CW00435678

The Form Book®
JUMPS ANNUAL
2015–2016

THE OFFICIAL FORM BOOK

Complete record of Jumps Racing
from 26 April 2015 to 23 April 2016

Published in 2016 by Raceform Ltd
27 Kingfisher Court, Hambridge Road, Newbury, Berkshire, RG14 5SJ

A catalogue record for this book is available from the British Library,

ISBN 978-1-910498-61-3

Printed and bound by the CPI Group (UK) Ltd, Croydon CR0 4YY

Full details of all Raceform services and publications are available from:

Tel: 01933 304858 • Fax: 01933 304796
Email: shop@racingpost.com
www.racingpost.com/shop

CONTENTS

The Official Scale of Weight, Age & Distance (Jumps)

The following scale should only be used in conjuction with the Official ratings published in this book. Use of any other scale will introduce errors into calculations. The allowances are expressed as the number of pounds that is deemed the average horse in each group falls short of maturity at different dates and distances.

N.B. Southern Hemisphere horses receive different allowances.

Scale of Weight for Age for Steeple Chases and Hurdle Races

HURDLE RACES

The allowances, assessed in lbs, which three-year-olds and four-year-olds will receive from five-year-olds and upwards

Distance		JAN		FEB		MAR		APR		MAY		JUNE		JULY		AUG		SEPT		OCT		NOV		DEC	
Miles	Age	1/15	16/31	1/14	15/29	1/15	16/31	1/15	16/30	1/15	16/31	1/15	16/30	1/15	16/31	1/15	16/31	1/15	16/30	1/15	16/31	1/15	16/30	1/15	16/31
2	3	–	–	–	–	–	–	–	–	22	22	21	21	20	20	19	19	18	18	17	17	16	15	14	13
	4	12	11	10	9	8	7	6	5	4	4	3	3	2	2	1	1	–	–	–	–	–	–	–	–
2½	3	–	–	–	–	–	–	–	–	23	23	22	22	21	21	20	20	19	19	18	18	17	16	15	14
	4	13	12	11	10	9	8	7	6	5	5	4	4	3	3	2	2	1	1	–	–	–	–	–	–
3	3	–	–	–	–	–	–	–	–	24	24	23	23	22	22	21	21	20	20	19	19	18	17	16	15
	4	14	13	12	11	10	9	8	7	6	6	5	5	4	4	3	3	2	2	1	1	–	–	–	–

STEEPLECHASES

The allowances, assessed in lbs, which four-year-olds and five-year-olds will receive from five-year-olds and upwards

Distance		JAN		FEB		MAR		APR		MAY		JUNE		JULY		AUG		SEPT		OCT		NOV		DEC	
Miles	Age	1/15	16/31	1/14	15/29	1/15	16/31	1/15	16/30	1/15	16/31	1/15	16/30	1/15	16/31	1/15	16/31	1/15	16/30	1/15	16/31	1/15	16/30	1/15	16/31
2	4	–	–	–	–	–	–	–	–	18	18	17	17	16	15	14	13	12	11	10	9	8	7	6	5
	5	4	3	2	1	–	–	–	–	–	–	–	–	–	–	–	–	–	–	–	–	–	–	–	–
2½	4	–	–	–	–	–	–	–	–	19	19	18	18	17	16	15	14	13	12	11	10	9	8	7	6
	5	5	4	3	2	1	–	–	–	–	–	–	–	–	–	–	–	–	–	–	–	–	–	–	–
3	4	–	–	–	–	–	–	–	–	20	20	19	19	18	17	16	15	14	13	12	11	10	9	8	7
	5	6	5	4	3	2	1	–	–	–	–	–	–	–	–	–	–	–	–	–	–	–	–	–	–

The Form Book Jumps Annual

Welcome to the 2015-2016 edition of *The Form Book Jumps Annual*, comprising the complete year's results from 26th April 2015 to 23rd April 2016.

Race details contain Racing Post Ratings assessing the merit of each individual performance, speed figures for every horse that clocks a worthwhile time, weight-for-age allowances, and the starting price percentage.

Race Focus comments are printed below of most races, along with the results of stewards' enquiries.

The official record

THE FORM BOOK records comprehensive race details of every domestic race, every major European Group race and every foreign event in which a British-trained runner participated.

MEETING BACK REFERENCE NUMBER is the Raceform number of the last meeting run at the track and is shown to the left of the course name. Abandoned meetings are signified by a dagger.

THE GOING, The Official going, shown at the head of each meeting, is recorded as follows: Turf: Hard; Firm; Good to firm; Good; Good to soft; Soft; Heavy. All-Weather: Fast; Standard to fast; Standard; Standard to slow; Slow. There may be variations for non-British meetings

Where appropriate, a note is included indicating track bias and any differences to the official going indicated by race times.

THE WEATHER is shown below the date for selected meetings.

THE WIND is given as a strength and direction at the Winning Post, classified as follows:
Strength: gale; v.str; str; fresh; mod; slt; almost nil; nil.
Direction: (half) against; (half) bhd; (half) across from or towards stands.

VISIBILITY is good unless otherwise stated.

RACE NUMBERS for Foreign races carry the suffix 'a' in the race header and in the index.

RACE TITLE is the name of the race as shown in the Racing Calendar.

COMPETITIVE RACING CLASSIFICATIONS are shown on a scale from Class 1 to Class 7. All graded races are Class 1.

THE RACE DISTANCE is given for all races to the nearest half-furlong. On All-Weather courses (F) for Fibresand or (P) for Polytrack indicates the nature of the artificial surface on which the race is run.

OFFICIAL RACE TIME as published in the Racing Calendar is followed in parentheses by the time when the race actually started. This is followed by the race class, age restrictions, handicap restrictions and the official rating of the top weight.

PRIZE MONEY shows penalty values down to sixth place (where applicable).

IN THE RACE RESULT, the figures to the far left of each horse (under FORM) show the most recent form figures. The figure in bold is the finishing position in this race as detailed below.

1...40 - finishing positions first to fortieth; b - brought down; c - carried out; f - fell; p - pulled up; r - refused; ro - ran out; s - slipped up; u - unseated rider; v - void race.

THE OFFICIAL DISTANCES between horses are shown on the left-hand side immediately after their position at the finish.

NUMBER OF DAYS SINCE PREVIOUS RUN is the superscript figure immediately following the horse name and suffix.

PREVIOUS RACEFORM RACE NUMBER is the boxed figure to the right of the horse's name.

THE HORSE'S AGE is shown immediately before the weight carried.

WEIGHTS shown are actual weights carried.

OFFICIAL RATING is the figure in bold type directly after the horse's name in the race result. This figure indicates the Official BHA rating, at entry, after the following adjustments had been made:
(i) Overweight carried by the rider.
(ii) The number of pounds out of the handicap (if applicable).
(iii) Penalties incurred after the publication of the weights.
However, no adjustments have been made for:
(i) Weight-for-age.
(ii) Riders' claims.

HEADGEAR is shown immediately before the jockey's name and in parentheses and expressed as: b (blinkers); v (visor); h (hood); e (eyeshield); p (sheepskin cheekpieces); t (tongue-tie).

THE JOCKEY is shown for every runner followed, in superscript, by apprentice allowances in parentheses.

CONDITIONAL JOCKEYS' ALLOWANCES The holders of conditional jockeys' licences, under the provisions of Rule 109(ii) (a) are permitted to claim the following allowances in Jumps races:

7lb until they have won 15 races;

thereafter 5lb until they have won 35 such races;

thereafter 3lb until they have won 65 such Jumps races.

These allowances can be claimed in the steeplechases, hurdle races and National Hunt flat races set out below, with the exception of races confined to conditional jockeys:
(a) All handicaps except the Grand National Steeplechase
(b) All selling races.
(c) All weight-for-age races classified 3, 4, 5, and 6.
(d) All National Hunt Flat races.

RACING POST RATINGS, which record the level of performance attained in this race for each horse, appear in the end column after each horse. These are the work of handicapper Steve Mason, who heads a dedicated team dealing with Jumps races for Raceform and sister publication, the Racing Post.

THE TRAINER is shown for every runner.

COMMENT-IN-RUNNING is shown for each horse in an abbreviated form. Details of abbreviations appear later in this section.

STARTING PRICES appear below the jockey in the race result. The favourite indicator appears to the right of the Starting Price; 1 for the favourite, 2 for the second-favourite and 3 for third-favourite. Joint favourites share the same number.

RACE TIMES in Great Britain are official times which are recorded to a tenth of a second. Figures in parentheses following the time show the number of seconds faster or slower than the Raceform Median Time for the course and distance.

RACEFORM MEDIAN TIMES are compiled from all races run over the course and distance in the preceding five years. Times equal to the median are shown as (0.00). Times under the median are preceded by minus, for instance, 1.8 seconds under the median would be shown (-1.8). Record times are displayed as follows (1.2 under best).

GOING CORRECTION appears against each race to allow for changing conditions of the ground. It is shown to a hundredth of a second and indicates the adjustment per furlong against the median time. The going based on the going correction is shown in parentheses and is recorded in the following stages: Turf: HD (Hard); F (Firm); GF (Good to firm); G (Good); GS (Good to soft); S (Soft); HVY (Heavy). All-Weather: FST (Fast); SF (Standard to fast); STD (Standard); SS (Standard to slow); SLW (Slow)

WEIGHT-FOR-AGE allowances are given where applicable for mixed-age races.

STARTING PRICE PERCENTAGE follows the going correction and weight-for-age details, and gives the total SP percentage of all runners that competed. It precedes the number of runners taking part in the race.

SELLING DETAILS (where applicable) and details of any claim are given. Friendly claims are not detailed.

SPEED RATINGS appear below the race time and going correction. They are the work of time expert Dave Bellingham and differ from conventional ratings systems in that they are an expression of a horse's ability in terms of lengths-per-mile, as opposed to pounds in weight. They are not directly comparable with BHA and Racing Post ratings.

The ratings take no account of the effect of weight, either historically or on the day, and this component is left completely to the user's discretion. What is shown is a speed rating represented in its purest form, rather than one that has been altered for weight using a mathematical formula that treats all types of horses as if they were the same.

A comparison of the rating achieved with the 'par' figure for the grade of race - the rating that should be achievable by an everage winner in that class of race- will both provide an at-a-glance indication of whether or not a race was truly run and also highlight the value of the form from a time perspective.

In theory, if a horse has a best speed figure five points superior to another and both run to their best form in a race over a mile, the first horse should beat the second by five lengths. In a race run over two miles, the margin should be ten lengths and so on.

Before the speed figures can be calculated, it is necessary to establish a set of standard or median times for every distance at every track, and this is done by averaging the times of all winners over a particular trip going back several years. No speed ratings are produced when insufficient races have been run over a distance for a reliable median time to be calculated.

Once a meeting has taken place, a raw unadjusted speed rating is calculated for each winner by calculating how many lengths per mile the winning time was faster or slower than the median for the trip. A difference of 0.2 of a second equals one length. The raw speed ratings of all winners on the card are then compared to the 'par' figure for the class of race. The difference between the 'raw' speed rating and the 'par' figure for each race is then noted, and both the fastest and slowest races are discarded before the rest are averaged to produce the going allowance or track variant. This figure gives an idea as to how much the elements, of which the going is one, have affected the final times of each race.

The figure representing the going allowance (track variant) is then used to adjust the raw speed figures and produce the final ratings, which represent how fast the winners would have run on a perfectly good surface with no external influences, including the weather. The ratings for beaten horses are worked out by taking the number of lengths they were behind the winner, adjusting that to take into account the distance of the race, and deducting from the winner's rating. The reader is left with a rating which provides an instant impression of the value of a time performance.

The speed 'pars' below act as benchmark with which to compare the speed figures earned by each horse in each race. A horse that has already exceeded the 'par' for the class he is about to run in, is of special interest, especially if he has done it more than once, as are horses that have consistently earned higher figures than their rivals.

Class 1 Grade One	117
Class 1 Grade Two	115
Class 1 Grade Three	113
Class 1 Listed	111
Class 2	109
Class 3	107
Class 4	105
Class 5	103
Class 6	101
Class 7	97

Allowances need to be made for younger horses and for fillies. These allowances are as follows.

MONTH	3yo
Jul / Aug	-3
Sep / Oct	-2
Nov / Dec	-1
Races contested by fillies and mares only	-3

Allowances are cumulative.

TOTE prices include £1 stake. Exacta dividends are shown in parentheses. The Computer Straight Forecast dividend is preceded by the letters CSF, Computer Tricast is preceded by CT and Tote Trifecta dividend is preceded by the word Trifecta. Jackpot, Placepot and Quadpot details appear at the end of the meeting to which they refer.

OWNER is followed by the breeder's name and the trainer's location.

STEWARDS' ENQUIRIES are included with the result, and any suspensions and/or fines incurred. Objections by jockeys and officials are included, where relevant.

HISTORICAL FOCUS details occasional points of historical significance.

FOCUS The Focus section has been enhanced to help readers distinguish good races from bad races and reliable form from unreliable form, by drawing together the opinions of handicapper, time expert and paddock watcher and interpreting their views in a punter-friendly manner.

Abbreviations and their meanings

Paddock comments

gd sort – well made, above average on looks
attr – attractive
gd bodied – good bodied, well put together
h.d.w – has done well, improved in looks
wl grwn – well grown, has filled to its frame
lengthy – longer than average for its height
tall – tall
rangy – lengthy and tall but in proportion.
cl cpld – close coupled
scope – scope for physical development
str – strong, powerful looking
w'like – workmanlike, ordinary in looks
lt-f – light-framed, not much substance
cmpt – compact
neat – smallish, well put together
leggy – long legs compared with body
angular – unfurnished behind the saddle, not filled to frame
unf – unfurnished in the midriff, not filled to frame
narrow – not as wide as side appearance would suggest
small – lacks any physical scope
nt grwn – not grown
lw – looked fit and well
bkwd – backward in condition
t – tubed
swtg – sweating
b (off fore or nr fore) – bandaged in front
b.hind (off or nr) – bandaged behind

At the start

stdd s – jockey purposely reins back the horse
dwlt – missed the break and left for a short time
s.s – slow to start, left longer than a horse that dwelt
s.v.s – started very slowly
s.i.s – started on terms but took time to get going
ref to r – does not jump off, or travels a few yards then stops
rel to r – tries to pull itself up in mid-race
w.r.s – whipped round start

Position in the race

led – in lead on its own
disp ld – upsides the leader
w ldr – almost upsides the leader
w ldrs – in a line of three or more disputing the lead
prom – on the heels of the leaders, in front third of the field
trckd ldr(s) – just in behind the leaders giving impression that it could lead if asked
chsd ldr – horse in second place
chsd clr ldrs – horse heads main body of field behind two clear leaders
chsd ldrs – horse is in the first four or five but making more of an effort to stay close to the pace than if it were tracking the leaders.
clsd – closed
in tch – close enough to have a chance
hdwy – making ground on the leader
gd hdwy – making ground quickly on the leader, could be a deliberate move
sme hdwy – making some ground but no real impact on the race
w.w – waited with
stdy hdwy – gradually making ground
ev ch – upsides the leaders when the race starts in earnest
rr – at the back of main group but not detached
bhd – detached from the main body of runners
hld up – restrained as a deliberate tactical move
nt rcvr – lost all chance after interference, mistake etc.
wknd – stride shortened as it began to tire
lost tch – had been in the main body but a gap appeared as it tired

lost pl – remains in main body of runners but lost several positions quickly

Riding

effrt – short-lived effort

pushed along – received urgings with hands only, jockey not using legs

rdn – received urgings from saddle, including use of whip

hrd rdn – received maximum assistance from the saddle including use of whip

drvn – received forceful urgings, jockey putting in a lot of effort and using whip

hrd drvn – jockey very animated, plenty of kicking, pushing and reminders

Finishing comments

jst failed – closing rapidly on the winner and probably would have led a stride after the line

r.o – jockey's efforts usually involved to produce an increase in pace without finding an appreciable turn of speed

r.o wl – jockey's efforts usually involved to produce an obvious increase in pace without finding an appreciable turn of speed

unable qckn – not visibly tiring but does not possess a sufficient change of pace

one pce – not tiring but does not find a turn of speed, from a position further out than unable qckn

nt r.o. – did not consent to respond to pressure

styd on – going on well towards the end, utilising stamina

nvr able to chal – unable to produce sufficient to reach a challenging position

nvr nr to chal – in the opinion of the racereader, the horse was never in a suitable position to challenge.

nrst fin – nearer to the winner in distance beaten than at any time since the race had begun in earnest

nvr nrr – nearer to the winner position-wise than at any time since the race had begun in earnest

rallied – responded to pressure to come back with a chance having lost its place

no ex – unable to sustain its run

bttr for r – likely to improve for the run and experience

rn green – inclined to wander and falter through inexperience

too much to do – left with too much leeway to make up

Winning comments

v.easily – a great deal in hand

easily – plenty in hand

comf – something in hand, always holding the others

pushed out – kept up to its work with hands and heels without jockey resorting to whip or kicking along and wins fairly comfortably

rdn out – pushed and kicked out to the line, with the whip employed

drvn out – pushed and kicked out to the line, with considerable effort and the whip employed

all out – nothing to spare, could not have found any more

jst hld on – holding on to a rapidly diminishing lead, could not have found any more if passed

unchal – must either make all or a majority of the running and not be challenged from an early stage

Complete list of abbreviations

a - always
abt - about
a.p - always prominent
appr - approaching
awrdd - awarded
b.b.v - broke blood-vessel
b.d - brought down
bdly - badly
bef - before
bhd - behind
bk - back
blkd - baulked
blnd - blundered
bmpd - bumped
bnd - bend
btn- beaten
bttr - better
c - came
ch - chance
chal - challenged
chse - chase
chsd - chased
chsng - chasing
circ - circuit
cl - close
clr - clear
clsd - closed
comf - comfortably
cpld - coupled
crse - course
ct - caught
def - definite
dismntd - dismounted
disp - disputed
dist - distance
div - division
drvn - driven
dwlt - dwelt
edgd - edged
effrt - effort
ent - entering
ev ch - every chance
ex - extra
f - furlong
fin - finished
fnd - found
fnl - final
fr - from
gd - good
gng - going
gp - group
grad - gradually
grnd - ground
hd - head
hdd - headed
hdwy - headway
hld - held
hmpd - hampered
imp - impression
ins - inside
j.b - jumped badly
j.w - jumped well
jnd - joined
jst - just
kpt - kept
l - length
ld - lead
ldr - leader
lft - left
mod - moderate
m - mile
m.n.s - made no show
mde - made
mid div - mid division
mstke - mistake
n.d - never dangerous
n.g.t - not go through
n.m.r - not much room
nk - neck
no ex - no extra
nr - near
nrr - nearer
nrst fin - nearest finish
nt - not
nvr - never
one pce - one pace
out - from finish
outpcd - outpaced
p.u - pulled up
pce - pace
pckd - pecked
pl - place

plcd - placed
plld - pulled
press - pressure
prog - progress
prom - prominent
qckly - quickly
qckn - quicken
r - race
racd - raced
rch - reach
rcvr - recover
rdn - ridden
rdr - rider
reard - reared
ref - refused
rn - ran
rnd - round
r.o - ran on
rr - rear
rspnse - response
rt - right
s - start
sddle - saddle
shkn - shaken
slt - slight
sme - some
sn - soo
spd- speed
st - straight
stmbld - stumbled
stdd - steadied
stdy - steady
strly - strongly
styd - stayed
styng - staying
s. u - slipped up
swtchd - switched
swvd - swerved
tk - took
t.k.h - took keen hold
t.o - tailed off
tch - touch
thrght - throughout
trbld - troubled
trckd - tracked
u.p - under pressure
u.str.p- under strong pressure
w - with
w.r.s - whipped round start
wd - wide
whn - when
wknd - weakened
wl - well
wnr - winner

Racing Post Ratings

Raceform Ratings for each horse are listed after the Starting Price and indicate the actual level of performance attained in that race. The figure in the back index represents the BEST public form that Raceform's Handicappers still believe the horse capable of reproducing.

To use the ratings constructively in determining those horses best-in in future events, the following procedures should be followed:

(i) In races where all runners are set to carry the same weight, no calculations are necessary. The horse with the highest rating is best in.

(ii) In races where all runners are set to carry different weights, add one point to the Raceform Rating for every pound less than 12 st to be carried; deduct one point for every pound more than 12 st.

For example,

Horse	Age & Weight	Adj. from 12st	RRbase rating	Adj. rating
Kid Cassidy	7-11-12	+2	150	152
Tanks For That	10-11-9	+5	147	152
Oiseau De Nuit	11-11-8	+6	147	153
Toubab	7-11-7	+7	145	152

Therefore Oiseau De Nuit is top-rated (best-in)

The following symbols are used in conjunction with the ratings:

++: almost certain to prove better

+: likely to prove better

d: disappointing (has run well below best recently)

?: form hard to evaluate

t: tentative rating based on race-time rating may prove unreliable

Weight adjusted ratings for every race are published daily in Raceform Private Handicap.

For subscription terms please contact the Subscription Department on 01933 304858.

Racereaders

Walter Glynn
Richard Lowther
Ian Mackenzie
Lee McKenzie
Tim Mitchell
Jonathan Neesom
Darren Owen
Steve Payne
Colin Roberts
Joe Rowntree
Andrew Sheret
Richard Young

Raceform median times

Some distances have been omitted where insufficient data exists to establish a reliable median time

AINTREE

MILDMAY

1m 7f 176y (C) 4m
2m 3f 200y (C) 5m 4.0s
2m 103y (H) 4m 6.2s
2m 209y (H) 4m 13.7s
2m 4f (H) 5m 0.7s
3m 149y (H) 6m 16.3s

NATIONAL

2m 5f 19y (C) 5m 37.0s
3m 210y (C) 6m 30.0s
3m 1f 188y (C) 6m 47.0s
4m 2f 74y (C) 9m 13.0s

ASCOT

2m 192y (C) 4m 14.6s
2m 2f 175y (C) 4m 46.4s
2m 5f 8y (C) 5m 26.0s
2m 7f 180y (C) 6m 3.5s
1m 7f 152y (H) 3m 47.4s
2m 3f 58y (H) 4m 44.7s
2m 5f 141y (H) 5m 26.0s
2m 7f 118y (H) 5m 56.0s
3m 97y (H) 6m 11.0s

AYR

1m 7f 112y (C) 4m 10.7s
3m 67y (C) 6m 49.9s
3m 2f 197y (C) 6m 54.3s
3m 7f 176y (C) 8m 53.0s
3m 70y (H) 6m 31.8s

BANGOR-ON-DEE

2m 1f 77y (C) 4m 22.1s
2m 4f 72y (C) 5m 9.1s
3m 30y (C) 6m 19.8s
3m 5f 142y (C) 7m 55.0s
2m 145y (H) 4m 10.9s
2m 3f 123y (H) 4m 52.0s
2m 7f 32y (H) 5m 51.0s

CARLISLE

1m 7f 207y (C) 4m 16.1s
2m 4f (C) 5m 27.4s
2m 4f 198y (C) 5m 37.0s
3m 110y (C) 6m 42.6s
3m 2f 34y (C) 7m 7.2s
2m 1f 33y (H) 4m 27.7s
2m 4f 8y (H) 5m 22.8s
3m 123y (H) 6m 39.0s

INNER

2m 1f (H) 4m 29.2s
2m 3f 61y (H) 5m 8.8s
3m 1f (H) 6m 39.0s

CARTMEL

2m 1f 61y (C) 4m 18.9s
2m 5f 34y (C) 5m 25.4s
3m 1f 107y (C) 6m 34.9s
3m 5f 80y (C) 7m 36.2s
2m 1f 46y (H) 4m 13.2s
2m 6f 31y (H) 5m 29.3s
3m 1f 83y (H) 6m 26.1s

CATTERICK

1m 7f 145y (C) 4m 0.1s
3m 1f 54y (C) 6m 42.0s
1m 7f 156y (H) 3m 52.5s
2m 3f 66y (H) 4m 36.1s
3m 1f 71y (H) 6m 27.6s

CHELTENHAM

OLD COURSE

1m 7f 199y (C) 3m 58.0s
2m 4f 78y (C) 5m 11.0s
3m 80y (C) 6m 18.3s
3m 1f (C) 6m 26.0s
3m 3f 71y (C) 7m 9.4s
3m 6f 37y (X-Country C) 8m 38.0s
3m 7f 170y (C) 8m 21.8s
2m 87y (H) 4m 2.0s
2m 3f 200y (H) 4m 50.0s
2m 5f 26y (H) 5m 13.4s
2m 7f 208y (H) 6m 3.4s
3m 1f 67y (H) 6m 26.1s

NEW COURSE

2m 62y (C) 4m 6.7s
2m 3f 198y (C) 5m 4.2s
2m 4f 166y (C) 5m 15.7s
3m 1f 56y (C) 6m 38.2s
3m 2f (C) 6m 46.0s
3m 2f 70y (C) 6m 53.8s
3m 4f 21y (C) 7m 25.0s
2m 179y (H) 4m 11.3s
2m 4f 56y (H) 4m 57.4s
2m 7f 213y (H) 6m 1.0s

CHEPSTOW

2m 11y (C) 4m 17.1s
2m 3f 98y (C) 5m 11.3s
2m 7f 131y (C) 6m 22.0s
3m 2f 54y (C) 7m 2.0s
2m 11y (H) 4m 10.6s
2m 3f 100y (H) 5m 1.8s
2m 7f 131y (H) 6m 2.2s

DONCASTER

2m 90y (C) 4m 5.0s
2m 3f 44y (C) 4m 49.0s
2m 4f 126y (C) 5m 12.0s
3m 6y (C) 6m 12.0s
3m 2f 14y (C) 6m 43.0s
2m 140y (H) 4m 4.7s
2m 3f 120y (H) 4m 51.3s
3m 96y (H) 5m 59.0s

EXETER

2m 1f 109y (C) 4m 19.0s
2m 3f 48y (C) 4m 57.3s
3m 54y (C) 6m 9.3s
3m 6f 153y (C) 7m 48.6s
2m 175y (H) 4m 15.5s
2m 2f 111y (H) 4m 42.7s
2m 5f 135y (H) 5m 33.0s
2m 7f 25y (H) 5m 59.0s

FAKENHAM

2m 59y (C) 4m 16.6s
2m 5f 44y (C) 5m 41.8s
3m 38y (C) 6m 35.7s
2m 3y (H) 4m 13.0s
2m 4f 1y (H) 5m 20.4s
2m 7f 95y (H) 6m 22.0s

FFOS LAS

2m 3f 83y (C) 5m 1.1s
2m 4f 199y (C) 5m 28.6s
2m 7f 177y (C) 6m 17.4s
3m 1f 60y (C) 6m 41.0s
1m 7f 202y (H) 3m 48.5s
2m 4f (OMS H) 4m 50.9s
2m 5f 192y (H) 5m 20.0s
2m 7f 191y (H) 5m 49.0s

FONTWELL

2m 1f 96y (C) 4m 34.7s
2m 3f 35y (C) 5m 7.3s
2m 5f 31y (C) 5m 43.0s
3m 1f 106y (C) 7m 1.1s
3m 3f 45y (C) 7m 27.3s
2m 1f 145y (H) 4m 34.3s
2m 3f 33y (H) 4m 59.4s
2m 5f 139y (H) 5m 42.5s
3m 1f 142y (H) 6m 52.8s

HAYDOCK

1m 7f 157y (C) 4m 11.0s
2m 67y (C) 4m 19.0s
2m 2f 211y (C) 5m 10.0s
2m 6f 204y (C) 6m 14.0s
3m 24y (C) 6m 30.5s
3m 3f 57y (C) 7m 16.0s
3m 4f 97y (C) 7m 31.6s
1m 7f 144y (H) 4m 4.2s
2m 2f 191y (Brush H) 4m 53.0s
2m 2f 191y (H) 4m 53.0s
2m 6f 177y (Brush H) ... 6m
2m 6f 177y (H) 6m

HEXHAM

1m 7f 133y (C) 4m 9.8s
2m 4f 15y (C) 5m 13.5s
3m 41y (C) 6m 32.2s
3m 7f 199y (C) 8m 55.4s
2m 48y (H) 4m 17.4s
2m 4f 28y (H) 5m 12.5s
2m 7f 63y (H) 6m 9.0s

HUNTINGDON

2m 104y (C) 4m 10.2s
2m 3f 189y (C) 5m 5.3s
2m 7f 129y (C) 6m 10.3s
3m 6f 162y (C) 8m 12.8s
1m 7f 171y (H) 3m 54.9s
2m 3f 137y (H) 4m 59.0s
2m 4f 145y (H) 5m 10.6s
3m 1f 10y (H) 6m 22.9s

KELSO

2m 1f 14y (C) 4m 18.0s
2m 5f 133y (C) 5m 29.2s
2m 7f 96y (C) 6m 8.0s
3m 2f 39y (C) 6m 47.2s
4m 90y (C) 8m 48.0s
2m 51y (H) 4m 1.8s
2m 2f 25y (H) 4m 27.0s
2m 4f 189y (H) 5m 8.0s
2m 6f 151y (H) 5m 41.0s
3m 1f 170y (H) 6m 40.0s

KEMPTON

2m (C) 3m 55.0s
2m 4f 110y (C) 5m 12.0s
3m (C) 6m 9.0s

SUMMER

2m (H) 3m 46.0s
2m 5f (H) 5m 3.0s
3m 110y (H) 6m 20.0s

WINTER

2m (H) 3m 58.0s
2m 5f (H) 5m 21.0s
3m 121y (H) 6m 20.0s

LEICESTER

1m 7f 201y (C) 4m 8.2s
2m 4f 45y (C) 5m 18.9s
2m 6f 151y (C) 6m 4.0s
1m 7f 113y (H) 4m 1.0s
2m 4f 110y (H) 5m 24.7s

LINGFIELD

2m (C) 4m 40.0s
2m 4f (C) 5m 35.0s
2m 7f 110y (C) 7m
2m (H) 4m 28.0s
2m 3f 110y (H) 5m 26.0s

LUDLOW

1m 7f 212y (C) 3m 58.5s
2m 4f 11y (C) 5m 4.4s
3m 1f 125y (C) 6m 35.3s
1m 7f 169y (H) 3m 49.5s
2m 5f 55y (H) 5m 14.8s
2m 7f 174y (H) 5m 52.3s

MARKET RASEN

2m 1f 43y (C) 4m 35.0s
2m 3f 34y (C) 5m 5.7s
2m 5f 89y (C) 5m 46.0s
2m 7f 191y (C) 6m 31.3s
3m 3f 123y (C) 7m 34.0s
2m 148y (H) 4m 6.7s
2m 2f 140y (H) 4m 39.4s
2m 4f 139y (H) 5m 8.8s
2m 7f 16y (H) 5m 50.5s

MUSSELBURGH

1m 7f 182y (C) 3m 52.4s
2m 3f 193y (C) 5m 1.2s
2m 7f 170y (C) 6m 3.4s
3m 2f 139y (C) 6m 48.8s
1m 7f 124y (H) 3m 48.4s
2m 3f 81y (H) 4m 51.5s
2m 7f 180y (H) 5m 42.1s
3m 2f 26y (H) 6m 15.1s

NEWBURY

2m 92y (C) 4m 8.0s
2m 2f 64y (C) 4m 30.0s
2m 3f 187y (C) 5m 3.0s
2m 6f 93y (C) 5m 47.0s
2m 7f 86y (C) 6m 6.0s
3m 1f 214y (C) 6m 46.0s
2m 69y (H) 4m 10.0s
2m 2f 183y (H) 4m 48.0s
2m 4f 118y (H) 5m 19.0s

NEWCASTLE

2m 75y (C) 4m 21.1s
2m 4f 19y (C) 5m 27.2s
2m 7f 91y (C) 6m 22.5s
4m 122y (C) 9m 7.8s
2m 98y (H) 4m 10.0s
2m 4f 133y (H) 5m 21.1s
2m 6f (H) 5m 36.0s
3m 10y (H) 6m 14.0s

NEWTON ABBOT

2m 75y (C) 4m 6.5s
2m 4f 216y (C) 5m 21.4s
3m 1f 170y (C) 6m 44.6s
2m 167y (H) 4m 5.7s
2m 2f 110y (H) 4m 30.0s
2m 5f 122y (H) 5m 20.2s
3m 2f 105y (H) 6m 41.0s

PERTH

2m 4f 20y (C) 5m 5.0s
2m 7f 180y (C) 6m 4.0s
3m 6f 121y (C) 7m 50.0s
2m 4f 35y (H) 5m 2.0s
2m 7f 207y (H) 6m 5.0s
3m 2f 127y (H) 6m 42.0s

PLUMPTON

2m 214y (C) 4m 23.0s
2m 3f 164y (C) 5m 7.3s
3m 1f 152y (C) 6m 50.7s
3m 4f 102y (C) 7m 38.0s
1m 7f 195y (H) 4m 0.8s
2m 1f 164y (H) 4m 30.9s
2m 4f 114y (H) 5m 17.0s
3m 217y (H) 6m 25.0s

SANDOWN

1m 7f 119y (C) 4m 1.8s
2m 4f 10y (C) 5m 18.4s
2m 6f 164y (C) 5m 53.4s
3m 37y (C) 6m 27.8s
3m 4f 166y (C) 7m 44.0s
1m 7f 216y (H) 4m 7.2s
2m 3f 173y (H) 4m 59.6s
2m 5f 110y (H) 5m 22.5s

SEDGEFIELD

2m 77y (C) 4m 14.0s
2m 3f 65y (C) 5m 3.0s
2m 5f 28y (C) 5m 33.0s
3m 2f 59y (C) 7m 11.0s
3m 5f 48y (C) 7m 59.0s
2m 178y (H) 4m 6.9s
2m 3f 34y (H) 4m 52.7s
2m 3f 188y (H) 4m 54.1s
2m 5f 34y (H) 5m 14.6s
3m 3f 9y (H) 6m 52.0s

SOUTHWELL

1m 7f 153y (C) 4m 2.0s
2m 4f 62y (C) 5m 17.0s
2m 7f 209y (C) 6m 23.0s
3m 1f 129y (C) 6m 46.0s
1m 7f 153y (H) 3m 57.0s
2m 4f 62y (H) 5m 13.0s
2m 7f 209y (H) 6m 15.0s

STRATFORD

2m 213y (C) 4m 7.1s
2m 3f 98y (C) 4m 50.0s
2m 4f 205y (C) 5m 15.0s
2m 6f 125y (C) 5m 39.2s
3m 3f 119y (C) 7m 3.0s
2m 70y (H) 3m 56.0s
2m 2f 148y (H) 4m 31.5s
2m 6f 7y (H) 5m 28.1s
3m 2f 83y (H) 6m 28.6s

TAUNTON

2m 12y (C) 4m 14.0s
2m 2f 40y (C) 4m 52.0s
2m 7f 3y (C) 6m 16.0s
3m 4f 85y (C) 7m 24.4s
2m 104y (H) 4m 8.0s
2m 3f 1y (H) 4m 46.0s
2m 7f 198y (H) 6m 4.0s

TOWCESTER

2m 70y (C) 4m 16.1s
2m 3f 179y (C) 5m 18.2s
2m 5f 153y (C) 5m 53.0s
3m 102y (C) 6m 36.9s
1m 7f 181y (H) 4m 7.9s
2m 3f 34y (H) 5m 9.6s
2m 4f 217y (H) 5m 27.2s
2m 7f 211y (H) 6m 15.0s

UTTOXETER

1m 7f 214y (C) 4m 1.4s
2m 4f (C) 5m 9.8s
2m 6f 105y (C) 5m 48.5s
2m 6f 108y (C) 5m 42.7s
3m 2y (C) 6m 8.1s
3m 2f 13y (C) 6m 38.8s
4m 1f 92y (C) 8m 43.6s
1m 7f 168y (H) 3m 57.4s
2m 3f 207y (H) 5m 3.2s
2m 7f 70y (H) 5m 58.8s

WARWICK

2m (C) 4m 10.0s
2m 4f (C) 5m 18.0s
3m (C) 6m 34.0s
3m 1f 100y (C) 6m 59.0s
3m 5f (C) 7m 56.0s
2m (H) 3m 51.0s
2m 3f (H) 4m 46.0s
2m 5f (H) 5m 21.0s
3m 2f (H) 6m 37.0s

INNER

2m (H) 3m 59.0s
2m 3f (H) 4m 46.0s
2m 5f (H) 5m 21.0s
3m 2f (H) 6m 37.0s

WETHERBY

1m 7f 36y (C) 3m 55.8s
2m 3f 85y (C) 5m 7.8s
2m 5f 75y (C) 5m 37.0s
3m 45y (C) 6m 48.0s
2m (H) 3m 55.8s
2m 3f 154y (H) 5m 7.0s
2m 5f 56y (H) 5m 26.8s
3m 26y (H) 6m 16.5s

WINCANTON

1m 7f 149y (C) 3m 59.9s
2m 4f 35y (C) 5m 17.5s
3m 1f 30y (C) 6m 39.5s
3m 2f 162y (C) 7m 8.2s
1m 7f 65y (H) 3m 48.9s
2m 5f 82y (H) 5m 26.5s

WORCESTER

2m 110y (C) 4m 5.0s
2m 4f (C) 5m 4.6s
2m 7f (C) 5m 49.9s
2m (H) 3m 50.6s
2m 4f (H) 4m 53.5s
2m 7f (H) 5m 38.6s

• Course descriptions

COURSE	COMMENT
AINTREE	Two left-handed courses. Grand National circuit, 2m2f, is flat and has bigf ences with a slight drop on the landing side of some and a long run-in.Mildmay Course, 1m3f, flat with conventional fences, is sharper than the hurdles course.
ASCOT	Right-handed, galloping, last mile mainly uphill, with stiff fences. Circuit1m5f.
AYR	Left-handed, mainly flat. Circuit 1m4f.
BANGOR	Left-handed, sharp and flat with a long run-in. Circuit 1m4f.
CARLISLE	Right-handed, undulating, stiff and galloping. Circuit 1m5f
CARTMEL	Left-handed, sharp and undulating, with stiff fences and a 4f run-in for chases. Circuit 1m.
CATTERICK	Left-handed, sharp and undulating, suiting handy types. Circuit 1m3f.
CHELTENHAM	Left-handed, galloping, undulating and testing track with stiff fences. (old course) Circuit 1m4f.
CHELTENHAM	Left-handed, galloping, undulating and testing track with stiff fences.(new course) Circuit 1m4½f.
CHEPSTOW	Left-handed and undulating. Going can be very testing. Circuit 1m7f.
DONCASTER	Left-handed, galloping, generally flat. Heavy ground rare. Circuit 2m.
EXETER	Right-handed and undulating. Stiff test of stamina. Circuit 2m.
FAKENHAM	Left-handed, sharp, undulating, suiting nippy types. Circuit 1m.
FFOS LAS	Left-handed, galloping, flat track. Circuit 1m6f.
FONTWELL	Left-handed hurdle course. Figure-of-eight chase course does not suit long-striding gallopers. Ground can be testing. Circuit 1m.
HAYDOCK	Left-handed, flat and galloping but with sharper bends since the course was re-aligned. Circuit 1m5f.
HEXHAM	Left-handed, severe and undulating, emphasis on stamina. Circuit 1m4f.

HUNTINGDON	Right-handed and galloping. Circuit 1m4f.
KELSO	Left-handed and undulating. Hurdles course of 1m1f is sharp, more so than 1m 3f chase track, which has 2f run-in.
KEMPTON	Triangular circuit 1m5f, practically flat. Circuit 1m5f.
LEICESTER	Right-handed and undulating, placing emphasis on stamina. Circuit 1m6f.
LINGFIELD	Left-handed, undulating and sharp. Chase circuit 1m5f, hurdles run on flat course.
LUDLOW	Right-handed. Chase course flat with sharp bends, circuit 1m4f. Hurdles track, 150y longer, slightly undulating, with easier bends.
MARKET RASEN	Right-handed oval, sharp and somewhat undulating. Circuit 1m2f.
MUSSELBURGH	Right-handed virtually flat track with sharp turns. Circuit 1m3f.
NEWBURY	Left-handed, flat and galloping, with stiff fences. Circuit 1m7f.
NEWCASTLE	Left-handed, with uphill finish. Going can be very testing. Circuit 1m6f.
NEWTON ABBOT	Left-handed oval, sharp with short run-in. Circuit 1m2f.
PERTH	Right-handed and flat, with tight bends. Chase course has long run-in. Circuit 1m 2f.
PLUMPTON	Left-handed, undulating, sharp. Circuit 1m1f.
SANDOWN	Right-handed with stiff uphill finish. Chase course tricky, especially for novices. Hurdles run on flat course. Circuit 1m5f.
SEDGEFIELD	Left-handed, undulating oval, sharp bends. Chase course has easy fences. Circuit 1m2f.
SOUTHWELL	Left-handed oval, approx 1m round, with six portable fences. Outside half of jumps course used in summer.
STRATFORD	Left-handed, flat and sharp, with short finishing straight. Circuit 1m2f.
TAUNTON	Right-handed oval, on the sharp side with short run-in. Circuit 1m2f.
TOWCESTER	Right-handed, with last mile uphill. Very testing. Circuit 1m6f.
UTTOXETER	Left-handed with some undulations. Hurdle course is inside chase course. Circuit 1m3f.
WARWICK	Left-handed, with tight turns and short run-in. Circuit 1m5f.
WETHERBY	Left-handed oval, with easy bends. Circuit 1m4f.
WINCANTON	Right-handed rectangular track, mainly flat. Circuit 1m3f.
WORCESTER	Left-handed 1m5f oval, flat with long straights and easy turns.

1-5a - (Foreign Racing) - See Raceform Interactive

PUNCHESTOWN (R-H)

Tuesday, April 28

OFFICIAL GOING: Hurdle & chase course - good to yielding; cross-country course - good (good to firm in places)

6a HERALD CHAMPION NOVICE HURDLE (GRADE 1) (9 hdls) 2m

4:20 (4:21) 5-Y-0+ **£44,186** (£13,992; £6,627; £2,209; £1,472)

RPR

1 **Douvan (FR)**[49] 4688 5-11-12 **160** ... RWalsh 159+
(W P Mullins, Ire) *chsd ldrs in 3rd: tk clsr order travelling wl fr 2 out and wnt 2nd between last 2: led on bit bef last and pushed clr run-in: easily* **1/6**[1]

2 *7 ½* **Sizing John**[49] 4688 5-11-12 **151** ... JJBurke 149
(Henry De Bromhead, Ire) *chsd ldr in 2nd: pressed ldr clly after 3 out and led after next: rdn and hdd bef last and no ch w easy wnr: kpt on same pce run-in* **5/1**[2]

3 *8* **Blair Perrone (IRE)**[22] 5223 6-11-12 **137** ... (t) DenisO'Regan 140+
(A J Martin, Ire) *hld up towards rr: nt fluent 1st: 5th 1/2-way: tk clsr order in mod 4th fr 2 out and wnt mod 3rd between last 2: kpt on same pce run-in: nvr trbld ldrs* **25/1**

4 *8* **Cardinal Palace (IRE)**[22] 5223 5-11-12 **0** ... DJCasey 132+
(J A Nash, Ire) *w.w in rr: j. sltly rt at times: wnt mod 5th fr 2 out and kpt on one pce into mod 4th run-in: nvr trbld ldrs* **66/1**

5 *16* **Velocity Boy (IRE)**[30] 5052 6-11-12 **126** ... BMCash 116
(William P Murphy, Ire) *led and clr tl reduced advantage after 3rd: slt mstke 5th: pressed clly after 3 out and slt mstke next: hdd after 2 out and wknd qckly bef last* **33/1**

P **Rich Coast**[22] 5223 7-11-12 **140** ... PaulCarberry
(Noel Meade, Ire) *hld up bhd ldrs in 4th: nt fluent 3rd: rdn in 4th bef 3 out and sn no ex: wknd to rr fr 2 out and p.u appr st* **20/1**[3]

4m 1.3s (-3.70) **Going Correction** -0.075s/f (Good) **6** Ran SP% **115.4**
Speed ratings: **106,102,98,94,86**
CSF £1.58 TOTE £1.10: £1.02, £1.30; DF 1.60 Trifecta £5.70.
Owner Mrs S Ricci **Bred** S A R L Haras De La Faisanderie **Trained** Muine Beag, Co Carlow

FOCUS
A facile victory for Douvan following on from his impressive Cheltenham success and leaves connections in an unenviable position as to next season's targets. The standard is rated around the third and fourth.

7a KILLASHEE H'CAP HURDLE (GRADE B) (9 hdls) 2m

4:55 (4:56) 4-Y-0+ **£25,193** (£7,364; £3,488; £1,162)

RPR

1 **Some Article (IRE)**[21] 5231 7-10-5 **125** ... NiallPMadden 135+
(Thomas Mullins, Ire) *chsd ldrs: cl 8th after 4 out: hdwy on outer after 2 out: rdn to chal in 2nd at last and kpt on wl run-in to ld clsng stages* **10/1**[3]

2 *¾* **Macnicholson (IRE)**[46] 4741 6-11-1 **135** ... (p) RobbiePower 144
(Mrs John Harrington, Ire) *settled bhd ldr: dropped to 9th after 4 out: hdwy again fr next to ld narrowly at last: strly pressed u.p run-in and hdd clsng stages* **20/1**

3 *½* **The Game Changer (IRE)**[17] 5276 6-11-7 **141** ... DavyRussell 150+
(Gordon Elliott, Ire) *in rr of mid-div: mstke 3rd: short of room on inner after 3 out and collided sltly w bush rail: hdwy after next to chse ldrs bef last where nt clr run: rdn into 3rd run-in and no ex clsng stages* **12/1**

4 *3 ¼* **Jebril (FR)**[41] 4847 5-10-6 **126** ... TomCannon 132
(Chris Gordon) *hld up in tch: rdn in 8th after 2 out and clsd u.p in 6th at last: kpt on wl run-in: nvr trbld ldrs* **33/1**

5 *1 ½* **Sizing Codelco (IRE)**[21] 5231 6-11-1 **135** ... (t) JJBurke 139
(Henry De Bromhead, Ire) *chsd ldrs: cl 5th after 4 out: rdn in 2nd into st and no ex u.p fr last: one pce run-in* **14/1**

6 *½* **Pivot Bridge**[21] 5231 7-9-10 **119** ... DavidSplaine(3) 123
(Adrian McGuinness, Ire) *chsd ldrs: rdn in 11th into st and no imp on ldrs u.p in 8th bef last: kpt on same pce run-in* **20/1**

7 *½* **Rupert Lamb**[22] 5222 9-10-3 **123** ... RWalsh 126
(W P Mullins, Ire) *chsd ldrs: cl 2nd 3 out and led narrowly fr next: strly pressed u.p bef last where hdd: wknd run-in* **14/1**

8 *nk* **Fethard Player (IRE)**[17] 5276 8-11-3 **137** ... (t) MarkEnright 140+
(W F Treacy, Ire) *mid-div: sme hdwy on inner after 2 out into 10th at last: kpt on same pce run-in: nvr nrr* **16/1**

9 *1 ½* **Waxies Dargle**[46] 4737 6-10-11 **131** ... PaulCarberry 132
(Noel Meade, Ire) *in rr of mid-div: 13th after 2 out: rdn and no imp on ldrs bef next: kpt on one pce run-in* **16/1**

10 *1* **Frontline (IRE)**[101] 3746 7-10-1 **121** ... APHeskin 121
(Peter Fahey, Ire) *hld up: hdwy after 2 out on outer to chse ldrs into st: rdn and no ex bef last: kpt on one pce run-in* **10/1**[3]

11 *1* **Viconte Du Noyer (FR)**[80] 4104 6-10-8 **128** ... (t) AELynch 127
(Henry De Bromhead, Ire) *in tch: rdn and no ex after 2 out: kpt on one pce* **33/1**

12 *¾* **Cliff House (IRE)**[30] 5051 5-10-13 **133** ... BrianO'Connell 131
(John J Walsh, Ire) *chsd ldrs: impr into 6th bef 3 out: rdn and no ex bef next: sn wknd* **16/1**

13 *1 ¾* **Morga (IRE)**[150] 2829 5-10-4 **124** ... DannyMullins 121
(Desmond McDonogh, Ire) *mid-div: rdn and no imp after 2 out* **33/1**

14 *5* **Xsquared (IRE)**[205] 1776 7-10-8 **128** ... (p) DenisO'Regan 120
(Sabrina J Harty, Ire) *hld up towards rr: no imp after 2 out: kpt on one pce fr last* **33/1**

15 *nk* **Henry Higgins (IRE)**[51] 4659 5-10-13 **133** ... MarkWalsh 124
(Charles O'Brien, Ire) *in rr of mid-div: sme hdwy after 2 out into 10th: rdn and no ex between last 2: one pce* **7/1**[1]

16 *hd* **Pink Coat**[21] 5231 8-10-8 **128** ... NoelFehily 119
(Ms Sandra Hughes, Ire) *hld up towards rr: sme hdwy after 4 out: rdn and no ex after 2 out* **25/1**

17 *½* **Indian Icon (FR)**[21] 5231 5-10-8 **128** ... MsNCarberry 119
(Ms Sandra Hughes, Ire) *chsd ldrs: 10th after 4 out: tk clsr order bhd ldrs on outer 2 out where mstke: sn rdn in 7th and no ex bef last: wknd* **33/1**

18 *1* **Astre De La Cour (FR)**[17] 5276 5-10-12 **137** ... DavidMullins(5) 127
(Robert Walford) *mid-div: clsr in 7th after 4 out: rdn and no ex after 2 out: sn wknd* **8/1**[2]

19 *½* **Mr Diablo (IRE)**[22] 5223 6-10-5 **130** ... LPDempsey(5) 119
(J P Dempsey, Ire) *mid-div: rdn and wknd after 2 out* **12/1**

20 *3 ½* **Mrs Mac Veale (IRE)**[23] 5168 10-10-2 **125** ... BrianHayes(3) 111
(Gavin Dower, Ire) *led: j. sltly lft at times: rdn and hdd narrowly fr 2 out: wknd into st* **25/1**

21 *5* **Dysios (IRE)**[23] 5178 7-10-2 **122** ... DJCasey 103
(Denis W Cullen, Ire) *chsd ldrs: cl 4th after 4 out: wknd next where nt fluent* **25/1**

22 *4 ¾* **Western Boy (IRE)**[21] 5231 6-11-4 **138** ... AlanCrowe 114
(P A Fahy, Ire) *a bhd: last 1/2-way: no imp after 2 out* **50/1**

23 *11* **Lucky Bridle (IRE)**[21] 5231 6-11-3 **137** ... PaulTownend 102
(W P Mullins, Ire) *chsd ldrs: tk clsr order bhd ldrs bef 3 out: rdn and wknd after next* **20/1**

24 *nk* **Cool Macavity (IRE)**[10] 5390 7-10-10 **130** ... DidielAOsorio 95
(Nicky Henderson) *a bhd: no imp 2 out* **20/1**

U **The Plan Man (IRE)**[21] 5231 5-10-12 **132** ... (t) BJCooper
(A J Martin, Ire) *hld up: mid-div whn blnd and uns rdr 4th* **14/1**

3m 59.8s (-5.20) **Going Correction** -0.075s/f (Good)
WFA 4 from 5yo+ 5lb **25** Ran SP% **142.1**
Speed ratings: **110,109,109,107,107 106,106,106,105,105 104,104,103,100,100 100,100,99,99,97 95,92,87,87,**
CSF £207.01 CT £2498.59 TOTE £10.00: £3.10, £5.40, £2.70, £11.50; DF 271.30 Trifecta £2295.20.
Owner John P McManus **Bred** Pat McLoughney **Trained** Goresbridge, Co Kilkenny

FOCUS
As competitive a handicap hurdle as you could care to see and it underlined the spring renaissance of the winner, who could really have put himself forward as a live contender for the Galway Hurdle later in the year.

8a BOYLESPORTS CHAMPION CHASE (GRADE 1) (11 fncs) 2m

5:30 (5:30) 5-Y-0+

£93,023 (£29,457; £13,953; £4,651; £3,100; £1,550)

RPR

1 **Felix Yonger (IRE)**[31] 5040 9-11-12 **158** ... DannyMullins 158
(W P Mullins, Ire) *hld up in tch: tk clsr order bhd ldrs on outer bef 3 out: rdn in 3rd bef 2 out where nt fluent: sn on terms and kpt on best run-in to ld cl home* **5/1**

2 *½* **Baily Green (IRE)**[26] 5123 9-11-12 **143** ... (tp) MarkEnright 157
(M F Morris, Ire) *chsd ldrs tl led after 1st: narrow advantage 1/2-way: jnd fr after 2 out: disp at last and kpt on wl run-in: hdd cl home* **40/1**

3 *16* **Hidden Cyclone (IRE)**[47] 4718 10-11-12 **158** ... (b[1]) AndrewJMcNamara 145
(John Joseph Hanlon, Ire) *disp early: lft in front briefly at 1st where slt mstke and settled bhd ldrs: clsr in 2nd at 1/2-way: mstke 4 out: rdn in 5th after next and no imp on ldrs whn nt fluent 2 out: kpt on same pce into mod 3rd run-in* **7/2**[2]

4 *¾* **Mallowney (IRE)**[21] 5229 9-11-12 **162** ... DavyRussell 142
(Timothy Doyle, Ire) *hld up: impr bhd ldrs 4 out and wnt 2nd after next: rdn and no ex u.p in 3rd fr 2 out: kpt on one pce* **4/1**[3]

5 *13* **Champagne Fever (IRE)**[18] 5252 8-11-12 **162** ... RWalsh 130
(W P Mullins, Ire) *chsd ldrs: mstke 1st: 3rd 1/2-way: rdn in 4th after 3 out and no imp on ldrs bef next: wknd* **3/1**[1]

6 *5 ½* **Twinlight (FR)**[21] 5229 8-11-12 **162** ... PaulTownend 122
(W P Mullins, Ire) *disp early: settled bhd ldr in 2nd fr 1st: slt mstke bhd ldrs at 5th: no imp in rr fr 3 out* **7/1**

7 *34* **Flemenstar (IRE)**[31] 5040 10-11-12 **158** ... KeithDonoghue 88
(A J Martin, Ire) *chsd ldrs: slt mstke in 5th at 2nd: in rr 4 out and no imp on ldrs next: one pce* **8/1**

P **Savello (IRE)**[21] 5229 9-11-12 **151** ... BJCooper
(A J Martin, Ire) *w.w in rr: mstke 1st where rdr lost iron and sddled slipped: p.u bef next* **28/1**

F **Oscar Hill (IRE)**[52] 4628 9-11-12 **144** ... TomO'Brien
(David Bridgwater) *disp early: narrow advantage whn fell 1st* **50/1**

4m 6.6s (-12.00) **Going Correction** -0.375s/f (Good) **9** Ran SP% **115.3**
Speed ratings: **115,114,106,106,99 97,80, ,**
CSF £150.28 CT £787.88 TOTE £5.10: £2.00, £7.00, £1.40; DF 202.00 Trifecta £794.60.
Owner Andrea & Graham Wylie **Bred** J Brophy **Trained** Muine Beag, Co Carlow
■ Stewards' Enquiry : Danny Mullins one-day ban: used whip in wrong place (tbn)

FOCUS
With no Vautour this race was both interesting and wide open, won by a horse that had been flying under the radar all season. The first two are rated to their best.

9a GOFFS LAND ROVER BUMPER INH FLAT RACE 2m

6:05 (6:05) 4-5-Y-0

£45,736 (£14,728; £6,976; £3,100; £1,550; £775)

RPR

1 **Petit Mouchoir (FR)**[73] 4-11-4 **0** ... [1] MrJJCodd 113
(Gordon Elliott, Ire) *chsd ldrs: 3rd 1/2-way: tk clsr order bhd ldrs over 3f out and led narrowly into st: rdn clr under 2f out and styd on strly* **4/1**[1]

2 *6 ½* **Policy Breach (IRE)**[59] 4506 4-11-1 **0** ... MissJMMangan(3) 106
(P Twomey, Ire) *led and disp tl led narrowly after 4f: jnd bef 1/2-way: remained prom tl rdn in 3rd into st: no imp on wnr over 1f out: kpt on u.p nr side into 2nd cl home* **25/1**

3 *½* **Tesseract (IRE)**[21] 5234 4-10-11 **0** ... MissSO'Brien(7) 106
(A P O'Brien, Ire) *led and disp: t.k.h early: settled bhd ldr in 2nd after 4f tl disp bef 1/2-way: rdn and hdd into st: no imp on wnr over 1f out: kpt on same pce ins fnl f and denied 2nd cl home* **20/1**

4 *2* **Red Giant (IRE)** 4-11-4 **0** ... MsNCarberry 104
(Noel Meade, Ire) *mid-div: tk clsr order in 8th over 5f out: rdn into 5th 2f out and no imp on wnr: kpt on same pce ins fnl f* **14/1**

5 *1* **Set In My Ways (IRE)** 4-11-4 **0** ... MrKEPower 103
(Jonjo O'Neill) *chsd ldrs: 5th 1/2-way: rdn in 3rd over 2f out and sn no imp on wnr: one pce fnl f* **12/1**

6 *nse* **Blast Of Koeman (IRE)** 4-11-4 **0** ... MrDerekO'Connor 102
(Robert Tyner, Ire) *in rr of mid-div: short of room briefly between horses over 5f out: hdwy fr 4f out to chse ldrs u.p in mod 6th under 2f out: kpt on one pce ins fnl f* **20/1**

7 *1 ½* **St Stephens Green (IRE)** 4-11-4 **0** ... MrPWMullins 101
(W P Mullins, Ire) *mid-div: 10th 5f out: tk clsr order fr 4f out: rdn into st and no imp on ldrs disputing 5th under 2f out: one pce after* **4/1**[1]

8 *2 ¾* **Last Goodbye (IRE)** 4-10-11 **0** ... MrFMaguire(7) 98
(Miss Elizabeth Doyle, Ire) *chsd ldrs: rdn and no ex 3f out: one pce fnl 2f* **16/1**

9 *nk* **Bingo Conti (FR)** 4-10-11 **0** ... MrJCBarry(7) 98
(C A Murphy, Ire) *mid-div: pushed along in 14th 3f out and no imp into st: kpt on one pce fnl 2f* **50/1**

10 *4 ½* **Art Of Synergy (IRE)**[31] 5037 4-10-13 **0** ... MrSClements(5) 93
(Ms Sandra Hughes, Ire) *settled bhd ldrs: 4th 1/2-way: rdn and wknd 3f out* **7/1**[2]

11 2 **Any Drama (IRE)** 4-11-4 0.......... MsKWalsh 91
(P A Fahy, Ire) *towards rr: rdn in 15th appr st and kpt on one pce fnl 2f* 25/1

12 hd **Ball D'Arc (FR)**[30] 5056 4-10-13 0.......... MrDGLavery(5) 91
(P M J Doyle, Ire) *chsd ldrs: rdn in 9th and no ex u.p appr st: wknd fnl 2f* 33/1

13 1 1/4 **Phar Island (IRE)** 4-11-1 0.......... MrMFahey(3) 90
(Thomas Mullins, Ire) *hld up: 21st 5f out: pushed along and struggling towards rr into st: sme hdwy fnl 2f* 33/1

14 shd **Rooster Byron (IRE)** 4-10-13 0.......... MrMNDoran(5) 90
(Paul Nolan, Ire) *chsd ldrs: rdn and wknd over 3f out* 25/1

15 1 **Rory's Valentine (IRE)**[45] 4776 4-10-6 0.......... MrNMcParlan(5) 82
(J Larkin, Ire) *towards rr: rdn and no imp over 3f out: one pce fnl 2f* 50/1

16 hd **Wingoldandwearit (IRE)** 4-10-13 0.......... MrJJKing(5) 89
(Ms Sandra Hughes, Ire) *in rr of mid-div for most: rdn and no imp over 3f out* 12/1

17 1 3/4 **Zagelle (IRE)** 5-11-9 0.......... MrDRoche(5) 97
(Henry De Bromhead, Ire) *in rr of mid-div for most: rdn and no imp over 3f out* 33/1

18 3 1/2 **Broken Soul (IRE)**[31] 4-11-1 0.......... MrRPQuinlan(3) 83
(P M J Doyle, Ire) *nvr bttr than mid-div: rdn in 12th into st and no ex: wknd fnl 2f* 33/1

19 hd **Twinkletoes (IRE)** 4-10-6 0.......... MissKHarrington(5) 76
(Mrs John Harrington, Ire) *a bhd: no imp 3f out* 20/1

20 3/4 **Bon Enfant (FR)**[27] 5104 4-11-4 0.......... MrSCrawford 82
(Warren Greatrex) *a bhd: no imp 3f out* 9/1[3]

21 23 **Can't Be Done (IRE)**[40] 4880 4-11-4 0.......... MrJPMcKeown 59
(W F Treacy, Ire) *nvr bttr than mid-div: racd keenly: no imp towards rr 3f out: t.o* 66/1

22 dist **Seano (IRE)** 4-10-11 0.......... MrBJFoley(7)
(Raymond Hurley, Ire) *chsd ldrs: 6th 1/2-way: wknd qckly fr over 5f out: completely t.o* 50/1

4m 8.1s (8.70) **Going Correction** -0.075s/f (Good)
WFA 4 from 5yo 5lb **22 Ran SP% 135.4**
Speed ratings: **75,71,71,70,70 69,69,67,67,65 64,64,63,63,63 63,62,60,60,59 48,**
CSF £117.93 CT £1897.54 TOTE £4.40: £2.20, £8.10, £6.40; DF 152.70 Trifecta £2093.30.
Owner Gigginstown House Stud **Bred** Philip Gueret **Trained** Longwood, Co Meath

FOCUS
This is always an informative affair and the rumour mill was doing overtime beforehand. The pace was only modest through the early stages and it paid to race prominently. The winner was much the best.

10a GROWISE CHAMPION NOVICE CHASE (GRADE 1) (17 fncs) 3m 1f
6:40 (6:40) 5-Y-0+ **£44,186** (£13,992; £6,627; £2,209; £1,472)

RPR

1 **Valseur Lido (FR)**[23] 5177 6-11-10 155.......... RWalsh 159
(W P Mullins, Ire) *w.w in 4th: hdwy after 3 out gng wl to chal on outer 2 out: rdn to ld bef last where edgd rt and kpt on wl run-in* 15/2[3]

2 2 1/4 **Wounded Warrior (IRE)**[48] 4703 6-11-10 153.......... PaulTownend 157
(Noel Meade, Ire) *led bef 1st and sn extended advantage: nt fluent 12th: pressed clly after 3 out and jnd next: rdn and hdd bef last: kpt on wl run-in wout matching wnr* 9/1

3 1 1/2 **Apache Stronghold (IRE)**[23] 5177 7-11-10 155.......... PaulCarberry 156
(Noel Meade, Ire) *w.w in rr: tk clsr order bhd ldrs stl in rr after 3 out: wnt 4th 2 out and no imp on wnr fr last where slt mstke: kpt on same pce into 3rd clsng stages: nt trble wnr* 5/1[2]

4 1/2 **Irish Cavalier (IRE)**[18] 5251 6-11-10 145.......... (p) NoelFehily 155
(Rebecca Curtis) *hld up bhd ldrs in 3rd: tk clsr order and wnt 2nd after 3 out: rdn to chal 2 out: no imp on wnr at last disputing 2nd: one pce run-in and dropped to 4th clsng stages* 25/1

5 6 1/2 **Don Poli (IRE)**[48] 4703 6-11-10 163.......... BJCooper 152
(W P Mullins, Ire) *settled bhd ldr in 2nd: nt fluent 12th: niggled along in cl 2nd bef 4 out: slt mstke next: sn rdn in 3rd and no ex in rr fr 2 out: wknd* 4/9[1]

6m 26.8s (-18.20) **Going Correction** -0.375s/f (Good) **5 Ran SP% 111.5**
Speed ratings: **114,113,112,112,110**
CSF £56.96 TOTE £7.00: £2.20, £2.30; DF 40.50 Trifecta £114.50.
Owner Gigginstown House Stud **Bred** M Contignon & Mme N Contignon **Trained** Muine Beag, Co Carlow

FOCUS
A small but select field. We had the RSA winner and the third. We also had the two who got closest to Vautour in the JLT at Cheltenham, while the quintet was completed by the winner of the novices' handicap chase at the Cheltenham Festival. The gallop was generous from the outset but they bunched up on the home turn. The odds-on favourite flopped but the runner-up looks a fair guide.

11a JLT INH FLAT RACE 2m
7:15 (7:15) 4-Y-0 **£5,883** (£1,364; £596; £341)

RPR

1 **Timing'severything (IRE)** 4-11-4 0.......... MissJMMangan(3) 116+
(P Twomey, Ire) *chsd ldrs: 5th 1/2-way: tk clsr order bhd ldrs over 3f out: led into st and rdn clr 2f out: kpt on wl u.p ins fnl f* 33/1

2 2 1/2 **Coeur Joyeux (IRE)**[59] 4506 4-11-7 0.......... MsKWalsh 113+
(Ms Sandra Hughes, Ire) *chsd ldrs: 4th 1/2-way: rdn into 3rd under 3f out and wnt 2nd u.p 2f out: no imp on wnr ins fnl f: kpt on wl* 5/2[1]

3 5 1/2 **Weyburn (IRE)** 4-11-7 0.......... MrSCrawford 108+
(S R B Crawford, Ire) *mid-div: hdwy into 5th 3f out and no imp on ldrs u.p in 4th 1 1/2f out: kpt on u.p into mod 3rd ent fnl f* 33/1

4 3 3/4 **Bobo Mac (IRE)** 4-11-0 0.......... MrRDeegan(7) 104+
(Michael Hourigan, Ire) *in rr of mid-div: rdn in mod 12th 2f out and kpt on wl u.p into mod 4th ins fnl f: nvr trbld ldrs* 50/1

5 1 **Bright Tomorrow (IRE)** 4-11-2 0.......... MissKHarrington(5) 103
(Mrs John Harrington, Ire) *chsd ldrs: 7th 1/2-way: tk clsr order under 4f out: rdn in 6th 3f out and sn no imp on wnr u.p in 4th: one pce ins fnl f where dropped to 5th* 12/1

6 nse **Man Of Conquest (IRE)**[69] 4310 4-11-0 0.......... MrJPDowling(7) 103
(Desmond McDonogh, Ire) *chsd ldrs: 3rd 1/2-way: rdn and lost pl appr st: no imp on ldrs u.p in 7th into st: kpt on one pce fnl 2f* 9/1

7 2 3/4 **Improver (IRE)**[38] 4935 4-11-0 0.......... MrKJBrouder(7) 100+
(J T Gorman, Ire) *hld up in tch: rdn in 9th 3f out and no imp on ldrs: kpt on one pce fnl 2f* 50/1

8 2 3/4 **Moon Over Germany (IRE)**[38] 4935 4-11-4 0.......... MrJTCarroll(3) 97
(Edward P Harty, Ire) *hld up in tch: racd keenly: rdn and short of room on inner appr st: mod 13th under 2f out: kpt on ins fnl f* 33/1

9 2 **Showem Silver (IRE)** 4-11-7 0.......... MsNCarberry 95
(Noel Meade, Ire) *mid-div: 8th 1/2-way: rdn and no ex under 3f out: one pce fnl 2f* 11/1

10 1/2 **Blood Crazed Tiger (IRE)**[16] 4-11-7 0.......... MrPWMullins 95
(P M J Doyle, Ire) *led: narrow advantage 1/2-way: rdn and hdd over 3f out: sn wknd* 5/1[2]

11 1 **Sweet Company (IRE)**[44] 4-11-2 0.......... MissEALalor(5) 94
(Miss Elizabeth Anne Lalor, Ire) *chsd ldr: cl 2nd 1/2-way: led narrowly over 3f out: hdd into st and sn no ex u.p in 3rd: wknd qckly fr over 1f out* 33/1

12 1/2 **Camlann (IRE)**[117] 3447 4-11-2 0.......... MrSClements(5) 93
(John Joseph Hanlon, Ire) *towards rr: sme hdwy fr over 5f out to chse ldrs appr st: rdn in 8th under 3f out and sn no ex: one pce fnl 2f* 12/1

13 1 1/2 **Alex Girl (IRE)**[18] 5270 4-10-7 0.......... MrFMaguire(7) 85
(W McCreery, Ire) *chsd ldrs: 6th 1/2-way: rdn over 3f out and sn no ex u.p: wknd fnl 2f* 20/1

14 1/2 **Our Boy Boru (IRE)**[51] 4664 4-11-0 0.......... MrPPower(7) 91
(J Woods, Ire) *mid-div best: rdn and no imp 3f out* 20/1

15 1 3/4 **Fair Wind** 4-11-2 0.......... MrDGLavery(5) 89
(Conor O'Dwyer, Ire) *towards rr: rdn and no imp 4f out* 33/1

16 1/2 **Burrows Lane (FR)** 4-11-7 0.......... MrJJCodd 89
(Miss Elizabeth Doyle, Ire) *hld up in tch: rdn in 11th over 3f out and sn no ex: wknd into st* 12/1

17 nk **Hogan's Alley (IRE)** 4-11-4 0.......... MrRPQuinlan(3) 89
(M F Morris, Ire) *towards rr: rdn and no imp 3f out* 25/1

18 hd **Our Jerry (IRE)** 4-11-2 0.......... MrJFO'Meara(5) 88
(Miss Evanna McCutcheon, Ire) *a bhd: no imp over 3f out* 66/1

19 7 **Startinfromscratch (IRE)** 4-11-7 0.......... (t) MrKEPower 81
(Jonjo O'Neill) *in rr of mid-div: rdn and wknd over 3f out* 13/2[3]

20 nk **Petite Gold (IRE)** 4-11-0 0.......... MsLO'Neill(7) 81
(Gordon Elliott, Ire) *a towards rr: no imp over 3f out* 20/1

21 nk **Baily Moon (IRE)**[51] 4-11-2 0.......... (t) MrJJKing(5) 81
(M F Morris, Ire) *in rr of mid-div: sme hdwy into 9th 5f out: rdn and wknd 3f out* 33/1

4m 1.7s (2.30) **Going Correction** -0.075s/f (Good) **21 Ran SP% 141.2**
Speed ratings: **91,89,87,85,84 84,83,81,80,80 80,79,79,78,77 77,77,77,73,73 73**
Pick Six @23,333.30. Tote aggregates 2014: @614,752.00; 2015: @590,919.33 CSF £115.74 CT £3027.67 TOTE £49.90: £8.40, £2.00, £13.80; DF 391.40.
Owner P Twomey **Bred** Ms Claire O'Connell **Trained** Cashel, Co Tipperary
■ Stewards' Enquiry : Mr P W Mullins 350 euro fine: passport

FOCUS
No form to go on and interestingly no Willie Mullins representative but plenty of good stables represented and chances are it was a good bumper. It usually is. Viewing of this race was compromised by a power cut.
T/Jkpt: @8,408.60. Pool: @48,049.47. T/Plt: @930.30. Pool: @77,793.83. **Brian Fleming**

CHELTENHAM (L-H)
Wednesday, April 29

OFFICIAL GOING: Good to soft (good in places)
Wind: light breeze Weather: sunny spells

12 JOHN ELLIS MEMORIAL HUNTERS' CHASE (14 fncs) 2m 62y
4:50 (4:52) (Class 5) 5-Y-0+ **£2,183** (£677; £338; £169)

Form RPR

2 1 **Sam Cavallaro (IRE)**[23] 9-11-3 0.......... DavidNoonan(7) 118
(Miss H Brookshaw) *bhd: hdwy 4 out: str run to ld flat* 7/1[3]

3F05 2 3/4 **Delta Borget (FR)**[11] 10-11-5 102.......... (p) MissJBuck(5) 117
(Mrs L J Jefford) *prom: led briefly flat: no ex cl home* 16/1

3-31 3 3 1/2 **Penmore Mill (IRE)**[18] 10-11-13 127.......... MrTEllis(3) 123+
(F A Hutsby) *prom: led 4 out: hit 2 out and last: hdd and no ex flat* 11/10[1]

1PP5 4 6 **Swallows Delight (IRE)**[54] 4609 10-11-13 103.......... MrDMansell 113
(Mrs Julie Mansell) *mstke 8th: cl up tl one pce u.p 2 out* 33/1

1-6 5 1 1/4 **Realt Ag Leimt (IRE)**[12] 5377 9-11-3 0.......... MrDPeters(7) 108
(D Peters) *midfield: no imp fr 2 out* 16/1

43FP 6 1 1/4 **Bay To Go (IRE)**[9] 5433 9-11-6 117.......... MissLWheeler(7) 110
(Mrs H M Kemp) *chsd ldrs: plodded on fr 2 out* 25/1

-110 7 4 **Popaway**[10] 10-11-4 105.......... (t) MrJDocker(5) 103
(Mrs Pauline Harkin) *effrt and mstke 4 out: sn rdn and no imp after* 11/2[2]

2PP/ 8 hd **Getaway Driver (IRE)**[17] 8-11-3 94.......... (bt[1]) MrNLawton(7) 103
(Mrs Janet Ackner) *bhd: blnd 4 out* 66/1

/P-2 9 1/2 **Caulkin (IRE)**[10] 12-11-7 105.......... MrDKemp(3) 102
(David Kemp) *handy tl fdd 4 out* 14/1

P 10 2 1/2 **Canshetrain (IRE)**[18] 8-11-5 0.......... MrBGibbs(5) 100
(J W Tudor) *bhd fr 1/2-way* 66/1

0P/3 11 25 **Loch Ard (IRE)**[34] 4994 7-11-10 0.......... MrWBiddick 93
(Miss S L Gould) *bhd: effrt 4 out: fdd next* 12/1

4-00 12 3 **Noble Ben (IRE)**[10] 13-11-5 89.......... (p) MrJMRidley(5) 75
(J M Ridley) *led tl 9th: fdd after 3 out* 66/1

405P U **Dr Anubis (IRE)**[4] 10-11-3 66.......... MrCGrant(7)
(Miss Hannah Taylor) *prom: led 9th: jst hdd whn blnd and uns rdr 4 out* 200/1

P P **Gather Round**[18] 8-11-5 0.......... (t) MrZBaker(5)
(Mrs K Lawther) *j.rt on outer: sn bhd: t.o and p.u 5 out* 150/1

4m 10.2s (3.50) **Going Correction** +0.20s/f (Yiel) **14 Ran SP% 114.1**
Speed ratings: **99,98,97,94,93 93,91,91,90,89 77,76, ,**
CSF £98.53 TOTE £6.90: £2.20, £4.40, £1.10; EX 132.00 Trifecta £478.90.
Owner Miss H Brookshaw **Bred** Edmond Vaughan **Trained** Whitchurch, Shropshire
■ Stewards' Enquiry : Mr D Mansell two-day ban: used whip above permitted level (May 13-14)

FOCUS
The ground after the opener was described by jockeys as "just on the soft side of good" and "a bit patchy but good ground." As expected, this was run at a solid gallop. The first two and the fifth set the level.

13 CONNOLLY'S RED MILLS PRECISION NUTRITION INTERMEDIATE P-T-P CHAMPIONSHIP FINAL HUNTERS' CHASE (21 fncs) 3m 1f 56y
5:25 (5:27) (Class 4) 5-Y-0+ **£4,367** (£1,354; £676; £338)

Form RPR

2321 1 **Mr Mercurial (IRE)**[12] 5377 7-11-10 117.......... (t) MrPGerety(5) 119+
(Mrs Sheila Crow) *effrt 1/2-way: wnt 2nd 3 out: delayed effrt tl led on bit after 2 out: drvn clr flat* 4/1[1]

0P5/ 2 4 1/2 **Repeat Business (IRE)**[25] 7-11-12 0.......... MrJETudor 109
(J W Tudor) *hdwy 11th: led gng wl 5 out: drvn and hdd after 2 out: no ex* 13/2[3]

233/ 3 1 **Empire Builder (IRE)**[18] 9-11-5 0.......... MrGGreenock(7) 109
(G T H Bailey) *led tl 12th: bmpd along 15th: outpcd 4 out: rallied and styd on gamely flat* 4/1[1]

The Form Book Jumps 2015-16, Raceform Ltd, Newbury, RG14 5SJ

36/1 **4** *6* **Legal Legend**[28] 5096 8-11-8 0........................ MrTAMcclorey(7) 107
(Christopher Henn) *cl up: rdn 3 out: one pce bef last* **9/2**[2]

5 *14* **Goodnight Vienna (IRE)**[38] 9-11-5 0........................ MrJoeHill(7) 90
(Mrs L Redman) *led 12th: hdd 5 out: wknd 2 out* **25/1**

6 *3 1/2* **Raffa**[3] 8-11-9 0........................ MrJFMathias(3) 87
(R Mitford-Slade) *lost tch w ldrs 5 out* **25/1**

7 *3/4* **Impact Area (IRE)**[46] 9-11-5 0........................(p) MrLouisMuspratt(7) 87
(Mrs Harriet Waight) *nt fluent: bhd and nvr gng wl enough* **33/1**

0-P3 **8** *7* **Fine Resolve**[5] 5511 6-11-7 95........................ MrMatthewBarber(5) 80
(Andrew Leyshon) *mstke 12th: struggling after* **28/1**

340- **9** *47* **Minella For Party (IRE)**[25] 8-11-9 0........................(p) MissHannahWatson(3) 38
(Miss V Collins) *struggling 5 out: t.o* **20/1**

2- **P** **Done A Runner (IRE)**[31] 9-11-5 0........................(t) MrDPeters(7)
(Alan Hill) *t.o and p.u 3 out* **12/1**

P **Out Of Range**[18] 8-11-5 0........................ MrPMann(7)
(Mrs Pauline Harkin) *lost tch bef 4 out: t.o and p.u 2 out* **40/1**

P **Remarkable Man (IRE)**[23] 9-11-12 0........................(p) MissGAndrews
(J P Owen) *mstke 12th: prom tl 4 out: t.o and p.u last* **20/1**

P **Carrigkerry (IRE)**[31] 8-11-5 0........................ MissPFuller(7)
(Mrs R Fuller) *mstke 11th: struggling 4 out: t.o and p.u 2 out* **66/1**

0 **P** **Supreme Danehill (IRE)**[15] 5337 7-11-12 0........................(p) MrDEdwards
(Gordon Edwards) *pckd 9th: bhd fr 1/2-way: t.o and p.u 2 out* **40/1**

5420 **P** **Minella Web (IRE)**[15] 5337 6-11-5 0........................(t) MrJLThomas(7)
(Mrs Kayley Woollacott) *in last pair and nvr travelling: t.o and p.u 2 out* **40/1**

P **Come On You (IRE)**[25] 7-11-5 96........................(tp) MrSDavies-Thomas(7)
(N Pearce) *prom tl 5 out: midfield and wl btn whn p.u 2 out* **33/1**

025- **P** **Gonalston Cloud (IRE)**[23] 8-11-5 92........................ MrTRFStrawson(7)
(R J Jackson) *dropped to rr 1/2-way: t.o and p.u in last* **14/1**

6m 41.0s (2.80) **Going Correction** +0.20s/f (Yiel) **17 Ran SP% 121.2**
Speed ratings: **103,101,101,99,95 94,93,91,77, , , , ,**
CSF £25.56 TOTE £4.50: £1.80, £2.40, £2.20; EX 25.90 Trifecta £97.90.
Owner David Rogers **Bred** Patrick Davern **Trained** Shrewsbury, Shropshire

FOCUS
A very competitive event for horses that have been placed in intermediate points this season. Most of these have been in good form between the flags this spring. The cosy winner set a decent standard and ran pretty much to his mark.

14 HUNT STAFF BENEFIT SOCIETY HUNTERS' CHASE (FOR THE UNITED HUNTS CHALLENGE CUP) (21 fncs) 3m 1f 56y
5:55 (5:59) (Class 4) 6-Y-0+ **£3,743** (£1,161; £580; £290)

Form RPR

5-64 **1** **Harbour Court**[40] 4886 9-12-0 122........................(tp) MrJETudor 127+
(Alan Hill) *mde all: drvn and fnd plenty to forge clr flat* **15/8**[2]

-312 **2** *4* **Following Dreams (IRE)**[25] 8-12-0 123........................ MrTWeston 124
(Alastair Ralph) *wnt prom 14th: chal 2 out: rdn and no imp flat* **5/4**[1]

6-0 **3** *6* **Barrick's Hill (IRE)**[31] 10-11-9 0........................ MrZBaker(5) 117
(Mrs Sarah J Bosley) *cl up: ev ch fr 4 out tl no ex bef last* **50/1**

4211 **4** *7* **Tugboat (IRE)**[10] 5409 7-11-9 118........................ MrJNixon(5) 111
(G Slade-Jones) *in rr and nvr really travelling: mstke 12th: effrt 4 out: cl up next: drvn and wknd 2 out* **4/1**[3]

5 *99* **Church Gallery (IRE)**[4] 8-11-7 84........................(v[1]) MrBCatton(7) 11
(S Rea) *blnd 11th: t.o and mstke 16th: eventually completed* **66/1**

65/- **P** **Credit Crunched (IRE)**[25] 10-11-11 96........................ MrTEllis(3)
(Miss L Thomas) *cl up: mstke 18th: sn t.o: p.u 2 out* **25/1**

205/ **U** **Midnight King**[23] 9-11-7 96........................(t) MrPMann(7)
(Mrs J M Mann) *prom tl blnd and uns rdr 10th* **25/1**

6m 48.5s (10.30) **Going Correction** +0.20s/f (Yiel) **7 Ran SP% 110.4**
Speed ratings: **92,90,88,86,56 ,**
CSF £4.44 TOTE £2.70: £1.50, £1.30; EX 6.10 Trifecta £79.00.
Owner Andrew West **Bred** Countess Goess-Saurau & A West **Trained** Aston Rowant, Oxfordshire
■ Stewards' Enquiry : Mr J E Tudor two-day ban: used whip above permitted level (May 13-14)

FOCUS
A decent hunter chase, if lacking strength in depth, and the pace wasn't great. The winner is rated to his best.

15 BONHAMS MEN'S OPEN POINT-TO-POINT CHAMPIONSHIP FINAL HUNTERS' CHASE (22 fncs) 3m 2f 70y
6:30 (6:33) (Class 4) 5-Y-0+ **£4,679** (£1,451; £725; £363)

Form RPR

202U **1** **Quinz (FR)**[20] 5239 11-11-5 123........................ MrJoeHill(7) 127+
(Alan Hill) *cl up: 2nd fr 12th: outj. 4 out and next: rallied to ld 2 out: drvn clr bef last* **5/1**[3]

U-11 **2** *3 3/4* **Moroman (IRE)**[23] 5192 8-12-1 127........................ MrDKemp(3) 128
(David Kemp) *j. sltly rt: led: drvn and hdd 2 out: outpcd flat* **11/4**[1]

120 **3** *4 1/2* **Temple Grandin (IRE)**[47] 4740 8-11-12 114........................ MrAlexEdwards(3) 121
(Philip Rowley) *chsd ldrs: mstke 18th: effrt 4 out: rdn and no real imp after* **6/1**

F-00 **4** *3/4* **Brackloon High (IRE)**[25] 10-11-5 117........................ MrABarlow(7) 116
(M Kehoe) *mstkes: prom tl 14th: lost pl: plugged on again fr 2 out* **20/1**

3-34 **5** *3 1/4* **Hameldown Tor**[3] 11-11-9 114........................(p) MrRGHenderson(3) 113
(E Walker) *bhd: short-lived effrt 4 out* **13/2**

20-1 **6** *15* **Doctor Kingsley**[17] 13-11-8 119........................ MrPMann(7) 102
(Mrs Pauline Harkin) *rn in snatches: drvn and dropped himself to rr 13th: no ch after* **3/1**[2]

/4-5 **7** *7* **Rosies Peacock**[11] 12-11-9 105........................ MrJFMathias(3) 93
(D H Llewellyn) *bhd: lost tch 5 out* **16/1**

14F- **8** *34* **Gotoyourplay (IRE)**[18] 11-11-11 117........................ MrGDisney(7) 68
(Mrs Dawn Woolf) *t.o 4th: sme hdwy 9th: t.o again 16th* **25/1**

2-P6 **P** **Princely Hero (IRE)**[25] 11-11-5 83........................(bt) MrCharlieMarshall(7)
(R Cummings) *v reluctant to set off: t.o tl p.u 13th* **100/1**

4141 **P** **Coombe Hill**[28] 5103 14-12-4 117........................ MrDEdwards
(Chris Honour) *t.o 4 out: p.u 2 out* **20/1**

6m 58.6s (4.80) **Going Correction** +0.20s/f (Yiel) **10 Ran SP% 116.2**
Speed ratings: **100,98,97,97,96 91,89,79, ,**
CSF £18.98 TOTE £5.30: £1.90, £1.70, £2.50; EX 13.70 Trifecta £120.20.
Owner Andrew L Cohen **Bred** Michael Blond **Trained** Aston Rowant, Oxfordshire

FOCUS
The third running of this series final at Cheltenham, and useful hunter chase form. Quinz ran to a similar level to Doncaster.

16 THOROUGHBRED BREEDERS' ASSOCIATION MARES' HUNTERS' CHASE (21 fncs) 3m 1f 56y
7:05 (7:06) (Class 4) 5-Y-0+ **£3,743** (£1,161; £580; £290)

Form RPR

515F **1** **Chosen Milan (IRE)**[20] 5239 8-11-7 123........................(t) MrEDavid(7) 125+
(R E Luke) *trckd ldrs: mstke 9th: led bef 4 out: 4 l clr 2 out: wnt lft and hit last: hung on gamely after: all out* **4/6**[1]

2 *nk* **Roseyroo (IRE)**[17] 8-11-5 0........................ CiaranGethings(3) 118+
(Miss L J Cabble) *bhd: effrt to press wnr 4 out: outpcd 2 out: rallied u.p last: jst hld fnl 100yds* **17/2**[3]

U/41 **3** *28* **Executive Benefit (IRE)**[25] 8-11-8 99........................ MrGCrow(3) 94
(J J O'Shea) *bhd: nt gng wl enough fr 4 out: 3rd and drvn and btn bef 2 out* **4/1**[2]

4F34 **4** *1/2* **Tandori**[15] 5337 13-11-1 82........................ MrDAndrews(7) 92
(Paul Phillips) *led at mod pce: hdd whn mstke 18th: rapidly lost tch* **33/1**

3-54 **F** **My Flora**[46] 11-11-8 114........................ MissHannahWatson(3)
(Miss V Collins) *2nd or 3rd tl fell heavily 16th* **14/1**

P **We Never Give Up (IRE)**[11] 9-11-1 0........................(p) MrTBetambeau(7)
(Mrs Pauline Harkin) *2nd or 3rd tl fdd rapidly 3 out: v tired whn p.u next* **66/1**

P **Miss Gotaway**[25] 6-11-1 0........................ MrJLThomas(7)
(Mrs Kayley Woollacott) *nt jump wl towards rr: dropped bk last 16th: t.o and p.u next* **9/1**

6m 48.0s (9.80) **Going Correction** +0.20s/f (Yiel) **7 Ran SP% 111.6**
Speed ratings: **92,91,83,83, ,**
CSF £7.00 TOTE £1.60: £1.20, £3.00; EX 7.30 Trifecta £22.60.
Owner D H Morgan **Bred** Mrs Ann Jenkins **Trained** Haverfordwest, Pembrokeshire

FOCUS
The first two finished well clear in this decent hunter chase for mares. The form is believable, with the winner 7lb off.

17 CHELTENHAM CLUB OPEN HUNTERS' CHASE (27 fncs) 4m 120y
7:40 (7:43) (Class 4) 5-Y-0+ **£3,743** (£1,161; £580; £290)

Form RPR

51U4 **1** **Major Malarkey (IRE)**[20] 5239 12-11-13 127........................(v) HarryBannister 129+
(Nigel Twiston-Davies) *wl in rr early: prog to midfield 17th: str run 2 out to go 2nd at last: kpt on stoutly u.p to ld cl home* **11/4**[2]

1-20 **2** *3/4* **Alskamatic**[18] 9-11-10 120........................(p) MissCVHart(3) 130+
(Richard J Bandey) *led 5th tl 16th: led again 22nd: drvn and hdd after 2 out: rallied flat: overwhelmed fnl 50yds* **5/2**[1]

3 *1 3/4* **Connies Cross (IRE)**[23] 8-11-5 0........................ MrPGerety(5) 123
(Mrs Sheila Crow) *taken steadily in rr: stdy prog 18th: wnt 2nd 3 out: led after next and looked in command: wknd flat: hdd fnl 50yds* **20/1**

50-5 **4** *38* **Findlay's Find (IRE)**[11] 9-11-10 103........................(p) MrDMansell 92
(Mrs Myfanwy Miles) *prom: mstke 8th: led 16th: hdd 22nd: furiously drvn after 3 out: sn fdd: fin v slowly* **33/1**

014F **5** *4* **Pentiffic (NZ)**[27] 5111 11-11-9 119........................(p[1]) MissLMTurner(7) 91
(P P C Turner) *bhd: t.o 18th: r.o strly up fnl hill whn r was over* **16/1**

0344 **6** *3 3/4* **Gale Force Oscar (IRE)**[10] 5409 10-11-8 96........ MrMatthewBarber(5) 85
(Sally Randell) *trckd ldrs 14th: ev ch 4 out: sn rdn: fdd next: t.o* **50/1**

153 **7** *5* **Bradley Brook (IRE)**[17] 9-11-13 111........................ MrDEdwards 80
(Miss Nicky Martin) *bhd and nvr travelling: mstke 12th: t.o 18th* **8/1**

3P0/ **8** *2* **Bubbly Breeze (IRE)**[38] 10-11-3 78........................ MissAGalliers-Pratt(7) 76
(Alastair Ralph) *led tl 4th: lost pl 7th: t.o 4 out* **66/1**

-412 **U** **Special Portrait (IRE)**[9] 5424 11-11-6 109........................(tp) MrRHogg(7)
(Mark Hughes) *hdwy to midfield whn mstke and uns rdr 12th* **12/1**

66-2 **U** **Charles Bruce (IRE)**[24] 5162 12-11-10 101........................ CharlieDeutsch
(A Campbell) *prom: 3rd and outpcd by ldng pair 17th: losing pl whn blnd and uns rdr 20th* **25/1**

0PP- **P** **Tarquinius (FR)**[23] 12-11-10 100........................(bt) MrMWall
(Miss K Frisby) *mstkes in rr: t.o 14th: p.u and collapsed bef 16th* **66/1**

/3P- **P** **Ben's Folly (IRE)**[25] 10-11-3 98........................(p) MrTommieMO'Brien(7)
(R A Owen) *mstkes: sn in midfield: struggling 17th: t.o and p.u 2 out* **66/1**

03P- **F** **Ace High**[23] 11-11-5 124........................ MrMatthewHampton(5)
(Mrs Janet Ackner) *led 4th tl 5th: 2nd and 8 l clr of rest at 17th: stl 2nd but pressed by chsng bunch whn fell 4 out* **5/1**[3]

3UPF **P** **Jim Job Jones**[41] 4865 11-11-13 84........................ MrJSole(3)
(Wyn Morris) *mstkes: dropped to rr 7th: t.o 15th: p.u 17th* **100/1**

/P-6 **P** **Reliable Richie (IRE)**[17] 9-11-3 0........................ MrSeanHoulihan(7)
(R G Chapman) *chsd ldrs: rdn and outpcd 22nd: t.o and p.u 2 out* **25/1**

8m 49.5s (-0.40) **Going Correction** +0.20s/f (Yiel) **15 Ran SP% 119.4**
Speed ratings: **108,107,107,98,97 96,95,94, , , , , , ,**
CSF £9.38 TOTE £3.90: £1.70, £1.80, £2.70; EX 12.20 Trifecta £68.60.
Owner Baker Dodd & Cooke **Bred** Bill Ronayne **Trained** Naunton, Gloucs
■ Midnight Haze was withdrawn. Price at time of withdrawal 25/1. Rule 4 does not apply.
■ Stewards' Enquiry : Harry Bannister seven-day ban: used whip above permitted level (May 13-15,19,22,24,25)

FOCUS
A terrific finish to this stamina test. The form is rated around the first two.

18 SPORTING ICONS EVENING WITH MCCOY LADIES' OPEN HUNTERS' CHASE (17 fncs) 2m 5f
8:15 (8:17) (Class 5) 5-Y-0+ **£2,183** (£677; £338; £169)

Form RPR

-10U **1** **Current Event (FR)**[20] 5239 8-11-3 135........................ MissBFrost(7) 134+
(Mrs Rose Loxton) *j.w: sn w ldr: led 5th: gng wl after: 5 l clr 2 out: styd on strly: eased flat* **2/1**[1]

U43P **2** *10* **Cottage Oak (IRE)**[17] 12-10-11 112........................ MissADalton(7) 119+
(J J O'Shea) *settled in midfield: effrt 4 out: chsd wnr bef 2 out: no imp: wl hld whn mstke last* **14/1**

3224 **3** *10* **Foundry Square (IRE)**[27] 5111 9-11-10 127........................ MissGAndrews 116
(Steve Flook) *rn in snatches: effrt and mstke 4 out: mstke next and drvn: poor 5th fr 2 out tl passed two faders after last* **9/2**[2]

5221 **4** *4 1/2* **Rockiteer (IRE)**[8] 5453 12-11-7 122........................(p) MissJCWilliams(3) 111
(Henry Daly) *prom: rdn after 4 out: 3rd and struggling bef 2 out* **11/2**[3]

0/4P **5** *1 3/4* **Fort George (IRE)**[11] 12-11-5 120........................(p) MissBHampson(5) 107
(Sally Randell) *prom tl rdn and wknd 3 out: lost poor 4th after last* **7/1**

4F32 **6** *9* **Tinelyra (IRE)**[37] 4968 9-11-4 93........................ MissAEStirling(3) 98
(Fergal O'Brien) *taken down early: led tl 5th: mstke 4 out and sn fdd* **25/1**

460P **7** *hd* **Theophrastus (IRE)**[9] 5433 13-11-1 99........................ MissAGoschen(3) 93
(J D Sole) *a towards rr: t.o 4 out* **100/1**

-3B2 **8** *3 1/4* **Archie Boy (IRE)**[12] 5377 13-11-1 103............................ MissCVHart(3) 90
(R D Potter) *hld up: effrt 1/2-way: rdn and wknd 4 out* **25/1**
9 *29* **Shanks A Bunch**[23] 7-10-13 0................................ MissJodieHughes(5) 64
(Miss A Griffiths) *sn bhd: t.o fr 12th* **80/1**
U-FP **10** *15* **Orang Outan (FR)**[18] 13-10-11 87................. MissEmily-JaneHarbour(7) 51
(Mrs R Hurley) *mstke 3rd: prom early: lost interest in rr 12th: sn t.o* **66/1**
540- **P** **Gauvain (GER)**[23] 13-11-1 0..........................(vt[1]) MissHannahWatson(3)
(Miss V Collins) *reluctant and nvr travelling in rr: t.o 12th: p.u next* **11/2[3]**
5m 24.0s (4.60) **Going Correction** +0.20s/f (Yiel) **11** Ran SP% **112.9**
Speed ratings: **99,95,91,89,89 85,85,84,73,67**
CSF £28.23 TOTE £2.80: £1.30, £4.40, £1.70; EX 46.20 Trifecta £221.60.
Owner Pearl Bloodstock Ltd **Bred** M L Bloodstock Limited **Trained** Bruton, Somerset
FOCUS
An impressive performance from the winner in this decent ladies' event. He was a 140+ horse at his best and may still be capable of matching that.
T/Plt: £4.80 to a £1 stake. Pool of £62136.66 - 9409.56 winning tickets. T/Qpdt: £3.20 to a £1 stake. Pool of £5722.65 - 1284.30 winning tickets. **Iain Mackenzie**

[5]PUNCHESTOWN (R-H)
Wednesday, April 29
OFFICIAL GOING: Good to yielding (yielding in places)

19a MARTINSTOWN OPPORTUNITY SERIES FINAL H'CAP HURDLE (12 hdls) 2m 4f
3:40 (3:42) (95-123,123) 4-Y-0+ **£14,360** (£4,197; £1,988; £662)

RPR
1 **Shamiran (IRE)**[23] 5222 10-11-3 **118**............................(p) AndrewRing(4) 129
(S T Nolan, Ire) *settled bhd ldrs: clsr in 3rd bef 7th: impr on outer and almost on terms 3 out: disp bef last and led narrowly u.p run-in: kpt on wl towards fin* **33/1**
2 *3/4* **Cassells Rock (IRE)**[60] 4502 5-11-8 **121**...................(t) ShaneShortall(2) 131
(A J Martin, Ire) *mid-div: tk clsr order bhd ldrs: bef 7th: impr fr 2 out to chal in 2nd into st: disp bef last: hdd narrowly run-in and kpt on wl towards fin wout matching wnr: jst hld 2nd* **11/1**
3 *shd* **Sir Ector (USA)**[38] 4950 8-11-6 **121**.....................(b) LiamMcKenna(4) 131+
(J J Lambe, Ire) *mid-div: tk clsr order after 2 out and gng wl in 11th into st: rdn and r.o wl fr bef last: nrst fin: jst hld for 2nd* **25/1**
4 *1/2* **Russian Bill (IRE)**[78] 4150 5-11-6 **119**.............................. GerFox(2) 129
(Noel Meade, Ire) *towards rr: tk clsr order after 3 out and impr into 7th appr st: rdn into 3rd fr last and kpt on wl towards fin: nvr trbld ldrs* **14/1**
5 *1 1/4* **Phantom Prince (IRE)**[43] 4843 6-11-4 **119**.................... RyanTreacy(4) 127
(Mrs John Harrington, Ire) *in rr of mid-div: hdwy after 3 out to chse ldrs in 9th appr st: kpt on same pce fr last: nvr trbld ldrs* **33/1**
6 *1 3/4* **Riviera Sun (IRE)**[31] 5050 6-11-10 **121**......................... JodyMcGarvey 128
(Henry De Bromhead, Ire) *hld up in tch: tk clsr order bhd ldrs after 3 out: rdn in 5th into st and sn no imp on ldrs: kpt on same pce md* **10/1[3]**
7 *nse* **Clonbanan Lad (IRE)**[22] 5228 9-11-7 **122**..............(p) DylanRobinson(4) 128
(Henry De Bromhead, Ire) *mid-div: tk clsr order bhd ldrs bef 7th: rdn in 10th appr st and no imp on ldrs bef last: kpt on one pce* **33/1**
8 *4 3/4* **Railway Tommy (IRE)**[34] 5006 7-11-6 **119**...................... ShaneButler(2) 121
(Peter Fahey, Ire) *hld up towards rr: tk clsr order on outer after 3 out: rdn after next and wnt 8th u.p appr st: no imp on ldrs and one pce bef last* **14/1**
9 *1/2* **Eight Till Late (IRE)**[19] 5266 7-11-7 **118**......................... StephenGray 119
(Peter Casey, Ire) *mid-div: hdd bef 4 out and almost on terms fr next: slt mstke 2 out and sn led gng wl: rdn and hdd bef last: sn wknd* **9/1[2]**
10 *hd* **Seskinane (IRE)**[23] 5222 9-11-10 **123**....................... PaddyKennedy(2) 124
(Brian M McMahon, Ire) *in tch: tk clsr order bhd ldrs after 4 out and led narrowly next: hdd 2 out and sn no ex u.p: wknd into st* **22/1**
11 *17* **Tarabiyn (IRE)**[45] 4793 4-10-11 **123**.................................... NiallKelly(4) 96
(W P Mullins, Ire) *hld up towards rr: hmpd 3rd and nt fluent in rr next: no imp and pushed along 3 out: kpt on one pce fr next* **16/1**
12 *3/4* **Pack The Punch (IRE)**[19] 5265 5-11-3 **118**.............(p) DonaghMeyler(4) 101
(Desmond McDonogh, Ire) *mid-div: tk clsr order bhd ldrs in 8th bef 7th: rdn and no ex 3 out: one pce fr next* **20/1**
13 *3 1/2* **Landau (IRE)**[202] 1811 5-11-5 **116**..............................(t) KevinSexton 96
(Gordon Elliott, Ire) *hld up towards rr: sme hdwy after 4 out to chse ldrs appr st: rdn and wknd bef last where slt mstke* **20/1**
14 *4 1/2* **Sea Beat**[22] 5231 5-11-8 **119**.. BenDalton 94
(A L T Moore, Ire) *mid-div: niggled along bef 7th: no imp 3 out* **20/1**
15 *14* **Captain Canada**[90] 3945 8-11-5 **116**................................ DavidSplaine 77
(Terence O'Brien, Ire) *led and disp: narrow advantage fr 4th: pushed along and hdd narrowly 3 out: wknd qckly fr next* **66/1**
16 *1 1/4* **Kylestyle (IRE)**[60] 4502 6-11-9 **120**.................................. DerekFox 80
(F Flood, Ire) *mid-div best: rdn and no imp bef 3 out* **10/1[3]**
17 *1 1/4* **Golden Boot (IRE)**[22] 5230 6-11-0 **115**..................(t) ShaneCrimin(4) 74
(Oliver McKiernan, Ire) *in rr of mid-div: sme hdwy after 4 out: rdn and no ex fr next* **33/1**
18 *30* **Westerners Son (IRE)**[24] 5167 7-11-7 **118**.................... ConorMaxwell 47
(Dermot Anthony McLoughlin, Ire) *sn disp and led narrowly bef 3rd: hdd fr next and remained prom tl wknd bef 7th: completely t.o* **14/1**
19 *10* **Nickname Exit (FR)**[27] 5120 5-11-12 **123**........................... BrianHayes 42
(W P Mullins, Ire) *settled in rr of mid-div: rdn and no imp towards rr bef 3 out: wknd next* **11/1**
20 *20* **Hurricane Ridge (IRE)**[12] 5385 6-11-3 **118**..............(p) AnthonyFox(4) 17
(Mrs John Harrington, Ire) *chsd ldrs: reminders after 1st: cl 2nd after 6th: j. sltly rt at times: rdn after 4 out and wknd next: completely t.o* **33/1**
21 *7* **Ange D'Or Javilex (FR)**[31] 5052 5-11-5 **120**................... AdamO'Neill(4) 12
(J R Barry, Ire) *hld up: pushed along towards rr after 4 out and no imp bef next: wknd: completely t.o* **33/1**
F **Waydownsouth (IRE)**[10] 3470 8-11-2 **115**.............. MatthewBowes(2)
(Patrick J Flynn, Ire) *chsd ldrs: disp 6th whn fell 3rd* **33/1**
F **Egyptian Warrior (IRE)**[31] 5052 6-11-7 **122**..............(b) ConorBrassil(4)
(A P O'Brien, Ire) *chsd ldrs: tk clsr order bhd ldrs after 7th: cl 4th 4 out: rdn and wknd after 2 out: trailing whn fell last* **25/1**
P **Lookslikeainted (IRE)**[17] 5288 8-11-3 **114**..............(bt) KillianMoore
(Sophie Leech) *hld up in tch: 7th 1/2-way: lost pl bef 7th and sn wknd: trailing whn p.u bef 3 out* **28/1**
B **Oscar Knight (IRE)**[22] 5230 6-11-5 **118**......................... DavidMullins(2)
(Thomas Mullins, Ire) *mid-div: hmpd and b.d 3rd* **7/2[1]** 5m 7.8s (1.80) **Going Correction** +0.275s/f (Yiel)
WFA 4 from 5yo+ 6lb **25** Ran SP% **144.8** Speed ratings: **107,106,106,106,105,105,105,103,103,103 96,95,94,92,87 86,86,74,70,62 59, , , ,**
CSF £350.07 CT £9022.70 TOTE £60.80: £10.70, £3.50, £13.00, £3.30; DF 796.40.
Owner John D McNally & Ms Julianne McNally **Bred** His Highness The Aga Khan's Studs Sc **Trained** Ballybrack, Co. Kildare
FOCUS
A fine finish to an ultra-competitive handicap and a fine training performance from Stephen Nolan to get this horse back in good enough shape to win this race for the second time.

20a (Foreign Racing) - See Raceform Interactive

21a IRISH DAILY MIRROR NOVICE HURDLE (GRADE 1) (14 hdls) 3m
4:55 (4:58) 4-Y-0+ **£44,186** (£13,992; £6,627; £2,209; £1,472; £736)

RPR
1 **Killultagh Vic (IRE)**[47] 4741 6-11-10 143........................ PaulTownend 157
(W P Mullins, Ire) *in rr: clsr in 8th fr 1/2-way: wnt 7th bef 3 out and impr into 3rd gng wl appr st: sn disp travelling wl and pushed clr bef last where mstke: rdn and all out towards fin where reduced ld: hld on* **8/1[3]**
2 *1/2* **Thistlecrack**[19] 5254 7-11-10 148.................................. TomScudamore 156+
(Colin Tizzard) *hld up in tch: 5th 1/2-way: 6th bef 5 out where slt mstke: clsr in 4th appr st: short of room on inner bef last: rdn in 2nd fr last and kpt on wl towards fin to strly press wnr: hld* **8/1[3]**
3 *8 1/2* **Shaneshill (IRE)**[24] 5176 6-11-10 154.................................... RWalsh 150
(W P Mullins, Ire) *w.w towards rr: slt mstke 5th: clsr in 7th at 1/2-way: hdwy in 6th gng wl bef 3 out into 2nd appr st: sn disp tl hdd u.p bef last: no ex and one pce in 3rd run-in* **11/8[1]**
4 *7* **Sub Lieutenant (IRE)**[18] 5271 6-11-10 139.....................(p) JJBurke 141
(Ms Sandra Hughes, Ire) *chsd ldrs: nt fluent 4th: 6th 1/2-way: cl 3rd bef 5 out and on terms fr 3 out: led after 2 out tl hdd u.p into st: wknd* **25/1**
5 *9* **No More Heroes (IRE)**[47] 4738 6-11-10 147.......................... BJCooper 134
(Gordon Elliott, Ire) *chsd ldrs: 4th 1/2-way: 5th bef 5 out: rdn and no ex after 2 out: kpt on one pce* **5/2[2]**
6 *34* **Roi Des Francs (FR)**[19] 5254 6-11-10 143...................... DannyMullins 98
(W P Mullins, Ire) *chsd ldrs: 3rd 1/2-way: 4th bef 5 out: led narrowly after next: jnd fr 3 out and hdd after next: sn wknd and eased: t.o* **20/1**
7 *36* **High Stratos**[45] 4802 6-11-10 125...................................... RobbiePower 62
(Mrs John Harrington, Ire) *chsd ldrs early: slt mstke 4th: nt fluent towards rr at 6th and 8th: wknd 3 out: completely t.o* **33/1**
8 *19* **Arctic Skipper (IRE)**[66] 4392 6-11-10 120.............................. AELynch 43
(Vincent Laurence Halley, Ire) *w.w towards rr: dropped to rr fr 1/2-way: rdn in rr after 4 out: wknd: completely t.o* **66/1**
9 *nk* **Binge Drinker (IRE)**[39] 4898 6-11-10 145......................... PaulCarberry 42
(Rebecca Curtis) *led tl jnd and hdd after 5th: cl 2nd 1/2-way: regained advantage after 8th hdd after 4 out: rdn and no ex next where nt fluent: wknd and eased: completely t.o* **20/1**
P **Fletchers Flyer (IRE)**[74] 4226 7-11-10 143........................(t) NoelFehily
(Harry Fry) *chsd ldr in 2nd tl led narrowly after 5th: hdd after 8th: rdn and wknd bef 3 out: trailing whn p.u bef last* **10/1**
6m 8.8s (1.80) **Going Correction** +0.275s/f (Yiel) **10** Ran SP% **119.8**
Speed ratings: **108,107,105,102,99 88,76,70,69,**
CSF £64.50 CT £142.10 TOTE £10.90: £2.60, £2.30, £1.02; DF 72.20 Trifecta £266.60.
Owner Mrs R Boyd, Mrs M J Armstrong & J B Anderson **Bred** F Boyd **Trained** Muine Beag, Co Carlow
FOCUS
A very high-class novice hurdle for the end of the season with not too many heavy hitters missing, won by a horse improving at the right time of the year and just about seeing out the trip. The second and fourth set the standard to their Aintree figures.

22a BIBBY FINANCIAL SERVICES IRELAND PUNCHESTOWN GOLD CUP (GRADE 1) (17 fncs) 3m 1f
5:30 (5:37) 5-Y-0+ **£93,023** (£29,457; £13,953; £4,651; £3,100)

RPR
1 **Don Cossack (GER)**[19] 5252 8-11-10 171.....................(t) PaulCarberry 181+
(Gordon Elliott, Ire) *hld up in tch: nt fluent and short of room towards rr at 11th: clsr in 6th after 5 out: rdn in 3rd after 3 out and clsd u.p to chal next: sn led narrowly and styd on strly to go clr fr last* **5/2[2]**
2 *7* **Djakadam (FR)**[47] 4739 6-11-10 168.. RWalsh 174
(W P Mullins, Ire) *chsd ldrs: racd keenly: clsr in 2nd bef 6th and led next: j.lft 8th and sn hdd: almost on terms 3 out and led narrowly bef next: hdd narrowly after 2 out where pckd sltly: no imp on wnr fr last* **2/1[1]**
3 *6 1/2* **Road To Riches (IRE)**[47] 4739 8-11-10 166.......................... BJCooper 168
(Noel Meade, Ire) *led: hdd narrowly 7th tl regained advantage after next: strly pressed fr 3 out and hdd bef next: no imp on ldrs u.p in 3rd bef last: kpt on same pce* **4/1[3]**
4 *2* **Cue Card**[19] 5252 9-11-10 160......................................(tp) AidanColeman 165
(Colin Tizzard) *chsd ldrs: slt mstke 12th: wnt 4th after 3 out: pushed along appr st and sn no imp on ldrs u.p: kpt on one pce* **12/1**
5 *24* **Boston Bob (IRE)**[47] 4739 10-11-10 157.................................. DJCasey 141
(W P Mullins, Ire) *hld up in rr: last 1/2-way: sltly hmpd 4 out: pushed along detached in rr bef next and no imp in mod 6th into st: lft mod 5th 2 out* **16/1**
F **The Giant Bolster**[47] 4739 10-11-10 156........................(b[1]) TomCannon
(David Bridgwater) *settled bhd ldr: 3rd bef 6th: cl 2nd at 11th where nt fluent: pushed along after 5 out and sn no imp on ldrs u.p in 5th after 3 out: no imp in mod 6th whn fell heavily 2 out* **33/1**
P **On His Own (IRE)**[24] 5170 11-11-10 164......................(p) PaulTownend
(W P Mullins, Ire) *settled bhd ldr tl dropped to 5th fr 6th: niggled along briefly bef 8th and tk clsr order bhd ldrs: cl 3rd after 5 out: rdn and wknd bef 3 out where mstke: lft mod 6th 2 out where slow: p.u bef last* **14/1**
F **Ballynagour (IRE)**[20] 5237 9-11-10 160.......................(t) TomScudamore
(David Pipe) *hld up towards rr: tk clsr order bhd ldrs after 5 out: stl gng wl in cl 5th whn fell 4 out* **9/1**
6m 22.1s (-22.90) **Going Correction** -0.475s/f (Good) **8** Ran SP% **115.1**
Speed ratings: **117,114,112,112,104 , ,**
CSF £8.41 CT £18.24 TOTE £3.10: £1.30, £1.20, £1.50; DF 8.70 Trifecta £21.50.
Owner Gigginstown House Stud **Bred** Gestut Etzean **Trained** Longwood, Co Meath

FOCUS
What a race. No disappointing performances, no excuses, potentially a race just as informative for next year's Betfred Cheltenham Gold Cup as Coneygree's performance in March. Don Cossack confirmed his status as the best chaser around.

23a ATTHERACES.COM CHAMPION INH FLAT RACE (GRADE 1) 2m
6:05 (6:11) 4-7-Y-0
£44,186 (£13,992; £6,627; £2,209; £1,472; £736)

RPR

1 **Bellshill (IRE)**[19] 5255 5-12-0 0 .... MrPWMullins 140+
(W P Mullins, Ire) *chsd ldrs early: 7th 1/2-way: gd hdwy bhd ldrs into 2nd gng wl under 4f out: led into st and rdn clr 2f out: kpt on wl ins fnl f* **8/1**

2 *3 1/4* **Disko (FR)**[70] 4310 4-11-4 0 .... MsNCarberry 127
(Noel Meade, Ire) *w.w towards rr: impr on outer 5f out: impr to chse ldrs in 3rd under 4f out: rdn in 5th into st and no imp on wnr in 3rd over 1f out: swtchd and kpt on same pce into 2nd cl home: nt trble wnr* **7/2**[1]

3 *3/4* **Modus**[49] 4708 5-12-0 0 .... MrDerekO'Connor 136
(Robert Stephens) *hld up towards rr: hdwy over 4f out gng wl to chse ldrs in 4th: rdn in 2nd and no imp on wnr under 2f out: kpt on same pce ins fnl f and dropped to 3rd cl home* **5/1**[2]

4 *2* **Charbel (IRE)**[31] 5056 4-11-4 0 .... MrKEPower 124
(Thomas Mullins, Ire) *hld up: hdwy in 10th over 3f out to chse ldrs 2f out: rdn in 4th over 1f out and kpt on same pce: nvr trbld ldrs* **7/1**

5 *shd* **Pylonthepressure (IRE)**[81] 4106 5-12-0 0 .... MissJMMangan 134
(W P Mullins, Ire) *chsd ldrs: 3rd 1/2-way: wnt 2nd after 1/2-way: rdn almost on terms over 3f out: dropped to 5th u.p into st and no imp on wnr after: kpt on same pce ins fnl f* **13/2**[3]

6 *2* **Altior (IRE)**[81] 4086 5-12-0 0 .... MissKHarrington 132
(Nicky Henderson) *settled in mid-div under dropped towards rr 1/2-way: hdwy in 12th 4f out: rdn into 6th appr st and no imp on ldrs: kpt on same pce* **14/1**

7 *13* **Bay Of Freedom (IRE)**[49] 4708 6-12-0 0 .... MrMFahey 119
(Peter Fahey, Ire) *chsd ldrs: 5th 1/2-way: pushed along in 4th under 4f out and sn wknd u.p* **50/1**

8 *2* **Livelovelaugh (IRE)**[23] 5227 5-12-0 0 .... MsKWalsh 117
(W P Mullins, Ire) *led: 1 l clr at 1/2-way: pressed clly over 3f out and hdd into st: wknd fnl 2f* **16/1**

9 *3 1/4* **Supasundae**[49] 4708 5-12-0 0 .... MrJJCodd 114
(Henry De Bromhead, Ire) *chsd ldrs: racd keenly: 6th 1/2-way: impr into 5th 5f out: rdn and no ex 3f out: sn wknd* **5/1**[2]

10 *4 3/4* **Au Quart De Tour (FR)**[23] 5227 5-12-0 0 .... MrSGCarey 109
(W P Mullins, Ire) *hld up towards rr: rdn over 4f out and sn no ex* **33/1**

11 *14* **Bordini (FR)**[49] 4708 5-12-0 0 .... MrDGLavery 95
(W P Mullins, Ire) *chsd ldrs: 4th 1/2-way: pushed along over 4f out and sn no ex u.p in 8th: wknd* **14/1**

12 *3 1/2* **Wade Harper (IRE)**[23] 5207 5-12-0 0 .... MrSClements 92
(David Dennis) *trckd ldrs: 2nd 1/2-way: dropped to 3rd after 1/2-way: rdn and wknd 4f out* **66/1**

13 *3/4* **Montana Belle (IRE)**[49] 4708 5-11-7 0 ....(t) MrSCrawford 84
(S R B Crawford, Ire) *hld up: rdn towards rr and no imp 4f out: wknd: scoped abnormally post r* **25/1**

4m 3.6s (4.20) **Going Correction** +0.275s/f (Yiel)
WFA 4 from 5yo+ 5lb **13 Ran SP% 122.0**
Speed ratings: **100,98,98,97,96 95,89,88,86,84 77,75,75**
CSF £36.02 CT £160.40 TOTE £10.00: £2.80, £1.70, £2.20; DF 48.60 Trifecta £400.10.
Owner Andrea & Graham Wylie **Bred** Frank Motherway **Trained** Muine Beag, Co Carlow

FOCUS
There was no Moon Racer but we did have the second, sixth, eighth, 13th, 15th and Bordini (pulled-up) from the Champion Bumper at Cheltenham as well as a pair of unbeaten and exciting four-year-olds. Plenty wanted to lead early but the gallop became sensible after a furlong or two. The result confused us more about this season's bumper crop. Bellshill has stepped forward with every start.

24a GUINNESS H'CAP CHASE (GRADE A) (14 fncs) 2m 4f
6:40 (6:41) 5-Y-0+
£46,511 (£14,728; £6,976; £2,325; £1,550; £775)

RPR

1 **Ballyadam Approach (IRE)**[24] 5178 10-9-7 **123** oh2.... DavidSplaine(3) 141+
(Terence O'Brien, Ire) *disp early: settled in 2nd fr 2nd: pressed ldr clly after 3 out and disp next: sn led and rdn clr bef last: styd on wl* **12/1**

2 *7 1/2* **Baby Mix (FR)**[20] 5240 7-10-6 **133** .... GavinSheehan 143
(Warren Greatrex) *disp early tl led fr 2nd: pressed clly after 3 out and jnd next: sn hdd and no imp on wnr u.p bef last: kpt on same pce* **9/1**[2]

3 *7* **Strongpoint (IRE)**[11] 5391 11-10-3 **130** .... PeterBuchanan 133+
(S R B Crawford, Ire) *mid-div: j. sltly rt at times: 8th bef 4 out: impr into 4th after next: no imp on ldrs in 3rd fr after 2 out: kpt on one pce* **14/1**

4 *3 3/4* **Turban (FR)**[19] 5253 8-11-10 **151** .... RWalsh 150+
(W P Mullins, Ire) *hld up towards rr: tk clsr order in 10th bef 4 out: impr into 7th after next and wnt 4th u.p fr 2 out: no imp on ldrs bef last: kpt on one pce* **12/1**

5 *1/2* **Foildubh (IRE)**[43] 4837 11-11-3 **144** .... PaulCarberry 143+
(John Patrick Ryan, Ire) *hld up towards rr: hdwy in 12th after 3 out: j. sltly rt 2 out and no imp on ldrs: rdn into mod 5th bef last and kpt on one pce: nvr trbld ldrs* **20/1**

6 *8* **Rathlin**[19] 5253 10-10-13 **145** ....(t) GerFox(5) 136+
(M F Morris, Ire) *chsd ldrs: mstke in 3rd at 9th: rdn after 3 out and no imp on ldrs bef next: kpt on one pce* **12/1**

7 *4 1/2* **Rubi Light (FR)**[18] 5275 10-11-7 **148** ....(t) AELynch 134+
(Robert Alan Hennessy, Ire) *hld up: rdn in 10th after 3 out and no imp on ldrs bef next: kpt on one pce* **16/1**

8 *3* **Bright New Dawn (IRE)**[32] 5040 8-11-9 **150** ....(p) BJCooper 133+
(Ms Sandra Hughes, Ire) *mid-div: clsr in 5th bef 4 out: rdn in 6th and no ex after next: kpt on one pce* **11/1**[3]

9 *2 3/4* **Ericht (IRE)**[48] 4721 9-10-2 **129** .... NicodeBoinville 110+
(Nicky Henderson) *chsd ldrs: cl 4th bef 4 out: rdn and no ex after next: wknd bef 2 out* **12/1**

10 *3 3/4* **You Must Know Me (IRE)**[27] 5123 9-10-9 **136** ....(p) JJBurke 113+
(Henry De Bromhead, Ire) *mid-div: clsr in 6th bef 4 out: rdn and no ex bef 2 out where nt fluent: wknd* **11/1**[3]

11 *3/4* **Klepht (IRE)**[48] 4720 10-10-9 **136** ....(t) MPFogarty 112+
(Thomas Mullins, Ire) *hld up towards rr: rdn and no imp after 3 out* **16/1**

12 *12* **Art Of Logistics (IRE)**[19] 5253 7-11-0 **141** ....(p) RogerLoughran 105+
(Ms Sandra Hughes, Ire) *settled bhd ldrs: nt fluent 4th: pushed along in 7th bef 4 out and no ex u.p fr next: wknd* **12/1**

P **Orpheus Valley (IRE)**[43] 4845 12-10-0 **127** ....(t) APHeskin
(Thomas Gibney, Ire) *chsd ldrs early: 6th bef 1/2-way: no imp towards rr bef 4 out and p.u bef next* **14/1**

P **Simply Wings (IRE)**[60] 4496 11-10-2 **129** .... MarkEnright
(Richard Lee) *mid-div: slt mstke 3rd: 9th bef 4 out: rdn and no imp fr next: p.u bef 2 out* **25/1**

P **Forty Foot Tom**[53] 4640 10-9-10 **123** oh2........................ NiallPMadden
(Daniel Miley, Ire) *nvr bttr than mid-div: mstke 8th and lost pl: dropped towards rr after 5 out and p.u bef next* **40/1**

P **Pass The Hat**[23] 5224 8-10-12 **139** ....(t) DJCasey
(A L T Moore, Ire) *nvr bttr than mid-div: slt mstke 4th: no imp towards rr bef 4 out: p.u bef next* **20/1**

P **King Vuvuzela (IRE)**[124] 3294 8-9-6 **124** .... LPDempsey(5)
(Paul Nolan, Ire) *nvr bttr than mid-div: no imp towards rr 4 out: p.u bef next* **11/1**[3]

P **Gold Bullet (IRE)**[27] 5123 7-10-13 **140** .... PaulTownend
(T J Taaffe, Ire) *mid-div: dropped towards rr 8th: pushed along bef next and sme hdwy on inner: no imp fr 3 out and trailing whn p.u bef next: sustained injury to rt pastern* **9/2**[1]

5m 12.4s (-11.60) **Going Correction** -0.475s/f (Good) **18 Ran SP% 132.6**
Speed ratings: **104,101,98,96,96 93,91,90,89,87 87,82,, , ,**
CSF £120.06 CT £1578.07 TOTE £12.40: £3.50, £2.00, £4.10, £3.20; DF 184.40 Trifecta £3322.50.
Owner William Horgan **Bred** N J Connors **Trained** Carrigtoohill, Co. Cork.

FOCUS
Deeply competitive, with the last three winners of the race in it, though there were some notable disappointments. A big personal best from the winner.

25a OLD HOUSE, KILL INH FLAT RACE 2m 2f
7:15 (7:17) 5-7-Y-0
£5,883 (£1,364; £596; £341)

RPR

1 **Champers On Ice (IRE)**[52] 5-12-0 0 .... MrJJCodd 123
(David Pipe) *dismntd bef s: cl up and disp briefly after 2f: cl 3rd 1/2-way: almost on terms 5f out and led over 3f out: strly pressed and jnd over 1f out: sn hdd narrowly tl rallied clsng stages to ld fnl strides: all out* **9/4**[1]

2 *hd* **First Figaro (GER)**[124] 3296 5-11-7 0 .... MrFMaguire(7) 123+
(D K Weld, Ire) *hld up in tch: 7th 5f out: gd hdwy on outer 4f out into 2nd under 3f out: sn disp and rdn to ld narrowly ins fnl f: all out clsng stages and hdd fnl strides* **7/2**[3]

3 *28* **Articulum (IRE)**[38] 5-11-7 0 .... MrPDCollins(7) 95
(Terence O'Brien, Ire) *mid-div: 7th 1/2-way: tk clsr order after 5f out: n.m.r between horses briefly appr st: rdn into mod 3rd over 1f out and no imp on clr ldrs: kpt on one pce* **7/1**

4 *hd* **Arkwrisht (FR)**[73] 4263 5-12-0 0 .... MrPWMullins 95
(W P Mullins, Ire) *hld up in tch: clsr in 5th at 1/2-way: rdn 3f out and sn no imp on clr ldrs: kpt on one pce in mod 4th ins fnl f* **3/1**[2]

5 *1/2* **Rocklander (IRE)** 6-11-9 0 .... MrSClements(5) 94
(Eoin Griffin, Ire) *mid-div and racd keenly early: 9th 5f out: rdn and no imp in mod 7th appr st: kpt on u.p ins fnl f into mod 5th* **20/1**

6 *6 1/2* **Raise A Tail (IRE)**[136] 5-11-9 0 .... MissKHarrington(5) 88
(Mrs John Harrington, Ire) *trckd ldrs: cl 2nd 1/2-way: disp 5f out: rdn under 4f out and no ex u.p in 4th appr st: wknd fnl 2f* **10/1**

7 *3 3/4* **Edwulf**[144] 6-12-0 0 .... MrDerekO'Connor 84
(Ben Pauling) *led tl jnd briefly after 2f: narrow advantage 1/2-way: jnd 5f out and hdd over 3f out: rdn and no imp in 3rd into st: wknd fnl 2f* **16/1**

8 *21* **Samiesosa (IRE)** 6-12-0 0 .... MrKEPower 63
(G A Kingston, Ire) *towards rr: clsr in 11th over 4f out: sn rdn and no imp on ldrs: one pce fnl 2f* **50/1**

9 *10* **Vertical Venture (IRE)**[17] 5-11-9 0 .... MrDGLavery(5) 53
(Conor O'Dwyer, Ire) *hld up: cl 8th 5f out: rdn and no ex 3f out: sn wknd* **66/1**

10 *32* **Llancillo Lord (IRE)**[22] 5234 5-11-7 0 .... MrRADevine(7) 21
(Thomas Mullins, Ire) *towards rr: sme hdwy over 5f out: rdn and no ex over 3f out: wknd: t.o* **20/1**

11 *9 1/2* **Railway Pearl (IRE)** 5-11-7 0 .... MrSCrawford 5
(Peter Fahey, Ire) *a bhd: rdn and no imp 4f out: t.o* **40/1**

12 *19* **Southerner (IRE)**[24] 5172 5-11-7 .... MrWTCronin(7)
(William Cronin, Ire) *chsd ldrs: 4th 1/2-way: rdn and wknd 4f out: t.o* **66/1**

13 *64* **Rosetub (IRE)**[289] 967 7-11-7 0 ....(p) MsKWalsh
(T J Corcoran, Ire) *chsd ldrs early: rdn in 10th over 5f out and no imp: sn wknd and eased: completely t.o* **20/1**

14 *1/2* **Lord De Beaufai (FR)**[7] 5488 7-12-0 0 .... MrJPMcKeown
(Georgios Pakidis, Ire) *hld up in tch: pushed along in 14th over 5f out and no ex: wknd and eased: completely t.o* **66/1**

15 *30* **Mugs Money (IRE)** 7-11-7 0 .... MrBJFoley(7)
(Garrett James Power, Ire) *chsd ldrs early: reminders towards rr bef 1/2-way: no imp after: wknd and eased fr 4f out: completely t.o* **33/1**

4m 37.3s (6.90) **Going Correction** +0.275s/f (Yiel) **15 Ran SP% 131.6**
Speed ratings: **95,94,82,82,82 79,77,68,63,49 45,36,8,8,**
Pick Six: Not Won. Pool of 1,873.50 carried forward to Punchestown on Thursday 30th April. Tote Aggregates: 2014: 809,784.00, 2015: 920,739.00 CSF £10.09 CT £52.31 TOTE £3.00: £1.50, £2.00, £2.50; DF 10.90 Trifecta £94.70.
Owner Professor Caroline Tisdall & Bryan Drew **Bred** Mrs Gail C List **Trained** Nicholashayne, Devon
■ Stewards' Enquiry : Mr J J Codd two-day ban: used whip with excessive frequency without giving gelding time to respond (tbn)

FOCUS
A really good scrap between two good horses in all likelihood as they pulled well clear.
T/Jkpt: @17,500.00. Pool of @25,000.00 - 1 winning units. T/Plt: @139.20.Pool of @102,554.62 - 515.36 winning units. **Brian Fleming**

NEWTON ABBOT (L-H)
Thursday, April 30

OFFICIAL GOING: Good to firm (good in places; 7.3)
Wind: almost nil Weather: sunny Rails: All moved out by 2 meters

26 NEWTONABBOTRACE ON TWITTER MAIDEN HURDLE (9 hdls) 2m 2f 110y
4:45 (4:45) (Class 4) 4-Y-0+
£3,328 (£1,033; £556)

Form RPR

F 1 **Take A Break (FR)**[72] 4286 4-10-8 0 .... TomScudamore 108
(Nigel Hawke) *trckd ldr: disp ld appr 2 out: rdn between last 2: led sn after last: r.o* **11/4**[2]

4523 **2** ¾ **Blandfords Gunner**[28] 5106 6-11-0 121 .... AdamWedge 114+
(Evan Williams) *led: pushed along whn jnd appr 2 out where nt fluent: mstke last: sn hdd: no ex* **4/11**[1]

0U **3** 67 **Astre Rose (FR)**[10] 5434 5-10-7 0 .... (tp) MrMatthewHampton(7) 53
(Victor Dartnall) *racd keenly: trckd ldng pair tl wknd appr 3 out: t.o whn wnt lft last 2* **16/1**[3]

5600 **P** **Pass On The Mantle**[25] 5155 7-11-0 0 .... MarkGrant
(Julian Smith) *trckd ldng trio: wnt 3rd whn hung bdly rt then veered lft 3 out: hung off crse and p.u sn after* **33/1**

4m 27.4s (-2.60) **Going Correction** -0.325s/f (Good)
WFA 4 from 5yo+ 5lb **4 Ran SP% 108.8**
Speed ratings (Par 105): **92,91,63,**
CSF £4.41 TOTE £3.40; EX 4.50 Trifecta £6.90.
Owner Pearce Bros Partnership **Bred** S C E A Des Prairies **Trained** Stoodleigh, Devon

FOCUS
All rail moved out 2metres. Something of a turn-up in this minor maiden hurdle, with the red-hot favourite defeated. The form is rated through the second.

27 SIS VIRTUAL MOBILE GAMES BEGINNERS' CHASE (16 fncs) 2m 4f 216y
5:15 (5:15) (Class 4) 5-Y-0+ **£4,328** (£1,574)

Form RPR

12F0 **1** **Vicente (FR)**[75] 4225 6-11-0 0 .... SamTwiston-Davies 136+
(Paul Nicholls) *mde all: nt fluent 7th: qcknd up and drew wl clr fr 8th: j.w and in n.d after: eased to a walk run-in* **1/5**[1]

-P53 **2** 51 **Veauce De Sivola (FR)**[13] 5368 6-11-0 112 .... (t) TomCannon 82
(Mark Gillard) *chsd wnr most of way: lost tch w wnr after 8th: continued to dispute modest 2nd fr next: clr 2nd 2 out: t.o* **14/1**[3]

P **Alefou D'Airy (FR)**[124] 5-11-0 121 .... JamesDavies
(Jimmy Frost) *chsd ldrs: nudged along fr 8th: lost tch w wnr but pressed for modest 2nd fr next: wknd after 4 out: t.o whn p.u after next* **11/2**[2]

0P00 **U** **Call Me Win (IRE)**[25] 5151 6-10-7 0 .... MrGTreacy(7) 77
(Paul Henderson) *chsd wnr most of way: lost tch w wnr after 8th: continued to dispute modest 2nd fr next tl wknd 2 out: nt fluent whn unseating rdr last* **66/1**

5m 17.5s (-3.90) **Going Correction** -0.325s/f (Good) **4 Ran SP% 106.9**
Speed ratings: **94,75, ,**
CSF £3.64 TOTE £1.50; EX 3.70 Trifecta £4.10.
Owner John Hales & Ian Fogg **Bred** Thierry Cypres & Jean-Francois Naudin **Trained** Ditcheat, Somerset

FOCUS
As expected this was a stroll in the park for the favourite. The time compares unfavourably with the later handicap.

28 ROYAL BRITISH LEGION, NEWTON ABBOT MARES' NOVICES' HURDLE (10 hdls) 2m 5f 122y
5:50 (5:51) (Class 4) 4-Y-0+ **£3,898** (£1,144; £572; £286)

Form RPR

0403 **1** **Miss Serious (IRE)**[29] 5098 5-10-12 0 .... NickScholfield 114+
(Jeremy Scott) *mde all: styd on wl fr 2 out: pushed out* **7/4**[2]

2P3 **2** 6 **Chantara Rose**[49] 4729 6-10-9 0 .... SeanBowen(3) 108+
(Peter Bowen) *racd keenly: trckd ldrs: squeezed up on bnd bef 7th: trckd wnr after 3 out: rdn whn rdr briefly lost reins after 2 out: styd on same pce* **6/5**[1]

6 **3** 17 **Rosie Revenue**[45] 4812 5-10-12 0 .... (t) RichardJohnson 93
(Philip Hobbs) *in tch: struggling to hold pl fr 4th: rdn in last after 6th: plugged on into hld 3rd bef 2 out: nvr gng pce to get involved* **10/1**[3]

6064 **4** 4½ **Burgundy Betty (IRE)**[10] 5430 5-10-12 0 .... DavidBass 87
(Ben Pauling) *hld up in tch: hdwy to dispute 4th 7th: rdn after 3 out: wknd next* **16/1**

FF02 **5** 7 **Element Quartet (IRE)**[11] 5415 6-10-12 0 .... TomCannon 83
(Brendan Powell) *trckd wnr tl rdn after 3 out: wknd bef next* **25/1**

/06- **6** 27 **Chambray Dancer (IRE)**[527] 2579 7-10-12 0 .... SamTwiston-Davies 56
(Simon Hodgson) *hld up in tch: hdwy to dispute 4th 7th: rdn after 3 out: sn wknd: t.o* **16/1**

06 **P** **Stage Twenty (IRE)**[24] 5181 5-10-12 0 .... BrendanPowell
(Jamie Snowden) *trckd ldrs: struggling 6th: wknd bef next: t.o whn p.u after 3 out* **25/1**

5m 16.5s (-3.70) **Going Correction** -0.325s/f (Good) **7 Ran SP% 110.4**
Speed ratings (Par 105): **93,90,84,83,80 70,**
CSF £4.03 TOTE £2.40: £1.10, £1.70; EX 5.00 Trifecta £12.00.
Owner Pillhead House Partners **Bred** Sean Galwey **Trained** Brompton Regis, Somerset

FOCUS
The market leaders predictably dominated this mares' hurdle. The winner built on a good Wincanton run.

29 NEWTONABBOTRACING.COM H'CAP CHASE (20 fncs) 3m 1f 170y
6:25 (6:25) (Class 3) (0-135,125) 5-Y-0+ **£6,498** (£1,908; £954; £477)

Form RPR

16P0 **1** **Chill Factor (IRE)**[71] 4294 6-11-9 122 .... (t) AidanColeman 138+
(Anthony Honeyball) *travelled best: trckd ldr fr 8th: led after 3 out: rdn clr: comf* **6/1**

4342 **2** 12 **Sin Bin (IRE)**[19] 5282 9-11-6 119 .... (tp) SamTwiston-Davies 126+
(Paul Nicholls) *j.rt: led: reminder after 13th: rdn after 4 out: hdd after next: sn hld by wnr: hit last: jst hld on for 2nd* **11/4**[2]

2631 **3** nk **Thomas Wild**[16] 5334 10-11-9 122 .... RichardJohnson 128
(Philip Hobbs) *trckd ldr tl 8th: sn nudged along in cl 3rd: hit 13th: cl enough whn rdn after 4 out: hld fr after next: styd on fr last* **3/1**[3]

2322 **4** ½ **Velator**[15] 5340 8-11-9 125 .... (p) SeanBowen(3) 131
(Peter Bowen) *trckd ldrs: nudged along fr 8th: cl enough whn rdn after 4 out: hld fr next: styd on fr last* **11/8**[1]

6m 30.6s (-14.00) **Going Correction** -0.325s/f (Good) **4 Ran SP% 108.1**
Speed ratings: **107,103,103,103**
CSF £21.03 TOTE £4.80; EX 22.00 Trifecta £52.30.
Owner Potwell Partners **Bred** Lorcan Allen **Trained** Mosterton, Dorset

FOCUS
A fair chase that was taken apart by the outsider of the field. The form makes sense.

30 FRED CHAMPION GROUNDWORKS LTD H'CAP HURDLE (10 hdls) 2m 5f 122y
7:00 (7:04) (Class 5) (0-100,100) 4-Y-0+ **£3,422** (£997; £499)

Form RPR

0005 **1** **Dubh Eile (IRE)**[45] 4810 7-11-5 93 .... RichardJohnson 105+
(Tim Vaughan) *mid-div: hdwy after 3 out: pushed along whn nt clr run turning in: led 2 out: r.o strly fr last: rdn out* **9/4**[1]

5005 **2** 5 **Handsome Horace (IRE)**[39] 4948 5-11-0 95 .... ConorSmith(7) 99
(Philip Hobbs) *mid-div: rdn and hdwy after 3 out: c wd ent st: styd on wl fr last: snatched 2nd fnl strides* **8/1**[3]

FP00 **3** nk **Ann's Lottery**[26] 5144 9-11-2 95 .... KieronEdgar(5) 100
(Tim Dennis) *mid-div: rdn and hdwy after 3 out: disp ld briefly bef next: 2nd and hld whn rchd for last: no ex whn lost 2nd fnl strides* **20/1**

3-50 **4** 3½ **Sterling Gent (IRE)**[19] 5280 8-11-2 90 .... (t) SamTwiston-Davies 91
(Liam Corcoran) *hld up towards rr: hdwy after 3 out: rdn and ev ch 2 out: no ex appr last* **6/1**[2]

26PP **5** 6 **Kentford Heiress**[52] 4685 5-10-4 85 .... KevinJones(7) 82
(Seamus Mullins) *trckd ldrs: rdn appr 2 out: sn one pce* **20/1**

P00 **6** 5 **Carhue (IRE)**[26] 5150 8-11-2 90 .... NickScholfield 82
(Paul Henderson) *hld up towards rr: rdn and hdwy after 3 out: no further imp fr next* **25/1**

5106 **7** 7 **Toe To Toe (IRE)**[212] 1672 7-10-12 86 .... (t) RhysFlint 71+
(John Flint) *racd too keenly: trckd ldrs: disp ld turning in: sn rdn and hdd: wknd between last 2* **11/1**

000 **8** 17 **Sangram (IRE)**[117] 3509 8-11-4 99 .... PaulO'Brien(7) 68
(Jimmy Frost) *trckd ldrs: rdn to chal after 3 out: wknd tamely bef next* **25/1**

30-0 **P** **Princess Annabelle**[16] 5335 6-11-2 90 .... JamesDavies
(Rod Millman) *a towards rr: struggling after 6th: t.o whn p.u bef 2 out* **16/1**

P304 **P** **Showboater (IRE)**[62] 4473 6-11-12 100 .... (p) DavidBass
(Ben Pauling) *led: jnd 3rd: rdn after 3 out: hdd bef next: wknd qckly: p.u bef last* **8/1**[3]

3003 **P** **Moncarno**[152] 2801 5-10-10 84 .... (t) TomScudamore
(David Pipe) *mid-div: hdwy 7th: rdn bef next: sn wknd: t.o whn p.u bef 2 out* **6/1**[2]

F500 **P** **Lanta's Legacy**[20] 5260 5-10-6 80 .... (t) LiamHeard
(Jeremy Scott) *a towards rr: t.o whn p.u bef 2 out* **16/1**

004 **P** **Madam Be**[16] 5332 5-10-8 89 .... WilliamFeatherstone(7)
(Brian Barr) *slowly away: disp fr 3rd: rdn and hdd after 3 out: sn wknd: p.u bef next* **9/1**

5m 11.9s (-8.30) **Going Correction** -0.325s/f (Good) **13 Ran SP% 128.9**
Speed ratings (Par 103): **102,100,100,98,96 94,92,86, ,**
CSF £21.74 CT £307.60 TOTE £3.40: £1.40, £3.80, £6.30; EX 27.00 Trifecta £428.10.
Owner Paul Bowtell **Bred** Kevin F O'Donnell **Trained** Aberthin, Vale of Glamorgan

FOCUS
There was a flag start for this moderate handicap hurdle. The winner was a bit better than bare the result and can win another.

31 SIS STREAMING H'CAP CHASE (16 fncs) 2m 4f 216y
7:35 (7:35) (Class 5) (0-100,96) 5-Y-0+ **£3,422** (£997; £499)

Form RPR

5PPP **1** **Louis Phillipe (IRE)**[28] 5117 8-10-0 70 oh6 .... (t) MarkQuinlan 81+
(Linda Blackford) *prom tl hit 5th: in tch: pushed along at times to hold pl: rdn after 10th: chsd ldr 3 out: led sn after last: styd on* **12/1**

33PP **2** 5 **Head Spin (IRE)**[44] 4822 7-11-12 96 .... (tp) AndrewThornton 104+
(Seamus Mullins) *in tch: hdwy 6th: led 4 out: rdn after 2 out: hit last: sn hdd: no ex* **8/1**

4545 **3** 6 **Beaujolais Bob**[55] 4606 7-10-0 70 oh1 .... (bt) BrendanPowell 70
(Richard Hawker) *trckd ldrs: rdn into 3rd 3 out: styd on same pce fr next* **7/1**[3]

2U34 **4** 9 **Bob Will (IRE)**[18] 5287 10-10-2 72 .... (bt[1]) WillKennedy 64
(John Flint) *led tl 4th: trcking ldrs whn hmpd 8th: rdn after 4 out: styd on same pce fr next* **8/1**

32U1 **5** 19 **Lamb's Cross**[26] 5149 9-10-10 87 .... PaulJohn(7) 67
(Mark Gillard) *in tch: rdn appr 4 out: sn wknd* **6/1**[2]

P5P1 **6** 31 **Captain Knock (IRE)**[183] 2129 12-10-12 82 .... JamesDavies 37
(Polly Gundry) *racd keenly: led 4th: hdd whn nt fluent 4 out: wknd next: t.o* **11/1**

505F **F** **Dancing Dik**[25] 5156 10-10-11 81 .... (b) TomO'Brien
(Paul Henderson) *trcking ldr whn fell 8th* **5/2**[1]

4P24 **B** **Vering (FR)**[26] 5149 9-10-4 77 .... (p) ConorShoemark(3)
(Polly Gundry) *in tch whn b.d 8th* **10/1**

P-PP **P** **Theroadtogorey (IRE)**[28] 5117 9-9-7 70 .... ThomasCheesman(7)
(Sarah Robinson) *hld up: in tch whn bdly hmpd 8th: rdn after 10th: nvr threatened ldrs: p.u after 2 out: fatally injured* **66/1**

-4F5 **P** **Hand On Bach (IRE)**[119] 3440 7-11-10 94 .... (vt[1]) RichardJohnson
(Tim Vaughan) *sn detached: lost tch fr 8th: t.o whn p.u 12th* **6/1**[2]

5m 16.1s (-5.30) **Going Correction** -0.325s/f (Good) **10 Ran SP% 118.5**
Speed ratings: **96,94,92,88,81 70, , , ,**
CSF £105.24 CT £733.96 TOTE £20.10: £3.70, £2.00, £2.50; EX 136.50 Trifecta £1137.80.
Owner Over The Last Racing **Bred** Shane O'Connor **Trained** Rackenford, Devon

FOCUS
An open handicap, made even more so after the favourite came down. The winner is rated back to form.

32 ATTHERACES.COM CONDITIONAL JOCKEYS' H'CAP HURDLE (8 hdls) 2m 167y
8:05 (8:06) (Class 4) (0-115,115) 4-Y-0+ **£3,898** (£1,144; £572; £286)

Form RPR

3606 **1** **Sunblazer (IRE)**[37] 1917 5-11-0 103 .... (t) ConorShoemark 104+
(Kim Bailey) *trckd ldrs: rdn into narrow advantage 2 out: hld on wl fr last: all out* **11/4**[1]

000 **2** ¾ **Race To Glory (FR)**[84] 4055 4-9-13 96 .... (tp) KieronEdgar(3) 92+
(David Pipe) *racd keenly: led 3rd: rdn whn narrowly hdd 2 out: ev ch whn mstke last: kpt on but no ex* **3/1**[2]

-303 **3** ½ **Destiny's Gold (IRE)**[31] 5065 5-11-12 115 .... SeanBowen 115
(George Baker) *hld up but in tch: rdn and hdwy appr 2 out: cl 3rd and ch last: kpt on* **10/3**[3]

5222 **4** 8 **Miss Fortywinks**[252] 1280 6-11-0 103 .... JeremiahMcGrath 95
(Seamus Mullins) *trckd ldrs: pressed ldr 5th tl rdn appr 2 out: sn outpcd* **8/1**

6040 **5** 2 **Ice Konig (FR)**[44] 4821 6-10-10 102 .... ThomasCheesman(3) 93
(Jimmy Frost) *prom: nt fluent 2nd: trckd ldrs fr next: rdn whn hmpd after 3 out: sn one pce* **10/1**

66 **6** 8 **On Alberts Head (IRE)**[52] 4683 5-11-5 108 .... (t) MattGriffiths 93
(Laura Young) *hld up: trckd ldrs 5th: hmpd after 3 out: sn rdn: wknd next* **28/1**

-063 **U** **Brinestine (USA)**[11] 5412 6-11-0 108 .... (t) HarrisonBeswick(5)
(Emma Baker) *led tl 3rd: trckd ldrs: mounting chal whn squeezed up: stmbld and uns rdr after 3 out* **6/1**

4m 4.1s (-1.60) **Going Correction** -0.325s/f (Good)
WFA 4 from 5yo+ 5lb **7 Ran SP% 112.7**
Speed ratings (Par 105): **90,89,89,85,84 80,**
CSF £11.38 CT £26.86 TOTE £4.40: £3.20, £1.20; EX 14.10 Trifecta £32.60.
Owner Kim Bailey Racing Partnership X **Bred** Michael G Daly **Trained** Andoversford, Gloucs
■ Stewards' Enquiry : Kieron Edgar six-day ban: careless riding (May 14-19)

FOCUS
The market leaders dominated this modest handicap, which was steadily run. The first two are entitled to rate a lot higher than this on Flat form.
T/Plt: £641.20 to a £1 stake. Pool of £42787.11 - 48.71 winning tickets. T/Qpdt: £156.70 to a £1 stake. Pool of £5633.15 - 26.60 winning tickets. **Tim Mitchell**

SEDGEFIELD (L-H)

Thursday, April 30

OFFICIAL GOING: Good to firm (good in places; hdl 8.9, chs 8.7)
Wind: strong 1/2 behind Weather: changeable, very breezy and cold

33 JENNINGS FORD TRANSIT 50TH ANNIVERSARY CONDITIONAL JOCKEYS' MAIDEN HURDLE (8 hdls) 2m 178y
1:45 (1:45) (Class 5) 4-Y-0+ **£2,469** (£725; £362; £181)

Form RPR
3445 **1** **Prince Khurram**[34] 5016 5-10-11 107..........(t) JamesCowley(6) 103+
(Donald McCain) *w ldr: led appr 3rd: briefly hdd 3 out: rdn between last 2: styd on* 13/8[2]
424 **2** 3 1/4 **Larmor (FR)**[13] 5378 4-10-7 108.......... RyanDay(5) 95+
(Micky Hammond) *hld up towards rr: stdy hdwy 3rd: 2nd appr 2 out: drvn and fnd little between last 2* 5/4[1]
004 **3** 6 **Ballalough**[25] 5158 5-11-0 0.......... DiarmuidO'Regan(3) 96+
(Chris Grant) *chsd ldrs: drvn 3 out: one pce* 9/2[3]
000 **4** 3 **Lucy Milan (IRE)**[51] 4701 6-10-7 0.......... JamieBargary(3) 84
(Andrew Crook) *in rr: hdwy 3 out: modest 4th appr last: one pce* 20/1
-6FU **5** 12 **Bertielicious**[10] 5421 7-11-3 61..........(p) GrahamWatters 80
(Jonathan Haynes) *led tl bef 3rd: cl 3rd whn mstke 3 out: wknd between last 2* 66/1
0PPP **6** 6 **Colonial Style (IRE)**[112] 3580 5-11-3 70.......... AdamNicol 73
(George Moore) *chsd ldrs: led briefly 3 out: wknd between last 2* 28/1
0000 **7** nk **Chasma**[10] 5419 5-10-10 0.......... ColmMcCormack 67
(Michael Easterby) *chsd ldrs: drvn 3 out: sn lost pl and bhd* 20/1
00P0 **8** 12 **Just My Luke**[34] 5009 6-10-9 0..........(t) JamesCorbett(8) 61
(Susan Corbett) *in rr: reminders sn after 3 out: sn bhd* 66/1
4m 5.1s (-1.80) **Going Correction** -0.45s/f (Good)
WFA 4 from 5yo+ 5lb **8 Ran SP% 116.7**
Speed ratings (Par 103): **86,84,81,80,74 71,71,65**
CSF £4.06 TOTE £2.80: £1.10, £1.10, £1.90; EX 5.00 Trifecta £7.20.
Owner T G Leslie **Bred** Ballygallon Stud Limited **Trained** Cholmondeley, Cheshire
FOCUS
Divided bends and Hurdles sited on outer. A weak maiden hurdle, steadily run on quick ground. The first two were around 7lb off.

34 NORTONTHORPE INDUSTRIAL ESTATE H'CAP HURDLE (8 hdls) 2m 178y
2:15 (2:15) (Class 5) (0-100,100) 4-Y-0+ **£2,469** (£725; £362; £181)

Form RPR
P052 **1** **Bertie Moon**[7] 5490 5-11-6 94.......... WilsonRenwick 99+
(Keith Dalgleish) *trckd ldrs: led 5th: drvn and styd on wl fr 2 out* 7/4[1]
-516 **2** 4 **Grand Vintage (IRE)**[47] 4761 9-11-12 100..........(tp) HenryBrooke 101
(Kenneth Slack) *led to 5th: reminders next: kpt on same pce fr 2 out: no imp* 8/1
0530 **3** 4 **Bob's Legend (IRE)**[41] 4888 9-11-7 95.......... PaddyBrennan 92
(Susan Corbett) *in rr: hdwy 3 out: kpt on same pce fr 2 out: tk 3rd post* 12/1
46P1 **4** shd **Jebulani**[25] 5163 5-10-11 85.......... BrianHarding 82
(Barry Murtagh) *hld up in rr: hdwy 3 out: styd on same pce to take 3rd last 100yds* 10/1
043 **5** 3 1/4 **Dynamic Drive (IRE)**[182] 2150 8-11-5 98..........(t) StephenMulqueen(5) 93
(Maurice Barnes) *mid-div: hdwy 5th: chsng ldrs next: one pce fr 2 out* 16/1
5U5P **6** 7 **Amir Pasha (UAE)**[10] 5421 10-10-3 87..........(b) FinianO'Toole(10) 75
(Micky Hammond) *chsd ldrs: wknd between last 2* 20/1
0452 **7** 2 3/4 **Morning With Ivan (IRE)**[49] 4722 5-11-4 95..........(p) GrahamWatters(3) 80
(Martin Todhunter) *chsd ldr: drvn 3 out: wknd next* 15/2[3]
4435 **8** 3 1/2 **Auto Mac**[159] 2668 7-10-0 77.......... AdamNicol(3) 60
(Mike Sowersby) *in rr: hdwy 5th: wknd 2 out* 16/1
PFFP **9** 1 3/4 **Toola Boola**[41] 4889 5-10-10 84.......... BrianHughes 65
(George Moore) *in rr: drvn 3 out: nvr a factor* 22/1
562P **10** 5 **District Attorney (IRE)**[202] 1827 6-10-10 87.......... JonathanEngland(3) 63
(Chris Fairhurst) *in rr: bhd fr 2 out* 20/1
-PP0 **11** 25 **Jimmie Brown (USA)**[16] 5325 7-10-7 84..........(bt[1]) JohnKington(3) 38
(Andrew Crook) *prom: lost pl 5th: bhd next: t.o* 33/1
3125 **F** **Mad For Road (IRE)**[34] 5019 6-11-12 100.......... AndrewTinkler 96
(Ben Haslam) *chsd ldrs: drvn 3 out: 6th and one pce whn fell last* 6/1[2]
3m 58.2s (-8.70) **Going Correction** -0.45s/f (Good) **12 Ran SP% 118.9**
Speed ratings (Par 103): **102,100,98,98,96 93,92,90,89,87 75,**
CSF £15.51 TOTE £3.10: £1.10, £3.30, £5.00; EX 20.70 Trifecta £196.40.
Owner Straightline Construction Ltd **Bred** M E Wates **Trained** Carluke, S Lanarks
FOCUS
A modest handicap run in a time around seven seconds quicker than the preceding maiden hurdle. The winner was well in on his recent run and ran to a similar level.

35 ALAN CASSELL RETIREMENT H'CAP CHASE (16 fncs) 2m 3f 65y
2:45 (2:46) (Class 4) (0-120,116) 5-Y-0+ **£3,798** (£1,122; £561; £280; £140)

Form RPR
6F21 **1** **Abricot De L'Oasis (FR)**[16] 5330 5-11-8 112.......... HenryBrooke 127+
(Donald McCain) *chsd ldr: led 12th: drvn rt out* 5/2[1]
5344 **2** 4 1/2 **Tahiti Pearl (IRE)**[16] 5328 11-11-12 116.......... SeanQuinlan 125
(Sue Smith) *led: reminders 7th: hdd 12th: drvn next: kpt on same pce fr 2 out: collapsed in unsaddling enclosure: fatally injured* 7/1[3]
-331 **3** 3/4 **Classinaglass**[57] 4557 8-11-1 110.......... HarryBannister(5) 118
(Michael Easterby) *hld up: hdwy and modest 3rd 11th: drvn 2 out: kpt on same pce* 5/2[1]
1444 **4** 10 **Claragh Native (IRE)**[17] 5309 10-10-13 106.......... GrahamWatters(3) 105
(Martin Todhunter) *in rr: hdwy and poor 4th 13th: chsng ldrs 2 out: wknd bef last* 8/1
3F04 **5** 15 **Indalo Return (IRE)**[51] 4695 9-10-5 95 ow1.......... JamesReveley 84
(Philip Kirby) *prom: hit 2nd: lost pl 8th: bhd fr 10th* 7/1[3]
132P **6** 11 **Solway Dornal**[8] 5473 10-10-1 98.......... RyanDay(7) 74
(Lisa Harrison) *chsd ldrs: pushed along 8th: reminders after next: wknd 11th: sn bhd* 12/1
5144 **P** **Auldthunder (IRE)**[18] 5298 8-9-13 96.......... JamieBargary(7)
(Micky Hammond) *detached in last: j. bdly: j. slowly 1st: blnd 3rd: sn t.o: p.u bef 7th* 13/2[2]
4m 46.9s (-16.10) **Going Correction** -0.825s/f (Firm) **7 Ran SP% 114.3**
Speed ratings: **99,97,96,92,86 82,**
CSF £19.93 TOTE £3.00: £1.90, £3.40; EX 17.20 Trifecta £48.10.
Owner Frank McAleavy **Bred** S Blanchais, N Blanchais Et Al **Trained** Cholmondeley, Cheshire
FOCUS
The form of this ordinary handicap chase seems sound enough. The winner should rate higher.

36 WILLS PROPERTY SERVICES H'CAP CHASE (13 fncs) 2m 77y
3:15 (3:15) (Class 4) (0-120,120) 5-Y-0+ **£3,833** (£1,157; £596; £315)

Form RPR
F410 **1** **Grey Life**[40] 4913 9-11-12 120.......... BrianHughes 128+
(Malcolm Jefferson) *trckd ldrs: handy 2nd 9th: rdn between last 2: narrow ld last: fnd ex nr fin* 11/4[2]
-361 **2** nk **Hotgrove Boy**[51] 4700 8-10-11 105.......... JamesReveley 112
(Stuart Coltherd) *trckd ldrs: led after 2nd: narrowly hdd last: no ex nr fin* 6/4[1]
3165 **3** 17 **Pamak D'Airy (FR)**[47] 4760 12-10-10 107..........(p) TonyKelly(3) 101
(Henry Hogarth) *chsd ldrs: outpcd 7th: reminders 9th: chsng ldng pair 3 out: sn btn* 11/1
1060 **4** 11 **Sleep In First (FR)**[13] 5361 9-11-4 117..........(tp) DaleIrving(5) 103
(James Ewart) *led tl after 2nd: blnd and reminders 10th: sn lost pl and bhd* 11/2
351U **U** **Gin Cobbler**[10] 5421 9-9-7 94 oh3.......... MissETodd(7)
(Victor Thompson) *in last but in tch whn blnd and uns rdr 1st* 4/1[3]
3m 59.1s (-14.90) **Going Correction** -0.825s/f (Firm) **5 Ran SP% 110.4**
Speed ratings: **102,101,93,88,**
CSF £7.66 TOTE £2.60: £1.40, £1.70; EX 7.40 Trifecta £27.70.
Owner D T Todd **Bred** Mrs C Teanby **Trained** Norton, N Yorks
FOCUS
The first two came clear in this fair handicap chase, which was run at a good clip. The form looks pretty solid.

37 PHOENIX SECURITY H'CAP HURDLE (10 hdls) 2m 5f 34y
3:45 (3:46) (Class 5) (0-100,100) 4-Y-0+ **£2,469** (£725; £362; £181)

Form RPR
5362 **1** **Danceintothelight**[24] 5206 8-10-5 86.......... JamieBargary(7) 96+
(Micky Hammond) *chsd ldrs: drvn appr 2 out: led between last 2: forged clr: eased in clsng stages* 9/2[1]
4104 **2** 11 **Whatsupjack (IRE)**[24] 5206 8-10-4 81..........(b) JonathanEngland(3) 82
(Shaun Harris) *trckd ldrs: led after 3 out: hdd between last 2: styd on same pce* 8/1[3]
0006 **3** 6 **Blast Martha (IRE)**[49] 4722 6-10-6 80.......... JamesReveley 76
(Michael Smith) *chsd ldrs: kpt on one pce between last 2: lft modest 3rd last* 11/1
066P **4** 4 **New Youmzain (FR)**[65] 4418 6-10-11 90.......... GrantCockburn(5) 80
(Lucy Normile) *mid-div: hdwy to chse ldrs 5th: one pce fr 3 out* 9/1
0500 **5** nse **Slipper Satin (IRE)**[17] 5315 5-11-12 100..........(t) HenryBrooke 90
(Simon West) *w ldr: led 2nd: hdd and hit 7th: one pce appr 2 out* 16/1
6200 **6** 7 **Mister Jones**[34] 5011 7-10-8 82.......... SeanQuinlan 66
(Sue Smith) *chsd ldrs: outpcd 3 out: sn btn* 17/2
P-P0 **7** 20 **Latest Fashion (IRE)**[34] 5015 9-9-9 74 oh5.......... StephenMulqueen(5) 40
(Christopher Wilson) *in rr: bhd fr 7th: t.o 2 out* 66/1
41P4 **8** 37 **Willie Hall**[16] 5324 11-10-12 93..........(p) RyanDay(7) 25
(Lisa Harrison) *in rr: hdwy 6th: sn drvn: lost pl 3 out: sn bhd: t.o* 8/1[3]
4000 **9** 1 3/4 **Mrs Grass**[34] 5011 8-9-9 74 oh2..........(vt) DiarmuidO'Regan(5) 5
(Jonathan Haynes) *in rr: bhd fr 6th: t.o 2 out* 25/1
0F54 **P** **Tennessee Bird**[25] 5163 7-9-11 74.......... AdamNicol(3)
(Mike Sowersby) *in rr: mstke 1st: reminders 4th: lost tch after next: t.o whn p.u after 6th: b.b.v* 9/1
4PP0 **P** **Izbushka (IRE)**[34] 5015 4-9-11 80..........(b) TonyKelly(3)
(David Thompson) *rr-div: bhd fr 3 out: poor 8th whn p.u bef last* 16/1
0506 **F** **Quest Magic (IRE)**[8] 5469 9-11-5 98..........(p) JonathonBewley(5) 97
(George Bewley) *led to 2nd: w ldrs: led 7th: hdd after next: 3rd and keeping on same pce whn fell last* 11/2[2]
50-P **P** **Rozener (IRE)**[11] 9-10-6 80.......... BrianHughes
(Mike Sowersby) *prom: lost pl 3rd: bhd fr 7th: t.o whn p.u bef 2 out* 12/1
5m 4.3s (-10.30) **Going Correction** -0.45s/f (Good)
WFA 4 from 5yo+ 6lb **13 Ran SP% 119.4**
Speed ratings (Par 103): **100,96,93,92,92 89,82,69,68, , ,**
CSF £40.74 CT £379.49 TOTE £2.40: £1.10, £2.70, £4.60; EX 23.80 Trifecta £84.50.
Owner Maybe The Last Time **Bred** Mrs David Low **Trained** Middleham, N Yorks
■ Stewards' Enquiry : Tony Kelly Fine: £80, completed course with others having been pulled up
FOCUS
A decidedly moderate event, but the pace was solid. The winner's best figure since 2013.

38 FREE BOOKMAKERS BETS AT BOOKMAKERS.CO.UK H'CAP CHASE (21 fncs) 3m 2f 59y
4:20 (4:20) (Class 4) (0-120,111) 5-Y-0+ **£3,833** (£1,157; £596; £315)

Form RPR
1144 **1** **Beau Dandy (IRE)**[26] 5135 10-10-8 98..........(p[1]) DiarmuidO'Regan(5) 100+
(Chris Grant) *trckd ldr: drvn 13th: led appr last: styd on wl* 6/1[3]
133P **2** 3 1/4 **Bennys Well (IRE)**[26] 5141 9-11-12 111.......... SeanQuinlan 112
(Sue Smith) *led: reminders 15th: hdd appr last: no ex* 8/1
4431 **3** 10 **Generous Chief (IRE)**[149] 2865 7-11-3 102..........(p) BrianHughes 91
(Chris Grant) *trckd ldrs: 2nd 17th: 2nd briefly 3 out: wknd between last 2* 11/4[2]
3063 **4** 12 **Senor Alco (FR)**[13] 5375 9-9-7 85 oh6.......... MissETodd(7) 67
(Victor Thompson) *chsd ldrs: blnd 4th: lost pl 3 out* 7/1
2221 **P** **Debt To Society (IRE)**[41] 4893 8-10-10 100..........(vt) HarryBannister(5)
(Richard Ford) *nt fluent in last: nvr gng wl: hit 8th: sme hdwy 13th: lost pl and hit 15th: sn t.o: p.u bef 4 out: b.b.v* 5/4[1]
6m 44.8s (-26.20) **Going Correction** -0.825s/f (Firm) **5 Ran SP% 109.0**
Speed ratings: **105,104,101,97,**
CSF £42.17 TOTE £6.40: £3.30, £2.60; EX 30.30 Trifecta £70.90.
Owner D Lofthouse E Lofthouse Mrs M Nicholas **Bred** George Cheatley **Trained** Newton Bewley, Co Durham

FOCUS
A modest staying event. The first two were pretty much to their marks.

39 FREE BETS ON YOUR MOBILE AT BOOKMAKERS.CO.UK STANDARD OPEN NATIONAL HUNT FLAT RACE 2m 178y
4:55 (4:55) (Class 6) 4-6-Y-O £1,559 (£457; £228; £114)

Form RPR
55 1 **Petapenko**[26] 5143 4-10-12 0 BrianHughes 98
(Malcolm Jefferson) *trckd ldrs: upsides 8f out: drvn over 3f out: rallied over 1f out: styd on to ld last 100yds* 9/2[2]
034 2 1 3/4 **Episode**[60] 4520 4-10-9 0 AdamNicol(3) 96
(Philip Kirby) *trckd ldrs: led over 1f out: hdd and no ex last 100yds* 9/2[2]
44 3 3 1/2 **Mr Witmore (IRE)**[34] 5020 5-11-3 0 HenryBrooke 98
(Michael Smith) *led: qcknd pce 7f out: hdd over 5f out: one pce fnl 3f* 6/1[3]
P 4 8 **Zakety Zak**[24] 5207 4-10-12 0 PeterBuchanan 85
(James Turner) *mid-div: drvn 6f out: sn outpcd: modest 4th over 1f out* 40/1
0 5 11 **Dorabaloo**[34] 5020 4-10-5 0 BrianHarding 67
(Tim Easterby) *trckd ldrs: lost pl over 4f out: wknd over 1f out* 20/1
6 13 **Danny The Dancer** 5-10-7 0 FinianO'Toole(10) 66
(Micky Hammond) *in rr: outpcd 6f out: sn bhd* 13/2
U 7 61 **Hello Pretty Ladys**[80] 4127 4-10-12 0 [1] DougieCostello
(Les Eyre) *t.k.h: sn trcking ldrs: lost pl 6f out: t.o 4f out: eventually completed* 14/1
4 P **John Dory (IRE)**[44] 4832 4-10-12 0 PaddyBrennan
(Alan Swinbank) *hld up towards rr: p.u after 4f: fatally injured* 13/8[1]

3m 58.5s (-2.80) **Going Correction** -0.45s/f (Good)
WFA 4 from 5yo 5lb 8 Ran SP% 115.9
Speed ratings: **88,87,85,81,76 70,41,**
CSF £25.43 TOTE £5.90: £1.90, £1.40, £1.10; EX 28.50 Trifecta £182.60.
Owner Richard Collins **Bred** Plantation Stud **Trained** Norton, N Yorks

FOCUS
This weak bumper was run at a steady initial pace. The form is rated around the second and third.
T/Jkpt: £7,100.00 to a £1 stake. Pool of £10000 - 1.00 winning ticket. T/Plt: £90.20 to a £1 stake. Pool of £59705.63 - 483.07 winning tickets. T/Qpdt: £32.50 to a £1 stake. Pool of £4133.81 - 93.95 winning tickets. **Walter Glynn**

TOWCESTER (R-H)
Thursday, April 30

OFFICIAL GOING: Good to firm
Wind: breezy Weather: sunny; 12 degrees

40 BET TOTEPLACEPOT H'CAP HURDLE (11 hdls) 2m 4f 217y
5:05 (5:06) (Class 5) (0-100,90) 4-Y-O+ £2,599 (£763; £381; £190)

Form RPR
0502 1 **Pennant Dancer**[24] 5185 8-11-7 85 (t) PaulMoloney 90+
(Debra Hamer) *last pair tl 8th: sn pushed along: stl 5th home turn: hrd drvn and styd on to catch idling ldr cl home* 7/2[1]
0P66 2 nk **Canarbino Girl**[13] 5371 8-10-11 75 (tp) JamesBest 79+
(Caroline Keevil) *cl up: led 3 out and qckly wnt 3 l clr: jnd and lft clr again next: over 2 l ahd whn hit last: rdn and fnd nil flat: jst ct* 9/1
P6PP 3 6 **Breezy Kin (IRE)**[35] 4996 7-11-5 90 MikeyHamill(7) 91
(Sean Curran) *mstkes: prom tl rdn 3 out: btn whn hmpd next: one pce whn hit last* 7/1[3]
6330 4 7 **Occasionally Yours (IRE)**[24] 5191 11-11-12 90 MarcGoldstein 82
(Alan Blackmore) *cl up: wnt 2nd at 5th: rdn 3 out: fdd bef next: mstke last* 9/1
0404 5 3 1/2 **Warsaw Pact (IRE)**[39] 4948 12-10-5 76 MrJamesKing(7) 66
(Steven Dixon) *trckd ldrs: rdn 3 out: no rspnse: btn bef next* 10/1
1322 6 24 **Rogue Dancer (FR)**[196] 1918 10-11-9 87 (t) TrevorWhelan 54
(Michael Banks) *cl up in midfield tl rdn 3 out: dropped out tamely: t.o* 7/1[3]
P20P 7 4 1/2 **Thefriendlygremlin**[49] 4733 7-10-1 70 ow3 (p) ConorRing(5) 33
(John Upson) *led at v mod pce tl rdn and hdd 3 out: immediately btn: t.o* 10/1
00PP 8 12 **Marina Bay**[92] 3925 10-9-9 64 JoeCornwall(5) 16
(Christopher Kellett) *bhd: rdn and struggling 8th: bdly t.o* 100/1
0P0P 9 49 **Bjornlucky (IRE)**[24] 5206 5-11-11 89 (p) HarrySkelton
(Caroline Fryer) *chsd ldrs tl 8th: rdn and t.o after next: eased 2 out* 20/1
0035 F **Pandy Wells**[24] 5185 6-10-10 74 GerardTumelty 78
(Graeme McPherson) *t.k.h towards rr: effrt 3 out: wnt 2nd and pushed along but looked to be gng best whn fell next* 4/1[2]

5m 26.3s (-0.90) **Going Correction** -0.975s/f (Hard) 10 Ran SP% 111.2
Speed ratings (Par 103): **62,61,59,56,55 46,44,40,21,**
CSF £33.14 CT £199.81 TOTE £4.50: £1.50, £3.50, £3.10; EX 42.80 Trifecta £544.80.
Owner P J Woolley **Bred** P J Woolley **Trained** Nantycaws, Carmarthens

FOCUS
Shared bends and Hurdle course dolled out to middle line. A weak handicap. It was run at an average gallop and saw late drama. The form is straightforward.

41 BET TOTEJACKPOT NOVICES' HURDLE (8 hdls) 1m 7f 181y
5:40 (5:46) (Class 4) 4-Y-O+ £3,898 (£1,144; £572; £286)

Form RPR
021 1 **Lochalsh (IRE)**[11] 5411 4-11-0 124 HarrySkelton 108+
(Dan Skelton) *racd keenly in last in slowly run r tl effrt bef 3 out: pushed along briefly: led sn after next: 5 l ahd last: easily* 1/4[1]
5PP3 2 8 **Ishusharella**[10] 5430 6-9-12 0 (t) FreddieMitchell(7) 84
(Clare Hobson) *led tl 3rd and 5th tl 3 out: sn rdn: outpcd 2 out: plodded into modest 2nd cl home* 6/1[2]
5 3 1/2 **Victory Rich (IRE)**[25] 5155 4-10-0 0 (t) MrFTett(7) 87
(Henry Tett) *plld hrd: led 3rd tl 5th and again 3 out: rdn and hdd sn after next: immediately outpcd by wnr: fin weakly to lose 2nd nr fin* 16/1
4 3 3/4 **Impeccability**[111] 5-10-5 0 (p) PeterCarberry 81
(John Mackie) *pressed ldng pair: chal briefly 3 out: sn rdn: wknd bef next* 14/1[3]
F **Fort Gabriel (FR)**[25] 4-10-7 0 SamJones 76
(Fiona Kehoe) *nt a fluent: pushed along 4th: in last and struggling 3 out: 10 l in last whn knuckled and fell 2 out* 16/1

3m 55.5s (-12.40) **Going Correction** -0.975s/f (Hard) 5 Ran SP% 112.7
Speed ratings (Par 105): **92,88,87,85,**
CSF £2.50 TOTE £1.20: £1.10, £2.10; EX 2.70 Trifecta £8.20.
Owner Craig Buckingham **Bred** J & L Young / Darlacher Ltd **Trained** Alcester, Warwicks
■ Gambol was withdrawn. Price at time of withdrawal 3/1. Rule 4 applies to bets struck prior to withdrawal but not to SP bets. Deduct 25p in the pound.

FOCUS
This was anything but competitive and it's lowly form, with the time slow. The third helps set the level.

42 BET TOTEQUADPOT H'CAP CHASE (11 fncs) 2m 70y
6:15 (6:16) (Class 5) (0-100,96) 5-Y-O+ £3,898 (£1,144; £572; £286)

Form RPR
0502 1 **Beauchamp Viking**[29] 5092 11-10-2 72 (t) DaveCrosse 81
(Hugo Froud) *led at brisk pce: jnd 5th tl lft in ld 7th: drvn and hdd bef 2 out: swtchd lft and rallied to ld again last: all out after but game* 9/2[3]
54P1 2 1/2 **Red Whisper**[29] 5092 11-11-2 91 (t) JakeHodson(5) 100
(Rob Summers) *trckd ldrs: wnt cl 2nd at 8th: led bef 2 out: sn drvn: hdd last: plugged on u.p but jst hld* 9/2[3]
410 3 13 **Grand Article (IRE)**[38] 4966 11-10-12 85 MissGAndrews(3) 82
(Paul Cowley) *pressed ldr tl 3rd: dropped bk last and swishing tail and nt keen 6th: sn lost tch: sme prog fr bef 2 out to go poor 3rd flat* 7/2[2]
1330 4 3 1/4 **Accessallareas (IRE)**[203] 1814 10-11-12 96 (tp) RobertDunne 90
(Sarah-Jayne Davies) *cl up tl rdn bef 3 out: sn struggling bhd ldng pair: lost poor 3rd after last* 6/1
0312 U **Ivans Back (IRE)**[16] 5326 10-11-3 90 MauriceLinehan(3)
(Nick Kent) *wnt 2nd at 3rd: jnd wnr 5th and gng wl tl misjudged 7th: blnd v bdly and uns rdr* 7/4[1]

3m 58.4s (-17.70) **Going Correction** -1.15s/f (Hard) 5 Ran SP% 109.2
Speed ratings: **95,94,88,87,**
CSF £22.88 TOTE £4.10: £1.60, £2.70; EX 13.60 Trifecta £41.40.
Owner Mrs Maureen Emery **Bred** E Penser **Trained** Bruton, Somerset

FOCUS
This moderate handicap was run at a solid gallop and the form is straightforward. The first two stepped up on recent C&D form.

43 BET TOTEEXACTA H'CAP HURDLE (8 hdls) 1m 7f 181y
6:50 (6:50) (Class 4) (0-110,110) 4-Y-O+ £3,898 (£1,144; £572; £286)

Form RPR
P2P0 1 **Drombeg West**[77] 4179 8-10-12 96 AndrewTinkler 106+
(Anna Brooks) *settled towards rr: prog 3 out: led gng best bef next: sn clr: unchal* 10/1
5P20 2 7 **Honour A Promise**[129] 3227 7-11-2 100 (p) LiamTreadwell 101
(Paul Webber) *prom: lft 3rd and rdn after 3 out: no ch w wnr fr next: plugged on into 10 l 2nd at last* 14/1
2326 3 3 1/2 **Hartside (GER)**[38] 4961 6-11-5 110 MrRWinks(7) 108
(Peter Winks) *towards rr: rdn and outpcd bef 3 out: urged along and styd on gamely fr next: wnt 3rd after last but nvr able to chal* 11/2[3]
PP3P 4 1/2 **Bunclody**[18] 5288 10-10-13 104 (p) MrZBaker(7) 101
(Barry Brennan) *rn in snatches: rdn and lost tch bef 3 out: kpt on same pce and no ch after* 16/1
4613 5 3 1/4 **Pembroke House**[20] 5260 8-11-0 105 (p) MichaelHeard(7) 100
(Sarah-Jayne Davies) *wnt 2nd at 3rd tl lft in ld 3 out: sn rdn: hdd bef next and immediately lost tch w wnr: 10 l 2nd and fading at last* 9/2[1]
0040 6 1 1/4 **Polstar (FR)**[28] 5115 6-10-11 102 PaulNO'Brien(7) 95
(Harry Whittington) *lost pl 3rd and dropped himself rt out: t.o 5th: plugged on* 5/1[2]
5006 7 shd **Rainman (IRE)**[28] 5106 5-11-7 105 (p) RichieMcLernon 98
(Jonjo O'Neill) *nt jump wl: bhd: rdn 5th: no ch w ldrs fr next* 16/1
111F 8 2 1/2 **Catchin Time (IRE)**[17] 5315 7-11-6 104 DaveCrosse 97
(Laura Hurley) *midfield tl mstke 3rd: reminders 4th: nt travelling after and lost tch 5th* 8/1
5213 P **Special Report (IRE)**[24] 1500 5-11-5 103 (bt) NoelFehily
(Neil Mulholland) *pressed ldrs and t.k.h: stl handy whn bdly hmpd 3 out: p.u and fatally injured* 6/1
0P0P F **Nervous Nineties**[26] 5148 6-10-0 84 oh6 (b[1]) AlainCawley
(Fergal O'Brien) *led at brisk pce: stl looked to be gng wl whn fell 3 out* 25/1
046 R **Ashkoun (FR)**[33] 5025 4-11-0 103 (t) MichaelByrne
(Tim Vaughan) *taken down early: t.k.h: disputing 3rd whn veered sharply lft at 5th: rn off crse and j. a chse fence* 8/1

3m 50.5s (-17.40) **Going Correction** -0.975s/f (Hard)
WFA 4 from 5yo+ 5lb 11 Ran SP% 118.1
Speed ratings (Par 105): **104,100,98,98,96 96,96,94, ,**
CSF £138.58 CT £854.69 TOTE £14.00: £4.70, £5.20, £2.20; EX 186.70 Trifecta £1035.30.
Owner Mrs J M Owen **Bred** Steve Hadley **Trained** Alderton, Northants

FOCUS
An ordinary handicap which proved eventful. The easy winner is on the upgrade.

44 BET TOTETRIFECTA CONDITIONAL JOCKEYS' TRAINING SERIES H'CAP CHASE (RACING EXCELLENCE INITIATIVE) (15 fncs) 2m 5f 153y
7:25 (7:25) (Class 5) (0-100,97) 5-Y-O+ £3,898 (£1,144; £572; £286)

Form RPR
P0-6 1 **Interpleader**[347] 10-10-3 79 (tp) MrMartinMcIntyre(5) 93+
(Sheila Lewis) *3rd tl wnt after 6th and 2nd at 11th: j. soundly: led 12th: rdn and kpt finding a bit more fr 2 out* 15/2
5541 2 6 **Royalracket (IRE)**[13] 5374 7-11-6 91 (b) JackSherwood 102+
(Paul Webber) *settled in midfield: nt fluent 6th: wnt 2nd 3 out: sn rdn to go clr of rest: wnt rt 2 out: racd awkwardly after: 2 l down and finding nthing whn wnt rt last and ungainly on landing: no imp after* 2/1[1]
P5PP 3 25 **Riddlestown (IRE)**[24] 5204 8-11-7 97 (b) MikeyHamill(5) 86
(Caroline Fryer) *blnd 1st: wnt 3rd at 11th: effrt and disputing 2nd whn mstke 3 out: rdn and sn lft bhd by ldng pair* 8/1
2630 4 10 **Around A Pound (IRE)**[16] 5324 10-10-9 85 PaulNO'Brien(5) 62
(Nick Kent) *led tl 11th: lost pl qckly bef 3 out: sn wl bhd: drvn into remote 4th flat* 9/2[3]
3P-3 5 3/4 **Ata Boy (IRE)**[55] 4606 9-10-0 74 (t) DanielHiskett(3) 50
(Richard Phillips) *in last pair: rdn bef 7th and nvr really travelling: brief effrt in 4th 3 out: sn struggling: 12 l 4th home turn: lost 4th cl home* 4/1[2]
P340 6 39 **Top Benefit (IRE)**[38] 4966 13-9-11 71 oh6 MichaelHeard(3) 12
(Richard Harper) *w ldr tl 3rd: lost 2nd after 6th and lost 3rd at 11th: sn struggling: t.o whn mstke 3 out: eventually completed* 25/1
6640 P **Dazzling Rita**[26] 5148 9-10-4 78 (t) FreddieMitchell(3)
(Sophie Leech) *in last mostly: j. slowly 3rd: mstkes 9th whn labouring 3 out: t.o and p.u next* 17/2

5m 21.5s (-31.50) **Going Correction** -1.15s/f (Hard) 7 Ran SP% 108.8
Speed ratings: **111,108,99,96,95 81,**
CSF £21.60 TOTE £10.10: £3.30, £1.70; EX 32.00 Trifecta £378.50.
Owner Brian Davies **Bred** David Brace **Trained** Brecon, Powys

FOCUS
A moderate handicap, confined to conditional riders. Only two mattered in the home straight. The form could be rated higher.

45 BET TOTESWINGER MARES' STANDARD OPEN NATIONAL HUNT FLAT RACE 1m 7f 181y
7:55 (7:55) (Class 6) 4-6-Y-0 **£1,949** (£572; £286; £143)

Form RPR
54 **1** **Kayla**[24] 5193 5-10-12 0 (t) SamJones 97
(Stuart Edmunds) *chsd ldrs: rdn and outpcd briefly 4f out: rallied to chse ldr over 2f out: urged along and clsd grad: got up 75yds out* **9/2**[3]

2 **2** ½ **Just A Feeling**[51] 4701 5-10-12 0 LiamTreadwell 97
(Paul Webber) *ldng pair: mde most for 6f: led again 4f out: rdn 2f out: kpt on steadily but worn down 75yds out* **7/2**[2]

3 3¼ **Kaddys Girl** 5-10-5 0 JosephPalmowski(7) 94
(Robin Dickin) *bhd: 6 l last and rdn 4f out: rallied 2f out: pressed ldng pair over 1f out: no imp after* **16/1**

0 **4** 6 **Palmaria**[140] 3037 5-10-12 0 JamesBest 89
(Caroline Keevil) *chsd ldrs: drvn 3f out: 4th and no ex wl over 1f out* **28/1**

4 **5** 19 **Kitty Power (IRE)**[33] 5035 6-10-7 0 (t) JackSherwood(5) 72
(Nigel Twiston-Davies) *plld hrd: sn w ldr: led 6f out and clr briefly: hdd 4f out: fdd rapidly 3f out: t.o* **6/1**

6 3¾ **Just The Way It Is** 5-10-12 0 PeterCarberry 68
(Nicky Henderson) *small light-framed: cl up tl drvn 4f out: fdd 3f out: sn t.o* **11/8**[1]

0 **7** 11 **Silver Djebel**[84] 4052 4-10-7 0 (t) MichealNolan 53
(Jamie Snowden) *chsd ldrs tl wknd qckly 3f out: sn t.o* **20/1**

3m 49.7s (-12.60) **Going Correction** -0.975s/f (Hard)
WFA 4 from 5yo+ 5lb **7 Ran SP% 110.9**
Speed ratings: **92,91,90,87,77 75,70**
CSF £19.27 TOTE £5.50: £2.00, £1.90; EX 23.60 Trifecta £264.50.
Owner Exors of the Late Mrs P Robeson **Bred** Mrs P Robeson **Trained** Newport Pagnell, Bucks

FOCUS
A modest mares' bumper, run at an uneven gallop. The second sets the level.
T/Plt: £95.80 to a £1 stake. Pool of £52701.56 - 401.17 winning tickets. T/Qpdt: £40.00 to a £1 stake. Pool of £5980.51 - 110.40 winning tickets. **Iain Mackenzie**

46a (Foreign Racing) - See Raceform Interactive

19 PUNCHESTOWN (R-H)
Thursday, April 30

OFFICIAL GOING: Hurdle & chase course -yielding; cross-country course - good

47a THREE.IE H'CAP CHASE (GRADE C) (11 fncs) 2m
4:15 (4:15) 4-Y-0+ **£25,193** (£7,364; £3,488; £1,162)

RPR
1 **Jacksonslady (IRE)**[82] 4101 10-10-9 **135** (p) MarkWalsh 147+
(J P Dempsey, Ire) *hld up tl tk clsr order bef 4 out: travelled wl into 2nd after next: led bef 2 out: rdn clr run-in* **10/1**

2 5 **Upazo (FR)**[23] 5228 7-10-9 **135** RWalsh 142
(W P Mullins, Ire) *hld up tl tk clsr order 3 out: rdn to press ldr in 2nd appr last: sn no imp: kpt on same pce* **11/2**[2]

3 2½ **Ned Buntline**[21] 5240 7-11-0 **140** PaulCarberry 145
(Noel Meade, Ire) *racd in mid-div tl clsr after 3 out: prog to chse ldr in 2nd 2 out: no imp appr last in 3rd: kpt on same pce* **7/2**[1]

4 8 **Usa (IRE)**[13] 5385 8-10-2 **128** PaulTownend 126
(S J Mahon, Ire) *hld up towards rr tl prog 4 out on outer: trckd ldrs in 3rd after next tl nt qckn in 4th bef last: sn one pce* **9/1**[3]

5 4½ **Treat Yourself (IRE)**[32] 5055 8-9-10 **122** (p) DJCasey 114
(A L T Moore, Ire) *racd in mid-div: rdn bef 2 out: kpt on into 5th run-in: nvr on terms* **14/1**

6 ¾ **One Term (IRE)**[11] 5406 8-10-10 **136** (b) JJBurke 127
(Rebecca Curtis) *t.k.h early to trck ldrs and sn disp: led 6th tl hdd bef 2 out: sn no ex* **20/1**

7 1 **Bold Henry**[48] 4742 9-10-6 **132** NiallPMadden 122
(Philip Hobbs) *hld up towards rr tl sme prog 3 out: no imp bef next* **14/1**

8 3¾ **Pires**[61] 4502 11-10-1 **132** ShaneShortall(5) 119
(A J Martin, Ire) *racd in mid-div: sme prog whn bdly hmpd 3 out: sn no ex* **16/1**

9 nk **Mount Colah (IRE)**[48] 4742 9-11-5 **150** MrNMcParlan(5) 136
(J G Cosgrave, Ire) *chsd ldrs early: mid-div whn mstke 6th: no threat after 3 out* **16/1**

10 8 **Enjoy Responsibly (IRE)**[21] 5240 6-10-2 **128** ow3 (tp) BJCooper 106
(Henry De Bromhead, Ire) *chsd ldrs: clsr in 4th after 1/2-way: wknd after 3 out* **11/1**

11 7 **Is Herself About (IRE)**[54] 4640 8-9-8 **123** BenDalton(3) 94
(David M O'Brien, Ire) *led to 1st: disp tl hdd 6th: wknd qckly* **20/1**

12 87 **Kates Benefit (IRE)**[82] 4101 9-9-10 **122** oh1 MarkEnright 6
(David Kenneth Budds, Ire) *disp early: trckd ldrs tl wknd 4 out and eased: t.o* **33/1**

U **Fosters Cross (IRE)**[32] 5055 13-9-13 **130** DavidMullins(5)
(Thomas Mullins, Ire) *racd towards rr: no imp whn bdly hmpd and uns rdr 3 out* **22/1**

P **Grey Gold (IRE)**[26] 5147 10-11-6 **146** DavyRussell
(Richard Lee) *chsd ldrs on inner whn bad blunder at 2nd: sn p.u* **14/1**

U **Dick Dundee**[48] 4742 10-10-4 **135** (b) LPDempsey(5)
(Paul Nolan, Ire) *chsd ldrs tl mstke and uns rdr 3 out* **14/1**

F **Ludo Et Emergo (IRE)**[32] 5055 8-10-10 **136** RobbieColgan
(Andrew Lee, Ire) *chsd ldrs on inner: gd hdwy to press ldrs 4 out: fell next* **12/1**

4m 9.1s (-9.50) **Going Correction** -0.35s/f (Good) **16 Ran SP% 128.0**
Speed ratings: **109,106,105,101,99 98,98,96,96,92 88,45, , ,**
CSF £65.43 CT £241.49 TOTE £7.40: £1.70, £1.80, £1.60, £1.80; DF 46.30 Trifecta £81.50.
Owner John P McManus **Bred** Tom Lawlor **Trained** Carbury, Co Kildare

FOCUS
A really competitive handicap chase run at a very decent clip, demonstrated by the fact that several horses that would normally front-run could get nowhere near the lead. It was won by a teak tough mare who's very likeable and posted a big personal best.

48a FBD CROSS COUNTRY CHASE FOR THE LA TOUCHE CUP 4m 1f
4:50 (4:52) 5-Y-0+ **£15,116** (£4,418; £2,093; £697)

RPR
1 **Uncle Junior (IRE)**[50] 4706 14-11-7 0 (p) MrPWMullins 133+
(W P Mullins, Ire) *hld up tl prog into mid-div at 9th: trckd ldrs whn lft 3rd 2 out: strly rdn to dispute appr last where nt fluent: kpt on gamely to ld cl home* **6/1**[3]

2 nk **Quantitativeeasing (IRE)**[50] 4706 10-11-7 0 (p) MsNCarberry 133+
(E Bolger, Ire) *racd in mid-div tl gd hdwy to press ldrs in 3rd at 23rd: led narrowly 3 out: strly pressed and jnd appr last: kpt on wl: hdd cl home* **13/8**[1]

3 16 **Keep On Track (IRE)**[39] 4952 8-11-12 107 AELynch 126
(I R Ferguson, Ire) *trckd ldr in 2nd tl led at 24th: hdd 3 out: lft 2nd 2 out: sn dropped to 3rd and no ex w principals: kpt on one pce* **7/1**

4 3 **Rose Of The Moon (IRE)**[50] 4706 10-11-12 0 JakeGreenall 119
(David O'Meara) *chsd ldrs tl nt qckn 7 out: no imp whn lft 5th 2 out* **20/1**

5 18 **Boxing Along (IRE)**[42] 4875 11-11-5 0 (t) MrPPower(7) 101
(Vincent Laurence Halley, Ire) *racd in mid-div tl prog to chse ldrs at 7th: nt qckn 7 out: no imp whn lft 5th 2 out* **33/1**

6 ¾ **Long Strand (IRE)**[88] 4002 11-11-0 0 (t) MissEvannaMcCutcheon(7) 95
(Miss Evanna McCutcheon, Ire) *sn trckd ldrs in 3rd: briefly on terms at 25th: mstke 3 out and sn wknd* **100/1**

R **Becauseicouldntsee (IRE)**[88] 12-11-2 0 MissEALalor(5)
(N F Glynn, Ire) *a towards rr: no threat whn ref 5 out* **33/1**

P **Rivage D'Or (FR)**[24] 5224 10-12-3 134 (t) BJCooper
(A J Martin, Ire) *a towards rr: nvr a factor: p.u bef 2 out* **8/1**

P **Prince Of Milan (IRE)**[196] 1928 10-11-7 108 BrianO'Connell
(Andrew Slattery, Ire) *chsd ldrs in 4th tl dropped towards rr at 8th: no imp whn p.u at 25th* **66/1**

U **Josies Orders (IRE)**[43] 4848 7-11-7 0 (p) MrDerekO'Connor 114+
(E Bolger, Ire) *racd in mid-div tl tk clsr order 6 out: prog into 5th whn bdly hmpd and uns rdr 2 out* **10/1**

U **Snooze (FR)**[20] 5269 9-11-7 113 (t) JohnCullen
(John Laurence Cullen, Ire) *chsd ldrs whn mstke and uns rdr 2nd* **33/1**

F **Ballyboker Bridge (IRE)**[88] 4002 8-11-5 0 (p) MrGLMurphy(7) 116+
(Peter Maher, Ire) *led tl mstke 22nd and dropped to mid-div: gd prog to press ldr in 2nd bef 2 out where fell* **12/1**

F **Dogora (FR)**[24] 5224 6-11-7 134 MsKWalsh
(W P Mullins, Ire) *racd towards rr tl prog 5 out: hdwy in 6th whn fell 2 out* **5/1**[2]

U **Murphys Filly (IRE)**[17] 5320 7-10-7 93 MrJRDoyle(7)
(Colin Bowe, Ire) *a in rr: no threat whn mstke and uns rdr at 25th* **100/1**

9m 12.8s (552.80) **14 Ran SP% 126.5**
CSF £17.08 CT £75.88 TOTE £6.20: £2.00, £1.20, £2.70; DF 13.80 Trifecta £155.90.
Owner Mrs M McMahon **Bred** Mrs Carmel O'Brien **Trained** Muine Beag, Co Carlow

FOCUS
A finish that brought a smile to the face as two grizzled and not always straightforward old veterans battled it out from the last, with the winner becoming the oldest horse ever to win the race. The third and sixth help with the standard.

49a LADBROKES WORLD SERIES HURDLE (GRADE 1) (14 hdls) 3m
5:30 (5:34) 4-Y-0+
£93,023 (£29,457; £13,953; £4,651; £3,100; £1,550)

RPR
1 **Jezki (IRE)**[21] 5238 7-11-10 169 MarkWalsh 165+
(Mrs John Harrington, Ire) *hld up tl travelled wl to take clsr order 4 out in 4th: trckd ldr in 2nd after 2 out and led bef last: styd on wl run-in* **5/2**[2]

2 1¾ **Hurricane Fly (IRE)**[51] 4691 11-11-10 168 RWalsh 163
(W P Mullins, Ire) *hld up tl tk clsr order after 3 out: wnt 3rd after next: rdn to chse wnr in 2nd bef last: kpt on wl wout getting on terms* **6/4**[1]

3 8 **Zabana (IRE)**[50] 4704 6-11-10 146 JJBurke 155+
(Andrew Lynch, Ire) *racd in mid-div: rdn and nt qckn after 2 out: kpt on fr last into 3rd in clsng stages* **20/1**

4 3¾ **Lieutenant Colonel**[49] 4719 6-11-10 151 BJCooper 152
(Ms Sandra Hughes, Ire) *trckd ldrs in 3rd: clsd to press ldr in 2nd bef 3 out: nt qckn after next in 4th: sn no ex* **7/1**[3]

5 3½ **Ttebbob (IRE)**[24] 5222 6-11-10 140 RobbiePower 148
(Mrs John Harrington, Ire) *t.k.h under restraint in rr tl sme hdwy into mid-div 3 out: no imp after next* **28/1**

6 ½ **Jetson (IRE)**[19] 5273 10-11-10 150 DavyRussell 148
(Mrs John Harrington, Ire) *chsd ldrs: gd hdwy to trck ldr in 2nd 3 out: led next tl hdd bef last and sn no imp on principals in 3rd: wknd run-in* **14/1**

7 2½ **Thousand Stars (FR)**[24] 5221 11-11-10 156 (p) PaulTownend 145
(W P Mullins, Ire) *led tl hdd bef 2 out where nt fluent: sn no ex* **9/1**

8 1¾ **Zaidpour (FR)**[24] 5221 9-11-10 150 (p) DJCasey 143
(W P Mullins, Ire) *trckd ldr in 2nd tl wknd bef 3 out* **33/1**

9 3¼ **Captainofthefleet (IRE)**[35] 5006 8-11-10 135 MrEO'Connell 140
(Eamonn O'Connell, Ire) *hld up: rdn and nt qckn after 3 out: sn no ex* **66/1**

10 16 **Lots Of Memories (IRE)**[24] 5224 8-11-10 148 PaddyKennedy 124
(P G Fahey, Ire) *racd in mid-div tl prog to chse ldrs in 4th w a circ to r: rdn in 5th after 4 out and sn wknd* **33/1**

11 dist **I Shot The Sheriff (IRE)**[24] 5222 8-11-10 146 (t) PaulCarberry
(A J Martin, Ire) *a towards rr: dropped to rr 5 out and sn no ex: eased: t.o* **12/1**

5m 51.9s (-15.10) **Going Correction** -0.20s/f (Good) **11 Ran SP% 121.0**
Speed ratings: **117,116,113,112,111 111,110,109,108,103**
CSF £6.71 CT £60.82 TOTE £3.80: £1.50, £1.20, £4.20; DF 6.50 Trifecta £92.20.
Owner John P McManus **Bred** Gerard M McGrath **Trained** Moone, Co Kildare
■ Stewards' Enquiry : Mark Walsh one-day ban: used whip in incorrect place (tbn)

FOCUS
A terrific race between these two old rivals. Despite Hurricane Fly's relative dominance of this duel there had never been very much between them either way. That was the race here once again which does make one believe that stamina wasn't something that really came into play. It was just a proper race between two top-class hurdlers and there's every chance that next season's campaigns for both horses will be in excess of two miles. The time was good.

50a DONOHUE MARQUEES H'CAP HURDLE (14 hdls) 3m
6:05 (6:07) 4-Y-O+ **£11,337** (£3,313; £1,569; £523)

RPR

1 **Avant Tout (FR)**^{48} 4738 5-11-8 **129**........ DannyMullins 145+
(W P Mullins, Ire) *racd in mid-div tl travelled wl to chse ldrs 2 out: led appr last: rdn clr run-in* **20/1**

2 *3 ¼* **Rogue Trader (IRE)**^{32} 5052 6-11-3 **123**........ MsNCarberry 137+
(T J Taaffe, Ire) *hld up tl prog into mid-div after 3 out: gd hdwy into 3rd appr last: kpt on wl into 2nd cl home: nt trble wnr* **8/1**^{3}

3 *1* **Pleasant Company (IRE)**^{23} 5230 7-11-4 **124**........ RWalsh 137
(W P Mullins, Ire) *chsd ldrs tl travelled wl into 2nd 2 out: led bef last but sn hdd: no imp on wnr after last and dropped to 3rd cl home* **9/4**^{1}

4 *8 ½* **Never Said That (IRE)**^{8} 5484 7-10-6 **112**........(p) AELynch 116
(Edward Cawley, Ire) *chsd ldrs: prog 4 out into 5th: rdn along in 4th after 2 out: no imp appr last: sn one pce* **16/1**

5 *¾* **Mine Now (IRE)**^{24} 5222 7-10-10 **121**........ DavidMullins$^{(5)}$ 125
(Peter Fahey, Ire) *hld up towards rr: stl plenty to do 2 out: gd hdwy into 5th at last: kpt on same pce: nvr nrr* **16/1**

6 *3 ¾* **No Secrets (IRE)**^{24} 5224 11-11-3 **123**........(t) DenisO'Regan 123
(A J Martin, Ire) *racd in mid-div tl tk clsr order to chse ldrs 3 out in 7th: nt qckn after next: kpt on one pce* **20/1**

7 *1* **Give Me A Break (IRE)**^{40} 4931 6-10-13 **126**........ DonaghMeyler$^{(7)}$ 125
(Michael Hourigan, Ire) *hld up tl prog into mid-div 2 out: sn one pce* **50/1**

8 *½* **Wicked Spice (IRE)**^{13} 5366 6-11-5 **130**........ GerFox$^{(5)}$ 128
(Nicky Richards) *chsd ldrs: rdn along in 7th after 2 out: no ex appr last* **20/1**

9 *4 ¾* **Abolitionist (IRE)**^{18} 5304 7-10-12 **121**........ BrianHayes$^{(3)}$ 115
(John Joseph Hanlon, Ire) *racd in mid-div: prog bef 2 out on outer: no imp appr last* **33/1**

10 *28* **Queens Wild (IRE)**^{23} 5230 5-11-0 **121**........ AndrewJMcNamara 86
(Edward P Harty, Ire) *hld up in rr tl sme hdwy on inner 2 out: sn no imp* **25/1**

11 *2 ½* **Kolaphos**^{23} 5231 7-11-0 **120**........(t) DJCasey 83
(Martin Brassil, Ire) *racd towards rr: sme hdwy bef 2 out: sn no imp* **16/1**

12 *3 ¾* **Horendus Hulabaloo (IRE)**^{24} 5222 6-11-3 **123**........(tp) BJCooper 82
(M F Morris, Ire) *trckd ldrs tl led 3rd: jnd 8th tl led again 4 out: hdd 2 out and sn wknd* **25/1**

13 *1* **Roll It Out (IRE)**^{40} 4931 6-10-10 **121**........ LPDempsey$^{(5)}$ 79
(Gordon Elliott, Ire) *a towards rr: no threat 3 out* **6/1**^{2}

14 *¾* **Subtle Ben (IRE)**^{102} 3759 8-10-13 **119**........ SeanFlanagan 77
(Miss Elizabeth Doyle, Ire) *hld up: nt fluent 8th: no threat 3 out* **25/1**

15 *8 ½* **Black Benny (IRE)**^{68} 4376 10-10-12 **118**........(t) APHeskin 67
(J P Broderick, Ire) *nvr bttr than mid-div: no threat bef 2 out* **33/1**

16 *¾* **Relentless Dreamer (IRE)**^{71} 4294 6-11-1 **121**........ JJBurke 69
(Rebecca Curtis) *chsd ldrs tl nt qckn bef 3 out: sn no ex* **33/1**

17 *3 ¼* **Shadow Play (IRE)**^{20} 5267 5-10-4 **111**........ RobbiePower 55
(Paul Nolan, Ire) *trckd ldrs: prog to dispute at 8th tl hdd 4 out: wknd 2 out: eased bef last* **25/1**

18 *38* **Aengus (IRE)**^{23} 5230 5-11-2 **123**........ PaulCarberry 29
(Noel Meade, Ire) *racd towards rr: reminders bef 1/2-way: no threat 4 out: eased: t.o* **20/1**

19 *2* **Killer Crow (IRE)**^{40} 4932 6-11-7 **127**........ MPFogarty 32
(W P Mullins, Ire) *hld up: nt fluent 5th: no threat bef 3 out: eased bef last: t.o* **33/1**

20 *37* **Phare Isle (IRE)**^{24} 5202 10-11-4 **124**........(tp) KielanWoods
(Ben Case) *hld up: no threat bef 3 out: t.o* **20/1**

21 *2 ¼* **Really Unique (IRE)**^{46} 4795 10-10-8 **114**........ BrianO'Connell
(John J Walsh, Ire) *chsd ldrs tl 4 out: sn wknd: t.o* **50/1**

P **Follow The Sign (IRE)**^{24} 5222 7-11-5 **125**........(t) MarkEnright
(Oliver McKiernan, Ire) *led to 3rd: trckd ldrs tl wknd qckly 4 out: p.u bef next* **50/1**

P **Heck Thomas (IRE)**^{23} 5230 7-11-0 **120**........ NiallPMadden
(Noel Meade, Ire) *nvr bttr than mid-div: rdn 1/2-way and sn towards rr: p.u bef 3 out* **33/1**

F **Sambremont (FR)**^{32} 5052 5-11-2 **123**........ PaulTownend
(W P Mullins, Ire) *trckd ldr in 2nd tl 3rd: racd in 3rd tl led briefly after 3 out tl hdd next: sn no ex: fell last* **12/1**

P **Rathpatrick (IRE)**^{23} 5230 7-11-3 **123**........ MarkWalsh
(Eoin Griffin, Ire) *chsd ldrs tl nt qckn after 4 out: sn no ex: p.u bef last* **16/1**

5m 57.1s (-9.90) **Going Correction** -0.20s/f (Good) **25 Ran SP% 147.2**
Speed ratings: **108,106,106,103,103 102,101,101,100,90 90,88,88,88,85 85,84,71,70,58 57,,,,**
CSF £166.01 CT £526.69 TOTE £21.20: £5.10, £2.00, £1.60, £3.60; DF 313.00 Trifecta £394.20.
Owner Supreme Horse Racing Club & Brett T Graham **Bred** Yves De Soultrait **Trained** Muine Beag, Co Carlow

FOCUS
Habitually competitive and it was run at a reasonable pace. The first three pulled away, the fourth and fifth are good yardsticks and the first two are particularly progressive.

51a RYANAIR NOVICE CHASE (GRADE 1) (11 fncs) 2m
6:40 (6:43) 5-Y-O+ **£53,488** (£16,937; £8,023; £2,674; £1,782)

RPR

1 **Un De Sceaux (FR)**^{51} 4689 7-11-10 **168**........ RWalsh 158+
(W P Mullins, Ire) *mde all: j. carefully at times: extended advantage 4 out: ld reduced appr last: pushed clr run-in: comf* **1/10**^{1}

2 *3* **Just Cameron**^{26} 5137 8-11-10 **148**........(t) JoeColliver 153
(Micky Hammond) *sn chsd ldr in clr 2nd: nt fluent 7th: rdn fr 3 out: clsr appr last: no imp on wnr run-in: kpt on same pce* **16/1**^{3}

3 *4 ½* **Ted Veale (IRE)**^{21} 5240 8-11-10 **140**........ PaulCarberry 149
(A J Martin, Ire) *hld up in rr: rdn fr 3 out: wnt 4th at next: kpt on same pce into 3rd at last: nvr nrr* **20/1**

4 *1 ¼* **Real Steel (IRE)**^{74} 4260 7-11-10 **140**........(t) BJCooper 147
(M F Morris, Ire) *hld up in 4th tl rdn clsr in 3rd after 3 out: sn no imp and dropped to 4th bef last* **20/1**

5 *21* **Melodic Rendezvous**^{68} 4359 9-11-10 **150**........ MrJJCodd 126
(Jeremy Scott) *chsd ldrs in 3rd tl no imp and dropped to 4th after 3 out: in rr at next* **12/1**^{2}

4m 4.5s (-14.10) **Going Correction** -0.35s/f (Good) **5 Ran SP% 114.0**
Speed ratings: **121,119,117,116,106**
CSF £3.79 TOTE £1.10: £1.10, £2.00; DF 3.70 Trifecta £16.30.
Owner Edward O'Connell **Bred** Haras De La Rousseliere Et Al **Trained** Muine Beag, Co Carlow
■ Smashing was withdrawn. Price at time of withdrawal 6/1. Rule 4 applies to all bets - deduct 10p in the pound.

FOCUS
We hoped to see something spectacular from the favourite, but it never really transpired despite his never being in danger of losing his perfect record when completing. He's rated 12lb below his best.

52a ORCHID TRANSPORT MARES NOVICE HURDLE (9 hdls) 2m
7:15 (7:16) 4-Y-O+ **£11,337** (£3,313; £1,569; £523)

RPR

1 **Whiteout (GER)**^{24} 5220 4-10-8 0........ PaulTownend 122+
(W P Mullins, Ire) *hld up towards rr tl tk clsr order after 3 out on outer: pressed ldrs after next: led bef last and styd on wl* **8/1**

2 *1* **Uranna (FR)**^{25} 5175 7-11-7 131........ RWalsh 134+
(W P Mullins, Ire) *hld up towards rr tl tk clsr order bef 2 out: sn pushed along in 3rd: rdn to press ldr in 2nd at last: kpt on wl run-in* **4/1**^{3}

3 *3 ¼* **Lyrical Theatre (IRE)**^{25} 5175 6-11-4 132........ MrPWMullins 128
(W P Mullins, Ire) *chsd ldrs in 4th tl lft 3rd at 5th: rdn and no imp in 4th appr last: kpt on same pce into 3rd run-in* **2/1**^{1}

4 *½* **Kabjoy (IRE)**^{18} 3292 4-10-8 116........(t) RobbiePower 118
(Mrs John Harrington, Ire) *hld up towards rr: bdly hmpd at 5th: rdn to chse ldrs in 3rd at last: no imp and dropped to 4th run-in* **9/1**

5 *2 ¾* **Melbourne Lady**^{89} 3989 7-11-2 127........ MatthewBowes$^{(5)}$ 128
(P Fegan, Ire) *led after 1st and sn clr: advantage reduced after 4 out: strly pressed 2 out and hdd bef last: sn no ex* **25/1**

6 *shd* **Hannah's Princess (IRE)**^{40} 4918 6-11-4 0........ GavinSheehan 125
(Warren Greatrex) *racd in rr: hmpd at 5th: kpt on fr bef last: nvr on terms* **7/2**^{2}

7 *3 ¼* **Annamatopoeia (IRE)**^{32} 5053 7-10-11 118........ MrBOWalsh$^{(7)}$ 121
(Brian Jordan, Ire) *chsd ldrs in 3rd tl lft 2nd at 5th: wknd bef last* **25/1**

8 *13* **Grange Hall (IRE)**^{10} 5419 8-10-11 112........ JonathanMoore$^{(7)}$ 108
(Paul Stafford, Ire) *chsd ldrs: 4th 4 out: rdn and nt qckn after 2 out: sn no ex* **66/1**

9 *4* **Storm Away (IRE)**^{15} 5349 6-10-11 123........ NiallKelly$^{(7)}$ 104
(Patrick J Flynn, Ire) *hld up: rdn and nt qckn after 2 out: sn one pce* **9/1**

10 *23* **West Montan (IRE)**^{181} 2180 5-11-4 119........(t) SeanFlanagan 81
(David Harry Kelly, Ire) *racd in mid-div tl rdn after 4 out: no imp 2 out where dropped to rr* **50/1**

F **Scooping (IRE)**^{24} 5220 4-10-5 117........ ConorMaxwell$^{(3)}$
(E D Delany, Ire) *led to 1st: racd in clr 2nd tl fell 5th* **33/1**

4m 4.1s (-0.90) **Going Correction** -0.20s/f (Good)
WFA 4 from 5yo+ 5lb **11 Ran SP% 120.8**
Speed ratings: **94,93,91,91,90 90,88,82,80,68**
CSF £40.05 CT £90.97 TOTE £9.80: £2.20, £1.70, £1.20; DF 31.20 Trifecta £47.20.
Owner David Lawlor **Bred** Gestut Karlshof **Trained** Muine Beag, Co Carlow

FOCUS
A reasonable mares' hurdle dominated by the Mullins runners. It became something of a sprint.

53a KILDARE POST INH FLAT RACE 2m
7:45 (7:45) 4-7-Y-O **£6,418** (£1,488; £651; £372)

RPR

1 **Yorkhill (IRE)**^{54} 4643 5-12-0 0........ MrPWMullins 135+
(W P Mullins, Ire) *chsd ldrs in 4th tl travelled wl to press ldrs 4f out: led 3f out and sn qcknd clr: styd on wl fnl f tl advantage reduced cl home* **5/4**^{1}

2 *2 ¼* **Ok Corral (IRE)**^{83} 4073 5-12-0 0........ MsNCarberry 131+
(Nicky Henderson) *hld up towards rr: rdn along in 5th 3f out: gd hdwy to chse clr wnr in 2nd fr 2f out: kpt on wl to reduce deficit cl home: nvr on terms* **6/1**

3 *17* **Up For Review (IRE)**^{50} 4708 6-12-0 0........ MsKWalsh 114
(W P Mullins, Ire) *disp tl led after 4f: jnd again 1/2-way tl hdd 3f out: sn no imp in 3rd: one pce* **11/1**

4 *¾* **Sandymount Duke (IRE)**^{193} 1977 6-11-9 0........ MissKHarrington$^{(5)}$ 113
(Mrs John Harrington, Ire) *disp for 4f and bk on terms 1/2-way: rdn along 4f out and sn hdd: nt qckn in 5th tl kpt on one pce into 4th ent fnl f* **20/1**

5 *5 ½* **Newsworthy (IRE)**^{83} 4072 5-12-0 0........ MrJJCodd 108
(Nicky Henderson) *hld up in rr: kpt on one pce fnl 2f: nvr a threat* **4/1**^{2}

6 *1 ½* **Solatentif (FR)**^{122} 3392 5-11-9 0........ MrDRoche$^{(5)}$ 106
(Henry De Bromhead, Ire) *chsd ldrs: 4th at 1/2-way: rdn 4f out and nt qckn under 3f out: wknd over 1f out* **11/2**^{3}

7 *14* **Alamein (IRE)**^{42} 4880 5-11-9 0........(t) MrDGLavery$^{(5)}$ 92
(M F Morris, Ire) *trckd ldrs in 3rd tl rdn and nt qckn over 3f out: sn wknd* **20/1**

8 *28* **Beau Et Sublime (FR)**^{125} 3290 5-11-2 0........ MrSClements$^{(5)}$ 57
(A J Martin, Ire) *a towards rr: no threat over 3f out: sn detached* **28/1**

3m 57.6s (-1.80) **Going Correction** -0.20s/f (Good) **8 Ran SP% 115.4**
Speed ratings: **96,94,86,86,83 82,75,61**
Pick Six. Not Won. Pool of 7,860.50 carried forward to Punchestown on Fri, 1st May. Tote Aggregates: 2014: 641,383.00; 2015: 705,744.17. CSF £9.04 CT £57.08 TOTE £2.20: £1.20, £1.50, £2.70; DF 8.10 Trifecta £48.10.
Owner Andrea & Graham Wylie **Bred** Patrick Keating **Trained** Muine Beag, Co Carlow

FOCUS
This looks a more decent bumper after the fact than beforehand possibly, the winner showing some gears to get to the front and probably winning with more authority than the margin of victory suggests.
T/Jkpt: @648.10. Pool of @25,000.00 - 27 winning units. T/Plt: @4.20. Pool of @105,887.46 - 17499.20 winning units. **Alan Hewison**

54a - (Foreign Racing) - See Raceform Interactive

BANGOR-ON-DEE (L-H)
Friday, May 1

OFFICIAL GOING: Good (6.9)
Wind: Light; half against Weather: Fine

55 GET LOGO'D H'CAP HURDLE (12 hdls) 2m 7f 32y
5:20 (5:21) (Class 5) (0-100,100) 4-Y-O+ **£3,249** (£954; £477; £238)

Form RPR

501- 1 **Billy Congo (IRE)**^{9} 5476 8-11-3 **91** 7ex........(t) MichealNolan 101+
(Adrian Wintle) *hld up towards rr: stdy hdwy 6th: trcking ldrs 8th: led appr last: pushed out* **4/1**^{2}

440- **2** *6* **Westerly Breeze (IRE)**34 5027 7-11-1 **92**........................(b) BenPoste(3) 96
(Edward Bevan) *chsd ldrs: led after 7th: hdd appr last: no ex* **9/1**

00P- **3** *3 ¼* **The Wee Midget**169 2462 10-10-8 **89**........................(b) ConorSmith(7) 89
(Arthur Whiting) *led tl after 7th: kpt on one pce fr 2 out* **9/1**

0P0- **4** *23* **Toast And Jam (IRE)**22 5245 6-11-0 **88**........................(t) TrevorWhelan 70
(Claire Dyson) *t.k.h: trckd ldrs: wkng whn blnd 2 out: sn bhd* **50/1**

521- **5** *17* **Pennies And Pounds**13 5398 8-11-0 **88**........................ MarkGrant 52
(Julian Smith) *prom: wknd bef 2 out: sn bhd* **9/2**3

PP5- **6** *3 ¼* **Nicky Nutjob (GER)**41 4928 9-9-7 **74** oh6........................(p) DavidPrichard(7) 35
(John O'Shea) *hld up in rr: sme hdwy 8th: sn wknd* **40/1**

003- **7** *20* **Horace Hazel**45 4825 6-11-11 **99**........................(b1) AidanColeman 42
(Anthony Honeyball) *nt jump wl in rr: reminders 7th: sn bhd: mstke 3 out: sn t.o* **9/4**1

553- **F** **Duke Of Monmouth (IRE)**31 5086 8-11-5 **100**........................ MrJNixon(7)
(Tom Symonds) *chsd ldrs: drvn 7th: lost pl and fell next* **11/2**

/54- **P** **Miss H Lewiss**43 4869 7-10-12 **93**........................ CiaranGethings(7)
(Steve Flook) *prom: lost pl 8th: sn bhd: t.o whn p.u bef 3 out* **20/1**

/3P- **P** **Magic Present**69 4355 8-11-6 **94**........................(b) RobertDunne
(Sarah-Jayne Davies) *chsd ldrs: lost pl after 9th: sn bhd: t.o whn p.u bef 2 out* **33/1**

306- **P** **Dolly Diamond**25 5194 6-11-7 **95**........................ GerardTumelty
(Graeme McPherson) *chsd ldrs: lost pl 5th: bhd whn nt fluent next: t.o whn hmpd 8th: t.o whn p.u bef 2 out* **40/1**

5m 58.9s (7.90) **Going Correction** +0.25s/f (Yiel) **11** Ran SP% **118.9**
Speed ratings (Par 103): **96,94,92,85,79 78,71,, ,**
CSF £37.32 CT £310.55 TOTE £6.10: £1.60, £3.10, £4.10; EX 56.50 Trifecta £560.50.
Owner Ron C Williams **Bred** Jimmy Howard **Trained** Westbury-On-Severn, Gloucs

FOCUS
Dry, overcast and cool for this evening meeting. The pace was ordinary for a moderate staying handicap where four drew clear from half a mile out. The cosy winner built on his recent victory.

56 EPDS RACING PARTNERSHIPS SUPPORTING RACING WELFARE NOVICES' HURDLE (11 hdls) 2m 3f 123y
5:50 (5:50) (Class 4) 4-Y-0+ **£3,898** (£1,144; £572; £286)

Form RPR

1 **Sign Manual**566 6-10-12 0........................ WilsonRenwick 112+
(Donald McCain) *towards rr: hdwy to chse ldrs 6th: led after 3 out: wnt clr between last 2: heavily eased last 100yds* **9/2**3

0- **2** *9* **Hillview Lad (IRE)**19 5293 7-10-12 0........................ AdamWedge 97
(Nick Kent) *in rr: hdwy 7th: chsng ldrs next: 2nd whn hit 2 out: no ch w wnr* **50/1**

606- **3** *12* **Uncle Monty (IRE)**26 5159 6-10-12 0........................(p) AdrianLane 86
(Donald McCain) *chsd ldrs: one pce appr 2 out* **50/1**

40- **4** *5* **Adam Du Breteau (FR)**37 4985 5-10-12 0........................ RichieMcLernon 80
(Jonjo O'Neill) *led: hdd after 3 out: hung rt and one pce bef next* **9/4**2

40- **5** *3 ¾* **Highland Life**32 5077 5-10-2 0........................(t) BenPoste(3) 71
(Steve Flook) *sn chsng ldrs: drvn 8th: fdd sn after 2 out* **100/1**

545- **6** *5* **Theflyingportrait (IRE)**29 5106 6-10-12 115........................ MarkGrant 72
(Jennie Candlish) *sn prom: drvn 3 out: fdd bef next* **8/1**

650- **7** *89* **Abijoe**25 5198 6-10-5 0........................ KielanWoods
(Pam Sly) *chsd ldrs: lost pl after 7th: sn bhd: t.o after 3 out: eventually completed* **25/1**

000- **8** *62* **David John**37 4984 4-10-7 0........................ RobertDunne
(Alexandra Dunn) *towards rr: bhd fr 6th: t.o next: eventually completed* **100/1**

0F4- **9** *nse* **Star Benefit (IRE)**32 5063 5-10-12 0........................ MichealNolan
(Adrian Wintle) *in rr: bhd fr 5th: reminders 7th: t.o 3 out: eventually completed* **33/1**

541- **P** **Forever Field (IRE)**40 4936 5-11-5 0........................ PeterCarberry
(Nicky Henderson) *chsd ldrs: wknd appr 2 out: 7th and bhd whn p.u bef last* **6/4**1

P **Time On Your Hands (IRE)** 5-10-12 0........................(t) MichaelByrne
(Tim Vaughan) *blnd 1st: sn in rr: bhd fr 5th: t.o whn p.u bef next* **20/1**

0- **P** **Midnight Owle**14 5380 5-10-12 0........................ TrevorWhelan
(Claire Dyson) *in rr: bhd fr 5th: t.o 7th: p.u bef 2 out* **100/1**

5m 1.3s (9.30) **Going Correction** +0.25s/f (Yiel)
WFA 4 from 5yo+ 19lb **12** Ran SP% **118.5**
Speed ratings (Par 105): **91,87,82,80,79 77,41,16,16, ,**
CSF £188.86 TOTE £5.20: £1.20, £22.90, £9.10; EX 125.30 Trifecta £1333.40 Part won..
Owner Graham & Carole Worsley **Bred** The Queen **Trained** Cholmondeley, Cheshire

FOCUS
Very little depth to this novice hurdle, the race fell apart and they finished well strung out. The winner looked out of the ordinary and is entitled to rate a lot higher on Flat form.

57 CHEESE WAREHOUSE NOVICES' H'CAP CHASE (15 fncs) 2m 4f 72y
6:25 (6:25) (Class 4) (0-105,105) 5-Y-0+ **£4,223** (£1,240; £620; £310)

Form RPR

333- **1** **Mor Brook**34 5029 7-11-8 **101**........................ DavidBass 112+
(Kim Bailey) *led: hit 1st: hdd after 4th: led 11th: styd on fr 2 out: drvn out* **85/40**1

446- **2** *3 ¼* **Miss Biscotti**50 4733 7-10-5 **91**........................(p) MrZBaker(7) 97+
(Martin Bosley) *chsd ldrs: led after 4th: hmpd by loose horse 6th: hdd 11th: keeping on same pce whn hit 2 out* **33/1**

445- **3** *6* **Lost In Newyork (IRE)**25 5206 8-10-2 **81**........................ AdamWedge 81
(Nick Kent) *hld up in rr: hdwy 10th: sn chsng ldrs: disputing 2nd 2 out: one pce* **20/1**

P54- **4** *25* **Bobble Boru (IRE)**44 4857 7-11-12 **105**........................ LiamTreadwell 85
(Venetia Williams) *in rr: nt fluent 3rd: sme hdwy 7th: lost pl bef 2 out* **12/1**

54P- **5** *9* **Blue Sea Of Ibrox (IRE)**13 5398 7-9-7 **79** oh5........................(b) GLavery(7) 47
(Alan Brown) *hmpd and lost pl 1st: reminders next: hdwy 6th: lost pl 9th: sn bhd* **40/1**

50F- **6** *51* **Siobhans Beauty (IRE)**97 3862 7-11-12 **105**........................ MichealNolan 28
(Jamie Snowden) *chsd ldrs: poor 4th and tired whn hit 2 out: sn wl bhd: t.o: eventually completed* **10/1**

/04- **7** *5* **French Canadian (FR)**13 5398 9-11-2 **95**........................ DougieCostello 13
(Heather Dalton) *trckd ldrs: lost pl 3rd: bhd fr 10th: t.o bef 2 out: eventually completed* **20/1**

600- **P** **Battleship Boy (IRE)**22 5245 7-10-7 **86**........................ RobertDunne
(Sarah-Jayne Davies) *chsd ldrs: lost pl 11th: t.o whn p.u bef 3 out* **66/1**

5P4- **U** **Bouggietopieces**14 5375 5-11-4 **97**........................ KielanWoods
(Pam Sly) *cl 2nd whn mstke and uns rdr 1st* **10/1**

646- **P** **Superior Fire (IRE)**19 5295 5-11-8 **101**........................(tp) AidanColeman
(Charlie Longsdon) *chsd ldrs: reminders 7th: lost pl 9th: sn bhd: t.o whn p.u bef 3 out* **6/1**3

6U3- **P** **Road To Freedom**11 5429 6-11-12 **105**........................ TomO'Brien
(Lucy Wadham) *nt jump wl in rr: blnd 10th: sn bhd: t.o whn p.u bef 3 out* **3/1**2

5m 10.7s (1.60) **Going Correction** +0.10s/f (Yiel) **11** Ran SP% **113.6**
Speed ratings: **100,98,96,86,83 64,62,, ,**
CSF £73.58 CT £1104.88 TOTE £3.00: £1.30, £4.80, £6.00; EX 92.00 Trifecta £1186.60 Part won..
Owner Mor Fun Partnership **Bred** Mrs Nicola Moores **Trained** Andoversford, Gloucs

FOCUS
A moderate novice handicap chase and a cosy winner, who can rate higher.

58 BANGORBET H'CAP CHASE (18 fncs) 3m 30y
7:00 (7:00) (Class 4) (0-110,109) 5-Y-0+ **£6,498** (£1,908; £954; £477)

Form RPR

P13- **1** **Trafficker (IRE)**54 4646 8-11-7 **104**........................ SamTwiston-Davies 115+
(Graeme McPherson) *hld up in rr: hdwy to chse ldrs 12th: 2nd 3 out: upsides whn lft in ld last: drvn out: fnd ex nr fin* **3/1**1

042- **2** *1* **Mission Complete (IRE)**13 5399 9-10-12 **105**........................(vt) JackSavage(10) 116
(Jonjo O'Neill) *reminders after 1st: hdwy 4th: drvn and dropped bk 8th: chsd ldrs 10th: lft 2nd sn after last: no ex clsng stages* **6/1**

3P3- **3** *3* **Uhlan Bute (FR)**37 4988 7-11-12 **109**........................ LiamTreadwell 117
(Venetia Williams) *trckd ldrs 4th: led after 9th: jnd and hrd drvn whn blnd last: kpt on one pce* **9/1**

032- **4** *10* **Musical Wedge**41 4925 11-10-5 **88**........................ TrevorWhelan 85
(Claire Dyson) *chsd ldrs: led 2nd tl after 9th: drvn 11th: fdd appr 2 out* **14/1**

511- **5** *33* **Tribal Dance (IRE)**26 5156 9-10-8 **91**........................(p) DaveCrosse 59
(John O'Shea) *led: hdd 2nd: reminders 5th: lost pl next: hdwy to chse ldrs 9th: lost pl 11th: t.o 3 out* **20/1**

23U- **6** *10* **Ready Token (IRE)**32 5073 7-11-8 **105**........................ AidanColeman 64
(Charlie Longsdon) *in rr: hdwy to chse ldrs 7th: reminders 12th: sn lost pl: bhd fr 14th: t.o 2 out* **5/1**3

FPF- **P** **Bringewood Belle**334 548 12-10-0 **83** oh3........................ TommyPhelan
(John Needham) *in rr: t.o 9th: p.u bef next* **25/1**

532- **P** **Roll The Dice (IRE)**31 5081 9-11-10 **107**........................ TomO'Brien
(Philip Hobbs) *chsd ldrs: drvn 12th: wknd next: sn bhd: t.o whn p.u bef 2 out* **13/2**

121- **P** **Harris (IRE)**13 5399 8-11-3 **103**........................(v) JonathanEngland(3)
(Alan Brown) *chsd ldrs: lost pl 7th: bhd 9th: t.o whn p.u bef 11th* **9/2**2

6m 19.5s (-0.30) **Going Correction** +0.10s/f (Yiel) **9** Ran SP% **112.7**
Speed ratings: **104,103,102,99,88 85,, ,**
CSF £21.17 CT £141.91 TOTE £3.70: £1.40, £2.00, £2.80; EX 24.10 Trifecta £226.00.
Owner R D Potter **Bred** River Side Farms **Trained** Upper Oddington, Gloucs

FOCUS
A relatively competitive, if low-grade staying handicap. Straightforward form.

59 NICOL HUGHES H'CAP HURDLE (9 hdls) 2m 145y
7:30 (7:31) (Class 4) (0-120,117) 4-Y-0+ **£5,523** (£1,621; £810; £405)

Form RPR

052- **1** **Another Journey**25 5189 6-11-2 **107**........................ RobertDunne 118+
(Sarah-Jayne Davies) *trckd ldrs: led 6th: drvn appr 2 out: forged clr between last 2: eased last 100yds* **25/1**

F12- **2** *6* **Tekthelot (IRE)**11 5422 9-11-3 **108**........................ JamesReveley 111
(Keith Reveley) *trckd ldrs: handy 2nd sn after 3 out: drvn bef next: kpt on same pce* **15/8**1

03U- **3** *6* **Short Takes (USA)**35 5019 7-11-7 **112**........................(b) WilsonRenwick 108
(Donald McCain) *led: hdd and drvn 6th: one pce bef 2 out: tk modest 3rd appr last* **20/1**

041- **4** *5* **Future Security (IRE)**10 5452 6-11-11 **116** 7ex........................(t) PaddyBrennan 108
(Anthony Middleton) *t.k.h: hdwy to trck ldrs 2nd: drvn 6th: one pce bef 2 out: modest 4th whn mstke last* **3/1**3

601- **5** *nk* **Songsmith**11 5427 7-11-12 **117**........................ MichealNolan 110
(Lucy Wadham) *trckd ldrs: drvn 3 out: wknd appr last* **2/1**2

6/0- **6** *68* **Grams And Ounces**20 5283 8-10-6 **97**........................(t) DougieCostello 27
(Adrian Wintle) *in last: outpcd and pushed along 5th: bhd next: t.o bef 2 out: sn eased: eventually completed* **12/1**

4m 12.6s (1.70) **Going Correction** +0.25s/f (Yiel) **6** Ran SP% **109.4**
Speed ratings (Par 105): **106,103,100,98,97 65**
CSF £70.28 TOTE £11.60: £4.00, £1.20; EX 76.70 Trifecta £202.30.
Owner Miss Sarah-Jayne Davies **Bred** Goldford Stud And D O Pickering **Trained** Leominster, H'fords

FOCUS
A fair race for the grade. Five were in contention three out, but the winner went well clear and the form should hold true, even though the winner was making a big step up..

60 JOHN HEWITT MEMORIAL NOVICES' HUNTERS' CHASE (18 fncs) 3m 30y
8:05 (8:06) (Class 6) 5-Y-0+ **£1,247** (£387; £193; £96)

Form RPR

502/ **1** **Don't Hang About**647 1083 10-11-11 102........................ MrGCrow(3) 106+
(Gary Hanmer) *trckd ldrs: 2nd sn after 3 out: upsides last: sn led: drvn out* **3/1**2

503/ **2** *¾* **Stratford Stroller (IRE)**13 11-11-7 89........................ MissJosephineBanks(7) 103
(Alastair Ralph) *t.k.h: trckd ldrs: led briefly after 7th: led 11th: jnd last: sn hdd and no ex* **9/2**3

3 *12* **Threapwood**27 8-11-11 0........................(b) MrEGlassonbury(3) 95
(Oliver Greenall) *chsd ldrs: lft 3rd and hmpd 15th: kpt on one pce fr 2 out: 3rd last* **9/2**3

603/ **4** *3 ¾* **Puyol (IRE)**5 13-11-7 92........................ MrBFurnival(7) 91
(Patricia Rigby) *in rr: hdwy 13th: 3rd 2 out: fdd last* **25/1**

P- **P** **Doctor Henry (IRE)**12 5409 9-11-7 0........................ MrTommieMO'Brien(7)
(Richard Mathias) *w ldrs: wknd 3 out: bhd whn p.u bef next* **12/1**

4/6- **U** **Miss Tilly Oscar (IRE)**30 5096 9-11-4 91........................ CiaranGethings(3)
(Steve Flook) *t.k.h: w ldr: led 5th: hdd briefly after 7th: cl 3rd whn blnd and uns rdr 15th* **12/1**

P **Cooladerry King (IRE)**19 7-12-0 0........................ MrWBiddick
(Mrs Sheila Crow) *led to 5th: lost pl 11th: hit next: sn bhd: t.o whn p.u bef 3 out* **2/1**1

6m 28.8s (9.00) **Going Correction** +0.10s/f (Yiel) **7** Ran SP% **113.9**
Speed ratings: **89,88,84,83, , ,**
CSF £17.00 TOTE £4.90: £2.20, £4.00; EX 22.40 Trifecta £57.80.
Owner F Lloyd **Bred** F Lloyd **Trained** Nantwich, Cheshire

FOCUS
A fair novice hunters' chase which saw a remarkable training performance. The winner can probably better this.
T/Plt: £590.60 to a £1 stake. Pool: £59,916.60 - 74.05 winning units T/Qpdt: £24.40 to a £1 stake. Pool: £7,319.70 - 221.95 winning units **Walter Glynn**

FONTWELL (L-H)

Friday, May 1

OFFICIAL GOING: Good (6.7)
Wind: Light; against Weather: Overcast

61 THIS ONE IS FOR EQUINITI LADIES! MAIDEN HURDLE (10 hdls) 2m 3f 33y
4:30 (4:30) (Class 5) 4-Y-O+ £2,339 (£686; £343; £171)

Form RPR

344- 1 **Towering (IRE)**[40] 4941 6-10-11 0 JeremiahMcGrath(3) 120+
(Nicky Henderson) *midfield: clsd after 6th: trcking ldrs and mstke 3 out: rdn bef next: cl 3rd and mstke last: sn swtchd rt and styd on wl to ld fnl 100yds: rdn out* 6/1[3]

443- 2 2 ¼ **Romulus Du Donjon (IRE)**[39] 4964 4-10-9 114 LeightonAspell 112
(Oliver Sherwood) *chsd ldrs: clsd and trckd ldng pair whn mstke 7th: led next: rdn after 2 out: blnd last: hdd and one pce fnl 100yds* 8/1

344- 3 1 ¼ **Sandygate (IRE)**[29] 5106 5-11-0 0 RichardJohnson 116
(Philip Hobbs) *hld up off the pce in midfield: j.big 2nd: clsd and in tch 7th: swtchd rt after next and hdwy to chse ldr 2 out: ev ch and rdn bef last: nt fluent last: outpcd fnl 100yds* 4/1[2]

403- 4 11 **Marden Court (IRE)**[40] 4947 5-11-0 119 BrendanPowell 106
(Colin Tizzard) *chsd ldrs: rdn after 6th: drvn bef 3 out: stl cl 4th bef 2 out: wknd last* 9/4[1]

653- 5 4 **Do We Like Him (IRE)**[26] 5151 5-11-0 0 NickScholfield 102
(Chris Gordon) *hld up wl off the pce in last trio: clsd after 6th: stmbld bnd after 3 out: no imp whn hung lft after next: swtchd rt last: plugged on past btn horses flat: nvr trbld ldrs* 14/1

6 2 ¼ **To Begin**[41] 4-10-9 0 NoelFehily 94
(Charlie Mann) *midfield: clsd after 6th: wnt 2nd after 3 out tl 2 out: rdn and btn bef last: wknd flat* 33/1

7 1 ¼ **Astrowolf**[99] 4-10-9 0 AndrewTinkler 94
(Mark H Tompkins) *midfield: clsd after 6th: mstke and rdn next: swtchd rt and hdwy sn after 3 out: no ex and btn bef last: mstke last: wknd flat* 80/1

8 22 **Cotton King**[710] 8-11-0 0 AndrewThornton 79
(Graham Mays) *hld up wl off the pce in last trio: nvr on terms: t.o 2 out* 20/1

05- 9 4 **Empty Marmalades (FR)**[14] 5373 4-10-9 0 WillKennedy 70
(Gary Moore) *a wl off the pce in last trio: nvr on terms: slipped bnd after 3 out: t.o whn blnd next* 33/1

U5U- 10 27 **Stars Royale (IRE)**[16] 5343 6-11-0 110 TomCannon 51
(Nick Gifford) *led tl 7th: rdn and lost pl sn after next: t.o and eased flat* 13/2

46- P **Hoist The Colours (IRE)**[33] 5043 4-10-9 0 (v) MarcGoldstein
(Gary Moore) *t.k.h: mstkes: w ldr tl led 7th: hdd next and sn lost pl u.p: t.o whn p.u last* 20/1

PFP- P **Abuelo (FR)**[79] 3960 5-11-0 0 [1] WayneHutchinson
(Zoe Davison) *midfield but nvr on terms: lost pl and mstke 5th: rdn and losing tch qckly after next: t.o whn p.u 7th* 100/1

505- P **Cool Fusion**[8] 5500 6-10-2 0 DannyBurton(5)
(Anthony Day) *hld up wl off the pce in rr: stmbld on landing and rdr lost iron 4th: nt rcvr and p.u bef next: sddle slipped* 100/1

4m 46.85s (-12.55) **Going Correction** -0.325s/f (Good)
WFA 4 from 5yo+ 18lb 13 Ran SP% 114.8
Speed ratings (Par 103): **112,111,110,106,104 103,103,94,92,82 , ,**
CSF £47.81 TOTE £6.50: £1.70, £3.20, £1.60; EX 49.90 Trifecta £187.10.
Owner Middleham Park Racing LIX **Bred** Liam O'Byrne **Trained** Upper Lambourn, Berks

FOCUS
Bottom bend common. Rail movement adding 60yds per circuit to chase course and 35yds per circuit to hurdles track. After riding in the opener Brendan Powell said: "It's good, good to firm in places. They're knocking the top off it, but it's quick underneath." A fair maiden hurdle to start with, in which the front three pulled clear. A step up on his bumper form from the winner.

62 "INTERNATIONAL PAYMENT-FIRST PAST THE POST" H'CAP CHASE (16 fncs) 2m 5f 31y
5:05 (5:05) (Class 4) (0-120,119) 5-Y-O+ £4,028 (£1,182; £591; £295)

Form RPR

01- 1 **Express Du Berlais (FR)**[9] 5465 6-11-7 114 (t) WillKennedy 128+
(Dr Richard Newland) *hld up in tch: hdwy to press ldr 7th: nt fluent 12th: led next: clr and in command next: pushed out flat* 5/4[1]

P43- 2 6 **Friendly Society (IRE)**[21] 5259 10-11-6 116 (v) JamesBanks(3) 122
(Noel Williams) *chsd ldrs: j. awkwardly 1st: rdn after 10th: j. into 2nd 13th: no imp next* 10/1

2U2- 3 3 ¾ **De Blacksmith (IRE)**[21] 5259 7-11-8 115 (tp) TomCannon 116
(Gary Moore) *chsd ldr: reminders after 4th: lost 2nd 7th: drvn after 10th: 4th and outpcd after 13th: 10 l down 3 out: no imp: wnt 3rd last* 11/2[3]

222- 4 7 **Bertie's Desire**[174] 2355 7-11-6 113 LeightonAspell 109
(Oliver Sherwood) *in tch: pushed along 9th: 3rd and rdn after 13th: no imp next: lost 3rd last* 10/3[2]

1U4- 5 41 **Strumble Head (IRE)**[173] 2377 10-11-12 119 DonalDevereux 76
(Peter Bowen) *led tl 13th: sn lost pl and bhd 3 out: lost tch next: t.o* 12/1

446- P **Burgess Dream (IRE)**[26] 5152 6-10-1 93 oh3 ow1 PaulMoloney
(Anna Newton-Smith) *a in rr: lost tch after 13th: t.o whn p.u last* 10/1

5m 41.5s (-1.50) **Going Correction** -0.10s/f (Good) 6 Ran SP% 108.8
Speed ratings: **98,95,94,91,77**
CSF £12.47 TOTE £2.10: £1.40, £4.10; EX 10.60 Trifecta £51.80.
Owner Dr R D P Newland **Bred** Jean-Marc Lucas **Trained** Claines, Worcs

FOCUS
A fair handicap chase. The winner looks to have more to offer.

63 "GET YOURSELF ON THE WINNER" H'CAP HURDLE (9 hdls) 2m 1f 145y
5:40 (5:40) (Class 3) (0-130,122) 4-Y-O £5,317 (£1,570; £785; £393; £196)

Form RPR

P42- 1 **Benbecula**[30] 5101 6-11-5 115 RichardJohnson 120+
(Richard Mitchell) *j.rt: mde all: rdn after 2 out: styd on wl flat: rdn out* 2/1[1]

F02- 2 2 ¼ **Kuda Huraa (IRE)**[32] 5070 7-11-8 118 (b) WayneHutchinson 121
(Alan King) *in tch: rdn and lost pl but stl wl in tch 6th: hdwy to chse ldrs after 2 out: wnt 2nd last: styd on same pce flat* 11/2

655- 3 ¾ **Watt Broderick (IRE)**[45] 4830 6-11-1 111 WillKennedy 111
(Ian Williams) *hld up in tch in rr: hdwy to chse ldrs 2 out: chsd wnr wl bef last: lost 2nd but stl cl enough last: one pce flat* 15/2

12- 4 5 **Aviator (GER)**[39] 4964 7-11-12 122 JackQuinlan 119
(James Eustace) *mostly chsd wnr: slipped bnd after 3 out: rdn bef next: lost 2nd and unable qck wl bef last: wknd flat* 12/1

0F3- 5 3 **City Supreme (IRE)**[65] 4439 5-10-13 109 (b[1]) NoelFehily 102
(Anthony Honeyball) *t.k.h: in tch in last pair: hdwy to chse ldrs after 5th: rdn and no ex bef 2 out: wknd bef last* 3/1[2]

334- 6 2 ½ **Ourmanmassini (IRE)**[14] 5369 7-11-3 113 (b) TomCannon 105
(Suzy Smith) *chsd ldrs tl after 6th: sn rdn: btn after 2 out: hung lft flat* 5/1[3]

4m 29.3s (-5.00) **Going Correction** -0.325s/f (Good) 6 Ran SP% 109.8
Speed ratings (Par 107): **97,96,95,93,92 91**
CSF £12.63 TOTE £2.40: £1.80, £2.40; EX 15.50 Trifecta £66.60.
Owner Mr And Mrs Andrew May **Bred** Floors Farming And Christopher J Heath **Trained** Piddletrenthide, Dorset

FOCUS
Not the strongest handicap for the grade, with the top weight rated 8lb below the ceiling. The form is rated around the second.

64 EQUINITI FINTECH FOR WEALTH SOLUTIONS H'CAP CHASE (13 fncs) 2m 1f 96y
6:15 (6:15) (Class 4) (0-115,113) 5-Y-O+ £4,028 (£1,182; £591; £295)

Form RPR

F33- 1 **Marie Des Anges (FR)**[32] 5064 7-11-5 113 (t) DavidNoonan(7) 124+
(Anthony Honeyball) *lft 2nd and hmpd 1st: led 4th tl after 7th: chsd ldr tl led again 10th: kpt on wl flat: rdn out* 6/1[3]

421- 2 4 **Very Noble (FR)**[14] 5369 6-11-8 109 (t) TomCannon 117
(Chris Gordon) *hld up in tch: effrt to chse wnr 3 out: rdn next: 2 l down whn mstke last: no imp u.p flat* 2/1[1]

2P5- 3 18 **Vision Des Champs (FR)**[25] 5211 6-11-2 103 (t) LeightonAspell 95
(Gary Moore) *hmpd 1st: chsd ldrs: effrt to chse wnr after 10th tl mstke 3 out: btn next: wknd bef last* 9/4[2]

0/ 4 7 **Darwins Theory (IRE)**[174] 2361 7-11-1 109 (t) MrMLegg(7) 96
(Fiona Shaw) *t.k.h early: hmpd 1st: in tch in last pair: rdn after 10th: sn struggling and wl hld next* 12/1

453- 5 12 **Keychain (IRE)**[156] 2733 5-11-1 102 (tp) BrendanPowell 84
(Brendan Powell) *nt a fluent: lft in ld 1st: hdd 4th: led again after 7th tl 10th: rdn and btn next: wknd between last 2: eased towards fin* 7/1

445- U **Miller Of Glanmire (IRE)**[53] 4670 7-10-8 105 (tp) TommyDowling(10)
(Charlie Mann) *led: j.lft: blnd and uns rdr 1st* 8/1

4m 38.1s (3.40) **Going Correction** -0.10s/f (Good) 6 Ran SP% 109.7
Speed ratings: **88,86,78,75,69**
CSF £18.25 TOTE £6.40: £1.70, £1.40; EX 8.50 Trifecta £32.50.
Owner Atlantic Racing & R W Huggins **Bred** Pegasus Breeding Ltd **Trained** Mosterton, Dorset

FOCUS
A modest handicap chase and the first two finished clear of the rest. The winner is rated to her best.

65 INVEST WITH CONFIDENCE AT SELFTRADE.CO.UK H'CAP HURDLE (11 hdls) 2m 5f 139y
6:50 (6:50) (Class 5) (0-100,97) 4-Y-O+ £2,339 (£686; £343; £171)

Form RPR

625- 1 **Hi Bronco**[27] 5148 8-10-1 72 (p) JamesDavies 77+
(John Ryall) *chsd ldr tl 3rd: wnt 2nd again and mstke 8th: led bef 2 out: styd on wl flat* 8/1

/06- 2 4 **Master Cardor Visa (IRE)**[354] 231 10-10-9 83 JamesBanks(3) 84
(Emma Baker) *wl in tch in midfield: chsd ldrs and rdn after 3 out: chsd wnr jst bef 2 out: styd on same pce flat* 14/1

262- 3 ¾ **Midnight Sequel**[29] 5118 6-11-4 89 (tp) NoelFehily 90
(Neil Mulholland) *wl in tch in midfield: hdwy to chse ldrs sn after 3 out: mstke last: styd on same pce flat* 7/2[1]

205- 4 nk **The Selector**[26] 5157 6-10-3 77 SeanBowen(3) 78
(Chris Gordon) *in tch in last pair: pushed along after 7th: swtchd rt bef 3 out: hdwy bef 2 out: kpt on flat: no threat to wnr* 6/1[3]

316- 5 2 ¼ **River Dancing (IRE)**[31] 5082 8-10-2 80 (t) MrMLegg(7) 80
(Anthony Honeyball) *hld up in tch: mstke 6th: effrt to chse ldrs and rdn after 3 out: no ex whn mstke and rdr dropped whip last: wknd flat* 9/2[2]

0P4- 6 32 **Kingscombe (USA)**[80] 3004 6-10-0 71 MarcGoldstein 40
(Linda Jewell) *hld up in tch in last pair: clsng and gng wl whn bdly hmpd bnd after 3 out: nt rcvr and hmpd again next: nt pushed after* 25/1

436- 7 5 **Dexter Benjamin (IRE)**[26] 5157 6-11-12 97 (p) TomCannon 61
(Nick Gifford) *chsd ldrs: rdn and lost pl 3 out: bhd next: t.o* 12/1

P00- 8 17 **Achemenes (FR)**[14] 5371 6-9-13 77 FreddieMitchell(7) 26
(Daniel Steele) *led: mstke 7th: hdd jst bef 2 out: sn wknd u.p: t.o flat* 33/1

134- 9 43 **Benability (IRE)**[80] 4147 5-11-10 95 RichardJohnson 5
(Tim Vaughan) *chsd ldr 3rd tl mstke 8th: rdn and hit next: sn dropped out: t.o and virtually p.u flat* 7/1

423- F **Golden Games (IRE)**[26] 5157 9-11-5 93 (p) ThomasGarner(3)
(Daniel O'Brien) *chsd ldrs: cl 6th and rdn whn n.m.r: clipped heels and fell heavily bnd sn after 3 out: fatally injured* 12/1

3/2- F **Titch Strider (IRE)**[40] 4948 10-11-10 95 BrendanPowell 95
(John Panvert) *hld up in tch: hdwy 3 out: 5 l 5th and drvn whn fell next* 10/1

000- P **Nicki's Nipper**[32] 5059 7-10-6 77 PaulMoloney
(Sophie Leech) *in tch in midfield: wd and lost pl bnd after 5th: rdn and lost tch after 7th: t.o whn p.u bef 2 out* 33/1

5m 34.9s (-7.60) **Going Correction** -0.325s/f (Good) 12 Ran SP% 119.2
Speed ratings (Par 103): **100,98,98,98,97 86,84,78,63, ,**
CSF £110.34 CT £464.57 TOTE £10.50: £3.10, £4.50, £1.90; EX 142.30 Trifecta £885.50.
Owner B J M Ryall **Bred** Mrs R C Ryall **Trained** Rimpton, Somerset

FOCUS
Only a moderate handicap. The first four are rated pretty much to their marks.

66 PEEL HUNT INDEPENDENT BROKING H'CAP CHASE (19 fncs) 3m 1f 106y
7:20 (7:23) (Class 5) (0-100,97) 5-Y-O+ £2,729 (£801; £400; £200)

Form RPR

3P3- 1 **I'm In Charge**[30] 5102 9-11-12 97 (t) NickScholfield 110+
(Grant Cann) *confidently rdn: hld up in rr: clsd steadily after 16th: led between last 2: sn pushed clr: comf* 15/2[3]

121- 2 6 **Charming Lad (IRE)**[7] 5512 10-11-6 96 7ex (bt) DannyBurton(5) 102
(Anthony Day) *hmpd 1st: in tch: clsd to chse ldrs 15th: rdn 3 out: no ch w wnr but kpt on u.p to go 2nd fnl 100yds* 2/1[1]

201- 3 1 ¾ **Red Anchor (IRE)**[53] 4672 11-10-10 84 (b) ThomasGarner(3) 87
(Linda Jewell) *in tch: hdwy to chse ldr 8th: led 14th: drvn and hrd pressed 3 out: hdd and outpcd between last 2: plugged on same pce after: lost 2nd fnl 100yds: eased last strides* 9/1

664- 4 hd **Silent Cliche (IRE)**[25] 5197 11-11-8 93 JackQuinlan 98
(Ms N M Hugo) *chsd ldrs: lost pl and rdn after 7th: rallied 15th: plugged on same pce fr 3 out: 5th and hld whn mstke last* 12/1

The Form Book Jumps 2015-16, Raceform Ltd, Newbury, RG14 5SJ

362- 5 ¾ **Roseneath (IRE)**51 4711 11-11-3 91 (bt) JamesBanks(3) 93
(Alex Hales) *in rr and niggled along early: hdwy into midfield 13th: chsd ldr 16th: drvn and ev ch 3 out: outpcd between last 2: lost 3 pls after last* 5/1²

543- 6 46 **Brunette'sonly (IRE)**25 5213 10-11-0 85 (p) AndrewThornton 45
(Seamus Mullins) *chsd ldr tl 8th: 5th and struggling 14th: lost tch bef 3 out: t.o* 16/1

P3P- 7 19 **Cypress Grove (IRE)**27 5149 12-10-0 71 oh2 (b) BrendanPowell 14
(John Ryall) *led tl 14th: sn drvn: lost pl after 16th: wknd next: t.o* 8/1

P32- P **Rivermouth**25 5213 10-10-7 78 (b) TomCannon
(Laura Mongan) *midfield: j.rt 1st: nvr jumping fluently after: rdn after 10th: bhd 14th: t.o whn p.u 3 out* 12/1

552- P **Dr Dreamy (IRE)**40 4938 8-10-4 75 (t) JamesDavies
(Claire Dyson) *chsd ldrs 5th tl lost pl u.p after 13th: lost tch 16th: t.o whn p.u next* 10/1

6m 56.4s (-4.70) **Going Correction** -0.10s/f (Good) 9 Ran SP% 113.2
Speed ratings: **102,100,99,99,99 85,80, ,**
CSF £23.47 CT £137.44 TOTE £5.90: £1.90, £1.40, £2.30; EX 18.70 Trifecta £124.50.
Owner J Grant Cann **Bred** Shade Oak Stud And D Jenks **Trained** Bath, Gloucestershire

FOCUS
A moderate handicap chase and a decisive winner. Fairly solid form.

67 EQUINITI SHAREVIEW.COM STANDARD OPEN NATIONAL HUNT FLAT RACE 1m 5f 143y
7:55 (7:56) (Class 6) 4-6-Y-O £1,559 (£457; £228; £114)

Form RPR

1 **Ilewin Geez** 5-11-2 0 NickScholfield 101+
(Gary Moore) *t.k.h: led tl 4f out: styd pressing ldrs tl led again over 2f out: rn green and hung rt ins fnl f: styd on wl* 20/1

2 ¾ **Toviere (IRE)** 4-10-12 0 LeightonAspell 96+
(Oliver Sherwood) *hld up in tch in midfield: hdwy jst over 2f out: chsd clr ldng pair over 1f out: styd on ins fnl f to go 2nd fnl 50yds* 8/1

3 1½ **Scorpion Princess (IRE)** 4-10-5 0 WillKennedy 86
(Charlie Longsdon) *t.k.h: chsd ldrs: rdn and chal jst over 2f out: clr w wnr over 1f out: carried rt ins fnl f: no ex and btn fnl 100yds: lost 2nd fnl 50yds* 14/1

4 6 **Kings Walk (IRE)** 4-10-12 0 DarylJacob 86
(Colin Tizzard) *w ldrs tl led 4f out: rdn and hdd over 2f out: 4th and outpcd 2f out: kpt on same pce after* 7/2¹

5 1¼ **Brown Bear (IRE)** 4-10-12 0 TomCannon 85
(Nick Gifford) *hld up in tch in rr: pushed along over 2f out: hdwy over 1f out: kpt on wl ins fnl f: nvr trbld ldrs* 8/1

6 1¾ **Earthwindorfire** 4-10-12 0 AndrewTinkler 83
(Geoffrey Deacon) *hld up in tch in rr: pushed along: rn green and outpcd 3f out: rallied and hdwy over 1f out: swtchd rt ins fnl f: kpt on: nvr trbld ldrs* 33/1

7 nse **Cor Wot An Apple** 4-10-12 0 BrendanPowell 82
(Colin Tizzard) *in tch in midfield: rdn over 2f out: sn outpcd and btn* 20/1

- 8 5 **Tonganui (IRE)** 4-10-12 0 NoelFehily 76
(Harry Fry) *chsd ldrs: rn green and outpcd over 2f out: wknd over 1f out* 17/2

0- 9 3¾ **Walk Of Shame**62 4499 4-10-12 0 JackQuinlan 72
(Phil McEntee) *t.k.h: chsd ldrs: 3rd and drvn 2f out: sn outpcd and btn over 1f out: wknd fnl f* 8/1

4- 10 7 **Lapalala (IRE)**19 5299 4-10-5 0 RichardJohnson 64
(Philip Hobbs) *hld up in tch in rr: effrt over 2f out: no imp: wknd over 1f out* 6/1³

11 9 **Ron Hegarty (IRE)** 4-10-12 0 ConorO'Farrell 60
(Seamus Durack) *in tch in midfield: slipped bnd over 3f out: sn rdn: wknd 2f out* 11/2²

0- 12 10 **Whatiknownow**34 5035 4-10-5 0 PaulMoloney 41
(Charlie Wallis) *in tch in rr: lost tch over 2f out: t.o* 50/1

50- 13 ½ **Honey'N'Spice**73 4283 6-10-9 0 JamesDavies 44
(George Margarson) *t.k.h: in tch in midfield: struggling whn hmpd bnd over 3f out: sn bhd: t.o* 66/1

- U **Alizee Javilex (FR)** 5-10-4 0 JackSherwood(5)
(Lucy Wadham) *t.k.h early: in tch in midfield: slipped and uns rdr bnd over 3f out* 25/1

3m 24.5s (-6.60) 14 Ran SP% 122.2
CSF £165.15 TOTE £20.60: £5.70, £4.00, £5.90; EX 85.10 Trifecta £1655.40 Part won..
Owner Tom Segrue **Bred** A W Buller **Trained** Lower Beeding, W Sussex
■ Stewards' Enquiry : Nick Scholfield one-day ban: careless riding (15 May)

FOCUS
The standard set by those with experience in this bumper wasn't a daunting one and the front three pulled a little way clear.
T/Plt: £37.40 to a £1 stake. Pool: £51,387.79 - 1,001.38 winning units T/Qpdt: £7.10 to a £1 stake. Pool: £6,015.65 - 624.35 winning units **Steve Payne**

68a (Foreign Racing) - See Raceform Interactive

46 PUNCHESTOWN (R-H)
Friday, May 1

OFFICIAL GOING: Good to yielding

69a EMS COPIERS NOVICE H'CAP CHASE (GRADE A) (15 fncs) 2m 5f
4:20 (4:20) 5-Y-O+ £46,511 (£14,728; £6,976; £2,325; £1,550; £775)

RPR

1 **Blood Cotil (FR)**49 4742 6-11-0 141 PaulTownend 154+
(W P Mullins, Ire) *hld up in mid-div: short of room and hmpd after 7th: gd prog to trck ldrs after 5 out: led on inner 2 out: nt fluent last: styd on wl* 11/1

2 2¾ **Irish Cavalier (IRE)**3 10 6-10-13 145 (p) LPDempsey(5) 155
(Rebecca Curtis) *trckd ldrs: prog to press ldr in 2nd 4 out: rdn and no imp on wnr in 2nd appr last: kpt on wl run-in* 9/1

3 4¾ **Dromnea (IRE)**52 4694 8-10-4 131 MarkEnright 136
(M F Morris, Ire) *led after 2nd: strly pressed after 4 out: hdd 2 out where dropped to 3rd: no ex appr last: kpt on same pce* 12/1

4 4¼ **Followmeuptocarlow (IRE)**76 4241 12-10-4 136 (t) GerFox(5) 137
(Thomas Foley, Ire) *racd towards rr: dropped to rr and nt fluent 7th: prog after 3 out in 8th: lft 4th 2 out: kpt on wl run-in* 33/1

5 16 **Azorian (IRE)**26 5177 7-10-5 137 (t) DavidMullins(5) 122
(Eoin Griffin, Ire) *hld up towards rr: prog bef 4 out: rdn along in 6th after 3 out: kpt on one pce into 5th run-in: nvr on terms* 25/1

6 ½ **Mister Hotelier (IRE)**26 5178 8-10-3 130 (t) DJCasey 115
(C A Murphy, Ire) *racd in mid-div: tk clsr order 4 out: wnt 5th after 3 out: briefly lft 4th 2 out: sn no imp* 33/1

7 7½ **Thomas Crapper**33 5044 8-10-11 138 CharliePoste 115
(Robin Dickin) *hld up tl tk clsr order bef 4 out: rdn and no imp after next* 7/1²

8 nk **Bishops Road (IRE)**33 5054 7-10-4 131 BJCooper 108
(Henry De Bromhead, Ire) *chsd ldrs early: mid-div 1/2-way: no imp and dropped towards rr 5 out: kpt on one pce fr 2 out* 10/1

9 1½ **Mr Fiftyone (IRE)**26 5178 6-10-4 131 RobbiePower 106
(Mrs John Harrington, Ire) *sn towards rr: pckd 7 out: kpt on one pce whn nt fluent 2 out: nvr on terms* 5/1¹

10 15 **Wuff (IRE)**42 4884 7-10-3 130 (t) TomScudamore 90
(Tom George) *trckd early ldrs on inner: chsd ldrs fr 1/2-way tl rdn and nt qckn after 4 out: sn no ex* 10/1

11 28 **Doing Fine (IRE)**52 4693 7-10-3 130 (bt) APHeskin 62
(Rebecca Curtis) *sn trckd ldrs: 2nd 1/2-way: rdn and wknd appr 3 out: t.o* 12/1

P **Tennis Cap (FR)**26 5171 8-10-13 140 DannyMullins
(W P Mullins, Ire) *hld up: nt fluent 5 out and sn dropped towards rr: mstke 4 out and p.u at next* 12/1

P **The King Of Brega (IRE)**186 2108 8-9-12 130 oh7 ShaneShortall(5)
(Patrick Downey, Ire) *racd in mid-div: dropped towards rr 5 out and sn detached: p.u bef next* 33/1

U **Silver Tassie (IRE)**25 5224 7-10-4 131 PaulCarberry 138+
(Noel Meade, Ire) *t.k.h in mid-div: clsr to chse ldrs 5 out: rdn in 4th after 3 out: trckd ldrs in 4th whn bad mstke and uns rdr 2 out* 25/1

P **Benemeade (IRE)**26 5178 7-10-3 130 oh3 NiallPMadden
(Noel Meade, Ire) *racd in mid-div: j.lft at times: no imp and dropped to rr 3 out: sn p.u* 40/1

F **Shanahan's Turn (IRE)**82 4117 7-11-2 143 JJBurke
(Henry De Bromhead, Ire) *led to 2nd: trckd ldrs tl fell 3 out* 8/1

P **Val De Ferbet (FR)**33 5054 6-11-10 151 RWalsh
(W P Mullins, Ire) *hld up: mstkes 4th and 5th: dropped to rr at 6th and sn p.u* 15/2³

5m 24.7s (-10.90) **Going Correction** -0.20s/f (Good) 17 Ran SP% 130.6
Speed ratings: **112,110,109,107,101 101,98,98,97,91 81, , , ,**
CSF £106.66 CT £1247.23 TOTE £11.50: £2.90, £2.60, £4.30, £8.70; DF 107.60 Trifecta £3912.20.
Owner Mrs S Ricci **Bred** Frederic Fisk **Trained** Muine Beag, Co Carlow

FOCUS
Deeply competitive and the right horses filled the placings. They went a pretty sensible gallop.

70a HANLON CONCRETE EUROPEAN BREEDERS FUND GLENCARRAIG LADY MARES H'CAP CHASE (GRADE C) (15 fncs) 2m 5f
4:55 (4:56) 4-Y-O+ £25,193 (£7,364; £3,488; £1,162)

RPR

1 **Mallards In Flight (IRE)**7 5533 9-9-5 110 oh8 (bt) LPDempsey(5) 119+
(Gavin Cromwell, Ire) *trckd ldrs in 4th tl lft 3rd 4 out: clsd to press ldr in 2nd at next: led 2 out and rdn clr appr last: kpt on wl* 8/1

2 5 **Speckled Wood (IRE)**14 5386 7-10-7 121 (tp) MarkWalsh 125
(C Roche, Ire) *hld up in mid-div: rdn to chse ldrs in 5th after 3 out: styd on wl into 2nd appr last: nt trble wnr* 7/1³

3 4¼ **Burn And Turn (IRE)**25 5225 9-11-10 138 (t) RobbiePower 138
(Mrs John Harrington, Ire) *hld up tl tk clsr order 4 out: clsd in 3rd 2 out: rdn and no imp whn nt fluent last: kpt on same pce* 7/2¹

4 2¾ **Indian Fairy (IRE)**19 5302 7-10-3 117 ¹ JJBurke 114
(Eoin Doyle, Ire) *t.k.h to press ldrs in 3rd tl led after 4th: strly pressed 3 out and hdd 2 out: no ex in 4th at last: kpt on one pce* 12/1

5 ½ **Annie Oakley (IRE)**10 5459 7-10-4 123 PaddyKennedy(5) 120
(Mrs John Harrington, Ire) *racd in mid-div: clsr 4 out: rdn after 3 out: no imp in 6th after 2 out* 9/1

6 1 **Perfect Promise (IRE)**47 4796 7-10-9 123 DavyRussell 119
(James Joseph Mangan, Ire) *trckd ldrs early: chsd ldrs in 4th fr 1/2-way: clsd in 3rd after 3 out: sn rdn and wknd appr last* 9/2²

7 18 **Elsie (IRE)**26 5178 8-9-12 112 AELynch 90
(Thomas Mullins, Ire) *a towards rr: rdn and no imp after 2 out* 7/1³

8 3½ **Dazzling Susie (IRE)**25 5225 10-10-9 123 DannyMullins 101+
(John F Phelan, Ire) *hld up: sme prog bef 4 out where bdly hmpd: nt rcvr* 16/1

9 17 **Lily Waugh (IRE)**15 5354 8-10-13 127 (t) RyanMahon 84
(Anthony Honeyball) *led to 4th: pressed ldr tl mstke 3 out: wknd qckly* 10/1

P **Way Up In The Air (IRE)**83 4103 8-10-7 121 DJCasey
(Robert Tyner, Ire) *sn in rr and jumping lft: no threat whn hmpd 4 out: j.lft again at next: p.u bef 2 out* 14/1

F **The Housekeeper (IRE)**72 4306 8-10-2 116 SeanFlanagan
(David Harry Kelly, Ire) *trckd ldrs: 3rd whn fell 4 out* 14/1

5m 28.0s (-7.60) **Going Correction** -0.20s/f (Good) 11 Ran SP% 122.5
Speed ratings: **106,104,102,101,101 100,94,92,86,**
CSF £66.27 CT £237.62 TOTE £9.10: £3.10, £2.40, £2.00; DF 82.10 Trifecta £373.00.
Owner Thomas Anthony Geoghegan **Bred** Thomas Anthony Geoghegan **Trained** Navan, Co. Meath

FOCUS
A pretty open renewal and great credit must go for connections for opting to run the winner, despite two clear negatives. She posted a personal best.

71a QUEALLY GROUP CELEBRATING 35 YEARS IN NAAS PUNCHESTOWN CHAMPION HURDLE (GRADE 1) (9 hdls) 2m
5:30 (5:30) 4-Y-O+ £93,023 (£29,457; £13,953; £4,651)

RPR

1 **Faugheen (IRE)**52 4691 7-11-12 173 RWalsh 173+
(W P Mullins, Ire) *mde all: advantage reduced at 5th: qcknd after 2 out: extended advantage appr last: styd on strly: easily* 1/6¹

2 8 **Arctic Fire (GER)**22 5238 6-11-12 169 PaulTownend 163
(W P Mullins, Ire) *chsd ldr in 2nd: clsd on ldr at 5th: rdn and no imp after 2 out: kpt on same pce fr last* 5/1²

3 8½ **Dell' Arca (IRE)**21 5249 6-11-12 142 (b) TomScudamore 154
(David Pipe) *racd in 3rd: nt fluent 4 out: rdn and no imp after 2 out: sn one pce* 50/1

4 19 **Tiger Roll (IRE)**50 4719 5-11-12 146 (bt) BJCooper 139
(Gordon Elliott, Ire) *a in rr: mstke 4th: rdn and detached after 3 out: no ex* 33/1³

3m 56.3s (-8.70) **Going Correction** -0.225s/f (Good) 4 Ran SP% 107.3
Speed ratings: **112,108,103,94**
CSF £1.50 TOTE £1.30; DF 1.40 Trifecta £2.70.
Owner Mrs S Ricci **Bred** Dr John Waldron **Trained** Muine Beag, Co Carlow

FOCUS
The first and second in what looked a fine Champion Hurdle clashed again, with the other pair an irrelevance. Faugheen is rated up 3lb.

72a TATTERSALLS IRELAND CHAMPION NOVICE HURDLE (GRADE 1) (12 hdls) 2m 4f
6:05 (6:06) 4-Y-O+ **£44,186** (£13,992; £6,627; £2,209; £1,472; £736)

RPR

1 **Nichols Canyon**[20] 5271 5-11-10 153 .... RWalsh 157+
(W P Mullins, Ire) *mde all: slt mstke 3 out: pressed after 2 out: sn qcknd to extend advantage and clr last: styd on wl: comf* **4/5**[1]

2 7 **Alpha Des Obeaux (FR)**[21] 5254 5-11-10 138 .... BJCooper 150
(M F Morris, Ire) *chsd ldr in 2nd: rdn to press ldr after 2 out: no imp bef last: kpt on same pce* **9/2**[2]

3 2 ¾ **Outlander (IRE)**[26] 5176 7-11-10 143 .... DannyMullins 147
(W P Mullins, Ire) *chsd ldrs in 4th on inner: prog into 3rd 4 out: rdn and nt qckn in 4th after 2 out: kpt on again into 3rd run-in* **13/2**[3]

4 2 ¾ **Sempre Medici (FR)**[25] 5223 5-11-10 147 .... PaulTownend 145
(W P Mullins, Ire) *hld up towards rr tl tk clsr order after 4 out: travelled wl into 3rd 2 out: rdn and no imp appr last: dropped to 4th run-in* **9/2**[2]

5 35 **McKinley**[20] 5271 5-11-10 139 .... (p) DJCasey 110
(W P Mullins, Ire) *chsd ldrs in 3rd tl rdn and dropped to 5th 3 out: wknd after 2 out* **25/1**

6 16 **Phil's Magic (IRE)**[25] 5223 5-11-10 133 .... JJBurke 94
(Ms Sandra Hughes, Ire) *in rr thrght: reminders fr 6th: detached 3 out: nvr a factor* **33/1**

4m 53.6s (-12.40) **Going Correction** -0.225s/f (Good) **6 Ran SP% 112.0**
Speed ratings: **115,112,111,110,96 89**
CSF £4.95 TOTE £1.60: £1.10, £2.20; DF 5.10 Trifecta £12.20.
Owner Andrea & Graham Wylie **Bred** Rabbah Bloodstock Limited **Trained** Muine Beag, Co Carlow

FOCUS
The form is rated around the third.

73a STAR BEST FOR RACING COVERAGE NOVICE HURDLE (9 hdls) 2m
6:40 (6:40) 4-Y-O+ **£11,337** (£3,313; £1,569; £523)

RPR

1 **Snake Eyes (IRE)**[103] 3760 7-11-12 128 .... MarkWalsh 135+
(Nicky Henderson) *chsd ldrs: clsr in 3rd 3 out: rdn to press ldr in 2nd appr last: led after last and rdn clr: styd on wl* **9/2**[2]

2 2 ¾ **Pyromaniac (IRE)**[27] 3183 5-11-12 128 .... (t) DenisO'Regan 132+
(A J Martin, Ire) *hld up towards rr whn mstke 1st: tk clsr order on inner 3 out: wnt 4th after 2 out: styd on strly run-in into 2nd clsng stages: nt rch wnr* **8/1**[3]

3 1 ½ **Tandem**[152] 2846 6-11-12 127 .... DavyRussell 131
(D K Weld, Ire) *sn chsd clr ldr in 2nd: travelled wl to press ldr after 2 out: led bef last: sn strly pressed and hdd after last: no ex and dropped to 3rd clsng stages* **9/2**[2]

4 3 ¾ **Blue Atlantic (USA)**[135] 3144 4-11-4 .... (b[1]) GavinSheehan 119
(Warren Greatrex) *led whn nt fluent 1st: sn clr tl advantage reduced 3 out: strly pressed after next and hdd bef last: sn one pce and dropped to 4th run-in* **33/1**

5 8 ½ **Alton Bay (IRE)**[223] 1060 7-11-12 .... JJBurke 118
(Peter Fahey, Ire) *hld up tl tk clsr order bef 3 out in 6th: rdn and nt qckn after 2 out: kpt on one pce into 5th run-in: nvr on terms* **9/2**[2]

6 shd **Aminabad (FR)**[68] 4395 5-11-12 136 .... BJCooper 118
(W P Mullins, Ire) *hld up: tk clsr order bef 3 out: rdn after 2 out in 5th: sn no imp: dropped to 6th after last* **10/1**

7 34 **Max Dynamite (FR)**[25] 5223 5-11-12 138 .... RWalsh 84
(W P Mullins, Ire) *sn chsd ldrs in 4th: prog into 3rd 1/2-way: niggled along bef 3 out: sn dropped to rr and no ex: eased bef last* **7/4**[1]

P **Kinnitty Castle (IRE)**[41] 4935 5-11-5 .... PaulTownend
(A J Martin, Ire) *sn in rr: slow at 3rd: detached fr 5 out and p.u bef 3 out* **33/1**

4m 2.8s (-2.20) **Going Correction** -0.225s/f (Good) **8 Ran SP% 117.0**
WFA 4 from 5yo+ 18lb
Speed ratings: **96,94,93,92,87 87,70,**
CSF £40.31 CT £169.98 TOTE £4.90: £1.60, £2.20, £1.50; DF 46.00 Trifecta £281.40.
Owner John P McManus **Bred** Aidan Aherne **Trained** Upper Lambourn, Berks
■ Stewards' Enquiry : Davy Russell caution: use of whip
Mark Walsh one-day ban: use of whip

FOCUS
A very interesting race and run at a proper gallop. The favourite was the first beaten.

75a RACING POST CHAMPION HUNTERS CHASE (17 fncs) 3m 1f
7:45 (7:47) 4-Y-O+ **£11,085** (£3,240; £1,534; £511)

RPR

1 **On The Fringe (IRE)**[22] 5239 10-12-0 0 .... MsNCarberry 139+
(E Bolger, Ire) *hld up in 5th tl travelled wl to trck ldr in 2nd after 3 out: led 2 out and sn clr: kpt gng hands and heels run-in: advantage reduced cl home* **4/11**[1]

2 1 **Noble Prince (GER)**[25] 5217 11-11-7 0 .... (p) MrGASpain[(7)] 135+
(Paul Nolan, Ire) *hld up towards rr tl tk clsr order 4 out: chsd ldrs in 3rd after next: nt qckn after 2 out: kpt on wl into 2nd run-in to cl on comfortable wnr cl home* **12/1**

3 2 ½ **Pearlysteps**[76] 4228 12-12-0 0 .... MrOGreenall 132
(Henry Daly) *trckd ldrs tl led fr 4th: strly pressed after 3 out: hdd 2 out and sn no match for wnr: nt fluent last and dropped to 3rd run-in* **7/1**[3]

4 13 **Warne (IRE)**[22] 5239 11-11-9 131 ....[1] MrDGLavery[(5)] 119
(B R Hamilton, Ire) *chsd ldrs: rdn into 4th after 3 out: no imp after next: kpt on one pce* **6/1**[2]

5 5 ½ **Vital Plot (USA)**[19] 11-12-0 0 .... (t) MrJJCodd 114
(Liam Kenny, Ire) *hld up towards rr: mstke 4 out and no ex fr next* **12/1**

6 ¾ **Sebadee (IRE)**[19] 11-11-7 0 .... MrJCBarry[(7)] 113
(Denis W Cullen, Ire) *led and sn jnd: trckd ldrs fr 4th tl rdn and nt qckn after 3 out: sn no ex* **28/1**

P **Onzo Mor (IRE)**[12] 11-11-7 0 .... (t) MrEannaCronin[(7)]
(J T R Dreaper, Ire) *a in rr: nt fluent at times: detached 1/2-way: p.u bef 2 out* **50/1**

P **Templemills (IRE)**[26] 10-12-0 0 .... (p) MrDerekO'Connor
(Thomas Cleary, Ire) *sn disp: trckd ldrs fr 4th tl wknd qckly bef 3 out: p.u bef 2 out* **50/1**

P **Need To Know (IRE)**[18] 5321 7-11-9 0 .... (t) MrSClements[(5)]
(John Paul Brennan, Ire) *hld up: nt fluent 6 out: nt qckn after 4 out: p.u bef 2 out* **25/1**

6m 36.3s (-8.70) **Going Correction** -0.20s/f (Good) **9 Ran SP% 126.7**
Speed ratings: **105,104,103,99,97 97, , ,**
Pick Six: Not won. Pool of @29,589.00 carried forward to Punchestown, Saturday 2nd May. Tote Aggregates: 2014 @865,233.71; 2015 @738,881.00 CSF £7.43 CT £20.49 TOTE £1.20: £1.02, £2.00, £1.50; DF 6.50 Trifecta £21.40.
Owner John P McManus **Bred** Pat Tobin **Trained** Bruree, Co Limerick

FOCUS
This was a smart renewal of the race, and the first three finished clear. On The Fringe didn't need to hit his best.
T/Jkpt: @179.40 Pool: @29,737.16 - 116.00 winning units T/Plt: @64.90 Pool: @88,999.38 - 958.50 winning units **Alan Hewison**

74a (Foreign Racing) - See Raceform Interactive

HEXHAM (L-H)
Saturday, May 2

OFFICIAL GOING: Good (good to soft in places; 6.8)
Wind: Fresh, half behind Weather: Overcast, showers

76 INDEPENDENT RACECOURSES LTD (IRL) NOVICES' CHASE (15 fncs) 2m 4f 15y
5:25 (5:27) (Class 4) 5-Y-O+ **£3,898** (£1,144; £572; £286)

Form RPR

3F4- 1 **Ueueteotl (FR)**[14] 5393 7-10-12 119 .... (p) LucyAlexander 123+
(James Ewart) *cl up: lft 2nd 4 out: led appr 2 out: rdn and styd on gamely fr last* **11/2**[3]

503- 2 2 ¼ **Super Collider**[19] 5315 8-10-5 0 .... (t) JamesCorbett[(7)] 120
(Susan Corbett) *in tch: stdy hdwy 1/2-way: lft in ld 4 out: hdd and sltly outpcd appr 2 out: rallied and ev ch last: one pce run-in* **20/1**

/50- 3 3 ½ **Take The Cash (IRE)**[28] 5133 6-10-12 0 .... WilsonRenwick 117
(Donald McCain) *in tch: stdy hdwy 3 out: effrt and rdn between last 2: kpt on same pce run-in* **9/4**[2]

560- 4 1 ½ **Rev Up Ruby**[15] 5366 7-10-0 0 .... JonathonBewley[(5)] 109
(George Bewley) *hld up: stdy hdwy to chse ldrs 4 out: outpcd 2 out: no imp fr last* **8/1**

202- 5 5 **Things Change (IRE)**[121] 3439 7-10-12 120 .... DougieCostello 112
(John Quinn) *cl up: effrt and disp ld 2 out: outpcd whn nt fluent last: sn btn* **5/4**[1]

10P- U **The Banastoir (IRE)**[14] 5401 6-10-9 115 .... TonyKelly[(3)]
(Rebecca Menzies) *mostly j.rt: led: hit 2nd: jst in front whn blnd and uns rdr 4 out* **25/1**

F3- F **Pekanheim (IRE)**[18] 5326 7-10-12 0 .... BrianHarding
(Martin Todhunter) *t.k.h: hld up: fell heavily 4 out* **25/1**

5m 20.7s (7.20) **Going Correction** -0.125s/f (Good) **7 Ran SP% 114.2**
Speed ratings: **81,80,78,78,76 ,**
CSF £82.80 TOTE £5.60: £1.70, £8.40; EX 88.80 Trifecta £338.60.
Owner Going Grey **Bred** William Ewart **Trained** Langholm, Dumfries & G'way

FOCUS
Bends and back straight moved on to fresh ground. Not a bad little novice chase and the fact the market leader pulled too hard and was a little disappointing shouldn't detract from the form as the first three all have futures over fences.

77 FRIENDS OF CHOLLERTON CHURCH (S) HURDLE (8 hdls) 2m 48y
6:00 (6:43) (Class 5) 4-Y-O+ **£2,395** (£698; £349)

Form RPR

435- 1 **King Of Strings (IRE)**[20] 5295 6-10-12 102 .... DougieCostello 99
(Mark Walford) *hld up: stdy hdwy and prom 1/2-way: ev ch 2 out: sn chsng ldr and rdn: led run-in: drvn out* **6/4**[1]

P66- 2 1 ¾ **The Ice Factor**[9] 5490 7-10-5 88 .... (p) JamieHamilton[(7)] 98
(Alison Hamilton) *led 1st: hdd after 3 out: regained ld next: rdn between last 2: hdd run-in: kpt on same pce towards fin* **9/1**[2]

5/P- 3 29 **Duhallowcountry (IRE)**[7] 9-10-5 89 .... (p) ThomasDowson[(7)] 73
(Victor Thompson) *chsd ldrs: drvn and outpcd 2 out: plugged on fr last: no ch w first two* **40/1**

PP5- 4 3 **Just Bee (IRE)**[8] 5514 6-10-0 0 .... (p) DaleIrving[(5)] 62
(Katie Scott) *nt fluent in rr: struggling 4th: rallied 2 out: no imp* **66/1**

00P- 5 ½ **Bobowen (IRE)**[21] 5274 9-10-12 126 .... (b[1]) WillKennedy 71
(Dr Richard Newland) *hld up in tch: stdy hdwy and cl up whn nt fluent 4th: led after 3 out: hdd and outpcd whn mstke next: sn btn* **6/4**[1]

3FP/ 6 2 ½ **Native Brian (IRE)**[139] 9-10-5 94 .... MrRWilson[(7)] 66
(Andrew Hamilton) *hld up: nt fluent 2nd: struggling 1/2-way: n.d after* **14/1**

6F0- 7 1 ½ **Seventeen Black (IRE)**[36] 5011 7-10-9 79 .... (v) DerekFox[(3)] 65
(Stuart Coltherd) *led tl j. slowly and hdd 1st: prom: struggling 1/2-way: n.d after* **12/1**[3]

006- 8 5 **Watchmego**[145] 2994 7-10-5 64 .... (t) MichaelMcAlister 53
(Maurice Barnes) *prom: outpcd bef 4 out: struggling fr next* **33/1**

464- 9 34 **Yourholidayisover (IRE)**[21] 4978 8-11-3 94 .... BrianHarding 35
(Patrick Holmes) *prom tl rdn and wknd qckly after 2 out: t.o* **20/1**

4m 10.2s (-7.20) **Going Correction** -0.225s/f (Good) **9 Ran SP% 116.0**
Speed ratings (Par 103): **107,106,92,91,90 89,89,86,70**
CSF £16.58 TOTE £2.40: £1.10, £2.50, £6.70; EX 16.70 Trifecta £418.60.The winner was bought in for 4,200gns
Owner F M & Mrs E Holmes **Bred** Cathal Ennis **Trained** Sherriff Hutton, N Yorks

FOCUS
The front two, both dropping in grade from handicap company, pulled a long way clear and are the only ones to take from this.

78 SOLAR SIGNS H'CAP CHASE (15 fncs) 2m 4f 15y
6:30 (7:01) (Class 5) (0-100,100) 5-Y-O+ **£2,600** (£758; £379)

Form RPR

406- 1 **Kai Broon (IRE)**[19] 5309 8-11-8 99 .... (p) CraigNichol[(3)] 119+
(Lucinda Russell) *chsd ldrs: wnt 2nd 4 out: led 2 out: sn clr: eased run-in* **20/1**

4P3- 2 20 **Everlasting (IRE)**[36] 5014 8-10-6 80 .... (b) DougieCostello 79
(Rose Dobbin) *led: rdn and hdd 2 out: kpt on: no ch w easy wnr* **9/2**[1]

U45- 3 5 **Thatildee (IRE)**[28] 5130 7-10-6 85 .... DiarmuidO'Regan[(5)] 78
(Chris Grant) *hld up on ins: outpcd 1/2-way: rallied 2 out: kpt on: nvr able to chal* **8/1**

032- 4 6 **Solway Legend**[18] 5330 8-9-13 80 .... RyanDay[(7)] 67
(Lisa Harrison) *hld up: stdy hdwy and in tch 10th: rdn bef 3 out: outpcd fr next* **5/1**[2]

P40- 5 3 1/4 **Odds On Dan (IRE)**[36] 5014 9-9-13 80........................(tp) DeanPratt(7) 64
(Lucinda Egerton) *bhd: struggling 1/2-way: rallied 3 out: no imp fr next* 11/1
U46- 6 hd **Forestside (IRE)**[39] 4974 10-10-0 74 oh6.................. LucyAlexander 58
(Barry Murtagh) *hld up in tch: outpcd 1/2-way: rallied 3 out: no imp fr next* 33/1
533- 7 4 1/2 **Brother Scott**[19] 5309 8-11-0 93........................ CallumBewley(5) 77
(Sue Smith) *chsd ldrs: mstke 7th: 3rd and pushed along whn mstke 2 out: sn btn* 13/2
6P4- 8 2 1/2 **Milan Royale**[12] 5421 10-10-8 85.......................... DerekFox(3) 63
(Kevin Hunter) *hld up towards rr: struggling 1/2-way: nvr on terms* 16/1
635- 9 9 **Emkae (IRE)**[18] 5330 7-11-7 95.............................. BrianHarding 65
(Alison Hamilton) *prom: drvn and outpcd 4 out: struggling fr next* 10/1
344- 10 3 1/2 **Carlos Fandango (IRE)**[28] 5132 9-11-12 100..........(tp) WilsonRenwick 66
(Martin Todhunter) *hld up: hit 9th: stdy hdwy and in tch whn hit 3 out: sn wknd* 11/2[3]
460- U **Cool Star (IRE)**[12] 5423 9-10-6 80....................(t) MichaelMcAlister
(Maurice Barnes) *chsd ldr: blnd 4 out: wknd bef next: btn whn blnd and uns rdr 2 out* 11/1
PPP- P **Cumbrian Farmer**[18] 5330 8-9-13 78..................(tp) JonathonBewley(5)
(George Bewley) *prom early: sn lost pl: lost tch and p.u 8th* 33/1
5m 10.0s (-3.50) **Going Correction** -0.125s/f (Good) **12 Ran SP% 117.0**
Speed ratings: **101,93,91,89,87 87,86,85,81,80 , ,**
CSF £107.56 CT £793.13 TOTE £21.30: £5.30, £1.30, £2.90; EX 93.20 Trifecta £997.20 Part won..
Owner John R Adam & Sons **Bred** Philip Brady **Trained** Arlary, Perth & Kinross

FOCUS
A pretty weak contest on paper and hard to know what to make of the winner's performance given he is thoroughly exposed as modest over fences with a poor strike-rate to boot.

79 STEVE JOHNSTON LAST LAP RETIREMENT DO NOVICES' HURDLE (8 hdls) 2m 48y
7:00 (7:25) (Class 4) 4-Y-O+ £3,422 (£997; £499)

Form RPR
212- 1 **Venue**[27] 5158 5-11-4 129.............................. WilsonRenwick 118+
(Donald McCain) *w ldr: led 2nd: qcknd clr between last 2: shkn up briefly run-in: easily* 2/5[1]
254- 2 6 **Towerburn (IRE)**[12] 5419 6-10-5 0.................. JamieHamilton(7) 100
(Alison Hamilton) *t.k.h: chsd ldrs: nt fluent 2nd: rdn and hdwy bef last: chsd (clr) wnr run-in: no imp* 7/1[3]
064- 3 3 1/4 **Destiny Awaits (IRE)**[145] 2994 6-10-7 67.............. CallumBewley(5) 97
(Keith Pollock) *hld up in tch: smooth hdwy to chse wnr after 2 out: rdn bef last: lost 2nd run-in: sn outpcd* 50/1
4 5 **My Escapade (IRE)**[26] 4-9-10 0........................ GrantCockburn(5) 83
(Simon Waugh) *in tch: hit 3 out: stdy hdwy bef next: rdn after 2 out: outpcd bef last* 66/1
404- 5 5 **The Late Shift**[18] 5327 5-10-9 0.......................... CraigNichol(3) 88
(Barry Murtagh) *hld up in tch: drvn and outpcd bef 2 out: no imp bef last* 12/1
405- 6 1 1/2 **Solway Prince**[10] 5471 6-10-5 0............................ RyanDay(7) 87
(Lisa Harrison) *led to 2nd: w wnr to 3 out: lost 2nd between last 2: sn btn* 8/1
- 7 12 **Parkie Boy** 4-10-8 0...................................... BrianHarding 72
(Nicky Richards) *nt fluent in rr: rdn and struggling after 3 out: btn fr next* 11/2[2]
060- P **Vodka Moon**[20] 5293 6-10-5 0........................ JosephPalmowski(7)
(Sharon Watt) *nt fluent in rr: struggling bef 2 out: sn btn: lost tch and p.u bef last* 20/1
4m 13.2s (-4.20) **Going Correction** -0.225s/f (Good) **8 Ran SP% 126.3**
WFA 4 from 5yo+ 18lb
Speed ratings (Par 105): **100,97,95,93,90 90,84,**
CSF £5.10 TOTE £1.20: £1.02, £3.30, £15.70; EX 2.80 Trifecta £6.90.
Owner Straightline Construction Ltd **Bred** Juddmonte Farms Ltd **Trained** Cholmondeley, Cheshire

FOCUS
A most uncompetitive novice hurdle.

80 EVE AITCHISON HEART OF ALL ENGLAND MAIDEN HUNTERS' CHASE (19 fncs) 3m 41y
7:30 (7:44) (Class 4) 5-Y-O+ £3,119 (£967; £483; £242)

Form RPR
F- 1 **Cave Hunter (IRE)**[13] 8-11-11 0....................(tp) MrTHamilton(3) 102
(Mrs Wendy Hamilton) *led or disp ld tl outpcd 2 out: rallied to ld last: styd on gamely run-in* 13/2[3]
6- 2 1 1/4 **Kalastar (IRE)**[19] 5311 6-12-0 0........................ MrJohnDawson 102+
(Katie Scott) *hld up: stdy hdwy and in tch 14th: rdn and outpcd 3 out: rallied bef last: kpt on to take 2nd cl home* 25/1
5- 3 hd **Dun Faw Good**[35] 8-12-0 0................................ MissCWalton 101
(Mrs C Walton) *led or disp ld tl wnt on 2 out: hdd last: rallied: no ex and lost 2nd cl home* 11/1
6P2- 4 46 **Newspage (IRE)**[13] 9-11-9 77........................(b) MrWEasterby(5) 59
(John Wade) *chsd ldrs tl rdn and wknd between last 2* 11/1
5- 5 1/2 **Sea Scout**[28] 12-11-7 0.................................. MissAWaugh(7) 59
(R A Ross) *midfield: drvn and outpcd 1/2-way: n.d after* 18/1
3F0- 6 44 **Little Fritz (FR)**[19] 5311 8-11-11 99.................. MissJWalton(3) 19
(L Kerr) *nt fluent in rr: struggling 1/2-way: sme hdwy after 4 out: struggling fr next: t.o* 14/1
0P0- 7 1/2 **Filbert Fox (IRE)**[12] 5423 9-11-7 63..............(p) MissRMcDonald(7) 19
(Ms Samantha Burns) *prom: lost pl 1/2-way: n.d after: t.o* 125/1
P/5- 8 4 1/2 **The Brig At Ayr**[19] 5311 11-11-7 79...................... RossChapman(7) 15
(S J Leadbetter) *towards rr: rdn along whn hit 4 out: sn btn: t.o* 33/1
2- 9 23 **Crazy Diamond**[19] 5311 11-11-11 0........................ MrGCrow(3)
(Miss J Mckie) *hld up: smooth hdwy and prom 1/2-way: rdn and wknd qckly fr 2 out: eased run-in* 2/1[1]
/4P- P **Know The Rules (IRE)**[13] 10-11-11 78................(p) MrCDawson(3)
(Mrs G Smith) *prom: outpcd fr 12th: t.o whn p.u bef 3 out* 33/1
P **Anddante (IRE)**[20] 7-11-7 0................................ MrJTeal(7)
(Miss G T Lee) *bhd: struggling fr 1/2-way: no ch whn p.u bef last* 33/1
2/3- P **Supreme Regime (IRE)**[28] 9-11-7 94...................[1] ThomasDowson(7)
(Miss G E J Anderson) *midfield: outpcd fr 13th: t.o whn p.u bef 2 out* 16/1
2F3- P **Darsi Dancer (IRE)**[19] 5311 7-11-7 92................(p) MrSWColtherd(7)
(Stuart Coltherd) *bhd and nvr travelling or jumping wl: lost tch and p.u 11th* 7/2[2]
3/4- P **Indigo Island (IRE)**[28] 6-11-7 86...................... MrWHRReed(7)
(R A Owen) *midfield: struggling bef 14th: lost tch and p.u bef 2 out* 50/1
P **Shannon Silver**[7] 6-11-7 0.............................. MrHMorshead(7)
(Mrs Anthea Morshead) *midfield on outside: drvn fr 1/2-way: lost tch and p.u 4 out* 66/1
6m 25.0s (-7.20) **Going Correction** -0.125s/f (Good) **15 Ran SP% 120.3**
Speed ratings: **106,105,105,90,90 76,76,74,67, , , , ,**
CSF £152.64 TOTE £8.50: £2.60, £5.70, £3.20; EX 404.20 Trifecta £408.60 Part won..
Owner Niel Manning **Bred** Paddy Crinion **Trained** Hawick, Borders

FOCUS
Three pulled a mile clear in this modest maiden hunter chase.

81 REDSCAR H'CAP CHASE (19 fncs) 3m 41y
8:00 (8:08) (Class 4) (0-120,117) 5-Y-O+ £5,328 (£1,564; £782; £391)

Form RPR
030- 1 **Pinerolo**[28] 5138 9-11-10 115......................(b[1]) SeanQuinlan 122
(Sue Smith) *chsd ldrs: chal 3rd: led next: mde rest: rdn and styd on wl fr 2 out* 8/1
52U- 2 6 **Big Sound**[19] 5313 8-11-3 108..........................(p) DougieCostello 111
(Mark Walford) *cl up: hit 4 out: effrt and chsd wnr 2 out: kpt on same pce fr last* 9/2[3]
331- 3 13 **Scarlet Fire (IRE)**[28] 5135 8-10-13 111..............(t) MissJRRichards(7) 102
(Nicky Richards) *sn pushed along in rr: hdwy to chse wnr 8th: rdn and lost 2nd 2 out: wknd bef last* 2/1[1]
610- 4 14 **Feast Of Fire (IRE)**[36] 5017 8-11-5 110.................. BrianHarding 88
(Mike Sowersby) *bhd and sn pushed along: hdwy and prom bef 3 out: rdn and wknd fr next* 16/1
3P4- 5 8 **Nosey Box (IRE)**[19] 5314 9-11-8 116.................(bt) DerekFox(3) 88
(Noel C Kelly, Ire) *hld up in tch: hit 5th: rdn whn mstke 14th: rdn and struggling bef 3 out: btn after next* 16/1
F44- 6 16 **Green Wizard (IRE)**[19] 5313 9-11-1 111.............. CallumBewley(5) 66
(Sue Smith) *prom: hit 7th: drvn 13th: wknd fr 3 out* 4/1[2]
110- P **Douglas Julian**[23] 5239 13-11-5 117...................... MrTHamilton(7)
(Katie Scott) *led to 4th: cl up: lost pl 9th: sn struggling: lost tch and p.u 3 out* 8/1
6m 24.8s (-7.40) **Going Correction** -0.125s/f (Good) **7 Ran SP% 105.5**
Speed ratings: **106,104,99,95,92 87,**
CSF £36.99 CT £80.13 TOTE £11.00: £4.00, £2.20; EX 35.00 Trifecta £237.60.
Owner McGoldrick Racing Syndicates (2) **Bred** W Goldie **Trained** High Eldwick, W Yorks
■ Northern Executive was withdrawn. Price at time of withdrawal 10-1. Rule 4 applies to all bets - deduction 5p in the pound.

FOCUS
Quite a competitive handicap chase on paper.

82 LINNELS H'CAP HURDLE (8 hdls) 2m 48y
8:30 (8:31) (Class 3) (0-125,125) 4-Y-O+ £5,848 (£1,717; £858; £429)

Form RPR
226- 1 **Vodka Wells (FR)**[15] 5361 5-11-5 125........................ GLavery(7) 131+
(Brian Ellison) *prom: hdwy to ld 2 out: rdn out fr last* 3/1[2]
032- 2 2 1/4 **Harvey's Hope**[4] 4761 9-10-12 111........................(t) JamesReveley 114+
(Keith Reveley) *cl up: hdwy to ld bef 4 out: hit next: hdd and rdn 2 out: kpt on fr last: nt pce of wnr* 11/4[1]
134- 3 12 **Walser (IRE)**[48] 4784 8-10-9 108.....................(b) WilsonRenwick 99
(John Wade) *hld up: pushed along after 3 out: rallied to chse clr ldng pair last: kpt on: no imp* 8/1
3/1- 4 2 1/4 **Age Of Glory**[48] 4784 6-11-3 116........................ AndrewTinkler 105
(Barbara Butterworth) *t.k.h: hld up: stdy hdwy and in tch bef 2 out: rdn and wknd bef last* 7/1
034- 5 hd **Tikkandemickey (IRE)**[28] 5130 9-11-7 125.............. CallumBewley(5) 115
(Raymond Shiels) *led to bef 4 out: rallied: rdn and ev ch 2 out: wknd bef last* 6/1[3]
106- 6 20 **Hunters Belt (IRE)**[10] 5475 11-10-10 114.........(bt) JonathonBewley(5) 88
(George Bewley) *bhd: outpcd 4th: struggling fr 3 out: t.o* 14/1
126- 7 37 **Groomed (IRE)**[285] 1041 7-11-4 117........................ SeanQuinlan 55
(Sue Smith) *prom: drvn and outpcd 1/2-way: struggling fr 3 out: t.o* 22/1
240- F **Mr Burgees (IRE)**[43] 4891 6-11-5 125...................... JamesCowley(7) 110
(Donald McCain) *in tch: effrt and pushed along 2 out: wknd between last 2: 16 l sixth whn fell last* 7/1
4m 10.5s (-6.90) **Going Correction** -0.225s/f (Good) **8 Ran SP% 113.1**
Speed ratings (Par 107): **107,105,100,99,99 89,72,**
CSF £11.75 CT £57.10 TOTE £4.80: £1.80, £1.40, £1.90; EX 14.40 Trifecta £71.90.
Owner Acorn Partners, Mike & Eileen Newbould **Bred** Berend Van Dalfsen **Trained** Norton, N Yorks

FOCUS
Reasonable form for the grade.
T/Plt: £374.80 to a £1 stake. Pool: £60,287.65 - 117.39 winning units. T/Qpdt: £52.40 to a £1 stake. Pool: £7153.35 - 100.90 winning units. **Richard Young**

UTTOXETER (L-H)
Saturday, May 2

OFFICIAL GOING: Good (good to firm in places) changing to good after race 5 (4.10) changing to good (good to soft in places) after race 7 (5.20)
Wind: Light behind Weather: Overcast, turning to rain after race 3

83 SENTINEL "NATIONAL HUNT" MAIDEN HURDLE (9 hdls) 2m
1:45 (1:45) (Class 4) 4-Y-O+ £3,378 (£992; £496; £248)

Form RPR
310- 1 **Midnight Shot**[134] 3170 5-11-0 0........................ RichardJohnson 118+
(Charlie Longsdon) *chsd ldrs: blnd 1st: nt fluent 6th: led 3 out: clr next: shkn up bef last: comf* 7/4[1]
002- 2 10 **Ballycamp (IRE)**[26] 5201 6-11-0 0........................ AdamPogson 106+
(Charles Pogson) *mid-div: hdwy after 5th: rdn 3 out: styd on same pce fr next* 9/1
222- 3 1 1/2 **Raise A Spark**[281] 1086 5-11-0 0.......................... AdrianLane 107
(Donald McCain) *hld up: hdwy 6th: chsd wnr 2 out: sn rdn: no ex last* 20/1
/10- 4 18 **Native Display (IRE)**[44] 4873 5-11-0 0.................. AndrewTinkler 93
(Nicky Henderson) *chsd ldr tl led 6th: hdd 2 out: rdn and wknd next: hit last* 5/1[3]
500- 5 6 **Fountains Blossom**[33] 5063 6-10-7 0...................... RachaelGreen 76
(Anthony Honeyball) *hld up: nvr on terms* 11/1
400- 6 38 **Octagon**[18] 5331 5-11-0 0................................ JamesReveley 49
(Dianne Sayer) *a in rr: bhd fr 3rd* 40/1
524- 7 2 **Monksgold (IRE)**[107] 3688 7-11-0 112....................(p) TomCannon 47
(David Bridgwater) *led to 6th: rdn and wknd bef next* 3/1[2]
U0- 8 7 **Double Cool**[26] 5181 6-10-7 0............................ RobertDunne 34
(Matt Sheppard) *mid-div: rdn and wknd after 6th* 100/1

225- 9 8 **It Is I (IRE)**[10] 5468 5-11-0 0 DenisO'Regan 34
(Don Cantillon) *hld up: a in rr: wknd 6th* 12/1
6/5- P **Anwyl House**[170] 2468 5-11-0 0 JamesDavies
(Jo Hughes) *chsd ldrs: mstke 4th: rdn and wknd 6th: bhd whn p.u bef 3 out* 66/1

3m 47.0s (-5.00) **Going Correction** -0.025s/f (Good) 10 Ran SP% 113.7
Speed ratings (Par 105): **111,106,105,96,93 74,73,69,65,**
CSF £17.64 TOTE £2.80: £1.50, £2.20, £2.50; EX 19.90 Trifecta £139.10.
Owner Alan Halsall **Bred** Overbury Partnership **Trained** Over Norton, Oxon

FOCUS
Hurdles on inside, divided bends. First fence in back straight was omitted due to ground under repair. The ground was described as largely good with a few quicker patches. An ordinary maiden hurdle where the first four came clear. The winner and third are rated in line with their best hurdles form.

84 SENTINEL MAY UN MAR LADY BEGINNERS' CHASE (11 fncs 1 omitted) 2m
2:20 (2:20) (Class 4) 5-Y-0+ £4,051 (£1,196; £598; £299; £149)

Form RPR
330- 1 **Germany Calling (IRE)**[154] 2806 6-11-0 0 AidanColeman 140+
(Charlie Longsdon) *mde all: clr fr 3 out: comf* 3/1[2]
006- 2 6 **Such A Legend**[35] 5022 7-11-0 0 DavidBass 132
(Kim Bailey) *a.p: chsd wnr 5th: rdn 3 out: styd on same pce fr next* 11/4[1]
/30- 3 13 **Paradise Valley (IRE)**[49] 4750 6-11-0 127 AndrewThornton 120
(Mick Channon) *nt fluent 1st: chsd wnr to 5th: remained handy: rdn appr 4 out: wknd next* 4/1[3]
FUU- 4 1 3/4 **Red Seventy**[50] 4746 6-11-0 0 JackQuinlan 119
(Sarah Humphrey) *prom: rdn appr 4 out: wknd next* 50/1
PP6- 5 51 **Sureness (IRE)**[16] 5353 5-10-7 0 (t) JamesDavies 66
(Charlie Mann) *hld up: hdwy and nt fluent 6th: rdn and wknd 4 out* 14/1
6 27 **Veroce (FR)**[849] 6-11-0 0 JakeGreenall 49
(Mark Walford) *hld up: a in rr: bhd fr 6th* 50/1
6/3- 7 10 **Don't Be Late (IRE)**[364] 87 7-11-0 0 RichieMcLernon 40
(Jonjo O'Neill) *mid-div: lost pl 5th: bhd fr next: hit 4 out* 15/2
153- 8 17 **Upsanddowns (IRE)**[11] 5448 7-11-0 0 (t) PaulMoloney 24
(Evan Williams) *hld up: hdwy 5th: rdn and wknd appr 4 out* 11/1
135- F **Collodi (GER)**[190] 1643 6-11-0 0 TomCannon
(David Bridgwater) *hld up: in rr whn fell 5th* 8/1

3m 48.3s (-6.70) **Going Correction** -0.025s/f (Good) 9 Ran SP% 113.5
Speed ratings: **115,112,105,104,79 65,60,52,**
CSF £11.97 TOTE £4.70: £1.80, £1.30, £1.80; EX 14.70 Trifecta £30.20.
Owner Tyrone Hanlon **Bred** Gabriel Fahy **Trained** Over Norton, Oxon

FOCUS
A fair beginners' chase dominated by the winner. He looks like being a better chaser than hurdler.

85 SENTINEL GREEN'UN H'CAP HURDLE (12 hdls) 3m
2:55 (2:55) (Class 4) (0-120,120) 4-Y-0+ £3,508 (£1,030; £515; £257)

Form RPR
4- 1 **Bold Conquest (IRE)**[22] 5258 7-11-3 111 BrendanPowell 117+
(Stuart Edmunds) *a.p: led appr 2 out: rdn bef last: styd on* 9/2[1]
3P2- 2 3 **Orby's Man (IRE)**[26] 5202 6-11-9 117 AidanColeman 119
(Charlie Longsdon) *chsd ldrs: led and nt fluent 9th: rdn and hdd appr 2 out: styd on* 7/1[3]
P56- 3 1 1/4 **Henri Parry Morgan**[14] 5400 7-11-7 115 DonalDevereux 116
(Peter Bowen) *w ldrs tl rdn after 3 out: styd on u.p* 5/1[2]
16P- 4 2 1/4 **Be Bop Boru (IRE)**[64] 4476 8-11-10 118 (t) RichardJohnson 119
(Tim Vaughan) *hld up: mstke 1st: hdwy 5th: rdn appr 2 out: no ex flat* 8/1
6P3- 5 1/2 **Castle Conflict (IRE)**[35] 5032 10-10-13 107 (b) TomO'Brien 106
(Henry Daly) *hld up: hdwy after 9th: pushed along after 3 out: kpt on towards fin* 12/1
PPU- 6 7 **Up For An Oscar (IRE)**[21] 5282 8-11-2 115 (vt) EdCookson[(5)] 107
(Kim Bailey) *hld up: drvn along after 7th: hdwy appr 2 out: nt trble ldrs* 12/1
400- 7 12 **Our Mick**[16] 5357 9-11-12 120 (p) HenryBrooke 105
(Donald McCain) *mde most to 8th: rdn after next: wkng whn hit 2 out* 10/1
P56- 8 26 **Royal Moll (IRE)**[30] 5112 8-11-2 110 (tp) DarylJacob 68
(Warren Greatrex) *w ldr tl led 8th: hdd next: rdn and wknd appr 2 out* 16/1
PF3- 9 8 **Boruma (IRE)**[19] 5312 5-11-5 113 JamesReveley 64
(Dianne Sayer) *hld up: hit 7th: rdn and wknd after 9th* 12/1
P25- 10 11 **Provincial Pride (IRE)**[236] 1479 8-10-5 106 (t) CharlieHammond[(7)] 47
(Mike Hammond) *mid-div: rdn and wknd after 9th* 14/1
231- 11 1 1/4 **Forgivienne**[44] 4864 8-11-1 109 AdamWedge 49
(Evan Williams) *chsd ldrs to 9th* 8/1
4- 12 11 **Zuccotti Park (IRE)**[44] 4861 7-10-13 107 RobertDunne 37
(Tom Lacey) *hld up: hdwy 8th: rdn and wknd next* 25/1

5m 45.7s (-4.30) **Going Correction** -0.025s/f (Good) 12 Ran SP% 118.1
Speed ratings (Par 105): **106,105,104,103,103 101,97,88,86,82 81,78**
CSF £36.29 CT £165.26 TOTE £5.70: £2.00, £2.20, £2.20; EX 32.70 Trifecta £169.30.
Owner Nick Brown Racing **Bred** Dan And Mrs Margaret O'Neill **Trained** Newport Pagnell, Bucks

FOCUS
This was run at a steady pace so there were several still battling it out turning for home. The winner was a 120+ chaser in Ireland and there may be more to come.

86 SENTINEL WAY WE WERE NOVICES' H'CAP CHASE (16 fncs 2 omitted) 3m
3:30 (3:30) (Class 4) (0-115,115) 5-Y-0 £4,051 (£1,196; £598; £299; £149)

Form RPR
444- 1 **Kilmurvy (IRE)**[44] 4864 7-11-12 115 (tp) NickScholfield 124+
(Jeremy Scott) *hld up in tch: lost pl 12th: rallied appr 2 out: chsd ldr bef last: led flat: rdn out* 4/1[2]
332- 2 3 **He's A Bully (IRE)**[26] 5194 6-11-1 104 RichardJohnson 113+
(Philip Hobbs) *led: nt fluent 1st and 2nd: shkn up appr 3 out: mstke last: hdd and unable qck flat* 2/1[1]
332- 3 5 **Still Believing (IRE)**[20] 5289 7-11-12 115 AdamWedge 117
(Evan Williams) *hld up: hdwy appr 3 out: styd on same pce fr next: wnt 3rd nr fin* 5/1
P11- 4 1/2 **Milly Malone (IRE)**[13] 5407 9-10-13 102 (t) AidanColeman 104
(Adrian Wintle) *chsd ldr: blnd 8th: lost 2nd 12th: rdn to go 2nd again 3 out tl appr last: no ex flat* 9/2[3]
P35/ 5 11 **Dancing Dude (IRE)**[25] 4984 8-10-9 98 AndrewTinkler 92
(Barry Leavy) *prom: chsd ldr 12th tl nt fluent 3 out: wknd bef next* 16/1
0F0- P **Arthur Mc Bride (IRE)**[47] 4811 6-11-4 107 PaddyBrennan
(Fergal O'Brien) *hld up: hdwy 12th: hit next: sn wknd: bhd whn p.u bef 2 out* 5/1

6m 11.5s (-3.60) **Going Correction** -0.025s/f (Good) 6 Ran SP% 110.7
Speed ratings: **105,104,102,102,98**
CSF £12.58 TOTE £5.30: £2.80, £1.50; EX 12.80 Trifecta £51.00.
Owner Ian Murray **Bred** Kevin Miller **Trained** Brompton Regis, Somerset

FOCUS
The forecast rain had arrived by this stage. The pace was ordinary, giving all of them a chance turning in, with the winner coming from last to first. He was well in on the best of his hurdle form and is rated to that sort of level.

87 SENTINEL CASHBACK H'CAP HURDLE (10 hdls) 2m 3f 207y
4:10 (4:10) (Class 3) (0-135,131) 4-Y-0 £5,443 (£1,608; £804; £402; £201)

Form RPR
163- 1 **Henllan Harri (IRE)**[151] 2870 7-11-3 125 SeanBowen[(3)] 130+
(Peter Bowen) *a.p: led appr 2 out: hit last: drvn out* 5/2[1]
60P/ 2 1 1/2 **Fountains Flypast**[28] 11-10-6 111 (t) RachaelGreen 114+
(Anthony Honeyball) *hld up: hdwy 6th: led 3 out: sn hdd: mstke next: styd on* 16/1
314- 3 hd **Flying Light (IRE)**[20] 5295 9-10-10 115 (b) KielanWoods 119+
(Graeme McPherson) *hld up: hdwy after 7th: rdn appr last: styd on* 9/1
234- 4 3 1/4 **Shear Rock (IRE)**[26] 5183 5-10-3 108 RichardJohnson 110
(Charlie Longsdon) *hld up: plld hrd: mstke 6th: hdwy appr 3 out: hit next: styd on: nt trble ldrs* 3/1[2]
212- 5 22 **Raktiman (IRE)**[28] 5139 8-11-9 131 JonathanEngland[(3)] 120
(Richard Drake) *hld up: hdwy 7th: hit 2 out: sn wknd* 11/2[3]
0F5- 6 3 1/4 **Hold Court (IRE)**[34] 5048 8-11-1 120 PaulMoloney 96
(Evan Williams) *prom tl rdn and wknd after 7th* 16/1
206- 7 10 **Get Home Now**[185] 2127 7-10-12 117 (t) DonalDevereux 84
(Peter Bowen) *w ldr tl led 7th: hdd next: sn rdn and wknd* 12/1
333- 8 14 **Maxie T**[35] 5022 4-10-11 121 RichieMcLernon 71
(Jonjo O'Neill) *nt fluent 2nd: mde most to 7th: sn rdn: wknd 3 out* 10/1
PU6- P **Hallings Comet**[30] 5116 6-11-6 125 AidanColeman
(Adrian Wintle) *plld hrd and prom: wknd after 6th: bhd whn p.u bef 3 out* 22/1

4m 56.2s (-7.00) **Going Correction** -0.025s/f (Good)
WFA 4 from 5yo+ 19lb 9 Ran SP% 111.9
Speed ratings (Par 107): **104,103,103,102,93 92,88,83,**
CSF £38.47 CT £305.02 TOTE £3.60: £1.40, £4.40, £3.00; EX 56.00 Trifecta £553.90.
Owner Einsley Harries **Bred** Paul Ryan **Trained** Little Newcastle, Pembrokes

FOCUS
Two duelling leaders ensured a good pace and both eventually dropped right out of it. The winner and second were well in on the best of their form.

88 SENTINEL #LOCALANDPROUD H'CAP CHASE (14 fncs 2 omitted) 2m 5f
4:45 (4:46) (Class 5) (0-100,95) 5-Y-0+ £2,859 (£839; £419; £209)

Form RPR
5PP- 1 **Mr Robinson (FR)**[218] 1625 8-10-3 72 JamesBest 86
(Rob Summers) *hld up: hdwy 4 out: led appr last: rdn out* 8/1
P31- 2 2 3/4 **Waddingtown Hero (IRE)**[10] 5463 8-11-7 90 (tp) GerardTumelty 104+
(Andy Turnell) *a.p: mstke 8th: hmpd 10th: chsd ldr 4 out: led next: j.lft 2 out: rdn and hdd bef last: styd on same pce flat* 5/2[1]
/64- 3 12 **Gran Torino (IRE)**[331] 595 10-11-5 88 PaulMoloney 88
(Evan Williams) *hld up: rdn appr 4 out: wnt 3rd flat: nvr trbld ldrs* 11/2[3]
533- 4 3 1/4 **Molko Jack (FR)**[12] 5421 11-11-4 90 BenPoste[(3)] 88
(Michael Mullineaux) *hld up: hdwy 8th: rdn and wknd appr 2 out* 14/1
P54- 5 16 **Dougalstar (FR)**[40] 4968 6-10-0 69 oh2 (b) HenryBrooke 59
(Jennie Candlish) *led and sn clr: wnt lft 2nd: c bk to the field 8th: wnt clr again and wnt lft next: rdn after 10th: hdd 3 out: wkng whn blnd next* 7/1
P66- P **Phoenix Des Mottes (FR)**[15] 5376 12-9-9 69 oh1 JoeCornwall[(5)]
(John Cornwall) *chsd ldrs: hmpd and lost pl 6th: drvn along 8th: sn wknd: bhd whn p.u bef 11th* 33/1
246- P **Rebel High (IRE)**[15] 5372 11-10-2 71 (v) LiamTreadwell
(Derek Frankland) *mid-div: j.lft 6th: hdwy and j.rt 8th: wknd 10th: bhd whn p.u bef 3 out* 16/1
63P- R **Noble Witness (IRE)**[15] 5374 12-11-12 95 (p) AdamPogson
(Charles Pogson) *chsd ldr tl after 8th: drvn along 10th: 5 l 3rd and keeping on whn hung lft and rn out last* 9/1
634- P **Definitely Better (IRE)**[23] 5247 7-11-12 95 PaddyBrennan
(Tom George) *hld up: hdwy 6th: chsd ldr after 8th: j.rt 10th: sn rdn: wknd bef next: bhd whn p.u bef 3 out* 4/1[2]

5m 20.0s (-2.80) **Going Correction** -0.025s/f (Good) 9 Ran SP% 113.1
Speed ratings: **104,102,98,97,91 , , ,**
CSF £28.87 CT £119.78 TOTE £9.80: £2.40, £1.40, £2.30; EX 47.40 Trifecta £276.30.
Owner Mrs Gill Summers **Bred** Haras De La Faisanderie & C Bouillette **Trained** Tanworth-in-Arden, Warwicks

FOCUS
An ordinary handicap.

89 WEEKEND SENTINEL NOVICES' H'CAP HURDLE (DIV I) (12 hdls) 3m
5:20 (5:20) (Class 5) (0-100,99) 4-Y-0+ £2,339 (£686; £343; £171)

Form RPR
6P1- 1 **Flemensbay**[21] 5280 7-11-11 98 (p) RichardJohnson 107+
(Richard Phillips) *chsd ldr tl led appr 3 out: sn clr: rdn bef next: styd on wl* 3/1[1]
303- 2 12 **Lord Aldervale (IRE)**[26] 5214 8-9-7 73 oh2 (t) GeorgeGorman[(7)] 71
(Luke Dace) *led and nt fluent 1st: rdn and hdd appr 3 out: sn outpcd: mstke next: hit last* 8/1
00F- 3 13 **Anda De Grissay (FR)**[33] 5063 5-11-12 99 (t) AidanColeman 83
(Anthony Honeyball) *hld up: hdwy appr 8th: hit next: sn rdn: wknd bef 3 out* 9/2[2]
306- 4 shd **Titans Approach (IRE)**[21] 5280 6-11-8 95 PaulMoloney 80
(Graeme McPherson) *hld up: nt fluent 2nd: drvn along after 7th: wkng whn hit 3 out* 7/1
064- 5 2 **Call Me Kate**[66] 4425 5-11-8 95 (p) JakeGreenall 78
(Henry Daly) *chsd ldrs to 9th* 8/1
644- 6 25 **Misteray**[21] 5281 5-10-13 91 (t) RyanWhile[(5)] 51
(Bill Turner) *chsd ldrs: hit 7th: rdn and wknd appr 3 out* 6/1[3]
0P5- P **Pembridge**[21] 5281 6-10-0 73 oh4 (t) AlainCawley
(Susan Johnson) *hld up: a in rr: lost tch 8th: bhd whn p.u bef 3 out* 16/1
FPP- P **Black Lily (IRE)**[39] 4977 7-11-11 98 TomMessenger
(Chris Bealby) *prom to 7th: bhd whn p.u bef 9th* 20/1
004- P **Very Live (FR)**[39] 4980 6-11-6 93 (p) LiamTreadwell
(Paul Webber) *hld up in tch: nt fluent 3rd and 4th: sn pushed along: wknd 7th: bhd whn p.u bef next* 8/1

5m 54.5s (4.50) **Going Correction** -0.025s/f (Good) 9 Ran SP% 113.9
Speed ratings (Par 103): **91,87,82,82,81 73, , ,**
CSF £26.89 CT £105.54 TOTE £3.10: £1.10, £3.70, £2.30; EX 26.80 Trifecta £226.50.
Owner Dozen Dreamers Partnership **Bred** Mrs J L Egan **Trained** Adlestrop, Gloucs

FOCUS
The going was changed to good after the rain. This turned into quite a test with the first two dominating throughout. Another big step up from the winner.

90 WEEKEND SENTINEL NOVICES' H'CAP HURDLE (DIV II) (12 hdls) 3m
5:55 (5:56) (Class 5) (0-100,99) 4-Y-O+ **£2,339** (£686; £343; £171)

Form RPR

634- **1** **Youngdocgallagher (IRE)**[51] 4733 6-11-7 **97**........ BenPoste(3) 110+
(Michael Mullineaux) *a.p: chsd ldr 5th: nt fluent 9th: sn led: rdn clr after 3 out: mstke last* **8/1**

060- **2** *14* **Lilly's Legend**[102] 3783 5-9-13 **75**........(p) SeanBowen(3) 74
(Mark Walford) *chsd ldrs: rdn appr 3 out: styd on same pce: wnt 2nd nr fin* **3/1**[1]

600- **3** *hd* **Catkin Copse**[41] 4944 7-10-11 **91**........(p) DanielHiskett(7) 90
(Richard Phillips) *hld up: hdwy 6th: chsd wnr after 9th: rdn 3 out: sn outpcd* **22/1**

4F0- **4** *8* **Vinegar Hill**[28] 5148 6-11-8 **95**........ DarylJacob 88
(Ben Case) *hld up: hdwy appr 3 out: sn rdn: wknd next* **9/2**[2]

533- **5** *15* **Diego Suarez (FR)**[15] 5379 5-11-1 **88**........(b) TomMessenger 66
(Chris Bealby) *mid-div: hit 3rd: rdn bef 8th: wknd bef 2 out* **13/2**[3]

024- **6** *21* **Allerton (IRE)**[21] 5280 8-11-5 **99**........(p) JamesO'Neill(7) 58
(Fergal O'Brien) *prom: nt fluent 3rd: pushed along 8th: wknd next* **7/1**

043- **P** **Dream N (IRE)**[45] 4853 7-11-11 **98**........ MarkGrant
(Sean Curran) *s.s: a in rr: bhd fr 4th: p.u bef 7th* **16/1**

0P0- **P** **Mountain Of Angels**[21] 5281 6-10-1 **74** oh6 ow1........ PaulMoloney
(Mary Evans) *chsd ldr to 5th: sn pushed along: lost pl next: bhd fr 7th: p.u bef 8th* **50/1**

000- **P** **League Of His Own (IRE)**[49] 4769 6-10-0 **73** oh3........(t) TrevorWhelan
(Claire Dyson) *led at str pce: clr after 4th: hit 8th: hdd & wknd after next: bhd whn p.u bef 3 out* **9/1**

600- **P** **Prince Of Thieves (IRE)**[77] 4234 5-11-7 **94**........(t) AidanColeman
(Anthony Honeyball) *hld up: hit 5th: rdn and wknd bef 9th: bhd whn p.u bef 3 out* **13/2**[3]

5m 53.9s (3.90) **Going Correction** -0.025s/f (Good) **10** Ran SP% **115.7**
Speed ratings (Par 103): **92,87,87,84,79 72,,,,**
CSF £32.73 CT £513.76 TOTE £13.00: £2.30, £1.20, £8.60; EX 48.60 Trifecta £956.00 Part won..
Owner Denis Gallagher **Bred** Patrick Kinsella **Trained** Alpraham, Cheshire

FOCUS
They were strung out early in this modest novice handicap. The second and third set the level.
T/Plt: £19.40 to a £1 stake. Pool: £59,557.60 - 2236.14 winning units. T/Qpdt: £8.70 to a £1 stake. Pool: £5037.99 - 425.45 winning units. **Colin Roberts**

91a (Foreign Racing) - See Raceform Interactive

68 PUNCHESTOWN (R-H)
Saturday, May 2
OFFICIAL GOING: Hurdle & chase course - soft; cross-country course - yielding

92a LADBROKES IRELAND H'CAP CHASE (21 fncs) 3m 6f
3:10 (3:11) (0-145,145) 5-Y-O+ **£15,116** (£4,418; £2,093; £697)

RPR

1 **Heathfield (IRE)**[48] 4804 8-9-13 **120**........ PaulTownend 138+
(A J Martin, Ire) *w.w: clsr in 11th 1/2-way: hdwy fr 12th to chse ldrs in 4th fr 4 out: clsr in 3rd after next: almost on terms 2 out where nt fluent: led travelling wl between last 2 and kpt on wl run-in* **4/1**[1]

2 *4 ¼* **Audacious Plan (IRE)**[10] 5464 6-10-1 **122**........(p) TomScudamore 133
(Rebecca Curtis) *hld up: tk clsr order bhd ldrs after 5 out and almost on terms fr next: led fr 3 out tl hdd u.p after next: sn no imp on wnr: kpt on same pce* **18/1**

3 *8* **Embracing Change (IRE)**[90] 4007 10-10-9 **130**........(bt) DJCasey 135
(Robert Tyner, Ire) *chsd ldrs: j. sltly rt at times: 4th bef 15th: almost on terms 4 out: rdn in 2nd into st and dropped to 3rd 2 out: no imp on ldrs u.p whn bad mstke last: kpt on u.p run-in to hold 3rd* **12/1**

4 *nk* **Urano (FR)**[20] 5303 7-10-10 **131**........ RWalsh 134
(W P Mullins, Ire) *w.w towards rr: prog after 5 out to chse ldrs in 5th gng wl after 3 out: wnt 4th bef next: rdn and no ex u.p after 2 out: kpt on one pce run-in: jst hld for 3rd* **11/1**

5 *15* **Bothair Clei (IRE)**[55] 4663 10-9-12 **119**........ MarkEnright 107
(Daniel G Murphy, Ire) *hld up in tch: tk clsr order 5 out: rdn in 4th after 3 out and sn no ex u.p in 5th: one pce fr 2 out* **16/1**

6 *4 ½* **Man With Van (IRE)**[14] 5392 9-10-12 **133**........(vt) AELynch 116
(S R B Crawford, Ire) *chsd ldrs: rdn in 6th after 3 out and no imp on ldrs bef next: one pce after* **25/1**

7 *4 ½* **Vasco Du Mee (FR)**[100] 3825 6-10-2 **126**........(bt) KevinSexton(3) 105
(Gordon Elliott, Ire) *mid-div: tk clsr order 4 out: rdn and no ex after next* **20/1**

8 *14* **Adrenalin Flight (IRE)**[18] 5334 9-9-13 **120**........(v) DannyMullins 85
(Seamus Mullins) *led and racd out wd: mstke 15th: jnd after 4 out and hdd u.p bef next: sn wknd* **12/1**

9 *2* **Top Dancer (FR)**[43] 4882 8-9-10 **117** oh1........ GavinSheehan 80
(Warren Greatrex) *chsd ldrs: rdn bef 4 out where slt mstke and no imp on ldrs: wknd* **10/1**

10 *2 ¾* **Milborough (IRE)**[14] 5392 9-11-4 **142**........ GrahamWatters(3) 102
(Ian Duncan) *chsd ldrs: 7th bef 15th: rdn and no ex after 4 out* **25/1**

11 *2* **More Madness (IRE)**[25] 5232 8-9-7 **117** oh3........(p) DavidSplaine(3) 75
(Terence O'Brien, Ire) *hld up in tch: rdn and wknd after 4 out* **33/1**

12 *29* **Portrait King (IRE)**[21] 5275 10-10-13 **134**........(p) AndrewJMcNamara 63
(M Phelan, Ire) *trckd ldr: j.lft 8th: cl 2nd 1/2-way: pushed along after 5 out and wknd fr next* **20/1**

P **Sword Fish (IRE)**[15] 5386 9-9-10 **117**........(tp) AlanCrowe
(C Roche, Ire) *nvr bttr than mid-div: reminders towards rr after 12th: trailing whn p.u after 16th* **33/1**

P **Thelobstercatcher**[25] 5232 11-9-10 **117** oh1........(bt) NiallPMadden
(P A Fahy, Ire) *settled in mid-div: wknd fr 15th and trailing whn p.u bef 4 out* **25/1**

P **Cross Appeal (IRE)**[210] 1752 9-10-2 **123**........ APHeskin
(Noel Meade, Ire) *mid-div: rdn and no imp 4 out where slt mstke: wknd and p.u bef 2 out* **25/1**

P **Groody Hill (IRE)**[76] 4259 9-10-4 **128**........(tp) JodyMcGarvey(3)
(C Roche, Ire) *towards rr: bad mstke 7th: p.u bef 2 out* **20/1**

P **Miss Xian (IRE)**[25] 5232 8-9-5 **117**........ AndrewRing(5)
(F Flood, Ire) *chsd ldrs: slt mstke 9th: 5th bef 12th: wknd bef next and p.u bef 15th: burst blood vessels* **25/1**

P **Forever Gold (IRE)**[26] 5222 8-9-5 **117** oh4........(p[1]) LPDempsey(5)
(Edward Cawley, Ire) *mid-div best: wknd fr 16th: p.u bef 2 out* **11/2**[2]

P **Rogue Angel (IRE)**[26] 5224 7-10-9 **130**........(b) BJCooper
(M F Morris, Ire) *sn chsd ldrs: racd out wd: wknd 4 out: p.u bef 2 out* **20/1**

P **Sizing Coal (IRE)**[26] 5224 7-10-12 **133**........ JJBurke
(J T R Dreaper, Ire) *in rr of mid-div: pushed along towards rr fr 12th: p.u bef 2 out* **8/1**[3]

8m 14.9s (28.60) **Going Correction** -0.10s/f (Good) **20** Ran SP% **134.6**
Speed ratings: **57,55,53,53,49 48,47,43,42,42 41,33,,,,,,,,**
CSF £64.67 CT £842.92 TOTE £4.30: £1.80, £3.60, £2.20, £2.20; DF 99.30 Trifecta £373.30.
Owner John P McManus **Bred** Denis Cleary **Trained** Summerhill, Co. Meath

FOCUS
This was a real test of stamina with the ground having deteriorated since the previous day. No fallers, but eight of the 20 were pulled up and the finishers were well strung out.

93a IRISH STALLION FARMS EUROPEAN BREEDERS FUND MARES CHAMPION HURDLE (GRADE 1) (11 hdls) 2m 2f
3:50 (3:52) 4-Y-O+
£46,511 (£14,728; £6,976; £2,325; £1,550; £775)

RPR

1 **Annie Power (IRE)**[53] 4692 7-11-7 162........ RWalsh 157+
(W P Mullins, Ire) *mde all: 2 l clr at 1/2-way: stl gng wl into st and extended advantage bef 2 out: pushed out run-in: easily* **2/9**[1]

2 *10* **Analifet (FR)**[26] 5221 5-11-7 142........ BJCooper 146
(W P Mullins, Ire) *w.w in rr: clsr in 6th after 4 out: impr to dispute 2nd 2 out where bad mstke and pckd: sn rdn in 3rd and wnt 2nd into st: no imp on easy wnr: kpt on same pce* **10/1**[3]

3 *11* **Kalane (IRE)**[42] 4918 6-11-7 129........ NoelFehily 132
(Charlie Longsdon) *chsd ldrs in 4th: rdn in 5th bef 2 out and no imp on easy wnr in 4th into st: kpt on u.p into mod 3rd run-in* **25/1**

4 *3* **Katie T (IRE)**[16] 3760 6-11-7 138........ BrianHughes 130
(Kevin Prendergast, Ire) *hld up towards rr: clsr in 5th 1/2-way: impr bhd ldrs fr 6th: nt fluent 3 out: rdn in 2nd after 2 out and no imp on easy wnr into st where dropped to 3rd: one pce after and dropped to mod 4th run-in* **7/1**[2]

5 *1 ¼* **Jennies Jewel (IRE)**[26] 5221 8-11-7 136........ IanMcCarthy 128
(Jarlath P Fahey, Ire) *chsd ldrs: 3rd 1/2-way: rdn fr bef 2 out and sn no ex u.p in 5th: wknd* **33/1**

6 *37* **Rock On The Moor (IRE)**[27] 5175 7-11-7 138........ RobbiePower 91
(Mrs John Harrington, Ire) *chsd ldrs: settled in rr fr 4th: pushed along in rr bef 3 out and no ex: wknd* **14/1**

7 *1 ¾* **Pass The Time**[27] 5154 6-11-7 137........(p) MarkWalsh 89
(Neil Mulholland) *settled bhd ldr in 2nd: nt fluent 1st and 3rd: pushed along fr 4 out where nt fluent and wknd u.p next bef next* **50/1**

4m 33.4s (-2.60) **Going Correction** +0.275s/f (Yiel) **7** Ran SP% **118.8**
Speed ratings: **116,111,106,105,104 88,87**
CSF £4.08 TOTE £1.10: £1.10, £2.30; DF 3.40 Trifecta £26.40.
Owner Mrs S Ricci **Bred** Eamon Cleary **Trained** Muine Beag, Co Carlow

FOCUS
Only one genuine Grade 1 performer in action and she put her rivals to the sword as expected.

94a AES CHAMPION FOUR YEAR OLD HURDLE (GRADE 1) (9 hdls) 2m
4:25 (4:27) 4-Y-O
£46,511 (£14,728; £6,976; £2,325; £1,550; £775)

RPR

1 **Petite Parisienne (FR)**[27] 5175 4-10-7 138........ BJCooper 143+
(W P Mullins, Ire) *chsd ldrs: 6th 1/2-way: tk clsr order after 4 out: rdn into 3rd after next and clsd on outer travelling best to ld: extended advantage and in command whn mstke last: styd on wl* **11/4**[1]

2 *8 ½* **Buiseness Sivola (FR)**[26] 5220 4-11-0 137........ RWalsh 139
(W P Mullins, Ire) *chsd ldrs: rdn after 2 out and no imp on ldrs u.p in 4th into st: kpt on u.p in 3rd fr last and wnt 2nd run-in: nt trble easy wnr* **9/2**[3]

3 *1 ¾* **Thunder Zone**[27] 5168 4-11-0 133........ PaulTownend 137
(Gordon Elliott, Ire) *trckd ldr: slt mstke in cl 2nd at 5th: disp 3 out and led narrowly after next where slt mstke: sn hdd and no imp on wnr bef last where nt fluent: one pce run-in and dropped to 3rd* **20/1**

4 *2 ½* **Stars Over The Sea (USA)**[23] 5236 4-11-0 138........(t) TomScudamore 135
(David Pipe) *led: narrow advantage 1/2-way: jnd 3 out and hdd after next: no ex u.p in 3rd bef last and one pce after* **10/1**

5 *4 ¾* **Pain Au Chocolat (FR)**[50] 4736 4-11-0 137........ WayneHutchinson 130
(Alan King) *hld up in tch: 7th 1/2-way: tk clsr order bef 3 out: rdn into 5th into st and no imp on ldrs: kpt on one pce* **12/1**

6 *7* **Prussian Eagle (IRE)**[26] 5220 4-11-0 134........ RobbiePower 123
(Charles O'Brien, Ire) *hld up in rr: last 1/2-way: slt mstke 5th and reminders after next: no imp on ldrs 3 out: kpt on u.p fr next: nvr trbld ldrs* **12/1**

7 *8* **Qualando (FR)**[52] 4707 4-11-0 139........ SamTwiston-Davies 115
(Paul Nicholls) *chsd ldrs: pushed along in 5th bef 3 out and sn no ex u.p in 7th: wknd* **7/2**[2]

8 *8* **Matorico (IRE)**[50] 4736 4-11-0 0........ MarkWalsh 107
(Jonjo O'Neill) *chsd ldrs: 4th 1/2-way: rdn on outer bef 2 out and no ex u.p in 6th into st: wknd* **14/1**

9 *1 ¼* **Lettre De Cachet**[26] 5220 4-10-7 120........ JJBurke 99
(Noel Meade, Ire) *hld up towards rr: mstke in 9th at 2nd: rdn and no imp 3 out* **33/1**

10 *14* **Fiscal Focus (IRE)**[97] 3890 4-11-0 138........ DannyMullins 92
(Desmond McDonogh, Ire) *hld up: 8th 1/2-way: rdn and no ex after 3 out: wknd* **7/1**

4m 9.3s (4.30) **Going Correction** +0.50s/f (Soft) **10** Ran SP% **118.4**
Speed ratings: **109,104,103,102,100 96,92,88,88,81**
CSF £15.76 CT £208.34 TOTE £3.50: £1.50, £1.80, £3.90; DF 14.70 Trifecta £462.00.
Owner Gigginstown House Stud **Bred** Thierry De La Heronniere **Trained** Muine Beag, Co Carlow

FOCUS
On paper the British challenge for this looked quite strong, but once again it was Willie Mullins who held the aces.

95a PALMERSTOWN HOUSE PAT TAAFFE H'CAP CHASE (GRADE B) (17 fncs) 3m 1f
5:00 (5:01) (0-150,150) 5-Y-O+ **£25,193** (£7,364; £3,488; £1,162)

RPR

1 **Gallant Oscar (IRE)**[53] 4690 9-10-9 **135**........ MarkWalsh 156+
(A J Martin, Ire) *w.w: tk clsr order in mid-div fr 1/2-way: hdwy bef 4 out to chse ldrs bef next: travelling wl in 3rd bef st and led after 2 out: sn clr and styd on wl: easily* **5/2**[1]

2 9 **Archie Meade (IRE)**[44] 4878 10-9-10 **122** oh6..............(tp) DanielHoward 131
(Daniel John Howard, Ire) *towards rr: sltly hmpd at 2nd: tk clsr order after 1/2-way: hdwy in 8th after 5 out to ld fr 3 out: strly pressed and hdd after next: no ch w easy wnr: kpt on same pce run-in* **16/1**

3 4 1/2 **Bless The Wings (IRE)**[22] 5253 10-10-8 **134**...............(p) MsNCarberry 139
(Gordon Elliott, Ire) *hld up in rr: prog after 5 out: rdn in 7th after 3 out and no imp on wnr u.p in 3rd fr next: kpt on one pce* **16/1**

4 3/4 **Ballycasey (IRE)**[21] 5275 8-11-10 **150**................................ RWalsh 154
(W P Mullins, Ire) *hld up towards rr: tk clsr order fr after 5 out and impr to chse ldrs after next: rdn disputing 4th 2 out and sn no imp on easy wnr: kpt on one pce* **10/1**

5 4 3/4 **Ballyculla (IRE)**[53] 4693 8-10-4 **130**..............(p) GavinSheehan 129
(Warren Greatrex) *mid-div: hdwy to chse ldrs after 5 out: almost on terms bef 3 out: rdn in 2nd into st and no ex in 3rd 2 out: one pce after* **14/1**

6 14 **Rule The World**[26] 5224 8-11-5 **145**..............................(p) BJCooper 130
(M F Morris, Ire) *mid-div: reminders in 9th after 4th: rdn in 6th after 3 out and sn no imp on ldrs: kpt on one pce fr 2 out* **8/1**[3]

7 14 **Cootamundra (IRE)**[46] 4845 12-10-0 **126**........................ MsKWalsh 97
(J A Berry, Ire) *hld up towards rr: clsr in 9th after 3 out: rdn and no imp on ldrs fr next: kpt on one pce* **25/1**

8 8 **First Lieutenant (IRE)**[21] 5275 10-11-5 **150**...............(bt) DavidMullins(5) 113
(M F Morris, Ire) *trckd ldr tl led bef 6th: hdd narrowly fr next tl regained advantage fr 11th: rdn and hdd fr 3 out: sn wknd* **14/1**

9 nk **Katnap (FR)**[48] 4804 8-9-10 **122** oh1..............................(t[1]) DannyMullins 85
(John Laurence Cullen, Ire) *trckd ldrs: clsr in 2nd bef 12th: rdn after 3 out and sn wknd* **11/2**[2]

P **Chartreux (FR)**[34] 5047 10-10-8 **134**..............................(t) TomScudamore
(Tom George) *led narrowly tl hdd narrowly bef 6th: regained advantage fr next tl hdd fr 11th: pushed along in 7th after 5 out and no imp on ldrs: wknd qckly and p.u after 3 out* **20/1**

P **Yes Tom (IRE)**[14] 5392 10-11-0 **140**...................................(p) RobbiePower
(S R B Crawford, Ire) *w.w: struggling in rr bef 8th and p.u bef next* **28/1**

U **Toon River (IRE)**[56] 4640 10-11-2 **142**...........................(t) MPFogarty
(Miss Mary Louise Hallahan, Ire) *chsd ldrs: disp 6th whn blnd and uns rdr 9th* **16/1**

P **Knock A Hand (IRE)**[42] 4910 10-11-1 **141**...........(b) SamTwiston-Davies
(Richard Lee) *chsd ldrs: rdn and wknd after 4 out: p.u after next* **25/1**

P **Aupcharlie (IRE)**[51] 4720 9-11-0 **140**.....................................(p) JJBurke
(Henry De Bromhead, Ire) *nvr bttr than mid-div: pushed along towards rr fr 12th and no imp fr 4 out: p.u after next* **20/1**

P **Daring Article (IRE)**[26] 5224 9-10-1 **127**..........................(bt) DJCasey
(Robert Tyner, Ire) *chsd ldrs: pushed along fr 10th and wknd fr after next: p.u after 4 out* **16/1**

P **Owega Star (IRE)**[21] 5275 8-10-11 **137**..........................(t) PaulTownend
(Peter Fahey, Ire) *hld up in mid-div: nt fluent 4th and at times after: no imp in rr fr 12th: p.u bef 4 out* **20/1**

P **The Crafty Butcher (IRE)**[26] 5224 8-10-0 **131**.............(b) LPDempsey(5)
(Michael Hourigan, Ire) *nvr bttr than mid-div: sltly hmpd 9th: wknd fr after 12th* **25/1**

P **The Job Is Right**[26] 5224 7-10-13 **139**...........................(b) MarkEnright
(Michael Hourigan, Ire) *hld up towards rr: mstkes 5th and next where reminder: mstke 5 out and p.u bef next* **10/1**

P **Kylecrue (IRE)**[15] 5386 8-9-7 **124** oh4 ow2..............(b) RyanTreacy(5) 34
(John Patrick Ryan, Ire) *hld up in tch: rdn and no ex fr 5 out: sn wknd and p.u bef 2 out* **66/1**

6m 34.6s (-10.40) **Going Correction** -0.10s/f (Good) **19 Ran SP% 140.9**
Speed ratings: **112,109,107,107,105 101,96,94,94, , , , , , , , ,**
CSF £43.64 CT £607.29 TOTE £3.20: £1.50, £3.40, £3.80, £2.20; DF 75.40 Trifecta £1163.00.
Owner John P McManus **Bred** Patricia And Marie Keating **Trained** Summerhill, Co. Meath

FOCUS
A strong handicap on paper, but a highly progressive staying chaser turned it into a procession.

96a SETANTA SPORTS H'CAP HURDLE (GRADE B) (12 hdls) 2m 4f
5:35 (5:38) 4-Y-0+
£46,511 (£14,728; £6,976; £2,325; £1,550; £775)

RPR

1 **Sort It Out (IRE)**[50] 4737 6-10-12 **136**............................... MarkWalsh 148
(Edward P Harty, Ire) *chsd ldrs: impr bhd ldrs bef 2 out where n.m.r briefly: sn pushed along and disp bef 2 out: sn led narrowly: strly pressed u.p fr last: kpt on wl towards fin* **6/1**[3]

2 1 **Arbre De Vie (FR)**[50] 4738 5-11-6 **144**.................................... RWalsh 155+
(W P Mullins, Ire) *hld up in mid-div: hdwy after 3 out to chse ldrs after next where stmbld sltly in 8th bef st: sn wnt 6th and rdn into 3rd bef last: kpt on wl run-in into 2nd cl home: nvr on terms* **5/1**[2]

3 1/2 **Clondaw Warrior (IRE)**[25] 5231 8-10-4 **128**........................ DJCasey 138
(W P Mullins, Ire) *chsd ldrs: tk clsr order in 5th appr st: rdn in 2nd bef last and kpt on wl run-in to strly press wnr: no ex cl home and dropped to 3rd* **16/1**

4 3 **Pleasant Company (IRE)**[2] 50 7-10-0 **124**..................... MsKWalsh 131+
(W P Mullins, Ire) *hld up towards rr: hdwy fr bef 2 out to chse ldrs in mod 5th bef last: no imp on ldrs run-in: kpt on u.p into 4th* **7/2**[1]

5 5 1/2 **Jimmy Two Times (IRE)**[25] 5230 6-10-4 **133**................. LPDempsey(5) 135
(B R Hamilton, Ire) *prom: cl 3rd bef 5 out: rdn after 2 out and no imp on ldrs u.p in 6th bef last: kpt on one pce* **11/1**

6 1 3/4 **Hammersly Lake (FR)**[52] 4704 7-11-4 **142**..................... PeterCarberry 143
(Nicky Henderson) *chsd ldrs: racd keenly: rdn after 2 out and no ex u.p in 4th bef last: one pce run-in where dropped to 6th* **20/1**

7 6 **Full Shift (FR)**[50] 4741 6-10-10 **134**................................ DavyRussell 128
(Nicky Henderson) *in rr of mid-div: 10th after 2 out where checked sltly on inner appr st: no imp on ldrs between last 2: kpt on one pce* **16/1**

8 2 **Monetaire (FR)**[22] 5253 9-10-11 **135**.......................(b[1]) TomScudamore 127
(David Pipe) *mid-div: rdn in 8th after 2 out and no imp on ldrs u.p bef last: one pce* **16/1**

9 4 3/4 **Daneking**[22] 5249 6-11-0 **138**.. PaulTownend 125
(W P Mullins, Ire) *mid-div: hdwy bef 5 out to chse ldrs: impr into 2nd 2 out gng wl: sn rdn in 3rd and no ex bef last where wknd and eased* **14/1**

10 2 1/2 **Ask Vic (IRE)**[146] 2979 6-10-4 **128**................................ DannyMullins 113
(W P Mullins, Ire) *in tch: rdn in 12th between last and no imp on ldrs bef last: kpt on one pce run-in* **16/1**

11 1 3/4 **Shantou Ed (IRE)**[70] 4376 6-10-2 **126**..........................(t) AlanCrowe 109
(P A Fahy, Ire) *hld up: no imp towards rr after 2 out: kpt on fr last: nvr nrr* **50/1**

12 shd **Mydor (FR)**[26] 5222 5-10-3 **132**.................................. ShaneShortall(5) 115
(A J Martin, Ire) *hld up towards rr: rdn after 2 out and sme hdwy bef last where nt clr run: no ex 13th bef last: one pce run-in* **8/1**

13 1 1/2 **Stonebrook (IRE)**[22] 5249 7-10-2 **126**................................... APHeskin 107
(Donald McCain) *towards rr: rdn and no imp into st: kpt on one pce* **16/1**

14 1/2 **The Saint James (FR)**[22] 5249 4-10-8 **141**...................(t) NiallPMadden 113
(Jonjo O'Neill) *sn chsd ldrs: rdn after 3 out and no ex fr next: wknd bef last* **12/1**

15 2 **King Of The Picts (IRE)**[76] 4258 6-10-9 **136**................ KevinSexton(3) 115
(John Patrick Shanahan, Ire) *sn led narrowly: jnd and hdd bef 4 out: remained prom tl wknd after 2 out where short of room on inner appr st* **66/1**

16 2 **Measureofmydreams (IRE)**[50] 4738 7-10-11 **135**................ BJCooper 112
(W P Mullins, Ire) *chsd ldrs: rdn to chse ldrs 5 out and led narrowly fr next: slt mstke 2 out and hdd: wknd* **20/1**

17 4 1/4 **Vulcanite (IRE)**[22] 5249 8-11-2 **145**................................. GerFox(5) 117
(Charlie Longsdon) *in rr of mid-div: rdn and no ex after 2 out* **66/1**

18 1 3/4 **Princely Conn (IRE)**[50] 4737 6-10-5 **134**...................... DavidMullins(5) 105
(Thomas Mullins, Ire) *nvr bttr than mid-div: rdn and wknd after 2 out* **14/1**

19 17 **Bally Longford (IRE)**[70] 4376 7-10-4 **128**............................. JJBurke 82
(Henry De Bromhead, Ire) *hld up in tch: cl 4th bef 5 out: disp bef 2 out: sn rdn in 2nd and wknd into st* **25/1**

20 7 1/2 **Hash Brown (IRE)**[202] 1871 6-10-11 **135**.......................... MarkEnright 81
(Michael Hourigan, Ire) *a bhd: rdn and no imp 2 out* **33/1**

21 14 **Ranjaan (FR)**[48] 4801 7-10-1 **125**.. AELynch 57
(S Wilson, Ire) *a bhd: rdn and no imp 2 out* **66/1**

22 11 **Courtncatcher (IRE)**[210] 1749 8-10-6 **133**................... JodyMcGarvey(3) 54
(Patrick J Duffy, Ire) *mid-div best: rdn and wknd 3 out* **66/1**

5m 10.3s (4.30) **Going Correction** +0.50s/f (Soft)
WFA 4 from 5yo+ 19lb **22 Ran SP% 147.3**
Speed ratings: **111,110,110,109,107 106,103,103,101,100 99,99,98,98,97 97,95,94,87,84 79,74**
CSF £39.91 CT £501.98 TOTE £5.90: £1.50, £2.30, £4.50, £2.50; DF 21.50 Trifecta £1032.30.
Owner John P McManus **Bred** Paul O'Dwyer **Trained** Curragh, Co Kildare

97a - (Foreign Racing) - See Raceform Interactive

KEMPTON (R-H)
Monday, May 4

OFFICIAL GOING: Good
Wind: light breeze Weather: bright and sunny; 17 degrees

98 JOIN THE RACING UK CLUB NOVICES' HURDLE (8 hdls) 2m
1:30 (1:30) (Class 4) 4-Y-0+ **£3,898** (£1,144; £572; £286)

Form RPR

31- 1 **Rock N Rhythm (IRE)**[35] 5063 5-11-5 125.................... RichardJohnson 126+
(Jonjo O'Neill) *pressed ldng pair: led 3 out: sn 4 l clr and in command: pushed out flat* **4/5**[1]

0/ 2 9 **Alfiboy**[408] 4964 5-10-12 0..[1] LiamTreadwell 107
(Paul Webber) *hit 1st: towards rr on outer and wl off pce: nt fluent 3 out: effrt despite awkward carriage bef next: plugged on into 2nd between last two: 7 l 2nd at last: no ch w wnr* **33/1**

055- 3 9 **Elkstone**[39] 4999 4-10-8 0.................................... WayneHutchinson 94
(Alan King) *t.k.h: towards rr and wl off pce: passed btn horses fr after 3 out: mod 3rd at last* **12/1**[3]

6- 4 2 **Jarlath**[33] 1589 4-10-1 0.. KevinJones(7) 92
(Seamus Mullins) *wl off pce in midfield: 20 l 4th at 5th: tried to cl after 3 out: sn no imp: mod 4th at last* **20/1**

35- 5 1 1/4 **Jupiter Storm**[14] 2248 6-10-12 0...............................(p) MarcGoldstein 96
(Gary Moore) *pressed ldr in breakaway gp of three: hit 3rd: led 4th: hdd 3 out: 4 l 2nd and tiring home turn* **16/1**

523- 6 3 3/4 **General Ginger**[129] 3282 5-10-12 0..................................(t) NoelFehily 94
(Harry Fry) *15 l 4th at 1st: nvr nr ldng trio: struggling after v slow jump 5th: mstke next* **11/4**[2]

46- 7 1 3/4 **Trojan Star (IRE)**[56] 4680 5-10-12 0............................ AidanColeman 89
(Kim Bailey) *wl off pce and nvr bttr than midfield: nudged along and wl btn bef 2 out* **40/1**

8 3 1/2 **Royal Battalion**[102] 4-10-8 0.. TomCannon 84
(Gary Moore) *small: wl off pce in rr: nt fluent 4th: struggling after 3 out* **16/1**

600- 9 1 1/4 **John Biscuit (IRE)**[54] 4710 7-10-7 0............................ DannyBurton(5) 85
(Jo Davis) *nt jump wl: led and clr w two others: hdd 4th: 10 l 3rd and fading qckly home turn* **50/1**

56- 10 11 **Rising Breeze (FR)**[28] 5198 4-10-8 0............................ PaddyBrennan 75
(Tom George) *sn wl bhd: no ch fr 3 out* **25/1**

500- 11 13 **Thehill Ofthe Rock (IRE)**[51] 4751 5-10-12 0........................ DarylJacob 61
(Jim Best) *poor last after 2nd: t.o after 3 out* **66/1**

P- P **Mansuri**[28] 5208 4-10-8 0..(t) GavinSheehan
(Warren Greatrex) *wl bhd: t.o after 3 out: p.u next* **33/1**

3m 50.4s (-7.70) **Going Correction** -0.55s/f (Firm)
WFA 4 from 5yo+ 18lb **12 Ran SP% 122.1**
Speed ratings (Par 105): **97,92,88,87,86 84,83,81,81,75 69,**
CSF £43.68 TOTE £1.50: £1.02, £5.70, £4.40; EX 41.30 Trifecta £250.70.
Owner Chanelle Medical UK Limited **Bred** Alan Dargan **Trained** Cheltenham, Gloucs

FOCUS
Dual bend alignment and all distances as advertised. The opening contest was a fair novice hurdle. They went a decent gallop on good ground. The easy winner was pretty much to his mark.

99 BETDAQ.COM £20 FREE BET NOVICES' CHASE (16 fncs) 2m 4f 110y
2:00 (2:00) (Class 3) 5-Y-0+ **£6,498** (£1,908; £954; £477)

Form RPR

151- 1 **Art Mauresque (FR)**[12] 5478 5-12-0 144............................ NickScholfield 147+
(Paul Nicholls) *mde all: j.lft occasionally: abt 5 l clr tl 10th: pressed by rival fr 3 out but stl gng strly: lft in full control next: heavily eased fr last* **11/10**[1]

11U- 2 23 **Cash And Go (IRE)**[25] 5235 8-12-0 145............................ LiamTreadwell 126
(Venetia Williams) *nt a fluent: struggling after blunder 11th: 12 l 4th home turn: lft remote 2nd 2 out* **11/4**[2]

6P2- 3 11 **Frampton (IRE)**[29] 5151 6-11-0 0..........................(p) RichardJohnson 100
(Charlie Longsdon) *nt a fluent: chsd ldr: slow 10th: 3rd and getting outpcd whn blnd 12th: lft remote 3rd 2 out* **7/1**

60F- 4 6 **Halling's Wish**[24] 5258 5-11-0 0...............................(t) MarcGoldstein 94
(Gary Moore) *t.k.h in last: easily lft bhd fr bef 3 out* **25/1**

The Form Book Jumps 2015-16, Raceform Ltd, Newbury, RG14 5SJ

110/ **U** **Billy Merriott (IRE)**[787] 4645 9-11-0 0...............................(t) NoelFehily 128+
(Harry Fry) *hld up: wnt 2nd at 12th: ev ch and clr of rest and stl gng wl but wnr gng even bttr whn stmbld: landed v awkwardly and uns rdr 2 out* **4/1**[3]
5m 2.8s (-13.80) **Going Correction** -0.55s/f (Firm) **5** Ran SP% **110.6**
Speed ratings: **104,95,91,88,**
CSF £4.72 TOTE £1.70: £1.10, £1.80; EX 3.70 Trifecta £12.80.
Owner Mrs Johnny de la Hey **Bred** Michel Parreau-Delhote **Trained** Ditcheat, Somerset
FOCUS
A decent little novice chase. They went a good gallop and the quick winning time suggests the ground is riding faster on the chase track. The winner was the form pick but this rates a step up.

100 BETDAQ.COM SERIOUS ABOUT HORSES NOVICES' HURDLE (10 hdls) 2m 5f
2:35 (2:35) (Class 4) 4-Y-0+ **£3,898** (£1,144; £572; £286)

Form RPR
22P- **1** **West Wizard (FR)**[58] 4633 6-10-12 129.............................. AndrewTinkler 129+
(Nicky Henderson) *settled trcking ldrs: wnt 2nd after 6th: led 3 out: rdn to assert between last two: 6 l clr at last: sn eased* **4/6**[1]
6/5- **2** *7* **One Big Love**[182] 2256 7-9-12 0.............................. GaryDerwin(7) 113+
(Harry Fry) *a ldng trio: led 4th tl blnd 3 out: sn rdn: outpcd by wnr between last two and flattered by proximity but a clr of rest: mstke last* **11/2**[3]
300- **3** *11* **Midnight Mint**[102] 3818 5-10-5 0..............................(t) TomScudamore 100
(Jeremy Scott) *midfield: 3rd and pushed along and n.d to ldng pair fr 3 out: 10 l 3rd at next: j.lft last* **16/1**
150- **4** *15* **Bobcatbilly (IRE)**[24] 5253 9-10-7 0.............................. RobMcCarth(5) 96
(Ian Williams) *led tl 4th: rdn and fading in 6 l 4th 3 out* **3/1**[2]
45- **5** *1 3/4* **Dadsintrouble (IRE)**[82] 4157 5-10-12 0.............................. RichardJohnson 94
(Tim Vaughan) *chsd ldrs: struggling whn hit 7th: remote 5th after blundering next* **12/1**
060- **6** *41* **Toohighforme (IRE)**[29] 5151 6-10-12 0.............................. TomCannon 55
(Nick Gifford) *towards rr: pushed along 6th: sn struggling: bdly t.o after 3 out* **40/1**
005- **7** *33* **Fairy Princess**[29] 5151 6-9-12 0.............................1 MrDGBurchell(7) 18
(Mark Hoad) *temperamental gng to s: dwlt and detached in last pl: mstke 1st: rdn 7th: bdly t.o bef next* **33/1**
8 *23* **Rahealty (IRE)**[716] 9-10-12 0.............................. DaveCrosse 5
(Dai Williams) *towards rr: hit 7th and struggling: bdly t.o after 3 out* **33/1**
5m 2.2s (-15.30) **Going Correction** -0.55s/f (Firm) **8** Ran SP% **122.3**
Speed ratings (Par 105): **197,104,100,94,93 78,65,56**
CSF £5.72 TOTE £2.00: £1.02, £1.80, £3.90; EX 5.10 Trifecta £65.00.
Owner Walters Plant Hire Ltd **Bred** Quadriga Gmbh **Trained** Upper Lambourn, Berks
FOCUS
A fair novice hurdle. They went a proper gallop. The easy winner stood out in this ordinary novice and is rated below his best.

101 BETDAQ.COM 50% COMMISSION REFUND H'CAP CHASE (18 fncs) 3m
3:10 (3:10) (Class 3) (0-140,140) 5-Y-0+ **£6,498** (£1,908; £954; £477)

Form RPR
000- **1** **Champion Court (IRE)**[53] 4720 10-11-12 140..........(p) RichardJohnson 156+
(Martin Keighley) *2nd pl fr 3rd and sn 12 l ahd of rest: led 12th: drew clr bef 3 out: pressed but lft clr again next: kpt on gamely after* **9/2**[2]
3P1- **2** *6* **Best Boy Barney (IRE)**[14] 5431 9-10-8 125..............(bt) MattGriffiths(3) 137+
(Jeremy Scott) *led tl 12th: rdn and outpcd bef 3 out: tried to rally for driving and 2 l down whn blnd next: a hld after* **13/2**[3]
0U3- **3** *4 1/2* **Sedgemoor Express (IRE)**[15] 5406 7-10-7 121.......(t) TomScudamore 128
(Nigel Hawke) *bhd: j. slowly 5th and 6th: hdwy 14th: wnt 7 l 3rd home turn: rdn and no imp on ldng pair after* **7/1**
/11- **4** *5* **Shuil Royale (IRE)**[45] 4882 10-11-1 129..............................(t) RyanMahon 131
(Harry Fry) *towards rr: struggling fr 14th: poor 5th home turn: plugged on* **4/1**[1]
/F6- **5** *20* **Brass Tax (IRE)**[17] 5370 9-11-4 132..............................(p) DarylJacob 114
(Ben Case) *2nd pl tl 3rd: sn in midfield w ldng pair clr: struggling fr 14th: t.o* **25/1**
600- **6** *1* **Dursey Sound (IRE)**[55] 4690 7-11-3 131.............................. DougieCostello 112
(Jonjo O'Neill) *detached and nt travelling in last: 25 l adrift at 6th: pushed next: t.o fr 14th* **10/1**
42F- **7** *3 1/4* **Wings Of Smoke (IRE)**[24] 5253 10-11-6 134................(t) MichaelByrne 113
(Tim Vaughan) *midfield and off pce: effrt 14th: 4th and rdn home turn: gng up and down on the spot after: t.o and eased last* **20/1**
613- **8** *6* **Gallery Exhibition (IRE)**[44] 4912 8-11-4 132..............(t) NickScholfield 105
(Kim Bailey) *chsd ldrs: 10 l 3rd at 1/2-way: wknd 14th: t.o 3 out: eased last* **7/1**
P00- **P** **Vino Griego (FR)**[23] 5274 10-11-7 135..............................(vt) TomCannon
(Gary Moore) *blnd bdly 3rd: rdn and nt travelling 9th: fading and nt keen whn slow 13th: t.o and p.u next* **10/1**
R02- **P** **Caulfields Venture (IRE)**[14] 5431 9-10-13 127...........(p) AidanColeman
(Emma Lavelle) *towards rr and off pce: mstke 11th: blnd bdly 15th: t.o and p.u next* **13/2**[3]
5m 55.9s (-19.50) **Going Correction** -0.55s/f (Firm) **10** Ran SP% **116.6**
Speed ratings: **110,108,106,104,98 97,96,94, ,**
CSF £34.35 CT £203.14 TOTE £4.80: £1.60, £2.00, £2.50; EX 34.50 Trifecta £208.40.
Owner M Boothright **Bred** Larry O'Connor **Trained** Condicote, Gloucs
FOCUS
A decent staying handicap chase. They went a good gallop. The winner is rated in line with his best form since 2014.

102 BETDAQ COMMISSION FREE FOOTBALL ON SATURDAYS H'CAP HURDLE (10 hdls) 2m 5f
3:45 (3:45) (Class 4) (0-120,120) 4-Y-0+ **£4,548** (£1,335; £667; £333)

Form RPR
401- **1** **Urcalin (FR)**[15] 5414 7-11-4 112..............................(t) TomCannon 128+
(David Arbuthnot) *bhd and smetimes pushed along: impr qckly to 3rd 3 out and 2nd bef next: led w ears pricked whn rdn 2 out: 4 l clr last: rdn out* **7/1**
0- **2** *15* **A Cor Et A Cri (FR)**[75] 4291 5-11-4 112..............................(t) NoelFehily 113
(Harry Fry) *trckd ldrs: wnt 2nd 3 out: led gng wl bef next where hdd: sn drvn and a finding less than wnr after: hld last: one pce* **9/1**
3/2- **3** *6* **Master Benjamin**[72] 4362 8-11-9 117..............................(p) NickScholfield 114
(Jeremy Scott) *last trio and hld up tl 6th: effrt and rdn 3 out: wnt 4 l 3rd 2 out: sn wknd* **5/1**[3]
6F0- **4** *4* **Buck Magic I (IRE)**[22] 5290 9-11-12 120..............................(p) MarkQuinlan 113
(Neil Mulholland) *led and abt 10 l clr at gd gallop: 5 l ahd whn hit 3 out: sn drvn: fdd tamely between last 2* **8/1**
601- **5** *nse* **Mont Royale**[166] 2588 7-11-0 108.............................. DougieCostello 100
(Jonjo O'Neill) *bhd: last at 6th: struggling 3 out: blnd last: nrly snatched poor 4th* **16/1**
400- **6** *12* **Our Chief (IRE)**[115] 3594 6-10-8 102..............................(p) TomScudamore 83
(David Pipe) *settled in midfield: effrt to press ldrs in 4th and rdn 3 out: fdd bef next: t.o* **10/3**[1]
U21- **7** *36* **Walkabout Creek (IRE)**[48] 4826 8-10-11 105.............................. LiamTreadwell 54
(Derek Frankland) *chsd clr ldr tl after 7th: fdd rapidly after next: bdly t.o* **25/1**
/41- **P** **Kalmbeforethestorm**[314] 796 7-11-6 114.............................. PaulMoloney
(Helen Nelmes) *last pair: nvr gng wl enough: t.o 3 out: p.u next* **12/1**
P11- **P** **Signed Request (IRE)**[28] 5183 8-11-1 112.............. JeremiahMcGrath(3)
(Henry Oliver) *chsd ldrs tl wknd 7th: t.o and p.u 2 out* **4/1**[2]
003- **P** **Loukhaar (IRE)**[14] 5428 7-10-9 103.............................. AidanColeman
(Jonathan Geake) *prom in chsng gp tl rdn 7th: fdd qckly: bdly t.o whn p.u 2 out* **33/1**
F00- **F** **Charlie Breekie (IRE)**[32] 5106 6-11-7 115.............................. KielanWoods
(Ben Pauling) *midfield: rdn and lost tch 3 out: 35 l 7th whn crashing fall last: winded but rcvrd* **16/1**
5m 1.4s (-16.10) **Going Correction** -0.55s/f (Firm) **11** Ran SP% **119.6**
Speed ratings (Par 105): **108,102,100,98,98 93,80, , ,**
CSF £69.61 CT £348.48 TOTE £9.50: £3.00, £3.80, £2.30; EX 81.10 Trifecta £896.20.
Owner A T A Wates & Mrs S Wates **Bred** Bernard-Louis Dutertre **Trained** Beare Green, Surrey
FOCUS
A fair handicap hurdle. They went a proper gallop. The winner was well in on his recent win but this rates another step up.

103 FREE TRADING SOFTWARE AVAILABLE ON BETDAQ.COM H'CAP CHASE (12 fncs) 2m
4:20 (4:20) (Class 2) 5-Y-0+ **£16,245** (£4,770; £2,385; £1,192)

Form RPR
020- **1** **Claret Cloak (IRE)**[25] 5240 8-11-12 151.............................. AidanColeman 156
(Emma Lavelle) *chsd ldrs: 2nd and rdn home turn: disp ld 2 out tl last where bttr jump: jst ahd flat and r.o gamely* **9/2**[3]
60F- **2** *1* **My Brother Sylvest**[16] 5391 9-10-12 137..............(b) TomScudamore 142
(David Pipe) *led at str pce fr 4th: drvn 3 out: w wnr 2 out tl hit last: kpt trying but a jst hld after* **11/1**
PFF- **3** *6* **Dunraven Storm (IRE)**[16] 5391 10-11-9 148.............. RichardJohnson 148
(Philip Hobbs) *racd wd: led briefly 2nd: lost pl bef 6th: detached last bef 3 out: styd on after but a too much to do* **8/1**
221- **4** *2* **Duke Of Navan (IRE)**[16] 5391 7-11-8 147.............................. BrianHarding 146+
(Nicky Richards) *bhd: last whn mstke 5th: effrt and nt fluent 8th: handy home turn but nvr really gng wl enough and rdn and no imp fr 3 out* **7/4**[1]
304- **5** *3 1/4* **Bellenos (FR)**[25] 5240 7-10-10 135..............................(bt) HarrySkelton 131+
(Dan Skelton) *plld hrd and cl up: gng wl 7th: 2 l 3rd at 9th: disputing 2nd whn mstke next and rdn: sn btn: hit last* **7/2**[2]
445- **6** *4* **De Faoithesdream (IRE)**[72] 4352 9-10-0 125.............................. PaulMoloney 115
(Evan Williams) *racd freely and mde most tl 4th: losing pl whn nt fluent 8th: btn bef 3 out* **7/1**
000- **7** *14* **Parsnip Pete**[25] 5240 9-11-3 142.............................. PaddyBrennan 130
(Tom George) *hdwy to 2nd at 7th: disputing 2nd but rdn whn mstke 3 out: dropped out qckly: eased last* **16/1**
3m 48.3s (-12.00) **Going Correction** -0.55s/f (Firm) **7** Ran SP% **114.6**
Speed ratings: **108,107,104,103,101 99,92**
CSF £47.44 TOTE £5.50: £2.50, £2.90; EX 75.50 Trifecta £156.70.
Owner Hawksmoor Partnership **Bred** W H Neville **Trained** Hatherden, Hants
FOCUS
The feature contest was a good quality handicap chase. They went a strong gallop and this is solid form.

104 MEHMET HASSAN MEMORIAL AMATEUR RIDERS' H'CAP HURDLE (8 hdls) 2m
4:50 (4:50) (Class 4) (0-115,112) 4-Y-0+ **£3,743** (£1,161; £580; £290)

Form RPR
122- **1** **Mr Lando**[14] 5427 6-11-3 110.............................. MrSHanson(7) 122+
(Alison Batchelor) *taken down early: led at brisk pce and abt 5 l clr: mstke 3 out: only one on bridle after: r.o stoutly and a in command fr next: hit last* **3/1**[2]
532- **2** *10* **Malanos (IRE)**[64] 4511 7-11-2 109.............................. MrMEnnis(7) 111
(Tony Carroll) *chsd wnr: rdn 3 out: nvr able to cl fr next: 5 l 2nd whn hit last* **10/1**
664- **3** *8* **Lucky Dottie**[15] 5412 4-10-3 100.............................. MrSeanHoulihan(7) 91
(Pat Phelan) *3rd or 4th thrght: hrd rdn 3rd and one pce fr bef 2 out* **8/1**[3]
06-1 **4** *18* **Sunblazer (IRE)**[4] 32 5-11-0 103..............................(t) CiaranGethings(3) 81
(Kim Bailey) *a 3rd or 4th: rdn and labouring fr bef 2 out* **11/8**[1]
5 *10* **Thepartysover**[43] 4953 10-10-7 100.............................. MrBParis-Crofts(7) 69
(Paul Henderson) *bhd: almost t.o at 5th but rdn and kpt plodding on to beat fading rivals* **20/1**
504- **6** *4 1/2* **Gold Medal (IRE)**[13] 4654 5-10-12 105.............................. MrJJO'Neill(7) 70
(Jonjo O'Neill) *midfield: struggling in 6th 3 out: t.o next* **8/1**[3]
0- **7** *8* **Daidaidai (FR)**[33] 5101 5-11-3 110.............................. MrWRussell(7) 67
(Gary Moore) *midfield: 12 l fr ldng quartet and rdn 3 out: t.o next* **50/1**
0PP- **8** *27* **Samizdat (FR)**[54] 4709 12-9-8 87 oh19 ow1.............................. MissGSwan(7) 20
(John O'Neill) *nt fluent 1st: bhd fr 3rd: bdly t.o fr 5th* **66/1**
116- **P** **Osgood**[202] 1889 8-11-5 112.............................. MrBCO'Shaughnessy(7)
(Gary Moore) *t.k.h early: bhd: struggling bef 3 out: bdly t.o whn p.u last* **20/1**
51U- **P** **Jumeirah Liberty**[37] 5030 7-9-11 86 oh1..............................(tp) MrFTett(3)
(Zoe Davison) *bhd and sn struggling: mstke 2nd: reminder 4th: t.o 3 out: p.u next* **16/1**
3m 45.9s (-12.20) **Going Correction** -0.55s/f (Firm)
WFA 4 from 5yo+ 18lb **10** Ran SP% **117.3**
Speed ratings (Par 105): **108,103,99,90,85 82,78,65, ,**
CSF £31.03 CT £220.84 TOTE £3.60: £1.20, £3.30, £2.40; EX 38.60 Trifecta £154.00.
Owner Mrs Alison Batchelor **Bred** Capitana Partnership **Trained** Petworth, W Sussex
FOCUS
The concluding contest was an ordinary handicap hurdle restricted to amateur riders. They went a decent gallop in a good time for the grade. The winner is rated in line with his upgraded C&D run.
T/Plt: £43.90 to a £1 stake. Pool: £56366.48 - 936.48 winning tickets. T/Qpdt: £27.60 to a £1 stake. Pool: £4125.96 - 110.46 winning tickets. **Iain Mackenzie**

WARWICK (L-H)

Monday, May 4

OFFICIAL GOING: Good to soft

Wind: Light; behind Weather: Cloudy

105 CALL STAR SPORTS ON 08000 521 321 NOVICES' HURDLE (9 hdls) 2m 3f

12:45 (12:45) (Class 4) 4-Y-0+ £3,249 (£954; £477; £238)

Form RPR

0- 1 **Montdragon (FR)**[24] 5250 5-11-0 0 (t) RichieMcLernon 132+
(Jonjo O'Neill) *hld up: hdwy 4th: nt clr run after 3 out: rdn to chse ldr bef next: led flat: styd on wl* 7/2[2]

421- 2 3 1/4 **Laurium**[42] 4964 5-11-6 127 DavidBass 132
(Nicky Henderson) *led: rdn after 3 out: hdd flat: styd on same pce* 10/11[1]

1- 3 13 **Faithful Mount**[29] 5155 6-11-6 0 WillKennedy 122
(Ian Williams) *prom: chsd ldr after 4th: mstke 3 out: sn rdn: wknd appr last* 7/2[2]

6- 4 15 **Being Global (FR)**[33] 5097 4-10-9 0 HarrySkelton 97
(Caroline Bailey) *hld up: hdwy appr 5th: sn wknd* 50/1

3- 5 5 **Apple Of Our Eye**[28] 5207 5-11-0 0 BrianHughes 96
(Charlie Longsdon) *chsd ldrs tl rdn and wknd after 3 out* 14/1[3]

6 67 **Lineman**[17] 5-11-0 0 PaulMoloney 36
(Sarah Hollinshead) *nt fluent and a in rr: lost tch after 4th* 33/1

P **Icancan** 7-10-10 0 ow3 MrJMartin(7)
(Alan Hollingsworth) *in rr whn mstke 3rd: sn hung rt: bhd whn j.rt next: sn p.u* 125/1

U **Tundridge**[140] 6-11-0 0 JamesBest
(John Spearing) *hld up in tch: mstke 4th: 10 l 5th whn uns rdr next* 100/1

P **Lord Emerson**[1301] 7-11-0 0 SamTwiston-Davies
(David Dennis) *hld up: bhd fr 5th: p.u bef 2 out* 33/1

00- P **Myroundorurs (IRE)**[39] 4999 5-11-0 0 TomO'Brien
(Robin Dickin) *hld up: a in rr: bhd fr 5th: p.u bef 2 out* 100/1

0P5- P **Wootsteps (IRE)**[15] 5410 7-10-9 0 (p) ConorRing(5)
(John Upson) *chsd ldr tl after 4th: wknd bef next: bhd whn p.u bef 2 out* 125/1

4m 32.1s (-10.60) **Going Correction** -0.30s/f (Good)
WFA 4 from 5yo+ 18lb 11 Ran SP% 114.9
Speed ratings (Par 105): **110,108,103,96,94 66,,,,**
CSF £7.05 TOTE £6.10: £1.30, £1.10, £1.70; EX 8.10 Trifecta £16.40.
Owner John P McManus **Bred** Csse Bertrand De Tarragon **Trained** Cheltenham, Gloucs

FOCUS
After 13mm of rain on Sunday and a further 6mm overnight, the going was changed to good to soft. All Hurdle races were on inner course. Rail out 3yds on hill and Stable bend: distances increased by about 10yds per circuit. There was little strength in depth in this novice hurdle but the three market leaders dominated. The winner posted a big step up on Aintree but in line with his French form.

106 STARSPORTSBET.CO.UK CONDITIONAL JOCKEYS' H'CAP HURDLE (9 hdls) 2m 3f

1:15 (1:15) (Class 5) (0-100,100) 4-Y-0+ £2,436 (£715; £357; £178)

Form RPR

F0U- 1 **Bennachie (IRE)**[98] 3903 6-10-10 90 (t) AlanJohns(6) 96+
(Tim Vaughan) *racd keenly: trckd ldr after 1st: led 2 out: rdn out* 5/1[2]

006- 2 3 1/2 **Good Value**[15] 5412 4-10-10 95 (bt) MichaelHeard(6) 92+
(David Pipe) *chsd ldrs: led 6th: rdn and hdd 2 out: no ex flat* 6/1[3]

066- 3 1/2 **Sea The Springs (FR)**[28] 5196 4-11-4 100 (p) BridgetAndrews(3) 96
(Dan Skelton) *prom: reminders after 4th: outpcd after 3 out: styd on flat* 13/2

236- 4 3/4 **Rolling Dough (IRE)**[125] 3407 7-11-2 90 (p) JamesBest 90
(Sophie Leech) *hld up: hdwy 6th: outpcd appr 2 out: styd on flat* 9/1

541- 5 6 **Walter De La Mare (IRE)**[226] 1383 8-11-12 100 MichealNolan 95
(Anabel K Murphy) *hld up: hdwy after 6th: wknd appr 2 out* 22/1

005- 6 1/2 **Sweet Summer**[17] 5378 4-10-7 86 ThomasGarner 76
(John Holt) *mid-div: blnd 2nd: rdn 4th: sn lost pl: bhd and drvn along next: styd on flat* 20/1

554- 7 nk **Lifetime (IRE)**[14] 5435 7-10-7 89 (tp) MrMartinMcIntyre(8) 83
(Neil Mulholland) *hld up: reminder bef 5th: nvr on terms* 5/1[2]

P63- 8 9 **Gwili Spar**[23] 5280 7-10-0 74 (t) KieronEdgar 64
(Laura Hurley) *hld up: mstke 6th: shkn up appr 2 out: wknd bef last* 12/1

000- 9 17 **Mr Mafia (IRE)**[116] 3586 6-11-4 98 NickSlatter(6) 69
(Tony Carroll) *prom tl rdn and wknd after 3 out* 50/1

P64- P **Blue Talisman (IRE)**[29] 5157 4-11-2 95 (tp) SeanBowen
(Peter Bowen) *led to 6th: wknd bef next: bhd whn p.u bef 2 out* 9/2[1]

P00- P **Spurned Girl**[283] 1081 5-10-1 75 BenPoste
(Robin Dickin) *chsd ldrs: rdn after 4th: in rr whn blnd next: bhd whn p.u bef 2 out* 66/1

0P0- P **Royal Supreme (IRE)**[87] 4068 5-11-9 97 (t) ConorShoemark
(Alex Hales) *mid-div: hdwy after 4th: rdn and wknd bef next: bhd whn p.u bef 2 out* 10/1

4m 35.1s (-7.60) **Going Correction** -0.30s/f (Good)
WFA 4 from 5yo+ 18lb 12 Ran SP% 118.5
Speed ratings (Par 103): **104,102,102,102,99 99,99,95,88,,,**
CSF £34.16 CT £199.82 TOTE £8.10: £3.10, £2.50, £2.90; EX 57.90 Trifecta £679.00.
Owner Oceans Racing **Bred** Michael Heskin **Trained** Aberthin, Vale of Glamorgan

FOCUS
The pace was not strong in this minor handicap but the winner scored with something in hand and the first four were clear of the rest. Solid enough form.

107 FOLLOW US ON TWITTER @STARSPORTS_BET NOVICES' H'CAP CHASE (12 fncs) 2m

1:45 (1:45) (Class 4) (0-120,120) 4-Y-0+ £3,898 (£1,144; £572; £286)

Form RPR

165- 1 **Notnowsam**[28] 5196 4-10-0 112 oh4 (p) HarrySkelton 115+
(Dan Skelton) *a.p: chsd ldr 7th: led 3 out: sn clr: comf* 4/1[3]

056- 2 5 **Celestino (FR)**[34] 5083 4-9-11 112 oh6 (t) SeanBowen(3) 106
(Paul Nicholls) *hld up: hdwy 3 out: wnt 2nd last: nt trble wnr* 7/2[2]

432- 3 4 1/2 **Alder Mairi (IRE)**[33] 5094 8-10-11 105 AndrewThornton 115+
(Seamus Mullins) *led to 3 out: sn rdn: no ex last* 11/2

113- 4 28 **Artifice Sivola (FR)**[15] 5405 5-11-6 114 LeightonAspell 97
(Lucy Wadham) *prom: racd keenly: wnt 2nd appr 3rd: hung rt fr next: lost 2nd 7th: wknd next* 5/1

245- 5 1 1/2 **Queen Olivia**[49] 4811 7-10-11 105 (t) RichieMcLernon 91
(Caroline Bailey) *hld up: hdwy 6th: wknd after 3 out: bhd whn blnd next* 10/1

320- P **Net Work Rouge (FR)**[30] 5139 6-11-12 120 DavidBass
(Kim Bailey) *chsd ldr tl appr 3rd: remained handy tl rdn and wknd 8th: bhd whn p.u bef 2 out* 11/4[1]

3m 55.7s (-9.90) **Going Correction** -0.45s/f (Good)
WFA 4 from 5yo+ 4lb 6 Ran SP% 110.0
Speed ratings (Par 105): **106,103,101,87,86**
CSF £17.73 TOTE £6.00: £2.80, £1.70; EX 20.10 Trifecta £106.60.
Owner Raymond Tooth **Bred** Aylesfield Farms Stud **Trained** Alcester, Warwicks

FOCUS
The two 4yos, who were out of the weights, filled the first two places in this handicap. A big step up on hurdle form from the winner.

108 QUANTUM MANUFACTURING H'CAP HURDLE (12 hdls) 3m 1f

2:20 (2:20) (Class 4) (0-110,110) 4-Y-0+ £3,249 (£954; £477; £238)

Form RPR

543- 1 **Crack Of Thunder (IRE)**[45] 4883 6-11-7 105 (p) BrianHughes 110+
(Charlie Longsdon) *mid-div: lost pl after 6th: pushed along 8th: hdwy 3 out: led next: drvn out* 4/1[1]

211- 2 7 **Sandynow (IRE)**[20] 5333 10-11-9 110 (vt) SeanBowen(3) 112+
(Peter Bowen) *chsd ldr to 6th: remained handy: hmpd 3 out: sn led: hdd next: no ex flat* 11/2[2]

660- 3 9 **Multimedia**[14] 5434 5-11-6 104 (t) ConorO'Farrell 93
(David Pipe) *hld up: hdwy appr 8th: ev ch after 3 out: rdn and no ex bef last* 33/1

455- 4 14 **Somemothersdohavem**[46] 4864 6-11-6 104 (b) AlainCawley 87
(Venetia Williams) *hld up: nt a fluent: hdwy 3 out: mstke next: wkng whn blnd last* 16/1

055- 5 6 **Shoofly Milly (IRE)**[28] 5181 6-11-10 108 LiamHeard 81
(Jeremy Scott) *hld up: rdn along after 7th: n.d* 33/1

622- 6 7 **The Cider Maker**[30] 5148 5-11-5 103 BrendanPowell 68
(Colin Tizzard) *chsd ldrs: ev ch after 3 out: sn rdn and wknd* 4/1[1]

434- 7 1 3/4 **Tyre Hill (IRE)**[30] 5146 6-11-5 103 (t) SamTwiston-Davies 67
(David Dennis) *hld up: rdn appr 8th: wknd after 3 out* 12/1[3]

343- 8 2 1/4 **Chance Taken**[28] 5194 7-11-0 101 ThomasGarner(3) 62
(Noel Williams) *prom: chsd ldr 8th: lft in ld 3 out: sn hdd & wknd* 12/1[3]

425- 9 6 **West End (IRE)**[174] 2429 8-11-9 107 (p) DavidBass 63
(Kim Bailey) *hld up: hdwy 8th: rdn and wknd after 3 out* 20/1

P00- P **Real Milan (IRE)**[14] 5437 10-11-12 110 (bt) TomO'Brien
(Anabel K Murphy) *chsd ldrs: rdn appr 8th: wkng whn blnd next: bhd whn p.u bef 2 out* 20/1

F56- P **Kudu Shine**[13] 5442 9-11-7 105 (p) AdamWedge
(Richard Woollacott) *led to 7th: rdn and wknd next: bhd whn p.u bef 3 out* 12/1[3]

22P- P **Presence Felt (IRE)**[144] 3042 7-11-6 104 (v) WillKennedy
(Jonjo O'Neill) *prom: reminders after 6th: wknd 9th: bhd whn p.u bef 2 out* 14/1

P45- P **Vinnie My Boy (IRE)**[14] 5437 7-11-5 110 MissADalton(7)
(Heather Dalton) *hld up: pushed along 7th: sn lost tch: bhd whn p.u bef 3 out* 50/1

435- F **Eastern Calm**[56] 4671 6-11-4 102 LeightonAspell
(Oliver Sherwood) *chsd ldrs: led 7th: slt ld whn fell 3 out* 16/1

055- P **Today Please (IRE)**[28] 5180 5-11-9 107 (t) RichieMcLernon
(Jonjo O'Neill) *hld up: rdn and wknd 7th: sn p.u* 16/1

6m 16.9s (1.90) **Going Correction** -0.30s/f (Good) 15 Ran SP% 120.1
Speed ratings (Par 105): **84,81,78,74,72 70,69,68,67,,,,,,**
CSF £24.14 CT £648.06 TOTE £5.90: £2.50, £2.10, £4.10; EX 33.50 Trifecta £787.10.
Owner Crack Of Thunder Partnership **Bred** Francis Small **Trained** Over Norton, Oxon

FOCUS
They finished well strung out in this staying handicap. A step up from the winner.

109 CALL STAR SPREADS ON 00353 1884 8114 H'CAP CHASE (17 fncs) 2m 4f 110y

2:55 (2:55) (Class 4) (0-120,118) 4-Y-0+ £5,198 (£1,526; £763; £381)

Form RPR

542- 1 **Prince Des Marais (FR)**[33] 5095 12-10-8 107 (t) MichaelHeard(7) 123
(Caroline Bailey) *chsd ldr to 4th: wnt 2nd again 6th: led 3 out: rdn out* 7/1[3]

316- 2 3 3/4 **Moorlands Jack**[195] 1990 10-11-5 111 (p) JamesDavies 125
(Jeremy Scott) *hld up: hdwy after 10th: rdn to chse wnr appr 2 out: styd on same pce flat* 16/1

P3P- 3 8 **Bob Tucker (IRE)**[30] 5141 8-11-12 118 BrianHughes 126
(Charlie Longsdon) *prom: chsd ldr 4th to 6th: remained handy tl outpcd 13th: rallied after 3 out: no ex last* 7/2[1]

2/5- 4 10 **Furrows**[51] 4768 10-11-7 113 LeightonAspell 113
(Oliver Sherwood) *hld up: hdwy 11th: rdn after 3 out: wknd bef last* 6/1[2]

U13- 5 13 **Unknown Legend (IRE)**[24] 5257 8-10-13 105 JackQuinlan 93
(Sarah Humphrey) *led: clr 4th: blnd and hdd 3 out: sn wknd* 16/1

5U4- 6 11 **No Likey (IRE)**[15] 5405 8-11-11 117 TomO'Brien 92
(Philip Hobbs) *prom tl rdn and mstke 12th: sn wknd: j.rt last* 15/2

PPP- P **Pilgrims Lane (IRE)**[145] 3021 11-11-9 115 (tp) SeanQuinlan
(Anthony Middleton) *hld up: bhd and pushed along 7th: p.u after 10th* 25/1

P2P- P **Frontier Spirit (IRE)**[30] 5141 11-10-13 112 JamieBargary(7)
(Nigel Twiston-Davies) *prom: blnd 7th: sn rdn: wknd 9th: bhd whn p.u bef 13th* 9/1

565- P **Greywell Boy**[17] 5370 8-11-4 117 (b1) LizzieKelly(7)
(Nick Williams) *hld up: rdn appr 8th: lost tch 10th: bhd whn p.u bef 14th* 7/1[3]

534- F **Saint Breiz (FR)**[28] 5182 9-11-9 115 (t) MichealNolan 87
(Carroll Gray) *chsd ldrs tl rdn and wknd appr 3 out: bhd whn fell last* 10/1

1U5- P **King Rolfe (IRE)**[84] 4133 7-11-12 118 (t) SamTwiston-Davies
(Tim Vaughan) *hld up: p.u after 3rd* 12/1

5m 9.8s (-11.20) **Going Correction** -0.45s/f (Good) 11 Ran SP% 115.7
Speed ratings (Par 105): **103,101,98,94,89 85,,,,**
CSF £106.10 CT £458.32 TOTE £7.10: £2.40, £3.90, £2.60; EX 36.70 Trifecta £490.20 Part won..
Owner C W Booth **Bred** Gaec Lancray **Trained** Holdenby, Northants

The Form Book Jumps 2015-16, Raceform Ltd, Newbury, RG14 5SJ

FOCUS
A revitalised veteran battled well to win this handicap. The first two were pretty much to their marks.

110 STARSPREADS.COM H'CAP HURDLE (8 hdls) 2m
3:30 (3:30) (Class 4) (0-120,111) 4-Y-0+ £3,249 (£954; £477; £238)

Form RPR
206- 1 **Cut The Corner (IRE)**[35] 5072 7-11-3 107 ChrisWard[(5)] 116+
(Dr Richard Newland) *a.p: led after 3 out: hit next: hung lft flat: r.o* 5/2[1]
451/ 2 4 **Shalambar (IRE)**[36] 4686 9-11-8 107 (v) SamTwiston-Davies 110
(Tony Carroll) *chsd ldrs: ev ch after 3 out: sn rdn: styd on same pce flat* 5/1[3]
55-3 3 3 3/4 **Watt Broderick (IRE)**[3] 63 6-11-12 111 (t) WillKennedy 111
(Ian Williams) *hld up: hdwy 5th: shkn up appr last: no ex flat* 5/1[3]
544- 4 7 **Benzanno (IRE)**[44] 4896 6-11-8 107 HenryBrooke 101
(Donald McCain) *chsd ldr tl led 4th: rdn and hdd after 3 out: wknd appr last* 9/1
420- 5 7 **Miracle Cure (IRE)**[51] 4764 6-11-11 110 AlainCawley 99
(Venetia Williams) *hld up in tch: rdn 3 out: wkng whn hit next* 25/1
406- 6 11 **New Tarabela**[15] 5404 4-11-2 105 LeeEdwards 81
(Tony Carroll) *prom: jnd ldrs after 3rd tl rdn bef next: wknd appr 3 out* 40/1
/65- 7 3 1/2 **Willow Island (IRE)**[308] 743 6-11-0 102 JonathanEngland[(3)] 77
(Sophie Leech) *hld up: nt fluent 3rd: wknd 5th* 66/1
P61- 8 43 **Third Act (IRE)**[10] 5513 6-11-9 108 (tp) BrendanPowell 43
(Colin Tizzard) *led to 4th: rdn and wknd after 3 out* 9/2[2]
9 3/4 **Hairy O'Malley (IRE)**[58] 4639 6-11-6 105 AdamWedge 40
(Evan Williams) *hld up: a in rr: wknd 5th* 6/1
00P- P **Ted Dolly (IRE)**[11] 5496 11-11-1 103 BenPoste[(3)]
(Tom Symonds) *hld up: effrt appr 5th: wknd next: bhd whn p.u bef 2 out* 33/1

3m 50.1s (-6.40) **Going Correction** -0.30s/f (Good)
WFA 4 from 6yo+ 18lb **10** Ran SP% **115.1**
Speed ratings (Par 105): **104,102,100,96,93 87,85,64,64,**
CSF £15.00 CT £57.48 TOTE £4.80: £1.70, £1.40, £1.60; EX 16.80 Trifecta £45.60.
Owner Paul L Drinkwater **Bred** P F Corbet **Trained** Claines, Worcs

FOCUS
They went a fair pace and the favourite scored in good style. The form is rated around the second and third.

111 THOROUGHBRED BREEDERS' ASSOCIATION MARES' "NATIONAL HUNT" MAIDEN HURDLE (8 hdls) 2m
4:05 (4:06) (Class 5) 4-Y-0+ £2,908 (£847; £424)

Form RPR
520- 1 **Surtee Du Berlais (IRE)**[58] 4634 5-11-2 0 LeightonAspell 118+
(Oliver Sherwood) *a.p: led appr 2 out: clr last: shkn up flat: styd on* 2/1[2]
6- 2 4 1/2 **Via Volupta**[80] 4207 5-11-2 0 GavinSheehan 112
(Warren Greatrex) *w ldr tl led after 2nd: hdd 5th: nt clr run after 3 out: styd on flat* 11/1
022- 3 1/2 **Storming Strumpet**[42] 4958 5-11-2 117 AlainCawley 112
(Tom George) *chsd ldrs: ev ch appr 2 out: rdn bef last: no ex flat* 7/4[1]
040- 4 8 **Vicky's Charm (IRE)**[34] 5090 6-10-13 0 JamesBanks[(3)] 103
(Barry Brennan) *led tl after 2nd: led again 5th: rdn and hdd appr 2 out: wknd bef last* 25/1
510- 5 14 **Amour D'Or**[58] 4634 4-10-5 0 LizzieKelly[(7)] 89
(Nick Williams) *prom: lost pl after 3rd: wknd after 3 out* 9/2[3]
460- 6 26 **Timon's Tara**[35] 5071 6-11-2 0 TomO'Brien 67
(Robin Dickin) *hld up: wknd 5th* 9/1
0P4- 7 4 1/2 **Overdo**[33] 5093 4-10-5 0 MrDSansom[(7)] 59
(Seamus Mullins) *hld up: bhd fr 5th* 33/1
P- P **Daisy Back**[53] 4729 7-11-2 0 JamesDavies
(Barry Brennan) *a in rr: bhd fr 4th: p.u bef 2 out* 100/1

3m 52.0s (-4.50) **Going Correction** -0.30s/f (Good)
WFA 4 from 5yo+ 18lb **8** Ran SP% **114.0**
Speed ratings (Par 103): **99,96,96,92,85 72,70,**
CSF £22.66 TOTE £3.70: £1.30, £2.60, £1.10; EX 24.40 Trifecta £69.10.
Owner Mrs Sue Griffiths **Bred** Mrs Kathryn Lillis **Trained** Upper Lambourn, Berks

FOCUS
The clear form pick was turned over but a hurdling newcomer scored in decent style. The winner is rated in line with his bumper mark but there should be more to come.
T/Plt: £53.60 to a £1 stake. Pool: £45,016.47 - 612.89 winning tickets. T/Qpdt: £22.70 to a £1 stake. Pool: £3,033.30 - 98.50 winning tickets. **Colin Roberts**

112-118a (Foreign Racing) - See Raceform Interactive

EXETER (R-H)
Tuesday, May 5
OFFICIAL GOING: Good (chs 8.9, hdl 8.3)
Wind: very strong behind Weather: overcast with showers

119 ANCHOR INN COCKWOOD MAIDEN HURDLE (8 hdls) 2m 175y
5:50 (5:50) (Class 4) 4-Y-0+ £3,249 (£954; £477; £238)

Form RPR
222- 1 **Sternrubin (GER)**[10] 5535 4-10-10 128 RichardJohnson 105+
(Philip Hobbs) *mde all: clr fr 2nd: awkward last: unchal* 1/2[1]
556- 2 15 **Doctor Look Here (IRE)**[36] 5063 5-10-11 0 LucyGardner[(3)] 92
(Sue Gardner) *trckd ldrs: rdn to chse wnr appr 3 out: nt fluent whn losing hld 2nd at the last: regained 2nd nring fin* 66/1
F4- 3 3/4 **Fashion Icon (FR)**[21] 5338 4-10-3 0 TomScudamore 79
(Nigel Hawke) *hld up: hdwy to chal for hld 2nd fr 3 out: wnt 2nd sn after last tl no ex nring fin* 28/1
006- 4 13 **Roderick Random**[40] 4999 5-11-0 0 RichieMcLernon 80
(Johnny Farrelly) *trckd ldrs: rdn appr 3 out: grad fdd* 66/1
4- 5 7 **Almaas (USA)**[65] 4507 6-10-11 0 SeanBowen[(3)] 72
(Kevin Bishop) *racd keenly: trckd wnr tl 2nd: rdn after 4th: wknd 3 out* 16/1
103- 6 26 **Pengo's Boy**[41] 4984 6-11-0 0 TomO'Brien 58
(Stuart Kittow) *racd keenly: trckd wnr fr 2nd tl rdn appr 3 out: sn wknd: t.o* 5/2[2]
U **Angus Glens**[28] 5-11-0 0 NoelFehily
(David Dennis) *veered bdly lft and rt whn unseating rdr bef 1st* 14/1[3]

4m 3.0s (-12.50) **Going Correction** -0.70s/f (Firm)
WFA 4 from 5yo+ 18lb **7** Ran SP% **114.2**
Speed ratings (Par 105): **101,93,93,87,84 71,**
CSF £43.65 TOTE £1.90: £1.10, £6.70; EX 26.10 Trifecta £85.10.
Owner Terry Warner **Bred** Gestut Karlshof **Trained** Withycombe, Somerset

FOCUS
Richard Johnson said of the ground: "It's good - there are some slightly slower patches but they are few and far between." Windy conditions didn't make it easy on the runners. Little depth to this maiden hurdle and the favourite strolled home. He had to be nowhere near his best.

120 LEY ARMS KENN MARES' "NATIONAL HUNT" NOVICES' HURDLE (10 hdls) 2m 2f 111y
6:20 (6:20) (Class 4) 4-Y-0+ £3,249 (£954; £477; £238)

Form RPR
421- 1 **Taylor (IRE)**[14] 5445 6-11-5 115 DarylJacob 99+
(Nicky Henderson) *mde all: in command fr 3 out: readily* 4/11[1]
505- 2 8 **Penzflo (IRE)**[24] 5278 9-10-12 0 AlainCawley 81
(Johnny Farrelly) *trckd ldr: rdn to chse wnr appr 3 out: kpt on but a being comf hld* 40/1
50- 3 10 **Tara's Rainbow**[23] 5299 5-10-12 0 (t) DavidBass 69
(Kim Bailey) *in tch: nt fluent 2nd: rdn to chse ldrs appr 3 out: styd on same pce: wnt 3rd run-in* 12/1
3/6- 4 3 3/4 **Scarlett Lady**[173] 2456 7-10-12 0 AidanColeman 65
(Ali Stronge) *trckd ldrs: rdn appr 3 out: sn one pce: no ex whn lost 3rd run-in* 7/1[3]
002- 5 8 **Ley Lady Grey**[195] 1998 5-10-12 0 MichealNolan 59
(Jamie Snowden) *trckd ldrs: hit 6th: rdn appr 3 out: wknd 2 out* 12/1
6- 6 7 **Appropriate (FR)**[15] 5430 5-10-5 0 BenFfrenchDavis[(7)] 50
(Dominic Ffrench Davis) *hld up in last: hit 6th: rdn appr 3 out: nvr any imp on ldrs* 33/1
7 3/4 **Dont Do That** 7-10-12 0 NoelFehily 50
(Richard Rowe) *hld up in last pair: nt fluent 7th: no imp whn stmbld 3 out: wknd next: mstke last* 25/1
026- 8 3/4 **Dashul (IRE)**[85] 4135 6-10-12 0 NickScholfield 49
(Jeremy Scott) *trcking ldr wnt wnt rt 1st: sn hld up in last trio: pushed along after 7th: wknd after 3 out* 9/2[2]

4m 36.6s (-6.10) **Going Correction** -0.70s/f (Firm) **8** Ran SP% **128.6**
Speed ratings (Par 105): **84,80,76,74,71 68,68,67**
CSF £30.72 TOTE £1.40: £1.02, £9.30, £2.90; EX 33.70 Trifecta £325.90.
Owner Simon Munir & Isaac Souede **Bred** Daniel Cotter **Trained** Upper Lambourn, Berks

FOCUS
This took little winning, with the favourite enjoying another easy success. The easy winner was a stone+ off her best in landing the odds.

121 HEAVITREE BREWERY H'CAP CHASE (15 fncs) 2m 3f 48y
6:50 (6:50) (Class 3) (0-140,136) 5-Y-0+ £6,498 (£1,908; £954; £477)

Form RPR
111- 1 **Brody Bleu (FR)**[11] 5509 8-11-5 129 DarylJacob 133
(Robert Walford) *led: rdn after 4 out: hdd 2 out: rallied gamely to regain ld nring fin: drvn out* 5/2[2]
2U2- 2 nk **Easily Pleased (IRE)**[13] 5480 9-10-5 118 [1] JeremiahMcGrath[(3)] 123
(Martin Hill) *racd keenly: hld up: hdwy 10th: rdn to chal 3 out: led next: no ex whn hdd nring fin* 13/2
443- 3 hd **Carrigmorna King (IRE)**[20] 5342 9-11-12 136 (t) RichardJohnson 143
(Philip Hobbs) *trckd ldrs: blnd 8th: cl 3rd whn mstke 4 out: sn rdn: styd on wl fr last: nrly snatched 2nd* 7/4[1]
400- 4 20 **Daymar Bay (IRE)**[29] 5195 9-10-13 123 (v) AidanColeman 109
(Emma Lavelle) *trckd wnr: pressed wnr 8th tl 10th: rdn after 11th: hld fr next: wknd 3 out* 4/1[3]
144- 5 9 **Sands Cove (IRE)**[29] 5195 8-10-12 122 (t) GavinSheehan 104
(Charlie Mann) *trckd ldrs: effrt after 11th: btn next* 7/1

4m 36.4s (-20.90) **Going Correction** -0.80s/f (Firm) **5** Ran SP% **110.8**
Speed ratings: **109,108,108,100,97**
CSF £17.14 TOTE £2.50: £1.20, £2.80; EX 10.20 Trifecta £37.80.
Owner R J Brown **Bred** Pierre Julienne **Trained** Child Okeford, Dorset

FOCUS
A cracking finish to this handicap, the form of which looks sound. Another step up from the winner.

122 BRUNSWICK ARMS DAWLISH H'CAP HURDLE (12 hdls) 2m 7f 25y
7:20 (7:20) (Class 3) (0-135,129) 4-Y-0+ £5,393 (£1,583; £791; £395)

Form RPR
135- 1 **Weather Babe**[257] 1277 7-11-8 125 (tp) ConorO'Farrell 131+
(David Pipe) *trckd ldr: led 2 out: clr whn rchd for last: styd on wl* 12/1
P23- 2 5 **Risk A Fine (IRE)**[11] 5507 6-11-6 123 RichardJohnson 124
(Philip Hobbs) *racd freely: led: clr tl 3 out: rdn and hdd 2 out: kpt on but no ex* 9/2[2]
3P3- 3 2 1/4 **More Buck's (IRE)**[26] 5245 5-10-13 116 (t[1]) SamTwiston-Davies 114
(Paul Nicholls) *mid-div: hdwy after 8th: cl 3rd 3 out: sn rdn: styd on same pce fr next* 5/1[3]
526- 4 7 **Houston Dynimo (IRE)**[37] 4752 10-11-5 122 (tp) TomScudamore 114
(David Pipe) *mid-div: hdwy to trck ldrs 3 out: rdn bef 2 out: sn one pce* 6/1
112- 5 2 **Tara Tavey (IRE)**[21] 5333 10-10-5 115 (t) CiaranGethings[(7)] 105
(Kevin Bishop) *trckd ldrs: pushed along fr after 7th: rdn appr 3 out: sn one pce* 5/1[3]
523- 6 4 **Cash Injection**[21] 5333 6-10-10 113 (t) DarylJacob 104
(Richard Woollacott) *hld up: hdwy to chse ldrs 3 out: rdn bef 2 out: nvr quite threatened: blnd last: fdd* 7/1
660- 7 dist **Rev It Up (IRE)**[52] 4759 9-11-5 129 AlanJohns[(7)] 75
(Tim Vaughan) *trckd ldr tl wknd 7th: t.o 3 out* 11/1
100- P **Dream Deal**[20] 5343 7-11-3 120 NickScholfield
(Jeremy Scott) *hld up: pushed along fr 7th: wknd 9th: t.o whn p.u bef 3 out* 4/1[1]

5m 37.2s (-21.80) **Going Correction** -0.70s/f (Firm) **8** Ran SP% **114.3**
Speed ratings (Par 107): **108,106,105,103,102 101,86,**
CSF £65.53 CT £309.23 TOTE £13.60: £3.80, £1.60, £2.50; EX 95.30 Trifecta £395.40.
Owner Wayne Clifford **Bred** Mrs S Clifford **Trained** Nicholashayne, Devon

FOCUS
A fair staying handicap, although a couple of the fancied runners failed to give their running. The winner ran to her best.

123 SHIP INN TEIGNMOUTH INTERMEDIATE HUNTERS' CHASE SERIES FINAL (18 fncs) 3m 54y
7:50 (7:50) (Class 6) 5-Y-0+ £1,996 (£619; £309; £154)

Form RPR
6/6- 1 **The Wealerdealer (IRE)**[37] 8-11-5 0 MrIChanin[(5)] 114+
(I Chanin) *mid-div: hdwy after 14th: rdn to chse ldr fr next: sn hanging lft: led run-in: drvn out* 11/4[2]

2- **2** 3 1/4 **Third Chance (IRE)**[21] 5337 8-11-3 0........................... DavidNoonan(7) 112+
(Miss S L Gould) *mid-div: trckd ldrs 7th: jnd ldr 11th tl 14th: ldng whn hit 4 out: sn rdn: hit last: no ex whn hdd run-in* **7/4**[1]

001- **3** 3 1/2 **Blinding Lights (IRE)**[21] 5337 10-11-7 104....(tp) MrMatthewHampton(5) 109
(Mary Sanderson) *trckd ldrs: rdn and ev ch appr 4 out: styd on same pce fr 3 out* **7/2**[3]

0- **4** 20 **What About Will (IRE)**[21] 5337 6-11-3 0....................(v1) MissVWade(7) 93
(N Harris) *led tl rdn 4 out: wknd 2 out: blnd last* **16/1**

5 18 **Carry On Nando (IRE)**[17] 8-11-3 0....................(p) MrSeanHoulihan(7) 72
(G Chambers) *hld up: mid-div 11th: rdn after 14th: sn wknd: t.o* **50/1**

6 1 1/4 **Way Before Dawn**[37] 8-11-3 0................................ MissLeandaTickle(7) 71
(Mrs Sarah Tickle) *racd keenly: trckd ldrs tl wknd 13th: t.o* **11/1**

5- **7** 20 **Mausefalle (IRE)**[15] 5440 8-11-7 0....................(p) MrRGHenderson(3) 53
(D Summersby) *a towards rr: t.o* **33/1**

8 38 **Sunken Secret (IRE)**[9] 10-11-3 0.............................. MissPGlanville(7) 18
(Mrs L Glanville) *a towards rr: t.o* **40/1**

P/3- **9** 25 **General Girling**[23] 8-11-3 0....................................(p) MrPhilipThomas(7)
(P M Bryant) *trckd ldrs tl 8th: towards rr 10th: t.o 14th* **20/1**

P **Fourstar River (IRE)**[23] 10-11-5 0........................ MrJoshuaNewman(5)
(S W Reddaway) *j.lft bdly at times: a in rr: t.o whn p.u bef 4 out* **12/1**

5m 52.5s (-16.80) **Going Correction** -0.80s/f (Firm) **10** Ran **SP% 119.3**
Speed ratings: **96,94,93,87,81 80,74,61,53,**
CSF £8.33 TOTE £4.50: £1.10, £1.40, £1.90; EX 15.60 Trifecta £20.10.
Owner Miss Rebecca Barnett **Bred** Mrs M Farrell **Trained** Tiverton, Devon

FOCUS
The market leaders dominated this modest hunter chase. The form makes sense.

124 HALF MOON INN CLYST ST MARY STANDARD OPEN NATIONAL HUNT FLAT RACE 2m 175y
8:20 (8:20) (Class 6) 4-6-Y-O **£1,624** (£477; £238; £119)

Form RPR

1 **Air Horse One** 4-10-12 0.. NoelFehily 99
(Harry Fry) *trckd ldrs: led over 2f out: sn rdn: hld on gamely fnl f: rdn out* **7/1**[3]

0- **2** hd **Pulling Power**[36] 5071 5-10-9 0..(t) DavidBass 96
(Kim Bailey) *trckd ldrs: pushed along 4f out: rdn over 2f out: ev ch over 1f out: styd on fnl f: jst hld* **25/1**

3 nk **Tapaculo** 4-10-12 0.. TomO'Brien 98+
(Philip Hobbs) *mid-div tl outpcd 3f out: hdwy 2f out: styd on strly fnl f: wnt 3rd nring fin* **14/1**

4 nk **Savoy Court (IRE)** 4-10-12 0.................................. GavinSheehan 98
(Warren Greatrex) *led for 7f: trckd ldrs: rdn over 2f out: ev ch over 1f out: styd on: lost 3rd fnl strides* **3/1**[2]

2- **5** 1 3/4 **Braavos**[38] 5028 4-10-12 0...................................... RichardJohnson 96
(Philip Hobbs) *mid-div: hdwy 3f out: sn rdn to chse ldrs: styd on same pce fnl 2f* **1/1**[1]

3- **6** nk **Motts Cross (IRE)**[12] 5501 4-10-12 0............................ JamesDavies 96
(Chris Down) *trckd ldrs: rdn wl over 2f out: styd on same pce* **16/1**

7 1 1/2 **Horse Force One (IRE)** 4-10-12 0............................ MichealNolan 95
(Philip Hobbs) *hld up towards rr: hdwy 3f out: rdn to chse ldrs 2f out: styd on same pce fnl f* **20/1**

40- **8** 3 3/4 **Innox Park**[152] 2908 5-11-2 0.................................... JamesBest 95
(Kevin Bishop) *hld up towards rr: hdwy whn bmpd 3f out: sn rdn: styd on but nt pce to get involved* **25/1**

9 9 **Lets Go Dutchess** 5-10-2 0.................................. CiaranGethings(7) 79
(Kevin Bishop) *racd keenly: hld up towards rr: hdwy over 6f out: rdn to chal wl over 2f out: wknd over 1f out* **33/1**

10 2 3/4 **Murifield** 5-10-9 0...(t) MrMLegg(7) 83
(Anthony Honeyball) *plld hrd: trckd ldr: led after 7f: hdd over 2f out: wknd qckly* **16/1**

5- **11** nk **Quarryman**[26] 5248 4-10-12 0.............................(p) AdamWedge 79
(Caroline Keevil) *struggling 5f out: a towards rr* **50/1**

0- **12** dist **Heavenly Magic**[239] 1481 6-10-13 0.............................. RobertWilliams(3)
(Bernard Llewellyn) *mid-div: hdwy to trck ldr after 7f: wknd wl over 2f out: t.o: virtually p.u* **50/1**

4m 0.9s (-7.90) **Going Correction** -0.70s/f (Firm)
WFA 4 from 5yo+ 4lb **12** Ran **SP% 125.2**
Speed ratings: **90,89,89,89,88 88,87,86,81,80 80,**
CSF £178.93 TOTE £11.40: £2.20, £5.50, £5.50; EX 187.40 Trifecta £1287.50.
Owner The Dons **Bred** Distillery Stud **Trained** Seaborough, Dorset

FOCUS
The favourite disappointed in what turned out to be quite an open bumper. The race should produce winners.
T/Plt: £91.10 to a £1 stake. Pool: £60,463.85 - 484.34 winning units. T/Qpdt: £54.50 to a £1 stake. Pool: £4,991.13 - 67.75 winning units. **Tim Mitchell**

FAKENHAM (L-H)
Tuesday, May 5

OFFICIAL GOING: Good
Wind: very strong blustery winds Weather: very changeable; 16 degrees

125 TOUR OF BRITAIN AT FAKENHAM 12TH SEPTEMBER (S) HURDLE (9 hdls) 2m 3y
2:00 (2:00) (Class 4) 4-Y-O+ **£3,249** (£954; £477; £238)

Form RPR

416- **1** **Barneys Honour (IRE)**[13] 5465 11-10-12 117........(p) MissBHampson(7) 123+
(Andy Turnell) *pressed ldng pair tl led and hit 5th: hit next: drew 8 l clr 3 out: kpt increasing advantage after: reminders between last two: totally unchal* **11/8**[1]

0P2- **2** 31 **Descaro (USA)**[17] 5023 9-10-12 101....................................(p) DaveCrosse 92
(John O'Shea) *led or disp ld tl 5th: sn furiously drvn: fnd nil: 12 l 3rd 3 out: wnt 15 l 2nd at next: continued remote* **7/1**[3]

030- **3** 27 **Carrowbeg (IRE)**[81] 4201 7-10-5 84.........................(vt) DanielHiskett(7) 63
(Lawney Hill) *nvr wnt a yard: lost tch 3rd: t.o 5th: wnt hopeless 3rd at last* **20/1**

046- **4** 6 **Luddsdenene (IRE)**[16] 5405 10-11-8 118..............................(t) RhysFlint 70
(Alexandra Dunn) *disp ld tl 5th: struggling to keep up w wnr 3 out: relegated 3rd and mstke next: gng v slowly after: lost t.o 3rd at last* **9/1**

5 4 1/2 **Bourbondi**[28] 4-10-8 0... JackQuinlan 49
(Conrad Allen) *mstkes: last mostly: 15 l adrift by 2nd: t.o fr 5th: eventually completed* **50/1**

050- **U** **Camachoice (IRE)**[11] 5508 5-11-5 117........................(b) BrendanPowell
(Jamie Snowden) *towards rr tl blnd bdly and uns rdr 2nd* **7/4**[2]

P/P- **P** **Cool Chief**[97] 3921 6-10-5 0...(t) GeorgeGorman(7)
(Alan Blackmore) *led or disp ld tl bmpd along vigorously and hit 5th: already t.o whn blnd next and p.u* **100/1**

4m 6.3s (-6.70) **Going Correction** -0.175s/f (Good)
WFA 4 from 5yo+ 18lb **7** Ran **SP% 108.7**
Speed ratings (Par 105): **108,93,80,77,75 ,**
CSF £10.26 TOTE £1.80: £1.20, £3.00; EX 10.90 Trifecta £80.60.There was no bid for the winner.
Owner Power Bloodstock Ltd **Bred** Mrs M Quinn **Trained** Broad Hinton, Wilts

FOCUS
Fresh ground provided all the way round on both tracks. Despite 10mm of overnight rain the ground remained good. An uncompetitive event that didn't take much winning after the second favourite unseated his rider early on. The gallop was an ordinary one. The winner was a 130+ hurdler at his peak and is still a lot better than this grade.

126 ORCHARD GROUP'S RACE FOR LIVVY H'CAP CHASE (16 fncs) 2m 5f 44y
2:30 (2:30) (Class 5) (0-100,99) 5-Y-O+ **£4,548** (£1,335; £667; £333)

Form RPR

2P2- **1** **Alright Benny (IRE)**[31] 5149 12-11-6 93......................... PaddyBrennan 102+
(Paul Henderson) *j. soundly: mde all: drew 6 l clr 3 out: plugged on u.p fr between last two: all out but remained in command* **5/1**[2]

31-2 **2** 11 **Waddingtown Hero (IRE)**[3] 88 8-11-3 90.............(tp) GerardTumelty 94
(Andy Turnell) *taken steadily towards rr: wnt 3rd at 13th and 2nd at next: brief effrt and 3 l down but rdn 2 out: no rspnse to urgings after: wl hld* **5/4**[1]

635- **3** 26 **Troubled (IRE)**[15] 5421 8-10-0 73 oh1.................................. JackQuinlan 49
(David Thompson) *mstkes towards rr: reminder bef 10th: nt travelling fr 12th: mstke next: t.o whn v slow 2 out: wnt 3rd bef last* **5/1**[2]

215- **4** 13 **My Silver Cloud (IRE)**[11] 5522 8-10-7 80...................(p) MarcGoldstein 44
(Paddy Butler) *chsd wnr fr 4th: mstke 11th and rdn: lost 2nd 3 out: lost remote 3rd bef last and fin slowly* **5/1**[2]

446- **5** 1 1/4 **Derryogue (IRE)**[45] 4927 10-11-12 99..................................(t) MarkGrant 62
(Zoe Davison) *mstkes: last v slow 7th and reminder: nt travelling after: t.o fr 12th* **20/1**

2P0- **6** 11 **Next Exit (IRE)**[23] 5295 10-11-0 92.............................. JoeCornwall(5) 45
(John Cornwall) *hit 2nd: slow 3rd: wnt 3rd fr 4th tl rdn 12th: fdd rapidly bef 3 out: bdly t.o* **40/1**

P1P- **P** **Thats Ben (IRE)**[18] 5372 10-10-6 79..................................(tp) JamesDavies
(Tom Gretton) *chsd ldrs tl 8th: dropped bk last and nt travelling at 11th: t.o whn mstke next and qckly p.u* **10/1**[3]

5m 44.6s (2.80) **Going Correction** +0.20s/f (Yiel) **7** Ran **SP% 110.7**
Speed ratings: **102,98,88,83,83 79,**
CSF £11.54 TOTE £4.10: £2.00, £1.40; EX 10.30 Trifecta £30.00.
Owner The Ray Of Hope Partnership **Bred** Miss D And P Keating **Trained** Whitsbury, Hants

FOCUS
Not much to dwell on behind the first two, who pulled clear in this low-grade handicap. The gallop was reasonable.

127 INDEPENDENT RACECOURSES LTD NOVICES' HURDLE (13 hdls) 2m 7f 95y
3:00 (3:00) (Class 3) 4-Y-O+ **£6,498** (£1,908; £954; £477)

Form RPR

304- **1** **Hunt Ball (IRE)**[25] 5253 10-10-13 0.................................. AndrewTinkler 133+
(Nicky Henderson) *j. fluently: led at slow pce: urged clr fr 2 out: 8 l ahd last* **10/11**[1]

52- **2** 8 **Shwaiman (IRE)**[112] 3659 5-10-13 0.................................. TrevorWhelan 127
(William Jarvis) *tended to lack fluency: pressed wnr tl 5th: rdn to go 2nd again 3 out: tried to chal 2 out: fnd little and sn brushed aside* **13/8**[2]

1- **3** 22 **Driftashore (IRE)**[23] 5286 8-10-12 0............................ MissBHampson(7) 111
(Andy Turnell) *racd keenly: pressed wnr fr 5th tl hit 3 out: rdn and sn lft bhd by ldng pair* **13/2**[3]

505- **4** 99 **Ballochmyle (IRE)**[29] 5201 5-10-13 0................................ RyanMahon 16
(Caroline Fryer) *a last: struggling 7th: t.o 10th: blnd 2 out: fin 2f bhd wnr* **125/1**

6m 13.4s (-8.60) **Going Correction** -0.175s/f (Good) **4** Ran **SP% 104.6**
Speed ratings (Par 107): **106,103,96,64**
CSF £2.57 TOTE £2.10; EX 2.90 Trifecta £3.60.
Owner Atlantic Equine **Bred** Michael Slevin **Trained** Upper Lambourn, Berks

FOCUS
Not a strong race for the money and the two market leaders had it between themselves in the last half mile. The pace was no more than fair. Hunt Ball was still 20lb+ off the best of last season's chase figures.

128 AT THE RACES NOVICES' CHASE (18 fncs) 3m 38y
3:30 (3:30) (Class 3) 5-Y-O+ **£7,797** (£2,289; £1,144; £572)

Form RPR

B35- **1** **Emerald Rose**[24] 5284 8-10-7 109....................................(p) MarkGrant 120+
(Julian Smith) *dwlt and lost 8 l s: sn rcvrd: nt fluent 2nd: effrt to ld 10th: jnd 2 out: rdn and outbattled rival after: over 2 l ahd and in command last* **10/3**[2]

512- **2** 6 **Morning Reggie**[40] 4998 6-11-5 122.................................. LeightonAspell 130+
(Oliver Sherwood) *settled in 3rd pl: blnd 15th: wnt 2nd and mstke next: chal 2 out: sn rdn and fnd nil: wl hld whn hit last* **4/9**[1]

53-2 **3** 35 **Veauce De Sivola (FR)**[5] 27 6-11-0 112..............................(t) TomCannon 97
(Mark Gillard) *led at slow pce tl 10th: rdn 14th: lost 2nd 3 out and sn wl bhd: t.o* **8/1**[3]

4P6- **4** 60 **The Jugopolist (IRE)**[50] 4808 8-10-9 86........................(v) JoeCornwall(5) 36
(John Cornwall) *several mod jumps: cl up tl v slow 9th and rdn: lost tch 12th: t.o 14th: climbed 2 out* **50/1**

6m 39.3s (3.60) **Going Correction** +0.20s/f (Yiel) **4** Ran **SP% 105.4**
Speed ratings: **102,100,88,69**
CSF £5.34 TOTE £4.70; EX 5.30 Trifecta £9.00.
Owner Grand Jury Partnership **Bred** Grand Jury Partnership **Trained** Tirley, Gloucs

FOCUS
A disappointing turnout for the money on offer. The gallop was an ordinary one and the two market leaders finished a long way clear. The form is rated around the first two.

129 IRL OPEN HUNTERS' CHASE (FOR THE TURNER FAMILY TROPHY) (18 fncs) 3m 38y
4:00 (4:00) (Class 6) 5-Y-O+ **£1,646** (£506; £253)

Form RPR

3U2- **1** **Neverownup (IRE)**[14] 5453 10-11-11 126.............. CharlieHammond(7) 120
(Dr Richard Newland) *hld up: effrt and mstke 12th and rdr unbalanced briefly: led next: hdd bef 15th: urged up to ld again 2 out: drew clr bef last whn rivals slowed bdly* **10/11**[1]

P/4- **2** 18 **Roby De Cimbre (FR)**[18] 5377 12-11-3 97..........(vt) MrTRFStrawson(7) 96
(S Robinson) *led at str gallop: hdd 12th: led bef 15th and 3 l clr briefly: drvn and hdd 2 out: fnd nil bef last and fin weakly* **25/1**

The Form Book Jumps 2015-16, Raceform Ltd, Newbury, RG14 5SJ

244/ **3** 4 ½ **See You Jack**[16] 10-11-10 0 MissGAndrews 93
(Mrs S Fryer) *rn in snatches: j. slowly 5th: cajoled along fr 13th: clsd for driving 3 out and 5 l 3rd whn slow next: sn trying to pull himself and wl bhd* **9/2**[3]

F/ **4** 1 **Baltic Blue**[16] 8-11-5 0 (p) MissCareyWilliamson(5) 91
(B Dowling) *detached bef 3rd: t.o fr 14th: plugging on fr 2 out but nvr any hope* **33/1**

/31- **U** **Master Workman (IRE)**[16] 9-11-9 110 (p) MrDKemp(3)
(David Kemp) *plld hrd: 3rd whn sltly squeezed for room and uns rdr 2nd* **10/3**[2]

0/2- **P** **Good Order**[17] 10-11-3 0 (t) MrRStearn(7)
(E Turner) *chsd ldrs: pushed along 7th: nt travelling fr 10th: lost tch and mstke 13th: nrly carried out by loose horse next but blnd over fence: continued t.o tl p.u 3 out* **11/1**

6m 43.2s (7.50) **Going Correction** +0.20s/f (Yiel) **6** Ran SP% **108.8**
Speed ratings: **96,90,88,88,**
CSF £18.60 TOTE £2.40: £1.30, £4.00; EX 19.60 Trifecta £90.20.
Owner Dr R D P Newland **Bred** Mark Donohoe **Trained** Claines, Worcs

FOCUS
An ordinary hunter chase and one in which the gallop was fair. There's a case for rating the form up to 9lb higher through the first two.

130 FAKENHAM LADIES RACEDAY 31ST MAY MARES' H'CAP HURDLE (10 hdls 1 omitted) 2m 4f 1y
4:30 (4:32) (Class 4) (0-110,110) 4-Y-O+ **£4,548** (£1,335; £667; £333)

Form RPR

425- **1** **Queen Spud**[14] 5451 6-11-6 **104** (p) JakeGreenall 109+
(Henry Daly) *cl up: lft in ld 4th: travelled wl after: gng best fr 2 out w only one in serious pursuit: clipped rail home turn: rdn and in command bef last* **5/2**[1]

445- **2** 4 **You've Been Mowed**[13] 5481 9-10-13 **97** TrevorWhelan 99
(Neil King) *hld up in rr: effrt bef 3 out: 2nd and u.p next: no imp after: 3 l 2nd whn mstke last* **5/1**[3]

55P- **3** 19 **Chasse En Mer (FR)**[175] 2418 5-11-9 **107** (t) AndrewTinkler 92
(Caroline Bailey) *hld up: rdn and effrt to go 2nd 3 out: fdd qckly next* **12/1**

030- **4** 2 ¼ **Come On Harriet**[18] 5371 6-10-8 **95** (t) JamesBanks(3) 77
(Alex Hales) *towards rr: effrt 7th: rdn and struggling after 3 out* **4/1**[2]

PPP- **5** 34 **Noir Girl**[44] 4937 6-10-3 **87** (p) MarkGrant 38
(Zoe Davison) *nt a fluent: bhd: rdn 7th: t.o 3 out* **33/1**

3U5- **6** 13 **Be My Witness (IRE)**[115] 3612 6-10-6 **97** JosephPalmowski(7) 37
(Robin Dickin) *hmpd 4th: cl up: 2nd fr 7th tl after 3 out: lost tch and blnd next: sn t.o* **8/1**

F00- **F** **Magic Money**[23] 5295 7-11-7 **110** EdCookson(5)
(Kim Bailey) *slt ld mostly tl fell 4th* **4/1**[2]

63P/ **P** **Strangelittlegirl**[709] 502 7-10-1 **85** JackQuinlan
(Giles Bravery) *w ldrs tl 5th: rdn and fdd rapidly 7th: sn t.o: p.u after 3 out* **25/1**

5m 14.3s (-6.10) **Going Correction** -0.175s/f (Good) **8** Ran SP% **110.8**
Speed ratings (Par 105): **104,102,95,94,81 76, ,**
CSF £14.68 CT £116.15 TOTE £2.90: £1.20, £1.90, £2.80; EX 10.80 Trifecta £57.60.
Owner Barlow, Brindley, Hanley & Russell **Bred** Mickley Stud **Trained** Stanton Lacy, Shropshire

FOCUS
A modest handicap, run at a fair pace, in which the first two pulled clear. The form is rated around the second.
T/Plt: £75.90 to a £1 stake. Pool: £46340.14 - 445.15 winning tickets. T/Qpdt: £31.60 to a £1 stake. Pool: £3051.18 - 71.4 winning tickets. **Iain Mackenzie**

33 SEDGEFIELD (L-H)
Tuesday, May 5

OFFICIAL GOING: Soft (chs 7.5, hdl 8.0)
Wind: fresh 1/2 behind Weather: overcast, very breezy, becoming fine

131 SEDGEFIELD RACECOURSE OWN A CASEIH 75CFARMALL NOVICES' HURDLE (8 hdls) 2m 178y
2:10 (2:10) (Class 4) 4-Y-O+ **£3,249** (£954; £477; £238)

Form RPR

1 **Captain Swift (IRE)**[81] 4-10-7 0 BrianHughes 102+
(John Mackie) *trckd ldng pair: cl 2nd appr 2 out: led appr last: j.lft: drvn out* **10/1**[2]

3- **2** 3 ¼ **Dynamo (IRE)**[30] 5155 4-10-7 0 HarrySkelton 97
(Dan Skelton) *trckd ldr: t.k.h: led appr 2 out: rdn and hdd appr last: kpt on same pce last 150yds* **11/10**[1]

F50- **3** 14 **Tokyo Brown (USA)**[82] 4182 6-10-8 0 (p) TonyKelly(3) 87
(James Moffatt) *trckd ldrs: drvn 3 out: outpcd appr 2 out: tk poor 3rd bef last* **40/1**[3]

14P- **4** 13 **Definite Dream (IRE)**[26] 5240 8-10-11 0 (t) PaulMoloney 79
(Evan Williams) *set stdy pce: increased pce 4th: reminders and hdd appr 2 out: sn btn: wl bhd whn eased clsng stages* **11/10**[1]

4m 23.3s (16.40) **Going Correction** +0.575s/f (Soft)
WFA 4 from 6yo+ 18lb **4** Ran SP% **106.8**
Speed ratings (Par 105): **84,82,75,69**
CSF £21.68 TOTE £7.90; EX 20.70 Trifecta £63.00.
Owner Mrs Sue Adams **Bred** Mrs Michele Craig White **Trained** Church Broughton , Derbys

FOCUS
Divided bends on fresh ground and Hurdles sited on outer. After 9mm of rain the ground was soft. This was run at an ordinary pace and the first two quickened away from the others in the straight. Not form to take seriously.

132 JOHN WADE GROUP "NATIONAL HUNT" NOVICES' HURDLE (10 hdls) 2m 3f 34y
2:40 (2:41) (Class 4) 4-Y-O+ **£3,249** (£954; £477; £238)

Form RPR

351- **1** **Sharp Rise (IRE)**[187] 2146 8-10-12 112 JamesReveley 125+
(Pauline Robson) *mde all: j. soundly: pushed out* **5/2**[2]

651- **2** 6 **Major Ivan (IRE)**[30] 5159 6-11-5 0 BrianHughes 127
(Malcolm Jefferson) *trckd ldng pair: 2nd 5th: drvn appr 2 out: 4 l down and wl hld whn hit last* **8/13**[1]

0P3- **3** 15 **Tickenwolf (IRE)**[39] 5016 5-10-12 109 HenryBrooke 107
(George Moore) *hld up in mid-div: handy 3rd sn after 6th: drvn after 3 out: wknd appr next* **8/1**[3]

3- **4** 34 **Milly Baloo**[184] 2223 4-10-0 0 DougieCostello 58
(Tim Easterby) *mid-div: t.k.h: hdwy to chse ldrs whn mstke 5th: wknd next: sn bhd: t.o* **33/1**

003- **5** 6 **Park House**[231] 1538 6-10-12 0 AndrewThornton 64
(Ray Craggs) *in rr: sme hdwy 7th: lost pl and reminders next: sn bhd: t.o* **50/1**

0/0- **6** 7 **Lukie**[166] 2617 7-10-12 0 BrianHarding 57
(Peter Niven) *nt fluent in rr: hdwy 7th: rdn and lost pl next: sn bhd: t.o* **50/1**

5/P- **P** **Amour Collonges (FR)**[22] 5308 5-10-7 0 (b[1]) DiarmuidO'Regan(5)
(Chris Grant) *chsd wnr: stmbld on landing 5th: drvn 7th: sn lost pl: t.o after next: p.u bef 2 out* **40/1**

4m 59.8s (7.10) **Going Correction** +0.575s/f (Soft)
WFA 4 from 5yo+ 18lb **7** Ran SP% **110.9**
Speed ratings (Par 105): **108,105,99,86,83 80,**
CSF £4.30 TOTE £3.00: £1.50, £1.20; EX 5.90 Trifecta £12.80.
Owner I Couldn't Switch Club **Bred** Mrs M Brophy **Trained** Kirkharle, Northumberland

FOCUS
Just a fair novice hurdle but the pace was true and the form should work out. The second and third were pretty close to their marks in the fastest of the hurdle races.

133 JARDINES CATERING H'CAP CHASE (12 fncs 9 omitted) 3m 2f 59y
3:10 (3:10) (Class 5) (0-100,97) 5-Y-O+ **£2,469** (£725; £362; £181)

Form RPR

150- **1** **Over And Above (IRE)**[15] 5423 9-10-7 **78** (tp) HenryBrooke 90+
(Henry Hogarth) *sn chsng ldrs: 2nd 7th: drvn to ld omitted 2 out: sn forged clr: eased clsng stages* **17/2**[3]

544- **2** 13 **Cara Court (IRE)**[56] 4699 9-10-2 **78** ow1 (p) MrJohnDawson(5) 77
(Joanne Foster) *w ldr: led 3rd: j.rt 8th: hdd omitted 2 out: one pce* **9/1**

503- **3** 9 **Strike Fast (IRE)**[31] 5135 10-11-1 **86** JamesReveley 76
(William Kinsey) *chsd ldrs: lost pl briefly 6th: drvn next: lost pl 10th* **7/4**[1]

PP3- **4** 1 ¾ **Westwire Toby (IRE)**[45] 4899 13-10-0 **71** oh13 SeanQuinlan 58
(Lynn Siddall) *in rr: pushed along 7th: poor 4th 10th* **100/1**

5P3- **5** 16 **Pyjama Game (IRE)**[30] 5162 9-11-5 **97** ThomasDowson(7) 67
(Rose Dobbin) *chsd ldrs: pushed along 7th: lost pl next: sn bhd* **10/3**[2]

2P6- **6** 11 ¼ **Acrai Rua (IRE)**[31] 5134 12-11-9 **94** (tp) BrianHughes 53
(Tim Fitzgerald) *led to 3rd: lost pl 9th: sn wl bhd* **10/1**

P35- **P** **Glenwood Prince (IRE)**[42] 4974 9-9-10 **72** (p) CallumBewley(5)
(Kevin Hunter) *in rr: pushed along 3rd: bhd 8th: t.o 10th: p.u bef last* **9/1**

P50- **U** **Top Cat Dj (IRE)**[21] 5329 7-10-5 **81** DiarmuidO'Regan(5)
(Chris Grant) *in rr: blnd and uns rdr 1st* **9/1**

7m 0.6s (-10.40) **Going Correction** -0.15s/f (Good) **8** Ran SP% **110.0**
Speed ratings: **109,105,102,101,97 93, ,**
CSF £72.70 CT £182.23 TOTE £11.40: £2.50, £1.70, £1.20; EX 96.40 Trifecta £195.80.
Owner Hogarth Racing **Bred** Leslie Tucker **Trained** Stillington, N Yorks

■ Stewards' Enquiry : Mr John Dawson seven-day ban: used whip above permitted level (May 19,22,24-28)

FOCUS
Just an ordinary staying handicap chase in which three fences per circuit were omitted and the normal third-last, the cross fence, was the final obstacle. The winner's effort could have been rated a lot higher.

134 JOHN WADE WASTE RECYCLING H'CAP CHASE (10 fncs 7 omitted) 2m 5f 28y
3:40 (3:42) (Class 4) (0-115,114) 5-Y-O+ **£3,798** (£1,122; £561; £280; £140)

Form RPR

133- **1** **Houndscourt (IRE)**[29] 5190 8-11-3 **105** DougieCostello 115+
(Joanne Foster) *chsd ldrs: mstke 6th: 2nd sn after omitted 2 out: led appr omitted last: drvn out* **11/2**[3]

426- **2** 2 ½ **Be A Dreamer**[21] 5330 7-10-0 **88** oh2 SeanQuinlan 93
(Sue Smith) *chsd ldrs: led appr 2 out: hdd appr omitted last: kpt on same pce* **4/1**[2]

413- **3** 6 **Cape York**[23] 5297 7-11-12 **114** (b) BrianHughes 113
(Malcolm Jefferson) *w ldrs: hit 1st: led 7th tl appr 2 out: rdn omitted 2 out: one pce* **2/1**[1]

162- **4** 1 ¼ **Smart Catch (IRE)**[23] 5297 9-11-5 **107** LeeEdwards 106
(Tony Carroll) *chsd ldrs: handy 4th 7th: reminders 2 out: one pce fr omitted 2 out* **13/2**

15P- **5** 58 **Redpender (IRE)**[123] 3485 9-11-1 **106** (p) TonyKelly(3) 46
(James Moffatt) *chsd ldrs: drvn 5th: sn lost pl: t.o 7th: eventually completed* **8/1**

5P5- **6** 7 **My Idea**[52] 4757 9-10-9 **102** (t) StephenMulqueen(5) 35
(Maurice Barnes) *led to 7th: lost pl and nt fluent next: sn bhd: t.o 2 out: eventually completed* **13/2**

600- **P** **Nobunaga**[11] 5515 10-10-8 **103** (v[1]) JamieHamilton(7)
(Andrew Hamilton) *chsd ldrs: drvn 6th: lost pl bef next: sn bhd: t.o 8th: p.u after 2 out* **40/1**

5m 33.2s (0.20) **Going Correction** -0.15s/f (Good) **7** Ran SP% **108.9**
Speed ratings: **93,92,89,89,68 65,**
CSF £25.37 CT £52.01 TOTE £6.00: £2.50, £2.30; EX 22.90 Trifecta £73.30.
Owner The Golden Syndicate **Bred** Ian Downey **Trained** Menston, W Yorks

FOCUS
Just an ordinary handicap chase in which the first four finished well clear. The pace was ordinary and the winner produced a chase best.

135 VIOLET STEAMS GOES AHEAD NOVICES' H'CAP CHASE (7 fncs 6 omitted) 2m 77y
4:10 (4:10) (Class 5) (0-100,100) 5-Y-O+ **£2,599** (£763; £381; £190)

Form RPR

034- **1** **Our Boy Ben**[21] 5329 6-11-4 **92** (b) BrianHughes 101
(Malcolm Jefferson) *chsd ldr: led sn after 2 out: rdn omitted 2 out: all out* **6/4**[1]

4PP- **2** nk **Dundee Blue (IRE)**[21] 5330 7-10-5 **82** (bt[1]) GrahamWatters(3) 91
(Henry Hogarth) *chsd ldrs: lft 3rd 5th: 2nd and drvn appr omitted 2 out: rallied omitted last: jst hld* **9/1**[2]

P13- **3** 24 **Shady Lane**[115] 3612 8-11-11 **99** (t) HarrySkelton 84
(Dan Skelton) *led: drvn 2 out: sn hdd: wknd omitted 2 out* **6/4**[1]

060- **4** 3 ¾ **King Of The Dark (IRE)**[18] 5379 8-11-5 **100** ThomasDowson(7) 81
(Victor Thompson) *a last: sn pushed along: bhd fr 4th: lft poor 4th next* **16/1**[3]

444- **F** **Missionaire (USA)**[60] 4603 8-10-9 **83** LeeEdwards
(Tony Carroll) *chsd ldrs: handy 3rd whn fell 5th* **9/1**[2]

4m 10.5s (-3.50) **Going Correction** -0.15s/f (Good) **5** Ran SP% **105.9**
Speed ratings: **102,101,90,88,**
CSF £12.35 TOTE £2.50: £1.70, £3.20; EX 17.30 Trifecta £37.40.
Owner P Nelson **Bred** P Nelson **Trained** Norton, N Yorks

FOCUS
Just a fair gallop to this novice handicap chase and the form is unlikely to prove anything special. The winner is rated in line with the best of his 2014 hurdle figures.

136 RITA CROSSLEY AT 60 H'CAP HURDLE (13 hdls) 3m 3f 9y
4:40 (4:40) (Class 5) (0-100,91) 4-Y-0+ £2,339 (£686; £343; £171)

Form RPR
044- 1 **Heart O Annandale (IRE)**[15] 5420 8-11-6 **85**..........(t) MichaelMcAlister 100+
(Maurice Barnes) *mde all: nt fluent 4 out: styd on wl fr 2 out: drvn out* 11/2[3]
050- 2 13 **Blue Cove**[54] 4726 10-10-0 **65** oh1..................................(t) SeanQuinlan 66
(Lynn Siddall) *in rr: hdwy 8th: outpcd 4 out: poor 5th 2 out: styd on: tk modest 2nd last 50yds* 15/2
040- 3 1 ½ **Sam Lord**[63] 4550 11-11-10 **89**...................................... BrianHughes 90
(James Moffatt) *chsd wnr: 2nd 3 out: one pce fr next* 9/1
4U3- 4 9 **Urban Gale (IRE)**[79] 4255 10-11-5 **89**....................(p) MrJohnDawson[(5)] 83
(Joanne Foster) *chsd ldrs: drvn 3 out: one pce appr 2 out* 3/1[2]
500- 5 1 ¾ **Master Murphy (IRE)**[54] 4726 10-11-5 **89**.......................... DaleIrving[(5)] 78
(Jane Walton) *prom: drvn 9th: one pce bef 2 out* 9/1
00P- 6 22 **Overtoyoulou**[54] 4726 7-11-1 **85**.............................. DiarmuidO'Regan[(5)] 52
(Chris Grant) *in rr: bhd and reminders 9th: nvr on terms* 20/1
P46- P **Kilcullen Article (IRE)**[24] 5281 7-11-8 **87**.......................... LiamTreadwell
(Michael Scudamore) *nt fluent: chsd ldrs: drvn 8th: wknd 4 out: sn bhd: t.o whn p.u after next: b.b.v* 11/4[1]
00F- P **Petre' Island (IRE)**[78] 4266 6-11-7 **86**.............................. HenryBrooke
(Michael Smith) *in tch: lost pl 10th: sn bhd: t.o whn p.u after 3 out* 18/1

7m 8.2s (16.20) **Going Correction** +0.575s/f (Soft) 8 Ran SP% 108.8
Speed ratings (Par 103): **99,95,94,92,91 85,,**
CSF £41.05 CT £326.39 TOTE £6.20: £2.30, £2.20, £2.10; EX 60.20 Trifecta £389.00.
Owner K Milligan Partnership **Bred** Frankie Powell **Trained** Farlam, Cumbria

FOCUS
A low-grade staying handicap hurdle run at a modest gallop.

137 CARLSBERG H'CAP HURDLE (8 hdls) 2m 178y
5:10 (5:10) (Class 5) (0-100,100) 4-Y-0+ £2,339 (£686; £343; £171)

Form RPR
543- 1 **Baraboy (IRE)**[38] 5030 5-11-1 **89**...................................... BrianHarding 94+
(Barry Murtagh) *trckd ldrs: led and wnt rt 2 out: drvn appr last: forged clr* 3/1[2]
353- 2 7 **First Of Never (IRE)**[62] 4559 9-10-0 **74** oh4........................ WillKennedy 73
(Lynn Siddall) *trckd ldrs: 2nd 4th: kpt on same pce between last 2* 4/1
106- 3 1 ¼ **Hi Dancer**[46] 4888 12-11-2 **95**......................................(p) KieronEdgar[(5)] 93
(Ben Haslam) *led: qcknd pce 4th: drvn next: hdd and swtchd lft 2 out: kpt on one pce* 7/2[3]
5P-6 4 16 **Amir Pasha (UAE)**[5] 34 10-10-2 **86**..............................(b) FinianO'Toole[(10)] 69
(Micky Hammond) *chsd ldrs: drvn appr 2 out: lost pl between last 2* 11/4[1]
323- 5 5 **Phase Shift**[217] 1669 7-11-9 **100**..............................(t) JonathanEngland[(3)] 76
(Harriet Bethell) *trckd ldrs: racd wd fr 5th: drvn after 3 out: lost pl bef next* 5/1

4m 15.7s (8.80) **Going Correction** +0.575s/f (Soft)
WFA 4 from 5yo+ 18lb 5 Ran SP% 110.6
Speed ratings (Par 103): **102,98,98,90,88**
CSF £14.89 TOTE £2.90: £1.50, £2.60; EX 14.90 Trifecta £39.60.
Owner Anthony White **Bred** Holborn Trust Co **Trained** Low Braithwaite, Cumbria

FOCUS
A moderately run race, which developed into a sprint up the straight.
T/Plt: £502.30 to a £1 stake. Pool: £56617.43 - 82.27 winning tickets. T/Qpdt: £22.40 to a £1 stake. Pool: £6390.58 - 210.28 winning tickets. **Walter Glynn**

KELSO (L-H)
Wednesday, May 6

OFFICIAL GOING: Good to soft (7.0)
Wind: Fresh, half against Weather: Overcast

138 BLACK BULL INN WOOLER NOVICES' CHASE (12 fncs) 2m 1f 14y
1:50 (1:50) (Class 4) 5-Y-0+ £4,548 (£1,335; £667; £333)

Form RPR
3U2- 1 **Pair Of Jacks (IRE)**[19] 5364 7-10-12 125.............................. BrianHughes 132
(Malcolm Jefferson) *chsd ldrs: stdy hdwy to ld 2 out: rdn and edgd lft bef last: hld on wl u.p run-in* 4/5[1]
2/4- 2 ¾ **Katachenko (IRE)**[172] 2504 6-10-12 128..........................[1] WilsonRenwick 132
(Donald McCain) *pressed ldr: led 5th: nt fluent 5 out: rdn and hdd 2 out: rallied and ev ch last: kpt on: hld towards fin* 2/1[2]
100/ 3 14 **Silk Hall (UAE)**[320] 759 10-10-12 130..............................(b) JamesReveley 122
(J J Lambe, Ire) *nt fluent on occasions: led to 5th: cl up tl nt fluent and outpcd 3 out: btn next* 13/2[3]
005- 4 9 **Neville Woods**[22] 5326 8-10-7 0...............................(tp) MrJohnDawson[(5)] 111
(J L Gledson) *bhd and sn outpcd: stdy hdwy 5th: rdn and struggling after 4 out: btn bef 2 out* 33/1

4m 13.9s (-4.10) **Going Correction** -0.025s/f (Good) 4 Ran SP% 105.2
Speed ratings: **108,107,101,96**
CSF £2.67 TOTE £1.90; EX 2.20 Trifecta £5.40.
Owner Mrs Rita Williams **Bred** Mary And Mrs Letty O'Sullivan **Trained** Norton, N Yorks

FOCUS
Rail dolled out 4yds on each bend and distances increased by about 25yds per circuit. The course was watered towards the end of the previous week and a further 10mm fell the day before. It was dry overnight, though, and the going looked in decent nick in the opener. The jockeys commented afterwards it rode as advertised. The winner set a fair standard and ran to his mark.

139 HUNTER REAL ESTATE INVESTMENT MANAGERS NOVICES' H'CAP HURDLE (11 hdls) 2m 6f 151y
2:20 (2:20) (Class 4) (0-110,107) 4-Y-0+ £4,548 (£1,335; £667; £333)

Form RPR
/46- 1 **Isaacstown Lad (IRE)**[22] 5324 8-10-12 **93**.......................... BrianHarding 109+
(Nicky Richards) *hld up: pushed along 1/2-way: hdwy after 4 out: led appr 2 out: sn clr: nt fluent last: pushed out* 10/3[1]
006- 2 3 ¼ **Hurricane Rita (FR)**[23] 5308 5-10-11 **97**.................... GrantCockburn[(5)] 109
(Stuart Coltherd) *hld up: pushed along bef 8th: outpcd and drvn 3 out: rallied to chse (clr) wnr whn nt fluent last: edgd lft run-in: kpt on* 25/1
465- 3 13 **Iora Glas (IRE)**[36] 5085 6-11-8 **103**.................................. SeanQuinlan 105
(Fergal O'Brien) *hld up: hdwy to chse (clr) ldr after 4 out: effrt and ch 2 out: chsd wnr briefly between last 2: nt fluent last: one pce* 7/2[2]
466- 4 6 **Lord Usher (IRE)**[46] 4909 8-11-4 **104**.......................(b[1]) CallumBewley[(5)] 101+
(George Charlton) *in tch: hdwy to ld 5 out: clr after 3 out: rdn and hdd appr 2 out: outpcd whn nt fluent last* 9/1
P06- 5 4 **Pegasus Walk (IRE)**[14] 5473 6-9-7 **81** oh1.............. ThomasDowson[(7)] 72
(Rose Dobbin) *hld up: hdwy and prom 5th: rdn after 4 out: no imp fr next* 16/1
U36- 6 2 ½ **Dutch Canyon (IRE)**[13] 5495 5-11-1 **96**........................(p) LucyAlexander 85
(N W Alexander) *bhd: drvn along 1/2-way: sme hdwy and edgd lft 2 out: nvr able to chal* 20/1
005- 7 23 **Wyfield Rose**[14] 5473 6-10-10 **91**....................................(p) BrianHughes 59
(Alistair Whillans) *chsd ldrs tl rdn and wknd fr 3 out* 10/1
050- 8 2 ½ **Proud Gamble (IRE)**[40] 5015 6-10-6 **90**........................(t) CraigNichol[(3)] 56
(Rose Dobbin) *mstkes in midfield: rdn after 4 out: wknd after next* 33/1
003- P **Zermatt (IRE)**[50] 4827 6-11-4 **99**..................................(p) DougieCostello
(John Quinn) *chsd ldrs: hit 4th: drvn and struggling 4 out: sn btn: t.o whn p.u bef last* 13/2[3]
005- P **Mr Hopeful (IRE)**[32] 5129 6-11-10 **105**.......................... WilsonRenwick
(Donald McCain) *cl up tl wknd fr 8th: lost tch and p.u bef 2 out* 20/1
222- P **Spoils Of War (IRE)**[55] 4728 6-11-12 **107**........................ PeterBuchanan
(Lucinda Russell) *led: hit 7th: hdd 5 out: wknd fr next: t.o whn p.u bef 2 out* 7/1
P **Mist One (IRE)**[59] 4662 7-11-4 **106**.............................. LiamMcKenna[(7)]
(J J Lambe, Ire) *in tch to 4th: sn lost pl: lost tch and p.u bef 8th* 33/1

5m 40.0s (-1.00) **Going Correction** -0.025s/f (Good) 12 Ran SP% 115.4
Speed ratings (Par 105): **100,98,94,92,90 90,82,81,,**
CSF £87.96 CT £306.13 TOTE £5.00: £1.60, £7.60, £2.30; EX 128.10 Trifecta £1255.30.
Owner M S Borders Racing Club & Partners **Bred** Patrick Cronin **Trained** Greystoke, Cumbria

FOCUS
A moderate novice handicap, run at an average gallop. The winner is rated in line with the best of his form for his old yard.

140 ANNE MACDONALD BIRTHDAY BASH (S) H'CAP CHASE (17 fncs) 2m 7f 96y
2:50 (2:50) (Class 5) (0-100,99) 5-Y-0+ £3,249 (£954; £477; £238)

Form RPR
212- 1 **My Friend George**[22] 5324 9-10-11 **84**..........................(p) HenryBrooke 96+
(Kenneth Slack) *hld up towards rr: stdy hdwy and prom 11th: effrt and swtchd rt after 2 out: led run-in: ears pricked: drvn out* 2/1[1]
55P- 2 2 ¼ **Winter Alchemy (IRE)**[32] 5134 10-11-2 **89**......................(p) BrianHarding 97
(Nicky Richards) *in tch: smooth hdwy to ld 2 out: rdn and hdd run-in: kpt on same pce* 9/1[3]
465- 3 6 **Chicago Outfit (IRE)**[16] 5423 10-10-8 **86**................(p) JonathonBewley[(5)] 89
(George Bewley) *led tl rdn and hdd 2 out: outpcd whn hit last: no ex* 5/1[2]
3PP- 4 2 ¾ **Brokethegate**[40] 5014 10-10-7 **85**............................ DiarmuidO'Regan[(5)] 84
(Chris Grant) *cl up: drvn and outpcd bef 2 out: no imp bef last* 16/1
6UP- 5 18 **Silent Snow (IRE)**[12] 5516 10-10-11 **91**.........................(p) MrWHRReed[(7)] 74
(W T Reed) *midfield on outside: drvn and outpcd 12th: rallied bef 2 out: sn no imp* 66/1
24P- 6 nk **Pistol Basc (FR)**[31] 5160 11-10-10 **86**................................ TonyKelly[(3)] 69
(Rebecca Menzies) *hld up: stdy hdwy 12th: rdn bef 4 out: wknd bef 2 out* 18/1
300- 7 nse **Saddle Pack (IRE)**[16] 5423 12-9-11 **77**.......................... JamieHamilton[(7)] 60
(James Walton) *bhd: pushed along 1/2-way: drvn along 5 out: nvr able to chal* 10/1
322- 8 8 **West Ship Master (IRE)**[16] 5423 11-11-5 **99**........(tp) JonathanMoore[(7)] 76
(Paul Stafford, Ire) *hld up: stdy hdwy whn hit 12th: rdn and wknd fr 3 out* 5/1[2]
5P2- 9 29 **Oxalido (FR)**[14] 5473 13-11-5 **95**.................................. JohnKington[(3)] 59
(Stuart Coltherd) *hld up: hdwy and in tch 5th: struggling 12th: rallied 4 out: wknd after next: t.o* 9/1[3]
PPF- P **Ultiep (FR)**[62] 4577 7-9-10 **74** oh9 ow1..............................(b) DaleIrving[(5)]
(Karen McLintock) *nt fluent: in tch: outpcd whn hit 11th: struggling fr next: t.o whn p.u bef 2 out* 40/1
5P6- P **War On (IRE)**[16] 5424 8-9-11 **77**..............................(b) ThomasDowson[(7)]
(Victor Thompson) *nt fluent on occasions: midfield: drvn along 12th: wknd after 5 out: t.o whn p.u bef 2 out* 25/1

6m 5.0s (-3.00) **Going Correction** -0.025s/f (Good) 11 Ran SP% 114.7
Speed ratings: **104,103,101,100,94 94,94,91,81,,**
CSF £19.94 CT £79.42 TOTE £2.50: £1.10, £2.60, £2.60; EX 20.40 Trifecta £95.00.There was no bid for the winner.
Owner A Slack **Bred** G A Slack And H D Sayer **Trained** Hilton, Cumbria

FOCUS
A typically weak handicap of its type. It was run at a fair gallop and only four mattered from the third-last. The winner is rated in line with the best of his 2013 form, the second to his mark.

141 BEDMAX H'CAP CHASE (19 fncs) 3m 2f 39y
3:20 (3:20) (Class 4) (0-115,115) 5-Y-0+ £7,797 (£2,289; £1,144; £572)

Form RPR
P4U- 1 **Winged Crusader (IRE)**[60] 4623 7-11-6 **109**......(v) SamTwiston-Davies 121+
(Nigel Twiston-Davies) *cl up: led 7th: rdn clr fr 2 out: readily* 5/1[3]
522- 2 14 **Viking Rebel (IRE)**[32] 5135 13-9-12 **94**........................(p) MrWHRReed[(7)] 92
(W T Reed) *led to 7th: cl up: outpcd 5 out: rallied to take 2nd 3 out: clsd on wnr bef last: outpcd between last 2* 9/1
5/F- 3 2 **Revocation**[74] 4364 7-11-12 **115**.................................... PeterBuchanan 110
(Lucinda Russell) *t.k.h in midfield: hdwy and prom whn mstke 9th: rdn along after 3 out: no imp fr next* 7/2[2]
215- 4 ½ **Gibbstown (IRE)**[32] 5134 9-10-9 **105**..................(p) JonathanMoore[(7)] 99
(Paul Stafford, Ire) *hld up: pushed along fr 12th: no imp fr 3 out* 16/1
P0- 5 2 ¼ **Stoney (IRE)**[32] 5135 8-9-7 **89** oh1.................................. MissETodd[(7)] 81
(Victor Thompson) *nt fluent on occasions: in tch: lost pl 5th: drvn along fr 12th: no imp fr 4 out* 33/1
/PP- 6 3 **Action Master**[25] 5274 9-11-5 **115**.................................... StevenFox[(7)] 106
(Sandy Thomson) *hld up: pushed along 12th: hdwy 13th: effrt and cl 3rd whn nt fluent 2 out: sn rdn and no ex* 16/1
611- 7 4 ½ **Resolute Reformer (IRE)**[16] 5423 6-10-13 **105**.................. DerekFox[(3)] 90
(Stuart Coltherd) *in tch: hdwy to chse wnr 5 out to after next: rdn and wknd after 3 out* 3/1[1]
305- 8 25 **Romany Ryme**[12] 5518 9-10-11 **105**..........................(v) GaryRutherford[(5)] 67
(George Bewley) *prom: lost pl 6th: rdn 1/2-way: n.d after: no ch whn blnd 2 out* 10/1
420- P **Jewellery (IRE)**[16] 5422 8-10-12 **108**..............................(t) JamieHamilton[(7)]
(Katie Scott) *nt fluent: a bhd: struggling fnl circ: t.o whn p.u bef 4 out* 16/1

The Form Book Jumps 2015-16, Raceform Ltd, Newbury, RG14 5SJ

214/ P **Farmer Matt (IRE)**[402] 5089 9-11-8 114....................(t) ConorShoemark(3)
(Fergal O'Brien) *in tch: rdn 12th: struggling 14th: t.o whn p.u bef 3 out*
10/1

6m 56.5s (9.30) **Going Correction** -0.025s/f (Good) **10** Ran SP% **112.7**
Speed ratings: **84,79,79,78,78 77,75,68,,**
CSF £47.38 CT £175.50 TOTE £4.80: £1.40, £2.90, £1.70; EX 58.30 Trifecta £177.30.
Owner Imperial Racing Partnership No 6 **Bred** Mrs Hugh Baird **Trained** Naunton, Gloucs

FOCUS

A modest staying handicap. This rates a step up from the winner.

142 PRINCIPAL & PROSPER CONDITIONAL JOCKEYS' H'CAP HURDLE (8 hdls) 2m 51y

3:55 (3:55) (Class 4) (0-120,118) 4-Y-O+ **£3,898** (£1,144; £572; £286)

Form RPR

/65- **1** **Turtle Watch**[19] 5361 7-11-4 **110**.................................... GrahamWatters 122+
(Jim Goldie) *hld up: nt fluent 3rd: hdwy after 4 out: rdn to ld appr 2 out: rdn clr* **15/8**[1]

320- **2** *12* **Peters Grey (IRE)**[19] 5361 5-11-6 **112**.......................... CallumBewley 110
(R Mike Smith) *hld up in tch: rdn and hdwy bef 2 out: chsd (clr) wnr between last 2: sn no imp* **7/2**[2]

233- **3** *nk* **Suprise Vendor (IRE)**[16] 4973 9-11-5 **111**.......................... DerekFox 109
(Stuart Coltherd) *led to 3rd: cl up: led briefly 3 out: rdn and outpcd bef next: rallied last: no imp* **5/1**[3]

140- **4** *7* **Cadore (IRE)**[46] 4914 7-11-1 **107**................................(p) AdamNicol 98
(Lucy Normile) *prom: effrt and rdn bef 2 out: edgd lft: outpcd bef last* **16/1**

134- **5** *3 ¾* **Politeness (FR)**[23] 5315 6-10-13 **105**.............................. CraigNichol 94
(Rose Dobbin) *hld up in tch: rdn bef 2 out: wknd bef last* **11/2**

P44/ **6** *6* **Shanroe Society (IRE)**[341] 532 9-10-2 **102**...........(b) LiamMcKenna(8) 85
(J J Lambe, Ire) *bhd: outpcd 1/2-way: no ch whn hmpd last* **16/1**

PPP/ **7** *43* **Kealigolane (IRE)**[394] 5210 11-11-12 **118**.......................... JoeColliver 62
(Barry Murtagh) *cl up: led 3rd to 3 out: rdn and wknd bef next: t.o* **40/1**

410- **F** **Stentorian (IRE)**[19] 5361 7-10-8 **100**.......................(v) DiarmuidO'Regan 89
(Linda Perratt) *prom: led after 3 out to appr next: sn outpcd: 10 l 5th whn fell last* **8/1**

3m 55.9s (-5.90) **Going Correction** -0.025s/f (Good) **8** Ran SP% **114.4**
Speed ratings (Par 105): **112,106,106,102,101 98,78,**
CSF £9.22 CT £27.09 TOTE £2.60: £1.10, £2.00, £2.70; EX 11.00 Trifecta £38.50.
Owner Mr & Mrs Raymond Anderson Green **Bred** Design And Planning Consultants Ltd **Trained** Uplawmoor, E Renfrews

FOCUS

This conditional riders' handicap looked competitive for the class and the placed horses set the level.

143 BERWICK SPEEDWAY EVERY SATURDAY KIDS FREE NOVICES' HUNTERS' CHASE (FOR THE CHARLIE BROWN TROPHY) (16 fncs) 2m 5f 133y

4:30 (4:30) (Class 5) 5-Y-O+ **£2,495** (£774; £386; £193)

Form RPR

533- **1** **Chanceofa Lifetime (IRE)**[16] 5420 8-11-5 113........ ThomasDowson(7) 102+
(Victor Thompson) *chsd ldrs: hdwy to ld 3 out: styd on wl u.p fr last* **11/4**[2]

U46- **2** *1 ¾* **Mister D (IRE)**[13] 5494 9-11-5 88.............................. MrNOrpwood(7) 98
(George Bewley) *cl up: chal 4 out: rdn 2 out: kpt on fr last* **12/1**

F3-P **3** *26* **Darsi Dancer (IRE)**[4] 80 7-11-5 92.......................... MrSWColtherd(7) 81
(Stuart Coltherd) *led to 4 out: drvn and wknd bef 2 out* **5/2**[1]

4- **4** *13* **Durban Gold**[11] 8-11-0 0.. MissJWalton(5) 56
(Mrs D Walton) *nt fluent: bhd and sn detached: nvr on terms* **5/2**[1]

00/ **P** **Mr Shahady (IRE)**[24] 10-11-5 0.................................... MissETodd(7)
(Victor Thompson) *prom: outpcd 10th: struggling fr next: 5th and btn whn hit 2 out: sn p.u* **33/1**

P **Afterclass (IRE)**[30] 7-11-9 97...............................(tp) MrKitAlexander(3)
(N W Alexander) *prom: outpcd 10th: struggling fr next: t.o whn p.u after 3 out* **13/2**[3]

P **Heckley Herbert**[24] 8-11-12 0.. MissCWalton
(James Walton) *bhd and nvr gng wl: t.o whn p.u bef 10th* **20/1**

5m 42.2s (13.00) **Going Correction** -0.025s/f (Good) **7** Ran SP% **112.5**
Speed ratings: **75,74,64,60,,**
CSF £31.02 TOTE £3.20: £1.60, £5.90; EX 36.10 Trifecta £110.90.
Owner V Thompson **Bred** Mrs Maura T Furlong **Trained** Alnwick, Northumbria

FOCUS

A weak novice hunter chase in which the first pair dominated from three out. The first two are rated in line with the best of their hurdle figures.

144 CHEERS BAR STANDARD OPEN NATIONAL HUNT FLAT RACE (DIV I) 2m 51y

5:05 (5:05) (Class 5) 4-6-Y-O **£2,599** (£763; £381; £190)

Form RPR

- **1** **Micklegate Run** 4-10-12 0.. PaulMoloney 104+
(Alan Swinbank) *t.k.h: prom: shkn up to ld over 1f out: sn drvn and edgd lft: hld on wl fnl f* **4/1**[2]

2- **2** *½* **Gully's Edge**[46] 4915 5-11-2 0..................................(t) BrianHughes 107+
(Malcolm Jefferson) *pressed ldr: rdn and ev ch over 1f out: kpt on u.p ins fnl f: hld nr fin* **1/1**[1]

1- **3** *2 ½* **Catching Shadows (IRE)**[110] 3721 6-11-7 0.................. DaleIrving(5) 115
(James Ewart) *plld hrd in midfield: stdy hdwy and ev ch over 1f out: sn rdn and hung rt: no ex ins fnl f* **6/1**[3]

4 *2 ¾* **Kalaniti (IRE)** 4-10-0 0.. DiarmuidO'Regan(5) 91
(Chris Grant) *hld up: stdy hdwy 3f out: shkn up and hung lft wl over 1f out: kpt on fnl f: no imp* **33/1**

661- **5** *5* **Benny's Secret (IRE)**[60] 4622 5-11-9 0.......................... LucyAlexander 105
(N W Alexander) *led: rdn and hdd over 1f out: sn wknd* **14/1**

6 *1* **Seven Devils (IRE)**[94] 5-10-13 0.................................... DerekFox(3) 96
(Lucinda Russell) *midfield: effrt and pushed along 3f out: outpcd fnl 2f* **8/1**

- **7** *6* **Lybowler** 5-10-13 0.. GrahamWatters(3) 90
(James Ewart) *t.k.h: hld up: n.m.r and stmbld bnd over 3f out: wknd over 2f out* **33/1**

05- **8** *½* **Herecomesnelson (IRE)**[46] 4915 6-10-9 0.................. JamieHamilton(7) 90
(Katie Scott) *t.k.h: chsd ldrs tl rdn and wknd over 2f out* **33/1**

9 *1 ½* **Red Story** 4-10-12 0.. BrianHarding 84
(Alistair Whillans) *t.k.h: hld up: struggling wl over 2f out: sn btn* **22/1**

10 *8* **Play Practice** 5-10-4 0.. MissCWalton(5) 73
(James Walton) *hld up: outpcd over 3f out: sn btn* **100/1**

000- **11** *10* **Turtleplex**[16] 5425 4-10-5 0.. HenryBrooke 59
(Michael Smith) *midfield on outside: struggling 3f out: sn btn* **100/1**

3m 58.8s (2.60) **Going Correction** -0.025s/f (Good)
WFA 4 from 5yo+ 4lb **11** Ran SP% **117.2**
Speed ratings: **92,91,90,89,86 86,83,83,82,78 74**
CSF £7.93 TOTE £4.70: £1.30, £1.30, £1.40; EX 10.20 Trifecta £38.60.
Owner Andrew Sparks **Bred** D Cantillon And E Cantillon **Trained** Melsonby, N Yorks

FOCUS

Not a bad bumper. It was run at a stop-start gallop and is rated around the second, fifth and eighth.

145 CHEERS BAR STANDARD OPEN NATIONAL HUNT FLAT RACE (DIV II) 2m 51y

5:40 (5:40) (Class 5) 4-6-Y-O **£2,599** (£763; £381; £190)

Form RPR

1 **Dante's Way (IRE)** 6-11-2 0.. BrianHughes 112+
(Malcolm Jefferson) *hld up bhd ldng gp: stdy hdwy 4f out: effrt and cl ldr over 1f out: rn green: led ins fnl f: hld on wl cl home* **9/4**[2]

3- **2** *shd* **Nuts Well**[16] 5425 4-10-9 0.. TonyKelly(3) 108+
(Ann Hamilton) *t.k.h: prom: smooth hdwy to ld over 2f out: rdn and edgd rt over 1f out: hdd ins fnl f: rallied: jst hld* **15/2**

3 *11* **Danmurphysdoor (IRE)**[151] 6-10-13 0.................... GrahamWatters(3) 102
(Tim Vaughan) *hld up in midfield: stdy hdwy to ld over 6f out: rdn and hdd over 2f out: edgd rt: outpcd over 1f out* **6/1**[3]

0- **4** *½* **Limos (GER)**[16] 5426 5-10-11 0.................................... DaleIrving(5) 102
(James Ewart) *hld up: smooth hdwy and prom over 2f out: sn rdn: outpcd over 1f out* **20/1**

03- **5** *8* **Tickanrun (IRE)**[47] 4894 5-10-11 0.......................... DiarmuidO'Regan(5) 94
(Chris Grant) *prom: drvn and outpcd over 4f out: edgd lft and rallied 2f out: nvr able to chal* **22/1**

231- **6** *5* **Down The Line (IRE)**[22] 5331 5-11-9 0.......................... PaulMoloney 97
(Alan Swinbank) *t.k.h: cl up: chal over 6f out: rdn and wknd over 2f out* **15/8**[1]

40- **7** *½* **Ange Des Malberaux (FR)**[16] 5425 5-11-2 0.................. LucyAlexander 89
(James Ewart) *hld up: rdn and outpcd over 5f out: n.d after* **50/1**

0- **8** *8* **Thisulldaeus**[18] 5395 4-10-12 0...................................... BrianHarding 78
(Jim Goldie) *led to over 6f out: rdn and wknd fr 3f out* **33/1**

9 *43* **Coachie Bear** 4-10-12 0.. WilsonRenwick 40
(Keith Dalgleish) *hld up in tch: struggling over 5f out: sn btn: eased whn no ch* **14/1**

3m 52.3s (-3.90) **Going Correction** -0.025s/f (Good)
WFA 4 from 5yo+ 4lb **9** Ran SP% **112.3**
Speed ratings: **108,107,102,102,98 96,96,92,72**
CSF £17.70 TOTE £3.60: £1.20, £3.20, £2.00; EX 17.40 Trifecta £112.90.
Owner Trevor Hemmings **Bred** Ms Margaret Treacy **Trained** Norton, N Yorks

FOCUS

This wasn't as strong as the preceding division. However, it was a more truly run affair and the first pair came well clear. The time was good for a bumper.

T/Plt: £61.30 to a £1 stake. Pool: £44,373.27 - 527.60 winning tickets T/Qpdt: £12.90 to a £1 stake. Pool: £3,843.65 - 219.70 winning tickets **Richard Young**

[83]UTTOXETER (L-H)

Wednesday, May 6

OFFICIAL GOING: Soft (heavy in places on chase course) changing to heavy after race 2 (6.00)

Wind: fresh 1/2 against Weather: overcast, heavy showers, cold, very breezy

146 32REDSPORT.COM "NATIONAL HUNT" NOVICES' HURDLE (12 hdls) 3m

5:30 (5:30) (Class 4) 4-Y-O+ **£3,378** (£992; £496; £248)

Form RPR

032- **1** **Robbie Rabbit (IRE)**[21] 5343 5-10-13 125.................... TomScudamore 124+
(Nigel Hawke) *nt fluent: led tl appr 2nd: sn pushed along: reminders 8th and appr 3 out: upsides 2 out: sn led and edgd lft: jst hld on* **4/11**[1]

5- **2** *hd* **Mustmeetalady (IRE)**[19] 5380 5-10-13 0...................... RichieMcLernon 123
(Jonjo O'Neill) *led appr 2nd: drvn 3 out: hdd and swtchd rt sn after 2 out: rallied run-in: jst hld* **12/1**

232- **3** *25* **Bryden Boy (IRE)**[22] 5325 5-10-13 114.................(p) PeterCarberry 103
(Jennie Candlish) *trckd ldrs: 3rd 7th: drvn appr 3 out: wknd appr 2 out* **4/1**[2]

2- **4** *87* **Callmenewtown (IRE)**[49] 4854 8-10-13 0....................(t) JamesDavies 11
(Graeme McPherson) *chsd ldrs: drvn 5th: lost pl 8th: sn bhd: t.o after next* **5/1**[3]

533- **5** *½* **Quincy Magoo (IRE)**[25] 5285 6-10-13 0.......................... MarkGrant 10
(Neil King) *in rr: reminders 7th: sn lost pl and bhd: mstke 9th: sn t.o* **20/1**

3/P- **6** *47* **Picodean**[24] 5293 7-10-13 0..(t[1]) RhysFlint
(Robert Stephens) *nt jump wl: chsd ldrs: j.lft 1st: lost pl 7th: t.o next: eventually completed* **33/1**

553- **F** **Princeton Royale (IRE)**[73] 4381 6-10-13 0.................... TrevorWhelan
(Neil King) *trckd ldrs: t.k.h: 4th 8th: reminders next: 4th and wl hld whn fell 3 out* **18/1**

0- **P** **Vizzy's Thunder**[30] 5180 7-10-13 0..................................(t) LeeEdwards
(Tony Carroll) *in rr: drvn 4th: reminders 6th: sn t.o: p.u bef 8th: b.b.v* **100/1**

6m 7.7s (17.70) **Going Correction** +0.925s/f (Soft) **8** Ran SP% **131.6**
Speed ratings (Par 105): **107,106,98,69,69 53,,**
CSF £8.88 TOTE £1.50: £1.02, £2.60, £2.10; EX 9.60 Trifecta £33.50.
Owner Mark J Phillips **Bred** Robert McCarthy **Trained** Stoodleigh, Devon

FOCUS

Hurdles had been moved in by 6yds to provide a fresh strip of ground. Once again, the first fence in the back straight was omitted in all chases. Intermittent rain fell during the day, the meeting started with heavy showers and the jockeys said the ground was "soft to heavy" and "pretty testing". A maiden novice hurdle in all but name, they got racing a long way from home and it looks to be only modest form. The winner was below his best.

147 32RED CONDITIONAL JOCKEYS' "NATIONAL HUNT" MAIDEN HURDLE (9 hdls) 2m

6:00 (6:00) (Class 5) 4-Y-O+ **£2,339** (£686; £343)

Form RPR

442- **1** **Curious Carlos**[14] 5462 6-11-0 0.. SeanBowen 116+
(Peter Bowen) *hld up in last: smooth hdwy 3 out: led appr last: pushed clr: v readily* **6/5**[1]

042- **2** *3* **Detroit Blues**[17] 5411 5-11-0 0.....(t) MichealNolan 108
(Jamie Snowden) *trckd ldr: led 2 out: sn drvn: hdd appr last: no ch w wnr* 9/4[2]

226- **3** *9* **Bobble Emerald (IRE)**[24] 5293 7-11-0 0..... ChrisWard 100
(Martin Keighley) *led: hit 2nd: pushed along and hit 3 out: hdd next: sn wknd* 5/2[3]

4m 8.5s (16.50) **Going Correction** +1.075s/f (Soft) **3** Ran SP% **104.8**
Speed ratings (Par 103): **101,99,95**
CSF £3.88 TOTE £2.10; EX 3.80 Trifecta £3.10.
Owner Carl Pyne **Bred** Carl Pyne **Trained** Little Newcastle, Pembrokes

FOCUS
All three of these held some sort of chance, they jumped in a line two out and the form shouldn't be disregarded because of the sparse line-up. The cosy winner is on the upgrade.

148 32RED CASINO H'CAP HURDLE (12 hdls) 3m
6:30 (6:30) (Class 5) (0-100,95) 4-Y-0+ **£2,339** (£686; £343; £171)

Form RPR

526- **1** **Earcomesthedream (IRE)**[55] 4735 12-11-5 **95**.....(b) ArchieBellamy(7) 108+
(Peter Pritchard) *rn in snatches: drvn along fr 3rd: lost pl next: hdwy to chse ldrs 6th: led sn after 9th: forged clr next: drew rt away drvn rt out* 14/1

PP4- **2** *30* **Fromthetop (IRE)**[30] 5185 9-10-5 **74**.....(v) TomScudamore 59
(Michael Scudamore) *chsd ldrs: drvn along 7th: lost pl next: hit 9th and reminders: styd on to chse wnr appr 2 out* 4/1[3]

523- **3** *5* **The Last Bridge**[49] 4855 8-11-1 **84**.....(p) RichardJohnson 62
(Susan Johnson) *chsd ldrs: drvn 7th: lost pl bef 3 out: distant 4th last: 3rd post* 7/2[2]

605- **4** *nse* **Cadgers Hole**[73] 4389 8-10-8 **77**.....(t[1]) WillKennedy 55
(Lynn Siddall) *hld up in rr: hdwy to chse ldrs 8th: clr 3rd 3 out: sn wl outpcd* 12/1

/53- **5** *6* **Young Lou**[163] 2716 6-9-9 **71**.....(p) JosephPalmowski(7) 43
(Robin Dickin) *led to 2nd: lost pl 7th: bhd fr next* 10/1

603- **P** **W Six Times**[30] 5185 9-11-3 **86**..... JackQuinlan
(Alistair Whillans) *w ldrs: lost pl bef 3 out: sn bhd: t.o whn p.u bef 2 out* 3/1[1]

P61- **P** **Comical Red**[42] 4989 7-11-4 **94**.....(b) PaulJohn(7)
(Mark Gillard) *led 2nd: reminders 9th: sn hdd: wknd rapidly next: t.o 2 out: p.u bef last* 5/1

410/ **P** **Rigolo Ville (FR)**[514] 2980 10-11-11 **94**..... AlainCawley
(Richard Hobson) *hld up: t.k.h: jnd ldrs 4th: clr 2nd bef 3 out: wknd rapidly appr 2 out: sn bhd: t.o whn p.u bef last: lame* 20/1

6m 14.8s (24.80) **Going Correction** +1.075s/f (Soft) **8** Ran SP% **112.1**
Speed ratings (Par 103): **101,91,89,89,87 , ,**
CSF £67.29 TOTE £9.70: £3.40, £1.60, £1.60; EX 60.80 Trifecta £354.10.
Owner Woodland Generators/Late DR Pritchard **Bred** Cornelius O'Riordan **Trained** Whatcote, Warwicks

FOCUS
Continuing rain resulted in an official ground change prior to this race to heavy. Well grouped for most of the way, but an eventual easy winner and this looks like weak form. Arguably a pb from the veteran winner.

149 £10 FREE AT 32RED.COM H'CAP CHASE (18 fncs 2 omitted) 3m 2f
7:00 (7:00) (Class 4) (0-120,119) 5-Y-0 **£3,798** (£1,122; £561; £280; £140)

Form RPR

364- **1** **Loughalder (IRE)**[46] 4925 9-10-12 **105**.....(bt[1]) CharliePoste 117+
(Matt Sheppard) *mde all: kpt on to forge clr fr 2 out: 8 l ahd whn mstke last: eased towards fin* 5/1

212- **2** *3 3/4* **Ultimatum Du Roy (FR)**[36] 5087 7-11-11 **118**.....(tp) NoelFehily 124
(Alex Hales) *trckd ldrs: cl 2nd 14th: 4 l down whn blnd and rdr lost iron 2 out: kpt on run-in* 3/1[1]

224- **3** *5* **King Massini (IRE)**[15] 5450 9-11-8 **115**..... AdamWedge 113
(Evan Williams) *in rr: chsd ldrs 14th: handy 3rd appr next: one pce fr 3 out* 9/2[3]

133- **4** *15* **Arbeo (IRE)**[66] 4510 9-11-6 **113**..... MarcGoldstein 101
(Diana Grissell) *chsd wnr: hit 5th: drvn along fr 9th: reminders 13th: wknd 4 out* 11/2

546- **5** *8* **As De Fer (FR)**[51] 4818 9-11-4 **111**.....(t) RyanMahon 86
(Anthony Honeyball) *trckd ldrs: drvn 14th: lost pl bef next: sn bhd* 7/1

541- **P** **Kingcora (FR)**[111] 3694 7-11-12 **119**..... AidanColeman
(Venetia Williams) *chsd ldrs: lost pl 14th: bhd bef next: t.o whn p.u bef 3 out* 7/2[2]

(13.60) **Going Correction** +0.675s/f (Soft) **6** Ran SP% **110.0**
Speed ratings: **106,104,103,98,96**
CSF £19.80 TOTE £6.70: £3.10, £1.80; EX 25.20 Trifecta £112.40.
Owner Simon Gegg & Tony Scrivin **Bred** Tom Burns **Trained** Eastnor, H'fords

FOCUS
The feature race on the card but it didn't looks the strongest 0-120 with a number of these having questions to answer. The winner was very well in on the best of last year's figures.

150 32RED ON THE APP STORE NOVICES' H'CAP CHASE (14 fncs 2 omitted) 2m 6f 105y
7:30 (7:30) (Class 5) (0-100,99) 5-Y-0+ **£2,729** (£801; £400; £200)

Form RPR

501- **1** **Courtown Oscar (IRE)**[22] 5324 6-11-12 **99**..... JamesReveley 119+
(Philip Kirby) *trckd ldrs: handy 2nd 9th: led 4 out: jnd last: fnd ex last 75yds* 6/5[1]

250- **2** *3 1/2* **Young Cheddar (IRE)**[16] 5429 8-11-4 **91**..... NickScholfield 103
(Polly Gundry) *in rr: hdwy to chse ldrs 6th: handy 3rd 10th: chsd wnr 4 out: upsides last: kpt on same pce* 5/1[3]

44P- **3** *29* **Wing Mira (IRE)**[17] 5407 7-10-0 **73** oh13.....(b) LiamTreadwell 62
(Venetia Williams) *led to 3rd: led after 7th: hdd 4 out: wknd next* 10/1

345- **4** *17* **Flash Tommie (IRE)**[103] 3838 7-11-5 **95**..... JonathanEngland(3) 61
(Michael Appleby) *chsd ldrs: led 3rd: hdd after 7th: lost pl bef 4 out: lft distant 4th 3 out* 9/2[2]

3F3- **R** **Houseparty**[19] 5372 7-9-10 **76**..... MissTWorsley(7)
(Diana Grissell) *in rr: mstke 5th: reminders next: chsd ldrs 10th: sn bhd: distant 4th whn ref 3 out* 9/1

PP0- **P** **Quintano (GER)**[22] 5324 7-10-12 **85**.....(b[1]) RhysFlint
(Heather Dalton) *t.k.h: trckd ldrs: wknd after 10th: distant 5th whn blnd 4 out: sn p.u* 18/1

5/4- **P** **Vauban Du Seuil (FR)**[340] 542 6-11-12 **99**..... KielanWoods
(Alex Hales) *in rr: bhd fr 8th: t.o whn j. slowly next: p.u bef 10th* 14/1

6m 13.9s (25.40) **Going Correction** +1.175s/f (Heav) **7** Ran SP% **111.3**
Speed ratings: **102,100,90,84, ,**
CSF £7.57 TOTE £2.20: £1.30, £2.10; EX 6.90 Trifecta £83.40.
Owner Nojab, Dolan & Sadler **Bred** Lorcan Allen **Trained** East Appleton, N Yorks

FOCUS
The contest took place with the rain lashing down and not many of these fancied it. Just moderate form. The winner built on his recent hurdle win and there's probably more to come.

151 MOUNT ARGUS OPEN HUNTERS' CHASE (14 fncs 2 omitted) 2m 6f 105y
8:00 (8:00) (Class 6) 5-Y-0+ **£1,247** (£387; £193; £96)

Form RPR

5/F- **1** **Owen Glendower (IRE)**[19] 5377 10-11-11 0..... CiaranGethings(3) 118+
(Sophie Leech) *hld up: hdwy to trck ldrs 10th: handy 3rd 3 out: led next: shkn up and styd on run-in* 8/1

250- **2** *3 3/4* **Rouge Et Blanc (FR)**[27] 5239 10-11-7 124..... MrLeoMahon(7) 113+
(Oliver Sherwood) *hld up in rr: hdwy to trck ldrs 9th: 2nd last: styd on same pce* 1/1[1]

326/ **3** *4* **Topaze Collonges (FR)**[66] 8-11-7 0..... MrJTeal(7) 109
(Mrs Emma Clark) *chsd ldrs: led 4 out: hdd 2 out: kpt on one pce appr last* 16/1

/50- **4** *10* **Brunswick Gold (IRE)**[27] 5239 10-11-13 122..... MrStuartRobinson(5) 105
(Miss Rose Grissell) *chsd ldrs: drvn 4 out: wknd fr 2 out* 15/2[3]

41-3 **5** *3 1/4* **Executive Benefit (IRE)**[7] 16 8-11-4 99..... MissADalton(7) 95
(J J O'Shea) *in rr: hdwy 9th: chsng ldrs next: drvn 4 out: wknd after next* 4/1[2]

P/P- **6** *23* **Mostly Bob (IRE)**[13] 5503 12-11-9 115.....(tp) MrRobertHawker(5) 73
(Sophie Leech) *chsd ldrs: led 2nd: hdd bef 4th: led 7th to next: sn drvn: outpcd and lost pl 10th: sn bhd* 16/1

132/ **7** *3 1/4* **Gemini Ahhs (IRE)**[30] 12-11-7 0..... MrTEley(7) 70
(Mrs S M McPherson) *prom: reminders 4th: sn lost pl: bhd and reminders 7th: t.o next* 33/1

/0P- **8** *2 1/4* **Woodlark Island (IRE)**[10] 9-11-7 0.....(b) MrHFNugent(7) 67
(A Campbell) *w ldrs: led bef 4th: hdd 7th: led next: hdd 4 out: sn lost pl end bhd* 100/1

3P/ **P** **Roskeen Boy (IRE)**[30] 10-12-0 0..... CharlieDeutsch
(W M Wanless) *chsd ldrs: lost pl 7th: sn bhd: t.o whn p.u bef 9th* 100/1

P **Parthian Empire**[10] 9-11-9 0..... MrJonathanBailey(5)
(W M Wanless) *in rr: bhd fr 9th: t.o whn p.u bef 3 out* 80/1

4U3- **P** **Hidden Future (IRE)**[19] 5377 9-11-7 98.....(v[1]) MrRichardCollinson(7)
(Mrs S J Stilgoe) *in rr: hdwy 5th: sn chsng ldrs: lost pl 8th: bhd 10th: t.o whn p.u bef 3 out* 16/1

6m 19.7s (31.20) **Going Correction** +1.175s/f (Heav) **11** Ran SP% **116.7**
Speed ratings: **92,90,89,85,84 76,75,74, ,**
CSF £17.11 TOTE £11.70: £2.70, £1.10, £3.50; EX 23.50 Trifecta £151.20.
Owner O'Brien,Mitchell,Frame,Lawton & Leech **Bred** Kenilworth House Stud **Trained** Elton, Gloucs

FOCUS
Solid hunter chase form, with the right horses coming to the fore. The second was 20lb below his best though.

152 32RED.COM MARES' STANDARD OPEN NATIONAL HUNT FLAT RACE 2m
8:30 (8:30) (Class 6) 4-6-Y-0 **£1,559** (£457; £228; £114)

Form RPR

1 **Mozo** 4-10-8 0..... TomScudamore 101+
(David Pipe) *hld up in rr: hdwy 7f out: sn trcking ldrs: 2nd over 3f out: led over 2f out: pushed out* 7/1[3]

3U- **2** *4 1/2* **Awesome Rosie**[48] 4866 4-10-8 0..... WayneHutchinson 96+
(Alan King) *hld up towards rr: hdwy 7f out: sn trcking ldrs: 3rd over 3f out: chsd wnr over 1f out: no imp* 9/4[1]

35- **3** *1 1/4* **Sainte Ladylime (FR)**[46] 4901 4-10-8 0..... NoelFehily 94
(Donald McCain) *w ldrs: led over 4f out: hdd over 2f out: kpt on same pce* 9/1

4 *7* **Colin's Sister** 4-10-8 0..... PaddyBrennan 87
(Fergal O'Brien) *mid-div: chsd ldrs 7f out: one pce fnl 3f* 16/1

4- **5** *11* **Omgnotanother (IRE)**[46] 4901 4-10-8 0..... AdamWedge 76
(Evan Williams) *mid-div: chsd ldrs 7f out: sn drvn: wknd fnl 3f* 25/1

6 *10* **Penny Option (IRE)** 6-10-12 0..... TomO'Brien 70
(Robert Stephens) *chsd ldrs: drvn over 4f out: sn outpcd: wknd over 2f out* 16/1

7 *8* **Potters Midnight** 5-10-12 0..... JackQuinlan 62
(Lucy Wadham) *w ldrs: drvn over 3f out: sn wknd* 25/1

- **8** *11* **Amber Alert** 5-10-12 0.....(t) AidanColeman 51
(Anthony Honeyball) *chsd ldrs: rdn over 4f out: sn wknd* 12/1

9 *26* **Bishopstone Girl (IRE)** 4-10-1 0..... MrZBaker(7) 21
(Paul Cowley) *mid-div: chsng ldrs whn hung rt bnd after 6f: hung bdly rt and lost pl 7f out: bhd fnl 5f: t.o* 50/1

10 *8* **Zakti (IRE)** 5-10-12 0..... BrendanPowell 17
(Jamie Snowden) *in rr: drvn after 6f: bhd 7f out: t.o 4f out* 16/1

11 *10* **It Was All A Dream (IRE)** 5-10-12 0..... RichardJohnson 7
(Adrian Wintle) *in rr: bhd and drvn over 5f out: t.o* 20/1

12 *1/2* **Kilty Caul (IRE)**[80] 6-10-12 0..... DavidBass 6
(Kim Bailey) *led: hdd over 4f out: sn wknd: bhd fnl 3f: t.o* 11/4[2]

4m 8.9s (22.50) **Going Correction** +1.075s/f (Soft)
WFA 4 from 5yo+ 4lb **12** Ran SP% **119.7**
Speed ratings: **86,83,83,79,74 69,65,59,46,42 37,37**
CSF £22.28 TOTE £9.30: £2.40, £1.60, £2.90; EX 29.10 Trifecta £128.20.
Owner R J H Geffen **Bred** R D And Mrs J S Chugg **Trained** Nicholashayne, Devon

FOCUS
An ordinary mares' bumper. They went no sort of pace and, despite being well grouped early, finished well strung out on this testing ground.

T/Plt: £19.10 to a £1 stake. Pool: £62,635.64 - 2,384.44 winning tickets T/Qpdt: £9.50 to a £1 stake. Pool: £6,114.07 - 475.39 winning tickets **Walter Glynn**

CARLISLE (R-H)
Thursday, May 7

OFFICIAL GOING: Hurdle course - good to soft (good in places); chase course - good (good to soft in places down the hill)
Wind: Fresh, half against Weather: Sunny, warm

153 APOLLOBET BEST ODDS GUARANTEED CONDITIONAL JOCKEYS' H'CAP HURDLE (11 hdls) 2m 3f 61y
5:40 (5:41) (Class 4) (0-105,105) 4-Y-0+ **£3,249** (£954; £477; £238)

Form RPR

PU0- **1** **Tara Mac**[13] 5516 6-11-3 **96**..... CraigNichol 106+
(Keith Dalgleish) *hld up bhd ldng gp: pushed along briefly 1/2-way: smooth hdwy 3 out: led next: sn pushed clr* 15/2[3]

232- **2** *8* **Separate Shadows (FR)**[15] 5479 7-11-12 **105**............ HarryChalloner 107
(Donald McCain) *t.k.h: prom: effrt bef 2 out: chsd wnr between last 2: kpt on run-in: no imp* **5/1**[2]

060- **3** *1 1/4* **Parles Pond (IRE)**[23] 5327 6-11-0 **93**............(p) GrahamWatters 94
(Martin Todhunter) *nt fluent on occasions in rr: stdy hdwy 3 out: rdn bef next: kpt on fr last: nt pce to chal* **14/1**

213- **4** *9* **Astaroland (FR)**[60] 4650 5-11-12 **105**............ ThomasGarner 99
(Jennie Candlish) *t.k.h early: hld up in tch: rdn and chsd wnr briefly between last 2: wknd run-in* **5/1**[2]

00-0 **5** *2 3/4* **Mrs Grass**[7] 37 8-10-0 **79** oh7............(vt) DiarmuidO'Regan 69
(Jonathan Haynes) *led tl hdd after 3 out: rdn and wknd bef next* **66/1**

634- **6** *3 1/4* **Brunello**[32] 5160 7-11-2 **95**............(b) AdamNicol 83
(Michael Smith) *t.k.h: prom on outside: outpcd whn mstke 3 out: drvn and no imp bef next* **11/1**

055- **7** *5* **Prince Of Pirates (IRE)**[23] 5325 10-11-8 **101**............(b) NicodeBoinville 87
(Ben Haslam) *t.k.h: cl up: hdwy to ld after 3 out: rdn and hdd next: wkng whn mstke last* **12/1**

40- **8** *16* **Caraline (FR)**[46] 4939 4-10-5 **92**............(v[1]) JoeColliver(3) 56
(Micky Hammond) *hld up on outside: hdwy and prom 1/2-way: rdn and outpcd 3 out: btn bef next* **10/1**

453- **9** *17* **Indepub**[23] 5325 6-10-9 **88**............ StephenMulqueen 41
(Lisa Harrison) *sn lost prom position: drvn and outpcd bef 4 out: lost tch next: t.o* **4/1**[1]

/P0- **P** **Agesilas (FR)**[65] 4550 7-10-0 **79** oh4............ JonathanEngland
(Andrew Crook) *bhd: drvn and flashed tail after 4th: struggling 6th: lost tch fr next: t.o whn p.u bef 2 out* **40/1**

4m 51.2s (-17.60) **Going Correction** -0.70s/f (Firm)
WFA 4 from 5yo+ 18lb 10 Ran SP% **109.8**
Speed ratings (Par 105): **107,103,103,99,98 97,95,88,82,**
CSF £42.02 CT £475.87 TOTE £9.90: £2.90, £1.80, £4.10; EX 53.30 Trifecta £784.40.
Owner Straightline Construction Ltd **Bred** Richard R Evans **Trained** Carluke, S Lanarks

FOCUS
Hurdle races on Inner course. Bends moved out, hurdles sited on outer. Chase bends moved out. Winning rider Craig Nichol said the ground was 'good' and the time was just over 12 seconds slower than standard. This was an open event, run at an ordinary gallop, but a decisive winner. The second and third set the level.

154 APOLLOBET WORLDWIDE LOTTERIES NOVICES' LIMITED H'CAP CHASE (11 fncs 1 omitted) 1m 7f 207y
6:10 (6:10) (Class 3) (0-125,122) 5-Y-0+ **£6,498** (£1,908; £954; £477)

Form RPR

243- **1** **Honourable Gent**[14] 5490 7-10-0 **103** oh3............ CraigNichol(3) 110+
(Rose Dobbin) *hld up: hdwy to chse ldrs 3rd: led after 3 out: pushed clr fr last: readily* **11/4**[1]

505- **2** *7* **Orsippus (USA)**[19] 5393 9-11-6 **120**............ BrianHughes 121
(Michael Smith) *mostly j.lft: led: hdd after 3 out: rallied: outpcd bef last* **11/4**[1]

U30- **3** *14* **Quick Brew**[24] 5315 7-10-12 **112**............(t) MichaelMcAlister 100
(Maurice Barnes) *j.lft: in tch: pushed along 1/2-way: rallied bef 4 out: outpcd fr next* **9/2**[2]

43-5 **4** *3 1/2* **Dynamic Drive (IRE)**[7] 34 8-9-12 **103** oh5............(t) StephenMulqueen(5) 91
(Maurice Barnes) *nt jump wl: hld up in tch: blnd bdly 5 out: rdn and outpcd next: n.d after* **17/2**[3]

142- **5** *21* **Plan Again (IRE)**[18] 5405 8-11-8 **122**............ WilsonRenwick 95
(Donald McCain) *cl up: ev ch and rdn 4 out: wknd 2 out: t.o* **11/4**[1]

4m 5.3s (-10.80) **Going Correction** -0.425s/f (Good) 5 Ran SP% **108.7**
Speed ratings: **110,106,99,97,87**
CSF £10.53 TOTE £2.90: £1.40, £1.90; EX 12.50 Trifecta £46.90.
Owner Mr & Mrs Duncan Davidson **Bred** Mrs P Wright **Trained** South Hazelrigg, Northumbria

FOCUS
This may not prove the most reliable of form, but the winner is should progress. A step up from the winner on his chasing debut.

155 APOLLOBET FREE DOWNLOAD APP NOVICES' HURDLE (11 hdls) 2m 3f 61y
6:40 (6:41) (Class 4) 4-Y-0+ **£3,249** (£954; £477; £238)

Form RPR

222- **1** **Wolf Sword (IRE)**[48] 4891 6-10-12 113............ HenryBrooke 111+
(George Moore) *hld up in tch: smooth hdwy to ld 2 out: qcknd clr on bit bef last: v easily* **8/15**[1]

104- **2** *9* **Luccombe Down**[68] 4479 5-10-12 0............ WilsonRenwick 95
(Donald McCain) *prom: effrt and rdn bef 2 out: chsd (clr) wnr run-in: kpt on: no imp* **3/1**[2]

00- **3** *1/2* **John Williams (IRE)**[47] 4915 6-10-12 0............ BrianHughes 95
(Sandy Thomson) *cl up: led 3 out: rdn and hdd next: kpt on same pce fr last* **16/1**

4 *23* **Cherry Princess**[122] 5-10-5 0............ SeanQuinlan 70
(Barbara Butterworth) *hld up: hdwy and in tch briefly bef 2 out: sn rdn: wknd between last 2* **33/1**

006- **5** *7* **Lady Vivona**[13] 5514 7-10-5 0............ BrianHarding 58
(Lisa Harrison) *prom to 4th: sn lost pl: struggling 4 out: nvr rchd ldrs* **100/1**

1/6- **6** *1 1/4* **Up The Bees**[181] 2326 5-10-9 0............ AdamNicol(3) 63
(Philip Kirby) *hld up in tch: drvn along 3 out: wknd bef next* **6/1**[3]

55P- **7** *5* **Desert Island Dusk**[15] 5469 4-10-7 0............(t) MichaelMcAlister 53
(Maurice Barnes) *racd wd: led to 6th: rdn and wknd bef 2 out* **33/1**

P **Bach To Before (IRE)**[25] 7-10-12 0............(p) JamesReveley
(Tom Gretton) *cl up: led 6th: hdd and rdn 3 out: wknd qckly and p.u bef next* **25/1**

4m 59.4s (-9.40) **Going Correction** -0.70s/f (Firm)
WFA 4 from 5yo+ 18lb 8 Ran SP% **121.1**
Speed ratings (Par 105): **90,86,86,77,74 73,71,**
CSF £2.73 TOTE £1.80: £1.10, £1.40, £4.40; EX 3.30 Trifecta £21.70.
Owner G R Orchard **Bred** Maurice Smiddy **Trained** Middleham Moor, N Yorks

FOCUS
An uncompetitive novice hurdle run at a modest gallop. The easy winner was the clear form pick and is rated to his mark.

156 APOLLOBET £50 SIGNUP BONUS H'CAP CHASE (17 fncs 2 omitted) 3m 2f 34y
7:10 (7:10) (Class 3) (0-130,129) 5-Y-0+ **£6,498** (£1,908; £954; £477)

Form RPR

562- **1** **Fill The Power (IRE)**[53] 4783 9-11-10 **127**............ SeanQuinlan 140+
(Sue Smith) *j.w: pressed ldr: chal 5th: led 7th: mde rest: rdn clr fr 3 out* **10/3**[1]

6P0- **2** *8* **Orange Nassau (FR)**[33] 5138 9-11-5 **122**............ BrianHarding 125
(Charlie Longsdon) *nt fluent on occasions: led to 7th: pressed wnr: rdn whn nt fluent 3 out: kpt on same pce fr next* **7/1**

U13- **3** *13* **Red Admirable (IRE)**[42] 5000 9-11-8 **125**............(p) WilsonRenwick 121
(Graeme McPherson) *hld up: blnd 4th: stdy hdwy and chsd ldrs 5 out: nrly 5 l down whn blnd next: sn rdn: outpcd fr 3 out* **10/1**

511- **4** *6* **Basford Ben**[33] 5134 7-10-10 **113**............(b) HenryBrooke 98
(Jennie Candlish) *racd wd: cl up: pushed along 1/2-way: wknd after 4 out* **4/1**[2]

F4P- **5** *63* **The Panama Kid (IRE)**[151] 2975 11-11-6 **123**............(b) BrianHughes 51
(Malcolm Jefferson) *in tch: drvn and outpcd after 10th: lost tch fr 5 out: t.o* **9/1**

35F- **P** **Mister Marker (IRE)**[73] 4401 11-10-13 **123**............ MissJRRichards(7)
(Nicky Richards) *t.k.h early: hld up in tch: outpcd after 9th: wknd and p.u after next* **9/2**[3]

PPP- **P** **Dark Glacier (IRE)**[117] 3617 10-11-12 **129**............(bt) DonalDevereux
(Peter Bowen) *hld up: rdn fr 6th: shortlived effrt bef 10th: struggling fr next: t.o whn p.u bef 2 out* **13/2**

654- **P** **Indian Voyage (IRE)**[50] 4851 7-11-5 **127**............(t) StephenMulqueen(5)
(Maurice Barnes) *hld up: pushed along and outpcd 10th: rallied u.p 5 out: no imp and wknd next: t.o whn p.u bef 2 out* **20/1**

6m 52.4s (-14.80) **Going Correction** -0.425s/f (Good) 8 Ran SP% **110.9**
Speed ratings: **105,102,98,96,77 , ,**
CSF £25.07 CT £199.29 TOTE £4.40: £1.50, £2.90, £2.20; EX 30.80 Trifecta £421.70.
Owner McGoldrick Racing Syndicates **Bred** Patrick Condon **Trained** High Eldwick, W Yorks

FOCUS
This looked quite competitive beforehand but for various reasons several ran below their best so it wouldn't be strong form. There's a case for rating the form a few pounds higher.

157 APOLLOBET HOME OF CASHBACKS SPECIAL H'CAP HURDLE (10 hdls) 2m 1f
7:40 (7:40) (Class 4) (0-110,110) 4-Y-0+ **£3,249** (£954; £477; £238)

Form RPR

26-3 **1** **Hartside (GER)**[7] 43 6-11-5 **110**............ MrRWinks(7) 110
(Peter Winks) *hld up: rdn and outpcd 3 out: rallied bef next: led after last: edgd lft: hld on wl towards fin* **4/1**[2]

536/ **2** *hd* **Miss Macnamara (IRE)**[11] 1043 6-10-2 **86**............ WilsonRenwick 86
(Martin Todhunter) *t.k.h: hld up in tch: hdwy and ev ch 2 out: rdn whn nt fluent last: kpt on wl u.p: jst hld* **11/4**[1]

232- **3** *2 1/4* **Hawdyerwheesht**[16] 5452 7-11-12 **110**............(t) BrianHughes 108
(David Dennis) *t.k.h: chsd ldrs: hdwy to ld 2 out: sn rdn and edgd lft: hdd after last: sn outpcd* **9/2**[3]

450- **4** *nk* **Pistol (IRE)**[24] 5310 6-11-0 **105**............ MrJDixon(7) 103
(John Dixon) *led to bef 4th: w ldr: hit but regained ld 3 out: hdd next: n.m.r briefly between last 2: sn one pce* **7/1**

000- **5** *5* **Raifteiri (IRE)**[12] 8-9-9 **84** oh12............ StephenMulqueen(5) 78
(William Young Jnr) *in tch: rdn and outpcd 3 out: rallied bef next: no imp between last 2* **125/1**

203- **6** *1 1/2* **Hatton Springs (IRE)**[32] 5158 4-11-3 **105**............ JamesReveley 93
(Stuart Coltherd) *in tch: stdy hdwy 3rd: effrt and ev ch 2 out: rdn and outpcd fr last* **14/1**

130- **7** *6* **Ever So Much (IRE)**[33] 5131 6-11-12 **110**............ AndrewTinkler 97
(Ben Haslam) *hld up: rdn after 3 out: wknd fr next* **12/1**

406- **8** *13* **Snowed In (IRE)**[17] 5422 6-11-5 **103**............(p) SeanQuinlan 82
(Barbara Butterworth) *pressed ldr: led bef 4th: hdd 3 out: rdn and wknd bef next* **6/1**

243- **9** *18* **Roll Of Thunder**[254] 1340 6-10-3 **92**............ MissCWalton(5) 51
(James Walton) *bhd: struggling 4 out: sn btn* **25/1**

325- **10** *88* **Al Musheer (FR)**[181] 2333 4-11-1 **103**............ AdrianLane
(Donald McCain) *midfield: struggling bef 4 out: lost tch next: t.o* **20/1**

4m 19.0s (-10.20) **Going Correction** -0.70s/f (Firm)
WFA 4 from 6yo+ 18lb 10 Ran SP% **115.4**
Speed ratings (Par 105): **96,95,94,94,92 91,88,82,74,32**
CSF £15.37 CT £50.77 TOTE £5.30: £1.70, £1.30, £1.80; EX 23.60 Trifecta £66.50.
Owner P Winks **Bred** Gestut Ammerland **Trained** Little Houghton, S Yorks
■ Stewards' Enquiry : Mr R Winks four-day ban: use of whip (22, 24-26 May)

FOCUS
Nine lengths covered the first six home in this handicap hurdle which was run at just an ordinary gallop. The winner was close to the best of his form from 2015.

158 APOLLOBET DAILY RACING SPECIALS NOVICES' H'CAP CHASE (15 fncs 1 omitted) 2m 4f
8:10 (8:10) (Class 4) (0-115,115) 5-Y-0+ **£3,994** (£1,240; £667)

Form RPR

5P4- **1** **Leanna Ban**[13] 5516 8-9-11 **89**............(t) JonathanEngland(3) 106+
(Tristan Davidson) *gifted 10 l s: j. bdly lft thrght: t.k.h: mde all: 35 l clr 8th (1/2-way): pushed along bef 3 out: kpt on: unchal* **7/4**[2]

611- **2** *14* **Narcissist (IRE)**[18] 5405 6-11-12 **115**............(b) DenisO'Regan 116
(Michael Easterby) *sed over 10 l bhd wnr: sn chsng (clr) wnr: 35 l down 8th (1/2-way): shkn up bef 2 out: sn no imp: hld on for 2nd towards fin* **5/4**[1]

/10- **3** *hd* **Lucematic**[47] 4914 9-11-11 **114**............ BrianHughes 115
(Chris Grant) *sed over 10 l bhd wnr: hld up in 3rd pl: shkn up and outpcd 3 out: kpt on fr last: no imp* **11/2**[3]

0F0- **P** **Rough King (IRE)**[98] 3935 6-11-2 **105**............(t) HenryBrooke
(Jennie Candlish) *sed 10 l bhd wnr: stdd in last pl: j.lft on occasions: struggling whn mstke 9th: btn bef 4 out: 4th and hld whn j. bdly lft 2 out: p.u bef last* **13/2**

5m 16.7s (-10.70) **Going Correction** -0.425s/f (Good) 4 Ran SP% **109.5**
Speed ratings: **104,98,98,**
CSF £4.56 TOTE £3.90; EX 5.90 Trifecta £10.00.
Owner E G Tunstall, P Nicholson, S M Grice **Bred** Mrs Claire Massey **Trained** Irthington, Cumbria

FOCUS
An unsatisfactory race from a form point of view as the winner was standing more than 10 lengths in front of the other three when the starter let them go and he was never headed. The winner is rated in line with the best of his hurdles form.

159 APOLLOBET MARES' STANDARD OPEN NATIONAL HUNT FLAT RACE 2m 1f
8:40 (8:40) (Class 6) 4-6-Y-0 **£1,559** (£457; £228; £114)

Form RPR

02- **1** **Boogie Life**[33] 5136 4-10-8 0............ JamesReveley 105+
(Jim Goldie) *chsd ldrs: shkn up to ld 2f out: edgd lft and pushed clr fr over 1f out* **5/1**[3]

2 10 **Klaazia (FR)** 4-10-8 0 AndrewTinkler 94
(Jeremy Gask) *hld up in midfield: hdwy to chse ldrs over 3f out: rdn and chsd (clr) wnr over 1f out: kpt on fnl f: no imp* **17/2**

45- 3 2 1/4 **Flower Power**[159] 2823 4-10-8 0 DenisO'Regan 92
(Tony Coyle) *chsd ldrs: effrt and drvn over 2f out: kpt on same pce fr over 1f out* **11/1**

433- 4 5 **Card Game (IRE)**[67] 4520 6-10-12 0 BrianHughes 94
(Malcolm Jefferson) *led: rdn and hdd 2f out: lost 2nd and outpcd over 1f out* **10/3**[2]

5- 5 5 **Question Of Faith**[58] 4701 4-10-8 0 WilsonRenwick 83
(Martin Todhunter) *hld up in midfield: drvn and outpcd over 3f out: rallied over 1f out: nvr able to chal* **20/1**

6 1 3/4 **Flemerina (IRE)** 6-10-2 0 StephenMcCarthy(10) 85
(Sue Smith) *in tch on outside: drvn and outpcd over 3f out: no imp fr 2f out* **11/1**

7 3 1/4 **Beyond Measure (IRE)** 4-10-8 0 NicodeBoinville 79
(Don Cantillon) *t.k.h: hld up: drvn and outpcd over 4f out: n.d after* **9/4**[1]

4- 8 16 **Daytripper**[33] 5136 4-10-5 0 CraigNichol(3) 64
(Lucinda Russell) *t.k.h: prom: pushed along and outpcd over 3f out: sn btn* **40/1**

9 30 **Olivia Joan** 4-10-8 0 BrianHarding 37
(Alistair Whillans) *hld up on outside: stdy hdwy 5f out: rdn and wknd over 3f out: eased whn no ch over 1f out: t.o* **25/1**

400- 10 28 **Comeonbonny**[13] 5520 6-10-5 0 JamieHamilton(7) 16
(Katie Scott) *reluctant to line up: hld up: struggling over 6f out: sn btn: t.o* **80/1**

11 4 **Little Miss Flossy** 6-10-9 0 JohnKington(3) 12
(Andrew Crook) *hld up in midfield: lost pl 1/2-way: struggling 5f out: t.o* **33/1**

12 99 **Flowalong (IRE)** 5-10-12 0 HenryBrooke
(Bruce Mactaggart) *bhd: lost tch 1/2-way: t.o* **50/1**

4m 14.8s (-8.80) **Going Correction** -0.70s/f (Firm)
WFA 4 from 5yo+ 4lb 12 Ran SP% **114.9**
Speed ratings: **94,89,88,85,83 82,81,73,59,46 44,**
CSF £41.88 TOTE £6.50: £2.00, £3.50, £3.80; EX 50.50 Trifecta £712.40.
Owner Mr & Mrs Raymond Anderson Green **Bred** Design And Planning Consultants Ltd **Trained** Uplawmoor, E Renfrews

FOCUS
A fair gallop to this mares' bumper which produced an interesting winner. Ordinary form.
T/Plt: £99.50 to a £1 stake. Pool of £49316.93 - 361.64 winning tickets. T/Qpdt: £23.00 to a £1 stake. Pool of £4725.53 - 151.50 winning tickets. **Richard Young**

[26]NEWTON ABBOT (L-H)

Thursday, May 7

OFFICIAL GOING: Soft (heavy in places: 5.0)
Wind: mild breeze across Weather: sunny with cloudy periods Rails: Hurdles pushed wide, chase course innermost position.

160 WALKINGTHECOURSES.COM "NATIONAL HUNT" MAIDEN HURDLE (9 hdls) 2m 2f 110y
2:00 (2:00) (Class 4) 4-Y-0+ **£3,898** (£1,144; £572; £286)

Form RPR

PP- 1 **Richardofdoccombe (IRE)**[86] 4142 9-10-7 0 (t) AliceMills(7) 97
(Gail Haywood) *disp ld tl clr ldr 2 out: kpt on gamely: pushed out* **40/1**

PF5- 2 1 1/2 **Grissom (FR)**[17] 5434 7-11-0 0 (t) JamesDavies 95
(Jimmy Frost) *hld up but wl in tch: rdn and hdwy after 3 out: wnt cl 2nd between last 2: ch last: kpt on same pce* **50/1**

/P5- 3 6 **Tuffstuff**[15] 5462 7-11-0 0 GavinSheehan 89
(Brian Barr) *trckd ldrs: rdn after 3 out: kpt on same pce fr next* **8/1**

533- 4 2 3/4 **Pauls Conn (IRE)**[23] 5338 6-10-7 0 (p) CiaranGethings(7) 86
(Mary Sanderson) *hld up but wl in tch: struggling after 5th: stl last w enough to do after 3 out: styd on fr 2 out: nvr rchd ldrs* **10/1**

2- 5 13 **Tricky (IRE)**[20] 5373 6-11-0 0 RichardJohnson 76
(Philip Hobbs) *racd keenly: trckd ldrs: disp ld 6th tl nt fluent 2 out: wknd qckly: mstke last* **2/1**[2]

2- 6 9 **Loch Garman (FR)**[31] 5180 4-10-9 0 JamesBest 59
(Nigel Hawke) *trckd ldrs: chal 6th tl next: sn rdn: wknd qckly* **13/8**[1]

P **Thady Quil (IRE)**[109] 5-11-0 0 WayneHutchinson
(Martin Keighley) *disp ld: reminders after 5th: rdn and hdd after next: wknd after 3 out: p.u bef next* **5/1**[3]

4m 46.9s (16.90) **Going Correction** +0.75s/f (Soft)
WFA 4 from 5yo+ 18lb 7 Ran SP% **112.7**
Speed ratings (Par 105): **94,93,90,89,84 80,**
CSF £798.75 TOTE £29.00: £9.30, £13.60; EX 235.50 Trifecta £1596.40.
Owner Romilly Stuart-Jervis **Bred** Edward Ryan **Trained** Moretonhampstead, Devon

FOCUS
Chase course at innermost position and hurdles pushed out wide. Unusually testing conditions for this venue following 52mm of rainfall in recent days and it's likely that led to a massive boil over in this opener. The third and fourth are probably the best guide.

161 SIS TOP ATA DELIVERY H'CAP CHASE (13 fncs) 2m 75y
2:30 (2:30) (Class 5) (0-100,100) 5-Y-0+ **£3,422** (£997; £499)

Form RPR

30-4 1 **Accessallareas (IRE)**[7] 42 10-11-8 **96** (tp) RichardJohnson 96+
(Sarah-Jayne Davies) *j.rt most of way: pressed ldr: led 6th: drew clr after next: reduced advantage 2 out: kpt on wl fr last: rdn out* **5/1**

4P6- 2 4 1/2 **Humbel Ben (IRE)**[78] 4300 12-11-9 **97** (p) NickScholfield 93
(Alan Jones) *hld up in last pair: wnt 15 l 2nd at the 9th: steadily clsd on wnr after 4 out: 4 l down 2 out: sn rdn: no further imp whn hit last: kpt on same pce* **6/1**

422- 3 30 **Olympian Boy (IRE)**[27] 5257 11-11-12 **100** (t) PaulMoloney 70
(Sophie Leech) *trckd ldrs: wnt 15 l 2nd at the 8th tl next: wknd 3 out: t.o* **5/2**[2]

533- 4 15 **Ballyegan (IRE)**[15] 5480 10-11-4 **92** LiamHeard 50
(Bob Buckler) *led: nt fluent 3rd: hdd 6th: rdn whn lost 2nd at the 8th: wknd after next: t.o* **9/2**[3]

5SU- P **Midnight Thomas**[20] 5376 6-10-9 **83** (t) WayneHutchinson
(Martin Keighley) *nvr fluent or really travelling: last most of way tl p.u whn losing tch after 7th* **9/4**[1]

4m 12.1s (5.60) **Going Correction** +0.475s/f (Soft) 5 Ran SP% **108.5**
Speed ratings: **105,102,88,81,**
CSF £29.74 TOTE £4.20: £2.80, £4.50; EX 38.80 Trifecta £94.00.
Owner Withers Winners **Bred** Mrs Gail Kidd **Trained** Leominster, H'fords

FOCUS
The majority of these appeared not to handle conditions. The winner was 118 chaser at his peak and may still be capable of better than this.

162 ATTHERACES.COM H'CAP HURDLE (8 hdls) 2m 167y
3:00 (3:00) (Class 3) (0-130,127) 4-Y-0+ **£5,523** (£1,621; £810; £405)

Form RPR

0P4- 1 **Quick Decisson (IRE)**[37] 5079 7-11-1 **112** RichardJohnson 117+
(Philip Hobbs) *mde all: styd on wl: rdn out* **11/4**[1]

P15- 2 2 3/4 **Come On Annie**[60] 4652 9-11-2 **118** MrsAlexDunn(5) 118
(Alexandra Dunn) *racd keenly: hld up in tch: hdwy 5th: trckd wnr after 3 out: rdn whn wnt lft 2 out: kpt on same pce* **16/1**

41P- 3 2 1/2 **Party Palace**[16] 5441 11-10-9 **106** GavinSheehan 104
(Stuart Howe) *racd wd: trckd ldrs: rdn whn outpcd after 3 out: styd on fr next but nt pce to get bk on terms: wnt 3rd run-in* **11/1**

341- 4 nk **Lucky Jim**[31] 5196 4-11-12 **127** NickScholfield 121
(David Dennis) *in tch: rdn to chse ldrs after 3 out: styd on same pce: lost 3rd run-in* **13/2**

0/P- 5 10 **Absolutlyfantastic**[131] 3316 8-11-6 **120** (t) JeremiahMcGrath(3) 108
(Martin Hill) *hld up in tch: effrt after 3 out: wknd between last 2* **20/1**

021- 6 hd **Ice Tres**[17] 5435 6-10-7 **104** (tp) JamesDavies 91
(Chris Down) *trckd ldrs: rdn appr 2 out: wknd between last 2* **5/1**[3]

365- 7 8 **Vosne Romanee**[12] 5535 4-11-6 **121** (tp) WillKennedy 98
(Dr Richard Newland) *in tch: blnd 5th: rdn after 3 out: wknd next* **3/1**[2]

/05- P **Too Scoops (IRE)**[22] 5345 8-11-9 **120** PaulMoloney
(Richard Woollacott) *chsd ldr tl after 4th: wknd next: tailing off whn p.u 3 out* **7/1**

4m 14.7s (9.00) **Going Correction** +0.75s/f (Soft) 8 Ran SP% **113.1**
Speed ratings (Par 107): **108,106,105,105,100 100,96,**
CSF £41.49 CT £415.87 TOTE £3.50: £1.10, £3.40, £3.80; EX 36.90 Trifecta £448.90.
Owner Owners For Owners: Quick Decisson **Bred** Oak Hill Stud **Trained** Withycombe, Somerset

FOCUS
A fair feature and the third race in succession where it paid to be up with the pace. The form makes sense.

163 TEIGNMOUTH NATIONAL COASTWATCH H'CAP CHASE (16 fncs) 2m 4f 216y
3:35 (3:35) (Class 4) (0-110,110) 5-Y-0+ **£3,898** (£1,144; £572; £286)

Form RPR

562- 1 **The Happy Warrior**[16] 5443 7-10-11 **95** LiamHeard 104+
(Bob Buckler) *trckd ldrs: hit 2nd: reminder after 8th: wnt 2nd after 10th: rdn after 4 out: 7 l down next: clsng on ldr whn hit 2 out: rchd for last: styd on wl to ld towards fin* **9/4**[1]

P11- 2 nk **Bang On Time (IRE)**[18] 5416 9-11-12 **110** (p) RichardJohnson 116
(Richard Woollacott) *led: 7 l clr after 3 out: rdn between last 2: 2 1/2 l up last: no ex whn hdd nring fin* **4/1**

534- 3 12 **Ray Diamond**[54] 4768 10-11-5 **110** (p) DavidNoonan(7) 104
(Jackie Du Plessis) *chsd ldr: pushed along at times: reminders after 9th: dropped to 4th 11th: nt fluent 3 out: wnt 3rd between last 2: styd on same pce* **3/1**[2]

223- 4 11 **Paddy The Stout (IRE)**[46] 4946 10-11-12 **110** (t) TomO'Brien 99
(Paul Henderson) *hld up 5th: wnt 4th at the 6th: rdn in 3rd after 4 out: wknd between last 2* **10/3**[3]

236/ P **Brannoc (IRE)**[625] 1328 10-9-7 **84** oh15 AliceMills(7)
(Gail Haywood) *trckd ldrs: nt fluent 5th: sn dropped to last and struggling: losing tch whn p.u bef 10th* **9/1**

5m 29.6s (8.20) **Going Correction** +0.475s/f (Soft) 5 Ran SP% **108.8**
Speed ratings: **104,103,99,95,**
CSF £11.11 TOTE £3.80: £1.50, £1.60; EX 9.50 Trifecta £33.30.
Owner Nick Elliott **Bred** H G Llewellyn **Trained** Henley, Somerset

FOCUS
This was arguably the most competitive race of the meeting and it served up a thrilling finish. The winner was on a good mark.

164 SIS VIRTUAL MOBILE GAMES NOVICES' H'CAP HURDLE (8 hdls) 2m 167y
4:10 (4:10) (Class 5) (0-100,100) 4-Y-0+ **£3,422** (£997; £499)

Form RPR

223- 1 **Billy My Boy**[17] 5434 6-11-5 **96** GilesHawkins(3) 106+
(Chris Down) *mde all: drew clr fr 2 out: wnt lft and hit last: styd on strly* **1/1**[1]

410- 2 10 **Galactic Power (IRE)**[19] 5397 5-10-7 **88** JosephPalmowski(7) 87
(Robin Dickin) *chsd ldng trio: outpcd after 5th: styd on after 3 out: chal for 2nd between last 2: wnt 2nd run-in: no ch w wnr* **9/2**[3]

000- 3 1 1/4 **Theionlady (IRE)**[128] 3407 5-10-10 **84** (t) WayneHutchinson 82
(Richard Woollacott) *trckd ldng pair: rdn to chse wnr after 3 out: hld fr next: no ex whn lost 2nd run-in* **8/1**

P24- 4 18 **Kahdian (IRE)**[51] 4821 5-11-5 **100** GaryDerwin(7) 88
(Helen Rees) *trckd wnr: rdn after 3 out: sn hld: wknd between last 2* **5/2**[2]

4m 23.7s (18.00) **Going Correction** +0.75s/f (Soft) 4 Ran SP% **107.9**
Speed ratings (Par 103): **87,82,81,73**
CSF £5.61 TOTE £1.70; EX 5.50 Trifecta £18.10.
Owner John Radford **Bred** J B Radford **Trained** Mutterton, Devon

FOCUS
This was won in good style by the heavily supported favourite, in a pretty slow time. The winner seems to be on the upgrade.

165 NEWTONABBOTRACING.COM (S) H'CAP HURDLE (10 hdls) 2m 5f 122y
4:45 (4:45) (Class 5) (0-100,100) 4-Y-0+ **£3,422** (£997; £499)

Form RPR

306- 1 **Y A Bon (IRE)**[15] 5476 7-10-5 **86** (b) MikeyHamill(7) 91+
(Alexandra Dunn) *led: jnd 3rd tl after 3 out: c wdst into st: drew clr after 2 out: rdn out* **5/1**[3]

54-0 2 8 **Lifetime (IRE)**[3] 106 7-11-1 **89** (tp) MarkQuinlan 87
(Neil Mulholland) *trckd ldrs: rdn in cl 2nd after 3 out: ev ch whn blnd 2 out: sn hld: kpt on same pce* **11/8**[1]

/P0- 3 1 1/4 **Railway Vic (IRE)**[59] 4685 8-9-7 **74** oh1 MissBFrost(7) 70
(Jimmy Frost) *trckd ldrs: ev ch appr 2 out: rdn between last 2: kpt on same pce* **6/1**

03F- 4 16 **The Sweetener (IRE)**[11] 6-11-5 **100** (tp) PaulJohn(7) 81
(Richard Woollacott) *disp ld fr 3rd tl rdn after 3 out: wknd bef next* **3/1**[2]

050- 5 12 **Barenger (IRE)**[26] 5281 8-11-2 **90** MichaelByrne 57
(Ali Stronge) *trckd ldrs: rdn after 3 out: wknd bef next* **10/1**

200/ 6 60 **Consult**[1062] 662 8-11-9 **97** (v[1]) AlainCawley 4
(Alan Phillips) *j.lft and nvr fluent: last but in tch tl wknd 3 out: t.o* **20/1**

5m 54.0s (33.80) **Going Correction** +0.75s/f (Soft) 6 Ran SP% **111.9**
Speed ratings (Par 103): **68,65,64,58,54 32**
CSF £12.72 CT £40.21 TOTE £9.20: £2.80, £1.50; EX 11.90 Trifecta £54.10.There was no bid for the winner.

The Form Book Jumps 2015-16, Raceform Ltd, Newbury, RG14 5SJ

Owner Ms Gill Butler **Bred** Gerard Samama **Trained** West Buckland, Somerset

FOCUS

This was extremely moderate, even by selling standards. The winner is rated in line with the best of his recent runs.

166 INDEPENDENT RACECOURSES LTD, IRL OPEN HUNTERS' CHASE (20 fncs) 3m 1f 170y

5:15 (5:15) (Class 6) 6-Y-0+ **£1,317** (£405; £202)

Form RPR

2U2- **1** **Indiana Bay (IRE)**[17] 5440 8-12-0 105 MrWBiddick 120+
(Mrs Jill Dennis) *a.p: led after 13th: drew wl clr fr 4 out: v easily* **5/6**[1]

/1P- **2** *32* **Iron Chancellor (IRE)**[31] 10-11-13 117 (b) MrRobertHawker[(5)] 90
(Mrs Sue Popham) *led tl after 13th: no ch w wnr fr 4 out: jst hld on for modest 2nd* **2/1**[2]

0/P- **3** *½* **Batu Ferringhi (FR)**[31] 9-11-7 105 (p) MrJLThomas[(7)] 86
(Mrs C Hitch) *trckd ldrs: slow 13th and reminders: lost tch w front pair whn dropped to 4th next: no ch fr 4 out: chal for modest 2nd run-in* **7/1**[3]

4/P- **P** **Buckstruther (IRE)**[19] 13-11-7 99 (p) DavidNoonan[(7)]
(Paul O J Hosgood) *chsd ldrs tl 14th: sn wknd: t.o whn p.u bef 16th* **16/1**

43P- **R** **Ifonlyalfie**[18] 10-11-7 76 (b) MrCHGDavies[(7)]
(C H G Davies) *hld up 5th: reminder after 12th: j.rt fr next: wnt 3rd 14th: no ch w front pair fr 15th: wknd after 4 out: t.o 4th whn ref last* **20/1**

6m 54.0s (9.40) **Going Correction** +0.475s/f (Soft) 5 Ran SP% **111.0**
Speed ratings: **105,95,95, ,**
CSF £3.05 TOTE £2.20: £1.50, £1.10; EX 2.90 Trifecta £6.30.
Owner Shirley Leslie, Exor CJ Rush **Bred** Mrs Mary Tynan Phelan **Trained** Bude, Cornwall

FOCUS

This was turned into a procession. Not an easy race to put a figure on.

T/Plt: £34,057.10 to a £1 stake. Pool of £46653.60 - 0.45 winning tickets. T/Qpdt: £15.50 to a £1 stake. Pool of £4950.40 - 235.90 winning tickets. **Tim Mitchell**

WINCANTON (R-H)

Thursday, May 7

OFFICIAL GOING: Good (good to firm in places)

Wind: Almost nil Weather: Cloudy

167 RACING TOGETHER H'CAP HURDLE (10 hdls) 2m 4f

5:50 (5:50) (Class 5) (0-100,97) 4-Y-0+ **£2,599** (£763; £381; £190)

Form RPR

22P/ **1** **Sir Dylan**[9] 6-11-0 85 NickScholfield 100+
(Polly Gundry) *t.k.h: in tch: chsd ldr 5th: led last: drvn and hung lft run-in: styd on* **14/1**

062- **2** *4 ½* **Henry Oliver (IRE)**[28] 5243 7-10-13 84 (tp) RichardJohnson 93
(Neil Mulholland) *led: slt mstke 5th: hrd rdn and hdd last: sn outpcd* **7/4**[1]

060- **3** *9* **Taroum (IRE)**[79] 4281 8-11-6 91 (bt) RhysFlint 94
(John Flint) *hld up in midfield: promising hdwy appr 2 out: 3rd and hld whn blnd last* **10/1**

0F0- **4** *1* **Wojciech**[49] 4860 5-11-5 90 (t) GavinSheehan 93+
(Warren Greatrex) *nt jump wl in rr: rdn and styd on fr 2 out: nvr nrr* **14/1**

30P- **5** *1 ½* **Dawnieriver (IRE)**[156] 2873 5-10-9 85 JackSherwood[(5)] 84
(Michael Scudamore) *mid-div: effrt appr 2 out: nvr rchd ldrs* **20/1**

303- **6** *2 ¼* **Daring Indian**[19] 5397 7-11-11 96 (t) PaulMoloney 93
(Graeme McPherson) *in tch on inner tl outpcd and btn appr 2 out* **14/1**

410- **7** *nk* **Anginola (IRE)**[19] 5397 6-10-5 81 (b) KieronEdgar[(5)] 77
(David Dennis) *chsd ldr tl 5th: remained prom tl wknd 2 out* **20/1**

600/ **8** *5* **Bright Light**[632] 1267 8-10-0 71 oh11 HarrySkelton 63
(Dan Skelton) *t.k.h: chsd ldrs tl wknd 2 out* **7/2**[2]

330- **9** *2 ¼* **Sun Quest**[43] 4987 11-10-1 79 (t) MrJamesKing[(7)] 70
(Steven Dixon) *towards rr: rdn appr 2 out: n.d* **20/1**

06P- **10** *5* **Eddy**[19] 5398 6-11-3 88 JamesDavies 73
(John Panvert) *prom tl wknd 3 out* **9/1**[3]

155- **11** *nk* **Ruby Valentine (FR)**[105] 3810 12-10-6 77 TomO'Brien 66
(Jim Wilson) *mid-div: 6th 5th: struggling towards rr 3 out* **33/1**

455- **12** *2 ½* **Vinceson (IRE)**[210] 1808 7-11-8 93 JamesBest 76
(Jess Westwood) *prom tl 3rd: in tch after: hrd rdn and wknd 7th* **33/1**

P01- **13** *24* **Tara Dove**[18] 5415 7-11-12 97 TomCannon 58
(Alison Batchelor) *a bhd: no ch 3 out* **14/1**

4m 38.7s (-18.10) **Going Correction** -0.85s/f (Firm) 13 Ran SP% **124.5**
Speed ratings (Par 103): **102,100,96,96,95 94,94,92,91,89 89,88,78**
CSF £38.82 CT £276.80 TOTE £11.00: £3.00, £1.70, £2.90; EX 76.90 Trifecta £757.30.
Owner M James & S Jarrett **Bred** Cavendish Bloodstock **Trained** Ottery St Mary, Devon

FOCUS

A combination of watering and rain the day before saw 10mm of water added to the track. A moderate handicap run at an ordinary pace saw the front two pull clear up the straight. The winner is rated in line with his recent Flat run.

168 WESSEX WASTE NOVICES' HURDLE (11 hdls) 2m 5f 82y

6:20 (6:20) (Class 4) 4-Y-0+ **£3,249** (£954; £477; £238)

Form RPR

4- **1** **Until Forever (IRE)**[31] 5200 5-10-5 0 (t) HarrySkelton 90+
(Dan Skelton) *trckd ldrs: shkn up 3 out: led next: wnt lft last: pushed clr: comf* **8/1**[3]

52- **2** *4* **Profit Commission (IRE)**[20] 5367 5-10-12 0 RyanMahon 92
(Harry Fry) *chsd ldr: slt ld after 3 out tl mstke next: one pce appr last* **4/5**[1]

344- **3** *1 ¼* **Velvet Cognac**[38] 5066 7-10-12 115 (t) GavinSheehan 91
(Warren Greatrex) *led: hmpd by loose horse 5th: hdd after 3 out: one pce fr next* **6/4**[2]

346- **4** *1 ½* **Trakeur (FR)**[175] 2467 8-10-12 67 NickScholfield 87
(Simon Hodgson) *hld up in tch: handy 4th and gng wl appr 2 out: rdn appr last: unable qck* **50/1**

050- **5** *2* **Ofcoursewecan (USA)**[15] 5476 5-10-12 82 TomCannon 85
(Mark Gillard) *chsd ldrs: rdn 8th: sn outpcd* **40/1**

0- **U** **Hill Forts Gypse (IRE)**[36] 5105 4-10-1 0 ow1 KevinJones[(7)]
(Seamus Mullins) *prom whn blnd and uns rdr 1st* **50/1**

5m 8.1s (-18.40) **Going Correction** -0.85s/f (Firm)
WFA 4 from 5yo+ 19lb 6 Ran SP% **113.0**
Speed ratings (Par 105): **99,97,97,96,95**
CSF £15.87 TOTE £8.50: £3.50, £1.10; EX 16.70 Trifecta £28.10.
Owner Howard Spooner & Ian Weaver **Bred** Paul Smith **Trained** Alcester, Warwicks

FOCUS

A steadily run novice hurdle that developed into a sprint, with the field finishing close together.

169 WINCANTON H'CAP CHASE (21 fncs) 3m 1f 30y

6:50 (6:50) (Class 3) (0-130,127) 5-Y-0+ **£6,498** (£1,908; £954; £477)

Form RPR

533- **1** **Steel Summit (IRE)**[19] 5401 6-11-5 120 GavinSheehan 135+
(David Dennis) *outpcd: hdwy 12th: sltly lost pl 17th: rallied and led 2 out: sn clr* **6/1**

P31- **2** *8* **Alberobello (IRE)**[26] 5284 7-11-4 122 (t) MattGriffiths[(3)] 127
(Jeremy Scott) *w ldr at str pce and clr of rest most of way tl 2 out: sn btn* **7/2**[2]

334- **3** *½* **Fruity O'Rooney**[20] 5370 12-11-12 127 (b) RichardJohnson 132
(Gary Moore) *mde most at str pce and clr w one rival most of way tl 2 out: no ex* **8/1**

004- **4** *16* **Ballybough Gorta (IRE)**[23] 5334 8-10-13 121 (v) CiaranGethings[(7)] 116
(Nick Mitchell) *chsd ldrs: blnd 11th: wknd appr 4 out* **11/4**[1]

032- **P** **Midnight Oscar (IRE)**[20] 5368 8-11-6 121 (v) DavidBass
(Kim Bailey) *nvr jumping fluently: sn wl bhd: p.u bef 14th* **4/1**[3]

4R2- **R** **Mighty Mobb (IRE)**[26] 5284 8-10-5 109 (b) JeremiahMcGrath[(3)]
(Seamus Mullins) *outpcd: hrd rdn and struggling 8th: mstke 11th: distant 5th whn ref next* **5/1**

6m 12.1s (-27.40) **Going Correction** -0.85s/f (Firm) 6 Ran SP% **111.0**
Speed ratings: **108,105,105,100, ,**
CSF £26.57 TOTE £6.40: £3.10, £1.60; EX 14.50 Trifecta £71.70.
Owner Rose Farm Developments(UK)Ltd & Partner **Bred** G T Greene **Trained** Hanley Swan, Worcestershire

FOCUS

Despite the small field this was run at a fierce gallop as Alberobello and Fruity O'Rooney duelled throughout, setting it up for the only other runner still in contention. The winner was back on the upgrade.

170 ROYAL BATH & WEST SHOW NOVICES' H'CAP CHASE (13 fncs) 1m 7f 149y

7:20 (7:20) (Class 4) (0-105,105) 5-Y-0+ **£4,548** (£1,335; £667; £333)

Form RPR

432- **1** **All But Grey**[17] 5438 9-11-8 101 (t) MichealNolan 105+
(Carroll Gray) *hld up: hdwy 6th: cl 2nd but hld whn lft in ld 2 out: drvn out* **4/1**[3]

546- **2** *1 ½* **No No Cardinal (IRE)**[6] 1814 6-10-0 79 oh6 (t) TommyPhelan 81
(Mark Gillard) *hld up in rr: hdwy 4 out: chal appr last: one pce run-in* **14/1**

400- **3** *17* **Positive Vibes**[46] 4948 6-10-12 91 (p) ConorO'Farrell 78
(Richard Woollacott) *in tch tl struggling in rr 9th: blnd 3 out: passed btn rivals and benefited fr fallers to rch modest 3rd run-in* **8/1**

541- **4** *6* **Golanova**[13] 5522 7-11-2 105 (v) GeorgeGorman[(10)] 87
(Gary Moore) *in tch: drvn along fr 5th: struggling 9th: bhd whn blnd 4 out* **9/2**

U61- **5** *¾* **Faith Jicaro (IRE)**[13] 5526 8-11-4 97 (p) TomScudamore 78
(David Bridgwater) *led tl 7th: lost pl and btn after 9th: lft modest 4th and blnd 2 out* **7/2**[2]

114- **F** **Agapanthus (GER)**[52] 4815 10-11-4 97 (b) MarkQuinlan 105+
(Neil Mulholland) *handy 3rd and gng wl: jnd ldr 9th: led 3 out: 2 l up and wl on top whn fell next* **10/1**

433- **U** **Alla Svelta (IRE)**[20] 5374 9-11-11 104 (p) TomCannon 99
(Brendan Powell) *sn chsng ldr: led 7th tl mstke 3 out: 3rd and btn whn j. bdly rt and uns rdr last* **5/2**[1]

3m 48.6s (-11.30) **Going Correction** -0.85s/f (Firm) 7 Ran SP% **115.8**
Speed ratings: **94,93,84,81,81**
CSF £51.08 TOTE £3.90: £2.40, £5.60; EX 70.70 Trifecta £1031.40.
Owner R J Napper and N P Searle **Bred** R Napper & N P Searle **Trained** Moorland, Somerset

171 WATCH RACING UK ON SKY 432 NOVICES' HURDLE (8 hdls) 1m 7f 65y

7:50 (7:50) (Class 4) 4-Y-0+ **£3,249** (£954; £477; £238)

Form RPR

233- **1** **Buy Back Bob (IRE)**[137] 3211 8-10-12 117 RichardJohnson 108+
(Tim Vaughan) *mde all: shkn up run-in: qcknd wl and sn clr* **6/5**[1]

2 *5* **Proofreader**[40] 6-10-12 NoelFehily 104
(Neil Mulholland) *t.k.h in rr: mstke 5th: smooth hdwy to trck wnr whn j.lft last: rdn and unable qck* **7/4**[2]

055- **3** *4 ½* **Age Of Discovery**[44] 4983 4-10-8 (t) HarrySkelton 94
(Dan Skelton) *chsd ldrs: briefly wnt 2nd 2 out: cl 3rd whn blnd last: nt rcvr* **5/1**[3]

4 *3 ½* **Footstepsintherain (IRE)**[42] 5-10-12 AidanColeman 93
(David Dennis) *t.k.h in 5th: effrt 2 out: hrd rdn and btn appr last* **8/1**

4- **5** *6* **Mazovian (USA)**[40] 5023 7-10-12 MarkQuinlan 87
(Neil Mulholland) *t.k.h: pressed wnr tl wknd 2 out* **16/1**

/P0- **6** *13* **Thymeandthymeagain**[17] 5428 6-10-5 DaveCrosse 67
(Hugo Froud) *chsd ldrs tl wknd 2 out* **66/1**

3m 36.9s (-12.00) **Going Correction** -0.85s/f (Firm) 6 Ran SP% **117.0**
Speed ratings (Par 105): **96,93,91,89,86 80**
CSF £3.98 TOTE £1.90: £1.10, £2.00; EX 3.50 Trifecta £10.10.
Owner R P B Michaelson & Robin Clay **Bred** Anamoine Ltd **Trained** Aberthin, Vale of Glamorgan

FOCUS

This proved easy pickings for the favourite, who was allowed to dominate. He's rated below his best.

172 RACING UK YOUR RACING HOME FROM HOME CONDITIONAL JOCKEYS' H'CAP HURDLE (8 hdls) 1m 7f 65y

8:20 (8:20) (Class 5) (0-100,95) 4-Y-0+ **£2,599** (£763; £381; £190)

Form RPR

4P5- **1** **Kentford Myth**[59] 4669 5-11-12 95 JeremiahMcGrath 97
(Seamus Mullins) *chsd ldr: led and hit last: hld on gamely: all out* **8/1**

/P0- **2** *½* **Vexillum (IRE)**[155] 2268 6-10-5 82 (p) MrMartinMcIntyre[(8)] 84
(Neil Mulholland) *hld up: effrt 2 out: r.o to press wnr fnl 100yds: jst hld* **7/2**[3]

P4P- **3** *nk* **The Kvilleken**[66] 4540 7-10-11 90 (be) ArchieBellamy[(10)] 91+
(Martin Keighley) *hld up: smooth hdwy on outer fr 3 out: drvn to chal whn nt fluent last: r.o* **2/1**[1]

462- **4** *1 ¼* **Heading To First**[15] 5481 8-11-4 87 (v) SeanBowen 86
(Jim Best) *in tch: mstke 5th: rdn to press ldrs appr last: kpt on run-in* **9/4**[2]

000- **5** *1 ½* **King Muro**[14] 5490 5-11-8 94 ConorShoemark[(3)] 91
(Fergal O'Brien) *sn led and r freely: clr tl 5th: hdd and blnd last: no ex fnl 100yds* **16/1**

005- **6** 3/4 **Bulletproof (IRE)**[45] 4967 9-11-4 **87**..............................(p) ChrisWard 84
(Ken Cunningham-Brown) *a in rr: in tch 3 out: rdn and btn appr next: styd on run-in* **8/1**

3m 35.5s (-13.40) **Going Correction** -0.85s/f (Firm) **6** Ran SP% **114.4**
Speed ratings (Par 103): **99,98,98,97,97 96**
CSF £36.70 TOTE £7.20: £3.00, £1.40; EX 33.00 Trifecta £132.30.
Owner D I Bare **Bred** D I Bare **Trained** Wilsford-Cum-Lake, Wilts

FOCUS
They finished in a heap in a steadily run handicap and this is not form to take seriously.
T/Plt: £202.90 to a £1 stake. Pool of £41870.86 - 150.64 winning tickets. T/Qpdt: £45.00 to a £1 stake. Pool of £4036.95 - 66.30 winning tickets. **Lee McKenzie**

WORCESTER (L-H)
Thursday, May 7

OFFICIAL GOING: Good to soft (good in places)
Wind: Light behind Weather: Cloudy with sunny spells

173 VISITWORCESTERSHIRE.ORG CONDITIONAL JOCKEYS' H'CAP CHASE (13 fncs) 2m 4f
1:50 (1:51) (Class 5) (0-100,100) 5-Y-O+ £2,599 (£763; £381; £190)

Form RPR

365- **1** **Thinger Licht (FR)**[72] 4419 6-10-9 **86**..............................(p) BridgetAndrews(3) 102+
(Dan Skelton) *chsd ldr: led briefly 8th: chalng whn lft in ld 4 out: clr last: comf* **6/4**[1]

463- **2** 5 **By The Boardwalk (IRE)**[31] 5197 7-11-9 **97**..............(t) ConorShoemark 103+
(Kim Bailey) *a.p: ev ch 3 out: rdn appr last: styd on same pce* **7/1**

32/- **3** 8 **Kap West (FR)**[561] 2023 10-10-8 **82**..............................(t) MattGriffiths 83
(Laura Young) *hld up: hdwy 4 out: mstke next: sn rdn: wknd flat* **18/1**

445- **4** 1 1/4 **Stafford Charlie**[13] 5512 9-9-11 **74** oh4......................(p) DavidPrichard(3) 73
(John O'Shea) *hld up: plld hrd: mstke 7th: hdwy after 9th: hmpd 4 out: pckd next: sn rdn: wknd last* **33/1**

035- **5** 11 **Thats Yer Man (IRE)**[15] 5463 7-10-9 **83**.............................. MichealNolan 73
(Linda Blackford) *chsd ldrs: rdn 3 out: wknd next* **16/1**

3P5- **F** **Nether Stream (IRE)**[40] 5024 11-11-4 **92**.............................. KieronEdgar
(David Dennis) *led: hmpd by loose horse after 7th: hdd briefly next: slt ld whn fell 4 out* **25/1**

F22- **F** **Who Am I**[15] 5467 9-11-8 **96**..............................(p) SeanBowen 86
(Debra Hamer) *hld up: pushed along whn hmpd 4 out: 7 l 6th whn fell 2 out* **9/2**[3]

002- **U** **Vujiyama (FR)**[15] 5463 6-11-4 **100**.............................. JackSavage(8)
(Jonjo O'Neill) *hld up: mstke and uns rdr 2nd* **4/1**[2]

5m 17.0s (17.00) **Going Correction** -0.025s/f (Good) **8** Ran SP% **108.6**
Speed ratings: **65,63,59,59,54 , ,**
CSF £11.40 CT £113.08 TOTE £2.60: £1.20, £1.70, £2.90; EX 14.40 Trifecta £142.60.
Owner Carl Hodgson **Bred** M Jacques Chapet & Mme Anne Dupont **Trained** Alcester, Warwicks

FOCUS
Far bend 12yds from inside line and Cathedral bend 8yds from inside line. 2m and 2m 1.5f races increased by 60yds and 2m 4f & 2m 7f increased by 96yds. The first fixture at Worcester since the autumn. Hurdles and fences were on the outside line, and times confirmed that the ground was riding on the easy side of good. They went a pretty steady pace in this ordinary handicap for conditionals. The winner is rated in line with the best of his form in the last year.

174 WORCESTER BETTING TIPS @ BOOKIES.COM H'CAP CHASE (16 fncs) 2m 7f
2:20 (2:20) (Class 4) (0-120,119) 5-Y-O+ £4,548 (£1,335; £667; £333)

Form RPR

432- **1** **Fond Memory (IRE)**[38] 5069 7-11-3 **110**..............(t) SamTwiston-Davies 122+
(Nigel Twiston-Davies) *hld up: hdwy appr 4 out: chsd ldr next: led and mstke last: drvn out* **11/4**[1]

2F3- **2** 2 3/4 **Sergeant Dick (IRE)**[16] 5450 10-11-4 **114**..............(tp) JamesBanks(3) 119
(Andy Turnell) *led: rdn and hdd last: styd on same pce flat* **4/1**[2]

4P1- **3** 26 **Royal Native (IRE)**[37] 5081 7-11-12 **119**..............(t) AidanColeman 103
(Anthony Honeyball) *hld up: hit 5th: pushed along and lost tch 11th: wnt poor 3rd flat* **5/1**[3]

11P- **4** 6 **Midnight Request**[21] 5358 6-11-8 **115**..............(v[1]) ConorO'Farrell 93
(Nigel Hawke) *mstkes: chsd ldr to 7th: wnt 2nd again next tl 9th: rdn appr 4 out: wknd 2 out* **13/2**

321- **5** 15 **Lord Landen (IRE)**[31] 5204 10-10-12 **108**..............(t) ConorShoemark(3) 71
(Fergal O'Brien) *hld up: hdwy 5th: chsd ldr 7th to 8th: wnt 2nd again next: rdn appr 4 out: wknd bef 2 out* **8/1**

423- **6** 2 1/4 **Worthy Award (IRE)**[23] 5336 7-11-9 **116**..............(p) RichieMcLernon 77
(Jonjo O'Neill) *sn prom: rdn after 12th: wknd 3 out* **13/2**

014- **P** **The Darling Boy**[38] 5062 10-11-5 **112**..............(tp) TomScudamore
(David Pipe) *chsd ldrs: lost pl 9th: sn bhd: p.u bef 2 out* **10/1**

5m 58.1s (10.10) **Going Correction** -0.025s/f (Good) **7** Ran SP% **110.2**
Speed ratings: **81,80,71,68,63 62,**
CSF £13.41 CT £46.83 TOTE £3.90: £2.20, £2.00; EX 11.80 Trifecta £71.10.
Owner The Stirling Partnership **Bred** C Kenneally **Trained** Naunton, Gloucs

FOCUS
This fair handicap was run at a reasonable gallop. The first two came well clear and the second sets the level.

175 DAILY RACING TIPS @ BOOKIES.COM H'CAP CHASE (12 fncs) 2m 110y
2:50 (2:50) (Class 4) (0-110,105) 5-Y-O+ £3,898 (£1,144; £572; £286)

Form RPR

005- **1** **Strongly Suggested**[175] 2466 8-11-12 **105**.............................. RichieMcLernon 117+
(Jonjo O'Neill) *a.p: chsd ldr 4 out: led next: shkn up flat: styd on wl* **10/3**[1]

125- **2** 2 3/4 **Sportsreport (IRE)**[32] 5153 7-11-12 **105**..............(p) AndrewThornton 112
(Seamus Mullins) *hld up: nt fluent 6th: hdwy after 9th: jnd wnr 3 out: shkn up: flat: styd on same pce* **9/2**[3]

050- **3** 5 **Regal D'Estruval (FR)**[160] 2786 10-11-6 **99**.............................. CharliePoste 103
(Matt Sheppard) *chsd ldr tl led after 9th: hit and hdd 3 out: styd on same pce fr next* **9/2**[3]

F55- **4** 23 **Imperial Plan (IRE)**[199] 1983 5-11-9 **102**..............(t) BrendanPowell 83
(Jamie Snowden) *prom tl rdn and wknd 4 out* **13/2**

310- **P** **Topthorn**[101] 3898 9-11-5 **105**..............................(p) MrZBaker(7)
(Martin Bosley) *chsd ldrs to 6th: sn bhd: p.u bef 4 out* **11/2**

221- **F** **Capisci (IRE)**[255] 1326 10-11-12 **105**.............................. RobertDunne 86
(Sarah-Jayne Davies) *led: hdd after 9th: wknd after 4 out: bhd whn fell last* **4/1**[2]

4m 11.3s (-2.70) **Going Correction** -0.025s/f (Good) **6** Ran SP% **108.2**
Speed ratings: **105,103,101,90,**
CSF £17.07 TOTE £4.90: £2.80, £3.30; EX 12.90 Trifecta £97.40.
Owner John P McManus **Bred** David Brace **Trained** Cheltenham, Gloucs

FOCUS
The pace was solid in this modest handicap. A chase best from the winner.

176 OGL NEIL MORRIS BIRTHDAY CELEBRATION (S) HURDLE (10 hdls) 2m 4f
3:25 (3:25) (Class 5) 4-7-Y-O £2,599 (£763; £381; £190)

Form RPR

015- **1** **Vif Argent (FR)**[25] 5290 6-11-0 120..............................(bt) TomScudamore 111+
(David Pipe) *mde all: nt fluent 5th: rdn appr last: styd on u.p* **1/1**[1]

530- **2** 1 3/4 **Fuzzy Logic (IRE)**[6] 1989 6-10-11 105..............(p) RobertWilliams(3) 109
(Bernard Llewellyn) *chsd wnr: rdn whn blnd 2 out: styd on u.p* **10/1**

030- **3** 6 **Whatthebutlersaw (IRE)**[52] 4813 6-10-7 0............ BenFfrenchDavis(7) 104
(Dominic Ffrench Davis) *hld up: hdwy 4th: rdn appr 2 out: j.rt last: styd on same pce* **9/1**

662- **4** 5 **Flash Crash**[13] 5523 6-11-0 115..............................(t) DarylJacob 98
(Jim Best) *hld up: hdwy 6th: rdn appr last: wknd flat* **7/2**[2]

50-U **5** 23 **Camachoice (IRE)**[2] 125 5-11-0 117..............................(p) BrendanPowell 80
(Jamie Snowden) *prom: nt fluent and lost pl 4th: rdn after 7th: wknd bef next* **5/1**[3]

442/ **6** 80 **Green And White (ITY)**[540] 2455 5-11-0 103.............................. LeeEdwards 5
(Dave Roberts) *hld up: mstkes 1st and 2nd: pushed along 5th: wknd bef 7th* **50/1**

/PP- **P** **Fanny Fantastic**[25] 5286 6-10-0 0.............................. MrJNixon(7)
(Miss Imogen Pickard) *chsd ldrs tl wknd appr 7th: bhd whn p.u bef 3 out* **100/1**

5m 1.5s (14.10) **Going Correction** +0.60s/f (Soft) **7** Ran SP% **110.9**
Speed ratings: **95,94,91,89,80 48,**
CSF £11.57 TOTE £1.80: £1.80, £4.00; EX 11.00 Trifecta £53.20.The winner was bought by A Reid for 11,500gns.
Owner Stef Stefanou **Bred** Francois Rimaud **Trained** Nicholashayne, Devon

FOCUS
The winner set a fair pace in this reasonable seller, and is rated below his best.

177 HEREFORDSHIRE AND WORCESTERSHIRE CHAMBER OF COMMERCE H'CAP HURDLE (10 hdls) 2m 4f
4:00 (4:01) (Class 4) (0-120,119) 4-Y-O+ £3,249 (£954; £477; £238)

Form RPR

/00- **1** **Fleet Dawn**[75] 4365 9-11-8 **115**..............................(t) FelixDeGiles 118
(Brian Ellison) *hld up: hdwy 7th: rdn to ld flat: r.o* **10/1**

244- **2** 1 **Singlefarmpayment**[60] 4651 5-11-7 **114**.............................. RobertDunne 116
(Tom Lacey) *chsd clr ldr: wnt rt 6th: tk clsr order bef 3 out: rdn to ld and edgd rt bef last: hdd flat: styd on* **13/2**[2]

024- **3** 1/2 **Lamblord (IRE)**[37] 5082 8-10-9 **102**..............(p) MichealNolan 104
(Carroll Gray) *led and sn clr: c bk to the field and rdn bef 3 out: hdd appr last: styd on* **14/1**

41P- **4** 3 3/4 **Definite Future (IRE)**[60] 4651 6-11-2 **109**.............................. JakeGreenall 108
(Richard Lee) *hld up: hdwy appr 3 out: rdn after next: styd on same pce flat* **16/1**

453- **5** 3 **Hawaii Five Nil (IRE)**[89] 4088 7-11-8 **115**.............................. RichieMcLernon 111
(Jonjo O'Neill) *chsd clr ldrs: tk clsr order 3 out: ev ch next: sn rdn: wknd flat* **8/1**[3]

460- **6** 1 1/4 **Arthur's Secret (FR)**[41] 5019 5-11-5 **112**..............(t) SamTwiston-Davies 107
(Nigel Twiston-Davies) *hld up: hdwy 3 out: sn rdn: no ex flat* **20/1**

335- **7** 1 3/4 **Twelve Strings (IRE)**[33] 5150 6-11-2 **109**..............(p) AidanColeman 102
(Venetia Williams) *hld up: hdwy appr 3 out: sn rdn: wknd last* **20/1**

446- **8** 6 **Iguacu**[19] 2021 11-10-7 **100**.............................. NoelFehily 88
(Richard Price) *hld up: rdn after 7th: nvr on terms* **20/1**

561- **9** 59 **Hi Tide (IRE)**[182] 2292 11-11-11 **118**.............................. DougieCostello 53
(J R Jenkins) *hld up: a in rr: wknd 7th* **33/1**

0F4- **10** 57 **Church Field (IRE)**[69] 4471 7-11-0 **110**.............................. MauriceLinehan(3)
(Jonjo O'Neill) *hld up: pushed along 5th: wknd 7th* **14/1**

4PP- **P** **Citizenship**[42] 4998 9-11-12 **119**.............................. LiamTreadwell
(Venetia Williams) *hld up: in rr whn mstke 5th: bhd fr 7th: p.u bef last* **25/1**

1F/ **B** **Malapie (IRE)**[811] 4230 7-11-5 **112**.............................. AdamPogson
(Caroline Bailey) *hld up: hdwy after 7th: 3 l 5th whn b.d 3 out* **9/1**

230- **P** **Looks Like Power (IRE)**[70] 4448 5-11-0 **110**.............................. SeanBowen(3)
(Debra Hamer) *racd in 3rd pl tl nt fluent 5th: wknd after next: bhd whn p.u bef 2 out* **10/1**

6/3- **P** **Benenden (IRE)**[25] 5295 7-11-9 **116**.............................. TomScudamore
(Michael Scudamore) *mid-div: rdn and wknd after 7th: bhd whn p.u bef 2 out* **13/2**[2]

133- **R** **The Geegeez Geegee (IRE)**[31] 5202 6-10-5 **105**..............(t) HarryCobden(7) 110+
(Anthony Honeyball) *hld up: hdwy appr 3 out: ev ch whn rn out last* **5/1**[1]

044- **F** **Smoking Jacket (IRE)**[40] 5025 5-11-3 **110**.............................. PaddyBrennan
(Tom George) *chsd clr ldrs: tk clsr in 2 l 4th but rdn whn fell 3 out* **16/1**

5m 3.6s (16.20) **Going Correction** +0.60s/f (Soft) **16** Ran SP% **128.8**
Speed ratings (Par 105): **91,90,90,88,87 87,86,84,60,37 , , , ,**
CSF £72.79 CT £945.43 TOTE £12.10: £3.20, £2.90, £3.60, £4.90; EX 133.80 Trifecta £1908.30.

Owner Prism Bloodstock **Bred** P Murphy **Trained** Norton, N Yorks
■ Stewards' Enquiry : Robert Dunne two-day ban: use of whip (21-22 May)

FOCUS
An ordinary but competitive handicap, run in a time 2.1sec slower than the earlier seller. The third home was clear from an early stage, and the pack didn't go a great gallop. The form looks sound.

178 POST YOUR BETS @ BOOKIES.COM MARES' MAIDEN HURDLE (DIV I) (8 hdls) 2m
4:35 (4:35) (Class 5) 4-Y-O+ £2,599 (£763; £381; £190)

Form RPR

1 **Taweyla (IRE)**[26] 4-10-10 0.............................. KielanWoods 105+
(Pam Sly) *chsd ldr: j.rt 5th led bef 3 out: rdn appr last: hung lft flat: styd on u.p* **10/1**

323- **2** 1 1/4 **Pandorica**[6] 5060 7-10-11 109..............................(p) RobertWilliams(3) 108
(Bernard Llewellyn) *mid-div: hdwy 4th: rdn and n.m.r flat: unable qck towards fin* **3/1**[2]

301- **3** 3 **Lolli (IRE)**[25] 5299 5-11-0 0.............................. NoelFehily 108+
(Nicky Henderson) *mid-div: hdwy 4th: ev ch fr 2 out tl mstke last: styd on same pce flat* **10/11**[1]

3/5- **4** 16 **Born To Benefit (IRE)**[15] 5466 9-11-0 99..............(t[1]) PaddyBrennan 94
(Fergal O'Brien) *led: racd keenly: hdd appr 3 out: wknd bef last* **6/1**[3]

65- **5** 15 **Sheer Poetry (IRE)**[33] 5144 4-10-10 0.............................. DarylJacob 73
(Richard Woollacott) *hld up: nvr on terms* **18/1**

00- **6** nk **Love Over Heels**[21] 5359 6-11-0 0.............................. RobertDunne 77
(Richard Price) *chsd ldrs tl rdn and wknd bef 3 out* **100/1**

\- **7** 15 **Quench Tara** 8-11-0 0.............................. LiamTreadwell 64
(Michael Scudamore) *nt fluent: a in rr* **12/1**

PP- P **Shining Grace**[49] 4860 6-11-0 0..............................(t) MarkGrant
(Sarah Robinson) *hld up: plld hrd: bhd fr 3rd: p.u bef 3 out* **150/1**

/05- P **Annies Idea**[40] 5035 6-11-0 0.............................. AdamPogson
(Mandy Rowland) *prom tl wknd after 4th: bhd whn p.u bef 3 out* **66/1**

06-P P **Stage Twenty (IRE)**[7] 28 5-11-0 0.............................. BrendanPowell
(Jamie Snowden) *hld up: j.lft 1st: bhd fr 3rd: blnd 5th: p.u bef 3 out* **50/1**

3m 54.4s (7.10) **Going Correction** +0.60s/f (Soft)
WFA 4 from 5yo+ 18lb **10 Ran SP% 118.8**
Speed ratings (Par 103): **106,105,103,95,88 88,80,,,**
CSF £41.94 TOTE £15.20: £3.40, £1.10, £1.10; EX 57.10 Trifecta £133.70.
Owner Pam's People **Bred** Darley **Trained** Thorney, Cambs

FOCUS
A weak event for mares, but the quickest of the three C&D times. The winner is a potential 110+ hurdler on Flat form.

179 POST YOUR BETS @ BOOKIES.COM MARES' MAIDEN HURDLE (DIV II) (8 hdls) 2m
5:05 (5:05) (Class 5) 4-Y-0+ **£2,599** (£763; £381; £190)

Form RPR

P02- 1 *nse* **Giveagirlachance (IRE)**[41] 4653 6-11-0 **107**.............. AndrewThornton 101+
(Seamus Mullins) *hld up: hdwy appr 3 out: chsd wnr and hmpd last: styd on u.p: fin 2nd: plcd 1st* **11/2**[3]

23- 2 **Nellies Quest**[18] 5411 6-11-0 **110**.............................. BrendanPowell 101+
(Brendan Powell) *hld up: hdwy and nt fluent 5th: led 2 out: rdn and wnt rt last: all out: fin 1st: plcd 2nd* **15/2**

242- 3 *7* **What A Scorcher**[59] 4682 4-10-10 **111**.............................. LeightonAspell 91
(Oliver Sherwood) *trckd ldrs: racd keenly: led after 5th: rdn and hdd 2 out: no ex flat* **7/4**[1]

02- 4 *4* **Miss Tongabezi**[40] 5035 6-11-0 0.............................. LiamTreadwell 90
(Paul Webber) *chsd ldr: rdn appr 3 out: styd on same pce fr next* **10/1**

3P0- 5 *17* **Tantalized**[19] 5397 6-11-0 70..............................(b) LeeEdwards 76
(Dave Roberts) *led: rdn and hdd after 5th: wknd next* **80/1**

04- 6 *9* **Rebekah Rabbit (IRE)**[44] 4981 5-11-0 0.............................. RobertDunne 66
(Tom Lacey) *chsd ldrs tl rdn and wknd after 3 out* **25/1**

7 *½* **Sawwala**[93] 5-11-0 0.............................. DougieCostello 65
(J R Jenkins) *hld up: wknd 5th* **66/1**

6- P **Southern Cross**[128] 3116 4-10-7 0.............................. JamesBanks(3)
(Andy Turnell) *hld up: wknd after 5th: bhd whn p.u bef 3 out* **66/1**

2P3- P **Saint Lucy**[72] 4416 4-10-10 119.............................. RichieMcLernon
(Jonjo O'Neill) *hld up in tch: rdn: wknd and p.u bef 3 out* **15/8**[2]

0- P **Hot Madras (IRE)**[176] 2447 7-10-7 0.............................. JoshWall(7)
(Trevor Wall) *hld up: bhd fr 4th: p.u bef 3 out* **100/1**

3m 55.8s (8.50) **Going Correction** +0.60s/f (Soft)
WFA 4 from 5yo+ 18lb **10 Ran SP% 116.4**
Speed ratings (Par 103): **101,102,98,96,87 83,83,,,**
CSF £43.67 TOTE £6.00: £3.50, £2.20, £1.10; EX 41.90 Trifecta £98.10.
Owner The Five Plus One Partnership **Bred** Pier House Stud **Trained** Wilsford-Cum-Lake, Wilts
■ Stewards' Enquiry : Brendan Powell seven-day ban: use of whip (21, 27 May)

FOCUS
Perhaps the weaker division, with the time slower. The placings of the first two were reversed by the stewards, with Giveagirlachance the best guide.

180 PREMIER LEAGUE DARTS TIPS @ BOOKIES.COM H'CAP HURDLE (8 hdls) 2m
5:35 (5:35) (Class 5) (0-100,100) 4-Y-0+ **£2,599** (£763; £381; £190)

Form RPR

0PU- 1 **Sir Note (FR)**[69] 4465 5-10-5 **79**..............................(t) RichieMcLernon 86
(Nick Littmoden) *hld up: hdwy appr 3 out: led bef next: drvn out* **16/1**

306- 2 *1 ¾* **Anton Dolin (IRE)**[63] 4576 7-11-5 **100**.............................. MrHFNugent(7) 106
(Michael Mullineaux) *hld up in tch: shkn up to chse wnr last: rdn and hung lft flat: kpt on* **14/1**

530/ 3 *3 ½* **Innoko (FR)**[34] 2975 5-11-6 **94**.............................. LeeEdwards 96
(Tony Carroll) *hld up: pushed along 5th: hdwy after 2 out: rdn and hung lft flat: styd on same pce* **20/1**

043- 4 *2* **Isdaal**[36] 5091 8-10-0 **74** oh2..............................(v[1]) AdamWedge 74
(Kevin Morgan) *mid-div: hdwy 4th: rdn and ev ch appr 2 out: nt clr run flat: styd on same pce* **11/1**

065- 5 *5* **L Stig**[19] 5397 5-11-7 **95**.............................. JakeGreenall 92
(Henry Daly) *hld up: rdn appr 2 out: no imp* **9/1**[3]

024- 6 *nk* **Symphony Of Pearls**[28] 5242 4-10-4 **82**.............................. RobertDunne 74
(Dai Burchell) *chsd ldrs: j.rt 3rd: rdn after 5th: wknd last* **11/1**

006- 7 *5* **Wolftrap (IRE)**[76] 4339 6-11-7 **95**..............................(t) DougieCostello 86
(Laura Young) *hld up: rdn after 5th: nvr trbld ldrs* **20/1**

P54- 8 *½* **Going Nowhere Fast (IRE)**[194] 2067 10-10-5 **86**........ JordanWilliams(7) 76
(Bernard Llewellyn) *prom: nt fluent 5th: rdn and wknd bef last* **14/1**

006- 9 *1 ¼* **Rockweiller**[30] 4390 8-10-5 **79**.............................. GerardTumelty 70
(Shaun Harris) *led to 4th: ev ch whn mstke 3 out: wkng whn j.rt last* **25/1**

604- 10 *10* **Empty The Tank (IRE)**[31] 5212 5-10-6 **80**.............. SamTwiston-Davies 60
(Nigel Twiston-Davies) *chsd ldrs tl rdn and wknd appr 2 out* **7/4**[1]

3P6- 11 *1 ¼* **All The Winds (GER)**[23] 5335 10-11-9 **97**..............................(t) PeterCarberry 78
(Shaun Lycett) *hld up in tch: rdn and ev ch after 3 out: mstke and wknd next* **16/1**

/0P- 12 *8* **General Ross (IRE)**[19] 5398 8-10-9 **83**..............................(b) BrendanPowell 55
(Adrian Wintle) *chsd ldr tl led 4th: hdd & wknd appr 2 out* **33/1**

/00- 13 *4* **Fine Jewellery**[105] 3810 6-10-9 **83**..............................(t[1]) FelixDeGiles 51
(Tom Gretton) *hld up: rdn and wknd appr 3 out* **50/1**

F13- P **Henri De Boistron (FR)**[64] 4560 5-11-8 **96**.............................. PaddyBrennan
(Tom George) *hld up: rdn 3rd: hdwy 5th: wknd bef next: bhd whn p.u flat* **15/2**[2]

3m 55.9s (8.60) **Going Correction** +0.60s/f (Soft)
WFA 4 from 5yo+ 18lb **14 Ran SP% 118.2**
Speed ratings (Par 103): **102,101,99,98,95 95,93,92,92,87 86,82,80,**
CSF £200.38 CT £4446.07 TOTE £35.70: £10.20, £4.10, £5.80; EX 699.90 Trifecta £1568.60 Part won. Pool of £2091.57 - 0.01 winning unit..
Owner G F Chesneaux **Bred** Jean-Pierre Coiffier **Trained** Newmarket, Suffolk

FOCUS
Modest handicap form, with a big step up from the winner.
T/Plt: £49.90, to a £1 stake. Pool of £52655.67 - 769.80 winning tickets. T/Qpdt: £20.80 to a £1 stake. Pool of £4400.99 - 156.0 winning tickets. **Colin Roberts**

MARKET RASEN (R-H)
Friday, May 8

OFFICIAL GOING: Good (8.5)
Wind: light 1/2 behind Weather: fine and warm, light rain race 5 onwards

181 WATCH RACING UK ON SKY CHANNEL 432 NOVICES' HURDLE (10 hdls) 2m 4f 139y
1:20 (1:21) (Class 4) 4-Y-0+ **£3,249** (£954; £477; £238)

Form RPR

332- 1 **Royalraise (IRE)**[43] 4996 6-10-12 **122**.............................. LeightonAspell 124+
(Oliver Sherwood) *mde all: drew readily clr appr 2 out: eased clsng stages* **10/11**[1]

341- 2 *10* **Oh Land Abloom (IRE)**[26] 5293 5-11-5 0..............................(t) TrevorWhelan 123+
(Neil King) *in rr: nt fluent 1st: drvn 3 out: chsng wnr appr next: kpt on same pce* **4/1**[3]

062- 3 *15* **Calin Du Brizais (FR)**[18] 5434 4-10-7 0..............................(t) TomScudamore 95
(Nigel Hawke) *chsd ldrs: 3rd 3 out: one pce* **12/1**

4 *4 ½* **Cool Runnings (IRE)**[931] 5-10-12 0.............................. AndrewTinkler 95
(Tim Fitzgerald) *in rr: drvn 6th: sme hdwy 3 out: modest 4th next* **66/1**

22- 5 *24* **Magnimity (IRE)**[161] 2781 5-10-9 0.............................. JeremiahMcGrath(3) 74
(Nicky Henderson) *chsd ldrs: 2nd 3 out: lost pl and poor 5th whn mstke 2 out: sn bhd* **5/2**[2]

653- 6 *10* **Catwalk Babe (IRE)**[19] 5410 5-10-5 0..............................(t) HarrySkelton 58
(Dan Skelton) *chsd ldrs: 3 out: sn wknd: t.o next* **25/1**

50- F **Fair To Middling**[41] 5028 5-10-12 0.............................. AidanColeman
(Charlie Longsdon) *chsd ldrs: outpcd 6th: rdn and lost pl 3 out: sn bhd: t.o whn fell heavily next* **80/1**

5m 15.6s (6.80) **Going Correction** +0.375s/f (Yiel)
WFA 4 from 5yo+ 19lb **7 Ran SP% 115.2**
Speed ratings (Par 105): **102,98,92,90,81 77,**
CSF £5.31 TOTE £1.90: £1.20, £2.40; EX 5.90 Trifecta £22.50.
Owner Ian Barratt, Stephen Short & Adam Signy **Bred** Stephen Roche **Trained** Upper Lambourn, Berks

FOCUS
Rail positioned 24 yards from innermost line, increasing circuit length by approximately 144 yards. A fair novice hurdle which was run at a steady initial pace, and in a time 18.6sec slower than the standard. Afterwards, Tom Scudamore reported the ground to be "good, maybe a bit bit quicker than that in places." The winner and third set the level.

182 MOLSON COORS "CARLING" CLASSIC H'CAP HURDLE (10 hdls) 2m 2f 140y
1:50 (1:52) (Class 4) (0-115,115) 4-Y-0 **£3,249** (£954; £477)

Form RPR

43-2 1 **Romulus Du Donjon (IRE)**[7] 61 4-11-11 **114**.............. LeightonAspell 120+
(Oliver Sherwood) *trckd ldr: upsides and pushed along 7th: led appr 2 out: drvn clr appr last* **5/4**[1]

245- 2 *8* **Mighty Missile (IRE)**[60] 4674 4-11-12 **115**..............................(tp) DougieCostello 115
(Warren Greatrex) *led: drvn 3 out: hdd appr last: sn btn* **5/2**[3]

640- 3 *16* **Master Dan**[41] 5025 4-11-3 **106**..............................(t) DavidBass 94
(Kim Bailey) *racd in last: trckd other 2: pushed along 5th: drvn 7th: reminders and lost pl appr 2 out: bhd whn eased sn after last* **2/1**[2]

4m 43.7s (4.30) **Going Correction** +0.375s/f (Yiel) **3 Ran SP% 106.3**
Speed ratings: **105,101,94**
CSF £4.29 TOTE £2.00; EX 2.70 Trifecta £2.90.
Owner Simon Munir & Isaac Souede **Bred** Pontchartrain Stud **Trained** Upper Lambourn, Berks

FOCUS
A disappointing turnout, but at least they went a reasonable gallop. The winner is on the upgrade.

183 RACING UK PROFITS RETURNED TO RACING NOVICES' H'CAP CHASE (14 fncs) 2m 5f 89y
2:20 (2:20) (Class 4) (0-110,105) 5-Y-0+ **£3,768** (£1,106; £553; £276)

Form RPR

3F2- 1 **The Purchaser (IRE)**[21] 5374 7-10-12 **91**..............................(b) TomMessenger 100+
(Chris Bealby) *mde all: drvn 3 out: kpt on wl run-in* **6/1**

612- 2 *3* **Thoresby (IRE)**[48] 4927 9-11-10 **103**..............................(p) DarylJacob 110
(Ben Case) *trckd ldrs: 2nd appr 3 out: hit last: kpt on same pce* **7/2**[1]

136- 3 *2 ¾* **Combustible Kate (IRE)**[155] 2893 9-10-2 **81**.............................. AdamWedge 85
(Nick Kent) *chsd ldrs: drvn 3 out: kpt on one pce between last 2* **12/1**

364- 4 *4 ½* **Cabaret Girl**[22] 5354 8-11-7 **100**.............................. AndrewThornton 99
(John O'Neill) *chsd ldrs: reminders after 5th: drvn to chse ldrs 11th: briefly upsides appr next: one pce: regained modest 4th nr fin* **11/2**[3]

146- 5 *1 ½* **Pagham Belle**[18] 5429 7-11-2 **95**..............................(bt) TomScudamore 94
(Nigel Hawke) *chsd ldrs: drvn appr 3 out: one pce: 4th last* **9/2**[2]

344- 6 *8* **The Society Man (IRE)**[32] 5203 8-10-13 **97**.............................. JoeCornwall(5) 91
(Michael Chapman) *in rr: outpcd 8th: lost pl 11th* **15/2**

364- 7 *65* **Finding Your Feet (IRE)**[113] 3694 7-11-12 **105**.............................. RichieMcLernon 37
(Jonjo O'Neill) *in rr: nt fluent and reminders 6th: lost pl 9th: bhd next: t.o bef 3 out: eventually ciompleted* **7/2**[1]

5m 33.45s (-12.55) **Going Correction** -0.675s/f (Firm) **7 Ran SP% 111.8**
Speed ratings: **94,92,92,90,89 87,64**
CSF £26.48 TOTE £6.30: £2.40, £2.10; EX 19.60 Trifecta £371.20.
Owner J H Henderson **Bred** Michael J Lee **Trained** Barrowby, Lincs

FOCUS
The winner set a fair gallop in this ordinary novice handicap. The first two are rated pretty much to their marks.

184 GO POINTING - FREE POINT-TO-POINT E-MAGAZINE H'CAP CHASE (14 fncs) 2m 3f 34y
2:50 (2:53) (Class 2) 5-Y-0+
£15,640 (£4,620; £2,310; £1,155; £577; £290)

Form RPR

P11- 1 **Anay Turge (FR)**[23] 5342 10-10-11 **135**..............................(t) TomScudamore 141+
(Nigel Hawke) *chsd ldrs: upsides 3 out: styd on to ld last 75yds* **6/1**[2]

204- 2 *1 ½* **Le Bacardy (FR)**[20] 5391 9-10-9 **133**.............................. HarrySkelton 139
(Dan Skelton) *hld up in rr: hdwy 10th: trcking ldrs next: upsides 3 out: led appr last: hdd and no ex last 75yds* **7/1**[3]

113- 3 *1 ½* **Brave Spartacus (IRE)**[21] 5363 9-10-11 **135**.............................. JamesReveley 140
(Keith Reveley) *trckd ldr: lft in ld 3rd: pestered by loose horse bnd after 7th: hdd 2 out: rallied run-in: no ex last 75yds* **12/1**

324- 4 *1 ¾* **Galway Jack (IRE)**[23] 5342 10-10-11 **135**..............................(t) AndrewThornton 140
(Caroline Bailey) *trckd ldrs: lft clr 2nd 3rd: led and blnd 2 out: sn hdd kpt on same pce last 100yds* **14/1**

PF2- **5** *14* **Freckle Face**[19] 5406 8-10-0 **124**........ MarkQuinlan 116
(Bill Turner) *in rr: hdwy 10th: fdd appr 3 out* **11/1**

2F1- **6** *1½* **Mountain King**[14] 5515 6-11-1 **139**........ RichardJohnson 128
(Philip Hobbs) *chsd ldrs: mstke 6th: sn lost pl: hdwy appr 3 out: kpt on: nvr a factor* **11/2**[1]

21U- **7** *4½* **Crookstown (IRE)**[40] 5046 8-10-12 **136**........ KielanWoods 122
(Ben Case) *in rr: hdwy and in tch whn mstke 10th: fdd appr 3 out* **12/1**

/02- **8** *hd* **Silver Roque (FR)**[85] 4191 9-11-2 **143**........ ConorShoemark(3) 128
(Fergal O'Brien) *chsd ldrs: lost pl after 10th* **8/1**

/PP- **9** *½* **Bar De Ligne (FR)**[20] 5393 9-9-13 **130**........(p) CraigGallagher(7) 114
(Brian Ellison) *in rr: bhd and drvn 11th: nvr on terms* **25/1**

F02- **10** *3½* **Alderbrook Lad (IRE)**[15] 5493 9-9-11 **124**........ JoeColliver(3) 105
(Micky Hammond) *chsd ldrs: lft 2nd 3rd: blnd 7th: lost pl 10th: sn bhd* **10/1**

06P- **11** *28* **Rum And Butter (IRE)**[59] 4694 7-10-9 **133**........(b[1]) RichieMcLernon 100
(Jonjo O'Neill) *in rr: hdwy 4th: lost pl 9th: sn bhd* **10/1**

F5U- **12** *22* **Anquetta (IRE)**[23] 5342 11-10-12 **139**........ MrSWaley-Cohen(3) 102
(Robert Waley-Cohen) *chsd ldrs: effrt 9th: lost pl 10th: sn bhd* **9/1**

604- **U** **Australia Day (IRE)**[29] 5246 12-11-12 **150**........ LiamTreadwell
(Paul Webber) *led: bluindered bdly: wnt rt and uns rdr 3rd* **25/1**

4m 46.4s (-19.30) **Going Correction** -0.675s/f (Firm) **13 Ran SP% 119.5**
Speed ratings: **111,110,109,109,103 102,101,101,100,99 88,79,**
CSF £48.57 CT £489.40 TOTE £5.80: £1.50, £3.60, £2.10; EX 45.10 Trifecta £551.30.
Owner Mrs K Hawke **Bred** Mme Annick Penouilh **Trained** Stoodleigh, Devon

FOCUS
A valuable handicap chase run at a sound pace, and this rates solid form with the first four all pretty much to their marks.

185 RASEN ROCKS 15TH AUGUST H'CAP HURDLE (12 hdls) 2m 7f 16y
3:25 (3:25) (Class 3) (0-130,130) 4-Y-0+ **£5,393** (£1,583; £791; £395)

Form RPR

521- **1** **The Road Ahead**[18] 5437 8-10-7 **114**........(p) SeanBowen(3) 123+
(Peter Bowen) *trckd ldrs: handy 2nd appr 2 out: reminders between last 2: upsides last: styd on wl u.p to ld clsng stages* **3/1**[1]

220- **2** *1* **Atlantic Gold (IRE)**[23] 5343 5-11-4 **122**........ AidanColeman 129
(Charlie Longsdon) *trckd ldrs: 2nd 3rd: led 7th: jnd last: hdd and no ex clsng stages* **7/2**[3]

004- **3** *6* **Master Of The Hall (IRE)**[26] 5297 11-11-3 **124**........ JoeColliver(3) 126
(Micky Hammond) *in rr: hdwy 9th: chsng ldrs next: handy 3rd appr 2 out: kpt on same pce* **12/1**

231- **4** *3¾* **Mercers Court (IRE)**[15] 5500 7-11-7 **125**........ TrevorWhelan 124
(Neil King) *hld up in rr: nt fluent 1st: hdwy 9th: handy 4th appr 2 out: one pce* **11/2**

F0F- **5** *2¾* **Touch Back (IRE)**[39] 5075 9-11-2 **123**........(v[1]) MauriceLinehan(3) 120
(Jonjo O'Neill) *chsd ldrs: reminders 6th: drvn 9th: one pce bef 2 out* **16/1**

3P6- **6** *4½* **Vandross (IRE)**[72] 4427 5-10-12 **123**........ LizzieKelly(7) 115
(Neil King) *led: hdd 7th: drvn next: wknd appr 2 out* **15/2**

166- **7** *16* **Quincy Des Pictons (FR)**[63] 4613 11-11-12 **130**........ RhysFlint 111
(Alan Jones) *t.k.h: trckd ldrs: drvn 3 out: lost pl bef next: sn bhd* **40/1**

222- **P** **Gone Forever**[49] 4892 5-11-7 **125**........ RichardJohnson 106
(Brian Ellison) *chsd ldrs: hit 4th: drvn 3 out: lost pl and modest 7th whn blnd 2 out: sn eased: p.u bef last* **10/3**[2]

6m 6.5s (16.00) **Going Correction** +0.375s/f (Yiel) **8 Ran SP% 113.5**
Speed ratings (Par 107): **88,87,85,84,83 82,76,**
CSF £14.06 CT £106.48 TOTE £4.80: £1.10, £1.60, £3.40; EX 14.00 Trifecta £103.10.
Owner F Lloyd **Bred** F Lloyd **Trained** Little Newcastle, Pembrokes

FOCUS
The pace for this fair staying handicap was only steady, and there were plenty still with hopes of winning on the home turn. The third sets the level.

186 MARKET RASEN RACECOURSE CARAVAN SITE H'CAP HURDLE (8 hdls) 2m 148y
4:00 (4:00) (Class 4) (0-115,115) 4-Y-0+ **£3,249** (£954; £477; £238)

Form RPR

345- **1** **Regulation (IRE)**[34] 3023 6-11-4 **107**........ TrevorWhelan 125+
(Neil King) *hld up in rr: smooth hdwy to trck ldrs 3 out: led appr next: clr whn hit last: v easily* **3/1**[2]

532- **2** *11* **A Little Bit Dusty**[38] 5088 7-11-7 **110**........(b) PaddyBrennan 116+
(Conor Dore) *chsd ldrs: hrd drvn: 2nd and hmpd bnd appr 2 out: no ch w wnr* **11/2**[3]

63-U **3** *4* **Brinestine (USA)**[8] 32 6-11-2 **108**........(t) JamesBanks(3) 105
(Emma Baker) *chsd ldrs: 4th whn bdly hmpd 2 out: modest 3rd appr last: kpt on one pce* **7/1**

3P5- **4** *1¼* **Fantasy King**[25] 5315 9-11-12 **115**........ BrianHughes 111
(James Moffatt) *hld up in tch: chsng ldrs 3 out: outpcd appr next: modest 4th appr last* **16/1**

401- **5** *9* **Yes Daddy (IRE)**[21] 5378 7-11-11 **114**........ TomO'Brien 105
(Robert Stephens) *j.lft: chsd ldrs: led briefly bef 2 out: 3rd whn j. bdly lft 2 out: wknd between last 2* **9/4**[1]

354- **6** *nk* **Vaihau (FR)**[36] 5112 6-11-6 **109**........ RichieMcLernon 97
(Jonjo O'Neill) *chsd ldrs: drvn 3 out: lost pl bef next* **8/1**

430- **7** *6* **Skyfire**[189] 2174 8-11-4 **107**........ AdamWedge 92
(Nick Kent) *led: hdd 4th: wknd bef 2 out* **33/1**

205- **8** *4* **Gud Day (IRE)**[38] 5088 7-11-4 **107**........(p) PeterCarberry 86
(Conor Dore) *in rr: bhd fr 4th* **40/1**

41P- **9** *3¼* **Relentless Pursuit (IRE)**[186] 2259 4-11-7 **114**........(t) GavinSheehan 86
(Warren Greatrex) *w ldrs: led 4th: hdd bef 2 out: sn lost pl* **16/1**

4m 15.7s (9.00) **Going Correction** +0.675s/f (Soft)
WFA 4 from 6yo+ 18lb **9 Ran SP% 111.9**
Speed ratings (Par 105): **105,99,97,97,93 92,90,88,86**
CSF £19.33 CT £102.96 TOTE £3.70: £1.10, £2.00, £2.00; EX 19.00 Trifecta £145.50.
Owner Amber Road Partnership **Bred** Barouche Stud (IRE) Ltd **Trained** Barbury Castle, Wiltshire

FOCUS
Rain began falling before this ordinary handicap, which produced a wide-margin winner. He's entitled to rate a lot higher on Flat form.

187 NEXT MEETING SUNDAY 17TH MAY STANDARD OPEN NATIONAL HUNT FLAT RACE (DIV I) 2m 148y
4:35 (4:35) (Class 6) 4-6-Y-0 **£1,559** (£457; £228; £114)

Form RPR

1 **Captain Bocelli (IRE)** 6-11-2 0........ RichieMcLernon 106
(Anabel K Murphy) *mid-div: hdwy over 5f out: 3rd over 2f out: 2nd 1f out: styd on to ld last 75yds: drvn out* **40/1**

2 *1* **Casper King (IRE)** 4-10-12 0........ RichardJohnson 101
(Philip Hobbs) *mid-div: hdwy 8f out: chsng ldrs 6f out: 2nd 3f out: led over 1f out: hdd and no ex last 75yds* **11/2**

3 *4* **Scarlett Peak (IRE)** 4-10-12 0........ JakeGreenall 97
(Michael Easterby) *in rr: drvn 6f out: sn outpcd: hdwy over 2f out: kpt on to take 3rd nr fin* **28/1**

1- **4** *1½* **Prince Of Poets**[164] 2724 4-11-5 0........ TomScudamore 104
(David Pipe) *led: t.k.h: hdd over 1f out: wknd towards fin* **5/1**[3]

5- **5** *¾* **Evening Stanley (IRE)**[58] 4715 5-11-2 0........ LeightonAspell 99
(Oliver Sherwood) *hld up in rr: t.k.h: hdwy 7f out: kpt on one pce fnl 2f* **9/1**

631- **6** *hd* **Kara Tara**[45] 4976 5-11-2 0........ DougieCostello 99
(Lawrence Mullaney) *mid-div: effrt over 4f out: kpt on one pce fnl 2f* **12/1**

3- **7** *18* **High Hopper (IRE)**[24] 5331 5-11-2 0........ BrianHughes 85
(Malcolm Jefferson) *trckd ldr: upsides 8f out: pushed along over 5f out: wknd over 2f out: bhd whn eased clsng stages* **3/1**[2]

- **8** *½* **Bestwork (FR)** 4-10-12 0........ DarylJacob 78
(Charlie Longsdon) *trckd ldrs: drvn over 5f out: wknd 2f out* **7/1**

00- **9** *12* **Early Boy (FR)**[97] 3986 4-10-9 0........ JohnKington(3) 67
(Andrew Crook) *in rr: lost pl 5f out: sn bhd: t.o 2f out* **66/1**

P **Fell Runner** 4-10-12 0........ NicodeBoinville
(Nicky Henderson) *chsd ldrs: hrd drvn after 6f: lost pl over 6f out: sn wl bhd: tailed rt off whn p.u over 3f out* **11/4**[1]

4m 10.0s (8.90) **Going Correction** +0.675s/f (Soft) **10 Ran SP% 121.3**
Speed ratings: **106,105,103,102,102 102,94,93,88,**
CSF £255.35 TOTE £55.40: £8.30, £2.60, £6.80; EX 587.00 Trifecta £1761.90.
Owner Mrs Diana L Whateley **Bred** Highfort Stud **Trained** Wilmcote, Warwicks

FOCUS
Probably a fair bumper, run at a relatively good pace. The time was very similar to that of division two and the form is rated around the fifth and sixth.

188 NEXT MEETING SUNDAY 17TH MAY STANDARD OPEN NATIONAL HUNT FLAT RACE (DIV II) 2m 148y
5:05 (5:05) (Class 6) 4-6-Y-0 **£1,559** (£457; £228; £114)

Form RPR

1- **1** **Brave Richard (IRE)**[32] 5200 4-11-5 0........ PaulMoloney 111+
(J R Jenkins) *hld up in rr: stdy hdwy on outside 6f out: upsides 4f out: led over 1f out: styd on wl* **11/2**[3]

2 *2* **Peppay Le Pugh (IRE)** 4-10-12 0........ NoelFehily 102
(Nicky Henderson) *hld up in rr: hdwy on inner over 4f out: chsng ldrs over 2f out: kpt on to atke 2nd last 75yds* **9/4**[2]

3 *hd* **Washed Ashore (IRE)** 4-10-12 0........ RichieMcLernon 102
(Jonjo O'Neill) *hld up in rr: hdwy on outer 6f out: chsng ldrs 3f out: edgd rt and tk 3rd last 75yds* **16/1**

4 *¾* **Byron Flyer** 4-10-12 0........ WillKennedy 101
(Ian Williams) *mid-div: drvn 7f out: chsng ldrs 4f out: kpt on to take 4th nr fin* **25/1**

5 *¾* **Alf 'N' Dor (IRE)** 4-10-9 0........ SeanBowen(3) 101
(Peter Bowen) *trckd ldrs: led over 5f out: hdd over 1f out:4th and keeping on one pce whn hmpd and swtchd lft clsng stages* **2/1**[1]

6 *1½* **Quieto Sol (FR)** 4-10-12 0........ AidanColeman 99
(Charlie Longsdon) *prom: hdwy to chse ldrs 4f out: upsides over 2f out: one pce over 1f out* **11/1**

7 *9* **Druids Lodge** 4-10-12 0........ DenisO'Regan 91
(Don Cantillon) *prom: effrt over 3f out: wknd over 1f out* **9/1**

8 *2¾* **Bonvilston Boy** 4-10-12 0........ RichardJohnson 89
(Tim Vaughan) *mid-div: drvn 7f out: upsides 4f out: wknd over 1f out* **12/1**

0- **9** *45* **Gifted Rose**[45] 4983 4-10-5 0........ DaveCrosse 41
(Christopher Kellett) *led: hdd over 7f out: lost pl 6f out: sn bhd: t.o 3f out* **100/1**

000/ **10** *¾* **Nataraja**[26] 6-11-2 0........(v[1]) LeightonAspell 52
(Conrad Allen) *trckd ldrs: led over 7f out: hdd over 5f out: sn lost pl and bhd: t.o 2f out* **50/1**

6- **11** *½* **King Simba (IRE)**[21] 5380 4-10-12 0........ DavidBass 47
(Kim Bailey) *trckd ldrs: upsides 6f out: lost pl over 3f out: sn bhd: eased whn t.o over 1f out* **20/1**

4m 10.3s (9.20) **Going Correction** +0.675s/f (Soft) **11 Ran SP% 123.0**
Speed ratings: **105,104,103,103,103 102,98,97,75,75 75**
CSF £18.64 TOTE £6.40: £2.40, £1.10, £2.90; EX 20.70 Trifecta £186.70.
Owner Miss A Finn **Bred** Suzanne Guise-Mist **Trained** Royston, Herts

FOCUS
This was run in a very similar time to the first division. It probably had the less depth of the two, but the winner looks useful. He probably improved a few pounds on his debut win.\n
T/Plt: £65.30 to a £1 stake. Pool: £37,831.29 - 422.54 winning tickets T/Qpdt: £21.20 to a £1 stake. Pool: £4,163.44 - 145.10 winning tickets **Walter Glynn**

189 - 195a (Foreign Racing) - See Raceform Interactive

HAYDOCK (L-H)
Saturday, May 9

OFFICIAL GOING: Soft (flat course 5.9) changing to good to soft on jumps courses after race 1 (1.45)
Wind: Moderate, against Weather: Cloudy

196 PERTEMPS NETWORK LONG DISTANCE H'CAP HURDLE (12 hdls) 2m 6f 177y
1:45 (1:45) (Class 2) 4-Y-0+
£18,768 (£5,544; £2,772; £1,386; £693; £348)

Form RPR

404- **1** **No Planning**[35] 5140 8-11-8 **138**........ SeanQuinlan 142
(Sue Smith) *mde all: rdn appr 2 out: jnd last and hrd pressed: styd on gamely and fnd more towards fin* **8/1**

122- **2** *1* **Alternatif (FR)**[24] 5341 5-11-2 **132**........(tp) TomScudamore 135
(David Pipe) *prom: wnt 2nd 4th: rdn appr last: sn upsides and chalng: hld towards fin* **5/1**[1]

411- **3** *2¼* **The Govaness**[23] 5355 6-11-12 **142**........ PaddyBrennan 144
(Fergal O'Brien) *hld up in tch: hdwy appr 3 out: chsng ldrs whn mstke 2 out: styd on run-in: nt rch front two* **6/1**[2]

P60- **4** *3½* **Pearl Swan (FR)**[29] 5249 7-11-7 **137**........(tp) SamTwiston-Davies 135
(Paul Nicholls) *midfield: hdwy 3 out: sn chsng ldrs: rdn bef last: kpt on same pce after* **10/1**

406- **5** *8* **Sybarite (FR)**[23] 5357 9-10-10 **133**........(t) JamieBargary(7) 125
(Nigel Twiston-Davies) *chsd ldr to 4th: rdn and lost pl 8th: bhd 4 out: struggling whn hit 3 out: stl in last pl at last: styd on run-in: tk 5th post* **9/1**

3P1- **6** *nse* **Dawn Commander (GER)**[16] 5498 8-11-12 **142**........ BrendanPowell 134
(Stuart Edmunds) *prom to 4th: rdn and outpcd bef 3 out: kpt on wout threatening fr 2 out* **8/1**

144- **7** *1¾* **Huff And Puff**[83] 4250 8-10-6 **122**........ AidanColeman 111
(Venetia Williams) *hld up: wnt into midfield bef 7th: rdn and outpcd bef 3 out: n.d after* **12/1**

/40- **8** *hd* **Edeymi (IRE)**[32] 5228 7-11-5 **135**....(t) BJCooper 124
(A J Martin, Ire) *hld up: hdwy after 4 out: chsd ldrs bef 3 out: no real imp after: wknd bef last* **7/1**[3]

220- **9** *1 1/4* **Serienschock (GER)**[30] 5241 7-11-10 **140**....(vt) ConorO'Farrell 128
(David Pipe) *hld up in midfield: lost pl and j. slowly 4th: rdn and outpcd bef 3 out: n.d after* **10/1**

410- **10** *5* **Milan Bound (IRE)**[23] 5357 7-11-1 **131**....(b) RichieMcLernon 116
(Jonjo O'Neill) *trckd ldrs: hit 3 out: wknd 2 out* **8/1**

5m 45.1s (-14.90) **Going Correction** -0.80s/f (Firm) **10** Ran SP% **112.7**
Speed ratings (Par 109): **92,91,90,89,87 87,86,86,86,84**
CSF £46.72 CT £256.48 TOTE £8.20: £2.30, £1.50, £1.80; EX 42.80 Trifecta £207.40.
Owner Mrs Jacqueline Conroy **Bred** Mrs S Johnson **Trained** High Eldwick, W Yorks
■ Stewards' Enquiry : Brendan Powell two-day ban: failed to ride out for 5th place (28-29 May)

FOCUS
Soft ground all round for this mixed meeting. The first two were always to the fore in this valuable staying handicap, which was run over 24 yards further than advertised. A hurdles best from the winner, rated around the balance of second to fourth.

197 PERTEMPS NETWORK H'CAP HURDLE (REGISTERED AS THE SWINTON HURDLE) (GRADE 3) (9 hdls) 1m 7f 144y
3:25 (3:25) (Class 1) 4-Y-O+
£34,170 (£12,822; £6,420; £3,198; £1,608; £804)

Form RPR

510- **1** **War Sound**[28] 5276 6-10-6 **140**.... CiaranGethings(7) 147+
(Philip Hobbs) *hld up: impr to midfield after 3rd: more prog 5th: led 3 out: rdn appr last: styd on wl to draw clr run-in* **6/1**[1]

640- **2** *3 1/4* **Barizan (IRE)**[19] 4741 9-10-8 **135**....(vt) BrendanPowell 138
(Brendan Powell) *midfield: hdwy and effrt appr 3 out: sn chsd ldrs: hit 2 out: edgd rt u.p on run-in: styd on to take 2nd fnl strides: no imp on wnr* **16/1**

105- **3** *nk* **Song Light**[34] 5154 5-9-11 **131** ow2.... KevinJones(7) 133
(Seamus Mullins) *hld up: hdwy bef 4 out: cl up chsng ldrs 2 out: wnt 2nd bef last: edgd rt run-in: no imp on wnr: lost 2nd fnl strides* **16/1**

000- **4** *1 1/4* **Ballyglasheen (IRE)**[28] 5276 5-10-8 **135**....(v) PaulMoloney 137
(Evan Williams) *hld up in midfield: lost pl bef 4th: rdn towards rr whn bmpd 4 out: rdn and sme hdwy appr 3 out: styd on under driving run-in: gng on at fin* **14/1**

44U- **5** *2 3/4* **The Plan Man (IRE)**[11] 7 5-10-7 **134**....(t) BJCooper 132
(A J Martin, Ire) *midfield: hdwy appr 3 out: sn chsd ldrs: hung lft and nt pick up bef last: styd on same pce fnl 100yds* **8/1**[3]

201- **6** *1/2* **Cheltenian (FR)**[21] 5390 9-11-12 **153**.... RichardJohnson 153
(Philip Hobbs) *hld up in rr: mstke 2nd: hdwy 4 out: chsd ldrs 3 out: nt fluent 2 out: sltly hmpd last: kpt on u.p tl no ex fnl 100yds* **8/1**[3]

004- **7** *5* **Fergall (IRE)**[38] 3124 8-10-11 **141**.... JeremiahMcGrath(3) 135
(Seamus Mullins) *led: hit and hdd 1st: chsd ldrs after: regained ld appr 4 out: hdd 3 out: stl cl up 2 out: rdn and no ex bef last: one pce run-in* **20/1**

6P1- **8** *1 3/4* **Arzal (FR)**[28] 5278 5-10-2 **136**.... PaulNO'Brien(7) 129
(Harry Whittington) *racd keenly: w ldr: nt fluent 5th: stl there 2 out: rdn and wknd appr last* **13/2**[2]

/24- **9** *4* **Handiwork**[21] 5390 5-10-12 **139**....(p) NicodeBoinville 127
(Steve Gollings) *nvr travelling: in rr: plugged on run-in: nvr able to get on terms w ldrs* **8/1**[3]

26-1 **10** *11* **Vodka Wells (FR)**[7] 82 5-9-12 **132**.... GLavery(7) 110
(Brian Ellison) *trckd ldrs: upsides after 4 out: rdn appr 3 out: wknd 2 out* **11/1**

000- **11** *13* **Sleepy Haven (IRE)**[29] 5249 5-10-9 **136**....(t) HenryBrooke 102
(Jennie Candlish) *in tch: pushed along and lost pl 5th: in rr whn j.lft u.p 4 out: n.d after* **25/1**

520- **12** *23* **Rayvin Black**[14] 5539 6-10-5 **135**....(p) ThomasGarner(3) 81
(Oliver Sherwood) *led after 1st: hit 5th: hdd appr 4 out: sn wknd* **11/1**

0/0- **P** **Lexi's Boy (IRE)**[29] 5249 7-10-3 **130**.... WilsonRenwick
(Donald McCain) *hld up: mstke 1st: hit 3rd: pushed along bef 5th: nvr on terms: wl bhd whn p.u bef 3 out* **12/1**

410- **P** **Royal Guardsman (IRE)**[50] 4885 8-10-2 **129**.... SamTwiston-Davies
(Ali Stronge) *in midfield: j.lft at 4th: rdn and lost pl after: bhd whn p.u bef 2 out* **22/1**

441- **U** **Last Supper**[17] 5475 6-9-12 **130**.... JackSherwood(5)
(James Bethell) *midfield: n.m.r whn uns rdr 4th* **16/1**

131- **P** **Rathealy (IRE)**[40] 5072 4-10-4 **135**.... TomScudamore
(David Pipe) *in tch: rdn and wknd after 4th: p.u bef 3 out* **20/1**

3m 46.2s (-18.00) **Going Correction** -0.80s/f (Firm)
WFA 4 from 5yo+ 18lb **16** Ran SP% **127.3**
Speed ratings (Par 113): **113,111,111,110,109 108,106,105,103,98 91,80, , ,**
CSF £97.02 CT £1500.12 TOTE £7.10: £2.20, £5.80, £4.90, £4.50; EX 155.70 Trifecta £3423.10.

Owner The Englands And Heywoods **Bred** Shaunagh Addinsell & Diana Blunt **Trained** Withycombe, Somerset
■ Stewards' Enquiry : Ciaran Gethings seven-day ban: use of whip (23-29 May) £600 fine: use of whip

FOCUS
The official ground description for the jumps track was changed to good to soft prior to this race. A prestigious and competitive handicap, it was run at a decent gallop. Solid form. The distance was 12 yards further than advertised.

198 PERTEMPS NETWORK INTERMEDIATE H'CAP CHASE (18 fncs) 2m 5f 64y
4:35 (4:35) (Class 2) 5-Y-O+ **£19,494** (£5,724; £2,862; £1,431)

Form RPR

353- **1** **Big Casino**[43] 5018 9-10-0 **124** oh3....(v) SamTwiston-Davies 132
(Nigel Twiston-Davies) *j.w: mde all: rdn appr 2 out: over 2 l up last: drvn out and styd on wl to draw clr fnl 150yds* **10/3**[2]

111- **2** *5* **Cloud Creeper (IRE)**[24] 5344 8-11-12 **150**.... RichardJohnson 153
(Philip Hobbs) *hld up: hdwy 12th: wnt 2nd 4 out: j.lft 3 out: over 2 l down last: kpt on same pce fnl 150yds* **3/1**[1]

116- **3** *11* **Ainsi Fideles (FR)**[29] 5251 5-11-11 **149**....(bt) TomScudamore 143
(David Pipe) *chsd wnr to 4 out: one pce bef 2 out: no ch after: all out to hold on for 3rd nr fin* **11/2**[3]

U66- **4** *1/2* **Back To Bracka (IRE)**[21] 5394 8-10-2 **129**.... DerekFox(3) 122
(Lucinda Russell) *hld up: outpcd fr 12th: styd on after last but no ch* **11/2**[3]

25F- **5** *1 3/4* **Hada Men (USA)**[35] 5140 10-10-0 **124**.... LiamTreadwell 115
(Venetia Williams) *prom: rdn along and lost pl bef 10th: bhd and toiling bef 4 out: styd on u.p fr last but no ch* **11/2**[3]

110- **6** *27* **It's A Gimme (IRE)**[283] 1131 8-11-3 **141**.... RichieMcLernon 108
(Jonjo O'Neill) *in tch: lost pl 10th: wkng whn mstke 4 out* **8/1**

P4- **U** **Lysino (GER)**[20] 5406 6-10-3 **127**.... WillKennedy
(Dr Richard Newland) *racd keenly: hld up in rr: hdwy 5th: shkn up abt 5 l off the pce in 4th whn blnd bdly: nrly fell and uns rdr 4 out* **13/2**

5m 31.1s (331.10) **Going Correction** -0.15s/f (Good) **7** Ran SP% **112.4**
Speed ratings: **112,110,106,106,105 95,**
CSF £13.73 TOTE £3.90: £2.10, £1.50; EX 16.80 Trifecta £47.40.
Owner The Jukes Family **Bred** Mrs M A Jukes **Trained** Naunton, Gloucs

FOCUS
The third running of this valuable prize. The winner is on the upgrade.

199 PERTEMPS NETWORK H'CAP CHASE (15 fncs) 2m 2f 211y
5:05 (5:05) (Class 3) (0-130,130) 5-Y-O+ **£8,122** (£2,385; £1,192; £596)

Form RPR

112/ **1** **Glen Countess (IRE)**[497] 3365 8-10-8 **112**.... SeanQuinlan 127+
(Sue Smith) *in tch: wnt 2nd 8th: led appr 4 out: drew clr bef 2 out: j. low at last: eased down run-in* **7/2**[2]

346- **2** *7* **Habbie Simpson**[26] 5313 10-11-4 **122**....(p) TomScudamore 121
(Pauline Robson) *hld up in rr: nt travelling wl bef 7th: wl outpcd and toiling bef 4 out: wnt 3rd 3 out: tk 2nd last: styd on fnl 150yds: no ch w wnr* **4/1**[3]

P51- **3** *9* **Bincombe**[28] 5279 7-11-12 **130**....(bt) RichardJohnson 123
(Philip Hobbs) *trckd ldrs: led appr 4th: hdd bef 4 out: unable to go w wnr bef 2 out: no ch after: lost 2nd last: no ex fnl 150yds* **7/2**[2]

34P- **4** *10* **Auvergnat (FR)**[42] 5026 5-11-9 **127**.... RichieMcLernon 111
(Jonjo O'Neill) *chsd ldr tl bef 4th: hit 10th: outpcd bef 4 out: bhd bef 2 out* **5/1**

22P- **P** **Noble Legend**[33] 5195 8-11-5 **123**.... AndrewThornton
(Caroline Bailey) *led: hdd appr 4th: rdn and lost pl bef 10th: p.u bef 11th* **5/2**[1]

5m 2.4s (-7.60) **Going Correction** -0.15s/f (Good) **5** Ran SP% **109.7**
Speed ratings: **109,106,102,98,**
CSF £16.95 TOTE £4.90: £2.00, £2.20; EX 17.60 Trifecta £78.30.
Owner The Naughty Partnership **Bred** David Pim **Trained** High Eldwick, W Yorks

FOCUS
This rather fell apart, and it remains to be seen what the form is worth. A personal best from the winner.
T/Plt: £1,551.00 to a £1 stake. Pool of £106026.35 - 49.90 winning tickets. T/Qpdt: £142.00 to a £1 stake. Pool of £6259.22 - 32.60 winning tickets. **Darren Owen**

76 HEXHAM (L-H)
Saturday, May 9

OFFICIAL GOING: Heavy
Wind: Fresh, half against Weather: Overcast

200 RAMSIDE EVENT CATERING NOVICES' HURDLE (8 hdls) 2m 48y
2:05 (2:07) (Class 4) 4-Y-O+ **£3,422** (£997; £499)

Form RPR

00-6 **1** **Octagon**[7] 83 5-10-12 0.... JamesReveley 117+
(Dianne Sayer) *hld up: stdy hdwy 1/2-way: rdn to ld bef last: drew clr run-in* **12/1**

22P- **2** *10* **Astrum**[65] 4580 5-10-12 106....(p) AdrianLane 104
(Donald McCain) *chsd ldr: hit 4th: effrt and pressed wnr bef last: sn rdn and edgd lft: outpcd run-in* **11/4**[2]

12-0 **3** *hd* **Grange Hall (IRE)**[9] 52 8-10-5 118.... JonathanMoore(7) 104
(Paul Stafford, Ire) *t.k.h: led to 1st: led 4th tl rdn and hdd bef last: outpcd run-in* **5/6**[1]

F3-F **4** *12* **Pekanheim (IRE)**[7] 76 7-10-9 0.... GrahamWatters(3) 94
(Martin Todhunter) *hld up in tch: stdy hdwy and cl up 3 out: rdn and wknd bef last* **9/1**[3]

044- **5** *18* **Soeur De Rois (IRE)**[60] 4701 5-10-2 0.... AdamNicol(3) 67
(Philip Kirby) *hld up: struggling 4th: lost tch after next: n.d after* **12/1**

6/ **P** **Sory**[1259] 2806 8-10-12 0.... BrianHarding
(Tina Jackson) *t.k.h: hld up: struggling bef 4 out: sn lost tch: t.o whn p.u bef last* **40/1**

FU-5 **P** **Bertielicious**[9] 33 7-10-9 61....(v) CraigNichol(3)
(Jonathan Haynes) *t.k.h: led 1st: hdd 4th: wknd qckly next: lost tch and p.u after 2 out* **100/1**

4m 31.4s (14.00) **Going Correction** +1.025s/f (Soft) **7** Ran SP% **110.0**
Speed ratings (Par 105): **108,103,103,97,89 ,**
CSF £42.53 TOTE £12.70: £6.50, £1.60; EX 45.60 Trifecta £125.60.
Owner Tony Ambler **Bred** Mrs J K M Oliver **Trained** Hackthorpe, Cumbria

FOCUS
Bends and back straight moved to fresh ground. Reasonable to assume the second and third have run somewhere near their best, so this represents a fair effort from the winner. The pace was predictably steady under very testing conditions.

201 RAMSIDE HALL HOTEL MAIDEN HURDLE (12 hdls) 2m 7f 63y
2:40 (2:41) (Class 5) 5-Y-O+ **£2,643** (£897)

Form RPR

342- **1** **Alto Des Mottes (FR)**[19] 5420 5-10-11 116.... TonyKelly(3) 111+
(Henry Hogarth) *led to bef 5th: regained ld 8th: drew clr after 2 out: easily* **1/5**[1]

05P- **2** *37* **Harleys Max**[25] 5324 6-10-7 86.... JamesCorbett(7) 81
(Susan Corbett) *t.k.h in tch: hdwy to ld bef 5th: hdd 8th: pressed wnr: rdn and wknd between last 2* **14/1**[3]

065- **P** **Native Optimist (IRE)**[25] 5324 8-10-11 81.... AdamNicol(3)
(Sheena Walton) *prom: hit and pushed along 3 out: wknd after next: p.u bef last* **13/2**[2]

0/ **P** **Attonburn (IRE)**[748] 5429 8-10-9 0.... CallumBewley(5)
(George Charlton) *mstkes: prom tl wknd 3 out: t.o whn p.u after next* **25/1**

6m 44.5s (35.50) **Going Correction** +1.375s/f (Heav) **4** Ran SP% **107.2**
Speed ratings: **95,82, ,**
CSF £3.76 TOTE £1.10; EX 3.60.
Owner Hogarth Racing **Bred** E A R L Ecurie Des Mottes **Trained** Stillington, N Yorks

FOCUS
This is an early contender for weakest maiden hurdle of the season. The facile winner stood out.

202 CWC HENDERSON 125TH YEAR ANNIVERSARY CONDITIONAL JOCKEYS' H'CAP CHASE (10 fncs 2 omitted) 1m 7f 133y
3:15 (3:15) (Class 4) (0-120,120) 5-Y-O+ **£4,106** (£1,197; £598)

Form RPR

03-2 **1** **Super Collider**[7] 76 8-10-13 **115**....(t) JamesCorbett(8) 120
(Susan Corbett) *chsd ldr: rdn after 2 out: rallied bef last: led run-in: pushed out* **3/1**[2]

021- **2** *1* **Amethyst Rose (IRE)**[26] 5314 8-11-4 **112**.................... GrantCockburn 116
(Stuart Coltherd) *led: rdn bef last: hdd run-in: kpt on: hld nr fin* **7/2[3]**
351- **3** *1 3/4* **Better B Quick (IRE)**[18] 5460 9-10-9 **108**.................... JonathanMoore(5) 110
(Paul Stafford, Ire) *t.k.h: trckd ldrs: pushed along and edgd rt bef last: kpt on same pce whn edgd rt last 100yds* **2/1[1]**
250- **4** *3/4* **Saddlers Deal (IRE)**[33] 5195 10-9-8 **94** oh1..............(p) CraigGallagher(6) 96
(Brian Ellison) *hld up: stdy hdwy bef 3 out: rdn and outpcd bef last: kpt on run-in: no imp* **15/2**
13P- **5** *1 1/4* **Ballycool (IRE)**[56] 4768 8-11-1 **112**....................(t) GrahamWatters(3) 112
(Lucinda Russell) *hld up in tch: smooth hdwy and cl up between last 2: drvn and outpcd run-in* **13/2**
5PP- **6** *11* **Sean Airgead (IRE)**[49] 4897 10-11-9 **120**....................(tp) StevenFox(3) 110
(Mark Michael McNiff, Ire) *hld up: struggling 3 out: wknd fr next* **16/1**
4m 32.0s (22.20) **Going Correction** +1.375s/f (Heav) 6 Ran SP% **111.5**
Speed ratings: **102,101,100,100,99 94**
CSF £13.90 TOTE £3.30: £2.60, £2.00; EX 11.30 Trifecta £30.40.
Owner Mrs Jordan Corbett **Bred** Newsells Park Stud **Trained** Otterburn, Northumberland

FOCUS
The pace was on the steady side here and the race effectively didn't begin in earnest until the third last, resulting in a relatively bunched finish. The winner is rated in line with his upgraded recent chase course run.

203 H MALONE & SONS H'CAP HURDLE (12 hdls) 2m 7f 63y
3:50 (3:50) (Class 4) (0-120,120) 4-Y-O+ **£6,498** (£1,908; £954; £477)

Form RPR
224- **1** **Manballandall (IRE)**[42] 5032 7-11-5 **120**....................(t) JamesCorbett(7) 128+
(Susan Corbett) *t.k.h: cl up: mstke 7th: led next to 3 out: regained ld appr 2 out: rdn and edgd rt bef last: styd on strly run-in* **5/2[1]**
42U- **2** *3* **Quel Elite (FR)**[35] 5133 11-11-2 **113**.................... TonyKelly(3) 117
(James Moffatt) *in tch: outpcd 1/2-way: rallied and cl up bef 2 out: drvn and ev ch between last 2: nt fluent last: one pce* **4/1[3]**
514- **3** *8* **Hartforth**[49] 4911 7-11-12 **120**.................... PeterBuchanan 115
(Donald Whillans) *led to 8th: led 3 out to appr next: ev ch tl wknd bef last* **11/4[2]**
/00- **4** *4 1/2* **Dusky Bob (IRE)**[17] 5473 10-10-1 **95**....................(p) DougieCostello 87
(Brian Ellison) *in tch: drvn and outpcd after 2 out: no imp bef last* **8/1**
343- **P** **George Fernbeck**[57] 4747 7-11-11 **119**....................(p) JamesReveley
(Brian Ellison) *w ldr: outpcd after 3 out: wknd fr next: p.u bef last* **13/2**
354- **P** **Knocklong (IRE)**[19] 5422 7-11-9 **117**.................... AndrewTinkler
(Ben Haslam) *hld up: stdy hdwy 3 out: rdn and wknd after next: p.u bef last* **8/1**
6m 42.1s (33.10) **Going Correction** +1.375s/f (Heav) 6 Ran SP% **110.8**
Speed ratings (Par 105): **99,98,95,93,**
CSF £12.60 CT £26.48 TOTE £3.60: £1.70, £2.00; EX 14.70 Trifecta £34.30.
Owner Mrs Jordan Corbett **Bred** Gerry Carroll **Trained** Otterburn, Northumberland

FOCUS
A fairly useful staying event, and the form makes sense.

204 DR HOWARD SCOTT MEMORIAL H'CAP CHASE (15 fncs 4 omitted) 3m 41y
4:25 (4:25) (Class 4) (0-110,87) 5-Y-O+ **£4,790** (£1,396; £698)

Form RPR
210- **1** **Flaming Thistle (IRE)**[19] 5423 11-11-0 **80**.................... GrantCockburn(5) 90
(John Hodge) *chsd ldr to 3rd: pushed along and outpcd next: hdwy 4 out: chsd clr ldr 2 out: rdn and sustained effrt to ld run-in: styd on wl* **11/2**
132- **2** *3* **Nalim (IRE)**[35] 5134 9-11-9 **87**....................(b) JonathanEngland(3) 94
(Harriet Bethell) *early reminders in rr: hdwy to chse clr ldr 3rd: led 3 out: clr next: sn rdn: hdd run-in: kpt on same pce* **13/8[1]**
500- **3** *dist* **The Shrimp (IRE)**[19] 5423 8-11-3 **78**....................(b) BrianHughes
(Sandy Thomson) *prom: outpcd 11th: struggling fr next: t.o whn lft 3rd between last 2* **7/4[2]**
P4-0 **P** **Willie Hall**[9] 37 11-11-4 **86**.................... RyanDay(7)
(Lisa Harrison) *led to 3 out: rdn and wknd next: 3rd and wl btn whn p.u between last 2* **9/2[3]**
7m 5.1s (32.90) **Going Correction** +1.375s/f (Heav) 4 Ran SP% **108.0**
Speed ratings: **102,101, ,**
CSF £14.81 TOTE £5.50; EX 18.70 Trifecta £23.90.
Owner Ms E Mercy C Hodge **Bred** John Noonan **Trained** Cumnock, Ayrshire
■ Stewards' Enquiry : Jonathan England two-day ban: use of whip (23-24 May)

FOCUS
A thorough test under the gruelling conditions. The top weight ran off a mark 23lb below the 110 limit. The first two were pretty much to their marks.

205 SPA AT RAMSIDE HALL HOTEL H'CAP HURDLE (8 hdls) 2m 48y
5:00 (5:01) (Class 4) (0-110,102) 4-Y-O+ **£3,898** (£1,144; £572; £286)

Form RPR
35-1 **1** **King Of Strings (IRE)**[7] 77 6-11-12 **102**....................(p) DougieCostello 107+
(Mark Walford) *hld up in tch: stdy hdwy whn hit 4 out: hit 2 out: rallied and led after last: drvn and styd on strly* **5/4[1]**
5P0- **2** *3 3/4* **Retrieve The Stick**[17] 5470 6-11-10 **100**....................(b) BrianHughes 99
(Malcolm Jefferson) *cl up: led 2 out: rdn and hdd after last: kpt on same pce* **11/4[2]**
442- **3** *13* **Persian Herald**[19] 5421 7-11-9 **99**....................(bt) JamesReveley 87
(Dianne Sayer) *cl up: drvn and outpcd 4th: lost tch 3 out: rallied to take modest 3rd after last: no ch w first two* **7/2[3]**
120- **4** *7* **Beyondtemptation**[25] 5325 7-10-12 **93**....................(t) DiarmuidO'Regan(5) 74
(Jonathan Haynes) *led: rdn and hdd 2 out: rallied: wkng whn hit last* **7/1**
P60- **5** *39* **Morning Time (IRE)**[26] 5309 9-11-12 **102**....................(tp) PeterBuchanan 63
(Lucinda Russell) *in tch: outpcd 1/2-way: sme hdwy after 3 out: wknd bef next: sn lost tch* **18/1**
4m 37.4s (20.00) **Going Correction** +1.375s/f (Heav) 5 Ran SP% **111.1**
Speed ratings (Par 105): **107,105,99,95,77**
CSF £5.32 TOTE £2.20: £1.10, £1.80; EX 7.90 Trifecta £9.90.
Owner F M & Mrs E Holmes **Bred** Cathal Ennis **Trained** Sherriff Hutton, N Yorks

FOCUS
A modest contest which was steadily run. The first two were pretty much to their marks.

206 NORTH EAST OYSTER FESTIVAL IN NEWCASTLE STANDARD OPEN NATIONAL HUNT FLAT RACE 2m 48y
5:30 (5:32) (Class 6) 4-6-Y-O **£1,642** (£478; £239)

Form RPR
2- **1** **Ryedale Racer**[19] 5426 4-10-12 0.................... BrianHughes 98
(Malcolm Jefferson) *prom: shkn up and stdy hdwy over 3f out: led 2f out: edgd rt and kpt on wl fnl f* **11/4[2]**
- **2** *7* **Smart Talk (IRE)**[76] 5-10-9 0.................... DougieCostello 88
(Brian Ellison) *cl up: led 1/2-way: rdn and hdd 2f out: sn outpcd: rallied fnl f: tk 2nd cl home: no ch w wnr* **6/5[1]**
654- **3** *nse* **Johnny Go**[15] 5520 5-10-9 0.................... RyanDay(7) 95
(Lisa Harrison) *chsd ldrs: chal 1/2-way to over 2f out: sn chsng wnr: rdn and one pce fnl f* **20/1**
65- **4** *32* **Temple Tiger**[19] 5425 5-11-2 0.................... PeterBuchanan 63
(James Turner) *hld up: struggling 1/2-way: shortlived effrt over 5f out: sn btn* **16/1**
5 *hd* **Court Baloo (IRE)** 4-10-9 0.................... CraigNichol(3) 59
(Alistair Whillans) *in tch: drvn and outpcd 1/2-way: nvr on terms after* **17/2**
00- **6** *dist* **Delgardo (IRE)**[25] 5331 6-11-2 0....................(b[1]) AlainCawley
(John David Riches) *led to 1/2-way: rdn and wknd over 5f out: t.o* **80/1**
7 *37* **Hasiteasy (IRE)**[29] 5270 4-9-12 0.................... JonathanMoore(7)
(Peter Croke, Ire) *prom tl rdn and wknd over 3f out: t.o* **4/1[3]**
4m 34.5s (21.80) **Going Correction** +1.375s/f (Heav)
WFA 4 from 5yo+ 4lb 7 Ran SP% **114.5**
Speed ratings: **103,99,99,84,84 ,**
CSF £6.45 TOTE £4.20: £2.20, £1.10; EX 8.10 Trifecta £57.70.
Owner Derek Gennard & Gillian Gennard **Bred** H Young **Trained** Norton, N Yorks

FOCUS
No depth to this bumper but the winner has made a promising start to his career. He and the third set the level.
T/Plt: £141.60 to a £1 stake. Pool of £42901.86 - 221.05 winning tickets. T/Qpdt: £47.80 to a £1 stake. Pool of £3614.89 - 55.92 winning tickets. **Richard Young**

[105]WARWICK (L-H)
Saturday, May 9

OFFICIAL GOING: Soft changing to soft (good to soft in places) after race 1 (5.25)
Wind: Fresh behind Weather: Cloudy with sunny spells

207 LUKE PURVIS 21ST BIRTHDAY CELEBRATION NOVICES' HURDLE (9 hdls) 2m 3f
5:25 (5:25) (Class 4) 4-Y-O+ **£3,249** (£954; £477; £238)

Form RPR
642- **1** **Benissimo (IRE)**[128] 3456 5-10-12 122.................... HarrySkelton 120+
(Dan Skelton) *mde all: clr appr last: comf* **1/1[1]**
626- **2** *10* **Wait A Second (IRE)**[78] 4336 5-10-9 0.................... MauriceLinehan(3) 107
(Jonjo O'Neill) *a.p: chsd wnr appr 2 out: styng on same pce whn nt fluent last* **3/1[2]**
3 *1 3/4* **All Together (FR)**[74] 4-10-7 0.................... NoelFehily 99
(Johnny Farrelly) *hld up: hdwy 5th: chsd wnr next tl rdn appr 2 out: styd on same pce* **5/1[3]**
04- **4** *6* **The Lion Man (IRE)**[47] 4964 5-10-12 0.................... CharliePoste 99
(Robin Dickin) *chsd ldrs: blnd 2nd: rdn after 3 out: wknd bef next* **16/1**
100- **5** *1/2* **Act Now**[35] 5144 6-10-5 0.................... RachaelGreen 92
(Anthony Honeyball) *hld up: nt fluent 4th: pushed along and outpcd next: n.d after* **7/1**
F00- **6** *2 3/4* **Gorman (FR)**[19] 5434 4-10-7 0.................... AdamWedge 90
(Evan Williams) *hld up and bhd: hdwy 3 out: wknd bef next* **25/1**
/06- **7** *23* **Tanner Hill (IRE)**[52] 4851 7-10-12 0....................(p) MarkQuinlan 72
(James Evans) *chsd wnr to 6th: sn rdn: wknd after 3 out* **80/1**
/00- **R** **Illusionary Star**[107] 3812 7-10-5 0.................... MarkGrant
(Julian Smith) *ref to r* **66/1**
4m 38.1s (-4.60) **Going Correction** -0.20s/f (Good)
WFA 4 from 5yo+ 18lb 8 Ran SP% **116.6**
Speed ratings (Par 105): **101,96,96,93,93 92,82,**
CSF £4.41 TOTE £2.30: £1.10, £1.10, £1.80; EX 5.10 Trifecta £9.20.
Owner A Chandler,L Westwood,D Balchin,K Jones **Bred** Michael Dillon **Trained** Alcester, Warwicks

FOCUS
Hurdle and INH Flat races run on Inner course and distances increased by 15yds per circuit. A warm, breezy evening. The going changed to soft, good to soft in places after a drying afternoon. A novice hurdle with little strength in depth strength and the market spoke correctly.

208 MIDSHIRE BUSINESS SYSTEMS - OFFICE TECHNOLOGY H'CAP HURDLE (9 hdls) 2m 3f
5:55 (5:55) (Class 3) (0-140,138) 4-Y-O+ **£6,498** (£1,908; £954; £477)

Form RPR
1 **Virgilio (FR)**[500] 6-10-6 **118**....................(t) HarrySkelton 135+
(Dan Skelton) *hld up: hdwy to chse ldr 6th: led appr 2 out: sn clr: easily* **7/2[1]**
504- **2** *12* **Handazan (IRE)**[41] 5048 6-11-4 **130**....................(b[1]) WayneHutchinson 130
(Alan King) *chsd ldrs: pushed along 5th: rdn to chse wnr appr 2 out: sn outpcd* **7/2[1]**
102- **3** *5* **Ruler Of All (IRE)**[22] 5361 9-11-0 **133**.................... MrRWinks(7) 131
(Peter Winks) *hld up: hdwy 5th: hmpd bnd after 3 out: rdn to go 3rd bef next: sn outpcd* **6/1[3]**
215- **4** *12* **Poker School (IRE)**[20] 5404 5-10-6 **118**.................... AidanColeman 103
(Ian Williams) *chsd ldrs: wnt 2nd after 4th tl 6th: cl up whn stmbld bnd after 3 out: sn rdn and wknd* **4/1[2]**
P45- **5** *15* **Willem (FR)**[30] 5245 5-10-13 **125**....................(bt[1]) ConorO'Farrell 94
(David Pipe) *led and sn clr: nt fluent 4th: c bk to the field next: hdd & wknd appr 2 out* **4/1[2]**
214- **P** **Up And Go (FR)**[69] 4518 7-11-4 **130**.................... NoelFehily
(Donald McCain) *chsd clr ldr: mstke 3rd: lost 2nd after next: rdn and wknd bef 5th: bhd whn p.u bef 3 out* **8/1**
4m 34.3s (-8.40) **Going Correction** -0.20s/f (Good) 6 Ran SP% **109.8**
Speed ratings (Par 107): **109,103,101,96,90**
CSF £15.48 CT £63.49 TOTE £4.80: £2.30, £2.80; EX 14.80 Trifecta £100.10.
Owner C J Edwards, D Futter, A H Rushworth **Bred** Francois-Marie Cottin **Trained** Alcester, Warwicks

FOCUS
A fair renewal of this decent handicap hurdle, although they finished well strung out.

209 WHITES OF COVENTRY - ALL THINGS METAL NOVICES' CHASE (17 fncs) 2m 4f 110y
6:25 (6:25) (Class 4) 5-Y-O+ **£3,898** (£1,144; £572; £286)

Form RPR
33P- **1** **Monkey Kingdom**[60] 4694 7-10-12 132....................(tp) LeightonAspell 122+
(Rebecca Curtis) *j.w: mde all: clr fr 14th: easily* **11/8[2]**

P24- **2** *10* **Kayf Moss**[76] 4380 7-10-12 0..........(b) RhysFlint 108+
(John Flint) *w wnr to 4th: mstke 6th: pushed along 12th: outpcd fr 14th* **4/5**[1]

054- **3** *11* **Webbswood (IRE)**[22] 5379 6-10-12 0.......... MarkGrant 96
(Sean Curran) *hld up: hdwy to go 3rd 7th: j.rt 12th and next: sn wknd* **14/1**[3]

44- **4** *1 1/2* **Conas Taoi (IRE)**[19] 5434 6-10-12 0.......... TomO'Brien 93
(Paul Morgan) *chsd ldrs: lost pl 7th: wknd 12th* **25/1**

5m 18.1s (-2.90) **Going Correction** -0.20s/f (Good) **4** Ran SP% **108.2**
Speed ratings: **97,93,89,88**
CSF £2.97 TOTE £2.30; EX 3.10 Trifecta £4.60.
Owner Carl Hinchy **Bred** R Aston **Trained** Newport, Pembrokeshire

FOCUS
A weak novice chase with the front two in the market contesting the finish.

210 WHITES - FOR AGGREGATE AND TOP SOIL H'CAP HURDLE (11 hdls) 2m 5f

6:55 (6:55) (Class 4) (0-120,115) 4-Y-0+ **£3,249** (£954; £477; £238)

Form RPR

633/ **1** **Ashbrittle**[581] 1766 8-11-11 **114**.......... TrevorWhelan 122+
(Neil King) *hld up: pushed along bef 6th: hdwy next: led appr 2 out: sn rdn: nt fluent last: hdd: rallied to ld towards fin* **4/1**[2]

221- **2** *1 1/2* **Brave Helios**[28] 5283 5-11-3 **113**.......... DanielHiskett(7) 116
(Richard Phillips) *a.p: led after 3 out: hdd bef next: led again flat: rdn and hdd towards fin* **6/1**

F13- **3** *1 3/4* **Easy Beesy**[71] 4477 7-11-9 **112**..........(b[1]) GavinSheehan 114
(Warren Greatrex) *chsd ldrs: mstke 5th: pushed along 7th: rdn appr 2 out: no ex towards fin* **10/3**[1]

520- **4** *22* **He's The Daddy**[33] 5183 8-11-2 **105**..........(vt) SamTwiston-Davies 84
(Nigel Twiston-Davies) *prom: rdn 8th: wknd after 3 out* **5/1**[3]

PU2- **5** *8* **Ugly Bug**[68] 4541 9-11-12 **115**.......... RobertDunne 86
(Alexandra Dunn) *led to 3rd: chsd ldr tl after 6th: led again 8th: hdd after 3 out: hung lft and wknd bef next* **12/1**

054- **6** *21* **Kamool (GER)**[33] 5198 5-11-12 **115**.......... WillKennedy 65
(Jonjo O'Neill) *hld up: rdn and wknd 3 out* **16/1**

606- **7** *9* **Springboks (IRE)**[40] 5068 5-10-11 **100**..........(p) WayneHutchinson 41
(Alan King) *hld up: mstke 7th: sn rdn and wknd* **7/1**

66- **F** **Rock Of Ages**[49] 4916 6-11-10 **113**.......... MarkGrant
(Neil King) *prom: chsd ldr after 6th tl 8th: rdn and wknd after 3 out: bhd whn fell next* **20/1**

340- **P** **Vaillant Creek (FR)**[33] 5191 6-11-3 **106**..........(tp) KielanWoods
(Alex Hales) *w ldr tl led 3rd: hdd 8th: rdn and wknd bef next: bhd whn p.u bef 2 out* **8/1**

5m 11.6s (-3.40) **Going Correction** -0.20s/f (Good) **9** Ran SP% **116.0**
Speed ratings (Par 105): **98,97,96,88,85 77,73, ,**
CSF £28.62 CT £88.38 TOTE £5.50: £1.70, £1.80, £2.00; EX 29.90 Trifecta £82.10.
Owner J L Rowsell **Bred** Ashbrittle Stud **Trained** Barbury Castle, Wiltshire

FOCUS
A modest handicap hurdle with changing fortunes near the finish. The form looks solid.

211 WHITES - FREE SKIPS FOR METAL CONDITIONAL JOCKEYS' H'CAP CHASE (18 fncs) 3m 110y

7:25 (7:25) (Class 5) (0-100,100) 5-Y-0+ **£2,599** (£763; £381; £190)

Form RPR

033- **1** **Moorlands George**[53] 4824 7-10-6 **80**..........(t) NicodeBoinville 94+
(Jeremy Scott) *chsd ldrs: led 3 out: rdn appr last: hung lft flat: styd on u.p* **10/3**[2]

65-1 **2** *1* **Thinger Licht (FR)**[2] 173 6-11-2 **93** 7ex..........(p) BridgetAndrews(3) 106+
(Dan Skelton) *w ldrs: plld hrd: chsd wnr after 3 out: sn rdn: nt fluent last: nt clr run flat: styd on* **11/8**[1]

PP0- **3** *8* **Volio Vincente (FR)**[52] 4855 8-10-3 **77**..........(b[1]) JamesBest 81
(Lydia Richards) *chsd ldr to 15th: sn rdn: styd on same pce fr 2 out* **25/1**

454- **4** *9* **Bebinn (IRE)**[15] 5512 8-11-3 **94**..........(p) JamieBargary(3) 89
(Ben Case) *led: hdd 3 out: rdn and wknd bef next* **16/1**

30-4 **5** *1 3/4* **Around A Pound (IRE)**[9] 44 10-10-2 **81**.......... PaulNO'Brien(5) 74
(Nick Kent) *hld up: hdwy after 11th: wknd 13th* **20/1**

431- **6** *shd* **Sir Lynx (IRE)**[48] 4938 8-11-7 **95**..........(tp) BenPoste 88
(Chris Bealby) *prom: rdn after 13th: wknd next* **16/1**

24U- **7** *26* **Royaume Bleu (FR)**[61] 4672 10-10-7 **81**..........(t) ConorShoemark 48
(Alex Hales) *hld up: mstke 10th: sme hdwy appr 12th: sn wknd: bhd whn blnd last* **10/1**

P0P- **P** **Petit Ecuyer (FR)**[20] 5407 9-11-1 **89**.......... ConorRing
(Dai Williams) *hld up: mstkes 6th and 9th: rdn and wknd after 11th: bhd whn p.u bef next* **33/1**

U43- **P** **Midnight Dove**[15] 5512 10-9-11 **74** oh3..........(v[1]) MichaelHeard(3)
(Andrew Price) *hld up: hdwy and j.rt 9th: rdn and wknd 14th: bhd whn p.u bef 2 out* **20/1**

PP3- **P** **Spanish Arch (IRE)**[20] 5407 8-10-11 **95**..........(tp) ArchieBellamy(10)
(Martin Keighley) *chsd ldrs: lost pl 5th: pushed along after next: mstke 9th: rdn and wknd after 11th: bhd whn p.u bef 2 out* **6/1**[3]

6m 21.9s (-5.10) **Going Correction** -0.20s/f (Good) **10** Ran SP% **116.6**
Speed ratings: **100,99,97,94,93 93,85, , ,**
CSF £8.26 CT £94.67 TOTE £4.90: £1.30, £1.30, £7.50; EX 12.60 Trifecta £194.90.
Owner Mrs Lynda M Williams **Bred** Mrs L M Williams **Trained** Brompton Regis, Somerset

FOCUS
They went a sensible gallop in this moderate handicap chase for conditional riders and the two best backed horses had it to themselves.

212 WHITES - FOR FACTORY AND WORK CLEARANCES MAIDEN HURDLE (12 hdls) 3m 1f

7:55 (7:55) (Class 5) 4-Y-0+ **£2,274** (£667; £333; £166)

Form RPR

652- **1** **Clancy's Cross (IRE)**[27] 5286 6-11-0 125..........(p) LeightonAspell 119+
(Rebecca Curtis) *w ldr tl led 8th: shkn up appr 2 out: clr last: idled flat: pushed out* **2/1**[1]

0- **2** *2* **Mad About The Boy**[128] 3454 5-11-0 0.......... PeterCarberry 118+
(Nicky Henderson) *trckd ldrs: racd keenly: nt fluent 8th: hmpd 3 out: sn chsng wnr: mstke next: sn rdn and hung rt: mstke last: styd on same pce flat* **6/1**

3- **3** *8* **Cul Dealga (IRE)**[27] 5293 6-10-7 0.......... TomMessenger 101
(Chris Bealby) *chsd ldrs: wnt 2nd 9th tl j.rt 3 out: sn rdn: styd on same pce* **8/1**

4 *11* **It'll Be Grand** 6-11-0 0.......... TomScudamore 96
(David Pipe) *hld up: pushed along 8th: rdn and wknd after 3 out* **3/1**[2]

/02- **5** *11* **Cleeve Hill Lad**[52] 4853 7-11-0 105.......... RobertDunne 85
(Tom Lacey) *led to 8th: rdn and wknd after 3 out* **14/1**

P50- **P** **Cleetons Turn**[33] 5180 8-10-9 0 ow2.......... MrJMartin(7)
(Alan Hollingsworth) *hld up: drvn along after 6th: wknd bef 8th: bhd whn p.u bef next* **100/1**

3- **P** **Get Involved (IRE)**[54] 4809 6-11-0 0.......... CharliePoste
(Robin Dickin) *chsd ldrs tl wknd 8th: bhd whn p.u bef next* **7/2**[3]

6m 31.3s (16.30) **Going Correction** -0.20s/f (Good) **7** Ran SP% **113.6**
Speed ratings (Par 103): **65,64,61,58,54 ,**
CSF £14.53 TOTE £3.50: £2.10, £3.90; EX 13.90 Trifecta £115.50.
Owner Carl Hinchy **Bred** Jimmy McCarthy **Trained** Newport, Pembrokeshire

FOCUS
An ordinary staying maiden hurdle and there was a lack of early pace.

213 WHITES - BEST BUYERS FOR COPPER AND BRASS STANDARD OPEN NATIONAL HUNT FLAT RACE 2m

8:25 (8:25) (Class 6) 4-6-Y-O **£1,624** (£477; £238; £119)

Form RPR

1 **Burlington Bert (FR)** 4-10-12 0.......... GavinSheehan 113+
(Warren Greatrex) *a.p: chsd ldr over 3f out: shkn up to ld over 1f out: r.o: comf* **9/2**[2]

2 *1 1/2* **Call To Order** 5-11-2 0.......... RichieMcLernon 116+
(Jonjo O'Neill) *hld up: hdwy over 5f out: rdn to chse wnr ins fnl f: styd on* **12/1**

2- **3** *2 3/4* **Mckenzie's Friend (IRE)**[49] 4921 4-10-12 0.......... LeightonAspell 109
(Oliver Sherwood) *hld up: hdwy 1/2-way: rdn over 1f out: styd on same pce ins fnl f* **2/1**[1]

4 *2 1/2* **Paddy's Field (IRE)** 5-11-2 0.......... DavidBass 111
(Ben Pauling) *chsd ldrs: led over 4f out: rdn and hdd over 1f out: no ex ins fnl f* **12/1**

5 *5* **Baron De Ligniere (FR)** 4-10-12 0.......... SamTwiston-Davies 102
(Paul Nicholls) *hld up: hdwy over 4f out: styd on same pce fnl 2f* **8/1**

3- **6** *1* **Will O'The West (IRE)**[76] 4391 4-10-12 0.......... RichardJohnson 101
(Henry Daly) *hld up: hdwy over 4f out: outpcd fnl 3f* **16/1**

5- **7** *9* **Bound Hill**[56] 4755 6-11-2 0.......... AidanColeman 96
(Fiona Shaw) *hld up: hdwy over 5f out: wknd over 3f out* **33/1**

8 *1/2* **Blue Comet** 4-10-12 0.......... WayneHutchinson 91
(Richard Phillips) *hld up: pushed along 7f out: nvr on terms* **33/1**

9 *4* **Poetry Emotion (IRE)** 4-10-12 0.......... NicodeBoinville 87
(Nicky Henderson) *prom: rdn over 5f out: n.m.r and wknd over 3f out* **7/1**[3]

10 *1 1/4* **The Artful Cobbler** 4-10-12 0.......... TomO'Brien 86
(Henry Daly) *mid-div: pushed along and lost pl over 6f out: n.d after* **20/1**

3- **11** *5* **Arctic Gold (IRE)**[40] 5077 4-10-9 0.......... ConorShoemark(3) 81
(Nigel Twiston-Davies) *plld hrd and prom: trckd ldr after 1f: rdn over 3f out: wknd over 2f out* **14/1**

5- **12** *3/4* **Better Days (IRE)**[42] 5028 4-10-5 0.......... JamieBargary(7) 80
(Nigel Twiston-Davies) *mid-div: hdwy over 5f out: rdn and wknd over 3f out* **40/1**

0- **13** *14* **Sugar Mix**[28] 5285 4-10-2 0.......... ArchieBellamy(10) 66
(Martin Keighley) *prom: racd keenly: rdn over 6f out: wknd over 4f out* **66/1**

6- **14** *15* **Stepover**[40] 5071 4-10-5 0.......... KielanWoods 44
(Alex Hales) *hld up: wknd over 5f out* **50/1**

3P- **15** *1 3/4* **Midtech Valentine**[23] 5359 4-10-0 0.......... RobMcCarth(5) 42
(Ian Williams) *led: hdd over 4f out: wknd over 3f out* **50/1**

0- **16** *69* **Samarinta**[54] 4812 6-10-9 0.......... TrevorWhelan
(Nicholas Pomfret) *chsd ldrs: pushed along 1/2-way: wknd over 6f out* **100/1**

3m 47.5s (-3.40) **Going Correction** -0.20s/f (Good)
WFA 4 from 5yo+ 4lb **16** Ran SP% **122.5**
Speed ratings: **100,99,97,96,94 93,89,88,86,86 83,83,76,68,68 33**
CSF £54.25 TOTE £4.60: £1.30, £3.20, £1.80; EX 94.00 Trifecta £306.10.
Owner Martin St Quinton & Tim Syder **Bred** Jean-Pierre Bichon **Trained** Upper Lambourn, Berks

FOCUS
An above-average bumper for the track which should produce a few subsequent winners.
T/Plt: £19.10 to a £1 stake. Pool of £38626.29 - 1471.51 winning tickets. T/Qpdt: £8.60 to a £1 stake. Pool of £3530.90 - 302.65 winning tickets. **Colin Roberts**

LUDLOW (R-H)

Sunday, May 10

OFFICIAL GOING: Good (8.3)
Wind: Light behind Weather: Cloudy with sunny spells

214 GWYN THOMAS BIRTHDAY CELEBRATION NOVICES' HURDLE (9 hdls) 1m 7f 169y

2:15 (2:15) (Class 4) 4-Y-0+ **£3,898** (£1,144; £572; £286)

Form RPR

0/2- **1** **Are They Your Own (IRE)**[19] 5448 7-10-7 0.......... NickSlatter(7) 113+
(Fergal O'Brien) *mde all: hung lft after 6th: shkn up appr last: styd on wl* **14/1**

2 *2 1/2* **Gambol (FR)**[245] 5-11-0 0.......... WillKennedy 112+
(Ian Williams) *chsd wnr: ev ch fr 3 out tl appr last: styd on same pce flat* **7/2**[2]

611- **3** *7* **Quebec**[28] 5294 4-11-1 132.......... CiaranGethings(7) 114
(Robert Stephens) *chsd ldrs: pushed along bef 3 out: mstke next: rdn whn nt fluent last: no ex flat* **1/1**[1]

4 *3/4* **Number One London (IRE)**[210] 5-11-0 0.......... RichardJohnson 105
(Tim Vaughan) *hld up: hdwy 3 out: sn outpcd: mstke next: styd on towards fin* **6/1**[3]

3- **5** *53* **Milestone (IRE)**[214] 1799 5-11-0 0..........(t) PaulMoloney 91+
(Evan Williams) *hld up: pushed along after 4th: effrt whn hmpd 3 out: no ch after* **13/2**

F **General Brook (IRE)**[22] 5-11-0 0.......... DaveCrosse
(John O'Shea) *trckd ldrs: racd keenly: ev ch whn fell 3 out* **33/1**

3m 41.6s (-7.90) **Going Correction** -0.70s/f (Firm) **6** Ran SP% **109.4**
Speed ratings (Par 105): **91,89,86,85,59**
CSF £58.80 TOTE £6.50: £4.10, £1.80; EX 28.10 Trifecta £35.40.
Owner Ian Slatter **Bred** William Neville **Trained** Naunton, Gloucs

FOCUS
Bottom bend out 5m increasing distances by 15m per circuit. Race times suggest the ground was definitely riding on the fast side of good, with this event only 3.6sec outside standard. An ordinary novice hurdle in which the winner dictated the pace.

215 TOTEPOOL BET ON ALL UK RACING NOVICES' LIMITED H'CAP CHASE (19 fncs) 3m
2:45 (2:45) (Class 3) (0-135,124) 5-Y-0+ **£7,797** (£2,289; £1,144; £572)

Form RPR
213- 1 **Belmount (IRE)**[45] 4991 6-11-0 **116**.......................... SamTwiston-Davies 132
(Nigel Twiston-Davies) *led to 2nd: chsd ldr tl led again 15th: mstke 2 out: sn rdn: stydon wl* **10/3**[1]
253- 2 *1* **Call Me Vic (IRE)**[62] 4676 8-11-8 **124**.......................... PaddyBrennan 139
(Tom George) *a.p: chsd wnr 4 out: ev ch fr next: mstke 2 out: sn rdn: styd on* **7/2**[2]
241- 3 *14* **Greenlaw**[44] 5018 9-10-10 **112**..........................(t) NoelFehily 113
(Charlie Longsdon) *led 2nd: clr 6th to 11th: mstke 13th: hdd 15th: rdn appr 3 out: wknd last* **9/2**[3]
32-3 4 *14* **Still Believing (IRE)**[8] 86 7-10-13 **115**.......................... AdamWedge 104
(Evan Williams) *hld up: hdwy 14th: rdn and wknd after 3 out* **10/1**
/03- 5 *6* **Lord Grantham (IRE)**[38] 5107 8-11-6 **122**.......................... JakeGreenall 107
(Henry Daly) *hld up: pushed along 15th: hdwy sn after: hit 4 out: wknd bef next* **7/2**[2]
/6-U 6 *5* **Miss Tilly Oscar (IRE)**[9] 60 9-10-0 **110** oh19.......................... BenPoste[(3)] 84
(Steve Flook) *hld up: pushed along 12th: rdn after 15th: wknd bef next* **66/1**
013- 7 *16* **Howaboutnow (IRE)**[42] 5048 8-11-4 **120**.......................... WillKennedy 85
(Ian Williams) *chsd ldrs: lost pl 14th: rdn and wknd wl bef 4 out* **6/1**

5m 48.3s (-20.00) **Going Correction** -0.65s/f (Firm) **7** Ran SP% **110.6**
Speed ratings: **107,106,102,97,95 93,88**
CSF £14.74 TOTE £4.10: £2.10, £1.30; EX 17.50 Trifecta £40.90.
Owner N A Twiston-Davies **Bred** Pamela Sweeney **Trained** Naunton, Gloucs

FOCUS
Not a particularly strong race for the grade, but the time was quick and the first two came clear. Nothing got involved from off the pace.

216 TOTEPOOL RACING'S BIGGEST SUPPORTER H'CAP HURDLE (11 hdls) 2m 5f 55y
3:15 (3:15) (Class 3) (0-125,125) 4-Y-0+ **£7,797** (£2,289; £1,144; £572)

Form RPR
/F1- 1 **Double Silver**[52] 4869 8-11-0 **113**.......................... PaddyBrennan 120+
(Fergal O'Brien) *hld up: hdwy after 8th: led and hung rt appr 2 out: rdn out* **8/1**
350- 2 *1 3/4* **Lava Lamp (GER)**[175] 2519 8-10-10 **109**.......................... PaulMoloney 113
(Evan Williams) *chsd ldr to 5th: remained handy: rdn and ev ch 2 out: styd on* **20/1**
U32- 3 *5* **Kalimantan (IRE)**[90] 3413 5-11-0 **113**.......................... RichardJohnson 111
(Tim Vaughan) *a.p: rdn appr last: no ex flat* **4/1**[2]
300- 4 *6* **Acertain Circus**[36] 5142 5-11-11 **124**..........................(t) KielanWoods 119
(Pam Sly) *chsd ldrs: nt fluent 5th: wnt 2nd 7th: ev ch 3 out: hmpd bef next: wknd last* **11/2**[3]
P35- 5 *2 1/4* **Brownville**[41] 5075 6-11-9 **122**..........................(t) SamTwiston-Davies 112
(Nigel Twiston-Davies) *led: rdn appr 3 out: hdd bef next: wknd flat* **7/2**[1]
6 *1 1/2* **Romeo Is Bleeding (IRE)**[34] 9-10-11 **110**.......................... AdamWedge 98
(David Rees) *hld up: effrt appr 3 out: mstke next: sn wknd* **12/1**
55-4 7 *1 1/2* **Somemothersdohavem**[6] 108 6-10-5 **104**..........................(b) LiamTreadwell 93
(Venetia Williams) *hld up: rdn appr 3 out hit next: sn wknd* **4/1**[2]
235- 8 *26* **Bonne Fee**[24] 5355 8-11-12 **125**..........................(p) DavidBass 86
(Kim Bailey) *chsd ldrs: wnt 2nd 5th to 7th: rdn and wknd appr 3 out* **7/1**

5m 3.4s (-11.40) **Going Correction** -0.70s/f (Firm) **8** Ran SP% **113.7**
Speed ratings (Par 107): **93,92,90,88,87 86,86,76**
CSF £131.86 CT £731.48 TOTE £7.00: £2.20, £4.30, £1.50; EX 39.90 Trifecta £747.90.
Owner R C Mayall **Bred** Ms Linda Redmond And Mrs Mary Mayall **Trained** Naunton, Gloucs

FOCUS
Fair handicap form.

217 WELSH GUARDS ASSOCIATION H'CAP HURDLE (9 hdls) 1m 7f 169y
3:45 (3:45) (Class 4) (0-120,117) 4-Y-0+ **£6,498** (£1,908; £954; £477)

Form RPR
P11- 1 **Frozen Over**[21] 5412 7-11-4 **106**..........................(t) JamesDavies 111+
(Chris Down) *hld up: hdwy to chse ldr 3 out: led appr last where mstke: rdn out* **4/1**[2]
22-1 2 *1* **Mr Lando**[6] 104 6-11-8 **117** 7ex.......................... MrSHanson[(7)] 120+
(Alison Batchelor) *led: rdn and hdd appr last: hmpd flat: styd on* **13/8**[1]
0F2- 3 *24* **Fairy Alisha**[18] 5466 7-10-10 **105**.......................... JoshWall[(7)] 85
(Trevor Wall) *chsd ldrs: mstke 6th: rdn appr 3 out: mstke and wknd next* **7/1**
2P5- 4 *1/2* **Candelita**[19] 5441 8-10-7 **102**.......................... MrStanSheppard[(7)] 82
(Matt Sheppard) *chsd ldrs: hit 2nd: rdn after 6th: wknd bef next* **8/1**
443- 5 *3/4* **Sword Of The Lord**[18] 5475 5-11-7 **109**..........................(tp) SamTwiston-Davies 89
(Nigel Twiston-Davies) *chsd ldr tl rdn appr 3 out: nt fluent next: sn wknd* **9/2**[3]
0/0- 6 *1 1/4* **Red Skipper (IRE)**[13] 213 10-11-6 **108**.......................... DaveCrosse 86
(John O'Shea) *hld up: hdwy after 6th: rdn bef next: wknd 2 out* **40/1**
004/ 7 *21* **Battlecat**[731] 176 8-11-12 **114**.......................... AdamWedge 73
(Evan Williams) *hld up: mstke 1st: rdn and wknd after 6th: bhd whn hit 2 out* **12/1**

3m 35.7s (-13.80) **Going Correction** -0.70s/f (Firm) course record **7** Ran SP% **110.0**
Speed ratings (Par 105): **106,105,93,93,92 92,81**
CSF £10.42 CT £38.43 TOTE £4.60: £2.80, £1.40; EX 12.90 Trifecta £40.20.
Owner O'Neill, Capps, Di Vincenzo **Bred** Manor Farm Packers Ltd **Trained** Mutterton, Devon

FOCUS
Two in-form handicappers dominated the finish of this soundly-run event, finishing clear.

218 MYTOTEPOOL.COM H'CAP CHASE (12 fncs) 1m 7f 212y
4:15 (4:15) (Class 3) (0-140,137) 5-Y-0+ **£12,996** (£3,816; £1,908; £954)

Form RPR
543- 1 **Bullet Street (IRE)**[42] 5046 7-11-0 **125**.......................... PaulMoloney 130+
(Evan Williams) *hld up: hdwy 4 out: shkn up to ld flat: rdn and edgd rt: r.o wl* **11/2**[3]
0F-2 2 *3 3/4* **My Brother Sylvest**[6] 103 9-11-12 **137**..........................(b) TomScudamore 139
(David Pipe) *led: racd freely: nt fluent 6th: rdn and hdd 2 out: ev ch last: styd on same pce flat* **6/1**
U2-2 3 *hd* **Easily Pleased (IRE)**[5] 121 9-10-7 **118**.......................... RichardJohnson 120
(Martin Hill) *hld up: hdwy 4 out: n.m.r appr last: styd on* **9/2**[2]
243- 4 *3/4* **Un Anjou (FR)**[21] 5413 7-10-12 **123**.......................... NoelFehily 124
(David Dennis) *chsd ldrs: wnt 2nd 4 out: led 2 out: rdn and hdd flat: no ex* **16/1**
31F- 5 *4* **Sir Valentino (FR)**[98] 3995 6-11-5 **130**..........................(t) PaddyBrennan 127
(Tom George) *hld up: hdwy 9th: rdn after 3 out: styd on same pce appr last* **13/2**
215- 6 *2* **Limpopo Tom (IRE)**[16] 5508 8-11-0 **125**..........................(p) DenisO'Regan 122
(David Rees) *sn bhd: nt fluent 4th: styd on fr 3 out: nt fluent next: nvr trbld ldrs* **25/1**
1U1- 7 *3 3/4* **Another Flutter (IRE)**[36] 5147 11-11-3 **135**..........................(tp) MrStanSheppard[(7)] 128
(Matt Sheppard) *hld up: hdwy 9th: mstke and wknd 2 out* **12/1**
63F- 8 *14* **Sonofagun (FR)**[21] 5406 9-10-8 **119**.......................... WillKennedy 99
(Ian Williams) *chsd ldrs: rdn after 9th: wknd 3 out* **14/1**
341- 9 *27* **Arkaim**[52] 4870 7-11-9 **134**..........................(tp) KielanWoods 89
(Pam Sly) *chsd ldr: nt a fluent: j.rt 3rd: mstkes 7th and 9th: wknd bef 3 out* **9/1**
111- P **Storm Of Swords (IRE)**[51] 4890 7-11-5 **130**.......................... HarrySkelton
(Dan Skelton) *chsd ldrs tl wknd after 9th: bhd whn p.u bef 3 out* **4/1**[1]

3m 47.3s (-11.20) **Going Correction** -0.65s/f (Firm) course record **10** Ran SP% **115.3**
Speed ratings: **102,100,100,99,97 96,94,87,74,**
CSF £38.61 CT £160.95 TOTE £8.80: £2.80, £1.50, £1.20; EX 45.00 Trifecta £179.70.
Owner Mrs Janet Davies & Mrs C Williams **Bred** Denis And Mrs Teresa Bergin **Trained** Llancarfan, Vale Of Glamorgan

FOCUS
A cracking handicap with a worthwhile prize, run at a strong gallop and in a record-equalling time.

219 TANNERS WINES NOVICES' HURDLE (11 hdls) 2m 5f 55y
4:45 (4:45) (Class 4) 4-Y-0+ **£3,898** (£1,144; £572; £286)

Form RPR
643- 1 **Promanco**[52] 4869 6-10-5 0..........................(t) RichardJohnson 112+
(Charlie Longsdon) *hld up: hdwy 8th: led appr and nt fluent 3 out: clr whn hit last: comf* **11/4**[3]
21- 2 *7* **Ballykan**[60] 4713 5-11-5 0..........................(t) SamTwiston-Davies 116
(Nigel Twiston-Davies) *chsd ldr and nt fluent 1st: led 2nd tl rdn appr 3 out: styd on same pce last* **2/1**[1]
6- 3 *3* **Babeny Bridge (IRE)**[26] 5337 6-10-5 0.......................... LizzieKelly[(7)] 107
(Nick Williams) *chsd ldrs tl wnt upsides 3rd: nt fluent 7th: rdn appr 3 out: styd on same pce fr next* **12/1**
41-4 4 *2 1/4* **Future Security (IRE)**[9] 59 6-11-5 118..........................(t) PaddyBrennan 111
(Anthony Middleton) *sn prom: after 2nd: rdn appr 3 out: styd on same pce fr next* **5/2**[2]
40-5 5 *16* **Highland Life**[9] 56 5-10-2 0..........................(t) BenPoste[(3)] 83
(Steve Flook) *led to 2nd: chsd ldrs tl rdn after 8th: wknd bef next* **50/1**
556/ 6 *2* **Mr Moss (IRE)**[526] 2822 10-10-12 0.......................... PaulMoloney 88
(Evan Williams) *prom tl rdn and wknd appr 3 out* **7/1**
050- 7 *85* **Bertie Lugg**[34] 5180 7-10-12 0.......................... RobertDunne 12
(Andrew Price) *hld up: rdn and wknd after 8th* **80/1**
050- P **Laughingalltheway**[39] 5097 4-10-7 0.......................... AndrewTinkler
(Martin Keighley) *hld up: mstke 5th: bhd fr next* **50/1**

5m 3.4s (-11.40) **Going Correction** -0.70s/f (Firm)
WFA 4 from 5yo+ 19lb **8** Ran SP% **113.9**
Speed ratings (Par 105): **93,90,89,88,82 81,49,**
CSF £8.89 TOTE £3.80: £1.10, £1.10, £2.80; EX 10.10 Trifecta £64.10.
Owner Mrs S Tainton **Bred** Mrs Jane Haywood **Trained** Over Norton, Oxon

FOCUS
A modest novice event.

220 ANN ESP MEMORIAL "NEWCOMERS" STANDARD OPEN NATIONAL HUNT FLAT RACE 1m 7f 169y
5:15 (5:15) (Class 5) 4-6-Y-0 **£3,249** (£954; £477; £238)

Form RPR
1 **Ascotdeux Nellerie (FR)** 5-11-4 0.......................... DavidBass 110+
(Kim Bailey) *hld up: hdwy 6f out: chsd ldr 4f out: led over 2f out: edgd rt and c clr fr over 1f out* **9/2**[3]
2 *9* **Handpicked** 4-10-7 0.......................... JakeGreenall 91+
(Henry Daly) *chsd ldrs: lost pl 10f out: hdwy over 3f out: r.o to go 2nd ins fnl f: no ch w wnr* **4/1**[2]
3 *3 3/4* **Round Robin (IRE)** 4-11-0 0.......................... TomO'Brien 95
(Henry Daly) *chsd ldrs: led over 7f out: rdn and hdd over 2f out: styd on same pce appr fnl f* **8/1**
4 *16* **Battle Master** 5-11-1 0.......................... BenPoste[(3)] 84
(Michael Mullineaux) *chsd ldrs tl wknd 5f out* **25/1**
5 *22* **Defiant Dazzler (IRE)** 6-10-11 0.......................... MissLBrooke[(7)] 64
(Lady Susan Brooke) *plld hrd and prom: led after 3f: hdd over 7f out: wknd over 3f out* **66/1**
6 *3 1/2* **Von Trappe (IRE)** 6-11-4 0.......................... AdamWedge 61
(Alan Phillips) *hld up: pushed along 1/2-way: sn lost tch* **33/1**
7 *1 3/4* **Teme Trixie** 5-10-11 0.......................... RobertDunne 53
(Andrew Price) *hld up: hdwy 1/2-way: chsd ldr briefly over 4f out: rdn and wknd over 2f out* **50/1**
8 *18* **Renfrew (IRE)** 5-11-4 0.......................... RichardJohnson 43
(Tim Vaughan) *led 3f: chsd ldrs: rdn and wknd over 3f out* **5/1**
U **Rather Be (IRE)** 4-11-0 0.......................... AndrewTinkler
(Nicky Henderson) *uns rdr s* **7/4**[1]

3m 38.2s (-5.70) **Going Correction** -0.70s/f (Firm)
WFA 4 from 5yo+ 4lb **9** Ran SP% **112.6**
Speed ratings: **86,81,79,71,60 58,58,49,**
CSF £21.55 TOTE £5.30: £1.90, £1.90, £2.30; EX 24.50 Trifecta £98.10.
Owner The Lucky Nelleries **Bred** M Huame, Mme M Huame Et Al **Trained** Andoversford, Gloucs

FOCUS
No previous form to go on in this bumper, but the winner could be useful.

T/Plt: £136.40 to a £1 stake. Pool: £61,617.52 - 329.70 winning units. T/Qpdt: £6.70 to a £1 stake. Pool: £6200.31 - 680.31 winning units. **Colin Roberts**

PLUMPTON (L-H)

Sunday, May 10

OFFICIAL GOING: Good (watered; hdl 8.3; chs 8.4) changing to good (good to firm in places) after race 3 (3.00)
Wind: light, half against Weather: dry, sunny spells

221 BAKER OF DELICIOUS HAPPINESS PUDDINGFAIRY.CO.UK MAIDEN HURDLE (9 hdls) 1m 7f 195y
2:00 (2:01) (Class 5) 4-Y-O+ **£2,794** (£820; £410; £205)

Form RPR
422- **1** **Ryeolliean**[6] 5154 4-10-10 **123**.................(p) NickScholfield 110+
(Gary Moore) *chsd ldr: upsides and travelling strly 3 out: led bef next and in command ent st: comf* **6/4**[1]

35- **2** *8* **Sebs Sensei (IRE)**[21] 5411 4-10-3 **0**.................. MrDGBurchell(7) 101
(Mark Hoad) *hld up in 5th: j.lft 3rd: clsd and in tch 6th: rdn after 3 out: wnt 2nd jst bef next: no imp: mstke last* **33/1**[3]

3 *8* **Asknotwhat (IRE)**[54] 4840 4-10-10 **0**.................(p) TomCannon 92
(David Bridgwater) *t.k.h: led tl rdn and hdd after 3 out: struggling and lost pl bef 2 out: lft 3rd 2 out: wknd bef last* **7/2**[2]

000- **4** *64* **Up Four It (IRE)**[35] 5151 7-10-11 **0**.................. JeremiahMcGrath(3) 37
(Jamie Poulton) *bhd: hmpd 1st: t.o after 5th: lft poor 4th and hmpd 2 out* **66/1**

F42- **U** **Ronaldinho (IRE)**[23] 5369 5-11-0 **119**.................(b) WayneHutchinson 107+
(Alan King) *chsd ldrs: effrt after 3 out: no imp ent st: 3rd and btn whn bdly hmpd by loose horse and uns rdr 2 out* **6/4**[1]

U **Modern Society**[670] 5-11-0 **0**.................. BrendanPowell
(Andrew Reid) *t.k.h: chsd ldrs tl 4th: sn lost pl: t.o after next: swvd arnd fallen jockey and uns rdr on landing 2 out* **100/1**

U **Mac's Superstar (FR)**[265] 5-11-0 **0**.................. AlainCawley
(Alan Coogan) *last pair whn veered sharply lft and uns rdr 1st* **33/1**[3]

3m 39.2s (-21.60) **Going Correction** -1.05s/f (Hard)
WFA 4 from 5yo+ 18lb 7 Ran SP% **110.6**
Speed ratings (Par 103): **112,108,104,72, , ,**
CSF £35.73 TOTE £1.90: £1.10, £7.50; EX 28.40 Trifecta £82.30.
Owner Bryan Fry **Bred** Dale Ablitt **Trained** Lower Beeding, W Sussex

FOCUS
Common bends used and consequently Chases increased by 90yds per circuit and Hurdles reduced by 10yds per circuit. An ordinary maiden.

222 STEVIE FISHER TRUST H'CAP HURDLE (14 hdls) 3m 217y
2:30 (2:30) (Class 5) (0-100,96) 4-Y-O+ **£2,924** (£858; £429; £214)

Form RPR
0PP- **1** **Band Of Thunder**[134] 3323 7-10-6 **79**.................(b) ThomasGarner(3) 87+
(Mark H Tompkins) *travelled strly: chsd ldrs: rdn to ld bef 2 out: sn clr: in command whn hit last: eased towards fin* **20/1**

411- **2** *8* **Flugzeug**[16] 5525 7-11-2 **93**.................. KevinJones(7) 92
(Seamus Mullins) *in tch in midfield: rdn after 11th: outpcd after next: kpt on u.p between last 2: wnt 2nd fnl 100yds: no ch w wnr* **5/1**[2]

2U0- **3** *nk* **Maccabees**[23] 5371 6-9-9 **72**.................(p) ThomasCheesman(7) 71
(Linda Jewell) *in tch towards rr: hdwy into midfield after 10th: rdn and no hdwy bef 3 out: outpcd bef 2 out: styd on again between last 2: wnt 3rd nr fin: no ch w wnr* **12/1**

66-2 **4** *1* **Canarbino Girl**[10] 40 8-10-10 **80**.................(tp) JamesBest 79
(Caroline Keevil) *travelled strly: in tch: hdwy to chse ldrs 10th: led after 3 out: rdn and hdd ent st: outpcd by wnr and hit 2 out: lost 2 pls fnl 100yds* **10/1**

330- **5** *1½* **Spanish Fork (IRE)**[189] 2229 6-11-5 **89**.................. MarcGoldstein 86
(Sheena West) *chsd ldr tl led bef 3 out: drvn and hdd wl bef 2 out: 3rd and btn 2 out: plugged on same pce after* **9/1**

214- **6** *11* **Bridal Suite (IRE)**[19] 5442 6-11-2 **96**.................(t) TommyDowling(10) 83
(Charlie Mann) *midfield whn mstke 1st: reminders after 4th: hdwy 7th: chsd ldrs and rdn bef 3 out: 4th and outpcd bef 2 out: wknd 2 out* **11/2**[3]

03-2 **7** *2¾* **Lord Aldervale (IRE)**[8] 89 8-9-9 **72**.................(t) GeorgeGorman(7) 56
(Luke Dace) *led tl rdn and hdd bef 3 out: mstke 3 out: wknd bef next: wl btn and mstke last* **6/1**

335- **8** *12* **The Kings Assassin (IRE)**[218] 1743 7-11-10 **94**.................. TomCannon 71
(Chris Gordon) *in tch in midfield: mstke 3rd: dropped to rr and niggled along 9th: nvr gng wl after: drvn and no rspnse after 11th: blnd next: sn lost tch* **10/3**[1]

450- **9** *19* **Conserve (IRE)**[19] 3602 5-11-8 **92**.................(b) TrevorWhelan 48
(Neil King) *nt fluent: hld up in tch in rr: hdwy after 10th: btn 3 out: sn wknd: t.o* **16/1**

603- **10** *24* **Petite Fantasie**[50] 4908 6-11-3 **87**.................. NickScholfield 22
(Mark Gillard) *chsd ldrs: j. slowly 2nd and 3rd: lost pl and rdn 11th: bhd next: t.o* **8/1**

000- **11** *5* **I'm Lucy (IRE)**[34] 5208 4-9-7 **76** oh15.................(t[1]) GaryDerwin(7)
(Linda Jewell) *hld up in rr: clsd and in tch 9th: rdn and struggling 11th: sn lost tch: t.o* **66/1**

6m 3.3s (-21.70) **Going Correction** -1.05s/f (Hard)
WFA 4 from 5yo+ 20lb 11 Ran SP% **119.4**
Speed ratings (Par 103): **91,88,88,88,87 84,83,79,73,66 64**
CSF £120.60 CT £1283.08 TOTE £31.50: £11.10, £2.00, £7.30; EX 188.50 Trifecta £1769.20 Part won..
Owner Mrs V Akehurst **Bred** John M Troy **Trained** Newmarket, Suffolk

FOCUS
A moderate staying handicap, run at a fair enough gallop and looks sound enough rated around the second.

223 SOPHIE MELLETT 18TH BIRTHDAY H'CAP CHASE (18 fncs) 3m 1f 152y
3:00 (3:01) (Class 5) (0-100,97) 5-Y-O+ **£3,573** (£1,049; £524; £262)

Form RPR
35P- **1** **Ya Hafed**[160] 2857 7-10-9 **80**.................. MarcGoldstein 87+
(Sheena West) *chsd ldrs: wnt 2nd bef 15th: rdn and hit rail after 3 out: clsd and j. into ld 2 out: clr between last 2: rdn out* **6/1**

21-2 **2** *1½* **Charming Lad (IRE)**[9] 66 10-11-7 **97**.................(bt) DannyBurton(5) 104+
(Anthony Day) *hld up in rr: hdwy 8th: mstke 10th: 3rd and effrt after 3 out: mstke and bmpd 2 out: sn drvn to chse wnr: styd on but nvr getting to wnr flat* **5/2**[1]

P52- **3** *16* **The Cat's Away (IRE)**[34] 5186 7-10-2 **73**.................(b) RichieMcLernon 69
(Richenda Ford) *racd wd: w ldr: mstke 2nd: led 9th: hdd: mstke and bmpd rival 2 out: 3rd and btn between last 2: wknd last* **11/4**[2]

4/4- **4** *10* **Roparta Avenue**[40] 5089 8-10-11 **82**.................. LeightonAspell 64
(Diana Grissell) *j.rt: in tch towards rr: rdn and struggling after 13th: no threat to ldrs after: plugged on: carried rt last: wnt modest 4th flat* **6/1**

354- **5** *hd* **What's For Tea**[16] 5525 10-9-11 **71** oh6.................. WayneKavanagh(3) 54
(Paddy Butler) *in rr fr 4th: nvr on terms after: no ch 14th: plugged on* **40/1**

01-3 **6** *¾* **Red Anchor (IRE)**[9] 66 11-10-10 **84**.................(b) ThomasGarner(3) 65
(Linda Jewell) *chsd ldrs: wnt 2nd after 10th tl after 14th: 3rd whn hmpd next: wknd u.p after 3 out: no ch whn j.rt last: lost 2 pls flat* **9/2**[3]

43-6 **7** *81* **Brunette'sonly (IRE)**[9] 66 10-10-12 **83**.................(p) AndrewThornton
(Seamus Mullins) *nt fluent: mde most tl hdd 9th: lost pl and reminders after 12th: bhd and lost tch after next: sn t.o* **10/1**

6m 39.7s (-11.00) **Going Correction** -0.35s/f (Good) 7 Ran SP% **113.5**
Speed ratings: **102,101,96,93,93 93,68**
CSF £21.83 TOTE £13.00: £6.10, £1.80; EX 33.00 Trifecta £99.10.
Owner Gerald West **Bred** Lady Bland & Miss Anthea Gibson-Fleming **Trained** Falmer, E Sussex

FOCUS
This was an ordinary handicap, but the form is solid with the first pair coming clear.

224 DOT HICKLING MEMORIAL H'CAP HURDLE (9 hdls) 1m 7f 195y
3:30 (3:30) (Class 5) (0-100,96) 4-Y-O+ **£2,924** (£858; £429; £214)

Form RPR
004- **1** **Zarawi (IRE)**[18] 5481 4-11-5 **93**.................(p) AidanColeman 101+
(Charlie Longsdon) *t.k.h: chsd ldrs: travelling strly but nt clr run after 3 out: shkn up and qcknd to ld 2 out: sn clr: eased towards fin: easily* **7/2**[1]

44F- **2** *10* **Lindsay's Dream**[16] 5527 9-11-5 **89**.................(p) MarkGrant 89
(Zoe Davison) *hld up in tch in rr: clsd to trck ldrs bef 3 out: rdn and chsd ldr bef 2 out: outpcd by wnr between last 2: kpt on u.p flat* **14/1**

323- **3** *1½* **Warrant Officer**[16] 5527 5-11-12 **96**.................. MarcGoldstein 96
(Sheena West) *led: rdn bef 2 out: hdd 2 out: sn outpcd by wnr: kpt on same pce after* **9/2**[3]

505- **4** *nk* **Tiger Feat**[34] 5212 5-11-4 **88**.................(b[1]) WayneHutchinson 87
(Alan King) *chsd ldrs: rdn and effrt after 3 out: outpcd by wnr between last 2: kpt on same pce flat* **4/1**[2]

641- **5** *4* **Hermosa Vaquera (IRE)**[16] 5527 5-11-4 **88**.................(tp) TomCannon 84
(Anna Newton-Smith) *chsd ldr: mstke 5th: rdn and ev ch after 3 out: no ex 2 out and sn outpcd: wknd last* **9/2**[3]

5P2- **6** *3* **Hawk Gold (IRE)**[16] 5527 11-10-1 **76**.................. JackSherwood(5) 69
(Michelle Bryant) *hld up in tch: effrt to chse ldrs after 3 out: btn whn mstke next: wknd flat* **11/2**

216- **7** *33* **Dorry K (IRE)**[231] 1595 6-11-4 **95**.................(t) JamieBargary(7) 57
(Jim Best) *in tch: rdn after 4th and nvr travelling after: lost tch after 3 out: t.o* **8/1**

3m 41.3s (-19.50) **Going Correction** -1.05s/f (Hard)
WFA 4 from 5yo+ 18lb 7 Ran SP% **111.7**
Speed ratings (Par 103): **106,101,100,100,98 96,80**
CSF £43.43 CT £218.89 TOTE £3.70: £1.40, £5.60; EX 45.80 Trifecta £125.30.
Owner Catchusifyoucan Partnership **Bred** His Highness The Aga Khan's Studs S C **Trained** Over Norton, Oxon

FOCUS
A weak handicap.

225 SPEEDCUT CONTRACTORS RACING EXCELLENCE CONDITIONAL JOCKEYS' TRAINING SERIES FINAL H'CAP HURDLE (12 hdls) 2m 4f 114y
4:00 (4:00) (Class 3) (0-135,130) 4-Y-O+ **£9,747** (£2,862; £1,431; £715)

Form RPR
210- **1** **Ossie's Dancer**[15] 5539 6-11-5 **126**.................. ThomasCheesman(3) 126+
(Martin Smith) *hld up in tch: mstke 2nd: clsd and gng wl after 3 out: led next: hit last: rdn out* **8/1**

32P- **2** *¾* **The Game Is A Foot (IRE)**[74] 4439 8-9-4 **104** oh2.................. JasonNuttall(10) 102
(Gary Moore) *hld up in rr: clsd after 3 out: rdn and cl 4th last: r.o to snatch 2nd last stride* **12/1**

31-4 **3** *shd* **Mercers Court (IRE)**[2] 185 7-11-4 **125**.................. AlanJohns(3) 124
(Neil King) *hld up in tch: hdwy after 5th: pressed ldr 9th: led sn after next: hdd and mstke 2 out: styd on same pce flat: lost 2nd last stride* **3/1**[3]

345- **4** *3¾* **Jayo Time (IRE)**[15] 5539 6-10-9 **113**.................. JackSherwood 109
(Dr Richard Newland) *wl in tch in midfield: rdn to chse ldrs bef 2 out: cl 3rd last: wknd flat* **11/4**[2]

341- **5** *11* **Blue Bear (IRE)**[62] 4667 6-11-4 **127**.................. ConorSmith(5) 112
(Diana Grissell) *chsd ldrs: wnt 2nd 3rd tl led after 8th: rdn and hdd sn after 3 out: wknd next* **10/1**

033- **6** *6* **Morestead Screamer**[23] 5367 6-10-2 **109**.................. PaulO'Brien(3) 88
(Chris Gordon) *chsd ldr tl mstke 3rd: styd chsng ldrs tl rdn and btn after 3 out: wknd 2 out* **16/1**

413- **7** *38* **Masterful Act (USA)**[53] 4849 8-10-13 **120**.................(t) BridgetAndrews(3) 85
(Dan Skelton) *led tl after 8th: mstke next and lost pl bef 3 out: lost tch bef 2 out: t.o* **5/2**[1]

4m 50.3s (-26.70) **Going Correction** -1.05s/f (Hard) 7 Ran SP% **114.0**
Speed ratings (Par 107): **108,107,107,106,102 99,85**
CSF £87.56 CT £352.29 TOTE £9.40: £3.20, £5.50; EX 116.80 Trifecta £646.60.
Owner Mrs V Garner **Bred** Verity Garner **Trained** Newmarket, Suffolk

FOCUS
Not a bad handicap and it was run at a sound tempo.

226 ANISE CATERING H'CAP CHASE (14 fncs) 2m 3f 164y
4:30 (4:33) (Class 4) (0-115,112) 5-Y-O+ **£5,523** (£1,621; £810; £405)

Form RPR
354- **1** **Venetian Lad**[30] 5259 10-11-5 **105**.................. MarcGoldstein 111
(Lydia Richards) *chsd ldrs: rdn and ev ch after 3 out: led narrowly next: j.lft and bmpd last: sn forged ahd: rdr lost iron flat but styd on wl* **6/1**

332- **2** *2¼* **Vikekhal (FR)**[34] 5209 6-11-12 **112**.................. NickScholfield 116
(Gary Moore) *hld up in rr: bustled along after 9th: clsd after next: pressed ldng pair sn after 3 out: finding little and swtchd rt bef last: drvn to go 2nd flat: no imp* **5/4**[1]

324/ **3** *1¾* **Speedy Bruere (FR)**[390] 5336 9-11-12 **112**.................. TomCannon 114
(David Bridgwater) *mde most: rdn and hrd pressed after 3 out: hdd next: stl ev ch whn j.rt and bmpd last: wknd and lost 2nd flat* **7/2**[2]

2FP- **4** *14* **Lily Little Legs (IRE)**[39] 5094 6-10-8 **99**.................. RobMcCarth(5) 89
(Ian Williams) *hld up in tch in last pair: clsd after 10th: cl 5th and short of room 3 out: bmpd sn after: n.d after* **9/2**[3]

45-U **5** *54* **Miller Of Glanmire (IRE)**[9] 64 7-10-9 **105**.......(tp) TommyDowling(10) 46
(Charlie Mann) *w ldr: reminder after 4th: lost pl 3 out: sn btn and lost tch bef 2 out: t.o* **8/1**

4m 57.8s (-9.50) **Going Correction** -1.05s/f (Hard) 5 Ran SP% **110.2**
Speed ratings: **105,104,103,97,76**
CSF £14.69 TOTE £8.20: £2.70, £1.30; EX 15.20 Trifecta £24.70.
Owner The Venetian Lad Partnership **Bred** Mrs Lydia Richards **Trained** Funtington, W Sussex

FOCUS
A modest handicap.

227 ANISE CATERING STANDARD OPEN NATIONAL HUNT FLAT RACE 2m 1f 164y
5:00 (5:02) (Class 6) 4-6-Y-0 £1,624 (£477; £238; £119)

Form RPR
53- 1 **Welluptoscratch (FR)**[23] 5373 4-10-12 0 TomCannon 97
(David Arbuthnot) *trckd ldrs: effrt on inner over 1f out: rdn to ld 1f out: r.o wl: rdn out* **3/1**[2]
4- 2 ¾ **Prince Oscar (IRE)**[39] 5097 6-10-11 0 RobMcCarth(5) 100
(Ian Williams) *chsd ldr: rdn and ev ch 2f out: stl ev ch and wnt lft ent fnl f: kpt on but a hld after* **8/1**
1 3 3¾ **Ilewin Geez**[9] 67 5-11-9 0 NickScholfield 104
(Gary Moore) *led: rdn over 1f out: hdd 1f out and sn bmpd: wknd fnl 100yds* **10/3**[3]
3- 4 2 **Pilgrims Bay (IRE)**[18] 5468 5-11-2 0 ConorO'Farrell 97+
(David Pipe) *taken down early: hld up in tch in rr: clsd to trck ldng trio over 1f out: nt clr run ent fnl f: sn flashed tail: wandered rt and lft and faltered 1f out: one pce after* **15/8**[1]
- 5 1¼ **The Golden Hour (IRE)**[77] 5-10-9 0 MarkGrant 87
(Zoe Davison) *hld up in tch in last pair: hdwy over 2f out: outpcd u.p over 1f out: keeping on same pce whn hmpd and swtchd lft ins fnl f* **20/1**
6 2¼ **Lunar Flow** 4-10-12 0 BrendanPowell 88
(Jamie Snowden) *chsd ldrs: drvn and unable qck 2f out: outpcd and btn over 1f out: kpt on same pce after* **10/1**
0- 7 7 **Betsy Boo Boo**[60] 4715 6-10-2 0 FreddieMitchell(7) 79
(Michael Roberts) *in tch in midfield: rdn over 3f out: wknd 2f out* **50/1**
6- 8 30 **Silver Ticket (IRE)**[39] 5105 4-10-12 0 AidanColeman 55
(Laura Mongan) *in tch in midfield: rdn and dropped to rr 3f out: sn lost tch: t.o* **16/1**

4m 10.5s (-14.80) **Going Correction** -1.05s/f (Hard)
WFA 4 from 5yo+ 4lb 8 Ran SP% **115.7**
Speed ratings: **90,89,88,87,86 85,82,69**
CSF £27.48 TOTE £5.00: £1.30, £2.30, £1.40; EX 30.20 Trifecta £95.00.
Owner A T A Wates & Mrs S Wates **Bred** Haras D'Etreham **Trained** Beare Green, Surrey
FOCUS
An ordinary bumper.
T/Jkpt: Not won. T/Plt: £1351.70 to a £1 stake. Pool: £84,991.22 - 45.90 winning units. T/Qpdt: £148.90 to a £1 stake. Pool: £7443.96 - 36.98 winning units. **Steve Payne**

228 - 230a (Foreign Racing) - See Raceform Interactive

KILLARNEY (L-H)
Sunday, May 10

OFFICIAL GOING: Good to yielding (yielding in places) changing to yielding to soft after race 1 (2.20) changing to soft after race 4 (3.50)

231a LADBROKES IRELAND H'CAP HURDLE (GRADE B) (10 hdls) 2m 1f
3:50 (3:50) 4-Y-0+ £25,193 (£7,364; £3,488; £1,162)

RPR
1 **Waxies Dargle**[12] 7 6-10-8 130 PaulTownend 140+
(Noel Meade, Ire) *trckd ldrs early: sn mid-div: tk clsr order bef 3 out: swtchd lft to outer to dispute appr 2 out: sn led: styd on wl to draw away cl home* **9/2**[1]
2 2½ **Mrs Mac Veale (IRE)**[12] 7 10-10-0 125 BrianHayes(3) 132
(Gavin Dower, Ire) *trckd ldrs on inner tl prog to dispute appr 2 out: sn narrowly hdd: kpt on wl tl no ex w wnr clsng stages* **14/1**
3 ¾ **Pivot Bridge**[12] 7 7-9-8 119 DavidSplaine(3) 125
(Adrian McGuinness, Ire) *sn pressed ldrs in 3rd: led 2 out but sn hdd: no imp on principals run-in: kpt on same pce* **9/2**[1]
4 2¼ **Misty Lady (IRE)**[35] 5168 6-9-5 118 oh5 AndrewRing(5) 122
(John Laurence Cullen, Ire) *led tl jnd at 3rd: nt fluent 3 out and hdd appr next: no ex in 4th at last: kpt on same pce* **8/1**[3]
5 shd **Rock The World (IRE)**[112] 3760 7-11-1 137 (t) RobbiePower 141
(Mrs John Harrington, Ire) *sn trckd ldr in 2nd and on terms 3rd: hdd 2 out: no ex in 5th at last: kpt on same pce* **8/1**[3]
6 1¾ **Elishpour (IRE)**[133] 3352 5-10-3 125 (t) APHeskin 127
(A J Martin, Ire) *hld up towards inner: tk clsr order to chse ldrs 3 out: no imp appr last* **14/1**
7 ½ **Solita (IRE)**[19] 5457 6-9-8 121 ow1 (t) LPDempsey(5) 123
(Paul Nolan, Ire) *hld up towards rr: kpt on one pce fr 2 out: nvr on terms* **10/1**
8 3¾ **Lilshane (IRE)**[35] 5174 7-9-10 118 oh12 (tp) DJCasey 116
(Thomas P O'Connor, Ire) *chsd ldrs in 4th tl rdn and nt qckn 3 out: sn one pce* **16/1**
9 3¼ **Western Boy (IRE)**[12] 7 6-10-13 135 AlanCrowe 130
(P A Fahy, Ire) *towards rr whn mstke 1st: no imp whn hmpd 3 out: kpt on one pce* **20/1**
10 4¼ **Thomas Edison (IRE)**[33] 5231 8-11-10 146 (t) NiallPMadden 137
(A J Martin, Ire) *racd in rr: nt fluent 4th: mod prog bef 3 out: sn no imp* **14/1**
11 7 **Cest Notre Gris (IRE)**[19] 5456 5-9-3 118 oh9 ShaneCrimin(7) 102
(Miss Elizabeth Doyle, Ire) *chsd ldrs tl nt qckn 3 out: sn no ex* **25/1**
12 12 **Courtncatcher (IRE)**[8] 96 8-10-6 131 JodyMcGarvey(3) 103
(Patrick J Duffy, Ire) *chsd ldrs early: mid-div 1/2-way: no threat fr 3 out* **33/1**
13 1¾ **Massini's Trap (IRE)**[22] 4950 6-10-8 130 RWalsh 100
(J A Nash, Ire) *hld up towards rr: no threat whn hmpd 3 out* **12/1**
F **Henry Higgins (IRE)**[12] 7 5-10-10 132 MarkWalsh
(Charles O'Brien, Ire) *racd in mid-div whn mstke 3rd: rdn and no imp towards rr whn fell 3 out* **7/1**[2]

4m 33.7s (27.30) 14 Ran SP% **125.3**
CSF £68.14 CT £310.58 TOTE £8.10: £3.20, £5.20, £2.60; DF 60.50 Trifecta £318.80.
Owner John P McManus **Bred** Adrian Smith **Trained** Castletown, Co Meath
FOCUS
A competitive contest, as expected, with the rain changing matters in favour of some, no more so than for the winner. According to his trainer at least.

232 - 235a (Foreign Racing) - See Raceform Interactive

LES LANDES
Sunday, May 10

OFFICIAL GOING: Good to firm

236a GEORGE & LEONORA SULLIVAN PERPETUAL HURDLE 2m
2:30 (2:35) 4-Y-0+ £1,460 (£525; £315)

RPR
1 **Red Four**[34] 5307 5-11-10 (p) MattieBatchelor 117
(George Baker) **4/7**[1]
2 7 **Pomander (IRE)**[34] 1474 12-9-10 JoshBaudains 82
(J Moon, Jersey) **5/1**[3]
3 shd **Dalmo**[43] 6-10-12 (b) MrRHodson 98
(K Kukk, Jersey) **6/4**[2]

Owner Lady Cobham **Bred** Lady Cobham **Trained** Manton, Wilts
■ Reach Out was withdrawn. Price at time of withdrawal 13/2. Rule 4 applies to all bets - deduction 10p in the pound.

[40] TOWCESTER (R-H)
Monday, May 11

OFFICIAL GOING: Good (good to firm in places; 8.9)
Wind: breezy Weather: bright and sunny; 21 degrees

237 HAYGAIN HAY STEAMERS CLEAN HEALTHY FORAGE H'CAP HURDLE (8 hdls) 1m 7f 181y
6:00 (6:00) (Class 4) (0-110,116) 4-Y-0+ £3,249 (£954; £477; £238)

Form RPR
463- 1 **Pied Du Roi (IRE)**[17] 5508 5-11-9 106 DarylJacob 111+
(Charlie Longsdon) *chsd ldrs: effrt in 2nd 3 out: rdn to ld last: grad edgd clr* **8/1**
605- 2 2 **Simple Assignment (IRE)**[58] 4753 6-11-7 104 GavinSheehan 106
(Warren Greatrex) *j.lft: hit 2nd: led at decent pce tl last where nt fluent and hdd: one pce after* **9/2**[2]
036- 3 2¾ **Acapulco Bay**[35] 5183 11-10-8 94 (p) RobertWilliams(3) 94
(Dai Burchell) *hld up in midfield: effrt bef 2 out: sn no imp: tk 3rd bef last* **25/1**
6-31 4 ¾ **Hartside (GER)**[4] 157 6-11-12 116 7ex MrRWinks(7) 115
(Peter Winks) *last early: rdn and effrt bef 2 out: no imp but kpt plugging on* **15/2**
226- 5 5 **Dainty Diva (IRE)**[40] 5101 7-11-4 101 NickScholfield 97
(Jeremy Scott) *midfield: rdn and effrt 3 out: btn next* **8/1**
4P-3 6 8 **The Kvilleken**[4] 172 7-10-7 90 (be) RichardJohnson 81
(Martin Keighley) *mstke 2nd: last tl bef 3 out: wnt 2nd bef next: drvn and sn v reluctant and dropped himself rt out* **11/4**[1]
3P-4 7 6 **Bunclody**[11] 43 10-10-12 102 (p) MrZBaker(7) 86
(Barry Brennan) *chsd ldrs: rdn 3 out: btn bef 2 out* **16/1**
445- P **Flashman**[49] 4961 6-11-9 106 (p) TomCannon
(Gary Moore) *pressed ldr tl 3 out: lost pl qckly: p.u bef 2 out* **11/2**[3]
024- P **Ride On Time (IRE)**[64] 4650 5-11-6 103 (p) DavidBass
(Ben Pauling) *rdn 3rd: fnd nil: chsd ldrs tl blnd 4th: t.o and p.u 2 out* **8/1**

3m 51.6s (-16.30) **Going Correction** -0.875s/f (Firm) 9 Ran SP% **115.1**
Speed ratings (Par 105): **105,104,102,102,99 95,92, ,**
CSF £44.30 CT £863.64 TOTE £7.00: £3.20, £2.10, £6.50; EX 45.70 Trifecta £1946.40 Part won..
Owner The Pantechnicons II **Bred** Long Acre Syndicate **Trained** Over Norton, Oxon
FOCUS
Shared bends and Hurdle course on middle line. This was run at a decent gallop on ever-quickening ground. The third and fourth have been rated to their marks.

238 HAYGAIN HAY STEAMERS CLEAN HEALTHY FORAGE MARES' MAIDEN HURDLE (11 hdls) 2m 4f 217y
6:30 (6:30) (Class 5) 4-Y-0+ £2,599 (£763; £381; £190)

Form RPR
433- 1 **What A Jewel (IRE)**[18] 5496 5-11-0 115 NicodeBoinville 115+
(Nicky Henderson) *mde all: rdn bef 2 out: in command last* **11/8**[1]
052- 2 6 **Susie Sheep**[41] 5090 5-11-0 0 (tp) TomScudamore 110
(David Pipe) *3rd tl wnt 2nd 3 out: rdn bef next: no imp after* **3/1**[2]
002- 3 17 **Hope's Wishes**[19] 5477 5-11-0 102 AidanColeman 96
(Emma Lavelle) *chsd ldrs: 7 l 3rd 3 out: rdn and struggling after* **8/1**
6-3 4 6 **Rosie Revenue**[11] 28 5-11-0 0 (t) RichardJohnson 90
(Philip Hobbs) *rdn bef 8th: mod 4th whn j.lft next* **12/1**
10- 5 2¼ **Trigger Point**[155] 2969 5-11-0 0 [1] TomO'Brien 87
(Hughie Morrison) *small: towards rr: last and struggling bef 3 out: b.b.v* **9/2**[3]
43-P 6 12 **Dream N (IRE)**[9] 90 7-11-0 96 MarkGrant 76
(Sean Curran) *mstkes: pressed wnr tl 8th: 20 l 4th and tiring next: t.o* **25/1**
/56- 7 2¾ **When In Roam (IRE)**[60] 4729 6-11-0 98 DaveCrosse 73
(John O'Shea) *bhd: rdn bef 7th: t.o 3 out* **33/1**
05-P 8 15 **Cool Fusion**[10] 61 6-10-9 0 DannyBurton(5) 60
(Anthony Day) *last mostly: lost tch bef 6th: t.o 3 out* **150/1**
P **Cearys (IRE)** 7-11-0 0 AndrewTinkler
(Martin Keighley) *j. slowly 2nd: cl up tl 6th: t.o and p.u 2 out* **40/1**

5m 17.7s (-9.50) **Going Correction** -0.875s/f (Firm) 9 Ran SP% **114.0**
Speed ratings (Par 103): **83,80,74,71,71 66,65,59,**
CSF £5.48 TOTE £2.00: £1.10, £1.90, £3.50; EX 7.00 Trifecta £28.40.
Owner Seven Barrows Limited **Bred** M C McDaniel-Stone **Trained** Upper Lambourn, Berks
FOCUS
Only a handful could be seriously considered. Two pulled well clear. The first four have all been rated pretty much to their marks in a straightforward mares' maiden.

239 GG.COM H'CAP CHASE (17 fncs) 3m 102y
7:00 (7:00) (Class 4) (0-115,115) 5-Y-0+ £4,548 (£1,335; £667; £333)

Form RPR
63-2 1 **By The Boardwalk (IRE)**[4] 173 7-10-5 97 (t) TomBellamy(3) 107+
(Kim Bailey) *pressed ldng pair gng wl: led sn after 3 out and easily asserted bef next* **4/1**[2]
122- 2 12 **Cosway Spirit (IRE)**[22] 5407 8-10-11 100 (p) DavidBass 101
(Ben Pauling) *led tl 2nd: nt fluent 4th: drvn fr 8th and mostly cl 2nd after tl level 14th: led next: hdd u.p after 3 out: styd on same pce* **3/1**[1]

The Form Book Jumps 2015-16, Raceform Ltd, Newbury, RG14 5SJ

50F- **3** *1 1/4* **On Trend (IRE)**[41] 5081 9-11-11 **114**..............................(bt) TomCannon 111
(Nick Gifford) *chsd ldrs tl 10th: j. slowly next: sn outpcd: 20 lenths fr ldrs and no ch 14th: wnt modd 3rd u.p cl home* **7/1**
623- **4** *3/4* **Jolly Boys Outing (IRE)**[49] 4968 12-9-11 **89** oh4............ BenPoste(3) 87
(Rosemary Gasson) *j. awkwardly 1st and sn v detached: impr to midfield at 11th: 10 fr ldng trio 14th: wnt 3rd but no ch fr 3 out tl fnl 75yds* **14/1**
621- **5** *58* **Kyles Faith (IRE)**[20] 5443 7-11-5 **108**......................(p) RichardJohnson 52
(Martin Keighley) *led 2nd: nt fluent 4th: jnd 14th: hdd next: rapidly lost tch 3 out: bdly t.o* **15/2**
443- **P** **High Kite (IRE)**[19] 5464 9-11-9 **112**.........................(b) GavinSheehan
(Warren Greatrex) *rdn 5th: in rr and nvr gng wl: mstke 8th: t.o and p.u 2 out* **6/1**
P52- **P** **Ifyousayso (IRE)**[18] 5497 8-11-12 **115**........................ TomScudamore
(David Bridgwater) *bhd: rdn and nt travelling 7th: t.o and p.u 13th* **5/1**[3]
64-0 **P** **Finding Your Feet (IRE)**[3] 183 7-11-2 **105**............(b[1]) RichieMcLernon
(Jonjo O'Neill) *blnd 2nd: midfield: rdn 11th: nt keen: t.o and p.u 3 out* **20/1**

6m 6.7s (-30.20) **Going Correction** -0.95s/f (Hard) **8** Ran SP% **111.6**
Speed ratings: **110,106,105,105,86 , ,**
CSF £16.21 CT £77.64 TOTE £3.80: £1.10, £1.80, £3.50; EX 18.50 Trifecta £149.90.
Owner J Perriss **Bred** Colman O'Flynn **Trained** Andoversford, Gloucs

FOCUS
This was run at a searching gallop and placed real emphasis on stamina. The winner has been rated as improving towards his hurdle mark, with the fourth to his mark.

240 VISIT THE FORUM ON GG.COM AMATEUR RIDERS' H'CAP HURDLE (10 hdls) 2m 3f 34y
7:30 (7:30) (Class 5) (0-100,100) 4-Y-O+ **£2,183** (£677; £338; £169)

Form RPR
412- **1** **Ruaraidh Hugh (IRE)**[24] 5379 6-10-3 **84**.........(b) MrTommieMO'Brien(7) 103+
(Chris Bealby) *settled trcking ldrs and gng wl: smooth prog on inner to ld sn after 3 out: wl in command after: 12 l ahd last* **10/3**[1]
343- **2** *13* **Sunshine Buddy**[30] 5281 8-10-7 **88**.....................(p) MrSeanHoulihan(7) 92+
(Chris Down) *midfield: styd on after 3 out: wnt 2nd at last: one pce and nvr nr wnr* **11/2**[3]
500- **3** *7* **Prince Pippin (IRE)**[32] 5243 9-11-0 **93**.......................(t) MsLucyJones(5) 91
(Lucy Jones) *pressed ldr: ev ch 3 out: rdn and sn outpcd by wnr: lost 2nd at last* **14/1**
434- **4** *3 3/4* **Shot In The Dark (IRE)**[32] 5243 6-10-8 **89**..............(p) MrTMcKeown(7) 84
(Jonathan Geake) *cl up: rdn 3 out: fading in 3rd on home turn* **12/1**
PPU- **5** *2 1/4* **Minority Interest**[17] 5527 6-10-9 **90**..........................(p) MrJPearce(7) 82
(Daniel O'Brien) *midfield: pushed along fr 5th: no ch fr 3 out: edgd lft flat* **33/1**
P5-6 **6** *5* **Nicky Nutjob (GER)**[10] 55 9-9-11 **74** oh6....................(p) MrMLegg(3) 62
(John O'Shea) *last early: struggling whn mstke 3 out* **20/1**
024- **7** *6* **Lady Of Longstone (IRE)**[22] 5414 5-10-11 **92**.........(bt) DavidNoonan(7) 74
(David Pipe) *cl up tl 3 out: rdn and sn dropped out bef next* **4/1**[2]
254- **8** *3/4* **Nouailhas**[17] 5527 9-10-0 **79**...............................(v) MissBHampson(5) 61
(Daniel O'Brien) *midfield: struggling after 3 out* **9/1**
6F1- **9** *7* **Wicklewood**[49] 4966 9-11-2 **97**.................................(t) MrTGillard(7) 72
(Mark Gillard) *midfield: pushed along bef 3 out: sn btn: t.o* **8/1**
06/ **10** *36* **Indubitably**[35] 9-10-0 **81**...(v[1]) HarryTeal(7) 24
(Roger Teal) *drvn along in last: t.o fr 1/2-way: eventually completed* **25/1**
000- **11** *4* **Tikkapick (IRE)**[51] 4900 5-11-7 **100**........................ MrSamPainting(5) 39
(Colin Tizzard) *midfield tl rdn 5th: no rspnse: eventually completed* **9/1**
P00- **12** *8* **Betty Borgia**[18] 5500 9-10-0 **81**.............................. MrGregoryWalters(7) 13
(Nicholas Pomfret) *in rr and struggling and racing awkwardly bef 6th: eventually completed* **100/1**
PP-0 **13** *53* **Marina Bay**[11] 40 10-9-7 **74** oh15.............................. MrMEnnis(7)
(Christopher Kellett) *chsd ldrs tl drvn bef 5th: t.o 7th: eventually completed* **125/1**
346- **P** **Monroe Park (IRE)**[17] 5527 10-10-7 **84**..................(p) MissAEStirling(3)
(Alan Blackmore) *led and abt 6 l clr: hdd sn after 3 out and slowed v bdly: t.o and p.u next* **33/1**

4m 46.9s (-22.70) **Going Correction** -0.875s/f (Firm) **14** Ran SP% **120.2**
Speed ratings (Par 103): **110,104,102,100,99 97,95,94,92,77 76,72,51,**
CSF £20.84 CT £231.95 TOTE £5.10: £2.50, £2.90, £5.10; EX 22.30 Trifecta £249.20.
Owner Paul L Read **Bred** Peter McCarthy **Trained** Barrowby, Lincs

FOCUS
This developed into a one-horse race. The second has been rated to the best of her recent form.

241 SOLOMONS FAMILY 25TH WEDDING ANNIVERSARY NOVICES' H'CAP CHASE (11 fncs) 2m 70y
8:00 (8:00) (Class 4) (0-120,120) 5-Y-O+ **£3,898** (£1,144; £572; £286)

Form RPR
P43- **1** **Gun Shy (IRE)**[41] 5080 7-11-8 **120**.............................. LeightonAspell 138+
(Gary Moore) *j. soundly: led tl bef 3rd and fr 4th: wnt 3 l clr 3 out: in full command bef next: eased flat* **4/1**[3]
255- **2** *7* **Rockmount River (IRE)**[22] 5405 6-10-10 **108**.............. TomScudamore 113
(David Bridgwater) *chsd ldrs: wnt 2nd sn after 3 out: rdn and unable to keep up w wnr wl bef next: one pce* **11/2**
513- **3** *4 1/2* **Town Mouse**[20] 5449 5-11-7 **119**.............................. TrevorWhelan 120
(Neil King) *taken down early: pushed along 4th: lost tl 7th: detached fr ldng quartet next: n.d after but drvn into mod 3rd after last* **6/1**
430- **4** *2 3/4* **Breaking The Bank**[206] 1936 6-11-8 **120**...................... DarylJacob 120
(Ben Case) *mstke 3rd: chsd ldrs: rdn 3 out: no rspnse: wnt wl hld 3rd 2 out tl after last* **7/2**[2]
252- **5** *29* **Yabadabadoo**[32] 5244 7-11-3 **115**............................ AidanColeman 87
(Emma Lavelle) *led bef 3rd tl next: pressed wnr tl rdn after 3 out: fdd bdly bef next: fin tired and t.o* **9/4**[1]
540- **P** **Sadma**[40] 5101 6-10-3 **101** oh6................................. GerardTumelty
(Nick Lampard) *blnd 1st: mstkes: t.k.h: cl up tl dropped bk last and mstke 7th: t.o and p.u 3 out* **14/1**

4m 0.1s (-16.00) **Going Correction** -0.95s/f (Hard) **6** Ran SP% **109.3**
Speed ratings: **99,95,93,92,78**
CSF £23.76 TOTE £5.90: £3.00, £2.40; EX 25.40 Trifecta £126.50.
Owner Paul Chapman **Bred** Pat Fenlon **Trained** Lower Beeding, W Sussex

FOCUS
This took little winning. The second and third have been rated to their marks.

242 DON'T MISS OUT WITH GG.COM ALERTS MAIDEN OPEN NATIONAL HUNT FLAT RACE 1m 7f 181y
8:30 (8:30) (Class 6) 4-6-Y-O **£1,949** (£572; £286; £143)

Form RPR
1 **Divine Spear (IRE)** 4-10-12 0................................... NicodeBoinville 107+
(Nicky Henderson) *trckd ldrs: led wl over 2f out: sn rdn clr: readily* **3/1**[2]
2- **2** *9* **Boy In A Bentley (IRE)**[35] 5207 5-11-2 0............................ DavidBass 101
(Kim Bailey) *chsd ldrs: rdn and sltly outpcd 3f out: wnt 2nd 1f out: kpt on but no match for wnr* **7/2**[3]
3- **3** *8* **Anti Cool (IRE)**[32] 5248 6-11-2 0................................ CharliePoste 94
(Robin Dickin) *t.k.h: rdn and hdd wl over 2f out: lost 2nd 1f out and kpt on same pce* **16/1**
6- **4** *4* **Justatenner**[116] 3689 4-10-5 0.............................. MrSamPainting(7) 86
(Colin Tizzard) *midfield: rdn and outpcd 3f out: plugged into poor 4th over 1f out* **20/1**
04- **5** *4* **False Accusation (IRE)**[32] 5248 6-11-2 0.............. SamTwiston-Davies 86
(Nigel Twiston-Davies) *plld hrd: prom: rdn 3f out: wknd over 2f out: t.o* **14/1**
6 *1 1/4* **Rhianna** 4-10-2 0.. TomBellamy(3) 74
(Kim Bailey) *towards rr: rdn and btn 3f out: t.o* **14/1**
4- **7** *1 1/4* **Triggitas**[77] 4411 5-11-2 0.. LeightonAspell 84
(Oliver Sherwood) *settled towards rr: effrt over 3f out: rdn and fdd over 2f out: t.o* **20/1**
8 *25* **The Bank Manager** 4-10-12 0.................................. TomScudamore 58
(David Pipe) *settled in midfield: shortlived effrt over 3f out: sn btn and labouring: bdly t.o* **2/1**[1]
20- **9** *14* **Norman The Red**[58] 4755 5-11-2 0.................................. TomO'Brien 49
(Jamie Poulton) *a bhd: t.o over 3f out: eventually completed* **25/1**
10 *6* **Alfloreda** 6-11-2 0... LiamTreadwell 44
(Nick Gifford) *plld hrd: prom 7f: t.o over 3f out: eventually completed* **50/1**
05- **U** **Viva Rafa (IRE)**[49] 4969 5-11-2 0................................ RichardJohnson
(Richard Phillips) *plld hrd towards rr: clipped heels and uns rdr over 5f out* **20/1**

3m 48.1s (-14.20) **Going Correction** -0.875s/f (Firm)
WFA 4 from 5yo+ 4lb **11** Ran SP% **119.9**
Speed ratings: **100,95,91,89,87 86,86,73,66,63**
CSF £13.05 TOTE £3.60: £1.30, £1.80, £4.30; EX 16.90 Trifecta £126.90.
Owner Middleham Park Racing LXII **Bred** Miss Elizabeth Kennedy **Trained** Upper Lambourn, Berks

FOCUS
They came home at long intervals in this finale. It's been rated around the balance of the second, third and fourth.
T/Plt: £87.00 to a £1 stake. Pool: £67,592.41 - 566.68 winning tickets T/Qpdt: £16.40 to a £1 stake. Pool: £7,177.87 - 322.56 winning tickets **Iain Mackenzie**

243 - 250a (Foreign Racing) - See Raceform Interactive

131 SEDGEFIELD (L-H)
Tuesday, May 12

OFFICIAL GOING: Good (8.0)
Wind: strong half behind Weather: Cloudy

251 PAXTONS FOR INDEPENDENT TWINE "KING OF STRING" MAIDEN HURDLE (10 hdls) 2m 5f 34y
2:15 (2:16) (Class 5) 4-Y-O+ **£2,469** (£725; £362; £181)

Form RPR
122- **1** **Black Jack Rover (IRE)**[37] 5159 6-11-0 107................ WilsonRenwick 115+
(Donald McCain) *trckd ldng pair: led appr 3 out: hit 2 out: sn nudged clr: easily* **5/6**[1]
334- **2** *15* **Lawless Island (IRE)**[73] 4485 6-11-0 0........................ MichaelByrne 99+
(Tim Vaughan) *trckd ldng pair: briefly pressed ldr after 3 out: rdn and outpcd appr 2 out: sn no ch w wnr after 2 out* **2/1**[2]
0/ **3** *12* **Have One For Me (IRE)**[10] 8-10-7 0..................... ThomasDowson(7) 84
(Victor Thompson) *led narrowly: hdd appr 3 out: grad wknd: lft poor 3rd 2 out* **40/1**
06-0 **4** *12* **Watchmego**[10] 77 7-10-7 64.................................(t) MichaelMcAlister 64
(Maurice Barnes) *w ldr: rdn 3 out: sn wknd* **50/1**
300- **5** *9* **Willie Whistle**[22] 5419 6-10-9 79..........................(t) StephenMulqueen(5) 62
(Maurice Barnes) *hld up in tch: rdn 6th: sn struggling* **33/1**
040- **P** **Wildest Dreams (IRE)**[29] 5310 6-11-0 94........................ BrianHarding
(Jane Walton) *hld up in tch: reminders 6th: sn struggling: t.o whn p.u bef 2 out* **10/1**[3]
00-4 **F** **Lucy Milan (IRE)**[12] 33 6-10-4 0.............................. JohnKington(3) 84
(Andrew Crook) *racd keenly in rr: hdwy after 7th: wnt 3rd appr 2 out: rdn and 6 l down whn fell 2 out* **20/1**

5m 13.8s (-0.80) **Going Correction** -0.275s/f (Good)
WFA 4 from 6yo+ 19lb **7** Ran SP% **109.1**
Speed ratings (Par 103): **90,84,80,75,72 ,**
CSF £2.43 TOTE £1.80: £1.10, £1.50; EX 2.90 Trifecta £31.90.
Owner Deva Racing Black Jack Partnership **Bred** John F Gibbons **Trained** Cholmondeley, Cheshire

FOCUS
Common bends dolled out towards centre and Hurdles sited on outer. The going was good though Wilson Renwick who rode the winner said there were some good to soft places. This was an uncompetitive maiden hurdle in which they bet big prices bar the first two and the gallop was ordinary. Arguably a step up from the winner.

252 PAXTONS & CASE IH MONEY WELL SPENT H'CAP HURDLE (8 hdls) 2m 178y
2:45 (2:49) (Class 5) (0-100,100) 4-Y-O+ **£2,469** (£725; £362; £181)

Form RPR
P22- **1** **Scorpions Sting (IRE)**[41] 5091 6-11-7 **100**................... DaleIrving(5) 108+
(James Ewart) *chsd ldr: led narrowly after 3 out: rdn to assert appr 2 out: 4 l up last: idled run-in* **9/4**[2]
P5P- **2** *1 3/4* **Wymeswold**[36] 5206 8-10-6 **83**................................. BenPoste(3) 86+
(Michael Mullineaux) *hld up: pushed along and hdwy after 3 out: sn chsd ldrs: wnt 2nd appr last: kpt on* **10/1**
35-0 **3** *11* **Auto Mac**[12] 34 7-10-0 **77**.. AdamNicol(3) 71
(Mike Sowersby) *in tch: trckd ldr 5th: pushed along and outpcd 3 out: 5th whn hit 2 out: plugged on into modest 3rd last* **9/1**
624- **4** *2* **Amtired**[28] 4284 9-11-9 **100**................................ JeremiahMcGrath(3) 91
(Marjorie Fife) *in tch: rdn to chse ldrs appr 2 out: outpcd after 2 out: plugged on fr last* **15/2**[3]
30-3 **5** *1 1/2* **Bob's Legend (IRE)**[12] 34 9-11-7 **95**......................(t) JamesReveley 85
(Susan Corbett) *led: hdd after 3 out: rdn bef 2 out: lost 2nd appr last: wknd* **2/1**[1]
034- **6** *10* **Stanley Bridge**[151] 3050 8-11-2 **90**............................ LucyAlexander 71
(Barry Murtagh) *hld up: sme hdwy 3 out: rdn appr 2 out: sn wknd* **11/1**
045- **7** *42* **Viva Star**[37] 5158 4-11-1 **93**...................................(t) JakeGreenall 32
(Michael Easterby) *hld up: rdn after 3 out: sn wknd* **14/1**

4m 0.2s (-6.70) **Going Correction** -0.275s/f (Good)
WFA 4 from 6yo+ 18lb **7** Ran SP% **110.0**
Speed ratings (Par 103): **104,103,98,97,96 91,71**
CSF £21.90 CT £155.24 TOTE £3.20: £1.90, £4.10; EX 31.80 Trifecta £218.40.

Owner DoddCarruthersKessonMurrillsPalmer **Bred** Mrs M O'Driscoll **Trained** Langholm, Dumfries & G'way
FOCUS
Mainly exposed sorts in this handicap hudle which was run at a decent gallop. A hurdle pb from the runner-up.

253 PAXTONS FOR JCB'S NEW FASTRAC 4000 NOVICES' CHASE (16 fncs) 2m 3f 65y
3:15 (3:15) (Class 4) 5-Y-O+ £4,158 (£1,221; £610; £305)

Form RPR
204- 1 **Mason Hindmarsh**[20] 5475 8-10-12 0 JamesReveley 115+
(Karen McLintock) *in tch: blnd 3rd: led 13th: rdn 2 out: 4 l up in and in command whn lft clr last* 7/2[3]
110- 2 11 **Enchanted Garden**[32] 5249 7-10-12 0 BrianHughes 104
(Malcolm Jefferson) *hld up: in tch fr 7th: nt fluent 4 out: hdwy to chse ldr appr 2 out: hit 2 out: sn drvn and btn in 3rd: lft 2nd and sltly hmpd by faller last* 6/5[1]
133- 3 6 **Master Dee (IRE)**[29] 5308 6-10-12 119 WilsonRenwick 99
(Donald McCain) *hld up in tch: pushed along and bit slow 3 out: nt fluent 2 out: sn drvn and no imp: lft 3rd last* 15/8[2]
5P- 4 20 **Castle Goer (IRE)**[72] 4524 6-10-5 0 (vt) PeterBuchanan 72
(Benjamin Arthey, Ire) *chsd ldr: rdn after 4 out: wknd after 2 out* 80/1
60-4 F **King Of The Dark (IRE)**[7] 135 8-10-5 100 ThomasDowson(7) 106
(Victor Thompson) *led: hdd 4 out: outpcd and dropped to 3rd appr 2 out: regained 2nd between last 2: 4 l down and keeping on whn fell last* 33/1
(-3.00) **Going Correction** -0.275s/f (Good) 5 Ran SP% **106.6**
Speed ratings: **95,90,88,80,**
CSF £8.00 TOTE £5.10: £2.70, £1.10; EX 8.60 Trifecta £13.00.
Owner Brian Chicken **Bred** Newsells Park Stud **Trained** Ingoe, Northumberland
FOCUS
Hard form to weigh up with two of the three chasing newcomers appearing not to run to their hurdles form. The gallop was no more than ordinary. There's a case for rating the race a lot higher through the hurdle marks of the first three.

254 PAXTONS SUPPORTING CUSTOMERS WITH PEREGRINE FINANCE NOVICES' HURDLE (8 hdls) 2m 178y
3:45 (3:45) (Class 4) 4-Y-O+ £3,638 (£1,068; £534; £267)

Form RPR
111- 1 **Gingili**[28] 5327 5-11-5 0 WilsonRenwick 107+
(Donald McCain) *in tch: pushed along and nt fluent 3 out: sn rdn: drvn appr 2 out: nt fluent 2 out: led between last 2: kpt on* 4/7[1]
2 1½ **Never Up (GER)**[196] 4-10-8 0 HenryBrooke 92
(George Moore) *hld up in tch: hdwy to trck ldr gng wl after 3 out: rdn and edgd lft between last 2: kpt on: hung lft towards fin* 5/1[3]
/P-3 3 11 **Duhallowcountry (IRE)**[10] 77 9-10-5 83 (p) JamieHamilton(7) 85
(Victor Thompson) *led: rdn appr 2 out: hdd between last 2: wknd* 100/1
24-2 4 16 **Larmor (FR)**[12] 33 4-10-5 106 CraigNichol(3) 65
(Micky Hammond) *trckd ldr: rdn appr 2 out: sn wknd* 3/1[2]
66- 5 20 **Strictly Glitz (IRE)**[124] 3579 4-9-12 0 AdamNicol(3) 38
(Mike Sowersby) *hld up: rdn after 3 out: sn wknd* 40/1
4m 3.1s (-3.80) **Going Correction** -0.275s/f (Good)
WFA 4 from 5yo+ 18lb 5 Ran SP% **108.7**
Speed ratings (Par 105): **97,96,91,83,74**
CSF £3.97 TOTE £2.10: £1.30, £1.90; EX 4.70 Trifecta £39.60.
Owner Paul & Clare Rooney **Bred** Mickley Stud, McCain & Hutchinson **Trained** Cholmondeley, Cheshire
FOCUS
Not form to get too excited about with the 83-rated Duhallowcountry beaten just over twelve lengths in third. The winner has again been rated well below his bumper mark.

255 PAXTONS USE ROMERO INSURANCE BROKERS H'CAP CHASE (16 fncs) 2m 3f 65y
4:15 (4:15) (Class 4) (0-120,119) 5-Y-O+ £4,158 (£1,221; £610; £305)

Form RPR
51-1 1 **Sharp Rise (IRE)**[7] 132 8-11-10 117 JamesReveley 140+
(Pauline Robson) *mde all: c clr on bit fr bef 2 out* 5/6[1]
423- 2 12 **Roseville Cottage (IRE)**[137] 3261 8-10-5 98 (b) BrianHughes 100
(John Wade) *trckd ldr: rdn bef 3 out: wnt 2nd between last 2: one pce* 5/1[3]
21P- 3 10 **Safari Journey (USA)**[45] 5034 11-11-3 110 (p) JakeGreenall 103
(Lucinda Egerton) *trckd ldr: rdn 3 out: sn outpcd by wnr: lost 2nd between last 2: wknd* 10/1
PPF- 4 75 **Sharivarry (FR)**[25] 5374 9-9-7 93 oh7 JamesCorbett(7) 19
(Victor Thompson) *hld up in rr: lost tch fr 11th: t.o* 33/1
314- F **Degooch (IRE)**[24] 5401 6-11-12 119 (p) WilsonRenwick
(Donald McCain) *racd keenly: trckd ldr: fell 7th* 10/3[2]
4m 58.1s (-4.90) **Going Correction** -0.275s/f (Good) 5 Ran SP% **106.3**
Speed ratings: **98,93,89,59,**
CSF £5.08 TOTE £1.60: £1.10, £2.00; EX 4.70 Trifecta £25.10.
Owner I Couldn't Switch Club **Bred** Mrs M Brophy **Trained** Kirkharle, Northumberland
FOCUS
No more than an ordianry gallop to this handicap chase in which the second favourite was an early casualty. The winner has been rated in line with his figure from the autumn when returning from a similar break.

256 PAXTONS FOR LELY, HORSCH AND MARSHALL H'CAP CHASE (13 fncs) 2m 77y
4:45 (4:45) (Class 5) (0-100,96) 5-Y-O+ £2,859 (£839; £419; £209)

Form RPR
40-5 1 **Odds On Dan (IRE)**[10] 78 9-9-13 76 (tp) DeanPratt(7) 86
(Lucinda Egerton) *hld up: slow 8th: rdn after 4 out: chsd ldrs bef 2 out: wnt 2nd last: styd on: led post* 10/3[1]
130- 2 nk **Carters Rest**[111] 3801 12-10-10 87 MissJWalton(7) 96
(George Bewley) *led: hdd 6th: remained prom: led again appr last: drvn and one pce run-in: hdd post* 8/1
3P6- 3 3 **Pindar (GER)**[22] 5421 11-10-6 76 (p) DougieCostello 83
(Joanne Foster) *in tch on outer: rdn after 8th: outpcd after 3 out: rallied between last 2: styd on* 5/1[3]
25F- 4 3 **Some Lad (IRE)**[29] 5309 10-11-5 96 JamieHamilton(7) 101
(Alison Hamilton) *in tch: hit 1st: chal 4 out: rdn to ld narrowly between last 2: hdd appr last: disputing 2nd whn hit last: wknd* 6/1
1U-U 5 3 **Gin Cobbler**[12] 36 9-11-0 91 JamesCorbett(7) 92
(Victor Thompson) *trckd ldr: led 6th: strly pressed fr 4 out: rdn after 3 out: hdd between last 2: wknd last* 4/1[2]
P-64 6 1¼ **Amir Pasha (UAE)**[7] 137 10-9-13 79 (b) FinianO'Toole(10) 78
(Micky Hammond) *hld up: hdwy to trck ldrs gng wl after 3 out: rdn after 2 out: sn wknd* 6/1
352- P **George Nympton (IRE)**[43] 5067 9-11-8 92 (tp) MarkGrant
(Zoe Davison) *in tch: slow 7th and lost pl: hit 9th: sn bhd: p.u bef 3 out* 17/2
4m 8.8s (-5.20) **Going Correction** -0.275s/f (Good) 7 Ran SP% **110.0**
Speed ratings: **101,100,99,98,96 96,**
CSF £26.44 TOTE £3.20: £1.90, £3.10; EX 30.50 Trifecta £164.90.
Owner Miss L Egerton **Bred** Martin C Fleming **Trained** Malton, North Yorks
FOCUS
This looked an open event with good recent form thin on the ground. It was run at an ordinary gallop and just over ten lengths covering the six finishers. The winner has been rated to his mark.

257 FURLONGER LIFE PAXTONS KVERNELAND GENUINE PARTS MAIDEN NATIONAL HUNT FLAT RACE (COND/AMATEURS) 2m 178y
5:15 (5:15) (Class 6) 4-6-Y-O £1,559 (£457; £228; £114)

Form RPR
054- 1 **Allycat**[22] 5425 5-10-13 0 DiarmuidO'Regan(5) 100
(Chris Grant) *prom: led over 4f out: sn strly pressed: drvn over 3f out: hdd appr fnl f: lft in narrow ld 50yds out* 4/1[2]
2 ½ **Burtredgipandgump (IRE)**[16] 6-10-11 0 MrJTeal(7) 100
(Malcolm Jefferson) *trckd ldrs: rdn and upsides fr wl over 3f out: led appr fnl f: hdd ins fnl f: one pce: lft cl 2nd 50yds out* 4/1[2]
3 14 **Pikarnia** 5-10-13 0 StephenMulqueen(5) 86
(John Wade) *trckd ldrs: rdn and outpcd over 3f out: plugged on fr over 1f out: lft modest 3rd 50yds out* 6/1[3]
4 63 **Lough Derg Cruise (IRE)**[51] 5-10-4 0 MichaelHeard(7) 16
(David Pipe) *led: hdd over 4f out: stopped qckly and sn bhd* 6/4[1]
5 15 **Molivias Lad** 4-10-9 0 MrJohnDawson(5) 4
(David Thompson) *hld up: wknd over 4f out: t.o* 25/1
0- 6 dist **Dream Place**[18] 5520 4-10-0 0 (t) LorcanMurtagh(7)
(Barry Murtagh) *hld up: bhd fr 1/2-way: t.o* 80/1
P- P **Correlate**[213] 1855 5-10-13 0 ColmMcCormack(5)
(John Wade) *hld up: lft bhd fr 1/2-way: p.u over 3f out* 33/1
00- P **Littlemissylennon**[49] 4975 4-10-0 0 (p) JamesCorbett(7)
(Kenny Johnson) *in tch on outer: reminders and dropped to rr 9f out: sn t.o: p.u over 3f out* 100/1
U **Dubai Shen (IRE)** 4-10-11 0 CraigNichol(3) 98+
(Alistair Whillans) *in tch: reminders and outpcd 6f out: rallied 4f out: wnt 3rd over 2f out: sn clsd down ldng pair: led ins fnl f: 2 l up and in command whn jinked rt and uns rdr 50yds out* 12/1
3m 56.8s (-4.50) **Going Correction** -0.30s/f (Good)
WFA 4 from 5yo+ 4lb 9 Ran SP% **111.0**
Speed ratings: **98,97,91,61,54 , , ,**
CSF £18.92 TOTE £4.60: £1.50, £2.50, £2.00; EX 22.30 Trifecta £111.30.
Owner Mickley Stud & Derrick Mossop **Bred** Riverside Stables and Mickley Stud **Trained** Newton Bewley, Co Durham
FOCUS
Just a modest bumper and one with an unsatisfactory conclusion. A small step up from the winner.
T/Plt: £26.70 to a £1 stake. Pool: £48,554.36 - 1,324.57 winning tickets. T/Qpdt: £6.50 to a £1 stake. Pool: £3,500.21 - 395.54 winning tickets. **Andrew Sheret**

SOUTHWELL (L-H)
Tuesday, May 12

OFFICIAL GOING: Good (7.9)
Wind: fresh 1/2 behind Weather: fine but breezy and very cool

258 SOUTHWELL RACING AND GOLF PACKAGE £20 H'CAP CHASE (16 fncs) 2m 4f 62y
5:20 (5:20) (Class 5) (0-100,101) 5-Y-O+ £2,599 (£763; £381; £190)

Form RPR
PP-3 1 **Riddlestown (IRE)**[12] 44 8-11-12 95 (b) HarrySkelton 105+
(Caroline Fryer) *trckd ldrs: led appr 3 out: sn clr: eased nr fin* 13/2
45-3 2 5 **Lost In Newyork (IRE)**[11] 57 8-10-12 81 AdamWedge 83
(Nick Kent) *in rr: hdwy to chse ldrs 10th: 2nd appr 3 out: one pce whn j.rt last* 4/1[2]
54-5 3 2¾ **Dougalstar (FR)**[10] 88 6-10-0 69 oh5 PeterCarberry 70
(Jennie Candlish) *led: j.lft 3rd: hdd next: drvn 13th: sn hmpd: modest 3rd bef 2 out* 4/1[2]
P0-6 4 20 **Next Exit (IRE)**[7] 126 10-11-4 92 JoeCornwall(5) 74
(John Cornwall) *prom: wknd 13th: distant 4th clsng stages* 66/1
305- 5 1 **Finch Flyer (IRE)**[21] 5449 8-10-0 69 (p) LeeEdwards 50
(Aytach Sadik) *chsd ldrs: outpcd 9th: reminders next: sn bhd* 14/1
0P4- 6 1¼ **Liars Poker (IRE)**[64] 4668 8-11-9 92 LeightonAspell 77
(Oliver Sherwood) *hld up: jnd ldrs 9th: led after 13th: hdd and blnd next: poor 4th whn hit 2 out* 11/4[1]
0-41 7 16 **Accessallareas (IRE)**[5] 161 10-11-11 101 7ex (tp) MrJMahot(7) 76
(Sarah-Jayne Davies) *j. bdly rt: chsd ldrs: hmpd 3rd: led next: hdd sn after 13th: sn lost pl and bhd* 9/2[3]
4P-5 P **Blue Sea Of Ibrox (IRE)**[11] 57 7-9-7 69 oh4 (b) GLavery(7)
(Alan Brown) *nt fluent: reminders 1st: drvn to chse ldrs: 2nd whn hmpd 7th: lost pl next: sn bhd: t.o whn p.u after 10th* 20/1
5m 17.9s (0.90) **Going Correction** +0.10s/f (Yiel) 8 Ran SP% **111.1**
Speed ratings: **102,100,99,91,91 90,84,**
CSF £31.46 CT £112.71 TOTE £6.70: £1.20, £2.20, £5.40; EX 33.40 Trifecta £233.50.
Owner J Ward **Bred** Jeremiah O'Brien **Trained** Wymondham, Norfolk
■ Stewards' Enquiry : Mr J Mahot two-day ban: careless riding (May 26-27)
FOCUS
The track received 10mm of water the previous day and the official going was good. The opener was a modest handicap chase and they finished well strung out. The second and third have been rated as improving in line with their hurdle marks.

259 18 TO 30 GOLF MEMBERSHIP £210 NOVICES' LIMITED H'CAP CHASE (16 fncs) 2m 4f 62y
5:50 (5:50) (Class 3) (0-135,131) 5-Y-O £6,330 (£1,870; £935; £468; £234)

Form RPR
1/1- 1 **Gray Hession (IRE)**[24] 5401 8-11-4 127 RichieMcLernon 133+
(Jonjo O'Neill) *hld up wl in tch: chsd ldrs 9th: cl 2nd appr 3 out: hit 2 out: styd on wl run-in despite being crowded: led towards fin* 13/8[1]

1P4- **2** *nk* **Owen Na View (IRE)**[18] 5515 7-11-8 **131**....................[1] PaddyBrennan 135
(Fergal O'Brien) *trckd ldrs: led sn after 13th: hung rt run-in: hdd cl home* **5/1**[3]

143- **3** *9* **Verano (GER)**[25] 5369 6-10-10 **119**..............................(t) LeightonAspell 117
(Charlie Mann) *w ldr: led 6th: hdd sn after 13th: 3rd and wkng whn hit 2 out* **11/2**

/06- **4** *8* **Figaro**[59] 4758 7-10-6 **115**..............................(t) AidanColeman 105
(Tim Vaughan) *chsd ldrs: lost pl appr 3 out* **14/1**

P30- **5** *17* **Abigail Lynch (IRE)**[26] 5353 7-10-9 **125**..................(t) JamieBargary(7) 101
(Nigel Twiston-Davies) *mde most to 6th: pushed along 9th: lost pl 12th: sn bhd* **10/1**

1P2- **F** **Emral Silk**[46] 5013 7-11-2 **125**.............................. SeanQuinlan
(Sue Smith) *trckd ldrs 10th: outpcd whn fell 12th: fatally injured* **3/1**[2]

5m 14.4s (-2.60) **Going Correction** +0.10s/f (Yiel) **6** Ran SP% **110.9**
Speed ratings: **108,107,104,101,94**
CSF £10.01 TOTE £2.70: £1.60, £3.30; EX 9.50 Trifecta £30.70.
Owner A D Gray **Bred** Seamus O'Farrell **Trained** Cheltenham, Gloucs
■ Stewards' Enquiry : Paddy Brennan caution: careless riding

FOCUS
Not the strongest event for the grade, but the first two pulled nicely clear. The second has been rated to his mark.

260 T FROST RACING SADDLERS OPEN HUNTERS' CHASE (MIDLANDS POINT-TO-POINT AREA) (16 fncs) 2m 4f 62y
6:20 (6:20) (Class 6) 5-Y-0+ **£1,871** (£580; £290; £145)

Form RPR

P31- **1** **Drom**[38] 12-11-11 115.............................. MrNOrpwood(7) 116+
(Mrs C Drury) *w ldr: led 2nd: drvn and styd on fr 3 out: forged clr next* **5/1**[2]

053/ **2** *7* **Cold Knight**[17] 9-12-0 0.............................. MrTWeston 104
(Tom Weston) *trckd ldrs: modest 2nd between last 2: kpt on same pce* **15/2**

B2-0 **3** *2* **Archie Boy (IRE)**[13] 18 13-11-7 103..................(p) MrJDrinkwater(7) 102
(R D Potter) *chsd ldrs: rdn bef 3 out: kpt on to take modest 3rd appr last: one pce* **16/1**

10-0 **4** *4 ½* **Popaway**[13] 12 10-11-10 105..............................(t) MrJDocker(5) 99
(Mrs Pauline Harkin) *in rr: effrt 13th: kpt on one pce: tk modest 4th clsng stages* **10/1**

/6-5 **5** *1* **Realt Ag Leimt (IRE)**[13] 12 9-11-7 0.............................. MrDPeters(7) 99
(D Peters) *blnd 1st: chsd ldrs 6th: 2nd 11th: modest 4th and wkng whn mstke last* **7/1**[3]

0/ **6** *33* **Play The Market (IRE)**[16] 8-11-9 0..................(t) MrJonathanBailey(5) 67
(Stuart Morris) *in rr: hdwy to chse ldrs 11th: drvn 13th: sn lost pl: bhd next: sn t.o* **20/1**

/4-2 **P** **Roby De Cimbre (FR)**[7] 129 12-11-7 97..............(vt) MrTRFStrawson(7)
(S Robinson) *led to 2nd: blnd 4th: drvn 9th: lost pl 11th: bhd whn p.u bef 3 out* **20/1**

225- **P** **Elsafeer (IRE)**[17] 10-11-7 113.............................. MrJSDay(7)
(D Russell) *chsd ldrs 6th: lost pl after 11th: sn bhd: t.o whn p.u bef 3 out* **25/1**

FP4- **P** **Shrewd Investment**[22] 5433 9-11-11 114..............(tp) MissKatyLyons(7)
(Miss L Thomas) *chsd ldrs: drvn 3rd: lost pl and reminders 6th: sn bhd: p.u bef 8th* **14/1**

14F/ **P** **Jimbill (IRE)**[533] 2716 9-11-9 122.............................. MrBGibbs(5)
(Tim Vaughan) *in rr: bhd whn p.u bef 3rd: lame* **13/8**[1]

5m 14.9s (-2.10) **Going Correction** +0.10s/f (Yiel) **10** Ran SP% **114.0**
Speed ratings: **108,105,104,102,102 89,,,,**
CSF £39.86 TOTE £3.70: £1.70, £2.80, £6.50; EX 37.60 Trifecta £469.90.
Owner Paul Drury **Bred** Miss Ellen Delaney **Trained** Sheriff Hutton, N Yorks

FOCUS
An ordinary hunter chase. It's been rated around the balance of the first three.

261 LIVE MUSIC AT SOUTHWELL 2ND JUNE H'CAP HURDLE (11 hdls) 2m 4f 62y
6:55 (6:56) (Class 4) (0-120,119) 4-Y-0+ **£3,249** (£954; £477; £238)

Form RPR

163- **1** **Bohemian Rhapsody (IRE)**[38] 1719 6-11-9 **116**........(p) GavinSheehan 123+
(Joseph Tuite) *mde all: drvn 5 l ahd last: rdn out* **16/1**

33-0 **2** *3* **The Geegeez Geegee (IRE)**[5] 177 6-10-5 **105**........(t) HarryCobden(7) 109+
(Anthony Honeyball) *hld up in rr: hdwy 7th: modest 5th 2 out: styd on wl and 2nd appr last: kpt on: nt rch wnr* **4/1**[2]

011- **3** *5* **Rocky Rebel**[13] 5379 7-11-5 **112**.............................. TomScudamore 113
(Michael Blake) *chsd ldrs: drvn appr 2 out: kpt on same pce* **8/1**

65-1 **4** *3 ¼* **Notnowsam**[8] 107 4-10-10 **108**..............................(p) HarrySkelton 101
(Dan Skelton) *in rr: hdwy 7th: chsng ldrs 3 out: 2nd and rdn whn hit 2 out: kpt on one pce* **5/2**[1]

421- **5** *2* **Vodka 'n Tonic (IRE)**[28] 5335 6-11-2 **112**.............. JeremiahMcGrath(3) 108
(Nicky Henderson) *hld up in rr: hdwy 6th: chsng ldrs next: kpt on one pce: stmbld landing last* **13/2**[3]

56F- **6** *21* **Ballythomas**[84] 4288 8-10-4 **100**.............................. JoeColliver(3) 76
(David Thompson) *chsd ldrs: lost pl 4th: bhd 6th: t.o 3 out: kpt on between last 2* **50/1**

365- **7** *1 ¾* **Trapper Peak (IRE)**[55] 4849 6-11-10 **117**.............................. AndrewThornton 91
(Caroline Bailey) *mid-div: chsd ldrs 5th: lost pl bef 2 out* **18/1**

P54- **8** *3 ¼* **Tidal Way (IRE)**[19] 5496 6-11-4 **111**..............................(p) AidanColeman 82
(Charlie Longsdon) *chsd ldrs: drvn 8th: lost pl after 3 out* **16/1**

661- **9** *6* **Mr Shantu (IRE)**[20] 5467 6-11-6 **116**.............................. MauriceLinehan(3) 82
(Jonjo O'Neill) *in rr: bhd fr 3 out* **8/1**

6PP- **P** **Yesyoucan (IRE)**[33] 5246 10-11-12 **119**.............................. LeightonAspell
(Neil Mulholland) *in rr: hdwy 7th: chsng ldrs 3 out: wknd qckly: t.o whn p.u bef last* **33/1**

450- **P** **Twojayslad**[53] 4887 6-11-1 **108**.............................. WillKennedy
(Ian Williams) *chsd ldrs: rdn 8th: lost pl next: sn bhd: t.o whn p.u bef last* **16/1**

SP2- **P** **Howwrongcanyoube**[30] 5293 6-11-5 **115**.............................. TomBellamy(3)
(Alan King) *sn chsng ldrs: blnd and reminders 2nd: lost pl 8th: bhd next: t.o whn p.u bef 2 out* **14/1**

5m 0.8s (-12.20) **Going Correction** -0.425s/f (Good)
WFA 4 from 6yo+ 19lb **12** Ran SP% **118.6**
Speed ratings (Par 105): **106,104,102,101,100 92,92,91,88,,,**
CSF £80.53 CT £567.08 TOTE £17.10: £4.50, £2.10, £2.20; EX 118.30 Trifecta £506.30.
Owner A A Byrne **Bred** Sweetmans Bloodstock **Trained** Great Shefford, Berks

FOCUS
A fair handicap hurdle and another all-the-way winner on the card. The second and third have been rated pretty much to their marks.

262 FULL GOLF CLUB MEMBERSHIP FOR £560 NOVICES' H'CAP HURDLE (11 hdls) 2m 4f 62y
7:25 (7:25) (Class 5) (0-100,100) 4-Y-0+ **£2,599** (£763; £381; £190)

Form RPR

0U-1 **1** **Bennachie (IRE)**[8] 106 6-10-9 **90**..............................(t) AlanJohns(7) 104+
(Tim Vaughan) *chsd ldrs: led after 3 out: drvn rt out* **7/4**[1]

000- **2** *2 ½* **Winged Express (IRE)**[42] 5083 6-10-7 **81**..............................(p) AdamWedge 93+
(Alexandra Dunn) *trckd ldrs: handy 2nd appr 2 out: styd on same pce run-in* **11/1**

6P1- **3** *28* **Bay Fortuna**[24] 5397 6-11-12 **100**.............................. DaveCrosse 90
(Mark Usher) *hld up in rr: hdwy to chse ldrs 6th: 3rd 2 out: wknd between last 2* **7/2**[2]

505- **4** *8* **Steps And Stairs (IRE)**[25] 5379 5-11-10 **98**.............. RichieMcLernon 77
(Jonjo O'Neill) *chsd ldrs: rdn 3 out: fdd appr next* **11/2**[3]

000- **5** *6* **Mister Chairman (IRE)**[31] 5280 7-11-5 **93**..............................(b[1]) DavidBass 67
(Nicky Henderson) *prom: mstke 8th: chsng ldrs next: wknd appr 2 out* **12/1**

P0-P **6** *6* **Izbushka (IRE)**[12] 37 4-9-11 **79** oh5..............................(b) JoeColliver(3) 43
(David Thompson) *led 2nd: hdd after 3 out: wknd appr last* **40/1**

0P5- **7** *38* **Jackfield**[22] 5428 5-10-10 **84**.............................. CharliePoste 18
(Robin Dickin) *in rr: mstke 1st: chsd ldrs 7th: lost pl bef 3 out: sn bhd: t.o 2 out* **50/1**

3P-P **8** *57* **Magic Present**[11] 55 8-11-1 **89**..............................(bt) RobertDunne
(Sarah-Jayne Davies) *trckd ldrs: lost pl 8th: sn bhd: t.o bef 2 out: eventually completed* **25/1**

04-2 **P** **Whatsupjack (IRE)**[12] 37 8-10-4 **81**..................(b) JonathanEngland(3)
(Shaun Harris) *led to 2nd: reminders 4th: lost pl 8th: sn bhd: t.o whn p.u bef 2 out* **9/1**

P3-2 **P** **Ishusharella**[12] 41 6-11-1 **96**..............................(t) FreddieMitchell(7)
(Clare Hobson) *mid-div: drvn 4th: bhd and reminders after next: p.u bef 7th* **25/1**

060- **P** **Primo Rossi**[45] 5027 6-10-4 **78**.............................. FelixDeGiles
(Tom Gretton) *mstkes in rr: bhd fr 4th: t.o whn p.u bef 7th* **33/1**

5m 2.3s (-10.70) **Going Correction** -0.425s/f (Good)
WFA 4 from 5yo+ 19lb **11** Ran SP% **115.0**
Speed ratings (Par 103): **103,102,91,88,86 83,69,47,,**
CSF £19.39 CT £62.08 TOTE £2.90: £2.10, £1.90, £1.40; EX 22.60 Trifecta £98.10.
Owner Oceans Racing **Bred** Michael Heskin **Trained** Aberthin, Vale of Glamorgan
■ Stewards' Enquiry : Alan Johns two-day ban: used whip in incorrect place (May 26-27)

FOCUS
A moderate handicap, in which only two mattered from some way out. A big hurdle pb from the second, but it looks believable.

263 BELVOIR EQUINE NUTRITION AND LASER THERAPY MAIDEN HURDLE (9 hdls) 1m 7f 153y
7:55 (7:56) (Class 5) 4-Y-0+ **£2,599** (£763; £381; £190)

Form RPR

U **1** **Angus Glens**[7] 119 5-11-0 0..............................(p) NoelFehily 121+
(David Dennis) *hld up in rr: hdwy 5th: trcking ldrs 3 out: led sn after 2 out: hit last: drvn out* **12/1**

1- **2** *2* **Holly Bush Henry (IRE)**[79] 4391 4-10-10 0.............. RichieMcLernon 112
(Jonjo O'Neill) *trckd ldrs: handy 2nd between last 2: styd pon same pce run-in* **11/4**[2]

/33- **3** *6* **Moidore**[25] 5378 6-11-0 115.............................. AdamPogson 111
(Charles Pogson) *w ldrs: hmpd 2nd: led briefly bef 2 out: kpt on one pce* **5/2**[1]

252- **4** *10* **Bigindie (IRE)**[46] 5016 5-10-11 0.............................. AdamNicol(3) 104
(John Weymes) *led and j.lft 2nd: hdd appr 2 out: wknd between last 2* **10/1**

00-6 **5** *20* **Mister Jones**[12] 37 7-10-4 78.............................. StephenMcCarthy(10) 84
(Sue Smith) *prom: lost pl after 6th: sn bhd* **25/1**

1/0- **6** *8* **Western Way (IRE)**[62] 4708 6-11-0 0.............................. DenisO'Regan 77
(Don Cantillon) *detached in last: shkn up after 4th: drvn and wl bhd next* **3/1**[3]

P- **P** **Daydreamer**[67] 3605 4-10-10 0.............................. AidanColeman
(Alan King) *chsd ldrs: lost pl 3 out: sn bhd: t.o whn p.u bef 2 out* **16/1**

P **P** **Lord Emerson**[8] 105 7-11-0 0.............................. TrevorWhelan
(David Dennis) *in rr: bhd fr 6th: t.o whn p.u bef 2 out* **50/1**

110/ **P** **Uncle Muf (USA)**[206] 5173 5-11-0 0..............................(t) GavinSheehan
(Ali Stronge) *mid-div: lost pl 6th: sn bhd: t.o whn p.u bef 2 out* **33/1**

P/P- **P** **Its A Story**[359] 357 8-10-4 0..............................(p) JonathanEngland(3)
(Mairi Wilson) *led to 2nd: lost pl 4th: sn bhd: t.o whn p.u bef next* **200/1**

5-3 **P** **Victory Rich (IRE)**[12] 41 4-10-3 0..............................(t) MrFTett(7)
(Henry Tett) *j.rt: chsd ldrs: mstke 5th: lost pl 3 out: sn bhd: p.u after next* **33/1**

P **Miss Moppet**[234] 4-9-10 0..............................[1] FreddieMitchell(7)
(Clare Hobson) *mid-div: lost pl 6th: sn bhd: t.o whn p.u bef 2 out* **40/1**

3m 50.3s (-6.70) **Going Correction** -0.425s/f (Good)
WFA 4 from 5yo+ 18lb **12** Ran SP% **117.5**
Speed ratings (Par 103): **99,98,95,90,80 76,,,,,,**
CSF £44.05 TOTE £12.40: £4.20, £2.70, £1.10; EX 66.20 Trifecta £217.80.
Owner Favourites Racing Ltd **Bred** Lady Bamford **Trained** Hanley Swan, Worcestershire

FOCUS
A maiden hurdle with little depth and two horses dominated the finish. The fourth and fifth have been rated close to their marks.

264 SUPPORT BEAUMOND HOUSE ON 2ND JUNE INTERMEDIATE NATIONAL HUNT FLAT RACE (COND/AMATEURS) 1m 7f 153y
8:25 (8:25) (Class 6) 4-6-Y-0 **£1,711** (£498; £249)

Form RPR

1 **Grandmaster George (IRE)** 6-11-1 0.............................. JeremiahMcGrath(3) 97
(Seamus Mullins) *w ldr: led after 3f: drvn and styd on fnl 2f: hld on towards fin* **12/1**

2 *nk* **Verygoodverygood (FR)** 4-11-0 0.............................. NicodeBoinville 93
(Nicky Henderson) *trckd ldrs: hdwy on ins over 4f out: effrt and chsd wnr over 2f out: rdn over 1f out: no ex clsng stages* **8/11**[1]

0/ **3** *4* **Grand Introduction (IRE)**[409] 5070 5-11-1 0.............. ConorShoemark(3) 93
(Fergal O'Brien) *hld up in last: hdwy to trck ldrs over 6f out: effrt and cl 3rd over 2f out: one pce appr fnl f* **13/2**[3]

4 *13* **May's Sister** 4-10-0 0..............................(t) GrahamCarson(7) 70
(Anthony Carson) *trckd ldrs: effrt over 2f: sn rdn: wknd over 1f out* **20/1**

5 59 **Sea Lion** 4-10-7 0........................ MrKWood(7) 24
(Tony Coyle) *led 3f: reminders over 5f out: lost pl over 4f out: sn bhd: t.o whn eased 2f out* 11/4[2]

3m 51.3s (-0.10) **Going Correction** -0.425s/f (Good)
WFA 4 from 5yo+ 4lb 5 Ran SP% 110.4
Speed ratings: **83,82,80,74,44**
CSF £21.89 TOTE £10.40: £4.00, £1.10; EX 24.50 Trifecta £52.10.
Owner Andrew Cocks And Tara Johnson **Bred** Mrs Christine Kelly **Trained** Wilsford-Cum-Lake, Wilts
■ Stewards' Enquiry : Jeremiah McGrath two-day ban: careless riding (tbn)

FOCUS
Little form to go in this bumper and a surprise winner.
T/Plt: £74.30 to a £1 stake. Pool: £53,201.93 - 522.68 winning tickets. T/Qpdt: £19.30 to a £1 stake. Pool: £6,370.28 - 243.60 winning tickets. **Walter Glynn**

[167]WINCANTON (R-H)

Tuesday, May 12

OFFICIAL GOING: Good (good to firm in places) changing to good to firm (good in places) after race 3 (3.05)
Wind: strong breeze across Weather: cloudy periods

265 RACING UK YOUR RACING HOME FROM HOME H'CAP HURDLE (11 hdls) 2m 5f 82y
2:05 (2:08) (Class 5) (0-100,100) 4-Y-O+ £2,274 (£667; £333; £166)

Form RPR
212- 1 **Karl Marx (IRE)**[23] 5414 5-10-13 87........................(b) TomCannon 93+
(Mark Gillard) *mde all: pushed along fr 8th: rdn after 3 out: styd on gamely fr last: drvn out* 9/2[2]
050- 2 ½ **Upton Wood**[56] 4822 9-11-10 98........................ JamesDavies 103
(Chris Down) *trckd ldrs: rdn after 3 out: ev ch after last: styd on* 11/2[3]
2-F 3 2 **Titch Strider (IRE)**[11] 65 10-11-7 95........................ ConorO'Farrell 97
(John Panvert) *hld up bhd: hdwy after 8th: rdn to chse ldng trio appr 2 out: styd on but nt pce to chal* 10/1
606- 4 8 **All Force Majeure (FR)**[22] 5434 5-11-12 100........................ TomScudamore 95
(David Pipe) *trckd ldr: rdn after 3 out: chalng whn nt fluent 2 out: sn hld: no ex run-in* 9/2[2]
P53- 5 ½ **Mr Cardle (IRE)**[21] 5442 6-11-0 95........................ MissCBoxall(7) 92
(Oliver Sherwood) *nt a fluent: pushed along in midfield fr 6th: plugged on fr 2 out: nvr a threat* 11/4[1]
04-5 6 3¾ **Warsaw Pact (IRE)**[12] 40 12-9-7 74 oh2........................ DavidNoonan(7) 65
(Steven Dixon) *in tch: pushed along fr 4th: reminders after next: nvr gng pce to get involved fr after 3 out* 14/1
00-6 7 16 **Carhue (IRE)**[12] 30 8-10-11 85........................ NickScholfield 66
(Paul Henderson) *a towards rr* 20/1
3P0- 8 36 **Businessmoney Judi**[36] 5183 9-10-12 93......(tp) MrMatthewHampton(7) 51
(Martin Hill) *nt a fluent: mid-div: pushed along fr 6th: rdn after 3 out: wknd bef 2 next: t.o* 10/1
6FP- P **On The Move**[25] 5371 7-10-9 90........................ MrMLegg(7)
(Fiona Shaw) *mid-div: struggling 6th: wknd 3 out: t.o whn p.u bef next* 50/1
306- P **Sirrah Star (IRE)**[19] 2759 7-11-8 96........................ MarkQuinlan
(Neil Mulholland) *whipped rnd and lft at s: latched on to main gp after 3rd: wknd 6th: t.o whn p.u 3 out* 50/1

5m 5.9s (-20.60) **Going Correction** -0.875s/f (Firm) 10 Ran SP% 111.9
Speed ratings (Par 103): **102,101,101,98,98 96,90,77, ,**
CSF £28.01 CT £230.11 TOTE £3.70: £1.60, £2.30, £3.20; EX 31.50 Trifecta £249.20.
Owner Sam Bartlett **Bred** George S O'Malley **Trained** Holwell, Dorset

FOCUS
The opening contest was a modest staying handicap hurdle. They went an ordinary gallop on ground officially described as good, good to firm in places. The first three have been rated pretty much to their marks.

266 WALKING THE COURSES H'CAP CHASE (21 fncs) 3m 1f 30y
2:35 (2:36) (Class 4) (0-120,117) 5-Y-O+ £3,994 (£1,240; £667)

Form RPR
/UP- 1 **Ruapehu (IRE)**[36] 9-11-4 116........................(t) KevinJones(7) 122
(Charles Whittaker) *led 3rd: mde rest: rdn whn strly chal fr 3 out: hld on wl fr last: drifted lft: all out* 7/1
P3-1 2 1 **I'm In Charge**[11] 66 9-11-1 106........................(t) NickScholfield 112
(Grant Cann) *hld up in tch: mstke 11th: lft 4th at the 12th: chal 3 out: rdn appr last: styd on w ev ch tl no ex nring fin* 7/2[2]
22F- 3 55 **Days Ahead (IRE)**[18] 5524 8-11-9 114........................(p) AndrewThornton 80
(Richenda Ford) *trckd ldrs: lft 2nd whn hmpd 12th: ev ch whn slow 4 out: sn wknd: lft btn 3rd next: t.o* 5/1
/3F- P **Allerford Jack**[33] 5239 11-11-8 113........................ MichealNolan
(Richard Woollacott) *hld up: p.u after 8th: fatally injured* 18/1
U16- F **Shy John**[22] 5431 9-11-12 117........................ JamesDavies 122
(Jennifer Mason) *trckd ldrs: wnt lft 1st: lft 3rd whn hmpd 12th: rdn along fr 17th: mounting chal whn fell 3 out* 4/1[3]
34P- F **The Chuckmeister (IRE)**[43] 5061 6-11-3 108........ SamTwiston-Davies
(Paul Nicholls) *led tl 3rd: trcking wnr whn fell 12th* 2/1[1]

6m 17.0s (-22.50) **Going Correction** -0.70s/f (Firm) 6 Ran SP% 110.0
Speed ratings: **106,105,88, ,**
CSF £30.30 TOTE £7.80: £3.40, £1.70; EX 39.90 Trifecta £139.80.
Owner C R Whittaker **Bred** Miss Mary McCabe **Trained** Radstock, Somerset

FOCUS
An ordinary staying handicap chase. They went an honest gallop. The second has been rated to his mark.

267 JOCKEY CLUB CATERING H'CAP HURDLE (8 hdls) 1m 7f 65y
3:05 (3:06) (Class 5) (0-100,100) 4-Y-O+ £2,274 (£667; £333; £166)

Form RPR
62-4 1 **Heading To First**[5] 172 8-10-13 87........................(v) DarylJacob 94+
(Jim Best) *hld up: hdwy after 3 out: led between last 2: pushed clr run-in: readily* 11/4[1]
644- 2 5 **Mount Vesuvius (IRE)**[28] 5335 7-11-2 90........................(t) TomO'Brien 90
(Paul Henderson) *hld up: hdwy after 3 out: led next: rdn and hdd bef last: kpt on same pce run-in* 10/3[2]
4- 3 2½ **Lions Charge (USA)**[71] 4531 8-11-7 95........................(t) MarkQuinlan 94
(Neil Mulholland) *trckd ldrs: rdn appr 2 out: keeping on at same pce whn awkward last* 8/1
603- 4 4 **Very Intense (IRE)**[22] 5435 4-11-5 97........................(b[1]) RobertDunne 87
(Tom Lacey) *trckd ldrs: rdn appr 2 out: kpt on but nt pce to chal* 10/3[2]
006- 5 2¾ **Catcharose (IRE)**[106] 3899 5-11-7 95........................(t) ConorO'Farrell 88
(Jennifer Mason) *hld up: rdn to chse ldrs 2 out: nt pce to chal: no ex fr last* 16/1
603- 6 2¼ **Swampfire (IRE)**[33] 5242 7-11-12 100........................(p) SamTwiston-Davies 90
(Barry Brennan) *disp ld: rdn and hdd after 3 out: one pce fr next* 11/2[3]
/00- 7 13 **Cloudy Lady**[66] 4624 7-11-6 94........................ JamesBest 72
(Caroline Keevil) *disp ld: rdn and hdd bef 2 out: wknd between last 2* 25/1

3m 35.4s (-13.50) **Going Correction** -0.875s/f (Firm) 7 Ran SP% 109.0
Speed ratings (Par 103): **98,95,94,92,90 89,83**
CSF £11.40 TOTE £3.90: £2.10, £1.60; EX 10.50 Trifecta £132.90.
Owner JAG Racing Elite **Bred** Darley **Trained** Lewes, E Sussex

FOCUS
A modest handicap hurdle. They went an even gallop, and the ground was changed to good to firm, good in places after this contest on a drying day. The second has been rated to his mark.

268 CHARLTON HOUSE CUP MARES' NOVICES' HURDLE (8 hdls) 1m 7f 65y
3:35 (3:35) (Class 4) 4-Y-O+ £3,249 (£954; £477; £238)

Form RPR
522- 1 **Bantam (IRE)**[26] 5353 5-10-11 130........................ RichardJohnson 115+
(Henry Daly) *trckd ldr: led 4th: in command 2 out: easily* 1/10[1]
05- 2 11 **Alottarain (IRE)**[32] 5262 5-10-4 0........................ MrDSansom(7) 100
(Seamus Mullins) *trckd ldrs: rdn to dispute 2nd after 3 out: wnt clr 2nd next but no ch w wnr* 50/1[3]
335- 3 14 **Bondi Mist (IRE)**[50] 4958 6-10-11 104........................ TomCannon 92
(Jonathan Geake) *trckd ldrs: pressed wnr 4th tl rdn after 3 out: wknd next* 9/1[2]
/0P- 4 107 **Ragtime Lady**[203] 1985 7-10-4 0........................ MrGTreacy(7)
(Steven Dixon) *led tl wnt lft and hdd 4th: sn t.o* 150/1

3m 32.9s (-16.00) **Going Correction** -0.875s/f (Firm) 4 Ran SP% 103.5
Speed ratings (Par 105): **105,99,92,**
CSF £5.22 TOTE £1.10; EX 6.40 Trifecta £9.70.
Owner Brooke Kelly Partnership **Bred** Airlie Stud And Sir Thomas Pilkington **Trained** Stanton Lacy, Shropshire

FOCUS
A fair, if uncompetitive, little mares' novices' hurdle. They went a respectable gallop. There's a case for rating the race at least 10lb higher through the winner and third, but not on time, and the second had previously shown nothing.

269 BATHWICK TYRES NOVICES' CHASE (21 fncs) 3m 1f 30y
4:05 (4:07) (Class 4) 5-Y-O+ £3,994 (£1,240; £667)

Form RPR
F0-1 1 **Vicente (FR)**[12] 27 6-11-5 0........................ SamTwiston-Davies 136+
(Paul Nicholls) *j.lft bdly at times: nt a fluent: mde all: rdn after 3 out: hit 2 out: styd on: rdn out* 2/9[1]
233- 2 3¼ **Chinatown Boy (IRE)**[45] 7-10-12 119........................(p) NickScholfield 122
(Charles Whittaker) *trckd ldrs: disp 2nd fr 10th: wnt clr 2nd 17th: rdn after 4 out: 6 l down 3 out: hit next: styd on but a being hld fr last* 4/1[2]
3-23 3 63 **Veauce De Sivola (FR)**[7] 128 6-10-12 112........................(t) TomCannon 65
(Mark Gillard) *trckd wnr tl 17th: sn rdn: wknd bef 3 out: t.o* 25/1[3]
/P5- P **Lupita (IRE)**[36] 5186 11-10-5 49........................(t) BrendanPowell
(Derrick Scott) *chsd ldrs tl 12th: sn t.o: p.u after 4 out* 100/1

6m 21.1s (-18.40) **Going Correction** -0.70s/f (Firm) 4 Ran SP% 106.7
Speed ratings: **100,99,79,**
CSF £1.57 TOTE £1.20; EX 1.50 Trifecta £2.20.
Owner Ian Fogg & John Hales **Bred** Thierry Cypres & Jean-Francois Naudin **Trained** Ditcheat, Somerset

FOCUS
A fairly decent, if uncompetitive, little staying novices' chase. They went an even gallop. The second has been rated in line with the best of last summer's form.

270 WESSEX OPEN HUNTERS' CHASE (17 fncs) 2m 4f 35y
4:35 (4:35) (Class 6) 5-Y-O+ £1,247 (£387; £193; £96)

Form RPR
/32- 1 **Parkam Jack**[8] 9-11-3 106........................ MrJLThomas(7) 119+
(Mrs Kayley Woollacott) *trckd ldrs: rdn to chal 3 out: led 2 out: styd on wl: rdn out* 3/1[2]
330- 2 5 **Mr Satco (IRE)**[64] 4678 7-11-9 118........................(p[1]) MrMWoodward(5) 118
(Ms Emma Oliver) *led: rdn after 4 out: hdd whn nt fluent 2 out: 2nd whn awkward last* 5/1[3]
U21/ 3 1 **Divine Intavention (IRE)**[10] 11-12-4 0........................ MrMWall 122+
(Miss Francesca Moller) *chsd ldr: hit 7th: pushed along fr 11th: rdn after 4 out: styd on same pce fr next* 5/4[1]
1/5- 4 12 **Theatre Evening (IRE)**[22] 5433 7-11-3 108........................ MrTBishop(7) 100
(Mrs Frances Bishop) *in tch: pushed along fr 9th: rdn after 13th: one pce fr after next* 10/1
F50- 5 1½ **Himalayan Express**[16] 11-11-5 103........................ MrJMartin(5) 102
(Mrs David Plunkett) *in tch: pushed along fr 8th: rdn after 13th: outpcd after next: no threat after* 25/1
FP-6 6 6 **Bay To Go (IRE)**[13] 12 9-11-7 114........................ MissLWheeler(7) 99
(Mrs H M Kemp) *trckd ldrs: rdn after 13th: nt pce to chal: wknd 2 out* 12/1
00P- P **Oscargo (IRE)**[9] 11-11-5 104........................(tp) MrRobertHawker(5)
(Mrs Sue Popham) *hld up: lost tch after 8th: t.o whn p.u 4 out* 25/1

5m 1.8s (-15.70) **Going Correction** -0.70s/f (Firm) 7 Ran SP% 110.6
Speed ratings: **101,99,98,94,93 91,**
CSF £17.22 TOTE £3.20: £1.50, £2.40; EX 17.90 Trifecta £38.20.
Owner J F Symes **Bred** Shade Oak Stud **Trained** South Molton, Devon

FOCUS
A fair hunters' chase. They went a respectable gallop. A pb from the winner, while the second has been rated close to his mark.

271 WINCANTON STANDARD OPEN NATIONAL HUNT FLAT RACE 1m 7f 65y
5:05 (5:05) (Class 6) 4-6-Y-O £1,624 (£477; £238; £119)

Form RPR
1 **Time Is Money** 6-10-9 0........................ DarylJacob 92+
(Emma Lavelle) *trckd ldrs: led over 2f out: sn rdn and strly pressed: kpt on wl fnl f: hld on: all out* 2/1[1]
2 nk **Hello Jazz** 5-10-2 0........................ MrMLegg(7) 92
(John Ryall) *in tch: hdwy on outer 4f out: rdn to chal over 2f out: ev ch thrght fnl f: jst hld* 20/1
65- 3 5 **Monkey Rum**[142] 3217 5-11-2 0........................ TomCannon 95
(Brendan Powell) *trckd ldrs: rdn over 2f out: wnt 3rd ent fnl f: styd on same pce* 6/1[3]

0/0- **4** 5 **Terra Firma**[52] 4921 5-11-2 0 .... BrendanPowell 90
(Brendan Powell) *led: rdn and hdd over 2f out: kpt pressing ldrs tl fdd jst over 1f out* **7/2**[2]
0- **5** ½ **Definately Vinnie**[54] 4873 5-10-11 0 .... ConorRing(5) 90
(Jane Mathias) *in tch: rdn wl over 2f out: sn one pce* **33/1**
20/ **6** ½ **Shout It Aloud**[437] 4547 6-11-2 0 .... RichardJohnson 89
(Tim Vaughan) *hld up: hdwy on outer fr 4f out: rdn over 2f out: sn one pce* **7/2**[2]
7 6 **Tombill (IRE)** 6-10-9 0 .... MrGTreacy(7) 84
(Paul Henderson) *hld up: rdn 3f out: nvr threatened ldrs* **16/1**
0- **8** 10 **Helenpark (IRE)**[79] 4384 6-10-9 0 .... TomO'Brien 68
(Paul Henderson) *veered lft s: sn pressing ldr: rdn wl over 3f out: sn wknd* **10/1**

3m 29.2s (-14.10) **Going Correction** -0.875s/f (Firm) **8** Ran SP% **114.7**
Speed ratings: **100,99,97,94,94 94,91,86**
CSF £45.78 TOTE £2.90: £1.40, £4.30, £1.30; EX 30.00 Trifecta £92.60.
Owner Cottage Stables Racing Club **Bred** David Jenks **Trained** Hatherden, Hants

FOCUS
The concluding contest was an ordinary bumper. They went an even gallop. It's been rated around the fourth and fifth.
T/Plt: £34.40 to a £1 stake. Pool: £36,515.18 - 774.56 winning tickets. T/Qpdt: £6.60 to a £1 stake. Pool: £2,005.84 - 223.30 winning tickets. **Tim Mitchell**

272 - 278a (Foreign Racing) - See Raceform Interactive

[98]KEMPTON (R-H)

Wednesday, May 13

OFFICIAL GOING: Good (watered; hdl 7.6, chs 8.0)
Wind: virtually nil Weather: dry, sunny

279 RACING UK ANYWHERE "NATIONAL HUNT" MAIDEN HURDLE (8 hdls) 2m
2:30 (2:30) (Class 5) 4-Y-0+ **£2,599** (£763; £381; £190)

Form RPR
23-6 **1** **General Ginger**[9] 98 5-11-0 0 .... (t) NoelFehily 108+
(Harry Fry) *mde virtually all: nt fluent 5th: gng best bef 2 out: rdn last: r.o wl and drew clr flat: readily* **9/4**[2]
03-3 **2** 4½ **Destiny's Gold (IRE)**[13] 32 5-11-0 120 .... AndrewTinkler 105+
(George Baker) *chsd ldrs: nt fluent 1st: rdn and effrt to chse wnr bef 2 out: drvn after 2 out: stl pressing wnr whn hit last: outpcd flat* **2/1**[1]
46-0 **3** 4½ **Trojan Star (IRE)**[9] 98 5-11-0 0 .... DavidBass 99
(Kim Bailey) *in tch in midfield: mstke 5th: effrt to chse ldrs after 3 out: 3rd and styd on same pce fr next* **25/1**
45-5 **4** 6 **Dadsintrouble (IRE)**[9] 100 5-11-0 0 .... MichaelByrne 94
(Tim Vaughan) *pressed ldr tl rdn and unable qck ent st: 4th and btn 2 out: wknd between last 2* **14/1**
05-0 **5** 8 **Empty Marmalades (FR)**[12] 61 4-10-10 0 .... WillKennedy 83
(Gary Moore) *hld up in tch: 7th and outpcd after 3 out: no threat to ldrs but styd on between last 2* **33/1**
/06- **6** 16 **Royal Roo**[23] 5428 6-10-7 0 .... GavinSheehan 65
(Mark Rimell) *chsd ldrs: struggling whn nt fluent 3 out: wknd bef next: t.o* **50/1**
7 5 **Art Libre (FR)** 4-10-10 0 .... MarcGoldstein 66
(Gary Moore) *in tch in midfield: hit 3 out: wknd bef next: t.o whn nt fluent last* **33/1**
300- **8** 12 **Admiral Miller**[21] 5469 5-11-0 0 .... NicodeBoinville 57
(Nicky Henderson) *in tch in midfield: lost pl and struggling 3 out: lost tch bef next: t.o* **10/1**
2/P- **9** 17 **Abitofbob**[170] 2709 6-11-0 0 .... AidanColeman 42
(Emma Lavelle) *t.k.h: hld up in rr: clsd after 4th: struggling next: sn lost tch: t.o: b.b.v* **3/1**[3]

3m 49.45s (-8.65) **Going Correction** -0.55s/f (Firm)
WFA 4 from 5yo+ 18lb **9** Ran SP% **116.5**
Speed ratings (Par 103): **99,96,94,91,87 79,77,71,62**
CSF £7.26 TOTE £2.30: £1.20, £1.10, £7.20; EX 8.30 Trifecta £67.50.
Owner Hazard Chase Racing **Bred** Miss E J Lucas **Trained** Seaborough, Dorset

FOCUS
Dual bend alignment was in operation for this meeting (distances were unaffected), while watering had taken place since the previous Tuesday to try and maintain good ground. Probably just a modest contest. The winner has been rated as improving to his bumper mark, with the fourth helping to set the level.

280 BET WITH YOUR RACING UK APP H'CAP CHASE (16 fncs) 2m 4f 110y
3:05 (3:05) (Class 5) (0-100,100) 5-Y-0+ **£2,599** (£763; £381; £190)

Form RPR
5-12 **1** **Thinger Licht (FR)**[4] 211 6-10-12 86 .... (p) HarrySkelton 106+
(Dan Skelton) *in tch in midfield: chsd ldrs after 9th: wnt 2nd and hit 13th: rdn and clsd to j. into ld 3 out: clr next: styd on* **4/7**[1]
233- **2** 12 **Lord Lir (IRE)**[19] 5522 9-10-11 85 .... (b) MichaelByrne 91
(Tim Vaughan) *j.w: w ldrs tl led 3rd: rdn and hdd 3 out: btn next: plugged to for clr 2nd* **14/1**
544- **3** 6 **Herecomesthetruth (IRE)**[19] 5522 13-11-10 98 .... TomCannon 100
(Chris Gordon) *w ldrs: chsd ldr 3rd tl 8th: chsd ldrs after: mstke 13th: rdn and wnt modest 3rd next: plugged on but no imp* **12/1**
P4-U **4** 2¾ **Bouggietopieces**[12] 57 5-11-9 97 .... KielanWoods 96
(Pam Sly) *hld up in rr: mstke 8th: hdwy into midfield next: mstke 12th: drvn and effrt after 13th: modest 4th and plugged on same pce fr 2 out* **12/1**
P2-1 **5** 4½ **Alright Benny (IRE)**[8] 126 12-11-12 100 7ex .... PaddyBrennan 96
(Paul Henderson) *w ldrs tl settled in 3rd fr 3rd: wnt 2nd 8th tl 13th: 4th and btn whn hit next: sn wknd* **7/1**[2]
624- **6** 37 **Where'd Ya Hide It (IRE)**[129] 3527 9-10-0 74 oh2 .... (bt) JamesBest 35
(Paul Henderson) *in tch in midfield: rdn and struggling whn mstke 10th: bhd after: lost tch bef 3 out* **25/1**
162- **7** 9 **Forresters Folly**[23] 5429 9-11-12 100 .... (tp) TrevorWhelan 53
(Claire Dyson) *m in snatches: a towards rr: nt fluent 7th: rdn and struggling 11th: lost tch bef 3 out: t.o whn virtually p.u flat* **8/1**[3]
P3P- **8** nk **Kayflin (FR)**[42] 5094 7-11-2 90 .... LeightonAspell 43
(Linda Jewell) *dropped to rr after blnd 3rd: a bhd after: lost tch bef 3 out: t.o whn virtually p.u flat* **25/1**

5m 8.2s (-8.40) **Going Correction** -0.475s/f (Good) **8** Ran SP% **117.0**
Speed ratings: **97,92,90,89,87 73,69,69**
CSF £10.51 CT £50.77 TOTE £1.70: £1.10, £2.50, £2.50; EX 10.80 Trifecta £65.10.
Owner Carl Hodgson **Bred** M Jacques Chapet & Mme Anne Dupont **Trained** Alcester, Warwicks

FOCUS
Probably just an ordinary race for the level despite four being fairly close to the ceiling rating for the contest. The easy winner stood out on recent form and has been rated to a similar level.

281 RACING UK 1 PRICE 3 DEVICES H'CAP HURDLE (8 hdls) 2m
3:35 (3:36) (Class 5) (0-105,105) 4-Y-0+ **£3,249** (£954; £477; £238)

Form RPR
223- **1** **Mr Fickle (IRE)**[15] 3658 6-11-7 100 .... TomCannon 110+
(Gary Moore) *hld up in tch in midfield: hdwy after 5th: rdn to ld bef 2 out: 3 l clr whn dived and blnd last: sn rcvrd and readily fnd enough flat: rdn out* **14/1**
050/ **2** 6 **Sleeping City (FR)**[500] 3390 8-11-0 93 .... (t) DenisO'Regan 96
(Victor Dartnall) *t.k.h: hld up in tch: hdwy and barging match after 3 out: wnt 2nd next: 3 l down and mstke last: no imp u.p flat* **9/2**[3]
456- **3** 1¼ **Drifter (IRE)**[41] 5114 4-11-1 105 .... PaulNO'Brien(7) 103
(Harry Whittington) *led: rdn and hdd bef 2 out: 3rd and kpt on same pce fr between last 2* **5/1**
443- **4** 11 **Ladies Dancing**[21] 5479 9-11-2 102 .... (p) CiaranGethings(7) 94
(Chris Down) *chsd ldrs: wnt 2nd 5th tl after next: 4th and unable qck ent st: wknd between last 2* **11/4**[1]
424- **5** 4½ **McCabe Creek (IRE)**[74] 4497 5-11-11 104 .... AidanColeman 91
(Alan King) *t.k.h: hld up in tch in midfield: 5th and drvn bef 2 out: sn btn: wknd 2 out* **10/3**[2]
1/2- **6** 12 **Flying Phoenix**[14] 4743 7-11-12 105 .... TomScudamore 85
(Michael Blake) *chsd ldr tl 5th: losing pl and barging match and hmpd bnd bef 2 out: sn wknd* **12/1**
60P- **7** 2½ **Love The Leader (IRE)**[23] 5435 7-11-11 104 .... AlainCawley 78
(Johnny Farrelly) *bhd: rdn after 4th: toiling and mstke 3 out: wl btn next: plugged on past btn horses flat* **25/1**
306- **8** ½ **Olymnia**[38] 5155 4-10-9 92 .... AdamWedge 62
(Anna Newton-Smith) *wl in tch in midfield: lost pl and reminders after 5th: lost tch after next: wl bhd last* **33/1**
505- **9** 3 **Softly She Treads (IRE)**[23] 5430 4-10-0 83 .... (v) JamesBest 50
(Pat Phelan) *wl in tch in midfield: nt fluent 1st: hdwy to chse ldrs 5th: rdn and wknd after next: wl bhd last* **14/1**
444/ **10** 2¼ **Hyperlink (IRE)**[261] 808 6-11-11 104 .... RhysFlint 73
(Heather Dalton) *t.k.h: in tch in midfield tl wknd bef 2 out: mstke 2 out: wl bhd last* **16/1**

3m 49.5s (-8.60) **Going Correction** -0.55s/f (Firm)
WFA 4 from 5yo+ 18lb **10** Ran SP% **118.3**
Speed ratings (Par 103): **99,96,95,89,87 81,80,80,78,77**
CSF £78.20 CT £368.46 TOTE £11.00: £3.50, £1.60, £2.20; EX 96.30 Trifecta £657.10.
Owner Gary Moore Racing **Bred** M Duffy **Trained** Lower Beeding, W Sussex

FOCUS
The pace was only respectable despite a noted front-runner being in the field. The winner was on a decent mark but this still rates a hurdle pb on better ground.

282 NEW RACING UK IPAD APP H'CAP CHASE (18 fncs) 3m
4:05 (4:06) (Class 4) (0-120,120) 5-Y-0+ **£3,898** (£1,144; £572; £286)

Form RPR
PP2- **1** **Ballybough Pat (IRE)**[44] 5061 8-11-12 120 .... (t) AidanColeman 136+
(David Dennis) *led: rdn: mstke and hdd 2 out: gd jump to ld again last: styd on wl: eased cl home* **11/8**[1]
/45- **2** 2½ **Double Handful (GER)**[53] 4907 9-11-0 108 .... (tp) NickScholfield 120
(Lawney Hill) *hld up in tch in rr: effrt to chal 3 out: outj. wnr to ld 2 out: outj. by wnr and hdd last: no ex and one pce flat* **9/2**[3]
111- **3** 23 **Milgen Bay**[22] 5447 9-11-7 115 .... LeightonAspell 106
(Oliver Sherwood) *chsd wnr tl 3 out: 3rd and btn next: wknd bef last* **4/1**[2]
F06- **4** 13 **Midnight Cataria**[37] 5195 6-11-5 113 .... DenisO'Regan 93
(Alan King) *chsd ldrs tl 3rd: styd wl in tch: 4th and rdn bef 3 out: sn btn: wknd after 3 out* **9/2**[3]
53P- **5** 3¾ **Trafalgar (FR)**[95] 4091 8-11-2 110 .... RobertDunne 86
(Sarah-Jayne Davies) *chsd ldrs 3rd tl after 15th: sn dropped to last and btn: wknd after 3 out* **8/1**

6m 0.15s (-15.25) **Going Correction** -0.475s/f (Good) **5** Ran SP% **109.6**
Speed ratings: **106,105,97,93,91**
CSF £7.85 TOTE £3.90: £1.50, £2.10; EX 8.40 Trifecta £25.20.
Owner Favourites Racing Ltd **Bred** Mrs Maryrose Kehoe **Trained** Hanley Swan, Worcestershire

FOCUS
The runner-up is the guide to the form, which suggests this was modest at best. There's a case for rating the race hgher through the well-beaten third, fourth and fifth.

283 NEW RACING UK ANDROID APP H'CAP HURDLE (10 hdls) 2m 5f
4:35 (4:36) (Class 4) (0-120,119) 4-Y-0+ **£3,249** (£954; £477; £238)

Form RPR
246- **1** **Kincora Fort (IRE)**[90] 4179 6-10-12 108 .... JamesBanks(3) 113+
(Noel Williams) *in tch in tch in midfield: clsd to chse ldrs bef 2 out: led wl bef last: hung rt u.p but r.o wl flat* **7/2**[2]
010- **2** 3¼ **New Horizons (IRE)**[28] 5343 5-11-4 111 .... DavidBass 114+
(Nicky Henderson) *chsd ldrs: rdn 3 out: kpt on and pressing ldrs next: mstke last: wnt 2nd and edgd lft u.p flat: no imp on wnr* **10/3**[1]
/32- **3** 1 **Keltic Rhythm (IRE)**[360] 362 8-11-7 114 .... TrevorWhelan 114
(Neil King) *chsd ldr tl led bef 2 out: sn u.p and hrd pressed: hdd wl bef last: stl cl enough last: styd on same pce flat* **14/1**
P12- **4** 1 **Exemplary**[26] 5371 8-11-1 108 .... (t) NoelFehily 107
(Johnny Farrelly) *hld up in rr: clsd after 3 out: rdn and chsd ldrs between last 2: cl 4th last: kpt on same pce flat* **8/1**
P24- **5** 12 **King's Request (IRE)**[44] 5068 5-11-12 119 .... TomCannon 107
(Laura Mongan) *in tch towards rr: clsd and pressing ldrs 3 out: 5th and btn next: wkng whn mstke last* **33/1**
2P0- **6** 8 **Changeofluck (IRE)**[43] 5086 7-11-3 110 .... (tp) NickScholfield 91
(Lawney Hill) *in tch in midfield: mstke 5th: rdn and btn after 3 out: wknd next* **14/1**
201- **7** 13 **Bostin (IRE)**[19] 5523 7-10-12 108 .... ThomasGarner(3) 80
(Daniel O'Brien) *t.k.h: in tch: hdwy to chse ldrs 4th: led 7th tl bef 2 out: sn wknd: mstke last: t.o* **12/1**
250- **P** **Pride In Battle (IRE)**[88] 4231 10-11-8 115 .... DenisO'Regan
(Alan King) *in tch in midfield: rdn and lost tch 3 out: t.o whn p.u next* **16/1**
345- **P** **Experimentalist**[23] 5429 7-10-11 104 .... (t) MichaelByrne
(Tim Vaughan) *in tch towards rr: dropped to last and rdn after 6th: lost tch next: t.o whn p.u 3 out* **20/1**
P0-1 **U** **Drombeg West**[13] 43 8-11-1 108 .... AndrewTinkler
(Anna Brooks) *last pair whn bdly hmpd and uns rdr 1st* **20/1**
323- **F** **Carry On Sydney**[26] 5366 5-11-9 116 .... LeightonAspell
(Oliver Sherwood) *midfield whn fell 1st* **11/2**[3]

40F- **P** **Spring Steel (IRE)**[31] 5295 6-11-3 **110**..........................(t) NicodeBoinville
(Ben Pauling) *led tl 7th: wknd bef next: t.o whn p.u 2 out* **12/1**
5m 2.6s (-14.90) **Going Correction** -0.55s/f (Firm) **12 Ran SP% 118.9**
Speed ratings (Par 105): **106,104,104,104,99 96,91,, ,**
CSF £15.55 CT £147.11 TOTE £5.80: £2.10, £1.80, £2.60; EX 17.00 Trifecta £136.80.
Owner EPDS Racing Partnership 8 **Bred** Neil O'Mahony **Trained** Blewbury, Oxon

FOCUS
This looked the most competitive race on the card, and the pace appeared to be respectable without being overly quick. The winner has been rated back to form, with the second similar to his C&D win and the fourth to his mark.

284 DOWNLOAD YOUR RACING UK APP H'CAP CHASE (12 fncs) 2m
5:05 (5:05) (Class 4) (0-110,107) 5-Y-0+ **£3,898** (£1,144; £572; £286)

Form RPR
14-F **1** **Agapanthus (GER)**[6] 170 10-11-2 **97**..............................(b) MarkQuinlan 104+
(Neil Mulholland) *nt fluent: in rr: reminders after 4th: more reminders after 7th: clsd to go 3rd 3 out: led and edgd lft between last 2: blnd last: drvn and a holding rival flat* **2/1**[1]
521- **2** *1 1/4* **Kayfton Pete**[31] 5298 9-11-12 **107**.............................. AdamPogson 111
(Charles Pogson) *t.k.h: trckd ldrs: wnt 2nd 7th: upsides and travelling wl 3 out: carried lft bef next: rdn and effrt jst bef last: drvn flat: one pce and a hld* **2/1**[1]
21-F **3** *8* **Capisci (IRE)**[6] 175 10-11-10 **105**.............................. RobertDunne 102
(Sarah-Jayne Davies) *led: mstke 8th: rdn after 3 out: wandered lft bef next: hdd wl bef last: sn btn and plugged on same pce after* **9/2**[3]
44F- **4** *10* **Wish In A Well (IRE)**[72] 4533 6-11-7 **102**..........(tp) KielanWoods 89
(Ben Case) *chsd ldr tl 7th: 4th and u.p after 9th: wknd bef 2 out* **7/2**[2]
3m 55.2s (-5.10) **Going Correction** -0.475s/f (Good) **4 Ran SP% 107.1**
Speed ratings: **93,92,88,83**
CSF £6.34 TOTE £2.10; EX 6.40 Trifecta £10.90.
Owner Stuart K Brown **Bred** Gestut Schlenderhan **Trained** Limpley Stoke, Wilts

FOCUS
Three of the four runners in this fell last time out, which suggests this form is worth treating with caution even at a moderate level. The second has been rated in line with his recent win.
T/Plt: £46.70 to a £1 stake. Pool: £47,182.46 - 736.76 winning tickets T/Qpdt: £33.00 to a £1 stake. Pool: £2,906.41 - 65.10 winning tickets **Steve Payne**

PERTH (R-H)
Wednesday, May 13

OFFICIAL GOING: Soft (heavy in places)
Wind: Breezy, half against Weather: Cloudy, bright

285 STRATHBRAAN BREWERY MAIDEN HURDLE (FOR THE ALAN NORMILE MEMORIAL TROPHY) (8 hdls 2 omitted) 2m 4f 35y
5:55 (5:56) (Class 5) 4-Y-0+ **£3,165** (£935; £467; £234; £117)

Form RPR
1 **Wind Of Hope (IRE)**[25] 6-10-11 0.............................. GrahamWatters(3) 118+
(Lucinda Russell) *hld up: stdy hdwy bef omitted 3 out: rdn bef next: rallied to ld run-in: styd on wl* **14/1**
/43- **2** *3/4* **Glacial Rock (IRE)**[39] 5129 9-11-0 115.............................. BrianHughes 117
(Alistair Whillans) *led: jinked lft sn after s: hdd 4th: rdn to ld whn mstke 2 out: hdd run-in: kpt on* **5/2**[2]
250- **3** *2 1/2* **Fort Smith (IRE)**[21] 5485 6-11-0 127..........................(tp) RichardJohnson 114
(Gordon Elliott, Ire) *j.lft: t.k.h in midfield: rdn bef 2 out: rallied and chsd ldrs last: kpt on same pce run-in* **5/4**[1]
245- **4** *2 3/4* **Badged**[20] 5495 6-10-9 109..............................(p) GrantCockburn(5) 111
(Lucy Normile) *chsd ldrs: effrt and ev ch 2 out: rdn and outpcd fr last* **6/1**[3]
600- **5** *16* **Welcome Ben (IRE)**[21] 5469 6-10-11 0.............................. TonyKelly(3) 95
(Jackie Stephen) *t.k.h: hld up: hdwy bef omitted 3 out: rdn and wknd bef next* **50/1**
OPP/ **6** *10* **Running Brook (IRE)**[18] 8-11-0 0.............................. WilsonRenwick 85
(R Mike Smith) *cl up: led 4th to bef 2 out: sn rdn and wknd* **100/1**
7 *1 1/2* **Farewelltocheyenne (IRE)**[276] 1202 7-11-0 0.............................. LucyAlexander 83
(N W Alexander) *t.k.h: nt fluent in rr: mstke and outpcd 3 out (usual 4 out): btn bef 2 out* **16/1**
8 *2 1/4* **Veinard (FR)** 6-11-0 0.............................. JamesReveley 85
(Iain Jardine) *t.k.h: sn cl up: rdn and led briefly bef 2 out: sn wknd* **28/1**
9 *2 1/4* **Craiganboy (IRE)**[564] 6-10-7 0.............................. AnthonyFox(7) 79
(S R B Crawford, Ire) *bhd: struggling 3 out (usual 4 out): nvr on terms* **66/1**
543- **10** *29* **Buckled**[50] 4976 5-11-0 0.............................. BrianHarding 50
(Sandy Thomson) *t.k.h: hld up: nt fluent 1st: blnd next: struggling 3 out (usual 4 out): nvr on terms* **16/1**
5m 15.1s (13.10) **Going Correction** +0.65s/f (Soft) **10 Ran SP% 113.6**
Speed ratings (Par 103): **101,100,99,98,92 88,88,87,86,75**
CSF £48.71 TOTE £15.60: £4.50, £1.30, £1.10; EX 72.30 Trifecta £274.20.
Owner Mrs Jo Tracey **Bred** Mrs Gail Kidd **Trained** Arlary, Perth & Kinross

FOCUS
All bends and hurdles moved on to fresh ground. After this race Richard Johnson said the ground was more soft, good to soft in places, but tiring ground. This was run at an ordinary gallop, the form is hard to access and but the first four finished clear of the remainder. The second and fourth set the level.

286 STEADFAST SCOTLAND NOVICES' H'CAP CHASE (12 fncs) 2m
6:25 (6:25) (Class 5) (0-100,100) 5-Y-0+ **£3,282** (£1,052; £584)

Form RPR
400- **1** **Throthethatch (IRE)**[21] 5469 6-11-7 **95**.............................. PeterBuchanan 108+
(Lucinda Russell) *mde virtually all: rdn whn hrd pressed bef 2 out: styd on gamely fr last* **15/8**[2]
223- **2** *3* **The Absent Mare**[5] 190 7-10-0 **74** oh2..........................(t) RichardJohnson 84
(Gordon Elliott, Ire) *t.k.h: in tch: smooth hdwy 4 out: effrt and rdn 2 out: kpt on same pce fr last* **6/5**[1]
00/P **3** *64* **Mr Shahady (IRE)**[7] 143 10-11-5 **100**.............................. MrWHRReed(7) 61
(Victor Thompson) *disp ld to 1/2-way: outpcd 4 out: lost tch fr next: no ch whn lft 3rd last* **50/1**
04P- **F** **Great Demeanor (USA)**[54] 4890 5-10-0 **74** oh2.................. HenryBrooke 84
(Dianne Sayer) *in tch: niggled and sltly outpcd 1/2-way: rallied 4 out: ev ch whn mstke 2 out: sn rdn: 3 l 3rd and one pce whn fell last* **6/1**[3]
056- **R** **The Village (IRE)**[29] 5326 6-9-11 **74** oh8..........................(t) DerekFox(3)
(Lucinda Russell) *ref to r* **9/1**
4m 6.3s (9.30) **Going Correction** +0.65s/f (Soft) **5 Ran SP% 106.5**
Speed ratings: **102,100,68,,**
CSF £4.41 TOTE £3.30: £1.80, £1.10; EX 5.10 Trifecta £43.80.
Owner Mrs Sandra Giles **Bred** Jerry Murphy **Trained** Arlary, Perth & Kinross

FOCUS
An ordinary novice handicap chase in which only two of the five were in the handicap. The winner has been rated up 8lb on the best of his hurdle runs.

287 ROA/RACING POST OWNERS JACKPOT H'CAP CHASE (15 fncs) 2m 4f 20y
6:55 (6:55) (Class 5) (0-100,93) 5-Y-0+ **£3,798** (£1,122; £561; £280; £140)

Form RPR
4U5- **1** **Just Awake**[62] 4725 8-10-13 **87**..............................(t) StevenFox(7) 109+
(Sandy Thomson) *nt fluent on occasions in rr: hld up: blnd 9th: stdy hdwy bef 4 out: led gng wl after next: drew clr on bit fr 2 out: v easily* **5/2**[1]
300- **2** *12* **Discoverie**[20] 5490 7-10-13 **80**.............................. SeanQuinlan 84
(Dianne Sayer) *nt fluent on occasions: led to 1st: pressed ldr: led after 8th: rdn and edgd lft 4 out: hdd after next: plugged on: no ch w easy wnr* **3/1**[2]
3P4- **3** *4 1/2* **Bescot Springs (IRE)**[50] 4974 10-11-9 **93**.............(b) GrahamWatters(3) 92
(Lucinda Russell) *hld up in tch: stdy hdwy 5 out: effrt and rdn 3 out: one pce next: 3rd and hld whn hit last* **9/2**[3]
2PP- **4** *10* **The Flaming Matron (IRE)**[62] 4724 9-10-9 **81**..(tp) StephenMulqueen(5) 71
(N W Alexander) *chsd ldrs: wnt 2nd 10th: rdn 4 out: wknd after next* **11/2**
P6-P **5** *22* **War On (IRE)**[7] 140 8-10-3 **77**.............................. MrWHRReed(7) 44
(Victor Thompson) *cl up: led 1st to after 7th: wknd 5 out: lost tch bef 3 out: t.o* **14/1**
/62- **P** **Lochore (IRE)**[287] 1125 9-10-3 **70**..............................(t) HenryBrooke
(Jean McGregor) *nt fluent: in tch: outpcd whn hmpd 9th: p.u bef next* **10/1**
64P- **U** **Prince Blackthorn (IRE)**[29] 5324 9-10-13 **80**.................. BrianHarding
(Barry Murtagh) *hld up: blnd and uns rdr 9th* **12/1**
5m 22.0s (17.00) **Going Correction** +0.65s/f (Soft) **7 Ran SP% 110.6**
Speed ratings: **93,88,86,82,74 ,**
CSF £10.10 TOTE £4.90: £2.20, £1.70; EX 11.80 Trifecta £46.10.
Owner Mrs A M Thomson **Bred** A M Thomson **Trained** Lambden, Berwicks

FOCUS
A weak handicap chase but the winning scored in good style. The easy winner was thrown in on last season's Kelso second and has been rated back to that level.

288 CHARLIE BIRD MEMORIAL NOVICES' H'CAP HURDLE (6 hdls 2 omitted) 2m 110y
7:25 (7:26) (Class 5) (0-100,92) 4-Y-0+ **£3,249** (£954; £477; £238)

Form RPR
F0-0 **1** **Seventeen Black (IRE)**[11] 77 7-10-3 **74**.................. GrantCockburn(5) 77+
(Stuart Coltherd) *hld up: nt fluent 3 out (usual 4 out): stdy hdwy bef next: effrt and ev ch whn carried lft bef last: edgd rt and led last 75yds: styd on wl* **3/1**[1]
05-6 **2** *1 3/4* **Solway Prince**[11] 79 6-11-5 **92**.............................. RyanDay(7) 91
(Lisa Harrison) *trckd ldrs: led 2 out: sn rdn: hung lft bef last: hdd and no ex last 75yds* **4/1**[2]
F00- **3** *3 1/2* **Jackofhearts**[20] 5489 7-10-11 **80**.............................. JonathanEngland(3) 77
(Jean McGregor) *in tch: stdy hdwy passing omitted 3 out: outpcd bef next: rallied and edgd lft run-in: kpt on: nt rch first two* **14/1**
/P2- **4** *5* **Marlee Massie (IRE)**[315] 834 6-11-0 **80**..........................(p) LucyAlexander 73
(N W Alexander) *mde most to 2 out: rdn and nt fluent last: sn btn* **8/1**
64-3 **5** *1* **Destiny Awaits (IRE)**[11] 79 6-10-3 **74**.............................. CallumBewley(5) 65
(Keith Pollock) *hld up in tch: stdy hdwy to chse ldrs 3 out (usual 4 out): effrt and rdn bef next: sn outpcd* **3/1**[1]
FP/6 **6** *31* **Native Brian (IRE)**[11] 77 9-11-2 **89**.............................. MrRWilson(7) 48
(Andrew Hamilton) *bhd: struggling 3 out (usual 4 out): lost tch bef next: t.o* **20/1**
P-33 **P** **Duhallowcountry (IRE)**[1] 254 9-10-10 **83**.................. MrWHRReed(7)
(Victor Thompson) *disp ld: drvn and outpcd 3 out (usual 4 out): lost tch and p.u bef next* **7/1**[3]
6PP- **P** **Presently Tipsy**[71] 4549 6-10-1 **77**..............................(t) BlairCampbell(10)
(N W Alexander) *unruly and loose bef s: t.k.h: cl up: hit 1st: outpcd 3 out (usual 4 out): lost tch and p.u bef next* **18/1**
4m 8.2s (10.20) **Going Correction** +0.65s/f (Soft) **8 Ran SP% 110.3**
Speed ratings (Par 103): **102,101,99,97,96 82,,**
CSF £14.58 CT £131.15 TOTE £4.50: £1.20, £1.30, £4.10; EX 16.20 Trifecta £72.50.
Owner Tony Whyte **Bred** Mrs A Keoghan **Trained** Selkirk, Borders

FOCUS
The gallop was fair but this was an ordinary contest and only around four lengths covered the first five at the last. The second has been rated as running a hurdle pb.

289 SALUTATION HOTEL PERTH H'CAP CHASE (18 fncs) 2m 7f 180y
7:55 (7:55) (Class 4) (0-120,116) 5-Y-0+ **£6,388** (£1,928; £993; £526)

Form RPR
06/ **1** **Russian Regent (IRE)**[59] 4805 11-11-2 **106**.................. RichardJohnson 122
(Gordon Elliott, Ire) *in tch: nt fluent 9th: smooth hdwy to ld after 3 out: rdn and edgd rt after last: styd on gamely* **7/2**[2]
/04- **2** *1 1/4* **Mister First (FR)**[25] 5399 9-11-12 **116**..............................(t) BrianHughes 131
(Robert Alan Hennessy, Ire) *hld up last but in tch: smooth hdwy to chse wnr 2 out: effrt and swtchd lft after last: kpt on: hld nr fin* **7/1**
6P5- **3** *18* **Settledoutofcourt (IRE)**[29] 5328 9-11-8 **115**.............. GrahamWatters(3) 112
(Lucinda Russell) *led to 4th: cl up: led 4 out: rdn and hdd after next: wknd bef last* **6/1**
244- **4** *23* **Bertie Milan (IRE)**[19] 5518 10-10-11 **101**..............................(v) LucyAlexander 75
(N W Alexander) *chsd ldrs: hdwy to ld 13th: hdd 4 out: wknd fr next* **4/1**[3]
4U-1 **P** **Winged Crusader (IRE)**[7] 141 7-11-12 **116** 7ex(v) SamTwiston-Davies
(Nigel Twiston-Davies) *cl up: led 4th: hit and hdd 13th: drvn after next: wknd bef 3 out: p.u bef next* **6/4**[1]
6m 23.3s (19.30) **Going Correction** +0.65s/f (Soft) **5 Ran SP% 109.0**
Speed ratings: **93,92,86,78,**
CSF £23.70 TOTE £4.90: £1.90, £2.50; EX 22.50 Trifecta £61.10.
Owner James J Reilly **Bred** Sean Breen **Trained** Longwood, Co Meath

FOCUS
An ordinary gallop to this staying handicap chase in which the first two finished clear. A step up from the winner, with the second rated to his best.

290 BRUCE FARMS OPEN HUNTERS' CHASE (FOR THE LINLITHGOW & STIRLINGSHIRE HUNT CHALLENGE TROPHY) (18 fncs) 2m 7f 180y
8:25 (8:25) (Class 6) 5-Y-0+ **£1,871** (£580; £290; £145)

Form RPR
33-1 **1** **Chanceofa Lifetime (IRE)**[7] 143 8-11-11 113.......... MrKitAlexander(3) 112+
(Victor Thompson) *trckd ldrs: smooth hdwy to chal whn lft 5 l clr 2 out: rdn and hung lft run-in: pushed out* **11/4**[2]
3/4- **2** *2* **Royal Chatelier (FR)**[11] 10-11-9 107.............................. MrJamieAlexander(7) 109
(N W Alexander) *chsd ldrs: outpcd 4 out: lft 3rd 2 out: chsd wnr bef last: kpt on run-in: nt pce to chal* **7/2**[3]

4P0- **3** *18* **Indian Print (IRE)**[11] 11-11-5 90........ MrWHRReed(7) 91
(Victor Thompson) *led: hdd whn blnd 3 out: sn outpcd: hld whn lft 11 l 3rd last* **14/1**
0/0- **4** *49* **Chandos (IRE)**[11] 7-11-9 73........ MrTHamilton(3) 38
(Sandy Thomson) *hld up in tch: outpcd 5 out: struggling fr next: t.o* **25/1**
12-U **U** **Special Portrait (IRE)**[14] [17] 11-11-9 109........(tp) MrNOrpwood(7) 114
(Mark Hughes) *pressed ldr: niggled fr 1/2-way: led bef 3 out: sn rdn: jnd whn blnd and uns rdr next* **15/8**[1]
2/3- **U** **Scrum V**[11] 11-11-12 97........ MrJohnDawson 97
(Mrs N Naughton) *nt fluent: hld up: stdy hdwy bef 4 out: rdn and hdwy whn lft 5 l 2nd 2 out: outpcd and 8 l 3rd whn blnd bdly and uns rdr last* **13/2**

6m 36.2s (32.20) **Going Correction** +0.65s/f (Soft) **6** Ran SP% **107.5**
Speed ratings: **72,71,65,49,**
CSF £11.85 TOTE £3.40: £2.40, £3.40; EX 12.40 Trifecta £82.40.
Owner V Thompson **Bred** Mrs Maura T Furlong **Trained** Alnwick, Northumbria

FOCUS
The pace was decrnt in what appeared an ordianry hunter chase, but it was an inconclusive result. A step up from the winner, with the second and third, together with the unseaters, rated to their marks.

291 SCOTTISH BERRIES H'CAP HURDLE (10 hdls 2 omitted) 2m 7f 207y
8:55 (8:55) (Class 4) (0-115,112) 4-Y-O+ £3,798 (£1,122; £561; £280; £140)

Form RPR
46-1 **1** **Isaacstown Lad (IRE)**[7] [139] 8-11-0 100 7ex........ BrianHarding 114+
(Nicky Richards) *hld up on ins: smooth hdwy to ld between last 2: shkn up and sn clr: eased run-in* **5/4**[1]
213- **2** *6* **Snapping Turtle (IRE)**[39] [5133] 10-11-9 109........ DougieCostello 111
(Donald Whillans) *led: rdn bef 2 out: hdd between last 2: no ch w easy wnr* **15/2**
P20- **3** *1 1/4* **Madame Allsorts**[37] [5185] 10-10-9 95........ PaulMoloney 95
(Willie Musson) *hld up: drvn and outpcd 3 out (usual 4 out): styd on fr next: nvr able to chal* **13/2**[2]
016/ **4** *1 3/4* **Ahhdehken**[697] [750] 10-10-0 86 oh7........ BrianHughes 84
(Alistair Whillans) *t.k.h: prom: nt fluent 6th: rdn bef 2 out: one pce between last 2* **25/1**
53-0 **5** *2 3/4* **Indepub**[6] [153] 6-9-11 88........ StephenMulqueen(5) 83
(Lisa Harrison) *hld up: rdn and hdwy bef 2 out: no imp fr last* **16/1**
056- **6** *9* **Daring Exit**[71] [4550] 6-9-10 87........ CallumBewley(5) 73
(Robert Bewley) *hld up in tch: drvn 2 out: sn wknd* **20/1**
526- **7** *3 1/2* **Golans Choice (IRE)**[30] [5310] 6-11-9 112........ CraigNichol(3) 95
(Rose Dobbin) *trckd ldrs: hit 3 out (usual 4 out): rdn and wknd fr next* **7/1**[3]
060- **8** *3 1/4* **Solway Sam**[21] [5473] 12-10-2 95........ RyanDay(7) 76
(Lisa Harrison) *t.k.h in tch: hit 6th: outpcd 3 out (usual 4 out): wknd bef next* **12/1**
524- **9** *4 1/2* **Ryton Runner (IRE)**[21] [5473] 7-10-13 102........(tp) DerekFox(3) 78
(Lucinda Russell) *chsd ldrs: rdn and outpcd whn nt fluent 2 out: sn btn* **10/1**

6m 23.7s (18.70) **Going Correction** +0.65s/f (Soft) **9** Ran SP% **113.3**
Speed ratings (Par 105): **96,94,93,93,92 89,88,87,85**
CSF £11.35 CT £43.93 TOTE £2.10: £1.10, £1.70, £1.90; EX 8.30 Trifecta £70.20.
Owner M S Borders Racing Club & Partners **Bred** Patrick Cronin **Trained** Greystoke, Cumbria

FOCUS
A fair gallop to this staying handicap hurdle which was won by a progressive sort. He's been rated as taking another step forward.
T/Plt: £26.50 to a £1 stake. Pool: £46,022.72 - 1,265.32 winning tickets T/Qpdt: £17.40 to a £1 stake. Pool: £3,494.78 - 148.00 winning tickets **Richard Young**

[61]FONTWELL (L-H)
Thursday, May 14

OFFICIAL GOING: Soft
Wind: blustery Weather: raining and chilly; 10 degrees

292 RACEBETS.COM - CLAIM YOUR £50 WELCOME BONUS! NOVICES' HUNTERS' CHS (GUY PEATE MEMORIAL CHALL TRPHY) (19 fncs) 3m 1f 106y
5:05 (5:07) (Class 6) 5-Y-O+ £1,247 (£387; £193; £96)

Form RPR
0 **1** **Impact Area (IRE)**[15] [13] 9-11-7 0........(p) MrLouisMuspratt(7) 106+
(Mrs Harriet Waight) *sme mstkes: a ldng pair: led tl 5th: blnd 11th: led again after 16th: drvn fr 2 out: hung on gamely flat* **3/1**[1]
P/ **2** *1/2* **Time Is Tickin**[12] 9-11-7 0........ OCdtOswaldWedmore(7) 103
(Miss Rose Grissell) *led 5th tl hit 16th: sn rdn and hdd: kpt pressing wnr hrd after: a jst hld fr 2 out* **25/1**
3 *14* **Heads Or Tails (IRE)**[25] 8-11-7 103........(p) MrJAndrews(7) 88
(S R Andrews) *pressed ldrs: 4 l 3rd and gng wl enough home turn: sn pushed along and grad outpcd by ldng pair* **4/1**[3]
2P- **4** *2 1/4* **John Daniell**[10] 10-11-7 0........ MissABush(7) 87
(Mrs O Bush) *hdwy 4th: 3rd and gng wl at 13th: 5 l 4th home turn: sn rdn and no ex* **7/2**[2]
F/0- **5** *6* **Behind The Scenes (IRE)**[12] 13-11-11 85........ MrPBull(3) 85+
(A Coveney) *j.rt and mstkes: chsd ldrs: last of five gng clr home turn: plugged on and no ch whn blnd 2 out* **12/1**
463/ **6** *2* **Alpha Native**[26] 11-11-7 0........ MissSusannahGill(7) 78
(Alan Hill) *midfield: outpcd 14th: sn wl bhd but plugging on after last* **10/1**
3/ **7** *2 1/4* **Rather Curious (IRE)**[19] 11-12-0 0........(p) MissGAndrews 76
(David Phelan) *chsd ldrs: j. slowly 8th: drvn 16th: sn fdd* **25/1**
5- **8** *13* **Shannon Smacker (IRE)**[38] 10-11-7 0........(v[1]) MrJPearce(7) 66
(Joshua Pearce) *j. erratically and sn wl bhd: nvr travelling: t.o fr 12th* **66/1**
004/ **P** **Broughton Green (IRE)**[38] 14-11-11 0........ MrPGHall(3)
(P G Hall) *mstkes: in rr and nvr travelling: t.o 14th: p.u last* **15/2**
P04/ **P** **Irish Rebel (IRE)**[33] 11-12-0 0........(t) MrTomDavid
(Clare Hobson) *cl up tl lost pl 7th: t.o 14th: p.u 3 out* **20/1**
P **Justforthebuzz (IRE)**[12] 10-11-7 0........ MrWRClarke(7)
(Chris Gordon) *mstkes: pckd bdly 10th: struggling after: t.o and p.u 3 out* **33/1**
060/ **P** **Boy Of Boru (IRE)**[38] 8-11-7 0........ MissRoseGrissell(7)
(Miss Rose Grissell) *mstkes in rr: t.o 12th: p.u last* **12/1**
F **A Country Mile**[18] 7-11-9 0........ MrMatthewBarber(5)
(Marc Barber) *t.k.h and racd wd: pressed ldrs tl fell heavily 10th* **12/1**
P **Printing Blue (IRE)**[32] 7-11-7 0........(p) MrGFBingham(7)
(Chris Gordon) *mstke 1st: bhd: t.o 12th: p.u 14th* **50/1**

7m 15.7s (14.60) **Going Correction** +0.65s/f (Soft) **14** Ran SP% **130.0**
Speed ratings: **104,103,99,99,97 96,96,92, , , , ,**
CSF £87.97 TOTE £4.60: £2.00, £15.30, £1.30; EX 154.60 Trifecta £1634.70.
Owner Miss Harriet Besent **Bred** Hugh J Holohan **Trained** Enford, Wilts

FOCUS
Fences sited on inner down the hill and outer in home straight. Rail movement increased distances by 40yds per circuit. The opening contest was a modest novice hunter chase. They went an honest gallop on ground officially changed to soft after this contest. The winner was building on his Cheltenham run, and there's a case for rating the race higher through the third and fourth, but this is probably high enough at this stage.

293 CALL STAR SPORTS ON 08000 521321 NOVICES' HUNTERS' CHASE (15 fncs) 2m 3f 35y
5:40 (5:41) (Class 6) 5-Y-O+ £935 (£290; £145; £72)

Form RPR
P **1** **Out Of Range**[15] [13] 8-11-7 0........ MrPMann(7) 94
(Mrs Pauline Harkin) *towards rr: rdn and outpcd 11th: 17 l 5th home turn: drvn along and styd on doggedly after: passed two rivals after last to get up on line* **10/1**
5- **2** *hd* **Slidecheck (IRE)**[40] 8-11-7 0........(tp) MrWRClarke(7) 96+
(N Pearce) *drvn along fr 5th: chsd ldrs: led after 12th: mstke 2 out: urged along and plugged on flat: pipped on post* **20/1**
00/ **3** *5* **Anglingforcharlie**[61] 6-11-7 0........ MrNLawton(7) 90
(Miss Beth Childs) *chsd ldrs: effrt 12th: chal 2 out: abt 1 l 2nd at last: rdn and wknd fnl 100yds* **14/1**
0/0- **4** *2* **Here I Am (IRE)**[40] 8-11-7 0........ MissRoseGrissell(7) 90
(Miss Rose Grissell) *t.k.h: led or cl 2nd: led fr 11th: hdd after next: mstke 3 out: blnd 2 out: bmpd along and nt qckn fr last* **9/2**[2]
P **P** **Remarkable Man (IRE)**[15] [13] 9-12-0 0........(p) MissGAndrews
(J P Owen) *pressed ldrs: mstke 5th: pushed along 11th: fdd tamely after next: t.o and p.u 2 out* **7/4**[1]
4P/ **P** **Haughtons Bridge (IRE)**[11] 7-11-7 0........ MrRichardCollinson(7)
(A Pennock) *nvr bttr than midfield: outpcd whn hit 10th: t.o and p.u 2 out* **5/1**[3]
P **Curraigflemens (IRE)**[25] 7-11-11 0........ MrPHall(3)
(David Kemp) *led or cl 2nd tl 12th: wknd qckly: t.o and p.u 2 out* **9/2**[2]
6R5/ **P** **Spiritofchartwell**[12] 7-12-0 0........ MrPYork
(P York) *mstke 4th: in tch: drvn 8th: lost tch 11th: t.o and p.u 2 out* **14/1**

5m 22.9s (15.60) **Going Correction** +0.85s/f (Soft) **8** Ran SP% **116.6**
Speed ratings: **102,101,99,99, , ,**
CSF £159.67 TOTE £15.70: £4.50, £5.10, £4.20; EX 191.70 Trifecta £998.60.
Owner C Padfield **Bred** Paddy Byrne **Trained** Chipping Warden, Northants

FOCUS
A moderate novice hunter chase. They went a respectable gallop.

294 STARSPORTSBET.CO.UK LADIES' OPEN HUNTERS' CHASE (FOR THE STUART ADAMSON MEMORIAL TROPHY) (16 fncs) 2m 5f 31y
6:15 (6:16) (Class 6) 5-Y-O+ £1,247 (£387; £193; £96)

Form RPR
342- **1** **Cygnet**[12] 9-11-5 0........(t) MissJodieHughes(5) 116+
(Mickey Bowen) *j. slowly 1st: pressed ldrs: led 11th tl 13th: rdn and cl 2nd whn mstke 3 out: urged ahd sn after next: readily drew clr* **4/1**[3]
24-3 **2** *9* **Foundry Square (IRE)**[15] [18] 9-12-4 127........ MissGAndrews 116+
(Steve Flook) *rn in snatches and sme mstkes: cl last tl hdwy bef 11th: gng wl enough 13th: 4 l 3rd and rdn home turn: immediately fnd nil and no imp after: 7 l 3rd at last: wnt modest 2nd flat* **11/10**[1]
0P-0 **3** *3 1/2* **Theophrastus (IRE)**[15] [18] 13-11-7 90........ MissAGoschen(3) 101
(J D Sole) *settled cl up in midfield: effrt on outer 11th: led 13th: rdn next: hdd sn after 2 out: plugged on: lost 2nd fnl 100yds* **20/1**
1P/ **4** *2 1/4* **Major Decision (IRE)**[10] 13-11-3 0........(p) MissKatyLyons(7) 99
(Miss J Wickens) *cl up tl hit 12th whn looking outpcd: 4th and struggling bef 3 out* **25/1**
4P-5 **5** *10* **Fort George (IRE)**[15] [18] 12-11-13 120........(p) MissBHampson(5) 98
(Sally Randell) *cl up: j. slowly 5th: hit 11th and nt gng wl enough after: struggling 13th* **11/4**[2]
555- **6** *44* **Wait No More (IRE)**[26] 10-11-3 89........ MissTWorsley(7) 44
(R Gurney) *mstke 6th: led at mod pce tl 11th: rdn and wknd 13th: t.o whn hopped over last: sn eased* **33/1**
2/0- **P** **Terra Bleu (IRE)**[12] 8-11-3 0........(tp) MissPFuller(7)
(W Smith) *cl 2nd tl 10th: drvn and dropped to rr 13th: t.o and p.u 3 out* **25/1**
134/ **P** **Joe The Rogue (IRE)**[19] 8-11-5 0........ MissJBuck(5)
(David Phelan) *reminders 7th: lost tch u.p 10th: t.o next: p.u 13th* **16/1**

6m 7.0s (24.00) **Going Correction** +1.05s/f (Soft) **8** Ran SP% **115.6**
Speed ratings: **98,94,93,92,89 73, ,**
CSF £9.03 TOTE £4.60: £1.40, £1.10, £3.40; EX 11.60 Trifecta £119.50.
Owner Mrs Karen Bowen **Bred** Charlie Wyatt **Trained** Haverfordwest, Pembrokes

FOCUS
A fairly decent hunter chase restricted to lady riders. They went a sensible gallop. The winner has been rated in line with last season's hurdle form.

295 POINTTOPOINT.CO.UK UNITED HUNTS OPEN CHAMPION HUNTERS' CHASE (21 fncs) 3m 3f 45y
6:45 (6:47) (Class 6) 6-Y-O+ £1,871 (£580; £290; £145)

Form RPR
200- **1** **Lets Get Serious (IRE)**[44] [5084] 9-11-3 110........ MrCJMiller(7) 130+
(Dai Williams) *blnd 3rd and 4th: bttr after: mde all: began to draw wl clr after 3 out: totally outstyd his rivals* **50/1**
/1-6 **2** *19* **Doctor Kingsley**[15] [15] 13-11-7 119........ MrPMann(7) 109
(Mrs Pauline Harkin) *wl bhd and nt travelling: 20 l 9th at 15th: t.o next: plugging on fr 3 out: lft remote 2nd at last* **6/1**
3P/F **3** *1* **Ace High**[15] [17] 11-11-5 124........ MrMatthewHampton(5) 114+
(Mrs Janet Ackner) *prom: rdn and gng clr w wnr bef 3 out: sn outpcd by him: 15 l 2nd whn tried to stop nring last and rdr flew into air and lost irons: lunged over and lost 2nd: plodded on* **7/2**[3]
5P1/ **4** *16* **Mr Bennett (IRE)**[38] 12-11-7 0........ MrPBull(3) 98
(Peter Bull) *mstkes: off pce in midfield: hdwy 15th: 5 l 3rd and bmpd along home turn: sn tired and fading: t.o* **16/1**
223- **5** *99* **Orfeo Conti (FR)**[26] 13-11-3 84........ OCdtOswaldWedmore(7)
(Miss Rose Grissell) *wl adrift and nt travelling: struggling fr 9th: bdly t.o bef 3 out* **28/1**
3/1- **P** **Start Royal (FR)**[40] 11-12-0 114........ MissGAndrews
(Alan Hill) *cl up early: lost pl and nt travelling 9th: struggling bdly whn p.u after 15th* **11/4**[1]
P/P- **P** **Showman (IRE)**[19] 12-11-3 54........ MrWHickman(7)
(M S Dilworth) *blnd 2nd and 9th: sn remote: eventually p.u after 15th* **66/1**

6/6- R Court Red Handed (IRE)[33] 10-11-3 115............(tp) MrMJPKendrick(7)
(Mrs S Case) *j. v erratically and a long way bhd: v slow 11th: bdly t.o fr next tl ref 15th* **8/1**
0/F- P Witch's Hat (IRE)[53] 12-12-10 79..............................(t) MrPYork
(R Gurney) *chsd ldrs tl mstke 11th: struggling 15th: t.o and p.u next* **66/1**
/36- P Rey Nacarado (IRE)[33] 10-11-3 109.......................(p) MrJAndrews(7)
(David Phelan) *racd keenly and prom: mstke 15th: ev ch tl 6 l 4th and wkng home turn: v tired whn p.u last* **16/1**
102/ F Adept Approach (IRE)[26] 9-11-7 0............................ MrPGHall(3)
(P G Hall) *pressed ldrs: hit 5th and 7th: slow 10th: effrt 15th: wnt 2nd and gng wl whn fell next* **3/1[2]**

7m 56.83s (29.53) **Going Correction** +1.25s/f (Heav) 11 Ran SP% 119.4
Speed ratings: **107,101,101,96,68** , , , ,
CSF £333.23 TOTE £26.20: £6.00, £2.70, £2.00; EX 232.60 Trifecta £1693.40.
Owner C J Miller **Bred** Stuart Weld **Trained** Broad Hinton, Wilts

FOCUS
The feature contest was a fairly good hunter chase. They went an honest gallop. The second has been rated a bit better than at Cheltenham but still well below last season's mark.

296 WEATHERBYS PRINTING OPEN HUNTERS' CHASE (FOR THE UNITED HUNTS CUP) (13 fncs) 2m 1f 96y
7:15 (7:20) (Class 6) 5-Y-O+ £1,247 (£387; £193; £96)

Form RPR
1F2- 1 Can Mestret (IRE)[38] 5188 8-12-2 111.......................... MissGAndrews 120+
(S R Andrews) *j. soundly and travelled wl: prom: 2nd at 7th: led 10th: cruised clr fr next: 25 l ahd and eased last* **9/4[2]**
1/3- 2 24 Samtheman[23] 5453 10-11-11 93.................................. MissABroome(7) 90
(M J Jackson) *j.rt 7th: led tl rdn and hdd 10th: lost tch w wnr next but remained wl clr of rest* **12/1[3]**
0P-0 3 12 Woodlark Island (IRE)[8] 151 9-11-7 0....................(p) MrHFNugent(7) 72
(A Campbell) *nt fluent and wl bhd: drvn 5th: struggling 7th: 25 l 4th 3 out: plodded on into remote 3rd* **25/1**
/2-0 4 13 Caulkin (IRE)[5] 12-11-7 105..................... MrRichardCollinson(7) 62
(David Kemp) *str reminders after 1st: in rr whn hmpd 4th: hdwy 7th: qckly lost tch w ldng pair after 10th: t.o last: fin v slowly* **12/1[3]**
U22/ P Quarrymount[38] 14-11-7 0.. MrJJCarden(7)
(E J Farrant) *bhd: drvn and reluctant and t.o fr 5th: p.u after 10th* **20/1**
0PP- P Tiermore (IRE)[12] 11-11-7 100...................... MrCharlieMarshall(7)
(Ian Cobb) *drvn and struggling in rr 5th: t.o 9th: p.u last* **25/1**
0- P Empyrean (USA)[19] 7-11-0 0.......................(p) MrTBetambeau(7)
(Mrs Annabel Wheatley) *prom tl 3rd and u.p 7th: lost tch and slow 10th: sn eased: t.o and p.u 2 out* **33/1**
1- U Desertmore View (IRE)[20] 5511 7-11-13 117................. MrJFMathias(3)
(Marc Barber) *2nd and taking a str hold whn pitched bdly and uns rdr 4th* **4/6[1]**

5m 0.9s (26.20) **Going Correction** +1.45s/f (Heav) 8 Ran SP% 121.5
Speed ratings: **99,88,83,77,** , , ,
CSF £25.59 TOTE £3.70: £1.20, £2.20, £5.90; EX 25.60 Trifecta £294.90.
Owner Cliff Myers **Bred** Francis Birrane **Trained** Luton, Beds
■ Stewards' Enquiry : Miss A Broome one-day ban: disobeyed starter (May 28)

FOCUS
An ordinary hunter chase. They went a proper gallop. The second is better on faster ground and has been rated a stone off his best, with the modest third close to his mark.

297 SIS LIVE MARES' HUNTERS' CHASE (19 fncs) 3m 1f 106y
7:50 (7:50) (Class 6) 5-Y-O+ £1,247 (£387; £193; £96)

Form RPR
5/2- 1 Kimora (IRE)[20] 5511 9-11-3 88...........................(t) MrMatthewBarber(5) 101+
(Marc Barber) *settled towards rr: wnt 4th at 7th: 2nd whn mstke 14th: blnd next: led after 16th: rdn and forged clr fr 3 out: all out but game flat* **11/4[2]**
F- 2 12 Cheyanwe (IRE)[26] 11-11-1 0...................(v[1]) MrRichardCollinson(7) 81
(David Kemp) *rn in snatches: prom tl rdn 12th: dropped to rr u.p next: rallied 15th: 2nd and v hrd rdn home turn: plugged on and no ch w wnr after* **9/4[1]**
2P0/ 3 22 Annie Confidential (IRE)[25] 12-11-1 68.................. MissABroome(7) 63
(M J Jackson) *mostly cl 2nd tl led 12th: hdd and lost footing bnd after 16th: lost 2nd bef next: fin tired* **16/1**
4 16 Running In Heels (IRE)[19] 6-11-8 0......................(p) MissGAndrews 51
(David Phelan) *chsd ldrs: blnd 15th: rdn and fdd rapidly after next: sn t.o: v tired whn blnd last: eased* **5/1**
P Zakharyina (IRE)[19] 10-11-1 0............................(p) MissTWorsley(7)
(Steve Spice) *mde most tl 12th: rdn and wknd rapidly bef 16th: t.o and p.u 2 out* **20/1**
/0P- P Kingsfold Flare[26] 8-11-1 0.. MrWRussell(7)
(W Russell) *nt jump wl in rr: rdn 13th: sn t.o: p.u 2 out* **4/1[3]**
P Triggywinkle (FR)[10] 6-11-1 0....................(tp) MissLeandaTickle(7)
(Roderick Chelton) *j. modly: racd in last trio: blnd 9th: rdn 14th: blnd next: t.o and p.u 16th* **14/1**

7m 49.1s (48.00) **Going Correction** +1.65s/f (Heav) 7 Ran SP% 111.4
Speed ratings: **94,90,83,79,** , ,
CSF £9.28 TOTE £3.50: £2.00, £2.60; EX 12.00 Trifecta £84.20.
Owner G M Barber **Bred** R McCarthy **Trained** Amroth, Pembrokes
■ Stewards' Enquiry : Mr Matthew Barber two-day ban: used whip when clearly winning (May 28-29)

FOCUS
A moderate mares' hunter chase. They went a sensible gallop. The winner has been rated as stepping up on her good Chepstow run.

298 STARSPREADS.COM MAIDEN HUNTERS' CHASE (FOR THE CUCKOO MAIDEN CHALLENGE CUP) (16 fncs) 2m 5f 31y
8:20 (8:21) (Class 6) 5-Y-O+ £935 (£290; £145; £72)

Form RPR
1 Full Trottle (IRE)[10] 6-11-9 0...........................(t) MrJonathanBailey(5) 96+
(Miss L Thomas) *hld up wl off the pce in rr: mstke 5th: stl last at 9th: prog in 4th at 13th: led bef next: hrd drvn fr 2 out: all out but a jst holding rivals fr last* **8/1**
/36- 2 1 3/4 Coeur Brule (FR)[24] 5433 9-11-9 93....................... MrDavidTurner(5) 94
(David Turner) *j. slowly 1st: racd v wd: hdwy 8th: led bef 11th: rdn and hdd bef 3 out: abt 2 l down last and no imp after: fin tired* **10/1**
54P/ 3 3/4 Star Of Massini (IRE)[33] 8-12-0 0.............................. MissGAndrews 91
(N W Padfield) *but mostly pressing ldrs: wnt 2nd briefly 13th: sn u.p: continued in 3rd and abt 3 l fr wnr but hld fnl 200yds* **7/2[1]**
4 3 Carnglave Cat (IRE)[12] 9-11-7 0.......................(tp) MissKatyLyons(7) 89
(T D B Underwood) *bhd early: blnd 10th: prog next: cl 5th and pushed along 13th: 4th and no imp fr next: fin tired* **8/1**

05/U 5 54 Midnight King[15] 14 9-11-7 96...............................(t) MrPMann(7) 73
(Mrs J M Mann) *towards rr early: blnd 8th: effrt in 3rd bef 11th: ev ch 13th: drvn and sn dropped out: t.o 2 out and heavily eased last* **4/1[2]**
0/ P Gallaflynn (IRE)[60] 10-11-9 94........................ MrMatthewBarber(5)
(Marc Barber) *chsd clr ldr: mstkes 5th and 6th: clsd on him 7th: led briefly after 10th: sn slowing alarmingly: t.o and blnd 11th: p.u 13th* **12/1**
466/ P Broken Eagle (USA)[61] 7-11-7 100.................................(t) MrJoeHill(7)
(Alan Hill) *led: 12 l clr at 4th: pressed whn mstke 7th: hdd after 10th: rapidly lost pl: t.o and p.u after 13th* **6/1[3]**
P5P/ P Conigre[12] 8-11-7 0.. HarryTeal(7)
(G E Burton) *p.u and dismntd bef 2nd* **33/1**
P P We Never Give Up (IRE)[15] 16 9-11-0 0............(p) MrTBetambeau(7)
(Mrs Pauline Harkin) *sn labouring in rr: last whn blnd 10th: t.o 12th: p.u 2 out* **33/1**
000/ U Sonoftheking (IRE)[18] 7-12-0 0.................................(t) MrDEdwards
(Miss Nicky Martin) *bhd whn blnd and uns rdr 10th* **8/1**
3- P Tompatpeg (IRE)[19] 8-11-7 0............................. MrCharlieMarshall(7)
(David Phelan) *midfield: lost tch u.p after 10th: t.o 12th: p.u 2 out* **16/1**
P Star Rise (IRE)[26] 6-11-11 0................................... MrJFMathias(3)
(Marc Barber) *cl up in gp chsng clr ldr tl 11th: fading qckly whn mstke 13th: t.o and p.u next* **25/1**

6m 20.9s (37.90) **Going Correction** +1.85s/f (Heav) 12 Ran SP% 122.2
Speed ratings: **105,104,104,103,83** , , , , ,
CSF £85.64 TOTE £10.00: £3.90, £4.10, £1.90; EX 107.10 Trifecta £1508.80 Part won..
Owner Norman Thomas **Bred** J O'Keeffe **Trained** Wroughton, Oxon
■ Stewards' Enquiry : Mr David Turner four-day ban: used whip above permitted level (May 28-29,Jun 13,28)

FOCUS
The concluding contest was a modest maiden hunter chase. They went a proper gallop. It's been rated through the second.
T/Plt: £267.00 to a £1 stake. Pool: £54971.58 - 150.26 winning units. T/Qpdt: £13.20 to a £1 stake. Pool: £7331.90 - 410.70 winning units. **Iain Mackenzie**

[285] PERTH (R-H)
Thursday, May 14
OFFICIAL GOING: Soft (good to soft in places)
Wind: Breezy, half against Weather: Overcast, dry

299 PENTLAND LAND ROVER NOVICES' HURDLE (10 hdls 2 omitted) 2m 7f 207y
2:30 (2:30) (Class 5) 4-Y-O+ £3,165 (£935; £467; £234)

Form RPR
1- 1 Antilope Du Seuil (FR)[22] 5469 5-10-12 125..................(p) DarylJacob 121+
(Gordon Elliott, Ire) *nt fluent on occasions: hld up in tch: stdy hdwy 1/2-way: led on bit 2 out: clr last: v easily* **1/3[1]**
564- 2 7 Calivigny (IRE)[22] 5471 6-10-13 116.......................... LucyAlexander 107
(N W Alexander) *t.k.h: prom: effrt and rdn bef 2 out: chsng (clr) wnr whn mstke last: no imp* **7/2[2]**
0/3 3 3 1/2 Have One For Me (IRE)[2] 251 8-10-6 0.................... MrWHRReed(7) 102
(Victor Thompson) *led at slow gallop: rdn and hdd 2 out: sn outpcd* **25/1**
052- 4 12 Kilquiggan (IRE)[123] 3637 7-10-13 95........................... BrianHarding 90
(Sandy Thomson) *nt fluent on occasions: chsd ldr: rdn and ev ch 2 out: sn rdn and wknd* **14/1[3]**

6m 31.0s (26.00) **Going Correction** +0.25s/f (Yiel) 4 Ran SP% 107.8
Speed ratings (Par 103): **68,65,64,60**
CSF £1.91 TOTE £1.40; EX 1.90 Trifecta £6.50.
Owner Simon Munir & Isaac Souede **Bred** Mme Catherine Boudot **Trained** Longwood, Co Meath

FOCUS
Bend on exit from Stands moved from previous day. According the Brian Harding the ground had dried out a little from the previous day but was still riding pretty 'dead'. This was an uncompetitive slowly-run staying novice hurdle. The second and fourth have been rated close to their marks.

300 BOND OFFSHORE HELICOPTERS NOVICES' CHASE (18 fncs) 2m 7f 180y
3:05 (3:09) (Class 5) 5-Y-O+ £3,898 (£1,144; £572)

Form RPR
34-5 1 Tikkandemickey (IRE)[12] 82 9-10-7 119.................... CallumBewley(5) 107+
(Raymond Shiels) *nt fluent: t.k.h: chsd ldr: chal 6th: led 9th: hit 13th: rdn 2 out: styd on wl to draw clr run-in* **5/4[1]**
4- 2 6 Ceithre Delta (IRE)[20] 5514 10-10-5 0.......................... PeterBuchanan 90
(S R B Crawford, Ire) *nt fluent on occasions: chsd ldrs: wnt 2nd 4 out: effrt and rdn bef 3 out: kpt on same pce fr last* **6/1[2]**
63-4 3 13 Senor Alco (FR)[14] 38 9-10-5 79............................... MrWHRReed(7) 83
(Victor Thompson) *j. hesitantly on occasions: led to 9th: chsd wnr to 4 out: rdn and wknd fr next* **10/1[3]**

6m 30.0s (26.00) **Going Correction** +0.45s/f (Soft) 3 Ran SP% 67.8
Speed ratings: **74,72,67**
CSF £2.46 TOTE £1.30; EX 3.20 Trifecta £3.50.
Owner R Shiels **Bred** Alistair Thompson **Trained** Jedburgh, Roxburgh
■ Spirit Oscar was withdrawn. Price at time of withdrawal 13-8. Rule 4 applies to all bets - deduction of 35p in the pound.

FOCUS
Following the withdrawal of Spirit Oscar who was proving mulish both on the way down and at the start this was an uncompetitive and largely uninformative event. The cosy winner has been rated to the level of his previous chase best, with the third to his mark.

301 DM HALL H'CAP HURDLE (FOR THE LADIES CUP FIRST PRESENTED IN 1844) (6 hdls 2 omitted) 2m 110y
3:35 (3:36) (Class 3) (0-130,125) 4-Y-O+
£9,384 (£2,772; £1,386; £693; £346; £174)

Form RPR
003- 1 Street Entertainer (IRE)[26] 5394 8-11-9 122..........(bt) TomScudamore 133+
(David Pipe) *t.k.h: cl up: nt fluent 3rd: led 3 out (usual 4 out): rdn and styd on wl fr 2 out* **7/2[3]**
5/- 2 4 1/2 Seeyouallincoppers (IRE)[14] 46 5-11-3 116........... RichardJohnson 121
(Gordon Elliott, Ire) *hld up: stdy hdwy 1/2-way: chsd wnr gng wl bef 2 out: sn rdn: swtchd rt and kpt on same pce after last* **15/8[1]**
420- 3 13 Thorpe (IRE)[33] 5276 5-11-12 125............................. PeterBuchanan 117
(Lucinda Russell) *hld up in tch: drvn and outpcd after 3 out (usual 4 out): rallied next: no ch w first two* **6/1**
3P6- 4 6 Gold Chain (IRE)[21] 5491 5-11-0 113........................... BrianHughes 99
(Dianne Sayer) *prom: drvn and outpcd fr 3rd: rallied bef last: nvr able to chal* **14/1**

The Form Book Jumps 2015-16, Raceform Ltd, Newbury, RG14 5SJ

20-2 **5** *7* **Peters Grey (IRE)**[8] 142 5-10-13 **112**.................. SamTwiston-Davies 91
(R Mike Smith) *prom: stdy hdwy after 3 out (usual 4 out): rdn and wknd fr next* **10/3**[2]

514- **6** *9* **Circus Star (USA)**[80] 4403 7-11-0 **120**.................. MrJDixon(7) 90
(John Dixon) *led at decent gallop: hdd 3 out (usual 4 out): rdn and wknd bef next* **10/1**

3m 58.4s (0.40) **Going Correction** +0.25s/f (Yiel) **6** Ran SP% **110.1**
Speed ratings (Par 107): **109,106,100,97,94 90**
CSF £10.40 TOTE £3.90: £2.00, £1.60; EX 12.30 Trifecta £43.00.

Owner Mrs Jo Tracey **Bred** Marston Stud And Fleming Thoroughbreds **Trained** Nicholashayne, Devon

FOCUS
Quite a competitive handicap hurdle run at a decent gallop and the first two were clear. The winner has been rated to his best, with the second close to the best of his Irish figures.

302 CLEAN HEELS CONDITIONAL JOCKEYS' H'CAP HURDLE (8 hdls 2 omitted) 2m 4f 35y

4:10 (4:10) (Class 4) (0-120,115) 4-Y-0+ **£3,165** (£935; £467; £234; £117)

Form RPR

221- **1** **Solway Dandy**[21] 5495 8-11-1 **112**.................. RyanDay(8) 118+
(Lisa Harrison) *t.k.h: hld up: stdy hdwy to chse ldrs 1/2-way: led gng wl 2 out: pushed out fr last* **9/4**[1]

/43- **2** *1 ¾* **Jack Albert (IRE)**[31] 5310 8-11-2 **105**..................(b) HarryChalloner 108
(Dianne Sayer) *nt fluent on occasions: led: rdn and hdd 2 out: kpt on fr last: nt rch wnr* **3/1**[2]

400- **3** *3 ¾* **Urban Kode (IRE)**[3] 5490 7-10-4 **96**..................(v) GrahamWatters(3) 95
(Lucinda Russell) *nt fluent on occasions: hld up in tch: stdy hdwy after 3 out (usual 4 out): rdn next: kpt on same pce bef last* **9/2**[3]

000- **4** *15* **Cool Baranca (GER)**[22] 5475 9-10-9 **101**.................. EmmaSayer(3) 89
(Dianne Sayer) *hld up: hdwy after 3 out (usual 4 out): rdn and wknd fr next* **9/1**

243- **5** *7* **Rock Relief (IRE)**[70] 4576 9-11-3 **109**..................(p) DiarmuidO'Regan(3) 85
(Chris Grant) *nt fluent: prom: lost pl and reminders 4th: struggling 3 out (usual 4 out): n.d after* **9/2**[3]

0P-U **6** *11* **The Banastoir (IRE)**[12] 76 6-11-12 **115**.................. CraigNichol 80
(Rebecca Menzies) *chsd ldr tl rdn and wknd bef 2 out* **11/1**

5m 13.1s (11.10) **Going Correction** +0.25s/f (Yiel) **6** Ran SP% **110.5**
Speed ratings (Par 105): **88,87,85,80,77 73**
CSF £9.31 TOTE £2.90: £1.80, £1.80; EX 7.20 Trifecta £27.20.

Owner David Alan Harrison **Bred** D A Harrison **Trained** Aldoth, Cumbria

FOCUS
There was a decent gallop to this handicap hurdle in which the first three finished clear. The second and third have been rated close to their marks.

303 TREND MAGAZINE H'CAP CHASE (18 fncs) 2m 7f 180y

4:40 (4:40) (Class 5) (0-100,93) 5-Y-0+ **£3,798** (£1,122; £561; £280; £140)

Form RPR

32-4 **1** **Solway Legend**[12] 78 8-10-3 **77**.................. RyanDay(7) 86
(Lisa Harrison) *t.k.h: hld up: smooth hdwy to ld 3 out: rdn bef last: hld on wl run-in* **4/1**[2]

236- **2** *½* **Sand Artist (IRE)**[34] 5257 7-10-6 **73**..................(t) RichardJohnson 81
(Gordon Elliott, Ire) *t.k.h: hld up: smooth hdwy and ev ch 2 out: rdn whn nt fluent last: kpt on u.p towards fin* **13/8**[1]

P4-3 **3** *7* **Bescot Springs (IRE)**[1] 287 10-11-9 **93**..................(b) GrahamWatters(3) 93
(Lucinda Russell) *chsd ldrs: rdn and outpcd appr 2 out: no imp fr last* **6/1**[3]

PP0- **4** *7* **Champagne Agent (IRE)**[24] 5423 9-10-10 **77**..................(b) DougieCostello 70
(Donald Whillans) *mde most to 3 out: rdn and wknd fr next* **12/1**

P0-5 **5** *½* **Stoney (IRE)**[8] 141 8-11-0 **88**.................. MrWHRReed(7) 81
(Victor Thompson) *w ldr: drvn after 4 out: wknd fr next* **14/1**

F20- **6** *7* **Marlee Mourinho (IRE)**[70] 4577 9-11-1 **82**..................(t) LucyAlexander 68
(N W Alexander) *chsd ldrs: outpcd 13th: rallied 4 out: wknd bef next* **7/1**

00-3 **7** *3* **The Shrimp (IRE)**[5] 204 8-10-4 **78**..................(b) MrTHamilton(7) 61
(Sandy Thomson) *chsd ldrs: drvn and outpcd 5 out: rallied next: wknd bef 3 out* **7/1**

6m 25.5s (21.50) **Going Correction** +0.45s/f (Soft) **7** Ran SP% **111.7**
Speed ratings: **82,81,79,77,77 74,73**
CSF £10.95 CT £35.96 TOTE £5.80: £2.70, £1.50; EX 12.80 Trifecta £61.70.

Owner Mr & Mrs Batey **Bred** D A Harrison **Trained** Aldoth, Cumbria

FOCUS
A low-grade handicap chase run at an ordinary gallop. The first two have been rated pretty much to their marks.

304 SMALL CITY BIG PERSONALITY VIP LOUNGE H'CAP CHASE (15 fncs) 2m 4f 20y

5:10 (5:10) (Class 4) (0-120,120) 5-Y-0 **£4,431** (£1,309; £654; £327; £163)

Form RPR

04-2 **1** **Mister First (FR)**[1] 289 9-11-8 **116**..................(t) BrianHughes 131+
(Robert Alan Hennessy, Ire) *hld up in last pl: smooth hdwy to chse ldr bef 2 out: nt fluent last: rdn to ld run-in: qcknd clr* **10/3**[2]

06/1 **2** *3 ½* **Russian Regent (IRE)**[1] 289 11-11-5 **113** 7ex.................. RichardJohnson 122
(Gordon Elliott, Ire) *mostly j.lft: cl up: led 8th: rdn bef 2 out: hdd run-in: kpt on same pce* **5/2**[1]

3P5- **3** *20* **Quito Du Tresor (FR)**[21] 5493 11-11-12 **120**..................(p) PeterBuchanan 108
(Lucinda Russell) *trckd ldrs tl rdn and wknd fr 2 out* **14/1**

0P6- **4** *hd* **Authinger (IRE)**[27] 5364 7-11-11 **119**.................. BrianHarding 108
(Barry Murtagh) *in tch: drvn and outpcd 5 out: n.d after* **25/1**

231- **5** *17* **Royal Macnab (IRE)**[20] 5517 7-11-7 **118**..................(t) TonyKelly(3) 89
(Rebecca Menzies) *t.k.h: led to 8th: cl up tl rdn and wknd after 3 out* **5/2**[1]

232- **P** **Silverton**[80] 4404 8-11-7 **115**.................. AdrianLane
(Lucy Normile) *cl up: hit 2nd: outpcd bef 10th: wknd and p.u bef 4 out* **4/1**[3]

5m 11.1s (6.10) **Going Correction** +0.45s/f (Soft) **6** Ran SP% **110.7**
Speed ratings: **106,104,97,96,90**
CSF £12.13 TOTE £5.00: £2.60, £1.40; EX 10.00 Trifecta £65.90.

Owner W Hennessy **Bred** Mlle Glwadis & Mlle Delphine Lardot **Trained** Ratoath, Co Meath

FOCUS
A fair gallop to this handicap chase in which the first two had finished first and second on the course the previous evening. The first two stood out on form over further from the previous day and have been rated to the same marks.

305 BREAKTHROUGH BREAST CANCER TOUCH LOOK CHECK MARES' STANDARD OPEN NATIONAL HUNT FLAT RACE 2m 110y

5:45 (5:47) (Class 6) 4-6-Y-0 **£2,053** (£598; £299)

Form RPR

1 **The Organist (IRE)** 4-10-8 0.................. MrSCrawford 96+
(S R B Crawford, Ire) *in tch: smooth hdwy to ld wl over 1f out: sn pushed clr: eased ins fnl f* **7/4**[1]

2 *3 ½* **Tara Mactwo** 5-10-9 0.................. CraigNichol(3) 92
(Keith Dalgleish) *cl up: rdn over 2f out: rallied and rn green over 1f out: sn chsng (clr) wnr: kpt on: no imp* **6/1**[3]

03- **3** *2 ¼* **Presenting Rose (IRE)**[20] 5520 5-10-7 0.................. StephenMulqueen(5) 89
(N W Alexander) *in tch: hdwy to ld over 4f out: rdn and hdd over 2f out: one pce whn edgd rt over 1f out* **16/1**

4 *1 ¼* **Milan Hart (IRE)** 5-10-12 0.................. WilsonRenwick 88
(Gavin Cromwell, Ire) *hld up: stdy hdwy over 3f out: rdn over 2f out: edgd lft and kpt on fnl f: no imp* **16/1**

5 *3 ¾* **Western Home (IRE)**[53] 5-10-12 0.................. RichardJohnson 84
(Gordon Elliott, Ire) *cl up: rdn and ev ch over 2f out: wknd over 1f out* **15/8**[2]

6- **6** *16* **Miss Joeking (IRE)**[72] 4555 4-10-3 0.................. GrantCockburn(5) 64
(Lucinda Russell) *bhd: pushed along after 5f: drvn and outpcd 5f out: sn struggling* **11/1**

5- **7** *3* **Miss Mackie (IRE)**[40] 5136 4-10-3 0.................. CallumBewley(5) 61
(R Mike Smith) *hld up: stdy hdwy over 4f out: rdn and wknd over 2f out* **18/1**

0- **8** *83* **Jane's Fantasy (IRE)**[72] 4555 5-10-12 0.................. LucyAlexander
(N W Alexander) *led to over 4f out: sn struggling: t.o* **25/1**

4m 0.6s (8.20) **Going Correction** +0.25s/f (Yiel)
WFA 4 from 5yo 4lb **8** Ran SP% **114.6**
Speed ratings: **90,88,87,86,84 77,76,36**
CSF £12.99 TOTE £3.20: £1.20, £2.70, £4.10; EX 13.90 Trifecta £120.80.
Owner Mrs Edith Crawford **Bred** John Browne **Trained** Larne, Co Antrim

FOCUS
Just a fair pace in this bumper in which the winner scored in good style. The third has been rated to her mark.
T/Plt: £14.90 to a £1 stake. Pool: £38,370.95 - 1879.06 winning units. T/Qpdt: £11.80 to a £1 stake. Pool: £2510.40 - 156.35 winning units. **Richard Young**

306 - 312a (Foreign Racing) - See Raceform Interactive

LE LION-D'ANGERS (R-H)

Thursday, May 14

OFFICIAL GOING: Turf: very soft

313a PRIX ANJOU-LOIRE CHALLENGE (CROSS-COUNTRY CHASE) (LISTED RACE) (6YO+) (TURF) 4m 4f 110y

5:30 (12:00) 6-Y-0+

£39,069 (£19,100; £11,286; £7,813; £4,341; £3,038)

RPR

1 **Kick On (FR)**[88] 6-10-10 0.................. DavidCottin 132
(P Cottin, France) **47/10**[3]

2 *8* **Kapville (FR)**[180] 2518 8-10-10 0..................(b) WilfridDenuault 124
(E Leenders, France) **13/2**

3 *shd* **Any Currency (IRE)**[64] 4706 12-10-10 0..................(p) AidanColeman 124
(Martin Keighley) *midfield: rdn after 3 out: styd on wl in st but nt pce of wnr* **11/2**

4 *8* **Quart De Lino (FR)**[102] 10-10-10 0.................. OlivierJouin 116
(P Peltier, France) **23/1**

5 *3* **Roselaine (FR)**[551] 2384 10-10-6 0..................(p) AlbanDesvaux 109
(G Chaignon, France) **49/1**

6 *1 ½* **Posilox (FR)**[102] 9-10-10 0..................(b) RomainJulliot 111
(W Menuet, France) **9/2**[2]

7 *6* **Star De La Prise (FR)**[236] 1588 9-10-10 0.................. SylvainDory 105
(S Dory, France) **57/1**

F **Phakos (FR)**[249] 1473 12-10-10 0.................. AlainDeChitray
(P Cottin, France) **18/1**

F **Toutancarmont (FR)**[64] 4706 8-10-10 0.................. JonathanPlouganou
(Mme I Pacault, France) **6/4**[1]

F **Ulodene (FR)**[19] 5543 7-10-6 0.................. PaulLucas
(P Cottin, France) **38/1**

Owner Magalen O Bryant & Miss Amanda Zetterholm **Bred** Mme M Bryant **Trained** France

AINTREE (L-H)

Friday, May 15

OFFICIAL GOING: Good (hdl 8.2, chs 8.1)
Wind: Moderate, across Weather: Cloudy

314 RACING UK MARES' H'CAP HURDLE (11 hdls) 2m 4f

5:25 (5:30) (Class 4) (0-120,121) 4-Y-0+ **£3,573** (£1,049; £524; £262)

Form RPR

05-1 **1** **Dubh Eile (IRE)**[15] 30 7-10-10 **104**.................. RichardJohnson 117+
(Tim Vaughan) *hld up in rr: mstke 1st: hdwy 3 out: led appr 2 out: asserted bef last: styd on wl to draw clr run-in: comf* **10/3**[2]

21-1 **2** *12* **The Road Ahead**[7] 185 8-11-10 **121** 7ex..................(p) SeanBowen(3) 122+
(Peter Bowen) *hld up: shkn up appr 3 out: rdn 2f out: hdwy whn edgd lft bef last: tk 2nd jst ins fnl f on run-in: kpt on but no ch w wnr* **9/4**[1]

23P- **3** *3 ¾* **Hannah Just Hannah**[104] 3979 6-11-6 **117**..................(t[1]) JamesBanks(3) 114
(Jo Hughes) *in tch: rdn to go 2nd 2 out: no imp on wnr whn nt fluent last: lost 2nd jst ins fnl f on run-in: kpt on same pce u.p* **12/1**

2P0- **4** *7* **Playhara (IRE)**[25] 5422 6-10-12 **109**..................(v) GrahamWatters(3) 99
(Martin Todhunter) *led: rdn and hdd appr 2 out: wknd u.p bef last* **8/1**

2/3- **5** *3* **Ginger Fizz**[38] 62 8-11-0 **108**..................(t) KielanWoods 96
(Ben Case) *in tch: effrt bef 2 out: sn outpcd and btn* **16/1**

222- **6** *4* **Whatdoesthefoxsay (IRE)**[26] 5408 6-11-5 **120**.......... JamieBargary(7) 103
(Donald McCain) *chsd ldrs: rdn and ev ch appr 3 out: lost pl bef 2 out: wknd after* **8/1**

25-1 **7** *1 ¼* **Queen Spud**[10] 130 6-11-3 **111** 7ex....................(p) JakeGreenall 93
(Henry Daly) *chsd ldr: ev ch 3 out: rdn and lost pl appr 2 out: wknd after: edgd lft whn no ch run-in* **6/1**[3]

/12- **P** **Indian Stream**[23] 5470 6-11-9 **117**.................... DougieCostello
(Neil Mulholland) *hld up: pushed along and lost grnd bef 6th: p.u after flight* **15/2**

4m 48.1s (-12.60) **Going Correction** -0.35s/f (Good) **8** Ran SP% **115.7**
Speed ratings (Par 105): **111,106,104,101,100 99,98,**
CSF £11.79 CT £78.33 TOTE £5.20: £1.80, £1.10, £3.70; EX 12.30 Trifecta £124.70.
Owner Paul Bowtell & Jonathan Shinton **Bred** Kevin F O'Donnell **Trained** Aberthin, Vale of Glamorgan

FOCUS
Hurdles sited on inside bends out slightly from inside line and Hurdles increased by 14yds per circuit, Chases by 25yds per circuit. Conditions were described by riders as good (but "probably a bit faster in places", according to Richard Johnson) after this opening mares' event, in which something of a sprint developed up the straight. A big step up from the impressive winner, who should go in again.

315 RACING TOGETHER H'CAP CHASE (16 fncs) 2m 3f 200y
6:00 (6:00) (Class 3) (0-130,127) 5-Y-0 **£6,279** (£1,871; £947; £485; £254)

Form RPR

225- **1** **Lucky Landing (IRE)**[43] 5109 9-11-9 **124**.................... DenisO'Regan 130+
(Tony Coyle) *hld up in rr: clsd and trcking ldrs gng wl 4 out: led appr last: edgd lft run-in: drvn out and kpt on gamely towards fin* **4/1**[2]

26U- **2** *¾* **Gleann Na Ndochais (IRE)**[21] 5517 9-10-13 **117**.................... CraigNichol[(3)] 123
(Alistair Whillans) *in tch: trckd ldrs fr 9th: ev ch fr 3 out: str chal appr last: nt qckn early on run-in: rallied towards fin but hld* **6/1**[3]

2PP- **3** *2 ½* **Lexicon Lad (IRE)**[299] 1024 10-11-3 **125**.................... MissADalton[(7)] 128
(Heather Dalton) *prom: wnt 2nd 5th: w ldr next: led 11th: rdn appr 2 out: hdd bef last: styd on same pce fnl 110yds* **16/1**

21-1 **4** *11* **Abricot De L'Oasis (FR)**[15] 35 5-11-5 **120**.................... HenryBrooke 115
(Donald McCain) *prom: hit 2nd: ev ch 3 out: stl cl 4th and jst coming u.p whn nt fluent 2 out: sn wknd* **11/8**[1]

332- **5** *15* **Chestnut Ben (IRE)**[21] 5509 10-11-1 **123**.................... MrRWinks[(7)] 108
(Peter Winks) *hld up: mstke 9th: pushed along appr 4 out: outpcd 3 out: lft bhd fr 2 out* **6/1**[3]

35P- **P** **Strobe**[21] 5516 11-10-2 **103**....................(p) DougieCostello
(Lucy Normile) *handy: lost pl and mistke 9th: toiling 11th: lost tch 12th: p.u bef last* **33/1**

P6P- **P** **Malibu Sun**[39] 5210 8-11-11 **126**....................(p) NicodeBoinville
(Ben Pauling) *led: hdd 11th: reamined prom tl rdn and wknd appr 2 out: bhd whn p.u bef last* **8/1**

54-P **P** **Indian Voyage (IRE)**[8] 156 7-11-7 **127**....................(t) StephenMulqueen[(5)]
(Maurice Barnes) *hld up in tch: mstke and lost pl 10th: struggling sn after: bhd whn p.u bef last* **20/1**

4m 59.3s (-4.70) **Going Correction** -0.05s/f (Good) **8** Ran SP% **115.4**
Speed ratings: **107,106,105,101,95 , ,**
CSF £28.51 CT £345.24 TOTE £5.10: £1.70, £1.70, £4.20; EX 30.00 Trifecta £304.40.
Owner Gary Dewhurst & Tony Coyle **Bred** James McGrath **Trained** Norton, N Yorks

FOCUS
Quite a well stocked 0-130, with the top six on the card separated by a mere 7lb. The winner has long been well handicapped.

316 DOUGIE PLEWS APPRECIATION NOVICES' HURDLE (9 hdls) 2m 209y
6:35 (6:36) (Class 4) 4-Y-0+ **£3,573** (£1,049; £524; £262)

Form RPR

1 **Hurricane Higgins (IRE)**[42] 7-10-12 0.................... NicodeBoinville 120+
(Nicky Henderson) *chsd ldr: rdn appr 2 out where upsides: led bef last: pressed by str travelling rival run-in: edgd lft and kpt on gamely towards fin* **1/1**[1]

42-1 **2** *1* **Curious Carlos**[9] 147 6-10-9 122.................... SeanBowen[(3)] 119+
(Peter Bowen) *hld up in rr: hdwy to trck ldrs after 1st: ev ch on bit last: upsides wnr: confidently rdn and stl travelling strly run-in: rdn fnl 110yds: edgd lft towards fin and no ex* **2/1**[2]

20- **3** *7* **Hepijeu (FR)**[64] 4731 4-10-8 115....................(t) AidanColeman 110
(Charlie Longsdon) *chsd ldrs: rdn and led narrowly 2 out: hdd appr last where stl ev ch: styd on same pce fnl 150yds* **14/1**

12-1 **4** *5* **Venue**[13] 79 5-11-12 129.................... WilsonRenwick 123
(Donald McCain) *jinked and w.r.s whn tape released but stl led: mstke 2nd: mstke 4 out: rdn whn hit and hdd 2 out: no ex bef last: wl btn run-in* **9/2**[3]

030- **5** *6* **Theatre Act**[33] 5299 4-9-10 0.................... DiarmuidO'Regan[(5)] 92
(Chris Grant) *hld up: outpcd bef 3 out: no imp after* **66/1**

4m 9.1s (-4.60) **Going Correction** -0.35s/f (Good)
WFA 4 from 5yo+ 18lb **5** Ran SP% **109.7**
Speed ratings (Par 105): **96,95,92,89,87**
CSF £3.38 TOTE £2.00: £1.30, £1.60; EX 3.60 Trifecta £17.00.
Owner A D Spence **Bred** Paul Nataf **Trained** Upper Lambourn, Berks

FOCUS
Two previous winners and a former classy Flat performer rendered this a respectable little novice hurdle for the time of year. The pace was fair. The winner is entitled to rate a lot higher on Flat form and should win more hurdles.

317 AINTREE GOLF COURSE H'CAP HURDLE (11 hdls) 2m 4f
7:05 (7:05) (Class 2) 4-Y-0+
£11,573 (£3,418; £1,709; £854; £427; £214)

Form RPR

1 **1** **Virgilio (FR)**[6] 208 6-10-5 **125** 7ex....................(t) HarrySkelton 137+
(Dan Skelton) *trckd ldrs: wnt 2nd after 4 out: led between last 2: outj. rival last: styd on wl to draw clr fnl 110yds* **11/8**[1]

430- **2** *6* **Sea Lord (IRE)**[27] 5390 8-11-12 **146**.................... AidanColeman 149
(John Ferguson) *prom: chsd ldr bef 3rd: lost 2nd after 4 out but stl there: rdn whn chalng 2 out: upsides wnr whn mstke last: no ex fnl 110yds* **8/1**

/2P- **3** *1 ¼* **River Maigue (IRE)**[140] 3246 8-11-6 **140**.................... PeterCarberry 141
(Nicky Henderson) *midfield: hdwy after 4 out: rdn whn chsng ldrs bef 2 out: wnt 3rd at last: kpt on but nt get to front two* **16/1**

/05- **4** *4* **Royal Irish Hussar (IRE)**[117] 3854 5-11-6 **140**....................(p) DavidBass 138
(Nicky Henderson) *racd keenly: led: nt fluent 6th: rdn and hdd between last 2: kpt on same pce after* **8/1**

00-0 **5** *1 ¾* **Vulcanite (IRE)**[13] 96 8-11-8 **142**.................... WillKennedy 139
(Charlie Longsdon) *trckd ldrs: hit 6th: lost pl bef 3 out: rdn and outpcd bef 2 out: kpt on u.p run-in but no ch* **22/1**

522- **6** *½* **Kayf Blanco**[21] 5508 6-10-5 **125**.................... PaulMoloney 120
(Graeme McPherson) *hld up in rr: hdwy appr 2 out: rdn whn chsng ldrs bef last: sn one pce and no imp* **16/1**

411- **7** *5* **Tanerko Emery (FR)**[22] 5491 9-11-5 **142**....................(t) SeanBowen[(3)] 134
(Peter Bowen) *hld up: pushed along appr 3 out: outpcd and n.d fr 2 out* **6/1**[2]

/P4- **8** *15* **Hazy Tom (IRE)**[70] 4609 9-10-5 **125**....................(p) NoelFehily 102
(Alan McCabe) *prom tl wknd 4 out* **33/1**

3P2- **9** *26* **Meadowcroft Boy**[23] 5475 6-10-11 **134**....................(t[1]) CraigNichol[(3)] 88
(Alistair Whillans) *hld up: hdwy into midfield 4 out: wknd 3 out* **20/1**

011/ **P** **Franciscan**[394] 5353 7-11-5 **139**.................... WilsonRenwick
(Donald McCain) *hld up: hit 5th: struggling after 4 out: t.o whn p.u bef 3 out* **33/1**

611- **U** **Remind Me Later (IRE)**[24] 5441 6-10-6 **126**.................... LeightonAspell 122
(Gary Moore) *midfield: hdwy after 4 out: shkn up in 4th abt 3 l off the pce whn blnd bdly and uns rdr 2 out* **13/2**[3]

4m 47.9s (-12.80) **Going Correction** -0.35s/f (Good) **11** Ran SP% **118.7**
Speed ratings (Par 109): **111,108,108,106,105 105,103,97,87,**
CSF £12.68 CT £124.88 TOTE £2.30: £1.20, £2.70, £6.10; EX 12.60 Trifecta £147.50.
Owner C J Edwards, D Futter, A H Rushworth **Bred** Francois-Marie Cottin **Trained** Alcester, Warwicks

FOCUS
A fairly strong renewal, but relatively few got into it off the decent pace and the well-handicapped bottomweight cleaned up. Solid-looking form.

318 RACING UK IPAD APP H'CAP CHASE (19 fncs) 3m 210y
7:40 (7:40) (Class 2) 5-Y-0+
£13,936 (£4,144; £2,076; £1,039; £526; £270)

Form RPR

206- **1** **Bear's Affair (IRE)**[36] 5241 9-11-5 **145**.................... FreddieMitchell[(7)] 152
(Nicky Henderson) *midfield: hdwy appr 12th: chsd ldrs bef 3 out: styd on to ld narrowly last: gamely prevailed in driving fin* **7/2**[1]

6F1- **2** *hd* **Samingarry (FR)**[39] 5184 8-11-7 **140**....................(vt) TomScudamore 147
(Nigel Hawke) *prom: led appr 3rd: hdd 14th: led again next: rdn after 2 out: hdd narrowly last: styd on gamely: jst hld in driving fin* **5/1**[2]

135- **3** *2 ¾* **Lamool (GER)**[62] 4752 8-11-0 **133**....................(t) RichardJohnson 137
(Tim Vaughan) *hld up: hdwy appr 3 out: rdn and no real imp bef last: styd on run-in: tk 3rd towards fin* **7/1**

420- **4** *¾* **Drop Out Joe**[27] 5392 7-11-1 **134**....................(t) GavinSheehan 140
(Charlie Longsdon) *led: hdd appr 3rd: remained prom: nt fluent 6th: led again 14th: hdd next: rdn along and sltly outpcd bef 4 out: rallied to chal bef 3 out: stl cl 3rd u.p last: no ex fnl 110yds* **11/2**[3]

01-1 **5** *9* **Express Du Berlais (FR)**[14] 62 6-10-5 **124**....................(t) WillKennedy 122
(Dr Richard Newland) *hld up: mstke and rdr briefly lost iron 2nd: in rr: reminders after 10th: hdwy 14th: rdn and hung lft appr 2 out: sn no imp: one pce and wl btn bef last* **7/2**[1]

435- **6** *5* **Benefit Cut (IRE)**[30] 5342 9-10-11 **130**....................(t) BrendanPowell 121
(Stuart Edmunds) *in tch: prom after 11th: wnt 2nd after 15th: lost 2nd bef 3 out: wknd bef 2 out* **14/1**

445- **7** *29* **Mwaleshi**[28] 5363 10-11-6 **139**.................... SeanQuinlan 104
(Sue Smith) *handy: mstke 2nd: rdn and wknd after 15th* **22/1**

0BP- **U** **Across The Bay (IRE)**[34] 5275 11-11-6 **139**....................(bt) WilsonRenwick
(Donald McCain) *midfield on outer whn j.lft and uns rdr 1st* **25/1**

125- **P** **Carrigdhoun (IRE)**[23] 5472 10-10-8 **132**....................(tp) StephenMulqueen[(5)]
(Maurice Barnes) *racd keenly: prom: j. slowly and lost pl 12th: wl bhd whn p.u bef 15th* **28/1**

0P1- **P** **Hollow Blue Sky (FR)**[41] 5141 8-9-10 **122**....................(tp) JamieBargary[(7)]
(Nigel Twiston-Davies) *nt jump wl: in tch: lost pl 5th: rdn appr 14th: wl bhd whn p.u bef 3 out* **15/2**

6m 21.5s (-8.50) **Going Correction** -0.05s/f (Good) **10** Ran SP% **119.1**
Speed ratings: **111,110,110,109,106 105,96, ,**
CSF £21.89 CT £118.26 TOTE £3.70: £1.80, £2.30, £2.80; EX 20.50 Trifecta £119.00.
Owner G B Barlow **Bred** T J Whitley **Trained** Upper Lambourn, Berks

FOCUS
A competitive heat once again, and sound form.

319 RACING UK IPAD APP RACINGUK.COM/MOBILE H'CAP HURDLE (13 hdls) 3m 149y
8:10 (8:12) (Class 3) (0-135,131) 4-Y-0+ **£5,523** (£1,621; £810; £405)

Form RPR

240- **1** **Masterofdeception (IRE)**[181] 2493 7-11-1 **120**....................(t[1]) WillKennedy 127+
(Dr Richard Newland) *midfield: hdwy 3 out: stmbld whn chsng ldrs 2 out: sn rdn: styd on strly run-in to ld nr fin* **14/1**

01-1 **2** *hd* **Urcalin (FR)**[11] 102 7-11-0 **119** 7ex....................(t) TomCannon 125
(David Arbuthnot) *in tch: tk clsr order 9th: chalng 3 out: rdn bef 2 out: styd on to ld fnl 150yds: hdd nr fin* **5/1**[3]

111- **3** *1 ¼* **Cowslip**[49] 5017 6-10-7 **112**.................... HenryBrooke 116
(George Moore) *hld up: hit 7th: hdwy 8th: rdn to ld 2 out: a hrd pressed: hdd fnl 150yds: kpt on gamely: no ex nr fin* **16/1**

541- **4** *2 ¼* **Aiaam Al Namoos**[130] 3545 6-10-10 **115**.................... BrianHughes 117
(John Wade) *midfield: hdwy appr 2 out: rdn bef last: styd on run-in but unable to chal ldrs* **10/1**

63-1 **5** *4 ½* **Henllan Harri (IRE)**[13] 87 7-11-9 **131**.................... SeanBowen[(3)] 130
(Peter Bowen) *mainly no bttr than midfield: pushed along and outpcd appr 3 out: hdwy 2 out: hit last whn chsng ldrs: one pce* **9/2**[2]

003- **6** *½* **Harristown**[24] 5451 5-11-2 **128**....................(p) GarethMalone[(7)] 127
(Charlie Longsdon) *prom: led 3 out: rdn and hdd 2 out: nt qckn appr last: no ex fnl 110yds* **20/1**

432- **7** *shd* **Kingsmere**[29] 5357 10-11-7 **126**.................... AndrewTinkler 123
(Henry Daly) *hld up: hdwy appr 3 out: rdn and outpcd bef 2 out: edgd lft u.p bef last and run-in: kpt on but nt trble ldrs* **8/1**

6U1- **8** *2 ½* **Lord Wishes (IRE)**[32] 5312 8-11-6 **125**....................(p) LucyAlexander 120
(James Ewart) *prom: rdn and outpcd bef 2 out: nt fluent whn uder press last: one pce* **25/1**

P11- **9** *¾* **Looking Well (IRE)**[32] 5310 6-11-1 **125**.................... DavidMullins[(5)] 119
(Nicky Richards) *hld up: rdn bef 2 out: plugged on fr last: nvr a threat* **3/1**[1]

P02- **10** *9* **Sealous Scout (IRE)**[27] 5400 7-11-3 **122**.................... WilsonRenwick 108
(Donald McCain) *hld up: hdwy into midfield 5th: lost pl 8th: n.m.r and hmpd on bnd after 4 out: n.d* **25/1**

614- **11** *1 ¼* **Rally**[33] 5290 6-11-5 **124**....................(vt) SamTwiston-Davies 109
(Nigel Twiston-Davies) *led: rdn fr 8th: hdd 3 out: wknd appr last* **10/1**

1P0- **P** **Letemgo (IRE)**[90] 4231 7-11-3 **122**....................(t) TomScudamore
(Giles Smyly) *prom: rdn after 4 out: sn wknd: bhd whn p.u bef 2 out* **25/1**

6m 6.0s (-10.30) **Going Correction** -0.35s/f (Good) **12** Ran SP% **118.0**
Speed ratings (Par 107): **102,101,101,100,99 99,99,98,98,95 94,**
CSF £79.24 CT £1133.81 TOTE £16.90: £5.00, £1.80, £3.20; EX 112.90 Trifecta £864.40.
Owner The Berrow Hill Partnership **Bred** Patrick Kinsella **Trained** Claines, Worcs

■ Stewards' Enquiry : Tom Cannon seven-day ban; used whip above permitted level (29th-31th May, 2nd-5th June)

The Form Book Jumps 2015-16, Raceform Ltd, Newbury, RG14 5SJ

Sean Bowen three-day ban; careless riding (29th-31st May)

FOCUS
A decent handicap. Any number of runners still with chances turning in, and a race of changing fortunes right to the end. A small pb from the winner.

320 DBS SPRING SALES "POINT-TO-POINT" BUMPER FINAL MAIDEN NATIONAL HUNT FLAT RACE (AMATEUR RIDERS) 2m 209y
8:45 (8:46) (Class 3) 4-6-Y-O
£6,256 (£1,848; £924; £462; £231; £116)

Form RPR

1 **Chap**[47] 5-11-5 0 MrLeoMahon(7) 112+
(Gabe Mahon) *hld up: hdwy over 3f out: led over 1f out: sn edgd lft: r.o wl to draw clr* **13/2**[3]

2 6 **Push Ahead (IRE)**[33] 6-11-12 0 MissGAndrews 105
(Gary Hanmer) *hld up: hdwy 6f out: led over 2f out: hdd over 1f out: outpcd by wnr fnl f* **20/1**

3 1 ¼ **Pinnacle Panda (IRE)**[12] 4-11-8 0 CharlieDeutsch 99
(Tom Lacey) *trckd ldrs: lost pl 6f out: rdn and hdwy over 2f out: hung rt over 1f out: styd on* **9/2**[2]

4 6 **Petite Power (IRE)**[75] 6-11-7 0 MrJoshuaNewman(5) 98
(Ali Stronge) *cl up: ev ch 2f out: rdn over 1f out: styd on same pce ins fnl f* **16/1**

5 1 **Brake Hill**[33] 6-11-5 0 (p) MrPMann(7) 97
(Mrs Julie Marles) *handy: rdn and nt qckn over 2f out: styd on ins fnl f: nt pce of ldrs* **50/1**

6 ½ **Quinto**[19] 5-11-5 0 MrMJohnson(7) 97
(N J Tinkler) *midfield: hdwy 6f out: ev ch over 2f out: one pce fnl f* **33/1**

7 ½ **Leith Hill Lad**[34] 5-11-9 0 MissCVHart(3) 96
(Miss C V Hart) *sn prom: rdn and ev ch over 2f out: one pce fnl f* **25/1**

8 ½ **Winter Garden (IRE)**[39] 6-11-5 0 MrSeanHoulihan(7) 96
(R G Chapman) *hld up: hdwy 4f out: travelled wl bhd ldrs over 2f out: sn rdn: btn fnl f* **40/1**

9 6 **Only Gorgeous (IRE)**[68] 6-11-7 0 MrMatthewHampton(5) 90
(Sue Gardner) *prom: rdn and wknd over 1f out* **25/1**

10 8 **Kalasaya (IRE)**[39] 4-11-5 0 MrAlexEdwards(3) 79
(Philip Rowley) *midfield: lost pl after 5f: hdwy and rdn 3f out: wknd over 1f out* **12/1**

11 3 ¼ **Play The Ace (IRE)**[11] 6-11-5 0 MrRichardCollinson(7) 80
(A Pennock) *midfield: rdn and lost pl over 4f out: n.d after* **8/1**

12 nk **Bishops Court**[75] 5-11-9 0 [1] MrIChanin(3) 80
(Neil Mulholland) *hld up: hdwy 1/2-way: prom 4f out: rdn 2f out: sn wknd* **10/1**

13 4 ½ **Charmix (FR)**[103] 5-11-12 0 MrWBiddick 76
(Harry Fry) *led: hdd over 4f out: led again over 3f out: hdd over 2f out: wknd over 1f out* **5/2**[1]

14 1 ¾ **The Dark Duchess**[33] 5-10-12 0 MrJTeal(7) 67
(C Brader) *trckd ldrs: lost pl after 5f: n.d* **25/1**

15 4 **Game As A Pheasant**[11] 5-11-12 0 MissCWalton 71
(Mrs C A Coward) *prom: led over 4f out: hdd over 3f out: wknd over 2f out* **50/1**

16 1 ½ **Havana Jack (IRE)**[20] 5-11-5 0 MrNOrpwood(7) 69
(L Kerr) *midfield: rdn 4f out: wknd over 3f out* **40/1**

17 3 ¾ **Twister Mix**[20] 4-11-3 0 MrJMRidley(5) 62
(J M Ridley) *hld up: rdn and outpcd 3f out: nvr a threat* **100/1**

18 shd **Next Surprise (IRE)**[11] 6-11-5 0 (t) DavidNoonan(7) 66
(Mrs Teresa Clark) *midfield: lost pl after 5f: sn in rr* **50/1**

19 25 **Braepark (IRE)**[33] 6-11-5 0 MrABartlett(7) 43
(D J Dickenson) *hld up: niggled along after 5f: sn in rr: t.o* **66/1**

20 20 **Repeal**[11] 5-11-9 0 [1] MissHannahWatson(3) 25
(S Allwood) *in tch: lost pl 10f out: t.o* **66/1**

3m 59.8s (-7.60) **Going Correction** -0.35s/f (Good)
WFA 4 from 5yo+ 4lb **20** Ran SP% **127.8**
Speed ratings: **103,100,99,96,96 96,95,95,92,89 87,87,85,84,82 81,80,79,68,58**
CSF £137.31 TOTE £6.80: £2.70, £4.40, £2.10; EX 131.90 Trifecta £818.20.
Owner Fruits Incorporated, P Castle, Mahon **Bred** John Allen **Trained** Stratford Upon Avon

FOCUS
A British equivalent to the longer-established Irish bumpers confined to horses previously only raced in point-to-points. All bar one had landed at least a maiden this season, and some promising types should emerge. The pace was better than the usual bumper crawl. Nothing to go on bar a fair time but the winner looks above average.
T/Plt: £51.90 to a £1 stake. Pool of £77456.39 - 1087.53 winning tickets. T/Qpdt: £8.00 to a £1 stake. Pool of £6261.01 - 572.05 winning tickets. **Darren Owen**

321 - 327a (Foreign Racing) - See Raceform Interactive

55 BANGOR-ON-DEE (L-H)
Saturday, May 16

OFFICIAL GOING: Good
Wind: fairly fresh 1/2 behind Weather: fine

328 BET ON YOUR MOBILE AT CORBETTSPORTS.COM NOVICES' H'CAP HURDLE (11 hdls) 2m 3f 123y
1:50 (1:50) (Class 5) (0-100,100) 4-Y-O+ **£2,599** (£763; £381; £190)

Form RPR

000- 1 **Dun Scaith (IRE)**[23] 5496 7-11-9 **100** KillianMoore(3) 114+
(Sophie Leech) *mde all: mstke 1st: clr 3 out: v easily* **7/1**

P06- 2 13 **Alwaysrecommended (IRE)**[50] 5011 6-10-2 **76** PeterBuchanan 77
(Jane Walton) *in rr: hdwy 7th: 2nd after 8th: kpt on: no ch w wnr* **4/1**[1]

53-5 3 8 **Young Lou**[10] 148 6-9-7 **74** oh5 (p) JosephPalmowski(7) 67
(Robin Dickin) *nt fluent: chsd ldrs: outpcd 7th: kpt on fr 2 out: tk poor 3rd nr fin* **6/1**[3]

63P- 4 ½ **Harriet's Ark**[42] 5148 8-10-8 **82** MarkGrant 74
(Julian Smith) *hld up in rr: hdwy 8th: poor 3rd appr 2 out: one pce* **12/1**

00-P 5 12 **League Of His Own (IRE)**[14] 90 6-10-0 **74** oh4 (t) TrevorWhelan 58
(Claire Dyson) *in rr: hdwy 7th: 3rd appr 2 out: sn wknd* **7/1**

0U4- 6 31 **Vasco Pierji (FR)**[74] 4549 6-10-13 **87** AdrianLane 39
(Donald McCain) *nt fluent: in tch: hit 6th and 8th: sn wknd: t.o bef 2 out* **6/1**[3]

000- 7 1 ¾ **Garde Freinet (IRE)**[150] 3137 6-9-13 **76** BenPoste(3) 26
(Steve Flook) *in rr: drvn 5th: bhd fr 7th: t.o bef 2 out* **25/1**

4FP- 8 7 **The Backup Plan (IRE)**[140] 3317 6-11-12 **100** WilsonRenwick 44
(Donald McCain) *chsd wnr fr 2nd: hit 8th: wknd next: t.o* **9/2**[2]

6/P- 9 11 **Tropical Bachelor (IRE)**[274] 330 9-10-1 **80** NickSlatter(5) 14
(Pippa Bickerton) *in rr: lost pl 7th: sn bhd: t.o bef 2 out* **10/1**

4m 52.6s (0.60) **Going Correction** -0.475s/f (Good) **9** Ran SP% **112.4**
Speed ratings (Par 103): **79,73,70,70,65 53,52,49,45**
CSF £34.56 CT £176.79 TOTE £4.40: £2.80, £1.20, £7.10; EX 34.20 Trifecta £340.40.
Owner G Doel, RS Liddington & C J Leech **Bred** J Devlin **Trained** Elton, Gloucs

FOCUS
It was fair to say that most of these didn't come into this race in particularly good form, but it was run at a quick pace. The winner returned to the level of his best Irish form.

329 BET LIVE AT CORBETTSPORTS.COM NOVICES' CHASE (12 fncs) 2m 1f 77y
2:20 (2:21) (Class 4) 5-Y-O+ **£3,898** (£1,144; £572; £286)

Form RPR

11- 1 **Long House Hall (IRE)**[31] 5341 7-10-12 0 (t) HarrySkelton 150+
(Dan Skelton) *trckd ldrs: led 8th: hit last: easily* **10/11**[1]

35P- 2 12 **Raven's Tower (USA)**[70] 4633 5-10-12 0 DavidBass 133
(Ben Pauling) *hld up in rr: hdwy 6th: 2nd 8th: kpt on: no ch w wnr* **28/1**

/P3- 3 4 ½ **Kilgefin Star (IRE)**[42] 5130 7-10-12 125 ConorO'Farrell 130
(Michael Smith) *chsd ldrs 3rd: upsides 7th: kpt on one pce fr 3 out* **6/1**[3]

010- 4 27 **Gold Futures (IRE)**[42] 5139 6-10-12 0 BrianHarding 104
(Nicky Richards) *nt fluent in rr: sn bhd: t.o 5th: hdwy 3 out: wnt poor 4th sn after 2 out* **15/2**

30-3 5 19 **Paradise Valley (IRE)**[14] 84 6-10-12 120 BrianHughes 94
(Mick Channon) *chsd ldrs: outpcd in 5th whn blnd 9th: sn wknd* **11/2**[2]

000- 6 6 **Chase The Wind (IRE)**[21] 5539 6-10-12 0 GavinSheehan 81
(Warren Greatrex) *prom early: lost pl 3rd: wl bhd fr 6th* **8/1**

7 30 **Midnight Wishes**[390] 10-10-5 0 LiamTreadwell 47
(Peter Hiatt) *led to 8th: sn lost pl and bhd: t.o 2 out* **100/1**

432/ P **Lisbon (IRE)**[618] 1504 7-10-12 124 (t) JamesReveley
(Patrick Griffin, Ire) *chsd ldrs: 6th and wkng whn mstke and hmpd 9th: sn bhd: p.u bef 2 out* **16/1**

4m 7.8s (-14.30) **Going Correction** -0.475s/f (Good) **8** Ran SP% **115.3**
Speed ratings: **112,106,104,92,84 81,68,**
CSF £26.70 TOTE £1.40: £1.20, £6.80, £1.70; EX 34.90 Trifecta £355.20.
Owner J D Duggan **Bred** R R Clarke **Trained** Alcester, Warwicks

FOCUS
This seemed quite a decent novice event, but it only concerned one horse late on. The winner's time looked noteworthy compared to other races over fences on the card.

330 FOLLOW YOUR BETS NOW @ CORBETTSPORTS.COM "NATIONAL HUNT" MAIDEN HURDLE (9 hdls) 2m 145y
2:55 (2:56) (Class 4) 4-Y-O+ **£3,249** (£954; £477; £238)

Form RPR

34-4 1 **Shear Rock (IRE)**[14] 87 5-11-0 108 RichardJohnson 114+
(Charlie Longsdon) *trckd ldr: led appr 3rd: drvn and styd on fr 2 out* **6/5**[1]

6- 2 13 **Monbeg Gold (IRE)**[150] 3149 5-11-0 0 RichieMcLernon 103
(Jonjo O'Neill) *trckd ldng pair: 2nd 5th: rdn appr 2 out: kpt on same pce: no imp* **2/1**[2]

04- 3 3 ¼ **Bletchley Castle (IRE)**[28] 5402 6-11-0 0 ConorO'Farrell 101
(Seamus Durack) *led tl appr 3rd: kpt on one pce fr 3 out* **7/1**[3]

5- 4 49 **Always On The Run (IRE)**[22] 5520 5-11-0 0 WilsonRenwick 55
(Donald McCain) *in rr: bhd fr 5th: distant 4th sn after 6th: t.o* **16/1**

46- 5 dist **Ho Lee Moses (IRE)**[24] 5462 5-11-0 0 PaulMoloney
(Evan Williams) *nt fluent in rr: mstke 1st: sn bhd: t.o 5th: distant 4th after 3 out: eventually completed* **33/1**

2/4- P **Bear Island Flint**[151] 3136 7-11-0 0 JamesReveley
(Patrick Holmes) *mid-div: hdwy 3rd: sn trcking ldrs: lost pl after 5th: blnd 6th: sn t.o: p.u bef 2 out* **12/1**

0- U **Saint Elm (FR)**[135] 3467 5-11-0 0 BrianHughes
(Patrick Griffin, Ire) *in rr: wl bhd 5th: blnd and uns rdr next* **50/1**

350- P **Wildmoor Boy**[77] 4499 4-10-10 0 CharliePoste
(Robin Dickin) *chsd ldrs: wknd 6th: t.o next: p.u bef 2 out* **16/1**

4m 4.4s (-6.50) **Going Correction** -0.475s/f (Good)
WFA 4 from 5yo+ 18lb **8** Ran SP% **115.6**
Speed ratings (Par 105): **96,89,88,65, , ,**
CSF £3.94 TOTE £1.80: £1.10, £1.10, £1.60; EX 6.70 Trifecta £18.10.
Owner Jones, Smith & Walsh **Bred** Cyril O'Hara **Trained** Over Norton, Oxon

FOCUS
Three came miles clear in a race that was probably just a modest event. The pace was good throughout. The winner set a fair standard and ran to his mark.

331 BET WITH CORBETTSPORTS H'CAP CHASE (15 fncs) 2m 4f 72y
3:30 (3:30) (Class 4) (0-115,114) 5-Y-O+ **£6,498** (£1,908; £954; £477)

Form RPR

50-4 1 **Saddlers Deal (IRE)**[7] 202 10-9-12 **93** (p) CraigGallagher(7) 105+
(Brian Ellison) *hld up in rr: hdwy to trck ldrs 10th: 2nd sn after 3 out: led between last 2: pushed out* **20/1**

/F-1 2 2 ¾ **Owen Glendower (IRE)**[10] 151 10-11-5 **114** CiaranGethings(7) 123+
(Sophie Leech) *hld up in rr: hdwy 10th: sn trcking ldrs: chsd wnr between last 2: kpt on same pce run-in* **3/1**[2]

54-4 3 7 **Bobble Boru (IRE)**[15] 57 7-11-1 **103** LiamTreadwell 105
(Venetia Williams) *w ldrs: led bef 2 out: hdd between last 2: sn fdd: lame* **18/1**

51-3 4 11 **Better B Quick (IRE)**[7] 202 9-10-13 **108** JonathanMoore(7) 100
(Paul Stafford, Ire) *trckd ldrs: rdn and wknd appr 2 out* **10/1**[3]

06-1 5 2 ¾ **Kai Broon (IRE)**[14] 78 8-11-9 **114** (p) GrahamWatters(3) 106
(Lucinda Russell) *w ldrs: led 7th: drvn 3 out: hdd bef next: sn wknd* **16/1**

P43- 6 14 **Kitegen (IRE)**[22] 5509 9-11-8 **110** CharliePoste 87
(Robin Dickin) *chsd ldrs: slipped bnd after 6th: outpcd and lost pl 3 out* **16/1**

634- 7 62 **River Purple**[49] 5034 8-11-8 **110** (t) BrianHughes 31
(John Mackie) *chsd ldrs: lost pl10th: sn bhd: t.o 3 out* **10/1**[3]

311- U **Have You Had Yours (IRE)**[33] 5309 9-11-4 **106** BrianHarding
(Jane Walton) *trcking ldrs whn slipped and uns rdr paddock bnd after 6th* **12/1**

33-1 P **Mor Brook**[15] 57 7-11-8 **110** DavidBass
(Kim Bailey) *nt fluent: led to 7th: pushed along 9th: lost pl 11th: sn bhd: p.u bef 3 out* **11/8**[1]

5m 1.6s (-7.50) **Going Correction** -0.475s/f (Good) **9** Ran SP% **116.6**
Speed ratings: **95,93,91,87,86 80,57, ,**
CSF £82.95 CT £1134.73 TOTE £31.10: £6.30, £2.70, £6.40; EX 109.50 Trifecta £1002.70 Part won. Pool of £1337.02 - 0.01 winning units..
Owner Ms Y Lowe & Brian Ellison **Bred** Patrick Hegarty **Trained** Norton, N Yorks

FOCUS
With four last-time-out winners in attendance, this should be decent form despite the fact that none of them managed to follow up their successes. The winner had slipped to a very good mark.

332 BET ON UK RACING AT CORBETTSPORTS H'CAP HURDLE (9 hdls) 2m 145y
4:05 (4:06) (Class 4) (0-120,120) 4-Y-O+ £3,898 (£1,144; £572; £286)

Form RPR
133- 1 **Good Of Luck**[242] 1539 6-11-4 112 GavinSheehan 123+
(Warren Greatrex) *hld up in rr: hdwy to trck ldrs 5th: led appr 2 out: drvn clr appr last: eased run-in* 8/1
124- 2 11 **Court Dismissed (IRE)**[57] 4891 5-11-11 119 HenryBrooke 116
(Donald McCain) *led tl after 2nd: led after 6th: hdd appr 2 out: kpt on same pce* 4/1[2]
615- 3 1 **There Is No Point (IRE)**[58] 4869 6-11-9 120 (t) MauriceLinehan(3) 116
(Jonjo O'Neill) *trckd ldrs: cl 2nd 3 out: kpt on same pce fr next* 14/1
05-P 4 1¼ **Too Scoops (IRE)**[9] 162 8-11-12 120 (t) DarylJacob 116
(Richard Woollacott) *chsd ldrs: drvn after 3 out: 4th and one pce whn mstke last* 14/1
413- 5 9 **Heist (IRE)**[29] 5382 5-11-7 115 (t) BrianHughes 103
(Patrick Griffin, Ire) *in rr: outpcd and pushed along 5th: lost pl next: modest 5th bef 2 out: nvr a factor* 5/2[1]
414- 6 40 **It's A Mans World**[29] 5361 9-11-3 118 GLavery(7) 69
(Brian Ellison) *last and sn drvn along: sme hdwy after 4th: lost pl 6th: sn bhd: t.o 3 out* 7/1
5-33 7 5 **Watt Broderick (IRE)**[12] 110 6-10-13 112 (t) RobMcCarth(5) 58
(Ian Williams) *w ldr: led after 2nd: hdd after 6th: sn lost pl and bhd: t.o 2 out* 9/2[3]
0 P **Hairy O'Malley (IRE)**[12] 110 6-10-11 105 PaulMoloney
(Evan Williams) *trckd ldrs: p.u after 4th* 12/1
4m 3.2s (-7.70) **Going Correction** -0.475s/f (Good) 8 Ran SP% 111.4
Speed ratings (Par 105): **99,93,93,92,88 69,67,**
CSF £38.42 CT £430.14 TOTE £6.90: £3.30, £1.80, £1.90; EX 34.60 Trifecta £151.00.
Owner Mr & Mrs Bernard Panton **Bred** Mrs G Slater **Trained** Upper Lambourn, Berks

FOCUS
The bend after passing the winning post was sanded after runners slipped up in the previous race at that point. These modest hurdlers were well grouped early on. A big step up from the winner.

333 CORBETTSPORTS AT WATERGATE STREET CHESTER H'CAP CHASE (18 fncs) 3m 30y
4:40 (4:40) (Class 5) (0-100,98) 5-Y-O+ £3,079 (£897; £449)

Form RPR
/11- 1 **It Is What It Is (IRE)**[262] 1350 8-11-10 96 WillKennedy 107+
(Jonjo O'Neill) *trckd ldrs: upsides 4th: led 13th: styd on strly: readily* 9/4[1]
/6-1 2 2½ **Interpleader**[16] 44 10-10-9 88 (tp) MrMartinMcIntyre(7) 101+
(Sheila Lewis) *trckd ldrs 3rd: hit 12th: clr 2nd 3 out: keeping on same pce and looking hld whn mstke last* 9/4[1]
52-P 3 24 **Dr Dreamy (IRE)**[15] 66 8-10-3 75 (t) TrevorWhelan 64
(Claire Dyson) *hld up: hdwy to chse ldrs 12th: outpcd 3 out: one pce* 9/1
1UP- 4 hd **Foot The Bill**[22] 5518 10-11-8 94 JamesReveley 81
(Patrick Holmes) *w ldr: led after 2nd: drvn and hdd 13th: outpcd 3 out: one pce* 11/2[2]
43-P 5 2¼ **Midnight Dove**[7] 211 10-9-7 72 oh4 MichaelHeard(7) 57
(Andrew Price) *led tl after 2nd: chsd ldrs: reminder 5th: drvn 8th: lost pl after 14th: sn bhd* 7/1[3]
01U- 6 13 **Solway Bay**[234] 1613 13-10-11 90 (t) RyanDay(7) 63
(Lisa Harrison) *hld up detached in last: effrt 12th: bhd fr 15th* 14/1
22-0 7 8 **West Ship Master (IRE)**[10] 140 11-11-5 98 (p) JonathanMoore(7) 67
(Paul Stafford, Ire) *hld up: chsd ldrs 9th: pushed along 11th: lost pl 14th: sn bhd* 8/1
6m 6.1s (-13.70) **Going Correction** -0.475s/f (Good) 7 Ran SP% 117.2
Speed ratings: **102,101,93,93,92 88,86**
CSF £7.78 CT £26.27 TOTE £2.70: £2.40, £2.20; EX 14.20 Trifecta £89.40.
Owner John P McManus **Bred** Bill Ronayne **Trained** Cheltenham, Gloucs
■ St Gregory was withdrawn. Price at time of withdrawal 4-1. Rule 4 applies to bets struck prior to withdrawal but not to SP bets - deduction 20p in the pound. New market formed.

FOCUS
Probably not a strong contest, and the two market leaders pulled well clear. The winner is on the upgrade and there should be more to come.

334 PROPERTY & THOROUGHBRED SERVICES LTD MARES' STANDARD OPEN NATIONAL HUNT FLAT RACE 2m 145y
5:15 (5:15) (Class 5) 4-6-Y-O £3,079 (£897; £449)

Form RPR
1 **The Nipper (IRE)** 4-10-8 0 GavinSheehan 117+
(Warren Greatrex) *mde all: wnt clr 6f out: shkn up over 2f out: styd on strly: unchal* 15/8[1]
32- 2 19 **Actinpieces**[40] 5193 4-10-3 0 BridgetAndrews(5) 98
(Pam Sly) *trckd wnr: kpt on same pce to regain 2nd appr fnl f* 8/1
223- 3 4½ **Ethelwyn**[228] 1681 5-10-12 0 BrianHughes 99
(Malcolm Jefferson) *trckd ldrs: modest 2nd over 3f out: fdd fnl f* 9/1
4 5 **Baby Bee Jay** 4-10-1 0 JamieBargary(7) 89
(Nigel Twiston-Davies) *hld up in mid-div: drvn 6f out: kpt on fnl 3f* 13/2[3]
5 1 **Midnight Gem** 5-10-12 0 WayneHutchinson 93
(Charlie Longsdon) *hld up in rr: hdwy 8f out: drvn 6f out: kpt on one pce fnl 4f* 8/1
6 3¾ **Myrtle Drive (IRE)** 4-10-8 0 AdrianLane 85
(Donald McCain) *mid-div: hdwy 6f out: sn chsng ldrs: wknd fnl 3f* 16/1
7 24 **Midnight Target** 5-10-9 0 HarryChalloner(3) 68
(John Groucott) *in rr: pushed along 8f out: bhd fnl 6f: t.o 3f out* 50/1
8 1¾ **Roztoc (IRE)** 5-10-12 0 RichardJohnson 66
(S R B Crawford, Ire) *in rr: sme hdwy 8f out: drvn 6f out: sn lost pl: bhd 3f out: t.o* 5/2[2]
9 8 **Cloudburst** 4-10-5 0 ThomasGarner(3) 55
(Oliver Sherwood) *in rr: bhd and drvn 6f out: sn t.o* 20/1
10 49 **Bonnie Black Rose** 5-10-12 0 NickScholfield 15
(Arthur Whiting) *prom: lost pl 7f out: sn bhd: tailed rt off 4f out: eventually completed* 40/1
0- 11 9 **Revoque Dokey**[24] 5468 4-10-8 0 (p) PeterCarberry 3
(Brian Eckley) *prom: reminders 7f out: sn lost pl and bhd: tailed rt off 4f out: eventually completed* 100/1
3m 54.6s (-10.70) **Going Correction** -0.475s/f (Good)
WFA 4 from 5yo+ 4lb 11 Ran SP% 124.9
Speed ratings: **106,97,94,92,92 90,79,78,74,51 47**
CSF £19.01 TOTE £3.50: £3.20, £2.20, £2.50; EX 29.70 Trifecta £121.70.
Owner Smith, Ratcliffe & Bowring **Bred** W L Smith & Partners **Trained** Upper Lambourn, Berks

FOCUS
Some leading stables had runners in this, but a well-fancied newcomer destroyed her rivals under front-running tactics. She looks a smart mare.
T/Plt: £32.60 to a £1 stake. Pool: £44898.81 - 1002.37 winning tickets. T/Qpdt: £13.90 to a £1 stake. Pool: £3619.41 - 191.5 winning tickets. **Walter Glynn**

[146]UTTOXETER (L-H)
Saturday, May 16

OFFICIAL GOING: Good
Wind: light breeze Weather: sunny; 16 degrees

335 PEKTRON NOVICES' HURDLE (10 hdls) 2m 3f 207y
5:30 (5:32) (Class 4) 4-Y-O+ £3,249 (£954; £477; £238)

Form RPR
52U- 1 **Berea Venture (IRE)**[22] 5510 7-10-12 119 DonalDevereux 118+
(Peter Bowen) *tall chsng type: mde all: set stdy pce: j.rt 2nd and 6th: gng best after next: hit 3 out: 4 l clr and in command last: rdn out* 7/4[1]
30- 2 2½ **Set List (IRE)**[193] 2263 6-10-12 0 AidanColeman 114
(Emma Lavelle) *t.k.h early: chsd wnr: shkn up bef 3 out: hrd drvn whn hit next: outpcd bef last and wl hld after* 7/4[1]
021- 3 7 **Dire Straits (IRE)**[22] 5521 4-10-7 115 (b) LizzieKelly(7) 113+
(Neil King) *pressed ldng pair: bdly hmpd by loose horse 4th: wnt rt and blnd bdly 6th: rdn bef 3 out: one pce and n.d fr next* 11/4[2]
2/0- 4 26 **Flashyfrank**[163] 2908 6-10-12 0 AndrewTinkler 86
(Tim Fitzgerald) *chsd ldrs: rdn and lost tch wl bef 3 out: mstke last: t.o* 16/1[3]
0- 5 3 **Sir Bentley**[23] 5501 5-10-12 0 AndrewThornton 81
(Caroline Bailey) *bhd: mstke 7th and drvn: sn lost tch: t.o next* 40/1
P0P- P **Bien Faire (IRE)**[61] 4816 5-10-12 0 (bt[1]) RachaelGreen
(Anthony Honeyball) *a last: drvn and lost tch 7th: sn bdly t.o: p.u bef last: injured* 66/1
0- U **Double Court (IRE)**[34] 5292 4-10-7 0 DaveCrosse
(Nigel Twiston-Davies) *bhd: blnd 1st: blnd again next and shot rdr out of sddle* 25/1
4m 58.3s (-4.90) **Going Correction** 0.0s/f (Good)
WFA 4 from 5yo+ 19lb 7 Ran SP% 113.1
Speed ratings (Par 105): **101,100,97,87,86 ,**
CSF £5.08 TOTE £3.10: £2.10, £2.20; EX 5.60 Trifecta £9.10.
Owner Ashley Hart **Bred** Mrs Liz O'Leary **Trained** Little Newcastle, Pembrokes

FOCUS
Hurdles moved in 4yds from meeting on May 6th and distances increased by 66yds per circuit. Divided bends on fresher ground. The opening contest was a fair novice hurdle. They went an initially modest gallop on good ground. Straightforward form.

336 CRABBIE'S ORIGINAL ALCOHOLIC GINGER BEER H'CAP HURDLE (9 hdls) 2m
6:00 (6:02) (Class 5) (0-100,100) 4-Y-O+ £2,339 (£686; £343; £171)

Form RPR
43-1 1 **Baraboy (IRE)**[11] 137 5-11-7 93 DiarmuidO'Regan(5) 99
(Barry Murtagh) *trckd ldrs: 4th and gng wl after 6th: produced to ld last: rdn and kpt on wl flat* 11/2[3]
552- 2 ¾ **Supernoverre (IRE)**[229] 1661 9-10-10 77 (b) BrendanPowell 82
(Alan Jones) *cl up: rdn to go 2nd and ev ch 2 out: urged along but a jst hld fr last* 8/1
540- 3 1 **Sambulando (FR)**[22] 5516 12-11-9 90 (p) AlainCawley 95
(Richard Hobson) *prom: jnd ldr 5th: led bef 3 out: rdn and nt fluent next: hdd last: one pce flat* 12/1
050- 4 1¼ **Multiview**[332] 733 6-11-0 84 BenPoste(3) 88
(Tom Symonds) *hit 5th: in last pair but wl in tch tl effrt bef 3 out: wnt 4th 2 out: styng on same pce whn awkward last* 50/1
465- 5 13 **Significant Move**[148] 3171 8-10-11 83 ChrisWard(5) 74
(Dr Richard Newland) *hld up towards rr: rdn after 3 out: no rspnse and btn next* 5/2[2]
54-0 6 1 **Going Nowhere Fast (IRE)**[9] 180 10-10-8 82 JordanWilliams(7) 73
(Bernard Llewellyn) *j. bdly: chsd ldrs: rdn 3 out: btn whn blnd next* 12/1
04-1 7 20 **Zarawi (IRE)**[6] 224 4-12-1 100 7ex (p) AidanColeman 68
(Charlie Longsdon) *racd freely in ld: jnd 5th: rdn and hdd 3 out: stopped v qckly: t.o* 7/4[1]
540- 8 20 **Roskilly (IRE)**[23] 5490 4-11-8 93 (bt) WilsonRenwick 43
(Donald McCain) *in tch tl last and drvn after 6th: fnd nil: t.o 2 out* 14/1
3m 52.5s (0.50) **Going Correction** 0.0s/f (Good) 8 Ran SP% 115.4
Speed ratings (Par 103): **98,97,97,96,90 89,79,69**
CSF £48.11 CT £506.82 TOTE £5.30: £1.80, £2.30, £3.50; EX 43.10 Trifecta £366.30.
Owner Anthony White **Bred** Holborn Trust Co **Trained** Low Braithwaite, Cumbria

FOCUS
A modest handicap hurdle. They went an honest gallop. The winner is rated in line with his recent win allowing for the jockey's claim.

337 SSJ ELECTRICAL H'CAP HURDLE (10 hdls) 2m 3f 207y
6:30 (6:30) (Class 5) (0-100,97) 4-Y-O+ £2,339 (£686; £343; £171)

Form RPR
566- 1 **Fire Tower**[55] 4948 7-11-10 95 (t) AidanColeman 101+
(Richard Phillips) *settled towards rr: smooth effrt in 3rd bef 3 out where jnd ldr: sn led: rdn bef last: styd on wl and comf on top fnl 100yds* 7/4[1]
000- 2 1¼ **Darnitnev**[35] 5281 5-11-12 97 AndrewTinkler 101
(Martin Keighley) *settled in last pair: 4 l 6th home turn: effrt to dispute 2nd 2 out: sn drvn: ev ch last: no ex fnl 100yds* 14/1
04-5 3 15 **The Late Shift**[14] 79 5-11-8 93 HenryBrooke 84
(Barry Murtagh) *cl up: rdn bef 3 out where w ldr: btn next: 7 l 3rd whn hit last* 10/1
63-0 4 10 **Gwili Spar**[12] 106 7-10-1 72 (t) DaveCrosse 56
(Laura Hurley) *settled in last pair: nt fluent 6th: shortlived effrt bef 3 out: sn racing awkwardly u.p: wl btn bef next* 7/1
003- 5 ¾ **Irish Octave (IRE)**[28] 5398 5-11-0 88 BenPoste(3) 69
(Rosemary Gasson) *t.k.h: nt fluent 1st: led at mod pce: 5 l clr after 5th: mstke 7th: hdd bef 3 out and rapidly dropped out* 5/1[3]
/02- 6 35 **Icanmotor**[350] 540 8-10-9 80 (tp) TrevorWhelan 29
(Claire Dyson) *2nd or 3rd tl led bef 3 out where hdd and drvn: rapidly dropped out: t.o* 9/1
30P- P **Laird Of Monksford (IRE)**[77] 4491 6-11-5 90 (t) WilsonRenwick
(Donald McCain) *kpt jumping awkwardly: 2nd or 3rd tl rdn 5th: sn bhd: dropped bk to last at 7th and qckly t.o: p.u 3 out* 4/1[2]
4m 59.5s (-3.70) **Going Correction** 0.0s/f (Good) 7 Ran SP% 111.3
Speed ratings (Par 103): **99,98,92,89,88 75,**
CSF £23.09 CT £183.72 TOTE £2.60: £1.70, £7.60; EX 30.30 Trifecta £353.60.

Owner The Firebirds **Bred** Mrs S C Welch **Trained** Adlestrop, Gloucs

FOCUS

A moderate handicap hurdle. They went an ordinary gallop. The winner rates back to her best.

338 SIR STANLEY CLARKE MEMORIAL H'CAP CHASE (11 fncs 1 omitted) 2m

7:00 (7:00) (Class 4) (0-120,118) 5-Y-0+ **£4,684** (£1,383; £691; £346; £173)

Form RPR

05-1 **1** **Strongly Suggested**[9] 175 8-11-7 **113**........................ RichieMcLernon 127+
(Jonjo O'Neill) *settled towards rr: effrt gng wl 8th: chal and hit 3 out: rdn and contested ld after: plld out a bit ex fnl 50yds* **9/2**[3]

UU-4 **2** *½* **Red Seventy**[14] 84 6-11-7 **113**........................ JackQuinlan 125
(Sarah Humphrey) *cl up: wnt 2nd at 6th: led after next: jnd 3 out and rdn: kpt battling on w ev ch tl no ex fnl 50yds* **12/1**

/5-4 **3** *1 ½* **Furrows**[12] 109 10-11-5 **111**........................ LeightonAspell 123
(Oliver Sherwood) *settled in midfield: effrt on inner whn hit 3 out: rdn and sn outpcd by ldng pair: styng on after last but n.d* **6/1**

452- **4** *3 ¾* **Ballybogey (IRE)**[40] 5203 9-11-9 **115**........................ AdamPogson 123
(Charles Pogson) *set decent gallop and mde most tl after 7th: rdn and ev ch 3 out: no ex between last two* **4/1**[2]

43-1 **5** *nse* **Honourable Gent**[9] 154 7-11-1 **110**........................ CraigNichol[(3)] 119
(Rose Dobbin) *hld up in rr: mstke 5th: effrt gng wl 8th and threatened briefly: u.p and little rspnse next: sn btn* **3/1**[1]

302- **6** *26* **Shooters Wood (IRE)**[34] 5298 11-10-12 **109**........................ JoeCornwall[(5)] 93
(David Pearson) *hit 4th: pressed ldrs tl rdn and lost pl qckly bef 8th: t.o 2 out* **20/1**

211- **7** *3* **Kerryhead Storm (IRE)**[71] 4608 10-11-9 **115**........................(t) CharliePoste 96
(Matt Sheppard) *w ldr or cl 2nd tl 6th: rdn after next: remained cl up tl lost pl bef 3 out: t.o next: eased: bttr for r* **8/1**

F54- **P** **Formal Bid (IRE)**[25] 5449 8-11-12 **118**........................(bt) FelixDeGiles
(Barry Brennan) *cl up: losing pl whn blnd 6th: sn last: p.u next* **33/1**

244- **P** **Dunowen Point (IRE)**[171] 2742 9-11-11 **117**........................(t) WilsonRenwick
(Donald McCain) *bhd: drvn and nt travelling 6th: t.o bef 8th: p.u next* **8/1**

3m 58.7s (3.70) **Going Correction** +0.375s/f (Yiel) 9 Ran SP% **115.1**

Speed ratings: **105,104,104,102,102 89,87, ,**

CSF £54.33 CT £326.28 TOTE £5.50: £1.90, £4.50, £2.50; EX 73.60 Trifecta £775.00.

Owner John P McManus **Bred** David Brace **Trained** Cheltenham, Gloucs

FOCUS

The feature contest was a fair handicap chase. They went an even gallop. The winner builto on his recent win.

339 ABACUS DECORATORS MARES' H'CAP HURDLE (12 hdls) 3m

7:30 (7:30) (Class 4) (0-120,120) 4-Y-0+ **£3,249** (£954; £477; £238)

Form RPR

345- **1** **Minnie Milan (IRE)**[29] 5371 6-10-1 **95**........................ TrevorWhelan 102+
(Neil King) *cl 2nd tl jnd ldr 7th: led bef 3 out: drvn and wandered rt between last two: drew 3 l clr at last and kpt on gamely* **5/1**

121- **2** *1 ½* **Ebony Empress (IRE)**[51] 5001 6-11-5 **120**........................(p) MrMartinMcIntyre[(7)] 126+
(Neil Mulholland) *last whn mstke 4th: stl 6th but on bridle and nt asked for effrt home turn: clsd fr 2 out and wnt 2nd at last: rdn and fin strly but too much to do* **13/2**

534- **3** *4* **Maypole Lass**[22] 5523 5-10-11 **105**........................(p) BrendanPowell 106
(Stuart Edmunds) *settled trcking ldrs: effrt gng wl bef 3 out: w wnr bef next: rdn and taken sltly rt and no ex between last two* **9/1**

52P- **4** *nk* **A Shade Of Bay**[54] 4965 7-11-12 **120**........................(p) DavidBass 121
(Kim Bailey) *towards rr: wnt 4th and pushed along bef 3 out: rdn and outpcd after next: styd on again after last wout threatening* **18/1**

331- **5** *5* **Mighty Minnie**[28] 5400 6-11-6 **114**........................ TomO'Brien 110
(Henry Daly) *hit 3rd: sn towards rr: last at 8th: drvn and btn bef 3 out: plugged on* **10/3**[2]

P1-1 **6** *21* **Flemensbay**[14] 89 7-10-12 **106**........................(p) RichardJohnson 83
(Richard Phillips) *t.k.h: led: jnd 7th: sn hrd drvn: hdd bef 3 out and dropped out v tamely: t.o* **11/4**[1]

044- **7** *nk* **Gaye Memories**[40] 5191 7-10-13 **107**........................ HarrySkelton 84
(Dan Skelton) *cl 3rd tl lost pl u.p wl bef 3 out: t.o whn mstke last* **9/2**[3]

5m 46.2s (-3.80) **Going Correction** 0.0s/f (Good) 7 Ran SP% **113.2**

Speed ratings (Par 105): **106,105,104,104,102 95,95**

CSF £35.50 TOTE £6.90: £3.00, £3.00; EX 30.20 Trifecta £209.10.

Owner Mark & Tracy Harrod,P Branigan,T Messom **Bred** S P Tindall **Trained** Barbury Castle, Wiltshire

FOCUS

A fair staying mares' handicap hurdle. They went a proper gallop. The form is rated around the second and third.

340 CRABBIE'S SCOTTISH RASPBERRY ALCOHOLIC GINGER BEER H'CAP CHASE (14 fncs 2 omitted) 2m 6f 105y

8:00 (8:00) (Class 5) (0-100,100) 5-Y-0+ **£2,599** (£763; £381; £190)

Form RPR

P/3- **1** **Caspian Piper (IRE)**[141] 3237 8-10-2 **76**........................(v) RichardJohnson 100+
(Tim Vaughan) *w ldr: led 8th: 6 l clr and gng wl 10th: sn only one lft on bridle: 20 l ahd and hacking fr 2 out tl heavily eased after last* **2/1**[1]

3P-0 **2** *13* **Noble Witness (IRE)**[14] 88 12-11-7 **95**........................(p) AdamPogson 100
(Charles Pogson) *led or disp ld tl 8th: dropped bk to 5th at 10th: rdn and n.d after: pluged on to take remote 2nd sn after last* **8/1**

PP-1 **3** *2* **Mr Robinson (FR)**[14] 88 8-10-7 **81**........................ JamesBest 84
(Rob Summers) *hld up in rr: effrt in 4th at 10th: tk 2nd bef next but wnr already clr: rdn and plodded on in vain pursuit: sn lost 2nd flat* **11/2**[3]

P5- **4** *10* **West Of The Edge (IRE)**[27] 5406 7-11-10 **98**........................ DaveCrosse 92
(Dai Williams) *cl up: wnt 2nd at 9th tl mstke next and rdn: sn dropped out* **16/1**

42F- **5** *12* **Kilcascan**[75] 4538 11-10-13 **90**........................(p) BenPoste[(3)] 75
(Rosemary Gasson) *prom tl rdn and dropped out qckly after 9th: t.o 11th* **12/1**

35/5 **P** **Dancing Dude (IRE)**[14] 86 8-11-3 **91**........................ AndrewTinkler
(Barry Leavy) *midfield: hit 8th: injured and p.u bef next* **10/1**

005- **P** **Balinderry (IRE)**[29] 5374 8-10-0 **74** oh1........................ AdamWedge
(Nick Kent) *pressed ldrs tl 8th: dropped to rr 10th: t.o and p.u 3 out* **11/1**

6/0- **P** **Steel Gold (IRE)**[198] 2152 9-9-12 **77** oh5 ow3........................ ConorRing[(5)]
(John Upson) *j. slowly in last and sn detached: nvr travelling: blnd 9th: t.o and p.u after next* **33/1**

02-U **P** **Vujiyama (FR)**[9] 173 6-11-12 **100**........................ RichieMcLernon
(Jonjo O'Neill) *plld hrd in rr: awkward 3rd: hdwy to 2nd at 10th: sn lost pl: t.o and p.u 2 out* **7/2**[2]

5m 55.1s (6.60) **Going Correction** +0.375s/f (Yiel) 9 Ran SP% **116.0**

Speed ratings: **103,98,97,94,90 , , ,**

CSF £18.91 CT £77.13 TOTE £2.70: £1.10, £3.00, £1.90; EX 20.30 Trifecta £126.50.

Owner Oceans Racing **Bred** R Guiry **Trained** Aberthin, Vale of Glamorgan

FOCUS

A modest handicap chase. They went an ordinary gallop. The wasy winner was a 110 hurdler at his peak and should win again.

341 PETER STOTT PLANT AND HAULAGE LTD STANDARD OPEN NATIONAL HUNT FLAT RACE 2m

8:30 (8:30) (Class 6) 4-6-Y-0 **£1,559** (£343; £343; £114)

Form RPR

1 **Robinesse (IRE)** 4-10-3 0........................ LeightonAspell 100+
(Oliver Sherwood) *last early: pushed along after 5f: hdwy but running green in st: rdn and stl 6th 1f out: penny fnlly dropped and late spurt to ld fnl strides* **16/1**

2 *nk* **Walkami (FR)** 4-10-10 0........................ RichieMcLernon 107
(Jonjo O'Neill) *hld up and bhd: prog over 4f out: rdn to ld wl over 1f out: narrow advantage tl hdd wl ins fnl f* **9/1**

2 *dht* **Winter Soldier**[34] 5-11-0 0........................ DarylJacob 111
(Richard Woollacott) *a in ldng trio: led over 2f out: drvn and hdd over 1f out: fought bk gamely to ld wl ins fnl f but pipped on post* **16/1**

4 *4* **Debece** 4-10-10 0........................ RichardJohnson 103
(Tim Vaughan) *tall: trckd ldrs: effrt to chal over 2f out: rdn and one pce fnl f* **8/1**

5- **5** *2 ½* **Aliandy (IRE)**[56] 4921 4-10-10 0........................ DavidBass 101
(Kim Bailey) *a abt same pce: rdn 2f out: btn over 1f out* **9/2**[2]

01- **6** *4* **Florrie Boy (IRE)**[22] 5520 4-10-10 0........................ JamieBargary[(7)] 104
(Nigel Twiston-Davies) *led or disp ld tl rdn 3f out: plugged on same pce and sn btn* **9/4**[1]

7 *9* **Oscar Bravo (IRE)** 4-10-3 0........................ MissADalton[(7)] 89
(Heather Dalton) *towards rr and outpcd 1/2-way: nvr on terms after* **33/1**

8 *1 ½* **Magic Mustard (IRE)** 4-10-10 0........................ AidanColeman 88
(Charlie Longsdon) *chsd ldrs 10f: t.o* **9/2**[2]

9 *4 ½* **Cracking Find (IRE)** 4-10-10 0........................ TomO'Brien 84
(Henry Daly) *chsd ldrs: rdn and effrt over 4f out: sn btn: t.o* **7/1**[3]

6 **10** *10* **Earthwindorfire**[15] 67 4-10-10 0........................ MarkGrant 75
(Geoffrey Deacon) *hld up towards rr: brief effrt 1/2-way: t.o* **16/1**

4- **11** *8* **Hey Up Ashey**[40] 5207 5-10-11 0........................ BenPoste[(3)] 72
(Michael Mullineaux) *led or prom tl rdn and wknd qckly 3f out: bdly t.o* **33/1**

0- **12** *79* **Adadream**[28] 5402 6-10-7 0........................ DanielHiskett[(7)] 1
(Claire Dyson) *dropped to rr after 7f and sn bdly t.o: fin eventually* **100/1**

3m 50.9s (4.50) **Going Correction** 0.0s/f (Good)

WFA 4 from 5yo+ 4lb 12 Ran SP% **123.2**

Speed ratings: **88,87,87,85,84 82,78,77,75,70 66,26**

WIN: 17.10; PL: 4.10, 3.60 Walkami, 4.70 Winter Soldier; EX: R & WS 77.20, R & Wa 66.50; CSF: R & WS 124.37, R & Wa 77.24; TF: 837.50 TRIFECTA Part won. Pool of £2233.52 - 0.03 winning units..

Owner A Taylor & The Three Underwriters **Bred** Lady Jennifer Fowler **Trained** Upper Lambourn, Berks

FOCUS

The concluding contest was a fair bumper won by the very useful hurdler Get Me Out Of Here on his debut in 2009. They went an even gallop.

T/Plt: £580.60 to a £1 stake. Pool: £50651.24 - 63.68 winning tickets. T/Qpdt: £67.00 to a £1 stake. Pool: £7342.76 - 81.07 winning tickets. **Iain Mackenzie**

342 - 348a (Foreign Racing) - See Raceform Interactive

[54]AUTEUIL (L-H)

Saturday, May 16

OFFICIAL GOING: Turf: very soft

349a PRIX LA BARKA (HURDLE) (GRADE 2) (5YO+) (TURF) 2m 5f 110y

2:08 (12:00) 5-Y-0+

£61,046 (£29,844; £17,635; £12,209; £6,782; £4,748)

RPR

1 **Ballynagour (IRE)**[17] 22 9-10-3 0........................ TomScudamore 149
(David Pipe) *w.w in midfield: clsd after 5 out: cl 3rd and ev ch 2 out: qcknd to ld last: drvn clr run-in* **7/1**

2 *5* **Val De Ferbet (FR)**[15] 69 6-10-3 0........................ RWalsh 144
(W P Mullins, Ire) *hld up towards rr: hdwy after 4 out: 7th and styng on bef 2 out: r.o u.p fr last: wnt 2nd cl home: no ch w wnr* **10/1**

3 *1* **Dos Santos (FR)**[48] 5058 5-10-3 0........................(p) MathieuCarroux 143
(Emmanuel Clayeux, France) *a cl up: led bef 2 out: hdd last: readily outpcd by wnr: lost 2nd cl home* **13/2**[3]

4 *2 ½* **Le Chateau (FR)**[20] 4 6-10-6 0........................ ErvanChazelle 144
(C Scandella, France) *w.w in tch: w ldng gp after 3 out: outpcd and rdn between last two flights: kpt on at same pce u.p run-in* **25/1**

5 *1* **Catmoves (FR)**[22] 8-9-13 0........................ JacquesRicou 136
(J-P Gallorini, France) *w.w in midfield: hdwy bef 6 out: led next: hdd bef 2 out: sn outpcd by ldrs: one pce u.p after last* **20/1**

6 *1* **Silsol (GER)**[83] 4380 6-10-6 0........................(p) SamTwiston-Davies 142
(Paul Nicholls) *prom: cl 3rd and scrubbed along fnl bnd bef 2 out: 5th and hrd rdn appr last: kpt on at same pce run-in* **7/1**

7 *2* **Gitane Du Berlais (FR)**[41] 5177 5-9-11 0........................ MlleNathalieDesoutter 131
(W P Mullins, Ire) *led: hdd 5 out: styd prom tl lost pl after 3 out: kpt on at one pce fr 2 out* **11/4**[1]

8 *2* **Defi D'Anjou (FR)**[24] 7-10-6 0........................ BertrandLestrade 138
(L Viel, France) *hld up in tch: rdn and btn fr 3 out* **9/1**

9 *1 ¾* **Dulce Leo (FR)**[20] 4 9-10-6 0........................(b) AngeloGasnier 136
(J-P Gallorini, France) *settled in midfield: rdn and no imp fr 3 out: nvr in contention* **33/1**

10 *1 ¾* **Hilton Du Berlais (FR)**[20] 4 5-9-11 0........................(p) FrancoisPamart 125
(A Chaille-Chaille, France) *hld up in midfield: lost pl after 3 out: kpt on again run-in: nvr trbld ldrs* **16/1**

11 *¾* **Saint Firmin (FR)**[20] 4 6-10-8 0........................ KevinNabet 135
(Robert Collet, France) *a towards rr: rdn and no imp after 3 out* **12/1**

12 *5* **Les Beaufs (FR)**[38] 6-10-3 0........................ JulienGuillochon 125
(Mme V Seignoux, France) *a among bkmarkers: nvr a factor* **25/1**

13 *8* **Roll On Has (FR)**[20] 4 5-10-1 0........................ VincentCheminaud 115
(J-P Gallorini, France) *hld up towards rr: rdn and effrt fnl bnd after 3 out: untidy 2 out: sn btn and eased run-in* **11/2**[2]

14 *dist* **Mon Bonbon (FR)**[9] 6-10-3 0........................(p) AnthonyLeJoncour
(J-C Bertin, France) *hld up in midfield: lost pl 8th: lost tch 6 out: t.o* **100/1**

5m 9.4s (309.40) 14 Ran SP% **129.4**

PARI-MUTUEL (all including 1 euro stake): WIN 16.90; PLACE 5.80, 6.20, 2.40; DF 167.60; SF 225.80.

Owner Allan Stennett **Bred** G T Morrow **Trained** Nicholashayne, Devon

350a PRIX D'ARLES PRESENTE PAR ELA (HURDLE) (LISTED RACE) (4-5YO FILLIES & MARES) (TURF) 2m 2f

2:40 (12:00) 4-5-Y-0 £31,627 (£15,813; £9,224; £6,259; £2,965)

RPR

1 **Turteene (FR)**[31] 5-11-3 0 .... BertrandLestrade 140
(Y-M Porzier, France) **19/5**[2]

2 6 **Analifet (FR)**[14] 93 5-10-10 0 .... BJCooper 127
(W P Mullins, Ire) *w.w towards rr: hdwy to chse ldng pair 4 out: cl 2nd and ev ch appr 2 out: kpt on u.p but nt match pce of wnr run-in* **6/4**[1]

3 1 1/2 **Linda's Charm (FR)**[24] 5-10-8 0 .... ErvanChazelle 124
(Mlle T Puitg, France) **25/1**

4 1 **Turn In Grey (FR)**[38] 5-10-10 0 .... DavidCottin 125
(Louis Baudron, Australia) **137/10**

5 1 1/4 **Aigrette De Loire (FR)**[16] 54 5-11-0 0 ....(b) ThomasBeaurain 127
(G Cherel, France) **172/10**

6 1 **Martalette (FR)**[16] 54 5-10-12 0 ....(b) GeoffreyRe 124
(Yannick Fouin, France) **91/10**[3]

7 2 1/2 **Miss Dixie (FR)**[20] 5-10-10 0 .... MathieuDelage 120
(A Lamotte D'Argy, France) **31/1**

8 nk **Bathilde (FR)**[22] 4-10-3 0 .... MorganRegairaz 112
(D Bressou, France) **37/1**

9 6 **Latyle (FR)**[16] 54 5-10-6 0 .... AnthonyLecordier 109
(D Windrif, France) **29/1**

10 1/2 **Nouma Jelois (FR)**[31] 4-10-8 0 .... KevinNabet 111
(Yannick Fouin, France) **15/1**

11 5 **Aguicheuse (FR)**[22] 5-10-8 0 .... JakeGreenall 106
(Francois Nicolle, France) **19/1**

12 20 **Boheme (FR)**[36] 4-10-8 0 ow2 .... JonathanPlouganou 86
(Emmanuel Clayeux, France) **111/10**

13 1 **Poprock Du Berlais (FR)**[31] 4-10-6 0 .... LudovicPhilipperon 83
(Robert Collet, France) **36/1**

P **Boscraie (FR)**[24] 4-10-3 0 ow2 .... MathieuCarroux
(Emmanuel Clayeux, France) **43/1**

4m 17.1s (257.10)
WFA 4 from 5yo 18lb **14 Ran SP% 120.5**
PARI-MUTUEL (all including 1 euro stake): WIN 4.80; PLACE 1.90, 1.50, 4.70; DF 5.90; SF 13.40.
Owner Suc Paul Sebag **Bred** B Compignie **Trained** France

351 - 352a (Foreign Racing) - See Raceform Interactive

[181] MARKET RASEN (R-H)

Sunday, May 17

OFFICIAL GOING: Good (chs 8.6, hdl 8.4)
Wind: moderate 1/2 against Weather: overcast becoming fine and sunny, very cool

353 BDN CONSTRUCTION MAIDEN HURDLE (7 hdls 1 omitted) 2m 148y

2:00 (2:00) (Class 4) 4-Y-0+ £3,249 (£954; £477; £238)

Form RPR

243- 1 **Countersign**[35] 5294 6-11-0 119 .... AdamPogson 109+
(Charles Pogson) *sn trcking ldrs: t.k.h: handy 2nd omitted 3 out: led appr 2 out: styd on: eased towards fin* **6/5**[1]

3-2 2 3 **Dynamo (IRE)**[12] 131 4-10-10 114 ....(t) HarrySkelton 99
(Dan Skelton) *chsd ldr: led 5th: drvn and hdd appr 2 out: kpt on same pce* **13/8**[2]

6- 3 1 1/2 **Bells Of Ailsworth (IRE)**[69] 4679 5-11-0 .... MichaelByrne 102
(Tim Vaughan) *chsd ldrs: wnt 2nd 5th: drvn appr 2 out: one pce whn j.rt last* **12/1**

4 1 1/4 **Keep Calm**[211] 5-11-0 0 .... BrianHughes 102
(John Mackie) *chsd ldrs: modest 4th bef 2 out: one pce* **14/1**

0PP- 5 48 **Rossington**[20] 3060 6-10-11 0 .... MauriceLinehan(3) 67
(John Wainwright) *led: t.k.h: wl clr after 1st: slowed up: j. slowly and jnd 4th: blnd bdly next: sn lost pl and bhd: t.o 2 out: b.b.v* **150/1**

050- 6 4 1/2 **Dounya's Boy**[41] 5201 6-11-0 ....(b) DaveCrosse 53
(Christopher Kellett) *in rr: bhd 4th: t.o omitted 3 out* **150/1**

7 81 **Satin Waters**[38] 4-10-3 0 .... BrendanPowell
(Christine Dunnett) *bhd 3rd: sme hdwy next: lost pl 5th: t.o omitted 3 out: eventually completed* **80/1**

F4- F **Sindarban (IRE)**[186] 2446 4-10-10 0 ....(t) WilsonRenwick
(Donald McCain) *mid-div: j.lft and fell 1st* **6/1**[3]

4m 16.0s (9.30) **Going Correction** +0.325s/f (Yiel)
WFA 4 from 5yo+ 18lb **8 Ran SP% 114.8**
Speed ratings (Par 105): **91,89,88,88,65 63,25,**
CSF £3.55 TOTE £1.80: £1.10, £1.10, £2.70; EX 2.90 Trifecta £15.80.
Owner C T Pogson **Bred** Hesmonds Stud Ltd **Trained** Farnsfield, Notts

FOCUS
Rail set 18yds from innermost position on Home bend and 26yds out on Stands bend consequently distances increased by 132yds per circuit. Only three of these looked to have an obvious chance of taking this, but one of those departed at the opening hurdle. That obstacle was missed out next time round. This was steadily run and the winner didn't need to improve.

354 MOUNT & MINSTER LINCOLNSHIRE PROPERTY PROFESSIONALS H'CAP HURDLE (8 hdls) 2m 148y

2:35 (2:36) (Class 4) (0-110,110) 4-Y-0+ £3,249 (£954; £477; £238)

Form RPR

600- 1 **Zarzal (IRE)**[182] 2519 7-11-10 108 .... AdamWedge 118+
(Evan Williams) *trckd ldrs: 2nd appr 2 out: sn led: drvn clr last 150yds* **4/1**[3]

505- 2 8 **Samoset**[125] 3653 5-11-7 105 ....(t) KielanWoods 109
(Charlie Longsdon) *led: hdd 2 out: kpt on same pce run-in* **20/1**

5-11 3 5 **King Of Strings (IRE)**[8] 205 6-11-11 109 ....(p) DougieCostello 107
(Mark Walford) *hld up towards rr: hdwy 3 out: modest 4th 2 out: kpt on to take 3rd last 150yds* **11/4**[1]

32-2 4 3 3/4 **A Little Bit Dusty**[9] 186 7-11-12 110 ....(b) PaddyBrennan 105
(Conor Dore) *chsd ldrs 3rd: modest 3rd 2 out: one pce* **7/2**[2]

00-5 5 12 **King Muro**[10] 172 5-10-5 92 .... ConorShoemark(3) 78
(Fergal O'Brien) *chsd ldr: hit 3 out: 5th and wkng whn mstke next* **8/1**

51/2 6 19 **Shalambar (IRE)**[13] 110 9-11-12 110 ....(v) WayneHutchinson 76
(Tony Carroll) *chsd ldrs: reminders 5th: lost pl next* **12/1**

153- 7 6 **Nefyn Bay**[26] 5452 6-11-10 108 ....(t) BrianHarding 69
(Donald McCain) *chsd ldrs: pushed along 4th: lost pl 3 out: sn bhd* **8/1**

06-6 8 21 **New Tarabela**[13] 110 4-10-12 100 .... LeeEdwards 38
(Tony Carroll) *prom: drvn 2nd: reminders and dropped bk detached last next: t.o 3 out* **25/1**

510- P **King's Road**[100] 4064 10-11-8 106 ....(t) TomScudamore
(Anabel K Murphy) *hld up in rr: hdwy 3rd: blnd and lost pl 5th: bhd and eased next: t.o whn p.u bef 2 out* **16/1**

4m 7.3s (0.60) **Going Correction** +0.325s/f (Yiel)
WFA 4 from 5yo+ 18lb **9 Ran SP% 113.3**
Speed ratings (Par 105): **111,107,104,103,97 88,85,75,**
CSF £72.21 CT £253.17 TOTE £5.60: £2.00, £5.90, £1.50; EX 84.20 Trifecta £889.10.
Owner Mrs Janet Davies **Bred** His Highness The Aga Khan's Studs S C **Trained** Llancarfan, Vale Of Glamorgan

FOCUS
Probably not the strongest race for the level, but two came away from the rest in the home straight. The winner was very well in on old form.

355 MOUNT & MINSTER LINCOLNSHIRE ESTATE AGENTS NOVICES' LIMITED H'CAP CHASE (17 fncs) 2m 7f 191y

3:05 (3:08) (Class 4) (0-120,118) 5-Y-0+ £3,963 (£1,163; £581; £290)

Form RPR

202- 1 **Silver Man**[193] 2288 8-11-8 118 ....(b) NicodeBoinville 127
(Jo Hughes) *mde all: edgd lft appr last: kpt on: all out* **7/4**[1]

U05- 2 shd **An Poc Ar Buile (IRE)**[99] 4092 6-11-5 115 .... PaddyBrennan 124
(Fergal O'Brien) *trckd ldng pair: drvn 4 out: cl 2nd between last 2: kpt on: jst denied* **2/1**[2]

056- 3 9 **Vesuvhill (FR)**[41] 5191 6-10-9 105 .... DarylJacob 106
(Ben Case) *trckd ldng pair: hit 6th: 2nd 12th: swtchd rt appr last: wknd last 150yds* **4/1**[3]

223- 4 66 **Askamore Darsi (IRE)**[29] 5399 6-11-5 115 ....(b) HenryBrooke 56
(Donald McCain) *chsd wnr: drvn 10th: reminders and struggling 12th: lost pl 4 out: sn wl bhd: t.o next: eventually completed* **4/1**[3]

6m 10.5s (-20.80) **Going Correction** -0.675s/f (Firm) **4 Ran SP% 109.7**
Speed ratings: **106,105,103,81**
CSF £5.79 TOTE £2.20; EX 4.50.
Owner John Wardle **Bred** T J Wardle **Trained** Lambourn. Berks

FOCUS
There were reasons to oppose all of these, so one would imagine this isn't particularly strong form. The winner is on the upgrade.

356 BDN CONSTRUCTION H'CAP HURDLE (10 hdls) 2m 4f 139y

3:40 (3:40) (Class 3) (0-125,124) 4-Y-0+ £6,498 (£1,908; £954; £477)

Form RPR

442- 1 **Sky Khan**[34] 5310 6-11-10 122 ....(p) PeterBuchanan 124
(Lucinda Russell) *trckd ldrs: 4th 1f out: swtchd lft and str run to ld nr fin* **13/2**[3]

404- 2 1/2 **Man Of Leisure**[46] 5099 11-11-4 123 ....(t) HarryCobden(7) 125
(Anthony Honeyball) *hld up in rr: smooth hdwy to trck ldrs 3 out: led narrowly last: no ex and hdd towards fin* **9/1**

424- 3 1 1/2 **Bowie (IRE)**[32] 5345 8-11-6 118 .... AdamWedge 120+
(Nick Kent) *hld up in mid-div: chsng ldrs 3 out: hit next: upsides whn mstke last: kpt on same pce* **10/1**

133- 4 1 **One For Hocky (IRE)**[24] 5495 7-11-3 115 .... BrianHarding 114
(Nicky Richards) *wore hood in paddock: stdd s: hld up in rr: hdwy 5th: trcking ldrs 3 out: upsides next: kpt on same pce run-in* **15/2**

06-0 5 3 **Get Home Now**[15] 87 7-11-0 115 ....(tp) SeanBowen(3) 111
(Peter Bowen) *led to 1st: chsd ldr: led 4th: hdd and drvn appr 3 out: one pce fr next* **4/1**[2]

215- 6 hd **Palm Grey (IRE)**[29] 5394 7-11-1 113 .... SeanQuinlan 109
(Sue Smith) *chsd ldrs: upsides and drvn appr 2 out: one pce* **9/1**

/01- 7 4 1/2 **Tiger O'Toole (IRE)**[33] 5325 10-11-4 119 .... JeremiahMcGrath(3) 112
(Henry Oliver) *trckd ldrs: led on bit appr 3 out: hdd last: eased whn btn last 100yds* **2/1**[1]

F3-0 8 67 **Boruma (IRE)**[15] 85 5-11-0 112 .... HenryBrooke 36
(Dianne Sayer) *led 1st: hdd 4th: upsides whn mstke 7th: wknd qckly: t.o next: eventually completed* **20/1**

5m 16.4s (7.60) **Going Correction** +0.325s/f (Yiel) **8 Ran SP% 112.3**
Speed ratings (Par 107): **98,97,97,96,95 95,93,68**
CSF £58.99 CT £574.63 TOTE £5.50: £2.20, £3.00, £2.60; EX 69.80 Trifecta £229.10.
Owner The Ormello Way **Bred** Heather Raw **Trained** Arlary, Perth & Kinross

FOCUS
The leader set just an ordinary gallop for this fair handicap, and it developed into a 2f sprint, so this is form to treat with plenty of caution. The third is probably the best guide.

357 BDN CONSTRUCTION H'CAP CHASE (12 fncs) 2m 1f 43y

4:10 (4:12) (Class 3) (0-140,140) 5-Y-0+ £12,996 (£3,816; £1,908; £954)

Form RPR

04-2 1 **Le Bacardy (FR)**[9] 184 9-11-7 135 .... HarrySkelton 137+
(Dan Skelton) *trckd ldng pair: upsides last: shkn up to ld last 150yds: drvn out* **11/8**[1]

F-22 2 3 **My Brother Sylvest**[7] 218 9-11-12 140 ....(b) TomScudamore 139
(David Pipe) *led: drvn and hdd appr 3 out: led appr last: hdd and no ex last 150yds* **7/2**[2]

150- 3 1 1/4 **Sew On Target (IRE)**[37] 5253 10-11-11 139 .... BrendanPowell 136
(Colin Tizzard) *trckd ldr: drvn to ld narrowly appr 3 out: hdd appr last: styd on same pce* **13/2**[3]

2F3- 4 1 1/4 **Sergeant Pink (IRE)**[23] 5515 9-10-0 114 oh1 .... BrianHughes 112
(Dianne Sayer) *in rr: hdwy to chse ldrs 5th: drvn 9th: 4th and styng on whn blnd 2 out: kpt on same pce run-in* **10/1**

201- 5 3/4 **Itsuptoyou (IRE)**[25] 5480 11-10-5 122 .... SeanBowen(3) 118
(Arthur Whiting) *t.k.h in rr-div: hdwy 7th: trcking ldrs in 4th 3 out: kpt on one pce between last 2* **11/1**

605- 6 20 **Shrapnel (IRE)**[29] 5391 9-10-8 122 ....(t) FelixDeGiles 103
(Brian Ellison) *in rr: outpcd and drvn 6th: rdn and j.lft 8th: in tch next: lost pl bef 3 out: sn bhd* **20/1**

33-1 U **Marie Des Anges (FR)**[16] 64 7-9-12 119 ....(t) DavidNoonan(7)
(Anthony Honeyball) *chsd ldrs: mstke and uns rdr 5th* **13/2**[3]

4m 18.3s (-16.70) **Going Correction** -0.675s/f (Firm) **7 Ran SP% 113.2**
Speed ratings: **110,108,108,107,107 98,**
CSF £6.85 TOTE £2.50: £1.50, £1.80; EX 7.40 Trifecta £35.90.
Owner Carl Hodgson **Bred** Jean-Charles Coude **Trained** Alcester, Warwicks

FOCUS
This was the best race on the card, and it was run at a decent gallop.

358 MOUNT & MINSTER CHARTERED AGRICULTURAL LAND AGENTS H'CAP CHASE (14 fncs) 2m 5f 89y
4:40 (4:41) (Class 4) (0-120,127) 5-Y-0+ **£4,548** (£1,335; £667; £333)

Form RPR
P2-1 **1** **Ballybough Pat (IRE)**[4] 282 8-11-12 **127** 7ex............(t) DavidNoonan[(7)] 138+
(David Dennis) *w ldrs: led 8th: hdd 10th: led after 11th: hdd narrowly 2 out: styd on u.p to ld last 75yds: all out* **2/1**[1]
PP2- **2** *¾* **Trillerin Minella (IRE)**[24] 5499 7-10-3 **102**........................ ConorRing[(5)] 113
(Graeme McPherson) *mstkes: trckd ldrs: led 10th: hdd narrowly after 11th: led and hit 2 out: hdd last 75yds: no ex clsng stages* **8/1**
04-3 **3** *8* **Master Of The Hall (IRE)**[9] 185 11-11-8 **119**.................. JoeColliver[(3)] 123
(Micky Hammond) *hld up in rr: trckd ldrs 5th: upsides 3 out: wknd appr last* **11/4**[2]
44-6 **4** *20* **Green Wizard (IRE)**[15] 81 9-10-13 **107**.............................(p) SeanQuinlan 92
(Sue Smith) *chsd ldrs: drvn 9th: lost pl and hit 11th: sn bhd* **7/1**
P05- **5** *26* **Count Salazar (IRE)**[22] 10-11-12 **120**........................(b[1]) NicodeBoinville 82
(Tracey L Bailey) *t.k.h: trckd ldrs: led 3rd: hdd 8th: lost pl after 10th: sn wl bhd* **11/1**
663- **P** **Imperial Vic (IRE)**[41] 5204 10-10-12 **106**.............................(t) PaddyBrennan
(Harriet Bethell) *lost pl 2nd: drvn 4th: bhd fr 7th: t.o whn p.u bef 9th* **5/1**[3]
P04- **P** **Book'em Danno (IRE)**[25] 5480 9-11-4 **112**...........................(t) DaveCrosse
(Laura Hurley) *led to 3rd: drvn 4th: reminders 6th: lost pl and hit next: sn bhd: t.o whn p.u bef 9th* **20/1**
5m 24.6s (-21.40) **Going Correction** -0.675s/f (Firm) **7 Ran SP% 113.4**
Speed ratings: **110,109,106,100,90 ,**
CSF £17.67 TOTE £3.50: £1.80, £3.20; EX 19.40 Trifecta £53.50.
Owner Favourites Racing Ltd **Bred** Mrs Maryrose Kehoe **Trained** Hanley Swan, Worcestershire
FOCUS
Quite a range of abilities on show for this handicap, with two rivals at either end of the weights fighting out the finish. The winner is a potential 140+ chaser.

359 MOUNT & MINSTER LINCOLNSHIRE LETTINGS AGENTS STANDARD OPEN NATIONAL HUNT FLAT RACE 2m 148y
5:15 (5:15) (Class 6) 4-6-Y-O **£1,559** (£457; £228; £114)

Form RPR
222- **1** **Simply Rouge**[35] 5299 5-10-9 0.. BrianHughes 104+
(Peter Niven) *trckd ldr: led 3f out: drvn clr 2f out: styd on strly: readily* **8/11**[1]
2 *8* **Wee Man (IRE)** 5-11-2 0.. BrianHarding 101
(Nicky Richards) *trckd ldrs: drvn over 3f out: kpt on to take 2nd 1f out: no ch w wnr* **10/3**[2]
4- **3** *3* **Lift The Lid (IRE)**[30] 5380 5-11-2 0.................................. DougieCostello 98
(Tony Coyle) *led: hdd 3f out: hung rt over 1f out: one pce* **5/1**[3]
4 *3 ½* **Maltese Doll** 5-10-9 0.. AdamWedge 88
(Nick Kent) *hld up in rr: drvn 6f out: one pce fnl 3f* **40/1**
5 *18* **Charm Park** 5-11-2 0.. AndrewThornton 77
(Geoffrey Harker) *hld up in rr: effrt 6f out: sn chsng ldrs: outpcd over 3f out: sn wknd* **12/1**
6 *1 ¾* **Emma Lee** 5-10-2 0.. MrRWinks[(7)] 68
(Peter Winks) *chsd ldrs: pushed along 7f out: reminders over 5f out: sn lost pl 4f out and sn bhd* **22/1**
4m 11.6s (10.50) **Going Correction** +0.325s/f (Yiel)
WFA 4 from 5yo+ 4lb **6 Ran SP% 112.1**
Speed ratings: **88,84,82,81,72 71**
CSF £3.41 TOTE £1.70: £1.40, £1.90; EX 3.90 Trifecta £7.30.
Owner Mrs J A Niven & Sandy Lodge Racing Club **Bred** Mrs J A Niven **Trained** Barton-le-Street, N Yorks
FOCUS
It was soon evident in the home straight that the market leader was going to win easily, as she charged clear throughout the final 2f. She didn't need to improve.
T/Plt: £64.20 to a £1 stake. Pool: £56,728.98 - 644.24 winning tickets. T/Qpdt: £16.20 to a £1 stake. Pool: £3,263.00 - 149.05 winning tickets. **Walter Glynn**

STRATFORD (L-H)
Sunday, May 17

OFFICIAL GOING: Good (good to firm in places) changing to good to firm (good in places) after race 4 (4.00)
Wind: virtually nil Weather: overcast, dry

360 RACHEL HAWKINS 30TH BIRTHDAY CHAMPAGNE NOVICES' HURDLE (8 hdls) 2m 70y
2:20 (2:20) (Class 4) 4-Y-0+ **£3,249** (£954; £477; £238)

Form RPR
210- **1** **San Benedeto (FR)**[32] 5345 4-11-1 129........................(t[1]) NickScholfield 127+
(Paul Nicholls) *mde all: drew clr w runner-up between last 2: shkn up and fnd ex bef last: r.o wl* **10/11**[1]
131- **2** *2* **Set The Trend**[26] 5448 9-11-12 138.. NoelFehily 137+
(David Dennis) *t.k.h: hld up in tch in midfield: clsd to chse ldrs 5th: wnt 2nd after next: mstke 2 out: sn drew clr w wnr: rdn to chal bef last: mstke last: one pce and hld after* **2/1**[2]
316- **3** *7* **Guard of Honour (IRE)**[25] 5467 4-11-1 116...............(b) LeightonAspell 119
(Rebecca Curtis) *in tch in midfield: mstke 3rd: clsd to chse ldrs bef 3 out: effrt in 3rd sn after 2 out: no imp and wl hld ent st* **5/1**[3]
1- **4** *21* **Hija**[43] 5144 4-10-3 0... AliceMills[(5)] 92
(Gail Haywood) *hld up in last: outpcd by ldrs after 5th: modest 6th 2 out: plugged on to go 4th bef last: nvr trbld ldrs* **14/1**
4-5 **5** *2 ¼* **Almaas (USA)**[12] 119 6-10-5 0...................................... ConorSmith[(7)] 94
(Kevin Bishop) *t.k.h: hld up in last quartet: lost tch w ldrs after 5th: mstke next: wnt modest 7th 2 out: plugged on to go 5th bef last: nvr trbld ldrs* **28/1**
06-4 **6** *13* **Roderick Random**[12] 119 5-10-12 0.............................. RichieMcLernon 85
(Johnny Farrelly) *chsd ldr tl bef 2 out: 4th and struggling sn after 2 out: wknd on long run between last 2: t.o* **50/1**
4- **7** *15* **Dover The Moon (IRE)**[218] 1437 4-10-8 0.............................. JamesDavies 65
(Tom Gretton) *chsd ldrs: 5th and struggling whn mstke 2 out: wknd on long run between last 2: t.o* **100/1**
8 *25* **Everlasting Spring (IRE)**[221] 2058 7-10-12 0.....................(t) AlainCawley 46
(Johnny Farrelly) *a bhd: t.o 3 out* **33/1**
0- **P** **My Scat Daddy (USA)**[28] 5411 6-10-5 0..................(t) FreddieMitchell[(7)]
(Daniel Steele) *in tch in midfield: struggling to hold pl whn blnd 5th: sn eased and p.u bef next* **200/1**
4- **P** **Captain Starlight (IRE)**[26] 5448 5-10-12 0........................ LiamTreadwell
(Aytach Sadik) *hld up in last quartet: outpcd after 5th: mstke 3 out: sn lost tch: t.o whn p.u last* **200/1**
00P- **P** **Neshikot (IRE)**[27] 5428 4-10-8 0.. GavinSheehan
(Jonathan Portman) *chsd ldrs tl wknd after 5th: mstke next: t.o whn p.u last* **150/1**
3m 50.75s (-5.25) **Going Correction** -0.10s/f (Good)
WFA 4 from 5yo+ 18lb **11 Ran SP% 120.0**
Speed ratings (Par 105): **108,107,103,93,92 86,79,67, ,**
CSF £3.06 TOTE £1.80: £1.10, £1.10, £1.50; EX 3.20 Trifecta £7.60.
Owner P J Vogt **Bred** E A R L Ecurie Haras Du Cadran Et Al **Trained** Ditcheat, Somerset
FOCUS
Hurdle races increased by 60yds per circuit and Chases by 33yds per circuit. Split bends. The going was good, good to firm in places after a dry night, despite selective watering, and both tracks were railed out to provide fresh ground. The jockeys said it was good to firm. Quite an interesting novices' hurdle; the betting suggested it was between just three, and that was how it worked out.

361 STRATFORDCARAVANS.CO.UK MARES' NOVICES' (S) HURDLE (8 hdls) 2m 70y
2:55 (2:55) (Class 5) 4-Y-0+ **£2,274** (£667; £333; £166)

Form RPR
3P0- **1** **Sudden Wish (IRE)**[6] 4673 6-10-10 97.........................(p) AidanColeman 107+
(Gary Moore) *in tch: clsd to trck ldrs after 5th: led and travelling strly on long run between last 2: sn drew clr: v easily* **11/4**[2]
550- **2** *21* **Bus Named Desire**[25] 5481 7-10-5 76.....................(tp) RobMcCarth[(5)] 85
(Ian Williams) *midfield: rdn after 5th: sltly hmpd 3 out: modest 6th 2 out: plugged on to go 2nd last: no ch w wnr* **16/1**
24-6 **3** *5* **Symphony Of Pearls**[10] 180 4-10-6 80................................ RobertDunne 76
(Dai Burchell) *t.k.h: in tch in midfield: effrt 3 out: outpcd by wnr on long run between last 2: wnt modest 2nd bnd bef last: lost 2nd and wknd last* **13/2**[3]
5P0- **4** *¾* **Stay Tuned (IRE)**[101] 4053 7-10-10 79...............................(tp) RhysFlint 79
(Alexandra Dunn) *chsd ldrs: rdn and outpcd by wnr sn after 2 out: wl btn 4th whn j.rt last* **40/1**
6-P **5** *11* **Southern Cross**[10] 179 4-10-3 0.................................(t) JamesBanks[(3)] 68
(Andy Turnell) *t.k.h: led: nt fluent 2nd: mstke 2 out: drvn and hdd on long run between last 2: lost 2nd and wkng whn hmpd and stmbld on bnd bef last* **33/1**
54-P **6** *3 ½* **Miss H Lewiss**[16] 55 7-10-3 92................................ CiaranGethings[(7)] 66
(Steve Flook) *chsd ldrs: lost pl u.p bef 3 out: wknd on long run between last 2: t.o* **9/1**
050- **7** *2* **Ginjo**[24] 5490 5-10-3 84...(t) JamieBargary[(7)] 65
(Nigel Twiston-Davies) *chsd ldr tl 2 out: sn struggling u.p: wknd on long run between last 2: mstke last: t.o* **10/1**
8 *17* **Desroches (GER)**[16] 7-10-10 0.. RichardJohnson 54
(C Von Der Recke, Germany) *nt jump wl: a in rr and nvr on terms: rdn bef 5th: no hdwy: t.o on long run between last 2* **15/8**[1]
P **Aglaja**[1008] 6-10-10 0..(e[1]) AndrewTinkler
(Steph Hollinshead) *a in rr: reminders after 3rd: rdn and lost tch qckly 5th: t.o whn p.u next* **100/1**
4 **F** **Impeccability**[17] 41 5-10-10 0...................................(p) PeterCarberry
(John Mackie) *in tch in midfield tl fell 3 out* **12/1**
04- **P** **Weston Super Mare**[28] 5410 5-10-10 0.............................. ConorO'Farrell
(Alexandra Dunn) *nvr gng wl: a towards rr: rdn after 2nd: lost tch 5th: t.o whn p.u 2 out* **100/1**
3m 51.65s (-4.35) **Going Correction** -0.10s/f (Good)
WFA 4 from 5yo+ 18lb **11 Ran SP% 114.8**
Speed ratings (Par 103): **106,96,93,93,88 86,85,77, ,**
CSF £42.28 TOTE £3.00: £1.30, £3.40, £1.90; EX 41.40 Trifecta £213.60.Winner bought in for 6,700gns.
Owner M&R Refurbishments Ltd **Bred** Catridge Farm Stud & S Von Schilcher **Trained** Lower Beeding, W Sussex
■ Stewards' Enquiry : Robert Dunne four-day ban: careless riding (May 31,Jun 2-4)
FOCUS
A low-grade mares' seller and an easy winner.

362 RIVERSIDE CARAVAN PARK H'CAP CHASE (14 fncs) 2m 3f 98y
3:25 (3:25) (Class 3) (0-140,139) 5-Y-0+ **£6,498** (£1,908; £954; £477)

Form RPR
43-3 **1** **Carrigmorna King (IRE)**[12] 121 9-11-9 **136**.............(t) RichardJohnson 145
(Philip Hobbs) *in tch: clsd to chse ldrs and mstke 11th: chsd ldr bef 2 out: styd on u.p to ld sn after last: drvn and hld on wl fnl 100yds* **9/4**[2]
/6-2 **2** *½* **Baby Mix (FR)**[18] 24 7-11-12 **139**.. GavinSheehan 147
(Warren Greatrex) *chsd ldrs tl 9th: styd in tch: hdwy to ld 3 out: rdn bnd bef last: hdd sn after last: battled on wl u.p: hld fnl 100yds* **11/8**[1]
420- **3** *10* **Buck Mulligan**[113] 3860 10-11-0 **127**.................................. PaulMoloney 129
(Evan Williams) *in tch in last pair: mstke 1st: clsd and mstke 10th: clsd 3rd 2 out: rdn and btn ent st: wknd last* **10/1**
PP0- **4** *15* **Mart Lane (IRE)**[26] 5450 10-10-13 **126**..........................(b) TomCannon 113
(Sophie Leech) *w ldr: led 3rd: rdn bef 11th: hdd 3 out: 4th and btn 2 out: wknd bef last* **11/1**
P1-6 **5** *6* **One Term (IRE)**[17] 47 8-11-10 **137**.........................(b) LeightonAspell 117
(Rebecca Curtis) *led tl mstke and hdd 3rd: pressed ldr after tl after 10th: btn after next: wknd 2 out* **11/2**[3]
262- **6** *16* **Passato (GER)**[263] 1355 11-10-6 **122**..............................(t) JamesBanks[(3)] 87
(Jo Davis) *racd wd: chsd ldrs: dropped to rr but styd in tch 4th: mstke 7th: rdn and struggling next: wknd 11th: t.o* **20/1**
4m 39.35s (-10.65) **Going Correction** -0.275s/f (Good) **6 Ran SP% 110.4**
Speed ratings: **110,109,105,99,97 91**
CSF £5.85 TOTE £2.20: £1.50, £1.20; EX 6.60 Trifecta £25.20.
Owner Robert & Janet Gibbs **Bred** Tom McCarthy **Trained** Withycombe, Somerset
FOCUS
The feature race and a decent handicap despite the small field, and it produced a terrific finish.

363 AVON CARAVAN PARK H'CAP HURDLE (FOR THE CHARLES LEA MEMORIAL TROPHY) (13 hdls) 3m 2f 83y
4:00 (4:00) (Class 4) (0-120,117) 4-Y-0+ **£3,898** (£1,144; £572; £286)

Form RPR
01-1 **1** **Billy Congo (IRE)**[16] 55 8-10-12 **103**..........................(t) MichealNolan 109+
(Adrian Wintle) *patiently rdn: hld up in rr: hdwy after 3 out: swtchd rt and clsd sn after next: chal and travelling wl bef last: sn led and wnt lft last: rdn hands and heels and fnd enough flat: r.o* **9/1**

056- **2** ½ **Rior (IRE)**[27] 5437 8-10-8 **99**........................ TomO'Brien 103
(Paul Henderson) *hld up in last trio: gd hdwy after 3 out: chsd ldrs on long run between last 2: drvn and wnt on w wnr bef last: kpt on u.p but a hld flat* **16/1**

0P6- **3** 11 **Wily Fox**[17] 4904 8-11-6 **111**........................(b) JackQuinlan 105
(James Eustace) *in tch in midfield: clsd to chse ldrs: 8th: ev ch 3 out: drvn after next: led bef last sn hdd: 3rd and btn whn mstke last* **20/1**

4-1 **4** 2 **Bold Conquest (IRE)**[15] 85 7-11-11 **116**........................ RichardJohnson 109
(Stuart Edmunds) *chsd ldrs: hdwy to join ldrs 10th: led next: hit 2 out: sn drvn: hdd bef last: sn btn: wknd flat* **15/8**[1]

100- **5** 31 **Tarvini (IRE)**[23] 5510 10-10-9 **110**........................(p) JackSavage[(10)] 74
(Jonjo O'Neill) *chsd ldrs: rn in snatches: rdn and struggling 2 out: wknd on long run between last 2: t.o* **12/1**

143- **6** 22 **Finish The Story (IRE)**[62] 4818 9-11-4 **109**........................(tp) NoelFehily 54
(Johnny Farrelly) *in tch in last trio: rdn after 9th: struggling bef 3 out: lost tch 2 out: t.o* **4/1**[2]

00/- **P** **Sainglend**[45] 1042 10-11-3 **115**........................(p) JamieBargary[(7)]
(Sean Curran) *mde most tl 3 out: sn drvn: lft cl 3rd next: sn wknd: t.o whn p.u last* **50/1**

24-3 **F** **Lamblord (IRE)**[10] 177 8-10-8 **106**........................(p) ConorSmith[(7)]
(Carroll Gray) *w ldr: rdn and ev ch 3 out: cl 3rd whn fell next* **13/2**[3]

PU-6 **P** **Up For An Oscar (IRE)**[15] 85 8-11-5 **110**........................(vt) DavidBass
(Kim Bailey) *in tch in midfield: mstke 7th: rdn 9th: struggling whn bdly hmpd 2 out: sn lost tch: t.o whn p.u last* **15/2**

/0P- **P** **Padre Tito (IRE)**[97] 4132 7-11-12 **117**........................ AidanColeman
(Emma Lavelle) *in tch in midfield: lft 5th 2 out: sn rdn and no imp: eased bnd bef last and p.u last* **20/1**

6m 28.9s (0.30) **Going Correction** -0.10s/f (Good) **10 Ran SP% 114.9**
Speed ratings (Par 105): **95,94,91,91,81 75,,,,**
CSF £128.59 CT £2772.30 TOTE £7.10: £2.20, £3.70, £3.80; EX 116.70 Trifecta £1817.60.
Owner Ron C Williams **Bred** Jimmy Howard **Trained** Westbury-On-Severn, Gloucs

FOCUS
A modest long-distance hurdle but a progressive winner.

364 STRATFORDCARAVANS.CO.UK NOVICES' H'CAP HURDLE (11 hdls) 2m 6f 7y

4:30 (4:30) (Class 4) (0-105,107) 4-Y-O+ **£3,898** (£1,144; £572; £286)

Form RPR

/44- **1** **Sukiyaki (IRE)**[25] 5467 6-11-8 **100**........................ CharliePoste 111+
(Charlie Longsdon) *mde virtually all: rdn 2 out: styd on strly and in command whn hit last: rdn out* **7/1**[3]

011- **2** 11 **Seymour Legend**[50] 5027 9-10-11 **89**........................ LiamTreadwell 89
(Jim Wilson) *t.k.h: in tch: chsd ldrs 5th: chsd wnr 8th: rdn after 2 out: 3rd and unable qck bnd bef last: wnt 2nd again sn after last: no imp* **11/4**[1]

406- **3** hd **Lawsons Thorns (IRE)**[42] 5153 6-11-7 **104**........................ BridgetAndrews[(5)] 104
(Dan Skelton) *t.k.h: hld up in tch: hdwy 7th: cl 5th 2 out: effrt in 4th bef last: no ch w wnr but battling for 2nd whn pckd last: 3rd and kpt on same pce flat* **9/1**

2P/1 **4** 5 **Sir Dylan**[10] 167 6-11-8 **100**........................ NickScholfield 97
(Polly Gundry) *t.k.h: hld up in tch in midfield: clsd to chse ldrs 3 out: effrt to chse wnr bnd bef last: sn drvn and fnd nil: btn whn hit last: sn lost 2 pls and wknd flat* **13/2**[2]

P0-4 **5** 14 **Toast And Jam (IRE)**[16] 55 6-10-10 **88**........................(t) TrevorWhelan 72
(Claire Dyson) *chsd ldrs: rdn after 2 out: wknd bnd bef last: wl btn whn mstke last* **14/1**

610- **6** 30 **Thomas Junior (FR)**[57] 4927 6-11-9 **101**........................ TomO'Brien 57
(Paul Morgan) *w wnr: mstke 4th: lost pl 8th and struggling u.p whn mstke next: wkng whn hit 2 out: t.o* **9/1**

005- **7** 21 **Stand Aside (IRE)**[54] 4980 5-11-10 **102**........................(p) RichieMcLernon 39
(Jonjo O'Neill) *mstkes: chsd ldrs: losing pl whn mstke 7th: lost tch 2 out: t.o* **14/1**

2P5- **8** 2½ **Mazurati (IRE)**[26] 5452 6-11-3 **102**........................(p) MrMJPKendrick[(7)] 37
(Ben Case) *midfield: dropped to rr and rdn 6th: nvr gng wl after: lost tch 2 out: t.o* **9/1**

65-0 **9** 14 **Willow Island (IRE)**[13] 110 6-11-2 **97**........................ KillianMoore[(3)] 19
(Sophie Leech) *a in rr: pushed along bef 3 out: lost tch bef 2 out: t.o* **25/1**

334- **P** **Douchkirk (FR)**[61] 4820 8-10-3 **88**........................(b) ConorSmith[(7)]
(Kevin Bishop) *a towards rr: rdn and struggling bef 3 out: lost tch bef 2 out: t.o whn p.u bef last* **7/1**[3]

5m 26.5s (-1.60) **Going Correction** -0.10s/f (Good) **10 Ran SP% 112.2**
Speed ratings (Par 105): **98,94,94,92,87 77,69,68,64,**
CSF £26.14 CT £173.41 TOTE £6.70: £1.10, £2.10, £3.20; EX 30.60 Trifecta £298.90.
Owner Robert Aplin **Bred** D H W Dobson **Trained** Over Norton, Oxon

FOCUS
A moderate novices' handicap hurdle and a decisive winner.

365 STRATFORDCARAVANS.CO.UK NOVICES' LIMITED H'CAP CHASE (14 fncs) 2m 3f 98y

5:00 (5:00) (Class 4) (0-120,120) 5-Y-O+ **£4,548** (£1,335; £667; £333)

Form RPR

45-4 **1** **Flash Tommie (IRE)**[11] 150 7-10-0 **101** oh7........(p) JonathanEngland[(3)] 107+
(Michael Appleby) *j.w: mde all: rdn and styd on wl bef last: nvr seriously chal: rdn out* **10/1**

014- **2** 11 **Sporting Boy (IRE)**[26] 5441 7-11-8 **120**........................(b) NoelFehily 117
(Johnny Farrelly) *chsd ldrs: chsd wnr 6th: rdn and mstke 2 out: sn drvn and no imp: plugged on* **9/4**[2]

103- **3** 1¾ **Andi'Amu (FR)**[25] 5477 5-11-1 **113**........................(t) GavinSheehan 109
(Warren Greatrex) *chsd wnr tl 6th: mstke 7th: 4th and sltly outpcd 3 out: rallied next: no ex in 3rd and btn bef last* **7/2**[3]

556- **4** 15 **River Deep (IRE)**[49] 5048 6-11-4 **116**........................ RichardJohnson 106
(Philip Hobbs) *mstkes: racd in 4th: niggled along 3rd: reminders after 5th: clsd to chse ldrs 11th: cl 3rd whn blnd 3 out: tried to rally next: 4th and btn bef last: wknd* **2/1**[1]

436- **P** **The Winking Prawn (IRE)**[23] 5510 8-10-4 **102**........................(t) PaulMoloney
(Graeme McPherson) *a in rr: mstke 3rd: struggling and mstke 8th: lost tch 10th: t.o whn p.u last* **5/1**

4m 42.8s (-7.20) **Going Correction** -0.275s/f (Good) **5 Ran SP% 112.1**
Speed ratings: **103,98,97,91,**
CSF £33.48 TOTE £8.60: £2.70, £1.90; EX 31.50 Trifecta £81.50.
Owner C L Bacon **Bred** Brian Griffin **Trained** Danethorpe, Notts
■ Muckle Roe (5-1) was withdrawn. Rule 4 applies to bets struck at board prices prior to withdrawal. Deduction - 15p in the pound. New market formed.

FOCUS
A modest novices' handicap chase and a surprise result.

366 RAYFORD CARAVAN PARK STANDARD OPEN NATIONAL HUNT FLAT RACE 2m 70y

5:35 (5:35) (Class 6) 4-6-Y-O **£1,949** (£572; £286; £143)

Form RPR

4- **1** **Top Priority (FR)**[24] 5501 4-10-9 **0**........................ MauriceLinehan[(3)] 102+
(Jonjo O'Neill) *in tch: clsd to chse ldrs 6f out: rdn and chsd wnr 2f out: pressing wnr on inner 1f out: led wl ins fnl f: r.o wl* **9/2**[2]

3- **2** ¾ **Vaillant Nonantais (FR)**[37] 5262 4-10-12 **0**........................ AndrewTinkler 100
(Nicky Henderson) *chsd ldrs tl wnt 2nd 1/2-way: led 7f out: rdn over 1f out: hdd and one pce wl ins fnl f* **7/4**[1]

4- **3** 7 **Zandino (FR)**[162] 2956 4-10-12 **0**........................ GavinSheehan 94
(Warren Greatrex) *in tch: rousted along after 3f: clsd to chse ldr 6f out tl 2f out: 3rd and outpcd over 1f out* **7/4**[1]

4 7 **The Drone (IRE)**[29] 4-10-12 **0**........................ RichardJohnson 88
(Liam Lennon, Ire) *hld up in tch: 4th and outpcd 4f out: plugged on same pce after* **7/1**[3]

4/ **5** 48 **Alys Rock (IRE)**[593] 1719 6-10-6 **0**........................ JonathanEngland[(3)] 42
(Michael Appleby) *t.k.h: chsd ldr tl led 9f out: hdd 1/2-way: rdn and lost pl 6f out: t.o fnl 3f* **14/1**

6- **6** dist **Sadiks Boy (IRE)**[26] 5454 6-11-2 **0**........................ LeeEdwards
(Aytach Sadik) *led tl 9f out: sn rdn: dropped to last 1/2-way and immediately t.o* **200/1**

3m 45.2s (-5.20) **Going Correction** -0.10s/f (Good)
WFA 4 from 6yo 4lb **6 Ran SP% 110.6**
Speed ratings: **108,107,104,101,78**
CSF £12.45 TOTE £7.30: £2.70, £1.70; EX 14.50 Trifecta £30.10.
Owner Jonjo O'Neill Racing Club **Bred** Jean-Louis Lucas **Trained** Cheltenham, Gloucs
■ Stewards' Enquiry : Andrew Tinkler two-day ban: careless riding (May 31,Jun 2)

FOCUS
A moderate looking bumper but a close finish.
T/Jkpt: Not won. T/Plt: £50.60 to a £1 stake. Pool: £74,412.00 - 1,071.79 winning tickets. T/Qpdt: £29.80 to a £1 stake. Pool: £5,015.00 - 124.35 winning tickets. **Steve Payne**

367 - 373a (Foreign Racing) - See Raceform Interactive

[349] AUTEUIL (L-H)

Sunday, May 17

OFFICIAL GOING: Turf: very soft

374a GRAS SAVOYE HIPCOVER - PRIX MARECHAL FOCH (CHASE) (CONDITIONS) (5YO+) (AMATEUR RIDERS) (TURF) 2m 6f

1:45 (12:00) 5-Y-O+ **£20,465** (£10,232; £5,968; £4,050; £1,918)

RPR

1 **Marinas (GER)**[1466] 8-10-10 **0**........................ KilianDubourg 128
(G Macaire, France) **37/10**[3]

2 shd **Viking De Balme (FR)**[727] 6-11-0 **0**........................ MrFTett 132
(Francois Nicolle, France) **41/1**

3 6 **United Park (FR)**[29] 7-10-12 **0**........................ MlleBarbaraGuenet 124
(G Macaire, France) **11/5**[1]

4 3 **Perfect Gentleman (IRE)**[41] 5224 10-11-5 **0** ow2........................ MrPWMullins 128
(W P Mullins, Ire) *w.w towards rr: hdwy on outer after 3 out: rdn and kpt on between last 2: got up for 4th cl home: nvr on terms w ldrs* **12/5**[2]

5 shd **Talk Will (FR)**[784] 8-10-8 **0**........................ MrGonzagueCottreau 117
(H De Lageneste, France) **184/10**

6 12 **Ultranet (FR)**[56] 7-11-0 **0**........................(b) MrJeromeFoucher 111
(G Chaignon, France) **49/1**

7 ¾ **Ballyrock (FR)**[17] 6-11-7 **0**........................ CCoste 117
(Y-M Porzier, France) **43/5**

U **Unzo Du Bara (FR)**[189] 2398 7-11-3 **0**........................ MrBenjaminCaron
(Francois Nicolle, France) **9/2**

5m 35.1s (-8.90) **8 Ran SP% 120.1**
PARI-MUTUEL (all including 1 euro stake): WIN 4.70; PLACE 1.60, 4.10, 1.40; DF 72.10; SF 96.50.
Owner Ecurie Sagara **Bred** Gestut Etzean **Trained** Les Mathes, France

375a GRAND STEEPLE-CHASE DE PARIS (CHASE) (GRADE 1) (5YO+) (TURF) 3m 6f

3:05 (12:00) 5-Y-O+

£296,511 (£144,961; £85,658; £59,302; £32,945; £23,062)

RPR

1 **Milord Thomas (FR)**[21] 3 6-10-10 **0**........................ JacquesRicou 160
(D Bressou, France) *cl up: led after 4th: slowed into 5th (water): scrambled over and hdd: settled in midfield: clsd 10th and trckd ldr: lft in front 5 out: rdn bef last: drvn clr run-in* **11/4**[1]

2 3½ **Shannon Rock (FR)**[21] 3 9-10-10 **0**........................(b) DavidCottin 157
(J-P Gallorini, France) *w.w in midfield: prom fr 8th: 2nd and ev ch after 2 out: nt fluent last: kpt on at same pce run-in* **6/1**[3]

3 20 **Saint Pistol (FR)**[28] 5418 7-10-10 **0**........................ ArnaudDuchene 137
(L Viel, France) *w.w towards rr: hdwy 5 out: chsd front two 2 out: sn rdn and btn: one pce u.p run-in* **12/1**

4 ½ **Sidi Bouknadel (FR)**[28] 5418 7-10-10 **0**........................ JonathanPlouganou 136
(J-L Guillochon, France) *w.w in fnl 3rd: clsd after 1/2-way: 5th and clsng 3 out: rdn and nt pce to go w ldrs bef 2 out: kpt on u.p run-in* **33/1**

5 1¼ **Tornade Precieuse (FR)**[25] 8-10-6 **0**........................(p) AlbanDesvaux 131
(Mme M Desvaux, France) *settled in midfield: hdwy to chse ldrs fr 3 out: sn rdn and nt pce of ldrs bef 2 out: sn btn* **40/1**

6 8 **Vieux Morvan (FR)**[21] 3 6-10-10 **0**........................(b) JamesReveley 127
(G Cherel, France) *racd in midfield: mstke 14th: tk clsr order 5 out: sn rdn and no further imp after 3 out* **20/1**

7 2 **On His Own (IRE)**[18] 22 11-10-10 **0**........................(b[1]) RWalsh 125
(W P Mullins, Ire) *prom: rdn and struggling whn blnd bdly 5 out (jockey did wl to stay on board): sn btn* **7/2**[2]

8 4½ **Messire Fontenail (FR)**[28] 5418 8-10-10 **0**........................(b) AnthonyLecordier 120
(C Aubert, France) *w.w in rr: rdn and no imp bef 3 out: nvr in contention* **50/1**

9 1½ **Royal Astarania (FR)**[44] 5128 6-10-10 **0**........................ OlivierJouin 119
(P Peltier, France) *w.w in midfield on inner: rdn and shortlived effrt after 5 out: sn btn* **12/1**

P **Bel La Vie (FR)**[21] 3 9-10-10 0 BertrandLestrade
(G Macaire, France) *trckd ldng gp: stl gng wl enough whn qckly lost pl and p.u bef 5 out* 7/1

U **Reglis Brunel (FR)**[25] 10-10-10 0 ThomasBeaurain
(E Lecoiffier, France) *w.w in midfield: lost pl after 1/2-way: towards rr whn blnd bdly and uns rdr 5 out* 20/1

P **Sire Collonges (FR)**[31] 5356 9-10-10 0 (b) SamTwiston-Davies
(Paul Nicholls) *led: hdd after 4th: led again 5th: hdd bef 8th: dropped into midfield: reminders 14th: scrubbed along bef 5 out: sn bhd: t.o whn p.u bef 2 out* 12/1

U **Pindare (FR)**[28] 5418 6-10-10 0 (b) AngeloGasnier
(J-P Gallorini, France) *in tch: led bef 8th: mstke and uns rdr 5 out* 20/1

U **Jemy Baie (FR)**[44] 5128 6-10-10 0 KevinNabet
(M Postic, France) *w.w in tch: cl 4th whn mstke and uns rdr 5 out* 12/1

7m 40.1s (460.10) **14** Ran SP% **128.1**
PARI-MUTUEL (all including 1 euro stake): WIN 3.00; PLACE 1.60, 1.90, 2.80; DF 6.60; SF 10.20.
Owner Magalen O Bryant **Bred** S Boucheron **Trained** France

376a - (Foreign Racing) - See Raceform Interactive

[237]TOWCESTER (R-H)

Monday, May 18

OFFICIAL GOING: Good to soft
Wind: fresh, across, changing to half against from race 5 Weather: cloudy with bright spells after morning rain

377 FLEXINEB NEBULISERS BREATHE FREELY H'CAP HURDLE (12 hdls) 2m 7f 211y

2:10 (2:10) (Class 4) (0-110,110) 4-Y-O+ **£3,249** (£954; £477; £238)

Form				RPR
54-6	**1**		**Vaihau (FR)**[10] 186 6-11-1 109 PatrickCowley(10)	121+
			(Jonjo O'Neill) *hld up in tch and a travelling wl: wnt 2nd 8th: led on bit bef 2 out: readily wnt clr bef last: easily* 7/2[3]	
460-	**2**	*19*	**Oscar Prairie (IRE)**[47] 5099 10-11-12 110 (p) GavinSheehan	105
			(Warren Greatrex) *led tl rdn and hdd bef 2 out: easily brushed aside bef last: plugged on for clr 2nd* 6/1	
03-0	**3**	*12*	**Horace Hazel**[17] 55 6-10-8 99 HarryCobden(7)	85
			(Anthony Honeyball) *chsd ldrs: reminder after 6th: 3rd and rdn after 3 out: no imp and wl hld next* 3/1[2]	
26-1	**4**	*4*	**Earcomesthedream (IRE)**[12] 148 12-11-3 108 (b) ArchieBellamy(7)	89
			(Peter Pritchard) *racd lazily: pressed ldr and on and off the bridle: lost 2nd 8th: dropped to last next: wl btn bef 2 out* 6/1	
032-	**P**		**Shady Glen (IRE)**[26] 5476 6-10-1 85 KielanWoods	
			(Graeme McPherson) *in tch: reminder after 5th: rdn and no rspnse after next: eased and p.u bef 7th* 15/8[1]	

6m 10.15s (-4.85) **Going Correction** -0.375s/f (Good) **5** Ran SP% **110.6**
Speed ratings (Par 105): **93,86,82,81,**
CSF £22.30 TOTE £4.30: £2.10, £2.90; EX 29.60 Trifecta £73.00.
Owner John P McManus **Bred** Charles Magnien **Trained** Cheltenham, Gloucs

FOCUS
Shared bends and Hurdle course on middle line. After persistent rain before racing the going was changed to good to soft, from good, good to firm in places, with Gavin Sheehan describing it as "dead, patchy and hard work". The opener was a modest handicap and they went a sensible gallop. A big step up from the easy winner, with the next two close to their marks.

378 FLEXINEB NEBULISERS BREATHE FREELY MAIDEN HURDLE (10 hdls) 2m 3f 34y

2:40 (2:41) (Class 5) 4-Y-O+ **£2,524** (£918)

Form				RPR
005-	**1**		**Little Mix**[100] 4093 4-10-9 0 GavinSheehan	98
			(Emma Lavelle) *mde most tl after 3 out: sn outpcd by wnr: 7 l down and plugging on whn lft 4 l clr last: pressed towards fin: hld on* 7/1	
35-0	**2**	*nk*	**Twelve Strings (IRE)**[11] 177 6-11-0 109 (p) LiamTreadwell	102
			(Venetia Williams) *in tch: 4th and outpcd by ldng trio 7th: no imp 3 out: wl hld whn lft 4 l 2nd last: plugged on and pressing ldr towards fin: hld cl home* 15/8[1]	
445/	**P**		**Alongthewatchtower (IRE)**[716] 589 7-11-0 0 SamTwiston-Davies	
			(Barry Brennan) *hld up in tch: struggling after 5th: lost tch and t.o bef 3 out: p.u 2 out* 14/1	
604-	**P**		**Masterplan (IRE)**[30] 5396 5-11-0 110 AidanColeman	
			(Charlie Longsdon) *w ldr: rdn and ev ch whn mstke 3 out: 3rd and fdd qckly on uphill run bef next: p.u 2 out* 9/4[2]	
F	**P**		**Fort Gabriel (FR)**[18] 41 4-10-9 0 TomMessenger	
			(Fiona Kehoe) *hld up in tch: struggling after 5th: lost tch and t.o bef 3 out: p.u 2 out* 33/1	
	F		**Fairlee Grey** 6-10-11 0 JeremiahMcGrath(3)	109+
			(Nicky Henderson) *t.k.h: chsd ldrs: led on bit sn after 3 out: clr whn j.lft and mstke next: hung rt bef last: 7 l clr whn fell heavily last* 11/4[3]	
	P		**Coxwell Crofter** 7-10-7 0 KevinJones(7)	
			(Jimmy Fox) *hld up in rr: mstke 2nd and 5th: sn lost tch: t.o whn tried to refuse 6th: immediately p.u* 50/1	

5m 2.1s (-7.50) **Going Correction** -0.375s/f (Good)
WFA 4 from 5yo+ 18lb **7** Ran SP% **116.3**
Speed ratings (Par 103): **100,99,,,,**
CSF £21.87 TOTE £6.60: £3.70, £1.60; EX 26.40.
Owner J R Lavelle & Dr Mark Scott **Bred** J R Lavelle & Dr Mark Scott **Trained** Hatherden, Hants

FOCUS
An uncompetitive maiden hurdle, in which only two finished, and there was late drama. The faller looked set to in easily, and there was a very slow finishing split from the winner.

379 FLEXINEB NEBULISERS BREATHE FREELY H'CAP CHASE (11 fncs) 2m 70y

3:10 (3:10) (Class 5) (0-100,95) 5-Y-O+ **£2,469** (£725; £362; £181)

Form				RPR
535-	**1**		**Heurtevent (FR)**[60] 4862 6-11-6 89 LeeEdwards	103+
			(Tony Carroll) *hld up in tch: clsd to press ldrs on outer after 2 out: led wl bef last: sn in command: rdn out* 16/1	
414-	**2**	*7*	**Moonlight Maggie**[31] 5376 8-11-3 86 (t) PaddyBrennan	93
			(Tom George) *hld up in tch: hdwy to join ldrs after 3 out: led next: sn hdd and unable qck: kpt on same pce after* 7/1	
0-51	**3**	*6*	**Odds On Dan (IRE)**[6] 256 9-10-7 83 7ex (tp) DeanPratt(7)	85
			(Lucinda Egerton) *hld up in tch in rr: clsd bef 3 out: rdn and wnt 3rd 2 out: no imp after* 7/1	
331-	**4**	*15*	**Table Bluff (IRE)**[207] 2024 6-11-12 95 NicodeBoinville	84
			(John Spearing) *chsd ldr: ev ch 3 out tl no ex and btn bef next: wknd 2 out* 4/1[2]	
553-	**5**	*nk*	**Thom Thumb (IRE)**[130] 3589 9-10-12 81 (tp) JamesBest	69
			(Paul Webber) *chsd ldrs: led bef 2 out: hdd 2 out and sn wknd: fin lame* 15/8[1]	
02-1	**6**	*1 1/2*	**Beauchamp Viking**[18] 42 11-10-5 74 (t) DaveCrosse	60
			(Hugo Froud) *led: rdn and hdd after 3 out: wknd 2 out* 12/1	
30P-	**P**		**Gainsborough's Art (IRE)**[51] 5024 10-9-7 69 oh14 (p) DanielHiskett(7)	
			(Harry Chisman) *dropped to rr 5th: lost tch 8th: t.o whn p.u 2 out* 66/1	
P1-2	**F**		**Red Whisper**[18] 42 11-11-3 91 (t) JakeHodson(5)	77
			(Rob Summers) *hld up in rr: hdwy into midfield whn mstke 8th: 7th and wkng whn fell 2 out* 5/1[3]	
303-	**U**		**Carobello (IRE)**[24] 5526 8-10-8 84 (bt) MrZBaker(7)	
			(Martin Bosley) *chsd ldrs tl mstke and uns rdr 3 out* 16/1	

4m 10.0s (-6.10) **Going Correction** -0.375s/f (Good) **9** Ran SP% **117.4**
Speed ratings: **99,95,92,85,85 84,,,**
CSF £123.90 CT £868.39 TOTE £16.50: £3.80, £2.00, £2.20; EX 108.40 Trifecta £1425.70.
Owner Layton T Cheshire **Bred** Gerard Ferron & Marc Cochet **Trained** Cropthorne, Worcs

FOCUS
A moderate handicap chase and they finished well strung out. A British pb from the winner though he did bigger figures in France.

380 HAYGAIN HAY STEAMERS CLEAN HEALTHY FORAGE H'CAP HURDLE (10 hdls) 2m 3f 34y

3:40 (3:41) (Class 4) (0-115,115) 4-Y-O+ **£3,249** (£954; £477; £238)

Form				RPR
65-3	**1**		**Iora Glas (IRE)**[12] 139 6-10-13 102 SeanQuinlan	110+
			(Fergal O'Brien) *hld up in tch: hdwy to chse ldrs 7th: chal after 3 out: rdn between last 2: led flat: styd on* 3/1[2]	
052-	**2**	*2*	**Knight Bachelor**[57] 4944 5-11-5 108 (t) GavinSheehan	115+
			(Warren Greatrex) *chsd ldrs: hdwy to ld 6th: rdn bef 2 out: hit last: hdd and no ex flat* 13/8[1]	
104-	**3**	*32*	**Miss Sassypants**[26] 5466 6-11-5 108 RyanMahon	85
			(Seamus Mullins) *hld up in tch in last pair: hdwy to chse ldrs 7th: cl 3rd 3 out: rdn and btn bef next: wknd 2 out* 12/1	
6FP-	**4**	*9*	**Bayley's Dream**[30] 5399 6-11-5 108 [1] LiamTreadwell	77
			(Paul Webber) *hld up in last pair: rdn and struggling 7th: t.o* 8/1	
055-	**5**	*1 3/4*	**Heroes Or Ghosts (IRE)**[53] 4996 6-11-6 112 JamesBanks(3)	80
			(Jo Davis) *chsd ldr tl 3 out: sn rdn and btn: wknd bef next: t.o* 10/1	
135-	**P**		**Bathwick Man**[221] 1807 10-11-11 114 ConorO'Farrell	
			(David Pipe) *in tch in midfield: rdn and dropped to last 7th: t.o 3 out: p.u next* 20/1	
136-	**P**		**Maller Tree**[24] 5523 8-11-12 115 (v) NoelFehily	
			(David Dennis) *led tl 6th: rdn and wknd bef 3 out: t.o whn p.u 2 out* 9/2[3]	

4m 59.3s (-10.30) **Going Correction** -0.375s/f (Good) **7** Ran SP% **113.9**
Speed ratings (Par 105): **105,104,91,87,87 ,**
CSF £8.53 CT £47.54 TOTE £4.40: £2.70, £1.70; EX 9.90 Trifecta £69.60.
Owner Imperial Racing Partnership **Bred** Mrs Mary Jane Roberts **Trained** Naunton, Gloucs

FOCUS
A fair handicap hurdle and the front two pulled a long way clear. Another step up from the winner.

381 HAYGAIN HAY STEAMERS CLEAN HEALTHY FORAGE H'CAP CHASE (13 fncs) 2m 3f 179y

4:10 (4:10) (Class 4) (0-110,110) 5-Y-O+ **£3,768** (£1,106; £553; £276)

Form				RPR
3-21	**1**		**By The Boardwalk (IRE)**[7] 239 7-11-3 104 7ex (t) TomBellamy(3)	124+
			(Kim Bailey) *hld up in tch: trckd ldrs 9th: led on bit bef 2 out: readily wnt clr and j.rt last: eased towards fin: v easily* 6/4[1]	
P-31	**2**	*23*	**Riddlestown (IRE)**[6] 258 8-11-4 102 7ex (b) HarrySkelton	101
			(Caroline Fryer) *chsd ldrs tl led 10th: rdn and hdd bef 2 out: sn rdn and btn: j.rt last: plugged on to hold 2nd flat* 9/4[2]	
1P-3	**3**	*5*	**Safari Journey (USA)**[6] 255 11-11-12 110 (p) JakeGreenall	104
			(Lucinda Egerton) *hld up in tch in rr: effrt in 4th after 3 out: no imp and btn next: wnt modest 3rd last* 12/1	
550-	**4**	*10*	**Temple Lord (FR)**[165] 2891 9-11-5 103 RichieMcLernon	91
			(Jonjo O'Neill) *in tch: mstke and lost pl 8th: hdwy to chse ldrs 3 out: j.rt next: sn rdn and btn: wknd and j.rt last* 8/1[3]	
F1-0	**P**		**Wicklewood**[7] 240 9-11-9 107 (bt) TomCannon	
			(Mark Gillard) *led tl 10th: struggling u.p 3 out: sn wknd: bhd whn p.u 2 out* 11/1	
53-5	**P**		**Keychain (IRE)**[17] 64 5-11-3 101 (v) BrendanPowell	
			(Brendan Powell) *chsd ldr tl 10th: dropped to last and struggling 3 out: sn lost tch and bhd whn p.u 2 out* 17/2	

5m 7.95s (-10.25) **Going Correction** -0.375s/f (Good) **6** Ran SP% **108.4**
Speed ratings: **105,95,93,89,,**
CSF £5.13 TOTE £2.70: £1.50, £1.50; EX 6.00 Trifecta £18.60.
Owner J Perriss **Bred** Colman O'Flynn **Trained** Andoversford, Gloucs

FOCUS
No more than a modest handicap chase but the winner was very impressive. Another step forward from the winner, in line with the best of his hurdle form.

382 HAYGAIN HAY STEAMERS CLEAN HEALTHY FORAGE NOVICES' CHASE (15 fncs) 2m 5f 153y

4:40 (4:40) (Class 4) 5-Y-O+ **£3,768** (£1,106; £553; £276)

Form				RPR
300-	**1**		**Vieux Lion Rouge (FR)**[66] 4741 6-10-12 0 TomScudamore	130+
			(David Pipe) *chsd ldr tl led bef 2 out: drvn and hdd between last 2: led again last: styd on: rdn out* 4/6[1]	
022-	**2**	*3*	**Simply The West (IRE)**[24] 5507 6-10-12 0 (t) AidanColeman	128+
			(Charlie Longsdon) *chsd ldrs: pckd 4th and reins ct up in tack afterwards: rdr dropped whip 6th: chal jst bef 2 out: led between last 2: hdd last: one pce flat* 6/1[3]	
242-	**3**	*7*	**Themanfrom Minella (IRE)**[53] 4993 6-10-5 0 (t) MrMJPKendrick(7)	122
			(Ben Case) *j. novicey: chsd ldrs: rdn 12th: plugged on same pce fr 2 out* 11/2[2]	
325-	**4**	*8*	**Rosa Fleet (IRE)**[56] 4965 7-10-5 108 LiamTreadwell	108
			(Venetia Williams) *t.k.h: hld up in last pair: j.rt and bmpd rival 1st: effrt bef 3 out: no imp bef 2 out* 25/1	
120-	**5**	*11*	**Greybougg**[33] 5341 6-10-12 0 ConorO'Farrell	108
			(Nigel Hawke) *led tl rdn and hdd after 3 out: 3rd and btn next: wknd between last 2* 6/1[3]	

523- **6** *23* **Amazing D'Azy (IRE)**[228] 1701 7-10-5 0........................ DavidBass 84
(Kim Bailey) *a in last pair: cannoned into 1st: struggling 12th: lost tch 3 out: t.o* **16/1**

5m 37.6s (-15.40) **Going Correction** -0.375s/f (Good) **6** Ran SP% **113.7**
Speed ratings: **113,111,109,106,102 94**
CSF £5.65 TOTE £2.30: £1.60, £2.10; EX 6.10 Trifecta £17.90.
Owner Prof Caroline Tisdall & John Gent **Bred** F M Cottin **Trained** Nicholashayne, Devon

FOCUS
An interesting novice chase and a workmanlike victory for the odds-on favourite. The winner was a 140 hurdler and there should be more to come.

383 HAYGAIN HAY STEAMERS CLEAN HEALTHY FORAGE CONDITIONAL JOCKEYS' MARES' H'CAP HURDLE (8 hdls) 1m 7f 181y
5:10 (5:10) (Class 5) (0-100,99) 4-Y-O+ **£2,274** (£667; £333; £166)

Form RPR

353- **1** **Carrigeen Lantana (IRE)**[155] 3107 6-11-3 **90**........................ CraigNichol 93+
(Donald McCain) *chsd ldrs: wnt 2nd bef 3 out: rdn and 5 l down whn lft in ld 2 out: hld on gamely flat: all out* **8/1**

0- **2** *hd* **Camillas Wish (IRE)**[44] 5131 6-11-2 **89**........................ JJBurke 90
(J T R Dreaper, Ire) *midfield: dropped to last after 3rd: rdn 5th: 6th and looked wl hld after 3 out: 10 l down whn lft 5 l 3rd 2 out: ev ch u.p last: one pce and hld fnl 100yds* **4/1**[1]

032- **3** *3 ½* **Cruise In Style (IRE)**[29] 5412 9-10-8 **86**........................(tp) ConorSmith(5) 85
(Kevin Bishop) *hld up in rr: hdwy into midfield 4th: chsd ldrs bef 3 out: rdn and no imp whn ev ch and j.lft 2 out: j.lft last: outpcd on flat* **13/2**[2]

U05- **4** *20* **Diamond Gesture (IRE)**[24] 5516 7-10-13 **89**........................ ConorShoemark(3) 71
(Fergal O'Brien) *t.k.h: hld up in rr: hdwy 4th: chsd ldrs 3 out: rdn and btn ent st: wkng whn lft 4th and hmpd 2 out* **7/1**[3]

P34- **5** *1 ¼* **Lady Ra (IRE)**[30] 5397 6-10-0 **76**........................ DeanPratt(3) 55
(Lucinda Egerton) *hld up in midfield: effrt 3 out: no imp bef 2 out: wknd 2 out* **8/1**

414- **P** **My Nosy Rosy**[259] 1420 7-11-8 **98**........................(t) JamieBargary(3)
(Ben Case) *hld up in tch: dropped to rr and rdn after 5th: no rspnse: fdd after next: t.o whn p.u 2 out* **14/1**

031- **P** **Passing Fiesta**[26] 5466 6-10-12 **88**........................(bt) MichaelHeard(3)
(Sarah-Jayne Davies) *chsd ldr: rdn after 4th: lost 2nd after next: losing pl whn mstke 3 out: sn fdd: bhd whn p.u 2 out* **8/1**

PP-5 **F** **Kentford Heiress**[18] 30 5-10-9 **82**........................ JeremiahMcGrath 89+
(Seamus Mullins) *led: 5 l clr and stl travelling wl whn fell 2 out* **4/1**[1]

F4-3 **P** **Fashion Icon (FR)**[13] 119 4-11-2 **93**........................(v[1]) TomBellamy
(Nigel Hawke) *t.k.h: chsd ldrs: rdn and losing pl whn mstke 3 out: t.o whn p.u next* **8/1**

4m 8.2s (0.30) **Going Correction** -0.375s/f (Good)
WFA 4 from 5yo+ 18lb **9** Ran SP% **116.9**
Speed ratings (Par 103): **84,83,82,72,71** , , ,
CSF £41.23 CT £224.00 TOTE £8.00: £2.70, £1.80, £2.20; EX 44.70 Trifecta £254.70.
Owner Paul & Clare Rooney **Bred** Mrs R H Lalor **Trained** Cholmondeley, Cheshire

FOCUS
A moderate handicap hurdle for mares and, for the second time on the card, there was a late twist. The faller was set to win, with the first three rated pretty much to form.
T/Plt: £97.90 to a £1 stake. Pool: £52,525.40 - 391.59 winning tickets. T/Qpdt: £9.80 to a £1 stake. Pool: £5,317.89 - 400.59 winning tickets. **Steve Payne**

384-386a (Foreign Racing) - See Raceform Interactive

[160]NEWTON ABBOT (L-H)
Tuesday, May 19

OFFICIAL GOING: Good to soft (good in places; 6.0)
Wind: mild across Weather: sunny with cloudy periods Rails: Chase bends moved out by 2 meters, Hurdle bends moved in by 2 meters.

387 PAIGNTON ZOO MARES' NOVICES' HURDLE (10 hdls) 2m 5f 122y
5:30 (5:30) (Class 4) 4-Y-O+ **£3,898** (£1,144; £572; £286)

Form RPR

03-1 **1** **Miss Serious (IRE)**[19] 28 5-11-4 115........................ NickScholfield 122+
(Jeremy Scott) *j. sltly rt at times: mde most: hdd after blundering 3 out: rdn to led again next: gd jump last: edgd lft: drvn out* **7/1**[3]

/5-2 **2** *½* **One Big Love**[15] 100 7-10-12 0........................ NoelFehily 115+
(Harry Fry) *trckd ldr: wnt lft 1st: bmpd whn chalng on inner after 7th: led narrowly next: hdd 2 out: stl upsides w ev ch whn nt fluent last: kpt on but hld after* **9/2**[2]

1- **3** *24* **Peggy Do (IRE)**[52] 5029 7-10-12 0........................ DarylJacob 96
(Nicky Henderson) *trckd ldrs: rdn after 3 out: nt pce to chal: wknd next (b.b.v)* **30/100**[1]

26-0 **4** *34* **Dashul (IRE)**[14] 120 6-10-12 0........................ LiamHeard 62
(Jeremy Scott) *trckd ldrs: wnt lft 1st: rdn after 7th: wknd after 3 out: t.o* **50/1**

500- **P** **Rebel Island (IRE)**[27] 5481 6-10-5 66........................ MissLeandaTickle(7)
(John Panvert) *hld up in tch: wknd qckly 7th: p.u bef next* **250/1**

444- **P** **Lucky Gal**[100] 4113 5-10-9 0........................ JeremiahMcGrath(3)
(Martin Hill) *hld up in tch: nt fluent 5th: struggling after 7th: wknd appr 2 out: p.u bef last* **33/1**

5m 24.6s (4.40) **Going Correction** +0.275s/f (Yiel) **6** Ran SP% **112.9**
Speed ratings (Par 105): **103,102,94,81,**
CSF £35.88 TOTE £6.20: £2.00, £2.50; EX 12.70 Trifecta £31.50.
Owner Pillhead House Partners **Bred** Sean Galwey **Trained** Brompton Regis, Somerset

FOCUS
Chase bends moved out 2m and Hurdle bends moved in by 2m but impact on distances not quantified. An upset in the opener as the long odds-on favourite ran well below expectations. The first two are rated pretty much to their marks in a fair race of its type.

388 SIS BEST IN OVICES' H'CAP CHASE (20 fncs) 3m 1f 170y
6:00 (6:00) (Class 4) (0-105,101) 5-Y-O+ **£3,898** (£1,144; £572; £286)

Form RPR

50-2 **1** **Young Cheddar (IRE)**[13] 150 8-11-4 **93**........................ NickScholfield 118+
(Polly Gundry) *trckd ldrs tl lost pl whn blundering bdly 8th: smooth hdwy 15th: led after 4 out: drew wl clr after next: v easily* **6/1**[3]

PP4- **2** *17* **Back In June**[43] 5190 7-11-12 **101**........................(b[1]) TomO'Brien 99
(Paul Henderson) *trckd ldrs: hit 2nd: rdn along whn lost pl 10th: plugged on past wkng horses fr 3 out: wnt 2nd bef last: nvr any ch w wnr* **12/1**

05-2 **3** *21* **Handsome Horace (IRE)**[19] 30 5-11-6 **95**........................ RichardJohnson 78
(Philip Hobbs) *hld up: hit 5th: hdwy 11th: hit 14th: led after 16th: rdn and hdd whn nt fluent 3 out: wknd next: lost 2nd sn after: wnt lft and awkward last: t.o* **2/1**[1]

112- **4** *10* **Clubs Are Trumps (IRE)**[25] 5512 6-11-11 **100**........................(p) WillKennedy 71
(Jonjo O'Neill) *prom: hit 7th: reminders: nt fluent 11th: hit 13th: sn drvn: no ch fr after 4 out: t.o* **4/1**[2]

F34/ **5** *1 ¾* **Molly Oscar (IRE)**[45] 9-11-3 **92**........................(b) NoelFehily 58
(Johnny Farrelly) *trckd ldrs: hit 11th: led after 16th: sn rdn: wknd 3 out: t.o* **10/1**

45-3 **6** *9* **Beaujolais Bob**[19] 31 7-10-0 **75** oh6........................(bt) BrendanPowell 33
(Richard Hawker) *hld up: rdn after 15th: nvr threatened: wknd after 4 out: t.o* **10/1**

252- **7** *30* **Driving Well (IRE)**[202] 2124 7-11-0 **89**........................ RobertDunne 20
(Arthur Whiting) *trckd ldrs: rdn after 16th: wknd after next: t.o* **25/1**

12-5 **P** **Tara Tavey (IRE)**[14] 122 10-11-1 **97**........................(tp) ConorSmith(7)
(Kevin Bishop) *nvr fluent or travelling: sn t.o: p.u bef 6th* **6/1**[3]

0-P **P** **Supreme Danehill (IRE)**[20] 13 7-11-8 **97**........................(p) DarylJacob
(Gordon Edwards) *hld up: nt fluent 9th: wkng whn slow jump 4 out: t.o next: p.u bef 2 out* **20/1**

6m 41.2s (-3.40) **Going Correction** +0.075s/f (Yiel) **9** Ran SP% **116.4**
Speed ratings: **108,102,96,93,93 90,81,** ,
CSF £71.97 CT £194.15 TOTE £9.70: £2.30, £1.80, £1.60; EX 63.70 Trifecta £872.10.
Owner G Carstairs **Bred** John & Donncha Cleary **Trained** Ottery St Mary, Devon

FOCUS
Few could have predicted the ease in which this handicap chase would be won. A big step up from the winner in what seems a good time.

389 AT THE RACES SKY 415 H'CAP HURDLE (10 hdls) 2m 5f 122y
6:30 (6:30) (Class 3) (0-135,132) 4-Y-O+ **£5,523** (£1,621; £810; £405)

Form RPR

1P0- **1** **Ustica (IRE)**[45] 5142 5-11-4 **124**........................(b[1]) RichieMcLernon 130+
(Jonjo O'Neill) *trckd ldrs: travelling strly whn chalng 3 out: led appr 2 out: sn rdn: styd on* **4/1**[2]

003- **2** *1 ¾* **St Dominick (IRE)**[49] 5083 8-10-1 **107**........................ JamesBest 109
(Jackie Du Plessis) *racd keenly: hld up: tk clsr order 7th: rdn after 3 out: ev ch appr 2 out tl no ex fr last* **10/3**[1]

22P- **3** *7* **My Legal Lady**[33] 5355 10-10-12 **118**........................(vt) TomScudamore 115
(Stuart Howe) *prom: led 7th: rdn and hdd appr 2 out: styd on same pce* **15/2**

F02- **4** *1* **Laughton Park**[43] 5210 10-10-4 **117**........................ FreddieMitchell(7) 112
(Suzy Smith) *trckd ldrs: rdn after 3 out: styd on same pce fr next* **5/1**[3]

F0-4 **5** *17* **Buck Magic I (IRE)**[15] 102 9-10-13 **119**........................ MarkQuinlan 101
(Neil Mulholland) *j. sltly rt: led: mstke 6th: hdd next: sn rdn: wknd after 3 out* **10/3**[1]

66-0 **6** *22* **Quincy Des Pictons (FR)**[11] 185 11-11-3 **123**........................ RhysFlint 83
(Alan Jones) *in tch: struggling after 6th: wknd after next: t.o* **10/1**

314- **7** *4 ½* **Raajih**[38] 5274 7-11-11 **131**........................(tp) DarylJacob 87
(Richard Woollacott) *trckd ldrs: nudged along fr 6th: lost pl next: wknd 3 out: t.o* **12/1**

5m 22.4s (2.20) **Going Correction** +0.275s/f (Yiel) **7** Ran SP% **111.4**
Speed ratings (Par 107): **107,106,103,103,97 89,87**
CSF £17.07 CT £91.07 TOTE £5.80: £3.50, £2.10; EX 24.80 Trifecta £147.20.
Owner Deep Sea Partnership **Bred** Desmond Devereux **Trained** Cheltenham, Gloucs

FOCUS
Recent winning form was thin on the ground and it's debatable as to the strength of this feature contest. The second and third set the level.

390 NEWTONABBOTRACING.COM H'CAP CHASE (16 fncs) 2m 4f 216y
7:00 (7:00) (Class 4) (0-120,120) 5-Y-O+ **£3,898** (£1,144; £572; £286)

Form RPR

11-2 **1** **Bang On Time (IRE)**[12] 163 9-11-6 **114**........................(p) DarylJacob 122
(Richard Woollacott) *trckd ldr: chal 10th: led after 4 out: drew clr fr 2 out: kpt up to work run-in* **4/1**[3]

F3-2 **2** *17* **Sergeant Dick (IRE)**[12] 174 10-11-6 **117**........................(tp) JamesBanks(3) 113
(Andy Turnell) *j.rt thrght and nvr that fluent: led: reminder after 8th: rdn after next: jnd 10th: hdd after 4 out: hld fr next: wknd between last 2* **11/10**[1]

4/P- **3** *39* **Ciceron (IRE)**[50] 5074 9-11-11 **119**........................(t) RichardJohnson 77
(Neil King) *trckd ldrs: rdn in cl 3rd after 4 out: wknd after next: t.o (b.b.v)* **2/1**[2]

P **4** *26* **Alefou D'Airy (FR)**[19] 27 5-11-12 **120**........................(b) JamesDavies 54
(Jimmy Frost) *trckd ldrs: rdn along fr 9th: hit 12th: sn wknd: t.o* **14/1**

5m 23.3s (1.90) **Going Correction** +0.075s/f (Yiel) **4** Ran SP% **107.6**
Speed ratings: **99,92,78,69**
CSF £9.10 TOTE £4.10; EX 6.50 Trifecta £9.10.
Owner Taunton Racecourse Owners Club **Bred** James M Kiernan **Trained** South Molton, Devon

FOCUS
This took little winnin, but seemingly another step forward from the winner.

391 NEWTON ABBOT RACECOURSE ON FACEBOOK H'CAP HURDLE (9 hdls) 2m 2f 110y
7:30 (7:30) (Class 5) (0-100,98) 4-Y-O+ **£3,422** (£997; £499)

Form RPR

50-2 **1** **Upton Wood**[7] 265 9-11-12 **98**........................(p) JamesDavies 110+
(Chris Down) *mde all but pressed for ld virtually thrght: rdn after 3 out: strly chal next: edgd sltly lft run-in: jst hld on: all out* **9/2**[3]

00-2 **2** *shd* **Winged Express (IRE)**[7] 262 6-10-9 **81**........................(p) AdamWedge 94+
(Alexandra Dunn) *mid-div: hdwy 6th: rdn for str chal appr 2 out: ev ch whn awkward on landing last: kpt on wl towards fin where short of room: jst hld* **6/4**[1]

6P6- **3** *7* **Dropzone (USA)**[63] 4822 6-10-6 **78**........................(b) ConorO'Farrell 85
(Brian Forsey) *mid-div: rdn after 3 out: wnt 3rd appr 2 out: styd on but nvr threatened ldrs* **25/1**

/50- **4** *19* **Whipcrackaway (IRE)**[63] 4821 6-11-9 **95**........................(b[1]) LeightonAspell 84
(Peter Hedger) *mid-div: pushed along after 6th: rdn after 3 out: wnt modest 4th between last 2: nvr threatened* **16/1**

000/ **5** *1 ¼* **Sylvan Legend**[403] 5262 7-10-5 **77**........................(p) NoelFehily 64
(Neil Mulholland) *chsd ldrs: rdn in cl 2nd briefly after 3 out: wknd bef next* **4/1**[2]

F46- **6** *23* **Mexican Border (GER)**[194] 2290 6-11-9 **98**........................[1] JeremiahMcGrath(3) 65
(Martin Hill) *chsd ldrs: rdn after 3 out: wknd qckly: t.o* **6/1**

/0-P **7** *4* **Princess Annabelle**[19] 30 6-10-8 **85**........................(b) AliceMills(5) 48
(Rod Millman) *racd keenly: pressed wnr most of way tl wknd appr 3 out: t.o* **33/1**

646- **8** *1* **Etheridge Annie**[64] 4814 6-11-9 **95**........................ DaveCrosse 57
(Hugo Froud) *in last pair: rdn along fr 5th: wknd 3 out: t.o* **16/1**

P/P- **P** **Exiles Return (IRE)**[378] 127 13-10-0 **72** oh8........................ MarkQuinlan
(Jackie Retter) *pressed wnr tl nt fluent 5th: sn wknd: t.o whn p.u bef 3 out* **80/1**

The Form Book Jumps 2015-16, Raceform Ltd, Newbury, RG14 5SJ

/40- **P** **Indiana Oscar**[38] [5280] 7-10-0 72 oh3 .... JamesBest
(Carroll Gray) j.rt at times: nvr travelling in last pair: tailing off 6th: p.u bef 2 out **25/1**
4m 36.7s (6.70) **Going Correction** +0.275s/f (Yiel) **10** Ran SP% **116.1**
Speed ratings (Par 103): **96,95,93,85,84 74,73,72,** ,
CSF £11.62 CT £150.35 TOTE £4.00: £1.20, £1.30, £6.30; EX 13.00 Trifecta £249.90.
Owner C J Down & C B Stevens **Bred** C J Down **Trained** Mutterton, Devon

FOCUS
This was run at a searching gallop and served up a thrilling finish. The winner is rated back to his very best.

392 SIS LIVE STANDARD OPEN NATIONAL HUNT FLAT RACE 2m 167y
8:00 (8:01) (Class 5) 4-6-Y-O **£1,711** (£498; £249)

Form RPR

U- **1** **One Cool Scorpion (IRE)**[91] [4283] 4-10-10 0 .... RichardJohnson 98
(Philip Hobbs) trckd ldrs: rdn to ld jst over 1f out: styd on wl: drvn out **3/1**[2]

5- **2** *nk* **Bindon Mill**[382] [70] 6-11-0 0 .... DenisO'Regan 101
(Victor Dartnall) led: jnd 4f out: rdn 2f out: hdd jst over 1f out: kpt on **8/1**

00- **3** *4 1/2* **Stand By Me (FR)**[110] [3944] 5-11-0 0 .... TomScudamore 97
(Alan Jones) mid-div: pushed along and stdy prog over 4f out: rdn in cl 4th over 2f out: styd on same pce fnl f **25/1**

4 *1* **Blu Cavalier** 5-11-0 0 .... ConorO'Farrell 96+
(Alexandra Dunn) rn green and a little unruly leaving the s: last: stdy prog fr 1/2-way: rdn in cl 5th over 2f out: styd on same pce fnl f **12/1**

26- **5** *3 3/4* **Bleu Et Noir**[45] [5143] 4-10-10 0 .... MichaelByrne 89
(Tim Vaughan) prom: disp ld 4f out tl rdn jst over 2f out: styd on same pce **5/1**

6 *16* **Pollyogan (IRE)** 5-10-7 0 .... NoelFehily 72
(Harry Fry) rn v green: sn pushed along in last trio: rdn wl over 7f out: sme late minor prog but nvr any danger **11/4**[1]

7 *3 3/4* **Virgile De Gene (FR)**[184] 6-11-0 0 .... TommyPhelan 75
(Nick Ayliffe) chsd ldrs tl 7f out **100/1**

8 *11* **Buy Me Out** 5-10-0 0 .... MrEDavid(7) 58
(Grace Harris) mid-div: hdwy to trck ldrs over 7f out: wknd over 3f out **40/1**

9 *1 3/4* **Never Learn (IRE)** 4-10-10 0 .... BrendanPowell 60
(Colin Tizzard) rn green: mid-div: towards rr whn rdn over 7f out: nvr a factor **4/1**[3]

00- **10** *19* **Norse Da**[39] [5262] 5-10-9 0 .... ConorRing(5) 47
(Helen Nelmes) chsd ldrs tl 5f out: sn wknd: t.o **100/1**

11 *27* **Garryduff Cross (IRE)** 5-11-0 0 .... PaulMoloney 22
(Helen Nelmes) mid-div tl 5f out: t.o **40/1**

12 *9* **Palmers Bridge**[16] 6-11-0 0 .... NickScholfield 14
(Linda Blackford) a towards rr: t.o **33/1**

4m 4.2s (4.10) **Going Correction** +0.275s/f (Yiel)
WFA 4 from 5yo+ 4lb **12** Ran SP% **120.8**
Speed ratings: **101,100,98,98,96 88,87,82,81,72 59,55**
CSF £26.55 TOTE £4.50: £1.80, £2.70, £4.50; EX 32.70 Trifecta £218.30.
Owner Louisville Syndicate II **Bred** F R Jarvey **Trained** Withycombe, Somerset

FOCUS
Some powerful yards were represented in this ordinary bumper. The fifth sets the level.

393 TOTNES AND BRIDGETOWN H'CAP HUNTERS' CHASE (16 fncs) 2m 4f 216y
8:30 (8:30) (Class 4) 5-Y-O+ **£3,743** (£1,161; £580; £290)

Form RPR

0U-1 **1** **Current Event (FR)**[20] [18] 8-12-0 135 .... MissBFrost(7) 146+
(Mrs Rose Loxton) mde all: jnd 3rd tl 10th: strly chal 4 out tl after next: jnd again briefly 2 out: qcknd clr: readily **6/5**[1]

U/4- **2** *5* **King Of Alcatraz (IRE)**[384] [21] 9-10-2 109 .... MissVWade(7) 114+
(N Harris) trckd ldrs: hit 2nd: chal 4 out tl rdn after 3 out: bk upsides next: hld whn awkward last **4/1**[2]

23U- **3** *8* **Ballytober**[26] [5503] 9-10-12 119 .... (t) MissCPrichard(7) 116
(Ian Prichard) hld up: hdwy 5th: rdn after 4 out: wnt 3rd after next: styd on same pce fr 2 out **9/2**[3]

/5-4 **4** *3/4* **Findlay's Find (IRE)**[20] [17] 9-10-2 107 oh4 .... (p) MissJodieHughes(5) 103
(Mrs Myfanwy Miles) chsd ldrs: pushed along fr 9th: outpcd after 4 out: styd on fr 2 out: wnt 4th run-in **14/1**

P3-0 **5** *nk* **Fine Resolve**[20] [13] 6-10-0 107 oh12 .... MrEDavid(7) 104
(Andrew Leyshon) j.lft at times: in tch: rdn after 4 out: sn one pce **33/1**

P5-4 **6** *3/4* **Swallows Delight (IRE)**[20] [12] 10-10-2 107 oh4 .... MrJNixon(5) 100
(Mrs Julie Mansell) disp 3rd tl 10th: rdn whn nt fluent 4 out: one pce fr next **12/1**

05-2 **7** *22* **Delta Borget (FR)**[20] [12] 10-10-4 109 .... (p) MissJBuck(5) 85
(Mrs L J Jefford) hld up in tch: rdn whn hit 3 out: sn wknd: t.o **7/1**

10P- **8** *2* **Bermuda Boy (FR)**[30] [5409] 10-10-0 107 .... (bt) DavidNoonan(7) 79
(Steve Flook) struggling in last but in tch fr 6th: wknd 3 out: t.o **25/1**

5m 21.1s (-0.30) **Going Correction** +0.075s/f (Yiel) **8** Ran SP% **117.3**
Speed ratings: **103,101,98,98,97 97,89,88**
CSF £7.17 CT £16.37 TOTE £2.20: £1.20, £1.60, £1.40; EX 7.10 Trifecta £34.60.
Owner Pearl Bloodstock Ltd **Bred** M L Bloodstock Limited **Trained** Bruton, Somerset

FOCUS
This revolved heavily around the favourite.
T/Plt: £315.00 to a £1 stake. Pool: £59,761.97 - 138.49 winning units. T/Qpdt: £35.80 to a £1 stake. Pool: £6,482.25 - 133.74 winning units. **Tim Mitchell**

[258]SOUTHWELL (L-H)
Wednesday, May 20
OFFICIAL GOING: Good (good to firm in places; 8.3)
Wind: fresh 1/2 behind Weather: fine and sunny

394 SUPPORT BEAUMOND HOUSE ON 2ND JUNE BEGINNERS' CHASE (19 fncs) 2m 7f 209y
5:50 (5:50) (Class 4) 5-Y-O+ **£3,898** (£1,144; £572; £286)

Form RPR

510- **1** **Royale Django (IRE)**[46] [5142] 6-11-0 0 .... RichardJohnson 138+
(Tim Vaughan) j.rt at times: chsd ldrs: 2nd 5th: led 4 out: pushed clr appr next: heavily eased run-in **7/2**[3]

111- **2** *20* **In The Rough (IRE)**[214] [1944] 6-11-0 0 .... WillKennedy 118+
(Jonjo O'Neill) chsd ldng pair 8th: pushed along 10th: drvn 4 out: 7 l down and wl hld whn blnd next **6/5**[1]

505- **3** *13* **Centasia**[33] [5365] 8-10-7 0 .... (t) GavinSheehan 98
(Warren Greatrex) w ldr: led after 3rd: blnd 14th: hdd 4 out: wknd bef next: hit 2 out **7/4**[2]

FF3/ **4** *58* **Roving Lad (IRE)**[31] 8-11-0 106 .... (t) PaulMoloney 51
(Paul John Gilligan, Ire) in rr: drvn 12th: sn lost tch: t.o 15th: vventually completed **33/1**

3-43 **5** *12* **Senor Alco (FR)**[6] [300] 9-10-7 79 .... MissETodd(7) 40
(Victor Thompson) led tl after 3rd: lost pl and pushed along 8th: bhd and reminders 12th: sn t.o: eventually completed **66/1**

6m 15.5s (-7.50) **Going Correction** +0.125s/f (Yiel) **5** Ran SP% **108.5**
Speed ratings: **117,110,106,87,84**
CSF £8.30 TOTE £3.90: £2.50, £1.10; EX 8.60 Trifecta £12.10.
Owner J Durston & N Harris **Bred** Paul Reynolds **Trained** Aberthin, Vale of Glamorgan

FOCUS
Fences sited 6yds inside the line raced on May 12th, bends moved to fresh ground. The opening contest was a fairly good beginners' chase. They went an initially modest gallop on ground officially described as good, good to firm in places. The impressive winner stepped up on the best of his hurdle form and looks a decent recruit.

395 SOUTHWELL RESIDENTS' EVENING 2ND JUNE H'CAP CHASE (16 fncs) 2m 4f 62y
6:20 (6:20) (Class 3) (0-130,130) 5-Y-O+ **£6,388** (£1,928; £993; £526)

Form RPR

U2-1 **1** **Pair Of Jacks (IRE)**[14] [138] 7-11-12 130 .... BrianHughes 134+
(Malcolm Jefferson) trckd ldrs: 2nd 9th: led 4 out: wnt clr between last 2: 12 l ahd last: eased: easily **3/1**[1]

455- **2** *7* **High Ron**[27] [5497] 10-10-12 116 .... (t) TomScudamore 110
(Caroline Bailey) led to 4 out: modest 2nd sn after 2 out: no ch w wnr **4/1**[2]

3 *10* **Glenwood For Ever (IRE)**[8] [277] 7-10-0 104 .... (t) PaulMoloney 93
(Paul John Gilligan, Ire) in rr: nt fluent 8th: sn pushed along and outpcd: drvn to chse ldrs sn after 4 out: lost pl next: modest 3rd last **9/2**[3]

00-6 **4** *7* **Dursey Sound (IRE)**[16] [101] 7-11-12 130 .... RichieMcLernon 112
(Jonjo O'Neill) chsd ldrs 3rd: hit 6th: 3 l 2nd and drvn 3 out: hit next: sn wknd **4/1**[2]

26-0 **F** **Groomed (IRE)**[18] [82] 7-10-11 115 .... SeanQuinlan
(Sue Smith) chsd ldr: fell 9th **14/1**

P36- **U** **Romeo Americo (IRE)**[25] [5539] 8-10-11 115 .... AndrewThornton
(Seamus Mullins) in rr: pushed along 6th: hmpd 9th: chsng ldrs next: handy 4th whn blnd and uns rdr 4 out: b.b.v **9/2**[3]

5m 20.3s (3.30) **Going Correction** +0.125s/f (Yiel) **6** Ran SP% **108.0**
Speed ratings: **98,95,91,88,**
CSF £14.22 TOTE £3.40: £1.40, £2.70; EX 17.80 Trifecta £46.40.
Owner Mrs Rita Williams **Bred** Mary And Mrs Letty O'Sullivan **Trained** Norton, N Yorks

FOCUS
The feature contest was a fairly decent handicap chase. They went an even gallop. The winner stood out on recent form and this was arguably another step up.

396 HAPPY 50TH BIRTHDAY D5 GLB "NATIONAL HUNT" NOVICES' HURDLE (9 hdls) 1m 7f 153y
6:50 (6:50) (Class 4) 4-Y-O+ **£3,249** (£954; £477; £238)

Form RPR

10-1 **1** **Midnight Shot**[18] [83] 5-11-5 0 .... RichardJohnson 123+
(Charlie Longsdon) led appr 2nd: pushed along appr 2 out: sn wl clr: v easily **30/100**[1]

55-3 **2** *20* **Age Of Discovery**[13] [171] 4-10-8 0 .... (t) HarrySkelton 94
(Dan Skelton) chsd wnr fr 3rd: drvn 3 out: no ch w wnr **5/1**[2]

50-P **3** *15* **Wildmoor Boy**[4] [330] 4-10-8 0 ....[1] CharliePoste 82
(Robin Dickin) hld up in rr: modest 3rd 6th: one pce whn hit next **33/1**

24-0 **4** *27* **Monksgold (IRE)**[18] [83] 7-10-12 112 ....[1] TomScudamore 60
(David Bridgwater) t.k.h: led: stdd and hdd appr 2nd: lost pl 6th: sn bhd: t.o next: b.b.v **15/2**[3]

00- **5** *59* **Tomsk (FR)**[104] [4055] 5-10-12 0 .... MichaelByrne 7
(Tim Vaughan) nt jump wl: chsd ldrs: outpcd 5th: sn bhd: t.o 3 out: eventually completed **40/1**

P- **P** **The Frugal Star**[79] [4539] 7-10-12 0 .... AdamPogson
(Caroline Bailey) chsd ldrs: outpcd 4th: drvn next: sn bhd: t.o 3 out: p.u bef next **100/1**

3m 56.5s (-0.50) **Going Correction** -0.325s/f (Good)
WFA 4 from 5yo+ 18lb **6** Ran SP% **111.7**
Speed ratings (Par 105): **88,78,70,57,27**
CSF £2.36 TOTE £1.30: £1.10, £2.30; EX 2.90 Trifecta £11.70.
Owner Alan Halsall **Bred** Overbury Partnership **Trained** Over Norton, Oxon

FOCUS
An ordinary novice hurdle. They went a respectable gallop after a dawdle over the first two obstacles. The impressive winner stood out.

397 LIVE MUSIC AT SOUTHWELL 2ND JUNE NOVICES' HURDLE (13 hdls) 2m 7f 209y
7:20 (7:20) (Class 4) 4-Y-O+ **£3,249** (£954; £477; £238)

Form RPR

U3-P **1** **Road To Freedom**[19] [57] 6-10-13 107 .... LeightonAspell 118+
(Lucy Wadham) trckd ldrs: led 2 out: sn drvn wl clr: heavily eased run-in **9/2**[3]

02-2 **2** *17* **Ballycamp (IRE)**[18] [83] 6-10-13 0 .... AdamPogson 101+
(Charles Pogson) tk fierce hold: trckd ldrs: hung violently rt thrght: led briefly appr 2 out: regain modest 2nd appr last **7/4**[1]

3 **3** *9* **Danmurphysdoor (IRE)**[14] [145] 6-10-13 0 .... RichardJohnson 95
(Tim Vaughan) hld up in rr: trckd ldrs 8th: 2nd whn stmbld on landing 2 out: wknd appr last **5/2**[2]

3-P **4** *2 1/2* **Get Involved (IRE)**[11] [212] 6-10-13 0 .... (t) CharliePoste 91
(Robin Dickin) led: hdd appr 2 out: one pce **5/1**

0/33 **5** *4* **Have One For Me (IRE)**[6] [299] 8-10-6 0 .... MissETodd(7) 87
(Victor Thompson) chsd ldr: lost pl 3 out: one pce **14/1**

/64- **P** **Ticinese**[52] [5043] 5-10-13 0 .... AndrewTinkler
(Heather Main) in rr: hdwy to chse ldrs 9th: lost pl 3 out: wl bhd whn mstke next: t.o whn p.u bef last **25/1**

6m 17.0s (2.00) **Going Correction** -0.325s/f (Good) **6** Ran SP% **110.3**
Speed ratings (Par 105): **83,77,74,73,72**
CSF £12.76 TOTE £9.10: £2.80, £1.60; EX 14.20 Trifecta £33.80.
Owner Richard S Keeley **Bred** Yorton Farm Stud **Trained** Newmarket, Suffolk

FOCUS
A fair novice hurdle. They went a modest gallop. A step up from the winner for the longer trip.

398 18 TO 30 GOLF MEMBERSHIP £210 H'CAP HURDLE (6 hdls 7 omitted) 2m 7f 209y
7:50 (7:50) (Class 5) (0-100,100) 4-Y-0+ £2,599 (£763; £381; £190)

Form RPR
13-5 1 **Unknown Legend (IRE)**[16] 109 8-11-11 **99**............ JackQuinlan 110+
(Sarah Humphrey) *mde all: t.k.h: clr 3rd (normal 7th): kpt on wl: unchal* **20/1**
6F-6 2 *10* **Ballythomas**[8] 261 8-11-9 **100**............ JoeColliver(3) 101
(David Thompson) *chsd ldrs: drvn and modest 2nd appr 2 out: kpt on same pce* **18/1**
00- 3 *5* **Urban Storm (IRE)**[54] 5017 5-11-12 **100**............(t) DavidBass 96
(Ben Pauling) *chsd ldrs: 2nd 3rd (normal 7th): one pce bef 2 out* **7/1**
PP-1 4 *4* **Band Of Thunder**[10] 222 7-10-9 **86** 7ex............(b) ThomasGarner(3) 78
(Mark H Tompkins) *chsd ldrs: drvn 7f out: one pce* **11/4**[1]
02-5 5 *7* **Element Quartet (IRE)**[20] 28 6-10-8 **82**............(t) BrendanPowell 68
(Brendan Powell) *mid-div: drvn 7f out: modest 5th bef 2 out: nvr a threat* **18/1**
PF-4 P **Sharivarry (FR)**[8] 255 9-10-10 **91**............ MissETodd(7)
(Victor Thompson) *chsd ldrs: lost pl 1/2-way: bhd fnl 6f: t.o 6th whn p.u between last 2* **66/1**
4FP- P **Trojan Sun**[104] 4051 9-11-9 **100**............(t) JeremiahMcGrath(3)
(Tom Symonds) *chaed ldrs: drvn and lost pl 8f out: sn bhd: t.o whn p.u bef 2 out* **14/1**
PP0- P **Blackwell Synergy (FR)**[50] 5086 9-11-7 **100**............(p) ConorRing(5)
(John Upson) *chsd ldrs: drvn and reminders circ to go: lost pl 8f out: sn bhd: t.o whn p.u bef 2 out* **25/1**
5/4- P **Storm To Pass**[373] 231 7-11-4 **97**............(t) BridgetAndrews(5)
(Caroline Fryer) *in rr: t.o w over a circ to go: p.u 9f out* **16/1**
113- P **Follow The Tracks (IRE)**[33] 5371 7-11-12 **100**............ GavinSheehan
(Brian Barr) *mid-div: bhd 8f out: t.o whn p.u bef 2 out* **7/2**[2]
0P- P **Agent Louise**[139] 3440 7-10-3 **80**............ AdamNicol(3)
(Mike Sowersby) *in rr: j.rt 1st (normal 2nd): brief effrt 7f out: sn lost pl and bhd: t.o 7th whn p.u bef 2 out* **16/1**
053- P **Essteepee**[58] 4963 6-11-4 **92**............ RichardJohnson
(Tim Vaughan) *in rr: mstke 2nd (normal 3rd): bhd 8f out: t.o 8th whn p.u bef 2 out* **5/1**[3]

6m 3.7s (-11.30) **Going Correction** -0.325s/f (Good) **12 Ran SP% 117.1**
Speed ratings (Par 103): **105,101,100,98,96 ,,,,,,,**
CSF £319.97 CT £2763.49 TOTE £21.10: £7.80, £9.30, £2.10; EX 193.30 Trifecta £1668.40 Part won..
Owner Yen Hall Farm Racing **Bred** Dan O'Brien **Trained** West Wratting, Cambs

FOCUS
A modest handicap hurdle. They went a proper gallop with the hurdles in the back straight omitted due to a low sun. The winner is rated in line with the best of his chase form.

399 SOUTHWELL RACING AND GOLF PACKAGE £20 H'CAP HURDLE (5 hdls 6 omitted) 2m 4f 62y
8:20 (8:20) (Class 5) (0-100,103) 4-Y-0+ £2,599 (£763; £381; £190)

Form RPR
30-4 1 **Occasionally Yours (IRE)**[20] 40 11-10-13 **87**............ MarcGoldstein 93
(Alan Blackmore) *led to 1st: chsd ldrs: modest 3rd and drvn bef 2 out: rallied between last 2: upsides last: styd on and led last 75yds* **12/1**
U-11 2 *1 1/4* **Bennachie (IRE)**[8] 262 6-11-8 **103** 7ex............(t) AlanJohns(7) 109
(Tim Vaughan) *hld up in rr: jnd ldrs 4th: drvn to ld bef 2 out: rdn between last 2: jnd last: hdd and no ex* **8/11**[1]
40-6 3 *7* **Polstar (FR)**[20] 43 6-11-11 **99**............ RichardJohnson 99
(Harry Whittington) *w ldr 2nd (normal 5th): led next: hdd appr 2 out: wknd appr last* **10/3**[2]
5-03 4 *27* **Auto Mac**[8] 252 7-10-0 **77**............ AdamNicol(3) 51
(Mike Sowersby) *chsd ldrs: lost pl after omitted 3 out: sn bhd: t.o* **10/1**
0/P3 P **Mr Shahady (IRE)**[7] 286 10-11-5 **100**............ MissETodd(7)
(Victor Thompson) *w ldrs: led 1st: hdd 3rd (normal 6th): reminders 8f out: sn lost pl: t.o 6th whn p.u bef 2 out* **50/1**
41-5 F **Walter De La Mare (IRE)**[16] 106 8-11-11 **99**............(t) RichieMcLernon
(Anabel K Murphy) *chsd ldrs: fell 1st: fatally injured* **8/1**[3]
0-P6 P **Izbushka (IRE)**[8] 262 4-9-11 **79** oh5............(bt) JoeColliver(3)
(David Thompson) *reluctant and v.s.a: hopelessly detached in last: t.o after 7f: p.u bef 2nd (normal 5th)* **25/1**
0P-0 P **Bjornlucky (IRE)**[20] 40 5-10-5 **79**............(p) HarrySkelton
(Caroline Fryer) *chsd ldrs: rdn and wknd rapidly omitted 3 out: t.o 5th whn p.u bef next* **20/1**

5m 4.0s (-9.00) **Going Correction** -0.325s/f (Good)
WFA 4 from 5yo+ 19lb **8 Ran SP% 119.4**
Speed ratings (Par 103): **104,103,100,90, , , ,**
CSF £22.93 CT £41.04 TOTE £15.40: £2.80, £1.10, £2.00; EX 32.60 Trifecta £129.90.
Owner A G Blackmore **Bred** Gerard Connolly **Trained** Little Berkhamsted, Herts

FOCUS
Another modest handicap hurdle. They went a respectable gallop and, once again, the hurdles in the back straight were omitted due to a low sun. The winner had slipped to a good mark and is rated in line with his best 2015 runs.

400 SOUTHWELL STANDARD OPEN NATIONAL HUNT FLAT RACE 1m 7f 153y
8:50 (8:50) (Class 6) 4-6-Y-0 £1,559 (£457; £228; £114)

Form RPR
0 1 **Potters Midnight**[14] 152 5-10-9 **0**............ LeightonAspell 88+
(Lucy Wadham) *hld up in rr: effrt over 4f out: rallied and handy 3rd over 1f out: styd on wl to ld nr fin* **8/1**
5- 2 *3/4* **Fields Of Glory (FR)**[380] 109 5-11-2 **0**............ RichardJohnson 94
(Tim Vaughan) *led: qcknd pce over 4f out: jnd and rdn 2f out: hdd and no ex nr fin* **9/2**[3]
0- 3 *1 1/2* **Bollin Beauty**[196] 2289 6-10-9 **0**............ BrianHughes 86
(Malcolm Jefferson) *trckd ldrs: effrt and upsides 2f out: kpt on same pce last 150yds* **14/1**
4 *9* **Glory For Rory (IRE)** 4-10-2 **0**............ PatrickCowley(10) 80
(Jonjo O'Neill) *hld up in last: hdwy on ins 7f out: sn trcking ldrs: effrt over 2f out: wknd over 1f out* **10/11**[1]
30- 5 *6* **Jessie Pinkman**[99] 4141 4-10-9 **0**............(p) AdamNicol(3) 74
(Philip Kirby) *trckd ldrs: drvn over 4f out: hung rt and lost pl over 1f out* **11/1**
6 *3/4* **Repeat The Feat (FR)** 4-10-12 **0**............ AidanColeman 73
(Charlie Longsdon) *chsd ldrs: drvn 4f out: lost pl over 1f out* **4/1**[2]

3m 57.1s (5.70) **Going Correction** -0.325s/f (Good)
WFA 4 from 5yo+ 4lb **6 Ran SP% 116.7**
Speed ratings: **72,71,70,66,63 63**
CSF £44.64 TOTE £7.50: £2.70, £1.20; EX 45.40 Trifecta £170.90.
Owner Mrs J May **Bred** F S And Mrs May **Trained** Newmarket, Suffolk

FOCUS
The concluding contest was an ordinary bumper. They went a modest gallop until the tempo increased on the home bend. The second is probably the best guide.
T/Plt: £56.20 to a £1 stake. Pool: £57,727.42 - 748.89 winning tickets T/Qpdt: £19.20 to a £1 stake. Pool: £4,525.91 - 174.10 winning tickets **Walter Glynn**

[207]WARWICK (L-H)
Wednesday, May 20

OFFICIAL GOING: Good to soft (hdl 6.1, chs 6.7)
Wind: Fresh across Weather: Overcast

401 ARDENCOTE "I DO" NOVICES' HURDLE (11 hdls) 2m 5f
2:10 (2:10) (Class 4) 4-Y-0+ £4,548 (£1,335; £667; £333)

Form RPR
6 1 **To Begin**[19] 61 4-10-9 **0**............(t) NoelFehily 107+
(Charlie Mann) *chsd ldr: shkn up whn mstke 2 out: j.lft last: rdn to ld fnl 110yds: styd on* **10/1**[2]
42-1 2 *1/2* **Benissimo (IRE)**[11] 207 5-11-7 122............ HarrySkelton 118
(Dan Skelton) *led: shkn up appr 2 out: j.lft last: rdn and hdd fnl 110yds: kpt on* **1/10**[1]
00- 3 *dist* **Finnegan's Garden (IRE)**[27] 5502 6-11-0 **0**............[1] MarkGrant 80
(Zoe Davison) *hld up: hdwy 8th: wknd after 3 out: mstke last* **150/1**
0 4 *4* **Cotton King**[19] 61 8-11-0 **0**............ LeightonAspell 79
(Graham Mays) *chsd ldrs: nt fluent: wknd 8th: bhd whn blnd last* **25/1**[3]

5m 10.1s (-4.90) **Going Correction** -0.05s/f (Good)
WFA 4 from 5yo+ 19lb **4 Ran SP% 104.5**
Speed ratings (Par 105): **107,106,93,91**
CSF £11.90 TOTE £12.90; EX 11.00 Trifecta £26.90.
Owner John Heron **Bred** Theakston Stud **Trained** Upper Lambourn, Berks

FOCUS
Hurdle and INH Flat races run on Inner course. Rail on Hill out 8yds, reservoir bend out 10yds and Stable bend on inside line. Races increased by about 14yds per circuit. Some results are difficult to explain from a form perspective, and this one ranks reasonably high in that list. The winner is rated up the best part of a stone on his debut run.

402 ROBERT WALTERS H'CAP CHASE (12 fncs) 2m
2:40 (2:40) (Class 3) (0-130,127) 5-Y-0+ £7,147 (£2,098; £1,049; £524)

Form RPR
623- 1 **Lough Kent**[35] 5345 6-11-9 **124**............ NicodeBoinville 147+
(Nicky Henderson) *chsd ldr tl led after 3 out: clr next: impressive* **7/4**[1]
43-4 2 *15* **Un Anjou (FR)**[10] 218 7-11-8 **123**............ NoelFehily 126
(David Dennis) *led: rdn and hdd after 3 out: sn outpcd* **6/1**[3]
136- 3 *5* **Jay Are (IRE)**[25] 5540 6-11-7 **122**............ LeightonAspell 122
(Gary Moore) *prom: nt fluent 8th: rdn after 3 out: styd on same pce: hit next* **9/4**[2]
/55- 4 *16* **Domtaline (FR)**[32] 8-11-12 **127**............ PaulMoloney 110
(Evan Williams) *chsd ldrs: lost pl 3rd: lost tch 6th: wnt 4th nr fin* **16/1**
162- 5 *3/4* **Boss In Boots (IRE)**[44] 5211 7-11-2 **117**............(b) AndrewThornton 101
(Seamus Mullins) *hld up: mstke 7th: nt fluent 9th: rdn and wknd after 3 out* **6/1**[3]
346/ 6 *10* **Red Riverman**[459] 4279 7-11-7 **122**............(v) SamTwiston-Davies 93
(Nigel Twiston-Davies) *hld up: plld hrd: hdwy 4th: pushed along 7th: wknd after 3 out* **12/1**

3m 53.5s (-12.10) **Going Correction** -0.375s/f (Good) **6 Ran SP% 109.3**
Speed ratings: **115,107,105,97,96 91**
CSF £11.78 TOTE £2.70: £1.40, £3.10; EX 10.70 Trifecta £28.70.
Owner Mrs Caroline Mould **Bred** Castlemartin Stud And Skymarc Farm **Trained** Upper Lambourn, Berks

FOCUS
This looked a solid race for the class, and the winner was most impressive. He's rated up over a stone on the best of his hurdle form.

403 ARDENCOTE "SPA" H'CAP CHASE (18 fncs) 3m 110y
3:10 (3:10) (Class 4) (0-115,114) 4-Y-0+ £3,898 (£1,144; £572; £286)

Form RPR
42-1 1 **Prince Des Marais (FR)**[16] 109 12-11-5 **114**............(t) MichaelHeard(7) 125
(Caroline Bailey) *a.p: chsd ldr 3rd: led 5th to appr 7th: led again 9th: drvn out* **9/1**
56P/ 2 *1 1/2* **Cardinal Rose**[380] 8-9-7 **88** oh3............ MissHannahWatson(7) 99
(Mark Wall) *hld up: hdwy 7th: chsd wnr 12th: rdn appr 2 out: styd on* **12/1**
PP-2 3 *8* **Head Spin (IRE)**[20] 31 7-10-10 **98**............(tp) AndrewThornton 101
(Seamus Mullins) *hld up: hdwy 11th: rdn after 3 out: styd on same pce fr next* **9/2**[2]
114- 4 *5* **Georgian King**[160] 3042 12-11-10 **112**............ RichardJohnson 111
(Martin Keighley) *chsd ldrs tl rdn and wknd after 3 out* **15/2**
42-2 5 *1/2* **Mission Complete (IRE)**[19] 58 9-10-10 **108**............(tp) JackSavage(10) 109
(Jonjo O'Neill) *prom: pushed along 4th: rdn after 11th: wknd bef 3 out* **5/1**[3]
344- P **Chac Du Cadran (FR)**[27] 5497 9-10-13 **101**............(p) TomMessenger
(Chris Bealby) *led tl after 1st: chsd ldrs: pushed along 4th: lost pl and rdn 8th: bhd fr next: p.u bef 12th* **11/2**
62-1 P **The Happy Warrior**[13] 163 7-10-13 **101**............ LiamHeard
(Bob Buckler) *hld up: nt fluent 1st and 5th: blnd next: sn rdn: hdwy 9th: wknd bef 12th: bhd whn p.u bef 13th* **9/1**
P3-3 P **Uhlan Bute (FR)**[19] 58 7-11-7 **109**............ LiamTreadwell
(Venetia Williams) *led after 1st: hdd 5th: led again appr 7th: hdd 9th: chsd wnr to 12th: mstke next: wknd 14th: bhd whn p.u bef 2 out* **7/2**[1]

6m 14.5s (-12.50) **Going Correction** -0.375s/f (Good) **8 Ran SP% 111.9**
Speed ratings (Par 105): **105,104,101,100,100 , ,**
CSF £97.47 CT £545.75 TOTE £6.10: £4.00, £3.30, £1.80; EX 108.40 Trifecta £788.50.
Owner C W Booth **Bred** Gaec Lancray **Trained** Holdenby, Northants

The Form Book Jumps 2015-16, Raceform Ltd, Newbury, RG14 5SJ

FOCUS
A couple of runners, including the winner, ensured this was a well-run race for the distance. The winner's best figure since 2012.

404 FELDON DUNSMORE BUILDING LEGAL SOLUTIONS H'CAP HURDLE (12 hdls) 3m 1f
3:40 (3:40) (Class 3) (0-140,135) 4-Y-0+
£9,071 (£2,679; £1,339; £669; £334; £168)

Form RPR
P14- 1 **Grape Tree Flame**[32] 5394 7-11-3 **129** (p) SeanBowen(3) 134+
(Peter Bowen) *chsd ldr: mstke 6th: rdn appr last: hung lft and r.o u.p to ld fnl 75yds* **9/2[3]**
56-3 2 *1 1/4* **Henri Parry Morgan**[18] 85 7-10-7 **116** (p) DonalDevereux 119
(Peter Bowen) *led: pushed along and nt fluent last: rdn and hdd fnl 75yds* **10/3[2]**
110- 3 *2* **Jennys Surprise (IRE)**[123] 3724 7-11-2 **125** PaddyBrennan 125
(Fergal O'Brien) *chsd ldr: disp fr 8th tl rdn appr last: no ex towards fin* **5/1**
641- 4 *3 1/2* **Allthegear No Idea (IRE)**[26] 5519 8-10-13 **122** SamTwiston-Davies 121
(Nigel Twiston-Davies) *hld up: nt fluent 8th: rdn next: hdwy after 3 out: styd on same pce appr last* **13/2**
005- 5 *3 3/4* **On The Bridge (IRE)**[34] 5357 10-11-7 **130** (p) NickScholfield 124
(Jeremy Scott) *hld up in tch: lost pl after 7th: pushed along after 3 out: no imp* **9/4[1]**
P6-6 6 *7* **Vandross (IRE)**[12] 185 5-10-11 **120** (b) TrevorWhelan 109
(Neil King) *hld up: rdn and hdwy after 7th: wknd bef 2 out* **9/1**
6m 18.7s (3.70) **Going Correction** -0.05s/f (Good) **6 Ran SP% 112.0**
Speed ratings (Par 107): **92,91,90,89,88 86**
CSF £19.82 CT £75.66 TOTE £5.50: £2.60, £1.70; EX 19.00 Trifecta £105.40.
Owner F Lloyd **Bred** F Lloyd **Trained** Little Newcastle, Pembrokes
FOCUS
Four non-runners meant this was less competitive than once looked likely, and it was only run at an ordinary gallop early. Being prominent was predictably an advantage. The second to fourth were pretty much to their marks.

405 WIGLEY GROUP FILLIES' 4-Y-O H'CAP HURDLE (8 hdls) 2m
4:10 (4:12) (Class 2) 4-Y-O **£25,024** (£7,392; £3,696; £1,848; £924)

Form RPR
4F4- 1 **Bella (FR)**[58] 4958 4-10-6 **112** (t) TomScudamore 111+
(David Pipe) *led to 3rd: chsd ldr tl led again 3 out: shkn up flat: styd on wl* **3/1[3]**
466- 2 *2 1/2* **Stoneham**[33] 2895 4-10-0 **106** oh4 ConorO'Farrell 103
(Mick Channon) *hld up: hdwy appr 2 out: rdn and wnt 2nd flat: nt rch wnr* **16/1**
214- 3 *2* **Nyanza (GER)**[88] 3858 4-11-12 **132** WayneHutchinson 127
(Alan King) *chsd ldrs: rdn and wnt 2nd appr 2 out: no ex flat* **5/2[2]**
3U4- 4 *1* **Magic Magnolia (IRE)**[72] 4682 4-10-1 **107** HarrySkelton 102
(Dan Skelton) *chsd wnr tl led 3rd: rdn and hdd after 3 out: styd on same pce appr last* **6/4[1]**
2F3- 5 *8* **Maid Of Tuscany (IRE)**[184] 2547 4-10-0 **106** oh1 (p) MarkQuinlan 95
(Neil Mulholland) *racd keenly: trckd ldrs tl rdn and wkng whn nt fluent last* **11/1**
3m 54.8s (-1.70) **Going Correction** -0.05s/f (Good) **5 Ran SP% 107.8**
Speed ratings: **102,100,99,99,95**
CSF £33.29 TOTE £3.40: £1.60, £5.00; EX 32.20 Trifecta £60.00.
Owner Prof Caroline Tisdall **Bred** Dr Vet R Y Simon & N Simon **Trained** Nicholashayne, Devon
FOCUS
A disappointing turnout for this valuable new event, in which all five fillies were making their handicap debuts. There was not much pace on early. The winner was heading for this sort of rating when falling at Taunton.

406 ARDENCOTE "HOLE IN ONE" H'CAP HURDLE (8 hdls) 2m
4:40 (4:40) (Class 3) (0-135,134) 4-Y-0+ **£6,498** (£1,908; £954; £477)

Form RPR
204- 1 **War Singer (USA)**[31] 4847 8-11-4 **126** (tp[1]) NoelFehily 130+
(Johnny Farrelly) *hld up: mstke 5th: hdwy after 3 out: led last: rdn out* **5/1[3]**
45-1 2 *3 1/4* **Regulation (IRE)**[12] 186 6-11-0 **122** TrevorWhelan 124+
(Neil King) *hld up: hdwy 4th: chsd ldr appr 2 out: ev ch whn blnd last: styd on same pce flat* **2/1[1]**
11-1 3 *2 1/2* **Frozen Over**[10] 217 7-10-5 **113** 7ex (t) JamesDavies 112
(Chris Down) *hld up: hdwy 4th: rdn after 3 out: styd on same pce last* **7/2[2]**
10F- 4 *1 1/4* **King Alfonso**[44] 5180 6-11-5 **127** RobertDunne 125
(Dai Burchell) *chsd clr ldr tl tk clsr order 4th: mstke next: led 3 out: rdn and hdd last: no ex flat* **10/1**
2-12 5 *18* **Mr Lando**[10] 217 6-10-12 **120** LeightonAspell 102
(Alison Batchelor) *racd keenly: led and sn clr: c bk to the field 4th: hdd 3 out: wkng whn nt fluent next* **11/2**
510- 6 *1 1/2* **Oyster Shell**[39] 5276 8-11-12 **134** JakeGreenall 113
(Henry Daly) *hld up: hdwy 4th: rdn and wknd after 3 out* **16/1**
35-F 7 *18* **Collodi (GER)**[18] 84 6-11-5 **127** TomCannon 90
(David Bridgwater) *hld up: mstke 5th: sn rdn and wknd* **16/1**
000- P **Dispour (IRE)**[28] 5475 5-11-6 **128** (t) WayneHutchinson
(Donald McCain) *hld up: bhd fr 4th: p.u bef 2 out* **20/1**
3m 51.9s (-4.60) **Going Correction** -0.05s/f (Good) **8 Ran SP% 113.2**
Speed ratings (Par 107): **109,107,106,105,96 95,86,**
CSF £15.59 CT £38.57 TOTE £7.30: £1.20, £2.00, £3.10; EX 22.20 Trifecta £69.60.
Owner The War Cabinet **Bred** Hertrich-McCarthy Livestock **Trained** Enmore, Somerset
FOCUS
A competitive contest, but the start was slightly odd, as Mr Lando and King Alfonso lined up a good five lengths in front of the remainder (Oyster Shell jogged in behind them at the last minute), and the former kicked on at a strong gallop. A hurdles best from the winner.

407 ARDENCOTE "CONFERENCE & EVENTS" INTERMEDIATE OPEN NATIONAL HUNT FLAT RACE 2m
5:10 (5:10) (Class 6) 4-6-Y-O **£1,949** (£572; £286; £143)

Form RPR
4- 1 **Ballinure (IRE)**[39] 5285 5-10-11 0 JeremiahMcGrath(3) 101+
(Nicky Henderson) *a.p: led over 3f out: rdn and hung rt ins fnl f: styd on* **3/1[2]**
3/1- 2 *1/2* **For Instance (IRE)**[27] 5502 5-11-7 0 NoelFehily 107
(Jonjo O'Neill) *racd keenly: led 1f: settled to trck ldrs: rdn to chse wnr over 1f out: styd on* **5/4[1]**
3 *1 1/2* **Pougne Bobbi (FR)** 4-10-10 0 AndrewTinkler 95
(Nicky Henderson) *prom: nt clr run and lost pl over 3f out: hdwy over 2f out: sn rdn: no ex wl ins fnl f* **12/1**
4 *8* **Lord Bryan (IRE)** 4-10-7 0 SeanBowen(3) 87
(Peter Bowen) *hld up: plld hrd: hdwy over 6f out: rdn and wknd over 1f out* **15/2**
5 *3/4* **Shan't Agree (IRE)**[46] 4-10-10 0 TomO'Brien 87
(Henry Daly) *chsd ldr after 1f tl led over 4f out: rdn and hdd over 3f out: wknd fnl f* **14/1**
3- 6 *12* **Captain Flash (IRE)**[347] 624 6-10-9 0 DannyBurton(5) 80
(Jo Davis) *prom tl rdn and wknd over 2f out* **25/1**
5- 7 *10* **Organ Morgan**[80] 4513 5-11-0 0 AidanColeman 71
(Richard Phillips) *hld up: wknd 5f out* **50/1**
8 *13* **Apache Pearl (IRE)** 4-10-10 0 JakeGreenall 55
(Warren Greatrex) *led after 1f: rdn and hdd over 4f out: wknd 3f out* **13/2[3]**
3m 48.5s (-2.40) **Going Correction** -0.05s/f (Good)
WFA 4 from 5yo+ 4lb **8 Ran SP% 114.7**
Speed ratings: **104,103,103,99,98 92,87,81**
CSF £7.13 TOTE £4.80: £1.20, £1.10, £2.80; EX 9.40 Trifecta £53.20.
Owner Mrs Mary-Anne Parker **Bred** N Murphy **Trained** Upper Lambourn, Berks
FOCUS
The early pace was sedate, and the whole field raced in a group for some way. Two with the most experienced dominated the outcome, and set the level.
T/Plt: £945.50 to a £1 stake. Pool: £42,991.74 - 33.19 winning tickets T/Qpdt: £42.10 to a £1 stake. Pool: £5,583.24 - 97.95 winning tickets **Colin Roberts**

408 - 414a (Foreign Racing) - See Raceform Interactive

WETHERBY (L-H)
Thursday, May 21
OFFICIAL GOING: Good (good to firm in places chs 9.3, hdl 9.1)
Wind: moderate 1/2 behind Weather: fine but very cool and breezy

415 BOOK YORKSHIRE POST LADIES EVENING HOSPITALITY MARES' MAIDEN HURDLE (9 hdls) 2m
2:00 (2:00) (Class 5) 4-Y-0+ **£2,395** (£698; £349)

Form RPR
21- 1 **Kayf Willow**[30] 5446 6-11-0 0 RichardJohnson 103+
(Philip Hobbs) *trckd ldrs: led appr 3 out: drvn out* **5/6[1]**
644- 2 *4* **Keep To The Beat**[23] 5016 4-10-10 **101** (p) NoelFehily 92
(Kevin Ryan) *trckd ldrs: 3rd whn edgd rt appr 2 out: 2nd last: no imp* **9/2[3]**
4 3 *1* **My Escapade (IRE)**[19] 79 4-10-3 0 MissAWaugh(7) 92
(Simon Waugh) *led: hdd appr 3 out: kpt on same pce* **20/1**
634- 4 *11* **Broadway Belle**[46] 5159 5-10-9 **84** DiarmuidO'Regan(5) 84
(Chris Grant) *chsd ldrs: outpcd and drvn 6th: modest 4th last* **50/1**
/13- 5 *3 1/2* **Chilly Miss**[43] 756 6-11-0 0 BrianHughes 81
(Malcolm Jefferson) *t.k.h: trckd ldrs: dropped bk 3rd: drvn 6th: sn btn* **11/4[2]**
6P6- 6 *4 1/2* **Miss Conway**[45] 5201 4-10-10 0 DougieCostello 72
(Mark Walford) *in rr: chsd ldrs 4th: lost pl 6th* **100/1**
44-5 P **Soeur De Rois (IRE)**[12] 200 5-10-11 0 AdamNicol(3)
(Philip Kirby) *in rr: p.u after 6th: fatally injured* **14/1**
3m 44.2s (-11.60) **Going Correction** -1.20s/f (Hard)
WFA 4 from 5yo+ 18lb **7 Ran SP% 113.8**
Speed ratings (Par 103): **79,77,76,71,69 67,**
CSF £5.18 TOTE £2.00: £1.80, £2.70; EX 5.20 Trifecta £35.60.
Owner Mrs S L Hobbs **Bred** R Johnson **Trained** Withycombe, Somerset
FOCUS
Shared Chase and Hurdle bends at both ends of track and located on inside line of each bend. A moderate mares' maiden but it threw up a fast-improving winner.

416 RACING UK ANYWHERE (S) HURDLE 2m 3f 154y
2:30 (2:30) (Class 5) 4-Y-0+ **£2,395** (£698; £349)

Form RPR
16-1 1 **Barneys Honour (IRE)**[16] 125 11-11-1 **120** (p) MissBHampson(7) 107
(Andy Turnell) *trckd ldrs: 2nd 4th: led bef 6th: drvn rt out* **15/8[2]**
/00- 2 *3/4* **Oneofapear (IRE)**[10] 5206 9-10-12 **94** BrianHughes 96
(Mike Sowersby) *trckd ldrs: 2nd 7th: styd on run-in: no ex in clsng stages* **20/1**
/6P- 3 *3 1/4* **Double Double (FR)**[119] 3817 9-11-1 **129** (p) SeanBowen(3) 100
(Peter Bowen) *nt fluent in rr: drvn 7th: 3rd 2 out: kpt on one pce* **10/11[1]**
654/ 4 *6* **Miss Chatterbox**[417] 10-10-0 0 DiarmuidO'Regan(5) 80
(Chris Grant) *chsd ldrs 3rd: outpcd appr 3 out: one pce and edgd lft run-in* **20/1**
P 5 *4 1/2* **Bach To Before (IRE)**[14] 155 7-10-12 0 DougieCostello 83
(Tom Gretton) *t.k.h: trckd ldrs 6th: modest 4th last: hung rt and wknd fnl 50yds* **33/1**
00P- 6 *14* **Takaatuf (IRE)**[11] 9-10-9 **87** (t) CraigNichol(3) 68
(Tina Jackson) *in rr: sme hdwy 8th: lost pl 2 out: sn bhd* **66/1**
6-P5 7 *17* **War On (IRE)**[8] 287 8-10-5 **73** MrJDixon(7) 51
(Victor Thompson) *led: hdd bef 6th: reminders and klost pl 8th: sn wl bhd* **33/1**
0/P- P **War Lord (IRE)**[23] 3260 5-10-12 **112** (t) HenryBrooke
(George Moore) *chsd ldr: mstke 3rd: reluctant: lost pl and reminders next: nt keen and bhd whn p.u after 5th* **13/2[3]**
4m 50.1s (-16.90) **Going Correction** -1.20s/f (Hard) **8 Ran SP% 117.4**
Speed ratings (Par 103): **84,83,82,80,78 73,66,**
CSF £35.12 TOTE £2.60: £1.20, £2.70, £1.10; EX 25.90 Trifecta £81.50.There was no bid for the winner.
Owner Power Bloodstock Ltd **Bred** Mrs M Quinn **Trained** Broad Hinton, Wilts
FOCUS
This seller is best rated around the runner-up.

417 YORKSHIRE POST LADIES EVENING - 28TH MAY H'CAP CHASE (13 fncs) 1m 7f 36y
3:05 (3:05) (Class 4) (0-120,117) 5-Y-0+ **£3,768** (£1,106; £553; £276)

Form RPR
44-4 1 **Claragh Native (IRE)**[21] 35 10-11-0 **105** NoelFehily 118+
(Martin Todhunter) *trckd ldrs 5th: shkn up 8th: led 2 out: drvn rt out* **7/2**
U-U5 2 *1 1/4* **Gin Cobbler**[9] 256 9-9-7 **91** MissETodd(7) 102
(Victor Thompson) *t.k.h: led 3rd: hdd 2 out: kpt on wl run-in* **7/1**
046- 3 *12* **Robin's Command (IRE)**[27] 5515 8-11-9 **117** CraigNichol(3) 119
(Rose Dobbin) *trckd ldrs: hit 9th: drvn next: wknd between last 2* **10/3[3]**
61-2 4 *8* **Hotgrove Boy**[21] 36 8-11-2 **107** JamesReveley 101
(Stuart Coltherd) *trckd ldrs 4th: pushed along 9th: wkng whn hit 3 out* **5/2[1]**

331- 5 9 **Civil Unrest (IRE)**[31] 5421 9-10-11 **107**............................(p) DaleIrving(5) 96
(James Ewart) *led to 3rd: pushed along 9th: lost pl next: bhd whn blnd bdly and rdr briefly lost iron 2 out* **3/1**[2]

3m 42.0s (-13.80) **Going Correction** -0.80s/f (Firm) **5** Ran SP% **111.4**
Speed ratings: **106,105,99,95,90**
CSF £24.39 TOTE £5.30: £2.50, £4.20; EX 28.00 Trifecta £106.00.
Owner Mrs S J Matthews **Bred** B Mellon **Trained** Orton, Cumbria

FOCUS
They got sorted out from the second-last in this modest handicap and the first pair came clear.

418 NEW RACING UK IPAD APP H'CAP HURDLE 2m 3f 154y
3:40 (3:40) (Class 3) (0-140,138) 4-Y-0+ **£5,393** (£1,583; £791; £395)

Form RPR
112- 1 **Chalk It Down (IRE)**[273] 1282 6-11-12 **138**.................... DougieCostello 143+
(Warren Greatrex) *hld up in rr: t.k.h: effrt 8th: modest 4th 2 out: 3rd last: str run to ld cl home* **12/1**

06-1 2 ½ **Cut The Corner (IRE)**[17] 110 7-9-12 **115**......................... ChrisWard(5) 121+
(Dr Richard Newland) *t.k.h: trckd ldrs: 3rd appr 3 out: led 2 out: hung lft: jst ct* **11/4**[1]

211- 3 1¾ **Avidity**[33] 5394 6-10-12 **129**...(t) DaleIrving(5) 133
(James Ewart) *trckd ldrs: 2nd appr 3 out: sn led: hdd 2 out: kpt on same pce run-in* **10/3**[2]

00-4 4 6 **Acertain Circus**[11] 216 5-10-12 **124**.................................(t) KielanWoods 124
(Pam Sly) *led: j.rt: hdd appr 2 out: fdd appr last* **15/2**

044- 5 1¾ **Unanimite (FR)**[26] 5535 4-11-3 **134**...(b) TomScudamore 127
(David Pipe) *chsd ldrs: drvn 8th: hung lft and lost pl bef next* **4/1**[3]

UP5- 6 33 **Doyly Carte**[28] 5491 7-10-13 **125**..................................(t) WayneHutchinson 91
(Donald McCain) *chsd ldrs: drvn 8th: lost pl bef next: t.o last* **18/1**

02-3 P **Ruler Of All (IRE)**[12] 208 9-11-0 **133**...................................... MrRWinks(7)
(Peter Winks) *in rr: lost pl 6th: sn wl bhd: t.o whn p.u after 8th* **12/1**

34-4 P **Blue Atlantic (USA)**[20] 73 4-10-10 **127**.....................................(p) GavinSheehan
(Warren Greatrex) *chsd ldrs: drvn 7th: reminders next: sn lost pl and bhd: t.o whn p.u bef next* **8/1**

4m 34.8s (-32.20) **Going Correction** -1.20s/f (Hard)
WFA 4 from 5yo+ 19lb **8** Ran SP% **113.3**
Speed ratings (Par 107): **113,112,112,109,109 96,,**
CSF £45.33 CT £137.12 TOTE £7.10: £1.70, £2.60, £1.20; EX 45.80 Trifecta £62.70.
Owner John P McManus **Bred** Michael Ryan **Trained** Upper Lambourn, Berks

FOCUS
This wasn't a bad handicap and it was truly run. Solid form, the winner making a small step up.

419 BET WITH YOUR RACING UK APP NOVICES' HURDLE 2m 3f 154y
4:15 (4:15) (Class 4) 4-Y-0+ **£3,249** (£954; £477; £238)

Form RPR
214- 1 **Go Odee Go (IRE)**[26] 5539 7-11-5 124...........................(p) HarrySkelton 115+
(Dan Skelton) *t.k.h: hld up in rr: trckd ldrs 4th: upsides 3 out: edgd rt appr 2 out: edgd rt and led last: drvn out* **4/5**[1]

1 2 2½ **Sign Manual**[20] 56 6-11-5 0.. NoelFehily 114+
(Donald McCain) *hld up in rr: nt fluent 6th: trckd ldrs 8th: led narrowly next: j.lft 2 out: crowded and hdd last: swtchd lft 100yds out: kpt on same pce* **2/1**[2]

620- 3 3½ **Bentons Lad**[55] 5016 4-10-7 109.......................................(t) HenryBrooke 97
(George Moore) *trckd ldng pair: pckd 2nd: lft in ld next: stdd pce 5th: hdd next: led and increased gallop 8th: hdd next: short of room appr 2 out: one pce* **18/1**

4 20 **Whimsical Notion** 5-10-12 0.. TomScudamore 82
(Nigel Hawke) *trckd ldrs: lft 2nd 3rd: led 6th: hdd 8th: lost pl appr next: sn bhd* **14/1**

U **Cobh National (IRE)**[19] 7-10-5 0.. MissETodd(7)
(Victor Thompson) *led: nt fluent 1st: j. slowly 2nd: wnt bdly rt and uns rdr 3rd* **100/1**

4- P **Ashes Corner (IRE)**[37] 5331 5-10-9 0...................................... TonyKelly(3)
(Julia Brooke) *w ldr: bdly hmpd: rdr lost irons: lost pl and p.u 3rd* **12/1**[3]

5m 3.0s (-4.00) **Going Correction** -1.20s/f (Hard)
WFA 4 from 5yo+ 19lb **6** Ran SP% **109.5**
Speed ratings (Par 105): **59,58,56,49,**
CSF £2.55 TOTE £1.80: £1.20, £1.20; EX 2.90 Trifecta £10.60.
Owner N W Lake **Bred** Patrick Hogan **Trained** Alcester, Warwicks

FOCUS
This was a falsely run novice event, although the form does make sense.

420 RACING UK H'CAP CHASE (18 fncs) 3m 1f
4:50 (4:50) (Class 3) (0-135,131) 5-Y-0+ **£6,498** (£1,908; £954; £477)

Form RPR
U3-3 1 **Sedgemoor Express (IRE)**[17] 101 7-11-2 **121**.......(p) TomScudamore 133+
(Nigel Hawke) *trckd ldrs: effrt 14th: handy 2nd 2 out: led appr last: wnt clr: v readily* **11/4**[1]

00-0 2 5 **Ericht (IRE)**[22] 24 9-11-11 **130**.. AndrewTinkler 135
(Nicky Henderson) *trckd ldrs: reminder 8th: led appr 4 out: hdd appr last: no ex* **13/2**

P25- 3 12 **Wolf Shield (IRE)**[33] 5388 8-11-7 **126**................................(t) HenryBrooke 120
(George Moore) *chsd ldrs: upsides 4 out: one pce fr 2 out* **4/1**[3]

36P- 4 6 **Susquehanna River (IRE)**[36] 5340 8-10-4 **109**..(p) SamTwiston-Davies 95
(Nigel Twiston-Davies) *w ldr: led 3rd: hdd appr 4 out: wknd appr 2 out* **5/1**

156- 5 43 **Allanard (IRE)**[65] 4831 11-10-11 **116**..(v) NoelFehily 64
(Martin Todhunter) *j.rt in rr: mstke 2nd: reminders 9th: sn outpcd: lost pl 11th: bhd fr 14th: t.o 4 out* **25/1**

13-3 6 25 **Cape York**[16] 134 7-10-9 **114**..(b) BrianHughes 39
(Malcolm Jefferson) *led to 3rd: hit 6th: lost pl 13th: sn bhd: t.o 4 out* **10/3**[2]

5m 54.4s (-15.00) **Going Correction** -0.80s/f (Firm) **6** Ran SP% **103.6**
Speed ratings: **92,90,86,84,70 62**
CSF £16.84 CT £50.77 TOTE £2.50: £1.20, £4.20; EX 16.90 Trifecta £43.90.
Owner Pearce Bros 2 **Bred** Seamus Cooney **Trained** Stoodleigh, Devon

■ Deciding Moment was withdrawn. Price at time of withdrawal 10-1. Rule 4 applies to all bets. Deduct 5p in the pound.

FOCUS
A modest staying handicap, run at a fair gallop. There's a case for rating this form 10lb+ higher.

421 YORKSHIRE POST LADIES NIGHT - 28TH MAY LADY RIDERS' H'CAP HURDLE (13 hdls) 3m 26y
5:20 (5:21) (Class 5) (0-100,100) 4-Y-0+ **£1,546** (£1,546; £349)

Form RPR
5U0- 1 **Minella Hero (IRE)**[65] 4828 7-11-3 **98**...................... MissBeckySmith(7) 106
(Micky Hammond) *trckd ldrs: cl 2nd 2 out: 3 l down last: styd on wl to dead-heat post* **13/2**[3]

60-2 1 dht **Lilly's Legend**[19] 90 5-9-7 **74** oh1...................................(p) MissETodd(7) 82
(Mark Walford) *t.k.h: trckd ldrs: led appr 3 out: jnd on line* **7/2**[2]

50-1 3 9 **Over And Above (IRE)**[16] 133 9-10-6 **87**.......................(tp) LizzieKelly(7) 87
(Henry Hogarth) *chsd ldrs: outpcd 10th: lft 5th 2 out: hung lft and kpty on to take modest 3rd last* **8/1**

3P0- 4 2 **Another Dimension (IRE)**[29] 5473 9-11-7 **100**...........(t) MissCWalton(5) 98
(Rose Dobbin) *mid-div: chsd ldrs 4th: lft 4th 2 out: one pce: crowded run-in* **14/1**

0P3- 5 10 **Azure Glamour (IRE)**[27] 5516 6-10-9 **90**..............(p) MissJRRichards(7) 81
(Nicky Richards) *t.k.h early: trckd ldrs: drvn 7th: lft 3rd 2 out: wknd appr last* **5/2**[1]

56-6 6 10 **Daring Exit**[8] 291 6-10-6 **87**.. MissKBryson(7) 67
(Robert Bewley) *in rr: blnd 8th: bhd fr 10th: j.lft and lft poor 6th 2 out* **10/1**

PP-0 7 2½ **Samizdat (FR)**[17] 104 12-9-9 **76** oh7 ow2............................ MissGSwan(7) 22
(John O'Neill) *in rr: hdwy 8th: sn chsng ldrs: lost pl bef 3 out* **100/1**

50-0 D dist **Abijoe**[20] 56 6-11-3 **94**.. MissGAndrews(3) 43
(Pam Sly) *chsd ldrs: drvn and lost pl 4th: sn bhd: t.o whn weight cloth c off bnd bef 3 out: rdr weighed in 9lb light: disqualified* **14/1**

5-66 U **Nicky Nutjob (GER)**[10] 240 9-9-7 **74** oh6.............(p) MissBHampson(7)
(John O'Shea) *nt fluent in rr: hdwy 9th: modest 7th whn blnd and uns rdr 3 out* **16/1**

500- U **Danehills Well (IRE)**[29] 5473 7-11-0 **95**....................(p) MissAEStirling(7) 101+
(Alison Hamilton) *led: hdd appr 3 out: 3rd and keeping on same pce whn blnd: swvd bdly lft and uns rdr 2 out* **8/1**

05-P U **Mr Hopeful (IRE)**[15] 139 6-11-12 **100**...................................(t) LucyAlexander
(Donald McCain) *mid-div: reminders 7th: outpcd whn rdr lost iron and uns rdr between 9th and 10th* **18/1**

5m 46.3s (-30.20) **Going Correction** -1.20s/f (Hard) **11** Ran SP% **120.9**
Speed ratings (Par 103): **102,102,99,98,95 92,80,,, 80**WIN: Lilly's Legend £2.00, Minella Hero £5.90 ; PL: £1.30 Lilly's Legend, £3.10 Minella Hero; EX: MH/LL £18.30, LL/MH £14.20; CSF: MH/LL £15.52, LL/MH £13.94; TC: MH/LL/OA £95.32, LL/MH/OA £87.45; TRIFECTA MH/LL/OA£111.50, LL/MH/OA £70.20,, £2.70 Trifecta £27 Owner Ball & Lees.
Owner N Skinner & J Grindal **Bred** Stewart Pike **Trained** Sherriff Hutton, N Yorks

FOCUS
This moderate staying handicap was made up of mainly lady amateur riders. It paid to race handily.
T/Plt: £13.20 to a £1 stake. Pool of £48048.08 - 2649.92 winning tickets. T/Qpdt: £11.70 to a £1 stake. Pool of £3260.02 - 206.13 winning tickets. **Walter Glynn**

422 - 428a (Foreign Racing) - See Raceform Interactive

[173]WORCESTER (L-H)
Friday, May 22

OFFICIAL GOING: Good (good to soft in places) changing to good after race 2 (6:20)
Wind: Almost nil Weather: Overcast Rails: Far bend approx 18yds from innermost position and Cathedral bend approx 6yds out. This adds approx 60yds to 2m races & 105yds to 2m 4f & 2m 7f. Jumps outside straights

429 HARGREAVE HALE INVESTMENT MANAGERS HUNTERS' CHASE (16 fncs) 2m 7f
5:50 (5:50) (Class 6) 5-Y-0+ **£935** (£290; £145; £72)

Form RPR
03/2 1 **Stratford Stroller (IRE)**[21] 60 11-11-3 97...... MissJosephineBanks(7) 103+
(Alastair Ralph) *a.p: racd keenly early: led after 8th: 6 l up whn lft wl clr 3 out* **6/5**[1]

5P-U 2 23 **Dr Anubis (IRE)**[5] 10-11-3 66.. MrEDavid(7) 82
(Miss Hannah Taylor) *prom: blnd and wknd 11th: lft remote 2nd 3 out: hit next* **20/1**

/2-U 3 48 **Charles Bruce (IRE)**[23] 17 12-11-3 101............................ MrHFNugent(7) 39
(A Campbell) *chsd ldrs: reminders 6th: wkng whn nt fluent 10th: hung rt and lft fr 4 out: wnt remote 3rd flat* **7/4**[2]

P 4 21 **Parthian Empire**[16] 151 9-11-3 0.. MrLeoMahon(7) 26
(W M Wanless) *led to 4th: chsd ldr tl led again 7th: hdd after next: chsd wnr to 10th: wknd bef 12th: lft remote 3rd 3 out: blnd last* **25/1**

0/5- U **Hall Kelly (IRE)**[12] 10-11-3 0..(bt) MissAPBanks(7) 82
(Mrs C Banks) *prom: chsd wnr 10th: rdn bef 4 out: 6 l down and looking hld whn j. slowly and uns rdr 3 out* **10/1**[3]

40P/ U **Jock Des Mottes (FR)**[6] 8-11-3 0.......................................(b[1]) MissTWorsley(7)
(Ms Sarah-Jayne Weaver) *hld up: mstke and uns rdr 5th* **20/1**

5 P **Church Gallery (IRE)**[12] 8-11-3 84...(vt) MrBCatton(7)
(S Rea) *chsd ldr tl led 4th: hdd 7th: rdn after next: wknd bef 9th: bhd whn p.u bef 12th* **20/1**

P **Gontdevon**[6] 10-11-5 0.. MrRobertHawker(5)
(R J Harraway) *hld up: a in rr: bhd fr 9th: p.u bef 4 out* **12/1**

6m 1.8s (13.80) **Going Correction** +0.275s/f (Yiel) **8** Ran SP% **116.7**
Speed ratings: **87,79,62,55, ,,**
CSF £28.06 TOTE £2.10: £1.10, £7.40, £1.10; EX 24.80 Trifecta £49.60.
Owner Mrs P Tollit **Bred** Spencer Hawkins **Trained** Ludlow, Shropshire

FOCUS
Rail movement increased 2m races by 60yds and 2m4f and 2m7f by 105yds. Jumps positioned to the outside of both straights. The ground was riding as advertised. Restricted to horses qualified with local hunts, this was a very weak hunter chase indeed.

430 LADBROKES NOVICES' CHASE (16 fncs) 2m 7f
6:20 (6:20) (Class 4) 5-Y-0+ **£3,898** (£1,144; £572; £286)

Form RPR
216- 1 **Deadly Sting (IRE)**[208] 2080 6-10-12 0..................................(p) NoelFehily 132+
(Neil Mulholland) *trckd ldrs: nt fluent 1st: chsd ldr 3 out: rdn to ld flat: styd on* **9/4**[1]

U2P- 2 1 **Atlantic Roller (IRE)**[69] 4765 8-10-12 125...........(p) SamTwiston-Davies 130
(Paul Nicholls) *led: rdn appr last: hung lft and hdd flat: styd on same pce* **11/4**[3]

110- 3 7 **Commitment**[189] 2481 6-10-12 0.. DougieCostello 125
(Neil Mulholland) *hld up: hdwy 3 out: rdn appr last: no ex flat* **10/1**

The Form Book Jumps 2015-16, Raceform Ltd, Newbury, RG14 5SJ

P2-2 **4** *17* **Orby's Man (IRE)**[20] 85 6-10-12 0.......................... AidanColeman 111
(Charlie Longsdon) *chsd ldr: rdn and ev ch 4 out: lost 2nd next: wknd 2 out* **5/2**[2]
P4-2 **5** *9* **Owen Na View (IRE)**[10] 259 7-11-1 131.................. ConorShoemark(3) 109
(Fergal O'Brien) *hld up in tch: rdn whn mstke 3 out: wknd next* **6/1**
5m 52.2s (4.20) **Going Correction** +0.275s/f (Yiel) **5** Ran SP% **109.4**
Speed ratings: **103,102,100,94,91**
CSF £8.84 TOTE £2.40: £1.10, £3.20; EX 8.60 Trifecta £53.10.
Owner Maxilead Limited **Bred** Michael Shanahan **Trained** Limpley Stoke, Wilts
■ Stewards' Enquiry : Noel Fehily nine-day ban: use of whip (5-7, 9, 11-13, 15-16 June)
FOCUS
A decent little novice chase, run at a reasonable gallop.

431 LADBROKES H'CAP CHASE (13 fncs) 2m 4f
6:50 (6:51) (Class 3) (0-130,131) 5-Y-0+ **£6,498** (£1,908; £954; £477)

Form RPR
431- **1** **Madame De Guise (FR)**[32] 5429 6-10-9 **112**.................. TomCannon 122+
(Laura Mongan) *led: blnd 8th: hdd 4 out: rdn to ld flat: styd on wl* **10/1**
3-1U **2** *1 3/4* **Marie Des Anges (FR)**[5] 357 7-10-9 **119**.................(t) DavidNoonan(7) 125
(Anthony Honeyball) *chsd ldrs: rdn appr 2 out: styd on to go 2nd nr fin* **10/1**
23-1 **3** *1/2* **Lough Kent**[2] 402 6-12-0 131 7ex.................................. NicodeBoinville 139+
(Nicky Henderson) *racd keenly: nt a fluent: trckd wnr: mstke 9th: led 4 out: rdn and hdd flat: no ex towards fin* **8/13**[1]
P5P- **4** *93* **Ackertac (IRE)**[104] 4098 10-11-12 **129**.......................(vt) RichardJohnson 51
(Tim Vaughan) *hld up: hdwy 6th: rdn and wknd 4 out* **5/1**[2]
F2-5 **U** **Freckle Face**[14] 184 8-11-6 **123**.................................. NickScholfield
(Bill Turner) *hld up: blnd and uns rdr 4th* **8/1**[3]
335/ **P** **Roger Beantown (IRE)**[396] 5456 10-11-0 **117**...............(p) MarkGrant
(Zoe Davison) *hld up: blnd 1st: bhd fr 7th: blnd 9th: sn p.u* **50/1**
5m 1.9s (1.90) **Going Correction** +0.275s/f (Yiel) **6** Ran SP% **109.8**
Speed ratings: **107,106,106,68,**
CSF £84.43 TOTE £7.90: £3.20, £2.30; EX 26.20 Trifecta £130.30.
Owner Mrs P J Sheen **Bred** Jean-Pierre Roussel & Diego Roussel **Trained** Epsom, Surrey
FOCUS
A fair handicap chase.

432 LADBROKES MARES' STANDARD OPEN NATIONAL HUNT FLAT RACE 2m
7:20 (7:20) (Class 6) 4-6-Y-O **£1,559** (£457; £228; £114)

Form RPR
3U-2 **1** **Awesome Rosie**[16] 152 4-10-10 0.......................... WayneHutchinson 96+
(Alan King) *trckd ldrs: led over 3f out: rdn out* **6/4**[1]
0-2 **2** *2 1/2* **Pulling Power**[17] 124 5-11-0 0..............................(t) DavidBass 98
(Kim Bailey) *a.p: rdn and ev ch over 2f out: styd on same pce ins fnl f* **3/1**[2]
3 *1 1/2* **Western Sunrise (IRE)** 6-11-0 0.......................... AlainCawley 96
(Johnny Farrelly) *hld up: hdwy over 5f out: rdn over 2f out: styd on same pce ins fnl f* **25/1**
4 *1* **Bitter Virtue** 4-10-10 0.. AidanColeman 92
(David Dennis) *hld up: hdwy 1/2-way: rdn over 2f out: no ex ins fnl f* **11/1**
3 **5** *4 1/2* **Kaddys Girl**[22] 45 5-10-7 0.............................. JosephPalmowski(7) 91
(Robin Dickin) *hld up: hdwy over 3f out: rdn over 2f out: styd on same pce fnl f* **16/1**
46- **6** *5* **Popular Opinion (IRE)**[156] 3143 5-11-0 0...................(t) NoelFehily 87
(Harry Fry) *w ldr tl rdn 4f out: wknd over 1f out* **4/1**[3]
00- **7** *nse* **Mari Me Oscar (IRE)**[331] 812 5-11-0 0.................... RichardJohnson 87
(Nikki Evans) *led: rdn and hdd over 3f out: wknd over 1f out* **33/1**
8 *4 1/2* **Bright Sunshine** 6-11-0 0.. RachaelGreen 83
(Anthony Honeyball) *hld up: hdwy over 5f out: rdn and wknd over 2f out* **14/1**
0- **9** *8* **Youllneverrunalone**[29] 5501 4-10-10 0........................ GerardTumelty 72
(Richard Price) *chsd ldrs tl wknd over 4f out* **100/1**
10 *2* **Dunnicks Delia** 6-10-11 0.................................. LucyGardner(3) 74
(Sue Gardner) *prom: lost pl over 6f out: wknd over 4f out* **50/1**
11 *28* **Dark Music** 4-10-7 0.. JamesBanks(3) 45
(Jo Davis) *hld up: effrt over 5f out: wknd over 4f out* **66/1**
3m 49.0s (7.30) **Going Correction** +0.325s/f (Yiel)
WFA 4 from 5yo+ 4lb **11** Ran SP% **117.1**
Speed ratings: **94,92,92,91,89 86,86,84,80,79 65**
CSF £5.66 TOTE £3.40: £1.40, £1.20, £7.10; EX 7.60 Trifecta £62.20.
Owner Mrs Gwen Meacham, A King & Withyslade **Bred** Meacham, King And Withyslade **Trained** Barbury Castle, Wilts
FOCUS
A modest mares' bumper.

433 LADBROKES "NATIONAL HUNT" NOVICES' HURDLE (8 hdls) 2m
7:50 (7:50) (Class 4) 4-Y-0+ **£3,249** (£954; £477; £238)

Form RPR
11-P **1** **Storm Of Swords (IRE)**[12] 218 7-11-7 130.............. BridgetAndrews(5) 133+
(Dan Skelton) *mde all: racd keenly: shkn up appr last: styd on wl* **4/6**[1]
10-5 **2** *5* **Amour D'Or**[18] 111 4-10-1 0.................................. RichardJohnson 103
(Nick Williams) *chsd wnr: nt fluent 1st: rdn appr 3 out: mstke next: styd on same pce flat* **5/1**[3]
22-3 **3** *6* **Raise A Spark**[20] 83 5-10-12 0..................................[1] AdrianLane 109
(Donald McCain) *hld up: plld hrd: hdwy 3 out: sn rdn: wknd flat* **4/1**[2]
56-2 **4** *9* **Doctor Look Here (IRE)**[17] 119 5-10-9 0.................. LucyGardner(3) 100
(Sue Gardner) *hld up: effrt 3 out: sn wknd* **10/1**
606- **5** *2 1/4* **Agha Des Mottes (FR)**[64] 4867 5-10-7 0.................. RobMcCarth(5) 98
(Ian Williams) *hld up: nt fluent 1st: effrt 3 out: wknd next* **16/1**
P-P **6** *dist* **Daisy Back**[18] 111 7-10-2 0.................................. JamesBanks(3) 55
(Barry Brennan) *chsd ldrs tl rdn and wknd 3 out* **100/1**
3m 51.2s (3.90) **Going Correction** +0.325s/f (Yiel)
WFA 4 from 5yo+ 18lb **6** Ran SP% **112.6**
Speed ratings (Par 105): **103,100,97,93,91 71**
CSF £4.71 TOTE £1.50: £1.10, £2.10; EX 4.90 Trifecta £14.30.
Owner The McKilocon Syndicate **Bred** Michael Ennis **Trained** Alcester, Warwicks
FOCUS
The winner set a brisk gallop in this modest novice hurdle.

434 DOWNLOAD THE LADBROKES APP NOVICES' HURDLE (12 hdls) 2m 7f
8:20 (8:20) (Class 4) 4-Y-0+ **£3,249** (£954; £477; £238)

Form RPR
04-1 **1** **Hunt Ball (IRE)**[17] 127 10-11-5 135.............................. AndrewTinkler 97+
(Nicky Henderson) *mde all: set stdy pce tl qcknd 8th: clr fr 3 out: canter* **1/12**[1]
004- **2** *8* **Goodacres Garden (IRE)**[193] 2412 8-10-13 69..............(t) PeterCarberry 66
(Shaun Lycett) *w wnr to 5th: remained handy: rdn appr 3 out: sn outpcd: nt fluent next* **16/1**[2]
0U-3 **3** *1 1/2* **Astre Rose (FR)**[22] 26 5-10-13 0..............................(tp) DenisO'Regan 67
(Victor Dartnall) *trckd ldrs: wnt upsides 5th tl nt fluent 7th: pushed along appr 3 out: sn outpcd: mstkes next and last* **20/1**[3]
0-P **4** *83* **Hot Madras (IRE)**[15] 179 7-9-13 0.................................. JoshWall(7)
(Trevor Wall) *hld up: plld hrd: rdn and wknd after 9th* **100/1**
6m 2.5s (34.50) **Going Correction** +0.325s/f (Yiel) **4** Ran SP% **104.0**
Speed ratings (Par 105): **53,50,49,20**
CSF £1.98 TOTE £1.02; EX 2.00 Trifecta £2.00.
Owner Atlantic Equine **Bred** Michael Slevin **Trained** Upper Lambourn, Berks
FOCUS
A very uncompetitive novice hurdle.

435 LADBROKES H'CAP HURDLE (10 hdls) 2m 4f
8:50 (8:50) (Class 5) (0-100,95) 4-Y-0+ **£2,599** (£763; £381; £190)

Form RPR
040- **1** **In The Crowd (IRE)**[46] 5185 6-11-9 **95**.....................(p) JamesBanks(3) 100
(Roy Brotherton) *mde all: set stdy pce tl qcknd appr 6th: drvn out* **12/1**
445- **2** *1/2* **Iktiview**[151] 3230 7-10-2 **78**..............................(bt) MrStanSheppard(7) 84+
(Matt Sheppard) *chsd wnr tl mstke 5th: remained handy: wnt 2nd again 2 out: rdn and ev ch whn mstke last: kpt on u.p* **4/1**[2]
10-2 **3** *2* **Galactic Power (IRE)**[15] 164 5-10-10 **86**.............. JosephPalmowski(7) 89
(Robin Dickin) *hld up: hdwy 3 out: rdn appr last: styd on: nt rch ldrs* **8/1**
PU-1 **4** *5* **Sir Note (FR)**[15] 180 5-11-3 **86**..............................(t) PaulMoloney 84
(Nick Littmoden) *hld up: mstke 7th: hdwy 3 out: rdn appr last: no ex flat* **3/1**[1]
6P-0 **5** *7* **Eddy**[15] 167 6-10-8 **84**..................................[1] ThomasCheesman(7) 75
(John Panvert) *hld up: hdwy after 6th: rdn after 2 out: wknd last* **7/1**
44-2 **6** *2 3/4* **Mount Vesuvius (IRE)**[10] 267 7-11-7 **90**.....................(t) TomO'Brien 78
(Paul Henderson) *hld up: hdwy 3 out: rdn and wknd last* **11/2**[3]
SU-P **7** *3 1/2* **Midnight Thomas**[15] 161 6-10-13 **82**.......................(t) AndrewTinkler 66
(Martin Keighley) *hld up: hdwy 7th: rdn and wknd appr last* **14/1**
0/5- **8** *8* **Oscar Jane (IRE)**[60] 4963 8-11-4 **87**.............................. AlainCawley 63
(Johnny Farrelly) *prom: chsd wnr 5th tl rdn after 3 out: wknd bef last* **16/1**
0/P- **9** *62* **Barney Rubble**[154] 3175 6-11-4 **87**.............................. CharliePoste 1
(Richard Lee) *chsd ldrs: lost pl after 7th: wknd bef next* **8/1**
5m 14.6s (27.20) **Going Correction** +0.325s/f (Yiel) **9** Ran SP% **115.3**
Speed ratings (Par 103): **58,57,57,55,52 51,49,46,21**
CSF £60.43 CT £414.25 TOTE £20.00: £6.20, £2.60, £2.60; EX 86.90 Trifecta £682.20.
Owner Mrs Tess Byrne **Bred** The Brook Stud Co Ltd **Trained** Elmley Castle, Worcs
■ Stewards' Enquiry : James Banks trainer said, regarding the apparent improvement of form, that the gelding may have benefitted from a wind op and also the change to front running tactics
FOCUS
A modest handicap hurdle. It wasn't truly run and the form may not prove all that solid.
T/Plt: £27.30 to a £1 stake. Pool: £528,27.7 - 1,410.28 winning tickets T/Qpdt: £14.10 to a £1 stake. Pool: £3,899.14 - 203.50 winning tickets **Colin Roberts**

374 AUTEUIL (L-H)
Friday, May 22

OFFICIAL GOING: Turf: very soft

436a PRIX DE LA MUETTE (HURDLE) (CONDITIONS) (5YO) (TURF) 2m 2f
3:25 (3:25) 5-Y-O **£20,465** (£10,232; £5,968; £4,050; £1,918)

RPR
1 **The Stomp (FR)**[37] 5-11-5 0.. JacquesRicou 128
(Francois Nicolle, France) **1/1**[1]
2 *3* **Ho Good Lord Has (FR)**[24] 5-9-11 0.......................... FrankieLeroy(4) 107
(J-P Gallorini, France) **13/1**
3 *2 1/2* **Another Dragon (FR)**[49] 5-10-8 0.............................. MorganRegairaz 111
(Yannick Fouin, France) **7/2**[2]
4 *1/2* **Quelle Miss (FR)**[22] 5-10-10 0.......................(b) JonathanPlouganou 113
(D Sourdeau De Beauregard, France) **54/10**[3]
5 *10* **A Dieu Vat (FR)**[172] 2859 5-10-8 0.............................. DavidCottin 101
(A Adeline De Boisbrunet, France) **127/10**
6 *9* **Let Me Alone (FR)**[439] 5-10-6 0.................................. AlbanDesvaux 90
(G Chaignon, France) **61/1**
7 *7* **Victorian Teo (FR)**[47] 5-10-1 0.................................. CedricSagot(5) 83
(E J O'Neill, France) **120/1**
8 *1 3/4* **Aniknam (FR)**[48] 5142 5-10-6 0.................................. TomScudamore 81
(Philip Kirby) *tk v t.k.h: hld up in tch: untidy 3rd: lft bhd by ldrs fr 6 out: btn whn awkward 2 out* **202/10**
9 *12* **Buck's Broker (FR)**[87] 5-10-8 0.............................. DamienMescam(4) 75
(E Lecoiffier, France) **36/1**
P **Positano Sud (FR)**[42] 5-10-10 0.................................. AlexisAcker
(M Rolland, France) **111/10**
P **Tel Sleepin (FR)**[30] 5-10-6 0.............................. Marc-AntoineBillard
(D Retif, France) **143/1**
4m 12.25s (252.25) **11** Ran SP% **121.1**
PARI-MUTUEL (all including 1 euro stake): WIN 2.00; PLACE 1.40, 2.40, 1.80; DF 14.10; SF 17.20.
Owner Jean-Claude Rouget **Bred** Haras D'Haspel **Trained** France

437a PRIX MELINOIR (HURDLE) (CONDITIONS) (5YO+) (TURF) 2m 2f
4:25 (4:25) 5-Y-O+ **£17,860** (£8,930; £5,209; £3,534; £1,674)

RPR
1 **Valkyri Colombe (FR)**[601] 6-11-0 0.............................. JacquesRicou 136
(P Peltier, France) **7/5**[1]
2 *nk* **Korfou De Maspie (FR)**[184] 2603 6-10-10 0.................. BertrandLestrade 132
(S Foucher, France) **54/10**[2]
3 *hd* **Katkeau (FR)**[71] 4717 8-11-0 0.................................. TomScudamore 136
(David Pipe) *led: rdn between last 2 flights: pckd last: rallied gamely u.p: hdd 75yds out: lost 2nd on line* **44/5**[3]
4 *6* **Ulysse Des Pictons (FR)**[539] 7-10-3 0.......................... BaptisteMeme(5) 124
(Yannick Fouin, France) **123/1**
5 *3* **Devil Inside (FR)**[165] 6-11-3 0.................................. ThomasViel(4) 134
(L Viel, France) **236/10**
6 *1* **Cantilien (IRE)**[81] 5-11-3 0.................................. StevanBourgois(4) 133
(Y-M Porzier, France) **54/10**[2]
7 *1* **Alabama Le Dun (FR)**[335] 771 5-10-3 0.......................... JulienMarquestau(5) 119
(J-P Gallorini, France) **118/10**

8 2 1/2 **Quat'Car (FR)**[216] 1960 11-10-8 0.............................. AlbanDesvaux 116
(G Chaignon, France) 60/1
9 8 **Wanaba (FR)**[24] 6-10-8 0..............................(b) Jean-LucBeaunez 108
(Mme P Butel, France) 136/10
10 20 **Hallssio**[749] 131 7-10-3 0..............................(b) JulienTabary(5) 88
(P Lenogue, France) 165/1
11 4 **Olofi (FR)**[42] 5249 9-10-12 0..............................(p) PaddyBrennan 88
(Tom George) *racd a little freely early on: hld up in tch: lost pl bef 3 out: wl bhd 2 out* 163/10
P **Pibrac (FR)**[24] 11-11-3 0.............................. ErvanChazelle
(C Scandella, France) 101/10
P **Seahorse (FR)** 5-10-3 0.............................. Marc-AntoineBillard
(S Jousselin, France) 121/1

4m 15.13s (255.13) 13 Ran SP% 120.5
PARI-MUTUEL (all including 1 euro stake): WIN 2.40; PLACE 1.40, 2.10, 2.50; DF 7.70; SF 9.90.
Owner Magalen O Bryant **Bred** C Boistier & B Vagne **Trained** France

FFOS LAS (L-H)
Saturday, May 23

OFFICIAL GOING: Good (watered)
Wind: moderate half behind Weather: fine

438 BET TOTEPLACEPOT H'CAP CHASE (17 fncs) 2m 4f 199y
5:50 (5:50) (Class 5) (0-100,94) 5-Y-O+ **£2,469** (£725; £362; £181)

Form RPR
/PU- 1 **Patricktom Boru (IRE)**[21] 8-11-1 **83**.............................. AdamWedge 98+
(Evan Williams) *hld up bhd ldrs: clsd to trck ldng pair 9th: wnt 2nd after 4 out: chal and hit 2 out: led narrowly last: r.o wl* 9/4[1]
PP-1 2 6 **Louis Phillipe (IRE)**[23] 31 8-10-10 **78**..............................(t) MarkQuinlan 89+
(Linda Blackford) *cl up: led 7th: hit 9th: hdd next: led after 13th: jnd 2 out: narrowly hdd whn mstke last: outpcd by wnr flat* 6/1
46-2 3 22 **Miss Biscotti**[22] 57 7-11-5 **94**..............................(p) MrZBaker(7) 82
(Martin Bosley) *cl up: led 5th to 7th: led 10th: hit 13th: sn hdd: rdn and lost 2nd after 4 out: wknd 2 out* 9/2[3]
645- 4 2 1/4 **Hopstrings**[77] 4623 7-11-7 **94**..............................(p) CharlieDeutsch(5) 79
(Tom Lacey) *hld up in tch: rdn and outpcd by ldng trio after 13th: plugged on but no ch* 8/1
032- 5 2 3/4 **Magical Man**[67] 4824 8-11-2 **84**..............................(p) PaddyBrennan 66
(Debra Hamer) *hld up in tch: rdn 11th: wknd after 13th* 10/3[2]
111/ P **Tom Bach (IRE)**[412] 5185 11-11-8 **90**..............................(b) JamesBest
(Hywel Evans) *led to 5th: losing pl whn mstke 9th: bhd fr 11th: t.o whn p.u bef 4 out* 10/1
34-4 P **Bob Will (IRE)**[23] 31 10-10-3 **71**..............................(tp) WillKennedy
(John Flint) *hld up bhd ldrs: rdn 10th: wknd after 13th: t.o whn p.u bef 4 out* 10/1

5m 14.2s (-14.40) **Going Correction** -0.65s/f (Firm) 7 Ran SP% 115.6
Speed ratings: **101,98,90,89,88**
CSF £16.58 CT £56.03 TOTE £3.20: £2.10, £4.10; EX 17.50 Trifecta £65.70.
Owner R W J Willcox **Bred** Mrs B M Browne **Trained** Llancarfan, Vale Of Glamorgan

FOCUS
Rail at innermost position on both tracks. Three pulled clear in a moderate handicap run at a fair pace. Winner in line with his best Rules form and runner-up close to best mark.

439 BET TOTEEXACTA H'CAP CHASE (18 fncs) 2m 7f 177y
6:20 (6:20) (Class 4) (0-120,119) 5-Y-O+ **£3,768** (£1,106; £553; £276)

Form RPR
564- 1 **Pigeon Island**[68] 4818 12-11-5 **112**.............................. SamTwiston-Davies 118
(Nigel Twiston-Davies) *hld up: chsd along briefly after 5th: clsd 9th: chsd ldrs and rdn after 13th: stl only 4th last: str run flat to ld nr fin* 6/1
/4-0 2 1 1/4 **Top Dancer (FR)**[21] 92 8-11-9 **116**.............................. GavinSheehan 122
(Warren Greatrex) *hld up in tch: mstke 2nd: hit 10th: rdn and hdwy after 13th: led appr last tl nr fin* 5/2[1]
U4-5 3 3 1/4 **Strumble Head (IRE)**[22] 62 10-11-11 **118**..............................(p) DonalDevereux 120
(Peter Bowen) *j.rt at times: cl up tl led 3rd: rdn 4 out: hdd appr last: one pce and lost 2nd flat* 14/1
5P2- 4 2 1/2 **Sir Mattie (IRE)**[338] 744 10-11-7 **114**.............................. PaulMoloney 118+
(David Rees) *hit 3rd: blnd bdly and lost grnd 7th: hdwy to trck ldrs after 13th: wnt 2nd 3 out where mstke: nt run on and one pce fr next* 12/1
133- 5 6 **Copper Birch (IRE)**[81] 4545 7-11-7 **119**.............................. ConorRing(5) 113
(Evan Williams) *prom: chsd ldr 11th to 3 out: wknd after 2 out* 4/1[2]
P5P- 6 19 **Shakalakaboomboom (IRE)**[38] 5340 11-11-10 **117**.............................. PeterCarberry 98
(Nicky Henderson) *chsd ldrs: mstke 12th: rdn after next: wknd 2 out* 5/1[3]
43-P 7 78 **High Kite (IRE)**[12] 239 9-11-5 **112**..............................(p) DougieCostello 19
(Warren Greatrex) *led to 3rd: trckd ldr after: drvn 10th: lost 2nd next: wknd after 13th: t.o* 14/1
331- P **Mac Le Couteau**[41] 5291 7-10-3 **96**.............................. AdamWedge
(Evan Williams) *mid-div: pckd 2nd: mstke 11th: sn wknd: t.o whn p.u bef 4 out: lame* 4/1[2]

6m 3.3s (-14.10) **Going Correction** -0.65s/f (Firm) 8 Ran SP% 120.5
Speed ratings: **97,96,95,94,92 86,60,**
CSF £23.55 CT £208.63 TOTE £8.70: £2.20, £1.40, £4.20; EX 24.80 Trifecta £829.50.
Owner H R Mould **Bred** Sir Eric Parker **Trained** Naunton, Gloucs

FOCUS
There were question marks over many of these, and it was a cagily-run affair that produced an exciting finish as the winner swooped late to collar the favourite near the line. Second and fourth ran to their marks.

440 BET TOTEQUADPOT NOVICES' HURDLE (8 hdls) 1m 7f 202y
6:50 (6:52) (Class 4) 4-Y-O+ **£3,249** (£954; £477; £238)

Form RPR
2-12 1 **Curious Carlos**[8] 316 6-10-9 122..............................(t) SeanBowen(3) 113+
(Peter Bowen) *mid-div: stdy hdwy 3 out: wnt 2nd on bit 2 out: rdn to ld 75yds out: hld on u.p: edgd rt nr fin* 4/5[1]
4P3- 2 hd **Canicallyouback**[31] 5462 7-10-7 0.............................. ConorRing(5) 112
(Evan Williams) *led to 2nd: chsd ldr tl led again after 2 out: sn rdn: hdd 75yds out: r.o u.p: carried rt nr fin* 14/1
2 3 11 **Gambol (FR)**[13] 214 5-10-12 0.............................. WillKennedy 101
(Ian Williams) *wnt to post early: t.k.h: chsd ldrs: rdn 2 out: unable qck* 7/2[2]
4 4 6 **Footstepsintherain (IRE)**[16] 171 5-10-12 0.............................. AidanColeman 96
(David Dennis) *led 2nd and set stdy pce: rdn 3 out: hdd after 2 out: grad wknd* 10/1

56P- 5 3 1/2 **King Of All Kings (IRE)**[214] 1985 5-10-12 0.............................. DonalDevereux 92
(Peter Bowen) *hld up in rr: outpcd 3 out: styd on u.p fr 2 out* 25/1
0- 6 1 1/2 **Rye House (IRE)**[77] 4624 6-10-12 0..............................(t) RichardJohnson 90
(Tim Vaughan) *chsd ldrs: nt fluent 4th: rdn appr 2 out: one pce* 9/2[3]
42/6 7 9 **Green And White (ITY)**[16] 176 5-10-12 97.............................. LeeEdwards 83
(Dave Roberts) *mid-div: rdn and outpcd 3 out: wknd next* 66/1
46-5 8 12 **Ho Lee Moses (IRE)**[7] 330 5-10-5 0.............................. MrConorOrr(7) 69
(Evan Williams) *t.k.h in rr: wknd 3 out* 50/1
4- 9 30 **Warrigal (IRE)**[29] 5507 5-10-12 0.............................. MichaelByrne 39
(Tim Vaughan) *hld up in rr: rdn and wknd appr 3 out: t.o* 25/1

3m 44.4s (-4.10) **Going Correction** -0.475s/f (Good) 9 Ran SP% 122.9
Speed ratings (Par 105): **91,90,85,82,80 79,75,69,54**
CSF £15.10 TOTE £1.60: £1.10, £3.70, £1.80; EX 11.90 Trifecta £39.20.
Owner Carl Pyne **Bred** Carl Pyne **Trained** Little Newcastle, Pembrokes
■ Stewards' Enquiry : Sean Bowen one-day ban: careless riding (Jun 6)

FOCUS
This developed into a sprint, with the favourite just getting home under a cheeky ride. Winner rated just below his best with runner-up taken to have improved slightly.

441 MYTOTEPOOL.COM NOVICES' HURDLE (10 hdls) 2m 4f
7:25 (7:25) (Class 4) 4-Y-O+ **£3,249** (£954; £477; £238)

Form RPR
21-2 1 **Laurium**[19] 105 5-11-5 130.............................. DavidBass 126+
(Nicky Henderson) *trckd ldr: chal 2 out: sn led: rdn out and wl on top flat* 4/6[1]
2U-1 2 3 3/4 **Berea Venture (IRE)**[7] 335 7-11-5 120.............................. DonalDevereux 121
(Peter Bowen) *led at stdy pce tl qcknd 3 out: rdn and jnd next: sn hdd: one pce flat* 2/1[2]
3-5 3 10 **Milestone (IRE)**[13] 214 5-10-12 0..............................(t) PaulMoloney 106
(Evan Williams) *nt a fluent: chsd ldng pair fr 3rd: shkn up after 7th: one pce and no imp fr 2 out* 7/1[3]
0-U 4 42 **Double Court (IRE)**[7] 335 4-10-7 0.............................. SamTwiston-Davies 72
(Nigel Twiston-Davies) *nt a fluent: last tl impr a pl 7th: rdn and wknd bef next: t.o* 25/1
345- U **Royal Craftsman (IRE)**[223] 1869 5-10-12 0.............................. TomO'Brien
(Peter Bowen) *t.k.h: j. bdly rt: in last pair fr 3rd: lost tch after 7th: t.o whn j.rt and uns rdr last* 12/1

4m 48.5s (-2.40) **Going Correction** -0.475s/f (Good)
WFA 4 from 5yo+ 19lb 5 Ran SP% 117.4
Speed ratings (Par 105): **85,83,79,62,**
CSF £2.67 TOTE £1.60: £1.10, £1.30; EX 2.80 Trifecta £4.10.
Owner The Ten From Seven **Bred** Oakhill Stud **Trained** Upper Lambourn, Berks

FOCUS
This proved a relatively straightforward task for a horse rated 10lb superior to his nearest challenger. First two home pretty much to their best marks.

442 TOTEPOOL BET ON ALL UK RACING H'CAP HURDLE (3 hdls 5 omitted) 1m 7f 202y
7:55 (7:58) (Class 3) (0-125,129) 4-Y-O+ **£5,393** (£1,583; £791; £395)

Form RPR
00-1 1 **Zarzal (IRE)**[6] 354 7-11-2 **115** 7ex.............................. AdamWedge 124+
(Evan Williams) *trckd ldrs: wnt 2nd 4f out: chal 3f out: sn rdn: led and hung lft over 1f out: drvn out* 7/4[1]
04/0 2 2 1/2 **Battlecat**[13] 217 8-10-5 **109**.............................. ConorRing(5) 116
(Evan Williams) *t.k.h: cl up: led 6f out: jnd and rdn 3f out: hdd over 1f out: no ex fnl f* 10/1
03-1 3 5 **Street Entertainer (IRE)**[9] 301 8-11-9 **129**..............................(bt) MichaelHeard(7) 132+
(David Pipe) *t.k.h: chsd ldrs: hmpd 1st: rdn 5f out: kpt on same pce fnl 3f* 9/4[2]
/0-6 4 21 **Red Skipper (IRE)**[13] 217 10-10-5 **104**.............................. DaveCrosse 87
(John O'Shea) *hld up in tch: hdwy 2nd where nt fluent: rdn and wknd over 3f out* 33/1
311- 5 25 **Mr Burbidge**[29] 5508 7-11-8 **121**..............................(p) MarkQuinlan 82
(Neil Mulholland) *cl up: led after 2f: pckd 2nd: rdn and hdd 6f out: wknd 4f out: t.o* 4/1[3]
0P-P 6 3 3/4 **Ted Dolly (IRE)**[19] 110 11-9-12 **100**.............................. BenPoste(3) 57
(Tom Symonds) *a bhd: niggled along after 3f: rdn and wknd 6f out: t.o* 20/1
236- P **Jolly Roger (IRE)**[29] 5508 8-10-6 **108**.............................. RobertWilliams(3)
(Bernard Llewellyn) *led 2f: cl up whn blnd bdly and rdr lost iron 1st: nt rcvr: p.u bef last (usual 4 out)* 7/1

3m 37.9s (-10.60) **Going Correction** -0.475s/f (Good) 7 Ran SP% 116.4
Speed ratings (Par 107): **107,105,103,92,80 78,**
CSF £19.71 CT £41.21 TOTE £2.60: £1.50, £4.20; EX 17.50 Trifecta £68.70.
Owner Mrs Janet Davies **Bred** His Highness The Aga Khan's Studs S C **Trained** Llancarfan, Vale Of Glamorgan

FOCUS
All the hurdles in the home straight were omitted due to low sun, meaning just three out of the eight were jumped. Back to form winner still well-in on old form; in-form third best guide to level of form.

443 BET TOTESWINGER MARES' H'CAP HURDLE (5 hdls 6 omitted) 2m 5f 192y
8:30 (8:31) (Class 5) (0-100,96) 4-Y-O+ **£2,274** (£667; £333; £166)

Form RPR
24-0 1 **Lady Of Longstone (IRE)**[12] 240 5-11-6 **90**..............................(b) TomScudamore 102
(David Pipe) *led: drvn and narrowly hdd appr fnl f: rallied to ld fnl 50yds* 3/1[2]
62-3 2 3/4 **Midnight Sequel**[22] 65 6-11-5 **89**..............................(tp) NoelFehily 100
(Neil Mulholland) *mid-div: hdwy to trck wnr last (usual 4 out): rdn to chal 2f out: sn tk narrow ld: hdd and no ex fnl 50yds* 2/1[1]
P0-5 3 12 **Tantalized**[16] 179 6-10-0 **70**..............................(b) LeeEdwards 71
(Dave Roberts) *chsd ldrs: rdn and lost pl 7f out: styd on fnl 2f: wnt 3rd nr fin* 12/1
11-4 4 1 **Milly Malone (IRE)**[21] 86 9-11-8 **92**..............................(t) AidanColeman 92
(Adrian Wintle) *hld up in last pair: rdn to chse ldng pair 6f out: one pce fnl 3f: lost 3rd nr fin* 9/2[3]
64-5 5 8 **Call Me Kate**[21] 89 5-11-1 **92**..............................(p) MrHFNugent(7) 84
(Henry Daly) *mid-div: hit 4th: sn rdn: one pce and no imp on ldrs fnl 4f* 7/1
0P-5 6 33 **Dawnieriver (IRE)**[16] 167 5-10-13 **83**.............................. LiamTreadwell 46
(Michael Scudamore) *trckd ldrs to last (usual 4 out): sn wknd: t.o* 11/2
0/ 7 dist **Luso's Way (IRE)**[183] 2140 7-11-5 **89**..............................(t) RichardJohnson
(Tim Vaughan) *hld up in last pair: lost tch appr last (usual 4 out): t.o and virtually p.u* 10/1

5m 24.4s (4.40) **Going Correction** -0.475s/f (Good) 7 Ran SP% 121.2
Speed ratings (Par 103): **73,72,68,68,65 53,**
CSF £10.60 CT £64.20 TOTE £4.80: £3.00, £1.60; EX 12.70 Trifecta £118.60.
Owner Miss S E Hartnell **Bred** David Crimmins **Trained** Nicholashayne, Devon

FOCUS
Once again all the flights in the home straight were omitted, leaving five to be jumped. The two market leaders battled it out all the way up the straight.Winner improving line line with the best of his bumper form.

444 BET TOTETRIFECTA STANDARD OPEN NATIONAL HUNT FLAT RACE 1m 7f 202y
9:00 (9:01) (Class 6) 4-6-Y-O **£1,559** (£457; £228; £114)

Form RPR
1 **Catcher On The Go (IRE)**[15] 195 5-10-13 0........... KeithDonoghue(3) 105+
(Mrs Gillian Callaghan, Ire) *trckd ldrs: wnt 2nd 4f out: led wl over 1f out: sn pushed clr: comf* **11/2**
0- 2 *6* **Majestic Touch (IRE)**[48] 5179 4-10-12 0.................. DenisO'Regan 93
(Don Cantillon) *hld up: n.m.r bnd over 4f out: hdwy 3f out: rdn 2f out: r.o fnl f: wnt 2nd nr fin* **6/1**
3 *½* **Chase End Charlie (IRE)**[19] 4-10-12 0...................... RobertDunne 93
(Tom Lacey) *t.k.h towards rr: rdn and hdwy 3f out: outpcd by ldrs over 1f out: styd on to go 3rd post* **16/1**
22- 4 *nse* **The Gipper (IRE)**[54] 5077 5-10-11 0........................ ConorRing(5) 96
(Evan Williams) *t.k.h: hdwy to ld after 4f and increased pce: rdn 2f out: sn hdd and outpcd by wnr: lost 2 pls nr fin* **2/1**[1]
5 *1 ¾* **Court King (IRE)** 4-10-9 0.. SeanBowen(3) 91
(Peter Bowen) *trckd ldrs: rdn 4f out: kpt on same pce fnl 3f* **5/2**[2]
0 6 *11* **Druids Lodge**[15] 188 4-10-12 0............................. RichardJohnson 80
(Don Cantillon) *led at stdy pce tl hdd after 4f: styd prom tl rdn and wknd over 3f out* **14/1**
7 *2 ¾* **Big Touch (FR)** 4-10-12 0.................................. SamTwiston-Davies 77
(Paul Morgan) *t.k.h in last: n.m.r bnd over 4f out: rdn 3f out: unable qck: wknd over 1f out* **5/1**[3]

3m 46.9s (4.00) **Going Correction** -0.475s/f (Good)
WFA 4 from 5yo 4lb **7 Ran SP% 120.8**
Speed ratings: **71,68,67,67,66 61,59**
CSF £40.47 TOTE £8.10: £4.10, £2.90; EX 40.00 Trifecta £855.60.
Owner Pearse Callaghan **Bred** Michael Woodlock And Seamus Kennedy **Trained** Kells, Co Meath
FOCUS
The race took shape leaving the back straight and the winner powered clear. Winner seemingly taking a big step up on Irish form with slight improvement form runner-up.
T/Plt: £15.20 to a £1 stake. Pool: £76,978.01 - 3,690.31 winning tickets. T/Qpdt: £4.20 to a £1 stake. Pool: £6,431.10 - 1,114.20 winning tickets. **Richard Lowther**

292 FONTWELL (L-H)
Sunday, May 24

OFFICIAL GOING: Good (7.3)
Wind: almost nil Weather: cloudy Rails: Rail movement adding; CH +60yds/circ and Hur +35yds/circ. Second fence in home straight omitted due to ground under repair. Fences outer down the hill, inner home straight. Hurdles middle outer.

445 BUTLINS DAY VISITS #YOURBESTBETFORAGRANDDAYOUT H'CAP HURDLE (13 hdls) 3m 1f 142y
2:20 (2:20) (Class 4) (0-120,114) 4-Y-O+ **£3,249** (£954; £477; £238)

Form RPR
001- 1 **Horsted Valley**[33] 5442 5-11-6 **108**......................... GavinSheehan 114+
(Warren Greatrex) *trckd ldrs: hit 9th: pushed along after next: rdn bef 2 out: swtchd rt bef last: led run-in: styd on: drvn out* **2/1**[1]
R2-R 2 *2* **Mighty Mobb (IRE)**[17] 169 8-11-7 **109**....................(b) AndrewThornton 112
(Seamus Mullins) *trckd ldrs: pushed along after 10th: led appr 2 out: rdn and hdd sn after last: styd on but no ex* **16/1**
1-11 3 *¾* **Billy Congo (IRE)**[7] 363 8-11-8 **110** 7ex.................. MichealNolan 113
(Adrian Wintle) *rn wout declared tongue-tie: hld up: hdwy after 9th: rdn after next: hung lft between last 2: cl 3rd whn nt fluent last: styd on same pce* **7/2**[3]
11-2 4 *25* **Sandynow (IRE)**[20] 108 10-11-5 **110**..........................(p) SeanBowen(3) 90
(Peter Bowen) *chsd ldrs: rdn whn dropped to last but stl in tch after 9th: wknd last* **3/1**[2]
13-3 5 *3 ¼* **Easy Beesy**[15] 210 7-11-12 **114**.............................. RichardJohnson 91
(Warren Greatrex) *led: nt fluent 7th: pushed along bef 9th: rdn and hdd appr 2 out: wknd last* **7/2**[3]

6m 30.7s (-22.10) **Going Correction** -0.725s/f (Firm) **5 Ran SP% 108.7**
Speed ratings (Par 105): **103,102,102,94,93**
CSF £23.89 TOTE £3.10: £1.10, £3.90; EX 25.90 Trifecta £54.60.
Owner The Broadwell Fox Partnership **Bred** G Deren **Trained** Upper Lambourn, Berks
FOCUS
Rail movement increased Chases by 60yds per circuit and Hurdles by 35yds per circuit. The second-last fence was omitted. Fences were on the outer down the hill and inner up the home straight. Hurdles were middle outer. Jockeys reported the ground to be riding 'beautifully'. Modest staying form, all of the runners being in with a chance rounding the final bend.

446 FAMILY FUN RACEDAY WITH EQUINITI H'CAP CHASE (11 fncs 2 omitted) 2m 1f 96y
2:50 (2:51) (Class 5) (0-100,99) 5-Y-O+ **£2,729** (£801; £400; £200)

Form RPR
F3-R 1 **Houseparty**[18] 150 7-9-11 **77** ow2.......................... MissTWorsley(7) 88+
(Diana Grissell) *chsd ldrs: rdn to chal between last 2: led sn after last: r.o wl* **10/1**
253- 2 *4* **Owner Occupier**[269] 1368 10-10-12 **85**..................... MarcGoldstein 92
(Chris Gordon) *disp ld tl clr ldr 3rd: rdn appr 2 out (usual 3 out): hdd sn after last: kpt on but no ex* **12/1**
132- 3 *3* **Star Presenter (IRE)**[30] 5526 7-11-12 **99**................... TomCannon 104
(Chris Gordon) *hung rt thrght: j. sltly rt at times: hld up: rdn and hdwy after 3 out (usual 4 out): ev ch last: sn no ex* **5/2**[2]
F3U- 4 *½* **Mac's Grey (IRE)**[202] 2260 8-10-0 **73**...................(t) GavinSheehan 77
(Ian Williams) *chsd ldrs: rdn appr 2 out (usual 3 out): styd on same pce (b.b.v)* **5/1**[3]
33-2 5 *16* **Lord Lir (IRE)**[11] 280 9-10-12 **85**...................(b) RichardJohnson 76
(Tim Vaughan) *disp tl 3rd: trckd ldr: rdn after 3 out (usual 4 out): wknd after next* **9/4**[1]
331- 6 *8* **The Informant**[37] 5372 9-11-2 **89**.....................(b) AndrewThornton 71
(Seamus Mullins) *chsd ldrs tl lost pl after 6th: rdn after 3 out (usual 4 out): wknd after next* **6/1**

45-4 P **Stafford Charlie**[17] 173 9-9-7 **73** oh3.......................(p) MichaelHeard(7)
(John O'Shea) *hld up: nt fluent 3rd: struggling after 6th: wknd after 8th: t.o whn p.u bef 2 out (usual 3 out)* **16/1**

4m 32.4s (-2.30) **Going Correction** -0.45s/f (Good) **7 Ran SP% 113.0**
Speed ratings: **87,85,83,83,76 73,**
CSF £103.65 TOTE £13.50: £4.80, £5.80; EX 160.70 Trifecta £739.00.
Owner Ms G Howell **Bred** Darley **Trained** Brightling, E Sussex
FOCUS
No hanging around here, with the duelling early leaders setting a good gallop in what was a moderate handicap.

447 TED DEAR - RETIREMENT CLASSIC "NATIONAL HUNT" MAIDEN HURDLE (9 hdls) 2m 1f 145y
3:25 (3:29) (Class 4) 4-Y-O+ **£3,249** (£954; £477; £238)

Form RPR
42-2 1 **Detroit Blues**[18] 147 5-11-0 118.........................(t) MichealNolan 107+
(Jamie Snowden) *trckd ldrs: rdn in cl 4th after 2 out: r.o wl to ld fnl 75yds: rdn out* **7/4**[1]
652- 2 *1* **Time And Again (FR)**[69] 4816 5-11-0 120.................. RichardJohnson 106
(Tim Vaughan) *led: rdn appr last: hdd fnl 75yds: kpt on but no ex* **2/1**[2]
600- 3 *½* **Shah Of Persia**[138] 3555 8-11-0 0.........................(t) GavinSheehan 106
(Warren Greatrex) *trckd ldr: rdn appr 2 out: ch last: styd on same pce* **17/2**
63F- 4 *2 ¾* **Glenariff**[96] 4278 6-10-7 109.................................. AndrewThornton 97
(Seamus Mullins) *trckd ldr: rdn after 2 out: ch whn nodded on landing last: hld after: styd on same pce* **3/1**[3]
56- 5 *17* **Itsaboutime (IRE)**[91] 4384 5-10-9 0.............................. ConorRing(5) 88
(Helen Nelmes) *hld up in last pair but in tch: nt a fluent and tended to jump lft: rdn after 3 out: wknd bef last* **25/1**
0 P **Art Libre (FR)**[11] 279 4-10-9 0...............................(t) MarcGoldstein
(Gary Moore) *hld up: rdn after 5th: sn lost tch: t.o whn p.u after 3 out* **20/1**

4m 27.3s (-7.00) **Going Correction** -0.725s/f (Firm)
WFA 4 from 5yo+ 18lb **6 Ran SP% 113.8**
Speed ratings (Par 105): **85,84,84,83,76**
CSF £5.93 TOTE £2.70: £1.60, £1.10; EX 4.30 Trifecta £25.20.
Owner Ade & The Winettes **Bred** R W Huggins **Trained** Lambourn, Berks
FOCUS
Modest maiden hurdle form.

448 SELFTRADE TRADE ANYWHERE MOBILE APP H'CAP CHASE (16 fncs 3 omitted) 3m 1f 106y
4:00 (4:00) (Class 3) (0-140,133) 5-Y-O **£6,330** (£1,870; £935; £468; £234)

Form RPR
42-0 1 **Adrenalin Flight (IRE)**[22] 92 9-11-0 **121**...............(v) AndrewThornton 132+
(Seamus Mullins) *trckd ldrs: led after 2 out (usual 3 out): styd on wl: rdn out* **7/2**[1]
04-4 2 *3* **Ballybough Gorta (IRE)**[17] 169 8-10-7 **117**...............(b) SeanBowen(3) 124
(Nick Mitchell) *rn in snatches: in last pair: nt fluent 8th: hdwy after 11th: chal after 3 out (usual 4 out): drvn to chse wnr after next: styd on same pce fr last* **5/1**[2]
02-P 3 *5* **Caulfields Venture (IRE)**[20] 101 9-11-6 **127**...........(p) GavinSheehan 129
(Emma Lavelle) *mid-div: in last trio 6th: rdn after 11th: hdwy after 3 out (usual 4 out): wnt 3rd bef last: styd on same pce run-in* **7/1**[3]
22P- 4 *13* **Master Rajeem (USA)**[74] 4706 6-11-2 **123**...................(p) MarkGrant 114
(Neil King) *disp ld most of way: clr ldr after 11th: rdn and hdd after 2 out: sn hld: no ex fr last* **17/2**
PU- 5 *¾* **American Spin**[34] 5431 11-11-5 **126**.....................(b) LeightonAspell 115
(Luke Dace) *hld up early: trckd ldrs fr 6th: rdn after 3 out (usual 4 out): wknd after next* **14/1**
P5-4 6 *11* **West Of The Edge (IRE)**[8] 340 7-9-7 **107** oh12.. ThomasCheesman(7) 86
(Dai Williams) *trckd ldrs: pushed along after 10th: rdn after 13th: wknd after next* **25/1**
41-P 7 *2 ¼* **Kingcora (FR)**[18] 149 7-10-12 **119**............................ LiamTreadwell 96
(Venetia Williams) *mid-div tl lost pl after 11th: nvr bk on terms* **8/1**
34-3 8 *5* **Fruity O'Rooney**[17] 169 12-11-5 **126**.........................(b) JamieMoore 101
(Gary Moore) *j.lft at times: disp ld most of way tl after 11th: blnd 13th: sn rdn: blnd 2 out: sn wknd* **5/1**[2]
130- 9 *25* **First Fandango**[143] 3445 8-11-12 **133**.....................(t) RichardJohnson 83
(Tim Vaughan) *mid-div: lost pl and struggling after 11th: wknd 3 out (usual 4 out)* **5/1**[2]
P0P- P **Life Of A Luso (IRE)**[38] 5356 11-11-5 **126**....................(t) TomO'Brien
(Paul Henderson) *struggling in last fr 6th: stmbld 8th: lost tch after 11th: t.o whn p.u after 13th* **25/1**

6m 43.6s (-17.50) **Going Correction** -0.45s/f (Good) **10 Ran SP% 120.7**
Speed ratings: **107,106,104,100,100 97,96,95,87,**
CSF £22.92 CT £116.68 TOTE £6.40: £2.50, £3.30, £3.20; EX 30.70 Trifecta £163.30.
Owner Mark Adams **Bred** Alex Heskin **Trained** Wilsford-Cum-Lake, Wilts
FOCUS
A good test at the distance and it was won by a thorough stayer.

449 EQUINITI INTERNATIONAL PAYMENTS H'CAP HURDLE (9 hdls) 2m 1f 145y
4:35 (4:35) (Class 4) (0-120,117) 4-Y-O+ **£3,249** (£954; £477; £238)

Form RPR
PP-P 1 **Yesyoucan (IRE)**[12] 261 10-11-10 **115**.................(p) LeightonAspell 122+
(Neil Mulholland) *trckd ldr: led after 3 out: clr between last 2: r.o wl: rdn out* **16/1**
1P0- 2 *6* **Baths Well (IRE)**[76] 4677 5-10-8 **109**.............. HarrisonBeswick(10) 110
(Ben Pauling) *trckd ldrs: pushed along after 5th: rdn after 3 out: chalng for hld 2nd whn nt fluent last: kpt on but a being hld by wnr* **16/1**
213- 3 *¾* **Epsom Flyer**[30] 5523 5-9-11 **98**.............................. PaddyBradley(10) 97
(Pat Phelan) *in tch: rdn to chse wnr whn wnt rt 2 out: styd on same pce fr last: lost 2nd nring fin* **4/1**[1]
46-0 4 *½* **Ashkoun (FR)**[24] 43 4-10-7 **103**.........................(t) RichardJohnson 97
(Tim Vaughan) *hld up towards rr: hdwy after 3 out: rdn between last 2: styd on fr last* **8/1**
F5-6 5 *1 ¼* **Hold Court (IRE)**[22] 87 8-11-12 **117**............................ PaulMoloney 114
(Evan Williams) *towards rr of midfield: rdn after 3 out: r.o strly fr last but nvr any ch* **8/1**
33-U 6 *nk* **Alla Svelta (IRE)**[17] 170 9-11-2 **107**............................. TomCannon 105
(Brendan Powell) *trckd ldrs: blnd bdly 4th: lost pl after 6th: kpt on same pce fr 2 out* **10/1**
205- 7 *5* **Taste The Wine (IRE)**[23] 5335 9-10-10 **104**......(tp) RobertWilliams(3) 98
(Bernard Llewellyn) *mid-div: rdn after 3 out: one pce fr next* **6/1**[3]
064- 8 *4* **Memphis Magic (GER)**[99] 4234 5-10-13 **104**................(t) JamesDavies 94
(Brendan Powell) *towards rr of midfield: rdn and hdwy after 3 out: wknd run-in* **14/1**

0-0 **9** *5* **Daidaidai (FR)**[20] 104 5-10-7 **105**............................ MrWRussell(7) 92
(Gary Moore) *in tch: pushed along after 3 out: one pce fr next* **50/1**

23-3 **10** *4 ½* **Warrant Officer**[14] 224 5-10-4 **95**............................ MarcGoldstein 76
(Sheena West) *led: rdn whn hdd after 3 out: wknd last* **11/2**[2]

16-P **11** *10* **Osgood**[20] 104 8-10-6 **107**............................ GeorgeGorman(10) 79
(Gary Moore) *racd keenly: mid-div: rdn after 3 out: wknd bef next* **16/1**

055- **12** *1 ¼* **Guards Chapel**[37] 5369 7-11-10 **115**............................(v) JamieMoore 85
(Gary Moore) *mid-div: struggling whn lost pl 6th: wknd bef 2 out* **12/1**

46-P **13** *7* **Hoist The Colours (IRE)**[23] 61 4-10-12 **108**............................ TomO'Brien 67
(Robert Walford) *nt a fluent: hld up towards rr: wknd 2 out* **12/1**

3F/ **F** **The Finger Post (IRE)**[630] 1483 8-11-2 **112**............................ ConorRing(5)
(Helen Nelmes) *hld up towards rr: nt a fluent: rdn after 3 out: no imp whn fell heavily next* **33/1**

4m 23.6s (-10.70) **Going Correction** -0.725s/f (Firm)
WFA 4 from 5yo+ 18lb **14** Ran SP% **125.6**
Speed ratings (Par 105): **93,90,90,89,89 89,87,85,83,81 77,76,73,**
CSF £256.60 CT £1241.02 TOTE £21.20: £4.90, £5.40, £2.10; EX 306.00 Trifecta £1204.60 Part won..
Owner Prism Bloodstock **Bred** Thomas Steele **Trained** Limpley Stoke, Wilts

FOCUS
Just an ordinary handicap, but it should produce winners.

450 EQUINITI "LEADERS IN TECHNOLOGY" H'CAP CHASE (14 fncs 2 omitted) 2m 5f 31y
5:05 (5:06) (Class 5) (0-100,100) 5-Y-0+ **£2,729** (£801; £400; £200)

Form RPR

0P4- **1** **La Madonnina (IRE)**[52] 5115 7-10-0 **74** oh5............................(p) JamesBest 92+
(Caroline Keevil) *in tch: trckd ldrs 6th: led after 3 out (usual 4 out): styd on wl to draw clr fr last: rdn out* **6/1**[3]

2F6- **2** *13* **Fast Exit (IRE)**[228] 1805 8-11-6 **94**............................(b) RichardJohnson 100
(Neil Mulholland) *in tch: disp 3rd 3 out (usual 4 out): sn rdn: kpt on to chse wnr between last 2: no ex fr last* **9/2**[2]

5F-F **3** *2 ¼* **Dancing Dik**[24] 31 10-10-7 **81**............................(p) TomO'Brien 86
(Paul Henderson) *led: j. sltly lft most of way: rdn and hdd after 3 out (usual 4 out): lost 2nd between last 2: styd on same pce* **7/2**[1]

PP4- **4** *41* **Gizzit (IRE)**[30] 5526 9-11-3 **91**............................(p) AndrewThornton 58
(Seamus Mullins) *hld up: hit 2nd: lost tch after 10th: lft t.o 4th bef 2 out (usual 3 out)* **10/1**

1P2/ **P** **Nomadic Warrior**[1238] 3548 10-11-11 **99**............................ MarcGoldstein
(Diana Grissell) *trcking ldrs whn lost action and p.u after 5th* **12/1**

4P-3 **P** **Wing Mira (IRE)**[18] 150 7-10-0 **74** oh14............................(b) LiamTreadwell
(Venetia Williams) *trckd ldr tl hit 9th: sn rdn: wknd after 3 out: p.u bef next* **13/2**

54F- **P** **On The Case**[57] 5024 7-11-2 **90**............................ PaddyBrennan
(Tom George) *trckd ldrs: rdn after 3 out (usual 4 out): wkng in 4th whn p.u bef next* **9/2**[2]

P6P- **P** **Family Motto**[76] 4668 6-11-12 **100**............................ TomCannon
(Chris Gordon) *a last: reminder after 3rd: nt fluent 6th: struggling 8th: losing tch whn p.u 10th* **8/1**

5m 41.4s (-1.60) **Going Correction** -0.45s/f (Good) **8** Ran SP% **114.1**
Speed ratings: **84,79,78,63, , , ,**
CSF £33.46 CT £108.40 TOTE £7.80: £2.20, £1.90, £1.70; EX 42.00 Trifecta £229.20.
Owner Mrs C J Dunn **Bred** Mrs Christopher Dunn **Trained** Motcombe, Dorset

FOCUS
Only half the field managed to complete in this low-grade chase.

451 CLUB-TOGETHER.ORG RACE WITH EQUINITI H'CAP HURDLE (11 hdls) 2m 5f 139y
5:35 (5:35) (Class 5) (0-100,100) 4-Y-0+ **£2,339** (£686; £343; £171)

Form RPR

364- **1** **Brass Monkey (IRE)**[48] 5204 8-11-5 **100**............................(v[1]) LizzieKelly(7) 111+
(Neil King) *trckd ldrs: led appr 8th: clr 2 out: kpt on wl: comf* **8/1**

4-56 **2** *13* **Warsaw Pact (IRE)**[12] 265 12-10-0 **74** oh5............................ JamieMoore 71
(Steven Dixon) *trckd ldrs: rdn along fr 7th: chsd wnr after 3 out: styd on same pce fr last* **20/1**

5 **3** *½* **Thepartysover**[20] 104 10-11-10 **98**............................ TomO'Brien 95
(Paul Henderson) *hld up towards rr: hdwy fr 8th: rdn into 3rd 2 out: chal for 2nd at the last: styd on same pce* **16/1**

43-0 **4** *10* **Chance Taken**[20] 108 7-11-12 **100**............................ RichardJohnson 88
(Noel Williams) *trckd ldrs: nt fluent 5th: mstke 8th: rdn after 3 out: styd on same pce fr next* **4/1**[2]

05-4 **5** *1 ½* **The Selector**[23] 65 6-10-0 **77**............................ SeanBowen(3) 63
(Chris Gordon) *mid-div: nt fluent 6th: rdn after 3 out: styd on steadily but nvr threatened to get on terms* **3/1**[1]

/P5- **6** *12* **Daizy (IRE)**[227] 1819 6-10-10 **84**............................ RobertDunne 59
(Hilary Parrott) *j.rt: led tl appr 8th: rdn after 3 out: wknd next* **14/1**

P4-6 **7** *¾* **Kingscombe (USA)**[23] 65 6-9-11 **74** oh3............................(p) ThomasGarner(3) 51
(Linda Jewell) *hld up towards rr: hdwy fr 7th: nt fluent next: rdn after 3 out: wknd between last 2* **25/1**

PP1- **8** *6* **Aaly**[232] 1743 8-10-3 **77**............................ MarcGoldstein 46
(Lydia Richards) *a towards rr* **16/1**

P0P- **9** *2 ½* **Al Guwair (IRE)**[37] 5367 5-10-10 **84**............................ LiamTreadwell 51
(Mark Hoad) *mid-div: hmpd 6th: hit next: rdn after 3 out: wknd next* **66/1**

/P5- **10** *7* **Mighty Thor**[55] 5066 5-10-9 **83**............................ LeightonAspell 44
(Lydia Richards) *mid-div: bdly hmpd 1st: wknd after 3 out* **22/1**

/65- **11** *25* **Comedy House**[23] 5260 7-10-1 **75**............................(v) PaddyBrennan 13
(Michael Madgwick) *a towards rr* **13/2**[3]

36-0 **12** *nk* **Dexter Benjamin (IRE)**[23] 65 6-11-7 **95**............................(tp) TomCannon 33
(Nick Gifford) *mid-div: wnt lft 1st: wknd 8th: t.o* **12/1**

000- **U** **Yes I Will**[37] 5371 6-11-2 **90**............................(t) AndrewThornton
(Linda Jewell) *hld up towards rr: stmbld and uns rdr 3 out* **20/1**

03-P **P** **Moncarno**[24] 30 5-10-5 **84**............................(bt[1]) KieronEdgar(5)
(David Pipe) *racd keenly: trckd ldrs: wnt 2nd 3rd tl rdn after 7th: wknd next: t.o whn p.u after 3 out* **14/1**

4PP- **P** **Underwood (FR)**[74] 4712 7-10-4 **85**............................(t) FreddieMitchell(7)
(Michael Roberts) *mid-div: rdn after 7th: wknd qckly: p.u bef next* **20/1**

5m 26.5s (-16.00) **Going Correction** -0.725s/f (Firm) **15** Ran SP% **126.2**
Speed ratings (Par 103): **98,93,93,89,89 85,84,82,81,79 70,70, , ,**
CSF £165.80 CT £2527.79 TOTE £7.40: £2.10, £6.50, £4.50; EX 263.60 Trifecta £876.00 Part won..
Owner The Ridgeway Racing For Fun Partnership **Bred** Oliver McDonnell **Trained** Barbury Castle, Wiltshire

FOCUS
This has looked quite competitive but the winner turned it into a rout.
T/Jkpt: Not won. T/Plt: £1,458.50 to a £1 stake. Pool: £85,616.02 - 42.85 winning tickets T/Qpdt: £14.00 to a £1 stake. Pool: £8,176.43 - 430.20 winning tickets **Tim Mitchell**

[138]KELSO (L-H)
Sunday, May 24

OFFICIAL GOING: Good (good to firm in places; 8.4)
Wind: Fresh, half against Weather: Overcast

452 LYNTOUN TAXIS & ANDERSONS BUTCHERS EAST LOTHIAN NOVICES' HURDLE (8 hdls) 2m 51y
2:10 (2:10) (Class 4) 4-Y-0+ **£5,198** (£1,526; £763; £381)

Form RPR

PP/6 **1** **Running Brook (IRE)**[11] 285 8-10-7 0............................ CallumBewley(5) 101
(R Mike Smith) *trckd ldrs: lft cl 2nd 3 out: rdn next: led after last: styd on wl* **40/1**

U1 **2** *nk* **Angus Glens**[12] 263 5-11-5 0............................(p) SamTwiston-Davies 109+
(David Dennis) *nt fluent on occasions: t.k.h early: hld up: stdy hdwy 1/2-way: lft cl 3rd 3 out: led gng wl next: nt fluent last: sn rdn and hdd: kpt on towards fin* **8/11**[1]

460- **3** *5* **Another Bygones (IRE)**[37] 5380 6-10-12 0............................ JamesReveley 96
(Karen McLintock) *hld up: hdwy and in tch 3 out: rdn and outpcd next: kpt on fr last: nt rch first two* **28/1**

3- **4** *½* **So Satisfied**[31] 5489 4-10-8 0............................ BrianHughes 91
(Sandy Thomson) *t.k.h: hld up in tch: hdwy and chsd ldrs 3 out: rdn next: kpt on same pce* **11/1**

5/5- **5** *2* **Naburn**[31] 5489 7-10-9 0............................ HarryChalloner(3) 93
(Andrew Wilson) *t.k.h: chsd ldrs: wnt 2nd 4th: cl 2nd whn lft in ld after 3 out: rdn and hdd next: sn outpcd* **16/1**

5- **6** *28* **Sky Full Of Stars (IRE)**[36] 5395 5-10-12 0............................ LucyAlexander 65
(James Ewart) *t.k.h: in tch: drvn along 3 out: 6th and struggling whn mstke next: sn btn* **9/2**[3]

7 *74* **Ballymorris (IRE)**[63] 6-10-5 0............................(p) ThomasDowson(7)
(Kenny Johnson) *nt fluent: chsd ldr to 4th: lost pl whn stmbld next: sn lost tch: t.o* **66/1**

464- **F** **Vital Evidence (USA)**[41] 5308 5-10-12 105............................ HenryBrooke 97+
(Donald McCain) *led at ordinary gallop: jst over 1 l in front and gng wl whn stmbld and fell after 3 out* **4/1**[2]

-0 **U** **Parkie Boy**[22] 79 4-10-8 0............................ BrianHarding
(Nicky Richards) *nt fluent in rr: struggling 1/2-way: no ch whn stmbld and uns rdr 2 out* **33/1**

3m 50.1s (-11.70) **Going Correction** -0.775s/f (Firm)
WFA 4 from 5yo+ 18lb **9** Ran SP% **120.6**
Speed ratings (Par 105): **96,95,93,93,92 79,44, ,**
CSF £75.52 TOTE £45.40: £13.80, £1.02, £6.50; EX 185.80 Trifecta £1915.70 Part won..
Owner Jamie Matheson **Bred** Mrs Sarah Martin **Trained** Galston, E Ayrshire

FOCUS
Rail dolled out and Hurdles increased by 45yds per circuit and Chases by 20yds per circuit. After the first Callum Bewley described the ground as on the fast side of good with a good covering of grass. This moderate novice hurdle produced an upset, with the odds-on favourite just edged out.

453 ELLIOT HENDERSON NOVICES' H'CAP CHASE (DIV I) (17 fncs) 2m 7f 96y
2:40 (2:40) (Class 4) (0-105,105) 5-Y-0+ **£3,898** (£1,144; £572; £286)

Form RPR

43-2 **1** **Jack Albert (IRE)**[10] 302 8-11-6 **99**............................(b) BrianHughes 113+
(Dianne Sayer) *cl up: led 3rd: mde rest: drew clr fr 2 out: j.rt last: styd on wl* **7/2**[1]

300- **2** *11* **Vision De La Vie (FR)**[58] 5011 5-11-1 **94**............................ JamesReveley 97
(Pauline Robson) *chsd ldrs: rdn bef 4 out: rallied bef 2 out: chsd (clr) wnr run-in: kpt on: no imp* **4/1**[2]

0-4F **3** *nk* **King Of The Dark (IRE)**[12] 253 8-11-0 **100**............................ ThomasDowson(7) 102
(Victor Thompson) *hld up in tch: stdy hdwy and chsd ldrs 9th: wnt 2nd 5 out: rdn bef 2 out: kpt on same pce run-in* **14/1**

35-0 **4** *2 ½* **Emkae (IRE)**[22] 78 7-10-13 **92**............................(t) BrianHarding 92
(Alison Hamilton) *hld up: hdwy and in tch whn hit 12th: outpcd 4 out: rallied bef 2 out: no imp bef last* **8/1**

50-U **5** *3 ¼* **Top Cat Dj (IRE)**[19] 133 7-9-11 **81**............................(v[1]) DiarmuidO'Regan(5) 78
(Chris Grant) *nt fluent on occasions: in tch: lost pl bef 1/2-way: drvn 5 out: rallied 2 out: nvr rchd ldrs* **8/1**

5PP- **6** *nse* **Reverse The Charge (IRE)**[34] 5420 8-10-0 **79** oh10............................ PeterBuchanan 75
(Jane Walton) *hld up towards rr: struggling fnl circ: kpt on fr 2 out: nvr able to chal* **25/1**

150- **7** *67* **Acordingtoscript (IRE)**[49] 5160 9-10-7 **89**............................ GrahamWatters(3) 24
(Martin Todhunter) *led to 3rd: chsd wnr tl hit and outpcd 5 out: lost tch after next: t.o: collapsed fatally after fin* **5/1**[3]

P/66 **F** **Native Brian (IRE)**[11] 288 9-9-12 **84**............................ RossChapman(7)
(Andrew Hamilton) *midfield on outside: mstke 9th: 5/ 5th whn fell next* **25/1**

U5-1 **F** **Just Awake**[11] 287 8-11-5 **105**............................(t) StevenFox(7)
(Sandy Thomson) *hld up: smooth hdwy and disputing 3rd pl (4 l down) whn fell 4 out* **4/1**[2]

5m 48.8s (-19.20) **Going Correction** -1.075s/f (Hard) **9** Ran SP% **115.5**
Speed ratings: **89,85,85,84,83 83,60, ,**
CSF £18.53 CT £168.46 TOTE £4.00: £1.40, £1.70, £2.50; EX 24.70 Trifecta £148.70.
Owner E G Tunstall **Bred** Miss Marie Harding **Trained** Hackthorpe, Cumbria

FOCUS
The winner dictated most of the pace, and eventually all the challengers dropped away.

454 ELLIOT HENDERSON NOVICES' H'CAP CHASE (DIV II) (17 fncs) 2m 7f 96y
3:10 (3:22) (Class 4) (0-105,101) 5-Y-0+ **£3,898** (£1,144; £572; £286)

Form RPR

P4-1 **1** **Leanna Ban**[17] 158 8-11-9 **101**............................(t) JonathanEngland(3) 124+
(Tristan Davidson) *cl up: led after 1st: mde rest: clr w runner-up fr 12th: rdn and styd on strly to draw clr after 2 out* **4/1**[2]

33-0 **2** *12* **Brother Scott**[22] 78 8-11-3 **92**............................ SeanQuinlan 106+
(Sue Smith) *prom: hdwy to chse wnr 1/2-way: clr of remainder fr 12th: effrt whn nt fluent 2 out: sn one pce* **11/2**

11-5 **3** *46* **Tribal Dance (IRE)**[23] 58 9-11-2 **91**............................(p) DaveCrosse 56
(John O'Shea) *nt fluent on occasions: chsd wnr to 1/2-way: sn drvn and outpcd: no imp whn lft modest 3rd after 3 out: no ch w first two* **16/1**

62-P **4** *22* **Lochore (IRE)**[11] 287 9-10-0 **75** oh5............................(t[1]) PeterBuchanan 18
(Jean McGregor) *nt fluent in rr: shortlived effrt 12th: struggling after next: t.o* **28/1**

2P2- **5** *56* **Coolanure (IRE)**[40] 5329 6-9-12 **80**............................(p) ThomasDowson(7)
(Kenny Johnson) *cl up tl outpcd bef 10th: struggling fr 12th: t.o* **9/4**[1]

00-2 **P** **Discoverie**[11] 287 7-10-2 **80**.............................. HarryChalloner(3)
(Dianne Sayer) *bhd and nvr jumping or gng wl: sturggling 1/2-way: t.o whn p.u bef 2 out* **5/1**[3]
06-3 **P** **Blast Martha (IRE)**[24] 37 6-10-3 **78**.............................. BrianHughes
(Michael Smith) *hld up bhd ldng gp: hdwy to chse ldrs 1/2-way: rdn 12th: 15 l 3rd 3 out: sn p.u and dismntd* **11/2**
000- **P** **Where's Malachy (IRE)**[30] 5516 7-10-6 **84**.............................. CraigNichol(3)
(Rose Dobbin) *hld up: stdy hdwy bef 12th: rdn bef 4 out: sn no imp: no ch whn p.u after 2 out* **25/1**
5m 40.3s (-27.70) **Going Correction** -1.075s/f (Hard) 8 Ran SP% **111.4**
Speed ratings: **103,99,83,76,57 , ,**
CSF £25.05 CT £303.87 TOTE £4.60: £1.80, £1.60, £3.10; EX 23.00 Trifecta £98.00.
Owner E G Tunstall, P Nicholson, S M Grice **Bred** Mrs Claire Massey **Trained** Irthington, Cumbria
FOCUS
There was a delay to this race while the groundsmen sanded the bends. This was more strongly run than the first division and they finished strung out.

455 KOSB NOVICES' H'CAP CHASE (12 fncs) 2m 1f 14y
3:45 (3:53) (Class 4) (0-105,105) 5-Y-O+ **£4,548** (£1,335; £667; £333)

Form RPR
663- **1** **Beidh Tine Anseo (IRE)**[32] 5474 9-11-0 **98**..........(tp) GrantCockburn(5) 106+
(Lucinda Russell) *in tch: outpcd 5 out: rallied bef 2 out: led run-in: drvn out* **7/1**[3]
4P-F **2** *2* **Great Demeanor (USA)**[11] 286 5-10-0 **79** oh5.............. BrianHughes 86+
(Dianne Sayer) *hld up: smooth hdwy to chse ldrs bef 2 out: rdn and swtchd rt run-in: sn chsng wnr: kpt on fin* **12/1**
5P0- **3** *1 1/2* **Clonleney (IRE)**[58] 5011 9-10-1 **87**..............................(t) JamieHamilton(7) 91
(Alison Hamilton) *t.k.h: in tch: rdn and sltly outpcd 2 out: kpt on fr last* **12/1**
22-1 **4** *nk* **Scorpions Sting (IRE)**[12] 252 6-11-7 **105**.............. DaleIrving(5) 110
(James Ewart) *nt fluent on occasions: cl up: led and rdn bef 2 out: hdd run-in: sn outpcd* **5/6**[1]
6B4- **5** *8* **Mwangaza (FR)**[50] 5131 5-11-3 **96**..............................(b) JamesReveley 93
(Pauline Robson) *led to bef 2 out: sn rdn: wknd between last 2* **3/1**[2]
00P- **6** *1/2* **No Such Number**[41] 5315 7-10-11 **97**.............................. MrTHamilton(7) 94
(Sandy Forster) *cl up: mstke 5th: rdn after 3 out: wknd fr next* **25/1**
56-R **7** *shd* **The Village (IRE)**[11] 286 6-10-0 **79** oh13.............. PeterBuchanan 75
(Lucinda Russell) *hld up on outside: rdn 4 out: no imp bef 2 out* **14/1**
4m 12.8s (-5.20) **Going Correction** -1.075s/f (Hard) 7 Ran SP% **118.0**
Speed ratings: **69,68,67,67,63 63,63**
CSF £74.40 CT £864.85 TOTE £8.60: £3.10, £3.30; EX 70.30 Trifecta £1094.10.
Owner Ian D Miller **Bred** J S Bolger **Trained** Arlary, Perth & Kinross
■ Neville Woods was withdrawn. Price at time of withdrawal 10/1. Rule 4 applies to bets placed prior to withdrawal but not to SP bets - deduction 5p in the pound.
FOCUS
A steady pace resulted in a bunched finish in this moderate handicap.

456 REECE, BEN, JESSICA & CHARLOTTE COPPOLA NOVICES' H'CAP HURDLE (10 hdls) 2m 2f 25y
4:20 (4:21) (Class 3) (0-125,120) 4-Y-O+ **£5,848** (£1,717; £858; £429)

Form RPR
246- **1** **Make It Happen (IRE)**[61] 4973 6-10-7 **106**.............. GrantCockburn(5) 106
(Lucinda Russell) *chsd ldrs: chal bef 6th: pckd next: effrt bef 2 out: styd on u.p to ld towards fin* **4/1**[3]
010- **2** *3/4* **Apachee Prince (IRE)**[31] 5495 6-11-10 **118**..............(t) BrianHughes 117
(Alistair Whillans) *prom: hdwy to ld bef 2 out: rdn and 3 l clr last: edgd rt run-in: hdd towards fin* **5/2**[1]
3-42 **3** *3 1/4* **Un Anjou (FR)**[4] 402 7-11-4 **119**.............................. MrShaneQuinlan(7) 115
(David Dennis) *t.k.h: led tl rn wd and hdd bnd bef 6th: regained ld after 3 out: rdn and hdd bef next: no ex fr last* **5/2**[1]
015- **4** *19* **Crinkle Crags (IRE)**[48] 5205 5-10-11 **105**.............. BrianHarding 84
(Nicky Richards) *nt fluent on occasions: hld up in tch: effrt after 3 out: wknd bef next* **7/2**[2]
050- **5** *1* **Silver Shuffle (IRE)**[65] 4891 8-10-9 **103**..............(p) JamesReveley 81
(Dianne Sayer) *cl up: led bnd bef 6th: hdd after 3 out: rdn and wknd bef next* **10/1**
/50- **U** **Ninepointsixthree**[23] 2489 5-10-13 **107**.............................. DaveCrosse
(John O'Shea) *cl up on outside whn jinked rt and uns rdr after 2nd* **25/1**
4m 18.0s (-9.00) **Going Correction** -0.775s/f (Firm) 6 Ran SP% **112.3**
Speed ratings (Par 107): **89,88,87,78,78**
CSF £14.73 TOTE £4.70: £2.50, £1.40; EX 12.10 Trifecta £40.80.
Owner Wright Mitchell Wilson **Bred** Stuart McPhee Bloodstock Ltd **Trained** Arlary, Perth & Kinross
FOCUS
This race opened up when Solway Dandy was a non-runner. It produced the second last-gasp winner for Lucinda Russell on the day.

457 ROYAL SCOTS DRAGOON GUARDS CHALLENGE CUP (AN OPEN HUNTERS' CHASE) (19 fncs) 3m 2f 39y
4:55 (4:58) (Class 4) 5-Y-O+ **£4,367** (£1,354; £676; £338)

Form RPR
F-1 **1** **Cave Hunter (IRE)**[22] 80 8-11-12 0..............................(tp) MrTHamilton(3) 121
(Mrs Wendy Hamilton) *led to 4th: cl up: led 13th to 3 out: rallied and regained ld next: edgd lft u.p run-in: styd on gamely* **10/3**[2]
32U- **2** *3* **Nowurhurlin (IRE)**[45] 5239 8-11-11 118.............................. MrNOrpwood(7) 122
(Mrs S J Stilgoe) *prom: nt fluent 12th: hdwy to chse wnr 5 out: led 3 out to next: rallied: nt clr run and swtchd rt run-in: kpt on same pce* **6/1**
P/5- **3** *11* **Young Hurricane (IRE)**[42] 9-11-5 112.............................. MrsFreyaBrewer(7) 106
(G C Brewer) *bhd and sn detached: sme hdwy bef 4 out: rdn and no imp after next* **8/1**
6-2 **4** *6* **Kalastar (IRE)**[22] 80 6-11-12 0.............................. MissCWalton 100
(Katie Scott) *bhd and sn detached: sme hdwy bef 4 out: rdn and no imp after next* **17/2**
21-4 **P** **Rockiteer (IRE)**[25] 18 12-12-1 122..............................(p) MissJCWilliams(3)
(Henry Daly) *t.k.h: cl up: led 4th to 13th: hit and outpcd 5 out: struggling next: lost tch and p.u bef 2 out* **11/4**[1]
323/ **F** **Dannanceys Hill (IRE)**[22] 8-11-5 0.............................. MissAWaugh(7)
(Miss A Waugh) *t.k.h: prom: mstke 5 out: 8 l seventh and outpcd whn fell next* **16/1**
161- **P** **Beggar's Velvet (IRE)**[34] 5424 9-11-11 112..........(p) MissRMcDonald(7)
(D Holmes) *hld up: struggling fr 8th: shortlived effrt after 5 out: wknd after next: t.o whn p.u after 2 out* **5/1**[3]
3-11 **F** **Chanceofa Lifetime (IRE)**[11] 290 8-12-1 113.......... MrKitAlexander(3) 112
(Victor Thompson) *prom: effrt and rdn 3 out: nrly 5 l 3rd and one pce whn fell next* **14/1**
6m 30.5s (-16.70) **Going Correction** -1.075s/f (Hard) 8 Ran SP% **114.9**
Speed ratings: **82,81,77,75, , ,**
CSF £23.91 TOTE £4.20: £1.80, £2.10, £2.80; EX 27.40 Trifecta £146.80.
Owner Niel Manning **Bred** Paddy Crinion **Trained** Hawick, Borders
■ Stewards' Enquiry : Mr T Hamilton three-day ban: careless riding (tbn)
FOCUS
After a sensible pace the first two pulled clear in a prolonged battle to the line.

458 BORDER FACILITIES H'CAP CHASE (FOR THE WILFRED & PATRICIA CRAWFORD MEMORIAL TROPHY) (19 fncs) 3m 2f 39y
5:25 (5:25) (Class 3) (0-125,125) 5-Y-O+ **£9,097** (£2,671; £1,335; £667)

Form RPR
FP4- **1** **Ballyben (IRE)**[37] 5366 7-11-3 **116**..............................(p) DerekFox 125
(Lucinda Russell) *pressed ldr: led appr 2 out: sn rdn: kpt on strly fr last* **11/1**
2U3- **2** *2 3/4* **Buddy Love**[38] 5354 8-10-2 **101**.............................. SamTwiston-Davies 107
(Nigel Twiston-Davies) *hld up in midfield: stdy hdwy after 5 out: effrt and chsd wnr between last 2: kpt on same pce run-in* **3/1**[1]
P12- **3** *3 1/4* **Beeves (IRE)**[41] 5313 8-11-9 **125**..............................(b) CraigNichol(3) 129
(Donald McCain) *led: rdn fr 1/2-way: rallied: hdd appr 2 out: kpt on same pce bef last* **7/1**
221- **4** *nk* **Lord Brendy**[41] 5313 7-11-8 **121**.............................. PeterBuchanan 124
(Kenny Johnson) *hld up: stdy hdwy and in tch bef 4 out: effrt bef 2 out: kpt on same pce between last 2* **5/1**[2]
132- **5** *17* **Full Jack (FR)**[30] 5518 8-11-5 **118**..............................(b) JamesReveley 109
(Pauline Robson) *chsd ldrs: effrt and rdn after 3 out: wknd after next* **5/1**[2]
532- **6** *1 3/4* **Purcell's Bridge (FR)**[31] 5492 8-11-1 **117**.............. GrahamWatters(3) 103
(Rose Dobbin) *hld up: smooth hdwy bef 4 out: rdn 2 out: wknd qckly* **9/1**
31-3 **7** *17* **Generous Chief (IRE)**[24] 38 7-10-2 **101**..............................(v) BrianHughes 72
(Chris Grant) *hld up in midfield: nt fluent 12th: rdn after 5 out: wknd fr next* **10/1**
303- **8** *7* **Mo Rouge (IRE)**[31] 5492 7-10-6 **108**.............................. TonyKelly(3) 73
(Jackie Stephen) *nt fluent in tch: lost pl 1/2-way: sn struggling: n.d after* **6/1**[3]
PP-6 **9** *1* **Action Master**[18] 141 9-10-11 **110**.............................. BrianHarding 74
(Sandy Thomson) *hld up: outpcd 13th: nvr on terms* **16/1**
6m 34.7s (-12.50) **Going Correction** -1.075s/f (Hard) 9 Ran SP% **118.4**
Speed ratings: **76,75,74,74,68 68,63,60,60**
CSF £46.80 CT £225.25 TOTE £14.60: £3.30, £1.60, £2.60; EX 84.50 Trifecta £590.30.
Owner Drew & Ailsa Russell **Bred** G Williams **Trained** Arlary, Perth & Kinross
■ Everaard was withdarwn. Price at time of withdrawal 16-1. Rule 4 does not apply.
FOCUS
A competitive handicap. The first three home in a handicap over C&D six weeks ago lined up again, though in they end they only fought out the minor placings.

459 JANE STURROCK 40TH BIRTHDAY BASH STANDARD OPEN NATIONAL HUNT FLAT RACE 2m 51y
5:55 (5:59) (Class 5) 4-6-Y-O **£2,599** (£763; £381; £190)

Form RPR
1 **Banks O' Houxty** 5-11-2 0.............................. SamTwiston-Davies 113+
(Karen McLintock) *in tch on outside: stdy hdwy to ld over 1f out: sn pushed along: clr whn edgd lft ins fnl f: kpt on strly* **8/1**
2 *7* **Show On The Road** 4-10-9 0.............................. CraigNichol(3) 103
(Keith Dalgleish) *t.k.h in midfield: effrt whn nt clr run briefly over 2f out: rallied and chsd (clr) wnr ins fnl f: nt pce to chal* **11/1**
02-1 **3** *3/4* **Boogie Life**[17] 159 4-10-12 0.............................. JamesReveley 102
(Jim Goldie) *pressed ldr: chal 1/2-way: led over 3f out: rdn and hdd over 1f out: edgd rt: one pce whn lost 2nd ins fnl f* **11/4**[2]
3-2 **4** *5* **Nuts Well**[18] 145 4-10-9 0.............................. TonyKelly(3) 99
(Ann Hamilton) *t.k.h: prom: effrt and rdn over 2f out: edgd lft over 1f out: sn outpcd* **5/2**[1]
6- **5** *3* **Fairy Theatre (IRE)**[40] 5331 4-10-5 0.............................. DougieCostello 88
(Iain Jardine) *hld up: pushed along over 3f out: edgd lft and kpt on fr 2f out: nt pce to chal* **20/1**
6 *hd* **Baysbrown (IRE)** 5-11-2 0.............................. BrianHarding 99
(Nicky Richards) *hld up: stdy hdwy on outside over 3f out: rdn and hung lft over 2f out: sn outpcd* **9/2**[3]
P-4 **7** *4* **Zakety Zak**[24] 39 4-10-12 0.............................. PeterBuchanan 91
(James Turner) *hld up towards rr: effrt and pushed along over 2f out: wknd over 1f out* **33/1**
5 **8** *2* **Court Baloo (IRE)**[15] 206 4-10-12 0.............................. SeanQuinlan 89
(Alistair Whillans) *chsd ldrs: drvn along 3f out: wknd 2f out* **50/1**
9 *12* **Mr Gillespie** 5-10-9 0.............................. MissAWaugh(7) 82
(Simon Waugh) *t.k.h: hld up: rdn over 2f out: sn btn* **50/1**
10 *2 1/2* **Another Job (IRE)** 5-10-9 0.............................. MissJRRichards(7) 80
(Nicky Richards) *hld up: outpcd over 6f out: sn struggling: n.d after* **9/1**
P-P **11** *36* **Correlate**[12] 257 5-11-2 0..............................[1] AdrianLane 48
(John Wade) *led: jnd 1/2-way: hdd and rdn over 3f out: sn wknd* **66/1**
0- **12** *7* **Lucky Touch (IRE)**[30] 5520 4-10-5 0.............................. BrianHughes 30
(Hugh Burns) *midfield: outpcd over 4f out: sn btn* **66/1**
0- **13** *34* **Ripasso**[30] 5520 6-11-2 0.............................. JonathanEngland(3) 14
(Jean McGregor) *cl up on outside: outpcd and hung rt 1/2-way: lost tch over 4f out: t.o* **200/1**
3m 42.3s (-13.90) **Going Correction** -0.775s/f (Firm)
WFA 4 from 5yo+ 4lb 13 Ran SP% **118.0**
Speed ratings: **101,97,97,95,93 93,91,90,85,83 66,63,47**
CSF £87.30 TOTE £12.00: £3.00, £3.10, £1.50; EX 99.00 Trifecta £514.90.
Owner W M Aitchison **Bred** Mrs E H Aitchison **Trained** Ingoe, Northumberland
FOCUS
An ordinary bumper.
T/Plt: £288.30 to a £1 stake. Pool: £60,058.86 - 152.06 winning tickets T/Qpdt: £92.90 to a £1 stake. Pool: £4,056.31 - 32.30 winning tickets **Richard Young**

335 UTTOXETER (L-H)
Sunday, May 24

OFFICIAL GOING: Good (chs 5.9, hdl 5.8)
Wind: light breeze Weather: overcast; 14 degrees

460 SIGNS 2000 MAIDEN HURDLE (12 hdls) 3m
2:00 (2:00) (Class 4) 5-Y-O+ **£3,508** (£1,030; £515; £257)

Form RPR
26-3 **1** **Bobble Emerald (IRE)**[18] 147 7-11-0 0.............................. AndrewTinkler 104+
(Martin Keighley) *mde all: set v slow pce: 3 l clr bef 3 out: sn rdn: hit 3 out and hrd pressed next: hit last: plodded on gamely and jst hld on: all out* **6/1**

03- **2** *nk* **Tir Dubh (IRE)**[34] 5439 6-10-7 0 RobertDunne 96+
(Robert Stephens) *chsd ldrs: 3rd at 7th: wnt 2nd at 9th: rdn whn hit next: chal 2 out and ev ch after: plugged on tl no ex cl home* **6/1**

3/4- **3** *44* **Maldivian Reef (IRE)**[64] 4900 7-11-0 0 WayneHutchinson 62
(Alan King) *hld up and bhd: hit 5th and nt a fluent: rdn and lost tch after 9th: remote fr next: tk t.o 3rd sn after last* **2/1[1]**

66-F **4** *7* **Rock Of Ages**[15] 210 6-11-0 109 TrevorWhelan 56
(Neil King) *chsd ldrs tl 10 l 3rd and hrd drvn and fading home turn: sn wl bhd: lost t.o 3rd sn after last* **3/1[2]**

5 *3½* **One Day Like This (IRE)**[133] 5-11-0 0 MichaelByrne 53
(Tim Vaughan) *awkward 1st: nt jump wl: pressed wnr: drvn after 7th: mstke 8th: lost pl 9th: t.o next* **9/2[3]**

P **P** **Icancan**[20] 105 7-10-11 0 JamesBanks(3)
(Alan Hollingsworth) *tall: unruly in paddock and threw rdr: j. and hung bdly rt in last: nvr travelling: t.o fr 4th tl p.u 6th* **100/1**

505- **U** **Tikketoride**[182] 2692 7-10-11 0 TomBellamy(3)
(Peter Pritchard) *j. awkwardly in 3rd tl uns rdr 3rd* **40/1**

00P- **P** **Solway Trigger**[32] 5469 6-10-9 0 StephenMulqueen(5)
(Lisa Harrison) *t.k.h: chsd ldrs tl bad mstke 8th and struggling: t.o and p.u after next* **40/1**

6m 0.9s (10.90) **Going Correction** -0.025s/f (Good) **8 Ran SP% 111.0**
Speed ratings: **80,79,65,62,61 , ,**
CSF £38.34 TOTE £5.30: £1.90, £1.90, £1.20; EX 31.40 Trifecta £128.20.
Owner D Bishop,C Bowkley,M Parker,D Thorpe **Bred** J S Bellingham **Trained** Condicote, Gloucs
■ Stewards' Enquiry : Andrew Tinkler two-day ban: used whip above permitted level (Jun 7,9)

FOCUS
Hurdles moved in 4yds from meeting on May 16th. Divided bends on fresher ground and races increased by 77yds per circuit. The ground had dried out a little from the overnight description, and jockeys in the first felt it was riding on the dead side of good. A weak maiden hurdle in which the first two fought out a good finish, having pulled clear of the rest. The time was nearly 24sec slower than standard.

461 PEKTRON NOVICES' CHASE (15 fncs) 2m 4f
2:30 (2:30) (Class 3) 5-Y-O+ **£6,279** (£1,871; £947; £485; £254)

Form RPR

F0-3 **1** **Dell' Arca (IRE)**[23] 71 6-10-12 0 (b) TomScudamore 142+
(David Pipe) *chsd ldr fr 6th: drvn and clsd grad fr 11th: led and nt fluent last: urged clr* **8/11[1]**

30-1 **2** *6* **Germany Calling (IRE)**[22] 84 6-11-4 134 AidanColeman 145+
(Charlie Longsdon) *led: nt fluent 10th: 4 l clr next: sn drvn: hdd and mstke last: wknd flat* **9/4[2]**

232- **3** *17* **Delgany Demon**[91] 4388 7-10-12 0 TrevorWhelan 126
(Neil King) *j.lft: chsd ldrs: effrt 9th: 4 l 3rd and rdn home turn: wknd after 11th: tired whn fumbled last* **10/1[3]**

560- **4** *18* **Muckle Roe (IRE)**[36] 5400 6-10-5 114 JamieBargary(7) 109
(Nigel Twiston-Davies) *t.k.h: 3rd mostly tl mstke 9th and rdn: 4th and struggling bef 11th: continued remote* **33/1**

6 **5** *26* **Veroce (FR)**[22] 84 6-10-12 0 JakeGreenall 82
(Mark Walford) *mstke 1st: bhd: rdn and lost tch 10th: sn t.o* **100/1**

200- **P** **Fighter Jet**[163] 3057 7-10-12 0 (p) WayneHutchinson
(Alan King) *bhd: struggling 9th: bdly t.o whn p.u 11th* **20/1**

/3-0 **P** **Don't Be Late (IRE)**[22] 84 7-10-12 0 (p) RichieMcLernon
(Jonjo O'Neill) *pressed ldr tl 6th: lost pl qckly: last whn p.u after next* **20/1**

4m 59.7s (-5.80) **Going Correction** -0.10s/f (Good) **7 Ran SP% 111.2**
Speed ratings: **107,104,97,90,80 ,**
CSF £2.53 TOTE £2.00: £1.10, £1.60; EX 2.90 Trifecta £5.70.
Owner Prof Caroline Tisdall **Bred** Bernhard & Brigitta Matusche **Trained** Nicholashayne, Devon

FOCUS
A decent novice chase run at a fair gallop. The time was seven seconds quicker than the later 0-120 handicap.

462 TUTBURY WINDOWS MARES' MAIDEN HURDLE (10 hdls) 2m 3f 207y
3:00 (3:00) (Class 4) 4-Y-O+ **£3,508** (£1,030; £515; £257)

Form RPR

442- **1** **Popping Along**[55] 5071 6-10-11 0 (t) MattGriffiths(3) 110
(Jeremy Scott) *chsd ldrs: nt fluent 6th: rdn and stdy prog fr 3 out: styd on to ld last: r.o gamely: all out* **7/1[3]**

01-3 **2** *nk* **Lolli (IRE)**[17] 178 5-11-0 0 NoelFehily 110+
(Nicky Henderson) *settled in 3rd or 4th pl: nt fluent 7th: wnt 2nd 3 out: drvn and disp ld sn after: nt fluent last: plugged on tl no ex fnl 100yds* **13/8[1]**

00-3 **3** *4½* **Midnight Mint**[20] 100 5-11-0 0 (t) LiamHeard 106
(Jeremy Scott) *trckd ldrs: nt fluent 6th: wnt 3rd next: tk narrow ld after 3 out: drvn and jnd next: stl ev ch last: sn wknd* **12/1**

600- **4** *6* **Arctic Dixie**[135] 3597 7-10-9 102 (t) JakeHodson(5) 101
(Rob Summers) *bhd: effrt bef 3 out: rdn and plugged on to go wl hld 4th bef last* **40/1**

52-2 **5** *29* **Susie Sheep**[13] 238 5-11-0 112 (tp) TomScudamore 77
(David Pipe) *led tl 3rd: pressed ldr tl rdn and lost pl rapidly 3 out* **5/2[2]**

/6-4 **6** *5* **Scarlett Lady**[19] 120 7-11-0 0 (t[1]) AidanColeman 69
(Ali Stronge) *mounted outside paddock and taken down early: a bhd: struggling fr 7th: t.o* **33/1**

30- **7** *1¾* **Margaret's Rose (IRE)**[50] 5144 5-10-7 0 JamieBargary(7) 68
(Nigel Twiston-Davies) *t.k.h: chsd ldrs: nt fluent 6th: sn rdn: struggling after next: t.o* **12/1**

5-P0 **8** *23* **Cool Fusion**[13] 238 6-10-9 0 DannyBurton(5) 47
(Anthony Day) *nt fluent: in last mostly: rdn 7th: sn t.o* **100/1**

22-4 **9** *21* **Miss Fortywinks**[24] 32 6-10-7 102 KevinJones(7) 77
(Seamus Mullins) *pressed ldr tl led 3rd: rdn and hdd sn after 3 out: fading whn blnd next: mod 5th whn nrly fell last: sn eased* **9/1**

50-3 **P** **Tara's Rainbow**[19] 120 5-11-0 0 (t) DavidBass
(Kim Bailey) *chsd ldng pair tl 1/2-way: wknd 7th: t.o and p.u next* **25/1**

4m 59.3s (-3.90) **Going Correction** -0.025s/f (Good) **10 Ran SP% 114.8**
Speed ratings (Par 105): **98,97,96,93,82 80,80,71,63,**
CSF £18.69 TOTE £9.90: £2.30, £1.10, £3.20; EX 22.40 Trifecta £200.50.
Owner Mrs Camilla Scott **Bred** Mrs C C Scott **Trained** Brompton Regis, Somerset

FOCUS
A very ordinary maiden hurdle.

463 GOLF WIDOWS H'CAP HURDLE (10 hdls) 2m 3f 207y
3:35 (3:35) (Class 4) (0-120,118) 4-Y-O+ **£3,508** (£1,030; £515; £257)

Form RPR

/44- **1** **Highpower (IRE)**[32] 5465 6-11-5 114 (p) MauriceLinehan(3) 118+
(Jonjo O'Neill) *pressed ldrs: disp 3rd and hrd drvn home turn: kpt on u.p to ld last: all out but jst kpt rivals at bay after* **9/1**

14-3 **2** *nk* **Flying Light (IRE)**[22] 87 9-11-11 117 (b) WayneHutchinson 122+
(Graeme McPherson) *bhd: stl 6th home turn: hrd drvn and effrt between last two: chal on inner last: w wnr 100yds out: no ex cl home* **13/2[3]**

32-3 **3** *hd* **Bryden Boy (IRE)**[18] 146 5-11-8 114 (p) PeterCarberry 117
(Jennie Candlish) *chsd ldrs: pushed along 5th: rdn and effrt on outer bef 3 out: chal and ev ch last: jst outpcd fnl 100yds* **7/1**

P43- **4** *10* **Kellys Brow (IRE)**[53] 5099 8-11-8 114 (p) DavidBass 110
(Ben Pauling) *led or disp ld: hrd drvn fr 7th: jst hdd and wkng whn mstke last* **12/1**

45-4 **5** *3¾* **Jayo Time (IRE)**[14] 225 6-11-7 113 WillKennedy 103
(Dr Richard Newland) *chsd ldrs: disp 3rd and rdn home turn: sn wknd* **4/1[2]**

115- **6** *29* **Java Rose**[44] 5258 6-11-11 117 (p) AidanColeman 81
(Charlie Longsdon) *prom: jnd ldr 6th and in dispute tl rdn and fdd tamely 3 out: t.o and eased* **9/1**

15-4 **7** *20* **Poker School (IRE)**[15] 208 5-11-5 116 RobMcCarth(5) 62
(Ian Williams) *j. v awkwardly in rr: last at 1/2-way: struggling after 7th: t.o and eased* **10/1**

21-1 **8** *27* **Taylor (IRE)**[19] 120 6-11-9 115 DarylJacob 37
(Nicky Henderson) *led tl hdd and mstke 7th and drvn: rapidly dropped bk to last: hacked on t.o fr 3 out* **3/1[1]**

30-3 **U** **Whatthebutlersaw (IRE)**[17] 176 6-10-6 105 BenFfrenchDavis(7)
(Dominic Ffrench Davis) *rn wout declared tongue-strap: unruly at s: bhd: pushed along 5th: struggling 7th: 20 l 7th whn veered rt and dislodged rdr 2 out* **14/1**

4m 56.7s (-6.50) **Going Correction** -0.025s/f (Good) **9 Ran SP% 114.3**
Speed ratings (Par 105): **103,102,102,99,97 86,78,68,**
CSF £65.48 CT £434.97 TOTE £14.50: £4.20, £2.00, £2.40; EX 75.50 Trifecta £998.80.
Owner John P McManus **Bred** Oliver And Salome Brennan **Trained** Cheltenham, Gloucs

FOCUS
An ordinary handicap hurdle, run at a fair gallop.

464 HANNAH MAY SPENDLOVE 21ST BIRTHDAY CELEBRATION H'CAP CHASE (15 fncs) 2m 4f
4:10 (4:10) (Class 4) (0-120,119) 5-Y-O+ **£3,924** (£1,159; £579; £290)

Form RPR

34-0 **1** **River Purple**[8] 331 8-11-0 107 (t) DarylJacob 117+
(John Mackie) *nt fluent 3rd: hld up 3rd or 4th: cajoled along bef 11th: clsd to ld 2 out: 6 l clr last: sn idling bdly and drvn out* **7/2[3]**

622- **2** *3½* **Larteta (FR)**[54] 5089 6-10-7 100 JackQuinlan 104
(Sarah Humphrey) *led at mod pce: drvn and hdd and hit 2 out: sn outpcd by wnr: plugged on* **11/8[1]**

3F-0 **3** *5* **Sonofagun (FR)**[14] 218 9-11-8 115 WillKennedy 114
(Ian Williams) *pressed ldr to 7th and fr next tl rdn and wknd bef 2 out: hit last* **7/2[3]**

44-5 **4** *22* **Sands Cove (IRE)**[19] 121 8-11-12 119 (bt[1]) NoelFehily 102
(Charlie Mann) *pressed ldr 7th tl next: rdn and lost tch bef 10th: t.o 3 out* **10/3[2]**

5m 6.8s (1.30) **Going Correction** -0.10s/f (Good) **4 Ran SP% 109.6**
Speed ratings: **93,91,89,80**
CSF £9.04 TOTE £5.10; EX 7.10 Trifecta £19.60.
Owner Sotby Farming Company Limited **Bred** Wood Farm Stud **Trained** Church Broughton , Derbys

FOCUS
Modest handicap form.

465 MOORLANDS RACING H'CAP HURDLE (9 hdls) 2m
4:45 (4:45) (Class 4) (0-115,112) 4-Y-O+ **£3,508** (£1,030; £515; £257)

Form RPR

40-3 **1** **Sambulando (FR)**[8] 336 12-10-6 92 (p) AlainCawley 96
(Richard Hobson) *rn in snatches and often lacked fluency: w ldr 3rd: lost pl and hit 6th: rallied on outer to go 2nd 3 out: chal and nt fluent next: rdn and outpcd bef last: rallied to catch idling ldr 100yds: drvn clr* **10/1**

23-1 **2** *1* **Billy My Boy**[17] 164 6-10-12 101 GilesHawkins(3) 105
(Chris Down) *mde most: almost jnd 2 out but drew 2 l clr and looked gng best last: sn idling: urged along and hdd 100yds out: kpt on whn hld cl home* **2/1[1]**

614- **3** *2¼* **Ogaritmo**[35] 5408 6-10-13 102 (t) JamesBanks(3) 103
(Alex Hales) *sn drvn along towards rr: 7th home turn: drvn into 3rd 2 out: styd on flat wout looking like getting in a blow* **16/1**

F2-3 **4** *6* **Fairy Alisha**[14] 217 7-10-11 104 JoshWall(7) 101
(Trevor Wall) *midfield: nt fluent 5th: effrt home turn: cl 4th 3 out: rdn and wl hld fr next* **10/1**

020- **5** *2¾* **Lean Burn (USA)**[5] 5206 9-10-0 86 (t) AndrewTinkler 79
(Barry Leavy) *hld up in rr: last after 6th: mod hdwy after 3 out: nvr trbld ldrs* **17/2[3]**

315- **6** *½* **Akula (IRE)**[35] 5412 8-11-2 109 AlanJohns(7) 102
(Tim Vaughan) *2nd or 3rd tl hrd drvn home turn: lost pl 3 out and wl hld next* **4/1[2]**

54-P **7** *12* **Formal Bid (IRE)**[8] 338 8-11-3 110 (bt) MrZBaker(7) 92
(Barry Brennan) *chsd ldrs: effrt 6th: rdn and dropped out qckly next: mstke last* **40/1**

45-6 **8** *2¼* **Theflyingportrait (IRE)**[23] 56 6-11-12 112 PeterCarberry 92
(Jennie Candlish) *prom tl 3rd and hrd drvn home turn: lost pl tamely* **17/2[3]**

460- **9** *6* **Barton Antix**[216] 1978 6-11-5 105 MichaelByrne 79
(Neil Mulholland) *towards rr: lost tch after 6th* **16/1**

00-6 **F** **Gorman (FR)**[15] 207 4-10-12 102 AdamWedge
(Evan Williams) *sn bhd: struggling whn fell 3 out* **10/1**

3m 53.5s (1.50) **Going Correction** -0.025s/f (Good)
WFA 4 from 6yo+ 18lb **10 Ran SP% 115.9**
Speed ratings (Par 105): **95,94,93,90,89 88,82,81,78,**
CSF £30.99 CT £327.32 TOTE £11.70: £2.80, £1.20, £5.20; EX 31.80 Trifecta £683.40.
Owner Richard Hobson **Bred** Earl Haras Du Camp Benard **Trained** Stow-On-The-Wold, Gloucs
■ Stewards' Enquiry : Alain Cawley four-day ban: used whip above permitted level (Jun 7,9,11,12)

FOCUS
There was a contested lead in this ordinary handicap.

466 DOUGLAS FAMILY NOVICES' H'CAP HURDLE (10 hdls) 2m 3f 207y
5:15 (5:15) (Class 5) (0-100,100) 4-Y-O+ **£2,599** (£763; £381; £190)

Form RPR

50-2 **1** **Bus Named Desire**[7] 361 7-9-11 76 (tp) RobMcCarth(5) 90+
(Ian Williams) *t.k.h in midfield: effrt 7th: led bef 3 out and only one travelling after: drew 6 l clr and wnt lft next: 10 l ahd and wnt lft again last and drvn: eased fnl 100yds* **11/4[2]**

06-2 **2** *13* **Good Value**[20] 106 4-11-4 **97**....................(vt) TomScudamore 92
(David Pipe) *pressed ldrs: wnt 3rd and rdn bef 3 out: sn chsng wnr: in vain pursuit fr next: hit last* **7/4**[1]

05-4 **3** *1 3/4* **Cadgers Hole**[18] 148 8-10-0 **74** oh1....................(t) WillKennedy 71
(Lynn Siddall) *taken down early: pressed ldr tl led 4th: rdn and hdd bef 3 out where mstke: sn outpcd by wnr and plugged on in 3rd after* **15/2**[3]

05-6 **4** *1 3/4* **Sweet Summer**[20] 106 4-10-6 **85**.................... JackQuinlan 76
(John Holt) *prom: rdn after 7th: wl btn next: plodded on* **20/1**

/5-4 **5** *1 1/4* **Born To Benefit (IRE)**[17] 178 9-11-8 **99**.................... ConorShoemark(3) 93
(Fergal O'Brien) *bhd: rdn and struggling bef 3 out* **8/1**

20-2 **6** *15* **Honour A Promise**[24] 43 7-11-9 **100**....................(p) TomBellamy(3) 86
(Paul Webber) *cl up: wnt 2nd at 7th: rdn bef 3 out where mstke whn fading v tamely* **10/1**

10-3 **P** **Grand Article (IRE)**[24] 42 11-10-5 **79**.................... AdamWedge
(Paul Cowley) *often swishing tail: led tl 4th: rdn and lost 2nd after next: drvn and qckly downed tools bef 7th: bdly t.o whn p.u 2 out* **16/1**

PP6- **P** **Haleo**[45] 5242 4-10-1 **80**....................(bt) RichieMcLernon
(Laura Young) *bhd: drvn 6th: no rspnse: t.o and p.u 2 out* **16/1**

06-5 **P** **Lady Vivona**[17] 155 7-10-0 **79**.................... StephenMulqueen(5)
(Lisa Harrison) *j. v poorly in last pair: drvn 6th: t.o next: p.u 3 out* **33/1**

5m 3.3s (0.10) **Going Correction** -0.025s/f (Good)
WFA 4 from 6yo+ 19lb **9** Ran SP% **114.5**
Speed ratings (Par 103): **90,85,84,83,83 77,,,**
CSF £8.13 CT £30.21 TOTE £3.70: £1.60, £1.30, £2.20; EX 10.70 Trifecta £47.80.
Owner The Ferandlin Peaches **Bred** Mrs P Grainger **Trained** Portway, Worcs

FOCUS
A weak event, but the pace was reasonable.
T/Plt: £133.00 to a £1 stake. Pool: £72,881.86 - 399.80 winning tickets T/Qpdt: £71.50 to a £1 stake. Pool: £4,691.08 - 48.50 winning tickets **Iain Mackenzie**

CARTMEL (L-H)
Monday, May 25

OFFICIAL GOING: Good to soft
Wind: moderate 1/2 against Weather: fine

467 CARTMEL 25TH ANNIVERSARY STICKY TOFFEE NOVICES' HURDLE (8 hdls) 2m 1f 46y
2:25 (2:25) (Class 4) 4-Y-O **£3,249** (£954; £477; £238)

Form RPR

2 **1** **Never Up (GER)**[13] 254 4-10-12 0.................... HenryBrooke 109+
(George Moore) *trckd ldrs: chal last: led narrowly elbow (1 1/2f out): all out* **4/1**[3]

3-21 **2** *hd* **Romulus Du Donjon (IRE)**[17] 182 4-11-5 119.................... LeightonAspell 115
(Oliver Sherwood) *led: hdd sn after last: kpt on: no ex nr fin* **8/11**[1]

21-3 **3** *11* **Dire Straits (IRE)**[9] 335 4-11-5 118....................(b) TrevorWhelan 104
(Neil King) *chsd ldr: drvn 3 out: wknd appr last* **11/4**[2]

4 *4* **Kauto Riko (FR)** 4-10-12 0.................... JamesDavies 93
(Tom Gretton) *nt fluent: j. slowly 1st: sn chsng ldrs: drvn 5th: wknd between last 2* **25/1**

4m 13.3s (0.10) **Going Correction** -0.05s/f (Good) **4** Ran SP% **108.4**
Speed ratings: **97,96,92,90**
CSF £7.72 TOTE £5.10; EX 7.40 Trifecta £14.10.
Owner Geoff & Sandra Turnbull **Bred** Wertheimer Et Frere **Trained** Middleham Moor, N Yorks

FOCUS
Rail at innermost position and all distances as advertised. The first Cartmel meeting of the year produced ground described as riding between good and good to soft. An interesting novice hurdle despite the small field. The two market leaders were dropping in trip after recent victories over further and this was a big step up from the winner.

468 TONY CONNELL MEMORIAL NOVICES' H'CAP HURDLE (11 hdls) 2m 6f 31y
3:00 (3:00) (Class 4) (0-110,110) 4-Y-O+ **£3,249** (£954; £477; £238)

Form RPR

16-2 **1** **Grand Vintage (IRE)**[25] 34 9-11-4 **102**....................(tp) HenryBrooke 108
(Kenneth Slack) *led: hdd last: edgd rt 1f out: styd on to ld last 50yds* **5/1**[3]

643- **2** *3/4* **Allbarnone**[37] 5400 7-11-8 **106**.................... DenisO'Regan 111
(William Kinsey) *hld up in mid-div: hdwy to trck ldrs 8th: led last: fnd little and hdd clsng stages* **3/1**[1]

06-2 **3** *7* **Hurricane Rita (FR)**[19] 139 5-11-1 **104**.................... GrantCockburn(5) 103
(Stuart Coltherd) *chsd ldrs: 3rd and one pce last* **9/2**[2]

5-62 **4** *3 1/2* **Solway Prince**[12] 288 6-10-4 **95**.................... RyanDay(7) 91
(Lisa Harrison) *hld up in rr: hdwy 3 out: kpt on to take modest 4th last 75yds* **6/1**

462- **5** *9* **Pulpitarian (USA)**[32] 5495 7-11-7 **105**....................(b) PeterBuchanan 93
(Lucinda Russell) *mid-div: hdwy 8th: chsng ldrs 2 out: wknd last* **8/1**

304/ **6** *3 3/4* **Lexington Bay (IRE)**[7] 4286 7-11-6 **104**....................(p) JamesReveley 90
(Philip Kirby) *chsd ldng pair: 2nd 6th: wknd appr last* **11/2**

206- **7** *17* **Dontupsettherhythm (IRE)**[38] 5379 10-9-13 **88**.......(b[1]) JoeCornwall(5) 57
(Michael Chapman) *chsd wnr: lost pl sn after 8th: sn bhd* **20/1**

50-3 **8** *93* **Tokyo Brown (USA)**[20] 131 6-11-2 **100**....................(v) BrianHughes
(James Moffatt) *in rr: bhd and reminders 5th: t.o 7th: eventually completed* **28/1**

2-4 **P** **Callmenewtown (IRE)**[19] 146 8-11-12 **110**....................(tp) JamesDavies
(Graeme McPherson) *chsd ldrs: drvn 5th: sn lost pl: t.o 7th: p.u between last 2* **20/1**

5m 24.6s (-4.70) **Going Correction** -0.05s/f (Good) **9** Ran SP% **113.6**
Speed ratings (Par 105): **106,105,103,101,98 97,91,57,**
CSF £19.91 CT £71.31 TOTE £6.20: £2.50, £1.30, £1.40; EX 22.90 Trifecta £86.90.
Owner A Slack **Bred** John Mulvaney **Trained** Hilton, Cumbria

FOCUS
Fortunes changed after the last as the long-time leader rallied to get back up near the line. The first two are on the upgrade.

469 BET TOTEEXACTA H'CAP CHASE (12 fncs) 2m 1f 61y
3:35 (3:36) (Class 3) (0-130,127) 5-Y-O+ **£7,797** (£2,289; £1,144; £572)

Form RPR

P5-4 **1** **Fantasy King**[17] 186 9-11-0 **118**.................... TonyKelly(3) 126+
(James Moffatt) *mid-div: wnt 2nd 8th: led next: drvn clr sn after last: drvn rt out* **11/2**

10F- **2** *4* **Vengeur De Guye (FR)**[38] 5364 6-11-12 **127**............(t[1]) TomScudamore 130
(Lucinda Russell) *in rr: hdwy to chse ldrs 8th: 2nd 3 out: kpt on sasme pce fnl f* **5/1**[3]

04-1 **3** *1 1/2* **Mason Hindmarsh**[13] 253 8-11-10 **125**.................... JamesReveley 129+
(Karen McLintock) *nt fluent: chsd ldr: j. slowly 1st and 8th: kpt on one pce fr 2 out* **10/3**[1]

3-21 **4** *1 3/4* **Super Collider**[16] 202 8-10-11 **119**....................(t) JamesCorbett(7) 118
(Susan Corbett) *nt fluent in rr: sn bhd: t.o 6th: hdwy next: modest 4th last: one pce* **7/1**

F3-4 **5** *1/2* **Sergeant Pink (IRE)**[8] 357 9-10-12 **113**.................... BrianHughes 113
(Dianne Sayer) *chsd ldrs: drvn and outpcd 9th: one pce fr 2 out* **7/2**[2]

32-5 **6** *15* **Chestnut Ben (IRE)**[10] 315 10-11-3 **121**.................... SeanBowen(3) 110
(Peter Winks) *mid-div: lost pl after 7th: sn bhd* **6/1**

665- **7** *58* **Master Of The Game (IRE)**[65] 4913 9-11-12 **127**...........(t) HenryBrooke 60
(Donald McCain) *led: drvn 6th: hdd 9th: sn lost pl and bhd: t.o last: virtually p.u clsng stages* **11/1**

4m 16.5s (-2.40) **Going Correction** -0.25s/f (Good) **7** Ran SP% **112.5**
Speed ratings: **95,93,92,91,91 84,59**
CSF £31.68 TOTE £7.70: £3.90, £2.90; EX 37.50 Trifecta £259.10.
Owner V R Vyner-Brooks **Bred** D R Tucker **Trained** Cartmel, Cumbria

FOCUS
Fair form. The winner ran to his course best.

470 BET TOTETRIFECTA H'CAP CHASE (14 fncs) 2m 5f 34y
4:10 (4:10) (Class 3) (0-135,131) 5-Y-O+ **£6,498** (£1,908; £954; £477)

Form RPR

02-0 **1** **Alderbrook Lad (IRE)**[17] 184 9-11-1 **123**.................... JoeColliver(3) 133
(Micky Hammond) *led: hdd 4 out: led last: sn 6 l clr: drvn rt out: all out* **15/2**

111- **2** *1* **Presenting Junior (IRE)**[38] 5363 8-11-9 **131**............ GrahamWatters(3) 140
(Martin Todhunter) *hld up towards rr: hdwy 9th: sn trcking ldrs: reminder bef 4 out: 2nd sn after last: 2 l down 1f out: kpt on* **11/2**[3]

324- **3** *14* **Iona Days (IRE)**[90] 4424 10-10-8 **113**.................... MarkGrant 110
(Julian Smith) *mid-div: chsd ldrs 4th: one pce appr last: tk modest 3rd over 2f out* **14/1**

122/ **4** *7* **Cruchain (IRE)**[397] 5516 12-10-8 **113**....................(p) RobertDunne 104
(Dai Burchell) *chsd ldrs 4th: led 4 out: hdd last: wknd fnl 2f* **9/1**

/00- **5** *1 3/4* **Silmi**[211] 2083 11-10-9 **114**.................... PaulMoloney 106
(Sophie Leech) *in rr: nt fluent and bhd 4th: kpt on fr 2 out: tk modest 5th post* **28/1**

50-2 **6** *hd* **Rouge Et Blanc (FR)**[19] 151 10-11-5 **124**.................... LeightonAspell 112
(Oliver Sherwood) *mid-div: hdwy and handy 4th whn mstke 3 out: one pce* **11/1**

10-P **7** *27* **Douglas Julian**[23] 81 13-10-4 **116**.................... MrTHamilton(7) 80
(Katie Scott) *drvn to chse wnr: lost pl 8th: bhd fr 10th: t.o* **20/1**

P6-4 **8** *52* **Authinger (IRE)**[11] 304 7-10-10 **115**....................(t) BrianHarding 32
(Barry Murtagh) *in rr: bhd fr 9th: t.o* **18/1**

12/1 **P** **Glen Countess (IRE)**[16] 199 8-11-2 **121**.................... SeanQuinlan
(Sue Smith) *chsd ldrs: lost pl 4 out: eased and bhd whn p.u bef 2 out* **9/2**[2]

5P-5 **P** **Redpender (IRE)**[20] 134 9-9-11 **105** oh1....................(v[1]) TonyKelly(3)
(James Moffatt) *in rr: mstke 6th: sn bhd: t.o whn p.u bef 8th* **20/1**

1-11 **U** **Sharp Rise (IRE)**[13] 255 8-11-11 **130**.................... JamesReveley
(Pauline Robson) *handy 3rd whn blnd and uns rdr 2nd* **5/2**[1]

5m 15.3s (-10.10) **Going Correction** -0.25s/f (Good) **11** Ran SP% **117.1**
Speed ratings: **108,107,102,100,99 99,89,70,,**
CSF £47.74 CT £571.36 TOTE £8.50: £2.70, £1.90, £4.10; EX 60.60 Trifecta £875.30.
Owner Masters Of The Hall **Bred** A Malone **Trained** Middleham, N Yorks

FOCUS
There was some early scrimmaging for the lead, which saw the favourite Sharp Rise depart at the second, but the winner soon dominated and was back to his best.

471 BURLINGTON STONE GRAND VETERANS' H'CAP CHASE (20 fncs) 3m 5f 80y
4:40 (4:40) (Class 3) (0-130,128) 10-Y-O+ **£9,747** (£2,862; £1,431; £715)

Form RPR

32P- **1** **Tullamore Dew (IRE)**[163] 3083 13-10-13 **118**.................... JoeColliver(3) 132+
(Micky Hammond) *hld up towards rr: hdwy to trck ldrs 9th: led 3 out: drvn rt out* **6/1**

620- **2** *8* **Hinton Indiana**[66] 4886 10-10-0 **102** oh2....................(t) HarrySkelton 110
(Dan Skelton) *in rr: hdwy 5th: lft cl 2nd 3 out: kpt on same pce run-in* **4/1**[3]

034- **3** *23* **Lackamon**[51] 5138 10-11-9 **125**.................... SeanQuinlan 116
(Sue Smith) *chsd ldrs: blnd 9th: blnd and lost pl 12th: sn bhd: sme hdwy 16th: distant 4th whn blnd 2 out: 3rd last 150yds* **7/2**[2]

40-4 **4** *5* **Rose Of The Moon (IRE)**[25] 48 10-11-12 **128**....................(p) JakeGreenall 112
(David O'Meara) *in rr: hdwy 10th: sn chsng ldrs: lost pl 15th: tk distant 4th fnl 100yds* **14/1**

311- **5** *8* **Gunna Be A Devil (IRE)**[32] 5492 11-11-3 **122**............(p) MattGriffiths(3) 104
(Jeremy Scott) *chsd ldrs: nt fluent 4th: led bef 15th: hdd 4 out: lft handy 3rd 3 out: sn wknd: tired and lost 2 pls last 150yds: collapsed fatally sn after line* **10/3**[1]

/63- **P** **Deal Done (FR)**[173] 2880 11-10-12 **117**...............(bt) JonathanEngland(3)
(Richard Drake) *led: wknd and hdd bef 15th: immediately p.u: lame* **14/1**

/P-6 **U** **Mostly Bob (IRE)**[19] 151 12-10-8 **110**....................(tp) JamesBest
(Sophie Leech) *in rr: drvn 8th: hdwy 14th: w ldrs next: led 4 out: hdd whn blnd and uns rdr next* **25/1**

114- **F** **Oh Right (IRE)**[258] 1491 11-10-0 **102** oh2....................(p) HenryBrooke
(Dianne Sayer) *in rr: hit 7th: hdwy 9th: lost pl and modest 8th whn fell 16th* **20/1**

133- **U** **Ballyvoneen (IRE)**[31] 5524 10-10-2 **104**.................... TrevorWhelan
(Neil King) *chsd ldrs: reminders 14th: lost pl next: modest 7th whn blnd and uns rdr 16th* **10/1**

44-1 **P** **Beau Dandy (IRE)**[25] 38 10-9-10 **103**....................(be) DiarmuidO'Regan(5)
(Chris Grant) *in rr: hdwy 14th: chasinfg ldrs next: reminders bef 4 out: lost pl and 5th whn mstke next: p.u bef 3 out: lame* **12/1**

7m 34.7s (-1.50) **Going Correction** -0.25s/f (Good) **10** Ran SP% **118.3**
Speed ratings: **92,89,83,82,80 ,,,,**
CSF £31.65 CT £98.32 TOTE £7.90: £2.20, £2.20, £1.60; EX 37.30 Trifecta £165.80.
Owner Give Every Man His Due **Bred** Michael Daly **Trained** Middleham, N Yorks

FOCUS
An incident-packed race from these experienced chasers, and only five finished. The winner was in line with his best form from last year.

472 HADWINS MAIDEN HUNTERS' CHASE (FOR THE FRASER CUP) (14 fncs) 2m 5f 34y
5:15 (5:16) (Class 6) 5-Y-O+ **£1,559** (£483; £241; £121)

Form RPR

0/P- **1** **Probably George**[8] 8-11-7 0.................... MissKBryson(5) 97
(Mrs K Lynn) *mid-div: hdwy 10th: chsng ldrs 3 out: cl 2nd over 3f out: led over 1f out: drvn out* **16/1**

P2-4 **2** *2 ¼* **Newspage (IRE)**[9] 9-11-7 77 ....(b) MrWEasterby(5) 95
(John Wade) *led to 2nd: led 3rd: drvn and hdd over 1f out: kpt on same pce* **7/2**[2]

46-2 **3** *12* **Mister D (IRE)**[19] [143] 9-11-9 95 .... MrTHamilton(3) 86
(George Bewley) *chsd ldrs: 2nd 5th: one pce fnl 3f* **9/4**[1]

4 *6* **Kilmacallogue Bay**[21] 9-11-9 0 .... MrCDawson(3) 79
(C T Dawson) *misd-div: hdwy 8th: sn chsng ldrs: handy 2nd 2 out: one pce* **9/2**

4U4/ **5** *shd* **Spitfire Ace (IRE)**[29] 7-11-12 0 ....(t) MrOGreenall 80
(Oliver Greenall) *mid-div: hdwy to chse ldrs 8th: one pce fr 2 out* **4/1**[3]

/24- **6** *18* **Tweedys Choice (IRE)**[8] 10-11-5 92 ....(b) MrTGreenwood(7) 65
(T O M Greenwood) *w ldrs: led 2nd: hdd and blnd next: lost pl and modest 6th whn blnd 2 out: sn wl bhd* **20/1**

F **Dead Ringa**[29] 10-11-5 0 .... MissETodd(7)
(Mrs E J Clark) *in rr whn fell 1st* **11/1**

000/ **P** **Colorado Kid (IRE)**[36] 9-11-5 0 .... MrSWColtherd(7)
(John Hellens) *in rr: drvn 6th: lost pl 8th: t.o whn p.u after 10th* **22/1**

P **Shepherd's Call (IRE)**[9] 7-11-5 0 ....(p) MrRLindsay(7)
(Andrew Nicholls) *sn detached in last: t.o 7th: p.u bef 10th* **50/1**

5m 24.2s (-1.20) **Going Correction** -0.25s/f (Good) **9** Ran **SP% 116.5**
Speed ratings: **92,91,86,84,84 78, , ,**
CSF £72.31 TOTE £12.60: £2.70, £1.60, £1.20; EX 69.30 Trifecta £256.40.
Owner Kenneth Lynn **Bred** Snowdrop Stud Co Ltd **Trained** Jedburgh, Borders
FOCUS
Five were in with a chance going to the last, but in the they finished strung out up the straight.

473 SWAN HOTEL & SPA H'CAP HURDLE (11 hdls) 2m 6f 31y
5:45 (5:45) (Class 3) (0-135,125) 4-Y-O+ **£5,848** (£1,717; £858; £429)

Form RPR

02-0 **1** **Sealous Scout (IRE)**[10] [319] 7-11-7 120 .... HenryBrooke 122
(Donald McCain) *chsd ldrs: led 8th: hdd narrowly 2 out: led last: drvn rt out* **8/1**

P60- **2** *1 ¾* **Stylish Chap (IRE)**[38] [5361] 5-11-0 113 .... PeterBuchanan 113
(Lucinda Russell) *hld up in rr: hdwy 8th: 3rd 2 out: upsides last: no ex last 75yds* **7/1**[3]

540- **3** *3 ¼* **Maybe I Wont**[42] [5312] 10-10-8 107 ....(v) BrianHughes 105
(James Moffatt) *trckd ldrs: outpcd between last 2: kpt on to take modest 3rd 1f out* **12/1**

4-61 **4** *11* **Vaihau (FR)**[7] [377] 6-10-10 116 7ex .... PatrickCowley(7) 109+
(Jonjo O'Neill) *hld up in rr: trckd ldrs 7th: led narrowly 2 out: hdd last: wknd bdly fnl 200yds: heavily eased nr fin* **1/1**[1]

50-4 **5** *nse* **Pistol (IRE)**[18] [157] 6-9-13 105 .... MrJDixon(7) 94
(John Dixon) *led: pushed along 7th: hdd next: sn wl outpcd and lost pl: wknd 2 out* **9/1**

24-1 **6** *hd* **Manballandall (IRE)**[16] [203] 7-11-5 125 ....(t) JamesCorbett(7) 112
(Susan Corbett) *trckd ldrs: outpcd and lost pl after 8th: wknd 2 out* **7/2**[2]

5m 26.7s (-2.60) **Going Correction** -0.05s/f (Good) **6** Ran **SP% 113.5**
Speed ratings (Par 107): **102,101,100,96,96 96**
CSF £58.31 TOTE £8.80: £3.30, £3.30; EX 63.10 Trifecta £206.80.
Owner T G Leslie **Bred** Mervyn Chamney **Trained** Cholmondeley, Cheshire
FOCUS
A game performance from the winner and a canny ride to give Henry Brooke a treble on the day.
T/Plt: £542.70 to a £1 stake. Pool: £70,663.49 - 95.04 winning tickets T/Qpdt: £42.60 to a £1 stake. Pool: £6,195.49 - 107.50 winning tickets **Walter Glynn**

474 - 480a (Foreign Racing) - See Raceform Interactive

200 HEXHAM (L-H)
Tuesday, May 26

OFFICIAL GOING: Good (6.4)
Wind: Fairly strong, half against Weather: Cloudy, bright

481 "FOLLOW US ON FACEBOOK" MAIDEN HURDLE (10 hdls) 2m 4f 28y
6:10 (6:11) (Class 5) 4-Y-O+ **£2,737** (£798; £399)

Form RPR

P3-3 **1** **Tickenwolf (IRE)**[21] [132] 5-10-11 109 .... JoeColliver(3) 104+
(George Moore) *in tch: effrt after 2 out: led bef last: rdn clr run-in* **7/4**[1]

4-35 **2** *4* **Destiny Awaits (IRE)**[13] [288] 6-10-9 72 .... CallumBewley(5) 97
(Keith Pollock) *in tch: hdwy to ld briefly between last 2: rdn and kpt on same pce fr last* **20/1**

33- **3** *3* **Mondlicht (USA)**[261] [1467] 5-11-0 0 .... JackQuinlan 94
(John Ferguson) *hld up: stdy hdwy after 3 out: chsng ldrs next: edgd lft and outpcd fr last* **15/8**[2]

P0-0 **4** *6* **Latest Fashion (IRE)**[26] [37] 9-10-2 64 ....(t) StephenMulqueen(5) 83
(Christopher Wilson) *nt fluent: cl up: outpcd after 4 out: rallied bef 2 out: wknd fr last* **100/1**

5 *30* **Suzy's Music (IRE)**[24] 7-10-7 0 .... PeterBuchanan 55
(S R B Crawford, Ire) *t.k.h: cl up: led 2nd to 3rd: prom tl rdn and wknd after 2 out* **20/1**

54-3 **6** *3 ¾* **Johnny Go**[17] [206] 5-10-7 0 .... RyanDay(7) 59
(Lisa Harrison) *nt jump wl: bhd: blnd 1st: drvn bef 3 out: wknd bef next* **12/1**

2P-2 **7** *1 ¼* **Astrum**[17] [200] 5-11-0 106 ....(b) AdrianLane 57
(Donald McCain) *nt fluent: t.k.h: led to 2nd: cl up: regained ld next: hdd 3 out: ev ch tl rdn and wknd qckly between last 2* **3/1**[3]

/55- **8** *32* **Touch Of Steel (IRE)**[51] [5159] 6-10-9 0 ....(p) DaleIrving(5) 29
(James Ewart) *cl up: chal 6th: led 3 out to between last 2: wknd qckly: t.o* **33/1**

U **P** **Cobh National (IRE)**[5] [419] 7-10-7 0 .... ThomasDowson(7)
(Victor Thompson) *bhd: struggling 4 out: lost tch after next: t.o whn p.u bef last* **100/1**

5m 11.6s (-0.90) **Going Correction** -0.175s/f (Good) **9** Ran **SP% 118.3**
Speed ratings (Par 103): **94,92,91,89,77 76,75,63,**
CSF £36.64 TOTE £2.40: £1.02, £6.10, £1.70; EX 40.10 Trifecta £167.50.
Owner G R Orchard **Bred** Denis J Reddan **Trained** Middleham Moor, N Yorks
FOCUS
Rail on bends moved to fresh ground and hurdles relocated. An ordinary maiden hurdle run at just a fair gallop and not easy form to assess, though the winner probably best guide to level.

482 HAPPY BIRTHDAY SARAH REAY LOOKING 25 MARES' H'CAP HURDLE (10 hdls) 2m 4f 28y
6:40 (6:41) (Class 4) (0-115,109) 4-Y-O+ **£4,448** (£1,296; £648)

Form RPR

344- **1** **Samedi Soir**[51] [5161] 5-11-0 97 .... JamesReveley 104+
(Keith Reveley) *t.k.h: in tch: nt fluent 4th: stdy hdwy 3 out: rdn to ld bef last: kpt on strly to go clr run-in* **9/2**[3]

5P-3 **2** *5* **Chasse En Mer (FR)**[21] [130] 5-11-8 105 ....(p) DougieCostello 104
(Caroline Bailey) *hld up in tch: hdwy to chse ldr 3 out: rdn and led briefly bef last: kpt on same pce run-in* **9/1**

423- **3** *1 ¾* **Sultana Belle (IRE)**[6] [190] 7-11-12 109 .... PeterBuchanan 106
(S R B Crawford, Ire) *hld up: mstke 3 out: hdwy to chse ldrs between last 2: sn rdn: kpt on same pce fr last* **7/1**

315- **4** *4* **Burnt Sienna (IRE)**[33] [5490] 5-10-8 94 ....(t) DerekFox(3) 88
(Noel C Kelly, Ire) *bhd: drvn and outpcd 1/2-way: rallied and prom bef last: no imp run-in* **4/1**[2]

0F1- **5** *1 ¼* **High Fair**[34] [5470] 9-10-10 100 .... MrTHamilton(7) 93
(Sandy Forster) *cl up: wnt 2nd 4 out to next: cl up tl rdn and outpcd bef last* **17/2**

00-5 **6** *½* **Slipper Satin (IRE)**[26] [37] 5-10-12 95 ....(t) HenryBrooke 88
(Simon West) *led: rdn and hdd bef last: wknd run-in* **13/2**

20-P **7** *11* **Jewellery (IRE)**[20] [141] 8-10-10 100 ....(t) JamieHamilton(7) 82
(Katie Scott) *sn pushed along to chse ldr: drvn along fr 1/2-way: wknd after 3 out: sn n.d* **20/1**

P0-4 **8** *6* **Playhara (IRE)**[11] [314] 6-11-7 107 ....(v) CraigNichol(3) 84
(Martin Todhunter) *chsd ldrs tl drvn and wknd qckly between last 2* **11/4**[1]

5m 6.4s (-6.10) **Going Correction** -0.175s/f (Good) **8** Ran **SP% 116.0**
Speed ratings (Par 105): **104,102,101,99,99 99,95,92**
CSF £43.74 CT £280.56 TOTE £6.60: £2.70, £4.20, £3.30; EX 46.70 Trifecta £256.40.
Owner Shade Oak Stud **Bred** Shade Oak Stud **Trained** Lingdale, Redcar & Cleveland
FOCUS
Just an ordinary mares' handicap hurdle, but the time was over five seconds quicker than the maiden hurdle and this was a step up from the cosy winner.

483 AGRICAL NOVICES' LIMITED H'CAP CHASE (19 fncs) 3m 41y
7:10 (7:10) (Class 4) (0-120,120) 5-Y-O+ **£3,898** (£1,144; £572; £286)

Form RPR

31-3 **1** **Scarlet Fire (IRE)**[24] [81] 8-10-6 111 ....(t) MissJRRichards(7) 116
(Nicky Richards) *cl up: led 7th: mde rest: rdn and hrd pressed last: styd on gamely run-in* **2/1**[1]

360- **2** *1 ¼* **Dr Moloney (IRE)**[38] [5394] 8-10-12 110 .... BrianHughes 115+
(S R B Crawford, Ire) *hld up in last pl: smooth hdwy bef 3 out: chalng whn nt fluent last: sn rdn: kpt on towards fin* **11/2**

F4-1 **3** *1* **Ueueteotl (FR)**[24] [76] 7-11-8 120 .... LucyAlexander 123+
(James Ewart) *in tch: pushed along 10th: rallied whn lft 3rd 4 out: ev ch briefly 2 out: rdn bef last: kpt on run-in* **7/2**[2]

60-4 **4** *12* **Rev Up Ruby**[24] [76] 7-10-7 110 .... JonathonBewley(5) 102
(George Bewley) *hld up in tch: hdwy to chse wnr bef 13th to 2 out: rdn and wknd bef last* **4/1**[3]

42U- **5** *20* **Spirit Oscar (IRE)**[43] [5314] 7-10-9 110 ....(t) DerekFox(3) 84
(Lucinda Russell) *nt fluent: led: hit 6th: mstke and hdd next: prom: drvn bef 3 out: wknd after next* **11/1**

4-51 **R** **Tikkandemickey (IRE)**[12] [300] 9-11-2 119 .... CallumBewley(5)
(Raymond Shiels) *prom: hdwy to chal 10th: cl 3rd whn rn out 4 out* **6/1**

6m 34.0s (1.80) **Going Correction** -0.10s/f (Good) **6** Ran **SP% 113.6**
Speed ratings: **93,92,92,88,82**
CSF £13.52 TOTE £2.90: £1.90, £2.40; EX 15.30 Trifecta £73.40.
Owner Miss J R Richards **Bred** Messrs E & A Delany **Trained** Greystoke, Cumbria
FOCUS
A fair gallop to this handicap chase. The winner ran to his mark.

484 DAD'S DAY H'CAP HURDLE (12 hdls) 2m 7f 63y
7:40 (7:41) (Class 5) (0-100,100) 4-Y-O+ **£2,729** (£801; £400; £200)

Form RPR

65-P **1** **Native Optimist (IRE)**[17] [201] 8-10-0 81 .... MrTHamilton(7) 87+
(Sheena Walton) *pressed ldr: led 3rd: mde rest: clr after 2 out: rdn: edgd lft and 2 l up last: kpt on wl run-in* **11/2**

255- **2** *1 ¾* **Verko (FR)**[118] [3928] 6-10-0 77 .... CraigNichol(3) 80
(Micky Hammond) *hld up in rr: smooth hdwy 4 out: effrt and chsd wnr between last 2: clsd and 2 l down last: rdn and kpt on run-in* **11/4**[1]

60-0 **3** *4* **Solway Sam**[13] [291] 12-10-9 90 .... RyanDay(7) 89
(Lisa Harrison) *led to 3rd: pressed wnr: drvn along bef 3 out: lost 2nd between last 2: kpt on same pce* **9/2**[2]

05-0 **4** *10* **Wyfield Rose**[20] [139] 6-10-13 87 ....(tp) BrianHughes 78
(Alistair Whillans) *in tch: stdy hdwy bef 3 out: rdn and outpcd after next: no imp bef last* **5/1**[3]

F-4P **5** *9* **Sharivarry (FR)**[6] [398] 9-10-10 91 .... ThomasDowson(7) 73
(Victor Thompson) *hld up: stdy hdwy after 3 out: drvn and outpcd next: n.d after* **25/1**

4-33 **6** *1* **Bescot Springs (IRE)**[12] [303] 10-11-5 100 ....(p) RossChapman(7) 81
(Lucinda Russell) *in tch: lost pl 5 out: rdn after 3 out: no imp bef next* **8/1**

4-0P **7** *6* **Willie Hall**[17] [204] 11-11-1 89 .... BrianHarding 66
(Lisa Harrison) *hld up on outside: stdy hdwy after 3 out: rdn and wknd fr next* **12/1**

00- **8** *69* **Cushcapple (IRE)**[18] [192] 8-10-10 87 .... DerekFox(3)
(Noel C Kelly, Ire) *t.k.h early: chsd ldrs: rdn bef 2 out: wknd qckly between last 2: t.o* **16/1**

/03- **P** **Castley Lane**[63] [4971] 9-11-2 97 ....(t) DeanPratt(7)
(Sara Ender) *towards rr: struggling bef 4 out: lost tch next: t.o whn p.u after 2 out* **28/1**

60-P **P** **Vodka Moon**[24] [79] 6-10-6 87 .... JosephPalmowski(7)
(Sharon Watt) *bhd: rdn after 3 out: wknd bef next: t.o whn p.u bef last* **25/1**

P45- **P** **Most Honourable**[77] [4699] 5-10-12 86 ....(v[1]) HenryBrooke
(Michael Smith) *chsd ldrs: rdn after 7th: wknd 4 out: t.o whn p.u bef 2 out* **9/1**

6m 6.7s (-2.30) **Going Correction** -0.175s/f (Good) **11** Ran **SP% 122.7**
Speed ratings (Par 103): **96,95,94,90,87 87,85,62, ,**
CSF £22.07 CT £77.06 TOTE £7.60: £4.10, £2.80, £2.40; EX 23.10 Trifecta £145.50.
Owner R H & S C Walton **Bred** Rodney Deacon **Trained** Hexham, Northumberland
FOCUS
Only a modest gallop to this low-grade staying handicap hurdle. This was a step up from the winner.

485 HEXHAM CARAVAN SITE H'CAP CHASE (12 fncs) 1m 7f 133y
8:10 (8:11) (Class 5) (0-100,100) 5-Y-O+ **£2,924** (£858; £429; £214)

Form RPR

-U52 **1** **Gin Cobbler**[5] [417] 9-10-9 90 .... ThomasDowson(7) 103+
(Victor Thompson) *j.w: mde all: sn clr: kpt on strly fr 2 out: unchal* **11/4**[2]

46-6 **2** *11* **Forestside (IRE)**[24] [78] 10-10-0 74 oh6 ....(p) LucyAlexander 75
(Barry Murtagh) *nt fluent on occasions: in tch: rdn bef 3 out: chsd (clr) wnr between last 2: no imp* **16/1**

The Form Book Jumps 2015-16, Raceform Ltd, Newbury, RG14 5SJ

00-0 **3** *7* **Saddle Pack (IRE)**[20] 140 12-9-8 **75**.................... JamieHamilton(7) 72
(James Walton) *midfield: outpcd 1/2-way: rallied after 2 out: no imp bef last* **15/2**

60-5 **4** *27* **Morning Time (IRE)**[17] 205 9-11-9 **97**....................(tp) PeterBuchanan 74
(Lucinda Russell) *chsd (clr) wnr tl drvn and outpcd between last 2: sn wknd* **15/2**

34P- **5** *15* **Tweedo Paradiso (NZ)**[51] 5160 7-10-5 **82**.................... GrahamWatters(3) 39
(Rose Dobbin) *hld up: pushed along bef 4 out: rdn and struggling fr next* **11/2**[3]

P4-0 **6** *1 3/4* **Milan Royale**[24] 78 10-10-3 **82**....................(t) CallumBewley(5) 37
(Kevin Hunter) *hld up in tch: struggling fr 1/2-way: nvr on terms* **9/1**

402- **7** *hd* **Roxyfet (FR)**[51] 5160 5-11-9 **100**....................(p) CraigNichol(3) 55
(Micky Hammond) *nt fluent in rr: struggling 1/2-way: nvr on terms* **9/4**[1]

U-5P **U** **Bertielicious**[17] 200 7-9-11 **74** oh18....................(p) JonathanEngland(3)
(Jonathan Haynes) *bhd whn mstke and uns rdr 1st* **28/1**

4m 7.0s (-2.80) **Going Correction** -0.10s/f (Good) **8** Ran SP% **115.7**
Speed ratings: **102,96,93,80,73 72,72,**
CSF £41.86 CT £299.32 TOTE £3.90: £1.30, £3.50, £2.70; EX 58.70 Trifecta £176.90.
Owner V Thompson **Bred** The Elms Stud Company Ltd **Trained** Alnwick, Northumbria

FOCUS
Although they went a decent gallop in this ordinary handicap chase the leader never looked like being caught.

486 ST JOHN LEE H'CAP CHASE (18 fncs 1 omitted) 3m 41y
8:40 (8:43) (Class 5) (0-100,99) 5-Y-O+ **£2,469** (£725; £362; £181)

Form RPR

65-3 **1** **Chicago Outfit (IRE)**[20] 140 10-10-8 **86**....................(p) JonathonBewley(5) 100+
(George Bewley) *mde all: clr bef 2 out (usual 3 out): styd on strly passing omitted last* **4/1**[1]

15U- **2** *15* **Mia's Anthem (IRE)**[18] 193 7-11-6 **96**.................... DerekFox(3) 95
(Noel C Kelly, Ire) *in tch: lost grnd 12th: rallied bef 2 out (usual 3 out): chsd (clr) wnr next: no imp bef omitted last* **12/1**

04-5 **3** *5* **Indalo Return (IRE)**[26] 35 9-11-3 **90**.................... JamesReveley 87
(Philip Kirby) *hld up: hmpd 13th: hdwy to chse wnr after 3 out (usual 4 out): outpcd fr last* **9/1**

P3-5 **4** *7* **Pyjama Game (IRE)**[21] 133 9-11-3 **97**.................... ThomasDowson(7) 85
(Rose Dobbin) *prom: nt fluent 2nd: chsd wnr 11th to after 3 out (usual 4 out): rdn and outpcd next: sn n.d* **7/1**[3]

35-P **5** *nk* **Glenwood Prince (IRE)**[21] 133 9-9-9 **73** oh9....................(tp) CallumBewley(5) 60
(Kevin Hunter) *prom: pushed along and outpcd after 3 out (usual 4 out): rallied last: sn n.d: btn bef omitted last* **20/1**

4F2- **6** *40* **Northern Executive (IRE)**[39] 5375 7-11-1 **93**....................(p) GrantCockburn(5) 44
(Karen McLintock) *hld up: pushed along 3 out (usual 4 out): lost tch fr next: t.o* **15/2**

F10- **7** *60* **Twice Lucky**[36] 5423 11-11-5 **92**.................... SeanQuinlan
(Sue Smith) *chsd wnr to 11th: rdn and struggling fr 14th: t.o* **7/1**[3]

5P-2 **P** **Winter Alchemy (IRE)**[20] 140 10-11-5 **92**.................... BrianHarding
(Nicky Richards) *bhd: struggling 1/2-way: t.o whn p.u after last (usual 2 out)* **9/2**[2]

1-22 **F** **Charming Lad (IRE)**[16] 223 10-11-7 **99**....................(bt) DannyBurton(5)
(Anthony Day) *prom: hdwy and disputing 2nd pl whn fell 13th* **7/1**[3]

00-5 **P** **Master Murphy (IRE)**[21] 136 10-10-10 **83**.................... PeterBuchanan
(Jane Walton) *bhd and nvr gng wl: struggling whn hmpd 13th: sn p.u* **10/1**

6m 29.2s (-3.00) **Going Correction** -0.10s/f (Good) **10** Ran SP% **119.0**
Speed ratings: **100,95,93,91,91 78,59,,,**
CSF £50.95 CT £414.20 TOTE £5.50: £2.30, £6.00, £5.10; EX 64.40 Trifecta £564.90.
Owner G T Bewley **Bred** Roger Ryan **Trained** Bonchester Bridge, Borders

FOCUS
A low-grade staying handicap chase run at a sound gallop, but the leader, who had slipped to a very good mark, had it sewn up a long way from home. The normal last fence was omitted on account of the low sun.

487 "FOLLOW US ON TWITTER" AMATEUR RIDERS' NOVICES' H'CAP HURDLE (8 hdls) 2m 48y
9:10 (9:10) (Class 5) (0-100,96) 4-Y-O+ **£2,502** (£769; £384)

Form RPR

3-F4 **1** **Pekanheim (IRE)**[17] 200 7-11-7 **96**.................... MrZBaker(5) 102
(Martin Todhunter) *in tch: hdwy bef 2 out: led and rdn bef last: hld on wl run-in* **12/1**

0-01 **2** *1/2* **Seventeen Black (IRE)**[13] 288 7-10-2 **79**.................... MrSWColtherd(7) 85
(Stuart Coltherd) *hld up: hdwy bef 2 out: effrt and ev ch whn crossed by loose horse appr last: drifted lft and ev ch run-in: kpt on: hld nr fin* **9/2**[3]

40-0 **3** *13* **Caraline (FR)**[19] 153 4-10-4 **85**....................(v) MrJoeWright(7) 76
(Micky Hammond) *t.k.h: sn chsng ldr: led 2 out to bef last: edgd lft and sn outpcd* **16/1**

0-65 **4** *3/4* **Mister Jones**[14] 263 7-10-1 **78**.................... MrRHogg(7) 71
(Sue Smith) *chsd ldrs: lost pl 3rd: struggling fr next: rallied between last 2: kpt on run-in: no imp* **11/2**

066- **5** *3/4* **Catchthemoonlight**[34] 5470 7-10-9 **86**.................... MrWHRReed(7) 79
(Lucinda Russell) *hld up in tch: effrt bef 2 out: rdn and outpcd between last 2* **10/1**

P1-4 **6** *2 1/4* **Jebulani**[26] 34 5-10-8 **85**.................... LorcanMurtagh(7) 76
(Barry Murtagh) *hld up: hdwy bef 2 out: sn rdn: no imp whn nt fluent last* **7/1**

P5-4 **7** *12* **Just Bee (IRE)**[24] 77 6-10-7 **80**....................(p) MrTHamilton(3) 60
(Katie Scott) *hld up towards rr: hdwy to chse ldrs 4th: rdn and wknd fr 2 out* **33/1**

8 *18* **Theo (IRE)**[114] 4003 5-11-3 **94**.................... MrConorOrr(7) 57
(S Donohoe, Ire) *nt fluent on occasions: hld up towards rr: hdwy to chse ldrs 3rd: rdn and ev ch 2 out: wknd bef last* **4/1**[2]

-33P **P** **Duhallowcountry (IRE)**[13] 288 9-10-13 **90**....................(p) ThomasDowson(7)
(Victor Thompson) *led: rdn and hdd 2 out: sn wknd: p.u bef last* **33/1**

050- **U** **Russian Royale**[32] 5516 5-11-4 **88**.................... MissCWalton
(Micky Hammond) *hld up: mstke and uns rdr 2nd* **11/4**[1]

4m 12.0s (-5.40) **Going Correction** -0.175s/f (Good)
WFA 4 from 5yo+ 18lb **10** Ran SP% **121.3**
Speed ratings (Par 103): **105,104,98,98,97 96,91,82,,**
CSF £68.93 CT £884.60 TOTE £9.10: £8.40, £4.00, £14.20; EX 64.10 Trifecta £1742.80.
Owner Andrew G Bell **Bred** Martin Hoste **Trained** Orton, Cumbria

FOCUS
A modest novice handicap hurdle run at a fair gallop and only around 5l covered the front eight going to the second-last.
T/Plt: £196.00 to a £1 stake. Pool of £72814.41 - 271.12 winning tickets. T/Qpdt: £82.50 to a £1 stake. Pool of £7126.34 - 63.87 winning tickets. **Richard Young**

HUNTINGDON (R-H)
Tuesday, May 26

OFFICIAL GOING: Chase course - good (good to firm in places; 6.8); hurdle course - good to firm (good in places; 6.9)
Wind: light, half behind Weather: dry, sunny spells

488 PAUL RACKHAM CHAMPION NOVICES' HUNTERS' CHASE (19 fncs) 2m 7f 129y
5:50 (5:51) (Class 6) 5-Y-O+ **£1,247** (£387; £193; £96)

Form RPR

P/P- **1** **Banksandditches (IRE)**[2] 9-11-12 0.................... MrTomDavid 98+
(Clare Hobson) *hld up in tch: hdwy and mstke 16th: chsd ldr next: led last: pushed clr flat* **12/1**

2 *9* **Hill Of Gold (IRE)**[22] 7-11-12 0....................(p) MissGAndrews 87
(David Kemp) *chsd ldr: led 13th: jnd whn j.lft and mstke 2 out: hdd last: sn btn* **7/1**

36-2 **3** *31* **Coeur Brule (FR)**[12] 298 9-11-7 93.................... MrDavidTurner(5) 67+
(David Turner) *s.i.s: j. bdly lft 1st: clsd and wl in tch in midfield: struggling whn j. bdly lft 3 out: sn wknd: no ch whn j. bdly lft next: wnt poor 3rd and wnt lft again last: t.o* **11/4**[2]

4 *51* **Native Pride (IRE)**[65] 7-11-5 0.................... MrMJPKendrick(7) 33
(Ms J Johnston) *chsd ldrs: almost uns rdr 2nd: rdn and struggling 3 out: sn lost tch: t.o whn j.lft and mstke last: fin lame* **2/1**[1]

3-P **P** **Tompatpeg (IRE)**[12] 298 8-11-5 0....................(p) MrCharlieMarshall(7)
(David Phelan) *in tch in rr: pushed along 4th: struggling 11th: tailing off whn p.u 13th* **25/1**

/60- **P** **Rocky Island (IRE)**[58] 7-11-7 89.................... MrTommieMO'Brien(5)
(T H Messenger) *led tl 13th: rdn and struggling 3 out: sn lost tch: t.o whn p.u next* **3/1**[3]

6m 1.95s (-8.35) **Going Correction** -0.575s/f (Firm) **6** Ran SP% **109.0**
Speed ratings: **90,87,76,59,**
CSF £79.21 TOTE £14.60: £3.80, £3.00; EX 54.90 Trifecta £374.60.
Owner Harry Hobson **Bred** Mrs Orlagh Sherry **Trained**

FOCUS
Chase bend out 2yds turning out of the back straight and into the home straight, adding approximately 6yds to chase circuit length. All other rail in innermost position. The ground was just on the quick side of good. Despite the title this was a very modest event.

489 FLEXITRANS LTD 10TH ANNIVERSARY CONDITIONAL JOCKEYS' H'CAP HURDLE (8 hdls) 1m 7f 171y
6:20 (6:21) (Class 5) (0-100,98) 4-Y-O+ **£2,274** (£667; £333; £166)

Form RPR

024- **1** **Celtic Artisan (IRE)**[14] 5189 4-11-10 **98**....................(p) BridgetAndrews 98+
(Rebecca Menzies) *t.k.h: hld up wl in tch in midfield: j. into 2nd 5th: led 2 out: styd on flat: rdn out* **11/2**

2-41 **2** *1 1/4* **Heading To First**[14] 267 8-11-10 **94**....................(v) NicodeBoinville 97
(Jim Best) *t.k.h: hld up in tch in last pair: hdwy to chse ldrs 3 out: sn rdn: wnt 2nd bef last: hanging in bhd wnr and styd on same pce flat* **15/8**[1]

63P- **3** *1 1/2* **Mix N Match**[106] 4134 11-10-0 **70** oh4.................... HarryChalloner 72
(Laura Young) *hld up in last pair: hdwy after 5th: 5th and rdn bef 2 out: 4th whn j.rt 2 out: lft 3rd sn after last: kpt on u.p flat* **9/1**

01P- **4** *14* **Mighty Mambo**[26] 5091 8-11-12 **96**....................(tp) SeanBowen 85
(Lawney Hill) *chsd ldr tl 5th: 4th and no ex bef 2 out: wknd between last 2* **9/2**[3]

653- **5** *3/4* **Cherry Tiger**[34] 5481 5-11-2 **86**....................(t) ConorRing 80
(Graeme McPherson) *led: rdn and jnd after 3 out: hdd 2 out: 3rd and btn whn blnd last: wknd flat* **4/1**[2]

004- **6** *11* **Smirfy's Silver**[37] 5404 11-11-6 **90**.................... BenPoste 71
(Michael Mullineaux) *in tch in midfield: mstke 4th: hit next: wknd qckly after next* **20/1**

5/6- **7** *6* **Mahayogin (USA)**[335] 810 7-10-11 **84**....................(t) MichaelHeard(3) 57
(Sarah-Jayne Davies) *in tch in midfield: rdn and wknd bef 2 out: sn bhd* **33/1**

050- **P** **Amirli (IRE)**[145] 3461 4-11-9 **97**....................(t) MauriceLinehan
(Donald McCain) *chsd ldrs: blnd and lost pl 3 out: sn wknd: bhd whn p.u after next* **14/1**

3m 44.75s (-10.15) **Going Correction** -0.575s/f (Firm)
WFA 4 from 5yo+ 18lb **8** Ran SP% **112.7**
Speed ratings (Par 103): **100,99,98,92,91 86,83,**
CSF £16.27 CT £89.53 TOTE £4.80: £1.60, £1.50, £2.20; EX 16.40 Trifecta £114.50.
Owner EPDS Racing Partnership 11 **Bred** Fortbarrington Stud **Trained** Stearsby, N Yorks

FOCUS
An ordinary handicap, run at a fair pace. The winner was well in on one Irish run.

490 SPA BREAKS AT WHITTLEBURYHALL.CO.UK H'CAP CHASE (16 fncs) 2m 3f 189y
6:50 (6:50) (Class 4) (0-110,114) 5-Y-O+ **£3,768** (£1,106; £553; £276)

Form RPR

44-3 **1** **Herecomesthetruth (IRE)**[13] 280 13-11-2 **97**.................... TomCannon 104+
(Chris Gordon) *chsd ldr tl after 5th: styd chsng ldrs: rdn bef 3 out: ev ch whn lft in ld 2 out: clr whn hung rt and idling flat: fnd a bit ex whn pressed towards fin* **10/1**

41-2 **2** *3/4* **Royalracket (IRE)**[26] 44 7-11-0 **95**....................(b) LiamTreadwell 100+
(Paul Webber) *chsd ldrs: wnt 2nd after 5th: mstke 9th: led sn after 3 out: rdn bef 2 out: hdd: hmpd and lft 2nd 2 out: plugged on same pce flat: pressing idling wnr towards fin: a hld* **11/4**[2]

2U1- **3** *16* **Isthereadifference (IRE)**[54] 5115 8-11-9 **104**....................(bt) NoelFehily 91
(Neil Mulholland) *hld up in tch in last pair: rdn and btn after 3 out: no ch whn lft 3rd 2 out* **7/2**[3]

1-F3 **4** *13* **Capisci (IRE)**[13] 284 10-11-7 **102**.................... TomScudamore 80
(Sarah-Jayne Davies) *led: mstke 13th: hdd sn after 3 out: sn wknd: wl btn whn lft 4th next* **17/2**

-211 **F** **By The Boardwalk (IRE)**[8] 381 7-12-2 **114** 7ex....................(t) TomBellamy(3) 124+
(Kim Bailey) *hld up in tch in last pair: mstke 10th: effrt and clsd on ldr after 3 out: led and fell 2 out* **11/8**[1]

4m 58.3s (-7.00) **Going Correction** -0.575s/f (Firm) **5** Ran SP% **110.6**
Speed ratings: **90,89,83,78,**
CSF £37.16 TOTE £9.80: £3.60, £1.60; EX 39.50 Trifecta £159.10.
Owner Mrs I Colderick **Bred** Thomas Cassidy **Trained** Morestead, Hampshire

FOCUS
Drama in the closing stages of this fair handicap chase. The winner is a bit better than the bare result.

491 BOOK ONLINE AT WHITTLEBURYHALL.CO.UK NOVICES' HURDLE (8 hdls) 1m 7f 171y
7:20 (7:20) (Class 4) 4-Y-0+ £3,249 (£954; £477; £238)

Form RPR

1 **Improvisation (IRE)**[769] 5-10-12 0 .... AidanColeman 132+
(John Ferguson) *travelled strly: hld up in midfield: clsd after 3rd: wnt 2nd and wandered 3 out: led on bit between last 2: cruised clr flat: v easily* **2/1**[2]

33-1 2 12 **Buy Back Bob (IRE)**[19] 171 8-11-5 117 .... RichardJohnson 120
(Tim Vaughan) *chsd ldr tl led 4th: hit next: rdn bef 2 out: hdd between last 2 and sn brushed aside by wnr: hld on for 2nd u.p flat* **6/4**[1]

1 3 ½ **Taweyla (IRE)**[19] 178 4-10-8 0 .... KielanWoods 110
(Pam Sly) *chsd ldrs: wnt 2nd after 5th tl j.rt next: 3rd and outpcd whn mstke 2 out: no ch w wnr but plugged on to battle for 2nd flat* **3/1**[3]

0 4 43 **Royal Battalion**[22] 98 4-10-8 0 .... JamieMoore 80
(Gary Moore) *hld up off the pce in last trio: clsd and handy 5th bef 3 out: mstke 3 out: sn wknd: t.o* **16/1**

605- 5 29 **Sturdy Dawn**[35] 5448 5-10-2 0 .... (b¹) BenPoste(3) 33
(Michael Mullineaux) *led tl 4th: rdn and lost 2nd after 5th: fdd rapidly after 3 out: t.o* **200/1**

6 75 **Bishop Of Ruscombe**[231] 4-10-8 0 .... MichealNolan
(Jamie Snowden) *t.k.h: hld up off the pce in last trio: clsd after 3rd: lost tch 5th: t.o whn mstke next* **14/1**

00P- P **Dj Gerry**[126] 3782 4-10-8 0 .... AdamWedge
(Nick Kent) *hld up in last trio: clsd and in tch after 3rd: struggling whn blnd and sddle slipped 5th: sn p.u* **250/1**

3m 40.9s (-14.00) **Going Correction** -0.575s/f (Firm)
WFA 4 from 5yo+ 18lb **7 Ran SP% 111.8**
Speed ratings (Par 105): **109,103,103,82,69 33,**
CSF £5.32 TOTE £3.20: £1.70, £1.20; EX 6.40 Trifecta £13.80.
Owner Bloomfields **Bred** Ennistown Stud **Trained** Cowlinge, Suffolk

FOCUS
An ordinary novice hurdle, but a very classy winner. The time was the best part of 4sec quicker than the earlier 0-100 handicap.

492 BOOK YOUR WHITTLEBURY HALL SPA DAY NOVICES' CHASE (12 fncs) 2m 104y
7:50 (7:53) (Class 4) 5-Y-0+ £3,768 (£1,106; £553; £276)

Form RPR

301- 1 **Fox Norton (FR)**[98] 4280 5-10-12 0 .... NoelFehily 130+
(Neil Mulholland) *hld up in midfield: clsd after 5th: wnt 2nd and 7th: mstke next: upsides ldr after 3 out: led on bit last: cruised clr flat: v easily* **8/15**[1]

13-3 2 6 **Town Mouse**[15] 241 5-11-5 118 .... TrevorWhelan 124
(Neil King) *chsd ldr tl led 4th: rdn and clr w cantering wnr after 3 out: hdd last: sn brushed aside: kpt on for clr 2nd* **8/1**[3]

532- 3 15 **Marju's Quest (IRE)**[12] 5441 5-10-12 0 .... AidanColeman 103
(David Dennis) *t.k.h: chsd clr ldng pair: clsd to chse ldrs 5th: 3rd and rdn after 3 out: no imp and hld whn mstke next: wknd last* **9/2**[2]

342- 4 hd **Lemony Bay**[35] 5444 6-10-12 0 .... LeightonAspell 103
(Oliver Sherwood) *hld up off the pce in last pair: clsd and in tch 6th: effrt in 4th 3 out: no imp u.p bef next: wknd between last 2* **8/1**[3]

44/0 5 14 **Hyperlink (IRE)**[13] 281 6-10-12 0 .... ¹ RhysFlint 89
(Heather Dalton) *hld up off the pce in last pair: clsd and in tch after 5th: effrt and mstke 3 out: sn no imp and wl btn 2 out* **66/1**

0 6 dist **Midnight Wishes**[10] 329 10-10-5 0 .... ¹ LiamTreadwell 31
(Peter Hiatt) *led tl 4th: chsd ldr tl 7th: steadily lost pl: last and lost tch after 3 out: t.o and eased flat* **100/1**

3m 56.05s (-14.15) **Going Correction** -0.575s/f (Firm) **6 Ran SP% 108.1**
Speed ratings: **110,107,100,100,93 69**
CSF £5.15 TOTE £1.40: £1.10, £3.00; EX 5.70 Trifecta £11.00.
Owner B Dunn **Bred** S A Scuderia Del Bargelo **Trained** Limpley Stoke, Wilts

FOCUS
Reasonable novice chase form. The winner was a 140+ hurdler.

493 LATEST OFFERS ONLINE AT WHITTLEBURYHALL.CO.UK H'CAP HURDLE (12 hdls) 3m 1f 10y
8:20 (8:21) (Class 4) (0-105,105) 4-Y-0+ £3,249 (£954; £477; £238)

Form RPR

45-1 1 **Minnie Milan (IRE)**[10] 339 6-11-8 101 .... TrevorWhelan 116+
(Neil King) *chsd ldrs: wnt 2nd 3rd tl led 2 out: r.o wl: comf* **5/2**[1]

53-5 2 5 **Mr Cardle (IRE)**[14] 265 6-11-2 95 .... LeightonAspell 102
(Oliver Sherwood) *in tch towards rr: pushed along 8th: rdn and hdwy after next: chsd wnr 2 out: no imp whn j.rt last: one pce flat* **3/1**[2]

36-3 3 4½ **Combustible Kate (IRE)**[18] 183 9-10-2 81 .... AdamWedge 84
(Nick Kent) *in tch in midfield: hdwy to chse ldrs after 8th: 3rd and rdn bef 3 out: outpcd between last 2: plugged on flat* **20/1**

30-5 4 16 **Spanish Fork (IRE)**[16] 222 6-10-9 88 .... (t) MarcGoldstein 77
(Sheena West) *rn in snatches: towards rr: reminder after 4th: mostly off the bridle after: cl enough in 7th whn mstke 3 out: outpcd and btn next: plugged on past btn horses bef last* **7/1**[3]

25-0 5 12 **West End (IRE)**[22] 108 8-11-9 102 .... (p) DavidBass 82
(Kim Bailey) *t.k.h: hld up in tch towards rr: mstke 5th: hdwy after 8th: rdn to go 2nd briefly but finding little bef 2 out: 4th and btn 2 out: fdd between last 2* **10/1**

/61- 6 3 **Demographic (USA)**[216] 1997 6-11-2 105 .... (v) RichieO'Dea(10) 80
(Emma Lavelle) *led: mstke 3 out: sn rdn and hdd: 5th and btn 2 out: fdd: t.o* **8/1**

23F- 7 3½ **Torran Sound**[233] 1758 8-11-3 96 .... (tp) AidanColeman 68
(Lawney Hill) *chsd ldr tl 3rd: chsd ldrs after tl lost pl qckly bef 3 out: wl btn bef 2 out: t.o* **16/1**

020- 8 8 **Freddy Fox (IRE)**[133] 3663 5-11-0 100 .... MrMJPKendrick(7) 65
(Ben Case) *in tch in midfield: hdwy to chse ldrs 4th: struggling u.p bef 3 out: wknd wl bef 2 out: t.o* **16/1**

55-0 9 47 **Vinceson (IRE)**[19] 167 7-10-6 85 .... JamesBest 7
(Jess Westwood) *in tch in midfield: reminder after 7th: lost pl u.p next: lost tch 9th: t.o 3 out* **12/1**

45-P P **Vinnie My Boy (IRE)**[22] 108 7-11-5 105 .... (t¹) MissADalton(7)
(Heather Dalton) *hld up in tch towards rr: rdn and lost tch 9th: t.o whn p.u 2 out* **28/1**

6m 5.5s (-17.40) **Going Correction** -0.575s/f (Firm) **10 Ran SP% 113.9**
Speed ratings (Par 105): **103,101,100,95,91 90,89,87,72,**
CSF £10.44 CT £116.67 TOTE £3.40: £1.50, £1.70, £2.10; EX 12.90 Trifecta £68.00.
Owner Mark & Tracy Harrod,P Branigan,T Messom **Bred** S P Tindall **Trained** Barbury Castle, Wiltshire
■ Stewards' Enquiry : Trevor Whelan caution: careless riding

FOCUS
A modest staying handicap. The cosy winner is on the upgrade.

494 SMITHS METAL CENTRES MAIDEN HURDLE (10 hdls) 2m 3f 137y
8:50 (8:51) (Class 5) 4-Y-0+ £2,274 (£667; £333; £166)

Form RPR

52-2 1 **Shwaiman (IRE)**[21] 127 5-11-0 125 .... TrevorWhelan 123+
(William Jarvis) *pressed ldr tl led 7th: qcknd 3 out: rdn bef last: r.o and a jst doing enough flat* **11/8**[2]

232- 2 ½ **Father Edward (IRE)**[139] 3570 6-11-0 127 .... (t) AidanColeman 123
(John Ferguson) *hld up in tch in midfield: effrt to go 2nd 3 out: ev ch and nt fluent next: sn rdn: kpt on but a jst hld flat* **8/11**[1]

6-4 3 26 **Being Global (FR)**[22] 105 4-10-9 0 .... HarrySkelton 91
(Caroline Bailey) *hld up in tch in last pair: clsd to chse ldrs 7th: 3rd and btn whn mstke 2 out: wknd bef last* **33/1**

0 4 15 **Astrowolf**[25] 61 4-10-9 0 .... AndrewTinkler 79
(Mark H Tompkins) *led: mstke 4th: hdd 7th: rdn and wknd qckly bef 2 out: t.o* **20/1**[3]

00-4 5 14 **Up Four It (IRE)**[16] 221 7-11-0 0 .... TomO'Brien 67
(Jamie Poulton) *chsd ldng pair tl outpcd 3 out: lost tch bef next: t.o* **100/1**

05-4 6 14 **Ballochmyle (IRE)**[21] 127 5-11-0 0 .... RyanMahon 53
(Caroline Fryer) *in tch in last pair: rdn and struggling whn mstke 6th: lost tch 3 out: t.o next* **100/1**

4m 45.65s (-13.35) **Going Correction** -0.575s/f (Firm)
WFA 4 from 5yo+ 19lb **6 Ran SP% 109.7**
Speed ratings (Par 103): **102,101,91,86,80 75**
CSF £2.68 TOTE £2.70: £1.10, £1.10; EX 2.60 Trifecta £7.30.
Owner M C Banks **Bred** Rabbah Bloodstock Limited **Trained** Newmarket, Suffolk

FOCUS
An ordinary maiden hurdle in which the first two came well clear. The form looks straightforward.
T/Plt: £132.60 to a £1 stake. Pool of £45423.14 - 250.03 winning tickets T/Qpdt: £9.90 to a £1 stake. Pool of £5165.09 - 382.94 winning tickets. **Steve Payne**

495 - 501a (Foreign Racing) - See Raceform Interactive

467 CARTMEL (L-H)

Wednesday, May 27

OFFICIAL GOING: Good changing to soft after race 4 (3.50)
Wind: moderate 1/2 behind Weather: overcast, cool, raining race 2 onwards

502 CHOOSESOUTHCUMBRIA.CO.UK H'CAP HURDLE (11 hdls) 2m 6f 31y
2:20 (2:20) (Class 5) (0-100,100) 4-Y-0+ £2,599 (£763; £381; £190)

Form RPR

P/1- 1 **Stags Leap (IRE)**[202] 2290 8-11-8 96 .... (p) HenryBrooke 109
(Julia Brooke) *mid-div: chsd ldrs 6th: led after 3 out: hit next: kpt on wl last 150yds* **15/2**[3]

00P- 2 1½ **Dumbarton (IRE)**[162] 3134 7-11-9 100 .... TonyKelly(3) 112
(James Moffatt) *hld up in rr: stdy hdwy 8th: upsides 2 out: no ex clsng stages* **9/1**

0F5- 3 14 **Volcanic Jack (IRE)**[6] 4650 7-9-9 74 oh5 .... JoeCornwall(5) 73
(Michael Chapman) *in rr: hdwy 8th: modest 3rd sn after 2 out: kpt on one pce* **6/1**[2]

3-05 4 10 **Indepub**[14] 291 6-10-6 87 .... RyanDay(7) 77
(Lisa Harrison) *mid-div: hmpd 7th: hdwy next: modest 4th between last 2: one pce* **15/2**[3]

000- 5 11 **Ardesia (IRE)**[87] 4519 11-9-11 74 oh1 .... (t) CraigNichol(3) 55
(Tina Jackson) *in rr: hdwy 8th: poor 5th between last 2: one pce* **16/1**

0-05 6 14 **Mrs Grass**[20] 153 8-9-9 74 oh5 .... (vt) DiarmuidO'Regan(5) 42
(Jonathan Haynes) *w ldr: led briefly appr 3 out: wknd between last 2* **33/1**

4-2P 7 hd **Whatsupjack (IRE)**[15] 262 8-10-4 81 .... (b) JonathanEngland(3) 49
(Shaun Harris) *prom: drvn 8th: lost pl and mstke next* **12/1**

0PF- 8 2 **Cloggy Powell (IRE)**[209] 2150 8-9-9 74 oh5 .... CallumBewley(5) 40
(Kevin Hunter) *in rr: sme hdwy 8th: wknd next* **100/1**

00-5 9 5 **Raifteiri (IRE)**[20] 157 8-9-13 80 .... MrJDixon(7) 41
(William Young Jnr) *chsd ldrs: drvn 6th: lost pl 8th* **14/1**

352- 10 36 **Omid**[88] 4491 7-11-9 100 .... (bt) HarryChalloner(3) 29
(Kenneth Slack) *sn drvn along: dropped to rr after 1st: bhd and reminders 3rd: nt keen: t.o 7th: b.b.v* **7/2**[1]

/00- P **Rare Coincidence**[277] 1310 14-9-11 74 oh7 .... JoeColliver(3)
(Alan Berry) *in rr: hmpd 7th: sme hdwy next: sn lost pl: t.o whn p.u between last 2* **50/1**

40-3 F **Sam Lord**[22] 136 11-11-0 88 .... BrianHughes
(James Moffatt) *chsd ldrs: 3rd whn fell 7th* **9/1**

46P- P **Turtle Cask (IRE)**[76] 4725 6-11-12 100 .... (p) JamesReveley
(Dianne Sayer) *led: hdd appr 3 out: sn eased: p.u bef 2 out* **8/1**

5m 18.5s (-10.80) **Going Correction** -0.425s/f (Good) **13 Ran SP% 117.3**
Speed ratings (Par 103): **102,101,96,92,88 83,83,82,81,67 , ,**
CSF £71.67 CT £435.20 TOTE £7.10: £3.10, £3.50, £2.80; EX 81.20 Trifecta £646.80.
Owner John & Billy Platts **Bred** P McCartan & Paddy Twomey **Trained** Middleham, North Yorks

FOCUS
It was dry and cloudy and the going was good. The Roadside had been watered with 6mm and the rail was moved out 3m on both bends providing fresh ground, increasing race distances by approx 19yds per circuit. Most of these are exposed as modest and this isn't strong form overall but the front two pulled a long way clear and the runner-up is a well-handicapped horse, so they are, by some distance, the two to take from the contest. A big step up from the winner, with the second rated in line with the best of his form from last year.

503 MILNER BOARDMAN PARTNERSHIP MARES' MAIDEN HURDLE (11 hdls) 2m 6f 31y
2:50 (2:59) (Class 5) 4-Y-0+ £2,599 (£763; £381; £190)

Form RPR

5 1 **Western Home (IRE)**[13] 305 5-11-0 0 .... TomScudamore 98
(Gordon Elliott, Ire) *hld up in tch: hdwy to chse ldrs 3 out: led last: drvn rt out: all out* **4/1**[3]

43P- 2 nk **Mrs Jordan (IRE)**[120] 3918 7-11-0 97 .... (t) PaulMoloney 98
(Sophie Leech) *chsd ldrs: handy 2nd sn after last: styd on fnl 75yds: jst hld* **7/2**[2]

3 5 **Classic Palace (IRE)**[84] 4570 6-11-0 0 .... BrianHughes 94
(J J Lambe, Ire) *led: hdd last: wknd fnl 50yds* **9/1**

543- 4 3 **Knockalyde Sno Cat (IRE)**[7] 409 6-11-0 108 .... (t) PeterBuchanan 91
(S R B Crawford, Ire) *hld up in tch: hdwy 3 out: sn chsng ldrs: 4th between last 2: kpt on one pce* **2/1**[1]

33P- **5** *4* **Blurred Lines (IRE)**[210] 2135 6-11-0 102 .... HenryBrooke 87
(Donald McCain) *chsd ldrs: drvn 3 out: one pce* **7/1**

4 **6** *4½* **Cherry Princess**[20] 155 5-11-0 0 .... SeanQuinlan 83
(Barbara Butterworth) *in rr: kpt on fr 2 out: nvr on terms* **25/1**

5 **7** *4* **Suzy's Music (IRE)**[1] 481 7-10-11 0 .... CraigNichol(3) 80
(S R B Crawford, Ire) *nt fluent in rr: nvr a factor* **22/1**

3/ **U** **Erica Starprincess**[19] 2168 5-10-11 0 .... JoeColliver(3)
(George Moore) *chsd ldrs: mstke and uns rdr 8th* **25/1**

603- **P** **Zabalee (IRE)**[33] 5514 5-10-11 87 .... HarryChalloner(3)
(Andrew Wilson) *trckd ldrs: drvn 7th: lost pl and bhd whn hmpd next: sn p.u: fatally injured* **22/1**

5m 29.3s **Going Correction** -0.425s/f (Good) **9** Ran SP% **114.4**
Speed ratings (Par 103): **83,82,81,79,78 76,75,** ,
CSF £17.50 TOTE £4.60: £1.80, £1.60, £2.10; EX 24.20 Trifecta £167.20.
Owner Raymond Burroughs **Bred** David Kennedy **Trained** Longwood, Co Meath

FOCUS
Modest maiden hurdle form but they went a reasonable gallop and and the unexposed winner has some potential over hurdles and then fences, being a point winner on her only start in that discipline. The second is probably the best guide to the level, but this is not form to be confident about.

504 CHAMPAGNE LOUIS ROEDERER H'CAP CHASE (12 fncs) 2m 1f 61y
3:20 (3:33) (Class 5) (0-100,95) 5-Y-O+ **£3,249** (£954; £477; £238)

Form RPR

30-2 **1** **Carters Rest**[15] 256 12-11-0 90 .... MissJWalton(7) 104+
(George Bewley) *t.k.h: led 2nd: drvn clr over 1f out: unchal* **12/1**

44-6 **2** *4½* **The Society Man (IRE)**[19] 183 8-11-7 95 .... JoeCornwall(5) 103
(Michael Chapman) *chsd ldrs: drvn 6th: 2nd 9th: kpt on same pce fnl 2f* **5/1**[3]

506- **3** *3¼* **King's Chorister**[33] 5516 9-11-0 83 ....(t) LucyAlexander 88
(Barry Murtagh) *hld up in rr but in tch: hdwy to chse ldrs 9th: kpt on one pce to take 3rd last 75yds* **14/1**

P6-3 **4** *½* **Pindar (GER)**[15] 256 11-10-7 76 ....(b) DougieCostello 81
(Joanne Foster) *chsd ldrs: pushed along 6th: outpcd sn after last: styd on fnl f: tk 4th last 50yds* **10/1**

-646 **5** *3¼* **Amir Pasha (UAE)**[15] 256 10-9-12 74 ....(b) JamieBargary(7) 77
(Micky Hammond) *chsd ldrs: wknd and last 2 pls last 100yds* **11/2**

23-2 **6** *12* **The Absent Mare**[14] 286 7-10-8 77 ....(t) TomScudamore 73
(Gordon Elliott, Ire) *in rr: blnd and lost pl 8th: hdwy to chse ldrs 3 out: lost pl over 2f out* **2/1**[1]

42-3 **7** *30* **Persian Herald**[18] 205 7-11-11 94 ....(b) JamesReveley 58
(Dianne Sayer) *nt fluent: led to 2nd: reminders and lost pl 3 out: sn bhd: t.o* **7/2**[2]

4m 22.9s (4.00) **Going Correction** -0.10s/f (Good) **7** Ran SP% **111.1**
Speed ratings: **87,85,83,83,81 76,63**
CSF £65.69 TOTE £7.80: £4.20, £2.50; EX 53.00 Trifecta £577.70.
Owner Mrs D Walton **Bred** A Dawson **Trained** Bonchester Bridge, Borders

FOCUS
With The Society Man rated 95 and only two of these rated above 90, this wouldn't be the strongest 0-100 event ever contested. The third has been rated in line with his recent hurdle form.

505 CARTMEL LODGE PARK BEGINNERS' CHASE (14 fncs) 2m 5f 34y
3:50 (3:58) (Class 4) 5-Y-O+ **£4,223** (£1,240; £620; £310)

Form RPR

2P-3 **1** **River Maigue (IRE)**[12] 317 8-11-0 135 ....(t) PaulMoloney 130+
(Sophie Leech) *chsd ldrs: 2nd appr last: styd on fnl 2f: led last 75yds* **9/2**[2]

22-2 **2** *1½* **Alternatif (FR)**[18] 196 5-11-0 0 ....(b[1]) TomScudamore 128
(David Pipe) *trckd ldrs: led 3 out: rdn 2 l clr over 1f out: fnd little and hdd last 75yds* **1/2**[1]

003- **3** *1¾* **Volcanic (FR)**[37] 5422 6-11-0 0 ....(t) HenryBrooke 128
(Donald McCain) *led: mstke and hdd 3 out: outpcd appr last: kpt on wl fnl 2f* **7/1**[3]

550- **4** *16* **Morning Royalty (IRE)**[37] 5422 8-11-0 125 .... BrianHughes 115
(James Moffatt) *chsd ldr: 3rd whn pckd 11th: wknd next: sn bhd: t.o* **20/1**

00/3 **P** **Silk Hall (UAE)**[21] 138 10-11-0 124 ....(b) JamesReveley
(J J Lambe, Ire) *nt fluent: chsd ldrs: hit 2nd: lost pl 6th: t.o 9th: p.u bef last* **20/1**

561/ **P** **Unex Picasso**[732] 476 7-11-0 0 .... LucyAlexander
(Barry Murtagh) *in last: hit 6th: sn bhd: t.o 9th: p.u after next* **50/1**

5m 18.0s (-7.40) **Going Correction** -0.10s/f (Good) **6** Ran SP% **108.8**
Speed ratings: **109,108,107,102,**
CSF £7.20 TOTE £6.60: £1.60, £1.30; EX 9.40 Trifecta £24.70.
Owner C J Leech **Bred** James Keegan **Trained** Elton, Gloucs

FOCUS
This looked all over when odds-on favourite Alternatif hit the front after the third-last fence, still travelling best, but he began to tread water on the long run-in. The first three have all done bigger figures over hurdles and this looks a fair novice for the track/time of year.

506 RACING UK DAY PASS OPEN HUNTERS' CHASE (FOR THE HORACE D. PAIN MEMORIAL TROPHY) (18 fncs) 3m 1f 107y
4:25 (4:25) (Class 6) 5-Y-O+ **£1,559** (£483; £241; £121)

Form RPR

42-1 **1** **Cygnet**[13] 294 9-11-11 0 ....(t) MissJodieHughes(5) 116+
(Mickey Bowen) *trckd ldrs: 2nd 3rd: led last: drvn clr over 1f out: styd on wl* **5/2**[1]

/24- **2** *11* **Forge Valley**[38] 11-11-5 107 ....(p) MrTGreenwood(7) 103
(Miss G Walton) *led: hit 10th: j. slowly 13th: hdd last: kpt on same pce fnl 2f* **8/1**

3 *2¾* **Abbeyview (IRE)**[31] 8-11-9 0 .... MrPGerety(3) 99
(Mrs Sheila Crow) *in rr: hdwy 8th: chaxsing ldrs 12th: modest 3rd last: one pce* **12/1**

3 **4** *7* **Threapwood**[26] 60 8-11-12 0 ....(b) MrOGreenall 92
(Oliver Greenall) *in rr: hdwy 9th: chsng ldrs 11th: one pce fr 14th* **16/1**

P0-3 **5** *shd* **Indian Print (IRE)**[4] 11-11-5 90 .... ThomasDowson(7) 91
(Victor Thompson) *chsd ldrs: lft 3rd 2 out: wknd last* **40/1**

03/4 **6** *12* **Puyol (IRE)**[10] 13-11-5 87 .... MrBFurnival(7) 79
(Patricia Rigby) *in rr: sme hdwy 6th: hdwy 12th: wknd 4 out* **28/1**

2-UU **U** **Special Portrait (IRE)**[14] 290 11-11-9 109 ....(tp) MrRHogg(7)
(Mark Hughes) *in rr: 8th and outpcd whn hmpd and uns rdr 14th* **9/1**

222- **U** **Railway Dillon (IRE)**[25] 10-11-5 114 ....(p) MissETodd(7) 105+
(Mrs C Drury) *chsd ldrs: handy 3rd whn mstke and uns rdr 2 out* **4/1**[3]

F/3- **F** **Third Of The Third**[10] 8-11-12 0 .... MissGAndrews
(Gary Hanmer) *mstke 1st: bhd: hdwy 12th: 5th and keeping on whn fell 13th* **3/1**[2]

0-55 **P** **Stoney (IRE)**[13] 303 8-11-9 85 .... MrKitAlexander(3)
(Victor Thompson) *in rr: bhd fr 12th: t.o whn p.u bef 3 out* **33/1**

6m 49.8s (14.90) **Going Correction** +0.75s/f (Soft) **10** Ran SP% **117.1**
Speed ratings: **107,103,102,100,100 96,** , , ,
CSF £23.00 TOTE £4.20: £1.40, £2.20, £4.70; EX 31.90 Trifecta £238.20.
Owner Mrs Karen Bowen **Bred** Charlie Wyatt **Trained** Haverfordwest, Pembrokes

FOCUS
The rain had clearly got into the ground because the official going was changed to soft from good before this race. An ordinary hunter, rated around the winner, second, fourth and fifth.

507 ROWLEYS CATERING AT CARTMEL H'CAP HURDLE (8 hdls) 2m 1f 46y
5:00 (5:00) (Class 5) (0-100,100) 4-Y-O+ **£2,924** (£858; £429; £214)

Form RPR

533- **1** **Van Mildert (IRE)**[52] 5163 6-10-0 74 oh4 ....(p) HenryBrooke 80+
(Kenneth Slack) *chsd ldrs: led after 2 out: drvn out* **9/1**

06-F **2** *3* **Quest Magic (IRE)**[27] 37 9-11-7 100 ....(p) JonathonBewley(5) 101
(George Bewley) *led tl appr 2nd: led 3 out: hdd after next: kpt on same pce fnl f* **9/1**

454- **3** *1¾* **Sendiym (FR)**[16] 5495 8-11-3 91 ....(p) BrianHughes 90
(Dianne Sayer) *chsd ldrs: kpt on between last 2: tk 3rd nr fin* **9/1**

65-5 **4** *hd* **L Stig**[20] 180 5-11-5 93 .... JakeGreenall 93
(Henry Daly) *mid-div: chsd ldrs 3rd: 3rd last: kpt on same pce* **7/1**[2]

34-6 **5** *8* **Stanley Bridge**[15] 252 8-10-11 85 .... LucyAlexander 77
(Barry Murtagh) *in rr: hdwy 5th: one pce fr 2 out* **12/1**

36-4 **6** *11* **Rolling Dough (IRE)**[23] 106 7-11-2 90 ....(p) PaulMoloney 70
(Sophie Leech) *mid-div: hdwy 5th: wknd 2 out* **4/1**[1]

0-35 **7** *¾* **Bob's Legend (IRE)**[15] 252 9-11-6 94 ....(t) DougieCostello 80+
(Susan Corbett) *in rr: hdwy 3 out: 6th and styng on whn blnd bdly last: sn eased* **10/1**

B05- **8** *5* **Tinseltown**[11] 3132 9-11-12 100 ....(p) TomScudamore 74
(Brian Rothwell) *in rr-div: sme hdwy 5th: wknd next* **33/1**

06-0 **9** *10* **Snowed In (IRE)**[20] 157 6-11-12 100 ....(p) SeanQuinlan 64
(Barbara Butterworth) *in rr: nvr on terms* **8/1**

/05- **10** *26* **Teescomponents Max**[368] 440 6-11-2 90 .... JamesReveley 28
(Keith Reveley) *trckd ldrs: led appr 2nd: hdd 3 out: sn eased and bhd: t.o between last 2: virtually p.u: t.o* **15/2**[3]

4P0- **P** **So Bazaar (IRE)**[180] 2787 8-9-11 74 oh6 ....(t) HarryChalloner(3)
(Andrew Wilson) *in rr: bhd fr 4th: t.o whn p.u bef 2 out* **28/1**

20-4 **P** **Beyondtemptation**[18] 205 7-10-11 90 ....(t) DiarmuidO'Regan(5)
(Jonathan Haynes) *chsd ldrs: drvn 5th: sn lost pl: t.o whn p.u bef last* **16/1**

34-5 **P** **Lady Ra (IRE)**[9] 383 6-9-10 77 ow1 .... DeanPratt(7)
(Lucinda Egerton) *in rr: bhd fr 4th: t.o whn p.u bef 2 out* **14/1**

4m 21.0s (7.80) **Going Correction** +0.50s/f (Soft) **13** Ran SP% **121.1**
Speed ratings (Par 103): **102,100,99,99,96 91,91,88,84,72** , ,
CSF £89.14 TOTE £13.90: £4.40, £3.70, £2.50; EX 157.90 Trifecta £1334.80.
Owner Mrs Evelyn Slack **Bred** Chesters Stud Ltd **Trained** Hilton, Cumbria

FOCUS
A weak race. A big step up from the winner, while the second, third and fourth help set the level.

508 ENGLISH LAKES ICE CREAM CONDITIONAL JOCKEYS' H'CAP HURDLE (8 hdls) 2m 1f 46y
5:35 (5:35) (Class 4) (0-120,118) 4-Y-O+ **£3,573** (£1,049; £524; £262)

Form RPR

52-0 **1** **Morning With Ivan (IRE)**[27] 34 5-10-2 94 ....(v[1]) GrahamWatters 101+
(Martin Todhunter) *chsd ldr: led 3rd: drvn out* **5/1**[3]

401- **2** *2* **Gurkha Brave (IRE)**[44] 5315 7-11-7 113 .... GrantCockburn 117
(Karen McLintock) *in rr-div: hdwy 3 out: 3rd between last 2: kpt on to take 2nd last 150yds* **2/1**[1]

551- **3** *1¾* **Captain Brown**[67] 4909 7-11-12 118 .... NicodeBoinville 120
(James Moffatt) *hld up in rr: hdwy 5th: 2nd between last 2: kpt on same pce* **9/2**[2]

50P- **4** *19* **Endeavor**[33] 5516 10-10-5 97 ....(p) HarryChalloner 82
(Dianne Sayer) *chsd ldrs: 2nd 3 out: wknd between last 2* **20/1**

60-4 **5** *3¾* **Sleep In First (FR)**[27] 36 9-11-8 117 ....(t) DaleIrving(3) 96
(James Ewart) *led to 3rd: drvn and lost pl 4th: wl bhd fr 3 out* **14/1**

3U-3 **6** *nse* **Short Takes (USA)**[26] 59 7-10-13 111 ....(b) JamesCowley(6) 90
(Donald McCain) *trckd ldrs: 2nd 4th: wknd after 3 out* **10/1**

22- **7** *69* **Amilliontimes (IRE)**[202] 2297 7-10-13 110 ....(t) RyanDay(5) 20
(Jackie Stephen) *chsd ldrs: outpcd and pushed along 4th: bhd next: t.o 2 out: eventually completed* **6/1**

625- **P** **Scotsbrook Legend**[79] 4677 7-11-9 115 .... ConorShoemark
(Shaun Lycett) *racd in last: detached whn p.u bef 5th: lame* **8/1**

4m 23.3s (10.10) **Going Correction** +0.50s/f (Soft) **8** Ran SP% **114.1**
Speed ratings (Par 105): **97,96,95,86,85 85,54,**
CSF £15.84 CT £47.49 TOTE £6.60: £1.70, £1.50, £1.70; EX 19.60 Trifecta £75.90.
Owner Leslie Richards **Bred** J S Bolger **Trained** Orton, Cumbria

FOCUS
The best quality handicap on the card, the pace was sound and this is form to be reasonably positive about. A pb from the second, with the third rated to his mark.
T/Plt: £346.80 to a £1 stake. Pool: £55,515.27 - 116.84 winning units. T/Qpdt: £49.80 to a £1 stake. Pool: £5,057.92 - 75.04 winning units. **Walter Glynn**

387 NEWTON ABBOT (L-H)
Wednesday, May 27

OFFICIAL GOING: Good (good to firm in places; 6.9)
Wind: almost nil Weather: cloudy periods Rails: Chase bends moved out 2 metres, Hurdles bends moved inwards 2 metres.

509 AT THE RACES SKY 415 NOVICES' HURDLE (10 hdls) 2m 5f 122y
6:00 (6:00) (Class 4) 4-Y-O+ **£3,898** (£1,144; £572; £286)

Form RPR

P3-3 **1** **More Buck's (IRE)**[22] 122 5-11-0 116 ....(t) SamTwiston-Davies 110+
(Paul Nicholls) *mde all: rdn whn chal appr 2 out: outj. runner-up last: in command run-in* **6/5**[2]

44-1 **2** *2* **Towering (IRE)**[26] 61 6-11-3 0 .... JeremiahMcGrath(3) 118+
(Nicky Henderson) *trckd ldrs: rdn after 3 out: hung lft next: ev ch whn nt fluent last: hld after* **10/11**[1]

50-5 **3** *19* **Ofcoursewecan (USA)**[20] 168 5-11-0 82 .... TomCannon 89
(Mark Gillard) *pressed wnr tl rdn after 3 out: wknd next* **25/1**

33-4 **4** *10* **Pauls Conn (IRE)**[20] 160 6-11-0 102 ....(p) TomO'Brien 79
(Mary Sanderson) *trckd ldrs: rdn after 3 out: sn wknd* **14/1**[3]

0-U 5 *dist* **Hill Forts Gypse (IRE)**[20] 168 4-10-9 0...................... AndrewThornton
(Seamus Mullins) *hld up bhd ldrs: lost tch after 6th: t.o (btn 173 l)* **66/1**
5m 16.0s (-4.20) **Going Correction** -0.10s/f (Good)
WFA 4 from 5yo+ 19lb **5** Ran SP% **109.8**
Speed ratings (Par 105): **103,102,95,91,**
CSF £2.72 TOTE £1.70: £1.20, £1.10; EX 2.60 Trifecta £9.30.
Owner The Stewart Family **Bred** Philip Hore Jnr **Trained** Ditcheat, Somerset

FOCUS
Chase bends had been moved out 2 metres, while hurdle bends were in 2 metres. Impact on distances not notified. Between 20-40mm of irrigation had been applied in the days leading up to this meeting, which resulted in an official going description of good, good to firm in places. Sam Twiston-Davies confirmed it was riding as such after the first saying it was, "good ground, with a few quicker places." Essentially a match race to open the card. It's been rated around the balance of the first three.

510 SUNFLOWER DAY NURSERY H'CAP CHASE (16 fncs) 2m 4f 216y
6:30 (6:30) (Class 4) (0-115,121) 5-Y-0+ **£3,994** (£1,240; £667)

Form RPR
042- **1** **Perfect Timing**[262] 1466 7-11-7 **109**...................................(b) NoelFehily 132+
(Neil Mulholland) *trckd ldr: led after 9th: jnd briefly 4 out: clr next: styd on wl: comf* **9/4**[2]
16-2 **2** *13* **Moorlands Jack**[23] 109 10-11-11 **113**...........................(p) JamesDavies 122
(Jeremy Scott) *trckd ldrs: cl 3rd 4 out: sn rdn: chsd wnr fr after next but a being hld* **9/2**
32-2 **3** *29* **He's A Bully (IRE)**[25] 86 6-11-5 **107**.................... RichardJohnson 98
(Philip Hobbs) *led tl after 9th: pushed along after next: chalng whn nt fluent 4 out: sn rdn: wknd after next* **7/4**[1]
0/4 **P** **Darwins Theory (IRE)**[26] 64 7-10-12 **107**......................(t) MrMLegg[(7)]
(Fiona Shaw) *chsd ldng 4: nudged along fr 5th: mstke 9th: wknd after next: tailing off whn p.u bef 12th* **25/1**
1-21 **P** **Bang On Time (IRE)**[8] 390 9-11-12 **121** 7ex..................(p) PaulJohn[(7)]
(Richard Woollacott) *trckd ldrs: reminders after 9th: lost action whn p.u bef next: dismntd* **7/2**[3]
5m 12.6s (-8.80) **Going Correction** -0.25s/f (Good) **5** Ran SP% **111.4**
Speed ratings: **106,101,90, ,**
CSF £12.43 TOTE £2.60: £1.80, £3.40; EX 13.00 Trifecta £30.50.
Owner Hanham Boys Racing Partnership **Bred** Mrs J L Egan **Trained** Limpley Stoke, Wilts

FOCUS
An interesting, if modest, small field handicap chase. A step up from the winner for his new yard, but the form could be up to 5lb out either way.

511 INDEPENDENT RACECOURSES LIMITED, IRL NOVICES' HURDLE (8 hdls) 2m 167y
7:00 (7:00) (Class 4) 4-Y-0+ **£3,898** (£1,144; £572; £286)

Form RPR
1 **Tercel (IRE)**[23] 4-10-8 0...(t[1]) SamTwiston-Davies 107+
(Paul Nicholls) *racd keenly: mid-div: hdwy 5th: edgd lft whn ldng 2 out: sn qcknd clr: comf* **4/1**[3]
221- **2** *4* **Dry Ol'Party**[210] 2130 5-10-5 0...................................... RichardJohnson 98
(Philip Hobbs) *trckd ldr: led whn hit 3 out: hdd whn wnt lft next: sn outpcd by wnr* **13/8**[1]
005- **3** *4 ½* **Bogoss Du Perret (FR)**[99] 4283 4-10-8 0.................... JamesDavies 96
(Jimmy Frost) *mid-div: hdwy 5th: rdn in 3rd after 3 out: kpt on same pce fr next* **25/1**
65-5 **4** *7* **Sheer Poetry (IRE)**[20] 178 4-10-1 0.............................. PaddyBrennan 84
(Richard Woollacott) *trckd ldrs: rdn after 3 out: styd on same pce fr next: mstke last* **8/1**
/2-1 **5** *17* **Are They Your Own (IRE)**[17] 214 7-10-13 125.............. NickSlatter[(5)] 87
(Fergal O'Brien) *led: mstke and hdd 3 out: sn rdn: wknd after next* **9/4**[2]
P/ **6** *64* **Dance With Me (IRE)**[10] 6-10-12 0..................................... MarkGrant 12
(Jonathan Geake) *hld up: lost tch after 5th: t.o* **50/1**
0 **P** **Virgile De Gene (FR)**[8] 392 6-10-12 0.......................... TommyPhelan
(Nick Ayliffe) *t.o 3rd: p.u after next* **66/1**
40-0 **U** **Innox Park**[22] 124 5-10-12 0.. JamesBest
(Kevin Bishop) *nvr that fluent: j. bdly lft most of way: hld up: lost tch after 5th: t.o whn mstke and uns rdr 2 out* **12/1**
4m 1.9s (-3.80) **Going Correction** -0.10s/f (Good)
WFA 4 from 5yo+ 18lb **8** Ran SP% **115.0**
Speed ratings (Par 105): **104,102,100,96,88 58, ,**
CSF £11.29 TOTE £4.00: £1.50, £1.02, £7.50; EX 13.80 Trifecta £97.10.
Owner Owners Group 007 **Bred** Ballymacoll Stud Farm Ltd **Trained** Ditcheat, Somerset

FOCUS
A typical novice hurdle and they were quickly strung out. It's been rated around the bumper form of the second and the fourth's hurdle form for the time being.

512 ATTHERACES.COM NOVICES' CHASE (13 fncs) 2m 75y
7:30 (7:30) (Class 3) 5-Y-0+ **£6,498** (£1,908; £954; £477)

Form RPR
010- **1** **Dormello Mo (FR)**[46] 5276 5-10-12 0...................(t) SamTwiston-Davies 133+
(Paul Nicholls) *trckd ldr: nt fluent 5th: chal 3 out: led narrowly 2 out: hdd narrowly last: kpt on wl u.str.p to regain ld fnl 50yds: won gng away* **11/10**[1]
0P2- **2** *½* **Union Saint (FR)**[37] 5436 7-10-12 125.................. RichardJohnson 130
(Jimmy Frost) *hld up bhd ldrs: smooth hdwy after 4 out: chal 2 out: led narrowly last: sn drvn: no ex whn hdd fnl 50yds* **3/1**[2]
P02- **3** *3 ¾* **Minella Present (IRE)**[35] 5478 6-10-12 0......................... NoelFehily 127
(Neil Mulholland) *hld up bhd ldrs: tk clsr order after 8th: mounting chal whn nt fluent 3 out: swtchd lft whn coming wd turning in: 1 l 3rd whn hit 2 out: kpt on but nt pce of ldrs run-in* **3/1**[2]
5-P4 **4** *4* **Too Scoops (IRE)**[11] 332 8-10-12 0.............................(t) DarylJacob 122
(Richard Woollacott) *led: rchd for 1st: rdn and hrd pressed after 3 out: hdd next: sn no ex* **10/1**[3]
00P- **5** *46* **Chill (IRE)**[25] 3511 7-10-12 110...................................(bt) TomO'Brien 76
(Paul Henderson) *trckd ldr tl pushed along after 8th: detached in 5th whn nt fluent 4 out: wknd next: t.o* **33/1**
4m 3.2s (-3.30) **Going Correction** -0.25s/f (Good) **5** Ran SP% **109.7**
Speed ratings: **97,96,95,93,71**
CSF £4.92 TOTE £1.70: £1.10, £2.50; EX 4.80 Trifecta £8.40.
Owner The Kyle & Stewart Families **Bred** E A R L Haras Du Taillis & H Poulsen **Trained** Ditcheat, Somerset

FOCUS
A good novice chase for the time of year, there was four in a line jumping two out, and the form should hold up. The second and fourth set the level.

513 SIS STREAMING MARES' H'CAP HURDLE (10 hdls) 2m 5f 122y
8:00 (8:00) (Class 5) (0-100,98) 4-Y-0+ **£3,422** (£997; £499)

Form RPR
024- **1** **Midnight Sapphire**[58] 5060 5-11-9 **95**.............................. DenisO'Regan 101+
(Victor Dartnall) *j.lft thrght bdly at times: hld up: lft 4th at the 7th: rdn after 3 out: upsides whn wnt lft 2 out: 1/2 l down last: led sn after: drvn out* **5/1**[3]
P5-1 **2** *½* **Kentford Myth**[20] 172 5-11-9 **98**.......................... JeremiahMcGrath[(3)] 103+
(Seamus Mullins) *trckd ldrs: led 3 out: rdn whn jnd and hmpd 2 out: 1/2 l advantage whn blnd last: sn hdd: nt time to rcvr* **6/1**
P0-0 **3** *21* **Businessmoney Judi**[15] 265 9-10-10 **89**.......(t) MrMatthewHampton[(7)] 74
(Martin Hill) *trckd ldr: rdn to chal after 3 out tl bef next: wknd between last 2* **12/1**
0-P0 **4** *8* **Princess Annabelle**[8] 391 6-10-13 **85**.........................(p) JamesDavies 63
(Rod Millman) *hld up: hmpd 1st: rdn after 7th: wnt hld 4th after 3 out: nvr trbld ldrs* **28/1**
000- **5** *28* **Milan Of Crystal (IRE)**[25] 6-11-5 **91**................................. TomO'Brien 44
(Jimmy Frost) *led tl nt fluent 3 out: sn rdn: wknd bef next: t.o* **16/1**
00-3 **6** *2 ¼* **Ann's Lottery**[27] 30 9-11-6 **97**.................................. KieronEdgar[(5)] 48
(Tim Dennis) *dwlt: a in rr: reminders after 2nd: wknd after 7th: t.o* **3/1**[2]
P/P- **P** **Newnham Flyer (IRE)**[37] 5440 13-9-7 **72** oh15.(b) ThomasCheesman[(7)]
(Sarah Robinson) *chsd ldrs tl 4th: sn struggling: lost tch after 6th: p.u bef next* **100/1**
2-32 **F** **Midnight Sequel**[4] 443 6-11-3 **89**.................................(bt) NoelFehily
(Neil Mulholland) *trckd ldrs: travelling strly in cl 4th whn fell 7th* **6/4**[1]
5m 22.2s (2.00) **Going Correction** -0.10s/f (Good) **8** Ran SP% **114.0**
Speed ratings (Par 103): **92,91,84,81,71 70, ,**
CSF £34.63 CT £339.11 TOTE £5.70: £1.60, £3.40, £2.60; EX 30.80 Trifecta £416.40.
Owner Rod Harding **Bred** Mrs Suzanne Hooper **Trained** Brayford, Devon

FOCUS
A real moderate mares' handicap. Small steps up from the first two.

514 HADDEN FROST, THE NEXT CHAPTER H'CAP CHASE (13 fncs) 2m 75y
8:30 (8:30) (Class 4) (0-105,105) 5-Y-0+ **£3,898** (£1,144; £572; £286)

Form RPR
46-2 **1** **No No Cardinal (IRE)**[20] 170 6-10-0 **79** oh2................(t) TommyPhelan 90+
(Mark Gillard) *mid-div: hdwy 7th: led after 4 out: kpt on wl: rdn out* **9/1**
41F- **2** *3 ½* **The Bay Bandit**[51] 5307 8-11-9 **102**..............................(p) NoelFehily 110+
(Neil Mulholland) *mid-div: nt fluent 7th: hdwy after 4 out: chalng for 2nd whn hmpd 2 out: sn rdn: wnt 2nd jst bef last: kpt on but a being hld* **13/2**[3]
2P5- **3** *4 ½* **Maizy Missile (IRE)**[173] 2920 13-10-5 **84**......................... AdamWedge 86
(Mary Evans) *mid-div: rdn to chse ldrs after 4 out: nt pce to get on terms but styd on to go 3rd nring fin* **33/1**
32-1 **4** *nk* **All But Grey**[20] 170 9-11-9 **102**...........................(t) MichealNolan 105
(Carroll Gray) *hld up: hdwy fr 7th: rdn to chse wnr after 3 out: wnt lft and bmpd next: lost 2nd bef last: no ex whn lost 3rd nring fin* **5/1**[1]
2-03 **5** *3* **Archie Boy (IRE)**[15] 260 13-11-7 **103**........................ KillianMoore[(3)] 102
(Sophie Leech) *chsd ldrs: led 6th tl after 4 out: sn rdn: one pce fr next* **10/1**
50-3 **6** *3* **Regal D'Estruval (FR)**[20] 175 10-11-6 **99**........................ CharliePoste 96
(Matt Sheppard) *prom: led 5th tl after next: chsd ldrs: rdn after 4 out: one pce fr next* **9/1**
7 *24* **Truckin All Night (IRE)**[104] 4196 9-11-11 **104**................(t) DenisO'Regan 79
(Don Cantillon) *hld up: rdn after 4 out: nvr gng pce to get on terms: wknd after next: t.o* **11/2**[2]
-410 **8** *7* **Accessallareas (IRE)**[15] 258 10-11-9 **102**............(bt[1]) RichardJohnson 70
(Sarah-Jayne Davies) *chsd ldrs tl 4 out: sn wknd: t.o* **10/1**
425- **9** *24* **Long John**[81] 4626 8-11-12 **105**.. JamesBest 52
(Jackie Du Plessis) *struggling 7th: a towards rr: t.o* **10/1**
0F-6 **10** *90* **Siobhans Beauty (IRE)**[26] 57 7-11-9 **102**..................... GavinSheehan
(Jamie Snowden) *led tl 5th: chsd ldrs: rdn whn nt fluent 3 out: wknd bef next: t.o* **5/1**[1]
00-3 **P** **Positive Vibes**[20] 170 6-10-11 **90**...........................(p) DarylJacob
(Richard Woollacott) *mid-div tl dropped to last 6th: sn struggling: t.o whn p.u bef 4 out* **16/1**
4m 1.5s (-5.00) **Going Correction** -0.25s/f (Good) **11** Ran SP% **118.1**
Speed ratings: **101,99,97,97,95 94,82,79,68,26**
CSF £67.59 CT £1857.21 TOTE £12.30: £3.10, £2.70, £5.30; EX 78.20 Trifecta £1356.20.
Owner Mrs J V Wilkinson **Bred** Mrs Eleanor Hadden **Trained** Holwell, Dorset

FOCUS
A run-of-the-mill low grade handicap chase where the betting suggested it was wide open. A small pb from the winner, with the second and fourth rated to their marks.

515 NEWTONABBOTRACING.COM H'CAP HURDLE (8 hdls) 2m 167y
9:00 (9:00) (Class 5) (0-100,100) 4-Y-0+ **£3,422** (£997; £499)

Form RPR
32-3 **1** **Cruise In Style (IRE)**[9] 383 9-10-12 **86**.........................(tp) JamesBest 89+
(Kevin Bishop) *mid-div: hdwy after 3 out: gd run on inner appr next: led bef last: drifted rt: hld on: drvn out* **12/1**
62-2 **2** *nk* **Henry Oliver (IRE)**[20] 167 7-11-3 **91**.................(tp) RichardJohnson 95+
(Neil Mulholland) *mid-div: hdwy 5th: awkward 3 out: nt clr run sn after: rdn and r.o appr last: wnt 2nd run-in but a being jst hld* **2/1**[1]
0PC- **3** *1* **Chankillo**[37] 5435 6-10-11 **85**................................ SamTwiston-Davies 86
(Sarah-Jayne Davies) *racd keenly: trckd ldr: rdn and ev ch after 3 out tl after next: kpt on but no ex run-in* **14/1**
43-4 **4** *nk* **Ladies Dancing**[14] 281 9-11-5 **100**.........................(b) KevinJones[(7)] 103+
(Chris Down) *led: rdn whn nt fluent 2 out: sn hdd: kpt on but no ex run-in* **6/1**[2]
4-26 **5** *¾* **Mount Vesuvius (IRE)**[5] 435 7-11-2 **90**...........................(t) TomO'Brien 92
(Paul Henderson) *mid-div: short of room whn mstke 3rd: hdwy 3 out: sn rdn: kpt on same pce fr 2 out: dived at last* **6/1**[2]
40-5 **6** *5* **Ice Konig (FR)**[27] 32 6-11-5 **100**................................ PaulO'Brien[(7)] 98
(Jimmy Frost) *chsd ldr: rdn after 3 out: ev ch whn mstke 2 out: hld whn awkward last* **9/1**
00-3 **7** *2* **Theionlady (IRE)**[20] 164 5-10-6 **80**..............................(t) DarylJacob 74
(Richard Woollacott) *hld up: rdn and hdwy after 3 out: no further imp fr next* **8/1**[3]
30-0 **8** *16* **Sun Quest**[20] 167 11-10-3 **77**.....................................(t) JamieMoore 56
(Steven Dixon) *chsd ldrs tl wknd after 3 out* **20/1**
P5-4 **9** *5* **Candelita**[17] 217 8-11-5 **100**...................................... MrStanSheppard[(7)] 75
(Matt Sheppard) *mid-div: rdn after 3 out: sn wknd* **10/1**

06P- P Indian Jack (IRE)[51] 5212 7-11-8 96 AndrewThornton
(Seamus Mullins) *a towards rr: wknd after 3 out: p.u next* 25/1
4m 3.1s (-2.60) **Going Correction** -0.10s/f (Good) 10 Ran SP% **115.1**
Speed ratings (Par 103): **102,101,101,101,100 98,97,90,87,**
CSF £36.84 CT £350.86 TOTE £7.10: £1.90, £1.50, £4.00; EX 36.00 Trifecta £425.40.
Owner Steve Atkinson **Bred** Swordlestown Stud **Trained** Spaxton, Somerset

FOCUS

Most of these find winning difficult and not form to dwell on. A small pb from the second, with the fifth rated to his mark.
T/Plt: £104.40 to a £1 stake. Pool: £63,786.13 - 445.77 winning units. T/Qpdt: £52.80 to a £1 stake. Pool: £5,610.70 - 78.57 winning units. **Tim Mitchell**

415 WETHERBY (L-H)

Thursday, May 28

OFFICIAL GOING: Good (good to firm in places; chs 9.0, hdl 8.8)
Wind: fresh 1/2 behind Weather: fine but cool and breezy

516 WETHERBYRACING.CO.UK MARES' NOVICES' HURDLE 2m 3f 154y

5:40 (5:41) (Class 4) 4-Y-0+ £3,411 (£1,001; £500; £250)

Form RPR
43-1 1 Promanco[18] 219 6-11-5 122 (t) RichardJohnson 122+
(Charlie Longsdon) *hld up in rr: mstke 2nd: nt fluent 6th: hdwy to trck ldrs 8th: led appr next: nt fluent last: easily* 1/4[1]
2 5 Western Breeze (IRE) 6-10-12 0 JakeGreenall 103
(Mark Walford) *chsd ldrs: 3rd appr 3 out: kpt on to take modest 2nd last 100yds* 20/1[3]
33-4 3 1 1/4 Card Game (IRE)[21] 159 6-10-12 0 BrianHughes 102
(Malcolm Jefferson) *hld up: hdwy to trck ldrs 5th: 2nd appr 3 out: kpt on same pce run-in* 9/2[2]
4-P6 4 27 Miss H Lewiss[11] 361 7-10-5 92 DavidNoonan(7) 78
(Steve Flook) *chsd ldrs: drvn appr 3 out: sn outpcd: tk poor 4th last 50yds* 25/1
FP-0 5 4 Toola Boola[28] 34 5-10-12 74 HenryBrooke 78
(George Moore) *led: hdd appr 3 out: poor 4th whn j.lft last: wknd in clsng stages* 28/1
66-5 6 24 Strictly Glitz (IRE)[16] 254 4-10-4 0 AdamNicol(3) 48
(Mike Sowersby) *chsd ldr: drvn 8th: lost pl bef next: t.o 2 out* 100/1
06P- P Little Wren[46] 5293 6-10-7 0 DiarmuidO'Regan(5)
(Chris Grant) *nt fluent: sn bhd: hit 3rd: j.rt and drvn next: sn t.o: p.u bef 3 out* 100/1
4m 48.1s (-18.90) **Going Correction** -0.875s/f (Firm)
WFA 4 from 5yo+ 19lb 7 Ran SP% **112.2**
Speed ratings (Par 105): **101,99,98,88,86 77,**
CSF £8.26 TOTE £1.20: £1.10, £6.90; EX 8.10 Trifecta £16.70.
Owner Mrs S Tainton **Bred** Mrs Jane Haywood **Trained** Over Norton, Oxon

FOCUS

Course alignment same as Thursday May 21st, i.e shared bends at both ends and both on inside line. However A1 bend moved out 3yds. A very weak mares' novice hurdle. The easy winner stood out and the third has been rated in line with her bumper form.

517 JAMES & MADDY GETTING MARRIED 06JUNE2015 NOVICES' CHASE (16 fncs 2 omitted) 3m 1f

6:10 (6:10) (Class 4) 5-Y-0+ £4,223 (£1,240; £620)

Form RPR
163- 1 Rathlin Rose (IRE)[63] 4993 7-10-12 0 (b1) TomScudamore 139+
(David Pipe) *w ldr: nt fluent 3rd: led next: hdd 8th: led next: wnt wl clr bef 4 out: j.lft 2 out: 42 l ahd last: eased run-in* 4/7[1]
14-0 2 40 Rally[13] 319 6-10-12 0 (vt) SamTwiston-Davies 98
(Nigel Twiston-Davies) *racd in last: hit 6th and reminders: hrd drvn fr 8th: looked reluctant: reminders 11th: hit next: tk poor 2nd last 75yds* 13/8[2]
6-U6 3 4 1/2 Miss Tilly Oscar (IRE)[18] 215 9-9-12 91 (t) DavidNoonan(7) 85
(Steve Flook) *led to 4th: led 8th to next: drvn 12th: one pce and lost 2nd last 75yds* 20/1[3]
6m 4.3s (-5.10) **Going Correction** -0.575s/f (Firm) 3 Ran SP% **106.5**
Speed ratings: **85,72,70**
CSF £1.87 TOTE £1.60; EX 1.80 Trifecta £1.30.
Owner Stef Stefanou **Bred** Cyril O'Hara **Trained** Nicholashayne, Devon

FOCUS

This staying novice chase fell apart and the form looks best rated around the third. The second has been rated two stone off, and the third is probably a better guide to the level.

518 LIFE & STYLE NOVICES' HURDLE (13 hdls) 3m 26y

6:45 (6:45) (Class 4) 4-Y-0+ £3,494 (£1,085; £584)

Form RPR
21-2 1 Ballykan[18] 219 5-11-5 122 (t) SamTwiston-Davies 116
(Nigel Twiston-Davies) *mde all: reminders bef 4th: drivcen 6th: j.rt last: kpt on* 1/2[1]
22-1 2 2 1/4 Black Jack Rover (IRE)[16] 251 6-11-5 114 HenryBrooke 115
(Donald McCain) *trckd wnr: rdr briefly lost iron 3 out: upsides next: crowded and swtchd lft last: kpt on same pce* 7/4[2]
00-0 3 dist Garde Freinet (IRE)[12] 328 6-9-13 71 DavidNoonan(7)
(Steve Flook) *in rr: drvn 6th: tk distant 3rd bef 3 out: eventually completed* 66/1
PP-6 P Colonial Style (IRE)[28] 33 5-10-10 70 AdamNicol(3)
(George Moore) *chsd ldng pair: rdn and wknd 9th: sn t.o: p.u bef next* 40/1
P Raknruin (IRE)[37] 5455 5-10-6 0 MrWEasterby(7)
(Joanne Foster) *nt fluent 1st 2 and reminders: drvn 7th and lost pl: t.o 9th: p.u bef next* 28/1[3]
5m 50.2s (-26.30) **Going Correction** -0.875s/f (Firm) 5 Ran SP% **110.4**
Speed ratings (Par 105): **107,106, , ,**
CSF £1.74 TOTE £1.20: £1.10, £1.20; EX 1.50 Trifecta £9.00.
Owner Simon Munir & Isaac Souede **Bred** Donhead Stud **Trained** Naunton, Gloucs

FOCUS

This was a essentially match and so it played out. The first two have been rated to their marks.

519 YORKSHIRE POST MAGAZINE H'CAP CHASE (16 fncs 2 omitted) 2m 5f 75y

7:20 (7:20) (Class 4) (0-105,103) 5-Y-0+ £4,223 (£1,240; £620; £310)

Form RPR
P3-2 1 Everylasting (IRE)[26] 78 8-10-0 80 (b) CraigNichol(3) 90
(Rose Dobbin) *w ldr: led 12th: drvn rt out* 5/1[3]
005- 2 3/4 Drumlister (IRE)[32] 9-11-0 98 MrTGreenwood(7) 108
(Dianne Sayer) *chsd ldrs: 2nd 3 out: kpt on run-in* 16/1
4P-6 3 3 1/4 Pistol Basc (FR)[22] 140 11-10-4 84 TonyKelly(3) 90
(Rebecca Menzies) *trckd ldrs: 2nd appr 4 out: kpt on one pce fr 2 out* 16/1
512- 4 24 Shady Sadie (IRE)[171] 2996 8-10-4 84 (t) HarryChalloner(3) 69
(Rose Dobbin) *mid-div: hdwy 12th: handy 4th 4 out: wknd 2 out* 20/1
12-1 5 10 My Friend George[22] 140 9-11-1 92 (p) HenryBrooke 68
(Kenneth Slack) *prom: 5th whn hmpd after 12th: wknd appr 3 out* 7/2[1]
UP-4 6 1/2 Foot The Bill[12] 333 10-11-1 92 JamesReveley 67
(Patrick Holmes) *in rr: sme hdwy 12th: nvr on terms* 9/1
P2-2 7 19 Trillerin Minella (IRE)[11] 358 7-11-6 102 ConorRing(5) 60
(Graeme McPherson) *chsd ldrs: reminders 5th: lost pl 7th: bhd 9th* 9/2[2]
23-2 8 2 3/4 Roseville Cottage (IRE)[16] 255 8-11-7 98 (b) BrianHughes 54
(John Wade) *mid-div: drvn 9th: sn bhd* 10/1
5-41 9 19 Flash Tommie (IRE)[11] 365 7-11-7 101 7ex (p) JonathanEngland(3) 40
(Michael Appleby) *led to 12th: sn lost pl and bhd* 5/1[3]
UP-5 10 18 Silent Snow (IRE)[22] 140 10-10-1 85 (p) MrWHRReed(7) 7
(W T Reed) *in rr: drvn 8th: bhd next* 50/1
0P-6 P Takaatuf (IRE)[7] 416 9-10-5 87 (t) StephenMulqueen(5)
(Tina Jackson) *in rr: bhd 12th: t.o whn p.u bef next* 50/1
00-P P Nobunaga[23] 134 10-11-5 103 (v) JamieHamilton(7)
(Andrew Hamilton) *in rr: bhd and rdn 8th: t.o whn p.u bef 4 out* 50/1
3PP- P Lord Redsgirth (IRE)[62] 5014 10-10-10 90 (p) AdamNicol(3)
(Lucy Normile) *nt jump wl: chsd ldrs: j. slowly 2nd: mstke and lost pl 3rd: sn bhd: t.o whn p.u bef 10th* 20/1
P0-0 P Jimmie Brown (USA)[28] 34 7-10-0 77 oh13 JamieBargary(7)
(Andrew Crook) *mid-div: sme hdwy 9th: lost pl 11th: t.o whn p.u bef 3 out* 33/1
5m 21.7s (-15.30) **Going Correction** -0.575s/f (Firm) course record 14 Ran SP% **122.9**
Speed ratings: **103,102,101,93,89 89,83,82,75,69 , , ,**
CSF £73.76 CT £1202.08 TOTE £8.00: £2.50, £4.50, £5.00; EX 143.60 Trifecta £1198.30.
Owner Miss C L Jones **Bred** Mr And Mrs Luke And Aileen Duggan **Trained** South Hazelrigg, Northumbria

FOCUS

A wide-open looking handicap, run at a decent gallop. The principals dominated in the home straight. A small pb from the winner, with the third 4lb off his best.

520 BE THE BEST DRESSED LADY H'CAP HURDLE (8 hdls 1 omitted) 2m

7:55 (7:55) (Class 4) (0-120,115) 4-Y-0+ £3,593 (£1,047; £523)

Form RPR
34-5 1 Politeness (FR)[22] 142 6-10-10 102 CraigNichol(3) 105
(Rose Dobbin) *mid-div: hdwy 6th: led appr last: drvn out* 8/1
334- 2 2 1/2 Knight In Purple[34] 5508 11-11-12 115 (vt) TomScudamore 115
(John Mackie) *w ldr: edgd lft omitted 2 out: kpt on same pce run-in* 13/2[3]
0-25 3 nk Peters Grey (IRE)[14] 301 5-11-7 110 RichardJohnson 110
(R Mike Smith) *hld up in rr: hdwy normal 3 out: 3rd last: kpt on same pce* 9/2[2]
/65- 4 1 3/4 King's Realm (IRE)[23] 3275 8-10-12 104 JonathanEngland(3) 102
(Tina Jackson) *in rr: outpcd normal 3 out: hdwy between last 2: styd on wl to take 4th post* 33/1
6-12 5 shd Cut The Corner (IRE)[7] 418 7-11-7 115 ChrisWard(5) 113
(Dr Richard Newland) *trckd ldrs: t.k.h: drvn normal 3 out: hung lft and one pce appr last* 5/4[1]
06-6 6 1/2 Hunters Belt (IRE)[17] 82 11-11-4 112 (bt) JonathonBewley(5) 111
(George Bewley) *led: bmpd omitted 2 out: sn hdd: one pce* 25/1
34-3 7 hd Walser (IRE)[26] 82 8-11-4 107 (b) BrianHughes 105
(John Wade) *chsd ldrs: hit 3rd: hung rt and one pce bef last* 10/1
4/0- 8 3 3/4 Cheshire Prince[359] 571 11-11-9 112 (t) TrevorWhelan 107
(Neil King) *trckd ldrs: wknd and eased last 100yds* 20/1
30-0 9 15 Ever So Much (IRE)[21] 157 6-11-4 107 (p) AndrewTinkler 88
(Ben Haslam) *in rr: nt fluent 4th: drvn and sme hdwy normal 3 out: lost pl omitted 2 out: eased whn bhd* 20/1
10-F F Stentorian (IRE)[6] 142 7-10-8 97 (v) DougieCostello
(Linda Perratt) *in rr: fell 2nd* 20/1
3m 42.6s (-13.20) **Going Correction** -0.875s/f (Firm) course record 10 Ran SP% **117.2**
Speed ratings (Par 105): **96,94,94,93,93 93,93,91,84,**
CSF £53.23 CT £265.73 TOTE £10.40: £3.00, £3.00, £2.30; EX 62.90 Trifecta £435.60.
Owner Mr & Mrs Duncan Davidson **Bred** R Monnier, Wertheimer Et Frere, Et Al **Trained** South Hazelrigg, Northumbria

FOCUS

A competitive handicap, rated around the veteran runner-up. A pb from the winner, while the second, third and sixth help set the level.

521 DOWNLOAD YOUR RACING UK APP OPEN HUNTERS' CHASE (14 fncs 2 omitted) 2m 3f 85y

8:25 (8:28) (Class 6) 5-Y-0+ £1,152 (£354; £177)

Form RPR
31-1 1 Drom[16] 260 12-12-1 117 MrNOrpwood(7) 118+
(Mrs C Drury) *mde all: kpt on wl run-in* 9/4[2]
3F3/ 2 2 Opera Og (IRE)[26] 9-11-7 0 MrSMurray(7) 110+
(Sean Murray) *prom: mstke and rdr temporarily lost iron 7th: hdwy 10th: trcking ldrs next: upsides 2 out: kpt on same pce run-in* 2/1[1]
/P5- 3 15 Son Of Flicka[12] 11-11-7 122 (b1) MrMJohnson(7) 94
(C Rae) *chsd ldrs: j.lft 2 out: sn wknd* 8/1[3]
4P-P 4 12 Know The Rules (IRE)[12] 10-11-11 75 (p) MrCDawson(3) 84
(Mrs G Smith) *chsd ldrs: outpcd 3 out: sn wknd: mstke last* 16/1
U3-P 5 10 Hidden Future (IRE)[22] 151 9-11-7 97 MrRichardCollinson(7) 73
(Mrs S J Stilgoe) *prom: lost pl 9th: sn bhd and drvn: distant 5th last* 12/1
00/- 6 3 1/4 Larkhall[12] 8-11-7 0 MrRLindsay(7) 70
(Mrs M Sowersby) *prom: outpcd after 10th: hit 3 out: sn bhd* 33/1
7 22 Silver O'Reilly[33] 9-11-7 0 MrDerekSmith(7) 50
(Mrs K M Diggle) *chsd ldrs: lost pl 8th: bhd fr 10th* 66/1
1FP- 8 20 Viking Ridge (IRE)[12] 8-11-11 115 MissSLKlug(7) 36
(Miss S L Klug) *in rr: blnd 1st: bhd fr 7th: t.o 10th* 10/1
431/ P Keki Buku (FR)[18] 12-12-0 0 MissCWalton
(I M Mason) *in rr: bhd fr 9th: t.o whn p.u bef 2 out* 8/1[3]
40P/ P Blackthirteen (IRE)[12] 11-11-7 0 MissJGillam(7)
(Michael B Jones) *mid-div: outpcd and lost pl bef 4 out: bhd whn p.u bef 2 out* 16/1
4m 54.3s (-13.50) **Going Correction** -0.575s/f (Firm) 10 Ran SP% **119.3**
Speed ratings: **102,101,95,90,87 85,77,69, ,**
CSF £7.75 TOTE £3.30: £1.20, £1.20, £2.80; EX 6.70 Trifecta £20.50.
Owner Paul Drury **Bred** Miss Ellen Delaney **Trained** Sheriff Hutton, N Yorks

FOCUS
Straightforward hunter chase form. The first two set a fair standard and have been rated close to their marks.

522 RACING UK ANYWHERE H'CAP HURDLE 2m 3f 154y
8:55 (8:57) (Class 5) (0-100,97) 4-Y-0+ **£2,599** (£763; £381; £190)

Form RPR
550- **1** **Craigdancer (IRE)**[41] 5379 6-10-11 **82**........................[1] DougieCostello 88+
(Joanne Foster) *in rr: detached and reminders 5th: hdwy 8th: 4th whn mstke 2 out: styd on run-in: led nr fin* **16/1**
36/2 **2** *nk* **Miss Macnamara (IRE)**[21] 157 6-11-4 **89**........................ BrianHarding 96+
(Martin Todhunter) *prom: upsides whn hmpd by loose horse 3 out and appr next: led 2 out: hdd and no ex in clsng stages* **3/1**[1]
55-0 **3** *3 ¼* **Prince Of Pirates (IRE)**[21] 153 10-11-12 **97**..............(b) AndrewTinkler 100
(Ben Haslam) *hld up in rr: hdwy 8th: trcking ldrs next: 2nd 2 out: kpt on same pce run-in* **8/1**
PP-P **4** *4* **Cumbrian Farmer**[26] 78 8-10-2 **80**..................(v[1]) MissJWalton(7) 79
(George Bewley) *chsd ldrs: led briefly appr 3 out: kpt on one pce: tk 4th nr fin* **33/1**
6P-4 **5** *nk* **New Youmzain (FR)**[28] 37 6-10-9 **85**............ GrantCockburn(5) 84
(Lucy Normile) *trckd ldrs: led 3 out: hdd next: fdd run-in* **9/2**[3]
06-5 **6** *3 ¾* **Pegasus Walk (IRE)**[22] 139 6-10-4 **78**................ CraigNichol(3) 73
(Rose Dobbin) *mid-div: drvn to chse ldrs 3 out: wknd appr last* **8/1**
03-5 **7** *11* **Park House**[23] 132 6-11-10 **95**............................. AndrewThornton 80
(Ray Craggs) *chsd ldrs: wknd between last 2* **33/1**
P-P **8** *3* **Agent Louise**[8] 398 7-10-6 **80**..................................(b[1]) AdamNicol(3) 62
(Mike Sowersby) *mid-div: hit 7th: hdwy next: wknd 2 out* **20/1**
034- **9** *3 ¾* **Saver**[210] 2153 6-11-12 **97**...(t) SamTwiston-Davies 76
(Nigel Twiston-Davies) *nt fluent in rr: hdwy 8th: rdn to chse ldrs next: sn lost pl* **16/1**
54-P **10** *28* **Tennessee Bird**[28] 37 7-10-3 **74**.................................. GavinSheehan 27
(Mike Sowersby) *t.k.h: led after 2nd: hdd 6th: drvn to ld 8th: hdd appr next: lost pl and eased 2 out: t.o* **9/1**
1/0- **11** *8* **Exit To Freedom**[365] 506 9-10-1 **79**...............................(p) GLavery(7) 25
(John Wainwright) *led tl after 2nd: led 6th tl 8th: lost pl appr next: sn bhd: heavily eased run-in: t.o* **40/1**
62-1 **U** **Danceintothelight**[5] 37 8-11-5 **97**............................(t) JamieBargary(7)
(Micky Hammond) *mid-div: mstke and uns rdr 2nd* **4/1**[2]
4m 47.2s (-19.80) **Going Correction** -0.875s/f (Firm) **12 Ran SP% 120.3**
Speed ratings (Par 103): **102,101,100,99,99 97,93,92,90,80 77,**
CSF £64.03 CT £431.85 TOTE £17.50: £2.80, £1.20, £3.10; EX 81.40 Trifecta £472.20.
Owner The Chessy Millers **Bred** Sean Culleton **Trained** Menston, W Yorks

FOCUS
This weak handicap saw the field strung out early, but the field bunched up turning for home. The first three have been rated pretty much to their marks.
T/Plt: £39.00 to a £1 stake. Pool of £43565.03 - 815.41 winning tickets. T/Qpdt: £19.20 to a £1 stake. Pool of £4832.05 - 185.57 winning tickets. **Walter Glynn**

429 WORCESTER (L-H)
Thursday, May 28
OFFICIAL GOING: Good (good to firm in places)
Wind: Light behind Weather: Cloudy with sunny spells

523 LADBROKES H'CAP CHASE (16 fncs) 2m 7f
2:10 (2:10) (Class 4) (0-120,121) 5-Y-0+ **£4,223** (£1,240; £620; £310)

Form RPR
41-3 **1** **Greenlaw**[18] 215 9-11-4 **112**...(t) NoelFehily 130+
(Charlie Longsdon) *led: hit 4th: j.rt next: hdd 7th: chsd ldr: led again 3 out: drvn out* **8/1**
325- **2** *6* **Guiding George (IRE)**[37] 5450 7-11-12 **120**..............(tp) HarrySkelton 132
(Dan Skelton) *chsd ldrs: led 10th: rdn and hdd 3 out: styd on same pce last* **5/2**[1]
32-1 **3** *20* **Fond Memory (IRE)**[21] 174 7-11-9 **117**...............(t) SamTwiston-Davies 114
(Nigel Twiston-Davies) *hld up: hdwy 12th: sn rdn: wnt 3rd and wknd 4 out* **7/2**[2]
22-4 **4** *38* **Bertie's Desire**[27] 62 7-11-4 **112**................................. LeightonAspell 72
(Oliver Sherwood) *prom: mstke 8th: sn pushed along: wknd appr 12th* **9/1**
32-2 **5** *41* **Vikekhal (FR)**[18] 226 6-11-4 **112**.................................... JamieMoore 35
(Gary Moore) *hld up: hdwy 8th: rdn after 12th: wknd bef next* **10/1**
P/0- **P** **Grouse Lodge (IRE)**[36] 5472 9-11-8 **116**.................. WayneHutchinson
(Donald McCain) *hld up: pushed along after 8th: wknd bef next: bhd whn p.u bef 4 out* **20/1**
2-1P **P** **The Happy Warrior**[8] 403 7-10-7 **101**.................................(p) LiamHeard
(Bob Buckler) *chsd wnr 2nd: led 7th: hdd 10th: rdn and wknd appr 12th: bhd whn p.u bef next* **28/1**
2P3- **P** **American Legend (IRE)**[44] 5334 7-11-8 **116**.............(v) RichieMcLernon
(Jonjo O'Neill) *prom: pushed along 11th: wknd after next: bhd whn p.u bef 4 out* **11/2**[3]
U20- **P** **King Boru (IRE)**[81] 4648 7-11-12 **120**...........................(v[1]) GavinSheehan
(Emma Lavelle) *hld up: a in rr: bhd whn hit 5th: sn rdn: lost tch after 8th: bhd whn p.u bef 10th* **14/1**
5m 53.6s (5.60) **Going Correction** +0.40s/f (Soft) **9 Ran SP% 111.3**
Speed ratings: **106,103,96,83,69 , , ,**
CSF £27.96 CT £80.45 TOTE £8.30: £1.90, £1.90, £1.60; EX 33.00 Trifecta £118.80.
Owner Simon and June Cadzow **Bred** Mrs J Cadzow **Trained** Over Norton, Oxon

FOCUS
Far bend 20yds from innermost position and the Cathedral bend 3yds from the inner for half the bend. 2m races increased by about 52yds and 2m 4f and 2m 7f by 111yds. The ground was on the fast side of good despite 6mm of water being put on the track in the morning. This looked quite a competitive heat on paper and the form could be useful, the front two coming clear of a previous winner who isn't fully exposed over staying trips. A big step up from the winner, with the third rated 8lb off his recent C&D win.

524 LADBROKES NOVICES' H'CAP CHASE (13 fncs) 2m 4f
2:40 (2:40) (Class 5) (0-100,98) 5-Y-0+ **£2,885** (£1,049)

Form RPR
20-P **1** **Minella Web (IRE)**[29] 13 6-11-10 **96**................................(t) DarylJacob 103+
(Richard Woollacott) *a.p: led 3 out: jnd whn lft wl clr last* **6/1**[3]
P-36 **2** *55* **The Kvilleken**[17] 237 7-11-2 **91**................................(b) ConorShoemark(3) 49
(Martin Keighley) *j.rt: chsd ldrs: led 3rd: clr after 5th tl 9th: rdn and hdd 4 out: wknd next: lft remote 2nd last* **12/1**
16-5 **P** **River Dancing (IRE)**[27] 65 8-10-7 **79**...........................(t) AidanColeman
(Anthony Honeyball) *hld up: rdn and wknd after 9th: bhd whn p.u bef 4 out* **4/1**[1]
60-3 **P** **Taroum (IRE)**[21] 167 8-11-5 **91**.......................................(tp) TomO'Brien
(John Flint) *prom: lost pl 4th: rdn and wknd after 7th: bhd whn p.u bef 3 out* **12/1**
03P- **U** **Adios Alonso (IRE)**[231] 1813 9-10-9 **84**............................ BenPoste(3) 84
(Rosemary Gasson) *prom: chsd ldr 3rd tl led 4 out: hdd next: styng on same pce whn lft 2nd: hmpd and uns rdr last* **20/1**
322- **F** **June French (FR)**[34] 5522 7-10-10 **82**..............................(p) NoelFehily 87
(Neil Mulholland) *hld up: hdwy 9th: chsd wnr 2 out: rdn and ev ch whn fell last* **6/1**[3]
34-P **P** **Definitely Better (IRE)**[26] 88 7-11-6 **92**....................... PaddyBrennan
(Tom George) *hld up: a in rr: bhd fr 6th: p.u bef 4 out* **11/1**
4F-4 **P** **Wish In A Well (IRE)**[15] 284 6-11-12 **98**........................(tp) KielanWoods
(Ben Case) *hld up: hit 5th: hdwy next: rdn and wknd 8th: bhd whn p.u bef 4 out* **20/1**
614- **P** **Seacon Beg (IRE)**[37] 5452 6-11-11 **97**.................(t) SamTwiston-Davies
(Nigel Twiston-Davies) *prom: rdn appr 4 out: sn wknd: blnd next: sn p.u* **5/1**[2]
/4-P **P** **Vauban Du Seuil (FR)**[22] 150 6-11-7 **96**....................... KillianMoore(3)
(Alex Hales) *hld up: drvn along 7th: sn wknd: bhd whn p.u bef 4 out* **50/1**
/00- **P** **Wilde And Willing (IRE)**[67] 4942 7-10-10 **82**.............. AndrewThornton
(Seamus Mullins) *hld up: led and hit 1st: sn hdd: lost pl 4th: wknd after 6th: bhd whn p.u bef 4 out* **25/1**
666- **P** **Routine Procedure (IRE)**[72] 4827 5-11-9 **95**..................(t) CharliePoste
(Robin Dickin) *led after 1st: j.rt next: hdd 3rd: wknd after 7th: bhd whn p.u bef 4 out* **16/1**
30-4 **P** **Come On Harriet**[23] 130 6-11-5 **94**...............................(t) JamesBanks(3)
(Alex Hales) *hld up: wknd 7th: bhd whn p.u bef 4 out* **25/1**
005- **F** **Edgar (GER)**[144] 3528 5-11-3 **94**..................................... JakeHodson(5) 89
(David Bridgwater) *hld up: hdwy 6th: rdn and wknd after 2 out: lft 10 l 2nd whn fell last* **40/1**
5m 15.3s (15.30) **Going Correction** +0.40s/f (Soft) **14 Ran SP% 116.5**
Speed ratings: **85,63, , , , , , , ,**
CSF £64.74 TOTE £6.10: £3.60, £6.90; EX 87.80.
Owner R M Harvey-Bailey **Bred** Noel Doyle **Trained** South Molton, Devon

FOCUS
It's not often 14 horses set off for a handicap chase on a sound surface and only two finish, but that's exactly what happened here, with three coming to grief at the final fence. A small step up on last year's course run from the winner.

525 LADBROKES STANDARD NATIONAL HUNT FLAT RACE (CONDITIONAL JOCKEYS' AND AMATEUR RIDERS' RACE) (DIV I) 2m
3:10 (3:11) (Class 6) 4-6-Y-0 **£1,559** (£457; £228; £114)

Form RPR
1 **Last Summer** 4-10-7 0.. MrAlexFerguson(7) 108+
(John Ferguson) *hld up: hdwy over 3f out: led over 1f out: r.o* **15/8**[2]
053- **2** *5* **Bendomingo (IRE)**[40] 5402 4-10-7 0.........................(t) JamieBargary(7) 101+
(Nigel Twiston-Davies) *led: rdn over 2f out: hdd over 1f out: styd on same pce ins fnl f* **6/1**[3]
3 *10* **Marquis Of Carabas (IRE)**[149] 5-10-13 0......................... KieronEdgar(5) 95
(David Dennis) *prom: chsd ldr over 6f out: ev ch over 2f out: sn rdn: wknd over 1f out* **11/1**
4- **4** *½* **Officer Hoolihan**[194] 2502 5-10-11 0............................... AlanJohns(7) 95
(Tim Vaughan) *trckd ldrs: rdn over 2f out: wknd over 1f out* **8/1**
60- **5** *7* **St Quintin**[44] 5331 5-10-13 0....................................... JackSherwood(5) 88
(David Brown) *w ldr over 5f: rdn over 5f out: wknd over 3f out* **20/1**
6 *1 ½* **New Providence (FR)** 4-11-0 0..................................... NicodeBoinville 83
(Nicky Henderson) *chsd ldrs: rdn over 3f out: wknd 2f out* **7/4**[1]
7 *shd* **Asian Ali (IRE)**[40] 6-10-11 0... MrRyanBird(7) 87
(Richard Lee) *s.s: a in rr* **33/1**
3m 43.9s (2.20) **Going Correction** +0.40s/f (Soft)
WFA 4 from 5yo+ 4lb **7 Ran SP% 112.6**
Speed ratings: **110,107,102,102,98 98,97**
CSF £13.16 TOTE £3.10: £1.70, £3.00; EX 16.30 Trifecta £60.90.
Owner Bloomfields **Bred** Darley **Trained** Cowlinge, Suffolk

FOCUS
Probably no better than ordinary summer bumper form. It's been rated around the balance of the second, fourth and fifth.

526 LADBROKES STANDARD NATIONAL HUNT FLAT RACE (CONDITIONAL JOCKEYS' AND AMATEUR RIDERS' RACE) (DIV II) 2m
3:40 (3:40) (Class 6) 4-6-Y-0 **£1,559** (£457; £228; £114)

Form RPR
64- **1** **Blackdown Hills**[185] 2717 5-10-4 0.. MrFTett(7) 95+
(Mark Bradstock) *a.p: chsd ldr over 3f out: rdn and ev ch whn lft in ld over 1f out: styd on* **7/1**[3]
2 *1 ¼* **Deshan (GER)** 4-10-7 0... MrBGibbs(7) 100+
(Tim Vaughan) *a.p: led over 4f out: rdn and slt ld whn swvd lft and nrly uns rdr over 1f out: sn hdd: rallied fnl 100yds: styd on* **13/8**[1]
U00- **3** *18* **My Diamond (IRE)**[47] 5285 4-10-11 0............................ MattGriffiths(3) 78
(Laura Young) *hld up: hdwy over 5f out: rdn over 2f out: wknd wl over 1f out* **50/1**
4 **4** *6* **Battle Master**[18] 220 5-11-1 0.. BenPoste(3) 76
(Michael Mullineaux) *led: rdn and hdd over 4f out: wknd over 2f out* **17/2**
0/ **5** *11* **Thyne River (IRE)**[460] 4417 5-10-11 0..........................(t) MichealNolan 59
(Robert Stephens) *hld up: hdwy over 4f out: wknd over 2f out* **14/1**
2- **6** *39* **Meyrem Ana**[39] 5417 5-10-4 0.. MrFFairchild(7) 24
(Natalie Lloyd-Beavis) *chsd ldr: wnt upsides 10f out tl rdn over 4f out: wknd over 3f out* **25/1**
5 **7** *53* **Defiant Dazzler (IRE)**[18] 220 6-10-11 0.............................. MrJNixon(7)
(Lady Susan Brooke) *chsd ldrs: rdn over 6f out: wknd over 4f out* **50/1**
P **Vabinsaru (FR)** 4-10-11 0.. MauriceLinehan(3)
(Jonjo O'Neill) *hld up: pushed along 1/2-way: wknd 6f out: bhd whn swvd rt over 4f out: sn p.u* **15/8**[2]
3m 50.7s (9.00) **Going Correction** +0.40s/f (Soft)
WFA 4 from 5yo+ 4lb **8 Ran SP% 110.3**
Speed ratings: **93,92,83,80,74 55,28,**
CSF £17.49 TOTE £8.10: £2.10, £1.10, £8.30; EX 18.80 Trifecta £516.10.
Owner Mrs P De W Johnson **Bred** P J Williams **Trained** Letcombe Bassett, Oxon

FOCUS
An eventful conclusion to this steadily-run bumper with Deshan seemingly blowing his chance when swerving to his right a furlong from home. The time was slow compared to the other division.

527 LADBROKES CLAIMING HURDLE (10 hdls) 2m 4f
4:10 (4:12) (Class 5) 4-Y-0+ £2,274 (£667; £333; £166)

Form RPR
11-0 **1** **Tanerko Emery (FR)**[13] 317 9-11-9 142......(t) SeanBowen(3) 134+
(Peter Bowen) *a.p: chsd ldr appr 3 out: led bef last: rdn out* **5/6[1]**
201- **2** *8* **Stow**[66] 4957 10-11-2 107......(b) TomCannon 115
(Michael Blake) *led: rdn and hdd appr last: no ex flat* **12/1**
04-2 **3** *11* **Man Of Leisure**[11] 356 11-11-5 123......(t) HarryCobden(7) 116
(Anthony Honeyball) *hld up: hdwy 7th: rdn appr 3 out: wkng whn mstke last* **3/1[2]**
212- **4** *3/4* **Macarthur**[251] 1573 11-11-4 115......(p) PaulMoloney 107
(David Rees) *hld up: hdwy 6th: rdn appr 3 out: wknd bef last* **12/1**
6-11 **5** *10* **Barneys Honour (IRE)**[7] 416 11-10-7 120......(p) MissBHampson(7) 93
(Andy Turnell) *chsd ldr tl rdn appr 3 out: wknd bef next* **9/2[3]**
0PP- **6** *48* **American World (FR)**[36] 5463 11-10-5 77...... MissLBrooke(7) 48
(Lady Susan Brooke) *prom: mstke 1st: rdn and wknd after 7th* **150/1**
P5 **7** *9* **Bach To Before (IRE)**[7] 416 7-11-0 0...... DougieCostello 42
(Tom Gretton) *hld up: rdn and wknd 7th* **80/1**
/P-P **P** **Exiles Return (IRE)**[9] 391 13-11-2 64...... JamesDavies
(Jackie Retter) *hld up: rdn and wknd after 5th: bhd whn p.u bef 3 out* **200/1**
0P-0 **P** **Bermuda Boy (FR)**[9] 393 10-10-12 107......(t) NoelFehily
(Steve Flook) *prom to 7th: bhd whn p.u bef next* **25/1**
P0-P **P** **Quintano (GER)**[22] 150 7-10-12 85......(tp) RichieMcLernon
(Heather Dalton) *hld up: nt fluent 1st: pushed along 5th: rdn and mstke 7th: sn wknd: bhd whn p.u bef next* **100/1**

5m 2.8s (15.40) **Going Correction** +0.40s/f (Soft) **10** Ran SP% **120.4**
Speed ratings (Par 103): **85,81,77,77,73 53,50, , ,**
CSF £13.72 TOTE £2.20: £1.20, £1.80, £1.20; EX 18.10 Trifecta £56.70.Stow was claimed by J Hughes for £5000. Tanerko Emery was claimed by A Turnell for £10000.
Owner Walters Plant Hire Ltd Egan Waste Ltd **Bred** Nicolas Taudon & Jean Taudon **Trained** Little Newcastle, Pembrokes

FOCUS
The winner stood out in this grade. The winner has been rated in line with his latest Aintree run.

528 LADBROKES MAIDEN HURDLE (8 hdls) 2m
4:40 (4:40) (Class 5) 4-Y-0+ £2,599 (£763; £381; £190)

Form RPR
524- **1** **Gioia Di Vita**[133] 3690 5-11-0 116...... WillKennedy 122+
(Dr Richard Newland) *chsd ldr tl led 4th: shkn up flat: r.o: comf* **7/4[1]**
0- **2** *8* **Eardisland**[38] 5439 5-10-7 0...... TomO'Brien 105
(Philip Hobbs) *chsd ldrs: nt fluent 1st: ev ch fr 3 out tl rdn appr last: no ex flat* **14/1**
0- **3** *13* **Rushvale (IRE)**[48] 5255 6-10-7 0...... MrMJPKendrick(7) 100
(Ben Case) *hld up: styd on fr 2 out: wnt 3rd flat: nvr nr to chal* **15/2[3]**
2 **4** *1 1/4* **Proofreader**[21] 171 6-11-0 0......[1] NoelFehily 100
(Neil Mulholland) *led: j.lft 1st: mstke and hdd 4th: remained handy tl wknd 2 out* **7/4[1]**
5 *15* **Gallic Destiny (IRE)**[287] 4-10-7 0......(t) JamesBanks(3) 81
(Jo Davis) *mid-div: effrt appr 3 out: wknd bef next* **16/1**
2-6 **6** *54* **Loch Garman (FR)**[21] 160 4-10-10 0...... JamesBest 33
(Nigel Hawke) *chsd ldrs: mstke 3rd: rdn and wknd appr 3 out* **7/1[2]**
P0-6 **7** *18* **Thymeandthymeagain**[21] 171 6-10-7 0...... DaveCrosse 14
(Hugo Froud) *hld up: wknd 5th* **100/1**
8 *30* **Foursquare Funtime**[31] 6-10-7 0......(t) JoshWall(7)
(Trevor Wall) *hld up: mstke 1st: wknd 5th* **100/1**
P **Bison Grass**[23] 5-11-0 0...... JackQuinlan
(Giles Bravery) *mid-div: wknd 4th: bhd whn j. slowly 3 out: sn p.u* **50/1**
400- **U** **Feisty Girl**[67] 4941 5-10-4 0...... BenPoste(3)
(Michael Mullineaux) *hld up: wknd 5th: bhd whn j.lft and uns rdr 3 out* **66/1**

3m 51.6s (4.30) **Going Correction** +0.40s/f (Soft)
WFA 4 from 5yo+ 18lb **10** Ran SP% **115.0**
Speed ratings (Par 103): **105,101,94,93,86 59,50,35, ,**
CSF £29.57 TOTE £3.30: £1.10, £3.10, £2.30; EX 25.60 Trifecta £164.20.
Owner Mark Albon & Chris Stedman **Bred** Hyphen Bloodstock **Trained** Claines, Worcs

FOCUS
This looked potentially quite a useful little maiden hurdle for the time of year but with the market leader proving disappointing and several of these racing keenly, it might prove only ordinary form. The winner has been rated in line with the best of last season's Flat turf form.

529 LADBROKES H'CAP HURDLE (10 hdls) 2m 4f
5:10 (5:12) (Class 4) (0-110,118) 4-Y-0+ £3,249 (£954; £477; £238)

Form RPR
0-11 **1** **Zarzal (IRE)**[5] 442 7-12-0 **118** 10ex...... MrConorOrr(7) 125+
(Evan Williams) *hld up: hdwy 7th: rdn to ld flat: edgd lft: r.o* **4/1[1]**
P0-2 **2** *2 1/2* **Baths Well (IRE)**[4] 449 5-11-2 **109**...... HarrisonBeswick(10) 114
(Ben Pauling) *chsd ldr tl led 3rd: rdn and hdd after 2 out: rallied to ld last: hdd flat: no ex towards fin* **10/1[3]**
241- **3** *1/2* **Over The Air**[238] 1701 7-11-7 **104**...... NicodeBoinville 108
(John Spearing) *a.p: led after 2 out: rdn and hdd last: styd on same pce flat* **20/1**
2P-2 **4** *8* **The Game Is A Foot (IRE)**[18] 225 8-10-13 **106**...... JasonNuttall(10) 103
(Gary Moore) *hld up: hdwy 3 out: sn rdn: hung lft flat: nt trble ldrs* **11/1**
06-2 **5** *1 3/4* **Anton Dolin (IRE)**[21] 180 7-11-0 **104**...... MrHFNugent(7) 101
(Michael Mullineaux) *hld up: hdwy 6th: rdn after 3 out: wnt rt last: wknd flat* **16/1**
13-4 **6** *14* **Astaroland (FR)**[21] 153 5-11-6 **103**...... PeterCarberry 89
(Jennie Candlish) *hld up: hdwy 7th: rdn after 3 out: wknd bef last* **16/1**
06-0 **7** *5* **Rainman (IRE)**[28] 43 5-11-6 **103**......(p) RichieMcLernon 81
(Jonjo O'Neill) *chsd ldrs: rdn appr 3 out: wknd bef next* **14/1**
44-1 **8** *7* **Sukiyaki (IRE)**[11] 364 6-11-10 **107** 7ex...... CharliePoste 81
(Charlie Longsdon) *prom: chsd ldr after 7th tl rdn appr 3 out: wknd after next* **5/1[2]**
25-0 **9** *4 1/2* **Provincial Pride (IRE)**[26] 85 8-11-1 **105**......(t) CharlieHammond(7) 73
(Mike Hammond) *chsd ldrs tl rdn and wknd appr 3 out* **25/1**
60-3 **10** *21* **Multimedia**[24] 108 5-11-1 **103**......(tp[1]) KieronEdgar(5) 52
(David Pipe) *hld up: effrt appr 3 out: sn wknd* **10/1[3]**
510- **11** *3 3/4* **Jigsaw Financial (IRE)**[170] 3004 9-11-3 **107**...... MrRobertHawker(7) 53
(Laura Young) *hld up: rdn and wknd after 7th* **33/1**
55-P **12** *3 3/4* **Today Please (IRE)**[24] 108 5-11-8 **105**......(t) DarylJacob 47
(Jonjo O'Neill) *hld up: hdwy appr 3 out: sn wknd* **33/1**
615- **13** *16* **Kastani Beach (IRE)**[34] 5523 9-11-4 **108**...... KevinJones(7) 36
(Seamus Mullins) *hld up: rdn and wknd after 6th* **40/1**
21-0 **P** **Walkabout Creek (IRE)**[24] 102 8-11-6 **103**...... LiamTreadwell
(Derek Frankland) *led to 3rd: remained handy tl rdn and wknd 7th: bhd whn p.u bef 3 out* **50/1**
530/ **P** **Never Says Never**[24] 7-11-7 **104**...... AidanColeman
(Anthony Honeyball) *mid-div: hdwy and hmpd after 4th: wknd 7th: bhd whn p.u bef 3 out* **5/1[2]**
220- **P** **Bajan Blu**[40] 7-11-5 **109**......(t[1]) MrBGibbs(7)
(David Brace) *mid-div: bhd fr 6th: p.u bef next* **14/1**

5m 1.3s (13.90) **Going Correction** +0.40s/f (Soft) **16** Ran SP% **123.8**
Speed ratings (Par 105): **88,87,86,83,82 77,75,72,70,62 60,59,52, , ,**
CSF £41.41 CT £738.50 TOTE £5.00: £1.80, £2.80, £4.80, £2.80; EX 46.80 Trifecta £879.30.
Owner Mrs Janet Davies **Bred** His Highness The Aga Khan's Studs S C **Trained** Llancarfan, Vale Of Glamorgan
■ Stewards' Enquiry : Mr Conor Orr two-day ban: used whip above permitted level (Jun 13,28)

FOCUS
A competitive handicap run at a sound pace, so this is form that should stand up. The winner has been a 129 hurdler at his best and has been rated as closing in on that level, with a small pb from the in-form second.

530 DOWNLOAD THE LADBROKES APP H'CAP HURDLE (12 hdls) 2m 7f
5:45 (5:46) (Class 5) (0-100,100) 4-Y-0+ £2,599 (£763; £381; £190)

Form RPR
02-1 **1** **Pennant Dancer**[28] 40 8-11-2 **90**......(t) PaulMoloney 102+
(Debra Hamer) *hld up: hdwy 9th: led appr 3 out: shkn up to go clr last: eased flat* **8/1**
05-4 **2** *9* **Steps And Stairs (IRE)**[16] 262 5-11-7 **95**......(p) DarylJacob 94
(Jonjo O'Neill) *prom: rdn bef 3 out: styd on same pce appr last* **4/1[2]**
F1F- **3** *2 1/4* **Modeligo (IRE)**[34] 5510 6-10-5 **86**......(t) MrStanSheppard(7) 84
(Matt Sheppard) *hld up: hdwy 7th: ev ch fr 3 out tl rdn after next: no ex flat* **11/2[3]**
160- **4** *3 1/4* **Tisfreetdream (IRE)**[61] 5027 14-10-11 **88**......(p) TomBellamy(3) 81
(Peter Pritchard) *hld up: hdwy 9th: rdn and wknd appr last* **28/1**
26P- **5** *1/2* **Minella Bliss (IRE)**[54] 5145 10-11-11 **99**......(b) MarkQuinlan 93
(James Evans) *hld up: hdwy 3 out: rdn and wknd appr last* **20/1**
40-2 **6** *6* **Westerly Breeze (IRE)**[27] 55 7-11-1 **92**......(b) BenPoste(3) 81
(Edward Bevan) *j.lft: disp ld tl rdn after 8th: wknd 2 out* **11/4[1]**
243- **7** *2 1/4* **Direct Flo (IRE)**[262] 1480 8-10-8 **87**...... JakeHodson(5) 72
(Rob Summers) *hld up: effrt appr 3 out: wknd bef next* **11/1**
430- **8** *30* **Legion D'Honneur (UAE)**[58] 5082 10-11-11 **99**......(t) JamesDavies 57
(Chris Down) *chsd ldrs: rdn after 8th: wknd appr 3 out* **17/2**
F3P- **9** *2 1/4* **Marmalade Man**[77] 4735 9-10-10 **84**......(b) AndrewThornton 40
(Seamus Mullins) *chsd ldrs: ev ch appr 3 out: rdn and wkng whn mstke next* **12/1**
10 *20* **Colley Row (IRE)**[24] 7-11-5 **100**......(b) MrBGibbs(7) 38
(Jess Westwood) *prom: led 9th: hdd bef next: sn wknd* **16/1**
2/6- **P** **Waltzing Tornado (IRE)**[211] 2134 11-11-12 **100**...... LiamTreadwell
(Liam Grassick) *hld up: wknd 8th: bhd whn p.u bef 3 out* **50/1**
600- **P** **Lady Knight (IRE)**[9] 4674 4-11-1 **95**...... DavidBass
(Sean Curran) *disp ld: mstke 8th: hdd whn blnd next: sn wknd: bhd whn p.u bef 3 out* **25/1**

5m 54.3s (26.30) **Going Correction** +0.40s/f (Soft)
WFA 4 from 5yo+ 19lb **12** Ran SP% **119.6**
Speed ratings (Par 103): **70,66,66,64,64 62,61,51,50,43 ,**
CSF £39.51 CT £196.18 TOTE £6.90: £2.40, £1.80, £2.20; EX 45.20 Trifecta £197.10.
Owner P J Woolley **Bred** P J Woolley **Trained** Nantycaws, Carmarthens

FOCUS
A open-looking finale in which a whole host still held realistic claims turning for home. A step up from the easy winner, with the second and third rated to their marks.
T/Plt: £80.20 to a £1 stake. Pool of £63876.58 - 580.99 winning tickets. T/Qpdt: £8.30 to a £1 stake. Pool of £5670.71 - 502.10 winning tickets. **Colin Roberts**

360 STRATFORD (L-H)
Friday, May 29

OFFICIAL GOING: Good
Wind: breezy Weather: sunshine and showers;; 10 degrees

531 SUBARU "RESTRICTED POINT-TO-POINT" SERIES FINAL (A NOVICES' HUNTERS' CHASE) (17 fncs) 2m 6f 125y
5:55 (5:57) (Class 3) 5-Y-0+ £6,239 (£1,935; £967; £484)

Form RPR
1 **Dabinett Moon**[20] 7-11-0 0...... MissCVHart(3) 112
(Mrs F Marriott) *hld up and bhd: stdy prog 14th: wnt 6 l 2nd 2 out: drvn and clsd to join ldr at last: asserted 100yds out and r.o gamely* **7/1[3]**
2 *2* **Flash Garden (IRE)**[47] 7-11-7 0...... MrTHamilton(3) 117
(J M B Cookson) *wnt 2nd after 8th: led 3 out: sn 6 l clr: drvn and jnd last: kpt trying but outstyd fnl 100yds* **12/1**
3 *17* **Its All Or Nothing**[25] 6-11-5 0...... DavidNoonan(5) 104
(Miss C Rowe) *nt a fluent: chsd ldrs: blnd 12th: rdn and outpcd 3 out: wknd next* **16/1**
53/2 **4** *7* **Cold Knight**[17] 260 9-11-10 0...... MrTWeston 96
(Tom Weston) *chsd ldrs: effrt 14th: rdn and disp 6 l 2nd 2 out: sn fdd* **7/1[3]**
F/4 **5** *5* **Baltic Blue**[24] 129 8-11-5 0......(p) MissCareyWilliamson(5) 93
(B Dowling) *bhd: hmpd 12th: plugged on fr 3 out: nvr nr ldrs* **100/1**
P1 **6** *29* **Out Of Range**[15] 293 8-11-6 0...... MrPMann(7) 68
(Mrs Pauline Harkin) *towards rr: struggling fr 13th: bdly t.o* **25/1**
303/ **7** *3* **Flicka's Witness (IRE)**[40] 10-11-3 0......(p) MrJGoss(7) 62
(Ms J Johnston) *in rr and nvr gng wl: t.o after bad blunder 14th* **50/1**
45P/ **P** **Merrydown Vintage (IRE)**[20] 8-11-10 0......(p) MrPYork
(Ray Fielder) *mstkes and sn detached: t.o and p.u 12th* **40/1**
4 **P** **Carnglave Cat (IRE)**[15] 298 9-11-3 0......(tp) MissKatyLyons(7)
(T D B Underwood) *midfield: rdn and wknd 13th: t.o and p.u last* **33/1**
P **Ruddy Article (IRE)**[19] 7-11-10 0...... MrWBiddick
(Jack R Barber) *led tl hdd 3 out: dropped out v rapidly: t.o and p.u after next* **9/4[1]**
P **Dandan (IRE)**[25] 7-11-10 0...... MrMWall
(Miss Francesca Moller) *pressed ldrs tl 10th: losing pl whn hmpd 12th: t.o and p.u 3 out* **15/2**

P **Road West (IRE)**[33] 6-11-3 0 MissImmyRobinson(7)
(Mrs C J Robinson) *prom tl lost pl and mstke 10th (water): t.o and p.u after 2 out* **33/1**

5-3 F **Dun Faw Good**[27] [80] 8-11-10 0 MissCWalton
(Mrs C Walton) *prom: 5th and looked abt to weaken whn fell heavily 12th* **9/2**[2]

5m 48.4s (9.20) **Going Correction** +0.45s/f (Soft) **13** Ran SP% **114.4**
Speed ratings: **102,101,95,92,91 81,80,, ,**
CSF £76.05 TOTE £8.30: £2.70, £3.50, £3.70; EX 100.70 Trifecta £556.30.
Owner C Marriott **Bred** Mrs F Marriott **Trained** Chipping Norton, Oxon

FOCUS
The ground had been selectively watered and there were split bends on fresh ground. The opener was for those who had won a restricted point-to-point or finished in the first three of a Subaru-sponsored restricted point-to-point qualifier. It was run at a good pace and two drew clear on the final circuit, ultimately giving the winner a target to aim at. The first two look fair hunters.

532 SIMS GARDEN MACHINERY H'CAP HURDLE (13 hdls) 3m 2f 83y
6:25 (6:25) (Class 3) (0-140,137) 4-Y-0+ **£5,848** (£1,717; £858; £429)

Form RPR

P02- **1** **Speed Master (IRE)**[38] [5451] 9-11-2 **127** (vt) SamTwiston-Davies 129
(Nigel Twiston-Davies) *cl 2nd mostly tl led bef 10th: drvn after 2 out: hdd bef last where galvanised to chal again and lft clr: styd on steadily whn in command flat* **9/2**[3]

35-1 **2** *3 ¼* **Weather Babe**[24] [122] 7-11-8 **133** (tp) ConorO'Farrell 134
(David Pipe) *trckd ldrs: hit 8th: effrt after 2 out: rdn to ld bef last where hrd pressed and blnd: nt rcvr* **11/2**

0/F- **3** *25* **Terminal (FR)**[303] [1131] 8-11-12 **137** NoelFehily 114
(David Dennis) *rn in snatches: cl up in last mostly: 6 l last and rdn bef 10th: rallied briefly 2 out: 5 l 3rd and btn home turn* **8/1**

P24- **4** *1 ¼* **Amigo (FR)**[41] [5392] 8-11-0 **132** (bt) DavidNoonan(7) 107
(David Pipe) *trckd ldrs: disp 3rd at 10th: rdn in 7 l 3rd and btn home turn* **2/1**[1]

1-15 **P** **Express Du Berlais (FR)**[14] [318] 6-10-13 **124** (t) WillKennedy
(Dr Richard Newland) *led and nt jump wl: slow 7th: hdd bef 10th: ev ch tl rdn and blnd next: blnd again 2 out and sn t.o: p.u last* **9/4**[2]

6m 31.3s (2.70) **Going Correction** +0.125s/f (Yiel) **5** Ran SP% **108.8**
Speed ratings (Par 107): **101,100,92,92,**
CSF £25.93 TOTE £4.10: £2.40, £2.10; EX 19.70 Trifecta £35.30.
Owner Spiers & Hartwell And N A Twiston-Davies **Bred** J Keegan And J Hamilton **Trained** Naunton, Gloucs

FOCUS
Just a small field but this produced a neck-and-neck battle from the last in the back straight. The first two ran pretty much to their marks.

533 POINTTOPOINT.CO.UK CHAMPION NOVICES' HUNTERS' CHASE (FOR THE JOHN CORBET CUP) (20 fncs) 3m 3f 119y
6:55 (6:56) (Class 2) 5-Y-0+
£11,992 (£3,746; £1,872; £936; £468; £236)

Form RPR

P- **1** **Lord Fingal (IRE)**[25] [117] 7-11-10 0 MrSClements 129
(J T R Dreaper, Ire) *trckd ldrs: wnt 2nd at 12th: lft in ld 15th: rdn and hrd pressed by two rivals at last: fnd ex to go 3 l clr flat: tired last 100yds but jst hld on* **5/1**[3]

3 **2** *hd* **Connies Cross (IRE)**[30] [17] 8-11-10 0 MrJNixon 129
(Mrs Sheila Crow) *trckd ldrs: mstke 10th: wnt 2nd at 16th: rdn 2 out: chal last: outpcd briefly flat but drvn and kpt on as ldr tired: jst failed* **12/1**

12-2 **3** *12* **Following Dreams (IRE)**[30] [14] 8-11-10 123 MrTWeston 122
(Alastair Ralph) *prom: j. slowly 11th: rdn to chal fr 2 out tl blnd last whn sing to weaken: no ch after* **11/4**[1]

21-1 **4** *13* **Mr Mercurial (IRE)**[30] [13] 7-11-10 118 (t) MrPGerety 108
(Mrs Sheila Crow) *hld up towards rr: nt fluent 8th: effrt 14th: rdn 3 out: little rspnse and wl hld fr 2 out* **3/1**[2]

U2-1 **5** *16* **Indiana Bay (IRE)**[22] [166] 8-11-10 120 MrWBiddick 92
(Mrs Jill Dennis) *towards rr: hit 14th: struggling whn blnd 3 out* **8/1**

33/3 **6** *8* **Empire Builder (IRE)**[30] [13] 9-11-10 0 MrGGreenock 88
(G T H Bailey) *led at stdy pce: slow 1st and 2nd: hit 8th: blnd 15th and hdd: lost pl next: t.o 2 out* **7/1**

511- **7** *60* **Wayupinthesky (IRE)**[36] [5494] 8-11-10 113 HarryBannister 31
(J P G Hamilton) *bhd and nvr gng wl enough: struggling 15th: t.o 3 out: eased last* **10/1**

34-4 **P** **Tandori**[30] [16] 13-11-3 82 MrDAndrews
(Paul Phillips) *pressed ldr tl 9th: in rr 13th: t.o and p.u 17th* **150/1**

4P/3 **P** **Star Of Massini (IRE)**[15] [298] 8-11-10 0 MissGAndrews
(N W Padfield) *often j. bdly and wl in rr: brief effrt 10th: in rr again 15th: t.o and p.u after blunder 16th* **80/1**

4- **P** **Moscow Blaze (IRE)**[26] 9-11-10 0 (p) MissPFuller
(Mrs R Fuller) *mstkes: 2nd or 3rd tl 15th: qckly lost pl: t.o and p.u 2 out* **66/1**

P **Blackwood Rover (IRE)**[15] [310] 7-11-10 0 MrBMLinehan
(J R Jenkins) *midfield: lost pl 14th: t.o and p.u 17th* **28/1**

7m 10.6s (7.60) **Going Correction** +0.45s/f (Soft) **11** Ran SP% **115.6**
Speed ratings: **107,106,103,99,95 92,75,, ,**
CSF £58.78 TOTE £4.30: £1.90, £3.10, £1.60; EX 30.70 Trifecta £237.90.
Owner Declan O'Farrell **Bred** J Mangan **Trained** Greenogue, Co Meath

FOCUS
After a steady early pace three emerged from the pack to fight out an exciting finish, with the winner just holding on. The first two are on the upgrade.

534 AGA LADIES OPEN POINT-TO-POINT CHAMPIONSHIP FINAL (A HUNTERS' CHASE FOR LADY RIDERS) (17 fncs) 2m 6f 125y
7:25 (7:25) (Class 3) 5-Y-0+ **£6,239** (£1,935; £967; £484)

Form RPR

P/5- **1** **What A Laugh**[41] 10-11-4 108 MissJCWilliams(3) 131+
(Gary Hanmer) *trckd ldrs: effrt 14th: wnt cl 2nd 2 out: led between last two: sn asserted: drvn out fr last* **14/1**

U-11 **2** *8* **Current Event (FR)**[10] [393] 8-11-6 135 MissBFrost(7) 129
(Mrs Rose Loxton) *hld up in 6th pl tl effrt 14th: 3rd 2 out: drvn and no ex between last two: wnt one pce 2nd bef last* **5/6**[1]

/15- **3** *7* **Bound For Glory (IRE)**[50] [5239] 9-11-5 122 MissHLewis(5) 122
(D M G Fitch-Peyton) *led at gd gallop tl hdd 11th: 4th and fading whn blnd 2 out: wnt 3rd bef last* **4/1**[3]

4 *74* **Trueflyingcolours (IRE)**[33] 9-11-0 0 (p) MissKatyLyons(7) 50
(S Penny) *2nd or 3rd tl led 11th: hdd and blnd 13th: sn t.o: lft v remote 4th after last* **66/1**

213- **5** *99* **His Excellency (IRE)**[19] 7-11-10 143 (t) MissCVHart(3) 125
(M N Dawson) *t.k.h in 2nd or 3rd: blnd 5th: mstke 10th (water): led 13th: slt advantage and drvn 2 out: hdd between last two and 10 l 4th and fading rapidly last: sn eased to a walk flat* **7/2**[2]

/2P- **U** **Invisible Man (FR)**[34] 10-11-0 122 (t) MissJosephineBanks(7)
(Alastair Ralph) *chsd ldrs: nt fluent 8th: 3rd and bmpd along 13th: blnd and uns rdr next* **16/1**

235- **F** **Academy General (IRE)**[19] 9-11-2 105 (t) MissJBuck(5)
(Patricia Shaw) *nt a fluent in last: struggling whn fell 14th* **66/1**

5m 48.2s (9.00) **Going Correction** +0.45s/f (Soft) **7** Ran SP% **112.3**
Speed ratings: **102,99,96,71,36 ,**
CSF £26.95 TOTE £12.90: £3.30, £1.40; EX 23.50 Trifecta £167.10.
Owner R P Davies-Cooke **Bred** Miss J C L Needham **Trained** Nantwich, Cheshire
■ he w
■ Stewards' Enquiry : Miss Josephine Banks two-day ban: careless riding (TBA)

FOCUS
This was run at an even pace, with three taking each other on going out on the final circuit, allowing the winner to make a late move. The winner threatened to be this good a few years back, while the second was below his recent level.

535 PERTEMPS NETWORK STRATFORD FOXHUNTERS CHAMPION HUNTERS' CHASE (THE 57TH RUNNING) (20 fncs) 3m 3f 119y
8:00 (8:00) (Class 2) 5-Y-0+
£14,990 (£4,682; £2,340; £1,170; £585; £295)

Form RPR

11-2 **1** **Moroman (IRE)**[30] [15] 8-12-0 127 MissGAndrews 140+
(David Kemp) *j.rt at times: led: rdn and hdd appr last where 4 l bhd: rallied u.p to ld nr fin: brilliant ride* **16/1**

134- **2** *hd* **Paint The Clouds**[34] [5538] 10-12-0 138 MrSWaley-Cohen 140
(Warren Greatrex) *mid-div: hdwy 7th: chsd wnr 2 out: rdn to ld appr last where 4 l clr and looked wnr: no ex and hdd nr fin* **5/6**[1]

212- **3** *10* **Pacha Du Polder (FR)**[50] [5239] 8-12-0 141 MrWBiddick 130
(Paul Nicholls) *hld up: hdwy 11th: rdn after 2 out: styd on same pce appr last* **4/1**[2]

116- **4** *8* **Twirling Magnet (IRE)**[50] [5239] 9-12-0 138 (p) MrMWalton 125
(Jonjo O'Neill) *hit 1st: prom: chsd wnr 13th tl 2 out: sn rdn: wkng whn mstke last* **14/1**

2U-1 **5** *½* **Quinz (FR)**[30] [15] 11-12-0 126 MrJoeHill 121
(Alan Hill) *hdwy 4th: drvn along 17th: wknd after 2 out* **20/1**

00-1 **6** *92* **Lets Get Serious (IRE)**[15] [295] 9-12-0 125 MrCJMiller 38
(Dai Williams) *prom: lost pl 7th: mstke 11th: t.o fr 14th* **66/1**

U4-1 **P** **Major Malarkey (IRE)**[30] [17] 12-12-0 127 (v) MrSClements
(Nigel Twiston-Davies) *prom: lost pl 10th: bhd fr 14th: sn t.o: p.u bef 17th* **16/1**

21/3 **P** **Divine Intavention (IRE)**[17] [270] 11-12-0 0 MrMWall
(Miss Francesca Moller) *hld up: a in rr: bhd fr 11th: p.u bef 14th* **50/1**

P/5- **U** **Sir Du Bearn (FR)**[13] 9-12-0 127 (p) MissJodieHughes
(Mickey Bowen) *chsd ldr: mstke 10th: lost 2nd 13th: mstke and wknd 16th: in rr whn blnd and uns rdr next* **33/1**

5-44 **P** **Findlay's Find (IRE)**[10] [393] 9-12-0 103 (b[1]) MrDMansell
(Mrs Myfanwy Miles) *prom: nt fluent 3rd: lost pl 5th: sn rdn and nt travelling: blnd 9th: t.o fr 12th: p.u bef 14th* **100/1**

5F-1 **P** **Chosen Milan (IRE)**[30] [16] 8-11-7 123 (t) MrEDavid
(R E Luke) *j. slowly 2nd: hld up: hdwy 8th: wknd after 16th: sn p.u* **8/1**[3]

4F-5 **P** **Pentiffic (NZ)**[30] [17] 11-12-0 119 (p) MissLMTurner
(P P C Turner) *hld up: bhd fr 5th: t.o 9th: p.u bef 14th* **100/1**

20-3 **P** **Temple Grandin (IRE)**[30] [15] 8-12-0 120 (t) MrPGerety
(Philip Rowley) *hld up: hdwy 8th: hit 10th: sn lost pl: blnd 15th: t.o whn p.u after 2 out* **50/1**

7m 8.2s (5.20) **Going Correction** +0.45s/f (Soft) **13** Ran SP% **119.2**
Speed ratings: **110,109,107,104,104 78,, , ,**
CSF £30.66 TOTE £16.00: £3.70, £1.10, £1.90; EX 58.10 Trifecta £203.10.
Owner B Belchem **Bred** Michael Whitty **Trained** Thetford, Norfolk
■ Stewards' Enquiry : Miss G Andrews two-day ban: use of whip (TBA)

FOCUS
Last year's winner Paint The Clouds lined up against some former smart handicap chasers for the 57th running of this Champion Hunters' Chase. It produced a dramatic finish with the favourite getting collared near the line. A step up from the winner.

536 TECHNICAIR AIR CONDITIONING & VENTILATION ENGINEERS OPEN HUNTERS' CHASE (12 fncs) 2m 213y
8:30 (8:32) (Class 6) 6-Y-0+ **£1,871** (£580; £290; £145)

Form RPR

34- **1** **Torn Asunder (IRE)**[25] 8-11-10 115 MrWBiddick 122
(Gary Hanmer) *hld up in last pair early: stdy prog fr 9th: 6 l 3rd 2 out: rdn to chal last: drvn ahd cl home* **16/1**

604- **2** *hd* **Joker Choker (IRE)**[38] [5453] 10-11-10 108 MrDEdwards 122
(Miss Nicky Martin) *w ldrs: led 7th: 5 l clr 2 out: rdn and jnd last: kpt on wl tl ct fnl strides* **16/1**

/UP- **3** *12* **Catch Tammy (IRE)**[13] 9-11-7 110 MissHannahWatson(3) 110
(Mrs I Barnett) *pressed ldrs: rdn and outpcd by ldng pair sn after 2 out: 12 l 3rd at last* **66/1**

/31- **4** *9* **Tataniano (FR)**[39] [5433] 11-11-9 133 (t) MrMatthewHampton(5) 106
(B A Sanderson) *bhd: rdn and outpcd bef 9th: plugged on to go poor 4th after last* **10/11**[1]

P-66 **5** *6* **Bay To Go (IRE)**[17] [270] 9-11-7 109 (b) MissKatyLyons(5) 101
(Mrs H M Kemp) *prom: led 5th tl 7th: stl 2nd 2 out: sn fdd* **40/1**

5-46 **6** *9* **Swallows Delight (IRE)**[10] [393] 10-12-0 103 MrDMansell 93
(Mrs Julie Mansell) *prom tl 8th: t.o* **33/1**

130/ **7** *1 ¾* **Silver Story**[117] 12-11-5 0 (t) MrBGibbs(5) 90
(William Vaughan) *mstke 1st: towards rr: t.o* **25/1**

/4-2 **8** *4* **King Of Alcatraz (IRE)**[10] [393] 9-11-3 109 MissVWade(7) 83
(N Harris) *w ldrs tl 3 out: 11 l 5th and fading next: t.o* **6/1**[3]

030- **9** *25* **Nishay (IRE)**[13] 8-11-3 0 (t) MissEmmaMoseley(7) 61
(R D L Glanville) *rdr nrly c off at 3rd: a bhd: t.o 3 out: nrly uns rdr at last* **100/1**

FP-0 **10** *9* **Orang Outan (FR)**[30] [18] 13-11-10 85 CharlieDeutsch 53
(Mrs R Hurley) *prom tl 9th: nt run on: t.o 3 out: eventually completed* **100/1**

4/6- **11** *17* **Maid Of Silk (IRE)**[19] 9-10-10 89 (tp) MrSLee(7) 31
(Mrs K Lee) *sn trailing: bdly t.o fr 8th: eventually completed* **150/1**

P-03 **U** **Woodlark Island (IRE)**[15] [296] 9-11-3 0 (b) MrHFNugent(7)
(A Campbell) *mde most tl 5th: nt run on: wl bhd whn uns rdr 3 out* **100/1**

644- **P** **Oranger (FR)**[40] [5407] 13-11-5 75 (b) MrJMartin(5)
(Andrew J Martin) *drvn and t.o 6th: p.u bef 2 out* **100/1**

P4-P **P** **Shrewd Investment**[17] 260 9-11-7 114.......(bt) MissPFuller(7)
(Miss L Thomas) mstkes: t.o 3 out: p.u next: fatally injured after r 50/1

06- **P** **Posh Trip**[47] 10-11-3 0.......(tp) MrJDrinkwater(7)
(Lady Blandford) nt jump wl and struggling in detached last: t.o and p.u after 6th 100/1

/3-2 **U** **Samtheman**[15] 296 10-11-7 93....... MissABroome(7)
(M J Jackson) chsng ldrson outer whn uns rdr 6th 40/1

F2-1 **P** **Can Mestret (IRE)**[15] 296 8-12-4 116....... MissGAndrews
(S R Andrews) nvr gng wl or bttr than midfield: strugling 9th: t.o and p.u last 7/2[2]

4m 20.1s (13.00) **Going Correction** +0.45s/f (Soft) **17 Ran SP% 121.4**
Speed ratings: **89,88,83,79,76 72,72,70,59,55 47,,,,,**
CSF £216.01 TOTE £13.40: £3.20, £4.00, £8.70; EX 183.70 Trifecta £853.40.
Owner R P Davies-Cooke **Bred** Lady Blaker **Trained** Nantwich, Cheshire
■ Stewards' Enquiry : Mr W Biddick two-day ban: use of whip

FOCUS
After a good early pace this produced yet another tight finish with the long-time leader trying to fend off the fast finisher. The form is rated in line with the second's best chase figure.

537 BRIGHTWELLS BLOODSTOCK AUCTIONEERS H'CAP HURDLE (9 hdls) 2m 2f 148y
9:00 (9:00) (Class 5) (0-100,98) 4-Y-O+ **£2,599** (£763; £381; £190)

Form RPR

46-0 **1** **Iguacu**[22] 177 11-11-12 **98**....... RichardJohnson 108+
(Richard Price) hld up: hdwy 6th: rdn to ld and hmpd last: r.o 9/1

34-4 **2** ½ **Shot In The Dark (IRE)**[18] 240 6-11-2 **88**.......(p) MarkGrant 97
(Jonathan Geake) sn led: rdn and hdd whn j.rt last: r.o 20/1

06-0 **3** 13 **Toe To Toe (IRE)**[29] 30 7-11-0 **86**.......(t) RhysFlint 84
(John Flint) hld up: hdwy 2 out: wknd last 12/1

22F- **4** 1½ **Fuse Wire**[176] 2902 8-10-8 **87**....... MissJodieHughes(7) 84
(Dai Burchell) prom: rdn after 2 out: wkng whn j.lft last 10/1

003/ **5** 2¼ **Cornish Beau (IRE)**[701] 681 8-10-9 **81**....... WillKennedy 76
(Dr Richard Newland) prom: hit 3 out: wknd appr last 12/1

0-21 **6** 3¼ **Bus Named Desire**[5] 466 7-10-8 **83** 7ex.......(tp) RobMcCarth(3) 74
(Ian Williams) mid-div: hdwy 5th: rdn and wknd appr last 5/2[1]

0-45 **7** 9 **Toast And Jam (IRE)**[12] 364 6-11-2 **88**.......(t) TrevorWhelan 70
(Claire Dyson) prom: rdn after 2 out: wknd appr last 25/1

015/ **8** ¾ **Oscar Leney (IRE)**[638] 1448 9-11-3 **89**.......(t) DougieCostello 71
(J T R Dreaper, Ire) hld up: pushed along after 2 out: nvr on terms 25/1

500/ **9** 7 **Umoristic (FR)**[34] 7-9-10 **75** ow3.......(t) MrStanSheppard(7) 50
(Matt Sheppard) mid-div: rdn after 3 out: wknd next 9/1

66-2 **10** 8 **The Ice Factor**[27] 77 7-10-11 **90**.......(p) JamieHamilton(7) 58
(Alison Hamilton) chsd ldrs: hit 3rd: rdn whn mstke 2 out: sn wknd 8/1[3]

/00- **11** 3 **Interior Minister**[334] 824 5-11-8 **94**.......(p) GavinSheehan 60
(Warren Greatrex) w ldr: rdn and ev ch whn nt fluent 2 out: sn wknd 11/2[2]

30P- **12** 3¾ **Maxdelas (FR)**[119] 3960 9-10-0 **75**.......(t) JamesBanks(3) 37
(Roy Brotherton) hld up: rdn and wknd after 2 out 33/1

0/0- **13** 27 **Markami (FR)**[10] 1661 5-10-9 **81**.......(bt) NoelFehily 19
(Johnny Farrelly) hld up: rdn appr 6th: bhd fr 3 out 25/1

55-0 **14** ¾ **Ruby Valentine (FR)**[22] 167 12-10-3 **75**....... LiamTreadwell 12
(Jim Wilson) hld up: effrt 6th: wknd bef next 25/1

4m 32.9s (1.40) **Going Correction** +0.125s/f (Yiel) **14 Ran SP% 122.6**
Speed ratings (Par 103): **102,101,96,95,94 93,89,89,86,82 81,80,68,68**
CSF £180.30 CT £2181.45 TOTE £5.30: £2.40, £4.40, £4.40; EX 131.00 Trifecta £393.80.
Owner Derek & Cheryl Holder **Bred** Cheveley Park Stud Ltd **Trained** Ullingswick, H'fords

FOCUS
Another tight finish saw two rivals fighting it out from the home turn. The pair came together and collided over the last, but it did not affect the result.
T/Plt: £2,175.80 to a £1 stake. Pool: £70192.81 - 23.55 winning tickets. T/Qpdt: £140.20 to a £1 stake. Pool: £6082.95 - 32.1 winning tickets. **Iain Mackenzie & Colin Roberts**

538 - 551a (Foreign Racing) - See Raceform Interactive

531
STRATFORD (L-H)
Saturday, May 30

OFFICIAL GOING: Good
Wind: Light across Weather: Overcast

552 LUXURIOUS BOUTIQUE WHITE SWAN HOTEL NOVICES' H'CAP HURDLE (11 hdls) 2m 6f 7y
5:55 (5:55) (Class 5) (0-100,96) 4-Y-O+ **£3,249** (£954; £477; £238)

Form RPR

PU-1 **1** **Patricktom Boru (IRE)**[7] 438 8-10-13 **83**....... AdamWedge 97+
(Evan Williams) a.p: chsd ldr after 5th: nt fluent 7th: mstke 3 out: sn rdn: led wl bef last: styd on u.p 13/8[1]

6U3- **2** 2 **Stay In My Heart (IRE)**[36] 5525 6-11-2 **86**.......(p) LeightonAspell 95
(Laura Mongan) chsd ldr to 2nd: remained handy: rdn and outpcd after 8th: rallied appr 2 out: chsd wnr bef last: styd on 11/1

0-P5 **3** 26 **League Of His Own (IRE)**[14] 328 6-10-0 **70**.......(t[1]) TrevorWhelan 56
(Claire Dyson) led: j.rt 3rd: clr 5th tl 3 out: rdn: hdd & wknd wl bef last 20/1

3P-4 **4** shd **Harriet's Ark**[14] 328 8-10-10 **80**....... MarkGrant 66
(Julian Smith) hld up: rdn appr 3 out: nvr on terms 16/1

06-2 **5** 5 **Master Cardor Visa (IRE)**[29] 65 10-10-11 **84**.......(p) JamesBanks(3) 65
(Emma Baker) prom: rdn appr 3 out: wknd after next: bhd whn mstke last 15/2[3]

003- **6** 16 **Steady Progress (IRE)**[69] 4940 7-10-8 **81**.......(tp) HarryChalloner(3) 48
(Richard Ford) prom: racd keenly: rdn and wknd appr 3 out 25/1

44-6 **7** 9 **Misteray**[28] 89 5-11-6 **90**.......(t) DenisO'Regan 49
(Bill Turner) mid-div: lost pl 3rd: mstke 6th: sn rdn: wknd 8th 16/1

3F0- **8** 12 **Sapphire Moon**[49] 5281 8-11-12 **96**....... RichardJohnson 44
(Richard Phillips) hld up: rdn and wknd after 7th 14/1

56-0 **U** **When In Roam (IRE)**[19] 238 6-11-1 **92**.......(v[1]) CiaranGethings(7)
(John O'Shea) hld up: pushed along 6th: wknd after next: bhd whn uns rdr bnd after 8th 25/1

25-1 **P** **Hi Bronco**[29] 65 8-10-7 **77**.......(p) JamesDavies
(John Ryall) prom: chsd ldr 2nd tl after 5th: rdn and wknd after 8th: bhd whn p.u bef last 11/4[2]

5m 25.8s (-2.30) **Going Correction** -0.275s/f (Good) **10 Ran SP% 115.7**
Speed ratings (Par 103): **93,92,83,83,81 75,72,68,,**
CSF £19.35 CT £255.35 TOTE £2.60: £1.30, £2.90, £5.90; EX 21.70 Trifecta £210.80.
Owner R W J Willcox **Bred** Mrs B M Browne **Trained** Llancarfan, Vale Of Glamorgan

FOCUS
One bend split and the other two shared. A moderate contest run at a slow tempo early. The winner was on a good mark and is rated similar to recent chase form.

553 AMG LOGISTICS H'CAP CHASE (20 fncs) 3m 3f 119y
6:25 (6:25) (Class 3) (0-125,125) 5-Y-O **£6,330** (£1,870; £935; £468; £234)

Form RPR

31-3 **1** **Thomas Wild**[30] 29 10-11-8 **121**....... RichardJohnson 130+
(Philip Hobbs) chsd ldrs: led 12th to next: rdn appr 2 out: led flat: styd on u.p 6/1[2]

31-2 **2** ½ **Alberobello (IRE)**[23] 169 7-11-6 **122**.......(t) MattGriffiths(3) 129
(Jeremy Scott) a.p: chsd ldr 3rd: led 9th to 12th: led 16th: rdn appr last: hdd flat: styd on u.p 6/1[2]

12P- **3** 15 **Universal Soldier (IRE)**[78] 4740 10-11-11 **124**....... CharliePoste 118
(Matt Sheppard) led: nt fluent 6th: sn pushed along: hdd 9th: led 13th to 16th: rdn and wknd appr last: wnt 3rd flat 11/4[1]

212- **4** ½ **Favoured Nation (IRE)**[38] 5464 8-11-5 **125**....... PatrickCowley(7) 124+
(Jonjo O'Neill) sn prom: mstke 2nd: hit 3 out: sn rdn: wkng whn mstke last 8/1[3]

33-5 **5** 6 **Copper Birch (IRE)**[7] 439 7-11-4 **117**.......(p) PaulMoloney 104
(Evan Williams) hld up: hdwy 17th: rdn and wknd after 2 out 8/1[3]

64-1 **6** 5 **Pigeon Island**[7] 439 12-11-5 **118**.......(t) SamTwiston-Davies 103
(Nigel Twiston-Davies) hld up: hdwy 16th: sn rdn: wknd after 2 out 10/1

P1P- **7** 32 **Quinton (FR)**[45] 5340 11-10-13 **112**....... NoelFehily 66
(Johnny Farrelly) prom: lost pl 3rd: in rr and drvn along 14th: sn lost tch 10/1

52-P **P** **Ifyousayso (IRE)**[19] 239 8-11-2 **115**....... TomScudamore
(David Bridgwater) hld up in tch: rdn 15th: wknd next: bhd whn p.u bef 4 out 14/1

05-2 **P** **An Poc Ar Buile (IRE)**[13] 355 6-11-4 **117**....... AlainCawley
(Fergal O'Brien) a in rr: pushed along 5th: bhd fr 9th: p.u bef 12th 8/1[3]

6m 48.8s (-14.20) **Going Correction** -0.375s/f (Good) **9 Ran SP% 113.4**
Speed ratings: **105,104,100,100,98 97,88,,**
CSF £41.36 CT £120.11 TOTE £4.80: £1.70, £2.30, £1.70; EX 19.50 Trifecta £117.60.
Owner C L T **Bred** Miss S J Turner **Trained** Withycombe, Somerset

FOCUS
A few of these came into this in fair heart, so this should be decent form at staying distances. Steps up from the first two.

554 STRATFORD HOME & GARDEN SHOW NOVICES' HURDLE (8 hdls) 2m 70y
6:55 (6:55) (Class 4) 4-Y-O+ **£3,249** (£954; £477; £238)

Form RPR

45-2 **1** **Mighty Missile (IRE)**[22] 182 4-10-8 113.......(tp) GavinSheehan 116+
(Warren Greatrex) mde all: rdn clr appr last: styd on wl 2/1[2]

2 22 **Ennistown**[203] 5-10-12 0....... AidanColeman 103+
(John Ferguson) trckd wnr: ev ch 2 out: rdn and wknd appr last 13/8[1]

3 4½ **Moulin Rouge (DEN)**[9] 4-10-1 0....... WillKennedy 85
(Ian Williams) hld up: hdwy 2 out: sn rdn and wknd 40/1

065- **4** ¾ **Kingdom (IRE)**[12] 4916 5-10-12 119.......(bt) JamieMoore 96
(Gary Moore) prom: rdn after 2 out: wknd wl bef last 10/1

0-6 **5** 23 **Rye House (IRE)**[7] 440 6-10-12 0....... RichardJohnson 80
(Tim Vaughan) chsd ldrs tl rdn and wknd 2 out 16/1

6-4 **6** 4 **Jarlath**[26] 98 4-10-8 0....... AndrewThornton 67
(Seamus Mullins) hld up: hdwy 3 out: rdn and wknd after next 22/1

7 17 **Dabuki (FR)**[189] 5-10-12 0....... AdamWedge 56
(Evan Williams) hld up: plld hrd: hdwy 2 out: sn rdn and wknd 40/1

0 **8** 5 **Everlasting Spring (IRE)**[13] 360 7-10-12 0.......(t) AlainCawley 51
(Johnny Farrelly) hld up: bhd fr 5th 100/1

04-5 **9** 1 **False Accusation (IRE)**[19] 242 6-10-12 0....... SamTwiston-Davies 50
(Nigel Twiston-Davies) hld up: nt fluent: rdn and wknd appr 3 out 33/1

41-P **P** **Forever Field (IRE)**[29] 56 5-11-5 118....... PeterCarberry
(Nicky Henderson) prom tl rdn and wknd 3 out: bhd whn p.u after next 9/2[3]

3m 51.9s (-4.10) **Going Correction** -0.275s/f (Good)
WFA 4 from 5yo+ 18lb **10 Ran SP% 117.7**
Speed ratings (Par 105): **98,87,85,85,74 72,64,62,61,**
CSF £5.67 TOTE £3.10: £1.10, £1.20, £5.70; EX 6.90 Trifecta £117.30.
Owner Bolingbroke Howard BJO Duthie Mercer **Bred** Gerry Flannery **Trained** Upper Lambourn, Berks

FOCUS
A pretty ordinary race of its type. The winner may prove to be the best guide to the level.

555 D W CLARK DRAINAGE H'CAP CHASE (FOR THE GAMBLING PRINCE TROPHY) (12 fncs) 2m 213y
7:25 (7:25) (Class 2) (0-150,142) 5-Y-O+
£11,573 (£3,418; £1,709; £854; £427; £214)

Form RPR

U1-0 **1** **Another Flutter (IRE)**[20] 218 11-11-3 **133**.......(tp) CharliePoste 141
(Matt Sheppard) chsd ldrs: led after 3 out: rdn whn nt fluent last: styd on u.p 12/1

10-6 **2** 1¼ **It's A Gimme (IRE)**[21] 198 8-11-10 **140**....... RichieMcLernon 146
(Jonjo O'Neill) hld up: hdwy 9th: rdn to chse wnr wl bef last: styd on 5/1

442- **3** 6 **Miss Tenacious**[41] 5413 8-10-0 **123**....... HarryCobden(7) 124
(Ron Hodges) hld up: mstkes 6th and 9th: r.o appr last: wnt 3rd flat: nvr nr to chal 8/1

221- **4** 5 **Surf And Turf (IRE)**[51] 5240 9-11-10 **140**....... BrianHughes 137
(Kevin Frost) hld up: hdwy 5th: chsd wnr after 3 out tl rdn after next: wknd last 4/1[2]

FU1- **5** 2 **Witness In Court (IRE)**[37] 5493 8-11-12 **142**....... WayneHutchinson 137
(Donald McCain) chsd ldrs: nt fluent 9th: sn rdn: wknd after 2 out 9/2[3]

-222 **6** 18 **My Brother Sylvest**[13] 357 9-11-10 **140**.......(b) TomScudamore 125
(David Pipe) w ldr and nt fluent 1st: led 2nd: mstke 3 out: sn hdd: rdn and wknd after next 3/1[1]

5U-0 **7** 36 **Anquetta (IRE)**[22] 184 11-11-4 **137**....... MrSWaley-Cohen(3) 108
(Robert Waley-Cohen) led to 2nd: chsd ldr to 3 out: rdn and wknd after next 16/1

212- **8** 9 **Sublime Talent (IRE)**[39] 5449 9-10-0 **116** oh2.......(t) PaulMoloney 53
(Evan Williams) hld up: bhd fr 7th 11/1

4m 0.5s (-6.60) **Going Correction** -0.375s/f (Good) **8 Ran SP% 112.9**
Speed ratings: **99,98,95,93,92 84,68,64**
CSF £69.25 CT £511.96 TOTE £4.40: £3.70, £2.20, £2.70; EX 95.20 Trifecta £344.10.
Owner Tony Scrivin **Bred** Eamon D Delany **Trained** Eastnor, H'fords

FOCUS
This was a strong race, run at a quick tempo. Another pb from the winner.

556 PORTLAND PLACE PROPERTIES H'CAP HURDLE (8 hdls) 2m 70y
7:55 (7:55) (Class 2) 4-Y-O+ £11,710 (£3,459; £1,729; £865; £432)

Form RPR
F00- 1 **Roman Flight (IRE)**[22] 5390 7-11-4 138 (v) NoelFehily 145+
(David Dennis) *hld up: hdwy after 3 out: led appr and blnd last: rdn out* **9/1**
502- 2 1 **Laudatory**[168] 3075 9-11-2 136 NicodeBoinville 141
(Nicky Henderson) *led: hit 4th: rdn and hdd wl bef last: ev ch whn nt fluent last: styd on* **10/1**
130- 3 1 1/4 **Dubai Prince (IRE)**[303] 1142 7-10-13 133 AidanColeman 136
(John Ferguson) *mid-div: hdwy 3 out: led wl bef last: rdn and hdd whn nt fluent last: no ex towards fin* **5/1**[1]
21-1 4 13 **Lochalsh (IRE)**[30] 41 4-10-0 124 HarrySkelton 110
(Dan Skelton) *hld up: hdwy 2 out: rdn: hung lft and no ex wl bef last* **10/1**
/1P- 5 3 1/4 **Alwaystheoptimist**[370] 468 12-10-2 122 PeterCarberry 109
(Shaun Lycett) *hld up: rdn after 2 out: nvr trbld ldrs* **50/1**
63P- 6 6 **Foxtail Hill (IRE)**[37] 5491 6-10-7 127 SamTwiston-Davies 109
(Nigel Twiston-Davies) *hld up: effrt after 2 out: n.d* **8/1**
22F- 7 hd **Western Diva (IRE)**[41] 5408 6-10-0 120 oh2 TomScudamore 102
(David Pipe) *hld up: mstke 1st: nvr nrr* **14/1**
52-1 8 3 1/4 **Another Journey**[29] 59 6-10-2 122 RobertDunne 101
(Sarah-Jayne Davies) *trckd ldrs: racd keenly: rdn and wknd 2 out* **33/1**
10-6 9 9 **Oyster Shell**[10] 406 8-10-12 132 TomO'Brien 103
(Henry Daly) *mid-div: pushed along 5th: wknd 3 out* **25/1**
22-1 10 4 1/2 **Ryeolliean**[20] 221 4-10-0 124 (p) JamieMoore 87
(Gary Moore) *chsd ldrs: nt fluent 2nd: chsd ldr whn blnd 2 out: sn rdn and wknd* **9/1**
0-05 11 2 1/4 **Vulcanite (IRE)**[15] 317 8-11-6 140 WillKennedy 105
(Charlie Longsdon) *mid-div: pushed along after 4th: wknd appr 2 out* **9/1**
20-1 12 9 **Claret Cloak (IRE)**[26] 103 8-11-12 146 GavinSheehan 103
(Emma Lavelle) *w ldr to 5th: rdn and wknd after 2 out* **6/1**[3]
42-1 13 3 1/2 **Benbecula**[29] 63 6-10-0 120 RichardJohnson 73
(Richard Mitchell) *prom tl rdn and wknd appr 2 out* **11/2**[2]
3-U3 14 3 1/2 **Brinestine (USA)**[22] 186 6-9-11 120 oh13 (t) JamesBanks(3) 70
(Emma Baker) *hld up: hdwy 5th: rdn and wknd after 2 out* **100/1**
5-F0 15 1 **Collodi (GER)**[10] 406 6-10-0 125 ow3 JakeHodson(5) 74
(David Bridgwater) *hld up: rdn after 3 out: wknd next* **40/1**

3m 46.6s (-9.40) **Going Correction** -0.275s/f (Good)
WFA 4 from 6yo+ 18lb **15 Ran SP% 124.5**
Speed ratings (Par 109): **111,110,109,103,102 99,99,97,93,91 90,86,84,82,82**
CSF £95.25 CT £512.71 TOTE £11.70: £3.20, £4.00, £2.50; EX 76.90 Trifecta £254.20.
Owner Favourites Racing Ltd **Bred** Jim Cockburn **Trained** Hanley Swan, Worcestershire

FOCUS
A competitive-looking contest, but three came well clear in the final stages. Solid handicap form.

557 LLEWELLYN HUMPHREYS H'CAP CHASE (15 fncs) 2m 4f 205y
8:25 (8:25) (Class 4) (0-120,120) 5-Y-O £3,798 (£1,122; £561; £280; £140)

Form RPR
14-2 1 **Sporting Boy (IRE)**[13] 365 7-11-12 120 (b) NoelFehily 130+
(Johnny Farrelly) *mde all: rdn appr last: all out* **4/1**[1]
135- 2 1/2 **Porters War (IRE)**[238] 1742 13-11-6 117 MattGriffiths(3) 126
(Jeremy Scott) *a.p: chsd wnr 10th to 12th: rdn to go 2nd again after 2 out: ev ch last: styd on u.p* **10/1**
P35- 3 17 **Kitchapoly (FR)**[43] 5364 5-11-9 117 WayneHutchinson 113
(Donald McCain) *hld up: hdwy 9th: chsd wnr 12th tl rdn after 2 out: wknd last* **12/1**
5PP- 4 42 **Papradon**[141] 3596 11-11-6 114 SamTwiston-Davies 80
(Nigel Twiston-Davies) *hld up: hdwy 9th: rdn and wknd appr 2 out* **8/1**
30-2 5 7 **Mr Satco (IRE)**[18] 270 7-11-4 112 (p) JamesDavies 62
(Chris Down) *chsd ldrs: j.lft 1st: hmpd 9th: sn rdn: wknd next* **9/2**[2]
P-55 P **Fort George (IRE)**[16] 294 12-11-2 117 (p) MissBHampson(7)
(Andy Turnell) *prom: lost pl after 5th: bhd fr 7th: p.u bef 9th* **11/2**
43-2 P **Friendly Society (IRE)**[29] 62 10-11-6 117 (v) JamesBanks(3)
(Noel Williams) *hld up: hit 4th: hdwy to chse wnr 6th: mstke 8th (water): hit next and 10th: wknd appr 4 out: bhd whn p.u bef next* **5/1**[3]
P12- P **Makadamia**[68] 4959 6-10-12 109 (p) MrSWaley-Cohen(3)
(Robert Waley-Cohen) *chsd ldrs: lost pl 5th: wknd 10th: bhd whn p.u bef last* **9/2**[2]

5m 3.4s (-11.60) **Going Correction** -0.375s/f (Good) **8 Ran SP% 116.3**
Speed ratings: **106,105,99,84,81 , ,**
CSF £42.09 CT £443.19 TOTE £5.50: £2.00, £3.10, £5.20; EX 45.10 Trifecta £369.30.
Owner Wayne Clifford **Bred** Joe & June Staunton **Trained** Enmore, Somerset

FOCUS
A modest contest run at a strong gallop. Four of these finished second on their previous outing. The winner improved to the level of his best hurdle form.

558 SEND YOUR MARE TO YORGUNNABELUCKY MAIDEN OPEN NATIONAL HUNT FLAT RACE 2m 70y
8:55 (8:57) (Class 5) 4-6-Y-O £2,274 (£667; £333; £166)

Form RPR
1 **Waterlord** 4-10-12 0 AidanColeman 123+
(John Ferguson) *hld up: hdwy over 5f out: led over 1f out: sn clr: easily* **9/4**[1]
3P-0 2 10 **Midtech Valentine**[21] 213 4-10-5 0 RichardJohnson 99
(Ian Williams) *chsd ldrs: led after 3f: rdn and hdd over 1f out: sn outpcd* **10/1**
3 7 **Grow Nasa Grow (IRE)** 4-10-5 0 MrRWinks(7) 99
(Peter Winks) *uns rdr on the way to s: hld up: styd on fnl 3f: wnt 3rd post: nrst fin* **25/1**
4 hd **I'dliketheoption (IRE)** 4-10-9 0 MauriceLinehan(3) 99
(Jonjo O'Neill) *trckd ldrs: plld hrd: wnt 2nd over 5f out tl rdn over 2f out: wknd over 1f out* **9/2**[3]
0-5 5 13 **Definately Vinnie**[18] 271 5-10-11 0 ConorRing(5) 90
(Jane Mathias) *mid-div: hdwy u.p over 4f out: wknd over 2f out* **40/1**
6 2 **Panopticon** 4-9-12 0 MrMJPKendrick(7) 77
(Giles Bravery) *hld up: pushed along and hdwy over 3f out: wknd over 2f out* **33/1**
/60- 7 4 **Star Of Salford**[352] 677 6-10-9 0 (t[1]) GavinSheehan 77
(Warren Greatrex) *hld up: nvr nrr* **10/1**
8 10 **Instingtive (IRE)** 4-10-12 0 NoelFehily 70
(Harry Fry) *prom: racd keenly: rdn and wknd over 2f out* **7/2**[2]
0 9 nk **The Bank Manager**[19] 242 4-10-12 0 TomScudamore 70
(David Pipe) *led 1f: chsd ldr tl over 5f out: wknd 3f out* **6/1**
10 3 3/4 **Uncle Chizza** 6-11-2 0 MarkGrant 70
(Sean Curran) *mid-div: rdn and wknd over 3f out* **50/1**
11 12 **Any Destination (IRE)** 4-10-9 0 JamesBanks(3) 54
(Andy Turnell) *prom: rdn over 5f out: wknd over 3f out* **33/1**
12 4 **Annie'sboydave** 5-10-13 0 TomBellamy(3) 54
(Peter Pritchard) *hld up: rdn over 5f out: wknd 4f out* **50/1**
6 13 4 **Von Trappe (IRE)**[20] 220 6-11-2 0 AdamWedge 50
(Alan Phillips) *hld up: plld hrd: pushed along 1/2-way: sn wknd* **66/1**

3m 48.4s (-2.00) **Going Correction** -0.275s/f (Good)
WFA 4 from 5yo+ 4lb **13 Ran SP% 121.2**
Speed ratings: **93,88,85,84,78 77,75,71,71,69 63,61,59**
CSF £25.65 TOTE £3.90: £1.40, £2.90, £7.30; EX 34.60 Trifecta £771.60.
Owner Bloomfields **Bred** Rabbah Bloodstock Limited **Trained** Cowlinge, Suffolk
■ Stewards' Enquiry : Maurice Linehan ten-day ban: failed to ride out for third (Jun 13,15-19,21, 23,24,26)

FOCUS
Not much pace on early for this bumper. It has been given a token rating but the winner looks a smart prospect.
T/Plt: £163.00 to a £1 stake. Pool: £68291.20 - 305.81 winning tickets. T/Qpdt: £156.50 to a £1 stake. Pool: £5161.14 - 24.4 winning tickets. **Colin Roberts**

559 - 565a (Foreign Racing) - See Raceform Interactive

125
FAKENHAM (L-H)
Sunday, May 31

OFFICIAL GOING: Good (good to firm in places; 7.8)
Wind: light, across Weather: dry, after rain earlier

566 ACTIVE FAKENHAM WEEK 22ND - 29TH AUGUST MAIDEN HURDLE (9 hdls) 2m 3y
2:30 (2:30) (Class 4) 4-Y-O+ £3,898 (£1,144; £572; £286)

Form RPR
1 **Mountain Fighter**[571] 4-10-12 0 AidanColeman 110+
(John Ferguson) *in tch in midfield: clsd to trck ldrs and hmpd 3 out: rdn to chal and wnt clr w runner-up between last two: forged ahd cl home* **11/4**[2]
3 2 hd **All Together (FR)**[22] 207 4-10-12 0 NoelFehily 110+
(Johnny Farrelly) *in tch in midfield: clsd to trck ldrs and hmpd 3 out: effrt to ld sn after next: sn rdn and wnt clr w wnr: kpt on u.p: hdd and no ex cl home* **11/4**[2]
P/ 3 26 **Sunny Bank**[13] 4039 6-11-2 0 (t) GerardTumelty 90
(Alan Coogan) *chsd ldrs: led after 3 out: blnd next and sn hdd: 3rd and btn ent st: wkng whn j. slowly last: fdd flat* **100/1**
2- 4 shd **Createur (IRE)**[76] 4814 4-10-12 0 RichardJohnson 85
(Tim Vaughan) *t.k.h: hld up in tch in rr: hdwy to trck ldrs 3 out: ev ch bef next: 4th and wknd u.p bef last* **9/4**[1]
/0-6 5 12 **Western Way (IRE)**[19] 263 6-11-2 0 DenisO'Regan 80
(Don Cantillon) *midfield: blnd 1st: rdn and struggling after 6th: losing tch and hmpd next* **4/1**[3]
P **Nifty Kier**[12] 6-11-2 0 JackQuinlan
(Phil McEntee) *led: hdd sn after 3 out: sn wknd: t.o whn p.u last* **50/1**
0 P **Satin Waters**[14] 353 4-10-5 0 TrevorWhelan
(Christine Dunnett) *hld up in tch in rr: rdn and struggling after mstke 5th: sn lost tch: t.o whn p.u 3 out* **100/1**
02-5 F **Ley Lady Grey**[26] 120 5-10-9 0 BrendanPowell
(Jamie Snowden) *chsd ldr: ev ch whn fell 3 out* **20/1**

4m 7.15s (-5.85) **Going Correction** -0.325s/f (Good)
WFA 4 from 5yo+ 18lb **8 Ran SP% 112.8**
Speed ratings (Par 105): **100,99,87,87,81 , ,**
CSF £10.62 TOTE £4.30: £1.40, £1.10, £5.50; EX 12.00 Trifecta £514.60.
Owner Bloomfields **Bred** Silfield Bloodstock & Qatar Bloodstock **Trained** Cowlinge, Suffolk

FOCUS
They went a sound gallop in this modest maiden and the first pair went clear from two out in a bobbing finish. Afterwards the rider's reported that morning rain had definitely got into the ground.

567 LIGHT DRAGOONS H'CAP CHASE (FOR THE PRINCE OF WALES CUP) (18 fncs) 3m 38y
3:00 (3:02) (Class 5) (0-100,100) 5-Y-O+ £4,548 (£1,335; £667; £333)

Form RPR
35-3 1 **Troubled (IRE)**[26] 126 8-10-0 74 oh2 (p) BrianHughes 83
(David Thompson) *chsd ldrs: wnt 2nd 13th tl 15th: bmpd next: drvn to chse ldr again after 3 out: 4 l down and hld whn lft 6 l clr and hmpd last: kpt on: rdn out* **10/1**
4U-0 2 4 1/2 **Royaume Bleu (FR)**[22] 211 10-10-1 78 (v[1]) JamesBanks(3) 82
(Alex Hales) *lft chsng ldr 2nd: led 5th: rdn and hdd 3 out: 4th and outpcd next: rallied u.p to go 3rd ent st: keeping on same pce whn lft 6 l 2nd and hmpd last: no imp flat* **10/1**
/06- 3 6 **No Principles**[160] 3230 12-11-12 100 (b) MarkGrant 99
(Julian Smith) *in tch: chsd ldrs 13th: j.rt 3 out: rdn and effrt in 2nd bef next: lost 2nd and wknd between last 2: lft 10 l 3rd last* **33/1**
4-62 4 19 **The Society Man (IRE)**[4] 504 8-11-2 95 JoeCornwall(5) 77
(Michael Chapman) *dropped to rr 2nd and nvr travelling after: lost tch after 13th: lft modest 4th last* **5/1**[3]
334- 5 6 **Lord Of The Dunes**[315] 1016 7-11-1 89 (bt) BrendanPowell 65
(Jamie Snowden) *j.lft: led tl after 1st: lft in ld 2nd tl hdd 5th: chsd ldr after tl 13th: struggling 3 out: wknd bef next* **9/1**
-233 6 36 **Veauce De Sivola (FR)**[19] 269 6-11-12 100 (t) TommyPhelan 44
(Mark Gillard) *nvr jumping fluently or travelling wl enough: in tch towards rr: rdn and lost tch after 13th: t.o* **20/1**
44/3 P **See You Jack**[15] 10-11-2 95 (p[1]) BridgetAndrews(5)
(Caroline Fryer) *dropped to rr after 2nd: mstke 5th and immediately p.u* **7/1**
0-64 P **Next Exit (IRE)**[19] 258 10-10-6 80 TomMessenger
(John Cornwall) *t.k.h: in tch in midfield: struggling and mstke 14th: sn bhd and lost tch: t.o whn p.u 2 out* **40/1**
44-6 U **Gale Force Oscar (IRE)**[32] 17 10-11-4 92 GerardTumelty
(Andy Turnell) *led after 1st: uns rdr 2nd* **7/2**[2]
P4-1 F **La Madonnina (IRE)**[7] 450 7-10-2 76 7ex (p) JamesBest 90+
(Caroline Keevil) *in tch in midfield: mstke 10th: hit 13th: rdn and hdwy to join ldrs after next: led 3 out: rdn and forged clr between last 2: 4 l ld and in command whn fell last* **11/4**[1]

6m 33.05s (-2.65) **Going Correction** -0.075s/f (Good) **10 Ran SP% 116.4**
Speed ratings: **101,99,97,91,89 78, , ,**
CSF £99.64 CT £3152.08 TOTE £12.40: £3.30, £3.60, £7.30; EX 107.80 Trifecta £1471.00.
Owner T J A Thompson **Bred** Grange Stud **Trained** Bolam, Co Durham

The Form Book Jumps 2015-16, Raceform Ltd, Newbury, RG14 5SJ

FOCUS
This weak handicap saw final-fence drama and the form has to be treated with some caution.

568 TOUR OF BRITAIN CYCLE RACE 12TH SEPT H'CAP CHASE (16 fncs) 2m 5f 44y
3:30 (3:31) (Class 3) (0-130,125) 5-Y-0+ £7,988 (£2,480; £1,335)

Form RPR
310- 1 **Benevolent (IRE)**[40] 5450 8-11-8 **121** TomMessenger 128
(Chris Bealby) *t.k.h: hld up in tch: lft 4th and hmpd 12th: rdn next: styd on to chse clr ldr after 3 out: 7 l down and plugging on whn lft in ld 2 out: kpt on u.p: drvn out* **7/2**[1]
20-3 2 *11* **Buck Mulligan**[14] 362 10-11-12 **125** PaulMoloney 122
(Evan Williams) *in tch in midfield: lft 2nd 12th: 8 l down next: 3rd and no imp whn lft 3 l 2nd last: no imp u.p whn mstke last: wknd flat* **6/1**[3]
62-6 3 *10* **Passato (GER)**[14] 362 11-11-4 **120** (t) JamesBanks(3) 108
(Jo Davis) *chsd ldrs: mstke and lost pl 6th: sn rdn: hdwy to chse ldrs 10th: lft 3rd and hmpd 12th: no imp and wl hld 4th whn lft 6 l 3rd 2 out: wknd bef last* **25/1**
2-5U F **Freckle Face**[9] 431 8-11-10 **123** AndrewThornton
(Bill Turner) *in tch in rr: fell 12th* **9/1**
35-6 U **Benefit Cut (IRE)**[16] 318 9-11-12 **125** [1] BrendanPowell
(Stuart Edmunds) *taken down early: chsd ldrs: wnt 2nd 7th tl mstke and uns rdr 12th* **7/2**[1]
3-51 U **Unknown Legend (IRE)**[11] 398 8-10-6 **105** JackQuinlan 110
(Sarah Humphrey) *taken down early: led and sn clr: 10 l clr and mstke 3 out: pushed along but stl 7 l ahd whn mstke and uns rdr 2 out* **7/2**[1]
1-14 F **Abricot De L'Oasis (FR)**[16] 315 5-11-7 **120** HenryBrooke
(Donald McCain) *mstkes: chsd ldr tl 7th: lost pl 9th: stl wl in tch whn fell 12th* **5/1**[2]

5m 38.35s (-3.45) **Going Correction** -0.075s/f (Good) **7** Ran SP% **111.5**
Speed ratings: **103,99,95, ,**
CSF £23.10 TOTE £5.10: £2.60, £1.80; EX 24.20 Trifecta £445.40.
Owner Paul Read & Dave Cook **Bred** Pierce Molony **Trained** Barrowby, Lincs

FOCUS
This was highly eventful and the form should be taken with a pinch of salt.

569 HOLKHAM COUNTRY FAIR 25TH & 26TH JULY NOVICES' H'CAP HURDLE (12 hdls 1 omitted) 2m 7f 95y
4:00 (4:00) (Class 5) (0-100,98) 4-Y-0+ £3,898 (£1,144; £572; £286)

Form RPR
-P6P 1 **Izbushka (IRE)**[11] 399 4-10-0 **78** oh4 (b) BrianHughes 82+
(David Thompson) *chsd ldrs: wnt 2nd 10th led bef 2 out: rdn clr between last 2: styd on: comf* **33/1**
44P- 2 *9* **Dynamic Idol (USA)**[13] 4051 8-11-6 **92** (bt) NoelFehily 95
(Johnny Farrelly) *chsd ldrs: clsd to trck ldrs bypassing 3 out: wnt 2nd next: sn drvn and btn: plugged on same pce after* **14/1**
44-4 3 *15* **Conas Taoi (IRE)**[22] 209 6-11-4 **90** TomO'Brien 79
(Paul Morgan) *midfield: hdwy after 6th: 3rd and drvn after 10th: no ex 2 out: sn wknd* **7/2**[2]
445- 4 *8* **Raid Stane (IRE)**[80] 4726 9-11-12 **98** (tp) HenryBrooke 78
(Julia Brooke) *dropped to rr 4th: drvn and no hdwy after 10th: no ch but styd on past btn horses between last 2* **8/1**
PP-3 5 *2* **Breezy Kin (IRE)**[31] 40 7-11-4 **90** RichardJohnson 69
(Sean Curran) *chsd clr ldr: clsd 7th: led after 9th: drvn and hdd bef 2 out: btn whn nt fluent next: sn wknd* **5/2**[1]
230- 6 *11* **Looks Like Magic**[49] 5295 6-11-7 **93** (v[1]) TrevorWhelan 65
(Neil King) *hld up towards rr: clsd 7th: rdn after 9th: 5th and stl cl enough bypassing 3 out: wknd u.p 2 out: t.o* **6/1**[3]
6-24 7 *9* **Canarbino Girl**[21] 222 8-10-8 **80** (tp) JamesBest 40
(Caroline Keevil) *a towards rr: rdn after 8th: struggling 10th: lost tch bypassing 3 out: t.o* **9/1**
21-5 8 *18* **Pennies And Pounds**[30] 55 8-11-2 **88** MarkGrant 32
(Julian Smith) *midfield: clsd 7th: 6th and rdn bypassing 3 out: sn btn and fdd 2 out: t.o* **8/1**
00-0 P **John Biscuit (IRE)**[27] 98 7-11-5 **94** (t) JamesBanks(3)
(Jo Davis) *led and sn clr: c bk to field 7th: mstke 9th and sn hdd: dropped out rapidly after next: t.o whn p.u 2 out* **14/1**
3P/P P **Strangelittlegirl**[26] 130 7-10-13 **85** JackQuinlan
(Giles Bravery) *midfield: dropped to rr and rdn 8th: lost tch after 10th: t.o whn p.u 2 out* **50/1**

6m 13.3s (-8.70) **Going Correction** -0.325s/f (Good)
WFA 4 from 6yo+ 19lb **10** Ran SP% **115.5**
Speed ratings (Par 103): **100,97,92,89,89 85,82,76, ,**
CSF £414.56 CT £2033.14 TOTE £24.60: £5.90, £4.60, £1.40; EX 200.90 Trifecta £2500.10.
Owner J A Moore **Bred** Mrs J Norris **Trained** Bolam, Co Durham

FOCUS
A weak novice handicap.

570 WELCOME TO NORFOLK PRINCESS CHARLOTTE NOVICES' LIMITED H'CAP CHASE (10 fncs 2 omitted) 2m 59y
4:30 (4:30) (Class 3) (0-135,130) 5-Y-0+ £6,657 (£2,067; £1,113)

Form RPR
U-42 1 **Red Seventy**[15] 338 6-10-9 **117** JackQuinlan 121
(Sarah Humphrey) *t.k.h: chsd ldrs: lft cl 2nd 9th: rdn and mstke next: drvn to ld bef last: forged clr: styd on* **5/2**[2]
0/1- 2 *3* **Jonnie Skull (IRE)**[15] 4743 9-10-8 **116** (t) BrianHughes 117
(Phil McEntee) *led: jnd 2 out: rdn and hdd bef last: no ex and btn whn j.rt last: one pce* **3/1**[3]
P6P- 3 *155* **Radsoc De Sivola (FR)**[241] 1696 10-9-12 **111** oh61 JoeCornwall(5)
(John Cornwall) *sn detached in last: t.o fr 7th* **50/1**
3-32 F **Town Mouse**[5] 492 5-10-10 **118** TrevorWhelan
(Neil King) *chsd ldr: mstke and rdn 7th: ev ch whn fell 9th* **10/11**[1]

4m 12.6s (-4.00) **Going Correction** -0.075s/f (Good) **4** Ran SP% **107.9**
Speed ratings: **106,104, ,**
CSF £9.78 TOTE £3.20; EX 8.00 Trifecta £31.70.
Owner Yen Hall Farm Racing **Bred** Sir Eric Parker **Trained** West Wratting, Cambs

FOCUS
This novice handicap was run at an average gallop.

571 AYLSHAM SHOW - AUGUST BANK HOLIDAY - LADY AMATEUR RIDERS' H'CAP HURDLE (11 hdls) 2m 4f 1y
5:00 (5:02) (Class 5) (0-100,100) 4-Y-0+ £3,951 (£1,215; £607)

Form RPR
0-41 1 **Occasionally Yours (IRE)**[11] 399 11-10-11 **92** MissTWorsley(7) 103+
(Alan Blackmore) *hld up in tch: hdwy to chse ldrs after 8th: wnt 2nd after 3 out: led and lft clr next: styd on wl and sn in command: readily* **5/1**[3]
242- 2 *13* **Weybridge Light**[10] 4534 10-11-9 **100** (b) MissAGoschen(3) 100
(David Thompson) *in tch in midfield: hdwy to chse ldrs 4th: wnt 2nd 8th tl after 3 out: lft 2nd 2 out: sn rdn and no imp: plugged on* **7/1**
F5-3 3 *12* **Volcanic Jack (IRE)**[4] 502 7-10-0 **74** oh5 AliceMills 62
(Michael Chapman) *chsd ldr tl 6th: reminder bef next: rdn and btn after 3 out: lft wl hld 3rd next: plugged on* **11/4**[1]
443- 4 *40* **Royal Etiquette (IRE)**[81] 4709 8-10-8 **89** (tp) MissKatyLyons(7) 41
(Lawney Hill) *in tch: effrt into midfield and hit 7th: rdn and no hdwy after 8th: lft poor 4th 2 out: t.o* **8/1**
-312 5 *24* **Riddlestown (IRE)**[13] 381 8-11-7 **95** (b) MissGAndrews 25
(Caroline Fryer) *in tch in midfield: mstke and reminder 4th: mstke next: rdn 6th: lost tch 8th: t.o bef 2 out* **4/1**[2]
PB3- 6 *2¾* **Indiefront**[183] 2797 6-10-10 **91** MissHStuckey(7) 18
(Jo Davis) *hld up in rr: lost tch 8th: t.o bef 2 out* **33/1**
P-00 P **Samizdat (FR)**[10] 421 12-9-7 **74** oh7 MissGSwan(7)
(John O'Neill) *a towards rr: lost tch 8th: t.o 3 out tl p.u last* **50/1**
53-2 P **Owner Occupier**[7] 446 10-9-8 **75** MissSKelk(7)
(Chris Gordon) *led: mstke and rdr lost irons 6th: hdd next: 5th and dropping out whn p.u arnd 3 out: rdr unable to stop: j. 2 out and uns rdr* **8/1**
46-P U **Monroe Park (IRE)**[20] 240 10-10-4 **81** (p) MissAEStirling(3) 69
(Alan Blackmore) *chsd ldrs: wnt 2nd 6th: led 7th tl hdd: mstke and uns rdr 2 out* **18/1**
/4-P P **Storm To Pass**[11] 398 7-10-11 **92** (t) MissKGowing(7)
(Caroline Fryer) *in tch: dropped to rr 6th: lost tch 8th and t.o whn p.u next* **14/1**

5m 9.5s (-10.90) **Going Correction** -0.325s/f (Good) **10** Ran SP% **114.9**
Speed ratings (Par 103): **107,102,97,82,73 72, , ,**
CSF £39.51 CT £114.78 TOTE £6.10: £4.10, £1.90, £1.50; EX 29.40 Trifecta £195.30.
Owner A G Blackmore **Bred** Gerard Connolly **Trained** Little Berkhamsted, Herts

FOCUS
A very weak handicap, confined to lady amateur riders.
T/Plt: £849.70 to a £1 stake. Pool: £104,160.72 - 89.48 winning units. T/Qpdt: £69.90 to a £1 stake. Pool: £9233.32 - 97.65 winning units. **Steve Payne**

572 - 587a (Foreign Racing) - See Raceform Interactive

394 SOUTHWELL (L-H)
Tuesday, June 2

OFFICIAL GOING: Good (7.9)
Wind: strong 1/2 behind Weather: fine but very breezy

588 ALEA EAST MIDLAND'S PREMIER ENTERTAINMENT VENUE H'CAP CHASE (13 fncs) 1m 7f 153y
5:05 (5:05) (Class 5) (0-100,100) 5-Y-0+ £2,599 (£763; £381; £190)

Form RPR
14-2 1 **Moonlight Maggie**[15] 379 8-10-12 **86** (t) PaddyBrennan 93
(Tom George) *hld up in mid-div: effrt appr 3 out: led last: drvn rt out* **6/1**
31-4 2 *¾* **Table Bluff (IRE)**[15] 379 6-11-6 **94** NicodeBoinville 100
(John Spearing) *mid-div: hdwy to chse ldrs 9th: led 2 out: kpt on towards fin* **9/2**[1]
552- 3 *2½* **Red Rosso**[46] 5376 10-10-0 **79** ow3 JakeHodson(5) 84
(Rob Summers) *hld up towards rr: hdwy 9th: mstke 3 out: 3rd last: kpt on same pce* **8/1**
00P/ 4 *½* **Go Teescomponents**[17] 8-10-0 **74** oh10 BrianHughes 76
(Keith Reveley) *chsd ldrs: kpt on same pce between last 2* **16/1**
4-53 5 *nk* **Dougalstar (FR)**[21] 258 6-10-0 **74** oh8 PeterCarberry 79+
(Jennie Candlish) *mstke 1st: chsd ldrs: mstke 7th: outpcd appr 3 out: 6th whn hit last: kpt on* **9/1**
5-32 6 *2½* **Lost In Newyork (IRE)**[21] 258 8-10-7 **81** AdamWedge 81
(Nick Kent) *mid-div: outpcd 10th: kpt on one pce* **5/1**[2]
/05- 7 *1¼* **Dancing Ecco (IRE)**[315] 1053 6-10-1 **80** ConorRing(5) 82+
(Evan Williams) *led: hdd 2 out: wkng whn hit last* **40/1**
P5P- 8 *16* **Wolf Hall (IRE)**[53] 5257 8-10-0 **74** DaveCrosse 58
(Violet M Jordan) *w ldr: j.rt 9th: lost pl 3 out: sn bhd* **33/1**
55-4 9 *16* **Imperial Plan (IRE)**[26] 175 5-11-9 **97** (t) BrendanPowell 67
(Jamie Snowden) *mid-div: hdwy 9th: sn chsng ldrs: drvn next: lost pl before 3 out: sn bhd* **10/1**
2P5- P **Tri Nations (UAE)**[46] 5376 10-10-12 **89** (tp) JonathanEngland(3)
(Harriet Bethell) *mid-div: lost pl 7th: sn bhd: t.o whn p.u bef last* **20/1**
440- P **Hopeand**[46] 5376 10-11-12 **100** (t) AdamPogson
(Charles Pogson) *in rr: lost pl 8th: bhd whn p.u bef 10th* **25/1**
512- P **Tempuran**[236] 1816 6-11-11 **99** TomScudamore
(David Bridgwater) *mid-div: sme hdwy 7th: lost pl 8th: bhd 10th: t.o whn p.u bef next* **11/2**[3]

4m 12.3s (10.30) **Going Correction** +0.70s/f (Soft) **12** Ran SP% **114.6**
Speed ratings: **102,101,100,100,99 98,98,90,82,**
CSF £31.41 CT £217.20 TOTE £7.80: £2.20, £1.70, £3.10; EX 28.60 Trifecta £203.10.
Owner Capt & Mrs J A George **Bred** Mrs Caroline George **Trained** Slad, Gloucs

FOCUS
Fences sited on outside. The opening contest was a moderate handicap chase. They went a respectable gallop on good ground. The form is rated around the first three.

589 HAMPSONS TO THE RESCUE H'CAP CHASE (16 fncs) 2m 4f 62y
5:35 (5:35) (Class 4) (0-110,110) 5-Y-0+ £3,898 (£1,144; £572; £286)

Form RPR
306- 1 **Sail And Return**[75] 4863 11-11-12 **110** (t) KielanWoods 120+
(Phil Middleton) *mid-div: trckd ldrs 6th: handy 2nd 13th: led appr 3 out: styd on wl* **5/1**[2]
0/4- 2 *4½* **Teddy's Reflection (IRE)**[77] 4831 12-11-2 **100** PaddyBrennan 104
(Harriet Bethell) *rr-div: nt fluent 8th: chsng ldrs next: blnd 12th: sn outpcd: kpt on fr 3 out: 3rd last: tk 2nd towards fin* **10/1**
50-4 3 *½* **Temple Lord (FR)**[15] 381 9-11-5 **103** (b) WillKennedy 105
(Jonjo O'Neill) *chsd ldrs: handy 3rd bef 3 out: 2nd between last 2: kpt on same pce* **11/1**

61-5 **4** *3 ¾* **Faith Jicaro (IRE)**[26] 170 8-10-13 **97**........................(p) TomScudamore 96
(David Bridgwater) *w ldr: led 6th: hdd appr 3 out: wknd last* **12/1**

36-P **5** *dist* **The Winking Prawn (IRE)**[16] 365 8-11-1 **99**...............(t) GavinSheehan
(Graeme McPherson) *chsd ldrs: j. slowly 3rd: 2nd whn blnd 10th: 3rd and wkng whn hit 13th: bhd next: t.o* **11/2**[3]

0-41 **6** *3 ¾* **Saddlers Deal (IRE)**[17] 331 10-10-11 **102**...............(p) CraigGallagher(7)
(Brian Ellison) *in rr: hdwy and prom 9th: lost pl after 12th: sn bhd: t.o* **13/2**

2U5- **P** **Killfinnan Castle (IRE)**[71] 4966 12-9-7 **84** oh13.... JosephPalmowski(7)
(Violet M Jordan) *led to 6th: reminders after 9th: lost pl 12th: sn bhd: t.o whn p.u bef 3 out* **66/1**

P6-4 **P** **The Jugopolist (IRE)**[28] 128 8-9-9 **84** oh1.................(v) JoeCornwall(5)
(John Cornwall) *in rr: hmpd 2nd: bhd fr 9th: t.o whn p.u bef 12th* **50/1**

44F- **P** **Goldie Horn**[66] 5033 7-11-6 **104**.............................(t) SamTwiston-Davies
(Nigel Twiston-Davies) *mid-div: reminders after 9th: sn bhd: t.o 13th: p.u bef next* **12/1**

12P- **F** **Pure Poteen (IRE)**[154] 3410 7-11-10 **108**.......................(t) MarkQuinlan
(Neil Mulholland) *chsd ldrs: fell 2nd* **2/1**[1]

5m 29.0s (12.00) **Going Correction** +0.70s/f (Soft) **10** Ran SP% **115.0**
Speed ratings: **104,102,102,100,86 85, , , ,**
CSF £52.59 CT £524.38 TOTE £6.40: £2.10, £2.60, £3.30; EX 27.40 Trifecta £384.70.
Owner P W Middleton **Bred** Andrew And Mrs S R B Davis **Trained** Dorton, Bucks

FOCUS
The feature contest was a modest handicap chase. They went an ordinary gallop. The winner was back to the level of last year's C&D win.

590 MORGAN TUCKER "NATIONAL HUNT" MAIDEN HURDLE (11 hdls) 2m 4f 62y
6:05 (6:05) (Class 5) 4-Y-O+ £2,599 (£763; £381; £190)

Form RPR

046- **1** **Just A Normal Day (IRE)**[86] 4653 5-11-0 108...............(p) HarrySkelton 110+
(Dan Skelton) *chsd ldrs: j.rt and reminders 5th: 2nd and reminders 7th: sn hrd drvn: 2 l down whn blnd 2 out: led appr last: 3 l clr and j.lft: idled: drvn rt out* **2/1**[1]

2 *1* **Cooper's Friend (IRE)**[44] 6-11-0 0...............................(t) AidanColeman 104
(Charlie Longsdon) *j.rt: w ldr: led 2nd: drvn appr 2 out: hdd appr last: rallied run-in: no ex clsng stages* **11/4**[2]

0- **3** *51* **Rebel Benefit (IRE)**[79] 7-11-0 0.................................... NoelFehily 58
(David Dennis) *in rr: j. slowly 2nd: lost pl 5th: bhd 7th: t.o 3 out: distant 3rd appr last* **6/1**

23-3 **4** *11* **Ethelwyn**[17] 334 5-10-7 0... BrianHughes 41
(Malcolm Jefferson) *hld up: hdwy 4th: handy 3rd sn after 7th: drvn 3 out: sn wknd: t.o next* **9/2**[3]

3-3 **P** **Anti Cool (IRE)**[22] 242 6-11-0 0...................................... CharliePoste
(Robin Dickin) *j.rt: led to 2nd: wknd 8th: sn wl bhd: t.o 3 out: p.u bef next* **20/1**

54-1 **P** **Allycat**[21] 257 5-10-9 0... DiarmuidO'Regan(5)
(Chris Grant) *chsd ldrs: unsighted: mstke and reminders 5th: lost pl 7th: sn bhd: t.o 3 out: p.u bef next* **10/1**

P **P** **Thady Quil (IRE)**[26] 160 5-11-0 0.................................. AndrewTinkler
(Martin Keighley) *in rr: drvn to chse ldrs 5th: reminders and lost pl after next: sn bhd: t.o 3 out: p.u bef next* **20/1**

5m 16.9s (3.90) **Going Correction** +0.30s/f (Yiel) **7** Ran SP% **111.1**
Speed ratings (Par 103): **104,103,83,78, ,**
CSF £7.40 TOTE £2.60: £1.60, £2.10; EX 8.70 Trifecta £41.90.
Owner CNC Routing Ltd **Bred** Mrs Grace Bracken **Trained** Alcester, Warwicks

FOCUS
An ordinary maiden hurdle. They went an even gallop. A step up from the idling winner.

591 PORSCHE CENTRE NOTTINGHAM MARES' NOVICES' HURDLE (9 hdls) 1m 7f 153y
6:35 (6:35) (Class 4) 4-Y-O+ £3,249 (£954; £477; £238)

Form RPR

33P- **1** **Tea In Transvaal (IRE)**[111] 4155 4-10-7 0........................ PaulMoloney 110+
(Evan Williams) *chsd ldr: nt fluent 4th: styd on fr 2 out: upsides last: led post* **7/1**[3]

6-2 **2** *hd* **Via Volupta**[29] 111 5-10-10 0....................................... GavinSheehan 112
(Warren Greatrex) *j.lft: led: drvn appr 2 out: hdd between last 2: led narrowly last: styd on: jst ct* **3/1**[2]

13-5 **3** *1 ¼* **Chilly Miss**[12] 415 6-10-10 0... BrianHughes 111
(Malcolm Jefferson) *trckd ldrs: led between last 2: hdd last: kpt on same pce last 50yds* **8/1**

22-1 **4** *21* **Bantam (IRE)**[21] 268 5-11-3 130.................................. RichardJohnson 102
(Henry Daly) *trckd ldng pair: 2nd 5th: drvn appr 2 out: rdn and wknd between last 2: j.lft last: sn eased* **4/9**[1]

P **5** *40* **Cearys (IRE)**[22] 238 7-10-10 0.................................... AndrewTinkler 50
(Martin Keighley) *chsd ldrs: outpcd: lost pl and reminders 3 out: sn bhd: diatsant 5th last: t.o* **50/1**

60-6 **6** *5* **Timon's Tara**[29] 111 6-10-10 0....................................... CharliePoste 45
(Robin Dickin) *in rr: hmpd 1st 2: hdwy 5th: sn chsng ldrs: wknd bef 3 out: sn bhd: t.o* **16/1**

0 **7** *7* **Sawwala**[26] 179 5-10-10 0... DougieCostello 38
(J R Jenkins) *j.lft 1st 2: in rr: bhd whn hit 4th: t.o 3 out* **50/1**

003- **P** **Simplified**[81] 4743 12-10-5 64......................................(t) JoeCornwall(5)
(Michael Chapman) *in rr: bhd 5th: t.o next: p.u bef 2 out* **200/1**

0-0 **P** **Silver Djebel**[33] 45 4-10-7 0...................................(t) BrendanPowell
(Jamie Snowden) *in rr: t.o and reminders 5th: p.u after 3 out: bromke blood vessel* **66/1**

4m 3.5s (6.50) **Going Correction** +0.30s/f (Yiel)
WFA 4 from 5yo+ 17lb **9** Ran SP% **129.7**
Speed ratings (Par 105): **95,94,94,83,63 61,57, ,**
CSF £32.44 TOTE £10.30: £1.70, £1.40, £2.20; EX 46.90 Trifecta £175.30.
Owner M J Haines **Bred** Summerville Bloodstock **Trained** Llancarfan, Vale Of Glamorgan

FOCUS
A fairly good mares' novice hurdle, if uncompetitive on paper, but the form horse disappointed badly. They went a steady pace with a fast finishing split.

592 RICHMOND RAMPAGE H'CAP HURDLE (9 hdls) 1m 7f 153y
7:05 (7:05) (Class 4) (0-120,118) 4-Y-O+ £3,249 (£954; £477; £238)

Form RPR

52-4 **1** **Bigindie (IRE)**[21] 263 5-11-3 **110**............................... AdamNicol(3) 115+
(John Weymes) *hld up: hdwy 6th: handy 3rd next: led appr 2 out: styd on wl appr last: heavily eased clsng stages* **15/2**

65-0 **2** *7* **Vosne Romanee**[26] 162 4-11-11 **118**...................(bt) WillKennedy 112
(Dr Richard Newland) *chsd ldrs 3rd: reminders 3 out: 2nd between last 2: kpt on same pce* **11/4**[1]

2/4- **3** *14* **Northern Meeting (IRE)**[385] 261 5-11-1 **105**..................... TomO'Brien 89
(Robert Stephens) *nt fluent: hdwy to chse ldrs 4th: drvn 3 out: 2nd 2 out: wknd and j.lft last* **8/1**

-330 **4** *11* **Watt Broderick (IRE)**[17] 332 6-11-3 **110**..................(tp) RobMcCarth(3) 85
(Ian Williams) *chsd ldr: upsides 5th: drvn appr 2 out: sn wknd* **5/1**[3]

61-0 **5** *25* **Hi Tide (IRE)**[26] 177 11-11-12 **116**................................ AidanColeman 68
(J R Jenkins) *in rr: bhd 4th: sme hdwy and drvn 3 out: sn lost pl and bhd: t.o* **12/1**

364- **P** **Wordy's Boy**[93] 4511 10-11-3 **107**................................... AdamPogson
(Charles Pogson) *j.lft 1st: in rr: handy 3rd whn blnd and lost pl 3rd: t.o after next: p.u bef 2 out* **7/2**[2]

05-2 **P** **Samoset**[16] 354 5-11-9 **113**...(t) KielanWoods
(Charlie Longsdon) *led: hdd appr 2 out: lost pl and modest 5th whn p.u bedore last* **5/1**[3]

4m 2.8s (5.80) **Going Correction** +0.30s/f (Yiel)
WFA 4 from 5yo+ 17lb **7** Ran SP% **112.8**
Speed ratings (Par 105): **97,93,86,81,68 ,**
CSF £28.20 TOTE £9.30: £3.80, £2.90; EX 27.70 Trifecta £261.60.
Owner R Lilley, Clarke, Highmoor Racing **Bred** Michael Downey & Roalso Ltd **Trained** Middleham Moor, N Yorks

FOCUS
A modest handicap hurdle. They went a respectable gallop. There's a case for rating the form up to 5lb higher.

593 STREETS CHARTERED ACCOUNTANTS H'CAP HURDLE (11 hdls) 2m 4f 62y
7:35 (7:36) (Class 4) (0-120,117) 4-Y-O+ £3,249 (£954; £477; £238)

Form RPR

01-5 **1** **Mont Royale**[29] 102 7-11-3 **108**................................. RichieMcLernon 116+
(Jonjo O'Neill) *mde all: drvn appr 2 out: styd on wl* **13/2**

12-P **2** *5* **Indian Stream**[18] 314 6-11-12 **117**............................. DougieCostello 119
(Neil Mulholland) *trckd ldrs: handy 2nd 8th: drvn appr 2 out: kpt on same pce* **16/1**

64-1 **3** *7* **Brass Monkey (IRE)**[9] 451 8-11-2 **107** 7ex...................(v) TrevorWhelan 104
(Neil King) *chsd ldrs: reminders 3rd: drvn and reminders 6th: lost pl 8th: modest 4th sn after 3 out: kpt on to take 3rd last* **3/1**[2]

-113 **4** *7* **King Of Strings (IRE)**[16] 354 6-10-13 **109**...............(p) JoeCornwall(5) 100
(Mark Walford) *in rr: hdwy 4th: pushed along 6th: modest 3rd and drvn appr 3 out: wknd last* **5/1**[3]

F30- **F** **Prettyasapicture**[57] 5210 6-11-0 **108**.......................(p) TomBellamy(3)
(Alan King) *trckd ldrs: cl 2nd whn fell 7th* **14/1**

52-2 **P** **Knight Bachelor**[15] 380 5-11-8 **113**............................(t) GavinSheehan
(Warren Greatrex) *chsd ldrs: mstke 5th: lost pl and reminders after 8th: sn bhd: t.o whn p.u bef 2 out* **15/8**[1]

5m 15.8s (2.80) **Going Correction** +0.30s/f (Yiel) **6** Ran SP% **102.3**
Speed ratings (Par 105): **106,104,101,98,**
CSF £66.84 CT £265.94 TOTE £7.80: £5.10, £3.60; EX 80.00 Trifecta £261.20.
Owner Phil Tufnell Racing Limited **Bred** D J And Mrs Deer **Trained** Cheltenham, Gloucs

■ Twelve Strings was withdrawn. Price at time of withdrawal 9/1. Rule 4 applies to all bets - deduction 10p in the pound.

FOCUS
Another ordinary handicap hurdle. They went an even gallop. A step up from the winner.

594 BLUEBIRD CARE PROVIDING HIGH QUALITY CARE MARES' STANDARD OPEN NH FLAT RACE (F&M) 1m 7f 153y
8:05 (8:05) (Class 6) 4-6-Y-O £1,559 (£457; £228; £114)

Form RPR

0/3- **1** **Native Princess**[203] 2426 5-11-0 0.............................. PaddyBrennan 100+
(Stuart Edmunds) *hld up in rr: hdwy 6f out: sn trcking ldrs: upsides over 2f out: led last 100yds: drvn out* **16/1**

12- **2** *½* **Princess Roania (IRE)**[43] 5439 4-11-1 0....................... SeanBowen(3) 104+
(Peter Bowen) *mid-div: hdwy to trck ldrs over 3f out: led over 2f out: hdd last 100yds: no ex towards fin* **5/2**[2]

3 *5* **Belcanto (IRE)** 5-11-0 0... BrendanPowell 96
(Jamie Snowden) *chsd ldrs: 3rd over 1f out: kpt on same pce* **33/1**

4 *7* **Stickee Fingers** 4-10-11 0... GavinSheehan 86
(Warren Greatrex) *mid-div: hdwy 7f out: chsng ldrs 4f out: wknd over 1f out* **9/4**[1]

0- **5** *6* **Martha's Benefit (IRE)**[17] 6-10-11 0............................. AdamNicol(3) 84
(Mike Sowersby) *mid-div: hdwy to chse ldrs 6f out: wknd fnl 2f* **100/1**

6 *8* **Blu Passione** 4-10-11 0... LeightonAspell 74
(Oliver Sherwood) *in rr: drvn and hdwy after 6f: chsng ldrs 6f out: wnt rt and lost pl over 2f out* **6/1**

7 *5* **Saffron's Song (IRE)**[100] 6-11-0 0............................. RichardJohnson 72
(Harry Whittington) *mid-div: chsng ldrs 6f out: drvn 3f out: sn lost pl* **5/1**[3]

6 **8** *2* **Penny Option (IRE)**[27] 152 6-11-0 0............................... TomO'Brien 70
(Robert Stephens) *led: hdd over 2f out: grad wknd* **20/1**

16- **9** *8* **Pixiepot**[245] 1681 5-11-7 0... DarylJacob 70
(Peter Niven) *chsd ldr: drvn over 3f out: lost pl over 2f out* **10/1**

-U **10** *36* **Alizee Javilex (FR)**[32] 67 5-10-4 0............................. LukeIngram(10) 31
(Lucy Wadham) *chsd ldrs: lost pl 4f out: sn bhd: t.o* **33/1**

50-0 **11** *2 ¼* **Honey'N'Spice**[32] 67 6-11-0 0.................................... HarrySkelton 29
(George Margarson) *chsd ldrs: lost pl 6f out: sn bhd: t.o over 3f out* **66/1**

0-0 **12** *21* **Gifted Rose**[25] 188 4-10-11 0....................................... DaveCrosse 7
(Christopher Kellett) *in rr: drvn along after 6f: bhd 8f out: sn tailed rt off* **150/1**

3m 54.5s (3.10) **Going Correction** +0.30s/f (Yiel)
WFA 4 from 5yo+ 3lb **12** Ran SP% **119.1**
Speed ratings: **104,103,101,97,94 90,88,87,83,65 64,53**
CSF £54.66 TOTE £13.30: £4.20, £1.20, £9.50; EX 65.00 Trifecta £1820.60.
Owner The Oakley Partnership **Bred** East Burrow Farm **Trained** Newport Pagnell, Bucks

FOCUS
The concluding contest was an ordinary mares' bumper. They went an even gallop and the winner stepped up.

T/Plt: £3,043.30 to a £1 stake. Pool: £66452.94 - 15.94 winning tickets. T/Qpdt: £327.20 to a £1 stake. Pool: £7297.64 - 16.5 winning tickets. **Walter Glynn**

[445]FONTWELL (L-H)

Wednesday, June 3

OFFICIAL GOING: Chase course - good to soft (good in places); hurdle course - good (good to soft in places)

Wind: light breeze behind Weather: cloudy with sunny periods Rails: Second fence in home straight omitted in all chases due to ground under repair.

595 ARUN BUSINESS PARTNERSHIP NOVICES' HURDLE (11 hdls) 2m 5f 139y

2:10 (2:10) (Class 4) 4-Y-O+ **£3,249** (£954; £477; £238)

Form RPR

332- **1** **Vivant Poeme (FR)**[44] 5437 6-10-12 120.............................(t) NoelFehily 126+
(Harry Fry) *patiently rdn on rr: kpt wd on far side: stdy prog fr 6th: wnt lft 3 out: shkn up to ld bef last: styd on wl: pushed out* **15/8**[1]

32-1 **2** *9* **Royalraise (IRE)**[26] 181 6-11-5 122............................ LeightonAspell 124
(Oliver Sherwood) *led: jnd 5th: rdn appr 2 out: hdd whn nt fluent last: styd on same pce* **2/1**[2]

1-43 **3** *4 1/2* **Mercers Court (IRE)**[24] 225 7-11-5 127.......................... TrevorWhelan 118
(Neil King) *trckd ldr: disp fr 5th: rdn whn nt fluent 2 out: hdd bef last: no ex run-in* **5/2**[3]

0 **4** *7* **Only Gorgeous (IRE)**[19] 320 6-10-9 0.......................... LucyGardner(3) 104
(Sue Gardner) *stmbld 1st: mid-div: rdn after 3 out: sn pone pce: lft 5th next: wnt 4th bef last* **33/1**

00- **5** *6* **Royale's Legacy**[65] 5063 6-10-12 0................................ AidanColeman 98
(Anthony Honeyball) *mid-div: rdn after 3 out: sn btn* **66/1**

34-2 **6** *1 1/2* **Lawless Island (IRE)**[22] 251 6-10-12 0......................... RichardJohnson 98
(Tim Vaughan) *trckd ldrs: rdn after 3 out: sn hld: wknd last (b.b.v)* **9/1**

00-3 **7** *51* **Finnegan's Garden (IRE)**[14] 401 6-10-12 0......................... MarkGrant 51
(Zoe Davison) *a towards rr: struggling 8th: wknd next: t.o* **100/1**

P **Nyetimber (USA)**[1189] 9-10-12 0..................................... PeterCarberry
(Sean Curran) *hmpd 1st: mid-div: wknd after 6th: p.u bef 8th* **100/1**

P/P- **P** **Court Finale**[179] 2938 14-10-12 64.................................. JamesBest
(Peter Purdy) *struggling 4th: lost tch next: p.u bef 8th (b.b.v)* **100/1**

4- **F** **Willshebetrying**[59] 5151 4-10-1 0............................... MarcGoldstein 98
(Laura Mongan) *wnt lft 1st: trckd ldrs: rdn after 3 out: disputing hld 4th whn wnt lft and fell 2 out* **66/1**

5m 28.7s (-13.80) **Going Correction** -0.30s/f (Good)
WFA 4 from 5yo+ 18lb **10** Ran SP% **115.6**
Speed ratings (Par 105): **113,109,108,105,103 102,84,, ,**
CSF £6.08 TOTE £2.90: £1.20, £1.10, £1.20; EX 7.20 Trifecta £10.10.
Owner Andy & Sharon Measham **Bred** Roger-Yves Simon **Trained** Seaborough, Dorset

FOCUS
Fences sited on outside down the hill and inside in home straight. Hurdles sited on inner. Rail movement increased Chases by 80yds per circuit and Hurdles by 50yds per circuit. The ground was slightly quicker on the hurdles track than the chase course. The form horses came to the fore in this ordinary novice hurdle, which was run at just a steady pace. The winner is rated in line with his Newton Abbot run.

596 PIGLETS PANTRY NOVICES' CHASE (11 fncs 2 omitted) 2m 1f 96y

2:40 (2:40) (Class 4) 5-Y-O+ **£3,898** (£1,144; £572; £286)

Form RPR

02-3 **1** **Minella Present (IRE)**[7] 512 6-10-12 0............................ NoelFehily 118+
(Neil Mulholland) *hld up in last trio: nt fluent 4th: clsd on ldng pair 6th: cl up after 3 out (usual 4 out): led bef last: rdn clr run-in* **6/5**[1]

61-0 **2** *5* **Third Act (IRE)**[30] 110 6-10-12 0.................................(bt[1]) DarylJacob 112+
(Colin Tizzard) *hld up in last trio: clsd on ldrs 6th: cl up whn hit 2 out (usual 3 out) and lost pl: styd on into 2nd run-in: no ch w wnr* **10/1**

/0-4 **3** *2 1/4* **Here I Am (IRE)**[20] 293 8-10-12 0............................... MarcGoldstein 108
(Diana Grissell) *led: j.w: rdn after 2 out (usual 3 out): hdd bef last: no ex run-in* **50/1**

5P-2 **4** *3/4* **Raven's Tower (USA)**[18] 329 5-10-12 0............................. DavidBass 107
(Ben Pauling) *hld up in last trio: clsd on ldng pair 6th: cl up whn pushed along after 3 out (usual 4 out): rdn after next: kpt on same pce* **9/4**[2]

43-1 **5** *26* **Gun Shy (IRE)**[23] 241 7-11-5 130................................. JamieMoore 103
(Gary Moore) *trckd clr ldr: clsd on ldr after 6th: rdn appr 2 out (usual 3 out): wknd last* **4/1**[3]

4m 39.4s (4.70) **Going Correction** +0.375s/f (Yiel) **5** Ran SP% **107.3**
Speed ratings: **103,100,99,99,87**
CSF £11.44 TOTE £2.60: £1.30, £2.80; EX 15.00 Trifecta £90.00.
Owner Lady Clarke **Bred** Paddy Kennedy **Trained** Limpley Stoke, Wilts

FOCUS
The second-last fence was omitted, as it was for the other two chases on the card. All five were in with a chance as they turned for home in this fair novice chase. The second is probably the best guide.

597 REGIS REMOVALS CONDITIONAL JOCKEYS' MARES' H'CAP HURDLE (9 hdls 2 omitted) 2m 5f 139y

3:10 (3:10) (Class 5) (0-100,102) 4-Y-O+ **£2,339** (£686; £343; £171)

Form RPR

2-F3 **1** **Titch Strider (IRE)**[22] 265 10-11-5 95................. ThomasCheesman(3) 101+
(John Panvert) *hld up: stdy prog after 7th (usual 8th): rdn appr 2 out: led last: styd on wl: rdn out* **8/1**

50-4 **2** *3 3/4* **Multiview**[18] 336 6-10-8 84.. BenPoste(3) 88
(Tom Symonds) *hld up: mid-div 4th: lost pl 7th: rdn and hdwy after by-passing omitted 3 out: ev ch last: styd on* **8/1**

0F-3 **3** *1 1/2* **Anda De Grissay (FR)**[32] 89 5-11-9 96...................(t) MichealNolan 98
(Anthony Honeyball) *trckd ldrs: rdn appr 2 out: ev ch last: styd on same pce* **8/1**

P-5F **4** *2 1/2* **Kentford Heiress**[16] 383 5-11-0 87.............................. TomBellamy 87
(Seamus Mullins) *led: rdn appr 2 out: hdd last: no ex* **6/1**[3]

00-3 **5** *2* **Catkin Copse**[32] 90 7-10-10 89.............................(p) DanielHiskett(6) 86
(Richard Phillips) *mid-div: hdwy 7th: rdn appr 2 out: styd on same pce* **11/1**

24-1 **6** *7* **Midnight Sapphire**[7] 513 5-11-12 102 7ex.............. CiaranGethings(3) 93
(Victor Dartnall) *hld up: rdn after by-passing omitted 3 out: nvr gng pce to get involved* **3/1**[1]

004/ **7** *3/4* **Oscar Baby (IRE)**[555] 2712 9-10-9 85..................... FreddieMitchell(3) 75
(Diana Grissell) *trckd ldr tl rdn appr 2 out: wknd bef last* **33/1**

/04- **8** *2* **Fifi L'Amour (IRE)**[58] 5214 9-10-2 75.......................... JackSherwood 63
(Linda Jewell) *mid-div: hdwy after 6th: rdn by-passing omitted 3 out: wknd between last 2* **16/1**

3P-0 **9** *27* **Kayflin (FR)**[21] 280 7-11-6 93.................................(p) ThomasGarner 57
(Linda Jewell) *hld up: hdwy after 6th: rdn after next: wknd by-passing omitted 3 out* **25/1**

634- **P** **Izzy Piccolina (IRE)**[60] 5144 7-11-12 99........................ NicodeBoinville
(Geoffrey Deacon) *mid-div tl wknd after 7th (usual 8th): t.o whn p.u bef 2 out* **25/1**

26-5 **U** **Dainty Diva (IRE)**[23] 237 7-11-8 98.............................. MattGriffiths(3)
(Jeremy Scott) *blnd bdly whn uns rdr 1st* **7/2**[2]

5m 37.3s (-5.20) **Going Correction** -0.30s/f (Good) **11** Ran SP% **119.7**
Speed ratings (Par 103): **97,95,95,94,93 90,90,89,80,**
CSF £70.10 CT £537.29 TOTE £8.20: £2.10, £3.40, £3.40; EX 95.60 Trifecta £2120.30 Part won..
Owner J F Panvert **Bred** Seamus O'Farrell **Trained** Stoodleigh, Devon

FOCUS
A modest handicap for mares. The time was 8.6sec slower than the opening novice hurdle. The winner is rated to her best.

598 GTR (GLOBAL TECHNOLOGIES RACING) LTD H'CAP CHASE (13 fncs 3 omitted) 2m 5f 31y

3:40 (3:41) (Class 4) (0-115,116) 5-Y-O+ **£3,898** (£1,144; £572; £286)

Form RPR

54-1 **1** **Venetian Lad**[24] 226 10-11-6 109.................................. MarcGoldstein 115
(Lydia Richards) *trckd ldrs: rdn after 3 out (usual 4 out): led narrowly last: styd on gamely: rdn out* **11/1**

113- **2** *1 3/4* **Ladfromhighworth**[242] 1740 10-11-6 112.................... MattGriffiths(3) 116
(Jeremy Scott) *trckd ldrs: pressed ldrs fr 9th: led 2 out: rdn and hdd last: no ex run-in* **7/2**[2]

0F-4 **3** *7* **Halling's Wish**[30] 99 5-11-12 115.................................(bt) JamieMoore 114
(Gary Moore) *hld up in tch: hdwy after 3 out (usual 4 out): rdn after next: wnt 3rd bef last: styd on same pce run-in* **16/1**

42-1 **4** *8* **Perfect Timing**[7] 510 7-11-13 116 7ex.................................(b) NoelFehily 112
(Neil Mulholland) *disp ld most of way: j. sltly rt at times: hit 7th: mstke 10th: rdn and hdd whn mstke 2 out (usual 3 out): sn btn* **1/1**[1]

544- **5** *10* **Forever My Friend (IRE)**[242] 1742 8-11-9 115.............. SeanBowen(3) 99
(Peter Bowen) *in tch: rdn along fr 8th: remained in tch but nvr threatened to get on terms: fdd run-in* **11/2**[3]

1- **P** **Ashanti Moon (IRE)**[384] 294 9-10-8 97......................... AndrewThornton
(Diana Grissell) *disp ld most of way: hdd after 10th: sn wknd: t.o whn p.u bef 2 out (usual 3 out)* **11/1**

5m 47.8s (4.80) **Going Correction** +0.375s/f (Yiel) **6** Ran SP% **110.2**
Speed ratings: **105,104,101,98,94**
CSF £47.12 TOTE £7.50: £2.80, £1.90; EX 41.70 Trifecta £200.80.
Owner The Venetian Lad Partnership **Bred** Mrs Lydia Richards **Trained** Funtington, W Sussex

FOCUS
A modest handicap chase. The first two are rated to their best.

599 CROWN PROPERTIES H'CAP HURDLE (13 hdls) 3m 1f 142y

4:10 (4:10) (Class 5) (0-100,93) 4-Y-O+ **£2,339** (£686; £343; £171)

Form RPR

35-0 **1** **The Kings Assassin (IRE)**[24] 222 7-11-9 93.............(p) SeanBowen(3) 99+
(Chris Gordon) *towards rr: pushed along whn veered lft 3rd: hdwy fr 7th: trckd ldrs 9th: rdn after 3 out: led sn after last: drifted rt: styd on* **5/2**[1]

0P-3 **2** *1 3/4* **The Wee Midget**[33] 55 10-11-0 88...........................(b) ConorSmith(7) 91
(Arthur Whiting) *led after 1st: hit 3 out: rdn whn narrowly hdd 2 out: sn regained ld: hdd sn after last: styd on but no ex* **13/2**

665- **3** *12* **Storm Alert**[43] 5442 8-11-6 90.................................... LucyGardner(3) 83
(Sue Gardner) *mid-div: hdwy after 9th: hit 3 out: sn rdn to chse ldrs: styd on into hld 3rd run-in* **11/2**[3]

23-3 **4** *2* **The Last Bridge**[28] 148 8-11-0 81...........................(p) RichardJohnson 70
(Susan Johnson) *led tl after 1st: trckd ldr: rdn along fr 9th: hld whn wnt lft 2 out: one pce after* **5/1**[2]

065- **5** *3/4* **Dreamisi (IRE)**[58] 5214 6-11-12 93................................... DavidBass 84
(Ben Pauling) *mid-div: hmpd 2nd: wnt 3rd 5th: led narrowly 2 out: sn rdn and hdd: 3rd jumping last: fdd and lost 2 pls run-in* **12/1**

0-54 **6** *9* **Spanish Fork (IRE)**[8] 493 6-11-7 88............................ MarcGoldstein 70
(Sheena West) *pushed along to chse ldrs early: drvn after 6th: bhd after 9th: last no ch 3 out: plugged on fr next* **8/1**

-66U **7** *9* **Nicky Nutjob (GER)**[13] 421 9-9-8 68.......................... MissBHampson(7) 41
(John O'Shea) *hld up: hdwy 9th: effrt after 3 out: sn wknd* **16/1**

11-2 **8** *25* **Flugzeug**[24] 222 7-11-5 93... KevinJones(7) 43
(Seamus Mullins) *trckd ldrs: rdn 7th: wknd 3 out: t.o* **6/1**

600/ **P** **Sam Whiskey (GER)**[423] 12-10-5 72.............................. AndrewThornton
(Diana Grissell) *reminders after 1st: slow 2nd: wnt rt 3rd: sn detached in last: t.o whn p.u bef 8th* **50/1**

0P-0 **P** **Al Guwair (IRE)**[10] 451 5-11-3 84................................. LiamTreadwell
(Mark Hoad) *mid-div: pushed along after 7th: wknd 10th: t.o whn p.u after 3 out* **66/1**

6m 44.1s (-8.70) **Going Correction** -0.30s/f (Good) **10** Ran SP% **116.4**
Speed ratings (Par 103): **101,100,96,96,95 93,90,82,,**
CSF £19.56 CT £82.36 TOTE £4.30: £1.80, £3.90, £3.80; EX 24.10 Trifecta £165.90.
Owner Fenton Ramsahoye **Bred** M Doran **Trained** Morestead, Hampshire

FOCUS
This moderate handicap was contested by some real characters. The form is rated around the second, the first two clear.

600 STONEPILLOW NOVICES' H'CAP CHASE (16 fncs 3 omitted) 3m 1f 106y

4:40 (4:45) (Class 4) (0-105,104) 5-Y-O+ **£3,898** (£1,144; £572; £286)

Form RPR

3U-6 **1** **Ready Token (IRE)**[33] 58 7-11-10 102..........................(t) AidanColeman 122+
(Charlie Longsdon) *mde all: rdn whn nt fluent last: styd on wl: game* **7/2**[2]

33-1 **2** *3 1/2* **Moorlands George**[25] 211 7-10-11 89......................(t) NicodeBoinville 104
(Jeremy Scott) *chsd ldrs: rdn along fr 13th: chsd wnr 3 out (usual 4 out): styd on fr next but a being hld* **13/8**[1]

P-35 **3** *13* **Breezy Kin (IRE)**[3] 569 7-10-5 90................................ MikeyHamill(7) 94
(Sean Curran) *hld up: brief hdwy whn mstke 8th: in last pair: rdn after 13th: wnt 3rd after 2 out (usual 3 out): wnt 3rd at the last: no threat to front pair* **7/1**

5P-1 **4** *2 1/4* **Ya Hafed**[24] 223 7-10-6 84.. MattieBatchelor 88
(Sheena West) *hld up: pushed along fr 11th: rdn after 3 out (usual 4 out): lft hld 4th briefly whn bdly hmpd next: regained 4th run-in* **9/1**

P/2 **5** *5* **Time Is Tickin**[20] 292 9-11-5 104........................ OCdtOswaldWedmore(7) 104
(Diana Grissell) *trckd wnr: pushed along appr 12th: rdn whn dropped to 4th after 3 out: lft hld 3rd next: fdd run-in* **5/1**[3]

60-6 **P** **Toohighforme (IRE)**[30] 100 6-10-7 85............................ LeightonAspell
(Nick Gifford) *trckd ldrs: mstke 8th: rdn after 12th: wknd 3 out (usual 4 out): p.u bef next* **16/1**

002- F **Born To Succeed (IRE)**[40] 5513 5-11-10 102 DavidBass
(Ben Pauling) *mid-div: pushed along 13th: gd hdwy 3 out (usual 4 out) to trck wnr: rdn and hld in 3rd whn fell next* 16/1

7m 8.4s (7.30) **Going Correction** +0.375s/f (Yiel) 7 Ran SP% 111.2
Speed ratings: **103,101,97,97,95** ,
CSF £9.54 CT £33.93 TOTE £3.70: £1.40, £1.50; EX 7.20 Trifecta £77.10.
Owner Charlie Longsdon **Bred** Sean Moran **Trained** Over Norton, Oxon

FOCUS
An ordinary event. A small chase best from the winner.

601 SUSSEX BY THE SEA STANDARD OPEN NATIONAL HUNT FLAT RACE (DIV I) 2m 1f 145y
5:10 (5:15) (Class 6) 4-6-Y-O £1,559 (£457; £228; £114)

Form RPR
1 **Lillian (IRE)** 4-10-3 0 TomBellamy(3) 97+
(Seamus Mullins) *trckd ldrs: led over 5f out: rdn clr over 2f out: styd on wl fnl f* 20/1

2 4 **Normandy King (IRE)** 4-10-13 0 RichardJohnson 101
(Tim Vaughan) *in tch: kpt wd far side last time: rdn to chse wnr 2f out: styd on but a being hld fnl f* 4/1[2]

3 ½ **Acajou Des Bieffes (FR)** 5-11-2 0 AidanColeman 103
(Anthony Honeyball) *hld up: hdwy over 2f out: wnt 3rd over 1f out: styd on fnl f* 13/2[3]

4 4½ **Dear Lottie (FR)** 4-10-6 0 JamieMoore 89
(Gary Moore) *in tch: rdn 3f out: styd on fnl 2f but nt pce to get on terms* 13/2[3]

5 3½ **Indian Leader (IRE)**[409] 6-10-13 0 SeanBowen(3) 96
(Peter Bowen) *trckd ldrs: kpt wd far side last time: rdn to chse wnr briefly over 2f out: one pce fr over 1f out* 8/1

1- 6 shd **Cougar Kid (IRE)**[47] 5373 4-11-6 0 SamTwiston-Davies 100
(Philip Hide) *hld up: hdwy 5f out: rdn to chal for 2nd briefly over 2f out: one pce fr over 1f out* 15/8[1]

6 7 19 **Lunar Flow**[24] 227 4-10-13 0 BrendanPowell 76
(Jamie Snowden) *prom: rdn over 3f out: wknd over 2f out* 10/1

-5 8 10 **The Golden Hour (IRE)**[24] 227 5-10-9 0 MarkGrant 63
(Zoe Davison) *led tl over 5f out: wknd over 3f out* 16/1

4m 29.5s (0.80) **Going Correction** -0.30s/f (Good) 8 Ran SP% 112.3
Speed ratings: **86,84,84,82,80 80,71,67**
CSF £94.69 TOTE £10.50: £2.40, £1.60, £1.80; EX 81.60 Trifecta £484.30.
Owner Andrew Cocks And Tara Johnson **Bred** Mrs Helen Power Wall **Trained** Wilsford-Cum-Lake, Wilts

FOCUS
An ordinary bumper run at a steady pace until the final half-mile. The time was 2.4sec slower than the second division.

602 SUSSEX BY THE SEA STANDARD OPEN NATIONAL HUNT FLAT RACE (DIV II) 2m 1f 145y
5:40 (5:41) (Class 6) 4-6-Y-O £1,559 (£457; £228; £114)

Form RPR
1 **Fountains Windfall** 5-11-2 0 RachaelGreen 113+
(Anthony Honeyball) *hld up bhd: smooth hdwy fr 3f out: led 2f out: pushed clr fnl f: easily* 3/1[2]

2- 2 11 **Our Three Sons (IRE)**[54] 5262 4-10-13 0 MichealNolan 100
(Jamie Snowden) *in tch: hdwy 5f out: rdn to ld briefly over 2f out: sn hld by wnr: kpt on same pce* 10/3[3]

3 4 **Midnight Folie** 5-10-9 0 DavidBass 93
(Ben Pauling) *led: rdn and hdd 2f out: sn one pce* 6/1

0- 4 16 **Maigh Dara (IRE)**[214] 2192 6-11-9 0 MarcGoldstein 92
(Lydia Richards) *trckd ldrs tl outpcd over 3f out: styd on into modest 4th fnl f* 6/1

5 7 **Dewberry** 4-10-6 0 MarkGrant 69
(Geoffrey Deacon) *in tch: rdn into 4th over 2f out: nvr threatened: wknd fnl f* 20/1

6 7 **Lovely Bubbly** 4-10-13 0 RichardJohnson 70
(Tim Vaughan) *trckd ldrs: rdn 3f out: wknd 2f out* 11/4[1]

0- 7 16 **Georgies Pip**[47] 5373 4-10-6 0 BrendanPowell 48
(Brendan Powell) *pressed ldr tl over 5f out: wknd over 3f out* 25/1

4m 27.1s (-1.60) **Going Correction** -0.30s/f (Good)
WFA 4 from 5yo+ 3lb 7 Ran SP% 111.9
Speed ratings: **91,86,84,77,74 71,63**
CSF £12.83 TOTE £4.40: £2.20, £2.00; EX 16.30 Trifecta £72.00.
Owner Mrs Marion Bowden **Bred** Mrs M Bowden **Trained** Mosterton, Dorset

FOCUS
The quicker division by 2.4sec and the winner looks a decent prospect.
T/Plt: £59.90 to a £1 stake. Pool: £60,503.87 - 736.91 winning tickets T/Qpdt: £22.40 to a £1 stake. Pool: £4,609.79 - 151.90 winning tickets **Tim Mitchell**

342 PUNCHESTOWN (R-H)
Wednesday, June 3

OFFICIAL GOING: Good

603a 15 EURO ADMISSION RATED CHASE (13 fncs) 2m 2f
6:00 (6:01) 5-Y-O+ £10,077 (£2,945; £1,395; £465)

RPR
1 **Savello (IRE)**[36] 8 9-11-7 150 DavidMullins(5) 157
(A J Martin, Ire) *sn chsd ldrs: 3rd 1/2-way: lft 2nd at 7th: disp 3 out and led bef next travelling wl: rdn clr fr 2 out and kpt on wl* 12/1

2 2½ **Darwins Fox (FR)**[55] 5240 9-11-6 144 AELynch 148
(Henry De Bromhead, Ire) *chsd ldrs: 4th 1/2-way: tk clsr order after 3 out: rdn in 2nd and no imp on wnr after 2 out: kpt on u.p towards fin: a hld* 13/2[3]

3 2 **Art Of Logistics (IRE)**[35] 24 7-11-2 139 JJBurke 142
(Ms Sandra Hughes, Ire) *hld up towards rr: 9th 1/2-way: pushed along in 6th bef 4 out and clsd u.p into 3rd after 2 out: no imp on wnr bef last: kpt on same pce* 8/1

4 8½ **Realt Mor (IRE)**[8] 500 10-11-6 144 KeithDonoghue 139
(Gordon Elliott, Ire) *led 1st: jnd at 6th and hdd narrowly bef next where lft in front: jnd 3 out and hdd bef next where nt fluent: sn no imp on wnr and one pce after* 25/1

5 1¼ **Foildubh (IRE)**[8] 500 11-11-3 141 PaulCarberry 133
(John Patrick Ryan, Ire) *hld up in tch: 5th 1/2-way: lft 3rd fr 7th: rdn and lost tch after 3 out: nt fluent in 6th at next: j.rt in 5th at last: kpt on one pce* 16/1

6 2 **French Opera**[49] 5342 12-11-10 148 RobbiePower 138
(Nicky Henderson) *hld up in tch: mstke in 6th at 6th: pushed along bef 4 out: dropped to 8th fr next and no imp: kpt on one pce fr 2 out* 10/1

7 2¾ **Indevan**[199] 2541 7-11-7 145 RWalsh 133
(W P Mullins, Ire) *w.w: slt mstke in 8th 5 out and pushed along: no imp on ldrs fr 4 out: slt mstke next: kpt on one pce fr 2 out* 9/2[2]

8 4½ **Gold Bullet (IRE)**[35] 24 7-11-2 140 (t) BrianO'Connell 123
(T J Taaffe, Ire) *chsd ldrs: cl 4th bef 4 out: rdn and wknd bef 2 out* 8/1

P **Shanpallas (IRE)**[200] 2492 7-11-7 145 MarkWalsh
(C Byrnes, Ire) *hld up: last 1/2-way: bdly hmpd by faller at 7th and almost uns rdr: no imp after and p.u bef next* 14/1

F **Real Steel (IRE)**[18] 345 7-11-5 143 (t) BJCooper
(M F Morris, Ire) *cl up nt fluent 2nd: almost on terms bef 6th and led narrowly bef next where fell: fatally injured* 11/4[1]

4m 32.9s (-8.40) 10 Ran SP% 113.6
CSF £86.23 TOTE £13.10: £3.80, £1.90, £2.10; DF 87.80 Trifecta £683.00.
Owner Gigginstown House Stud **Bred** Anthony Walsh **Trained** Summerhill, Co. Meath

FOCUS
A return to form for the winner, a horse that had been running against the best 2-milers and looked as though he appreciated the drop in class.

604 - 609a (Foreign Racing) - See Raceform Interactive

438 FFOS LAS (L-H)
Thursday, June 4

OFFICIAL GOING: Good
Wind: moderate half across Weather: fine but cloudy

610 THOMAS MARTIN TRUST NOVICES' H'CAP CHASE (18 fncs) 2m 7f 177y
5:50 (5:50) (Class 4) (0-105,105) 5-Y-O+ £3,768 (£1,106; £553; £276)

Form RPR
422/ 1 **Celtic Intrigue (IRE)**[31] 8-10-9 88 (tp) TomScudamore 102+
(David Bridgwater) *chsd ldrs: nt fluent 10th: rdn 3 out: led 2 out: pushed clr flat* 5/1[2]

65P- 2 7 **Killimordaly (IRE)**[211] 2287 6-11-4 100 (tp) JamesBanks(3) 104
(Andy Turnell) *tended to jump lft: cl up: led 3rd: rdn and hdd 3 out: kpt on tl no ex appr last* 20/1

U-11 3 1½ **Patricktom Boru (IRE)**[5] 552 8-10-13 92 AdamWedge 99+
(Evan Williams) *chsd ldrs: rdn to ld 4 out: hdd and mstke next: hit 2 out: one pce* 11/8[1]

3/4- 4 15 **Mortlestown (IRE)**[189] 2764 7-11-12 105 (p) AndrewTinkler 97
(Martin Keighley) *cl up: disp ld 5th tl rdn 4 out: wknd 2 out* 12/1

50-4 5 6 **Sterling Gent (IRE)**[35] 30 8-10-10 89 (t) SamTwiston-Davies 76
(Liam Corcoran) *hld up in tch: blnd 1st: rdn appr 4 out: wknd 3 out* 6/1[3]

/05- P **Bedrock Fred**[39] 9-10-4 88 (p) DannyBurton(5)
(David Weston) *wnt to post early: midfield tl dropped to rr 3rd: reminders after 5th: struggling fr 9th: lost tch 12th: t.o whn p.u bef 4 out* 8/1

34/5 P **Molly Oscar (IRE)**[16] 388 9-10-11 90 (b) NoelFehily
(Johnny Farrelly) *led: mstke 3rd: hdd 3rd: styd cl up tl lost pl 10th: wknd 13th: t.o whn p.u bef 4 out* 8/1

062/ P **Divine Folly (IRE)**[40] 10-11-0 93 (t) AidanColeman
(Lawney Hill) *hld up: mstke 4th and reminder: nvr gng after: hit 6th: last whn nt fluent 9th: sn p.u* 12/1

5m 55.1s (-22.30) **Going Correction** -0.825s/f (Firm) 8 Ran SP% 115.4
Speed ratings: **104,101,101,96,94**
CSF £83.56 CT £208.39 TOTE £5.50: £1.70, £6.20, £1.10; EX 131.10 Trifecta £369.00.
Owner Mrs Jan Smith **Bred** Hardys Of Kilkeel Ltd **Trained** Icomb, Gloucs

FOCUS
The opening contest was a modest novice handicap chase. They went a proper gallop on officially good ground which is riding on the quick side of that description. The winner is rated to his best.

611 M HIORNS BUILDING CONTRACTOR LTD H'CAP CHASE (18 fncs) 2m 7f 177y
6:20 (6:21) (Class 3) (0-130,128) 5-Y-O+ £6,498 (£1,908; £954; £477)

Form RPR
33-1 1 **Steel Summit (IRE)**[28] 169 6-11-12 128 AidanColeman 141+
(David Dennis) *j. sltly rt: mde all: qckNd clr appr 4 out: in command whn nt fluent 2 out: easily* 6/1

P2-4 2 8 **Sir Mattie (IRE)**[12] 439 10-10-11 113 RichardJohnson 118
(David Rees) *hld up: hdwy 12th: mstke 4 out: wnt 2nd next: one pce and no real imp on easy wnr* 9/2[3]

123- 3 2¾ **Buachaill Alainn (IRE)**[53] 5289 8-11-2 121 (vt) SeanBowen(3) 124
(Peter Bowen) *trckd wnr: j. slowly 1st: j. slowly 10th and lost pl: sn drvn: no ch after: styd on u.p fr 3 out: tk 3rd last* 11/4[2]

26-4 4 9 **Houston Dynimo (IRE)**[30] 122 10-11-7 123 (tp) TomScudamore 120
(David Pipe) *hld up: hdwy 14th: briefly in 2nd 4 out: one pce fr next: lost 3rd last* 6/1

61P- 5 40 **Bandit Country (IRE)**[82] 4765 6-11-10 126 (tp) NoelFehily 83
(Jonjo O'Neill) *trckd ldrs: chsd wnr 10th tl wknd 4 out: t.o whn j.lft last* 9/4[1]

56/6 6 2 **Mr Moss (IRE)**[25] 219 10-11-11 127 PaulMoloney 83
(Evan Williams) *hld up bhd ldrs: mstke 6th: mstke and dropped to rr 11th: wknd 14th: t.o whn j.rt 4 out* 12/1

5m 57.1s (-20.30) **Going Correction** -0.825s/f (Firm) 6 Ran SP% 111.9
Speed ratings: **100,97,96,93,80 79**
CSF £31.90 TOTE £4.90: £3.00, £3.70; EX 40.30 Trifecta £114.40.
Owner Rose Farm Developments(UK)Ltd & Partner **Bred** G T Greene **Trained** Hanley Swan, Worcestershire

FOCUS
The feature contest was a fair handicap chase. They went an ordinary gallop. The form is rated around the second, leaving the winner's rating too high based on the race time.

612 STRADEY PARK HOTEL H'CAP CHASE (17 fncs) 2m 4f 199y
6:55 (6:55) (Class 5) (0-100,103) 5-Y-O+ £2,469 (£725; £362; £181)

Form RPR
/3-1 1 **Caspian Piper (IRE)**[19] 340 8-11-8 93 (v) RichardJohnson 103+
(Tim Vaughan) *mde all: drvn 3 out: styd on* 5/2[2]

P-12 2 1¾ **Louis Phillipe (IRE)**[12] 438 8-10-9 80 (t) MarkQuinlan 89
(Linda Blackford) *chsd ldrs: mstke 6th: wnt 2nd 4 out: kpt on u.p: nt fluent last: one pce flat* 3/1[3]

224- 3 13 **Zama Zama**[43] 5463 8-11-2 94 MrConorOrr(7) 89
(Evan Williams) *trckd ldrs: chsd wnr 11th to 4 out: wknd between last 2* 8/1

0-P1 4 15 **Minella Web (IRE)**[7] 524 6-12-4 103 7ex (t) DarylJacob 85
(Richard Woollacott) *hld up in last pair: bmpd 13th: sn clsd on ldrs: rdn 4 out: wknd next* 9/4[1]

525- **5** ½ **Celtic Fella (IRE)**[203] 2467 8-10-0 **71** oh4..........(t) TrevorWhelan 52
(Debra Hamer) *trckd wnr: j. slowly 9th: mstke next and lost 2nd: sn rdn: wknd 4 out* **11/1**

35-1 **6** 31 **Heurtevent (FR)**[17] 379 6-11-12 **97**.......... LeeEdwards 50
(Tony Carroll) *hld up in last pair: mstke 6th: j.lft 13th: sn rdn: wknd appr 4 out: t.o* **10/1**

5m 10.5s (-18.10) **Going Correction** -0.825s/f (Firm) **6** Ran SP% **112.9**
Speed ratings: **101,100,95,89,89 77**
CSF £10.86 TOTE £2.70: £1.10, £2.40; EX 10.40 Trifecta £15.40.
Owner Oceans Racing **Bred** R Guiry **Trained** Aberthin, Vale of Glamorgan

FOCUS
A modest handicap chase. They went an even gallop. and the winner confirmed the merit of his recent easy win.

613 RAYMOND'S GARAGE SEAT NOVICES' HURDLE (8 hdls) 1m 7f 202y
7:30 (7:30) (Class 4) 4-Y-0+ **£3,249** (£954; £477; £238)

Form RPR

354- **1** **In On The Act**[43] 5462 5-10-12 0.......... PaulMoloney 118+
(Evan Williams) *mid-div: hdwy to chse ldrs 5th: rdn 3 out: nt fluent next: stl 3rd last: str run flat to ld fnl 75yds* **7/1**[2]

P3-2 **2** 1¼ **Canicallyouback**[12] 440 7-10-7 121.......... ConorRing(5) 115
(Evan Williams) *led to 2nd: styd prom: wnt 2nd 3 out: chal last: ev ch flat: r.o* **15/8**[1]

101- **3** ½ **Bengali (IRE)**[18] 367 6-10-5 0..........(t) TomScudamore 108
(Patrick Griffin, Ire) *cl up: j.lft 1st: led 2nd tl appr next: styd cl up: led again after 5th: wandered and rdn bef 2 out: hdd and no ex fnl 75yds* **15/8**[1]

4 20 **Nordical (IRE)** 5-10-3 0 ow1..........(t) LewisGordon(10) 100
(Evan Williams) *towards rr: sme hdwy 5th: rdn bef next: kpt on steadily fr 2 out: tk 4th last: no ch w ldng trio* **25/1**

F **5** 6 **General Brook (IRE)**[25] 214 5-10-12 0.......... DaveCrosse 91
(John O'Shea) *t.k.h in mid-div: hdwy to ld appr 3rd: hdd after 5th: lost 2nd 3 out: wknd next* **12/1**[3]

45-U **6** 12 **Royal Craftsman (IRE)**[12] 441 5-10-12 0.......... DonalDevereux 80
(Peter Bowen) *j.rt: a towards rr: lost tch after 5th: t.o* **25/1**

0-U4 **7** 16 **Double Court (IRE)**[12] 441 4-10-9 0.......... SamTwiston-Davies 63
(Nigel Twiston-Davies) *a in rr: lost tch after 5th: t.o* **33/1**

6P-5 **8** 15 **King Of All Kings (IRE)**[12] 440 5-10-9 0.......... SeanBowen(3) 52
(Peter Bowen) *t.k.h: chsd ldrs: nt fluent 3rd: j. slowly next: rdn after 5th: wknd 3 out: t.o* **7/1**[2]

4-0 **P** **Warrigal (IRE)**[12] 440 5-10-12 0.......... MichaelByrne
(Tim Vaughan) *chsd ldrs tl mstke 4th: wknd next: t.o whn p.u bef last* **33/1**

3m 41.9s (-6.60)
WFA 4 from 5yo+ 17lb **9** Ran SP% **115.8**
CSF £20.53 TOTE £9.60: £2.20, £1.10, £1.10; EX 19.90 Trifecta £49.50.
Owner R E R Williams **Bred** J A And Mrs M A Knox **Trained** Llancarfan, Vale Of Glamorgan

FOCUS
A fair novice hurdle. They went a respectable gallop. The winner produced a big step up on his recent hurdle run.

614 RAY GRAVELL & FRIENDS CHARITABLE TRUST H'CAP HURDLE (12 hdls) 2m 7f 191y
8:05 (8:05) (Class 4) (0-120,118) 4-Y-0+ **£3,249** (£954; £477; £238)

Form RPR

6P-4 **1** **Be Bop Boru (IRE)**[33] 85 8-11-12 **118**..........(t) RichardJohnson 127+
(Tim Vaughan) *hld up in rr: hdwy 8th: led appr 2 out: drew clr bef last: eased nr fin* **7/2**[1]

P3-5 **2** 5 **Castle Conflict (IRE)**[33] 85 10-11-1 **107**..........(b) TomO'Brien 108
(Henry Daly) *chsd ldrs: led bef 3 out tl appr 2 out: kpt on but no ch w wnr* **7/1**

2-34 **3** 2¼ **Still Believing (IRE)**[25] 215 7-11-0 **113**.......... MrConorOrr(7) 112
(Evan Williams) *hld up: shkn up 8th: hdwy after next: wnt 3rd 2 out: kpt on same pce* **8/1**

3PP- **4** 3½ **Primo Capitano (IRE)**[80] 4809 7-11-9 **115**..........(p) AndrewTinkler 112
(Martin Keighley) *chsd ldrs: cl 2nd whn nt fluent 3 out: one pce fr next* **20/1**

0P/2 **5** 2¼ **Fountains Flypast**[33] 87 11-11-7 **113**..........(t) RachaelGreen 108
(Anthony Honeyball) *hld up: clsd 9th: rdn 3 out: one pce* **5/1**[3]

22-F **6** 9 **Who Am I**[28] 173 9-10-9 **104**..........(p) SeanBowen(3) 90
(Debra Hamer) *hld up: mstke 5th: rdn and wknd appr 3 out* **6/1**

20-4 **P** **He's The Daddy**[26] 210 8-10-10 **102**..........(vt) SamTwiston-Davies
(Nigel Twiston-Davies) *led to 3rd: styd cl up tl led again appr 9th: hdd & wknd qckly bef next: t.o whn p.u bef 2 out* **6/1**

532- **P** **Magheral Express (IRE)**[41] 5510 6-11-8 **114**..........(p) RichieMcLernon
(Jonjo O'Neill) *cl up: led 3rd tl appr 9th: wknd rapidly: p.u bef next* **4/1**[2]

5m 39.4s (-9.60) **Going Correction** -0.25s/f (Good) **8** Ran SP% **115.8**
Speed ratings (Par 105): **106,104,103,102,101 98, ,**
CSF £28.40 CT £183.23 TOTE £4.10: £3.00, £1.90, £2.20; EX 32.00 Trifecta £187.10.
Owner The Oak Syndicate **Bred** Robert McCarthy **Trained** Aberthin, Vale of Glamorgan

FOCUS
An ordinary handicap hurdle. They went a respectable gallop and the winner stepped up on his Uttoxeter effort.

615 WRW GROUP H'CAP HURDLE (9 hdls 1 omitted) 2m 4f
8:40 (8:40) (Class 5) (0-100,100) 4-Y-0+ **£2,274** (£667; £333; £166)

Form RPR

505- **1** **Mac Bertie**[43] 5465 6-11-9 **97**..........(p) AdamWedge 107+
(Evan Williams) *chsd ldrs: wnt 2nd 7th: chal gng best 2 out (usual 3 out): led over 1f out: rdn out* **12/1**

4-01 **2** 3¼ **Lady Of Longstone (IRE)**[12] 443 5-11-9 **97**..........(b) TomScudamore 102
(David Pipe) *led 1st: rdn 2 out (usual 3 out): jnd next: hdd over 1f out: kpt on u.p* **9/2**[2]

234- **3** 3½ **Dipity Doo Dah**[261] 1543 11-10-9 **86**..........(p) SeanBowen(3) 88
(Peter Bowen) *hld up: hdwy to chse ldrs 7th: no imp fr 2 out (usual 3 out): tk 3rd run-in* **8/1**

P1-3 **4** 2¼ **Bay Fortuna**[23] 262 6-11-11 **99**..........(p) DaveCrosse 101
(Mark Usher) *mid-div: hdwy to chse ldrs 6th: rdn after next: one pce fr 2 out (usual 3 out): lost 3rd run-in* **7/1**

0U0- **5** 38 **Strictly The One (IRE)**[164] 2268 5-11-3 **91**.......... NoelFehily 57
(Neil Mulholland) *mid-div: hdwy whn mstke 6th: rdn appr 2 out (usual 3 out): sn wknd: t.o* **14/1**

2-11 **6** 7 **Pennant Dancer**[7] 530 8-11-9 **97** 7ex..........(t) PaulMoloney 57
(Debra Hamer) *hld up towards rr: mstke 6th: rdn and wknd after next: t.o* **4/1**[1]

00-3 **7** 1¼ **Prince Pippin (IRE)**[24] 240 9-10-12 **93**..........(t) MsLucyJones(7) 51
(Lucy Jones) *mid-div: mstke 2nd: wnt prom next: wknd after 7th: t.o* **14/1**

50P- **8** 11 **Benefitofhindsight**[211] 2280 6-10-0 **74**.......... JamesBest 22
(Hywel Evans) *in rr: rdn along after 4th: sme hdwy 6th: wknd after next: t.o* **20/1**

/0-6 **9** 17 **Grams And Ounces**[34] 59 8-11-7 **95**..........(t) MichealNolan 28
(Adrian Wintle) *hld up: rdn 5th: lost tch 7th: t.o* **6/1**[3]

P0-4 **10** 2 **Stay Tuned (IRE)**[18] 361 7-9-12 **79**..........(tp) MikeyHamill(7) 10
(Alexandra Dunn) *prom: rdn 7th: sn wknd: t.o* **33/1**

10-6 **11** 22 **Thomas Junior (FR)**[18] 364 6-11-12 **100**..........(b[1]) SamTwiston-Davies 12
(Paul Morgan) *led tl hit 1st: chsd ldrs: reminder after 3rd: rdn and lost pl 5th: wknd after 7th: t.o* **16/1**

0P-0 **P** **General Ross (IRE)**[28] 180 8-10-6 **80**..........(b) RichardJohnson
(Adrian Wintle) *hld up towards rr: struggling 6th: lost tch next: t.o whn p.u bef last (usual 2 out)* **25/1**

6-46 **P** **Roderick Random**[18] 360 5-11-2 **90**..........(p) RichieMcLernon
(Johnny Farrelly) *prom tl rdn and wknd after 7th: t.o whn p.u bef last (usual 2 out)* **12/1**

4m 44.8s (284.80) **13** Ran SP% **122.2**
CSF £66.44 CT £474.39 TOTE £12.60: £6.20, £1.40, £2.20; EX 77.00 Trifecta £466.50.
Owner Keith And Sue Lowry **Bred** Mrs S Lowry **Trained** Llancarfan, Vale Of Glamorgan

FOCUS
A moderate handicap hurdle with the final flight bypassed. They went a decent gallop. The winner was well in on the best of his 2014 form and is rated back to that level.

616 PROJECT 13 H'CAP HURDLE (8 hdls) 1m 7f 202y
9:10 (9:11) (Class 5) (0-100,100) 4-Y-0+ **£2,274** (£667; £333; £166)

Form RPR

0-63 **1** **Polstar (FR)**[15] 399 6-11-3 **98**.......... PaulNO'Brien(7) 104+
(Harry Whittington) *t.k.h early: trckd ldr: hit 4th: led after next: drew clr appr last: eased fin* **2/1**[1]

602- **2** 3¾ **Spin Cast**[94] 4531 7-11-4 **99**..........(t) ConorSmith(7) 98
(Alan Jones) *mid-div: clsd after 5th: wnt 2nd appr 2 out: sn outpcd by wnr* **7/1**[3]

4-06 **3** 6 **Going Nowhere Fast (IRE)**[19] 336 10-9-13 **80**....(p) JordanWilliams(7) 73
(Bernard Llewellyn) *t.k.h in rr: rdn and hdwy 3 out: tk 3rd after 2 out: no imp on ldng pair* **8/1**

4-3 **4** 3¾ **Lions Charge (USA)**[23] 267 8-11-5 **93**..........(tp) MarkQuinlan 84
(Neil Mulholland) *hld up: rdn and clsd after 5th: briefly in 3rd 2 out: one pce u.p* **7/2**[2]

/2-6 **5** 12 **Flying Phoenix**[22] 281 7-11-12 **100**.......... TomScudamore 79
(Michael Blake) *chsd ldrs tl wknd 3 out* **8/1**

50C- **6** 2¾ **Blue Top**[16] 5435 6-10-8 **85**.......... RobertWilliams(3) 68
(Dai Burchell) *chsd ldrs: cl 2nd whn rdn 3 out: wknd next* **7/2**[2]

P05- **7** 41 **Worldor (FR)**[66] 5062 9-11-7 **95**..........(t) AdamWedge 35
(Alexandra Dunn) *led: clr after 2nd to 4th: hdd after 5th: sn wknd: t.o* **20/1**

3m 45.6s (-2.90) **7** Ran SP% **117.3**
CSF £17.08 CT £94.15 TOTE £3.30: £2.20, £2.70; EX 19.40 Trifecta £143.30.
Owner Dixon,Ellis,Lynds,Travers,Watkins **Bred** Comte Jean-Jacques De La Rochette **Trained** Sparsholt, Oxfordshire

FOCUS
The concluding contest was another moderate handicap hurdle. They went an even gallop. The cosy winner was on a good mark.
T/Plt: £37.70 to a £1 stake. Pool: £71,848.12 - 1389.55 winning units. T/Qpdt: £9.50 to a £1 stake. Pool: £6,776.85 - 525.80 winning units. **Richard Lowther**

617 - 619a (Foreign Racing) - See Raceform Interactive

[353]MARKET RASEN (R-H)
Friday, June 5

OFFICIAL GOING: Good changing to good (good to firm in places) after race 2 (14:25)
Wind: moderate 1/2 against Weather: fine and sunny, becoming overcast last 2

620 WATCH RACING UK ON SKY CHANNEL 432 NOVICES' HURDLE (8 hdls) 2m 148y
1:50 (1:50) (Class 4) 4-Y-0+ **£3,249** (£954; £477; £238)

Form RPR

31-2 **1** **Set The Trend**[19] 360 9-11-12 135.......... GavinSheehan 139+
(David Dennis) *trckd ldrs: clr 2nd 3rd: upsides 3 out: led appr next: 8 l clr last: pushed out* **2/1**[2]

2 2 **Tiger Twenty Two**[11] 4-10-9 0.......... AndrewTinkler 115+
(Brian Rothwell) *towards rr: hdwy 5th: modest 4th sn after 3 out: 3rd appr 2 out: 2nd last: styd on wl* **33/1**

1-P1 **3** 14 **Storm Of Swords (IRE)**[14] 433 7-12-0 134.......... BridgetAndrews(5) 129
(Dan Skelton) *led: hdd appr 2 out: kpt on one pce* **6/4**[1]

1 **4** ¾ **Captain Swift (IRE)**[31] 131 4-11-2 0.......... BrianHughes 110
(John Mackie) *chsd ldrs: one pce fr 3 out* **10/1**

4 **5** 3¼ **Keep Calm**[19] 353 5-10-12 0.......... HenryBrooke 102
(John Mackie) *chsd ldrs: drvn after 3rd: lost pl next: reminders 3 out: modest 5th appr 2 out* **14/1**

43-1 **6** 8 **Countersign**[19] 353 6-11-5 118.......... AdamPogson 104
(Charles Pogson) *hld up in mid-div: blnd 5th: wknd appr 2 out* **3/1**[3]

0P- **7** 12 **Outtillalhours (IRE)**[52] 5327 7-10-12 0..........[1] DougieCostello 84
(Joanne Foster) *hld up in rr: bhd whn hit 3 out* **100/1**

PP-5 **8** 33 **Rossington**[19] 353 6-10-9 0.......... MauriceLinehan(3) 54
(John Wainwright) *chsd ldr to 3rd: 3rd whn blnd 7th: wknd next: sn bhd: t.o whn heavily eased run-in* **100/1**

/P-P **P** **Its A Story**[24] 263 8-10-2 0..........(p) JonathanEngland(3)
(Mairi Wilson) *nt jump wl in last: t.o 3rd: p.u bef next* **100/1**

0P-P **P** **Dj Gerry**[10] 491 4-10-9 0.......... AdamWedge
(Nick Kent) *nt jump wl towards rr: bhd 5th: sn t.o: p.u bef 2 out* **100/1**

4m 1.1s (-5.60) **Going Correction** -0.25s/f (Good)
WFA 4 from 5yo+ 17lb **10** Ran SP% **121.0**
Speed ratings (Par 105): **103,102,95,95,93 89,84,68, ,**
CSF £57.78 TOTE £2.70: £1.20, £4.40, £1.10; EX 93.40 Trifecta £439.90.
Owner Corbett Stud **Bred** Old Suffolk Stud **Trained** Hanley Swan, Worcestershire

FOCUS
Rail movements added approximately 174yds to races 1, 4, 5 and 7, and 258yds to races 2, 3 and 6. Quickish ground on a warm day. They went a fair pace in what was a decent novice hurdle for the time of year. The winner and third dominated from a long way out. The winner set a decent standard but this arguably his best run over hurdles to date.

621 B EYRE AND SONS LTD FORD NOVICES' HURDLE (10 hdls) 2m 4f 139y
2:25 (2:25) (Class 4) 4-Y-0+ £3,249 (£954; £477; £238)

Form RPR
12-4 1 **Aviator (GER)**[35] 63 7-11-4 122 .... JackQuinlan 124
(James Eustace) *chsd ldrs: 2nd 5th: led appr 2 out: kpt on run-in: hld on towards fin* 9/2[3]
41-2 2 ½ **Oh Land Abloom (IRE)**[28] 181 5-11-4 120 .... (t) TrevorWhelan 124+
(Neil King) *trckd ldrs: cl 2nd appr 2 out: upsides run-in: jst hld* 2/1[1]
U4-4 3 4 **Magic Magnolia (IRE)**[16] 405 4-10-0 107 .... (t) HarrySkelton 102
(Dan Skelton) *led 1st: qcknd pce 6th: hdd appr 2 out: kpt on one pce run-in* 3/1[2]
1-3 4 25 **Faithful Mount**[32] 105 6-11-4 124 .... WillKennedy 105
(Ian Williams) *in rr: hdwy 3 out: handy 4th whn blnd next: sn wknd* 3/1[2]
/P-P 5 17 **Amour Collonges (FR)**[31] 132 5-10-11 0 .... (bt) BrianHughes 75
(Chris Grant) *led to 1st: wknd 7th: sn bhd: t.o 2 out* 66/1
4-5 6 37 **Mazovian (USA)**[29] 171 7-10-11 0 .... MarkQuinlan 42
(Neil Mulholland) *chsd ldrs: lost pl 5th: sn bhd: t.o 3 out* 25/1
P **Anis Des Malberaux (FR)** 5-10-11 0 .... TomScudamore
(Nigel Hawke) *nt fluent in last: reminders 3rd: t.o 6th: p.u bef 3 out* 20/1

5m 9.3s (0.50) **Going Correction** -0.25s/f (Good)
WFA 4 from 5yo+ 18lb 7 Ran SP% **111.6**
Speed ratings (Par 105): **89,88,87,77,71 57,**
CSF £13.60 TOTE £7.30: £2.80, £1.90; EX 14.30 Trifecta £60.60.
Owner The MacDougall Two **Bred** Gestut Hof Ittlingen **Trained** Newmarket, Suffolk
FOCUS
An ordinary event, run at a sound pace. The first two are rated to their marks.

622 RASEN ROCKS SATURDAY 15TH AUGUST BEGINNERS' CHASE (14 fncs) 2m 5f 89y
3:00 (3:00) (Class 4) 5-Y-0+ £3,768 (£1,106; £553; £276)

Form RPR
23-2 1 **Risk A Fine (IRE)**[31] 122 6-11-0 0 .... RichardJohnson 139+
(Philip Hobbs) *sn led: blnd 10th: hit next: styd on and 8 l clr last: drvn out* 7/4[1]
320- 2 17 **Stephen Hero (IRE)**[41] 5539 5-11-0 0 .... HarrySkelton 126+
(Dan Skelton) *chsd ldrs: cl 2nd whn hit 3 out: kpt on same pce between last 2* 7/2[2]
20-5 3 13 **Greybougg**[18] 382 6-11-0 0 .... TomScudamore 114
(Nigel Hawke) *led early: chsd wnr: cl 3rd whn hit 3 out: sn wknd: fin tired* 7/2[2]
P2-3 4 2¼ **Frampton (IRE)**[32] 99 6-11-0 0 .... (p) AidanColeman 109
(Charlie Longsdon) *in rr: hdwy and modest 4th appr 3 out: one pce* 5/1[3]
02P- 5 15 **Factor Fifty (IRE)**[41] 5539 6-11-0 0 .... JamesReveley 96
(Philip Kirby) *prom: lost pl 8th: sn bhd: t.o 11th* 6/1
04U- 6 1¾ **I'm A Joker**[66] 5085 6-11-0 0 .... JackQuinlan 93
(Sarah Humphrey) *hld up in rr: lost pl 8th: poor 4th 11th: bhd whn hit next* 50/1

5m 18.6s (-27.40) **Going Correction** -0.925s/f (Hard) 6 Ran SP% **113.7**
Speed ratings: **115,108,103,102,97 96**
CSF £8.72 TOTE £2.40: £1.30, £2.20; EX 8.90 Trifecta £19.40.
Owner Mrs Diana L Whateley **Bred** Mrs Fintina Kealey **Trained** Withycombe, Somerset
FOCUS
The going description was amended to Good, good to firm in places before this race. A dominant winner in this beginners' chase, who looks like proving much better over fences than hurdles.

623 MALTON MARQUEES H'CAP CHASE (14 fncs) 2m 3f 34y
3:35 (3:35) (Class 4) (0-115,115) 5-Y-0+ £3,768 (£1,106; £553; £276)

Form RPR
UU5- 1 **Great Link**[91] 4599 6-11-12 115 .... HarrySkelton 130+
(Dan Skelton) *trckd ldrs: 2nd 11th: upsides next: rallied and upsides last: styd on wl to ld last 50yds* 6/5[1]
43-6 2 2½ **Kitegen (IRE)**[20] 331 9-11-5 108 .... CharliePoste 118
(Robin Dickin) *trckd ldrs: 2nd 3rd: led 11th: jnd next: hdd and no ex last 50yds* 9/1
12-U 3 7 **Ivans Back (IRE)**[36] 42 10-10-1 90 .... AdamWedge 98
(Nick Kent) *hld up: mstke 5th: trckd ldrs 10th: cl 3rd 3 out: one pce* 11/2[2]
P1- 4 19 **Tiquer (FR)**[69] 5034 7-11-5 108 .... BrendanPowell 103+
(Alan Jones) *in rr: hmpd and lost pl 7th: drvn next: hdwy 11th: 4th and prom whn blnd and lost pl next: wl bhd whn eased run-in: t.o* 8/1
516- 5 32 **Mister Wiseman**[54] 5297 13-11-1 104 .... (t) TomScudamore 77
(Nigel Hawke) *led: hdd 11th: sn lost pl and bhd: t.o last: heavily eased: t.o* 9/1
21-2 F **Kayfton Pete**[23] 284 9-11-6 109 .... AdamPogson
(Charles Pogson) *trckd ldrs: fell 7th* 7/1[3]
06-4 P **Figaro**[24] 259 7-11-10 113 .... (t) RichardJohnson
(Tim Vaughan) *in rr: blnd bdly and one of rdr's leathers snapped 4th: sn p.u* 15/2

4m 45.5s (-20.20) **Going Correction** -0.925s/f (Hard) 7 Ran SP% **116.2**
Speed ratings: **105,103,101,93,79**
CSF £13.06 TOTE £1.70: £1.40, £6.40; EX 23.50 Trifecta £112.40.
Owner Carl Hodgson **Bred** Granham Farm And P Hearson Bloodstock **Trained** Alcester, Warwicks
FOCUS
An ordinary handicap chase. The third and fourth help set the level.

624 DOWNLOAD THE RACING UK IPAD APP H'CAP HURDLE (10 hdls) 2m 2f 140y
4:10 (4:10) (Class 3) (0-125,125) 4-Y-0+ £6,498 (£1,908; £954; £477)

Form RPR
4-41 1 **Shear Rock (IRE)**[20] 330 5-10-9 108 .... RichardJohnson 110+
(Charlie Longsdon) *led: clr 3rd tl after 5th: nt fluent 7th: hdd narrowly sn after 3 out: led next: styd on gamely run-in: all out* 11/10[1]
24-3 2 nk **Bowie (IRE)**[19] 356 8-11-6 119 .... AdamWedge 120
(Nick Kent) *hld up: hdwy and handy 3rd 3 out: upsides fr next: no ex clsng stages* 5/1[2]
262/ 3 6 **Scoglio**[672] 1185 7-11-2 115 .... LeeEdwards 111
(Dave Roberts) *hld up in rr: hdwy to trck ldrs 7th: kpt on fr 2 out: one pce and tk modest 3rd last 75yds* 33/1
P33- 4 1½ **Kodicil (IRE)**[28] 5205 7-10-13 112 .... (b) DougieCostello 106
(Mark Walford) *chsd wnr: narrow ld sn after 3 out: hdd and hung lft next: one pce appr last* 5/1[2]
045- 5 20 **Earls Quarter (IRE)**[34] 2205 9-11-12 125 .... (t) WillKennedy 103
(Ian Williams) *chsd ldrs 3rd: drvn 7th: reminders next: lost pl bef 2 out: sn bhd: j.lft last* 16/1
P-P1 6 2 **Yesyoucan (IRE)**[12] 449 10-11-9 122 7ex .... (p) LeightonAspell 96
(Neil Mulholland) *chsd ldrs: drvn 3 out: lost pl bef next: sn bhd* 11/2[3]
3-22 7 13 **Dynamo (IRE)**[19] 353 4-10-11 114 .... (t) HarrySkelton 72
(Dan Skelton) *in rr: pushed along 6th: lost pl bef 2 out: bhd whn eased clsng stages* 9/1

4m 31.3s (-8.10) **Going Correction** -0.25s/f (Good)
WFA 4 from 5yo+ 17lb 7 Ran SP% **115.2**
Speed ratings (Par 107): **107,106,104,103,95 94,88**
CSF £7.58 CT £110.97 TOTE £2.20: £1.20, £3.00; EX 6.00 Trifecta £131.50.
Owner Jones, Smith & Walsh **Bred** Cyril O'Hara **Trained** Over Norton, Oxon
FOCUS
The form for this fair handicap looks solid enough, the first two pretty much to their marks.

625 MARKET RASEN INTERACTIVE H'CAP HURDLE (12 hdls) 2m 7f 16y
4:55 (4:56) (Class 3) (0-125,125) 4-Y-0+ £5,393 (£1,583; £791; £395)

Form RPR
110- 1 **Kilfinichen Bay (IRE)**[223] 2050 7-11-1 114 .... RichardJohnson 113
(Charlie Longsdon) *trckd ldrs: t.k.h: effrt appr 2 out: lft 3rd last: swtchd lft run-in: styd on strly to ld last 50yds* 10/3[2]
116- 2 1 **Border Breaker (IRE)**[48] 5393 6-11-12 125 .... (tp) TomScudamore 123
(David Pipe) *led: increased pce 8th: jnd 2 out: hdd and no ex last 50yds* 7/2[3]
11-0 3 ¾ **Phare Isle (IRE)**[36] 50 10-11-5 125 .... (tp) MrMJPKendrick[(7)] 122
(Ben Case) *trckd ldrs: upsides 2 out: kpt on last 75yds* 8/1
06-3 4 2 **Lawsons Thorns (IRE)**[19] 364 6-10-5 104 .... BrianHughes 102
(Mike Sowersby) *hld up in last: stdy hdwy appr 3 out: lft 4th and hmpd last: kpt on* 16/1
/00- 5 11 **Topolski (IRE)**[9] 5210 9-11-5 118 .... AidanColeman 105
(David Arbuthnot) *chsd ldrs: hit 3 out: outpcd appr next: sn wknd* 12/1
2P-4 6 2¾ **Master Rajeem (USA)**[12] 448 6-11-2 115 .... (p) MarkGrant 100
(Neil King) *chsd ldrs: drvn 3 out: lost pl appr next* 8/1
0-1U 7 15 **Drombeg West**[23] 283 8-10-9 108 .... AndrewTinkler 85
(Anna Brooks) *t.k.h in rr: hdwy 3 out: outpcd and lost pl appr next: sn bhd* 10/1
6-05 F **Get Home Now**[19] 356 7-10-12 114 .... (tp) SeanBowen[(3)] 112+
(Peter Bowen) *chsd ldrs: drvn upsides 2 out: cl 3rd whn fell last* 3/1[1]

5m 45.8s (-4.70) **Going Correction** -0.25s/f (Good) 8 Ran SP% **115.2**
Speed ratings (Par 107): **98,97,97,96,92 91,86,**
CSF £15.95 CT £85.13 TOTE £3.70: £1.50, £1.30, £2.80; EX 14.70 Trifecta £65.00.
Owner Cracker Syndicate **Bred** Brian Kearney **Trained** Over Norton, Oxon
FOCUS
They went a steady initial pace in this reasonable handicap hurdle. The form is rated around the first four.

626 RACING UK PROFITS RETURNED TO RACING NOVICES' H'CAP HURDLE (10 hdls) 2m 2f 140y
5:30 (5:30) (Class 5) (0-100,100) 4-Y-0+ £2,274 (£667; £333; £166)

Form RPR
12-1 1 **Ruaraidh Hugh (IRE)**[25] 240 6-11-2 97 .... (b) MrTommieMO'Brien[(7)] 105+
(Chris Bealby) *hld up: drvn and hdwy to chse ldrs appr 2 out: led last: wnt clr last 150yds* 10/11[1]
0-23 2 8 **Galactic Power (IRE)**[14] 435 5-10-7 88 .... JosephPalmowski[(7)] 89
(Robin Dickin) *in rr: drvn 7th: chsng ldrs appr 2 out: upsides last: kpt on to take modest 2nd last 50yds* 11/4[2]
00-2 3 1 **Oneofapear (IRE)**[15] 416 9-11-12 100 .... BrianHughes 99
(Mike Sowersby) *trckd clr ldr: led narrowly appr 2 out: hdd last: kpt on same pce* 8/1
6/P- 4 2½ **The Yank**[55] 292 6-10-12 86 .... RichardJohnson 83
(Tony Carroll) *hld up: hdwy 7th: chsng ldrs appr 2 out: sn upsides: kpt on one pce run-in* 6/1[3]
P-0P P **Bjornlucky (IRE)**[16] 399 5-10-0 74 oh5 .... (b[1]) HarrySkelton
(Caroline Fryer) *best away: sn wl clr: coming bk to field whn blnd 3 out: hdd appr next: sn heavily eased: p.u bef 2 out* 14/1

4m 37.1s (-2.30) **Going Correction** -0.25s/f (Good)
WFA 4 from 5yo+ 17lb 5 Ran SP% **111.1**
Speed ratings (Par 103): **94,90,90,89,**
CSF £4.04 TOTE £1.90: £1.10, £2.50; EX 4.50 Trifecta £10.20.
Owner Triumph In Mind **Bred** Peter McCarthy **Trained** Barrowby, Lincs
FOCUS
There were four in line over the last, the exception being the outsider who had been a long way clear at one stage. The winner was well in on his recent win and ran to a similar level.
T/Plt: £32.00 to a £1 stake. Pool: £41,880.43 - 953.65 winning tickets T/Qpdt: £17.00 to a £1 stake. Pool: £2,886.40 - 125.15 winning tickets **Walter Glynn**

627 - 633a (Foreign Racing) - See Raceform Interactive

[481] HEXHAM (L-H)
Saturday, June 6

OFFICIAL GOING: Good (good to firm in places; 7.6)
Wind: Very strong, half against Weather: Cloudy, bright

634 GREATRUN.ORG (S) HURDLE (6 hdls 2 omitted) 2m 48y
2:05 (2:07) (Class 5) 4-Y-0+ £2,737 (£798; £399)

Form RPR
162/ 1 **Celtic Monarch (IRE)**[412] 5421 6-10-11 112 .... DerekFox[(3)] 95+
(Mark Michael McNiff, Ire) *chsd ldrs: hdwy to ld bef omitted last: edgd lft: rdn clr* 9/4[2]
-350 2 6 **Bob's Legend (IRE)**[10] 507 9-10-12 94 .... (t) JamesCorbett[(7)] 95
(Susan Corbett) *hld up: hdwy to join ldr 2 out (usual 3 out): led briefly and rdn bef omitted last: kpt on same pce* 7/4[1]
3 5 **Butlergrove King (IRE)**[91] 6-10-7 0 .... (t) MissADalton[(7)] 86
(Heather Dalton) *led: jnd 2 out (usual 3 out): hdd bef omitted last: sn outpcd* 4/1[3]
0- 4 1¼ **Rocky Two (IRE)**[12] 2507 5-11-0 0 .... JamesReveley 84
(Philip Kirby) *in tch: stead hdwy after 2 out (usual 3 out): rdn and outpcd bef omitted last* 10/1
5PF- 5 7 **Momkinzain (USA)**[6] 8-11-0 99 .... (vt[1]) PeterBuchanan 78
(Lucinda Russell) *chsd ldr to 2 out (usual 3 out): rdn and wknd bef omitted last* 7/1
0P-P 6 41 **Solway Trigger**[13] 460 6-10-7 0 .... RyanDay[(7)] 41
(Lisa Harrison) *hld up in tch: rdn and outpcd 2 out (usual 3 out): sn btn: t.o* 66/1

The Form Book Jumps 2015-16, Raceform Ltd, Newbury, RG14 5SJ

UP 7 1¾ **Cobh National (IRE)**[11] 481 7-10-7 0........ ThomasDowson(7) 40
(Victor Thompson) *in tch: outpcd whn nt fluent 3 out (usual 4 out): lost tch fr next: t.o* **100/1**

8 47 **Cash Is King**[24] 5-11-0 0........ DougieCostello
(Kenny Johnson) *bhd: struggling 3 out (usual 4 out): sn btn: t.o* **25/1**

4m 9.6s (-7.80) **Going Correction** -0.675s/f (Firm) **8** Ran SP% **115.1**
Speed ratings (Par 103): **92,89,86,85,82 61,61,37**
CSF £6.85 TOTE £3.00: £1.20, £1.10, £1.80; EX 8.00 Trifecta £26.80.No bid for the winner.
Owner John Watters **Bred** Airlie Stud **Trained** Coolaney, Co. Sligo

FOCUS
Fresh ground on bends. It was very windy and there was some doubt about whether racing could take place. The final flight of hurdles and the final fence were omitted. The winner was a 110+ horse at best but was nowhere near that level in this modest seller.

635 JUNIOR GREAT NORTH RUN NOVICES' CHASE (13 fncs 2 omitted) 2m 4f 15y
2:40 (2:41) (Class 4) 5-Y-0+ **£3,898** (£1,144; £572; £286)

Form RPR

10-4 1 **Gold Futures (IRE)**[21] 329 6-10-12 0........ BrianHarding 127+
(Nicky Richards) *in tch: stdy hdwy 5th: effrt and wnt 2nd last (usual 2 out): led bef omitted last: edgd lft: drvn clr* **9/4**[2]

03-3 2 8 **Volcanic (FR)**[10] 505 6-10-12 0........(t) HenryBrooke 119
(Donald McCain) *led tl rdn and hdd bef omitted last: sn drvn: rallied to take 2nd pl cl home* **7/4**[1]

10-2 3 nk **Enchanted Garden**[25] 253 7-10-12 0........ BrianHughes 121+
(Malcolm Jefferson) *cl up: blnd 2nd: nt fluent 3 out (usual 4 out): effrt and wnt 2nd bef omitted last: one pce last 100yds: lost 2nd cl home* **4/1**[3]

-214 4 13 **Super Collider**[12] 469 8-10-5 118........(t) JamesCorbett(7) 106
(Susan Corbett) *hld up: stdy hdwy 1/2-way: rdn and outpcd 2 out (usual 3 out): n.d after* **11/2**

6-66 5 7 **Daring Exit**[16] 421 6-10-7 0........ CallumBewley(5) 100
(Robert Bewley) *hld up: stdy hdwy and in tch 1/2-way: nt fluent 3 out (usual 4 out): wknd after next* **66/1**

-4F3 6 12 **King Of The Dark (IRE)**[13] 453 8-10-5 100........ ThomasDowson(7) 87
(Victor Thompson) *hld up in tch: hdwy to chse ldrs bef 1/2-way: nt fluent 3 out (usual 4 out): wknd fr next* **25/1**

0 7 69 **Ballymorris (IRE)**[13] 452 6-10-5 0........(p) RossChapman(7) 18
(Kenny Johnson) *chsd ldrs: outpcd whn hit 8th: lost tch after next: t.o* **150/1**

0-04 F **Latest Fashion (IRE)**[11] 481 9-10-0 0........(t) StephenMulqueen(5)
(Christopher Wilson) *hld up: fell 3rd* **100/1**

U **Fresh By Nature (IRE)**[43] 5532 8-10-9 0........ JonathanEngland(3)
(Harriet Bethell) *prom: nt fluent 3rd: mstke and lost pl next: struggling 1/2-way: no ch whn mstke and uns rdr 3 out (usual 4 out)* **12/1**

U **My Lady West (IRE)**[62] 6-9-12 0........(p) MrJDixon(7)
(Victor Thompson) *bhd whn stmbld and uns rdr 1st* **100/1**

5m 12.0s (-1.50) **Going Correction** -0.225s/f (Good) **10** Ran SP% **118.2**
Speed ratings: **94,90,90,85,82 77,50,,,**
CSF £7.03 TOTE £3.20: £1.20, £1.30, £1.90; EX 8.20 Trifecta £26.50.
Owner Mrs C A Torkington **Bred** D W Macauley **Trained** Greystoke, Cumbria

FOCUS
Quite an interesting novice chase, with the winner one to follow this summer. The winner was a 133 hurdler and should at least match that over fences.

636 FILM NOVA JUVENILE HURDLE (6 hdls 2 omitted) 2m 48y
3:15 (3:17) (Class 4) 3-Y-0 **£3,969** (£1,157; £578)

Form RPR

1 **Egmont**[11] 3-10-12 0........ BrianHughes 92+
(George Moore) *hmpd 1st: in tch: hdwy to join ldr 3rd: effrt and led bef omitted last: styd on wl run-in* **9/1**

2 1¾ **Mojawiz**[122] 3-10-12 0........ AidanColeman 89
(John Ferguson) *t.k.h: led to after 1st: led next: sn jnd: rdn and hdd bef omitted last: kpt on u.p run-in* **4/7**[1]

3 7 **The Name's Bond**[19] 3-10-12 0........ JamesReveley 85
(Keith Reveley) *cl up whn hesitated bdly and lost pl 1st: prom: nt fluent and outpcd last (usual 2 out): no imp passing omitted last* **9/2**[2]

4 4½ **Ace Of Marmalade (IRE)**[25] 3-10-5 0........ CraigGallagher(7) 79
(Brian Ellison) *plld hrd: chsd ldrs tl nt fluent and outpcd 2 out (uusal 3 out): hit last: no imp* **18/1**

5 99 **Fortuna Glas (IRE)**[240] 3-10-12 0........ HenryBrooke
(Donald McCain) *plld hrd: nt fluent: led after 1st to next: lost tch 3 out (usual 4 out): t.o* **5/1**[3]

4m 18.2s (0.80) **Going Correction** -0.675s/f (Firm) **5** Ran SP% **113.8**
Speed ratings: **71,70,66,64,14**
CSF £16.11 TOTE £12.00: £2.70, £2.00; EX 20.30 Trifecta £59.30.
Owner T S Ingham **Bred** Whatton Manor Stud **Trained** Middleham Moor, N Yorks

FOCUS
The first juvenile hurdle of the season and it was run at a modest pace, with most pulling hard early on. The last flight was omitted on both circuits so they only jumped six. Nothing to judge the form on bar a very slow time.

637 GREAT NORTH SWIM H'CAP CHASE (18 fncs 1 omitted) 3m 41y
3:50 (3:50) (Class 5) (0-100,98) 5-Y-0+ **£3,285** (£957; £479)

Form RPR

5-31 1 **Chicago Outfit (IRE)**[11] 486 10-11-7 98........(p) JonathonBewley(5) 116+
(George Bewley) *mde all: drew clr after last (usual 2 out): unchal* **11/4**[2]

2-41 2 21 **Solway Legend**[23] 303 8-10-5 84........ RyanDay(7) 85
(Lisa Harrison) *hld up: stdy hdwy and in tch 1/2-way: cl 3rd whn pckd and outpcd last (usual 2 out): rallied to chse wnr passing omitted last: no imp* **9/1**

F2-6 3 ¾ **Northern Executive (IRE)**[11] 486 7-11-2 88........(p) PaddyBrennan 86
(Karen McLintock) *cl up: wnt 2nd 4 out (usual 5 out): rdn last (usual 2 out): sn outpcd: lost 2nd passing omitted last* **15/2**

/66F 4 1¼ **Native Brian (IRE)**[13] 453 9-10-5 84........ RossChapman(7) 82
(Andrew Hamilton) *sn towards rr: stdy hdwy 1/2-way: rdn and outpcd 3 out (usual 4 out): plugged on fr last: no imp* **50/1**

316- 5 15 **Highlander Ted**[47] 5423 7-11-7 93........(p) DougieCostello 79
(Mark Walford) *in tch: outpcd whn hit 4 out (usual 5 out): struggling after next* **5/2**[1]

00-2 6 21 **Vision De La Vie (FR)**[13] 453 5-11-8 94........ JamesReveley 74
(Pauline Robson) *chsd wnr to 4 out (usual 5 out): wknd qckly 2 out (usual 3 out): eased whn btn* **6/1**[3]

5-46 7 21 **West Of The Edge (IRE)**[13] 448 7-11-2 95........ ThomasCheesman(7) 41
(Dai Williams) *in tch: drvn 1/2-way: wknd bef 14th: t.o* **12/1**

5-04 8 36 **Emkae (IRE)**[13] 453 7-11-4 90........(t) BrianHarding 4
(Alison Hamilton) *hld up: struggling bef 12th: sn lost tch: t.o* **7/1**

5-P5 P **Glenwood Prince (IRE)**[11] 486 9-9-9 72 oh8........(p) CallumBewley(5)
(Kevin Hunter) *in tch: reminders and outpcd 9th: lost tch and p.u bef 4 out* **20/1**

6m 23.2s (-9.00) **Going Correction** -0.225s/f (Good) **9** Ran SP% **118.2**
Speed ratings: **106,99,98,98,93 86,79,67,**
CSF £28.34 CT £170.17 TOTE £3.60: £1.90, £1.90, £2.30; EX 25.70 Trifecta £160.10.
Owner G T Bewley **Bred** Roger Ryan **Trained** Bonchester Bridge, Borders

FOCUS
Not a strong handicap chase but the winner is in great form at present. The winner is rated in line with his old best.

638 GREAT NORTH CITY GAMES H'CAP HURDLE (6 hdls 2 omitted) 2m 48y
4:45 (4:47) (Class 3) (0-130,130) 4-Y-0+
£6,568 (£1,940; £970; £485; £242; £121)

Form RPR

01-2 1 **Gurkha Brave (IRE)**[10] 508 7-10-11 115........ PaddyBrennan 116
(Karen McLintock) *hld up in tch: stdy hdwy 3rd: rdn and outpcd last (usual 2 out): rallied passing omitted last: styd on wl to ld nr fin* **7/2**[1]

6-10 2 ½ **Vodka Wells (FR)**[28] 197 5-11-5 130........ JamieBargary(7) 131
(Micky Hammond) *prom: hdwy to ld last (usual 2 out): hdd bef omitted last: rallied and regained ld last 150yds: kpt on: hdd nr fin* **6/1**

12-2 3 nk **Tekthelot (IRE)**[36] 59 9-10-11 115........ JamesReveley 116
(Keith Reveley) *hld up in rr: smooth hdwy bef last (usual 2 out): led bef omitted last: rdn: hung lft and hdd laslt 150yds: kpt on* **4/1**[2]

P43- 4 23 **Restraint Of Trade (IRE)**[77] 4896 5-10-12 116........(t) PeterCarberry 96
(Jennie Candlish) *hld up bhd ldng gp: rdn and outpcd 2 out (usual 3 out): rallied bef omitted last: sn no imp* **13/2**

002- 5 6 **Midnight Game**[7] 5394 8-11-5 130........ CraigGallagher(7) 105
(Brian Ellison) *prom: effrt and ev ch last (usual 2 out): wknd bef omitted last* **18/1**

02-2 6 2¾ **Kuda Huraa (IRE)**[36] 63 7-10-11 118........(t) JonathanEngland(3) 90
(Harriet Bethell) *hld up: rdn and outpcd 2 out (usual 3 out): n.d after* **18/1**

/00- 7 8 **Broughton (GER)**[211] 2337 5-11-9 127........(t) AidanColeman 94
(John Ferguson) *cl up: rdn whn nt fluent last: sn btn* **9/2**[3]

6-66 8 1 **Hunters Belt (IRE)**[9] 520 11-10-1 110........(vt) JonathonBewley(5) 74
(George Bewley) *sn pressing ldr: led 3rd to last (usual 2 out): sn wknd* **20/1**

105- 9 10 **Satanic Beat (IRE)**[15] 5475 6-11-12 130........ BrianHarding 85
(Jedd O'Keeffe) *led: hdd 3rd: cl up: mstke 2 out (usual 3 out): wknd bef next* **18/1**

/54- 10 7 **Rockabilly Riot (IRE)**[12] 1005 5-10-1 108........ CraigNichol(3) 57
(Martin Todhunter) *hld up: rdn after 2 out (usual 3 out): sn wknd* **25/1**

165- 11 9 **Rockawango (FR)**[26] 3322 9-10-13 122........(tp) DaleIrving(5) 63
(James Ewart) *in tch: rdn 3rd: wknd fr 2 out (usual 3 out)* **22/1**

4m 2.8s (-14.60) **Going Correction** -0.675s/f (Firm) **11** Ran SP% **116.8**
Speed ratings (Par 107): **109,108,108,97,94 92,88,88,83,79 75**
CSF £24.21 CT £87.63 TOTE £4.00: £1.40, £2.40, £1.90; EX 27.30 Trifecta £72.90.
Owner Alan Lamont **Bred** Miss Penny Downes **Trained** Ingoe, Northumberland

FOCUS
An open handicap run at a good pace that produced an exciting finish with three engaged in a close battle. The winner posted a small pb.

639 GREAT NORTH RUN H'CAP CHASE (14 fncs 1 omitted) 2m 4f 15y
5:20 (5:21) (Class 5) (0-100,105) 5-Y-0+ **£2,599** (£763; £381; £190)

Form RPR

-F41 1 **Pekanheim (IRE)**[11] 487 7-11-10 105........ MrZBaker(7) 115+
(Martin Todhunter) *hld up in tch: smooth hdwy to chse ldr 3 out (usual 4 out): rdn clr bef last* **3/1**[1]

345- 2 16 **Mister Wall Street (FR)**[238] 1851 10-11-0 91........(tp) TonyKelly(3) 85
(Rebecca Menzies) *hld up in tch: hdwy to chse wnr after last (usual 2 out): hung lft passing omitted last: sn outpcd* **4/1**[2]

4P-U 3 10 **Prince Blackthorn (IRE)**[24] 287 9-10-6 80........ BrianHarding 65
(Barry Murtagh) *bhd: outpcd 1/2-way: plugged on fr last (usual 2 out): no ch w first two* **14/1**

P-50 4 14 **Silent Snow (IRE)**[9] 519 10-9-11 78........(p) MrWHRReed(7) 51
(W T Reed) *in tch: outpcd 1/2-way: no imp whn hit 3 out (usual 4 out): sn n.d* **20/1**

P0-4 5 hd **Champagne Agent (IRE)**[23] 303 9-10-0 74........(b) DougieCostello 46
(Donald Whillans) *sn wl bhd: rdn 1/2-way: nvr on terms* **11/2**[3]

U521 6 21 **Gin Cobbler**[11] 485 9-11-2 97........ ThomasDowson(7) 50
(Victor Thompson) *led: hit 9th: sn hdd: wknd fr 2 out (usual 3 out)* **3/1**[1]

-4P5 U **Sharivarry (FR)**[11] 484 9-10-5 86........(p) MrJDixon(7)
(Victor Thompson) *in tch: 5th and outpcd whn mstke and uns rdr 8th* **25/1**

-5PU U **Bertielicious**[11] 485 7-9-9 74 oh18........ DiarmuidO'Regan(5)
(Jonathan Haynes) *led and clr tl hit 9th: sn hdd: 4th and outpcd whn mstke and uns rdr last (usual 2 out)* **66/1**

P2-5 U **Coolanure (IRE)**[13] 454 6-9-13 80........(p) RossChapman(7)
(Kenny Johnson) *pressed ldr: hit and uns rdr 1st* **7/1**

5m 12.5s (-1.00) **Going Correction** -0.225s/f (Good) **9** Ran SP% **114.7**
Speed ratings: **93,86,82,77,76 68,,,**
CSF £15.46 CT £142.45 TOTE £4.90: £1.90, £1.20, £3.70; EX 19.60 Trifecta £310.70.
Owner Andrew G Bell **Bred** Martin Hoste **Trained** Orton, Cumbria

FOCUS
A moderate handicap in which the wind took its toll as they finished strung out. The winner impressed in a good time for the grade and can win again.

640 GREAT RUN COMPANY STANDARD OPEN NATIONAL HUNT FLAT RACE 2m 48y
5:55 (5:56) (Class 6) 4-6-Y-0 **£1,779** (£518; £259)

Form RPR

401- 1 **Emperor Sakhee**[47] 5426 5-11-9 0........ JamesReveley 113+
(Karen McLintock) *hld up: hdwy 1/2-way: w ldrs 4f out: led 2f out: styd on wl to draw clr ins fnl f* **10/11**[1]

0-3 2 13 **Bollin Beauty**[17] 400 6-10-9 0........ BrianHughes 86
(Malcolm Jefferson) *hld up bhd ldrs: effrt 2f out: wnt 2nd u.p over 1f out: no imp on wnr fnl f* **3/1**[2]

3 3 5 **Pikarnia**[25] 257 5-10-11 0........ StephenMulqueen(5) 88
(John Wade) *racd keenly: disp ld: def advantage bef 1/2-way: rdn and hdd 2f out: wl btn fnl f* **8/1**

6 4 22 **Danny The Dancer**[37] 39 5-10-6 0........ FinianO'Toole(10) 66
(Micky Hammond) *racd keenly: w ldrs: pushed along and wknd over 3f out* **25/1**

6 5 4 **Myrtle Drive (IRE)**[21] 334 4-10-6 0........ AdrianLane 52
(Donald McCain) *hld up in rr: rdn wl over 2f out: sn btn* **11/1**

6 38 **Cairnshill (IRE)**[27] 235 4-10-10 0........................ DerekFox(3) 21
(Mark Michael McNiff, Ire) *disp ld tl bef 1/2-way: lost pl 6f out: t.o* **13/2**[3]

4m 5.5s (-7.20) **Going Correction** -0.675s/f (Firm)
WFA 4 from 5yo+ 3lb **6 Ran SP% 114.0**
Speed ratings: **91,84,82,71,69 50**
CSF £3.96 TOTE £1.70: £1.10, £1.70; EX 5.00 Trifecta £14.80.
Owner 06 Zoo Ltd **Bred** Mrs J J Shaw **Trained** Ingoe, Northumberland

FOCUS
A moderate bumper. Three pulled clear leaving the back until the winner left them well behind. The easy winner built on his course win, with the next three close to their marks.
T/Plt: £16.40 to a £1 stake. Pool: £52,269.41 - 2,319.09 winning tickets. T/Qpdt: £14.20 to a £1 stake. Pool: £3,336.08 - 173.10 winning tickets. **Richard Young**

[523]WORCESTER (L-H)

Saturday, June 6

OFFICIAL GOING: Good to firm (good in places)
Wind: Fresh across Weather: Cloudy with sunny spells

641 HAZELTON MOUNTFORD RACEHORSE TRAINERS INSURANCE NOVICES' CHASE (16 fncs) 2m 7f
1:45 (1:45) (Class 4) 5-Y-O+ **£5,198** (£1,526; £763; £381)

Form RPR
10-1 **1** **Royale Django (IRE)**[17] 394 6-11-4 0........................ RichardJohnson 137+
(Tim Vaughan) *hld up: hit 11th: hdwy to chse ldr appr 4 out: led bef next: rdn and swvd rt bef last: drvn out* **4/7**[1]

00-6 **2** ¾ **Chase The Wind (IRE)**[21] 329 6-10-12 0..................(t[1]) GavinSheehan 129+
(Warren Greatrex) *w ldr tl led 5th: hdd appr 3 out: rdn whn nt clr run and hung rt bef last: styd on u.p* **5/1**[3]

4P6- **3** 13 **Rothman (FR)**[76] 4945 5-10-12 0........................ SamTwiston-Davies 116
(Paul Nicholls) *chsd ldrs: rdn appr 3 out: nt fluent next: wknd flat* **7/2**[2]

200- **4** 25 **Lock Towers (IRE)**[134] 3838 6-10-12 0........................ NicodeBoinville 92
(Ben Pauling) *j.rt: led to 5th: chsd ldr tl rdn appr 4 out: sn wknd* **14/1**

5m 45.6s (-4.30) **Going Correction** -0.30s/f (Good) **4 Ran SP% 109.2**
Speed ratings: **95,94,90,81**
CSF £3.93 TOTE £1.50; EX 3.40 Trifecta £7.40.
Owner J Durston & N Harris **Bred** Paul Reynolds **Trained** Aberthin, Vale of Glamorgan

FOCUS
With all starts at the track having been moved, no speed figures will be compiled for Worcester until sufficient data is available. Far bend 6yds from inner line and Cathedral bend 3yds. Races 1, 2, 5, 6, 7 & 8 increased by 54yds, races 3 & 4 by 27yds. Richard Johnson described the ground as "good to firm and bit quicker down the far side." The obstacles in the home straight were positioned down the middle line. A fair novice chase in which the stewards looked into an incident at the last. The winner set a decent standard and is rated similar to his Southwell form.

642 WINNING BRANDS, STYLISH SHOPPING AT CROWNGATE H'CAP CHASE (13 fncs) 2m 4f
2:20 (2:20) (Class 3) (0-135,132) 5-Y-O+ **£7,797** (£2,289; £1,144; £572)

Form RPR
2F-0 **1** **Wings Of Smoke (IRE)**[33] 101 10-11-12 **132**..........(t) RichardJohnson 139+
(Tim Vaughan) *hld up: hdwy after 9th: rdn to ld fnl 110yds: styd on wl* **5/1**[2]

U4-6 **2** ¾ **No Likey (IRE)**[33] 109 8-10-9 **115**........................ TomO'Brien 120
(Philip Hobbs) *chsd ldrs: led appr 3 out: rdn whn mstke last: hdd 110yds out: kpt on* **10/3**[1]

01-5 **3** 15 **Itsuptoyou (IRE)**[20] 357 11-11-2 **122**........................ DarylJacob 115
(Arthur Whiting) *prom: hmpd and lost pl after 3rd: hdwy 9th: rdn and ev ch 3 out: wknd appr last* **10/1**

PP0- **4** 1 ¼ **Foundation Man (IRE)**[47] 5431 8-11-7 **127**..................(tp) WillKennedy 116
(Jonjo O'Neill) *led tl after 5th: chsd ldr tl rdn after 9th: wknd appr last* **8/1**[3]

3P6- **5** 1 ¾ **Uriah Heep (FR)**[65] 5109 6-11-5 **125**........................ WayneHutchinson 116
(Alan King) *chsd ldrs: mstke 3rd: rdn appr 3 out: wknd bef last* **5/1**[2]

01P- **6** ½ **Kadalkin (FR)**[44] 5499 9-11-0 **120**........................(vt[1]) TomScudamore 109
(Nigel Hawke) *chsd ldr tl led after 5th: rdn and hdd appr 3 out: wkng whn j.rt last* **12/1**

0-64 **7** 58 **Dursey Sound (IRE)**[17] 395 7-11-7 **127**........................ RichieMcLernon 62
(Jonjo O'Neill) *hld up: hdwy 5th: hit 9th: sn rdn: wknd bef next* **5/1**[2]

P0-4 **8** 13 **Mart Lane (IRE)**[20] 362 10-10-13 **122**........................ KillianMoore(3) 45
(Sophie Leech) *hld up in tch: reminder after 5th: drvn along 7th: wknd appr 9th* **10/1**

060- **P** **Drumlang (IRE)**[52] 5341 9-11-4 **127**........................ RobMcCarth(3)
(Ian Williams) *hld up: a in rr: wknd 8th: bhd whn p.u bef 3 out* **16/1**

4m 54.0s (-10.60) **Going Correction** -0.30s/f (Good) **9 Ran SP% 115.9**
Speed ratings: **109,108,102,102,101 101,78,72,**
CSF £22.92 CT £160.86 TOTE £4.80: £2.30, £1.50, £2.30; EX 19.30 Trifecta £189.80.
Owner Pearn's Pharmacies Ltd **Bred** Fred Mackey **Trained** Aberthin, Vale of Glamorgan

FOCUS
A decent handicap chase in which the first two came clear. The winner is rated back to his best.

643 JOHN BURKE MEMORIAL NOVICES' H'CAP CHASE (12 fncs) 2m 110y
2:55 (2:55) (Class 4) (0-120,120) 5-Y-O+ **£4,873** (£1,431; £715; £357)

Form RPR
133- **1** **Sergeant Thunder**[328] 937 6-11-10 **118**..........(t) SamTwiston-Davies 127+
(Paul Nicholls) *hld up: hdwy 7th: chsd ldr after 4 out: led 2 out: drvn out* **11/8**[1]

30-4 **2** 1 ¼ **Breaking The Bank**[26] 241 6-11-10 **118**........................ DarylJacob 124
(Ben Case) *chsd ldrs: led 4 out: hdd 2 out: styd on u.p* **9/2**[2]

662- **3** 14 **Vinnie The Fish (IRE)**[279] 1405 7-11-2 **110**........................ RobertDunne 105
(Dai Burchell) *hld up: hdwy 7th: ev ch 4 out: wknd 2 out* **12/1**

01-0 **4** 38 **Tara Dove**[30] 167 7-9-12 **95**........................ ConorShoemark(3) 66
(Alison Batchelor) *prom: chsd ldr and mstke 5th: led next: rdn and hdd 4 out: wknd next* **25/1**

45P- **P** **Life And Soul (IRE)**[102] 4415 8-11-12 **120**..................(p) WayneHutchinson
(Donald McCain) *chsd ldr: j.rt 2nd: lost 2nd 5th: rdn and wknd 8th: bhd whn p.u bef next* **8/1**[3]

52-5 **P** **Yabadabadoo**[26] 241 7-10-9 **113**........................ RichieO'Dea(10)
(Emma Lavelle) *led: j.rt: hdd and pckd 6th: wknd after next: bhd whn p.u bef 4 out* **9/2**[2]

020- **P** **Powderonthebonnet (IRE)**[56] 5283 7-10-6 **100**........................ AlainCawley
(Richard Phillips) *hld up: a in rr: bhd fr 5th: p.u bef 7th* **9/1**

4m 2.1s (-2.90) **Going Correction** -0.30s/f (Good) **7 Ran SP% 111.1**
Speed ratings: **94,93,86,68, ,**
CSF £7.86 TOTE £2.00: £1.60, £2.20; EX 6.70 Trifecta £42.20.
Owner C G Roach **Bred** Springcombe Park Stud **Trained** Ditcheat, Somerset

FOCUS
Ordinary form. A step up from the winner on his best hurdles figures, and the second was ion line with his hurdling best.

644 HOMEXPERTSUK.COM EXCEPTIONAL ESTATE AND LETTING AGENTS INTERMEDIATE OPEN NATIONAL HUNT FLAT RACE 2m
3:30 (3:30) (Class 6) 4-6-Y-O **£1,819** (£534; £267; £133)

Form RPR
1 **London Prize** 4-10-11 0........................ SamTwiston-Davies 101+
(John Ferguson) *hld up: hdwy over 3f out: chsd ldr over 2f out: led over 1f out: r.o wl: eased nr fin* **1/1**[1]

2 9 **Thehossbehind (IRE)** 4-10-11 0........................ RichardJohnson 87
(Ian Williams) *a.p: rdn over 2f out: chsd wnr fnl f: styd on same pce* **12/1**

00- **3** 1 ½ **Midnight Gypsy**[51] 5359 5-10-7 0........................[1] TomScudamore 82
(Stuart Kittow) *hld up: hdwy over 2f out: nt rch ldrs* **16/1**

0 **4** ¾ **Cor Wot An Apple**[36] 67 4-10-11 0........................ BrendanPowell 85
(Colin Tizzard) *chsd ldr tl led over 3f out: rdn and hdd over 1f out: wknd ins fnl f* **16/1**

4 **5** ¾ **Petite Power (IRE)**[22] 320 6-11-0 0........................ GavinSheehan 87
(Ali Stronge) *prom: rdn over 2f out: wknd over 1f out* **11/2**[3]

6 1 **Mr Kite** 4-10-11 0........................ AndrewThornton 83
(Mick Channon) *hld up: shkn up over 2f out: nvr on terms* **3/1**[2]

0- **7** 2 ¾ **Aspecialpresent (IRE)**[216] 2230 5-11-0 0........................ MichealNolan 84
(Adrian Wintle) *hld up: effrt over 5f out: wknd over 2f out* **50/1**

8 shd **Red Rust**[56] 6-11-0 0........................ TomO'Brien 83
(Robert Stephens) *led: hdd over 3f out: rdn and wknd over 1f out* **22/1**

6- **9** 15 **Foxy Mistress**[61] 5207 5-10-7 0........................[1] DarylJacob 61
(Ali Stronge) *chsd ldrs: rdn over 3f out: wknd over 2f out* **25/1**

0 **10** 23 **Palmers Bridge**[18] 392 6-10-7 0........................(t) ConorSmith(7) 45
(Linda Blackford) *hld up in tch: plld hrd: rdn and wknd over 2f out* **50/1**

6-6 **11** 11 **Sadiks Boy (IRE)**[20] 366 6-11-0 0........................ LeeEdwards 34
(Aytach Sadik) *mid-div: plld hrd: lost pl over 7f out: wknd over 5f out* **100/1**

3m 43.1s (-1.90) **Going Correction** -0.175s/f (Good)
WFA 4 from 5yo+ 3lb **11 Ran SP% 122.9**
Speed ratings: **97,92,91,91,91 90,89,89,81,70 64**
CSF £16.01 TOTE £1.90: £1.10, £2.60, £3.80; EX 15.10 Trifecta £114.40.
Owner Bloomfields **Bred** P And Mrs A G Venner **Trained** Cowlinge, Suffolk

FOCUS
The favourite proved far too good for some weak opposition. The form is rated around the third, fourth and fifth.

645 BRI WEALTH MANAGEMENT H'CAP HURDLE (10 hdls) 2m 4f
4:05 (4:05) (Class 3) (0-140,133) 4-Y-O+ **£6,498** (£1,908; £954; £477)

Form RPR
4-32 **1** **Flying Light (IRE)**[13] 463 9-10-13 **120**..................(b) WayneHutchinson 127
(Graeme McPherson) *hld up: hdwy appr 3 out: ev ch fr next: styd on u.p to ld post* **11/2**

012- **2** nse **Aficionado**[156] 3458 5-10-10 **117**........................(p) WillKennedy 123
(Dr Richard Newland) *hld up: hdwy 5th: led appr last: rdn flat: hdd post* **9/2**[2]

50-2 **3** 2 ¾ **Lava Lamp (GER)**[27] 216 8-10-6 **113**........................ PaulMoloney 117
(Evan Williams) *chsd ldrs: outpcd 7th: rallied appr last: r.o to go 3rd towards fin* **8/1**

642- **4** 1 ¼ **Valco De Touzaine (FR)**[50] 5370 6-11-9 **130**.......(t) SamTwiston-Davies 133
(Paul Nicholls) *hld up: hdwy appr 3 out: rdn after next: styd on same pce flat* **3/1**[1]

140- **5** 6 **Mile House (IRE)**[57] 5249 7-11-7 **128**........................ TomO'Brien 126
(Robert Stephens) *chsd ldr tl led 5th: rdn and hdd appr last: wknd flat* **5/1**[3]

13- **6** 17 **Perspicace**[56] 5278 4-10-11 **122**........................ TomScudamore 103
(David Pipe) *hld up: hdwy 6th: rdn and wknd appr last* **7/1**

/13- **7** 13 **Rumble Of Thunder (IRE)**[29] 1009 9-11-9 **133**..................(p) AdamNicol(3) 103
(Philip Kirby) *chsd ldrs: lost pl after 5th: rdn and wknd after 7th* **20/1**

160- **8** 14 **Skint**[233] 1920 9-10-8 **115**........................(p) GavinSheehan 73
(Ali Stronge) *prom tl rdn and wknd appr 3 out* **16/1**

35-P **F** **Bathwick Man**[19] 380 10-9-12 **112**........................ DavidNoonan(7) 113
(David Pipe) *led to 5th: chsd ldr: ev ch 3 out: sn rdn: cl 4th whn fell next: fatally injured* **14/1**

4m 45.1s (-8.40) **Going Correction** -0.175s/f (Good)
WFA 4 from 5yo+ 18lb **9 Ran SP% 116.2**
Speed ratings (Par 107): **109,108,107,107,104 98,92,87,**
CSF £31.12 CT £198.33 TOTE £6.70: £1.90, £1.70, £2.50; EX 32.50 Trifecta £135.60.
Owner The McPherson Racing Partnership **Bred** John McEnery **Trained** Upper Oddington, Gloucs

FOCUS
A decent handicap hurdle, if not the strongest for the grade. The pace was sound and the form should hold up. The winner was back to the level of his best Irish form.

646 GREENLIGHTING, THE UK HOUSE BUILDER'S CHOICE NOVICES' H'CAP HURDLE (12 hdls) 2m 7f
5:00 (5:00) (Class 5) (0-100,99) 4-Y-O+ **£2,599** (£763; £381; £190)

Form RPR
406- **1** **Tobefair**[81] 4825 5-10-8 **81**........................(p) TrevorWhelan 97+
(Debra Hamer) *hld up: hdwy after 9th: chsd ldr bef 3 out: led appr 2 out: j.lft last: pushed out* **11/2**[3]

0-26 **2** 4 ½ **Westerly Breeze (IRE)**[9] 530 7-11-5 **92**..................(b) RichardJohnson 103
(Edward Bevan) *chsd ldr tl pushed along and mstke 3 out: rdn to chse wnr appr last: styd on same pce flat* **9/4**[1]

32-P **3** 16 **Shady Glen (IRE)**[19] 377 6-10-12 **85**........................(p) KielanWoods 82
(Graeme McPherson) *mid-div: hdwy 7th: rdn appr 3 out: wknd after next* **5/1**[2]

P5-0 **4** 2 ¼ **Mazurati (IRE)**[20] 364 6-11-5 **99**........................(b[1]) MrMJPKendrick(7) 93
(Ben Case) *led: rdn and hdd appr 2 out: wknd bef last* **16/1**

46-5 **5** ¾ **Pagham Belle**[29] 183 7-11-7 **94**........................(vt[1]) DaveCrosse 87
(Nigel Hawke) *hld up: pushed along and sme hdwy appr 3 out: wknd bef next* **9/1**

025- **6** 1 ¼ **Dan's Quest**[49] 5398 5-11-4 **91**........................ CharliePoste 83
(Robin Dickin) *hld up: hdwy appr 3 out: rdn and wknd bef next* **16/1**

/0-P **7** 7 **Steel Gold (IRE)**[21] 340 9-9-9 **73** oh4........................ ConorRing(5) 58
(John Upson) *chsd ldrs tl rdn and wknd appr 3 out* **100/1**

0-53 **8** 10 **Tantalized**[14] 443 6-10-0 **73** oh4........................(b) LeeEdwards 49
(Dave Roberts) *hld up: rdn after 9th: sn wknd* **14/1**

9 7 **Distant Sound (IRE)**[21] 8-11-12 **99**........................ MichealNolan 69
(Adrian Wintle) *prom tl wknd appr 3 out* **12/1**

253- **10** *12* **Midnight Mustang**[76] 4937 8-10-7 87 ow3........................ MrJMartin(7) 46
(Andrew J Martin) *prom: pushed along after 8th: rdn and wknd after next* **10/1**

/6-P **P** **Waltzing Tornado (IRE)**[9] 530 11-11-8 95.................. LiamTreadwell
(Liam Grassick) *hld up: a in rr: bhd whn p.u bef 3 out* **40/1**

5m 41.3s (2.70) **Going Correction** -0.175s/f (Good) **11 Ran SP% 118.1**
Speed ratings (Par 103): **88,86,80,80,79 79,76,73,71,66**
CSF £18.79 CT £67.14 TOTE £9.10: £2.60, £1.70, £2.10; EX 32.70 Trifecta £273.40.
Owner Down The Quay Club **Bred** Mickley Stud **Trained** Nantycaws, Carmarthens

FOCUS
A distinctly moderate event, run at a fairly steady gallop. The form looks believable.

647 TRAMPS & VELVET NIGHTCLUB MAIDEN HURDLE (DIV I) (10 hdls) 2m 4f
5:30 (5:30) (Class 4) 4-Y-0+ **£3,898** (£1,144; £572; £286)

Form RPR

32-2 **1** **Father Edward (IRE)**[11] 494 6-11-0 125..............(t) SamTwiston-Davies 123+
(John Ferguson) *chsd ldrs: led 3 out: clr last: pushed out* **4/11**[1]

6-3 **2** *13* **Bells Of Ailsworth (IRE)**[20] 353 5-11-0 0.............. RichardJohnson 107
(Tim Vaughan) *hld up: mstke 1st: hdwy 6th: rdn and ev ch 3 out: styd on same pce appr last* **5/1**[2]

0P-P **3** *hd* **Padre Tito (IRE)**[20] 363 7-11-0 117.............................. GavinSheehan 106
(Emma Lavelle) *led to 3rd: chsd ldr tl led again 6th: rdn and hdd 3 out: styd on same pce appr last* **7/1**[3]

/2P- **4** *2 ½* **Paddocks Lounge (IRE)**[78] 4883 8-11-0 110.................. PaulMoloney 105
(Sophie Leech) *hld up: plld hrd: hdwy 7th: ev ch 3 out: sn rdn: styd on same pce appr last* **10/1**

544- **5** *17* **Sparkling Ice (IRE)**[75] 4960 4-10-0 104..................... MattGriffiths(3) 77
(Laura Young) *hld up: mstke 2nd: hdwy 7th: rdn and wknd next* **10/1**

6 *5* **Diamond Reign (IRE)**[61] 9-10-7 0.................................... LiamHeard 77
(Bob Buckler) *hld up: hdwy 6th: rdn and wknd after 3 out* **50/1**

50-P **7** *91* **Laughingalltheway**[27] 219 4-10-10 0........................(p) AndrewTinkler
(Martin Keighley) *chsd ldrs: reminders 6th: rdn and wknd bef 3 out* **33/1**

000/ **P** **On The Raz**[617] 1671 8-10-7 0.. MarkQuinlan
(Jackie Retter) *bhd fr 3rd: p.u bef 3 out* **100/1**

50-U **P** **Ninepointsixthree**[13] 456 5-11-0 107.............................. DaveCrosse
(John O'Shea) *chsd ldr tl led 3rd: clr next: blnd 5th: hdd next: sn rdn: wknd 7th: sn p.u* **16/1**

05-U **U** **Tikketoride**[13] 460 7-10-11 0.................................... TomBellamy(3)
(Peter Pritchard) *mid-div: hung rt and then lft whn uns rdr 3rd* **100/1**

4m 48.2s (-5.30) **Going Correction** -0.175s/f (Good)
WFA 4 from 5yo+ 18lb **10 Ran SP% 133.4**
Speed ratings (Par 105): **103,97,97,96,89 87,51, , ,**
CSF £3.82 TOTE £1.50: £1.02, £1.70, £2.30; EX 4.10 Trifecta £12.70.
Owner Bloomfields **Bred** Hugh Fitzpatrick **Trained** Cowlinge, Suffolk

FOCUS
A very modest event, but it was 2.2sec quicker than division two. The winner set a decent standard and was close to his mark.

648 TRAMPS & VELVET NIGHTCLUB MAIDEN HURDLE (DIV II) (10 hdls) 2m 4f
6:05 (6:05) (Class 4) 4-Y-0+ **£3,898** (£1,144; £572; £286)

Form RPR

5-4 **1** **Always On The Run (IRE)**[21] 330 5-11-0 0..............[1] WayneHutchinson 116+
(Donald McCain) *hld up: hdwy 6th: led 2 out: drvn out* **16/1**

30-2 **2** *1 ½* **Set List (IRE)**[21] 335 6-11-0 117.............................. GavinSheehan 116
(Emma Lavelle) *led to 3rd: chsd ldr tl led again after 6th: nt fluent 3 out: rdn and hdd next: styd on same pce flat* **6/5**[1]

350- **3** *14* **Dear Darling**[138] 3772 5-10-7 105...............................(bt[1]) BrendanPowell 95
(Colin Tizzard) *chsd ldrs: rdn and hung rt after 2 out: wknd last* **7/2**[2]

0/0- **4** *7* **Jeans Lady**[361] 660 6-10-7 0...................................... AndrewTinkler 90
(Martin Keighley) *chsd ldrs: rdn appr 3 out: wkng whn mstke next* **50/1**

343- **5** *30* **Poetic Presence (IRE)**[253] 1631 5-10-7 0.................... RichardJohnson 62
(Adrian Wintle) *prom tl wknd after 7th* **14/1**

3- **6** *48* **Newton Geronimo**[211] 2325 6-10-4 0...................... HarrisonBeswick(10) 26
(Ben Pauling) *chsd ldr tl led 3rd: hdd after 6th: mstke next: sn rdn: hung rt and wknd* **15/2**[3]

22-5 **P** **Magnimity (IRE)**[29] 181 5-11-0 0.............................. NicodeBoinville
(Nicky Henderson) *hld up: wknd 5th: p.u bef next* **7/2**[2]

P- **P** **The Banshee**[182] 2936 9-10-7 0.................................... AlainCawley
(Liam Grassick) *in rr: pushed along 4th: wknd bef next: bhd whn p.u bef 6th* **66/1**

-0 **F** **Quench Tara**[30] 178 8-10-7 0..................................... LiamTreadwell
(Michael Scudamore) *nt jump wl in rr: bhd whn fell 2 out* **33/1**

4m 50.4s (-3.10) **Going Correction** -0.175s/f (Good) **9 Ran SP% 120.6**
Speed ratings (Par 105): **99,98,92,90,78 58, , ,**
CSF £38.62 TOTE £14.10: £3.80, £1.10, £1.50; EX 61.90 Trifecta £345.40.
Owner Straightline Construction Ltd **Bred** Island Bridge Racing Club **Trained** Cholmondeley, Cheshire

FOCUS
The weaker division on paper, and the slower by 2.2sec. Not form to be confident about.
T/Plt: £39.80 to a £1 stake. Pool: £54,495.19 - 997.95 winning tickets T/Qpdt: £16.80 to a £1 stake. Pool: £4,196.29 - 184.80 winning tickets **Colin Roberts**

649 - 655a (Foreign Racing) - See Raceform Interactive

299 PERTH (R-H)
Sunday, June 7

OFFICIAL GOING: Good (good to firm in places; 8.5)
Wind: fresh half behind Weather: cloudy

656 LAND ROVER DEFENDER NOVICES' HURDLE (FOR THE PROVOST'S PLATE CHALLENGE TROPHY) (10 hdls) 2m 4f 35y
2:10 (2:10) (Class 4) 4-Y-0+ **£3,165** (£935; £467; £234; £117)

Form RPR

1-1 **1** **Antilope Du Seuil (FR)**[24] 299 5-11-5 125...............(p) RichardJohnson 115+
(Gordon Elliott, Ire) *in tch: hdwy to ld 2 out: pushed clr between last 2: kpt on* **5/6**[1]

00-5 **2** *5* **Welcome Ben (IRE)**[25] 285 6-10-11 0............................ TonyKelly(3) 104
(Jackie Stephen) *trckd ldr: rdn 2 out: hit last but sn 2nd: kpt on* **33/1**

1 **3** *½* **Wind Of Hope (IRE)**[25] 285 6-11-3 0...................... GrahamWatters(3) 109
(Lucinda Russell) *led: rdn whn hdd 2 out: hit last and lost 2nd: one pce* **4/1**[2]

1-3 **4** *1 ¾* **Catching Shadows (IRE)**[32] 144 6-11-0 0.................... JakeGreenall 101
(James Ewart) *in tch: rdn bef 2 out: kpt on* **9/2**[3]

3-4 **5** *3* **So Satisfied**[14] 452 4-10-10 112..................................... BrianHughes 94
(Sandy Thomson) *midfield: in tch 3 out: rdn bef next: one pce* **20/1**

5- **6** *1 ¾* **Drumhart (IRE)**[22] 342 6-11-0 99.............................. DenisO'Regan 97
(C A McBratney, Ire) *trckd ldr: rdn bef 2 out: grad wknd after 2 out* **14/1**

4-2 **7** *17* **Ceithre Delta (IRE)**[24] 300 10-10-7 0.......................... PeterBuchanan 74
(S R B Crawford, Ire) *midfield: rdn 3 out: sn wknd* **28/1**

4-36 **8** *17* **Johnny Go**[12] 481 5-10-7 0.. RyanDay(7) 66
(Lisa Harrison) *in tch on outer: rdn after 7th: wknd after 3 out* **33/1**

50 **9** *dist* **Suzy's Music (IRE)**[11] 503 7-10-7 0.............................. AELynch 28
(S R B Crawford, Ire) *hld up: bhd fr 7th* **50/1**

10 *7* **Coppelia (IRE)** 7-10-7 0.. BrianHarding 21
(Nicky Richards) *hld up: hit 7th: sn wknd* **22/1**

0-0 **11** *16* **Ripasso**[14] 459 6-11-0 0.. HenryBrooke 14
(Jean McGregor) *hld up: hit 2nd: a in rr* **200/1**

05/ **12** *17* **Thehoodlum**[693] 962 8-10-11 0............................. JonathanEngland(3)
(Jean McGregor) *hld up: nt fluent 5th: hit 6th: sn bhd* **200/1**

0- **P** **Persian Fashion (IRE)**[156] 3487 6-10-4 0......................(t) CraigNichol(3)
(Ian Duncan) *hld up: hit 1st: bhd after 6th: p.u bef 2 out* **100/1**

5m 0.7s (-1.30) **Going Correction** -0.30s/f (Good)
WFA 4 from 5yo+ 18lb **13 Ran SP% 121.8**
Speed ratings (Par 105): **90,88,87,87,85 85,78,71,57,54 48,41,**
CSF £44.44 TOTE £2.00: £1.10, £6.40, £1.60; EX 54.10 Trifecta £205.80.
Owner Simon Munir & Isaac Souede **Bred** Mme Catherine Boudot **Trained** Longwood, Co Meath

FOCUS
Hurdles and bends moved to fresh ground. Actual race distance of the opener was 2m4f114y. The general view of jockeys riding in the first was that the ground was good with the odd bit of good to firm. A fair novice hurdle in which they didn't go much of a gallop.

657 RANGE ROVER SPORT H'CAP CHASE (15 fncs) 2m 4f 20y
2:45 (2:46) (Class 3) (0-140,133) 5-Y-0+ **£6,963** (£2,057; £1,028; £514; £257)

Form RPR

155- **1** **Vesperal Dream (FR)**[43] 5540 6-11-5 129.................(tp) SeanBowen(3) 139+
(Paul Nicholls) *in tch: hdwy after 3 out: rdn to chal last: led 110yds out: kpt on* **7/2**[2]

6/12 **2** *1 ½* **Russian Regent (IRE)**[9] 543 11-10-10 117.............. RichardJohnson 126
(Gordon Elliott, Ire) *trckd ldr: mstke 2nd: nt fluent 11th: rdn after 3 out: led narrowly last: sn drvn: hdd 110yds out: one pce* **11/2**

33-3 **3** *½* **Strongpoint (IRE)**[39] 24 11-11-12 133...................... PeterBuchanan 140
(S R B Crawford, Ire) *led: hit 9th: rdn after 3 out: hdd last: one pce* **11/4**[1]

112- **4** *9* **Bearly Legal (IRE)**[50] 5401 9-11-1 129..........................(t) MrJCBarry(7) 128
(Karl Thornton, Ire) *trckd ldr: nt fluent 4 out: drvn 3 out: wknd after 2 out* **7/2**[2]

4-21 **5** *1 ½* **Mister First (FR)**[24] 304 9-11-4 125..............................(t) BrianHughes 123
(Robert Alan Hennessy, Ire) *hld up in tch: rdn 3 out: wknd 2 out* **5/1**[3]

46-2 **6** *6* **Habbie Simpson**[29] 199 10-10-8 122.......................... MrTHamilton(7) 115
(Pauline Robson) *in tch: rdn and lost pl bef 4 out: wknd after 3 out* **14/1**

4/P- **7** *32* **Back To Balloo (IRE)**[22] 345 9-11-9 130.................. DenisO'Regan 94
(C A McBratney, Ire) *hld up in rr: hit 9th: pushed along 4 out: a bhd* **33/1**

4m 52.8s (-12.20) **Going Correction** -0.375s/f (Good) **7 Ran SP% 112.8**
Speed ratings: **109,108,108,104,104 101,88**
CSF £22.21 CT £58.69 TOTE £4.70: £2.80, £3.40; EX 24.00 Trifecta £97.30.
Owner The Loving Insurance Partnership **Bred** Bernard Delvigne **Trained** Ditcheat, Somerset

FOCUS
They went a solid gallop in this decent handicap chase. Five of the seven runners came from Ireland.

658 PETER PRICE MEMORIAL NOVICES' H'CAP HURDLE (8 hdls) 2m 47y
3:20 (3:20) (Class 4) (0-105,105) 4-Y-0+ **£3,165** (£935; £467; £234; £117)

Form RPR

50-U **1** **Russian Royale**[12] 487 5-10-6 88.................................... CraigNichol(3) 98+
(Micky Hammond) *in tch: smooth hdwy after 5th: led gng wl bef 2 out: rdn to assert between last 2: nt fluent last: kpt on* **9/4**[1]

000- **2** *6* **Tangolan (IRE)**[34] 7-11-11 104.................................... PaddyBrennan 110+
(Fergal O'Brien) *in tch: hdwy to trck ldrs 3 out: rdn to go 2nd 2 out: kpt on but sn no ch w wnr: eased towards fin* **13/2**

6-F2 **3** *2 ¼* **Quest Magic (IRE)**[11] 507 9-11-5 103...............(p) JonathonBewley(5) 105
(George Bewley) *led: rdn whn hdd bef 2 out: sn one pce in 3rd* **9/2**[3]

-012 **4** *6* **Seventeen Black (IRE)**[12] 487 7-10-3 87.................. GrantCockburn(5) 85
(Stuart Coltherd) *hld up: rdn after 3 out: plugged on after 2 out: nvr threatened* **4/1**[2]

00-3 **5** *¾* **Jackofhearts**[25] 288 7-9-12 80...........................(p) JonathanEngland(3) 76
(Jean McGregor) *hld up: nt fluent 5th: sn pushed along: plugged on after 2 out: nvr threatened* **16/1**

P2-4 **6** *1* **Marlee Massie (IRE)**[25] 288 6-10-0 79..................(p) LucyAlexander 74
(N W Alexander) *trckd ldr: nt fluent 3rd: rdn and already lost pl whn nt fluent 2 out: no threat after* **12/1**

534- **7** *2 ¼* **Wot A Shot (IRE)**[51] 5364 6-11-4 97............................ PeterBuchanan 90
(C A McBratney, Ire) *hld up: hdwy whn hit 3 out: sn rdn: wknd 2 out* **14/1**

4-3P **8** *13* **Fashion Icon (FR)**[20] 383 4-10-11 93............................(v) JamieMoore 71
(Nigel Hawke) *trckd ldr: rdn after 3 out: wknd bef 2 out* **16/1**

5P0- **P** **Star Date (IRE)**[55] 5315 6-11-9 105................................. DerekFox(3)
(Lucinda Russell) *in tch: wknd after 3 out: in rr whn wnt wrong and p.u and dismntd jst bef 2 out* **22/1**

3m 54.2s (234.20)
WFA 4 from 5yo+ 17lb **9 Ran SP% 112.8**
CSF £17.13 CT £59.34 TOTE £4.10: £1.40, £2.00, £1.70; EX 19.10 Trifecta £95.70.
Owner Richard & Katherine Gilbert **Bred** Mrs P A & M J Reditt **Trained** Middleham, N Yorks

FOCUS
Actual race distance 2m 114y. Decidedly modest fare.

659 FUGRO SUBSEA SERVICES NOVICES' CHASE (12 fncs) 2m
3:50 (3:50) (Class 4) 5-Y-0+ **£4,540** (£1,418; £763)

Form RPR

4-25 **1** **Owen Na View (IRE)**[16] 430 7-11-5 135.......................... PaddyBrennan 135+
(Fergal O'Brien) *mde all: shkn up 3 out: sn clr: unchal* **7/2**[2]

5- **2** *20* **Swantykay (IRE)**[9] 549 6-10-12 115.............................. RichardJohnson 115
(Gordon Elliott, Ire) *in tch in 3rd: lft 2nd 4 out: rdn 3 out: sn no ch w wnr* **9/2**[3]

45-4 **3** *74* **Badged**[25] 285 6-10-7 0...(p) GrantCockburn(5) 43
(Lucy Normile) *hld up in 4th: bhd after 8th: lft remote 3rd 4 out* **28/1**

30-2 **F** **Sea Lord (IRE)**[23] 317 8-10-12 0..................................... AidanColeman
(John Ferguson) *trckd ldr in 2nd: 4 l down whn fell 4 out* **4/7**[1]

3m 55.1s (235.10) **4 Ran SP% 107.5**
CSF £16.49 TOTE £3.80; EX 11.10 Trifecta £29.20.
Owner The Yes No Wait Sorries **Bred** Brian Walsh **Trained** Naunton, Gloucs

FOCUS
Actual race distance 2m54y. The favourite's fall left the other three to come home at wide intervals.

660 PENTLAND LAND ROVER PERTH GOLD CUP H'CAP CHASE (FOR THE CITY OF PERTH GOLD CUP) (18 fncs) 2m 7f 180y
4:25 (4:25) (Class 2) 5-Y-0+ **£15,825** (£4,675; £2,337; £1,170; £585)

Form RPR
231- **1** **Kilbree Kid (IRE)**[47] 5450 8-10-6 **128**..........(tp) PaddyBrennan 136
(Tom George) *trckd ldrs: led 4 out: lft 3 l up 3 out: sn rdn: drvn and kpt on run-in: all out* **7/2**[2]
41F- **2** *1* **Runswick Royal (IRE)**[50] 5388 6-11-10 **146**.......................... BrianHughes 153
(Ann Hamilton) *in tch: rdn after 4 out: lft in dispute of 2nd 3 out: 2 l down last: kpt on run-in* **13/2**[3]
20-3 **3** *nk* **Bless The Wings (IRE)**[36] 95 10-10-12 **134**.........(p) RichardJohnson 141
(Gordon Elliott, Ire) *hld up: hdwy 14th: lft in dispute of 2nd 3 out: sn rdn: 2 l down last: kpt on run-in* **7/2**[2]
66P- **4** *30* **Kasbadali (FR)**[90] 4684 10-9-13 **124**.................(p) ThomasGarner(3) 104
(Oliver Sherwood) *led: hdd 5th: led again 9th: hdd 4 out: sn rdn: wknd after 3 out* **10/1**
PP-0 **5** *½* **Bar De Ligne (FR)**[30] 184 9-9-12 **127**......................(p) CraigGallagher(7) 107
(Brian Ellison) *midfield: rdn and outpcd 14th: wknd after 3 out* **25/1**
6-06 **P** **Quincy Des Pictons (FR)**[19] 389 11-11-5 **141**.......................... RhysFlint
(Alan Jones) *hld up in rr: nt fluent 12th: sn pushed and struggling: p.u bef next* **40/1**
022- **F** **Aerial (FR)**[47] 5450 9-10-5 **130**..(p) SeanBowen(3) 137
(Paul Nicholls) *trckd ldr: led 5th to 9th: yet to be asked for effrt in cl 2nd whn fell 3 out* **7/4**[1]
10-P **P** **Yes Tom (IRE)**[36] 95 10-11-5 **141**.................................(p) PeterBuchanan
(S R B Crawford, Ire) *midfield: mstke 13th: sn lost pl and struggling: p.u bef 3 out* **25/1**

5m 54.8s (-9.20) **Going Correction** -0.375s/f (Good) **8 Ran SP% 113.4**
Speed ratings: **100,99,99,89,89** , ,
CSF £25.14 CT £83.79 TOTE £4.10: £1.60, £1.60, £1.60; EX 23.70 Trifecta £82.50.
Owner Five Valleys Racing Partnership **Bred** John O'Mahony **Trained** Slad, Gloucs

FOCUS
Actual race distance 3m41y. Not the race it had been in the morning, with six taken out due to the drying ground, but still a good contest for this valuable prize. The first three finished clear of the remainder.

661 CRABBIE'S ALCOHOLIC GINGER BEER H'CAP HURDLE (10 hdls) 2m 4f 35y
4:55 (4:58) (Class 4) (0-110,109) 4-Y-O **£3,798** (£1,122; £561; £280; £140)

Form RPR
1 **Topper Thornton (IRE)**[22] 343 6-11-6 **103**...................(p) BrianHughes 111+
(C A McBratney, Ire) *in tch: trckd ldr gng wl after 3 out: upsides on bit whn nt fluent last: pushed along to ld towards fin* **5/2**[1]
456- **2** *¾* **Los Nadis (GER)**[9] 5519 11-11-5 **102**.......................(v[1]) HenryBrooke 106
(Jim Goldie) *led: clr after 2nd: reduced advantage 3 out: sn rdn: jnd after 2 out: kpt on: hdd towards fin* **16/1**
00-3 **3** *6* **Urban Kode (IRE)**[24] 302 7-10-12 **98**.................(v) GrahamWatters(3) 97
(Lucinda Russell) *midfield: hdwy after 3 out: rdn bef 2 out: kpt on same pce* **14/1**
-624 **4** *3¼* **Solway Prince**[13] 468 6-10-5 **95**.................................... RyanDay(7) 91
(Lisa Harrison) *midfield: rdn bef 3 out: plugged on after 2 out: nvr threatened* **11/2**[3]
362- **5** *3½* **Maraweh (IRE)**[44] 5516 5-10-6 **92**.....................................(v) DerekFox(3) 87
(Lucinda Russell) *hld up: mstke 2nd: rdn along in rr after 6th: plugged on after 2 out: nvr threatened* **9/2**[2]
22-0 **6** *12* **Amilliontimes (IRE)**[11] 508 7-11-6 **106**..........................(t) TonyKelly(3) 91
(Jackie Stephen) *chsd clr ldr: rdn after 3 out: wknd after 2 out* **9/1**
P-P4 **7** *10* **Cumbrian Farmer**[10] 522 8-9-7 **83** oh4.....................(v) MissJWalton(7) 56
(George Bewley) *midfield: rdn 3 out: already wkng whn hit 2 out* **11/1**
200- **8** *dist* **Dotties Dilema (IRE)**[46] 5473 7-11-1 **103**................(tp) GrantCockburn(5) 40
(Lucinda Russell) *hld up: rdn 3 out: sn wknd* **25/1**
/56- **F** **Bowdler's Magic**[13] 2812 8-11-5 **102**...........................(t) BrianHarding 88
(David Thompson) *in tch: rdn 3 out: wknd after 2 out: wl btn whn fell last* **11/2**[3]

4m 54.4s (-7.60) **Going Correction** -0.30s/f (Good)
WFA 4 from 5yo+ 18lb **9 Ran SP% 112.3**
Speed ratings (Par 105): **103,102,100,99,97 92,88,72,**
CSF £38.77 CT £460.36 TOTE £3.50: £1.50, £2.90, £2.40; EX 44.00 Trifecta £327.80.
Owner R P Behan/Steven Wylie **Bred** Patrick Wilmott **Trained** Crossgar, Co. Down

FOCUS
Actual race distance 2m4f114y. Most of the runners were exposed in this modest handicap.

662 RANGE ROVER EVOQUE STANDARD OPEN NATIONAL HUNT FLAT RACE 2m 13y
5:30 (5:30) (Class 6) 4-6-Y-O **£2,053** (£598; £299)

Form RPR
020- **1** **Chitu (IRE)**[58] 5255 5-11-0..................................... MrSCrawford 108+
(S R B Crawford, Ire) *hld up in tch: smooth hdwy over 3f out: led on bit over 1f out: pushed clr: comf* **11/10**[1]
2 *4½* **Blessed King (IRE)**[50] 5-11-0............................. RichardJohnson 101
(Gordon Elliott, Ire) *trckd ldr: led over 3f out: rdn over 2f out: hdd over 1f out: kpt on but no ch w wnr* **5/2**[2]
5- **3** *2¼* **Carinena (IRE)**[193] 2745 6-10-7.............................. BrianHarding 92
(Nicky Richards) *in tch: chal over 3f out: rdn over 2f out: one pce in 3rd fr over 1f out* **7/2**[3]
06- **4** *31* **Mayze Bell**[212] 2339 6-10-4.................................. CraigNichol(3) 64
(Alistair Whillans) *led: rdn whn hdd over 3f out: sn wknd* **40/1**
5 *99* **Recycle Rob** 6-10-11...(t) AdamNicol(3)
(David Thompson) *hld up in rr: rdn over 6f out: sn bhd: t.o* **33/1**
6 *1¼* **Kettle** 4-10-4.. DougieCostello
(Donald Whillans) *hld up: bhd fr 1/2-way: t.o* **16/1**

3m 48.8s (228.80)
WFA 4 from 5yo+ 3lb **6 Ran SP% 109.7**
CSF £3.84 TOTE £2.50: £1.20, £1.80; EX 3.90 Trifecta £6.20.
Owner Graham Slesser **Bred** Michael Coburn **Trained** Larne, Co Antrim

FOCUS
Actual race distance 2m114y. Three came well clear in this modest bumper. The first two are both sons of Desert King.
T/Plt: £83.00 to a £1 stake. Pool: £109,061.50 - 958.37 winning units. T/Qpdt: £19.20 to a £1 stake. Pool: £7825.15 - 300.70 winning units. **Andrew Sheret**

586 # AUTEUIL (L-H)
Sunday, June 7
OFFICIAL GOING: Turf: very soft

663a GRANDE COURSE DE HAIES D'AUTEUIL (HURDLE) (GRADE 1) (5YO+) (TURF) 3m 1f 110y
2:08 (12:00) 5-Y-0+
£129,069 (£63,100; £37,286; £25,813; £14,341; £10,038)

RPR
1 **Un Temps Pour Tout (IRE)**[57] 5273 6-10-10...........(b) JamesReveley 164+
(David Pipe) *mde all: j.w: set decent pce: clr ld thrght: asserted bef last: unchal: impressive* **10/1**
2 *10* **Thousand Stars (FR)**[38] 49 11-10-10..........................(p) MsKWalsh 154
(W P Mullins, Ire) *w.w towards rr: 10th and plenty to do bef 2 out: clsd u.p bef last: styd on to go 2nd run-in: no ch w wnr* **14/1**
3 *3* **Zarkandar (IRE)**[57] 5273 8-10-10.......................(b) SamTwiston-Davies 151
(Paul Nicholls) *settled bhd ldrs: tk clsr order 3 out: 3rd and rdn 2 out: one pce fr last* **7/1**[3]
4 *2* **Dos Santos (FR)**[22] 349 5-10-6..........................(p) BertrandLestrade 145
(Emmanuel Clayeux, France) *racd midfield: tk clsr order 3 out: styd on to go 3rd between last 2: kpt on same pce fr last* **16/1**
5 *¾* **Ballynagour (IRE)**[22] 349 9-10-10...................... TomScudamore 148
(David Pipe) *w.w in midfield: tk clsr order bef 4 out: chsd ldr after 3 out: 4 l 2nd 2 out: rdn and no imp between last 2: fdd run-in* **6/1**[2]
6 *1½* **Hurricane Fly (IRE)**[38] 49 11-10-10........................... RWalsh 147
(W P Mullins, Ire) *settled in midfield: niggled along after 3 out: 5th and rdn 2 out: sltly hmpd and swtchd between last 2: plugged on at same pce: nvr in contention* **6/4**[1]
7 *12* **Le Chateau (FR)**[22] 349 6-10-10........................... ErvanChazelle 135
(C Scandella, France) *prom in main gp: rdn and effrt bef 3 out: hrd rdn 2 out: btn whn mstke last* **50/1**
8 *2* **Attila De Sivola (FR)**[21] 5-10-7 ow1........................ DavidCottin 130
(Y-M Porzier, France) *a cl up in main gp bhd clr ldr: tk wd crse 2nd circ but remained in tch: effrt turning for home: rdn and btn bef 2 out* **50/1**
9 *8* **Activial (FR)**[42] 4 5-10-6.................................... DarylJacob 121
(Harry Fry) *chsd clr ldr: shkn up and nt qckn bef 3 out: grad wknd* **10/1**
P **Rameur (FR)**[38] 54 10-10-10................................ PACarberry
(Louisa Carberry, France) *towards rr: wl bhd whn p.u bef 7th* **66/1**
F **Lamego (FR)**[22] 8-10-10.................................. Jean-LucBeaunez
(Mme P Butel, France) *towards rr: effrt u.p bef 2 out: sharing 7th and btn whn fell last* **100/1**
P **Defi D'Anjou (FR)**[22] 349 7-10-10.......................... ArnaudDuchene
(L Viel, France) *w.w in fnl 3rd: among bkmarkers 4 out: sn t.o: p.u bef 2 out* **50/1**
P **Voiladenuo (FR)**[42] 4 6-10-10.............................(p) WilfridDenuault
(Guy Denuault, France) *midfield: rdn and struggling 4 out: bhd whn p.u bef 2 out* **9/1**
P **Nando (FR)**[42] 4 5-10-6...(b) RegisSchmidlin
(F-M Cottin, France) *a among bkmarkers: t.o whn p.u bef 2 out* **66/1**
P **Val De Ferbet (FR)**[22] 349 6-10-10.......................... PaulTownend
(W P Mullins, Ire) *midfield on outer: lost pl 7th: bhd whn mstke 8th: p.u bef next* **14/1**

6m 5.8s (365.80) **15 Ran SP% 124.0**
PARI-MUTUEL (all including 1 euro stake): WIN 10.90; PLACE 3.60, 6.70, 2.90; DF 117.90; SF 247.00.
Owner Professor Caroline Tisdall & Bryan Drew **Bred** Felix Talbot **Trained** Nicholashayne, Devon

664a PRIX DES DRAGS (CHASE) (GRADE 2) (5YO+) (TURF) 2m 6f
3:15 (3:15) 5-Y-0+
£83,720 (£40,930; £24,186; £16,744; £9,302; £6,511)

RPR
1 **Bel La Vie (FR)**[21] 375 9-10-6............................ BertrandLestrade 136
(G Macaire, France) *a cl up: 4th and pushed along 2 out: rdn to chal last: sustained run u.p to ld cl home* **13/8**[1]
2 *¾* **Reglis Brunel (FR)**[21] 375 10-10-8 ow5............ JonathanPlouganou 137
(E Lecoiffier, France) *towards rr: hdwy after 3 out: 6th and rdn 2 out: styd on to chal after last: led 150yds out: hdd cl home* **14/1**
3 *1½* **Vent Sombre (FR)**[38] 54 6-10-8.....................................(b) DavidCottin 136
(G Cherel, France) *a cl up: 3rd and mstke 5 out: j.lft 4 out: 2nd and rdn whn swtchd rnd ldr appr last: kpt on u.p run-in: no ex cl home* **16/1**
4 *5* **Lachlan Bridge (GER)**[42] 3 7-10-6..................... FrancoisPamart 129
(A Chaille-Chaille, France) *settled midfield: mstke 6th: tk clsr order 3 out: 6th last: styd on u.p run-in: nrest at fin* **16/1**
5 *3* **Rasique (FR)**[42] 3 5-10-1.................................... ErvanChazelle 121
(C Scandella, France) *trckd ldr: led 11th: 2 l ld and rdn appr last: hdd 150yds out: no ex* **50/1**
6 *3* **Anaking (FR)**[44] 5-10-3 ow4..........................(p) FelixDeGiles 120
(Emmanuel Clayeux, France) *a towards rr: mstkes early: hit 5 out: rdn and btn bef 2 out* **40/1**
7 *nk* **Pindare (FR)**[21] 375 6-10-6............................(p) ArnaudDuchene 122
(J-P Gallorini, France) *racd in midfield: 6th and travelling wl enough 5 out: rdn and no imp 3 out: styd on after last: nvr on terms* **5/1**[3]
8 *1½* **Varabad Du Buisson (FR)**[31] 6-10-3........................... KevinNabet 118
(M Postic, France) *led: remained cl up after being hdd bef 11th: mstke 4 out: wknd after 2 out* **12/1**
9 *6* **On His Own (IRE)**[21] 375 11-10-10...................................(b) RWalsh 119
(W P Mullins, Ire) *midfield: lost pl 5 out: sn scrubbed along and no imp: wl hld fr 2 out* **9/2**[2]
10 *20* **Royale Flag (FR)**[65] 5128 5-9-13............................ RegisSchmidlin 88
(F-M Cottin, France) *in rr: hdwy 3 out: wl hld fr 2 out* **16/1**
F **Tiot Cas (FR)**[44] 8-10-3.................................... ChristopheHerpin
(P Chemin, France) *w.w towards rr: moved into midfield bef 11th: tk clsr order 5 out: 3rd fnl bnd after 3 out: mstke 2 out: wkng whn fell last* **50/1**
U **Perfect Gentleman (IRE)**[21] 374 10-10-3......................... PaulTownend
(W P Mullins, Ire) *prom: mstke 10th (water) and uns rdr* **12/1**
F **Iroufcar Has (FR)**[46] 5-9-13................................... JacquesRicou
(J-P Gallorini, France) *w.w towards rr: fell 10th (water)* **9/1**

5m 27.2s (-16.80) **13 Ran SP% 129.0**
PARI-MUTUEL (all including 1 euro stake): WIN 2.30 (combined with Vente Sombre & Anaking); PLACE 1.60, 3.50, 4.30; DF 20.10; SF 29.80.
Owner Mme Patrick Papot **Bred** Mme Marie-Christine Gabeur **Trained** Les Mathes, France

665a PRIX ALAIN DU BREIL - COURSE DE HAIES D'ETE DES QUATRE ANS (HURDLE) (GRADE 1) (4YO) (TURF) 2m 3f 110y

3:45 (3:45) 4-Y-O

£94,186 (£46,046; £27,209; £18,837; £10,465; £7,325)

RPR

1 **Blue Dragon (FR)**[22] [351] 4-10-8 0 VincentCheminaud 146
(G Cherel, France) *mde all: clr thrght: won unchal* **11/4**[2]

2 6 **Bosseur (FR)**[42] [2] 4-10-8 0 DavidCottin 140
(G Cherel, France) *prom in main gp: 4th and rdn 2 out: keeping on whn wnt rt last: styd on run-in: no ch w wnr* **40/1**

3 5 **Yoko (FR)**[22] [351] 4-10-8 0 KevinNabet 135
(J-P Gallorini, France) *in rr early: gd hdwy fr 2 out: r.o flat: nvr in contention* **50/1**

4 1 1/4 **Bonito Du Berlais (FR)**[42] [2] 4-10-8 0 FrancoisPamart 134
(A Chaille-Chaille, France) *prom in main gp: racd on outside bk st: plenty to do appr 2 out: one pce u.p* **4/7**[1]

5 1 1/2 **Buiseness Sivola (FR)**[36] [94] 4-10-8 0 RWalsh 132
(W P Mullins, Ire) *chsd clr ldr: rdn and no imp 2 out: one pce u.p fr bef last* **14/1**

6 3/4 **Clovis Du Berlais (FR)**[22] [351] 4-10-8 0 (p) LudovicPhilipperon 132
(Robert Collet, France) *towards rr: clsd 5 out: mod 5th fnl bnd bef 2 out: kpt on u.p run-in: nvr trbld ldrs* **22/1**

7 3 **Champ De Bataille (FR)**[65] [5127] 4-10-8 0 DamienMescam 129
(F-M Cottin, France) *w.w towards rr: rdn and no imp 3 out: sme modest hdwy bef last: nvr in contention* **50/1**

8 dist **Tin Soldier (FR)**[49] 4-10-8 0 (p) JonathanPlouganou
(M Seror, France) *midfield: towards rr 4 out: wl bhd fr 2 out* **100/1**

9 10 **Petite Parisienne (FR)**[36] [94] 4-10-3 0 BJCooper
(W P Mullins, Ire) *cl up in main gp bhd clr ldr: dropped into midfield 6th: pushed along 4 out: mstke next and sn struggling: wl bhd fr 2 out* **5/1**[3]

P **Nicknos (FR)**[22] [351] 4-10-8 0 AnthonyLecordier
(Mlle I Gallorini, France) *a in rr: t.o 4 out: p.u bef 2 out* **50/1**

4m 31.6s (-23.40) **10 Ran SP% 127.3**
PARI-MUTUEL (all including 1 euro stake): WIN 2.70; PLACE 1.70, 5.30, 8.40; DF 43.10; SF 61.20.
Owner Magalen O Bryant, D Powell & D Baer **Bred** Mme M Bryant, D Baer & Eurl Chene **Trained** France

666 - 668a (Foreign Racing) - See Raceform Interactive

595 FONTWELL (L-H)

Tuesday, June 9

OFFICIAL GOING: Good
Wind: breezy Weather: overcast with sunny spells; 16 degrees

669 CALL STAR SPORTS ON 08000 521 321 H'CAP HURDLE (10 hdls) 2m 3f 33y

2:10 (2:10) (Class 4) (0-120,120) 4-Y-O+ £3,249 (£954; £477; £238)

Form RPR

340- 1 **Antony (FR)**[186] [2928] 5-11-2 110 JamieMoore 121+
(Gary Moore) *t.k.h in midfield: stl 7th after 3 out: impr qckly next to ld between last two: sn rdn clr: heavily eased fnl 100yds* **7/1**

2-23 2 9 **Easily Pleased (IRE)**[30] [218] 9-10-13 107 RichardJohnson 107
(Martin Hill) *t.k.h in last pl: effrt after 3 out: rdn to go 7 l 2nd at last: plugged on but nvr nr easy wnr* **4/1**[1]

36P- 3 nk **Hi Note**[46] [5523] 7-11-4 112 MarcGoldstein 112
(Sheena West) *chsd ldrs: rdn fr 6th: no imp whn hit 2 out: kpt on steadily but no ch w wnr* **10/1**

33-3 4 1 **Mondlicht (USA)**[14] [481] 5-10-12 113 (p) MrAlexFerguson(7) 112
(John Ferguson) *towards rr: passed btn horses fr 3 out: nvr gng wl enough to mount any sort of chal* **8/1**

3-U6 5 2 1/4 **Alla Svelta (IRE)**[16] [449] 9-10-12 106 (t) LeightonAspell 104
(Brendan Powell) *racd keenly and trckd ldrs: effrt gng wl after 3 out: led bef next: rdn and hdd between last two: fnd little and lost mod 2nd at last* **13/2**

041- 6 1 1/2 **Sir Frank Morgan (IRE)**[49] [5444] 5-11-7 115 (p) TomScudamore 113
(David Pipe) *2nd or 3rd but nt a fluent: led after 3 out: sn drvn: hdd bef next: fdd between last two* **5/1**[2]

P5-3 7 21 **Tuffstuff**[33] [160] 7-10-11 105 (tp) CharliePoste 85
(Brian Barr) *led 4th tl bef 7th: hit next and drvn: sn dropped out* **16/1**

0/0- 8 3/4 **Moveable Asset (IRE)**[108] [4362] 7-11-5 120 (vt) MrFTett(7) 96
(Henry Tett) *chsd ldrs tl rdn and lost pl and mstke 3 out: wl bhd next* **33/1**

01-0 9 1 **Bostin (IRE)**[27] [283] 7-10-11 105 TomCannon 80
(Daniel O'Brien) *led tl 4th and bef 7th tl drvn and hdd after 3 out: lost pl qckly bef next* **11/2**[3]

6-P0 10 2 **Hoist The Colours (IRE)**[16] [449] 4-10-7 105 (p) DarylJacob 74
(Robert Walford) *last pair: urged along and nt travelling 7th: t.o* **16/1**

6-P0 11 22 **Osgood**[16] [449] 8-10-1 105 GeorgeGorman(10) 59
(Gary Moore) *t.k.h in midfield: rdn and struggling 3 out: hit next: t.o* **25/1**

4m 48.5s (-10.90) **Going Correction** -0.575s/f (Firm)
WFA 4 from 5yo+ 17lb **11 Ran SP% 116.6**
Speed ratings (Par 105): **99,95,95,94,93 93,84,83,83,82 73**
CSF £35.50 CT £283.08 TOTE £7.70: £2.90, £1.70, £3.40; EX 36.00 Trifecta £457.90.
Owner The Winning Hand **Bred** Madame Marie-Laure Besnouin **Trained** Lower Beeding, W Sussex

FOCUS
Fences were outside down the hill; inside in the home straight. Second-last fence omitted, ground under repair. Hurdles on outer. Rail movements added 60yds per circuit to chases and 40yds per circuit to hurdle races. Genuine good ground, and no non-runners on the card. The initial pace was steady enough for this ordinary handicap hurdle, but three of the first four came from the rear. A big step up from the easy winner, the third to sixth helping to set the level.

670 CALL STAR SPREADS ON 0808 234 9709 H'CAP CHASE (FOR THE ALAN ARNELL TROPHY) (16 fncs 3 omitted) 3m 1f 106y

2:40 (2:40) (Class 4) (0-120,118) 5-Y-O+ £4,548 (£1,335; £667; £333)

Form RPR

2-25 1 **Vikekhal (FR)**[12] [523] 6-11-4 110 (b[1]) JamieMoore 122+
(Gary Moore) *settled towards rr but wl in tch: gng strly fnl circ: wnt 2nd after 3 out: rdn to ld last: sn drvn clr* **7/1**

4-53 2 8 **Strumble Head (IRE)**[17] [439] 10-11-12 118 (p) DonalDevereux 124
(Peter Bowen) *led fr 4th: rdn and hdd last: sn outpcd by wnr flat* **13/2**[3]

23-5 3 13 **Orfeo Conti (FR)**[26] [295] 13-9-7 92 oh8 OCdtOswaldWedmore(7) 85
(Diana Grissell) *towards rr: effrt 11th: 2nd briefly 3 out: bmpd along and wknd next* **16/1**

P4-2 4 1 1/4 **Back In June**[21] [388] 7-10-9 101 (b) TomO'Brien 94
(Paul Henderson) *slt ld tl 4th: nt fluent 6th: pressed ldr tl rdn 12th: wknd 3 out* **3/1**[1]

515- 5 36 **Green Bank (IRE)**[243] [1809] 9-11-7 113 RichardJohnson 88
(Charlie Longsdon) *chsd ldrs: rdn 3 out: no rspnse and wknd next (usual 3 out): eased last: t.o* **7/2**[2]

502- B **Spirit River (FR)**[322] [1047] 10-10-13 105 LeeEdwards
(Dave Roberts) *nt a fluent in reat: in tch bef 2 out (usual 3 out) where b.d whn nt apparently gng wl enough* **25/1**

PP2- P **Leg Iron (IRE)**[46] [5524] 10-11-8 114 (p) MarcGoldstein
(Sheena West) *prom early but sn drvn and nvr travelling: dropped himself to rr 9th: t.o and p.u after 11th* **8/1**

P-23 F **Head Spin (IRE)**[20] [403] 7-10-6 98 (tp) AndrewThornton
(Seamus Mullins) *cl up: wnt 2nd at 12th tl 3 out: 4 l 4th but rdn and finding nthing whn fell 2 out* **7/2**[2]

6m 45.4s (-15.70) **Going Correction** -0.475s/f (Good) **8 Ran SP% 116.1**
Speed ratings: **106,103,99,98,87 , ,**
CSF £51.86 CT £705.59 TOTE £8.70: £2.20, £1.90, £3.70; EX 44.40 Trifecta £521.60.
Owner N J Roach **Bred** E A R L Guittet-Desbois Et Al **Trained** Lower Beeding, W Sussex

FOCUS
The first two finished clear in this modest handicap chase. A small step up from the winner and there may be a bit more to come.

671 STARSPORTS.CO.UK NOVICES' HURDLE (10 hdls) 2m 3f 33y

3:10 (3:14) (Class 4) 4-Y-O+ £3,249 (£954; £477; £238)

Form RPR

5 1 **Gallic Destiny (IRE)**[12] [528] 4-10-5 0 (t) JamesBanks(3) 111
(Jo Davis) *hit most of the flights: pressed ldr fr 3rd tl led 7th: drvn fr 2 out: edgd lft flat: hld on wl but all out* **20/1**

24-1 2 1 3/4 **Gioia Di Vita**[12] [528] 5-11-5 116 WillKennedy 121
(Dr Richard Newland) *cl up: wnt 2nd 3 out: 4 l bhd ldr and drvn home turn: effrt and blnd 2 out: ev ch u.p tl hld fnl 100yds* **4/5**[1]

3-6 3 25 **Captain Flash (IRE)**[20] [407] 6-10-12 0 MarcGoldstein 91
(Jo Davis) *prom tl 5 l 3rd and drvn home turn where wl clr of rest: sn lost tch w ldng pair* **50/1**

04 4 15 **Royal Battalion**[14] [491] 4-10-8 0 JamieMoore 78+
(Gary Moore) *taken steadily and nvr nr ldrs: poor 6th after 3 out: eased next: mstke last: can do bttr* **12/1**

53-F 5 hd **Princeton Royale (IRE)**[34] [146] 6-10-12 0 TrevorWhelan 82
(Neil King) *chsd ldrs: blnd 3rd: rdn and last of five gng clr after 3 out: struggling after* **7/1**

/6P- 6 1 1/4 **Snippetydoodah**[131] [3932] 7-10-5 0 [1] TomO'Brien 69
(Michael Roberts) *wl bhd: nt fluent 6th: remote after 3 out but kpt plugging on* **100/1**

04 7 4 1/2 **Cotton King**[20] [401] 8-10-12 0 LeightonAspell 72
(Graham Mays) *chsd ldrs: drvn bef 7th: sn struggling: t.o after next* **50/1**

0 8 74 **Dont Do That**[35] [120] 7-10-5 0 JamesDavies
(Richard Rowe) *chsd ldrs tl rdn and wknd bef 7th: t.o next: fin eventually* **66/1**

9 8 **Fair Lucky**[44] 6-10-12 0 AndrewGlassonbury
(Gary Moore) *nt fluent and wl bhd: t.o fr 7th: fin eventually* **33/1**

05/ 10 1 **Tanner Bet**[675] [1196] 7-9-12 0 DavidNoonan(7)
(Polly Gundry) *sn bhd and nt fluent: mstke 5th: t.o 7th: fin eventually* **100/1**

11 17 **Merry Mast (USA)**[81] [654] 6-10-5 0 MrGTreacy(7)
(Paul Henderson) *labouring in last: cumbersme jumper: t.o fr 5th: fin eventually* **66/1**

61 12 11 **To Begin**[20] [401] 4-11-1 0 (t) GavinSheehan
(Charlie Mann) *led tl rdn and jnd after 6th: hdd next: lost pl rapidly: eased and fin eventually* **6/1**[3]

2-21 P **Detroit Blues**[16] [447] 5-11-5 118 (t) MichealNolan
(Jamie Snowden) *pressed ldrs tl drvn 3 out: poor 4th whn p.u bef next: dismntd* **4/1**[2]

0P- P **Madame Evelyn**[80] [4902] 4-10-1 0 PaddyBrennan
(Suzy Smith) *small: nvr travelling and wl bhd: bdly t.o whn p.u after 6th* **100/1**

4m 45.1s (-14.30) **Going Correction** -0.575s/f (Firm)
WFA 4 from 5yo+ 17lb **14 Ran SP% 127.6**
Speed ratings (Par 105): **107,106,95,89,89 88,86,55,52,51 44,40, ,**
CSF £39.52 TOTE £26.20: £3.50, £1.40, £9.10; EX 77.50 Trifecta £2373.50.
Owner Dr Philip Brown **Bred** Good Breeding **Trained** East Garston, Berks

FOCUS
A modest novice hurdle. The first two finished well clear and a big step up from the winner.

672 SHOREHAM PORT H'CAP CHASE (11 fncs 2 omitted) 2m 1f 96y

3:40 (3:40) (Class 4) (0-120,119) 5-Y-O+ £3,768 (£1,106; £553; £276)

Form RPR

113- 1 **Noble Friend (IRE)**[50] [5438] 7-11-0 107 TomCannon 118+
(Chris Gordon) *settled in last pl: mstke 5th: effrt gng wl whn gd jump 3 out (normal 4 out): led bef last and sn urged clr* **3/1**[2]

-1U2 2 6 **Marie Des Anges (FR)**[18] [431] 7-11-5 119 (t) DavidNoonan(7) 126
(Anthony Honeyball) *settled trcking ldrs: j. slowly 7th: mstke whn effrt 3 out (normal 4 out): gng wl tl rdn to chse wnr bef last where 2 l bhd: sn no imp* **9/2**

0-43 3 13 **Here I Am (IRE)**[6] [596] 8-10-2 95 MarcGoldstein 91
(Diana Grissell) *led tl hdd bef 7th: lft in ld again next: rdn and hdd 2 out (normal 3 out): sn outpcd and plugged on: tk poor 3rd sn after last* **15/8**[1]

62-5 4 9 **Boss In Boots (IRE)**[20] [402] 7-11-8 115 (b) JamieMoore 103
(Seamus Mullins) *hit 3rd: cl up: effrt 3 out: led next (normal 3 out): urged and hdd bef last: fnd nil and plodded on after* **6/1**

03-3 5 43 **Andi'Amu (FR)**[23] [365] 5-11-5 112 (tp) RichardJohnson 59
(Warren Greatrex) *nt fluent 6th: off bridle and reminders: pressed ldr: led bef 7th tl clambered over next: qckly lost interest and wl bhd in last after next* **4/1**[3]

4m 30.1s (-4.60) **Going Correction** -0.475s/f (Good) **5 Ran SP% 112.3**
Speed ratings: **91,88,82,77,57**
CSF £16.26 TOTE £2.90: £1.80, £3.00; EX 9.70 Trifecta £31.40.
Owner Mrs Kate Digweed **Bred** D Mitchell **Trained** Morestead, Hampshire

FOCUS
Just a fair handicap chase and the race was run to suit the winner.

673 STARSPREADS.COM NOVICES' H'CAP HURDLE (9 hdls) 2m 1f 145y
4:10 (4:10) (Class 4) (0-105,105) 4-Y-0+ £3,249 (£954; £477; £238)

Form RPR
4-10 1 **Zarawi (IRE)**[24] 336 4-11-12 105..........(p) RichardJohnson 106+
(Charlie Longsdon) *settled in rr tl effrt wd after 6th: 2 l 3rd and shkn up home turn: rdn to ld after 2 out: 3 l clr last but nt doing much in front: outstyd rivals* 9/4[2]
2/60 2 9 **Green And White (ITY)**[17] 440 5-11-7 97.......... LeeEdwards 93
(Dave Roberts) *midfield: mstke 5th: effrt 3 out: led and blnd next: sn hdd and outpcd by wnr: plugged on although looking tired flat* 25/1
00-2 3 3¾ **Race To Glory (FR)**[40] 32 4-11-10 103..........(tp) TomScudamore 92
(David Pipe) *j. v modly at times: cl 2nd tl led bef 6th: hrd drvn home turn: hdd 2 out: nt run on: poor 3rd at last* 2/1[1]
65-0 4 11 **Comedy House**[16] 451 7-10-0 76 oh1..........(v) MarcGoldstein 57
(Michael Madgwick) *midfield: drvn and outpcd whn impeded 6th: continued wl bhd* 9/2[3]
05-0 5 3¼ **Fairy Princess**[36] 100 6-10-1 84.......... MrDGBurchell(7) 62
(Mark Hoad) *12 l last after 3rd: wl bhd fr 1/2-way: plodded rnd* 25/1
06-5 6 58 **Catcharose (IRE)**[28] 267 5-11-1 91..........(t) JamesDavies 17
(Jennifer Mason) *nt fluent 2nd: pressed ldng pair tl 1/2-way: poor 4th and u.p after mstke 3 out: t.o and eased next* 11/2
P-00 F **Kayflin (FR)**[6] 597 7-11-3 93..........(p) TomCannon
(Linda Jewell) *led: mstke 4th: drvn and hdd bef 6th where fell whn looking abt to struggle* 14/1

4m 29.6s (-4.70) **Going Correction** -0.575s/f (Firm) 7 Ran SP% 112.0
Speed ratings (Par 105): **87,83,81,76,75 49,**
CSF £43.65 TOTE £3.30: £2.50, £11.50; EX 49.00 Trifecta £130.20.
Owner Catchusifyoucan Partnership **Bred** His Highness The Aga Khan's Studs S C **Trained** Over Norton, Oxon

FOCUS
A pretty weak event, but the pace was good. The winner was building on his recent Plumpton win.

674 FOLLOW US ON TWITTER @STARSPORTS_BET H'CAP CHASE (12 fncs 4 omitted) 2m 5f 31y
4:40 (4:41) (Class 5) (0-100,99) 5-Y-0+ £2,469 (£725; £362; £181)

Form RPR
0/P- 1 **Tachbury**[399] 128 11-10-0 73 oh3..........(p) RichardJohnson 88+
(Tim Vaughan) *mstkes: bhd tl rapid prog to ld after 8th: blnd 10th and hdd: rallied on v long run to last where led and blnd: hrd rdn and plugged on gamely: all out* 9/2[2]
00P- 2 1¼ **Knockyoursocksoff (IRE)**[38] 5-10-12 85..........(b[1]) JamieMoore 97+
(Gary Moore) *sn led and racd keenly: hdd briefly after 8th where gng clr w wnr: 4 l ahd home turn: drvn and hdd bef last and hit fence: nt qckn fnl 100yds* 13/8[1]
F53- 3 3 **Rusty Nail (IRE)**[49] 5443 10-10-0 80.......... MissBFrost(7) 88+
(Jimmy Frost) *bhd: mod 8th and one of few nt off bridle 1/2-way: styd on wl up home st: st 8 l 3rd at last: fin best but too much to do* 10/1
4-31 4 16 **Herecomesthetruth (IRE)**[14] 490 13-11-12 99.......... TomCannon 93
(Chris Gordon) *prom early: lost pl to 7th and drvn 1/2-way: struggling after* 12/1
15-4 5 5 **My Silver Cloud (IRE)**[35] 126 8-10-5 78..........(p) MarcGoldstein 67
(Paddy Butler) *fell over lining up bef s: prom: rdn 9th: sn btn: 20 l 4th home turn: remote 3rd bef last: collapsed after fin: fatally injured* 14/1
46-4 6 2¼ **Trakeur (FR)**[33] 168 8-9-7 73 oh2.......... ThomasCheesman(7) 60
(Simon Hodgson) *towards rr: 9th and struggling 1/2-way: plodded on w no ch* 14/1
P/U- 7 1 **Captain Crackers (IRE)**[45] 11-10-6 82.......... ThomasGarner(3) 68
(Linda Jewell) *t.k.h: prom tl 5th and drvn and losing pl 1/2-way: t.o home turn* 50/1
4-1F 8 3½ **La Madonnina (IRE)**[9] 567 7-11-1 88..........(p) JamesBest 71
(Caroline Keevil) *cl up tl 3rd and rdn 1/2-way: no rspnse: struggling in 20 l 3rd home turn* 11/2[3]
3-R1 9 11 **Houseparty**[16] 446 7-10-4 84.......... MissTWorsley(7) 57
(Diana Grissell) *bhd: 7th and drvn 1/2-way: no ch after: t.o* 14/1
P1-6 10 14 **Captain Knock (IRE)**[40] 31 12-10-8 81.......... JamesDavies 42
(Polly Gundry) *hit 5th: chsd ldrs tl 7th: 9th and drvn after next: sn t.o* 25/1
54-5 P **What's For Tea**[30] 223 10-9-11 73 oh8..........(b[1]) WayneKavanagh(3)
(Paddy Butler) *in rr and rdn 7th: t.o and p.u after next* 66/1
65P- F **Baltic Pathfinder (IRE)**[77] 4972 11-11-0 94.......... MrJamesSmith(7)
(Martin Smith) *j. v stickily in last tl fell heavily 7th* 25/1

5m 37.4s (-5.60) **Going Correction** -0.475s/f (Good) 12 Ran SP% 119.6
Speed ratings: **91,90,89,83,81 80,80,78,74,69**
CSF £12.52 CT £71.28 TOTE £7.20: £2.10, £1.60, £2.90; EX 16.80 Trifecta £134.10.
Owner Ms Julie Williams **Bred** Terry Harman **Trained** Aberthin, Vale of Glamorgan

FOCUS
Two ex-pointers dominated in a race lacking depth. The second-last (normal three out) was bypassed on the final circuit as it was damaged.

675 FOLLOW US ON TWITTER @STARSPREADS_BET H'CAP HURDLE (11 hdls) 2m 5f 139y
5:10 (5:11) (Class 5) (0-100,96) 4-Y-0+ £2,339 (£686; £343; £171)

Form RPR
/23- 1 **Archie Rice (USA)**[70] 5078 9-11-2 93.......... MissBFrost(7) 102+
(Jimmy Frost) *settled towards rr: prog 7th: 3rd home turn: clsd gng best to ld and hit 2 out: 3 l clr last: pushed out* 8/1
P6-3 2 8 **Dropzone (USA)**[21] 391 6-10-10 80..........(b) TomO'Brien 81
(Brian Forsey) *midfield: effrt 7th: rdn and outpcd 3 out: 10 l 5th home turn: rallied to chse wnr after last: one pce and no imp* 9/2[1]
PU-5 3 nk **Minority Interest**[29] 240 6-11-3 87..........(tp) GavinSheehan 88
(Daniel O'Brien) *bhd: plugged on past btn horses fr 2 out: tried to catch 2nd cl home but nvr nr wnr* 6/1[2]
05-6 4 2 **Bulletproof (IRE)**[33] 172 9-11-0 84..........(p) PaddyBrennan 85
(Ken Cunningham-Brown) *hld up and bhd: effrt 3 out: 2nd home turn: chal and hit 2 out: btn bef last: fin weakly to lose two pls flat* 8/1
000- 5 7 **Lyssio (GER)**[48] 5481 8-10-13 90.......... MrDGBurchell(7) 86
(Mark Hoad) *j. awkwardly at times: bhd tl rapid prog after 5th: led next: mstke 7th: 3 l clr home turn: bmpd along and hdd 2 out: fdd bef last* 10/1
P2-6 6 10 **Hawk Gold (IRE)**[30] 224 11-10-4 74.......... MarcGoldstein 58
(Michelle Bryant) *wl bhd tl sme prog to midfield 3 out: sn urged w no rspnse: btn next* 20/1
006- 7 3¾ **All Riled Up**[51] 5408 7-10-7 84.......... DanielHiskett(7) 65
(Harry Chisman) *led or contested ld tl 7th: sn drvn: 9 l 4th home turn: fdd bef 2 out* 25/1
0F0- 8 2 **Kavestorm**[66] 5148 9-10-0 70 oh2.......... JamesBest 49
(Polly Gundry) *midfield: rdn 7th: btn after 3 out* 8/1
000- 9 4½ **Uranox (FR)**[92] 4673 7-10-2 72..........(t[1]) WillKennedy 47
(Michael Roberts) *wl off pce in last pair: nvr gng wl enough* 20/1
-562 10 ¾ **Warsaw Pact (IRE)**[16] 451 12-10-4 74.......... JamieMoore 48
(Steven Dixon) *chsd ldrs but sn drvn along: downed tools completely and dropped himself bk to last after 7th* 13/2[3]
626/ 11 11 **Pepito Collonges (FR)**[931] 2544 12-9-12 71.......... ConorShoemark(3) 35
(Laura Mongan) *cl up tl 7th: sn lost pl: t.o and eased* 22/1
0-00 12 7 **Sun Quest**[13] 515 11-9-9 72..........(t) DavidNoonan(7) 30
(Steven Dixon) *led or contested ld tl 7th: dropped out rapidly after 3 out: bdly t.o* 14/1
6P-P P **Family Motto**[16] 450 6-11-12 96..........[1] TomCannon
(Chris Gordon) *prom tl hit 6th: sn lost pl: t.o and p.u 2 out* 12/1

5m 27.5s (-15.00) **Going Correction** -0.575s/f (Firm) 13 Ran SP% 120.3
Speed ratings (Par 103): **104,101,100,100,97 94,92,91,90,90 86,83,**
CSF £42.38 CT £237.70 TOTE £6.70: £2.10, £2.20, £2.70; EX 36.40 Trifecta £306.10.
Owner Frost Racing Club **Bred** Baltusrol Thoughbreds Llc Et Al **Trained** Buckfast, Devon

FOCUS
A race devoid of progressive types, but the winner was on a good mark.
T/Plt: £269.30 to a £1 stake. Pool: £90801.59 - 246.07 winning tickets. T/Qpdt: £17.90 to a £1 stake. Pool: £5914.98 - 243.5 winning tickets. **Iain Mackenzie**

588 SOUTHWELL (L-H)
Tuesday, June 9

OFFICIAL GOING: Good (7.7)
Wind: moderate 1/2 against Weather: fine but breezy and cool

676 NIS SIGNS H'CAP CHASE (16 fncs 3 omitted) 2m 7f 209y
4:50 (4:50) (Class 4) (0-110,110) 5-Y-0+ £3,994 (£1,240; £667)

Form RPR
3-P0 1 **High Kite (IRE)**[17] 439 9-11-12 110..........(b) NicodeBoinville 114
(Jo Hughes) *chsd ldrs 3rd: 2nd bef 11th: 10 l down whn lft clr last: eased clsng stages* 9/1
2-25 2 23 **Mission Complete (IRE)**[20] 403 9-10-13 107..........(tp) JackSavage(10) 88
(Jonjo O'Neill) *in rr: drvn 3rd: sn bhd: poor 4th appr 2 out: 3rd between last 2: lft distant 2nd last* 4/1[2]
62-0 3 67 **Forresters Folly**[27] 280 9-11-2 100..........(tp) BrendanPowell 21
(Claire Dyson) *chsd ldrs: modest 3rd after 13th: rdn next: wknd appr 2 out: tailed rt off* 20/1
1-0P P **Wicklewood**[22] 381 9-11-7 105..........(t) TommyPhelan
(Mark Gillard) *chsd ldrs: blnd 1st: drvn 7th: lost pl next: t.o whn p.u bef 11th* 33/1
325/ P **The Ferbane Man (IRE)**[9] 11-11-0 105..........(p) CharlieHammond(7)
(Mike Hammond) *in tch: pushed along 3rd: lost pl 11th: t.o whn p.u bef 14th: b.b.v* 9/1
63-P P **Imperial Vic (IRE)**[23] 358 10-11-5 106..........(bt[1]) JonathanEngland(3)
(Harriet Bethell) *j.rt: led: hdd bef 9th: lost pl 12th: sn bhd: t.o whn p.u bef 2 out* 12/1
3-02 F **Brother Scott**[16] 454 8-10-8 92.......... SeanQuinlan 106+
(Sue Smith) *chsd ldr: led bef 9th: reminders 14th: 10 l ahd whn fell last* 11/4[1]
2P-F P **Pure Poteen (IRE)**[7] 589 7-11-10 108..........(t[1]) MarkQuinlan
(Neil Mulholland) *nt fluent: blnd 2nd: bhd: sme hdwy whn hit 11th: modest 3rd next: wknd bef 14th: tailed rt off in last whn p.u bef last* 9/2[3]
1-30 P **Generous Chief (IRE)**[16] 458 7-11-0 98..........(v) BrianHughes
(Chris Grant) *chsd ldrs: reminders 8th: lost pl 10th: sn bhd: t.o whn p.u bef 13th* 7/1

6m 31.4s (8.40) **Going Correction** +0.40s/f (Soft) 9 Ran SP% 112.7
Speed ratings: **102,94,72, , ,**
CSF £44.88 CT £700.34 TOTE £10.80: £2.70, £2.40, £6.40; EX 50.90 Trifecta £819.50.
Owner Mrs Joanna Hughes **Bred** Harold Byrne **Trained** Lambourn, Berks

FOCUS
Fences sited inside the line race on June 2nd. Both bends moved to fresh ground, but impact on distances not quantified. Course officials had applied around 17mm of water in the past two days in an attempt to maintain good going. This moderate handicap was run at a solid gallop and, after changing fortunes coming to the last, only three completed. The lucky winner is rated in line with the best of his 2014 form.

677 TONY MARTIN LTD H'CAP CHASE (13 fncs 3 omitted) 2m 4f 62y
5:20 (5:20) (Class 4) (0-115,115) 5-Y-0+ £3,898 (£1,144; £572; £286)

Form RPR
52-4 1 **Ballybogey (IRE)**[24] 338 9-11-12 115.......... AdamPogson 123+
(Charles Pogson) *chsd ldrs: 2nd 10th: led bef 2 out: drvn out* 11/2[2]
24/3 2 1¼ **Speedy Bruere (FR)**[30] 226 9-11-3 111.......... JakeHodson(5) 115
(David Bridgwater) *chsd ldrs: pushed along 7th: 3rd and outpcd bef 2 out: 2nd appr last: kpt on same pce* 10/1
-035 3 ¾ **Archie Boy (IRE)**[13] 514 13-10-10 102..........(t) KillianMoore(3) 105
(Sophie Leech) *in rr: mstke 1st: hdwy 10th: 3rd next: handy 2nd bef 2 out: kpt on one pce between last 2* 13/2[3]
P00- 4 19 **Speedy Tunes (IRE)**[81] 4882 8-11-10 113.......... AndrewTinkler 101
(Simon Waugh) *in rr: hit 8th: bhd 11th: lft distant 4th appr 2 out* 25/1
6-4P P **Figaro**[4] 623 7-11-10 113..........(t) AidanColeman
(Tim Vaughan) *j.rt: mstkes: chsd ldrs: wknd qckly 11th: t.o last whn p.u appr last* 12/1
3125 P **Riddlestown (IRE)**[9] 571 8-11-1 104..........(b) HarrySkelton
(Caroline Fryer) *in rr: hdwy to chse ldrs 5th: reminders 8th: lost pl next: bhd whn p.u bef 11th* 10/1
35-3 P **Kitchapoly (FR)**[10] 557 5-11-12 115.......... WayneHutchinson
(Donald McCain) *in rr: hdwy to chse ldrs 5th: drvn 8th: lost pl 10th: sn bhd: t.o whn p.u bef 2 out* 7/1
132- P **Less Time (IRE)**[64] 5204 6-11-9 112.......... RichieMcLernon
(Jonjo O'Neill) *nt fluent: led: hdd bef 2 out: wknd qckly and bhd whn sn p.u* 6/4[1]

5m 22.1s (5.10) **Going Correction** +0.40s/f (Soft) 8 Ran SP% 110.9
Speed ratings: **105,104,104,96, , ,**
CSF £52.63 CT £349.39 TOTE £8.40: £1.70, £2.40, £2.30; EX 39.40 Trifecta £332.50.
Owner James Callow Charles Pogson **Bred** Michael Lee **Trained** Farnsfield, Notts

FOCUS
A modest handicap chase. It was run at a sound gallop and the principals dominated from two out. The winner had a bit in hand and could be rated higher.

678 THANK YOU STEVE HILLYER TRANSPORT H'CAP HURDLE (11 hdls) 2m 4f 62y
5:50 (5:50) (Class 4) (0-115,114) 4-Y-O+ £3,249 (£954; £477; £238)

Form RPR
032- **1** **Ubaldo Des Menhies (FR)**[250] 1691 7-11-8 **110**......(p) RichieMcLernon 120+
(Jonjo O'Neill) *chsd ldrs: 2nd 3rd: led 2 out: hung lft: drvn rt out* **8/1**

05-0 **2** *4* **Tinseltown**[13] 507 9-10-10 **98**.. DougieCostello 102
(Brian Rothwell) *in rr: hdwy 6th: outpcd and modest 4th 3 out: styd on to take 2nd appr last: kpt on same pce* **25/1**

00-1 **3** *6* **Dun Scaith (IRE)**[24] 328 7-11-7 **112**.............................. KillianMoore(3) 112
(Sophie Leech) *led: hdd 2 out: wknd appr last* **11/4**[1]

36-P **4** *1* **Maller Tree**[22] 380 8-11-10 **112**..............................(v) SamTwiston-Davies 110
(David Dennis) *chsd ldrs: drvn appr 2 out: wknd appr last* **9/2**[3]

6-4P **5** *44* **The Jugopolist (IRE)**[7] 589 8-10-1 **94**.............................. JoeCornwall(5) 53
(John Cornwall) *in rr: drvn 2nd: reminders 4th and 6th: bhd fr 8th: distant 6th whn hmpd 3 out: sn t.o* **66/1**

650- **6** *29* **General Montgomery (IRE)**[179] 3048 6-11-11 **113**.......... MarkQuinlan 45
(Neil Mulholland) *chsd ldrs: mstke and lost pl 8th: sn bhd: t.o 2 out: virtually p.u run-in* **11/2**

3PP- **P** **Run On Sterling**[64] 5202 6-11-3 **105**..............................(vt[1]) LiamTreadwell
(Paul Webber) *reminders 1st: chsd ldrs next: reminders 4th: lost pl after 6th: sn t.o p.u after next* **7/1**

66-3 **F** **Sea The Springs (FR)**[36] 106 4-10-10 **102**..............................(b[1]) HarrySkelton
(Dan Skelton) *chsd ldrs: 5th whn fell 3 out* **3/1**[2]

5m 14.4s (1.40) **Going Correction** +0.20s/f (Yiel)
WFA 4 from 6yo+ 18lb **8 Ran SP% 114.2**
Speed ratings (Par 105): **105,103,101,100,83 71, ,**
CSF £154.14 CT £686.63 TOTE £7.80: £3.00, £4.20, £2.40; EX 129.10 Trifecta £2124.30.
Owner Jackdaws Castle Crew **Bred** J L Glotin **Trained** Cheltenham, Gloucs

FOCUS
An ordinary handicap, run at a fair gallop.

679 DCH LAW MARES' MAIDEN HURDLE (11 hdls) 2m 4f 62y
6:20 (6:20) (Class 5) 4-Y-O+ £2,599 (£763; £381; £190)

Form RPR
2 **1** **Western Breeze (IRE)**[12] 516 6-11-0 0.............................. JakeGreenall 111
(Mark Walford) *mde all: drvn and styd on fr 2 out: hld on gamely* **4/1**[3]

1-32 **2** *1 3/4* **Lolli (IRE)**[16] 462 5-11-0 111.............................. NicodeBoinville 110
(Nicky Henderson) *trckd ldrs: 2nd 5th: upsides 2 out: drvn between last 2: kpt on same pce run-in* **4/7**[1]

3-43 **3** *6* **Card Game (IRE)**[12] 516 6-11-0 0.............................. BrianHughes 104
(Malcolm Jefferson) *hld up towards rr: hdwy to trck ldrs 8th: handy 3rd after next: one pce whn hit last* **3/1**[2]

P6-6 **4** *22* **Miss Conway**[19] 415 4-10-10 0.............................. DougieCostello 77
(Mark Walford) *in rr: drvn to chse ldrs 3 out: outpcd and modest 4th appr next* **50/1**

3/U **5** *1* **Erica Starprincess**[13] 503 5-11-0 0.............................. RichieMcLernon 80
(George Moore) *in rr: hdwy to chse ldrs 8th: drvn next: sn outpcd* **16/1**

P66- **6** *1 1/2* **Lady Busanda**[56] 5327 5-11-0 0.............................. HenryBrooke 79
(George Moore) *chsd ldrs: drvn 3 out: sn lost pl and bhd: distant 5th whn mstke last* **33/1**

0-66 **7** *27* **Timon's Tara**[7] 591 6-11-0 0..............................[1] AidanColeman 52
(Robin Dickin) *in rr: hdwy 6th: lost pl after 8th: sn wl bhd: t.o whn eased run-in* **16/1**

506/ **P** **All For Lily**[466] 4528 6-11-0 0..............................(p) AdamPogson
(Charles Pogson) *t.k.h: j.rt: chsd wnr: 3rd whn mstke 6th: drvn next: sn lost pl: t.o 3 out: p.u bef next* **33/1**

0/P- **P** **Midnight Memories**[221] 2167 5-11-0 0..............................(p[1]) AndrewTinkler
(Steph Hollinshead) *chsd ldrs: lost pl after 8th: sn wl bhd: t.o whn p.u bef 2 out* **66/1**

5m 20.2s (7.20) **Going Correction** +0.20s/f (Yiel)
WFA 4 from 5yo+ 18lb **9 Ran SP% 129.8**
Speed ratings (Par 103): **93,92,89,81,80 80,69, ,**
CSF £7.82 TOTE £5.10: £1.30, £1.10, £1.20; EX 11.50 Trifecta £22.40.
Owner Andrew Nicholls **Bred** Mrs Patricia Furlong **Trained** Sherriff Hutton, N Yorks

FOCUS
A typically uncompetitive mares' maiden for the time of year. Straightforward form.

680 SARAH NEWBY'S 21ST BIRTHDAY "NATIONAL HUNT" NOVICES' HURDLE (9 hdls) 1m 7f 153y
6:50 (6:50) (Class 4) 4-Y-O+ £3,249 (£954; £477; £238)

Form RPR
123- **1** **Paolozzi (IRE)**[234] 1950 6-10-12 0.............................. BrianHughes 116+
(Seamus Durack) *trckd ldng pair: hit 3 out: led appr next: rdn appr last: styd on* **8/11**[1]

333- **2** *2* **Cochinillo (IRE)**[53] 5380 6-10-12 0.............................. DarylJacob 112+
(Ben Case) *trckd ldrs 5th: j.lft 6th: handy 2nd sn after 2 out: kpt on same pce appr last* **7/1**[3]

503- **3** *20* **Bleu Et Or (FR)**[46] 5513 4-10-9 0.............................. AdrianLane 88
(Donald McCain) *hdwy to chse ldrs 5th: 2nd 2 out: wknd between last 2* **33/1**

04-3 **4** *1 1/4* **Bletchley Castle (IRE)**[24] 330 6-10-7 0.............................. NickSlatter(5) 89
(Seamus Durack) *chsd ldr: wknd between last 2* **8/1**

52-2 **5** *10* **Time And Again (FR)**[16] 447 5-10-12 117.............................. MichaelByrne 83
(Tim Vaughan) *led: mstke 4th: hdd appr 2 out: sn lost pl* **4/1**[2]

0-P3 **P** **Wildmoor Boy**[20] 396 4-10-9 0.............................. AidanColeman
(Robin Dickin) *detached in last: sme hdwy 3rd: lost pl bef next: sn bhd: t.o whn pulled up bef 3rd* **20/1**

4m 0.8s (3.80) **Going Correction** +0.20s/f (Yiel)
WFA 4 from 5yo+ 17lb **6 Ran SP% 109.2**
Speed ratings (Par 105): **98,97,87,86,81**
CSF £6.13 TOTE £1.50: £1.10, £2.80; EX 5.40 Trifecta £67.10.
Owner C Wilkinson **Bred** Mrs V Wilkinson **Trained** Upper Lambourn, Berkshire

FOCUS
A moderate novice hurdle in which there was no hanging about. Two came clear near the finish and the winner can do even better.

681 NEXT PLC LEICESTER H'CAP HURDLE (6 hdls 7 omitted) 2m 7f 209y
7:25 (7:27) (Class 3) (0-140,140) 4-Y-O+ £5,523 (£1,621; £810; £405)

Form RPR
6-32 **1** **Henri Parry Morgan**[20] 404 7-10-4 **118**..............................(p) DonalDevereux 125+
(Peter Bowen) *trckd ldrs: hit 4th (normal 8th): led over 4f out: j.lft last: drvn out* **9/4**[1]

/30- **2** *7* **Crack Away Jack**[59] 5273 11-11-7 **135**.............................. AidanColeman 135
(Emma Lavelle) *chsd ldrs: handy 2nd appr 2 out: kpt on same pce run-in* **11/4**[3]

P1-6 **3** *20* **Dawn Commander (GER)**[31] 196 8-11-12 **140**.............................. BrendanPowell 122
(Stuart Edmunds) *in rr: reminders 3rd (normal 8th): bhd 6f out: distant 4th 2 out: poor 3rd last* **5/2**[2]

00-P **4** *12* **Fighter Jet**[16] 461 7-10-9 **123**..............................(b) WayneHutchinson 98
(Alan King) *chsd ldrs: reminders 2nd (normal 3rd): rdn 6f out: outpcd and lost pl over 4f out: distant 4th whn hit last: hung lft and wknd* **8/1**

30-0 **5** *4 1/2* **First Fandango**[16] 448 8-11-10 **138**..............................(t) MichaelByrne 105
(Tim Vaughan) *chsd ldrs: reminders 2nd (normal 3rd): drvn 4th (normal 8th): lost pl over 5f out* **25/1**

U-5 **6** *1 1/2* **American Spin**[16] 448 11-10-5 **126**..............................(b) GeorgeGorman(7) 92
(Luke Dace) *drvn to ld: j.rt 2nd (normal 3rd): sn hrd drvn and reluctant: j.rt and hdd 3rd (normal 7th): lost pl over 5f out: sn bhd* **22/1**

01P- **7** *8* **Shantou Tiger (IRE)**[234] 1944 6-10-9 **130**.............................. JamesCowley(7) 88
(Donald McCain) *chsd ldrs: reminders 7f out: lost pl over 4f out: sn bhd* **12/1**

6-0F **8** *nk* **Groomed (IRE)**[20] 395 7-10-0 **114** oh1.............................. SeanQuinlan 72
(Sue Smith) *chsd ldr: led 3rd (normal 7th): hdd over 4f out: wknd qckly 2 out: sn bhd* **33/1**

6m 13.4s (-1.60) **Going Correction** +0.20s/f (Yiel) **8 Ran SP% 115.9**
Speed ratings (Par 107): **110,107,101,97,95 95,92,92**
CSF £9.10 CT £15.81 TOTE £2.90: £1.20, £1.20, £1.50; EX 10.30 Trifecta £18.40.
Owner Ednyfed & Elizabeth Morgan **Bred** J R Bryan **Trained** Little Newcastle, Pembrokes

FOCUS
This was a fair staying handicap. They went an average sort of gallop and only two mattered off the home bend. The winner has been rated in line with his best novice form.

682 CONGRATULATIONS ON YOUR RETIREMENT PB STANDARD OPEN NATIONAL HUNT FLAT RACE 1m 7f 153y
7:55 (7:56) (Class 6) 4-6-Y-O £1,949 (£572; £286; £143)

Form RPR
1-1 **1** **Brave Richard (IRE)**[32] 188 4-11-7 0.............................. PaulMoloney 100+
(J R Jenkins) *t.k.h in 5th: trckd ldrs: effrt over 2f out: styd on wl to ld jst ins fnl f: drvn out* **1/1**[1]

2 *3* **Tullow Tonic (IRE)** 4-10-4 0.............................. AidanColeman 80+
(Charlie Longsdon) *trckd ldrs in 4th: effrt and 2nd over 2f out: led over 1f out: hdd jst ins fnl f: kpt on same pce* **7/2**[2]

56- **3** *2* **Jaslamour (FR)**[50] 5425 4-10-11 0.............................. BrianHarding 85
(Micky Hammond) *set v stdy pce: qcknd gallop 4f out: sn hdd: rallied over 2f out: kpt on same pce* **33/1**

6 **4** *3/4* **Flemerina (IRE)**[33] 159 6-9-11 0.............................. StephenMcCarthy(10) 80
(Sue Smith) *trckd ldr: led over 3f out: hdd over 2f out: kpt on same pce fnl f* **20/1**

5 *5* **Tour De Ville (IRE)** 5-11-0 0.............................. BrianHughes 82
(Seamus Durack) *trckd ldrs in 5th: drvn over 2f out: wknd over 1f out* **6/1**[3]

6 *1 3/4* **Breath Of Life** 5-10-7 0.............................. SamTwiston-Davies 73
(Mark Rimell) *trckd ldrs in 3rd: drvn 3f out: wknd over 1f out* **18/1**

7 *2 1/2* **Last Wish (IRE)** 4-10-11 0.............................. JakeGreenall 75
(Richard Guest) *t.k.h in 6th: effrt 3f out: lost pl over 1f out* **7/1**

4m 12.9s (21.50) **Going Correction** +0.20s/f (Yiel) **7 Ran SP% 112.0**
Speed ratings: **54,52,51,51,48 47,46**
CSF £4.41 TOTE £1.30: £1.10, £1.70; EX 4.10 Trifecta £51.50.
Owner Miss A Finn **Bred** Suzanne Guise-Mist **Trained** Royston, Herts

FOCUS
The runners crawled early on in this bumper and it developed into a dash from 2f out.
T/Plt: £45.70 to a £1 stake. Pool: £59,084.36 - 942.95 winning units. T/Qpdt: £3.20 to a £1 stake. Pool: £7,087.05 - 1636.10 winning units. **Walter Glynn**

683 - 689a (Foreign Racing) - See Raceform Interactive

460
UTTOXETER (L-H)
Thursday, June 11

OFFICIAL GOING: Good (good to firm in places; 8.1)
Wind: Almost nil Weather: Fine

690 UKOPS JUVENILE HURDLE (9 hdls) 1m 7f 168y
6:10 (6:11) (Class 4) 3-Y-O £3,249 (£954; £477; £238)

Form RPR
1 **Dominada (IRE)**[8] 3-10-12 0.............................. RichardJohnson 98+
(Brian Ellison) *mde all: nt fluent 3rd: mstke last: rdn out* **11/8**[1]

2 *7* **Directional**[181] 3-10-12 0.............................. SamTwiston-Davies 90
(John Ferguson) *chsd ldrs: rdn appr 2 out: styd on same pce last* **5/1**[3]

3 *99* **Fast Scat (USA)**[9] 3-10-5 0.............................. SeanQuinlan
(David Evans) *hld up: plld hrd early: nt fluent: bhd fr 3rd* **33/1**

4 *65* **Bleu Astral (FR)**[191] 3-10-12 0.............................. AdamWedge
(Alexandra Dunn) *hld up: plld hrd: hit 1st: bhd fr 4th* **11/1**

C **Ventura Castle**[34] 3-10-12 0.............................. BrendanPowell
(Jamie Snowden) *prom to 6th: bhd whn hmpd by loose horse and rn out 3 out* **9/2**[2]

U **Smugglers Lane (IRE)**[5] 3-10-12 0.............................. PeterCarberry
(David Evans) *prom: j. slowly: hmpd and uns rdr 2nd* **7/1**

P **Royal Street**[19] 3-10-12 0..............................(t) GavinSheehan
(Warren Greatrex) *nt fluent 1st: j. slowly and lost pl next: bhd 4th: p.u bef 3 out* **14/1**

C **Auld Fyffee (IRE)**[16] 3-10-5 0.............................. JamesDavies
(Tom Gretton) *in rr and hmpd 2nd: bhd fr 4th: ref 3 out* **25/1**

F **Rokbaan**[10] 3-10-12 0..............................(v) DaveCrosse
(Mark Usher) *hld up: plld hrd: hdwy and hmpd 2nd: wknd 6th: bhd whn fell last* **33/1**

3m 57.7s (0.30) **Going Correction** +0.10s/f (Yiel) **9 Ran SP% 114.2**
Speed ratings: **103,99,50,17,**
CSF £8.24 TOTE £2.40: £1.20, £2.10, £4.20; EX 9.70 Trifecta £220.40.
Owner Julie & Keith Hanson **Bred** Glending Bloodstock **Trained** Norton, N Yorks

FOCUS
First meeting with new advertised distances. Common bends and rail out further 3yds from previous meeting. Hurdle races increased by 84yds per circuit and chases on inner line. Some starts have been moved at this track following remeasuring, so some races will not have speed figures until there is sufficient data to calculate updated median times. Plenty of these were strung out at wide distances from a very early stage, and two pulled miles clear. The winner is probably a fair early-season juvenile.

691 LISA OLDHAM NOVICES' H'CAP CHASE (15 fncs) 2m 4f
6:40 (6:42) (Class 4) (0-120,120) 5-Y-0+ **£3,938** (£1,262; £701)

Form RPR
525- **1** **Gone Too Far**[77] 4998 7-11-11 **119** WayneHutchinson 128+
(Alan King) *chsd ldrs: led 3 out: rdn and 3 l up whn lft wl clr last* **11/4**[1]
33-4 **2** *18* **One For Hocky (IRE)**[25] 356 7-11-7 **115** BrianHarding 109
(Nicky Richards) *hld up: pushed along 8th: hdwy 10th: rdn and wknd after 3 out: wnt 2nd flat* **10/3**[2]
00-1 **3** *17* **Fleet Dawn**[35] 177 9-11-12 **120** (t) FelixDeGiles 110
(Brian Ellison) *hld up: nt fluent 3rd: mstke 9th: hdwy appr 4 out: sn rdn: wknd appr 2 out: lft poor 2nd whn hmpd last* **9/2**
13-0 **P** **Masterful Act (USA)**[32] 225 8-11-10 **118** (t) HarrySkelton
(Dan Skelton) *chsd ldrs: pushed along after 4th: lost pl appr 10th: rdn and wknd bef next: bhd whn p.u bef 2 out* **7/1**
2U1- **P** **Oscatara (IRE)**[50] 5474 8-11-11 **119** HenryBrooke
(Donald McCain) *led: rdn and hdd 4 out: wknd bef next: bhd whn p.u bef 2 out* **10/1**
1P-4 **F** **Definite Future (IRE)**[35] 177 6-11-1 **109** JakeGreenall 113
(Richard Lee) *chsd ldr tl led 4 out: hdd next: rdn after 2 out: 3 l down whn fell last* **7/2**[3]

5m 9.8s **Going Correction** +0.10s/f (Yiel) **6** Ran SP% **111.7**
Speed ratings: **104,96,90, ,**
CSF £12.45 TOTE £3.20: £1.90, £2.20; EX 14.20 Trifecta £43.60.
Owner John P McManus **Bred** Richard Evans Bloodstock **Trained** Barbury Castle, Wilts

FOCUS
The winner was on a fair mark and is rated to his best. The faller was heading for a small step up on best hurdles form.

692 MEDIA RESOURCES H'CAP HURDLE (8 hdls 1 omitted) 1m 7f 168y
7:10 (7:10) (Class 5) (0-100,105) 4-Y-0+ **£2,339** (£686; £343; £171)

Form RPR
1F-3 **1** **Modeligo (IRE)**[14] 530 6-10-6 **85** (t) MrStanSheppard(7) 96+
(Matt Sheppard) *mde virtually all: shkn up appr 2 out: styd on wl* **5/1**[3]
52-2 **2** *3 ¾* **Supernoverre (IRE)**[26] 336 9-10-8 **80** (b) RichardJohnson 87
(Alan Jones) *hld up: hdwy after 5th: ev ch 3 out: sn rdn: mstke last: styd on same pce* **4/1**[2]
634- **3** *3 ½* **Fred Le Macon (FR)**[83] 4887 6-11-2 **98** JamieInsole(10) 101
(Alan King) *a.p: rdn bef 3 out: styd on same pce appr last* **6/1**
4-P0 **4** *1* **Tennessee Bird**[14] 522 7-10-0 **72** oh3 GavinSheehan 77+
(Mike Sowersby) *hld up: hdwy whn blnd 3 out: styd on same pce appr last* **10/1**
3P-3 **5** *2 ¾* **Mix N Match**[16] 489 11-9-11 **72** oh1 HarryChalloner(3) 71
(Laura Young) *hld up: hdwy after 3 out: sn rdn: no imp last* **14/1**
-631 **6** *nk* **Polstar (FR)**[7] 616 6-11-12 **105** 7ex PaulNO'Brien(7) 104
(Harry Whittington) *chsd ldrs: rdn whn j.lft 2 out: wknd bef last* **11/4**[1]
030- **7** *26* **Ullswater (IRE)**[219] 2268 7-11-10 **96** (t) SamTwiston-Davies 77
(Emma Lavelle) *chsd ldrs tl rdn and wknd appr 3 out* **7/1**
P-P6 **8** *½* **Ted Dolly (IRE)**[19] 442 11-11-3 **92** BenPoste(3) 80+
(Tom Symonds) *hld up: hdwy whn hmpd 2 out: sn rdn and wknd* **25/1**
60-P **9** *28* **Primo Rossi**[30] 262 6-10-0 **72** oh3 (p) JamesDavies 22
(Tom Gretton) *w ldr to 5th: sn rdn: wknd bef next* **22/1**

3m 55.7s (-1.70) **Going Correction** +0.10s/f (Yiel) **9** Ran SP% **114.1**
Speed ratings (Par 103): **108,106,104,103,102 102,89,89,75**
CSF £25.46 CT £121.63 TOTE £6.00: £1.90, £1.50, £2.80; EX 35.70 Trifecta £188.00.
Owner Simon Gegg **Bred** Edward And Joseph McCormack **Trained** Eastnor, H'fords

FOCUS
The stewards held an enquiry following concerns expressed by the riders after race 1 about the siting of the first hurdle in the back straight and gave permission for it to be omitted in this contest plus the fifth and sixth races. This looked a competitive race for the level, but the early pace was far from quick and the winner was in an ideal position to strike. The winner stepped up a bit on this drop back in trip.

693 CRABBIES ALCOHOLIC GINGER BEER H'CAP CHASE (18 fncs) 3m 2y
7:40 (7:40) (Class 4) (0-120,119) 5-Y-0+ **£3,861** (£1,198; £645)

Form RPR
2U-2 **1** **Big Sound**[40] 81 8-11-1 **108** (p) DougieCostello 119+
(Mark Walford) *led to 2nd: led 4th: hung lft flat: drvn out* **7/2**[1]
55-2 **2** *4* **High Ron**[22] 395 10-11-9 **116** (t) TomScudamore 121
(Caroline Bailey) *sn prom: chsd wnr 4 out: sn rdn: styd on same pce last* **7/2**[1]
33-1 **3** *36* **Houndscourt (IRE)**[37] 134 8-11-5 **112** BrianHughes 84
(Joanne Foster) *a.p: chsd ldr 10th tl rdn 4 out: wknd next* **10/1**
2PP- **P** **Everaard (USA)**[68] 5138 9-11-8 **115** (tp) HenryBrooke
(Micky Hammond) *sn pushed along towards rr: bhd fr 5th: p.u bef 12th* **18/1**
-55P **P** **Fort George (IRE)**[12] 557 12-11-0 **114** (p) MissBHampson(7)
(Andy Turnell) *bhd fr 5th: p.u bef 4 out* **16/1**
06-4 **P** **Midnight Cataria**[29] 282 6-11-3 **110** WayneHutchinson
(Alan King) *mid-div: j.rt 8th: rdn 11th: wkng whn j.rt next: bhd whn p.u bef 4 out* **10/1**
253- **P** **Book Of Excuses (IRE)**[225] 2125 7-11-6 **113** (t) SamTwiston-Davies
(Donald McCain) *led 2nd to 4th: chsd ldr to 10th: rdn and wknd bef 4 out: bhd whn p.u bef next* **8/1**
56-4 **P** **River Deep (IRE)**[25] 365 6-11-7 **114** (p) RichardJohnson
(Philip Hobbs) *hld up: a in rr: bhd whn p.u bef 9th* **6/1**[3]
2-24 **P** **Orby's Man (IRE)**[20] 430 6-11-12 **119** (p) AidanColeman
(Charlie Longsdon) *prom: mstke 2nd: rdn 11th: wknd next: bhd whn p.u bef 3 out* **11/2**[2]

6m 6.8s (-1.30) **Going Correction** +0.10s/f (Yiel) **9** Ran SP% **114.6**
Speed ratings: **106,104,92, , , , ,**
CSF £16.64 CT £109.84 TOTE £4.00: £1.60, £1.60, £3.00; EX 19.60 Trifecta £128.80.
Owner Hanson & Hamilton **Bred** Mr & Mrs W Hodge **Trained** Sherriff Hutton, N Yorks

FOCUS
Considering the distance, this was run at a decent gallop and plenty were in trouble early on. Step up from winner, the second on a good mark and 10lb better than this in 2014, but rated in line with best of 2015 form for the time being.

694 NANCY BASKERVILLE MEMORIAL NOVICES' H'CAP HURDLE (8 hdls 1 omitted) 1m 7f 168y
8:10 (8:11) (Class 5) (0-100,100) 4-Y-0+ **£2,339** (£686; £343; £171)

Form RPR
U-14 **1** **Sir Note (FR)**[20] 435 5-10-12 **86** (t) PaulMoloney 94+
(Nick Littmoden) *chsd ldrs: hmpd after 5th: led appr 2 out: j.rt last: rdn out* **4/1**[1]
4-63 **2** *2 ¾* **Symphony Of Pearls**[25] 361 4-9-10 **80** MissJodieHughes(7) 83+
(Dai Burchell) *a.p: hmpd after 5th: rdn to chse wnr appr last: styd on same pce flat* **9/1**
64B- **3** *2 ½* **Osorios Trial**[190] 2882 8-10-8 **82** (tp) BrianHughes 84
(Kevin Frost) *hld up: hdwy appr 2 out: styd on to go 3rd flat: nt rch ldrs* **15/2**
5P-2 **4** *1 ¼* **Wymeswold**[30] 252 8-10-8 **85** BenPoste(3) 87
(Michael Mullineaux) *hld up: styd on fr 2 out: nt rch ldrs* **9/1**
1-46 **5** *1 ¾* **Jebulani**[16] 487 5-10-9 **83** BrianHarding 82
(Barry Murtagh) *hld up: hdwy appr 3 out: rdn bef last: no ex flat* **14/1**
53-1 **6** *2* **Carrigeen Lantana (IRE)**[24] 383 6-11-4 **92** WayneHutchinson 90
(Donald McCain) *led: hit 4th: rdn and hdd appr 2 out: wknd flat* **5/1**[2]
-034 **7** *2 ½* **Auto Mac**[22] 399 7-9-11 **74** oh1 AdamNicol(3) 71
(Mike Sowersby) *hld up in tch: rdn after 3 out: wknd flat* **12/1**
F3-5 **8** *8* **Maid Of Tuscany (IRE)**[22] 405 4-11-9 **100** (p) MarkQuinlan 85
(Neil Mulholland) *hld up: hdwy 3 out: rdn and wknd next* **16/1**
0-03 **9** *22* **Caraline (FR)**[16] 487 4-10-1 **85** (v) JamieBargary(7) 50
(Micky Hammond) *chsd ldr tl hmpd after 5th: rdn and wknd next* **6/1**[3]
05-4 **P** **Diamond Gesture (IRE)**[24] 383 7-10-13 **87** PaddyBrennan
(Fergal O'Brien) *hld up: hdwy u.p appr 3 out: sn wknd: bhd whn p.u bef next* **13/2**
00-0 **P** **Fine Jewellery**[35] 180 6-10-3 **77** (t) JamesDavies
(Tom Gretton) *prom: racd keenly: rdn and wknd after 5th: bhd whn p.u bef next* **33/1**

3m 57.8s (0.40) **Going Correction** +0.10s/f (Yiel)
WFA 4 from 5yo+ 17lb **11** Ran SP% **119.2**
Speed ratings (Par 103): **103,101,100,99,98 97,96,92,81, ,**
CSF £40.75 CT £264.44 TOTE £5.50: £2.10, £3.20, £2.50; EX 53.40 Trifecta £401.70.
Owner G F Chesneaux **Bred** Jean-Pierre Coiffier **Trained** Newmarket, Suffolk

FOCUS
The winner is back on the upgrade, the second posted a small pb, and the third was well in on best of 2014 form.

695 ST14 CONSTRUCTION H'CAP HURDLE (8 hdls 2 omitted) 2m 3f 207y
8:40 (8:41) (Class 5) (0-100,100) 4-Y-0+ **£2,339** (£686; £343; £171)

Form RPR
0-3P **1** **Taroum (IRE)**[14] 524 8-11-3 **91** (bt) RhysFlint 98+
(John Flint) *w ldr tl led 5th: hdd whn lft wl clr 3 out: blnd last: easily* **20/1**
2-1U **2** *9* **Danceintothelight**[14] 522 8-10-13 **97** (t) FinianO'Toole(10) 85
(Micky Hammond) *hld up: stmbld 2nd: bhd and rdn appr 5th: styd on to go 2nd flat: no ch w wnr* **6/1**[2]
6/6- **3** *½* **Highland River**[54] 5398 9-10-0 **74** oh8 LeeEdwards 60
(Dave Roberts) *hld up: bhd and rdn after 4th: styd on flat: nvr nrr* **40/1**
03/5 **4** *9* **Cornish Beau (IRE)**[13] 537 8-10-5 **79** WillKennedy 57
(Dr Richard Newland) *hld up: hdwy 4th: rdn appr 3 out: sn btn* **5/1**[1]
P-40 **5** *¾* **Bunclody**[31] 237 10-11-9 **100** (p) JamesBanks(3) 78
(Barry Brennan) *led to 5th: rdn and wknd bef 3 out* **25/1**
04-2 **6** *49* **Goodacres Garden (IRE)**[20] 434 8-10-0 **74** oh5 (t) PeterCarberry 8
(Shaun Lycett) *hld up: hit 4th: sn rdn: wknd bef next* **14/1**
36P- **7** *2 ½* **Paddy Mulligan (IRE)**[109] 4385 6-11-2 **97** MrAlexFerguson(7) 28
(John Ferguson) *prom to 5th* **6/1**[2]
45-2 **F** **Iktiview**[20] 435 7-10-1 **82** (bt) MrStanSheppard(7) 89+
(Matt Sheppard) *sn prom: led and fell 3 out* **5/1**[1]
00/5 **P** **Sylvan Legend**[23] 391 7-10-0 **74** (tp) TomScudamore
(Neil Mulholland) *prom: blnd and lost pl 1st: hdwy after 4th: rdn 3 out: wknd and p.u bef next* **5/1**[1]
222- **P** **Forget And Forgive (IRE)**[130] 7-11-0 **95** (p) KevinJones(7)
(Sophie Leech) *hld up: rdn after 4th: sn bhd: p.u bef last* **12/1**[3]
505- **P** **Send For Katie (IRE)**[87] 4809 7-11-6 **94** (t) TomMessenger
(Chris Bealby) *prom to 5th: bhd whn p.u bef 3 out* **14/1**
05-2 **P** **Penzflo (IRE)**[37] 120 9-11-12 **100** RichardJohnson
(Johnny Farrelly) *sn prom: mstke and lost pl 4th: wknd bef next: bhd whn p.u bef 3 out* **12/1**[3]

5m 9.5s (6.30) **Going Correction** +0.10s/f (Yiel) **12** Ran SP% **118.3**
Speed ratings (Par 103): **91,87,87,83,83 63,62, , ,**
CSF £134.63 CT £4741.95 TOTE £22.90: £7.50, £2.50, £10.70; EX 205.30 Trifecta £2124.40.
Owner J L Flint **Bred** His Highness The Aga Khan's Studs S C **Trained** Kenfig Hill, Bridgend

FOCUS
Not for the first time on the card, it paid to race prominently. The winner is rated to the level of his 2014 best. The faller probably would have won and is rated close to best of 2014 form, case for rating fair bit higher through the second.

696 DOVE VALLEY OUTDOOR EVENTS MARES' STANDARD OPEN NATIONAL HUNT FLAT RACE 1m 7f 168y
9:10 (9:10) (Class 6) 4-6-Y-0 **£1,559** (£457; £228; £114)

Form RPR
1 **Which One Is Which** 4-10-9 0 RichieMcLernon 109+
(Jonjo O'Neill) *hld up: hdwy over 3f out: led over 1f out: shkn up and r.o wl* **11/4**[2]
5 **2** *14* **Midnight Gem**[26] 334 5-10-12 0 WayneHutchinson 95
(Charlie Longsdon) *led: racd keenly: hung rt over 10f out: hdd over 8f out: led again over 3f out: rdn and hdd over 1f out: sn outpcd* **7/1**[3]
3 *¾* **Lemtara Bay** 4-10-9 0 LeightonAspell 91
(Oliver Sherwood) *chsd ldrs: rdn over 2f out: no ex fr over 1f out* **5/2**[1]
3 **4** *¾* **Western Sunrise (IRE)**[20] 432 6-10-12 0 RichardJohnson 94
(Johnny Farrelly) *hld up: hdwy over 3f out: sn rdn: styd on same pce fr over 1f out* **11/4**[2]
0-5 **5** *3 ¼* **Martha's Benefit (IRE)**[9] 594 6-10-9 0 AdamNicol(3) 90
(Mike Sowersby) *chsd ldrs: rdn and ev ch over 2f out: wknd over 1f out* **20/1**
6 *13* **River Wye** 4-10-9 0 RachaelGreen 74
(Anthony Honeyball) *hld up: rdn and hung rt over 4f out: sn wknd* **8/1**

7 *dist* **Jump And Jump (IRE)**[17] 5-10-12 0................................ CharliePoste 32
(Robin Dickin) *w ldr: hmpd over 10f out: led over 8f out: rdn and hdd over 3f out: wknd over 2f out* **20/1**

3m 59.1s (7.30) **Going Correction** +0.10s/f (Yiel)
WFA 4 from 5yo+ 3lb **7** Ran SP% **115.0**
Speed ratings: **85,78,77,77,75 69,**
CSF £22.36 TOTE £3.70: £1.70, £4.40; EX 27.10 Trifecta £103.10.
Owner John P McManus **Bred** Aiden Murphy & Alan Peterson **Trained** Cheltenham, Gloucs

FOCUS
Although this developed into a sprint, the winner impressed and readily disposed of her rivals. This is rated around the second, fourth and fifth.
T/Plt: £159.50 to a £1 stake. Pool £82,444.45 - 377.25 winning units. T/Qpdt: £29.40 to a £1 stake. Pool £8,208.89 - 206.45 winning units. **Colin Roberts**

[641]WORCESTER (L-H)
Thursday, June 11

OFFICIAL GOING: Good to firm (6.9)
Wind: light breeze Weather: very hot and sunny; 23 degrees

697 MYRACING.COM BEGINNERS' CHASE (13 fncs) 2m 4f
1:40 (1:41) (Class 4) 5-Y-0+ **£4,548** (£1,335; £667; £333)

Form RPR
20-2 **1** **Stephen Hero (IRE)**[6] [622] 5-11-0 0................................(t) HarrySkelton 126+
(Dan Skelton) *led 3rd: given a few reminders fr bef 9th onwards: 6 l clr 2 out: drvn and holding rivals after* **10/11**[1]

40-F **2** *9* **Mr Burgees (IRE)**[40] [82] 6-11-0 0................................ WayneHutchinson 119+
(Donald McCain) *trckd ldrs: wnt 2nd bef 9th: hit next: sn rdn: nvr making any imp fr 3 out* **17/2**

0F-4 **3** *7* **King Alfonso**[22] [406] 6-11-0 0................................ RobertDunne 112
(Dai Burchell) *3rd most of way: ev ch bef 10th: sn rdn: one pce and wl hld fr next* **3/1**[2]

12-4 **4** *5* **Macarthur**[14] [527] 11-11-0 0................................ PaulMoloney 107
(David Rees) *hld up trcking ldrs: last of four gng clr bef 10th: sn rdn and fnd nil: wl btn 3 out* **20/1**

00-0 **5** *3 ½* **Mr Mafia (IRE)**[38] [106] 6-11-0 0................................ LeeEdwards 104
(Tony Carroll) *hld up last tl 9th: sn rdn: lost tch w ldng quartet bef next: wl bhd whn mstke 3 out: plodded on after last* **200/1**

36-U **6** *28* **Romeo Americo (IRE)**[22] [395] 8-11-0 115................................ JamieMoore 79
(Seamus Mullins) *towards rr: rdn and lost tch bef 10th: t.o and eased whn hopped over last* **5/1**[3]

7 *32* **Tony (IRE)**[46] 8-10-7 0................................ MissTWorsley[(7)] 50
(Ken Wingrove) *led tl 3rd: pressed wnr tl blnd 8th: drvn in last after next: sn t.o* **150/1**

5m 12.0s (7.40) **Going Correction** +0.45s/f (Soft) **7** Ran SP% **110.5**
Speed ratings: **103,99,96,94,93 82,69**
CSF £8.66 TOTE £1.70: £1.10, £2.90; EX 9.00 Trifecta £21.80.
Owner Three Celts **Bred** Peter Jones And G G Jones **Trained** Alcester, Warwicks

FOCUS
All starts have been moved at this track following remeasuring, so there will be no speed figures here until there is sufficient data to calculate updated median times. A warm day. Harry Skelton described it as "good ground, they have done a good job", and Wayne Hutchinson said: "It's nearer good than good to firm." The fences and hurdles were down the middle line in the home straight. The winner set a fair standard and is rated to his mark. The second and third did bigger figures over hurdles but are probably plenty high enough, with the fifth a concern.

698 MYRACING.COM FOR FREE TIPS H'CAP CHASE (16 fncs) 2m 7f
2:10 (2:11) (Class 5) (0-100,100) 5-Y-0+ **£2,924** (£858; £429; £214)

Form RPR
4-0P **1** **Finding Your Feet (IRE)**[31] [239] 7-11-12 100................(v) WillKennedy 111+
(Jonjo O'Neill) *hld up and bhd: mstke 11th: stl 7th after 12th: clsd next: rdn and wnt 2nd 3 out: led despite slipping sddle at last: urged clr* **9/1**

2F-5 **2** *6* **Kilcascan**[26] [340] 11-10-9 86................................(p) BenPoste[(3)] 91
(Rosemary Gasson) *2nd tl led 6th: hdd last: pushed along and outpcd flat* **16/1**

25-5 **3** *12* **Celtic Fella (IRE)**[7] [612] 8-10-0 74 oh7................................(vt) TrevorWhelan 70
(Debra Hamer) *pressed ldrs: looked unsighted 6th and blnd: lost pl: blnd bdly 12th: 6th and drvn after: no ch fr next but plodded into 15 l 3rd at last* **12/1**

PP-6 **4** *8* **American World (FR)**[14] [527] 11-10-3 84................................ MissLBrooke[(7)] 70
(Lady Susan Brooke) *wnt 2nd briefly at 7th: 5th and pushed along after 12th: struggling next* **100/1**

-U63 **5** *9* **Miss Tilly Oscar (IRE)**[14] [517] 9-10-10 91................(t) DavidNoonan[(7)] 70
(Steve Flook) *cl up: wnt 2nd bef 9th: rdn bef 13th: lost 2nd 3 out and losing tired 15 l 3rd whn mstke last* **12/1**

U0- **6** *11* **Dream Bolt (IRE)**[18] 7-11-12 100................................ PaulMoloney 69
(David Rees) *hld up last tl 1/2-way: wnt 3rd and looked to be gng wl after 12th: lost pl next* **7/1**

1P-P **P** **Thats Ben (IRE)**[37] [126] 10-10-2 76................................(tp) JamesDavies
(Tom Gretton) *unruly at s: led tl hdd and hmpd 6th: cl up tl 12th: drvn and fdd tamely: t.o and p.u 3 out* **25/1**

4-6U **P** **Gale Force Oscar (IRE)**[11] [567] 10-11-4 92................................ GerardTumelty
(Andy Turnell) *midfield: rdn 7th: hmpd bnd after next: drvn and lost tch 12th: t.o and p.u next* **6/1**[3]

F6-2 **P** **Fast Exit (IRE)**[18] [450] 8-11-6 94................................(b) RichardJohnson
(Neil Mulholland) *bhd: blnd 8th and rdn in last after: j. slowly next: t.o and p.u 13th* **10/3**[1]

45-4 **P** **Hopstrings**[19] [438] 7-10-12 91................................(p) CharlieDeutsch[(5)]
(Tom Lacey) *chsd ldrs tl rdn and dropped to rr 11th: t.o and p.u 3 out* **8/1**

52-0 **U** **Driving Well (IRE)**[23] [388] 7-10-12 86................................ RobertDunne
(Arthur Whiting) *blnd and uns rdr 1st* **11/2**[2]

6m 0.2s (10.30) **Going Correction** +0.45s/f (Soft) **11** Ran SP% **112.5**
Speed ratings: **100,97,93,90,87 84, , , ,**
CSF £131.28 CT £1715.95 TOTE £13.10: £2.80, £5.00, £3.60; EX 142.70 Trifecta £777.30.
Owner John P McManus **Bred** L Wright **Trained** Cheltenham, Gloucs

FOCUS
A low-grade handicap chase. The winner posted a chase pb but was 115 hurdler and can match that over fences. The second is probably best guide to level.

699 DOWNLOAD MY RACING RESULTS FREE IPHONE APP H'CAP CHASE (12 fncs) 2m 110y
2:40 (2:42) (Class 5) (0-100,99) 5-Y-0+ **£2,924** (£858; £429; £214)

Form RPR
13-3 **1** **Shady Lane**[37] [135] 8-11-10 97................................(t) HarrySkelton 115+
(Dan Skelton) *cl up: led 7th: gng wl after next: tending to jump sltly rt after: 9 l ahd whn crashed through last: kpt rt up to work tl eased fnl 75yds* **3/1**[1]

023/ **2** *15* **Wak A Turtle (IRE)**[25] 7-11-6 93................................ DarylJacob 98
(Richard Woollacott) *led 5th tl 7th: pressed wnr after: drew clr w him 3 out: rdn and hld whn nt fluent next: plugged on after* **3/1**[1]

P-U2 **3** *2 ¼* **Dr Anubis (IRE)**[20] [429] 10-9-7 73 oh7................................(p) MissJodieHughes[(7)] 74
(Dai Burchell) *prom in 3rd or 4th: rdn bef 9th: 8 l 3rd and wl hld 3 out* **4/1**[2]

F4/- **4** *39* **Darnborough (IRE)**[40] 9-9-7 73................................(p) DavidNoonan[(7)] 39
(Mark Shears) *midfield: rdn fr 7th: struggling bef 9th: t.o* **25/1**

4/05 **5** *1* **Hyperlink (IRE)**[16] [492] 6-11-12 99................................(t) RhysFlint 64
(Heather Dalton) *midfield: rdn 7th: 4th briefly bef 9th: sn lost tch: t.o and fin weakly* **14/1**

1-2F **6** *2 ¼* **Red Whisper**[24] [379] 11-10-13 91................................(t) JakeHodson[(5)] 54
(Rob Summers) *dropped out last tl 1/2-way: mod prog to 5th and rdn bef 9th: struggling next: t.o* **9/1**

2-16 **7** *hd* **Beauchamp Viking**[24] [379] 11-10-1 74................................(t) DaveCrosse 37
(Hugo Froud) *led tl 5th: dropped bk last u.p after 8th: sn t.o* **16/1**

P4U- **P** **Surprise Us**[23] [3215] 8-10-1 74 oh3 ow1................................(p) TommyPhelan
(Mark Gillard) *t.k.h: chsd ldrs tl 8th: wknd and mstke next: t.o and p.u 3 out: dismntd* **14/1**

14-P **F** **My Nosy Rosy**[24] [383] 7-11-8 95................................(t) KielanWoods
(Ben Case) *dropping to rr whn fell 7th* **6/1**[3]

4m 8.6s (3.60) **Going Correction** +0.45s/f (Soft) **9** Ran SP% **117.3**
Speed ratings: **109,101,100,82,82 81,80, ,**
CSF £13.25 CT £36.13 TOTE £3.80: £1.50, £1.50, £2.00; EX 15.10 Trifecta £55.80.
Owner Mrs S C Welch **Bred** Mrs S C Welch **Trained** Alcester, Warwicks

FOCUS
A very moderate handicap. The winner was well in on best of hurdle form and is rated to a similar level.

700 EPDS RACING WELFARE BTO SERIES 2015 INTERMEDIATE OPEN NATIONAL HUNT FLAT RACE 2m
3:15 (3:16) (Class 6) 4-6-Y-0 **£1,559** (£457; £228; £114)

Form RPR
1 **Mont Choisy (FR)**[48] 5-11-0 0................................ SamTwiston-Davies 90+
(Nigel Twiston-Davies) *trckd ldng pair: rdn and effrt and n.m.r over 2f out: hrd drvn and sustained run fr over 1f out: forced ahd fnl strides* **10/11**[1]

2 *shd* **Rollo's Reflection (IRE)**[96] 5-10-7 0................................ MrMJPKendrick[(7)] 90+
(Ben Case) *settled trcking ldrs: effrt 3 out: led wl over 1f out: pushed along fnl f and fending off wnr tl ct cl home* **15/2**[3]

3 *10* **Epic Warrior (IRE)**[60] 6-11-0 0................................[1] TomScudamore 80
(David Pipe) *big: led at slow pce: drvn over 2f out: hdd wl over 1f out: carried hd awkwardly after: btn 1f out* **6/4**[2]

0 **4** *9* **Buy Me Out**[23] [392] 5-10-7 0................................[1] DarylJacob 64
(Grace Harris) *v reluctant to line up: t.k.h and pressed ldr at slow pce tl rdn 3f out: looked reluctant and wl hld over 2f out* **25/1**

6-60 **5** *99* **Sadiks Boy (IRE)**[5] [644] 6-11-0 0................................ LeeEdwards
(Aytach Sadik) *in last pair: drvn 7f out: qckly t.o* **150/1**

3m 49.6s (4.60) **Going Correction** +0.25s/f (Yiel)
WFA 4 from 5yo+ 3lb **5** Ran SP% **108.7**
Speed ratings: **98,97,92,88,38**
CSF £8.18 TOTE £2.20: £1.10, £3.30; EX 7.70 Trifecta £10.50.
Owner N A Twiston-Davies **Bred** Scea Ecurie Domaine De Baune **Trained** Naunton, Gloucs

FOCUS
A very modest bumper. The first three are all former pointers.

701 FOLLOW @MYRACINGTIPS ON TWITTER H'CAP HURDLE (10 hdls) 2m 4f
3:50 (3:50) (Class 3) (0-130,130) 4-Y-0+ **£6,498** (£1,908; £954; £477)

Form RPR
3-13 **1** **Street Entertainer (IRE)**[19] [442] 8-11-11 129................(bt) TomScudamore 136+
(David Pipe) *racd keenly: led at brisk pce and sn 15 l clr: advantage down to 5 l at 7th but stl gng wl: rdn 2 out and readily maintained avantage: kpt up to work tl eased fnl 50yds* **7/2**[2]

-125 **2** *5* **Cut The Corner (IRE)**[14] [520] 7-10-11 120................................ ChrisWard[(5)] 121
(Dr Richard Newland) *chsd wnr after 4th: rdn after 3 out: racing awkwardly next: stl 5 l bhd at last and nvr making any imp but remained clr of rest* **7/2**[2]

06P- **3** *17* **Aalim**[167] [3250] 5-11-12 130................................(b) AidanColeman 119
(John Ferguson) *trckd ldrs: rdn to chse ldng pair 3 out: sn fnd nil and no imp after: 15 l 3rd at last* **3/1**[1]

P2-P **4** *12* **Lookslikerainted (IRE)**[43] [19] 8-10-11 115................(tp) PaulMoloney 92
(Sophie Leech) *midfield: mstke 4th: drvn and outpcd bef 3 out: plodded on* **10/1**

320- **5** *4 ½* **Avel Vor (IRE)**[135] [3917] 4-10-9 117................................(p) TomO'Brien 84
(Philip Hobbs) *midfield: untidy 5th: wnt 3rd and looked to be gng wl 7th: pushed along and struggling after next* **12/1**

15-6 **6** *13* **Limpopo Tom (IRE)**[32] [218] 8-10-13 117................................(p) DenisO'Regan 76
(David Rees) *bhd: rdn and lost tch 7th: t.o next* **12/1**

00U- **7** *16* **First Avenue**[52] [5432] 10-11-11 129................................ TomCannon 74
(Laura Mongan) *last mostly: nt fluent 6th: rdn and struggling whn mstke 7th: sn t.o: eased* **6/1**[3]

004/ **8** *51* **Staigue Fort**[416] [5451] 7-11-2 120................................ DarylJacob 19
(Emma Lavelle) *t.k.h: prom tl lost pl bef 6th: t.o after next: sn eased* **16/1**

4m 54.3s (0.80) **Going Correction** +0.25s/f (Yiel)
WFA 4 from 5yo+ 18lb **8** Ran SP% **114.1**
Speed ratings (Par 107): **108,106,99,94,92 87,81,60**
CSF £16.47 CT £39.81 TOTE £5.20: £1.50, £1.30, £1.90; EX 15.70 Trifecta £40.80.
Owner Mrs Jo Tracey **Bred** Marston Stud And Fleming Thoroughbreds **Trained** Nicholashayne, Devon

FOCUS
The all-the-way winner set a sound pace in this fair handicap. There was a small pb from the winner, with the second to his mark and the third again well below his best.

702 WORCESTER NEWS MAIDEN HURDLE (DIV I) (8 hdls) 2m
4:20 (4:20) (Class 4) 4-Y-0+ £3,573 (£1,049; £524; £262)

Form RPR
1 **Black Iceman**[42] 7-11-0 0 JackQuinlan 104
(Lydia Pearce) *racd keenly and trckd ldrs in slow r: disp 3rd home turn: 3 l 3rd and rdn whn lft in ld last: drvn and styd on gamely after* **33/1**
F4-F 2 1 1/4 **Sindarban (IRE)**[25] [353] 4-10-11 0 (t) AdrianLane 102+
(Donald McCain) *plld hrd: cl up: 3rd 3 out: chal and untidy next: led and blnd last and wnt rt: sn hdd: one pce u.p after* **12/1**
3 3 1/2 **Fauve (IRE)**[310] 4-10-11 0 RichieMcLernon 99+
(Paul Webber) *prom: led narrowly 3 out: sn rdn: jnd and mstke next: rdn and cl 2nd whn blnd last: nt rcvr* **6/1**[2]
02- 4 5 **Hill Fort**[58] [5338] 5-11-0 0 TomScudamore 95
(Ronald Harris) *midfield: effrt 3 out: sn rdn and plugged on same pce* **10/1**
210- 5 6 **Bumble Bay**[301] [1222] 5-11-0 0 TomO'Brien 90
(Robert Stephens) *t.k.h on outer: chsd ldrs: pushed along bef 3 out: sn outpcd* **7/1**[3]
0- 6 1 **Mr McGuiness (IRE)**[221] [2230] 5-10-11 0 BenPoste(3) 89
(Rosemary Gasson) *t.k.h: cl 2nd mostly tl led 4th: set slow pce: rdn and hdd 3 out: fdd steadily* **28/1**
0P0- 7 3 3/4 **The Doom Bar (IRE)**[81] [4942] 6-11-0 0 MichealNolan 86
(Philip Hobbs) *towards rr: pushed along and struggling bef 3 out* **14/1**
8 10 **Dubai Star (IRE)**[225] 4-10-11 0 AidanColeman 76
(John Ferguson) *plld hrd in midfield: disp 3rd and looked to be gng wl home turn: sn rdn and fnd nil: wl btn 2 out* **11/10**[1]
9 63 **Gardiners Hill (IRE)**[18] 5-11-0 0 PaulMoloney 20
(David Rees) *mde most at slow pce tl mstke 4th: t.o after next* **11/1**
P- 10 5 **Hoy Hoy (IRE)**[34] [4653] 4-10-11 0 RhysFlint 12
(Alexandra Dunn) *hld up last: rdn 4th: mstke 5th: sn t.o* **100/1**

3m 58.3s (7.70) **Going Correction** +0.25s/f (Yiel)
WFA 4 from 5yo+ 17lb **10 Ran SP% 113.6**
Speed ratings (Par 105): **90,89,87,85,82 81,79,74,43,40**
CSF £362.49 TOTE £29.10: £5.70, £2.50, £2.30; EX 276.10 Trifecta £915.20.
Owner Mrs Jennifer Marsh **Bred** Graham Wilson **Trained** Newmarket, Suffolk
FOCUS
A weak maiden hurdle run at a very steady pace and in a slow time. Not form to take too seriously.

703 WORCESTER NEWS MAIDEN HURDLE (DIV II) (8 hdls) 2m
4:55 (4:57) (Class 4) 4-Y-0+ £3,573 (£1,049; £524; £262)

Form RPR
6-46 1 **Jarlath**[12] [554] 4-10-4 0 KevinJones(7) 109
(Seamus Mullins) *t.k.h in remote 3rd tl clsd bef 5th where nt fluent: rdn to chse ldr wl bef next: looked hld tl lft in ld after last: styd on steadily w clr advantage fnl 100yds* **8/1**
20-3 2 3 **Hepijeu (FR)**[27] [316] 4-10-11 115 (t) AidanColeman 114+
(Charlie Longsdon) *hld up in pursuit of ldr: clsd bef 5th: led gng wl sn after: hanging rt st: 5 l ahd whn j. bdly rt 2 out: veered rt at last and nrly dislodged rdr: hdd after last: stened up but ch gone* **6/4**[1]
1-4 3 15 **Prince Of Poets**[34] [187] 4-10-11 0 TomScudamore 98+
(David Pipe) *midfield: nt fluent 4th: mstke next: rdn: last of six gng clr bef next: drvn and sn btn: wnt 10 l 3rd whn mstke 2 out* **3/1**[2]
4 20 **Chasing The Light (IRE)** 5-11-0 0 RichieMcLernon 78
(Jonjo O'Neill) *tall chser type: cl up: wnt 3rd after 5th: rdn and wknd next: fin v tired* **10/1**
2-5 5 22 **Tricky (IRE)**[35] [160] 6-11-0 0 TomO'Brien 58
(Philip Hobbs) *midfield: in tch tl rdn and fdd v tamely 3 out: t.o and fin v tired* **7/1**[3]
4-P 6 19 **Captain Starlight (IRE)**[25] [360] 5-11-0 0 LeeEdwards 41
(Aytach Sadik) *mstkes: midfield to 4th: t.o after next* **100/1**
7 1 **Black Vale (IRE)**[19] 4-10-11 0 TomCannon 37
(Ralph J Smith) *bolted off into 40 l ld: c bk to field after 5th and hdd sn after flight: continued t.o and virtually p.u fr bef next* **33/1**
46/ 8 3/4 **Prairie Hawk (USA)**[1008] [1501] 10-11-0 0 MichealNolan 39
(Adrian Wintle) *bhd: last and struggling 4th: t.o after next* **66/1**
5- F **Xclusive**[12] [5338] 5-10-11 0 ThomasGarner(3)
(Ronald Harris) *plld hrd in last tl crashing fall 1st* **100/1**

3m 56.3s (5.70) **Going Correction** +0.25s/f (Yiel)
WFA 4 from 5yo+ 17lb **9 Ran SP% 104.1**
Speed ratings (Par 105): **95,93,86,76,65 55,55,54,**
CSF £17.47 TOTE £11.30: £2.60, £1.10, £1.30; EX 19.80 Trifecta £58.70.
Owner Phoenix Bloodstock **Bred** D & C Bloodstock **Trained** Wilsford-Cum-Lake, Wilts
FOCUS
Another weak race, run in a time two seconds quicker than the preceding division. The rest ignored Black Vale, who raced into a very long lead. This was a step up from the winner, but entitled to rate higher on Flat form.

704 MYRACING.COM FOR FREE ROYAL ASCOT TIPS CONDITIONAL JOCKEYS' H'CAP HURDLE (10 hdls) 2m 4f
5:25 (5:26) (Class 5) (0-100,100) 4-Y-0+ £2,599 (£763; £381; £190)

Form RPR
4-42 1 **Shot In The Dark (IRE)**[13] [537] 6-11-7 95 (p) NicodeBoinville 102
(Jonathan Geake) *j.rt: slt ld tl 6th: led again bef 3 out: drvn and jst hdd last: battled on gamely: led again on nod* **9/2**[3]
600- 2 nse **Bedouin Bay**[114] [4281] 8-11-4 97 (p) ConorSmith(5) 104
(Johnny Farrelly) *settled in midfield: smooth prog fr 6th: 3rd and gng strly home turn: wnt 2nd 3 out: rdn and led narrowly last: ct fnl strides* **4/1**[2]
3-04 3 13 **Gwili Spar**[26] [337] 7-10-0 74 oh4 (t) KieronEdgar 69
(Laura Hurley) *hld up detached in last tl effrt wd after 7th: coaxed onto heels of ldrs 2 out: plugged on to go 7 l 3rd last: fnd nthing after* **20/1**
5-00 4 1 1/2 **Provincial Pride (IRE)**[14] [529] 8-11-4 100 (t) CharlieHammond(8) 94
(Mike Hammond) *prom: disp 3rd and rdn after 7th: no imp fr next and styd on same pce* **11/1**
12-1 5 2 **Karl Marx (IRE)**[30] [265] 5-11-2 90 (b) SeanBowen 82
(Mark Gillard) *sn off bridle and drvn along: chsd ldrs tl no rspnse to press after 7th: btn bef 2 out* **3/1**[1]
40-1 6 shd **In The Crowd (IRE)**[20] [435] 6-11-9 100 (p) JamieBargary(3) 93
(Roy Brotherton) *cl 2nd tl led 6th: rdn and hdd bef 3 out: 3rd and btn whn nt fluent next* **10/1**
-450 7 1 1/4 **Toast And Jam (IRE)**[13] [537] 6-10-6 83 (t) DanielHiskett(3) 74
(Claire Dyson) *chsd ldrs: effrt after 7th: drvn bef next: sn struggling* **16/1**
054- 8 7 **Amuse Me**[214] [2370] 9-10-12 94 (t) PatrickCowley(8) 78
(Jonjo O'Neill) *chsd ldrs: mstke 5th: rdn 7th: no rspnse: wl btn 2 out: mstke last* **9/1**
02-3 9 5 **Hope's Wishes**[31] [238] 5-11-4 100 RichieO'Dea(8) 80
(Emma Lavelle) *hld up and bhd: rdn and btn bef 3 out* **14/1**
524- 10 dist **Unwanted Gift (IRE)**[25] 10-10-10 84 MichealNolan 19
(Alan Phillips) *prom tl rdn and fdd bef 3 out: t.o next* **25/1**
3/P- 11 8 **Roseini (IRE)**[167] [3266] 9-10-0 74 ConorShoemark 2
(Rob Summers) *unruly and did nt want to line up: bhd: shkn up 5th: drvn 7th: sn lost tch: t.o bef 2 out* **50/1**
0P-0 P **Benefitofhindsight**[7] [615] 6-10-0 74 (t) KillianMoore
(Hywel Evans) *bhd: rdn and t.o after 7th: p.u next* **28/1**

5m 2.9s (9.40) **Going Correction** +0.25s/f (Yiel) **12 Ran SP% 117.2**
Speed ratings (Par 103): **91,90,85,85,84 84,83,81,79, ,**
CSF £21.99 CT £328.50 TOTE £3.00: £1.10, £2.60, £8.10; EX 34.80 Trifecta £493.10.
Owner Mrs P D Gulliver **Bred** Littleton Stud **Trained** East Kennett, Wilts
FOCUS
They went an ordinary pace in this modest handicap. The winner stepped up on a good recent run, the second was very well in on best of 2014 form, and the third is rated in line with best of recent runs.
T/Plt: £225.10 to a £1 stake. Pool: £50,028.57 - 162.21 winning units. T/Qpdt: £15.80 to a £1 stake. Pool: £5,721.65 - 267.50 winning units. **Iain Mackenzie**

[314] AINTREE (L-H)
Friday, June 12

OFFICIAL GOING: Good (mildmay 8.1; hdl 8.1)
Wind: light 1/2 behind Weather: fine

705 MEGA SPORT ODDS CONDITIONAL JOCKEYS' H'CAP HURDLE (13 hdls) 3m 149y
5:40 (5:41) (Class 4) (0-120,120) 4-Y-0+ £3,898 (£1,144; £572; £286)

Form RPR
21-2 1 **Brave Helios**[34] [210] 5-11-3 117 DanielHiskett(6) 126
(Richard Phillips) *chsd ldrs: led between last 2: kpt on towards fin* **14/1**
11-3 2 nk **Cowslip**[28] [319] 6-11-9 117 AdamNicol 125
(George Moore) *hld up towards rr: hdwy 8th: drvn appr 3 out: 2nd between last 2: upsides whn hit last: no ex clsng stages* **13/2**
404- 3 7 **What A Steel (IRE)**[49] [5519] 11-10-11 105 DaleIrving 107
(Alistair Whillans) *chsd ldrs: led 3 out: hdd between last 2: sn fdd* **25/1**
P6-3 4 3 1/2 **Wily Fox**[26] [363] 8-11-1 109 (b) KieronEdgar 109
(James Eustace) *hld up in rr: hdwy 8th: sn trcking ldrs: hit 10th: drvn next: wknd between last 2* **6/1**[3]
4PP/ 5 12 **Regal Diamond (IRE)**[455] [4786] 7-11-12 120 (p) SeanBowen 113+
(Peter Bowen) *nt fluent: w ldr: led 6th: hdd 3 out: wknd 2 out: hit last* **7/4**[1]
34-1 6 9 **Youngdocgallagher (IRE)**[41] [90] 6-10-13 107 BenPoste 89
(Michael Mullineaux) *chsd ldrs: mstke 8th: sn drvn: lost pl appr next* **7/1**
3-21 7 8 **Jack Albert (IRE)**[19] [453] 8-11-1 109 (b) ColmMcCormack 82
(Dianne Sayer) *led: hdd 6th: wknd 3 out* **20/1**
/5P- P **Bit Of A Jig (IRE)**[225] [2149] 8-11-10 118 NicodeBoinville
(Donald McCain) *in rr: bhd and drvn 7th: t.o 10th: p.u bef next* **33/1**
41-4 P **Aiaam Al Namoos**[28] [319] 6-11-10 118 DiarmuidO'Regan
(John Wade) *chsd ldrs: blnd and lost pl 1st: bhd and shkn up 4th: t.o 10th: p.u bef next* **9/2**[2]

6m 10.7s (-5.60) **Going Correction** -0.225s/f (Good) **9 Ran SP% 112.9**
Speed ratings (Par 105): **99,98,96,95,91 88,86, ,**
CSF £96.12 CT £2242.01 TOTE £13.90: £2.50, £1.90, £6.50; EX 72.50 Trifecta £987.20.
Owner Mrs June Watts **Bred** Oscar Stud **Trained** Adlestrop, Gloucs
FOCUS
All bends moved out to fresh ground. Race 1 increased by 54yds, races 2 & 4 by 35yds, race 3 by 72yds, race 5 by 48yds and races 6 & 7 by 47yds. A modest staying handicap hurdle in which two came clear. This was another step forward from the winner, with the second posting a pb in defeat.

706 TRANMERE ROVERS BOUNCING BACK MAIDEN HURDLE (9 hdls) 2m 209y
6:10 (6:12) (Class 4) 4-Y-0+ £3,898 (£1,144; £572; £286)

Form RPR
64- 1 **Cardinal Palace (IRE)**[12] [6] 5-11-0 135 DJCasey 134+
(J A Nash, Ire) *j.rt: mde all: wnt clr run-in: v readily* **5/4**[1]
2 7 **Nabucco**[259] 6-11-0 0 AidanColeman 124+
(John Ferguson) *trckd ldrs: 2nd appr 3 out: kpt on same pce appr last* **11/8**[2]
3 10 **Dare To Achieve**[267] 5-11-0 0 PaddyBrennan 116+
(Tom George) *t.k.h in last: hdwy and handy 3rd appr 3 out: wknd appr last* **9/2**[3]
05-5 4 41 **Sturdy Dawn**[17] [491] 5-10-4 0 BenPoste(3) 65
(Michael Mullineaux) *chsd wnr: lost pl appr 3 out: sn bhd: t.o* **125/1**
34-2 5 8 **Episode**[43] [39] 4-10-11 0 JamesReveley 61
(Philip Kirby) *chsd ldrs 4th: lost pl appr 3 out: sn bhd: t.o* **25/1**

4m 6.4s (-7.30) **Going Correction** -0.225s/f (Good)
WFA 4 from 5yo+ 17lb **5 Ran SP% 109.4**
Speed ratings (Par 105): **108,104,100,80,76**
CSF £3.38 TOTE £2.10: £1.10, £1.20; EX 3.40 Trifecta £4.00.
Owner J & T Partnership **Bred** J Murphy **Trained** The Curragh, Co. Kildare
FOCUS
A small field but some interesting sorts in this maiden hurdle. The cosy winner set a decent standard and is rated to his mark.

707 MEGA SPORT ODDS H'CAP CHASE (19 fncs) 3m 210y
6:45 (6:45) (Class 3) (0-135,133) 5-Y-0+
£6,256 (£1,848; £924; £462; £231; £116)

Form RPR
02-1 1 **Silver Man**[26] [355] 8-11-0 121 (b) NicodeBoinville 141+
(Jo Hughes) *chsd ldrs: led 3 out: wnt clr bef last: eased clsng stages* **6/1**[3]
3-31 2 16 **Sedgemoor Express (IRE)**[22] [420] 7-11-3 131 (p) CiaranGethings(7) 135
(Nigel Hawke) *chsd ldrs: styd on to take modest 2nd last: no ch w wnr* **6/1**[3]
2-11 3 5 **Ballybough Pat (IRE)**[26] [358] 8-11-12 133 (t) AidanColeman 136
(David Dennis) *led 2nd: hdd 3 out: wknd last* **9/2**[1]
21-4 4 5 **Lord Brendy**[19] [458] 7-11-0 121 PeterBuchanan 118
(Kenny Johnson) *rn in snatches: hdwy and prom whn hit 15th: one pce fr 3 out* **17/2**

6U-2 **5** *2 ¾* **Gleann Na Ndochais (IRE)**[28] 315 9-10-10 **120**........... CraigNichol(3) 113
(Alistair Whillans) *chsd ldrs: one pce fr 3 out* **14/1**
412- **6** *21* **Candide (IRE)**[57] 5358 8-10-10 **120**..............................(p) JamesBanks(3) 97
(Andy Turnell) *chsd ldrs: pushed along 7th: blnd 11th: lost pl 13th* **5/1**[2]
PP-P **7** *14* **Dark Glacier (IRE)**[36] 156 10-11-2 **126**.......................(bt) SeanBowen(3) 87
(Peter Bowen) *in rr: reminders 11th: bhd 14th: t.o 3 out: eased clsng stages* **14/1**
P4-1 **8** *12* **Ballyben (IRE)**[19] 458 7-11-2 **123**...............................(p) BrianHughes 73
(Lucinda Russell) *led to 2nd: chsd ldrs: lost pl after 15th: t.o 3 out: eased clsng stages* **8/1**
30U- **U** **Deciding Moment (IRE)**[63] 5253 9-11-10 **131**........(t) WayneHutchinson
(Ben De Haan) *in rr: blnd and uns rdr 12th* **20/1**
25-3 **P** **Wolf Shield (IRE)**[22] 420 8-11-4 **125**............................(tp) HenryBrooke
(George Moore) *in rr: hit 6th: bhd and reminders 9th: t.o whn p.u bef 13th* **8/1**

6m 19.2s (-10.80) **Going Correction** -0.225s/f (Good) **10** Ran SP% **114.3**
Speed ratings: **108,102,101,99,98 92,87,83, ,**
CSF £41.61 CT £176.74 TOTE £6.60: £2.40, £2.70, £1.80; EX 37.40 Trifecta £121.50.
Owner John Wardle **Bred** T J Wardle **Trained** Lambourn, Berks

FOCUS
One of the feature events and a decent handicap chase for the time of year and three last-time-out winners dominated, suggesting the form is solid. This was a big step forward from the impressive winner, with the second and third close to their marks and a case for rating higher through the fourth and fifth.

708 MEGA SPORT ODDS H'CAP HURDLE (9 hdls) 2m 103y
7:15 (7:17) (Class 3) (0-135,132) 4-Y-0+ **£5,848** (£1,717; £858; £429)

Form RPR
13- **1** **Buckwheat**[140] 3835 5-11-10 **130**.................................(t) AidanColeman 143+
(John Ferguson) *hld up in rr: smooth hdwy appr 3 out: sn 2nd: led appr last: cruised clr: v easily* **9/4**[1]
0-45 **2** *4 ½* **Sleep In First (FR)**[16] 508 9-10-3 **114**.........................(t) DaleIrving(5) 115
(James Ewart) *led: hit 1st: hdd and mstke next: led 3rd: hdd whn blnd last: no ch w wnr* **14/1**
261- **3** *3 ¾* **Purple 'n Gold (IRE)**[86] 4847 6-11-2 **127**.......................(p) KieronEdgar(5) 123
(David Pipe) *hld up: effrt appr 3 out: 3rd out: kpt on same pce* **11/4**[2]
33-1 **4** *4* **Good Of Luck**[27] 332 6-11-5 **125**...............................(p) GavinSheehan 118
(Warren Greatrex) *chsd ldrs: one pce fr 3 out* **9/2**[3]
/32- **5** *¾* **Dovils Date**[20] 1309 6-11-1 **128**.. AlanJohns(7) 120
(Tim Vaughan) *t.k.h: w ldr: led 2nd: hdd next: one pce fr 3 out* **5/1**
233- **6** *52* **Swaledale Lad (IRE)**[85] 4870 8-11-9 **132**..................... HarryChalloner(3) 97
(Richard Ford) *in rr: sme hdwy 6th: drvn and lost pl next: sn bhd: t.o whn eased clsng stages* **8/1**

3m 59.2s (-7.00) **Going Correction** -0.225s/f (Good) **6** Ran SP% **110.1**
Speed ratings (Par 107): **108,105,103,101,101 75**
CSF £27.27 TOTE £2.20: £1.20, £4.50; EX 28.00 Trifecta £126.10.
Owner Bloomfields **Bred** Darley **Trained** Cowlinge, Suffolk

FOCUS
This handicap was run at a fair pace and produced an impressive winner, who has the potential to rate higher still on Flat form. The second is on a good mark and back to form, with the third to the level of his Haydock win. Form that should work out.

709 INKERMAN LONDON H'CAP CHASE (12 fncs) 1m 7f 176y
7:50 (7:50) (Class 3) (0-135,130) 5-Y-0**£6,256** (£1,848; £924; £462; £231)

Form RPR
U6B- **1** **Kings Grey (IRE)**[63] 5253 11-11-10 **128**.........................(tp) JamesReveley 135+
(Philip Kirby) *best away: clr to 3rd: j. soundly: rdn after 2 out: styd on: drvn rt out* **11/4**[1]
4-41 **2** *1 ½* **Claragh Native (IRE)**[22] 417 10-10-9 **113**............................ BrianHarding 118
(Martin Todhunter) *trckd clr ldr: handy 2nd 4th: drvn and kpt on fr 2 out: unable chal* **6/1**
125- **3** *2 ¾* **Falcarragh (IRE)**[238] 1931 8-11-12 **130**.......................... RichardJohnson 132
(Tim Vaughan) *hld up in rr: effrt and modest 4th 3 out: 3rd appr last: kpt on same pce* **7/2**[3]
25-1 **4** *10* **Lucky Landing (IRE)**[28] 315 9-11-11 **129**........................... DenisO'Regan 125
(Tony Coyle) *racd in 3rd: trckd ldng pair 5th: effrt appr 3 out: wknd appr last* **10/3**[2]
0F-2 **5** *3 ½* **Vengeur De Guye (FR)**[18] 469 6-11-7 **128**..........................(t) DerekFox(3) 118
(Lucinda Russell) *in rr: effrt appr 3 out: nvr on terms: wknd bef last* **7/2**[3]

4m 0.4s (0.40) **Going Correction** -0.225s/f (Good) **5** Ran SP% **108.5**
Speed ratings: **90,89,87,82,81**
CSF £17.14 TOTE £4.00: £2.30, £2.90; EX 16.80 Trifecta £51.00.
Owner B Dunn **Bred** Fred Mackey **Trained** East Appleton, N Yorks

FOCUS
A tightly knit handicap chase that was reflected in the betting, but a race dictated from the front. The winner was a 139 chaser at his best and came back to form under a good ride, with the second and third close to their marks.

710 AINTREE GOLF DRIVING RANGE NOVICES' HURDLE (11 hdls) 2m 4f
8:25 (8:25) (Class 4) 4-Y-0+ **£3,898** (£1,144; £572; £286)

Form RPR
35-3 **1** **Lamool (GER)**[28] 318 8-10-12 129.........................(t) RichardJohnson 134+
(Tim Vaughan) *mde all: shkn up between last 2: sn wnt clr: v easily* **8/11**[1]
42/ **2** *11* **Oculist**[639] 1561 7-10-12 104.. WayneHutchinson 118
(Ben De Haan) *hld up: hdwy to trck ldrs 4th: 2nd appr 3 out: kpt on same pce fr 2 out: no ch ww inner* **28/1**
U12 **3** *4 ½* **Angus Glens**[19] 452 5-11-5 125... AidanColeman 120
(David Dennis) *hld up in rr: hdwy 8th: 3rd 3 out: kpt on one pce* **8/1**[3]
0-61 **4** *5* **Octagon**[34] 200 5-11-5 0.. JamesReveley 117
(Dianne Sayer) *hldf up in last: hdwy 7th: 4th 3 out: one pce and j.lft last* **12/1**
21 **5** *12* **Never Up (GER)**[18] 467 4-11-1 113.................................... HenryBrooke 100
(George Moore) *hld up in tch: effrt appr 3 out: wknd between last 2* **16/1**
6 *17* **Olympiad (IRE)**[607] 7-10-12 0... BrianHarding 81
(Martin Todhunter) *t.k.h: trckd wnr: lost pl 8th: t.o next* **11/1**
434- **7** *7* **Roc D'Apsis (FR)**[83] 4897 6-10-12 0................................ PaddyBrennan 75
(Tom George) *chsd ldrs: drvn 6th: lost pl appr 3 out: sn bhd: t.o whn eased run-in* **4/1**[2]

4m 49.1s (-11.60) **Going Correction** -0.225s/f (Good)
WFA 4 from 5yo+ 18lb **7** Ran SP% **114.4**
Speed ratings (Par 105): **114,109,107,105,101 94,91**
CSF £22.63 TOTE £1.60: £1.50, £6.40; EX 37.40 Trifecta £139.00.
Owner J H Frost **Bred** Frau M U W Lohmann **Trained** Aberthin, Vale of Glamorgan

FOCUS
Three recent winners and a couple returning from absences featured in this novice hurdle. The easy winner was a 139 chaser and might match that over hudles. This was a big step up from the second, with the third to his mark and the fourth a bit below after not quite getting home.

711 NORTH WEST MARES' H'CAP HURDLE (11 hdls) 2m 4f
9:00 (9:00) (Class 4) (0-120,120) 4-Y-0+ **£3,898** (£1,144; £572; £286)

Form RPR
00-4 **1** **Cool Baranca (GER)**[8] 302 9-10-1 **98**.............................. EmmaSayer(3) 109+
(Dianne Sayer) *hld up detached in last: hdwy appr 3 out: upsides whn carried rt 2 out: led between last 2: wnt clr run-in: eased towards fin* **12/1**
010- **2** *11* **Jackies Solitaire**[121] 4159 7-11-6 **117**..........................(tp) SeanBowen(3) 119
(Peter Bowen) *t.k.h: w ldrs: kpt on fr 3 out: 2nd between last 2: kpt on same pce* **3/1**[2]
44-2 **3** *3 ¾* **Keep To The Beat**[22] 415 4-10-3 **101**..................................... BrianHughes 94
(Kevin Ryan) *chsd ldetrs: kpt on one pce fr 2 out: tk modest 3rd last 150yds* **9/1**
233- **4** *4 ½* **Dardanella**[54] 5414 8-10-13 **107**..............................(p) WayneHutchinson 102
(Alan King) *trckd ldrs: j.rt 6th: led and j.rt 2 out: sn hdd: modest 3rd whn hit last: sn wknd* **2/1**[1]
2-01 **5** *7* **Morning With Ivan (IRE)**[16] 508 5-10-3 **100**.........(v) GrahamWatters(3) 89
(Martin Todhunter) *w ldrs: led 7th: hdd 2 out: sn wknd* **10/3**[3]
22-6 **6** *12* **Whatdoesthefoxsay (IRE)**[28] 314 6-11-5 **120**............ JamesCowley(7) 95
(Donald McCain) *led to 7th: reminders appr 3 out: sn wknd* **8/1**

4m 56.3s (-4.40) **Going Correction** -0.225s/f (Good)
WFA 4 from 5yo+ 18lb **6** Ran SP% **110.2**
Speed ratings (Par 105): **99,94,93,91,88 83**
CSF £46.30 TOTE £17.70: £5.20, £2.10; EX 56.10 Trifecta £149.30.
Owner Dennis J Coppola **Bred** Stiftung Gestut Fahrhof **Trained** Hackthorpe, Cumbria

FOCUS
An ordinary mares' handicap hurdle but an easy winner - she was a 115+ horse last summer and might win another. The second and third are rated pretty much to their marks.
T/Plt: £55.30 to a £1 stake. Pool: £59,049.17 - 779.10 winning tickets T/Qpdt: £11.30 to a £1 stake. Pool: £5,152.73 - 336.83 winning tickets **Walter Glynn**

[509]NEWTON ABBOT (L-H)
Friday, June 12

OFFICIAL GOING: Good changing to good (good to soft in places) after race 3 (2.50) changing to good to soft after race 6 (4.30)
Wind: mild breeze Weather: rain heavy at times Rails: Shared bends. Rail movement has added approximately: 45yds to race 2, 57yds to race 4, 75yds to race 6.

712 HAPPY 60TH BIRTHDAY PHIL MCGRATH NOVICES' H'CAP HURDLE (9 hdls) 2m 2f 110y
1:50 (1:50) (Class 5) (0-100,100) 4-Y-0+ **£3,422** (£997; £499)

Form RPR
2F-4 **1** **Fuse Wire**[14] 537 8-10-13 **87**.. RobertDunne 91+
(Dai Burchell) *hld up: tk clsr order 6th: rdn after 3 out: 2 l 2nd whn lft ld 2 out where hmpd and rdr lost irons: kpt on wl* **11/2**[3]
P-05 **2** *3* **Eddy**[21] 435 6-10-0 **81**.. ThomasCheesman(7) 80
(John Panvert) *travelled wl in tch: rdn whn lft 3rd and hmpd 2 out: wnt 2nd at the last: kpt on but a hld by wnr* **4/1**[2]
5-54 **3** *1* **Sheer Poetry (IRE)**[16] 511 4-11-8 **100**................................ DarylJacob 96+
(Richard Woollacott) *trckd ldrs: rdn appr 2 out: lft 2nd whn bdly hmpd 2 out: kpt on but no ex fr last* **9/1**
PC-3 **4** *13* **Chankillo**[16] 515 6-10-11 **85**.................................... SamTwiston-Davies 73
(Sarah-Jayne Davies) *led: rdn and hdd after 3 out: hld in 5th whn hmpd and lft 4th next* **15/2**
6-22 **5** *3 ½* **Good Value**[19] 466 4-11-5 **97**...(vt) TomScudamore 78
(David Pipe) *rousted along early: chsd ldr fr 2nd untl drvn after 3 out: sn btn* **7/2**[1]
00-5 **6** *8* **Milan Of Crystal (IRE)**[16] 513 6-10-4 **85**................................ MissBFrost(7) 60
(Jimmy Frost) *pushed along fr 4th: a towards rr* **25/1**
002- **7** *hd* **Staff Sergeant**[119] 4201 8-11-12 **100**.................................... PaulMoloney 75
(Jim Best) *a towards rr* **10/1**
0-45 **8** *25* **Up Four It (IRE)**[17] 494 7-10-11 **85**...................................... TomO'Brien 38
(Jamie Poulton) *in tch tl 6th: sn bhd: t.o* **20/1**
4/ **P** **Lets Get Cracking (FR)**[620] 1700 11-9-7 **74** oh9.......... JamieBargary(7)
(Alan Jones) *in tch: effrt after 3 out: sn wknd: in rr whn hmpd next: p.u bef last* **11/2**[3]
323- **F** **Faustina Pius (IRE)**[183] 3036 7-11-0 **88**........................(p) CharliePoste 95+
(Matt Sheppard) *trckd ldrs: led after 3 out: 2 l clr whn fell 2 out* **14/1**

4m 32.7s (2.70) **Going Correction** +0.20s/f (Yiel)
WFA 4 from 6yo+ 17lb **10** Ran SP% **119.1**
Speed ratings (Par 103): **102,100,100,94,93 90,89,79, ,**
CSF £29.01 CT £198.81 TOTE £8.50: £2.60, £2.70, £2.40; EX 39.00 Trifecta £744.00.
Owner P Webb **Bred** A W Buller **Trained** Briery Hill, Blaenau Gwent

FOCUS
Shared bends; race 2 increased by 45yds, race 4 by 57yds and race 6 by 75yds. The course had been watered over the previous week; rain had set in prior to the first race and jockeys reported the ground to be on the soft side of good. The winner was on a good mark and is rated to form, though the faller was on an even better mark and looked set to win. The second was very well in on his best form but was below that level again.

713 AT THE PAR INN, STILL NOT MARRIED NOVICES' H'CAP CHASE (13 fncs) 2m 75y
2:20 (2:20) (Class 5) (0-100,100) 5-Y-0+ **£3,249** (£954; £477; £238)

Form RPR
0-64 **1** **Red Skipper (IRE)**[20] 442 10-11-12 **100**................................ DaveCrosse 111+
(John O'Shea) *trckd ldrs: lost 3 out: hit next: styd on wl: rdn out* **25/1**
3-25 **2** *4 ½* **Lord Lir (IRE)**[19] 446 9-10-10 **84**.................................(b) MichaelByrne 89
(Tim Vaughan) *led: j.rt at times: rdn and hdd 3 out: styd on same pce fr next* **7/2**[2]
3 *2 ¼* **Mad Money (IRE)**[131] 9-10-13 **87**.. PaulMoloney 92
(Sophie Leech) *hld up: hdwy 3 out: sn rdn to chse ldng pair: styd on same pce fr next* **12/1**
-063 **4** *6* **Going Nowhere Fast (IRE)**[8] 616 10-10-3 **80**........ RobertWilliams(3) 79
(Bernard Llewellyn) *in tch: rdn after 4 out: wnt 4th after next: styd on same pce fr 2 out* **15/2**
6-21 **5** *61* **No No Cardinal (IRE)**[16] 514 6-11-0 **88**..........................(t) TommyPhelan 56
(Mark Gillard) *trckd ldrs: rdn in 3rd after 4 out: nt fluent next: sn wknd: tired whn awkward last: t.o* **2/1**[1]

425- **6** *11* **El Toreros (USA)**^{226} [2129] 7-11-1 **89**....................(tp) DavidBass 22
(Lawney Hill) *chsd ldrs: pushed along fr 6th: wknd 9th: t.o* **7/2**^{2}

000- **P** **Paper Lady (IRE)**^{73} [5082] 7-10-11 **85**.................... FelixDeGiles
(Jimmy Frost) *hld up: nt a fluent: struggling 8th: lost tch next: t.o whn p.u bef 2 out* **6/1**^{3}

4m 11.2s (4.70) **Going Correction** +0.45s/f (Soft) **7** Ran SP% **115.4**
Speed ratings: **106,103,102,99,69 63,**
CSF £113.20 TOTE £12.60: £3.40, £3.50; EX 73.70 Trifecta £226.80.

Owner K W Bell **Bred** Keith Moran **Trained** Elton, Gloucs

FOCUS
With two of the market leaders flopping, this did not take that much winning. The winner was better than this over hurdles at his peak.

714 "STATION ROAD" PLAYING AFTER RACING MARES' NOVICES' HURDLE (8 hdls) 2m 167y
2:50 (2:50) (Class 3) 4-Y-0+ **£5,523** (£1,621; £810; £405)

Form RPR

23-2 **1** **Pandorica**^{36} [178] 7-10-9 109....................(p) RobertWilliams$^{(3)}$ 108+
(Bernard Llewellyn) *trckd ldr in chsng gp: pressed ldr fr 5th: led after 3 out: rdn whn nt fluent last: kpt on* **11/4**^{2}

305- **2** *1* **Rest And Be (IRE)**^{183} [3033] 8-10-12 98.................... TomScudamore 105
(Alan Jones) *hld up in chsng gp: hdwy 5th: rdn to chse wnr appr 2 out: kpt on but a being hld* **8/1**^{3}

05-2 **3** *19* **Alottarain (IRE)**^{31} [268] 5-10-5 0.................... MrDSansom$^{(7)}$ 90
(Seamus Mullins) *trckd ldrs in chsng gp: rdn whn sltly outpcd after 3 out: n.d after: regained modest 3rd run-in* **25/1**

42-1 **4** *¾* **Popping Along**^{19} [462] 6-11-1 0....................(t) MattGriffiths$^{(3)}$ 94
(Jeremy Scott) *hld up in chsng gp: hdwy 5th: rdn to chse ldng pair 2 out: sn no ex: lost modest 3rd run-in* **2/1**^{1}

21-2 **5** *3* **Dry Ol'Party**^{16} [511] 5-10-12 0.................... TomO'Brien 87
(Philip Hobbs) *led chsng gp: led bef 5th: hdd after 3 out: sn rdn: wknd after next* **2/1**^{1}

3 **6** *1½* **Moulin Rouge (DEN)**^{13} [554] 4-10-9 0.................... WillKennedy 81
(Ian Williams) *hld up in chsng gp: hdwy 5th: effrt after 3 out: nvr threatened: btn whn awkward next* **14/1**

0P-4 **7** *dist* **Ragtime Lady**^{31} [268] 7-10-5 0.................... MrGTreacy$^{(7)}$
(Steven Dixon) *led: sn wl clr: hdd bef 5th: wknd qckly: t.o* **200/1**

4m 4.1s (-1.60) **Going Correction** +0.20s/f (Yiel)
WFA 4 from 5yo+ 17lb **7** Ran SP% **115.5**
Speed ratings (Par 107): **111,110,101,101,99 99,**
CSF £24.66 TOTE £4.70: £1.90, £3.30; EX 24.50 Trifecta £262.70.

Owner B J Llewellyn **Bred** Ambersham Stud **Trained** Fochriw, Caerphilly

■ Stewards' Enquiry : Mr G Treacy five-day ban; carelss riding (tba)

FOCUS
With the field chasing the tearaway Ragtime Lady, the early pace was quite strong and two finished well clear. The winner set a fair standard and is probably the best guide to the level.

715 WEATHERBYS PRINTING H'CAP CHASE (16 fncs) 2m 4f 216y
3:25 (3:25) (Class 3) (0-135,131) 5-Y-0+ **£6,498** (£1,908; £954; £477)

Form RPR

4-21 **1** **Sporting Boy (IRE)**^{13} [557] 7-11-5 **124**....................(b) BrendanPowell 130+
(Johnny Farrelly) *j.w: mde all: rdn after 3 out: styd on gamely: rdn out* **10/3**^{2}

2P-2 **2** *1¼* **Atlantic Roller (IRE)**^{21} [430] 8-11-6 **125**....................(p) SamTwiston-Davies 130
(Paul Nicholls) *trckd ldrs: chsd wnr fr 11th: rdn after 4 out: 3 l down 2 out: edging lft but ev ch last: no ex run-in* **6/5**^{1}

42-3 **3** *2½* **Miss Tenacious**^{13} [555] 8-10-11 **123**.................... HarryCobden$^{(7)}$ 127
(Ron Hodges) *hld up: hdwy into cl 3rd after 11th: rdn after 3 out: 2 1/2 l down 2 out: no ex fr last* **8/1**

11-1 **4** *83* **Brody Bleu (FR)**^{38} [121] 8-11-12 **131**.................... FelixDeGiles 58
(Robert Walford) *trckd wnr tl 11th: sn rdn: wknd after next: t.o* **7/2**^{3}

3-0P **P** **Don't Be Late (IRE)**^{19} [461] 7-11-3 **122**....................(p) RichieMcLernon
(Jonjo O'Neill) *trckd ldrs: struggling after 9th: wknd 11th: t.o whn p.u bef 4 out* **10/1**

5m 27.1s (5.70) **Going Correction** +0.45s/f (Soft) **5** Ran SP% **111.0**
Speed ratings: **107,106,105,73,**
CSF £8.25 TOTE £3.90: £1.40, £2.00; EX 8.20 Trifecta £36.60.

Owner Wayne Clifford **Bred** Joe & June Staunton **Trained** Enmore, Somerset

FOCUS
Quite a competitive handicap with several coming into this in good form, though the softening ground seemed to have an impact. This was another small pb from the winner, with the second and third pretty much to their marks.

716 BELATED BIRTHDAY GREETING SEAN DOONER H'CAP HURDLE (12 hdls) 3m 2f 105y
4:00 (4:00) (Class 4) (0-105,104) 4-Y-0+ **£3,898** (£1,144; £572; £286)

Form RPR

3-03 **1** **Horace Hazel**^{25} [377] 6-11-3 **95**.................... SamTwiston-Davies 99+
(Anthony Honeyball) *travelled wl: trckd ldrs: led narrowly 2 out: clr last: drifted lft: pushed out* **4/1**^{3}

56-2 **2** *2¼* **Rior (IRE)**^{26} [363] 8-11-11 **103**.................... TomO'Brien 103
(Paul Henderson) *cl up: rdn whn briefly outpcd after 3 out: kpt on between last 2: wnt 2nd at the last: styd on but a being hld* **11/4**^{2}

06-4 **3** *1¼* **All Force Majeure (FR)**^{31} [265] 5-11-7 **99**....................(b^{1}) TomScudamore 100
(David Pipe) *led: hit 5th: nt fluent 7th: rdn after 3 out: hdd next: nt fluent last: no ex* **5/2**^{1}

43-6 **4** *8* **Finish The Story (IRE)**^{26} [363] 9-11-5 **104**.........(bt) MrRobertHawker$^{(7)}$ 97
(Johnny Farrelly) *pressed ldr: nt fluent 9th: sn pushed along: nt fluent 3 out: sn drvn: one pce fr next* **11/4**^{2}

3-44 **5** *33* **Pauls Conn (IRE)**^{16} [509] 6-11-9 **101**....................(p) JamesBest 71
(Mary Sanderson) *chsd ldrs: pushed along fr 4th: rdn after 9th: stl cl up 3 out: wkng whn awkward 2 out* **16/1**

P **Did You Ever (IRE)**^{19} 9-11-3 **95**....................(p) MarcGoldstein
(Jamie Poulton) *chsd ldrs: nt fluent 2nd: pushed along fr 6th: lost tch next: p.u after 8th* **28/1**

6m 44.1s (3.10) **Going Correction** +0.20s/f (Yiel) **6** Ran SP% **111.2**
Speed ratings (Par 105): **103,102,101,99,89**
CSF £15.36 CT £30.61 TOTE £5.90: £3.50, £1.40; EX 16.00 Trifecta £36.90.

Owner T C Frost **Bred** T C Frost **Trained** Mosterton, Dorset

FOCUS
The softening ground and the extended distance took its toll in this moderate handicap. This was a big hurdles pb from the winner but he was still below best of bumper figures and probably more to come. The second is rated to his mark, the third posted a hurdles pb but is another who did bigger figure in bumper.

717 WEATHERBYS HAMILTON H'CAP CHASE (20 fncs) 3m 1f 170y
4:30 (4:31) (Class 5) (0-100,95) 5-Y-0+ **£3,422** (£997; £499)

Form RPR

22/1 **1** **Celtic Intrigue (IRE)**^{8} [610] 8-12-0 **95** 7ex....................(p) TomScudamore 109+
(David Bridgwater) *trckd ldrs: wnt 2nd after 16th: led 3 out: idling but in command after: rdn out* **9/4**^{1}

24-6 **2** *2¼* **Where'd Ya Hide It (IRE)**^{30} [280] 9-10-5 **72**....................(bt) TomO'Brien 83
(Paul Henderson) *prom: led 7th: blnd bdly 13th: rdn after 4 out: hdd next: styd on same pce fr 2 out* **14/1**

P0-3 **3** *16* **Volio Vincente (FR)**^{34} [211] 8-10-10 **77**....................(b) JamesBest 74
(Lydia Richards) *nt a fluent: disp ld tl 7th: pressed ldr tl 15th: sn rdn: lost 2nd after next: grad fdd fr 3 out* **9/2**^{3}

6-12 **4** *27* **Interpleader**^{27} [333] 10-11-5 **93**....................(tp) MrMartinMcIntyre$^{(7)}$ 63
(Sheila Lewis) *trckd ldrs: pushed along fr 9th: rdn after 16th: wknd 3 out: t.o* **3/1**^{2}

6-5P **P** **River Dancing (IRE)**^{15} [524] 8-10-3 **77**....................(tp) MrMLegg$^{(7)}$
(Anthony Honeyball) *nvr travelling: in tch: pushed along fr 5th: reminders after 8th: losing tch whn p.u after 14th* **9/2**^{3}

64-3 **P** **Gran Torino (IRE)**^{41} [88] 10-11-6 **87**.................... PaulMoloney
(Mary Evans) *in tch tl lost pl qckly after 13th: p.u bef next* **8/1**

7m 2.4s (17.80) **Going Correction** +0.45s/f (Soft) **6** Ran SP% **109.9**
Speed ratings: **90,89,84,76,**
CSF £26.47 TOTE £2.50: £1.60, £5.00; EX 27.50 Trifecta £99.70.

Owner Mrs Jan Smith **Bred** Hardys Of Kilkeel Ltd **Trained** Icomb, Gloucs

FOCUS
This was run at a steady pace, but one by one the ground found them out. There's a case for rating this a bit higher through the third.

718 WEATHERBYS BLOODSTOCK CONDITIONAL JOCKEYS' H'CAP HURDLE (8 hdls) 2m 167y
5:05 (5:05) (Class 4) (0-115,115) 4-Y-0+ **£3,898** (£1,144; £572; £286)

Form RPR

1 **Monte Wildhorn (IRE)**^{76} [5038] 7-10-13 **108**.................... JakeHodson$^{(6)}$ 116+
(David Bridgwater) *trckd ldrs: led after 3 out: styd on: rdn out* **9/2**^{3}

3-12 **2** *7* **Billy My Boy**^{19} [465] 6-11-1 **104**....................(p) GilesHawkins 106+
(Chris Down) *j.lft: led tl rdn after 3 out: hld in 2nd whn rchd for 2 out: kpt on same pce* **4/1**^{2}

5-45 **3** *6* **Jayo Time (IRE)**^{19} [463] 6-11-5 **111**....................(b^{1}) ChrisWard$^{(3)}$ 107
(Dr Richard Newland) *mid-div: hdwy into cl 3rd briefly 3 out: sn drvn: hld in bef 4th next: wnt 3rd run-in* **9/4**^{1}

50/2 **4** *2½* **Sleeping City (FR)**^{30} [281] 8-10-5 **94**....................(t) ConorShoemark 86
(Victor Dartnall) *mid-div: hdwy 3 out: sn rdn to chse ldng pair: hld whn awkward 2 out: wandering u.p bef last: lost 3rd run-in* **11/2**

32-3 **5** *1¼* **Hawdyerwheesht**^{36} [157] 7-10-13 **110**....................(t) MrShaneQuinlan$^{(8)}$ 103
(David Dennis) *in tch: nt fluent 2nd: bdly hmpd 3rd: rdn after 3 out: sn one pce* **6/1**

35-F **6** *7* **Academy General (IRE)**^{14} [534] 9-11-7 **110**....................(t) MichealNolan 94
(Patricia Shaw) *mid-div: rdn after 3 out: sn btn* **50/1**

1P-3 **7** *3¼* **Party Palace**^{21} [162] 11-11-0 **106**.................... ThomasCheesman$^{(3)}$ 87
(Stuart Howe) *in tch tl wnt wd on bnd u.p after 4th: bhd: sme late prog but nvr any danger after* **14/1**

54U- **8** *1¾* **Tenby Jewel (IRE)**^{218} [2308] 10-10-6 **101**....................(t) PaulJohn$^{(6)}$ 81
(Mark Gillard) *trckd ldrs: rdn after 3 out: sn wknd* **25/1**

46-4 **9** *49* **Luddsdenene (IRE)**^{38} [125] 10-11-4 **115**....................(t) MikeyHamill$^{(8)}$ 51
(Alexandra Dunn) *taken to s early: hld up last: drvn along after 4th: sn wknd: t.o* **33/1**

2-31 **U** **Cruise In Style (IRE)**^{16} [515] 9-10-0 **89**....................(tp) ThomasGarner
(Kevin Bishop) *trcking ldrs whn blnd bdly and uns rdr 3rd* **12/1**

4m 6.9s (1.20) **Going Correction** +0.20s/f (Yiel)
WFA 4 from 5yo+ 17lb **10** Ran SP% **121.7**
Speed ratings (Par 105): **105,101,98,97,97 93,92,91,68,**
CSF £24.10 CT £52.17 TOTE £7.30: £2.10, £1.30, £1.70; EX 30.20 Trifecta £133.50.

Owner Building Bridgies **Bred** Dr Mariann And Richard Klay **Trained** Icomb, Gloucs

FOCUS
A fairly competitive handicap run at a good pace in the conditions and the first five in the betting pulled clear. The winner stepped up on best of Irish form for new yard, the second posted a small pb, with the third close to his mark.
T/Plt: £184.30 to a £1 stake. Pool: £56,182.32 - 222.43 winning tickets T/Qpdt: £17.10 to a £1 stake. Pool: £5,455.40 - 235.10 winning tickets **Tim Mitchell**

719 - 725a (Foreign Racing) - See Raceform Interactive

634
HEXHAM (L-H)
Saturday, June 13

OFFICIAL GOING: Good (7.0)
Wind: Virtually nil Weather: Cloudy, drizzle before 4th

726 MARIE CURIE AMATEUR RIDERS' H'CAP HURDLE (12 hdls) 2m 7f 63y
1:50 (1:50) (Class 4) (0-120,117) 4-Y-0+ **£3,119** (£725; £725; £242)

Form RPR

U0-1 **1** **Minella Hero (IRE)**^{23} [421] 7-10-5 **103**.................... MrJoeWright$^{(7)}$ 116+
(Micky Hammond) *in tch: hdwy to trck ldr 8th: led appr last: rdn clr: easily* **5/2**^{2}

00-U **2** *20* **Danehills Well (IRE)**^{23} [421] 7-10-7 **98**....................(p) HarryBannister 94
(Alison Hamilton) *led: rdn whn hdd appr last: wknd run-in* **9/1**

5-P1 **2** *dht* **Native Optimist (IRE)**^{18} [484] 8-9-7 **91** oh4.................... MrSWColtherd$^{(7)}$ 87
(Sheena Walton) *trckd ldr: rdn after 2 out: outpcd in 3rd whn hit last: one pce* **11/2**^{3}

60-2 **4** *6* **Oscar Prairie (IRE)**^{26} [377] 10-10-12 **110**....................(b) MrTGreatrex$^{(7)}$ 100
(Warren Greatrex) *trckd ldr: rdn after 2 out: sn wknd* **13/2**

60-3 **5** *7* **Parles Pond (IRE)**^{37} [153] 6-10-0 **96** ow3.................... MrZBaker$^{(5)}$ 82
(Martin Todhunter) *hld up: hdwy and in tch 2 out: rdn after 2 out sn wknd* **9/4**^{1}

01-2 **6** *21* **Stow**^{16} [527] 10-11-5 **117**....................(b) MrJamesHughes$^{(7)}$ 86
(Jo Hughes) *hld up: wnt in snatches: a in rr* **9/1**

435 **7** *12* **Senor Alco (FR)**^{24} [394] 9-9-7 **91** oh12....................(p) MrWHRReed$^{(7)}$ 45
(Victor Thompson) *hld up: pushed along after 7th: sn struggling* **50/1**

3P0- 8 *shd* **Court Of Law (IRE)**[54] 5420 7-10-7 **105**.................. MrTGillard[(7)] 59
(Donald McCain) *trckd ldr: rdn after 3 out: sn wknd* **28/1**

5m 54.6s (-14.40) **Going Correction** -0.80s/f (Firm) **8** Ran SP% **113.5**
Speed ratings (Par 105): **93,86,86,83,81 74,70,70**
PL: Native Optimist 2.00, Danehills Well 1.70; EX: MH&DW 13.60, MH&NO 7.90; CSF: MH&DW12.25, MH&NO 8.33; TC: MH&DW&NO 56.16, MH&NO&DW 52.12; TF: MH&DW&NO 59.50, MH&NO&DW 33.90; TOTE £3.60: £1.50.
Owner Ball & Lees **Bred** L G Vambeck **Trained** Middleham, N Yorks
■ Stewards' Enquiry : Harry Bannister Fine: £140, failed to report reason for easing gelding when weighing in

FOCUS
A cool, overcast day. The ground had been watered to provide good going, with fresh ground on the bends. An open-looking amateur handicap run at a moderate pace. A big step up from the winner with Danehills Well on Wetherby form.

727 ANDY CALVERT CELEBRATION NOVICES' HURDLE (8 hdls) 2m 48y
2:25 (2:25) (Class 3) 4-Y-0+ **£5,817** (£1,695; £848)

Form RPR
1 **Penglai Pavilion (USA)**[231] 5-11-0 0.................. AidanColeman 138+
(John Ferguson) *midfield: in tch after 3rd: stdy hdwy to trck ldr gng wl bef 2 out: led appr last: pushed clr* **2/1**[1]

32P- 2 *13* **Mercoeur (FR)**[49] 5535 4-10-11 115..................(b) GavinSheehan 118
(Warren Greatrex) *led at gd pce: rdn whn hdd appr last: sn no ch w wnr* **5/2**[3]

60-3 3 *32* **Another Bygones (IRE)**[20] 452 6-11-0 0.................. JamesReveley 94
(Karen McLintock) *midfield: hit 3rd: rdn bef 2 out: plugged on into poor 3rd last* **14/1**

46 4 *6* **Cherry Princess**[17] 503 5-10-7 0.................. SeanQuinlan 78
(Barbara Butterworth) *midfield: rdn bef 2 out: plugged on: nvr threatened* **66/1**

P/61 5 *hd* **Running Brook (IRE)**[20] 452 8-11-0 119.................. CallumBewley[(5)] 90
(R Mike Smith) *trckd ldr: rdn and outpcd by ldng pair after 2 out: wknd appr last* **11/1**

6 *1 ½* **Jimmy Crackle (IRE)**[7] 4-10-4 0.................. CraigGallagher[(7)] 80
(Brian Ellison) *midfield: reminders after 4th: plugged on fr appr last: nvr threatened* **40/1**

2-14 7 *3* **Venue**[29] 316 5-11-5 127.................. CraigNichol[(3)] 89
(Donald McCain) *trckd ldr: rdn and outpcd bef 3 out: wknd after 2 out* **9/4**[2]

55-0 8 *32* **Touch Of Steel (IRE)**[18] 481 6-10-9 0..................(p) DaleIrving[(5)] 52
(James Ewart) *in tch: rdn and lost pl 5th: sn struggling* **66/1**

9 *½* **Ping (IRE)** 4-10-11 0.................. BrianHarding 48
(Nicky Richards) *a towards rr* **22/1**

0-P 10 *70* **Persian Fashion (IRE)**[6] 656 6-10-4 0..................(t) GrahamWatters[(3)]
(Ian Duncan) *a bhd* **250/1**

11 *45* **Reeflex**[331] 4-10-11 0.................. HenryBrooke
(Jennie Candlish) *a bhd* **100/1**

3m 59.6s (-17.80) **Going Correction** -0.80s/f (Firm)
WFA 4 from 5yo+ 17lb **11** Ran SP% **118.8**
Speed ratings (Par 107): **112,105,89,86,86 85,84,68,67,32 10**
CSF £7.46 TOTE £4.00: £1.40, £1.20, £3.70; EX 10.10 Trifecta £38.80.
Owner Bloomfields **Bred** Darley **Trained** Cowlinge, Suffolk

FOCUS
It was tight at the head of the market in this interesting novice, but they were strung out after a good early pace and the winner came clear in impressive style. He looks a smart recruit.

728 ST MARTINS CARE H'CAP CHASE (12 fncs) 1m 7f 133y
3:00 (3:01) (Class 5) (0-100,100) 5-Y-0+ **£2,599** (£763; £381; £190)

Form RPR
5216 1 **Gin Cobbler**[7] 639 9-11-2 **97**.................. ThomasDowson[(7)] 106+
(Victor Thompson) *trckd ldr: led gng wl appr 3 out: rdn bef last: kpt on* **9/1**

6-62 2 *3 ¾* **Forestside (IRE)**[18] 485 10-10-0 **74** oh5..................(p) LucyAlexander 79
(Barry Murtagh) *hld up: rdn and hdwy after 3 out: wnt 2nd last: styd on* **11/1**

540- 3 *1 ½* **Shine A Diamond (IRE)**[54] 5421 7-10-13 **90**..........(tp) GrahamWatters[(3)] 92
(Lucinda Russell) *trckd ldr: rdn 2 out: one pce* **15/2**[3]

0-03 4 *5* **Saddle Pack (IRE)**[18] 485 12-9-7 **74** oh4.................. JamieHamilton[(7)] 72
(James Walton) *hld up in rr: hit 1st: nt fluent 8th: rdn and hdwy after 2 out: plugged on* **9/1**

440- 5 *3 ½* **Roc De Prince**[25] 1957 6-11-7 **100**..................(p) DaleIrving[(5)] 96
(James Ewart) *midfield: rdn 3 out: one pce and nvr threatened* **11/2**[2]

6465 6 *7* **Amir Pasha (UAE)**[17] 504 10-9-7 **74** oh2..................(v) JamieBargary[(7)] 62
(Micky Hammond) *hld up: rdn after 3 out: nvr threatened* **10/1**

5PUU 7 *1* **Bertielicious**[7] 639 7-9-9 **74** oh18.................. DiarmuidO'Regan[(5)] 63
(Jonathan Haynes) *led: hdd bef 3 out: rdn 2 out: wknd appr last* **50/1**

34-1 8 *1 ½* **Our Boy Ben**[39] 135 6-11-11 **99**..................(b) BrianHughes 87
(Malcolm Jefferson) *in tch: hit 3 out: sn lost pl and btn* **2/1**[1]

3-54 9 *19* **Dynamic Drive (IRE)**[37] 154 8-10-13 **92**..........(t) StephenMulqueen[(5)] 61
(Maurice Barnes) *in tch: blnd 2 out: wknd* **15/2**[3]

00-P U **Where's Malachy (IRE)**[20] 454 7-10-4 **81**.................. CraigNichol[(3)]
(Rose Dobbin) *hld up: mstke 1st: blnd and uns rdr 6th* **16/1**

3m 58.5s (-11.30) **Going Correction** -0.65s/f (Firm) **10** Ran SP% **117.5**
Speed ratings: **102,100,99,96,95 91,91,90,80,**
CSF £101.26 CT £784.91 TOTE £6.20: £1.50, £3.60, £2.50; EX 66.60 Trifecta £374.00 Part won..
Owner V Thompson **Bred** The Elms Stud Company Ltd **Trained** Alnwick, Northumbria

FOCUS
A moderate handicap with the warm favourite failing to run to form. Low-grade form but solid enough at its level.

729 TERESA DUCHETT H'CAP HURDLE (10 hdls) 2m 4f 28y
3:35 (3:36) (Class 3) (0-140,130) 4-Y-0+ **£5,848** (£1,717; £858; £429)

Form RPR
4-33 1 **Master Of The Hall (IRE)**[27] 358 11-10-12 **123**.......... JamieBargary[(7)] 127+
(Micky Hammond) *in tch in 3rd: chsd ldr after 2 out: rdn appr last: led last: drvn and kpt on* **5/2**[1]

0/3P 2 *4* **Silk Hall (UAE)**[17] 505 10-11-12 **130**..................(v[1]) RichardJohnson 130
(J J Lambe, Ire) *led: rdn appr last: hdd last: one pce* **3/1**[3]

225- 3 *5* **Northside Prince (IRE)**[141] 3829 9-10-11 **115**.................. PaulMoloney 113
(Alan Swinbank) *hld up in 4th: hdwy to trck ldr after 2 out: rdn appr last: sn one pce: hld in 3rd whn hit last* **11/4**[2]

122- 4 *42* **Clues And Arrows (IRE)**[329] 1006 7-11-7 **125**.................. BrianHughes 95
(John Wade) *trckd ldr in 2nd: rdn and lost pl qckly after 2 out: eased* **5/2**[1]

5m 3.1s (-9.40) **Going Correction** -0.80s/f (Firm) **4** Ran SP% **108.8**
Speed ratings (Par 107): **86,84,82,65**
CSF £9.87 TOTE £3.10; EX 8.50 Trifecta £16.60.
Owner Masters Of The Hall **Bred** Sweetmans Bloodstock **Trained** Middleham, N Yorks

FOCUS
A tight handicap, as reflected in the betting, and approaching the final climb they were all vying for position off a steady pace. The winner is rated in line with the best of his Market Rasen hurdle runs.

730 HADRIAN HEALTHCARE NOVICES' HURDLE (12 hdls) 2m 7f 63y
4:10 (4:10) (Class 3) 4-Y-0+ **£5,523** (£1,621; £810; £405)

Form RPR
3 1 **Classic Palace (IRE)**[17] 503 6-10-7 0.................. BrianHughes 104+
(J J Lambe, Ire) *trckd ldr: led jst bef 2 out: sn rdn clr: 12 l up last: idled run-in* **8/1**[3]

2 *1 ½* **Lowanbehold (IRE)**[21] 8-10-7 0.................. JamieHamilton[(7)] 107
(Sandy Forster) *hld up: in tch 1/2-way: rdn and outpcd in 4th after 3 out: styd on fr appr last* **16/1**

44-1 3 *22* **Heart O Annandale (IRE)**[39] 136 8-11-0 98......(t) StephenMulqueen[(5)] 95
(Maurice Barnes) *led: hdd jst bef 2 out: hit 2 out: sn rdn: wknd appr last* **9/1**

04-2 4 *3* **Luccombe Down**[37] 155 5-11-0 107.................. WayneHutchinson 85
(Donald McCain) *j. none too fluently: in tch: rdn after 3 out: wknd appr last* **2/1**[2]

546- F **Uncle Tone (IRE)**[91] 4769 6-11-0 120.................. MichealNolan
(Tim Vaughan) *hld up: fell 3rd* **11/10**[1]

4-1P P **Allycat**[11] 590 5-10-9 0.................. DiarmuidO'Regan[(5)]
(Chris Grant) *in tch: lost pl after 8th: hit 9th: sn bhd: p.u bef last* **25/1**

U P **My Lady West (IRE)**[7] 635 6-10-0 0.................. ThomasDowson[(7)]
(Victor Thompson) *hld up in tch: wknd after 9th: p.u bef last* **80/1**

6m 2.4s (-6.60) **Going Correction** -0.80s/f (Firm) **7** Ran SP% **113.0**
Speed ratings (Par 107): **79,78,70,69,**
CSF £104.74 TOTE £6.50: £2.70, £4.20; EX 68.40 Trifecta £270.20.
Owner James Callow **Bred** Mrs Winefride Crean-Murphy **Trained** Dungannon, Co Tyrone

FOCUS
With market leader Uncle Tone an early faller, this steadily-run contest did not take that much winning. The winner built on her Cartmel form.

731 MARIE CURIE H'CAP CHASE (15 fncs) 2m 4f 15y
4:45 (4:45) (Class 5) (0-100,100) 5-Y-0+ **£2,599** (£763; £381; £190)

Form RPR
60-U 1 **Cool Star (IRE)**[42] 78 9-9-11 **74**..................(t) JonathanEngland[(3)] 88+
(Maurice Barnes) *mde all: rdn appr last: styd on* **7/1**[3]

45-2 2 *8* **Mister Wall Street (FR)**[7] 639 10-11-0 **91**..................(tp) TonyKelly[(3)] 97
(Rebecca Menzies) *prom: trckd wnr after 2 out: rdn appr last: sn one pce and hld in 2nd* **11/4**[1]

12-4 3 *3 ¼* **Shady Sadie (IRE)**[16] 519 8-10-6 **83**..................(t) HarryChalloner[(3)] 86
(Rose Dobbin) *midfield: hdwy to trck ldrs 12th: rdn after 3 out: plugged on* **7/1**[3]

-504 4 *10* **Silent Snow (IRE)**[7] 639 10-10-0 **74** oh3..................(p) PeterBuchanan 68
(W T Reed) *prom: rdn 3 out: grad wknd after 2 out* **16/1**

4-53 5 *1* **Indalo Return (IRE)**[18] 486 9-10-3 **87**.......... HugoThompsonBrown[(10)] 84+
(Philip Kirby) *hld up: hit 2nd: mstke 10th: rdn 4 out: nvr threatened* **4/1**[2]

06-3 6 *26* **King's Chorister**[17] 504 9-10-9 **83**..................(t) LucyAlexander 53
(Barry Murtagh) *hld up: a towards rr* **12/1**

02-0 7 *12* **Roxyfet (FR)**[18] 485 5-11-9 **100**..................(b) CraigNichol[(3)] 59
(Micky Hammond) *trckd ldrs: rdn after 3 out: sn wknd* **10/1**

2-5U 8 *5* **Coolanure (IRE)**[7] 639 6-9-13 **80**..................(p) RossChapman[(7)] 34
(Kenny Johnson) *trckd ldrs: rdn appr 3 out: sn wknd* **18/1**

P5-6 P **My Idea**[39] 134 9-11-5 **98**..................(t) StephenMulqueen[(5)]
(Maurice Barnes) *hld up: p.u after 4th* **8/1**

0-0P P **Jimmie Brown (USA)**[16] 519 7-9-7 **74** oh10..........(t) JamieBargary[(7)]
(Andrew Crook) *hld up: lost tch after 10th: p.u bef 3 out* **28/1**

5m 8.0s (-5.50) **Going Correction** -0.65s/f (Firm) **10** Ran SP% **114.2**
Speed ratings: **85,81,80,76,76 65,60,58,,**
CSF £27.02 CT £140.33 TOTE £6.70: £1.70, £1.10, £1.90; EX 30.60 Trifecta £405.80.
Owner D Carr & M Carlyle **Bred** C Amerian **Trained** Farlam, Cumbria

FOCUS
The first and second from this race last year lined up again, but they were bettered by an unconsidered improver. The winner was well in on the best of his 2014 form and is rated back to that sort of level.

732 TERESA DUCHETT STANDARD OPEN NATIONAL HUNT FLAT RACE 2m 48y
5:20 (5:21) (Class 6) 4-6-Y-0 **£1,779** (£518; £259)

Form RPR
-1 1 **Micklegate Run**[38] 144 4-11-7 0.................. PaulMoloney 110+
(Alan Swinbank) *trckd ldng pair: rdn and briefly outpcd over 2f out: led appr fnl f: styd on* **9/4**[1]

422- 2 *1 ¾* **Australasia (IRE)**[54] 5425 5-11-3 0..................(p) JamesReveley 105
(Karen McLintock) *trckd ldng pair: rdn 4f out: led over 2f out: hdd appr fnl f: one pce* **9/4**[1]

0/ 3 *5* **Mullinavat (IRE)**[23] 428 6-11-3 0.................. AidanColeman 100
(Jennie Candlish) *led narrowly: rdn whn hdd over 2f out: one pce* **10/1**

4-3 4 *½* **Zandino (FR)**[27] 366 4-11-0 0..................(p) GavinSheehan 96
(Warren Greatrex) *w ldr: rdn over 2f out: one pce* **3/1**[2]

5 *12* **King Of Fashion (IRE)** 5-11-0 0.................. GrahamWatters[(3)] 87
(Ian Duncan) *hld up in tch: rdn over 3f out: wknd 2f out* **40/1**

5/0- 6 *74* **Spinning Scooter**[260] 1628 5-10-12 0..................(t) StephenMulqueen[(5)] 13
(Maurice Barnes) *hld up in tch: rdn 6f out: sn wknd: t.o* **50/1**

7 *1 ¾* **Sheriff's Star (IRE)** 4-11-0 0.................. BrianHughes 8
(J J Lambe, Ire) *hld up: sn pushed along: wknd over 4f out: t.o* **7/1**[3]

4m 2.0s (-10.70) **Going Correction** -0.80s/f (Firm) **7** Ran SP% **112.5**
Speed ratings: **94,93,90,90,84 47,46**
CSF £7.23 TOTE £3.00: £1.70, £1.70; EX 6.10 Trifecta £37.20.
Owner Andrew Sparks **Bred** D Cantillon And E Cantillon **Trained** Melsonby, N Yorks

FOCUS
An open-looking contest. The pace was fair and the first four home, all with previous bumper form, pulled clear. The second and fourth set the level.

T/Plt: £670.60 to a £1 stake. Pool: £52,136.66 - 56.75 winning tickets T/Qpdt: £77.70 to a £1 stake. Pool: £4,087.62 - 38.90 winning tickets **Andrew Sheret**

733 - 739a (Foreign Racing) - See Raceform Interactive

236 LES LANDES
Saturday, June 13

OFFICIAL GOING: Good

740a MIDSUMMER H'CAP HURDLE 2m 2f
6:30 (6:30) 4-Y-O+ **£1,460** (£525; £315)

RPR
1 **Agapanthus (GER)**[31] [284] 10-11-7 ....(b) MarkQuinlan 106
(Neil Mulholland) **21/20**[1]
2 *1* **The Kvilleken**[16] [524] 7-10-2 ....(p) MrFTett 86
(Martin Keighley) **11/4**[3]
3 *12* **Pomander (IRE)**[20] [236] 12-10-7 .... MrRHodson 79
(J Moon, Jersey) **16/1**
4 *dist* **Dalmo**[20] [236] 6-11-10 ....(b) ThomasGarner
(K Kukk, Jersey) **14/1**
F **Rossetti**[20] 7-11-6 .... MattieBatchelor
(Mrs A Malzard, Jersey) **6/5**[2]

Owner Stuart K Brown **Bred** Gestut Schlenderhan **Trained** Limpley Stoke, Wilts

676 SOUTHWELL (L-H)
Monday, June 15

OFFICIAL GOING: Good changing to good to soft after race 1 (2.30)
Wind: light 1/2 against Weather: fine

741 SOUTHWELL LADIES DAY DISCOUNTED TICKETS NOVICES' H'CAP CHASE (16 fncs 3 omitted) 2m 7f 209y
2:30 (2:30) (Class 4) (0-105,102) 5-Y-O+ **£3,898** (£1,144; £572; £286)

Form RPR
6P/2 1 **Cardinal Rose**[26] [403] 8-11-1 **91** .... KielanWoods 104+
(Mark Wall) *j.rt: led to 3rd: w ldr: led 5th: drvn clr between last 2* **5/4**[1]
-353 2 *10* **Breezy Kin (IRE)**[12] [600] 7-10-7 **90** .... MikeyHamill(7) 94
(Sean Curran) *w ldr: led 3rd: hdd 5th: kpt on same pce fr 2 out* **7/2**[2]
-64P 3 *48* **Next Exit (IRE)**[15] [567] 10-9-9 **76** oh7 ....(t) JoeCornwall(5) 44
(John Cornwall) *chsd ldrs: lost pl after 10th: modest 3rd 14th: one pce* **40/1**
2-P3 4 *15* **Dr Dreamy (IRE)**[30] [333] 8-10-0 **76** oh2 ....(t) TrevorWhelan 23
(Claire Dyson) *mstke 2nd: chsd ldrs next: outpcd 13th: poor 4th next: sn t.o* **8/1**
5 *13* **Icthec (IRE)**[78] 8-11-5 **95** ....(t) JamesDavies 31
(Jennifer Mason) *j.rt: chsd ldrs: outpcd and lost pl 13th: sn bhd: t.o bef 2 out* **40/1**
20-0 6 *3 ¾* **Freddy Fox (IRE)**[20] [493] 5-10-12 **95** ....(t) MrMJPKendrick(7) 27
(Ben Case) *chsd ldrs: reminders 4th and 10th: outpcd and lost pl 13th: sn bhd: t.o bef 2 out* **7/1**
1-44 P **Milly Malone (IRE)**[23] [443] 9-11-12 **102** ....(t) AidanColeman
(Adrian Wintle) *in rr: drvn and lost pl 12th: sn bhd: p.u bef 14th* **6/1**[3]

6m 30.2s (7.20) **Going Correction** +0.425s/f (Soft) **7 Ran SP% 109.4**
Speed ratings: **105,101,85,80,76 75,**
CSF £5.78 TOTE £2.40: £1.40, £2.00; EX 7.40 Trifecta £110.20.
Owner M J Wall **Bred** Coln Valley Stud **Trained** Cheltenham, Gloucs

FOCUS
Fences were inside the line raced on the 9th June. Both bends were moved to provide fresh ground. Middle fence omitted in all chases. A moderate chase that didn't take a great deal of winning, with little getting involved. The winner looked to step up from his Warwick run.

742 SEE PEPPA PIG FAMILY FUN DAY H'CAP CHASE (11 fncs 2 omitted) 1m 7f 153y
3:00 (3:00) (Class 4) (0-120,117) 5-Y-O+ **£3,898** (£1,144; £572; £286)

Form RPR
5-43 1 **Furrows**[30] [338] 10-11-8 **113** .... LeightonAspell 124+
(Oliver Sherwood) *chsd ldng pair: 2nd 6th: led sn after 9th: clr next: 15 l ahd last: eased* **13/8**[1]
4PP- 2 *12* **Jack The Gent (IRE)**[80] [5018] 11-10-13 **104** .... HenryBrooke 99+
(George Moore) *led: hit 8th: hdd and reminders sn after next: one pce appr 2 out* **11/4**[2]
05-6 3 *½* **Shrapnel (IRE)**[29] [357] 9-11-12 **117** .... AidanColeman 109
(Brian Ellison) *chsd ldrs: reminders 3rd and 6th: outpcd and lost pl 8th: poor 4th whn hit 2 out: 3rd last* **9/2**
1-2F 4 *13* **Kayfton Pete**[10] [623] 9-11-4 **109** .... AdamPogson 97
(Charles Pogson) *in last: pushed along 4th: modest 3rd 7th: reminders next: sn lost pl: wknd last: sn eased* **3/1**[3]

4m 6.4s (4.40) **Going Correction** +0.425s/f (Soft) **4 Ran SP% 107.9**
Speed ratings: **106,100,99,93**
CSF £6.34 TOTE £2.50; EX 7.70 Trifecta £18.70.
Owner Furrows Ltd **Bred** John Coward & Mrs Rachael Downey **Trained** Upper Lambourn, Berks

FOCUS
This didn't take much winning and the well-handicapped winner is rated back to his best.

743 COLLABRO LIVE ON FAMILY FUN DAY H'CAP CHASE (16 fncs 3 omitted) 2m 7f 209y
3:30 (3:30) (Class 5) (0-100,98) 5-Y-O+ **£2,599** (£763; £381; £190)

Form RPR
0/0- 1 **Call Me Mulligan (IRE)**[15] 11-10-8 **87** .... MrABartlett(7) 93
(Patrick Holmes) *w ldr: led 8th: jnd between last 2: hit last: fnd ex in clsng stages* **14/1**
0/-6 2 *1 ¾* **Larkhall**[18] [521] 8-10-0 **72** oh10 .... BrianHughes 75
(Mike Sowersby) *hld up: trckd ldrs 9th: cl 2nd gng wl appr 2 out: rdn appr last: no ex last 50yds* **8/1**
44-2 3 *9* **Cara Court (IRE)**[41] [133] 9-10-5 **77** ....(p) DougieCostello 73
(Joanne Foster) *j.rt: chsd ldng pair: stdd 3rd: chsng ldrs 6th: drvn 14th: sn wl outpcd* **3/1**[2]
06-3 4 *10* **No Principles**[15] [567] 12-11-12 **98** ....(b) MarkGrant 86
(Julian Smith) *chsd ldrs 6th: 2nd 10th: drvn 14th: lost pl appr next* **11/2**[3]
P-02 5 *72* **Noble Witness (IRE)**[30] [340] 12-11-9 **95** ....(p) AdamPogson 16
(Charles Pogson) *led: hdd 8th: reminders and lost pl 10th: bhd: next: t.o 14th: eventually completed* **11/4**[1]
62-5 P **Roseneath (IRE)**[45] [66] 11-11-4 **90** ....(bt) KielanWoods
(Alex Hales) *hld up: chsd ldrs 8th: reminder next: lost pl 14th: wl hld whn j.rt next: poor 5th whn p.u bef last* **3/1**[2]

6m 30.6s (7.60) **Going Correction** +0.425s/f (Soft) **6 Ran SP% 109.8**
Speed ratings: **104,103,100,97,73**
CSF £101.31 TOTE £16.00: £6.70, £3.50; EX 62.90 Trifecta £353.80.
Owner N Mechie **Bred** Chris McDonnell **Trained** Middleham, N Yorks

FOCUS
The front pair came clear in what was quite a lowly handicap, with a couple of the market leaders disappointing. The winner was recording his best figure since 2013.

744 18 TO 30 GOLF MEMBERSHIP £210 MARES' H'CAP HURDLE (9 hdls) 1m 7f 153y
4:00 (4:00) (Class 4) (0-120,117) 4-Y-O+ **£3,249** (£954; £477; £238)

Form RPR
04-3 1 **Miss Sassypants**[28] [380] 6-11-4 **106** .... RyanMahon 111
(Seamus Mullins) *trckd ldrs 4th: led narrowly 2 out: drvn rt out* **10/1**
/3-5 2 *1 ½* **Ginger Fizz**[31] [314] 8-11-3 **105** ....(t) KielanWoods 110
(Ben Case) *trckd ldrs 4th: led briefly appr 2 out: styd on same pce run-in* **5/1**
3-31 3 *½* **Shady Lane**[4] [699] 8-11-5 **107** ....(t) HarrySkelton 111
(Dan Skelton) *chsd ldr: led after 2nd: j.rt 5th and 7th: hdd and reminders appr 2 out: swtchd rt and rallied between last 2: kpt on wl run-in* **15/8**[1]
14-3 4 *11* **Ogaritmo**[22] [465] 6-11-0 **102** ....(t) TrevorWhelan 96
(Alex Hales) *chsd ldrs 4th: drvn next: reminders and lost pl 7th: poor 4th between last 2* **9/2**[3]
F4-1 5 *25* **Bella (FR)**[26] [405] 4-11-12 **117** ....(t[1]) TomScudamore 97
(David Pipe) *led tl after 2nd: chsd ldr: pushed along 6th: reminders and lost pl next: sn bhd: eased between last 2: t.o* **5/2**[2]

4m 1.9s (4.90) **Going Correction** +0.475s/f (Soft) **5 Ran SP% 107.3**
Speed ratings (Par 105): **106,105,105,99,87**
CSF £50.95 TOTE £8.40: £3.00, £1.70; EX 30.70 Trifecta £104.40.
Owner J T Brown **Bred** J T Brown And Miss Kirsten Rausing **Trained** Wilsford-Cum-Lake, Wilts

FOCUS
Quite a competitive little heat and it went to the outsider of the field. The race has been rated around the balance of the first three.

745 SOUTHWELL RACING AND GOLF PACKAGE £20 MAIDEN HURDLE (9 hdls) 1m 7f 153y
4:30 (4:30) (Class 5) 4-Y-O+ **£2,599** (£763; £381; £190)

Form RPR
2-40 1 **Miss Fortywinks**[22] [462] 6-10-7 100 .... RyanMahon 111
(Seamus Mullins) *chsd ldr: led narrowly appr 2 out: game and fnd ex nr fin* **10/1**[3]
222- 2 *nk* **Jalingo (IRE)**[128] [4087] 4-10-11 123 .... AidanColeman 115
(John Ferguson) *led: hdd appr 2 out: upsides last: no ex cl home* **4/7**[1]
3-32 3 *7* **Destiny's Gold (IRE)**[33] [279] 5-11-0 120 .... AndrewTinkler 114
(George Baker) *trckd ldrs 3rd: handy 3rd sn after 3 out: one pce appr next* **9/4**[2]
4 *3* **Irondale Express**[33] 4-10-4 0 ....(p) PaulMoloney 98
(Des Donovan) *chsd ldrs 3rd: pushed along 3 out: one pce* **40/1**
/46- 5 *22* **Hold The Fort (IRE)**[258] [1667] 8-11-0 0 ....(t) AlainCawley 90
(Johnny Farrelly) *hld up in rr: sme hdwy 3 out: poor 5th whn blnd 2 out: hit last: sn eased* **66/1**
4-0 6 *12* **Dover The Moon (IRE)**[29] [360] 4-10-11 0 .... JamesDavies 71
(Tom Gretton) *trckd ldrs: outpcd 6th: lost pl bef 2 out: sn bhd* **100/1**
U 7 *½* **Tundridge**[42] [105] 6-11-0 0 ....(p) NicodeBoinville 74
(John Spearing) *trckd ldrs 2nd: nt fluent 4th: pushed along next: drvn and lost pl 3 out: sn bhd* **25/1**

4m 6.1s (9.10) **Going Correction** +0.475s/f (Soft)
WFA 4 from 5yo+ 17lb **7 Ran SP% 112.3**
Speed ratings (Par 103): **96,95,92,90,79 73,73**
CSF £16.69 TOTE £6.90: £2.70, £1.60; EX 23.80 Trifecta £31.50.
Owner J T Brown **Bred** J T Brown **Trained** Wilsford-Cum-Lake, Wilts

FOCUS
A maiden hurdle that looked to concern only two, but there was a bit of a turn-up. This was a big step up from the winner.

746 FULL GOLF CLUB MEMBERSHIP FOR £560 H'CAP HURDLE (13 hdls) 2m 7f 209y
5:00 (5:00) (Class 4) (0-115,113) 4-Y-O+ **£3,249** (£954; £477; £238)

Form RPR
10-2 1 **New Horizons (IRE)**[33] [283] 5-11-12 **113** .... JackQuinlan 114+
(Caroline Fryer) *w ldr: led sn after 3 out: hdd narrowly between last 2: led sn after last: jst hld on* **11/2**
00-5 2 *nk* **Tarvini (IRE)**[29] [363] 10-10-11 **108** ....(p) JackSavage(10) 108
(Jonjo O'Neill) *chsd ldrs: pushed along 4th: 3rd whn hit 9th: lost pl bef 3 out: styd on fr 2 out: 4th last: fin wl to take cl 2nd fnl strides* **15/2**
42-2 3 *hd* **Weybridge Light**[15] [571] 10-10-13 **100** ....(b) PaddyBrennan 101
(David Thompson) *chsd ldrs: pushed along 9th: drvn and upsides 2 out: led narrowly between last 2: awkward jump last: sn hdd: no ex in clsng stages* **5/1**[3]
35-F 4 *18* **Eastern Calm**[42] [108] 6-11-1 **102** ....(b[1]) LeightonAspell 89
(Oliver Sherwood) *trckd ldrs: t.k.h: wknd between last 2: hit last* **9/2**[2]
FP-4 5 *nk* **Bayley's Dream**[28] [380] 6-11-5 **106** .... LiamTreadwell 91
(Paul Webber) *led: hit 3 out: sn hdd: wknd appr 2 out: lft poor 5th last* **8/1**
20-P 6 *21* **Powderonthebonnet (IRE)**[9] [643] 7-10-13 **100** .... AlainCawley 64
(Richard Phillips) *hld up in rr: effrt 10th: sn drvn and wknd: t.o bef 2 out* **7/1**
-113 P **Billy Congo (IRE)**[22] [445] 8-11-12 **113** ....(t) MichealNolan
(Adrian Wintle) *in last: drvn 9th: nvr on terms: bhd 3 out: t.o whn p.u bef next* **4/1**[1]
20-3 F **Bentons Lad**[25] [419] 4-11-4 **110** ....(t) HenryBrooke 94
(George Moore) *hld up in rr: sme hdwy 10th: chsng ldrs in 4th whn mstke 2 out: wknd and modest 5th whn fell heavily last* **12/1**

6m 30.6s (15.60) **Going Correction** +0.475s/f (Soft)
WFA 4 from 5yo+ 19lb **8 Ran SP% 113.3**
Speed ratings (Par 105): **93,92,92,86,86 79, ,**
CSF £44.50 CT £217.67 TOTE £5.90: £1.80, £4.90, £1.80; EX 40.10 Trifecta £233.00.
Owner Miss Caroline Fryer **Bred** Mrs Sheila O'Shea **Trained** Wymondham, Norfolk

FOCUS
Run at a fair pace, several had their chance in what was just a modest handicap. The winner ran to his mark in a slow-motion finish.

747 SOUTHWELL CONDITIONAL JOCKEYS' H'CAP HURDLE (11 hdls) 2m 4f 62y
5:30 (5:30) (Class 4) (0-110,110) 4-Y-0+ **£3,249** (£954; £477; £238)

Form RPR
0/P- **1** **Ebazan (USA)**[80] 5019 6-11-3 **101** NicodeBoinville 110+
(Brian Ellison) *chsd ldrs: drvn 3 out: 6th and outpcd next: styd on to ld bef last: drvn out* **11/4**[2]
66-1 **2** *3 ¼* **Fire Tower**[30] 337 7-10-13 **103**....................(t) DanielHiskett(6) 109+
(Richard Phillips) *hld up in rr: hdwy on outside to trck ldrs 8th: 2nd between last 2: kpt on same pce run-in* **8/1**[3]
01P- **3** *6* **Vivacissimo (IRE)**[106] 4508 8-11-1 **102**.................... BridgetAndrews(3) 103+
(Dan Skelton) *hld up towards rr: t.k.h: hdwy to trck ldrs 4th: cl 3rd appr last: one pce* **6/4**[1]
006- **4** *1 ½* **Stormbay Bomber (IRE)**[80] 5019 6-10-8 **92**.................... AdamNicol 91
(George Moore) *w ldrs: led 7th: hdd bef last: one pce* **20/1**
F4-0 **5** *1 ¾* **Church Field (IRE)**[39] 177 7-11-4 **110**....................(p) PatrickCowley(8) 107
(Jonjo O'Neill) *chsd ldrs: 2nd appr 2 out: one pce between last 2* **11/1**
65-4 **6** *5* **King's Realm (IRE)**[18] 520 8-11-5 **103**.................... JonathanEngland 95
(Tina Jackson) *hld up in rr: hdwy 4th: drvn 3 out: wknd 2 out* **16/1**
12-4 **7** *1 ½* **Exemplary**[33] 283 8-11-10 **108**....................(t) KieronEdgar 98
(Johnny Farrelly) *hld up in rr: hdwy after 8th: drvn and wknd 2 out* **10/1**
5-10 **8** *3 ¾* **Queen Spud**[31] 314 6-11-12 **110**....................(p) SeanBowen 97
(Henry Daly) *led: hdd 7th: lost pl appr 2 out: hung rt run-in* **10/1**
-4P5 **9** *23* **The Jugopolist (IRE)**[6] 678 8-10-7 **94**.................... JoeCornwall(3) 58
(John Cornwall) *chsd ldrs: drvn 7th: lost pl next: bhd 3 out: eased run-in* **150/1**

5m 25.2s (12.20) **Going Correction** +0.475s/f (Soft) **9** Ran SP% **115.6**
Speed ratings (Par 105): **94,92,90,89,89 87,86,84,75**
CSF £25.21 CT £43.69 TOTE £4.30: £1.60, £1.90, £1.30; EX 27.20 Trifecta £64.50.
Owner Mrs Claire Ellison **Bred** His Highness The Aga Khan Studs Sc **Trained** Norton, N Yorks

FOCUS
Reasonable form for the level and the winner was subject of a gamble. The right horses came to the fore.
T/Plt: £2,650.40 to a £1 stake. Pool of £59470.86 - 16.38 winning tickets. T/Qpdt: £307.10 to a £1 stake. Pool of £4732.30 - 11.40 winning tickets. **Walter Glynn**

552 STRATFORD (L-H)
Tuesday, June 16

OFFICIAL GOING: Chase course- good; hurdle course- good changing to good (good to firm places) after race 1 (2.10)
Wind: almost nil Weather: very hot and sunny; 22 degrees

748 ALVESTON MARES' NOVICES' HURDLE (9 hdls) 2m 2f 148y
2:10 (2:10) (Class 4) 4-Y-0+ **£3,249** (£954; £477; £238)

Form RPR
4-43 **1** **Magic Magnolia (IRE)**[11] 621 4-10-3 107....................(t) BridgetAndrews(5) 88+
(Dan Skelton) *awkward at s: mstke 2nd: hit 4th: disp 2nd pl: hrd drvn and outpcd by ldr fr 2 out: stl 5 l down and hrd rdn last: wore down rival cl home* **2/1**[2]
21-1 **2** *½* **Kayf Willow**[26] 415 6-11-5 0.................... RichardJohnson 97+
(Philip Hobbs) *led: set slow pce tl 1/2-way and nt a fluent: drew 5 l clr and looked to be gng best fr 2 out: rdn bef last: flagged flat and ct nr fin* **4/6**[1]
00-P **3** *16* **Spurned Girl**[43] 106 5-10-9 69....................(t[1]) BenPoste(3) 73
(Robin Dickin) *t.k.h in last: rdn and tried to cl bef 3 out: nvr trbld ldng pair but tk poor 3rd at last* **150/1**
01 **4** *8* **Potters Midnight**[27] 400 5-10-12 0.................... LeightonAspell 70
(Lucy Wadham) *chsd ldrs: blnd 7th: 5 l 3rd bef next: sn rdn: outpcd by ldng pair fr 2 out and losing tired 3rd whn slow at last* **17/2**[3]
5/0- **5** *47* **Choral Bee**[154] 3659 6-10-12 83.................... TomO'Brien 18
(Alan Jessop) *prom tl rdn bef 6th: t.o fr 2 out* **50/1**
0P- **6** *5* **Rainbow Lollipop**[99] 4682 4-10-8 0....................(t) JamesDavies 9
(Tom Gretton) *small: in rr but in tch tl outpcd and slow next: sn t.o after 2 out* **125/1**

4m 35.2s (3.70) **Going Correction** -0.30s/f (Good)
WFA 4 from 5yo+ 17lb **6** Ran SP% **107.3**
Speed ratings (Par 105): **80,79,73,69,49 47**
CSF £3.48 TOTE £2.80: £1.20, £1.10; EX 4.10 Trifecta £88.80.
Owner Dan Skelton **Bred** Storeway Ltd **Trained** Alcester, Warwicks

FOCUS
Split bends on fresh ground. Race 1 increased by 54yds, races 2, 4 & 6 by 42yds, race 3 by 60yds, race 5 by 39yds. Richard Johnson said after the opener that the ground was "heading towards good to firm." A modest event for mares run at a slow initial gallop.

749 TEMPLE GRAFTON NOVICES' HURDLE (8 hdls) 2m 70y
2:45 (2:46) (Class 4) 4-Y-0+ **£3,249** (£954; £477; £238)

Form RPR
1 **Miner's Lamp (IRE)**[234] 4-10-9 0.................... AidanColeman 113+
(John Ferguson) *tall powerful: racd keenly and pressed ldr gng wl: mstke 5th: rdn to ld bef last: wl in command flat* **13/8**[2]
5-21 **2** *3 ¼* **Mighty Missile (IRE)**[17] 554 4-11-2 120....................(tp) GavinSheehan 114
(Warren Greatrex) *led: drvn after 2 out: hdd bef last: kpt on same pce* **5/4**[1]
1-14 **3** *4* **Lochalsh (IRE)**[17] 556 4-11-4 122.................... BridgetAndrews(5) 116
(Dan Skelton) *chsd ldng pair and sn clr of rest: 2 l 3rd bef 3 out: rdn and wl hld fr next but did keep on steadily after* **4/1**[3]
04- **4** *40* **Crashing Thew Life**[15] 1457 5-10-12 0.................... MarcGoldstein 69
(Sheena West) *sn wl off pce: blnd 3rd: struggling next: t.o 3 out* **40/1**
P **5** *shd* **Nyetimber (USA)**[13] 595 9-10-12 0.................... MarkGrant 69
(Sean Curran) *sweating profusely: t.k.h in detached 4th pl: 20 l 4th at 4th: t.o 3 out* **200/1**
6 *31* **Goonjim (IRE)**[31] 4-10-9 0.................... AdamWedge 38
(Alexandra Dunn) *j. v awkwardly and wl off pce in last pair: blnd 3rd: struggling after: t.o 3 out* **25/1**
0/0- **7** *2 ¾* **Padova**[166] 3449 9-10-12 0.................... TommyPhelan 39
(Dr Jeremy Naylor) *small: sweating and on his toes: j. awkwardly: 20 l 5th at 2nd: t.o 3 out* **200/1**

3m 47.4s (-8.60) **Going Correction** -0.30s/f (Good) **7** Ran SP% **109.8**
Speed ratings (Par 105): **109,107,105,85,85 69,68**
CSF £3.81 TOTE £3.10: £1.60, £1.10; EX 5.30 Trifecta £6.80.
Owner Bloomfields **Bred** Mrs C L Weld **Trained** Cowlinge, Suffolk

FOCUS
Actual race distance 2m112yds. The ground was officially good and faster in places by now. The pace was brisk in this ordinary novice event and the first three were quickly clear. The winner can rate higher.

750 JENKINSONS CATERERS H'CAP CHASE (17 fncs) 2m 6f 125y
3:20 (3:20) (Class 4) (0-120,120) 5-Y-0+ **£4,548** (£1,335; £667; £333)

Form RPR
06-1 **1** **Sail And Return**[14] 589 11-11-6 **117**....................(t) ConorShoemark(3) 122+
(Phil Middleton) *settled in midfield: hmpd bnd bef 12th: rdn to go 2 l 3rd whn blnd 2 out: sn 6 l fr ldr in 3rd and no imp tl last: styd on gamely flat and drvn ahd fnl 50yds* **6/1**
615- **2** *¾* **Balinroab (IRE)**[290] 1393 8-11-1 **109**.................... NicodeBoinville 112
(Mark Bradstock) *pressed ldr: drvn to chal and lft in front last: kpt on steadily tl collared cl home* **4/1**[1]
F-12 **3** *2* **Owen Glendower (IRE)**[31] 331 10-11-2 **117**.................... CiaranGethings(7) 120+
(Sophie Leech) *settled in midfield: effrt and blnd 3 out: rdn and tried to rally and awkward next: 7 l 4th and outpcd home turn: kpt on wl after last to snatch 3rd* **9/2**[2]
03-5 **4** *hd* **Lord Grantham (IRE)**[37] 215 8-11-12 **120**.................... JakeGreenall 122+
(Henry Daly) *racd keenly in 3rd pl: led 3 out: wnt 2 l clr home turn: rdn and jnd whn mstke last: nt rcvr: lost 3rd nr fin* **11/2**[3]
34-3 **5** *18* **Ray Diamond**[40] 163 10-10-8 **109**.................... DavidNoonan(7) 94
(Jackie Du Plessis) *prom: nt fluent 4th: sn dropped to rr: rdn and nt travelling 7th: wl bhd 14th* **20/1**
43P- **6** *20* **According To Sarah (IRE)**[208] 2622 7-11-0 **108**.......... RichardJohnson 74
(Philip Hobbs) *towards rr: pushed along 11th: sn struggling: t.o* **10/1**
53 **7** *1 ½* **Thepartysover**[23] 451 10-11-1 **109**....................(t) TomO'Brien 73
(Paul Henderson) *last pair: nt travelling fr 8th: t.o whn mstke 3 out* **20/1**
22/4 **P** **Cruchain (IRE)**[22] 470 12-11-4 **112**....................(p) RobertDunne
(Dai Burchell) *tended to jump slowly: chsd ldrs: slow 14th and sn rdn and struggling: p.u after 2 out* **17/2**
0-36 **F** **Regal D'Estruval (FR)**[20] 514 10-10-3 **97**.................... CharliePoste 92
(Matt Sheppard) *led: hdd 3 out: rdn and sn lost pl: plodding on in 5th whn fell last: fatally injured* **12/1**
42P- **U** **Silent Knight (IRE)**[230] 2131 6-11-8 **116**.................... GavinSheehan
(Warren Greatrex) *last and rdn at 5th: blnd v bdly and uns rdr next* **9/1**

5m 30.8s (-8.40) **Going Correction** -0.20s/f (Good) **10** Ran SP% **114.7**
Speed ratings: **106,105,105,104,98 91,91, , ,**
CSF £30.63 CT £116.49 TOTE £6.00: £1.50, £2.40, £2.10; EX 51.00 Trifecta £229.90.
Owner P W Middleton **Bred** Andrew And Mrs S R B Davis **Trained** Dorton, Bucks

FOCUS
Actual race distance 2m6f185yds. A fair, competitive handicap chase with a dramatic finish. The first four all made errors over the last few fences.

751 FSW GROUP 50TH GOLDEN ANNIVERSARY H'CAP HURDLE (8 hdls) 2m 70y
3:55 (3:55) (Class 4) (0-120,119) 4-Y-0+ **£4,548** (£1,335; £667; £333)

Form RPR
061- **1** **Kapstadt (FR)**[83] 4987 5-10-9 **102**.................... WillKennedy 113+
(Ian Williams) *in rr and rdn after 2nd: smooth prog 3 out: led over 2f out (wl bef last): sn asserted and styd on wl* **4/1**[1]
-F00 **2** *2* **Collodi (GER)**[17] 556 6-11-12 **119**.................... TomScudamore 127
(David Bridgwater) *hld up towards rr: effrt 3 out: rdn to chse wnr 2f out: one pce and no imp fr last* **10/1**
6-01 **3** *13* **Iguacu**[18] 537 11-10-13 **106**.................... RichardJohnson 102
(Richard Price) *settled towards rr: n.m.r bef 5th: effrt next: rdn and outpcd 2 out: lft mod 3rd at last* **9/2**[2]
/P-5 **4** *10* **Absolutlyfantastic**[40] 162 8-11-8 **115**....................(t) NicodeBoinville 106+
(Martin Hill) *racd keenly and chsd ldrs: effrt to go 2nd bef 3 out: upsides whn mstke next: rdn and fnd little between last two: sn lost pl and btn* **6/1**[3]
3-34 **5** *20* **Mondlicht (USA)**[7] 669 5-10-13 **113**....................(p) MrAlexFerguson(7) 82
(John Ferguson) *chsd ldrs: wnt 2nd at 3rd tl hit next: urged along and lost pl bef 3 out: fnd nil and sn btn: t.o* **6/1**[3]
3-30 **6** *7* **Warrant Officer**[23] 449 5-10-2 **95**.................... MarcGoldstein 58
(Sheena West) *2nd or 3rd tl rdn bef 3 out: lost pl after next: sn wknd: t.o* **10/1**
34-2 **7** *1 ¼* **Knight In Purple**[19] 520 11-11-8 **115**....................(vt) PeterCarberry 77
(John Mackie) *cl up tl 1/2-way: rdn and lost pl bef 3 out: nt run on: t.o* **8/1**
41R- **8** *5* **Nikos Extra (FR)**[233] 2079 11-11-10 **117**.................... AdamWedge 74
(Alexandra Dunn) *reluctant to s and lost 20 l: nvr on tems: stl last whn blnd 5th: t.o next* **25/1**
6-25 **F** **Anton Dolin (IRE)**[19] 529 7-10-4 **104**.................... MrHFNugent(7) 106
(Michael Mullineaux) *midfield: effrt 3 out: rdn after next: plodding on in 10 l 3rd whn fell last* **9/1**
3304 **F** **Watt Broderick (IRE)**[14] 592 6-10-12 **108**.................... RobMcCarth(3) 99
(Ian Williams) *led: rdn and jnd whn mstke 2 out: hdd over 2f out: disputing 15 l 4th whn fell last* **14/1**

3m 44.1s (-11.90) **Going Correction** -0.30s/f (Good) **10** Ran SP% **116.6**
Speed ratings (Par 105): **117,116,109,104,94 91,90,87, ,**
CSF £43.40 CT £187.93 TOTE £3.90: £1.10, £4.00, £1.90; EX 56.50 Trifecta £177.50.
Owner Anchor Men **Bred** Charles Barel **Trained** Portway, Worcs

FOCUS
Actual race distance 2m212yds. Sound form, with the first two clear, and a big step up from the winner with more to come.

752 BIDFORD-ON-AVON NOVICES' H'CAP CHASE (15 fncs) 2m 4f 205y
4:35 (4:35) (Class 4) (0-105,102) 5-Y-0+ **£3,898** (£1,144; £572; £286)

Form
3P-U **1** **Adios Alonso (IRE)**[19] 524 9-10-5 **84**.................... BenPoste(3) 102+
(Rosemary Gasson) *racd in 2nd or 3rd pl: chal 2 out: urged ahd bef last: a holding rival fr last* **8/1**
0P-2 **2** *7* **Knockyoursocksoff (IRE)**[7] 674 5-10-9 **85**....................(v[1]) JamieMoore 100+
(Gary Moore) *t.k.h in 2nd or 3rd: led 8th: blnd 12th: pressed whn hit 2 out: sn hrd drvn: hdd bef last and over 2 l bhd and hld whn hit fence* **11/10**[1]
54-3 **3** *24* **Webbswood (IRE)**[38] 209 6-11-12 **102**.................... MarkGrant 93
(Sean Curran) *nt a fluent: last whn j. slowly 6th: wnt 4th at 12th: effrt short-lived: wnt poor 3rd after 2 out* **9/2**[2]
00/0 **4** *5* **Bright Light**[40] 167 8-10-0 **76** oh15.................... HarrySkelton 61
(Dan Skelton) *settled towards rr: effrt in 3rd at 11th and 2nd briefly next: rdn and fdd tamely bef 2 out* **11/1**
P4 **5** *28* **Parthian Empire**[25] 429 9-10-6 **89**.................... MrDSansom(7) 56
(Seamus Mullins) *chsd ldrs: rdn bef 7th: nt travelling after: tailing off whn blnd bdly 3 out* **20/1**

F-F3 **P** **Dancing Dik**[23] 450 10-10-5 **81**..............................(b) TomO'Brien
(Paul Henderson) *led tl 8th: dropping out qckly whn blnd 10th and p.u* **5/1**[3]

P00- **P** **Killshannon (IRE)**[159] 3591 6-11-7 **97**.............................. TomScudamore
(David Bridgwater) *handy tl blnd 3rd: rdr lost iron and sn p.u* **16/1**

5m 6.6s (-8.40) **Going Correction** -0.20s/f (Good) 7 Ran SP% **112.6**
Speed ratings: **108,105,96,94,83 ,**
CSF £17.71 CT £44.80 TOTE £11.10: £4.90, £1.90; EX 22.90 Trifecta £86.70.
Owner Mrs Rosemary Gasson **Bred** Robert Finnegan **Trained** Balscote, Oxon

FOCUS
Actual race distance 2m2f177yds. A modest novice handicap with the winner rated up a few pounds on best hurdle figures.

753 GREENWAY INTERMEDIATE OPEN NATIONAL HUNT FLAT RACE 2m 70y
5:10 (5:10) (Class 6) 4-6-Y-O **£1,949** (£572; £286; £143)

Form RPR

2- **1** **Amirr (IRE)**[114] 4391 5-11-2 **0**.............................. AidanColeman 110+
(John Ferguson) *tall powerful: settled cl up: lft 2nd 6f out: led over 2f out: rdn over 1f out: a jst holding persistent chalr fnl 100yds* **1/5**[1]

2 *½* **Tilinisi (IRE)** 5-10-9 **0**.............................. KielanWoods 100+
(Phil Middleton) *hld up: effrt 3f out: chsd wnr wl over 1f out: drvn and tried hrd to overtake ins fnl f but a jst hld* **7/1**[2]

50 **3** *15* **Court Baloo (IRE)**[23] 459 4-10-10 **0**.............................. CraigNichol[(3)] 89
(Alistair Whillans) *led tl hung rt bnd after 6f: lft in front again 6f out: rdn and hdd over 2f out: sn wknd* **20/1**

4 *27* **Dancing Admiral** 4-10-3 **0**..............................(p) GrahamCarson[(10)] 62
(Anthony Carson) *a last: pushed along after 7f: lost tch 6f out: t.o fnl 3f* **20/1**

4- **R** **Miss Lucarno**[55] 5468 5-10-4 **0**.............................. ConorRing[(5)]
(Evan Williams) *2nd tl lft in ld 1/2-way: hung violently rt over 6f out and fnlly uns rdr passing wing of hurdle* **10/1**[3]

3m 47.1s (-3.30) **Going Correction** -0.30s/f (Good)
WFA 4 from 5yo+ 3lb 5 Ran SP% **114.4**
Speed ratings: **96,95,88,74,**
CSF £2.57 TOTE £1.30: £1.10, £1.70; EX 3.00 Trifecta £15.20.
Owner Bloomfields **Bred** Breeding Capital Plc **Trained** Cowlinge, Suffolk

FOCUS
Actual race distance 2m112yds. A bumper weakened by four non-runners. It was steadily run.
T/Plt: £4.10 to a £1 stake. Pool: £50593.09 - 8817.89 winning tickets. T/Qpdt: £3.90 to a £1 stake. Pool: £3598.06 - 671.84 winning tickets. **Iain Mackenzie**

690 UTTOXETER (L-H)
Wednesday, June 17

OFFICIAL GOING: Good (chs 8.8; hdl 8.5)
Wind: breezy Weather: overcast; 20 degrees

754 BROWN RECYCLING "NATIONAL HUNT" MAIDEN HURDLE (9 hdls) 1m 7f 168y
2:10 (2:10) (Class 4) 4-Y-O+ **£3,249** (£954; £477; £238)

Form RPR

4 **1** **I'dliketheoption (IRE)**[18] 558 4-10-11 **0**.............................. RichieMcLernon 108+
(Jonjo O'Neill) *trckd ldr: blnd 3 out: gng strly after: led between last two: 4 l clr last: easily* **11/2**[3]

4-34 **2** *4* **Bletchley Castle (IRE)**[8] 680 6-10-9 **98**.............................. NickSlatter[(5)] 103
(Seamus Durack) *led and abt 5 l clr and racing keenly: drvn bef 2 out: hdd between last two: one pce and wl hld after* **5/1**[2]

0/ **3** *4 ½* **Mighty Leader (IRE)**[33] 7-11-0 **0**.............................. JamesDavies 98
(Henry Oliver) *settled in 3rd: pushed along 3 out: n.d to ldng pair fr next but kpt on steadily* **16/1**

45-3 **4** *hd* **Flower Power**[41] 159 4-10-4 **0**.............................. DenisO'Regan 90
(Tony Coyle) *small: hld up and bhd: prog 5th: disputing 5 l 3rd and no imp on ldrs whn hit 2 out and wl hld whn blnd last: plugged on* **8/1**

46-F **5** *19* **Uncle Tone (IRE)**[4] 730 6-11-0 **120**.............................. MichealNolan 87
(Tim Vaughan) *mstkes: blnd 2nd: prom tl 6 l 3rd home turn: sn lost pl tamely* **13/8**[1]

4 **6** *19* **Whimsical Notion**[27] 419 5-11-0 **0**.............................. TomScudamore 66
(Nigel Hawke) *mstkes in rr: t.o bef 3 out* **6/1**

5/0- **7** *14* **Wistari Rocks (IRE)**[131] 4065 6-11-0 **0**.............................. RichardJohnson 51
(Tim Vaughan) *bhd tl impr qckly to chse ldrs bef 3 out where blnd and dropped out rapidly: t.o* **12/1**

546- **8** *8* **Bricbracsmate**[249] 1855 7-10-11 **0**.............................. BenPoste[(3)] 44
(Michael Mullineaux) *mstkes in rr: t.o 3 out* **66/1**

3m 50.9s (-6.50) **Going Correction** -0.325s/f (Good)
WFA 4 from 5yo+ 17lb 8 Ran SP% **110.6**
Speed ratings (Par 105): **103,101,98,98,89 79,72,68**
CSF £31.07 TOTE £4.10: £1.60, £1.60, £3.10; EX 26.50 Trifecta £321.20.
Owner John P McManus **Bred** Stephen O'Flynn **Trained** Cheltenham, Gloucs

FOCUS
Hurdles sited on fresh ground on inside with Hurdle track at its shortest. Chase bends dolled out 6.5yds and distances increased by 44yds per circuit. Some starts have been moved at this track following remeasuring, so some races will not have speed figures until there is sufficient data to calculate updated median times. This weak opener was won in runaway fashion by an easy-to-back hurdling debutant.

755 STAFFORDSHIRE'S LARGEST SKIP HIRE SERVICES CONDITIONAL JOCKEYS' (S) HURDLE (10 hdls) 2m 3f 207y
2:45 (2:45) (Class 5) 4-7-Y-O **£2,339** (£686; £343; £171)

Form RPR

-453 **1** **Jayo Time (IRE)**[5] 718 6-11-5 **111**..............................(b) ChrisWard[(3)] 114+
(Dr Richard Newland) *plld hrd: wnt prom and awkward 5th: led 7th: urged clr after hitting 3 out: 8 lebgths ahd whn hit last: doing v little in front on flat and kpt up to work* **5/4**[1]

114/ **2** *8* **Stand To Reason (IRE)**[32] 3778 7-10-6 **0**.............................. NickSlatter[(6)] 97
(Tony Carroll) *t.k.h: hld up in tch: effrt 7th: wnt 1 l 2nd bef next where mstke: sn drvn: no imp on v long run fr 2 out* **4/1**[3]

4-PP **3** *19* **Storm To Pass**[17] 571 7-10-7 **88**..............................(tp) MikeyHamill[(5)] 78
(Caroline Fryer) *hit 5th: prom tl rdn and outpcd bef 3 out: gng v slowly fr next* **33/1**

-P64 **4** *11* **Miss H Lewiss**[20] 516 7-10-2 **90**.............................. CiaranGethings[(3)] 61
(Steve Flook) *sweating and unruly at s: led at brisk early gallop: hit 7th and drvn: swished tail whn losing pl next: nt keen in remote 4th after* **25/1**

/PP- **5** *45* **Tinctoria**[37] 1269 5-10-5 **79**..............................(p) BenPoste 20
(Adrian Wintle) *bhd: drvn 6th: no rspnse: t.o after next* **66/1**

P **Encouraging (IRE)**[18] 6-10-12 **0**..............................(b[1]) AdamNicol
(Mike Sowersby) *mstkes: t.k.h early: prom tl wnt wd and lost pl qckly bef 6th: t.o next: p.u 3 out* **50/1**

6-66 **F** **Vandross (IRE)**[28] 404 5-10-12 **115**..............................(b) SeanBowen
(Neil King) *fell 1st* **15/8**[2]

0 **P** **Dabuki (FR)**[18] 554 5-10-9 **0**.............................. ConorRing[(3)]
(Evan Williams) *w.r.s and lost 15 l: sn dashed up to rr of bunch: mstke 3rd: slow 6th and struggling: t.o next: p.u 3 out* **16/1**

4m 54.1s (-9.10) **Going Correction** -0.325s/f (Good) 8 Ran SP% **115.4**
Speed ratings: **105,101,94,89,71 , ,**
CSF £6.83 TOTE £2.50: £1.10, £1.40, £4.70; EX 8.10 Trifecta £102.00.winner bought in for 4600gns
Owner Paul Jenkins **Bred** E J P Kane **Trained** Claines, Worcs

FOCUS
This took very little winning, even by selling standards. They came home at long intervals.

756 BROWN SCRAP METAL NOVICES' H'CAP CHASE (14 fncs 2 omitted) 2m 6f 108y
3:20 (3:20) (Class 4) (0-120,120) 5-Y-O+ **£3,768** (£1,106; £553; £276)

Form RPR

1-12 **1** **Urcalin (FR)**[33] 319 7-11-9 **117**..............................(t) TomCannon 128+
(David Arbuthnot) *cl 2nd or 3rd tl rdn to ld sn after 3 out: hdd and untidy next: 2 l down last: drvn and rallied gamely to ld again fnl 50yds: ears pricked passing line* **3/1**[2]

2-25 **2** *1* **Susie Sheep**[24] 462 5-11-4 **112**..............................(b[1]) TomScudamore 122+
(David Pipe) *hld up in last: effrt 8th: wnt 2nd sn after 3 out: led and hit next: drvn bef last where 2 l ahd: outbattled and passed cl home* **7/1**

15P- **3** *11* **Take A Bow**[179] 3178 6-11-7 **115**..............................(t) AidanColeman 116
(Lawney Hill) *2nd or 3rd pl: rdn after 9th: drvn and lost tch w ldng pair wl bef 2 out* **17/2**

44-1 **4** *5* **Highpower (IRE)**[24] 463 6-11-12 **120**..............................(p) NoelFehily 117
(Jonjo O'Neill) *mstke 1st: settled trcking ldrs: rdn after 9th: sn no rspnse: poor 4th 2 out* **13/8**[1]

3-36 **5** *38* **Cape York**[27] 420 7-11-6 **114**..............................(b) BrianHughes 74
(Malcolm Jefferson) *racd freely in ld at decent pce: nt fluent: rdn and hdd sn after 3 out: surrendered v meekly: t.o whn mstke last* **9/2**[3]

23-6 **P** **Amazing D'Azy (IRE)**[30] 382 7-11-7 **115**.............................. DavidBass
(Kim Bailey) *rn in snatches: sn pushed along: last and reminder 7th: fnd nil: t.o after 9th: p.u after next* **18/1**

5m 39.9s (-2.80) **Going Correction** +0.025s/f (Yiel) 6 Ran SP% **109.6**
Speed ratings: **106,105,101,99,86**
CSF £21.53 TOTE £3.60: £1.70, £2.50; EX 17.40 Trifecta £100.80.
Owner A T A Wates & Mrs S Wates **Bred** Bernard-Louis Dutertre **Trained** Beare Green, Surrey

FOCUS
A competitive, if select field for the inaugural running of this race. The winner was well in on his recent hurdle best.

757 BROWN WASTE MANAGEMENT H'CAP HURDLE (DIV I) (12 hdls) 2m 7f 70y
3:55 (3:55) (Class 4) (0-105,105) 4-Y-O+ **£3,249** (£954; £477; £238)

Form RPR

P0-P **1** **Blackwell Synergy (FR)**[28] 398 9-10-11 **95**.............................. ConorRing[(5)] 104+
(John Upson) *led after 2nd tl 4th: pressed ldr tl led again bef 3 out: 2 l clr and hrd drvn fr 2 out: kpt plugging on and hld on gamely cl home: all out* **66/1**

5-05 **2** *1 ¼* **West End (IRE)**[22] 493 8-11-6 **99**..............................(tp) DavidBass 105
(Kim Bailey) *t.k.h in rr tl rdn and no rspnse after 7th: 6th and plenty to do 3 out: decided to rally and wnt 2 l 2nd but racing awkwardly bef last: no imp fnl 100yds* **8/1**[3]

13-1 **3** *7* **Trafficker (IRE)**[47] 58 8-11-12 **105**.............................. WillKennedy 106
(Dr Richard Newland) *trckd ldrs: rdn bef 8th: wnt 3rd next: nt really gng wl enough after: pressed wnr 3 out tl bef last: plugged on* **11/10**[1]

00-4 **4** *1* **Arctic Dixie**[24] 462 7-11-5 **103**..............................(tp) JakeHodson[(5)] 104
(Rob Summers) *last whn nt fluent 2nd: prog 9th: 3rd next: sn rdn: nt qckn after: btn 4th whn mstke last* **16/1**

6P-5 **5** *1* **Minella Bliss (IRE)**[20] 530 10-10-10 **96**..............................(b) CharlieHammond[(7)] 95
(James Evans) *settled in rr: hdwy 9th: 5th and flattered 3 out: drvn and plodded on fr next and nvr making any imp* **12/1**

34-3 **6** *23* **Maypole Lass**[32] 339 5-11-12 **105**..............................(p) BrendanPowell 82
(Stuart Edmunds) *chsd ldrs: rdn after 9th: struggling next: t.o* **11/2**[2]

/4-3 **7** *6* **Maldivian Reef (IRE)**[24] 460 7-11-11 **104**.............................. DenisO'Regan 76
(Alan King) *chsd ldrs: rdn and btn bef 3 out: t.o* **20/1**

04-6 **8** *nk* **Gold Medal (IRE)**[44] 104 5-10-11 **100**..............................(p) JackSavage[(10)] 72
(Jonjo O'Neill) *midfield: effrt in 4th pl at 9th: flattered briefly 3 out: lost pl qckly: t.o* **16/1**

3-53 **9** *4* **Young Lou**[32] 328 6-9-7 **79** oh10..............................(p) JosephPalmowski[(7)] 47
(Robin Dickin) *mde most tl after 2nd: prom tl 7th: t.o 3 out: blnd last* **25/1**

4-55 **10** *3* **Call Me Kate**[25] 443 5-10-1 **87**..............................(p) MrHFNugent[(7)] 52
(Henry Daly) *chsd ldrs tl nt fluent 4th and next: drvn and nt travelling after: dropped to rr 2 out: t.o next* **11/1**

F0-0 **11** *1 ¼* **Sapphire Moon**[18] 552 8-10-6 **90**..............................(v[1]) DanielHiskett[(5)] 54
(Richard Phillips) *led 4th tl rdn and hdd bef 3 out: lost pl rapidly: t.o* **33/1**

60-4 **P** **Tisfreetdream (IRE)**[20] 530 14-10-0 **86**..............................(p) JamieBargary[(7)]
(Peter Pritchard) *bhd: rdn and struggling after 7th: t.o and p.u after 9th* **25/1**

5m 50.6s (-8.20) **Going Correction** -0.325s/f (Good) 12 Ran SP% **118.8**
Speed ratings (Par 105): **101,100,98,97,97 89,87,87,85,84 84,**
CSF £512.18 CT £1114.08 TOTE £51.00: £12.60, £2.10, £1.40; EX 1063.10 Trifecta £3498.00 Part won..
Owner The Peter Partnership **Bred** Erick Bec De La Motte **Trained** Maidford, Northants

FOCUS
This was a deal more competitive than the market suggested, though few could have predicted this outcome. The winner was a 130+ hurdler at his peak.

758 BROWN WASTE MANAGEMENT H'CAP HURDLE (DIV II) (12 hdls) 2m 7f 70y
4:35 (4:35) (Class 4) (0-105,105) 4-Y-O+ **£3,249** (£954; £477; £238)

Form RPR

1-16 **1** **Flemensbay**[32] 339 7-11-12 **105**..............................(p) RichardJohnson 109
(Richard Phillips) *mde all: 3 l clr home turn: drvn and looked vulnerable fr 3 out: kpt outbattling rivals after and styd on stoutly flat* **9/2**[3]

5-42 **2** *1 ¼* **Steps And Stairs (IRE)**[20] 530 5-11-2 **95**..............................(p) DarylJacob 99
(Jonjo O'Neill) *settled in 3rd or 4th pl: gng strly 9th: tk 2nd home turn: hit 3 out and next and drvn: looked hld whn mstke last: no imp after* **9/4**[1]

-P0 **3** *5* **Agent Louise**[20] 522 7-9-11 **79** oh5..............................(b) AdamNicol[(3)] 77
(Mike Sowersby) *towards rr: stl 7th at 9th: rdn and styd on fr 2 out: tk 3rd flat and kpt on wl but nt rch ldrs* **16/1**

00-6 **4** *2 ¼* **Our Chief (IRE)**[44] 102 6-11-7 **100**.........................(bt[1]) TomScudamore 97
(David Pipe) *settled towards rr: effrt gng wl after 9th: cl 3rd home turn: rdn 3 out: fnd nil fr next and sn no imp: lost 3rd after last* **7/2**[2]
6-14 **5** *13* **Earcomesthedream (IRE)**[30] 377 12-11-5 **105**......(b) ArchieBellamy[(7)] 90
(Peter Pritchard) *racd lazily and often rdn: pressed wnr tl lost pl wl bef 3 out: sn no ch* **16/1**
21-5 **6** *20* **Kyles Faith (IRE)**[37] 239 7-11-7 **103**......................... ConorShoemark[(3)] 70
(Martin Keighley) *prom tl rdn 9th: dropping rt out whn mstke next: t.o* **10/1**
405- **7** *47* **Bob's Call (IRE)**[229] 2178 6-10-7 **96**...................... JakeHolliday[(10)] 20
(Tony Coyle) *in tch tl 7th: rdn and struggling 9th: t.o and virtually p.u flat* **8/1**
46-P **P** **Kilcullen Article (IRE)**[43] 136 7-10-8 **87**...................... LiamTreadwell
(Michael Scudamore) *sn drvn in last: nvr wnt a yard: lost tch 7th: t.o next: p.u 3 out* **17/2**

5m 54.7s (-4.10) **Going Correction** -0.325s/f (Good) **8 Ran SP% 113.7**
Speed ratings (Par 105): **94,93,91,91,86 79,63,**
CSF £15.31 CT £145.27 TOTE £5.00: £1.70, £1.50, £4.20; EX 16.20 Trifecta £186.60.
Owner Dozen Dreamers Partnership **Bred** Mrs J L Egan **Trained** Adlestrop, Gloucs

FOCUS
This looked the stronger of the two divisions and was run at a sound gallop.

759 BROWNRECYCLING.CO.UK MARES' H'CAP HURDLE (10 hdls) 2m 3f 207y
5:10 (5:10) (Class 5) (0-100,100) 4-Y-0+ **£2,339** (£686; £343; £171)

Form RPR
133/ **1** **Ivebeenthinking**[588] 2291 7-10-1 **78**.............................. BenPoste[(3)] 86+
(Tom Symonds) *looked fit: s.s and lost 20 l: sn in tch in rr: effrt bef 3 out where mstke: sn led and 5 l clr: wl in command bef last: pushed out* **16/1**
-530 **2** *3 ¼* **Tantalized**[11] 646 6-10-0 **74** oh5.................................(v) LeeEdwards 78+
(Dave Roberts) *hit 1st: drvn most of way fr 3rd: midfield: outpcd bef 3 out: 4th next: kpt on u.p to go 8 l 2nd at last: nvr looked like catching wnr* **25/1**
0-03 **3** *6* **Businessmoney Judi**[21] 513 9-10-12 **86**.........................(t) DarylJacob 84
(Martin Hill) *midfield: mstke 5th: rdn bef 7th: 3rd but making no imp whn hit 2 out* **9/1**
U5-6 **4** *1 ¼* **Be My Witness (IRE)**[43] 130 6-11-0 **95**.............. JosephPalmowski[(7)] 90
(Robin Dickin) *chsd ldrs: rdn and outpcd bef 3 out: unable to chal after* **25/1**
02-6 **5** *7* **Icanmotor**[32] 337 8-10-2 **76**.......................................(tp) TrevorWhelan 64
(Claire Dyson) *cl up: wnt cl 3rd and looked to be gng wl home turn: led briefly 3 out: sn rdn and little rspnse: lost three pls fr after next* **16/1**
0-21 **6** *hd* **Lilly's Legend**[27] 421 5-10-8 **82**.............................(p) DougieCostello 70
(Mark Walford) *led or cl 2nd tl rdn bef 7th: drvn and fading bef 3 out* **3/1**[2]
-012 **7** *7* **Lady Of Longstone (IRE)**[13] 615 5-11-12 **100**........(b) TomScudamore 82
(David Pipe) *led or cl 2nd tl drvn home turn: dropped out tamely* **11/4**[1]
-5F4 **8** *3 ¾* **Kentford Heiress**[14] 597 5-10-6 **87**........................ KevinJones[(7)] 67
(Seamus Mullins) *settled in 3rd pl tl led bef 7th: rdn and hdd after 3 out: dropped out qckly* **13/2**[3]
54/4 **9** *49* **Miss Chatterbox**[27] 416 10-10-8 **87**...................... MrJohnDawson[(5)] 21
(Chris Grant) *towards rr: rdn and lost tch bef 7th: t.o 3 out* **28/1**
0P0- **P** **Ifits A Fiddle**[68] 5260 6-10-10 **84**.............................(t) RichardJohnson
(Richard Phillips) *in last pair: struggling after 7th: wl bhd whn p.u 2 out* **8/1**
/5-0 **P** **Oscar Jane (IRE)**[26] 435 8-10-6 **80**.............................. AlainCawley
(Johnny Farrelly) *towards rr: lost tch bef 7th: t.o and p.u after 9th* **14/1**

4m 54.5s (-8.70) **Going Correction** -0.325s/f (Good)
WFA 4 from 5yo+ 18lb **11 Ran SP% 115.7**
Speed ratings (Par 103): **104,102,100,99,97 96,94,92,73,**
CSF £339.07 CT £3772.89 TOTE £13.80: £3.50, £7.70, £2.10; EX 474.10 Trifecta £3056.70.
Owner Mrs V J Norbury **Bred** Mrs V J Norbury **Trained** Harewood End, H'fords

FOCUS
This was run at a suicidal early gallop and suited those held up. The winner has been rated in line with her 2013 form.

760 ZERO TO LANDFILL H'CAP CHASE (17 fncs 3 omitted) 3m 2f 13y
5:45 (5:45) (Class 4) (0-120,120) 5-Y-0+ **£3,768** (£1,106; £553; £276)

Form RPR
1-31 **1** **Greenlaw**[20] 523 9-11-12 **120**.....................................(t) NoelFehily 132+
(Charlie Longsdon) *racd keenly and gng wl: trckd ldrs: last of five gng clr at 11th: rdn to chse ldr after 3 out: styd on to ld last: sn drvn clr* **5/2**[2]
45-2 **2** *3 ¾* **Double Handful (GER)**[35] 282 9-11-4 **112**........................(tp) DavidBass 120
(Lawney Hill) *settled towards rr: effrt gng wl in 2nd at 11th: led after next: 3 l clr and rdn whn nt fluent 2 out: hdd and nt fluent last: nt qckn flat* **10/1**
P3-P **3** *1* **American Legend (IRE)**[20] 523 7-11-6 **114**...................(v) WillKennedy 120
(Jonjo O'Neill) *settled towards rr: rdn and effrt 3 out: kpt on steadily fr next but nvr really looked like getting in a blow* **17/2**
PP4- **4** *26* **Master Neo (FR)**[67] 5284 9-11-0 **115**.............................(vt) MrLDrowne[(7)] 98
(Nigel Hawke) *slt ld mostly tl 6th: rdn bef 10th: cl 2nd tl led after 11th tl after next: drvn and qckly 3 out: fin tired* **8/1**[3]
14-4 **5** *2* **Georgian King**[28] 403 12-11-3 **111**.............................(p) AndrewTinkler 92
(Martin Keighley) *cl up tl dropped out qckly bef 12th: sn wl bhd* **14/1**
15-5 **6** *59* **Green Bank (IRE)**[8] 670 9-11-5 **113**........................... RichardJohnson 41
(Charlie Longsdon) *chsd ldrs tl lost tch qckly 10th: sn t.o: hacked on* **9/1**
3U5- **7** *5* **Wither Yenot (IRE)**[24] 8-10-8 **109**...........................(p) MrMJPKendrick[(7)] 32
(Ben Case) *nt fluent 6th and rdn: struggling in last at next: t.o fr 11th* **25/1**
5-22 **P** **High Ron**[6] 693 10-11-8 **116**.. TomScudamore
(Caroline Bailey) *mostly cl 2nd tl led narrowly after 6th: hdd 11th: 7 lebgths 5th and fading whn stmbld bdly 3 out: sn t.o* **2/1**[1]

6m 40.0s (1.20) **Going Correction** +0.025s/f (Yiel) **8 Ran SP% 113.1**
Speed ratings: **99,97,97,89,88 70,69,**
CSF £26.24 CT £182.28 TOTE £3.00: £1.20, £2.50, £2.50; EX 12.20 Trifecta £236.60.
Owner Simon and June Cadzow **Bred** Mrs J Cadzow **Trained** Over Norton, Oxon

FOCUS
This was a proper test and produced a likeable performance from the progressive winner.

761 BROWN RECYCLING STANDARD OPEN NATIONAL HUNT FLAT RACE 1m 7f 168y
6:15 (6:15) (Class 6) 4-6-Y-0 **£1,559** (£457; £228; £114)

Form RPR
2 **1** **Winter Soldier**[32] 341 5-11-0... DarylJacob 112+
(Richard Woollacott) *cl up in 3rd or 4th pl: led over 3f out: rdn over 1f out: kpt on gamely to hold rival fnl f* **11/4**[1]
2 *1 ¼* **Galveston (IRE)**[92] 6-11-0.. PaddyBrennan 112+
(Fergal O'Brien) *cl up bhd ldng pair: hmpd on inner over 4f out: chsd wnr fnl 3f: chal w rdr looking arnd 2f out: rdn 1f out: one pce and rn green and nt qckn after* **14/1**
3-4 **3** *8* **Pilgrims Bay (IRE)**[38] 227 5-11-0.. ConorO'Farrell 104
(David Pipe) *taken down early: led or cl 2nd tl reluctant and swished tail u.p over 3f out: plugged on same pce after: btn over 1f out* **6/1**[3]
31- **4** *1 ¾* **Muthabir (IRE)**[85] 4983 5-11-7.. RichardJohnson 109
(Richard Phillips) *racd keenly in rr: effrt 3f out: one pce fnl 2f* **7/2**[2]
5 *2 ½* **Bruce Of Crionaich (IRE)** 5-11-0..................................... AidanColeman 101
(John Ferguson) *chsng type: chsd ldrs: drvn and racing awkwardly wl over 2f out: hung lft and no imp after* **11/4**[1]
6 *1* **Ablazing (IRE)** 4-10-11... NoelFehily 97
(Johnny Farrelly) *midfield: effrt 4f out: 3rd 3f out: rdn and wknd wl over 1f out* **10/1**
7 *25* **Heighnow** 4-10-4.. PaulMoloney 67
(Conrad Allen) *chsd ldrs early: lost pl over 4f out: t.o fnl 3f* **28/1**
8 *1 ¾* **St Lewis** 5-11-0.. SeanQuinlan 75
(Sophie Leech) *tall: rngy: t.k.h in midfield: wknd over 4f out: t.o fnl 3f* **33/1**
9 *46* **Present Accord (IRE)**[17] 6-10-7.......................................(b[1]) KielanWoods 27
(Michael Mullineaux) *led or disp ld tl rdn 4f out: fnd nil and sn t.o* **100/1**
10 *32* **Mayden Massini** 4-10-11... LeeEdwards 2
(Tony Carroll) *small: racd in last pl: rdn 6f out: sn t.o* **50/1**

3m 46.7s (-5.10) **Going Correction** -0.325s/f (Good)
WFA 4 from 5yo+ 3lb **10 Ran SP% 114.9**
Speed ratings: **99,98,94,93,92 91,79,78,55,39**
CSF £41.37 TOTE £3.70: £1.50, £4.20, £2.90; EX 45.80 Trifecta £193.00.
Owner R Mitford-Slade & Lucy Johnson **Bred** Mrs Lucy Fielding-Johnson **Trained** South Molton, Devon

FOCUS
An informative bumper, in which two pulled nicely clear.
T/Plt: £187.40 to a £1 stake. Pool: £61,195.24 - 238.26 winning units. T/Qpdt: £60.30 to a £1 stake. Pool: £4,747.65 - 58.20 winning units. **Iain Mackenzie**

762 - 769a (Foreign Racing) - See Raceform Interactive

610
FFOS LAS (L-H)
Thursday, June 18

OFFICIAL GOING: Good to firm (good in places)
Wind: light breeze Weather: hot and sunny; 18 degrees

770 LLANMOOR HOMES NOVICES' H'CAP CHASE (17 fncs) 2m 4f 199y
6:05 (6:05) (Class 4) (0-105,105) 5-Y-0+ **£3,768** (£1,106; £553; £276)

Form RPR
1-22 **1** **Waddingtown Hero (IRE)**[44] 126 8-11-1 **94**..................(tp) GerardTumelty 110+
(Andy Turnell) *pressed ldng pair: effrt gng bttr than them to chal 3 out: led next: rdn and forged 4 l clr last: kpt on wl* **4/1**[2]
24-3 **2** *6* **Zama Zama**[14] 612 8-10-6 **92**...................................... MrConorOrr[(7)] 101
(Evan Williams) *cl 2nd tl slt ld fr 7th: drvn 14th: jnd next: hdd 2 out: outpcd by wnr bef last* **6/1**[3]
3-11 **3** *3 ¼* **Caspian Piper (IRE)**[14] 612 8-11-5 **98**........................(v) RichardJohnson 105
(Tim Vaughan) *slt ld tl 7th: remained cl 2nd: drvn 14th: ev ch 2 out: no ex bef last* **5/4**[1]
-004 **4** *2 ¼* **Provincial Pride (IRE)**[7] 704 8-10-11 **100**.........(t) CharlieHammond[(10)] 105
(Mike Hammond) *nt a fluent: wnt cl up bef 8th: rdn after 13th: 6 l 4th and btn 3 out: plugged on* **10/1**
34-3 **5** *13* **Dipity Doo Dah**[14] 615 11-10-7 **86**...........................(p) DonalDevereux 78
(Peter Bowen) *settled in rr and in tch: effrt bef 14th: sn drvn: no rspnse and btn next* **7/1**
4F-P **6** *10* **Goldie Horn**[16] 589 7-11-8 **101**..............................(t) SamTwiston-Davies 84
(Nigel Twiston-Davies) *hit 2nd: towards rr but in tch: rdn after 13th: struggling next* **14/1**
B3-6 **P** **Indiefront**[18] 571 6-9-11 **79**...(bt) JamesBanks[(3)]
(Jo Davis) *numerous mstkes: chsd ldrs tl lost tch after 13th: t.o and p.u next* **20/1**
2-4P **P** **Callmenewtown (IRE)**[24] 468 8-11-12 **105**........................ JamesDavies
(Graeme McPherson) *trckd ldrs: hit 9th: last next: blnd 11th: sn t.o: p.u 14th* **25/1**

5m 17.1s (-11.50) **Going Correction** -0.675s/f (Firm) **8 Ran SP% 115.6**
Speed ratings: **94,91,90,89,84 80, ,**
CSF £28.56 CT £45.81 TOTE £5.70: £2.00, £2.00, £1.30; EX 27.40 Trifecta £52.50.
Owner L M Power **Bred** Michael Rafter **Trained** Broad Hinton, Wilts

FOCUS
Warm and sunny conditions for Ffos Las's oldest meeting, first hosted six years ago to the very date. Very few got into this opener and this was a step up from the winner.

771 IWEC INTERNATIONAL H'CAP CHASE (18 fncs) 2m 7f 177y
6:35 (6:35) (Class 4) (0-110,110) 5-Y-0+ **£3,768** (£1,106; £553; £276)

Form RPR
12-4 **1** **Clubs Are Trumps (IRE)**[30] 388 6-11-1 **99**...................(p) WillKennedy 112+
(Jonjo O'Neill) *pressed ldng pair: mstke 11th: pushed along bef 15th: led 3 out: hrd rdn and trying to edge to lft fr next: idling but hld on wl in driving fin* **9/2**[3]
6P-4 **2** *nk* **Susquehanna River (IRE)**[28] 420 8-11-9 **107**...... SamTwiston-Davies 117
(Nigel Twiston-Davies) *lft in narrow ld 1st and set str pce: hdd 6th: remained cl 2nd: hrd drvn fr 3 out: pressed wnr after and kpt on wl cl home: jst hld* **3/1**[1]
U-61 **3** *nk* **Ready Token (IRE)**[15] 600 7-11-10 **108**.........................(t) AidanColeman 119
(Charlie Longsdon) *led tl j. slowly 1st: nt a fluent: led 6th: slow 10th: drvn and hdd 3 out: remained w ev ch and styd on wl flat* **7/2**[2]
1P-0 **4** *23* **Quinton (FR)**[19] 553 11-11-12 **110**...................................... NoelFehily 101
(Johnny Farrelly) *chsd ldrs: rdn after 9th: lost tch w ldng trio bef 15th* **8/1**
5 *22* **All Fired Up (IRE)**[48] 68 8-11-11 **109**............................... PaulMoloney 79
(Evan Williams) *j. slowly 3rd: mstke 7th: hld up and bhd: lost tch after 14th* **9/1**
231- **6** *4* **Ravens Brook (IRE)**[67] 5287 9-11-5 **103**........................(b) TrevorWhelan 69
(Neil King) *midfield: rdn and struggling after 14th: t.o 3 out* **7/1**
30/0 **7** *½* **Silver Story**[20] 536 12-11-7 **105**..................................(t) RichardJohnson 70
(Tim Vaughan) *in a last pair: rdn and lost tch after 14th: t.o 3 out* **8/1**
11/P **P** **Tom Bach (IRE)**[26] 438 11-10-4 **88**...................................(b) JamesBest
(Hywel Evans) *hit 2nd and 4th: nvr travelling in rr: hrd drvn 9th: last 11th: t.o whn climbed next two and p.u* **14/1**

5m 58.4s (-19.00) **Going Correction** -0.675s/f (Firm) **8 Ran SP% 116.8**
Speed ratings: **104,103,103,96,88 87,87,**
CSF £19.54 CT £52.68 TOTE £4.50: £1.60, £2.40, £1.20; EX 13.60 Trifecta £32.00.
Owner John P McManus **Bred** S & S Hubbard Rodwell **Trained** Cheltenham, Gloucs
■ Stewards' Enquiry : Will Kennedy caution: careless riding

FOCUS
The early pace in this fair 0-110 handicap looked generous and not many ever featured. The first three in the market finished miles clear and this looks straightforward form.

772 OBRIEN & PARTNERS H'CAP CHASE (15 fncs) 2m 3f 83y
7:10 (7:11) (Class 4) (0-120,120) 5-Y-O+ **£3,768** (£1,106; £553; £276)

Form RPR
6-22 1 **Moorlands Jack**[22] 510 10-11-5 **113**..............(p) JamesDavies 122+
(Jeremy Scott) *trckd ldrs: wnt 3rd at 11th: rdn 3 out: pressed ldng pair and 2 l bhd ldr fr next tl drvn and fnd ex to ld after last: forged clr* 9/2[3]
-343 2 *1* **Still Believing (IRE)**[14] 614 7-11-5 **113**.................. AdamWedge 120
(Evan Williams) *cl 3rd tl wnt 2nd at 11th: rdn and ev ch fr 3 out tl last: nt qckn fnl 150yds* 7/2[2]
6-44 3 *1 1/2* **Houston Dynimo (IRE)**[14] 611 10-11-12 **120**.........(bt) TomScudamore 126
(David Pipe) *led: rdn 3 out: hrd pressed after: hdd after last: nt qckn flat* 3/1[1]
45-P 4 *14* **Experimentalist**[36] 283 7-10-8 **102**..........................(t) RichardJohnson 97
(Tim Vaughan) *blnd 1st: nt a fluent: in last pair: rdn and outpcd bef 12th: no ch after but drvn into mod 4th cl home* 5/1
0-43 5 *nk* **Temple Lord (FR)**[16] 589 9-10-9 **103**........................(b) WillKennedy 97
(Jonjo O'Neill) *mstke 2nd: chsd ldrs tl lost pl and reminder 9th: rdn and no rspnse 12th: mod 4th fr next tl nr fin* 13/2
12-0 6 *15* **Sublime Talent (IRE)**[19] 555 9-10-10 **114**..............(t) LewisGordon(10) 93
(Evan Williams) *in last pair: lost tch 12th: racing awkwardly next* 16/1
00-4 7 *14* **Daymar Bay (IRE)**[44] 121 9-11-12 **120**......................(b[1]) AidanColeman 87
(Emma Lavelle) *pressed ldr: blnd 8th: rdn and lost pl after 11th: t.o 3 out* 7/1

4m 48.7s (-12.40) **Going Correction** -0.675s/f (Firm) **7 Ran SP% 113.8**
Speed ratings: 99,98,97,92,91 85,79
CSF £20.84 TOTE £4.80: £2.60, £2.10; EX 22.60 Trifecta £74.50.
Owner Mrs Lynda M Williams **Bred** Mrs L M Williams **Trained** Brompton Regis, Somerset

FOCUS
Not run at the frenetic gallop that might have been expected, but once again there were three a long way clear at the finish. The first two ran pretty much to their marks.

773 THOMAS CARROLL NOVICES' HURDLE (12 hdls) 2m 7f 191y
7:45 (7:45) (Class 4) 4-Y-O+ **£3,249** (£954; £477; £238)

Form RPR
3-53 1 **Milestone (IRE)**[26] 441 5-10-12 0..............................(t) PaulMoloney 110+
(Evan Williams) *settled trcking ldrs: nt fluent 3rd: effrt bef 3 out: chal and blnd next: edging rt bef last where led and nt fluent: drvn and kpt on wl flat* 7/1[2]
PP0- 2 *2* **Troyan (IRE)**[59] 5429 8-10-5 107.................................... DavidNoonan(7) 107
(Steve Flook) *hld up in last trio: effrt bef 3 out: styng on wl after: rdn in 3 l 4th at last: wnt 2nd flat: no imp fnl 100yds* 20/1
530- 3 *2 1/2* **Kinari (IRE)**[110] 4479 5-10-12 0.................................... TomO'Brien 104
(Peter Bowen) *cl 2nd tl led and mstke 7th: rdn bef 3 out: hdd and n.m.r last: lost 2nd and one pce flat* 16/1
-433 4 *3/4* **Mercers Court (IRE)**[15] 595 7-11-5 124...................... TrevorWhelan 110
(Neil King) *settled towards rr: wnt 4th home turn: sn rdn: sltly outpcd 2 out: kpt on wout threatening after last* 6/4[1]
52-2 5 *1 3/4* **Profit Commission (IRE)**[42] 168 5-10-12 120.................. NoelFehily 103
(Harry Fry) *plld hrd and chsd ldrs: wnt 2nd bef 3 out: rdn next: ev ch last: sn btn* 6/4[1]
5-U6 6 *7* **Royal Craftsman (IRE)**[14] 613 5-10-12 0...................... DonalDevereux 96
(Peter Bowen) *midfield: shkn up 8th: handy 6th but looking outpcd whn mstke 3 out: rdn and no imp after* 50/1
5/ 7 *63* **Sovinnie (IRE)**[655] 1489 6-10-7 0..............................(t) ConorRing(5) 39
(Jane Mathias) *small: mstkes early: in last trio: rdn bef 7th: lost tch next: t.o bef 3 out* 66/1
05-1 8 *1 3/4* **Little Mix**[31] 378 4-11-0 0.. GavinSheehan 39
(Emma Lavelle) *t.k.h in 3rd pl tl 1/2-way: dropped out rapidly 9th: t.o next* 10/1[3]
5 9 *6* **One Day Like This (IRE)**[25] 460 5-10-12 0.................. RichardJohnson 32
(Tim Vaughan) *nt a fluent: led: reminder after 6th: hdd next: lost pl and mstke 9th: sn t.o* 20/1

5m 56.4s (7.40) **Going Correction** 0.0s/f (Good)
WFA 4 from 5yo+ 19lb **9 Ran SP% 120.5**
Speed ratings (Par 105): 87,86,85,85,84 82,61,60,58
CSF £121.06 TOTE £8.20: £1.70, £5.20, £4.20; EX 159.80 Trifecta £2136.80.
Owner R J Gambarini **Bred** Barronstown Stud **Trained** Llancarfan, Vale Of Glamorgan
■ Stewards' Enquiry : Gavin Sheehan vet said gelding finished distressed

FOCUS
The decent early gallop subsided to let the field bunch to around 8l at halfway, to the detriment of at least one of the joint-favourites. The was a case for rating the race higher.

774 HUGH JAMES SOLICITORS H'CAP HURDLE (6 hdls 6 omitted) 2m 7f 191y
8:15 (8:18) (Class 3) (0-125,125) 4-Y-O+ **£5,393** (£1,583; £791; £395)

Form RPR
10-1 1 **Kilfinichen Bay (IRE)**[13] 625 7-11-6 **119**.................... RichardJohnson 122+
(Charlie Longsdon) *plld hrd and cl up: led over 4f out: hrd drvn fnl 3f: kpt finding plenty: in command fnl f: v game* 5/2[1]
140- 2 *1 1/4* **Listen And Learn (IRE)**[222] 2347 7-11-8 **121**..............(v) WillKennedy 123+
(Jonjo O'Neill) *settled in 3rd pl: led bef 2 out (one m fr home): mstke last (normal 4 out): rdn and hdd over 4f out: hld fnl f* 8/1
126/ 3 *3/4* **Berea Boru (IRE)**[551] 3081 7-11-11 **124**...................(t) DonalDevereux 124
(Peter Bowen) *towards rr: rdn 4f out: wnt 3rd 2f out: kpt on ins fnl f but no real imp* 7/1
0-23 4 *3 3/4* **Lava Lamp (GER)**[12] 645 8-10-7 **113**........................ MrConorOrr(7) 110
(Evan Williams) *midfield: drvn in 6 l 4th 4f out: btn 2f out* 7/2[2]
3-52 5 *2* **Castle Conflict (IRE)**[14] 614 10-10-10 **109**...................(b) TomO'Brien 104
(Henry Daly) *pressed ldr tl rdn and lost pl over 4f out: plugged on after* 5/1[3]
P2-P 6 *2* **Howwrongcanyoube**[37] 261 6-11-2 **115**...............(p) WayneHutchinson 108
(Alan King) *chsd ldrs: 3 l 3rd home turn: rdn 3f out: one pce and no imp after* 9/1
0-16 7 *49* **Lets Get Serious (IRE)**[20] 535 9-11-12 **125**.................. DaveCrosse 74
(Dai Williams) *led: hdd bef 2 out (normal 5 out) where mstke whn wkng: sn t.o* 33/1
232- 8 *33* **Dais Return (IRE)**[281] 1514 11-9-13 **105**..............(t) CiaranGethings(7) 25
(John Coombe) *in tch: rdn 1/2-way: t.o fnl 4f: eased* 13/2

5m 44.4s (-4.60) **Going Correction** 0.0s/f (Good) **8 Ran SP% 117.3**
Speed ratings (Par 107): 107,106,106,105,104 103,87,76
CSF £23.41 CT £126.12 TOTE £2.80: £1.60, £3.40, £4.00; EX 26.40 Trifecta £70.40.
Owner Cracker Syndicate **Bred** Brian Kearney **Trained** Over Norton, Oxon

FOCUS
The feature event on the evening, but not for the first time a Ffos Las event diminished as a spectacle by the omission of all hurdles in the home straight due to low sun. The winner is on the upgrade and probably more to come.

775 CASTELL HOWELL H'CAP HURDLE (4 hdls 6 omitted) 2m 4f
8:45 (8:47) (Class 4) (0-120,118) 4-Y-O+ **£3,249** (£954; £477; £238)

Form RPR
46-1 1 **Just A Normal Day (IRE)**[16] 590 5-11-2 **108**................(p) HarrySkelton 113+
(Dan Skelton) *hld up: effrt in 4th home turn: sn rdn to chse wnr: wore him down fnl 100yds* 5/2[1]
1-51 2 *1/2* **Mont Royale**[16] 593 7-11-10 **116**.............................. RichieMcLernon 121+
(Jonjo O'Neill) *led: hrd rdn over 2f out: racing rather awkwardly after: hdd and no ex fnl 100yds* 9/2[2]
5-65 3 *17* **Hold Court (IRE)**[25] 449 8-11-11 **117**.............................. PaulMoloney 105
(Evan Williams) *disp 5 l last home turn: rdn and sn lft bhd by ldng pair* 6/1
2F-0 4 *1/2* **Western Diva (IRE)**[19] 556 6-11-12 **118**.................... TomScudamore 105
(David Pipe) *t.k.h in last pl: brief effrt over 4f out: t.o* 10/1
30-F 5 *4* **Prettyasapicture**[16] 593 6-11-2 **108**..................(p) WayneHutchinson 91
(Alan King) *chsd ldrs: rdn in 3rd home turn: sn n.d* 10/1
P-30 6 *3 1/2* **Party Palace**[6] 718 11-11-0 **106**................................ GavinSheehan 86
(Stuart Howe) *midfield: rdn and lost pl home turn: sn wl bhd* 14/1
U0-1 7 *2 1/2* **Tara Mac**[42] 153 6-10-12 **104**.................................... MichaelByrne 81
(Tim Vaughan) *chsd ldrs: rdn 10f out: wknd 4f out: t.o* 5/1[3]
0-22 8 *15* **Baths Well (IRE)**[21] 529 5-11-7 **113**.............................. DavidBass 75
(Ben Pauling) *t.k.h in 2nd tl rdn home turn: dropped out tamely: t.o* 6/1

4m 47.6s (287.60) **8 Ran SP% 116.8**
CSF £14.92 CT £61.05 TOTE £4.40: £1.90, £1.50, £2.30; EX 15.70 Trifecta £80.70.
Owner CNC Routing Ltd **Bred** Mrs Grace Bracken **Trained** Alcester, Warwicks
■ Stewards' Enquiry : Harry Skelton four-day ban: used whip above permitted level (Jul 2,3,5,6)

FOCUS
Just four hurdles out of the ten were jumped due to the low sun and the moderate gallop resulted into something of a 6f sprint.

776 CP HIRE H'CAP HURDLE (3 hdls 5 omitted) 1m 7f 202y
9:15 (9:19) (Class 4) (0-110,109) 4-Y-O+ **£3,249** (£954; £477; £238)

Form RPR
0/6- 1 **Little Pop**[266] 1622 7-11-11 **107**.........................(t) SamTwiston-Davies 113+
(Nigel Twiston-Davies) *mde all: drew clr 4f out: 4 l ahd 1f out: rdn and a looked to be holding on to diminishing advantage after* 7/2[2]
3-46 2 *1* **Astaroland (FR)**[21] 529 5-11-6 **102**............................ PeterCarberry 105
(Jennie Candlish) *chsd ldrs: rdn to go 2nd 2f out: styd on steadily ins fnl f but nvr looked getting past wnr* 7/2[2]
0-60 3 *2 1/2* **Grams And Ounces**[5] 615 8-10-9 **91**........................(t) MichealNolan 92
(Adrian Wintle) *hld up: effrt 3f out: rdn to take 3rd cl home: nvr looked like chalng wnr* 16/1
6-04 4 *nk* **Ashkoun (FR)**[25] 449 4-11-4 **103**........................(t) RichardJohnson 100
(Tim Vaughan) *hld up: effrt 4f out: drvn 2f out: sn no imp: lost 3rd nr fin* 8/1
05-1 5 *1 3/4* **Mac Bertie**[14] 615 6-11-8 **104**..................................(p) AdamWedge 103
(Evan Williams) *pressed wnr tl rdn and lost pl 4f out: plugged on steadily* 5/2[1]
P2-2 6 *1 1/4* **Descaro (USA)**[44] 125 9-10-12 **101**........................ JamesO'Neill(7) 99
(John O'Shea) *dropped towards rr 5f out: sme late prog but no ch* 25/1
0/0- 7 *14* **Makethedifference (IRE)**[55] 5508 7-11-12 **108**.............. MichaelByrne 96
(Tim Vaughan) *mstke 2nd: t.o* 14/1
5-32 8 *3* **Age Of Discovery**[29] 396 4-11-6 **105**........................(t) HarrySkelton 84
(Dan Skelton) *prom tl hrd drvn and wknd over 4f out: t.o* 6/1[3]
-U65 9 *nk* **Alla Svelta (IRE)**[9] 669 9-11-10 **106**.................(t) BrendanPowell 88
(Brendan Powell) *blnd bdly 1st: nvr travelling after: t.o fnl 6f* 8/1
0-6F 10 *1 1/2* **Gorman (FR)**[25] 465 4-11-1 **100**.............................. PaulMoloney 78
(Evan Williams) *t.k.h in rr: brief effrt 4f out: t.o* 10/1
40F- 11 *1 1/4* **Say When**[210] 2618 7-10-10 **102**.............................. JamieInsole(10) 82
(Alan King) *lost tch 4f out: t.o* 33/1

3m 43.6s (-4.90)
WFA 4 from 5yo+ 17lb **11 Ran SP% 124.4**
CSF £30.60 CT £361.82 TOTE £5.40: £1.40, £2.80, £9.10; EX 33.10 Trifecta £674.40.
Owner S Such & Cg Paletta **Bred** Jethro Bloodstock **Trained** Naunton, Gloucs

FOCUS
Only three hurdles were jumped in this finale. The winner threatened this sort of figure as a novice.
T/Plt: £400.90 to a £1 stake. Pool of £52611.92 - 95.80 winning tickets. T/Qpdt: £84.50 to a £1 stake. Pool of £4784.75 - 41.90 winning tickets. **Iain Mackenzie**

620 MARKET RASEN (R-H)
Friday, June 19

OFFICIAL GOING: Good (watered; chs 8.5, hdl 8.6)
Wind: light 1/2 against Weather: overcast

777 SVITZER NOVICES' H'CAP HURDLE (8 hdls) 2m 148y
2:10 (2:12) (Class 5) (0-100,100) 4-Y-O+ **£2,274** (£667; £333; £166)

Form RPR
0-U1 1 **Russian Royale**[12] 658 5-11-4 **95** 7ex........................ CraigNichol(3) 105+
(Micky Hammond) *trckd ldrs: led narrowly 2 out: edgd rt and drvn clr run-in* 4/5[1]
-P04 2 *5* **Tennessee Bird**[8] 692 7-10-0 **74** oh5........................ GavinSheehan 77
(Mike Sowersby) *t.k.h detached in last: hdwy 3 out: handy 3rd appr next: kpt on same pce: tk modest 2nd nr fin* 7/2[2]
0-23 3 *3/4* **Oneofapear (IRE)**[14] 626 9-11-9 **100**.....................(p) AdamNicol(3) 102
(Mike Sowersby) *trckd ldr: led 4th: hdd 2 out: kpt on one pce* 7/1
/6-0 4 *22* **Mahayogin (USA)**[24] 489 7-10-7 **81** ow2..................(t) RobertDunne 63
(Sarah-Jayne Davies) *chsd ldrs: 4th and wkng appr 2 out* 25/1
600- 5 *6* **Aregra (FR)**[232] 2145 5-10-8 **82**................................ BrianHughes 59
(Peter Niven) *chsd ldrs: nt fluent 2nd: lost pl 3 out: sn bhd* 16/1
6 *1 1/4* **See It As It Is (IRE)**[82] 8-11-5 **100**.......................... MissTWorsley(7) 76
(Diana Grissell) *bolted gng to s: led: pushed along and hdd 4th: wknd 3 out: sn bhd* 40/1
03-P 7 *37* **Simplified**[17] 591 12-9-9 **74** oh10...........................(t) JoeCornwall(5) 16
(Michael Chapman) *in rr: nt fluent 3rd: sn pushed along: bhd fr 5th: sn t.o: eventually completed* 100/1
0P0- F **Northern Oscar (IRE)**[273] 1576 7-11-0 **88**...................... AdamPogson
(Charles Pogson) *t.k.h: mstke 1st: chsd ldrs: outpcd whn fell 5th* 16/1

The Form Book Jumps 2015-16, Raceform Ltd, Newbury, RG14 5SJ

6P-0 **U** **Paddy Mulligan (IRE)**[8] 695 6-11-2 **97**.................... MrAlexFerguson(7)
(John Ferguson) *chsd ldrs: swvd bdly lft: attempted to run out and uns rdr 5th* **13/2**[3]

4m 10.5s (3.80) **Going Correction** +0.275s/f (Yiel) 9 Ran SP% **122.7**
Speed ratings (Par 103): **102,99,99,88,86 85,68,,**
CSF £4.75 CT £12.97 TOTE £1.60: £1.10, £1.20, £1.50; EX 5.00 Trifecta £19.20.
Owner Richard & Katherine Gilbert **Bred** Mrs P A & M J Reditt **Trained** Middleham, N Yorks
■ Stewards' Enquiry : Robert Dunne twelve-day ban: 12 Aug-29 Aug (weighed in 2lb over)

FOCUS
Rail set out 18 yards on the wood bend and 30 yards on the stands' bend, adding approximately 198 yards to races 1, 2, 3 and 7, and approximately 288 yards to races 4, 5 and 6. Good ground that had been watered. This was a weak race of its type and another step up from the winner.

778 GBA GROUP JUVENILE HURDLE (8 hdls) 2m 148y
2:45 (2:45) (Class 4) 3-Y-0 **£3,249** (£954; £477; £238)

Form RPR
1 **Mountainside**[209] 3-10-12 0.. AidanColeman 93+
(John Ferguson) *in rr: drvn 5th: hdwy after next: 2nd appr 2 out: styd on wl run-in: led last 75yds: forged clr* **5/2**[2]

1 **2** *3 ¼* **Dominada (IRE)**[8] 690 3-11-5 0.................................. RichardJohnson 98+
(Brian Ellison) *nt jump wl: led: lft clr 3rd: mstke 2 out: over 1 l ahd last: hdd last 75yds: fdd towards fin* **4/6**[1]

4 **3** *¾* **Ace Of Marmalade (IRE)**[13] 636 3-10-5 0................ CraigGallagher(7) 88
(Brian Ellison) *chsd ldrs: drvn 3 out: 2nd bef next: kpt on same pce run-in* **40/1**

3 **4** *6* **Fast Scat (USA)**[8] 690 3-10-5 0.................................. SeanQuinlan 78
(David Evans) *chsd ldrs: lost pl appr 2 out: wkng whn hung rt run-in* **50/1**

U **5** *9* **Smugglers Lane (IRE)**[8] 690 3-10-12 0............................ JamieMoore 75
(David Evans) *in rr: drvn 5th: sme hdwy next: lost pl appr 2 out* **16/1**

6 *60* **Chic Name (FR)**[17] 3-10-12 0.. AlainCawley 21
(Richard Hobson) *chsd ldng pair: lft 2nd 3rd: drvn 5th: wknd next: sn t.o: eventually completed* **12/1**[3]

U **Whisky Marmalade (IRE)**[24] 3-10-5 0.............................. AndrewTinkler
(Ben Haslam) *t.k.h: trckd ldr: j.rt and uns rdr 3rd* **14/1**

4m 11.0s (4.30) **Going Correction** +0.275s/f (Yiel) 7 Ran SP% **113.2**
Speed ratings: **100,98,98,95,91 62,**
CSF £4.58 TOTE £4.10: £1.10, £1.30; EX 5.30 Trifecta £54.20.
Owner Bloomfields **Bred** Darley **Trained** Cowlinge, Suffolk

FOCUS
A modest juvenile hurdle. The time was half a second slower than the preceding race, but the winner should go on to rate higher.

779 DFDS SEAWAYS NOVICES' CHASE (14 fncs) 2m 3f 34y
3:20 (3:24) (Class 4) 5-Y-0+ **£3,861** (£1,198; £645)

Form RPR
00-1 **1** **Vieux Lion Rouge (FR)**[32] 382 6-11-5 0.......................... TomScudamore 138+
(David Pipe) *gifted long ld s: mde all: coasted home* **1/3**[1]

6P-3 **2** *7* **Aalim**[8] 701 5-10-12 0..(p) AidanColeman 122+
(John Ferguson) *hld up: wnt distant 2nd at 2nd: effrt and reminders appr 3 out: 7 l down at last: no ch w wnr* **9/4**[2]

00P- **3** *87* **Joyful Motive**[79] 5091 6-10-5 0.................................. ThomasCheesman(7) 43
(Michael Chapman) *distant 3rd 3rd: drvn 6th: reminders next: t.o 11th: eventually completed* **50/1**

6P-3 **R** **Radsoc De Sivola (FR)**[19] 570 10-10-12 50.......................... AdamPogson
(John Cornwall) *ref to r: lft at s* **80/1**

06-0 **P** **Dontupsettherhythm (IRE)**[25] 468 10-10-7 85.............. MrJohnDawson(5)
(Michael Chapman) *distant last fr 3rd: t.o whn p.u bef 10th: lame* **20/1**[3]

4m 52.8s (-12.90) **Going Correction** -0.70s/f (Firm) 5 Ran SP% **113.7**
Speed ratings: **99,96,59,,**
CSF £1.63 TOTE £1.20: £1.10, £1.40; EX 1.50 Trifecta £6.10.
Owner Prof Caroline Tisdall & John Gent **Bred** F M Cottin **Trained** Nicholashayne, Devon

FOCUS
A farcical start saw the favourite left in an unassailable lead. Form to ignore.

780 ABP H'CAP HURDLE (10 hdls) 2m 4f 139y
3:55 (3:55) (Class 4) (0-120,120) 4-Y-0+ **£3,249** (£954; £477; £238)

Form RPR
2-11 **1** **Ruaraidh Hugh (IRE)**[14] 626 6-10-4 **105**........(b) MrTommieMO'Brien(7) 116+
(Chris Bealby) *hld up: trckd ldrs 5th: stmbld on landing 7th: drvn to ld 2 out: forged clr bef last: rdn out* **9/4**[2]

0F-P **2** *10* **Spring Steel (IRE)**[37] 283 6-11-2 **110**..........................(t) NicodeBoinville 111
(Ben Pauling) *led to 1st: chsd ldr: led briefly appr 2 out: kpt on same pce between last 2* **13/2**[3]

40-1 **3** *1 ¾* **Antony (FR)**[10] 669 5-11-9 **117** 7ex.................................. JamieMoore 118+
(Gary Moore) *hld up in rr: hdwy to trck ldrs 3 out: 3rd and drvn: blnd 2 out: one pce* **13/8**[1]

2-22 **4** *4* **Ballycamp (IRE)**[30] 397 6-11-12 **120**.................................. AdamPogson 115
(Charles Pogson) *trckd ldrs: t.k.h: 2nd 6th: led next: hdd appr 2 out: wknd between last 2* **16/1**

/1-4 **5** *8* **Age Of Glory**[48] 82 6-11-8 **116**.. SeanQuinlan 106
(Barbara Butterworth) *in rr: chsd ldrs 5th: lost pl 3 out: sn bhd* **14/1**

3-00 **6** *8* **Boruma (IRE)**[33] 356 5-11-2 **110**...................................... HenryBrooke 95
(Dianne Sayer) *led 1st: hdd 7th: lost pl next: bhd whn j. bdly lft and blnd last* **14/1**

6-34 **7** *13* **Lawsons Thorns (IRE)**[14] 625 6-10-10 **104**........................ BrianHughes 73
(Mike Sowersby) *hld up in rr: bhd fr 3 out* **8/1**

5m 15.1s (6.30) **Going Correction** +0.275s/f (Yiel) 7 Ran SP% **112.5**
Speed ratings (Par 105): **99,95,94,93,89 86,81**
CSF £16.60 CT £28.27 TOTE £3.30: £1.30, £4.30; EX 16.70 Trifecta £85.20.
Owner Triumph In Mind **Bred** Peter McCarthy **Trained** Barrowby, Lincs

FOCUS
Fair handicap form and the winner is on the upgrade.

781 PD PORTS H'CAP CHASE (14 fncs) 2m 5f 89y
4:35 (4:36) (Class 3) (0-140,127) 5-Y-0+ **£7,797** (£2,289; £1,144; £572)

Form RPR
P-05 **1** **Bar De Ligne (FR)**[12] 660 9-11-12 **127**........................(p) RichardJohnson 134+
(Brian Ellison) *chsd ldrs: 2nd 7th: hit 3 out: edgd rt and led last 150yds: hld on towards fin* **9/4**[1]

P33- **2** *nk* **Harrys Whim**[230] 2194 10-10-6 **110**..........................(t) JonathanEngland(3) 116
(Maurice Barnes) *led: edgd lft 2 out: hdd and edgd rt last 150yds: kpt on clsng stages* **6/1**

0P5/ **3** *7* **King's Legacy (IRE)**[12] 11-11-4 **119**................................(t) AidanColeman 119
(Lawney Hill) *in rr: hdwy to chse ldrs 10th: 3rd 2 out: one pce* **11/1**

1-53 **4** *6* **Itsuptoyou (IRE)**[13] 642 11-11-7 **122**................................ TomScudamore 116
(Arthur Whiting) *hdwy and handy 3rd 8th: drvn appr 3 out: wknd between last 2* **9/2**

343- **5** *10* **Tregaro (FR)**[169] 3439 9-10-4 **105**....................................(t) BrianHughes 92
(Mike Sowersby) *hld up in rr: hdwy to chse ldrs 11th: wknd 2 out* **4/1**[3]

-210 **6** *37* **Jack Albert (IRE)**[7] 705 8-10-9 **110**................................(b) BrianHarding 62
(Dianne Sayer) *chsd ldr to 7th: pushed along next: reminders and lost pl 10th: sn bhd: t.o 2 out* **7/2**[2]

5m 32.0s (-14.00) **Going Correction** -0.70s/f (Firm) 6 Ran SP% **113.8**
Speed ratings: **98,97,95,92,89 75**
CSF £16.00 TOTE £3.10: £1.60, £3.50; EX 19.80 Trifecta £122.30.
Owner P J Martin **Bred** Neustrian Associates **Trained** Norton, N Yorks

FOCUS
Not a strong race for the grade with the winner, under top weight, running off 13lb below the race ceiling. The pace was decent.

782 GP SHIPPING NOVICES' H'CAP CHASE (17 fncs) 2m 7f 191y
5:10 (5:10) (Class 4) (0-105,105) 5-Y-0+ **£3,768** (£1,106; £553; £276)

Form RPR
50-P **1** **Twojayslad**[38] 261 6-11-12 **105**.. WillKennedy 118+
(Ian Williams) *chsd ldrs: led sn after 15th: pushed out* **8/1**

6-33 **2** *6* **Combustible Kate (IRE)**[24] 493 9-10-1 **80**.......................... AdamWedge 85
(Nick Kent) *chsd ldrs: drvn appr 3 out: kpt on same pce to take 2nd last 150yds* **6/1**[3]

F2-1 **3** *1 ½* **The Purchaser (IRE)**[42] 183 7-11-4 **97**......................(b) TomMessenger 100
(Chris Bealby) *mde most tl sn after 4 out: kpt on one pce appr last* **7/2**[1]

-624 **4** *6* **The Society Man (IRE)**[19] 567 8-10-13 **97**.................... JoeCornwall(5) 94
(Michael Chapman) *chsd ldrs: one pce fr 3 out* **16/1**

1-22 **5** *18* **Royalracket (IRE)**[24] 490 7-11-2 **95**............................(b) LiamTreadwell 76
(Paul Webber) *mid-div: lost pl 12th: hit 14th: sn bhd* **9/2**[2]

00-4 **6** *hd* **Lock Towers (IRE)**[13] 641 6-11-12 **105**............................(t) NicodeBoinville 86
(Ben Pauling) *in rr: hdwy 12th: chsng ldrs 14th: wknd 2 out* **9/1**

5/P- **7** *9* **Tipsy Gypsy (IRE)**[412] 89 8-11-10 **103**.............................. TomCannon 76
(Nick Gifford) *w ldr: lost pl bef 3 out: sn bhd* **14/1**

12-2 **P** **Thoresby (IRE)**[42] 183 9-11-12 **105**....................................(p) DarylJacob
(Ben Case) *chsd ldrs: p.u bef 11th: fatally injured* **6/1**[3]

04/0 **P** **Oscar Baby (IRE)**[16] 597 9-10-1 **80**.............................. MarcGoldstein
(Diana Grissell) *in rr: reminders 7th: bhd 9th: t.o whn p.u sn after 14th* **14/1**

2PP/ **P** **Foxes Bridge**[33] 7-11-2 **95**.. GavinSheehan
(Nick Mitchell) *chsd ldrs: drvn and lost pl 4th: bhd whn mstke 10th: t.o 12th: p.u sn after 14th* **25/1**

2-0U **P** **Driving Well (IRE)**[8] 698 7-10-7 **86**.................................. RobertDunne
(Arthur Whiting) *prom: lost pl 11th: bhd whn eased and p.u bef 13th* **16/1**

6m 12.7s (-18.60) **Going Correction** -0.70s/f (Firm) 11 Ran SP% **119.0**
Speed ratings: **103,101,100,98,92 92,89,,,**
CSF £57.05 CT £202.05 TOTE £10.20: £2.60, £3.60, £1.70; EX 78.20 Trifecta £606.50.
Owner J Tredwell **Bred** J Tredwell **Trained** Portway, Worcs

FOCUS
A competitive race of its type, run at a fair gallop. The winner was stepping up on his hurdles form.

783 SEA-CARGO STANDARD OPEN NATIONAL HUNT FLAT RACE 2m 148y
5:45 (5:45) (Class 6) 4-6-Y-0 **£1,559** (£457; £228; £114)

Form RPR
6 **1** **Mr Kite**[13] 644 4-10-13 0.. GavinSheehan 95+
(Mick Channon) *mde all: drvn over 3f out: clr over 1f out: rdn out* **11/2**[2]

2 *9* **Kendari King (IRE)** 4-10-13 0...................................... RichardJohnson 87
(Tim Vaughan) *chsd ldng pair: drvn over 5f out: kpt on to take modest 2nd 1f out* **8/1**

3 *2 ¼* **Presenting Streak (IRE)**[46] 6-10-9 0.............................. MrRWinks(7) 88
(Peter Winks) *mid-div: hdwy to chse ldrs after 4f: drvn over 5f out: kpt on one pce to take modest 3rd last 150yds* **20/1**

4 *2* **Junior Package** 4-10-13 0.. TomScudamore 83
(David Pipe) *trckd wnr: effrt over 3f out: rdn over 1f out: sn wknd* **5/6**[1]

5 *17* **Balkato Des Bois (FR)**[89] 4-10-13 0.................................. RobertDunne 68
(Tom Lacey) *t.k.h in rr: hdwy 7f out: drvn over 5f out: lost pl over 2f out: heavily eased fnl f* **15/2**[3]

6 *91* **Noble Air** 5-11-2 0.. DougieCostello
(Tony Coyle) *mid-div: pushed along after 4f: reminders over 6f out: sn lost pl and bhd: tailed rt off over 4f out: eventually fin* **20/1**

7 *2 ½* **Farang Ber Song** 4-10-13 0.. TomO'Brien
(Declan Carroll) *hld up in rr: t.k.h: brief effrt 6f out: sn lost pl and bhd: tailed rt off over 4f out: eventually fin* **10/1**

8 *15* **Twosons** 5-11-2 0.. BrianHughes
(Malcolm Jefferson) *in rr: drvn 6f out: sn lost pl tailed rt off over 4f out: eventually fin* **9/1**

4m 4.1s (3.00) **Going Correction** +0.275s/f (Yiel)
WFA 4 from 5yo+ 3lb 8 Ran SP% **121.4**
Speed ratings: **103,98,97,96,88 45,44,37**
CSF £51.46 TOTE £5.60: £2.70, £2.40, £4.40; EX 38.80 Trifecta £161.00.
Owner M Channon **Bred** R W K Lewis **Trained** West Ilsley, Berks

FOCUS
The winner set a reasonable gallop in this modest bumper.
T/Plt: £18.80 to a £1 stake. Pool: £40,514.95 - 1,566.37 winning tickets T/Qpdt: £19.10 to a £1 stake. Pool: £2,021.76 - 78.00 winning tickets **Walter Glynn**

784 - 797a (Foreign Racing) - See Raceform Interactive

726

HEXHAM (L-H)
Sunday, June 21

OFFICIAL GOING: Good (good to soft in places; 6.8)
Wind: fresh against Weather: Cloudy

798 TOTEPLACEPOT RACING'S FAVOURITE BET CONDITIONAL JOCKEYS' (S) HURDLE (12 hdls) 2m 7f 63y
2:30 (2:30) (Class 4) 4-Y-0+ **£3,627** (£1,057; £528)

Form RPR
04-3 **1** **What A Steel (IRE)**[9] 705 11-11-0 105..........................(p) CraigNichol 109
(Alistair Whillans) *trckd ldr: led narrowly 3 out: rdn appr last: styd on and c clr run-in* **15/2**

5-2P **2** *4 ½* **An Poc Ar Buile (IRE)**[22] 553 6-11-2 0.......................... ConorShoemark(3) 113
(Fergal O'Brien) *hld up: tk clsr order 5th: prom fr 9th: upsides whn slow 2 out: sn rdn: l down whn hit last: edgd lft and no ex run-in* **4/1**[3]

62/1 **3** *11* **Celtic Monarch (IRE)**[15] 634 6-11-5 112.............................. DerekFox 100
(Mark Michael McNiff, Ire) *hld up: hdwy after 3 out: wnt 3rd 2 out: sn rdn: no imp* **7/1**

4-23 **4** *4* **Man Of Leisure**[24] 527 11-11-5 125........................(t) CiaranGethings(3) 100
(Anthony Honeyball) *hld up in rr: hdwy after 3 out: wnt 4th after 2 out: rdn appr last: no imp* **7/2**[2]
-654 **5** *4* **Mister Jones**[26] 487 7-10-4 78.............................. StephenMcCarthy(10) 88
(Sue Smith) *hld up: hdwy into midfield 7th: rdn and outpcd after 3 out: plugged on fr appr last* **33/1**
21-P **6** *shd* **Debt To Society (IRE)**[52] 38 8-11-9 110.............(vt) HarryChalloner(3) 100
(Richard Ford) *midfield: hdwy into 3rd after 3 out: lost 3rd 2 out: wknd appr last* **22/1**
4P5U **7** *61* **Sharivarry (FR)**[15] 639 9-10-11 81............................ JamieHamilton(3) 33
(Victor Thompson) *midfield: wknd after 3 out* **100/1**
P-P6 **8** *5* **Solway Trigger**[15] 634 6-10-6 0.. RyanDay(8) 29
(Lisa Harrison) *hld up: hdwy to trck ldrs 8th: wknd after 3 out* **150/1**
P-6P **P** **Takaatuf (IRE)**[24] 519 9-11-0 82...............................(t) JonathanEngland
(Tina Jackson) *trckd ldrs: lost pl after 8th: sn struggling: t.o whn p.u bef last* **125/1**
602- **F** **Arctic Court (IRE)**[65] 5366 11-11-5 121........................ GrahamWatters
(Jim Goldie) *midfield: fell 5th* **13/8**[1]
03-P **P** **Castley Lane**[26] 484 9-11-0 91..................................(tp) KillianMoore
(Sara Ender) *prom: lost pl after 8th: sn struggling: t.o whn p.u bef last* **100/1**
00 **P** **Ballymorris (IRE)**[15] 635 6-11-0 0...............................(b[1]) DiarmuidO'Regan
(Kenny Johnson) *led: hit 3 out and hdd: sn wknd: p.u bef last* **200/1**

6m 6.6s (-2.40) **Going Correction** -0.25s/f (Good) **12** Ran SP% **115.8**
Speed ratings (Par 105): **94,92,88,87,85 85,64,62, , ,**
CSF £36.74 TOTE £8.60: £2.90, £2.10, £2.60; EX 53.10 Trifecta £339.40.There was no bid for the winner. An Poc Ar Buile was claimed by Mrs S. V. O. Leech for £6,000.
Owner J D Wright **Bred** D Dean **Trained** Newmill-On-Slitrig, Borders

FOCUS
Fresh ground on all bends. The going was good, good to soft in places after 2mm of overnight rain. A long distance selling hurdle and the first two had it between them from some way out.

799 TOTEPOOL SPONSORING EVERY UK RACE TODAY NOVICES' HURDLE (8 hdls) 2m 48y
3:00 (3:01) (Class 4) 4-Y-0+ **£4,790** (£1,396; £698)

Form RPR
-251 **1** **Owen Na View (IRE)**[14] 659 7-10-12 0........................ PaddyBrennan 106+
(Fergal O'Brien) *mde all: rdn after 2 out: pressed appr last: styd on and a in command run-in* **6/4**[1]
6- **2** *3¾* **Galizzi (USA)**[171] 3461 4-10-9 0................................. JackQuinlan 101+
(John Ferguson) *trckd ldr: chal appr last: upsides whn mstke last: rdn and no ex* **11/4**[3]
023- **3** *1* **Lockedoutaheaven (IRE)**[47] 4970 4-10-6 102.......(t) JonathanEngland(3) 97
(Maurice Barnes) *midfield: pckd on landing 3 out: rdn and hdwy after 2 out: wnt 3rd appr last: styd on: edgd lft run-in* **14/1**
0-4 **4** *3* **Rocky Two (IRE)**[15] 634 5-10-9 0................................ AdamNicol(3) 97
(Philip Kirby) *in tch: rdn and outpcd bef 2 out: styd on fr appr last* **33/1**
/615 **5** *4* **Running Brook (IRE)**[8] 727 8-11-0 117...................... CallumBewley(5) 101
(R Mike Smith) *trckd ldr: rdn after 2 out: wknd appr last* **20/1**
10-2 **6** *2* **Apachee Prince (IRE)**[28] 456 6-11-5 120....................(p) BrianHughes 100
(Alistair Whillans) *trckd ldr: rdn after 2 out: wknd appr last* **9/4**[2]
-360 **7** *13* **Johnny Go**[14] 656 5-10-5 0... RyanDay(7) 80
(Lisa Harrison) *midfield: rdn after 3 out: wknd after 2 out* **100/1**
64 **8** *3¼* **Flemerina (IRE)**[12] 682 6-10-5 0.................................... SeanQuinlan 70
(Sue Smith) *midfield: hit 5th: rdn after 3 out: wknd after 2 out* **25/1**
0 **9** *14* **Coppelia (IRE)**[14] 656 7-10-5 0.................................... BrianHarding 58
(Nicky Richards) *hld up: pushed along after 3 out: sn wknd* **66/1**
0-U **10** *6* **Saint Elm (FR)**[12] 684 5-10-9 0..................................... DerekFox(3) 59
(Patrick Griffin, Ire) *hld up: wknd after 2 out* **200/1**
0- **11** *29* **Run To The Rhythm**[123] 4296 5-10-12 0.......................... JakeGreenall 33
(Michael Easterby) *v.s.a: a in rr* **80/1**
12 *1½* **Megansfield**[56] 6-9-12 0.. MrWHRReed(7) 25
(Kenny Johnson) *in tch: lost pl after 4th: bhd after 3 out* **200/1**
000- **P** **Nowreyna**[15] 3501 4-9-12 0 ow1....................................... MissCWalton(5)
(Kenny Johnson) *a in rr: p.u bef 2 out* **200/1**

4m 13.2s (-4.20) **Going Correction** -0.25s/f (Good)
WFA 4 from 5yo+ 17lb **13** Ran SP% **120.9**
Speed ratings (Par 105): **100,98,97,96,94 93,86,85,78,75 60,59,**
CSF £5.93 TOTE £2.50: £1.10, £1.70, £3.10; EX 7.60 Trifecta £53.70.
Owner The Yes No Wait Sorries **Bred** Brian Walsh **Trained** Naunton, Gloucs

FOCUS
A couple of fair sorts in this novices' hurdle but only three mattered in the betting and two of those dominated. Fair form for the time of year.

800 TOTEQUADPOT FOUR PLACES IN FOUR RACES H'CAP CHASE (19 fncs) 3m 41y
3:30 (3:31) (Class 3) (0-130,128) 5-Y-0+ **£7,797** (£2,289; £1,144; £572)

Form RPR
-311 **1** **Chicago Outfit (IRE)**[15] 637 10-10-3 110.............(p) JonathonBewley(5) 124+
(George Bewley) *mde all: jnd 13th: rdn after 2 out: asserted appr last: styd on* **7/2**[3]
4-64 **2** *1¾* **Green Wizard (IRE)**[35] 358 9-10-3 105.......................... SeanQuinlan 115
(Sue Smith) *trckd ldr: jnd ldr 13th: hit 4 out: rdn after 2 out: outpcd by wnr appr last: styd on run-in* **7/1**
F411 **3** *31* **Pekanheim (IRE)**[15] 639 7-10-5 114.............................. MrZBaker(7) 97
(Martin Todhunter) *midfield: rdn in 4th whn blnd 2 out: plugged on into remote 3rd after last* **10/3**[2]
-331 **4** *¾* **Master Of The Hall (IRE)**[8] 729 11-10-10 119............ JamieBargary(7) 99
(Micky Hammond) *midfield: wnt modest 3rd bef 3 out: sn rdn: wknd last: lost 3rd run-in* **11/4**[1]
4/P- **5** *2* **Problema Tic (FR)**[401] 319 9-11-9 128.......................(t) TonyKelly(3) 107
(Jackie Stephen) *wl bhd tl plugged on fr appr last* **20/1**
12-3 **6** *2¾* **Beeves (IRE)**[28] 458 8-11-9 125.................................(b) HenryBrooke 101
(Donald McCain) *chsd clr ldng pair: pushed along and lost pl after 13th: wknd after 2 out* **5/1**
2144 **P** **Super Collider**[15] 635 8-10-9 118..............................(t) JamesCorbett(7)
(Susan Corbett) *a in rr: p.u bef 2 out* **22/1**
65P- **P** **Dystonia's Revenge (IRE)**[58] 5518 10-10-3 112............ MrTHamilton(7)
(Sheena Walton) *hld up: pushed along after 12th: sn struggling: t.o whn p.u bef last* **18/1**

6m 25.9s (-6.30) **Going Correction** -0.05s/f (Good) **8** Ran SP% **115.5**
Speed ratings: **108,107,97,96,96 95, ,**
CSF £28.27 CT £88.09 TOTE £5.40: £1.50, £4.40, £1.50; EX 30.90 Trifecta £142.80.
Owner G T Bewley **Bred** Roger Ryan **Trained** Bonchester Bridge, Borders

FOCUS
The feature race and a decent contest for the time of year. The first two went off at a good lick and nothing else could get near them.

801 MYTOTEPOOL.COM NOVICES' CHASE (12 fncs) 1m 7f 133y
4:00 (4:01) (Class 4) 5-Y-0+ **£5,848** (£1,717; £858; £429)

Form RPR
-102 **1** **Vodka Wells (FR)**[15] 638 5-10-5 0............................... JamieBargary(7) 131+
(Micky Hammond) *in tch: hit 4 out: nt fluent 3 out: smooth hdwy after 2 out: led last: rdn and kpt on* **6/5**[1]
0-41 **2** *2¼* **Gold Futures (IRE)**[15] 635 6-11-5 0............................... BrianHarding 134+
(Nicky Richards) *trckd ldr: led 5th tl 7th: rdn after 2 out: led again appr last: hdd last: drvn and one pce* **7/4**[2]
4-13 **3** *3½* **Mason Hindmarsh**[27] 469 8-11-5 125............................ PaddyBrennan 129
(Karen McLintock) *prom: led 7th: rdn after 2 out: hdd appr last: plugged on* **11/2**[3]
32/P **4** *16* **Lisbon (IRE)**[13] 666 7-10-12 124..................................(t) BrianHughes 106
(Patrick Griffin, Ire) *led tl 5th: trckd ldr: rdn after 3 out: wknd after 2 out* **12/1**
5 *12* **Longueville Flier (IRE)**[20] 584 6-10-2 0........................ FinianO'Toole(10) 94
(Micky Hammond) *hld up: rdn bef 3 out: wknd 2 out* **40/1**
003- **6** *39* **Captain Sharpe**[76] 4826 7-10-5 0................................ ThomasDowson(7) 55
(Kenny Johnson) *hld up in rr: nt fluent 4 out: sn pushed along: wknd 3 out* **66/1**

4m 5.2s (-4.60) **Going Correction** -0.05s/f (Good) **6** Ran SP% **108.8**
Speed ratings: **109,107,106,98,92 72**
CSF £3.56 TOTE £1.80: £1.10, £1.90; EX 4.00 Trifecta £8.30.
Owner The Newboulds **Bred** Berend Van Dalfsen **Trained** Middleham, N Yorks

FOCUS
An interesting novices' chase in which only three mattered in the betting and they finished clear.

802 TOTEEXACTA PICK THE 1ST AND 2ND H'CAP HURDLE (10 hdls) 2m 4f 28y
4:30 (4:30) (Class 4) (0-120,117) 4-Y-0+ **£5,523** (£1,621; £810; £405)

Form RPR
020- **1** **Serenity Now (IRE)**[30] 3079 7-10-10 108.................... CraigGallagher(7) 113+
(Brian Ellison) *hld up: pushed along and gd hdwy after 2 out: led bef last: sn rdn to assert: idled fnl 110yds* **12/1**
342- **2** *3* **Ballyvoque (IRE)**[69] 5315 9-11-6 111............................ JanFaltejsek 112
(George Charlton) *trckd ldr: jnd ldr 3 out: led appr 2 out: rdn whn hdd bef last: hit last: one pce* **5/1**[2]
32-2 **3** *hd* **Harvey's Hope**[15] 82 9-11-4 114..........................(t) MrJohnDawson(5) 114
(Keith Reveley) *midfield: hdwy after 2 out: sn trckd ldr: rdn and ev ch appr last: one pce run-in* **10/1**[3]
-1U2 **4** *½* **Danceintothelight**[10] 695 8-9-11 95.............................. JamieBargary(7) 94
(Micky Hammond) *trckd ldr: rdn after 2 out: one pce* **5/1**[2]
-660 **5** *25* **Hunters Belt (IRE)**[15] 638 11-10-11 107.............(bt) JonathonBewley(5) 84
(George Bewley) *w ldr: rdn after 2 out: sn wknd* **12/1**
002- **6** *15* **All That Remains (IRE)**[241] 2012 10-11-3 115..........(t) JamesCorbett(7) 78
(Susan Corbett) *hld up: a towards rr* **20/1**
-0F0 **7** *9* **Groomed (IRE)**[12] 681 7-11-5 110.................................. SeanQuinlan 65
(Sue Smith) *led: rdn whn hdd appr 2 out: sn wknd* **20/1**
2-23 **F** **Tekthelot (IRE)**[15] 638 9-11-12 117.............................. BrianHughes
(Keith Reveley) *midfield on inner: fell 7th* **11/10**[1]

5m 8.7s (-3.80) **Going Correction** -0.25s/f (Good) **8** Ran SP% **115.0**
Speed ratings (Par 105): **97,95,95,95,85 79,75,**
CSF £71.25 CT £623.75 TOTE £14.10: £3.40, £1.10, £2.40; EX 82.00 Trifecta £636.30.
Owner J M Basquill **Bred** Citadel Stud **Trained** Norton, N Yorks

FOCUS
A modest handicap hurdle but a race of changing fortunes.

803 TOTETRIFECTA WIN BIG MONEY H'CAP CHASE (19 fncs) 3m 41y
5:00 (5:01) (Class 5) (0-100,100) 5-Y-0+ **£4,223** (£1,240; £620; £310)

Form RPR
-412 **1** **Solway Legend**[15] 637 8-10-3 84.. RyanDay(7) 97+
(Lisa Harrison) *midfield: hdwy to trck ldrs 14th: led last: rdn and styd on wl* **15/2**
5-31 **2** *4* **Troubled (IRE)**[21] 567 8-10-4 78...................................(p) BrianHughes 85
(David Thompson) *prom: rdn after 2 out: kpt on* **6/1**[2]
3-54 **3** *½* **Pyjama Game (IRE)**[26] 486 9-10-12 93...................... ThomasDowson(7) 101
(Rose Dobbin) *led: rdn 2 out: nt fluent and hdd last: no ex* **8/1**
5U-2 **4** *shd* **Mia's Anthem (IRE)**[26] 486 7-11-3 94.............................. DerekFox(3) 100
(Noel C Kelly, Ire) *trckd ldrs: rdn after 2 out: plugged on* **9/2**[1]
350 **5** *2½* **Senor Alco (FR)**[8] 726 9-9-12 79................................. MrWHRReed(7) 83
(Victor Thompson) *midfield: rdn after 2 out: plugged on* **28/1**
-30P **6** *½* **Generous Chief (IRE)**[12] 676 7-11-3 96..........(b[1]) DiarmuidO'Regan(5) 101
(Chris Grant) *hld up: nt fluent 9th: rdn after 2 out: styd on fr last: nvr threatened* **20/1**
0-03 **7** *3* **Solway Sam**[26] 484 12-10-5 84..................................... CallumBewley(5) 85
(Lisa Harrison) *midfield: rdn after 2 out: no imp* **6/1**[2]
P-U3 **8** *21* **Prince Blackthorn (IRE)**[15] 639 9-10-4 78...................... BrianHarding 60
(Barry Murtagh) *hld up: hdwy bef 3 out: rdn after 2 out: wknd appr last* **25/1**
/P0- **9** *14* **Just Talking (IRE)**[21] 13-10-1 82.........................(bt) MissRMcDonald(7) 52
(Sara Ender) *trckd ldrs: rdn after 3 out: sn wknd* **80/1**
0-35 **P** **Indian Print (IRE)**[25] 506 11-10-9 90............................ RossChapman(7)
(Victor Thompson) *prom: lost pl qckly after 13th: p.u bef 15th* **22/1**
-04F **U** **Latest Fashion (IRE)**[15] 635 9-9-10 75 oh10 ow1(tp) StephenMulqueen(5)
(Christopher Wilson) *midfield: blnd and uns rdr 12th* **40/1**
4-13 **P** **Heart O Annandale (IRE)**[8] 730 8-10-13 90.........(t) JonathanEngland(3)
(Maurice Barnes) *hld up: dropped to rr after 10th: p.u bef 13th* **7/1**[3]
03-6 **P** **Steady Progress (IRE)**[22] 552 7-10-7 81.......................(t) PaddyBrennan
(Richard Ford) *hld up: hit 3 out: sn wknd: p.u bef last* **16/1**
3P-2 **P** **Mrs Jordan (IRE)**[25] 503 7-11-9 100...............................(t) KillianMoore(3)
(Sophie Leech) *a in rr: p.u bef last* **7/1**[3]

6m 34.0s (1.80) **Going Correction** -0.05s/f (Good) **14** Ran SP% **120.6**
Speed ratings: **95,93,93,93,92 92,91,84,79, , , ,**
CSF £48.83 CT £378.26 TOTE £8.90: £3.10, £2.20, £4.20; EX 49.00 Trifecta £688.40.
Owner Mr & Mrs Batey **Bred** D A Harrison **Trained** Aldoth, Cumbria

FOCUS
A low-grade handicap chase but ultimately a clear-cut winner.

804 TOTEPOOL RACING'S BIGGEST SUPPORTER H'CAP HURDLE (DIV I) (8 hdls) 2m 48y

5:30 (5:31) (Class 5) (0-100,100) 4-Y-0+ **£3,832** (£1,117; £558)

Form RPR

3-11 **1** **Baraboy (IRE)**[13] 336 5-11-7 **100** DiarmuidO'Regan[(5)] 105+
(Barry Murtagh) *midfield: pushed along and hdwy after 2 out: led appr last: rdn and kpt on* **2/1**[1]

6-20 **2** *2 ½* **The Ice Factor**[23] 537 7-10-6 **87** (p) JamieHamilton[(7)] 87
(Alison Hamilton) *led: rdn after 2 out: hdd appr last: kpt on* **4/1**[2]

43 **3** *1 ½* **My Escapade (IRE)**[31] 415 4-11-2 **100** MissAWaugh[(7)] 96
(Simon Waugh) *trckd ldr: rdn after 2 out: plugged on* **16/1**

3502 **4** *1* **Bob's Legend (IRE)**[15] 634 9-10-13 **94** (t) JamesCorbett[(7)] 92
(Susan Corbett) *hld up in rr: gd hdwy after 3 out to trck ldr 2 out: rdn and ev ch appr last: no ex run-in* **4/1**[2]

P2/- **5** *9* **Minkie Moon (IRE)**[557] 3024 7-9-11 **74** oh5 (t) JonathanEngland[(3)] 64
(Mark Campion) *bhd tl styd on fr appr last* **50/1**

0-50 **6** *2* **Raifteiri (IRE)**[25] 502 8-9-11 **76** StephenMulqueen[(5)] 65
(William Young Jnr) *trckd ldr: rdn 2 out: wknd bef last* **12/1**

05-0 **7** *¾* **Teescomponents Max**[25] 507 6-10-6 **85** MrJohnDawson[(5)] 73
(Keith Reveley) *in tch: rdn after 2 out: wknd appr last* **8/1**[3]

B4-5 **8** *1* **Mwangaza (FR)**[28] 455 5-11-1 **92** GrahamWatters[(3)] 79
(Pauline Robson) *hld up: nt fluent 3 out: rdn after 2 out: sn btn* **10/1**

4P-5 **9** *17* **Tweedo Paradiso (NZ)**[26] 485 7-10-1 **78** CraigNichol[(3)] 49
(Rose Dobbin) *in tch: rdn after 3 out: sn wknd* **12/1**

PP-P **10** *11* **Presently Tipsy**[39] 288 6-10-0 **74** oh1 LucyAlexander 35
(N W Alexander) *a towards rr* **40/1**

4m 12.6s (-4.80) **Going Correction** -0.25s/f (Good)
WFA 4 from 5yo+ 17lb **10** Ran SP% **119.2**
Speed ratings (Par 103): **102,100,100,99,95 94,93,93,84,79**
CSF £11.14 CT £101.47 TOTE £2.80: £1.40, £2.10, £2.70; EX 13.70.
Owner Anthony White **Bred** Holborn Trust Co **Trained** Low Braithwaite, Cumbria

FOCUS
The first division of this moderate handicap hurdle and a win for an in-form gelding.

805 TOTEPOOL RACING'S BIGGEST SUPPORTER H'CAP HURDLE (DIV II) (8 hdls) 2m 48y

6:00 (6:01) (Class 5) (0-100,98) 4-Y-0+ **£3,832** (£1,117; £558)

Form RPR

43-0 **1** **Roll Of Thunder**[45] 157 6-10-6 **83** MissCWalton[(5)] 85
(James Walton) *mde all: rdn after 2 out: kpt on* **25/1**

064- **2** *1 ¼* **Poppies Milan (IRE)**[357] 817 6-11-3 **92** TonyKelly[(3)] 93
(Rebecca Menzies) *hld up in rr: rdn and hdwy after 2 out: styd on wl: wnt 2nd towards fin* **14/1**

6/22 **3** *½* **Miss Macnamara (IRE)**[8] 522 6-11-8 **94** BrianHarding 96+
(Martin Todhunter) *midfield: hdwy to trck ldr gng wl after 3 out: rdn appr last: l down whn mstke last: one pce: lost 2nd towards fin* **5/4**[1]

66-5 **4** *7* **Catchthemoonlight**[26] 487 7-10-10 **85** DerekFox[(3)] 79
(Lucinda Russell) *hld up in rr: rdn after 2 out: styd on fr appr last: nvr threatened* **7/1**[2]

00-5 **5** *nk* **Ardesia (IRE)**[25] 502 11-9-11 **72** HarryChalloner[(3)] 65
(Tina Jackson) *midfield: rdn after 2 out: no imp* **16/1**

-540 **6** *1* **Dynamic Drive (IRE)**[8] 728 8-11-4 **93** (t) JonathanEngland[(3)] 86
(Maurice Barnes) *trckd ldr: hit 2 out: sn rdn: wknd after last* **8/1**[3]

FPP- **7** *2* **Stand Clear**[36] 10-9-10 **75** (t) ThomasDowson[(7)] 66
(Chris Grant) *hld up: rdn after 2 out: nvr threatened* **16/1**

44/6 **8** *10* **Shanroe Society (IRE)**[27] 478 9-11-12 **98** (v[1]) BrianHughes 80
(J J Lambe, Ire) *midfield: rdn after 2 out: sn wknd* **7/1**[2]

-030 **9** *11* **Caraline (FR)**[10] 694 4-9-12 **80** (v) JamieBargary[(7)] 49
(Micky Hammond) *prom: rdn after 2 out: sn wknd* **8/1**[3]

4m 12.9s (-4.50) **Going Correction** -0.25s/f (Good)
WFA 4 from 6yo+ 17lb **9** Ran SP% **113.9**
Speed ratings (Par 103): **101,100,100,96,96 95,94,89,84**
CSF £311.43 CT £767.91 TOTE £27.50: £4.40, £3.40, £1.20; EX 224.00 Trifecta £965.80.
Owner Messrs F T Walton **Bred** A W Robson **Trained** Thropton, Northumberland

FOCUS
The second leg of this handicap hurdle was run 0.3 secs slower than the first division.
T/Jkpt: £34,745.90 to a £1 stake. Pool: £73,406.97 - 1.50 winning tickets T/Plt: £51.40 to a £1 stake. Pool: £111,030.92 - 1,574.43 winning tickets T/Qpdt: £14.80 to a £1 stake. Pool: £7,753.41 - 387.55 winning tickets **Andrew Sheret**

697 WORCESTER (L-H)

Sunday, June 21

OFFICIAL GOING: Good (6.6)
Wind: Light across Weather: Fine

806 TOTEPLACEPOT RACING'S FAVOURITE BET H'CAP CHASE (DIV I) (13 fncs) 2m 4f

2:20 (2:22) (Class 5) (0-100,100) 5-Y-0+ **£2,599** (£763; £381; £190)

Form RPR

235- **1** **Croco Mister (IRE)**[102] 4714 8-10-2 **79** (t) BenPoste[(3)] 88
(Rosemary Gasson) *hld up: pushed along 6th: hdwy appr 3 out: nt clr run last: led flat: drvn out* **10/1**

34-5 **2** *¾* **Lord Of The Dunes**[21] 567 7-10-12 **86** (bt) BrendanPowell 94
(Jamie Snowden) *hld up: hdwy 9th: chsd ldr 4 out: led appr 2 out: j.lft last: rdn and hdd flat: styd on* **8/1**

1-54 **3** *½* **Faith Jicaro (IRE)**[19] 589 8-11-8 **96** (tp) TomScudamore 104
(David Bridgwater) *a.p: rdn after 9th: ev ch last: styd on u.p* **7/1**[3]

3-2P **4** *8* **Owner Occupier**[21] 571 10-10-13 **87** TomCannon 90
(Chris Gordon) *chsd ldrs: rdn after 9th: styd on same pce appr last* **10/1**

-535 **5** *34* **Dougalstar (FR)**[19] 588 6-10-0 **74** oh1 RichieMcLernon 54
(Jennie Candlish) *in rr: hdwy 5th: rdn after 9th: wknd bef next* **8/1**

23F- **6** *38* **The Omen**[171] 3457 9-11-5 **100** AlanJohns[(7)] 36
(Tim Vaughan) *led 2nd: hdd appr 9th: wknd 4 out* **10/1**

05-5 **7** *35* **Finch Flyer (IRE)**[40] 258 8-10-0 **74** oh7 (p) LeeEdwards
(Aytach Sadik) *plld hrd and prom: mstke and lost pl 5th: wknd after 7th* **40/1**

1-60 **P** **Captain Knock (IRE)**[12] 674 12-10-5 **79** JamesDavies
(Polly Gundry) *prom: rdn appr 4 out: wkng whn wnt wrong and p.u after next* **16/1**

53-3 **P** **Rusty Nail (IRE)**[12] 674 10-10-1 **82** MissBFrost[(7)]
(Jimmy Frost) *led: hdd and hit 2nd: chsd ldr to 6th: rdn and wknd 9th: bhd whn p.u bef 3 out* **5/1**[2]

6-03 **P** **Toe To Toe (IRE)**[23] 537 7-10-7 **81** (t) RhysFlint
(John Flint) *hld up: hdwy 7th: led appr 9th: rdn and hdd bef 2 out: wkng whn p.u bef last* **11/4**[1]

5m 16.5s (11.90) **Going Correction** +0.65s/f (Soft) **10** Ran SP% **113.6**
Speed ratings: **102,101,101,98,84 69,55,,,**
CSF £84.90 CT £597.68 TOTE £12.50: £2.70, £2.60, £2.50; EX 105.40 Trifecta £1425.50.
Owner Mrs Rosemary Gasson **Bred** Corbally Stud **Trained** Balscote, Oxon

FOCUS
All starts have been moved at this track following remeasuring, so there will be no speed figures here until there is sufficient data to calculate updated median times. There had been 6.5mm of rain the previous day, which had fallen on watered ground. Consequently the going was officially good (GoingStick 6.4). Dry with sunny spells. The first division of a weak handicap and it appeared an open contest. They went a fair gallop and the complexion changed when they turned in. Winner and third set the level.

807 TOTEPLACEPOT RACING'S FAVOURITE BET H'CAP CHASE (DIV II) (13 fncs) 2m 4f

2:50 (2:50) (Class 5) (0-100,99) 5-Y-0+ **£2,599** (£763; £381; £190)

Form RPR

4-43 **1** **Conas Taoi (IRE)**[21] 569 6-10-13 **86** TomO'Brien 93
(Paul Morgan) *hld up: bhd and pushed along 6th: hdwy appr 2 out: lft 10 l 2nd last: styd on u.p to ld post* **9/4**[1]

/P-1 **2** *hd* **Tachbury**[12] 674 11-10-9 **82** (p) RichardJohnson 92+
(Tim Vaughan) *chsd ldrs: wnt 2nd 6th tl hit 8th: wnt 2nd again appr 4 out: led 2 out: clr last: rdn flat: hdd post* **3/1**[2]

-326 **3** *11* **Lost In Newyork (IRE)**[19] 588 8-10-6 **79** AdamWedge 76
(Nick Kent) *hld up: rdn 7th: effrt appr 4 out: sn outpcd: blnd 2 out: wnt 3rd flat* **7/2**[3]

6-P5 **4** *9* **The Winking Prawn (IRE)**[19] 589 8-11-12 **99** KielanWoods 93
(Graeme McPherson) *chsd ldr: mstke 2nd: nt fluent 5th: lost 2nd next: chsd ldr again 8th tl rdn appr 4 out: wknd 2 out: lft poor 3rd briefly last* **9/1**

150- **P** **Massachusetts**[209] 2716 8-10-0 **73** (t) TrevorWhelan
(Rob Summers) *hld up: bhd and pushed along 6th: effrt appr 4 out: sn wknd: bhd whn p.u bef 2 out* **33/1**

22-F **P** **June French (FR)**[24] 524 7-10-13 **86** (b) NoelFehily
(Neil Mulholland) *hld up: sme hdwy appr 6th: rdn after 8th: wknd bef 4 out: bhd whn p.u bef next* **9/2**

3-6P **F** **Indiefront**[3] 770 6-10-3 **79** JamesBanks[(3)] 76
(Jo Davis) *led: rdn and hdd whn blnd 2 out: 5 l down and wkng whn fell last* **22/1**

5m 23.4s (18.80) **Going Correction** +0.65s/f (Soft) **7** Ran SP% **113.5**
Speed ratings: **88,87,83,79,, ,**
CSF £9.69 CT £21.68 TOTE £4.00: £2.40, £2.20; EX 11.20 Trifecta £35.60.
Owner All Stars Sports Racing **Bred** Martin McCaughey **Trained** Ystrad, Rhondda C Taff

FOCUS
The second division of the modest handicap chase was run at a genuine pace and again saw wholly changing fortunes over the last four fences and only four finised. Winner ran to his pre-race mark.

808 TOTEPOOL SPONSORING EVERY UK RACE TODAY NOVICES' CHASE (16 fncs) 2m 7f

3:20 (3:20) (Class 4) 5-Y-0+ **£3,898** (£1,144; £572; £286)

Form RPR

P-31 **1** **River Maigue (IRE)**[25] 505 8-11-5 135 (t) PaulMoloney 130+
(Sophie Leech) *a.p: hit 7th: chsd ldr after next tl 12th: remained handy: stmbld bnd appr 4 out: led flat: drvn out* **11/8**[1]

P4P/ **2** *2 ¾* **Amber Flush**[22] 6-10-5 0 TrevorWhelan 110
(Martin Smith) *hld up: hdwy appr 9th: chsd ldr 12th: rdn whn mstke 3 out: led next: hdd flat: styd on same pce* **33/1**

16-2 **3** *4* **Border Breaker (IRE)**[16] 625 6-10-12 0 (bt[1]) TomScudamore 115
(David Pipe) *led and sn clr: j.rt: c bk to the field after 12th: rdn and hdd 2 out: wknd flat* **2/1**[2]

6P0- **4** *24* **Annamult (IRE)**[50] 7-9-12 0 MrAlexEdwards[(7)] 84
(Alan Phillips) *mid-div: sme hdwy after 8th: wknd next: bhd whn j.lft 2 out* **25/1**

U635 **5** *56* **Miss Tilly Oscar (IRE)**[10] 698 9-9-12 87 (t) DavidNoonan[(7)] 34
(Steve Flook) *hld up: a in rr: rdn after 8th: bhd fr next* **33/1**

0 **U** **Tony (IRE)**[10] 697 8-10-5 0 MissTWorsley[(7)]
(Ken Wingrove) *chsd ldrs: lost pl after 4th: bhd fr 8th: blnd and uns rdr 2 out* **100/1**

460/ **P** **Storm Lantern**[155] 6-10-9 0 MrSWaley-Cohen[(3)]
(Robert Waley-Cohen) *chsd clr ldr tl after 8th: wknd next: in rr whn blnd 11th: sn p.u* **7/1**

4-02 **P** **Rally**[24] 517 6-10-12 120 (vt) SamTwiston-Davies
(Nigel Twiston-Davies) *hld up: rdn after 7th: wknd 9th: bhd whn p.u bef 12th* **11/2**[3]

044- **P** **Just Skittles**[22] 7-10-5 0 MrMJPKendrick[(7)]
(Richard Harper) *mid-div: lost pl after 4th: bhd fr 8th: p.u bef 11th* **100/1**

6m 4.3s (14.40) **Going Correction** +0.65s/f (Soft) **9** Ran SP% **115.0**
Speed ratings: **100,99,97,89,69 ,,,**
CSF £45.20 TOTE £2.90: £1.10, £5.80, £1.80; EX 48.20 Trifecta £299.40.
Owner C J Leech **Bred** James Keegan **Trained** Elton, Gloucs

FOCUS
An uncompetitive novice chase, but the gallop was sound enough. Winner could be rated higher with fourth taken to have run to old hurdle form.

809 TOTEQUADPOT FOUR PLACES IN FOUR RACES H'CAP CHASE (13 fncs) 2m 4f

3:50 (3:50) (Class 3) (0-140,137) 5-Y-0+ **£7,027** (£2,121; £1,092; £579)

Form RPR

42-4 **1** **Valco De Touzaine (FR)**[15] 645 6-11-12 **137** (t) SamTwiston-Davies 144+
(Paul Nicholls) *chsd ldr tl led 7th: drvn out* **5/2**[1]

4-62 **2** *1 ¼* **No Likey (IRE)**[15] 642 8-10-7 **118** (tp) TomO'Brien 122
(Philip Hobbs) *a.p: chsd wnr appr 4 out: styd on u.p* **3/1**[2]

0-21 **3** *26* **Stephen Hero (IRE)**[10] 697 5-11-5 **130** (t) HarrySkelton 116
(Dan Skelton) *wnt prom 2nd: nt fluent 9th: sn rdn: hung rt after 4 out: wkng whn hit 2 out* **7/2**[3]

4/32 **4** *9* **Speedy Bruere (FR)**[12] 677 9-10-2 **113** (p) TomScudamore 90
(David Bridgwater) *chsd ldrs: nt fluent and lost pl 2nd: j. slowly 8th: rdn after next: wknd bef 4 out* **7/2**[3]

U-00 **P** **Anquetta (IRE)**[22] 555 11-11-7 **135**........................ MrSWaley-Cohen(3)
(Robert Waley-Cohen) *led: j.rt: hdd whn pckd 7th: wknd and p.u bef 4 out* **16/1**

53-0 **P** **Upsanddowns (IRE)**[50] 84 7-11-5 **130**........................(t) PaulMoloney
(Evan Williams) *hld up: bhd fr 6th: p.u bef 4 out* **10/1**

5m 12.3s (7.70) **Going Correction** +0.65s/f (Soft) **6** Ran **SP% 113.0**
Speed ratings: **110,109,99,95,**
CSF £10.88 TOTE £3.10: £1.80, £2.80; EX 12.00 Trifecta £24.80.
Owner The Gi Gi Syndicate **Bred** Daniel Jandard & Mme Andree Jandard **Trained** Ditcheat, Somerset

FOCUS
A fairly decent, small-field handicap run at a sound clip and only four finished. Small PB for winners and runner-up taken to have run to mark.

810 MYTOTEPOOL.COM H'CAP HURDLE (8 hdls) 2m
4:20 (4:20) (Class 4) (0-120,120) 4-Y-O+ **£3,249** (£954; £477; £238)

Form RPR

53-5 **1** **Hawaii Five Nil (IRE)**[45] 177 7-11-6 **114**..................(p) RichieMcLernon 118+
(Jonjo O'Neill) *hld up: in tch: nt fluent 2 out: sn rdn: styd on u.p to ld fnl 100yds* **7/2**[2]

2-P2 **2** ½ **Indian Stream**[19] 593 6-11-9 **117**........................(t) DougieCostello 119
(Neil Mulholland) *a.p: chsd ldr 3rd: led 2 out: rdn appr last: hdd fnl 100yds: styd on* **9/1**

3-44 **3** *hd* **Ladies Dancing**[25] 515 9-10-6 **100**........................(b) JamesDavies 102
(Chris Down) *a.p: racd keenly: rdn after 2 out: styd on* **14/1**

1 **4** 1¾ **Monte Wildhorn (IRE)**[9] 718 7-11-8 **116**..............(p) TomScudamore 116
(David Bridgwater) *chsd ldr to 3rd: led after 5th: rdn and hdd 2 out: ev ch last: no ex towards fin* **2/1**[1]

/30- **5** 14 **Royal Skies (IRE)**[218] 2489 5-11-7 **115**....................(t) AidanColeman 103
(John Ferguson) *chsd ldrs tl rdn and wknd appr last* **7/2**[2]

1-05 **6** 5 **Hi Tide (IRE)**[19] 592 11-11-5 **113**........................ BrendanPowell 96
(J R Jenkins) *in rr: pushed along after 2nd: sme hdwy appr 3 out: wknd next* **25/1**

4/02 **7** 61 **Battlecat**[29] 442 8-11-5 **113**........................ AdamWedge 41
(Evan Williams) *led and mstke 1st: hdd after 5th: sn rdn: wknd bef next* **13/2**[3]

163/ **P** **Mighty Snazy**[449] 11-10-4 **103**........................[1] MrsAlexDunn(5)
(Alexandra Dunn) *hld up: bhd 3rd: sme hdwy after 4th: wknd after next: bhd whn p.u bef last* **66/1**

3m 54.2s (3.60) **Going Correction** +0.375s/f (Yiel) **8** Ran **SP% 113.1**
Speed ratings (Par 105): **106,105,105,104,97 95,64,**
CSF £33.28 CT £387.33 TOTE £5.80: £1.90, £1.70, £3.90; EX 38.70 Trifecta £489.50.
Owner Regulatory Finance Solutions Limited **Bred** John Supple **Trained** Cheltenham, Gloucs

FOCUS
The pace was genuine for this moderate handicap hurdle, which provided a tight finish. Winner made most of a fair mark and runner-up and fourth efforts in line with good recent runs.

811 TOTEEXACTA PICK THE 1ST AND 2ND NOVICES' H'CAP HURDLE (8 hdls) 2m
4:50 (4:50) (Class 5) (0-100,100) 4-Y-O+ **£2,599** (£763; £381; £190)

Form RPR

U06- **1** **Kalifourchon (FR)**[97] 4816 4-11-6 **97**........................ TomScudamore 109+
(David Pipe) *hld up: hdwy 4th: led last: rdn clr flat* **3/1**[1]

00/0 **2** 9 **Umoristic (FR)**[23] 537 7-9-7 **74** oh2........................(t) DavidNoonan(7) 80
(Matt Sheppard) *chsd ldrs: led 4th: rdn and hdd last: styd on same pce flat* **10/1**

502/ **3** 2 **Rose Red**[527] 3636 8-10-1 **80**........................ JakeHodson(5) 85+
(Rob Summers) *plld hrd and sn prom: chsd ldr appr 3 out: rdn bef last: hung lft and no ex flat* **16/1**

-412 **4** 9 **Heading To First**[11] 489 8-11-9 **97**........................(t) PaulMoloney 93
(Jim Best) *hld up: hung lft fr 3 out: mstke next: nt trble ldrs* **6/1**[2]

14-P **5** 9 **Seacon Beg (IRE)**[24] 524 6-11-9 **97**........................(t) DarylJacob 85
(Richard Woollacott) *hld up: hdwy appr 3 out: rdn: hung lft and wknd bef next* **6/1**[2]

02-0 **6** ½ **Staff Sergeant**[9] 712 8-11-12 **100**........................ NoelFehily 88
(Jim Best) *hld up: hdwy 4th: mstke 3 out: sn wknd* **12/1**

C-34 **7** 6 **Chankillo**[9] 712 6-10-11 **85**........................ SamTwiston-Davies 67
(Sarah-Jayne Davies) *prom lost pl after 4th: n.d after* **8/1**[3]

-P53 **8** 3 **League Of His Own (IRE)**[22] 552 6-10-0 **74** oh4........(t) TrevorWhelan 53
(Claire Dyson) *racd keenly: led 2nd to 3rd: chsd ldrs tl wknd appr 3 out* **11/1**

000- **9** 16 **Bobonyx**[245] 1967 5-10-0 **74** oh3........................ DaveCrosse 39
(Dai Williams) *led to 2nd: led 3rd to next: wknd appr 3 out* **20/1**

64-0 **10** 1¼ **Memphis Magic (GER)**[28] 449 5-11-12 **100**..........(t) BrendanPowell 64
(Brendan Powell) *hld up: hdwy after 5th: wknd bef next* **10/1**

4-P6 **11** *nk* **Captain Starlight (IRE)**[10] 703 5-10-5 **79**..........(bt[1]) LeeEdwards 43
(Aytach Sadik) *hld up: hdwy 4th: rdn and wknd bef 3 out: mstke next* **66/1**

0PP/ **P** **Backhomeinderry (IRE)**[436] 5259 10-10-11 **92**..........(t) MissCBoxall(7)
(Dominic Ffrench Davis) *hld up: bhd fr 3rd: p.u bef 3 out* **50/1**

0/0 **P** **Luso's Way (IRE)**[29] 443 7-11-0 **88**........................(t) RichardJohnson
(Tim Vaughan) *w ldrs to 3rd: wknd after next: bhd whn p.u bef 3 out* **16/1**

3m 55.8s (5.20) **Going Correction** +0.375s/f (Yiel)
WFA 4 from 5yo+ 17lb **13** Ran **SP% 118.9**
Speed ratings (Par 103): **102,97,96,92,87 87,84,82,74,74 73, ,**
CSF £32.89 CT £420.58 TOTE £4.50: £1.90, £4.20, £4.00; EX 60.80 Trifecta £800.40.
Owner CHM Partnership **Bred** I , J P , G & C Garcon **Trained** Nicholashayne, Devon

FOCUS
A weak novice handicap. Big personal best by winner and race rated through the fourth horse.

812 TOTETRIFECTA WIN BIG MONEY H'CAP HURDLE (10 hdls) 2m 4f
5:20 (5:20) (Class 2) (0-150,143) 4-Y-O+ **£12,660** (£3,740; £1,870; £936; £468)

Form RPR

00-1 **1** **Champion Court (IRE)**[48] 101 10-11-12 **143**..............(p) AndrewTinkler 148
(Martin Keighley) *led: racd wd: nt fluent 2nd: reminder after 5th: rdn appr 3 out: edgd rt after next: hdd last: rallied to ld post* **16/1**

12-2 **2** *hd* **Aficionado**[15] 645 5-10-3 **120**........................(b[1]) WillKennedy 126
(Dr Richard Newland) *hld up: hdwy after 7th: led last: rdn 2 l ahd flat: idled towards fin: hdd post* **5/1**[1]

5-11 **3** 14 **Dubh Eile (IRE)**[37] 314 7-10-3 **120**........................ RichardJohnson 113
(Tim Vaughan) *hld up: hdwy after 5th: stmbld next: rdn after 2 out: wknd last* **5/1**[1]

-050 **4** 3¾ **Vulcanite (IRE)**[22] 556 8-11-3 **137**........................ GerFox(3) 129+
(Charlie Longsdon) *prom: chsd wnr 3 out: ev ch whn mstke next: wknd last* **5/1**[1]

10-1 **5** 8 **Ossie's Dancer**[42] 225 6-10-4 **128**........................ ThomasCheesman(7) 111
(Martin Smith) *hld up: hdwy after 6th: rdn and wknd after 2 out* **12/1**

6P-0 **6** 3 **Rum And Butter (IRE)**[44] 184 7-11-4 **135**..............(p) DougieCostello 116
(Jonjo O'Neill) *hld up: mstke 4th: effrt whn mstke 3 out: sn wknd* **33/1**

14-1 **7** 16 **Go Odee Go (IRE)**[31] 419 7-10-7 **124**........................(p) HarrySkelton 89
(Dan Skelton) *hld up: rdn after 6th: effrt appr 3 out: sn wknd* **6/1**[2]

00-4 **8** 8 **Ballyglasheen (IRE)**[22] 197 5-11-5 **136**........................(v) PaulMoloney 97
(Evan Williams) *prom: jnd wnr after 4th tl rdn after 7th: wknd 3 out* **10/1**[3]

-05F **9** 29 **Get Home Now**[16] 625 7-9-11 **117** oh1..............(tp) SeanBowen(3) 48
(Peter Bowen) *chsd ldrs tl wknd after 5th* **20/1**

02-2 **P** **Laudatory**[22] 556 9-11-9 **140**........................ NicodeBoinville
(Nicky Henderson) *chsd wnr tl after 4th: wknd after 6th: bhd whn p.u bef 3 out* **10/1**[3]

210- **P** **My Direction**[239] 2056 5-11-4 **135**........................ AidanColeman
(John Ferguson) *chsd ldrs tl rdn and wknd after 7th: bhd whn p.u bef next* **11/1**

412- **F** **Vayland**[72] 5256 6-10-3 **120**........................[1] TomScudamore
(David Pipe) *hld up: bhd fr 5th: fell 7th* **16/1**

5m 0.1s (6.60) **Going Correction** +0.375s/f (Yiel) **12** Ran **SP% 118.0**
Speed ratings (Par 109): **101,100,95,93,90 89,83,79,68, ,**
CSF £95.11 CT £469.46 TOTE £11.80: £3.90, £2.30, £1.90; EX 144.20 Trifecta £733.20.
Owner M Boothright **Bred** Larry O'Connor **Trained** Condicote, Gloucs

FOCUS
A competitive renewal of this decent handicap hurdle and, not for the first time, the long run-in helped produce another cracking finish. Winner rated 5lb off recent chase win, though a case for rating a few lbs higher through third.

813 TOTEPOOL RACING'S BIGGEST SUPPORTER CONDITIONAL JOCKEYS' MARES' MAIDEN HURDLE (8 hdls) 2m
5:50 (5:50) (Class 4) 4-Y-O+ **£3,249** (£954; £477; £238)

Form RPR

66-2 **1** **Stoneham**[16] 405 4-10-13 109........................ KieronEdgar 97
(Mick Channon) *hld up: hdwy appr 3 out: rdn to ld fnl 100yds: styd on wl* **5/1**[3]

0-52 **2** 2¼ **Amour D'Or**[30] 433 4-10-10 0........................ LizzieKelly(3) 94
(Nick Williams) *hld up: rdn appr last: hdd fnl 100yds: styd on same pce* **7/4**[1]

-0F **3** 4 **Quench Tara**[15] 648 8-11-2 0........................[1] JackSherwood 95
(Michael Scudamore) *hld up: mstkes 4th and 5th: sn rdn: styd on fr 2 out: wnt 3rd flat: nt rch ldrs* **66/1**

/00- **4** 2¼ **Big Night Out**[36] 9-10-11 90........................(t) MikeyHamill(5) 91
(Laura Hurley) *prom: chsd ldr after 3rd: rdn and ev ch appr 3 out: no ex last* **25/1**

5 8 **Micras**[48] 4-10-7 0........................ AlanJohns(6) 81
(Tim Vaughan) *chsd ldrs: rdn appr 3 out: wknd next* **16/1**

0/6- **6** 68 **Cara Carlotta**[78] 5144 6-10-13 0........................(t) MichealNolan(3) 23
(Philip Hobbs) *hld up: hdwy appr 5th: sn wknd* **11/2**

P **P** **Miss Moppet**[40] 263 4-10-10 0........................ FreddieMitchell(3)
(Clare Hobson) *prom: lost pl after 2nd: hdwy 4th: rdn and wknd after next: bhd whn p.u bef 3 out* **66/1**

3F-4 **P** **Glenariff**[28] 447 6-11-2 108........................ SeanBowen
(Seamus Mullins) *chsd ldrs tl rdn and wknd bef 4th: bhd whn p.u bef next* **5/2**[2]

00-U **P** **Feisty Girl**[24] 528 5-11-2 0........................[1] BenPoste
(Michael Mullineaux) *chsd ldrs tl rdn and wknd after 4th: bhd whn p.u bef 3 out* **50/1**

P-P **P** **The Banshee**[15] 648 9-10-13 0........................ DanielHiskett(3)
(Liam Grassick) *chsd ldr tl after 3rd: wknd bef next: bhd whn p.u bef 5th* **100/1**

3m 57.9s (7.30) **Going Correction** +0.375s/f (Yiel)
WFA 4 from 5yo+ 17lb **10** Ran **SP% 112.7**
Speed ratings (Par 105): **96,94,92,91,87 53, , ,**
CSF £13.87 TOTE £4.50: £1.30, £1.80, £7.20; EX 13.70 Trifecta £405.30.
Owner Insignia Racing **Bred** Norman Court Stud **Trained** West Ilsley, Berks

FOCUS
A weak maiden hurdle for mares and conditional riders. The pace was solid enough. Winner and fourth best guide to the level of this race.
T/Plt: £216.80 to a £1 stake. Pool: £84,728.82 - 285.18 winning tickets T/Qpdt: £41.40 to a £1 stake. Pool: £6,821.19 - 121.92 winning tickets **Colin Roberts**

814 - 822a (Foreign Racing) - See Raceform Interactive

[712] NEWTON ABBOT (L-H)
Tuesday, June 23

OFFICIAL GOING: Good (good to firm in places, 6.8)
Wind: light breeze across Weather: sunny Rails: Rail movements changed race distances as follows: Races 1 & 2 add 17yds; Races 3 & 5 add 121yds; Race 4 add 16yds; Race 6 add 13yds; water jump omitted in all chases.

823 LEE ANDREWS 40TH BIRTHDAY BASH MAIDEN HURDLE (10 hdls) 2m 5f 122y
6:00 (6:00) (Class 5) 4-Y-O+ **£3,422** (£997; £499)

Form RPR

4 **1** **Number One London (IRE)**[44] 214 5-11-0 0........................ RichardJohnson 116+
(Tim Vaughan) *hld up bhd: hdwy after 6th: trckd ldrs next: led appr 2 out: kpt on: rdn out* **9/4**[1]

00-3 **2** 1¼ **Shah Of Persia**[30] 447 8-11-0 115........................(t) GavinSheehan 113
(Warren Greatrex) *trckd ldrs: rdn after 3 out: styd on to chse wnr between last 2: kpt on but a being hld run-in* **11/2**

P **3** 7 **Ruddy Article (IRE)**[25] 531 7-11-0 0..............(t) SamTwiston-Davies 107
(Paul Nicholls) *j.lft thrght: led: rdn and hdd appr 2 out: sn one pce* **10/3**[3]

0-33 **4** 16 **Midnight Mint**[30] 462 5-10-7 105........................(t) LiamHeard 85
(Jeremy Scott) *trckd ldrs: rdn after 3 out: sn outpcd: wnt hld 4th between last 2* **5/2**[2]

-445 **5** 1 **Pauls Conn (IRE)**[11] 716 6-11-0 100........................ JamesBest 92
(Mary Sanderson) *prom: pushed along fr 6th: rdn to chse ldr after 3 out tl wknd bef next* **20/1**

6 1¼ **Wintour Leap**[188] 4-10-3 0........................ TomO'Brien 80
(Robert Stephens) *trckd ldrs: rdn after 3 out: wknd bef next* **22/1**

05-3 **7** 50 **Bogoss Du Perret (FR)**[27] 511 4-10-10 0........................ JamesDavies 41
(Jimmy Frost) *struggling 6th wknd next: a towards rr: t.o* **14/1**

0 **8** 3½ **Asian Ali (IRE)**[26] 525 6-11-0 0........................[1] JamieMoore 42
(Richard Lee) *a towards rr: t.o after 3 out* **50/1**

9 22 **Ujagar (IRE)**[98] 4-10-10 0........................(t) KielanWoods 18
(Graeme McPherson) *trckd ldrs: nt fluent 4th: wknd 7th: t.o* **33/1**

The Form Book Jumps 2015-16, Raceform Ltd, Newbury, RG14 5SJ

05/0 **P** **Tanner Bet**[14] 671 7-10-0 0................................ DavidNoonan(7)
(Polly Gundry) *chsd ldrs tl after 6th: sn t.o: p.u bef next* **200/1**

5m 6.1s (-14.10) **Going Correction** -0.65s/f (Firm)
WFA 4 from 5yo+ 18lb **10** Ran SP% **119.0**
Speed ratings (Par 103): **99,98,96,90,89 89,71,69,61,**
CSF £14.89 TOTE £3.70: £1.40, £2.50, £1.40; EX 17.90 Trifecta £89.60.
Owner D J Wallis **Bred** Irish National Stud **Trained** Aberthin, Vale of Glamorgan

FOCUS
Shared bends moved out since last meeting affecting race distances as follows; Race 1 & 2 add 17y, Race 3 & 5 add 121y, Race 4 add 16y and Race 6 add 13y. A fair maiden hurdle run at a steady gallop. The first two are on the upgrade.

824 DAVID CHILLERY 70TH BIRTHDAY CELEBRATION (S) H'CAP HURDLE (10 hdls) 2m 5f 122y
6:30 (6:30) (Class 5) (0-100,100) 4-Y-0+ **£3,422** (£997; £499)

Form RPR
0-56 **1** **Ice Konig (FR)**[27] 515 6-11-2 **97**................................ PaulO'Brien(7) 101
(Jimmy Frost) *hld up towards rr: nudged along after 6th: hdwy next: led appr 2 out: kpt on wl: rdn out* **9/2**[2]

00P- **2** *1½* **Peaceful Gardens**[179] 3280 6-9-7 **74**................................ DavidPrichard(7) 76
(Jeremy Scott) *hld up towards rr: stdy hdwy after 3 out: rdn to chse ldrs bef next: styd on to go 2nd nring fin* **20/1**

465- **3** *nk* **Unefille De Guye (FR)**[112] 4548 7-10-4 **78**................................(t) DenisO'Regan 80
(Victor Dartnall) *hld up towards rr: hdwy fr 7th: rdn to chse wnr between last 2: no ex whn lost 2nd nring fin* **8/1**

4P-2 **4** *3* **Dynamic Idol (USA)**[23] 569 8-11-4 **92**................................(bt) NoelFehily 94
(Johnny Farrelly) *trckd ldrs: nt fluent 6th and briefly lost pl: rdn whn nt fluent 3 out: one pce after* **7/2**[1]

06-1 **5** *1¼* **Y A Bon (IRE)**[47] 165 7-10-11 **92**................................(b) MikeyHamill(7) 91
(Alexandra Dunn) *prom: led after 3 out: rdn and hdd whn nt fluent next: fdd* **15/2**

30-0 **6** *16* **Legion D'Honneur (UAE)**[26] 530 10-11-9 **97**................................(t) JamesDavies 81
(Chris Down) *mid-div: outpcd after 3 out: no threat after* **12/1**

5-00 **7** *8* **Willow Island (IRE)**[37] 364 6-11-7 **95**................................(t) PaulMoloney 77
(Sophie Leech) *hld up: rdn and sme prog after 3 out: nvr threatened: wknd next* **25/1**

6 **8** *10* **Diamond Reign (IRE)**[17] 647 9-10-11 **85**................................ LiamHeard 53
(Bob Buckler) *mid-div: nt fluent 1st: rdn appr 7th: wknd after 3 out* **25/1**

550- **9** *40* **Scripturist**[146] 3921 6-10-9 **90**................................(b) JordanWilliams(7) 22
(Bernard Llewellyn) *mid-div: rdn to chse ldrs after 6th tl next: sn bhd: t.o whn blnd last* **33/1**

-5PP **P** **River Dancing (IRE)**[11] 717 8-10-4 **78**................................(bt[1]) SamTwiston-Davies
(Anthony Honeyball) *led tl rdn after 3 out: sn wknd: t.o whn p.u bef last* **11/2**[3]

3/2- **P** **Mia's Vic (IRE)**[38] 10-11-12 **100**................................(t) RichardJohnson
(Tim Vaughan) *trcking ldrs whn lost action and p.u after 2nd: fatally injured* **6/1**

4-26 **U** **Goodacres Garden (IRE)**[12] 695 8-9-11 **74** oh5.(t) ConorShoemark(3)
(Shaun Lycett) *trckd ldrs: rdn after 7th: losing pl whn stmbld and uns rdr after 3 out* **20/1**

5m 8.4s (-11.80) **Going Correction** -0.65s/f (Firm) **12** Ran SP% **120.8**
Speed ratings (Par 103): **95,94,94,93,92 86,84,80,65, ,**
CSF £94.53 CT £713.11 TOTE £7.00: £2.70, £7.90, £3.00; EX 105.10 Trifecta £3022.60.No bid for the winner.
Owner Geoff Martin **Bred** S A R L Ecurie Haras De Quetieville **Trained** Buckfast, Devon

FOCUS
The gallop was steady for this modest handicap. The winner and third set the level.

825 "BEAU" NOVICES' CHASE (14 fncs 2 omitted) 2m 4f 216y
7:00 (7:00) (Class 3) 5-Y-0+ **£6,498** (£1,908; £954; £477)

Form RPR
10-1 **1** **Dormello Mo (FR)**[27] 512 5-11-4 0................................(t) SamTwiston-Davies 145+
(Paul Nicholls) *mde all: j.w but sltly rt thrght: qcknd clr appr 2 out: easily* **1/5**[1]

2P-3 **2** *13* **My Legal Lady**[35] 389 10-10-5 0................................(vt) TomScudamore 107
(Stuart Howe) *trckd wnr: rdn appr 2 out: sn outpcd* **5/1**[2]

30-2 **3** *4* **Fuzzy Logic (IRE)**[35] 176 6-10-9 0................................(p) RobertWilliams(3) 111
(Bernard Llewellyn) *trckd wnr: blnd 4th: rdn after 3 out (usual 4 out): sn one pce* **16/1**[3]

2336 **4** *35* **Veauce De Sivola (FR)**[23] 567 6-10-12 **95**................................(t) TomCannon 75
(Mark Gillard) *trckd wnr tl dropped to 4th at the 6th: sn nudged along: wknd 3 out (usual 4 out)* **25/1**

5m 18.6s (-2.80) **Going Correction** +0.125s/f (Yiel) **4** Ran SP% **109.7**
Speed ratings: **110,105,103,90**
CSF £1.91 TOTE £1.20; EX 1.80 Trifecta £3.40.
Owner The Kyle & Stewart Families **Bred** E A R L Haras Du Taillis & H Poulsen **Trained** Ditcheat, Somerset

FOCUS
Much of the interest was taken out of this contest with the late withdrawal of the second favourite. Dormello Mo should go on to rate higher.

826 ST AUSTELL BREWERY H'CAP HURDLE (8 hdls) 2m 167y
7:30 (7:31) (Class 3) (0-140,136) 4-Y-0+ **£6,498** (£1,908; £954; £477)

Form RPR
30-3 **1** **Dubai Prince (IRE)**[24] 556 7-11-12 **136**................................ AidanColeman 149+
(John Ferguson) *trckd ldrs: led 2 out: qcknd clr: v easily* **5/2**[2]

45-5 **2** *9* **Willem (FR)**[45] 208 5-11-0 **124**................................ TomScudamore 123
(David Pipe) *trckd ldrs: wnt 3rd 2 out: rdn bef last: r.o to go 2nd run-in but no ch w wnr* **9/2**[3]

61-3 **3** *¾* **Purple 'n Gold (IRE)**[11] 708 6-10-12 **127**................................(p) KieronEdgar(5) 125
(David Pipe) *trckd ldrs: chal after 3 out: led briefly bef next: rdn between last 2: sn outpcd by wnr: no ex whn lost 2nd run-in* **8/1**

-306 **4** *6* **Party Palace**[5] 775 11-9-9 **110** oh4................................ AliceMills(5) 103
(Stuart Howe) *trckd ldr tl outpcd after 3 out: styd on again between last 2: wnt 4th run-in* **33/1**

0-60 **5** *hd* **Oyster Shell**[24] 556 8-11-7 **131**................................ JakeGreenall 123
(Henry Daly) *led: rdn and hdd bef 2 out: sn one pce: no ex whn lost 4th run-in* **25/1**

1-13 **6** *3* **Frozen Over**[34] 406 7-10-5 **115**................................(t) JamesDavies 105
(Chris Down) *hld up bhd ldrs: rdn after 3 out: nvr finding pce to get involved* **6/1**

F002 **7** *nk* **Collodi (GER)**[7] 751 6-10-9 **119**................................ TomCannon 110
(David Bridgwater) *chsd ldrs: hit 5th: rdn after 3 out: sn one pce* **2/1**[1]

3m 50.4s (-15.30) **Going Correction** -0.65s/f (Firm) **7** Ran SP% **112.3**
Speed ratings (Par 107): **110,105,105,102,102 101,100**
CSF £13.82 TOTE £3.20: £1.80, £3.60; EX 17.20 Trifecta £76.30.
Owner Bloomfields **Bred** Mrs Eithne Hamilton **Trained** Cowlinge, Suffolk

FOCUS
A competitive handicap run at a sound gallop. A big step up from the winner but there should be more to come.

827 REMEMBERING BARRY AND JOE EDWARDS H'CAP CHASE (16 fncs) 2m 4f 216y
8:00 (8:00) (Class 4) (0-115,114) 5-Y-0+ **£3,898** (£1,144; £572; £286)

Form RPR
U1-3 **1** **Istheresadifference (IRE)**[28] 490 8-11-1 **103**................................(bt) NoelFehily 112+
(Neil Mulholland) *trckd ldrs: nt fluent 2nd: led appr 2 out: kpt on wl fr last: drvn out* **8/1**

610- **2** *1¾* **Etania**[64] 5429 7-10-4 **92**................................ TomO'Brien 97
(Ian Williams) *trckd ldrs: rdn after 3 out (usual 4 out): styd on fr last: wnt 2nd nring fin* **12/1**

5-23 **3** *¾* **Handsome Horace (IRE)**[35] 388 5-10-7 **95**................................ RichardJohnson 100
(Philip Hobbs) *led: rdn and hdd appr 2 out: rallied briefly run-in: hld fnl 50yds: lost 2nd nring fin* **5/2**[2]

13-2 **4** *3* **Ladfromhighworth**[20] 598 10-11-9 **114**................................ MattGriffiths(3) 118
(Jeremy Scott) *cl up: nudged along in last pair after 8th: rdn to chal briefly on outer on bnd after 3 out (usual 4 out): styd on same pce fr next* **7/2**[3]

0353 **5** *2½* **Archie Boy (IRE)**[14] 677 13-10-12 **103**................................(t) KillianMoore(3) 102
(Sophie Leech) *hld up but wl in tch: rdn after 3 out (usual 4 out): nt pce to get on terms* **10/1**

6 *2¼* **Railway Storm (IRE)**[229] 2311 10-9-12 **93**................................ MissBFrost(7) 92
(Jimmy Frost) *hld up but wl in tch: mstke 10th: rdn after 3 out: nt gng pce to get involved* **25/1**

500- **7** *26* **Cinevator (IRE)**[29] 8-11-8 **110**................................(p) DarylJacob 94
(Richard Woollacott) *prom: rdn after 11th: chal on outer on bnd after 3 out (usual 4 out): wknd bef next* **9/4**[1]

5m 21.3s (-0.10) **Going Correction** +0.125s/f (Yiel) **7** Ran SP% **113.3**
Speed ratings: **105,104,104,102,101 101,91**
CSF £84.39 CT £307.74 TOTE £7.10: £5.00, £6.80; EX 118.20 Trifecta £144.50.
Owner The Colony Stable LLC **Bred** Daryl Deacon **Trained** Limpley Stoke, Wilts

FOCUS
The pace was steady for this fair handicap. The winner rates a small personal best.

828 BOYZONE/ALESHA HERE THIS SUNDAY LADY AMATEUR RIDERS' H'CAP HURDLE (9 hdls) 2m 2f 110y
8:35 (8:35) (Class 4) (0-105,105) 4-Y-0+ **£3,743** (£1,161; £580; £290)

Form RPR
23-1 **1** **Archie Rice (USA)**[14] 675 9-11-2 **100**................................ MissBFrost(5) 106+
(Jimmy Frost) *led after 1st: rdn and hdd 2 out: regained ld bef last: styd on wl* **9/2**[2]

4/F- **2** *4½* **Quadriller (FR)**[326] 174 8-11-6 **104**................................(t) MissNatalieParker(5) 108+
(Philip Hobbs) *mid-div: hdwy appr 6th: str chal after 3 out: led 2 out: rdn and hdd bef last: no ex* **8/1**

F-41 **3** *1¼* **Fuse Wire**[11] 712 8-10-10 **92**................................ MissJodieHughes(3) 93
(Dai Burchell) *mid-div: hdwy 4th: trckd ldrs next: rdn after 3 out: styd on same pce fr next* **10/3**[1]

10-0 **4** *½* **Jigsaw Financial (IRE)**[26] 529 9-11-5 **103**................................ MissVWade(5) 102
(Laura Young) *in tch: rdn to chse ldrs after 3 out: styd on same pce fr next* **25/1**

5F3- **5** *1¼* **Regal One (IRE)**[289] 1466 7-11-3 **96**................................ MissAEStirling 97+
(David Bridgwater) *hld up towards rr: hmpd 3rd: bdly hmpd on bnd appr 6th: stdy prog after 3 out: styd on between last 2: nt rch ldrs* **12/1**

155- **6** *3½* **Key To Milan**[65] 5414 9-11-7 **103**................................(tp) MissBHampson(3) 99
(Chris Down) *led tl after 1st: trckd ldrs: rdn after 3 out: styd on same pce* **7/1**[3]

0-65 **7** *1¾* **Rye House (IRE)**[24] 554 6-11-3 **99**................................ MissLBrooke(3) 93
(Tim Vaughan) *a in mid-div* **8/1**

236/ **8** *16* **Louis Ludwig (IRE)**[17] 10-10-1 **87**................................ MissGSwan(7) 66
(Tim Vaughan) *a towards rr* **40/1**

30-0 **9** *14* **Nishay (IRE)**[25] 536 8-9-12 **84**................................(t) MissEmmaMoseley(7) 50
(David Rees) *a towards rr: t.o* **33/1**

03/- **10** *nse* **Diddypurptoon**[23] 9-10-11 **97**................................ MissOliviaHutchings(7) 63
(Jackie Du Plessis) *towards rr: lost tch 5th: t.o* **50/1**

4100 **11** *2¾* **Accessallareas (IRE)**[27] 514 10-11-0 **100**................................ MissABroome(7) 64
(Sarah-Jayne Davies) *mid-div tl wknd after 3 out: t.o* **66/1**

/05- **P** **Minneapolis**[11] 1026 10-10-9 **88**................................(t) MissCVHart
(Sophie Leech) *in tch: trcking ldrs whn lost action and p.u sn after 3 out* **20/1**

34P- **U** **Dance**[19] 1213 6-10-7 **93**................................ MissPGlanville(7)
(Rod Millman) *mid-div: sddle slipped after being hmpd on bnd bef 6th: uns rdr sn after* **12/1**

2UP- **P** **Dont Call Me Oscar (IRE)**[64] 5435 8-11-7 **105**................................(t) MissTWorsley(5)
(Mark Gillard) *prom: rdn whn short of room and collided w rail on bnd bef 6th: sn lost pl: t.o whn p.u after 3 out* **25/1**

1-4 **P** **Hija**[37] 360 4-11-7 **104**................................ AliceMills
(Gail Haywood) *sn detached in rr: wnt bdly lft 3rd: tailing off whn p.u after 5th* **12/1**

-225 **P** **Good Value**[11] 712 4-10-12 **95**................................ MrsAlexDunn
(David Pipe) *a towards rr: t.o after 5th and p.u* **8/1**

4m 20.9s (-9.10) **Going Correction** -0.65s/f (Firm) **16** Ran SP% **131.5**
Speed ratings (Par 105): **93,91,90,90,89 88,87,80,75,74 73, , , ,**
CSF £41.42 CT £143.56 TOTE £3.10: £1.50, £3.50, £2.00, £7.10; EX 33.40 Trifecta £151.40.
Owner Frost Racing Club **Bred** Baltusrol Thoughbreds Llc Et Al **Trained** Buckfast, Devon

FOCUS
A modest contest run at a fair pace. The first two are rated to their best.
T/Jkpt: Part won. £7,341.00 to a £1 stake. Pool: £10,321.17 - 0.50 winning tickets. T/Plt: £187.50 to a £1 stake. Pool: £98,118.43 - 381.55 winning tickets. T/Qpdt: £26.70 to a £1 stake. Pool: £7,598.75 - 210.30 winning tickets. **Tim Mitchell**

806 WORCESTER (L-H)
Wednesday, June 24

OFFICIAL GOING: Good (good to firm in places; 6.7)
Wind: almost nil Weather: hot and sunny; 22 degrees

829 THURSFIELDS SOLICITORS NOVICES' CHASE (13 fncs) 2m 4f
2:20 (2:20) (Class 4) 5-Y-0+ **£3,898** (£1,144; £572)

Form RPR
10-3 **1** **Commitment**[33] 430 6-10-12 0................................ DougieCostello 125
(Neil Mulholland) *mde all: j. sltly rt: set mod pce: rdn whn mstke 3 out: over 2 l clr last: drvn and hung on gamely: distressed after* **7/4**[2]

-131 **2** ½ **Street Entertainer (IRE)**[13] [701] 8-10-12 0..............(bt) TomScudamore 125
(David Pipe) *a 2nd: 3 l bhd and drvn 3 out: clsd grad fr last but nvr really looked like getting past wnr* **4/7**[1]

25-0 **3** *dist* **It Is I (IRE)**[53] [83] 5-10-12 0.. DenisO'Regan
(Don Cantillon) *coasted rnd in detached last: 6 l bhd whn nt fluent 6th: bdly t.o after 9th* **20/1**[3]

5m 6.3s (1.70) **Going Correction** +0.375s/f (Yiel) **3** Ran SP% **104.8**
Speed ratings: **111,110,**
CSF £3.16 TOTE £2.40; EX 2.90 Trifecta £3.00.
Owner Mrs H R Cross **Bred** Cheveley Park Stud Ltd **Trained** Limpley Stoke, Wilts

FOCUS
All starts have been moved at this track following remeasuring, so there will be no speed figures here until there is sufficient data to calculate updated median times. Both bends were dolled out from the inside line and races 1, 5 & 6 increased by about 130yds and races 2, 3, 4 & 7 increased by 75yds. According to the jockeys it was good ground in the main, but on the easy side of good in places. The fences were on the outside of the track, the same line used for the meeting on Sunday. This race was won a year ago by It's A Gimme, who went on to land the Listed Summer Plate at Market Rasen. The first two are fairly useful novices. A small step up from the winner, with the second 7lb below his hurdles form.

830 SUCKLING TRANSPORT H'CAP CHASE (12 fncs) 2m 110y
2:50 (2:50) (Class 3) (0-140,140) 5-Y-0 **£6,330** (£1,870; £935; £468; £234)

Form RPR

21-4 **1** **Surf And Turf (IRE)**[25] [555] 9-11-12 **140**......................... BrianHughes 143
(Kevin Frost) *settled 4th w ldng pair clr: effrt bef 9th: led 2 out: hrd drvn and responded gamely flat: jst hld on* **11/2**[3]

2-33 **2** *hd* **Miss Tenacious**[12] [715] 8-10-1 **122**.............................. HarryCobden(7) 125+
(Ron Hodges) *settled nr rr of bunch: delayed effrt tl after 3 out: stl nrly 4 l 4th at last: urged along and styd on gamely fnl 100yds: too much to do and jst failed* **4/1**[2]

20P- **3** 2¼ **Fair Dilemma (IRE)**[193] [3068] 10-11-11 **139**....................... TomO'Brien 140
(Paul Henderson) *led tl after 4th: led again 3 out: rdn and hdd next: ev ch last: one pce and lost 2nd fnl 50yds* **10/1**

F-43 **4** *4* **King Alfonso**[13] [697] 6-10-11 **125**........................... RobertDunne 123
(Dai Burchell) *mstke 3rd: nt fluent 7th: chsd ldrs: effrt after 8th: rdn and keeping on same pce whn nt fluent 2 out* **7/2**[1]

-431 **5** *7* **Furrows**[9] [742] 10-10-6 **120** 7ex.............................. LeightonAspell 112
(Oliver Sherwood) *chsd clr ldng pair: pushed along 6th and nvr really looked gng wl enough after: effrt after 8th: rdn and btn 3 out: plodded on* **4/1**[2]

32-3 **6** *19* **Marju's Quest (IRE)**[29] [492] 5-11-1 **129**............................. NoelFehily 110+
(David Dennis) *plld hrd: led after 4th where 10 l clr w one rival: pressed fr 8th: edging rt up st: hdd 3 out: fdd next* **15/2**

5-41 **U** **Fantasy King**[30] [469] 9-10-7 **124**.................................. TonyKelly(3)
(James Moffatt) *blnd and uns rdr 2nd* **8/1**

4m 8.4s (3.40) **Going Correction** +0.375s/f (Yiel) **7** Ran SP% **109.6**
Speed ratings: **107,106,105,103,100 91,**
CSF £25.68 TOTE £4.80: £2.10, £2.80; EX 18.80 Trifecta £88.20.
Owner Carl Hinchy **Bred** J P Murphy & M Barry Murphy **Trained** Red Hill, Warwickshire

FOCUS
A decent handicap chase run at a brisk gallop. Most of these still held a chance two out, and the form has a solid look to it. It's rated around the first two.

831 EFG HARRIS ALLDAY MARES' STANDARD OPEN NATIONAL HUNT FLAT RACE 2m
3:20 (3:21) (Class 6) 4-6-Y-0 **£1,559** (£457; £228; £114)

Form RPR

1 **Epic Ethel** 4-10-9 0.. RichardJohnson 88+
(Philip Hobbs) *small wl-mde: chsd ldrs: rdn 6f out: hrd drvn fnl 4f: responded generously fnl f: led 100yds out and sn outbattled rival* **5/1**[2]

00-3 **2** 3½ **Midnight Gypsy**[18] [644] 5-10-12 0................................ PaddyBrennan 88+
(Stuart Kittow) *plld hrd in last: effrt wd fr 4f out: led over 1f out: reluctant and wandered whn rdn and hdd 100yds out: sn btn* **8/1**[3]

3 3¼ **Violets Girl** 5-10-12 0.. AndrewTinkler 84
(Warren Greatrex) *w ldr: rdn 3f out: hdd over 1f out: sn no ex* **11/4**[1]

1 **4** 2¾ **Time Is Money**[43] [271] 6-11-5 0.................................. DarylJacob 88
(Emma Lavelle) *chsd ldrs: rdn over 4f out: plugged on same pce and wl hld fnl 2f: edgd rt over 1f out* **5/1**[2]

0- **5** ½ **Honey Brown**[139] [4052] 4-10-9 0................................. RobertDunne 78
(Tom Lacey) *small: prom: rdn 6f out: edgd lft 4f out: wl hld fnl 2f* **33/1**

6 1½ **Brenda De Ronceray (FR)** 4-10-9 0............................ TomScudamore 76
(David Pipe) *small: chsd ldrs: rdn and outpcd 5f out: plugged on fnl 2f* **11/4**[1]

7 *12* **Cottonwool Baby (IRE)**[74] 4-10-9 0............................... LiamTreadwell 66
(Michael Scudamore) *midfield: short-lived effrt 5f out: t.o* **25/1**

8 *9* **Sultan's Dancer** 6-10-12 0... BrendanPowell 58
(Brendan Powell) *narrow ld mostly tl rdn 4f out: sn wknd: t.o* **14/1**

0 **9** *8* **Bishopstone Girl (IRE)**[49] [152] 4-10-9 0................. WayneHutchinson 47
(Paul Cowley) *small: sweating and unruly s: t.k.h in rr: struggling over 4f out: t.o* **66/1**

0 **10** *47* **Teme Trixie**[45] [220] 5-10-5 0.................................. MichaelHeard(7) 3
(Andrew Price) *t.k.h in rr: rdn 5f out: t.o fnl 3f* **100/1**

4m 8.4s (23.40) **Going Correction** +0.375s/f (Yiel)
WFA 4 from 5yo+ 3lb **10** Ran SP% **113.7**
Speed ratings: **56,54,52,51,51 50,44,39,35,12**
CSF £42.05 TOTE £5.10: £2.50, £2.80, £1.10; EX 42.20 Trifecta £239.30.
Owner L J McGuinness **Bred** Steve Hadley **Trained** Withycombe, Somerset

FOCUS
A modest mares' bumper. They went no pace early and the second, fourth and fifth help with the form.

832 DINOSAUR DASH WMSP.CO.UK NOVICES' HURDLE (8 hdls) 2m
3:55 (3:55) (Class 4) 4-Y-0+ **£3,249** (£954; £477; £238)

Form RPR

23-1 **1** **Paolozzi (IRE)**[15] [680] 6-11-5 0................................(t) ConorO'Farrell 120+
(Seamus Durack) *led after 2nd: set stdy pce: pressed whn nt fluent 2 out and whn lunged at last: drvn and kpt finding ex flat* **13/8**[1]

1 **2** 1¼ **Tercel (IRE)**[28] [511] 4-11-2 0...............................(t) SamTwiston-Davies 114+
(Paul Nicholls) *plld hrd towards rr: effrt after 5th: chsd wnr bef 2 out: sn hrd drvn: no imp fnl 100yds* **11/4**[3]

0-32 **3** *5* **Hepijeu (FR)**[13] [703] 4-10-9 115...............................(t) AidanColeman 103
(Charlie Longsdon) *pressed ldrs: rdn and chsd ldng pair fr 2 out: nvr making any imp and 5 l 3rd at last* **9/4**[2]

3-6 **4** *11* **Newton Geronimo**[18] [648] 6-10-12 0............................. NicodeBoinville 94+
(Ben Pauling) *plld hrd in last pair: mod prog after 5th: tk 15 l 4th bef last: nvr nr ldrs* **50/1**

6-50 **5** 1½ **Ho Lee Moses (IRE)**[32] [440] 5-10-12 0.............................. PaulMoloney 93
(Evan Williams) *t.k.h in 3rd pl tl lost position bef 3 out: no ch whn taken rt between last two* **100/1**

6 *11* **Moreece (IRE)**[158] [3746] 6-10-12 116................................ RichardJohnson 82
(Tim Vaughan) *led tl after 2nd: pressed ldr tl nt fluent 3 out and drvn: wknd qckly next* **8/1**

7 *5* **Honourable Exit (IRE)**[31] 8-10-12 0................................ AdamWedge 77
(Alexandra Dunn) *nvr bttr than midfield: lost tch 3 out* **33/1**

0-0U **8** *2* **Innox Park**[28] [511] 5-10-12 0.....................................(p) JamesBest 75
(Kevin Bishop) *towards rr: rdn and struggling bef 3 out* **66/1**

6-P5 **9** *13* **Southern Cross**[27] [361] 4-10-2 0.................................. DaveCrosse 52
(Dai Williams) *hld up in last pair: lost tch after 5th: t.o next* **100/1**

3m 59.1s (8.50) **Going Correction** +0.375s/f (Yiel)
WFA 4 from 5yo+ 17lb **9** Ran SP% **115.0**
Speed ratings (Par 105): **93,92,89,84,83 78,75,74,68**
CSF £6.54 TOTE £3.20: £1.50, £1.10, £1.10; EX 7.00 Trifecta £9.60.
Owner C Wilkinson **Bred** Mrs V Wilkinson **Trained** Upper Lambourn, Berkshire

FOCUS
A fair novice hurdle for the time of year. The early pace was sedate and the first three finished clear. The form is rated around the first two.

833 THURSFIELDS SOLICITORS H'CAP HURDLE (12 hdls) 2m 7f
4:30 (4:30) (Class 3) (0-140,134) 4-Y-0+ **£5,393** (£1,583; £791; £395)

Form RPR

61-0 **1** **Mr Shantu (IRE)**[43] [261] 6-10-1 **116**..........................(t) PatrickCowley(7) 124
(Jonjo O'Neill) *settled in last pair: rdn and effrt after 9th: clsd 2 out to chal ldng pair last: sn surged ahd and steadily forged clr* **13/2**

3-15 **2** 3¾ **Henllan Harri (IRE)**[40] [319] 7-11-5 **130**............................ SeanBowen(3) 135
(Peter Bowen) *2nd or 3rd pl tl led 3 out: jnd next and drvn: hdd sn after last: kpt on same pce* **5/2**[1]

05-5 **3** 2¾ **On The Bridge (IRE)**[35] [404] 10-11-2 **127**..................(tp) MattGriffiths(3) 132+
(Jeremy Scott) *racd on outer and t.k.h: several positions: cl up fr 7th: rdn to join ldr and blnd 2 out: stl ev ch whn mstke last: hld in 3rd fnl 150yds* **11/4**[2]

5-12 **4** *7* **Weather Babe**[26] [532] 7-11-12 **134**...........................(tp) TomScudamore 130
(David Pipe) *chsd ldrs: 4th and hrd drvn home turn: no imp fr 3 out* **4/1**[3]

43-2 **5** *18* **Allbarnone**[30] [468] 7-10-5 **113**.................................... DenisO'Regan 93
(William Kinsey) *towards rr: rdn and lost tch bef 3 out* **7/1**

6-31 **6** *17* **Bobble Emerald (IRE)**[31] [460] 7-10-9 **117**.......................... AndrewTinkler 91
(Martin Keighley) *t.k.h: led bef 3rd: hdd and mstke 3 out: disputing 3rd and rdn next: tiring and wl btn whn wnt lft last: t.o* **14/1**

2FP- **7** *43* **Prince Tom**[107] [4684] 11-11-8 **130**.............................. ConorO'Farrell 56
(Alexandra Dunn) *led tl bef 3rd: prom tl lost pl and nt fluent 9th: sn u.p and t.o* **25/1**

5m 46.1s (7.50) **Going Correction** +0.375s/f (Yiel) **7** Ran SP% **111.6**
Speed ratings (Par 107): **101,99,98,96,90 84,69**
CSF £22.53 TOTE £6.90: £3.10, £2.20; EX 27.20 Trifecta £114.60.
Owner Local Parking Security Limited **Bred** Victor Connolly **Trained** Cheltenham, Gloucs

FOCUS
A fair handicap hurdle run at a reasonable gallop. The first two are rated to their best.

834 CLARENDON CARE WORCESTERSHIRE NOVICES' HURDLE (10 hdls) 2m 4f
5:05 (5:06) (Class 4) 4-Y-0+ **£3,249** (£954; £477; £238)

Form RPR

1 **Applesandpierres (IRE)**[51] 7-10-12 0.............................. HarrySkelton 118+
(Dan Skelton) *small: trckd ldrs: effrt in 3rd after 7th: led 3 out: 5 l clr and awkward last: drvn out and a in command* **7/4**[1]

5-41 **2** *9* **Always On The Run (IRE)**[18] [648] 5-11-5 120........ WayneHutchinson 114
(Donald McCain) *hld up in rr: prog after 7th: rdn to chse wnr after 3 out: no imp fr next* **2/1**[2]

0-3 **3** *8* **Rebel Benefit (IRE)**[22] [590] 7-10-12 0................................ NoelFehily 101
(David Dennis) *sn led and set mod gallop: jnd after 7th: hdd next: rdn and grad wknd: 10 l 3rd at last* **12/1**

4 *9* **Panis Angelicus (FR)**[239] 6-10-12 0............................ RichardJohnson 94
(Tim Vaughan) *pressed ldr: upsides after 7th tl rdn 3 out: fdd fr next* **4/1**[3]

5 *11* **Sturmwind (GER)**[31] 4-10-8 0....................................... LeightonAspell 79
(Alison Batchelor) *hld up and bhd: mod prog bef 3 out: sn btn* **80/1**

6 *4* **Crosslanes (IRE)**[78] 4-10-1 0.................................... TomMessenger 67
(Chris Bealby) *small: bhd: rdn and lost tch bef 3 out: t.o* **20/1**

04 **7** 3¾ **Buy Me Out**[13] [700] 5-10-5 0... PaulMoloney 68
(Grace Harris) *awkward at s: t.k.h but wnt in snatches: disp 3rd home turn: sn drvn and dropped out: t.o* **50/1**

4 **8** *55* **Chasing The Light (IRE)**[13] [703] 5-10-12 0.............(t) RichieMcLernon 25
(Jonjo O'Neill) *t.k.h: chsd ldrs tl 7th: struggling next: t.o and eased* **8/1**

0 **9** *7* **Merry Mast (USA)**[15] [671] 6-10-12 0................................. TomO'Brien 19
(Paul Henderson) *chsd ldrs tl 5th: t.o 3 out: eased* **100/1**

50 **P** **Defiant Dazzler (IRE)**[27] [526] 6-10-5 0............................. MissLBrooke(7)
(Lady Susan Brooke) *mstkes in rr: last whn slow 5th and 6th: t.o and p.u after next* **200/1**

5m 2.2s (8.70) **Going Correction** +0.375s/f (Yiel)
WFA 4 from 5yo+ 18lb **10** Ran SP% **117.9**
Speed ratings (Par 105): **97,93,90,86,82 80,79,57,54,**
CSF £5.67 TOTE £2.40: £1.10, £1.30, £2.40; EX 5.70 Trifecta £35.00.
Owner M Rozenbroek **Bred** John Doyle **Trained** Alcester, Warwicks

FOCUS
A modest event run at an ordinary gallop. The winner can rate higher.

835 NICKLIN CONDITIONAL JOCKEYS' H'CAP HURDLE (8 hdls) 2m
5:35 (5:35) (Class 4) (0-110,110) 4-Y-0+ **£3,249** (£954; £477; £238)

Form RPR

354- **1** **At First Light**[95] [4902] 6-11-1 **99**................................... NicodeBoinville 111+
(David Weston) *settled trcking ldrs: effrt in 3rd 3 out: led between last two: 3 l clr last: rdn and kpt on gamely after* **16/1**

2-35 **2** *4* **Hawdyerwheesht**[12] [718] 7-11-4 **110**.......................... MrShaneQuinlan(8) 116
(David Dennis) *ldng trio: led 4th tl next: drvn and disp ld 2 out: hdd between last two: btn and finding little whn hung lft bef last* **9/2**[3]

56-3 **3** 1½ **Drifter (IRE)**[42] [281] 4-10-10 **105**................................... PaulNO'Brien(8) 107
(Harry Whittington) *hld up and bhd: 7th home turn: rdn and racing awkwardly after: plugged on after last to take wl hld 3rd cl home* **7/2**[2]

-443 **4** ½ **Ladies Dancing**[3] [810] 9-11-2 **100**...............................(b) KieronEdgar 105
(Chris Down) *t.k.h: chsd ldrs: led 5th: rdn and jnd 2 out: hdd and edgd rt between last two: no ex flat and lost 3rd nr fin* **15/8**[1]

3-5P **5** *16* **Keychain (IRE)**[37] [381] 5-11-2 **100**...............................(v) ThomasGarner 91
(Brendan Powell) *hld up and bhd: effrt after 5th: chsd ldrs briefly 3 out: sn rdn and btn* **33/1**

U-36 **6** *8* **Short Takes (USA)**[28] 508 7-11-4 **108** (b) JamesCowley[(6)] 91
(Donald McCain) *nt a fluent: led tl after 2nd: mstke 4th: rdn and dropped out tamely after next* **16/1**

30-0 **7** *1 1/2* **Ullswater (IRE)**[13] 692 7-10-10 **94** (vt[1]) SeanBowen 75
(Emma Lavelle) *led after 2nd tl 4th: remained prom tl rdn and wknd qckly 3 out* **8/1**

6-14 **8** *29* **Sunblazer (IRE)**[51] 104 5-11-12 **110** (t) ConorShoemark 65
(Kim Bailey) *cl up: hrd drvn after 5th: fnd nil: wl btn next: t.o* **9/1**

6-40 **9** *1 1/2* **Luddsdenene (IRE)**[12] 718 10-11-4 **110** (t) MikeyHamill[(8)] 64
(Alexandra Dunn) *sn last: t.o after 5th* **40/1**

3m 55.0s (4.40) **Going Correction** +0.375s/f (Yiel)
WFA 4 from 5yo+ 17lb **9** Ran **SP% 113.4**
Speed ratings (Par 105): **104,102,101,101,93 89,88,73,73**
CSF £86.06 CT £313.98 TOTE £25.40: £4.10, £2.20, £2.50; EX 123.10 Trifecta £377.20.
Owner Miss E J Tanner **Bred** D J Weston **Trained** Marlborough, Wilts

FOCUS
A moderate handicap, and not form to take too seriously. A big step up from the winner.
T/Plt: £48.40 to a £1 stake. Pool: £58,703.70 - 884.90 winning units T/Qpdt: £4.90 to a £1 stake. Pool: £6,417.76 - 953.10 winning units **Iain Mackenzie**

821 AUTEUIL (L-H)
Thursday, June 25

OFFICIAL GOING: Turf: soft

836a PRIX DAWN RUN (HURDLE) (LISTED RACE) (5YO+) (TURF) 2m 3f 110y
2:05 (12:00) 5-Y-O+ **£31,627** (£15,813; £9,224; £6,259; £2,965)

RPR

1 **Prince Philippe (FR)**[71] 5-10-10 0 BertrandLestrade 136
(P Bourgeais, France) **103/10**

2 *1/2* **Password (FR)**[18] 6-11-0 0 ErvanChazelle 140
(Mlle T Puitg, France) **17/5**[1]

3 *15* **Tango Lima (FR)**[39] 7-10-10 0 (p) ThomasBeaurain 121
(J-P Gallorini, France) **39/10**[2]

4 *shd* **Anemos (FR)**[39] 8-10-12 0 JonathanNattiez 122
(B Duchemin, France) **174/10**

5 *4* **Katkeau (FR)**[34] 437 8-10-8 0 TomScudamore 114
(David Pipe) *trckd ldng pair: disp ld 5 out: nudged along and hdd bef 2 out: outpcd between last 2: mstke last and wknd* **41/10**[3]

6 *1 3/4* **High Policy (FR)**[398] 7-10-8 0 RichardLeStang 113
(Stephen Ramsay, France) **60/1**

7 *20* **Singapore Sling (FR)**[25] 4 6-10-12 0 (p) MorganRegairaz 97
(A Bonin, France) **47/10**

8 *2 1/2* **Franche Alliance (FR)**[71] 6-10-12 0 (p) JonathanPlouganou 94
(A De Watrigant, France) **53/10**

P **Le Bel Anjou (FR)**[39] 7-10-12 0 RegisSchmidlin
(F-M Cottin, France) **135/10**

4m 37.1s (-17.90) **9** Ran **SP% 119.0**
PARI-MUTUEL (all including 1 euro stake): WIN 11.30; PLACE 2.60, 1.90, 1.60; DF 21.80; SF 50.10.
Owner Mme Marie-France Besnard **Bred** P Bourgeais & Mme M-F Besnard **Trained** France

502 CARTMEL (L-H)
Friday, June 26

OFFICIAL GOING: Good to firm (good in places) changing to good after race 2 (2:40)
Wind: moderate 1/2 behind Weather: overcast, breezy, light rain

837 RACING UK MAIDEN HURDLE (11 hdls) 2m 6f 31y
2:10 (2:10) (Class 5) 4-Y-O+ **£2,599** (£763; £381; £190)

Form RPR

1 **Thatshowhedidit (IRE)**[65] 5488 6-11-2 0 ow3 (t) KeithDonoghue[(3)] 117+
(Mrs Gillian Callaghan, Ire) *hld up towards rr: hdwy 8th: trcking ldrs whn nt fluent next: led sn after last: wnt clr: v readily* **5/1**[2]

546- **2** *10* **Dr Robin (IRE)**[193] 3117 5-11-2 100 DonalDevereux 99
(Peter Bowen) *chsd ldrs: upsides 4th: led 8th: hdd between last 2: kpt on same pce last 200yds* **8/1**

3 *nse* **Spicy Fruity (IRE)**[21] 633 5-11-2 0 RichardJohnson 100
(Gordon Elliott, Ire) *t.k.h in mid-div: trckd ldrs 6th: hit 2 out: styd on last 150yds* **5/1**[2]

2-33 **4** *1 3/4* **Bryden Boy (IRE)**[33] 463 5-11-2 119 (p) PeterCarberry 98
(Jennie Candlish) *led: hdd 8th: rdn to ld between last 2: hdd sn after last: kpt on one pce* **11/8**[1]

42-U **5** *2 1/2* **Ronaldinho (IRE)**[6] 221 5-11-2 119 BrianHughes 95
(Dianne Sayer) *chsd ldrs: one pce appr last* **7/1**[3]

4/40 **6** *3 3/4* **Miss Chatterbox**[9] 759 10-10-4 87 MrJohnDawson[(5)] 84
(Chris Grant) *chsd ldrs: one pce between last 2* **100/1**

7 *3 1/2* **Benarty Hill (IRE)**[81] 5-10-13 0 GrahamWatters[(3)] 89
(Liam Lennon, Ire) *hld up towards rr: hdwy 8th: hmpd bnd sn after 2 out: modest 7th and hld whn hit last* **66/1**

3/U5 **8** *1* **Erica Starprincess**[17] 679 5-10-9 0 HenryBrooke 80
(George Moore) *hld up in rr: gd hdwy 8th: trcking ldrs 2 out: sn hmpd on bnd: one pce* **25/1**

0-30 **9** *18* **Tokyo Brown (USA)**[32] 468 6-10-13 95 (p) TonyKelly[(3)] 68
(James Moffatt) *hld up in rr: bhd fr 8th* **40/1**

0- **10** *45* **Warksburn Boy**[205] 2881 5-11-2 0 BrianHarding 23
(Sheena Walton) *mid-div: chsd ldrs 3rd: reminders 7th: lost pl next: sn bhd: t.o 2 out: eventually completed* **200/1**

04 **U** **Only Gorgeous (IRE)**[23] 595 6-10-13 0 LucyGardner[(3)]
(Sue Gardner) *trckd ldrs: t.k.h: j. sltly lft and uns rdr 1st* **10/1**

5m 26.3s (-3.00) **Going Correction** -0.525s/f (Firm) **11** Ran **SP% 117.4**
Speed ratings (Par 103): **84,80,80,79,78 77,76,75,69,52**
CSF £42.83 TOTE £7.30: £2.00, £2.60, £1.80; EX 64.50 Trifecta £359.20.
Owner Ms Sarah Connolly **Bred** Mrs Mary McRedmond **Trained** Kells, Co Meath
■ Stewards' Enquiry : Peter Carberry two-day ban: careless riding (Jul 12, 15)

FOCUS
The rail was on the inner line and all distances as advertised. Fair form in this maiden hurdle, the winner doing it easily. The gallop wasn't strong, a number still in contention at the second-last. The winenr is rated in line with his best bumper figures.

838 HADWINS H'CAP HURDLE (12 hdls) 3m 1f 83y
2:40 (2:41) (Class 5) (0-100,100) 4-Y-O+ **£2,599** (£763; £381; £190)

Form RPR

/05- **1** **Redclue (IRE)**[28] 550 6-11-9 100 (tp) KeithDonoghue[(3)] 116+
(Mrs Gillian Callaghan, Ire) *trckd ldrs: 2nd 3 out: led between last 2: wnt clr sn after last: eased fnl 150yds* **7/2**[1]

50-1 **2** *9* **Craigdancer (IRE)**[29] 522 6-11-0 88 DougieCostello 89
(Joanne Foster) *in rr: hdwy 7th: 5th last: styd on wl last 100yds: tk 2nd post* **17/2**

P6P1 **3** *nse* **Izbushka (IRE)**[26] 569 4-10-9 88 (b) BrianHughes 83
(David Thompson) *chsd ldrs: rdn 2 out: one pce appr last* **7/1**[3]

-P12 **4** *nk* **Native Optimist (IRE)**[13] 726 8-10-8 87 MissCWalton[(5)] 88
(Sheena Walton) *w ldr: led 3 out: hdd between last 2: fdd clsng stages* **8/1**

45-4 **5** *hd* **Raid Stane (IRE)**[26] 569 9-11-6 94 (b) HenryBrooke 95
(Julia Brooke) *mid-div: outpcd appr 2 out: modest 6th last: styd on wl last 100yds* **12/1**

P6P- **6** *2* **Triumph Davis (IRE)**[66] 5442 6-11-12 100 RichardJohnson 100
(Gordon Elliott, Ire) *nt fluent in rr: hdwy 9th: handy 4th whn blnd last: styd on last 100yds* **7/2**[1]

65-3 **7** *4 1/4* **Storm Alert**[23] 599 8-10-13 90 LucyGardner[(3)] 84
(Sue Gardner) *hld up in rr: hdwy 9th: lost pl 2 out* **6/1**[2]

61/P **8** *43* **Unex Picasso**[30] 505 7-11-12 100 LucyAlexander 55
(Barry Murtagh) *led: hdd 3 out: sn reminders and lost pl: t.o last: eventually completed* **20/1**

PF-0 **9** *38* **Cloggy Powell (IRE)**[30] 502 8-9-11 76 oh5 ow2 CallumBewley[(5)]
(Kevin Hunter) *chsd ldrs: lost pl bef 2 out: sn wl bhd: t.o last: eventually completed* **100/1**

P03 **P** **Agent Louise**[9] 758 7-9-11 74 (b) AdamNicol[(3)]
(Mike Sowersby) *nt fluent in rr: sme hdwy 8th: lost pl after next: sn bhd: t.o whn p.u bef last* **7/1**[3]

6m 11.5s (-14.60) **Going Correction** -0.525s/f (Firm)
WFA 4 from 6yo+ 19lb **10** Ran **SP% 118.8**
Speed ratings (Par 103): **102,99,99,99,98 98,96,83,71,**
CSF £34.24 CT £201.25 TOTE £3.60: £1.80, £3.50, £2.30; EX 44.10 Trifecta £206.80.
Owner E R Syndicate **Bred** John Mounsey **Trained** Kells, Co Meath
■ Stewards' Enquiry : Callum Bewley one-day ban: weighed-in 2lb heavy (Jul 12)

FOCUS
The looked quite competitive beforehand but turned out to be anything but, the winner bolting up. The second to sixth were all pretty close to their marks.

839 CUMBRIA GRAND HOTEL AT GRANGE H'CAP HURDLE (11 hdls) 2m 6f 31y
3:10 (3:12) (Class 4) (0-120,122) 4-Y-O+ **£3,898** (£1,144; £572; £286)

Form RPR

/1-1 **1** **Stags Leap (IRE)**[30] 502 8-10-9 103 (p) HenryBrooke 106+
(Julia Brooke) *mid-div: blnd bdly and lost pl 5th: hdwy to chse ldrs 8th: 2nd 2 out: led sn after last: idled: drvn rt out* **3/1**[2]

0- **2** *1 1/4* **From Frost**[6] 796 4-11-10 122 7ex (tp) RichardJohnson 118
(Gordon Elliott, Ire) *mid-div: hdwy 8th: 4th and drvn 2 out: kpt on to take 2nd last 50yds* **11/4**[1]

41P/ **3** *1/2* **Ongenstown Lad (IRE)**[17] 687 11-11-9 120 (p) KeithDonoghue[(3)] 120
(Mrs Gillian Callaghan, Ire) *trckd ldrs: led appr 3 out: hdd sn after last: kpt on same pce* **14/1**

6-21 **4** *2* **Grand Vintage (IRE)**[32] 468 9-11-2 110 (tp) DougieCostello 108
(Kenneth Slack) *led: clr 2nd: hdd appr 3 out: outpcd 2 out: modest 5th last: rallied and styd on last 150yds* **10/1**

306- **5** *2 3/4* **Handmaid**[168] 3597 6-11-0 111 SeanBowen[(3)] 106
(Peter Bowen) *chsd ldrs: drvn 8th: outpcd appr 2 out: modest 6th last: kpt on* **4/1**[3]

3-31 **6** *11* **Tickenwolf (IRE)**[31] 481 5-10-12 109 AdamNicol[(3)] 96
(George Moore) *chsd ldrs: drvn appr 2 out: wknd appr last* **10/1**

40-3 **7** *3/4* **Maybe I Wont**[32] 473 10-10-13 107 (v) BrianHughes 92
(James Moffatt) *prom: drvn 3 out: lost pl next* **22/1**

02-B **8** *7* **Spirit River (FR)**[17] 670 10-10-11 105 LeeEdwards 83
(Dave Roberts) *in rr: hdwy 8th: nt fluent and lost pl next* **50/1**

014- **9** *9* **Tayarat (IRE)**[371] 755 10-9-12 97 JoeCornwall[(5)] 67
(Michael Chapman) *in rr: bhd and drvn 7th: nvr on terms* **66/1**

2-23 **10** *4* **Weybridge Light**[11] 746 10-10-6 100 (b) PaddyBrennan 72
(David Thompson) *in rr: bhd and drvn 8th: blnd last* **14/1**

6-P4 **11** *18* **Maller Tree**[17] 678 8-11-3 111 (p) GavinSheehan 62
(David Dennis) *chsd ldrs: drvn 7th: lost pl next: sn bhd* **10/1**

5m 19.1s (-10.20) **Going Correction** -0.275s/f (Good) **11** Ran **SP% 120.1**
Speed ratings (Par 105): **107,106,106,105,104 100,100,97,94,93 86**
CSF £12.16 CT £101.46 TOTE £4.30: £1.40, £1.50, £5.10; EX 15.50 Trifecta £179.10.
Owner John & Billy Platts **Bred** P McCartan & Paddy Twomey **Trained** Middleham, North Yorks

FOCUS
A fair handicap. The going was changed to good before this race. The winner was 3lb off his recent C&D win.

840 NIKKI'S CELEBRATION BEGINNERS' CHASE (18 fncs) 3m 1f 107y
3:45 (3:46) (Class 4) 5-Y-O+ **£3,994** (£1,240; £667)

Form RPR

50-4 **1** **Morning Royalty (IRE)**[30] 505 8-11-0 122 BrianHughes 123+
(James Moffatt) *hld up in last: hdwy 12th: handy 3rd 14th: 2nd 2 out: led 2f out: pushed out* **3/1**[2]

224- **2** *10* **Supapowers (IRE)**[240] 2135 9-10-7 0 (t) RichardJohnson 108
(Robert Stephens) *chsd ldng pair: hit 7th and 12th: 2nd 13th: led 3 out: hdd 2f out: kpt on same pce* **9/1**

3-32 **3** *6* **Volcanic (FR)**[20] 635 6-11-0 0 (t) HenryBrooke 112
(Donald McCain) *led: drvn and hdd 3 out: one pce* **4/5**[1]

P **Without Wings (IRE)**[27] 7-10-4 0 (t) GrahamWatters[(3)]
(Liam Lennon, Ire) *chsd ldr: blnd 12th: blnd and dropped bk last 14th: sn bhd: t.o whn p.u sn after 3 out* **9/2**[3]

6m 16.1s (-18.80) **Going Correction** -0.575s/f (Firm) **4** Ran **SP% 108.7**
Speed ratings: **107,103,101,**
CSF £20.59 TOTE £3.70; EX 15.80 Trifecta £25.10.
Owner Mrs Eileen M Milligan **Bred** Miss Marie Murphy **Trained** Cartmel, Cumbria

FOCUS
A race which almost certainly took little winning, the favourite disappointing. The winner is rated to the level of previous chase runs.

841 DANIEL THWAITES H'CAP CHASE (14 fncs) 2m 5f 34y
4:20 (4:20) (Class 5) (0-100,96) 5-Y-O+ £3,249 (£954; £477; £238)

Form RPR
0-U1 1 **Cool Star (IRE)**[13] 731 9-10-10 83.......................(t) JonathanEngland(3) 116+
(Maurice Barnes) *mde all: j. soundly: pushed clr 3f out: eased clsng stages* **15/2[3]**
/-62 2 29 **Larkhall**[11] 743 8-9-11 70 oh8.............................. AdamNicol(3) 77
(Mike Sowersby) *hld up in rr: hdwy to chse ldrs 5th: 2nd 9th: drvn last: one pce* **11/1**
P-63 3 1 1/4 **Pistol Basc (FR)**[29] 519 11-10-13 86.............................. TonyKelly(3) 90
(Rebecca Menzies) *prom: outpcd 8th: modest 3rd 3 out: one pce* **14/1**
2-15 4 10 **My Friend George**[29] 519 9-11-8 92.....................(p) HenryBrooke 87
(Kenneth Slack) *chsd ldrs: drvn 10th: wknd last* **4/1[2]**
4-23 5 3 3/4 **Cara Court (IRE)**[11] 743 9-10-4 79 ow2..................(p) MrJohnDawson(5) 71
(Joanne Foster) *chsd ldrs in 3rd: drvn 10th: one pce fr next* **10/1**
45P- 6 18 **Peak Seasons (IRE)**[105] 4744 12-9-9 70 oh8................. JoeCornwall(5) 45
(Michael Chapman) *chsd ldrs: drvn and lost pl 8th: sn bhd* **80/1**
0P/4 7 1 1/2 **Go Teescomponents**[24] 588 8-10-1 74.................. HarryChalloner(3) 48
(Keith Reveley) *mid-div outpcd 8th: bhd fr 10th* **16/1**
6-34 8 dist **Pindar (GER)**[30] 504 11-10-6 76.............................. DougieCostello
(Joanne Foster) *in rr: bhd fr 8th: tailed rt off whn blnd last: eased and eventually completed* **20/1**
0-2P P **Discoverie**[33] 454 7-10-10 80..............................(p) SeanQuinlan
(Dianne Sayer) *mid-div: reminders after 2nd: sn lost pl: bhd 8th: t.o whn p.u bef next* **20/1**
3-20 P **Roseville Cottage (IRE)**[29] 519 8-11-12 96.................(b) BrianHughes
(John Wade) *chsd ldrs: blnd and lost pl 4th: sn bhd: t.o 8th: p.u bef next* **12/1**
F44- P **Home For Tea**[77] 5257 6-10-10 80.............................. RichardJohnson
(Gordon Elliott, Ire) *in rr: mstke 4th: bhd whn mstke 9th: p.u bef next* **11/8[1]**

5m 10.4s (-15.00) **Going Correction** -0.575s/f (Firm) **11** Ran SP% **122.3**
Speed ratings: **105,93,93,89,88 81,80, , ,**
CSF £86.07 CT £1149.22 TOTE £9.10: £2.40, £4.10, £3.40; EX 79.80 Trifecta £778.60.
Owner D Carr & M Carlyle **Bred** C Amerian **Trained** Farlam, Cumbria

FOCUS
A one-sided handicap, the winner having everything else in trouble a long way out. The time was good for the grade.

842 FURNESS FISH & GAME H'CAP CHASE (18 fncs) 3m 1f 107y
4:55 (4:56) (Class 5) (0-100,100) 5-Y-O+ £3,249 (£954; £477; £238)

Form RPR
0-13 1 **Over And Above (IRE)**[36] 421 9-10-10 87..........(tp) GrahamWatters(3) 95
(Henry Hogarth) *chsd ldrs: drvn 12th: outpcd and reminders next: 4 l 2nd over 1f out: styd on to ld towards fin* **5/1[2]**
1U-6 2 1 **Solway Bay**[41] 333 13-10-6 87..............................(tp) RyanDay(7) 95+
(Lisa Harrison) *hld up in rr: hdwy 12th: chsng ldrs next: led 2f out: sn 4 l clr: no ex and hdd clsng stages* **12/1**
/0-1 3 6 **Call Me Mulligan (IRE)**[11] 743 11-10-13 94 7ex............ MrABartlett(7) 97
(Patrick Holmes) *chsd ldrs: pushed along 7th: 2nd 12th: chalng whn blnd last: 3rd and one pce over 1f out* **13/2**
3-21 4 12 **Everylasting (IRE)**[29] 519 8-10-10 87.........................(b) CraigNichol(3) 78
(Rose Dobbin) *w ldrs: led 4th: hdd 2f out: wknd qckly over 1f out* **11/4[1]**
14-F 5 41 **Oh Right (IRE)**[32] 471 11-11-12 100..............................(b) HenryBrooke 53
(Dianne Sayer) *hld up towards rr: hdwy 8th: chsng ldrs 13th: wknd 3 out: sn bhd: t.o* **11/1**
30P6 6 14 **Generous Chief (IRE)**[5] 803 7-11-3 96.............(b) DiarmuidO'Regan(5) 36
(Chris Grant) *chsd ldrs: 2nd 8th: hit 13th: drvn next lost pl next: sn bhd: t.o* **11/2[3]**
/PP- 7 25 **Apache Blue (IRE)**[41] 11-11-6 94..............................(p) BrianHughes 12
(John Wade) *nt jump wl: lost pl 6th: bhd whn mstke 12th: t.o 15th* **14/1**
4PP- 8 nse **Bayfirth (IRE)**[90] 12-9-7 74.. MrWHRReed(7)
(Andrew Hamilton) *in rr: bhd 7th: t.o 15th* **50/1**
P-2P P **Winter Alchemy (IRE)**[31] 486 10-11-4 92...................(b[1]) BrianHarding
(Nicky Richards) *led: hdd 4th: reminders and lost pl next: bhd 9th: t.o whn p.u bef 14th* **6/1**
PP-6 P **Reverse The Charge (IRE)**[33] 453 8-10-0 74 oh5........ PeterBuchanan
(Jane Walton) *in rr: hit 4th: bhd 12th: t.o whn p.u bef 3 out* **14/1**

6m 26.4s (-8.50) **Going Correction** -0.575s/f (Firm) **10** Ran SP% **117.7**
Speed ratings: **90,89,87,83,70 66,58,58, ,**
CSF £62.08 CT £397.54 TOTE £7.20: £2.60, £4.20, £2.60; EX 50.30 Trifecta £495.00.
Owner Hogarth Racing **Bred** Leslie Tucker **Trained** Stillington, N Yorks

FOCUS
A modest contest. The complexion of the race changed dramatically on the long run-in, the runner-up throwing it away. The first two are rated pretty much to their marks.

843 KINGSTONE PRESS CIDER NOVICES' H'CAP HURDLE (8 hdls) 2m 1f 46y
5:30 (5:30) (Class 4) (0-105,104) 4-Y-O+ £3,249 (£954; £477; £238)

Form RPR
4-23 1 **Keep To The Beat**[14] 711 4-10-13 101.............................. RyanDay(7) 104
(Kevin Ryan) *chsd ldrs: led 2 out: drvn and styd on run-in* **11/1**
3-26 2 3 1/4 **The Absent Mare**[30] 504 7-10-0 78 oh1....................(t) RichardJohnson 81
(Gordon Elliott, Ire) *hld up in rr: hdwy 5th: trcking ldrs next: 2nd 2 out: pushed along appr last: hung lft and styd on same pce* **3/1[1]**
25-F 3 2 1/4 **Mad For Road (IRE)**[57] 34 6-11-8 100.............................. DougieCostello 101
(Ben Haslam) *in rr: hdwy 3 out: 3rd appr last: kpt on same pce* **13/2**
340- 4 19 **Perennial**[20] 1679 6-11-12 104..............................(b) AdamNicol(3) 91
(Philip Kirby) *mid-div: hdwy 5th: reminders appr 2 out: sn outpcd: poor 4th 1f out* **5/1[2]**
004- 5 9 **Dalby Spook (IRE)**[9] 2400 5-10-10 88.............................. BrianHughes 64
(Dianne Sayer) *mid-div: chsd ldrs 5th: handy 3rd sn after 2 out: sn wknd* **11/1**
P06- 6 3/4 **Dr Dalwhinny**[153] 3864 6-10-13 98..............................(p) JamesCowley(7) 74
(Donald McCain) *chsd ldrs: reminders 3rd: lost pl after 5th* **8/1**
/602 7 2 1/4 **Green And White (ITY)**[17] 673 5-11-5 97.............................. LeeEdwards 70
(Dave Roberts) *nt fluent towards rr: sme hdwy 5th: sn lost pl* **12/1**
6-04 8 2 1/4 **Mahayogin (USA)**[7] 777 7-9-8 79..............................(t) HenryBrooke 43
(Sarah-Jayne Davies) *led to 4th: lost pl bef 3 out* **25/1**
5-00 9 18 **Touch Of Steel (IRE)**[13] 727 6-10-4 87..............................(p) DaleIrving(5) 42
(James Ewart) *chsd ldrs: nt fluent and lost pl 5th: sn bhd* **16/1**
P/P- 10 4 1/2 **Palus San Marco (IRE)**[15] 2501 6-10-12 90..................(b[1]) PeterCarberry 41
(Jennie Candlish) *w ldr: led 4th: sn pushed along: hdd 2 out: sn lost pl and bhd* **20/1**
-465 11 8 **Jebulani**[15] 694 5-10-4 82.............................. BrianHarding 26
(Barry Murtagh) *in rr: sme hdwy 5th: sn lost pl: bhd whn heavily eased run-in* **11/2[3]**

4m 5.0s (-8.20) **Going Correction** -0.275s/f (Good)
WFA 4 from 5yo+ 17lb **11** Ran SP% **120.3**
Speed ratings (Par 105): **108,106,105,96,92 91,90,89,81,79 75**
CSF £46.12 CT £242.05 TOTE £12.90: £2.80, £1.30, £2.70; EX 55.60 Trifecta £177.80.
Owner Hambleton Racing Ltd XXIX **Bred** Hopeful **Trained** Hambleton, N Yorks

FOCUS
A modest contest, though it was at least soundly run. The winner is closing in on the level expected from her Flat form.
T/Plt: £824.90 to a £1 stake. Pool: £51,835.24 - 45.87 winning tickets T/Qpdt: £95.30 to a £1 stake. Pool: £5,323.26 - 41.30 winning tickets **Walter Glynn**

740 LES LANDES
Friday, June 26

OFFICIAL GOING: Good to firm

844a EL PRESIDENTE H'CAP HURDLE (TURF) 2m 1f
6:30 (6:30) 4-Y-O+ £1,460 (£525; £315)

1 **Rossetti**[13] 740 7-11-6.............................. MattieBatchelor 107
(Mrs A Malzard, Jersey) **4/5[1]**
2 5 **Agapanthus (GER)**[13] 740 10-11-10..............................(b) MarkQuinlan 106
(Neil Mulholland) **5/4[2]**
3 10 **Dalmo**[13] 740 6-11-4..............................(p) ThomasGarner 90
(K Kukk, Jersey) **15/2[3]**

Owner Sheikh A'Leg Racing **Bred** Bricklow Ltd **Trained** St Ouen, Jersey

837 CARTMEL (L-H)
Sunday, June 28

OFFICIAL GOING: Good (good to soft in places)
Wind: moderate 1/2 behind Weather: fine

845 BROWN HORSE WINSTER VALLEY BREWERY H'CAP HURDLE (11 hdls) 2m 6f 31y
2:10 (2:10) (Class 5) (0-100,107) 4-Y-O+ £2,599 (£763; £381; £190)

Form RPR
05-1 1 **Redclue (IRE)**[2] 838 6-12-2 107 7ex..................(tp) KeithDonoghue(3) 119+
(Mrs Gillian Callaghan, Ire) *in rr: hmpd and rdr briefly lost iron 2nd: hdwy 8th: sn drvn: chsd ldrs next: upsides last: sn led: eased last 50yds* **10/11[1]**
0-56 2 1 1/2 **Slipper Satin (IRE)**[8] 482 5-11-4 92..............................(t) HenryBrooke 96
(Simon West) *led: drvn between last 2: hdd and no excctra sn after last* **17/2[3]**
5-30 3 1 1/2 **Storm Alert**[2] 838 8-10-13 90.............................. LucyGardner(3) 92
(Sue Gardner) *chsd ldrs: kpt on same pce between last 2* **9/1**
54-3 4 4 1/2 **Sendiym (FR)**[32] 507 8-11-4 92..............................(b) BrianHughes 91
(Dianne Sayer) *chsd ldrs: one pce fr 2 out* **9/1**
P05- 5 6 **The Last Leg (IRE)**[69] 5420 6-11-8 96..............................(v) PaddyBrennan 89
(Karen McLintock) *prom: drvn 3 out: one pce* **15/2[2]**
-352 6 7 **Destiny Awaits (IRE)**[33] 481 6-11-1 92.............................. DerekFox(3) 78
(Keith Pollock) *mid-div: drvn 8th: wknd 2 out* **16/1**
0-35 7 16 **Parles Pond (IRE)**[15] 726 6-11-2 93.............................. GrahamWatters(3) 65
(Martin Todhunter) *in rr: reminders 6th: nvr on terms* **14/1**
650- 8 1 1/2 **Maggie Blue (IRE)**[93] 5017 7-11-4 97.............................. CallumBewley(5) 68
(Harriet Graham) *chsd ldrs: lost pl 3 out* **22/1**
464 9 1 3/4 **Cherry Princess**[15] 727 5-11-8 96.............................. SeanQuinlan 65
(Barbara Butterworth) *in rr: bhd fr 8th* **50/1**
-2PP 10 11 **Discoverie**[2] 841 7-10-12 89..............................(p) HarryChalloner(3) 48
(Dianne Sayer) *chsd ldrs: drvn 7th: lost pl after next* **33/1**
4-65 P **Stanley Bridge**[32] 507 8-10-8 82.............................. LucyAlexander
(Barry Murtagh) *in rr: drvn 3rd: sn bhd: t.o whn p.u bef 8th* **40/1**
5-04 P **Wyfield Rose**[33] 484 6-10-7 84..............................(tp) CraigNichol(3)
(Alistair Whillans) *j. slowly 2nd: in rr: bhd fr 8th: t.o whn p.u between last 2* **20/1**

5m 25.8s (-3.50) **Going Correction** -0.225s/f (Good) **12** Ran SP% **123.7**
Speed ratings (Par 103): **97,96,95,94,92 89,83,83,82,78 , ,**
CSF £9.57 CT £51.36 TOTE £2.30: £1.20, £2.90, £3.50; EX 14.30 Trifecta £62.70.
Owner E R Syndicate **Bred** John Mounsey **Trained** Kells, Co Meath

FOCUS
Rails moved out 4yds on both bends and distances increased by 15yds per circuit. This moderate contest was run at a decent gallop throughout and the winner was confirming the merit of his recent course win.

846 BURLINGTON STONE MARES' MAIDEN HURDLE (8 hdls) 2m 1f 46y
2:40 (2:40) (Class 5) 4-Y-O+ £2,924 (£858; £429; £214)

Form RPR
2- 1 **Miss Dinamic (IRE)**[30] 546 6-11-0 0.............................. RichardJohnson 121+
(Gordon Elliott, Ire) *wander and j. slowly 1st 2: mde all: pushed clr sn after last: eased clsng stages* **6/5[1]**
3-53 2 11 **Chilly Miss**[26] 591 6-11-0 0.............................. BrianHughes 107
(Malcolm Jefferson) *trckd ldrs: drvn 2 out: sn 2nd: no ch w wnr* **4/1[3]**
4 3 3 3/4 **Irondale Express**[13] 745 4-10-11 0..............................(p) PaulMoloney 101
(Des Donovan) *awkward s and slowly away: in rr: hdwy to chse ldrs 5th: 4th whn nt fluent 2 out: 3rd between last 2: kpt on one pce* **16/1**
4 25 **Auntie Annie (IRE)**[9] 784 4-10-11 0..............................(t) AlainCawley 81
(Mrs Gillian Callaghan, Ire) *chsd wnr: wknd sn after 2 out: sn bhd* **12/1**
16-0 5 28 **Pixiepot**[26] 594 5-11-0 0.............................. GavinSheehan 56
(Peter Niven) *j. slowly 1st: nt fluent 3rd: in tch: lost pl 4th: sn bhd: t.o 3 out* **20/1**
6 11 **Petite Madame (IRE)**[22] 4-10-11 0.............................. HenryBrooke 43
(David Thompson) *in rr: mstke 4th: sn bhd: t.o 3 out* **100/1**
01-3 P **Bengali (IRE)**[9] 784 6-10-11 0..............................(t) CraigNichol(3)
(Patrick Griffin, Ire) *sltly hmpd s: sn chsng ldrs: handy 4th whn p.u bef 2 out: sddle slipped* **3/1[2]**

6-6 **U** **Miss Joeking (IRE)**[45] 305 4-10-11 0 PeterBuchanan
(Lucinda Russell) *in rr: last whn mstke and uns rdr 2nd* **28/1**
4m 9.6s (-3.60) **Going Correction** -0.225s/f (Good)
WFA 4 from 5yo+ 17lb 8 Ran SP% **113.2**
Speed ratings (Par 103): **99,93,92,80,67 61, ,**
CSF £6.25 TOTE £2.20: £1.10, £1.80, £3.50; EX 7.40 Trifecta £42.40.
Owner C Flattery **Bred** Charles Flattery **Trained** Longwood, Co Meath

FOCUS
One would imagine that this is just modest form, and the winner, who was seemingly taking a big step up, had it all her own way from the front.

847 CHAMPAGNE LOUIS ROEDERER H'CAP CHASE (18 fncs) 3m 1f 107y
3:10 (3:10) (Class 4) (0-115,115) 5-Y-0+ **£3,898** (£1,144; £572; £286)

Form RPR
144/ **1** **Pena Dorada (IRE)**[414] 8-10-7 **103** MissRMcDonald[(7)] 115+
(Alistair Whillans) *mde all: j. soundly: rdn and styd on fnl f* **8/1**
6244 **2** *5* **The Society Man (IRE)**[9] 782 8-10-1 **95** JoeCornwall[(5)] 103
(Michael Chapman) *chsd ldrs: drvn after 12th: 2nd 3 out: kpt on same pce run-in* **15/2**
05-2 **3** *13* **Drumlister (IRE)**[31] 519 9-10-7 **103** MrTGreenwood[(7)] 104+
(Dianne Sayer) *chsd ldrs: hit 10th: modest 3rd last: one pce* **11/4**[1]
-P01 **4** *1 ½* **High Kite (IRE)**[19] 676 9-11-7 **110** (b) PaddyBrennan 106
(Jo Hughes) *chsd ldrs: 2nd whn hit 3 out: lost pl appr last: kpt on fnl f* **4/1**[3]
P-6U **P** **Mostly Bob (IRE)**[34] 471 12-11-7 **110** (tp) PaulMoloney
(Sophie Leech) *w ldrs: nt fluent: lost pl and reminders 6th: t.o 8th: p.u bef 13th* **8/1**
P **Local Celebrity (IRE)**[44] 11-11-12 **115** (b[1]) RichardJohnson
(Gordon Elliott, Ire) *nt jump wl: blnd 2nd: chsd ldrs 6th: lost pl 10th: sn bhd: t.o whn p.u bef 13th* **3/1**[2]
P-5P **F** **Redpender (IRE)**[34] 470 9-11-1 **104** (vt) BrianHughes
(James Moffatt) *in rr: hdwy to chse ldrs 7th: wknd 13th: sn bhd: fell 3 out* **14/1**
6m 30.2s (-4.70) **Going Correction** -0.05s/f (Good) 7 Ran SP% **112.3**
Speed ratings: **105,103,99,98,**
CSF £60.28 CT £205.72 TOTE £10.60: £4.70, £4.90; EX 46.00 Trifecta £144.20.
Owner Alan J Brown **Bred** J P Dwan **Trained** Newmill-On-Slitrig, Borders

FOCUS
A really good performance by the winner who was back to his best following a break.

848 PSR MARQUEES H'CAP CHASE (12 fncs) 2m 1f 61y
3:45 (3:45) (Class 4) (0-120,120) 5-Y-0+ **£4,873** (£1,431; £715; £357)

Form RPR
134- **1** **Toledo Gold (IRE)**[232] 2344 9-11-9 **120** (t) JonathanEngland[(3)] 124
(Maurice Barnes) *mde all: sn clr to 7th: rdn and kpt on fnl 2f: jst hld on* **13/2**
0-21 **2** *nk* **Carters Rest**[32] 504 12-9-11 **98** MissJWalton[(7)] 102
(George Bewley) *chsd ldrs: drvn last: 2nd over 2f out: styd on towards fin: jst hld* **4/1**[2]
2-00 **3** *2 ¼* **Roxyfet (FR)**[15] 731 5-10-3 **97** (p) HenryBrooke 99
(Micky Hammond) *in rr: hdwy 8th: 4th next: 3rd 1f out: kpt on one pce* **9/1**
3-45 **4** *1* **Sergeant Pink (IRE)**[34] 469 9-11-4 **112** (p) BrianHughes 114
(Dianne Sayer) *chsd ldrs: hit 8th: outpcd next: kpt on and 4th last: one pce* **7/2**[1]
2161 **5** *6* **Gin Cobbler**[15] 728 9-10-4 **105** ThomasDowson[(7)] 100
(Victor Thompson) *chsd ldrs: 2nd 5th: wknd fnl f* **13/2**
5-63 **6** *8* **Shrapnel (IRE)**[13] 742 9-11-7 **115** (p) GavinSheehan 103
(Brian Ellison) *chsd ldrs: mstke 6th: sn lost pl and reminders: hdwy 8th: sn outpcd: in rr whn mstke last* **6/1**[3]
1-24 **7** *23* **Hotgrove Boy**[38] 417 8-10-6 **107** MrSWColtherd[(7)] 80
(Stuart Coltherd) *chsd ldrs: pushed along 6th: outpcd 9th: wknd last: sn bhd: eased fnl f: t.o* **4/1**[2]
4m 19.2s (0.30) **Going Correction** -0.05s/f (Good) 7 Ran SP% **113.2**
Speed ratings: **97,96,95,95,92 88,77**
CSF £32.18 TOTE £7.10: £2.80, £2.60; EX 34.00 Trifecta £352.60.
Owner M Barnes, Scott Lowther **Bred** Rathbarry Stud **Trained** Farlam, Cumbria

FOCUS
Quite a varying amount of ability on show for this handicap judged on official figures. The first three ran pretty much to their marks.

849 OAKMERE HOMES H'CAP CHASE (14 fncs) 2m 5f 34y
4:20 (4:20) (Class 2) (0-150,142) 5-Y-0+ **£12,512** (£3,696; £1,848; £924; £462)

Form RPR
2-01 **1** **Alderbrook Lad (IRE)**[34] 470 9-10-4 **130** FinianO'Toole[(10)] 140+
(Micky Hammond) *mde all: j. soundly: drvn and styd on fnl 2f* **9/4**[1]
230- **2** *5* **Definite Ruby (IRE)**[227] 2473 7-10-11 **127** (p) RichardJohnson 133
(Gordon Elliott, Ire) *hdwy to chse ldrs 5th: 2nd 3 out: drvn and kpt on same pce run-in* **10/3**[2]
11-2 **3** *2 ¾* **Presenting Junior (IRE)**[34] 470 8-11-4 **137** GrahamWatters[(3)] 140
(Martin Todhunter) *chsd ldrs: pushed along 10th: outpcd last: kpt on fnl 2f* **9/4**[1]
140- **4** *21* **Sudski Star (IRE)**[74] 5351 7-10-4 **120** BrianHughes 103
(Harriet Graham) *in rr: outpcd 9th: sme hdwy 3 out: lost pl last* **15/2**[3]
U1-5 **5** *2* **Witness In Court (IRE)**[29] 555 8-11-5 **142** JamesCowley[(7)] 123
(Donald McCain) *chsd wnr: drvn 3 out: outpcd last: wknd over 2f out* **15/2**[3]
5m 18.3s (-7.10) **Going Correction** -0.05s/f (Good) 5 Ran SP% **108.1**
Speed ratings: **111,109,108,100,99**
CSF £9.75 TOTE £3.20: £1.90, £1.50; EX 7.40 Trifecta £17.90.
Owner Masters Of The Hall **Bred** A Malone **Trained** Middleham, N Yorks

FOCUS
Not for the first time on the card, a horse sent straight into the lead made every yard. This was a small personal best from the winner.

850 OAKMERE HOMES H'CAP HURDLE (8 hdls) 2m 1f 46y
4:55 (4:55) (Class 2) 4-Y-0+
£12,512 (£3,696; £1,848; £924; £462; £232)

Form RPR
15U- **1** **Commissioned (IRE)**[79] 5250 5-10-9 **140** (p) MikeyEnnis[(5)] 154+
(John Ferguson) *trckd ldrs: led sn after 2 out: sn drvn clr: rdn rt out* **7/2**[1]
00-1 **2** *18* **Roman Flight (IRE)**[29] 556 7-11-3 **143** (v) GavinSheehan 139
(David Dennis) *chsd ldrs: drvn 5th: 4th 2 out: kpt on to take modest 2nd 1f out* **4/1**[2]
13-3 **3** *1 ¾* **Brave Spartacus (IRE)**[51] 184 9-9-11 **126** oh1 HarryChalloner[(3)] 121
(Keith Reveley) *led: hdd sn after 2 out: modest 2nd whn blnd last: kpt on same pce* **10/1**
-111 **4** *nk* **Zarzal (IRE)**[31] 529 7-10-0 **126** oh1 AdamWedge 121
(Evan Williams) *chsd ldrs: drvn and 3rd 2 out: kpt on same pce* **5/1**
101- **5** *1* **Smart Ruler (IRE)**[37] 2337 9-10-0 **126** oh3 BrianHughes 119
(James Moffatt) *mid-div: outpcd bef 2 out: modest 5th between last 2: kpt on same pce* **16/1**
1-21 **6** *7* **Gurkha Brave (IRE)**[22] 638 7-9-10 **127** oh7 ow1 DaleIrving[(5)] 113
(Karen McLintock) *mid-div: drvn 5th: nvr a factor* **9/2**[3]
51-3 **7** *2 ¼* **Captain Brown**[32] 508 7-9-9 **126** oh7 DiarmuidO'Regan[(5)] 110
(James Moffatt) *in rr: effrt 5th: nvr on terms* **20/1**
5-33 **8** *9* **Volcanic Jack (IRE)**[10] 571 7-9-9 **126** oh57 JoeCornwall[(5)] 101
(Michael Chapman) *chsd ldr: drvn 5th: lost pl appr next* **250/1**
546- **9** *1 ¼* **Court Minstrel (IRE)**[64] 5537 8-11-12 **152** PaulMoloney 127
(Evan Williams) *in rr: hdwy 5th: lost pl after next* **11/2**
/P6- **10** *56* **Trucking Along (IRE)**[141] 4104 9-10-4 **130** RichardJohnson 47
(S R B Crawford, Ire) *stdd s: detached in last: drvn 5th: sn bhd: t.o whn eased run-in: virtually p.u* **25/1**
F00- **11** *nk* **Lucky Bridle (IRE)**[61] 7 6-10-11 **137** HenryBrooke 54
(Chris Grant) *chsd ldrs: mstke 1st: lost pl after 5th: sn bhd: t.o whn eased run-in: virtually p.u* **33/1**
4m 2.1s (-11.10) **Going Correction** -0.225s/f (Good) 11 Ran SP% **119.4**
Speed ratings (Par 109): **117,108,107,107,107 103,102,98,97,71 71**
CSF £17.96 CT £130.13 TOTE £4.10: £2.10, £1.60, £2.50; EX 18.50 Trifecta £99.80.
Owner Bloomfields **Bred** Kilfrush Stud **Trained** Cowlinge, Suffolk

FOCUS
This was the first open handicap to be run at the track and they were rewarded with a strong field, with five of the runners officially rated 130 or higher. The pace was sound from the start. and this was a massive step up from the impressive winner.

851 ANGLO IRISH AMATEUR CHALLENGE H'CAP HURDLE (8 hdls) 2m 1f 46y
5:25 (5:25) (Class 4) (0-115,115) 4-Y-0+ **£3,119** (£967; £483; £242)

Form RPR
43-4 **1** **Restraint Of Trade (IRE)**[22] 638 5-11-12 **115** (vt[1]) MrRDeegan 120+
(Jennie Candlish) *mde all: t.k.h: sn clr: drvn and kpt on run-in: unchal* **11/4**[2]
-111 **2** *10* **Baraboy (IRE)**[7] 804 5-11-4 **107** 7ex MrZBaker 104
(Barry Murtagh) *hld up in mid-div: hdwy and modest 3rd 3 out: 2nd over 1f out: styd on: nt rch wnr* **13/8**[1]
450- **3** *3* **May's Boy**[37] 3133 7-11-7 **110** (p) MissJWalton 102
(James Moffatt) *mid-div: hdwy 5th: one pce and hung rt fnl 100yds: tk modest 3rd nr fin* **9/1**
0P-4 **4** *½* **Endeavor**[32] 508 10-10-8 **97** (p) LorcanMurtagh 89
(Dianne Sayer) *chsd ldrs: modest 2nd sn after 5th: one pce and hung rt clsng stages* **14/1**
2-30 **5** *3 ¾* **Persian Herald**[23] 504 7-10-8 **97** (b) MissCWalton 85
(Dianne Sayer) *chsd ldrs: drvn 3 out: one pce* **14/1**
000- **6** *25* **Viking Warrior (IRE)**[198] 3060 8-10-0 **89** oh3 MrSWColtherd 55
(Shaun Harris) *detached in last: bhd fr 5th: t.o 2 out* **20/1**
-015 **7** *12* **Morning With Ivan (IRE)**[16] 711 5-10-11 **100** (v) MissBHampson 55
(Martin Todhunter) *chsd clr ldr: reminders and lost pl 5th: sn wl bhd: t.o 2 out* **7/2**[3]
4m 13.0s (-0.20) **Going Correction** -0.225s/f (Good)
WFA 4 from 5yo+ 17lb 7 Ran SP% **115.1**
Speed ratings (Par 105): **91,86,84,84,82 71,65**
CSF £8.04 CT £33.07 TOTE £3.90: £2.00, £1.60; EX 10.30 Trifecta £47.40.
Owner Alan Baxter **Bred** Kildaragh Stud **Trained** Basford Green, Staffs

FOCUS
A modest contest taken by another horse to make all on the card. The winner is on a good mark, but this was still a small personal best.
T/Plt: £165.90 to a £1 stake. Pool: £69,431.81 - 305.40 winning tickets T/Qpdt: £151.20 to a £1 stake. Pool: £4,497.94 - 22.00 winning tickets **Walter Glynn**

[754] UTTOXETER (L-H)
Sunday, June 28

OFFICIAL GOING: Good (good to soft in places; 8.5)
Wind: Fresh half-against Weather: Cloudy with sunny spells

852 BET365 MAIDEN HURDLE (10 hdls) 2m 3f 207y
2:00 (2:00) (Class 4) 4-Y-0+ **£3,924** (£1,159; £579; £290; £145)

Form RPR
42/2 **1** **Oculist**[16] 710 7-11-0 120 WayneHutchinson 110
(Ben De Haan) *hld up in tch: jnd ldr 2 out: sn rdn: led flat: edgd lft: drvn out* **7/4**[1]
2 *1 ¼* **Air Glider (IRE)**[63] 5-11-0 0 HarrySkelton 109
(Dan Skelton) *hld up: hdwy 7th: rdn to ld 2 out: hdd flat: styd on same pce* **15/8**[2]
45 **3** *4 ½* **Keep Calm**[23] 620 5-11-0 0 DarylJacob 105
(John Mackie) *chsd ldrs: led after 7th: rdn and hdd 2 out: no ex last* **17/2**
/P-P **4** *23* **Midnight Memories**[19] 679 5-10-7 0 RobertDunne 82
(Steph Hollinshead) *led: rdn and hdd after 7th: wknd bef 2 out* **100/1**
- **5** *15* **Beat The Tide**[278] 5-11-0 0 AidanColeman 74
(Tim Vaughan) *prom: chsd ldr 3rd: mstke 5th: lost 2nd after 7th: wknd 3 out* **7/1**[3]
6 *14* **Aza Run (IRE)**[154] 3887 5-10-11 0 ConorShoemark[(3)] 63
(Fergal O'Brien) *hld up: wkng whn hmpd 3 out* **8/1**
7 *7* **Barra Rotha (IRE)**[406] 8-11-0 0 DaveCrosse 52
(Laura Hurley) *prom: mstke 1st: hmpd 5th: rdn and wknd after 7th* **100/1**
0 **8** *13* **Red Rust**[22] 644 6-11-0 0 TomO'Brien 40
(Robert Stephens) *hld up: a in rr: rdn and wknd after 7th* **33/1**
0-55 **F** **Martha's Benefit (IRE)**[17] 696 6-10-4 0 AdamNicol[(3)]
(Mike Sowersby) *chsd ldr to 3rd: remained handy: rdn after 7th: wkng whn fell 3 out* **28/1**
P **Run Of The Mill (IRE)** 5-11-0 0 TomMessenger
(Chris Bealby) *hld up: j.rt and a in rr: rdn and wknd after 6th: bhd whn p.u bef 2 out* **33/1**
5m 4.0s (0.80) **Going Correction** -0.20s/f (Good) 10 Ran SP% **116.6**
Speed ratings (Par 105): **90,89,87,78,72 66,64,58, ,**
CSF £5.31 TOTE £2.60: £1.10, £1.10, £2.60; EX 6.10 Trifecta £23.60.
Owner Mrs F Walwyn **Bred** Mrs G Kindersley **Trained** Lambourn, Berks

FOCUS
Some starts have been moved at this track following remeasuring, so some races will not have speed figures until there is sufficient data to calculate updated median times. Good ground with some good to soft places ahead of this bumper eight-race card. Hurdles were moved 4-5yds off the inside rail to fresher ground, adding 23yds per circuit. On the chase course, the fences were all opened up to full width, while fence five (first in back straight) was omitted as the ground is under repair. Not much depth to this maiden hurdle and, despite the pace not looking overly strong, they finished well strung out and it looked fairly slow-motion stuff on the run-in. The winner was the form pick, but has been rated below his Aintree mark.

853 BET365 NOVICES' HURDLE (9 hdls) 1m 7f 168y
2:30 (2:31) (Class 4) 4-Y-0+ **£4,051** (£1,196; £598; £299; £149)

Form RPR
1 **Theatre Flame (IRE)**[38] 423 5-10-12 0 TomScudamore 116+
(David Bridgwater) *mde all: hit 4th: mstke 3 out: rdn appr last: styd on wl* **11/8**[1]
2 3 **Silent Movie (IRE)**[604] 5-10-12 0 AidanColeman 113+
(John Ferguson) *a.p: chsd wnr and mstke 3 out: rdn and ev ch appr last: styd on same pce flat* **5/2**[2]
20/6 3 16 **Shout It Aloud**[47] 271 6-10-5 0 (t) AlanJohns(7) 99
(Tim Vaughan) *chsd wnr: mstke 5th: lost 2nd appr 3 out: wkng whn mstke next* **16/1**
4 15 **Cabin Fever**[265] 4-10-2 0 LiamTreadwell 75
(Tom Lacey) *hld up: styd on fr 2 out: nvr on terms* **66/1**
14 5 6 **Captain Swift (IRE)**[23] 620 4-11-2 120 DarylJacob 83
(John Mackie) *prom: rdn after 3 out: wknd bef next* **9/2**[3]
5 6 10 **Micras**[7] 813 4-10-4 0 ow2 MichaelByrne 62
(Tim Vaughan) *hld up: rdn and wknd after 6th* **12/1**
U/0- 7 19 **Smiley Miley (IRE)**[371] 785 7-9-12 0 MissJodieHughes(7) 46
(Dai Burchell) *hld up: bhd fr 5th* **100/1**
6 8 11 **Goonjim (IRE)**[12] 749 4-10-9 0 SamTwiston-Davies 40
(Alexandra Dunn) *hld up: rdn after 5th: wknd next* **40/1**
6 P **Jimmy Crackle (IRE)**[15] 727 4-10-2 0 CraigGallagher(7)
(Brian Ellison) *hld up: hdwy 5th: hit 3 out: sn wknd: bhd whn p.u bef last* **25/1**
P P **Vabinsaru (FR)**[31] 526 4-10-9 0[1] RichieMcLernon
(Jonjo O'Neill) *prom to 6th: bhd whn p.u bef next* **16/1**
3m 52.8s (-4.60) **Going Correction** -0.20s/f (Good) **10 Ran SP% 117.1**
Speed ratings (Par 105): **103,101,93,86,83 78,68,63, ,**
CSF £4.94 TOTE £3.20: £1.10, £1.50, £4.40; EX 7.50 Trifecta £45.10.
Owner CWB LLP **Bred** Liam Brady **Trained** Icomb, Gloucs

FOCUS
Not much depth once again but the front two, who dominated the market, pulled well clear and both should be kept on side in the near future. The winner has been rated similar to the best of his Irish form.

854 BET365 H'CAP HURDLE (9 hdls) 1m 7f 168y
3:00 (3:00) (Class 3) (0-140,134) 4-Y-0+
£9,384 (£2,772; £1,386; £693; £346; £174)

Form RPR
121- 1 **Ittirad (USA)**[295] 1454 7-11-12 134 (p) AidanColeman 138+
(John Ferguson) *chsd ldr to 4th: remained handy: wnt 2nd again after 6th: ev ch whn lft in ld 3 out: rdn out* **3/1**[1]
2-3P 2 2 3/4 **Ruler Of All (IRE)**[38] 418 9-11-1 130 MrRWinks(7) 132
(Peter Winks) *a.p: rdn after 2 out: styd on to go 2nd towards fin* **8/1**
026- 3 2 **Oliver's Gold**[20] 1898 7-10-10 118 DougieCostello 118
(Mark Walford) *hld up: hdwy to chse ldr 4th: lost 2nd after 6th: ev ch fr 3 out tl rdn and edgd lft appr last: sn swtchd rt: no ex flat* **15/2**
053- 4 8 **Skylander (IRE)**[68] 5441 6-10-12 120 (tp) TomScudamore 114
(David Pipe) *prom: rdn after 2 out: wknd bef last* **3/1**[1]
104- 5 15 **Honey Pound (IRE)**[198] 3048 7-11-3 125 MichaelByrne 109
(Tim Vaughan) *hld up: effrt whn hmpd 3 out: sn wknd* **16/1**
550- 6 10 **Laser Blazer**[74] 5345 7-11-7 129 WayneHutchinson 99
(Alan King) *hld up: hdwy 5th: blnd next: sn rdn: wknd 3 out* **6/1**[3]
P6-5 7 4 **Sureness (IRE)**[57] 84 5-11-5 127 (t) NoelFehily 94
(Charlie Mann) *prom: nt fluent and lost pl 3rd: wknd 3 out* **20/1**
-P13 F **Storm Of Swords (IRE)**[23] 620 7-11-7 134 BridgetAndrews(5)
(Dan Skelton) *led: jnd whn fell 3 out* **11/2**[2]
3m 50.6s (-6.80) **Going Correction** -0.20s/f (Good) **8 Ran SP% 113.2**
Speed ratings (Par 107): **109,107,106,102,95 90,88,**
CSF £26.31 CT £162.27 TOTE £3.20: £1.30, £2.20, £2.30; EX 29.10 Trifecta £322.80.
Owner Bloomfields **Bred** Darley **Trained** Cowlinge, Suffolk

FOCUS
Not a particularly strong race for the grade with the winner carrying top weight despite being rated 6lb below the ceiling rating, and none of these having major scope for improvement. A small personal best from the winner after a break.

855 JOHN SMITH'S SUMMER CUP (A H'CAP CHASE) (LISTED RACE) (18 fncs 2 omitted) 3m 2f 13y
3:35 (3:35) (Class 1) 5-Y-0+
£33,762 (£12,720; £6,366; £3,180; £1,596; £798)

Form RPR
11-4 1 **Shuil Royale (IRE)**[55] 101 10-10-6 130 ow1 (t) NoelFehily 143+
(Harry Fry) *hld up: hdwy 7th: led appr 2 out: rdn out* **8/1**[2]
2-11 2 5 **Silver Man**[16] 707 8-10-11 135 (b) NicodeBoinville 141
(Jo Hughes) *chsd ldr: led 3rd: hdd after next: remained w ldr: led 6th to 7th: led again 12th: hdd appr 2 out: styd on same pce last* **6/1**[1]
2-01 3 2 **Adrenalin Flight (IRE)**[35] 448 9-10-5 129 (v) JamieMoore 134
(Seamus Mullins) *hld up: hdwy 6th: rdn appr last: styd on same pce* **14/1**
1F2- 4 1 3/4 **Harangue (IRE)**[6] 819 7-9-7 124 5ex oh8 (tp) ThomasCheesman(7) 127
(Paul John Gilligan, Ire) *a.p: rdn after 4 out: styd on same pce fr 2 out* **40/1**
02-1 5 shd **Speed Master (IRE)**[30] 532 9-10-4 128 (vt) SamTwiston-Davies 132
(Nigel Twiston-Davies) *chsd ldrs: led after 4th: hdd 6th: led again next: hdd 12th: ev ch 4 out: sn rdn: styd on same pce fr 2 out* **17/2**[3]
16-4 6 7 **Twirling Magnet (IRE)**[30] 535 9-10-13 137 (tp) RichieMcLernon 134
(Jonjo O'Neill) *hld up: hdwy 4 out: rdn and wknd appr last* **8/1**[2]
6-11 7 6 **Sail And Return**[12] 750 11-9-7 124 oh3 (t) HarryCobden(7) 115
(Phil Middleton) *hld up: rdn appr 4 out: nvr on terms* **16/1**
P1P- 8 1/2 **The Package**[64] 5538 12-11-9 147 (bt) ConorO'Farrell 137
(David Pipe) *hld up: dropped to rr 12th: rdn 4 out: n.d* **16/1**
1-31 9 19 **Thomas Wild**[29] 553 10-10-2 126 MichealNolan 99
(Philip Hobbs) *hld up: rdn appr 4 out: n.d* **20/1**
06-1 10 7 **Bear's Affair (IRE)**[44] 318 9-11-5 150 FreddieMitchell(7) 117
(Nicky Henderson) *hld up: mstke 5th: hdwy 12th: wknd 4 out* **8/1**[2]
-312 11 1 **Sedgemoor Express (IRE)**[16] 707 7-10-0 131 CiaranGethings(7) 97
(Nigel Hawke) *hld up: hmpd 5th: wknd 13th* **12/1**
U55- 12 15 **Midnight Appeal**[99] 4898 10-10-5 132 (tp) KillianMoore(3) 85
(Sophie Leech) *led to 3rd: remained handy tl rdn and wknd after 4 out* **25/1**
PFP- 13 hd **Benbane Head (USA)**[73] 5356 11-10-6 133 (p) ConorShoemark(3) 85
(Martin Keighley) *chsd ldrs: rdn 14th: mstke and wknd 4 out* **16/1**
2P-3 P **Universal Soldier (IRE)**[29] 553 10-10-2 126 ow2 (p) CharliePoste
(Matt Sheppard) *hld up: bhd fr 10th: p.u bef 3 out* **11/1**
P1-P P **Hollow Blue Sky (FR)**[44] 318 8-9-9 124 oh2 (tp) HarryBannister(5)
(Nigel Twiston-Davies) *hld up: j.rt 5th: wknd after 12th: bhd whn p.u bef 2 out* **25/1**
F1-2 P **Samingarry (FR)**[44] 318 8-11-6 144 (vt) JamesBest
(Nigel Hawke) *chsd ldrs: rdn and lost pl appr 12th: wknd bef next: bhd whn p.u bef 2 out* **10/1**
16-3 P **Ainsi Fideles (FR)**[50] 198 5-11-9 147 (bt) TomScudamore
(David Pipe) *prom: hit 6th and 12th: wknd appr 4 out: bhd whn p.u bef next* **14/1**
6m 33.1s (-5.70) **Going Correction** +0.10s/f (Yiel) **17 Ran SP% 129.1**
Speed ratings: **112,110,109,109,109 107,105,105,99,97 96,92,92,**
CSF £57.04 CT £691.50 TOTE £10.20: £2.30, £2.30, £4.50, £9.70; EX 74.50 Trifecta £629.60.
Owner Phil Fry **Bred** Greenville House Stud And M Morgan **Trained** Seaborough, Dorset

FOCUS
Ultra-competitive as you would expect for a £60,000 pot at this time of the year, and this looks very strong summer chasing form. A big step up from the cosy winner.

856 BET365 SUPPORTING THE INJURED JOCKEYS FUND H'CAP HURDLE (9 hdls) 1m 7f 168y
4:10 (4:12) (Class 5) (0-100,104) 4-Y-0+ **£2,729** (£801; £400; £200)

Form RPR
30/3 1 **Innoko (FR)**[15] 180 5-11-12 94 LeeEdwards 104
(Tony Carroll) *hld up: nt fluent 3rd: pushed along after next: hdwy appr 2 out: led flat: edgd lft: styd on wl* **20/1**
06-1 2 2 **Kalifourchon (FR)**[7] 811 4-12-5 104 7ex TomScudamore 109
(David Pipe) *chsd ldrs: led 3 out: hdd next: rdn appr last: styd on same pce flat* **7/4**[1]
65-5 3 1 1/4 **Significant Move**[43] 336 8-10-8 81 ChrisWard(5) 89
(Dr Richard Newland) *hld up: hdwy appr 3 out: led next: rdn and hung lft bef last: hdd and no ex flat* **7/2**[2]
-632 4 9 **Symphony Of Pearls**[17] 694 4-10-5 83 MissJodieHughes(7) 79
(Dai Burchell) *prom: rdn after 2 out: wknd bef last* **12/1**
5-64 5 4 1/2 **Bulletproof (IRE)**[19] 675 9-11-1 83 (p) TomCannon 80
(Ken Cunningham-Brown) *chsd ldrs: mstke 3rd: led appr 6th: hdd and mstke 3 out: sn rdn: wknd after next* **16/1**
P0-2 6 9 **Vexillum (IRE)**[52] 172 6-11-2 84 (p) NoelFehily 73
(Neil Mulholland) *hld up: hdwy after 6th: ev ch 3 out: wknd next* **6/1**[3]
41-5 7 8 **Hermosa Vaquera (IRE)**[49] 224 5-11-5 87 JamieMoore 66
(Gary Moore) *mid-div: hdwy 5th: rdn appr 3 out: wknd next* **16/1**
P-35 8 13 **Mix N Match**[17] 692 11-10-2 70 DougieCostello 38
(Laura Young) *chsd ldrs: mstke 4th: rdn and wknd appr 3 out* **33/1**
0/24 9 1 1/4 **Sleeping City (FR)**[16] 718 8-11-12 94 (t) DenisO'Regan 61
(Victor Dartnall) *hld up: hit 3 out: sn wknd* **7/1**
05-0 10 68 **Worldor (FR)**[24] 616 9-11-11 93 RhysFlint
(Alexandra Dunn) *led: hdd appr 6th: sn wknd* **50/1**
-265 P **Mount Vesuvius (IRE)**[32] 515 7-11-8 90 (tp) TomO'Brien
(Paul Henderson) *mid-div: wknd 6th: bhd whn p.u bef last* **14/1**
6-56 P **Strictly Glitz (IRE)**[31] 516 4-10-11 85 AdamNicol(3)
(Mike Sowersby) *a bhd: p.u bef 3 out* **100/1**
3m 55.1s (-2.30) **Going Correction** -0.20s/f (Good) **12 Ran SP% 122.1**
Speed ratings (Par 103): **97,96,95,90,88 84,80,73,73,39 ,**
CSF £57.45 CT £165.58 TOTE £28.00: £6.60, £1.30, £1.90; EX 110.60 Trifecta £1866.90.
Owner Mill House Racing Syndicate **Bred** Marquise Soledad De Moratalla **Trained** Cropthorne, Worcs

FOCUS
Modest hurdle form, but the pace looked quite strong and the first three finished nicely clear. A prrsonal best from the winner over hurdles.

857 BET365 H'CAP CHASE (11 fncs 1 omitted) 1m 7f 214y
4:45 (4:45) (Class 4) (0-120,120) 5-Y-0+
£6,256 (£1,848; £924; £462; £231; £116)

Form RPR
032- 1 **Ulis De Vassy (FR)**[136] 4180 7-11-3 111 HarrySkelton 134+
(Dan Skelton) *chsd ldrs: led 3rd: clr after 4 out: blnd next: nt fluent 2 out: easily* **13/8**[1]
3-62 2 23 **Kitegen (IRE)**[23] 623 9-11-3 111 CharliePoste 112
(Robin Dickin) *prom: chsd wnr 7th: rdn appr 4 out: wknd bef next* **13/2**
1F-2 3 6 **The Bay Bandit**[32] 514 8-10-13 107 (p) NoelFehily 103
(Neil Mulholland) *hld up: hdwy 7th: wknd after 4 out* **5/1**[3]
0-42 4 2 1/4 **Breaking The Bank**[22] 643 6-11-12 120 DarylJacob 113
(Ben Case) *hld up: hit 5th: effrt after 7th: sn wknd* **9/2**[2]
P/5- 5 7 **Cayman Islands**[113] 4635 7-11-4 119 MrAlexFerguson(7) 105
(John Ferguson) *prom tl wknd after 4 out* **9/1**
0-40 6 3/4 **Mart Lane (IRE)**[22] 642 10-11-6 117 (v) KillianMoore(3) 102
(Sophie Leech) *chsd ldr to 3rd: wknd bef 5th* **25/1**
0 7 5 **Truckin All Night (IRE)**[32] 514 9-10-8 102 (t) DenisO'Regan 83
(Don Cantillon) *hld up: wknd bef 5th* **14/1**
1P-6 P **Kadalkin (FR)**[22] 642 9-11-9 117 (vt) TomScudamore
(Nigel Hawke) *j.rt: led: mstke 2nd: hdd next: chsd wnr to 7th: wknd 4 out: bhd whn blnd 2 out: p.u bef last* **14/1**
3m 59.3s (-2.10) **Going Correction** +0.10s/f (Yiel) **8 Ran SP% 113.5**
Speed ratings: **109,97,94,93,89 89,87,**
CSF £12.83 CT £42.89 TOTE £2.30: £1.10, £2.10, £2.40; EX 13.50 Trifecta £56.80.
Owner Len&White,Hewlett,Robinson,Banyard&Booth **Bred** Nicolas Ferrand **Trained** Alcester, Warwicks

FOCUS
This looked fairly open on paper, but the market screamed the winner on his first run for Dan Skelton and it proved more than accurate as the 7yo absolutely bolted up. This rates as a big step up from him.

858 CASINO AT BET365 H'CAP HURDLE (DIV I) (10 hdls) 2m 3f 207y
5:15 (5:15) (Class 5) (0-100,100) 4-Y-0+ **£2,729** (£801; £400; £200)

Form RPR
0P-0 1 **Thefriendlygremlin**[59] 40 7-9-11 76 oh10 ow2 (p) ConorRing(5) 80
(John Upson) *chsd ldr: drvn along after 7th: styd on to ld last: all out* **33/1**

052 **2** *nk* **Eddy**[16] 712 6-10-0 **81**................................ ThomasCheesman(7) 85
(John Panvert) *hld up: hdwy 5th: rdn after 2 out: r.o to go 2nd towards fin: nt quite rch wnr* **9/2**[3]

-342 **3** *2 1/4* **Bletchley Castle (IRE)**[11] 754 6-11-5 **98**................... NickSlatter(5) 100
(Seamus Durack) *led: nt fluent 2nd: rdn and hdd last: styd on same pce flat* **4/1**[2]

005- **4** *shd* **Solstice Star**[88] 5091 5-11-1 **92**................................ KillianMoore(3) 94
(Martin Keighley) *hld up: hdwy after 6th: chsd ldr 2 out: rdn and ev ch bef last: styd on same pce flat* **5/1**

20-5 **5** *2 1/4* **Lean Burn (USA)**[13] 465 9-10-7 **84**.......................(bt) SeanBowen(3) 85
(Barry Leavy) *hld up: hdwy appr 3 out: drvn along after next: styd on: nt rch ldrs* **8/1**

4P0- **6** *4 1/2* **Spending Time**[143] 4053 6-11-12 **100**.......................(t) TomScudamore 97
(David Pipe) *hld up: hdwy 5th: hit 3 out: sn rdn: styd on same pce appr last* **7/2**[1]

5302 **7** *10* **Tantalized**[11] 759 6-10-2 **76**..(v) LeeEdwards 63
(Dave Roberts) *hld up: pushed along 5th: nvr on terms* **12/1**

55- **P** **Charging Indian (IRE)**[118] 4531 9-11-5 **93**.......................... TomO'Brien
(Paul Henderson) *chsd ldrs: rdn after 5th: wknd bef next: bhd whn p.u bef 2 out* **33/1**

65-5 **P** **Dreamisi (IRE)**[25] 599 6-11-3 **91**................................ NicodeBoinville
(Ben Pauling) *prom: drvn along after 6th: wknd and p.u bef next* **6/1**

5m 5.3s (2.10) **Going Correction** -0.20s/f (Good) **9** Ran SP% **116.0**
Speed ratings (Par 103): **87,86,85,85,85 83,79, ,**
CSF £178.43 CT £738.64 TOTE £31.40: £4.60, £1.60, £1.90; EX 310.30 Trifecta £379.90.
Owner The Nap Hand Partnership **Bred** Mr & Mrs M White **Trained** Maidford, Northants

FOCUS
A real slow-motion finish to this modest handicap and the form looks particularly weak given 64-rated winner was able to win from 10lb out of the handicap. He has been rated back to the best of his old form.

859 CASINO AT BET365 H'CAP HURDLE (DIV II) (10 hdls) 2m 3f 207y
5:45 (5:45) (Class 5) (0-100,98) 4-Y-0+ £2,729 (£801; £400; £200)

Form RPR

P042 **1** **Tennessee Bird**[9] 777 7-10-3 **75**................................ DougieCostello 86+
(Mike Sowersby) *hld up: hdwy 4th: chsd ldr 2 out: led last: edgd lft flat: rdn out* **7/1**

P/5- **2** *3/4* **Hassadin**[416] 169 9-10-12 **84**.. NoelFehily 94
(Michael Blake) *chsd ldr tl led 3 out: rdn and hdd last: nt clr run and swtchd rt flat: styd on u.p* **6/1**[3]

6-32 **3** *23* **Dropzone (USA)**[19] 675 6-10-8 **80**..........................(b) ConorO'Farrell 70
(Brian Forsey) *chsd ldrs: nt fluent and lost pl 3rd: outpcd after 7th: styd on to go 3rd post* **7/2**[2]

5-22 **4** *shd* **Mister Wall Street (FR)**[15] 731 10-11-7 **96**.................(tp) TonyKelly(3) 87
(Rebecca Menzies) *led: hdd 3 out: rdn and wknd bef last* **5/1**

25-6 **5** *4 1/2* **El Toreros (USA)**[16] 713 7-11-5 **91**.........................(tp) AidanColeman 76
(Lawney Hill) *chsd ldrs tl wknd 3 out* **16/1**

FP0- **6** *2 1/2* **Watchmetail (IRE)**[111] 4681 9-9-7 **72** oh8............. ThomasCheesman(7) 55
(John Panvert) *hld up: hdwy appr 3 out: wknd bef next* **12/1**

0-64 **7** *34* **Our Chief (IRE)**[11] 758 6-11-12 **98**..........................(bt) TomScudamore 71
(David Pipe) *prom tl rdn and wknd 3 out* **85/40**[1]

334/ **P** **Lukeys Luck**[677] 1327 9-11-12 **98**...............................(p) PeterCarberry
(Jennie Candlish) *hld up: a in rr: rdn after 6th: bhd whn p.u after next* **12/1**

5m 3.3s (0.10) **Going Correction** -0.20s/f (Good) **8** Ran SP% **114.8**
Speed ratings (Par 103): **91,90,81,81,79 78,65,**
CSF £48.37 CT £172.05 TOTE £9.10: £3.60, £2.10, £1.50; EX 48.70 Trifecta £216.20.
Owner Queens Head Racing Club **Bred** Mrs J Wiltschinsky **Trained** Goodmanham, E Yorks

FOCUS
Slightly stronger than the first division, but still very modest form with the winner breaking his duck at the 36th attempt. The first two were on decent marks.
T/Jkpt: £3,843.20 to a £1 stake. Pool: £16,239.07 - 3.00 winning tickets T/Plt: £10.20 to a £1 stake. Pool: £125,739.23 - 8,992.64 winning tickets T/Qpdt: £8.20 to a £1 stake. Pool: £8,220.82 - 741.20 winning tickets **Colin Roberts**

748 STRATFORD (L-H)
Tuesday, June 30

OFFICIAL GOING: Good (good to firm in places; 7.9)
Wind: Nil Weather: Fine

860 19TH OF JULY IS LADIES DAY MAIDEN HURDLE (8 hdls) 2m 70y
6:30 (6:30) (Class 5) 4-Y-0+ £2,599 (£763; £381; £190)

Form RPR

223- **1** **El Massivo (IRE)**[22] 774 5-11-0 **119**.............................. RichardJohnson 114+
(Brian Ellison) *a.p: shkn up to ld last: styd on wl* **5/4**[1]

2 *3* **Personable**[629] 5-11-0 .... AidanColeman 112+
(John Ferguson) *chsd ldr: rdn and ev ch whn nt fluent: last: styd on same pce* **7/4**[2]

5-2P **3** *1* **Samoset**[28] 592 5-11-0 **110**.......................................(t) KielanWoods 109
(Charlie Longsdon) *led: rdn and hdd last: no ex flat* **6/1**[3]

4-55 **4** *17* **Almaas (USA)**[44] 360 6-10-7 **0**................................ ConorSmith(7) 93
(Kevin Bishop) *mid-div: hdwy 5th: rdn and wknd bef last* **16/1**

P/3 **5** *2 1/2* **Sunny Bank**[30] 566 6-11-0 **0**...................................(t) GerardTumelty 90
(Alan Coogan) *chsd ldrs: rdn after 2 out: wknd bef last* **66/1**

6 *2* **Uncle Bernie (IRE)**[88] 5-11-0 **0**.................................... PaulMoloney 88
(Sarah Hollinshead) *hld up: hdwy and mstke 5th: wknd wl bef last* **12/1**

4/5 **7** *5* **Alys Rock (IRE)**[44] 366 6-10-4 **0**........................... JonathanEngland(3) 76
(Michael Appleby) *hld up: blnd 1st: nt fluent next: hdwy after 2 out: wknd wl bef last* **66/1**

50- **8** *6* **Its A Dizzy Life**[99] 4969 5-11-0 **0**............................... LeightonAspell 77
(Peter Hedger) *hld up: hdwy 3 out: wknd after next* **80/1**

/0-4 **9** *8* **Jeans Lady**[24] 648 6-10-7 **0**.. AndrewTinkler 62
(Martin Keighley) *prom: mstke 4th: sn pushed along: wknd 3 out* **33/1**

10 *13* **Filament Of Gold (USA)**[357] 4-10-8 **0**........................... JamesBanks(3) 53
(Roy Brotherton) *mid-div: wknd after 3 out* **33/1**

11 *4* **New Decade**[62] 6-10-7 **0**.. CiaranGethings(7) 52
(Milton Bradley) *hld up: wknd after 2 out* **200/1**

12 *1* **Berwin (IRE)**[118] 6-10-0 **0**..................................... ThomasCheesman(7) 44
(Sarah Robinson) *hld up: a in rr: nt fluent: mstke and wknd 3 out* **200/1**

3m 51.5s (-4.50) **Going Correction** -0.35s/f (Good)
WFA 4 from 5yo+ 17lb **12** Ran SP% **119.8**
Speed ratings (Par 103): **97,95,95,86,85 84,81,78,74,68 66,65**
CSF £3.68 TOTE £2.20: £1.10, £1.10, £2.40; EX 4.70 Trifecta £9.10.
Owner D Gilbert, M Lawrence, A Bruce **Bred** Laundry Cottage Stud Farm **Trained** Norton, N Yorks

FOCUS
A hot and humid evening and lively underfoot conditions, despite 72mm of water having been placed on the track by officials during the past week. Split bends on fresh ground. Rails were positioned on an outer line to provide fresh racing ground; this added the following distances to the following races: Races 1, 3 and 6 - 45 yards; Race 2 - 78 yards; Race 4 - 57 yards; Race 5 - 66 yards. Punters were rewarded for favouring experience over potential in this apparent match. This is rated around the winner, third, fourth and fifth.

861 SHEPPARD FAMILY NOVICES' CHASE (FOR THE GAY, EVE AND TIM SHEPPARD MEMORIAL CUP) (17 fncs) 2m 6f 125y
7:00 (7:00) (Class 3) 5-Y-0+ £6,498 (£1,908; £954)

Form RPR

53-2 **1** **Call Me Vic (IRE)**[51] 215 8-11-0 **129**................................ PaddyBrennan 139+
(Tom George) *mde all: rdn clr after 2 out: styd on wl* **4/9**[1]

0-62 **2** *38* **Chase The Wind (IRE)**[24] 641 6-11-0 **0**.......................(t) GavinSheehan 119
(Warren Greatrex) *chsd wnr to 6th: blnd next: wnt 2nd again 9th: rdn whn pckd 2 out: wkng whn j. slowly last: eased flat* **2/1**[2]

00-P **3** *45* **Killshannon (IRE)**[14] 752 6-11-0 **97**.............................. TomScudamore 89
(David Bridgwater) *hld up in tch: chsd wnr 6th tl 9th: mstke next: rdn and wknd 2 out* **18/1**[3]

5m 33.5s (-5.70) **Going Correction** -0.275s/f (Good) **3** Ran SP% **107.8**
Speed ratings: **98,84,69**
CSF £1.76 TOTE £1.20; EX 2.00 Trifecta £1.50.
Owner C B Compton **Bred** R P Walshe **Trained** Slad, Gloucs

FOCUS
A disappointing turn out and it proved a straightforward task for the odds-on favourite. There's a case for rating this a bit higher through the second.

862 JENKINSONS CATERERS H'CAP HURDLE (8 hdls) 2m 70y
7:30 (7:30) (Class 4) (0-120,120) 4-Y-0+ £3,249 (£954; £477; £238)

Form RPR

1P-3 **1** **Vivacissimo (IRE)**[15] 747 8-10-8 **102**................................ HarrySkelton 106+
(Dan Skelton) *led: rdn after 2 out: hdd bef last: rallied to ld flat: styd on gamely* **11/10**[1]

45-1 **2** *1/2* **Prince Khurram**[61] 33 5-11-2 **110**...................................(t) NoelFehily 114
(Donald McCain) *chsd wnr: wnt upsides after 2 out: led on bit bef last: rdn and hdd flat: nt qckn* **15/2**

1P-5 **3** *7* **Alwaystheoptimist**[31] 556 12-11-12 **120**........................ TomScudamore 117
(Shaun Lycett) *chsd ldrs: ev ch 2 out: sn rdn: styd on same pce* **5/1**[3]

-101 **4** *1/2* **Zarawi (IRE)**[21] 673 4-11-4 **115**.....................................(p) RichardJohnson 110
(Charlie Longsdon) *hld up: mstke 3 out: sn drvn along: hdwy to go 3rd appr last: wknd flat* **2/1**[2]

3m 47.7s (-8.30) **Going Correction** -0.35s/f (Good)
WFA 4 from 5yo+ 17lb **4** Ran SP% **109.4**
Speed ratings (Par 105): **106,105,102,102**
CSF £8.37 TOTE £2.60; EX 7.30 Trifecta £24.00.
Owner Carl Hodgson **Bred** Haras De Bourgeauville **Trained** Alcester, Warwicks

FOCUS
A couple of notable absentees meant this was deal weaker than originally advertised. The winner was thrown in on his French form and the second came back to form.

863 PORSCHE CENTRE SOLIHULL H'CAP CHASE (14 fncs) 2m 3f 98y
8:00 (8:00) (Class 3) (0-130,128) 4-Y-0 £6,330 (£1,870; £935; £468; £234)

Form RPR

13-1 **1** **Noble Friend (IRE)**[21] 672 7-10-12 **114**.............................. TomCannon 127+
(Chris Gordon) *hld up: hdwy 10th: chsd ldr 3 out: led last: rdn out* **11/4**[1]

55-4 **2** *2 1/2* **Domtaline (FR)**[41] 402 8-11-7 **123**................................... PaulMoloney 132
(Evan Williams) *a.p: chsd ldr after 5th: led 10th: hdd last: styd on same pce flat* **7/1**

65-0 **3** *12* **Master Of The Game (IRE)**[36] 469 9-11-7 **123**.................(t) NoelFehily 125
(Donald McCain) *hld up: hit 9th: hdwy 11th: rdn after 2 out: wkng whn nt fluent last* **20/1**

35-2 **4** *13* **Porters War (IRE)**[31] 557 13-11-0 **119**.......................... MattGriffiths(3) 111
(Jeremy Scott) *chsd ldrs: lost pl whn hit 6th: hdwy after 3 out: rdn and wknd bef last* **11/4**[1]

2-63 **5** *17* **Passato (GER)**[30] 568 11-10-9 **114**...........................(t) JamesBanks(3) 85
(Jo Davis) *chsd ldr to 4th: pushed along after next: remained handy tl wknd 11th* **11/1**

305/ **P** **Gentleman Anshan (IRE)**[655] 1576 11-11-3 **122**...................... BenPoste(3)
(Rosemary Gasson) *prom: chsd ldr 4th tl after next: remained handy tl rdn and wknd after 2 out: p.u bef last: dismntd* **11/2**[3]

-410 **P** **Flash Tommie (IRE)**[33] 519 7-10-5 **110**..............(p) JonathanEngland(3)
(Michael Appleby) *led to 10th: wkng whn hit 3 out: sn p.u* **5/1**[2]

4m 41.0s (-9.00) **Going Correction** -0.275s/f (Good) **7** Ran SP% **111.0**
Speed ratings (Par 107): **107,105,100,95,88 ,**
CSF £20.45 CT £301.01 TOTE £2.70: £1.70, £2.70; EX 23.40 Trifecta £142.80.
Owner Mrs Kate Digweed **Bred** D Mitchell **Trained** Morestead, Hampshire

FOCUS
This was strongly run and represents solid form for the grade. The second and third were thrown in on best of old form and could be rated higher with the fourth a stone off recent course run. Biggish pb from the winner.

864 HAPPY TRAVELS DOUG AND JEAN H'CAP HURDLE (11 hdls) 2m 6f 7y
8:30 (8:32) (Class 5) (0-100,100) 4-Y-0+ £2,599 (£763; £381; £190)

Form RPR

000- **1** **Annaroe (IRE)**[97] 4987 6-10-0 **74**.................................... AdamWedge 81+
(Alexandra Dunn) *mid-div: hdwy 4th: led flat: drvn out* **14/1**

2 *4* **Kilcross Boy (IRE)**[53] 191 10-11-6 **94**.........................(bt) NoelFehily 100+
(Neil Mulholland) *hld up: lost pl after 6th: hdwy 3 out: led after next: rdn whn mstke last: sn hdd: styd on same pce* **4/1**[2]

U3-2 **3** *1/2* **Stay In My Heart (IRE)**[31] 552 6-11-4 **92**....................... LeightonAspell 95
(Laura Mongan) *hld up: pushed along 5th: hdwy after 3 out: chsd wnr after next: rdn appr last: hung rt flat: styd on same pce* **8/1**[3]

0-42 **4** *7* **Multiview**[27] 597 6-10-13 **87**.. RichardJohnson 84
(Tom Symonds) *hld up: hdwy 3 out: rdn after next: wknd bef last* **3/1**[1]

43-0 **5** *10* **Direct Flo (IRE)**[33] 530 8-10-6 **85**.................................. JakeHodson(5) 73
(Rob Summers) *prom: chsd ldr 6th rdn and ev ch 2 out: wknd wl bef last* **12/1**

-216 **6** *2 1/2* **Bus Named Desire**[32] 537 7-10-13 **87**........................(tp) WillKennedy 72
(Ian Williams) *hld up: hdwy 8th: rdn and wknd wl bef last* **8/1**[3]

0-16 **7** *2 3/4* **In The Crowd (IRE)**[19] 704 6-11-9 **100**.........................(p) JamesBanks(3) 84
(Roy Brotherton) *prom: rdn whn mstke 2 out: sn wknd* **10/1**

43-5 **8** *18* **Poetic Presence (IRE)**[24] 648 5-10-6 **80**............................ MichealNolan 47
(Adrian Wintle) *hld up: wknd 8th* **33/1**

50-4 **9** *18* **Whipcrackaway (IRE)**[42] 391 6-11-5 **93**.......................(b) JamieMoore 44
(Peter Hedger) *hld up: drvn along after 6th: wknd 8th* **20/1**

P/0- **10** *9* **Midnight Whisper**[91] 5082 9-11-12 **100**..........................(t) DarylJacob 42
(Richard Woollacott) *prom tl rdn and wknd after 2 out* **25/1**

03-6 **11** *10* **Daring Indian**[15] 167 7-11-5 **93**..........................(tp) KielanWoods 26
(Graeme McPherson) *chsd ldr: led 2nd: rdn and hdd after 2 out: sn wknd* **10/1**

0F6- **P** **Pattara**[111] 4712 6-11-3 **91**.......................... GerardTumelty
(Noel Williams) *hld up: hdwy 7th: wknd 3 out: bhd whn p.u bef last* **33/1**

F52- **P** **Vinaigrette**[67] 5525 6-10-0 **74**..........................(t) SeanQuinlan
(Richard Phillips) *led to 2nd: chsd ldr to 6th: wknd after next: bhd whn p.u bef 3 out* **14/1**

5m 17.5s (-10.60) **Going Correction** -0.35s/f (Good) **13** Ran SP% **120.9**
Speed ratings (Par 103): **105,103,103,100,97 96,95,88,82,78 75, ,**
CSF £68.61 CT £491.94 TOTE £23.10: £7.80, £1.70, £3.30; EX 123.70 Trifecta £1837.90 Part won..
Owner W A Thomas **Bred** James Wickham **Trained** West Buckland, Somerset

FOCUS
They went a brisk gallop throughout and this took plenty of getting. The winner is rated back to the level of her Fontwell second, with the runner-up better than the result and similar to Irish form. The third and fourth were close to their marks.

865 BORDEAUX UNDISCOVERED STANDARD NATIONAL HUNT FLAT RACE (CONDITIONAL JOCKEYS' AND AMATEUR RIDERS') 2m 70y
9:00 (9:00) (Class 6) 4-6-Y-O **£1,949** (£572; £286; £143)

Form RPR

1 **Alyasan (IRE)** 4-10-12 0.......................... SeanBowen[3] 102+
(Seamus Durack) *hld up: hdwy over 2f out: led over 1f out: edgd lft ins fnl f: pushed out* **9/4**[1]

05-U **2** *1* **Viva Rafa (IRE)**[50] 242 5-10-13 0.......................... DanielHiskett[5] 104
(Richard Phillips) *led: rdn and hdd over 1f out: n.m.r ins fnl f: styd on* **25/1**

/61- **3** *4 ½* **War On The Rocks (IRE)**[113] 4680 6-11-8 0.......................... ConorShoemark[3] 107
(Fergal O'Brien) *hld up: hdwy over 5f out: rdn over 1f out: styd on same pce fnl f* **5/1**[3]

4 *1 ½* **Oh So Gigolo (IRE)** 5-10-11 0.......................... MrRO'Reilly[7] 100+
(Nicky Henderson) *hld up: hdwy over 3f out: nt clr run wl over 1f out: styd on* **5/1**[3]

5 *shd* **Bare Necessities (IRE)**[57] 5-11-4 0.......................... NicodeBoinville 99
(Shaun Lycett) *prom: rdn over 3f out: no ex fnl f* **11/2**

24- **6** *¾* **Lincoln County**[135] 4256 4-10-8 0.......................... MrAlexFerguson[7] 95
(John Ferguson) *chsd ldr: rdn over 2f out: hung lft over 1f out: no ex fnl f* **7/2**[2]

7 *4 ½* **Airpur Desbois (FR)** 5-10-13 0.......................... HarryBannister[5] 94
(Charlie Mann) *hld up: hdwy 6f out: rdn over 2f out: wknd over 1f out* **25/1**

8 *23* **Flick Knife (IRE)**[764] 6-11-1 0.......................... KillianMoore[3] 73
(Mark Wall) *prom: pushed along 1/2-way: wknd wl over 3f out* **14/1**

6 **9** *1 ½* **Panopticon**[31] 558 4-10-1 0.......................... MrMJPKendrick[7] 62
(Giles Bravery) *prom: pushed along over 6f out: wknd wl over 2f out* **50/1**

0- **10** *15* **Four Plus**[23] 4-10-1 0.......................... MrPhilipThomas[7] 48
(Hugo Froud) *hld up and a bhd* **66/1**

3m 46.4s (-4.00) **Going Correction** -0.35s/f (Good)
WFA 4 from 5yo+ 3lb **10** Ran SP% **119.5**
Speed ratings: **96,95,93,92,92 92,89,78,77,70**
CSF £68.13 TOTE £4.70: £1.30, £7.20, £1.60; EX 60.90 Trifecta £245.10.
Owner The Alyasan Partnership **Bred** His Highness The Aga Khan's Studs S C **Trained** Upper Lambourn, Berkshire

FOCUS
Ordinary bumper rated around the third and sixth, with a big step up from the second.
T/Plt: £32.60 to a £1 stake. Pool: £71,826.70 - 1,606.63 winning tickets. T/Qpdt: £29.60 to a £1 stake. Pool: £6,604.60 - 164.92 winning tickets. **Colin Roberts**

656 PERTH (R-H)
Wednesday, July 1

OFFICIAL GOING: Good (good to firm in places)
Wind: Breezy, half against Weather: Cloudy, warm

866 STRONGBOW DARK FRUIT NOVICES' HURDLE (STRONGBOW DARK FRUIT SCOTTISH HURDLE SERIES QUALIFIER) (8 hdls) 2m 47y
2:10 (2:10) (Class 4) 4-Y-O+ **£3,165** (£935; £467; £234)

Form RPR

1 **1** **Improvisation (IRE)**[36] 491 5-11-5 0.......................... AidanColeman 135+
(John Ferguson) *trckd ldrs: wnt 2nd 3rd: led on bit 2 out: qcknd clr fr last: v easily* **1/9**[1]

2 *9* **Pershing**[11] 793 4-10-10 116..........................(tp) BrianHughes 111
(Robert Alan Hennessy, Ire) *cl up: led bef 2nd: rdn and hdd 2 out: no ch w wnr* **10/1**[2]

2 **3** *26* **Lowanbehold (IRE)**[18] 730 8-10-5 0.......................... JamieHamilton[7] 87
(Sandy Forster) *led to bef 2nd: cl up: drvn and outpcd 4 out: wnt modest 3rd 2 out: no imp* **20/1**[3]

6-6U **4** *6* **Miss Joeking (IRE)**[3] 846 4-10-3 0.......................... PeterBuchanan 73
(Lucinda Russell) *nt fluent on occasions: in tch: drvn and outpcd 4 out: struggling fr next* **125/1**

4m 0.5s (240.50)
WFA 4 from 5yo+ 15lb **4** Ran SP% **104.7**
CSF £1.70 TOTE £1.10; EX 1.70 Trifecta £2.10.
Owner Bloomfields **Bred** Ennistown Stud **Trained** Cowlinge, Suffolk

FOCUS
Bends and Hurdles moved to fresh ground. Races 1 & 7 increased by 54yds, races 2 & 3 by 82yds, race 4 by 115yds, race 5 by 66yds and race 6 by 79. The ground was officially good, good to firm in places but Aidan Coleman who rode the winner said it was good to soft down the far side and good in the straight. This was an uncompetitive and laregely uninformative event. The winner is rated similar to his Huntington form, with the second to his mark.

867 CREAMY BY NATURE H'CAP CHASE (18 fncs) 2m 7f 180y
2:40 (2:40) (Class 4) (0-110,110) 4-Y-O+ **£3,833** (£1,157; £596; £315)

Form RPR

/ **1** **St Maxime (IRE)**[17] 738 7-10-4 **95**..........................(b) JBKane[7] 111+
(Gavin Cromwell, Ire) *pressed ldr: led 5 out: rdn whn mstke and pckd last: hung rt: styd on strly* **4/1**[2]

331- **2** *7* **Xaarcet (IRE)**[75] 5371 8-11-9 **107**..........................(tp) RichardJohnson 116
(Gordon Elliott, Ire) *trckd ldrs: wnt 2nd bef 4 out: effrt and ev ch 2 out: sn rdn: one pce whn hit last: sn btn* **9/5**[1]

2-43 **3** *14* **Shady Sadie (IRE)**[18] 731 8-9-11 **84** oh2..........................(t) HarryChalloner[3] 81
(Rose Dobbin) *hld up: hdwy and prom 5 out: rdn and effrt bef 3 out: wknd bef next* **11/2**

44-4 **4** *51* **Bertie Milan (IRE)**[49] 289 10-11-0 **98**..........................(p) BrianHarding 48
(N W Alexander) *led to 5 out: sn drvn along: wknd bef 3 out: t.o* **13/2**

2-P4 **P** **Lochore (IRE)**[38] 454 9-10-0 **84** oh14..........................(t) HenryBrooke
(Jean McGregor) *nt fluent in rr: struggling fr 12th: t.o whn p.u after 4 out* **80/1**

00-4 **P** **Speedy Tunes (IRE)**[22] 677 8-11-7 **110**..........................(p) CallumBewley[5]
(Simon Waugh) *nt fluent: prom: drvn and outpcd 5 out: struggling after next: t.o whn p.u bef last* **18/1**

0-44 **U** **Rev Up Ruby**[36] 483 7-11-2 **105**.......................... JonathonBewley[5] 53
(George Bewley) *hld up: drvn along after 5 out: nvr rchd ldrs: 37 l 4th whn blnd and uns rdr last* **9/2**[3]

6m 4.4s (0.40) **Going Correction** +0.025s/f (Yiel) **7** Ran SP% **109.1**
Speed ratings (Par 105): **100,97,93,76, ,**
CSF £11.05 TOTE £4.70: £1.60, £2.30; EX 13.00 Trifecta £44.30.
Owner DT Racing Club **Bred** Gerrardstown House Stud **Trained** Navan, Co. Meath
■ A first winner in Britain for Irish-based Brien Kane.

FOCUS
Just an ordnary staying handicap chase. The gallop was fair and they finished well strung out. First two improved chase ratings in line with best of their hurdles form and there's a case for rating a bit higher through the third.

868 GROSVENOR CASINOS H'CAP CHASE (FOR THE STIRLING CUP) (18 fncs) 2m 7f 180y
3:10 (3:10) (Class 3) (0-140,139) 4-Y-O **£9,495** (£2,805; £1,402; £702; £351)

Form RPR

230- **1** **Maggio (FR)**[82] 5253 10-11-12 **139**..........................(t) BrianHughes 144+
(Patrick Griffin, Ire) *pressed ldr: led 4 out: drvn along after 2 out: hung rt run-in: kpt on wl towards fin* **14/1**

31-1 **2** *½* **Kilbree Kid (IRE)**[24] 660 8-11-5 **132**..........................(tp) PaddyBrennan 136
(Tom George) *prom: effrt and chsd wnr 2 out: drvn next: edgd lft and kpt on wl run-in* **7/5**[1]

0-33 **3** *5* **Bless The Wings (IRE)**[24] 660 10-11-7 **134**..........................(p) RichardJohnson 134
(Gordon Elliott, Ire) *hld up in tch: nt fluent 10th: smooth hdwy bef 5 out: effrt and rdn bef 2 out: outpcd fr last* **13/8**[2]

33-2 **4** *24* **Harrys Whim**[12] 781 10-9-11 **113**..........................(t) JonathanEngland[3] 89
(Maurice Barnes) *led: rdn and hdd 4 out: rallied: wknd bef 2 out* **17/2**[3]

/P-5 **5** *3 ¼* **Problema Tic (FR)**[10] 800 9-10-12 **128**..........................(t) TonyKelly[3] 102
(Jackie Stephen) *nt fluent in rr: shortlived effrt u.p 5 out: struggling fr next* **12/1**

1U5/ **P** **Organisedconfusion (IRE)**[886] 3881 10-11-10 **137**...... PeterBuchanan
(C A McBratney, Ire) *nt fluent on occasions: outpcd whn hit 5 out: sn struggling: t.o whn p.u bef 3 out* **20/1**

5m 58.1s (-5.90) **Going Correction** +0.025s/f (Yiel) **6** Ran SP% **109.4**
Speed ratings (Par 107): **110,109,108,100,99**
CSF £34.09 TOTE £9.80: £2.70, £1.60; EX 23.60 Trifecta £76.30.
Owner D G Pryde/James Beaumont **Bred** Haras Du Reuilly **Trained** Oldtown, Co Dublin

FOCUS
A competitive handicap chase run at a sound gallop and the form should prove solid. The winner is rated to his best, with the second making a small step up on recent course win.

869 VISIT BEAUTIFUL PERTH H'CAP HURDLE (12 hdls) 2m 7f 207y
3:40 (3:40) (Class 4) (0-120,115) 4-Y-O **£3,798** (£1,122; £561; £280; £140)

Form RPR

05-0 **1** **Romany Ryme**[56] 141 9-11-4 **107**.......................... RichardJohnson 115+
(Gordon Elliott, Ire) *hld up in tch: smooth hdwy to ld bef 2 out: rdn bef last: hld on wl run-in* **5/2**[2]

2 *hd* **Caledon Craic (IRE)**[22] 688 8-11-2 **110**.......................... MatthewBowes[5] 118+
(Lady Jane Gillespie, Ire) *hld up: smooth hdwy 3 out: effrt and chsd wnr after next: sn rdn: kpt on wl u.p fr last: jst hld* **7/4**[1]

56-2 **3** *14* **Los Nadis (GER)**[24] 661 11-11-2 **105**..........................(v) HenryBrooke 99
(Jim Goldie) *led: clr 2nd to 7th: rdn and hdd bef 2 out: wknd bef last* **9/2**[3]

F1-5 **4** *3 ½* **High Fair**[36] 482 9-10-2 **98**.......................... MrTHamilton[7] 89
(Sandy Forster) *prom: drvn and outpcd 3 out: n.d after* **9/1**

1/6- **5** *27* **Degenerous (IRE)**[123] 4481 7-10-9 **98**.......................... BrianHarding 65
(Sarah Dawson, Ire) *hld up: nt fluent 3rd: smooth hdwy and prom 3 out: rdn and wknd bef next* **16/1**

-13P **6** *1 ¼* **Heart O Annandale (IRE)**[10] 803 8-10-6 **98**.......(t) JonathanEngland[3] 64
(Maurice Barnes) *nt fluent: chsd ldr: hit and outpcd 3 out: wknd bef next* **11/1**

5P-P **P** **Bit Of A Jig (IRE)**[19] 705 8-11-5 **115**..........................(p) JamesCowley[7]
(Donald McCain) *in tch: drvn and struggling fr 1/2-way: lost tch and p.u 3 out* **25/1**

5m 57.6s (-7.40) **Going Correction** -0.175s/f (Good) **7** Ran SP% **111.2**
Speed ratings (Par 105): **105,104,100,99,90 89,**
CSF £7.10 CT £16.00 TOTE £3.00: £1.60, £1.70; EX 9.10 Trifecta £15.10.
Owner Five Men Syndicate **Bred** Graindale And Quinnies Stud **Trained** Longwood, Co Meath

FOCUS
A staying handicap hurdle run at a true gallop and the first two were clear. The winner is rated back to his best on debut for new yard.

870 GREEN HOTEL (S) H'CAP HURDLE (10 hdls) 2m 4f 35y
4:10 (4:10) (Class 5) (0-100,99) 4-Y-O+ **£3,165** (£935; £467; £234; £117)

Form RPR

500- **1** **An Capall Mor (IRE)**[12] 787 9-11-3 **90**..........................(bt) RichardJohnson 105+
(Gordon Elliott, Ire) *cl up: led bef 2 out: clr 2 out: shkn up and kpt on wl fr last* **4/5**[1]

-405 **2** *7* **Bunclody**[20] 695 10-11-1 **95**.......................... MrZBaker[7] 101
(Barry Brennan) *hld up in tch: hdwy to chse wnr 3 out: rdn next: one pce whn hit last* **5/1**[2]

-P40 **3** *27* **Cumbrian Farmer**[24] 661 8-10-1 **79**..........................(vt) GaryRutherford[5] 63
(George Bewley) *cl up: drvn and outpcd 3 out: 3rd and no imp whn hit next* **7/1**[3]

0P0/ **4** *5* **Grand Diamond (IRE)**[23] 5546 11-10-13 **91**.......................... DaleIrving[5] 68
(Jim Goldie) *hld up: stdy hdwy bef 3 out: rdn and wknd bef next* **16/1**

P0-P **5** *6* **So Bazaar (IRE)**[35] 507 8-10-0 **73** oh5..........................(t) BrianHarding 45
(Andrew Wilson) *hld up: stdy hdwy after 4 out: rdn and wknd bef 2 out* **25/1**

/UP- **P** **Reland (FR)**[402] 458 10-9-7 **73** oh5..........................(t) JamieHamilton[7]
(Jackie Stephen) *chsd ldrs: lost pl 4th: struggling fnl circ: t.o whn p.u bef 2 out* **25/1**

PP-4 **P** **The Flaming Matron (IRE)**[49] 287 9-11-7 **99**..(tp) StephenMulqueen[5]
(N W Alexander) *led to bef 4 out: struggling bef next: t.o whn p.u bef 2 out* **12/1**

5-40 **P** **Just Bee (IRE)**[36] 487 6-9-10 **74**....(p) CallumBewley[(5)]
(Katie Scott) *prom: mstke 5th: struggling next: t.o whn p.u bef 2 out* **18/1**
5m 0.2s (-1.80) **Going Correction** -0.175s/f (Good) **8** Ran SP% **111.3**
Speed ratings (Par 103): **96,93,82,80,78** , ,
CSF £5.26 CT £14.87 TOTE £1.90: £1.10, £1.60, £2.70; EX 6.10 Trifecta £18.20.There was no bid for the winner.
Owner T Howley Jnr/Oliver Jack Murphy **Bred** Paul Cleary **Trained** Longwood, Co Meath
FOCUS
An ordinary selling handicap hurdle featuring mainly hard-to-win with sorts and they finished strung out. The winner and second were 120 hurdlers at their peak.

871 GREENVALE NOVICES' H'CAP CHASE (15 fncs) 2m 4f 20y
4:40 (4:41) (Class 4) (0-105,105) 4-Y-0 **£3,798** (£1,122; £561; £280; £140)

Form RPR
5-1F **1** **Just Awake**[38] 453 8-11-5 **105**....(t) StevenFox[(7)] 110+
(Sandy Thomson) *nt fluent on occasions: hld up: stdy hdwy bef 4 out: effrt after next: led run-in: drvn out* **9/2**[3]
4-U4 **2** *1 ¼* **Bouggietopieces**[17] 738 5-11-2 **95**.... RichardJohnson 99+
(Gordon Elliott, Ire) *t.k.h early: cl up: led 7th: mstke and rdn 2 out: hdd run-in: kpt on at same pce towards fin* **15/8**[1]
-622 **3** *2 ¾* **Forestside (IRE)**[18] 728 10-10-0 **79** oh5....(p) BrianHughes 79
(Barry Murtagh) *chsd ldrs: pushed along bef 3 out: kpt on fr last: nt rch first two* **10/1**
6-23 **4** *nse* **Mister D (IRE)**[37] 472 9-10-11 **95**.... JonathonBewley[(5)] 95
(George Bewley) *t.k.h early: prom: hdwy to chse ldr 3 out to last: outpcd run-in* **7/2**[2]
0-45 **5** *3 ½* **Champagne Agent (IRE)**[25] 639 9-10-0 **79** oh11....(b) DougieCostello 76
(Donald Whillans) *led to 7th: chsd ldr to 3 out: rdn and outpcd fr next* **14/1**
63-1 **6** *59* **Beidh Tine Anseo (IRE)**[38] 455 9-11-4 **102**....(tp) GrantCockburn[(5)] 46
(Lucinda Russell) *hld up in tch: outpcd 10th: lost tch fr 3 out* **10/1**
P0-3 **P** **Clonleney (IRE)**[38] 455 9-10-1 **87**....(t) JamieHamilton[(7)]
(Alison Hamilton) *hld up: outpcd whn blnd 10th: p.u bef 4 out* **9/1**
5m 9.0s (4.00) **Going Correction** +0.025s/f (Yiel) **7** Ran SP% **110.0**
Speed ratings (Par 105): **93,92,91,91,89 66,**
CSF £12.93 TOTE £3.70: £2.90, £1.20; EX 13.80 Trifecta £48.10.
Owner Mrs A M Thomson **Bred** A M Thomson **Trained** Lambden, Berwicks
FOCUS
A modest novice handicap chase run at a fair gallop and the winner came from last to first. The first four have been rated pretty much to their marks.

872 SCOTTISH GAME FAIR 3RD 4TH & 5TH JULY H'CAP HURDLE (8 hdls) 2m 47y
5:10 (5:10) (Class 4) (0-110,108) 3-Y-0+ **£3,165** (£935; £467; £234; £117)

Form RPR
4-51 **1** **Politeness (FR)**[34] 520 6-11-7 **106**.... CraigNichol[(3)] 116+
(Rose Dobbin) *hld up: stdy hdwy after 4 out: effrt and led bef 2 out: sn clr: pushed out* **7/2**[1]
5406 **2** *4 ½* **Dynamic Drive (IRE)**[10] 805 8-10-4 **93**....(t) RyanDay[(7)] 98
(Maurice Barnes) *hld up in tch: hdwy and ev ch bef 2 out: kpt on fr last: nt gng pce of wnr* **7/1**
4-P0 **3** *4* **Formal Bid (IRE)**[38] 465 8-11-0 **103**....(bt) MrZBaker[(7)] 105
(Barry Brennan) *hld up: hdwy to chal 4 out: led next to bef 2 out: sn outpcd: plugged on fr last: no imp* **25/1**
P/ **4** *3 ¼* **Coney Choice (IRE)**[71] 5458 7-11-2 **103**....(t) MatthewBowes[(5)] 101
(Lady Jane Gillespie, Ire) *hld up in midfield: smooth hdwy and cl up 3 out: rdn and ev ch bef next: sn outpcd* **11/2**
30- **5** *1* **Ashjar (FR)**[26] 629 5-11-12 **108**....(b) BrianHughes 106
(C A McBratney, Ire) *hld up: rdn and effrt after 3 out: drvn and no imp bef next* **22/1**
2-06 **6** *nk* **Amilliontimes (IRE)**[24] 661 7-11-6 **105**....(t) TonyKelly[(3)] 103
(Jackie Stephen) *cl up: led 4 out to next: rdn and wknd bef 2 out* **9/1**
00-2 **7** *8* **Tangolan (IRE)**[24] 658 7-11-12 **108**.... PaddyBrennan 101
(Fergal O'Brien) *t.k.h: in tch: drvn and outpcd after 4 out: no imp bef 2 out* **4/1**[2]
-506 **8** *39* **Raifteiri (IRE)**[10] 804 8-9-9 **82** oh6.... StephenMulqueen[(5)] 37
(William Young Jnr) *cl up: drvn along bef 4 out: wknd bef next: t.o* **40/1**
3/5- **9** *7* **Agricultural**[388] 632 9-10-12 **94**.... DougieCostello 43
(Lucy Normile) *bhd: outpcd whn nt fluent 4 out: sn lost tch: t.o* **33/1**
-202 **P** **The Ice Factor**[10] 804 7-9-12 **87**....(p) JamieHamilton[(7)]
(Alison Hamilton) *led to 4 out: sn drvn along: wknd after next: t.o whn p.u bef last* **9/2**[3]
3m 57.9s (237.90) **10** Ran SP% **111.9**
CSF £25.58 CT £514.37 TOTE £4.10: £1.10, £3.30, £7.10; EX 20.50 Trifecta £370.90.
Owner Mr & Mrs Duncan Davidson **Bred** R Monnier, Wertheimer Et Frere, Et Al **Trained** South Hazelrigg, Northumbria
FOCUS
Quite a competitive handicap hurdle for the grade and though the pace was fair most were still in with a chance on the turn for home.
T/Plt: £9.50 to a £1 stake. Pool of £41428.39 - 3150.70 winning tickets. T/Qpdt: £6.70 to a £1 stake. Pool of £3212.69 - 354.75 winning tickets. **Richard Young**

829 WORCESTER (L-H)
Wednesday, July 1

OFFICIAL GOING: Good to firm
Wind: Light across Weather: Cloudy with sunny spells

873 WINTERFOLD HOUSE SCHOOL H'CAP CHASE (16 fncs) 2m 7f
2:20 (2:23) (Class 4) (0-115,114) 4-Y-0+ **£4,223** (£1,240; £620; £310)

Form RPR
10-2 **1** **Etania**[8] 827 7-10-4 **92**.... TomO'Brien 101+
(Ian Williams) *hld up: mstke 1st: hdwy 12th: rdn to ld flat: styd on* **7/1**[2]
53-P **2** *1 ¼* **Book Of Excuses (IRE)**[20] 693 7-11-8 **110**....(t) NoelFehily 116
(Donald McCain) *a.p: chsd ldr 5th: led 3 out: rdn and hdd flat: styd on* **10/1**
-24P **3** *¾* **Orby's Man (IRE)**[20] 693 6-11-7 **114**....(p) DanielHiskett[(5)] 119
(Charlie Longsdon) *chsd ldrs: wnt 2nd 2 out: sn rdn: styd on* **8/1**[3]
0-46 **4** *18* **Lock Towers (IRE)**[12] 782 6-11-0 **102**....(tp) NicodeBoinville 96+
(Ben Pauling) *hld up: j.rt: hdd 3 out: wknd last* **9/1**
2-42 **5** *4 ½* **Sir Mattie (IRE)**[27] 611 10-11-11 **113**.... PaulMoloney 98
(David Rees) *hld up: hdwy 11th: mstke 3 out: sn rdn: wknd after next* **12/1**
3-13 **6** *13* **Trafficker (IRE)**[14] 757 8-11-8 **110**....(p) WillKennedy 83
(Dr Richard Newland) *hld up: pushed along after 8th: hdwy next: drvn along 11th: wknd after next* **2/1**[1]

-252 **7** *1 ½* **Mission Complete (IRE)**[22] 676 9-10-10 **105**....(tp) PatrickCowley[(7)] 78
(Jonjo O'Neill) *a in rr: mstke 2nd: reminder after 7th: wknd 11th* **7/1**[2]
U5-0 **8** *dist* **Wither Yenot (IRE)**[14] 760 8-10-9 **104**....(b[1]) MrMJPKendrick[(7)] 44
(Ben Case) *prom wkng whn mstke 10th* **50/1**
PP-4 **P** **Papradon**[32] 557 11-11-9 **111**....(v) SamTwiston-Davies
(Nigel Twiston-Davies) *chsd ldr to 5th: remained handy tl rdn and wknd after 12th: bhd whn p.u bef 3 out* **16/1**
44-5 **P** **Forever My Friend (IRE)**[28] 598 8-11-11 **113**.... JamieMoore
(Peter Bowen) *hld up in tch: rdn after 12th: wknd bef next: bhd whn p.u bef 2 out* **14/1**
5m 43.7s (-6.20) **Going Correction** -0.375s/f (Good) **10** Ran SP% **110.7**
Speed ratings (Par 105): **95,94,94,88,86 81,81, , ,**
CSF £69.38 CT £545.52 TOTE £5.10: £2.20, £3.20, £2.80; EX 74.20 Trifecta £1087.40.
Owner Mr & Mrs H Parmar **Bred** Mrs S Horne **Trained** Portway, Worcs
FOCUS
All starts have been moved at this track following remeasuring, so there will be no speed figures here until there is sufficient data to calculate updated median times. Rail movements increased distances of all races by approximately 42yds, with the exception of race 3 (the bumper) which increased by 26yds. It was hard work for the horses on this hot and humid day. Winner stepped up for this longer trip, the second was close to his mark, with the third in line with hurdles form.

874 LISTERS VOLKSWAGEN WORCESTER, UNBELIEVABLE VALUE H'CAP CHASE (13 fncs) 2m 4f
2:50 (2:53) (Class 5) (0-100,97) 4-Y-0+ **£2,599** (£763; £381; £190)

Form RPR
23/2 **1** **Wak A Turtle (IRE)**[20] 699 7-11-8 **93**.... DarylJacob 106+
(Richard Woollacott) *a.p: chsd ldr 7th: led 2 out: rdn and edgd rt flat: styd on* **11/4**[2]
54-0 **2** *5* **Amuse Me**[20] 704 9-11-12 **97**....(t) RichieMcLernon 104
(Jonjo O'Neill) *chsd ldrs: rdn and edgd lft flat: styd on same pce* **14/1**
4-52 **3** *3 ½* **Lord Of The Dunes**[10] 806 7-11-1 **86**....(bt) BrendanPowell 91
(Jamie Snowden) *hld up: hdwy 8th: j.lft 3 out: sn rdn: styd on same pce appr last: wnt 3rd nr fin* **15/8**[1]
FP-4 **4** *1 ¼* **Lily Little Legs (IRE)**[52] 226 6-11-11 **96**.... WillKennedy 99
(Ian Williams) *led: rdn and hdd 2 out: wknd flat* **11/2**[3]
F-P6 **5** *6* **Goldie Horn**[13] 770 7-11-11 **96**....(tp) SamTwiston-Davies 94
(Nigel Twiston-Davies) *hld up: hdwy 8th: rdn after 3 out: wknd bef last* **16/1**
4-PF **6** *30* **My Nosy Rosy**[20] 699 7-11-10 **95**....(tp) KielanWoods 65
(Ben Case) *hld up: hdwy 9th: rdn and wknd 3 out* **20/1**
2-03 **7** *32* **Forresters Folly**[22] 676 9-11-12 **97**....(tp) TrevorWhelan 38
(Claire Dyson) *prom: rdn after 9th: wknd 4 out* **16/1**
4/-4 **P** **Darnborough (IRE)**[20] 699 9-9-7 **71** oh2....(p) DavidNoonan[(7)]
(Mark Shears) *chsd ldr: pushed along 6th: sn lost pl: wknd appr 8th: bhd whn p.u bef 4 out* **40/1**
5 **P** **Icthec (IRE)**[16] 741 8-11-2 **87**....(t) JamesDavies
(Jennifer Mason) *prom: pushed along after 5th: wknd 8th: bhd whn p.u bef 4 out* **12/1**
4m 55.7s (-8.90) **Going Correction** -0.375s/f (Good) **9** Ran SP% **110.2**
Speed ratings (Par 103): **102,100,98,98,95 83,70, ,**
CSF £36.07 CT £81.32 TOTE £3.30: £1.10, £2.70, £1.10; EX 34.40 Trifecta £86.30.
Owner J Pike **Bred** Mrs A S O'Brien **Trained** South Molton, Devon
FOCUS
A modest handicap chase. The winner stepped up for the longer trip, with the third and fourth close to their marks.

875 FRANCIS OF MALVERN, FURNITURE BEDS FLOORING STANDARD OPEN NATIONAL HUNT FLAT RACE 2m
3:20 (3:22) (Class 6) 4-6-Y-0 **£1,754** (£515; £257; £128)

Form RPR
120- **1** **Joe Farrell (IRE)**[137] 4221 6-11-7 0.... SamTwiston-Davies 116+
(John Ferguson) *trckd ldr tl led over 2f out: sn clr: eased ins fnl f* **1/7**[1]
0-0 **2** *20* **Aspecialpresent (IRE)**[25] 644 5-11-0 0.... MichealNolan 84
(Adrian Wintle) *trckd ldrs: pushed along over 4f out: wknd over 2f out: wnt 2nd ins fnl f* **33/1**
0 **3** *7* **Ron Hegarty (IRE)**[61] 67 4-10-12 0....(t) ConorO'Farrell 76
(Seamus Durack) *led at stdy pce tl rdn and hdd over 2f out: wknd over 1f out* **14/1**[3]
4 *13* **Backoftherock**[68] 6-11-0 0.... PaulMoloney 64
(David Rees) *hld up in tch: pushed along 6f out: wknd over 3f out* **12/1**[2]
3m 40.4s (-4.60) **Going Correction** -0.375s/f (Good) **4** Ran SP% **104.8**
Speed ratings: **96,86,82,76**
CSF £5.96 TOTE £1.10; EX 5.10 Trifecta £11.70.
Owner Bloomfields **Bred** Mrs E A Pendarves **Trained** Cowlinge, Suffolk
FOCUS
An uncompetitive little bumper, won by a useful performer. He didn't need to run to his best, with the second to his C&D mark.

876 BLAZING SAVILLS H'CAP HURDLE (10 hdls) 2m 4f
3:50 (3:53) (Class 3) (0-135,126) 4-Y-0+ **£5,523** (£1,621; £810; £405)

Form RPR
40-5 **1** **Mile House (IRE)**[25] 645 7-11-11 **125**.... TomO'Brien 130
(Robert Stephens) *j.rt at times: trckd ldr tl led 3rd: shkn up appr last: rdn and hung lft flat: styd on u.p* **7/1**
2-22 **2** *½* **Aficionado**[10] 812 5-11-6 **120**....(p) WillKennedy 126+
(Dr Richard Newland) *prom to 4th: wnt cl up again 6th: chsd wnr last: hmpd flat: swtchd rt: styd on* **7/4**[1]
41-3 **3** *8* **Over The Air**[34] 529 7-10-8 **108**.... NicodeBoinville 105
(John Spearing) *trckd ldrs tl lost tch w ldng pair 4th: tk clsr order 6th: rdn after 2 out: no ex flat* **8/1**
/1F- **4** *3 ¼* **Fort Worth (IRE)**[115] 4645 6-11-12 **126**.... RichieMcLernon 120
(Jonjo O'Neill) *hld up: hdwy after 2 out: rdn and wknd flat* **5/1**[3]
6P5- **5** *2* **Byron Blue (IRE)**[137] 4233 6-11-11 **125**.... TomCannon 118
(Mark Gillard) *racd keenly: led to 3rd: trckd wnr tl rdn appr last: wknd flat* **16/1**
21P- **6** *30* **Zip Top (IRE)**[116] 4633 6-11-12 **126**.... SamTwiston-Davies 92
(John Ferguson) *hld up: pushed along appr 3 out: rdn and wknd bef next* **3/1**[2]
6-U6 **7** *43* **Romeo Americo (IRE)**[20] 697 8-11-4 **118**.... JamieMoore 45
(Seamus Mullins) *hld up: rdn after 6th: wknd appr 3 out* **50/1**
4m 42.3s (-11.20) **Going Correction** -0.375s/f (Good) **7** Ran SP% **109.5**
Speed ratings (Par 107): **107,106,103,102,101 89,72**
CSF £18.61 TOTE £9.80: £4.00, £1.20; EX 24.00 Trifecta £149.50.
Owner Castle Farm Racing **Bred** Mrs J O'Gorman **Trained** Penhow, Newport
■ Stewards' Enquiry : Tom O'Brien two-day ban: use of whip (18-19 Jul)

FOCUS
A decent handicap hurdle. The pace was solid with two, including the winner, racing clear of the remainder. The winner was back to the level of his Fontwell success, with the runner-up in line with his recent C&D second. There's a case for rating this a bit higher through the third.

877 FOR GREAT SERVICE VISIT VOLKSWAGEN WORCESTER NOVICES' HURDLE (12 hdls) 2m 7f
4:20 (4:24) (Class 4) 4-Y-0+ **£3,249** (£954; £477; £238)

Form RPR
4-12 **1** **Towering (IRE)**[35] 509 6-11-5 122.................................... NicodeBoinville 119+
(Nicky Henderson) *led at stdy pce tl qcknd 7th: nt fluent 3 out: shkn up whn hung rt bef last: hdd whn mstke last: rallied to ld nr fin* **11/10**[1]
2-12 **2** ½ **Black Jack Rover (IRE)**[34] 518 6-11-5 120.............................. NoelFehily 115+
(Donald McCain) *chsd wnr: pckd 3 out: rdn to ld last: hdd nr fin* **7/4**[2]
3 4½ **Part And Parcel (IRE)**[18] 7-10-5 0.............................. MrAlexEdwards[(7)] 102
(Alan Phillips) *a.p: hung lft appr 3 out: sn rdn: mstke last: styd on same pce* **20/1**
P0-2 **4** 9 **Troyan (IRE)**[13] 773 8-10-5 110..............................(t) DavidNoonan[(7)] 95
(Steve Flook) *hld up: hdwy 9th: rdn 2 out: wkng whn hung lft flat* **9/2**[3]
3 **5** 9 **Butlergrove King (IRE)**[25] 634 6-10-12 0........................ AndrewTinkler 88
(Natalie Lloyd-Beavis) *hld up: outpcd 7th: mstke next: styd on appr last* **16/1**
6 dist **Carbon Emission (IRE)**[31] 12-10-5 0..........................(b) MissABroome[(7)] 45
(John Needham) *wnt prom 2nd: rdn and wknd appr 9th* **80/1**
P **7** 9 **Blackwood Rover (IRE)**[33] 533 7-10-12 0............................ PaulMoloney 37
(J R Jenkins) *prom tl rdn and wknd after 3 out* **20/1**
0-P4 **8** 3½ **Hot Madras (IRE)**[40] 434 7-9-12 0.................................. JoshWall[(7)] 27
(Trevor Wall) *hld up: wknd 8th: bhd whn mstke next: blnd 3 out* **125/1**
5-UU **P** **Tikketoride**[25] 647 7-10-5 0..................................(b[1]) ArchieBellamy[(7)]
(Peter Pritchard) *plld hrd and prom: nt fluent 2nd and 3rd: pushed along 6th: wknd next: bhd whn p.u bef 8th* **150/1**
5m 38.7s (0.10) **Going Correction** -0.375s/f (Good) **9 Ran SP% 120.3**
Speed ratings (Par 105): **84,83,82,79,76 , , ,**
CSF £3.46 TOTE £1.90: £1.10, £1.10, £7.40; EX 3.50 Trifecta £26.80.
Owner Middleham Park Racing LIX **Bred** Liam O'Byrne **Trained** Upper Lambourn, Berks
■ Stewards' Enquiry : Mr Alex Edwards two-day ban: use of whip (15 & 23 Jul)
FOCUS
The winner set his own pace in this modest event. He's rated close to his mark along with the second and fifth.

878 BETTINGGODS.COM HORSE RACING TIPS NOVICES' H'CAP HURDLE (DIV I) (12 hdls) 2m 7f
4:50 (4:53) (Class 5) (0-100,100) 4-Y-0+ **£2,599** (£763; £381; £190)

Form RPR
06-1 **1** **Tobefair**[25] 646 5-11-7 95.. TrevorWhelan 109+
(Debra Hamer) *hld up: hdwy 9th: led 2 out: wnt lft last: styd on wl* **11/4**[1]
0120 **2** 11 **Lady Of Longstone (IRE)**[14] 759 5-11-12 100........(b) TomScudamore 102
(David Pipe) *chsd ldr: nt fluent 6th: led after 9th: hdd 2 out: sn rdn: no ex last* **11/2**[2]
2P-P **3** 10 **Presence Felt (IRE)**[58] 108 7-11-11 99..........................(v) WillKennedy 91
(Jonjo O'Neill) *prom: lost pl 2nd: hdwy after 9th: rdn and wknd appr 2 out* **10/1**
-0UP **4** 9 **Driving Well (IRE)**[12] 782 7-10-9 86.............................. SeanBowen[(3)] 70
(Arthur Whiting) *chsd ldrs: rdn appr 3 out: wknd next* **7/1**
U-53 **5** 14 **Minority Interest**[22] 675 6-10-13 87..........................(bt) GavinSheehan 58
(Daniel O'Brien) *prom: rdn appr 3 out: wknd bef next* **6/1**[3]
60 **6** 14 **Diamond Reign (IRE)**[8] 824 9-10-11 85................................ LiamHeard 44
(Bob Buckler) *led: rdn and hdd after 9th: wknd after 3 out* **50/1**
00-0 **7** 56 **Bobonyx**[10] 811 5-10-0 74 oh3.. DaveCrosse
(Dai Williams) *prom: drvn along appr 7th: wknd 9th* **100/1**
P-24 **P** **Dynamic Idol (USA)**[8] 824 8-11-4 92..............................(bt) NoelFehily
(Johnny Farrelly) *hld up in tch: racd wd tl after 3rd: pushed along after 6th: wknd bef next: bhd whn p.u bef 8th* **11/2**[2]
000- **P** **Fountains Cider**[153] 3938 7-10-12 93..........................(t) DavidNoonan[(7)]
(Anthony Honeyball) *hld up: drvn along 7th: sn wknd: bhd whn p.u after next* **6/1**[3]
5m 32.5s (-6.10) **Going Correction** -0.375s/f (Good) **9 Ran SP% 110.5**
Speed ratings (Par 103): **95,91,87,84,79 74,55, ,**
CSF £17.32 CT £121.18 TOTE £4.00: £1.70, £1.80, £3.50; EX 11.20 Trifecta £53.40.
Owner Down The Quay Club **Bred** Mickley Stud **Trained** Nantycaws, Carmarthens
FOCUS
An ordinary event run in a time 6.2sec quicker than the previous novice event. The first two drew clear off the home turn. This was another big step up from the winner and the second sets the level.

879 BETTINGGODS.COM HORSE RACING TIPS NOVICES' H'CAP HURDLE (DIV II) (12 hdls) 2m 7f
5:20 (5:22) (Class 5) (0-100,100) 4-Y-0+ **£2,599** (£763; £381; £190)

Form RPR
-113 **1** **Patricktom Boru (IRE)**[27] 610 8-11-4 92................................ AdamWedge 99+
(Evan Williams) *hld up in tch: blnd 3rd: chsd ldr appr 3 out: mstke next: styd on u.p to ld towards fin* **3/1**[1]
-262 **2** 1¼ **Westerly Breeze (IRE)**[25] 646 7-11-9 100....................(b) BenPoste[(3)] 105+
(Edward Bevan) *w ldrs: led 8th: mstke 3 out: rdn flat: hdd towards fin* **4/1**[2]
P-12 **3** 23 **Tachbury**[10] 807 11-9-7 74......................................(p) AlanJohns[(7)] 57
(Tim Vaughan) *chsd ldrs: rdn after 3 out: wknd bef last* **11/2**[3]
05-0 **4** 1¼ **Stand Aside (IRE)**[45] 364 5-11-12 100..........................(p) DarylJacob 82
(Jonjo O'Neill) *hld up: hdwy 9th: rdn and wknd appr 2 out* **16/1**
2-P3 **5** 9 **Shady Glen (IRE)**[25] 646 6-10-11 85............................(p) KielanWoods 59
(Graeme McPherson) *chsd ldrs: led 5th to 8th: rdn and wknd 3 out* **7/1**
6-25 **6** 12 **Master Cardor Visa (IRE)**[32] 552 10-10-6 83..........(p) JamesBanks[(3)] 46
(Emma Baker) *hld up: bhd fr 7th* **11/1**
-124 **7** 41 **Interpleader**[19] 717 10-10-5 86..........................(tp) MrMartinMcIntyre[(7)] 12
(Sheila Lewis) *prom: nt fluent 2nd and next: rdn and wknd appr 8th* **14/1**
0 **8** 25 **Distant Sound (IRE)**[25] 646 8-11-7 95.............................. MichealNolan
(Adrian Wintle) *hld up: a in rr: wknd 8th* **50/1**
5-04 **P** **Mazurati (IRE)**[25] 646 6-11-2 97..........................(bt) MrMJPKendrick[(7)]
(Ben Case) *led to 5th: remained handy tl wknd qckly and p.u after 9th* **12/1**
0-35 **P** **Catkin Copse**[28] 597 7-10-8 87..............................(p) DanielHiskett[(5)]
(Richard Phillips) *hld up: hdwy 8th: rdn and wknd 3 out: bhd whn p.u bef last* **11/1**
5m 31.1s (-7.50) **Going Correction** -0.375s/f (Good) **10 Ran SP% 111.8**
Speed ratings (Par 103): **98,97,89,89,86 81,67,58, ,**
CSF £15.02 CT £59.87 TOTE £3.50: £1.40, £2.20, £1.50; EX 12.20 Trifecta £34.70.
Owner R W J Willcox **Bred** Mrs B M Browne **Trained** Llancarfan, Vale Of Glamorgan

FOCUS
The quickest of the three C&D races, this was run in a time 1.4sec quicker than the first division. The first two finished a long way clear. The winner was on a decent mark but this still rates a small step up, with the second to his best.

880 WORCESTER NEWS CONDITIONAL JOCKEYS' NOVICES' H'CAP HURDLE (10 hdls) 2m 4f
5:50 (5:54) (Class 4) (0-115,113) 4-Y-0+ **£3,249** (£954; £477; £238)

Form RPR
26-2 **1** **Wait A Second (IRE)**[53] 207 5-11-9 113..................(p) MauriceLinehan[(3)] 112
(Jonjo O'Neill) *a.p: chsd ldr 3 out: rdn to ld flat: styd on u.p* **4/1**[1]
464- **2** ¾ **Zephyr**[137] 4229 4-10-11 104.. LizzieKelly[(3)] 99
(Nick Williams) *chsd ldr tl led 7th: rdn and hdd flat: styd on* **4/1**[1]
33-6 **3** 1¼ **Morestead Screamer**[52] 225 6-11-6 107............................ SeanBowen 104
(Chris Gordon) *prom: lost pl after 6th: rallied appr last: r.o* **15/2**
532- **4** 13 **Bold Duke**[25] 5496 7-11-11 112.. BenPoste 99
(Edward Bevan) *hld up: plld hrd: hdwy 6th: rdn after 2 out: wknd flat* **7/1**[3]
F-P2 **5** 11 **Spring Steel (IRE)**[12] 780 6-11-9 110..........................(t) NicodeBoinville 85
(Ben Pauling) *led: nt fluent 5th: hdd 7th: rdn and wknd appr last* **4/1**[1]
005- **6** 6 **Flabello (IRE)**[107] 4814 5-10-10 103.............................. MichaelHeard[(6)] 73
(David Pipe) *hld up: hdwy after 7th: rdn and wknd 2 out* **8/1**
0-23 **7** 17 **Race To Glory (FR)**[22] 673 4-10-9 102......................(vt[1]) KieronEdgar[(3)] 54
(David Pipe) *prom: rdn after 7th: mstke 3 out: wknd bef next* **13/2**[2]
4m 49.3s (-4.20) **Going Correction** -0.375s/f (Good)
WFA 4 from 5yo+ 16lb **7 Ran SP% 108.7**
Speed ratings (Par 105): **93,92,92,87,82 80,73**
CSF £18.47 TOTE £3.00: £2.00, £2.00; EX 12.90 Trifecta £168.80.
Owner John P McManus **Bred** Mrs Noreen McManus **Trained** Cheltenham, Gloucs
FOCUS
This modest event was run at a steady gallop, and all seven were still in with a shout turning for home. This was a step up from the winner in headgear, with the second to his mark.
T/Plt: £14.00 to a £1stake. Pool of £63555.09 - 3305.23 winning tickets. T/Qpdt: £2.80 to a £1 stake. Pool of £5357.75 - 1368.65 winning tickets. **Colin Roberts**

866 PERTH (R-H)
Thursday, July 2

OFFICIAL GOING: Good (good to soft in places)
Wind: Breezy, half against Weather: Overcast

881 STRONGBOW DARK FRUIT MAIDEN HURDLE (STRONGBOW DARK FRUIT SCOTTISH HURDLE RACE SERIES QUALIFIER) (10 hdls) 2m 4f 35y
2:30 (2:30) (Class 5) 4-Y-0+ **£3,165** (£935; £467; £234; £117)

Form RPR
22-2 **1** **Jalingo (IRE)**[17] 745 4-10-11 123.................................... AidanColeman 114+
(John Ferguson) *t.k.h early: cl up: led 2 out: sn drvn and edgd lft: clr last: eased towards fin* **10/11**[1]
10- **2** 3 **Dancing Meadows (IRE)**[49] 306 5-10-7 0.............................. NoelFehily 105+
(Gordon Elliott, Ire) *hld up in rr: stdy hdwy gng wl bef 2 out: shkn up and chsd (clr) wnr last: kpt on: nvr nr to chal* **7/2**[2]
0-52 **3** 9 **Welcome Ben (IRE)**[25] 656 6-10-11 110............................ TonyKelly[(3)] 105
(Jackie Stephen) *pressed ldr: nt fluent 4 out: rdn to ld bef 2 out: hdd 2 out: outpcd fr last* **7/1**[3]
5-6 **4** ½ **Drumhart (IRE)**[25] 656 6-11-0 108.................................. PaddyBrennan 103
(C A McBratney, Ire) *trckd ldrs: drvn along bef 2 out: sn outpcd* **12/1**
3-45 **5** 11 **So Satisfied**[25] 656 4-10-11 110...................................... BrianHughes 94
(Sandy Thomson) *hld up bhd ldng gp: blnd 4 out: sn rdn along: wknd bef 2 out* **9/1**
/5-5 **6** 13 **Naburn**[39] 452 7-11-0 0.. BrianHarding 81
(Andrew Wilson) *led tl rdn and hdd bef 2 out: sn btn* **33/1**
552- **7** 5 **Lucky Buttons (IRE)**[34] 540 7-10-4 110.......................... CraigNichol[(3)] 71
(S R B Crawford, Ire) *prom on outside tl rdn and wknd after 3 out* **33/1**
8 2¼ **Drop A Gear (IRE)**[59] 5-11-0 0...................................... PeterBuchanan 74
(Lucinda Russell) *hld up on ins: drvn along after 4 out: struggling fr next* **25/1**
9 32 **Tish Hall (IRE)** 5-10-4 0...................................... GrahamWatters[(3)] 39
(S R B Crawford, Ire) *bhd: nt fluent 6th: struggling fr next: t.o* **40/1**
0-00 **P** **Ripasso**[25] 656 6-11-0 0.. HenryBrooke
(Jean McGregor) *nt fluent in rr: p.u and dismntd bef 5th* **250/1**
5m 0.9s (-1.10) **Going Correction** +0.175s/f (Yiel)
WFA 4 from 5yo+ 16lb **10 Ran SP% 117.4**
Speed ratings (Par 103): **109,107,104,104,99 94,92,91,78,**
CSF £4.13 TOTE £1.70: £1.10, £1.70, £1.80; EX 5.20 Trifecta £19.40.
Owner Bloomfields **Bred** Gerrardstown House Stud **Trained** Cowlinge, Suffolk
FOCUS
Rail movement increased race 1 by 66yds, race 2 by 54yds, race 3by 115yds, race 4 by 39yds, races 5 & 6 by 79yds and race 7 by 82yds. Some starts have been moved at this track following remeasuring, so some races will not have speed figures until there is sufficient data to calculate updated median times. There was 4mm of rain overnight and the going was changed to good, good to soft in places. This was a weakish maiden hurdle in which the winner had the best credentials. It's rated around the winner, and the third to fifth. The second is improving towards her bumper mark.

882 FROM SKY TO SCOOP NOVICES' H'CAP HURDLE (8 hdls) 2m 47y
3:00 (3:00) (Class 4) (0-105,103) 3-Y-0+ **£3,165** (£935; £467; £234; £117)

Form RPR
-262 **1** **The Absent Mare**[6] 843 7-10-0 77..............................(t) RichardJohnson 81+
(Gordon Elliott, Ire) *hld up: hdwy to chse ldrs bef 2 out: jst led whn lft 3 l clr last: rdn out* **9/4**[1]
2 8 **Canova (IRE)**[18] 735 4-11-2 98..................................(t) KevinSexton[(3)] 95+
(Gordon Elliott, Ire) *chsd ldrs: effrt and rdn bef 2 out: one pce whn lft 3 l 2nd and checked by faller last: no imp* **28/1**
3-01 **3** 1¼ **Roll Of Thunder**[11] 805 6-10-8 90 7ex.............................. MissCWalton[(5)] 85
(James Walton) *led to bef 2 out: rdn and one pce whn lft 5 l 3rd last* **7/1**
40-3 **4** 1¼ **Shine A Diamond (IRE)**[19] 728 7-10-9 89..........(tp) GrahamWatters[(3)] 83
(Lucinda Russell) *prom: rdn and outpcd bef 2 out: plugged on fr last: no imp* **12/1**
534- **5** 8 **Dalstontosiloth (IRE)**[203] 3026 7-10-9 86........................(t) BrianHughes 75
(Barry Murtagh) *hld up in tch: mstke 6th: rdn and wknd bef 2 out* **8/1**
5-4P **6** 9 **Diamond Gesture (IRE)**[21] 694 7-10-2 82.............. ConorShoemark[(3)] 61
(Fergal O'Brien) *hld up: rdn after 3 out: wknd bef next* **8/1**
-F23 **F** **Quest Magic (IRE)**[25] 658 9-11-7 103..................(p) JonathonBewley[(5)] 105
(George Bewley) *chsd ldr: led bef 2 out: jst hdd whn fell last* **11/2**[3]

23-3 **U** **Lockedoutaheaven (IRE)**[11] 799 4-11-6 **102**.....(t) JonathanEngland(3)
(Maurice Barnes) *in tch: swvd: sprawled bdly and uns rdr appr first* **9/2**[2]

3m 59.58s (239.58)
WFA 4 from 6yo+ 15lb **8** Ran **SP% 110.2**
CSF £49.41 CT £356.52 TOTE £2.60: £1.20, £7.20, £1.60; EX 46.90 Trifecta £167.60.
Owner T Howley Jnr/Oliver Jack Murphy **Bred** Beautiful Losers Bloodstock & R Hobson **Trained** Longwood, Co Meath

FOCUS
Not a strong novice handicap hurdle but the pace was sound. The winner is rated in line with her recent Cartmel run, with the second, third and faller to their marks.

883 BOOK YOUR CHRISTMAS PARTY AT PERTH RACECOURSE NOVICES' H'CAP HURDLE (12 hdls) 2m 7f 207y
3:30 (3:30) (Class 4) (0-105,105) 4-Y-0+ **£3,165** (£935; £467; £234; £117)

Form RPR

004- **1** **Broughtons Bandit**[18] 735 8-10-12 **91**........................ RichardJohnson 99+
(Gordon Elliott, Ire) *hld up in midfield: hdwy bef 3 out: led bef next: rdn and hung rt between last 2: kpt on strly fr last* **7/2**[2]

6244 **2** *3* **Solway Prince**[25] 661 6-11-1 **94**........................ BrianHarding 97+
(Lisa Harrison) *hld up: hdwy and ev ch bef 2 out: rdn and kpt on fr last: nt pce of wnr* **9/1**

0-35 **3** *2* **Jackofhearts**[25] 658 7-9-11 **79**........................ JonathanEngland(3) 80
(Jean McGregor) *hld up: rdn and hdwy bef 2 out: kpt on fr last: nrst fin* **22/1**

64-2 **4** *3/4* **Poppies Milan (IRE)**[11] 805 6-10-10 **92**..............(t) TonyKelly(3) 93
(Rebecca Menzies) *hld up: rdn and hdwy bef 2 out: kpt on same pce fr last* **15/2**

-1F1 **5** *6* **Just Awake**[1] 871 8-10-12 **98**..............(t) StevenFox(7) 95+
(Sandy Thomson) *hld up: mstke 6th: effrt and hdwy on outside after 3 out: rdn and no imp fr next* **10/3**[1]

62-5 **6** *2* **Maraweh (IRE)**[25] 661 5-10-10 **92**..............(v) DerekFox(3) 85
(Lucinda Russell) *led: rdn clr after 3 out: hdd bef next: hung rt and wknd bef last* **9/1**

P-45 **7** *8* **New Youmzain (FR)**[35] 522 6-10-0 **84**........................ GrantCockburn(5) 71
(Lucy Normile) *t.k.h: sn trcking ldrs: rdn after 3 out: wknd bef next* **6/1**[3]

4P0- **8** *22* **Presented (IRE)**[80] 5313 8-11-4 **104**........................ RyanDay(7) 70
(Lisa Harrison) *trckd ldrs: rdn after 3 out: wknd bef next* **10/1**

/PP- **P** **Dr Paddy (IRE)**[118] 4598 8-9-11 **81**..............(p) StephenMulqueen(5)
(Lucy Normile) *chsd ldrs: drvn and lost pl after 5th: lost tch and p.u after next* **80/1**

0/3- **P** **Master Butcher (IRE)**[70] 5494 8-11-5 **105**........................ MrKitAlexander(7)
(N W Alexander) *prom: rdn after 3 out: wknd and p.u after next* **12/1**

54P- **P** **Son Of Feyan (IRE)**[22] 5516 4-10-9 **92**........................ DougieCostello
(Lucy Normile) *t.k.h: sn pressing ldr: rdn and wknd after 3 out: p.u bef next* **80/1**

6m 7.0s (2.00) **Going Correction** +0.175s/f (Yiel)
WFA 4 from 5yo+ 17lb **11** Ran **SP% 115.0**
Speed ratings (Par 105): **103,102,101,101,99 98,95,88, ,**
CSF £33.84 CT £595.41 TOTE £4.20: £1.40, £4.00, £5.90; EX 32.40 Trifecta £661.80.
Owner Twenty Syndicate **Bred** M E Broughton **Trained** Longwood, Co Meath

FOCUS
Not strong form, but the pace was sound. The winner was on a good mark and is rated close to his best, with the second posting a small pb. The third is rated to his mark.

884 BLACKHILLS CLINIC H'CAP CHASE (12 fncs) 2m
4:00 (4:00) (Class 4) (0-110,110) 4-Y-0 **£3,798** (£1,122; £561; £280; £140)

Form RPR

4052 **1** **Bunclody**[1] 870 10-10-4 **95**..............(p) MrZBaker(7) 108+
(Barry Brennan) *mde all: rdn bef 2 out: styd on wl run-in* **9/4**[1]

3-15 **2** *4 1/2* **Honourable Gent**[47] 338 7-11-9 **110**........................ CraigNichol(3) 119
(Rose Dobbin) *trckd ldrs: wnt 2nd bef 4 out: effrt whn hit 2 out: kpt on same pce fr last* **9/4**[1]

4-21 **3** *9* **Moonlight Maggie**[30] 588 8-10-6 **90**..............(t) PaddyBrennan 90
(Tom George) *prom: nt fluent 4 out: rdn after next: outpcd fr 2 out* **7/2**[2]

34-0 **4** *4* **Wot A Shot (IRE)**[25] 658 6-11-0 **98**........................ PeterBuchanan 95
(C A McBratney, Ire) *hld up: hdwy after 4 out: effrt and rdn next: outpcd fr 2 out* **8/1**[3]

-034 **5** *10* **Saddle Pack (IRE)**[19] 728 12-9-7 **84** oh14........................ JamieHamilton(7) 73
(James Walton) *w ldr to 1/2-way: cl up: rdn after 4 out: wknd bef next* **12/1**

6-R0 **6** *31* **The Village (IRE)**[39] 455 6-9-11 **84** oh18........................ DerekFox(3) 50
(Lucinda Russell) *s.v.s: hdwy after 3rd: rdn and struggling 5 out: sn btn: t.o* **16/1**

3m 58.1s (238.10) **6** Ran **SP% 108.4**
CSF £7.48 TOTE £4.30: £1.50, £2.00; EX 9.70 Trifecta £33.80.
Owner F J Brennan **Bred** Mrs A M O'Sullivan **Trained** Upper Lambourn, Berks
■ Stewards' Enquiry : Derek Fox four-day ban; improper riding (18th-20th, 23rd July)

FOCUS
The winner was a 120+ performer at his best and is rated up a bit on the previous day's hurdles run, with the second to his mark. There's a case for rating this a little higher.

885 DIAGEO H'CAP CHASE (15 fncs) 2m 4f 20y
4:30 (4:30) (Class 4) (0-120,118) 4-Y-0 **£6,330** (£1,870; £935; £468; £234)

Form RPR

/122 **1** **Russian Regent (IRE)**[25] 657 11-11-12 **118**........................ RichardJohnson 135+
(Gordon Elliott, Ire) *hld up: stdy hdwy 1/2-way: led 5 out: shkn up and drew clr fr 3 out: easily* **1/1**[1]

131- **2** *22* **Peachey Moment (USA)**[275] 1677 10-11-2 **108**........................ NoelFehily 100
(Nicky Richards) *prom: pushed along after 4 out: rallied to chse (clr) wnr 2 out: sn no imp* **3/1**[2]

5P-P **3** *6* **Strobe**[15] 315 11-10-3 **95**..............(p) DougieCostello 80
(Lucy Normile) *prom: hit and outpcd 9th: struggling fr next: plugged on fr 2 out: no ch w first two* **16/1**

6-15 **4** *1 1/4* **Kai Broon (IRE)**[47] 331 8-11-3 **112**..............(p) GrahamWatters(3) 98
(Lucinda Russell) *led to 5 out: rallied and ev ch next: rdn and wknd fr 2 out* **6/1**[3]

5-43 **5** *14* **Badged**[25] 659 6-10-13 **110**..............(p) GrantCockburn(5) 81
(Lucy Normile) *hld up: hdwy and prom 1/2-way: rdn and wknd bef 3 out* **14/1**

/31- **P** **Humphrey Bee (IRE)**[365] 832 12-11-4 **110**..............(p) BrianHarding
(N W Alexander) *t.k.h: trckd ldrs: outpcd whn nt fluent 8th: lost tch and p.u bef 10th* **10/1**

5m 6.4s (1.40) **Going Correction** +0.225s/f (Yiel) **6** Ran **SP% 110.9**
Speed ratings (Par 105): **106,97,94,94,88**
CSF £4.56 CT £23.50 TOTE £1.70: £1.10, £2.40; EX 3.40 Trifecta £27.00.
Owner James J Reilly **Bred** Sean Breen **Trained** Longwood, Co Meath

FOCUS
A reasonable pace to this handicap chase. This seemed a step up from the winner, but it's not a race to be confident about.

886 VISIT SCONE PALACE CONDITIONAL JOCKEYS' H'CAP HURDLE (10 hdls) 2m 4f 35y
5:00 (5:00) (Class 4) (0-120,120) 4-Y-0 **£3,798** (£1,122; £561; £280; £140)

Form RPR

1 **Bank Bonus**[47] 344 6-10-8 **105**........................ KevinSexton(3) 116+
(Gordon Elliott, Ire) *hld up: smooth hdwy bef 2 out: led between last 2: gng clr whn flattened last: kpt on strly* **6/4**[1]

21-1 **2** *3 1/4* **Solway Dandy**[49] 302 8-11-6 **120**........................ RyanDay(6) 124
(Lisa Harrison) *t.k.h: hld up: hdwy bef 2 out: chsd wnr between last 2: kpt on run-in: no imp* **9/2**[3]

20P- **3** *4* **Spitz (FR)**[110] 4761 7-10-12 **106**........................ CraigNichol 106
(Rose Dobbin) *hld up in tch: pushed along after 3 out: kpt on same pce fr next* **15/2**

0-33 **4** *hd* **Urban Kode (IRE)**[25] 661 7-10-0 **97**..............(v) DerekFox(3) 97
(Lucinda Russell) *led at stdy pce: hdd 4 out: rallied and ev ch tl outpcd fr 2 out* **9/1**

1 **5** *1 1/2* **Topper Thornton (IRE)**[25] 661 6-11-7 **115**........................ GrahamWatters 113
(C A McBratney, Ire) *cl up: led 4 out to between last 2: sn wknd* **3/1**[2]

/24- **6** *12* **Karingo**[236] 2340 8-10-0 **94**........................ GrantCockburn 80
(Lucy Normile) *prom: rdn along 3 out: wknd bef next* **22/1**

453/ **7** *4* **Andhaar**[52] 1340 9-11-1 **109**........................ StephenMulqueen 91
(N W Alexander) *prom: drvn along after 3 out: struggling bef next: sn btn* **50/1**

5m 18.4s (16.40) **Going Correction** +0.175s/f (Yiel) **7** Ran **SP% 111.3**
Speed ratings (Par 105): **74,72,71,71,70 65,64**
CSF £8.45 CT £35.00 TOTE £2.10: £1.40, £2.00; EX 7.90 Trifecta £50.90.
Owner John F O'Shea **Bred** The Queen **Trained** Longwood, Co Meath

FOCUS
A slow pace to this handicap hurdle and it developed into a spint up the straight. The winner was well in and the second seemed to step up, with the third to fifth close to their marks.

887 SCOTTISH GAME FAIR STARTING TOMORROW STANDARD OPEN NATIONAL HUNT FLAT RACE 2m 47y
5:30 (5:30) (Class 5) 4-6-Y-0 **£2,053** (£598; £299)

Form RPR

1 **1** **Waterlord**[33] 558 4-11-7 0........................ AidanColeman 135+
(John Ferguson) *hld up: smooth hdwy to chse clr ldr 1/2-way: led gng wl over 3f out: sn drew clr on bit: v easily* **1/3**[1]

2 *36* **Touch A Million (IRE)**[12] 797 5-11-2 0..............(bt) RichardJohnson 91
(Gordon Elliott, Ire) *led and sn clr: rdn along and hdd over 3f out: no ch w v easy wnr: fin lame* **4/1**[2]

5 **3** *4 1/2* **King Of Fashion (IRE)**[19] 732 5-10-13 0........................ GrahamWatters(3) 87
(Ian Duncan) *chsd ldrs: drvn and outpcd over 5f out: rallied over 3f out: sn no imp* **50/1**

4 *48* **Emdale Ruby (IRE)** 5-10-9 0........................ BrianHarding 37
(Sarah Dawson, Ire) *chsd clr ldr to 1/2-way: sn struggling: nvr on terms after: t.o* **33/1**

5 *39* **Miss High Time (IRE)** 4-10-2 0........................ GrantCockburn(5)
(Lucinda Russell) *hld up in tch: drvn and struggling over 5f out: sn btn: t.o* **10/1**[3]

3m 54.4s (234.40) **5** Ran **SP% 109.0**
CSF £1.94 TOTE £1.30: £1.10, £1.50; EX 2.00 Trifecta £9.50.
Owner Bloomfields **Bred** Rabbah Bloodstock Limited **Trained** Cowlinge, Suffolk

FOCUS
An uncompetitive bumper run at a fair gallop and a very interesting winner. He was building on his easy debut win and looks smart. This could be rated higher through the second, but it's rated through the third for the time being.

888 - 890a (Foreign Racing) - See Raceform Interactive

823
NEWTON ABBOT (L-H)
Friday, July 3

OFFICIAL GOING: Good to soft (soft in places; 6.1)
Wind: mild breeze half against Weather: sunny with cloudy periods Rails: Bends divided. Rail moved outwards, effecting distances; Races 1,2&5, adds 28yds Race 3, adds 47yds Race 4, adds 30yds Race 6, adds 15yds Race 7, adds 52yds.

891 AT THE RACES SKY 415 JUVENILE HURDLE (8 hdls) 2m 167y
2:10 (2:10) (Class 4) 3-Y-0 **£3,898** (£1,144; £572; £286)

Form RPR

1 **Doubly Clever (IRE)**[28] 3-10-10 0........................ NoelFehily 98+
(Michael Blake) *racd keenly: trckd ldr: led 2 out: edgd lft: clr last: easily* **4/1**[2]

2 **2** *5* **Mojawiz**[27] 636 3-10-10 0........................ AidanColeman 91
(John Ferguson) *racd keenly: led: hdd 2 out: sn rdn and hld: kpt on same pce* **8/15**[1]

C **3** *10* **Auld Fyffee (IRE)**[22] 690 3-10-3 0........................ JamesDavies 73
(Tom Gretton) *trckd ldrs: rdn to chse ldng pair after 3 out: kpt on same pce fr next* **33/1**

4 *26* **Londonia**[51] 3-10-10 0........................ KielanWoods 54
(Graeme McPherson) *trckd ldrs: nt fluent 2nd: rdn after 5th: wknd bef 2 out* **11/1**

C **5** *9* **Ventura Castle**[22] 690 3-10-10 0........................ BrendanPowell 45
(Jamie Snowden) *trckd ldr fr 2nd: struggling 5th: wknd after 3 out* **6/1**[3]

4m 5.6s (-0.10) **Going Correction** -0.225s/f (Good) **5** Ran **SP% 110.8**
Speed ratings (Par 102): **91,88,83,71,67**
CSF £6.96 TOTE £4.90: £2.40, £1.10; EX 7.30 Trifecta £58.10.
Owner Francise Tieman **Bred** Gigginstown House Stud **Trained** Trowbridge, Wilts

FOCUS
The course endured a lot of rainfall the previous day (28mm) and the going was on the easy side of good. This was a typically moderate juvenile hurdle for the time of year and only two mattered off the home turn. The time was slow compared with other races over the trip.

892 JAN HINES 60TH BIRTHDAY NOVICES' H'CAP HURDLE (8 hdls) 2m 167y
2:40 (2:41) (Class 5) (0-100,100) 3-Y-0+ **£3,422** (£997; £499)

Form RPR

000- **1** **Honkytonktennessee (IRE)**[97] 5025 6-11-12 **100**.............. DaveCrosse 110+
(Hugo Froud) *mde all: nt fluent 5th: 9 l clr 3 out: rdn bef next: 5 l clr and in command whn awkward last: rdn out* **16/1**

54-1 **2** *3* **At First Light**[9] 835 6-11-11 **99**.. NicodeBoinville 104
(David Weston) *j.rt: chsd clr ldrs: pushed along after 5th: wnt 9 l 2nd 3 out: sn rdn: 5 l down next: styd on but a being hld* **10/11**[1]

02-2 **3** *17* **Spin Cast**[29] 616 7-11-5 **100**..(t) ConorSmith(7) 89
(Alan Jones) *hld up: rdn after 5th: no on terms w ldng pair but wnt wl hld 3rd after 3 out: nvr any danger* **7/2**[2]

3-50 **4** *13* **Maid Of Tuscany (IRE)**[22] 694 4-11-7 **97**....................(p) NoelFehily 72
(Neil Mulholland) *hld up in tch: rdn after 5th: sn btn: wnt modest 4th bef last* **15/2**[3]

6-56 **5** *7* **Catcharose (IRE)**[24] 673 5-10-6 **87**..............................(t) LewisGordon(7) 58
(Jennifer Mason) *chsd wnr clr of remainder tl 5th: wkng in btn 4th whn blnd 2 out* **16/1**

0P-0 **6** *2 ½* **Love The Leader (IRE)**[51] 281 7-11-11 **99**........................ AlainCawley 68
(Johnny Farrelly) *a towards rr* **20/1**

4P-U **7** *13* **Dance**[10] 828 6-11-5 **93**.. JamesDavies 50
(Rod Millman) *in tch: nt fluent 2nd: rdn after 3 out: sn wknd* **14/1**

4m 1.9s (-3.80) **Going Correction** -0.225s/f (Good)
WFA 4 from 5yo+ 15lb **7** Ran SP% **109.6**
Speed ratings (Par 103): **99,97,89,83,80 79,72**
CSF £29.88 CT £60.57 TOTE £16.60: £5.20, £1.30; EX 48.10 Trifecta £120.10.
Owner Ms Gill Langford **Bred** Ardobrien Stud Ltd **Trained** Bruton, Somerset

FOCUS
An uncompetitive novice handicap and suspect form. The winner is rated in line with the best of his bumper form.

893 NEWTONABBOTRACE ON TWITTER MAIDEN HURDLE (10 hdls) 2m 5f 122y
3:10 (3:11) (Class 4) 4-Y-0+ **£3,249** (£954; £477; £238)

Form RPR

6-32 **1** **Bells Of Ailsworth (IRE)**[27] 647 5-11-0 111........................ RichardJohnson 107+
(Tim Vaughan) *led: rdn and hdd appr 2 out: regained narrow ld whn nt fluent last: styd on wl to assert run-in* **5/2**[1]

04U **2** *2* **Only Gorgeous (IRE)**[7] 837 6-10-11 0........................ LucyGardner(3) 106+
(Sue Gardner) *trckd wnr: led appr 2 out: rdn between last 2: hdd last: no ex* **11/2**

4/4- **3** *14* **Marlpit Oak**[26] 10-10-0 0.. MrDSansom(7) 87
(Seamus Mullins) *mid-div: hdwy after 6th: trckd ldrs after next: rdn to chse ldng pair appr 2 out: styd on same pce* **50/1**

4 *32* **Almagest**[252] 7-11-0 0.. TomO'Brien 63
(Robert Stephens) *trckd ldrs: rdn after 3 out: sn wknd: t.o* **7/2**[3]

50-3 **5** *10* **Dear Darling**[27] 648 5-10-7 102..(bt) BrendanPowell 47
(Colin Tizzard) *trckd ldrs: rdn after 3 out: sn wknd: t.o* **3/1**[2]

6 *3 ½* **I'llhavealook (IRE)**[48] 10-10-11 0........................ RobertWilliams(3) 50
(Katie Stephens) *a towards rr: t.o 7th* **22/1**

00 **P** **Merry Mast (USA)**[9] 834 6-10-7 0.. MrGTreacy(7)
(Paul Henderson) *mid-div: lost tch 6th: hit next: sn p.u* **100/1**

3/0- **P** **Too Trigger Happy**[194] 3217 6-10-4 0........................(p) WayneKavanagh(3)
(Dr Jeremy Naylor) *t.k.h in midfield early: hit 4th: in rr whn wnt rt 5th: tailing off whn p.u after next* **66/1**

/62- **P** **Quick N' Easy (IRE)**[131] 4384 5-11-0 0........................[1] MichealNolan
(Sue Gardner) *a towards rr: t.o whn p.u bef 7th* **22/1**

P **Intercooler Turbo (IRE)**[54] 6-10-9 0........................ BridgetAndrews(5)
(Dan Skelton) *in tch: trckd ldrs 5th: rdn after 7th: wknd next: t.o whn p.u bef 2 out* **8/1**

5m 12.1s (-8.10) **Going Correction** -0.225s/f (Good) **10** Ran SP% **115.4**
Speed ratings (Par 105): **105,104,99,87,83 82,,,,**
CSF £15.94 TOTE £3.00: £1.20, £2.20, £7.10; EX 15.30 Trifecta £366.70.
Owner S Grys & M O'Boyle **Bred** Sean Gorman **Trained** Aberthin, Vale of Glamorgan

FOCUS
A weak maiden, run at an average gallop and the first pair dominated from the third-last. The first two are rated similar to recent runs.

894 SIMON BISHOP LAST CHANCE NOVICES' H'CAP CHASE (16 fncs) 2m 4f 216y
3:45 (3:45) (Class 3) (0-125,125) 5-Y-0+ **£6,498** (£1,908; £954; £477)

Form RPR

/4-4 **1** **Mortlestown (IRE)**[29] 610 7-10-6 105........................(p) AndrewTinkler 124+
(Martin Keighley) *j.w: trckd ldrs: led after 4 out: rdn clr after 3 out: eased run-in* **8/1**[3]

42-4 **2** *13* **Lemony Bay**[38] 492 6-11-0 **113**........................ LeightonAspell 117
(Oliver Sherwood) *hld up in tch: rdn in 4th after 12th: wnt 3rd after 4 out: styd on same pce fr next: wnt 2nd run-in: no ch w wnr* **14/1**

3-31 **3** *¾* **More Buck's (IRE)**[37] 509 5-11-3 **116**........................(t) SamTwiston-Davies 120
(Paul Nicholls) *disp ld: clr ldr 3rd: rdn and hdd after 4 out: hld fr after next: no ex whn lost 2nd run-in* **11/4**[2]

25-1 **4** *11* **Gone Too Far**[22] 691 7-11-12 **125**........................ WayneHutchinson 121
(Alan King) *hld up bhd ldrs: rdn into 3rd after 12th tl after 4 out: wknd between last 2* **11/10**[1]

P-32 **5** *4 ½* **My Legal Lady**[10] 825 10-11-5 **118**........................(vt) TomScudamore 107
(Stuart Howe) *chsd ldrs tl outpcd 11th: nvr bk on terms: wknd between last 2* **12/1**

P6P/ **P** **Knight Pass (IRE)**[76] 9-11-3 **116**........................ RichardJohnson
(Jimmy Frost) *disp ld tl 3rd: chsd ldr tl 7th: lost tch after 9th: p.u bef next* **8/1**[3]

5m 13.0s (-8.40) **Going Correction** -0.225s/f (Good) **6** Ran SP% **110.9**
Speed ratings: **107,102,101,97,95**
CSF £84.89 TOTE £9.50: £3.10, £5.60; EX 98.50 Trifecta £539.90.
Owner M Boothright **Bred** Jan Kennedy **Trained** Condicote, Gloucs

FOCUS
An ordinary novice handicap which fell apart on the far side. The winner was up a stone on the best of his hurdle figures.

895 NEWTONABBOTRACING.COM H'CAP HURDLE (8 hdls) 2m 167y
4:20 (4:20) (Class 4) (0-115,115) 3-Y-0+ **£3,898** (£1,144; £572; £286)

Form RPR

3P-1 **1** **Tea In Transvaal (IRE)**[31] 591 4-11-6 **111**........................ PaulMoloney 124+
(Evan Williams) *nvr that fluent: kpt wd most of way: prom in chsng gp: disp 2nd 5th: led 2 out: clr last: comf* **9/1**

30-5 **2** *9* **Royal Skies (IRE)**[12] 810 5-11-12 **115**........................(vt[1]) AidanColeman 120+
(John Ferguson) *set decent pce: clr ldr after 2nd: nt fluent 4th: reduced advantage 3 out: rdn and hdd whn awkward 2 out: sn no ex* **5/1**[2]

-122 **3** *6* **Billy My Boy**[21] 718 6-10-13 **105**........................(p) GilesHawkins(3) 106
(Chris Down) *chsd clr ldrs in 3rd: disp 2nd 3 out: rdn and hld in 3rd whn nt fluent 2 out: styd on same pce* **15/8**[1]

P-54 **4** *3 ½* **Absolutlyfantastic**[17] 751 8-11-9 **112**........................(t) RichardJohnson 106
(Martin Hill) *disp ld tl after 2nd: chsd ldr tl 3 out: sn rdn: wknd bef next* **7/1**

20-5 **5** *5* **Avel Vor (IRE)**[22] 701 4-11-2 **114**........................(p) CiaranGethings(7) 101
(Philip Hobbs) *in tch in chsng gp: hdwy 5th: rdn to chse ldrs after 3 out: nvr threatened: wknd bef next* **9/1**

300- **6** *7* **Sweet World**[70] 5508 11-10-9 **101**........................ RobertWilliams(3) 84
(Bernard Llewellyn) *a towards rr* **25/1**

030- **7** *5* **Sinndar's Man**[72] 5465 4-11-10 **115**........................ NoelFehily 91
(Michael Blake) *hld up: struggling after 4th: nvr a factor* **11/2**[3]

-345 **8** *1 ½* **Mondlicht (USA)**[17] 751 5-11-0 **110**........................(p) MrAlexFerguson(7) 87
(John Ferguson) *struggling 3rd: a towards rr* **10/1**

4U-0 **9** *25* **Tenby Jewel (IRE)**[21] 718 10-10-7 **96**........................(t) TomCannon 50
(Mark Gillard) *in tch in chsng gp tl struggling appr 5th: wknd bef 3 out: t.o* **28/1**

3m 58.1s (-7.60) **Going Correction** -0.225s/f (Good)
WFA 4 from 5yo+ 15lb **9** Ran SP% **115.7**
Speed ratings (Par 105): **108,103,100,99,96 93,91,90,78**
CSF £54.14 CT £121.24 TOTE £6.20: £1.90, £2.10, £1.30; EX 34.70 Trifecta £132.70.
Owner M J Haines **Bred** Summerville Bloodstock **Trained** Llancarfan, Vale Of Glamorgan

FOCUS
A modest handicap, run at a decent gallop thanks to front-running Royal Skies. A big step up from the winner, who is entitled to be this good on the best of her Flat form.

896 FRANCIS CLARK H'CAP CHASE (13 fncs) 2m 75y
4:55 (4:56) (Class 4) (0-120,119) 4-Y-0+ **£3,898** (£1,144; £572)

Form RPR

-232 **1** **Easily Pleased (IRE)**[24] 669 9-11-12 **119**........................ RichardJohnson 125
(Martin Hill) *led 2nd: rchd for 3rd: strly chal after 4 out: narrowly hdd sn after last: rallied cl home: all out to win on nod* **1/1**[1]

-641 **2** *nse* **Red Skipper (IRE)**[21] 713 10-11-0 **107**........................ DaveCrosse 114
(John O'Shea) *trckd wnr fr 2nd: rdn for str chal fr after 4 out: tk v narrow advantage sn after last: lost on nod* **4/1**[3]

1-02 **3** *57* **Third Act (IRE)**[30] 596 6-11-3 **110**........................(bt) DarylJacob 77
(Colin Tizzard) *led tl 2nd: sn chsng ldng pair: nt travelling or that fluent fr 6th: btn 4 out: t.o* **6/4**[2]

3m 59.9s (-6.60) **Going Correction** -0.225s/f (Good) **3** Ran SP% **110.0**
Speed ratings (Par 105): **107,106,78**
CSF £4.65 TOTE £2.00; EX 6.00 Trifecta £3.90.
Owner Roger Oliver & Claire Harding **Bred** Mrs Eleanor Hadden **Trained** Littlehempston, Devon

FOCUS
This was a moderate little handicap and only two ever really counted. The winner is rated to his mark with the second improving in line with his hurdle mark.

897 HELEN HAMBLY HAPPY 40TH BIRTHDAY H'CAP HURDLE (12 hdls) 3m 2f 105y
5:30 (5:30) (Class 4) (0-120,118) 4-Y-0+ **£3,898** (£1,144; £572; £286)

Form RPR

PUF- **1** **Decimus (IRE)**[210] 2921 8-11-9 **118**........................ MattGriffiths(3) 122+
(Jeremy Scott) *hld up in last trio: rousted along after 2nd: hdwy after 8th: trckd ldrs next: led after 3 out: rdn and strly pressed fr 2 out where wnt rt: nt fluent last: hld on wl: all out* **15/2**

-031 **2** *½* **Horace Hazel**[21] 716 6-10-13 **105**........................ SamTwiston-Davies 108
(Anthony Honeyball) *cl up on outer: prom 8th: rdn for str chal appr 2 out where bmpd: ev ch last: no ex nring fin* **3/1**[1]

5-01 **3** *4* **The Kings Assassin (IRE)**[30] 599 7-10-8 **100**........................(p) TomCannon 98
(Chris Gordon) *trckd ldrs: rdn after 3 out: wnt 3rd bef next: styd on same pce* **9/2**[3]

3-64 **4** *16* **Finish The Story (IRE)**[21] 716 9-10-10 **102**........................(bt) NoelFehily 86
(Johnny Farrelly) *pressed ldr: led after 8th tl after 3 out: sn rdn and outpcd: regained 4th run-in* **4/1**[2]

6-22 **5** *1 ½* **Rior (IRE)**[21] 716 8-10-13 **105**........................ RichardJohnson 87
(Paul Henderson) *hld up in last trio: hdwy 9th: rdn to chse ldrs after 3 out: wknd between last 2* **4/1**[2]

0P-P **6** *2 ¾* **Life Of A Luso (IRE)**[40] 448 11-10-4 **96**........................(t) TomO'Brien 76
(Paul Henderson) *hld up in last trio: sme prog after 9th: rdn after 3 out: wknd between last 2* **20/1**

PP-4 **7** *11* **Primo Capitano (IRE)**[29] 614 7-11-6 **112**........................(p) AndrewTinkler 82
(Martin Keighley) *trckd ldrs: rdn after 8th: wknd 3 out* **8/1**

5/P- **P** **Getmeouthedoldrums**[403] 10-10-3 **95**........................(t) KielanWoods
(Mark Wall) *led tl after 8th: sn rdn: wknd after next: t.o whn p.u after 3 out* **33/1**

-66F **P** **Vandross (IRE)**[16] 755 5-11-9 **115**........................(b) TrevorWhelan
(Neil King) *m in snatches: chsd ldrs: hit 4th: lost pl after 8th: bhd fr next: t.o whn p.u after 3 out* **18/1**

6m 31.8s (-9.20) **Going Correction** -0.225s/f (Good) **9** Ran SP% **119.0**
Speed ratings (Par 105): **105,104,103,98,98 97,94,,**
CSF £31.99 CT £116.42 TOTE £11.50: £2.50, £1.50, £1.90; EX 41.30 Trifecta £234.30.
Owner The Ten 2 One Gang **Bred** Mrs Sheila Kelleher **Trained** Brompton Regis, Somerset

FOCUS
A moderate staying handicap, run a steady gallop. Straightforward form.
T/Plt: £114.90 to a £1 stake. Pool: £59,063.73 - 375.24 winning units. T/Qpdt: £66.20 to a £1 stake. Pool: £4308.62 - 48.10 winning units. **Tim Mitchell**

898 - 911a (Foreign Racing) - See Raceform Interactive

777

MARKET RASEN (R-H)
Sunday, July 5

OFFICIAL GOING: Good (8.5)
Wind: fine and sunny Weather: light 1/2 behind Rails: Rail out 20yds on Wood Bend and 30yds on Stands bend. Races 1, 2, 3 & 7 increased by about 210yds and races 4, 5, &6 by about 300yds.

912 DON NOBLE BETTING NOVICES' HURDLE (10 hdls) 2m 2f 140y
2:15 (2:15) (Class 4) 4-Y-0+ **£3,249** (£954; £477; £238)

Form RPR

2 **1** **Nabucco**[23] 706 6-10-12 0........................ AidanColeman 124+
(John Ferguson) *trckd ldng pair: t.k.h: upsides appr 2 out: led on bit 2 out: pushed clr appr last: easily* **4/9**[1]

1-33 **2** *6* **Dire Straits (IRE)**[41] 467 4-11-2 117........................(bt) TrevorWhelan 116
(Neil King) *chsd ldr: drvn to ld narrowly appr 2 out: sn hdd: kpt on: no ch w wnr* **16/1**

2 **3** *1 ¼* **Tiger Twenty Two**[30] 620 4-10-9 0........................ AndrewTinkler 107
(Brian Rothwell) *t.k.h: trckd ldng trio: effrt 3 out: handy 3rd appr next: kpt on same pce* **5/1**[2]

P-P **4** *8* **Daydreamer**[26] 263 4-10-9 0........................ WayneHutchinson 100
(Alan King) *t.k.h in rr: hdwy 3 out: modest 4th next: kpt on* **33/1**

0/3 5 14 **Mullinavat (IRE)**[22] 732 6-10-12 0 (t) RichardJohnson 95
(Jennie Candlish) *led: drvn 3 out: hdd and wkng 5th whn mstke 2 out* 13/2[3]

6 41 **Beedee**[36] 5-10-12 0 MichaelByrne 54
(Tim Vaughan) *nt fluent in rr: bhd fr 6th: t.o 3 out* 50/1

P6P/ 7 6 **Monzino (USA)**[4] 5190 7-10-7 0 JoeCornwall(5) 48
(Michael Chapman) *in rr: pushed along 5th: bhd next: t.o 3 out* 200/1

4m 43.8s (4.40) **Going Correction** +0.475s/f (Soft) 7 Ran SP% 110.5
Speed ratings (Par 105): **109,106,105,102,96 79,76**
CSF £8.37 TOTE £1.30: £1.02, £4.70; EX 6.00 Trifecta £11.00.
Owner Bloomfields **Bred** Darley **Trained** Cowlinge, Suffolk

FOCUS
Rail out 20yds on Wood Bend and 30yds on Stands bend. Races 1, 2, 3 & 7 increased by about 210yds and races 4, 5, & 6 by about 300yds. An uncompetitive novice hurdle, rated around the penalised runner-up. The easy winner is rated in line with his debut run.

913 DONNOBLE.CO.UK BEGINNERS' CHASE (14 fncs) 2m 3f 34y
2:45 (2:46) (Class 4) 4-Y-0+ **£3,898** (£1,144; £572; £286)

Form RPR

0-23 1 **Enchanted Garden**[29] 635 7-11-10 0 (b[1]) BrianHughes 112+
(Malcolm Jefferson) *mde all: j.lft: mstke 2 out: drvn clr last: rdn out* 11/8[1]

311- 2 6 **Dino Mite**[74] 5477 4-10-0 0 MichealNolan 81
(Jamie Snowden) *chsd wnr fr 3rd: drvn 11th: briefly upsides appr next: 4 l down and wl hld whn hit last* 11/8[1]

-330 3 ½ **Volcanic Jack (IRE)**[7] 850 7-11-5 0 JoeCornwall(5) 103
(Michael Chapman) *chsd ldng pair: pushed along 8th: kpt on fr 3 out: styd on run-in* 50/1

4P/2 4 8 **Amber Flush**[14] 808 6-11-3 0 TrevorWhelan 89
(Martin Smith) *chsd ldrs: wnt 3rd briefly bef 3 out: wknd 2 out* 9/2[2]

5-46 5 45 **King's Realm (IRE)**[20] 747 8-11-7 0 JonathanEngland(3) 55
(Tina Jackson) *a last: pushed along 9th: lost pl and hit next: t.o 10th* 28/1[3]

4m 52.4s (-13.30) **Going Correction** -0.725s/f (Firm)
WFA 4 from 6yo+ 2lb 5 Ran SP% 107.8
Speed ratings (Par 105): **99,96,96,92,73**
CSF £3.59 TOTE £2.30: £1.40, £1.10; EX 3.70 Trifecta £27.50.
Owner Mrs D W Davenport **Bred** Mrs S Camacho **Trained** Norton, N Yorks

FOCUS
A moderate beginners' chase. There's a case for rating the form a lot higher but the third is a worry.

914 MANNY BERNSTEIN H'CAP CHASE (12 fncs) 2m 1f 43y
3:20 (3:20) (Class 4) (0-105,102) 4-Y-0+ **£3,898** (£1,144; £572; £286)

Form RPR

3U-4 1 **Mac's Grey (IRE)**[42] 446 8-10-0 **76** oh3 (t) WillKennedy 86
(Ian Williams) *chsd ldrs: led 9th: hdd next: upsides last: led post* 9/2[3]

P-0U 2 nse **Paddy Mulligan (IRE)**[16] 777 6-11-5 **95** AidanColeman 106
(John Ferguson) *chsd ldrs: led narrowly 3 out: hdd and no ex post* 7/1

2-U3 3 3¼ **Ivans Back (IRE)**[30] 623 10-11-0 **90** AdamWedge 98
(Nick Kent) *t.k.h towards rr: nt fluent 2nd: hdwy to trck ldrs 9th: upsides next and last: kpt on same pce last 150yds* 3/1[1]

023- 4 11 **Jackthejourneyman (IRE)**[87] 5244 6-11-12 **102** (t[1]) RichardJohnson 103
(Tom Gretton) *led tl after 2nd: chsd ldrs: 4th and rdn whn mstke 3 out: one pce* 10/3[2]

1000 5 12 **Accessallareas (IRE)**[12] 828 10-11-10 **100** RobertDunne 86
(Sarah-Jayne Davies) *in rr: chsd ldrs 3rd: led appr 8th: hdd next: lost pl bef 3 out* 25/1

5/2- 6 9 **Manger Hanagment (IRE)**[414] 339 10-11-3 **100** MrZBaker(7) 78
(Barry Brennan) *chsd ldrs: drvn 5th: lost pl next: sn bhd* 10/1

3F-6 7 18 **The Omen**[14] 806 9-10-12 **95** AlanJohns(7) 57
(Tim Vaughan) *w ldrs: led after 2nd: hdd: lost pl and blnd 8th: sn bhd* 7/1

P5-P 8 24 **Tri Nations (UAE)**[33] 588 10-10-4 **83** (tp) JonathanEngland(3) 23
(Harriet Bethell) *in rr: modest 5th and drvn 9th: lost pl bef next: sn bhd: t.o* 14/1

4m 21.0s (-14.00) **Going Correction** -0.725s/f (Firm) 8 Ran SP% 110.9
Speed ratings (Par 105): **103,102,101,96,90 86,77,66**
CSF £33.27 CT £103.18 TOTE £4.80: £1.80, £1.60, £1.50; EX 40.30 Trifecta £157.50.
Owner Macable Partnership **Bred** Arctic Tack Stud **Trained** Portway, Worcs

FOCUS
The principals jumped the last as one in this ordinary handicap and the third sets the level. A pb from the winner.

915 DON NOBLE BETTING H'CAP CHASE (14 fncs) 2m 5f 89y
3:50 (3:51) (Class 3) (0-135,137) 4-Y-0+ **£6,498** (£1,908; £954; £477)

Form RPR

2-14 1 **Perfect Timing**[32] 598 7-10-11 **120** (b) NoelFehily 129+
(Neil Mulholland) *mde all: jnd 3 out: fnd ex and forged clr last 150yds* 6/4[1]

332- 2 6 **Tindaro (FR)**[43] 1248 8-11-12 **135** (t) RichieMcLernon 140
(Paul Webber) *chsd ldng pair: 2nd sn after 11th: upsides next: upsides whn hit last: fnd little and fdd last 100yds* 15/2[3]

3314 3 2½ **Master Of The Hall (IRE)**[14] 800 11-10-1 **117** JamieBargary(7) 119
(Micky Hammond) *hld up in rr: hdwy 9th: handy 3rd appr 3 out: sn drvn kpt on one pce* 13/8[2]

43-5 4 10 **Tregaro (FR)**[16] 781 9-10-0 **109** oh6 (t) BrianHughes 100
(Mike Sowersby) *hld up in rr: hdwy to trck ldrs 8th: lost pl appr 3 out* 11/1

60-0 5 46 **Skint**[29] 645 9-11-0 **123** (p) GavinSheehan 68
(Ali Stronge) *mid-div: pushed along 7th: lost pl next: sn bhd: t.o 11th* 12/1

14-0 P **Tayarat (IRE)**[9] 839 10-9-9 **109** oh6 JoeCornwall(5)
(Michael Chapman) *j.lft: chsd wnr: lost pl sn after 11th: eased and poor 5th whn p.u bef next: lame* 25/1

5m 30.6s (-15.40) **Going Correction** -0.725s/f (Firm) 6 Ran SP% 109.7
Speed ratings (Par 107): **100,97,96,92,75**
CSF £12.15 CT £17.61 TOTE £2.20: £1.10, £3.00; EX 8.50 Trifecta £18.10.
Owner Hanham Boys Racing Partnership **Bred** Mrs J L Egan **Trained** Limpley Stoke, Wilts

FOCUS
A modest handicap. The winner is rated back to form.

916 MANNYBERNSTEIN.CO.UK H'CAP HURDLE (12 hdls) 2m 7f 16y
4:25 (4:25) (Class 2) (0-150,142) 4-Y-0+ **£9,747** (£2,862; £1,431; £715)

Form RPR

P-32 1 **Aalim**[16] 779 5-10-12 **128** (p) AidanColeman 133+
(John Ferguson) *hld up: hdwy to trck ldrs 6th: nt clr run appr 2 out: led last: drvn out* 9/2[2]

2-41 2 1¼ **Aviator (GER)**[30] 621 7-10-6 **122** JackQuinlan 125
(James Eustace) *chsd ldrs 5th: led appr 2 out and j.rt: hdd: awkward last: sddle slipped and rdr lost iron: kpt on towards fin* 10/1

130- 3 9 **Teak (IRE)**[15] 5358 8-10-11 **127** (p) RichardJohnson 123
(Ian Williams) *in rr: drvn and sme hdwy 3 out: 3rd sn after last: kpt on same pce* 7/4[1]

1-63 4 ½ **Dawn Commander (GER)**[26] 681 8-11-8 **138** BrendanPowell 131
(Stuart Edmunds) *chsd ldrs 5th: kpt on same pce appr 2 out* 12/1

254- 5 1¾ **Kelvingrove (IRE)**[127] 4482 5-10-10 **129** (p) MauriceLinehan(3) 122
(Jonjo O'Neill) *chsd ldrs: drvn 3 out: led briefly bef next: hung lft and one pce fr 2 out* 15/2[3]

1-03 6 3½ **Phare Isle (IRE)**[30] 625 10-10-2 **125** (tp) MrMJPKendrick(7) 115
(Ben Case) *chsd ldrs 5th: cl 2nd appr 2 out: fdd last 75yds* 10/1

1PP- 7 20 **Pantxoa (FR)**[92] 5140 8-11-5 **135** WayneHutchinson 106
(Alan King) *led: hdd bef 2 out: sn lost pl snd bhd* 25/1

/F-3 8 65 **Terminal (FR)**[37] 532 8-11-2 **132** NoelFehily 44
(David Dennis) *chsd ldrs: lost pl 5th: sn bhd: t.o whn blnd 3 out: virtually p.u: eventually completed* 9/1

0-05 P **First Fandango**[26] 681 8-11-5 **135** (t) MichaelByrne
(Tim Vaughan) *chsd ldrs: lost pl bef 6th: bhd whn p.u after 7th* 50/1

1-01 P **Tanerko Emery (FR)**[38] 527 9-11-5 **142** (t) MissBHampson(7)
(Andy Turnell) *in rr: hdwy to chse ldrs whn hit 8th: lost pl and p.u sn after 3 out: lame* 16/1

5m 54.8s (4.30) **Going Correction** +0.475s/f (Soft) 10 Ran SP% 113.9
Speed ratings (Par 109): **111,110,107,107,106 105,98,75, ,**
CSF £47.30 CT £106.30 TOTE £6.40: £1.80, £2.70, £1.10; EX 36.40 Trifecta £134.20.
Owner Bloomfields **Bred** Darley **Trained** Cowlinge, Suffolk

FOCUS
A fair handicap hurdle. Small pbs from the first two.

917 TOM HALLIDAY MEMORIAL CONDITIONAL JOCKEYS' H'CAP HURDLE (10 hdls) 2m 4f 139y
5:00 (5:02) (Class 4) (0-120,120) 4-Y-0+ **£3,249** (£954; £477; £238)

Form RPR

-121 1 **Thinger Licht (FR)**[53] 280 6-9-11 **94** oh1 BridgetAndrews(3) 101+
(Dan Skelton) *chsd ldrs: led narrowly 2 out: forged clr run-in* 5/4[1]

-220 2 3½ **Baths Well (IRE)**[17] 775 5-10-11 **113** (p) HarrisonBeswick(8) 116
(Ben Pauling) *gave problems gng to s: led: j. slowly 1st: narrowly hdd 2 out: styd on same pce run-in* 14/1

1252 3 3½ **Cut The Corner (IRE)**[24] 701 7-11-9 **120** ChrisWard(3) 119
(Dr Richard Newland) *t.k.h in rr: hdwy 5th: cl 3rd 2 out: hung bdly lft: kpt on fnl 100yds* 9/4[2]

1-56 4 14 **Kyles Faith (IRE)**[18] 758 7-9-10 **98** (p) ArchieBellamy(8) 84
(Martin Keighley) *w ldr: reminders 8th: sn outpcd* 18/1

2P-5 5 ¾ **Factor Fifty (IRE)**[30] 622 6-11-9 **120** AdamNicol(3) 106
(Philip Kirby) *chsd ldrs: nt fluent and lost pl 6th: sn bhd* 11/1

430/ 6 16 **Kings Bayonet**[29] 5128 8-11-1 **117** WilliamFeatherstone(8) 88
(Alan King) *hld up in rr: t.k.h: hdwy 5th: cl 2nd 3 out: wknd j.lft next: sn eased* 7/1[3]

5-14 7 8 **Lucky Landing (IRE)**[23] 709 9-11-0 **118** JakeHolliday(10) 82
(Tony Coyle) *in rr: bhd fr 5th* 16/1

U 8 23 **Fresh By Nature (IRE)**[29] 635 8-11-2 **110** JonathanEngland 53
(Harriet Bethell) *prom: pushed along 3rd: sn bhd: t.o 3 out* 33/1

5m 23.9s (15.10) **Going Correction** +0.475s/f (Soft) 8 Ran SP% 116.8
Speed ratings (Par 105): **90,88,87,82,81 75,72,63**
CSF £19.65 CT £38.21 TOTE £2.10: £1.20, £3.00, £1.20; EX 23.30 Trifecta £74.90.
Owner Carl Hodgson **Bred** M Jacques Chapet & Mme Anne Dupont **Trained** Alcester, Warwicks

FOCUS
A modest handicap for conditional riders. The first three are rated pretty much to their marks.

918 DON NOBLE BETTING LADY AMATEUR RIDERS' H'CAP HURDLE (8 hdls) 2m 148y
5:30 (5:32) (Class 5) (0-100,100) 3-Y-0+ **£2,183** (£677; £338; £169)

Form RPR

3/54 1 **Cornish Beau (IRE)**[24] 695 8-10-2 **76** (p) MissCWalton 94+
(Dr Richard Newland) *chsd ldrs: led after 3 out: wnt clr between last 2: v readily* 3/1[1]

5-40 2 12 **Imperial Plan (IRE)**[33] 588 5-11-4 **99** (p) MissPFuller(7) 105
(Jamie Snowden) *led: hdd after 3 out: kpt on same pce between last 2* 16/1

0-55 3 6 **Ardesia (IRE)**[14] 805 11-9-7 **74** oh5 (p) MissRMcDonald(7) 74
(Tina Jackson) *chsd ldr: one pce appr 2 out: lft modest 3rd sn after 2 out: hit last* 10/1

-233 4 ¾ **Oneofapear (IRE)**[16] 777 9-11-7 **100** (p) MissKBryson(5) 100
(Mike Sowersby) *chsd ldrs: drvn 3 out: one pce: lft modest 4th sn after 2 out* 11/2[3]

133- 5 ½ **Speed Check (IRE)**[248] 2158 8-10-12 **93** MissAGalliers-Pratt(7) 90
(Don Cantillon) *hld up towards rr: hdwy 4th: drvn next: outpcd 3 out: kpt on between last 2* 6/1

2-66 6 2½ **Hawk Gold (IRE)**[26] 675 11-9-8 **75** oh2 ow1 MissTWorsley(7) 70
(Michelle Bryant) *mid-div: hdwy 3rd: outpcd 3 out: no threat after* 16/1

3-P0 7 6 **Simplified**[16] 777 12-9-9 **74** oh10 MissBeckySmith(5) 64
(Michael Chapman) *in rr: bhd fr 4th* 80/1

4124 8 1 **Heading To First**[9] 811 8-11-5 **96** (v) MissAEStirling(3) 85
(Jim Best) *hld up in rr: hdwy 5th: chsng ldrs whn hit next: sn lost pl* 11/2[3]

36/0 9 6 **Louis Ludwig (IRE)**[12] 828 10-10-4 **85** MissRPLeyshon(7) 69
(Tim Vaughan) *in rr: sme hdwy 5th: sn lost pl and bhd* 25/1

U-P0 P **Midnight Thomas**[44] 435 6-10-2 **79** (t) MissCVHart(3)
(Martin Keighley) *stdd s: nt fluent in last: bhd 4th: hdwy next: modestr 3rd 2 out: sn p.u: lame* 9/2[2]

4m 15.5s (8.80) **Going Correction** +0.475s/f (Soft) 10 Ran SP% 114.2
Speed ratings (Par 103): **98,92,89,89,88 87,84,84,81,**
CSF £47.79 CT £425.52 TOTE £4.00: £1.70, £3.30, £3.50; EX 59.40 Trifecta £749.70.
Owner The London Foot & Ankle Centre **Bred** Thomas Heatrick **Trained**

FOCUS
A typically moderate handicap for amateur riders. There's probably more to come from the winner.

T/Plt: £3.80 to a £1 stake. Pool: £78,274.44 - 14,745.06 winning tickets. T/Qpdt: £3.20 to a £1 stake. Pool: £7,185.30 - 1,653.77 winning tickets. **Walter Glynn**

919 - 925a (Foreign Racing) - See Raceform Interactive

873 WORCESTER (L-H)

Monday, July 6

OFFICIAL GOING: Good to firm (good in places) changing to good after race 1 (2.20)

Wind: light breeze Weather: overcast; 18 degrees

926 LATIMER COURT H'CAP CHASE (16 fncs) 2m 7f
2:20 (2:20) (Class 5) (0-100,100) 4-Y-0+ **£2,599** (£763; £381; £190)

Form RPR

PP/P **1** **Foxes Bridge**[17] 782 7-11-3 **91**.....................(v[1]) GavinSheehan 110+
(Nick Mitchell) *bhd: disputing last and hrd drvn after 8th: hit next: gd prog after 12th: 3rd bef next: chal u.p and j.lft 2 out: wnt cl 2nd at last: led fnl 75yds: all out* **33/1**

1131 **2** *nk* **Patricktom Boru (IRE)**[5] 879 8-11-4 **92**..................... AdamWedge 110+
(Evan Williams) *trckd ldrs: effrt gng wl in 2nd after 12th: sn contesting ld: slt advantage last: hrd drvn and battled on v gamely tl hdd 75yds out: jst hld* **11/8**[1]

F-52 **3** *15* **Kilcascan**[25] 698 11-10-9 **86**.....................(p) BenPoste[(3)] 91
(Rosemary Gasson) *ldng trio: led 8th: jnd 13th: stl upsides ldr tl hit last and wknd: eased fnl 100yds* **10/1**[3]

-P34 **4** *29* **Dr Dreamy (IRE)**[21] 741 8-10-0 **74** oh1.....................(t) TrevorWhelan 51
(Claire Dyson) *towards rr: prog in 4th after 12th: rdn and lost tch w ldng trio next: wnt remote 4th after last* **50/1**

P-32 **5** *1 1/2* **The Wee Midget**[33] 599 10-10-4 **85**.....................(b) ConorSmith[(7)] 61
(Arthur Whiting) *sn prom: pressed ldr 8th tl 12th: drvn and dropped out qckly bef next: t.o* **11/1**

-314 **6** *3* **Herecomesthetruth (IRE)**[27] 674 13-11-10 **98**..................... TomCannon 71
(Chris Gordon) *cl up tl 3rd and rdn home turn: racing idly after: 15 l 4th 2 out: t.o* **20/1**

1U6- **7** *6* **Always Bold (IRE)**[110] 4855 10-11-12 **100**.....................(p) AndrewTinkler 68
(Martin Keighley) *prom tl rdn and dropped himself out bef 9th: lost tch and blnd 11th: sn t.o* **16/1**

-025 **8** *2* **Noble Witness (IRE)**[21] 743 12-11-7 **95**.....................(p) AdamPogson 61
(Charles Pogson) *a towards rr: t.o whn hmpd 13th* **25/1**

1240 **9** *1* **Interpleader**[5] 879 10-11-3 **91**.....................(tp) HenryBrooke 56
(Sheila Lewis) *midfield: hit 10th: rdn 12th: sn fdd: t.o next* **20/1**

U-02 **10** *21* **Royaume Bleu (FR)**[36] 567 10-10-0 **77**.....................(v) JamesBanks[(3)] 23
(Alex Hales) *t.k.h to post and in r: led tl hdd and mstke 8th: nt run on fr next: t.o bef 13th* **10/1**[3]

0/00 **P** **Silver Story**[18] 771 12-11-11 **99**.....................(t) MichaelByrne
(Tim Vaughan) *a wl in rr: hit 9th: t.o and p.u after 12th* **33/1**

3532 **U** **Breezy Kin (IRE)**[21] 741 7-10-9 **90**..................... MikeyHamill[(7)]
(Sean Curran) *mstke 3rd: rn in snatches: wnt 3rd at 9th: dropped to rr 12th: t.o whn uns rdr next* **6/1**[2]

P-2P **P** **Mrs Jordan (IRE)**[15] 803 7-11-12 **100**.....................(t) PaulMoloney
(Sophie Leech) *chsd ldrs: blnd 6th: rdn next: nt travelling in last after: t.o 10th: p.u after 12th* **25/1**

5m 49.9s **Going Correction** +0.05s/f (Yiel) **13 Ran SP% 113.8**
Speed ratings (Par 103): **102,101,96,86,86 85,82,82,81,74 , ,**
CSF £74.27 CT £522.11 TOTE £37.80: £5.30, £1.30, £2.60; EX 109.20 Trifecta £2797.30 Part won.
Owner Glanvilles Stud Partners **Bred** Wriggle Valley Thoroughbreds **Trained** Piddletrenthide, Dorset

FOCUS
All starts have been moved at this track following remeasuring, so there will be no speed figures here until there is sufficient data to calculate updated median times. A total of 6mm of rain the previous day helped the going and the rail was dolled out on both bends adding approximately 81yds to races 1, 2 & 5, and 51yds to races 3, 4, 6 & 7. This moderate staying handicap was run at a fair gallop and they got sorted out from the fifth-last. The winner has been rated in line with his old hurdle mark.

927 BARCHESTER HEALTHCARE H'CAP CHASE (13 fncs) 2m 4f
2:50 (2:51) (Class 3) (0-140,130) 4-Y-0+ **£6,330** (£1,870; £935; £468; £234)

Form RPR

5F0- **1** **Valleyofmilan (IRE)**[215] 2885 8-10-11 **122**..................... JamesCowley[(7)] 129+
(Donald McCain) *pressed ldr: hit 6th: led after 9th: jumping sltly rt after: rdn bef 2 out: hit last: hung on wl flat* **6/1**[3]

6/66 **2** *1 1/2* **Mr Moss (IRE)**[32] 611 10-11-4 **122**..................... PaulMoloney 127
(Evan Williams) *hld up: hit 8th: outpcd briefly after next: rallied 3 out: disp 2nd at last: rdn and no imp flat* **8/1**

25-3 **3** *3 3/4* **Falcarragh (IRE)**[24] 709 8-11-12 **130**..................... RichardJohnson 132
(Tim Vaughan) *mstke 5th: hld up last tl effrt 1/2-way: wnt 3rd and looked to be gng wl after 9th: rdn 3 out: 2nd and ev ch whn nt fluent next: fnd little and wl hld fr last* **11/4**[2]

P0-4 **4** *11* **Foundation Man (IRE)**[30] 642 8-11-7 **125**.....................(tp) WillKennedy 118
(Jonjo O'Neill) *led: reminder after 8th: drvn and hdd after next: dropped out tamely* **9/4**[1]

1U22 **5** *1* **Marie Des Anges (FR)**[27] 672 7-10-8 **119**.....................(t) DavidNoonan[(7)] 109
(Anthony Honeyball) *trckd ldrs: bustled up fr 7th: rdn 10th: btn next* **11/4**[2]

5m 7.7s (3.10) **Going Correction** +0.05s/f (Yiel) **5 Ran SP% 109.5**
Speed ratings (Par 107): **95,94,92,88,88**
CSF £42.50 TOTE £7.90: £3.30, £5.10; EX 53.20 Trifecta £130.20.
Owner Tim & Miranda Johnson **Bred** Kenneth William Quinn **Trained** Cholmondeley, Cheshire

FOCUS
A tight handicap, rated around the third. The winner has been rated back to the level of last summer's Bangor win.

928 WORCESTERSHIRE ASSOCIATION OF CARERS STANDARD OPEN NATIONAL HUNT FLAT RACE 2m
3:20 (3:20) (Class 6) 4-6-Y-0 **£1,559** (£457; £228; £114)

Form RPR

4- **1** **Morthanalegend**[105] 4969 6-11-0 0..................... BrendanPowell 109+
(Brendan Powell) *trckd ldrs: wnt 2nd over 3f out: rdn after: led 300yds out: plugged on steadily fnl f* **12/1**

2 *3/4* **Dusk Till Dawn (IRE)**[176] 6-11-0 0..................... [1] TomScudamore 108
(David Pipe) *gd-sized: led at fair gallop: rdn over 3f out: hdd fnl 300yds: racd awkwardly and a jst hld after* **5/4**[1]

2 **3** *14* **Klaazia (FR)**[60] 159 4-10-5 0..................... AndrewTinkler 86+
(Jeremy Gask) *towards rr: rdn and outpcd 4f out: wnt poor 3rd ins fnl f* **4/1**[2]

4 *1* **Oneforthenure (IRE)**[73] 6-10-7 0..................... DarylJacob 87
(Richard Woollacott) *pressed ldr tl rdn over 3f out: dropped out grad and lost poor 3rd ins fnl f* **20/1**

5 *7* **Lovefromabove (IRE)**[90] 4-10-0 0..................... BridgetAndrews[(5)] 79
(Dan Skelton) *small: pressed ldrs tl stmbld bef home turn: sn rdn: n.d after: t.o* **4/1**[2]

6- **6** *28* **Menace**[182] 3541 4-10-9 0..................... JamesBanks[(3)] 61
(Noel Williams) *midfield: bmpd bef home turn and sn dropped rt out: t.o over 2f out* **50/1**

7 *47* **Mixit** 6-11-0 0..................... RichardJohnson 20
(Henry Daly) *t.k.h in last: drvn 6f out: bdly t.o fnl 3f* **7/1**[3]

R **Gentle Nature** 4-10-12 0..................... RhysFlint
(John Flint) *unruly leaving s: veered lft: crashed into ser's rostrum and fell* **66/1**

3m 50.7s (5.70) **Going Correction** +0.05s/f (Yiel)
WFA 4 from 6yo 2lb **8 Ran SP% 112.9**
Speed ratings: **87,86,79,79,75 61,38,**
CSF £26.94 TOTE £15.80: £3.90, £1.10, £1.70; EX 38.80 Trifecta £153.10.
Owner R H Kerswell **Bred** R H Kerswell **Trained** Upper Lambourn, Berks

FOCUS
The going was changed to good all over after the second, and riders were claiming it rode easier than that description. This was a modest bumper, run at an average gallop and the first pair dominated from the furlong marker.

929 HIGH HABBERLEY HOUSE CARE HOME (S) HURDLE (8 hdls) 2m
3:50 (3:50) (Class 5) 4-7-Y-0 **£2,599** (£763; £381; £190)

Form RPR

4531 **1** **Jayo Time (IRE)**[19] 755 6-10-7 110.....................(b) ChrisWard[(5)] 107
(Dr Richard Newland) *racd freely towards rr: wnt 3rd at 1/2-way: 2nd gng wl home turn: led 3 out: rdn 3 l clr last: hrd drvn after: plld out a little more whn almost jnd fnl 100yds* **1/3**[1]

F3-5 **2** *shd* **Regal One (IRE)**[13] 828 7-10-7 96..................... JakeHodson[(5)] 107
(David Bridgwater) *settled towards rr: effrt 5th: wnt 3rd home turn and 2nd 2 out: rdn and no imp under wnr idled flat: rnged upsides 100yds out but jst hld cl home* **6/1**[3]

-366 **3** *16* **Short Takes (USA)**[12] 835 7-10-12 105.....................(b) NoelFehily 93
(Donald McCain) *led tl 1st: pressed ldr tl led after 5th: sn rdn: hdd next: wknd 2 out and 9 l 3rd at last* **11/2**[2]

30-3 **4** *20* **Carrowbeg (IRE)**[32] 125 7-10-12 84.....................(bt) AidanColeman 75
(Lawney Hill) *chsd ldrs tl lost tch tamely u.p after 5th: nrly 20 l 5th at next* **25/1**

-P50 **5** *9* **Southern Cross**[12] 832 4-10-3 78..................... DaveCrosse 58
(Dai Williams) *bhd: reminders 4th: lost tch qckly after next: racing awkwardly fr 3 out* **100/1**

50P **6** *nk* **Defiant Dazzler (IRE)**[12] 834 6-10-5 0.....................(p) MissLBrooke[(7)] 66
(Lady Susan Brooke) *towards rr: rdn 5th: wnt 3rd briefly bef home turn: dropped out qckly 3 out: t.o* **150/1**

/0-0 **7** *93* **Smiley Miley (IRE)**[8] 853 7-9-12 0..................... MissJodieHughes[(7)]
(Dai Burchell) *fly j. s: plld hrd and led at 1st: hdd after 5th and slowed rapidly u.p: sn bdly t.o: blnd 3 out* **150/1**

3m 55.5s (4.90) **Going Correction** +0.05s/f (Yiel)
WFA 4 from 6yo+ 15lb **7 Ran SP% 110.8**
Speed ratings: **89,88,80,70,66 66,19**
CSF £2.76 TOTE £1.40: £1.10, £1.90; EX 3.10 Trifecta £4.10.
Owner Paul Jenkins **Bred** E J P Kane **Trained** Claines, Worcs

FOCUS
A typically weak seller. The winner has been rated 7lb off the best of his recent figures.

930 HOLLYFIELDS CARE HOME NOVICES' HURDLE (10 hdls) 2m 4f
4:20 (4:21) (Class 4) 4-Y-0+ **£3,249** (£954; £477; £238)

Form RPR

4-12 **1** **Gioia Di Vita**[27] 671 5-11-5 116..................... WillKennedy 126+
(Dr Richard Newland) *pressed ldr: slt ld 3 out tl drew 3 l clr w ears pricked last: rdn out whn in command flat* **11/8**[1]

33-2 **2** *7* **Cochinillo (IRE)**[27] 680 6-10-12 0..................... DarylJacob 112
(Ben Case) *pressed ldng pair: rdn and ev ch whn mstke 2 out: wnt 2nd after last and plugged on but no match for wnr* **3/1**[3]

044 **3** *1 1/4* **Royal Battalion**[27] 671 4-10-9 0..................... JamieMoore 108
(Gary Moore) *settled towards rr: effrt after 7th: 3 l 4th home turn: drvn 2 out: wnt 2nd briefly by wnr at last: no ex fnl 100yds* **10/1**

201- **4** *3/4* **She's Late**[24] 5496 5-11-5 125..................... NoelFehily 117
(Jonjo O'Neill) *led at mod pce tl jst hdd 3 out: sn rdn: ev ch of wl hld 2nd at last: plugged on* **9/4**[2]

610 **5** *29* **To Begin**[27] 671 4-11-2 0.....................(t) GavinSheehan 88
(Charlie Mann) *midfield: struggling whn mstke 7th and rdn: no ch after* **16/1**

6P-6 **6** *nk* **Snippetydoodah**[27] 671 7-10-5 0..................... TomO'Brien 77
(Michael Roberts) *t.k.h in midfield: rdn and dropped out qckly after 7th* **66/1**

U0 **7** *11* **Tundridge**[21] 745 6-10-12 0.....................(p) NicodeBoinville 74
(John Spearing) *t.k.h and pressed ldrs: mstkes 5th and 6th and rdn: lost tch bef 3 out: t.o* **66/1**

P5 **8** *73* **Nyetimber (USA)**[20] 749 9-10-12 0..................... MarkGrant 8
(Sean Curran) *nt fluent in last pair: lost tch 6th: bdly t.o after next* **100/1**

5m 1.7s (8.20) **Going Correction** +0.05s/f (Yiel)
WFA 4 from 5yo+ 16lb **8 Ran SP% 116.8**
Speed ratings (Par 105): **85,82,81,81,69 69,65,36**
CSF £6.26 TOTE £3.70: £1.20, £1.10, £2.10; EX 6.90 Trifecta £29.00.
Owner Mark Albon & Chris Stedman **Bred** Hyphen Bloodstock **Trained** Claines, Worcs

FOCUS
A modest novice hurdle, run at an ordinary gallop. The winner has been rated in line with his Fontwell run.

931 LATIMER COURT CARE HOME H'CAP HURDLE (8 hdls) 2m
4:50 (4:50) (Class 4) (0-120,120) 3-Y-0+ **£3,249** (£954; £477; £238)

Form RPR

-352 **1** **Hawdyerwheesht**[12] 835 7-11-2 **110**.....................(tp) NoelFehily 123+
(David Dennis) *trckd ldrs: nt fluent 3rd: wnt 2nd after 5th: w ldr 3 out: rdn to go 3 l clr whn hung lft bef last: kpt up to work whn in command flat* **11/2**

0-52 **2** *8* **Royal Skies (IRE)**[3] 895 5-11-5 **113**.....................(vt) AidanColeman 120
(John Ferguson) *prom: led 3rd: nt fluent 5th: gng wl whn jnd next tl hdd u.p between last two: fnd nil after and wl hld fr last* **6/4**[1]

/0-0 **3** *21* **Moveable Asset (IRE)**[27] 669 7-11-0 **115**.....................(vt) MrFTett[(7)] 103
(Henry Tett) *chsd ldrs: nt fluent 4th: rdn and outpcd next: 4th and struggling home turn: 25 l down bef last* **66/1**

0/3 **4** *8* **Mighty Leader (IRE)**[19] 754 7-10-0 **94**..................... JamesDavies 74
(Henry Oliver) *bhd: effrt to midfield but off pce whn rdn 5th: sn wl bhd: snatched remote 4th* **7/2**[2]

/6-1 5 3 1/4 **Little Pop**18 [776] 7-11-5 **113**........................(t) SamTwiston-Davies 91
(Nigel Twiston-Davies) *racd freely in ld: hdd 3rd: nt fluent 4th: rdn and lost 2nd after 5th: 8 l and 3rd and wkng next: lost remote 3rd bef last* **9/2**3

-P00 6 26 **Osgood**27 [669] 8-9-11 **101**........................ GeorgeGorman(10) 55
(Gary Moore) *t.k.h early: towards rr: rdn 1/2-way: struggling after: t.o 3 out* **50/1**

-056 7 33 **Hi Tide (IRE)**15 [810] 11-11-2 **110**........................(p) BrendanPowell 34
(J R Jenkins) *last pair: shkn up 3rd: nvr travelling: bdly t.o 3 out* **16/1**

-505 8 19 **Ho Lee Moses (IRE)**12 [832] 5-10-8 **102**........................ PaulMoloney 9
(Evan Williams) *bhd: lost tch 5th: bdly t.o next* **20/1**

5P-P P **Life And Soul (IRE)**30 [643] 8-11-5 **120**........................(p) JamesCowley(7)
(Donald McCain) *pressed ldr tl bef 3rd: dropped out rapidly: t.o and p.u 5th* **33/1**

3m 48.3s (-2.30) **Going Correction** +0.05s/f (Yiel) **9 Ran SP% 112.8**
Speed ratings (Par 105): **107,103,92,88,86 73,57,47,**
CSF £13.95 CT £478.08 TOTE £5.90: £1.90, £1.10, £7.40; EX 17.60 Trifecta £573.80.
Owner Favourites Racing Ltd **Bred** Baldernock Bloodstock Ltd **Trained** Hanley Swan, Worcestershire

FOCUS
The first pair came right away in this run-of-the-mill handicap. A pb from the winner, with the third in line with his 2014 mark.

932 WWW.BARCHESTER.COM MAIDEN HURDLE (8 hdls) 2m
5:20 (5:20) (Class 5) 4-Y-0+ **£2,599** (£763; £381; £190)

Form RPR

2 1 **Ennistown**37 [554] 5-11-0 0........................ AidanColeman 122+
(John Ferguson) *cl up and gng strly: delayed effrt tl unleashed to ld last: sn dashed clr: hrd hld fnl 100yds* **5/4**1

3-64 2 12 **Newton Geronimo**12 [832] 6-11-0 0........................ NicodeBoinville 107+
(Ben Pauling) *t.k.h in rr: effrt on outside fr 4th: disp 5th home turn: 5 l fr ldr at last: drvn and kpt on wl after to snatch 2nd but wnr in a different league: game effrt* **14/1**

3 3 nk **Fauve (IRE)**25 [702] 4-10-12 0........................ RichieMcLernon 102
(Paul Webber) *led at slow pce: shkn up 3 out: hdd next and rdn: no ex fr last and jst lost wl btn 2nd* **6/1**3

3-22 4 nk **Canicallyouback**32 [613] 7-11-0 121........................ PaulMoloney 104
(Evan Williams) *pressed ldr: rdn and outpcd bef 2 out: tried to rally last: kpt on steadily at same pce flat* **5/2**2

2-55 5 5 **Tricky (IRE)**25 [703] 6-11-0 0........................ RichardJohnson 99
(Philip Hobbs) *settled towards rr: stdy prog 4th: chal on inner 3 out: led next: hanging bdly lft and difficult to control bef last where hdd: kpt hanging flat and sn wknd* **10/1**

0-6 6 10 **Mr McGuiness (IRE)**25 [702] 5-10-11 0........................ BenPoste(3) 94+
(Rosemary Gasson) *midfield: wnt prom at 5th: disp 3rd home turn: disputing 4th and fading whn blnd last: eased fnl 100yds* **50/1**

56 7 7 **Micras**8 [853] 4-10-5 0........................ MichaelByrne 73
(Tim Vaughan) *a towards rr: lost tch bef 3 out* **33/1**

6 8 1 3/4 **Crosslanes (IRE)**12 [834] 4-10-5 0........................ TomMessenger 71
(Chris Bealby) *hld up towards rr: lost tch bef 3 out* **66/1**

9 1 **Prince Of Silver** 9-10-11 0........................(t) JamesBanks(3) 79
(Andy Turnell) *tall: rngy: pressed ldrs tl rdn 4th: struggling bef 3 out* **66/1**

-0U0 10 1 1/2 **Innox Park**12 [832] 5-11-0........................(p) JamesBest 78
(Kevin Bishop) *chsd ldrs tl 1/2-way: struggling bef 3 out* **66/1**

6 11 15 **Bishop Of Ruscombe**41 [491] 4-10-12 0........................(t1) BrendanPowell 61
(Jamie Snowden) *mstke 3rd: t.o bef 3 out* **40/1**

0P/ 12 25 **Skating Home (IRE)**23 9-10-7 0........................ MrRobertHawker(7) 38
(Richard Hawker) *midfield tl rdn 3rd: t.o bef 5th* **100/1**

0 13 45 **New Decade**6 [860] 6-10-7 0........................ CiaranGethings(7)
(Milton Bradley) *plld hrd: cl up tl drvn after 5th: bdly t.o next* **200/1**

3m 50.6s **Going Correction** +0.05s/f (Yiel)
WFA 4 from 5yo+ 15lb **13 Ran SP% 116.4**
Speed ratings (Par 103): **102,96,95,95,93 88,84,83,83,82 75,62,40**
CSF £20.21 TOTE £2.50: £1.10, £3.30, £2.10; EX 22.40 Trifecta £82.30.
Owner Bloomfields **Bred** Darley **Trained** Cowlinge, Suffolk
■ Stewards' Enquiry : Tom Messenger eight-day ban: failing to take all reasonable and permissible measures to obtain the best possible placing (23-31 Jul)

FOCUS
An ordinary maiden hurdle, but it saw a promising winner. A big step up from the easy winner, with the third rated to his mark.
T/Plt: £44.20 to a £1 stake. Pool: £74,008.35 - 1221.54 winning units. T/Qpdt: £2.40 to a £1 stake. Pool: £7146.48 - 2181.61 winning units. **Iain Mackenzie**

852 UTTOXETER (L-H)
Tuesday, July 7

OFFICIAL GOING: Good to firm (good in places; 8.9)
Wind: light 1/2 behind Weather: fine and sunny

933 DOUGLAS FAMILY CONDITIONAL JOCKEYS' NOVICES' HURDLE (9 hdls) 1m 7f 168y
6:10 (6:10) (Class 4) 4-Y-0+ **£3,249** (£954; £477; £238)

Form RPR

5-12 1 **Regulation (IRE)**32 [406] 6-10-13 126........................ LizzieKelly(6) 120+
(Neil King) *hld up: t.k.h in rr: smooth hdwy and 2nd 2 out: led on bit between last 2: wnt clr: v easily* **5/6**1

2 8 **Lilac Tree**366 5-10-12 0........................ NicodeBoinville 100+
(John Ferguson) *t.k.h: trckd ldrs 3rd: led appr 3 out: hdd between last 2: no ch w wnr* **9/4**2

/0-0 3 1 1/4 **Wistari Rocks (IRE)**20 [754] 6-10-6 0........................ AlanJohns(6) 97
(Tim Vaughan) *in rr: hdwywhn hit 2 out: 4th last: kpt on one pce to take modest 3rd nr fin* **66/1**

-461 4 1/2 **Jarlath**26 [703] 4-11-3 110........................ ConorRing 101
(Seamus Mullins) *bdly hmpd 1st: chsd ldrs next: one pce appr 2 out: modest 3rd last* **6/1**3

5/6- 5 1 3/4 **Howaboutnever (IRE)**410 [430] 7-10-12 0........................ MauriceLinehan 95
(Ian Williams) *ld to 2nd: chsd ldrs: 3rd whn blnd 3 out: one pce fr next* **12/1**

-1PP 6 15 **Allycat**24 [730] 5-10-9 0........................ DiarmuidO'Regan(3) 79
(Chris Grant) *led 2nd: hdd appr 3 out: lost pl between last 2* **25/1**

7 5 **Keep On Walking (IRE)**298 4-10-3 0........................ AdamShort(7) 72
(Peter Croke, Ire) *t.k.h: trckd ldrs 4th: lost pl bef 2 out* **40/1**

4-0 8 16 **Triggitas**57 [242] 5-10-4 0........................1 BenFfrenchDavis(8) 58
(Oliver Sherwood) *nt jump wl: chsd ldrs: j. bdly lft 1st: lost pl bef 3 out: sn bhd: b.b.v* **25/1**

3m 57.8s (0.40) **Going Correction** -0.55s/f (Firm) **8 Ran SP% 118.9**
Speed ratings (Par 105): **77,73,72,72,71 63,61,53**
CSF £3.10 TOTE £1.90: £1.10, £1.20, £8.60; EX 3.20 Trifecta £130.30.
Owner Amber Road Partnership **Bred** Barouche Stud (IRE) Ltd **Trained** Barbury Castle, Wiltshire

FOCUS
Some starts have been moved at this track following remeasuring, so some races will not have speed figures until there is sufficient data to calculate updated median times. Hurdles sited 8-10yds off inside rail and distances increased by 47yds per circuit. Lizzie Kelly described the ground as: "Quite quick, good to firm", and Nico De Boinville added: "It's what they say - good to firm and good in places. An ordinary novice hurdle in which the gallop was sedate until lifting on the home turn. The time was a full ten seconds slower than the later Class 5 handicap. The third has been rated close to the best of his bumper figures, while the fourth helps set the level.

934 NEVILLE LUMB 50TH ANNIVERSARY NOVICES' H'CAP CHASE (15 fncs) 2m 4f
6:40 (6:40) (Class 5) (0-100,99) 4-Y-0+ **£2,599** (£763; £381; £190)

Form RPR

0-05 1 **Mr Mafia (IRE)**26 [697] 6-11-3 **90**........................(t) LeeEdwards 108+
(Tony Carroll) *rr-div: hdwy 8th: led and j.lft 3 out: clrbef last: eased clsng stages* **9/1**

0/5P 2 7 **Sylvan Legend**26 [695] 7-10-1 **74**........................(tp) MarkQuinlan 82
(Neil Mulholland) *mid-div: chsd ldrs 8th: 2nd 4 out: sn led: hdd: bmpd and rdr lost irons next: kpt on same pce* **15/2**3

P-U1 3 nk **Adios Alonso (IRE)**21 [752] 9-11-3 **93**........................ BenPoste(3) 102+
(Rosemary Gasson) *chsd ldrs: blnd 3 out: kpt on run-in: tk 3rd nr fin* **5/1**1

3263 4 1/2 **Lost In Newyork (IRE)**16 [807] 8-10-5 **78**........................(p) AdamWedge 84
(Nick Kent) *rr-div: hdwy 8th: chsng ldrs 4 out: kpt on run-in: tk 4th clsng stages* **9/1**

-622 5 1 **Larkhall**11 [841] 8-10-0 **73**........................ BrianHughes 78
(Mike Sowersby) *hld up in rr: hdwy 10th: 3rd 3 out: one pce* **11/2**2

4500 6 17 **Toast And Jam (IRE)**26 [704] 6-10-5 **78**........................(t) TrevorWhelan 68
(Claire Dyson) *j.rt: chsd ldrs: outpcd 10th: lost pl 4 out* **9/1**

UP0- 7 nk **Alta Rock (IRE)**353 [1003] 10-11-2 **89**........................ SeanQuinlan 80
(Sue Smith) *in rr: drvn 8th: hdwy to chse ldrs out: sn wknd* **33/1**

P/40 8 17 **Go Teescomponents**11 [841] 8-10-0 **73** oh2........................ GavinSheehan 49
(Keith Reveley) *chsd ldr: hit 11th: sn led: hdd sn after 4 out: sn wknd* **14/1**

0-26 9 1 1/2 **Honour A Promise**44 [466] 7-11-5 **92**........................(v1) JamesBest 65
(Paul Webber) *chsd ldrs: lost pl 11th: sn bhd* **25/1**

5355 10 34 **Dougalstar (FR)**16 [806] 6-10-0 **73**........................ PeterCarberry 15
(Jennie Candlish) *chsd ldrs: mstke 6th: drvn 10th: lost pl next: sn bhd: t.o and eased 2 out* **12/1**

3-6P 11 1/2 **Steady Progress (IRE)**16 [803] 7-10-3 **79**........................(t1) HarryChalloner(3) 21
(Richard Ford) *racd freely: led: drvn 8th: hdd after 11th: sn lost pl and bhd: t.o 2 out* **25/1**

5-P4 P **Experimentalist**19 [772] 7-11-12 **99**........................(tp) RichardJohnson
(Tim Vaughan) *j. bdly detached in last: sn wl bhd: t.o 4th: p.u bef 7th* **9/1**

5-45 P **Born To Benefit (IRE)**44 [466] 9-11-10 **97**........................ PaddyBrennan
(Fergal O'Brien) *detached in rr: blnd bdly 8th: sn t.o: p.u bef 4 out* **16/1**

5-00 P **Vinceson (IRE)**42 [493] 7-10-7 **80**........................(p) MichealNolan
(Jess Westwood) *in tch: drvn 7th: sn bhd: t.o 10th: p.u bef 4 out* **20/1**

4m 55.8s (-14.00) **Going Correction** -0.55s/f (Firm) **14 Ran SP% 119.5**
Speed ratings (Par 103): **106,103,103,102,102 95,95,88,88,74 74, , ,**
CSF £71.73 CT £381.57 TOTE £16.00: £5.80, £4.40, £3.30; EX 116.20 Trifecta £1192.30.
Owner Three Counties Racing **Bred** Ivan Hamilton **Trained** Cropthorne, Worcs

FOCUS
Quite a competitive novice handicap chase. It was run at a decent clip and the form looks sound enough. The second has been rated to his hurdles mark, with the fourth and fifth close to their marks.

935 DOUGLAS FAMILY NOVICES' H'CAP HURDLE (10 hdls) 2m 3f 207y
7:15 (7:15) (Class 5) (0-100,98) 4-Y-0+ **£2,339** (£686; £343; £171)

Form RPR

2P/- 1 **Regal Park (IRE)**47 [4734] 8-10-8 **80**........................(b) WillKennedy 89+
(Dr Richard Newland) *nt fluent in rr: gd hdwy appr 3 out: upsides last: sn led and drvn clr: readily* **9/4**1

0-P0 2 3 1/2 **Steel Gold (IRE)**31 [646] 9-9-12 **75** oh3 ow3........................ ConorRing(5) 77
(John Upson) *led to 1st: chsd ldrs: 2nd and drvn appr 2 out: kpt on to chse wnr last 50yds: no imp* **20/1**

0421 3 1 1/4 **Tennessee Bird**9 [859] 7-10-10 **82** 7ex........................ GavinSheehan 84
(Mike Sowersby) *hld up in rr: hdwy 3 out: kpt on to take 3rd clsng stages* **5/1**2

5-5P 4 1 1/2 **Dreamisi (IRE)**9 [858] 6-11-5 **91**........................(p) NicodeBoinville 90
(Ben Pauling) *led 1st: j.rt: jnd last: sn hdd: kpt on same pce* **14/1**

3526 5 1 3/4 **Destiny Awaits (IRE)**9 [845] 6-11-1 **92**........................ CallumBewley(5) 90
(Keith Pollock) *mid-div: hdwy to chse ldrs 7th: hit 2 out: kpt on same pce* **20/1**

-P60 6 4 **Solway Trigger**16 [798] 6-9-11 **76**........................ RyanDay(7) 69
(Lisa Harrison) *in rr: drvn appr 3 out: kpt on fr 2 out: nvr a factor* **66/1**

2-65 7 1 **Icanmotor**20 [759] 8-10-1 **73**........................(tp) TrevorWhelan 66
(Claire Dyson) *chsd ldrs: 2nd 3 out: sn drvn: 4th last: wknd last 75yds* **16/1**

4-60 8 2 **Misteray**38 [552] 5-10-10 **87**........................(t) RyanWhile(5) 77
(Bill Turner) *chsd ldrs: drvn appr 3 out: wknd appr 2 out* **18/1**

60-0 9 8 **Barton Antix**44 [465] 6-11-12 **98**........................(p) NoelFehily 80
(Neil Mulholland) *t.k.h: trckd ldrs: stdd 6th: lost pl after 3 out* **9/1**

P530 10 1 **League Of His Own (IRE)**16 [811] 6-10-0 **72** oh2........(t) BrendanPowell 53
(Claire Dyson) *in rr: hdwy 5th: lost pl bef 3 out* **22/1**

06-4 11 2 3/4 **Stormbay Bomber (IRE)**22 [747] 6-11-5 **91**........................ HenryBrooke 70
(George Moore) *chsd ldrs: drvn 7th: wknd next* **8/1**

P0-0 12 66 **The Doom Bar (IRE)**26 [702] 6-11-3 **89**........................(t) RichardJohnson
(Philip Hobbs) *t.k.h in rr: nt fluent and dropped out 7th: sn detached last: t.o 3 out: eventually completed* **6/1**3

4m 55.5s (-7.70) **Going Correction** -0.55s/f (Firm) **12 Ran SP% 116.0**
Speed ratings (Par 103): **93,91,91,90,89 88,87,87,83,83 82,55**
CSF £51.08 CT £208.59 TOTE £3.90: £1.50, £9.50, £1.50; EX 61.90 Trifecta £1010.80 Part won.

Owner J A Provan **Bred** Lodge Park Stud **Trained** Claines, Worcs

FOCUS
This modest novice handicap was run at a steady pace, and in a time five seconds slower than the later mares' handicap. A big hurdle pb from the runner-up, with the third and fourth rated close to their marks.

936 SAINT GOBAIN 350TH ANNIVERSARY H'CAP CHASE (12 fncs) 1m 7f 214y
7:45 (7:45) (Class 4) (0-120,118) 4-Y-0 **£3,798** (£1,122; £561; £280; £140)

Form				RPR
32-1	1		**Ulis De Vassy (FR)**[9] 857 7-11-12 118 7ex... HarrySkelton (Dan Skelton) *trckd ldr: led 4th: styd on fr 2 out: drvn out* 5/6[1]	133+
1-	2	3 ¾	**Five O'clock Tea (FR)**[39] 543 8-10-10 102...(t) RichardJohnson (A J Martin, Ire) *jnd ldrs 8th: 2nd appr 3 out: upsides whn blnd 2 out: kpt on same pce* 7/2[2]	116+
2/P4	3	8	**Lisbon (IRE)**[16] 801 7-11-9 115...(t) BrianHughes (Patrick Griffin, Ire) *in rr: hdwy 4 out: modest 3rd appr 2 out: one pce* 20/1	119
P-4F	4	12	**Definite Future (IRE)**[26] 691 6-11-6 112... JamieMoore (Kerry Lee) *chsd ldng pair: j. v big: 2nd and drvn 8th: wknd appr 3 out* 7/1[3]	107
-32F	5	9	**Town Mouse**[37] 570 5-11-12 118... TrevorWhelan (Neil King) *t.k.h: led to 4th: drvn 7th: lost pl after next* 14/1	106
226-	6	4 ½	**Vasco D'Ycy (FR)**[84] 5328 6-11-2 108... HenryBrooke (Julia Brooke) *in rr: bhd fr 8th* 8/1	89

3m 53.1s (-8.30) **Going Correction** -0.55s/f (Firm) 6 Ran SP% 111.8
Speed ratings (Par 105): **98,96,92,86,81 79**
CSF £4.43 TOTE £1.70: £1.10, £1.90; EX 4.60 Trifecta £35.40.
Owner Len&White,Hewlett,Robinson,Banyard&Booth **Bred** Nicolas Ferrand **Trained** Alcester, Warwicks

FOCUS
A fair handicap chase in which they went a reasonable gallop. The winner has been rated a bit below his recent win, but biggish steps up from the second and third.

937 DON AMOTT LEISURE H'CAP HURDLE (9 hdls) 1m 7f 168y
8:15 (8:15) (Class 5) (0-100,100) 3-Y-0+ **£2,339** (£686; £343; £171)

Form				RPR
0340	1		**Auto Mac**[26] 694 7-9-11 74 oh5... AdamNicol(3) (Mike Sowersby) *hld up in rr: hdwy 3 out: 2nd between last 2: styd on to ld post* 14/1	81
02/3	2	nse	**Rose Red**[16] 811 8-10-1 80... JakeHodson(5) (Rob Summers) *hld up towards rr: hdwy appr 3 out: led appr 2 out: hdd post* 10/1	88
5-53	3	3 ¼	**Significant Move**[9] 856 8-10-2 81...(b) ChrisWard(5) (Dr Richard Newland) *chsd ldrs: drvn and outpcd 6th: styd on fr 2 out: tk 3rd clsng stages* 6/4[1]	86
5-00	4	nk	**Teescomponents Max**[16] 804 6-10-8 82... JamesReveley (Keith Reveley) *trckd ldrs: kpt on same pce between last 2* 12/1	86
4B-3	5	3 ¼	**Osorios Trial**[26] 694 8-10-9 83...(p) BrianHughes (Kevin Frost) *mid-div: hdwy to chse ldrs 6th: one pce fr 2 out* 8/1[3]	84
-03P	6	2 ½	**Toe To Toe (IRE)**[16] 806 7-10-12 86...(t) RhysFlint (John Flint) *in rr: hdwy to chse ldrs 6th: one pce fr 3 out* 7/1[2]	85
5F40	7	3 ¾	**Kentford Heiress**[20] 759 5-10-12 86... JamieMoore (Seamus Mullins) *led to 2nd: hit 4th: led appr 5th: hdd appr 2 out: wknd between last 2* 16/1	82
010-	8	15	**Perseid (IRE)**[112] 4833 5-10-13 87... SeanQuinlan (Sue Smith) *w ldrs: led briefly 2nd: chsd ldrs: wknd sn after 2 out* 9/1	69
5-54	9	8	**Sturdy Dawn**[25] 706 5-9-5 75... LewisStones(10) (Michael Mullineaux) *chsd ldrs: hit 5th: sn drvn: lost pl next: sn bhd* 66/1	50
000/	10	57	**Weet In Nerja**[964] 2434 9-9-7 74 oh9...(p) MissTWorsley(7) (Ken Wingrove) *t.k.h: hdwy to ld after 2nd: hdd appr 5th: lost pl after 6th: sn bhd: t.o 2 out: virtually p.u: eventually completed* 100/1	
-603	P		**Grams And Ounces**[19] 776 8-11-3 91...(t) MichealNolan (Adrian Wintle) *in rr: struck into himself 6th: sn p.u* 8/1[3]	
23P-	P		**Nellie The Elegant**[166] 3814 4-11-3 93...(t) RichardJohnson (Tim Vaughan) *in rr: dropped bk 7th: sn bhd: t.o next: p.u bef 2 out: b.b.v* 16/1	

3m 47.6s (-9.80) **Going Correction** -0.55s/f (Firm)
WFA 4 from 5yo+ 15lb 12 Ran SP% 122.4
Speed ratings (Par 103): **102,101,100,100,98 97,95,87,83,55 ,**
CSF £150.85 CT £339.45 TOTE £11.70: £2.50, £3.30, £1.30; EX 172.50 Trifecta £759.00.
Owner Mounted Gamess Assoc Syndicate **Bred** Roger Ingram **Trained** Goodmanham, E Yorks

FOCUS
A moderate handicap hurdle. The pace was reasonable and the first two came from the rear. The time was ten seconds slower than the opening novices' hurdle, in which they crawled. The winner has been rated back to the best of his 2014 figures, with the second down to the sixth all rated pretty much to their marks.

938 HEXAGON LEASING MARES' H'CAP HURDLE (10 hdls) 2m 3f 207y
8:45 (8:45) (Class 4) (0-115,115) 4-Y-0+ **£3,249** (£954; £477; £238)

Form				RPR
360-	1		**Welcometothejungle**[178] 3612 7-10-12 101...(t) NoelFehily (Harry Fry) *trckd ldrs: hit 3rd: led appr 3 out: hit 3 out: jnd last: fnd ex clsng stages* 13/8[1]	107+
4-31	2	nk	**Miss Sassypants**[22] 744 6-11-8 111... RyanMahon (Seamus Mullins) *in rr: effrt 78th: chsng ldrs next: upsides last: no ex nr fin* 12/1	116
546-	3	7	**Always Managing**[97] 5093 6-10-9 98...(t) AndrewTinkler (Warren Greatrex) *chsd ldrs: effrt 3 out: kpt on same pce between last 2* 14/1	97
15-6	4	8	**Java Rose**[44] 463 6-11-12 115...(tp) AidanColeman (Charlie Longsdon) *mstkes: chsd ldrs: 2nd whn hit 2 out: sn wknd* 10/1	106
44-1	5	¾	**Samedi Soir**[42] 482 5-11-4 107... JamesReveley (Keith Reveley) *hld up towards rr: effrt appr 3 out: one pce fr 2 out* 9/2[2]	97
3-52	6	1 ¾	**Ginger Fizz**[22] 744 8-11-4 107...(t) KielanWoods (Ben Case) *chsd ldrs: lost pl bef 2 out* 9/1	95
234-	7	10	**Goldray**[92] 5181 9-11-6 109... CharliePoste (Kerry Lee) *chsd ldrs: drvn 7th: lost pl 3 out* 25/1	87
-431	8	1 ¼	**Magic Magnolia (IRE)**[21] 748 4-10-13 105...(t) HarrySkelton (Dan Skelton) *in rr: hmpd 1st: mstke next: hdwy 7th: lost pl bef next* 7/1[3]	79
-100	9	18	**Queen Spud**[22] 747 6-11-6 109...(p) RichardJohnson (Henry Daly) *led: hdd appr 3 out: in rr whn eased 2 out: sn wl bhd: virtually p.u run-in* 11/1	82
4-15	P		**Bella (FR)**[22] 744 4-11-9 115...(t) TomScudamore (David Pipe) *in rr: j.rt 2nd: drvn 7th: bhd next: last whn p.u bef last* 20/1	

4m 50.5s (-12.70) **Going Correction** -0.55s/f (Firm)
WFA 4 from 5yo+ 16lb 10 Ran SP% 119.2
Speed ratings (Par 105): **103,102,100,96,96 95,91,91,84,**
CSF £22.73 CT £214.28 TOTE £2.60: £1.30, £2.70, £4.20; EX 26.70 Trifecta £310.50.
Owner Withyslade **Bred** David Bond **Trained** Seaborough, Dorset

FOCUS
An ordinary handicap, confined to mares. It was five seconds quicker than the earlier novice handicap. The second has been rated to her mark.

939 DOVE VALLEY EVENTS H'CAP HURDLE (12 hdls) 2m 7f 70y
9:15 (9:15) (Class 4) (0-110,110) 4-Y-0+ **£3,249** (£954; £477; £238)

Form				RPR
2442	1		**Solway Prince**[5] 883 6-10-3 94... RyanDay(7) (Lisa Harrison) *prom: 5th 3 out: styd on to ld appr last: forged clr* 5/2[1]	105+
0-P1	2	6	**Blackwell Synergy (FR)**[20] 757 9-10-11 100... ConorRing(5) (John Upson) *chsd ldrs: drvn 8th: 4th last: kpt on to take 2nd nr fin* 10/1	105
4-45	3	1 ¾	**Georgian King**[20] 760 12-11-0 108...(p) ArchieBellamy(10) (Martin Keighley) *w ldrs: led 2nd: drvn 4th: hdd 7th: led 9th: hdd 2 out: swvd violently lft appr last: tk 3rd nr fin* 25/1	113
3-52	4	nk	**Mr Cardle (IRE)**[42] 493 6-10-11 95...(b[1]) LeightonAspell (Oliver Sherwood) *chsd ldrs: blnd and rdr lost irons 9th: led and blnd 2 out: hdd appr last: one pce* 7/2[2]	102+
0-44	5	14	**Arctic Dixie**[20] 757 7-10-13 102...(tp) JakeHodson(5) (Rob Summers) *in rr: j.rt 3rd: jhdwy 8th: chsng ldrs appr 3 out: sn outpcd: tk poor 5th last* 25/1	93
-161	6	3	**Flemensbay**[20] 758 7-11-12 110...(p) RichardJohnson (Richard Phillips) *chsd ldrs: led 7th: hdd 9th: wknd 2 out* 5/1[3]	98
4-16	7	5	**Youngdocgallagher (IRE)**[25] 705 6-11-4 105... BenPoste(3) (Michael Mullineaux) *chsd ldrs: lost pl 3 out* 8/1	88
15/0	8	10	**Oscar Leney (IRE)**[39] 537 9-9-7 84...(t) MissAileenO'Sullivan(7) (J T R Draper, Ire) *in tch: lost pl 4th: bhd fr 6th* 20/1	58
164/	9	1 ¼	**Koultas King (IRE)**[593] 2624 8-11-5 103... MichaelByrne (Tim Vaughan) *in rr: nt fluent 4th: hdwy to chse ldrs 7th: wknd appr 3 out: bhd whn hit 2 out: sn eased* 20/1	76
55-2	10	16	**Verko (FR)**[42] 484 6-9-11 84 oh2... CraigNichol(3) (Micky Hammond) *in rr: bhd and drvn 7th* 7/1	43
P03P	P		**Agent Louise**[11] 838 7-9-11 84 oh6...(b) AdamNicol(3) (Mike Sowersby) *in rr: bhd and drvn 5th: t.o 9th: p.u bef last* 33/1	

5m 43.7s (-15.10) **Going Correction** -0.55s/f (Firm) 11 Ran SP% 120.3
Speed ratings (Par 105): **104,101,101,101,96 95,93,90,89,84**
CSF £25.62 CT £523.29 TOTE £4.20: £1.60, £2.70, £5.80; EX 35.30 Trifecta £647.50.
Owner David Alan Harrison **Bred** D A Harrison **Trained** Aldoth, Cumbria

FOCUS
There was no shortage of drama in this moderate handicap. A hurdle pb from the winner, with the second rated to his mark.
T/Plt: £11.00 to a £1 stake. Pool: £78,128.13 - 5,157.01 winning tickets. T/Qpdt: £6.20 to a £1 stake. Pool: £7,373.59 - 877.35 winning tickets. **Walter Glynn**

940 - 953a (Foreign Racing) - See Raceform Interactive

617 TIPPERARY (L-H)
Saturday, July 11

OFFICIAL GOING: Good (good to firm in places on flat course)

954a KEVIN MCMANUS BOOKMAKER GRIMES HURDLE (GRADE 3) (9 hdls) 2m
4:25 (4:25) 4-Y-0+ **£31,492** (£9,205; £4,360; £1,453)

			RPR
1		**Diakali (FR)**[398] 638 6-11-0 153... RWalsh (W P Mullins, Ire) *hld up bhd ldrs: clsr in 2nd after 4th: racd keenly: disp fr bef 4 out and led fr next: travelling wl into st and extended advantage fr 2 out: easily* 4/5[1]	160+
2	10	**Thousand Stars (FR)**[34] 663 11-11-9 153...(p) PaulTownend (W P Mullins, Ire) *sn disp tl settled in cl 2nd fr 2nd: lost pl after 4th: 4th at 1/2-way: nt fluent on outer 3 out and reminders after: impr into 2nd bef st: no imp on easy wnr fr 2 out: kpt on one pce* 10/3[2]	151
3	3 ½	**Mrs Mac Veale (IRE)**[38] 608 10-10-11 126... BrianHayes (Gavin Dower, Ire) *prom: sn settled bhd ldrs: 3rd 1/2-way: rdn bef 2 out and no imp on easy wnr fr 2 out: kpt on one pce* 28/1	136
4	1 ¼	**Taglietelle**[48] 5241 6-11-7 148...(p) BJCooper (Gordon Elliott, Ire) *w.w in rr: last 1/2-way: slt mstke 3 out and reminder after: no imp on easy wnr in 4th whn nt fluent next: kpt on one pce* 6/1	144
5	19	**Darwins Fox (FR)**[38] 603 9-11-4 141...(p) AELynch (Henry De Bromhead, Ire) *sn led tl jnd bef 1st: narrow advantage fr next: jnd fr bef 4 out and hdd fr next: sn pushed along in 2nd and wknd bef st: eased bef last* 5/1[3]	122

3m 50.6s (230.60) 5 Ran SP% 113.0
CSF £4.10 TOTE £1.80: £1.40, £1.02; DF 3.60 Trifecta £29.10.
Owner Wicklow Bloodstock (Ireland) Ltd **Bred** Haras De Son Altesse L'Aga Khan S C E A **Trained** Muine Beag, Co Carlow

FOCUS
A good renewal and, while the winner was entitled to score at the weights, it was still hard not to be impressed. The proviso is that the third has a mark of 126.

956a (Foreign Racing) - See Raceform Interactive

881 PERTH (R-H)
Sunday, July 12

OFFICIAL GOING: Good (good to soft in places)
Wind: Breezy, half behind Weather: Fine, dry

957 TOTETRIFECTA PICK THE 1,2,3 NOVICES' HURDLE (STRONGBOW DARK FRUIT SCOTTISH HURDLE SERIES QUALIFIER) (10 hdls) 2m 4f 35y
2:00 (2:00) (Class 4) 4-Y-0+ **£3,898** (£1,144; £572; £286)

Form				RPR
-11U	1		**Sharp Rise (IRE)**[48] 470 8-11-5 130... RichardJohnson (Pauline Robson) *nt fluent on occasions: mde all: shkn up bef 2 out: kpt on strly* 9/4[2]	130+
1-12	2	3 ½	**Solway Dandy**[10] 886 8-10-12 123... RyanDay(7) (Lisa Harrison) *t.k.h: chsd ldrs: rdn and outpcd whn nt fluent 2 out: rallied to chse wnr appr last: kpt on: nt pce to chal* 7/2[3]	125
2-21	3	7	**Father Edward (IRE)**[36] 647 6-11-5 130...(t) AidanColeman (John Ferguson) *t.k.h early: pressed wnr: drvn and ch briefly bef 2 out: lost 2nd and outpcd appr last: edgd rt and btn run-in* 1/1[1]	120
6155	4	41	**Running Brook (IRE)**[21] 799 8-11-0 115... CallumBewley(5) (R Mike Smith) *prom: drvn and outpcd 3 out: lost tch fr next: t.o* 40/1	86
	5	57	**Raw Condition (IRE)**[56] 7-10-12 0... HenryBrooke (Julia Brooke) *bhd: mstke and outpcd 6th: lost tch after next: t.o* 100/1	23

The Form Book Jumps 2015-16, Raceform Ltd, Newbury, RG14 5SJ

F Crofton Trail (IRE)[401] 613 6-10-5 0............................(t) PeterCarberry
(Patrick Griffin, Ire) *t.k.h: in tch: blnd 4th: fell next* **22/1**
5m 4.7s (2.70) **Going Correction** +0.225s/f (Yiel) **6** Ran SP% **110.8**
Speed ratings (Par 105): **103,101,98,82,59**
CSF £10.12 TOTE £2.70: £1.20, £2.20; EX 9.40 Trifecta £13.10.
Owner I Couldn't Switch Club **Bred** Mrs M Brophy **Trained** Kirkharle, Northumberland

FOCUS
Some starts have been moved at this track following remeasuring, so some races will not have speed figures until there is sufficient data to calculate updated median times. The rails were in the outer most position and distances were revised as follows: 2m Hurdle/Flat run over 2m139yds; 2m4f Hurdle run over 2m4f143yds; 2m4f chase run over 2m4f110yds; 2m7f Hurdle run over 3m117yds; 2m7f chase run over 3m66yds. Richard Johnson said of the ground: "It's good to soft mostly but there are one or two soft patches". The winner improving his hurdle mark but was still below his best chase figure.

958 TOTEEXACTA PICK THE 1ST AND 2ND H'CAP HURDLE (12 hdls) 2m 7f 207y
2:30 (2:30) (Class 4) (0-115,114) 4-Y-0+ **£5,198** (£1,526; £763; £381)

Form RPR
-030 **1** **Solway Sam**[21] 803 12-9-9 **90**..............................(p) RyanDay(7) 96+
(Lisa Harrison) *chsd ldr: led after 4 out: rdn 2 out: pricked ears and hld on gamely run-in* **7/2**[2]
643- **2** *nk* **Le Grand Chene (FR)**[28] 738 9-10-3 **91**..................(bt) RichardJohnson 95+
(Gordon Elliott, Ire) *hld up: stdy hdwy on outside 4 out: pressed ldr gng wl bef 2 out: shkn up whn nt fluent last: kpt on towards fin* **85/40**[1]
-44U **3** *7* **Rev Up Ruby**[11] 867 7-11-3 **110**............................ JonathonBewley(5) 109
(George Bewley) *hld up: smooth hdwy and prom whn stmbld bnd bef 2 out: sn rdn: kpt on same pce fr 2 out* **12/1**
6-23 **4** *16* **Los Nadis (GER)**[11] 869 11-11-3 **105**..........................(v) HenryBrooke 89
(Jim Goldie) *led: hdd after 4 out: sn rdn along: rallied: wknd 2 out* **9/2**[3]
4-31 **5** *7* **What A Steel (IRE)**[21] 798 11-11-8 **113**..................(p) CraigNichol(3) 90
(Alistair Whillans) *chsd ldrs: outpcd 6th: rallied next: drvn bef 3 out: wknd bef next* **13/2**
200- **6** *13* **Bollin Fiona**[122] 4726 11-10-7 **95**................................ AdrianLane 64
(Donald Whillans) *hld up in tch: stdy hdwy after 7th: blnd and outpcd 4 out: n.d after* **20/1**
P0-0 **7** *10* **Presented (IRE)**[10] 883 8-10-12 **100**............................ BrianHarding 57
(Lisa Harrison) *chsd ldrs tl rdn and lost pl after 7th: lost tch fr 4 out: t.o* **16/1**
4U0- **8** *5* **Ballygrooby Bertie (IRE)**[327] 1264 7-11-12 **114**............ PeterBuchanan 66
(S R B Crawford, Ire) *hld up: stdy hdwy bef 4 out: pushed along and outpcd whn nt fluent next: wknd qckly: t.o* **12/1**
6m 8.8s (3.80) **Going Correction** +0.225s/f (Yiel) **8** Ran SP% **111.8**
Speed ratings (Par 105): **102,101,99,94,91 87,84,82**
CSF £11.16 CT £74.92 TOTE £4.50: £1.70, £1.10, £3.20; EX 13.90 Trifecta £153.10.
Owner David Alan Harrison **Bred** D A Harrison **Trained** Aldoth, Cumbria

FOCUS
The market leaders came clear late on with the winner proving most game to deny the favourite. The third sets the level.

959 TOTEPOOL RACING'S BIGGEST SUPPORTER NOVICES' H'CAP CHASE (18 fncs) 2m 7f 180y
3:05 (3:05) (Class 4) (0-120,116) 4-Y-0+ **£6,498** (£1,908; £954; £477)

Form RPR
/1 **1** **St Maxime (IRE)**[11] 867 7-10-7 **104**............................(b) JBKane(7) 120+
(Gavin Cromwell, Ire) *j.w: mde all at stdy pce: qcknd clr 2 out: rdn and edgd rt run-in: kpt on wl* **4/1**[3]
210/ **2** *8* **Gee Hi (IRE)**[817] 5340 9-11-1 **105**............................ AidanColeman 113
(Warren Greatrex) *hld up: pushed along and hdwy 3 out: chsd (clr) wnr last: kpt on: no imp* **10/3**[2]
4121 **3** *6* **Solway Legend**[21] 803 8-9-7 **90**.................................. RyanDay(7) 92
(Lisa Harrison) *t.k.h: chsd ldrs: wnt 2nd 10th to 13th: effrt and regained 2nd 3 out to last: edgd rt and one pce* **11/2**
3-42 **4** *3 ¼* **One For Hocky (IRE)**[31] 691 7-11-11 **115**.................... BrianHarding 114
(Nicky Richards) *wore hood in paddock: hld up: stdy hdwy bef 4 out: drvn along bef next: wknd fr 2 out* **15/2**
-U42 **5** *13* **Bouggietopieces**[11] 871 5-10-8 **98**.......................... RichardJohnson 86
(Gordon Elliott, Ire) *t.k.h: chsd ldrs: rdn after 4 out: wknd bef next* **11/4**[1]
F-62 **6** *1* **Ballythomas**[53] 398 8-10-9 **99**.................................. HenryBrooke 86
(David Thompson) *chsd wnr tl mstke 10th: regained 2nd 13th: ev ch 4 out: rdn and wknd fr next* **10/1**
13 **7** *8* **Wind Of Hope (IRE)**[35] 656 6-11-9 **116**.................. GrahamWatters(3) 93
(Lucinda Russell) *nt fluent in rr: rdn and struggling after 4 out: wknd bef next* **14/1**
6m 17.2s (13.20) **Going Correction** +0.225s/f (Yiel) **7** Ran SP% **112.7**
Speed ratings (Par 105): **87,84,82,81,76 76,73**
CSF £17.63 TOTE £3.90: £2.50, £2.10; EX 27.40 Trifecta £107.30.
Owner DT Racing Club **Bred** Gerrardstown House Stud **Trained** Navan, Co. Meath

FOCUS
Little pace on here, with the winner dominating from the front. She's rated in line with the best of her hurdles figures.

960 ACTION GLEN MAIDEN HURDLE (8 hdls) 2m 47y
3:40 (3:41) (Class 4) 4-Y-0+ **£3,798** (£1,122; £561; £280; £140)

Form RPR
6-2 **1** **Galizzi (USA)**[21] 799 4-10-12 0..................................(t) AidanColeman 119+
(John Ferguson) *pressed ldr: led 4 out: qcknd clr bef 2 out: v easily* **10/11**[1]
2 *22* **Chaz Michaels (IRE)**[56] 5-10-11 0................................ DerekFox(3) 94
(Lucinda Russell) *in tch: drvn and outpcd 1/2-way: rallied bef 2 out: chsd (clr) wnr last: plugged on: no imp* **8/1**[3]
2- **3** *1 ½* **Iffjack (IRE)**[23] 785 5-11-0 0............................(t) RichardJohnson 95+
(Gordon Elliott, Ire) *hld up: stdy hdwy to chse ldrs whn blnd 3 out: effrt and chsd (clr) wnr 2 out to last: no ex* **3/1**[2]
5- **4** *3 ¼* **Bawnogues Bahri (IRE)**[8] 909 6-10-12 0.................. GrantCockburn(5) 82
(Paul Stafford, Ire) *prom: drvn and outpcd bef 2 out: sn n.d* **100/1**
4-F2 **5** *1 ¼* **Sindarban (IRE)**[31] 702 4-10-12 110..............................(t) AdrianLane 86
(Donald McCain) *hld up: pushed along and outpcd bef 3 out: no imp bef next* **10/1**
0-33 **6** *9* **Another Bygones (IRE)**[29] 727 6-11-0 109...................... HenryBrooke 83
(Karen McLintock) *led to 4 out: chsd wnr tl wknd 2 out* **12/1**
00 **7** *15* **Coppelia (IRE)**[21] 799 7-10-7 0.................................. BrianHarding 59
(Nicky Richards) *midfield: drvn and outpcd 1/2-way: n.d after* **66/1**
0 **8** *7* **Tish Hall (IRE)**[10] 881 5-10-7 0................................ PeterBuchanan 53
(S R B Crawford, Ire) *hld up: rdn and struggling after 4 out: btn bef 2 out* **50/1**
- **P** **Archipeligo**[31] 4-10-9 0.. CraigNichol(3)
(Iain Jardine) *bhd: struggling 4 out: no ch whn p.u bef 2 out* **14/1**

P **Pirate's Penny (IRE)**[46] 4-10-9 0............................ JonathanEngland(3)
(Hugh Burns) *bhd: lost tch bef 4th: t.o whn p.u next* **33/1**
4m 8.6s (248.60)
WFA 4 from 5yo+ 15lb **10** Ran SP% **119.3**
CSF £9.70 TOTE £2.00: £1.10, £2.70, £1.60; EX 11.80 Trifecta £21.10.
Owner Bloomfields **Bred** Darley **Trained** Cowlinge, Suffolk

FOCUS
This took little winning, with the favourite bolting up. There's a case for rating the form a bit higher but not on time.

961 SKY TO SCOOP PERTH SILVER CUP H'CAP CHASE (FOR THE PERTH SILVER CUP) (15 fncs) 2m 4f 20y
4:10 (4:10) (Class 3) (0-130,130) 4£13,814 (£4,116; £2,083; £1,067; £559)

Form RPR
5F5/ **1** **Run With The Wind (IRE)**[23] 786 9-11-9 **127**..........(t) PeterBuchanan 134+
(S R B Crawford, Ire) *t.k.h early: prom: effrt and chsd ldr bef 2 out: ev ch whn blkd run-in: styd on wl to ld cl home* **20/1**
-123 **2** *shd* **Owen Glendower (IRE)**[26] 750 10-10-6 **117**........(tp) CiaranGethings(7) 123
(Sophie Leech) *hld up: hdwy and cl up 7th: wnt 2nd 10th: led 3 out: pushed along and edgd rt next: hrd pressed and blkd run-in: kpt on: hdd cl home* **11/2**[3]
U-25 **3** *9* **Gleann Na Ndochais (IRE)**[30] 707 9-10-12 **119**.......... CraigNichol(3) 117
(Alistair Whillans) *hld up: hdwy to chse ldr 9th to next: drvn and outpcd 4 out: plugged on fr last: nt rch first two* **9/1**
0521 **4** *15* **Bunclody**[10] 884 10-10-0 **104** oh1..................................(p) AidanColeman 93
(Barry Brennan) *led: rdn and hdd 3 out: 9 l 3rd and outpcd whn blnd last* **6/1**
1221 **5** *27* **Russian Regent (IRE)**[10] 885 11-11-12 **130**.............. RichardJohnson 95
(Gordon Elliott, Ire) *in tch on outside: blnd and lost pl 5th: struggling whn hit 9th: sn lost tch: t.o* **7/2**[2]
-133 **P** **Mason Hindmarsh**[21] 801 8-11-7 **125**.............................. BrianHarding
(Karen McLintock) *prom tl p.u bef 5th* **10/1**
1211 **P** **Thinger Licht (FR)**[7] 917 6-9-9 **104** oh3...............(p) BridgetAndrews(5)
(Dan Skelton) *chsd ldr: rdn 7th: lost pl whn hit next: sn struggling: lost tch and p.u after 9th* **7/4**[1]
5m 7.5s (2.50) **Going Correction** +0.225s/f (Yiel) **7** Ran SP% **112.1**
Speed ratings (Par 107): **104,103,100,94,83**
CSF £117.32 TOTE £16.30: £6.20, £3.60; EX 150.90 Trifecta £982.30.
Owner John B O'Hagan **Bred** King Bloodstock And R Scarborough **Trained** Larne, Co Antrim

FOCUS
The front pair came clear up the straight and, having come close on the run-in, there was little between them as they hit the line. Straightforward form.

962 CRABBIES ALCOHOLIC GINGER BEER CONDITIONAL JOCKEYS' H'CAP HURDLE (8 hdls) 2m 47y
4:45 (4:46) (Class 4) (0-105,105) 3-Y-0+ **£3,898** (£1,144; £572; £286)

Form RPR
03-6 **1** **Swampfire (IRE)**[61] 267 7-11-0 **98**.............................. MikeyHamill(5) 109+
(Barry Brennan) *prom: hdwy to ld bef 3 out: rdn clr fr next* **6/1**[3]
3600 **2** *14* **Johnny Go**[21] 799 5-10-7 **92**.. RyanDay(6) 91
(Lisa Harrison) *chsd ldrs: nt fluent and rdn 3 out: rallied to chse wnr next: kpt on fr last: no imp* **6/1**[3]
1112 **3** *9* **Baraboy (IRE)**[14] 851 5-11-12 **105**.......................... GrahamWatters 96
(Barry Murtagh) *hld up: smooth hdwy to dispute 2nd pl bef 2 out: sn rdn: 3rd and outpcd whn nt fluent last* **5/2**[2]
32-2 **4** *12* **Separate Shadows (FR)**[66] 153 7-11-6 **105**.............. JamesCowley(6) 86
(Donald McCain) *chsd ldrs: drvn and outpcd bef 2 out: sn btn* **2/1**[1]
445- **5** *12* **Claude Carter**[129] 4576 11-11-12 **105**.............................. CraigNichol 73
(Alistair Whillans) *led to 3rd: chsd ldrs: hit next: struggling fr 4 out* **10/1**
3-16 **6** *30* **Beidh Tine Anseo (IRE)**[11] 871 9-11-2 **98**..........(tp) GrantCockburn(3) 39
(Lucinda Russell) *hld up: rdn and outpcd 4th: lost tch fr next: t.o* **16/1**
P **Harry's Summer (USA)**[10] 889 4-10-13 **97**..........(bt) CiaranGethings(3)
(Gordon Elliott, Ire) *cl up: led 3rd: drvn and hdd bef 3 out: sn wknd: t.o whn p.u between last 2* **9/1**
4m 2.2s (242.20)
WFA 4 from 5yo+ 15lb **7** Ran SP% **115.4**
CSF £41.42 CT £113.05 TOTE £8.10: £4.10, £3.80; EX 44.70 Trifecta £102.00.
Owner F J Brennan **Bred** Kilboy Estate **Trained** Upper Lambourn, Berks

FOCUS
Moderate handicap form. The winner's best figure since 2013.

963 SILVER CUP DAY STANDARD OPEN NATIONAL HUNT FLAT RACE 2m 47y
5:20 (5:20) (Class 5) 4-6-Y-0 **£2,053** (£598; £299)

Form RPR
2-1 **1** **Amirr (IRE)**[26] 753 5-11-9 0.. AidanColeman 119+
(John Ferguson) *mde all: qcknd clr over 3f out: shkn up over 1f out: kpt on wl: unchal* **1/2**[1]
5-3 **2** *5* **Carinena (IRE)**[35] 662 6-10-6 0.................................... CraigNichol(3) 98
(Nicky Richards) *chsd wnr thrght: rdn and outpcd over 3f out: rallied over 1f out: nt pce to chal* **4/1**[2]
4- **3** *19* **Paddy's Yarn (IRE)**[290] 1624 5-11-2 0..........................(t) PeterBuchanan 88
(S R B Crawford, Ire) *hld up in tch: drvn and outpcd over 4f out: plugged on fr 2f out: no ch w first two* **10/1**
4 *16* **Bellas Rock (IRE)**[23] 790 4-11-0 0.............................. RichardJohnson 72
(Gordon Elliott, Ire) *chsd ldrs: drvn and struggling over 3f out: btn fnl 2f* **7/1**[3]
5 *23* **Sandy Grey (IRE)** 6-10-6 0.. DerekFox(3) 46
(Paul Stafford, Ire) *hld up in tch: struggling over 4f out: sn btn: t.o* **33/1**
6 *8* **Lady From Milan (IRE)** 6-10-6 0.................................. GrahamWatters(3) 39
(Ian Duncan) *hld up: rdn and outpcd 5f out: sn struggling: t.o* **25/1**
4m 0.7s (240.70)
WFA 4 from 5yo+ 2lb **6** Ran SP% **115.0**
CSF £3.05 TOTE £1.50: £1.10, £2.00; EX 2.90 Trifecta £9.30.
Owner Bloomfields **Bred** Breeding Capital Plc **Trained** Cowlinge, Suffolk

FOCUS
Little depth to this bumper and it went the way the market suggested it would. The winner built on his recent victory.

T/Plt: £842.20 to a £1 stake. Pool: £73591.90 - 63.78 winning tickets. T/Qpdt: £418.80 to a £1 stake. Pool: £4584.74 - 8.1 winning tickets. **Richard Young**

[741] SOUTHWELL (L-H)

Sunday, July 12

OFFICIAL GOING: Good (good to firm in places) changing to good after race 1 (2.10)

Wind: light 1/2 behind Weather: fine

964 SHANE W DARBY MEMORIAL H'CAP CHASE (13 fncs) 1m 7f 153y

2:10 (2:10) (Class 5) (0-100,96) 4-Y-0+ **£2,599** (£763; £381; £190)

Form RPR

F24/ **1** **Walden Prince (IRE)**[474] 5017 8-11-8 **92**.................(tp) TomScudamore 123+
(David Bridgwater) *led 3rd: j.rt fr 7th: hit 10th: clr bef next: heavily eased run-in* **9/4**[1]

U-41 **2** *28* **Mac's Grey (IRE)**[7] 914 8-10-10 **80** 7ex..........................(t) WillKennedy 80
(Ian Williams) *chsd ldrs: 2nd 6th: drvn after 10th: one pce* **3/1**[2]

1-42 **3** *4* **Table Bluff (IRE)**[40] 588 6-11-12 **96**..........................(p) NicodeBoinville 94
(John Spearing) *chsd ldrs: lost pl and hit 10th: sme hdwy 9th: one pce fr next* **9/4**[1]

64P3 **4** *43* **Next Exit (IRE)**[27] 741 10-9-9 **70** oh1........................... JoeCornwall(5) 28
(John Cornwall) *in tch: drvn 8th: lost pl next: sn bhd and reminders: t.o 9th: distant 4th 2 out* **20/1**

-340 **P** **Pindar (GER)**[16] 841 11-10-4 **74**..................................(p) DougieCostello
(Joanne Foster) *nt fluent in last: drvn 4th: bhd 6th: t.o next: p.u bef 8th* **11/1**

05-0 **P** **Dancing Ecco (IRE)**[40] 588 6-10-3 **78**..............................(t) ConorRing(5)
(Evan Williams) *led tl hdd bef 3rd: 3rd whn mstke 9th: wknd next: t.o 3 out: distant 4th whn hit 2 out: last whn p.u bef last* **7/1**[3]

4m 2.8s (0.80) **Going Correction** 0.0s/f (Good) **6** Ran SP% **112.1**
Speed ratings (Par 103): **98,84,82,60,**
CSF £9.71 CT £15.41 TOTE £3.90: £2.00, £2.10; EX 12.30 Trifecta £19.50.

Owner Gary Attwood **Bred** John McEnery **Trained** Icomb, Gloucs

FOCUS
The fences were situated on the inside rail. A moderate contest started off the meeting, which appeared to be run at solid gallop.

965 BILLY SOLOMAN MEMORIAL NOVICES' CHASE (19 fncs) 2m 7f 209y

2:40 (2:40) (Class 4) 5-Y-0+ **£3,898** (£1,144; £572; £286)

Form RPR

3-21 **1** **Call Me Vic (IRE)**[12] 861 8-11-5 132.............................. PaddyBrennan 139+
(Tom George) *mde all: hit 8th: qckd pce 12th: drvn appr 3 out: 6 l ahd whn blnd last: drvn rt out* **4/6**[1]

-152 **2** *2* **Henllan Harri (IRE)**[18] 833 7-10-9 0............................ SeanBowen(3) 131+
(Peter Bowen) *trckd wnr: mstke 14th: rallied and nt fluent 3 out: kpt on run-in* **6/5**[2]

0U **3** *89* **Tony (IRE)**[21] 808 8-10-5 0.. MissTWorsley(7) 48
(Ken Wingrove) *trckd ldrs: outpcd and drvn 12th: reminders and lost pl next: bhd and reminders 15th: t.o next: tk distant 3rd last 50yds* **50/1**

4P50 **4** *11* **The Jugopolist (IRE)**[27] 747 8-10-7 76........................... JoeCornwall(5) 43
(John Cornwall) *chsd ldng pair: pushed along 5th: reminders 9th: outpcd and lost pl 12th: t.o 16th: nt fluent and sddle slipped last: wknd and lost distant 3rd clsng stages* **33/1**[3]

6m 22.5s (-0.50) **Going Correction** 0.0s/f (Good) **4** Ran SP% **110.3**
Speed ratings: **100,99,69,66**
CSF £1.95 TOTE £1.40; EX 1.90 Trifecta £6.00.

Owner C B Compton **Bred** R P Walshe **Trained** Slad, Gloucs

FOCUS
This looked a match pre-race and that's how it played out.

966 NOTTINGHAM CITY TRANSPORT H'CAP HURDLE (13 hdls) 2m 7f 209y

3:15 (3:15) (Class 5) (0-100,100) 4-Y-0+ **£2,599** (£763; £381; £190)

Form RPR

OPF/ **1** **French Seventyfive**[63] 8-9-7 **74** oh4................................... MissETodd(7) 81+
(Keith Reveley) *chsd ldrs: led sn after 3 out: jnd last: jst hld on* **6/1**[2]

-P02 **2** *nse* **Steel Gold (IRE)**[5] 935 9-9-11 **76** oh5 ow2........................ ConorRing(5) 85+
(John Upson) *chsd ldrs: handy 2nd whn hit 2 out: upsides whn nt fluent last: kpt on towards fin: jst hld* **9/2**[1]

PP-0 **3** *6* **Stand Clear**[21] 805 10-9-9 **74** oh4..............................(t) HarryBannister(5) 75
(Chris Grant) *in rr: chsd ldrs 9th: 2nd after 3 out: kpt on one pce appr last* **14/1**

-435 **4** *1 3/4* **Temple Lord (FR)**[24] 772 9-11-9 **97**..............................(vt) WillKennedy 97
(Jonjo O'Neill) *mid-div: lost pl and reminders 8th: hdwy 10th: modest 4th whn mstke 2 out: styd on same pce* **9/1**

P1-0 **5** *30* **Aaly**[49] 451 8-10-3 **77**.. MarcGoldstein 49
(Lydia Richards) *in rr: hdwy 9th: lost pl 3 out: sn bhd* **20/1**

P-P5 **6** *1 1/4* **Amour Collonges (FR)**[37] 621 5-9-10 **75**................(bt) DiarmuidO'Regan(5) 46
(Chris Grant) *led after 1st: hdd sn after 3 out: sn lost pl and bhd* **16/1**

2-55 **7** *6* **Element Quartet (IRE)**[53] 398 6-10-5 **79**......................(t) BrendanPowell 44
(Brendan Powell) *in rr: pushed along 3rd: hdwy to chse ldrs 9th: lost pl 3 out: sn bhd* **7/1**[3]

252/ **8** *8* **Miss Mayfair (IRE)**[474] 5022 8-10-6 **83**...................... ConorShoemark(3) 41
(Lawney Hill) *chsd ldrs: drvn 3 out: sn lost pl and bhd* **16/1**

/00- **9** *9* **Transfer**[27] 662 10-10-11 **88**... BenPoste(3) 38
(Tom Symonds) *chsd ldrs: reminders 10th: sn lost pl and bhd* **20/1**

031- **P** **Moon Melody (GER)**[299] 1541 12-11-0 **88**............................. BrianHughes
(Mike Sowersby) *led tl after 1st: drvn and lost pl 6th: bhd 9th: sn t.o and p.u* **6/1**[2]

4-35 **P** **Dipity Doo Dah**[24] 770 11-10-9 **86**..(tp) SeanBowen(3)
(Peter Bowen) *nt fluent in rr and j.rt: bhd 8th: p.u sn after 3 out* **7/1**[3]

03-6 **P** **Captain Sharpe**[21] 801 7-11-5 **100**..............................(p) ThomasDowson(7)
(Kenny Johnson) *nt jump wl in rr: reminders 5th: bhd whn blnd 7th: t.o whn p.u after next* **33/1**

-216 **P** **Lilly's Legend**[25] 759 5-10-8 **82**..(p) DougieCostello
(Mark Walford) *prom: lost pl bef 3 out: wl bhd whn p.u bef 2 out* **6/1**[2]

6m 13.0s (-2.00) **Going Correction** 0.0s/f (Good) **13** Ran SP% **126.9**
Speed ratings (Par 103): **103,102,100,100,90 89,87,85,82, , ,**
CSF £35.10 CT £380.78 TOTE £8.30: £2.50, £2.80, £3.50; EX 42.60 Trifecta £827.70.

Owner Miss G Boanas **Bred** Mrs O Tunstall **Trained** Lingdale, Redcar & Cleveland

FOCUS
A moderate but interesting handicap. The three runners running from out of the weights filled the first three positions.

967 LINCS&NOTTS AIR AMBULANCE 21ST ANNIVERSARY H'CAP HURDLE (13 hdls) 2m 7f 209y

3:50 (3:50) (Class 4) (0-120,120) 4-Y-0+ **£3,249** (£954; £477; £238)

Form RPR

46-2 **1** **Dr Robin (IRE)**[16] 837 5-10-5 **102**.. SeanBowen(3) 111+
(Peter Bowen) *w ldr: led 10th: drvn rt out* **10/3**[1]

-052 **2** *3 1/4* **West End (IRE)**[25] 757 8-10-8 **105** ow2.....................(tp) TomBellamy(3) 111
(Kim Bailey) *t.k.h: in tch: hdwy 9th: 2nd 2 out: kpt on same pce appr last* **7/2**[2]

4-36 **3** *11* **Maypole Lass**[25] 757 5-10-10 **104**...................................(b[1]) BrendanPowell 102
(Stuart Edmunds) *trckd ldrs: cl 3rd whn hit 2 out: one pce* **10/1**

3432 **4** *2 3/4* **Still Believing (IRE)**[24] 772 7-11-2 **115**................................ ConorRing(5) 109
(Evan Williams) *in tch: reminder 6th: pushed along 8th: jnd ldrs 10th: one pce fr 2 out* **15/2**[3]

10-4 **5** *12* **Feast Of Fire (IRE)**[71] 81 8-11-2 **110**.. BrianHughes 93
(Mike Sowersby) *hld up in tch: hdwy 3 out: rdn and lost pl bef next: poor 5th last* **10/1**

U-21 **6** *29* **Big Sound**[31] 693 8-11-3 **111**......................................(p) DougieCostello 68
(Mark Walford) *led: nt fluent 1st 2: hdd 10th: lost pl appr 2 out: t.o whn eased run-in* **10/3**[1]

222- **7** *3 1/4* **Always Archie**[321] 1318 8-11-12 **120**.. RhysFlint 74
(Robert Stephens) *in tch: chsd ldrs 8th: nt fluent 9th: lost pl next: sn bhd: t.o: fin lame* **16/1**

41-6 **8** *1/2* **Sir Frank Morgan (IRE)**[33] 669 5-11-6 **114**...............(b) TomScudamore 67
(David Pipe) *chsd ldrs: reminders and lost pl 3 out: sn bhd: t.o* **8/1**

6m 9.3s (-5.70) **Going Correction** 0.0s/f (Good) **8** Ran SP% **115.3**
Speed ratings (Par 105): **109,107,104,103,99 89,88,88**
CSF £15.97 CT £104.14 TOTE £3.70: £1.90, £1.70, £3.80; EX 20.20 Trifecta £245.30.

Owner David Robbins & Karen Bowen **Bred** Michael Ronayne **Trained** Little Newcastle, Pembrokes

■ Stewards' Enquiry : Tom Bellamy three-day ban: weighed in 2lb heavy (Jul 27-28)

FOCUS
Quite a range of abilities on show when considering official ratings for this staying handicap, but it was dominated by those towards the foot of the weights.

968 BETBONUS.COM CLAIM YOUR FREE BETS NOW NOVICES' (S) HURDLE (11 hdls) 2m 4f 62y

4:20 (4:20) (Class 4) 4-Y-0+ **£3,606** (£1,311)

Form RPR

P5-6 **1** **Daizy (IRE)**[49] 451 6-10-12 77..(p) WillKennedy 94+
(Hilary Parrott) *led 1st: hdd next: chsd ldr: 2nd sn after 3 out: 3 l 2nd 2 out: led between last 2: j.rt and hit last: drvn out* **18/1**

2334 **2** *5* **Oneofapear (IRE)**[7] 918 9-10-12 100..............................(p) BrianHughes 91
(Mike Sowersby) *trckd ldrs: upsides 8th: led sn after next: clr whn wandered appr 2 out: hdd between last 2: fnd little* **7/2**[2]

6B-1 **P** **Kings Grey (IRE)**[30] 709 11-10-9 0...............................(tp) BrianToomey(3)
(Philip Kirby) *led to 1st: led 2nd: hdd sn after 3 out: wknd qckly: t.o 3rd whn p.u bef next* **1/3**[1]

0/3- **P** **Novel Dancer**[38] 1707 7-10-12 99.. MarcGoldstein
(Lydia Richards) *in rr: reminders 6th: sn bhd: t.o whn p.u after 8th* **12/1**[3]

P **Plettenburg Bay (IRE)**[49] 10-10-12 0.. MarkGrant
(Sean Curran) *in rr: reminders 5th: drvn and outpcd next: lost pl and reminders 3 out: sn t.o: p.u bef 2 out* **33/1**

5m 16.2s (3.20) **Going Correction** 0.0s/f (Good) **5** Ran SP% **113.1**
Speed ratings (Par 105): **93,91, , ,**
CSF £77.50 TOTE £13.90: £6.30, £1.40; EX 47.70.There was no bid for the winner.

Owner T J & Mrs H Parrott **Bred** Patrick Doyle **Trained** Redmarley, Gloucs

■ Brian Toomey's first ride since suffering life-threatening head injuries in a fall two years ago.

FOCUS
This had the look of an uncompetitive contest before the off, but the long odds-on favourite was pulled up some way from home.

969 HAPPY BIRTHDAY JOAN ROBINSON H'CAP HURDLE (11 hdls) 2m 4f 62y

4:55 (4:55) (Class 4) (0-120,118) 3-Y-0+ **£3,249** (£954; £477; £238)

Form RPR

-111 **1** **Ruaraidh Hugh (IRE)**[23] 780 6-11-1 **114**........(b) MrTommieMO'Brien(7) 124+
(Chris Bealby) *chsd ldrs: pushed along 5th: wnt 2nd appr 2 out: upsides last: styd on to ld last 50yds* **4/1**[3]

32-1 **2** *1 1/4* **Ubaldo Des Menhies (FR)**[33] 678 7-11-10 **116**.....(p) RichieMcLernon 124
(Jonjo O'Neill) *trckd ldr: led bef 2 out: jnd last: hdd and no ex clsng stages* **7/4**[1]

2-23 **3** *10* **Harvey's Hope**[21] 802 9-11-4 **115**...............................(t) MrJohnDawson(5) 116
(Keith Reveley) *trckd ldrs: handy 3rd appr 2 out: j.rt and hit last: sn wknd* **8/1**

-653 **4** *10* **Hold Court (IRE)**[24] 775 8-11-9 **115**.. PaulMoloney 105
(Evan Williams) *chsd ldrs: pushed along 6th: lost pl 3 out: hung rt 2 out: poor 4th last* **6/1**

53-4 **5** *12* **Skylander (IRE)**[14] 854 6-11-12 **118**...........................(bt) TomScudamore 97
(David Pipe) *led: hdd bef 2 out: sn lost pl and bhd* **10/3**[2]

-340 **6** *1 3/4* **Lawsons Thorns (IRE)**[23] 780 6-10-10 **102**.............................. BrianHughes 80
(Mike Sowersby) *hld up in rr: hdwy 3 out: lost pl bef next: sn bhd* **14/1**

5m 11.5s (-1.50) **Going Correction** 0.0s/f (Good) **6** Ran SP% **111.5**
Speed ratings (Par 105): **103,102,98,94,89 89**
CSF £11.65 TOTE £4.80: £2.10, £1.80; EX 12.40 Trifecta £26.00.

Owner Triumph In Mind **Bred** Peter McCarthy **Trained** Barrowby, Lincs

FOCUS
This wasn't run that quickly early and the pace steadily increased on the final circuit.

970 MRFREEBET.CO.UK ON YOUR MOBILE MARES' STANDARD OPEN NATIONAL HUNT FLAT RACE 1m 7f 153y

5:30 (5:30) (Class 6) 4-6-Y-0 **£1,949** (£572; £286; £143)

Form RPR

2 **1** **Tilinisi (IRE)**[26] 753 5-10-12 0... KielanWoods 99+
(Phil Middleton) *trckd ldrs: 2nd over 1f out: styd on wl to ld fnl strides* **2/1**[1]

12-2 **2** *hd* **Princess Roania (IRE)**[40] 594 4-11-0 0............................. SeanBowen(3) 104+
(Peter Bowen) *w ldrs: led on ins over 2f out: 3 l clr 1f out: veered bdly rt: hdd fnl strides* **5/2**[2]

3 *3* **Donttellthemissis (IRE)** 4-10-10 0.............................. TomScudamore 94
(Gary Hanmer) *mid-div: effrt 4f out: kpt on to take 3rd last 150yds* **16/1**

4 *3 1/4* **A Touch Of Sass (IRE)**[48] 5-10-12 0.................................... JamieMoore 93
(John Spearing) *hld up in rr: hdwy 4f out: kpt on same pce fnl 2f: tk 4th last 100yds* **12/1**

3 **5** *2 ¼* **Belcanto (IRE)**[40] 594 5-10-12 0 BrendanPowell 91
(Jamie Snowden) *chsd ldrs: drvn over 2f out: one pce* **10/1**

0- **6** *hd* **Pretty Rose (IRE)**[91] 5299 5-10-12 0 DarylJacob 91
(Ben Case) *mid-div: chsd ldrs 7f out: one pce fnl 3f* **33/1**

0-32 **7** *½* **Bollin Beauty**[36] 640 6-10-12 0 BrianHughes 91
(Malcolm Jefferson) *w ldrs: led 9f out: hdd over 2f out: one pce* **14/1**

0-5 **8** *¾* **Honey Brown**[18] 831 4-10-10 0 RobertDunne 88
(Tom Lacey) *mid-div: hdwy 9f out: chsng ldrs 7f out: one pce fnl 3f* **33/1**

0- **9** *19* **Coral Queen**[248] 2309 4-10-10 0 AndrewTinkler 71
(Peter Niven) *hld up in rr: hdwy on inner over 3f out: wknd over 1f out: eased clsng stages* **40/1**

6 **10** *6* **Blu Passione**[40] 594 4-10-10 0 LeightonAspell 66
(Oliver Sherwood) *chsd ldrs: pushed along 8f out: lost pl 4f out: sn bhd* **14/1**

11 *9* **Kilcullen Lady (IRE)**[70] 5-10-12 0 DougieCostello 59
(Henry Hogarth) *racd wd: w ldrs: led after 3f: hdd 9f out: lost pl over 3f out: sn bhd* **8/1**[3]

6- **12** *9* **My Teescomponents**[208] 3136 5-10-7 0 MrJohnDawson(5) 51
(Keith Reveley) *hld up in rr: t.k.h: brief effrt over 3f out: sn lost pl and bhd* **33/1**

13 *3 ½* **Sailors Legend** 6-10-12 0 LiamTreadwell 48
(Michael Scudamore) *led 3f: chsd ldrs: lost pl 5f out: sn bhd* **25/1**

35 **14** *2 ¼* **Kaddys Girl**[51] 432 5-10-5 0 JosephPalmowski(7) 46
(Robin Dickin) *in rr: bhd fnl 4f* **25/1**

3m 51.1s (-0.30) **Going Correction** 0.0s/f (Good) **14 Ran SP% 128.0**
Speed ratings: **100,99,98,96,95 95,95,94,85,82 77,73,71,70**
CSF £6.76 TOTE £2.70: £1.30, £1.60, £3.20; EX 10.10 Trifecta £172.40.
Owner P W Middleton **Bred** Woodview Stud **Trained** Dorton, Bucks

FOCUS
This had the look of an interesting race of its type, but only time will tell how good the form proves to be.
T/Plt: £270.10 to a £1 stake. Pool: £70086.98 - 189.4 winning tickets. T/Qpdt: £83.80 to a £1 stake. Pool: £4758.90 - 42.0 winning tickets. **Walter Glynn**

860 STRATFORD (L-H)
Sunday, July 12

OFFICIAL GOING: Good (good to soft in places)
Wind: light breeze Weather: sunshine and heavy showers; 20 degrees

971 SHAKESPEARE MARTINEAU "NATIONAL HUNT" NOVICES' HURDLE (8 hdls) 2m 70y
2:20 (2:20) (Class 4) 4-Y-0+ **£3,898** (£1,144; £572; £286)

Form RPR

54-1 **1** **In On The Act**[38] 613 5-11-5 123 PaulMoloney 125+
(Evan Williams) *nt a fluent: cl up in chsng bunch: clsd 3 out: wnt 2nd gng wl 3f out: rdn to ld and hit last: sn asserted flat: drvn out* **11/2**[3]

3-11 **2** *2 ¾* **Paolozzi (IRE)**[18] 832 6-11-12 129 (t) ConorO'Farrell 127+
(Seamus Durack) *settled in 2nd or 3rd: clsd 3 out: led after next (3f out): rdn and hdd nring last: nt qckn flat* **2/1**[2]

0-65 **3** *17* **Western Way (IRE)**[42] 566 6-10-12 0 DenisO'Regan 98
(Don Cantillon) *last pair: virtually t.o 3 out: cajoled along after next: tk 20 l 3rd at last: nvr nr ldrs but signs of promise* **16/1**

14 **4** *8* **Monte Wildhorn (IRE)**[21] 810 7-10-7 116 JakeHodson(5) 91
(David Bridgwater) *led: sn 6 l clr: 12 l ahd 5th: clsd on after next: rdn and hdd after 2 out (3f out): fdd to lose poor 3rd at last* **6/5**[1]

10-5 **5** *2 ¼* **Bumble Bay**[31] 702 5-10-12 0 TomO'Brien 89
(Robert Stephens) *cl up in chsng gp tl rdn and wknd sn after 2 out: lost remote 4th bef last* **12/1**

0P/0 **6** *23* **Skating Home (IRE)**[6] 932 9-10-5 0 MrRobertHawker(7) 68
(Richard Hawker) *prom tl rdn and fdd rapidly bef 3 out: sn t.o* **100/1**

00- **U** **Pennant Lady**[141] 4356 5-10-5 0 TrevorWhelan
(Debra Hamer) *small: j. v erratically in last: lost tch 3rd: t.o whn slow 5th and uns rdr* **100/1**

4m 0.1s (4.10) **Going Correction** +0.175s/f (Yiel) **7 Ran SP% 109.7**
Speed ratings (Par 105): **96,94,86,82,81 69,**
CSF £16.02 TOTE £5.70: £2.80, £1.70; EX 11.90 Trifecta £83.10.
Owner David M Williams **Bred** J A And Mrs M A Knox **Trained** Llancarfan, Vale Of Glamorgan

FOCUS
Shared bend entering back straight and rail movement increased races 1, 3, 5, & 7 by 87yds, race 2 by 60yds and races 4 & 6 by 42yds. After heavy rain before racing, the going description was changed to good with good to soft places. A fair novice hurdle in which the first two came clear.

972 PEUGEOT CITROEN H'CAP CHASE (17 fncs) 2m 6f 125y
2:50 (2:50) (Class 5) (0-100,100) 4-Y-0+ **£3,898** (£1,144; £572; £286)

Form RPR

-633 **1** **Pistol Basc (FR)**[16] 841 11-10-9 86 TonyKelly(3) 94+
(Rebecca Menzies) *t.k.h and settled towards rr: effrt 14th: wnt cl 2nd 2 out: sn rdn: led w ears pricked last: idling and drvn rt out to forge clr fnl 100yds* **11/2**

-122 **2** *2 ½* **Louis Phillipe (IRE)**[38] 612 8-10-8 82 (t) MichealNolan 89
(Linda Blackford) *w ldr or prom tl led narrowly 3 out: drvn and jnd next: hdd last: kpt trying tl wknd fnl 75yds* **6/4**[1]

22-P **3** *28* **Forget And Forgive (IRE)**[31] 695 7-11-3 91 (p) SeanQuinlan 77
(Sophie Leech) *mstke 6th: mde most tl drvn and hdd 3 out: 3rd whn j. slowly next and lost tch rapidly* **17/2**

0UP4 **4** *dist* **Driving Well (IRE)**[11] 878 7-10-2 76 (b) JamesBest 25
(Arthur Whiting) *cl up: led briefly 6th: blnd 12th and dropped out u.p: t.o after blunder 14th: j. bdly lft last but wnt 4th nr fin* **9/2**[3]

P-PP **5** *1 ¼* **Thats Ben (IRE)**[31] 698 10-10-2 76 (tp) JamesDavies 24
(Tom Gretton) *tended to lack fluency: cl up tl 12th: struggling whn blnd 14th: sn t.o: hit 3 out: fin v weakly and lost 4th cl home* **20/1**

0005 **P** **Accessallareas (IRE)**[7] 914 10-11-12 100 RobertDunne
(Sarah-Jayne Davies) *trckd ldrs tl drvn 13th: qckly lost tch: t.o and p.u 2 out* **25/1**

P-13 **P** **Mr Robinson (FR)**[57] 340 8-10-2 81 JakeHodson(5)
(Rob Summers) *tended to jump slowly in last: nvr gng wl enough: struggling whn hit 11th and reminders: sn t.o: p.u 14th* **4/1**[2]

5m 42.0s (2.80) **Going Correction** +0.175s/f (Yiel) **7 Ran SP% 112.7**
Speed ratings (Par 103): **102,101,91,79,78 ,**
CSF £14.50 CT £67.78 TOTE £6.90: £2.90, £1.50; EX 14.80 Trifecta £93.40.
Owner Panther Racing Ltd **Bred** Sebastien & Alain Dufrancatel **Trained** Stearsby, N Yorks

FOCUS
A weak handicap chase in which the first two finished a long way clear.

973 PRIDE OF BIRMINGHAM H'CAP HURDLE (FOR THE STRATFORD SUMMER SALVER) (8 hdls) 2m 70y
3:25 (3:25) (Class 3) (0-130,130) 3-Y-£7,596 (£2,244; £1,122; £561; £280)

Form RPR

3-14 **1** **Good Of Luck**[30] 708 6-11-6 124 (p) GavinSheehan 128+
(Warren Greatrex) *racd in 2nd or 3rd: rdn after 2 out: pressed ldr between last two: led after last: r.o gamely to edge clr* **10/1**

2-21 **2** *1 ¾* **Jalingo (IRE)**[10] 881 4-11-8 128 SamTwiston-Davies 128
(John Ferguson) *racd keenly: settled cl up: chal gng wl 2 out: led between last two but sn drvn: stl had ears pricked w slt advantage last: outbattled whn hdd flat* **4/1**[2]

26-3 **3** *2* **Oliver's Gold**[14] 854 7-10-9 120 JamieHamilton(7) 120
(Mark Walford) *midfield: drvn and effrt after 2 out: wnt 3rd bef last where nt fluent: no imp on ldrs flat* **7/1**

1-33 **4** *8* **Purple 'n Gold (IRE)**[19] 826 6-11-3 126 (p) KieronEdgar(5) 122+
(David Pipe) *hld up and bhd: impeded and stmbld bef 5th: effrt 3 out: rdn and outpcd next: tk wl hld 4th after last* **6/1**[3]

23-1 **5** *2 ½* **El Massivo (IRE)**[12] 860 5-11-1 119 TomCannon 115+
(Brian Ellison) *cl up: 4th and drvn after 2 out: 3 l 4th and btn whn blnd last* **10/3**[1]

146- **6** *hd* **Don Padeja**[9] 1513 5-11-0 121 (p) MauriceLinehan(3) 111
(Jonjo O'Neill) *racd freely in ld: rdn after 2 out: hdd between last two: fdd u.p bef last* **12/1**

/020 **7** *5* **Battlecat**[21] 810 8-10-9 113 AdamWedge 99
(Evan Williams) *plld hrd in midfield: mstke 5th and dropped out qckly u.p: plugged on after 2 out* **14/1**

50-6 **8** *48* **Laser Blazer**[14] 854 7-11-6 124 WayneHutchinson 67
(Alan King) *towards rr: shkn up 3rd: drvn 5th: sn lost tch: t.o 2 out* **8/1**

13-0 **F** **Rumble Of Thunder (IRE)**[36] 645 9-11-9 130 (p) AdamNicol(3)
(Philip Kirby) *cl up: 5 l 5th and rdn and looking hld whn fell 2 out* **20/1**

04-5 **U** **Honey Pound (IRE)**[14] 854 7-11-4 122 MichaelByrne
(Tim Vaughan) *mounted on crse: hld up last and t.k.h: rdn and lost tch 2 out: 15 l 7th whn landed awkwardly and uns rdr last* **20/1**

3m 53.7s (-2.30) **Going Correction** +0.175s/f (Yiel)
WFA 4 from 5yo+ 15lb **10 Ran SP% 113.9**
Speed ratings (Par 107): **112,111,110,106,104 104,102,78, ,**
CSF £49.57 CT £298.96 TOTE £13.00: £3.60, £1.40, £2.10; EX 55.40 Trifecta £278.80.
Owner Bernard & Jane Panton **Bred** Mrs G Slater **Trained** Upper Lambourn, Berks

FOCUS
A fair handicap, and form that looks sound enough.

974 PRIDE OF COVENTRY H'CAP CHASE (FOR THE STRATFORD SUMMER CUP) (12 fncs) 2m 213y
4:00 (4:00) (Class 2) (0-150,144) 4-Y-0+
£12,512 (£3,696; £1,848; £924; £462; £232)

Form RPR

-421 **1** **Red Seventy**[42] 570 6-10-2 120 JackQuinlan 127+
(Sarah Humphrey) *trckd ldrs: chal gng wl 2 out: sn led: 5 l clr last: pushed along and kpt on wl* **15/2**

-332 **2** *3* **Miss Tenacious**[18] 830 8-9-13 124 HarryCobden(7) 128
(Ron Hodges) *tended to jump deliberately: off pce in 6th pl: effrt 9th: mstke next: 4 l 4th 2 out where j. slowly: pushed along bef last: styd on willingly to go 2nd flat but wnr had already asserted* **10/3**[1]

0P-3 **3** *3 ¾* **Fair Dilemma (IRE)**[18] 830 10-11-7 139 TomO'Brien 141
(Paul Henderson) *2nd tl led 6th: hdd bef 9th: rdn and ev ch 2 out: no ex bef last: lost 2nd and eased whn btn flat* **10/3**[1]

2226 **4** *3 ¼* **My Brother Sylvest**[43] 555 9-11-0 139 (b) MichaelHeard(7) 136
(David Pipe) *sweating and kpt wl away fr rest at s: led at fast pce tl hdd 6th: outj. next: led again bef 9th: hrd rdn and hdd sn after 2 out: lost 3rd bef last: eased whn btn flat* **7/2**[2]

5-66 **5** *10* **Limpopo Tom (IRE)**[31] 701 8-10-6 124 (p) DenisO'Regan 112
(David Rees) *detached in last: mstkes 4th and 6th: t.o 8th: styd on wl after 2 out: no ch of rching ldrs* **10/1**

1-01 **6** *2 ½* **Another Flutter (IRE)**[43] 555 11-11-7 139 (tp) CharliePoste 125
(Matt Sheppard) *pressed ldrs tl 9th: sn rdn: wl bhd after 2 out* **6/1**[3]

1R-0 **R** **Nikos Extra (FR)**[26] 751 11-10-9 127 AdamWedge
(Alexandra Dunn) *ref to r* **14/1**

4m 6.5s (-0.60) **Going Correction** +0.175s/f (Yiel) **7 Ran SP% 110.2**
Speed ratings (Par 109): **108,106,104,103,98 97,**
CSF £30.91 CT £92.80 TOTE £8.20: £5.20, £1.60; EX 25.70 Trifecta £99.10.
Owner Yen Hall Farm Racing **Bred** Sir Eric Parker **Trained** West Wratting, Cambs

FOCUS
This decent handicap was run at a strong gallop.

975 ALLSOPPANDALLSOPP INTERNATIONAL AWARD WINNERS JUVENILE HURDLE (8 hdls) 2m 70y
4:30 (4:30) (Class 4) 3-Y-O **£3,898** (£1,144; £572; £286)

Form RPR

1 **Leoncavallo (IRE)**[76] 3-10-12 0 SamTwiston-Davies 110+
(John Ferguson) *often j. nimbly and travelled wl: led after 2nd: hit 2 out and hdd briefly but sn gng clr of rest: asserting whn rn green bef last and rdn and clipped flight: wl in command flat* **9/4**[2]

2 *7* **Paddys Runner**[20] 3-10-12 0 NoelFehily 102+
(Alan King) *settled in rr: effrt 3 out: chal and lft in ld briefly next: gng wl w ev ch tl rdn between last two: 3 l 2nd and btn whn blnd last* **11/10**[1]

3 *16* **Racing Spirit**[47] 3-10-12 0 GavinSheehan 84
(John Quinn) *hld up and bhd: drvn bef 5th: poor 5th home turn: kpt on to take remote 3rd nr fin* **14/1**

43 **4** *1* **Ace Of Marmalade (IRE)**[23] 778 3-10-5 0 CraigGallagher(7) 83
(Brian Ellison) *t.k.h and led at stdy pce tl restrained after 2nd: cl up tl 2 out: wknd to 10 l 3rd and drvn home turn: lost remote 3rd cl home* **16/1**

5 *5* **Loom Of Life (IRE)**[8] 3-10-12 0 DenisO'Regan 78
(Richard Fahey) *drvn briefly 1st: prom tl drvn 3 out: struggling sn after next* **25/1**

P **St Paul's Square (IRE)**[33] 3-10-12 0 TomCannon
(Chris Gordon) *j. v stickily in rr: lost tch and slow 4th and 5th: continued t.o tl p.u after 2 out* **50/1**

P **Solstalla**[31] 3-10-5 0 TrevorWhelan
(William Jarvis) *hit 2nd: cl up tl rdn and wknd qckly sn after 2 out: t.o and p.u last* **5/1**[3]

3m 58.3s (2.30) **Going Correction** +0.175s/f (Yiel) **7 Ran SP% 113.4**
Speed ratings (Par 102): **101,97,89,89,86 ,**
CSF £5.20 TOTE £3.60: £2.00, £1.20; EX 6.50 Trifecta £43.00.

Owner Bloomfields **Bred** Darley **Trained** Cowlinge, Suffolk
FOCUS
A juvenile hurdle lacking depth, but the first two look decent recruits.

976 MARCO'S NEW YORK ITALIAN STRATFORD H'CAP CHASE (14 fncs) 2m 3f 98y
5:05 (5:05) (Class 5) (0-100,100) 4-Y-O+ **£3,898** (£1,144; £572; £286)

Form RPR
4-32 **1** **Zama Zama**[24] 770 8-11-4 92 ....(v) AdamWedge 108+
(Evan Williams) *settled cl up: led after 11th: rdn clr after 2 out: 7 l ahd and idling last: kpt up to work but was a gng to hold on* **4/1**[2]
-543 **2** *3* **Faith Jicaro (IRE)**[21] 806 8-11-5 98 ....(p) JakeHodson(5) 108
(David Bridgwater) *midfield: rdn 8th: nt fluent 10th and sn drvn and outpcd: 10 l 3rd 2 out: rallied bef last and styd on to go 2nd flat but flattered by proximity to idling wnr* **7/1**
U0-6 **3** *2 1/4* **Dream Bolt (IRE)**[31] 698 7-11-9 97 .... DenisO'Regan 105
(David Rees) *settled trcking ldrs: wnt 2nd 3 out: clr of rest next: sn rdn: outpcd by wnr bef last: lost 2nd flat* **8/1**
-224 **4** *3 3/4* **Mister Wall Street (FR)**[14] 859 10-11-0 91 ....(vt[1]) TonyKelly(3) 97
(Rebecca Menzies) *bhd and nt a fluent: brief effrt 11th: rdn and btn after next: plodded on* **6/1**[3]
-F34 **P** **Capisci (IRE)**[47] 490 10-11-11 99 ....(p) SamTwiston-Davies
(Sarah-Jayne Davies) *led 2nd: t.k.h: hdd and blnd 3 out: dropped out rapidly: t.o and p.u last* **9/1**
52-3 **P** **Red Rosso**[40] 588 10-10-5 79 .... TrevorWhelan
(Rob Summers) *last pair and tended to lack fluency: hit 9th and struggling: lost tch whn drvn bef 3 out: t.o and p.u last* **7/1**
P **Tiger D'Oust (FR)**[29] 6-11-7 100 ....(p) KieronEdgar(5)
(Chris Down) *led tl 2nd: cl 2nd tl mstke 10th: wkng whn mstke 3 out: blnd next: t.o and p.u last* **16/1**
P-44 **P** **Lily Little Legs (IRE)**[11] 874 6-11-6 94 .... TomO'Brien
(Ian Williams) *hit 3rd: handy tl mstke 7th (water): last and nt travelling after: t.o and p.u 3 out* **11/4**[1]
4m 52.1s (2.10) **Going Correction** +0.175s/f (Yiel) **8 Ran SP% 112.9**
Speed ratings (Par 103): **102,100,99,98, , ,**
CSF £30.90 CT £210.85 TOTE £5.10: £2.10, £2.00, £3.00; EX 16.50 Trifecta £102.00.
Owner Tony Cromwell & Partner **Bred** Cheveley Park Stud Ltd **Trained** Llancarfan, Vale Of Glamorgan
FOCUS
Modest handicap form.

977 BIRMINGHAM MAIL CONDITIONAL JOCKEYS' H'CAP HURDLE (8 hdls 1 omitted) 2m 2f 148y
5:40 (5:40) (Class 5) (0-100,98) 4-Y-O+ **£2,599** (£763; £381; £190)

Form RPR
06-0 **1** **All Riled Up**[33] 675 7-10-1 76 .... DanielHiskett(3) 84
(Harry Chisman) *led after 1st: hdd 4th: chsd ldrs: 4th home turn: rdn to ld and crossed by loose horse bef last where 2 l ahd: sn clr and plugged on gamely* **16/1**
-350 **2** *5* **Mix N Match**[14] 856 11-9-11 72 oh4 .... ThomasCheesman(3) 75
(Laura Young) *bhd: clsd after normal 3 out: disp 2nd and drvn between last two: ch tl nt qckn bef last but got up for wl hld 2nd cl home* **33/1**
-5P5 **3** *nk* **Keychain (IRE)**[18] 835 5-11-11 97 ....(bt[1]) ThomasGarner 101
(Brendan Powell) *cl up: led 4th: drvn and hdd and racd awkwardly bef last: jst lost r for wl hld 2nd* **20/1**
34-3 **4** *7* **Fred Le Macon (FR)**[31] 692 6-11-2 98 .... JamieInsole(10) 96
(Alan King) *towards rr: rdn and struggling whn blnd normal 3 out: plodded on after* **6/1**[3]
50-P **5** *3* **Massachusetts**[21] 807 8-10-1 73 ....(t) JakeHodson 67
(Rob Summers) *wl bhd most of way: mod and short-lived effrt after omitted 2 out: nvr nr ldrs* **33/1**
46/0 **F** **Prairie Hawk (USA)**[31] 703 10-10-4 76 ....(t) BenPoste
(Adrian Wintle) *chsd ldrs: disputing 4th whn stmbld and fell 6th* **33/1**
PP/P **P** **Backhomeinderry (IRE)**[21] 811 10-10-10 87(v[1])
WilliamFeatherstone(5)
(Dominic Ffrench Davis) *effrt to midfield 5th but sn u.p: no rspnse: t.o and p.u after omitted 2 out* **50/1**
/541 **U** **Cornish Beau (IRE)**[7] 918 8-10-8 83 7ex ....(p) ChrisWard(3)
(Dr Richard Newland) *hmpd after 2nd: t.k.h in midfield tl hmpd and uns rdr 6th* **10/11**[1]
-033 **P** **Businessmoney Judi**[25] 759 9-10-8 85 ....(t) MrMatthewHampton(5)
(Martin Hill) *prom whn p.u after 2nd: fatally injured* **10/1**
-040 **P** **Mahayogin (USA)**[16] 843 7-9-11 72 ....(t) MichaelHeard(3)
(Sarah-Jayne Davies) *t.k.h and prom on outer tl rdn after 5th: t.o and p.u bef normal 3 out* **50/1**
40P/ **P** **Micquus (IRE)**[520] 4132 6-11-3 89 ....(v) ConorShoemark
(Jonathan Geake) *last and drvn after 4th: fnd nil: t.o and p.u bef normal 3 out* **40/1**
5-2F **U** **Iktiview**[31] 695 7-10-7 82 ....(bt) JamieBargary(3) 86
(Matt Sheppard) *led tl after 1st: bdly hmpd next: prom: pressed ldr fr 5th: bmpd along after omitted 2 out: wknd bef last and 5 l 4th whn pitched and uns rdr* **4/1**[2]
-00F **P** **Kayflin (FR)**[33] 673 7-11-4 90 ....(p) JackSherwood
(Linda Jewell) *prom: rdn and lost pl 6th: t.o and p.u last* **40/1**
4m 38.3s (6.80) **Going Correction** +0.175s/f (Yiel) **13 Ran SP% 124.0**
Speed ratings (Par 103): **92,89,89,86,85 , , , ,**
CSF £428.99 CT £10129.10 TOTE £21.20: £4.20, £7.90, £4.00; EX 560.30 Trifecta £3369.50 Part won.
Owner McClean Baker Grabham Flint Wood Welch **Bred** R Robinson **Trained** Maugersbury, Gloucs
FOCUS
Just a moderate handicap hurdle, but a dramatic race. Not many became involved. The second-last flight was bypassed, leaving a very long run to the final flight. A group of four were clear at that stage.
T/Jkpt: Not won T/Plt: £21.60 to a £1 stake. Pool: £92112.45 - 3111.3 winning tickets. T/Qpdt: £11.00 to a £1 stake. Pool: £6265.74 - 421.4 winning tickets. **Iain Mackenzie**

978 - 984a (Foreign Racing) - See Raceform Interactive

[844] LES LANDES
Sunday, July 12
OFFICIAL GOING: Good (good to firm in places)

985a DALLAS BURSTON GROUP CHAMPION HURDLE 2m 1f
2:30 (2:30) 4-Y-O+ **£1,900** (£685; £415)

RPR
1 **Rossetti**[16] 844 7-11-2 .... MattieBatchelor 114
(Mrs A Malzard, Jersey) **4/6**[1]
2 *10* **The Bay Bandit**[14] 857 8-11-2 ....(p) MarkQuinlan 104
(Neil Mulholland) **5/4**[2]
3 *15* **Steely**[16] 7-11-2 ....(p) MrRBirkett 89
(K Kukk, Jersey) **12/1**
4 *12* **Eightfold**[16] 6-11-2 ....(p) MrFTett 77
(Mrs A Corson, Jersey) **5/1**[3]
5 *7* **Pomander (IRE)**[29] 740 12-10-11 .... MrRHodson 65
(J Moon, Jersey) **16/1**
P **Dalmo**[16] 844 6-11-2 ....(p) MrPCollington
(K Kukk, Jersey) **9/1**
Owner Sheikh A'Leg Racing **Bred** Bricklow Ltd **Trained** St Ouen, Jersey

986 - 998a (Foreign Racing) - See Raceform Interactive

[933] UTTOXETER (L-H)
Wednesday, July 15
OFFICIAL GOING: Good
Wind: light breeze Weather: hot and sunny; 20 degrees

999 ASHLEIGH BUILDERS CONDITIONAL JOCKEYS' MAIDEN HURDLE (10 hdls) 2m 3f 207y
2:20 (2:20) (Class 5) 4-Y-O+ **£2,339** (£686; £343; £171)

Form RPR
PP/5 **1** **Regal Diamond (IRE)**[33] 705 7-11-0 120 ....(v[1]) SeanBowen 123+
(Peter Bowen) *nt a too fluent: settled chsng tearaway ldr: clsd after 7th: led bef next: 17 l clr last: sn heavily eased* **8/13**[1]
2P-4 **2** *12* **Paddocks Lounge (IRE)**[39] 647 8-10-11 110 ....[1] KillianMoore(3) 105
(Sophie Leech) *hld up in last tl after 6th: plodded on after next: lft remote 3rd 3 out: 20 l 3rd at last but drvn into 2nd cl home* **9/1**
660- **3** *3/4* **Little Windmill (IRE)**[159] 4073 5-10-8 0 .... LizzieKelly(6) 104
(Neil King) *settled cl up bhd long ldr: effrt after 7th to 6 l 3rd home turn: lft 2nd 3 out but wnr sn wl clr: rdn and lost 2nd nr fin* **50/1**
4 **4** *17* **Almagest**[12] 893 7-10-11 0 .... DavidPrichard(3) 96
(Robert Stephens) *towards rr: rdn after 7th: sn lost tch: remote fr 3 out* **8/1**[3]
F54- **U** **Bringithomeminty**[82] 5513 6-11-0 0 .... KieronEdgar
(David Evans) *wore a nose net: led and sn tore 20 l clr: reduced advantage fr 6th: hdd bef 3 out and 3rd and slowing rapidly whn uns at flight: collapsed after r but got to his feet abt 20 minutes later* **12/1**
04 **P** **Astrowolf**[50] 494 4-10-11 0 .... ThomasGarner
(Mark H Tompkins) *bhd: rdn 6th: t.o next: sn p.u* **25/1**
6/0- **P** **Alco Sivola (FR)**[407] 574 5-11-0 115 ....(t) NicodeBoinville
(Nick Williams) *hit 4th: cl up in chsng gp tl rdn and fdd bef 3 out where hmpd: t.o and p.u next* **6/1**[2]
4m 49.7s (-13.50) **Going Correction** -0.525s/f (Firm)
WFA 4 from 5yo+ 16lb **7 Ran SP% 110.8**
Speed ratings (Par 103): **106,101,100,94, ,**
CSF £6.62 TOTE £1.60: £1.30, £3.10; EX 6.80 Trifecta £67.10.
Owner Roddy Owen,Paul Fullagar & Karen Bowen **Bred** Brittas House Stud **Trained** Little Newcastle, Pembrokes
FOCUS
Some starts have been moved at this track following remeasuring, so some races will not have speed figures until there is sufficient data to calculate updated median times. Hurdles had been moved to the inside rail, with the course at its shortest. Divided bends. The track had been extensively watered to maintain good ground. After the second race the winning jockey Nick Slatter said, "I thought it would be quick but it is good the whole way round", while Richard Johnson stated, "It is just on the slow side of good." A weak maiden hurdle, restricted to conditional jockeys. It's been rated around the second, to his mark.

1000 SMITH COOPER NOVICES' HURDLE (9 hdls) 1m 7f 168y
2:50 (2:50) (Class 4) 4-Y-O+ **£3,249** (£954; £477; £238)

Form RPR
2-15 **1** **Are They Your Own (IRE)**[49] 511 7-11-0 123 .... NickSlatter(5) 121+
(Fergal O'Brien) *led tl 4th: cl 2nd tl led again 3 out: rdn next: nrly 2 l clr last: hung on gamely: all out* **8/1**[3]
41 **2** *3/4* **Number One London (IRE)**[22] 823 5-11-5 120 .... RichardJohnson 121+
(Tim Vaughan) *trckd ldng pair: wnt 2nd sn after 3 out: hrd drvn fr next: kpt on after last but wnr a fending him off* **2/1**[2]
2 **3** *17* **Silent Movie (IRE)**[17] 853 5-10-12 0 .... AidanColeman 100
(John Ferguson) *hld up: rdn bef 3 out and already floundering whn hit flight: 8 l 3rd and btn and racing awkwardly next: plodded on: hit last* **1/1**[1]
4 **4** *6* **Cabin Fever**[17] 853 4-10-3 0 .... RobertDunne 87
(Tom Lacey) *t.k.h in 2nd tl led 4th: hdd and blnd 3 out: dropped out qckly and mstke next: lost two shoes* **50/1**
0/35 **5** *5* **Mullinavat (IRE)**[10] 912 6-10-12 0 ....(t) HenryBrooke 87
(Jennie Candlish) *chsd ldrs: rdn and struggling bef 3 out* **33/1**
6 **6** *4* **Uncle Bernie (IRE)**[15] 860 5-10-12 0 ....[1] PaulMoloney 84
(Sarah Hollinshead) *detached in last whn hit 4th: blnd 6th and no ch after but kpt plugging on fr 2 out* **25/1**
145 **F** **Captain Swift (IRE)**[17] 853 4-11-3 115 .... BrianHughes
(John Mackie) *hld up towards rr tl fell 5th* **14/1**
3m 48.2s (-9.20) **Going Correction** -0.525s/f (Firm)
WFA 4 from 5yo+ 15lb **7 Ran SP% 109.9**
Speed ratings (Par 105): **102,101,93,90,87 85,**
CSF £23.08 TOTE £8.20: £3.20, £1.70; EX 25.70 Trifecta £35.80.
Owner Ian Slatter **Bred** William Neville **Trained** Naunton, Gloucs

FOCUS
A modest, uncompetitive novice hurdle. They went a decent pace, but it paid to be prominent. The first two are rated to their marks.

1001 PSP WEALTH MANAGEMENT (S) HURDLE (9 hdls) 1m 7f 168y
3:20 (3:20) (Class 5) 4-7-Y-0 **£2,339** (£686; £343; £171)

Form | | | | RPR
334- **1** **Roja Dove (IRE)**[187] [3597] 6-10-5 119..........................(v) TrevorWhelan 104+
(Neil King) *plld hrd in 2nd tl led gng best nring 3 out: abt 2 l ahd whn hit last: rdn and jst hld on* **11/10**[1]
3-61 **2** *hd* **Swampfire (IRE)**[3] [962] 7-10-10 98.................................. MikeyHamill(7) 114
(Barry Brennan) *chsd clr ldng pair: effrt in 2nd 3 out: hrd drvn fr next: blnd last: r.o u.p: jst hld* **2/1**[2]
0-55 **3** *17* **King Muro**[59] [354] 5-10-12 90..............................(t[1]) PaddyBrennan 94
(Fergal O'Brien) *settled in midfield: 5 l home turn: sn rdn and no rspnse: poor 3rd at next* **8/1**[3]
P **4** *38* **Intercooler Turbo (IRE)**[12] [893] 6-10-12 0..................(b[1]) RyanMahon 60
(Dan Skelton) *led: slow 2nd: rdn and hdd bef 3 out: stopped v qckly and sn t.o* **20/1**
P/35 **P** **Sunny Bank**[7] [860] 6-10-12 0...........................(t) GerardTumelty
(Alan Coogan) *10 l 3rd after 4th: lost action and p.u 6th: dismntd* **50/1**
U **El Duque**[22] 4-10-5 0.. RyanWhile(5)
(Bill Turner) *bhd: hit 4th: v slow next: rdn and sn t.o: rdr c adrift 3 out* **28/1**
P-50 **P** **King Of All Kings (IRE)**[41] [613] 5-10-9 0..................(b[1]) SeanBowen(3)
(Peter Bowen) *15 l 4th after 4th: v slow next and lost action: p.u and dismntd 6th* **12/1**

3m 46.4s (-11.00) **Going Correction** -0.525s/f (Firm)
WFA 4 from 5yo+ 15lb **7 Ran SP% 109.9**
Speed ratings: **106,105,97,78, ,**
CSF £3.24 TOTE £2.10: £1.50, £1.70; EX 4.40 Trifecta £15.80.The winner was bought in 4200gns.
Owner Barry Williams & Donald Caldwell **Bred** Bernard Cooke **Trained** Barbury Castle, Wiltshire

FOCUS
A weak seller and not form to dwell on, although the time was faster than the previous novice event. The winner was a stone+ off her mark.

1002 KEN BOULTON 50TH ANNIVERSARY H'CAP HURDLE (FOR THE KEN BOULTON MEMORIAL TROPHY) (12 hdls) 2m 7f 70y
3:50 (3:50) (Class 4) (0-120,120) 4-Y-0+ **£3,249** (£954; £477; £238)

Form | | | | RPR
5-11 **1** **Minnie Milan (IRE)**[50] [493] 6-11-2 110............................ TrevorWhelan 122+
(Neil King) *trckd ldrs: clsd to ld 7th: rdn to forge clr fr 2 out: 5 l ahd whn hit last: readily: v game* **11/4**[1]
0-P4 **2** *6* **Fighter Jet**[36] [681] 7-11-12 120....................................(p) BrianHughes 125
(John Mackie) *a 2nd or 3rd pl: chsd wnr fr 3 out but sn hrd drvn: no imp fr next* **9/1**
2-P4 **3** *7* **Lookslikerainted (IRE)**[34] [701] 8-11-4 112....................(tp) PaulMoloney 112
(Sophie Leech) *pressed ldrs: 3rd and drvn 3 out: wandering lft and rt after next whn making no imp* **9/1**
-614 **4** *shd* **Vaihau (FR)**[51] [473] 6-11-12 120.................................. NoelFehily 119
(Jonjo O'Neill) *settled towards rr: effrt bef 3 out: sn drvn: one pce fr next: disp wl hld 3rd fr last* **9/2**[2]
0-22 **5** *¾* **Set List (IRE)**[39] [648] 6-11-9 117................................ AidanColeman 116
(Emma Lavelle) *mstke 1st: v slow 3rd: several positions: nt fluent 8th: rdn bef 3 out: plugged on and n.d after* **11/2**[3]
05F0 **6** *1 ¾* **Get Home Now**[24] [812] 7-11-3 114............................(tp) SeanBowen(3) 110
(Peter Bowen) *pressed ldr tl lost pl 7th: outpcd in rr bef 3 out: plugged on sltly after next: no ch w ldrs* **8/1**
-224 **7** *½* **Ballycamp (IRE)**[26] [780] 6-11-9 117................................ AdamPogson 113+
(Charles Pogson) *sweating: tk fierce hold in midfield tl after 9th: rdn bef next: btn bef 2 out* **14/1**
05-5 **8** *12* **Count Salazar (IRE)**[59] [358] 10-11-0 115..............(p) MissBHampson(7) 105
(Andy Turnell) *led: j.rt and ofter violently so: set modest pce tl hdd 7th: w wnr tl 9th: wknd next* **22/1**
2-40 **9** *3 ¼* **Exemplary**[30] [747] 8-10-7 108..........................(t) MrRobertHawker(7) 90
(Johnny Farrelly) *hld up in rr of tight knit bunch: drvn bef 3 out: sn btn: eased flat* **17/2**

5m 49.3s (-9.50) **Going Correction** -0.525s/f (Firm) **9 Ran SP% 112.9**
Speed ratings (Par 105): **95,92,90,90,90 89,89,85,84**
CSF £26.94 TOTE £3.20: £1.50, £3.00, £2.50; EX 26.50 Trifecta £251.60.
Owner Mark & Tracy Harrod,P Branigan,T Messom **Bred** S P Tindall **Trained** Barbury Castle, Wiltshire
■ Stewards' Enquiry : Adam Pogson ten-day ban: failed to take all reasonable and permissable measures to obtain best possible placing (Jul 29-31,Aug 2,12,13,15,16,19,20)

FOCUS
A fair handicap hurdle. They were well grouped until late on, but nothing came from behind. Another step up from the winner and there's probably more to come.

1003 SMITH COOPER "NEWCOMERS" STANDARD OPEN NATIONAL HUNT FLAT RACE 1m 7f 168y
4:20 (4:20) (Class 6) 4-6-Y-0 **£1,559** (£457; £228; £114)

Form | | | | RPR
1 **Improved (IRE)** 5-10-11 0.................................... AdamNicol(3) 95+
(Philip Kirby) *wl mde: mde all: v slow pce for 10f: shkn up 3f out: rdn clr over 1f out: styd on gamely* **12/1**
2 *4 ½* **Golden Thread** 5-11-0 0.................................... TrevorWhelan 91
(Neil King) *trckd ldrs: effrt home turn: rnged upsides wnr 3f out tl rdn and wknd over 1f out* **10/1**
3 *¾* **That's Gonna Sting (IRE)** 4-10-9 0........................ MattGriffiths(3) 88
(Jeremy Scott) *tall: in midfield: rdn and outpcd 3f out: tried to rally over 1f out: looked green but kpt on steadily ins fnl f: grad catching runner-up after* **4/1**[3]
4 *4* **Mountyfirth** 5-10-7 0.................................... LizzieKelly(7) 86
(Nick Williams) *chsd ldrs: rdn 3f out: one pce and btn wl over 1f out* **10/3**[2]
5 *18* **Common Practice (IRE)** 4-10-12 0............................ NoelFehily 66
(Jonjo O'Neill) *settled towards rr: rdn over 3f out: btn over 2f out: t.o* **2/1**[1]
6 *1 ¼* **Golden Feet** 4-10-12 0..........................(t) MichaelByrne 65
(Tim Vaughan) *chsd ldrs: rdn 3f out: sn btn: t.o* **13/2**
7 *8* **Gold Thief (IRE)** 5-11-0 0.................................... TomCannon 59
(Laura Young) *small: pressed ldr at sedate pce tl rdn and fdd rapidly 3f out: t.o* **16/1**

3m 47.3s (-4.50) **Going Correction** -0.525s/f (Firm)
WFA 4 from 5yo 2lb **7 Ran SP% 112.4**
Speed ratings: **90,87,87,85,76 75,71**
CSF £115.50 TOTE £13.60: £5.70, £5.30; EX 106.10 Trifecta £290.90.
Owner Mrs Philippa Kirby **Bred** Miss Susan Heath **Trained** East Appleton, N Yorks

FOCUS
A bumper confined to horses who have not run under any code of racing. There was little pace on and the winner made all in a slow time.

1004 SIGNS 2000 NOVICES' H'CAP CHASE (18 fncs) 3m 2y
4:50 (4:51) (Class 5) (0-100,100) 4-Y-0+ **£2,729** (£801; £400; £200)

Form | | | | RPR
P/-1 **1** **Regal Park (IRE)**[8] [935] 8-10-6 80............................(b) WillKennedy 91+
(Dr Richard Newland) *settled towards rr: prog gng wl 15th: led and hit last: rdn and kpt on stoutly* **2/1**[1]
56- **2** *1* **Top Chief**[38] 7-11-12 93.................................(t) CiaranGethings(7) 100
(Anthony Honeyball) *mstke 2nd: prom and often j. boldly: led 10th tl 12th: led again bef 15th: drvn next: hdd last: jst outpcd flat* **14/1**
24-2 **3** *1 ¼* **Supapowers (IRE)**[19] [840] 9-11-12 100............................(t) TomO'Brien 105
(Robert Stephens) *cl up in 3rd or 4th pl: rdn 3 out: ev ch next: nt qckn bef last but kpt trying flat* **10/1**
-P35 **4** *½* **Shady Glen (IRE)**[14] [879] 6-10-9 83............................(p) KielanWoods 87
(Graeme McPherson) *chsd ldrs: effrt bef 15th: sn rdn: last of four gng clr bef 2 out: kpt on u.p flat but a hld* **16/1**
P0-4 **5** *9* **Annamult (IRE)**[24] [808] 7-10-6 80.................................... AdamWedge 76
(Alan Phillips) *chsd ldrs: rdn bef 15th: plugged on same pce and n.d after* **20/1**
2-13 **6** *nse* **The Purchaser (IRE)**[26] [782] 7-11-2 97..........(p) MrTommieMO'Brien(7) 93
(Chris Bealby) *led tl after 2nd: w ldr tl led again 12th: rdn and hdd bef 15th: btn 2 out: wnt lft and eased flat* **13/2**[3]
-P54 **7** *½* **The Winking Prawn (IRE)**[24] [807] 8-11-1 94..................(t) ConorRing(5) 90
(Graeme McPherson) *chsd ldrs: rdn 15th: nt qckn bef 2 out and wl hld after* **22/1**
P344 **8** *6* **Dr Dreamy (IRE)**[9] [926] 8-10-0 74 oh1..........................(t) TrevorWhelan 64
(Claire Dyson) *midfield: drvn bef 15th: sn btn: hit last* **33/1**
2 **9** *7* **Kilcross Boy (IRE)**[15] [864] 10-11-9 97............................(tp) NoelFehily 81
(Neil Mulholland) *blnd 4th: nvr bttr than midfield: rdn and little rspnse bef 15th: sn btn* **11/2**[2]
532U **10** *7* **Breezy Kin (IRE)**[9] [926] 7-10-9 90............................(p) MikeyHamill(7) 68
(Sean Curran) *mstkes: slt ld after 2nd tl 10th: wknd 14th: remote after next* **25/1**
-312 **11** *dist* **Troubled (IRE)**[24] [803] 8-10-6 80............................(p) BrianHughes 22
(David Thompson) *prom tl 10th: wknd 12th: t.o 15th: b.b.v* **9/1**
4-P **12** *3 ¼* **Madam Be**[76] [30] 5-10-10 84.................................... GavinSheehan 23
(Brian Barr) *in last pair: struggling 11th: t.o 14th* **20/1**
0P-3 **P** **Joyful Motive**[26] [779] 6-9-7 74 oh8........................ ThomasCheesman(7)
(Michael Chapman) *bhd and nvr travelling: rdn 4th: t.o 10th: p.u 12th* **100/1**
05-0 **P** **Bob's Call (IRE)**[28] [758] 6-11-7 95................................ DenisO'Regan
(Tony Coyle) *midfield: rdn 10th: t.o 14th: p.u after next* **28/1**
/55- **P** **Sgt Bull Berry**[319] [1392] 8-9-12 79............................ JamieHamilton(7)
(Peter Maddison) *chsd ldrs tl 1/2-way: t.o 14th: p.u 2 out* **25/1**

6m 9.4s (1.30) **Going Correction** -0.40s/f (Good) **15 Ran SP% 122.6**
Speed ratings (Par 103): **81,80,80,80,77 77,76,74,72,70 , , , ,**
CSF £26.35 CT £242.67 TOTE £2.90: £1.40, £5.20, £3.00; EX 32.70 Trifecta £264.30.
Owner J A Provan **Bred** Lodge Park Stud **Trained** Claines, Worcs

FOCUS
Just moderate form, but it was competitive enough, and the first four came clear. The winner should go in again.

1005 WHITLEY GROUNDWORKS H'CAP CHASE (15 fncs) 2m 4f
5:20 (5:21) (Class 4) (0-120,120) 4-Y-0 **£3,924** (£1,159; £579; £290; £145)

Form | | | | RPR
4-41 **1** **Mortlestown (IRE)**[12] [894] 7-11-7 115............................(p) AndrewTinkler 122+
(Martin Keighley) *j. slowly 1st: ldng trio: led fr 10th: rdn 3 out: fnd ex to forge clr after last: gamely* **5/2**[1]
4-01 **2** *1* **River Purple**[52] [464] 8-11-6 114....................................(t) DarylJacob 119
(John Mackie) *hld up in rr: effrt 12th: disp 2nd 3 out: rdn and ev ch last: jst outpcd fnl 100yds* **9/1**
2-41 **3** *6* **Ballybogey (IRE)**[36] [677] 9-11-12 120................................ AdamPogson 121
(Charles Pogson) *ldng trio and often vying for ld: hit 9th: pressed wnr bef 12th: rdn 3 out: lost 2nd after next and wknd bef last* **17/2**
-252 **4** *½* **Susie Sheep**[28] [756] 5-11-10 118............................(b) TomScudamore 118
(David Pipe) *hld up towards rr of bunch: effrt 12th: u.p 3 out: fnd nil: btn next* **5/1**[3]
3-54 **5** *4* **Tregaro (FR)**[10] [915] 9-10-9 103................................(t) BrianHughes 99
(Mike Sowersby) *settled in last pair: stl last at 11th: effrt next: rdn and btn after 3 out* **9/1**
055- **6** *2* **Highway Code (USA)**[18] [4607] 9-11-12 120........................(t) JamieMoore 114
(Kerry Lee) *midfield: rdn 12th: one pce and btn next* **9/1**
22-2 **7** *3 ¼* **Larteta (FR)**[52] [464] 6-10-6 100.................................... JackQuinlan 91
(Sarah Humphrey) *contested ld w two others tl slt advantage 7th tl 10th: rdn and wknd 12th* **9/2**[2]
1-31 **8** *5* **Isthereadifference (IRE)**[22] [827] 8-11-0 108..................(bt) MarkQuinlan 95
(Neil Mulholland) *midfield: drvn bef 12th: sn remote* **9/1**

4m 58.8s (-11.00) **Going Correction** -0.40s/f (Good) **8 Ran SP% 113.9**
Speed ratings (Par 105): **106,105,103,103,101 100,99,97**
CSF £24.59 CT £164.71 TOTE £2.70: £1.10, £3.30, £3.50; EX 27.40 Trifecta £221.20.
Owner M Boothright **Bred** Jan Kennedy **Trained** Condicote, Gloucs
■ Stewards' Enquiry : Daryl Jacob two-day ban: used whip above permitted level (Jul 29-30)

FOCUS
A good, competitive 0-120 chase with no horse going off a double-figure price. Straightforward form.
T/Plt: £273.00 to a £1 stake. Pool of £52910.74 - 141.45 winning tickets. T/Qpdt: £78.60 to a £1 stake. Pool of £4529.46 - 42.60 winning tickets. **Iain Mackenzie**

[926]WORCESTER (L-H)

Wednesday, July 15

OFFICIAL GOING: Good (good to firm in places)

Wind: Light behind Weather: Fine

1006 PP ELECTRICAL SYSTEMS NOVICES' CHASE (13 fncs) 2m 4f

5:50 (5:50) (Class 4) 4-Y-O+ £3,768 (£1,106; £553; £276)

Form RPR

3-21 **1** **Risk A Fine (IRE)**[40] 622 6-11-10 0 RichardJohnson 137+
(Philip Hobbs) *mde all: j.rt: nt fluent 1st and 7th: shkn up after 2 out: drvn out* **8/13**[1]

P6-3 **2** 3 3/4 **Rothman (FR)**[39] 641 5-11-3 0 (t[1]) SamTwiston-Davies 124
(Paul Nicholls) *a.p: hit 1st: chsd wnr 7th: nt fluent 3 out and next: sn rdn: j.rt and mstke last: styd on same pce* **9/2**[2]

151- **3** 15 **Garnock (IRE)**[321] 1359 7-10-5 0 JakeHodson(5) 102
(David Bridgwater) *chsd wnr to 7th: wknd 4 out* **11/1**[3]

1P-0 **4** 47 **Shantou Tiger (IRE)**[36] 681 6-10-10 0 JamesCowley(7) 66
(Donald McCain) *hld up and a in rr: bhd fr 6th* **9/2**[2]

5m 1.2s (-3.40) **Going Correction** +0.075s/f (Yiel) **4 Ran SP% 106.6**
Speed ratings (Par 105): **109,107,101,82**
CSF £3.69 TOTE £1.30; EX 3.00 Trifecta £8.70.
Owner Mrs Diana L Whateley **Bred** Mrs Fintina Kealey **Trained** Withycombe, Somerset

FOCUS

All starts have been moved at this track following remeasuring, so there will be no speed figures here until there is sufficient data to calculate updated median times. The home bend was out approximately 12 yards and the Cathedral bend 9 yards, adding approximately 53 yards to a 2m race. The run-in was on the stands' side. Quickish ground on a warm evening. Not the most competitive of events, but the winner is a useful novice. The form is rated around the first two.

1007 HOMEXPERTSUK.COM EXCEPTIONAL ESTATE AND LETTING AGENTS H'CAP CHASE (16 fncs) 2m 7f

6:20 (6:20) (Class 4) (0-115,115) 4-Y-O+ £3,768 (£1,106; £553; £276)

Form RPR

3-P3 **1** **American Legend (IRE)**[28] 760 7-11-12 **115** (v) RichardJohnson 125+
(Jonjo O'Neill) *hld up: hmpd 1st: hdwy 9th: led 3 out: rdn clr flat: eased nr fin* **15/8**[1]

3-24 **2** 1 1/4 **Ladfromhighworth**[22] 827 10-11-11 **114** SamTwiston-Davies 115
(Jeremy Scott) *chsd ldr tl led 6th: hdd 9th: ev ch 4 out: sn rdn: no ex last: fin 3rd: plcd 2nd* **3/1**[2]

3P-6 **3** 15 **According To Sarah (IRE)**[29] 750 7-10-11 **107** ConorSmith(7) 105
(Philip Hobbs) *chsd ldrs: wnt 2nd 7th tl led 9th: rdn and hdd 3 out: wknd last: fin 4th: plcd 3rd* **9/1**

UF6- **4** 7 **King Fontaine (IRE)**[51] 12-11-9 **112** (t) AidanColeman 106
(Lawney Hill) *chsd ldrs: rdn 11th: wknd after next: fin 5th: pl 4th* **7/1**[3]

/324 **5** 13 **Speedy Bruere (FR)**[24] 809 9-11-4 **112** (t) JakeHodson(5) 95
(David Bridgwater) *led to 6th: pushed along and dropped in rr after 8th: wknd appr 12th: fin 6th: plcd 5th* **14/1**

-644 **6** 7 **Finish The Story (IRE)**[12] 897 9-11-11 **114** (bt) BrendanPowell 115
(Johnny Farrelly) *hld up: hdwy after 8th: outpcd 12th: rallied appr 4 out: lost weightcloth after 4 out: rdn 2 out: styd on same pce: wnt 2nd nr fin: fin 2nd: disqualified and plcd last: rdr failed to draw the correct weight* **7/1**[3]

3-6P **F** **Amazing D'Azy (IRE)**[28] 756 7-11-4 **110** (p) TomBellamy(3)
(Kim Bailey) *fell 1st* **18/1**

5m 51.9s (2.00) **Going Correction** +0.075s/f (Yiel) **7 Ran SP% 106.7**
Speed ratings (Par 105): **99,96,90,88,83 96,**
CSF £7.09 TOTE £2.30; £1.10, £3.10; EX 8.10 Trifecta £68.20.
Owner John P McManus **Bred** David Fenton **Trained** Cheltenham, Gloucs

FOCUS

Fair handicap form.

1008 MAZAK & POWER PANELS GOING FORWARD TOGETHER NOVICES' H'CAP CHASE (12 fncs) 2m 110y

6:55 (6:55) (Class 4) (0-120,119) 4-Y-O+ £3,768 (£1,106; £553; £276)

Form RPR

-P22 **1** **Indian Stream**[24] 810 6-11-12 **119** (t) NoelFehily 127+
(Neil Mulholland) *chsd ldr tl led appr 4 out: mstke last: rdn out* **3/1**[2]

-323 **2** 4 **Hepijeu (FR)**[21] 832 4-10-6 **115** (t) AidanColeman 105+
(Charlie Longsdon) *hld up: hdwy 4 out: chsd wnr and j.rt next: wnt rt again 2 out: sn rdn: mstke last: styd on same pce flat* **5/2**[1]

-220 **3** 1 3/4 **Dynamo (IRE)**[40] 624 4-10-3 **112** (t) RyanMahon 99
(Dan Skelton) *chsd ldrs: nt fluent 2nd: outpcd after 3 out: rallied flat: styd on wl towards fin* **8/1**

/3F- **4** 10 **Tour D'Argent (FR)**[85] 5449 8-11-8 **115** WayneHutchinson 109
(Donald McCain) *trckd ldrs: plld hrd: rdn appr 4 out: wknd after next* **9/1**

2-44 **5** 20 **Macarthur**[34] 697 11-11-8 **115** (p) PaulMoloney 89
(David Rees) *hld up: hmpd 3rd: pushed along after 8th: lost tch bef next* **22/1**

/5-5 **F** **Cayman Islands**[17] 857 7-11-1 **115** MrAlexFerguson(7)
(John Ferguson) *led: mstke 4th: rdn and hdd appr 4 out: 3 l 3rd whn hmpd and fell 3 out* **9/1**

3-51 **U** **Hawaii Five Nil (IRE)**[24] 810 7-11-10 **117** (p) RichieMcLernon
(Jonjo O'Neill) *hld up: hdwy 6th: rdn after 4 out: disputing 4th and looking hld whn hmpd and uns rdr 3 out* **7/2**[3]

4m 5.9s (0.90) **Going Correction** +0.075s/f (Yiel)
WFA 4 from 6yo+ 2lb **7 Ran SP% 111.3**
Speed ratings (Par 105): **100,98,97,92,83 ,**
CSF £10.76 TOTE £4.00: £2.10, £2.00; EX 14.40 Trifecta £68.20.
Owner Mrs G Davies **Bred** A W Buller **Trained** Limpley Stoke, Wilts

FOCUS

A fair novice handicap. The winner is the sort to rate higher over fences.

1009 MAZAK & POWER PANELS TOGETHER SUCCESS MARES' MAIDEN HURDLE (8 hdls) 2m

7:30 (7:30) (Class 5) 4-Y-O+ £2,274 (£667; £333; £166)

Form RPR

-322 **1** **Lolli (IRE)**[36] 679 5-10-12 110 NoelFehily 108+
(Nicky Henderson) *hld up: hdwy appr 3 out: led last: edgd rt flat: styd on wl* **5/4**[1]

43 **2** 2 1/2 **Irondale Express**[17] 846 4-10-10 0 PaulMoloney 102
(Des Donovan) *a.p: led after 2 out: hdd and mstke last: rdn and nt clr run flat: styd on same pce* **11/1**

1-25 **3** 3 3/4 **Dry Ol'Party**[33] 714 5-10-12 0 RichardJohnson 100
(Philip Hobbs) *chsd ldrs: led appr 3 out: rdn and hdd after next: no ex flat* **5/2**[2]

5-23 **4** 1 1/4 **Alottarain (IRE)**[33] 714 5-10-5 104 MrDSansom(7) 100
(Seamus Mullins) *hld up in tch: racd keenly: rdn after 3 out: styng on same pce whn mstke last* **12/1**

60-0 **5** 3 1/4 **Star Of Salford**[46] 558 6-10-12 0 (t) GavinSheehan 96
(Warren Greatrex) *led to 3rd: remained handy: rdn and ev ch 2 out: wknd flat* **25/1**

6 **6** 7 **Wintour Leap**[22] 823 4-10-10 0 TomO'Brien 87
(Robert Stephens) *chsd ldrs: led after 5th: hdd bef 3 out: sn rdn: wknd appr last* **16/1**

7 8 **Arthur's Queen (FR)**[87] 4-10-10 0 MichealNolan 81
(Carroll Gray) *hld up: wknd appr 2 out* **25/1**

0-32 **8** 7 **Midnight Gypsy**[21] 831 5-10-12 0 TomScudamore 76
(Stuart Kittow) *hld up: hdwy appr 3 out: wknd next* **7/1**[3]

P505 **9** 9 **Southern Cross**[9] 929 4-10-10 78 DaveCrosse 66
(Dai Williams) *hld up: rdn and wknd bef 3 out* **100/1**

P5 **P** **Cearys (IRE)**[43] 591 7-10-12 0 AndrewTinkler
(Martin Keighley) *trckd ldr tl led 3rd: hdd after 5th: sn lost pl: p.u bef next* **100/1**

3m 48.8s (-1.80) **Going Correction** +0.075s/f (Yiel)
WFA 4 from 5yo+ 15lb **10 Ran SP% 117.1**
Speed ratings (Par 103): **107,105,103,103,101 98,94,90,86,**
CSF £16.45 TOTE £2.10: £1.10, £3.50, £1.10; EX 14.40 Trifecta £52.70.
Owner Potensis Bloodstock Ltd & J Palmer Brown **Bred** Mick McGinn **Trained** Upper Lambourn, Berks

FOCUS

They went a modest gallop in this ordinary mares' hurdle and half a dozen were in with a chance turning for home. The form is sound enough.

1010 PARTEX T-800 PROMARK PRINTER (S) H'CAP HURDLE (10 hdls) 2m 4f

8:05 (8:05) (Class 5) (0-100,98) 4-Y-O+ £2,274 (£667; £333; £166)

Form RPR

0 **1** **Colley Row (IRE)**[48] 530 7-11-9 **95** (b) RichardJohnson 100+
(Tim Vaughan) *hld up: hdwy appr 3 out: led bef next: drvn out* **8/1**

-645 **2** 3 1/4 **Bulletproof (IRE)**[17] 856 9-10-10 **82** (p) PaddyBrennan 84
(Ken Cunningham-Brown) *hld up: hdwy appr 3 out: chsd wnr and mstke next: rdn and edgd lft flat: styd on same pce* **6/1**[1]

3 2 1/4 **Vinnie Trenta (IRE)**[72] 7-11-6 **95** SeanBowen(3) 94
(Alan Phillips) *hld up: hdwy 7th: nt fluent and outpcd 3 out: rallied flat: wnt 3rd nr fin* **7/1**[3]

-564 **4** 1 **Kyles Faith (IRE)**[10] 917 7-11-12 **98** (p) AndrewTinkler 95
(Martin Keighley) *chsd ldr to 3rd: remained handy: led appr 3 out: rdn and hdd bef next: no ex last* **9/1**

2166 **5** nk **Bus Named Desire**[15] 864 7-10-13 **85** (t) WillKennedy 82
(Ian Williams) *hld up: hdwy 5th: rdn appr 3 out: styd on same pce appr last* **13/2**[2]

0-00 **6** 1 3/4 **Bobonyx**[14] 878 5-9-7 **72** oh3 (v[1]) ThomasCheesman(7) 68
(Dai Williams) *hld up: nt fluent 2nd: hdwy 5th: rdn appr 3 out: styd on same pce appr last* **66/1**

-600 **7** 22 **Misteray**[8] 935 5-10-10 **87** (t) RyanWhile(5) 68
(Bill Turner) *w ldr: led 5th: rdn and hdd bef 3 out: wknd appr last* **16/1**

U-00 **8** 25 **Tenby Jewel (IRE)**[12] 895 10-10-12 **91** (bt) PaulJohn(7) 44
(Mark Gillard) *led to 5th: rdn appr 3 out: wknd next* **20/1**

-043 **9** 36 **Gwili Spar**[34] 704 7-10-1 **73** oh2 ow1 (t) DaveCrosse
(Laura Hurley) *hld up: hdwy 6th: wknd next* **9/1**

63/P **P** **Mighty Snazy**[24] 810 11-11-7 **98** MrsAlexDunn(5)
(Alexandra Dunn) *hld up: a in rr: bhd fr 6th: p.u bef 3 out* **33/1**

0-53 **P** **Ofcoursewecan (USA)**[25] 509 5-11-4 **90** TomCannon
(Mark Gillard) *chsd clr ldrs: nt fluent 3rd: mstke 5th: rdn and wknd after next: bhd whn p.u bef 3 out* **7/1**[3]

06-6 **P** **Dr Dalwhinny**[19] 843 6-11-8 **94** (p) AdrianLane
(Donald McCain) *mid-div: rdn and wknd 6th: bhd whn p.u bef 3 out* **16/1**

4-P5 **P** **Seacon Beg (IRE)**[24] 811 6-11-9 **95** DarylJacob
(Richard Woollacott) *mid-div: wknd 7th: bhd whn blnd 2 out: sn p.u* **7/1**[3]

4m 54.9s (1.40) **Going Correction** +0.075s/f (Yiel) **13 Ran SP% 117.2**
Speed ratings (Par 103): **100,98,97,97,97 96,87,77,63, , ,**
CSF £54.07 CT £356.84 TOTE £7.10: £3.30, £2.60, £2.40; EX 81.90 Trifecta £1091.10 Part won..
Owner Geraint Anstee **Bred** Roger Hume **Trained** Aberthin, Vale of Glamorgan

FOCUS

This was run at a brisk gallop, a trio going out clear, and the first three both came from the back. The winner is rated in line with his best Irish bumper figure.

1011 COTSWOLD SCAFFOLDING MAIDEN HURDLE (12 hdls) 2m 7f

8:35 (8:35) (Class 4) 4-Y-O+ £3,249 (£954; £477; £238)

Form RPR

6-F5 **1** **Uncle Tone (IRE)**[28] 754 6-11-0 116 MichealNolan 118+
(Tim Vaughan) *hld up: hdwy 7th: led and mstke 2 out: rdn out* **12/1**

32-P **2** 1 1/4 **Magheral Express (IRE)**[41] 614 6-11-0 114 (t) RichieMcLernon 117+
(Jonjo O'Neill) *hld up: hdwy appr 3 out: chsd wnr after next: ev ch whn mstke last: styd on u.p* **5/1**

0-32 **3** 11 **Shah Of Persia**[22] 823 8-11-0 115 (t) GavinSheehan 106
(Warren Greatrex) *mid-div: hdwy 7th: rdn appr 2 out: wknd bef last* **4/1**[3]

03-2 **4** nse **Tir Dubh (IRE)**[52] 460 6-10-7 0 TomO'Brien 99
(Robert Stephens) *chsd ldrs: led appr 3 out: hdd next: rdn and wknd bef last* **10/1**

35 **5** 13 **Butlergrove King (IRE)**[14] 877 6-11-0 0 (t) AndrewTinkler 96
(Natalie Lloyd-Beavis) *prom: led 8th to next: rdn and ev ch 2 out: wknd bef last* **20/1**

2-25 **6** 21 **Profit Commission (IRE)**[27] 773 5-11-0 120 (t) NoelFehily 75
(Harry Fry) *hld up: hdwy 8th: rdn after 3 out: wknd next* **7/2**[2]

2622 **7** 12 **Westerly Breeze (IRE)**[14] 879 7-11-0 105 (b) RichardJohnson 65
(Edward Bevan) *prom: chsd ldr 3rd: led 9th: rdn and hdd appr 3 out: wknd bef next* **3/1**[1]

8 22 **Rush House (IRE)**[45] 7-10-4 0 MattGriffiths(3) 38
(Jeremy Scott) *mid-div: hdwy 5th: rdn and wknd appr 3 out* **66/1**

4 **P** **Backoftherock**[14] 875 6-11-0 0 PaulMoloney
(David Rees) *hld up: a in rr: mstke 4th: bhd fr 6th: p.u bef 3 out* **50/1**

-UUP **P** **Tikketoride**[14] 877 7-10-7 0 (b) ArchieBellamy(7)
(Peter Pritchard) *mid-div: plld hrd: lost pl 3rd: bhd fr 6th: p.u bef 3 out* **200/1**

P **Coote Street (IRE)**[452] 7-11-0 0..................................(p) NicodeBoinville
(Mark Bradstock) *led: j.lft 2nd: j.lft and hdd 8th: sn rdn and wknd: bhd whn p.u bef 3 out* **20/1**

P5-P P **Wootsteps (IRE)**[72] 105 7-10-9 0.............................. ConorRing(5)
(John Upson) *prom: lost pl 3rd: nt fluent next: rdn and wknd bef 7th: bhd whn p.u bef 3 out* **200/1**

P P **Run Of The Mill (IRE)**[17] 852 5-11-0 0.......................... TomMessenger
(Chris Bealby) *chsd ldr to 3rd: remained handy: reminder after 6th: wknd after 8th: bhd whn p.u bef 3 out* **100/1**

5m 38.6s **Going Correction** +0.075s/f (Yiel) **13 Ran SP% 115.6**
Speed ratings (Par 105): **103,102,98,98,94 86,82,75, , ,**
CSF £67.21 TOTE £17.20: £4.00, £2.10, £2.30; EX 87.90 Trifecta £571.80.
Owner Kings Head Duffield Racing Partnership **Bred** Michael J Bowe **Trained** Aberthin, Vale of Glamorgan

FOCUS
A very ordinary maiden hurdle in which the first two finished clear. The first two and the fourth and fifth are rated pretty much to their marks.

1012 PAL50 MARKER KITS BY PARTEX H'CAP HURDLE (8 hdls) 2m
9:10 (9:10) (Class 4) (0-120,119) 3-Y-O+ **£3,249** (£954; £477; £238)

Form RPR

4-12 1 **At First Light**[12] 892 6-10-11 **104**........................ NicodeBoinville 111
(David Weston) *prom: lost pl 2nd: pushed along and hdwy 5th: rdn and outpcd bef next: rallied after 2 out: chsd ldr and hmpd last: styd on to ld towards fin* **11/4**[1]

3521 2 1 **Hawdyerwheesht**[9] 931 7-11-10 **117** 7ex..........................(tp) NoelFehily 123
(David Dennis) *w ldr to 2nd: remained handy: led after 5th: rdn and j.lft last: hdd towards fin* **7/2**[3]

1-12 3 3 3/4 **Kayf Willow**[29] 748 6-11-4 **111**.............................. RichardJohnson 115
(Philip Hobbs) *trckd ldrs: rdn after 2 out: styd on same pce flat* **3/1**[2]

6-33 4 2 1/4 **Drifter (IRE)**[21] 835 4-10-3 **105**............................ PaulNO'Brien(7) 104
(Harry Whittington) *hld up: plld hrd: hdwy 3 out: rdn appr last: styd on same pce* **4/1**

U650 5 1 1/4 **Alla Svelta (IRE)**[27] 776 9-10-9 **102**........................(p) BrendanPowell 102
(Brendan Powell) *hld up: plld hrd: hdwy to trck ldr after 2nd tl 5th: rdn appr last: wknd flat* **8/1**

0-03 6 40 **Moveable Asset (IRE)**[9] 931 7-11-1 **115**........................(vt) MrFTett(7) 79
(Henry Tett) *led tl after 5th: rdn and wknd bef next* **16/1**

3m 49.7s (-0.90) **Going Correction** +0.075s/f (Yiel)
WFA 4 from 5yo+ 15lb **6 Ran SP% 110.9**
Speed ratings (Par 105): **105,104,102,101,100 80**
CSF £12.58 CT £27.81 TOTE £3.30: £1.40, £2.20; EX 13.80 Trifecta £24.90.
Owner Miss E J Tanner **Bred** D J Weston **Trained** Marlborough, Wilts

FOCUS
This ordinary handicap was run 0.9sec slower than the earlier mares' maiden. The winner is rated to her C&D mark.
T/Plt: £23.20 to a £1 stake. Pool of £56767.38 - 1783.09 winning tickets. T/Qpdt: £10.40 to a £1 stake. Pool of £6589.64 - 465.20 winning tickets. **Colin Roberts**

1013 - 1029a (Foreign Racing) - See Raceform Interactive

845
CARTMEL (L-H)
Saturday, July 18

OFFICIAL GOING: Good (good to firm in places)
Wind: fresh 1/2 behind Weather: overcast, breezy and cool

1030 HADWINS NOVICES' HURDLE (11 hdls) 2m 6f 31y
2:05 (2:07) (Class 4) 4-Y-O+ **£3,898** (£1,144; £572; £286)

Form RPR

31 1 **Classic Palace (IRE)**[35] 730 6-10-12 110......................... BrianHughes 108+
(J J Lambe, Ire) *mde all: wnt clr between last 2: rdn out* **2/1**[1]

-412 2 12 **Always On The Run (IRE)**[24] 834 5-11-5 120.................. HenryBrooke 103
(Donald McCain) *hld up in last: t.k.h in rr: hdwy 3 out: rdn to go 2nd next: no ch w wnr* **2/1**[1]

51 3 5 **Western Home (IRE)**[29] 784 5-10-12 0........................ RichardJohnson 91
(Gordon Elliott, Ire) *t.k.h in mid-div: hdwy 3 out: drvn next: modest 3rd and one pce appr last* **85/40**[2]

6P/0 4 13 **Monzino (USA)**[13] 912 7-10-7 74............................ JoeCornwall(5) 78
(Michael Chapman) *nt fluent: prom: drvn 5th: lost pl 8th: sn bhd: kpt on run-in: tk poor 4th post* **100/1**

-300 5 shd **Tokyo Brown (USA)**[22] 837 6-10-9 92..........................(p) TonyKelly(3) 78
(James Moffatt) *chsd wnr: drvn 3 out: wknd appr last* **12/1**

1PP6 6 3/4 **Allycat**[11] 933 5-10-7 0...................................... DiarmuidO'Regan(5) 77
(Chris Grant) *chsd ldrs: reminders 6th: lost pl bef 2 out* **9/1**[3]

0-0 7 1/2 **Warksburn Boy**[22] 837 5-10-5 0.............................. JamieHamilton(7) 77
(Sheena Walton) *chsd ldrs: wknd 2 out* **125/1**

00-6 P **Delgardo (IRE)**[70] 206 6-10-12 0..................................(t) AlainCawley
(John David Riches) *uns rdr and rn loose bef s: in rr: drvn 4th: bhd whn p.u bef 6th* **125/1**

5m 20.8s (-8.50) **Going Correction** -0.725s/f (Firm) **8 Ran SP% 118.9**
Speed ratings (Par 105): **86,81,79,75,75 74,74,**
CSF £6.99 TOTE £2.80: £1.10, £1.20, £1.10; EX 7.10 Trifecta £12.90.
Owner James Callow **Bred** Mrs Winefride Crean-Murphy **Trained** Dungannon, Co Tyrone

FOCUS
A windy afternoon. The going was good with good to firm places and the roadside, bends and home straight had been watered. It was tight at the head of the market, with the three previous hurdle winners dominating. Another big step up from the winner.

1031 RACING UK DAY PASS H'CAP CHASE (12 fncs) 2m 1f 61y
2:40 (2:40) (Class 5) (0-100,97) 4-Y-O+ **£3,249** (£954; £477; £238)

Form RPR

-252 1 **Lord Lir (IRE)**[36] 713 9-11-0 85..................................(b) RichardJohnson 108+
(Tim Vaughan) *mde all: sn clr: j. boldly: 12 l ahd last: eased fnl 75yds* **6/4**[1]

6223 2 24 **Forestside (IRE)**[17] 871 10-10-9 80..........................(p) DenisO'Regan 79
(Barry Murtagh) *chsd wnr tl appr 9th: kpt on to take modest 2nd last 75yds* **11/2**

P-F2 3 4 1/2 **Great Demeanor (USA)**[12] 455 5-10-10 81........................ BrianHughes 80
(Dianne Sayer) *chsd ldng pair: modest 2nd appr 9th: rdn whn stmbld bdly crossing sn after last: wknd fnl 100yds* **4/1**[3]

-003 4 11 **Roxyfet (FR)**[20] 848 5-11-2 97..................................(p) FinianO'Toole(10) 85
(Micky Hammond) *nt fluent: outpcd and lost pl 8th: sn bhd* **9/5**[2]

4m 10.9s (-8.00) **Going Correction** -0.725s/f (Firm) **4 Ran SP% 111.1**
Speed ratings (Par 103): **94,82,80,75**
CSF £9.08 TOTE £2.20; EX 10.50 Trifecta £30.80.
Owner Two Gents & An Orange Bloke Racing **Bred** Killian Lynch **Trained** Aberthin, Vale of Glamorgan

FOCUS
This turned into a procession with the favourite dominating. There's a case for rating the form around 7lb higher.

1032 HEATHER'S 18TH & LANCE'S 65TH BIRTHDAY H'CAP CHASE (14 fncs) 2m 5f 34y
3:15 (3:15) (Class 4) (0-115,113) 4-Y-O+ **£3,898** (£1,144; £572; £286)

Form RPR

5P-P 1 **Dystonia's Revenge (IRE)**[27] 800 10-11-0 **108**........ JamieHamilton(7) 117
(Sheena Walton) *chsd ldrs: 2nd 3rd: led 10th: drvn out* **25/1**

-234 2 6 **Mister D (IRE)**[17] 871 9-10-3 **95**........................ JonathonBewley(5) 100
(George Bewley) *chsd ldrs: mstke 2nd: wnt 2nd over 2f out: kpt on same pce* **11/1**

5-01 3 3/4 **Romany Ryme**[17] 869 9-11-10 **111**.............................. RichardJohnson 115
(Gordon Elliott, Ire) *hld up in rr: hdwy to chse ldrs 9th: drvn 3 out: 3rd over 2f out: kpt on same pce* **85/40**[1]

2442 4 1 **The Society Man (IRE)**[20] 847 8-10-3 **95**.................. JoeCornwall(5) 98
(Michael Chapman) *chsd ldrs: drvn 3 out: 2nd whn hit last: sn crowded on bnd: kpt on same pce* **8/1**

4-34 5 12 **Sendiym (FR)**[20] 845 8-10-5 **92**..................................(p) BrianHughes 83
(Dianne Sayer) *in rr: sme hdwy 8th: lost pl bef 11th* **7/1**[3]

-U11 6 2 1/2 **Cool Star (IRE)**[22] 841 9-11-0 **104**..........................(t) JonathanEngland(3) 96
(Maurice Barnes) *led: nt fluent 4th: j. slowly and hdd 10th: rallied and 2nd sn after last: wknd over 2f out* **11/4**[2]

PP-2 7 5 **Jack The Gent (IRE)**[33] 742 11-11-1 **102**........................ DarylJacob 87
(George Moore) *chsd ldrs: drvn 11th: hmpd on inner bnd sn after last: sn lost pl* **10/1**

532- 8 3 3/4 **Welsh Bard (IRE)**[253] 2336 6-11-12 **113**.......................... HenryBrooke 94
(Donald McCain) *in rr: hit 9th: bhd next* **12/1**

3-13 9 52 **Houndscourt (IRE)**[37] 693 8-11-11 **112**........................ DougieCostello 46
(Joanne Foster) *chsd ldrs: lost pl 5th: sn bhd: t.o 9th* **20/1**

5m 11.0s (-14.40) **Going Correction** -0.725s/f (Firm) **9 Ran SP% 116.0**
Speed ratings (Par 105): **103,100,100,100,95 94,92,91,71**
CSF £261.28 CT £841.15 TOTE £37.20: £10.30, £3.90, £1.40; EX 383.90 Trifecta £620.80 Part won..
Owner John Blacklock & Margaret Rogerson **Bred** Winston Honner **Trained** Hexham, Northumberland

FOCUS
Something of an upset as the outsider of the field powered clear from the last. He's rated to his best.

1033 BURLINGTON STONE H'CAP CHASE (18 fncs) 3m 1f 107y
3:50 (3:50) (Class 3) (0-135,130) 4-Y-O+
£6,881 (£2,032; £1,016; £508; £254; £127)

Form RPR

44/1 1 **Pena Dorada (IRE)**[20] 847 8-9-13 **110**.................. MissRMcDonald(7) 120+
(Alistair Whillans) *chsd ldrs: led last: drvn rt out* **7/2**[2]

23-3 2 2 1/4 **Buachaill Alainn (IRE)**[44] 611 8-10-13 **120**..................(t) SeanBowen(3) 129
(Peter Bowen) *rn in snatches: chsd ldrs: lost pl 3rd: drvn 6th: hdwy to chse ldrs 13th: outpcd and lost pl 3 out: styd on and modest 4th over 2f out: tk 2nd last 50yds* **3/1**[1]

3143 3 1 1/4 **Master Of The Hall (IRE)**[13] 915 11-10-2 **116**......... FinianO'Toole(10) 123
(Micky Hammond) *hld up towards rr: hdwy to chse ldrs 13th: 2nd over 1f out: kpt on same pce* **11/2**

55-0 4 3/4 **Midnight Appeal**[20] 855 10-11-9 **130**..........................(t) KillianMoore(3) 136
(Sophie Leech) *chsd ldr: led 3 out: hdd last: kpt on same pce* **12/1**

P-55 5 7 **Problema Tic (FR)**[17] 868 9-11-3 **124**..........................(t) TonyKelly(3) 124
(Jackie Stephen) *in rr: hdwy to chse ldrs 13th: sn drvn: outpcd 15th: modest 5th 2f out* **14/1**

-642 6 8 **Green Wizard (IRE)**[27] 800 9-10-6 **110**........................ SeanQuinlan 103
(Sue Smith) *chsd ldrs: drvn 14th: wknd sn after last* **4/1**[3]

3111 7 8 **Chicago Outfit (IRE)**[27] 800 10-10-10 **119**.........(p) JonathonBewley(5) 105
(George Bewley) *led: hdd 3 out: lost pl last* **4/1**[3]

6m 17.8s (-17.10) **Going Correction** -0.725s/f (Firm) **7 Ran SP% 117.0**
Speed ratings (Par 107): **103,102,101,101,99 96,94**
CSF £15.50 CT £56.50 TOTE £4.40: £3.20, £1.90; EX 15.20 Trifecta £44.50.
Owner Alan J Brown **Bred** J P Dwan **Trained** Newmill-On-Slitrig, Borders

FOCUS
A competitive handicap run at a good pace. The winner built on his recent C&D win.

1034 BANKS LYON JEWELLERS LADY RIDERS' H'CAP HURDLE (7 hdls 1 omitted) 2m 1f 46y
4:25 (4:25) (Class 3) (0-135,135) 3-Y-O+
£6,256 (£1,848; £924; £462; £231; £116)

Form RPR

0- 1 **Tempo Mac (IRE)**[14] 908 5-10-3 **119**........................ MsLO'Neill(7) 131+
(Gordon Elliott, Ire) *hld up in rr: smooth hdwy to trck ldrs 2 out: led last: rdn clr* **5/2**[1]

-511 2 8 **Politeness (FR)**[17] 872 6-9-13 **113**.......................... MissCWalton(5) 118
(Rose Dobbin) *mid-div: styd on fr 2 out: 2nd over 1f out: no ch w wnr* **6/1**[3]

0-41 3 3 1/2 **Cool Baranca (GER)**[5] 711 9-9-11 **109**........................ EmmaSayer(3) 111
(Dianne Sayer) *mid-div: lost pl 4th: hdwy between last 2: styd on to take 3rd last 50yds* **4/1**[2]

50-3 4 1 3/4 **May's Boy**[20] 851 7-9-7 **109** oh2..........................(p) MissRMcDonald(7) 109
(James Moffatt) *chsd ldrs: hmpd 3rd: upsides 5th: led 2 out: hdd last: kpt on one pce* **14/1**

01-5 5 3/4 **Smart Ruler (IRE)**[20] 850 9-10-11 **123**.......................... MissGAndrews(3) 123
(James Moffatt) *hld up in rr: hdwy 5th: sn chsng ldrs: one pce appr last* **14/1**

P-31 6 2 1/4 **Vivacissimo (IRE)**[18] 862 8-9-9 **109** oh4...............(t) BridgetAndrews(5) 108
(Dan Skelton) *led to 1st: chsd ldrs: j.lft 3rd: reminders after next: lost pl 5th: kpt on one pce between last 2* **7/1**

1312 7 1 1/2 **Street Entertainer (IRE)**[24] 829 8-11-5 **135**.....(bt) MissJodieHughes(7) 132
(David Pipe) *chsd ldrs: led 3rd: hdd 2 out: fdd last* **8/1**

-214 8 20 **Grand Vintage (IRE)**[22] 839 9-9-9 **111**..........(tp) MissHannahWatson(7) 89
(Kenneth Slack) *led 1st: hdd 3rd: lost pl after 5th: sn bhd* **6/1**[3]

6 9 31 **Moreece (IRE)**[24] 832 6-9-10 **112**............................ MissRPLeyshon(7) 62
(Tim Vaughan) *in rr: bhd fr 5th: t.o whn blnd 2 out* **50/1**

3m 58.4s (-14.80) **Going Correction** -0.725s/f (Firm) **9 Ran SP% 116.0**
Speed ratings (Par 107): **105,101,99,98,98 97,96,87,72**
CSF £18.40 CT £58.23 TOTE £3.10: £1.10, £2.80, £1.80; EX 21.80 Trifecta £34.90.
Owner John P McGovern **Bred** Padraig Williams **Trained** Longwood, Co Meath

FOCUS
A valuable race restricted to lady riders, with the winning jockey receiving the added bonus of a diamond necklace. It was run at a ferocious pace and the leaders all weakened out of it. Solid form, the winner on the upgrade.

1035 TOTEPOOL CUMBRIA CRYSTAL TROPHY H'CAP HURDLE (11 hdls) 2m 6f 31y
5:00 (5:00) (Class 3) (0-140,136) 4-Y-0+
£16,265 (£4,804; £2,402; £1,201; £600; £301)

Form RPR
0-11 **1** **Kilfinichen Bay (IRE)**[30] 774 7-11-1 **125**................... RichardJohnson 130+
(Charlie Longsdon) *chsd ldrs: led last: drvn rt out* **5/1**[2]
-212 **2** 2 ¼ **Jalingo (IRE)**[6] 973 4-11-1 **128**...............................(p) JackQuinlan 128
(John Ferguson) *trckd ldrs: handy 4th last: styd on to take 2nd post* **5/1**[2]
6-11 **3** nse **Just A Normal Day (IRE)**[30] 775 5-10-3 **118**.......(p) BridgetAndrews(5) 121
(Dan Skelton) *prom: drvn 3 out: 3rd last: styd on same pce* **6/1**[3]
130- **4** nk **Mister Fizz**[9] 5271 7-11-12 **136**................................ RobertDunne 139
(Miss Imogen Pickard) *chsd ldrs: led 2 out: hdd last: styd on same pce* **25/1**
1-30 **5** 5 **Captain Brown**[20] 850 7-10-3 **118**..................... DiarmuidO'Regan(5) 116
(James Moffatt) *in rr: hdwy 8th: styd on run-in: tk 5th clsng stages* **25/1**
-222 **6** 1 ¼ **Aficionado**[17] 876 5-11-3 **127**...............................(p) DarylJacob 124
(Dr Richard Newland) *mid-div: chsd ldrs 7th: one pce fr 2 out* **9/2**[1]
/3P2 **7** 5 **Silk Hall (UAE)**[35] 729 10-11-6 **130**......................(v) DenisO'Regan 123
(J J Lambe, Ire) *w ldr: led 8th: hdd 2 out: wknd last* **25/1**
1-44 **8** 1 ½ **Future Security (IRE)**[69] 219 6-10-8 **118**...............(t) DougieCostello 110
(William Kinsey) *nt fluent in rr: sme hdwy 2 out: nvr a factor* **25/1**
0-15 **9** 5 **Ossie's Dancer**[27] 812 6-10-10 **127**..................... ThomasCheesman(7) 114
(Martin Smith) *mid-div: chsd ldrs 8th: sn drvn: wknd sn after 2 out* **16/1**
10-2 **10** 3 ¾ **Jackies Solitaire**[36] 711 7-10-4 **117**......................(tp) SeanBowen(3) 100
(Peter Bowen) *in rr: sme hdwy 7th: nvr on terms* **12/1**
1-21 **11** 4 **Brave Helios**[36] 705 5-10-9 **124**........................... DanielHiskett(5) 104
(Richard Phillips) *mid-div: drvn 8th: lost pl next* **20/1**
/12- **12** 1 ½ **Goldan Jess (IRE)**[24] 1323 11-11-6 **133**..................... KyleJames(3) 111
(Philip Kirby) *led: hdd 8th: wknd sn after 2 out* **12/1**
5-52 **13** 1 ½ **Willem (FR)**[25] 826 5-10-7 **124**......................(p) MichaelHeard(7) 101
(David Pipe) *mid-div: hdwy 7th: chsng ldrs 3 out: lost pl after next* **9/1**
1114 **14** ½ **Zarzal (IRE)**[20] 850 7-11-1 **125**................................ AdamWedge 102
(Evan Williams) *mid-div: chsng ldrs 7th: drvn next: lost pl bef 2 out* **14/1**
2-01 **15** 22 **Sealous Scout (IRE)**[54] 473 7-11-0 **124**........................ HenryBrooke 81
(Donald McCain) *in rr: nt fluent 4th: bhd fr 8th: t.o 2 out* **20/1**
25P- **16** 1 ½ **Baileys Concerto (IRE)**[14] 5392 9-11-9 **133**...................... BrianHughes 88
(Dianne Sayer) *in rr: bhd fr 7th: t.o 2 out* **20/1**
5m 14.6s (-14.70) **Going Correction** -0.725s/f (Firm) **16** Ran SP% **133.4**
WFA 4 from 5yo+ 16lb
Speed ratings (Par 107): 97,96,96,96,94 93,91,91,89,88 86,86,85,85,77 76
CSF £30.34 CT £157.94 TOTE £5.20: £1.50, £2.00, £2.10, £6.90; EX 39.30 Trifecta £283.70.
Owner Cracker Syndicate **Bred** Brian Kearney **Trained** Over Norton, Oxon

FOCUS
A fiercely competitive handicap for the track's most valuable hurdle prize. Four came clear off a good mid-race pace. Solid form with a progressive winner.

1036 WILLOW WATER MARES' H'CAP HURDLE (8 hdls) 2m 1f 46y
5:30 (5:31) (Class 4) (0-115,115) 3-Y-0+ **£3,898** (£1,144; £572; £286)

Form RPR
-532 **1** **Chilly Miss**[20] 846 6-11-7 **108**.................................. BrianHughes 116
(Malcolm Jefferson) *hld up in mid-div: effrt appr 2 out: cl 2nd last: led 1f out: drvn rt out* **9/2**[3]
-U11 **2** 2 ½ **Russian Royale**[23] 777 5-11-0 **104**............................ CraigNichol(3) 110
(Micky Hammond) *chsd ldrs: upsides 3 out: sn led: jnd last: hdd 1f out: kpt on same pce* **15/8**[1]
-313 **3** 10 **Shady Lane**[33] 744 8-11-2 **108**......................(t) BridgetAndrews(5) 105
(Dan Skelton) *led: hdd sn after 3 out: one pce fr next* **10/3**[2]
453- **4** 2 ¾ **Announcement**[147] 4368 4-11-12 **115**......................... RichardJohnson 108
(Brian Ellison) *stdd s: hld up in last: hdwy and drvn 5th: 4th between last 2: one pce* **7/1**
0150 **5** 20 **Morning With Ivan (IRE)**[20] 851 5-10-11 **98**..................(p) HenryBrooke 75
(Martin Todhunter) *chsd ldr: drvn appr 3 out: wknd appr 2 out: sn bhd* **12/1**
P6-4 **6** 47 **Gold Chain (IRE)**[17] 301 5-11-5 **109**...........................(b) EmmaSayer(3) 43
(Dianne Sayer) *in rr: bhd and drvn 5th: reminders and t.o bef next: eased after 2 out: eventually completed* **11/2**
4m 2.5s (-10.70) **Going Correction** -0.725s/f (Firm) **6** Ran SP% **111.6**
Speed ratings (Par 105): 96,94,90,88,79 57
CSF £13.62 TOTE £4.40: £2.20, £1.30; EX 11.90 Trifecta £17.30.
Owner Racegoers Club Owners Group **Bred** Lesley Winn And Reveley Farms **Trained** Norton, N Yorks

FOCUS
This produced a good battle up the straight with the winner getting on top near the line. A step up from her.
T/Plt: £28.00 to a £1 stake. Pool: £52,758.52 - 1,371.68 winning tickets T/Qpdt: £10.60 to a £1 stake. Pool: £3,639.12 - 252.00 winning tickets **Walter Glynn**

[912] MARKET RASEN (R-H)
Saturday, July 18

OFFICIAL GOING: Good (8.5)
Wind: moderate against Weather: mostly sunny; 22 degrees

1037 BETFRED "RACING'S BIGGEST SUPPORTER" JUVENILE HURDLE (8 hdls) 2m 148y
1:45 (1:45) (Class 4) 3-Y-0 **£3,249** (£954; £477; £238)

Form RPR
1 **Retro Valley (IRE)**[18] 3-10-12 0.................................. NoelFehily 84+
(David Dennis) *hld up: pckd 2nd: wnt 2nd at 4th: blnd next: nt fluent 3 out: led wl bef 2 out and sn in command but j. markedly lft fnl two* **4/9**[1]
2 6 **Robben**[37] 3-10-12 0...(p) PaddyBrennan 76
(John Mackie) *nt fluent: in last pair: wnt 2nd bef 2 out: abt 3 l bhd wnr after: sn rdn: wl hld whn mstke last* **5/1**[2]
4 **3** 17 **Londonia**[15] 891 3-10-12 0.................................. KielanWoods 60
(Graeme McPherson) *led at mod pce and j. stickily: rdn and hdd wl bef 2 out: sn struggling in poor 3rd: fin weakly* **10/1**
4 66 **Penny Boo (IRE)**[38] 3-10-5 0.................................. GavinSheehan
(Brian Ellison) *pressed ldr tl mstke 4th: lost tch and mstke next: drvn and t.o after 3 out* **11/2**[3]
4m 11.8s (5.10) **Going Correction** -0.05s/f (Good) **4** Ran SP% **110.4**
Speed ratings (Par 102): **86,83,75,44**
CSF £3.28 TOTE £1.60; EX 3.20 Trifecta £6.90.
Owner Favourites Racing Ltd **Bred** Hardys Of Kilkeel Ltd **Trained** Hanley Swan, Worcestershire

FOCUS
Rail moved out 15yds on Wood Bend and 25yds on Stands Bend. Races 1, 3, 5 and 7 increased by 165yds and races 2, 4 &6 by 240yds. The absence of morning favourite Mountainside robbed this renewal of much of its interest. The slowest race over the trip and modest though guessy form.

1038 BETFRED "SUPPORTS JACK BERRY HOUSE" H'CAP HURDLE (10 hdls) 2m 4f 139y
2:20 (2:20) (Class 2) (0-150,146) 4-Y-0+
£11,260 (£3,326; £1,663; £831; £415; £208)

Form RPR
0-2F **1** **Sea Lord (IRE)**[41] 659 8-11-12 **146**............................ AidanColeman 152+
(John Ferguson) *settled in last trio: shkn up at times fr 6th: effrt and mstke 3 out: led bef next: rdn and mstke last: idling sltly in front and kpt up to work but a holding rival* **3/1**[1]
32-1 **2** 1 ¾ **Vivant Poeme (FR)**[45] 595 6-10-6 **126**..............................(t) NoelFehily 130
(Harry Fry) *hld up in last: hmpd 7th: effrt gng wl after next: chsd wnr bef 2 out: rdn and tried to cl fr last: kpt on but nvr able to reduce abt 2 l deficit* **3/1**[1]
0-51 **3** 14 **Mile House (IRE)**[17] 876 7-10-10 **130**............................ TomO'Brien 123
(Robert Stephens) *hit 1st: pressed ldr tl led 6th: rdn and hdd bef 2 out where hmpd whn wkng: mstke last* **7/2**[2]
02-5 **4** ¾ **Midnight Game**[42] 638 8-10-8 **128**.............................. GavinSheehan 118
(Brian Ellison) *hld up in last trio: effrt gng wl 3 out: rdn and nt qckn bef next* **16/1**
4-10 **5** nk **Go Odee Go (IRE)**[27] 812 7-10-3 **123**.........................(p) HarrySkelton 113
(Dan Skelton) *chsd ldrs tl drvn and wknd bef 2 out where hmpd* **7/1**
-0PP **6** 19 **Don't Be Late (IRE)**[36] 715 7-10-7 **127**......................(p) WillKennedy 104
(Jonjo O'Neill) *chsd ldrs tl blnd bdly 7th and lost all ch: t.o next but styng on wl after last* **14/1**
-113 **7** ¾ **Dubh Eile (IRE)**[27] 812 7-9-7 **120**............................ AlanJohns(7) 92
(Tim Vaughan) *midfield: shkn up 6th: nt gng wl enough after: struggling u.p 3 out* **6/1**[3]
2-36 **8** 67 **Marju's Quest (IRE)**[24] 830 5-10-9 **129**............... SamTwiston-Davies 40
(David Dennis) *racd freely in ld tl hdd 6th: blnd next: sn t.o and hacked on* **16/1**
0-26 **F** **Apachee Prince (IRE)**[27] 799 6-10-0 **120** oh1..............(t) BrianHarding 115
(Alistair Whillans) *3rd pl tl wnt 2nd at 6th: relegated abt 3 l 3rd: rdn and looking hld whn fell 2 out* **20/1**
5m 4.0s (-4.80) **Going Correction** -0.05s/f (Good) **9** Ran SP% **121.4**
Speed ratings (Par 109): **107,106,101,100,100 93,93,67,**
CSF £13.61 CT £33.63 TOTE £3.50: £1.60, £1.30, £1.80; EX 11.60 Trifecta £44.40.
Owner Bloomfields **Bred** Darley **Trained** Cowlinge, Suffolk

FOCUS
The fourth time this has been run as a 0-150, although with only one horse rated within 20lb of the ceiling this didn't look quite as deep as last year's renewal. Only two mattered from two out. The first two are on the upgrade, with a career best from the winner.

1039 BETFRED TV SUMMER HURDLE (A H'CAP) (LISTED RACE) (8 hdls) 2m 148y
2:55 (2:55) (Class 1) 3-Y-0+
£19,932 (£7,479; £3,745; £1,865; £938; £469)

Form RPR
132- **1** **Gran Maestro (USA)**[26] 5539 6-10-1 **127**.....................(bt) WillKennedy 130
(Dr Richard Newland) *pressed ldr fr 3rd: gng wl after 3 out: tk slt advantage home turn: disp ld 2 out: cl 2nd at last: fought on wl flat despite flapping lft rein: jst prevailed nr fin* **16/1**
06-6 **2** nk **Hammersly Lake (FR)**[77] 96 7-11-2 **142**..................... BarryGeraghty 145
(Nicky Henderson) *racd keenly and prom: drew abt 3 l clr w wnr bef 2 out: slt advantage last: hrd drvn and hdd and no ex cl home* **7/1**
13- **3** 2 **Manhattan Swing (IRE)**[8] 1845 5-10-4 **130**...............(b) GavinSheehan 131
(Brian Ellison) *hld up in last trio: effrt 3 out: 7th home turn: drvn and kpt on stoutly after last but nvr rchd ldng pair* **11/1**
2-2P **4** ½ **Laudatory**[27] 812 9-11-0 **140**.................................. NicodeBoinville 142
(Nicky Henderson) *racd keenly: led after 1st: hit 3rd and 5th: rdn and hdd bef 2 out: nt qckn fr last* **28/1**
-121 **5** 5 **Gioia Di Vita**[12] 930 5-10-0 **126** oh1..................... SamTwiston-Davies 122
(Dr Richard Newland) *chsd ldrs: disp 3rd home turn: sn hrd drvn: kpt on fr 2 out but nvr looked winning* **9/1**
-121 **6** 5 **Regulation (IRE)**[11] 933 6-10-0 **126**.............................. TrevorWhelan 119
(Neil King) *hld up chsng ldrs: effrt 3 out: 6th home turn: rdn and pressing ldrs whn mstke 2 out: kpt on same pce after* **10/1**
5U-1 **7** ½ **Commissioned (IRE)**[20] 850 5-11-7 **152**.....................(p) MikeyEnnis(5) 143
(John Ferguson) *hld up: lost pl bef 3 out: kpt on same pce and n.d fr next* **13/2**[3]
141- **8** 1 ½ **Hurricane Hollow**[94] 5345 5-10-10 **136**........................... HarrySkelton 126
(Dan Skelton) *trckd ldrs: effrt bef 3 out: rdn and one pce bef next* **11/2**[2]
13-1 **9** ½ **Buckwheat**[36] 708 5-11-3 **143**...................................(t) AidanColeman 133
(John Ferguson) *pressed ldrs: rdn after 4th: disp 3rd home turn: lost pl bef 2 out: one pce and n.d after* **5/1**[1]
0020 **10** 1 ¼ **Collodi (GER)**[25] 826 6-10-0 **126** oh1........................ BrendanPowell 115
(David Bridgwater) *towards rr whn n.m.r bnd after 3rd: rdn and btn after 3 out* **20/1**
331- **11** shd **Silver Duke (IRE)**[13] 4320 4-9-8 **136** oh3 ow1..................... AlanJohns(7) 109
(Jim Goldie) *last trio: mstke 3 out whn last: no ch after but plugged on* **33/1**
0-12 **12** 1 **Roman Flight (IRE)**[20] 850 7-11-3 **143**.............................(v) NoelFehily 130
(David Dennis) *nvr bttr than midfield: rdn and btn after 3 out* **20/1**
0P5- **13** ½ **Kie (IRE)**[167] 3995 7-10-3 **129**...............................(t) TomScudamore 117
(David Pipe) *plld hrd: led tl after 1st: mstke 3 out whn losing pl: no ch after* **14/1**
3-41 **14** ¾ **Restraint Of Trade (IRE)**[20] 851 5-10-0 **126** oh2..........(vt) PeterCarberry 113
(Jennie Candlish) *racd keenly: cl up: nt a fluent: drvn after 3 out: sn lost pl* **40/1**
-334 **15** 6 **Purple 'n Gold (IRE)**[6] 973 6-9-11 **128** ow2..................(p) KieronEdgar(5) 109
(David Pipe) *hit 2nd: racd on outer: rdn 3 out: sn struggling* **22/1**
46-0 **16** 32 **Court Minstrel (IRE)**[20] 850 8-11-8 **148**......................... PaulMoloney 100
(Evan Williams) *last trio: nt travelling fr 4th: t.o bef 2 out: sn eased* **20/1**

1-41 **17** *nk* **Surf And Turf (IRE)**[24] 830 9-10-8 **134**.......................... JamesReveley 86
(Kevin Frost) *nvr trbld ldrs: struggling after 3 out: sn t.o: eased* **20/1**

3m 59.5s (-7.20) **Going Correction** -0.05s/f (Good)
WFA 4 from 5yo+ 15lb **17 Ran SP% 130.1**
Speed ratings (Par 111): **114,113,112,112,110 107,107,107,106,106 106,105,105,105,102 87,87**
CSF £117.45 CT £1328.82 TOTE £26.80: £5.00, £2.90, £3.30, £8.70; EX 206.50 Trifecta £3279.40.
Owner ValueRacingClub.co.uk **Bred** Darley **Trained** Claines, Worcs

FOCUS
Another strong renewal of this now long-established contest, featuring eight last-time hurdles winners. The pace was quick but didn't burn all of those that got involved with it by any means. Solid form, the winner improving in line with his Flat level.

1040 BETFRED SUMMER PLATE (A H'CAP CHASE) (LISTED RACE) (14 fncs) 2m 5f 89y

3:30 (3:32) (Class 1) 4-Y-0+
£28,475 (£10,685; £5,350; £2,665; £1,340; £670)

Form RPR

3-33 **1** **Brave Spartacus (IRE)**[20] 850 9-10-12 **135**.................. JamesReveley 148+
(Keith Reveley) *led after 1st: racd v enthusiastically and j. really wl: set str gallop: drawing 7 l clr whn hit 2 out: drvn out and remained wl in command* **12/1**

6-22 **2** *7* **Baby Mix (FR)**[62] 362 7-11-3 **140**........................ GavinSheehan 147
(Warren Greatrex) *settled in midfield: effrt gng wl after 11th: rdn and outpcd bef next: rallied to go 2nd but hanging rt and hit 2 out: chsd wnr vainly after* **5/1**[2]

2-41 **3** *5* **Valco De Touzaine (FR)**[27] 809 6-11-5 **142**.......(t) SamTwiston-Davies 145+
(Paul Nicholls) *midfield: nt a fluent: drvn and effrt after 11th: hit next: no imp fr 2 out* **9/1**

411- **4** *¾* **Pumped Up Kicks (IRE)**[86] 5499 8-10-9 **132**................... HarrySkelton 133+
(Dan Skelton) *settled in midfield: 5th after 11th: drvn and nvr looked like getting in a blow fr after 3 out* **9/2**[1]

250- **5** *1 ¾* **Hollow Penny**[92] 5363 7-11-5 **142**..................... WayneHutchinson 141
(Alan King) *towards rr: rdn and outpcd 11th: styd on steadily to make grnd fr 2 out but no ch w ldrs* **12/1**

0-62 **6** *1 ¾* **It's A Gimme (IRE)**[49] 555 8-11-6 **143**........................(t) BarryGeraghty 140
(Jonjo O'Neill) *trckd ldrs: effrt in 4th gng wl enough after 11th: drvn bef next: fnd little after* **11/2**[3]

56P- **7** *1 ½* **Lost Legend (IRE)**[84] 5538 8-11-4 **141**......................(p) RichieMcLernon 137
(Jonjo O'Neill) *trckd ldrs: chal gng wl 10th: 2nd but rdn home turn: little rspnse: wknd 2 out* **11/1**

-051 **8** *8* **Bar De Ligne (FR)**[29] 781 9-10-9 **132**..........................(p) AidanColeman 121
(Brian Ellison) *prom tl hrd drvn and wknd bef 3 out* **20/1**

304- **9** *3 ¾* **Conquisto**[92] 5363 10-10-13 **143**..........................(t) CraigGallagher(7) 128
(Brian Ellison) *towards rr: rdn 8th: struggling after* **20/1**

F-01 **10** *10* **Wings Of Smoke (IRE)**[42] 642 10-11-1 **138**.................(t) MichaelByrne 114
(Tim Vaughan) *lacked fluency and wl in rr: struggling 9th: t.o* **33/1**

3-31 **11** *13* **Carrigmorna King (IRE)**[62] 362 9-11-2 **139**................(t) MichealNolan 104
(Philip Hobbs) *midfield: struggling fr 11th: t.o* **12/1**

-311 **12** *19* **Greenlaw**[31] 760 9-10-4 **127**...(t) PaulMoloney 75
(Charlie Longsdon) *racd freely in 2nd pl tl 10th: dropped out qckly: t.o 3 out: eased next* **8/1**

PP-0 **P** **Pantxoa (FR)**[13] 916 8-10-13 **139**............................ TomBellamy(3)
(Alan King) *led tl after 1st: prom tl rdn bef 8th: hit next two: t.o and p.u 11th* **25/1**

-141 **P** **Perfect Timing**[13] 915 7-10-5 **128**...................................(b) NoelFehily
(Neil Mulholland) *rdn to begin: nvr travelling in rr: rdn and lost tch 8th: t.o and p.u 11th* **8/1**

5m 19.2s (-26.80) **Going Correction** -1.45s/f (Hard) **14 Ran SP% 130.2**
Speed ratings (Par 111): **93,90,88,88,87 86,86,83,81,77 73,65, ,**
CSF £75.13 CT £594.88 TOTE £13.90: £3.70, £1.80, £3.90; EX 98.20 Trifecta £521.20.
Owner Richard Collins **Bred** Dan O'Regan **Trained** Lingdale, Redcar & Cleveland

FOCUS
A maximum field at the overnight stage for the eighth time in the last nine seasons, and one of the deepest renewals with nothing rated lower than 127. Even more so than with the preceding feature hurdle, playing a part in the strong pace didn't prove a bar to success this time. The winner is up 8lb but there may still be more to come.

1041 B EYRE AND SONS LTD FORD NOVICES' HURDLE (8 hdls) 2m 148y

4:05 (4:05) (Class 4) 4-Y-0+ **£3,249** (£954; £477; £238)

Form RPR

-332 **1** **Dire Straits (IRE)**[13] 912 4-11-3 120...............................(bt) TrevorWhelan 116
(Neil King) *sent ahd 1st: rdn bef 2 out: gd jump last and kpt on u.p despite idling: jst hld on* **7/2**[2]

40- **2** *shd* **Brigadoon**[24] 3342 8-10-12 0.. JamieMoore 112
(Michael Appleby) *str: t.k.h: wnt 3rd 3 out: 4 l 3rd home turn: sn drvn: no real imp after hitting 2 out tl styd on u.p after last: jst failed* **16/1**

1 **3** *1* **Miner's Lamp (IRE)**[32] 749 4-11-3 0............................... AidanColeman 116+
(John Ferguson) *plld hrd cl up: wnt 2nd 3 out: rdn bef next: little rspnse although remained w ev ch tl nt fluent last: no ex fnl 100yds* **8/13**[1]

6-05 **4** *24* **Pixiepot**[20] 846 5-10-5 0.. WayneHutchinson 81
(Peter Niven) *last pair: lost tch and slow 5th: t.o next: poor 4th whn hmpd last* **33/1**

6P **5** *2* **Jimmy Crackle (IRE)**[20] 853 4-10-10 0..........................(p) GavinSheehan 82
(Brian Ellison) *wnt 2nd at 4th tl next: rdn and tamely dropped to rr 3 out: t.o next* **25/1**

23 **F** **Tiger Twenty Two**[13] 912 4-10-10 115............................ AndrewTinkler 92
(Brian Rothwell) *v small: mostly 2nd in muddling r tl 1/2-way: nt fluent 3 out and drvn: sn dropped out: abt 20 l 4th whn fell 2 out* **11/2**[3]

4m 6.4s (-0.30) **Going Correction** -0.05s/f (Good) **6 Ran SP% 112.2**
Speed ratings (Par 105): **98,97,97,86,85**
CSF £45.57 TOTE £4.90: £1.70, £8.30; EX 52.10 Trifecta £115.10.
Owner D S Lee **Bred** Noel Carter **Trained** Barbury Castle, Wiltshire

FOCUS
Not an especially deep contest, and a winning time nearly eight seconds slower than that of the Summer Hurdle. Suspect form, the third and fifth helping with the level.

1042 BETFRED RACING "FOLLOW US ON TWITTER" NOVICES' LIMITED H'CAP CHASE (14 fncs) 2m 5f 89y

4:40 (4:40) (Class 3) (0-125,125) 4-Y-0+ **£6,498** (£1,908; £954; £477)

Form RPR

0-20 **1** **Tangolan (IRE)**[17] 872 7-10-5 **108**.......................(t) PaddyBrennan 118+
(Fergal O'Brien) *settled in 3rd pl: nt fluent 8th: led after 11th: rdn to qckn clr next: nrly 4 l ahd 2 out tl last: drvn and hld on gamely flat* **10/1**

-512 **2** *1 ½* **Mont Royale**[30] 775 7-11-8 **125**.................................. RichieMcLernon 133
(Jonjo O'Neill) *2nd tl led 9th: hdd after 11th: drvn and sltly outpcd fr next tl hrd rdn and styd on after last: a had jst too much to do* **7/1**

3-11 **3** *3 ¼* **Noble Friend (IRE)**[18] 863 7-11-5 **122**............................ TomCannon 127
(Chris Gordon) *settled in rr: effrt bef 3 out: sn cajoled along: 3rd and no imp fr 2 out* **7/2**[2]

6-50 **4** *4 ½* **Sureness (IRE)**[20] 854 5-11-3 **120**............................(t) GavinSheehan 121
(Charlie Mann) *hld up towards rr: awkward 11th: effrt bef 3 out: sn rdn and a hld fr next* **25/1**

3-54 **5** *¾* **Lord Grantham (IRE)**[32] 750 8-11-3 **120**............................ TomO'Brien 121
(Henry Daly) *cl up: rdn and no ex fr 3 out* **10/3**[1]

5311 **6** *11* **Jayo Time (IRE)**[12] 929 6-10-7 **110**.................................... WillKennedy 105
(Dr Richard Newland) *settled in rr: last whn blnd bdly 4th: stl in rr whn bmpd and blnd 11th: no ch after* **7/2**[2]

5-22 **7** *3* **Double Handful (GER)**[31] 760 9-10-11 **114**..................(tp) NickScholfield 102
(Lawney Hill) *towards rr: rdn after 11th: sn lost tch* **4/1**[3]

410P **8** *62* **Flash Tommie (IRE)**[18] 863 7-10-5 **108**............................(p) JamieMoore 40
(Michael Appleby) *led: awkward 2nd: rdn and hdd 9th: lost pl rapidly next: t.o fr 11th and hacked on* **12/1**

5m 25.3s (-20.70) **Going Correction** -1.45s/f (Hard) **8 Ran SP% 120.7**
Speed ratings (Par 107): **81,80,79,77,77 73,71,48**
CSF £79.82 CT £300.29 TOTE £18.00: £4.30, £1.60, £1.20; EX 95.20 Trifecta £384.40.
Owner The Yes No Wait Sorries **Bred** Brian McManus **Trained** Naunton, Gloucs

FOCUS
A fair 0-125 run over the Summer Plate C&D, and a winning time not surprisingly 6.1 seconds slower than that strongly run feature. The winner is rated in line with the best of his hurdles form.

1043 BETFRED "KEEP IT FUN" H'CAP CHASE (12 fncs) 2m 1f 43y

5:15 (5:15) (Class 4) (0-120,117) 4-Y-0+ **£3,898** (£1,144; £572; £286)

Form RPR

-P03 **1** **Formal Bid (IRE)**[17] 872 8-11-6 **114**..........................(bt) JamesBanks(3) 121
(Barry Brennan) *chsd ldrs: drvn bef 3 out: outpcd whn mstke 2 out: stl 5 l 3rd at last: r.o u.p to get up on nod* **9/1**

32F5 **2** *½* **Town Mouse**[11] 936 5-11-12 **117**..................................(p) TrevorWhelan 124
(Neil King) *walked to post early: racd freely and prom: hit 8th: chal for ld after next: shkn up bef 3 out: outpcd next: hrd drvn and rallied after last: led 50yds out: jst ct* **10/3**[2]

5-3P **3** *nse* **Kitchapoly (FR)**[39] 677 5-11-5 **110**............................ WayneHutchinson 117
(Donald McCain) *pressed ldng pair: led bef 3 out and looked to be gng best: abt 3 l clr 2 out tl last: urged along and doing little in front flat: hdd 50yds out and lost 2nd fnl stride* **7/2**[3]

F34P **4** *25* **Capisci (IRE)**[6] 976 10-10-8 **99**............................(p) SamTwiston-Davies 89
(Sarah-Jayne Davies) *led at brisk pce: blnd 5th and rdr lost iron briefly: drvn 7th: blnd again 9th: hrd rdn and hdd & wknd bef next* **3/1**[1]

-2F4 **5** *3 ¼* **Kayfton Pete**[33] 742 9-11-3 **108**.. AdamPogson 90
(Charles Pogson) *taken down v early: plld hrd: towards rr: v awkward 3rd: rdn and wknd tamely bef 3 out* **5/1**

2/3- **6** *99* **Spock (FR)**[427] 339 10-11-2 **112**.................................(b) MrsAlexDunn(5) 4
(Alexandra Dunn) *dropped bk last and struggling bef 6th: sn bdly t.o* **8/1**

-4PP **P** **Figaro**[39] 677 7-11-5 **110**...(t) MichaelByrne
(Tim Vaughan) *blnd 2nd and continued last: detached and drvn 5th: blnd next and t.o after: p.u after 9th* **10/1**

4m 15.8s (-19.20) **Going Correction** -1.45s/f (Hard) **7 Ran SP% 117.2**
Speed ratings (Par 105): **87,86,86,74,73 26,**
CSF £41.20 TOTE £9.40: £3.90, £2.30; EX 36.90 Trifecta £144.60.
Owner David Gibbons **Bred** Neville O'Byrne & John Weld **Trained** Upper Lambourn, Berks

FOCUS
A well-run finale, with the result in doubt until the final stride. The first three ran pretty much to their marks.
T/Jkpt: Not won. T/Plt: £558.50 to a £1 stake. Pool: £83,020.92 - 108.50 winning tickets T/Qpdt: £260.00 to a £1 stake. Pool: £5,798.59 - 16.50 winning tickets **Iain Mackenzie**

891 NEWTON ABBOT (L-H)

Sunday, July 19

OFFICIAL GOING: Good (good to firm in places; 7.0)
Wind: almost nil Weather: sunny with cloudy periods Rails: Bends moved out by 2 metres altering race distances as follows: Race 1 add 83yds; Races 2 & 4 add 30yds; Race 3 add 62yds; Race 5 & 7 add 55yds; Race 6 add 85yds.

1044 IN MEMORY OF LENA PACKMAN MAIDEN HURDLE (10 hdls) 2m 5f 122y

1:45 (1:45) (Class 4) 4-Y-0+ **£4,223** (£1,240; £620; £310)

Form RPR

P3 **1** **Ruddy Article (IRE)**[26] 823 7-11-0 0...................(t) SamTwiston-Davies 115+
(Paul Nicholls) *led 1st: mde rest: shkn up appr 2 out: styd on wl: pushed out* **6/4**[1]

1 **2** *4* **Mont Choisy (FR)**[38] 700 5-10-7 0.................................. JamieBargary(7) 113+
(Nigel Twiston-Davies) *trckd ldrs: rdn after 3 out: chsd wnr next: styd on to draw wl clr of the 3rd but a being hld by wnr* **6/1**[2]

2 **3** *38* **Air Glider (IRE)**[21] 852 5-11-0 0... HarrySkelton 86
(Dan Skelton) *mid-div: hdwy after 6th: trckd wnr next: rdn after 3 out: wknd bef next: t.o* **6/4**[1]

3 **4** *10* **Part And Parcel (IRE)**[18] 877 7-10-7 0.......................... MrAlexEdwards(7) 67
(Alan Phillips) *mid-div: hdwy after 6th: rdn to chse ldrs after 3 out: sn wknd: t.o* **17/2**[3]

5 *10* **Cecile De Volanges**[63] 7-10-2 0............................ CharlieDeutsch(5) 51
(Ronald Harris) *hld up towards rr: hdwy after 6th: rdn to chse ldrs after 3 out: sn wknd: t.o* **20/1**

6 *3 ½* **Polo The Mumm (FR)**[76] 5-10-7 112................................ MissHWelch(7) 55
(Jimmy Frost) *mid-div: struggling after 6th: wknd 3 out: t.o* **66/1**

62-P **7** *nse* **Quick N' Easy (IRE)**[16] 893 5-11-0 0................................ MichealNolan 55
(Sue Gardner) *mid-div tl wknd after 3 out: t.o* **50/1**

5 **8** *22* **Sturmwind (GER)**[25] 834 4-10-11 0.................................. LeightonAspell 32
(Alison Batchelor) *a towards rr: t.o 3 out* **66/1**

00P **9** *5* **Merry Mast (USA)**[16] 893 6-10-7 0.................................. MrGTreacy(7) 31
(Paul Henderson) *a towards rr: lost tch bef 7th: t.o* **200/1**

40-P **P** **Indiana Oscar**[61] 391 7-11-0 67...(b[1]) JamesBest
(Carroll Gray) *chsd ldrs: wknd after 6th: t.o whn p.u bef 3 out* **200/1**

P **Indian Dancer (IRE)**[92] 8-11-0 0...(p) JamieMoore
(Katie Stephens) *led tl awkward 1st: trckd ldr: lost pl u.p after 6th: t.o next: p.u after 3 out* **50/1**

P **Botney Bay (IRE)**[91] 5-11-0 0 TomCannon
(Robert Walford) *in tch: drvn along fr 4th: wknd bef 7th: t.o whn p.u bef last* 33/1

5m 8.8s (-11.40) **Going Correction** -0.375s/f (Good)
WFA 4 from 5yo+ 16lb 12 Ran SP% 120.4
Speed ratings (Par 105): **105,103,89,86,82 81,81,73,71, ,**
CSF £12.07 TOTE £2.20: £1.10, £1.90, £1.10; EX 12.40 Trifecta £19.20.
Owner A J Powell **Bred** Dorothy M H Murdoch **Trained** Ditcheat, Somerset

FOCUS
All Bends moved out 2m and race 1 increased by 83yds, races 2 & 4 by 30yds, race 3 by 62yds, races 5 & 7 by 55yds and race 6 by 85yds. Not a bad maiden hurdle for the time of year but the race was littered with jumping errors from all quarters, not least from the runner-up, who must have quite a lot of ability to run so well despite doing so much wrong.

1045 INDEPENDENT RACECOURSES LIMITED, IRL H'CAP CHASE (13 fncs) 2m 75y
2:20 (2:20) (Class 5) (0-100,99) 4-Y-O+ **£3,249** (£954; £477; £238)

Form RPR
24/1 **1** **Walden Prince (IRE)**[7] 964 8-12-0 **99** 7ex (tp) TomScudamore 124+
(David Bridgwater) *j.rt at times: prom: disp 6th tl clr ldr 8th: drew further clr after 3 out: easily* 8/11[1]
P5-3 **2** *14* **Maizy Missile (IRE)**[53] 514 13-10-13 **84** PaulMoloney 92
(Mary Evans) *chsd ldrs: j.rt at times: disp 6th tl after next: pushed along to chse wnr fr 8th: rdn after 4 out: hld fr next* 12/1
005P **3** *9* **Accessallareas (IRE)**[7] 972 10-11-12 **97** RobertDunne 96
(Sarah-Jayne Davies) *trckd ldrs: disp ld 6th tl 8th: rdn after 4 out: sn hld: regained 3rd 2 out* 22/1
/5P2 **4** *10* **Sylvan Legend**[12] 934 7-10-4 **75** (tp) SamTwiston-Davies 66
(Neil Mulholland) *trckd ldrs: rdn to dispute 2nd after 4 out tl next: wknd appr 2 out* 5/2[2]
215 **5** *10* **No No Cardinal (IRE)**[37] 713 6-11-3 **88** (t) TomCannon 72
(Mark Gillard) *hld up bhd ldrs: making hdwy whn propped on landing 4 out: sn rdn: wknd next* 10/1[3]
F-60 **6** *21* **The Omen**[14] 914 9-11-8 **93** MichaelByrne 55
(Tim Vaughan) *led tl 6th: struggling in detached 6th after next: t.o after 4 out* 20/1

4m 1.3s (-5.20) **Going Correction** -0.50s/f (Good) 6 Ran SP% 112.4
Speed ratings (Par 103): **93,86,81,76,71 61**
CSF £9.90 TOTE £1.50: £1.10, £3.30; EX 9.90 Trifecta £65.20.
Owner Gary Attwood **Bred** John McEnery **Trained** Icomb, Gloucs

FOCUS
This was pretty much done and dusted around three fences from home.

1046 PACKEXE EDGE H'CAP HURDLE (9 hdls) 2m 2f 110y
2:50 (2:50) (Class 3) (0-135,130) 4-Y-O£7,912 (£2,337; £1,168; £585; £292)

Form RPR
-234 **1** **Lava Lamp (GER)**[31] 774 8-10-9 **113** PaulMoloney 117
(Evan Williams) *in tch: pushed along in last pair after 5th: hdwy u.p after 3 out: led last: r.o: drvn out* 8/1
P5-5 **2** *1 3/4* **Byron Blue (IRE)**[18] 876 6-11-4 **122** TomCannon 125
(Mark Gillard) *led: rdn after 3 out: hdd last: kpt on but no ex* 8/1
P-06 **3** *6* **Rum And Butter (IRE)**[28] 812 7-11-12 **130** (p) BarryGeraghty 128
(Jonjo O'Neill) *trckd ldrs: dropped to last trio and nudged along after 5th: stdy prog after 3 out where pushed wd on bnd by wnr: styd on fr next: wnt 3rd run-in* 3/1[1]
0-13 **4** *1* **Dun Scaith (IRE)**[40] 678 7-10-5 **112** (t) KillianMoore[(3)] 108
(Sophie Leech) *pressed ldr: ev ch 3 out: sn rdn: hld next: kpt on same pce* 20/1
3-11 **5** *2 1/2* **Archie Rice (USA)**[26] 828 9-9-9 **106** MissBFrost[(7)] 100
(Jimmy Frost) *trckd ldrs: rdn after 3 out: styd on same pce fr next* 4/1[2]
-143 **6** *19* **Lochalsh (IRE)**[33] 749 4-11-1 **122** HarrySkelton 96
(Dan Skelton) *in tch: rdn after 6th: no imp: wknd bef 2 out* 7/1[3]
3064 **7** *6* **Party Palace**[26] 826 11-9-9 **104** AliceMills[(5)] 75
(Stuart Howe) *in tch: drvn along in detached last after 5th: no threat after* 25/1
-605 **8** *7* **Oyster Shell**[26] 826 8-11-9 **127** (t) TomScudamore 95
(Henry Daly) *trckd ldrs: rdn after 6th: wknd after next* 10/1
1P-6 **P** **Zip Top (IRE)**[18] 876 6-11-8 **126** (p) AidanColeman
(John Ferguson) *travelled wl trcking ldrs tl rdn after 6th: wknd tamely next: p.u bef 2 out* 4/1[2]

4m 21.7s (-8.30) **Going Correction** -0.375s/f (Good)
WFA 4 from 6yo+ 15lb 9 Ran SP% 117.4
Speed ratings (Par 107): **102,101,98,98,97 89,86,83,**
CSF £70.56 CT £237.63 TOTE £8.90: £2.30, £3.30, £1.20; EX 89.40 Trifecta £555.50.
Owner Mrs Janet Davies **Bred** Graf And Grafin Von Stauffenberg **Trained** Llancarfan, Vale Of Glamorgan

FOCUS
They got racing a long way out here. and although it looked for a while like those in behind weren't going to get in a blow,

1047 GILL AND TERRY WEDDING CELEBRATION, 31 JULY NOVICES' CHASE (13 fncs) 2m 75y
3:25 (3:25) (Class 4) 4-Y-O+ **£5,198** (£1,526; £763; £381)

Form RPR
0-31 **1** **Dubai Prince (IRE)**[26] 826 7-11-1 0 AidanColeman 144+
(John Ferguson) *hld up: hdwy to trck ldrs 6th: hit next: wnt 2nd after 8th: led appr 2 out: sn in command: comf* 10/11[1]
0-11 **2** *8* **Dormello Mo (FR)**[26] 825 5-12-1 0 (t) SamTwiston-Davies 150+
(Paul Nicholls) *trckd ldrs: led 7th: nt fluent 3 out: rdn and hdd bef next: sn hld* 9/4[2]
363- **3** *9* **Russian Bolero (GER)**[123] 4854 4-10-0 0[1] TomScudamore 106
(David Bridgwater) *trckd ldrs: lost pl briefly after 7th: regained 3rd after next: outpcd by front pair 3 out* 8/1[3]
3P-6 **4** *5* **Foxtail Hill (IRE)**[50] 556 6-10-8 0 JamieBargary[(7)] 117
(Nigel Twiston-Davies) *hld up: wnt 4th after 9th: hit 3 out: nvr threatened ldrs: styd on same pce* 14/1
-125 **5** *20* **Mr Lando**[60] 406 6-11-1 0 LeightonAspell 96
(Alison Batchelor) *led tl 7th: wknd after 4 out* 20/1
F5-2 **6** *7* **Grissom (FR)**[73] 160 7-11-1 110 (t) JamesDavies 89
(Jimmy Frost) *cl up: in last pair but in tch 6th: struggling fr 9th: wknd after 4 out* 50/1
0-55 **7** *1 1/4* **Avel Vor (IRE)**[16] 895 4-10-0 110 (p) JamesBest 73
(Philip Hobbs) *trckd ldrs tl after 7th: wknd 4 out* 25/1

3m 56.6s (-9.90) **Going Correction** -0.50s/f (Good)
WFA 4 from 5yo+ 2lb 7 Ran SP% 111.5
Speed ratings (Par 105): **104,100,95,93,83 79,78**
CSF £3.17 TOTE £1.90: £1.10, £1.50; EX 2.80 Trifecta £8.40.
Owner Bloomfields **Bred** Mrs Eithne Hamilton **Trained** Cowlinge, Suffolk

FOCUS
A decent little novices' chase in which Dormello Mo set a good standard on his chase form.

1048 RACING TOGETHER H'CAP HURDLE (8 hdls) 2m 167y
4:00 (4:00) (Class 4) (0-110,106) 3-Y-O+ **£4,223** (£1,240; £620; £310)

Form RPR
-462 **1** **Astaroland (FR)**[31] 776 5-11-10 **104** PeterCarberry 115+
(Jennie Candlish) *mid-div: hdwy after 4th: hit next: led sn after 2 out: in command whn mstke last: rdn out* 5/1[2]
55-6 **2** *2* **Key To Milan**[26] 828 9-11-6 **103** (tp) GilesHawkins[(3)] 111
(Chris Down) *j.lft at times: led: rdn after 3 out: hdd sn after 2 out: styng on at same pce whn sltly hmpd last* 8/1
4434 **3** *11* **Ladies Dancing**[25] 835 9-11-6 **100** (b) JamesDavies 97
(Chris Down) *mid-div: hdwy after 3 out: sn rdn: wnt 3rd between last 2: styd on same pce* 9/1
-31U **4** *13* **Cruise In Style (IRE)**[37] 718 9-10-9 **89** (tp) JamesBest 76
(Kevin Bishop) *trckd ldr tl rdn after 3 out: wknd appr last* 14/1
05-0 **5** *4 1/2* **Taste The Wine (IRE)**[19] 449 9-11-3 **100** (p) RobertWilliams[(3)] 84
(Bernard Llewellyn) *cl up: lost pl u.p after 5th: hmpd next: wknd bef 2 out* 6/1[3]
52-1 **6** *2* **Bertie Moon**[20] 34 5-11-10 **104** TomScudamore 85
(Polly Gundry) *trckd ldrs: hmpd 3 out: sn rdn: wknd bef next* 2/1[1]
02-4 **7** *3 3/4* **Hill Fort**[38] 702 5-11-2 **101** MikeyEnnis[(5)] 77
(Ronald Harris) *hld up towards rr: hdwy appr 5th: trckd ldrs 3 out: sn rdn: wknd bef next* 18/1
5-00 **8** *4* **Worldor (FR)**[21] 856 9-10-11 **91** SamTwiston-Davies 64
(Alexandra Dunn) *hld up towards rr: hmpd 3 out: wknd bef next* 25/1
-4PP **9** *12* **Callmenewtown (IRE)**[31] 770 8-11-4 **105** (b[1]) MissBHampson[(7)] 67
(Katie Stephens) *nt fluent 1st and 2nd: towards rr: struggling after 4th: hmpd 3 out: wknd* 50/1
55-P **10** *12* **Charging Indian (IRE)**[21] 858 9-10-8 **88** (p) JamieMoore 39
(Paul Henderson) *trckd ldr: rdn after 4th: wknd after next: hmpd 3 out: t.o* 33/1
6316 **F** **Polstar (FR)**[38] 692 6-11-5 **106** PaulNO'Brien[(7)]
(Harry Whittington) *cl up: travelling strly bhd ldr whn fell 3 out* 6/1[3]

3m 57.8s (-7.90) **Going Correction** -0.375s/f (Good) 11 Ran SP% 120.4
Speed ratings (Par 105): **103,102,96,90,88 87,85,84,78,72**
CSF £45.14 CT £357.33 TOTE £6.00: £1.80, £3.30, £3.40; EX 59.10 Trifecta £515.10.
Owner Paul Beck **Bred** Mlle Marie-Laure Besnouin **Trained** Basford Green, Staffs

FOCUS
A wide-open handicap hurdle run at what looked a sound pace, but few brought compelling recent claims, so it's hard to know whether the form will work out.

1049 PACKEXE FLEECE H'CAP CHASE (20 fncs) 3m 1f 170y
4:30 (4:32) (Class 4) (0-110,110) 4-Y-O+ **£5,198** (£1,526; £763; £381)

Form RPR
2/11 **1** **Celtic Intrigue (IRE)**[37] 717 8-11-5 **103** (b[1]) TomScudamore 119+
(David Bridgwater) *trckd ldrs: led 15th: in command but idling fr 3 out: kpt up to work: styd on wl* 2/1[1]
20-2 **2** *4 1/2* **Hinton Indiana**[55] 471 10-11-4 **102** (t) HarrySkelton 110
(Dan Skelton) *hld up: hdwy 13th: rdn 15th: chsd wnr fr next: styd on same pce fr 3 out* 11/4[2]
-325 **3** *11* **The Wee Midget**[13] 926 10-9-7 **84** oh4 (b) ThomasCheesman[(7)] 84
(Arthur Whiting) *trckd ldrs: disp 2nd after 15th tl 4 out: sn rdn: styd on same pce fr next* 14/1
-F3P **4** *dist* **Dancing Dik**[33] 752 10-10-0 **84** oh4 (b) JamieMoore 46
(Paul Henderson) *led: rchd for 15th: sn hdd: wknd after 4 out: t.o* 16/1
P-42 **5** *1 1/4* **Susquehanna River (IRE)**[31] 771 8-11-11 **109** SamTwiston-Davies 70
(Nigel Twiston-Davies) *trckd ldrs: pushed along after 10th: drvn in last trio after 13th: wknd bef 4 out: t.o* 10/3[3]
00-0 **6** *44* **Cinevator (IRE)**[26] 827 8-11-3 **108** (p) MrMatthewHampton[(7)] 29
(Richard Woollacott) *trckd ldr tl 13th: sn rdn: lost tch fr after next: t.o* 8/1
-1F0 **P** **La Madonnina (IRE)**[40] 674 7-10-4 **88** (p) JamesBest
(Caroline Keevil) *hld up: pushed along fr 9th: detached 13th: tailing off whn blnd bdly 15th: p.u bef next* 16/1

6m 28.6s (-16.00) **Going Correction** -0.50s/f (Good) 7 Ran SP% 112.6
Speed ratings (Par 105): **104,102,99,86,86 73,**
CSF £8.05 CT £55.50 TOTE £3.10: £1.50, £2.30; EX 7.40 Trifecta £66.90.
Owner Mrs Jan Smith **Bred** Hardys Of Kilkeel Ltd **Trained** Icomb, Gloucs

FOCUS
Not a particularly competitive handicap chase.

1050 AT THE RACES VIRGIN 534 MAIDEN OPEN NATIONAL HUNT FLAT RACE 2m 167y
5:05 (5:05) (Class 5) 4-6-Y-O **£1,711** (£498; £249)

Form RPR
24-6 **1** **Lincoln County**[19] 865 4-11-0 0 (p) AidanColeman 102+
(John Ferguson) *travelled wl trcking ldrs: led over 2f out: sn clr: pushed out* 2/1[1]
5 **2** *10* **Tour De Ville (IRE)**[40] 682 5-11-2 0 ConorO'Farrell 95
(Seamus Durack) *hld up: hdwy fr 3f out: hung rt fnl bnd: rdn to chse wnr over 2f out: kpt on but nvr threatened to get on terms* 4/1[3]
6 **3** *11* **Brenda De Ronceray (FR)**[25] 831 4-10-7 0 TomScudamore 76
(David Pipe) *led: rdn and hdd over 2f out: sn one pce* 3/1[2]
4 *17* **Mollylikestoboogie** 5-10-9 0 SamTwiston-Davies 68
(Linda Blackford) *trckd ldrs: chal over 3f out: rdn over 2f out: sn wknd* 8/1
0 **5** *1 3/4* **Tombill (IRE)**[68] 271 6-10-9 0 MrGTreacy[(7)] 68
(Paul Henderson) *trckd ldrs tl wknd over 3f out* 25/1
2 **6** *7* **Kendari King (IRE)**[30] 783 4-11-0 0 MichaelByrne 60
(Tim Vaughan) *trckd ldr: rdn over 5f out: wknd over 3f out* 6/1
7 *nk* **Thrilling Moments** 4-10-0 0 ThomasCheesman[(7)] 53
(John Panvert) *hld up: struggling fnl circ: wknd over 3f out* 33/1
0 **8** *1* **Zakti (IRE)**[74] 152 5-10-9 0 (t) BrendanPowell 54
(Jamie Snowden) *trckd ldrs tl 6f out: sn bhd: t.o* 20/1

3m 54.7s (-5.40) **Going Correction** -0.375s/f (Good)
WFA 4 from 5yo+ 2lb 8 Ran SP% 115.3
Speed ratings: **97,92,87,79,78 75,74,74**
CSF £10.11 TOTE £3.00: £1.20, £1.20, £1.70; EX 9.00 Trifecta £35.40.
Owner Bloomfields **Bred** Darley **Trained** Cowlinge, Suffolk

FOCUS
Unlikely this will turn out to be anything other than ordinary bumper form.
T/Plt: £19.70 to a £1 stake. Pool: £79,398.61 - 2,933.72 winning tickets T/Qpdt: £11.80 to a £1 stake. Pool: £5,214.49 - 324.40 winning tickets **Tim Mitchell**

971 STRATFORD (L-H)
Sunday, July 19

OFFICIAL GOING: Chase course - good; hurdle course - good (good to firm in places) changing to good to firm after race 1 (2:10)
Wind: light breeze Weather: hot and sunny; 20 degrees

1051 SHAKESPEARE MEDIA (S) HURDLE (9 hdls) 2m 2f 148y
2:10 (2:10) (Class 5) 4-Y-0+ £2,599 (£763; £381; £190)

Form RPR
-234 1 **Man Of Leisure**[28] 798 11-11-12 123..............................(t) NoelFehily 126+
(Anthony Honeyball) *settled wl off pce tl stdy prog 4th: wnt 2nd after 2 out: rdn to ld bef last where 4 l clr w ears pricked: kpt idling flat but a doing enough* **4/1**[3]
3-0P 2 2 1/4 **Masterful Act (USA)**[38] 691 8-11-1 118..............(bt[1]) BridgetAndrews[(5)] 116
(Dan Skelton) *set str pce: sn 6 l clr: nt fluent 1st and 2nd: hit 2 out and drvn: hdd sme way bef last: hrd drvn and plugged on flat but a outbattled* **5/2**[2]
-665 3 5 **Limpopo Tom (IRE)**[7] 974 8-11-6 112..............(v[1]) DenisO'Regan 111
(David Rees) *hld up and wl bhd tl sme prog in 12 l 4th whn blnd 2 out: tk mod 3rd bef last and kpt plugging on flat* **8/1**
/F-2 4 9 **Quadriller (FR)**[26] 828 8-10-13 105..............(t) CiaranGethings[(7)] 104
(Philip Hobbs) *prom in gp of three chsng clr ldr: rdn fr 6th: struggling 2 out: lost mod 3rd bef last* **9/2**
33P/ 5 50 **Aughcarra (IRE)**[714] 1206 10-11-1 72.............. DanielHiskett[(5)] 57
(Harry Chisman) *prom in gp of three chsng clr ldr tl 5th: fdd v rapidly next: bdly t.o 2 out* **66/1**
00/0 6 nk **Weet In Nerja**[12] 937 9-10-7 65..............(p) MissTWorsley[(7)] 51
(Ken Wingrove) *last trio and a wl bhd: bdly t.o 3 out* **100/1**
0/4- P **Mister Green (FR)**[1] 4360 9-10-7 0..............(bt) BenFfrenchDavis[(7)]
(David Flood) *a struggling in last: mstke 3rd: t.o 6th: p.u after 2 out* **50/1**
45-5 P **Earls Quarter (IRE)**[44] 624 9-11-10 123..............(vt[1]) RichardJohnson
(Ian Williams) *prom in gp of three chsng clr ldr tl rdn and wnt bdly wrong after 6th: sn p.u: fatally injured* **9/4**[1]

4m 18.3s (-13.20) **Going Correction** -0.775s/f (Firm) 8 Ran SP% 113.1
Speed ratings (Par 103): **96,95,92,89,68 67, ,**
CSF £14.47 TOTE £4.60: £2.00, £1.10, £3.20; EX 16.50 Trifecta £71.40.The winner was bought in for 5,700gns.
Owner Anthony Honeyball Racing Club Ltd **Bred** Mrs Nerys Dutfield **Trained** Mosterton, Dorset

FOCUS
Divided bends on fresh ground. Inner line used. The ground was riding fast on a warm day and there were some very quick times. Not a bad seller, run at a strong pace thanks to the runner-up. It resulted in a record time, 1.4sec inside the previous best.

1052 AMBER SECURITY NOVICES' HURDLE (8 hdls) 2m 70y
2:40 (2:41) (Class 4) 4-Y-0+ £3,898 (£1,144; £572; £286)

Form RPR
1 1 **Penglai Pavilion (USA)**[36] 727 5-11-5 0.............. NoelFehily 136+
(John Ferguson) *chsd clr ldr in fast early r: clsd to ld bef 5th: 10 l ahd after 2 out: easily increased advantage and hrd hld fr last: impressive* **4/9**[1]
2 22 **No Win No Fee**[42] 5-10-12 0.............. WillKennedy 105+
(Dr Richard Newland) *off pce at rr of midfield: effrt 3 out: wnt 2nd after 2 out: rdn and nvr nr wnr after* **5/1**[3]
3 3 7 **Presenting Streak (IRE)**[30] 783 6-10-5 0.............. MrRWinks[(7)] 93
(Peter Winks) *tall scope: qckly lost tch: t.o at 3rd: began to stay on after 2 out: wnt remote 3rd bef last: urged along and fin v strly and looked full of running* **20/1**
4 11 **Lee Side Lady (IRE)**[105] 5-9-12 0.............. MrMartinMcIntyre[(7)] 75
(Neil Mulholland) *wl bhd: virtually t.o 5th: plugged on but nvr remotely in contention* **33/1**
P- 5 9 **Iwanabebobbiesgirl**[178] 3818 5-10-5 0..............(t[1]) LiamTreadwell 66
(David Brace) *small: tk ferocious hold and led and sn 7 l clr: nt fluent 3rd: hdd bef 5th: fdd bef 2 out: sn t.o* **40/1**
6 19 **Sharp Sword (IRE)**[41] 4-10-10 0.............. GavinSheehan 52
(Neil Mulholland) *a wl bhd: t.o fr 5th* **16/1**
0 7 13 **Filament Of Gold (USA)**[19] 860 4-10-7 0.............. JamesBanks[(3)] 39
(Roy Brotherton) *off pce in midfield: lost tch after 5th: t.o 2 out* **40/1**
0-0 8 10 **Four Plus**[19] 865 4-10-3 0.............. MarkGrant 22
(Hugo Froud) *chsd clr ldng trio tl wknd 1/2-way: t.o 2 out* **66/1**
3 P **Dare To Achieve**[37] 706 5-10-12 0..............[1] PaddyBrennan
(Tom George) *settled in 3rd and plld hrd: sn 12 l clr of rest: mstke 4th: wnt 2nd bef 3 out tl after next: mod 3rd whn p.u last: dismntd* **5/2**[2]

3m 43.4s (-12.60) **Going Correction** -0.775s/f (Firm)
WFA 4 from 5yo+ 15lb 9 Ran SP% 134.4
Speed ratings (Par 105): **100,89,85,80,75 66,59,54,**
CSF £4.54 TOTE £1.40: £1.02, £1.30, £6.50; EX 5.10 Trifecta £33.40.
Owner Bloomfields **Bred** Darley **Trained** Cowlinge, Suffolk

FOCUS
Before this event the official going description was changed to Good to firm over hurdles and Good on the chase course. Another strongly run race, in which the field was quickly spread out. Another quick time.

1053 HAT LADY OF ALCESTER H'CAP CHASE (17 fncs) 2m 6f 125y
3:15 (3:15) (Class 3) (0-130,130) 4-Y-£9,495 (£2,805; £1,402; £702; £351)

Form RPR
024- 1 **Danandy (IRE)**[262] 2156 8-11-0 118..............(p) RichardJohnson 125+
(Philip Hobbs) *settled in 4th pl: mstke 9th: effrt in 2nd at 12th: led 14th: rdn 2 l clr 2 out: styd on gamely to increase advantage bef last: drvn out* **13/2**
0-32 2 8 **Buck Mulligan**[49] 568 10-11-0 123.............. ConorRing[(5)] 122
(Evan Williams) *a 2nd or 3rd pl: rdn to chse wnr bef 2 out: outpcd appr last: rdn out* **9/2**[3]
35-1 3 8 **Croco Mister (IRE)**[28] 806 8-9-11 104 oh20..............(t) BenPoste[(3)] 95
(Rosemary Gasson) *towards rr: effrt in 8 l 4th 3 out: sn pushed along and outpcd: tk mod 3rd bef last and kpt trying vainly flat* **33/1**
-110 4 14 **Sail And Return**[21] 855 11-11-0 121..............(t) ConorShoemark[(3)] 99
(Phil Middleton) *midfield: drvn and outpcd after 13th: struggling whn hit next: snatched poor 4th* **6/1**
-211 5 nk **Sporting Boy (IRE)**[37] 715 7-11-9 127..............(b) NoelFehily 105
(Johnny Farrelly) *led at brisk pce fr 3rd tl hdd 14th: rdn and lost 2nd bef 2 out: wknd and lost 4th cl home* **7/2**[2]
5-24 6 36 **Porters War (IRE)**[19] 863 13-10-13 117.............. NickScholfield 62
(Jeremy Scott) *led tl 3rd: pressed ldr tl 10th: dropped himself to rr 12th: t.o 3 out: eased last* **12/1**
1232 F **Owen Glendower (IRE)**[7] 961 10-10-6 117..............(t) CiaranGethings[(7)]
(Sophie Leech) *in rr whn fell 2nd (water)* **3/1**[1]
2-P3 P **Caulfields Venture (IRE)**[56] 448 9-11-9 127..............(p) GavinSheehan
(Emma Lavelle) *last whn j. slowly 2nd (water) and 3rd: detached last and nvr travelling: rdn 8th: t.o 12th: p.u 14th* **8/1**

5m 22.8s (-16.40) **Going Correction** -0.50s/f (Good) 8 Ran SP% 114.8
Speed ratings (Par 107): **108,105,102,97,97 84, ,**
CSF £36.45 CT £895.94 TOTE £7.60: £1.90, £2.10, £8.10; EX 43.30 Trifecta £795.10 Part won.
Owner P J Hobbs **Bred** Mrs Mary Motherway **Trained** Withycombe, Somerset

FOCUS
This decent handicap chase was run over 66yds further than advertised. It was run at a good clip and in a time a second inside the course record, despite the extra yardage.

1054 102 TOUCH FM NOVICES' H'CAP HURDLE (9 hdls) 2m 2f 148y
3:50 (3:50) (Class 4) (0-110,110) 4-Y-0+ £3,898 (£1,144; £572; £286)

Form RPR
3622 1 **The Kvilleken**[36] 740 7-10-7 91..............(p) AndrewTinkler 94
(Martin Keighley) *hld up in rr in slow r: stl 8 l last bef 3 out and 6 l 4th home turn: kidded to chal last: sn led as others capitulated: edgd rt after* **17/2**
5-15 2 1 3/4 **Mac Bertie**[31] 776 6-11-5 103..............(p) AdamWedge 105
(Evan Williams) *settled in 2nd or 3rd in slow r: rdn after 2 out: drew upsides last: sn hdd and plugged on same pce* **5/2**[1]
F4P- 3 1 1/2 **Cousin Guillaume (FR)**[121] 4890 6-11-5 103..............(b[1]) HenryBrooke 103
(Donald McCain) *led at slow pce: u.p after 2 out: jnd and hit last: plodded on after* **16/1**
-044 4 1 3/4 **Ashkoun (FR)**[31] 776 4-11-2 103..............(t) RichardJohnson 98
(Tim Vaughan) *settled in rr: effrt after 2 out: rdn and little rspnse bef last where j.lft* **7/2**[2]
3-F5 5 nk **Princeton Royale (IRE)**[40] 671 6-11-7 105.............. TrevorWhelan 104
(Neil King) *chsd ldrs: nt fluent 4th: rdn and hit 2 out: one pce and nvr looked dangerous after* **6/1**[3]
-401 6 8 **Miss Fortywinks**[34] 745 6-11-12 110.............. RyanMahon 101
(Seamus Mullins) *prom: wnt 2nd at 6th: ev ch 2f out: drvn and fdd bef last* **8/1**
U50/ 7 2 1/4 **Swincombe Stone**[551] 3693 8-10-12 96.............. DarylJacob 84
(Robert Walford) *nt a fluent: wl in tch tl rdn and fdd fr 3 out* **10/1**
44 8 19 **Footstepsintherain (IRE)**[57] 440 5-11-7 105.............. NoelFehily 74
(David Dennis) *plld hrd: chsd ldrs tl 3 out: t.o and eased bef last* **8/1**

4m 23.2s (-8.30) **Going Correction** -0.775s/f (Firm)
WFA 4 from 5yo+ 15lb 8 Ran SP% 112.8
Speed ratings (Par 105): **86,85,84,83,83 80,79,71**
CSF £30.04 CT £334.49 TOTE £10.10: £2.90, £1.10, £5.80; EX 29.70 Trifecta £663.80.
Owner Mrs Belinda Keighley **Bred** A M Tombs **Trained** Condicote, Gloucs

FOCUS
This moderate event was run at a very steady gallop, which only really increased at the second-last. This isn't form to treat seriously.

1055 IVOR HUCKERBY MEMORIAL H'CAP HURDLE (11 hdls) 2m 6f 7y
4:20 (4:20) (Class 4) (0-115,112) 4-Y-0+ £3,898 (£1,144; £572; £286)

Form RPR
-544 1 **Absolutlyfantastic**[16] 895 8-11-10 110..............(t) NicodeBoinville 119+
(Martin Hill) *mde all: drew 5 l clr at 7th: 10 l clr after 2 out: rdn wl bef last: fnd plenty and a holding rival flat* **17/2**
4-16 2 7 **Midnight Sapphire**[46] 597 5-11-0 100..............(t) DenisO'Regan 104
(Victor Dartnall) *last tl 5th: gd prog after 8th to go 8 l 4th 2 out: chsd wnr and drvn between last two: no imp whn j. bdly rt last: kpt on valiantly flat* **9/1**
-013 3 10 **Iguacu**[33] 751 11-11-6 106.............. RichardJohnson 100
(Richard Price) *settled in rr: hdwy 7th: chsd wnr vainly 3 out tl drvn after next: wknd bef last* **13/2**[3]
P-P3 4 8 **Padre Tito (IRE)**[43] 647 7-11-11 111.............. GavinSheehan 98
(Emma Lavelle) *prom tl lost pl 5th: wl bhd 8th: plugged on after 2 out and snatched remote 4th* **11/1**
-421 5 1 **Shot In The Dark (IRE)**[38] 704 6-11-2 102..............(p) MarkGrant 88
(Jonathan Geake) *chsd wnr and sn clr of rest: outpcd by him after 7th: lost 2nd 3 out: wknd between last two and jst lost remote 4th* **12/1**
00-2 6 3 1/2 **Bedouin Bay**[38] 704 8-10-10 103.............. MrRobertHawker[(7)] 86
(Johnny Farrelly) *bhd: sme prog in 15 l 5th after 7th: struggling bef 3 out* **7/1**
235- 7 3 1/4 **Hazzaat (IRE)**[120] 4926 5-11-6 111.............. JakeHodson[(5)] 94
(Rob Summers) *chsd ldrs tl 5th: dropping rt out whn hmpd 8th: continued t.o* **25/1**
4-10 8 11 **Sukiyaki (IRE)**[52] 529 6-11-10 110..............(p) CharliePoste 80
(Charlie Longsdon) *midfield: hit 5th and 6th: 11 l 3rd at 7th: rdn and nvr travelling after: lost tch after 3 out: t.o* **11/2**[2]
-U66 9 8 **Royal Craftsman (IRE)**[31] 773 5-10-13 99..............(t) DonalDevereux 62
(Peter Bowen) *rn in snatches: dropping rt out whn hmpd 8th: t.o after* **16/1**
32P- P **Leath Acra Mor (IRE)**[92] 5399 9-11-2 112..............(v) TobyWheeler[(10)]
(Ian Williams) *last after 5th: nt travelling after and sn rdn: t.o 8th: p.u after 2 out* **12/1**
-112 F **Bennachie (IRE)**[60] 399 6-10-13 106..............(t) AlanJohns[(7)]
(Tim Vaughan) *chsd ldrs: disputing 4th (but wnr sme way clr) whn fell 8th* **3/1**[1]

5m 8.0s (-20.10) **Going Correction** -0.775s/f (Firm) 11 Ran SP% 120.2
Speed ratings (Par 105): **105,102,98,95,95 94,93,89,86,**
CSF £84.30 CT £537.82 TOTE £10.90: £3.30, £3.80, £1.90; EX 92.70 Trifecta £464.70.
Owner Fantastic Four **Bred** Mrs James Wigan & London TB Services Ltd **Trained** Littlehempston, Devon

FOCUS
Another strongly run event.

1056 JACKIE EBSWORTH MEMORIAL NOVICES' H'CAP CHASE (12 fncs) 2m 213y
4:55 (4:55) (Class 4) (0-105,105) 4-Y-0+ £4,548 (£1,335; £667; £333)

Form RPR
-321 1 **Zama Zama**[7] 976 8-11-6 99 7ex..............(v) AdamWedge 111+
(Evan Williams) *mde all: rdn after 3 out: drvn after next: swtchd lft whn almost jnd bef last: fnd ex to forge clr flat* **5/2**[2]
23-F 2 4 **Faustina Pius (IRE)**[37] 712 7-11-0 100..............(p) MrStanSheppard[(7)] 108
(Matt Sheppard) *cl up: outpcd 8th: rallied after 2 out: bmpd along to chal on inner bef last: sn hmpd: outpcd flat* **11/2**[3]

-051 **3** *8* **Mr Mafia (IRE)**[12] 934 6-11-8 **101**....................(t) LeeEdwards 104
(Tony Carroll) *hld up chsng ldrs: hit 4th and 7th: blnd next: wnt 2nd bef 3 out: chal and nt fluent next: rdn and wknd bef last: eased flat* **2/1**[1]

5-64 **4** *22* **Be My Witness (IRE)**[32] 759 6-11-0 **93**....................(t) CharliePoste 73
(Robin Dickin) *pressed wnr tl 9th: rdn and struggling 2 out* **12/1**

-P65 **5** *8* **Goldie Horn**[18] 874 7-10-11 **93**....................(t) ConorShoemark(3) 66
(Nigel Twiston-Davies) *j. slowly 1st: cl up: wnt 2nd at 8th tl rdn bef 3 out: wl btnwhn mstke next: t.o* **7/1**

2-24 **6** *24* **Separate Shadows (FR)**[7] 962 7-11-12 **105**.................... HenryBrooke 56
(Donald McCain) *j. slowly in last: sn detached and nt travelling: clambered over 9th and continued t.o* **6/1**

4m 2.2s (-4.90) **Going Correction** -0.50s/f (Good)
WFA 4 from 6yo+ 2lb **6** Ran SP% **111.8**
Speed ratings (Par 105): **91,89,85,75,71 59**
CSF £16.07 CT £30.63 TOTE £2.30: £1.60, £3.80; EX 16.80.
Owner Tony Cromwell & Partner **Bred** Cheveley Park Stud Ltd **Trained** Llancarfan, Vale Of Glamorgan
■ Stewards' Enquiry : Adam Wedge four-day ban: careless riding (2, 12, 13 and 15 Aug)
FOCUS
Race run over 51yds further than advertised. A fair novice handicap for the grade.

1057 RETRO REBEL MARES' STANDARD OPEN NATIONAL HUNT FLAT RACE — 2m 70y
5:25 (5:25) (Class 6) 4-6-Y-O **£1,949** (£572; £286; £143)

Form RPR

3 **1** **Violets Girl**[25] 831 5-10-12 0.................... AndrewTinkler 100+
(Warren Greatrex) *mde all and travelled wl: hrd pressed 2f out tl pushed clr fnl f: readily* **5/2**[2]

256/ **2** *4½* **Jazz Thyme (IRE)**[592] 2892 6-10-12 0.................... RhysFlint 96
(Robert Stephens) *settled towards rr: effrt in 2nd 6f out: 3rd and drvn over 2f out: one pce over 1f out but styd on to go wl hld 2nd ins fnl f* **12/1**

21 **3** *4½* **Tilinisi (IRE)**[7] 970 5-11-2 0.................... ConorShoemark(3) 99
(Phil Middleton) *tall: bhd: effrt 6f out: wnt 2nd 3f out: sn drvn: chal briefly home turn: wknd 1f out and lost 2nd ins fnl f* **11/10**[1]

4 *10* **DreamingofreveIry** 4-10-5 0.................... NickSlatter(5) 81
(Tony Carroll) *chsd ldrs: rdn and wknd 2f out* **20/1**

4 **5** *29* **Oneforthenure (IRE)**[13] 928 6-10-12 0....................(t) DarylJacob 57
(Richard Woollacott) *prom tl rdn and wknd over 4f out: t.o* **10/1**

50- **6** *1* **Chosen Destiny (IRE)**[104] 5193 5-10-7 0....................(t) BridgetAndrews(5) 56
(Dan Skelton) *t.k.h early: pressed ldrs tl rdn and lost tch 3f out: t.o* **6/1**[3]

6 **7** *8* **Emma Lee**[63] 359 5-10-5 0.................... MrRWinks(7) 49
(Peter Winks) *tall rngy: in last pair: pushed along after 5f: outpcd after: t.o fnl 4f* **20/1**

00- **8** *62* **Vitarra**[94] 5359 6-10-12 0....................(p) LiamTreadwell
(Jim Wilson) *prom tl wknd qckly 1/2-way: sn bdly t.o* **40/1**

3m 39.1s (-11.30) **Going Correction** -0.775s/f (Firm)
WFA 4 from 5yo+ 2lb **8** Ran SP% **119.2**
Speed ratings: **97,94,92,87,73 72,68,37**
CSF £32.11 TOTE £4.20: £1.20, £3.30, £1.10; EX 38.60.
Owner Harry Redknapp **Bred** Harry Redknapp **Trained** Upper Lambourn, Berks
FOCUS
A modest bumper for mares.
T/Jkpt: Not won. T/Plt: £93.10 to a £1 stake. Pool: £85,527.98 - 670.41 winning tickets T/Qpdt: £29.00 to a £1 stake. Pool: £6,385.04 - 162.40 winning tickets **Iain Mackenzie**

1058 - 1064a (Foreign Racing) - See Raceform Interactive

1030 CARTMEL (L-H)
Monday, July 20

OFFICIAL GOING: Good to soft (good in places) changing to good to soft (soft in places) after race 5 (4:25)
Wind: moderate 1/2 behind Weather: heavy shower race 1 & 5

1065 BETFAIR PRICE RUSH MAIDEN HURDLE (8 hdls) — 2m 1f 46y
2:10 (2:10) (Class 5) 4-Y-O+ **£2,599** (£763; £381; £190)

Form RPR

1 **Altruism (IRE)**[436] 5-11-0 0.................... BrianHughes 113+
(James Moffatt) *hld up in rr: t.k.h: hdwy 5th: trcking ldrs next: led between last 2: stmbld on landing on last: drvn out* **8/1**[3]

2-U5 **2** *3¾* **Ronaldinho (IRE)**[24] 837 5-11-0 115....................(t) HenryBrooke 107
(Dianne Sayer) *chsd ldrs: drvn 3 out: 2nd last: kpt on same pce* **11/4**[2]

2-4 **3** *4½* **Createur (IRE)**[50] 566 4-10-12 0....................(t) RichardJohnson 101
(Tim Vaughan) *hld up towards rr: hdwy 5th: chsng ldrs next: one pce appr last* **9/4**[1]

3005 **4** *16* **Tokyo Brown (USA)**[2] 1030 6-10-9 92....................(p) DiarmuidO'Regan(5) 89
(James Moffatt) *led: hdd between last 2: sn wknd* **11/1**

40- **5** *8* **Louloumills**[206] 3263 5-10-0 0.................... ThomasDowson(7) 77
(Maurice Barnes) *nt fluent in rr: lost pl 3 out: bhd next* **22/1**

00P- **6** *13* **Hope For Glory**[204] 3339 6-10-11 74....................(t) JonathanEngland(3) 70
(Maurice Barnes) *led: hdd between last 2: sn lost pl and bhd* **33/1**

F-00 **7** *12* **Cloggy Powell (IRE)**[24] 838 8-10-9 69.................... CallumBewley(5) 59
(Kevin Hunter) *chsd ldrs: drvn 3 out: lost pl next: sn bhd* **100/1**

P **L'Orfeo**[306] 5-11-0 0.................... AidanColeman
(John Ferguson) *mid-div: chsd ldrs 3 out: lost pl next: sn bhd: t.o whn p.u bef last* **9/4**[1]

4m 17.6s (4.40) **Going Correction** +0.45s/f (Soft)
WFA 4 from 5yo+ 15lb **8** Ran SP% **115.6**
Speed ratings (Par 103): **107,105,103,95,91 85,80,**
CSF £30.97 TOTE £8.20: £2.50, £1.10, £1.20; EX 29.20 Trifecta £120.30.
Owner V R Vyner-Brooks, K Bowron **Bred** Kevin & Meta Cullen **Trained** Cartmel, Cumbria
FOCUS
Rail realignment increased races 1, 6 & 7 by 26yds, races 2 & 4 by 45yds and races 3 & 5 by 54yds. The opening contest was an ordinary maiden hurdle. They went a respectable gallop on easing ground officially described as good to soft, good in places on a murky day. The winner has the potential to rate higher.

1066 UNSWORTH'S YARD MARES' H'CAP HURDLE (11 hdls) — 2m 6f 31y
2:45 (2:45) (Class 5) (0-100,98) 4-Y-O+ **£2,599** (£763; £381; £190)

Form RPR

-562 **1** **Slipper Satin (IRE)**[7] 845 5-11-12 **95**....................(t) HenryBrooke 106+
(Simon West) *best away: mde all: 10 l ahd last: drvn and styd on tl eased clsng stages* **2/1**[1]

203- **2** *8* **Pixie Cut (IRE)**[9] 5470 5-11-8 **94**....................(p) CraigNichol(3) 97
(Alistair Whillans) *mid-div: hdwy 3 out: kpt on to take modest 2nd fnl 200yds* **15/2**

3 *7* **Urban Dusk (IRE)**[8] 982 6-11-10 **98** 7ex.................... MrNMcParlan(5) 99
(Mark Michael McNiff, Ire) *trckd ldng pair: 2nd sn after 2 out: one pce* **11/4**[2]

3-16 **4** *17* **Carrigeen Lantana (IRE)**[39] 694 6-11-9 **92**.................... WayneHutchinson 76
(Donald McCain) *trckd wnr: reminders bef 3 out: 2nd whn hit 2 out: wknd between last 2* **8/1**

4640 **5** *10* **Cherry Princess**[22] 845 5-11-6 **89**.................... SeanQuinlan 61
(Barbara Butterworth) *chsd ldrs: drvn 8th: wknd next* **50/1**

065- **6** *2½* **Honeychile Ryder**[130] 4722 4-11-2 **88**.................... BrianHughes 55
(Dianne Sayer) *t.k.h: trckd ldrs: lost pl 8th: sn bhd* **50/1**

P-03 **7** *6* **Stand Clear**[8] 966 10-9-10 **70**....................(t) HarryBannister(5) 35
(Chris Grant) *in rr: bhd fr 3 out* **7/2**[3]

/U50 **8** *6* **Erica Starprincess**[24] 837 5-11-0 **83**.................... RichieMcLernon 42
(George Moore) *in rr: sme hdwy 8th: sn lost pl and bhd* **16/1**

000- **P** **Spring Back**[206] 3257 7-10-3 **75**.................... TonyKelly(3)
(Edwin Tuer) *in rr: reminders 6th: bhd 8th: t.o whn p.u bef 2 out* **28/1**

5m 39.7s (10.40) **Going Correction** +0.45s/f (Soft)
WFA 4 from 5yo+ 16lb **9** Ran SP% **118.4**
Speed ratings (Par 103): **99,96,93,87,83 82,80,78,**
CSF £17.92 CT £41.79 TOTE £2.50: £1.10, £2.70, £1.40; EX 16.90 Trifecta £54.40.
Owner Mrs J M L Milligan **Bred** J Murphy **Trained** Middleham Moor, N Yorks
FOCUS
A modest mares' staying handicap hurdle, but a hurdle personal best from the winner who has the potential to rate higher. They went an even gallop and the light rain continued.

1067 PRIORY HOTEL H'CAP HURDLE (12 hdls) — 3m 1f 83y
3:20 (3:20) (Class 4) (0-110,110) 4-Y-O+ **£3,249** (£954; £477; £238)

Form RPR

44U3 **1** **Rev Up Ruby**[8] 958 7-11-7 **110**.................... JonathonBewley(5) 117+
(George Bewley) *chsd ldrs: 2nd 7th: led appr 2 out: drvn out* **13/2**

50-0 **2** *5* **Maggie Blue (IRE)**[22] 845 7-10-6 **95**.................... CallumBewley(5) 94
(Harriet Graham) *chsd ldr tl 7th: 2nd between last 2: kpt on same pce* **12/1**

6002 **3** *1¾* **Johnny Go**[8] 962 5-10-1 **92**.................... RyanDay(7) 89
(Lisa Harrison) *in rr: hdwy 9th: 3rd last: kpt on same pce* **3/1**[2]

0-30 **4** *4½* **Maybe I Wont**[24] 839 10-11-7 **105**....................(v) BrianHughes 99
(James Moffatt) *in rr: drvn and sme hdwy 9th: modest 4th 1f out* **8/1**

2PP0 **5** *6* **Discoverie**[22] 845 7-10-0 **84** oh1.................... SeanQuinlan 75
(Dianne Sayer) *led tl bef 2 out: sn wknd* **33/1**

P-55 **6** *17* **Minella Bliss (IRE)**[33] 757 10-10-4 **95**....................(b) CharlieHammond(7) 71
(James Evans) *hld up in rr: t.k.h: hdwy 8th: hung rt wknd after next* **5/1**[3]

7 *10* **Goodoldhonkytonk (IRE)**[402] 690 7-11-12 **110**.................... LiamTreadwell 73
(James Evans) *chsd ldrs: lost pl 5th: sn bhd* **33/1**

23 **P** **Lowanbehold (IRE)**[19] 866 8-11-2 **107**.................... JamieHamilton(7)
(Sandy Forster) *in rr: hdwy to chse ldrs 4th: wknd 3 out: t.o whn p.u bef last* **11/1**

0-12 **P** **Craigdancer (IRE)**[24] 838 6-10-4 **88**.................... DougieCostello
(Joanne Foster) *chsd ldrs: lost pl 3rd: sn bhd: t.o whn p.u bef 2 out* **11/4**[1]

6m 34.4s (8.30) **Going Correction** +0.45s/f (Soft) **9** Ran SP% **114.7**
Speed ratings (Par 105): **104,102,101,100,98 93,89,,**
CSF £77.71 CT £278.82 TOTE £7.70: £2.10, £4.20, £1.40; EX 98.40 Trifecta £516.20.
Owner A Kerr, L Kerr, K Twentyman & Bewley **Bred** Mrs J A Niven **Trained** Bonchester Bridge, Borders
FOCUS
An ordinary staying handicap hurdle and a surprise hurdling personal best from the winner. They went an even gallop.

1068 MSP TECHNOLOGIES BEGINNERS' CHASE (14 fncs) — 2m 5f 34y
3:55 (3:56) (Class 4) 4-Y-O+ **£3,898** (£1,144; £572; £286)

Form RPR

0-F2 **1** **Mr Burgees (IRE)**[39] 697 6-11-9 120.................... WayneHutchinson 110+
(Donald McCain) *chsd ldrs: upsides last: sn led: drvn out* **3/1**[3]

22-4 **2** *3½* **Clues And Arrows (IRE)**[37] 729 7-11-9.................... BrianHughes 106
(John Wade) *chsd ldrs: 2nd over 2f out: kpt on same pce* **5/1**

3303 **3** *16* **Volcanic Jack (IRE)**[15] 913 7-11-4 97.................... JoeCornwall(5) 93
(Michael Chapman) *led: drvn 10th: hdd sn after last: sn wknd* **20/1**

42-2 **4** *2¾* **Ballyvoque (IRE)**[29] 802 9-11-9.................... JanFaltejsek 91+
(George Charlton) *chsd ldr: blnd and lost pl 10th: bhd whn mstke last* **5/2**[2]

PP-0 **5** *2¼* **Bayfirth (IRE)**[24] 842 12-11-2 66.................... MrWHRReed(7) 84
(Andrew Hamilton) *in rr: bhd fr 10th* **150/1**

PP- **P** **Tom's Article (IRE)**[45] 630 6-11-9 122.................... RichardJohnson
(Gordon Elliott, Ire) *j. bdly in rr: j. bdly lft 7th: sn t.o whn p.u after next* **15/8**[1]

5m 35.5s (10.10) **Going Correction** +0.50s/f (Soft) **6** Ran SP% **110.4**
Speed ratings (Par 105): **100,98,92,91,90**
CSF £17.36 TOTE £3.10: £1.40, £3.10; EX 14.80 Trifecta £69.20.
Owner Paul & Clare Rooney **Bred** Walter Crean **Trained** Cholmondeley, Cheshire
FOCUS
A fair beginners' chase. They went a proper gallop.

1069 WEATHERBYS HAMILTON H'CAP CHASE (18 fncs) — 3m 1f 107y
4:25 (4:25) (Class 5) (0-100,100) 4-Y-O+ **£3,249** (£954; £477; £238)

Form RPR

U-24 **1** **Mia's Anthem (IRE)**[29] 803 7-10-13 **94**.................... StevenFox(7) 116+
(Noel C Kelly, Ire) *chsd ldrs: led 14th: clr 2 out: eased clsng stages* **9/2**[2]

0P66 **2** *16* **Generous Chief (IRE)**[24] 842 7-11-1 **94**....................(b) DiarmuidO'Regan(5) 101
(Chris Grant) *mid-div: hdwy to chse ldrs 14th: 2nd 3 out: kpt on same pce* **10/1**

-131 **3** *16* **Over And Above (IRE)**[24] 842 9-11-2 **93**....................(tp) GrahamWatters(3) 85
(Henry Hogarth) *led 2nd to 6th: outpcd 3 out: poor 3rd over 1f out* **5/1**[3]

5P-6 **4** *2¾* **Peak Seasons (IRE)**[24] 841 12-9-9 **74** oh12.................... JoeCornwall(5) 63
(Michael Chapman) *in rr: hdwy 12th: sn chsng ldrs: 2nd 3 out: wknd fnl 3f* **66/1**

P6-6 **5** *4½* **Acrai Rua (IRE)**[76] 133 12-11-1 **89**....................(tp) BrianHughes 74
(Tim Fitzgerald) *led to 12nd: w ldrs: wknd 3 out* **9/1**

U3-4 **6** *3¾* **Urban Gale (IRE)**[76] 136 10-11-1 **89**....................(p) DougieCostello 71
(Joanne Foster) *sn drvn along in rr: nvr on terms* **4/1**[1]

U-62 **7** *32* **Solway Bay**[24] 842 13-10-10 **91**....................(tp) RyanDay(7) 44
(Lisa Harrison) *sn bhd* **5/1**[3]

4-F5 **8** *36* **Oh Right (IRE)**[24] 842 11-11-8 **96**....................(p) HenryBrooke 17
(Dianne Sayer) *led to 2nd: led 6th to 14th: wknd next: eased clsng stages: t.o* **14/1**

-6UP **9** *1¼* **Gale Force Oscar (IRE)**[39] 698 10-11-4 **92**....................(t) GerardTumelty 11
(Sean Curran) *in rr: bhd fr 12th: easede clsng stages: t.o* **12/1**

P- **P** **Ard Agus Fada (IRE)**[165] 4051 12-10-6 **80**.......................... SeanQuinlan
(Joanne Foster) *chsd ldrs: lost pl 6th: sn bhd: t.o whn p.u after 12th* **50/1**
-U30 **P** **Prince Blackthorn (IRE)**[29] 803 9-10-0 **76** ow1............ CraigNichol(3)
(Barry Murtagh) *in rr: bhd fr 8th: t.o whn p.u after 14th* **25/1**
-5PF **P** **Redpender (IRE)**[22] 847 9-11-9 **100**..................................(t) TonyKelly(3)
(James Moffatt) *in rr: bhd fr 8th: t.o 12th: p.u bef 3 out* **16/1**

6m 45.6s (10.70) **Going Correction** +0.50s/f (Soft) **12** Ran SP% **118.1**
Speed ratings (Par 103): **102,96,91,90,89 88,78,66,66,**
CSF £48.12 CT £236.03 TOTE £6.60: £2.10, £2.70, £2.30; EX 54.70 Trifecta £248.80.
Owner Don't Ask Now Syndicate **Bred** Cornelius Walsh **Trained** Draperstown, Co. Derry

FOCUS
A modest staying handicap chase and a big step up from the easy winner. They went a proper gallop and the ground was officially changed to good to soft, soft in places after this race.

1070 BETFAIR CASH OUT H'CAP CHASE (12 fncs) 2m 1f 61y
4:55 (4:57) (Class 3) (0-135,132) 4-Y-0 **£6,279** (£1,871; £947; £485; £254)

Form RPR
2/4P **1** **Cruchain (IRE)**[34] 750 12-10-0 **109**...................................(p) SeanBowen(3) 121+
(Dai Burchell) *chsd ldrs: styd on to ld over 1f out: drvn out* **3/1**[1]
33-6 **2** *7* **Swaledale Lad (IRE)**[38] 708 8-11-9 **132**.................. HarryChalloner(3) 137
(Richard Ford) *w ldr: led briefly 6th led 9th: hdd and kpt on same pce over 1f out* **10/3**[2]
62-3 **3** *nk* **Vinnie The Fish (IRE)**[44] 643 7-10-4 **110**..........................(p) RobertDunne 114
(Dai Burchell) *chsd ldrs: 2nd last: kpt on same pce* **6/1**
34-1 **4** *13* **Toledo Gold (IRE)**[22] 848 9-11-1 **124**..................(t) JonathanEngland(3) 118
(Maurice Barnes) *led to 9th: wknd 3f out: sn bhd* **13/2**
000- **5** *10* **Peckhamecho (IRE)**[130] 4717 9-11-8 **128**............................ PaulMoloney 114
(Sophie Leech) *in rr: hdwy 6th: sn chsng ldrs: wknd 3 out* **4/1**[3]
-454 **R** **Sergeant Pink (IRE)**[6] 848 9-10-5 **111**............................(p) BrianHughes
(Dianne Sayer) *j. slowly in rr: bhd 4th: sme hdwy 7th: sn lost pl and bhd: t.o whn heavily eased and p.u after 2 out* **5/1**

4m 27.0s (8.10) **Going Correction** +0.725s/f (Soft) **6** Ran SP% **112.4**
Speed ratings (Par 107): **109,105,105,99,94**
CSF £13.67 CT £53.97 TOTE £3.40: £1.60, £1.90; EX 16.10 Trifecta £93.80.
Owner Mr & Mrs A J Mutch **Bred** Dunmanway Breeding Club **Trained** Briery Hill, Blaenau Gwent
■ Fantasy King was withdrawn. Prices at time of withdrawal 6-1. Rule 4 applies to all bets - deduction 10p in the pound.

FOCUS
The feature contest was a fairly decent handicap chase. The winner was well in and was back to his best 2014 form. They went a proper gallop.

1071 GLOBAL RADIO H'CAP HURDLE (8 hdls) 2m 1f 46y
5:25 (5:25) (Class 5) (0-100,100) 3-Y-0+ **£2,599** (£763; £381; £190)

Form RPR
-553 **1** **Ardesia (IRE)**[15] 918 11-9-11 **74** oh5..................(p) JonathanEngland(3) 78
(Tina Jackson) *mde all: drvn 5th: hld on clsng stages* **11/1**
P-44 **2** *½* **Endeavor**[22] 851 10-11-6 **94**.. BrianHughes 97
(Dianne Sayer) *mid-div: chsd ldrs 3 out: 2nd between last 2: no ex clsng stages* **15/2**
1505 **3** *1 ¼* **Morning With Ivan (IRE)**[2] 1036 5-11-10 **98**................... HenryBrooke 101
(Martin Todhunter) *hld up in rr: hdwy to chse ldrs 5th: styng on same pce whn n.m.r last 100yds* **10/1**
-65P **4** *21* **Stanley Bridge**[22] 845 8-9-13 **78**........................... DiarmuidO'Regan(5) 62
(Barry Murtagh) *in rr: hdwy to chse ldrs 5th: 2nd whn hit 2 out: wknd between last 2* **7/1**[3]
020- **5** *4* **Kathlatino**[7] 3801 8-9-8 **75**...............................(v) JamieBargary(7) 55
(Micky Hammond) *in rr: reminders 4th: sme hdwy after 5th: sn wknd* **11/2**[2]
4062 **6** *1 ¾* **Dynamic Drive (IRE)**[19] 872 8-11-0 **95**............................(t) RyanDay(7) 75
(Maurice Barnes) *mid-div: hdwy to chse ldrs 4thy: wknd appr 2 out* **5/2**[1]
060 **7** *11* **Raifteiri (IRE)**[19] 872 8-9-10 **74** oh1 ow1..................(p) CallumBewley(5) 43
(William Young Jnr) *w ldrs: reminders and lost pl 3rd: bhd 5th* **16/1**
6/00 **8** *23* **Louis Ludwig (IRE)**[15] 918 10-10-4 **78**......................... RichardJohnson 25
(Tim Vaughan) *in rr: bhd fr 5th* **12/1**
6-00 **9** *¾* **Snowed In (IRE)**[54] 507 6-11-10 **98**.............................(p) SeanQuinlan 45
(Barbara Butterworth) *w wnr: lost pl after 5th: sn bhd* **17/2**
25P- **10** *13* **Mulligan's Man (IRE)**[263] 2147 8-11-12 **100**...................... DavidEngland 35
(Clare Ellam) *chsd ldrs: wknd 3 out: sn bhd* **8/1**

4m 25.1s (11.90) **Going Correction** +0.675s/f (Soft) **10** Ran SP% **120.9**
Speed ratings (Par 103): **99,98,98,88,86 85,80,69,69,63**
CSF £93.93 CT £867.45 TOTE £9.80: £2.80, £2.50, £3.50; EX 63.20 Trifecta £391.70.
Owner A Jackson **Bred** Patrick J Farrington **Trained** Liverton, Cleveland
■ Stewards' Enquiry : Jonathan England two-day ban: used whip above permitted level (Aug 12-13)
Brian Hughes six-day ban: improper riding (Aug 12-13,15-16,19-20)

FOCUS
The concluding contest was another modest handicap hurdle. They went an honest gallop.
T/Plt: £30.90 to a £1 stake. Pool: £63,445.36 - 1,496.24 winning tickets T/Qpdt: £16.00 to a £1 stake. Pool: £5,232.94 - 241.98 winning tickets **Walter Glynn**

1072 - 1078a (Foreign Racing) - See Raceform Interactive

1006 WORCESTER (L-H)
Thursday, July 23

OFFICIAL GOING: Good to firm (good in places; watered; 7.0)
Wind: Light behind Weather: Cloudy

1079 WALKING THE COURSES H'CAP CHASE (16 fncs) 2m 7f
2:10 (2:10) (Class 4) (0-105,104) 4-Y-0+ **£3,768** (£1,106; £553; £276)

Form RPR
2-41 **1** **Clubs Are Trumps (IRE)**[35] 771 6-11-11 **103**.................(p) WillKennedy 116
(Jonjo O'Neill) *mid-div: hdwy 5th: chsd ldr 4 out: styd on u.p to ld towards fin* **6/1**[3]
-523 **2** *¾* **Kilcascan**[17] 926 11-10-5 **86**...(p) BenPoste(3) 98
(Rosemary Gasson) *chsd ldrs: led 7th: rdn flat: hdd towards fin* **8/1**
P40 **3** *4 ½* **Maller Tree**[27] 839 8-11-8 **100**.........................(v) SamTwiston-Davies 108
(David Dennis) *hld up: drvn along 10th: hdwy appr 4 out: blnd last: styd on same pce* **14/1**
1312 **4** *7* **Patricktom Boru (IRE)**[17] 926 8-11-7 **99**............................ AdamWedge 103
(Evan Williams) *prom: hmpd bnd after 8th: hit 11th: rdn after next: wknd appr last* **11/4**[1]
1-24 **5** *12* **Sandynow (IRE)**[60] 445 10-11-9 **104**..............................(vt) SeanBowen(3) 98
(Peter Bowen) *mid-div: hdwy 4th: lost pl whn mstke 9th: hdwy appr 4 out: wknd 2 out* **9/1**
5006 **6** *27* **Toast And Jam (IRE)**[16] 934 6-10-0 **78** oh2...............(t) BrendanPowell 45
(Claire Dyson) *mde most to 7th: chsd ldrs: rdn after 12th: wkng whn j.rt 4 out* **16/1**
6-2P **7** *11* **Fast Exit (IRE)**[42] 698 8-11-2 **94**...(b) NoelFehily 51
(Neil Mulholland) *hld up: hdwy 10th: chsd ldr after 12th tl next: wknd 3 out: sn hung rt* **14/1**
-02F **P** **Brother Scott**[44] 676 8-11-7 **99**.. SeanQuinlan
(Sue Smith) *hld up: mstke 6th: hdwy 10th: wknd 12th: bhd whn p.u bef last* **12/1**
-00P **P** **Vinceson (IRE)**[16] 934 7-10-0 **78** oh1......................................(p) JamesBest
(Jess Westwood) *chsd ldrs tl rdn and wknd appr 4 out: bhd whn p.u bef last* **66/1**
5P-2 **P** **Killimordaly (IRE)**[49] 610 6-11-8 **103**........................(tp) JamesBanks(3)
(Andy Turnell) *chsd ldrs: nt fluent 5th: mstke 8th: hmpd bnd bef next: sn wknd: bhd whn p.u bef 4 out* **4/1**[2]

5m 53.9s (4.00) **Going Correction** +0.075s/f (Yiel) **10** Ran SP% **110.5**
Speed ratings (Par 105): **96,95,94,91,87 78,74,,,**
CSF £49.90 CT £606.44 TOTE £5.90: £1.80, £1.70, £4.20; EX 53.40 Trifecta £711.30.
Owner John P McManus **Bred** S & S Hubbard Rodwell **Trained** Cheltenham, Gloucs

FOCUS
All starts have been moved at this track following remeasuring, so there will be no speed figures here until there is sufficient data to calculate updated median times. Both bends railed out from innermost line and races 3 & 5 increased by 72yds and the rest by 114yds. Sam Twiston-Davies said of the ground: "There's more good out there than good to firm." The day's feature, this was a competitive handicap chase. The winner is rated similar to his recent win with the second to his mark.

1080 CELEBRATING 200 WINNERS FOR THE HITCHINGS FAMILY H'CAP CHASE (13 fncs) 2m 4f
2:40 (2:41) (Class 5) (0-100,99) 4-Y-0+ **£2,469** (£725; £362; £181)

Form RPR
4-02 **1** **Amuse Me**[22] 874 9-11-12 **99**......................................(tp) RichardJohnson 112+
(Jonjo O'Neill) *hld up: hdwy 8th: led 2 out: styd on wl* **11/2**[3]
2-F6 **2** *3 ¼* **Who Am I**[49] 614 9-11-9 **96**...(p) RobertDunne 106
(Debra Hamer) *a.p: led 8th: hdd 2 out: styd on same pce flat* **12/1**
-U13 **3** *6* **Adios Alonso (IRE)**[16] 934 9-11-3 **93**................................. BenPoste(3) 99
(Rosemary Gasson) *chsd ldrs: mstke and rdr lost iron 7th: rdn appr last: no ex flat* **7/2**[1]
2634 **4** *1 ¼* **Lost In Newyork (IRE)**[16] 934 8-10-5 **78**.......................(p) AdamWedge 81
(Nick Kent) *hld up: hdwy appr 4 out: rdn after 2 out: styd on same pce* **7/1**
5-4P **5** *2 ¼* **Stafford Charlie**[60] 446 9-10-0 **73** oh6.............................(p) PeterCarberry 74
(John O'Shea) *hld up: hdwy 9th: rdn appr 2 out: wknd last* **20/1**
-0U2 **6** *2* **Paddy Mulligan (IRE)**[18] 914 6-11-11 **98**......................(p) AidanColeman 97
(John Ferguson) *hld up: mstke 1st: hdwy 6th: rdn and wknd appr last* **5/1**[2]
53P- **7** *4* **Alba King (IRE)**[369] 1002 9-10-10 **83**.................................. SeanQuinlan 80
(Sue Smith) *led to 8th: rdn and wknd appr last* **16/1**
-PF6 **8** *¾* **My Nosy Rosy**[22] 874 7-11-3 **90**..(tp) DarylJacob 85
(Ben Case) *hld up: plld hrd: hdwy 9th: rdn and wknd after 2 out* **25/1**
/00P **9** *25* **Silver Story**[17] 926 12-11-5 **92**..(t) MichaelByrne 64
(Tim Vaughan) *hld up: pushed along after 5th: rdn and wknd after 9th* **20/1**
06P- **10** *46* **A Keen Sense (GER)**[143] 4538 6-10-1 **74**........................ GavinSheehan 5
(David Dennis) *prom: lost pl 2nd: bhd fr 8th* **11/2**[3]
P0-0 **P** **Just Talking (IRE)**[32] 803 13-9-7 **73**..........................(bt) MissRMcDonald(7)
(Sara Ender) *chsd ldr: mstke 2nd: lost 2nd 4th: wknd after 6th: bhd whn p.u bef 9th* **66/1**
-030 **P** **Forresters Folly**[22] 874 9-11-7 **94**..................................(p) BrendanPowell
(Claire Dyson) *hld up: rdn after 9th: wknd bef next: bhd whn p.u bef 2 out* **25/1**

5m 4.6s **Going Correction** +0.075s/f (Yiel) **12** Ran SP% **114.4**
Speed ratings (Par 103): **103,101,99,98,97 97,95,95,85,66 ,**
CSF £59.48 CT £262.52 TOTE £5.30: £2.30, £2.00, £2.30; EX 66.50 Trifecta £244.40.
Owner John P McManus **Bred** Whatton Manor Stud **Trained** Cheltenham, Gloucs

FOCUS
A modest handicap chase, but competitive enough. The winner was rated 118 at his peak so could still be competitive when reassessed.

1081 LISTERS VOLKSWAGEN WORCESTER, UNBELIEVABLE VALUE NOVICES' HURDLE (8 hdls) 2m
3:15 (3:16) (Class 4) 4-Y-0+ **£3,249** (£954; £477; £238)

Form RPR
21 **1** **Ennistown**[17] 932 5-11-5 130.. AidanColeman 127+
(John Ferguson) *hld up: racd keenly: hdwy appr 3 out: led after next: comf* **2/7**[1]
66 **2** *4* **Wintour Leap**[8] 1009 4-10-3 0.. RobertDunne 101
(Robert Stephens) *a.p: ev ch after 2 out: styd on same pce flat* **12/1**
60- **3** *2 ½* **Trader Jack**[25] 5250 6-10-12 0...................................... StephenCraine 106
(David Flood) *hld up: racd keenly: hdwy 2 out: styd on same pce last* **8/1**[3]
1 **4** *13* **Black Iceman**[36] 702 7-11-5 0.. JackQuinlan 100
(Lydia Pearce) *chsd ldrs: ev ch fr 3 out tl rdn after next: wknd bef last* **5/1**[2]
336- **5** *2 ½* **The Western Force (IRE)**[213] 3229 5-10-12 0................. DavidEngland 91
(Dan Skelton) *disp ld at stdy pce tl wnt on 4th: hdd next: rdn and wknd appr last* **16/1**
0-55 **6** *shd* **Bumble Bay**[11] 971 5-10-12 0.. TomO'Brien 90
(Robert Stephens) *hld up: hdwy 4th: led next: rdn and hdd after 2 out: wknd bef last* **12/1**
6 **7** *5* **Beedee**[18] 912 5-10-12 0... MichaelByrne 85
(Tim Vaughan) *nt fluent 1st: disp ld at stdy pce to 4th: lost pl after next: wknd bef 3 out* **66/1**
0 **8** *1* **Prince Of Silver**[17] 932 9-10-9 0..................................(t) JamesBanks(3) 84
(Andy Turnell) *prom tl rdn and wknd appr 2 out* **66/1**

3m 54.8s (4.20) **Going Correction** +0.075s/f (Yiel)
WFA 4 from 5yo+ 15lb **8** Ran SP% **129.8**
Speed ratings (Par 105): **92,90,88,82,81 80,78,77**
CSF £7.69 TOTE £1.30: £1.02, £2.90, £2.10; EX 7.60 Trifecta £48.70.
Owner Bloomfields **Bred** Darley **Trained** Cowlinge, Suffolk

FOCUS
They didn't go much of a gallop in this ordinary novice hurdle. The easy winner was building on his recent win.

1082 FOR GREAT SERVICE VISIT VOLKSWAGEN WORCESTER NOVICES' HURDLE (10 hdls) 2m 4f
3:50 (3:50) (Class 4) 4-Y-0+ £3,249 (£954; £477; £238)

Form RPR
-213 1 **Father Edward (IRE)**[11] 957 6-11-5 130 ... (tp) AidanColeman 123+
(John Ferguson) *chsd ldrs: led after 2 out: sn rdn clr: eased nr fin* 13/8[1]
5-03 2 7 **It Is I (IRE)**[29] 829 5-10-12 0 ... (v[1]) DenisO'Regan 107
(Don Cantillon) *chsd ldrs: rdn appr 2 out: styd on same pce: wnt 2nd flat* 25/1
-212 3 3 **Romulus Du Donjon (IRE)**[59] 467 4-11-2 119 ... DarylJacob 108
(Oliver Sherwood) *chsd ldr tl after 4th: wnt 2nd again 7th: rdn after 2 out: j.lft last: wknd flat* 10/3[3]
1 4 6 **Theatre Flame (IRE)**[25] 853 5-11-5 124 ... TomScudamore 107
(David Bridgwater) *led: mstke 2 out: sn rdn and hdd: wknd bef last* 7/4[2]
3P3- 5 8 **Moyode Wood**[152] 4364 10-10-5 0 ... CraigGallagher[(7)] 91
(Brian Ellison) *hld up in tch: rdn and wknd appr 3 out* 16/1
0 6 7 **Barra Rotha (IRE)**[25] 852 8-10-7 0 ... KieronEdgar[(5)] 84
(Laura Hurley) *hld up: sme hdwy appr 3 out: wknd bef next* 150/1
5/0 7 19 **Sovinnie (IRE)**[35] 773 6-10-7 0 ... ConorRing[(5)] 67
(Jane Mathias) *hld up: rdn and wknd after 7th* 100/1
R5/P 8 1 1/4 **Spiritofchartwell**[70] 293 7-10-12 0 ... TomCannon 66
(Raymond York) *prom: chsd ldr after 4th tl appr 7th: sn rdn and wknd* 66/1
FP 9 46 **Fort Gabriel (FR)**[66] 378 4-10-9 0 ... GerardTumelty 22
(Fiona Kehoe) *hld up: wknd 6th* 150/1
10 hd **Generous Pet (IRE)**[68] 6-10-12 0 ...[1] JamieMoore 25
(Kevin Bishop) *hld up: rdn and wknd after 7th* 33/1
00-U P **Pennant Lady**[11] 971 5-10-5 0 ... (p) TrevorWhelan
(Debra Hamer) *in rr: bhd fr 4th: p.u bef 3 out* 200/1
P **Gunner Gotya** 6-10-2 0 ... HarrisonBeswick[(10)]
(Ben Pauling) *in rr: bhd fr 4th: p.u bef 3 out* 66/1

4m 56.1s (2.60) **Going Correction** +0.075s/f (Yiel)
WFA 4 from 5yo+ 16lb 12 Ran SP% 116.0
Speed ratings (Par 105): **97,94,93,90,87 84,77,76,58,58**
CSF £40.00 TOTE £2.40: £1.10, £7.80, £1.40; EX 46.80 Trifecta £143.50.
Owner Bloomfields **Bred** Hugh Fitzpatrick **Trained** Cowlinge, Suffolk

FOCUS
Not much depth to this novice hurdle, which was run at a decent gallop. The cosy winner is rated to his mark.

1083 NATIONAL TYRES & AUTOCARE H'CAP HURDLE (8 hdls) 2m
4:25 (4:27) (Class 4) (0-120,117) 3-Y-0+ £3,249 (£954; £477; £238)

Form RPR
4343 1 **Ladies Dancing**[4] 1048 9-10-9 100 ... (b) JamesDavies 107
(Chris Down) *chsd ldr to 3rd: remained handy: led last: drvn out* 7/2[3]
01-5 2 1 **Yes Daddy (IRE)**[20] 186 7-11-9 114 ... TomO'Brien 119
(Robert Stephens) *trckd ldrs: wnt 2nd 3rd: led 3 out: rdn and hdd last: styd on* 10/3[2]
-522 3 3/4 **Royal Skies (IRE)**[17] 931 5-11-12 117 ... (vt) AidanColeman 120
(John Ferguson) *trckd ldrs: rdn and ev ch last: no ex towards fin* 9/4[1]
5-12 4 12 **Prince Khurram**[23] 862 5-11-8 113 ... (t) NoelFehily 107
(Donald McCain) *led at stdy pce tl qckd 4th: hdd 3 out: rdn appr last: wknd flat* 6/1
0560 5 21 **Hi Tide (IRE)**[17] 931 11-11-2 107 ... BrendanPowell 80
(J R Jenkins) *hld up: nt fluent 4th: rdn and wknd 3 out* 25/1
-642 6 2 3/4 **Newton Geronimo**[17] 932 6-11-9 114 ... RichardJohnson 85
(Ben Pauling) *reluctant to s and lost many l: clsd up to the field 3rd: wknd wl bef 3 out* 11/2

3m 49.4s (-1.20) **Going Correction** +0.075s/f (Yiel) 6 Ran SP% 109.6
Speed ratings (Par 105): **106,105,105,99,88 87**
CSF £14.90 TOTE £6.10: £1.80, £1.80; EX 17.50 Trifecta £56.50.
Owner Upton Racing **Bred** P And Mrs Venner And Trickledown Stud **Trained** Mutterton, Devon

FOCUS
This fair handicap hurdle didn't appear to be strongly run, but the pace did pick up and the time was 5.4sec quicker than the earlier novice hurdle. The winner had long been on a good mark.

1084 BETTINGGODS.COM FREE RACING TIPS H'CAP HURDLE (10 hdls) 2m 4f
4:55 (4:56) (Class 5) (0-100,99) 4-Y-0+ £2,274 (£667; £333; £166)

Form RPR
0/34 1 **Mighty Leader (IRE)**[17] 931 7-11-5 92 ... JamesDavies 101+
(Henry Oliver) *a.p: led 2 out: edgd lft flat: drvn out* 5/1[1]
-323 2 3/4 **Dropzone (USA)**[25] 859 6-10-7 80 ... TomO'Brien 88
(Brian Forsey) *hld up: hdwy bef 3 out: chsd wnr appr last: styd on u.p* 8/1[3]
10-0 3 8 **Perseid (IRE)**[16] 937 5-10-9 82 ... SeanQuinlan 83
(Sue Smith) *hld up: hdwy appr 3 out: sn rdn: styd on to go 3rd towards fin: nt rch ldrs* 8/1[3]
-650 4 3 1/4 **Icanmotor**[16] 935 8-10-0 73 oh4 ... (tp) BrendanPowell 72
(Claire Dyson) *hld up in tch: rdn after 2 out: hung lft and wknd flat* 25/1
042- 5 2 3/4 **Mrs Burbidge**[11] 4276 5-9-9 75 ... (tp) MrMartinMcIntyre[(7)] 72
(Neil Mulholland) *plld hrd: trckd ldr 2nd: led 7th: sn hdd: nt fluent 2 out: wknd last* 5/1[1]
6/0F 6 3/4 **Prairie Hawk (USA)**[11] 977 10-10-3 76 ... (t) MichealNolan 71
(Adrian Wintle) *hld up: hdwy appr 3 out: rdn and wknd bef last* 66/1
-5P4 7 4 1/2 **Dreamisi (IRE)**[16] 935 6-11-3 90 ... (b[1]) NicodeBoinville 81
(Ben Pauling) *prom: led after 7th: hdd 2 out: wkng whn hung lft flat* 9/1
F6-P 8 26 **Pattara**[23] 864 6-10-12 85 ... GerardTumelty 52
(Noel Williams) *hld up: hdwy appr 3 out: wknd bef next* 33/1
-160 9 26 **In The Crowd (IRE)**[23] 864 6-11-9 99 ... (p) JamesBanks[(3)] 43
(Roy Brotherton) *chsd ldrs: drvn along after 7th: sn wknd* 16/1
05-4 10 1 1/2 **Tiger Feat**[74] 224 5-11-0 87 ... GavinSheehan 30
(Ali Stronge) *hld up: pushed along after 5th: wknd next* 16/1
300- 11 nk **Wheelavit (IRE)**[105] 5243 12-10-0 78 oh8 ... (t) LeeEdwards 15
(Claire Dyson) *led to 7th: sn rdn and wknd* 100/1
-565 12 12 **Catcharose (IRE)**[20] 892 5-10-5 85 ... (tp) LewisGordon[(7)] 16
(Jennifer Mason) *hld up: rdn after 6th: sn wknd* 66/1
3502 B **Mix N Match**[11] 977 11-9-7 73 oh5 ... ThomasCheesman[(7)]
(Laura Young) *b.d 1st* 14/1
06/6 P **Chambray Dancer (IRE)**[84] 28 7-10-7 80 ... (t) SamTwiston-Davies
(Simon Hodgson) *hld up: bhd fr 6th: p.u bef next* 33/1
3/21 P **Wak A Turtle (IRE)**[22] 874 7-11-10 97 ... DarylJacob
(Richard Woollacott) *hld up: p.u after 5th* 6/1[2]
362- P **Stitched In Time (IRE)**[386] 832 8-11-3 95 ... NathanMoscrop[(5)]
(Sara Ender) *prom: rdn after 5th: wknd after next: bhd whn p.u bef 3 out* 20/1
06-0 F **Olymnia**[71] 281 4-10-10 86 ... (p) JamieMoore
(Gary Moore) *fell 1st* 14/1

4m 54.4s (0.90) **Going Correction** +0.075s/f (Yiel)
WFA 4 from 5yo+ 16lb 17 Ran SP% 123.4
Speed ratings (Par 103): **101,100,97,96,95 94,93,82,72,71 71,66, , ,**
CSF £42.60 CT £325.29 TOTE £6.30: £1.50, £2.60, £3.30, £7.30; EX 47.50 Trifecta £497.30.
Owner Oscar Singh & Miss Priya Purewal **Bred** John Hore **Trained** Abberley, Worcs

FOCUS
A large field for this very modest handicap, which was run 1.7sec quicker than the earlier novice hurdle. The winner was on a good mark and there is probably more to come.

1085 WORCESTER NEWS AMATEUR RIDERS' H'CAP HURDLE (DIV I) (12 hdls) 2m 7f
5:25 (5:26) (Class 5) (0-100,100) 4-Y-0+ £2,183 (£677; £338; £169)

Form RPR
P-P3 1 **Presence Felt (IRE)**[22] 878 7-11-0 95 ... (v) MrMWalton[(7)] 103
(Jonjo O'Neill) *chsd ldrs: led appr 9th: rdn out* 9/2[2]
-32F 2 1 **Midnight Sequel**[57] 513 6-11-4 95 ... (bt) MissBHampson[(3)] 102
(Neil Mulholland) *hld up: hdwy after 8th: chsd wnr and j.lft 2 out: mstke last: styd on* 8/1
00-1 3 27 **Annaroe (IRE)**[23] 864 6-10-2 81 ... MrTommieMO'Brien[(5)] 64
(Alexandra Dunn) *chsd ldrs: rdn appr 3 out: wknd next* 4/1[1]
46 4 1/2 **Trakeur (FR)**[44] 674 8-10-3 84 ... MrMSBastyan[(7)] 66
(Simon Hodgson) *hld up: racd keenly: hdwy 7th: chsd wnr 3 out tl hmpd next: sn wknd* 40/1
1202 5 4 **Lady Of Longstone (IRE)**[22] 878 5-11-7 100 ... (b) DavidNoonan[(5)] 79
(David Pipe) *disp ld tl after 7th: sn rdn: wknd appr 3 out* 5/1[3]
6PP- 6 6 **Tokyo Javilex (FR)**[114] 5081 8-10-11 92 ... (t) MrLDrowne[(7)] 65
(Nigel Hawke) *a bhd* 9/1
2-15 7 8 **Karl Marx (IRE)**[42] 704 5-11-0 95 ... (b) MrTGillard[(7)] 61
(Mark Gillard) *prom: pushed along and lost pl 5th: wknd bef 7th* 12/1
0F-0 8 20 **Say When**[35] 776 7-11-2 97 ... HarryTeal[(7)] 45
(Alan King) *hld up: hdwy 6th: ev ch appr 3 out: sn rdn and wknd* 33/1
43P/ P **Viel Gluck (IRE)**[439] 12-10-4 78 ... (t) CharlieDeutsch
(Lawney Hill) *hld up: a in rr: bhd fr 6th: p.u bef 3 out* 16/1
2-26 P **Descaro (USA)**[13] 776 9-11-4 99 ... MrDSymes-Meineck[(7)]
(John O'Shea) *hld up: hdwy 6th: rdn and lost pl bef next: wknd 8th: bhd whn p.u bef 3 out* 22/1
043- P **Newton Martini**[92] 5476 6-10-5 79 ... (p) MrTomDavid
(Ben Pauling) *disp ld tl wnt on after 7th: hdd bef 9th: sn rdn and wknd: bhd whn p.u bef last* 11/2

5m 46.2s (7.60) **Going Correction** +0.075s/f (Yiel) 11 Ran SP% 114.6
Speed ratings (Par 103): **89,88,79,79,77 75,72,65, ,**
CSF £38.57 CT £154.96 TOTE £5.70: £2.10, £2.10, £1.70; EX 49.50 Trifecta £144.60.
Owner Mrs Peter Bond **Bred** Pete Roche **Trained** Cheltenham, Gloucs
■ Michael Walton's first winner under rules.

FOCUS
Two came clear in this low-grade handicap for amateurs. It looked the stronger division on paper. The winner is a 115 hurdler/chaser at best.

1086 WORCESTER NEWS AMATEUR RIDERS' H'CAP HURDLE (DIV II) (12 hdls) 2m 7f
5:55 (5:57) (Class 5) (0-100,100) 4-Y-0+ £2,183 (£677; £338; £169)

Form RPR
4354 1 **Temple Lord (FR)**[11] 966 9-11-2 97 ... (vt) MrJJO'Neill[(7)] 104+
(Jonjo O'Neill) *a.p: stmbld 2nd: chsd ldr after 2 out: rdn flat: styd on to ld nr fin* 7/2[2]
2 nk **Ennisnag (IRE)**[186] 10-11-0 95 ... MrBParis-Crofts[(7)] 102+
(Paul Henderson) *hld up: racd keenly: hdwy appr 7th: led 3 out: rdn flat: hdd nr fin* 25/1
-2FU 3 4 1/2 **Iktiview**[11] 977 7-10-1 82 ... (bt) MrStanSheppard[(7)] 85
(Matt Sheppard) *hld up: hdwy 8th: rdn appr 2 out: styd on* 11/4[1]
0-00 4 1 1/2 **Nishay (IRE)**[30] 828 8-9-13 80 ... MissEmmaMoseley[(7)] 81
(David Rees) *hld up: hdwy after 6th: rdn appr last: no ex flat* 40/1
-2P4 5 11 **Owner Occupier**[32] 806 10-9-8 75 ... (p) MissSKelk[(7)] 66
(Chris Gordon) *hld up in tch: racd keenly: chsd ldr 8th: led after next: hdd 3 out: wknd bef last* 6/1[3]
0-06 6 14 **Legion D'Honneur (UAE)**[30] 824 10-11-0 95 ... (tp) MrSeanHoulihan[(7)] 73
(Chris Down) *hld up: hdwy appr 3 out: sn rdn: wkng whn hmpd 2 out* 8/1
P0-0 7 hd **Court Of Law (IRE)**[40] 726 7-11-5 100 ... CaiWilliams[(7)] 78
(Donald McCain) *prom tl rdn and wknd after 9th* 33/1
5050 8 32 **Southern Cross**[8] 1009 4-9-7 78 ... MrMEnnis[(7)] 23
(Dai Williams) *hld up: a in rr: wknd after 9th* 33/1
F5-P 9 31 **Hand On Bach (IRE)**[84] 31 7-11-0 93 ... (bt) MrBGibbs[(5)] 14
(Tim Vaughan) *chsd ldr 2nd tl led 4th: hdd appr 9th: sn rdn and wknd* 14/1
P04/ F **Overlay**[739] 969 11-10-4 78 ... CharlieDeutsch 77
(Lawney Hill) *chsd ldrs: rdn appr 3 out: 4 l 4th and looking hld whn fell 2 out* 20/1
0-06 P **Freddy Fox (IRE)**[38] 741 5-11-0 95 ... (b[1]) MrJMPKendrick[(7)]
(Ben Case) *prom: lost pl 3rd: sn given reminders: dropped to rr 6th: wknd next: bhd whn p.u bef 3 out* 11/1
05-6 P **Flabello (IRE)**[22] 880 5-11-7 100 ... DavidNoonan[(5)]
(David Pipe) *led to 4th: chsd ldr to 8th: sn rdn: wknd after next: bhd whn p.u bef 3 out* 12/1

5m 46.4s (7.80) **Going Correction** +0.075s/f (Yiel)
WFA 4 from 5yo+ 16lb 12 Ran SP% 113.9
Speed ratings (Par 103): **89,88,87,86,82 78,78,66,56, ,**
CSF £90.06 CT £272.11 TOTE £4.30: £2.00, £2.10, £1.50; EX 130.40 Trifecta £792.60.
Owner John P McManus **Bred** M L Bloodstock Limited **Trained** Cheltenham, Gloucs
■ The first winner under rules for Jonjo O'Neill junior.
■ Stewards' Enquiry : Mr J J O'Neill four-day ban: used whip above permitted level (tbn)
Mr B Paris-Crofts two-day ban: used whip above permitted level (tbn)

FOCUS
This was probably the weaker division, although the time was almost identical. The first two were very well in on the best of their old form.
T/Jkpt: £7,374.40 to a £1 stake. Pool: £10,386. - 1.00 winning tickets. T/Plt: £114.50 to a £1 stake. Pool: £79,353.05 - 505.41 winning tickets. T/Qpdt: £13.50 to a £1 stake. Pool: £6,723.52 - 368.40 winning tickets. **Colin Roberts**

The Form Book Jumps 2015-16, Raceform Ltd, Newbury, RG14 5SJ

1087 - 1093a (Foreign Racing) - See Raceform Interactive

^{999}UTTOXETER (L-H)

Friday, July 24

OFFICIAL GOING: Good (good to firm in places) changing to good after race 1 (1.40)

Wind: Light across Weather: Light rain

1094 INDIAN SPICE MARES' MAIDEN HURDLE (8 hdls 2 omitted) 2m 3f 207y

1:40 (1:40) (Class 5) 4-Y-0+ **£2,339** (£686; £343; £171)

Form RPR

5-34 **1** **Flower Power**^{37} [754] 4-10-11 0 DenisO'Regan 106+
(Tony Coyle) *sn prom: led and mstke 3 out: nt fluent next: styd on wl* **5/1**^{3}

2-22 **2** *2* **Princess Roania (IRE)**^{12} [970] 4-10-8 0 SeanBowen(3) 104+
(Peter Bowen) *hld up: hdwy appr 3 out: chsd wnr bef next: rdn flat: styd on same pce* **5/6**^{1}

-2PP **3** *15* **Mrs Jordan (IRE)**^{18} [926] 7-11-0 102 (tp) PaulMoloney 95
(Sophie Leech) *chsd ldr: led 3rd: nt fluent 5th: hdd 3 out: rdn and wknd appr last* **7/2**^{2}

0-6 **4** *3 ½* **Pretty Rose (IRE)**^{12} [970] 5-11-0 0 DarylJacob 93
(Ben Case) *hld up: hmpd bnd bef 3 out: hdwy sn after: wknd next* **12/1**

4/50 **5** *nk* **Alys Rock (IRE)**^{24} [860] 6-10-11 0 JonathanEngland(3) 94
(Michael Appleby) *hld up: mstke 5th: hmpd bnd appr 3 out: sn rdn: hit last: nvr trbld ldrs* **40/1**

6 *8* **Housewives Choice**^{287} 4-10-8 0 KyleJames(3) 83
(James Bethell) *hld up: hmpd 1st: mstke next: hdwy 5th: rdn and wknd appr 2 out* **25/1**

0-50 **7** *1 ¼* **Honey Brown**^{12} [970] 4-10-11 0 RobertDunne 84
(Tom Lacey) *prom: nt fluent 1st and 2nd: hit rails and lost pl appr 3 out* **25/1**

P-P4 **8** *99* **Midnight Memories**^{26} [852] 5-11-0 94 DougieCostello
(Steph Hollinshead) *led to 3rd: remained handy: rdn and wknd appr 3 out* **20/1**

/PP- **P** **Falcon's Legend**^{150} [4416] 5-10-9 0 NathanMoscrop(5)
(John Weymes) *chsd ldrs: pushed along after 5th: sn wknd: bhd whn p.u bef next* **100/1**

P **Hooray Hebe** 8-11-0 0 KielanWoods
(Mark Wall) *prom: mstke and lost pl 2nd: bhd whn mstke 4th: p.u bef 3 out* **100/1**

5m 2.8s (-0.40) **Going Correction** -0.10s/f (Good)
WFA 4 from 5yo+ 16lb **10** Ran SP% **118.0**
Speed ratings (Par 103): **96,95,89,87,87 84,83,44, ,**
CSF £9.64 TOTE £7.60: £1.70, £1.10, £1.40; EX 13.10 Trifecta £34.60.
Owner Ms Margaret Matheson **Bred** Margaret Matheson **Trained** Norton, N Yorks

FOCUS
Some starts have been moved at this track following remeasuring, so some races will not have speed figures until there is sufficient data to calculate updated median times. Hurdles moved out on to fresh ground and hurdle races increased by 83yds per circuit. Common bends and chase fences narrowed down from inside. The first hurdle in the back straight was omitted. A dry morning left the going unchanged. A moderate maiden with the first two running right away from the 102-rated third. A big step up from the winner.

1095 HOAR CROSS HALL SPA HOTEL NOVICES' H'CAP HURDLE (DIV I) (8 hdls 1 omitted) 1m 7f 168y

2:10 (2:11) (Class 5) (0-100,96) 3-Y-0+ **£2,339** (£686; £343; £171)

Form RPR

04-0 **1** **Empty The Tank (IRE)**^{78} [180] 5-10-9 **79** RichardJohnson 89+
(Lucy Wadham) *hld up: hdwy after 2 out: nt clr run flat: r.o u.p to ld nr fin* **7/4**^{1}

-553 **2** *½* **King Muro**^{9} [1001] 5-11-6 **90** (t) PaddyBrennan 100+
(Fergal O'Brien) *hld up: plld hrd: hdwy appr 3 out: chsd ldr next: led last: rdn flat: hdd nr fin* **10/3**^{2}

-504 **3** *5* **Maid Of Tuscany (IRE)**^{21} [892] 4-11-9 **95** (b^{1}) NoelFehily 98
(Neil Mulholland) *w ldr: hit 2nd: led 4th to next: led again 3 out: rdn and hdd last: no ex flat* **12/1**

000- **4** *2* **Private Jones**^{157} [4281] 6-11-2 **86** RobertDunne 89
(Miss Imogen Pickard) *s.i.s: hld up: rdn 3 out: hdwy next: styd on: nt trble ldrs* **33/1**

2/32 **5** *5* **Rose Red**^{17} [937] 8-10-12 **87** JakeHodson(5) 86
(Rob Summers) *hld up: hmpd 1st: hdwy 5th: rdn and wknd 2 out* **6/1**^{3}

245- **6** *1* **Gin And Tonic**^{273} [2043] 5-11-12 **96** JackQuinlan 93
(Michael Wigham) *led: hit 2nd: hdd 4th: led again next: rdn and hdd 3 out: wknd last* **14/1**

34-5 **7** *3* **Dalstontosiloth (IRE)**^{22} [882] 7-10-8 **83** CallumBewley(5) 78
(Barry Murtagh) *chsd ldrs: rdn after 3 out: wknd appr last* **7/1**

/U0- **8** *6* **Youm Jamil (USA)**^{107} [2027] 8-9-9 **70** oh1 (t) NickSlatter(5) 59
(Tony Carroll) *prom tl wknd after 2 out* **20/1**

U00 **9** *41* **Tundridge**^{18} [930] 6-11-0 **84** NicodeBoinville 36
(John Spearing) *mid-div: j.lft 1st: lost pl 4th: rdn and wknd appr 3 out* **16/1**

3m 56.4s (-1.00) **Going Correction** -0.10s/f (Good)
WFA 4 from 5yo+ 15lb **9** Ran SP% **114.2**
Speed ratings (Par 103): **98,97,95,94,91 91,89,86,66**
CSF £8.23 CT £50.60 TOTE £3.30: £1.10, £2.20, £2.60; EX 11.40 Trifecta £111.50.
Owner Asinus Verendus Syndicate **Bred** Michael O'Dwyer **Trained** Newmarket, Suffolk

FOCUS
This developed into a sprint from three out with the favourite storming home to grab victory on the line. A hurdles pb from the winner, in a faster time than the other division.

1096 HOAR CROSS HALL SPA HOTEL NOVICES' H'CAP HURDLE (DIV II) (8 hdls 1 omitted) 1m 7f 168y

2:40 (2:40) (Class 5) (0-100,95) 3-Y-0+ **£2,339** (£686; £343; £171)

Form RPR

/240 **1** **Sleeping City (FR)**^{26} [856] 8-11-9 **92** (tp) DenisO'Regan 102+
(Victor Dartnall) *hld up: hdwy appr 3 out: led last: sn clr: comf* **7/1**

/P-4 **2** *10* **The Yank**^{49} [626] 6-11-3 **86** (t) TomScudamore 84
(Tony Carroll) *hld up: hdwy 5th: led 2 out: hdd and mstke last: no ex flat* **5/1**^{3}

540- **3** *3 ½* **Ovilia (IRE)**^{214} [3227] 6-11-4 **87** AdrianLane 83
(Donald McCain) *led: nt fluent 3 out: rdn and hdd next: wknd flat* **25/1**

3401 **4** *2 ¾* **Auto Mac**^{17} [937] 7-10-10 **82** AdamNicol(3) 75
(Mike Sowersby) *hld up: hdwy 2 out: rdn and wknd flat* **8/1**

0/02 **5** *9* **Umoristic (FR)**^{33} [811] 7-9-13 **75** (t) MrStanSheppard(7) 62
(Matt Sheppard) *hld up in tch: rdn appr 3 out: sn wknd: hmpd next* **7/2**^{2}

P0-F **6** *1* **Northern Oscar (IRE)**^{35} [777] 7-11-5 **88** (t) AdamPogson 72
(Charles Pogson) *chsd ldr to 3 out: wknd bef next* **25/1**

B-35 **F** **Osorios Trial**^{17} [937] 8-11-0 **83** (p) BrianHughes 74
(Kevin Frost) *trckd ldrs: racd keenly: 4th and wkng whn fell 2 out* **6/1**

-141 **P** **Sir Note (FR)**^{43} [694] 5-11-12 **95** (t) PaulMoloney
(Nick Littmoden) *prom tl pushed along and lost pl bef 5th: p.u sn after* **9/4**^{1}

3m 57.4s **Going Correction** -0.10s/f (Good) **8** Ran SP% **115.2**
Speed ratings (Par 103): **96,91,89,87,83 82, ,**
CSF £42.33 CT £817.34 TOTE £9.50: £2.40, £2.20, £6.00; EX 58.60 Trifecta £1095.30.
Owner Edge Of Exmoor **Bred** Mlle Frederique Brion Et Al **Trained** Brayford, Devon

FOCUS
The pace was slightly stronger than for the first division, and with the favourites flopping the race opened up. The winner's best figure since 2013.

1097 UKOPS BEGINNERS' CHASE (16 fncs) 2m 6f 108y

3:15 (3:15) (Class 4) 5-Y-0+ **£3,798** (£1,122; £561)

Form RPR

-124 **1** **Weather Babe**^{30} [833] 7-10-7 0 (tp) TomScudamore 132+
(David Pipe) *chsd ldr tl led 12th: clr whn mstke 3 out: comf* **8/11**^{1}

-323 **2** *6* **Volcanic (FR)**^{28} [840] 6-11-0 123 (t) HenryBrooke 128
(Donald McCain) *led to 12th: rdn bef next: styd on same pce fr 2 out* **5/2**^{2}

3 *24* **Go On Henry (IRE)**^{47} 7-11-0 0 (t) RichardJohnson 116
(Philip Hobbs) *hld up: effrt whn nt fluent 4 out: hit next: sn wknd* **7/2**^{3}

5m 40.1s (-2.60) **Going Correction** +0.175s/f (Yiel) **3** Ran SP% **108.7**
Speed ratings: **111,108,100**
CSF £2.89 TOTE £1.80; EX 2.30 Trifecta £2.60.
Owner Wayne Clifford **Bred** Mrs S Clifford **Trained** Nicholashayne, Devon

FOCUS
This provided an easy introduction to fences for the well-backed favourite, who is rated similar to his hurdles mark.

1098 HOAR CROSS HALL UNDER SPA-TERS ORDERS H'CAP HURDLE (10 hdls 2 omitted) 2m 7f 70y

3:50 (3:50) (Class 5) (0-100,100) 4-Y-0+ **£2,339** (£686; £343; £171)

Form RPR

P022 **1** **Steel Gold (IRE)**^{12} [966] 9-9-11 **76** ConorRing(5) 85+
(John Upson) *a.p: chsd ldr 3 out: rdn to ld flat: styd on wl* **7/1**

0-P6 **2** *1 ¾* **Powderonthebonnet (IRE)**^{39} [746] 7-11-7 **95** AlainCawley 103+
(Richard Phillips) *hld up: hdwy 7th: led appr 3 out: rdn and hdd flat: styd on same pce* **9/2**^{2}

P606 **3** *19* **Solway Trigger**^{17} [935] 6-9-7 **74** oh1 RyanDay(7) 67
(Lisa Harrison) *hld up: hdwy after 7th: mstke 3 out: wkng whn nt fluent next* **12/1**

P/21 **4** *17* **Cardinal Rose**^{39} [741] 8-11-5 **93** KielanWoods 69
(Mark Wall) *chsd ldr to appr 3 out: wknd appr 2 out* **4/1**^{1}

3 **5** *nse* **Vinnie Trenta (IRE)**^{9} [1010] 7-11-4 **95** SeanBowen(3) 70
(Alan Phillips) *hld up: hdwy whn mstke 3 out: sn wknd* **8/1**

00-5 **6** *½* **Aregra (FR)**^{35} [777] 5-10-3 **77** (p) BrianHughes 51
(Peter Niven) *led: hdd appr 3 out: wknd bef next* **20/1**

1-34 **7** *2 ¼* **Bay Fortuna**^{50} [615] 6-11-9 **97** (p) RichardJohnson 69
(Mark Usher) *hld up: hdwy 7th: rdn and wknd bef 3 out* **9/2**^{2}

5300 **8** *7* **League Of His Own (IRE)**^{17} [935] 6-10-0 **74** oh5 (t) BrendanPowell 40
(Claire Dyson) *prom: rdn after 7th: wknd bef next* **50/1**

5-F3 **9** *2 ¾* **Mad For Road (IRE)**^{28} [843] 6-11-12 **100** AndrewTinkler 63
(Ben Haslam) *hld up: hdwy appr 7th: rdn and wknd sn after* **14/1**

3-50 **10** *24* **Poetic Presence (IRE)**^{24} [864] 5-10-1 **75** (t) AidanColeman 17
(Adrian Wintle) *hld up: rdn and wknd after 6th* **25/1**

31-P **P** **Moon Melody (GER)**^{12} [966] 12-10-11 **88** (tp) AdamNicol(3)
(Mike Sowersby) *chsd ldrs: mstke 2nd: pushed along 4th: rdn and wknd appr 7th: bhd whn p.u bef next* **28/1**

/5-2 **P** **Hassadin**^{26} [859] 9-11-1 **89** NoelFehily
(Michael Blake) *prom: rdn after 7th: sn wknd: bhd whn p.u bef 3 out* **13/2**^{3}

5m 55.1s (-3.70) **Going Correction** -0.10s/f (Good) **12** Ran SP% **121.7**
Speed ratings (Par 103): **102,101,94,88,88 88,87,85,84,76 ,**
CSF £38.66 CT £383.22 TOTE £5.20: £2.50, £1.20, £5.20; EX 45.60 Trifecta £404.40.
Owner The Marron Partnership **Bred** John Kenny **Trained** Maidford, Northants

FOCUS
A modest staying handicap hurdle. A step[up from the winner, with the first two clear.

1099 MATTHEW CURTIS HAIR HOAR CROSS HALL H'CAP CHASE (12 fncs) 1m 7f 214y

4:25 (4:25) (Class 4) (0-120,112) 4-Y-0 **£3,671** (£1,084; £542; £271; £135)

Form RPR

4/11 **1** **Walden Prince (IRE)**^{5} [1045] 8-11-6 **106** 14ex (tp) TomScudamore 124+
(David Bridgwater) *chsd ldr tl led 2nd: nt fluent 8th: clr fr 2 out: easily* **8/15**^{1}

2-06 **2** *6* **Sublime Talent (IRE)**^{36} [772] 9-11-2 **112** (t) LewisGordon(10) 118
(Evan Williams) *hld up: hdwy 8th: chsd wnr 3 out: sn rdn: styd on same pce fr next* **14/1**

-452 **3** *5* **Sleep In First (FR)**^{42} [708] 9-11-12 **112** (tp) RichardJohnson 116
(James Ewart) *chsd ldrs: nt fluent 2nd: j.rt next: chsd wnr 6th tl rdn 3 out: wknd next* **3/1**^{2}

04- **4** *4 ½* **Giant O Murchu (IRE)**^{292} [1754] 11-11-2 **107** ConorRing(5) 104
(John Upson) *prom tl rdn and wknd after 3 out* **25/1**

0P-5 **5** *1 ¼* **Chill (IRE)**^{58} [512] 7-11-10 **110** (b) TomO'Brien 106
(Paul Henderson) *led to 2nd: chsd wnr tl j. slowly 6th: sn given reminder: dropped to rr after 8th: rdn and wknd appr 3 out* **10/1**^{3}

4m 2.1s (0.70) **Going Correction** +0.175s/f (Yiel) **5** Ran SP% **109.8**
Speed ratings (Par 105): **105,102,99,97,96**
CSF £7.95 TOTE £1.40: £1.10, £3.50; EX 7.30 Trifecta £14.10.
Owner Gary Attwood **Bred** John McEnery **Trained** Icomb, Gloucs

FOCUS
As the only in-form horse in the field, the hat-trick-seeking favourite completely dominated the betting, and it was a similar story in the race. He was thrown in on recent form.

1100 NAGS AND GLAD RAGS SPA DAY H'CAP HURDLE (8 hdls 2 omitted) 2m 3f 207y

4:55 (4:55) (Class 4) (0-120,119) 4-Y-0+ **£3,249** (£954; £477; £238)

Form RPR

P-53 **1** **Alwaystheoptimist**^{24} [862] 12-11-10 **115** (t) RichardJohnson 118+
(Shaun Lycett) *hld up: hdwy 3 out: jnd ldrs whn stmbld next: styd on u.p to ld nr fin* **12/1**

2202 **2** ¾ **Baths Well (IRE)**[19] 917 5-11-1 116..................(p) HarrisonBeswick[(10)] 116
(Ben Pauling) *sn led: hdd 5th: led again bef next: rdn flat: hdd nr fin* **11/1**

0/- **3** 1¼ **Benefits Well (IRE)**[639] 2018 8-11-5 110.................. GavinSheehan 109
(Warren Greatrex) *hld up: pushed along after 4th: hdwy appr 2 out: nt clr run flat: styd on to go 3rd nr fin* **5/1**[3]

13-6 **4** ½ **Perspicace**[48] 645 4-11-11 119.................. TomScudamore 114
(David Pipe) *a.p: ev ch 2 out: sn rdn: no ex towards fin* **11/1**

30-0 **5** 1¼ **Sinndar's Man**[21] 895 4-11-2 110.................. NickScholfield 104
(Michael Blake) *prom: rdn appr 2 out: styd on same pce flat* **16/1**

052- **6** 7 **A Hairy Koala (FR)**[129] 4825 5-10-9 105..................(tp) KieronEdgar[(5)] 97
(David Pipe) *chsd ldrs: rdn appr 3 out: wknd last* **4/1**[2]

0-00 **7** hd **Ever So Much (IRE)**[57] 520 6-10-11 102..................(p) AndrewTinkler 94
(Ben Haslam) *hld up: hdwy appr 3 out: rdn and wknd bef next* **14/1**

124- **8** 3¼ **Cusheen Bridge (IRE)**[265] 2186 7-11-12 117..................(t) AdamPogson 106
(Charles Pogson) *hld up: hdwy 3 out: wknd next* **16/1**

50-6 **9** 17 **General Montgomery (IRE)**[45] 678 6-11-5 110..................(p) NoelFehily 83
(Neil Mulholland) *prom: rdn appr 3 out: wknd next* **16/1**

2-12 **10** 2¼ **Ubaldo Des Menhies (FR)**[12] 969 7-11-11 116....(p) RichieMcLernon 87
(Jonjo O'Neill) *sn chsng ldr: led 5th: rdn and hdd bef next: sn wknd* **9/4**[1]

5m 3.2s **Going Correction** -0.10s/f (Good)
WFA 4 from 5yo+ 16lb **10** Ran **SP% 116.1**
Speed ratings (Par 105): **96,95,95,95,94 91,91,90,83,82**
CSF £133.21 CT £751.00 TOTE £7.60: £2.40, £3.00, £2.00; EX 102.60 Trifecta £431.10.
Owner Alan Bosley **Bred** Crandon Park Stud **Trained** Clapton-on-the-Hill, Gloucs

FOCUS
An exciting finish with five fighting it out from the last. A small step up from the winner on his recent run.

1101 BURTON KIA STANDARD OPEN NATIONAL HUNT FLAT RACE 1m 7f 168y
5:25 (5:25) (Class 6) 4-6-Y-O **£1,559** (£457; £228; £114)

Form RPR

11 **1** **Waterlord**[22] 887 4-11-8 0.................. AidanColeman 122+
(John Ferguson) *hld up: hdwy over 2f out: led over 1f out: shkn up and sn clr: comf* **8/15**[1]

1-11 **2** 7 **Brave Richard (IRE)**[45] 682 4-11-5 0.................. MrBMLinehan[(7)] 115+
(J R Jenkins) *hld up: hdwy over 2f out: rdn to chse wnr over 1f out: sn outpcd* **3/1**[2]

2/1- **3** 3 **Magna Cartor**[274] 2028 5-11-7 0.................. KielanWoods 108
(Ronald Thompson) *chsd ldrs: led over 3f out: rdn and hdd over 1f out: styd on same pce* **5/1**[3]

26- **4** 1½ **The Clonlisk Bug (IRE)**[92] 5501 5-11-0 0.................. BrianHughes 99
(Kevin Frost) *hld up: hdwy over 3f out: rdn and edgd lft over 1f out: styd on same pce* **16/1**

0 **5** 2 **Last Wish (IRE)**[45] 682 4-10-12 0..................[1] DougieCostello 95
(Richard Guest) *prom: rdn over 2f out: styd on same pce fr over 1f out* **20/1**

6- **6** 6 **Teals Lad**[324] 1436 6-11-0 0.................. JakeGreenall 92
(Michael Easterby) *chsd ldrs: rdn over 2f out: wknd over 1f out* **50/1**

0 **7** 11 **Flick Knife (IRE)**[24] 865 6-10-11 0.................. KillianMoore[(3)] 82
(Mark Wall) *wnt lft s: sn led: hdd over 11f out: chsd ldr tl rdn over 3f out: wknd over 2f out* **33/1**

8 7 **Irish Ranger (IRE)**[53] 4-10-9 0.................. BenPoste[(3)] 74
(Rosemary Gasson) *w ldr tl led over 11f out: rdn and hdd over 3f out: wknd over 2f out* **100/1**

6- **9** 9 **Kayf Tiger**[195] 3618 6-11-0 0.................. CharliePoste 67
(Robin Dickin) *hld up: rdn and wknd over 3f out* **28/1**

10 1 **Lochwell Lad (IRE)**[131] 6-10-11 0..................(t) TonyKelly[(3)] 67
(Rebecca Menzies) *hld up: rdn and wknd over 3f out* **100/1**

11 20 **Generous Past** 5-10-11 0.................. BrianToomey[(3)] 49
(Michael Mullineaux) *prom: pushed along 6f out: wknd 4f out* **50/1**

3m 52.1s (0.30) **Going Correction** -0.10s/f (Good) **11** Ran **SP% 129.8**
Speed ratings: **95,91,90,89,88 85,79,76,71,71 61**
CSF £2.70 TOTE £1.90: £1.02, £1.30, £1.70; EX 3.00 Trifecta £4.60.
Owner Bloomfields **Bred** Rabbah Bloodstock Limited **Trained** Cowlinge, Suffolk

FOCUS
This was run at a good pace, with the market leaders coming to the fore in a fair bumper. The winner set a very high standard and didn't need to be at his best.
T/Plt: £58.60 to a £1 stake. Pool: £62,182.85 - 773.56 winning units. T/Qpdt: £40.20 to a £1 stake. Pool: £4175.29 - 76.80 winning units. **Colin Roberts**

1102 - 1108a (Foreign Racing) - See Raceform Interactive

1094 UTTOXETER (L-H)
Sunday, July 26

OFFICIAL GOING: Good to soft changing to soft after race 1 (2:30)
Wind: Fresh behind Weather: Raining

1109 BURTON ALBION MARES' NOVICES' HURDLE (9 hdls) 1m 7f 168y
2:30 (2:31) (Class 4) 4-Y-O+ **£3,798** (£1,122; £561; £280; £140)

Form RPR

P-11 **1** **Tea In Transvaal (IRE)**[23] 895 4-11-8 125.................. PaulMoloney 129+
(Evan Williams) *chsd ldr tl led appr 2 out: rdn out* **11/10**[2]

2 1½ **Tahira (GER)**[29] 5-10-10 0.................. BrianHughes 116+
(John Quinn) *a.p: nt fluent 2nd: chsd wnr appr 2 out: nt fluent last: rdn and swtchd lft flat: styd on* **1/1**[1]

44 **3** 33 **Cabin Fever**[11] 1000 4-10-8 0.................. RobertDunne 84
(Tom Lacey) *led: hdd appr 2 out: wknd wl bef last* **20/1**[3]

640 **4** 2¼ **Flemerina (IRE)**[35] 799 6-10-10 0.................. SeanQuinlan 80
(Sue Smith) *hld up: rdn and wknd appr 3 out* **50/1**

5 5 **Annskert Lady (IRE)**[12] 991 5-10-10 0.................. PaddyBrennan 75
(Anthony McCann, Ire) *hld up: hdwy 6th: rdn and wknd 3 out* **22/1**

1-4P **6** 1 **Hija**[33] 828 4-10-10 104.................. AliceMills[(5)] 79
(Gail Haywood) *a in rr: hit 1st: bhd fr 3rd* **25/1**

60 **7** dist **Crosslanes (IRE)**[20] 932 4-10-8 0..................[1] RichieMcLernon 32
(Chris Bealby) *prom: reminders after 5th: wknd after next* **80/1**

3m 52.8s (-4.60) **Going Correction** -0.10s/f (Good) **7** Ran **SP% 113.8**
Speed ratings (Par 105): **107,106,89,88,86 85,**
CSF £2.49 TOTE £2.20: £1.20, £1.10; EX 3.30 Trifecta £10.90.
Owner M J Haines **Bred** Summerville Bloodstock **Trained** Llancarfan, Vale Of Glamorgan

FOCUS
All starts in use at this fixture had been moved following remeasuring, so there will be no speed figures here until there is sufficient data to calculate updated median times. Hurdles moved in 6yds on to fresher ground and divided bends. 2m hurdle races increased by 60yds, 2m4f by 90yds, 2m7.5f by 120yds. Chase fences narrowed down from inside. Prolonged rain had eased the going to soft after the first. The two market leaders pulled right away from a moderate field.

1110 BREWERS BEGINNERS' CHASE (15 fncs) 2m 4f
3:00 (3:00) (Class 4) 4-Y-O+ **£4,431** (£1,309; £654; £327; £163)

Form RPR

-120 **1** **Roman Flight (IRE)**[8] 1039 7-11-9 0..................(v) NoelFehily 122+
(David Dennis) *hld up: hdwy 4 out: shkn up to ld flat: r.o: comf* **8/15**[1]

2-42 **2** nk **Lemony Bay**[23] 894 6-11-9 113.................. LeightonAspell 120
(Oliver Sherwood) *led to 2nd: w ldr tl led again 4th: hdd 7th: led again next: rdn appr last: hdd flat: styd on* **3/1**[2]

0-23 **3** 4 **Fuzzy Logic (IRE)**[33] 825 6-11-6 110..................(p) RobertWilliams[(3)] 115
(Bernard Llewellyn) *chsd ldrs: nt fluent 5th: wnt 2nd 11th tl rdn appr last: no ex flat* **16/1**

000- **4** 32 **The Shropshire Lad**[198] 3594 5-11-9 0.................. HarrySkelton 83
(Dan Skelton) *prom: rdn whn mstke 4 out: wknd bef next* **25/1**

504/ **5** ½ **Koup De Kanon (FR)**[912] 3853 9-11-9 0.................. WayneHutchinson 83
(Donald McCain) *prom tl rdn and wknd appr 2 out* **10/1**[3]

B43/ **6** 19 **Optical High**[576] 3334 6-11-9 0.................. SeanQuinlan 64
(Sue Smith) *led 2nd to 4th: led again 7th tl next: chsd ldr to 11th: sn rdn and wknd* **50/1**

5m 16.5s (6.70) **Going Correction** +0.075s/f (Yiel) **6** Ran **SP% 111.0**
Speed ratings (Par 105): **89,88,87,74,74 66**
CSF £2.60 TOTE £1.50: £1.10, £1.40; EX 2.50 Trifecta £6.60.
Owner Favourites Racing Ltd **Bred** Jim Cockburn **Trained** Hanley Swan, Worcestershire

FOCUS
Three were still in it up the home straight, though in the end the winner showed a bit more class.

1111 BURTON ALBION COMMUNITY TRUST JUVENILE HURDLE (9 hdls) 1m 7f 168y
3:35 (3:35) (Class 4) 3-Y-O **£3,898** (£1,144; £572; £286)

Form RPR

1 **1** **Doubly Clever (IRE)**[23] 891 3-11-4 0.................. NoelFehily 101+
(Michael Blake) *trckd ldr: racd keenly: led after 2 out: hit last: rdn out* **4/9**[1]

1 **2** 3½ **Egmont**[50] 636 3-11-4 0.................. HenryBrooke 92
(George Moore) *led at stdy pce tl qckng appr 3 out: sn rdn: hdd after 2 out: hit last: styd on same pce flat* **7/2**[2]

C3 **3** 4 **Auld Fyffee (IRE)**[23] 891 3-10-5 0.................. JamesDavies 75
(Tom Gretton) *chsd ldrs: rdn bef 2 out: styd on same pce appr last* **25/1**

4 46 **Naval Action**[41] 3-10-12 0.................. SamTwiston-Davies 36
(Sandy Thomson) *hld up: nt fluent 1st and 4th: j. slowly 6th: sn rdn: wknd bef next* **8/1**[3]

3m 58.8s (1.40) **Going Correction** +0.125s/f (Yiel) **4** Ran **SP% 106.4**
Speed ratings (Par 102): **101,99,97,74**
CSF £2.31 TOTE £1.30; EX 2.30 Trifecta £6.00.
Owner Francise Tieman **Bred** Gigginstown House Stud **Trained** Trowbridge, Wilts

FOCUS
tactical affair between two previous hurdles winners, with the favourite showing a fair turn of foot.

1112 BEN ROBINSON H'CAP CHASE (15 fncs) 2m 4f
4:10 (4:10) (Class 2) 4-Y-O+
£14,138 (£4,176; £2,088; £1,044; £522; £262)

Form RPR

0-11 **1** **Champion Court (IRE)**[35] 812 10-11-12 148..................(p) AndrewTinkler 159+
(Martin Keighley) *mde all: j.rt at times: hung rt after 10th: rdn appr 4 out: styd on wl* **9/4**[1]

2-11 **2** 6 **Ulis De Vassy (FR)**[19] 936 7-10-7 129.................. HarrySkelton 134+
(Dan Skelton) *chsd wnr: nt clr run and nt fluent 9th: rdn appr 4 out: wknd flat* **5/2**[2]

-221 **3** ½ **Moorlands Jack**[38] 772 10-10-0 122 oh5..................(p) JamesDavies 125
(Jeremy Scott) *hld up: nt fluent 4 out: hdwy to go 3rd after next: sn rdn: styd on flat: nrst fin* **14/1**

0-31 **4** 12 **Commitment**[32] 829 6-10-5 127.................. AidanColeman 118
(Neil Mulholland) *chsd ldrs: lost pl 3rd: rdn 11th wknd bef next* **4/1**[3]

-622 **5** nk **No Likey (IRE)**[35] 809 8-9-7 122 oh2..................(tp) ThomasCheesman[(7)] 113
(Philip Hobbs) *nt fluent 1st: wnt prom 3rd: rdn appr 4 out: wknd after next* **5/1**

-443 **6** 23 **Houston Dynimo (IRE)**[38] 772 10-10-0 122 oh2....(bt) TomScudamore 98
(David Pipe) *hld up: hdwy 5th: rdn appr 4 out: wknd next* **9/1**

5m 9.8s **Going Correction** +0.30s/f (Yiel) **6** Ran **SP% 112.7**
Speed ratings (Par 109): **112,109,109,104,104 95**
CSF £8.72 CT £58.70 TOTE £2.90: £1.50, £1.70; EX 8.50 Trifecta £49.40.
Owner M Boothright **Bred** Larry O'Connor **Trained** Condicote, Gloucs

FOCUS
With four non-runners this valuable handicap lost some of its competitiveness, but the morning favourites held their ground and they produced a stirring battle to cheer up a gloomy day.

1113 #BAFCANDPROUD H'CAP HURDLE (12 hdls) 2m 7f 70y
4:45 (4:45) (Class 4) (0-120,120) 4-Y-O **£3,924** (£1,159; £579; £290; £145)

Form RPR

-P12 **1** **Blackwell Synergy (FR)**[19] 939 9-10-3 102.................. ConorRing[(5)] 109+
(John Upson) *a.p: chsd ldr 8th: led after next: rdn appr 2 out: all out* **15/2**

U0 **2** ½ **Fresh By Nature (IRE)**[21] 917 8-10-8 105.................. JonathanEngland[(3)] 109
(Harriet Bethell) *hld up: bhd and pushed along whn hit 7th: hdwy after 9th: rdn appr last: r.o* **66/1**

06-5 **3** nk **Handmaid**[30] 839 6-10-13 110.................. SeanBowen[(3)] 114
(Peter Bowen) *mid-div: lost pl after 7th: nt fluent 9th: sn rdn: hdwy 2 out: r.o u.p flat* **13/2**[3]

4421 **4** 3¼ **Solway Prince**[19] 939 6-10-0 101.................. RyanDay[(7)] 102
(Lisa Harrison) *hld up: hdwy 8th: nt fluent and outpcd 3 out: rallied appr last: styd on* **7/2**[1]

42U- **5** 11 **Taradrewe**[125] 4959 8-11-7 115..................(t) AidanColeman 106
(Anthony Honeyball) *hld up: hdwy 8th: rdn and wknd appr last* **10/1**

6-21 **6** 12 **Wait A Second (IRE)**[25] 880 5-11-7 118..................(p) MauriceLinehan[(3)] 95
(Jonjo O'Neill) *prom tl rdn and wknd after 2 out: mstke last* **5/1**[2]

F6F- **7** ¾ **Standing Ovation (IRE)**[107] 5253 8-11-12 120.........(tp) TomScudamore 97
(David Pipe) *hld up: mstke 6th: hdwy after 8th: rdn and wknd appr 3 out* **8/1**

0-45 **8** 1¾ **Feast Of Fire (IRE)**[14] 967 8-10-13 107.................. BrianHughes 82
(Mike Sowersby) *hld up: hdwy after 9th: sn rdn: wknd next* **33/1**

4 **9** *11* **Solstice Star**[28] 858 5-9-11 **94**................................[1] KillianMoore(3) 58
(Martin Keighley) *chsd ldrs tl rdn and wknd 3 out: hit next* **8/1**
-400 **10** *4 ½* **Exemplary**[11] 1002 8-10-12 **106**................................(bt[1]) BrendanPowell 65
(Johnny Farrelly) *hld up: hit 5th: effrt appr 3 out: sn wknd* **33/1**
64/0 **11** *11* **Koultas King (IRE)**[19] 939 8-10-9 **103**................................(t) RichardJohnson 51
(Tim Vaughan) *hld up: rdn and wknd bef 9th* **12/1**
32-0 **P** **Dais Return (IRE)**[38] 774 11-10-3 **104**................................(t) CiaranGethings(7)
(John Coombe) *led tl after 2nd: remained w ldr tl pushed along 8th: wknd bef next: bhd whn p.u bef 3 out* **25/1**
5-3P **P** **Wolf Shield (IRE)**[44] 707 8-11-9 **117**................................(t) HenryBrooke
(George Moore) *w ldr tl led after 2nd: nt fluent 6th: hdd after 9th: wknd and p.u bef next* **20/1**
6m 4.5s (5.70) **Going Correction** +0.35s/f (Yiel) **13** Ran SP% **119.0**
Speed ratings (Par 105): **104,103,103,102,98 94,94,93,89,88 84,** ,
CSF £432.53 CT £3366.83 TOTE £8.50: £2.90, £10.50, £2.90; EX 338.30 Trifecta £3661.50 Part won..
Owner The Peter Partnership **Bred** Erick Bec De La Motte **Trained** Maidford, Northants
FOCUS
he winner was the first to commit for home and had to fend off two strong-finishing rivals.

1114 BURTON ALBION 65TH ANNIVERSARY H'CAP CHASE (18 fncs) 3m 2y
5:20 (5:20) (Class 4) (0-120,119) 4-Y-O **£4,431** (£1,309; £654; £327; £163)

Form RPR
-22P **1** **High Ron**[39] 760 10-11-12 **119**................................(t) HarrySkelton 131+
(Caroline Bailey) *led 2nd to 3rd: led 6th to 8th: led 12th: clr fr 14th: easily* **5/1[2]**
5-56 **2** *28* **Green Bank (IRE)**[39] 760 9-11-3 **110**................................(bt) RichardJohnson 90
(Charlie Longsdon) *led to 2nd: led 3rd to 6th: led 8th to 12th: rdn after 14th: wknd bef next* **12/1**
6442 **3** *4* **Finish The Story (IRE)**[11] 1007 9-11-7 **114**................................(bt) NoelFehily 89
(Johnny Farrelly) *chsd ldrs: rdn after 14th: wknd bef next* **11/2[3]**
4-5P **4** *9* **Forever My Friend (IRE)**[25] 873 8-11-0 **110**................................ SeanBowen(3) 76
(Peter Bowen) *hld up: hmpd 5th: sme hdwy after 14th: wknd bef next* **11/1**
4-16 **5** *¾* **Pigeon Island**[57] 553 12-11-11 **118**................................ SamTwiston-Davies 83
(Nigel Twiston-Davies) *hld up: hit 3rd: a in rr* **8/1**
0522 **6** *½* **West End (IRE)**[14] 967 8-11-3 **110**................................(tp) TomScudamore 75
(Kim Bailey) *hld up: hdwy 8th: rdn and wknd bef 4 out* **4/1[1]**
6426 **7** *1 ½* **Green Wizard (IRE)**[8] 1033 9-11-3 **110**................................ SeanQuinlan 73
(Sue Smith) *chsd ldrs tl rdn and wknd wl bef 4 out* **8/1**
U6-0 **P** **Always Bold (IRE)**[20] 926 10-10-5 **98**................................(p) AndrewTinkler
(Martin Keighley) *prom: rdn 11th: sn wknd: bhd whn p.u bef 3 out* **6/1**
113- **P** **West Cork Flash (IRE)**[182] 11-11-5 **112**................................(p) TomO'Brien
(Paul Henderson) *prom: rdn and lost pl 7th: wknd next: bhd whn p.u bef 3 out* **25/1**
11-3 **P** **Milgen Bay**[74] 282 9-11-8 **115**................................ LeightonAspell
(Oliver Sherwood) *hld up: a in rr: bhd fr 7th: p.u bef 11th* **12/1**
4P3/ **P** **Balding Banker (IRE)**[586] 3146 9-11-7 **117**................................ TonyKelly(3)
(Rebecca Menzies) *hld up: effrt after 13th: sn wknd: bhd whn p.u bef 3 out* **28/1**
6m 30.3s (22.20) **Going Correction** +0.525s/f (Soft) **11** Ran SP% **119.6**
Speed ratings (Par 105): **84,74,73,70,70 69,69,** ,
CSF £63.52 CT £346.96 TOTE £6.00: £2.30, £3.90, £2.20; EX 78.30 Trifecta £701.00.
Owner Mrs Gillian Burke **Bred** Gillian & Micheal Burke **Trained** Holdenby, Northants
FOCUS
The conditions really took their toll and the race fell apart.

1115 PIRELLI STADIUM'S 10TH ANNIVERSARY H'CAP HURDLE (9 hdls) 1m 7f 168y
5:50 (5:52) (Class 5) (0-100,100) 3-Y-O+ **£2,729** (£801; £400; £200)

Form RPR
F-31 **1** **Modeligo (IRE)**[45] 692 6-10-13 **94**................................(t) MrStanSheppard(7) 102+
(Matt Sheppard) *a.p: mstke 6th: chsd ldr 3 out: led appr last: styd on wl* **9/4[1]**
0/ **2** *6* **Authorative (IRE)**[12] 992 5-11-10 **98**................................(p) PaddyBrennan 99
(Anthony McCann, Ire) *hld up: hdwy appr 3 out: rdn whn nt fluent last: styd on same pce* **20/1**
-533 **3** *½* **Significant Move**[19] 937 8-10-5 **84**................................(b) ChrisWard(5) 84
(Dr Richard Newland) *led to 2nd: chsd ldr tl led again 6th: rdn and hdd appr last: no ex flat* **5/2[2]**
603P **4** *½* **Grams And Ounces**[6] 937 8-11-3 **91**................................(t) MichealNolan 92
(Adrian Wintle) *hld up: hdwy 5th: ev ch whn blnd 2 out: sn rdn: nt fluent last: styd on same pce* **10/1[3]**
-650 **5** *42* **Rye House (IRE)**[33] 828 6-11-10 **98**................................(t) RichardJohnson 55
(Tim Vaughan) *hld up: rdn and wknd appr 3 out* **5/2[2]**
-P60 **6** *16* **Ted Dolly (IRE)**[45] 692 11-11-1 **92**................................(p) BenPoste(3) 33
(Tom Symonds) *hld up: hdwy 5th: lost pl after next: wknd bef 3 out* **33/1**
0- **P** **Columbanus (IRE)**[50] 342 4-10-7 **83**................................ TomScudamore
(Kevin Bishop) *led and mstke 2nd: nt fluent 4th: hdd 6th: rdn and wknd 3 out: bhd whn p.u bef next* **40/1**
4m 5.8s (8.40) **Going Correction** +0.575s/f (Soft)
WFA 4 from 5yo+ 15lb **7** Ran SP% **107.1**
Speed ratings (Par 103): **102,99,98,98,77 69,**
CSF £33.67 CT £99.20 TOTE £2.80: £1.50, £5.40; EX 38.70 Trifecta £144.50.
Owner Simon Gegg **Bred** Edward And Joseph McCormack **Trained** Eastnor, H'fords
FOCUS
Only a couple came into this in any form but it was run at a fair pace and four finished clear.
T/Plt: 35.30 Pool: T/Qpdt: 52.20 Pool: **Colin Roberts**

1044 NEWTON ABBOT (L-H)
Monday, July 27

OFFICIAL GOING: Good to soft (soft in places; 5.8)
Wind: mild breeze across Weather: overcast Rails: All bends moved outwards. Adjusted race distances as follows: Race 1 add 104 yards; Race 2 & 7 add 71 yards; Race 3 add 87 yards; Race 4 & 5 add 81 yards; Race 6 add 76 yards.

1116 SUMMERTIME NOVICES' HURDLE (10 hdls) 2m 5f 122y
2:15 (2:15) (Class 4) 4-Y-O+ **£3,898** (£1,144; £572; £286)

Form RPR
5-31 **1** **Lamool (GER)**[45] 710 8-11-4 134................................(t) RichardJohnson 118+
(Tim Vaughan) *mde all: wl in command fr 3 out: easily* **1/10[1]**
2 *10* **Theatre Goer**[120] 6-10-2 0................................ JamesBanks(3) 85
(Noel Williams) *cl up: rdn to dispute 3rd after 3 out: wnt 2nd next but no ch w wnr: styd on same pce* **14/1[3]**
-5 **3** *7* **Beat The Tide**[29] 852 5-10-5 0................................ AlanJohns(7) 87
(Tim Vaughan) *trckd wnr: rdn after 3 out: lost 2nd next: one pce after* **8/1[2]**
6 **4** *2 ½* **I'llhavealook (IRE)**[24] 893 10-10-9 0................................(p) RobertWilliams(3) 82
(Katie Stephens) *trckd ldrs: rdn in disp 3rd after 3 out: one pce fr next* **50/1**
4 **5** *32* **Lee Side Lady (IRE)**[8] 1052 5-10-5 0................................ MarkQuinlan 43
(Neil Mulholland) *trckd ldrs: rdn 3 out: sn wknd: t.o* **16/1**
P/ **P** **Milburn**[477] 5182 9-10-7 0................................ AliceMills(5)
(Gail Haywood) *in tch: reminders after 4th: sn detached: t.o whn p.u bef 7th* **20/1**
5m 26.2s (6.00) **Going Correction** +0.50s/f (Soft) **6** Ran SP% **121.3**
Speed ratings (Par 105): **109,105,102,101,90**
CSF £4.45 TOTE £1.10: £1.10, £4.60; EX 4.90 Trifecta £12.80.
Owner J H Frost **Bred** Frau M U W Lohmann **Trained** Aberthin, Vale of Glamorgan
FOCUS
All bends moved out and race 1 increased by 104yds, races 2 & 7 by 71yds, race 3 by 87yds, races 4 &5 by 81yds and race 6 by 76yds. Following 13mm the previous day, the going was good to soft, soft in places. An uncompetitive affair, which presented an easy opportunity for the short-priced favourite, who was in a different class to the rest of these.

1117 AT THE RACES MAIDEN HURDLE (8 hdls) 2m 167y
2:45 (2:45) (Class 4) 4-Y-O+ **£3,898** (£1,144; £572; £286)

Form RPR
2 **1** **Lilac Tree**[20] 933 5-11-2 0................................[1] AidanColeman 113+
(John Ferguson) *mid-div: hdwy after 4th: trckd ldr 3 out: led sn after 2 out: sn clr: readily* **9/2[3]**
0/63 **2** *7* **Shout It Aloud**[29] 853 6-11-2 0................................(t) RichardJohnson 108+
(Tim Vaughan) *led: rdn whn mstke 2 out: sn hdd and hld by wnr but wl clr of remainder: nt fluent last* **14/1**
44 **3** *11* **Almagest**[12] 999 7-11-2 0................................ RhysFlint 96
(Robert Stephens) *trckd ldrs: rdn after 3 out: styd on same pce* **33/1**
1-43 **4** *3 ½* **Prince Of Poets**[46] 703 4-11-0 0................................ TomScudamore 91
(David Pipe) *mid-div: hdwy 5th: rdn after 3 out: nvr threatened front pair: styd on same pce* **9/1**
6 **5** *½* **Polo The Mumm (FR)**[8] 1044 5-10-9 112................................ MissHWelch(7) 92
(Jimmy Frost) *trckd ldrs: rdn after 3 out: styd on same pce* **100/1**
0 **6** *11* **Arthur's Queen (FR)**[12] 1009 4-10-7 0................................ MichealNolan 74
(Carroll Gray) *mid-div: hdwy 5th: rdn after 3 out: wknd between last 2* **66/1**
2 **7** *6* **No Win No Fee**[8] 1052 5-11-2 0................................ WillKennedy 78
(Dr Richard Newland) *mid-div: struggling 3 out: nvr threatened: wknd bef next* **3/1[1]**
4/P **8** *11* **Lets Get Cracking (FR)**[45] 712 11-11-2 65................................ NickScholfield 67
(Alan Jones) *mid-div tl wknd 3 out* **100/1**
5 **9** *nk* **Bare Necessities (IRE)**[27] 865 5-11-2 0................................ PeterCarberry 67
(Shaun Lycett) *trckd ldrs: losing pl u.p whn hit 5th: wknd next* **12/1**
-653 **10** *15* **Western Way (IRE)**[15] 971 6-11-2 0................................ DenisO'Regan 53
(Don Cantillon) *a towards rr* **9/2[3]**
2-P0 **11** *4* **Quick N' Easy (IRE)**[8] 1044 5-10-13 0................................ LucyGardner(3) 50
(Sue Gardner) *a towards rr* **100/1**
12 *18* **Kisha Lad (IRE)**[159] 4309 8-10-9 0................................ MrMatthewHampton(7) 34
(Richard Woollacott) *a towards rr* **80/1**
6 **13** *40* **Sharp Sword (IRE)**[8] 1052 4-11-0 0................................ MarkQuinlan
(Neil Mulholland) *mstke 1st and rdr lost iron: nt fluent next: a bhd: t.o* **40/1**
0 **14** *9* **Uncle Chizza**[58] 558 6-11-2 0................................ MarkGrant
(Sean Curran) *mid-div tl wknd 5th: t.o* **150/1**
P **Marshgate Lane (USA)**[465] 6-11-2 0................................(t) NoelFehily
(Neil Mulholland) *mid-div: hdwy to trck ldrs 5th: effrt after 3 out: sn btn: p.u bef next (dismntd)* **10/3[2]**
P **Brean Splash Susie**[34] 4-10-4 0................................ JamesBanks(3)
(Bill Turner) *a towards rr: t.o whn p.u bef 2 out* **150/1**
4m 8.6s (2.90) **Going Correction** +0.50s/f (Soft)
WFA 4 from 5yo+ 15lb **16** Ran SP% **121.2**
Speed ratings (Par 105): **113,109,104,102,102 97,94,89,89,82 80,71,53,48,**
CSF £62.65 TOTE £4.20: £2.00, £4.60, £7.40; EX 42.80 Trifecta £1192.40.
Owner Bloomfields **Bred** Biddestone Stud Ltd **Trained** Cowlinge, Suffolk
FOCUS
Probably a modest maiden, despite the numbers run at a sensible gallop in the ground. The winner stepped up on his debut but is entitled to rate a lot higher on Flat form, and the second is rated in line with best bumper figures. The third and fourth help set the ordinary level.

1118 PAUL SHERRIFF 60TH BIRTHDAY H'CAP CHASE (20 fncs) 3m 1f 170y
3:15 (3:15) (Class 5) (0-100,99) 4-Y-O+ **£3,422** (£997; £499)

Form RPR
P/P1 **1** **Foxes Bridge**[21] 926 7-11-12 **99**................................(v) GavinSheehan 113+
(Nick Mitchell) *hld up: hmpd 2nd: nt fluent 11th: pushed along and hdwy whn mstke 14th: rdn after 4 out: nt clr run after 3 out: led between last 2: blnd and hdd last: rallied wl to regain ld run-in: drvn rt out* **6/1**
6 **2** *¾* **Railway Storm (IRE)**[34] 827 10-10-11 **91**................................ MissBFrost(7) 100
(Jimmy Frost) *in tch: tk clsr order 14th: pckd 4 out: sn rdn: str chal 2 out: ev ch fr last: styd on* **10/1**
5- **3** *1 ¼* **Distracted (IRE)**[59] 550 7-11-9 **96**................................(p) TomO'Brien 103
(Robert Stephens) *j.rt at times: in tch: reminders after 8th: led after 3 out: rdn and hdd between last 2: led briefly sn after last: no ex nring fin* **9/2[3]**
4-62 **4** *22* **Where'd Ya Hide It (IRE)**[45] 717 9-10-3 **76**................................(bt) PaddyBrennan 69
(Paul Henderson) *chsd ldrs: led after 14th: rdn and hdd after 3 out: wknd between last 2* **6/1**
56-2 **5** *11* **Top Chief**[12] 1004 7-11-2 **96**................................(t) CiaranGethings(7) 73
(Anthony Honeyball) *trckd ldrs: rdn in cl 3rd after 4 out: wkng whn mstke 2 out* **10/3[1]**
0-45 **6** *17* **Annamult (IRE)**[12] 1004 7-9-12 **78**................................ MrAlexEdwards(7) 40
(Alan Phillips) *in tch: rdn after 15th: sn wknd: t.o* **10/1**
/2-1 **7** *55* **Kimora (IRE)**[51] 9-10-13 **93**................................(t) MrMatthewBarber(7) 6
(Debra Hamer) *nt fluent 4th: a detached in last: t.o fr 13th* **4/1[2]**
P/06 **P** **Skating Home (IRE)**[15] 971 9-10-5 **78**................................(b[1]) JamesBest
(Richard Hawker) *chsd ldr tl rdn after 9th: sn struggling in last pair: tailing off whn p.u after 13th* **50/1**
6UP0 **P** **Gale Force Oscar (IRE)**[7] 1069 10-11-5 **92**................................(bt[1]) GerardTumelty
(Sean Curran) *led: sn clr: hdd after 14th: wknd qckly next: p.u bef 16th* **22/1**
6m 49.5s (4.90) **Going Correction** +0.25s/f (Yiel) **9** Ran SP% **114.3**
Speed ratings (Par 103): **102,101,101,94,91 86,69,** ,
CSF £61.66 CT £294.49 TOTE £7.70: £2.80, £2.80, £1.80; EX 76.90 Trifecta £326.70.
Owner Glanvilles Stud Partners **Bred** Wriggle Valley Thoroughbreds **Trained** Piddletrenthide, Dorset
■ Stewards' Enquiry : Gavin Sheehan two-day ban: used whip above permitted level (Aug 12-13)

FOCUS
An ordinary handicap chase. A good gallop was set by Gale Force Oscar, who ran freely. The winner is on the upgrade, the second stepped up on his reappearance and the third is rated in line with her Irish form.

1119 NEWTONABBOTRACING.COM H'CAP HURDLE (9 hdls) 2m 2f 110y
3:45 (3:45) (Class 2) (0-150,141) 4-Y-0+
£11,573 (£3,418; £1,709; £854; £427; £214)

Form RPR
21-1 1 **Ittirad (USA)**[29] 854 7-11-12 **141**....................(p) AidanColeman 147+
(John Ferguson) *trckd ldrs: led 2 out: kpt on wl: pushed out* **7/2**[3]
0-40 2 *2* **Ballyglasheen (IRE)**[6] 812 5-10-10 **135**....................(p) LewisGordon(10) 139
(Evan Williams) *trckd ldrs: rdn after 3 out: wnt 2nd between last 2: kpt on but a being hld by wnr* **9/4**[1]
5441 3 *2 1/4* **Absolutlyfantastic**[8] 1055 8-10-2 **117** 7ex....................(t) RichardJohnson 120
(Martin Hill) *led: hit 2nd: rdn after 3 out: sn hdd: styd on same pce fr next* **5/2**[2]
603- 4 *4 1/2* **Low Key (IRE)**[116] 5113 8-10-9 **124**.................... TomScudamore 124
(David Pipe) *hld up wl in tch: trckd ldr after 5th: rdn to ld after 3 out: hdd whn mstke 2 out: fdd bef last* **8/1**
2341 5 *2 3/4* **Lava Lamp (GER)**[8] 1046 8-10-5 **120** 7ex....................(v) PaulMoloney 115
(Evan Williams) *trckd ldrs: pushed along after 5th: rdn and sltly detached in 5th after 3 out: styd on into 4th between last 2: nt pce to trble ldrs* **9/2**
0-P5 6 *52* **Massachusetts**[15] 977 8-10-0 **115** oh44....................(t) TrevorWhelan 64
(Rob Summers) *trckd ldr tl 5th: sn rdn: wknd next: t.o* **150/1**
4m 36.2s (6.20) **Going Correction** +0.50s/f (Soft) **6** Ran SP% **111.5**
Speed ratings (Par 109): **106,105,104,102,101 79**
CSF £11.95 TOTE £3.10: £1.60, £1.60; EX 12.30 Trifecta £33.40.
Owner Bloomfields **Bred** Darley **Trained** Cowlinge, Suffolk

FOCUS
The feature contest wasn't the strongest for the grade, with the top-weight/winner running from a mark 9lb below the ceiling. Nonetheless, there were a trio of recent winners present and the pace was decent. The third and fourth help set the level.

1120 NORTH DEVON HOSPICE H'CAP HURDLE (9 hdls) 2m 2f 110y
4:20 (4:20) (Class 5) (0-100,99) 3-Y-0+ **£3,422** (£997; £499)

Form RPR
F400 1 **Kentford Heiress**[20] 937 5-10-2 **82**.................... KevinJones(7) 94+
(Seamus Mullins) *mid-div: hdwy 6th: led appr 2 out: sn clr: easily* **5/1**[2]
P44- 2 *9* **Boher Lad (IRE)**[126] 4963 8-9-7 **73**.................... MrAlexEdwards(7) 75
(Alan Phillips) *mid-div: hdwy after 6th: rdn after 3 out: styd on fr next: snatched 2nd fnl strides: no ch w wnr* **15/2**
46-5 3 *nk* **Hold The Fort (IRE)**[42] 745 8-11-8 **95**....................(t) NoelFehily 98
(Johnny Farrelly) *mid-div: hdwy 6th: rdn in disp 2nd appr 2 out: nt pce to get on terms w wnr: no ex whn lost 2nd fnl strides* **11/1**
F0-4 4 *3* **Wojciech**[81] 167 5-11-3 **90**.................... GavinSheehan 89
(Martin Hill) *in tch: wnt 3rd after 5th: rdn after 3 out: styd on same pce fr next* **9/2**[1]
2-23 5 *6* **Spin Cast**[24] 892 7-11-5 **99**....................(t) JamieBargary(7) 93
(Alan Jones) *mid-div: hdwy 3 out: sn rdn: one pce fr next* **8/1**
502B 6 *2 1/4* **Mix N Match**[4] 1084 11-10-0 **73** oh1.................... RichieMcLernon 64
(Laura Young) *hld up towards rr: hdwy 3 out: rdn to chse ldrs bef 2 out: fdd bef last* **11/1**
560 7 *29* **Micras**[21] 932 4-11-3 **93**....................(v) RichardJohnson 51
(Tim Vaughan) *tended to jump lft at times: prom fr 2nd: led after 3 out: rdn and hdd bef next: wknd* **11/2**[3]
36/P P **Brannoc (IRE)**[81] 163 10-9-9 **73** oh4....................(t) AliceMills(5)
(Gail Haywood) *led tl 2nd: prom tl rdn after 4th: sn bhd: t.o whn p.u bef 6th* **40/1**
0/2- P **Ravens Nest**[336] 1331 5-11-7 **94**.................... NickScholfield
(Lawney Hill) *in tch: rdn after 6th: sn wknd: t.o whn p.u bef 2 out* **6/1**
5-0P P **Oscar Jane (IRE)**[40] 759 8-10-2 **75**....................(p) AlainCawley
(Johnny Farrelly) *led 2nd: rdn and hdd after 3 out: wknd qckly: p.u bef next* **20/1**
0U00 U **Innox Park**[21] 932 5-11-7 **94**....................(p) JamesBest
(Kevin Bishop) *hld up towards rr: awkward and uns rdr 2nd* **25/1**
-3P0 P **Fashion Icon (FR)**[50] 658 4-11-0 **90**....................(t) TomScudamore
(Nigel Hawke) *a towards rr: struggling 6th: t.o whn p.u bef 2 out* **16/1**
4m 40.8s (10.80) **Going Correction** +0.50s/f (Soft)
WFA 4 from 5yo+ 15lb **12** Ran SP% **121.0**
Speed ratings (Par 103): **97,93,93,91,89 88,76,,,**
CSF £42.63 CT £403.01 TOTE £5.70: £2.70, £3.60, £3.50; EX 56.00 Trifecta £1016.70.
Owner D I Bare **Bred** D I Bare **Trained** Wilsford-Cum-Lake, Wilts

FOCUS
Several unexposed types in an ordinary handicap for the grade. The pace was fair. The winner was potentially well in on her Towcester fall but this still rates a step up. The second and third set the level.

1121 PAIGNTON ZOO H'CAP CHASE (16 fncs) 2m 4f 216y
4:55 (4:55) (Class 5) (0-100,106) 4-Y-0+ **£3,422** (£997; £499)

Form RPR
0-63 1 **Dream Bolt (IRE)**[15] 976 7-11-9 **97**.................... PaulMoloney 113+
(David Rees) *trckd ldrs: wnt 2nd 9th: led sn after 2 out: pushed clr: easily* **2/1**[1]
3211 2 *10* **Zama Zama**[8] 1056 8-12-4 **106** 7ex....................(v) AdamWedge 111
(Evan Williams) *led: rdn and hdd after 2 out: sn hld* **7/2**[3]
465- 3 *6* **Matrow's Lady (IRE)**[106] 5287 8-11-3 **91**....................(tp) NoelFehily 91
(Neil Mulholland) *trckd ldrs: rdn in cl 3rd after 3 out: styd on same pce fr next* **3/1**[2]
24-B 4 *29* **Vering (FR)**[88] 31 9-10-3 **77**....................(t) MichealNolan 60
(Carroll Gray) *hld up: rdn in cl 4th after 3 out: wknd next* **12/1**
0P3- P **North London**[114] 5149 8-10-0 **74** oh4.................... JamesDavies
(Jimmy Frost) *hld up: struggling 7th: lost tch after 10th: t.o whn p.u bef 4 out* **9/1**
113/ P **Badgers Retreat**[793] 472 9-11-12 **100**.................... TomScudamore
(Nick Mitchell) *trckd ldr tl 9th: sn wknd: bhd whn p.u after next* **6/1**
5m 33.3s (11.90) **Going Correction** +0.25s/f (Yiel) **6** Ran SP% **112.5**
Speed ratings (Par 103): **87,83,80,69,**
CSF £9.74 TOTE £2.90: £1.40, £1.50; EX 9.10 Trifecta £26.40.
Owner D A Rees & N Adams **Bred** John Brennan **Trained** Clarbeston, Pembrokes

FOCUS
An average handicap in which Zama Zama took them along at a sensible gallop. The winner is on the upgrade, the second is rated in line with latest win, and the third posted a chase pb but was still below her old hurdles form.

1122 IRL INDEPENDENT RACECOURSES LTD INTERMEDIATE OPEN NATIONAL HUNT FLAT RACE 2m 167y
5:25 (5:26) (Class 5) 4-6-Y-O **£1,711** (£498; £249)

Form RPR
1 **Arthur Burrell** 6-11-0 0.................... JamesBest 99+
(Jackie Du Plessis) *hld up: hdwy 3f out: drifted rt 2f out: sn led: kpt on wl: rdn out* **28/1**
60- 2 *1* **Josie Jump**[199] 3604 6-10-7 0.................... TomO'Brien 91+
(Paul Henderson) *hld up: rdn and stdy prog fr 3f out: chsd ldrs over 1f out: styd on wl ins fnl f: wnt 2nd towards fin* **33/1**
3- 3 *1* **Wilde Oak (IRE)**[228] 3037 5-11-0 0....................(t) NoelFehily 97+
(Anthony Honeyball) *hld up: hdwy fr 3f out: rdn to ld briefly 2f out: ev ch ins fnl f: no ex fnl 75yds* **4/6**[1]
4 4 *3 3/4* **Junior Package**[38] 783 4-10-12 0.................... TomScudamore 91
(David Pipe) *trckd ldr: led 3f out tl rdn 2f out: kpt on same pce fnl f* **4/1**[2]
0 5 *1* **Airpur Desbois (FR)**[27] 865 5-11-0 0.................... GavinSheehan 92
(Charlie Mann) *hld up: pushed along over 6f out: rdn 3f out: styd on fnl 2f but nt pce to get on terms* **14/1**[3]
6 *12* **Black Kettle (IRE)** 5-11-0 0.................... KielanWoods 80
(Ronald Thompson) *trckd ldrs: rdn over 2f out: wknd over 1f out* **16/1**
7 *21* **Wy Worry (IRE)**[134] 5-10-11 0.................... KillianMoore(3) 59
(Mark Wall) *led tl 3f out: sn wknd* **28/1**
8 *15* **Good Rhythm** 5-11-0 0.................... TrevorWhelan 44
(Neil King) *trckd ldrs: pushed along over 6f out: wknd 3f out* **4/1**[2]
4m 10.0s (9.90) **Going Correction** +0.50s/f (Soft)
WFA 4 from 5yo+ 2lb **8** Ran SP% **122.4**
Speed ratings: **96,95,95,93,92 87,77,70**
CSF £681.83 TOTE £26.30: £7.90, £6.30, £1.10; EX 810.40 Trifecta £1753.80.
Owner Miss J Du Plessis **Bred** Miss J Du Plessis **Trained** Trehan, Cornwall

FOCUS
The concluding contest wasn't the strongest of bumpers and there was a shock result. It's rated around the balance of the third to fifth.
T/Plt: £121.00 to a £1 stake. Pool: £72978.09 - 440.02 winning tickets. T/Qpdt: £35.70 to a £1 stake. Pool: £6716.51 - 139.0 winning tickets. **Tim Mitchell**

1123 - 1125a (Foreign Racing) - See Raceform Interactive

957 PERTH (R-H)
Tuesday, July 28
1126 Meeting Abandoned - waterlogged

1079 WORCESTER (L-H)
Tuesday, July 28

OFFICIAL GOING: Good
Wind: light breeze Weather: sunny spells; 18 degrees

1133 WIDMER LTD, PERSHORE H'CAP CHASE (12 fncs) 2m 110y
5:35 (5:35) (Class 5) (0-100,96) 4-Y-0+ **£2,469** (£725; £362; £181)

Form RPR
2521 1 **Lord Lir (IRE)**[10] 1031 9-11-12 **96**....................(b) RichardJohnson 108+
(Tim Vaughan) *led and set decent pce: 10 l clr at 4th: rdn after 2 out: drvn to readily maintain 4 l advantage fr last* **3/1**[2]
-340 2 *3 3/4* **Chankillo**[37] 811 6-10-9 **79**.................... SamTwiston-Davies 87
(Sarah-Jayne Davies) *midfield: effrt 8th: 4 l 4th home turn: rdn 2 out: wnt 2nd at last but wnr a maintaining advantage* **16/1**
03P6 3 *13* **Toe To Toe (IRE)**[21] 937 7-10-8 **78**....................(t) RhysFlint 73
(John Flint) *chsd wnr: effrt after 8th: rdn and hld 2 out: lost 4 l 2nd at last and fin weakly* **7/4**[1]
2-3P 4 *1 1/2* **Red Rosso**[16] 976 10-10-7 **77**.................... TrevorWhelan 73
(Rob Summers) *midfield: hit 5th and 8th: nvr gng wl enough: 15 l 6th and btn home turn* **16/1**
05P3 5 *12* **Accessallareas (IRE)**[9] 1045 10-11-11 **95**.................... RobertDunne 80
(Sarah-Jayne Davies) *towards rr: effrt 8th: 6 l 4th home turn: rdn and fdd 3 out* **25/1**
-P0P 6 *11* **Midnight Thomas**[23] 918 6-10-13 **83**....................(t) AndrewTinkler 56
(Martin Keighley) *hit 4th: chsd ldrs tl rdn after 8th: fnd nil: 10 l 5th home turn: no ch after: t.o* **11/1**
5-P0 P **Tri Nations (UAE)**[23] 914 10-10-6 **79**....................(tp) JonathanEngland(3)
(Harriet Bethell) *lost pl and rdn 5th: nt keen after: t.o 8th: p.u next* **16/1**
0P0/ P **Grand Fella (IRE)**[686] 1547 10-9-7 **70** oh8....................(p) MissTWorsley(7)
(Ken Wingrove) *a in last: t.o 7th: p.u 3 out* **200/1**
-412 P **Mac's Grey (IRE)**[16] 964 8-10-10 **80**....................(t) WillKennedy
(Ian Williams) *prom in chsng gp tl lost pl 1/2-way: rdn 8th: t.o and p.u 3 out* **11/2**[3]
-45P P **Born To Benefit (IRE)**[21] 934 9-11-8 **92**.................... PaddyBrennan
(Fergal O'Brien) *nt jump wl in rr: blnd 3rd and 6th: struggling whn p.u next* **10/1**
4m 2.4s (-2.60) **Going Correction** -0.175s/f (Good) **10** Ran SP% **116.2**
Speed ratings (Par 103): **99,97,91,90,84 79,,,,**
CSF £47.75 CT £107.71 TOTE £2.50: £1.20, £3.70, £1.10; EX 43.40 Trifecta £235.60.
Owner Two Gents & An Orange Bloke Racing **Bred** Killian Lynch **Trained** Aberthin, Vale of Glamorgan

FOCUS
Both bends railed out from inner line and races 1, 3 & 7 increased by 36yds and races 2, 4, 5 &6 by 60yds. Richard Johnson called it "consistently good ground". A modest handicap chase in which the winner set a decent pace. The time was five seconds slower than the later 0-140 event. Lord Lir is rated in line with his recent win, with the second similar to his hurdles mark and the third 10lb+ off his recent hurdles form.

1134 MIDSHIRE COMMUNICATIONS BEGINNERS' CHASE (16 fncs) 2m 7f
6:05 (6:05) (Class 4) 4-Y-0+ **£3,898** (£1,144; £572; £286)

Form RPR
060/ 1 **Oscara Dara (IRE)**[843] 5175 10-11-7 0....................(p) NoelFehily 125+
(Neil Mulholland) *settled in midfield: effrt 13th: wnt 2nd bef 13th: did nt cl tl after last but styd on gamely to ld over 100yds out and readily asserted: dismntd sn after fin* **2/5**[1]

P-04 **2** *2* **Shantou Tiger (IRE)**[13] 1006 6-11-7 120 WayneHutchinson 118
(Donald McCain) *alternated in ld tl led bef 9th: rdn 3 out: 3 l clr at last: kpt on wl tl hdd and no ex fnl 100yds* **12/1**

P/24 **3** *24* **Amber Flush**[23] 913 6-10-7 0 MrJamesSmith(7) 90
(Martin Smith) *last whn hit 2nd: a bhd: rdn and struggling bef 13th: j.lft next: wnt poor 3rd bef last* **10/1**[3]

5 **4** *4 ½* **Cecile De Volanges**[9] 1044 7-10-7 0 MrRobertHawker(7) 85
(Ronald Harris) *cl up: wnt 2nd at 10th tl bef 13th: sn lost tch w ldng pair: plugged on in 3rd tl bef last* **33/1**

P **Turnover (FR)**[800] 8-11-4 0 (p) BenPoste(3)
(Alan Phillips) *j. slowly 3rd: nt travelling in rr: rdn fr 6th: t.o after 8th and p.u next* **66/1**

51-3 **P** **Garnock (IRE)**[13] 1006 7-11-0 116 TomScudamore
(David Bridgwater) *alternated in ld tl hdd bef 9th: lost 2nd at next: sn struggling: t.o and p.u 13th* **4/1**[2]

P **Kerry Mganga**[58] 9-11-7 0 (t) TomO'Brien
(Robert Stephens) *j. sltly rt and nt a fluent: dropped bk last and blnd 9th: t.o and p.u sn after 12th* **40/1**

5m 49.5s (-0.40) **Going Correction** -0.175s/f (Good) **7** Ran SP% **115.1**
Speed ratings (Par 105): **93,92,83,82,** ,
CSF £6.65 TOTE £1.60: £1.10, £3.20; EX 7.00 Trifecta £26.60.
Owner BG Racing Partnership **Bred** Tom And P Phelan **Trained** Limpley Stoke, Wilts

FOCUS
They went a steady pace in this beginners' chase. It lacked depth, but the winner is pretty useful. He was a 150+ hurdler, the second is rated similar to his hurdles mark and the third was again well below her Market Rasen mark.

1135 PERSHORE PLUM FESTIVAL LAND O'PLUMS H'CAP CHASE (12 fncs) 2m 110y
6:35 (6:35) (Class 3) (0-140,139) 4-Y-O £6,330 (£1,870; £935; £468; £234)

Form RPR

5-11 **1** **Strongly Suggested**[73] 338 8-10-11 124 RichardJohnson 130+
(Jonjo O'Neill) *settled trcking ldrs: effrt after 8th: led sn after 3 out: rdn and grad forged clr fr next* **2/1**[1]

2264 **2** *7* **My Brother Sylvest**[16] 974 9-11-10 137 (b) TomScudamore 136
(David Pipe) *led: rdn after 8th: hdd sn after 3 out: wl hld by wnr fr next but clr of rest* **13/2**

1-55 **3** *10* **Witness In Court (IRE)**[30] 849 8-11-12 139 WayneHutchinson 128
(Donald McCain) *prom: ev ch 9th: rdn and qckly lost tch w ldng pair next: plodded on* **9/1**

4211 **4** *3* **Red Seventy**[16] 974 6-10-11 124 JackQuinlan 111
(Sarah Humphrey) *chsd ldrs tl rdn after 8th: btn next: mod 4th whn mstke last* **4/1**[2]

-016 **5** *3 ¾* **Another Flutter (IRE)**[16] 974 11-11-4 138 (tp) MrStanSheppard(7) 121
(Matt Sheppard) *towards rr: rdn fr 7th: styd on one pce wout threatening fr 9th* **12/1**

-423 **6** *22* **Un Anjou (FR)**[65] 456 7-10-10 123 NoelFehily 85
(David Dennis) *pressed ldr tl 8th: dropped out v tamely bef next: t.o* **9/2**[3]

1P1- **7** *49* **Fairyinthewind (IRE)**[22] 1405 6-10-9 122 (t) BrendanPowell 40
(Brendan Powell) *chsd ldrs on outer: losing pl whn nt fluent 5th: in last and rdn 8th: t.o whn blnd last* **11/1**

3m 57.5s (-7.50) **Going Correction** -0.175s/f (Good) **7** Ran SP% **110.9**
Speed ratings (Par 107): **110,106,102,100,98 88,65**
CSF £14.42 TOTE £2.70: £1.80, £2.80; EX 15.00 Trifecta £48.70.
Owner John P McManus **Bred** David Brace **Trained** Cheltenham, Gloucs

FOCUS
This decent summer handicap was run at a solid gallop, and in a time almost five seconds quicker than the earlier 0-100 handicap chase. This was another step forward from the winner, with the second 3lb off his best.

1136 PICKLED PLUM PUB PERSHORE "NATIONAL HUNT" NOVICES' HURDLE (10 hdls) 2m 4f
7:05 (7:05) (Class 4) 4-Y-O+ £3,249 (£954; £477; £238)

Form RPR

103/ **1** **Werenearlyoutofit (IRE)**[623] 2432 7-10-12 0 KielanWoods 119+
(Graeme McPherson) *str: midfield in slow r: effrt 3 out: chal next: led last: rdn to steadily draw clr after* **5/1**[3]

-F51 **2** *4 ½* **Uncle Tone (IRE)**[13] 1011 6-11-5 116 MichealNolan 120+
(Tim Vaughan) *settled in last pair: 5 l 6th home turn: sn rdn w little rspnse: stl 4th at last: plugged into 2nd flat but no ch w wnr* **11/4**[1]

044- **3** *5* **Sky Watch (IRE)**[126] 4977 8-10-12 114 (t) RichardJohnson 108
(Brian Barr) *led at mod pce: rdn and jnd whn nt fluent 2 out: hdd last: sn btn and lost 2nd flat* **15/2**

2-14 **4** *5* **Popping Along**[46] 714 6-10-9 110 (tp) MattGriffiths(3) 103
(Jeremy Scott) *cl up: effrt 3 out: rdn next: ev ch bef last: sn btn* **11/4**[1]

5 *4 ½* **Mollyanna (IRE)**[69] 409 6-10-12 110 BrendanPowell 98
(Jamie Snowden) *chser type: trckd ldrs: rdn bef 3 out: no ex between last 2: wknd flat* **3/1**[2]

311- **6** *25* **Try Catch Me (IRE)**[279] 1994 10-10-12 101 LeightonAspell 73
(Alison Batchelor) *pressed ldr: rdn and losing pl whn mstke 2 out: eased and t.o* **20/1**

5/00 **7** *3 ½* **Sovinnie (IRE)**[5] 1082 6-10-7 0 ConorRing(5) 69
(Jane Mathias) *midfield: rdn bef 3 out: sn struggling: t.o whn blnd next* **100/1**

6-6 **8** *76* **Appropriate (FR)**[84] 120 5-10-5 0 MarkGrant
(Dominic Ffrench Davis) *hld up in last: lost tch wl bef 3 out: sn bdly t.o* **100/1**

4m 53.4s (-0.10) **Going Correction** +0.025s/f (Yiel) **8** Ran SP% **113.5**
Speed ratings (Par 105): **101,99,97,95,93 83,82,51**
CSF £19.27 TOTE £8.50: £1.90, £1.10, £4.40; EX 20.30 Trifecta £148.10.
Owner The Ladies Of Martins Hill **Bred** John O'Callaghan **Trained** Upper Oddington, Gloucs

FOCUS
They went just a steady initial gallop in this modest novice hurdle. The winner is rated in line with his 2013 form, with the second probably still on the upgrade and the third close to his mark.

1137 ANGEL HOTEL PERSHORE PENSHAM (S) HURDLE (10 hdls) 2m 4f
7:35 (7:35) (Class 5) 4-7-Y-O £2,274 (£667; £333; £166)

Form RPR

35-0 **1** **Hazzaat (IRE)**[9] 1055 5-10-12 111 TrevorWhelan 103
(Rob Summers) *settled in 3rd or 4th: outpcd and looked struggling bef 6th: plugged on fr 2 out: 8 l 3rd at last: kpt gng steadily to overtake reluctant rivals flat and drvn ahd 50yds out* **9/2**[3]

-P4P **2** *½* **Experimentalist**[21] 934 7-10-12 99 (vt) MichaelByrne 103
(Tim Vaughan) *chsd ldr: nt fluent 7th: sn upsides tl rdn bef 3 out: little rspnse: 5 l 2nd at last: sn hung lft: lft in front 100yds out but doing nthing and jst ct* **10/1**

5644 **3** *3 ½* **Kyles Faith (IRE)**[13] 1010 7-10-12 97 (p) RichardJohnson 102+
(Martin Keighley) *led: 5 l clr tl rdn fr bef 5th: began to draw clr again fr 3 out: 5 l l ahd last: reluctant u.p and sn veered rt: hdd 100yds out and nt run on* **15/8**[1]

3-52 **4** *27* **Regal One (IRE)**[22] 929 7-10-7 101 JakeHodson(5) 75
(David Bridgwater) *hld up in last: pushed along and lost tch bef 6th: t.o 3 out* **2/1**[2]

6 **5** *16* **Aza Run (IRE)**[30] 852 5-10-9 107 (t) ConorShoemark(3) 60
(Fergal O'Brien) *settled in 3rd or 4th: rdn and lost tch qckly bef 3 out: t.o last at last* **8/1**

4m 51.2s (-2.30) **Going Correction** +0.025s/f (Yiel) **5** Ran SP% **106.5**
Speed ratings: **105,104,103,92,86**
CSF £36.07 TOTE £3.90: £2.40, £5.00; EX 26.90 Trifecta £60.80.The winner was bought by C Coley for 4200 gns.
Owner C R Taylor **Bred** Tribesmen Syndicate **Trained** Tanworth-in-Arden, Warwicks
■ Stewards' Enquiry : Michael Byrne six-day ban: used whip above permitted level without giving gelding time to respond (Aug 12-13,15-16,19-20)

FOCUS
Not a strong seller, but it was run at a decent gallop. The winner rated below best in slow-motion finish, with the second setting the level.

1138 TIDDESLEY WOOD YELLOW EGG PLUM H'CAP HURDLE (12 hdls) 2m 7f
8:05 (8:05) (Class 3) (0-140,136) 4-Y-O+ £5,393 (£1,583; £791; £395)

Form RPR

5-53 **1** **On The Bridge (IRE)**[34] 833 10-11-3 127 (tp) NickScholfield 135+
(Jeremy Scott) *hld up in last but gng wl: effrt and n.m.r bef 3 out: wnt 3rd next: taken rt to ld bef last: idling but sn clr flat: styd on wl* **9/2**[3]

2523 **2** *5* **Cut The Corner (IRE)**[23] 917 7-10-10 120 WillKennedy 122
(Dr Richard Newland) *trckd ldrs: wnt prom 8th: gng wl whn disp ld after next: rdn and hanging between last two: hdd bef last and sn outpcd* **7/1**

F-30 **3** *3 ¾* **Terminal (FR)**[23] 916 8-11-3 127 (p) NoelFehily 126
(David Dennis) *settled towards rr: pushed along 7th: drvn after next: outpcd 3 out: styd on after last wout threatening: tk wl btn 3rd cl home* **33/1**

-453 **4** *¾* **Georgian King**[21] 939 12-9-4 110 oh2 (p) ArchieBellamy(10) 108
(Martin Keighley) *t.k.h: led at stdy pce: rdn after 9th: hdd bef next: styd on same pce wout threatening fr 2 out: mstke last* **12/1**

-05P **5** *nk* **First Fandango**[23] 916 8-11-6 130 (t) MichaelByrne 127
(Tim Vaughan) *pressed ldr tl rdn after 9th: one pce and no imp fr bef 2 out* **50/1**

0-11 **6** *shd* **Royale Django (IRE)**[52] 641 6-11-1 125 RichardJohnson 123
(Tim Vaughan) *prom: effrt to dispute ld bef 3 out: rdn and hdd bef last: no ex: lost three pls cl home* **2/1**[1]

-634 **7** *36* **Dawn Commander (GER)**[23] 916 8-11-12 136 (p) BrendanPowell 100
(Stuart Edmunds) *chsd ldrs tl rdn and racd awkwardly bef 7th: sn lost tch: t.o* **10/1**

1F-4 **F** **Fort Worth (IRE)**[27] 876 6-11-1 125 DougieCostello
(Jonjo O'Neill) *hld up and t.k.h in rr tl stmbld and fell after 5th* **5/2**[2]

5m 38.0s (-0.60) **Going Correction** +0.025s/f (Yiel) **8** Ran SP% **114.3**
Speed ratings (Par 107): **102,100,98,98,98 98,86,**
CSF £35.45 CT £916.81 TOTE £7.00: £1.70, £2.00, £4.20; EX 22.20 Trifecta £393.50.
Owner Kit James **Bred** J & D Melody **Trained** Brompton Regis, Somerset

FOCUS
The pace increased with a circuit to run in this decent handicap hurdle. The winner had slipped to a good mark, the second posted a small pb and the third was well in on old form. There's a case for this being a bit higher through the fourth.

1139 SKETTS QUALITY EVENTS SKETTS.CO.UK "NATIONAL HUNT" MAIDEN HURDLE (8 hdls) 2m
8:35 (8:35) (Class 5) 4-Y-O+ £2,274 (£667; £333; £166)

Form RPR

-224 **1** **Canicallyouback**[22] 932 7-11-0 120 PaulMoloney 118+
(Evan Williams) *pressed ldr gng wl: led on bit 2 out: edgd rt and lft bef last where 12 l ahd: hrd hld* **8/15**[1]

4P-3 **2** *14* **Cousin Guillaume (FR)**[9] 1054 6-11-0 103 (b) NoelFehily 99
(Donald McCain) *led: blnd bdly 2nd: set mod pce: shkn up bef 3rd: rdn and hdd 2 out: sn btn: mstke last: all out to hold poor 2nd* **11/4**[2]

/6-5 **3** *1 ¼* **Howaboutnever (IRE)**[21] 933 7-11-0 0 WillKennedy 98
(Ian Williams) *in last pair: outpcd and rdn whn blnd 5th: last bef 3 out: wnt poor 3rd cl home* **11/2**[3]

00- **4** *½* **Scartare (IRE)**[141] 4679 4-10-9 0 BenPoste(3) 94
(Rosemary Gasson) *unruly in preliminaries: mstkes in last: nrly 15 l fr ldr at 3rd: effrt in 3rd bef 3 out: rdn next: tried to chal for poor 2nd whn yet anther mstke last: no ex flat and jst lost 3rd* **66/1**

3m 50.1s (-0.50) **Going Correction** +0.025s/f (Yiel)
WFA 4 from 6yo+ 15lb **4** Ran SP% **108.8**
Speed ratings (Par 103): **102,95,94,94**
CSF £2.44 TOTE £1.40; EX 2.30 Trifecta £2.40.
Owner Mrs D E Cheshire **Bred** Charles And David Hodge **Trained** Llancarfan, Vale Of Glamorgan

FOCUS
The favourite set a decent standard and proved much too good in this weakly contested maiden hurdle.
T/Plt: £122.10 to a £1 stake. Pool of £76947.47 - 459.70 winning tickets. T/Qpdt: £83.80 to a £1 stake. Pool of £7735.24 - 68.30 winning tickets. **Iain Mackenzie**

1140 - 1141a (Foreign Racing) - See Raceform Interactive

957 PERTH (R-H)
Wednesday, July 29
1142 Meeting Abandoned - waterlogged

1149 - (Foreign Racing) - See Raceform Interactive

1140
GALWAY (R-H)
Wednesday, July 29

OFFICIAL GOING: Jumps courses - good; flat course - yielding (yielding to soft in places)

1150a DOWNLOAD THE TOTE MOBILE APP EUROPEAN BREEDERS FUND MARES H'CAP HURDLE (9 hdls) 2m
3:35 (3:35) 4-Y-0+ £10,581 (£3,093; £1,465; £488)

RPR

1 **Lilly The Lioness (IRE)**[10] 1061 8-11-2 108 .... MarkEnright 120
(Garrett James Power, Ire) *chsd ldrs: nt fluent 3rd: pushed along bef 2 out and clsd u.p on outer to ead between last 2: kpt on wl fr last and edgd rt run-in: all out* 8/1[2]

2 1 1/4 **Crystal Earth (IRE)**[27] 766 8-10-13 105 .... RWalsh 116+
(Peter Fahey, Ire) *hld up: hdwy fr 3 out to chse ldrs on outer bef next: rdn in 3rd bef last and wnt 2nd u.p run-in: kpt on wl towards fin to press wnr: hld* 11/2[1]

3 5 1/2 **Damefirth (IRE)**[12] 1025 6-11-3 116 .... DylanRobinson(7) 121
(Henry De Bromhead, Ire) *sltly hmpd s: hld up: hdwy on outer to chse ldrs after 3 out: led narrowly fr next tl hdd between last 2: no ex u.p in 3rd fr after last: kpt on one pce to jst hold 3rd* 11/2[1]

4 shd **Give Her Bach (IRE)**[13] 1017 6-10-8 105 ....(t) PierceGallagher(5) 110
(Patrick Cronin, Ire) *chsd ldrs: cl up bhd ldrs bef 2 out: lost pl and rdn in 7th after 2 out and no imp on ldrs bef last: kpt on u.p into 4th run-in: jst hld for 3rd* 11/1

5 3/4 **Colla Pier (IRE)**[27] 890 6-10-7 99 .... RobertDunne 103
(Patrick Mooney, Ire) *mid-div: pushed along in 10th after 2 out and clsd u.p fr last where nt fluent into mod 5th cl home: nvr trbld ldrs* 14/1

6 1 1/2 **Dazzling Susie (IRE)**[15] 996 10-11-8 114 .... DannyMullins 117
(John F Phelan, Ire) *led: jnd bef 1/2-way and hdd bef 4 out: remained prom tl rdn after 2 out and no imp on ldrs bef last: one pce run-in* 20/1

7 1 **Blackandamber Vic (IRE)**[8] 1074 8-9-6 89 ow2........(t) ShaneShortall(5) 91
(Norman Lee, Ire) *chsd ldrs: rdn in 6th after 2 out and no imp on ldrs fr last: kpt on one pce* 12/1

8 4 **Lost Book (IRE)**[8] 1076 7-10-3 95 ....(tp) RobbieColgan 93
(S J Mahon, Ire) *mid-div: tk clsr order bhd ldrs fr 3 out: rdn in 8th after next and no imp on ldrs bef last where mstke: one pce run-in* 10/1[3]

9 nk **The Nutcracker (IRE)**[40] 784 5-11-9 115 .... AELynch 112
(Thomas Gibney, Ire) *hld up in rr of mid-div: hdwy fr 3 out to chse ldrs bef next where short of room on inner: rdn in 9th after 2 out and no imp on ldrs bef fr last: one pce run-in* 12/1

10 1 3/4 **Queen Matilda (IRE)**[12] 1024 4-9-7 94 oh1........ ConorMaxwell(3) 84
(Donal Kinsella, Ire) *rrd and lost grnd s: settled towards rr: tk clsr order after 1/2-way: mstke in 11th after 2 out and rdn: no imp on ldrs bef last: kpt on one pce* 40/1

11 1/2 **Supreme Vic (IRE)**[8] 1074 9-11-2 113 .... AdamO'Neill(5) 108
(Norman Lee, Ire) *chsd ldr tl disp at 1/2-way: led narrowly bef 4 out where slt mstke: mstke 2 out and hdd: sn wknd* 8/1[2]

12 15 **Anotherlady (IRE)**[105] 5348 7-10-2 94 ....(bt[1]) JJBurke 74
(J P Dempsey, Ire) *towards rr: no imp bef 2 out: kpt on one pce fr last* 33/1

13 7 **Annagh Haven (IRE)**[5] 5036 5-11-0 109 ....(t) LPDempsey(3) 82
(Michael Mulvany, Ire) *in rr of mid-div: pushed along in 11th after 3 out and no ex u.p bef next* 20/1

14 4 3/4 **Madaboy Cross (IRE)**[16] 986 5-10-0 99 .... JonathanMoore(7) 67
(Thomas P O'Connor, Ire) *chsd ldrs: rdn and wknd after 3 out* 50/1

15 18 **I'm All You Need (IRE)**[42] 762 5-11-1 114 .... JackKennedy(7) 64
(Paul Nolan, Ire) *mid-div best: rdn and no imp towards rr bef 2 out* 11/2[1]

16 18 **Havana Dancer (IRE)**[56] 607 6-10-10 102 ow2........ JohnCullen 34
(Anthony John Black, Ire) *chsd ldrs early: dropped to mid-div at 1/2-way: rdn bef 4 out and no ex: wknd next: t.o* 25/1

P **Red Four**[80] 236 5-11-8 114 ....(p) AndrewTinkler
(George Baker) *hld up: in rr and detached whn hmpd at 5th: t.o whn p.u bef 3 out* 25/1

F **Catimini (IRE)**[12] 1025 7-11-4 110 ....(b) KevinSexton
(Sean Byrne, Ire) *mid-div: 10th whn fell 5th* 33/1

3m 50.7s (-6.00)
WFA 4 from 5yo+ 15lb **18 Ran SP% 135.3**
CSF £52.25 CT £280.34 TOTE £9.50: £2.30, £1.40, £2.20, £3.00; DF 54.20 Trifecta £391.80.
Owner P McCarthy **Bred** P McCarthy **Trained** Windgap, Co. Kilkenny

FOCUS
A race that didn't really change complexion that much, even given that it was a very competitive handicap hurdle, but when it did change complexion it happened quickly and decisively.

1151a - (Foreign Racing) - See Raceform Interactive

1152a THETOTE.COM GALWAY PLATE (HANDICAP CHASE) (GRADE A) (14 fncs) 2m 6f 111y
5:30 (5:32) 4-Y-0+ £102,480 (£32,558; £15,503; £5,271; £3,565; £1,860)

RPR

1 **Shanahan's Turn (IRE)**[15] 996 7-10-10 142 .... JJBurke 154+
(Henry De Bromhead, Ire) *chsd ldrs: clsr in 2nd bef 2nd: nt fluent next and lost pl: clsr in 2nd again after 6th and led bef 5 out: extended advantage fr next: nt fluent 2 out where reduced ld: styd on wl u.p run-in: eased cl home* 16/1

2 5 1/2 **The Paparrazi Kid (IRE)**[243] 2793 8-10-8 140 .... PaulTownend 146
(W P Mullins, Ire) *led tl jnd after 3rd and hdd next: bad mstke in 2nd at 5th: 4th bef 5 out: rdn into 2nd fr last and no imp on wnr into st: kpt on same pce clsng stages to jst hold 2nd* 12/1

3 1/2 **Sadler's Risk (IRE)**[91] 20 7-10-8 140 .... AELynch 145
(Henry De Bromhead, Ire) *chsd ldrs: hmpd bef last: rdn in 3rd after last and no imp on wnr into st: kpt on same pce clsng stages: jst hld for 2nd* 16/1

4 hd **Alderwood (IRE)**[114] 5224 11-10-10 142 .... NiallPMadden 147+
(Thomas Mullins, Ire) *settled in mid-div: prog bef 2 out and wnt 5th u.p fr last: no imp on wnr u.p in 4th clsng stages: kpt on* 20/1

5 3 3/4 **Shanpallas (IRE)**[56] 603 7-10-13 145 .... BarryGeraghty 146
(C Byrnes, Ire) *mid-div: nt fluent 6th: sme hdwy after 3 out to chse ldrs in 5th bef next: hmpd bef last and rdn in 6th after last: kpt on one pce run-in: nt trble wnr* 6/1[2]

6 hd **Alelchi Inois (FR)**[19] 948 7-11-1 147 .... RWalsh 148
(W P Mullins, Ire) *hld up: 11th after 3 out: rdn in 8th after last and kpt on u.p into mod 6th fnl strides: nvr nrr* 7/2[1]

7 hd **Perfect Gentleman (IRE)**[52] 664 10-10-7 139 .... DJCasey 140
(W P Mullins, Ire) *in tch: rdn in 11th after 3 out and no imp on ldrs in 9th after last: kpt on u.p clsng stages: nvr nrr* 25/1

8 3 3/4 **Savello (IRE)**[56] 603 9-11-5 154 .... DavidMullins(3) 151
(A J Martin, Ire) *chsd ldrs: mstke 4th: nt fluent 7th: 6th after 3 out: rdn in 4th after last and no imp on wnr into st where wknd* 20/1

9 2 **It's A Gimme (IRE)**[11] 1040 8-10-8 140 ....(t) RobbiePower 135
(Jonjo O'Neill) *in rr of mid-div: tk clsr order in 8th bef 2 out: rdn and no ex after last: kpt on one pce* 20/1

10 7 **Letter Of Credit (IRE)**[80] 234 10-10-8 140 .... RobbieColgan 128
(James Joseph Mangan, Ire) *hld up towards rr: hmpd 1st and 2nd: rdn after 3 out and no imp whn mstke 2 out: kpt on one pce run-in* 18/1

11 1 1/4 **Marito (GER)**[86] 116 9-10-11 143 ....(p) APHeskin 130
(C A McBratney, Ire) *mid-div: rdn and no imp bef 2 out* 25/1

12 30 **Spring Heeled (IRE)**[109] 5275 8-11-1 147 ....(v[1]) BrianO'Connell 104
(J H Culloty, Ire) *in tch: wknd bef 5 out where slt mstke: hmpd bef last: kpt on one pce run-in* 16/1

13 3/4 **Boston Bob (IRE)**[91] 22 10-11-10 156 .... MrPWMullins 112
(W P Mullins, Ire) *a bhd: mstke 1st: rdn in rr fr 5 out and no imp fr next* 16/1

14 2 1/4 **Texas Jack (IRE)**[80] 234 9-11-2 151 ....(p) GerFox(3) 105
(Noel Meade, Ire) *w.w towards rr: bdly hmpd 2nd: slt mstke 5 out: sme hdwy bef next: no ex in 12th fr 2 out: wknd run-in* 25/1

15 8 **Rathlin**[40] 789 10-10-7 142 ....(t) LPDempsey(3) 88
(M F Morris, Ire) *chsd ldrs: 3rd bef 5 out: rdn and wknd after 3 out: t.o* 25/1

16 7 **Baily Green (IRE)**[56] 604 9-11-4 150 ....(tp) MarkEnright 89
(M F Morris, Ire) *chsd ldrs: clsr in 2nd after 3rd and led next: hdd bef 5 out: rdn and wknd after 3 out: t.o* 25/1

17 6 **Jacksonslady (IRE)**[90] 47 10-10-9 141 ....(p) MarkWalsh 74
(J P Dempsey, Ire) *mid-div: rdn and no ex bef 2 out: wknd run-in: t.o* 10/1

F **Foildubh (IRE)**[9] 603 11-10-3 140 .... RyanTreacy(5)
(John Patrick Ryan, Ire) *in rr of mid-div: hmpd 1st: fell 2nd: fatally injured* 50/1

F **Colour Squadron (IRE)**[139] 4716 9-10-11 143 .... AndrewJMcNamara
(E Bolger, Ire) *in rr of mid-div: fell 2nd* 12/1

U **Make A Track (IRE)**[56] 604 9-10-12 144 ....(tp) MPFogarty
(Gordon Elliott, Ire) *hld up in rr of mid-div: mstke and uns rdr 1st: fatally injured* 16/1

S **Rule The World**[88] 95 8-10-12 144 ....(p) DavyRussell
(M F Morris, Ire) *chsd ldrs: slt mstke 5 out: wnt 2nd after 3 out: ev ch whn stmbld and slipped up bef last* 8/1[3]

F **Indevan**[19] 948 7-10-12 144 .... DannyMullins
(W P Mullins, Ire) *chsd ldrs: fell 1st* 25/1

5m 22.3s (-17.70) **22 Ran SP% 146.1**
CSF £199.23 CT £3204.33 TOTE £21.70: £7.30, £2.80, £5.60, £7.70; DF 297.20 Trifecta £4408.00.
Owner Ann & Alan Potts Partnership **Bred** Bluegate Stud **Trained** Knockeen, Co Waterford

FOCUS
Beautiful jumping ground for a renewal that seemed up to scratch, even if precious few of the runners appeared capable of improving much beyond the ratings they have. Very little got into it and there were plenty of early casualties. The form is rated around the first six.

1051
STRATFORD (L-H)
Thursday, July 30

OFFICIAL GOING: Good to soft (good in places) changing to good (good to soft in places) after race 2 (2.10)
Wind: Light across Weather: Cloudy with sunny periods

1153 BHEST RACING TO SCHOOLS MAIDEN HURDLE (9 hdls) 2m 2f 148y
1:40 (1:40) (Class 5) 4-Y-0+ £3,119 (£915; £457; £228)

Form RPR

3232 1 **Hepijeu (FR)**[15] 1008 4-11-0 116 ....(tp) AidanColeman 119+
(Charlie Longsdon) *led to 1st: chsd ldr tl led again 4th: clr fr 6th: mstke 3 out: in n.d after* 2/1[2]

4 2 6 **Panis Angelicus (FR)**[36] 834 6-11-3 0 .... RichardJohnson 113
(Tim Vaughan) *hld up: mstke 3 out: hdwy after next: wnt 2nd and hit last: no ch w wnr* 11/1

0-66 3 8 **Mr McGuiness (IRE)**[24] 932 5-11-0 0 .... BenPoste(3) 104
(Rosemary Gasson) *hld up: hdwy after 6th: chsd wnr who was clr 2 out tl wknd appr last* 33/1

33 4 3 1/4 **Presenting Streak (IRE)**[11] 1052 6-10-10 0 .... MrRWinks(7) 101+
(Peter Winks) *sn bhd: r.o flat: nvr nrr* 20/1

60-3 5 2 1/4 **Little Windmill (IRE)**[15] 999 5-11-3 0 .... TrevorWhelan 99
(Neil King) *chsd ldrs: wnt 2nd 3 out tl next: sn rdn and wknd* 18/1

325- 6 5 **Surf In September (IRE)**[266] 2307 6-10-10 0 .... MarkGrant 87
(Dominic Ffrench Davis) *hld up: hdwy 6th: rdn and wknd appr 2 out* 66/1

00 7 14 **Everlasting Spring (IRE)**[61] 554 7-11-3 0 ....(t) AlainCawley 82
(Johnny Farrelly) *mid-div: pckd 4th: rdn 3 out: wknd next* 20/1

44/ 8 37 **Hustle (IRE)**[1751] 1832 10-10-10 0 .... FreddieMitchell(7) 49
(Clare Hobson) *prom: j.rt 5th: rdn appr 3 out: sn wknd* 66/1

P-5 9 7 **Iwanabebobbiesgirl**[11] 1052 5-10-10 0 ....[1] LiamTreadwell 35
(David Brace) *plld hrd: led 1st tl 4th: wknd after 6th* 150/1

33 10 6 **Fauve (IRE)**[24] 932 4-11-0 114 .... RichieMcLernon 34
(Paul Webber) *prom: chsd ldr after 5th tl 3 out: wknd bef next* 13/2[3]

36- U **Swivel**[204] 3567 4-10-7 0 .... MrAlexFerguson(7)
(John Ferguson) *mid-div: nt clr run: blnd and uns rdr 5th* 6/4[1]

26 P **Kendari King (IRE)**[11] 1050 4-11-0 0 .... MichaelByrne
(Tim Vaughan) *sn bhd: j. slowly 1st: p.u bef 3 out* 66/1

4m 22.6s (-8.90) **Going Correction** -0.40s/f (Good)
WFA 4 from 5yo+ 15lb **12 Ran SP% 117.9**
Speed ratings (Par 103): **102,99,96,94,93 91,85,70,67,64**
CSF £22.31 TOTE £2.60: £1.10, £3.10, £7.40; EX 17.80 Trifecta £1185.40.
Owner Countrywide Vehicle Rentals Taxi Hire **Bred** Mlle Francoise Perree **Trained** Over Norton, Oxon

The Form Book Jumps 2015-16, Raceform Ltd, Newbury, RG14 5SJ

FOCUS
Split bends just off inner line and race 1 increased by 51yds, races 2 & 4 by 42yds, race 3 by 60yds, race 5 by 39yds race 6 by 66yds and race 7 by 48yds. At the overnight stage, the going was given as good to soft, soft in places but by the second race that had been revised to good, good to soft in places. The betting suggested that this maiden hurdle concerned only three, but one of those disappointed and another failed to complete. The pace seemed sound from the outset, with quite a few getting behind early. The third and fourth are probably the best guide.

1154 BIDVEST FOODSERVICE (S) HURDLE (8 hdls) 2m 70y
2:10 (2:10) (Class 5) 4-7-Y-0 £2,274 (£667; £333; £166)

Form RPR
612 1 **Swampfire (IRE)**[15] 1001 7-11-3 112 JamesBanks(3) 111
(Barry Brennan) *chsd ldr 2nd: led after 2 out: rdn and hdd bef last: rallied to ld towards fin* 5/2[2]
50P- 2 *nk* **Clock On Tom**[121] 5088 5-11-0 104 JackQuinlan 105
(Denis Quinn) *a.p: led appr last: rdn flat: hdd towards fin* 20/1
34-1 3 *3 1/4* **Roja Dove (IRE)**[15] 1001 6-10-13 119 (v) TrevorWhelan 102
(Neil King) *chsd ldr tl nt fluent 2nd: remained handy: rdn and ev ch appr last: no ex flat* 6/5[1]
0- 4 *4 1/2* **Idlewild**[38] 817 5-11-3 119 (t) DerekFox(3) 104
(Mark Michael McNiff, Ire) *bhd: hdwy after 2 out: rdn appr last: hung lft and wknd flat* 9/1
-524 5 *13* **Regal One (IRE)**[2] 1137 7-10-9 101 (bt[1]) JakeHodson(5) 88
(David Bridgwater) *led and sn clr: j.rt 4th: c bk to the field next: j.rt 2 out: sn hdd: wknd wl bef last* 9/2[3]
-P60 6 *72* **Captain Starlight (IRE)**[39] 811 5-11-0 73 LeeEdwards 22
(Aytach Sadik) *a bhd: rdn and lost tch bef 3 out* 200/1
3m 49.0s (-7.00) **Going Correction** -0.40s/f (Good) 6 Ran SP% **107.5**
Speed ratings: **101,100,99,96,90 54**
CSF £35.85 TOTE £4.20: £1.90, £6.10; EX 36.90 Trifecta £69.20.
Owner F J Brennan **Bred** Kilboy Estate **Trained** Upper Lambourn, Berks
FOCUS
Considering official figures, this was a pretty decent race for the level. The first two were close to their marks, with the third similar to her recent win but again well below best.

1155 ARTHUR J GALLAGHER GEORGE BURROWS H'CAP CHASE (17 fncs) 2m 6f 125y
2:45 (2:45) (Class 5) (0-100,100) 4-Y-0+ £2,599 (£763; £381; £190)

Form RPR
3-12 1 **Moorlands George**[57] 600 7-11-3 91 (t) NicodeBoinville 102+
(Jeremy Scott) *w ldr tl led 7th: hdd 9th: led again 11th: rdn appr last: styd on u.p* 15/8[1]
0044 2 *1 3/4* **Provincial Pride (IRE)**[42] 770 8-10-12 96 (tp) CharlieHammond(10) 106
(Mike Hammond) *a.p: chsd wnr after 11th: mstke 14th: sn rdn: styd on same pce flat* 10/1
5-13 3 *nk* **Croco Mister (IRE)**[11] 1053 8-10-7 84 (t) BenPoste(3) 92
(Rosemary Gasson) *hld up: hdwy 9th: rdn appr 2 out: styd on towards fin* 10/3[2]
6331 4 *6* **Pistol Basc (FR)**[18] 972 11-11-0 91 TonyKelly(3) 94
(Rebecca Menzies) *chsd ldrs: rdn appr 2 out: styd on same pce appr last* 6/1
1-53 5 *25* **Tribal Dance (IRE)**[67] 454 9-11-2 90 (p) DaveCrosse 71
(John O'Shea) *led to 7th: pushed along and led again 9th: hdd 11th: sn rdn: wkng whn j.lft 13th* 20/1
463- 6 *1 3/4* **Xenophon**[301] 1695 7-9-9 74 oh2 AliceMills(5) 53
(Michael Chapman) *hld up: hdwy and nt fluent 13th: sn rdn and wknd* 50/1
0/ 7 *35* **Preswell Lad (IRE)**[83] 193 12-11-9 100 (p) MPButler(3) 47
(Michael Butler, Ire) *hld up: hmpd 13th: rdn and wknd bef next* 20/1
P504 P **The Jugopolist (IRE)**[18] 965 8-9-11 76 (v) JoeCornwall(5)
(John Cornwall) *in rr whn hmpd 3rd: bhd and pushed along 6th: p.u bef 3 out* 40/1
-013 F **The Kings Assassin (IRE)**[27] 897 7-11-8 96 (p) TomCannon
(Chris Gordon) *prom tl fell 3rd* 9/2[3]
5m 37.5s (-1.70) **Going Correction** 0.0s/f (Good) 9 Ran SP% **113.3**
Speed ratings (Par 103): **102,101,101,99,90 89,77, ,**
CSF £18.69 CT £58.21 TOTE £2.70: £1.30, £3.00, £1.10; EX 18.80 Trifecta £98.80.
Owner Mrs Lynda M Williams **Bred** Mrs L M Williams **Trained** Brompton Regis, Somerset
FOCUS
Although this was a moderate race, it contained plenty of horses running well, so the form should be strong for the class. The first four were all in decent form and close to their marks.

1156 BIDVEST FOODSERVICE H'CAP HURDLE (8 hdls) 2m 70y
3:20 (3:20) (Class 3) (0-125,120) 3-Y-0+ £5,523 (£1,621; £810; £405)

Form RPR
14/2 1 **Stand To Reason (IRE)**[43] 755 7-10-11 105 LeeEdwards 110+
(Tony Carroll) *hld up: hdwy appr 2 out: hung lft and led appr last: sn lft clr* 5/1[3]
46-6 2 *6* **Don Padeja**[18] 973 5-11-9 117 (t) RichardJohnson 119+
(Jonjo O'Neill) *led: rdn and hdd whn blnd last: no ex* 7/2[2]
5212 3 *nk* **Hawdyerwheesht**[15] 1012 7-11-12 120 (tp) NoelFehily 119
(David Dennis) *chsd ldr and clr of the rest: mstke 4th: rdn bef 2 out: styd on same pce appr last* 7/2[2]
41 4 *10* **Bigindie (IRE)**[58] 592 5-11-8 119 AdamNicol(3) 108
(John Weymes) *hld up: drvn along 5th: nvr on terms* 10/3[1]
-136 5 *9* **Frozen Over**[37] 826 7-11-5 113 (t) JamesDavies 94
(Chris Down) *hld up: hdwy appr 2 out: rdn and wknd wl bef last* 6/1
60 6 *24* **Moreece (IRE)**[12] 1034 6-10-11 105 MichaelByrne 65
(Tim Vaughan) *hld up: mstke 3rd: hit 3 out: a bhd* 33/1
5-54 F **L Stig**[64] 507 5-10-0 94 oh1 DaveCrosse
(John O'Shea) *chsd clr ldrs: nt fluent 3rd: rdn appr 3 out: disputing 4th and wkng whn fell next* 11/1
3m 46.9s (-9.10) **Going Correction** -0.40s/f (Good) 7 Ran SP% **109.8**
Speed ratings (Par 107): **106,103,102,97,93 81,**
CSF £21.24 TOTE £6.60: £2.70, £1.90; EX 20.90 Trifecta £82.70.
Owner Montpellier Racing **Bred** Coleman Bloodstock Limited **Trained** Cropthorne, Worcs
FOCUS
The winner was thrown in on his old form, there was a pb from the second, and the third was close to his mark.

1157 BIDVEST FOODSERVICE NOVICES' CHASE (12 fncs) 2m 213y
3:55 (3:55) (Class 4) 5-Y-0+ £3,768 (£1,106; £553)

Form RPR
00-0 1 **Broughton (GER)**[54] 638 5-11-0 0 (bt) AidanColeman 137+
(John Ferguson) *last but cl up: nt fluent: led bef 9th: clr fr 2 out: easily* 7/4[2]
3120 2 *19* **Street Entertainer (IRE)**[12] 1034 8-11-0 0 (bt) TomScudamore 115
(David Pipe) *chsd ldr: upsides wnr 9th: rdn and wknd after 2 out* 8/13[1]
5-6P 3 *46* **Flabello (IRE)**[7] 1086 5-10-9 0 (b[1]) KieronEdgar(5) 74
(David Pipe) *led tl appr 9th: wknd qckly* 16/1[3]
4m 6.8s (-0.30) **Going Correction** 0.0s/f (Good) 3 Ran SP% **104.2**
Speed ratings: **100,91,69**
CSF £3.21 TOTE £2.00; EX 3.40 Trifecta £2.70.
Owner Bloomfields **Bred** Gestut Westerberg **Trained** Cowlinge, Suffolk
FOCUS
In the grand scheme of things, this result probably means little, but it gave the three runners some valuable chasing experience with the potential of picking up prize money. The winner was a decent hurdler at his peak and there's a case for rating this a lot higher through the second, but it's not one to be confident about.

1158 ROR RACECOURSE TO RACECOURSE RIDE NOVICES' H'CAP HURDLE (11 hdls) 2m 6f 7y
4:30 (4:30) (Class 5) (0-100,98) 4-Y-0+ £2,599 (£763; £381; £190)

Form RPR
P540 1 **The Winking Prawn (IRE)**[15] 1004 8-11-12 98 (t) KielanWoods 110+
(Graeme McPherson) *hld up: hdwy 8th: led after 2 out: sn clr: rdn flat: all out* 12/1
32F2 2 *1* **Midnight Sequel**[7] 1085 6-11-2 95 (bt) MissBHampson(7) 105+
(Neil Mulholland) *hld up: hdwy 2 out: nt clr run and swtchd lft sn after: sn outpcd: rallied to go 10 l 2nd last: str run flat: nt rch wnr: too much to do* 9/4[1]
-123 3 *7* **Tachbury**[29] 879 11-10-2 74 (p) RichardJohnson 76
(Tim Vaughan) *chsd ldrs: rdn after 2 out: styd on same pce appr last* 7/1[3]
03-5 4 *6* **Irish Octave (IRE)**[75] 337 5-10-10 85 BenPoste(3) 81
(Rosemary Gasson) *chsd ldrs: rdn after 8th: wknd wl bef last* 10/1
52/0 5 *1 1/4* **Miss Mayfair (IRE)**[18] 966 8-10-11 83 (p) NickScholfield 78
(Lawney Hill) *w ldr tl led 2nd: nt fluent next: rdn and hdd after 2 out: sn wknd* 20/1
522 6 *19* **Eddy**[32] 858 6-10-5 84 ThomasCheesman(7) 62
(John Panvert) *mid-div: mstke 8th: sn rdn: wknd appr 2 out* 3/1[2]
-006 7 *1* **Bobonyx**[15] 1010 5-9-7 73 oh4 (v) MissPFuller(7) 49
(Dai Williams) *prom: ev ch fr 3 out tl rdn and wknd after next* 20/1
P/04 8 *14* **Monzino (USA)**[12] 1030 7-9-11 74 JoeCornwall(5) 39
(Michael Chapman) *hld up: rdn and wknd 8th* 16/1
-06P 9 *2* **Freddy Fox (IRE)**[7] 1086 5-11-2 95 MrMJPKendrick(7) 58
(Ben Case) *hld up: in rr and pushed along 6th: bhd fr next* 33/1
6-15 10 *9* **Y A Bon (IRE)**[37] 824 7-11-6 92 (b) LeeEdwards 47
(Aytach Sadik) *chsd ldrs tl rdn and wknd after 8th* 16/1
P50 U **Nyetimber (USA)**[24] 930 9-10-10 82 (t) MarkGrant
(Sean Curran) *rrd and uns rdr s* 33/1
0-30 P **Thelonlady (IRE)**[64] 515 5-10-5 77 (tp) PaddyBrennan
(Richard Woollacott) *hld up: rdn and wknd 3 out: bhd whn p.u bef last* 9/1
060- P **Bo's Return**[194] 3737 5-10-12 84 MichaelByrne
(Tim Vaughan) *led to 2nd: chsd ldr tl rdn and wknd 3 out: bhd whn p.u bef last* 50/1
5m 20.7s (-7.40) **Going Correction** -0.40s/f (Good) 13 Ran SP% **124.2**
Speed ratings (Par 103): **97,96,94,91,91 84,84,79,78,75 , ,**
CSF £39.61 CT £218.69 TOTE £12.10: £3.20, £1.40, £2.40; EX 50.70 Trifecta £395.90.
Owner James Daly & Graeme McPherson **Bred** James And Joe Ryan **Trained** Upper Oddington, Gloucs
FOCUS
The winner was well in but this still rates a pb on return to hurdles.

1159 BIDVEST FOODSERVICE H'CAP CHASE (14 fncs) 2m 3f 98y
5:05 (5:05) (Class 5) (0-100,100) 4-Y-0+ £2,599 (£763; £381; £190)

Form RPR
3-F2 1 **Faustina Pius (IRE)**[11] 1056 7-11-5 100 (p) MrStanSheppard(7) 111+
(Matt Sheppard) *hld up: hit 11th: hdwy 3 out: led appr last: rdn out* 5/1
5432 2 *2 1/2* **Faith Jicaro (IRE)**[18] 976 8-11-7 100 (p) JakeHodson(5) 108+
(David Bridgwater) *chsd ldr: hmpd 2nd: nt fluent 8th: led next: rdn and hdd appr last: styd on same pce flat* 7/1
P0 3 *3 1/4* **Blackwood Rover (IRE)**[29] 877 7-11-1 89 PaulMoloney 92
(J R Jenkins) *a.p: rdn bef 2 out: styd on same pce appr last* 8/1
-F62 4 *3 1/2* **Who Am I**[7] 1080 9-11-8 96 (p) RobertDunne 99
(Debra Hamer) *chsd ldrs: mstke 2nd: wnt 2nd and hmpd 10th: rdn 2 out: wknd bef last* 3/1[1]
040P 5 *6* **Mahayogin (USA)**[18] 977 7-9-12 75 oh5 ow1 JamesBanks(3) 71
(Sarah-Jayne Davies) *hld up: mstke 4th: hdwy next: rdn and wknd after 2 out* 40/1
-523 6 *5* **Lord Of The Dunes**[29] 874 7-11-1 89 (bt) BrendanPowell 80
(Jamie Snowden) *led: j.lft 2nd: hdd 9th: j.lft next: rdn 3 out: wknd next* 9/2[3]
036- 7 *12* **If It Be Your Will**[130] 4940 5-11-8 96 (t) RyanMahon 75
(Dan Skelton) *prom: lost pl 5th: wknd bef 11th* 7/2[2]
4P34 P **Next Exit (IRE)**[18] 964 10-9-9 74 oh8 JoeCornwall(5)
(John Cornwall) *hld up: pushed along 9th: wknd after next: bhd whn p.u bef last* 66/1
4m 49.7s (-0.30) **Going Correction** 0.0s/f (Good) 8 Ran SP% **109.6**
Speed ratings (Par 103): **100,98,97,96,93 91,86,**
CSF £35.96 CT £251.80 TOTE £6.70: £1.90, £1.60, £2.60; EX 24.00 Trifecta £190.20.
Owner Lost In The Summer Wine **Bred** Pearse Mee **Trained** Eastnor, H'fords
FOCUS
The winner was on a decent mark and is rated to her best, with the second to the level of her recent C&D run.
T/Plt: £151.40 to a £1 stake. Pool: £47,097.47 - 227.08 winning units. T/Qpdt: £24.00 to a £1 stake. Pool: £4,126.38 - 126.80 winning units. **Colin Roberts**

1160 - 1162a (Foreign Racing) - See Raceform Interactive

1149
GALWAY (R-H)
Thursday, July 30

OFFICIAL GOING: Jumps courses - good; flat course - good to yielding

1163a GUINNESS GALWAY HURDLE H'CAP (GRADE A) (9 hdls) 2m
4:45 (4:45) 4-Y-0+
£139,922 (£44,573; £21,317; £7,364; £5,038; £2,713)

RPR

1 **Quick Jack (IRE)**[85] 4737 6-10-4 **136** DenisO'Regan 152+
(A J Martin, Ire) *chsd ldrs: 6th 1/2-way: tk clsr order bhd ldrs 3 out and wnt 2nd bef next where slt mstke on inner: led narrowly travelling wl between last 2: jnd at last where lft clr and pushed out run-in: comf* **9/2**[2]

2 2 1/4 **Max Dynamite (FR)**[33] 73 5-10-1 **136** DavidMullins(3) 147+
(W P Mullins, Ire) *hld up in rr of mid-div: tk clsr order bef 4 out: rdn in 12th after 2 out where slt mstke and hdwy bhd ldrs bef last where swtchd lft in 8th: r.o wl into 2nd clsng stages: nvr on terms* **10/1**

3 2 1/4 **Ted Veale (IRE)**[3] 244 8-10-7 **144** ShaneShortall(5) 151
(A J Martin, Ire) *hld up towards rr: tk clsr order after 3 out: hdwy in 10th fr next to chse ldrs at last where lft 2nd: no imp on wnr run-in and dropped to 3rd clsng stages: kpt on same pce* **16/1**

4 3 1/4 **Hidden Cyclone (IRE)**[21] 8 10-10-2 **137** (p) BrianHayes(3) 141
(John Joseph Hanlon, Ire) *settled bhd ldrs: slt mstke 3rd and led briefly bef 4th where mstke and hdd: 4th 1/2-way: hdwy to ld bef 2 out: rdn and hdd between last 2: no imp on wnr in 3rd at last where lft 2nd briefly: one pce run-in* **6/1**[3]

5 2 **Marchese Marconi (IRE)**[26] 905 6-10-6 **138** (tp) MarkWalsh 140
(A P O'Brien, Ire) *mid-div: 9th bef 2 out: prog on inner after 2 out: lft 5th at last and sltly hmpd: kpt on one pce* **16/1**

6 3 1/2 **Thousand Stars (FR)**[19] 954 11-11-7 **153** (b[1]) MsKWalsh 151
(W P Mullins, Ire) *towards rr: sme hdwy bef 2 out where slt mstke: lft 8th at last and kpt on u.p run-in* **33/1**

7 3 1/4 **Macnicholson (IRE)**[24] 576 6-10-7 **139** (b[1]) MsNCarberry 140
(Mrs John Harrington, Ire) *in tch: 7th 1/2-way: tk clsr order on outer in 2nd bef 2 out: sn rdn and no imp on wnr disputing 3rd at last where bdly hmpd by faller and dropped to 7th: one pce run-in* **25/1**

8 *hd* **Stephanie Frances (IRE)**[105] 5353 7-10-6 **138** HarrySkelton 133
(Dan Skelton) *mid-div: tk clsr order bhd ldrs: 2 out: rdn in 6th bef last and no imp on wnr whn bdly hmpd by faller: one pce after* **20/1**

9 2 1/2 **Bayan (IRE)**[20] 948 6-10-11 **150** (bt) JackKennedy(7) 142
(Gordon Elliott, Ire) *chsd ldrs: cl 3rd at 1/2-way: rdn in 2nd wl bef 2 out and sn no ex between horses: wknd bef last where mstke and hmpd by faller: one pce run-in* **20/1**

10 4 1/2 **Plinth (IRE)**[3] 498 5-10-3 **138** (bt) JodyMcGarvey(3) 126
(A P O'Brien, Ire) *sn chsd ldrs tl led fr 4th: narrow advantage at 1/2-way: rdn and hdd bef 2 out: sn wknd* **50/1**

11 2 **Wicklow Brave**[40] 4737 6-11-7 **153** PaulTownend 139
(W P Mullins, Ire) *mid-div: tk clsr order on outer bef 2 out: rdn and no ex after 2 out: eased bef last where hmpd by faller* **12/1**

12 1 1/2 **The Game Changer (IRE)**[7] 1090 6-10-11 **143** (t) DavyRussell 127
(Gordon Elliott, Ire) *settled bhd ldrs: 5th 1/2-way: slt mstke 5th: rdn and wknd 2 out* **10/1**

13 19 **Diakali (FR)**[19] 954 6-11-7 **153** RWalsh 118
(W P Mullins, Ire) *in tch: tk clsr order on outer in 7th after 3 out: rdn and no ex bef next: wknd and eased* **4/1**[1]

14 8 1/2 **Aminabad (FR)**[9] 1075 5-10-1 **136** 1ex LPDempsey(3) 93
(W P Mullins, Ire) *in rr of mid-div: pushed along after 4th: reminders after next and no ex u.p fr 4 out where slt mstke: wknd fr next and eased bef 2 out* **33/1**

15 3 **Rich Coast**[93] 6 7-10-7 **139** PaulCarberry 93
(Noel Meade, Ire) *led narrowly fr 1st: slt mstke 3rd: hdd bef next: cl 2nd at 1/2-way: slt mstke 4 out and wknd bef next: eased bef 2 out* **33/1**

16 1 1/2 **Hisaabaat (IRE)**[27] 4704 7-10-5 **137** (v) JJBurke 89
(D K Weld, Ire) *towards rr: pushed along after 4 out and no imp* **20/1**

17 39 **Snake Eyes (IRE)**[90] 73 7-10-4 **136** NiallPMadden 49
(Nicky Henderson) *towards rr: nt fluent 1st: pushed along after 4 out and no imp whn j.lft next: eased: completely t.o* **12/1**

U **Rawnaq (IRE)**[26] 908 8-10-4 **143** KevinSmith(7)
(Matthew J Smith, Ire) *hld up: towards rr whn blnd and uns rdr 3rd* **20/1**

F **Thomas Edison (IRE)**[81] 231 8-11-0 **146** (t) BarryGeraghty 155
(A J Martin, Ire) *mid-div: nt fluent 5th: impr bhd ldrs bef 2 out where n.m.r: hdwy after 2 out and swtchd lft in 3rd between last 2: got on terms and ev ch whn fell last* **14/1**

P **Rae's Creek**[16] 990 5-10-3 **135** MarkBolger
(Mrs John Harrington, Ire) *towards rr: slt mstke 2nd: last 1/2-way: rdn and no imp after 3 out: t.o whn p.u bef 2 out* **33/1**

3m 36.5s (-20.20) **20 Ran SP% 141.1**
CSF £49.45 CT £719.95 TOTE £4.90: £1.50, £3.10, £4.10, £2.10; DF 76.30 Trifecta £1956.40.
Owner John Breslin **Bred** Newtown Anner Stud **Trained** Summerhill, Co. Meath

FOCUS
Actual race distance 2m60yds. What a race for trainer Tony Martin, unluckily denied having first, second and fourth, but first and third is far from a bad result in a race of such a competitive nature. A step up from the winner in line with his Flat form.

1164 - (Foreign Racing) - See Raceform Interactive

328
BANGOR-ON-DEE (L-H)
Friday, July 31

OFFICIAL GOING: Good (6.7)
Wind: moderate 1/2 behind Weather: fine

1165 BANGORBET MARES' MAIDEN HURDLE (11 hdls) 2m 3f 123y
1:40 (1:40) (Class 5) 4-Y-0+ £2,737 (£798; £399)

Form RPR

/223 1 **Miss Macnamara (IRE)**[23] 805 6-11-0 98 HenryBrooke 109+
(Martin Todhunter) *trckd ldrs: t.k.h: led 3 out: rdn clr between last 2: eased towards fin* **7/2**[2]

34-0 2 5 **Goldray**[24] 938 9-11-0 107 RichardJohnson 104+
(Kerry Lee) *trckd ldrs: mstke 3rd: 2nd and drvn sn after 3 out: hit next: kpt on one pce between last 2: regained modest 2nd clsng stages* **7/2**[2]

3P-5 3 *nk* **Blurred Lines (IRE)**[65] 503 6-11-0 100 WayneHutchinson 102
(Donald McCain) *led: jnd 3 out: sn hdd: kpt on to regain modest 2nd appr last: one pce* **13/2**

-363 4 13 **Maypole Lass**[19] 967 5-11-0 102 (b) BrendanPowell 90
(Stuart Edmunds) *chsd ldrs: outpcd appr 3 out* **10/3**[1]

-320 5 4 **Bollin Beauty**[19] 970 6-11-0 0 BrianHughes 89
(Malcolm Jefferson) *mid-div: chsng ldrs whn hit 6th: outpcd appr 3 out* **20/1**

6 33 **Tortueuse (IRE)**[24] 944 8-11-0 105 (p) RobertDunne 56
(Dermot Anthony McLoughlin, Ire) *j.rt 1st: chsd ldrs: drvn and lost pl 6th: bhd 3 out: t.o next* **12/1**

F 7 1 **Crofton Trail (IRE)**[19] 957 6-11-0 0 (t) SamTwiston-Davies 55
(Patrick Griffin, Ire) *chsd ldrs: drvn 6th: lost pl next: sn bhd: t.o 2 out: lame* **9/2**[3]

5-4 8 15 **Bawnogues Bahri (IRE)**[19] 960 6-10-9 94 GrantCockburn(5) 42
(Paul Stafford, Ire) *j.lft in rr: bhd and drvn 6th: t.o 8th* **80/1**

0-UP 9 2 **Feisty Girl**[40] 813 5-10-11 0 BenPoste(3) 40
(Michael Mullineaux) *nt fluent in rr: drvn 6th: sn bhd: t.o 8th* **100/1**

4m 41.6s (-10.40) **Going Correction** -0.925s/f (Hard) **9 Ran SP% 113.7**
Speed ratings (Par 103): **83,81,80,75,74 60,60,54,53**
CSF £16.10 TOTE £3.80: £1.10, £1.10, £3.50; EX 17.70 Trifecta £102.10.
Owner Javas Charvers **Bred** Airlie Stud **Trained** Orton, Cumbria

FOCUS
Races 1, 2, 4, &6 increased by 42yds, race 7 by 57yds, race 3 reduced by 12yds and race 5 reduced by 9yds. A moderate mares' only race to start proceedings. It was run at a steady gallop. The winner is entitled to rate higher on Flat form.

1166 RACING UK H'CAP HURDLE (9 hdls) 2m 145y
2:10 (2:12) (Class 4) (0-110,111) 3-Y-0+ £3,249 (£954; £477; £238)

Form RPR

4621 1 **Astaroland (FR)**[12] 1048 5-11-13 **111** 7ex PeterCarberry 118+
(Jennie Candlish) *chsd ldrs: led between last 2: hit last: kpt on wl* **3/1**[1]

-526 2 2 3/4 **Ginger Fizz**[24] 938 8-11-9 **107** (tp) KielanWoods 110
(Ben Case) *w ldrs: led after 6th: hdd between last 2: kpt on same pce* **14/1**

-25F 3 3 1/2 **Anton Dolin (IRE)**[45] 751 7-10-13 **104** MrHFNugent(7) 104
(Michael Mullineaux) *mid-div: drvn 5th: chsng ldrs 3 out: kpt on same pce next* **16/1**

5333 4 3/4 **Significant Move**[5] 1115 8-10-0 **84** (b) WillKennedy 83
(Dr Richard Newland) *in tch: reminders and chsd ldrs 5th: kpt on one pce fr 2 out* **7/2**[2]

260- 5 1 **Nafaath (IRE)**[138] 4784 9-11-8 **106** WayneHutchinson 103
(Donald McCain) *chsd ldrs: reminders after 1st: outpcd 3 out: kpt on fr next* **20/1**

0-U0 6 1 **Saint Elm (FR)**[40] 799 5-10-3 **87** BrianHughes 83
(Patrick Griffin, Ire) *stdd s: in rr: hdwy 6th: chsng ldrs 3 out: one pce* **50/1**

2-34 7 11 **Fairy Alisha**[68] 465 7-10-12 **103** JoshWall(7) 89
(Trevor Wall) *in rr: hdwy 5th: one pce appr 2 out* **20/1**

6020 8 8 **Green And White (ITY)**[35] 843 5-10-13 **97** (p) LeeEdwards 76
(Dave Roberts) *unruly s: mid-div: drvn 4th: reminders 6th: sn lost pl and bhd* **33/1**

3P6- 9 5 **Carnaross**[132] 4928 6-10-4 **88** (t) PaulMoloney 63
(Sophie Leech) *hld up in rr: sme hdwy 5th: lost pl bef 3 out* **6/1**

0/ 10 8 **Flight Control (IRE)**[704] 1408 10-10-11 **95** (vt[1]) SamTwiston-Davies 63
(Peter Croke, Ire) *led: hdd after 6th: sn lost pl: bhd fr 2 out* **66/1**

-334 11 17 **Drifter (IRE)**[16] 1012 4-11-4 **104** RichardJohnson 54
(Harry Whittington) *chsd ldrs: hit 6th: sn lost pl: bhd whn eased between last 2* **4/1**[3]

00-1 F **Honkytonktennessee (IRE)**[28] 892 6-11-12 **110** DaveCrosse
(Hugo Froud) *chsd ldrs: fell 5th* **9/1**

3m 57.2s (-13.70) **Going Correction** -0.925s/f (Hard)
WFA 4 from 5yo+ 15lb **12 Ran SP% 120.0**
Speed ratings (Par 105): **95,93,92,91,91 90,85,81,79,75 67,**
CSF £41.31 CT £592.88 TOTE £3.70: £1.20, £4.60, £4.40; EX 37.20 Trifecta £441.10.
Owner Paul Beck **Bred** Mlle Marie-Laure Besnouin **Trained** Basford Green, Staffs

FOCUS
This looked competitive on paper, but it featured very few regular winners. The winner comfirmed the merit of his improved recent win.

1167 CLOGAU GOLD TREE OF LIFE H'CAP CHASE (18 fncs) 3m 30y
2:45 (2:46) (Class 3) (0-130,130) 4-Y-0+ £6,844 (£1,995; £998)

Form RPR

-412 1 **Gold Futures (IRE)**[40] 801 6-11-12 **130** BrianHarding 142+
(Nicky Richards) *hld up: hdwy to trck ldrs 9th: led between last 2: styd on wl* **9/2**[2]

-532 2 3 1/2 **Strumble Head (IRE)**[52] 670 10-11-0 **118** (b) DonalDevereux 124
(Peter Bowen) *led to 5th: led 11th: hdd between last 2: styd on same pce* **10/1**

25-2 3 3 3/4 **Guiding George (IRE)**[64] 523 7-11-7 **125** (tp) HarrySkelton 129
(Dan Skelton) *chsd ldrs: kpt on one pce fr 2 out* **11/4**[1]

55-6 4 *hd* **Highway Code (USA)**[16] 1005 9-10-13 **117** (t) RichardJohnson 120
(Kerry Lee) *hld up in rr: hdwy 13th: sn chsng ldrs: kpt on one pce fr 2 out* **20/1**

5-04 5 1/2 **Midnight Appeal**[13] 1033 10-11-8 **129** (t) KillianMoore(3) 131
(Sophie Leech) *hld up in rr: hdwy 10th: one pce fr 2 out* **11/1**

-425 6 3/4 **Sir Mattie (IRE)**[30] 873 10-10-7 **111** TomScudamore 113
(David Rees) *in rr: hdwy 12th: sn chsng ldrs: one pce fr 2 out* **10/1**

/662 7 4 1/2 **Mr Moss (IRE)**[25] 927 10-11-7 **125** (v[1]) PaulMoloney 123
(Evan Williams) *chsd ldrs: outpcd 12th: kpt on one pce appr 2 out* **8/1**

F0-1 8 3 1/4 **Valleyofmilan (IRE)**[25] 927 8-11-3 **128** JamesCowley(7) 123
(Donald McCain) *chsd ldrs: wknd 2 out* **12/1**

P5/3 9 12 **King's Legacy (IRE)**[42] 781 11-11-1 **119** (t) NickScholfield 103
(Lawney Hill) *nt jump wl detached in last: nvr on terms* **25/1**

F6-5 10 3/4 **Brass Tax (IRE)**[88] 101 9-11-4 **125** (p) MrMJPKendrick(7) 112
(Ben Case) *w ldr: led 5th to 11th: lost pl appr 2 out* **25/1**

2-B0 11 1 **Spirit River (FR)**[35] 839 10-10-1 **105** LeeEdwards 87
(Dave Roberts) *in rr: hdwy 14th: sn chsng ldrs: lost pl appr 2 out: sn bhd* **40/1**

1P-5 12 2 1/2 **Bandit Country (IRE)**[57] 611 6-11-7 **125** (bt[1]) NoelFehily 105
(Jonjo O'Neill) *prom: hit 8th: outpcd 12th: lost pl bef 2 out* **7/1**[3]

5m 52.3s (-27.50) **Going Correction** -0.925s/f (Hard) **12 Ran SP% 117.6**
Speed ratings (Par 107): **108,106,105,105,105 105,103,102,98,98 97,97**
CSF £45.67 CT £147.23 TOTE £5.30: £2.00, £3.90, £1.70; EX 60.50 Trifecta £312.80.
Owner Mrs C A Torkington **Bred** D W Macauley **Trained** Greystoke, Cumbria

FOCUS
This was run at a stern pace and placed plenty of emphasis on stamina. The winner remains unexposed and should go on to bigger and better things. The cosy winner is on the upgrade and there is probably more to come.

1168 DEVA RACING NOVICES' HURDLE (9 hdls) 2m 145y
3:20 (3:22) (Class 4) 4-Y-0+ £3,249 (£954; £477; £238)

Form RPR
-212 1 **Mighty Missile (IRE)**30 749 4-11-3 120....................(tp) GavinSheehan 123+
(Warren Greatrex) *mde all: drvn after 3 out: jnd next: fnd ex between last 2: 3 l clr last: drvn rt out* **2/1**2

13 2 ¾ **Miner's Lamp (IRE)**13 1041 4-11-3 119..........................1 AidanColeman 120
(John Ferguson) *hld up towards rr: hdwy 5th: trcking ldrs next: drvn bef 2 out: kpt on to take 2nd last: styd on* **15/8**1

2 3 1 ¼ **Pershing**6 981 4-10-10 116..............................(tp) BrianHughes 112
(Robert Alan Hennessy, Ire) *trckd wnr: upsides 2 out: kpt on same pce appr last* **9/1**

-124 4 1 ¼ **Prince Khurram**8 1083 5-10-12 113..............................(t) NoelFehily 114
(Donald McCain) *trckd ldrs: effrt 3 out: one pce appr next* **7/1**

41 5 13 **I'dliketheoption (IRE)**44 754 4-11-3 0.................. RichieMcLernon 108
(Jonjo O'Neill) *trckd ldrs: drvn 3 out: wknd appr next* **4/1**3

/355 6 31 **Mullinavat (IRE)**16 1000 6-10-12 0..............................(t) HenryBrooke 73
(Jennie Candlish) *chsd ldrs: drvn and lost pl 6th: bhd 2 out: sn t.o* **66/1**

0-03 P **Wistari Rocks (IRE)**24 933 6-10-12 0.................. RichardJohnson
(Tim Vaughan) *in rr: pushed along 4th: bhd 6th: t.o next: p.u bef 2 out* **33/1**

0 P **Keep On Walking (IRE)**24 933 4-10-10 0........... SamTwiston-Davies
(Peter Croke, Ire) *j.lft 1st: drvn and lost pl after 4th: sn bhd: t.o 3 out: p.u bef next* **80/1**

3m 51.2s (-19.70) **Going Correction** -0.925s/f (Hard) 8 Ran SP% **116.3**
Speed ratings (Par 105): **109,108,108,107,101 86,,**
CSF £6.51 TOTE £3.60: £1.30, £1.30, £2.30; EX 6.40 Trifecta £42.00.
Owner Bolingbroke Howard BJO Duthie Mercer **Bred** Gerry Flannery **Trained** Upper Lambourn, Berks

FOCUS
A fair running of this contest, which had been won by Donald McCain-trained horses in three of the previous four years. The first two are on the upgrade.

1169 BILL AND JOAN WOODWARD 70TH WEDDING ANNIVERSARY H'CAP CHASE (12 fncs) 2m 1f 77y
3:55 (3:55) (Class 4) (0-120,118) 4-Y-0+ £4,223 (£1,240; £620; £310)

Form RPR
P-20 1 **Jack The Gent (IRE)**13 1032 11-10-8 100.................. RichieMcLernon 115+
(George Moore) *mde all: drvn appr 2 out: styd on wl: unchal* **16/1**

/P43 2 8 **Lisbon (IRE)**24 936 7-11-9 115..............................(t) BrianHughes 124
(Patrick Griffin, Ire) *chsd ldrs: 2nd and drvn 3 out: styd on same pce between last 2* **4/1**2

3116 3 2 ¾ **Jayo Time (IRE)**13 1042 6-11-4 110.................................. WillKennedy 115
(Dr Richard Newland) *hld up in mid-div: chsd ldrs 6th: 3rd last: one pce* **9/2**3

-445 4 6 **Macarthur**16 1008 11-11-4 110..............................(p) PaulMoloney 110
(David Rees) *in rr-div: hdwy to chse ldrs 6th: modest 3rd 2 out: wknd last* **25/1**

2203 5 2 ½ **Dynamo (IRE)**16 1008 4-10-5 112..............................(t) HarrySkelton 97
(Dan Skelton) *nt fluent in rr: drvn 7th: outpcd and nt fluent 9th: kpt on fr 2 out* **5/2**1

-424 6 2 ½ **Breaking The Bank**33 857 6-11-12 118............................ DarylJacob 115
(Ben Case) *chsd ldrs: hit 4th: lost pl 9th: kpt on between last 2* **8/1**

3F-4 7 2 **Tour D'Argent (FR)**16 1008 8-11-7 113..............................(p) NoelFehily 107
(Donald McCain) *chsd wnr: j.lft 2nd: drvn 9th: one pce fr next* **15/2**

-412 8 11 **Claragh Native (IRE)**49 709 10-11-8 114.................. HenryBrooke 98
(Martin Todhunter) *chsd ldrs: lost pl appr 2 out: sn bhd* **10/1**

514- 9 25 **Marky Bob (IRE)**373 1067 10-10-13 105.............................. DaveCrosse 66
(Hugo Froud) *a in last: bhd fr 7th* **16/1**

4m 3.5s (-18.60) **Going Correction** -0.925s/f (Hard)
WFA 4 from 6yo+ 2lb 9 Ran SP% **114.3**
Speed ratings (Par 105): **106,102,100,98,96 95,94,89,77**
CSF £80.09 CT £342.65 TOTE £24.30: £5.30, £1.50, £2.00; EX 97.40 Trifecta £781.40.
Owner J B Wallwin **Bred** P O'Connor **Trained** Middleham Moor, N Yorks

FOCUS
Few got competitive in this feature handicap chase as the giant winner ran them into submission. The time was good for the grade.

1170 GRAHAM BOYS CELEBRATORY H'CAP HURDLE (11 hdls) 2m 3f 123y
4:30 (4:30) (Class 4) (0-120,120) 4-Y-0+ £3,249 (£954; £477; £238)

Form RPR
/14- 1 **Chebsey Beau**371 1085 5-11-0 115.............................. DeanPratt(7) 123+
(John Quinn) *hld up in mid-div: hdwy 6th: sn trcking ldrs: upsides travelling wl 2 out: shkn up to ld between last 2: rdn clr* **18/1**

5-64 2 4 **Java Rose**24 938 6-11-5 113..............................(tp) AidanColeman 115
(Charlie Longsdon) *best away: led: drvn 3 out: hdd between last 2: styd on same pce* **7/1**

543- 3 3 ½ **Workbench (FR)**108 5332 7-11-8 116..............................(t) HarrySkelton 114
(Dan Skelton) *hld up in rr: hdwy to chse ldrs 6th: 3rd last: kpt on one pce* **7/1**

0P-3 4 3 ½ **Spitz (FR)**29 886 7-10-8 105.............................. CraigNichol(3) 99
(Rose Dobbin) *chsd ldrs: hit 5th: kpt on one pce fr 2 out: lame* **6/1**3

13-5 5 nk **Heist (IRE)**26 921 5-11-4 112..............................(vt1) SamTwiston-Davies 106
(Patrick Griffin, Ire) *chsd ldr: drvn 3 out: hung lft between last 2: one pce* **12/1**

5053 6 1 ½ **Morning With Ivan (IRE)**11 1071 5-10-2 96.................. HenryBrooke 88
(Martin Todhunter) *in rr: hdwy 7th: drvn appr 2 out: one pce* **20/1**

5321 7 shd **Chilly Miss**13 1036 6-11-7 115.............................. BrianHughes 109
(Malcolm Jefferson) *t.k.h: trckd ldrs: drvn appr 2 out: fdd last* **5/1**2

P/- 8 7 **Maoi Chinn Tire (IRE)**13 1780 8-11-7 115..................(tp) PeterCarberry 100
(Jennie Candlish) *hld up in rr: hdwy 3 out: nvr on terms* **33/1**

9 ½ **Gold Class**27 906 4-10-6 103..............................(tp) RichardJohnson 86
(Robert Alan Hennessy, Ire) *chsd ldrs: wknd 2 out* **4/1**1

F-04 10 3 **Western Diva (IRE)**43 775 6-11-7 115.................. TomScudamore 97
(David Pipe) *t.k.h in rr: hdwy to trck ldrs 6th: lost pl sn after 3 out* **16/1**

0-26 11 1 ¼ **Bedouin Bay**12 1055 8-10-9 103.............................. AlainCawley 83
(Johnny Farrelly) *mid-div: lost pl 8th* **28/1**

01- 12 33 **Revolutionary Road**235 2993 7-10-8 105.................. TonyKelly(3) 52
(Rebecca Menzies) *in rr: drvn 7th: lost pl next: sn bhd: eased whn t.o: lame* **20/1**

6534 13 73 **Hold Court (IRE)**19 969 8-11-5 113.............................. PaulMoloney
(Evan Williams) *hld up in rr: hdwy to chse ldrs 6th: hung rt and lost pl next: sn bhd: tailed rt off bef 2 out* **11/1**

4m 38.3s (-13.70) **Going Correction** -0.925s/f (Hard)
WFA 4 from 5yo+ 16lb 13 Ran SP% **119.0**
Speed ratings (Par 105): **90,88,87,85,85 84,84,82,81,80 80,66,37**
CSF £132.87 CT £984.48 TOTE £23.50: £4.40, £3.30, £2.90; EX 217.20 Trifecta £2709.80.
Owner Kent & Greaves **Bred** Mickley Stud & M A Greaves **Trained** Settrington, N Yorks

FOCUS
This was strongly contested and produced an impressive winner. A step up from him with the second to his mark.

1171 R W HOUGH & SONS CONDITIONAL JOCKEYS' H'CAP HURDLE (12 hdls) 2m 7f 32y
5:05 (5:05) (Class 5) (0-100,100) 4-Y-0+ £2,737 (£798; £399)

Form RPR
-P62 1 **Powderonthebonnet (IRE)**7 1098 7-11-4 95.............. DanielHiskett(3) 106+
(Richard Phillips) *chsd ldrs: nt fluent 4th: lost pl 8th: rallied 3 out: 2nd appr 2 out: led appr last: readily* **11/10**1

-2PP 2 2 **Winter Alchemy (IRE)**35 842 10-11-0 88.............. StephenMulqueen 92
(Nicky Richards) *led to 9th: drvn to regain ld next: hdd appr last: styd on same pce* **16/1**

630- 3 13 **Western Goose (IRE)**105 5379 8-11-7 100.............. FinianO'Toole(5) 93
(Heather Dalton) *in rr: hdwy 8th: sn chsng ldrs: 3rd 2 out: one pce* **33/1**

-021 4 6 **Amuse Me**8 1080 9-10-9 91..............................(tp) JackSavage(8) 78
(Jonjo O'Neill) *rn in snatches: outpcd bef 2 out: one pce* **3/1**2

000 5 6 **Coppelia (IRE)**19 960 7-10-11 85.............................. CraigNichol 67
(Nicky Richards) *hld up in rr: t.k.h: hdwy 7th: chsng ldrs next: wknd appr 2 out* **33/1**

-620 6 54 **Solway Bay**11 1069 13-10-11 91..............................(tp) RyanDay(6) 24
(Lisa Harrison) *prom: pushed along 6th: lost pl 9th: sn bhd: t.o bef 2 out* **20/1**

-P40 7 11 **Hot Madras (IRE)**30 877 7-9-11 74 oh5.............. ThomasCheesman(3)
(Trevor Wall) *t.k.h in rr: drvn and lost pl 7th: sn bhd: t.o after 3 out* **100/1**

5-PU 8 2 ¾ **Mr Hopeful (IRE)**71 421 6-11-6 100..............................(bt1) JamesCowley(6) 20
(Donald McCain) *chsd ldrs: drvn 7th: reminders next: sn lost pl and bhd: t.o after 3 out* **16/1**

3-PP P **Moncarno**68 451 5-9-13 79..............................(bt) MichaelHeard(6)
(David Pipe) *chsd ldrs: lost pl after 9th: sn bhd: t.o whn p.u bef 2 out* **10/1**

6-40 P **Stormbay Bomber (IRE)**24 935 6-11-3 91.............................. AdamNicol
(George Moore) *chsd ldrs: lost pl bef 2 out: t.o 6th whn p.u bef last* **17/2**3

5m 36.8s (-14.20) **Going Correction** -0.925s/f (Hard) 10 Ran SP% **115.6**
Speed ratings (Par 103): **87,86,81,79,77 58,55,54,,**
CSF £18.10 CT £383.19 TOTE £2.00: £1.10, £3.60, £7.80; EX 19.70 Trifecta £255.70.
Owner W McLuskey **Bred** Vincent Finn **Trained** Adlestrop, Gloucs

FOCUS
The market proved a good guide to this weak finale. The winner should still be competitive when reassessed.
T/Plt: £112.00 to a £1 stake. Pool: £46,895.90 - 305.53 winning tickets T/Qpdt: £21.70 to a £1 stake. Pool: £4,438.14 - 151.30 winning tickets **Walter Glynn**

1172-1174a - (Foreign Racing) - See Raceform Interactive

1172 GALWAY (R-H)
Saturday, August 1

OFFICIAL GOING: Yielding (soft in places)

1175a LADBROKES H'CAP HURDLE (GRADE B) (13 hdls) 2m 5f 124y
3:15 (3:18) 4-Y-0+
£37,209 (£11,782; £5,581; £1,860; £1,240; £620)

RPR
1 **Valyssa Monterg (FR)**27 920 6-10-8 122.............................. RWalsh 138+
(W P Mullins, Ire) *racd in mid-div: gd prog bef last in 5th: styd on strly on outer to ld ins fnl 100yds: gng away at fin* **8/1**

2 2 ¾ **Argentino (FR)**17 1014 5-10-8 122..............................(p) MPFogarty 131
(W P Mullins, Ire) *trckd ldrs on inner in 3rd tl led 3 out: strly rdn after last: hdd ins fnl 100yds and sn no match for wnr* **25/1**

3 4 ½ **Massini's Trap (IRE)**4 231 6-11-1 129.............................. DJCasey 134+
(J A Nash, Ire) *hld up: prog towards inner bef 2 out where mstke: wnt 7th at last: styd on strly on outer run-in into 3rd clsng stages: nrst fin* **33/1**

4 1 ¾ **Gusty Rocky (IRE)**16 1018 6-10-9 123.............................. JJBurke 126
(Patrick J Flynn, Ire) *racd in mid-div tl clsr order to chse ldrs after 1/2-way: travelled wl in 4th appr 2 out: rdn to chse ldr in 2nd at last: sn no imp and dropped to 4th clsng stages* **12/1**

5 1 ¾ **Some Article (IRE)**95 7 7-11-4 132.............................. NiallPMadden 133
(Thomas Mullins, Ire) *chsd ldrs: clsr to trck ldrs in 3rd 4 out: rdn briefly in 2nd 2 out: no imp in 3rd at last: no ex run-in* **9/1**

6 1 ¾ **Eight Till Late (IRE)**28 908 7-10-11 125.............................. AELynch 124
(Peter Casey, Ire) *hld up in rr tl travelled wl into mid-div bef 3 out: wnt 5th at next: sn rdn and no imp at last: kpt on one pce* **12/1**

7 20 **Pyromaniac (IRE)**69 274 5-11-5 133..............................(tp) DenisO'Regan 112
(A J Martin, Ire) *hld up towards rr tl tk clsr order 4 out: wnt 6th 2 out: sn rdn and no imp bef last: no ex* **11/4**1

8 8 ½ **Silver Tassie (IRE)**15 1028 7-10-9 123.............................. PaulCarberry 94
(Noel Meade, Ire) *hld up: rdn along towards rr after 3 out: styd on wl fr last: nvr on terms* **20/1**

9 2 ¾ **Erlkonig (GER)**17 1014 5-10-13 130.............................. DavidMullins(3) 98
(Anthony Mullins, Ire) *racd towards rr: sme prog in mid-div 4 out: rdn and no imp after 2 out: kpt on one pce* **14/1**

10 ¾ **Phantom Prince (IRE)**42 796 6-11-0 128..............................(p) RobbiePower 95
(Mrs John Harrington, Ire) *trckd ldr in 2nd tl rdn and wknd after 2 out: sn no ex* **25/1**

11 20 **Coffee (IRE)**366 1142 8-11-2 133.............................. GerFox(3) 80
(E Bolger, Ire) *hld up towards rr: kpt on fr bef last: nvr nrr* **33/1**

12 6 ½ **Bishops Road (IRE)**13 1063 7-10-9 128..............................(p) AdamO'Neill(5) 69
(Henry De Bromhead, Ire) *led tl hdd 3 out: wknd qckly bef next* **20/1**

13 nk **Prince Rudi (IRE)**54 667 13-11-2 135..............................(v) AndrewRing(5) 75
(S T Nolan, Ire) *chsd ldrs tl rdn and nt qckn bef 3 out: sn no ex* **33/1**

14 2 ¼ **Cantlow (IRE)**117 5224 10-11-5 133..............................(tp) BarryGeraghty 71
(Paul Webber) *racd in mid-div: bit clsr after 4 out: rdn and no imp bef 2 out* **14/1**

15 nk **Cape Glory (IRE)**42 796 5-10-8 129..............................(tp) JackKennedy(7) 67
(Gordon Elliott, Ire) *chsd ldrs tl nt qckn after 4 out: sn one pce* **16/1**

16 2 ½ **Ibsen (IRE)**[25] 941 6-10-9 **123**........................ PaulTownend 58
(Gordon Elliott, Ire) *hld up: towards rr 1/2-way: nvr a factor* **7/1**[3]
17 9 ½ **Knight's Parade (IRE)**[5] 114 5-10-11 **128**..................(t) LPDempsey(3) 54
(Gordon Elliott, Ire) *a in rr: nvr a factor* **25/1**
18 38 **Elishpour (IRE)**[46] 231 5-10-10 **124**..............................(t) APHeskin 12
(A J Martin, Ire) *racd in mid-div: rdn after 4 out: no imp after next: sn eased* **13/2**[2]
P **Western Boy (IRE)**[17] 231 6-11-4 **132**.............................. MarkWalsh
(P A Fahy, Ire) *racd in mid-div on outer tl gd hdwy to chse ldrs bef 2 out: wknd qckly and sn p.u* **12/1**

5m 15.7s (315.70) **19 Ran SP% 145.8**
CSF £214.80 CT £6290.14 TOTE £14.10: £2.70, £8.50, £13.10, £3.50; DF 289.80.
Owner Mrs S Ricci **Bred** S C E A Haute Perriere **Trained** Muine Beag, Co Carlow

FOCUS
Exceptionally competitive, something of a race for those who missed the Galway Hurdle, and the two reserves coming in only added to the depth of the race. The pace was good.

1176 - (Foreign Racing) - See Raceform Interactive

1037

MARKET RASEN (R-H)
Sunday, August 2

OFFICIAL GOING: Good (8.4)
Wind: light 1/2 behind Weather: fine and sunny

1177 COMPASS ESTATE AGENTS MARKET RASEN JUVENILE HURDLE (8 hdls) 2m 148y
2:20 (2:21) (Class 4) 3-Y-O **£3,898** (£1,144; £572; £286)

Form RPR
1 1 **Retro Valley (IRE)**[15] 1037 3-11-4 0.............................. NoelFehily 103+
(David Dennis) *j.lft: trckd ldrs: 2nd whn stmbld on landing 4th: led appr 2 out: edgd rt sn after last: drvn rt out* **11/10**[1]
2 ¾ **Our Kylie (IRE)**[12] 3-10-5 0.............................. DenisO'Regan 87
(Tony Coyle) *chsd ldrs: 1 l 2nd last: sn swtchd lft and styd on: no ex clsng stages* **12/1**
3 4 ½ **Arabian Oasis**[96] 3-10-12 0.............................. AidanColeman 93+
(John Ferguson) *trckd ldrs: reminders and upsides whn bmpd 2 out: 1 l down whn mstke last: kpt on same pce* **15/8**[2]
2 4 8 **Robben**[15] 1037 3-10-12 0..............................(p) PaddyBrennan 83
(John Mackie) *chsd ldrs: pushed along 5th: nt fluent and lost pl 2 out* **5/1**[3]
5 17 **Boldbob (IRE)**[13] 3-10-2 0.............................. FinianO'Toole(10) 68
(Micky Hammond) *t.k.h: led: hit 2nd: clr 2nd: j.rt 5th: hdd appr 2 out: sn wknd* **33/1**
6 13 **Toboggan's Gift**[13] 3-10-5 0.............................. HenryBrooke 49
(Ann Duffield) *in rr: j.rt: reminders and hdwy 3 out: sn chsng ldrs: lost pl bef next: sn bhd* **66/1**
43 7 11 **Londonia**[15] 1037 3-10-12 0.............................. KielanWoods 46
(Graeme McPherson) *in rr: bhd fr 4th: t.o 3 out* **20/1**
8 22 **Wagstaff (IRE)**[52] 3-10-12 0.............................. BrianHughes 26
(Mick Channon) *chsd ldrs to 3rd: lost pl next and sn bhd: t.o 3 out* **33/1**
P **La Vien Zen (IRE)**[24] 3-10-2 0.............................. JonathanEngland(3)
(Jim Goldie) *nt jump wl in rr: t.o whn j. slowly 4th: p.u sn after next* **66/1**

4m 11.9s (5.20) **Going Correction** +0.025s/f (Yiel) **9 Ran SP% 120.4**
Speed ratings (Par 102): **88,87,85,81,73 67,62,52,**
CSF £15.26 TOTE £2.50: £1.10, £3.30, £1.10; EX 14.80 Trifecta £45.40.
Owner Favourites Racing Ltd **Bred** Hardys Of Kilkeel Ltd **Trained** Hanley Swan, Worcestershire

FOCUS
Rail on Hurdles track set out 18yds on Wood Bend and 22yds on Stand Bend. Races 1, 2, 4 & 6 increased by 174yds and races 3 & 5 by 240yds. 16mm of rain last weekend and another 16mm applied over the past three days left good ground with a decent covering of grass. All-hurdles card while drainage work undertaken on chase track. Some decent performances from the front three in this interesting juvenile contest, with a big step up from the winner.

1178 DOUBLE M NOVICES' HURDLE (8 hdls) 2m 148y
2:55 (2:56) (Class 4) 4-Y-O+ **£3,573** (£1,049; £524; £262)

Form RPR
223- 1 **Scrafton**[117] 4222 4-10-11 122.............................. BrianHughes 122+
(John Quinn) *hld up in mid-div: handy 3rd 3 out: 2nd appr next: qcknd to ld last 100yds: pushed out* **15/8**[2]
2511 2 1 ½ **Owen Na View (IRE)**[42] 799 7-11-5 125.............................. PaddyBrennan 126
(Fergal O'Brien) *chsd clr ldr 2nd: led sn after 3 out: rdn between last 2: hdd last 100yds: kpt on same pce* **11/8**[1]
40-2 3 8 **Brigadoon**[15] 1041 8-10-9 112.............................. JonathanEngland(3) 113
(Michael Appleby) *hld up in mid-div: drvn and modest 3rd bef 2 out: one pce: mstke last* **11/4**[3]
0P/ 4 10 **Mr Selby**[76] 6-10-9 0.............................. AdamNicol(3) 103
(Philip Kirby) *led: clr after 1st: j. slowly 4th: lft next 2: hdd sn after 3 out: wknd bef next* **50/1**
5 3 ¼ **Bearskin (IRE)**[22] 4-10-11 0.............................. HenryBrooke 96
(Ann Duffield) *hld up in rr: hdwy to chse ldrs 3 out: lost pl bef next* **50/1**
-054 6 15 **Pixiepot**[15] 1041 5-10-5 0.............................. DenisO'Regan 75
(Peter Niven) *nt fluent in rr: brief effrt 3 out: sn bhd* **20/1**
00 7 53 **Flick Knife (IRE)**[9] 1101 6-10-9 0.............................. KillianMoore(3) 29
(Mark Wall) *chsd ldrs: lost pl 4th: sn bhd: t.o 3 out* **50/1**
60 P **Beedee**[10] 1081 5-10-12 0.............................. MichaelByrne
(Tim Vaughan) *towards rr: p.u sn after 3rd: fatally injured* **66/1**
P **Furas (IRE)**[69] 4-10-11 0.............................. JakeGreenall
(Ruth Carr) *in rr: j.lft 1st: bhd fr 4th: t.o 2 out: p.u bef last* **20/1**

4m 8.5s (1.80) **Going Correction** +0.025s/f (Yiel) **9 Ran SP% 120.5**
WFA 4 from 5yo+ 13lb
Speed ratings (Par 105): **96,95,91,86,85 78,53,,**
CSF £5.01 TOTE £3.00: £1.10, £1.10, £1.20; EX 5.70 Trifecta £10.50.
Owner Fletcher, Outhart, Moran & Maddison **Bred** Bearstone Stud Ltd **Trained** Settrington, N Yorks

FOCUS
A fair novice hurdle run at an even pace. The winner improved in line with his Flat form.

1179 VICTOR LUCAS MEMORIAL NOVICES' HURDLE (10 hdls) 2m 4f 139y
3:30 (3:31) (Class 4) 4-Y-O+ **£3,898** (£1,144; £572; £286)

Form RPR
-201 1 **Tangolan (IRE)**[15] 1042 7-10-12 108..............................(t) PaddyBrennan 117+
(Fergal O'Brien) *mde all: drvn sn after 3 out: edgd lft run-in: hld on towards fin* **11/4**[2]
5- 2 ¾ **Morning Symphony (IRE)**[173] 4148 6-10-12 0..............................(t) DenisO'Regan 116+
(Warren Greatrex) *trckd wnr: drvn 3 out: 3 l down whn nt fluent next: rallied last 75yds: jst hld* **5/1**[3]
2131 3 22 **Father Edward (IRE)**[10] 1082 6-11-12 130..............................(tp) AidanColeman 116+
(John Ferguson) *trckd ldng pair: hit 6th: drvn 3 out: outpcd appr next: wknd run-in: heavily eased clsng stages* **8/11**[1]
40-5 4 23 **Louloumills**[13] 1065 5-9-12 0.............................. RyanDay(7) 67
(Maurice Barnes) *in rr: pushed along and bhd fr 6th: distant 4th last* **100/1**
-P00 5 nk **Quick N' Easy (IRE)**[6] 1117 5-10-12 0.............................. MichealNolan 74
(Sue Gardner) *chsd ldng trio: j.lft 2nd: wknd bef 2 out: sn wl bhd* **100/1**
0-35 6 28 **Little Windmill (IRE)**[3] 1153 5-10-12 0.............................. TrevorWhelan 49
(Neil King) *in rr: bhd fr 6th: distant 4th 2 out* **10/1**
/505 7 46 **Alys Rock (IRE)**[9] 1094 6-10-2 0.............................. JonathanEngland(3)
(Michael Appleby) *t.k.h in last: bhd fr 5th: t.o whn eased 2 out* **40/1**

5m 10.0s (1.20) **Going Correction** +0.025s/f (Yiel) **7 Ran SP% 114.7**
Speed ratings (Par 105): **98,97,89,80,80 69,52**
CSF £16.72 TOTE £3.60: £1.60, £2.60; EX 17.20 Trifecta £53.50.
Owner The Yes No Wait Sorries **Bred** Brian McManus **Trained** Naunton, Gloucs

FOCUS
The three market leaders went clear from an early stage off a decent pace. The winner is rated to his mark.

1180 HEMSWELL SURFACING LIMITED H'CAP HURDLE (10 hdls) 2m 2f 140y
4:05 (4:06) (Class 3) (0-130,130) 4-Y-O+ **£7,797** (£2,289; £1,144; £572)

Form RPR
034- 1 **Poetic Verse**[36] 2503 5-10-8 119.............................. DeanPratt(7) 126+
(John Quinn) *trckd ldrs: 2nd 2 out: shkn up to ld appr last: eased fnl 75yds: v comf* **11/4**[2]
04-U 2 4 **Australia Day (IRE)**[50] 184 12-11-12 130.............................. DenisO'Regan 126
(Paul Webber) *led: clr 4th: edgd rt between last 2: sn hdd: no ch w wnr* **11/2**
/53- 3 2 ¼ **Downtown Boy (IRE)**[89] 3884 7-10-5 109..............................(p) BrianHughes 105
(Ray Craggs) *trckd ldrs: hmpd 4th: handy 2nd sn after 3 out: keeping on same pce whn short of room appr last* **5/1**[3]
11-2 4 3 ½ **Dino Mite**[28] 913 4-11-4 124.............................. MichealNolan 113
(Jamie Snowden) *in rr: pushed along 6th: modest 4th bef 2 out: one pce* **8/1**
U112 5 19 **Russian Royale**[15] 1036 5-10-1 108.............................. CraigNichol(3) 82
(Micky Hammond) *chsd ldrs: lft 2nd 4th: hit 7th: lost pl bef 2 out: sn bhd* **5/2**[1]
-360 6 36 **Marju's Quest (IRE)**[15] 1038 5-11-9 127.............................. NoelFehily 68
(David Dennis) *trckd ldr: blnd 4th: lost pl after 7th: sn bhd: t.o 2 out* **7/1**

4m 35.1s (-4.30) **Going Correction** +0.025s/f (Yiel)
WFA 4 from 5yo+ 13lb **6 Ran SP% 110.9**
Speed ratings (Par 107): **110,108,107,105,97 82**
CSF £17.29 CT £66.94 TOTE £3.40: £1.90, £2.80; EX 18.20 Trifecta £135.10.
Owner J N Blackburn **Bred** The Links Partnership **Trained** Settrington, N Yorks

FOCUS
An open-looking handicap run at a good pace. The winner is a potenial 135 hurdler on Flat form.

1181 JENNISON H'CAP HURDLE (12 hdls) 2m 7f 16y
4:35 (4:36) (Class 4) (0-120,120) 4-Y-O+ **£4,548** (£1,335; £667; £333)

Form RPR
5-50 1 **Count Salazar (IRE)**[18] 1002 10-10-8 105..............................(p) JamesBanks(3) 111+
(Andy Turnell) *led to 3rd: led 7th: hit 3 out: hrd pressed run-in: hld on towards fin: all out* **16/1**
4-05 2 ½ **Church Field (IRE)**[48] 747 7-11-0 108..............................(p) RichieMcLernon 112
(Jonjo O'Neill) *hld up towards rr: hdwy to trck ldrs 7th: drvn bef 2 out: cl 3rd last: styd on to take 2nd last 75yds: jst hld* **15/2**
05-5 3 shd **The Last Leg (IRE)**[35] 845 6-10-0 94..............................(v) PaddyBrennan 99
(Karen McLintock) *in rr: hdwy 3 out: modest 4th bef next: nt fluent last: styd on wl run-in: tk cl 3rd last 50yds* **11/2**[3]
-111 4 1 **Minnie Milan (IRE)**[18] 1002 6-11-12 120.............................. TrevorWhelan 125+
(Neil King) *chsd ldrs: hit 7th: cl 2nd bef 3 out: 2nd whn hit last: fdd nr fin* **9/2**[2]
6443 5 8 **Kyles Faith (IRE)**[5] 1137 7-10-3 97..............................(b) IanPopham 97+
(Martin Keighley) *chsd ldrs: mstke 9th: outpcd appr 2 out* **12/1**
-424 6 3 ¼ **One For Hocky (IRE)**[21] 959 7-11-7 115.............................. BrianHarding 110
(Nicky Richards) *last whn nt fluent 1st: hdwy 7th: drvn bef 3 out: fdd next* **8/1**
P-55 7 16 **Factor Fifty (IRE)**[28] 917 6-11-7 118.............................. AdamNicol(3) 97
(Philip Kirby) *in rr: modest 7th bef 2 out: nvr on terms* **18/1**
3-24 8 1 **Harrys Whim**[32] 868 10-10-7 104..............................(t) JonathanEngland(3) 82
(Maurice Barnes) *mid-div: lost pl 7th: wknd 3 out* **20/1**
-234 9 12 **Los Nadis (GER)**[21] 958 11-10-9 103..............................(v) HenryBrooke 72
(Jim Goldie) *chsd ldr: led 3rd: hdd 7th: hmpd 9th: sn lost pl and bhd: eased between last 2* **20/1**
4U2 10 98 **Only Gorgeous (IRE)**[30] 893 6-10-13 110.............................. LucyGardner(3)
(Sue Gardner) *prom: wkng whn mstke 9th: sn bhd: tailed rt off 2 out* **9/1**
/P-P P **Getmeouthedoldrums**[30] 897 10-9-11 94 oh4..............................(t) KillianMoore(3)
(Mark Wall) *lost pl 2nd: bhd whn reminders 4th: t.o whn p.u after 7th* **66/1**
6-21 P **Dr Robin (IRE)**[21] 967 5-11-1 112.............................. SeanBowen(3)
(Peter Bowen) *chsd ldrs: drvn after 7th: bit slipped and sn bhd: t.o 3 out: p.u bef next* **10/3**[1]

5m 47.6s (-2.90) **Going Correction** +0.025s/f (Yiel) **12 Ran SP% 119.4**
Speed ratings (Par 105): **106,105,105,105,102 101,95,95,91,57 ,**
CSF £129.72 TOTE £19.10: £5.40, £3.10, £2.50; EX 158.90 Trifecta £2031.60.
Owner The Gentlemen Of Salazar **Bred** Mrs Catherine Barry **Trained** Broad Hinton, Wilts

FOCUS
This produced an exciting finish with four bunched crossing the line. Solid form.

1182 BRAYFORD PLASTICS ANNIVERSARY H'CAP HURDLE (8 hdls) 2m 148y
5:05 (5:07) (Class 5) (0-100,100) 3-Y-O+ **£2,599** (£763; £381; £190)

Form RPR
6221 1 **The Kvilleken**[14] 1054 7-11-7 95..............................(p) AndrewTinkler 102+
(Martin Keighley) *hld up in rr: hdwy whn hmpd bnd appr 2 out: chsng ldrs whn nt clr run appr last: hit last: styd on to ld towards fin* **5/1**[2]
0626 2 nk **Dynamic Drive (IRE)**[13] 1071 8-11-0 95..............................(t) RyanDay(7) 99
(Maurice Barnes) *hld up in mid-div: hdwy to chse ldrs 3 out: led narrowly last 75yds: no ex and hdd towards fin* **8/1**
3 3 nse **Mad Money (IRE)**[51] 713 9-10-13 87.............................. PaulMoloney 92
(Sophie Leech) *in rr: hdwy 6th: chsng ldrs next: hmpd last: styd on wl to snatch 3rd clsng stages* **13/2**[3]
P6-0 4 1 ¾ **Carnaross**[2] 1166 6-10-11 88..............................(t) KillianMoore(3) 91
(Sophie Leech) *chsd ldrs: reminders 3 out: led narrowly next: hdd and no ex last 75yds* **15/2**
541U 5 ¾ **Cornish Beau (IRE)**[21] 977 8-11-3 91..............................(p) WillKennedy 94
(Dr Richard Newland) *chsd ldrs: upsides last: kpt on same pce last 75yds* **2/1**[1]

002/ **6** *12* **Until The Man (IRE)**384 5143 8-9-12 **75**........................(b) JamesBanks(3) 66
(Barry Brennan) *prom: drvn appr 2 out: wknd between last 2* **22/1**
45U- **7** *6* **Lord Brantwood**191 3836 4-10-12 **87**........................ MichaelByrne 72
(Tim Vaughan) *in rr: hdwy to chse ldrs 3 out: wknd next* **50/1**
-402 **8** *6* **Imperial Plan (IRE)**28 918 5-11-12 **100**........................(p) BrendanPowell 81
(Jamie Snowden) *led tl after 1st: chsd ldr: led bef 3 out: hit 3 out: hdd next: sn wknd* **8/1**
4PP- **9** *19* **Moving Waves (IRE)**163 4339 4-11-1 **90**........................(t) NoelFehily 53
(Johnny Farrelly) *trckd ldrs: nt fluent 2nd: lost pl whn hmpd 2 out* **9/1**
52P- **P** **Saint Brieuc (FR)**392 868 6-11-7 **95**........................(p) HenryBrooke
(Simon West) *nt fluent: led after 1st: clr 4th: hdd bef 3 out: sn lost pl and bhd: p.u bef next* **12/1**
4-06 **F** **Dover The Moon (IRE)**48 745 4-11-0 **89**........................(t) JamesDavies 72
(Tom Gretton) *prom: chsng ldrs 3 out: wkng whn fell next* **66/1**

4m 7.2s (0.50) **Going Correction** +0.025s/f (Yiel)
WFA 4 from 5yo+ 13lb **11** Ran SP% **122.8**
Speed ratings (Par 103): **99,98,98,98,97 92,89,86,77,**
CSF £46.27 CT £270.57 TOTE £4.40: £1.60, £3.00, £3.20; EX 41.80 Trifecta £257.20.
Owner P Spittle **Bred** A M Tombs **Trained** Condicote, Gloucs

FOCUS
Another exciting finish with five fighting it out to the line and the rest a long way back. Solid enough form.
T/Plt: £211.40 to a £1 stake. Pool: £70,423.80 - 243.11 winning tickets. T/Qpdt: £111.90 to a £1 stake. Pool: £4,068.99 - 26.9 winning tickets. **Walter Glynn**

1183a - (Foreign Racing) - See Raceform Interactive

1174 GALWAY (R-H)
Sunday, August 2

OFFICIAL GOING: Soft

1184a GALWAY SHOPPING CENTRE H'CAP HURDLE (14 hdls) 2m 7f 128y
2:45 (2:46) (81-123,123) 4-Y-0+ **£9,627** (£2,232; £976; £558)

RPR

1 **Slygufftou (IRE)**9 1104 6-10-0 **100**........................(p) LPDempsey(3) 116
(Michael McCullagh, Ire) *chsd ldrs: 5th 1/2-way: pushed along after 3 out to go 3rd next: kpt on steadily u.p to ld 50yds out: styd on wl* **16/1**
2 *1 3/4* **Harangue (IRE)**14 1063 7-10-2 **99**........................(tp) JJBurke 113
(Paul John Gilligan, Ire) *led: hdd after 2nd: styd cl-up: 3rd 1/2-way: led again appr 2 out: jnd at last: led again run-in: no ex fnl 50yds and hdd cl home* **20/1**
3 *1* **Medinah Gold (IRE)**17 1019 6-9-8 **98**........................ JackKennedy(7) 111
(Peter Fahey, Ire) *chsd ldrs: 4th 1/2-way: slt mstke 4 out: pushed along after next to go cl 2nd 2 out: disp at last whn stmbld after flight and hdd: sn no ex* **16/1**
4 *2 1/2* **Redclue (IRE)**35 845 6-10-10 **107**........................(tp) RobbieColgan 118
(Mrs Gillian Callaghan, Ire) *mid-div: slt mstke 4 out: hdwy to go 4th 2 out: no ex u.p fr bef last and kpt on same pce* **9/1**3
5 *12* **Top Of The Town (IRE)**19 993 7-10-9 **106**........................ PaulTownend 105
(C Byrnes, Ire) *in rr of mid-div: tk clsr order after 3 out to go 5th next: no ex u.p bef last and sn one pce* **10/1**
6 *1 1/4* **Abolitionist (IRE)**28 922 7-11-6 **120**........................ BrianHayes(3) 117
(John Joseph Hanlon, Ire) *in rr: pushed along appr 2 out: kpt on wl u.p fr bef last but nvr nr to chal* **25/1**
7 *7 1/2* **St Maxime (IRE)**16 1026 7-9-12 **102**........................(b) JBKane(7) 92
(Gavin Cromwell, Ire) *mid-div: 9th 1/2-way: rdn appr 2 out: no ex u.p between last 2: one pce* **12/1**
8 *3/4* **Dawerann (IRE)**12 1076 6-10-8 **105**........................ MarkEnright 94
(Michael Hourigan, Ire) *towards rr: pushed along after 3 out and sme hdwy: kpt on steadily fr next but nvr nr to chal* **16/1**
9 *nk* **Ravished (IRE)**16 1028 7-11-3 **117**........................(t) DavidMullins(3) 106
(M F Morris, Ire) *a cl-up: 2nd 1/2-way: led 5 out: bad mstke 3 out and hdd appr next: sn drvn in 3rd and lost pl: wknd* **7/2**1
10 *nk* **Seskinane (IRE)**41 817 9-11-1 **119**........................ MrJCBarry(7) 107
(Brian M McMahon, Ire) *in rr of mid-div: tk clsr order fr 5 out: drvn after 3 out: no ex fr 2 out* **16/1**
11 *1* **Never Said That (IRE)**94 50 7-11-1 **112**........................(p) AELynch 99
(Edward Cawley, Ire) *chsd ldrs: 6th 1/2-way: pushed along in 6th appr 2 out: sn no imp and wknd* **10/1**
12 *34* **Nautical Nitwit (IRE)**29 909 6-10-10 **110**........................ GerFox(3) 63
(R P Burns, Ire) *towards rr: u.p fr 3 out: nvr a factor: t.o* **33/1**
13 *2 1/4* **Xaarcet (IRE)**32 867 8-10-11 **108**........................(tp) PaulCarberry 59
(Gordon Elliott, Ire) *a towards rr: nvr in contention: t.o* **16/1**
14 *4 3/4* **Your Busy (IRE)**18 1014 12-11-12 **123**........................(t) RWalsh 69
(J A Nash, Ire) *cl-up: led after 2nd: hdd 5 out: pushed along fr next: sn no ex and wknd: t.o* **14/1**
15 *14* **Top Spin (IRE)**6 1060 8-10-6 **103**........................(tp) MarkWalsh 35
(C A Murphy, Ire) *a towards rr: rdn and no imp fr 3 out: sn bhd: t.o* **20/1**
16 *11* **Our Sox (IRE)**22 955 6-10-6 **103**........................(t) DJCasey 24
(A J Martin, Ire) *wl in rr: rdn and no imp fr 3 out: t.o* **10/1**
17 *3 1/2* **Phangio (USA)**29 910 6-10-2 **99**........................ APHeskin 17
(Colin Bowe, Ire) *mid-div: 8th 1/2-way: pushed along and wknd fr 4 out: t.o* **25/1**
P **Sinbad The Sailor**18 572 10-10-10 **114**........................(v) CiaranGethings(7)
(George Baker) *a towards rr: bhd fr 3 out: p.u bef next* **33/1**
P **Steel King (IRE)**26 943 6-11-4 **115**........................ DavyRussell
(Paul W Flynn, Ire) *a towards rr: bhd fr 3 out: p.u bef next* **7/1**2

6m 2.8s (15.40)
WFA 4 from 5yo+ 15lb **19** Ran SP% **138.9**
CSF £326.93 CT £5185.97 TOTE £19.90: £3.30, £4.20, £4.90, £2.50; DF 667.50.
Owner I R Kidd **Bred** I R Kidd **Trained** Bagnelstown, Carlow
■ Stewards' Enquiry : L P Dempsey two-day ban: use of whip (TBA)

FOCUS
A proper staying handicap run at a generous pace.

1185a AT THE RACES CHASE (14 fncs) 2m 6f 111y
3:55 (3:55) 5-Y-0+ **£11,841** (£3,461; £1,639; £546)

RPR

1 **Cailin Annamh (IRE)**18 1014 7-11-3 **138**........................(bt1) RobbiePower 143
(Mrs John Harrington, Ire) *led: j. sltly to lft at times: in cl to 4 out and dropped to 3rd after next: pushed along to go 2nd again last where nt fluent: kpt on wl u.p on long run-in to ld cl home* **14/1**
2 *2 3/4* **Rebel Fitz (FR)**301 1774 10-11-3 **155**........................ DavyRussell 140+
(Michael Winters, Ire) *trckd ldrs: cl 4th 1/2-way: led narrowly 3 out: rdn clr bef next: stl 4 l clr after last: reduced advantage u.p run-in and wknd: hdd cl home* **9/10**1
3 *13* **Colour Squadron (IRE)**4 1152 9-10-13 **144**........................ BarryGeraghty 123
(E Bolger, Ire) *settled in 5th: prog to go 2nd after 3 out: pushed along bef next: rdn and dropped to 3rd after last: no ex u.p and wknd run-in* **4/1**2
4 *5 1/2* **Conquisto**15 1040 10-11-3 **139**........................ GavinSheehan 122
(Brian Ellison) *cl-up: 2nd 1/2-way: drvn in 4th after 3 out and no imp on principals: kpt on same pce* **14/1**
5 *12* **Aranhill Chief (IRE)**2 1173 8-11-7 **123**........................(t) LPDempsey(3) 117
(S J Mahon, Ire) *settled towards rr: 6th 1/2-way: rdn after 3 out and sn no imp on principals: styd on same pce* **16/1**
6 *shd* **Balnaslow (IRE)**16 1028 8-11-3 **135**........................ RWalsh 110
(W P Mullins, Ire) *settled towards rr: 7th 1/2-way: rdn after 3 out and sme hdwy to go 5th next: no imp on principals run-in and kpt on same pce* **5/1**3
7 *81* **Indevan**4 1152 7-11-10 **144**........................ PaulTownend 36
(W P Mullins, Ire) *in rr: nt fluent at times: 8th 1/2-way: no imp fr 3 out and sn bhd: t.o* **8/1**
8 *24* **Hurricane Ridge (IRE)**15 19 6-11-10 **123**........................(p) MarkBolger 12
(Mrs John Harrington, Ire) *trckd ldr in 2nd: slt mstke 5 out: drvn bef next and lost pl: sn bhd: t.o* **33/1**

5m 35.0s (-5.00) **8** Ran SP% **122.6**
CSF £30.91 TOTE £15.70: £2.50, £1.50, £1.90; DF 54.80 Trifecta £187.90.
Owner Flyers Syndicate **Bred** A J Nevin **Trained** Moone, Co Kildare

FOCUS
A cracker of a race and fitness seemingly won the day.

1186a LORD HEMPHILL MEMORIAL H'CAP CHASE (12 fncs) 2m 2f 54y
4:30 (4:30) 4-Y-0+ **£16,375** (£4,786; £2,267; £755)

RPR

1 **Bally Longford (IRE)**92 96 7-11-3 **128**........................ BarryGeraghty 135
(Henry De Bromhead, Ire) *trckd ldr in 2nd: stl cl 2nd at last and pushed into ld run-in: wnt clr: reduced advantage 100yds out but r.o gamely u.p to hold on* **8/1**
2 *1* **Un Beau Roman (FR)**19 996 7-11-6 **131**........................ RWalsh 137
(W P Mullins, Ire) *attempted to make all: hdd after last and sn 3 l bhd in 2nd: rallied u.p to cl on wnr again cl home but no ex and hld* **10/1**
3 *1 3/4* **Mr Fiftyone (IRE)**19 996 6-11-7 **132**........................(p) RobbiePower 136
(Mrs John Harrington, Ire) *chsd ldrs: 6th at 7th: prog after 3 out and wnt 3rd at last: kpt on strly u.p and clsd gap on front pair run-in but hld cl home* **6/1**2
4 *3 3/4* **Valours Minion (IRE)**19 997 12-9-10 **107** oh1........................(t) MarkEnright 108+
(V T O'Brien, Ire) *mid-div: mstke 6th: gd prog fr 3 out to cl on principals: kpt on steadily run-in to go 4th cl home: nrst fin* **8/1**
5 *1/2* **Midnight Game**15 1038 8-10-13 **124**........................ GavinSheehan 124+
(Brian Ellison) *mid-div: 8th at 7th: pushed along after 3 out and 6th 2 out: kpt on same pce run-in but no ex* **20/1**
6 *6 1/2* **Pires**28 920 11-10-13 **131**........................ DonaghMeyler(7) 126
(A J Martin, Ire) *mid-div: pushed along and sme prog to go 6th at last where mstke: sn rdn and one pce* **14/1**
7 *3 1/4* **Mister Hotelier (IRE)**19 996 8-11-3 **128**........................(t) MPFogarty 118
(C A Murphy, Ire) *chsd ldrs: 4th at 7th: mstke 5 out: sn wnt 3rd: no ex fr last and wknd run-in* **14/1**
8 *10* **Sizing Solution (IRE)**19 996 7-11-0 **125**........................(t) JJBurke 105
(J T R Dreaper, Ire) *chsd ldrs: 5th 1/2-way: pushed along in 4th after 3 out: no imp fr next and wknd* **6/1**2
9 *9 1/2* **Fosters Cross (IRE)**5 479 13-10-13 **127**........................ DavidMullins(3) 98
(Thomas Mullins, Ire) *mid-div: wnt 7th at 7th: pushed along and no ex fr 4 out* **11/1**
10 *7* **Klepht (IRE)**18 1014 10-11-10 **135**........................(t) DavyRussell 99
(Thomas Mullins, Ire) *in rr of mid-div: rdn after 3 out and sme prog but no ex and kpt on same pce fr last* **20/1**
11 *12* **Kates Benefit (IRE)**17 1018 9-10-8 **119**........................ AELynch 71
(David Kenneth Budds, Ire) *in rr of mid-div: no imp after 3 out and sn bhd: nvr a factor* **25/1**
12 *18* **Holeinthewall Bar (IRE)**4 1151 7-9-8 **108**........................ LPDempsey(3) 42
(Michael Hourigan, Ire) *towards rr: no imp fr 4 out and nvr in contention* **7/1**3
13 *10* **Georgie**12 1077 10-9-5 **107** oh18........................(bt) AndrewRing(5) 31
(M O Cullinane, Ire) *towards rr: no imp fr 4 out: nvr in contention* **28/1**
14 *30* **Usa (IRE)**19 996 8-11-3 **128**........................ PaulCarberry 22
(S J Mahon, Ire) *a in rr: nvr a factor: t.o* **20/1**
15 *32* **Coldstonesober (IRE)**4 1151 9-10-8 **119**........................ PaulTownend
(J R Finn, Ire) *wl in rr: last at 7th: nvr in contention: t.o* **11/2**1
P **Kings Grey (IRE)**21 968 11-11-2 **130**........................(bt1) BrianToomey(3)
(Philip Kirby) *chsd ldrs: collided in air w rival 4th: rdn and lost pl fr 4 out: p.u bef 2 out* **25/1**
U **Mitebeall Forluck**281 2069 7-10-2 **113**........................ DJCasey
(A L T Moore, Ire) *chsd ldrs whn mstke and uns rdr 2nd* **20/1**

4m 27.5s (-8.00) **17** Ran SP% **139.6**
CSF £88.37 CT £544.00 TOTE £13.20: £2.50, £3.10, £2.00, £1.60; DF 91.20 Trifecta £599.10.
Owner Ann & Alan Potts Partnership **Bred** J J Fisher **Trained** Knockeen, Co Waterford

FOCUS
Few got into this competitive handicap in which - a bit like the Plate - not many looked well handicapped by any means.

1187 - 1222a (Foreign Racing) - See Raceform Interactive

313 LE LION-D'ANGERS (R-H)
Sunday, August 9

OFFICIAL GOING: Turf: good

1223a PRIX PIANO DE LA JUIVERIE (CHASE) (CONDITIONS) (5YO+) (TURF) 2m 6f
1:15 (12:00) 5-Y-0+ **£8,186** (£4,093; £2,387; £1,620; £767)

RPR

1 **Neofito (FR)**437 522 7-11-0 **0**........................(b) DavidCottin
(P Cottin, France) **7/5**1
2 *6* **Ulysse De Touzaine (FR)**166 7-11-0 **0**........................(p) ArnoldCisel
(A Le Clerc, France) **81/10**
3 *3/4* **Cover Story (FR)**1029 8-10-8 **0**........................ JulienMorel
(L Godard, France) **173/10**

4 nk **Ryvalo Des Brosses (FR)**[437] 10-10-12 0 .... OlivierJouin
(Jean-Paul Gasnier, France) **164/10**

5 nk **Quality John (FR)**[2274] 11-11-5 0 .... MrFTett
(Christian Le Galliard, France) **9/2**[2]

6 dist **Rosabi (FR)**[364] 1203 8-11-0 0 .... (b) NicolasPaysan
(H Paysan, France) **118/10**

7 dist **Cornas (NZ)**[106] 5543 13-10-12 0 .... JamesReveley
(Nick Williams) *t.k.h early: prom: lost pl 17th and dropped into fnl trio: wl bhd bef 3 out: t.o* **26/5**[3]

U **Reventful (FR)**[406] 10-11-0 0 .... StephanePaillard
(E Leray, France) **73/10**

U **Ange Du Lemo (FR)**[798] 616 8-10-6 0 .... AlexandreLethuillier
(A Le Clerc, France) **40/1**

\n\x\x PARI-MUTUEL (all including 1 euro stake): WIN 2.40; PLACE 1.50, 2.20, 3.10;

Owner Jacques Detre **Bred** G Dufour, MME C Dufour **Trained** France

1224 - 1230a (Foreign Racing) - See Raceform Interactive

1223

LE LION-D'ANGERS (R-H)

Monday, August 10

OFFICIAL GOING: Turf: good

1231a PRIX FRANCOIS DE QUATREBARBES (HURDLE) (CONDITIONS) (4YO FILLIES) (TURF) 2m 2f 110y

7:40 (12:00) 4-Y-O **£7,813** (£3,906; £2,279; £1,546; £732)

RPR

1 **Amour D'Or**[50] 813 4-10-6 0 .... StephanePaillard
(Nick Williams) *a.p: sltly outpcd and scrubbed along after 3 out: rallied to chse ldrs 2 out: 2nd and styng on u.p whn lft in ld last: rdn clr* **5/2**[2]

2 10 **Jolila (FR)** 4-10-12 0 .... RomainBonnet
(G Lassausaye, France) **5/1**

3 4 **La Baghera (FR)**[250] 4-10-3 0 .... HugoLucas
(E Leray, France) **104/10**

4 2 **Brise D'Allier (FR)** 4-10-3 0 .... OlivierJouin
(Guy Denuault, France) **26/1**

5 dist **Baguette D'Or (FR)** 4-9-13 0 .... MaximeGorieu(4)
(Gabriel Leenders, France) **35/1**

F **Calcite (FR)** 4-10-6 0 .... (p) BenoitClaudic(4)
(G Mousnier, France) **106/10**

F **Quadriviae (FR)** 4-10-10 0 .... DavidCottin
(D Sourdeau De Beauregard, France) **43/10**[3]

F **Belle Ile (FR)** 4-10-8 0 .... (p) NicolasEven
(P Peltier, France) **21/10**[1]

\n\x\x PARI-MUTUEL (all including 1 euro stake): WIN 3.50; PLACE 1.90, 2.10, 3.00;

Owner French Gold **Bred** T H Chadney **Trained** George Nympton, Devon

1116

NEWTON ABBOT (L-H)

Wednesday, August 12

OFFICIAL GOING: Good to soft (soft in places; 6.2)

Wind: light breeze Weather: hot and sunny; 23 degrees

1232 NEWTONABBOTRACING.COM GRADUATE JUVENILE HURDLE (8 hdls) 2m 167y

2:10 (2:10) (Class 4) 3-Y-O **£3,898** (£1,144; £572; £286)

Form RPR

1 1 **Leoncavallo (IRE)**[31] 975 3-11-5 0 .... AidanColeman 115+
(John Ferguson) *led tl mstke 2nd: pressed ldr: nt fluent 3 out: sn led: sauntered 10 l clr 2 out: v easily* **2/9**[1]

2 18 **Secrets Safe (IRE)**[12] 3-10-12 0 .... (p) RichardJohnson 86
(John Joseph Hanlon, Ire) *pressed ldng pair: pushed along to go 2nd after 3 out: nvr any ch w effrtless wnr after* **10/1**[3]

3 20 **La Voix (FR)**[73] 3-9-12 0 .... MissBFrost(7) 58
(Jimmy Frost) *lft in ld 2nd: hdd after 3 out: sn rdn: tired 20 l 3rd whn hit 2 out: hit last: t.o* **14/1**

4 2 3/4 **Idle Talker (IRE)**[7] 3-10-12 0 .... JamesDavies 64
(Jose Santos) *j. poorly: slow 5th: struggling next: t.o whn blnd last* **5/1**[2]

P **Whistler Mountain**[47] 3-10-12 0 .... TomCannon
(Mark Gillard) *small: j. deliberately 1st: nt fluent 4th: last pair: rdn bef 5th: sn t.o: p.u 2 out* **33/1**

4m 1.0s (-4.70) **Going Correction** -0.325s/f (Good) **5 Ran SP% 117.2**

Speed ratings (Par 102): **98,89,80,78,**

CSF £4.28 TOTE £1.20: £1.02, £4.40; EX 4.50 Trifecta £15.60.

Owner Bloomfields **Bred** Darley **Trained** Cowlinge, Suffolk

FOCUS

All, except the bend after the winning post, on shared bends. This added 62 yards to race 2, 102 yards to race 4 and 80 yards to race 6. The jockeys after the opener said the ground was 'on the soft side of good' and 'there is plenty of juice in it.' The winner of the opener looks an above-average juvenile who can rate higher.

1233 ACTUATE MARKETING, PLYMOUTH H'CAP CHASE (13 fncs) 2m 75y

2:40 (2:40) (Class 4) (0-120,119) 4-Y-0+ **£3,898** (£1,144; £572; £286)

Form RPR

P432 1 **Lisbon (IRE)**[12] 1169 7-11-8 115 .... (t) TomScudamore 125+
(Patrick Griffin, Ire) *pressed ldr: led 8th: drew at least 7 l clr fr 10th: wl in command whn dived at last* **15/8**[1]

14-0 2 7 **Marky Bob (IRE)**[12] 1169 10-10-8 101 .... DaveCrosse 102
(Hugo Froud) *racd freely: lft in ld 2nd: hdd 8th: plodded on and no ch w wnr fr 10th* **11/1**

-062 3 12 **Sublime Talent (IRE)**[19] 1099 9-10-9 112 .... (t) LewisGordon(10) 104
(Evan Williams) *chsd ldng pair: struggling 10th: 15 l 3rd 3 out* **6/1**

-550 4 14 **Avel Vor (IRE)**[24] 1047 4-10-3 110 .... (b[1]) TomO'Brien 76
(Philip Hobbs) *bhd: blnd 7th: last whn blnd next: struggling after: mstke 9th and continued remote: b.b.v* **7/2**[3]

4-B4 5 20 **Vering (FR)**[16] 1121 9-10-0 93 oh18 .... (t) JamesBest 53
(Carroll Gray) *last pair: struggling 9th: t.o last at next* **66/1**

0/0- F **It's All An Act (IRE)**[59] 737 7-11-12 119 .... RichardJohnson
(John Joseph Hanlon, Ire) *led: j. bdly rt 1st: ditto and fell 2nd* **5/2**[2]

4m 4.5s (-2.00) **Going Correction** -0.325s/f (Good)

WFA 4 from 7yo+ 1lb **6 Ran SP% 109.7**

Speed ratings (Par 105): **92,88,82,75,65**

CSF £19.23 TOTE £2.60: £1.20, £5.80; EX 20.80 Trifecta £89.10.

Owner M Deren **Bred** George And Myrtle Grothier **Trained** Oldtown, Co Dublin

FOCUS

A modest contest, in which there was early drama. The winner is rated similar to good recent Bangor run.

1234 IN MEMORY OF MIKE SWIFT NOVICES' HURDLE (8 hdls) 2m 167y

3:10 (3:10) (Class 4) 4-Y-0+ **£3,898** (£1,144; £572; £286)

Form RPR

1 **Anomaly**[680] 6-10-12 0 .... AidanColeman 125+
(John Ferguson) *tall: hld up tl prog 4th: a gng strly after: effrt after 3 out to ld bef next: sn drew rt away on bridle* **11/4**[1]

1 2 15 **Catcher On The Go (IRE)**[81] 444 5-10-12 0 .... PaulMoloney 106+
(Evan Williams) *a.p: 4th and rdn bef 2 out: chsd v easy wnr bef last* **11/4**[1]

-105 3 2 3/4 **Go Odee Go (IRE)**[25] 1038 7-11-7 122 .... (p) BridgetAndrews(5) 118
(Dan Skelton) *prom: ev ch home turn: rdn in 2nd whn mstke 2 out: nt qckn after* **3/1**[2]

040 4 1/2 **Buy Me Out**[49] 834 5-9-12 0 .... AlanJohns(7) 96
(Grace Harris) *chsd ldrs: j.lft 3rd: hrd drvn and effrt bef 2 out where j. awkwardly: n.d after* **100/1**

56- 5 3 1/2 **Cry Fury**[20] 5065 7-10-9 0 .... KillianMoore(3) 98
(Sophie Leech) *a chsng ldrs: rdn and no ex bef 2 out* **25/1**

64 6 hd **I'llhavealook (IRE)**[16] 1116 10-10-5 0 .... (p) JordanWilliams(7) 99
(Katie Stephens) *mstke 1st: towards rr: effrt after 3 out: rdn and wl hld next: plodded on* **50/1**

0- 7 1/2 **Agenor (GER)**[228] 3311 4-10-11 0 .... BrendanPowell 97
(Jamie Snowden) *chsd ldrs tl 3 out: rdn and btn bef next* **8/1**[3]

8 32 **Senor George (IRE)**[21] 8-10-12 0 .... NickScholfield 66
(Simon Hodgson) *hld up wl off pce: sme prog 5th: fdd wl bef 2 out: t.o* **28/1**

9 1 1/4 **Bold Runner**[18] 4-10-11 0 .... JamesDavies 63
(Jose Santos) *midfield: hmpd 5th: struggling after: t.o* **16/1**

10 31 **Gilmer (IRE)**[10] 4-10-11 0 .... (t) JamesBest 32
(Laura Young) *taken down early and mounted on crse: prom and t.k.h: rdn and wknd wl bef 2 out: t.o* **66/1**

05/ P **Hector's Chance**[14] 3141 6-10-12 0 .... AndrewTinkler
(Heather Main) *racd much too freely in ld: hdd bef 2 out and stopped v qckly: p.u 2 out* **33/1**

06 U **Arthur's Queen (FR)**[16] 1117 4-10-4 0 .... MichealNolan 90
(Carroll Gray) *settled wl off pce: effrt 3 out: 6th and btn bef next where nrly fell and uns rdr* **66/1**

\- P **Art Of War (IRE)**[89] 4-10-11 0 .... (v[1]) TomScudamore
(David Pipe) *cl up but j. bdly: losing pl whn nrly fell 5th and p.u* **10/1**

-320 P **Midnight Gypsy**[28] 1009 5-10-5 0 .... (t[1]) PaddyBrennan
(Stuart Kittow) *hld up wl off pce: slt prog 4th: fnd nil 3 out: t.o and p.u next* **16/1**

P **Highridge Princess (IRE)** 7-10-5 0 .... AlainCawley
(Johnny Farrelly) *small: hld up wl off pce: t.o bef 5th: p.u 2 out* **100/1**

P **Shecaughtmyeye** 7-10-5 0 .... TomO'Brien
(Polly Gundry) *v small: hld up wl off pce: t.o bef 5th: p.u 2 out* **66/1**

3m 57.7s (-8.00) **Going Correction** -0.325s/f (Good)

WFA 4 from 5yo+ 13lb **16 Ran SP% 129.0**

Speed ratings (Par 105): **105,97,96,96,94 94,94,79,78,64 , , , ,**

CSF £10.81 TOTE £3.20: £1.30, £1.80, £1.50; EX 13.90 Trifecta £32.10.

Owner Bloomfields **Bred** Darley **Trained** Cowlinge, Suffolk

FOCUS

For quite a while plenty of these raced in a pack, suggesting the early pace wasn't quick. However, one horse proved to be in a different class to his rivals when the race started to unfold.

1235 PAIGNTON ZOO NOVICES' CHASE (20 fncs) 3m 1f 170y

3:45 (3:45) (Class 3) 4-Y-0+ **£6,657** (£2,067; £1,113)

Form RPR

1522 1 **Henllan Harri (IRE)**[31] 965 7-10-13 0 .... (p) SeanBowen(3) 130+
(Peter Bowen) *v slow into 1st and slow at 3rd: j. bttr after: wnt 3rd at 12th: cl up 15th: led bef 3 out and sn 4 l clr: j.rt 2 out and drvn: j.rt again last: all out* **13/8**[2]

4-06 2 2 1/4 **Abolitionist (IRE)**[10] 1184 7-11-12 0 .... RichardJohnson 134
(John Joseph Hanlon, Ire) *pushed along early: pressed ldrs: wnt cl up 15th: chsd wnr u.p after 3 out: one pce and nvr really looked like catching him* **7/2**[3]

P31 3 99 **Ruddy Article (IRE)**[24] 1044 7-11-2 0 .... (t) SamTwiston-Davies 89
(Paul Nicholls) *led tl hdd bef 3 out: stopped v rapidly and sn t.o: virtually walking fr last* **6/4**[1]

-325 P **My Legal Lady**[40] 894 10-10-9 113 .... (vt) TomScudamore
(Stuart Howe) *cl up tl dropped out qckly u.p after 13th and hung rt: p.u next* **14/1**

64 P **Trakeur (FR)**[20] 1085 8-11-2 61 .... NickScholfield
(Simon Hodgson) *last and sn detached: nvr travelling: wl bhd 9th: bdly t.o whn p.u 2 out* **100/1**

355 P **Butlergrove King (IRE)**[28] 1011 6-10-9 0 .... FreddieMitchell(7)
(Natalie Lloyd-Beavis) *cl 2nd: w ldr briefly 7th: stl 2nd at 15th: stopped qckly 17th and continued t.o: p.u 2 out* **25/1**

6m 32.1s (-12.50) **Going Correction** -0.325s/f (Good) **6 Ran SP% 111.8**

Speed ratings (Par 107): **106,105,74, ,**

CSF £7.96 TOTE £2.50: £1.10, £2.40; EX 6.80 Trifecta £11.20.

Owner Einsley Harries **Bred** Paul Ryan **Trained** Little Newcastle, Pembrokes

FOCUS

Not a particularly strong contest, but the winner can make into a good handicapper.

1236 SIS H'CAP HURDLE (10 hdls) 2m 5f 122y

4:15 (4:15) (Class 5) (0-100,100) 4-Y-0+ **£3,422** (£997; £499)

Form RPR

46-3 1 1 3/4 **Always Managing**[36] 938 6-11-10 98 .... (t) AndrewTinkler 107+
(Warren Greatrex) *chsd ldrs: rdn to go 2nd bef 2 out: chalng on inner and got to win abt a nk but jst hld whn squeezed for room 50yds out: nt rcvr and swtchd rt: fin 2nd: awrdd the r* **6/1**[2]

4001 2 **Kentford Heiress**[16] 1120 5-11-2 95 .... KevinJones(5) 104+
(Seamus Mullins) *towards rr: gd prog 6th: led 3 out: drew clr w one rival next and gng best but allowed to drift lft: ears pricked and running on gamely whn barged rival 50yds out: lft clr: fin 1st: disqualified and plcd 2nd* **9/1**

20 3 4 1/2 **Kilcross Boy (IRE)**[28] 1004 10-11-9 97 .... (tp) NoelFehily 100
(Neil Mulholland) *midfield: hdwy 3 out: rdn bef next: one pce and sn no imp on ldrs* **6/1**[2]

226 4 1 3/4 **Eddy**[13] 1158 6-10-3 84 .... ThomasCheesman(7) 85
(John Panvert) *trckd ldrs: effrt 3 out: 4th and rdn bef next: kpt on same pce* **10/1**

4UP/ **5** *17* **Sutton Storm**[241] 10-10-8 **89** .... MrMLegg(7) 75
(John Ryall) *chsd ldrs: effrt after 3 out: rdn bef next: sn lost tch w ldrs* **40/1**

-066 **6** *1 1/2* **Legion D'Honneur (UAE)**[20] 1086 10-11-2 **90** ....(bt[1]) JamesDavies 75
(Chris Down) *prom: rdn and fdd bef 2 out* **16/1**

4P/P **7** *nse* **Haughtons Bridge (IRE)**[90] 293 7-11-10 **98** ....(t) NicodeBoinville 85
(Martin Hill) *pressed ldr tl blnd 3 out: rdn and fdd bef next* **12/1**

P3-P **8** *3* **North London**[16] 1121 8-9-8 **75** ....(bt[1]) MissBFrost(7) 57
(Jimmy Frost) *bhd and nt travelling: rdn 4th: nvr nr ldrs fr 7th* **22/1**

2025 **9** *9* **Lady Of Longstone (IRE)**[20] 1085 5-11-7 **100** ....(b) KieronEdgar(5) 74
(David Pipe) *prom: rdn 7th: no rspnse: fdd 3 out* **14/1**

65-3 **10** *17* **Unefille De Guye (FR)**[50] 824 7-10-6 **80** ....(t) DenisO'Regan 39
(Victor Dartnall) *bhd and nt travelling: detached w one other at 4th: t.o whn mstke 3 out* **7/1**[3]

P0-6 **11** *2 1/4* **Spending Time**[45] 858 6-11-10 **98** ....(bt[1]) TomScudamore 55
(David Pipe) *led tl hdd 3 out: rdn and nt run on: t.o* **9/2**[1]

0-56 **12** *2 3/4* **Milan Of Crystal (IRE)**[61] 712 6-10-6 **80** .... PaddyBrennan 34
(Jimmy Frost) *a towards rr: t.o after 3 out* **20/1**

/0-0 **13** *12* **Midnight Whisper**[43] 864 9-11-10 **98** ....(t) RichardJohnson 41
(Richard Woollacott) *cl up tl rdn and fdd after 6th: t.o after 3 out* **25/1**

-260 **14** *28* **Bedouin Bay**[12] 1170 8-11-5 **100** .... MrRobertHawker(7) 18
(Johnny Farrelly) *bhd: drvn and nt travelling after 6th: t.o after 3 out* **14/1**

F3P4 **15** *1/2* **Dancing Dik**[24] 1049 10-10-8 **82** ....[1] TomO'Brien
(Paul Henderson) *cl up tl dropped out qckly u.p 6th: t.o fr next* **16/1**

5050 **P** **Ho Lee Moses (IRE)**[37] 931 5-11-0 **95** .... MrConorOrr(7)
(Evan Williams) *a wl bhd: t.o and p.u 2 out* **50/1**

5m 11.8s (-8.40) **Going Correction** -0.325s/f (Good) **16** Ran SP% **128.5**
Speed ratings (Par 103): **101,102,99,99,92 92,92,91,87,81 80,79,75,65,65**
CSF £59.11 CT £352.64 TOTE £7.50: £2.20, £2.60, £2.00, £2.90; EX 41.60 Trifecta £617.70.
Owner Harry Redknapp **Bred** Harry Redknapp **Trained** Upper Lambourn, Berks
■ Stewards' Enquiry : Kevin Jones five-day ban: careless riding (Aug 27,29,31,Sep 1-2)

FOCUS
A big field lined up for this moderate contest, but it's debatable how many of them came into it anywhere near their best. There was messy ending, which prompted the original result to be overturned.

1237 THANK YOU FOR 25 WONDERFUL YEARS H'CAP CHASE (16 fncs) 2m 4f 216y
4:50 (4:50) (Class 5) (0-100,100) 4-Y-O+ **£3,422** (£997; £499)

Form RPR

3/0- **1** **Down Time (USA)**[15] 738 5-11-11 **99** ....(p) RichardJohnson 111+
(John Joseph Hanlon, Ire) *cl up: led and mstke 12th: 4 l clr 3 out: sn drvn and idling: a maintaining advantage* **7/1**

6505 **2** *7* **Alla Svelta (IRE)**[28] 1012 9-11-12 **100** ....(p) BrendanPowell 107
(Brendan Powell) *nt fluent 2nd: settled in midfield: effrt 11th: drvn to chse wnr 3 out: nvr making any imp after* **6/1**[3]

1222 **3** *4* **Louis Phillipe (IRE)**[13] 972 8-10-10 **84** ....(t) MichealNolan 86
(Linda Blackford) *racd keenly in 2nd: led 9th: hdd 12th: 5 l 3rd and wkng 3 out* **2/1**[1]

6P-0 **4** *18* **A Keen Sense (GER)**[20] 1080 6-9-7 **74** oh3 ....(p) JamieBargary(7) 65
(David Dennis) *prom: mstke 5th: 10 l 4th and rdn 3 out: struggling after: mstke next* **12/1**

-4P5 **5** *10* **Stafford Charlie**[20] 1080 9-10-2 **76** oh7 ow2 ....(p) DaveCrosse 55
(John O'Shea) *midfield: in tch tl mstke 12th: no ch and kpt jumping modly after* **22/1**

3-3P **6** *6* **Rusty Nail (IRE)**[52] 806 10-10-1 **82** .... MissBFrost(7) 53
(Jimmy Frost) *nt fluent 2nd and 7th: bhd: nvr really travelling: no ch fr 10th: t.o bef 3 out* **4/1**[2]

PF-P **P** **Bringewood Belle**[103] 58 12-10-0 **74** .... PeterCarberry
(John Needham) *hld up: losing pl and rdn whn j. slowly 6th: sn last: t.o and p.u 10th* **20/1**

0/0 **P** **Flight Control (IRE)**[12] 1166 10-11-5 **93** ....(t) JamesDavies
(Peter Croke, Ire) *sn bhd: rdn and losing tch 9th: bdly t.o whn p.u 12th* **50/1**

6/PP **P** **Brannoc (IRE)**[16] 1120 10-9-9 **74** oh5 ....(t) AliceMills(5)
(Gail Haywood) *j. slowly 4th and reminders: bhd and nt travelling after: t.o 10th: p.u next* **40/1**

2-P3 **P** **Forget And Forgive (IRE)**[31] 972 7-10-11 **88** ....(vt) KillianMoore(3)
(Sophie Leech) *led tl 9th: drvn and no rspnse: sn lost pl: t.o and p.u 2 out* **9/1**

P **P** **Tiger D'Oust (FR)**[31] 976 6-11-2 **95** ....(p) KieronEdgar(5)
(Chris Down) *a wl bhd: lost tch 9th: t.o 12th: p.u 2 out* **17/2**

5m 22.2s (0.80) **Going Correction** -0.325s/f (Good) **11** Ran SP% **121.8**
Speed ratings (Par 103): **85,82,80,73,70 67,,,,**
CSF £48.89 CT £117.58 TOTE £7.40: £2.00, £1.50, £1.70; EX 35.70 Trifecta £101.40.
Owner Mrs A F Mee **Bred** Brookdale & Ted Folkerth **Trained** Bagenalstown, Co Carlow

FOCUS
A pretty weak race, in which the two highest-rated on official figures came home first and second. The winner is improving in line with his best hurdles form.

1238 LIVING COASTS CONDITIONAL JOCKEYS' H'CAP HURDLE (9 hdls) 2m 2f 110y
5:20 (5:21) (Class 4) (0-120,120) 4-Y-O+ **£3,898** (£1,144; £572; £286)

Form RPR

4-5U **1** **Honey Pound (IRE)**[31] 973 7-11-4 **117** .... AlanJohns(6) 124+
(Tim Vaughan) *on his toes in preliminaries: trckd ldrs: tk narrow ld after 3 out and sn gng clr w one other: rdn whn clipped next: a holding rival after* **9/1**

60-1 **2** *2 1/4* **Welcometothejungle**[36] 938 7-10-12 **110** ....(t) LiamMcKenna(5) 114
(Harry Fry) *2nd tl led 5th: hdd bef next: pressed wnr hrd fr after 3 out: rdn and edgd rt whn making no imp between last two* **5/2**[1]

3-45 **3** *2 1/2* **Skylander (IRE)**[31] 969 6-11-2 **115** .... MichaelHeard(6) 118
(David Pipe) *settled towards rr: stdy prog 6th: wnt 5 l 3rd after 3 out: drvn and hld fr bef next* **11/2**[2]

0640 **4** *6* **Party Palace**[8] 1046 11-10-10 **103** .... SeanBowen 99
(Stuart Howe) *midfield: rdn and outpcd after 3 out: plugged on for wl hld 4th fr next* **22/1**

5-62 **5** *3 1/4* **Key To Milan**[24] 1048 9-11-3 **110** ....(tp) GilesHawkins 103
(Chris Down) *kpt wl away fr rest at s: prom: led bef 6th tl after 3 out: rdn and wknd wl bef next* **15/2**[3]

-134 **6** *14* **Dun Scaith (IRE)**[24] 1046 7-11-2 **112** ....(t) KillianMoore(3) 93
(Sophie Leech) *led tl hdd bef 6th: dropped out qckly* **12/1**

4236 **7** *7* **Un Anjou (FR)**[15] 1135 7-11-9 **119** .... JamieBargary(3) 94
(David Dennis) *bhd: wl btn 3 out* **25/1**

1436 **8** *7* **Lochalsh (IRE)**[24] 1046 4-11-8 **120** .... BridgetAndrews(3) 86
(Dan Skelton) *midfield: rdn bef 3 out: sn wl btn: t.o* **12/1**

4000 **9** *3 1/4* **Exemplary**[17] 1113 8-10-3 **104** ....(bt) MrRobertHawker(8) 69
(Johnny Farrelly) *t.k.h and prom tl lost pl 6th: t.o* **16/1**

2022 **10** *3 1/2* **Baths Well (IRE)**[19] 1100 5-11-3 **118** ....(p) HarrisonBeswick(8) 80
(Ben Pauling) *slow to go and rdn: reluctant and sn tailed himself off* **11/1**

5340 **11** *14* **Hold Court (IRE)**[12] 1170 8-11-2 **112** .... ConorRing(3) 62
(Evan Williams) *a wl to rr: t.o 3 out* **18/1**

50/- **12** *8* **School For Scandal (IRE)**[845] 5376 7-10-4 **100** .... PaulO'Brien(3) 42
(Jimmy Frost) *bhd: rdn after 5th: t.o 3 out* **40/1**

64-2 **13** *nk* **Zephyr**[42] 880 4-10-10 **108** .... LizzieKelly(3) 48
(Nick Williams) *wl bhd: rdn and no rspnse 5th: sn t.o* **15/2**[3]

4m 24.9s (-5.10) **Going Correction** -0.325s/f (Good)
WFA 4 from 5yo+ 13lb **13** Ran SP% **123.0**
Speed ratings (Par 105): **97,96,95,92,91 85,82,79,77,76 70,67,67**
CSF £32.75 CT £143.38 TOTE £10.70: £2.90, £1.60, £1.90; EX 44.70 Trifecta £375.40.
Owner D&S Luke & Great Northern Partnership II **Bred** Islanmore Stud **Trained** Aberthin, Vale of Glamorgan

FOCUS
An ordinary race, but the form looks fairly strong for the level with the winner on a good mark.
T/Jkpt: £3541.80 to a £1 stake. Pool: £82,310.95 - 16.50 winning units. T/Plt: £11.00 to a £1 stake. Pool: £70,862.62 - 4672.29 winning units. T/Qpdt: £3.40 to a £1 stake. Pool: £6,114.85 - 1307.49 winning units. **Iain Mackenzie**

669 FONTWELL (L-H)
Thursday, August 13

OFFICIAL GOING: Good to soft (good in places) changing to good to soft after race 1 (1.15)
Wind: light breeze Weather: overcast after heavy rain; brightening and muggy later; 19 degrees

1239 SARA TIARA HAT WEAR H'CAP HURDLE (9 hdls) 2m 1f 145y
1:15 (1:15) (Class 4) (0-120,120) 3-Y-O+ **£3,249** (£954; £477; £238)

Form RPR

0443 **1** **Royal Battalion**[38] 930 4-10-12 **107** ....(p) TomCannon 108
(Gary Moore) *chsd ldrs: shkn up 6th: rdn 3 out: sltly outpcd bef next but rallied u.p to ld last: sn asserted and r.o gamely* **7/1**

-121 **2** *1 1/4* **At First Light**[29] 1012 6-11-0 **108** .... NicodeBoinville 109
(David Weston) *prom: nt fluent 5th: wnt 2nd briefly whn rdn 3 out: sltly outpcd between last two: 5th at last: styd on: hld by wnr flat but tried hrd* **5/2**[2]

1014 **3** *2* **Zarawi (IRE)**[28] 862 4-11-5 **114** ....(p) RichardJohnson 112
(Charlie Longsdon) *settled towards rr: effrt on outer fr 2 out: drvn and tried to chal last: one pce flat* **17/2**

5223 **4** *3* **Royal Skies (IRE)**[21] 1083 5-11-9 **117** ....(vt) AidanColeman 115
(John Ferguson) *t.k.h and trckd ldrs: effrt 3 out: wnt 2nd home turn: rdn to ld 2 out: fnd v little and hdd last: sn btn and eased* **9/4**[1]

3-64 **5** *3 3/4* **Perspicace**[20] 1100 4-11-11 **120** .... TomScudamore 114
(David Pipe) *2nd tl led and mstke 6th: rdn and hdd 2 out: fnd little and wknd bef last* **6/1**[3]

055- **6** *3/4* **Mandy's Boy (IRE)**[17] 5283 5-10-8 **102** .... WillKennedy 94
(Ralph J Smith) *hld up last tl 3 out: stdy prog after: rdn to chal and flattered last: sn wknd flat* **20/1**

342- **7** *1 3/4* **Goal (IRE)**[10] 2466 7-11-1 **116** ....(t) MissBHampson(7) 107
(Andy Turnell) *bhd: rdn after 3 out: plugged on and n.d fr next* **14/1**

6653 **8** *24* **Limpopo Tom (IRE)**[25] 1051 8-11-4 **112** .... DenisO'Regan 81
(David Rees) *nt fluent: led tl 6th: last after next: t.o 2 out* **14/1**

4m 31.3s (-3.00) **Going Correction** -0.025s/f (Good)
WFA 4 from 5yo+ 13lb **8** Ran SP% **114.7**
Speed ratings (Par 105): **105,104,103,102,100 100,99,88**
CSF £25.65 CT £152.11 TOTE £6.10: £2.40, £1.60, £2.20; EX 29.40 Trifecta £251.30.
Owner Heart Of The South Racing **Bred** Newsells Park Stud **Trained** Lower Beeding, W Sussex

FOCUS
Bottom bend common, hurdles on inner. Rail movements added 45 yards to each circuit on the chase course and 15 yards to each circuit of the hurdles track. Persistent rain fell prior to racing, which changed the overnight going of good, good to firm in places to good to soft, good in places before the first. The front pair in this ordinary handicap are on the upgrade.

1240 GEORGE DIGWEED SPORTING AGENCY NOVICES' HURDLE (9 hdls) 2m 1f 145y
1:45 (1:46) (Class 4) 4-Y-O+ **£3,249** (£954; £477; £238)

Form RPR

415 **1** **I'dliketheoption (IRE)**[13] 1168 4-11-4 0 .... RichieMcLernon 117+
(Jonjo O'Neill) *settled towards rr in slowly run r: hit 6th: effrt 2 out: rdn to dispute 2nd at last: led 100yds out: hld on wl* **13/2**

0-13 **2** *nk* **Antony (FR)**[55] 780 5-11-5 120 .... RichardJohnson 117
(Gary Moore) *settled in midfield: effrt gng wl after 3 out: led bef next: sn rdn: hdd fnl 100yds: kpt on u.p but jst hld* **5/4**[1]

3 *2 1/4* **Bedale**[414] 4-10-11 0 ....(v[1]) AidanColeman 106
(John Ferguson) *settled in midfield: effrt bef 2 out: rdn and disp cl 2nd at last: no ex fnl 100yds* **11/4**[2]

-113 **4** *5* **Noble Friend (IRE)**[26] 1042 7-10-12 117 .... TomCannon 103
(Chris Gordon) *trckd ldrs: wnt 2nd bef 2 out: drvn and dropped bk 4th at last: wl hld after* **10/3**[3]

45 **5** *12* **Lee Side Lady (IRE)**[17] 1116 5-10-5 0 .... MarkQuinlan 83
(Neil Mulholland) *slt ld at slow pce tl 3rd: hit 6th: remained prom w ev ch tl rdn and lost pl bef 2 out* **66/1**

50 **6** *8* **Sturmwind (GER)**[25] 1044 4-10-11 0 .... LeightonAspell 82
(Alison Batchelor) *slt ld 3rd tl rdn and hdd bef 2 out: sn wknd* **100/1**

00 **7** *16* **Prince Of Silver**[21] 1081 9-10-9 0 ....(t) JamesBanks(3) 66
(Andy Turnell) *j. deliberately 2nd: in last trio: rdn and lost tch after 3 out: t.o and tired whn hit next* **100/1**

60 **8** *3/4* **Sharp Sword (IRE)**[17] 1117 4-10-11 0 .... NoelFehily 64
(Neil Mulholland) *t.k.h in last: shkn up and lost tch after 3 out: t.o next: may do bttr* **50/1**

36-5 **9** *3 3/4* **The Western Force (IRE)**[21] 1081 5-10-12 0 .... HarrySkelton 62
(Dan Skelton) *small: w ldng pair tl rdn 6th: dropped out tamely: t.o bef 2 out* **20/1**

4m 34.7s (0.40) **Going Correction** -0.025s/f (Good)
WFA 4 from 5yo+ 13lb **9** Ran SP% **117.7**
Speed ratings (Par 105): **98,97,96,94,89 85,78,78,76**
CSF £15.82 TOTE £7.30: £1.70, £1.10, £1.70; EX 18.50 Trifecta £61.40.
Owner John P McManus **Bred** Stephen O'Flynn **Trained** Cheltenham, Gloucs

FOCUS
The going was changed to good to soft all over prior to this interesting novice hurdle. The early pace wasn't strong and it turned into a sprint heading to the second-last.

1241 AVIATOR BAR AND RESTAURANT BOGNOR REGIS H'CAP CHASE (13 fncs) 2m 1f 96y
2:15 (2:15) (Class 4) (0-120,120) 4-Y-O+ **£4,183** (£1,521)

Form RPR

U225 **1** **Marie Des Anges (FR)**[38] [927] 7-11-4 **119**.................(t) DavidNoonan(7) 126+
(Anthony Honeyball) *cl up: led gng wl 9th: hrd pressed but stl travelling comf whn lft almost solo 2 out: pushed out* **5/2**[2]

11-6 **2** *59* **Try Catch Me (IRE)**[16] [1136] 10-10-12 **106**...................(b) LeightonAspell 73
(Alison Batchelor) *led tl 9th: drvn and sn fdd: lft remote 2nd and mstke 2 out: eased last* **9/2**

P031 **P** **Formal Bid (IRE)**[26] [1043] 8-11-6 **117**...........................(bt) JamesBanks(3)
(Barry Brennan) *immediately rdn and nvr gng w any zest: u.p 5th: lost tch completely 10th and p.u wl bef next* **4/1**[3]

-631 **F** **Dream Bolt (IRE)**[17] [1121] 7-11-1 **109**............................ PaulMoloney 116
(David Rees) *cl up and t.k.h: nt fluent 3rd: mstke 9th: effrt and pressing wnr w ev ch whn fell 2 out* **11/8**[1]

4m 41.3s (6.60) **Going Correction** +0.55s/f (Soft) **4** Ran SP% **108.9**
Speed ratings (Par 105): **106,78, ,**
CSF £12.33 TOTE £2.30; EX 11.00 Trifecta £11.20.
Owner Atlantic Racing & R W Huggins **Bred** Pegasus Breeding Ltd **Trained** Mosterton, Dorset

FOCUS
Quite a bit of interest was lost in this when Walden Prince was taken out prior to the race, and it produced an unsatisfactory finish, with one of the pair who drew well clear falling two from home, leaving the winner a long way clear. The winner has been rated to his mark.

1242 WIN A FOOTBALL FORTUNE WITH SCOOP6SOCCER H'CAP HURDLE (11 hdls) 2m 5f 139y
2:45 (2:45) (Class 4) (0-120,118) 4-Y-O+ **£3,249** (£954; £477; £238)

Form RPR

022- **1** **For 'N' Against (IRE)**[135] [5082] 6-11-3 **109**.................(t) TomScudamore 122+
(David Pipe) *settled trcking ldrs: led 3 out: immediately drew clr: unchal fr next where nt fluent: heavily eased after hitting last* **3/1**[2]

0-05 **2** *25* **Skint**[39] [915] 9-11-4 **110**...(p) AidanColeman 96
(Ali Stronge) *settled cl up: effrt to 2nd after 3 out but sn hrd drvn and wnr gng clr: 12 l down whn hit 2 out: plodded on in vain pursuit and v flattered by fnl proximity* **12/1**

6P-3 **3** *6* **Hi Note**[29] [669] 7-11-6 **112**... MarcGoldstein 90
(Sheena West) *sticky 1st: prom tl rdn after 7th: struggling next: plugged on into poor 3rd bef last* **7/1**[3]

3-63 **4** *½* **Morestead Screamer**[43] [880] 6-11-4 **110**........................ TomCannon 88
(Chris Gordon) *led at modest pce: hdd 4th: mstke 5th: rdn to ld after 7th: hdd 3 out: lost tch w ldng pair u.p bef next: mstke last* **7/1**[3]

0-2 **P** **A Cor Et A Cri (FR)**[101] [102] 5-11-6 **112**..........................(t) NoelFehily
(Harry Fry) *wnt 2nd at 3rd: led next: hdd after 7th: fdd v tamely after 3 out: t.o and p.u last* **1/1**[1]

5m 39.0s (-3.50) **Going Correction** -0.025s/f (Good) **5** Ran SP% **107.7**
Speed ratings (Par 105): **105,95,93,93,**
CSF £28.35 TOTE £3.20: £1.80, £2.80; EX 22.50 Trifecta £78.20.
Owner E A P Scouller **Bred** P A D Scouller **Trained** Nicholashayne, Devon

FOCUS
Four non-runners meant this was far weaker than it had looked at the overnight stage, and the market leader proved to be very disappointing. Seemingly a big step up from the easy winner.

1243 MAUREEN STURT LADIES DAY NOVICES' H'CAP CHASE (16 fncs) 2m 5f 31y
3:15 (3:15) (Class 5) (0-100,100) 4-Y-O+ **£2,469** (£725; £362; £181)

Form RPR

5P24 **1** **Sylvan Legend**[25] [1045] 7-10-1 **75**...........................(tp) MarkQuinlan 87+
(Neil Mulholland) *mounted outside paddock: settled towards rr of cl bunch: effrt in 2nd 3 out: led next: 3 l clr last: drvn and all out after* **13/2**

3253 **2** *1¼* **The Wee Midget**[25] [1049] 10-9-13 **80**...................(b) ThomasCheesman(7) 90
(Arthur Whiting) *cl 2nd tl led 11th: hdd next: 3rd and drvn after 3 out: outpcd briefly: wnt 2nd at last and tried to cl: no imp fnl 100yds* **9/2**[2]

P03 **3** *10* **Blackwood Rover (IRE)**[14] [1159] 7-11-2 **90**.......................... PaulMoloney 91
(J R Jenkins) *trckd ldrs: led gng wl bef 3 out: hdd next and rdn: fdd tamely bef last* **5/1**[3]

32U0 **4** *nk* **Breezy Kin (IRE)**[29] [1004] 7-10-8 **85**...........................(p) JamesBanks(3) 88
(Andy Turnell) *mstkes 7th and 9th: mde most but frequently drvn along: hdd u.p bef 3 out: btn next* **11/4**[1]

-624 **5** *1¾* **Where'd Ya Hide It (IRE)**[17] [1118] 9-10-4 **78** ow2...........(t[1]) TomO'Brien 77
(Paul Henderson) *midfield: stl cl 5th after 13th but bmpd along and sn dropped out* **15/2**

5236 **6** *nk* **Lord Of The Dunes**[14] [1159] 7-10-13 **87**...................(bt) BrendanPowell 86
(Jamie Snowden) *towards rr but cl up: rdn after 7th: nvr looked to be gng wl enough: rdn and lost tch bef 3 out* **8/1**

4/0P **P** **Oscar Baby (IRE)**[55] [782] 9-10-1 **75**.............................. MarcGoldstein
(Diana Grissell) *rdn 4th: lost tch and mstke 5th: sn t.o: p.u 8th* **16/1**

00PP **P** **Vinceson (IRE)**[21] [1079] 7-10-0 **74** oh2..............................(bt) JamesBest
(Jess Westwood) *mounted outside paddock: chsd ldrs: mstke 9th: nt keen after: t.o next: p.u 12th* **25/1**

5-40 **P** **Tiger Feat**[21] [1084] 5-10-12 **86**..(b) AidanColeman
(Ali Stronge) *towards rr: mstke 6th: struggling whn p.u 9th* **25/1**

5PP- **F** **Kerry Maur**[129] [5212] 6-10-6 **80**.. TomCannon
(Chris Gordon) *bhd tl fell 2nd* **10/1**

5m 53.8s (10.80) **Going Correction** +0.55s/f (Soft) **10** Ran SP% **120.4**
Speed ratings (Par 100): **101,100,96,96,95 95, , , ,**
CSF £38.03 CT £159.83 TOTE £8.60: £2.50, £2.20, £1.90; EX 43.80 Trifecta £200.20.
Owner Brian Derrick **Bred** Larkinglass Ltd **Trained** Limpley Stoke, Wilts

FOCUS
A moderate but competitive race and a step up from the winner.

1244 £50 WELCOME BONUS AT RACEBETS.COM H'CAP HURDLE (DIV I) (10 hdls) 2m 3f 33y
3:45 (3:45) (Class 5) (0-100,98) 4-Y-O+ **£2,339** (£686; £343; £171)

Form RPR

P006 **1** **Osgood**[38] [931] 8-11-2 **98**.............................(v) GeorgeGorman(10) 106+
(Gary Moore) *t.k.h: pressed ldrs: nt fluent 3rd: gng bttr than most bef 2 out where wnt 2nd: led last: urged clr flat* **20/1**

3146 **2** *2¾* **Herecomesthetruth (IRE)**[38] [926] 13-11-5 **91**.................. TomCannon 96
(Chris Gordon) *cl 2nd: drvn 3 out: sn led but idling: hdd and stl had ears pricked last: outbattled fnl 100yds* **14/1**

5-65 **3** *2¼* **El Toreros (USA)**[46] [859] 7-11-0 **86**...........................(tp) AidanColeman 89
(Lawney Hill) *led: rdn and hdd after 3 out: ev ch tl nt qckn bef last* **12/1**

6452 **4** *2½* **Bulletproof (IRE)**[29] [1010] 9-10-12 **84**...........................(p) RichardJohnson 85
(Ken Cunningham-Brown) *chsd ldrs: rdn after 3 out: tried to chal between last two: tiring flat* **7/2**[1]

41U5 **5** *1½* **Cornish Beau (IRE)**[11] [1182] 8-11-5 **91**.............................(p) WillKennedy 92
(Dr Richard Newland) *prom: hit 3 out: sn rdn: continued to press ldrs tl wknd last* **9/2**[3]

00-5 **6** *6* **Lyssio (GER)**[65] [675] 8-10-8 **87**.. MrDGBurchell(7) 83
(Mark Hoad) *last pair: bmpd along and sme hdwy bef 2 out: plugged on but nvr nr ldrs* **7/2**[1]

6-53 **7** *6* **Hold The Fort (IRE)**[17] [1120] 8-11-9 **95**..................................(t) NoelFehily 84
(Johnny Farrelly) *a towards rr: wknd bef 2 out* **4/1**[2]

6PU- **8** *20* **Tang Royal (FR)**[145] [4903] 8-10-3 **75**..................................(t) PaddyBrennan 46
(Richard Rowe) *last pair: rdn bef 7th: t.o after next* **14/1**

0060 **9** *5* **Bobonyx**[14] [1158] 5-9-7 **72** oh3...(v) MissPFuller(7) 38
(Dai Williams) *chsd ldrs: beginning to struggle whn mstke 7th: fdd qckly and t.o after next* **16/1**

4m 56.4s (-3.00) **Going Correction** -0.025s/f (Good) **9** Ran SP% **114.3**
Speed ratings (Par 103): **105,103,102,101,101 98,96,87,85**
CSF £253.28 CT £3473.60 TOTE £15.90: £4.30, £3.30, £3.60; EX 143.80 Trifecta £650.30.
Owner G L Moore **Bred** Eurostrait Ltd **Trained** Lower Beeding, W Sussex

FOCUS
A weak race for moderate performers, run at a respectable gallop. The winner was well in on course form from last August.

1245 £50 WELCOME BONUS AT RACEBETS.COM H'CAP HURDLE (DIV II) (10 hdls) 2m 3f 33y
4:15 (4:15) (Class 5) (0-100,97) 4-Y-O+ **£2,339** (£686; £343; £171)

Form RPR

06P- **1** **Shalianzi (IRE)**[17] [5212] 5-11-3 **88**.......................(b) AndrewGlassonbury 102+
(Gary Moore) *trckd ldrs: effrt to dispute 2nd and hrd drvn after 3 out: led next: drew 10 l clr last: sn heavily eased* **10/1**

5P53 **2** *16* **Keychain (IRE)**[32] [977] 5-11-12 **97**...........................(bt) BrendanPowell 91
(Brendan Powell) *cl up: led 7th: rdn and hdd and nt fluent 2 out: immediately outpcd by wnr: wobbling arnd fr last but managed to cling on to remote 2nd* **7/2**[2]

P-0P **3** *1* **Al Guwair (IRE)**[71] [599] 5-10-6 **77**.. MarcGoldstein 69
(Mark Hoad) *bhd: rdn 6th: 10 l 6th home turn: kpt on to try for remote 2nd fr last but v one pce* **25/1**

2P45 **4** *2½* **Owner Occupier**[21] [1086] 10-9-7 **74**.............................(p) MrWRClarke(10) 63
(Chris Gordon) *led tl 7th: rdn after next: btn 2 out: plodded on* **7/2**[2]

3334 **5** *¾* **Significant Move**[13] [1166] 8-10-8 **84**..................................(b) ChrisWard(5) 76
(Dr Richard Newland) *t.k.h and cl up: rdn after 3 out: no rspnse: btn whn blnd next* **6/4**[1]

/4-3 **6** *41* **Marlpit Oak**[41] [893] 10-10-13 **91**.. MrDSansom(7) 43
(Seamus Mullins) *bhd and sn rdn: nt fluent 3rd: struggling 6th: t.o after 3 out* **16/1**

00-U **P** **Yes I Will**[81] [451] 6-11-0 **90**...(tp) JackSherwood(5)
(Linda Jewell) *pressed ldr tl rdn and fdd rapidly 6th: t.o after next: p.u 2 out* **8/1**[3]

1-04 **P** **Tara Dove**[68] [643] 7-11-10 **95**.. LeightonAspell
(Alison Batchelor) *cl up tl rdn 5th: dropped out rapidly next: t.o 7th: p.u after 3 out* **25/1**

4m 55.5s (-3.90) **Going Correction** -0.025s/f (Good) **8** Ran SP% **118.2**
Speed ratings (Par 103): **107,100,99,98,98 81, ,**
CSF £47.27 CT £857.44 TOTE £8.50: £2.40, £1.60, £3.20; EX 53.60 Trifecta £430.00.
Owner Ashley Head **Bred** His Highness The Aga Khan's Studs S C **Trained** Lower Beeding, W Sussex

FOCUS
Not form to dwell on, even though the winner won with ease.

1246 MAUREEN STURT MEMORIAL STANDARD OPEN NATIONAL HUNT FLAT RACE 2m 1f 145y
4:45 (4:45) (Class 6) 4-6-Y-O **£1,559** (£457; £228; £114)

Form RPR

1 **Nicely Indeed (IRE)**[256] 5-10-9 0.. MikeyHamill(7) 113+
(Seamus Durack) *cl-cpld: pressed ldrs: wnt 2nd gng wl 5f out: led gng best 2f out: sn rdn and green but a holding rival fnl f* **7/1**[3]

2-11 **2** *3* **Amirr (IRE)**[32] [963] 5-11-5 0.. MrAlexFerguson(7) 119+
(John Ferguson) *2nd tl led 6f out: rdn and hdd 2f out: stuck on wl enough fnl f but a hld* **10/11**[1]

6-6 **3** *2½* **Menace**[38] [928] 4-10-12 0.. JamesBanks(3) 105+
(Noel Williams) *bhd: outpcd 5f out: rdn to go 10 l 3rd home turn: no imp tl styd on strly fnl 100yds* **40/1**

4 **4** *24* **Oh So Gigolo (IRE)**[44] [865] 5-10-9 0.................................... FreddieMitchell(7) 84
(Nicky Henderson) *pressed ldng pair: rdn 6f out: floundering wl over 2f out: t.o* **3/1**[2]

5 *10* **Native Robin (IRE)**[75] 5-11-2 0.. HarrySkelton 75
(Dan Skelton) *led tl hdd 6f out: sn rdn: lost tch 3f out: t.o* **12/1**

6 *1½* **Tinkers Hill Tommy (IRE)** 4-11-1 0...................................... RichardJohnson 73
(Tom Lacey) *small: burly: towards rr: pushed along 7f out: t.o over 2f out* **8/1**

P- **7** *1¾* **Leith Hill (IRE)**[364] [1222] 5-11-2 0.. TomCannon 72
(Laura Mongan) *in tch tl rdn 7f out: sn t.o* **50/1**

4m 24.8s (-3.90) **Going Correction** -0.025s/f (Good)
WFA 4 from 5yo 1lb **7** Ran SP% **113.1**
Speed ratings: **107,105,104,93,89 88,88**
CSF £13.54 TOTE £9.80: £3.20, £1.10; EX 23.50 Trifecta £230.10.
Owner Gary Tardi & ownaracehorse.co.uk **Bred** R Guiry **Trained** Upper Lambourn, Berkshire

FOCUS
Hardly any of these featured, as two same well clear. The winner looks a decent prospect.

T/Plt: £409.40 to a £1 stake. Pool: 53,897.78 - 96.09 winning tickets. T/Qpdt: £164.20 to a £1 stake. Pool: 4,637.88 - 20.9 winning tickets. **Iain Mackenzie**

1247 - 1259a (Foreign Racing) - See Raceform Interactive

1177

MARKET RASEN (R-H)

Saturday, August 15

OFFICIAL GOING: Good (8.2)
Wind: light 1/2 against Weather: fine and sunny

1260 MANTERFIELD DRILLING NOVICES' HURDLE (10 hdls) 2m 4f 139y
5:40 (5:42) (Class 4) 4-Y-0+ £3,249 (£954; £477; £238)

Form RPR
0P/4 1 **Mr Selby**[13] 1178 6-10-9 0 AdamNicol[(3)] 111
(Philip Kirby) *led: hdd narrowly 2 out: rallied run-in: led nr fin* **25/1**
36-U 2 ½ **Swivel**[16] 1153 4-10-10 0 (p) AidanColeman 109
(John Ferguson) *trckd ldrs: led narrowly 2 out: hdd and no ex nr fin* **4/1**[3]
334 3 ¾ **Presenting Streak (IRE)**[16] 1153 6-10-5 0 MrRWinks[(7)] 110
(Peter Winks) *mid-div: chsd ldrs 5th: drvn 3 out: 6th last: hung bdly lft run-in: styd on to take 3rd clsng stages* **11/1**
000- 4 1 ¾ **Dr Irv**[11] 2776 6-10-2 107 FinianO'Toole[(10)] 109
(Micky Hammond) *chsd ldrs: hung rt and kpt on same pce run-in* **8/1**
453 5 3 ¾ **Keep Calm**[48] 852 5-10-12 110 HenryBrooke 105
(John Mackie) *chsd ldrs: upsides 2 out: fdd run-in* **14/1**
1-2 6 1 ½ **Holly Bush Henry (IRE)**[95] 263 4-10-10 0 RichieMcLernon 103
(Jonjo O'Neill) *mid-div: chsd ldrs 6th: fdd last* **5/4**[1]
60-5 7 4 **St Quintin**[79] 525 5-10-12 0 PaddyBrennan 103
(David Brown) *nt fluent in rr: hdwy appr 2 out: wknd between last 2* **66/1**
51F/ 8 2 ¼ **Knightly Escapade**[35] 4941 7-10-12 112 RichardJohnson 101
(Brian Ellison) *in rr: blnd 5th: hdwy to chse ldrs whn hit 3 out: sn drvn: wknd between last 2* **7/2**[2]
6105 9 20 **To Begin**[40] 930 4-11-3 115 (t) NoelFehily 86
(Charlie Mann) *in rr: bhd fr 3 out: t.o* **25/1**
P- 10 39 **L'Es Fremantle (FR)**[10] 941 4-10-5 0 JoeCornwall[(5)] 44
(Michael Chapman) *chsd ldrs: drvn 7th: lost pl after next: sn bhd: tailed rt off* **100/1**

5m 20.3s (11.50) **Going Correction** +0.15s/f (Yiel) 10 Ran SP% **123.0**
Speed ratings (Par 105): **84,83,83,82,81 81,79,78,71,56**
CSF £128.62 TOTE £40.60: £11.10, £1.80, £3.40; EX 292.70 Trifecta £2044.50 Part won..
Owner P Kirby **Bred** Jim McNaught **Trained** East Appleton, N Yorks

FOCUS
Drainage works continuing on chase track meant another all-hurdle card. Rail moved out 20yds on each bend, adding approximately 180yds to races 2, 4 & 6 and 240yds to races 1, 3 & 5. Of those with previous hurdles form, five were rated between 107 and 115, which meant it was a fair standard but beatable. They finished in a bit of a heap, but this was a step up from the winner.

1261 BETHANY AND FAYE MANTERFIELD "HANDS AND HEELS" (S) HURDLE (COND' JOCKEYS & AMATEUR RIDERS) (8 hdls) 2m 148y
6:10 (6:13) (Class 5) 4-Y-0+ £2,274 (£667; £333; £166)

Form RPR
U44- 1 **Fair Loch**[9] 5155 7-10-9 115 HarryCobden[(3)] 115+
(Brian Ellison) *mde all: drvn clr appr last* **8/1**
4-13 2 6 **Roja Dove (IRE)**[16] 1154 6-10-12 119 (v) MrZBaker 110
(Neil King) *in rr: hdwy 5th: chsd wnr appr 2 out: kpt on same pce between last 2* **9/2**[3]
/04- 3 ¾ **Changing The Guard**[417] 798 9-10-9 131 (tp) CharlieHammond[(3)] 111
(Dr Richard Newland) *chsd ldrs 3rd: mstke 3 out: kpt on one pce appr 2 out* **13/8**[1]
1- 4 3 ¼ **Grey Monk (IRE)**[316] 1724 7-11-2 120 (t) ThomasDowson[(3)] 113
(Sara Ender) *chsd ldrs 2nd: one pce appr 2 out* **10/1**
45-5 5 12 **Claude Carter**[34] 962 11-11-3 102 (p) MrGaryBeaumont[(5)] 105
(Alistair Whillans) *chsd wnr: drvn 3 out: lost pl bef next* **20/1**
5245 6 nk **Regal One (IRE)**[16] 1154 7-10-12 100 ow3 MrJLaunchbury[(3)] 98
(David Bridgwater) *trckd ldrs: t.k.h: wknd 2 out: lame* **20/1**
3-15 7 1 ½ **El Massivo (IRE)**[7] 973 5-11-5 119 MrKWood 102
(Brian Ellison) *in rr: hdwy 3 out: chsng ldrs appr next: sn wknd* **3/1**[2]
0P-2 8 1 ¾ **Clock On Tom**[16] 1154 5-10-12 109 LiamMcKenna 92
(Denis Quinn) *mid-div: chsng ldrs 3 out: wknd appr next* **12/1**
0P5/ 9 10 **Kheskianto (IRE)**[32] 2323 9-10-2 0 (t) MissKatyLyons[(3)] 76
(Michael Chapman) *in rr: hdwy 3rd: lost pl bef 2 out: sn bhd* **100/1**
35P 10 34 **Sunny Bank**[31] 1001 6-10-7 0 (t) LukeIngram[(5)] 52
(Alan Coogan) *in rr: bhd fr 4th: t.o next* **66/1**
0 P **Cash Is King**[70] 634 5-10-7 0 RossChapman[(5)]
(Kenny Johnson) *in rr: bhd whn blnd 5th: sn t.o: p.u bef 2 out* **66/1**
3P0P U **Fashion Icon (FR)**[19] 1120 4-10-4 85 (tp) ConorSmith
(Nigel Hawke) *towards rr whn uns rdr bhd after 1st* **33/1**

4m 7.7s (1.00) **Going Correction** +0.15s/f (Yiel)
WFA 4 from 5yo+ 13lb 12 Ran SP% **125.6**
Speed ratings (Par 103): **103,100,99,98,92 92,91,90,86,70** ,
CSF £44.70 TOTE £9.40: £2.40, £1.70, £1.40; EX 65.50 Trifecta £177.60.The winner was bought in for 5,200gns.
Owner Mrs J A Martin **Bred** Steve Hadley **Trained** Norton, N Yorks

FOCUS
This was run at a fair pace with the winner making all. The winner was a 123-rated hurdler at his peak, but this was more in line with his 2015 runs.

1262 JANE CLUGSTON CHALLENGE CUP NOVICES' HURDLE (12 hdls) 2m 7f 16y
6:45 (6:45) (Class 4) 4-Y-0+ £3,249 (£954; £477; £238)

Form RPR
6F-0 1 **Standing Ovation (IRE)**[20] 1113 8-10-13 117 (bt) TomScudamore 125+
(David Pipe) *mde all: qckn pce 7th: drvn clr appr 2 out: heavily eased last 150yds* **9/4**[2]
2PP3 2 13 **Mrs Jordan (IRE)**[22] 1094 7-10-6 102 (t) PaulMoloney 101
(Sophie Leech) *in rr: pushed along 9th: outpcd next: 4th 2 out: kpt on to take modest 2nd clsng stages* **11/1**[3]
P-50 3 ¾ **Bandit Country (IRE)**[15] 1167 6-10-13 0 (bt) NoelFehily 107
(Jonjo O'Neill) *in rr: effrt and 3rd whn j.lft 2 out: one pce* **2/1**[1]
-121 4 3 **Towering (IRE)**[45] 877 6-11-6 122 FreddieMitchell[(7)] 121
(Nicky Henderson) *trckd wnr: drvn appr 2 out: wknd run-in* **2/1**[1]
0-05 P **Star Of Salford**[31] 1009 6-10-6 0 (t) GavinSheehan
(Warren Greatrex) *chsd wnr: pushed along 8th: hit 3 out: sn lost pl: bhd whn p.u bef next* **14/1**

5m 57.2s (6.70) **Going Correction** +0.15s/f (Yiel) 5 Ran SP% **112.4**
Speed ratings (Par 105): **94,89,89,88,**
CSF £22.23 TOTE £3.40: £1.50, £3.90; EX 28.40 Trifecta £81.80.
Owner The Bravo Partnership **Bred** Patrick McGrath **Trained** Nicholashayne, Devon

FOCUS
Four horses were rated between 117 and 124, but the race was not as strong as the ratings suggested and the winner ran away with it. A big hurdles personal best from the winner, but he is a 136-rated chaser at his best.

1263 GEOFF AND ANDY MANTERFIELD H'CAP HURDLE (8 hdls) 2m 148y
7:15 (7:16) (Class 3) (0-135,133) 3-Y-0+ £6,498 (£1,908; £954; £477)

Form RPR
13-3 1 **Manhattan Swing (IRE)**[28] 1039 5-11-10 131 (b) RichardJohnson 138+
(Brian Ellison) *hld up: hdwy 5th: 2nd appr 2 out: led 2 out: hit last: drvn clr* **9/4**[1]
-216 2 2 ¼ **Gurkha Brave (IRE)**[48] 850 7-10-12 119 PaddyBrennan 122
(Karen McLintock) *trckd ldr: led after 3 out: hdd next: hung lft and kpt on same pce run-in* **3/1**[2]
216 3 13 **Regulation (IRE)**[28] 1039 6-10-11 125 LizzieKelly[(7)] 117
(Neil King) *t.k.h towards rr: hit 3 out: drvn appr next: kpt on one pce: modest 3rd appr last* **7/2**[3]
4-U2 4 4 ½ **Australia Day (IRE)**[13] 1180 12-11-9 130 DenisO'Regan 117
(Paul Webber) *led: hdd after 3 out: one pce* **7/1**
6-62 5 9 **Don Padeja**[16] 1156 5-10-12 119 (t) NoelFehily 98
(Jonjo O'Neill) *chsd ldrs: drvn and hung rt appr 2 out: sn lost pl* **5/1**
-3P2 U **Ruler Of All (IRE)**[48] 854 9-11-5 133 MrRWinks[(7)]
(Peter Winks) *chsd ldrs: blnd and uns rdr 5th: fatally injured* **9/1**

4m 5.6s (-1.10) **Going Correction** +0.15s/f (Yiel) 6 Ran SP% **117.2**
Speed ratings (Par 107): **108,106,100,98,94**
CSF £10.24 TOTE £2.70: £1.80, £2.40; EX 11.20 Trifecta £29.50.
Owner Mrs J A Martin **Bred** Gerrardstown House Stud **Trained** Norton, N Yorks

FOCUS
Confirmed front-runner Australia Day ensured this was run at a sound pace, although this was the first race of the evening not to be won from the front. A step up from the winner on recent course form, but he is a potential 145-rated hurdler on Flat form.

1264 DENNIS MEECH "MAGIC MOMENTS" MEMORIAL H'CAP HURDLE (6 hdls 6 omitted) 2m 7f 16y
7:45 (7:48) (Class 4) (0-115,115) 4-Y-0+ £3,249 (£954; £477; £238)

Form RPR
-501 1 **Count Salazar (IRE)**[13] 1181 10-11-0 110 (p) MissBHampson[(7)] 115+
(Andy Turnell) *mde all: drvn appr omitted 2 out: jst hld on* **13/2**[2]
6-53 2 nse **Handmaid**[20] 1113 6-11-9 115 (p) SeanBowen[(3)] 119
(Peter Bowen) *chsd ldrs: cl 2nd appr 2 out: styd on towards fin: jst hld* **7/2**[1]
2FP- 3 2 ¾ **Handsome Dan (IRE)**[119] 5399 9-11-11 114 PaulMoloney 115
(Sarah Hollinshead) *in rr: hdwy normal 3 out: chsng ldrs omitted 2 out: fdd clsng stages* **14/1**
3-24 4 1 **Tir Dubh (IRE)**[31] 1011 6-11-2 105 TomO'Brien 106
(Robert Stephens) *mid-div: hdwy normal 3 out: chsng ldrs omitted 2 out: kpt on same pce fnl 2f* **10/1**
P3-5 5 2 ½ **Moyode Wood**[23] 1082 10-10-8 104 CraigGallagher[(7)] 102
(Brian Ellison) *mid-div: hdwy to chse ldrs normal 3 out: one pce fnl 2f* **22/1**
-550 6 2 ½ **Call Me Kate**[59] 757 5-10-0 89 oh6 (p) PaddyBrennan 86
(Henry Daly) *in rr: hdwy normal 3 out: one pce fnl 3f* **16/1**
4214 7 nk **Solway Prince**[20] 1113 6-11-1 104 BrianHarding 100
(Lisa Harrison) *rr-div: hdwy normal 3 out: one pce fnl 3f* **7/1**[3]
-450 8 6 **Feast Of Fire (IRE)**[20] 1113 8-11-3 106 (b[1]) GavinSheehan 96
(Mike Sowersby) *in rr: hdwy on wd outside to chse ldrs appr omitted 2 out: sn wknd* **20/1**
2520 9 3 ½ **Mission Complete (IRE)**[45] 873 9-11-6 109 (tp) RichardJohnson 96
(Jonjo O'Neill) *chsd ldrs: drvn normal 3 out: sn outpcd: wknd fnl 2f* **7/1**[3]
52-6 10 14 **A Hairy Koala (FR)**[22] 1100 5-11-2 105 (bt) TomScudamore 80
(David Pipe) *chsd ldrs: 2nd whn hit normal 3 out: wknd omitted 2 out* **13/2**[2]
03-0 11 ¾ **Mo Rouge (IRE)**[83] 458 7-11-2 108 TonyKelly[(3)] 82
(Jackie Stephen) *mid-div: lost pl w a circ to go: sn t.o: kpt on fnl 2f* **11/1**
0301 12 5 **Solway Sam**[34] 958 12-10-4 100 RyanDay[(7)] 69
(Lisa Harrison) *in rr-div: drvn bef half way: wl bhd normal 3 out* **11/1**
-315 13 1 ¾ **What A Steel (IRE)**[34] 958 11-11-4 110 CraigNichol[(3)] 78
(Alistair Whillans) *chsd ldrs: drvn normal 3 out: sn lost pl* **16/1**

5m 50.7s (0.20) **Going Correction** +0.15s/f (Yiel) 13 Ran SP% **127.2**
Speed ratings (Par 105): **105,104,104,103,102 101,101,99,98,93 93,91,91**
CSF £32.09 CT £326.04 TOTE £8.70: £2.50, £1.70, £4.80; EX 33.70 Trifecta £537.90.
Owner The Gentlemen Of Salazar **Bred** Mrs Catherine Barry **Trained** Broad Hinton, Wilts

FOCUS
The hurdles in the home straight were removed due to the low sun, leaving a 6f run-in from the last in the back. It produced a photo finish, with the winner another to make all, just holding on. The winner was in line with his recent win, but there may still be more to come.

1265 MDLUTILITIES.CO.UK H'CAP HURDLE (6 hdls 4 omitted) 2m 2f 140y
8:15 (8:19) (Class 4) (0-110,110) 4-Y-0+ £3,249 (£954; £477; £238)

Form RPR
6530 1 **Western Way (IRE)**[19] 1117 6-11-11 109 (b) DenisO'Regan 115+
(Don Cantillon) *trckd ldrs: led appr omitted 2 out: drvn rt out* **9/1**
6-0 2 1 ¼ **Top Spin (IRE)**[13] 1184 8-11-12 110 (t) RichardJohnson 112
(Jonjo O'Neill) *rr-div: hdwy to chse ldrs normal 3 out: 2nd over 2f out: styd on same pce* **3/1**[1]
25F3 3 nk **Anton Dolin (IRE)**[15] 1166 7-10-13 104 MrHFNugent[(7)] 106
(Michael Mullineaux) *mid-div: hdwy normal 3 out: 3rd over 1f out: styd on same pce* **12/1**
/0-0 4 4 **Makethedifference (IRE)**[58] 776 7-10-12 103 AlanJohns[(7)] 101
(Tim Vaughan) *hld up in rr: n.m.r bnd sn after normal 3 out: hdwy appr omitted 2 out: modest 6th omitted last: styd on to take 4th post* **11/2**[2]
304F 5 shd **Watt Broderick (IRE)**[60] 751 6-11-9 107 (t) WillKennedy 105
(Ian Williams) *in rr: gd hdwy appr omitted 2 out: kpt on same pce fnl 2f* **8/1**
316F 6 9 **Polstar (FR)**[27] 1048 6-11-5 106 SeanBowen[(3)] 98
(Harry Whittington) *chsd ldrs: 2nd appr omitted 2 out: wknd fnl 2f* **13/2**
4213 7 1 ½ **Tennessee Bird**[39] 935 7-10-0 84 oh2 GavinSheehan 73
(Mike Sowersby) *chsd ldrs: edgd lft and wknd over 2f out* **9/1**
-P43 8 3 ½ **Lookslikerainted (IRE)**[31] 1002 8-11-12 110 (tp) PaulMoloney 97
(Sophie Leech) *prom: lost pl sn after normal 3 out* **12/1**
-434 9 6 **Prince Of Poets**[19] 1117 4-11-1 101 TomScudamore 79
(David Pipe) *hld up towards rr: hdwy normal 4 out: wknd appr omitted 2 out* **6/1**[3]
P-6P 10 15 **Kadalkin (FR)**[48] 857 9-11-10 108 (tp) DaveCrosse 75
(Nigel Hawke) *mid-div: lost pl normal 3 out* **25/1**

63-6 **11** *1* **Xenophon**[16] 1155 7-9-9 **84** oh12 AliceMills(5) 50
(Michael Chapman) *chsd ldr: led 3rd: hdd sn after normal 3 out: sn lost pl* **50/1**
62-P **12** *1 ¾* **Stitched In Time (IRE)**[23] 1084 8-10-1 **90** NathanMoscrop(5) 54
(Sara Ender) *in rr: j.rt: bhd early fnl circ: t.o normal 3 out* **28/1**
-523 **13** *5* **Welcome Ben (IRE)**[44] 881 6-11-9 **110** TonyKelly(3) 70
(Jackie Stephen) *led to 3rd: chsd ldr: lost pl sn after normal 3 out: sn bhd* **14/1**
-336 **14** *4* **Another Bygones (IRE)**[34] 960 6-11-7 **105** PaddyBrennan 61
(Karen McLintock) *chsd ldrs: drvn 8f out: lost pl sn after normal 3 out: bhd whn eased fnl f* **16/1**

4m 44.1s (4.70) **Going Correction** +0.15s/f (Yiel)
WFA 4 from 6yo+ 13lb **14** Ran SP% **136.3**
Speed ratings (Par 105): **96,95,95,93,93 89,89,87,85,78 78,77,75,73**
CSF £41.30 CT £357.52 TOTE £13.40: £4.10, £2.00, £4.50; EX 71.40 Trifecta £898.50.
Owner Don Cantillon **Bred** Don Cantillon **Trained** Newmarket, Suffolk
■ Stewards' Enquiry : Dave Crosse five-day ban: 29, 31 Aug-3 Sep (used whip when out of contention)
Nathan Moscrop five-day ban: Aug 29, Aug 31-Sep 3 (used whip when out of contention)

FOCUS
The market was strong for Top Spin, but he was readily held by a quietly supported handicap debutant. A big hurdles personal best from the winner, though he ran an RPR of 118 in blinkers in bumpers.
T/Plt: £475.50 to a £1 stake. Pool: 60,168.57 - 92.37 winning tickets. T/Qpdt: £52.70 to a £1 stake. Pool: 6,230.56 - 87.4 winning tickets. **Walter Glynn**

964 SOUTHWELL (L-H)
Sunday, August 16

OFFICIAL GOING: Good to firm (good in places; 8.5)
Wind: almost nil Weather: fine

1266 LOVE TO SPA AT EDEN HALL NOVICES' CHASE (13 fncs) 1m 7f 153y
2:00 (2:00) (Class 4) 4-Y-O+ **£3,898** (£1,144; £572; £286)

Form RPR
-311 **1** **Dubai Prince (IRE)**[28] 1047 7-11-6 0 (t) AidanColeman 129+
(John Ferguson) *hld up in last: hit 5th: led 2 out: qcknd clr run-in: easily* **1/3**[1]
-P25 **2** *3 ¾* **Spring Steel (IRE)**[46] 880 6-11-0 110 (t) NicodeBoinville 113
(Ben Pauling) *mde most: hit 10th: hdd 2 out: kpt on: no ch w wnr* **33/1**
P221 **3** *1* **Indian Stream**[32] 1008 6-10-13 124 (t) NoelFehily 110
(Neil Mulholland) *w ldr: drvn 3 out: outpcd next: kpt on wl run-in* **4/1**[2]
-545 **4** *18* **Midnight Game**[14] 1186 8-11-0 127 RichardJohnson 99
(Brian Ellison) *j.rt: chsd ldrs: mstke 8th: drvn 10th: lost pl 3 out: bhd whn eased run-in* **13/2**[3]

4m 2.2s (0.20) **Going Correction** -0.15s/f (Good)
WFA 4 from 6yo+ 1lb **4** Ran SP% **111.3**
Speed ratings (Par 105): **93,91,90,81**
CSF £8.37 TOTE £1.10; EX 10.70 Trifecta £28.20.
Owner Bloomfields **Bred** Mrs Eithne Hamilton **Trained** Cowlinge, Suffolk

FOCUS
Fences and hurdles sited in centre of track. As expected this was easy pickings for the classy winner. Afterwards Nico de Boinville said: "The ground is good to firm" and Aidan Coleman said: "It is good and a shade quicker in places."

1267 LADBROKES H'CAP CHASE (16 fncs) 2m 4f 62y
2:30 (2:30) (Class 4) (0-120,119) 4-Y-O+ **£3,768** (£1,106; £553; £276)

Form RPR
-243 **1** **Ladfromhighworth**[32] 1007 10-11-6 113 NickScholfield 124
(Jeremy Scott) *chsd ldr: lft in clr ld 2nd: mde rest: blnd 7th: styd on wl fr 2 out* **11/4**[1]
-545 **2** *3 ¼* **Tregaro (FR)**[32] 1005 9-10-7 100 (t) TomScudamore 107
(Mike Sowersby) *hld up: effrt appr 3 out: sn chsng wnr: kpt on same pce appr last* **9/1**
1433 **3** *9* **Master Of The Hall (IRE)**[29] 1033 11-10-13 116 FinianO'Toole(10) 117
(Micky Hammond) *chsd ldrs: hmpd 2nd: 2nd 13th: rdn next: wknd 2 out* **3/1**[2]
0F00 **4** *nk* **Groomed (IRE)**[56] 802 7-11-8 115 SeanQuinlan 114
(Sue Smith) *lft 2nd at 2nd: hit 7th: pushed along 10th: drvn 13th: lost pl bef next* **16/1**
-012 **5** *18* **River Purple**[32] 1005 8-11-12 119 (t) DarylJacob 101
(John Mackie) *lft 3rd 2nd: blnd 11th: drvn next: lost pl bef 3 out: bhd whn eased run-in* **8/1**
-201 **F** **Jack The Gent (IRE)**[16] 1169 11-11-2 109 RichieMcLernon
(George Moore) *led: fell 2nd* **4/1**[3]
-504 **U** **Sureness (IRE)**[29] 1042 5-11-11 118 (tp) GavinSheehan
(Charlie Mann) *towards rr whn bdly hmpd and uns rdr 2nd* **5/1**

5m 22.0s (5.00) **Going Correction** -0.15s/f (Good) **7** Ran SP% **115.3**
Speed ratings (Par 105): **84,82,79,78,71 ,**
CSF £26.57 TOTE £4.40: £2.30, £4.60; EX 32.80 Trifecta £136.80.
Owner Mrs H J Manners **Bred** H J Manners **Trained** Brompton Regis, Somerset

FOCUS
A modest handicap, run at a sound gallop.

1268 AMBITIONS PERSONNEL H'CAP CHASE (16 fncs) 2m 4f 62y
3:00 (3:00) (Class 2) 4-Y-O+
£14,388 (£4,250; £2,125; £1,062; £531; £266)

Form RPR
/1-1 **1** **Gray Hession (IRE)**[96] 259 8-11-7 **133** RichieMcLernon 142+
(Jonjo O'Neill) *mid-div: hdwy 10th: chsng ldrs 13th: 2nd 2 out: styd on to ld nr fin* **4/1**[1]
-011 **2** *nk* **Alderbrook Lad (IRE)**[49] 849 9-11-2 **138** FinianO'Toole(10) 146
(Micky Hammond) *led tl after 3rd: w ldr: led 5th: jnd last: hdd and no ex nr fin* **14/1**
5112 **3** *14* **Owen Na View (IRE)**[14] 1178 7-11-9 **135** PaddyBrennan 131
(Fergal O'Brien) *chsd ldrs: one pce fr 2 out* **10/1**
32-2 **4** *1 ¼* **Tindaro (FR)**[42] 915 8-11-9 **135** (t) LiamTreadwell 129
(Paul Webber) *in rr: hdwy 7th: outpcd appr 3 out: kpt on to take modest 4th last* **14/1**
232F **5** *3 ½* **Owen Glendower (IRE)**[28] 1053 10-10-1 **120** (tp) CiaranGethings(7) 111
(Sophie Leech) *hld up in rr: hdwy 9th: modest 5th and drvn 3 out: one pce* **10/1**
-322 **6** *6* **Buck Mulligan**[28] 1053 10-10-6 **123** ConorRing(5) 111
(Evan Williams) *chsd ldrs: drvn and outpcd appr 3 out* **7/1**
-314 **7** *1* **Commitment**[21] 1112 6-10-13 **125** NoelFehily 110
(Neil Mulholland) *j.rt: in rr: hdwy 9th: lost pl next: bhd fr 12th* **6/1**[3]
2642 **8** *4* **My Brother Sylvest**[19] 1135 9-11-11 **137** (b) TomScudamore 124
(David Pipe) *t.k.h: sn trcking ldrs: 2nd at 2nd: sn led: j.rt next: hdd bef 5th: hit 13th: wknd 2 out: 6th whn j. slowly and blnd last* **12/1**
2213 **9** *4 ½* **Moorlands Jack**[21] 1112 10-10-8 **120** (p) JamesDavies 98
(Jeremy Scott) *hld up in rr: hdwy 9th: drvn and outpcd 13th: sn lost pl* **8/1**
11P- **10** *12* **Montoya's Son (IRE)**[128] 5253 10-11-4 **133** CraigNichol(3) 99
(Keith Dalgleish) *chsd ldrs: drvn 11th: lost pl next: wl bhd 13th* **10/1**
-112 **F** **Ulis De Vassy (FR)**[21] 1112 7-11-3 **129** HarrySkelton
(Dan Skelton) *rr-div whn fell 1st* **5/1**[2]

5m 8.7s (-8.30) **Going Correction** -0.15s/f (Good) **11** Ran SP% **122.9**
Speed ratings (Par 109): **110,109,104,103,102 99,99,97,96,91**
CSF £59.94 CT £539.52 TOTE £3.40: £1.10, £4.80, £4.30; EX 63.30 Trifecta £392.50.
Owner A D Gray **Bred** Seamus O'Farrell **Trained** Cheltenham, Gloucs

FOCUS
A fair handicap and two came a long way clear.

1269 FIREWALL LTD H'CAP HURDLE (11 hdls) 2m 4f 62y
3:30 (3:30) (Class 4) (0-120,120) 4-Y-O+ **£3,573** (£1,049; £524; £262)

Form RPR
6-12 **1** **Kalifourchon (FR)**[49] 856 4-10-12 **108** TomScudamore 115+
(David Pipe) *trckd ldrs: led 7th: j.lft last: fnd ex clsng stages: cosily* **7/2**[1]
-152 **2** *1 ¼* **Mac Bertie**[28] 1054 6-10-11 **105** (p) AdamWedge 110
(Evan Williams) *trckd ldrs: 2 l 2nd appr last: styd on same pce: no real imp* **7/1**
-312 **3** *4 ½* **Miss Sassypants**[40] 938 6-11-7 **115** RyanMahon 116
(Seamus Mullins) *hld up: trckd ldrs 4th: kpt on same pce between last 2* **9/2**[2]
P14- **4** *1* **Mawaqeet (USA)**[18] 5202 6-11-7 **115** (p) RichardJohnson 115
(Michael Appleby) *hld up in rr: effrt appr 2 out: kpt on to take modest 4th last 100yds* **9/2**[2]
-216 **5** *1 ¼* **Wait A Second (IRE)**[21] 1113 5-11-7 **118** (p) MauriceLinehan(3) 117
(Jonjo O'Neill) *chsd ldrs: cl 2nd 3 out: one pce fr next* **6/1**[3]
0-04 **6** *14* **Jigsaw Financial (IRE)**[54] 828 9-10-9 **103** SamTwiston-Davies 91
(Laura Young) *chsd ldrs: drvn and outpcd appr 2 out: wknd between last 2* **8/1**
0-05 **7** *21* **Sinndar's Man**[23] 1100 4-11-0 **110** NickScholfield 75
(Michael Blake) *led: blnd and hdd 7th: lost pl next: sn bhd* **12/1**
P **P** **Local Celebrity (IRE)**[49] 847 11-11-5 **120** MissBHampson(7)
(Andy Turnell) *j.rt: w ldr: wknd 3 out: t.o whn p.u between last 2* **50/1**
0-2P **P** **A Cor Et A Cri (FR)**[3] 1242 5-11-4 **112** (tp) NoelFehily
(Harry Fry) *hld up in rr: rdn 8th: no rspnse and sn bhd: t.o whn p.u bef 2 out* **8/1**

5m 5.9s (-7.10) **Going Correction** -0.15s/f (Good)
WFA 4 from 5yo+ 14lb **9** Ran SP% **117.2**
Speed ratings (Par 105): **108,107,105,105,104 99,90, ,**
CSF £28.84 CT £112.91 TOTE £4.20: £1.40, £2.70, £2.00; EX 33.40 Trifecta £150.10.
Owner CHM Partnership **Bred** I , J P , G & C Garcon **Trained** Nicholashayne, Devon

FOCUS
A competitive handicap for the grade. It was run at a fair gallop and the first pair dominated from two out.

1270 PORSCHE CENTRE NOTTINGHAM H'CAP HURDLE (13 hdls) 2m 7f 209y
4:05 (4:05) (Class 3) (0-140,127) 4-Y-O+ **£5,848** (£1,717; £858; £429)

Form RPR
3-11 **1** **Miss Serious (IRE)**[89] 387 5-11-8 **123** NickScholfield 127+
(Jeremy Scott) *hld up in last: hdwy 10th: clr 3rd next: 2nd appr 2 out: led appr last: pushed out* **4/1**[2]
5-52 **2** *4* **Byron Blue (IRE)**[28] 1046 6-11-12 **127** TomCannon 125
(Mark Gillard) *t.k.h: led: j.lft: clr 6th: hit 9th: drvn appr 2 out: hdd appr last: kpt on same pce* **9/2**[3]
5232 **3** *2 ¾* **Cut The Corner (IRE)**[19] 1138 7-11-5 **120** (p) WillKennedy 115
(Dr Richard Newland) *chsd ldrs: 2nd 9th: drvn 3 out: one pce appr next* **9/4**[1]
-233 **4** *21* **Harvey's Hope**[35] 969 9-10-9 **115** MrJohnDawson(5) 92
(Keith Reveley) *chsd ldrs: lost pl 10th: distant 4th 2 out* **6/1**
-550 **5** *7* **Factor Fifty (IRE)**[14] 1181 6-10-11 **115** AdamNicol(3) 86
(Philip Kirby) *chsd ldrs: dropped bk 3rd: drvn 8th: bhd fr 10th* **11/2**
-303 **6** *3 ¼* **Terminal (FR)**[19] 1138 8-11-10 **125** (tp) NoelFehily 91
(David Dennis) *chsd ldr: drvn 10th: lost pl next: sn wl bhd* **6/1**

6m 5.5s (-9.50) **Going Correction** -0.15s/f (Good) **6** Ran SP% **112.9**
Speed ratings (Par 107): **109,107,106,99,97 96**
CSF £22.12 TOTE £4.00: £2.50, £2.30; EX 14.50 Trifecta £33.50.
Owner Pillhead House Partners **Bred** Sean Galwey **Trained** Brompton Regis, Somerset

FOCUS
This modest staying handicap was run at a decent gallop and proved a real test of the distance.

1271 NEWARK ADVERTISER MARES' NOVICES' HURDLE (9 hdls) 1m 7f 153y
4:35 (4:35) (Class 4) 4-Y-O+ **£3,573** (£1,049; £524; £262)

Form RPR
2-14 **1** **Bantam (IRE)**[75] 591 5-11-3 130 RichardJohnson 126+
(Henry Daly) *t.k.h: mde all: wl clr bef 2 out: heavily eased run-in: v easily* **4/9**[1]
432 **2** *17* **Irondale Express**[32] 1009 4-10-9 0 PaulMoloney 95
(Des Donovan) *chsd ldng pair: pushed along 5th: hit next: outpcd and j.rt 3 out: j.rt next: tk poor 2nd clsng stages* **5/2**[2]
3 *1 ½* **Jumpandtravel (IRE)**[105] 6-10-0 0 FinianO'Toole(10) 96
(Micky Hammond) *chsd wnr: pushed along 5th: drvn 3 out: poor 2nd whn hit last* **10/1**[3]
6404 **4** *5* **Flemerina (IRE)**[21] 1109 6-10-10 0 SeanQuinlan 90
(Sue Smith) *outpcd and poor 4th fr 5th* **16/1**
-P00 **P** **Simplified**[42] 918 12-10-5 64 JoeCornwall(5)
(Michael Chapman) *in rr: bhd and drvn 4th: sn t.o: p.u bef last* **100/1**
P **P** **Highridge Princess (IRE)**[4] 1234 7-10-10 0 AlainCawley
(Johnny Farrelly) *detached in last: hit 3rd: sn drvn: t.o 6th: p.u after next* **50/1**

3m 52.2s (-4.80) **Going Correction** -0.15s/f (Good)
WFA 4 from 5yo+ 13lb **6** Ran SP% **115.7**
Speed ratings (Par 105): **106,97,96,94,**
CSF £2.11 TOTE £1.40: £1.10, £1.60; EX 2.30 Trifecta £5.40.
Owner Brooke Kelly Partnership **Bred** Airlie Stud And Sir Thomas Pilkington **Trained** Stanton Lacy, Shropshire

FOCUS
An uncompetitive mare's novice event.

1272 COOPERS MARQUEES LTD H'CAP HURDLE (DIV I) (13 hdls) 2m 7f 209y
5:05 (5:05) (Class 5) (0-100,100) 4-Y-0+ **£2,599** (£763; £381; £190)

Form RPR
55-P **1** **Sgt Bull Berry**[32] [1004] 8-9-7 **74** oh1.................... JamieHamilton(7) 79
(Peter Maddison) *led bef 2nd: mde rest: hld on nr fin* **20/1**
6206 **2** *nk* **Solway Bay**[16] [1171] 13-10-6 **87**..............................(t) RyanDay(7) 92
(Lisa Harrison) *in rr: hdwy 6th: chsng ldrs and drvn 3 out: outpcd appr next: styd on between last 2: 4th last: str run last 75yds: tk 2nd nr fin: jst hld* **20/1**
PF/1 **3** *¾* **French Seventyfive**[35] [966] 8-9-13 **80**.................... MissETodd(7) 84
(Keith Reveley) *in rr: hdwy to chse ldrs 6th: cl 2nd last: no ex last 50yds* **11/8**[1]
/243 **4** *nk* **Amber Flush**[19] [1134] 6-10-13 **94**.................... MrJamesSmith(7) 98
(Martin Smith) *mid-div: chsd ldrs 6th: cl 3rd last: no ex last 75yds* **8/1**
0-56 **5** *13* **Aregra (FR)**[23] [1098] 5-10-1 **75**..............................(p) GavinSheehan 68
(Peter Niven) *chsd ldrs: wknd between last 2* **7/1**[3]
5-02 **6** *44* **Tinseltown**[25] [678] 9-11-12 **100**..........................(p) TomScudamore 52
(Brian Rothwell) *in rr: sme hdwy 10th: lost pl sn after next: t.o 2 out* **7/1**[3]
252- **7** *14* **Orsm**[316] [1743] 8-11-10 **98**...(t) TomCannon 38
(Laura Mongan) *trckd ldrs: drvn 3 out: lost pl bef next: sn bhd: t.o* **6/1**[2]
1-PP **P** **Moon Melody (GER)**[23] [1098] 12-10-8 **85**....................(tp) AdamNicol(3)
(Mike Sowersby) *led tl bef 2nd: reminders 3rd: lost pl after 8th: sn bhd: t.o whn p.u bef 2 out* **16/1**
/040 **P** **Monzino (USA)**[17] [1158] 7-9-9 **74** oh5............................ JoeCornwall(5)
(Michael Chapman) *detached last: pushed along 4th: t.o whn blnd 9th: p.u bef 3 out* **33/1**
5-0P **P** **Bob's Call (IRE)**[32] [1004] 6-10-11 **95**....................(p) JakeHolliday(10)
(Tony Coyle) *chsd ldrs: rdn 3 out: sn lost pl: t.o whn p.u sn after 2 out* **12/1**

6m 11.4s (-3.60) **Going Correction** -0.15s/f (Good) **10** Ran SP% **118.5**
Speed ratings (Par 103): **100,99,99,99,95 80,75, , ,**
CSF £325.18 CT £921.68 TOTE £34.30: £4.90, £4.60, £1.10; EX 777.80 Trifecta £645.10.
Owner Peter Maddison **Bred** P Maddison **Trained** Skewsby, N Yorks
■ Stewards' Enquiry : Mr James Smith caution: careless riding

FOCUS
It paid to race handily in this moderate staying handicap.

1273 COOPERS MARQUEES LTD H'CAP HURDLE (DIV II) (13 hdls) 2m 7f 209y
5:35 (5:37) (Class 5) (0-100,99) 4-Y-0+ **£2,599** (£763; £381; £190)

Form RPR
-422 **1** **Steps And Stairs (IRE)**[60] [758] 5-11-8 **95**..................(p) DarylJacob 101+
(Jonjo O'Neill) *mid-div: blnd 7th: chsng ldrs next: led between last 2: drvn out* **15/8**[1]
0-03 **2** *2 ¼* **Perseid (IRE)**[24] [1084] 5-10-9 **82**.................... SeanQuinlan 83
(Sue Smith) *chsd ldrs: drvn 9th: cl 2nd last: styd on same pce* **3/1**[2]
PP-6 **3** *hd* **Tokyo Javilex (FR)**[24] [1085] 8-10-7 **87**..................(t) MrLDrowne(7) 89
(Nigel Hawke) *in rr: hdwy to chse ldrs 8th: led bef 2 out: hdd between last 2: 3rd and keeping on same pce whn hit last* **12/1**
6063 **4** *¾* **Solway Trigger**[23] [1098] 6-9-7 **73**.................... JamieHamilton(7) 74
(Lisa Harrison) *t.k.h: trckd ldr 2nd: led after next: j.rt: mstke 3 out: hdd bef next: hung rt appr last: styd on same pce last 75yds* **6/1**
6225 **5** *dist* **Larkhall**[40] [934] 8-9-11 **73**.................... AdamNicol(3) 37
(Mike Sowersby) *hld up in rr: hdwy to trck ldrs 8th: drvn 3 out: sn lost pl: t.o whn eased* **16/1**
0221 **6** *40* **Steel Gold (IRE)**[23] [1098] 9-10-10 **88**.................... ConorRing(5) 16
(John Upson) *chsd ldrs: drvn 8th: lost pl next: sn bhd: t.o 3 out* **4/1**[3]
3406 **7** *3 ¾* **Lawsons Thorns (IRE)**[35] [969] 6-11-12 **99**.................... GavinSheehan 24
(Mike Sowersby) *t.k.h in rr: lost pl 8th: sn bhd: t.o 3 out* **14/1**
P43- **P** **Feeling Peckish (USA)**[279] [2408] 11-9-9 **73** oh17........(b) JoeCornwall(5)
(Michael Chapman) *chsd ldrs: drvn 4th: lost pl 7th: sn bhd: t.o whn p.u after next* **50/1**
/0-0 **P** **Exit To Freedom**[80] [522] 9-10-1 **77**..............................(p) CraigNichol(3)
(John Wainwright) *led tl after 3rd: blnd 4th: drvn 10th: sn lost pl: t.o whn p.u bef 2 out* **33/1**

6m 13.4s (-1.60) **Going Correction** -0.15s/f (Good) **9** Ran SP% **119.2**
Speed ratings (Par 103): **96,95,95,94,81 68,67, ,**
CSF £8.62 CT £52.78 TOTE £2.60: £1.30, £1.50, £3.80; EX 8.70 Trifecta £82.70.
Owner Mark Dunphy **Bred** Liam & Michael Flavin **Trained** Cheltenham, Gloucs

FOCUS
The second division of an ordinary staying handicap and again only four mattered in the home straight.
T/Plt: £53.90 to a £1 stake. Pool: £83,026.13 - 1,123.31 winning tickets. T/Qpdt: £9.80 to a £1 stake. Pool: £6,907.07 - 517 winning tickets. **Walter Glynn**

1274 - 1286a (Foreign Racing) - See Raceform Interactive

1133 WORCESTER (L-H)
Wednesday, August 19

OFFICIAL GOING: Good (good to firm in places) changing to good after race 1 (5.00) changing to good (good to soft in places) after race 3 (6.00)
Wind: Light against Weather: Light rain

1287 UNDER STARTIN ORDERS H'CAP CHASE (16 fncs) 2m 7f
5:00 (5:00) (Class 5) (0-100,100) 4-Y-0+ **£2,469** (£725; £362; £181)

Form RPR
3440 **1** **Dr Dreamy (IRE)**[35] [1004] 8-10-0 **74** oh4.....................(t) BrendanPowell 84
(Claire Dyson) *hld up: hdwy 12th: chsd ldr 4 out: led 2 out: drvn out* **33/1**
3124 **2** *½* **Patricktom Boru (IRE)**[27] [1079] 8-11-10 **98**.................... AdamWedge 108
(Evan Williams) *hld up: nt fluent 1st: hmpd 12th: hdwy appr 4 out: rdn and r.o wl flat: nt quite rch wnr* **9/2**[1]
P-22 **3** *2 ¼* **Knockyoursocksoff (IRE)**[64] [752] 5-11-3 **91**..................(b) WillKennedy 100
(Gary Moore) *a.p: ev ch whn pckd last: sn rdn: styd on same pce flat* **6/1**[2]
36-2 **4** *4 ½* **Sand Artist (IRE)**[10] [1221] 7-10-4 **78**..........................(t) RichardJohnson 81
(Gordon Elliott, Ire) *hld up: hdwy after 12th: rdn appr last: styd on same pce flat* **7/1**[3]
5 *5* **Admiral Barton (IRE)**[36] [997] 9-11-9 **97**..................(bt) TomScudamore 96
(Paul W Flynn, Ire) *mid-div: hdwy 4 out: rdn and wknd appr last* **7/1**[3]
321- **6** *12* **Local Present (IRE)**[318] [1765] 12-10-9 **83**..................(b) TomCannon 73
(Denis Quinn) *prom: chsd ldr after 12th: led 4 out: rdn and hdd 2 out: wknd bef last* **22/1**
2-63 **7** *14* **Northern Executive (IRE)**[74] [637] 7-11-0 **88**..................(p) PaddyBrennan 67
(Karen McLintock) *mid-div: nt fluent 3rd: hit 7th: hdwy next: rdn 11th: wknd 4 out* **9/1**
UP44 **8** *7* **Driving Well (IRE)**[38] [972] 7-9-7 **74** oh5...........(bt) ThomasCheesman(7) 47
(Arthur Whiting) *hld up: hdwy 9th: j.rt 11th wknd 4 out* **25/1**
5232 **9** *16* **Kilcascan**[27] [1079] 11-10-13 **90**..............................(p) BenPoste(3) 45
(Rosemary Gasson) *chsd ldrs: led and mstke 4th: hdd next: led again 9th tl 12th: rdn and wkng whn hmpd appr 4 out* **9/1**
/06P **10** *1 ½* **Skating Home (IRE)**[23] [1118] 9-10-0 **74** oh1.................... MarkQuinlan 28
(Richard Hawker) *led to 4th: chsd ldrs: drvn along 11th: sn wknd* **100/1**
P403 **11** *12* **Maller Tree**[27] [1079] 8-11-12 **100**..................(v) SamTwiston-Davies 43
(David Dennis) *chsd ldrs: led 5th: hdd 9th: rdn after 11th: wknd next* **8/1**
-136 **12** *14* **The Purchaser (IRE)**[35] [1004] 7-11-8 **96**..................(b) TomMessenger 26
(Chris Bealby) *prom: led 12th: hdd 4 out: wknd next* **14/1**
-2P0 **P** **Fast Exit (IRE)**[27] [1079] 8-11-3 **91**..............................(b) NoelFehily
(Neil Mulholland) *hld up: mstke 1st: rdn and wknd 10th: bhd whn p.u bef 4 out* **16/1**
36-0 **P** **If It Be Your Will**[20] [1159] 5-11-5 **93**..............................(t) HarrySkelton
(Dan Skelton) *hld up: a in rr: hdwy fr 6th: p.u bef 4 out* **16/1**

5m 42.1s (-7.80) **Going Correction** -0.375s/f (Good) **14** Ran SP% **119.1**
Speed ratings (Par 103): **98,97,97,95,93 89,84,82,76,76 72,67, ,**
CSF £175.63 CT £1045.73 TOTE £51.80: £9.80, £1.60, £2.50; EX 385.80 Trifecta £829.40.
Owner Guy Sainsbury & Partner **Bred** H S Kenny **Trained** Cleeve Prior, Worcs

FOCUS
All starts have been moved at this track following remeasuring, so there will be no speed figures here until there is sufficient data to calculate updated median times. The course had been watered during the week and the weather was damp. A competitive handicap run at a good pace with the winning outsider coming from off the pace. The third, fourth and fifth have been rated pretty much to their marks.

1288 HALLMARKHULME H'CAP CHASE (16 fncs) 2m 7f
5:30 (5:30) (Class 3) (0-140,140) 4-Y-0+ **£6,498** (£1,908; £954; £477)

Form RPR
3-32 **1** **Buachaill Alainn (IRE)**[32] [1033] 8-10-3 **120**..................(vt) SeanBowen(3) 134+
(Peter Bowen) *chsd ldrs: hit 6th: led 2 out: styd on wl* **7/2**[2]
-P31 **2** *9* **American Legend (IRE)**[35] [1007] 7-10-6 **120**..........(v) RichardJohnson 125
(Jonjo O'Neill) *hld up: hdwy bef 4 out: rdn appr last: styd on same pce flat* **7/4**[1]
P1-2 **3** *½* **Best Boy Barney (IRE)**[107] [101] 9-10-13 **130**..........(bt) MattGriffiths(3) 135+
(Jeremy Scott) *led: j.rt: rdn and hdd 2 out: no ex flat* **7/1**
3110 **4** *11* **Greenlaw**[32] [1040] 9-10-12 **126**..............................(t) NoelFehily 121
(Charlie Longsdon) *chsd ldrs: wnt 2nd 4 out: rdn and wknd appr last* **9/2**[3]
4534 **5** *2* **Georgian King**[22] [1138] 12-9-4 **114** oh5..................(p) ArchieBellamy(10) 108
(Martin Keighley) *chsd ldr: rdn after 12th: lost 2nd bef next: wknd 3 out* **16/1**
6620 **6** *49* **Mr Moss (IRE)**[19] [1167] 10-10-10 **124**..............................(v) PaulMoloney 73
(Evan Williams) *hld up: rdn after 10th: wknd next* **10/1**
5P-4 **P** **Ackertac (IRE)**[89] [431] 10-10-4 **125**..............................(bt) AlanJohns(7)
(Tim Vaughan) *hld up: rdn after 9th: sn outpcd: sme hdwy bef 4 out: sn wknd: bhd whn p.u bef 2 out* **14/1**

5m 36.2s (-13.70) **Going Correction** -0.375s/f (Good) **7** Ran SP% **110.9**
Speed ratings (Par 107): **108,104,104,100,100 83,**
CSF £9.90 CT £36.26 TOTE £4.60: £2.30, £1.10; EX 11.70 Trifecta £33.50.
Owner Roddy Owen & Paul Fullagar **Bred** T F Duggan **Trained** Little Newcastle, Pembrokes

FOCUS
With topweight In The Rough a non-runner, the ceiling was lowered by 10lb. There was steady rain by this point, which had a bearing on the result. There's a case for rating the race a few pounds higher through the second.

1289 STARTIN SKODA STANDARD OPEN NATIONAL HUNT FLAT RACE 2m
6:00 (6:00) (Class 6) 4-6-Y-0 **£1,559** (£457; £228; £114)

Form RPR
1 **Roadie Joe (IRE)**[171] 6-10-4 0.................... LewisGordon(10) 104+
(Evan Williams) *hld up: hdwy over 4f out: led over 2f out: shkn up and clr over 1f out: comf* **20/1**
2 *5* **Fisherman Frank** 4-10-6 0..............................(t) FreddieMitchell(7) 97
(Natalie Lloyd-Beavis) *hld up: pushed along over 6f out: rdn over 3f out: hdwy over 1f out: r.o to go 2nd wl ins fnl f: no ch w wnr* **20/1**
3 *4* **Moontripper**[95] 6-10-2 0.................... MrBMoorcroft(5) 87
(Phillip Dando) *racd keenly: led: hdd over 14f out: trckd ldr tl over 7f out: rdn and ev ch over 2f out: styd on same pce fr over 1f out* **33/1**
4 *½* **Tara Potter** 5-10-7 0.................... HarrySkelton 87
(Dan Skelton) *prom: racd keenly: rdn and ev ch whn hmpd over 2f out: styd on same pce fr over 1f out* **2/1**[1]
26-4 **5** *½* **The Clonlisk Bug (IRE)**[26] [1101] 5-11-0 0.................... LeeEdwards 93
(Kevin Frost) *prom: racd keenly: rdn over 3f out: outpcd fr over 2f out* **12/1**
00- **6** *8* **Marley Joe (IRE)**[163] [4680] 4-10-13 0....................[1] AndrewTinkler 85
(Martin Keighley) *hld up: hdwy over 2f out: rdn and wknd over 1f out* **40/1**
233- **7** *nk* **Rustamabad (FR)**[226] [3541] 5-11-0 0.................... RichardJohnson 86
(Tim Vaughan) *chsd ldrs: wnt 2nd over 7f out: rdn and ev ch over 2f out: wknd over 1f out* **2/1**[1]
8 *1 ¾* **Lilbourne Legacy**[185] 4-10-13 0.................... TomScudamore 83
(David Pipe) *w ldr tl led over 14f out: rdn and hung lft 3f out: hdd over 2f out: wknd fnl f* **6/1**[2]
4 **9** *¾* **A Touch Of Sass (IRE)**[38] [970] 5-10-7 0.................... NicodeBoinville 76
(John Spearing) *hld up: plld hrd: hdwy 10f out: rdn over 4f out: wknd over 2f out* **10/1**[3]

3m 45.4s (0.40) **Going Correction** +0.125s/f (Yiel)
WFA 4 from 5yo+ 1lb **9** Ran SP% **112.6**
Speed ratings: **104,101,99,99,99 95,94,93,93**
CSF £323.14 TOTE £16.90: £3.70, £5.30, £5.10; EX 293.00 Trifecta £714.10.
Owner Billy Bates **Bred** Michael McEvoy **Trained** Llancarfan, Vale Of Glamorgan

FOCUS
The winner made quite an impression in an ordinary bumper.

1290 HALLMARKHULME NOVICES' HURDLE (10 hdls) 2m 4f
6:30 (6:32) (Class 4) 4-Y-0+ **£3,249** (£954; £477; £238)

Form RPR
1212 **1** **At First Light**[6] [1239] 6-10-12 108.................... NicodeBoinville 110+
(David Weston) *a.p: drvn along 6th: chsd wnr 3 out: 10 l 2nd and btn whn lft clr and mstke last: kpt on* **4/1**[2]
-53 **2** *1 ¾* **Beat The Tide**[23] [1116] 5-10-5 0.................... AlanJohns(7) 105
(Tim Vaughan) *chsd ldrs: nt fluent 2nd: rdn appr 3 out: outpcd after next out: lft 6 l 2nd last: hung lft u.p flat: styd on* **25/1**
05 **3** *2 ½* **Airpur Desbois (FR)**[23] [1122] 5-10-12 0.................... NoelFehily 105+
(Charlie Mann) *hld up: hdwy after 7th: outpcd bef next: lft 3rd and styng on whn hmpd by loose horse last: nt trble ldrs* **33/1**

-21P 4 9 **Detroit Blues**[71] 671 5-11-5 118........(t) MichealNolan 102
(Jamie Snowden) *hld up: hdwy 6th: rdn appr 3 out: sn wknd* **14/1**[3]

00P/ 5 1 **On Your Max**[73] 7-10-7 0........MrPYork(5) 95
(Raymond York) *led to 6th: rdn and wknd after 2 out* **100/1**

6 27 **Drop In The Ocean** 5-10-12 0........RichieMcLernon 70
(Jonjo O'Neill) *hld up: rdn and wknd appr 3 out* **14/1**[3]

F **Great Fighter**[403] 5-10-12 0........AidanColeman 120+
(John Ferguson) *trckd ldr tl wnt upsides 3rd: led 6th: wnt readily clr bef 3 out: shkn up after next: 10 l ahd whn fell last* **5/2**[1]

4-0 P **Miss Lucarno**[64] 753 5-10-5 0........AdamWedge
(Evan Williams) *hld up: a bhd: p.u bef 3 out* **33/1**

4m 53.7s (0.20) **Going Correction** +0.125s/f (Yiel) **8 Ran SP% 72.6**
Speed ratings (Par 105): **104,103,102,98,98 87, ,**
CSF £34.12 TOTE £3.40: £1.10, £4.00, £6.30; EX 39.70 Trifecta £304.80.
Owner Miss E J Tanner **Bred** D J Weston **Trained** Marlborough, Wilts
■ Dancing Meadows was withdrawn. Price at time of withdrawal 5/4F. Rule 4 applies to all bets - deduct 40p in the pound.

FOCUS
A dramatic race. There's a case for rating the race up to 6lb higher through the winner and fourth.

1291 HALLMARKHULME CLAIMING HURDLE (10 hdls) 2m 4f
7:00 (7:00) (Class 5) 4-Y-O+ £2,274 (£667; £333; £166)

Form RPR

5PP- 1 **Big Generator**[223] 3584 9-11-1 109........(t) HarrySkelton 115
(Caroline Bailey) *chsd ldr after 1st: led 5th: drvn out* **16/1**

2341 2 3 **Man Of Leisure**[31] 1051 11-11-7 125........(t) NoelFehily 119
(Anthony Honeyball) *hld up: hdwy 7th: chsd wnr 3 out: rdn appr last: styd on same pce flat* **5/2**[1]

1163 3 8 **Jayo Time (IRE)**[19] 1169 6-11-0 110........(b) ChrisWard(5) 109
(Dr Richard Newland) *prom: racd keenly: chsd wnr 7th to 3 out: sn rdn: styd on same pce appr last* **7/2**[2]

5-01 4 2 3/4 **Hazzaat (IRE)**[22] 1137 5-11-9 105........(t) PaddyBrennan 111
(Fergal O'Brien) *hld up: hdwy 7th: rdn and wknd last* **9/2**[3]

PP-6 5 1 1/2 **Sean Airgead (IRE)**[13] 1204 10-11-5 110........(tp) RichardJohnson 107
(Mark Michael McNiff, Ire) *hld up: plld hrd: nt fluent 3 out: hdwy next: sn rdn: wknd last* **9/1**

506/ 6 39 **Millksheikh**[87] 8-11-8 0........MrPYork(5) 79
(Raymond York) *chsd ldr tl after 1st: remained handy: nt fluent 2nd: rdn appr 3 out: wknd bef next* **66/1**

02-F 7 10 **Arctic Court (IRE)**[59] 798 11-11-3 121........JamesReveley 60
(Jim Goldie) *led to 5th: rdn and wknd after 7th* **5/2**[1]

4m 52.4s (-1.10) **Going Correction** +0.125s/f (Yiel) **7 Ran SP% 114.9**
Speed ratings (Par 103): **107,105,102,101,100 85,81**
CSF £57.74 TOTE £14.30: £4.70, £2.30; EX 61.40 Trifecta £324.00.Jayo Time was claimed by K Lee for £7000.
Owner G T H Bailey **Bred** Jethro Bloodstock **Trained** Holdenby, Northants

FOCUS
This produced a convincing winner under a positive ride in a fair claimer. There's a case for rating the race a bit higher through the second, but the fourth is probably a better guide to the level.

1292 HALLMARKHULME H'CAP HURDLE (12 hdls) 2m 7f
7:30 (7:30) (Class 3) (0-125,125) 4-Y-O+ £5,393 (£1,583; £791; £395)

Form RPR

-21P 1 **Dr Robin (IRE)**[17] 1181 5-10-11 **110**........SeanBowen(3) 119+
(Peter Bowen) *disp ld to 4th: pushed along and mstke 8th: rdn after next: outpcd bef 3 out: rallied 2 out: styd on to ld fnl 100yds* **9/2**[2]

4-14 2 1 1/4 **Highpower (IRE)**[63] 756 6-11-10 **120**........(p) RichardJohnson 127
(Jonjo O'Neill) *a.p: pushed along after 8th: led 3 out: rdn and hdd after next: led again last: hdd and unable qck fnl 100yds* **5/1**[3]

1-33 3 7 **Over The Air**[49] 876 7-10-12 **108**........NicodeBoinville 110
(John Spearing) *hld up: hdwy appr 3 out: led after next: hdd last: no ex flat* **15/2**

22-1 4 4 1/2 **For 'N' Against (IRE)**[6] 1242 6-11-6 **116** 7ex........(t) TomScudamore 114
(David Pipe) *hld up: hdwy 8th: nt fluent 2 out: sn rdn: wknd last* **11/10**[1]

-010 5 5 **Sealous Scout (IRE)**[32] 1035 7-11-12 **122**........NoelFehily 115
(Donald McCain) *hld up in tch: rdn appr 3 out: wknd bef last* **10/1**

34 6 17 **Part And Parcel (IRE)**[31] 1044 7-10-5 **108**........MrAlexEdwards(7) 85
(Alan Phillips) *disp ld to 4th: chsd ldr tl rdn appr 3 out: wknd bef next* **25/1**

-316 7 52 **Bobble Emerald (IRE)**[56] 833 7-11-2 **112**........AndrewTinkler 42
(Martin Keighley) *trckd ldrs: racd keenly: led 4th: mstke 7th: rdn and hdd 3 out: wknd next* **14/1**

5-F6 8 5 **Academy General (IRE)**[68] 718 9-10-6 **105**........(t) LucyGardner(3) 30
(Patricia Shaw) *hld up: a in rr: wknd after 9th* **33/1**

5m 37.2s (-1.40) **Going Correction** +0.125s/f (Yiel) **8 Ran SP% 116.8**
Speed ratings (Par 107): **107,106,104,102,100 94,76,75**
CSF £28.07 CT £166.06 TOTE £6.50: £2.00, £1.80, £1.90; EX 36.00 Trifecta £187.90.
Owner David Robbins & Karen Bowen **Bred** Michael Ronayne **Trained** Little Newcastle, Pembrokes
■ Stewards' Enquiry : Sean Bowen two-day ban: used whip in incorrect place (Sep 2-3)

FOCUS
Four went clear in an exciting finish. A pb from the second, and the third has been rated close to her mark.

1293 STARTIN HONDA H'CAP HURDLE (12 hdls) 2m 7f
8:00 (8:00) (Class 5) (0-100,100) 4-Y-O+ £2,274 (£667; £333; £166)

Form RPR

45P/ 1 **Rainbow Haze**[95] 9-10-4 **83** ow5........MrBMoorcroft(5) 90
(Phillip Dando) *hld up: hdwy 3 out: rdn to ld flat: edgd rt: styd on* **9/1**

042/ 2 1 **Bob Lewis**[472] 9-10-7 **81**........NickScholfield 89
(Stuart Kittow) *hld up: hdwy appr 3 out: led bef last: rdn and hdd flat: styd on* **10/1**

0513 3 6 **Mr Mafia (IRE)**[31] 1056 6-11-6 **94**........(t) LeeEdwards 97
(Tony Carroll) *hld up: mstke 3rd: hdwy after 9th: rdn appr last: styd on same pce flat* **9/2**[1]

/000 4 1/2 **Sovinnie (IRE)**[22] 1136 6-10-7 **86**........ConorRing(5) 88
(Jane Mathias) *hld up: hdwy 8th: rdn appr 3 out: edgd lft flat: styd on same pce* **66/1**

43-P 5 3/4 **Newton Martini**[27] 1085 6-10-5 **79**........(bt[1]) NicodeBoinville 80
(Ben Pauling) *prom: led 2 out: hdd bef last: no ex flat* **10/1**

2FU3 6 9 **Iktiview**[27] 1086 7-10-1 **82**........(bt) MrStanSheppard(7) 78
(Matt Sheppard) *hld up: hdwy 8th: blnd and rdr lost iron next: sn lost pl: rallied bef next: rdn and wknd after 2 out* **13/2**[3]

2 7 nk **Ennisnag (IRE)**[27] 1086 10-11-11 **99**........RichardJohnson 93
(Paul Henderson) *hld up: hdwy appr 2 out: sn rdn: wknd flat* **10/1**

-303 8 4 **Storm Alert**[52] 845 8-11-1 **92**........LucyGardner(3) 82
(Sue Gardner) *chsd ldrs: pushed along 8th: wknd 2 out* **6/1**[2]

0-13 9 1 1/4 **Annaroe (IRE)**[27] 1085 6-10-0 **81**........MikeyHamill(7) 69
(Alexandra Dunn) *chsd ldr to 4th: remained handy: 4th: ev ch 3 out: wknd after next* **12/1**

3232 10 hd **Dropzone (USA)**[27] 1084 6-10-13 **87**........TomO'Brien 75
(Brian Forsey) *hld up: effrt 3 out: wknd next* **8/1**

5/P0 11 5 **Spiritofchartwell**[27] 1082 7-11-2 **95**........MrPYork(5) 79
(Raymond York) *prom: led appr 3 out: rdn and hdd next: wknd bef last* **50/1**

FUP- 12 2 **Monty's Revenge (IRE)**[135] 5186 10-10-2 **76**........(p) IanPopham 58
(Martin Keighley) *mid-div: rdn and lost pl bef 9th: wknd appr 3 out* **20/1**

00 13 39 **Distant Sound (IRE)**[49] 879 8-10-9 **90**........(p) AlanJohns(7) 37
(Adrian Wintle) *prom: chsd ldr 4th: led 7th: rdn and hdd bef 3 out: sn wknd* **33/1**

U00U 14 26 **Innox Park**[23] 1120 5-11-6 **94**........(p) JamesBest 17
(Kevin Bishop) *hld up in tch: rdn and wknd bef 3 out* **28/1**

P-53 P **Blurred Lines (IRE)**[19] 1165 6-11-5 **100**........JamesCowley(7)
(Donald McCain) *led to 7th: rdn and wknd appr 3 out: bhd whn p.u bef last* **16/1**

5m 39.5s (0.90) **Going Correction** +0.125s/f (Yiel) **15 Ran SP% 122.4**
Speed ratings (Par 103): **103,102,100,100,100 97,96,95,95,95 93,92,79,69,**
CSF £92.34 CT £467.95 TOTE £9.40: £3.50, £4.00, £2.50; EX 101.10 Trifecta £1278.80.
Owner Phillip Dando & Dr Michael Armitage **Bred** Phillip C And Mrs Kathryn M Dando **Trained** Peterston-Super-Ely, S Glamorg
■ Stewards' Enquiry : Mr B Moorcroft three-day ban: weighed-in 2lb heavier (tbn)

FOCUS
An open-looking handicap with two hold-up horses coming through to dominate. The fifth has been rated to her mark.
T/Plt: £1,186.40 to a £1 stake. Pool of £54122.57 - 33.30 winning tickets. T/Qpdt: £374.00 to a £1 stake. Pool of £6217.13 - 12.30 winning tickets. **Colin Roberts**

1153

STRATFORD (L-H)
Thursday, August 20

OFFICIAL GOING: Good (good to firm in places; chs 7.4, hdl 7.5)
Wind: Fresh across Weather: Overcast

1294 H.L. BARNES & SONS JUVENILE HURDLE (8 hdls) 2m 70y
2:20 (2:20) (Class 4) 3-Y-O £3,249 (£954; £477; £238)

Form RPR

11 1 **Leoncavallo (IRE)**[8] 1232 3-11-12 0........AidanColeman 114+
(John Ferguson) *led to 2nd: chsd ldr tl shkn up to ld again appr last: sn clr: eased nr fin* **30/100**[1]

C33 2 3 3/4 **Auld Fyffee (IRE)**[25] 1111 3-10-5 0........JamesDavies 84
(Tom Gretton) *led 2nd: rdn and hdd appr last: sn outpcd* **25/1**

12 3 6 **Egmont**[25] 1111 3-11-5 0........HenryBrooke 92
(George Moore) *chsd ldrs: rdn after 2 out: wkng whn blnd last* **12/1**[3]

4 11 **Champagne Ransom (FR)**[63] 3-10-5 0........NicodeBoinville 67
(Nicky Henderson) *prom: nt fluent 3rd: j. path bef next: rdn after 2 out: wknd wl bef last* **9/2**[2]

5 5 14 **Fortuna Glas (IRE)**[75] 636 3-10-12 0........NoelFehily 60
(Donald McCain) *hld up: nt fluent 5th: rdn appr 3 out: wknd next* **20/1**

6 8 **Layerthorpe (IRE)**[119] 3-10-12 0........DonalDevereux 52
(Debra Hamer) *prom tl rdn and wknd after 2 out* **50/1**

P 7 27 **Whistler Mountain**[8] 1232 3-10-12 0........TomCannon 25
(Mark Gillard) *hld up: mstke 1st: nt fluent 4th: wknd after next* **200/1**

3m 58.4s (2.40) **Going Correction** +0.025s/f (Yiel) **7 Ran SP% 113.9**
Speed ratings (Par 102): **95,93,90,84,77 73,60**
CSF £12.57 TOTE £1.30: £1.10, £9.00; EX 11.20 Trifecta £30.70.
Owner Bloomfields **Bred** Darley **Trained** Cowlinge, Suffolk

FOCUS
After watering earlier in the week and 4mm of rain overnight the going had eased slightly. After the first jockeys described the going as 'good'. Shared bend by 2m start. Chase track on innermost line and Hurdle track out wide on one bend. Races 1, 6 & 7 increased by 21yds, races 2 & 4 by 42yds. An interesting juvenile hurdle that did not heat up until the last down the back.

1295 EDWARD BRAIN PLANT HIRE NOVICES' HURDLE (11 hdls) 2m 6f 7y
2:55 (2:55) (Class 4) 4-Y-O+ £3,249 (£954; £477; £238)

Form RPR

42 1 **Panis Angelicus (FR)**[21] 1153 6-10-12 111........RichardJohnson 116+
(Tim Vaughan) *disp ld at stdy pce tl wnt on 8th: rdn clr appr last* **11/10**[1]

443 2 18 **Almagest**[24] 1117 7-10-12 105........TomO'Brien 96
(Robert Stephens) *prom: mstke 8th: sn chsng wnr: rdn after 2 out: wknd appr last* **15/8**[2]

33 3 34 **Danmurphysdoor (IRE)**[92] 397 6-10-12 0........(t) AidanColeman 63
(Tim Vaughan) *hld up: hdwy 4th: rdn and wknd after 2 out* **4/1**[3]

0 4 22 **Sultan's Dancer**[57] 831 6-10-5 0........BrendanPowell 31
(Brendan Powell) *hld up: hdwy appr 3 out: rdn and wknd next* **50/1**

0-P0 5 20 **Laughingalltheway**[75] 647 4-10-10 0........AndrewTinkler 16
(Martin Keighley) *nt fluent 3rd: disp ld to 8th: wknd bef next* **80/1**

6 88 **Double Dan (IRE)**[91] 423 6-10-12 0........RhysFlint
(Alexandra Dunn) *prom: lost pl 4th: sn pushed along: bhd fr 6th* **25/1**

5m 28.9s (0.80) **Going Correction** +0.025s/f (Yiel)
WFA 4 from 6yo+ 14lb **6 Ran SP% 109.4**
Speed ratings (Par 105): **99,92,80,72,64 32**
CSF £3.35 TOTE £1.90: £1.10, £1.50; EX 3.30 Trifecta £5.00.
Owner Oceans Racing **Bred** Erick Bec De La Motte Et Al **Trained** Aberthin, Vale of Glamorgan

FOCUS
A moderate novice hurdle run at a crawl until the winner injected some pace heading out on the final circuit.

1296 WALLS AND CEILINGS INTERNATIONAL H'CAP CHASE (14 fncs) 2m 3f 98y
3:30 (3:30) (Class 3) (0-130,130) 4-Y-O+ £6,498 (£1,908; £954; £477)

Form RPR

6225 1 **No Likey (IRE)**[25] 1112 8-11-2 **120**........(tp) TomO'Brien 126
(Philip Hobbs) *a.p: led 3 out: rdn appr last: styd on* **4/1**[2]

2F52 2 3/4 **Town Mouse**[33] 1043 5-11-1 **119**........(p) TrevorWhelan 124
(Neil King) *chsd ldr tl led after 11th: hdd next: rdn and ev ch last: nt clr run and swtchd lft flat: styd on* **8/1**

-531 3 4 1/2 **Alwaystheoptimist**[27] 1100 12-11-4 **122**........(t) TomScudamore 123
(Shaun Lycett) *hld up: nt fluent 7th (water): hdwy after 3 out: rdn appr last: styd on same pce flat* **7/1**

5-42 4 3 1/4 **Domtaline (FR)**[51] 863 8-11-9 **127**........PaulMoloney 125
(Evan Williams) *chsd ldrs: lost pl after 11th: rallied appr 2 out: rdn bef last: no ex flat* **5/2**[1]

-213 **5** *9* **Stephen Hero (IRE)**[60] 809 5-11-12 **130**.......................(t) HarrySkelton 119
(Dan Skelton) *hld up: mstke 6th: hdwy 10th: rdn after 2 out: wkng whn nt fluent last* **6/1**[3]

4454 **F** **Macarthur**[20] 1169 11-10-4 **108**..(b) AdamWedge
(David Rees) *hld up: mstke 2nd: fell 4th* **11/1**

0PP/ **P** **Mr Cracker (IRE)**[525] 4768 10-11-7 **125**................. RichardJohnson
(Tim Vaughan) *hld up: bhd fr 6th: p.u bef 10th* **9/1**

-00P **P** **Anquetta (IRE)**[60] 809 11-11-9 **130**......................(p) MrSWaley-Cohen(3)
(Robert Waley-Cohen) *led: hdd appr 11th: wknd 3 out: bhd whn p.u bef last* **16/1**

4m 42.7s (-7.30) **Going Correction** -0.10s/f (Good) **8** Ran SP% **110.7**
Speed ratings (Par 107): **111,110,108,107,103** , ,
CSF £32.79 CT £204.52 TOTE £5.30: £1.60, £2.10, £2.00; EX 30.70 Trifecta £143.10.
Owner The Country Side **Bred** R A Steele **Trained** Withycombe, Somerset

FOCUS
An open-looking handicap. The first two went clear and came close together bypassing the water on the run-in, with the result unchanged after a stewards' enquiry.

1297 JON PINFOLD INDUSTRIAL CLEANERS NOVICES' H'CAP HURDLE (9 hdls) 2m 2f 148y
4:05 (4:05) (Class 5) (0-100,100) 4-Y-0+ **£2,274** (£667; £333; £166)

Form RPR

6P-1 **1** **Shalianzi (IRE)**[7] 1245 5-11-7 **95** 7ex.....................(b) AndrewGlassonbury 102
(Gary Moore) *a.p: rdn after 2 out: hung lft appr last: hung rt flat: styd on to ld towards fin* **7/4**[1]

4-34 **2** *½* **Fred Le Macon (FR)**[39] 977 6-11-0 **98**............................... JamieInsole(10) 105
(Alan King) *a.p: chsd ldr 6th: led flat: rdn and hdd towards fin* **7/1**[2]

-306 **3** *3¾* **Warrant Officer**[15] 751 5-11-4 **92**.................................... MarcGoldstein 96
(Sheena West) *led: mstke 3 out: rdn and hdd and no ex flat* **16/1**

25-6 **4** *1* **Surf In September (IRE)**[21] 1153 6-11-6 **94**.................... MarkGrant 96
(Dominic Ffrench Davis) *hld up: rdn after 6th: r.o appr last: nt rch ldrs* **33/1**

0-00 **5** *5* **Barton Antix**[44] 935 6-11-10 **98**......................................(p) NoelFehily 96
(Neil Mulholland) *hld up: hdwy 6th: rdn and wkng whn mstke last* **7/1**[2]

6-01 **6** *3¾* **All Riled Up**[39] 977 7-10-3 **82**.. DanielHiskett(5) 75
(Harry Chisman) *chsd ldr to 6th: mstke 2 out: sn rdn: wknd wl bef last* **7/1**[2]

-54F **7** *23* **L Stig**[21] 1156 5-11-5 **93**.. DaveCrosse 63
(John O'Shea) *hld up: hdwy 6th: rdn and wknd after 2 out* **20/1**

0500 **8** *51* **Southern Cross**[8] 1086 4-9-7 **76** oh7..............(v[1]) ThomasCheesman(7)
(Dai Williams) *chsd ldrs: mstke 3rd: rdn after 6th: wknd bef next* **66/1**

4/ **9** *4½* **Man Of God (IRE)**[370] 1229 7-11-12 **100**................... RichardJohnson 15
(Tim Vaughan) *hld up: rdn and wknd after 6th* **14/1**

/2-P **10** *3* **Ravens Nest**[24] 1120 5-11-5 **93**.. NickScholfield 5
(Lawney Hill) *hld up: rdn and wknd appr 3 out* **33/1**

/0F6 **P** **Prairie Hawk (USA)**[28] 1084 10-9-11 **74** oh1..................(t) BenPoste(3)
(Adrian Wintle) *hld up: rdn after 6th: wknd bef next: bhd whn p.u and dismntd after 2 out* **12/1**

P65- **P** **My Renaissance**[19] 4923 5-10-5 **79**...................................(t) KielanWoods
(Ben Case) *hld up: nt fluent 4th: hit next: hdwy 6th: wknd appr 2 out: bhd whn p.u bef last* **9/1**[3]

0P-6 **P** **Rainbow Lollipop**[65] 748 4-10-0 **76** oh2........................(tp) JamesDavies
(Tom Gretton) *prom: mstke 4th: wknd after 6th: bhd whn p.u after 2 out* **50/1**

4m 29.5s (-2.00) **Going Correction** +0.025s/f (Yiel)
WFA 4 from 5yo+ 13lb **13** Ran SP% **118.2**
Speed ratings (Par 103): **105,104,103,102,100 99,89,67,66,64** , ,
CSF £13.67 CT £151.83 TOTE £3.00: £1.40, £2.50, £2.70; EX 16.90 Trifecta £103.50.
Owner Ashley Head **Bred** His Highness The Aga Khan's Studs S C **Trained** Lower Beeding, W Sussex

FOCUS
After a good early pace three were left to fight out the finish. The favourite looked an unlikely winner turning for home.

1298 JOHN SMITH'S H'CAP CHASE (17 fncs) 2m 6f 125y
4:40 (4:40) (Class 4) (0-110,109) 4-Y-0+ **£3,898** (£1,144; £572; £286)

Form RPR

-F21 **1** **Faustina Pius (IRE)**[21] 1159 7-11-3 **107**................(p) MrStanSheppard(7) 121+
(Matt Sheppard) *hld up: hdwy 12th: led and mstke 3 out: shkn up flat: styd on wl* **10/1**

5226 **2** *8* **West End (IRE)**[25] 1114 8-11-8 **108**..............................(tp) TomBellamy(3) 111
(Kim Bailey) *hld up: hdwy 14th: chsd wnr 2 out: rdn appr last: styd on same pce flat* **9/2**[1]

0214 **3** *6* **Amuse Me**[20] 1171 9-11-10 **107**.......................................(tp) WillKennedy 104
(Jonjo O'Neill) *hld up: mstke 2nd (water): hdwy after 14th: rdn after 2 out: no ex last* **16/1**

13/P **4** *18* **Badgers Retreat**[24] 1121 9-11-0 **97**.................................... GavinSheehan 76
(Nick Mitchell) *hld up: hdwy after 14th: hmpd 3 out: wknd wl bef last* **16/1**

435 **5** *14* **Kyles Faith (IRE)**[18] 1181 7-11-10 **107**..............................(p) IanPopham 72
(Martin Keighley) *prom: pushed along and lost pl 8th: bhd fr 12th* **16/1**

2-23 **6** *4½* **He's A Bully (IRE)**[85] 510 6-11-8 **105**............................ RichardJohnson 66
(Philip Hobbs) *hld up: hdwy 9th: led 13th: hdd 3 out: nt fluent next: rdn and wknd after 2 out* **5/1**[2]

P-4P **P** **Papradon**[50] 873 11-11-10 **107**...................................(v) SamTwiston-Davies
(Nigel Twiston-Davies) *chsd ldrs: drvn along after 13th: wknd next: bhd whn p.u bef 2 out* **16/1**

3/0- **P** **Michigan Assassin (IRE)**[436] 656 13-11-1 **98**............(p) DonalDevereux
(Debra Hamer) *led 2nd: hdd 12th: rdn and wknd appr 14th: bhd whn p.u bef 2 out* **33/1**

5 **P** **Admiral Barton (IRE)**[1] 1287 9-11-0 **97**........................(bt) TomScudamore
(Paul W Flynn, Ire) *mstke 1st: chsd ldr 3rd: led 12th: j.rt and hdd next: wknd after 14th: bhd whn p.u bef 2 out* **11/2**[3]

U133 **F** **Adios Alonso (IRE)**[28] 1080 9-10-7 **93**............................ BenPoste(3)
(Rosemary Gasson) *mid-div: hdwy 8th: ev ch whn fell 3 out* **11/2**[3]

-316 **P** **Vivacissimo (IRE)**[33] 1034 8-11-12 **109**...........................(t) HarrySkelton
(Dan Skelton) *led to 2nd: chsd ldrs: pckd 9th: sn rdn: wknd 13th: sn p.u* **5/1**[2]

5m 35.3s (-3.90) **Going Correction** -0.10s/f (Good) **11** Ran SP% **117.8**
Speed ratings (Par 105): **102,99,97,90,86 84**, , , ,
CSF £56.18 CT £727.25 TOTE £12.80: £3.70, £2.00, £4.50; EX 52.20 Trifecta £314.90.
Owner Lost In The Summer Wine **Bred** Pearse Mee **Trained** Eastnor, H'fords

FOCUS
An ordinary handicap with the only last-time-out winner in the field following up with ease.

1299 MOLLY OLLY'S WISHES WALK AMATEUR RIDERS' H'CAP HURDLE (8 hdls) 2m 70y
5:15 (5:15) (Class 5) (0-100,97) 3-Y-0+ **£2,183** (£677; £338; £169)

Form RPR

03P4 **1** **Grams And Ounces**[25] 1115 8-11-1 **91**........................(t) DavidNoonan(5) 106
(Adrian Wintle) *a.p: rdn to ld appr last: styd on wl* **5/1**[2]

265P **2** *10* **Mount Vesuvius (IRE)**[53] 856 7-10-9 **87**....................(tp) MrGTreacy(7) 90
(Paul Henderson) *hld up: hdwy after 2 out: sn rdn: styng on same pce whn lft 2nd last* **8/1**[3]

0-26 **3** *1½* **Vexillum (IRE)**[8] 856 6-10-10 **84**..(p) MrMLegg(3) 86
(Neil Mulholland) *hld up: hdwy appr 3 out: rdn after next: styd on same pce appr last* **5/1**[2]

-26P **4** *2* **Descaro (USA)**[28] 1085 9-11-5 **97**...................(tp) MrDSymes-Meineck(7) 97
(Fergal O'Brien) *prom: rdn after 3 out: outpcd after next* **17/2**

02/6 **5** *nk* **Until The Man (IRE)**[18] 1182 8-9-13 **73**................................ MrZBaker(3) 74
(Barry Brennan) *chsd ldrs: rdn after 2 out: hmpd and wknd last* **14/1**

3P/5 **6** *nk* **Aughcarra (IRE)**[32] 1051 10-9-12 **72**.......................... MissAEStirling(3) 71
(Harry Chisman) *hld up: effrt after 3 out: rdn and outpcd after next: kpt on flat* **25/1**

/025 **7** *6* **Umoristic (FR)**[27] 1096 7-9-13 **75**..........................(tp) MrStanSheppard(5) 68
(Matt Sheppard) *led to 5th: ev ch 2 out: sn rdn: wkng whn hmpd last* **9/2**[1]

443 **8** *6* **Cabin Fever**[25] 1109 4-11-1 **87**....................................[1] MissGAndrews 73
(Tom Lacey) *chsd ldr tl led 5th: hit 2 out: sn hdd: wknd wl bef last* **8/1**[3]

000- **9** *44* **Bells Of Castor (IRE)**[237] 3257 5-11-5 **97**......................(t) MrEDavid(7) 40
(Tim Vaughan) *hld up: blnd and wknd 3 out* **20/1**

155 **10** *5* **No No Cardinal (IRE)**[32] 1045 6-9-13 **77**............................ MrTGillard(7) 15
(Mark Gillard) *chsd ldrs tl rdn and wknd after 2 out* **16/1**

5043 **F** **Maid Of Tuscany (IRE)**[27] 1095 4-11-6 **95**............(b) MissBHampson(3) 97
(Neil Mulholland) *a.p: led after 2 out: hdd and 3 l down whn fell last* **8/1**[3]

3m 54.2s (-1.80) **Going Correction** +0.025s/f (Yiel) **11** Ran SP% **116.5**
Speed ratings (Par 103): **105,100,99,98,98 97,94,91,69,67**
CSF £44.55 CT £211.31 TOTE £6.60: £2.90, £3.40, £1.90; EX 54.10 Trifecta £271.50.
Owner Ron C Williams **Bred** Brook Stud Bloodstock Ltd **Trained** Westbury-On-Severn, Gloucs

FOCUS
A moderate handicap.

1300 BORDEAUX UNDISCOVERED STANDARD OPEN NATIONAL HUNT FLAT RACE 2m 70y
5:45 (5:45) (Class 6) 4-6-Y-0 **£1,624** (£477; £238; £119)

Form RPR

1 **1** **Alyasan (IRE)**[51] 865 4-11-5 0...................................(t) SeanBowen(3) 106+
(Seamus Durack) *hld up: plld hrd: hdwy 7f out: chsd ldr over 1f out: sn swtchd lft: shkn up to ld ins fnl f: r.o* **8/11**[1]

/1-3 **2** *1¾* **Magna Cartor**[27] 1101 5-11-9 0......................................[1] KielanWoods 103
(Ronald Thompson) *led at stdy pce but sn clr: c bk to the field 7f out: qckng over 5f out: rdn over 1f out: hdd ins fnl f: styd on same pce* **15/8**[2]

3 *3¼* **Miliair** 5-10-4 0.. JakeHodson(5) 86
(David Bridgwater) *chsd ldr: pushed along over 3f out: lost 2nd over 1f out: styd on same pce* **16/1**[3]

0 **4** *5* **Good Rhythm**[24] 1122 5-11-2 0.. TrevorWhelan 88+
(Neil King) *hld up: outpcd 5f out: rdn over 1f out: styd on to go 4th ins fnl f: nvr on terms* **20/1**

4 **5** *8* **Mollylikestoboogie**[32] 1050 5-10-9 0............................... TomScudamore 73
(Linda Blackford) *chsd ldrs: rdn over 2f out: wknd over 1f out* **25/1**

3m 56.9s (6.50) **Going Correction** +0.025s/f (Yiel)
WFA 4 from 5yo 1lb **5** Ran SP% **107.2**
Speed ratings: **84,83,81,79,75**
CSF £2.12 TOTE £1.70: £1.10, £1.20; EX 3.00 Trifecta £7.40.
Owner The Alyasan Partnership **Bred** His Highness The Aga Khan's Studs S C **Trained** Upper Lambourn, Berkshire

FOCUS
Little depth to this bumper.
T/Plt: £26.10 to a £1 stake. Pool: £48,510.65 - 1,356.73 winning tickets T/Qpdt: £20.10 to a £1 stake. Pool: £3,440.14 - 126.40 winning tickets **Colin Roberts**

1301 - 1304a (Foreign Racing) - See Raceform Interactive

1165 BANGOR-ON-DEE (L-H)
Friday, August 21

OFFICIAL GOING: Good changing to good to soft after race 3 (3:20)
Wind: Fresh across Weather: Overcast turning to rain for race 3

1305 EXTERION MEDIA MAIDEN HURDLE (9 hdls) 2m 145y
2:10 (2:11) (Class 5) 4-Y-0+ **£2,737** (£798; £399)

Form RPR

0-0 **1** **Agenor (GER)**[9] 1234 4-10-13 0...................................(b[1]) BrendanPowell 122+
(Jamie Snowden) *mde all: sn clr: c bk to the field 4th: wnt clr again bef 2 out: comf* **10/1**

222- **2** *13* **Sacred Square (GER)**[39] 2126 5-11-0 113..............(b) WayneHutchinson 108
(Donald McCain) *hld up: mstkes: hdwy 6th: sn rdn: wnt 2nd appr 2 out: styd on same pce* **7/2**[3]

3 *11* **Moontime**[301] 4-10-13 0.. AidanColeman 96
(John Ferguson) *hld up: j.lft 2nd: nt fluent 4th: pushed along 6th: nvr on terms* **5/2**[1]

4 **4** *1* **Nordical (IRE)**[78] 613 5-11-0 0......................................(t) AdamWedge 96
(Evan Williams) *hld up: drvn along after 5th nvr on terms* **16/1**

2-43 **5** *1½* **Createur (IRE)**[32] 1065 4-10-13 109...............................(t) RichardJohnson 94
(Tim Vaughan) *chsd ldrs: lft 2nd 3 out: rdn and wknd bef next* **11/4**[2]

10-4 **F** **Native Display (IRE)**[111] 83 5-11-0 0.................................. NoelFehily
(Nicky Henderson) *chsd wnr who was sn clr: tk clsr order 5th: jnd wnr next tl fell 3 out* **9/2**

4m 2.1s (-8.80) **Going Correction** -0.55s/f (Firm)
WFA 4 from 5yo 13lb **6** Ran SP% **110.6**
Speed ratings (Par 103): **98,91,86,86,85**
CSF £43.20 TOTE £15.60: £3.50, £1.90; EX 48.60 Trifecta £215.50.
Owner Sir Chips Keswick **Bred** Gestut Am Schlossgarten Gbr **Trained** Lambourn, Berks

FOCUS
Despite a sharp shower before racing the official going remained good. The opener was a modest maiden hurdle and the winner made all.

1306 MINT STAFFING SOLUTIONS H'CAP CHASE (15 fncs) 2m 4f 72y
2:45 (2:45) (Class 4) (0-105,105) 4-Y-0+ **£4,548** (£1,335; £667; £333)

Form RPR
P-P3 **1** **Strobe**[13] 885 11-10-7 **89**.....(p) AdamNicol[(3)] 99
(Lucy Normile) *led to 5th: led again next: hdd 10th: rdn to chse ldr appr 2 out: styd on u.p to ld post* **20/1**
P-64 **2** *nse* **According To Sarah (IRE)**[37] 1007 7-11-12 **105**..... RichardJohnson 115
(Philip Hobbs) *chsd ldr 4th tl led next: hdd 6th: led again 10th: rdn appr last: hdd post* **9/2**[2]
-245 **3** *7* **Sandynow (IRE)**[29] 1079 10-11-6 **102**.....(vt) SeanBowen[(3)] 105
(Peter Bowen) *chsd ldrs: lost pl 6th: rallied appr 2 out: styd on to go 3rd flat* **9/2**[2]
0-21 **4** *6* **Etania**[51] 873 7-11-4 **97**..... TomO'Brien 94
(Ian Williams) *chsd ldr to 2nd: remained handy tl outpcd 9th: rallied appr 2 out: styd on* **13/2**[3]
00-4 **5** *shd* **The Shropshire Lad**[26] 1110 5-11-4 **97**..... HarrySkelton 94
(Dan Skelton) *hld up in tch: chsd ldr 12th tl rdn appr 2 out: wknd flat* **12/1**
P6-2 **6** *2¼* **Humbel Ben (IRE)**[106] 161 12-11-4 **97**.....(p) NickScholfield 92
(Alan Jones) *hld up: hdwy 12th: rdn appr 2 out: wknd last* **11/1**
-221 **7** *15* **Waddingtown Hero (IRE)**[64] 770 8-11-9 **102**.....(tp) GerardTumelty 82
(Andy Turnell) *hld up: hdwy 6th: rdn 11th: wknd after 3 out* **4/1**[1]
-P3P **8** *4* **Forget And Forgive (IRE)**[9] 1237 7-10-9 **88**.....(p) AdamWedge 64
(Sophie Leech) *hld up: hdwy 9th: rdn and wknd after 3 out* **22/1**
432- **9** *hd* **Cool Bob (IRE)**[134] 5247 12-9-9 **81** ow2.....(tp) MrStanSheppard[(7)] 56
(Matt Sheppard) *chsd ldr 3rd to 4th: remained handy tl mstke and lost pl 8th: rdn and wknd appr 2 out* **8/1**
-13P **10** *25* **Mr Robinson (FR)**[40] 972 8-10-0 **79**..... JamesBest 29
(Rob Summers) *hld up: pushed along 10th: wknd 3 out* **16/1**
4m 56.1s (-13.00) **Going Correction** -0.70s/f (Firm) **10** Ran SP% **111.8**
Speed ratings (Par 105): **98,97,95,92,92 91,85,84,84,74**
CSF £106.02 CT £480.34 TOTE £13.10: £5.20, £1.70, £1.80; EX 141.80 Trifecta £2953.40.
Owner Miss P A & P J Carnaby **Bred** Old Mill Stud **Trained** Duncrievie, Perth & Kinross
FOCUS
A modest, open-looking handicap chase, in which it paid to race prominently.

1307 EVANS HALSHAW FORD COMMERCIALS BRETTON NOVICES' H'CAP HURDLE (9 hdls) 2m 145y
3:20 (3:22) (Class 4) (0-105,105) 3-Y-0+ **£3,422** (£997; £499)

Form RPR
5532 **1** **King Muro**[28] 1095 5-11-2 **95**.....(t) PaddyBrennan 111+
(Fergal O'Brien) *hld up and bhd: hdwy to ld after 3 out: sn clr: mstke last: easily* **5/2**[1]
45-6 **2** *14* **Gin And Tonic**[28] 1095 5-11-0 **93**..... JackQuinlan 89
(Michael Wigham) *hld up: hdwy 3 out: rdn to chse wnr appr 2 out: sn outpcd: mstke last* **7/1**
3 *¾* **The Bugler (IRE)**[288] 2315 8-11-5 **98**.....(t) PaulMoloney 93
(Evan Williams) *hld up: hdwy 6th: rdn after 3 out: styd on same pce* **11/2**[3]
P-24 **4** *1* **Wymeswold**[71] 694 8-10-3 **85**..... BenPoste[(3)] 79
(Michael Mullineaux) *chsd clr ldrs: tk clsr order appr 3 out: sn rdn and btn* **9/2**[2]
440 **5** *½* **Footstepsintherain (IRE)**[18] 1054 5-11-9 **102**.....(t) AidanColeman 96
(David Dennis) *chsd ldrs: nt fluent 2nd: rdn after 3 out: sn btn* **14/1**
5-56 **6** *7* **Naburn**[50] 881 7-11-10 **103**..... BrianHarding 90
(Andrew Wilson) *hld up: bhd fr 5th* **20/1**
P-32 **7** *8* **Cousin Guillaume (FR)**[24] 1139 6-11-10 **103**.....(b) WayneHutchinson 82
(Donald McCain) *led to 3rd: led again 5th: clr next: hdd & wknd after 3 out* **11/2**[3]
5-60 **P** **Theflyingportrait (IRE)**[89] 465 6-11-12 **105**.....(tp) PeterCarberry
(Jennie Candlish) *chsd ldr tl led 3rd: hdd 5th: wknd next: bhd whn mstke 3 out: p.u bef next* **8/1**
4m 1.5s (-9.40) **Going Correction** -0.55s/f (Firm) **8** Ran SP% **112.6**
Speed ratings (Par 105): **100,93,93,92,92 89,85,**
CSF £19.75 CT £86.23 TOTE £2.60: £1.30, £1.90, £2.00; EX 17.80 Trifecta £139.70.
Owner The General Asphalte Company Ltd **Bred** Stourbank Stud **Trained** Naunton, Gloucs
FOCUS
A modest novice handicap hurdle and a wide-margin winner.

1308 GOLDEN SUNSET HOLIDAYS NOVICES' HURDLE (11 hdls) 2m 3f 123y
3:55 (3:55) (Class 4) 4-Y-0+ **£3,249** (£954; £477; £238)

Form RPR
-121 **1** **Curious Carlos**[90] 440 6-11-2 122..... SeanBowen[(3)] 132+
(Peter Bowen) *a.p: chsd ldr 7th: led appr 2 out: shkn up flat: styd on wl* **11/4**[2]
21 **2** *3½* **Lilac Tree**[25] 1117 5-11-5 120..... AidanColeman 127
(John Ferguson) *chsd ldrs: chsd wnr appr 2 out: rdn bef last: styd on same pce flat* **15/8**[1]
2321 **3** *19* **Hepijeu (FR)**[22] 1153 4-11-3 118.....(tp) RichardJohnson 106
(Charlie Longsdon) *led: rdn and hdd appr 2 out: edgd lft and wknd bef last* **4/1**[3]
1244 **4** *7* **Prince Khurram**[21] 1168 5-10-12 111.....(t) WayneHutchinson 94
(Donald McCain) *hld up: hdwy 8th: blnd 3 out: sn rdn and wknd* **6/1**
-151 **5** *9* **Are They Your Own (IRE)**[37] 1000 7-11-7 125..... NickSlatter[(5)] 99
(Fergal O'Brien) *chsd ldr to 7th: wknd after 3 out* **10/1**
6 *99* **Little Dream (IRE)**[819] 8-10-5 0..... PaulMoloney
(Evan Williams) *nt fluent and a bhd* **50/1**
3-16 **R** **Countersign**[77] 620 6-11-5 117..... AdamPogson
(Charles Pogson) *nt fluent in rr: bhd whn rn out and uns rdr 7th* **20/1**
4m 41.4s (-10.60) **Going Correction** -0.55s/f (Firm)
WFA 4 from 5yo+ 14lb **7** Ran SP% **111.5**
Speed ratings (Par 105): **99,97,90,87,83 44,**
CSF £8.17 TOTE £3.40: £1.20, £2.50; EX 8.60 Trifecta £22.50.
Owner Carl Pyne **Bred** Carl Pyne **Trained** Little Newcastle, Pembrokes
FOCUS
Following persistent rain the ground was changed to good to soft before this race. An interesting novice hurdle and they were well strung out, with the two principals pulling a long way clear.

1309 GENESIS WEALTH MANAGEMENT H'CAP CHASE (18 fncs) 3m 30y
4:30 (4:30) (Class 4) (0-120,120) 4-Y-0+ **£6,498** (£1,908; £954; £477)

Form RPR
40P- **1** **Dreamsoftheatre (IRE)**[261] 2885 7-11-9 **117**.....(t) RichardJohnson 134
(Jonjo O'Neill) *hld up: hdwy 8th: led 14: clr fr 2 out: styd on wl* **5/1**[3]
4/11 **2** *7* **Pena Dorada (IRE)**[34] 1033 8-11-0 **115**..... MissRMcDonald[(7)] 123
(Alistair Whillans) *hld up: hdwy 10th: chsd wnr after 2 out: styd on same pce* **9/2**[2]
-246 **3** *13* **Porters War (IRE)**[33] 1053 13-11-7 **115**..... NickScholfield 110
(Jeremy Scott) *hld up: hdwy 12th: rdn 15th: wknd after 2 out* **20/1**
0-22 **4** *½* **Hinton Indiana**[33] 1049 10-10-8 **102**.....(t) HarrySkelton 97
(Dan Skelton) *hld up: hdwy 8th: chsd ldr 10th tl rdn and wknd after 2 out* **7/2**[1]
4256 **5** *10* **Sir Mattie (IRE)**[21] 1167 10-11-2 **110**..... PaulMoloney 95
(David Rees) *hld up: sme hdwy 4 out: sn wknd* **11/1**
5322 **6** *7* **Strumble Head (IRE)**[21] 1167 10-11-12 **120**.....(b) DonalDevereux 98
(Peter Bowen) *led to 13th: wknd 15th* **8/1**
-216 **7** *8* **Big Sound**[40] 967 8-11-8 **116**.....(p) JakeGreenall 86
(Mark Walford) *chsd ldrs tl rdn and wknd 15th* **12/1**
F6-5 **P** **King Fontaine (IRE)**[37] 1007 12-10-13 **110**.....(tp) SeanBowen[(3)]
(Lawney Hill) *a in rr: bhd whn p.u bef 13th* **14/1**
5-64 **P** **Highway Code (USA)**[21] 1167 9-11-9 **117**.....(t) TomCannon
(Kerry Lee) *hld up: sme hdwy 10th: wknd bef 12th: bhd whn p.u bef 3 out* **11/1**
-562 **P** **Green Bank (IRE)**[26] 1114 9-11-2 **110**.....(bt) AidanColeman
(Charlie Longsdon) *chsd ldrs: drvn along 11th: wknd bef 13th: bhd whn p.u bef 2 out* **11/1**
P-2P **P** **Killimordaly (IRE)**[29] 1079 6-10-6 **103**.....(tp) JamesBanks[(3)]
(Andy Turnell) *sn pushed along and prom: chsd ldr 3rd to 10th: wknd 13th bhd whn p.u bef 15th* **16/1**
5m 55.3s (-24.50) **Going Correction** -0.70s/f (Firm) **11** Ran SP% **118.2**
Speed ratings (Par 105): **112,109,105,105,101 99,96,, ,**
CSF £28.76 CT £419.06 TOTE £4.90: £2.30, £2.00, £9.70; EX 35.00 Trifecta £965.30.
Owner John P McManus **Bred** Kieran Gleeson **Trained** Cheltenham, Gloucs
FOCUS
A fair handicap chase run at a decent gallop.

1310 UTILITIES CONNECTIONS MANAGEMENT LTD H'CAP HURDLE (11 hdls) 2m 3f 123y
5:05 (5:05) (Class 5) (0-100,100) 4-Y-0+ **£2,599** (£763; £381; £190)

Form RPR
-000 **1** **Ever So Much (IRE)**[28] 1100 6-11-12 **100**.....(p) AndrewTinkler 106
(Ben Haslam) *hld up: hdwy 8th: r.o u.p to ld towards fin* **7/2**[2]
00P- **2** *1½* **Secret Dancer (IRE)**[206] 3919 10-11-7 **95**..... RhysFlint 100
(Alan Jones) *hld up: hdwy 8th: rdn to chse ldr and j.lft 2 out: sn led: hdd towards fin* **9/1**
5-61 **3** *3¼* **Daizy (IRE)**[40] 968 6-10-10 **84**.....(p) WillKennedy 85
(Hilary Parrott) *led to 8th: ev ch 3 out: sn rdn: styd on same pce last* **5/2**[1]
0-P0 **4** *1¼* **Primo Rossi**[71] 692 6-10-0 **74** oh12.....(p) JamesDavies 74
(Tom Gretton) *trckd ldrs: racd keenly: mstke 5th: led 8th: rdn and hdd after 2 out: no ex flat* **40/1**
6504 **5** *8* **Icanmotor**[29] 1084 8-10-0 **74** oh4.....(tp) BrendanPowell 66
(Claire Dyson) *chsd ldrs: rdn after 3 out: wknd bef last* **13/2**
1665 **6** *5* **Bus Named Desire**[37] 1010 7-10-11 **85**.....(tp) TomScudamore 72
(Ian Williams) *prom: rdn after 3 out: sn wknd* **5/1**[3]
P0-P **7** *23* **Royal Supreme (IRE)**[109] 106 5-11-4 **92**..... KielanWoods 56
(Alex Hales) *nt fluent 2nd: w ldr to 8th: sn rdn: wknd 2 out* **11/1**
-164 **8** *19* **Carrigeen Lantana (IRE)**[32] 1066 6-11-3 **91**..... WayneHutchinson 36
(Donald McCain) *hld up in tch: blnd 8th: sn wknd* **7/1**
4m 49.8s (-2.20) **Going Correction** -0.55s/f (Firm) **8** Ran SP% **116.6**
Speed ratings (Par 103): **82,81,80,79,76 74,65,57**
CSF £28.60 CT £71.59 TOTE £3.70: £1.60, £2.90, £1.10; EX 32.70 Trifecta £221.20.
Owner John P McManus **Bred** Mrs Noreen McManus **Trained** Middleham Moor, N Yorks
■ Stewards' Enquiry : Rhys Flint four-day ban; used his whip above the permitted level (4th-8th Sept)
FOCUS
Just a moderate handicap hurdle.
T/Plt: £77.20 to a £1 stake. Pool: £42,842.53 - 404.67 winning tickets T/Qpdt: £9.00 to a £1 stake. Pool: £4,333.83 - 355.31 winning tickets **Colin Roberts**

1311 - 1320a (Foreign Racing) - See Raceform Interactive

1232 NEWTON ABBOT (L-H)
Saturday, August 22

OFFICIAL GOING: Good to soft (good in places; 5.9) changing to good to soft after race 5 (4.15)
Wind: almost nil Weather: sunny periods with showers Rails: Divided bends. Rail movements, altered race distances as follows: Race 1, add 35yds; Race 2, add 26yds; Race 3, add 43yds, Race 4, add 35yds; Race 5, add 58yds; Race 6, add 26yds; Race 7, add 13yds.

1321 TOTEPLACEPOT JUVENILE HURDLE (8 hdls) 2m 167y
1:55 (1:55) (Class 3) 3-Y-O **£6,330** (£1,870; £935; £468)

Form RPR
11 **1** **Doubly Clever (IRE)**[27] 1111 3-11-8 0..... NoelFehily 119+
(Michael Blake) *trckd ldrs: wnt cl 2nd after 3 out: chal between last 2: led last: r.o: rdn out* **9/5**[2]
1 **2** *1¼* **Mountainside**[64] 778 3-11-4 0.....(tp) SamTwiston-Davies 114
(John Ferguson) *disp ld tl 3rd: trckd ldr: led after 3 out: rdn and hung lft whn chal between last 2: hdd last: no ex* **11/8**[1]
11 **3** *22* **Retro Valley (IRE)**[20] 1177 3-11-1 122.....(p) JamieBargary[(7)] 96
(David Dennis) *disp ld tl clr ldr 3rd: rdn and hdd after 3 out: wknd next* **11/4**[3]
3 **4** *28* **La Voix (FR)**[10] 1232 3-9-12 0..... MissBFrost[(7)] 51
(Jimmy Frost) *disp tl 2nd: chsd ldrs: struggling and detached after 4th: t.o bef 2 out* **22/1**
4m 3.0s (-2.70) **Going Correction** 0.0s/f (Good) **4** Ran SP% **108.8**
Speed ratings (Par 104): **106,105,95,81**
CSF £4.82 TOTE £2.40; EX 4.70 Trifecta £4.60.
Owner Francise Tieman **Bred** Gigginstown House Stud **Trained** Trowbridge, Wilts

FOCUS
Divided bends. Rail movement increased races 1 & 4 by 35yds, races 2 & 6 by 26yds, race 3 by 43yds, race 5 by 58yds and race 7 by 13yds. The going was Good to soft, good in places and the jockeys said it was riding much as the official description. A fair juvenile hurdle despite the small field featuring three previous winners and two came clear.

1322 LORD MILDMAY MEMORIAL H'CAP CHASE (LISTED RACE) (16 fncs) 2m 4f 216y
2:30 (2:36) (Class 1) 4-Y-0+
£22,780 (£8,548; £4,280; £2,132; £1,072; £536)

Form RPR
F-01 1 **Standing Ovation (IRE)**[7] 1262 8-10-0 **130** oh3.......(bt) TomScudamore 137
(David Pipe) *j. sltly rt at times: prom: led 9th: rdn whn strly pressed after 3 out: styd on wl fr last: rdn out* **6/1**
-413 2 *1* **Valco De Touzaine (FR)**[35] 1040 6-10-12 **142**..............(t) NickScholfield 148
(Paul Nicholls) *trckd ldrs: chal after 4 out: rdn and ev ch fr after next: styd on but no ex run-in* **10/1**
4121 3 *7* **Gold Futures (IRE)**[22] 1167 6-10-9 **139**.......................... BrianHarding 138
(Nicky Richards) *sweating: mid-div: trckd ldrs 10th: rdn to chse ldng pair after 3 out: styd on but nt pce to chal* **9/2**[2]
0-10 4 *3* **Claret Cloak (IRE)**[84] 556 8-11-12 **156**........................ GavinSheehan 152
(Emma Lavelle) *mid-div: struggling towards rr 12th: styd on fr 3 out: wnt 4th bef last: no further imp on ldrs run-in* **20/1**
43-3 5 *7* **Workbench (FR)**[22] 1170 7-10-0 **130** oh2..................(t) HarrySkelton 119
(Dan Skelton) *hld up: hdwy 11th: rdn after 4 out: grad fdd fr next* **12/1**
141P 6 *7* **Perfect Timing**[35] 1040 7-10-0 **130** oh3.......................(b) BrendanPowell 112
(Neil Mulholland) *trckd ldrs: nt fluent 4 out: sn rdn: wknd after next* **14/1**
55-1 7 *6* **Vesperal Dream (FR)**[76] 657 6-10-0 **133**..................(tp) SeanBowen[(3)] 109
(Paul Nicholls) *mid-div: pushed along after 10th: sme prog after 12th: rdn after 4 out: wknd after next* **4/1**[1]
-045 8 *13* **Midnight Appeal**[22] 1167 10-9-11 **130** oh1..................(tp) KillianMoore[(3)] 93
(Sophie Leech) *mid-div: rdn after 12th: wknd 3 out* **16/1**
14-0 9 *nk* **Raajih**[95] 389 7-10-9 **139**...(bt) DarylJacob 102
(Richard Woollacott) *led tl 9th: rdn after 12th: wknd next* **33/1**
6P-0 10 *11* **Lost Legend (IRE)**[35] 1040 8-10-9 **139**..................(v) RichieMcLernon 91
(Jonjo O'Neill) *towards rr of mid-div: rdn after 10th: sn btn* **8/1**
-111 U **Strongly Suggested**[25] 1135 8-10-3 **133**.......................... WillKennedy
(Jonjo O'Neill) *hld up: uns rdr 5th* **12/1**
-112 U **Dormello Mo (FR)**[34] 1047 5-11-0 **144**..................(t) SamTwiston-Davies
(Paul Nicholls) *hld up: awkward whn unseating rdr 2nd* **11/2**[3]

5m 10.2s (-11.20) **Going Correction** +0.10s/f (Yiel) 12 Ran SP% **123.7**
Speed ratings (Par 111): **113,112,109,108,106 103,101,96,96,91**
CSF £67.52 CT £303.42 TOTE £5.40: £2.20, £3.90, £2.20; EX 81.30 Trifecta £524.50.
Owner The Bravo Partnership **Bred** Patrick McGrath **Trained** Nicholashayne, Devon

FOCUS
Decent prizemoney resulted in a very good handicap chase for the time of year and a good finish.

1323 PLAY THE NEW SCOOP6SOCCER TODAY H'CAP HURDLE (9 hdls) 2m 2f 110y
3:05 (3:05) (Class 5) (0-100,100) 4-Y-0+ £3,898 (£1,144; £572; £286)

Form RPR
31U4 1 *nse* **Cruise In Style (IRE)**[34] 1048 9-11-0 **88**..................(tp) JamesBest 96
(Kevin Bishop) *mid-div: smooth hdwy 3 out: led 2 out: idled bef last and narrowly hdd: kpt on towards fin: jst hld* **6/1**[2]
02B6 2 *14* **Mix N Match**[26] 1120 11-10-0 **74** oh4........................ RichieMcLernon 68
(Laura Young) *hld up: mstke 4th: hdwy 6th: rdn after 3 out: styd on but nt pce to chal* **14/1**
P0-6 3 *2¾* **Watchmetail (IRE)**[55] 859 9-9-7 **74** oh10............ ThomasCheesman[(7)] 65
(John Panvert) *mid-div: rdn to chse ldrs after 3 out: styd on same pce* **14/1**
44-2 4 *nk* **Boher Lad (IRE)**[26] 1120 8-9-7 **74** oh1.................. MrAlexEdwards[(7)] 65
(Alan Phillips) *trckd ldrs: lost pl and rdn 3 out: styd on fr next but n.d* **15/8**[1]
-000 5 *¾* **Tenby Jewel (IRE)**[38] 1010 10-10-7 **86**..................(tp) JakeHodson[(5)] 76
(Mark Gillard) *trckd ldr clr of remainder: rdn after 3 out: sn one pce* **14/1**
-30P 6 *16* **Theionlady (IRE)**[23] 1158 5-10-3 **77**..................(bt[1]) PaddyBrennan 51
(Richard Woollacott) *led: rdn and hdd after 3 out: sn wknd* **8/1**
P0-3 7 *8* **Railway Vic (IRE)**[107] 165 8-10-0 **74** oh1..................... JamesDavies 40
(Jimmy Frost) *chsd ldrs tl rdn appr 6th: wknd 3 out* **12/1**
606 8 *8* **Moreece (IRE)**[23] 1156 6-11-12 **100**.......................... MichaelByrne 58
(Tim Vaughan) *mid-div tl dropped to last pair after 5th: nvr bk on terms* **14/1**
/P0 U **Lets Get Cracking (FR)**[26] 1117 11-9-7 **74** oh9.....(tp) JordanWilliams[(7)]
(Alan Jones) *towards rr: struggling 5th: stl in rr whn mstke and uns rdr 3 out* **9/1**
-P5P D **Seacon Beg (IRE)**[38] 1010 6-11-5 **93**..........................(t) DarylJacob 101
(Richard Woollacott) *trckd ldrs: tk narrow advantage after 3 out: rdn and hdd next: led narrowly last: jst hld on: all out* **7/1**[3]
00P0 P **Merry Mast (USA)**[34] 1044 6-10-11 **85**..........................(p) TomO'Brien
(Paul Henderson) *a towards rr: t.o whn p.u 2 out* **20/1**

4m 35.2s (5.20) **Going Correction** 0.0s/f (Good) 11 Ran SP% **121.8**
Speed ratings (Par 103): **88,83,81,81,81 74,71,68, ,89**
CSF £51.04 CT £586.50 TOTE £9.00: £2.80, £1.10, £3.00; EX 45.90 Trifecta £309.10 Part won..
Owner Steve Atkinson **Bred** Swordlestown Stud **Trained** Spaxton, Somerset

FOCUS
This moderate handicap hurdle resulted in a desperate finish.

1324 PLAY SCOOP6SOCCER IN BETFRED SHOPS NOVICES' H'CAP HURDLE (8 hdls) 2m 167y
3:40 (3:40) (Class 4) (0-110,108) 3-Y-0+ £5,198 (£1,526; £763; £381)

Form RPR
2401 1 **Sleeping City (FR)**[29] 1096 8-11-9 **105**..................(tp) DenisO'Regan 110+
(Victor Dartnall) *trckd ldrs: led 2 out: drifted rt bef last: pushed out: readily* **6/1**
/36- 2 *1½* **Arty Campbell (IRE)**[24] 1842 5-10-13 **98**.................. RobertWilliams[(3)] 101
(Bernard Llewellyn) *hld up: hdwy after 4th: chal after 3 out: rdn to chse wnr bef last: kpt on same pce* **7/2**[1]
/632 3 *2¾* **Shout It Aloud**[26] 1117 6-11-5 **108**..........................(t) AlanJohns[(7)] 108
(Tim Vaughan) *led: rdn and hdd 2 out: styd on same pce* **5/1**[3]
-555 4 *1* **Tricky (IRE)**[47] 932 6-11-5 **108**.......................... CiaranGethings[(7)] 107
(Philip Hobbs) *hld up: hdwy after 3 out: c wd into st: hung lft u.p in cl 4th between last 2: styd on same pce* **14/1**
4340 5 *8* **Prince Of Poets**[7] 1265 4-11-2 **99**..........................(b[1]) TomScudamore 89
(David Pipe) *hld up: nudged along after 5th: hdwy next: sn rdn: nvr threatened* **7/1**
-311 6 *2¾* **Modeligo (IRE)**[27] 1115 6-11-1 **104**..........................(t) MrStanSheppard[(7)] 93
(Matt Sheppard) *trckd ldrs: rdn after 3 out: wknd bef last* **4/1**[2]
00-2 7 *hd* **Darnitnev**[98] 337 5-11-6 **102**.......................... AndrewTinkler 90
(Martin Keighley) *mid-div: rdn after 3 out: nt pce to get involved* **12/1**
U20 8 *1* **Only Gorgeous (IRE)**[20] 1181 6-11-8 **107**.......................... LucyGardner[(3)] 94
(Sue Gardner) *trckd ldrs: rdn after 3 out: wknd next* **16/1**
65 9 *10* **Polo The Mumm (FR)**[26] 1117 5-11-2 **105**.......................... MissHWelch[(7)] 82
(Jimmy Frost) *trckd ldrs: rdn appr 3 out: sn wknd* **20/1**
2-16 10 *27* **Bertie Moon**[20] 1048 5-11-8 **104**.......................... NickScholfield 54
(Polly Gundry) *mid-div tl dropped to last pair after 4th: rdn after 3 out: sn wknd: t.o* **10/1**

4m 3.8s (-1.90) **Going Correction** 0.0s/f (Good)
WFA 4 from 5yo+ 13lb 10 Ran SP% **119.8**
Speed ratings (Par 105): **104,103,102,101,97 96,96,95,91,78**
CSF £28.71 CT £115.67 TOTE £6.30: £2.10, £1.70, £1.90; EX 22.90 Trifecta £185.90.
Owner Edge Of Exmoor **Bred** Mlle Frederique Brion Et Al **Trained** Brayford, Devon

FOCUS
This modest novices' handicap hurdle was run at an ordinary gallop and the time was slower than the opening juvenile hurdle.

1325 TOTESWINGER H'CAP HURDLE (10 hdls) 2m 5f 122y
4:15 (4:15) (Class 2) 4-Y-0+
£22,521 (£6,652; £3,326; £1,663; £831; £417)

Form RPR
30-4 1 **Mister Fizz**[8] 1035 7-10-11 **140**.......................... SeanBowen[(3)] 144
(Miss Imogen Pickard) *trckd ldrs: led appr 2 out: kpt on wl: rdn out* **14/1**
2-12 2 *3¾* **Vivant Poeme (FR)**[35] 1038 6-10-6 **132** ow2..........................(t) NoelFehily 132
(Harry Fry) *kpt off inner: hld up bhd: smooth hdwy fr 7th: trckd ldr 2 out: sn rdn: kpt on but nt pce to chal* **11/2**[2]
-311 3 *nk* **Lamool (GER)**[26] 1116 8-10-8 **134**..........................(t) MichaelByrne 134
(Tim Vaughan) *trckd ldr: led after 3 out: rdn and hdd bef next: kpt on same pce* **9/1**
-412 4 *1¼* **Aviator (GER)**[48] 916 7-10-0 **126** oh1.......................... JackQuinlan 125
(James Eustace) *mid-div: hdwy 7th: rdn to chse ldrs after 3 out: kpt on same pce fr next* **9/1**
-111 5 *¾* **Miss Serious (IRE)**[6] 1270 5-10-2 **128** 5ex.......................... JamesDavies 126
(Jeremy Scott) *cl up: prom 4th: rdn after 3 out: styd on same pce fr next* **6/1**[3]
P5-0 6 *10* **Kie (IRE)**[18] 1039 7-10-0 **126** oh2..........................(tp) TomScudamore 114
(David Pipe) *led: rdn and hdd after 3 out: fdd fr next* **16/1**
-402 7 *2* **Ballyglasheen (IRE)**[26] 1119 5-10-0 **136**..........................(p) LewisGordon[(10)] 122
(Evan Williams) *hld up towards rr: rdn and sme prog after 3 out but nvr threatened to get involved* **8/1**
-531 8 *4* **On The Bridge (IRE)**[25] 1138 10-10-9 **135**..........................(tp) NickScholfield 117
(Jeremy Scott) *hld up bhd: rdn 7th: nvr any imp on ldrs but plugged on past btn horses fr 2 out* **7/1**
-063 9 *nk* **Rum And Butter (IRE)**[34] 1046 7-10-4 **130**..........................(p) WillKennedy 112
(Jonjo O'Neill) *mid-div: hdwy 7th: rdn after 3 out: wknd next* **8/1**
-2F1 10 *2* **Sea Lord (IRE)**[35] 1038 8-11-12 **152**.......................... SamTwiston-Davies 132
(John Ferguson) *mid-div: struggling after 6th: nvr any imp: wknd 2 out* **4/1**[1]
500- P **Thundering Home**[129] 5345 8-10-0 **126** oh3..........................(t) NicodeBoinville
(Richard Mitchell) *hld up: rdn 7th: wknd after 3 out: p.u bef next* **20/1**

5m 14.5s (-5.70) **Going Correction** 0.0s/f (Good) 11 Ran SP% **121.7**
Speed ratings (Par 109): **110,108,108,108,107 104,103,101,101,101**
CSF £93.29 CT £752.07 TOTE £16.60: £4.30, £1.70, £3.00; EX 139.30 Trifecta £844.60 Part won..
Owner Mrs Margaret J Wilson **Bred** Mrs Margaret J Wilson **Trained** Kingsland, Herefordshire

FOCUS
Another good prize produced a decent handicap hurdle good winner for a small yard. With in-form horses close up, the form looks sound.

1326 FOLLOW @ TOTEPOOL ON TWITTER NOVICES' H'CAP CHASE (20 fncs) 3m 1f 170y
4:50 (4:50) (Class 5) (0-100,99) 4-Y-0+ £4,548 (£1,335; £667; £333)

Form RPR
P-04 1 **A Keen Sense (GER)**[10] 1237 6-9-8 **74** oh2 ow1.....(v[1]) JamieBargary[(7)] 82
(David Dennis) *trckd ldrs: led 3 out: rdn clr between last 2: styd on: rdn out* **16/1**
62 2 *1* **Railway Storm (IRE)**[26] 1118 10-11-1 **95**.......................... MissBFrost[(7)] 102
(Jimmy Frost) *trckd ldrs: mstke 10th: rdn after 4 out: disp 3rd 2 out: styd on fr last: wnt 2nd cl home* **9/2**[3]
-121 3 *hd* **Moorlands George**[23] 1155 7-11-12 **99**..........................(t) NicodeBoinville 106
(Jeremy Scott) *mid-div: mstke 13th: hdwy 4 out: rdn to chal after 3 out: looked hld between last 2: styd on fr last* **11/4**[2]
-431 4 *3¼* **Conas Taoi (IRE)**[62] 807 6-11-4 **91**.......................... TomO'Brien 95
(Paul Morgan) *trckd ldrs: nudged along after 13th: rdn after 4 out: styd on same pce fr 2 out* **5/2**[1]
6245 5 *8* **Where'd Ya Hide It (IRE)**[9] 1243 9-10-3 **76**..........................(bt) PaddyBrennan 72
(Paul Henderson) *hld up: rdn and styd on fr 3 out: wnt hld 5th after 2 out: nvr trbld ldrs* **10/1**
52-3 6 *17* **The Cat's Away (IRE)**[104] 223 7-10-0 **73**..........................(b) RichieMcLernon 52
(Richenda Ford) *led: rdn and hdd 3 out: wknd between last 2* **10/1**
0-00 7 *5* **Midnight Whisper**[10] 1236 9-11-3 **90**..........................(tp) DarylJacob 64+
(Richard Woollacott) *mid-div: blnd 6th and dropped in rr: reminders: hdwy after 13th: rdn after 4 out: disputing cl 3rd whn mstke 2 out: sn wknd* **20/1**
P-56 8 *5* **Dawnieriver (IRE)**[91] 443 5-10-8 **81**.......................... TomScudamore 50
(Michael Scudamore) *mid-div: trckd ldrs 12th: rdn after 16th: wknd after 4 out* **12/1**
P-PP 9 *1¾* **Getmeouthedoldrums**[20] 1181 10-11-3 **90**..........................(t) KielanWoods 57
(Mark Wall) *trckd ldr: rdn after 16th: wknd after 4 out* **33/1**
5-53 P **Celtic Fella (IRE)**[72] 698 8-10-0 **73** oh6..........................(vt) TrevorWhelan
(Debra Hamer) *a towards rr: lost tch after 13th: p.u bef 15th* **16/1**
6-60 P **Appropriate (FR)**[25] 1136 5-10-5 **78**.......................... MarkGrant
(Dominic Ffrench Davis) *a in rr: lost tch after 14th: p.u 3 out* **50/1**

6m 48.2s (3.60) **Going Correction** +0.10s/f (Yiel) 11 Ran SP% **120.7**
Speed ratings (Par 103): **98,97,97,96,94 88,87,85,85,**
CSF £89.49 CT £266.80 TOTE £17.90: £4.00, £1.70, £1.40; EX 108.70 Trifecta £487.50.
Owner Superdream Racing LLP **Bred** Stall Tralopp **Trained** Hanley Swan, Worcestershire

FOCUS
After a shower before the previous race the going was changed to Good to soft. A low-grade novices' handicap chase and a surprise result.

1327 LIKE TOTEPOOL ON FACEBOOK H'CAP CHASE (13 fncs) 2m 75y
5:25 (5:25) (Class 3) (0-125,124) 4-Y-£8,229 (£2,431; £1,215; £608; £304)

Form RPR
2321 1 **Easily Pleased (IRE)**[50] [896] 9-11-5 120 JeremiahMcGrath(3) 130
(Martin Hill) *hld up: hdwy 8th: led 4 out: jnd whn lft clr 2 out: rdn out* 7/4[1]
0623 2 2 1/2 **Sublime Talent (IRE)**[10] [1233] 9-10-6 111 (t) MrConorOrr(7) 118
(Evan Williams) *in tch: rdn and hdwy after 4 out: lft 2nd and hmpd 2 out: kpt on but a being hld* 11/1
2251 3 1 3/4 **Marie Des Anges (FR)**[9] [1241] 7-11-1 120 (t) DavidNoonan(7) 124
(Anthony Honeyball) *led: hdd 4 out: sn rdn: styd on same pce fr next: regained 3rd between last 2* 4/1[3]
-51U 4 6 **Hawaii Five Nil (IRE)**[38] [1008] 7-11-5 117 (p) RichieMcLernon 115
(Jonjo O'Neill) *trckd ldrs: rdn after 4 out: stmbld whn lft 3rd 2 out: wknd run-in* 5/2[2]
2360 5 7 **Un Anjou (FR)**[10] [1238] 7-11-11 123 (p) NoelFehily 114
(David Dennis) *in tch: effrt after 4 out: wknd after next* 10/1
4315 F **Furrows**[59] [830] 10-11-5 120 ThomasGarner(3) 125
(Oliver Sherwood) *trckd ldrs: rdn after 3 out: disputing ld whn fell 2 out* 9/1

4m 8.3s (1.80) **Going Correction** +0.10s/f (Yiel)
WFA 4 from 6yo+ 1lb 6 Ran SP% 112.4
Speed ratings (Par 107): **99,97,96,93,90**
CSF £19.05 CT £67.19 TOTE £2.80: £1.90, £4.30; EX 12.90 Trifecta £33.00.
Owner Roger Oliver & Claire Harding **Bred** Mrs Eleanor Hadden **Trained** Littlehempston, Devon

FOCUS
A fair handicap chase that was weakened by the withdrawal of the expected market leaders.
T/Plt: £114.20 to a £1 stake. Pool of £43667.73 - 278.93 winning tickets. T/Qpdt: £15.10 to a £1 stake. Pool of £3893.57 - 189.70 winning tickets. **Tim Mitchell**

[957]PERTH (R-H)
Saturday, August 22

OFFICIAL GOING: Good (good to firm in places; 8.2)
Wind: virtually nil Weather: overcast

1328 KEYLINE NOVICES' HURDLE (STRONGBOW DARK FRUIT SCOTTISH HURDLE SERIES QUAL) (8 hdls) 2m 47y
3:15 (3:18) (Class 4) 4-Y-0+ £3,165 (£935; £467; £234; £117)

Form RPR
1 **Maputo**[569] 5-10-12 0 AidanColeman 115+
(John Ferguson) *racd keenly in midfield: nt fluent 1st: mstke 4th: stdy hdwy after 3 out: led on bit between last 2: rdn out run-in* 11/10[1]
1- 2 2 1/4 **Mr Steadfast (IRE)**[8] [1255] 5-11-5 115 (t) RichardJohnson 119
(Gordon Elliott, Ire) *hld up: hdwy after 3 out to chse ldrs 2 out: sn rdn: wnt 2nd jst after last: kpt on* 5/2[2]
46-3 3 3 **Robin's Command (IRE)**[93] [417] 8-10-9 117 CraigNichol(3) 109
(Rose Dobbin) *trckd ldr: led after 3rd: rdn whn hdd between last 2: one pce run-in* 9/1[3]
4 8 **Lady Clitico (IRE)**[8] [3358] 4-10-1 113 TonyKelly(3) 102
(Rebecca Menzies) *trckd ldrs: rdn to chal 2 out: ev ch whn slithered on landing last: nt rcvr* 10/1
5 5 **Where's Tiger**[21] 4-10-6 0 GrantCockburn(5) 95
(Lucinda Russell) *hld up in midfield: pushed along and wknd after 3 out* 22/1
0 6 1 3/4 **Drop A Gear (IRE)**[51] [881] 5-10-12 0 PeterBuchanan 94
(Lucinda Russell) *midfield: pushed along and wknd after 3 out* 12/1
0-00 7 2 1/4 **Warksburn Boy**[35] [1030] 5-10-5 0 JamieHamilton(7) 92
(Sheena Walton) *trckd ldr: lft in front 2nd: hdd after 3rd: remained cl up tl wknd after 3 out* 66/1
2 8 7 **Chaz Michaels (IRE)**[41] [960] 5-10-9 0 DerekFox(3) 85
(Lucinda Russell) *a towards rr* 14/1
6 R **Housewives Choice**[29] [1094] 4-10-1 0 AdamNicol(3)
(James Bethell) *tk str hold: led: sddle slipped and rn out bef 2nd* 33/1
06-4 U **Mayze Bell**[76] [662] 6-10-5 0 HenryBrooke
(Alistair Whillans) *hld up in rr: j.lft 1st: j. bdly rt and uns rdr 3rd* 66/1

3m 49.4s (229.40)
WFA 4 from 5yo+ 13lb 10 Ran SP% 119.9
CSF £4.03 TOTE £1.90: £1.20, £1.10, £1.90; EX 4.60 Trifecta £18.10.
Owner Bloomfields **Bred** Darley **Trained** Cowlinge, Suffolk

FOCUS
Rail at inner position and distances as advertised. Some starts have been moved at this track following remeasuring, so some races will not have speed figures until there is sufficient data to calculate updated median times.

1329 SPM SCOTLAND NOVICES' H'CAP HURDLE (STRONGBOW DARK FRUIT SCOTTISH HURDLE SERIES QUAL) (12 hdls) 2m 7f 207y
3:50 (3:50) (Class 4) (0-105,104) 4-Y-0+ £3,165 (£935; £467; £234; £117)

Form RPR
2-56 1 **Maraweh (IRE)**[51] [883] 5-10-9 90 (v) DerekFox(3) 99
(Lucinda Russell) *trckd ldrs: briefly lost pl bef 3 out: rdn and hdwy appr 2 out: upsides 2 out: led last: edgd rt: kpt on* 7/1[3]
0023 2 1 3/4 **Johnny Go**[33] [1067] 5-11-0 92 BrianHughes 99
(Lisa Harrison) *trckd ldr: led narrowly appr 2 out: rdn between last 2: hit last and hdd: one pce* 7/1[3]
6-34 3 6 **Rosie Revenue**[13] [1219] 5-11-8 100 (t) RichardJohnson 101
(Gordon Elliott, Ire) *midfield on inner: hdwy to chse ldng pair whn hit 2 out: sn rdn: one pce* 5/2[1]
5265 4 nk **Destiny Awaits (IRE)**[46] [935] 6-10-7 90 CallumBewley(5) 91
(Keith Pollock) *hld up: rdn and sme hdwy bef 2 out: disp 3rd last: one pce* 18/1
-353 5 1 1/2 **Jackofhearts**[51] [883] 7-10-2 80 HenryBrooke 79
(Jean McGregor) *hld up in midfield: rdn bef 2 out: one pce and nvr threatened* 10/1
6P-6 6 1/2 **Triumph Davis (IRE)**[57] [838] 6-11-5 100 (p) CraigNichol(3) 99
(Gordon Elliott, Ire) *midfield: rdn bef 2 out: no imp* 11/2[2]
2140 7 4 **Solway Prince**[7] [1264] 6-11-7 104 StephenMulqueen(5) 99
(Lisa Harrison) *midfield on outside: rdn bef 2 out: wknd last* 11/2[2]
-013 8 2 3/4 **Roll Of Thunder**[51] [882] 6-10-7 90 MissCWalton(5) 82
(James Walton) *hld up in rr: rdn after 3 out: nvr threatened* 16/1
U116 9 dist **Cool Star (IRE)**[35] [1032] 9-11-1 96 (t) JonathanEngland(3) 43
(Maurice Barnes) *led: nt fluent 3 out: hdd appr 2 out: wknd and eased* 14/1
PP66 10 21 **Allycat**[35] [1030] 5-10-9 92 (v[1]) DiarmuidO'Regan(5) 18
(Chris Grant) *in tch: trckd ldr after 7th: rdn after 3 out: already wkng whn hit 2 out: eased* 20/1

5m 53.4s (-11.60) **Going Correction** -0.725s/f (Firm) 10 Ran SP% 116.0
Speed ratings (Par 105): **90,89,87,87,86 86,85,84,69,62**
CSF £55.18 CT £156.71 TOTE £14.90: £3.10, £1.60, £1.60; EX 66.10 Trifecta £333.90.
Owner Tay Valley Chasers Racing Club **Bred** Shadwell Estate Company Limited **Trained** Arlary, Perth & Kinross

FOCUS
This was run at a dawdle until halfway down the back; the field were still bunched heading for the straight before two of the handily-ridden horses drew clear.

1330 VISIT MYTOTEPOOL.COM NOVICES' H'CAP CHASE (15 fncs) 2m 4f 20y
4:25 (4:26) (Class 4) (0-115,115) 4-Y-0 £6,330 (£1,870; £935; £468; £234)

Form RPR
1-20 1 **Xaarcet (IRE)**[20] [1184] 8-11-9 112 (tp) RichardJohnson 121
(Gordon Elliott, Ire) *mde all: rdn after 2 out: kpt on* 11/4[1]
5-5F 2 2 1/4 **Cayman Islands**[38] [1008] 7-11-12 115 AidanColeman 121
(John Ferguson) *prom: rdn bef 2 out: kpt on but a hld by wnr* 8/1
F-40 3 1 1/2 **Tour D'Argent (FR)**[22] [1169] 8-11-6 109 WayneHutchinson 113
(Donald McCain) *racd keenly: hld up: sme hdwy bef 4 out: rdn after 3 out: kpt on run-in: wnt 3rd towards fin* 14/1
1213 4 hd **Solway Legend**[41] [959] 8-9-10 90 DiarmuidO'Regan(5) 94
(Lisa Harrison) *chsd ldng pair: rdn 3 out: sn one pce: lost 3rd towards fin* 4/1[2]
-152 5 20 **Honourable Gent**[51] [884] 7-11-4 110 CraigNichol(3) 94
(Rose Dobbin) *hld up in rr: hdwy bef 4 out: mstke 3 out: sn rdn: hit 2 out: wknd* 4/1[2]
00/ 6 9 **Kilmainham (IRE)**[46] [944] 7-10-9 98 HenryBrooke 73
(Martin Todhunter) *midfield: rdn after 4 out: sn wknd* 14/1
5-64 7 hd **Drumhart (IRE)**[25] [1141] 6-11-7 110 BrianHughes 85
(C A McBratney, Ire) *midfield: mstke 1st: stl to be asked for effrt whn blnd 3 out: sn wknd* 14/1
2342 8 3 1/2 **Mister D (IRE)**[35] [1032] 9-10-1 95 JonathonBewley(5) 66
(George Bewley) *hld up: rdn bef 4 out: sn struggling* 13/2[3]
/5-0 9 9 **Agricultural**[52] [872] 9-10-2 94 AdamNicol(3) 56
(Lucy Normile) *in tch: pushed along and lost pl after 5 out: wknd after 3 out* 25/1
24-6 P **Karingo**[51] [886] 8-9-12 92 GrantCockburn(5)
(Lucy Normile) *nt fluent: hld up: lost tch after 8th: p.u bef 10th* 25/1

4m 52.1s (-12.90) **Going Correction** -0.725s/f (Firm) 10 Ran SP% 118.8
Speed ratings (Par 105): **96,95,94,94,86 82,82,81,77,**
CSF £26.04 CT £260.80 TOTE £4.30: £1.70, £1.50, £5.10; EX 21.80 Trifecta £247.00.
Owner Brendan Scully **Bred** Denis McDonnell **Trained** Longwood, Co Meath

FOCUS
A strong front-running performance from the winner. The running order barely changed throughout the race.

1331 CPS GLOBAL RACING H'CAP HURDLE (10 hdls) 2m 4f 35y
5:00 (5:01) (Class 3) (0-125,119) 4-Y-0+ £4,548 (£1,335; £667; £333)

Form RPR
2340 1 **Los Nadis (GER)**[20] [1181] 11-10-8 101 (v) HenryBrooke 106
(Jim Goldie) *mde all: clr 4th tl 6th: rdn after 3 out: jnd between last 2: kpt on wl run-in* 7/2[3]
5112 2 6 **Politeness (FR)**[35] [1034] 6-11-7 117 CraigNichol(3) 116
(Rose Dobbin) *hld up: hdwy bef 3 out: hit 3 out but sn trckd ldr gng wl: rdn to go upsides between last 2: wknd run-in* 15/8[1]
P25- 3 17 **Kumbeshwar**[169] [4600] 8-11-0 117 (p) RossChapman(10) 99
(Lucinda Russell) *hld up in tch: chsd ldr after 4th: rdn after 3 out: sn wknd* 9/1
-26F 4 2 **Apachee Prince (IRE)**[35] [1038] 6-11-12 119 (t) BrianHughes 99
(Alistair Whillans) *chsd ldr: rdn after 3 out: wknd between last 2* 5/2[2]
24-0 P **Ryton Runner (IRE)**[101] [291] 7-10-5 101 (tp) DerekFox(3)
(Lucinda Russell) *chsd ldr: lost pl after 4th: bhd after 6th: p.u bef 3 out* 7/1

4m 45.6s (-16.40) **Going Correction** -0.725s/f (Firm)
WFA 4 from 6yo+ 14lb 5 Ran SP% 108.1
Speed ratings (Par 107): **103,100,93,93,**
CSF £10.33 TOTE £4.50: £2.10, £1.20; EX 7.60 Trifecta £40.90.
Owner Ian G M Dalgleish **Bred** Stiftung Gestut Fahrhof **Trained** Uplawmoor, E Renfrews

FOCUS
A game front-running performance from a Perth standing dish.

1332 TOTEPOOL RACING'S BIGGEST SUPPORTER H'CAP CHASE (18 fncs) 2m 7f 180y
5:35 (5:35) (Class 4) (0-120,120) 4-Y-0+ £9,747 (£2,862; £1,431; £715)

Form RPR
P3/P 1 **Balding Banker (IRE)**[27] [1114] 9-11-2 113 TonyKelly(3) 123
(Rebecca Menzies) *led: hdd 12th: remained cl up: rdn bef 3 out: sn dropped to 3rd: rallied between last 2: led again run-in: styd on* 16/1
5011 2 1 1/4 **Count Salazar (IRE)**[7] [1264] 10-11-4 115 (p) JamesBanks(3) 124
(Andy Turnell) *trckd ldr: led 12th: 4 l up and seemingly stl gng wl 2 out: reduced advantage last: sn drvn: hdd run-in: one pce* 3/1[1]
2062 3 3 **Solway Bay**[6] [1272] 13-9-7 94 oh4 (t) MissRMcDonald(7) 100
(Lisa Harrison) *midfield: rdn after 4 out: wnt 3rd last: edgd lft: kpt on* 9/1
0-00 4 1 1/2 **Presented (IRE)**[41] [958] 8-10-12 111 CallumBewley(5) 116
(Lisa Harrison) *midfield: rdn after 4 out: styd on fr between last 2: wnt 4th post* 28/1
-253 5 hd **Gleann Na Ndochais (IRE)**[41] [961] 9-11-6 117 CraigNichol(3) 121
(Alistair Whillans) *midfield: pushed along and hdwy to go 3rd 4 out: rdn to chse ldr 3 out: wknd and lost 3 pls fr appr last* 5/1[3]
-013 6 23 **Romany Ryme**[18] [1199] 9-11-3 111 RichardJohnson 92
(Gordon Elliott, Ire) *hld up: rdn after 4 out: sn struggling: hit last* 4/1[2]
-154 7 64 **Kai Broon (IRE)**[51] [885] 8-11-2 110 (p) PeterBuchanan 27
(Lucinda Russell) *midfield: hit 10th: rdn 4 out: mstke 3 out: sn wknd: eased* 16/1
4-44 P **Bertie Milan (IRE)**[52] [867] 10-10-2 96 (v) LucyAlexander
(N W Alexander) *hld up: nvr gng w much fluency: bhd fr 11th: p.u bef 13th* 14/1
32F5 U **Owen Glendower (IRE)**[6] [1268] 10-11-12 120 (tp) PaulMoloney
(Sophie Leech) *hld up in rr: blnd and uns rdr 5th* 9/1

The Form Book Jumps 2015-16, Raceform Ltd, Newbury, RG14 5SJ

P-P1 P **Dystonia's Revenge (IRE)**[35] 1032 10-10-12 113...... JamieHamilton(7)
(Sheena Walton) *trckd ldr: lost pl after 5 out: sn wknd: p.u bef 2 out* 8/1
5m 50.0s (-14.00) **Going Correction** -0.725s/f (Firm) 10 Ran SP% 114.7
Speed ratings (Par 105): **94,93,92,92,92 84,63, , ,**
CSF £65.02 CT £470.54 TOTE £16.70: £4.00, £1.70, £2.50; EX 64.40 Trifecta £766.10.
Owner Club Racing Banker Partnership **Bred** Peter And Ann Downes **Trained** Stearsby, N Yorks

FOCUS
This was run at a good pace with fortunes changing up the straight as the favourite, who had gone four lengths clear two out, ran out of steam and was headed.

1333 CRABBIE'S ALCOHOLIC GINGER BEER STV APPEAL SUMMER HURDLE (H'CAP) (FOR THE GOVERNORS CUP) (8 hdls) 2m 47y
6:05 (6:05) (Class 2) 3-Y-0+
£12,512 (£3,696; £1,848; £924; £462; £232)

Form RPR
6-00 1 **Court Minstrel (IRE)**[35] 1039 8-11-4 145................ PaulMoloney 148
(Evan Williams) *hld up in tch: hdwy bef 2 out: rdn to chse ldng pair between last 2: l down in 3rd last: kpt on: led post* 6/1
U-10 2 *nse* **Commissioned (IRE)**[35] 1039 5-11-5 151..............(p) MikeyEnnis(5) 154
(John Ferguson) *trckd ldng pair: led bef 2 out: sn rdn: strly pressed between last 2: kpt on: hdd post* 9/4[2]
1-11 3 *hd* **Ittirad (USA)**[26] 1119 7-11-4 145..................(p) AidanColeman 148
(John Ferguson) *trckd ldng pair: rdn to chal strly between last 2: kpt on* 15/8[1]
30-0 4 *6* **King Of The Picts (IRE)**[23] 96 6-10-7 139.............. JackSherwood(5) 136
(John Patrick Shanahan, Ire) *midfield: rdn bef 2 out: one pce* 4/1[3]
P6-0 5 *16* **Trucking Along (IRE)**[55] 850 9-10-4 131 oh6............ PeterBuchanan 112
(S R B Crawford, Ire) *hld up in rr: pushed along after 3 out: nvr threatened* 25/1
00-0 6 *2 3/4* **Lucky Bridle (IRE)**[55] 850 6-10-5 132.................. BrianHughes 110
(Chris Grant) *led: hdd bef 2 out: sn wknd* 20/1
610- 7 *1/2* **Calton Entry (IRE)**[34] 1062 6-10-4 131 oh21............ HenryBrooke 109
(Linda Perratt) *hld up in tch: rdn bef 2 out: wknd after 2 out* 50/1
11/P 8 *17* **Franciscan**[99] 317 7-10-8 135.......................(b) WayneHutchinson 96
(Donald McCain) *prom: rdn 3 out: wknd and eased* 14/1
3m 40.2s (220.20) 8 Ran SP% 117.1
CSF £20.62 CT £35.32 TOTE £8.20: £2.20, £1.20, £1.10; EX 23.70 Trifecta £57.10.
Owner Mrs Janet Davies **Bred** William Flood **Trained** Llancarfan, Vale Of Glamorgan

FOCUS
Plenty of pace on but despite the decent prize money few came into this in any form. Nevertheless, it produced a stirring blanket finish befitting the prize.

1334 BOOK YOUR CHRISTMAS PARTY AT PERTH RACECOURSE MARES' STANDARD OPEN NATIONAL HUNT FLAT RACE 2m 47y
6:35 (6:36) (Class 6) 4-6-Y-0 £1,899 (£561; £280; £140; £70)

Form RPR
5-32 1 **Carinena (IRE)**[41] 963 6-10-9 0...................... CraigNichol(3) 98
(Nicky Richards) *mde all: rdn over 2f out: pressed over 1f out: hld on wl* 15/8[1]
2 *1/2* **Tara Time** 4-10-8 0...................... AdamNicol(3) 97
(Philip Kirby) *trckd ldr: rdn to chal over 1f out: kpt on but a jst hld* 3/1[2]
46- 3 *7* **Blayney Queen (IRE)**[361] 1345 6-10-12 0.................. PeterBuchanan 91
(S R B Crawford, Ire) *hld up: rdn over 3f out: styd on fnl 2f: wnt 3rd ins fnl f* 11/1
5- 4 *3* **Cosmic Tigress**[224] 3625 4-10-11 0...................... BrianHughes 87
(John Quinn) *midfield: hdwy into 3rd over 3f out: rdn over 2f out: wknd ins fnl f* 6/1[3]
5 *15* **Lucy Mc (IRE)**[26] 1125 4-10-11 0...................... RichardJohnson 72
(Gordon Elliott, Ire) *racd keenly: hld up in midfield: rdn 3f out: nvr threatened* 7/1
6 *5* **Solway Berry** 4-10-6 0...................... StephenMulqueen(5) 67
(Lisa Harrison) *hld up: rdn 4f out: nvr threatened* 25/1
7 *1 1/4* **Worcester Pearmain** 5-10-12 0...................... AidanColeman 66
(Rose Dobbin) *hld up in midfield: dropped to rr over 6f out: no threat after* 20/1
8 *14* **Skiddaw Poppy** 4-10-1 0...................... ThomasDowson(10) 51
(Maurice Barnes) *in tch: rdn over 3f out: sn wknd* 50/1
9 *58* **Overbury Queen** 5-10-12 0...................... PaulMoloney
(Alan Swinbank) *midfield: dropped to rr qckly on home bnd over 3f out: eased and t.o* 6/1[3]
3m 44.9s (224.90)
WFA 4 from 5yo+ 1lb 9 Ran SP% 119.8
CSF £7.69 TOTE £2.90: £1.30, £1.60, £2.20; EX 9.50 Trifecta £91.50.
Owner Mrs C A Torkington **Bred** Cecil And Martin McCracken **Trained** Greystoke, Cumbria

FOCUS
This looked an ordinary mares' bumper.
T/Plt: £11.60 to £1 stake. Pool of £42681.91 - 2666.72 winning tickets. T/Qpdt: £8.10 to a £1 stake. Pool of £2219.63 - 202.20 winning tickets. **Andrew Sheret**

1335 - 1342a (Foreign Racing) - See Raceform Interactive

1287 WORCESTER (L-H)
Sunday, August 23

OFFICIAL GOING: Good to soft changing to soft after race 2 (2.30)
Wind: Light against Weather: Raining

1343 BET TOTEPLACEPOT NOVICES' CHASE (12 fncs) 2m 110y
2:00 (2:01) (Class 4) 4-Y-0+ £3,898 (£1,144; £572; £286)

Form RPR
3340 1 **Purple 'n Gold (IRE)**[24] 1039 6-11-4 0................(p) TomScudamore 132
(David Pipe) *a.p: chsd ldr 4 out: rdn to ld fnl 100yds: r.o* 5/1[3]
0-01 2 *1 1/4* **Broughton (GER)**[24] 1157 5-11-10 0................(bt) AidanColeman 137
(John Ferguson) *chsd ldr: mstke 4th: led wl bef 4 out: rdn appr 2 out: hdd fnl 100yds: styd on same pce* 10/11[1]
123 3 *47* **Hawdyerwheesht**[24] 1156 7-11-4 0....................(tp) NoelFehily 98
(David Dennis) *got loose on the way to post: chsd ldrs: mstke 2nd: hit 4th: blnd 7th: rdn and wkng whn lft 3rd 4 out: bhd whn j.lft next* 8/1
0600 4 *65* **Bobonyx**[10] 1244 5-11-4 0............................(v) DaveCrosse 30
(Dai Williams) *hld up: bhd fr 5th: j.rt 7th and last* 100/1
1123 U **Owen Na View (IRE)**[7] 1268 7-11-9 135.................. JamesO'Neill(7)
(Fergal O'Brien) *led: hdd wl bef 4 out: disputing cl 2nd but rdn whn uns rdr 4 out* 11/4[2]
4m 3.8s (-1.20) **Going Correction** +0.20s/f (Yiel) 5 Ran SP% 107.8
Speed ratings (Par 105): **110,109,87,56,**
CSF £10.18 TOTE £5.40: £1.90, £1.20; EX 10.70 Trifecta £37.90.
Owner Mrs Lynne Webb **Bred** Stonethorn Stud Farms Ltd **Trained** Nicholashayne, Devon

FOCUS
All starts have been moved at this track following remeasuring, so there will be no speed figures here until there is sufficient data to calculate updated median times. This wasn't a bad novice chase for the time of year. It was run in driving rain at an average gallop and only two mattered from the penultimate fence.

1344 BET TOTEEXACTA H'CAP CHASE (12 fncs) 2m 110y
2:30 (2:31) (Class 2) (0-150,144) 4-Y-0+
£12,512 (£3,696; £1,848; £924; £462; £232)

Form RPR
P1-0 1 **Fairyinthewind (IRE)**[26] 1135 6-10-1 119..................(t) BrendanPowell 125
(Brendan Powell) *prom: mstke and lost pl 3rd: reminder after next: hdwy and hmpd 4 out: chsd ldr next: rdn to ld after 2 out: styd on wl* 25/1
3322 2 *4* **Miss Tenacious**[42] 974 8-9-13 124...................... HarryCobden(7) 126
(Ron Hodges) *hld up: hdwy appr 4 out: chsd wnr last: sn rdn: styd on same pce* 7/1
6420 3 *1 1/2* **My Brother Sylvest**[7] 1268 9-10-12 137..................(bt) MichaelHeard(7) 138
(David Pipe) *led: j.rt: nt fluent 6th: rdn and hdd after 2 out: styd on same pce flat* 13/2
2/1- 4 *3 1/4* **Nearest The Pin (IRE)**[15] 1214 10-11-8 140..............(p) RichardJohnson 138
(John Joseph Hanlon, Ire) *hld up: hdwy 8th: hmpd 3 out: styd on same pce appr last* 5/1[3]
112F 5 *12* **Ulis De Vassy (FR)**[7] 1268 7-10-11 129.................. HarrySkelton 119
(Dan Skelton) *chsd ldr to 4th: wnt 2nd again 5th tl rdn appr 4 out: wknd appr 2 out* 9/4[1]
0165 6 *22* **Another Flutter (IRE)**[26] 1135 11-10-12 137..........(tp) MrStanSheppard(7) 104
(Matt Sheppard) *hld up: pushed along after 7th: rdn and wknd bef 4 out* 16/1
/111 P **Walden Prince (IRE)**[30] 1099 8-10-2 120..................(tp) TomScudamore
(David Bridgwater) *prom: chsd ldr 4th to next: wnt 2nd again whn blnd 4 out: p.u bef next* 11/4[2]
4m 4.0s (-1.00) **Going Correction** +0.20s/f (Yiel) 7 Ran SP% 109.7
Speed ratings (Par 109): **110,108,107,105,100 89,**
CSF £164.96 CT £1196.56 TOTE £14.10: £5.50, £3.80; EX 143.40 Trifecta £389.30.
Owner R Delnevo **Bred** J Cullinan **Trained** Upper Lambourn, Berks

FOCUS
A modest handicap, run at a decent gallop and it's straightforward to assess through the runner-up.

1345 BET TOTEQUADPOT INTERMEDIATE OPEN NATIONAL HUNT FLAT RACE 2m
3:00 (3:00) (Class 6) 4-6-Y-0 £1,624 (£477; £238; £119)

Form RPR
52 1 **Tour De Ville (IRE)**[35] 1050 5-11-0 0....................(t) BrianHughes 101
(Seamus Durack) *hld up: plld hrd: hdwy 6f out: led over 2f out: hung rt over 1f out: rdn out* 11/4[2]
44 2 *3 1/4* **Junior Package**[27] 1122 4-10-13 0....................(t) TomScudamore 97
(David Pipe) *hld up: hdwy over 4f out: rdn and ev ch over 2f out: styd on same pce ins fnl f* 6/1[3]
3-3 3 *7* **Wilde Oak (IRE)**[27] 1122 5-11-0 0........................(t) NoelFehily 91
(Anthony Honeyball) *hld up: plld hrd: hdwy 6f out: rdn: hung lft and ev ch over 2f out: wknd over 1f out* 10/11[1]
6 4 *3 3/4* **Black Kettle (IRE)**[27] 1122 5-11-0 0...................... KielanWoods 87
(Ronald Thompson) *led and sn clr: c bk to the field 10f out: rdn: hdd and hung rt over 2f out: wknd over 1f out* 33/1
5 *18* **Thate Hiana Juelli** 4-10-13 0...................... TomCannon 68
(William Knight) *chsd clr ldr: tk clsr order 10f out: rdn and hung rt over 3f out: wknd over 2f out* 8/1
0/ 6 *60* **Lily Marie**[718] 1499 6-9-11 0...................... CharlieHammond(10)
(Mike Hammond) *chsd ldrs tl rdn over 6f out: hmpd and wknd sn after* 66/1
3m 44.8s (-0.20) **Going Correction** -0.025s/f (Good)
WFA 4 from 5yo+ 1lb 6 Ran SP% 108.9
Speed ratings: **99,97,93,92,83 53**
CSF £17.86 TOTE £3.70: £1.50, £1.70; EX 20.70 Trifecta £39.30.
Owner Hey Ho Let's Go **Bred** Mrs Meliosa Walshe **Trained** Upper Lambourn, Berkshire

FOCUS
A moderate bumper.

1346 TOTEPOOL RACING'S BIGGEST SUPPORTER (S) HURDLE (8 hdls) 2m
3:30 (3:30) (Class 5) 4-7-Y-0 £2,599 (£763; £381; £190)

Form RPR
3606 1 **Marju's Quest (IRE)**[21] 1180 5-10-12 125...................... NoelFehily 120+
(David Dennis) *mde all: hung rt almost thrght: j.rt fnl 3 flights: shkn up flat: r.o wl* 6/4[2]
P-20 2 *9* **Clock On Tom**[8] 1261 5-10-12 109...................... WillKennedy 112
(Denis Quinn) *a.p: chsd wnr appr 3 out: mstke last: rdn and no ex flat* 10/1[3]
P655 3 *19* **Goldie Horn**[35] 1056 7-10-5 96.................(t) SamTwiston-Davies 88
(Nigel Twiston-Davies) *chsd wnr tl rdn after 5th: wknd bef next* 10/1[3]
144 4 *6* **Monte Wildhorn (IRE)**[42] 971 7-10-12 115.............(tp) TomScudamore 90
(David Bridgwater) *chsd ldrs: pushed along 4th: wnt 2nd after next tl rdn appr 3 out: sn wknd* 11/8[1]
14 5 *hd* **Black Iceman**[19] 1081 7-10-12 108...................... JackQuinlan 92
(Lydia Pearce) *hld up: hdwy 3 out: wknd next: blnd last* 10/1[3]
3m 47.6s (-3.00) **Going Correction** -0.025s/f (Good) 5 Ran SP% 109.4
Speed ratings: **106,101,92,89,88**
CSF £14.35 TOTE £2.50: £1.20, £3.30; EX 18.00 Trifecta £83.50.
Owner Favourites Racing (Syndication) Ltd 1 **Bred** Derrinstown Stud Ltd **Trained** Hanley Swan, Worcestershire

FOCUS
A typically weak seller.

1347 PLAY SCOOP6SOCCER AT BETFRED.COM H'CAP HURDLE (8 hdls) 2m
4:00 (4:00) (Class 3) (0-130,125) 3-Y-0+ £5,523 (£1,621; £810; £405)

Form RPR
3/ 1 **Baby Jake (IRE)**[27] 1124 6-10-11 110...................... RichardJohnson 118
(John Joseph Hanlon, Ire) *hld up: plld hrd: nt fluent 4th: hdwy to go 2nd 5th: led sn after: drvn out* 7/4[1]
414/ 2 *1 1/2* **Nesterenko (GER)**[473] 5172 6-11-12 125...................... NicodeBoinville 131
(Nicky Henderson) *plld hrd: trckd ldr 2nd to 5th: chsd wnr appr 3 out: styd on u.p* 3/1[2]
-645 3 *11* **Perspicace**[10] 1239 4-11-5 119......................(b1) TomScudamore 114
(David Pipe) *hld up: hdwy appr 3 out: nt fluent next: wknd last* 9/2

0200 **4** *6* **Battlecat**[42] 973 8-10-6 **110**............ ConorRing(5) 100
(Evan Williams) *led: hdd after 5th: rdn and wknd appr 2 out* **7/2**[3]
316- **5** *11* **Della Sun (FR)**[317] 1836 9-10-11 **117**............ JoshWall(7) 97
(Arthur Whitehead) *chsd ldrs: rdn after 5th: wknd bef next* **10/1**
3m 47.1s (-3.50) **Going Correction** -0.025s/f (Good)
WFA 3 from 4yo 19lb 4 from 6yo+ 13lb 5 Ran SP% **110.9**
Speed ratings (Par 107): **107,106,100,97,92**
CSF £7.58 TOTE £2.80: £1.30, £1.90; EX 7.40 Trifecta £11.40.
Owner Mrs Nanette Wheatley **Bred** Mrs N Wheatley **Trained** Bagenalstown, Co Carlow

FOCUS
An ordinary handicap where two came clear late in the day.

1348 WIN A FOOTBALL FORTUNE WITH SCOOP6SOCCER MARES' H'CAP HURDLE (10 hdls) 2m 4f
4:30 (4:30) (Class 4) (0-120,119) 4-Y-O+ **£3,249** (£954; £477; £238)

Form RPR
2U-5 **1** **Taradrewe**[28] 1113 8-11-6 **113**............(t) AidanColeman 123
(Anthony Honeyball) *chsd clr ldr: tk clsr order 5th: led appr 2 out: rdn out* **5/2**[1]
662 **2** *3 ¾* **Wintour Leap**[31] 1081 4-10-9 **104**............ TomO'Brien 108
(Robert Stephens) *hld up: hdwy 3 out: rdn appr last: styd on to go 2nd towards fin* **9/2**[3]
4324 **3** *½* **Still Believing (IRE)**[42] 967 7-11-6 **113**............ AdamWedge 118
(Evan Williams) *hld up: mstke 3rd: hdwy 6th: rdn to chse wnr last: styd on same pce flat: lost 2nd towards fin* **4/1**[2]
-642 **4** *14* **Java Rose**[23] 1170 6-11-8 **115**............(tp) RichardJohnson 113
(Charlie Longsdon) *led and sn clr: pushed along and c bk to the field 5th: rdn and hdd appr 2 out: wknd last* **5/2**[1]
-040 **F** **Western Diva (IRE)**[23] 1170 6-11-5 **112**............ TomScudamore 117
(David Pipe) *hld up: hdwy 3 out: disputing 2 l 3rd whn fell 2 out* **6/1**
4m 52.9s (-0.60) **Going Correction** -0.025s/f (Good)
WFA 4 from 5yo+ 14lb 5 Ran SP% **109.6**
Speed ratings (Par 105): **100,98,98,92,**
CSF £13.41 TOTE £3.30: £1.70, £1.90; EX 13.00 Trifecta £43.20.
Owner Frosties Friends II **Bred** T C Frost **Trained** Mosterton, Dorset

FOCUS
A run-of-the-mill mares' handicap.

1349 MYTOTEPOOL.COM CONDITIONAL JOCKEYS' MAIDEN HURDLE (12 hdls) 2m 7f
5:00 (5:00) (Class 5) 4-Y-O+ **£2,599** (£763; £381; £190)

Form RPR
12 **1** **Mont Choisy (FR)**[35] 1044 5-10-13 0............ RyanHatch(3) 120+
(Nigel Twiston-Davies) *chsd ldr to 5th: remained handy: j.lft 3 out: mstke next: rdn to ld appr last: styd on u.p* **13/8**[1]
3 **2** *2 ½* **Epic Warrior (IRE)**[73] 700 6-10-13 0............ KieronEdgar(3) 116
(David Pipe) *a.p: rdn appr 2 out: styd on* **14/1**
44-3 **3** *5* **Sky Watch (IRE)**[26] 1136 8-11-2 111............(t) SeanBowen 111
(Brian Barr) *led tl after 6th: chsd ldr tl after 9th: sn rdn: outpcd bef next: rallied appr last: styd on same pce flat* **4/1**[3]
/U0- **4** *1 ¾* **Johnny Og**[134] 6-11-2 110............ DanielHiskett 109
(Martin Keighley) *prom: chsd ldr 5th: led after next: rdn and hdd appr last: wknd flat* **9/1**
34P- **P** **Neville**[154] 4946 7-10-10 120............ CiaranGethings(6)
(Philip Hobbs) *hld up: rdn after 8th: sn wknd: bhd whn p.u bef 3 out* **9/4**[2]
P **The Mustang** 8-10-13 0............ LizzieKelly(3)
(Nick Williams) *sn pushed along in rr: rdn and wknd after 6th: bhd whn p.u bef 8th* **20/1**
5m 44.1s (5.50) **Going Correction** -0.025s/f (Good) 6 Ran SP% **110.3**
Speed ratings (Par 103): **89,88,86,85,**
CSF £21.70 TOTE £2.90: £1.60, £4.00; EX 17.20 Trifecta £38.70.
Owner Mrs N Unsworth **Bred** Scea Ecurie Domaine De Baune **Trained** Naunton, Gloucs

FOCUS
A modest staying maiden.
T/Plt: £311.60 to a £1 stake. Pool: £68,966 - 161.55 winning units. T/Qpdt: £24.40 to a £1 stake. Pool: £5575.30 - 168.93 winning units. **Colin Roberts**

1239 FONTWELL (L-H)
Tuesday, August 25

OFFICIAL GOING: Soft
Wind: strong half behind Weather: overcast with sunny periods Rails: Fences Inner. Hurdles Middle Inner. Rail movement adding; Top bend 27yds. Bottom bend 42yds.

1350 INTERNATIONAL PAYMENT-FIRST PAST THE POST H'CAP HURDLE (11 hdls) 2m 5f 139y
4:50 (4:50) (Class 4) (0-120,115) 4-Y-O+ **£3,249** (£954; £477; £238)

Form RPR
-052 **1** **Church Field (IRE)**[23] 1181 7-11-9 **112**............(p) RichieMcLernon 115
(Jonjo O'Neill) *disp ld: rdn into clr ld bef 2 out: narrowly hdd bef last: rallied gamely to ld fnl 50yds: drvn out* **4/1**[2]
-F31 **2** *½* **Titch Strider (IRE)**[83] 597 10-10-6 **102**............ ThomasCheesman(7) 104
(John Panvert) *hld up in tch: hdwy after 3 out: rdn to take narrow advantage between last 2: kpt on but no ex whn hdd fnl 50yds* **15/2**
/-3 **3** *4 ½* **Benefits Well (IRE)**[32] 1100 8-11-7 **110**............ NoelFehily 108
(Warren Greatrex) *trckd ldrs: rdn appr 2 out: styd on same pce* **15/8**[1]
P-33 **4** *4 ½* **Hi Note**[12] 1242 7-11-7 **110**............ MarcGoldstein 104
(Sheena West) *trckd ldrs: rdn to chse ldng pair appr 2 out tl bef last: no ex run-in* **8/1**
-F55 **5** *2 ½* **Princeton Royale (IRE)**[37] 1054 6-11-0 **103**............ TrevorWhelan 95
(Neil King) *hld up in tch: hit 9th: rdn after 3 out: wkng whn mstke last* **13/2**
-635 **6** *13* **Passato (GER)**[56] 863 11-11-5 **108**............(t) RichardJohnson 88
(Jo Davis) *disp ld tl rdn bef 2 out: wknd between last 2* **22/1**
F-43 **7** *½* **Halling's Wish**[13] 598 5-11-12 **115**............(t) TomCannon 95
(Gary Moore) *hld up last but in tch: pushed along after 8th: rdn appr 2 out: nvr threatened: wknd last* **5/1**[3]
5m 49.2s (6.70) **Going Correction** +0.15s/f (Yiel) 7 Ran SP% **112.0**
Speed ratings (Par 105): **93,92,91,89,88 83,83**
CSF £31.29 CT £71.89 TOTE £4.40: £2.30, £3.00; EX 25.50 Trifecta £103.40.
Owner John P McManus **Bred** Mrs Eleanor Hadden **Trained** Cheltenham, Gloucs

FOCUS
Fences sited on Inner, Hurdles middle. Top bend movement added 27yds and bottom bend 42yds. Significant rainfall saw a change to soft ground, a far cry from that at declaration time, and there were non-runners aplenty. The opening handicap hurdle was run at a steady pace and all seven runners held a chance as the field turned for home, the winner confirming the promise of his previous start at Market Rasen. The winner is getting back to his 2013 level and the third has been rated close to his latest.

1351 INVEST WITH CONFIDENCE AT SELFTRADE.CO.UK BEGINNERS' CHASE (16 fncs) 2m 5f 31y
5:20 (5:20) (Class 4) 4-Y-O+ **£3,768** (£1,106; £553; £276)

Form RPR
6-32 **1** **Rothman (FR)**[41] 1006 5-11-7 123............(t) SamTwiston-Davies 127+
(Paul Nicholls) *trckd ldr: led 10th: qcknd pce next: drew clr fr 3 out: eased run-in* **2/1**[2]
-513 **2** *12* **Mile House (IRE)**[38] 1038 7-11-7 0............ TomO'Brien 113
(Robert Stephens) *j. sltly rt at times: trckd ldrs: wnt 2nd after 10th: rdn appr 3 out: sn no ch w wnr* **4/6**[1]
5FP- **3** *43* **Johns Luck (IRE)**[180] 4456 6-11-7 0............ NoelFehily 74
(Neil Mulholland) *trckd ldrs: hit 11th: rdn after 4 out: sn wknd* **8/1**[3]
6 **4** *20* **See It As It Is (IRE)**[67] 777 8-11-0 100............ MissTWorsley(7) 56
(Diana Grissell) *led tl 10th: chsd ldrs tl wknd after 4 out: hmpd 2 out* **40/1**
6m 1.6s (18.60) **Going Correction** +1.075s/f (Soft)
WFA 4 from 5yo+ 2lb 4 Ran SP% **106.9**
Speed ratings (Par 105): **107,102,86,78**
CSF £3.85 TOTE £3.00; EX 3.50 Trifecta £5.10.
Owner Mrs J Hitchings **Bred** Lydie Cottin & Margaux Cottin **Trained** Ditcheat, Somerset

FOCUS
Three non-runners left a field of four and the two best hurdlers dominating proceedings. The winner has been rated to his chase latest.

1352 EQUINITI FINTECH FOR WEALTH SOLUTIONS MARES' NOVICES' HURDLE (9 hdls) 2m 1f 145y
5:50 (5:50) (Class 4) 4-Y-O+ **£3,249** (£954; £477)

Form RPR
/3-1 **1** **Native Princess**[84] 594 5-10-10 0............ PaddyBrennan 103
(Stuart Edmunds) *racd keenly: j. sltly rt at times: trckd ldr: hit 3rd: chal 5th: kpt wd on far side 2nd time: rdn to ld appr 2 out: drifted lft run-in: kpt on strly* **9/4**[2]
-253 **2** *2 ¼* **Dry Ol'Party**[41] 1009 5-10-10 107............ RichardJohnson 100
(Philip Hobbs) *led: kpt to inner on far side 2nd time: hit 3 out: hdd bef next where nt fluent: sn rdn: hit last: styd on but a being hld* **10/11**[1]
/4-3 **3** *1* **Northern Meeting (IRE)**[33] 592 5-10-10 105............ TomO'Brien 100
(Robert Stephens) *racd keenly: trckd ldng pair: rdn appr 2 out where nt fluent: hit last: kpt on but nt pce to chal* **7/2**[3]
4m 51.6s (17.30) **Going Correction** +0.15s/f (Yiel) 3 Ran SP% **105.4**
Speed ratings (Par 105): **67,66,65**
CSF £4.63 TOTE £3.00; EX 4.00 Trifecta £3.50.
Owner The Oakley Partnership **Bred** East Burrow Farm **Trained** Newport Pagnell, Bucks

FOCUS
A modest event run at a slow pace and certainly not form to be getting carried away with - the winner the best long-term prospect in the field. The winner has been rated to a similar level to her bumper win, while the third has been rated to form.

1353 EQUINITI SHAREVIEW.COM H'CAP CHASE (13 fncs) 2m 1f 96y
6:20 (6:20) (Class 4) (0-105,105) 4-Y-O+ **£3,768** (£1,106; £553; £276)

Form RPR
F-24 **1** **Quadriller (FR)**[25] 1051 8-11-12 **105**............(t) RichardJohnson 112
(Philip Hobbs) *hld up: hdwy fr 8th: led after 3 out: pushed out* **9/4**[1]
P454 **2** *3 ¾* **Owner Occupier**[12] 1245 10-10-8 **87**............(p) TomCannon 90
(Chris Gordon) *pressed ldr most of way tl led 7th: jnd whn nt fluent 3 out: sn rdn and hdd: styd on same pce fr next* **5/1**[3]
P/25 **3** *3 ¾* **Time Is Tickin**[83] 600 9-11-3 **103**............ OCdtOswaldWedmore(7) 104
(Diana Grissell) *chsd ldrs: wnt 2nd after 9th: rdn after 4 out: ev ch next: hld 2 out: no ex run-in* **9/2**[2]
1-62 **4** *23* **Try Catch Me (IRE)**[12] 1241 10-11-9 **105**............ ConorShoemark(3) 84
(Alison Batchelor) *hld up: hdwy after 7th: rdn after 9th: wknd after 4 out: t.o* **17/2**
F112 **5** *2* **Agapanthus (GER)**[44] 844 10-11-9 **102**............(b) MarkQuinlan 79
(Neil Mulholland) *led: reminders after 6th: hdd next: drvn after 8th: wknd after 4 out: t.o* **9/2**[2]
4-02 **P** **Marky Bob (IRE)**[13] 1233 10-11-8 **101**............ DaveCrosse
(Hugo Froud) *chsd ldrs: hit 5th: rdn after 7th: sn detached: t.o whn p.u bef 3 out* **5/1**[3]
4m 56.6s (21.90) **Going Correction** +1.075s/f (Soft) 6 Ran SP% **111.0**
Speed ratings (Par 105): **91,89,87,76,75**
CSF £13.46 TOTE £3.30: £2.00, £2.40; EX 14.00 Trifecta £41.60.
Owner P J Hobbs **Bred** Brian Moran **Trained** Withycombe, Somerset

FOCUS
A modest handicap but run at a stronger pace than some of the earlier races on the card. A small pb from the winner, with the second and third to their marks.

1354 SELFTRADE SIMPLY SMARTER INVESTING H'CAP HURDLE (10 hdls) 2m 3f 33y
6:50 (6:50) (Class 4) (0-120,120) 3-Y-O+ **£3,249** (£954; £477)

Form RPR
-144 **1** **Popping Along**[28] 1136 6-10-12 **109**............(tp) MattGriffiths(3) 112
(Jeremy Scott) *trckd ldrs: wnt cl 2nd after 2 out: led sn after last: pushed clr* **2/1**[2]
4431 **2** *4* **Royal Battalion**[12] 1239 4-11-3 **113**............(p) TomCannon 110
(Gary Moore) *chsd clr ldr: clsd on ldr 5th: chalng whn blnd 3 out: rdn to ld next: hit last: sn hdd: kpt on same pce* **1/1**[1]
453- **3** *35* **Tijori (IRE)**[5] 5467 7-11-3 **114**............(p) RobertWilliams(3) 82
(Bernard Llewellyn) *sn pushed into clr ld: reduced advantage 5th: hit 7th: rdn: hdd and hld whn blnd 2 out* **3/1**[3]
4m 59.8s (0.40) **Going Correction** +0.15s/f (Yiel)
WFA 4 from 6yo+ 13lb 3 Ran SP% **108.3**
Speed ratings (Par 105): **105,103,88**
CSF £4.44 TOTE £2.90; EX 4.50 Trifecta £3.70.
Owner Mrs Camilla Scott **Bred** Mrs C C Scott **Trained** Brompton Regis, Somerset

FOCUS
A farcical start to the race with none of the trio wanting to go on - the field stationary for some time after the tapes went up before Tijori was sent into a 20 length lead. A small pb from the winner, with the runner-up rated to his previous win here over shorter.

1355 EQUINITI INTERNATIONAL PAYMENT H'CAP CHASE (19 fncs) 3m 1f 106y
7:20 (7:20) (Class 5) (0-100,100) 4-Y-0+ **£2,529** (£785; £422)

Form RPR
-3P6 **1** **Rusty Nail (IRE)**[13] 1237 10-10-0 **81**.................................... MissBFrost(7) 94
(Jimmy Frost) *hld up bhd ldrs: hdwy 13th: led after 4 out: sn in command: hit last: pushed out* **9/2**[3]
2532 **2** *20* **The Wee Midget**[12] 1243 10-10-4 **85**..................(b) ThomasCheesman(7) 80
(Arthur Whiting) *disp ld most of way: rdn after 15th: hdd after 4 out: styd on same pce fr next* **2/1**[1]
3-53 **3** *31* **Orfeo Conti (FR)**[77] 670 13-10-3 **84**.............. OCdtOswaldWedmore(7) 51
(Diana Grissell) *trckd ldrs: rdn after 13th: awkward next: wknd after 4 out: lft 4th next: lft 3rd at the last: t.o* **6/1**
00P0 **P** **Silver Story**[33] 1080 12-10-10 **84**..............................(t) MichaelByrne
(Tim Vaughan) *prom tl 3rd: trckd ldng pair: rdn whn mstke 14th: wknd after 4 out: tailing off in 4th whn clambered over 3 out: sn p.u* **4/1**[2]
F-PP **U** **Bringewood Belle**[13] 1237 12-10-0 **74** oh2.............................. PeterCarberry
(John Needham) *blnd and uns rdr 1st* **11/1**
2/5- **P** **Mansonien L'As (FR)**[235] 3484 9-11-4 **92**............................(p) AdrianLane
(Donald McCain) *j. sltly lft at times: disp ld most of way tl rdn and hdd after 4 out: wknd after 3 out: tired 3rd whn p.u bef last* **5/1**

7m 33.9s (32.80) **Going Correction** +1.075s/f (Soft) **6** Ran SP% **110.8**
Speed ratings (Par 103): **90,83,73, ,**
CSF £14.10 CT £50.01 TOTE £4.70: £2.20, £1.90; EX 15.30 Trifecta £88.00.
Owner Frost Racing Club **Bred** Mrs Barbara Beattie **Trained** Buckfast, Devon

FOCUS
The defection of Spirit River and Caspian Piper left the top weight rated just 92 and this is not strong form, for all that the winner won as he pleased. The winner has been rated back to form.

1356 EQUINITI WEALTH SOLUTIONS FINAL H'CAP HURDLE (9 hdls) 2m 1f 145y
7:50 (7:50) (Class 5) (0-100,107) 3-Y-0+ **£2,396** (£744; £400)

Form RPR
455 **1** **Lee Side Lady (IRE)**[12] 1240 5-11-2 **90**.................................. NoelFehily 97+
(Neil Mulholland) *mde all: styd on wl fr 2 out: rdn out* **5/2**[2]
P532 **2** *4 ½* **Keychain (IRE)**[12] 1245 5-11-9 **97**..............................(bt) BrendanPowell 100
(Brendan Powell) *trckd wnr: rdn after 2 out: kpt on but nt pce to chal* **15/8**[1]
00-6 **3** *5* **Sweet World**[5] 895 11-11-5 **96**.. RobertWilliams(3) 95
(Bernard Llewellyn) *trckd ldrs: rdn after 3 out: sn one pce* **17/2**[3]
335- **F** **Drummond**[5] 3280 6-9-12 **75**..(bt) SeanBowen(3)
(Bernard Llewellyn) *hld up 4th: tk clsr order 5th: jinked rt appr 3 out where fell* **15/8**[1]

4m 47.5s (13.20) **Going Correction** +0.15s/f (Yiel) **4** Ran SP% **108.7**
Speed ratings (Par 103): **76,74,71,**
CSF £7.62 TOTE £3.70; EX 5.60 Trifecta £14.40.
Owner The Affordable (2) Partnership **Bred** Michael Lane **Trained** Limpley Stoke, Wilts

FOCUS
Another weak event but the one unexposed runner in the field landed the spoils. A pb from the winner on her handicap debut, with the runner-up rated to her latest.
T/Plt: £176.80 to a £1 stake. Pool: £43,547.73 - 179.77 winning tickets. T/Qpdt: £25.80 to a £1 stake. Pool: £4,848.40 - 138.90 winning tickets. **Tim Mitchell**

1357 - 1364a (Foreign Racing) - See Raceform Interactive

251 SEDGEFIELD (L-H)
Thursday, August 27

OFFICIAL GOING: Good to firm (good in places) changing to good to firm after race 1 (5:00)
Wind: fresh 1/2 behind Weather: fineand sunny, breezy

1365 GROSVENOR CASINO NEWCASTLE "NATIONAL HUNT" NOVICES' HURDLE (BETFRED HURDLE SERIES QUALIFIER) (8 hdls) 2m 178y
5:00 (5:00) (Class 4) 4-Y-0+ **£3,898** (£1,144; £572; £286)

Form RPR
2- **1** **Viens Chercher (IRE)**[131] 4-10-11 0....................................... DannyCook 127+
(Brian Ellison) *trckd ldr: led after 5th: clr between last 2: eased last 100yds* **8/15**[1]
2-33 **2** *19* **Raise A Spark**[97] 433 5-10-12 110.................................... AdrianLane 109
(Donald McCain) *t.k.h: wnt modest 3rd 4th: drvn to chse wnr 3 out: reminders bef next: kpt on same pce* **11/4**[2]
3 **3** *11* **Jumpandtravel (IRE)**[11] 1271 6-9-12 0........................ JamieBargary(7) 90
(Micky Hammond) *t.k.h: trckd ldng pair 3rd: modest 3rd and drvn 3 out: one pce* **8/1**[3]
4- **4** *21* **Sackett**[298] 2223 4-10-8 0.. HarryChalloner(3) 76
(Dianne Sayer) *mid-div: poor 4th 3 out: sn bhd* **18/1**
33PP **5** *38* **Duhallowcountry (IRE)**[93] 487 9-10-5 82....................(p) MrWHRReed(7) 43
(Victor Thompson) *led: hdd sn after 5th: lost pl next: sn wl bhd: t.o* **100/1**
P **Dinky Dave** 4-10-8 0.. JonathanEngland(3)
(Richard Drake) *j. poorly in detached last: reminders after 1st: t.o after 3rd: j. slowly and p.u immediately after 5th* **33/1**

3m 52.8s (-14.10) **Going Correction** -1.20s/f (Hard)
WFA 4 from 5yo+ 13lb **6** Ran SP% **112.2**
Speed ratings (Par 105): **85,76,70,61,43**
CSF £2.40 TOTE £1.60: £1.10, £1.60; EX 2.40 Trifecta £5.80.
Owner P J Martin **Bred** P Ryan **Trained** Norton, N Yorks

FOCUS
Not a bad race of its type considering the small field, run at a medium pace. The second helps set the level.

1366 MTREC RECRUITMENT NOVICES' HURDLE (BETFRED HURDLE SERIES QUALIFIER) 2m 3f 188y
5:30 (5:30) (Class 4) 4-Y-0+ **£3,898** (£1,144; £572; £286)

Form RPR
2444 **1** **Prince Khurram**[6] 1308 5-10-5 111..............................(t) JamesCowley(7) 109+
(Donald McCain) *trckd ldng pair: 2nd 5th: led after 3 out: styd on fr next: rdn rt out: hld on wl* **7/4**[2]
12-F **2** *1* **Vayland**[67] 812 6-11-5 120.. DarylJacob 116
(David Pipe) *hld up in tch: trckd ldng pair 6th: 2nd appr 2 out: 1 l down and rdn last: styd on sme pce* **5/4**[1]
1346 **3** *14* **Dun Scaith (IRE)**[15] 1238 7-10-12 110...........................(t) CiaranGethings(7) 102
(Sophie Leech) *t.k.h: led: hdd after 3 out: wknd between last 2* **10/3**[3]
0P **4** *12* **Cash Is King**[12] 1261 5-10-12 0......................................(t) PeterBuchanan 82
(Kenny Johnson) *in rr: modest 4th 7th: sn outpcd* **200/1**
5 *20* **Great Anticipation (IRE)**[96] 6-10-9 0............................ CraigNichol(3) 62
(Lynsey Kendall) *chsd ldr to 5th: wknd 7th: sn wl bhd* **28/1**

4m 40.05s (-14.05) **5** Ran SP% **107.8**
CSF £4.28 TOTE £2.30: £1.30, £1.10; EX 4.40 Trifecta £5.90.
Owner T G Leslie **Bred** Ballygallon Stud Limited **Trained** Cholmondeley, Cheshire

FOCUS
The three main contenders had established a fair level of form. The leader went clear by halfway but the pace wasn't testing. A hurdle pb from the second.

1367 ROFLOW ENVIRONMENTAL ENGINEERING - SUPPORTING GNAA H'CAP CHASE (13 fncs) 2m 77y
6:00 (6:01) (Class 4) (0-110,110) 4-Y-0+ **£4,548** (£1,335; £667; £333)

Form RPR
-232 **1** **The Bay Bandit**[46] 985 8-11-8 **106**.....................................(p) NoelFehily 112+
(Neil Mulholland) *hld up: trckd ldrs 5th: handy 3rd 9th: produced between horses to ld last: drvn out* **7/2**[2]
-345 **2** *½* **Sendiym (FR)**[9] 1032 8-10-6 **90**.. HenryBrooke 95
(Dianne Sayer) *trckd ldrs: 2nd 8th: upsides fr 10th: kpt on same pce last 50yds* **11/2**[3]
4523 **3** *nk* **Sleep In First (FR)**[34] 1099 9-11-7 **110**........................(t) DaleIrving(5) 115
(James Ewart) *led: j.rt: jnd 10th: hdd last: kpt on same pce last 75yds* **7/2**[2]
3P-0 **4** *27* **Alba King (IRE)**[35] 1080 9-9-9 **84** oh4............................ DiarmuidO'Regan(5) 64
(Sue Smith) *chsd ldr: nt fluent 7th: drvn next: lost pl bef 10th: sn bhd* **6/1**
0034 **5** *6* **Roxyfet (FR)**[40] 1031 5-10-1 **95**.. FinianO'Toole(10) 70
(Micky Hammond) *racd in last: outpcd 6th: hit 9th: sn bhd* **9/1**
2035 **U** **Dynamo (IRE)**[27] 1169 4-10-13 **110**................................(t) HarrySkelton
(Dan Skelton) *trckd ldrs: blnd and uns rdr 4th* **5/2**[1]

4m 3.9s (-10.10) **Going Correction** -1.20s/f (Hard)
WFA 4 from 5yo+ 1lb **6** Ran SP% **112.7**
Speed ratings (Par 105): **77,76,76,63,60**
CSF £22.28 TOTE £3.70: £2.40, £1.90; EX 20.40 Trifecta £54.90.
Owner Neil Mulholland Racing Club **Bred** Darley **Trained** Limpley Stoke, Wilts

FOCUS
The early pace was good but it soon steadied, and the first three all still had a chance at the last. A small pb from the winner, with the second in line with his previous course best.

1368 GROSVENOR CASINO SUNDERLAND NOVICES' H'CAP HURDLE 2m 3f 188y
6:30 (6:32) (Class 5) (0-100,91) 3-Y-0+ **£2,599** (£763; £381; £190)

Form RPR
-12P **1** **Craigdancer (IRE)**[38] 1067 6-11-9 **88**................................ DougieCostello 89
(Joanne Foster) *in rr: hdwy omitted 4 out: sn chsng ldrs: led bef 2 out: edgd rt last 100yds: all out* **7/2**[1]
3-50 **2** *nk* **Park House**[91] 522 6-11-11 **90**.. BrianHughes 89
(Ray Craggs) *chsd ldrs: 2nd omitted 3 out: no ex last 50yds* **7/1**
2P-0 **3** *nk* **District Attorney (IRE)**[21] 34 6-11-2 **84**.............. JonathanEngland(3) 85+
(Chris Fairhurst) *hld up in rr: hdwy omitted 3 out: upsides 2 out: crowded and no ex last 50yds* **9/2**[2]
2P-P **4** *9* **Saint Brieuc (FR)**[25] 1182 6-11-12 **91**.................................. HenryBrooke 82
(Simon West) *hld up towards rr: hdwy to chse ldrs omitted 4 out: wknd last* **12/1**
4650 **5** *6* **Jebulani**[23] 843 5-11-3 **82**.. BrianHarding 68
(Barry Murtagh) *trckd ldrs: drvn appr 2 out: wknd last 150yds* **6/1**[3]
U0-5 **6** *13* **Strictly The One (IRE)**[36] 615 5-11-8 **87**......................(bt) NoelFehily 61
(Neil Mulholland) *t.k.h: trckd ldrs: led omitted 4 out: hdd bef 2 out: wknd between last 2* **7/2**[1]
PUU0 **P** **Bertielicious**[75] 728 7-9-9 **65** oh4..................... DiarmuidO'Regan(5)
(Jonathan Haynes) *led: hdd omitted 4 out: sn lost pl and bhd: t.o whn p.u bef 2 out* **16/1**
P-6P **P** **Colonial Style (IRE)**[52] 518 5-10-2 **70**.............................. CraigNichol(3)
(George Moore) *w ldr: wknd qckly omitted 3 out: sn bhd: t.o whn p.u bef 2 out* **9/1**

4m 34.6s (-19.50) **8** Ran SP% **113.0**
CSF £27.29 CT £110.14 TOTE £4.10: £1.80, £1.70, £1.50; EX 36.50 Trifecta £189.00.
Owner The Chessy Millers **Bred** Sean Culleton **Trained** Menston, W Yorks

FOCUS
The two hurdles in the back straight were omitted because of low sun, so it wasn't much of test of jumping. The pace was solid and six still had a chance at the second-last. The first three have been rated pretty much to their marks.

1369 ROFLOW SPECIALIST VENTILATION SYSTEMS H'CAP HURDLE 2m 3f 188y
7:00 (7:00) (Class 4) (0-120,120) 4-Y-0+ **£3,898** (£1,144; £572; £286)

Form RPR
3P41 **1** **Grams And Ounces**[7] 1299 8-9-13 **98** 7ex.......................(t) DavidNoonan(7) 108+
(Adrian Wintle) *hld up towards rr: hdwy omitted 4 out: 3rd and drvn appr 2 out: cl 2nd last: sn led: edgd rt: drvn out* **13/8**[1]
224- **2** *1* **Waterclock (IRE)**[14] 4288 6-11-4 **110**...............................(v) BrianHarding 120
(Jedd O'Keeffe) *trckd ldrs: led sn after omitted 3 out: hdd sn after last: styd on same pce* **9/4**[2]
1125 **3** *8* **Russian Royale**[25] 1180 5-10-13 **108**.................................. CraigNichol(3) 110
(Micky Hammond) *hld up in rr: hdwy to chse ldrs omitted 4 out: 2nd appr 2 out: fdd last* **9/1**
5-55 **4** *14* **Claude Carter**[12] 1261 11-10-5 **102**.............................(p) KieronEdgar(5) 91
(Alistair Whillans) *racd wd: w ldr: led normal 3rd: hdd sn after omitted 3 out: wknd 2 out* **12/1**
614- **5** *1 ¾* **Cooking Fat**[238] 3461 4-11-12 **120**...................................... HenryBrooke 107
(Dianne Sayer) *hld up in rr: hdwy omitted 4 out: 5th and outpcd whn hit 2 out: sn wknd* **20/1**
-365 **6** *10* **Cape York**[71] 756 7-11-10 **116**...(b) BrianHughes 95
(Malcolm Jefferson) *led tl normal 3rd: drvn omitted 3 out: lost pl bef 2 out: sn bhd* **15/2**[3]
363- **7** *37* **Come On Sunshine**[39] 4323 4-11-8 **116**..............................(p) DannyCook 59
(Brian Ellison) *chsd ldrs: drvn a circ fr home: lost pl omitted 4 out: sn bhd: t.o 2 out* **11/1**

4m 32.8s (-21.30) **7** Ran SP% **111.4**
CSF £5.58 CT £21.11 TOTE £2.20: £1.70, £1.70; EX 5.40 Trifecta £24.60.
Owner Ron C Williams **Bred** Brook Stud Bloodstock Ltd **Trained** Westbury-On-Severn, Gloucs

FOCUS
Not a bad race of its type, though the two flights in the back straight were again omitted. The second has been rated to his best.

1370 ALBERT HILL COMMERCIALS NOVICES' H'CAP CHASE (8 fncs 8 omitted) 2m 3f 65y
7:30 (7:31) (Class 5) (0-100,98) 4-Y-O+ £3,249 (£954; £477; £238)

Form RPR
FP-0 1 **The Backup Plan (IRE)**103 328 6-11-9 95 BrianHarding 106+
(Donald McCain) *led after 1st: mde rest: styd on fr 3 out: drvn rt out* 12/1
-113 2 7 **Caspian Piper (IRE)**70 770 8-11-5 98 (v) AlanJohns(7) 103
(Tim Vaughan) *chsd wnr sn after 1st: hit 2 out: kpt on same pce* 9/4[1]
P-3P 3 2 1/4 **Joyful Motive**43 1004 6-9-7 72 oh6 ThomasCheesman(7) 74
(Brian Ellison) *sn chsng ldrs: kpt on same pce bef 2 out: 4th whn bmpd last: kpt on* 8/1
-455 4 3/4 **Champagne Agent (IRE)**57 871 9-10-0 72 oh4 (b) DougieCostello 75
(Donald Whillans) *sn chsng ldrs: 3rd 3 out: j.lft last: one pce* 8/1
2232 5 3/4 **Forestside (IRE)**40 1031 10-10-5 77 (p) LucyAlexander 79
(Barry Murtagh) *hld up towards rr: hdwy circ to go: 4th and one pce whn mstke 2 out* 14/1
43/6 6 26 **Optical High**32 1110 6-10-0 72 SeanQuinlan 50
(Sue Smith) *chsd ldrs: drvn omitted 11th: reminders and lost pl omitted 4 out: sn bhd* 9/2[2]
P/2- 7 8 **Alf The Audacious**415 894 9-11-11 97 DannyCook 67
(Sue Smith) *in rr: hdwy omitted 8th: blnd next: lost pl omitted 11th: sn bhd: t.o 3 out* 13/2[3]
1U24 F **Danceintothelight**24 802 8-10-13 95 FinianO'Toole(10) 97
(Micky Hammond) *hld up in rr: sme hdwy circ to go: one pce fr 3 out: modest 6th whn fell last* 7/1
0-0P F **Exit To Freedom**11 1273 9-10-2 77 (p) CraigNichol(3)
(John Wainwright) *in rr: blnd and uns rdr 1st* 40/1

4m 38.8s (-24.20) **Going Correction** -1.20s/f (Hard) course record 9 Ran SP% 113.8
Speed ratings (Par 103): **102,99,98,97,97 86,83, ,**
CSF £40.39 CT £234.55 TOTE £11.90: £3.80, £1.50, £2.60; EX 44.50 Trifecta £466.00.
Owner N.Y.P.D Racing **Bred** Miss Sharon Spillane **Trained** Cholmondeley, Cheshire

FOCUS
All four fences in the back straight were omitted because of the low sun, leaving just eight to jump. In an otherwise moderate chase, the winner looked progressive. The second, fourth and fifth help set the level.

1371 GROSVENOR CASINO STOCKTON H'CAP HURDLE (13 hdls) 3m 3f 9y
8:00 (8:00) (Class 5) (0-100,100) 4-Y-O+ £2,599 (£763; £381; £190)

Form RPR
52-0 1 **Omid**33 502 7-11-9 100 (tp) JohnKington(3) 105+
(Kenneth Slack) *w ldr: led 5th to 8th: led 10th: drvn and styd on fr 3 out: forged clr run-in* 11/2[3]
2 7 **Derryfadda (IRE)**123 6-11-4 95 HarryChalloner(3) 94
(Richard Ford) *trckd ldng pair: lft 2nd after 10th: 1 l down 2 out: rdn bef last: kpt on one pce run-in* 5/2[1]
5-20 3 19 **Verko (FR)**51 939 6-10-5 82 CraigNichol(3) 64
(Micky Hammond) *hld up in rr: hdwy 5th: chsng ldrs after 9th: drvn bef 2 out: wknd between last 2* 7/2[2]
4-23 4 3 3/4 **Supapowers (IRE)**43 1004 9-11-5 100 (t) CiaranGethings(7) 79
(Robert Stephens) *chsd ldng pair: drvn 3 outer: wknd bef next* 5/2[1]
-PPP P **Moon Melody (GER)**11 1272 12-10-11 85 (bt) BrianHughes
(Mike Sowersby) *led to 5th: ld 8th: hdd 10th: sn p.u: lame* 14/1
-P4P P **Lochore (IRE)**57 867 9-10-0 74 oh4 (t) HenryBrooke
(Jean McGregor) *in rr: reminders 6th and 8th: chsng ldrs 9th: sn lost pl and p.u after next: lame* 28/1
04P- P **Dizoard**19 5379 5-11-6 94 BrianHarding
(Ollie Pears) *mid-div: nt fluent 4th: reminders 9th: sn bhd: t.o 3 out: p.u bef next* 33/1

6m 20.9s (-31.10) **Going Correction** -1.20s/f (Hard) 7 Ran SP% 107.8
Speed ratings (Par 103): **98,95,90,89, ,**
CSF £17.82 CT £46.35 TOTE £6.80: £3.00, £1.80; EX 20.40 Trifecta £67.60.
Owner Mrs Evelyn Slack **Bred** Silfield Bloodstock **Trained** Hilton, Cumbria

FOCUS
A modest race but the tempo was good. A small pb from the winner.
T/Plt: £10.80 to a £1 stake. Pool: £39,528.29 - 2,654.61 winning tickets T/Qpdt: £10.40 to a £1 stake. Pool: £3,849.51 - 273.33 winning tickets **Walter Glynn**

1266 SOUTHWELL (L-H)
Thursday, August 27

OFFICIAL GOING: Good (8.0)
Wind: Light behind Weather: Cloudy with sunny spells

1372 MRFREEBET.CO.UK ON YOUR MOBILE NOVICES' H'CAP CHASE (19 fncs) 2m 7f 209y
1:50 (1:50) (Class 4) (0-120,118) 4-Y-O+ £3,898 (£1,144; £572; £286)

Form RPR
-422 1 **Lemony Bay**32 1110 6-11-5 114 ThomasGarner(3) 120+
(Oliver Sherwood) *mde all: nt fluent 3 out: rdn appr last: styd on wl* 13/2
5P-3 2 3 **Take A Bow**71 756 6-11-9 115 (t) NickScholfield 118
(Lawney Hill) *chsd wnr: nt fluent 11th: lost 2nd next: sn given a reminder: wnt 2nd again 4 out: rdn appr last: styd on same pce flat* 15/2
10/2 3 38 **Gee Hi (IRE)**46 959 9-10-13 105 SamTwiston-Davies 76
(Warren Greatrex) *trckd ldrs: mstkes 4th and 11th: chsd wnr 14th: nt fluent next: lost 2nd 4 out: rdn and wkng whn mstke 3 out* 2/1[1]
02FP 4 7 **Brother Scott**35 1079 8-10-3 95 SeanQuinlan 57
(Sue Smith) *chsd ldrs: wnt 2nd 12th: hit next: lost 2nd 14th: wknd bef 4 out* 10/1
-0P1 5 2 1/4 **Finding Your Feet (IRE)**77 698 7-11-2 108 (v) WillKennedy 68
(Jonjo O'Neill) *hld up: nt fluent 1st: mstke 7th: hit 10th: mstke next: bhd and rdn 12th: wknd 14th* 7/2[2]
3P4- P **Whats Left (IRE)**173 4625 7-11-12 118 NoelFehily
(Neil Mulholland) *hld up: wknd 15th: bhd whn p.u after 4 out* 9/2[3]
04U P **Sureness (IRE)**11 1267 5-11-12 118 (tp) DarylJacob
(Charlie Mann) *hld up: j.rt 8th and next: wknd 15th: bhd whn p.u bef 2 out* 25/1

6m 18.7s (-4.30) **Going Correction** -0.025s/f (Good) 7 Ran SP% 111.8
Speed ratings (Par 105): **106,105,92,90,89 ,**
CSF £48.98 CT £129.77 TOTE £7.70: £3.40, £2.90; EX 44.00 Trifecta £232.50.
Owner R Waters **Bred** G R Waters **Trained** Upper Lambourn, Berks
■ Stewards' Enquiry : Nick Scholfield two-day ban: use of whip (14 & 16 Sept)

FOCUS
Rail movement reduced 2m races by 12yds and 2m 4f and 3m races by 24yds. Only two mattered from the final bend in what was a modest chase. A small pb from the winner.

1373 18 TO 30 GOLF MEMBERSHIP £210 NOVICES' H'CAP CHASE (13 fncs) 1m 7f 153y
2:20 (2:20) (Class 5) (0-100,99) 4-Y-O+ £2,599 (£763; £381; £190)

Form RPR
P-42 1 **The Yank**34 1096 6-10-13 86 1 TomCannon 111+
(David Bridgwater) *mde all: mstke 4th: nt fluent next: clr fr 4 out: easily* 9/2[1]
0634 2 6 **Going Nowhere Fast (IRE)**76 713 10-10-3 79 RobertWilliams(3) 88
(Bernard Llewellyn) *hld up: hdwy 7th: rdn after 4 out: wnt 2nd next: styd on: no ch w wnr* 10/1
P033 3 8 **Blackwood Rover (IRE)**14 1243 7-11-3 90 PaulMoloney 93
(J R Jenkins) *prom: hmpd 9th: rdn after 4 out: styd on same pce* 9/2[1]
3402 4 5 **Chankillo**30 1133 6-10-10 83 SamTwiston-Davies 79
(Sarah-Jayne Davies) *hld up: rdn after 4 out: n.d* 6/1[2]
5024 5 1 **Bob's Legend (IRE)**67 804 9-11-7 94 BrendanPowell 89
(Jamie Snowden) *chsd wnr: rdn after 4 out: wknd next* 9/2[1]
40P5 P **Mahayogin (USA)**28 1159 7-10-0 73 oh4 PeterCarberry
(Sarah-Jayne Davies) *a in rr: hit 3rd: bhd fr 5th: mstke 8th: p.u bef 3 out* 28/1
/400 P **Go Teescomponents**51 934 8-10-0 73 oh2 BrianHughes
(Keith Reveley) *chsd ldrs: lost pl 3rd: wknd 8th: bhd whn p.u bef 3 out* 7/1[3]
F624 F **Who Am I**28 1159 9-11-12 99 (v1) TomO'Brien
(Debra Hamer) *chsd ldrs: j.rt 6th and 9th: rdn after 4 out: disputing 3rd and wkng whn fell 3 out* 7/1[3]
-6PF P **Indiefront**67 807 6-10-0 76 (t) JamesBanks(3)
(Jo Davis) *hld up: bhd fr 4th: p.u bef last* 18/1
-04P U **Tara Dove**14 1245 7-10-11 87 ConorShoemark(3) 82
(Alison Batchelor) *mid-div: hdwy 8th: rdn after 4 out: wknd bef next: poor 5th whn blnd and uns rdr 2 out* 33/1

4m 0.4s (-1.60) **Going Correction** -0.025s/f (Good) 10 Ran SP% 114.6
Speed ratings (Par 103): **103,100,96,93,93 , , , ,**
CSF £47.42 CT £213.15 TOTE £4.50: £1.90, £3.90, £2.20; EX 70.50 Trifecta £217.70.
Owner Gary Attwood **Bred** Mrs J L Egan **Trained** Icomb, Gloucs

FOCUS
A moderate handicap that played out in similar fashion to the opener, with the winner making all. A big jumps pb from the winner, with the second in line with his hurdle mark.

1374 MANSFIELD TOWN FC RACEDAY 2ND SEPTEMBER MARES' NOVICES' HURDLE (11 hdls) 2m 4f 62y
2:50 (2:50) (Class 4) 4-Y-O+ £3,249 (£954; £477; £238)

Form RPR
0-12 1 **Welcometothejungle**15 1238 7-11-5 113 (t) NoelFehily 119+
(Harry Fry) *trckd ldrs: mstkes 2nd and 3rd: rdn to ld appr last: styd on wl* 10/11[1]
33-1 2 2 1/2 **What A Jewel (IRE)**14 1247 5-11-2 115 MPButler(3) 114
(Eoin Doyle, Ire) *chsd ldr who wnt clr fr 2nd: tk clsr order 7th: led after 3 out: rdn bef next: hdd appr last: styd on same pce flat* 9/4[2]
-341 3 4 1/2 **Flower Power**34 1094 4-11-3 120 DenisO'Regan 110
(Tony Coyle) *a.p: ev ch after 3 out: rdn whn mstke next: styd on same pce appr last* 7/1[3]
3205 4 7 **Bollin Beauty**27 1165 6-10-12 0 BrianHughes 98
(Malcolm Jefferson) *hld up: hdwy 5th: rdn appr 2 out: wknd bef last* 25/1
56/2 5 6 **Jazz Thyme (IRE)**39 1057 6-10-12 0 TomO'Brien 91
(Robert Stephens) *hld up: hdwy 3 out: rdn and wknd appr last* 8/1
0 6 24 **Desroches (GER)**102 361 7-10-12 0 BrendanPowell 70
(Robin Dickin) *led: clr fr 2nd: mstke 5th: c bk to the field 7th: rdn and hdd after 3 out: wknd bef next* 50/1
0-64 7 1 3/4 **Pretty Rose (IRE)**34 1094 5-10-12 0 KielanWoods 68
(Ben Case) *s.i.s: sn prom: wknd after 8th* 20/1
600 8 67 **Crosslanes (IRE)**32 1109 4-10-10 0 (t) TomMessenger 6
(Chris Bealby) *s.i.s: a in rr: pushed along 5th: lost tch 7th* 100/1
4-0P 9 nk **Miss Lucarno**8 1290 5-10-12 0 AdamWedge 8
(Evan Williams) *hld up: wknd after 7th* 80/1

5m 3.2s (-9.80) **Going Correction** -0.25s/f (Good)
WFA 4 from 5yo+ 14lb 9 Ran SP% 119.6
Speed ratings (Par 105): **109,108,106,103,101 91,90,63,63**
CSF £3.28 TOTE £1.90: £1.10, £1.30, £1.60; EX 3.80 Trifecta £7.00.
Owner Withyslade **Bred** David Bond **Trained** Seaborough, Dorset

FOCUS
Little depth to this and the market leaders dominated. The winner has been rated as running a pb, with the second close to her mark.

1375 RUBY CONGRATULATIONS STEVE & WENDY EDMUNDSONS ELECTRICAL H'CAP HURDLE (13 hdls) 2m 7f 209y
3:20 (3:20) (Class 4) (0-105,105) 4-Y-O+ £3,249 (£954; £477; £238)

Form RPR
F555 1 **Princeton Royale (IRE)**2 1350 6-11-3 103 (v1) LizzieKelly(7) 121+
(Neil King) *hld up: racd keenly: hdwy 7th: led after 3 out: clr last: comf* 10/1
-P31 2 9 **Presence Felt (IRE)**35 1085 7-11-10 103 (v) WillKennedy 113
(Jonjo O'Neill) *disp ld tl wnt on 9th: hdd after 3 out: rdn appr last: no ex* 8/1
5401 3 11 **The Winking Prawn (IRE)**28 1158 8-11-12 105 (t) KielanWoods 106
(Graeme McPherson) *hld up: hdwy 10th: rdn appr 2 out: styd on same pce* 7/1[3]
P-63 4 nk **Tokyo Javilex (FR)**11 1273 8-10-1 87 (t) MrLDrowne(7) 89
(Nigel Hawke) *w ldrs tl mstke 4th: nt fluent and lost pl 6th: r.o flat* 8/1
F/13 5 1 1/2 **French Seventyfive**11 1272 8-9-8 80 MissETodd(7) 78
(Keith Reveley) *hld up in tch: lost pl after 6th: n.d after* 6/1[2]
2F22 6 6 **Midnight Sequel**28 1158 6-11-8 101 (bt) NoelFehily 94
(Neil Mulholland) *hld up: hdwy 9th: rdn and wknd 2 out* 17/2
-032 7 4 1/2 **Perseid (IRE)**11 1273 5-10-3 82 SeanQuinlan 71
(Sue Smith) *mid-div: hdwy 6th: lost pl 9th: rallied after 3 out: rdn and wknd bef next* 5/1[1]
4423 8 1 1/2 **Finish The Story (IRE)**32 1114 9-11-8 101 (bt) BrendanPowell 89
(Johnny Farrelly) *disp ld tl rdn appr 9th: wknd bef 2 out* 14/1
3556 9 9 **Mullinavat (IRE)**27 1168 6-11-5 98 (t) HenryBrooke 77
(Jennie Candlish) *trckd ldrs: racd keenly: rdn and wknd appr 2 out* 14/1
U660 10 29 **Royal Craftsman (IRE)**39 1055 5-11-3 99 (p) SeanBowen(3) 52
(Peter Bowen) *prom: rdn after 8th: wknd next* 16/1

3541 **11** 1 1/4 **Temple Lord (FR)**[35] 1086 9-11-9 **102**..........(vt) RichieMcLernon 54
(Jonjo O'Neill) *prom tl rdn and wknd after 3 out* **14/1**
2-0P **P** **Dais Return (IRE)**[32] 1113 11-11-2 **102**..........(tp) FreddieMitchell[(7)]
(John Coombe) *mstke 1st: prom: rdn after 8th: wknd next: bhd whn p.u bef 2 out* **33/1**
-116 **P** **Pennant Dancer**[84] 615 8-11-9 **102**..........(t) PaulMoloney
(Debra Hamer) *hld up: bhd fr 9th: blnd 3 out: p.u bef next* **33/1**
5-00 **P** **Wither Yenot (IRE)**[57] 873 8-11-5 **105**..........(p) MrMJPKendrick[(7)]
(Ben Case) *hld up: pushed along 7th: rdn after next: wknd 9th: bhd whn p.u bef 2 out* **66/1**

6m 6.7s (-8.30) **Going Correction** -0.25s/f (Good) **14 Ran SP% 118.5**
Speed ratings (Par 105): **103,100,96,96,95 93,92,91,88,79 78, , ,**
CSF £86.06 CT £605.07 TOTE £13.90: £4.30, £2.70, £3.50; EX 123.90 Trifecta £1181.50.
Owner D Nott, P Beadles, R Clarke **Bred** Brett Merry **Trained** Barbury Castle, Wiltshire

FOCUS
This had looked quite open and the winner improved for the fitting of a visor. A step up from the winner and second, and there's a case for rating the race a few pounds higher through the third and fourth.

1376 AUTUMN JUMPS AT SOUTHWELL RACECOURSE (S) HURDLE (9 hdls) 1m 7f 153y
3:50 (3:50) (Class 5) 4-Y-O+ **£2,599** (£763; £381; £190)

Form RPR
2-24 **1** **A Little Bit Dusty**[10] 354 7-11-4 109..........(b) PaddyBrennan 121+
(Conor Dore) *trckd ldrs: racd keenly: led after 5th: hdd after 3 out: led appr last: shkn up flat: styd on* **7/1**
04-3 **2** 3/4 **Changing The Guard**[12] 1261 9-10-7 126..........(tp) ChrisWard[(5)] 114
(Dr Richard Newland) *chsd ldr: nt fluent 3rd: led after 3 out: rdn and hdd appr last: styd on* **6/4**[1]
3 7 **Akinspirit (IRE)**[56] 890 11-10-9 107..........(t) MPButler[(3)] 107
(Michael Butler, Ire) *hld up: hdwy after 3 out: shkn up and ev ch appr last: styd on same pce* **14/1**
132 **4** 1 1/2 **Roja Dove (IRE)**[12] 1261 6-10-11 118..........(v) TrevorWhelan 105
(Neil King) *hld up: hdwy 5th: rdn and hung lft bef 2 out: styd on same pce appr last* **3/1**[2]
246/ **5** 8 **Renoyr (FR)**[753] 1203 10-10-12 107.......... BrianHughes 101+
(Malcolm Jefferson) *prom: mstke 3rd: rdn appr 2 out: wknd bef last* **7/2**[3]
2F45 **6** 25 **Kayfton Pete**[40] 1043 9-11-4 0.......... AdamPogson 82
(Charles Pogson) *led: plld hrd: wnt clr after 2nd: hdd after 5th: rdn and wknd after 3 out* **20/1**
44/0 **P** **Hustle (IRE)**[28] 1153 10-10-5 0.......... FreddieMitchell[(7)]
(Clare Hobson) *chsd ldrs: nt fluent 3rd: mstke and wknd 6th: bhd whn p.u and dismntd after 3 out* **66/1**

3m 52.3s (-4.70) **Going Correction** -0.25s/f (Good) **7 Ran SP% 112.6**
Speed ratings (Par 103): **101,100,97,96,92 79,**
CSF £18.04 TOTE £6.30: £2.80, £1.50; EX 19.80 Trifecta £148.30.There was no bid fChanging The Guard was claimed by Mr F. J. Brennan for £5,000. Roja Dove was claimed by Mr David W. Thompson for £5,000.
Owner David Baldwin & Chris Marsh **Bred** T O C S Limited **Trained** Hubbert's Bridge, Lincs

FOCUS
The front pair pulled clear late in a weak seller. Arguably a pb from the winner, with the second in line with his recent win. The third and fourth help set the level.

1377 JOHN AND BARBARA DIAMOND ANNIVERSARY H'CAP HURDLE (9 hdls) 1m 7f 153y
4:20 (4:23) (Class 4) (0-120,115) 3-Y-O+ **£3,249** (£954; £477; £238)

Form RPR
24-0 **1** **Cusheen Bridge (IRE)**[34] 1100 7-11-12 **115**..........(t) AdamPogson 117+
(Charles Pogson) *chsd ldr tl led 2 out: rdn flat: r.o: eased nr fin* **6/1**[3]
1522 **2** 2 1/2 **Mac Bertie**[11] 1269 6-11-2 **105**..........(p) AdamWedge 103
(Evan Williams) *led: hdd 2 out: sn rdn: styd on same pce flat* **15/8**[2]
4614 **3** 2 3/4 **Jarlath**[47] 933 4-11-6 **110**.......... RyanMahon 105
(Seamus Mullins) *hld up: hdwy appr 2 out: rdn and hung lft bef last: styd on same pce* **8/1**
21-5 **4** 1 **Vodka 'n Tonic (IRE)**[107] 261 6-11-6 **112**.......... JeremiahMcGrath[(3)] 107
(Nicky Henderson) *hld up in tch: racd keenly: rdn appr 2 out: styd on same pce last* **7/4**[1]
42-0 **5** 7 **Goal (IRE)**[14] 1239 7-11-3 **113**..........(t) MissBHampson[(7)] 101
(Andy Turnell) *hld up: sme hdwy appr 2 out: wknd bef last* **11/1**
30-0 **6** 12 **Skyfire**[41] 186 8-10-11 **105**.......... CharlieDeutsch[(5)] 83
(Nick Kent) *chsd ldrs: rdn after 3 out: wknd bef next* **16/1**

3m 55.9s (-1.10) **Going Correction** -0.25s/f (Good)
WFA 4 from 6yo+ 13lb **6 Ran SP% 110.8**
Speed ratings (Par 105): **92,90,89,88,85 79**
CSF £17.71 TOTE £5.50: £2.40, £1.20; EX 21.00 Trifecta £95.70.
Owner Wordingham Plant Hire **Bred** Gfe Agri Ltd **Trained** Farnsfield, Notts

FOCUS
Modest handicap form. The cosy winner has been rated back to his best, with the second in line with his form over this trip and the third to his mark.

1378 SOUTHWELL "NEWCOMERS" STANDARD OPEN NATIONAL HUNT FLAT RACE 1m 7f 153y
4:55 (4:55) (Class 6) 4-6-Y-O **£1,949** (£572; £286; £143)

Form RPR
1 **What A Lark (IRE)** 4-10-9 0.......... DenisO'Regan 91+
(Tony Coyle) *trckd ldrs: rdn over 1f out: r.o to ld nr fin* **5/2**[2]
2 1/2 **Throckley** 4-11-2 0.......... RichieMcLernon 97
(John Davies) *hld up: hdwy over 3f out: led wl over 1f out: sn rdn: hdd nr fin* **33/1**
3 3 1/2 **Nabateo** 4-10-13 0.......... AdamNicol[(3)] 93
(Philip Kirby) *chsd ldr: led over 2f out: rdn and hdd over 1f out: styd on same pce fnl f* **15/8**[1]
4 10 **Glimpse Of Gold** 4-11-2 0.......... PaulMoloney 83
(Tim Vaughan) *prom: rdn over 2f out: wknd over 1f out* **3/1**[3]
5 5 **Dr Izzymoo (IRE)** 6-11-3 0.......... KielanWoods 79
(Jennie Candlish) *led: rdn and hdd over 2f out: wknd over 1f out* **10/1**
6 11 **Balade Mail (FR)** 4-10-9 0.......... PeterCarberry 60
(Shaun Lycett) *rn green towards rr: rdn over 6f out: wknd over 3f out* **16/1**
7 5 **Lexi Lou (IRE)** 5-10-10 0.......... SamTwiston-Davies 56
(David Thompson) *hld up: rdn over 6f out: wknd over 4f out* **20/1**

3m 55.2s (3.80) **Going Correction** -0.25s/f (Good)
WFA 4 from 5yo+ 1lb **7 Ran SP% 111.0**
Speed ratings: **80,79,78,73,70 65,62**
CSF £65.27 TOTE £3.90: £1.60, £8.10; EX 54.50 Trifecta £230.00.
Owner Craig Buckingham **Bred** Miss Susan Flanagan **Trained** Norton, N Yorks

FOCUS
A fairly moderate bumper. There's nothing to go on, bar a modest time, by which to rate the race.
T/Plt: £84.20 to a £1 stake. Pool: £54,991.40 - 476.73 winning tickets T/Qpdt: £9.30 to a £1 stake. Pool: £5,409.54 - 427.65 winning tickets **Colin Roberts**

[1294] STRATFORD (L-H)
Thursday, August 27

OFFICIAL GOING: Good (good to soft in places; 6.8)
Wind: breezy Weather: sunshine and showers; 18 degrees

1379 GRUNDON WASTE MANAGEMENT MAIDEN HURDLE (9 hdls) 2m 2f 148y
2:10 (2:10) (Class 4) 4-Y-O+ **£3,249** (£954; £477; £238)

Form RPR
03-4 **1** **Low Key (IRE)**[31] 1119 8-11-1 124.......... TomScudamore 130+
(David Pipe) *small: v slow 1st: pressed ldr: nt fluent 6th: led 2 out: drew 6 l clr home turn and easily continued to increase advantage: eased after last* **8/11**[1]
0404 **2** 19 **Buy Me Out**[15] 1234 5-10-1 0.......... AlanJohns[(7)] 102
(Grace Harris) *hld up tl effrt in 3rd after 2 out: 14 l 3rd and rdn home turn: wnt poor 2nd wl bef last but nvr any hope of catching wnr* **16/1**
3 **3** 5 **Bedale**[14] 1240 4-10-13 0..........(v) AidanColeman 102
(John Ferguson) *settled trcking ldrs: wnt 2nd 2 out: sn drvn and fnd nil: lost poor 2nd wl bef last* **2/1**[2]
56-5 **4** nk **Cry Fury**[15] 1234 7-10-12 104.......... KillianMoore[(3)] 105
(Sophie Leech) *t.k.h: impeded 1st: prom tl rdn and lost tch w ldng trio sn after 2 out: plugged on flat* **14/1**
5 12 **The Mythologist (IRE)**[130] 7-11-1 0.......... RichardJohnson 95
(Tim Vaughan) *tall rngy chser type: led at modest pce and nt a fluent: hdd 2 out and rapidly lost pl* **6/1**[3]
PP- **6** 29 **Berry De Carjac (FR)**[200] 4107 4-10-13 0..........(t) JamesBest 65
(Nigel Hawke) *hld up towards rr: lost tch bef 3 out: sn t.o* **66/1**
P-0 **7** 13 **L'Es Fremantle (FR)**[12] 1260 4-10-8 0.......... JoeCornwall[(5)] 54
(Michael Chapman) *nt fluent 4th: chsd ldrs tl rdn after 6th: blnd bdly next and continued t.o* **200/1**
/FF- **P** **Just Lewis**[124] 8-10-8 0.......... WilliamFeatherstone[(7)]
(Nikki Evans) *wnt cl up after 4th tl rdn bef 3 out: fdd v tamely: t.o and p.u last* **200/1**
6-0 **P** **Kayf Tiger**[34] 1101 6-11-1 0.......... CharliePoste
(Robin Dickin) *nt jump wl in rr: labouring 4th: t.o after next: p.u after 2 out* **50/1**

4m 33.8s (2.30) **Going Correction** -0.075s/f (Good)
WFA 4 from 5yo+ 13lb **9 Ran SP% 122.5**
Speed ratings (Par 105): **92,84,81,81,76 64,59, ,**
CSF £16.71 TOTE £2.10: £1.02, £3.20, £1.30; EX 14.50 Trifecta £52.80.
Owner G Thompson **Bred** Christoph Berglar **Trained** Nicholashayne, Devon

FOCUS
All bends moved on to fresh ground. Shared bend by the 2m start. The Chase track used the inside line while the following distances were added to the hurdles track: Races 1 & 6 - 99 yards, race 3 - 72 yards, race 5 - 108 yards. They went a very steady initial pace in this modest maiden hurdle. Afterwards both Tom Scudamore and Aidan Coleman described the ground as "good to soft". The winner stood out in this grade. There's a case for rating the race up to 7lb higher through the third, but not on time compared with the last race.

1380 HAPPY BIRTHDAY DI NOVICES' H'CAP CHASE (17 fncs) 2m 6f 125y
2:40 (2:40) (Class 5) (0-100,100) 4-Y-O+ **£2,599** (£763; £381; £190)

Form RPR
5-P1 **1** **Sgt Bull Berry**[11] 1272 8-9-7 **74** oh1.......... JamieHamilton[(7)] 82+
(Peter Maddison) *tall rngy: settled towards rr: effrt 14th: hit next: styd on dourly whn drvn fr 2 out: wnt 5 l 2nd at last: v game effrt to ld cl home* **5/1**
4/00 **2** 1/2 **Koultas King (IRE)**[32] 1113 8-11-12 **100**..........(t) MichaelByrne 108+
(Tim Vaughan) *2nd mostly: mstke 3 out: rdn next: led bef last: urged along and ct nr fin* **20/1**
0-00 **3** 3 1/2 **Court Of Law (IRE)**[35] 1086 7-11-2 **90**.......... WayneHutchinson 93
(Donald McCain) *trckd ldrs: effrt 14th: led and looked gng wl bef next: 4 l clr but rdn 2 out: hdd bef last: plodded on in 3rd after* **16/1**
-535 **4** 8 **Tribal Dance (IRE)**[28] 1155 9-11-1 **89**..........(p) DaveCrosse 87
(John O'Shea) *led: drvn 12th: hdd bef 3 out: dropped out tamely to 4th and mstke next: mstke last* **14/1**
6-25 **5** 11 **Top Chief**[31] 1118 7-11-7 **95**..........(t) AidanColeman 81
(Anthony Honeyball) *chsd ldrs tl drvn and dropped himself to rr 12th: nt travelling after and wl bhd 14th* **11/4**[2]
6-24 **6** 3 1/2 **Sand Artist (IRE)**[8] 1287 7-10-4 **78**..........(t) RichardJohnson 61
(Gordon Elliott, Ire) *nt a fluent: chsd ldrs tl wknd and mstke 13th: sn wl bhd* **2/1**[1]
P241 **P** **Sylvan Legend**[14] 1243 7-10-9 **83**..........(tp) MarkQuinlan
(Neil Mulholland) *hit 6th and 8th: last and bad mstke next: fnd nil after: t.o and p.u 14th* **9/2**[3]

5m 44.7s (5.50) **Going Correction** -0.025s/f (Good) **7 Ran SP% 112.2**
Speed ratings (Par 103): **89,88,87,84,81 79,**
CSF £73.95 TOTE £6.10: £2.80, £5.60; EX 80.00 Trifecta £865.30.
Owner Peter Maddison **Bred** P Maddison **Trained** Skewsby, N Yorks

FOCUS
The pace was solid in this novice handicap and the form ought to work out. The fourth has been rated close to his mark.

1381 GEORGE PRAGNELL H'CAP HURDLE (8 hdls) 2m 70y
3:10 (3:10) (Class 3) (0-140,138) 3-Y-O+ **£5,523** (£1,621; £810; £405)

Form RPR
212 **1** **Lilac Tree**[6] 1308 5-10-8 **120**.......... AidanColeman 127+
(John Ferguson) *settled trcking ldrs: effrt 3 out: led gng best between last two: sn shkn up: 4 l clr and ears pricked whn hit last: won w smething in hand* **11/8**[1]
532- **2** 1 3/4 **Desert Recluse (IRE)**[130] 5404 8-10-11 **123**.......... JamesDavies 125
(Henry Oliver) *settled cl up: rdn to ld 2 out: hdd between last two: no imp on wnr but stuck on gamely despite hitting last* **7/1**
05-4 **3** 10 **Royal Irish Hussar (IRE)**[72] 317 5-11-12 **138**..........(p) DavidBass 132
(Nicky Henderson) *led and t.k.h early: 5 l clr whn hit 5th: drvn and hdd 2 out: wl hld 3rd and awkward hd carriage fr bef last* **3/1**[2]
-141 **4** 35 **Good Of Luck**[46] 973 6-11-3 **129**..........(p) GavinSheehan 90
(Warren Greatrex) *pressed ldr: rdn and lost pl bef 3 out: wnt rt whn struggling next: sn t.o* **7/2**[3]

5 32 **Alf Wright (IRE)**[468] 324 9-10-13 **125** .... JamesBest 57
(Philip Hobbs) *a in last: rdn bef 3 out: sn t.o* **11/1**

3m 50.7s (-5.30) **Going Correction** -0.075s/f (Good) **5** Ran SP% **110.2**
Speed ratings (Par 107): **110,109,104,86,70**
CSF £10.71 TOTE £2.00: £1.10, £3.30; EX 10.70 Trifecta £24.10.
Owner Bloomfields **Bred** Biddestone Stud Ltd **Trained** Cowlinge, Suffolk

FOCUS
A decent little handicap run at a fair pace. A small hurdle pb from the second, with the third rated 6lb off.

1382 PAUL WEBBER RACING H'CAP CHASE (14 fncs) 2m 3f 98y
3:40 (3:40) (Class 3) (0-140,138) 4-Y-O+ **£6,498** (£1,908; £954; £477)

Form RPR

520- 1 **Al Alfa**[166] 4752 8-11-0 **126** .... RichardJohnson 134+
(Philip Hobbs) *j. soundly: mde all: rdn 4 l clr bef last: drvn and styd on stoutly flat* **13/8**[1]

-553 2 4 ½ **Witness In Court (IRE)**[30] 1135 8-11-12 **138** .... WayneHutchinson 142
(Donald McCain) *cl up: wnt 2nd sn after 2 out: rdn and no imp on wnr fr bef last* **7/1**[3]

F0P- 3 18 **Dresden (IRE)**[124] 5540 7-11-9 **135** .... JamesDavies 122
(Henry Oliver) *pressed wnr fr 3rd: outj. 3 out and drvn next: sn btn in 3rd* **9/4**[2]

-010 4 2 ½ **Wings Of Smoke (IRE)**[40] 1040 10-11-11 **137** ....(t) MichaelByrne 122
(Tim Vaughan) *a towards rr: rdn 11th: wknd bef 2 out* **10/1**

P430 5 2 **Lookslikerainted (IRE)**[12] 1265 8-10-9 **124** ....(tp) KillianMoore(3) 108
(Sophie Leech) *towards rr: drvn and outpcd 10th: rallied next: lost tch bef 2 out* **14/1**

114 P **Red Seventy**[30] 1135 6-10-12 **124** .... JackQuinlan
(Sarah Humphrey) *cl up tl nt fluent 7th (water): lost pl and nt fluent next: last whn mstke 9th and rdn: nt run on: t.o 11th: p.u last* **15/2**

4m 44.6s (-5.40) **Going Correction** -0.025s/f (Good) **6** Ran SP% **108.9**
Speed ratings (Par 107): **110,108,100,99,98**
CSF £12.20 TOTE £2.50: £1.80, £1.80; EX 7.60 Trifecta £31.80.
Owner James Drummond **Bred** Countess Goess-Saurau **Trained** Withycombe, Somerset

FOCUS
A fair handicap chase in which the winner made all. Arguably a small pb from the winner.

1383 MURPHY SALISBURY H'CAP HURDLE (11 hdls) 2m 6f 7y
4:10 (4:10) (Class 5) (0-100,100) 4-Y-O+ **£2,599** (£763; £381; £190)

Form RPR

4P0/ 1 **Duke's Affair**[493] 5432 7-10-3 **80** .... MattGriffiths(3) 90+
(Jeremy Scott) *on his toes at s: plld hrd in last: mstke 7th: effrt after 3 out: 5th and rdn but styng on next: kpt on to ld last: sn in command despite idling sltly flat* **4/1**[2]

5-2P 2 1 ¼ **Hassadin**[34] 1098 9-11-1 **89** ....(p) NickScholfield 94
(Michael Blake) *led at stdy pce tl 5th: pressed ldr: drvn after 2 out: led bef last where hdd: v one pce flat* **9/1**

0-60 3 1 ½ **Spending Time**[15] 1236 6-11-8 **96** ....(t) TomScudamore 100
(David Pipe) *pressed ldrs: cl 4th after 2 out: sn rdn: remained w ev ch tl fnd little bef last: plugged on* **5/1**[3]

2211 4 9 **The Kvilleken**[25] 1182 7-11-12 **100** ....(p) AndrewTinkler 98
(Martin Keighley) *hit 1st: hld up last but one tl 8th: effrt gng wl in 3rd after 2 out: sn rdn: kpt covered up on heels of ldrs tl reluctant to go through bef last: sn btn* **11/4**[1]

P/P0 5 10 **Haughtons Bridge (IRE)**[15] 1236 7-11-5 **93** .... NicodeBoinville 80
(Martin Hill) *cl 2nd tl led 5th: rdn and hdd bef last: lost pl tamely* **4/1**[2]

UP/5 6 7 **Sutton Storm**[15] 1236 10-10-7 **88** .... MrMLegg(7) 73
(John Ryall) *pressed ldrs but hit several flights: rdn and wkng whn j. slowly 2 out* **11/1**

5600 7 2 **Micras**[31] 1120 4-11-0 **90** ....(b[1]) MichaelByrne 67
(Tim Vaughan) *mstkes in midfield: rdn befor 3 out: sn lost tch* **20/1**

-P56 8 42 **Massachusetts**[31] 1119 8-9-11 **74** oh3........(bt) KillianMoore(3) 15
(Rob Summers) *in tch tl dropped bk last bef 3 out: sn t.o* **14/1**

5m 28.8s (0.70) **Going Correction** -0.075s/f (Good)
WFA 4 from 6yo+ 14lb **8** Ran SP% **113.1**
Speed ratings (Par 103): **95,94,94,90,87 84,83,68**
CSF £37.72 CT £181.33 TOTE £4.70: £1.10, £3.40, £2.00; EX 60.60 Trifecta £246.00.
Owner Mrs Helen L Stoneman **Bred** Mrs J Munnis And Mrs E Hockenhull **Trained** Brompton Regis, Somerset

FOCUS
There were five still in contention heading to the final flight. Ordinary form. The second and third set the level in a straightforward handicap.

1384 JENKINSONS CATERERS MARES' H'CAP HURDLE (9 hdls) 2m 2f 148y
4:40 (4:40) (Class 5) (0-100,100) 3-Y-O+ **£2,599** (£763; £381; £190)

Form RPR

2-30 1 **Hope's Wishes**[77] 704 5-11-4 **95** .... JamesBanks(3) 100+
(Barry Brennan) *cl up: led jst after 2 out: sn rdn: 3 l clr last: kpt up to work whn in control flat* **11/1**

34-P 2 3 ¼ **Izzy Piccolina (IRE)**[85] 597 7-11-5 **93** .... MarkGrant 95
(Geoffrey Deacon) *hld up and bhd: prog whn veered and nrly hit doll after 2 out: 6 l 3rd and rdn home turn: wnt 2nd bef last but nvr making much imp on wnr* **25/1**

0-40 3 2 **Jeans Lady**[58] 860 6-11-7 **95** .... RichardJohnson 94
(Martin Keighley) *chsd ldrs: disp btn 4th and rdn home turn: lft 3rd at last: plugged on* **10/1**

4 20 **Think Of Me (IRE)**[94] 476 6-11-4 **92** .... AlainCawley 73
(Fergal O'Brien) *settled towards rr: prog 3 out: disp 4th and rdn home turn: sn wknd* **11/2**[3]

C332 5 ¾ **Auld Fyffee (IRE)**[7] 1294 3-10-0 **94** .... JamesDavies 55
(Tom Gretton) *small: disp 2nd tl rdn and dropped out rapidly 2 out* **7/2**[1]

42-5 6 ¾ **Mrs Burbidge**[35] 1084 5-10-1 **75** ....(tp) MarkQuinlan 55
(Neil Mulholland) *midfield: rdn 2 out: sn btn* **9/2**[2]

/325 7 2 ½ **Rose Red**[34] 1095 8-10-13 **87** .... JamesBest 65
(Rob Summers) *midfield: drvn bef 3 out: struggling after* **9/1**

06U 8 15 **Arthur's Queen (FR)**[15] 1234 4-11-7 **97** .... MichealNolan 59
(Carroll Gray) *midfield: rdn after 6th: sn struggling: t.o* **16/1**

P5/0 9 nk **Kheskianto (IRE)**[9] 1261 9-10-9 **88** ....(t) JoeCornwall(5) 52
(Michael Chapman) *last mostly: rdn and mstke 6th: t.o 2 out* **100/1**

-340 U **Fairy Alisha**[27] 1166 7-11-5 **100** .... JoshWall(7) 99
(Trevor Wall) *hld up and bhd: smooth prog 3 out: wnt cl 2nd after next: rdn and wknd bef last and clipped it and rdr c adrift whn 4 l 3rd* **10/1**

40-3 P **Ovilia (IRE)**[34] 1096 6-10-11 **85** .... WayneHutchinson
(Donald McCain) *led: rdn and hdd jst after 2 out: lost pl rapidly: sn eased: t.o and p.u last* **7/1**

0-60 P **Thymeandthymeagain**[91] 528 6-10-10 **84** .... DaveCrosse
(Hugo Froud) *cl up: lost pl 6th: t.o 3 out: p.u after next* **50/1**

4m 37.5s (6.00) **Going Correction** -0.075s/f (Good)
WFA 3 from 4yo 19lb 4 from 5yo+ 13lb **12** Ran SP% **117.5**
Speed ratings (Par 103): **84,82,81,73,73 72,71,65,65, ,**
CSF £232.73 CT £2819.24 TOTE £11.70: £3.50, £9.00, £2.80; EX 372.10 Trifecta £1342.30.
Owner M J Hills **Bred** Edward Spurrier **Trained** Upper Lambourn, Berks

FOCUS
This very moderate mares' handicap began in a heavy downpour. They went a reasonable gallop. A small pb from the winner, with small steps up from the second and third.
T/Plt: £2,047.10 to a £1 stake. Pool: £55,245.51 - 19.70 winning tickets T/Qpdt: £95.90 to a £1 stake. Pool: £4,264.94 - 32.90 winning tickets **Iain Mackenzie**

1385 - 1398a (Foreign Racing) - See Raceform Interactive

[1065] CARTMEL (L-H)
Saturday, August 29

OFFICIAL GOING: Good to soft (good in places)
Wind: fresh 1/2 behind Weather: mainly fine and sunny

1399 E-CATERING NOVICES' HURDLE (8 hdls) 2m 1f 46y
2:05 (2:05) (Class 4) 4-Y-O+ **£3,249** (£954; £477; £238)

Form RPR

1 1 **Altruism (IRE)**[40] 1065 5-11-2 0 .... RichardJohnson 124+
(James Moffatt) *t.k.h in rr: hdwy to trck ldrs 3rd: led bef 3 out: rdn clr fnl f* **7/4**[2]

23-1 2 12 **Scrafton**[27] 1178 4-11-1 124 .... BrianHughes 111
(John Quinn) *trckd ldrs: in 2nd 2 out: sn rdn: kpt on same pce run-in* **1/1**[1]

P0- 3 5 **Stanley (GER)**[174] 4654 4-10-9 0 ....(t) WayneHutchinson 102
(Donald McCain) *hld up in rr: hdwy to trck ldrs 5th: 3rd 2 out: kpt on one pce* **11/1**

53 4 11 **King Of Fashion (IRE)**[58] 887 5-10-7 0 .... GrahamWatters(3) 90
(Ian Duncan) *chsd ldrs: wknd and modest 4th between last 2* **16/1**

0054 5 7 **Tokyo Brown (USA)**[40] 1065 6-10-5 92 ....(p) DiarmuidO'Regan(5) 83
(James Moffatt) *led: hdd bef 3 out: wknd between last 2* **12/1**

F/P- 6 9 **Stormont Bridge**[39] 1548 7-10-0 0 ....(t) ThomasDowson(10) 74
(Maurice Barnes) *mid-div: drvn 5th: lost pl 2 out* **100/1**

U- 7 35 **Killiecrankie**[188] 4387 7-10-10 0 .... HenryBrooke 39
(Kenneth Slack) *t.k.h in rr: nt fluent 3rd: bhd fr 2 out: sn t.o* **8/1**[3]

0 8 4 **Sheriff's Star (IRE)**[48] 978 4-10-2 0 .... LiamMcKenna(7) 34
(J J Lambe, Ire) *nt jump wl: mid-div: lost pl 5th: bhd 2 out: sn t.o* **25/1**

4m 9.7s (-3.50) **Going Correction** -0.125s/f (Good)
WFA 4 from 5yo+ 13lb **8** Ran SP% **124.2**
Speed ratings (Par 105): **103,97,95,89,86 82,65,63**
CSF £4.46 TOTE £2.40: £1.10, £1.10, £2.90; EX 4.60 Trifecta £19.50.
Owner V R Vyner-Brooks, K Bowron **Bred** Kevin & Meta Cullen **Trained** Cartmel, Cumbria

FOCUS
Rail at innermost configuration and distances as advertised. The meeting started with an interesting novice hurdle. Easy winner built on CD win and could arguably be rated a stone higher, but time slow.

1400 HADWINS H'CAP HURDLE (11 hdls) 2m 6f 31y
2:40 (2:40) (Class 5) (0-100,100) 4-Y-O+ **£2,599** (£763; £381; £190)

Form RPR

0232 1 **Johnny Go**[7] 1329 5-11-4 **97** .... CallumBewley(5) 104+
(Lisa Harrison) *trckd ldrs: upsides 2 out: led sn after last: pushed 3 l clr: idled last 75yds: kpt rt up to work* **11/4**[1]

2-46 2 ¾ **Marlee Massie (IRE)**[83] 658 6-10-3 **77** ....(p) LucyAlexander 80
(N W Alexander) *led tl after 2nd: upsides ldr: led 8th: jnd last: sn hdd: rallied last 50yds: jst hld* **14/1**

-304 3 1 ¼ **Maybe I Wont**[40] 1067 10-11-12 **100** .... TomScudamore 102
(James Moffatt) *hld up in rr: hdwy 7th: chsng ldrs 3 out: kpt on and 3rd last 75yds* **11/2**[3]

U425 4 1 ½ **Bouggietopieces**[25] 1199 5-11-9 **97** .... RichardJohnson 99
(Gordon Elliott, Ire) *hld up in rr: hdwy after 8th: chsng ldrs 2 out: kpt on same pce run-in* **4/1**[2]

15-4 5 4 **Burnt Sienna (IRE)**[14] 482 5-11-3 **94** ....(tp) DerekFox(3) 91
(Noel C Kelly, Ire) *mid-div: lost pl 6th: hdwy 3 out: one pce fr next* **6/1**

P403 6 12 **Cumbrian Farmer**[59] 870 8-9-13 **78** ....(tp) GaryRutherford(5) 64
(George Bewley) *chsd ldrs: drvn 7th: wknd between last 2* **20/1**

0536 7 14 **Morning With Ivan (IRE)**[29] 1170 5-11-10 **98** .... HenryBrooke 74
(Martin Todhunter) *in rr: hdwy after 7th: lost pl 2 out* **11/1**

P660 8 6 **Allycat**[7] 1329 5-10-12 **86** ....(b[1]) WayneHutchinson 54
(Chris Grant) *prom: hit 5th: lost pl 2 out* **20/1**

600 9 22 **Raifteiri (IRE)**[40] 1071 8-9-7 **74** oh1........(p) MrJDixon(7) 23
(William Young Jnr) *t.k.h: jnd ldr 2nd: sn led: hdd 8th: sn lost pl and bhd: t.o between last 2* **20/1**

6P13 10 10 **Izbushka (IRE)**[47] 838 4-10-12 **88** ....(b) BrianHughes 26
(David Thompson) *chsd ldrs: reminders 7th: lost pl 3 out: sn bhd: t.o between last 2* **8/1**

U500 P **Erica Starprincess**[40] 1066 5-10-4 **81** .... AdamNicol(3)
(George Moore) *in rr: bhd whn p.u bef 3 out: lame* **20/1**

5m 30.0s (0.70) **Going Correction** -0.125s/f (Good)
WFA 4 from 5yo+ 14lb **11** Ran SP% **120.6**
Speed ratings (Par 103): **93,92,92,91,90 85,80,78,70,67**
CSF £38.39 CT £205.89 TOTE £3.70: £1.40, £4.50, £2.10; EX 51.20 Trifecta £590.80.
Owner J B Harrison **Bred** J B Harrison **Trained** Aldoth, Cumbria

FOCUS
A moderate contest, with few of these coming into this off a decent effort. Big improvement by winner with third and fourth setting the level.

1401 BURLINGTON STONE EBF STALLIONS BEGINNERS' CHASE (14 fncs) 2m 5f 34y
3:15 (3:15) (Class 4) 4-Y-O+ **£3,768** (£1,106; £553; £276)

Form RPR

3232 1 **Volcanic (FR)**[36] 1097 6-11-7 123 ....(t) WayneHutchinson 128+
(Donald McCain) *w ldr: led after 2nd: drvn clr last: reminders over 2f out: drvn rt out* **1/1**[1]

3P20 2 8 **Silk Hall (UAE)**[23] 1203 10-11-7 122 ....(p) RichardJohnson 122
(J J Lambe, Ire) *led tl after 2nd: chsd wnr: j.lft and mstke 7th: j.lft 2 out: outpcd last: rallied 2f out: kpt on same pce* **11/4**[3]

2-42 3 21 **Clues And Arrows (IRE)**[40] 1068 7-11-7 0 .... BrianHughes 102
(John Wade) *wnt modest 3rd 8th: drvn 10th: lost pl 3 out* **9/4**[2]

-150 4 41 **Y A Bon (IRE)**[30] 1158 7-11-7 0 ....(b) LeeEdwards 63
(Aytach Sadik) *nt jump wl in rr: t.o 8th: distant 4th last* **33/1**

6004 **5** *12* **Bobonyx**[6] 1343 5-11-0 0 ThomasCheesman(7) 52
(Dai Williams) *chsd ldng pair to 8th: drvn next: sn lost pl and bhd: t.o 10th* **150/1**

/32- **P** **Mystified (IRE)**[458] 503 12-11-7 74 BrianHarding
(Alan Berry) *in rr: bhd fr 4th: t.o 8th: p.u bef 10th* **40/1**

5m 18.4s (-7.00) **Going Correction** -0.125s/f (Good) **6** Ran SP% **113.5**
Speed ratings (Par 105): **108,104,96,81,76**
CSF £4.44 TOTE £2.00: £1.20, £2.00; EX 4.10 Trifecta £6.90.
Owner Elite Racing Club **Bred** Guy Cherel And Emmanuel Cherel **Trained** Cholmondeley, Cheshire

FOCUS
Only three of the field made serious appeal, and they ended up coming miles clear of the rest. First three home in line with previous chase form.

1402 GRANT THORNTON H'CAP CHASE (14 fncs) 2m 5f 34y
3:50 (3:50) (Class 5) (0-100,97) 4-Y-0+ **£3,249** (£954; £477; £238)

Form RPR

P-05 **1** **Bayfirth (IRE)**[40] 1068 12-9-7 71 oh5 MrWHRReed(7) 84+
(R Mike Smith) *w ldr: led bef 3rd: hdd 2 out: rallied to regain ld 3f out: drvn clr fnl f* **10/3**[2]

-606 **2** *9* **The Omen**[41] 1045 9-11-4 89 MichaelByrne 94
(Tim Vaughan) *stdd s: hld up in rr: hdwy 10th: 2nd next: led 2 out: hdd 3f out: wknd fnl f* **9/1**

416- **3** *2* **Lord Fox (IRE)**[139] 5287 8-10-13 87 JonathanEngland(3) 90
(Shaun Harris) *hld up in rr: hdwy 10th: 3rd sn after last: one pce* **4/1**[3]

3-60 **4** *9* **Xenophon**[14] 1265 7-9-8 72 ThomasCheesman(7) 68
(Michael Chapman) *led tl bef 3rd: chsd ldr: hit 8th: outpcd 3 out: wknd last* **14/1**

-235 **5** *7* **Cara Court (IRE)**[64] 841 9-10-3 74 (p) HenryBrooke 63
(Joanne Foster) *chsd ldrs: drvn 4 out: wknd last* **3/1**[1]

3314 **6** *5* **Pistol Basc (FR)**[30] 1155 11-11-3 91 TonyKelly(3) 77
(Rebecca Menzies) *chsd ldrs: lost pl 3 out* **9/2**

PP3- **7** *76* **Azerodegree (IRE)**[294] 2346 6-10-8 84 CallumBewley(5)
(Harriet Graham) *prom: drvn 5th: lost pl 9th: hit next: sn bhd: t.o 3 out: eventually completed* **12/1**

5m 23.2s (-2.20) **Going Correction** -0.125s/f (Good) **7** Ran SP% **110.6**
Speed ratings (Par 103): **99,95,94,91,88 86,57**
CSF £29.14 CT £115.76 TOTE £4.40: £2.40, £4.00; EX 41.10 Trifecta £224.60.
Owner A B Hamilton **Bred** Pat Browne **Trained** Galston, E Ayrshire

FOCUS
Nothing more than a run-of-the-mill low-grade handicap. Winner rated in line with recent CD run in stronger race. Runner-up close to best mark.

1403 TOTEPOOL RACING'S BIGGEST SUPPORTER H'CAP CHASE (FOR THE SADIK MEMORIAL TROPHY) (18 fncs) 3m 1f 107y
4:25 (4:26) (Class 4) (0-105,103) 4-Y-0+ **£4,418** (£1,297; £648; £324)

Form RPR

3-46 **1** **Urban Gale (IRE)**[40] 1069 10-10-9 86 (p) HenryBrooke 96+
(Joanne Foster) *mde all: drvn rt out* **9/2**

3120 **2** *3 ¾* **Troubled (IRE)**[45] 1004 8-10-3 80 (p) LeeEdwards 87
(Aytach Sadik) *chsd wnr thrght: outpcd sn after last: rallied over 1f out: kpt on same pce* **8/1**

5200 **3** *16* **Mission Complete (IRE)**[14] 1264 9-11-11 102 (tp) RichardJohnson 98
(Jonjo O'Neill) *in rr: hdwy to chse ldrs 10th: drvn 13th: lft 3rd 3 out: wknd last* **7/2**[2]

2134 **4** *22* **Solway Legend**[7] 1330 8-10-13 90 BrianHughes 73
(Lisa Harrison) *trckd ldng pair 6th: 3rd and drvn whn blnd 3 out: sn wknd* **3/1**[1]

PP **5** *24* **Imperial Vic (IRE)**[81] 676 10-11-9 103 JonathanEngland(3) 54
(Harriet Bethell) *chsd ldrs: lost pl and reminders 8th: brief effrt 13th: sn lost pl and bhd* **11/1**

4424 **6** *22* **The Society Man (IRE)**[42] 1032 8-10-13 95 JoeCornwall(5) 26
(Michael Chapman) *chsd ldrs: outpcd 10th: lost pl 13th: sn bhd* **8/1**

P662 **P** **Generous Chief (IRE)**[40] 1069 7-10-12 94 (b) DiarmuidO'Regan(5)
(Chris Grant) *hit 1st: in tch: drvn and lost pl 12th: bhd 4 out: t.o last p.u bef last: b.b.v* **4/1**[3]

6m 33.5s (-1.40) **Going Correction** -0.125s/f (Good) **7** Ran SP% **116.0**
Speed ratings (Par 105): **97,95,90,83,75 68,**
CSF £38.84 TOTE £5.20: £2.40, £4.50; EX 49.70 Trifecta £260.50.
Owner P Foster **Bred** M Wiseman **Trained** Menston, W Yorks

FOCUS
This was dominated by the two lowest-weighted runners in the field, who raced prominently pretty much throughout. Winner well-in on 2014 chase form and capable of better still.

1404 TOTEPOOL CARTMEL CUP (HANDICAP HURDLE) (8 hdls) 2m 1f 46y
4:55 (4:57) (Class 3) (0-130,125) 3-Y-0+
£6,256 (£1,848; £924; £462; £231; £116)

Form RPR

-305 **1** **Captain Brown**[42] 1035 7-11-0 118 DiarmuidO'Regan(5) 125
(James Moffatt) *in rr: hdwy 3 out: handy 3rd appr last: led 2f out: drvn out* **10/1**

14-1 **2** *3 ¼* **Chebsey Beau**[15] 1170 5-11-5 125 DeanPratt(7) 129
(John Quinn) *trckd ldrs: led last: sn hdd and no ex* **10/3**[2]

2231 **3** *5* **Miss Macnamara (IRE)**[7] 1165 6-10-6 105 HenryBrooke 105
(Martin Todhunter) *chsd clr ldr: lft in ld bnd sn after 4th: hdd last: kpt on one pce* **5/1**[3]

41U **4** *10* **Fantasy King**[23] 830 9-11-2 115 TomScudamore 106
(James Moffatt) *in rr: hdwy 5th: one pce fr 2 out* **15/2**

3210 **5** *6* **Chilly Miss**[29] 1170 6-11-2 115 BrianHughes 100
(Malcolm Jefferson) *chsd ldrs: lft 2nd sn after 5th: wknd sn after last* **8/1**

-5U1 **6** *35* **Honey Pound (IRE)**[17] 1238 7-11-11 124 RichardJohnson 88
(Tim Vaughan) *chsd ldrs: lft 3rd sn after 5th: wknd 2 out* **3/1**[1]

545/ **7** *17* **Dartford Warbler (IRE)**[504] 5272 8-10-6 115 StephenMcCarthy(10) 53
(Sue Smith) *prom: lost pl 4th: sn bhd: t.o 3 out* **11/1**

0-34 **U** **May's Boy**[42] 1034 7-10-1 107 (p) MissRMcDonald(7)
(James Moffatt) *in rr: hdwy 5th: sn outpcd: modest 7th whn mstke 2 out: 6th and keeping on whn blnd bdly and uns rdr last* **12/1**

050- **P** **Spot The Pro (IRE)**[23] 2973 6-10-10 112 (v[1]) TonyKelly(3)
(Rebecca Menzies) *best away: set str pce and sn clr: reluctant: hung bdly lft and hdd bnd sn after 5th: nt keen and sn t.o: p.u after next: b.b.v* **28/1**

4m 7.7s (-5.50) **Going Correction** -0.125s/f (Good) **9** Ran SP% **116.2**
Speed ratings (Par 107): **107,105,103,98,95 79,71,,**
CSF £44.57 CT £190.51 TOTE £13.30: £3.00, £1.60, £2.00; EX 58.60 Trifecta £334.50.
Owner K Bowron **Bred** Mr & Mrs A E Pakenham **Trained** Cartmel, Cumbria

FOCUS
Some in-form types lined up for this handicap, and it was run at a reasonably gallop, even though the field pretty much ignored tearaway leader \bSpot The Pro\p. PB for winner and second's effort in line with recent Flat run.

1405 EWGA RACING EXCELLENCE "HANDS AND HEELS" H'CAP HURDLE (FOR CONDITIONAL JOCKEYS & AMATEUR RIDERS) (8 hdls) 2m 1f 46y
5:30 (5:30) (Class 5) (0-100,100) 3-Y-0+ **£2,599** (£763; £381; £190)

Form RPR

6-04 **1** **Carnaross**[27] 1182 6-11-0 88 (t) MrZBaker 102+
(Julia Brooke) *prom: chsng ldrs 5th: led sn after 2 out: drew clr fnl 2f* **10/3**[2]

6-36 **2** *12* **King's Chorister**[19] 731 9-10-6 83 (t) LorcanMurtagh(3) 83
(Barry Murtagh) *in rr: hdwy to chse ldrs 5th: 2nd sn after 2 out: kpt on same pce run-in* **14/1**

5PFP **3** *12* **Redpender (IRE)**[40] 1069 9-11-6 97 MissRMcDonald(3) 86
(James Moffatt) *hld up detached in last: hdwy 3 out: 4th appr last: one pce and modest 3rd nr fin* **12/1**

45-P **4** *hd* **Most Honourable**[15] 1257 5-11-8 99 HarryCobden(3) 88
(John Joseph Hanlon, Ire) *chsd ldrs: 3rd and drvn sn after 2 out: wknd fnl 2f* **9/4**[1]

26P4 **5** *3 ½* **Descaro (USA)**[9] 1299 9-11-3 96 (bt) MrDSymes-Meineck(5) 82
(Fergal O'Brien) *w ldrs: led 2nd: hdd briefly 5th: hdd sn after 2 out: wknd last* **10/1**

3663 **6** *2 ½* **Short Takes (USA)**[54] 929 7-11-9 100 (b) MrTGillard(3) 84
(Donald McCain) *chsd ldrs: hung rt sn after 4th: sn drvn: lost pl between last 2* **8/1**

5531 **7** *31* **Ardesia (IRE)**[40] 1071 11-10-1 78 (p) FinianO'Toole(3) 34
(Tina Jackson) *led to 2nd: w ldr: drvn 5th: lost pl next: sn wl bhd: t.o* **5/1**[3]

333 **8** *23* **Danmurphysdoor (IRE)**[9] 1295 6-11-7 98 (t) MrEDavid(3) 33
(Tim Vaughan) *trckd ldrs: t.k.h: led briefly 5th: wknd qckly between last 2: sn wl bhd: tailed rt off* **17/2**

4m 12.9s (-0.30) **Going Correction** -0.125s/f (Good) **8** Ran SP% **115.6**
Speed ratings (Par 103): **95,89,83,83,81 80,66,55**
CSF £46.22 CT £501.32 TOTE £4.40: £1.30, £2.90, £4.00; EX 38.90 Trifecta £886.60.
Owner Chrissy's Passion Racing & Nobaj Ltd **Bred** Mrs L M Edwards **Trained** Middleham, North Yorks

FOCUS
A moderate event but the winner won with authority. Easy winner improving in line with bumper form; runner-up close to best mark.
T/Plt: £234.80 to a £1 stake. Pool: £60,927.14 - 189.40 winning tickets T/Qpdt: £85.20 to a £1 stake. Pool: £2,637.68 - 22.90 winning tickets **Walter Glynn**

1406 - 1413a (Foreign Racing) - See Raceform Interactive

1399 CARTMEL (L-H)
Monday, August 31

OFFICIAL GOING: Good (good to soft in places)
Wind: light 1/2 behind Weather: fine

1414 CARTMEL 25TH ANNIVERSARY STICKY TOFFEE PUDDING NOVICES' HURDLE (11 hdls) 2m 6f 31y
2:15 (2:16) (Class 4) 4-Y-0+ **£3,249** (£954; £477; £238)

Form RPR

-142 **1** **Highpower (IRE)**[12] 1292 6-11-5 123 (v[1]) RichardJohnson 128+
(Jonjo O'Neill) *trckd ldng pair: t.k.h: upsides 2 out: led last: drvn clr over 1f out* **6/4**[1]

11U1 **2** *3 ½* **Sharp Rise (IRE)**[50] 957 8-11-12 130 JamesReveley 133
(Pauline Robson) *led: hit 6th: hdd last: styd on same pce* **2/1**[2]

311 **3** *22* **Classic Palace (IRE)**[44] 1030 6-11-5 130 BrianHughes 110
(J J Lambe, Ire) *trckd ldrs: drvn 3 out: wknd after next* **11/4**[3]

0545 **4** *43* **Tokyo Brown (USA)**[2] 1399 6-10-7 92 (p) DiarmuidO'Regan(5) 60
(James Moffatt) *chsd ldng trio: pushed along 6th: outpcd next: lost pl 8th: bhd 2 out: t.o* **14/1**

6PP- **P** **Kaylan's Rose**[324] 1850 5-10-5 0 HenryBrooke
(Dianne Sayer) *nt fluent in last: drvn 8th: sn lost pl and bhd: t.o whn p.u bef 2 out* **33/1**

5m 27.4s (-1.90) **Going Correction** -0.125s/f (Good) **5** Ran SP% **109.6**
Speed ratings (Par 105): **98,96,88,73,**
CSF £4.93 TOTE £2.40: £1.20, £1.50; EX 4.70 Trifecta £6.20.
Owner John P McManus **Bred** Oliver And Salome Brennan **Trained** Cheltenham, Gloucs

FOCUS
Rail moved out 3yds on both bends. Hurdles increased by 16yds per circuit and Chases by 4yds per circuit. The opening contest was a fair staying novices' hurdle. They went a respectable gallop on ground officially described as good, good to soft in places. A small step up from the winner.

1415 WICKS WASTE SERVICES JUVENILE HURDLE (8 hdls) 2m 1f 46y
2:50 (2:51) (Class 4) 3-Y-0 **£3,249** (£954; £477; £238)

Form RPR

5 **1** **Boldbob (IRE)**[29] 1177 3-10-2 0 FinianO'Toole(10) 99+
(Micky Hammond) *t.k.h: mde all: j.rt last: drvn rt out* **12/1**

2 **2** *1 ½* **Secrets Safe (IRE)**[19] 1232 3-10-12 0 (p) RichardJohnson 98
(John Joseph Hanlon, Ire) *chsd ldrs: 2nd 3 out: 3 l down whn mstke last: kpt on: nt rch wnr* **9/4**[2]

2 **3** *14* **Our Kylie (IRE)**[29] 1177 3-10-5 0 DenisO'Regan 79
(Tony Coyle) *chsd ldrs: shkn up 3rd: drvn 5th: 3rd bef 2 out: wknd run-in* **1/1**[1]

4 *8* **Sarafina**[11] 3-10-5 0 SeanQuinlan 70
(David Thompson) *hld up in rr: gd hdwy to trck ldrs 5th: wknd between last 2* **25/1**

5 *32* **Azyaan (IRE)**[63] 3-10-5 0 BrianHughes 41
(Kevin Ryan) *trckd wnr: hit 2nd: drvn 3 out: lost pl bef next: sn wl bhd: t.o* **5/1**[3]

6 *8* **Seraffimo**[104] 3-10-12 0 HenryBrooke 41
(Sharon Watt) *in rr: bhd fr 5th: t.o 2 out* **22/1**

4m 15.8s (2.60) **Going Correction** -0.125s/f (Good) **6** Ran SP% **113.3**
Speed ratings (Par 102): **88,87,80,76,61 58**
CSF £40.62 TOTE £16.30: £5.60, £1.70; EX 43.30 Trifecta £133.10.
Owner M H O G 2 **Bred** Matthew Duffy **Trained** Middleham, N Yorks

FOCUS
An ordinary juvenile hurdle. They went a proper gallop. A big step up from the winner, with the second on the upgrade.

1416 MICHAEL ENNIS MEMORIAL H'CAP CHASE (12 fncs) 2m 1f 61y
3:25 (3:25) (Class 4) (0-115,112) 4-Y-O+ £4,223 (£1,240; £620; £310)

Form RPR
-442 1 **Endeavor**[4] 1071 10-10-11 97 BrianHughes 107
(Dianne Sayer) *chsd ldrs: nt fluent 2nd: drvn 3 out: rallied run-in: led over 1f out: styd on* 7/2[2]
-3P3 2 2¾ **Kitchapoly (FR)**[44] 1043 5-11-7 112 JamesCowley(5) 119
(Donald McCain) *trckd ldrs: 2nd 3rd: led briefly 2f out: kpt on same pce fnl f* 9/4[1]
2-33 3 1¾ **Vinnie The Fish (IRE)**[42] 1070 7-11-10 110 (tp) RobertDunne 115
(Dai Burchell) *chsd ldrs 6th: upsides last: kpt on same pce fnl f* 9/4[1]
4120 4 1¼ **Claragh Native (IRE)**[31] 1169 10-11-12 112 HenryBrooke 116
(Martin Todhunter) *hld up last but wl in tch: trckd ldrs 14th: outpcd over 2f out: kpt on fnl f: tk 4th last 50yds* 15/2
6232 5 4½ **Sublime Talent (IRE)**[9] 1327 9-11-11 111 (t) PaulMoloney 113
(Evan Williams) *led: hdd 2f out: wknd fnl f* 11/2[3]
4m 28.1s (9.20) **Going Correction** +0.20s/f (Yiel) 5 Ran SP% 110.9
Speed ratings (Par 105): **86,84,83,83,81**
CSF £12.12 TOTE £3.20: £2.60, £2.00; EX 19.20 Trifecta £54.00.
Owner Mrs Margaret Coppola **Bred** Bradmill Meat Ltd **Trained** Hackthorpe, Cumbria
FOCUS
A modest handicap chase. They went quite steadily in the formative stages of this contest. The form is rated around the second and third.

1417 CORAL BOOKMAKERS CAVENDISH CUP H'CAP CHASE (18 fncs) 3m 1f 107y
4:00 (4:00) (Class 2) (0-150,144) 4-Y-O+
£11,573 (£3,418; £1,709; £854; £427; £214)

Form RPR
0P-1 1 **Dreamsoftheatre (IRE)**[10] 1309 7-10-9 127 (t) RichardJohnson 132+
(Jonjo O'Neill) *chsd ldrs: hit 7th: 2nd 3 out: sn drvn: styd on to ld last 50yds: jst hld on* 2/1[1]
-062 2 shd **Abolitionist (IRE)**[19] 1235 7-10-12 130 TomScudamore 134
(John Joseph Hanlon, Ire) *chsd ldrs 7th: 2nd 13th: mstke 3 out: styd on over 1f out: jst hld: fin lame* 9/4[2]
4/P- 3 hd **Danimix (IRE)**[204] 4110 10-9-11 118 (t) SeanBowen(3) 122
(Peter Bowen) *chsd ldrs: hit 10th: outpcd 14th: lost pl 3 out: styd on wl fnl 3f: handy 4th over 1f out: kpt on wl fin* 7/2[3]
0112 4 1¾ **Alderbrook Lad (IRE)**[15] 1268 9-11-2 144 FinianO'Toole(10) 146
(Micky Hammond) *led: hit 3 out: drvn clr 3f out: stl 4 l ahd 1f out: wknd and ct last 50yds* 15/2
5P-0 5 4½ **Baileys Concerto (IRE)**[11] 1035 9-11-3 135 BrianHughes 134+
(Dianne Sayer) *hld up in rr: hit 6th: handy 4th 14th: wknd over 1f out* 12/1
0-10 6 9 **Valleyofmilan (IRE)**[31] 1167 8-10-2 125 JamesCowley(5) 116
(Donald McCain) *chsd ldrs: outpcd 14th: bhd 3 out* 14/1
6m 32.8s (-2.10) **Going Correction** +0.20s/f (Yiel) 6 Ran SP% 112.4
Speed ratings (Par 109): **111,110,110,110,108 106**
CSF £7.28 TOTE £2.60: £2.00, £1.10; EX 7.40 Trifecta £17.80.
Owner John P McManus **Bred** Kieran Gleeson **Trained** Cheltenham, Gloucs
FOCUS
A decent staying handicap chase in which they went an even gallop. The winner is rated to the level of his recent win.

1418 MILLER HOWE HOTEL H'CAP CHASE (14 fncs) 2m 5f 34y
4:35 (4:38) (Class 3) (0-130,128) 4-Y-O+
£6,256 (£1,848; £924; £462; £231; £116)

Form RPR
-5P4 1 **Forever My Friend (IRE)**[36] 1114 8-10-3 108 (p) SeanBowen(3) 116+
(Peter Bowen) *mde all: j. boldly: drvn and styd on fr 3 out: unchal* 7/2[3]
1U4 2 3½ **Fantasy King**[2] 1404 9-11-3 124 DiarmuidO'Regan(5) 128
(James Moffatt) *hld up in rr but wl in tch: hit 8th: chsd ldrs 10th: 2nd sn after last: kpt on same pce over 1f out* 3/1[2]
-640 3 11 **Dursey Sound (IRE)**[86] 642 7-11-7 123 TomScudamore 117
(Jonjo O'Neill) *chsd ldrs: 2nd 11th: wknd fnl 2f* 11/4[1]
/4P1 4 7 **Cruchain (IRE)**[42] 1070 12-11-1 117 (p) RobertDunne 105
(Dai Burchell) *sn chsng wnr: outpcd 3 out: wknd next* 11/2
5-33 5 8 **Falcarragh (IRE)**[56] 927 8-11-12 128 RichardJohnson 113
(Tim Vaughan) *t.k.h in rr: nt fluent: mstke 3rd: blnd 9th: lost pl and bhd whn mstke 11th* 5/1
40-4 6 36 **Sudski Star (IRE)**[64] 849 7-11-2 118 (tp) BrianHughes 66
(Harriet Graham) *chsd ldrs: pushed along 9th: lost pl 11th: sn bhd: t.o whn eased over 1f out* 11/1
5m 24.2s (-1.20) **Going Correction** +0.20s/f (Yiel) 6 Ran SP% 114.3
Speed ratings (Par 107): **110,108,104,101,98 85**
CSF £15.10 CT £31.90 TOTE £5.00: £2.40, £1.70; EX 20.60 Trifecta £95.40.
Owner Mrs J H Docker **Bred** Eamon Fitzgerald **Trained** Little Newcastle, Pembrokes
FOCUS
A fair handicap chase. They went an even gallop once again. The winner is rated to the best of his chase figures in the last year.

1419 CORAL.CO.UK H'CAP HURDLE (12 hdls) 3m 1f 83y
5:10 (5:12) (Class 2) 4-Y-O+
£11,573 (£3,418; £1,709; £854; £427; £214)

Form RPR
12-0 1 **Goldan Jess (IRE)**[14] 1035 11-11-6 130 KyleJames(3) 136+
(Philip Kirby) *mde all: drvn 9th: styd on wl: unchal* 10/1
1202 2 9 **Street Entertainer (IRE)**[10] 1157 8-11-12 133 (bt) TomScudamore 131
(David Pipe) *hld up towards rr: hdwy 8th: hit next: 3rd 2 out: 2nd between last 2: no imp whn nt fluent last* 11/1
-532 3 18 **Handmaid**[16] 1264 6-10-8 118 (p) SeanBowen(3) 100
(Peter Bowen) *chsd ldrs: outpcd after 9th: kpt on clsng stages: tk poor 3rd nr line* 11/4[2]
3415 4 ½ **Lava Lamp (GER)**[35] 1119 8-10-8 120 ConorRing(5) 101
(Evan Williams) *chsd ldrs: 2nd after 9th: wknd between last 2: tired and lost poor 3rd nr line* 8/1
421 5 5 **Panis Angelicus (FR)**[11] 1295 6-10-4 111 RichardJohnson 88
(Tim Vaughan) *in rr: pushed along 8th: lost pl next* 9/4[1]
060- 6 12 **Bell Weir**[12] 5139 7-10-9 116 HenryBrooke 82
(Dianne Sayer) *trckd ldrs: effrt bef 3 out: sn lost pl and bhd* 16/1
UF-1 P **Decimus (IRE)**[59] 897 8-11-1 125 (p) MattGriffiths(3)
(Jeremy Scott) *nt fluent in rr: reminders 4th: reminders and lost pl 7th: sn bhd: t.o whn p.u after next* 5/1[3]

P **Oscar Fiain (IRE)**[131] 5484 7-10-5 112 MichaelByrne
(Tim Vaughan) *t.k.h in rr: drvn after 7th: bhd 9th: t.o whn p.u sn after 3 out* 14/1
6m 16.9s (-9.20) **Going Correction** -0.125s/f (Good) 8 Ran SP% 115.2
Speed ratings (Par 109): **109,106,100,100,98 94, ,**
CSF £108.00 CT £386.43 TOTE £11.00: £2.60, £2.60, £1.20; EX 74.80 Trifecta £316.00.
Owner The Jessies,Colin Fletcher,Brian Cobbett **Bred** Bendis Partnership **Trained** East Appleton, N Yorks
FOCUS
A fairly decent staying handicap hurdle. They went an honest gallop and the winner posted a pb.

1420 SWAN HOTEL & SPA MARES' H'CAP HURDLE (11 hdls) 2m 6f 31y
5:40 (5:41) (Class 4) (0-110,107) 4-Y-O+ £3,249 (£954; £477; £238)

Form RPR
/05- 1 **Binowagh Bay (IRE)**[27] 1197 7-10-13 97 (p) JeremiahMcGrath(3) 104+
(Brian M McMahon, Ire) *chsd ldrs: led last: drvn clr* 9/2[3]
4-15 2 11 **Samedi Soir**[55] 938 5-11-10 105 JamesReveley 103
(Keith Reveley) *trckd ldrs: led 4th: hdd last: kpt on same pce* 5/1
403- 3 3 **Mistress Mole (IRE)**[162] 4944 6-11-11 106 (p) RichardJohnson 100
(Gordon Elliott, Ire) *trckd ldrs: hit 2nd: one pce run-in* 11/4[1]
03-2 4 nk **Pixie Cut (IRE)**[7] 1066 5-10-11 95 (p) CraigNichol(3) 89
(Alistair Whillans) *w ldrs: one pce run-in* 4/1[2]
0005 5 hd **Coppelia (IRE)**[31] 1171 7-10-1 82 BrianHarding 77
(Nicky Richards) *hld up towards rr: hit 7th: drvn to chse ldrs 3 out: one pce: lame* 14/1
U/ 6 14 **Cinder Rua (IRE)**[25] 1205 8-11-5 107 LiamMcKenna(7) 91
(J J Lambe, Ire) *hld up in rr: hit 4th: effrt 8th: chsng ldrs 2 out: wknd last* 10/1
0-02 7 33 **Maggie Blue (IRE)**[42] 1067 7-11-0 95 LucyAlexander 47
(Harriet Graham) *led: hdd 4th: drvn 8th: sn lost pl and bhd: t.o 2 out* 6/1
5-40 P **Candelita**[18] 515 8-10-13 97 KyleJames(3)
(Alan Berry) *hld up towards rr: t.k.h: lost pl 3 out: sn bhd: t.o whn p.u bef last* 33/1
5m 32.4s (3.10) **Going Correction** -0.125s/f (Good) 8 Ran SP% 114.5
Speed ratings (Par 105): **89,85,83,83,83 78,66,**
CSF £27.49 CT £72.40 TOTE £5.80: £2.10, £2.10, £1.30; EX 28.00 Trifecta £118.70.
Owner Michael Feeney **Bred** Patrick Keane **Trained** Strandhill, Co. Sligo
FOCUS
The concluding contest was an ordinary mares' handicap hurdle. They went an, at best, respectable gallop. The winner is rated back to the level of his Irish form.
T/Plt: £62.30 to a £1 stake. Pool: £50329.49 - 588.97 winning tickets T/Qpdt: £17.90 to a £1 stake. Pool: £2753.29 - 113.4 winning tickets **Walter Glynn**

488 HUNTINGDON (R-H)
Monday, August 31

OFFICIAL GOING: Good to soft (good in places; chs 7.4, hdl 7.5) changing to good to soft after race 3 (1.30)
Wind: Medium; half behind Weather: Rain until Race 5

1421 BDN CONSTRUCTION LTD H'CAP HURDLE (8 hdls) 1m 7f 171y
12:30 (12:32) (Class 4) (0-110,110)
3-Y-O+ £3,249 (£954; £477; £238)

Form RPR
16F6 1 **Polstar (FR)**[16] 1265 6-10-12 103 PaulNO'Brien(7) 111+
(Harry Whittington) *t.k.h: hld up in tch in midfield: hdwy travelling wl after 3 out: ev ch 2 out: led between last 2: gng clr and mstke last: r.o strly: comf* 15/2
55-6 2 6 **Mandy's Boy (IRE)**[18] 1239 5-11-2 100 WillKennedy 102
(Ralph J Smith) *hld up in rr: hdwy and travelling wl after 3 out: led bef next: hdd and rdn between last 2: sn outpcd: no ch w wnr flat but kpt on for clr 2nd* 8/1
5F33 3 7 **Anton Dolin (IRE)**[16] 1265 7-10-13 104 MrHFNugent(7) 100
(Michael Mullineaux) *in tch in midfield: clsd to chse ldrs whn j.rt and nt fluent 3 out: outpcd and j.rt again next: 3rd and wl hld whn j.rt and mstke last* 8/1
65P2 4 1¼ **Mount Vesuvius (IRE)**[11] 1299 7-10-5 89 (tp) TomO'Brien 84
(Paul Henderson) *in tch in rr: hdwy after 5th: rdn and chsng ldr after 3 out: struggling and bmpd 2 out: sn outpcd and wl hld 4th last* 6/1[3]
60-5 5 2½ **Nafaath (IRE)**[31] 1166 9-11-7 105 (p) WayneHutchinson 98
(Donald McCain) *chsd ldr tl after 1st: styd handy: wnt 2nd again 5th: ev ch whn hit 3 out: sn u.p and unable qck: wknd between last 2* 6/1[3]
145- 6 2¾ **Tiradia (FR)**[185] 2842 8-11-12 110 AidanColeman 100
(J R Jenkins) *hld up in tch: effrt and sme hdwy after 3 out: btn next: wknd between last 2* 9/2[2]
-202 7 4½ **Clock On Tom**[8] 1346 5-11-11 109 JackQuinlan 94
(Denis Quinn) *t.k.h: chsd ldrs: j. into ld 4th: drvn and hdd bef 2 out: sn wknd* 9/1
-03P 8 53 **Wistari Rocks (IRE)**[31] 1168 6-10-11 102 AlanJohns(7) 40
(Tim Vaughan) *t.k.h: hld up in rr: rapid hdwy on outer to ld and wandering arnd 2nd: out j. and hdd 4th: wknd qckly bef 3 out: t.o 2 out* 20/1
356- P **Yul Finegold (IRE)**[21] 4548 5-11-4 102 PaddyBrennan
(Conor Dore) *t.k.h: led tl 2nd: chsd ldrs: pushed along after 5th: cl 3rd whn slipped and lost pl bnd bef 3 out: wknd wl bef 2 out: wl bhd and p.u last* 4/1[1]
3m 48.75s (-6.15) **Going Correction** -0.375s/f (Good) 9 Ran SP% 115.5
Speed ratings (Par 105): **100,97,93,92,91 90,88,61,**
CSF £65.26 CT £494.90 TOTE £9.50: £3.00, £2.40, £2.80; EX 79.20 Trifecta £311.00.
Owner Dixon,Ellis,Lynds,Travers,Watkins **Bred** Comte Jean-Jacques De La Rochette **Trained** Sparsholt, Oxfordshire
FOCUS
Rail at innermost position and distances as advertised. The overnight going description of good (good to firm in places) was changed followed several hours of rain. In a race featuring some inconsistent types, the pace was average but good enough in the conditions to set the race up for the hold-up runners. The winner is rated back to his 2014 level.

1422 MCCARTHY & STONE ELM TREE COURT H'CAP CHASE (12 fncs) 2m 104y
1:00 (1:02) (Class 5) (0-100,100) 4-Y-O+ £2,469 (£725; £362; £181)

Form RPR
23-4 1 **Jackthejourneyman (IRE)**[57] 914 6-11-12 100 (t) JamesDavies 110+
(Tom Gretton) *mde all: bmpd 2nd: rdn bef 2 out: kpt on u.p flat: rdn out* 10/3[1]

PF60 **2** *4* **My Nosy Rosy**[39] 1080 7-10-13 **87**......................(tp) DarylJacob 93
(Ben Case) *t.k.h: hld up in tch in last pair: smooth hdwy to trck ldr bef 2 out: rdr delayed effrt tl sn after last: fnd nil for press and sn btn: plugged on* **8/1**

-3P4 **3** *9* **Red Rosso**[34] 1133 10-10-1 **75**...................... TrevorWhelan 74
(Rob Summers) *rn wout declared tongue strap: hld up in last pair: hdwy 9th: wnt cl 3rd and rdn bef 2 out: sn btn and mstke 2 out: no ch w ldng pair and battling for 3rd flat: plugged on* **6/1**

5P35 **4** *nk* **Accessallareas (IRE)**[34] 1133 10-11-1 **92**...................... JamesBanks[(3)] 89
(Sarah-Jayne Davies) *in tch in midfield: lft chsng ldrs 2nd: wnt 2nd 7th tl outpcd u.p bef 2 out: wl hld 3rd last: lost 3rd towards fin* **8/1**

34P4 **5** *16* **Capisci (IRE)**[44] 1043 10-11-9 **97**......................(b[1]) SamTwiston-Davies 83
(Sarah-Jayne Davies) *chsd ldrs: lft chsng wnr 2nd: drvn after 5th: lost 2nd 7th: struggling bef 3 out: wknd on long run to 2 out* **12/1**

33-4 **6** *2½* **Molko Jack (FR)**[121] 88 11-10-11 **88**...................... BenPoste[(3)] 73
(Michael Mullineaux) *in tch in last trio: j. slowly 6th and nvr travelling after: j. slowly 7th: losing tch whn blnd 3 out* **11/2**

/P-0 **7** *1¾* **Tipsy Gypsy (IRE)**[73] 782 8-11-9 **97**...................... TomCannon 77
(Nick Gifford) *chsd wnr: j.rt and collided w wnr 2nd: midfield but stl wl in tch after: struggling in 6th 8th: lost tch sn after 3 out* **5/1[3]**

4m 9.4s (-0.80) **Going Correction** +0.125s/f (Yiel) **7 Ran SP% 111.6**
Speed ratings (Par 103): **107,105,100,100,92 91,90**
CSF £27.27 CT £148.71 TOTE £3.70: £2.10, £3.90; EX 31.00 Trifecta £201.90.
Owner Edmund O'Reilly Hyland **Bred** John Connolly **Trained** Holberrow Green, Worcs

FOCUS
The winner made all at a decent gallop and, in a low-grade race, only the first two home showed enough to be of interest next time. The winner is rated back to his Taunton level.

1423 MCCARTHY & STONE - RETIREMENT LIVING H'CAP HURDLE (10 hdls) 2m 3f 137y
1:30 (1:30) (Class 5) (0-100,97) 4-Y-O+ **£2,274** (£667; £333; £166)

Form RPR

6-P0 **1** **Pattara**[39] 1084 6-11-2 **80**......................(t[1]) GerardTumelty 94+
(Noel Williams) *chsd ldr: upsides 6th: led wl bef 3 out: drew clr on bit after 3 out: eased towards fin: v easily* **7/1**

2B63 **2** *12* **Mix N Match**[9] 1323 11-10-6 **70**...................... RichieMcLernon 70
(Laura Young) *hld up in tch in last pair: hdwy 6th: chsd ldrs bef 3 out: wnt 2nd sn after 3 out but sn brushed aside by wnr: no ch but plugged on for clr 2nd* **7/1**

4-25 **3** *1½* **Boher Lad (IRE)**[9] 1323 8-10-1 **72**......................(b[1]) MrAlexEdwards[(7)] 71
(Alan Phillips) *in tch in midfield tl dropped to rr and rdn after 5th: nvr gng wl after: no ch but plugged on to press for 3rd whn rdr dropped whip between last 2: wnt 3rd last* **2/1[1]**

2/65 **4** *2¼* **Until The Man (IRE)**[11] 1299 8-10-6 **73**......................(b) JamesBanks[(3)] 74+
(Barry Brennan) *chsd ldrs: blnd and lost pl 6th: struggling u.p bef 3 out: no ch w wnr and plugged on same pce fr next* **9/2[3]**

0-56 **5** *1¼* **Lyssio (GER)**[18] 1244 8-11-0 **85**...................... MrDGBurchell[(7)] 84
(Mark Hoad) *nt fluent: chsd ldrs: wnt 2nd after 7th tl wl bef 2 out: sn nudged along and wl btn 3rd next: wknd last* **4/1[2]**

-666 **6** *22* **Hawk Gold (IRE)**[57] 918 11-10-5 **69**......................(v[1]) MarcGoldstein 45
(Michelle Bryant) *hld up in last pair: shortlived effrt bef 3 out: sn btn: t.o 2 out* **11/1**

00-0 **7** *1¼* **Wheelavit (IRE)**[39] 1084 12-10-1 **68** oh3......................(t) BrendanPowell 40
(Claire Dyson) *led tl sn after 7th: sn lost pl u.p: t.o 2 out* **14/1**

040/ **P** **Stadium Of Light (IRE)**[10] 3141 8-10-12 **76**......................(v[1]) JamesDavies
(Christopher Kellett) *t.k.h: chsd ldrs tl 5th: dropped to last and lost tch on long run to next: t.o whn p.u 7th* **50/1**

4m 50.35s (-8.65) **Going Correction** -0.375s/f (Good) **8 Ran SP% 113.5**
Speed ratings (Par 103): **102,97,96,95,95 86,85,**
CSF £53.36 CT £133.16 TOTE £9.00: £2.30, £1.70, £1.10; EX 87.80 Trifecta £487.60.
Owner J E Garrett **Bred** Mrs P Conway-Garrett **Trained** Blewbury, Oxon

FOCUS
A modest line-up of largely out-of-form runners, run at an undemanding pace. A step up from the winner, the form rated around the next four.

1424 BDN CONSTRUCTION LTD H'CAP CHASE (16 fncs) 2m 3f 189y
2:05 (2:07) (Class 4) (0-115,115) 4-Y-O+ **£3,768** (£1,106; £553; £276)

Form RPR

2011 **1** **Tangolan (IRE)**[29] 1179 7-11-12 **115**......................(t) PaddyBrennan 126+
(Fergal O'Brien) *led tl blnd bdly and hdd 1st: rcvrd to ld again next tl out j. and hdd 3rd: chsd ldr after tl led again after 3 out: kpt on u.p flat: drvn out* **3/1[1]**

256/ **2** *1¼* **Shockingtimes (IRE)**[508] 5228 8-11-12 **115**...................... BrendanPowell 122
(Jamie Snowden) *hmpd 1st: in tch: effrt to chse ldrs and hit 2 out: drvn between last 2: kpt on u.p flat: wnt 2nd last strides* **10/1**

4246 **3** *nk* **Breaking The Bank**[31] 1169 6-11-12 **115**...................... DarylJacob 121
(Ben Case) *chsd wnr tl led 1st: hdd next and chsd ldrs after: wnt 2nd after 3 out: rdn bef next: drvn between last 2: plugged on same pce last: lost 2nd flat* **6/1[3]**

-310 **4** *8* **Isthereadifference (IRE)**[47] 1005 8-11-4 **107**......................(bt) NoelFehily 108
(Neil Mulholland) *hld up in tch: hdwy 12th: 4th and rdn after 3 out: mstke next: sn btn and wknd bef last* **13/2**

-622 **5** *18* **Kitegen (IRE)**[64] 857 9-11-8 **111**...................... CharliePoste 96
(Robin Dickin) *in tch in midfield: mstke 11th: 6th and rdn 12th: wknd bef 2 out* **9/2[2]**

6 *7* **Treacy Hotels Boy (IRE)**[43] 1061 8-11-4 **107**...................... TomO'Brien 87
(Paul Henderson) *hld up in rr: rdn and struggling after 11th: n.d after: wl btn and mstke last* **12/1**

32-P **P** **Less Time (IRE)**[83] 677 6-11-9 **112**...................... RichieMcLernon
(Jonjo O'Neill) *chsd ldrs tl j. into ld 3rd: rdn and hdd after 3 out: sn dropped out and wl btn: t.o whn p.u 2 out* **3/1[1]**

5m 5.3s **Going Correction** +0.125s/f (Yiel) **7 Ran SP% 112.6**
Speed ratings (Par 105): **105,104,104,101,93 91,**
CSF £29.54 CT £166.96 TOTE £3.30: £1.80, £4.40; EX 30.00 Trifecta £275.70.
Owner The Yes No Wait Sorries **Bred** Brian McManus **Trained** Naunton, Gloucs

FOCUS
Run at a medium pace, this well-contested chase went to an improver. The winner is rated better than the bare result.

1425 BANDMPALLETSUPPLIES.CO.UK MAIDEN HURDLE (8 hdls) 1m 7f 171y
2:40 (2:42) (Class 4) 4-Y-O+ **£3,249** (£954; £477; £238)

Form RPR

1 **Vancouverite**[200] 5-11-0 **0**...................... AidanColeman 121+
(John Ferguson) *hld up in midfield: nt fluent 1st: hdwy to chse ldrs after 5th: mstke next: ev ch 2 out: led: wnt rt and cannoned into rival last: sn hdd: rdn and qcknd to ld again flat: sn in command: r.o* **1/1[1]**

2240 **2** *1¾* **Ballycamp (IRE)**[47] 1002 6-11-0 117......................(t) AdamPogson 115
(Charles Pogson) *led: clr after 3rd: rdn and jnd 2 out: hdd and bmpd last: sn led again: hdd and styd on same pce flat* **9/2[2]**

50 **3** *1¼* **Bare Necessities (IRE)**[35] 1117 5-11-0 **0**...................... PeterCarberry 113
(Shaun Lycett) *midfield: clsd on ldrs 4th: rdn bef 3 out: kpt on wl tl unable qck between last 2: styd on same pce flat* **33/1**

4 *½* **Dynamic Ranger (USA)**[26] 4-10-13 **0**...................... MarcGoldstein 112
(Gary Moore) *hld up in last pair: gd hdwy after 5th and trcking ldrs next: rdn bef 2 out: styd on same pce between last 2* **100/1**

23 **5** *6* **Gambol (FR)**[51] 440 5-11-0 120...................... WillKennedy 109
(Ian Williams) *taken down early and led to post: chsd ldrs: wnt 2nd 5th: ev ch and drvn bef 2 out: struggling and hit 2 out: wknd bef last* **7/1**

0-23 **6** *1¼* **Brigadoon**[29] 1178 8-10-11 112...................... JonathanEngland[(3)] 108
(Michael Appleby) *chsd ldr: mstke 4th: lost 2nd and drvn and mstke next: rdn and lost pl bef 3 out: wl hld and plugged on same pce fr bef 2 out* **5/1[3]**

6-63 **7** *34* **Menace**[18] 1246 4-10-10 **0**...................... JamesBanks[(3)] 74
(Noel Williams) *racd in last quartet: rdn and btn after 5th: lost tch after 3 out: t.o* **16/1**

P-P4 **P** **Daydreamer**[57] 912 4-10-13 **0**...................... WayneHutchinson
(Alan King) *hld up in last pair: rdn and struggling after 5th: sn bhd: t.o whn p.u 2 out* **14/1**

4/0P **P** **Hustle (IRE)**[4] 1376 10-10-7 **0**...................... FreddieMitchell[(7)]
(Clare Hobson) *a in rr: rdn and lost tch after 5th: t.o whn p.u 2 out* **100/1**

00- **P** **Dabadiyan (IRE)**[23] 5250 5-11-0 **0**......................(b) TomCannon
(Gary Moore) *midfield: mstke 3rd and 5th: clsd on ldrs bef next: struggling u.p whn hit 3 out: sn wknd and wl btn whn p.u 2 out* **20/1**

3m 46.1s (-8.80) **Going Correction** -0.375s/f (Good)
WFA 4 from 5yo+ 13lb **10 Ran SP% 119.6**
Speed ratings (Par 105): **107,106,105,105,102 101,84, , ,**
CSF £5.93 TOTE £1.80: £1.10, £1.60, £5.50; EX 8.40 Trifecta £126.00.
Owner Bloomfields **Bred** Darley **Trained** Cowlinge, Suffolk

FOCUS
There was some depth to this race, and the pace was good, so the form looks solid. The winner should go on to rate higher.

1426 PALLETS WANTED AT BM PALLETS H'CAP HURDLE (12 hdls) 3m 1f 10y
3:15 (3:16) (Class 5) (0-100,100) 4-Y-O+ **£2,274** (£667; £333; £166)

Form RPR

2/05 **1** **Miss Mayfair (IRE)**[32] 1158 8-10-6 **80**......................(p) TomCannon 94+
(Lawney Hill) *mde all: rdn and drew wl clr after 3 out: in n.d next: styd on: unchal* **14/1**

-44P **2** *16* **Lily Little Legs (IRE)**[50] 976 6-11-11 **99**...................... WillKennedy 99
(Ian Williams) *hld up in midfield: effrt to chse ldng pair bef 3 out: hrd drvn and chsd clr wnr bef 2 out: no imp* **14/1**

3010 **3** *4* **Solway Sam**[16] 1264 12-11-6 **99**...................... CallumBewley[(5)] 94
(Lisa Harrison) *midfield: 4th and drvn after 9th: struggling and btn whn mstke next: plugged on to go modest 3rd flat* **14/1**

-556 **4** *¾* **Minella Bliss (IRE)**[42] 1067 10-11-4 **92**......................(b) LiamTreadwell 88
(James Evans) *hld up in rr: clsd bef 9th: effrt bef 3 out: 3rd and no imp u.p bef 2 out: lost 3rd flat* **9/1**

-546 **5** *2¼* **Spanish Fork (IRE)**[89] 599 6-10-11 **85**...................... MarcGoldstein 77
(Sheena West) *rn in snatches: chsd ldr tl 3rd: styd chsng ldrs: rdn and mstke 9th: sn drvn: wl btn next* **7/1**

01 **6** *dist* **Colley Row (IRE)**[47] 1010 7-11-5 **100**......................(b) MrBGibbs[(7)] 56
(Tim Vaughan) *hld up in last pair: mstke 1st: shortlived effrt whn mstke 9th: sn wl btn: t.o after 3 out* **5/1[2]**

P-P6 **P** **Life Of A Luso (IRE)**[59] 897 11-11-6 **94**......................(t) TomO'Brien
(Paul Henderson) *midfield: reminders after 7th: lost pl and drvn next: lost tch bef 3 out: t.o whn p.u 2 out* **20/1**

4221 **P** **Steps And Stairs (IRE)**[15] 1273 5-11-11 **99**......................(p) DarylJacob
(Jonjo O'Neill) *midfield: hdwy to chse ldrs 8th: rdn after next: sn btn and fading whn mstke 3 out: t.o whn p.u 2 out* **2/1[1]**

3-P5 **P** **Newton Martini**[12] 1293 6-10-5 **79**......................(bt) NicodeBoinville
(Ben Pauling) *chsd ldrs: wnt 2nd 3rd: rdn and mstke 3 out: lost 2nd and fdd rapidly bnd bef 2 out: 6th and p.u 2 out* **11/2[3]**

6m 14.1s (-8.80) **Going Correction** -0.375s/f (Good) **9 Ran SP% 112.6**
Speed ratings (Par 103): **99,93,92,92,91 78, , ,**
CSF £178.14 CT £2763.58 TOTE £21.00: £4.30, £2.20, £4.20; EX 188.70 Trifecta £1143.80.
Owner Alan Hill **Bred** John B O'Connor **Trained** Aston Rowant, Oxon

FOCUS
In a modest staying race, the pace was solid for the trip, making it a good test of stamina. The winner improved in line with the best of her bumper form.

1427 BRIAN MARTIN PALLETS CORBY NORTHANTS NOVICES' H'CAP HURDLE (10 hdls) 2m 4f 145y
3:50 (3:51) (Class 5) (0-100,99) 4-Y-O+ **£2,274** (£667; £333; £166)

Form RPR

6-53 **1** **Howaboutnever (IRE)**[34] 1139 7-11-12 **99**...................... WillKennedy 109+
(Ian Williams) *mde all: rdn and asserting whn wandered bef 2 out: mstke and landed awkwardly 2 out: in command last: rdn out* **7/2[2]**

-35P **2** *7* **Catkin Copse**[61] 879 7-10-9 **87**......................(p) DanielHiskett[(5)] 87
(Richard Phillips) *hld up in tch in last trio: rdn after 7th: hdwy past btn horses after 3 out: wnt 3rd next: kpt on u.p flat to go 2nd towards fin: no ch w wnr* **5/1[3]**

0634 **3** *½* **Solway Trigger**[15] 1273 6-9-9 **73**...................... CallumBewley[(5)] 74
(Lisa Harrison) *hld up in tch in rr: hdwy 9th: rdn and mstke next: 3rd and no imp bef next: plugged on* **9/4[1]**

5050 **4** *½* **Alys Rock (IRE)**[29] 1179 6-11-9 **99**...................... JonathanEngland[(3)] 100
(Michael Appleby) *chsd ldr: j. slowly 1st and lost pl: in tch in midfield: hdwy to chse wnr after 9th: rdn bef 2 out: btn whn mstke 2 out: plugged on same pce: lost 2 pls towards fin* **14/1**

-0P3 **5** *22* **Al Guwair (IRE)**[18] 1245 5-10-3 **76**...................... MarcGoldstein 57
(Mark Hoad) *chsd ldrs: rdn after 9th: sn wknd bef 2 out* **5/1[3]**

P-06 **6** *7* **Love The Leader (IRE)**[59] 892 7-11-8 **95**...................... AlainCawley 68
(Johnny Farrelly) *hld up in tch in last trio: rdn and struggling after 9th: wl btn next: sn wknd: t.o* **14/1**

506 **7** *1½* **Sturmwind (GER)**[18] 1240 4-11-0 **89**...................... LeightonAspell 59
(Alison Batchelor) *lft 2nd 1st: jnd ldr after 5th tl lost pl u.p bef 3 out: sn bhd and lost tch bef 2 out: t.o* **10/1**

5P0 **8** *21* **Sunny Bank**[16] 1261 6-11-7 **94**......................(t) BrendanPowell 47
(Alan Coogan) *chsd ldrs 3rd: rdn and after 9th: wkng next: sn wl bhd: t.o* **20/1**

5m 10.8s (0.20) **Going Correction** -0.375s/f (Good)
WFA 4 from 5yo+ 14lb **8 Ran SP% 113.5**
Speed ratings (Par 103): **84,81,81,80,72 69,69,61**
CSF £21.26 CT £46.39 TOTE £3.60: £1.30, £1.80, £1.10; EX 19.80 Trifecta £74.80.
Owner Brannon, Dick, Hernon & Holden **Bred** Mrs A Connolly **Trained** Portway, Worcs

FOCUS
This was a modest race, run at an ordinary tempo, but the unexposed winner has some potential. The winner improved to the level of his bumper form.
T/Jkpt: Not won. T/Plt: £318.10 to a £1 stake. Pool: £38,851.79 - 89.16 winning units T/Qpdt: £51.30 to a £1 stake. Pool: £3,764.66 - 54.25 winning units **Steve Payne**

1428 - 1437a (Foreign Racing) - See Raceform Interactive

[1321] NEWTON ABBOT (L-H)
Tuesday, September 1

1438 Meeting Abandoned - Unsafe ground following heavy rain

[1372] SOUTHWELL (L-H)
Wednesday, September 2

OFFICIAL GOING: Good changing to good to soft after race 2 (2.40)
Wind: light 1/2 behind Weather: heavy shower 1st 2 races, shower race 4 & 5

1444 SIS H'CAP CHASE (16 fncs) 2m 4f 62y
2:10 (2:10) (Class 4) (0-120,120) 4-Y-0+ **£4,548** (£1,335; £667; £333)

Form RPR
5452 1 **Tregaro (FR)**[17] 1267 9-10-8 **102**.....(t) BrianHughes 109+
(Mike Sowersby) *hld up: hdwy to trck ldrs 13th: 2nd 2 out: sn led: idled and pushed out clsng stages* **7/2[2]**
2143 2 ¾ **Amuse Me**[13] 1298 9-10-13 **107**.....(tp) RichardJohnson 112
(Jonjo O'Neill) *chsd ldng pair: 2nd 10th: drvn to ld briefly appr 2 out: kpt on clsng stages* **5/2[1]**
P5-3 3 3 ¼ **Quito Du Tresor (FR)**[111] 304 11-11-9 **117**.....(p) PeterBuchanan 118
(Lucinda Russell) *chsd clr ldr: pushed along 11th: one pce fr 2 out* **9/1**
1-3P 4 11 **Milgen Bay**[38] 1114 9-11-5 **113**..... LeightonAspell 108
(Oliver Sherwood) *led and sn clr: mstke 4th: jnd 13th: hdd appr 2 out: hit fence: wl btn whn pckd landing last: eased clsng stages* **4/1[3]**
2-PP F **Less Time (IRE)**[2] 1424 6-11-4 **112**.....(t[1]) RichieMcLernon
(Jonjo O'Neill) *nt jump wl in last: hdwy and in tch 13th: outpcd and lost pl whn fell 2 out* **5/2[1]**
5m 15.1s (-1.90) **Going Correction** +0.075s/f (Yiel) 5 Ran SP% **109.4**
Speed ratings (Par 105): **106,105,104,100,**
CSF £12.62 TOTE £4.60: £1.40, £2.10; EX 11.50 Trifecta £41.90.
Owner Alan R Lyons **Bred** Jean-Charles Haimet & J-Pascal Liberge **Trained** Goodmanham, E Yorks

FOCUS
Fences and hurdles sited inside the line used on August 27. After the first winning jockey Brian Hughes described the going as on the soft side of good. An open contest run at a steady pace giving most of them a chance entering the straight. The winner built on his good recent C&D run.

1445 SOUTHWELL RACECOURSE BEER FESTIVAL 12TH DECEMBER NOVICES' CHASE (19 fncs) 2m 7f 209y
2:40 (2:40) (Class 4) 4-Y-0+ **£5,049** (£1,836)

Form RPR
2213 1 **Indian Stream**[17] 1266 6-10-13 124.....(t) NoelFehily 132
(Neil Mulholland) *trckd ldng pair: 2nd 9th: upsides 3 out: drvn whn lft 8 l clr next* **2/1[2]**
-121 2 15 **Urcalin (FR)**[77] 756 7-11-6 125.....(t) TomCannon 131
(David Arbuthnot) *chsd ldr: hit 6th: hmpd 9th: outpcd 16th: 8 l down and wl hld whn lft 2nd 2 out* **3/1[3]**
12-0 F **Lily Waugh (IRE)**[124] 70 8-10-13 127.....(t) AidanColeman 137+
(Anthony Honeyball) *led: j.rt: hit 2nd: drvn and jnd 3 out: fell next* **11/10[1]**
3000 U **League Of His Own (IRE)**[40] 1098 6-11-0 0.....(t) LeeEdwards
(Claire Dyson) *t.k.h in last: in tch: blnd bdly and uns rdr 4th* **100/1**
6m 19.3s (-3.70) **Going Correction** +0.075s/f (Yiel) 4 Ran SP% **106.9**
Speed ratings (Par 105): **109,104,,**
CSF £7.91 TOTE £2.70; EX 6.60 Trifecta £6.10.
Owner Mrs G Davies **Bred** A W Buller **Trained** Limpley Stoke, Wilts

FOCUS
The finishers are rated to their marks, with the faller looking set to win.

1446 18 TO 30 GOLF MEMBERSHIP £210 H'CAP HURDLE (9 hdls) 1m 7f 153y
3:10 (3:10) (Class 5) (0-100,100) 3-Y-0+ **£3,573** (£1,049; £524; £262)

Form RPR
4-01 1 **Empty The Tank (IRE)**[40] 1095 5-11-0 **88**.....[1] LeightonAspell 98+
(Jim Boyle) *trckd ldng pair: cl 2nd 2 out: led narrowly last: fnd ex clsng stages* **7/2[2]**
-40P 2 ½ **Stormbay Bomber (IRE)**[33] 1171 6-10-11 **88**..... AdamNicol[(3)] 96
(George Moore) *mde most tl hdd narrowly last: no ex clsng stages* **5/1**
3P-P 3 10 **Nellie The Elegant**[57] 937 4-10-12 **93**.....(t[1]) AlanJohns[(7)] 92
(Tim Vaughan) *chsd ldr: one pce fr 2 out* **33/1**
65-P 4 ½ **My Renaissance**[13] 1297 5-10-0 **74**.....(t) TrevorWhelan 72
(Ben Case) *chsd ldrs: drvn appr 2 out: one pce* **16/1**
5605 5 7 **Hi Tide (IRE)**[41] 1083 11-11-12 **100**..... AidanColeman 92
(J R Jenkins) *hld up in rr: effrt and chsng ldrs bef 2 out: rdn and lost pl bef last* **9/1**
00-4 6 hd **Private Jones**[40] 1095 6-10-13 **87**.....(p) RobertDunne 80
(Miss Imogen Pickard) *rr-div: hdwy to chse ldrs 3 out: sn drvn: lost pl bef last* **9/1**
33 7 5 **Mad Money (IRE)**[31] 1182 9-11-2 **90**.....(p) PaulMoloney 77
(Sophie Leech) *in rr: hdwy to chse ldrs 3 out: sn drvn: lost pl bef next* **9/2[3]**
3345 P **Significant Move**[20] 1245 8-10-2 **81**.....(b) ChrisWard[(5)]
(Dr Richard Newland) *nt fluent: chsd ldrs: hit 4th: shkn up next: lost pl and j.rt 6th: sn bhd: t.o whn p.u bef 2 out* **11/4[1]**
3m 52.0s (-5.00) **Going Correction** -0.20s/f (Good)
WFA 4 from 5yo+ 11lb 8 Ran SP% **112.6**
Speed ratings (Par 103): **104,103,98,98,95 94,92,**
CSF £20.88 CT £481.40 TOTE £3.70: £1.70, £1.80, £3.00; EX 25.70 Trifecta £931.50.
Owner The 'In Recovery' Partnership **Bred** Michael O'Dwyer **Trained** Epsom, Surrey

FOCUS
A modest race. The winner is on the upgrade.

1447 SOUTHWELL-RACECOURSE.CO.UK MAIDEN HURDLE (13 hdls) 2m 7f 209y
3:40 (3:40) (Class 4) 4-Y-0+ **£3,898** (£1,144; £572; £286)

Form RPR
32 1 **Epic Warrior (IRE)**[10] 1349 6-10-9 0.....(p[1]) KieronEdgar[(5)] 126+
(David Pipe) *trckd ldr: led 3 out: drew clr fr next* **9/4[1]**
3343 2 15 **Presenting Streak (IRE)**[18] 1260 6-10-7 110..... MrRWinks[(7)] 110
(Peter Winks) *trckd ldrs: kpt on same pce fr 2 out: hung lft and tk modest 2nd run-in* **11/4[2]**
PP- 3 2 ¼ **Jimmy Shan (IRE)**[223] 3816 7-11-0 110..... MichaelByrne 107
(Tim Vaughan) *j.rt: led to 3 out: kpt on one pce fr next* **12/1**
-356 4 8 **Little Windmill (IRE)**[31] 1179 5-11-0 108..... TrevorWhelan 103+
(Neil King) *chsd ldrs: hmpd bnd and lost pl after 6th: chsd ldrs 3 out: one pce and modest 4th last* **12/1**
5 7 **Fearsome Fred**[130] 6-11-0 0..... HarrySkelton 95
(Caroline Bailey) *hld up in rr: chsd ldrs 8th: wknd last* **8/1**
6 6 18 **Tinkers Hill Tommy (IRE)**[20] 1246 4-10-12 0..... RobertDunne 75
(Tom Lacey) *in rr: hmpd and lost pl bnd after 6th: chsng ldrs 8th: lost pl 3 out: bhd next* **50/1**
06/6 7 18 **Millksheikh**[14] 1291 8-10-9 0.....(t) MrPYork[(5)] 61
(Raymond York) *in rr: drvn to chse ldrs bef 9th: lost pl 3 out: sn bhd* **100/1**
P-40 P **Primo Capitano (IRE)**[61] 897 7-11-0 111.....(p) AndrewTinkler
(Martin Keighley) *chsd ldrs: shkn up 4th: reminders 6th: lost pl after 8th: sn bhd: t.o whn p.u bef 10th* **3/1[3]**
PP-P P **Falcon's Legend**[40] 1094 5-10-4 0.....(t) AdamNicol[(3)]
(John Weymes) *chsd ldrs: lost pl 7th: wl bhd whn p.u bef next* **150/1**
6m 7.1s (-7.90) **Going Correction** -0.20s/f (Good)
WFA 4 from 5yo+ 13lb 9 Ran SP% **112.5**
Speed ratings (Par 105): **105,100,99,96,94 88,82,,**
CSF £8.57 TOTE £3.30: £1.20, £1.50, £2.80; EX 9.50 Trifecta £30.10.
Owner Stuart & Simon Mercer & Peter Green **Bred** Thomas Hannon **Trained** Nicholashayne, Devon

FOCUS
Those filling the minor places were rated 108-110, but the winner was far superior and ran away with it. This rates a step up.

1448 MRFREEBET.CO.UK ON YOUR MOBILE H'CAP HURDLE (11 hdls) 2m 4f 62y
4:10 (4:10) (Class 3) (0-140,130) 4-Y-0 **£6,330** (£1,870; £935; £468; £234)

Form RPR
PP-1 1 **Big Generator**[14] 1291 9-11-1 **119**.....(t) HarrySkelton 124+
(Caroline Bailey) *racd wd: chsd ldrs to 4th: chsd ldrs 8th: 2nd next: sn led: 3 l ahd last: drvn rt out* **9/1**
01-5 2 1 ¾ **Songsmith**[26] 59 7-11-6 **124**..... LeightonAspell 127
(Lucy Wadham) *trckd ldrs: handy 2nd bef 2 out: styd on same pce run-in* **8/1**
3-0F 3 5 **Rumble Of Thunder (IRE)**[52] 973 9-11-8 **129**.....(p) AdamNicol[(3)] 127
(Philip Kirby) *hld up towards rr: hdwy 7th: trcking ldrs next: 3rd appr 2 out: kpt on same pce* **14/1**
-331 4 20 **Brave Spartacus (IRE)**[46] 1040 9-11-12 **130**..... JamesReveley 110
(Keith Reveley) *led: nt fluent 6th: hdd sn after 3 out: wknd appr next* **3/1[2]**
-112 5 4 ½ **Paolozzi (IRE)**[52] 971 6-11-11 **129**.....(t) ConorO'Farrell 104
(Seamus Durack) *chsd ldrs to 4th: drvn 7th: chsng ldrs next: lost pl 3 out* **4/1[3]**
412- 6 9 **Champagne Present (IRE)**[162] 4980 5-11-8 **126**..... RichieMcLernon 93
(Jonjo O'Neill) *t.k.h in rr: hdwy 7th: trcking ldrs next: drvn 3 out: sn lost pl* **5/2[1]**
-P16 7 11 **Yesyoucan (IRE)**[89] 624 10-11-6 **124**.....(p) DannyCook 81
(Neil Mulholland) *chsd ldr to 3 out: sn lost pl: bhd whn blnd 2 out: sn eased* **9/1**
5m 4.9s (-8.10) **Going Correction** -0.20s/f (Good) 7 Ran SP% **111.3**
Speed ratings (Par 107): **108,107,105,97,95 91,87**
CSF £70.29 TOTE £9.70: £4.20, £3.40; EX 53.10 Trifecta £560.00.
Owner G T H Bailey **Bred** Jethro Bloodstock **Trained** Holdenby, Northants

FOCUS
A competitive handicap. The winner is rated in line with the best of his Irish form.

1449 AUTUMN JUMPS AT SOUTHWELL RACECOURSE MAIDEN OPEN NATIONAL HUNT FLAT RACE 1m 7f 153y
4:40 (4:40) (Class 6) 4-6-Y-0 **£2,274** (£667; £333; £166)

Form RPR
1 **Who You For (IRE)**[150] 5-11-4 0..... JackQuinlan 104+
(Sarah Humphrey) *chsd ldrs: handy 2nd over 2f out: led over 1f out: edgd rt: drvn clr fnl 100yds* **14/1**
40- 2 4 ½ **Rebel Collins (IRE)**[158] 5028 4-11-4 0..... DenisO'Regan 100
(David Evans) *chsd ldrs: led over 5f out: hdd over 1f out: swtchd rt 100yds out: kpt on same pce* **10/1**
442 3 4 ½ **Junior Package**[10] 1345 4-10-11 0.....(bt[1]) DavidNoonan[(7)] 96
(David Pipe) *hld up in mid-div: hdwy 4f out: sn outpcd: modest 4th over 2f out: kpt on over 1f out: tk modest 3rd nr fin* **5/1[3]**
4 ½ **Mahlerdramatic (IRE)**[129] 5-11-4 0..... DannyCook 95
(Brian Ellison) *trckd ldrs: drvn 5f out: clr 3rd over 2f out: wknd fnl f* **9/4[1]**
0- 5 4 ½ **Due East**[183] 4555 5-10-1 0..... FinianO'Toole[(10)] 84
(Micky Hammond) *in rr: reminders 9f out: outpcd over 4f out: styd on fnl 2f* **50/1**
6 4 ½ **Christmas Twenty (IRE)**[185] 5-11-4 0..... NickScholfield 87
(Stuart Edmunds) *chsd ldrs: outpcd and lost pl over 3f out* **5/1[3]**
40- 7 5 **The White Duke (IRE)**[413] 978 6-11-4 0..... AdamWedge 82
(Nick Kent) *in rr: sme hdwy 7f out: lost pl over 4f out* **40/1**
2 8 shd **Golden Thread**[49] 1003 5-11-4 0..... TrevorWhelan 82
(Neil King) *in rr: hdwy on outside over 8f out: chsng ldrs 7f out: lost pl over 3f out* **4/1[2]**
64 9 9 **Black Kettle (IRE)**[10] 1345 5-11-1 0.....(t) TomBellamy[(3)] 74
(Ronald Thompson) *w ldr: t.k.h: led after 2f: hdd over 5f out: sn lost pl and bhd* **33/1**
6-6 10 7 **Teals Lad**[40] 1101 6-11-4 0..... JakeGreenall 68
(Michael Easterby) *mid-div: drvn 6f out: lost pl over 4f out* **25/1**
0- 11 5 **Miss Eyelash (IRE)**[158] 5028 5-10-8 0..... SeanBowen[(3)] 56
(Peter Bowen) *led 2f: chsd ldrs: lost pl over 5f out: sn lost pl and bhd* **9/1**
0- 12 57 **Dawlish**[295] 2419 4-11-1 0.....(p) JohnKington[(3)] 12
(Noel Wilson) *chsd ldrs: drvn after 4f: lost pl 6f out: sn bhd: t.o whn eased 2f out* **100/1**
3m 43.2s (-8.20) **Going Correction** -0.20s/f (Good)
WFA 4 from 5yo+ 11lb 12 Ran SP% **122.0**
Speed ratings: **112,109,107,107,105 102,100,100,95,92 89,61**
CSF £144.90 TOTE £14.60: £3.50, £3.50, £1.80; EX 157.00 Trifecta £1069.40.
Owner The Doc Partnership **Bred** Katie McCarthy **Trained** West Wratting, Cambs

FOCUS
A moderate maiden bumper with the runners finishing strung out. The time wasn't bad.
T/Plt: £694.10 to a £1 stake. Pool: £57,199.11 - 60.15 winning tickets. T/Qpdt: £114.60 to a £1 stake. Pool: £4,677.19 - 30.2 winning tickets. **Walter Glynn**

[1343]WORCESTER (L-H)

Wednesday, September 2

OFFICIAL GOING: Good to soft (soft in places)

Wind: Light behind Weather: Cloudy

1450 EVENTSI MARQUEE HIRE, VISIT EVENTSIMARQUEES.CO.UK NOVICES' H'CAP CHASE (16 fncs) 2m 7f

5:10 (5:10) (Class 4) (0-120,120) 4-Y-0+ **£3,898** (£1,144; £572; £286)

Form RPR

-411 1 **Clubs Are Trumps (IRE)**[41] 1079 6-11-1 **109**..................(p) WillKennedy 119+
(Jonjo O'Neill) *chsd ldr 2nd to 6th: remained handy: mstke 12th: wnt 2nd again 4 out: led flat: drvn out* **9/4**[1]

2323 2 1 3/4 **Cut The Corner (IRE)**[17] 1270 7-11-12 **120**........... SamTwiston-Davies 127
(Dr Richard Newland) *hld up: nt fluent 10th: hdwy appr 4 out: led next: rdn: hung lft and hdd flat: styd on same pce* **4/1**[3]

/P11 3 2 1/4 **Foxes Bridge**[37] 1118 7-10-11 **105**..............................(v) GavinSheehan 111
(Nick Mitchell) *led: j.lft 5th: hdd next: mstke and lost pl 8th: drvn along bef next: rallied 4 out: j.lft next: styd on u.p* **11/4**[2]

30-3 4 18 **Kinari (IRE)**[76] 773 5-10-13 **107**.............................. TomO'Brien 95
(Peter Bowen) *chsd ldr tl led 6th: hdd next: remained handy: rdn appr 4 out: wknd next* **17/2**

2-14 5 12 **For 'N' Against (IRE)**[14] 1292 6-11-12 **120**..............(tp[1]) TomScudamore 102
(David Pipe) *hld up: hdwy 5th: led 7th: hdd whn hmpd 3 out: sn wknd* **4/1**[3]

5m 53.2s (3.30) **Going Correction** +0.30s/f (Yiel) **5 Ran SP% 108.0**
Speed ratings (Par 105): **106,105,104,98,94**
CSF £10.92 TOTE £2.50: £1.60, £2.00; EX 8.20 Trifecta £25.30.
Owner John P McManus **Bred** S & S Hubbard Rodwell **Trained** Cheltenham, Gloucs

FOCUS
All starts have been moved at this track following remeasuring, so there will be no speed figures here until there is sufficient data to calculate updated median times. Both bends were dolled out from the inside line, adding approximately 78yds to races 1 & 6, and 48yds to races 2, 3, 4 & 5. Will Kennedy said of the ground: "It's good to soft but softer on the Cathedral bend past the stands", and Sam Twiston-Davies called it "good to soft with the odd softer patch." This fair handicap chase was run at a steady early gallop. A small pb from the winner, with the second in line with his hurdles form.

1451 COUNTRYWIDE MOBILITY WORCESTERSHIRE'S PREMIER SUPPLIER H'CAP CHASE (12 fncs) 2m 110y

5:40 (5:40) (Class 3) (0-135,126) 4-Y-0+ **£6,498** (£1,908; £954; £477)

Form RPR

3222 1 **Miss Tenacious**[10] 1344 8-11-4 **124**.............................. HarryCobden[(7)] 130
(Ron Hodges) *trckd ldrs: racd keenly: wnt 2nd 3rd: hmpd 8th: led flat: rdn out* **6/1**

2-54 2 1 3/4 **Boss In Boots (IRE)**[85] 672 7-11-2 **115**..................(b) RichardJohnson 121+
(Seamus Mullins) *hld up in tch: mstke 3 out: led next: nt fluent last: sn rdn and hdd: no ex towards fin* **3/1**[2]

111P 3 5 **Walden Prince (IRE)**[10] 1344 8-11-7 **120**..................(tp) TomScudamore 120+
(David Bridgwater) *led: j.rt: rdn and hdd 2 out: no ex flat* **4/1**[3]

1-01 4 3/4 **Fairyinthewind (IRE)**[10] 1344 6-11-13 **126** 7ex.............(t) BrendanPowell 125
(Brendan Powell) *chsd ldr to 3rd: j.rt next: sn lost pl: pushed along and mstke 5th: j.rt 7th: rallied appr 4 out: rdn after next: styd on same pce appr last* **6/1**

510/ 5 hd **Noche De Reyes (FR)**[521] 5091 6-11-12 **125**................. PaddyBrennan 123+
(Tom George) *hld up: hdwy 4 out: ev ch next: mstke 2 out: no ex last* **15/8**[1]

4m 9.5s (4.50) **Going Correction** +0.30s/f (Yiel) **5 Ran SP% 108.4**
Speed ratings (Par 107): **101,100,97,97,97**
CSF £23.09 TOTE £5.50: £2.80, £1.70; EX 25.90 Trifecta £71.20.
Owner John Frampton & Paul Frampton **Bred** Frampton Farms & Widdin Stud **Trained** Charlton Mackrell, Somerset

FOCUS
A fair handicap chase, and sound form. A small pb from the ultra-consistent winner.

1452 SSAFA LIFELONG SUPPORT FOR OUR FORCES JUVENILE MAIDEN HURDLE (8 hdls) 2m

6:10 (6:10) (Class 5) 3-Y-O **£2,599** (£763; £381; £190)

Form RPR

1 **Hadfield (IRE)**[107] 3-11-0 0.............................. AidanColeman 106+
(John Ferguson) *hld up: hdwy after 5th: chsd ldr 3 out: rdn to ld appr last: edgd lft and drvn clr flat* **4/6**[1]

6 2 4 1/2 **Chic Name (FR)**[75] 778 3-11-0 90..................(p) AlainCawley 100
(Richard Hobson) *led: nt fluent 2nd: rdn and hdd appr last: styd on same pce flat* **25/1**

4 3 7 **Champagne Ransom (FR)**[13] 1294 3-10-7 0.............. NicodeBoinville 86
(Nicky Henderson) *chsd ldrs: rdn appr last: styd on same pce* **9/2**[3]

4 10 **Dylan's Storm (IRE)**[21] 3-11-0 0.............................. NoelFehily 84
(David Dennis) *hld up: rdn and wknd appr 3 out* **4/1**[2]

6 5 7 **Layerthorpe (IRE)**[13] 1294 3-11-0 0.............................. PaulMoloney 78
(Debra Hamer) *chsd ldrs tl rdn and wknd 3 out* **28/1**

6 24 **Big McIntosh (IRE)**[7] 3-11-0 0.............................. MattieBatchelor 56
(John Ryan) *trckd ldrs: racd keenly: rdn and wknd appr 3 out* **7/1**

P0 7 60 **Whistler Mountain**[13] 1294 3-11-0 0.............................. TomCannon
(Mark Gillard) *chsd ldr tl rdn after 5th: wknd bef next* **80/1**

P **Ourlittle Senorita**[34] 3-10-7 0.............................. RobertDunne
(Miss Imogen Pickard) *hld up: racd keenly: mstke 4th: wknd appr next: bhd whn p.u bef 3 out* **66/1**

3m 50.6s **Going Correction** +0.25s/f (Yiel) **8 Ran SP% 120.7**
Speed ratings (Par 101): **110,107,104,99,95 83,53,**
CSF £22.59 TOTE £1.70: £1.10, £3.30, £1.60; EX 17.70 Trifecta £71.00.
Owner Bloomfields **Bred** Mrs Renata Coleman **Trained** Cowlinge, Suffolk

FOCUS
An ordinary juvenile hurdle, but the winner is capable of better. It was the quickest of the three C&D times and the third may prove the best guide.

1453 WORCESTER NEWS MAIDEN HURDLE (8 hdls) 2m

6:40 (6:40) (Class 5) 4-Y-0+ **£2,599** (£763; £381; £190)

Form RPR

1 1 **Roadie Joe (IRE)**[14] 1289 6-11-0 0.............................. PaulMoloney 116+
(Evan Williams) *lft in ld 1st: nt fluent 3rd: wnt clr appr last: easily* **9/4**[2]

000- 2 12 **Air Of Glory (IRE)**[18] 3413 5-11-0 100..................(p) WillKennedy 101
(Martin Bosley) *w wnr 2nd tl after 5th: j.rt last 3 flights: styd on same pce appr last* **25/1**

063- 3 6 **The Big Dipper**[132] 5500 6-11-0 0.............................. NoelFehily 96
(David Dennis) *hld up: hdwy after 5th: styd on same pce fr 3 out* **7/1**

0 4 19 **Generous Pet (IRE)**[41] 1082 6-11-0 0.............................. TomScudamore 78
(Kevin Bishop) *chsd ldrs: lost pl bef 3rd: sn bhd* **66/1**

0 5 1 3/4 **Gilmer (IRE)**[21] 1234 4-11-0 0..............................(t) JamesBest 76
(Laura Young) *hld up: rdn and wknd bef 3 out* **33/1**

F **Golden Heritage**[300] 4-11-0 0.............................. AidanColeman 111+
(John Ferguson) *trckd ldrs: 3 l 3rd and gng okay whn fell 3 out* **6/4**[1]

1-32 U **Magna Cartor**[13] 1300 5-11-0 0.............................. KielanWoods
(Ronald Thompson) *led: stmbld on landing: sddle slipped and uns rdr after 1st* **7/2**[3]

3m 53.7s (3.10) **Going Correction** +0.25s/f (Yiel)
WFA 4 from 5yo+ 11lb **7 Ran SP% 113.8**
Speed ratings (Par 103): **102,96,93,83,82 ,**
CSF £42.85 TOTE £3.40: £1.60, £5.50; EX 43.10 Trifecta £219.60.
Owner Billy Bates **Bred** Michael McEvoy **Trained** Llancarfan, Vale Of Glamorgan

FOCUS
A modest maiden hurdle. The easy winner built on his bumper win.

1454 BETTINGGODS.COM MARES' H'CAP HURDLE (8 hdls) 2m

7:10 (7:10) (Class 4) (0-110,108) 3-Y-0+ **£3,249** (£954; £477; £238)

Form RPR

6622 1 **Wintour Leap**[10] 1348 4-11-8 **104**.............................. TomO'Brien 112+
(Robert Stephens) *a.p: shkn up appr last: rdn to ld flat: r.o* **5/2**[1]

1U42 2 1 1/4 **Cruise In Style (IRE)**[11] 1323 9-10-11 **93**..................(tp) JamesBest 97
(Kevin Bishop) *hld up: pushed along 4th: hdwy 3 out: ev ch flat: nt qckn towards fin* **8/1**

340U 3 3/4 **Fairy Alisha**[6] 1384 7-10-11 **100**.............................. JoshWall[(7)] 103
(Trevor Wall) *hld up: hdwy 3 out: led last: rdn and hdd flat: styd on same pce* **8/1**

-231 4 2 1/2 **Keep To The Beat**[25] 843 4-11-10 **106**.............................. BrianHughes 108
(Kevin Ryan) *w ldr to 5th: remained handy: ev ch fr 2 out: sn hung rt: rdn and no ex flat* **6/1**

5262 5 3/4 **Ginger Fizz**[33] 1166 8-11-12 **108**..................(tp) KielanWoods 108
(Ben Case) *led: rdn and hdd appr 2 out: hung rt after 2 out: swtchd lft appr last: styd on same pce flat* **4/1**[2]

0-F5 6 2 1/2 **Prettyasapicture**[76] 775 6-11-9 **105**..................(p) WayneHutchinson 104
(Alan King) *chsd ldrs: led appr 2 out: hdd last: wknd towards fin* **9/2**[3]

4322 7 7 **Irondale Express**[17] 1271 4-11-12 **108**.............................. PaulMoloney 102
(Des Donovan) *prom: rdn after 5th: wkng whn mstke last* **10/1**

3m 53.4s (2.80) **Going Correction** +0.25s/f (Yiel) **7 Ran SP% 112.4**
Speed ratings (Par 105): **103,102,102,100,100 99,95**
CSF £21.33 TOTE £3.40: £2.10, £3.20; EX 23.30 Trifecta £113.80.
Owner Paul Cooper **Bred** D J And Mrs Deer **Trained** Penhow, Newport

FOCUS
Quite a competitive mares' handicap hurdle. They went a steady early gallop and all of them still had some sort of a chance two from home.

1455 SSAFA SUPPORTING ARMED FORCES AND FAMILIES H'CAP HURDLE (10 hdls) 2m 4f

7:40 (7:40) (Class 4) (0-115,112) 4-Y-0+ **£3,249** (£954; £477; £238)

Form RPR

333 1 **Over The Air**[14] 1292 7-11-8 **107**.............................. NicodeBoinville 112
(John Spearing) *hld up: hdwy 3 out: chsd ldr after next: rdn to ld flat: styd on* **4/1**[3]

/341 2 3/4 **Mighty Leader (IRE)**[41] 1084 7-11-1 **100**.............................. JamesDavies 104
(Henry Oliver) *led at stdy pce tl qcknd bef 3 out: mstke next: rdn and hdd flat: styd on* **7/4**[1]

631F 3 3 3/4 **Dream Bolt (IRE)**[20] 1241 7-11-5 **104**.............................. PaulMoloney 105
(David Rees) *plld hrd early: a.p: rdn appr last: styd on same pce flat* **11/2**

404- 4 7 **Bassarabad (FR)**[231] 3671 4-11-10 **110**.............................. RichardJohnson 104
(Tim Vaughan) *hld up: hdwy 6th: rdn bef 3 out: wknd appr last* **14/1**

246- 5 3/4 **Bourne**[180] 4601 9-11-11 **110**..............................(b) AdrianLane 106
(Donald McCain) *chsd ldr: ev ch whn mstke 3 out: rdn and wknd appr last* **10/1**

6-U2 6 8 **Swivel**[18] 1260 4-11-5 **112**..............................(b[1]) MrAlexFerguson[(7)] 100
(John Ferguson) *chsd ldrs: pckd 4th: nt fluent and lost pl 6th: mstke next: wkng whn mstke 3 out* **3/1**[2]

5m 12.1s (18.60) **Going Correction** +0.25s/f (Yiel)
WFA 4 from 6yo+ 12lb **6 Ran SP% 112.5**
Speed ratings (Par 105): **72,71,70,67,67 63**
CSF £11.87 CT £36.67 TOTE £4.50: £2.40, £1.80; EX 13.20 Trifecta £38.30.
Owner Mrs Peter Badger **Bred** Mrs P Badger **Trained** Kinnersley, Worcs

FOCUS
They went a very steady gallop in this ordinary handicap hurdle. The winner is rated in line with his recent C&D run.
T/Plt: £74.00 to a £1 stake. Pool: £67,476.66 - 664.94 winning tickets. T/Qpdt: £14.50 to a £1 stake. Pool: £7,502.49 - 382.45 winning tickets. **Colin Roberts**

[1365]SEDGEFIELD (L-H)

Thursday, September 3

OFFICIAL GOING: Good to firm (good in places; 7.4)

Wind: fresh behind Weather: Cloudy

1456 PIERCY PROPERTIES JUVENILE HURDLE (BETFRED HURDLE SERIES QUALIFIER) (8 hdls) 2m 178y

2:20 (2:20) (Class 4) 3-Y-O **£3,898** (£1,144; £572; £286)

Form RPR

1 **Cooper**[16] 3-10-12 0.............................. BrianHughes 102+
(Kevin Ryan) *in tch: hdwy to stalk ldr after 3 out: led appr last: hit last: pushed clr run-in: comf* **6/4**[1]

113 2 8 **Retro Valley (IRE)**[12] 1321 3-11-5 122..................(p) JamieBargary[(7)] 106
(David Dennis) *led: hdd after 1st: lft in front again 2nd: rdn bef 2 out: hdd appr last: hit last: one pce and no ch w wnr run-in* **7/4**[2]

123 3 7 **Egmont**[14] 1294 3-11-5 110.............................. HenryBrooke 92
(George Moore) *chsd ldr: hit 3rd: reminder after 5th: rdn and one pce in 3rd after 3 out* **11/4**[3]

55 4 23 **Fortuna Glas (IRE)**[14] 1294 3-10-7 0.............................. JamesCowley[(5)] 63
(Donald McCain) *trckd ldr: rdn after 3 out: sn btn* **22/1**

5 1 1/2 **Well I Never** 3-10-9 0.............................. TonyKelly[(3)] 62
(Ray Craggs) *hld up: a in rr* **150/1**

R **Hey Bob (IRE)**[26] 3-10-7 0........................ DiarmuidO'Regan(5)
(Chris Grant) *tk str hold: led after 1st: rn out 2nd* 125/1

3m 52.4s (-14.50) **Going Correction** -0.925s/f (Hard) **6** Ran SP% **108.8**
Speed ratings (Par 103): **97,93,89,79,78**
CSF £4.30 TOTE £2.30: £1.60, £1.20; EX 4.80 Trifecta £6.20.
Owner Guy Reed Racing **Bred** G Reed **Trained** Hambleton, N Yorks

FOCUS
Hurdles sited on outer and rail realignment increased distances by 10yds per circuit. This had the look of a fair contest, but two of the market leaders were disappointing, so the winner didn't have a hard task if staying upright. The winner should go on to rate higher and win again.

1457 SEDGEFIELD BOOKMAKERS CONDITIONAL JOCKEYS' NOVICES' HURDLE (BETFRED HURDLE SERIES QUALIFIER) 2m 3f 188y
2:50 (2:50) (Class 4) 4-Y-O+ **£3,508** (£1,030; £515; £257)

Form RPR
3113 **1** **Lamool (GER)**[12] 1325 8-11-6 134........................(t) AlanJohns(6) 132+
(Tim Vaughan) *mde all: c clr on bit after 3 out* 2/9[1]
0-44 **2** *15* **Rocky Two (IRE)**[8] 799 5-10-9 107........................ AdamNicol(3) 97
(Philip Kirby) *hld up in tch: mstke 3 out: rdn to go modest 2nd jst after last: no threat wnr* 22/1[3]
0-54 **3** *3 ¾* **Louloumills**[32] 1179 5-9-11 0........................ ThomasDowson(8) 86
(Maurice Barnes) *chsd ldr: rdn bef 2 out: already one pce and hld whn mstke 2 out: lost 2nd jst after last* 150/1
3321 **4** *5* **Dire Straits (IRE)**[47] 1041 4-11-5 120........................(bt) LizzieKelly(6) 101
(Neil King) *chsd ldr: slow 4 out: sn pushed along: wknd after last: p.u and dismntd after line* 9/2[2]

4m 42.4s (-11.70)
WFA 4 from 5yo+ 12lb **4** Ran SP% **105.0**
CSF £5.21 TOTE £1.30; EX 4.80 Trifecta £19.60.
Owner J H Frost **Bred** Frau M U W Lohmann **Trained** Aberthin, Vale of Glamorgan

FOCUS
On official figures this was a one-sided affair, and so it proved. The easy winner was value for further.

1458 PHOENIX SECURITY H'CAP CHASE (17 fncs) 2m 5f 28y
3:20 (3:21) (Class 4) (0-120,115) 4-Y-O+ **£4,548** (£1,335; £667; £333)

Form RPR
32-0 **1** **Welsh Bard (IRE)**[47] 1032 6-11-6 109........................(b) WayneHutchinson 122+
(Donald McCain) *trckd ldr: pressed ldr 9th: led 11th: rdn bef 2 out: styd on to go clr appr last* 5/2[1]
F004 **2** *17* **Groomed (IRE)**[18] 1267 7-11-6 114........................ DiarmuidO'Regan(5) 112
(Sue Smith) *hld up: hdwy bef 4 out: wnt 2nd bef 3 out: rdn bef 2 out: wknd and hld in 2nd fr appr last* 11/1
-052 **3** *20* **Skint**[21] 1242 9-11-12 115........................(p) AidanColeman 95
(Ali Stronge) *hld up: hdwy into 3rd 10th: rdn bef 3 out: sn wknd* 15/2
-240 **4** *4* **Harrys Whim**[32] 1181 10-11-6 112........................(t) JonathanEngland(3) 88
(Maurice Barnes) *led: jnd after 9th: hdd 11th: lost 2nd bef 3 out: sn wknd* 5/1[3]
2160 **5** *½* **Big Sound**[13] 1309 8-11-12 115........................(p) DougieCostello 91
(Mark Walford) *trckd ldr: hit 6th: grad lost pl after: nt fluent 12th: sn btn* 11/4[2]
4322 **6** *1 ½* **Faith Jicaro (IRE)**[22] 1159 8-11-0 103........................(p) TomScudamore 77
(David Bridgwater) *hld up: hit 4th and dropped to rr: nvr gng w much fluency after: bhd fr 12th* 5/1[3]

5m 17.1s (-15.90) **Going Correction** -1.10s/f (Hard) **6** Ran SP% **108.7**
Speed ratings (Par 105): **86,79,71,70,70 69**
CSF £24.33 TOTE £3.60: £1.80, £5.40; EX 26.20 Trifecta £115.40.
Owner George Tobitt & Richard Gurney **Bred** Whisperview Trading Ltd **Trained** Cholmondeley, Cheshire

FOCUS
A modest contest, and plenty of these were seen off well before heading into the home straight for the final time. The form could be 5lb+ out either way.

1459 HENRY FAMILY MEMORIAL H'CAP HURDLE (8 hdls) 2m 178y
3:55 (3:56) (Class 3) (0-130,130) 3-Y-O+ **£5,588** (£1,640; £820; £410)

Form RPR
4F5- **1** **Mighty Whitey (IRE)**[19] 1017 9-9-12 105........................(t) DerekFox(3) 108
(Noel C Kelly, Ire) *mde all: rdn after 2 out: hrd pressed appr last: kpt on wl* 22/1
3/1 **2** *1 ¾* **Baby Jake (IRE)**[11] 1347 6-10-13 117 7ex........................ RichardJohnson 118
(John Joseph Hanlon, Ire) *midfield: hdwy to trck ldr after 3 out: rdn to chal strly appr last: drvn and one pce run-in* 11/10[1]
420- **3** *1 ¾* **Push Me (IRE)**[26] 1955 8-10-0 104 oh2........................ AdrianLane 103
(Iain Jardine) *hld up: hdwy to trck ldng pair appr 2 out: nt fluent 2 out: sn rdn: one pce* 10/1
/54- **4** *shd* **Sailors Warn (IRE)**[24] 498 8-11-4 122........................(t) KielanWoods 121
(Ronald Thompson) *hld up: hdwy after 3 out: rdn to chse ldng pair 2 out: one pce* 80/1
53-3 **5** *20* **Downtown Boy (IRE)**[32] 1180 7-10-4 108........................(p) BrianHughes 94
(Ray Craggs) *midfield: nt fluent 3 out: sn pushed along: btn whn hit 2 out* 4/1[2]
00-P **6** *6* **Dispour (IRE)**[106] 406 5-11-5 123........................(bt) WayneHutchinson 99
(Donald McCain) *trckd ldr: rdn appr 2 out: sn wknd* 16/1
3-62 **7** *6* **Swaledale Lad (IRE)**[45] 1070 8-11-9 130........................ HarryChalloner(3) 101
(Richard Ford) *in tch: wknd appr 2 out* 9/2[3]
23F **8** *8* **Tiger Twenty Two**[10] 1041 4-10-8 112........................ AndrewTinkler 75
(Brian Rothwell) *hld up: rdn after 3 out: sn wknd* 20/1

3m 47.6s (-19.30) **Going Correction** -0.925s/f (Hard)
WFA 4 from 5yo+ 11lb **8** Ran SP% **111.1**
Speed ratings (Par 107): **108,107,106,106,96 94,91,87**
CSF £46.05 CT £265.22 TOTE £18.70: £8.40, £1.10, £2.50; EX 63.70 Trifecta £1253.50.
Owner Mrs Christina Kelly **Bred** Miss Carmel Whelan **Trained** Draperstown, Co. Derry

FOCUS
The early gallop wasn't overly strong in this handicap. The second to fourth were pretty much to their marks.

1460 PAXTONS FOR CASE IH TRACTORS NOVICES' H'CAP CHASE (13 fncs) 2m 77y
4:25 (4:25) (Class 4) (0-120,120) 4-Y-O+ **£4,548** (£1,335; £667; £333)

Form RPR
3-55 **1** **Heist (IRE)**[34] 1170 5-11-2 110........................(t) BrianHughes 111
(Patrick Griffin, Ire) *hld up in rr: reminders after 4th: rdn 5 out: stl 12 l down in 5th 2 out: clsd appr last: lft 2nd last: sn led: kpt on* 13/2
6-33 **2** *5* **Oliver's Gold**[24] 973 7-11-12 120........................ DougieCostello 121+
(Mark Walford) *hld up in tch: rdn to go 2nd between last 2: lft in front last but hmpd and sn hdd: nt rcvr* 9/1
-F21 **3** *7* **Mr Burgees (IRE)**[45] 1068 6-11-12 120........................ WayneHutchinson 110
(Donald McCain) *hld up in tch: nt fluent 4th: rdn after 5 out: wknd after 2 out: lft poor 3rd last* 5/1[3]
6-15 **4** *27* **Little Pop**[59] 931 7-11-2 110........................(t) SamTwiston-Davies 83
(Nigel Twiston-Davies) *led: mstke 5th: jnd 8th: hdd 4 out: rdn after 3 out: mstke 2 out: wknd* 3/1[2]
-421 **F** **The Yank**[7] 1373 6-10-0 93 7ex........................ TomScudamore 100+
(David Bridgwater) *trckd ldr: pressed ldr 8th: led 4 out: asserted on bit bef 2 out: hld together and 4 l up whn fell last* 5/4[1]

3m 59.7s (-14.30) **Going Correction** -1.10s/f (Hard) **5** Ran SP% **109.4**
Speed ratings (Par 105): **91,88,85,71,**
CSF £48.90 TOTE £7.60: £2.70, £3.70; EX 56.70 Trifecta £136.30.
Owner M Deren **Bred** Whisperview Trading Ltd **Trained** Oldtown, Co Dublin

FOCUS
Two horses that like to get on with things ensured this was run at a good gallop, and there was plenty of drama at the final fence. The fortunate winner was a bit below the best of his hurdles form.

1461 DAILY RACING TIPS @BOOKIES.COM H'CAP HURDLE (8 hdls) 2m 178y
4:55 (4:55) (Class 5) (0-100,100) 4-Y-O+ **£2,599** (£763; £381; £190)

Form RPR
-263 **1** **Vexillum (IRE)**[14] 1299 6-10-10 84........................(p) NoelFehily 100
(Neil Mulholland) *hld up in midfield: smooth hdwy after 3 out: trckd ldr 2 out: rdn between last 2: styd on to ld 110yds out* 11/2[2]
-041 **2** *1 ½* **Carnaross**[5] 1405 6-11-0 88........................(t) HenryBrooke 102
(Julia Brooke) *trckd ldrs: led appr 2 out: rdn between last 2: one pce: hdd 110yds out* 5/6[1]
6262 **3** *6* **Dynamic Drive (IRE)**[32] 1182 8-10-13 97........................(t) ThomasDowson(10) 107
(Maurice Barnes) *hld up in midfield: hdwy 4th: prom on bit after 3 out: rdn 2 out: no ex run-in* 6/1[3]
P-05 **4** *13* **Toola Boola**[59] 516 5-9-11 74........................ AdamNicol(3) 71
(George Moore) *prom: led narrowly jst after 3 out: hdd appr 2 out: wknd* 18/1
06-3 **5** *1 ¼* **Hi Dancer**[91] 137 12-11-4 92........................ AndrewTinkler 88
(Ben Haslam) *trckd ldrs: rdn and outpcd after 3 out: no threat after* 25/1
0-P5 **6** *11* **So Bazaar (IRE)**[64] 870 8-10-0 74 oh6........................(tp) BrianHarding 60
(Andrew Wilson) *hld up: rdn after 3 out: sn btn* 100/1
400- **7** *1* **Mitcd (IRE)**[225] 3801 4-10-13 90........................ GrahamWatters(3) 75
(Martin Todhunter) *midfield: rdn after 3 out: sn wknd* 66/1
4-50 **8** *5* **Dalstontosiloth (IRE)**[41] 1095 7-10-6 80........................(tp) BrianHughes 61
(Barry Murtagh) *led: hdd jst after 3 out: wknd* 9/1
-06F **9** *6* **Dover The Moon (IRE)**[32] 1182 4-10-10 84........................ JamesDavies 59
(Tom Gretton) *in tch: hit 3rd: wknd after 3 out* 125/1
4405 **10** *13* **Footstepsintherain (IRE)**[13] 1307 5-11-5 100........................(t) JamieBargary(7) 64
(David Dennis) *hld up: hit 3 out: wknd* 18/1

3m 50.3s (-16.60) **Going Correction** -0.925s/f (Hard)
WFA 4 from 5yo+ 11lb **10** Ran SP% **111.9**
Speed ratings (Par 103): **102,101,98,92,91 86,86,83,80,74**
CSF £10.29 CT £26.87 TOTE £7.00: £1.80, £1.10, £2.10; EX 13.40 Trifecta £46.70.
Owner John Heaney **Bred** Rathasker Stud **Trained** Limpley Stoke, Wilts

FOCUS
A moderate race but the three that headed the market came right away. The third helps set the level.

1462 TIPS ON THIS RACE @BOOKIES.COM H'CAP CHASE (21 fncs) 3m 2f 59y
5:25 (5:25) (Class 5) (0-100,100) 4-Y-O+ **£3,249** (£954; £477; £238)

Form RPR
P0-0 **1** **Alta Rock (IRE)**[58] 934 10-10-11 85........................ SeanQuinlan 92
(Sue Smith) *midfield: hdwy to trck ldrs after 14th: rdn after 4 out: led between last 2: styd on* 16/1
3/4- **2** *1 ½* **Duroob**[25] 1221 13-10-12 86........................(v) RichardJohnson 92
(Anthony McCann, Ire) *hld up: rdn and hdwy after 4 out: chsd ldrs 2 out: wnt 2nd jst after last: styd on* 13/2[3]
5 **3** *1 ½* **Longueville Flier (IRE)**[74] 801 6-10-10 94........................ FinianO'Toole(10) 100
(Micky Hammond) *hld up: mstke 1st and 11th: hdwy 5 out: rdn to ld appr 2 out: hdd between last 2: no ex run-in* 13/2[3]
P354 **4** *11* **Shady Glen (IRE)**[50] 1004 6-10-12 86........................(p) KielanWoods 82
(Graeme McPherson) *midfield: trckd ldrs 10th: led after 14th: rdn whn hdd appr 2 out: wknd between last 2* 7/2[2]
1313 **5** *21* **Over And Above (IRE)**[45] 1069 9-11-2 93........................(tp) GrahamWatters(3) 69
(Henry Hogarth) *w ldr: rdn after 5 out: sn struggling* 9/1
-051 **6** *4* **Bayfirth (IRE)**[5] 1402 12-9-7 73 7ex........................ MrWHRReed(7) 46
(R Mike Smith) *midfield: trckd ldrs 10th: rdn after 5 out: wknd after 3 out* 9/4[1]
-PP0 **P** **Getmeouthedoldrums**[12] 1326 10-10-8 85........................(t) KillianMoore(3)
(Mark Wall) *led narrowly: hdd 14th: reminders and sn struggling: t.o whn p.u bef 3 out* 9/1
-2PP **P** **Killimordaly (IRE)**[13] 1309 6-11-5 100........................(b[1]) MissBHampson(7)
(Andy Turnell) *trckd ldrs: already lost pl whn hit 5 out: sn bhd: slow 3 out and p.u bef next* 10/1

6m 40.7s (-30.30) **Going Correction** -1.10s/f (Hard) **8** Ran SP% **114.6**
Speed ratings (Par 103): **102,101,101,97,91 90, ,**
CSF £113.79 CT £752.78 TOTE £28.60: £3.50, £1.70, £2.40; EX 97.30 Trifecta £452.40.
Owner Mrs S Smith **Bred** M W Hickey **Trained** High Eldwick, W Yorks
■ Stewards' Enquiry : Miss B Hampson two-day ban: careless riding (tbn)

FOCUS
With the first two either out of form and/or without a win for a long time, this isn't a result to be following. The second and third are the best guides.
T/Plt: £60.60 to a £1 stake. Pool of £62167.56 - 748.19 winning tickets. T/Qpdt: £33.30 to a £1 stake. Pool of £4044.69 - 89.80 winning units. **Andrew Sheret**

1463 - 1476a (Foreign Racing) - See Raceform Interactive

836
AUTEUIL (L-H)
Friday, September 4

OFFICIAL GOING: Soft

1477a PRIX DE L'ORLEANAIS (HURDLE) (CONDITIONS) (5YO+) (TURF) 2m 2f
3:25 (12:00) 5-Y-0+ **£18,604** (£9,302; £5,426; £3,682; £1,744)

RPR
1 **Milord Thomas (FR)**[110] 375 6-11-3 0........................ JacquesRicou 141
(D Bressou, France) 5/2[1]
2 *2* **Iroufícar Has (FR)**[89] 664 5-10-10 0........................ AngeloGasnier 132
(J-P Gallorini, France) 187/10

The Form Book Jumps 2015-16, Raceform Ltd, Newbury, RG14 5SJ

3 nse **Buck's Bank (FR)**[81] 7-10-8 0................................(b) GeoffreyRe 130
(Yannick Fouin, France) **107/10**

4 6 **Bel La Vie (FR)**[89] 664 9-10-10 0.............................. BertrandLestrade 126
(G Macaire, France) **17/5**[2]

5 1 1/4 **Vladimir (FR)**[86] 6-10-10 0.............................. DavidCottin 125
(P Peltier, France) **48/10**[3]

6 3 **Reglis Brunel (FR)**[89] 664 10-10-8 0.............................. SylvainDehez 120
(E Lecoiffier, France) **128/10**

7 1 1/4 **Kahyadam (FR)**[150] 7-10-12 0.............................. FrancoisPamart 122
(A Chaille-Chaille, France) **15/2**

8 7 **Viky Du Reponet (FR)**[81] 6-10-8 0.............................. StephanePaillard 111
(S Foucher, France) **186/10**

9 5 **Gevrey Chambertin (FR)**[151] 5184 7-10-8 0.............(b) TomScudamore 106
(David Pipe) *t.k.h: hld up in midfield: j. slowly 5 out: shkn up and no imp bef 3 out: rdn and wl hld fr 2 out* **154/10**

10 3 **Un Regard (FR)**[285] 7-10-8 0..............................(p) JamesReveley 103
(Guy Denuault, France) **51/1**

11 2 1/2 **Los Banderos (FR)**[537] 6-10-10 0.............................. JonathanGiron(4) 107
(F-X De Chevigny, France) **50/1**

12 20 **Gaelic Joy (FR)**[285] 5-10-12 0.............................. OlivierJouin 85
(G Taupin, France) **77/1**

P **Jaguy De Cimbre (FR)**[866] 5446 11-10-3 0.............................. ThomasViel(5)
(L Viel, France) **53/1**

4m 6.1s (246.10) **13 Ran SP% 119.4**
PARI-MUTUEL (all including 1 euro stake): WIN 3.50; PLACE 2.10, 4.00, 3.40; DF 38.70; SF 50.00.
Owner Magalen O Bryant **Bred** S Boucheron **Trained** France

1379 STRATFORD (L-H)
Saturday, September 5

OFFICIAL GOING: Chase course - good to soft (soft in places); hurdle course - good (good to soft in places)
Wind: light breeze Weather: overcast; 14 degrees

1478 KATIE FALLON HAPPY 40TH BIRTHDAY CONDITIONAL JOCKEYS' (S) H'CAP HURDLE (9 hdls) 2m 2f 148y
2:05 (2:06) (Class 5) (0-100,100) 4-7-Y-0 **£2,274** (£667; £333; £166)

Form RPR

000- 1 **Triple Eight (IRE)**[16] 2168 7-10-8 **85**.............................. AdamNicol(3) 93
(Philip Kirby) *pressed ldrs: 3rd and gng wl after 6th: 4th home turn: drvn to join ldr last: sustained duel and all out flat: jst prevailed* **9/2**[3]

P5P1 2 nse **Seacon Beg (IRE)**[14] 1323 6-11-4 **100**.............(t) MrMatthewHampton(8) 109
(Richard Woollacott) *settled in 3rd or 4th tl wnt 2nd after 2 out: led bef last and hit flight: u.p: w wnr after: tried hrd but btn on nod* **4/1**[2]

P5-P 3 8 **Pembridge**[126] 89 6-10-0 **74** oh6..............................(t) BenPoste 75
(Adrian Wintle) *settled towards rr: effrt after 2 out: cl 3rd whn unbalanced home turn: no ex bef last where regained 3rd* **20/1**

6636 4 1 1/4 **Short Takes (USA)**[7] 1405 7-11-1 **95**..............................(p) JamesCowley(6) 95
(Donald McCain) *led briefly 1st: pressed ldr tl led again 3 out: rdn after next: hdd bef last and fnd little: nt hrd rdn whn btn: lost 3rd and hit last* **11/2**

0/-0 5 2 1/4 **School For Scandal (IRE)**[24] 1238 7-11-4 **95**.............................. PaulO'Brien(3) 93
(Jimmy Frost) *midfield: rdn 6th: chsd ldrs tl no ex between last two* **16/1**

355 6 1 1/4 **Kyles Faith (IRE)**[16] 1298 7-11-0 **96**..............................(p) ArchieBellamy(8) 94
(Martin Keighley) *led after 1st: drvn and hdd and hit 3 out: lost 2nd after next: 5 l 5th whn impeded home turn: plugged on* **7/2**[1]

35-F 7 1 1/2 **Drummond**[11] 1356 6-9-12 **75**..............................(bt) RobertWilliams(3) 71
(Bernard Llewellyn) *bhd: awkward bnd bef 6th: drvn after 2 out: sn btn* **9/1**

54F0 8 12 **L Stig**[16] 1297 5-11-3 **91**..............................(tp) KillianMoore 75
(John O'Shea) *last pair: rdn bef 3 out: lost tch after next* **11/1**

6553 9 3 1/2 **Goldie Horn**[13] 1346 7-11-5 **96**..............................(t) RyanHatch(3) 79
(Nigel Twiston-Davies) *dropped to rr after 4th: t.o between last two* **8/1**

4m 30.2s (-1.30) **Going Correction** -0.15s/f (Good) **9 Ran SP% 115.9**
Speed ratings: **96,95,92,92,91 90,89,84,83**
CSF £23.40 CT £326.07 TOTE £4.90: £2.10, £2.10, £6.20; EX 21.40 Trifecta £729.20 Part won. Pool: £972.33 - 0.94 winning units..The winner was bought in for 4,700 guineas. Seacon Beg was claimed by Mrs Nikki Evans for £7,000.
Owner RedHotGardogs **Bred** Moyglare Stud Farm Ltd **Trained** East Appleton, N Yorks
■ Stewards' Enquiry : Ben Poste one-day ban; careless riding (20th Sept)

FOCUS
All bends and hurdles moved to fresh ground. Races 1 & 2 increased by 60yds, races 3, 5, 6 & 7 by 51yds and race 4 by 84yds. The track had taken 30mm of rain since the start of the previous weekend but none in the second half of this week, and all remaining soft patches had dried out by the morning. A weak selling handicap to begin with, but two recent winners came to the fore. The winner was close to his best.

1479 JAGUAR LANDROVER BEGINNERS' CHASE (14 fncs) 2m 3f 98y
2:40 (2:40) (Class 4) 4-Y-0+ **£3,898** (£1,144; £572; £286)

Form RPR

3213 1 **Hepijeu (FR)**[15] 1308 4-10-7 116..............................(tp) AidanColeman 126+
(Charlie Longsdon) *looked wl: led: sn clr: drew rt away w one pursuer 2 out and sn brushed him aside: racing sltly awkwardly bef last and hit fence: pushed out* **3/1**[2]

53- 2 14 **Voix D'Eau (FR)**[180] 4677 5-11-6 0..............................(t) NoelFehily 128+
(Harry Fry) *trckd ldrs gng wl: wnt 2nd at 11th: ev ch 2 out: rdn and no rspnse: 7 l 2nd whn stmbld sltly last* **7/4**[1]

5454 3 16 **Midnight Game**[20] 1266 8-11-6 122..............................(p) WillKennedy 111
(Brian Ellison) *nt a fluent: trckd ldrs: wnt 2nd at 9th tl 11th: sn rdn: 6 l 3rd and fading 3 out* **8/1**

35-0 4 2 1/2 **Bonne Fee**[118] 216 8-10-13 0..............................(p) DavidBass 104
(Kim Bailey) *tended to lack fluency in 5th: brief effrt 11th: rdn and struggling next: plugged on flat* **8/1**

63-3 5 4 **Russian Bolero (GER)**[48] 1047 4-10-7 0.............................. TomScudamore 96
(David Bridgwater) *mstkes: chsd wnr 2nd tl rdn 9th: dropped out tamely 11th* **7/2**[3]

-233 6 29 **Fuzzy Logic (IRE)**[16] 1110 6-11-3 110..............................(p) RobertWilliams(3) 79
(Bernard Llewellyn) *lost tch and rdn 3rd: j. modly: t.o 10th* **20/1**

4m 46.2s (-3.80) **Going Correction** +0.15s/f (Yiel) **6 Ran SP% 110.6**
WFA 4 from 5yo+ 11lb
Speed ratings (Par 105): **114,108,101,100,98 86**
CSF £8.81 TOTE £3.70: £2.00, £1.60; EX 8.20 Trifecta £30.30.
Owner Countrywide Vehicle Rentals Taxi Hire **Bred** Mlle Francoise Perree **Trained** Over Norton, Oxon

FOCUS
An okay beginners' chase, but very few still meaningfully involved late on. The winner was back to the level of his course hurdle win.

1480 BLOOMING MARVELLOUS CHRISTMAS FAYRE NOVICES' HURDLE (8 hdls) 2m 70y
3:15 (3:15) (Class 4) 4-Y-0+ **£3,249** (£954; £477; £238)

Form RPR

1 **Francis Of Assisi (IRE)**[191] 5-10-12 0..............................[1] AidanColeman 122+
(John Ferguson) *hld up in 4th pl: j. slowly 2nd and 4th: nt fluent 3 out: clsd on bit after next: led bef last: immediately asserted and 5 l clr whn nt fluent at flight* **7/4**[2]

2/5- 2 6 **Closest Friend**[444] 729 6-10-12 0..............................(t) HarrySkelton 112
(Dan Skelton) *settled 3rd: wnt 2nd after 2 out: sn rdn and edgd rt: chsng wnr vainly whn pckd last* **7/1**

1515 3 6 **Are They Your Own (IRE)**[15] 1308 7-11-7 125..............................(t) NickSlatter(5) 121
(Fergal O'Brien) *led at mod pce: rdn after 2 out: hdd bef last: sn btn* **13/2**[3]

0-01 4 20 **Agenor (GER)**[15] 1305 4-11-5 128..............................(b) BrendanPowell 99
(Jamie Snowden) *pressed ldr tl rdn after 2 out: dropped out v tamely and floundering bef home turn* **5/4**[1]

0F- F **Run Hurricane (IRE)**[147] 5278 7-10-12 0..............................(t[1]) DaveCrosse
(John O'Shea) *hld up last: struggling 3 out: t.o next: fell last* **33/1**

3m 52.5s (-3.50) **Going Correction** -0.15s/f (Good)
WFA 4 from 5yo+ 11lb **5 Ran SP% 109.6**
Speed ratings (Par 105): **102,99,96,86,**
CSF £13.04 TOTE £2.20: £1.30, £3.20; EX 14.40 Trifecta £18.70.
Owner Bloomfields **Bred** Queen Cleopatra Syndicate **Trained** Cowlinge, Suffolk

FOCUS
The two 120s-rated performers were not at their best, but respectable form nevertheless and a winning effort worth upgrading. The early pace was moderate.

1481 KEOGH AND HOWS H'CAP CHASE (17 fncs) 2m 6f 125y
3:50 (3:50) (Class 3) (0-140,140) 4-Y-0+ **£6,388** (£1,925; £993; £526)

Form RPR

5-06 1 **Kie (IRE)**[14] 1325 7-11-9 **137**.............................. TomScudamore 148
(David Pipe) *settled trcking ldrs: wnt 2nd bef 3 out: rdn to ld bef last: urged clr flat and styd on gamely* **6/1**[3]

5122 2 6 **Mont Royale**[49] 1042 7-11-0 **128**.............................. RichieMcLernon 134
(Jonjo O'Neill) *cl 2nd: jnd ldr 5th tl led 7th: nt fluent next two: nt fluent 2 out whn 2 l clr: rdn and hdd bef last: fnd little and sn outpcd* **85/40**[1]

4-04 3 4 **Conquisto**[34] 1185 10-11-12 **140**..............................(p) AidanColeman 140
(Brian Ellison) *led 2nd tl jnd 5th: hdd 7th: rdn and lost 2nd bef 3 out: drvn and one pce between last two* **11/4**[2]

3036 4 55 **Terminal (FR)**[20] 1270 8-11-11 **139**..............................(tp) NoelFehily 90
(David Dennis) *j. slowly 3rd: rdn and lost tch 9th: t.o 12th: hacked on* **9/1**

3226 F **Buck Mulligan**[20] 1268 10-10-6 **120**.............................. PaulMoloney
(Evan Williams) *hld up last tl fell 7th* **11/4**[2]

5m 36.9s (-2.30) **Going Correction** +0.15s/f (Yiel) **5 Ran SP% 109.6**
Speed ratings (Par 107): **110,107,106,87,**
CSF £19.28 TOTE £8.00: £2.50, £1.50; EX 18.90 Trifecta £57.20.
Owner Allan Stennett **Bred** Azienda Agricola La Selvatica **Trained** Nicholashayne, Devon

FOCUS
Not quite the event it might have been following Carrigmorna King's non-participation, and \bBuck Mulligan\p's uncharacteristic fall detracted from it further. The winner is rated back to his best.

1482 HIBBERT FAMILY H'CAP HURDLE (8 hdls) 2m 70y
4:25 (4:25) (Class 2) (0-150,140) 3-Y-**£9,384** (£2,772; £1,386; £693; £346)

Form RPR

-012 1 **Broughton (GER)**[13] 1343 5-10-11 **125**..............................(bt) AidanColeman 131+
(John Ferguson) *rn in snatches: led bef 5th: hdd and mstke 3 out: led again after next: drew clr home turn but rdr did nt let up: nrly 4 l ahd and idling bdly whn j. slowly last: rdn out* **9/4**[1]

-2P4 2 2 1/4 **Laudatory**[49] 1039 9-11-12 **140**.............................. NicodeBoinville 142
(Nicky Henderson) *racd keenly: led after 2nd tl bef 5th: led again 3 out tl rdn and hdd after next: kpt on steadily but a hld fr between last two: mstke last* **10/3**[2]

000- 3 12 **Cool Macavity (IRE)**[130] 7 7-11-3 **131**.............................. DavidBass 123
(Nicky Henderson) *3rd much of way: drvn after 2 out: btn between last two* **7/2**[3]

4-11 4 10 **In On The Act**[55] 971 5-10-11 **125**.............................. PaulMoloney 105
(Evan Williams) *last pair: pushed along 3rd: rdn 5th: lost tch bef 2 out* **7/2**[3]

P-33 5 1 **Fair Dilemma (IRE)**[55] 974 10-11-1 **129**.............................. TomO'Brien 108
(Paul Henderson) *led tl after 2nd: dropped to rr and rdn 5th: last and struggling bef 2 out* **17/2**

3m 49.4s (-6.60) **Going Correction** -0.15s/f (Good) **5 Ran SP% 108.8**
Speed ratings (Par 109): **110,108,102,97,97**
CSF £9.85 TOTE £2.90: £1.70, £2.20; EX 11.20 Trifecta £25.50.
Owner Bloomfields **Bred** Gestut Westerberg **Trained** Cowlinge, Suffolk

FOCUS
A nice prize and a decent little race, for all that just one of these came into the race rated within fewer than 19lb of the ratings ceiling. There was a decent, if contested, early pace. The idling winner was value for further.

1483 MARGOT FYFE 80TH BIRTHDAY H'CAP CHASE (12 fncs) 2m 213y
5:00 (5:00) (Class 4) (0-115,115) 4-Y-0+ **£3,898** (£1,144; £572; £286)

Form RPR

U0-4 1 **Johnny Og**[13] 1349 6-11-2 **105**..............................(b[1]) AndrewTinkler 110
(Martin Keighley) *mde all: set stdy pce: rdn between last two: hld on gamely flat: all out* **13/2**

51U4 2 nk **Hawaii Five Nil (IRE)**[14] 1327 7-11-12 **115**.............(b[1]) RichieMcLernon 121
(Jonjo O'Neill) *pressed wnr tl 7th: blnd 9th: regained 2nd bef 2 out: rdn between last two: cajoled along to cl fr last: nvr really looked like getting past wnr* **11/4**[3]

-241 3 5 **Quadriller (FR)**[11] 1353 8-11-7 **110**..............................(t) RichardJohnson 112
(Philip Hobbs) *j. slowly 3rd and 5th (water): last tl wnt 4th at 7th and 3rd 2 out: sn drvn and one pce: no imp whn mstke last* **9/4**[1]

2112 4 7 **Zama Zama**[40] 1121 8-11-4 **107**..............................(v) AdamWedge 102
(Evan Williams) *3rd tl wnt 2nd at 7th: rdn 3 out: dropped out bef next* **5/2**[2]

454F 5 10 **Macarthur**[16] 1296 11-11-5 **108**..............................(p) PaulMoloney 95
(David Rees) *4th tl last at 7th: mstke next: sn rdn and no rspnse: plodded on* **10/1**

4m 10.6s (3.50) **Going Correction** +0.15s/f (Yiel) **5 Ran SP% 108.4**
Speed ratings (Par 105): **97,96,94,91,86**
CSF £23.70 TOTE £8.00: £2.40, £2.10; EX 28.20 Trifecta £115.80.
Owner T Hanlon M Boothright S Hanlon N Martin **Bred** R T Crellin **Trained** Condicote, Gloucs

FOCUS
A decent contest for the grade despite the small field, and a finish fought out by two horses sporting first-time blinkers. The first two are rated in line with their hurdles marks.

1484 ANDY TOWNSEND MEMORIAL STANDARD OPEN NATIONAL HUNT FLAT RACE 2m 70y
5:35 (5:41) (Class 6) 4-6-Y-O **£1,949** (£572; £286; £143)

Form RPR
1 **1** **Nicely Indeed (IRE)**[23] 1246 5-11-0 0.......................... MikeyHamill(7) 113+
(Seamus Durack) *prom: rdn 3f out: chal fr wl over 1f out but awkward and v green: led 120yds out: urged clr* **8/11**[1]

01- **2** *1 3/4* **Amber Spyglass**[148] 5262 5-11-7 0.......................... JackQuinlan 107
(Giles Bravery) *2nd or 3rd tl led 3f out: drvn over 1f out: kpt on gamely tl hdd and no ex fnl 120yds* **11/2**[2]

3 *3 3/4* **Crimson Ark (IRE)**[167] 5-10-4 0.......................... RichieO'Dea(10) 98
(Emma Lavelle) *tall rngy: v awkward to post: overshot s: dismntd several times bef fnlly arriving there: led and settled at slow pce: hdd 3f out: rdn and wknd over 1f out: eased whn btn* **6/1**[3]

4 *6* **Grand Enterprise** 5-11-0 0.......................... PaddyBrennan 91
(Tom George) *on his toes: pressed ldrs tl rdn and wknd over 2f out* **7/1**

0- **5** *1/2* **Run Bob Run**[264] 3122 4-11-0 0.......................... WillKennedy 90
(John Flint) *midfield: rdn 6f out: fdd over 2f out* **20/1**

6 *6* **Hard Toffee (IRE)**[126] 97 4-10-11 0.......................... MPButler(3) 84
(Michael Butler, Ire) *settled in rr: rdn 4f out: sn lost tch* **14/1**

7 *24* **Indimoon** 5-10-9 0.......................... JakeHodson(5) 60
(David Bridgwater) *on his toes: bhd: lost tch 6f out: t.o over 2f out* **33/1**

0 **8** *21* **Gentle Nature**[61] 928 4-11-0 0.......................... RobertDunne 39
(John Flint) *small: midfield: rdn and wknd 6f out: t.o over 2f out: sn eased* **50/1**

9 *43* **Justice Is Done** 5-11-0 0.......................... PeterCarberry
(Shaun Lycett) *small: v unruly and taken down early: kpt wl away fr rest at s: prom 6f: dropped out rapidly and bdly t.o fnl 7f* **20/1**

3m 50.4s **Going Correction** -0.15s/f (Good)
WFA 4 from 5yo 11lb 9 Ran SP% 121.2
Speed ratings: **94,93,91,88,88 85,73,62,41**
CSF £5.23 TOTE £1.40: £1.10, £1.90, £2.30; EX 5.70 Trifecta £15.70.
Owner Gary Tardi & ownaracehorse.co.uk **Bred** R Guiry **Trained** Upper Lambourn, Berkshire

FOCUS
No pace on at all for the first half of this bumper, but the market got this spot on and the form looks pretty straightforward. The winner is a fair sort for this time of year.
T/Plt: £82.90 to a £1 stake. Pool: £56,082.38 - 493.26 winning tickets. T/Qpdt: £27.90 to a £1 stake. Pool: £3,893.09 - 103.20 winning tickets. **Iain Mackenzie**

1350 FONTWELL (L-H)
Sunday, September 6

OFFICIAL GOING: Good (good to firm in places; 7.2)
Wind: Virtually nil Weather: Mainly sunny, light cloud

1485 M.S SOCIETY NOVICES' HURDLE (9 hdls) 2m 1f 145y
2:20 (2:20) (Class 4) 4-Y-O+ **£3,898** (£1,144; £572; £286)

Form RPR
1215 **1** **Gioia Di Vita**[26] 1039 5-11-12 125.......................... WillKennedy 131+
(Dr Richard Newland) *mde all: rdn and hit 2 out: edgd lft u.p flat: styd on wl: rdn out* **7/2**[3]

132 **2** *3 1/2* **Antony (FR)**[24] 1240 5-11-5 120.......................... RichardJohnson 120
(Gary Moore) *t.k.h: chsd ldrs: effrt to press wnr and hit 2 out: drvn between last 2: unable qck and swtchd rt: wknd fnl 150yds* **9/4**[2]

F **3** *3 1/4* **Great Fighter**[18] 1290 5-10-12 0.......................... AidanColeman 111
(John Ferguson) *chsd wnr: j. slowly 2nd: mstke 4th and 5th: dropped to 3rd and pushed along bef 2 out: drvn and unable qck between last 2: wl hld flat* **4/5**[1]

4 *55* **Hedge End (IRE)**[16] 4-10-2 0.......................... JamesBanks(3) 52
(Jimmy Fox) *j. slowly 2nd and dropped to last: detached and j. slowly next: lost tch 6th: t.o next: wnt poor 4th flat* **33/1**

F4/ **5** *18* **Dark Justice (IRE)**[13] 1271 5-10-5 0..........................(b) MarcGoldstein 36
(Michael Madgwick) *in tch in 4th: rdn and struggling 6th: lost tch next: t.o bef 2 out: lost 4th and eased flat* **150/1**

4m 25.4s (-8.90) **Going Correction** -0.65s/f (Firm)
WFA 4 from 5yo+ 11lb 5 Ran SP% 112.2
Speed ratings (Par 105): **93,91,90,65,57**
CSF £12.19 TOTE £4.80: £1.90, £1.80; EX 12.20 Trifecta £10.70.
Owner Mark Albon & Chris Stedman **Bred** Hyphen Bloodstock **Trained** Claines, Worcs

FOCUS
Not a bad novice. There's a case for rating the form up to 4lb higher.

1486 ALEXANDER KITCHENS, BATHROOMS AND BEDROOMS JUVENILE HURDLE (9 hdls) 2m 1f 145y
2:50 (2:50) (Class 4) 3-Y-O **£3,249** (£954; £477; £238)

Form RPR
12 **1** **Mountainside**[15] 1321 3-11-5 129..........................(tp) AidanColeman 105+
(John Ferguson) *mde all: clr 6th: awkward hd carriage and racing v awkwardly bef 2 out: pressed 2 out: sn drvn: hung lft but asserted u.p flat: rdn out* **2/11**[1]

2 *2 3/4* **Jersey Bull (IRE)**[9] 3-10-12 0.......................... MarcGoldstein 94
(Michael Madgwick) *t.k.h: hld up in last: mstke 1st and 5th: effrt and cl up 2 out: wnt 2nd and hit last: styd on same pce flat* **20/1**[3]

3 *5* **Fazenda's Girl**[25] 3-10-5 0.......................... WillKennedy 81
(Ian Williams) *t.k.h: chsd wnr: j. slowly and dropped to 3rd 2nd: wnt 2nd again bef 2 out: ev ch 2 out: dropped to 4th but stl cl enough last: wknd flat* **50/1**

4 **4** *nk* **Dylan's Storm (IRE)**[4] 1452 3-10-12 0..........................(t) NoelFehily 87
(David Dennis) *chsd ldrs: wnt 2nd after 1st tl bef 2 out: cl 3rd and rdn next: wnt 2nd again between last 2 tl mstke last: wknd flat* **5/1**[2]

4m 34.15s (-0.15) **Going Correction** -0.65s/f (Firm) 4 Ran SP% 108.0
Speed ratings (Par 103): **74,72,70,70**
CSF £4.79 TOTE £1.10; EX 4.60 Trifecta £15.20.
Owner Bloomfields **Bred** Darley **Trained** Cowlinge, Suffolk

FOCUS
A straightforward opportunity for the favourite but he made hard enough work of it. Suspect form.

1487 MIKE BENNETT BESTDOITNOW BEFORE IPEGOUT MEMORIAL H'CAP CHASE (16 fncs) 2m 5f 31y
3:25 (3:25) (Class 4) (0-110,108) 4-Y-O+ **£4,260** (£1,322; £712)

Form RPR
1462 **1** **Herecomesthetruth (IRE)**[24] 1244 13-11-0 96.......................... TomCannon 104+
(Chris Gordon) *chsd ldrs: hit 12th: rdn to chse ldr after next: led and j.rt 2 out: idling and wandering between last 2: over 1 l ahd whn lft wl clr last: rdn out* **6/1**

-255 **2** *26* **Top Chief**[10] 1380 7-10-11 93..........................(bt[1]) AidanColeman 77
(Anthony Honeyball) *racd keenly: chsd ldr tl led 2nd tl 6th: mstke 11th: rdn and wknd bef 3 out: lft poor 2nd and blnd last* **7/2**[3]

2262 **3** *49* **West End (IRE)**[17] 1298 8-11-12 108..........................(vt) DavidBass 48
(Kim Bailey) *led tl 2nd: chsd ldr tl led again 6th: mstke 12th: hdd 3 out: sn btn and fdd: lft poor 3rd last: t.o* **15/8**[1]

5052 **F** **Alla Svelta (IRE)**[25] 1237 9-11-4 100..........................(tp) BrendanPowell 106
(Brendan Powell) *hld up in tch: clsd to trck ldrs 11th: wnt 2nd 3 out: rdn and pressing wnr next: jst over 1 l down whn fell heavily last* **11/4**[2]

/253 **P** **Time Is Tickin**[12] 1353 9-10-13 102.......................... OCdtOswaldWedmore(7)
(Diana Grissell) *sn dropped to last and detached: nvr travelling or on terms after: t.o whn p.u last* **7/1**

5m 38.1s (-4.90) **Going Correction** -0.125s/f (Good) 5 Ran SP% 110.5
Speed ratings (Par 105): **104,94,75,,**
CSF £26.22 TOTE £5.70: £2.70, £1.70; EX 21.50 Trifecta £70.40.
Owner Mrs I Colderick **Bred** Thomas Cassidy **Trained** Morestead, Hampshire

FOCUS
The front pair had drawn clear when Alla Svelta came down at the last, leaving it to the winner. The form is rated around the two.

1488 STEPHANIE REES RAINBOW CHILD FOUNDATION H'CAP HURDLE (8 hdls 2 omitted) 2m 3f 33y
3:55 (3:55) (Class 3) (0-130,129) 4-Y-O+ **£6,498** (£1,908; £954; £477)

Form RPR
3-41 **1** **Low Key (IRE)**[10] 1379 8-11-12 129.......................... TomScudamore 135+
(David Pipe) *chsd ldrs tl led bef 3 out: hit next (actual last): sn rdn: hdd fnl 100yds: battled bk gamely u.p to ld again last stride* **4/1**[2]

14- **2** *shd* **Mantou (IRE)**[227] 3815 4-11-7 125..........................(t) AidanColeman 129
(John Ferguson) *hld up in tch in midfield: clsd to join ldr 2 out (actual last): rdn bypassing last: drvn to ld fnl 100yds: hdd last stride* **10/1**

1134 **3** *5* **Noble Friend (IRE)**[24] 1240 7-10-6 109.......................... TomCannon 109
(Chris Gordon) *hld up in rr: hdwy after 3 out: wnt 3rd (actual last): drvn and styd on same pce bypassing last* **8/1**

0143 **4** *3 1/4* **Zarawi (IRE)**[24] 1239 4-10-12 116..........................(p) RichardJohnson 112
(Charlie Longsdon) *hld up in tch in rr: effrt bef 2 out (actual last): drvn no imp bypassing last: plugged on* **12/1**

-121 **5** *2* **Welcometothejungle**[10] 1374 7-11-3 120..........................(t) NoelFehily 115
(Harry Fry) *mostly chsd ldr tl dropped to 3rd and rdn bef 2 out (actual last): wknd bypassing last* **11/4**[1]

1-10 **6** *10* **Taylor (IRE)**[105] 463 6-10-12 115.......................... DarylJacob 101
(Nicky Henderson) *hld up in last: rdn after 3 out: wknd after next (actual last)* **7/1**

-522 **7** *48* **Byron Blue (IRE)**[21] 1270 6-11-10 127.......................... TomO'Brien 70
(Mark Gillard) *j.lft: led tl bef 3 out: sn rdn and dropped out: wl bhd next (actual last): t.o* **7/1**

360- **F** **Uptendownone (IRE)**[169] 4904 6-10-7 110.......................... LeightonAspell
(Gary Moore) *hld up towards rr: fell heavily 2nd* **11/2**[3]

4m 42.8s (-16.60) **Going Correction** -0.65s/f (Firm)
WFA 4 from 6yo+ 11lb 8 Ran SP% 114.9
Speed ratings (Par 107): **108,107,105,104,103 99,79,**
CSF £42.09 CT £305.05 TOTE £5.00: £1.60, £1.90, £3.10; EX 21.50 Trifecta £344.90.
Owner G Thompson **Bred** Christoph Berglar **Trained** Nicholashayne, Devon

FOCUS
The front pair came a few lengths clear in what was a fair little handicap. The final hurdle had to be omitted on the final two circuits. The winner has the potential to rate higher yet on his best Flat form.

1489 COMMUNITY SPIRIT LIVES ON H'CAP CHASE (13 fncs) 2m 1f 96y
4:30 (4:30) (Class 5) (0-100,92) 4-Y-O+ **£2,859** (£839; £419; £209)

Form RPR
4542 **1** **Owner Occupier**[12] 1353 10-11-7 87..........................(p) TomCannon 92+
(Chris Gordon) *mde virtually all: rdn after 10th: racing lazily but finding enough for press to forge ahd between last 2: drvn out* **11/4**[2]

/P00 **2** *2 1/2* **Spiritofchartwell**[18] 1293 7-11-5 85.......................... KielanWoods 87
(Raymond York) *in tch: rdn after 7th: clsd to press ldrs and mstke 10th: rdn and j.rt next: dived last: sn chsng wnr: styd on same pce after* **11/2**

P354 **3** *3 1/2* **Accessallareas (IRE)**[6] 1422 10-11-9 92..........................(p) JamesBanks(3) 91
(Sarah-Jayne Davies) *pressed wnr: rdn after 10th: ev ch next: hrd drvn and no rspnse between last 2: mstke last: 3rd and wknd fnl 150yds* **4/1**[3]

0245 **4** *23* **Bob's Legend (IRE)**[10] 1373 9-11-12 92.......................... BrendanPowell 74
(Jamie Snowden) *chsd ldrs: mstke 8th: rdn and struggling after mstke 10th: wknd after next* **9/4**[1]

-B45 **P** **Vering (FR)**[25] 1233 9-10-9 75..........................(t) MichealNolan
(Carroll Gray) *in tch towards rr: hit 3rd: clsd to chse ldrs after 7th: struggling and mstke 10th: sn btn: t.o whn p.u last* **9/1**

0045 **P** **Bobonyx**[8] 1401 5-9-7 66 oh5..........................(t) ThomasCheesman(7)
(Dai Williams) *in tch towards rr: mstke 5th: detached and j. slowly next: losing tch and j. slowly again 7th: tailing off whn p.u bef next* **9/1**

4m 38.5s (3.80) **Going Correction** -0.125s/f (Good) 6 Ran SP% 112.8
Speed ratings (Par 103): **86,84,83,72,**
CSF £17.88 CT £58.37 TOTE £2.50: £1.40, £3.00; EX 14.80 Trifecta £57.90.
Owner A W Spooner **Bred** Bearstone Stud Ltd **Trained** Morestead, Hampshire

FOCUS
Lowly chasing form. The winner is rated to his best.

1490 FONTWELL PARK RACECOURSE SUPPORTS M.S. SOCIETY MARES' H'CAP HURDLE (11 hdls) 2m 5f 139y
5:00 (5:00) (Class 4) (0-115,118) 4-Y-O+ **£3,378** (£992; £496; £248)

Form RPR
U-51 **1** **Taradrewe**[14] 1348 8-12-1 118..........................(t) AidanColeman 127+
(Anthony Honeyball) *hld up in tch towards rr: hdwy 8th: wnt 2nd bef 2 out: rdn to ld 2 out: clr between last 2: styd on strly: rdn out* **5/1**[2]

5-64 **2** *5* **Surf In September (IRE)**[17] 1297 6-10-5 **94**........................ MarkGrant 96
(Dominic Ffrench Davis) *in tch in midfield: clsd to chse ldrs after 7th: pressing ldrs 3 out: 4th and outpcd u.p bef next: kpt on to go 2nd fnl 100yds: no threat to wnr* **20/1**

6-32 **3** *2 1/2* **Always Managing**[25] 1236 6-11-1 **104**............................(t) AndrewTinkler 106+
(Warren Greatrex) *wl in tch in midfield: clsd to chse ldrs 7th: upsides ldr after 8th: led after 3 out: hdd and rdn 2 out: btn whn wnt lft last: lost 2nd fnl 100yds* **5/1**[2]

3-23 **4** *1/2* **Stay In My Heart (IRE)**[68] 864 6-10-6 **95**........................(p) TomCannon 94
(Laura Mongan) *in tch towards rr: rdn and struggling after 7th: wl hld in 7th whn j.rt 2 out: kpt on u.p to go 4th last: no threat to wnr* **12/1**

F312 **5** *3 3/4* **Titch Strider (IRE)**[12] 1350 10-10-10 **106**............. ThomasCheesman(7) 102
(John Panvert) *hld up in tch in rr: clsd 8th: rdn after 3 out: drvn and no imp bef next: wl hld and plugged on same pce between last 2* **17/2**

-634 **6** *3 1/2* **Morestead Screamer**[24] 1242 6-10-9 **108**.................... MrWRClarke(10) 101
(Chris Gordon) *chsd ldrs: pushed along after 6th: stl cl enough and rdn 3 out: outpcd bef next: wknd between last 2* **14/1**

6404 **7** *12* **Party Palace**[4] 1238 11-10-13 **102**.. GavinSheehan 84
(Stuart Howe) *led tl after 3rd: chsd ldr tl led again 7th: rdn and hdd after 3 out: wknd next* **20/1**

-6PF **8** *8* **Amazing D'Azy (IRE)**[53] 1007 7-11-12 **115**...........................(p) DavidBass 92
(Kim Bailey) *in tch in rr: dropped to last and detached after 4th: nvr on terms after: rdn after 7th: no ch after 3 out* **22/1**

31-5 **9** *5* **Mighty Minnie**[113] 339 6-11-9 **112**.................................... RichardJohnson 82
(Henry Daly) *chsd ldrs tl hdwy to ld after 3rd: hdd 7th: lost pl qckly 3 out: wl btn next: eased flat: t.o* **3/1**[1]

/0PP **10** *3* **Oscar Baby (IRE)**[24] 1243 9-10-0 **89** oh12...................(p) MarcGoldstein 57
(Diana Grissell) *chsd ldr: nt fluent 1st: lost 2nd but styd chsng ldrs after 3rd: lost pl and j.big 8th: bhd after next: t.o* **66/1**

546/ **B** **Lady From Geneva**[537] 4884 8-10-0 **89** oh7.................(t) BrendanPowell
(Brendan Powell) *in tch towards rr tl b.d 3rd* **16/1**

-244 **F** **Tir Dubh (IRE)**[22] 1264 6-11-2 **105**.. TomO'Brien
(Robert Stephens) *in tch in midfield tl fell 3rd* **6/1**[3]

5m 27.2s (-15.30) **Going Correction** -0.65s/f (Firm) **12 Ran SP% 118.8**
Speed ratings (Par 105): **101,99,98,98,96 95,91,88,86,85 ,**
CSF £101.81 CT £531.48 TOTE £5.70: £2.00, £6.90, £2.10; EX 127.60 Trifecta £379.60.
Owner Frosties Friends II **Bred** T C Frost **Trained** Mosterton, Dorset

FOCUS
A modest mares' handicap won in dominant fashion by the top weight. Straightforward form.

1491 EQUINITI FINTECH FOR WEALTH SOLUTIONS STANDARD OPEN NATIONAL HUNT FLAT RACE 1m 5f 143y
5:30 (5:30) (Class 6) 4-6-Y-O £1,949 (£572; £286; £143)

Form RPR

35 **1** **Belcanto (IRE)**[56] 970 5-10-12 0.. BrendanPowell 97+
(Jamie Snowden) *t.k.h: led after 3f: mde rest: rdn over 2f out: kpt on u.p and forged ahd ins fnl f: rdn out* **4/1**[3]

2 *1* **Fishy Story** 5-10-12 0.. TomScudamore 97+
(David Pipe) *led for 3f: chsd wnr after: effrt to press wnr but rn green over 2f out: wandering abt over 1f out: ev ch 1f out: no ex and styd on same pce fnl 100yds* **15/8**[2]

3 *hd* **Primrose Court (IRE)** 5-10-12 0.. KielanWoods 96
(Shaun Lycett) *hld up in tch: effrt 3f out: swtchd rt over 1f out: cl 3rd and n.m.r 1f out: kpt on ins fnl f* **9/2**

4 **4** *5* **Tara Potter**[18] 1289 5-10-12 0.. HarrySkelton 90
(Dan Skelton) *t.k.h: trckd ldrs: effrt over 2f out: hung lft and no imp over 1f out: wknd ins fnl f* **7/4**[1]

5 *25* **Verax** 4-10-5 0.. MrSamPainting(7) 60
(Raymond York) *in tch: dropped to last 7f out: sn rdn: lost tch 3f out* **50/1**

3m 23.25s (-7.85) **5 Ran SP% 111.3**
CSF £12.08 TOTE £3.70: £1.80, £1.90; EX 12.30 Trifecta £32.90.
Owner Jamie Snowden Racing Club **Bred** James L O'Toole **Trained** Lambourn, Berks

FOCUS
A modest bumper and the winner's past experience made the difference. She and the fourth are rated similar to their debut runs.
T/Plt: £88.50 to a £1 stake. Pool: £78,161.83. 644.63 winning tickets. T/Qpdt: £26.60 to a £1 stake. Pool: £7,985.27. 221.60 winning tickets. **Steve Payne**

1328 PERTH (R-H)
Monday, September 7
OFFICIAL GOING: Good to firm (good in places)
Wind: Almost nil Weather: Sunny, hot

1492 STRONGBOW DARK FRUIT H'CAP CHASE (15 fncs) 2m 4f 20y
2:10 (2:10) (Class 5) (0-100,98) 4-Y-O+ £3,249 (£954; £477; £238)

Form RPR

4254 **1** **Bouggietopieces**[9] 1400 5-11-12 **98**.................................. RichardJohnson 111
(Gordon Elliott, Ire) *trckd ldrs: rdn 3 out: led next: sn hrd pressed: hld on gamely u.p towards fin* **9/4**[1]

/2-6 **2** *nk* **Manger Hanagment (IRE)**[64] 914 10-11-7 **96**...............(p) JamesBanks(3) 110
(Barry Brennan) *mostly j.ft: led: mstke 8th (water): rdn and hdd 2 out: rallied and ev ch fr last: kpt on: jst hld* **7/1**

0-34 **3** *24* **Shine A Diamond (IRE)**[67] 882 7-11-0 **89**...........(tp) GrahamWatters(3) 80
(Lucinda Russell) *hld up: smooth hdwy to chse ldrs 4 out: rdn whn hit next: sn outpcd: nt fluent 2 out: sn no imp* **9/2**[2]

3420 **4** *4 1/2* **Mister D (IRE)**[16] 1330 9-11-2 **93**............................... JonathonBewley(5) 80
(George Bewley) *in tch: hdwy and ev ch 3 out: sn rdn: wknd after next* **8/1**

4554 **5** *8* **Champagne Agent (IRE)**[11] 1370 9-10-0 **72** oh3..........(b) HenryBrooke 52
(Donald Whillans) *chsd ldrs: drvn and outpcd 5 out: struggling fr next* **6/1**[3]

U30P **6** *21* **Prince Blackthorn (IRE)**[49] 1069 9-10-0 **72**........................ BrianHughes 33
(Barry Murtagh) *hld up: hit and outpcd 5 out: btn fnl 3* **11/1**

-P31 **P** **Strobe**[17] 1306 11-11-6 **95**..(p) AdamNicol(3)
(Lucy Normile) *pressed ldr to 7th: sn lost pl: struggling fr 9th: lost tch and p.u appr 5 out* **11/1**

4-6P **F** **Karingo**[16] 1330 8-11-3 **89**.. AdrianLane
(Lucy Normile) *bhd: nt fluent 1st and 2nd: fell next* **28/1**

4m 55.8s (-9.20) **Going Correction** -0.40s/f (Good) **8 Ran SP% 111.1**
Speed ratings (Par 103): **102,101,92,90,87 78, ,**
CSF £17.44 CT £61.67 TOTE £2.90: £1.30, £2.00, £1.80; EX 15.90 Trifecta £64.70.
Owner Twenty Times Two Syndicate **Bred** Mrs P Sly **Trained** Longwood, Co Meath

FOCUS
Rail moved for fresh ground. Race 1 increased by 50yds, race 2 by 49yds, races 3 and 4 by 41yds, races 5 and 6 by 59yds. The opener was a moderate handicap chase and the two principals pulled well clear. This was a step up from the winner.

1493 MACKIES ICE CREAM H'CAP HURDLE (10 hdls) 2m 4f 35y
2:40 (2:40) (Class 4) (0-110,106) 4-Y-O+ £3,249 (£954; £477; £238)

Form RPR

3340 **1** **Drifter (IRE)**[38] 1166 4-11-1 **103**.................................. PaulNO'Brien(7) 107+
(Harry Whittington) *mde all: rdn 2 out: styd on wl fr last* **9/2**[3]

112F **2** *2* **Bennachie (IRE)**[50] 1055 6-11-7 **106**..............................(t) AlanJohns(5) 109
(Tim Vaughan) *t.k.h early: w wnr to 2 out: rdn and edgd rt run-in: kpt on* **11/4**[2]

-334 **3** *2 3/4* **Urban Kode (IRE)**[67] 886 7-10-13 **96**.....................(v) GrahamWatters(3) 97
(Lucinda Russell) *prom: effrt and rdn bef 2 out: one pce bef last* **8/1**

2321 **4** *13* **Johnny Go**[9] 1400 5-11-3 **102**.. CallumBewley(5) 93
(Lisa Harrison) *nt fluent: prom: drvn and outpcd appr 2 out: btn bef last* **6/4**[1]

3360 **5** *2 3/4* **Another Bygones (IRE)**[23] 1265 6-11-6 **100**.................... PaddyBrennan 87
(Karen McLintock) *hld up: stdy hdwy after 4 out: rdn bef 2 out: sn wknd* **14/1**

6-40 **6** *65* **Authinger (IRE)**[35] 470 7-11-7 **106**.......................(b[1]) DiarmuidO'Regan(5) 34
(Barry Murtagh) *hld up in tch: nt fluent 2nd: struggling after 4 out: lost tch after next: t.o* **28/1**

4m 51.8s (-10.20) **Going Correction** -0.40s/f (Good)
WFA 4 from 5yo+ 12lb **6 Ran SP% 106.1**
Speed ratings (Par 105): **104,103,102,96,95 69**
CSF £15.58 TOTE £5.50: £2.40, £1.30; EX 18.10 Trifecta £77.60.
Owner The Boardwalk Partnership **Bred** Churchtown, Lane & Orpendale Bloodstock **Trained** Sparsholt, Oxfordshire

FOCUS
A modest handicap hurdle, in which the first two were in front rank throughout. The first three ran pretty much to their marks.

1494 SODEXO PRESTIGE VENUES AND EVENTS H'CAP CHASE (12 fncs) 2m
3:10 (3:10) (Class 4) (0-120,119) 4-Y-O+ £6,498 (£1,908; £954; £477)

Form RPR

6-33 **1** **Robin's Command (IRE)**[16] 1328 8-11-5 **115**.................... CraigNichol(3) 126+
(Rose Dobbin) *mde all: nt fluent 1st: rdn and drew clr fr 3 out: unchal* **12/5**[2]

221- **2** *7* **Muwalla**[329] 1886 8-10-10 **108**....................................(t) CallumBewley(5) 115
(Lisa Harrison) *in tch: hdwy to chse wnr whn mstke 3 out: sn rdn: edgd rt after next: kpt on same pce* **9/1**

031P **3** *9* **Formal Bid (IRE)**[25] 1241 8-11-7 **117**.............................(bt) JamesBanks(3) 115
(Barry Brennan) *chsd wnr to bef 3 out: outpcd whn nt fluent next: sn btn* **15/2**

1204 **4** *8* **Claragh Native (IRE)**[7] 1416 10-11-5 **112**........................ HenryBrooke 103
(Martin Todhunter) *hld up: nt fluent and outpcd 5 out: btn fnl 3* **8/1**

/0-F **5** *15* **It's All An Act (IRE)**[26] 1233 7-11-12 **119**...................... RichardJohnson 100
(John Joseph Hanlon, Ire) *hld up: stdy hdwy bef 4 out: rdn and outpcd bef next: btn fnl 2* **9/4**[1]

04/5 **F** **Koup De Kanon (FR)**[43] 1110 9-11-8 **115**........................ WayneHutchinson 84
(Donald McCain) *cl up: drvn after 5 out: wknd fr next: last and no ch whn fell last* **11/2**[3]

3m 48.0s (228.00) **6 Ran SP% 108.4**
CSF £20.42 CT £121.65 TOTE £2.90: £1.40, £3.40; EX 17.50 Trifecta £76.80.
Owner M Hunter, J Matterson & R Jacobs **Bred** Gregory Lawler **Trained** South Hazelrigg, Northumbria

FOCUS
A fair handicap chase and the winner was never headed. He was well in on his old form.

1495 ISLE OF SKYE 8YO SCOTCH BLENDED WHISKY JUVENILE HURDLE (8 hdls) 2m 47y
3:40 (3:40) (Class 4) 3-Y-O £3,165 (£935; £467)

Form RPR

1 **Officer Sydney (IRE)**[21] 1281 3-11-5 0.............................. RichardJohnson 109+
(Gordon Elliott, Ire) *pressed ldr: nt fluent 1st: led 4th: nt fluent next: qcknd clr after next: pushed along and 18 l up whn blnd last: unchal* **30/100**[1]

2 *15* **Sunny Purchase (IRE)**[21] 1281 3-10-12 0........................(bt[1]) GavinSheehan 83
(John C McConnell, Ire) *led: mstke 2nd: hdd 4th: drvn along 4 out: outpcd after next: no ch w wnr* **14/1**[3]

3 *nk* **Pariyan (FR)**[76] 3-10-12 0.. WayneHutchinson 82
(Donald McCain) *t.k.h: nt fluent: chsd ldrs: shkn up and outpcd 3 out: no imp fr next* **7/2**[2]

3m 55.2s (235.20) **3 Ran SP% 105.8**
CSF £3.83 TOTE £1.30; EX 5.70 Trifecta £3.90.
Owner Mr & Mrs P Rooney Partnership **Bred** Catesby W Clay **Trained** Longwood, Co Meath

FOCUS
An uncompetitive juvenile hurdle in which the winner stood out.

1496 CRABBIE'S ALCOHOLIC GINGER BEER NOVICES' H'CAP CHASE (18 fncs) 2m 7f 180y
4:10 (4:10) (Class 4) (0-105,104) 4-Y-O+ £4,548 (£1,335; £667; £333)

Form RPR

1344 **1** **Solway Legend**[9] 1403 8-10-12 **90**.. BrianHughes 105+
(Lisa Harrison) *hld up in tch: blnd 8th: stdy hdwy 4 out: effrt 2 out: rdn to ld after last: kpt on strly* **9/4**[1]

-003 **2** *3* **Court Of Law (IRE)**[11] 1380 7-10-12 **90**........................ WayneHutchinson 100
(Donald McCain) *t.k.h: prom: hit 13th: hdwy to ld 4 out: rdn and edgd rt after 2 out: hung rt and hdd after last: kpt on same pce* **7/2**[3]

-630 **3** *10* **Northern Executive (IRE)**[19] 1287 7-10-7 **85**..............(p) PaddyBrennan 86
(Karen McLintock) *cl up: chal 5th: led 5 out to next: drvn and outpcd fr 2 out* **11/4**[2]

00/6 **4** *30* **Kilmainham (IRE)**[16] 1330 7-11-4 **96**................................ HenryBrooke 68
(Martin Todhunter) *hld up in tch: reminders after 5 out: struggling after next: t.o* **11/1**

5-00 **5** *3* **Agricultural**[16] 1330 9-10-9 **90**.. AdamNicol(3) 59
(Lucy Normile) *chsd ldrs: drvn along 5 out: wknd fr next: t.o* **16/1**

1160 **P** **Cool Star (IRE)**[16] 1329 9-11-2 **104**.....................(t) ThomasDowson(10)
(Maurice Barnes) *led: jnd 5th: hdd 5 out: wkng whn hit 3 out: sn lost tch: p.u and dismntd after next* **13/2**

5m 58.5s (-5.50) **Going Correction** -0.40s/f (Good) **6 Ran SP% 107.2**
Speed ratings (Par 105): **93,92,88,78,77**
CSF £9.75 TOTE £3.10: £2.00, £1.60; EX 8.60 Trifecta £15.80.
Owner Mr & Mrs Batey **Bred** D A Harrison **Trained** Aldoth, Cumbria

■ Stewards' Enquiry : Wayne Hutchinson two-day ban: use of whip (22-23 Sept)

FOCUS

A modest, open-looking novice handicap chase. The winner was stepping up and there is probably more to come.

1497 SAVILLS NOVICES' H'CAP HURDLE (12 hdls) 2m 7f 207y

4:40 (4:40) (Class 5) (0-100,100) 4-Y-O+ £3,165 (£935; £467; £234; £117)

Form				RPR
-561	1		**Maraweh (IRE)**[16] 1329 5-11-6 **97**......(v) DerekFox(3)	102+
			(Lucinda Russell) *pressed ldr: lost pl and outpcd 7th: rallied after 4 out: drvn and led 2 out: styd on wl* 11/4[2]	
6343	2	2 3/4	**Solway Trigger**[7] 1427 6-10-0 **74** oh1...... BrianHughes	78
			(Lisa Harrison) *in tch: stdy hdwy bef 3 out: chal gng wl bef next: sn rdn: chsd wnr run-in: kpt on* 9/4[1]	
-343	3	2	**Rosie Revenue**[16] 1329 5-11-12 **100**......(tp) RichardJohnson	101
			(Gordon Elliott, Ire) *led at stdy pce: rdn and hdd 2 out: kpt on same pce fr last* 3/1[3]	
3535	4	6	**Jackofhearts**[16] 1329 7-10-3 **80**...... JonathanEngland(3)	79
			(Jean McGregor) *prom: chal 7th to 4 out: sn rdn: outpcd bef 2 out* 6/1	
P-P4	5	33	**Saint Brieuc (FR)**[11] 1368 6-11-1 **89**...... HenryBrooke	55
			(Simon West) *hld up in tch: stdy hdwy bef 3 out: rdn and wkng whn nt fluent next: sn btn and eased* 8/1	

6m 7.9s (2.90) **Going Correction** -0.40s/f (Good) 5 Ran SP% **107.8**
Speed ratings (Par 103): **79,78,77,75,64**
CSF £9.10 TOTE £4.00: £1.50, £1.70; EX 11.70 Trifecta £25.70.
Owner Tay Valley Chasers Racing Club **Bred** Shadwell Estate Company Limited **Trained** Arlary, Perth & Kinross

FOCUS

Only a moderate handicap hurdle, but the winner is progressive.
T/Plt: £31.00 to a £1 stake. Pool of £46543.37 - 1095.10 winning tickets. T/Qpdt: £6.90 to a £1 skake. Pool of £2673.66 - 285.92 winning tickets. **Richard Young**

[1492] PERTH (R-H)

Tuesday, September 8

OFFICIAL GOING: Good to firm (good in places) changing to good after race 2 (5.40)

Wind: Almost nil Weather: Overcast

1498 OLD MOUT CIDER NOVICES' HURDLE (A STRONGBOW DARK FRUIT SCOTTISH HURDLE RACE SERIES QUALIFIER) (10 hdls) 2m 4f 35y

5:10 (5:11) (Class 4) 4-Y-O+ £3,165 (£935; £467; £234; £117)

Form				RPR
5230	1		**Welcome Ben (IRE)**[24] 1265 6-10-9 110...... TonyKelly(3)	107+
			(Jackie Stephen) *chsd ldr: hdwy to ld after 2 out: rdn whn pckd last: styd on strly* 5/1[2]	
1-2	2	2	**Mr Steadfast (IRE)**[17] 1328 5-11-5 119......(t) RichardJohnson	113+
			(Gordon Elliott, Ire) *in tch: stdy hdwy 1/2-way: nt fluent 4 out and next: effrt and ev ch whn nt fluent 2 out: sn rdn: kpt on same pce fr last* 4/11[1]	
4	3	7	**Lough Derg Cruise (IRE)**[119] 257 5-9-12 0...... MissRMcDonald(7)	92
			(Sandy Thomson) *t.k.h: led: nt fluent 3rd: qcknd bef 4 out: rdn whn mstke 2 out: sn hdd: outpcd bef last* 18/1	
06	4	4 1/2	**Drop A Gear (IRE)**[17] 1328 5-10-12 0...... PeterBuchanan	94
			(Lucinda Russell) *hld up: stdy hdwy after 4 out: rdn and outpcd bef 2 out: sn btn* 9/1[3]	
05/0	5	57	**Thehoodlum**[93] 656 8-10-9 0...... JonathanEngland(3)	37
			(Jean McGregor) *prom: lost pl 1/2-way: lost tch fr 4 out: t.o* 250/1	

5m 11.7s (9.70) **Going Correction** +0.15s/f (Yiel) 5 Ran SP% **105.6**
Speed ratings (Par 105): **86,85,82,80,57**
CSF £7.05 TOTE £4.30: £1.90, £1.10; EX 8.50 Trifecta £20.10.
Owner Ben's Men **Bred** Dermot Cross **Trained** Inverurie, Aberdeens

FOCUS

Rail moved out on bends. 2m races increased by 41yds, 2m 4f by 50yds and 2m 7f and 3m by 59yds. This is form to take with a pinch of salt as they crawled around before sprinting for home around two out. The winner ran to his best.

1499 GREEN HOTEL NOVICES' HURDLE (A STRONGBOW DARK FRUIT SCOTTISH HURDLE RACE SERIES QUALIFIER) (8 hdls) 2m 47y

5:40 (5:40) (Class 4) 4-Y-O+ £3,165 (£935; £467; £234; £117)

Form				RPR
0-1	1		**Tempo Mac (IRE)**[39] 1172 5-12-5 132...... RichardJohnson	131+
			(Gordon Elliott, Ire) *t.k.h: chsd ldrs: wnt 2nd after 4th: nt fluent next: led bef 2 out: sn hrd pressed: keeping on wl whn lft 4 l clr last: drvn out* 15/8[2]	
4	2	5	**Lady Clitico (IRE)**[17] 1328 4-10-2 113...... TonyKelly(3)	98
			(Rebecca Menzies) *t.k.h: prom: effrt and rdn bef 2 out: one pce whn lft 4 l 2nd last: no imp* 6/1[3]	
	3	15	**Hitman Hearns (IRE)**[191] 6-10-9 0...... CraigNichol(3)	91
			(Keith Dalgleish) *pressed ldr: led bef 4th: rdn after next: hdd bef 2 out: sn outpcd: no imp whn lft 15 l 3rd last* 25/1	
	4	7	**Laajooj (IRE)**[913] 7-10-12 0......[1] AidanColeman	87+
			(John Ferguson) *nt fluent: t.k.h early in rr: pushed along and hdwy after 3 out: rdn and wknd next: lft 17 l 4th last* 11/8[1]	
-U52	5	16	**Ronaldinho (IRE)**[12] 1065 5-10-12 115...... HenryBrooke	75
			(Dianne Sayer) *hld up: pushed along and outpcd bef 3 out: sn btn* 10/1	
	6	10	**Here Comes Molly (IRE)**[9] 1407 4-10-5 0...... TomScudamore	54
			(John Joseph Hanlon, Ire) *bhd: struggling fr 1/2-way: nvr on terms* 40/1	
00	7	1 3/4	**Tish Hall (IRE)**[11] 1393 5-10-5 0...... PeterBuchanan	53
			(S R B Crawford, Ire) *bhd: hit and struggling 4 out: sn btn* 150/1	
5	F		**Where's Tiger**[17] 1328 4-10-7 0...... GrantCockburn(5)	100
			(Lucinda Russell) *in tch: pushed along and outpcd bef 2 out: lft 10 l 3rd and fell last* 33/1	
	P		**Gotcha**[156] 4-10-0 0...... StephenMulqueen(5)	
			(N W Alexander) *t.k.h: led to bef 4th: struggling next: p.u bef 3 out* 80/1	
3-34	F		**Ethelwyn**[98] 590 5-10-5 0...... BrianHughes	102+
			(Malcolm Jefferson) *hld up: hit 4th: hdwy 3 out: chalng whn hit next: sn rdn: ev ch whn fell last* 28/1	

3m 52.0s (232.00)
WFA 4 from 5yo+ 11lb 10 Ran SP% **114.8**
CSF £12.44 TOTE £3.10: £1.20, £1.60, £6.00; EX 12.30 Trifecta £153.50.
Owner J P McGovern **Bred** Padraig Williams **Trained** Longwood, Co Meath

FOCUS

A modest novice hurdle, best rated around the runner-up.

1500 ORION GROUP H'CAP CHASE (18 fncs) 2m 7f 180y

6:10 (6:10) (Class 4) (0-115,115) 4-Y-O+ £3,898 (£1,144; £572; £286)

Form				RPR
-004	1		**Presented (IRE)**[17] 1332 8-11-2 **110**...... CallumBewley(5)	119
			(Lisa Harrison) *chsd ldrs: hmpd 1st: led 5 out: hrd pressed fr 3 out: drifted lft run-in: styd on wl u.p* 4/1[3]	
2453	2	3/4	**Sandynow (IRE)**[18] 1306 10-10-10 **102**......(vt) SeanBowen(3)	112+
			(Peter Bowen) *led to 2nd: nt fluent next (water): led 6th: nt fluent 11th (water): hdd 5 out: blkd bnd bef 3 out: chal bef next: sn rdn: carried lft run-in: kpt on same pce towards fin* 3/1[1]	
44P-	3	7	**Donapollo**[142] 5407 7-10-5 **97**...... CraigNichol(3)	100
			(Rose Dobbin) *cl up: led 2nd to 6th: w ldr to 5 out: rdn whn blkd bnd bef 3 out: drvn and outpcd next: no imp whn edgd rt run-in* 3/1[1]	
/0-1	4	36	**Down Time (USA)**[19] 1303 5-11-4 **107**......(p) RichardJohnson	91
			(John Joseph Hanlon, Ire) *hld up in tch: stdy hdwy 11th: mstke 13th: rdn after 4 out: wknd fr next* 7/2[2]	
5/30	F		**King's Legacy (IRE)**[39] 1167 11-11-12 **115**......(t) AidanColeman	117
			(Lawney Hill) *hld up in tch: effrt and rdn bef 3 out: no imp fr next: 5 l down and disputing 3rd whn fell last* 11/2	

6m 9.6s (5.60) **Going Correction** -0.025s/f (Good) 5 Ran SP% **107.6**
Speed ratings (Par 105): **89,88,86,74,**
CSF £15.47 TOTE £4.70: £2.10, £1.50; EX 18.50 Trifecta £60.00.
Owner Abbadis Racing Club & Partner **Bred** Miss Catherine M Walsh **Trained** Aldoth, Cumbria
■ Stewards' Enquiry : Callum Bewley one-day ban: careless riding (Sep 22)

FOCUS

Only two mattered from the penultimate fence in this ordinary staying handicap. The winner was on a very good mark.

1501 SALUTATION HOTEL H'CAP HURDLE (8 hdls) 2m 47y

6:40 (6:40) (Class 4) (0-110,110) 3-Y-O+ £3,898 (£1,144; £572; £286)

Form				RPR
0-04	1		**Makethedifference (IRE)**[24] 1265 7-11-3 **101**...... MichaelByrne	115+
			(Tim Vaughan) *in tch: hdwy and cl up whn hit 2 out: led last: rdn out* 7/2[1]	
2623	2	1 3/4	**Dynamic Drive (IRE)**[5] 1461 8-10-3 **97**......(t) ThomasDowson(10)	109
			(Maurice Barnes) *chsd ldrs: smooth hdwy to ld 2 out: rdn and hdd last: kpt on same pce run-in* 7/2[1]	
10-0	3	11	**Calton Entry (IRE)**[17] 1333 6-11-9 **110**...... SeanBowen(3)	112
			(Linda Perratt) *chsd ldr: led briefly appr 2 out: rdn and outpcd between last 2* 5/1[3]	
/05-	4	4	**Call Of Duty (IRE)**[20] 1547 10-10-0 **84** oh1...... HenryBrooke	83
			(Dianne Sayer) *hld up: drvn and outpcd bef 3 out: rallied next: no imp* 12/1	
	5	7	**Old Storm (IRE)**[127] 113 6-11-4 **102**......(t) RichardJohnson	94
			(John Joseph Hanlon, Ire) *led: rdn and hdd appr 2 out: sn wknd* 4/1[2]	
2-05	6	3 1/2	**Goal (IRE)**[12] 1377 7-11-5 **110**......(t) MissBHampson(7)	99
			(Andy Turnell) *hld up: shortlived effrt 3 out: sn rdn and wknd* 12/1	
-U06	7	14	**Saint Elm (FR)**[39] 1166 5-10-3 **87**...... BrianHughes	63
			(Patrick Griffin, Ire) *bhd: mstke and rdn 4 out: struggling fr next* 6/1	

3m 53.5s (233.50) 7 Ran SP% **110.8**
CSF £15.37 CT £56.28 TOTE £3.20: £2.10, £1.70; EX 15.30 Trifecta £89.90.
Owner Brian Jones **Bred** Tipper House Stud **Trained** Aberthin, Vale of Glamorgan

FOCUS

This moderate handicap was run at a sound gallop. The second is a decent benchmark and the winner was taking a big step up from Market Rasen.

1502 MACKIES FROM SKY TO SCOOP H'CAP CHASE (FOR THE INVERNESS CUP) (15 fncs) 2m 4f 20y

7:10 (7:10) (Class 3) (0-140,137) 4-Y-O+ £9,747 (£2,862; £1,431; £715)

Form				RPR
6-23	1		**Border Breaker (IRE)**[79] 808 6-11-0 **125**......(tp) TomScudamore	130+
			(David Pipe) *chsd ldrs: pushed along whn lft 2 l 2nd and checked 3 out: rallied after next: styd on wl u.p to ld towards fin* 9/4[1]	
2215	2	hd	**Russian Regent (IRE)**[58] 961 11-11-5 **130**...... RichardJohnson	135
			(Gordon Elliott, Ire) *chsd ldr: hit 4 out: 1 l down whn lft 2 l clr next: sn rdn: edgd rt run-in: kpt on: hdd towards fin* 7/2[2]	
F5/1	3	16	**Run With The Wind (IRE)**[39] 1173 9-11-6 **131**......(t) PeterBuchanan	121
			(S R B Crawford, Ire) *t.k.h early: prom: drvn and outpcd whn lft 4 l 3rd 3 out: wknd fr next* 4/1[3]	
/1-4	4	1/2	**Nearest The Pin (IRE)**[9] 1409 10-11-12 **137**...... GavinSheehan	125
			(John Joseph Hanlon, Ire) *t.k.h: hld up in last pl: drvn and outpcd whn lft 8 l 4th 3 out: sn btn* 9/2	
-231	F		**Enchanted Garden**[34] 913 7-11-10 **135**......(b) BrianHughes	138+
			(Malcolm Jefferson) *led: 1 l in front and gng wl whn fell 3 out* 4/1[3]	

4m 59.4s (-5.60) **Going Correction** -0.025s/f (Good) 5 Ran SP% **111.2**
Speed ratings (Par 107): **110,109,103,103,**
CSF £10.57 TOTE £3.00: £1.50, £1.90; EX 10.30 Trifecta £42.70.
Owner Jimmy Hack Racing Partners 1 **Bred** Mrs B D Byrne **Trained** Nicholashayne, Devon

FOCUS

A fair little handicap with the winner on the upgrade.

1503 CRABBIE'S ALCOHOLIC GINGER BEER AMATEUR RIDERS' H'CAP HURDLE (12 hdls) 2m 7f 207y

7:40 (7:40) (Class 4) (0-115,115) 4-Y-O+ £3,119 (£967; £483; £242)

Form				RPR
5301	1		**Western Way (IRE)**[24] 1265 6-11-12 **115**......(b) MrDerekO'Connor	123+
			(Don Cantillon) *chsd ldrs: rdn bef 2 out: edgd rt and led between last 2: nt fluent last: drvn out* 9/4[2]	
-453	2	2 1/4	**Skylander (IRE)**[27] 1238 6-11-5 **115**...... MrTGreatrex(7)	119
			(David Pipe) *hld up: stdy hdwy after 3 out: rdn next: rallied to chse wnr run-in: kpt on* 11/8[1]	
0112	3	1/2	**Count Salazar (IRE)**[17] 1332 10-11-8 **114**......(p) MissBHampson(3)	118
			(Andy Turnell) *led: rdn bef 2 out: hdd between last 2: rallied: kpt on same pce run-in* 4/1[3]	
0623	4	10	**Solway Bay**[17] 1332 13-9-9 **89**......(t) MissRMcDonald(5)	83
			(Lisa Harrison) *chsd ldr: rdn and ev ch 2 out: hung lft and wknd fr last* 8/1	
000/	5	16	**Blue Cannon (IRE)**[11] 1394 7-11-12 **115**......(p) MrSClements	94
			(S R B Crawford, Ire) *nt fluent: hld up in tch: drvn and struggling bef 2 out: sn wknd* 16/1	

6m 5.5s (0.50) **Going Correction** +0.15s/f (Yiel) 5 Ran SP% **109.9**
Speed ratings (Par 105): **105,104,104,100,95**
CSF £5.94 TOTE £3.20: £1.50, £1.50; EX 5.50 Trifecta £7.90.
Owner Don Cantillon **Bred** Don Cantillon **Trained** Newmarket, Suffolk

FOCUS
Not a bad staying handicap, confined to amateur riders. The winner stepped up for the longer trip and is the type to rate higher.
T/Plt: £15.50 to a £1 stake. Pool: £51,391.91 - 2,414.04 winning tickets T/Qpdt: £4.50 to a £1 stake. Pool: £5,553.51 - 912.58 winning tickets **Richard Young**

1450 WORCESTER (L-H)
Tuesday, September 8

OFFICIAL GOING: Good to firm (7.4)
Wind: light breeze Weather: overcast; 14 degrees

1504 LEWIS BADGES NOVICES' H'CAP CHASE (13 fncs) 2m 4f
2:10 (2:11) (Class 4) (0-120,118) 4-Y-0+ **£3,768** (£1,106; £553; £276)

Form RPR
-225 **1** **Set List (IRE)**[55] 1002 6-11-11 **117**........ DarylJacob 129+
(Emma Lavelle) *cl up: lost pl 6th: j. slowly next: rallied on inner 10th: led after 3 out: 2 l clr last: pushed out: comf* **10/3**[1]
5133 **2** *6* **Mr Mafia (IRE)**[20] 1293 6-10-9 **101**........(t) LeeEdwards 107
(Tony Carroll) *settled towards rr: mstke 8th: effrt in 3rd bef 10th: led next: sn hdd: urged along and nt qckn fr last* **7/2**[2]
2004 **3** *1 3/4* **Battlecat**[16] 1347 8-10-8 **105**........ ConorRing(5) 110+
(Evan Williams) *t.k.h in midfield: rdn and flattered 3 out: no imp next: 6 l 3rd whn pckd bdly last: plugged on* **12/1**
-5F2 **4** *14* **Cayman Islands**[17] 1330 7-11-4 **117**........ MrAlexFerguson(7) 110
(John Ferguson) *led: hdd 3 out: dropped out v tamely after next* **4/1**[3]
-4F4 **5** *29* **Definite Future (IRE)**[63] 936 6-11-4 **110**........ TomCannon 87
(Kerry Lee) *pressed ldr: mstke 9th: rdn bef next: wkng whn blnd 3 out: t.o and eased last* **7/2**[2]
104- **6** *30* **Rayak (IRE)**[17] 5432 5-11-12 **118**........ RichieMcLernon 56
(Jonjo O'Neill) *plld hrd in last pair: j. hesitantly early: stl wl in tch and gng strly 9th: bmpd along briefly: t.o bef 3 out* **16/1**
23-6 **P** **Cash Injection**[126] 122 6-11-4 **110**........(t) NoelFehily
(Richard Woollacott) *last pair: rdn 9th: lost tch next: t.o and p.u 10th* **10/1**
4m 47.8s (-16.80) **Going Correction** -0.675s/f (Firm) **7 Ran SP% 110.2**
Speed ratings (Par 105): **106,103,102,97,85 73,**
CSF £14.63 CT £112.34 TOTE £4.40: £1.70, £3.00; EX 20.40 Trifecta £114.30.
Owner Tim Syder **Bred** Mrs Kathleen And James Wickham **Trained** Hatherden, Hants
FOCUS
All starts have been moved at this track following remeasuring, so there will be no speed figures here until there is sufficient data to calculate updated median times. The rail was positioned 5 metres from the innermost line on the far bend, adding approximately 30yds to races 1, 4, 6 & 7, and 15yds to races 2, 3 & 5. Good to firm ground that had been watered. A fair novice handicap chase run at a reasonable gallop with the winner taking a big step up on his hurdle form.

1505 WORCESTER NEWS NOVICES' CHASE (12 fncs) 2m 110y
2:40 (2:40) (Class 4) 4-Y-0+ **£3,768** (£1,106; £553; £276)

Form RPR
-113 **1** **Ittirad (USA)**[17] 1333 7-11-5 0........ SamTwiston-Davies 132+
(John Ferguson) *sn chsng ldr: led on bit 2 out: 5 l clr last: effrtlessly* **30/100**[1]
211- **2** *6* **Lyric Street (IRE)**[403] 1145 7-11-5 0........ WayneHutchinson 116
(Donald McCain) *t.k.h and j.rt early: rdn and hdd 2 out: immediately outpcd: hit last hrd* **4/1**[2]
-036 **3** *17* **Moveable Asset (IRE)**[55] 1012 7-11-5 0........ BrendanPowell 101
(Henry Tett) *sn settled in 3rd pl: rdn bef 9th: struggling after* **25/1**
4 *dist* **Shaky Gift (IRE)**[142] 6-10-12 0........ MarkQuinlan
(Neil Mulholland) *led in s: j.rt and ambled rnd in detached last becoming progively more remote: j. last after wnr fin* **20/1**[3]
4m 2.1s (-2.90) **Going Correction** -0.675s/f (Firm) **4 Ran SP% 105.5**
Speed ratings (Par 105): **79,76,68,**
CSF £1.87 TOTE £1.10; EX 1.70 Trifecta £4.20.
Owner Bloomfields **Bred** Darley **Trained** Cowlinge, Suffolk
FOCUS
Not much depth to this, but a very promising winner who is value for further. All four were making their chasing debut.

1506 SIS MARES' MAIDEN HURDLE (8 hdls) 2m
3:10 (3:10) (Class 5) 4-Y-0+ **£2,274** (£667; £333; £166)

Form RPR
4-33 **1** **Northern Meeting (IRE)**[14] 1352 5-11-0 105........ TomO'Brien 100+
(Robert Stephens) *t.k.h: travelled wl and a had ears pricked: mde most at mod pce: steadily drew clr fr 2 out: over 2 l in front and edging rt whn landed in a heap at last: urged along and a holding rival flat* **2/1**[1]
54-1 **2** *6* **Kayla**[131] 45 5-11-0 0........(t) PaddyBrennan 95+
(Stuart Edmunds) *trckd ldrs: wnt 2nd after 5th: drew upsides 3 out tl next: sn rdn and nt qckn: hld whn edgd lft flat* **2/1**[1]
3 *9* **Miss Tiger Lily**[476] 5-11-0 0........ BrendanPowell 85
(Jamie Snowden) *small: settled in cl 3rd or 4th: rdn and outpcd by ldng pair bef 2 out: plugged on for mod 3rd* **9/1**[3]
P5P **4** *3 1/2* **Cearys (IRE)**[55] 1009 7-11-0 0........(p) AndrewTinkler 81
(Martin Keighley) *bhd: last and rdn 5th: passed btn horses whn rdn fr next: tk mod 4th at last: nvr looked like landing a blow* **100/1**
6 **5** *3 3/4* **Little Dream (IRE)**[18] 1308 8-11-0 0........ PaulMoloney 78
(Evan Williams) *small: on her toes: t.k.h in midfield: pushed along and outpcd bef 3 out: hit last* **25/1**
-640 **6** *3 1/2* **Pretty Rose (IRE)**[12] 1374 5-11-0 0........ DarylJacob 76
(Ben Case) *small: prom tl 5 l 3rd and rdn home turn: btn after3 out: plugged on fr next* **5/1**[2]
7 *3 1/2* **Alianca (IRE)**[453] 4-11-0 0........ NickScholfield 73
(Lawney Hill) *towards rr: rdn and btn bef 3 out: blnd next* **25/1**
000- **8** *3 1/2* **Bronwydd**[173] 4869 5-11-0 0........ TrevorWhelan 70
(Debra Hamer) *w ldr whn blnd 2nd: t.k.h: prom tl drvn and fdd bef 3 out* **250/1**
63 **9** *3 1/2* **Brenda De Ronceray (FR)**[51] 1050 4-10-7 0........ MichaelHeard(7) 65
(David Pipe) *cl up: w ldr briefly 4th: rdn and dropped out rapidly wl bef 3 out* **9/1**[3]
P **10** *8* **Brean Splash Susie**[15] 1117 4-10-9 0........ RyanWhile(5) 58
(Bill Turner) *towards rr: rdn 5th: sn struggling: t.o* **66/1**
60/ **P** **Youmaysee**[648] 2796 5-10-7 0........ MrStanSheppard(7)
(Matt Sheppard) *plld hrd: led or prom tl mstke 3rd: stopped rapidly next: t.o and p.u after 5th* **100/1**
3m 42.8s (-7.80) **Going Correction** -0.475s/f (Good)
WFA 4 from 5yo+ 11lb **11 Ran SP% 114.9**
Speed ratings (Par 103): **100,97,92,90,88 87,85,83,81,77**
CSF £5.55 TOTE £2.70: £1.10, £1.20, £2.80; EX 8.30 Trifecta £31.20.
Owner The Go Slow Club **Bred** Ballymacoll Stud Farm Ltd **Trained** Penhow, Newport
FOCUS
A weak mares' maiden hurdle run at a fairly modest tempo. The winner was the hurdle form pick.

1507 BETTINGGODS.COM NOVICES' HURDLE (12 hdls) 2m 7f
3:40 (3:40) (Class 4) 4-Y-0+ **£3,249** (£954; £477; £238)

Form RPR
4-11 **1** **Hunt Ball (IRE)**[109] 434 10-11-12 135........ AndrewTinkler 134+
(Nicky Henderson) *racd enthusiastically in cl 2nd tl mde most fr 6th: wnt 2 l clr 3 out: rdn next: edgd lft after last: all out after but hld on tenaciously* **6/4**[2]
121 **2** *3/4* **Mont Choisy (FR)**[16] 1349 5-10-12 118........ SamTwiston-Davies 120+
(Nigel Twiston-Davies) *set stdy pce tl nt fluent 6th: drvn and sltly outpcd bef 3 out: rallied after next: tried to chal on inner and mstke last: taken outside and styd on u.p: a jst hld fnl 100yds* **11/10**[1]
053 **3** *16* **Airpur Desbois (FR)**[20] 1290 5-10-12 0........ PaddyBrennan 105
(Charlie Mann) *last tl drvn into 3rd bef 3 out: sn outpcd by ldng pair: plugged on* **25/1**
01-4 **4** *6* **She's Late**[64] 930 5-11-5 124........(p) NoelFehily 108
(Jonjo O'Neill) *3rd tl 8 l last and rdn bef 3 out: btn whn hit next: edgd rt bef last: eased flat* **5/1**[3]
5m 35.4s (-3.20) **Going Correction** -0.475s/f (Good) **4 Ran SP% 108.1**
Speed ratings (Par 105): **86,85,80,78**
CSF £3.65 TOTE £2.20; EX 4.20 Trifecta £11.70.
Owner Atlantic Equine **Bred** Michael Slevin **Trained** Upper Lambourn, Berks
FOCUS
The pace lifted on the second circuit and the first two came clear. The first three ran pretty much to their marks.

1508 CLARE CHIPPING RETIREMENT H'CAP HURDLE (8 hdls) 2m
4:10 (4:10) (Class 4) (0-120,120) 3-Y-0+ **£3,249** (£954; £477; £238)

Form RPR
5321 **1** **King Muro**[18] 1307 5-10-13 **107**........(t) PaddyBrennan 118+
(Fergal O'Brien) *t.k.h and travelled wl: hld up last tl 4th: effrt in last of five gng clr home turn: clsd grad on outer tl reminder to ld last: drvn and kpt on steadily flat* **3/1**[1]
04F5 **2** *1 3/4* **Watt Broderick (IRE)**[24] 1265 6-10-11 **105**........(t) WillKennedy 112
(Ian Williams) *led: rdn 2 out: hdd last: kpt on same pce and a hld flat* **5/1**[2]
3431 **3** *4 1/2* **Ladies Dancing**[47] 1083 9-10-9 **103**........(b) JamesDavies 106
(Chris Down) *prom: disp 2nd and rdn 3 out: nt qckn fr next and wl hld after* **8/1**
F333 **4** *2 1/4* **Anton Dolin (IRE)**[8] 1421 7-10-3 **104**........ MrHFNugent(7) 106
(Michael Mullineaux) *nt fluent 3rd: trckd ldrs: wnt 2nd 1/2-way: rdn and disp 2nd 3 out: fnd little and no real danger fr next* **8/1**
45-6 **5** *9* **Tiradia (FR)**[8] 1421 8-10-11 **110**........ MikeyEnnis(5) 104
(J R Jenkins) *hld up towards rr: effrt after 5th: 4th and rdn home turn: struggling after 3 out* **17/2**
145- **6** *15* **Zip Wire (IRE)**[419] 973 6-11-7 **115**........ WayneHutchinson 97
(Donald McCain) *chsd ldrs: mstke 4th: drvn and struggling after next: wl bhd whn blnd 2 out* **14/1**
0-1F **7** *hd* **Honkytonktennessee (IRE)**[39] 1166 6-11-2 **110**........ DaveCrosse 90
(Hugo Froud) *pressed ldr tl wnt rt 4th: dropped bk 7th and losing tch qckly home turn* **9/1**
P5U- **8** *5* **Talkin Thomas (IRE)**[171] 9-10-11 **105**........ SeanQuinlan 80
(Michael Appleby) *midfield: lost tch after 5th* **7/1**[3]
1444 **9** *12* **Monte Wildhorn (IRE)**[16] 1346 7-10-12 **111**........ JakeHodson(5) 75
(David Bridgwater) *chsd ldrs tl lost pl rapidly 4th: sn wl detached* **14/1**
120 **P** **Ubaldo Des Menhies (FR)**[46] 1100 7-11-12 **120**....(p) RichieMcLernon
(Jonjo O'Neill) *chsd ldrs tl blnd 5th: nt rcvr and sn lost tch: wl bhd whn p.u last* **8/1**
3m 40.5s (-10.10) **Going Correction** -0.475s/f (Good) **10 Ran SP% 121.4**
Speed ratings (Par 105): **106,105,102,101,97 89,89,87,81,**
CSF £19.73 CT £112.58 TOTE £4.10: £1.60, £2.30, £2.90; EX 33.40 Trifecta £160.30.
Owner The General Asphalte Company Ltd **Bred** Stourbank Stud **Trained** Naunton, Gloucs
■ Stewards' Enquiry : Paddy Brennan two-day ban: used whip without giving gelding time to respond (Sep 22-23)
FOCUS
This modest handicap was run in a time 2.3sec quicker than the earlier mares' maiden. The form looks sound with another step up from the winner and more to come.

1509 NEW HOPE "HANDS AND HEELS" H'CAP HURDLE (FOR CONDITIONAL JOCKEYS AND AMATEUR RIDERS) (DIV I) (10 hdls) 2m 4f
4:40 (4:42) (Class 5) (0-100,98) 4-Y-0+ **£2,469** (£725; £362; £181)

Form RPR
30-3 **1** **Western Goose (IRE)**[39] 1171 8-11-9 **98**........ FinianO'Toole(3) 105+
(Heather Dalton) *settled remote 3rd: wnt 2nd at 7th and sn clsd on tearaway ldr: led 3 out: 2 l clr last: pushed along after: bit in hand* **9/1**
6656 **2** *4* **Bus Named Desire**[18] 1310 7-10-8 **83**........(tp) TobyWheeler(3) 85
(Ian Williams) *hld up in midfield: effrt 7th: 3rd home turn: rdn 2 out: kpt on same pce: wnt 2nd fnl 75yds* **11/2**[3]
20 **3** *2 1/4* **Ennisnag (IRE)**[20] 1293 10-11-8 **97**........ MrGTreacy(3) 98
(Paul Henderson) *hld up in rr: prog after 7th: wnt 2nd bef 2 out: fnd nil whn rdn: plugged on: lost 2nd clsng stages* **16/1**
4551 **4** *3 1/4* **Lee Side Lady (IRE)**[14] 1356 5-11-7 **93**........ MrMartinMcIntyre 90
(Neil Mulholland) *hld up towards rr: effrt after 7th: 4th and rdn and hld whn edgd rt after 2 out* **4/1**[2]
-550 **5** *2 1/2* **Element Quartet (IRE)**[58] 966 6-10-3 **75**........(t) LiamMcKenna 70
(Brendan Powell) *chsd long ldr tl hit 7th: rdn and outpcd after next* **11/2**[3]
4-36 **6** *2* **Marlpit Oak**[26] 1245 10-10-11 **88**........ MrDSansom(5) 82
(Seamus Mullins) *off pce in midfield: rdn bef 3 out: plodded on and n.d after* **33/1**
FU36 **7** *3 1/2* **Iktiview**[20] 1293 7-10-8 **80**........(bt) MrStanSheppard 70
(Matt Sheppard) *bhd: last and drvn after 7th: nt keen and no ch after* **7/2**[1]
P440 **8** *6* **Driving Well (IRE)**[20] 1287 7-9-11 **72** oh1........ MrJamesKing(3) 56
(Arthur Whiting) *bhd: rdn after 7th: no rspnse and sn wl btn* **6/1**
4U-P **9** *16* **Surprise Us**[22] 699 8-10-3 **78**........(p) MrTGillard(3) 48
(Mark Gillard) *on his toes: set off too fast and sn 25 l clr: mstke 4th: maintained advantage tl rdn after 7th: hdd and blnd 3 out: lost pl rapidly and dropped bk to last at last* **25/1**
4m 46.6s (-6.90) **Going Correction** -0.475s/f (Good) **9 Ran SP% 109.9**
Speed ratings (Par 103): **94,92,91,90,89 88,87,84,78**
CSF £53.87 CT £728.73 TOTE £7.70: £2.20, £2.00, £3.00; EX 52.80 Trifecta £726.40.
Owner Ms Heather Dalton **Bred** Joseph Tierney **Trained** Childs Ercall, Shropshire

FOCUS
Very moderate form though a biggish step up from the winner, but it was the quicker division by four seconds. The remainder of the field ignored the tearaway leader Surprise Us, who came back to them on the home turn.

1510 NEW HOPE "HANDS AND HEELS" H'CAP HURDLE (FOR CONDITIONAL JOCKEYS AND AMATEUR RIDERS) (DIV II) (10 hdls) 2m 4f
5:15 (5:17) (Class 5) (0-100,98) 4-Y-O+ £2,469 (£725; £362; £181)

Form RPR
P20- 1 **King's Song (FR)**[150] 5281 5-11-8 93 MrZBaker 97
(David Dennis) *settled towards rr: effrt in 4th home turn: led narrowly after 2 out: wnt 2 l clr and rdn along after last: hld on wl* **9/2**[2]
-005 2 nk **Barton Antix**[19] 1297 6-11-11 96 (p) MrMartinMcIntyre 100
(Neil Mulholland) *t.k.h in slowly run r: cl up: nt fluent 6th: wnt 3rd home turn: bmpd along and outpcd 2 out: rallied after last: wnt 2nd 100yds out and styd on wl: too much to do* **9/2**[2]
B632 3 3 ½ **Mix N Match**[8] 1423 11-9-11 71 oh1 HarryCobden(3) 72
(Laura Young) *hld up last tl 6th: stdy prog 3 out: chal fr next: rdn and w wnr last: lost 2nd fnl 100yds and wknd* **5/1**[3]
5P24 4 9 **Mount Vesuvius (IRE)**[8] 1421 7-11-1 89 (tp) MrGTreacy(3) 82
(Paul Henderson) *t.k.h in slowly run r: wnt 2nd at 3rd: led after 7th: hdd after 2 out: dropped out steadily: fin weakly flat* **8/1**
64P 5 3 ½ **Trakeur (FR)**[27] 1235 8-10-2 78 MrMSBastyan(5) 68
(Simon Hodgson) *bhd: last and nt fluent 6th: struggling after* **12/1**
3405 6 6 **Prince Of Poets**[17] 1324 4-11-12 98 (b) DavidNoonan 81
(David Pipe) *2nd or 3rd tl rdn and ev ch 2 out: fnd nil and dropped out tamely* **7/2**[1]
-P5P 7 16 **Newton Martini**[8] 1426 6-10-5 79 (bt) HarrisonBeswick(3) 49
(Ben Pauling) *led at sedate pce: rdn after 7th: sn hdd and dropped herself out* **9/2**[2]
4m 50.8s (-2.70) **Going Correction** -0.475s/f (Good) 7 Ran SP% **112.2**
Speed ratings (Par 103): **86,85,84,80,79 77,70**
CSF £24.08 CT £102.79 TOTE £4.80: £2.60, £2.60; EX 31.90 Trifecta £135.50.
Owner Favourites Racing (Syndication) Ltd 2 **Bred** Keith Bradley **Trained** Hanley Swan, Worcestershire
■ Stewards' Enquiry : Mr Z Baker seven-day ban: used whip contrary to race rules (Sep 30, Oct 1,8,10,20,22,23)

FOCUS
They took things very steadily in the initial part of the race and the time was four seconds slower than division one. A small step up from the first two.
T/Plt: £59.60 to a £1 stake. Pool: £53,369.10 - 653.55 winning tickets. T/Qpdt: £19.70 to a £1 stake. Pool: £3,917.50 - 146.63 winning tickets. **Iain Mackenzie**

1511 - 1514a (Foreign Racing) - See Raceform Interactive

1183 GALWAY (R-H)
Tuesday, September 8

OFFICIAL GOING: Good (good to firm in places)
Rails: Actual race distances: 4.25 & 7.25- 2m125y; 4.55 & 5.25- 2m5f50y; 5.55 - 2m2f174y

1515a BALLYBRIT NOVICE CHASE (GRADE 3) (12 fncs) 2m 2f 54y
6:25 (6:25) 4-Y-O+ £15,116 (£4,418; £2,093; £697)

RPR
1 **Rock The World (IRE)**[40] 1161 7-11-1 140 (t) BarryGeraghty 147+
(Mrs John Harrington, Ire) *led: pressed clly bef 2 out and pushed along after last: rdn w narrow advantage appr st and hdd ent fnl f: rallied far side to regain advantage fnl 100yds: styd on wl to extend advantage cl home* **11/10**[1]
2 2 **The Game Changer (IRE)**[40] 1163 6-11-8 144 (t) BJCooper 152+
(Gordon Elliott, Ire) *settled bhd ldr in 2nd: nt fluent 7th: gng best in cl 2nd after last: rdn to ld ent fnl f: hdd u.p fnl 100yds and sn no ex in 2nd* **7/4**[2]
3 22 **Upazo (FR)**[19] 1302 7-11-5 137 RWalsh 127
(W P Mullins, Ire) *w.w bhd ldrs in 3rd: no imp on ldrs in mod 3rd 2 out: pushed along after last and no ex run-in: one pce* **7/2**[3]
4 76 **Battling Boru (IRE)**[25] 1253 9-11-1 0 (p) DannyMullins 47
(Anthony Mullins, Ire) *in rr thrght: detached fr 1st and nvr involved: completely t.o* **25/1**
4m 21.6s (-13.90) 4 Ran SP% **110.1**
CSF £3.60 TOTE £1.90; DF 2.80 Trifecta £4.80.
Owner Michael Buckley **Bred** D Donegan **Trained** Moone, Co Kildare

FOCUS
A cracking spectacle, just like when the front two clashed earlier in the campaign at Roscommon. At the weights, the form should have been reversed though it looked more a case of the winner wanting it more here.

1516 - 1517a (Foreign Racing) - See Raceform Interactive

1109 UTTOXETER (L-H)
Wednesday, September 9

OFFICIAL GOING: Good (8.2)
Wind: moderate 1/2 behind Weather: fine

1518 BETFRED RACING "FOLLOW US ON TWITTER" MAIDEN HURDLE (DIV I) (10 hdls) 2m 3f 207y
1:40 (1:40) (Class 5) 4-Y-O+ £2,469 (£725; £362; £181)

Form RPR
1 **Samtu (IRE)**[57] 4-10-13 0 (t) HarrySkelton 117+
(Dan Skelton) *led tl after 1st: chsd ldr: led bef 3 out: hit last 2: drvn out* **9/2**
2 6 **Teviot Prince (IRE)**[442] 807 5-10-7 0 MrZBaker(7) 111
(Martin Bosley) *chsd ldng pair: 3rd whn blnd 2 out: modest 2nd last: kpt on same pce* **150/1**
235 3 ½ **Gambol (FR)**[9] 1425 5-11-0 120 RichardJohnson 112
(Ian Williams) *led after 1st: chsd ldr: hdd bef 3 out: 2nd whn blnd 2 out: kpt on same pce* **4/1**[3]
62-4 4 5 **Flash Crash**[114] 176 6-10-11 112 JamesBanks(3) 107
(Barry Brennan) *rr-div: drvn after 5th: hdwy 3 out: kpt on between last 2* **10/1**
213 5 12 **Tilinisi (IRE)**[52] 1057 5-10-7 0 KielanWoods 93+
(Phil Middleton) *mid-div: modest 4th 5th: drvn bef 3 out: lost pl bef 2 out: eased run-in* **10/3**[1]
5 6 ½ **Native Robin (IRE)**[27] 1246 5-11-0 0 NickScholfield 94
(Jeremy Scott) *in rr: t.o 7th: nvr on terms* **66/1**
6-03 7 nk **Trojan Star (IRE)**[119] 279 5-11-0 0 DavidBass 96
(Kim Bailey) *in rr: sme hdwy 5th: drvn 7th: nvr on terms* **16/1**
0 8 11 **Lilbourne Legacy**[21] 1289 4-10-13 0 TomScudamore 83
(David Pipe) *in rr: bhd fr 7th* **50/1**
152- 9 14 **Champagne Chaser**[200] 4350 5-11-0 0 MichaelByrne 71
(Tim Vaughan) *in rr: hit 2nd: sme hdwy 5th: lost pl next: t.o 7th* **8/1**
1/ P **Tom Lamb**[566] 4384 5-11-0 0 WillKennedy
(Jonjo O'Neill) *nt fluent: mid-div: reminders and lost pl bef 6th: t.o 7th: p.u bef 3 out* **7/2**[2]
4m 58.4s (-4.80) **Going Correction** -0.35s/f (Good)
WFA 4 from 5yo+ 12lb 10 Ran SP% **113.7**
Speed ratings (Par 103): **95,92,92,90,85 85,85,80,75,**
CSF £426.43 TOTE £5.10: £2.00, £26.20, £1.50; EX 402.20 Trifecta £1440.10 Part won..
Owner Craig Buckingham **Bred** Rabbah Bloodstock Limited **Trained** Alcester, Warwicks

FOCUS
Some starts have been moved at this track following remeasuring, so some races will not have speed figures until there is sufficient data to calculate updated median times. The 2m chute was not in use due to drainage works, therefore there was a temporary start for the 2m hurdle races at the end of the back straight. The hurdles were 9yds off the inside rail, which added 46yds per circuit. As a result the 2m and 2m 4f hurdle races were extended by 69yds and the 2m 7.5f hurdle race was 92yds longer. The going was given as good all over and had been watered the day prior to racing. After the first both Richard Johnson and Harry Skelton agreed that it was riding exactly as the official description. The first division of a modest maiden hurdle in which they went a good pace and were quickly strung out.

1519 BETFRED RACING "FOLLOW US ON TWITTER" MAIDEN HURDLE (DIV II) (10 hdls) 2m 3f 207y
2:10 (2:10) (Class 5) 4-Y-O+ £2,469 (£725; £362; £181)

Form RPR
4535 1 **Keep Calm**[25] 1260 5-11-0 107 HenryBrooke 105+
(John Mackie) *chsd ldng trio: lost pl and reminders 7th: hdwy 3 out: cl 3rd 2 out: led last: drvn rt out* **9/1**[3]
6-45 2 1 **The Clonlisk Bug (IRE)**[21] 1289 5-11-0 0 BrianHughes 104
(Kevin Frost) *in rr: pushed along 6th: hdwy 3 out: chsng ldrs next: styd on run-in: tk 2nd post* **20/1**
0-50 3 nse **St Quintin**[25] 1260 5-11-0 0 PaddyBrennan 103
(David Brown) *in rr: drvn 7th: chsng ldrs 2 out: kpt on same pce run-in: n.m.r and eased fnl strides: lost 2nd post* **20/1**
2 4 2 ½ **Dusk Till Dawn (IRE)**[65] 928 6-11-0 0 TomScudamore 101
(David Pipe) *chsd ldr: drvn bef 3 out: one pce appr last* **13/8**[2]
F- 5 1 **Ashtown (IRE)**[308] 2277 8-11-0 0 MarkQuinlan 100
(Malcolm Jones) *chsd ldng pair: led narrowly 2 out: hdd last: one pce* **25/1**
6 1 ¼ **A Little Magic (IRE)** 4-10-13 0 RichieMcLernon 99
(Jonjo O'Neill) *t.k.h in rr: hdwy 4th: chsng ldrs bef 6th: drvn 3 out: one pce appr last* **25/1**
P **Dragon City**[695] 5-11-0 0 (t) NoelFehily
(Charlie Mann) *t.k.h towards rr: sme hdwy 6th: drvn next: sn lost pl: bhd whn p.u bef 3 out* **14/1**
43- P **Deadly Move (IRE)**[305] 2353 6-11-0 0 RichardJohnson 95
(Charlie Longsdon) *led: hdd and blnd 2 out: stl chsng ldrs whn eased and p.u appr last: b.b.v* **11/8**[1]
F **Seeanythingyoulike (IRE)** 4-10-13 0 LiamHeard
(Jeremy Scott) *t.k.h in rr: fell 1st* **66/1**
4m 56.2s (-7.00) **Going Correction** -0.35s/f (Good)
WFA 4 from 5yo+ 12lb 9 Ran SP% **115.6**
Speed ratings (Par 103): **100,99,99,98,98 97, , ,**
CSF £149.34 TOTE £9.10: £2.10, £3.20, £4.60; EX 110.20 Trifecta £2090.60 Part won..
Owner Derbyshire Racing VI **Bred** Aislabie Bloodstock Ltd **Trained** Church Broughton , Derbys

FOCUS
Two seconds quicker than the first division, but also a modest race. Strong market moves suggested this was a two-horse affair, but both those prominent in the market blew out, which led to a messy bunched finish.

1520 BETFRED "RACING'S BIGGEST SUPPORTER" BEGINNERS' CHASE (18 fncs) 3m 2y
2:40 (2:40) (Class 4) 4-Y-O+ £3,938 (£1,262; £701)

Form RPR
1-21 1 **Ballykan**[104] 518 5-11-7 0 (t) DarylJacob 130+
(Nigel Twiston-Davies) *chsd ldr: led 4 out: rdn appr last: forged clr run-in* **3/1**[2]
-042 2 7 **Shantou Tiger (IRE)**[43] 1134 6-11-7 120 WayneHutchinson 124
(Donald McCain) *led: hdd 4 out: rdn bef 2 out: 2 l down last: kpt on same pce* **7/1**
3 3 23 **Go On Henry (IRE)**[47] 1097 7-11-7 0 (t) RichardJohnson 109
(Philip Hobbs) *in rr: lft modest 3rd 12th: lost tch 4 out: eased run-in* **12/1**
5132 U **Mile House (IRE)**[15] 1351 7-11-7 130 TomO'Brien
(Robert Stephens) *handy 3rd 8th: mstke and uns rdr 12th* **5/1**[3]
24P- U **Parish Business (IRE)**[152] 5254 7-11-7 0 (t) AidanColeman
(Emma Lavelle) *trckd ldng pair: blnd and uns rdr 7th* **5/4**[1]
160 P **Bobble Emerald (IRE)**[21] 1292 7-11-7 110 [1] AndrewTinkler
(Martin Keighley) *nt fluent in last: bhd fr 7th: t.o whn p.u bef 14th* **40/1**
6m 5.9s (-2.20) **Going Correction** -0.35s/f (Good) 6 Ran SP% **108.7**
Speed ratings (Par 105): **89,86,79, ,**
CSF £21.20 TOTE £3.00: £2.00, £3.20; EX 15.40 Trifecta £50.30.
Owner Simon Munir & Isaac Souede **Bred** Donhead Stud **Trained** Naunton, Gloucs

FOCUS
Most of these had shown fair form in hurdles or points, so on paper it looked an above-average beginners' chase. However, the race rather fell apart with the departure of two of the first three in the market. The winner was up a stone on the best of his hurdle figures.

1521 BETFRED "BE PART OF THE ACTION" H'CAP HURDLE (10 hdls) 2m 3f 207y
3:15 (3:15) (Class 3) (0-140,126) 4-Y-O £5,317 (£1,570; £785; £393; £196)

Form RPR
-121 1 **Kalifourchon (FR)**[24] 1269 4-11-2 117 TomScudamore 124+
(David Pipe) *trckd ldr: led 7th: pushed along appr next: 3 l clr last: eased clsng stages: v readily* **7/4**[1]
21P4 2 4 **Detroit Blues**[21] 1290 5-11-3 117 (t) MichealNolan 118
(Jamie Snowden) *chsd ldrs: 2nd 3 out: styd on same pce between last 2* **20/1**
12-6 3 6 **Champagne Present (IRE)**[7] 1448 5-11-12 126 (t) RichardJohnson 123
(Jonjo O'Neill) *led: hdd 7th: swtchd rt appr last: one pce* **11/4**[2]
2251 4 9 **No Likey (IRE)**[20] 1296 8-11-6 120 (t) TomO'Brien 111
(Philip Hobbs) *chsd ldrs: mstke and lost pl 6th: wknd 3 out* **9/1**
5 7 **High Counsel (IRE)**[107] 6-11-1 120 BridgetAndrews(5) 104
(Gary Hanmer) *t.k.h in last: j.lft 2nd: chsd ldrs 7th: wknd next* **7/2**[3]

The Form Book Jumps 2015-16, Raceform Ltd, Newbury, RG14 5SJ

5- **P** **Itshard To No (IRE)**[31] 1216 6-11-5 **119**..........................(t) CharliePoste
(Kerry Lee) *towards rr: lost pl 7th: sn bhd: t.o whn eased 2 out: p.u bef last* **10/1**
4m 52.6s (-10.60) **Going Correction** -0.35s/f (Good)
WFA 4 from 5yo+ 12lb **6** Ran SP% **109.1**
Speed ratings (Par 107): **107,105,103,99,96**
CSF £27.18 TOTE £2.10: £1.20, £6.60; EX 30.70 Trifecta £100.50.
Owner CHM Partnership **Bred** I , J P , G & C Garcon **Trained** Nicholashayne, Devon
FOCUS
A 0-140 handicap, in which the top-rated runner had an official mark of 126 and everything else was 120 or below, so nothing came close to the ceiling rating. The first two are on the upgrade, though.

1522 BETFRED "SUPPORTS JACK BERRY HOUSE" H'CAP HURDLE (12 hdls) 2m 7f 70y
3:50 (3:51) (Class 4) (0-120,120) 4-Y-O+ **£3,249** (£954; £477; £238)

Form RPR
5551 **1** **Princeton Royale (IRE)**[13] 1375 6-11-2 **115**..................(v) LizzieKelly(5) 130+
(Neil King) *hld up in rr: hdwy 9th: handy 3rd next: led last: drvn out* **4/1**[2]
3412 **2** 2 ¾ **Mighty Leader (IRE)**[7] 1455 7-10-6 **100**.......................... JamesDavies 110
(Henry Oliver) *chsd ldr: narrow ld 2 out: hdd last: styd on same pce run-in* **9/2**[3]
-011 **3** ½ **Standing Ovation (IRE)**[18] 1322 8-11-12 **120**.........(bt) TomScudamore 130
(David Pipe) *led: pushed along 8th: drvn appr 3 out: hdd 2 out: styd on same pce run-in* **9/4**[1]
40-4 **4** 22 **Adam Du Breteau (FR)**[131] 56 5-11-0 **108**............(p) RichardJohnson 101
(Jonjo O'Neill) *chsd ldrs: wknd 2 out: poor 4th whn blnd last* **5/1**
U2/ **5** 1 ¾ **Murchu (IRE)**[720] 1611 9-10-13 **107**........................(t) AidanColeman 97
(Tim Vaughan) *mid-div: drvn and outpcd 9th: lost pl bef next* **12/1**
/1-P **6** 10 **Sinbad The Sailor**[38] 1184 10-11-9 **117**........................(vt) TrevorWhelan 97
(George Baker) *in rr: hdwy and in tch 9th: sn given reminders: lost pl bef next: sn bhd* **20/1**
P46- **7** 9 **Tales Of Milan (IRE)**[187] 4612 8-11-7 **118**...................(vt) TomBellamy(3) 90
(Phil Middleton) *chsd ldrs: drvn 9th: lost pl appr next* **14/1**
P61- **8** 9 **Madrasa (IRE)**[13] 4827 7-10-2 **103**...........................(p) JoshWall(7) 66
(Tony Forbes) *hld up towards rr: rapid hdwy 5th: w ldr next: lost pl appr 3 out: sn bhd* **25/1**
54-P **9** 7 **Knocklong (IRE)**[123] 203 7-11-6 **114**.......................... RichieMcLernon 71
(Ben Haslam) *in rr: drvn 8th: bhd fr 3 out* **33/1**
PP/P **P** **Mr Cracker (IRE)**[20] 1296 10-11-4 **112**.......................... MichaelByrne
(Tim Vaughan) *in rr: mstke 4th: bhd and reminders 8th: t.o whn p.u bef next* **50/1**
5m 48.6s (-10.20) **Going Correction** -0.35s/f (Good) **10** Ran SP% **113.5**
Speed ratings (Par 105): **103,102,101,94,93 90,87,83,81,**
CSF £21.05 CT £48.85 TOTE £4.80: £1.50, £1.90, £1.60; EX 23.40 Trifecta £64.50.
Owner D Nott, P Beadles, R Clarke **Bred** Brett Merry **Trained** Barbury Castle, Wiltshire
FOCUS
A decent race for the grade where they went a fair pace throughout. The winner is on the upgrade in the visor.

1523 BETFRED SCOOP6SOCCER H'CAP CHASE (15 fncs) 2m 4f
4:20 (4:20) (Class 4) (0-120,120) 4-Y-O **£3,798** (£1,122; £561; £280; £140)

Form RPR
1633 **1** **Jayo Time (IRE)**[21] 1291 6-10-9 **110**......................(p) CiaranGethings(7) 125+
(Kerry Lee) *sn trcking ldrs: hit 10th: 2nd next: led sn after 3 out: 6 l ahd last: drvn out* **7/2**[3]
2 3 ¼ **Valadom (FR)**[206] 6-11-3 **111**.. AlainCawley 124+
(Richard Hobson) *led: hit 6th: hit 3 out: sn hdd: j.rt next: kpt on run-in* **12/1**
-642 **3** 24 **According To Sarah (IRE)**[19] 1306 7-11-2 **110**.......... RichardJohnson 105
(Philip Hobbs) *chsd ldrs: wknd 3 out: j.rt next: eased run-in* **2/1**[2]
2431 **4** 21 **Ladfromhighworth**[24] 1267 10-11-12 **120**.......................... NickScholfield 100
(Jeremy Scott) *chsd ldrs: drvn 11th: lost pl bef next: sn wl bhd* **15/8**[1]
0125 **5** 21 **River Purple**[24] 1267 8-11-9 **117**..(t) DarylJacob 68
(John Mackie) *racd in last: pushed along 10th: lost pl next: sn wl bhd* **8/1**
4m 59.5s (-10.30) **Going Correction** -0.35s/f (Good) **5** Ran SP% **109.1**
Speed ratings (Par 105): **106,104,95,86,78**
CSF £32.37 TOTE £4.50: £2.40, £3.10; EX 33.10 Trifecta £110.50.
Owner S R Holt & Mrs B M Ayres **Bred** E J P Kane **Trained** Byton, H'fords
■ Kerry Lee's first winner.
FOCUS
Just a modest chase with a personal best from the winner.

1524 BETFRED "HOME OF GOALS GALORE" H'CAP HURDLE (DIV I) (8 hdls 1 omitted) 1m 7f 215y
4:55 (4:55) (Class 5) (0-100,100) 3-Y-O+ **£2,469** (£725; £362; £181)

Form RPR
-000 **1** **Worldor (FR)**[52] 1048 9-10-13 **87**..(t) AdamWedge 102+
(Alexandra Dunn) *hld up in rr: hdwy 5th: handy 2nd bef 2 out: led appr last: drvn out* **9/1**
-011 **2** 3 ½ **Empty The Tank (IRE)**[7] 1446 5-11-7 **95** 7ex.............. RichardJohnson 102
(Jim Boyle) *trckd ldrs: led bef 3 out: hdd appr last: kpt on same pce* **11/8**[1]
5-62 **3** 7 **Mandy's Boy (IRE)**[9] 1421 5-11-12 **100**.......................... TomScudamore 100
(Ralph J Smith) *hld up towards rr: hdwy to chse ldrs 5th: 3rd appr 2 out: kpt on one pce* **8/1**
2-22 **4** 1 ¾ **Supernoverre (IRE)**[90] 692 9-10-9 **83**..............................(p) AidanColeman 81
(Alan Jones) *towards rr: bhd 5th: hdwy 3 out: 4th bef 2 out: one pce* **9/1**
-P04 **5** 14 **Primo Rossi**[19] 1310 6-10-0 **74** oh1..(p) JamesDavies 58
(Tom Gretton) *chsd ldrs: lost pl bef 2 out* **16/1**
215- **6** 2 **Operateur (IRE)**[37] 1887 7-11-5 **93**.......................... RichieMcLernon 75
(Ben Haslam) *chsd ldrs: lost pl 3 out* **16/1**
2114 **7** 20 **The Kvilleken**[13] 1383 7-11-10 **98**..............................(p) AndrewTinkler 60
(Martin Keighley) *in rr: bhd fr 5th* **7/1**[3]
1U55 **8** 5 **Cornish Beau (IRE)**[27] 1244 8-11-2 **90**..............................(b) WillKennedy 47
(Dr Richard Newland) *led: j.lft 4th: hdd bef 3 out: sn lost pl and bhd* **6/1**[2]
PP-0 **9** 6 **Moving Waves (IRE)**[38] 1182 4-10-13 **87**..............................(bt[1]) BrendanPowell 38
(Johnny Farrelly) *chsd ldrs: lost pl 3 out: sn bhd* **25/1**
3m 50.5s (230.50) **Going Correction** -0.35s/f (Good)
WFA 4 from 5yo+ 11lb **9** Ran SP% **115.6**
Speed ratings (Par 103): **103,101,97,96,89 88,78,76,73**
CSF £22.55 CT £107.23 TOTE £12.50: £2.30, £1.50, £2.30; EX 35.50 Trifecta £200.80.
Owner Nigel Berbillion **Bred** Jean-Pierre Claudic & Valerie Claudic **Trained** West Buckland, Somerset

FOCUS
A weak race in which the winner was supported from an overnight price of 50-1. He was a 120-rated hurdler in Ireland.

1525 BETFRED "HOME OF GOALS GALORE" H'CAP HURDLE (DIV II) (8 hdls 1 omitted) 1m 7f 215y
5:25 (5:26) (Class 5) (0-100,99) 3-Y-O+ **£2,469** (£725; £362; £181)

Form RPR
U422 **1** **Cruise In Style (IRE)**[7] 1454 9-11-6 **93**..........................(tp) JamesBest 104+
(Kevin Bishop) *hld up towards rr: hdwy 4th: sn trcking ldrs: handy 2nd appr last: led last: pushed out* **5/1**[2]
0-63 **2** 3 ¼ **Sweet World**[15] 1356 11-11-0 **90**.......................... RobertWilliams(3) 96
(Bernard Llewellyn) *mid-div: chsng ldrs 5th: led appr 3 out: hdd last: styd on same pce* **9/1**
5P-0 **3** 5 **Mulligan's Man (IRE)**[51] 1071 8-11-8 **95**.......................... DavidEngland 96
(Clare Ellam) *chsd ldrs: 2nd 3 out: kpt on one pce appr next* **16/1**
U0-0 **4** 9 **Youm Jamil (USA)**[34] 1095 8-10-0 **73** oh6..........................(t) PaddyBrennan 67
(Tony Carroll) *in rr: hdwy appr 3 out: modest 4th appr 2 out: nvr a factor* **16/1**
-556 **5** 21 **Bumble Bay**[48] 1081 5-11-12 **99**.. TomO'Brien 73
(Robert Stephens) *chsd ldrs 3rd: lost pl appr 3 out* **7/2**[1]
0-46 **6** 2 ½ **Private Jones**[7] 1446 6-11-0 **87**.. RobertDunne 60
(Miss Imogen Pickard) *led: hdd after 4th: led briefly bef 3 out: hit 3 out: lost pl bef 2 out* **6/1**[3]
-40P **7** 9 **Candelita**[9] 1420 8-11-7 **97**.. KyleJames(3) 60
(Alan Berry) *chsd ldr: led after 4th: drvn next: reminders and hdd bef 3 out: sn lost pl* **40/1**
-244 **8** 36 **Wymeswold**[19] 1307 8-10-12 **85**.. RichardJohnson 16
(Michael Mullineaux) *chsd ldrs: blnd 5th: sn lost pl: bhd next: sn t.o* **7/2**[1]
540/ **P** **King's Opus (IRE)**[502] 5547 6-11-1 **88**..........................(t) DavidBass
(Kim Bailey) *mid-div: chsd ldrs 5th: drvn appr next: sn lost pl: poor 7th whn p.u sn after 2 out: lame* **6/1**[3]
3m 54.7s (234.70) **Going Correction** -0.35s/f (Good) **9** Ran SP% **113.9**
Speed ratings (Par 103): **92,90,87,83,72 71,67,49,**
CSF £47.89 CT £665.04 TOTE £4.20: £2.00, £2.50, £3.50; EX 34.60 Trifecta £186.20.
Owner Steve Atkinson **Bred** Swordlestown Stud **Trained** Spaxton, Somerset
FOCUS
This division of a moderate contest was four seconds slower than the previous race. The in-form winner is rated back to her best.
T/Plt: £1433.80 to a £1 stake. Pool: £86,298.91 - 43.93 winning units. T/Qpdt: £29.40 to a £1 stake. Pool: £6,823.18 - 171.60 winning units. **Walter Glynn**

1526 - 1543a (Foreign Racing) - See Raceform Interactive

[1478] STRATFORD (L-H)
Monday, September 14

OFFICIAL GOING: Good (good to firm in places) changing to good (good to soft in places) after race 1 (2.20) changing to good to soft after race 2 (2.50)
Weather: Frequent showers

1544 SIS NOVICES' HURDLE (9 hdls) 2m 2f 148y
2:20 (2:20) (Class 4) 4-Y-O+ **£3,249** (£954; £477; £238)

Form RPR
1 **1** **Maputo**[23] 1328 5-11-5 0..[1] AidanColeman 137+
(John Ferguson) *mostly chsd ldr: cruised up on bit to ld bef last: flicked last and sn wl clr wout being asked: easily* **8/11**[1]
0111 **2** 18 **Tangolan (IRE)**[14] 1424 7-11-5 115..........................(t) PaddyBrennan 118+
(Fergal O'Brien) *led: j.big and out to the rt 2nd where nrly shot rdr out of sddle: j.big after: hdd bef last: kpt on one pce* **11/4**[2]
0/2 **3** 9 **Authorative (IRE)**[10] 1471 5-10-12 99.......................... BrendanPowell 101
(Anthony McCann, Ire) *in tch: prog to chse ldng pair 3 out: cl up next: sn drvn and outpcd* **25/1**
01-6 **4** 12 **Florrie Boy (IRE)**[121] 341 4-10-11 0.......................... SamTwiston-Davies 87
(Nigel Twiston-Davies) *nt fluent: t.k.h on inner: in tch: outpcd in 6th after 3 out: no ch after: kpt on* **8/1**
5 ¾ **Linguine (FR)**[325] 5-10-12 0.. ConorO'Farrell 90
(Seamus Durack) *mostly trckd ldng pair to 3 out: wknd next* **7/1**[3]
5-2 **6** 17 **Fields Of Glory (FR)**[117] 400 5-10-12 0.......................... RichardJohnson 75
(Tim Vaughan) *chsd ldrs: outpcd fr 3 out: wknd after next* **16/1**
5 **7** 21 **The Mythologist (IRE)**[18] 1379 7-10-12 0.......................... MichaelByrne 53
(Tim Vaughan) *hld up wl in rr: outpcd whn mstke 3 out: nvr involved* **50/1**
05 **8** 12 **Gilmer (IRE)**[12] 1453 4-10-11 0..(t) JamesBest 42
(Laura Young) *hld up wl in rr: mstke 5th and lost tch: t.o* **100/1**
P/ **9** 47 **Greek Islands (IRE)**[19] 2417 7-10-12 0.......................... MarkQuinlan
(Neil Mulholland) *trckd ldrs and t.k.h: wknd qckly fr 3 out: t.o* **66/1**
10 22 **Whitstable Native**[755] 7-10-12 0.. PaulMoloney
(Sophie Leech) *hld up wl in rr: wl bhd bef 3 out: sn wknd: t.o* **100/1**
P-50 **U** **Iwanabebobbiesgirl**[46] 1153 5-10-5 0.......................... LiamTreadwell
(Debra Hamer) *hld up wl in rr: disputing 9th whn mstke and uns rdr 6th* **100/1**
4m 32.9s (1.40) **Going Correction** +0.40s/f (Soft)
WFA 4 from 5yo+ 11lb **11** Ran SP% **124.3**
Speed ratings (Par 105): **113,105,101,96,96 89,80,75,55,46**
CSF £3.22 TOTE £1.80: £1.10, £1.30, £4.70; EX 3.40 Trifecta £16.40.
Owner Bloomfields **Bred** Darley **Trained** Cowlinge, Suffolk
FOCUS
The way the track was railed resulted in the following distances being added to each race: Races 1, 2 & 6 - 42 yds, Race 3 - 84 yds, Race 4 - 54 yds & Race 5 - 51 yds. 5mm of rain fell over the weekend and Paddy Brennan described the ground as "bordering on soft". Not the most competitive novice hurdle with the favourite a league apart. He looks a decent novice.

1545 IRL RACECOURSES H'CAP HURDLE (11 hdls) 2m 6f 7y
2:50 (2:51) (Class 4) (0-110,110) 4-Y-O+ **£5,198** (£1,526; £763; £381)

Form RPR
500/ **1** **Our Folly**[25] 5138 7-10-8 **92**..(t) TomScudamore 96
(Stuart Kittow) *wl in tch: prog to ld 2 out: hdd bef last: led again last 110yds: hld on wl* **3/1**[1]
-162 **2** 1 ¼ **Midnight Sapphire**[57] 1055 5-11-4 **102**..........................(t) DenisO'Regan 106
(Victor Dartnall) *hld up on inner in tch: hdwy to chse ldr and led bef last: mstke last and hdd 110yds out: kpt on wl* **9/2**[2]
3432 **3** 1 ½ **Presenting Streak (IRE)**[12] 1447 6-11-3 **108**.......................... MrRWinks(7) 111
(Peter Winks) *chsd ldrs: mstke 3 out: drvn in 6th after 2 out: clsd bef last: kpt on but nvr quite able to chal* **5/1**[3]

-342 **4** *3 1/4* **Fred Le Macon (FR)**[25] 1297 6-10-9 **103**.................... JamieInsole(10) 104
(Alan King) *hld up in rr but in tch: tk clsr order fr 3 out where slt mstke: pressed ldrs after 2 out: rdn and kpt on same pce after* **6/1**

61-6 **5** *2 1/4* **Demographic (USA)**[111] 493 6-11-7 **105**..............(v) RichieMcLernon 102
(Emma Lavelle) *trckd ldrs: narrow ld 3 out tl hdd 2 out: one pce and hld whn mstke last* **9/1**

4030 **6** *21* **Maller Tree**[26] 1287 8-11-3 **108**..............................(v) JamieBargary(7) 91
(David Dennis) *disp ld to 7th: sn u.p: wknd after 3 out* **14/1**

-625 **7** *34* **Key To Milan**[33] 1238 9-11-5 **110**...........................(tp) CiaranGethings(7) 58
(Chris Down) *disp ld: rdn after 8th and hdd: wknd qckly: t.o* **8/1**

PP32 **8** *48* **Mrs Jordan (IRE)**[30] 1262 7-11-4 **102**.......................(tp) PaulMoloney 6
(Sophie Leech) *towards rr: rdn and wknd 8th: t.o* **16/1**

26/0 **P** **Pepito Collonges (FR)**[97] 675 12-10-0 **84** oh13.......... BrendanPowell
(Laura Mongan) *in tch: hit 6th: wknd 8th: t.o whn p.u bef 2 out* **100/1**

-6UP **P** **Mostly Bob (IRE)**[78] 847 12-10-10 **97**......................(tp) KillianMoore(3)
(Sophie Leech) *j. slowly 1st: sn dropped to last and gng bdly: t.o whn p.u bef 8th* **25/1**

5m 42.3s (14.20) **Going Correction** +0.75s/f (Soft) **10** Ran SP% **112.6**
Speed ratings (Par 105): **104,103,103,101,101 93,81,63, ,**
CSF £16.62 CT £63.32 TOTE £4.20: £1.60, £1.60, £2.00; EX 17.40 Trifecta £63.20.
Owner Midd Shire Racing **Bred** D R Tucker **Trained** Blackborough, Devon

FOCUS
A competitive handicap hurdle and the market leaders came to the fore. A big hurdles pb from the winner but he's entitled to rate higher on Flat form.

1546 PAUL WEBBER STABLES VISIT TOMORROW NOVICES' H'CAP CHASE (17 fncs) 2m 6f 125y
3:20 (3:20) (Class 5) (0-100,100) 4-Y-O+ **£3,249** (£954; £477; £238)

Form RPR

2U04 **1** **Breezy Kin (IRE)**[32] 1243 7-10-10 **84**............................(b1) WillKennedy 99+
(Andy Turnell) *mde all: 15 l ahd 7th: reduced ld at 1/2-way: lft clr 13th: hrd rdn and pressed after 2 out: kpt on wl: all out* **10/3**[2]

42/2 **2** *1 1/4* **Bob Lewis**[26] 1293 9-11-0 **88**.. NickScholfield 101
(Stuart Kittow) *hld up in last pair: awkward 4th: stdy prog gng wl to chse wnr 3 out: clsd next: hrd rdn and tried to chal bef last: kpt on but hld* **9/4**[1]

-604 **3** *12* **Xenophon**[16] 1402 7-9-9 **74** oh5.. AliceMills(5) 77
(Michael Chapman) *chsd ldrs: mstke 11th: sn struggling: tk modest 3rd after 2 out: kpt on but n.d* **16/1**

/P05 **4** *31* **Haughtons Bridge (IRE)**[18] 1383 7-11-8 **99**.......... JeremiahMcGrath(3) 72
(Martin Hill) *chsd ldrs: no imp bef 4 out: wknd next: t.o* **9/2**[3]

000 **5** *3 1/4* **Midnight Whisper**[23] 1326 9-10-13 **87**.............................(tp) DarylJacob 57
(Richard Woollacott) *in tch: lft in 2nd after 13th to 3 out: wknd: t.o* **10/1**

0-UP **6** *19* **Yes I Will**[32] 1245 6-10-11 **85**.......................................(tp) JamesBest 45
(Linda Jewell) *in tch: prog to trck wnr 9th: upsides and clr of rest whn blnd and nrly fell 13th: nt rcvr: t.o* **25/1**

64 **7** *32* **See It As It Is (IRE)**[20] 1351 8-11-5 **100**...................... MissTWorsley(7) 24
(Diana Grissell) *chsd wnr to 9th: rdn and wknd 11th: t.o* **33/1**

46/B **P** **Lady From Geneva**[8] 1490 8-10-13 **87**.............................(t) BrendanPowell
(Brendan Powell) *in tch: no imp 4 out: wkng whn mstke next: t.o whn p.u bef 2 out* **9/1**

P3P0 **P** **Forget And Forgive (IRE)**[24] 1306 7-10-9 **83**..............(tp) SeanQuinlan
(Sophie Leech) *hld up in last: shkn up and lost tch 9th: bhd after: p.u bef 4 out* **12/1**

6m 1.7s (22.50) **Going Correction** +1.05s/f (Soft) **9** Ran SP% **111.5**
Speed ratings (Par 103): **102,101,97,86,85 78,67, ,**
CSF £11.16 CT £96.77 TOTE £3.70: £1.60, £1.40, £3.20; EX 9.60 Trifecta £104.10.
Owner Paul Mannion **Bred** Michael C Griffin **Trained** Broad Hinton, Wilts

FOCUS
The two at the head of the market dominated this moderate novice handicap, with the winner making all. He and the third are the best guides.

1547 BLOOMING MARVELLOUS CHRISTMAS FAYRE H'CAP HURDLE (13 hdls) 3m 2f 83y
3:50 (3:50) (Class 4) (0-110,106) 4-Y-O+ **£3,898** (£1,144; £572; £286)

Form RPR

-603 **1** **Spending Time**[18] 1383 6-11-1 **95**...................................(t) TomScudamore 108+
(David Pipe) *trckd ldrs gng wl: led 2 out: rdn and pressed last: urged along and kpt on wl* **9/2**[1]

450- **2** *2* **Vendredi Trois (FR)**[148] 5414 6-11-6 **100**...................... GavinSheehan 106
(Emma Lavelle) *hld up towards rr: prog fr 3 out to chse wnr after next: hrd rdn and 1 l down last: one pce and hld after* **13/2**[3]

/4-2 **3** *10* **Duroob**[11] 1462 13-10-7 **87**..(v) RichardJohnson 85
(Anthony McCann, Ire) *led to 3rd: remained prom: pushed along at 1/2-way in 5th: outpcd bef 2 out: kpt on again to take 3rd after last* **17/2**

5564 **4** *2* **Minella Bliss (IRE)**[14] 1426 10-10-10 **90**..................(b) LiamTreadwell 85
(James Evans) *prom: mde most fr 4th to 2 out: fdd bef last* **12/1**

2434 **5** *11* **Amber Flush**[29] 1272 6-11-1 **95**.. TrevorWhelan 80
(Martin Smith) *hld up in rr: prog at 1/2-way to chse ldrs: cl up gng wl 3 out: sn wknd qckly* **14/1**

0250 **6** *nk* **Lady Of Longstone (IRE)**[33] 1236 5-10-10 **97**..........(b) MichaelHeard(7) 82
(David Pipe) *prom: rdn bef 3 out: wknd next* **12/1**

244F **7** *2 1/4* **Tir Dubh (IRE)**[8] 1490 6-11-11 **105**.................................... TomO'Brien 88
(Robert Stephens) *led 3rd to 4th: mstke 6th: pressed ldr tl wknd after 3 out* **8/1**

-225 **8** *22* **Rior (IRE)**[73] 897 8-11-11 **105**.. NickScholfield 68
(Paul Henderson) *hld up in last trio: stl wl in rr but in tch 3 out: sn wknd* **14/1**

5506 **9** *2 3/4* **Call Me Kate**[30] 1264 5-9-12 **85**...............................(p) MrHFNugent(7) 46
(Henry Daly) *mid-div: hrd rdn and wknd bef 3 out: t.o* **10/1**

-F60 **P** **Academy General (IRE)**[26] 1292 9-11-3 **100**..............(t) LucyGardner(3)
(Patricia Shaw) *a in rr: struggling whn mstke 3 out: p.u bef last* **66/1**

05-1 **P** **Binowagh Bay (IRE)**[14] 1420 7-11-9 **106**..............(p) JeremiahMcGrath(3)
(Brian M McMahon, Ire) *midfield: reminder 5th: wknd 10th: t.o whn p.u bef last* **6/1**[2]

013F **P** **The Kings Assassin (IRE)**[46] 1155 7-11-7 **101**...............(p) TomCannon
(Chris Gordon) *in tch tl wknd qckly after 9th: sn t.o: p.u bef last* **8/1**

6m 58.5s (29.90) **Going Correction** +0.90s/f (Soft) **12** Ran SP% **116.7**
Speed ratings (Par 105): **90,89,86,85,82 82,81,74,73, ,**
CSF £33.58 CT £241.31 TOTE £5.00: £2.10, £2.60, £2.70; EX 29.40 Trifecta £107.50.
Owner Brocade Racing **Bred** Patrick And Roslyn Burling **Trained** Nicholashayne, Devon

FOCUS
This proved a good test and the front pair had it to themselves from a fair way out. The winner looked to have a bit in hand.

1548 STRATFORD RACECOURSE BUSINESS CLUB H'CAP CHASE (12 fncs) 2m 213y
4:20 (4:20) (Class 5) (0-100,96) 4-Y-O+ **£2,599** (£763; £381; £190)

Form RPR

6342 **1** **Going Nowhere Fast (IRE)**[18] 1373 10-10-7 **80**........ RobertWilliams(3) 106+
(Bernard Llewellyn) *hld up off str pce: slow at 1st: prog to dispute ld bef 4 out where mstke: led full of running 3 out: pressed on and increased advantage fr 2 out: comf* **6/1**[3]

F602 **2** *31* **My Nosy Rosy**[14] 1422 7-11-5 **89**...................................(tp) DarylJacob 93
(Ben Case) *hld up off str pce: prog 4 out: chsd wnr 2 out and in tch: sn rdn and wknd* **7/1**

3543 **3** *40* **Accessallareas (IRE)**[8] 1489 10-11-6 **90**.................(p) RichardJohnson 52
(Sarah-Jayne Davies) *led to 2nd: chsd ldr to 8th: wknd qckly 3 out: t.o* **4/1**[2]

3P63 **4** *13* **Toe To Toe (IRE)**[48] 1133 7-10-8 **78**..............................(tp) WillKennedy 28
(John Flint) *led 2nd at str pce: hdd 3 out: wknd rapidly next: t.o* **9/4**[1]

2-62 **P** **Manger Hanagment (IRE)**[7] 1492 10-11-9 **96**...........(p) JamesBanks(3)
(Barry Brennan) *tried to ld but unable to: dropped to last pl 5th and reluctant: t.o whn p.u after 7th* **9/4**[1]

4m 24.4s (17.30) **Going Correction** +1.05s/f (Soft) **5** Ran SP% **108.3**
Speed ratings (Par 103): **101,86,67,61,**
CSF £38.60 TOTE £5.10: £2.80, £4.20; EX 28.80 Trifecta £70.50.
Owner Alan J Williams **Bred** J Dowling **Trained** Fochriw, Caerphilly

FOCUS
They came home at long intervals in this low-grade chase. A big step up from the winner, who should go in again.

1549 BORDEAUX UNDISCOVERED H'CAP HURDLE (9 hdls) 2m 2f 148y
4:50 (4:50) (Class 4) (0-120,120) 3-Y-O+ **£3,249** (£954; £477; £238)

Form RPR

151/ **1** **Cousin Khee**[68] 3695 8-11-10 **118**.. TomO'Brien 132+
(Hughie Morrison) *a gng wl: in tch: moved onto heels of ldrs bef 2 out: eased into ld bef last: sn clr* **11/4**[1]

233 **2** *11* **Hawdyerwheesht**[22] 1343 7-11-5 **120**........................(tp) JamieBargary(7) 121
(David Dennis) *trckd ldrs: chal 3 out: led after next: rdn and hdd bef last: no ch w wnr* **8/1**

313 **3** *20* **Alwaystheoptimist**[25] 1296 12-11-9 **117**........................(t) TomScudamore 100
(Shaun Lycett) *hld up in rr: lost tch 6th: bhd next: plugged on fr 2 out to take remote 3rd nr fin* **6/1**

-236 **4** *1 1/2* **Brigadoon**[14] 1425 8-11-4 **112**.................................... SamTwiston-Davies 94
(Michael Appleby) *chsd clr ldr: led 3 out: rdn and hdd after 2 out: wknd qckly* **15/2**

0133 **5** *19* **Iguacu**[12] 1055 11-10-8 **105**.. SeanBowen(3) 70
(Richard Price) *in tch: rdn 6th: sn struggling in rr: t.o* **11/2**[3]

-663 **6** *5* **Mr McGuiness (IRE)**[46] 1153 5-10-6 **103**............................ BenPoste(3) 63
(Rosemary Gasson) *in tch in rr to 3 out: sn wknd: t.o* **9/1**

6323 **P** **Shout It Aloud**[23] 1324 6-11-1 **109**..............................(t) RichardJohnson
(Tim Vaughan) *led and clr: blnd 3rd: hdd 3 out: wkng rapidly whn blnd 2 out: t.o whn p.u bef last* **7/2**[2]

4m 45.7s (14.20) **Going Correction** +0.90s/f (Soft) **7** Ran SP% **111.4**
Speed ratings (Par 105): **106,101,92,92,84 82,**
CSF £22.89 CT £116.96 TOTE £3.30: £2.00, £3.40; EX 21.70 Trifecta £50.50.
Owner Raymond Tooth **Bred** Miss B Swire **Trained** East Ilsley, Berks

FOCUS
A fair handicap won in good style by the favourite, who was posting a big hurdling best.
T/Plt: £15.80 to a £1 stake. Pool: £79,422.34 - 3668.64 winning units. T/Qpdt: £16.00 to a £1 stake. Pool: £4,940.95 - 228.40 winning units. **Cathal Gahan**

452 KELSO (L-H)
Wednesday, September 16

OFFICIAL GOING: Good to firm (8.2)
Wind: Breezy, half behind Weather: Cloudy, bright

1550 BARBARA MCLEOD MAIDEN HURDLE (10 hdls 1 omitted) 2m 4f 189y
4:40 (4:40) (Class 4) 4-Y-O+ **£3,249** (£954; £477; £238)

Form RPR

24-2 **1** **Waterclock (IRE)**[20] 1369 6-11-0 115.............................(v) BrianHarding 126
(Jedd O'Keeffe) *cl up: effrt and chal last (usual 2 out): led passing omitted last: drvn and hld on gamely* **2/1**[2]

1- **2** *1* **Fingerontheswitch (IRE)**[177] 4969 5-11-0 0............................ NoelFehily 126
(Neil Mulholland) *t.k.h: cl up: led 6th: nt fluent next: rdn whn jnd last (usual 2 out): hdd passing omitted last: kpt on: hld nr fin* **6/4**[1]

102- **3** *26* **Professor Plum (IRE)**[156] 5308 5-10-11 0...................... CraigNichol(3) 104
(Rose Dobbin) *pckd 1st: hld up in midfield: rdn and outpcd after 3 out (usual 4 out): rallied to chse clr ldng pair last (usual 2 out): no imp* **13/2**[3]

-503 **4** *2 1/4* **St Quintin**[7] 1519 5-11-0 0.. RichardJohnson 103
(David Brown) *led to 6th: cl up: hit and rdn 3 out (usual 4 out): wknd bef last (usual 2 out)* **16/1**

1/1- **5** *10* **Theatrical Style (IRE)**[430] 929 6-11-0 0................. WayneHutchinson 91
(Donald McCain) *hld up: hdwy to chse ldrs 1/2-way: rdn and wknd bef last (usual 2 out)* **13/2**[3]

3- **6** *6* **Beechroad Ally (IRE)**[200] 4486 6-10-4 0..............................(t) DerekFox(3) 79
(Sandy Thomson) *in tch: stdy hdwy after 3 out (usual 4 out): rdn and wknd bef last (usual 2 out)* **16/1**

0P4 **7** *61* **Cash Is King**[20] 1366 5-11-0 0..(t) PeterBuchanan 31
(Kenny Johnson) *bhd: nt fluent 1st: struggling 3 out (usual 4 out): nvr on terms* **125/1**

5/05 **8** *11* **Thehoodlum**[8] 1498 8-11-0 0.. HenryBrooke 21
(Jean McGregor) *nt fluent in rr: struggling fnl circ: nvr on terms* **200/1**

-543 **U** **Louloumills**[13] 1457 5-9-11 82.. ThomasDowson(10)
(Maurice Barnes) *chsd ldrs: stmbld and uns rdr 6th* **66/1**

4m 49.5s (-18.50) **Going Correction** -1.075s/f (Hard) **9** Ran SP% **114.5**
Speed ratings (Par 105): **92,91,81,80,77 74,51,47,**
CSF £5.54 TOTE £2.70: £1.20, £1.10, £2.30; EX 7.60 Trifecta £22.20.
Owner Caron & Paul Chapman **Bred** The Rt Hon Lord Rothschild **Trained** Middleham Moor, N Yorks

FOCUS
All distances as advertised. Ever-quickening ground awaited the runners for this average maiden hurdle. The final flight was bypassed due to an injured rider receiving medical treatment. The finish was dominated by those towards the head of the betting. The winner has the potential to rate higher on Flat form.

1551 FARNE SALMON & TROUT H'CAP CHASE (16 fncs) 2m 5f 133y
5:10 (5:10) (Class 4) (0-110,109) 4-Y-0+ **£3,898** (£1,144; £572; £286)

Form RPR
0136 1 **Romany Ryme**[25] 1332 9-11-12 **109** RichardJohnson 117+
(Gordon Elliott, Ire) *nt fluent: in tch: hdwy to chse ldr 10th: led gng wl bef 2 out: rdn bef last: kpt on wl* **3/1**[2]
6234 2 2 **Solway Bay**[8] 1503 13-10-6 **94** (t) CallumBewley[(5)] 99+
(Lisa Harrison) *bhd: outpcd 1/2-way: rallied bef 4 out: hit next: styd on wl fr last to take 2nd cl home: nt rch wnr* **9/1**
3104 3 *nse* **Isthereadifference (IRE)**[16] 1424 8-11-10 **107** (bt) NoelFehily 110
(Neil Mulholland) *in tch: rdn 4 out: rallied bef 2 out: effrt and chsd wnr last: kpt on same pce last 100yds: lost 2nd cl home* **11/2**
-214 4 5 **Everlasting (IRE)**[82] 842 8-10-1 **87** (b) CraigNichol[(3)] 85
(Rose Dobbin) *led to bef 2 out: sn rdn: wknd after last* **9/4**[1]
3452 5 ¾ **Sendiym (FR)**[20] 1367 8-10-7 **90** BrianHughes 91
(Dianne Sayer) *chsd ldrs: drvn 11th: outpcd 3 out: n.d after* **7/2**[3]
0-P0 P **Jewellery (IRE)**[113] 482 8-11-1 **105** (t) PaulJohn[(7)]
(Katie Scott) *pressed ldr: outpcd after 9th: rallied: struggling 4 out: wknd after next: p.u bef last* **10/1**

5m 19.8s (-9.40) **Going Correction** -0.90s/f (Hard) 6 Ran SP% **112.5**
Speed ratings (Par 105): **81,80,80,78,78**
CSF £26.85 TOTE £3.80: £1.40, £4.60; EX 34.70 Trifecta £90.90.
Owner Five Men Syndicate **Bred** Graindale And Quinnies Stud **Trained** Longwood, Co Meath

FOCUS
The first chase of Kelso's new season and a winning raid for Irish trainer Gordon Elliott, who was scoring with his first runner at the track. Ordinary form, rated around the first three.

1552 PRINCIPAL & PROSPER H'CAP HURDLE (11 hdls) 2m 4f 189y
5:40 (5:40) (Class 5) (0-100,100) 4-Y-0+ **£3,898** (£1,144; £572; £286)

Form RPR
-000 1 **Touch Of Steel (IRE)**[82] 843 6-10-1 **79** (b[1]) DaleIrving[(5)] 84+
(James Ewart) *a cl up: effrt 2 out: led run-in: drvn out* **9/1**
0130 2 ¾ **Roll Of Thunder**[25] 1329 6-10-12 **90** MissCWalton[(5)] 92
(James Walton) *led: rdn after 2 out: hdd run-in: rallied: hld nr fin* **6/1**[1]
-000 3 5 **Snowed In (IRE)**[33] 1071 6-11-7 **94** SeanQuinlan 92
(Barbara Butterworth) *hld up in midfield: outpcd 4 out: rallied after next: chsd clr ldng pair last: kpt on: no imp* **8/1**[3]
-566 4 1 **Naburn**[26] 1307 7-11-12 **99** BrianHarding 96
(Andrew Wilson) *hld up: stdy hdwy and in tch bef 2 out: sn rdn and edgd lft: kpt on same pce fr last* **14/1**
063- 5 8 **Attention Please (IRE)**[186] 4762 5-11-2 **92** CraigNichol[(3)] 83
(Rose Dobbin) *chsd ldrs: nt fluent and pushed along 3 out: rdn and ch next: outpcd whn nt fluent last: sn btn* **7/1**[2]
P-03 6 *nk* **District Attorney (IRE)**[20] 1368 6-10-11 **87** JohnKington[(3)] 77
(Chris Fairhurst) *midfield: effrt and pushed along after 3 out: rdn and wknd fr next* **6/1**[1]
P2-0 7 1¼ **Oxalido (FR)**[133] 140 13-11-6 **93** BrianHughes 81
(Hugh Burns) *in tch: drvn after 3 out: wknd bef next* **14/1**
-P45 8 ¾ **Saint Brieuc (FR)**[9] 1497 6-10-9 **89** MrTommieMO'Brien[(7)] 77
(Simon West) *hld up: hdwy and cl up 1/2-way: rdn and wknd bef 2 out* **8/1**[3]
06- 9 15 **Late For Supper (IRE)**[312] 2345 6-11-0 **90** HarryChalloner[(3)] 64
(Richard Ford) *bhd: struggling after 4 out: btn bef 2 out* **14/1**
433 10 2¾ **My Escapade (IRE)**[87] 804 4-11-5 **100** MissAWaugh[(7)] 71
(Simon Waugh) *t.k.h: cl up tl rdn and wknd 3 out* **10/1**
61F- 11 4 **Slaney Star (IRE)**[396] 1239 7-11-8 **95** (v) HenryBrooke 63
(Jean McGregor) *hld up: stdy hdwy 1/2-way: rdn and wknd after 3 out* **14/1**
-030 12 25 **Stand Clear**[58] 1066 10-9-10 **74** (t) DiarmuidO'Regan[(5)] 20
(Chris Grant) *bhd: struggling 4 out: lost tch fr next: t.o* **8/1**[3]

4m 55.2s (-12.80) **Going Correction** -1.075s/f (Hard)
WFA 4 from 5yo+ 12lb 12 Ran SP% **120.2**
Speed ratings (Par 103): **81,80,78,78,75 75,74,74,68,67 66,56**
CSF £63.79 CT £459.94 TOTE £11.90: £3.00, £2.30, £3.40; EX 100.80 Trifecta £1053.90.
Owner Mrs Hugh Fraser **Bred** Frances Galloway **Trained** Langholm, Dumfries & G'way

FOCUS
This was hugely competitive, but featured some moderate and mostly frustrating sorts. The market was headed by a now 34-race maiden. A big step up from the winner.

1553 STRAIGHTLINE CONSTRUCTION H'CAP CHASE (12 fncs) 2m 1f 14y
6:10 (6:10) (Class 3) (0-140,132) 4-Y-0+ **£7,797** (£2,289; £1,144; £572)

Form RPR
-331 1 **Robin's Command (IRE)**[9] 1494 8-10-13 **122** 7ex CraigNichol[(3)] 138+
(Rose Dobbin) *chsd ldr and sn clr of rest: led 6th: mde rest: drew clr bef 2 out: kpt on strly* **4/1**[3]
21-2 2 8 **Muwalla**[9] 1494 8-9-11 **108** (t) CallumBewley[(5)] 115
(Lisa Harrison) *hld up: stdy hdwy to chse clr ldng pair 6th: clsd 5 out: effrt and wnt 2nd 3 out: rdn and no imp fr next* **7/2**[2]
3401 3 3¾ **Purple 'n Gold (IRE)**[24] 1343 6-11-9 **129** (p) TomScudamore 132
(David Pipe) *nt fluent on occasions: hld up: stdy hdwy and in tch 5 out: rdn after 3 out: outpcd fr next* **3/1**[1]
201F 4 24 **Jack The Gent (IRE)**[31] 1267 11-10-6 **112** RichieMcLernon 93
(George Moore) *hld up in tch: drvn and outpcd 7th: struggling fr 4 out* **10/1**
4-14 5 22 **Toledo Gold (IRE)**[58] 1070 9-10-8 **124** (t) HenryBrooke 86
(Maurice Barnes) *led at decent gallop: hdd 6th: rallied: rdn and wknd after 3 out* **20/1**
U42 F **Fantasy King**[16] 1418 9-11-0 **125** DiarmuidO'Regan[(5)]
(James Moffatt) *hld up: pushed along 1/2-way: hit and struggling 4 out: nrly 20 l down and no ch whn fell 2 out* **5/1**
6P4- P **Swift Arrow (IRE)**[227] 3995 9-11-10 **130** (t) WayneHutchinson
(Donald McCain) *hld up: stdy hdwy and in tch 5 out: blnd and struggling 3 out: sn btn: p.u bef next* **14/1**
-620 P **Swaledale Lad (IRE)**[13] 1459 8-11-9 **132** HarryChalloner[(3)]
(Richard Ford) *chsd clr ldng pair: nt fluent 5th: sn p.u* **9/1**

3m 58.6s (-19.40) **Going Correction** -0.90s/f (Hard) 8 Ran SP% **114.4**
Speed ratings (Par 107): **109,105,103,92,81 , ,**
CSF £19.02 CT £46.85 TOTE £6.10: £1.50, £1.60, £1.20; EX 24.70 Trifecta £119.70.
Owner M Hunter, J Matterson & R Jacobs **Bred** Gregory Lawler **Trained** South Hazelrigg, Northumbria

FOCUS
A strong turn out for this handicap chase, which was run at a stern early gallop. The form looks rock solid, with a big career best from the winner and the next two to their marks.

1554 BRUCE FARMS SUPPORTING WORLD HORSE WELFARE H'CAP HURDLE (8 hdls) 2m 51y
6:40 (6:40) (Class 2) (0-150,130) 3-Y-0+ **£9,747** (£2,862; £1,431; £715)

Form RPR
-041 1 **Makethedifference (IRE)**[8] 1501 7-10-3 **107** 6ex MichaelByrne 113+
(Tim Vaughan) *t.k.h: hld up in tch: stdy hdwy 4 out: led between last 2: j.lft last: sn rdn: kpt on strly run-in* **6/4**[1]
3051 2 2¼ **Captain Brown**[18] 1404 7-11-1 **124** DiarmuidO'Regan[(5)] 125
(James Moffatt) *hld up in last pl: effrt and rdn bef 2 out: chsd wnr run-in: kpt on: no imp* **11/4**[2]
4-32 3 *nk* **Changing The Guard**[20] 1376 9-10-8 **115** (tp) JamesBanks[(3)] 117
(Barry Brennan) *led and clr to 4th: rdn and hdd between last 2: cl 2nd whn hmpd last: kpt on same pce* **11/1**
4321 4 1½ **Lisbon (IRE)**[35] 1233 7-11-6 **124** (t) TomScudamore 123
(Patrick Griffin, Ire) *chsd ldrs: effrt and wnt 2nd briefly bef 2 out: rdn and outpcd fr last* **9/2**[3]
-332 5 3 **Oliver's Gold**[13] 1460 7-11-2 **120** (p) DougieCostello 119
(Mark Walford) *chsd ldr: lost 2nd whn nt fluent 2 out: wknd bef last* **15/2**
1/P0 6 16 **Franciscan**[25] 1333 7-11-12 **130** (b) WayneHutchinson 114
(Donald McCain) *t.k.h: hld up in tch: pushed along 3 out: wknd and eased next* **25/1**

3m 41.1s (-20.70) **Going Correction** -1.075s/f (Hard)
WFA 4 from 7yo+ 11lb 6 Ran SP% **108.8**
Speed ratings (Par 109): **108,106,106,105,104 96**
CSF £5.82 CT £25.24 TOTE £2.20: £1.60, £1.60; EX 6.50 Trifecta £31.80.
Owner Brian Jones **Bred** Tipper House Stud **Trained** Aberthin, Vale of Glamorgan

FOCUS
A slightly disappointing line-up for this valuable feature contest, with the top weight rated 20lb below the ceiling mark of 150. Solid handicap form.

1555 RACING UK SCOTTISH SEASON TICKET MAIDEN OPEN NATIONAL HUNT FLAT RACE 2m 51y
7:10 (7:10) (Class 6) 4-6-Y-0 **£1,949** (£572; £286; £143)

Form RPR
1 **Meet The Legend** 4-10-13 0 CraigNichol[(3)] 124+
(Keith Dalgleish) *t.k.h: trckd ldrs: led after 4f: mde rest: qcknd clr 2f out: kpt on wl fnl f: readily* **11/4**[2]
2 7 **Dubai Angel (IRE)** 4-11-2 0 BrianHughes 118+
(Malcolm Jefferson) *hld up in tch: stdy hdwy to chse (clr) wnr over 1f out: sn pushed along and hung lft: kpt on fnl f: nvr able to chal* **5/1**[3]
223- 3 5 **Mardale (IRE)**[215] 4207 5-10-9 0 (t) BrianHarding 106
(Nicky Richards) *t.k.h: in tch: stdy hdwy over 2f out: rdn over 1f out: kpt on same pce* **9/4**[1]
4 6 **Jethro (IRE)**[163] 4-10-9 0 CraigGallagher[(7)] 109
(Brian Ellison) *hld up: drvn and outpcd 4f out: rallied over 2f out: no imp over 1f out* **18/1**
5 3¼ **Barney Dwan (IRE)**[164] 5-11-2 0 WayneHutchinson 105
(Donald McCain) *t.k.h: cl up: drvn along over 3f out: wknd fr 2f out* **9/1**
2 6 10 **Throckley**[20] 1378 4-11-2 0 RichieMcLernon 96
(John Davies) *hld up: pushed along and outpcd over 2f out: btn over 1f out* **8/1**
6-5 7 4½ **Fairy Theatre (IRE)**[115] 459 4-10-9 0[1] RichardJohnson 85
(Iain Jardine) *t.k.h: hld up on outside: struggling wl over 2f out: sn btn* **15/2**
0- 8 16 **Pickle And Tickle (IRE)**[328] 2014 5-10-11 0 JonathonBewley[(5)] 77
(George Bewley) *led 4f: cl up: drvn and outpcd over 3f out: sn wknd* **50/1**

3m 34.4s (-21.80) **Going Correction** -1.075s/f (Hard) 8 Ran SP% **114.2**
Speed ratings: **111,107,105,102,100 95,93,85**
CSF £16.93 TOTE £3.70: £1.70, £1.60, £1.30; EX 18.60 Trifecta £71.20.
Owner Straightline Construction Ltd **Bred** B G Hellyer & H D J Daly **Trained** Carluke, S Lanarks

FOCUS
An informative bumper, in which the market leader set a fair standard. A well above average bumper for the track and time of year.
T/Plt: £29.00 to a £1 stake. Pool: £56,490.70 - 1,417.62 winning tickets T/Qpdt: £6.50 to a £1 stake. Pool: £6,393.33 - 721.22 winning tickets **Richard Young**

1537 LISTOWEL (L-H)
Wednesday, September 16

OFFICIAL GOING: Heavy

1556a GUINNESS KERRY NATIONAL H'CAP CHASE (GRADE A) (18 fncs) 3m
4:20 (4:20) 4-Y-0+
£81,589 (£25,968; £12,403; £4,263; £2,906; £1,550)

RPR
1 **Rogue Angel (IRE)**[3] 1542 7-10-4 **133** (bt) GerFox[(3)] 143
(M F Morris, Ire) *chsd ldrs on outer tl led after 1st: nt fluent 3rd and next: pressed clly bef 2 out where hdd: rallied u.p fr last and styd on wl run-in to ld fnl stride* **8/1**[3]
2 *shd* **Urano (FR)**[7] 1530 7-10-8 **134** PaulTownend 144
(W P Mullins, Ire) *settled in mid-div: hdwy bef 4 out where slt mstke on outer in 5th: wnt cl 3rd after 3 out: rdn to ld bef last and wnt clr: one pce run-in and all out clsng stages: hdd fnl stride* **12/1**
3 3½ **Rule The World**[49] 1152 8-11-4 **147** (p) DavidMullins[(3)] 153
(M F Morris, Ire) *chsd ldrs: disp 2nd 5 out: rdn in cl 2nd bef 2 out where led narrowly: sn hdd and no ex u.p in 3rd fr last: kpt on same pce* **8/1**[3]
4 11 **The Paparazzi Kid (IRE)**[49] 1152 8-11-5 **145** RWalsh 141
(W P Mullins, Ire) *hld up in tch: clsr bhd ldrs 4 out: cl 4th after 3 out: rdn in 4th bef next and sn no imp on ldrs: one pce after* **6/1**[2]
5 3¼ **Shesaportrait (IRE)**[48] 1161 7-10-4 **130** (b) PhillipEnright 123
(Patrick Neville, Ire) *on toes behand: chsd ldrs: slt mstke 3rd: wnt cl 2nd fr 9th: jnd for 2nd 5 out: lost pl next and pushed along in 4th bef 3 out: rdn in 5th bef next and no imp on ldrs: one pce after* **16/1**
6 ½ **Dare To Endeavour**[17] 1409 8-10-6 **132** MarkBolger 124
(E McNamara, Ire) *mid-div: pckd sltly at 2nd: rdn in 9th after 4 out and no imp on ldrs in 8th bef next: sn rdn and kpt on one pce into mod 6th run-in: nvr nrr* **25/1**

7 ¾ **Colour Squadron (IRE)**[25] 1339 9-11-0 **140** MarkWalsh 131
(E Bolger, Ire) *mid-div: hdwy towards rr fr 1/2-way to chse ldrs: slt mstke in 6th 3 out: no ex u.p bef next: kpt on one pce* **12/1**

8 47 **Indevan**[26] 1312 7-11-3 **143** DannyMullins 87
(W P Mullins, Ire) *hld up in rr of mid-div: hmpd 9th: rdn and no imp 5 out: sn wknd and eased: t.o* **33/1**

9 4 ½ **Un Beau Roman (FR)**[7] 1531 7-10-8 **134** MPFogarty 73
(W P Mullins, Ire) *w.w towards rr: slt mstke 5th: sltly hmpd 9th: sme hdwy after next: rdn in 9th bef 3 out where slt mstke: sn wknd and eased: t.o* **25/1**

P **Your Busy (IRE)**[16] 1435 12-10-10 **136** (t) MsKWalsh
(J A Nash, Ire) *led tl hdd after 1st: dropped to 3rd fr 9th: lost pl after 11th: towards rr whn bdly hmpd at 12th: trailing whn p.u after next* **20/1**

F **Cantlow (IRE)**[46] 1175 10-10-10 **136** (tp) BarryGeraghty
(Paul Webber) *hld up towards rr early: clsr in 4th bef 1/2-way: disp 4th whn fell 9th* **14/1**

B **Owega Star (IRE)**[14] 1337 8-10-8 **134** (t) JJBurke
(Peter Fahey, Ire) *settled bhd ldrs early: pushed along in 8th after 10th and no ex u.p after next: towards rr whn hmpd and b.d at 12th: fatally injured* **8/1**[3]

P **Bridgets Pet (IRE)**[9] 998 8-10-4 **130** APHeskin
(Alan Fleming, Ire) *hld up towards rr: slt mstke 8th: bdly hmpd in rr at 12th: no imp after: trailing whn p.u bef 2 out* **16/1**

P **Alelchi Inois (FR)**[49] 1152 7-11-7 **147** DJCasey
(W P Mullins, Ire) *hld up in mid-div: tk clsr order after 1/2-way: slt mstke in 6th at 12th: wknd after 5 out and p.u bef next* **16/1**

F **Lots Of Memories (IRE)**[16] 1435 8-10-3 **134** PaddyKennedy[5]
(P G Fahey, Ire) *mid-div: sltly hmpd 9th: stl in tch in mid-div whn fell 12th: fatally injured* **11/2**[1]

P **Ravished (IRE)**[45] 1184 7-10-9 **135** (t) BJCooper
(M F Morris, Ire) *hld up: sltly hmpd towards rr at 9th: pushed along in rr after next and no imp fr 12th: trailing whn p.u bef 3 out* **12/1**

F **Horendus Hulabaloo (IRE)**[64] 998 6-10-2 **135** (p) DonaghMeyler[7]
(M F Morris, Ire) *mid-div: tk clsr order bhd ldrs after 3rd: j.big in 5th 5 out: pushed along in 6th after 4 out and wknd in 7th fr next: fell 2 out* **12/1**

6m 2.2s (2.30) **17 Ran SP% 133.5**
CSF £104.61 CT £825.81 TOTE £11.40: £2.30, £3.00, £2.40, £2.30; DF 134.20 Trifecta £1881.40.
Owner Gigginstown House Stud **Bred** Mrs R H Lalor **Trained** Fethard, Co Tipperary
■ Stewards' Enquiry : Ger Fox severe caution: used whip without giving gelding time to respond and, furthermore, continued after winning post

FOCUS
A stirring finish at the end of three miles and a race with plenty of twists and turns, no more so than between the last two fences between the two principals. Sound form, the first three clear.

1557 - 1564a (Foreign Racing) - See Raceform Interactive

1556 LISTOWEL (L-H)
Thursday, September 17
OFFICIAL GOING: Flat course - soft to heavy; jumps courses - soft

1565a LADBROKES ISLAND H'CAP HURDLE (GRADE B) (10 hdls) 2m
5:00 (5:01) 5-Y-O+
£27,906 (£8,837; £4,186; £1,395; £930; £465)

RPR

1 **Misty Lady (IRE)**[10] 608 6-10-6 **117** SeanFlanagan 123
(John Laurence Cullen, Ire) *led: over 1 l clr at 1/2-way: pressed clly after 3 out: rdn w narrow advantage fr 2 out and hdd bef last: kpt on wl u.p in cl 2nd run-in to regain advantage on line* **10/1**

2 nse **Lilly The Lioness (IRE)**[8] 1528 8-10-4 **115** PaulTownend 121
(Garrett James Power, Ire) *chsd ldrs: 3rd 1/2-way: clsr in 2nd bef 3 out: almost on terms next and rdn to ld narrowly bef last: strly pressed u.p run-in and hdd on line* **10/1**

3 ¾ **The Nutcracker (IRE)**[21] 1385 5-10-3 **114** AELynch 120
(Thomas Gibney, Ire) *mid-div: nt fluent in 5th at 1st: tk clsr order on outer 3 out: cl 3rd appr st: pushed along bef 2 out where nt fluent: sn rdn and swtchd lft after last: kpt on same pce in 3rd clsng stages* **14/1**

4 ½ **Dollar And A Dream (IRE)**[46] 1183 6-9-10 **107** oh1 (t) PhillipEnright 112+
(A J Martin, Ire) *hld up towards rr: 7th 1/2-way: gng wl bhd ldrs into st where brought wd: j.big nr side 2 out and pckd sltly: rdn between last 2 and kpt on u.p in 4th clsng stages: hld* **6/4**[1]

5 2 **Gentleman Duke (IRE)**[65] 996 7-10-3 **114** (p) PaulCarberry 117
(A L T Moore, Ire) *settled bhd ldr in 2nd: lost pl bef 3 out: pushed along disputing 4th into st: rdn after 2 out and slt mstke last: kpt on one pce in 5th clsng stages* **12/1**

6 hd **Draco**[27] 1319 6-11-10 BarryGeraghty 138
(A P O'Brien, Ire) *chsd ldrs: 4th 1/2-way: pushed along disputing 4th into st: no imp on ldrs fr last where nt fluent: kpt on one pce* **7/2**[2]

7 12 **West Montan (IRE)**[20] 1394 5-9-12 **116** (t) JonathanMoore[7] 107
(David Harry Kelly, Ire) *w.w in rr: last at 1/2-way: pushed along into 7th bef st: rdn and no ex bef 2 out: wknd* **25/1**

8 16 **Whatsforuwontgobyu (IRE)**[46] 408 5-10-8 **119** MarkWalsh 94
(A J Martin, Ire) *mid-div: 6th 1/2-way: pushed along in 7th after 3 out and no imp on ldrs in rr bef st: wknd and eased bef 2 out* **9/2**[3]

4m 3.7s (-3.00) **8 Ran SP% 116.8**
CSF £101.86 CT £1404.04 TOTE £10.70: £2.50, £2.30, £2.60; DF 116.40 Trifecta £2161.50.
Owner Mrs Imelda M Lynch **Bred** James Canty **Trained** Bunclody, Co. Wexford

FOCUS
A terrific finish at the end of this valuable contest, with the winner overcoming an obstacle or two to register a very game success. The runner-up helps with the standard.

1566 - 1567a (Foreign Racing) - See Raceform Interactive

798 HEXHAM (L-H)
Friday, September 18
OFFICIAL GOING: Good (good to firm in places; 7.9)
Wind: almost nil Weather: fine

1568 FIRST TWILIGHT MAIDEN HURDLE (8 hdls) 2m 48y
4:30 (4:31) (Class 5) 4-Y-O+ **£2,274** (£667; £333; £166)

Form RPR

F3 1 **Great Fighter**[12] 1485 5-10-7 0 MrAlexFerguson[7] 122+
(John Ferguson) *hld up in midfield: hdwy appr 2 out: 2nd between last 2: led appr last: pushed clr: eased clsng stages* **11/10**[1]

125- 2 14 **Summer Storm**[309] 2458 5-10-11 0 TonyKelly[3] 106
(Rebecca Menzies) *chsd ldrs: 2nd appr 2 out: kpt on same pce between last 2: chsd wnr fnl f* **5/1**[3]

22-2 3 1 ¾ **Sacred Square (GER)**[28] 1305 5-10-9 113 (b) JamesCowley[5] 105
(Donald McCain) *chsd ldrs: one pce between last 2: tk 3rd clsng stages* **9/2**[2]

3 4 1 **Hitman Hearns (IRE)**[10] 1499 6-10-11 0 CraigNichol[3] 106+
(Keith Dalgleish) *chsd ldr: led 3rd: j.rt 5th: clr appr 2 out: hdd appr last: wknd last 100yds* **5/1**[3]

43 5 9 **Lough Derg Cruise (IRE)**[10] 1498 5-10-7 0 JamesReveley 90
(Sandy Thomson) *in rr: hdwy after 3 out: wknd between last 2* **16/1**

-6U4 6 21 **Miss Joeking (IRE)**[79] 866 4-10-7 0 PeterBuchanan 70
(Lucinda Russell) *in rr: t.o 5th* **66/1**

7 4 ½ **Green Zone (IRE)**[10] 4-11-0 0 AndrewTinkler 72
(Nigel Tinkler) *mid-div: lost pl after 3rd: sn bhd: t.o* **28/1**

/P-6 8 15 **Stormont Bridge**[20] 1399 7-10-4 83 (t) ThomasDowson[10] 59
(Maurice Barnes) *mid-div: lost pl sn after 3 out: sn bhd t.o* **100/1**

9 9 **Bold Henmie (IRE)**[4] 617 4-10-11 0 BrianToomey[3] 51
(Philip Kirby) *led to 3rd: chsd ldr: j.rt 5th: lost pl bef 2 out: sn bhd: t.o whn eased appr last* **14/1**

P P **Dinky Dave**[22] 1365 4-11-0 0 DavidEngland
(Richard Drake) *nt fluent in rr: bhd and reminders 4th: t.o: p.u between last 2* **200/1**

4m 6.9s (-10.50) **Going Correction** -0.55s/f (Firm) **10 Ran SP% 118.1**
Speed ratings (Par 103): **104,97,96,95,91 80,78,70,66,**
CSF £7.25 TOTE £1.50: £1.50, £1.40, £1.60; EX 8.40 Trifecta £16.60.
Owner Bloomfields **Bred** Darley **Trained** Cowlinge, Suffolk

FOCUS
Both bends dolled out races 1, 3 & 5 increased by 111yds, race 2 by 103yds, race 4 by 138yds and race 6 by 148yds. An uncompetitive maiden hurdle run at a sound gallop. The winner is rated in line with his debut fall, and there's a case for rating it a few pounds higher.

1569 NORTHUMBERLAND COLLEGE H'CAP CHASE (15 fncs) 2m 4f 15y
5:05 (5:07) (Class 5) (0-100,92) 4-Y-O+ **£2,924** (£858; £429; £214)

Form RPR

2FP4 1 **Brother Scott**[22] 1372 8-11-12 **92** SeanQuinlan 100
(Sue Smith) *chsd ldrs: 2nd 3 out: kpt on run-in: led nr fin* **9/2**[2]

21-6 2 nk **Local Present (IRE)**[30] 1287 12-11-2 **82** (b) DougieCostello 90
(Denis Quinn) *t.k.h: w ldr: led 2nd to 7th: led 10th: hdd next: led 12th: rdn and hung lft run-in: edgd rt and hdd nr fin* **9/2**[2]

/135 3 1 ½ **French Seventyfive**[22] 1375 8-10-8 **81** MissETodd[7] 88
(Keith Reveley) *hld up in rr: chsd ldrs 9th: outpcd 11th: drvn and hdwy 3 out: handy 3rd appr last: kpt on same pce last 50yds* **2/1**[1]

P-04 4 6 **Alba King (IRE)**[22] 1367 9-10-8 **79** DiarmuidO'Regan[5] 81
(Sue Smith) *rr-div: reminders 8th: chsng ldrs next: outpcd 11th: kpt on one pce fr 2 out: hit last: tk modest 4th last 75yds* **11/2**[3]

2325 5 5 **Forestside (IRE)**[22] 1370 10-10-8 **74** (p) LucyAlexander 74
(Barry Murtagh) *chsd ldrs 9th: led 11th: hdd next: reminders 3 out: 4th and wkng whn hit last: eased nr fin* **9/1**

454/ P **Areuwitmenow (IRE)**[526] 5248 10-11-9 **89** (t) HenryBrooke
(Jennie Candlish) *led to 2nd: led 7th to 10th: lost pl next: sn bhd: t.o whn p.u bef 3 out* **9/2**[2]

5m 14.5s (1.00) **Going Correction** -0.55s/f (Firm) **6 Ran SP% 113.3**
Speed ratings (Par 103): **88,87,87,84,82**
CSF £24.81 TOTE £2.60: £2.00, £3.60; EX 22.20 Trifecta £79.00.
Owner Mrs S Smith **Bred** C P E Brooks **Trained** High Eldwick, W Yorks
■ Stewards' Enquiry : Sean Quinlan four-day ban; used whip above the permitted level (2nd-5th Spt)

FOCUS
A modest handicap. The winner was very well in on a couple of runs in the summer and is rated back to that sort of level.

1570 WEDDING CONGRATULATIONS MR & MRS READER NOVICES' HURDLE (10 hdls) 2m 4f 28y
5:35 (5:37) (Class 4) 4-Y-O+ **£3,573** (£1,049; £524; £262)

Form RPR

-152 1 **Samedi Soir**[18] 1420 5-10-12 105 JamesReveley 122+
(Keith Reveley) *best away: mde all: hit 6th: cruised clr bef last: eased fnl f: v easily* **9/4**[2]

412 2 37 **Number One London (IRE)**[51] 1000 5-11-5 124 (p) MichaelByrne 99+
(Tim Vaughan) *trckd wnr: rdn 2 out: no imp: wl btn whn eased last 100yds* **10/11**[1]

3 34 **Landmeafortune (IRE)**[299] 6-10-12 0 HenryBrooke 53
(Martin Todhunter) *in rr: nt fluent 3rd: drvn 6th: sn bhd: tk distant 3rd appr last* **100/1**

3PP5 4 29 **Duhallowcountry (IRE)**[22] 1365 9-10-5 82 (p) MrWHRReed[7] 27
(Victor Thompson) *rr-div: sme hdwy 5th: lft modest 3rd 7th: sn lost tch: lost distant 3rd appr last: sn t.o* **100/1**

5 5 28 **Great Anticipation (IRE)**[22] 1366 6-10-9 0 CraigNichol[3] 2
(Lynsey Kendall) *in rr: drvn 4th: bhd 7th: t.o next* **100/1**

/23- P **Mister Hendre**[431] 952 7-10-5 84 JamesCorbett[7]
(Susan Corbett) *chsd ldrs: outpcd whn mstke 6th: sn bhd: t.o 3 out: p.u between last 2* **28/1**

124/ F **Cloudy Joker (IRE)**[546] 4941 7-10-12 0 AdrianLane
(Donald McCain) *trckd ldrs: 3rd 3rd: fell 7th* **7/2**[3]

5m 6.5s (-6.00) **Going Correction** -0.55s/f (Firm) **7 Ran SP% 111.8**
Speed ratings (Par 105): **90,75,61,50,38 ,**
CSF £4.66 TOTE £2.90: £1.30, £1.30; EX 5.40 Trifecta £60.50.
Owner Shade Oak Stud **Bred** Shade Oak Stud **Trained** Lingdale, Redcar & Cleveland

FOCUS
A sound gallop for this uncompetitive novices hurdle. Seemingly a big step up from the winner, but not form to be confident about.

1571 CHARLES ENDERBY HAPPY BIRTHDAY H'CAP CHASE (19 fncs) 3m 41y
6:05 (6:08) (Class 4) (0-120,119) 4-Y-O+ **£5,523** (£1,621; £810; £405)

Form RPR

1110 1 **Chicago Outfit (IRE)**[62] 1033 10-11-7 **119** (p) JonathonBewley[5] 130+
(George Bewley) *mde most: drvn 3 out: 6 l ahd last: styd on gamely: eased nr fin* **8/1**

4260 2 2 **Green Wizard (IRE)**[54] 1114 9-11-0 **107** SeanQuinlan 115+
(Sue Smith) *hit 2nd: chsd ldrs 7th: hit 4 out: chsd wnr sn after 2 out: styd on run-in: no real imp* **7/1**[3]

1605 3 23 **Big Sound**[15] 1458 8-11-6 **113** (p) DougieCostello 98
(Mark Walford) *uns rdr and rn loose bef s: in rr: hdwy 14th: sn outpcd: modest 4th 3 out: kpt on to take 3rd last 100yds* **9/1**

3-55 **4** *3* **Moyode Wood**[34] 1264 10-11-2 109.................................. DannyCook 94
(Brian Ellison) *chsd ldrs: upsides 6th: drvn 4 out: hit 2 out: sn wknd: hung lft and lost 3rd last 100yds* **7/1**[3]

53 **5** *17* **Longueville Flier (IRE)**[15] 1462 6-10-1 94..................(p) PaddyBrennan 66
(Micky Hammond) *mstkes: in rr: hdwy 14th: drvn and outpcd next: wkng whn mstke 3 out* **2/1**[1]

3226 **6** *1 1/2* **Strumble Head (IRE)**[28] 1309 10-11-9 119..................(b) SeanBowen(3) 85
(Peter Bowen) *chsd ldrs: lost pl 8th: reminders 13th: sn bhd* **6/1**[2]

43-P **7** *3/4* **George Fernbeck**[132] 203 7-11-2 119......................(p) FinianO'Toole(10) 84
(Micky Hammond) *in rr: outpcd 14th: sn bhd* **11/1**

P5-3 **U** **Settledoutofcourt (IRE)**[128] 289 9-11-8 115................ PeterBuchanan
(Lucinda Russell) *chsd ldrs: 4th whn blnd and uns rdr 11th* **7/1**[3]

6m 17.9s (-14.30) **Going Correction** -0.55s/f (Firm) 8 Ran SP% **114.6**
Speed ratings (Par 105): **107,106,98,97,92 91,91,**
CSF £61.47 CT £515.10 TOTE £6.10: £1.30, £2.30, £3.40; EX 79.50 Trifecta £296.20.
Owner G T Bewley **Bred** Roger Ryan **Trained** Bonchester Bridge, Borders

FOCUS
A fair handicap run at a solid gallop. The winner stepped up on the second on their C&D form from June.

1572 TYNEDALE HOSPICE AT HOME H'CAP HURDLE (8 hdls) 2m 48y
6:35 (6:38) (Class 4) (0-110,105) 3-Y-O+ **£4,548** (£1,335; £667; £333)

Form RPR
6232 **1** **Dynamic Drive (IRE)**[10] 1501 8-10-8 97.....................(t) ThomasDowson(10) 114+
(Maurice Barnes) *mid-div: hdwy 4th: trcking ldrs 6th: led sn after 2 out: drvn clr run-in* **9/2**[2]

1525 **2** *11* **Honourable Gent**[27] 1330 7-11-8 104............................ CraigNichol(3) 112+
(Rose Dobbin) *in rr: hdwy 4th: drvn next: sn chsng ldrs: upsides 2 out: kpt on same pce run-in* **11/2**[3]

0001 **3** *8* **Worldor (FR)**[9] 1524 9-11-1 94 7ex...............................(t) RhysFlint 93
(Alexandra Dunn) *hld up in rr: hdwy 4th: trcking ldrs 3 out: upsides next: one pce appr last* **5/2**[1]

6605 **4** *6* **Hunters Belt (IRE)**[89] 802 11-11-7 105..................(vt) JonathonBewley(5) 99
(George Bewley) *chsd ldr: 2nd 4th: drvn 3 out: led briefly appr next: wknd bef last* **14/1**

5-45 **5** *2 1/4* **Burnt Sienna (IRE)**[20] 1400 5-10-10 92.........................(tp) DerekFox(3) 83
(Noel C Kelly, Ire) *chsd ldrs: outpcd 5th: lost pl after next* **7/1**

00-0 **6** *1* **Mitcd (IRE)**[15] 1461 4-10-5 84.. HenryBrooke 75
(Martin Todhunter) *in rr: bhd 5th: kpt on between last 2: nvr on terms* **66/1**

606- **7** *1 3/4* **Mac N Cheese (IRE)**[151] 5419 5-11-2 95........................... BrianHarding 84
(Rose Dobbin) *chsd ldrs: lost pl 4th: bhd fr 3 out* **7/1**

0-4P **8** *42* **Beyondtemptation**[114] 507 7-10-5 89......................(t) DiarmuidO'Regan(5) 40
(Jonathan Haynes) *led: hdd appr 2 out: sn lost pl and bhd: t.o last: eventually completed* **33/1**

66-4 **P** **Lord Usher (IRE)**[135] 139 8-11-11 104..................................(b) JanFaltejsek
(George Charlton) *prom: drvn 4th: lost pl after 3 out: sn bhd: t.o whn p.u bef last* **11/1**

P **Millen Dollar Man (IRE)**[28] 1318 6-10-5 84..................(b[1]) BrianHughes
(Karl Thornton, Ire) *chsd ldrs: wknd qckly bef 2 out: sn bhd: t.o whn p.u bef last* **15/2**

4m 7.0s (-10.40) **Going Correction** -0.55s/f (Firm)
WFA 4 from 5yo+ 11lb 10 Ran SP% **118.3**
Speed ratings (Par 105): **104,98,94,91,90 89,89,68,,**
CSF £30.41 CT £75.85 TOTE £4.20: £2.10, £1.70, £1.50; EX 22.50 Trifecta £56.00.
Owner Ring Of Fire **Bred** Pendley Farm **Trained** Farlam, Cumbria

FOCUS
Not a strong handicap, but the pace was good. The winner is rated similarly to his latest run.

1573 CHOLLERFORD CONDITIONAL JOCKEYS' H'CAP HURDLE (12 hdls) 2m 7f 63y
7:05 (7:06) (Class 5) (0-100,100) 4-Y-O+ **£2,599** (£763; £381; £190)

Form RPR
-336 **1** **Bescot Springs (IRE)**[115] 484 10-11-4 95..............(p) GrahamWatters(3) 104
(Lucinda Russell) *led to 3rd: chsd ldr: led appr 2 out: kpt on game fnl f* **16/1**

/002 **2** *2* **Koultas King (IRE)**[22] 1380 8-11-12 100....................(tp) SeanBowen 108
(Tim Vaughan) *jnd ldrs 3rd: led 8th: hit next: hdd appr 2 out: upsides 1f out: kpt on same pce* **9/2**[2]

-241 **3** *3 1/4* **Mia's Anthem (IRE)**[28] 1316 7-11-9 100............................ StevenFox(3) 105
(Noel C Kelly, Ire) *chsd ldrs: outpcd 9th: styd on and handy 4th 2 out: kpt on one pce appr last* **5/1**[3]

3432 **4** *24* **Solway Trigger**[11] 1497 6-10-0 74 oh1................................. CallumBewley 56
(Lisa Harrison) *in rr: hdwy 9th: handy 3rd 2 out: wknd qckly bef last* **2/1**[1]

-203 **5** *32* **Verko (FR)**[22] 1371 6-10-6 80.. CraigNichol 34
(Micky Hammond) *in rr: hdwy 8th: handy 5th 2 out: wknd between last 2* **5/1**[3]

6000 **6** *21* **Raifteiri (IRE)**[20] 1400 8-10-0 74 oh2................................(p) DerekFox 9
(William Young Jnr) *t.k.h towards rr: sme hdwy 8th: lost pl next: bhd fr 2 out: sn t.o* **28/1**

20-1 **7** *51* **King's Song (FR)**[10] 1510 5-11-9 100 7ex........................ JamieBargary(3)
(David Dennis) *in rr: hdwy 7th: chsng ldrs next: lost pl after 3 out: sn bhd: t.o last* **7/1**

2-P0 **P** **Stitched In Time (IRE)**[34] 1265 8-10-10 87............(p) NathanMoscrop(3)
(Sara Ender) *t.k.h in rr: hdwy to trck ldrs 2nd: sddle slipped 4th: eased and bhd whn p.u bef next* **16/1**

-056 **P** **Mrs Grass**[114] 502 8-10-0 74 oh5...................................(t) DiarmuidO'Regan
(Jonathan Haynes) *sn w ldr: led 3rd: hdd and hung rt 8th: sn lost pl and bhd: t.o whn p.u between last 2* **40/1**

6m 3.8s (-5.20) **Going Correction** -0.55s/f (Firm) 9 Ran SP% **115.0**
Speed ratings (Par 103): **87,86,85,76,65 58,40,,**
CSF £87.18 CT £420.26 TOTE £13.90: £3.80, £2.20, £1.10; EX 131.00 Trifecta £257.10.
Owner Kelso Lowflyers & PJS Russell **Bred** Pat Tobin **Trained** Arlary, Perth & Kinross

FOCUS
A modest contest run at a steady gallop, it paid to race handy. Fairly solid form at the level.
T/Plt: £29.30 to a £1 stake. Pool: £58,518.00 - 1,456.99 winning tickets T/Qpdt: £12.50 to a £1 stake. Pool: £6,307.70 - 371.60 winning tickets **Walter Glynn**

1321

NEWTON ABBOT (L-H)
Friday, September 18

OFFICIAL GOING: Good (6.6)
Wind: almost nil Weather: cloudy Rails: Re-alignment means correct race distances are as follows: Race 1 - add 65yds, Races 2 & 4 - add 19yds, Races 3 & 6 - add 85yds, Race 5 - add 56yds.

1574 WEATHERBYS PRINTING MARES' NOVICES' HURDLE (9 hdls) 2m 2f 110y
1:50 (1:50) (Class 4) 4-Y-O+ **£3,898** (£1,144; £572; £286)

Form RPR
2532 **1** **Dry Ol'Party**[24] 1352 5-10-10 107.. TomO'Brien 113+
(Philip Hobbs) *trckd ldrs: led appr 2 out: sn in command: comf* **4/1**[3]

-141 **2** *6* **Bantam (IRE)**[33] 1271 5-11-8 130................................... RichardJohnson 118
(Henry Daly) *led: rdn and hdd bef 2 out: sn hld: kpt on same pce* **10/11**[1]

3 *6* **Precision Five**[35] 6-10-10 0.. WayneHutchinson 105+
(Alan King) *trckd ldrs: rdn in cl 3rd after 3 out: hld fr next: disputing 2nd whn blnd bdly last* **5/2**[2]

320P **4** *20* **Midnight Gypsy**[37] 1234 5-10-10 0..................................(t) TomScudamore 83
(Stuart Kittow) *mid-div: hdwy 6th: wnt 4th and hit 3 out: sn rdn: nvr threatened to get on terms w ldrs* **18/1**

PP **5** *6* **Highridge Princess (IRE)**[33] 1271 7-10-3 0...................(t) DavidNoonan(7) 78
(Johnny Farrelly) *mid-div: plugged on past btn horses after 3 out: nvr a danger* **200/1**

0-4 **6** *2 3/4* **Palmaria**[141] 45 5-10-10 0.. JamesBest 75
(Caroline Keevil) *hld up towards rr: midfield 6th: sn rdn: nvr threatened* **50/1**

3/ **7** *5* **Heartening**[1039] 2402 7-10-3 0... MrDAndrews(7) 71
(Paul Phillips) *mid-div: rdn after 3 out: wknd bef next* **33/1**

OP0 **8** *32* **Miss Lucarno**[22] 1374 5-10-10 0... AdamWedge 42
(Evan Williams) *wnt rt 1st: a towards rr: t.o* **100/1**

0/0- **9** *40* **Starlight Sonata**[193] 4687 5-10-10 0................................. RichieMcLernon 6
(Emma Lavelle) *trckd ldrs tl rdn after 6th: sn wknd: t.o* **20/1**

P **Beauchamp Bella**[486] 5-10-3 0.. MrMLegg(7)
(John Ryall) *nt fluent: a in rr: t.o whn p.u after 3 out* **100/1**

06/ **P** **Tambalong**[660] 2745 7-10-10 0...(t) IanPopham
(Caroline Keevil) *hit 1st: a in rr: tailing off whn p.u after 5th* **100/1**

0-UP **P** **Pennant Lady**[57] 1082 5-10-10 0...................................(v[1]) TrevorWhelan
(Debra Hamer) *hmpd 1st: a in rr: tailing off whn p.u after 5th* **200/1**

00- **P** **Dont Call Me Doris**[183] 4866 5-10-10 0................................ MichealNolan
(Jess Westwood) *trckd ldrs: wnt lft 3rd: wknd after 5th: t.o whn p.u after 3 out* **150/1**

4m 36.3s (6.30) **Going Correction** +0.20s/f (Yiel) 13 Ran SP% **120.5**
Speed ratings (Par 105): **94,91,88,80,78 76,74,61,44,,,,**
CSF £8.29 TOTE £6.00: £1.10, £1.10, £1.60; EX 10.00 Trifecta £22.60.
Owner Woodmore Racing **Bred** Woodmore Racing **Trained** Withycombe, Somerset

FOCUS
Rail movement increased races 1 by 65yds, 2 & 4 by 19yds, 3 & 6 by 85yds and race 5 by 56yds. The three clear market leaders predictably dominated this opening mares' novice. Semmingly a step up from the winner but the second is rated a stone off.

1575 RIVIERA STONEMASONS, NOVICES' CHASE (13 fncs) 2m 75y
2:20 (2:20) (Class 4) 4-Y-O+ **£3,898** (£1,144; £572; £286)

Form RPR
112U **1** **Dormello Mo (FR)**[27] 1322 5-11-12 144................(t) SamTwiston-Davies 150+
(Paul Nicholls) *trckd ldr: led after 2 out: kpt on wl to draw clr after last: rdn out* **15/8**[2]

3111 **2** *8* **Dubai Prince (IRE)**[33] 1266 7-11-12 0..........................(t) AidanColeman 147+
(John Ferguson) *trckd ldng pair: hit 7th: nudged along fr 4 out: mounting chal whn hit 2 out: ev ch whn mstke last: sn rdn and hld* **4/5**[1]

322- **3** *2 1/2* **Nicolas Chauvin (IRE)**[151] 5428 7-11-0 0........................ NicodeBoinville 129+
(Nicky Henderson) *led: jnd whn hit 2 out: sn hdd: no ex* **5/1**[3]

/-05 **4** *87* **School For Scandal (IRE)**[13] 1478 7-10-7 0................. PaulO'Brien(7) 49
(Jimmy Frost) *chsd ldrs: struggling after 8th: lost tch 4 out: t.o* **100/1**

4m 2.2s (-4.30) **Going Correction** +0.025s/f (Yiel) 4 Ran SP% **108.0**
Speed ratings (Par 105): **111,107,105,62**
CSF £3.94 TOTE £3.20; EX 4.70 Trifecta £4.60.
Owner The Kyle & Stewart Families **Bred** E A R L Haras Du Taillis & H Poulsen **Trained** Ditcheat, Somerset

FOCUS
An interesting novice chase and there was no hanging about. The first two are a couple of smart early-seaason novices.

1576 BISHOPS CHARTER NOVICES' HURDLE (10 hdls) 2m 5f 122y
2:55 (2:55) (Class 4) 4-Y-O+ **£3,898** (£1,144; £572; £286)

Form RPR
20-1 **1** **Al Alfa**[22] 1382 8-10-12 0.. RichardJohnson 125
(Philip Hobbs) *mde all: rdn whn chal after 3 out: kpt on gamely to assert fr last* **13/8**[2]

1131 **2** *1 1/4* **Lamool (GER)**[15] 1457 8-11-5 134..................................(t) AlanJohns(5) 136
(Tim Vaughan) *trckd ldrs: chal after 3 out: sn rdn: ev ch fr next tl no ex fr last* **5/6**[1]

56 **3** *55* **Native Robin (IRE)**[9] 1518 5-10-12 0.............................. NickScholfield 75
(Jeremy Scott) *hld up in last pair wl in tch: tk clsr order after 6th: rdn after 3 out: sn wknd: t.o* **16/1**

004/ **4** *3 1/4* **Boxatrix**[128] 7-10-5 0.. MrDAndrews(7) 72
(Paul Phillips) *cl up: dropped to last and struggling but stl in tch 7th: wknd after 3 out: t.o* **66/1**

0/ **5** *1 3/4* **Looking For Mick**[103] 6-10-9 0................................... GilesHawkins(3) 70
(Chris Down) *chsd ldrs tl rdn after 3 out: sn wknd: t.o* **25/1**

BP4- **P** **Tresor De La Vie (FR)**[150] 5443 8-10-12 0.................(t) TomScudamore
(Stuart Howe) *chsd ldrs tl 6th: qckly lost tch u.p: p.u bef next* **50/1**

00 **F** **Lilbourne Legacy**[9] 1518 4-10-4 0................................ DavidNoonan(7)
(David Pipe) *trckd ldrs: pushed along 5th: fell 7th* **25/1**

2 **U** **Theatre Goer**[53] 1116 6-10-2 0.. JamesBanks(3)
(Noel Williams) *hld up in tch: bdly hmpd whn uns rdr 7th* **6/1**[3]

5m 19.1s (-1.10) **Going Correction** +0.20s/f (Yiel)
WFA 4 from 5yo+ 12lb 8 Ran SP% **124.0**
Speed ratings (Par 105): **110,109,89,88,87 ,,**
CSF £3.76 TOTE £2.00: £1.10, £1.10, £3.50; EX 4.50 Trifecta £21.80.
Owner James Drummond **Bred** Countess Goess-Saurau **Trained** Withycombe, Somerset

FOCUS
This essentially looked a match and so it played out entering the home straight. A hurdles pb from the winner and the second set a decent standard.

1577 PETER GOORD TRAVEL & KUONI H'CAP CHASE (13 fncs) 2m 75y
3:30 (3:30) (Class 3) (0-125,123) 4-Y-0+ **£6,498** (£1,908; £954; £477)

Form RPR
31F3 1 **Dream Bolt (IRE)**[16] 1455 7-10-12 **109**.................................. PaulMoloney 119+
(David Rees) *trckd ldrs: led between last 2: rdn clr: kpt on wl* **9/2**[3]
3211 2 *8* **Easily Pleased (IRE)**[27] 1327 9-11-8 **122**.............. JeremiahMcGrath(3) 126+
(Martin Hill) *plld hrd: j.rt: hld up: hdwy to ld 5th: clr 7th: rdn and hdd after 2 out: no ex fr last* **11/4**[2]
33-1 3 *5* **Sergeant Thunder**[104] 643 6-11-12 **123**..............(t) SamTwiston-Davies 121
(Paul Nicholls) *hld up last bhd ldrs: wnt 3rd 4 out: mounting chal whn sltly hmpd 2 out: sn rdn and qckly btn* **7/4**[1]
6225 4 *5* **Kitegen (IRE)**[18] 1424 9-10-12 **109**.................................. CharliePoste 104
(Robin Dickin) *trckd ldr: led 3rd tl 5th: trckd ldrs: rdn after 4 out: styd on same pce fr next* **7/1**
-P44 5 *62* **Too Scoops (IRE)**[114] 512 8-11-9 **120**..........................(t) DarylJacob 58
(Richard Woollacott) *led tl 3rd: chsd ldrs tl 4 out: sn wknd: t.o* **9/2**[3]

4m 6.9s (0.40) **Going Correction** +0.025s/f (Yiel) **5 Ran SP% 111.9**
Speed ratings (Par 107): **100,96,93,91,60**
CSF £17.45 TOTE £6.90: £2.40, £2.30; EX 16.40 Trifecta £41.50.
Owner D A Rees & N Adams **Bred** John Brennan **Trained** Clarbeston, Pembrokes

FOCUS
A modest handicap, run at a sound gallop. The form is rated around the firt two.

1578 ALPHA LOGIC (S) H'CAP HURDLE (8 hdls) 2m 167y
4:05 (4:05) (Class 5) (0-100,98) 3-Y-0+ **£3,422** (£997; £499)

Form RPR
4524 1 **Bulletproof (IRE)**[36] 1244 9-10-11 **83**..................................(p) TomCannon 92
(Ken Cunningham-Brown) *hld up towards rr: hdwy after 3 out: nt fluent whn ldng last: kpt on wl: pushed out* **5/1**[2]
-632 2 *1 ¼* **Sweet World**[9] 1525 11-11-1 **90**.................................. RobertWilliams(3) 98
(Bernard Llewellyn) *mid-div: hdwy appr 3 out: led bef 2 out: rdn and hdd last: styd on same pce* **4/1**[1]
-0PP 3 *5* **Oscar Jane (IRE)**[53] 1120 8-10-0 **72** oh3......................(bt¹) AlainCawley 76
(Johnny Farrelly) *led 2nd: rdn and hdd after 3 out: hld next: styd on to regain 3rd run-in* **22/1**
4056 4 *2 ¾* **Prince Of Poets**[10] 1510 4-11-12 **98**..........................(tp) TomScudamore 102+
(David Pipe) *trckd ldr: led after 3 out: rdn and hdd whn nt fluent next: awkward last: no ex* **5/1**[2]
0006 5 *1 ¾* **Tenby Jewel (IRE)**[27] 1323 10-10-10 **82**..........................(tp) TomO'Brien 81
(Mark Gillard) *mid-div: hdwy 5th: rdn after 3 out: styd on same pce* **14/1**
-224 6 *¾* **Supernoverre (IRE)**[9] 1524 9-10-11 **83**.................................. (b) AidanColeman 83
(Alan Jones) *hld up towards rr: hdwy into midfield 5th: sn rdn: hung lft appr 2 out: nvr trbld ldrs* **5/1**[2]
5-F0 7 *8* **Drummond**[13] 1478 6-9-7 **72** oh1..........................(tp) JordanWilliams(7) 64
(Bernard Llewellyn) *led tl 2nd: chsd ldrs: rdn 3 out: fdd next* **12/1**
0-30 8 *2* **Railway Vic (IRE)**[27] 1323 8-9-8 **73** oh1 ow1.................................. MissBFrost(7) 63
(Jimmy Frost) *pushed along after 4th: a towards rr* **12/1**
235 9 *1 ¾* **Spin Cast**[53] 1120 7-11-4 **97**..........................(bt) ThomasCheesman(7) 85
(Alan Jones) *struggling 5th: a towards rr* **14/1**
2454 10 *17* **Bob's Legend (IRE)**[12] 1489 9-11-6 **92**..........................(p) BrendanPowell 65
(Jamie Snowden) *in tch: rdn after 3 out: wknd bef next: t.o* **10/1**[3]
P-P3 P **Nellie The Elegant**[16] 1446 4-11-7 **93**..........................(t) RichardJohnson
(Tim Vaughan) *mid-div: rdn after 5th: sn hung lft: wknd next: bhd whn p.u bef 2 out* **12/1**

4m 8.2s (2.50) **Going Correction** +0.20s/f (Yiel) **11 Ran SP% 119.8**
Speed ratings (Par 103): **102,101,99,97,96 96,92,91,91,83**
CSF £26.39 CT £411.63 TOTE £5.50: £2.30, £1.70, £4.40; EX 29.00 Trifecta £779.90.There was no bid for the winner.
Owner Danebury Racing Stables **Bred** Miss Laura Duggan **Trained** Danebury, Hants

FOCUS
This weak affair was run at a solid gallop and it saw changing fortunes late in the piece. The first two were on decent marks and are rated in line with their best recent runs.

1579 CLIMATIC ENGINEERING LTD H'CAP HURDLE (10 hdls) 2m 5f 122y
4:40 (4:40) (Class 4) (0-120,118) 4-Y-0+ **£3,898** (£1,144; £572; £286)

Form RPR
4532 1 **Skylander (IRE)**[10] 1503 6-11-6 **115**.................................. KieronEdgar(3) 117
(David Pipe) *mid-div most of way: nt clr run whn clsng on ldrs after 3 out: wnt 2nd w clr run next: led last: drvn out: hld on* **4/1**[2]
4013 2 *shd* **The Winking Prawn (IRE)**[22] 1375 8-10-13 **105**.............(t) KielanWoods 108
(Graeme McPherson) *hld up: smooth hdwy 7th: led after 3 out: rdn: hung rt and hdd last: kpt on towards fin: jst hld* **8/1**
41-P 3 *8* **Kalmbeforethestorm**[137] 102 7-10-13 **110**.............................. ConorRing(5) 105
(Helen Nelmes) *mid-div: hdwy after 3 out: sn rdn: styd on but nt pce to chal* **12/1**
-046 4 *½* **Jigsaw Financial (IRE)**[33] 1269 9-10-9 **101**........... SamTwiston-Davies 95
(Laura Young) *chsd ldrs: outpcd after 3 out: styd on again fr next* **18/1**
6453 5 *½* **Perspicace**[26] 1347 4-11-11 **118**..........................(bt) TomScudamore 111
(David Pipe) *hld up: midfield 3rd: wnt 2nd 3 out: rdn and eev ch briefly bef next: sn one pce* **10/1**
4U4- 6 *½* **Well Rewarded (IRE)**[224] 4069 5-11-0 **106**..........................(p) AidanColeman 99
(Emma Lavelle) *mid-div: struggling towards rr after 6th: plugged on ent st but nvr any threat* **10/3**[1]
646 7 *5* **I'llhavealook (IRE)**[37] 1234 10-10-8 **103**..........................(p) RobertWilliams(3) 92
(Katie Stephens) *trckd ldrs: rdn after 3 out: sn one pce* **50/1**
220- 8 *3 ¼* **Sirop De Menthe (FR)**[180] 4945 5-11-1 **110**.............................. LucyGardner(3) 97
(Sue Gardner) *led: rdn and hdd after 3 out: fdd* **16/1**
421- 9 *3 ½* **Kublai (FR)**[161] 5258 5-11-3 **116**.............................. CiaranGethings(7) 99
(Philip Hobbs) *mid-div: mstke 4th: smooth hdwy 3 out: upsides sn after: rdn bef 2 out: wknd tamely* **9/2**[3]
2320 P **Dropzone (USA)**[30] 1293 6-10-0 **92** oh5.............................. ConorO'Farrell
(Brian Forsey) *a towards rr: struggling 4th: t.o 6th: p.u after 3 out* **25/1**
4413 P **Absolutlyfantastic**[14] 1119 8-11-12 **118**..........................(t) NicodeBoinville
(Martin Hill) *prom: rdn after 7th: wknd qckly next: sn p.u* **6/1**

5m 23.3s (3.10) **Going Correction** +0.20s/f (Yiel)
WFA 4 from 5yo+ 12lb **11 Ran SP% 120.4**
Speed ratings (Par 105): **102,101,99,98,98 98,96,95,94,**
CSF £37.33 CT £361.22 TOTE £4.30: £1.80, £2.70, £3.60; EX 34.80 Trifecta £590.70.
Owner The Trap Team Partnership **Bred** M Sheehy **Trained** Nicholashayne, Devon

FOCUS
An ordinary handicap and another race where two came clear in the home straight. The winner is rated close to his best but the second probably should have won.

T/Plt: £48.40 to a £1 stake. Pool: £60,674.15 - 914.39 winning tickets T/Qpdt: £9.60 to a £1 stake. Pool: £3,913.28 - 299.10 winning tickets **Tim Mitchell**

1580 - 1589a (Foreign Racing) - See Raceform Interactive

221 PLUMPTON (L-H)
Sunday, September 20

OFFICIAL GOING: Good (8.0)
Wind: Light, against Weather: Fine, warm

1590 MID SUSSEX FLOORING & CARPETS NOVICES' HURDLE (10 hdls) 2m 1f 164y
2:00 (2:01) (Class 4) 4-Y-0+ **£4,548** (£1,335; £667; £333)

Form RPR
222- 1 **Argot**[152] 5065 4-10-12 119..........................(p) NoelFehily 118+
(Charlie Longsdon) *mostly trckd ldr: led 3 out: 2 l up and in command whn blnd last: drvn and styd on wl whn pressed fnl 100yds* **2/1**[1]
1 2 *½* **Mountain Fighter**[112] 566 4-11-5 0.................................. AidanColeman 123
(John Ferguson) *trckd ldrs: wnt 2nd bef 2 out: looked hld tl wnr blnd last: chal fnl 100yds: r.o but hld nr fin* **11/4**[3]
4 3 *10* **Dynamic Ranger (USA)**[20] 1425 4-10-12 0.................................. JamieMoore 107
(Gary Moore) *hld up: prog after 7th to join ldrs 3 out: cl up bef next: steadily fdd* **12/1**
5153 4 *1* **Are They Your Own (IRE)**[15] 1480 7-11-7 125..............(t) NickSlatter(5) 121
(Fergal O'Brien) *led to 3 out: lost 2nd and fdd bef 2 out* **12/1**
-630 5 *6* **Menace**[20] 1425 4-10-9 0.................................. JamesBanks(3) 101
(Noel Williams) *hld up: lost tch w main gp after 6th: lost no further grnd though poor 9th whn mstke 3 out: pushed along and kpt on steadily after: nt disgracd* **66/1**
6 *6* **See The Rock (IRE)**[322] 5-10-12 0.................................. RichardJohnson 101+
(Jonjo O'Neill) *t.k.h: mstke 1st and nt a fluent: hld up tl prog and prom 6th: wnt 2nd briefly next: cl up whn blnd 3 out: wknd* **9/4**[2]
0P/5 7 *nk* **On Your Max**[32] 1290 7-10-8 0 ow1.................................. MrPYork(5) 96
(Raymond York) *prom to 7th: rdn and lost tch w ldrs bef 3 out: one pce after* **80/1**
-32U 8 *24* **Magna Cartor**[18] 1453 5-10-12 0.................................. KielanWoods 73
(Ronald Thompson) *t.k.h: racd wd: in tch: mstke 3rd: on terms bef 3 out: wknd sn after: eased fr last* **16/1**
F4/5 9 *23* **Dark Justice (IRE)**[14] 1485 5-10-5 79..........................(b) MarcGoldstein 46
(Michael Madgwick) *in tch to 7th: wkng whn blnd 3 out: t.o* **100/1**
10 *23* **Jopaan (IRE)**[161] 8-10-9 0.................................. ThomasGarner(3) 32
(Brian Barr) *fractious bef s: hld up in last: lost tch 6th: t.o* **80/1**
11 *18* **Seayoujimmy** 5-10-5 0.................................. MrJPearce(7) 16
(Daniel O'Brien) *nt convincing at the jumps: prom to 4th: wknd 6th: t.o* **100/1**

4m 12.1s (-18.80) **Going Correction** -1.225s/f (Hard)
WFA 4 from 5yo+ 11lb **11 Ran SP% 118.0**
Speed ratings (Par 105): **92,91,87,86,84 81,81,70,60,50 42**
CSF £8.11 TOTE £2.90: £1.40, £1.70, £2.50; EX 8.70 Trifecta £26.10.
Owner Westbourne Racing Club **Bred** Millsec Limited **Trained** Over Norton, Oxon

FOCUS
Common bends. Race 1 reduced by 48yds, 2, 4 & 7 by 36yds, race 5 by 60yds. Race 3 increased by 108yds and race 6 by 72yds. A modest novice hurdle in which two came clear. The third and fourth set the level in a fair novice for the track and time of year.

1591 MOLLY MILAM 90TH BIRTHDAY H'CAP HURDLE (9 hdls) 1m 7f 195y
2:30 (2:30) (Class 3) (0-135,135) 3-Y-0+ **£8,447** (£2,480; £1,240; £620)

Form RPR
00-3 1 **Cool Macavity (IRE)**[15] 1482 7-11-4 **127**.................................. DavidBass 133
(Nicky Henderson) *trckd ldng pair: wnt 2nd bef 3 out: led 2 out: narrow ld last: drvn ahd flat* **10/3**[1]
-430 2 *2 ¼* **Halling's Wish**[26] 1350 5-10-2 **111**..........................(bt) JamieMoore 115
(Gary Moore) *t.k.h: led and allowed easy advantage: breather 4th: kicked on again 6th: hdd 2 out: w wnr last: one pce flat* **7/1**
4020 3 *nk* **Ballyglasheen (IRE)**[29] 1325 5-11-12 **135**..........................(b¹) PaulMoloney 139
(Evan Williams) *trckd ldr tl bef 3 out: shkn up and lost pl: disp 4th 2 out: rallied last: styd on wl nr fin* **5/1**[3]
3211 4 *2 ¾* **King Muro**[12] 1508 5-10-6 **115**..........................(t) PaddyBrennan 117
(Fergal O'Brien) *t.k.h: hld up in last trio and off the pce: nt fluent 4th: stl keen in rr after 6th: clsd fr 3 out: pushed along and one pce fr 2 out* **10/3**[1]
4011 5 *1 ¼* **Sleeping City (FR)**[29] 1324 8-10-3 **112**..........................(tp) RichardJohnson 112
(Victor Dartnall) *trckd ldng trio: clsd 3 out: cl 3rd bef 2 out: fdd bef last* **7/2**[2]
54-4 6 *12* **Sailors Warn (IRE)**[17] 1459 8-10-13 **122**..........................(t) KielanWoods 112
(Ronald Thompson) *hld up in last and off the pce: pushed along and no prog bef 3 out: no ch after* **14/1**
5-65 7 *14* **Tiradia (FR)**[12] 1508 8-10-0 **109** oh2.................................. AidanColeman 86
(J R Jenkins) *hld up in last pair and off the pce: pushed along and no prog after 6th: wknd bef 2 out* **12/1**

3m 39.0s (-21.80) **Going Correction** -1.225s/f (Hard) **7 Ran SP% 111.9**
Speed ratings (Par 107): **105,103,103,102,101 95,88**
CSF £24.99 TOTE £3.90: £1.90, £4.70; EX 20.70 Trifecta £229.50.
Owner Triermore Stud **Bred** C O P Hanbury **Trained** Upper Lambourn, Berks

FOCUS
Not a bad handicap for the time of year, but it was relatively steadily run. The first three are rated pretty much to their marks.

1592 ANDREW "SUPER WACK" JACKSON MEMORIAL H'CAP CHASE (18 fncs) 3m 1f 152y
3:00 (3:00) (Class 4) (0-115,108) 4-Y-0+ **£4,548** (£1,335; £667; £333)

Form RPR
6-5P 1 **King Fontaine (IRE)**[30] 1309 12-11-9 **105**..........................(p) NickScholfield 118
(Lawney Hill) *trckd ldr to 2nd and fr 11th: clr of rest after 13th tl 4 out: rdn bef 2 out: led bef last: styd on wl and drvn clr* **14/1**
562P 2 *7* **Green Bank (IRE)**[30] 1309 9-11-11 **107**..........................(bt) AidanColeman 115
(Charlie Longsdon) *mde most: kicked on after 13th and had most in trble: drvn bef 2 out: hdd bef last: wknd flat: jst hld on for 2nd* **4/1**[3]
4532 3 *hd* **Sandynow (IRE)**[12] 1500 10-11-6 **105**..........................(t¹) SeanBowen(3) 112
(Peter Bowen) *in tch: slow jump 2nd: outpcd after 13th: tried to cl fr 4 out: wnt 3rd bef 2 out: kpt on flat: nrly snatched 2nd* **7/2**[2]
4-33 4 *4 ½* **Sky Watch (IRE)**[28] 1349 8-11-4 **103**..........................(t) ThomasGarner(3) 106
(Brian Barr) *in tch: lost pl 7th: outpcd w others after 13th: rdn and tried to cl fr 4 out: no imp after next* **6/1**
33-U 5 *9* **Ballyvoneen (IRE)**[118] 471 10-11-8 **104**.................................. TrevorWhelan 99
(Neil King) *in tch: rdn fr 13th: effrt to chse ldng pair 4 out: lost 3rd and wknd bef 2 out* **7/1**

The Form Book Jumps 2015-16, Raceform Ltd, Newbury, RG14 5SJ

253P **6** *3* **Time Is Tickin**[14] 1487 9-10-10 **99** OCdtOswaldWedmore(7) 93
(Diana Grissell) *chsd ldr fr 2nd: narrow ld whn blnd 10th: lost pl next: outpcd after 13th but nt pushed: reminder after 4 out: wknd after next* **10/1**

3/2- **7** *6* **Jayandbee (IRE)**[495] 262 8-11-12 **108** (p) RichardJohnson 99
(Philip Hobbs) *several slow jumps and often j.rt as wl: a last: outpcd 13th: pushed along after 4 out: no ch* **5/2**[1]

6m 40.5s (-10.20) **Going Correction** -0.85s/f (Firm) **7 Ran SP% 113.3**
Speed ratings (Par 105): **81,78,78,77,74 73,71**
CSF £67.98 TOTE £13.60: £5.70, £2.30; EX 95.10 Trifecta £518.10.
Owner R J Hewitt **Bred** Peter McCarthy **Trained** Aston Rowant, Oxon
■ Stewards' Enquiry : Nick Scholfield two-day ban: used whip above permitted level (Oct 4-5)

FOCUS
A moderate staying handicap. Straightforward form.

1593 AWARD WINNING EXTECH IT JUVENILE HURDLE (9 hdls) 1m 7f 195y
3:30 (3:30) (Class 4) 3-Y-O **£4,548** (£1,335; £667; £333)

Form RPR
2 **1** **Paddys Runner**[17] 975 3-10-12 0 WayneHutchinson 105+
(Alan King) *mde all: pushed along and drew rt away after 3 out* **1/3**[1]

2 *29* **Zabeel Star (IRE)**[29] 3-10-12 0 KielanWoods 83
(Graeme McPherson) *a 2nd: cl up whn nt fluent 3 out: sn shkn up: wknd bef next* **11/4**[2]

3 *31* **Caramba (IRE)**[32] 3-10-2 0 JamesBanks(3) 44
(Brendan Powell) *a 3rd: lost tch w ldng pair after 6th: wknd 3 out: t.o* **40/1**

4 *28* **Konnos Bay**[85] 3-10-12 0 BrendanPowell 26
(Brendan Powell) *w.r.s: t.o whn j. slowly 1st: nvr able to rcvr* **25/1**[3]

3m 44.0s (-16.80) **Going Correction** -1.225s/f (Hard) **4 Ran SP% 108.0**
Speed ratings (Par 103): **93,78,63,49**
CSF £1.65 TOTE £1.20; EX 2.10 Trifecta £4.80.
Owner Let's Live Racing **Bred** Miss K Rausing **Trained** Barbury Castle, Wilts

FOCUS
A very weak juvenile event after the withdrawal, but the winner set a decent standard for the time of year and is rated similarly to his debut run.

1594 MIDSUSSEXFLOORING.CO.UK H'CAP HURDLE (14 hdls) 3m 217y
4:00 (4:01) (Class 3) (0-140,133) 4-Y-O+ **£9,097** (£2,671; £1,335; £667)

Form RPR
-111 **1** **Kilfinichen Bay (IRE)**[64] 1035 7-11-11 **132** RichardJohnson 136
(Charlie Longsdon) *trckd ldrs: lft in 2nd pl 5th: led after 3 out: rdn next: hrd pressed after last: jst hld on* **7/2**[1]

5511 **2** *nse* **Princeton Royale (IRE)**[11] 1522 6-11-2 **123** (v) TrevorWhelan 127
(Neil King) *w.w: prog after 11th: wnt 2nd bef 2 out: drvn to chal after last: styd on wl: jst failed* **9/2**[2]

40-2 **3** *3 1/2* **Listen And Learn (IRE)**[94] 774 7-10-9 **123** (v) PatrickCowley(7) 126+
(Jonjo O'Neill) *w.w: sltly hmpd 5th: trckd ldrs fr 3 out: wnt 3rd next: cl up but looked hld whn mstke last: kpt on* **13/2**

-321 **4** *3 3/4* **Henri Parry Morgan**[103] 681 7-11-6 **130** (p) SeanBowen(3) 128
(Peter Bowen) *trckd ldr: led and mstke 5th: hmpd by loose horse fr 10th: hdd after 3 out: fdd fr next* **7/2**[1]

5310 **5** *nk* **On The Bridge (IRE)**[29] 1325 10-11-12 **133** (tp) NickScholfield 129
(Jeremy Scott) *w.w in last pair: effrt 3 out and cl up bhd ldrs: one pce bef next* **8/1**

-531 **6** *52* **Milestone (IRE)**[94] 773 5-10-4 **111** (t) PaulMoloney 77
(Evan Williams) *in tch: blnd 10th: no prog whn mstke 3 out: wkng whn mstke 2 out: virtually p.u fr last* **6/1**[3]

344- **F** **Cannon Fodder**[157] 5357 8-10-10 **117** MarcGoldstein
(Sheena West) *led: hdd and fell 5th* **7/1**

6m 4.1s (-20.90) **Going Correction** -1.225s/f (Hard) **7 Ran SP% 113.9**
Speed ratings (Par 107): **84,83,82,81,81 64,**
CSF £19.54 TOTE £2.90: £1.70, £2.70; EX 12.60 Trifecta £61.20.
Owner Cracker Syndicate **Bred** Brian Kearney **Trained** Over Norton, Oxon

FOCUS
A fair staying handicap. Another step up from the winner, the next three close to their marks.

1595 ANISE CATERING NOVICES' H'CAP CHASE (14 fncs) 2m 3f 164y
4:30 (4:30) (Class 4) (0-105,104) 4-Y-O+ **£4,223** (£1,240; £620; £310)

Form RPR
3P40 **1** **Dancing Dik**[39] 1236 10-10-0 **78** oh1 (b) PaddyBrennan 96+
(Paul Henderson) *mde all: drew clr 7th: 12 l up fr 11th: drvn 2 out: kpt on wl: unchal* **7/1**

0043 **2** *11* **Battlecat**[12] 1504 8-11-7 **104** ConorRing(5) 113+
(Evan Williams) *settled in midfield: prog 7th: chsd clr wnr 11th: nt fluent 3 out: rdn and no imp after* **11/4**[1]

P002 **3** *14* **Spiritofchartwell**[14] 1489 7-10-7 **85** LeightonAspell 79
(Raymond York) *hld up in last pair: stl there and wl off the pce 11th: prog 4 out: shkn up and styd on fr 2 out to take 3rd last strides: nvr a threat* **9/2**[2]

115- **4** *hd* **Ashcott Boy**[332] 2027 7-11-5 **97** MarkQuinlan 91
(Neil Mulholland) *hld up in last trio: stdy prog fr 10th: chsd clr ldng pair 4 out: pushed along and no imp: lost 3rd last strides* **5/1**[3]

-60P **5** *16* **Appropriate (FR)**[29] 1326 5-10-0 **78** oh3 (t[1]) MarkGrant 58
(Dominic Ffrench Davis) *chsd ldrs: lost pl 8th: struggling fr 11th: no ch after* **66/1**

3226 **6** *3/4* **Faith Jicaro (IRE)**[17] 1458 8-11-6 **103** (p) JakeHodson(5) 83
(David Bridgwater) *chsd wnr to 2nd: lost pl fr 10th: struggling next: no ch after* **14/1**

2-FP **P** **June French (FR)**[91] 807 7-10-8 **86** (p) NoelFehily
(Neil Mulholland) *nt fluent 4th and 5th: struggling towards rr 8th: wl btn after 11th: p.u bef last* **5/1**[3]

3P0P **P** **Forget And Forgive (IRE)**[6] 1546 7-10-2 **83** (bt[1]) JamesBanks(3)
(Sophie Leech) *chsd wnr 2nd to 10th: wknd rapidly after 4 out: wl bhd whn p.u bef 2 out* **10/1**

4-00 **P** **Memphis Magic (GER)**[18] 811 5-11-8 **100** (t) BrendanPowell
(Brendan Powell) *set off in last pair: nvr in it: wl adrift 11th: t.o whn p.u bef last* **12/1**

4m 59.6s (-7.70) **Going Correction** -0.85s/f (Firm) **9 Ran SP% 115.6**
Speed ratings (Par 105): **81,76,71,70,64 64, , ,**
CSF £27.67 TOTE £7.70: £2.30, £1.90, £2.30; EX 33.70 Trifecta £167.30.
Owner The Ray Of Hope Partnership **Bred** Usk Valley Stud **Trained** Whitsbury, Hants

FOCUS
A weak handicap in which they finished strung out. The winner was heading for this sort of figure when falling here in the spring and should still be well treated when reassessed.

1596 ANISE CATERING H'CAP HURDLE (9 hdls) 1m 7f 195y
5:00 (5:00) (Class 5) (0-100,100) 3-Y-O+ **£2,274** (£667; £333; £166)

Form RPR
0112 **1** **Empty The Tank (IRE)**[11] 1524 5-11-12 **100** LeightonAspell 106+
(Jim Boyle) *trckd ldrs: rdn to chal bef 2 out: led last: drvn and styd on wl* **11/4**[1]

06P- **2** *1* **Nebula Storm (IRE)**[13] 4709 8-10-12 **86** (v) JamieMoore 90
(Gary Moore) *in tch disputing 5th: clsd on ldrs and mstke 3 out: drvn to chal next: chsd wnr after last: styd on but hld nr fin* **12/1**

1-50 **3** *1* **Hermosa Vaquera (IRE)**[6] 856 5-10-11 **85** (p) JoshuaMoore 89
(Gary Moore) *prom: trckd ldr 4th: rdn to ld bef 2 out but sn pressed: hdd and nt fluent last: one pce flat* **9/2**[2]

3063 **4** *12* **Warrant Officer**[31] 1297 5-11-6 **94** MarcGoldstein 86
(Sheena West) *led: tried to kick on 6th: hdd & wknd bef 2 out* **6/1**[3]

3 **5** *3 1/2* **The Bugler (IRE)**[30] 1307 8-11-9 **97** (t) PaulMoloney 86
(Evan Williams) *wl in tch disputing 5th: nudged along and no imp on ldng quartet after 3 out: nvr really involved* **8/1**

P244 **6** *7* **Mount Vesuvius (IRE)**[12] 1510 7-10-13 **87** (t) RichardJohnson 72
(Paul Henderson) *hld up and immediately bhd in last trio: mstke 1st: no prog tl pushed along and modest hdwy after 3 out: nvr involved* **6/1**[3]

6666 **7** *1 1/4* **Hawk Gold (IRE)**[20] 1423 11-9-7 **74** oh7 (p) PaddyBradley(7) 56
(Michelle Bryant) *hld up and immediately bhd in last trio: nvr involved: pushed along and no prog after 3 out* **33/1**

32-3 **8** *3 3/4* **Star Presenter (IRE)**[119] 446 7-11-11 **99** TomCannon 77
(Chris Gordon) *hld up and immediately bhd in last trio: urged along after 6th: awkward 3 out: no prog* **15/2**

5-04 **9** *8* **Comedy House**[47] 673 7-10-0 **74** oh3 (v) BrendanPowell 45
(Michael Madgwick) *chsd ldr to 4th: wknd fr 6th: no ch 3 out* **12/1**

3m 41.5s (-19.30) **Going Correction** -1.225s/f (Hard) **9 Ran SP% 114.6**
Speed ratings (Par 103): **99,98,98,92,90 86,86,84,80**
CSF £34.63 CT £144.01 TOTE £3.10: £1.10, £4.50, £2.10; EX 39.30.
Owner The 'In Recovery' Partnership **Bred** Michael O'Dwyer **Trained** Epsom, Surrey

FOCUS
A moderate handicap. The form makes sense.
T/Plt: £62.40 to a £1 stake. Pool: £68,505.76 - 801.01 winning tickets. T/Qpdt: £22.30 to a £1 stake. Pool: £3,700.87 - 122.45 winning tickets. **Jonathan Neesom**

1518 UTTOXETER (L-H)
Sunday, September 20

OFFICIAL GOING: Good (8.1)
Wind: light 1/2 against Weather: overcast

1597 SENTINEL MAIDEN HURDLE (10 hdls) 2m 3f 207y
1:40 (1:40) (Class 5) 4-Y-O+ **£2,599** (£763; £381; £190)

Form RPR
2 **1** **Cooper's Friend (IRE)**[110] 590 6-11-0 0 (t) DarylJacob 110+
(Charlie Longsdon) *mde all j.rt: drvn and styd on fr 2 out* **5/4**[1]

6-2 **2** *1 1/4* **Monbeg Gold (IRE)**[127] 330 5-11-0 0 WillKennedy 108
(Jonjo O'Neill) *trckd ldrs: handy 2nd appr 2 out: hung lft: styd on same pce run-in* **9/4**[2]

3 *5* **Medieval Bishop (IRE)**[24] 6-10-7 0 JoshWall(7) 104
(Tony Forbes) *stdd s: hld up in rr: hdwy 7th: chsng ldrs next: handy 3rd appr 2 out: kpt on same pce between last 2* **33/1**

-452 **4** *5* **The Clonlisk Bug (IRE)**[11] 1519 5-11-0 0 BrianHughes 99
(Kevin Frost) *chsd ldrs: pushed along 6th: one pce appr 2 out* **13/2**[3]

2F- **5** *3/4* **An Tarbh Og (IRE)**[288] 2936 7-11-0 0 JamesBest 97
(Caroline Keevil) *chsd ldrs: one pce fr 3 out* **7/1**

FF-P **6** *33* **Just Lewis**[24] 1379 8-10-7 0 WilliamFeatherstone(7) 64
(Nikki Evans) *hld up in rr: hdwy 7th: chsng ldrs next: sn wknd: t.o last* **200/1**

7 *45* **Westerly**[24] 4-10-6 0 (p) HenryBrooke 11
(John Mackie) *chsd ldrs: outpcd 5th: drvn to chse ldrs 7th: wd bnd and lost pl bef next: sn bhd: t.o 2 out: eventually completed* **20/1**

5m 1.3s (-1.90) **Going Correction** -0.075s/f (Good) **7 Ran SP% 109.2**
WFA 4 from 5yo+ 12lb
Speed ratings (Par 103): **100,99,97,95,95 82,64**
CSF £3.92 TOTE £2.30: £1.40, £2.10; EX 5.40 Trifecta £68.60.
Owner The Stewkley Shindiggers Partnership **Bred** Gerry Moore **Trained** Over Norton, Oxon

FOCUS
Some starts have been moved at this track following remeasuring, so some races will not have speed figures until there is sufficient data to calculate updated median times. Hurdles moved out from lined raced last week. Races 1, 2 & 3 increased by 105yds and races 5 & 7 by 70yds. An ordinary maiden hurdle in which they went a sensible gallop on ground officially described as good. The winner is rated to his mark.

1598 SENTINEL "MAY UN MAR LADY" NOVICES' H'CAP HURDLE (DIV I) (12 hdls) 2m 7f 70y
2:10 (2:10) (Class 5) (0-100,102) 4-Y-O+ **£2,599** (£763; £381; £190)

Form RPR
-214 **1** **Etania**[30] 1306 7-11-3 **91** TomO'Brien 101
(Ian Williams) *trckd ldrs: upsides 3 out: styd on to ld clsng stages* **13/2**[2]

35P2 **2** *hd* **Catkin Copse**[20] 1427 7-10-8 **87** (p) DanielHiskett(5) 97
(Richard Phillips) *hld up in mid-div: hdwy 7th: sn chsng ldrs: led narrowly appr 3 out: hdd and no ex clsng stages* **11/1**

-634 **3** *7* **Tokyo Javilex (FR)**[24] 1375 8-10-6 **87** (t) MrLDrowne(7) 91
(Nigel Hawke) *hld up towards rr: hdwy to chse ldrs 8th: upsides 3 out: outpcd between last 2: styd on run-in: tk 3rd nr fin* **7/1**[3]

2130 **4** *3/4* **Tennessee Bird**[36] 1265 7-10-8 **82** GavinSheehan 85
(Mike Sowersby) *hld up in rr: gd hdwy to chse ldrs 3 out: kpt on one pce fr next* **12/1**

0-31 **5** *2* **Western Goose (IRE)**[12] 1509 8-11-7 **102** FinianO'Toole(7) 104
(Heather Dalton) *trckd ldrs: upsides 3 out: one pce fr next* **7/1**[3]

5045 **6** *2 1/2* **Icanmotor**[30] 1310 8-9-11 **74** oh4 (tp) ConorShoemark(3) 75
(Claire Dyson) *chsd ldrs: 3rd and one pce whn blnd 2 out* **25/1**

55P- **7** *4 1/2* **Ask A Bank (IRE)**[169] 5148 5-11-4 **92** SamTwiston-Davies 87
(David Dennis) *mid-div: hdwy 8th: chsng ldrs appr 3 out: wknd appr last* **10/1**

P0/1 **8** *6* **Duke's Affair**[24] 1383 7-10-8 **85** MattGriffiths(3) 75
(Jeremy Scott) *t.k.h in rr: effrt appr 3 out: sn drvn: nvr a factor* **4/1**[1]

P-01 **9** *5* **Thefriendlygremlin**[84] 858 7-10-1 **80**......................(p) HarryBannister(5) 66
(John Upson) *led to 3rd: led 5th to 8th: lost pl 3 out* **10/1**
224- **10** *20* **Mist The Boat**[458] 745 7-11-10 **98**...................................... MichaelByrne 65
(Tim Vaughan) *in rr: drvn 9th: bhd next* **16/1**
P400 **11** *10* **Hot Madras (IRE)**[51] 1171 7-9-7 **74** oh5.................. ThomasCheesman(7) 32
(Trevor Wall) *hld up in rr: hdwy 8th: drvn next: lost pl bef 3 out: sn wl bhd* **100/1**
0-56 **12** *18* **Strictly The One (IRE)**[24] 1368 5-10-10 **84**................(bt) DougieCostello 26
(Neil Mulholland) *t.k.h: trckd ldrs: lost pl appr 3 out: sn wl bhd* **25/1**
5-04 **13** *49* **Stand Aside (IRE)**[81] 879 5-11-7 **95**........................(p) DarylJacob
(Jonjo O'Neill) *w ldr: led 3rd to 5th: led 8th: hdd appr 3 out: sn lost pl and wl bhd: tailed rt off: virtually p.u* **9/1**

6m 2.5s (3.70) **Going Correction** -0.075s/f (Good) **13** Ran SP% **117.1**
Speed ratings (Par 103): **90,89,87,87,86 85,84,82,80,73 69,63,46**
CSF £73.06 CT £518.86 TOTE £7.70: £3.20, £3.20, £3.20; EX 59.40 Trifecta £418.90.
Owner Mr & Mrs H Parmar **Bred** Mrs S Horne **Trained** Portway, Worcs

FOCUS
A modest, but more competitive affair than the second division. The pace was fair, though they were tightly grouped, plenty holding chances entering the straight. The winner was well in on her best chase form.

1599 SENTINEL "MAY UN MAR LADY" NOVICES' H'CAP HURDLE (DIV II) (12 hdls) 2m 7f 70y
2:40 (2:40) (Class 5) (0-100,100) 4-Y-0+ **£2,599** (£763; £381; £190)

Form RPR
0320 **1** **Perseid (IRE)**[24] 1375 5-10-8 **82**.. SeanQuinlan 96+
(Sue Smith) *trckd ldr: led 8th: wnt clr sn after 3 out: 10 l ahd last: heavily eased last 100yds* **11/4**[1]
6562 **2** *6* **Bus Named Desire**[12] 1509 7-10-1 **85** ow2..............(tp) TobyWheeler(10) 88
(Ian Williams) *trckd ldrs: t.k.h: 4th 2 out: kpt on to take modest 2nd last* **9/2**[2]
0-20 **3** *2* **Darnitnev**[29] 1324 5-11-12 **100**..[1] AndrewTinkler 101
(Martin Keighley) *hld up in rr: hdwy 8th: drvn next: 3rd 2 out: kpt on one pce* **8/1**
0004 **4** *3* **Sovinnie (IRE)**[32] 1293 6-10-13 **87**.................................. AdamWedge 85
(Jane Mathias) *trckd ldrs: chsd wnr 3 out: one pce fr next* **12/1**
0P-2 **5** *22* **Peaceful Gardens**[89] 824 6-9-8 **75**........................ DavidPrichard(7) 54
(Jeremy Scott) *hld up in rr: sme hdwy 8th: drvn after next: nvr on terms* **9/2**[2]
000- **6** *5* **Barneby (FR)**[205] 4472 4-11-9 **99**..................................(t) TomScudamore 73
(David Pipe) *trckd ldrs: 3rd 3 out: lost pl bef next* **6/1**[3]
P130 **7** *6* **Izbushka (IRE)**[22] 1400 4-10-12 **88**..............................(b) BrianHughes 55
(David Thompson) *chsd ldrs: drvn 7th: lost pl 7th: bhd next* **14/1**
-P40 **8** *12* **Midnight Memories**[58] 1094 5-11-3 **91**.......................... RobertDunne 49
(Steph Hollinshead) *led to 8th: lost pl 3 out: sn bhd: t.o whn eased clsng stages* **33/1**
-240 **9** *22* **Canarbino Girl**[112] 569 8-10-6 **80**..................................(t) JamesBest 18
(Caroline Keevil) *in rr: hdwy 7th: drvn 9th: sn lost pl: t.o* **25/1**
-066 **10** *16* **Love The Leader (IRE)**[20] 1427 7-11-2 **90**........................ AlainCawley 14
(Johnny Farrelly) *mid-div: lost pl after 8th: t.o 3 out* **28/1**
UUPP **11** *½* **Tikketoride**[67] 1011 7-9-7 **74** oh5....................................(bt) ArchieBellamy(7)
(Peter Pritchard) *prom: t.k.h: hit 5th: lost pl next: sn bhd: t.o 9th* **100/1**
P6U- **P** **Giveimachance (IRE)**[176] 5027 7-10-7 **84**.............(t) ConorShoemark(3)
(Claire Dyson) *trckd ldrs: t.k.h: lost pl 8th: sn bhd: t.o whn p.u bef next: lame* **40/1**

6m 5.0s (6.20) **Going Correction** -0.075s/f (Good)
WFA 4 from 5yo+ 12lb **12** Ran SP% **116.5**
Speed ratings (Par 103): **86,83,83,82,74 72,70,66,58,53 53,**
CSF £14.67 CT £87.98 TOTE £3.80: £2.10, £2.10, £2.80; EX 18.00 Trifecta £155.80.
Owner Mrs S Smith **Bred** P Connell **Trained** High Eldwick, W Yorks

FOCUS
Less competitive than the first division and run in a slower time. Once again, the field were bunched and the pace was moderate. The easy winner improved towards the level of his best bumper form.

1600 SENTINEL GREEN 'UN H'CAP HURDLE (10 hdls) 2m 3f 207y
3:10 (3:12) (Class 4) (0-120,118) 4-Y-0+ **£3,378** (£992; £496; £248)

Form RPR
45/0 **1** **Dartford Warbler (IRE)**[22] 1404 8-11-4 **110**...................... DannyCook 117+
(Sue Smith) *mde all: jnd 3 out: fnd ex clsng stages* **8/1**[3]
001 **2** *1* **Ever So Much (IRE)**[30] 1310 6-11-0 **106**....................(p) AndrewTinkler 111
(Ben Haslam) *trckd ldrs 3rd: 2nd 3 out: upsides fr next: no ex nr fin* **3/1**[1]
5-05 **3** *7* **Taste The Wine (IRE)**[31] 1048 9-9-13 **98**..............(t) JordanWilliams(7) 98
(Bernard Llewellyn) *trckd ldrs: 3rd 3 out: one pce* **10/1**
524- **4** *15* **Ballyrath (IRE)**[190] 4769 5-11-6 **112**.......................... SamTwiston-Davies 97
(Nigel Twiston-Davies) *chsd ldrs: drvn appr 3 out: lost pl bef 2 out* **7/2**[2]
6144 **5** *nk* **Vaihau (FR)**[67] 1002 6-11-2 **118**.................................. JackSavage(10) 105
(Jonjo O'Neill) *in rr: blnd and rdr lost iron 2nd tl appr next: hdwy 7th: sn drvn: poor 4th bef 2 out* **7/2**[2]
4F45 **6** *nk* **Definite Future (IRE)**[12] 1504 6-11-3 **109**..................(tp) JakeGreenall 94
(Kerry Lee) *trckd ldrs 2nd: drvn after 8th: lost pl appr next* **12/1**
16-5 **7** *7* **Della Sun (FR)**[28] 1347 9-10-13 **112**.............................. JoshWall(7) 91
(Arthur Whitehead) *chsd ldrs: drvn 5th: lost pl 7th: wl bhd whn mstke 2 out* **9/1**
5PP- **P** **Polarbrook (IRE)**[306] 2561 8-10-10 **102**..........................(p) JamesDavies
(Derek Shaw) *in rr: lost pl 7th: sn bhd: t.o whn p.u bef next* **40/1**
63-0 **P** **Come On Sunshine**[24] 1369 4-10-11 **111**..................(p) CraigGallagher(7)
(Brian Ellison) *chsd ldrs: mstke 3rd: drvn next: lost pl and reminders 6th: sn bhd: t.o 3 out: p.u bef next* **25/1**

4m 57.8s (-5.40) **Going Correction** -0.075s/f (Good)
WFA 4 from 5yo+ 12lb **9** Ran SP% **113.6**
Speed ratings (Par 105): **107,106,103,97,97 97,94, ,**
CSF £32.47 CT £243.53 TOTE £10.40: £2.60, £1.80, £2.70; EX 38.40 Trifecta £226.60.
Owner Mrs S Smith **Bred** John O'Dwyer **Trained** High Eldwick, W Yorks

FOCUS
An average handicap hurdle in which they went only a moderate gallop. Once again those at the head of affairs came out best. The form is rated around the second.

1601 SENTINEL WAY WE WERE H'CAP CHASE (15 fncs) 2m 4f
3:40 (3:40) (Class 4) (0-120,120) 4-Y-0 **£3,924** (£1,159; £579; £290; £145)

Form RPR
33-4 **1** **Kodicil (IRE)**[25] 624 7-11-9 **117**..............................(p) DougieCostello 130
(Mark Walford) *led: hdd narrowly sn after 3 out: led last: drvn out* **8/1**
6331 **2** *1 ¾* **Jayo Time (IRE)**[11] 1523 6-11-2 **117**....................(p) CiaranGethings(7) 129
(Kerry Lee) *trckd ldrs: cl 2nd 3 out: sn led: mstke next: hdd last: styd on same pce last 75yds* **10/3**[1]
3232 **3** *1* **Cut The Corner (IRE)**[18] 1450 7-11-12 **120**.................... WillKennedy 130
(Dr Richard Newland) *chsd ldrs: swtchd lft sn after last: styd on same pce* **9/2**[2]
226F **4** *6* **Buck Mulligan**[15] 1481 10-11-12 **120**................................. AdamWedge 126
(Evan Williams) *in rr: hdwy appr 4 out: outpcd 3 out: modest 4th appr last* **12/1**
F46- **5** *4* **Withoutdefavourite (IRE)**[190] 4754 7-10-13 **107**.............. JamesDavies 109
(Henry Oliver) *w ldr: outpcd 3 out: wkng whn hit next* **5/1**[3]
2130 **6** *1* **Moorlands Jack**[35] 1268 10-11-9 **117**.....................(p) NicodeBoinville 118
(Jeremy Scott) *prom: pushed along 9th: chsng ldrs 11th: lost pl appr 3 out* **13/2**
60-4 **7** *22* **Muckle Roe (IRE)**[119] 461 6-11-6 **114**................... SamTwiston-Davies 94
(Nigel Twiston-Davies) *chsd ldrs: drvn 4 out: lost pl next: sn bhd* **6/1**
1255 **8** *15* **River Purple**[11] 1523 8-11-7 **115**......................................(t) DarylJacob 82
(John Mackie) *prom: lost pl appr 4 out: sn bhd* **25/1**
4521 **9** *7* **Tregaro (FR)**[18] 1444 9-10-12 **106**..............................(t) BrianHughes 67
(Mike Sowersby) *hld up: hdwy to trck ldrs 8th: lost pl appr 3 out: sn bhd* **16/1**

5m 1.8s (-8.00) **Going Correction** -0.25s/f (Good) **9** Ran SP% **114.1**
Speed ratings (Par 105): **106,105,104,102,100 100,91,85,82**
CSF £35.56 CT £135.53 TOTE £9.20: £2.70, £1.60, £1.50; EX 27.40 Trifecta £126.50.
Owner The Elephant Group **Bred** Tally-Ho Stud **Trained** Sheriff Hutton, N Yorks

FOCUS
Four course winners were among the numbers for this fair handicap. The theme of the afternoon continued with another well-judged front-running ride. A small pb from the winner.

1602 SENTINEL CASHBACK H'CAP HURDLE (8 hdls 1 omitted) 1m 7f 168y
4:10 (4:10) (Class 4) (0-120,125) 3-Y-0+ **£3,378** (£992; £496; £248)

Form RPR
51/1 **1** **Cousin Khee**[6] 1549 8-12-4 **125** 7ex..........................(p) TomO'Brien 131+
(Hughie Morrison) *hld up wl in tch: hdwy to trck ldrs 5th: effrt 3 out: cl 2nd appr 2 out: rdn to ld between last 2: clr whn reminder clsng stages* **4/6**[1]
115- **2** *7* **While You Wait (IRE)**[36] 4957 6-11-8 **115**...................... JamesDavies 113
(Paul Fitzsimons) *in rr but wl in tch: shkn up 4th: drvn to chse ldrs next: disputing 2nd whn hit last: kpt on same pce* **33/1**
2/6- **3** *½* **Breaking Bits (IRE)**[487] 394 8-11-5 **112**..................... MichealNolan 110
(Jamie Snowden) *trcking ldrs: t.k.h: narrow ld 5th: hit 2 out: hdd between last 2: kpt on same pce* **9/2**[2]
14 **4** *6* **Bigindie (IRE)**[52] 1156 5-11-12 **119**............................ TomScudamore 110
(John Weymes) *w ldr: drvn appr 3 out: fdd between last 2* **6/1**[3]
5 *46* **Beau Bay (FR)**[43] 4-11-8 **115**.......................................(t) RhysFlint 65
(Alan Jones) *chsd ldrs: mstke and lost pl 5th: sn bhd: t.o next* **8/1**
1PP/ **6** *8* **He's A Hawker (IRE)**[696] 2050 10-10-2 **105**.................. LewisStones(10) 48
(Michael Mullineaux) *led: hdd 5th: sn drvn: lost pl bef 3 out: sn bhd: t.o 2 out* **20/1**

3m 53.4s (-4.00) **Going Correction** -0.075s/f (Good)
WFA 4 from 5yo+ 11lb **6** Ran SP% **111.3**
Speed ratings (Par 105): **107,103,103,100,77 73**
CSF £18.34 TOTE £1.40: £1.20, £6.20; EX 17.60 Trifecta £68.70.
Owner Raymond Tooth **Bred** Miss B Swire **Trained** East Ilsley, Berks

FOCUS
An uncompetitive handicap that revolved around the odds-on favourite, who is rated close to his recent win. They went a sound enough gallop.

1603 SENTINEL #LOCALANDPROUD H'CAP CHASE (12 fncs) 1m 7f 214y
4:40 (4:40) (Class 5) (0-100,89) 4-Y-0+ **£2,859** (£839; £419; £209)

Form RPR
3421 **1** **Going Nowhere Fast (IRE)**[6] 1548 10-11-7 **87** 7ex.... RobertWilliams(3) 101+
(Bernard Llewellyn) *trckd ldrs 6th: cl 2nd appr 4 out: upsides fr 3 out: styd on to ld clsng stages* **2/1**[1]
4024 **2** *1 ¼* **Chankillo**[24] 1373 6-11-4 **81**.............................(p) SamTwiston-Davies 92
(Sarah-Jayne Davies) *t.k.h: led: jnd 3 out: hdd and no ex nr fin* **5/1**[3]
5-32 **3** *6* **Maizy Missile (IRE)**[63] 1045 13-11-7 **84**........................ AdamWedge 90
(Mary Evans) *chsd ldrs 6th: 3rd 3 out: kpt on one pce* **7/1**
2255 **4** *3* **Larkhall**[35] 1273 8-10-10 **73**.. BrianHughes 76
(Mike Sowersby) *hld up wl in tch: hdwy and handy 4th 4 out: one pce fr 3 out: hit last* **13/2**
-3P3 **5** *29* **Joyful Motive**[24] 1370 6-10-0 **70**............................ ThomasCheesman(7) 49
(Brian Ellison) *w ldrs: drvn 8th: lost pl 4 out* **10/3**[2]
3-46 **6** *12* **Molko Jack (FR)**[20] 1422 11-11-4 **84**................................ BenPoste(3) 50
(Michael Mullineaux) *chsd ldrs: drvn 8th: lost pl 4 out* **12/1**
-2F6 **7** *2 ¾* **Red Whisper**[101] 699 11-11-12 **89**.....................................(t) JamesBest 53
(Rob Summers) *in rr: nt fluent 2nd: hdwy 7th: sn chsng ldrs: lost pl 4 out* **16/1**

4m 1.4s **Going Correction** -0.25s/f (Good) **7** Ran SP% **112.5**
Speed ratings (Par 103): **90,89,86,84,70 64,63**
CSF £12.27 TOTE £3.10, £2.40; EX 13.80 Trifecta £44.90.
Owner Alan J Williams **Bred** J Dowling **Trained** Fochriw, Caerphilly

FOCUS
A weak handicap for the grade, featuring some infrequent winners, but they went a good pace. The winner is rated below his recent win.

1604 WEEKEND SENTINEL NOVICES' H'CAP HURDLE (8 hdls 1 omitted) 1m 7f 168y
5:10 (5:10) (Class 5) (0-100,100) 3-Y-0+ **£2,599** (£763; £381; £190)

Form RPR
5-62 **1** **Gin And Tonic**[30] 1307 5-11-5 **93**...................................... JackQuinlan 101+
(Michael Wigham) *hld up off pce: stdy hdwy after 5th: upsides 2 out: led and hit last: rdr lost whip run-in: drvn rt out* **10/3**[2]
00-1 **2** *hd* **Triple Eight (IRE)**[15] 1478 7-10-13 **90**............................ AdamNicol(3) 97+
(Philip Kirby) *trckd ldng pair: led narrowly appr 2 out: hdd last: no ex nr fin* **3/1**[1]
-530 **3** *3 ¼* **Hold The Fort (IRE)**[38] 1244 8-11-6 **94**..........................(t) AlainCawley 97
(Johnny Farrelly) *chsd ldng pair: pushed along 5th: upsides 2 out: one pce run-in* **5/1**[3]
4 *9* **Shaiyzar (IRE)**[30] 1318 6-11-12 **100**..............................(p) BrianHughes 97
(David Thompson) *chsd ldng pair: led narrowly and wandered lft appr 3 out: hdd appr 2 out: wknd and hit last* **8/1**
00U0 **5** *20* **Innox Park**[32] 1293 5-11-2 **90**.. JamesBest 67
(Kevin Bishop) *in rr: drvn 4th: chsng ldrs whn n.m.r appr 3 out: lost pl appr 2 out* **8/1**
4P45 **6** *17* **Capisci (IRE)**[20] 1422 10-10-11 **85**.............................. TomScudamore 50
(Sarah-Jayne Davies) *led: hdd and losing pl whn blnd 3 out: sn bhd* **8/1**
4F00 **7** *2 ¾* **L Stig**[15] 1478 5-10-5 **86**.. CiaranGethings(7) 45
(John O'Shea) *w ldr: lost pl 3 out: sn bhd* **6/1**

0F-F **8** *28* **Run Hurricane (IRE)**[15] 1480 7-11-8 **96**..........................[1] DaveCrosse 30
(John O'Shea) *hld up in last: drvn 4th: reminders next: sn bhd: t.o 2 out: eased run-in* **25/1**

3m 55.1s (-2.30) **Going Correction** -0.075s/f (Good) **8** Ran SP% **116.2**
Speed ratings (Par 103): **102,101,100,95,85 77,75,61**
CSF £14.43 CT £48.86 TOTE £4.10: £1.50, £1.50, £2.30; EX 9.20 Trifecta £38.70.
Owner The Gin & Tonic Partnership **Bred** Winterbeck Manor Stud **Trained** Newmarket, Suffolk

FOCUS
The concluding contest produced another thrilling finish, with the patiently ridden winner benefiting from a strong pace.
T/Jkpt: £19,125.00 to a £1 stake. Pool: £40,406.30 - 1.50 winning tickets. T/Plt: £33.70 to a £1 stake. Pool: £8,7352.31 - 1,887.46 winning tickets. T/Qpdt: £5.70 to a £1 stake. Pool: £5,079.97 - 653.08 winning tickets. **Walter Glynn**

1605 - 1611a (Foreign Racing) - See Raceform Interactive

401 WARWICK (L-H)
Tuesday, September 22

OFFICIAL GOING: Good (good to soft in places back straight)
Wind: Light half-behind Weather: Showers clearing

1612 WINNER.CO.UK CASINO NOVICES' HURDLE (DIV I) (8 hdls) 2m
2:10 (2:10) (Class 4) 4-Y-0+ **£3,249** (£954; £477; £238)

Form RPR
163 **1** **Regulation (IRE)**[38] 1263 6-11-0 123..........................(p) LizzieKelly(5) 125+
(Neil King) *hld up: hdwy 5th: led flat: styd on wl* **15/8**[1]
2241 **2** *1* **Canicallyouback**[56] 1139 7-11-5 121.......................... PaulMoloney 123
(Evan Williams) *chsd ldrs: shkn up and ev ch appr last: styd on* **7/1**
P- **3** *3 ½* **Crickel Wood (FR)**[212] 4387 5-10-12 0..........................(t) AidanColeman 114+
(Charlie Longsdon) *chsd ldr to 4th: remained handy: ev ch whn lft in ld after 2 out: hdd flat: styd on same pce* **11/4**[2]
4 *7* **Silver Dixie (USA)**[11] 5-10-12 0.......................... LeightonAspell 107
(Peter Hedger) *hld up: hdwy and mstke 3 out: styd on same pce fr next* **25/1**
00-6 **5** *12* **Marley Joe (IRE)**[34] 1289 4-10-12 0.......................... SamTwiston-Davies 94
(Martin Keighley) *hld up: hdwy appr 4th: wknd 2 out* **80/1**
P3/ **6** *3 ¾* **Ifan (IRE)**[28] 994 7-10-12 0.......................... RichardJohnson 92
(Tim Vaughan) *j.big early: led to 5th: wknd appr 2 out* **20/1**
4- **7** *55* **Mr Ooosh**[219] 4249 5-10-12 0.......................... DavidBass 35
(Tom Symonds) *hld up: nt fluent 1st: wknd appr 4th* **25/1**
P- **P** **Ruggero**[193] 2066 5-10-9 0.......................... JamesBanks(3)
(Roy Brotherton) *prom: mstke and lost pl 3rd: wknd 5th: bhd whn p.u bef 2 out* **100/1**
222- **F** **Clemency**[154] 5454 4-10-5 0.......................... AndrewTinkler 106+
(Nicky Henderson) *chsd ldrs: led 5th: rdn and jnd whn fell 2 out* **7/2**[3]

3m 43.5s (-15.50) **Going Correction** -0.925s/f (Hard)
WFA 4 from 5yo+ 11lb **9** Ran SP% **110.9**
Speed ratings (Par 105): **101,100,98,95,89 87,59,,**
CSF £13.85 TOTE £2.60: £1.10, £1.60, £1.20; EX 11.60 Trifecta £34.70.
Owner Amber Road Partnership **Bred** Barouche Stud (IRE) Ltd **Trained** Barbury Castle, Wiltshire

FOCUS
Some starts have been moved at this track following remeasuring, so some races will not have speed figures until there is sufficient data to calculate updated median times. A damp and gloomy afternoon and steadily deteriorating ground following 9mm of rain in the past 24 hours. This was arguably the deeper of the two divisions. The first two set a fair standard and were close to their marks.

1613 WINNER.CO.UK CASINO NOVICES' HURDLE (DIV II) (8 hdls) 2m
2:40 (2:42) (Class 4) 4-Y-0+ **£3,249** (£954; £477; £238)

Form RPR
11 **1** **Roadie Joe (IRE)**[20] 1453 6-11-5 0.......................... PaulMoloney 122+
(Evan Williams) *chsd ldrs: wnt 2nd 3rd: led appr 2 out: mstke last: drvn out* **9/4**[1]
6 **2** *1 ¼* **A Little Magic (IRE)**[13] 1519 4-10-12 0..........................[1] WillKennedy 111+
(Jonjo O'Neill) *hld up: plld hrd: hdwy 3 out: chsd wnr bef next: rdn appr last: r.o* **14/1**
P3/ **3** *10* **Spa's Dancer (IRE)**[56] 2007 8-10-12 0.......................... JackQuinlan 103
(James Eustace) *trckd ldrs: plld hrd: led 4th: hdd appr 2 out: wknd bef last* **4/1**[3]
0-4F **4** *15* **Native Display (IRE)**[32] 1305 5-10-12 0.......................... AndrewTinkler 93
(Nicky Henderson) *prom: mstke 2nd: wknd appr 2 out* **8/1**
5 *11* **Imperial Glance**[423] 5-10-12 0.......................... RichardJohnson 82
(Nick Williams) *hld up: plld hrd: blnd 4th: nvr on terms* **14/1**
P **6** *8* **Dragon City**[13] 1519 5-10-12 0..........................(t) NoelFehily 71
(Charlie Mann) *chsd ldr to 3rd: remained handy tl wknd after 3 out* **50/1**
156- **7** *15* **Arthamint**[208] 4444 7-10-12 0..........................(t) HarrySkelton 67
(Dan Skelton) *racd keenly: led to 4th: wkng whn mstke 3 out* **7/2**[2]
06- **8** *20* **Vodka Island (IRE)**[243] 3818 6-10-5 0.......................... MichaelByrne 32
(Tim Vaughan) *mid-div: nt fluent 3rd: wknd next* **66/1**
41- **9** *1 ¾* **Burma (FR)**[219] 4264 4-10-5 0.......................... JamesBest 31
(Paul Webber) *hld up: effrt 5th: wkng whn mstke 3 out* **25/1**

3m 40.8s (-18.20) **Going Correction** -0.925s/f (Hard)
WFA 4 from 5yo+ 11lb **9** Ran SP% **104.7**
Speed ratings (Par 105): **108,107,102,94,89 85,77,67,67**
CSF £27.77 TOTE £2.30: £1.20, £3.90, £1.60; EX 25.50 Trifecta £31.30.
Owner Billy Bates **Bred** Michael McEvoy **Trained** Llancarfan, Vale Of Glamorgan
■ Northandsouth was withdrawn. Price at time of withdrawal 8/1. Rule 4 applies to all bets. Deduct 10p in the pound.

FOCUS
This was run at a stronger gallop than the first division and had them sorted out from a relatively early stage. The winner set a fair standard and stepped up on that.

1614 WINNER SPORTS H'CAP CHASE (17 fncs) 2m 4f
3:10 (3:11) (Class 5) (0-100,94) 4-Y-0+ **£2,599** (£763; £381; £190)

Form RPR
0032 **1** **Court Of Law (IRE)**[15] 1496 7-11-11 93..........................(p) WayneHutchinson 102
(Donald McCain) *led to 6th: led again 8th: rdn appr last: jst hld on* **3/1**[2]
3/P4 **2** *hd* **Badgers Retreat**[33] 1298 9-11-12 94..........................[1] GavinSheehan 103
(Nick Mitchell) *chsd ldrs: pushed along 11th: lft 2nd 13th: rdn appr 2 out: styd on wl: sddle slipped* **5/1**
B4P- **3** *41* **Shades Of Autumn (IRE)**[341] 1918 10-10-9 77..........................(v) MichealNolan 52
(Linda Blackford) *chsd ldrs: lost pl 5th: slipped appr 8th: hdwy next: wknd 12th: lft 3rd next* **8/1**
6344 **4** *8* **Lost In Newyork (IRE)**[61] 1080 8-10-9 77.......................... AdamWedge 42
(Nick Kent) *hld up: hdwy 7th: slipped bef next: wknd 12th* **7/2**[3]
-644 **5** *2 ½* **Be My Witness (IRE)**[65] 1056 6-11-9 91.......................... CharliePoste 53
(Robin Dickin) *hld up: hdwy after 5th: mstke and lost pl 7th: wknd 10th* **12/1**
544 **F** **Shady Glen (IRE)**[19] 1462 6-11-1 83..........................(p) KielanWoods
(Graeme McPherson) *chsd wnr tl led 6th to 8th: upsides whn stmbld and fell 13th* **11/4**[1]

5m 1.6s (-16.40) **Going Correction** -0.925s/f (Hard) **6** Ran SP% **109.4**
Speed ratings (Par 103): **95,94,78,75,74**
CSF £17.01 TOTE £2.50: £1.50, £2.30; EX 12.20 Trifecta £113.60.
Owner D McCain Jnr **Bred** William Flood **Trained** Cholmondeley, Cheshire

FOCUS
This was only moderate but it was run at a decent gallop and served up a thrilling finish between those at the head of the weights. The winner is rated similar to Perth.

1615 WINNER HEAD OR LESS PROMO H'CAP HURDLE (12 hdls) 3m 2f
3:40 (3:43) (Class 4) (0-120,120) 4-Y-0+ **£3,249** (£954; £477; £238)

Form RPR
1-01 **1** **Mr Shantu (IRE)**[90] 833 6-11-5 120..........................(t) PatrickCowley(7) 133+
(Jonjo O'Neill) *hld up: hdwy 9th: led appr last: wnt clr flat* **8/1**
20-P **2** *6* **King Boru (IRE)**[117] 523 7-11-12 120..........................(t) HarrySkelton 123
(Dan Skelton) *chsd ldrs: lost pl 4th: hdwy after 7th: lft 2nd next: led 2 out: sn rdn and hdd: mstke last: styd on same pce* **7/2**[1]
4-14 **3** *5* **Bold Conquest (IRE)**[128] 363 7-11-8 116.......................... BrendanPowell 114
(Stuart Edmunds) *hld up: hdwy 8th: rdn after 3 out: styd on same pce fr next* **17/2**
21P1 **4** *½* **Dr Robin (IRE)**[34] 1292 5-11-9 120..........................(p) SeanBowen(3) 119+
(Peter Bowen) *led: nt fluent 4th: rdn and hdd 2 out: wknd flat* **7/1**[3]
5P/1 **5** *7* **Rainbow Haze**[34] 1293 9-10-0 94 oh1.......................... PaddyBrennan 85
(Phillip Dando) *hld up: hdwy 9th: rdn and wknd appr 2 out* **10/1**
4500 **6** *shd* **Feast Of Fire (IRE)**[38] 1264 8-10-9 103.......................... BrianHughes 94
(Mike Sowersby) *prom tl rdn and wknd appr 2 out* **33/1**
P0-6 **7** *10* **Changeofluck (IRE)**[132] 283 7-10-13 107..........................(tp) NickScholfield 89
(Lawney Hill) *chsd ldr to 5th: remained handy tl rdn and wknd after 3 out* **8/1**
46-0 **8** *15* **Tales Of Milan (IRE)**[13] 1522 8-11-4 115..........................(vt) TomBellamy(3) 83
(Phil Middleton) *hld up: hdwy after 4th: lost pl after 7th: wknd 9th* **16/1**
4PP/ **9** *2* **Start Me Up (IRE)**[807] 909 11-10-10 104.......................... JackQuinlan 70
(Conor Dore) *chsd ldrs: hit 6th: wknd bef 8th* **33/1**
U02 **10** *6* **Fresh By Nature (IRE)**[58] 1113 8-10-11 110.......................... HarryBannister(5) 71
(Harriet Bethell) *hld up: hdwy after 7th: wknd bef next* **25/1**
1-50 **11** *23* **Mighty Minnie**[16] 1490 6-11-4 112.......................... RichardJohnson 52
(Henry Daly) *hld up: hdwy after 4th: lost pl after 7th: sn bhd* **14/1**
50-2 **U** **Vendredi Trois (FR)**[8] 1547 6-10-6 100.......................... GavinSheehan
(Emma Lavelle) *prom: chsd ldr 5th tl stmbld and uns rdr 8th* **9/2**[2]
F512 **P** **Uncle Tone (IRE)**[56] 1136 6-11-12 120.......................... MichealNolan
(Tim Vaughan) *hld up: hdwy 9th: wknd and p.u after 3 out* **16/1**

6m 8.6s (-28.40) **Going Correction** -0.925s/f (Hard) **13** Ran SP% **122.9**
Speed ratings (Par 105): **106,104,102,102,100 100,97,92,91,90 83,,**
CSF £37.27 CT £251.87 TOTE £9.00: £3.40, £1.70, £3.00; EX 40.40 Trifecta £392.90.
Owner Local Parking Security Limited **Bred** Victor Connolly **Trained** Cheltenham, Gloucs

FOCUS
A lively betting heat and solid handicap form. The winner is on the upgrade.

1616 WINNER.CO.UK H'CAP CHASE (20 fncs) 3m 1f 100y
4:10 (4:11) (Class 3) (0-140,136) 4-Y-0+ **£7,797** (£2,289; £1,144; £572)

Form RPR
6403 **1** **Dursey Sound (IRE)**[22] 1418 7-10-12 122.......................... RichardJohnson 131+
(Jonjo O'Neill) *hld up: hdwy 4 out: led appr last: hdd flat: rallied to ld nr fin* **7/1**
13-1 **2** *½* **Belmount (IRE)**[135] 215 6-11-1 125.......................... SamTwiston-Davies 135+
(Nigel Twiston-Davies) *chsd ldrs: mstke 2nd: led 7th to next: led 4 out: nt fluent next: hdd appr last: rallied to ld flat: hdd towards fin* **3/1**[2]
UU5- **3** *19* **Garrahalish (IRE)**[159] 5358 7-11-8 132.......................... CharliePoste 122
(Robin Dickin) *hld up: hdwy after 13th: rdn and wknd appr 2 out* **8/1**
1-12 **4** *1 ¾* **Kilbree Kid (IRE)**[83] 868 8-11-12 136..........................(tp) PaddyBrennan 125
(Tom George) *chsd ldrs: led 10th to 4 out: ev ch after next: sn rdn: wknd last* **6/1**[3]
3U1- **5** *13* **Allthekingshorses (IRE)**[152] 5497 9-11-4 128..........................(tp) JamesBest 105
(Philip Hobbs) *chsd ldrs: led 5th to 7th: remained handy: rdn appr 14th: wknd 16th* **12/1**
P00- **6** *hd* **Lamboro Lad (IRE)**[293] 2885 10-10-11 124..........................(t) SeanBowen(3) 100
(Peter Bowen) *sn prom: chsd ldr 12th tl appr 14th: wknd 16th* **16/1**
504- **7** *59* **Highland Lodge (IRE)**[267] 3381 9-11-3 127.......................... DarylJacob 50
(Emma Lavelle) *led to 5th: led again 8th tl 10th: slipped bef next: lost pl 12th: rdn and wknd 15th* **2/1**[1]
0364 **P** **Terminal (FR)**[17] 1481 8-11-8 132..........................(tp) NoelFehily
(David Dennis) *hld up: nt fluent 5th: mstke next: sn bhd: p.u bef 12th* **33/1**

6m 30.1s (-28.90) **Going Correction** -0.925s/f (Hard) **8** Ran SP% **112.7**
Speed ratings (Par 107): **109,108,102,102,98 97,79,**
CSF £28.43 CT £170.81 TOTE £6.00: £2.10, £1.50, £2.20; EX 31.70 Trifecta £350.90.
Owner John P McManus **Bred** Billy Kenneally **Trained** Cheltenham, Gloucs

FOCUS
A strong inaugural running of this handicap chase. It produced an electrifying finish between two of the best jockeys in the business. The winner should still be competitive when reassessed.

1617 DOWNLOAD THE WINNER APP H'CAP CHASE (17 fncs) 2m 4f
4:40 (4:42) (Class 3) (0-135,135) 4-Y-0+ **£6,498** (£1,908; £954; £477)

Form RPR
5-14 **1** **Gone Too Far**[81] 894 7-11-2 125.......................... WayneHutchinson 131
(Alan King) *chsd ldr tl led 3 out: drvn out* **3/1**[2]
1222 **2** *1 ¼* **Mont Royale**[17] 1481 7-11-5 128.......................... RichieMcLernon 134+
(Jonjo O'Neill) *a.p: chsd wnr after 3 out: nt fluent next: mstke last: styd on u.p* **6/1**
P43- **3** *19* **Creepy (IRE)**[189] 4829 7-11-12 135.......................... AndrewTinkler 124
(Martin Keighley) *led: mstke 4 out: hdd next: sn rdn: wknd appr last* **5/4**[1]
2-13 **4** *½* **Fond Memory (IRE)**[117] 523 7-10-8 117..........................(t) SamTwiston-Davies 105
(Nigel Twiston-Davies) *hld up: hit 4th: rdn and wknd 12th* **4/1**[3]
3133 **5** *37* **Alwaystheoptimist**[8] 1549 12-10-13 122..........................(t) TomScudamore 86
(Shaun Lycett) *chsd ldrs: rdn appr 11th: wknd next* **12/1**

4m 55.6s (-22.40) **Going Correction** -0.925s/f (Hard) course record **5** Ran SP% **111.4**
Speed ratings (Par 107): **107,106,98,98,83**
CSF £19.31 TOTE £4.30: £2.60, £1.90; EX 16.40 Trifecta £29.70.
Owner John P McManus **Bred** Richard Evans Bloodstock **Trained** Barbury Castle, Wilts

FOCUS
Two pulled nicely clear in this fascinating feature. Small pbs from the first two, but Creepy disappointed.

1618 WINNER BET AND WATCH MARES' H'CAP HURDLE (9 hdls) 2m 3f
5:10 (5:10) (Class 4) (0-110,110) 3-Y-0+ **£3,249** (£954; £477; £238)

Form RPR
-334 **1** **Midnight Mint**[91] 823 5-11-7 **105**...(t) LiamHeard 113+
(Jeremy Scott) *hld up: hdwy 6th: led 2 out: styd on wl* **14/1**
00-F **2** *9* **Magic Money**[140] 130 7-11-12 **110**... DavidBass 111
(Kim Bailey) *led: hdd appr 2nd: chsd ldr: rdn to ld after 3 out: hdd next: mstke last: wknd flat* **10/1**
6406 **3** *4* **Pretty Rose (IRE)**[14] 1506 5-11-0 **98**... DarylJacob 93
(Ben Case) *hld up: hdwy after 3 out: styd on same pce fr next* **28/1**
03-3 **4** *1* **Mistress Mole (IRE)**[22] 1420 6-11-7 **105**... RichardJohnson 101
(Gordon Elliott, Ire) *hld up: hdwy 3 out: rdn bef next: styd on same pce* **7/2**[1]
-331 **5** *10* **Northern Meeting (IRE)**[14] 1506 5-11-10 **108**...(v[1]) TomO'Brien 94
(Robert Stephens) *led appr 2nd: rdn and hdd after 3 out: wknd bef last* **6/1**[3]
060- **6** *5* **Dunmallet Belle**[166] 5243 6-10-10 **94**... JamesDavies 75
(Tom Symonds) *chsd ldrs tl rdn and wknd after 3 out* **8/1**
2314 **7** *2 ½* **Keep To The Beat**[20] 1454 4-11-0 **106**... RyanDay(7) 84
(Kevin Ryan) *trckd ldrs: racd keenly: rdn and wknd after 3 out* **10/1**
660- **U** **Teochew (IRE)**[157] 5400 7-11-7 **110**...(t) CallumBewley(5)
(Richard Drake) *prom: losing pl whn hmpd and uns rdr 5th* **20/1**
-F56 **P** **Prettyasapicture**[20] 1454 6-11-4 **102**...(p) WayneHutchinson
(Alan King) *hld up: hmpd 4th: sme hdwy bef next: wknd 6th: bhd whn p.u bef 2 out* **5/1**[2]
44P2 **F** **Lily Little Legs (IRE)**[22] 1426 6-11-1 **99**... BrianHughes
(Mike Sowersby) *hld up: hdwy whn fell 5th* **12/1**
-403 **U** **Jeans Lady**[26] 1384 6-11-0 **98**... AndrewTinkler
(Martin Keighley) *blnd and uns rdr 1st* **14/1**
P00- **S** **Walk Of Gleams**[252] 3660 6-10-10 **94**... AdamWedge
(Anna Newton-Smith) *hld up: bhd fr 3rd: hmpd and slipped up 5th* **100/1**
4042 **U** **Buy Me Out**[26] 1379 5-10-11 **100**... AlanJohns(5)
(Grace Harris) *prom whn j. slowly and uns rdr 4th* **12/1**

4m 25.6s (-20.40) **Going Correction** -0.925s/f (Hard)
WFA 4 from 5yo+ 11lb **13** Ran SP% **120.4**
Speed ratings (Par 105): **105,101,99,99,94 92,91,,, ,,**
CSF £145.35 CT £3851.83 TOTE £23.80: £5.80, £3.40, £7.20; EX 135.80 TRIFECTA Not won..
Owner London Erratics Racing Club **Bred** Pitchall Stud **Trained** Brompton Regis, Somerset
FOCUS
An incident-packed finale. A step up from the unexposed winner.
T/Plt: £57.40 to a £1 stake. Pool of £58129.20 - 738.51 winning tickets T/Qpdt: £26.40 to a £1 stake. Pool of £3453.83 - 96.60 winning tickets. **Colin Roberts**

1619 - 1626a (Foreign Racing) - See Raceform Interactive

1498 PERTH (R-H)
Wednesday, September 23

OFFICIAL GOING: Good to soft (soft in places; 6.8)
Wind: Breezy, half behind Weather: Overcast

1627 BARCLAYS MARES' NOVICES' HURDLE (10 hdls) 2m 4f 35y
2:20 (2:20) (Class 4) 4-Y-0+ **£3,165** (£935; £467; £234; £117)

Form RPR
2-1 **1** **Miss Dinamic (IRE)**[27] 1385 6-11-12 125... RichardJohnson 130+
(Gordon Elliott, Ire) *mde all: qcknd clr on bit bef 2 out: v easily* **8/15**[1]
-321 **2** *14* **Carinena (IRE)**[32] 1334 6-10-9 0... CraigNichol(3) 101+
(Nicky Richards) *nt fluent: pressed wnr: ev ch and rdn bef 2 out: sn outpcd* **11/4**[2]
54- **3** *14* **La Dama De Hierro**[200] 4622 5-10-12 0... BrianHughes 87
(Malcolm Jefferson) *nt fluent on occasions: in tch: outpcd after 4 out: plugged on fr 2 out: n.d* **20/1**
6U46 **4** *10* **Miss Joeking (IRE)**[5] 1568 4-10-11 0... PeterBuchanan 79
(Lucinda Russell) *hld up: rdn and outpcd 4 out: no imp fr next: 4th and hld whn mstke last* **80/1**
220- **5** *10* **Innis Shannon (IRE)**[165] 5277 5-10-7 0... JonathonBewley(5) 73
(George Bewley) *nt fluent: hld up in tch: outpcd 4 out: sn btn* **9/1**[3]
/05- **6** *17* **Toarmandowithlove (IRE)**[8] 463 7-10-5 0... JamesCorbett(7) 53
(Susan Corbett) *hld up: hdwy to chse ldrs 3rd: outpcd after 4 out: wknd after next* **80/1**
7 *11* **Nelly La Rue (IRE)**[129] 8-10-5 0...(p) MrWHRReed(7) 43
(Victor Thompson) *t.k.h: hld up: struggling 6th: sn lost tch* **50/1**

5m 18.8s (16.80) **Going Correction** +0.75s/f (Soft)
WFA 4 from 5yo+ 12lb **7** Ran SP% **111.1**
Speed ratings (Par 105): **96,90,84,80,76 70,65**
CSF £2.15 TOTE £1.40: £1.10, £1.30; EX 2.30 Trifecta £7.70.
Owner C Flattery **Bred** Charles Flattery **Trained** Longwood, Co Meath
FOCUS
The course was at its outermost position, meaning race distances were revised as follows: 2m Hdle & Bumper - now 2m 175yds, 2m Chse - 2m 128yds, 2m4f Hdle - 2m 4f 187yds, 2m 4f Chse - 2m 4f 173yds, 2m 7f Hdle - 3m 175yds, 2m 7f Chse - 3m 148yds. Richard Johnson agreed with the going description of good to soft, although felt it would get slower as the day went on. Little depth to this opening mares' hurdle.

1628 JM IFA CLAIMING HURDLE (8 hdls) 2m 47y
2:55 (2:55) (Class 4) 4-Y-0+ **£3,194** (£964; £496; £263)

Form RPR
2022 **1** **Street Entertainer (IRE)**[23] 1419 8-12-0 133...(bt) TomScudamore 129+
(David Pipe) *mde all: rdn whn hit 2 out: styd on strly fr last* **10/11**[1]
25-3 **2** *5* **Kumbeshwar**[32] 1331 8-10-13 115...(p) MrWHRReed(7) 114
(Lucinda Russell) *t.k.h: chsd ldrs: wnt 2nd 3rd: effrt bef 2 out: kpt on same pce bef last* **9/1**
3 *1 ¼* **The Scourge (IRE)**[27] 1390 4-10-12 113...(p) RichardJohnson 105
(Gordon Elliott, Ire) *hld up in tch: stdy hdwy bef 3 out: rdn and effrt bef next: kpt on same pce bef last* **9/2**[2]
25-3 **4** *5* **Northside Prince (IRE)**[6] 729 9-11-6 113... PaulMoloney 110
(Alan Swinbank) *nt fluent early: hld up: stdy hdwy after 4 out: rdn bef 2 out: sn btn* **11/2**[3]
2-F0 **P** **Arctic Court (IRE)**[35] 1291 11-10-10 120... BrianHarding
(Jim Goldie) *chsd wnr to 3rd: drvn and outpcd bef next: lost tch and p.u bef 3 out* **13/2**

4m 9.3s (249.30)
WFA 4 from 8yo+ 11lb **5** Ran SP% **109.3**
CSF £9.16 TOTE £1.60: £1.10, £2.60; EX 4.90 Trifecta £29.00.The winner was claimed by Sarah Jane Stilgoe for £12,000
Owner Mrs Jo Tracey **Bred** Marston Stud And Fleming Thoroughbreds **Trained** Nicholashayne, Devon
FOCUS
Not the most competitive claiming hurdle.

1629 WEATHERBYS PRIVATE BANKING H'CAP CHASE (18 fncs) 2m 7f 180y
3:30 (3:31) (Class 4) (0-105,105) 4-Y-0+ **£3,898** (£1,144; £572; £286)

Form RPR
-44P **1** **Bertie Milan (IRE)**[32] 1332 10-10-13 **92**...(p) LucyAlexander 106
(N W Alexander) *cl up: led 11th to 4 out: rallied and regained ld next: rdn and styd on strly fr 2 out* **12/1**
2541 **2** *6* **Bouggietopieces**[16] 1492 5-11-12 **105**... RichardJohnson 114
(Gordon Elliott, Ire) *in tch: stdy hdwy bef 4 out: trcking ldrs whn hit next: sn rdn: chsd wnr 2 out: kpt on same pce fr last* **7/2**[2]
0-14 **3** *6* **Down Time (USA)**[15] 1500 5-11-9 **105**...(p) BrianHayes(3) 110
(John Joseph Hanlon, Ire) *in tch: hit and lost pl 6th: rallied to chse ldrs 13th: led 4 out to next: rdn and outpcd between last 2* **16/1**
3441 **4** *4 ½* **Solway Legend**[16] 1496 8-11-4 **97**... BrianHughes 97
(Lisa Harrison) *hld up: stdy hdwy and prom 5 out: rdn after next: outpcd bef 2 out* **4/1**[3]
16-3 **5** *10* **Lord Fox (IRE)**[25] 1402 8-10-7 **86**...(b) TrevorWhelan 79
(Shaun Harris) *led to 2nd: chsd ldrs: drvn along and outpcd after 5 out: btn fnl 3* **8/1**
-005 **U** **Agricultural**[16] 1496 9-10-0 **82**... AdamNicol(3)
(Lucy Normile) *cl up: led 2nd to 11th: wknd next: last and struggling whn blnd and uns rdr 13th* **28/1**
-433 **P** **Shady Sadie (IRE)**[84] 867 8-9-12 **80**...(t) HarryChalloner(3)
(Rose Dobbin) *hld up: mstke 3rd: pushed along 11th: struggling fr next: t.o whn p.u 4 out* **6/1**
64F- **P** **Bar A Mine (FR)**[242] 3863 6-11-11 **104**... SamTwiston-Davies
(Nigel Twiston-Davies) *nt fluent: prom: blnd and lost pl 12th: sn struggling: t.o whn p.u after 4 out* **5/2**[1]

6m 21.9s (17.90) **Going Correction** +0.90s/f (Soft) **8** Ran SP% **113.2**
Speed ratings (Par 105): **106,104,102,100,97 , ,**
CSF £54.02 CT £680.21 TOTE £16.70: £4.00, £1.40, £5.00; EX 69.70 Trifecta £522.80.
Owner Turcan Barber Douglas Miller Dunning **Bred** Brian Curley **Trained** Kinneston, Perth & Kinross
FOCUS
Moderate handicap form, with a couple of the fancied runners disappointing.

1630 WEATHERBYS PRIVATE BANKING NOVICES' H'CAP CHASE (12 fncs) 2m
4:05 (4:05) (Class 4) (0-110,110) 4-Y-0 **£3,798** (£1,122; £561; £280; £140)

Form RPR
336- **1** **Monbeg River (IRE)**[200] 4618 6-11-7 **105**... HenryBrooke 117+
(Martin Todhunter) *chsd ldr: led 3 out: rdn and drew clr after next: eased towards fin* **9/2**
2-3 **2** *11* **Iffjack (IRE)**[14] 1526 5-11-12 **110**...(tp) RichardJohnson 109
(Gordon Elliott, Ire) *hld up: stdy hdwy 4 out: effrt next: lft nrly 7 l 3rd 2 out: chsd (clr) wnr run-in: no imp* **7/2**[2]
-066 **3** *6* **Amilliontimes (IRE)**[84] 872 7-11-1 **102**...(t) TonyKelly(3) 98
(Jackie Stephen) *hld up: pushed along whn mstke 4 out: sn drvn and struggling: kpt on fr last: no ch w first two* **4/1**[3]
-154 **4** *1 ¾* **Little Pop**[20] 1460 7-11-9 **107**...(t) SamTwiston-Davies 100+
(Nigel Twiston-Davies) *led: rdn and hdd 3 out: nrly 8 l down whn mstke last: sn wknd* **5/2**[1]
2- **5** *13* **Island Villa (IRE)**[19] 1471 6-11-3 **108**...(b) FinianO'Toole(7) 92
(Denis Gerard Hogan, Ire) *hld up: stdy hdwy and prom after 4 out: rdn next: outpcd whn hmpd and lft 4th 2 out: sn btn* **14/1**
05-4 **6** *63* **Call Of Duty (IRE)**[15] 1501 10-9-13 **86**... HarryChalloner(3) 9
(Dianne Sayer) *nt jump wl: chsd ldrs tl lost pl 3rd: struggling fnl circ: t.o* **12/1**
-F23 **U** **Great Demeanor (USA)**[67] 1031 5-10-0 **84** oh5... BrianHughes 77
(Dianne Sayer) *chsd ldrs: jst over 6 l 3rd and rdn along whn blnd and uns rdr 2 out* **10/1**

4m 8.5s (248.50) **7** Ran SP% **112.4**
CSF £20.33 TOTE £5.90: £2.40, £1.70; EX 21.40 Trifecta £89.80.
Owner V Vyner-Brookes & Bill Hazeldean **Bred** Ballycrane Stud **Trained** Orton, Cumbria
FOCUS
Not the strongest of races, although it was run at a decent gallop.

1631 CRABBIE'S ALCOHOLIC GINGER BEER JUVENILE HURDLE (8 hdls) 2m 47y
4:40 (4:41) (Class 4) 3-Y-0 **£3,165** (£935; £467; £234; £117)

Form RPR
1 **Persiflage**[26] 1392 3-10-5 0... RichardJohnson 98+
(Gordon Elliott, Ire) *hld up: stdy hdwy 4 out: effrt and led between last 2: kpt on strly to draw clr run-in* **6/1**[3]
1 **2** *6* **Hadfield (IRE)**[21] 1452 3-11-5 0... AidanColeman 106
(John Ferguson) *trckd ldrs: hit 2 out: effrt and chal next: sn rdn: kpt on same pce fr last* **5/4**[1]
3 *5* **The Compeller (IRE)**[65] 3-10-12 0... PeterBuchanan 95+
(Lucinda Russell) *led: rdn and hdd between last 2: kpt on same pce* **17/2**
4 *nk* **Impulsive American**[13] 3-10-12 0... TomScudamore 96+
(David Pipe) *t.k.h: hld up: nt fluent 3rd: hdwy and prom whn nt fluent 4 out: drvn bef 2 out: outpcd between last 2* **3/1**[2]
5 *32* **Moon Arc (IRE)**[47] 3-10-9 0... CraigNichol(3) 64
(Keith Dalgleish) *t.k.h: hld up towards rr: drvn and outpcd 3 out: rallied bef next: sn no imp* **25/1**
6 *2 ¼* **Armistice Day (IRE)**[37] 1281 3-10-2 0...(p) BrianHayes(3) 55
(John Joseph Hanlon, Ire) *chsd ldrs: nt fluent 4 out: drvn and outpcd after next: btn fnl 2* **25/1**
7 *2 ½* **Social Climber (IRE)**[26] 1392 3-10-9 0...(b[1]) ConorShoemark(3) 60
(Fergal O'Brien) *w ldr tl rdn and wknd bef 2 out* **9/1**
8 *3* **Danny O'Ruairc (IRE)**[30] 3-10-12 0... BrianHughes 57
(James Moffatt) *hld up: drvn and outpcd 3 out: btn whn mstke next* **50/1**
9 *25* **Bond Starprincess**[65] 3-10-2 0... AdamNicol(3) 28
(George Moore) *hld up: stdy hdwy into midfield after 3rd: rdn and outpcd after 4 out: struggling fr next: t.o* **100/1**

4 **10** *nk* **Sarafina**[23] 1415 3-10-5 0.......................... SeanQuinlan 27
(David Thompson) *bhd: mstke 4th: struggling fr next: t.o* **100/1**
4m 11.2s (251.20) **10** Ran SP% **115.5**
CSF £14.00 TOTE £5.90: £1.40, £1.10, £2.20; EX 13.90 Trifecta £152.30.
Owner G Elliott/T Cromwell/Mrs B McConnell **Bred** Mr & Mrs A E Pakenham **Trained** Longwood, Co Meath

FOCUS
Not a bad juvenile hurdle and it should produce winners.

1632 ISLE OF SKYE 8YO BLEND H'CAP CHASE (FOR THE DUKE OF ATHOLL CHALLENGE CUP) (18 fncs) 2m 7f 180y
5:15 (5:15) (Class 3) (0-130,130) 4-Y-0+ **£7,147** (£2,098; £1,049; £524)

Form RPR
211F **1** **By The Boardwalk (IRE)**[120] 490 7-10-13 **120**..........(t) TomBellamy(3) 134+
(Kim Bailey) *trckd ldrs gng wl: smooth hdwy to ld last: shkn up and qcknd clr: eased nr fin: readily* **9/2**[2]
P1F- **2** *9* **King Of The Wolds (IRE)**[172] 5140 8-11-12 **130**.............. BrianHughes 133
(Malcolm Jefferson) *trckd ldrs: hdwy and ev ch 4 out: led 2 out to last: sn rdn and hung rt: no ch w wnr* **5/1**[3]
-231 **3** *6* **Border Breaker (IRE)**[15] 1502 6-11-11 **129**..............(t) TomScudamore 127
(David Pipe) *led: rdn along 4 out: hdd 2 out: outpcd bef last* **3/1**[1]
4-10 **4** *5* **Ballyben (IRE)**[103] 707 7-11-1 **122**..............................(p) DerekFox(3) 114
(Lucinda Russell) *w ldr: mstke 3rd (water): nt fluent 11th (water): ev ch tl rdn and outpcd bef 2 out* **16/1**
0041 **5** *6* **Presented (IRE)**[15] 1500 8-10-6 **115**.......................... CallumBewley(5) 102
(Lisa Harrison) *in tch: drvn and outpcd bef 5 out: n.d after* **11/2**
2P6- **6** *16* **Five Star Wilsham (IRE)**[154] 5472 11-11-2 **120**..... SamTwiston-Davies 91
(Nigel Twiston-Davies) *hld up: rdn and outpcd after 4 out: struggling fr next* **9/1**
-201 **7** *28* **Xaarcet (IRE)**[15] 1513 8-11-2 **120**..............................(tp) RichardJohnson 66
(Gordon Elliott, Ire) *hld up in tch: drvn after 5 out: struggling after next: btn fnl 2* **13/2**
/12- **P** **Billfromthebar (IRE)**[437] 931 8-11-7 **125**.......................... BrianHarding
(Donald McCain) *bhd and nvr gng wl: outpcd whn mstke 12th: sn struggling: t.o whn p.u 4 out* **12/1**
6m 20.8s (16.80) **Going Correction** +0.90s/f (Soft) **8** Ran SP% **112.1**
Speed ratings (Par 107): **108,105,103,101,99 94,84,**
CSF £26.47 CT £76.21 TOTE £4.50: £1.80, £1.90, £1.50; EX 34.40 Trifecta £90.20.
Owner J Perriss **Bred** Colman O'Flynn **Trained** Andoversford, Gloucs

FOCUS
A good little handicap and the form looks solid, with the right horses coming to the fore.

1633 BET WITH THE DEWHURST BOOKMAKERS H'CAP HURDLE (12 hdls) 2m 7f 207y
5:45 (5:46) (Class 3) (0-140,135) 4-Y-0+ **£5,523** (£1,621; £810; £405)

Form RPR
0105 **1** **Sealous Scout (IRE)**[35] 1292 7-10-12 **121**............. SamTwiston-Davies 125+
(Donald McCain) *mde all: rdn whn hrd pressed 2 out: asserting whn nt fluent last: drvn out* **13/2**
42-1 **2** *3 ¼* **Sky Khan**[129] 356 6-11-2 **125**..............................(p) PeterBuchanan 124
(Lucinda Russell) *hld up: smooth hdwy to chse wnr after 4 out: ev ch gng wl 2 out: sn rdn: edgd lft and one pce run-in* **11/2**[3]
141- **3** *18* **Sun Cloud (IRE)**[154] 5472 8-11-12 **135**.............................. BrianHughes 121
(Malcolm Jefferson) *hld up: stdy hdwy after 4 out: pushed along and outpcd bef 2 out: sn no imp* **15/2**
4-16 **4** *7* **Manballandall (IRE)**[121] 473 7-10-9 **125**..................(t) JamesCorbett(7) 102
(Susan Corbett) *in tch: pushed along after 4 out: wknd fr next* **15/2**
321 **5** *10* **Epic Warrior (IRE)**[21] 1447 6-11-2 **125**......................(p) TomScudamore 95
(David Pipe) *chsd wnr to after 4 out: rdn and wknd after next* **15/8**[1]
3/0 **6** *12* **Andhaar**[28] 886 9-10-0 **109** oh4.. LucyAlexander 66
(N W Alexander) *t.k.h: chsd ldrs: hit 4 out: sn rdn: wknd bef next* **40/1**
10-0 **P** **Knight's Parade (IRE)**[24] 1410 5-11-8 **131**..................(bt) RichardJohnson
(Gordon Elliott, Ire) *hld up in tch: drvn and outpcd whn nt fluent 8th: sn struggling: t.o whn p.u bef 4 out* **7/2**[2]
6m 17.5s (12.50) **Going Correction** +0.75s/f (Soft) **7** Ran SP% **111.7**
Speed ratings (Par 107): **109,107,101,99,96 92,**
CSF £39.31 CT £268.59 TOTE £9.80: £3.70, £2.50; EX 55.00 Trifecta £460.30.
Owner T G Leslie **Bred** Mervyn Chamney **Trained** Cholmondeley, Cheshire

FOCUS
The front pair came clear in this fair handicap.
T/Plt: £13.70 to a £1 stake. Pool: £55,863.64 - 2973.68 winning units. T/Qpdt: £11.30 to a £1 stake. Pool: £3,798.16 - 246.82 winning units. **Richard Young**

1627 PERTH (R-H)
Thursday, September 24

OFFICIAL GOING: Good to soft (soft in places; 6.8)
Wind: Fresh, half behind Weather: Cloudy, bright

1634 WALKING THE COURSES NOVICES' HURDLE (8 hdls) 2m 47y
2:10 (2:11) (Class 4) 4-Y-0+ **£3,165** (£935; £467; £234; £117)

Form RPR
5F **1** **Where's Tiger**[16] 1499 4-10-7 0.............................. GrantCockburn(5) 116
(Lucinda Russell) *mde all: clr to 3 out: rdn whn nt fluent next: nt fluent last: drvn and styd on wl* **20/1**
1 **2** *1 ½* **Vancouverite**[24] 1425 5-11-5 0.. AidanColeman 121
(John Ferguson) *t.k.h early: nt fluent on occasions: cl up in chsng gp: chsd wnr after 3 out: effrt and rdn next: kpt on fr last* **4/7**[1]
3 *12* **Frederic Chopin**[29] 4-10-12 0.. BrianHughes 105
(James Moffatt) *hld up: hdwy to chse ldrs bef 2 out: outpcd whn nt fluent last* **10/1**[3]
1-22 **4** *5* **Mr Steadfast (IRE)**[16] 1498 5-11-5 120..................(t) RichardJohnson 105
(Gordon Elliott, Ire) *hld up: hdwy and cl up 3 out: rdn and wknd fr next* **5/2**[2]
3-0 **5** *2 ½* **Arctic Gold (IRE)**[138] 213 4-10-12 0........................ SamTwiston-Davies 98
(Nigel Twiston-Davies) *hld up in tch: drvn and outpcd after 3 out: wknd bef next* **12/1**
6 **6** *22* **Seven Devils (IRE)**[141] 144 5-10-9 0.............................. DerekFox(3) 76
(Lucinda Russell) *chsd ldrs: wnt 2nd 3rd to 3 out: sn rdn and wknd* **16/1**
4-4 **7** *45* **Sackett**[28] 1365 4-10-9 0.. HarryChalloner(3) 36
(Dianne Sayer) *t.k.h early: hld up towards rr: struggling fr 4th: t.o* **50/1**
46/ **P** **Katies Choice (IRE)**[654] 2998 7-10-7 0.......................... CallumBewley(5)
(R Mike Smith) *chsd (clr) wnr to 3rd: struggling after next: lost tch and p.u bef 2 out* **50/1**

P- **P** **Centre Haafhd**[101] 2333 4-10-12 0.. HenryBrooke
(Barry Murtagh) *hld up: outpcd fr 1/2-way: t.o whn p.u bef 2 out* **100/1**
4m 12.3s (252.30)
WFA 4 from 5yo+ 11lb **9** Ran SP% **124.6**
CSF £35.72 TOTE £27.30: £4.10, £1.10, £2.40; EX 80.30 Trifecta £1241.80.
Owner Michael & Lady Jane Kaplan **Bred** Michael E Broughton **Trained** Arlary, Perth & Kinross

FOCUS
Races 1, 5 & 7 increased by 128yds, race 2 by 188yds and races 3, 4 & 6 by 152yds. An unhappy start for most punters as the odds-on favourite lost out in a tactical battle. The winner took a big step up, with the second similar to his recent win.

1635 INVESTEC NOVICES' HURDLE (12 hdls) 2m 7f 207y
2:45 (2:45) (Class 4) 4-Y-0+ **£3,194** (£964; £496; £263)

Form RPR
235- **1** **Tradewinds (FR)**[28] 1390 7-11-0 0.............................. GrantCockburn(5) 121+
(Lucinda Russell) *mde all: hung lft fr 1/2-way: rdn bef 2 out: hrd pressed last: styd on strly* **3/1**[2]
2 *3 ½* **Mustadrik (USA)**[24] 1431 4-11-10 114......................(tp) RichardJohnson 122
(Gordon Elliott, Ire) *hld up: stdy hdwy bef 3 out: effrt and chsd wnr next: rdn and ev ch last: kpt on same pce run-in* **16/1**
51-2 **3** *1* **Major Ivan (IRE)**[142] 132 6-11-5 129.................................. BrianHughes 116
(Malcolm Jefferson) *hld up in tch: smooth hdwy to chse wnr after 3 out to next: sn rdn: kpt on same pce fr last* **3/1**[2]
1- **4** *68* **Ballywilliam (IRE)**[215] 4356 5-10-12 0.............................. TomScudamore 66
(David Pipe) *nt fluent thrght: chsd ldrs: rdn after 3 out: wknd qckly bef next: t.o* **7/4**[1]
2- **P** **Kerisper (FR)**[189] 4873 6-10-12 0.............................. SamTwiston-Davies
(Nigel Twiston-Davies) *nt fluent on occasions: chsd wnr to after 3 out: sn rdn and wknd qckly: p.u bef next* **9/2**[3]
6m 21.9s (16.90) **Going Correction** +0.80s/f (Soft) **5** Ran SP% **110.4**
Speed ratings (Par 105): **103,101,101,78,**
CSF £34.61 TOTE £3.90: £1.90, £4.10; EX 29.60 Trifecta £48.50.
Owner Gerry McGladery **Bred** Mlle Katherine Aalen **Trained** Arlary, Perth & Kinross

FOCUS
An informative staying contest, though it's debatable how reliable this form will prove. The winner is rated similarly to his recent victory.

1636 TIMOTHY HARDIE JEWELLERS NOVICES' CHASE (FOR THE CENTENARY SILVER PLATE) (15 fncs) 2m 4f 20y
3:20 (3:20) (Class 3) 4-Y-0+ **£6,881** (£2,032; £1,016)

Form RPR
111- **1** **Cyrus Darius**[167] 5250 6-11-2 0.. BrianHughes 130+
(Malcolm Jefferson) *trckd ldr: chalng whn nt fluent 8th (water): mstke next: gd jump to ld 5 out: jst over 5 l up whn blnd 3 out: rdn and hung rt bef last: hung rt and hrd pressed run-in: stened: hld on wl* **1/6**[1]
3/0- **2** *nk* **Shadow Catcher**[14] 1312 7-11-8 128..........................(tp) RichardJohnson 133
(Gordon Elliott, Ire) *led: hdd whn hit 5 out: jst over 5 l down 3 out: rallied next: effrt and swtchd lft run-in: sn ev ch and carried lft: kpt on: hld nr fin* **13/2**[2]
3 **3** *dist* **The Scourge (IRE)**[1] 1628 4-10-4 114.................................. SeanQuinlan
(Gordon Elliott, Ire) *nt fluent on occasions: sn struggling in rr: no ch fnl circ: t.o* **14/1**[3]
5m 9.9s (4.90) **Going Correction** +0.475s/f (Soft)
WFA 4 from 5yo+ 1lb **3** Ran SP% **105.7**
Speed ratings (Par 107): **109,108,**
CSF £1.73 TOTE £1.10; EX 1.50 Trifecta £1.60.
Owner Mr & Mrs G Calder & P M Warren **Bred** Lingbourne Stud **Trained** Norton, N Yorks

FOCUS
This looked an ideal starting point over fences for the long odds-on favourite. However, those that got involved with Malcolm Jefferson's Grade 2-winning hurdler endured anything but a comfortable ride. He's sure to rate higher.

1637 STRONGBOW DARK FRUIT SCOTTISH HURDLE SERIES FINAL (A NOVICES' H'CAP HURDLE) (10 hdls) 2m 4f 35y
3:50 (3:50) (Class 2) 4-Y-0+ **£9,747** (£2,862; £1,431; £715)

Form RPR
3214 **1** **Johnny Go**[17] 1493 5-10-0 **104** oh2..............................(p) BrianHughes 107+
(Lisa Harrison) *chsd ldr: 2 l down and rdn along whn lft 2 l in front 2 out: hrd pressed last: styd on wl u.p* **4/1**[3]
1400 **2** *2 ¾* **Solway Prince**[33] 1329 6-9-9 **104** oh1..........................(p) CallumBewley(5) 105
(Lisa Harrison) *chsd ldrs: rdn and outpcd after 3 out: rallied and lft 2 l 2nd 2 out: ev ch last: kpt on same pce run-in* **4/1**[3]
5354 **3** *1 ¾* **Jackofhearts**[17] 1497 7-10-0 **104** oh25.............................. SeanQuinlan 104
(Jean McGregor) *hld up in tch: effrt and rdn whn lft 3 l 3rd 2 out: kpt on same pce fr last* **150/1**
0- **4** *15* **Be Seeing You**[28] 1388 4-11-1 **120**..........................(tp) RichardJohnson 107
(Gordon Elliott, Ire) *hld up in tch: nt fluent 4 out: rdn next: wkng whn lft 4th 2 out* **7/2**[2]
5611 **5** *6* **Maraweh (IRE)**[17] 1497 5-9-11 **104** oh2..............................(v) DerekFox(3) 87
(Lucinda Russell) *hld up: pushed along and outpcd bef 4 out: no imp bef 2 out* **4/1**[3]
U525 **6** *31* **Ronaldinho (IRE)**[16] 1499 5-10-9 **113**..........................(bt) HenryBrooke 66
(Dianne Sayer) *trckd ldrs tl rdn and wknd bef 2 out* **25/1**
1U12 **F** **Sharp Rise (IRE)**[24] 1414 8-11-12 **130**.............................. JamesReveley 133+
(Pauline Robson) *led: 2 l in front and gng wl whn fell 2 out* **3/1**[1]
5m 14.6s (12.60) **Going Correction** +0.80s/f (Soft)
WFA 4 from 5yo+ 12lb **7** Ran SP% **111.7**
Speed ratings (Par 109): **106,104,104,98,95 83,**
CSF £19.57 CT £1961.59 TOTE £4.90: £2.10, £2.00; EX 19.40 Trifecta £705.20.
Owner J B Harrison **Bred** J B Harrison **Trained** Aldoth, Cumbria

FOCUS
A strong renewal of this series final, in which Lisa Harrison saddled a notable 1-2. The first two are rated pretty much to their marks.

1638 CELEBRATING SAM'S 27 YEARS H'CAP HURDLE (8 hdls) 2m 47y
4:25 (4:25) (Class 4) (0-120,120) 3-Y-0+ **£3,898** (£1,144; £572; £286)

Form RPR
F66- **1** **Jet Master (IRE)**[181] 5013 9-11-11 **119**.............................. LucyAlexander 125
(N W Alexander) *hld up: smooth hdwy 3 out: led next: rdn out fr last* **12/1**
533- **2** *1 ½* **Jack Steel (IRE)**[160] 5361 5-11-1 **109**.............................. TomScudamore 113
(Lucinda Russell) *hld up in midfield: hdwy and ev ch 2 out: sn rdn: kpt on fr last* **7/2**[2]
43-5 **3** *5* **Sword Of The Lord**[23] 217 5-10-13 **107**..................... SamTwiston-Davies 108
(Nigel Twiston-Davies) *led: rdn and hdd 2 out: kpt on same pce fr last* **9/2**

5- **4** *13* **Miss North Light (IRE)**[27] 1393 6-11-2 **110**..............(t) RichardJohnson 98
(Gordon Elliott, Ire) *hld up: effrt on ins after 3 out: rdn and outpcd bef 2 out: plugged on fr last: no imp* **14/1**

-413 **5** *6* **Cool Baranca (GER)**[20] 1034 9-10-12 **109**.................... EmmaSayer(3) 92
(Dianne Sayer) *hld up: rdn after 3 out: nvr rchd ldrs* **20/1**

1122 **6** *2 1/4* **Politeness (FR)**[33] 1331 6-11-6 **117**.......................... CraigNichol(3) 98
(Rose Dobbin) *hld up: hdwy to dispute 2nd pl after 3 out: rdn and wknd fr next* **4/1**[3]

5-31 **7** *4* **Iora Glas (IRE)**[129] 380 6-11-3 **111**........................ PaddyBrennan 92
(Fergal O'Brien) *w.r.s: hld up in tch: stdy hdwy 1/2-way: rdn whn mstke 3 out: wknd bef next* **5/2**[1]

0/ **8** *23* **Roman Numeral (IRE)**[41] 1253 7-11-9 **117**.................. BrianHughes 73
(David Thompson) *chsd ldr to after 3 out: sn rdn: wknd bef next* **22/1**

1554 **P** **Running Brook (IRE)**[74] 957 8-10-13 **112**.................. CallumBewley(5)
(R Mike Smith) *chsd ldrs: lost pl after 4 out: struggling fr next: t.o whn p.u bef 2 out* **40/1**

4m 9.7s (249.70) **9** Ran SP% **114.9**
CSF £53.25 CT £221.87 TOTE £15.30: £4.00, £1.80, £2.00; EX 72.80 Trifecta £311.20.
Owner H W Turcan & Sir Simon Dunning **Bred** Roger G English **Trained** Kinneston, Perth & Kinross

FOCUS
This looks solid form, particularly from the first two who pulled nicely clear. The winner will probably still be competitive when reassessed.

1639 ANDERSON ANDERSON & BROWN H'CAP CHASE (15 fncs) 2m 4f 20y
5:00 (5:00) (Class 4) (0-115,115) 4-Y-O+ **£3,898** (£1,144; £572; £286)

Form RPR

2623 **1** **West End (IRE)**[18] 1487 8-11-1 **107**.............................(tp) TomBellamy(3) 118
(Kim Bailey) *t.k.h: chsd ldrs: effrt bef 2 out: led last: rdn and hung lft run-in: kpt on wl* **5/1**[3]

535 **2** *2 1/4* **Gleann Na Ndochais (IRE)**[33] 1332 9-11-9 **115**.............. CraigNichol(3) 125
(Alistair Whillans) *cl up: gng wl 2 out: ev ch and rdn last: kpt on same pce last 100yds* **11/4**[1]

5F24 **3** *5* **Cayman Islands**[16] 1504 7-11-12 **115**........................... AidanColeman 121
(John Ferguson) *led: rdn and hdd last: short of room briefly run-in: edgd rt and sn outpcd* **11/4**[1]

5-33 **4** *19* **Quito Du Tresor (FR)**[22] 1444 11-11-12 **115**..............(p) PeterBuchanan 103
(Lucinda Russell) *hld up in tch: rdn bef 3 out: wknd bef next* **8/1**

4113 **5** *1/2* **Pekanheim (IRE)**[95] 800 7-11-11 **114**......................... HenryBrooke 101
(Martin Todhunter) *hld up: pushed along and outpcd after 4 out: wknd fr next* **7/2**[2]

4421 **6** *2* **Endeavor**[24] 1416 10-10-13 **102**....................................... BrianHughes 87
(Dianne Sayer) *t.k.h: prom: drvn and outpcd bef 3 out: sn wknd* **14/1**

1615 **F** **Gin Cobbler**[88] 848 9-10-9 **105**.. MrWHRReed(7)
(Victor Thompson) *t.k.h: prom: fell 5th* **28/1**

5m 17.5s (12.50) **Going Correction** +0.475s/f (Soft) **7** Ran SP% **113.4**
Speed ratings (Par 105): **94,93,91,83,83 82,**
CSF £19.46 CT £44.48 TOTE £6.40: £3.30, £2.20; EX 25.50 Trifecta £81.30.
Owner Dan Hall **Bred** Clody & Lucy Norton **Trained** Andoversford, Gloucs

FOCUS
This lacked regular winners and represents only ordinary chase form. The winner had slipped to a very good mark.

1640 DAVE SMART BIG 70 STANDARD OPEN NATIONAL HUNT FLAT RACE 2m 47y
5:30 (5:30) (Class 6) 4-6-Y-O **£2,053** (£598; £299)

Form RPR

3- **1** **Fagan**[170] 5-11-2 0... RichardJohnson 117+
(Gordon Elliott, Ire) *t.k.h: in tch: smooth hdwy to ld over 2f out: shkn up and clr over 1f out: easily* **11/8**[1]

2 *9* **Celtic Flames (IRE)**[158] 5-10-13 0............................... GrahamWatters(3) 107
(Lucinda Russell) *t.k.h: hld up: hdwy over 3f out: effrt and chsd wnr 2f out: sn one pce* **17/2**

3 *6* **Ballinvegga (IRE)**[130] 5-10-13 0.................................. TonyKelly(3) 101
(Jackie Stephen) *trckd ldrs: ev ch over 4f out: rdn over 2f out: sn one pce* **22/1**

3- **4** *3* **Trespassers Will (IRE)**[176] 5105 4-11-2 0..................... PaddyBrennan 98
(Fergal O'Brien) *hld up: hdwy over 3f out: rdn over 2f out: sn no imp* **4/1**[3]

55-1 **5** *1 1/2* **Petapenko**[147] 39 4-11-9 0..(b[1]) BrianHughes 104
(Malcolm Jefferson) *cl up: led over 4f out to over 2f out: edgd rt and wknd over 1f out* **14/1**

6 *2 1/2* **Solway Lark** 4-10-11 0.. StephenMulqueen(5) 94
(Lisa Harrison) *hld up: stdy hdwy over 4f out: rdn and wknd over 2f out* **50/1**

3- **7** *1* **Wicked Willy (IRE)**[173] 5143 4-11-2 0.......................... SamTwiston-Davies 94
(Nigel Twiston-Davies) *hld up in midfield: stdy hdwy over 4f out: rdn over 2f out: sn wknd* **3/1**[2]

8 *25* **Solway Sunrise** 4-10-4 0.. CallumBewley(5) 64
(Lisa Harrison) *hld up: struggling over 4f out: sn wknd: t.o* **50/1**

0- **9** *27* **Silva Samourai**[184] 4975 6-10-9 0................................. JamesCorbett(7) 47
(Susan Corbett) *t.k.h: led to over 4f out: rdn and wknd over 3f out: t.o* **100/1**

4m 10.2s (250.20) **9** Ran SP% **113.6**
CSF £13.75 TOTE £2.30: £1.20, £2.50, £5.00; EX 12.30 Trifecta £119.20.
Owner R A Bartlett **Bred** J R Weston **Trained** Longwood, Co Meath

FOCUS
The final race of Perth's season produced an emphatic winner, who looks destined for bigger and better things. The form is rated around the fourth, fifth and seventh.
T/Plt: £104.70 to a £1 stake. Pool: £58826.1 - 409.84 winning tickets T/Qpdt: £14.20 to a £1 stake. Pool: £4038.46 - 210.0 winning tickets **Richard Young**

1504 WORCESTER (L-H)
Friday, September 25

OFFICIAL GOING: Good (7.3)
Wind: almost nil Weather: fine

1641 RYBROOK, NOBODY KNOWS BMW BETTER H'CAP CHASE (12 fncs 1 omitted) 2m 4f
1:50 (1:50) (Class 4) (0-120,120) 4-Y-O+ **£3,898** (£1,144; £572; £286)

Form RPR

2 **1** **Valadom (FR)**[16] 1523 6-11-5 **113**...................................... AlainCawley 130+
(Richard Hobson) *racd keenly: mde all: pushed clr fr 2 out: easily* **9/4**[1]

4314 **2** *11* **Ladfromhighworth**[16] 1523 10-11-12 **120**......................... NickScholfield 122
(Jeremy Scott) *chsd wnr thrght: rdn appr 4 out: sn one pce: no ch w wnr fr 2 out* **10/1**

0UP- **3** *2* **Cloudy Bob (IRE)**[157] 5450 8-11-11 **119**......................... LeightonAspell 120
(Pat Murphy) *hld up in rr: hdwy 7th: rdn 4 out: styd on fr 2 out* **13/2**[3]

5PP- **4** *19* **Gus Macrae (IRE)**[225] 4191 11-10-9 **113**....................(tp) ConorBrassil(10) 96
(Rebecca Curtis) *chsd ldrs: rdn 4 out: wknd 2 out* **7/1**

4P14 **5** *3/4* **Cruchain (IRE)**[25] 1418 12-11-9 **117**..............................(p) RobertDunne 100
(Dai Burchell) *mid-div: hdwy 7th: rdn after 9th: wknd 3 out* **22/1**

6530 **6** *3* **Limpopo Tom (IRE)**[43] 1239 8-11-11 **119**........................(p) PaulMoloney 99
(David Rees) *hld up and a in rr: struggling fr 9th* **25/1**

UF4- **P** **My Lad Percy**[329] 2177 7-11-2 **110**................................. AndrewTinkler
(Martin Keighley) *trckd ldrs: mstke 5th: j. slowly and lost pl next: sn in rr: p.u bef 9th* **17/2**

1U42 **P** **Hawaii Five Nil (IRE)**[20] 1483 7-11-10 **118**....................(b) RichardJohnson
(Jonjo O'Neill) *mid-div: hdwy to chse ldng pair 6th: rdn 4 out: wknd next: bhd whn p.u bef last: lame* **3/1**[2]

624F **P** **Who Am I**[29] 1373 9-10-5 **99**..(p) TomO'Brien
(Debra Hamer) *hld up towards rr: sme hdwy 5th: struggling fr 8th: bhd whn p.u bef 3 out* **14/1**

4m 54.8s (-9.80) **Going Correction** -0.325s/f (Good) **9** Ran SP% **116.1**
Speed ratings (Par 105): **106,101,100,93,92 91, , ,**
CSF £25.12 CT £129.34 TOTE £3.30: £1.40, £2.00, £2.20; EX 29.10 Trifecta £93.70.
Owner Richard Hobson **Bred** Mme C Montaudoin & J Montaudoin **Trained** Stow-On-The-Wold, Gloucs

FOCUS
All starts have been moved at this track following remeasuring, so there will be no speed figures here until there is sufficient data to calculate updated median times. Both bends railed out from innermost line. Races 1, 2, 6 & 8 increased by about 60yds and races 3, 4, 5 & 7 by 36yds. A fair handicap chase, though half of the field had little recent form. The pace was respectable throughout. The winner was well in on his recent run but this rates a step up.

1642 BOB LOVE "KING OF THE DIRT" MEMORIAL BEGINNERS' CHASE (14 fncs 2 omitted) 2m 7f
2:20 (2:20) (Class 4) 4-Y-O+ **£3,898** (£1,144; £572; £286)

Form RPR

243- **1** **Vintage Vinnie (IRE)**[180] 5043 6-11-6 0.......................... LeightonAspell 143+
(Rebecca Curtis) *mde all: 8 l clr 10th: steadily increased advantage fr 4 out: unchal: eased nr fin* **14/1**

520- **2** *29* **Upswing (IRE)**[174] 5139 7-11-6 130............................... BarryGeraghty 116+
(Jonjo O'Neill) *hld up towards rr: hdwy to chse ldrs 10th: rdn after 12th: styd on same pce to take mod 2nd last: no ch w wnr* **3/1**[2]

4P-U **3** *7* **Parish Business (IRE)**[16] 1520 7-11-6 0........................(t) AidanColeman 108
(Emma Lavelle) *prom: chsd wnr fr 5th: rdn appr 4 out: one pce and no imp: lost mod 2nd last* **9/4**[1]

-323 **4** *2 1/4* **Shah Of Persia**[72] 1011 8-11-6 0..................................(t) GavinSheehan 103
(Warren Greatrex) *mid-div: lost tch w principals after 12th: rdn 4 out: styd on steadily* **28/1**

1F0- **5** *24* **Kilronan High (IRE)**[162] 5355 6-10-13 0...............(t) SamTwiston-Davies 74
(Nigel Twiston-Davies) *mid-div: hdwy 8th: rdn after 12th: wkng whn j.rt 4 out and 3 out: t.o* **10/1**

510- **6** *22* **John Louis**[86] 4088 7-11-6 0.. LiamTreadwell 61
(Venetia Williams) *t.k.h: chsd ldrs: j.lft, mstke and lost pl 5th: rdn 10th: sn wknd: t.o whn j.rt 3 out and last* **25/1**

20-P **7** *23* **Net Work Rouge (FR)**[144] 107 6-11-6 120.......................(t) DavidBass 40
(Kim Bailey) *hld up in last: nt fluent 1st: bdly hmpd and rdr lost iron 5th: no ch after: t.o* **13/2**

132U **F** **Mile House (IRE)**[16] 1520 7-11-6 130.............................. TomO'Brien
(Robert Stephens) *mid-div: hmpd and fell 5th* **4/1**[3]

-P34 **P** **Padre Tito (IRE)**[68] 1055 7-11-6 0..............................(v[1]) RichieMcLernon
(Emma Lavelle) *hld up in rr: mstke 6th: rdn 11th: sn lost tch: t.o whn p.u bef 4 out: b.b.v* **25/1**

050/ **P** **Venez Horace (FR)**[618] 3716 6-11-6 0.............................. TomCannon
(Giles Smyly) *trckd wnr to 5th: mstke 7th: j.rt next: sn struggling: lost tch 11th: t.o whn p.u bef 4 out* **150/1**

5m 39.2s (-10.70) **Going Correction** -0.325s/f (Good) **10** Ran SP% **116.7**
Speed ratings (Par 105): **105,94,92,91,83 75,67, , ,**
CSF £56.23 TOTE £12.90: £3.30, £1.70, £1.60; EX 85.70 Trifecta £266.00.
Owner Trembath, Hyde, Outhart & Hill **Bred** Miss Carmel Hennessy **Trained** Newport, Pembrokeshire

FOCUS
The winner set off to make all at a solid gallop and ran some promising but equally inexperienced chasers into the ground. He looks a decent recruit.

1643 RYBROOK, NOBODY KNOWS MINI BETTER H'CAP CHASE (11 fncs 1 omitted) 2m 110y
2:55 (2:55) (Class 3) (0-135,135) 4-Y-O+
£6,256 (£1,848; £924; £462; £231; £116)

Form RPR

4013 **1** **Purple 'n Gold (IRE)**[9] 1553 6-11-6 **129**.......................(p) TomScudamore 137
(David Pipe) *chsd ldrs: rdn and lost pl 8th: rallied 4 out: led 2 out: in command and pushed out flat* **5/1**[3]

5-6U **2** *3 1/4* **Benefit Cut (IRE)**[117] 568 9-11-2 **125**.................... SamTwiston-Davies 130
(Stuart Edmunds) *led tl rdn and hdd appr 4 out: ev ch next: hld in 3rd last: rallied flat* **5/1**[3]

0P-3 **3** *2 1/4* **Dresden (IRE)**[29] 1382 7-11-12 **135**............................... JamesDavies 138
(Henry Oliver) *trckd wnr tl rdn to ld appr 4 out: j.rt 3 out: hdd 2 out: no ex and lost 2nd flat* **4/1**[2]

1-44 **4** *7* **Nearest The Pin (IRE)**[17] 1502 10-11-9 **135**.........(tp) BrianHayes(3) 133
(John Joseph Hanlon, Ire) *hld up towards rr: hdwy 7th: rdn 4 out: one pce fr next* **12/1**

-014 **5** *3 1/2* **Fairyinthewind (IRE)**[23] 1451 6-11-1 **124**.....................(vt[1]) BrendanPowell 119
(Brendan Powell) *tended to jump rt: chsd ldrs: rdn 4 out: one pce fr 2 out* **14/1**

111U **6** *5* **Strongly Suggested**[34] 1322 8-11-10 **133**....................... BarryGeraghty 122
(Jonjo O'Neill) *mid-div: hdwy 7th: rdn after next: wknd after 3 out* **3/1**[1]

10/5 **7** *2 1/2* **Noche De Reyes (FR)**[23] 1451 6-11-2 **125**....................(t) PaddyBrennan 114
(Tom George) *hld up towards rr: nt fluent 3rd: hdwy 4th: wknd 4 out* **8/1**

10P- **8** *12* **Teenage Dream (IRE)**[61] 2886 7-10-0 **116**.................(t) CraigGallagher(7) 92
(Brian Ellison) *a in last pair: drvn 8th: mstke 4 out: wknd next* **33/1**

-434 **9** *18* **King Alfonso**[93] 830 6-11-0 **123**.. RobertDunne 83
(Dai Burchell) *a in last pair: wknd 4 out: t.o* **10/1**

3m 58.8s (-6.20) **Going Correction** -0.325s/f (Good) **9** Ran SP% **115.8**
Speed ratings (Par 107): **101,99,98,95,93 91,89,84,75**
CSF £30.88 CT £109.72 TOTE £6.30: £2.00, £2.10, £2.20; EX 42.40 Trifecta £292.00.
Owner Mrs Lynne Webb **Bred** Stonethorn Stud Farms Ltd **Trained** Nicholashayne, Devon

FOCUS
A competitive race, run at a medium gallop, in which all nine still had a chance around the home turn. The form is rated around the first three.

1644 HAZELTON MOUNTFORD RACEHORSE TRAINERS INSURANCE INTERMEDIATE OPEN NATIONAL HUNT FLAT RACE (DIV I) 2m
3:30 (3:30) (Class 6) 4-6-Y-O **£1,624** (£477; £238; £119)

Form RPR
1 **Vive Le Roi (IRE)** 4-11-0 0 RichardJohnson 106+
(Charlie Longsdon) *hld up: hdwy 3f out: led 2f out: pushed out* **2/1**[1]
40-2 2 2 ¾ **Rebel Collins (IRE)**[23] 1449 4-11-0 0 DenisO'Regan 103+
(David Evans) *trckd ldrs: rdn over 2f out: sn wnt 2nd: one pce appr fnl f* **9/2**[3]
1- 3 11 **Preseli Star (IRE)**[159] 5417 5-11-7 0 AndrewTinkler 101
(George Baker) *disp ld tl def advantage 5f out: rdn and hdd 2f out: one pce* **7/1**
4 3 ¾ **Will Take Charge (IRE)** 4-11-0 0 BarryGeraghty 90
(Jonjo O'Neill) *hld up towards rr: hdwy 6f out: rdn 4f out: one pce fnl 2f* **7/2**[2]
44 5 2 **Oh So Gigolo (IRE)**[43] 1246 5-10-7 0 FreddieMitchell[(7)] 88
(Nicky Henderson) *t.k.h: chsd ldrs: rdn 6f out: wknd over 2f out* **16/1**
6 6 2 ¾ **Ablazing (IRE)**[100] 761 4-11-0 0 NoelFehily 85
(Johnny Farrelly) *hld up in tch towards rr: rdn 3f out: one pce* **25/1**
43- 7 1 ¾ **Holy Cross (IRE)**[157] 5446 4-11-0 0 LeightonAspell 84
(Rebecca Curtis) *t.k.h in mid-div: rdn and wknd 3f out* **17/2**
0- 8 7 **Up The Junction**[228] 4135 4-11-0 0 MichaelByrne 78
(Tim Vaughan) *disp ld tl hdd 5f out: wknd 3f out* **40/1**
0 9 1 ½ **Indimoon**[20] 1484 5-10-9 0 (p) JakeHodson[(5)] 76
(David Bridgwater) *mid-div: rdn along 7f out: wknd over 4f out* **100/1**
P **La Premiere Dame (FR)** 4-10-7 0[1] GavinSheehan
(Emma Lavelle) *chsd ldrs tl rdn and wknd 5f out: t.o whn p.u 3f out* **16/1**

3m 43.7s (-1.30) **Going Correction** -0.20s/f (Good)
WFA 4 from 5yo 11lb 10 Ran SP% **115.8**
Speed ratings: **95,93,88,86,85 83,83,79,78,**
CSF £10.83 TOTE £3.20: £1.50, £1.70, £2.20; EX 18.80 Trifecta £55.90.
Owner Thomas Richens **Bred** Anngrove Stud **Trained** Over Norton, Oxon

FOCUS
The gallop wasn't bad for a bumper and only two were in it in the last 2f. The slower division, but the winner can rate higher.

1645 HAZELTON MOUNTFORD RACEHORSE TRAINERS INSURANCE INTERMEDIATE OPEN NATIONAL HUNT FLAT RACE (DIV II) 2m
4:05 (4:05) (Class 6) 4-6-Y-O **£1,624** (£477; £238; £119)

Form RPR
1 **Wholestone (IRE)** 4-11-0 0 SamTwiston-Davies 115+
(Nigel Twiston-Davies) *chsd ldrs: led over 3f out: pushed along 2f out: drvn out and styd on wl fnl f* **14/1**
2- 2 2 ¾ **Western Miller (IRE)**[155] 5501 4-11-0 0 RichardJohnson 111+
(Charlie Longsdon) *hld up towards rr: hdwy and prom 5f out: rdn over 3f out: sn wnt 2nd: unable qck fnl f* **6/4**[1]
3 12 **Still Together (IRE)**[180] 5-10-11 0 BrianToomey[(3)] 100
(David Pipe) *mid-div: hdwy 6f out: led over 4f out tl over 3f out: sn hld: plugged on to take modest 3rd 1f out* **20/1**
3 4 nk **Crimson Ark (IRE)**[20] 1484 5-11-0 0[1] AidanColeman 100
(Emma Lavelle) *racd keenly: prom: rdn and ev ch over 2f out: sn one pce: wknd and lost modest 3rd 1f out* **15/2**
5 16 **Beggar's Wishes (IRE)** 4-10-11 0 SeanBowen[(3)] 86
(Peter Bowen) *chsd ldrs tl rdn and wknd over 4f out* **3/1**[2]
6 9 **Rosskerrig (IRE)**[124] 5-11-0 0 (t) HarrySkelton 78
(Dan Skelton) *t.k.h: led tl rdn and hdd over 4f out: sn wknd* **16/1**
0- 7 7 **Singing Hinnie**[192] 4832 4-10-7 0 AndrewTinkler 64
(Mark H Tompkins) *hld up in rr: rdn 7f out: wknd 4f out* **50/1**
8 28 **Kanturk Bank (IRE)**[167] 5-11-0 0 LeightonAspell 46
(Rebecca Curtis) *prom: pushed along whn hmpd and lost pl 5f out: sn wknd: t.o* **5/1**[3]
9 39 **Just Nobby** 4-11-0 0 HenryBrooke 11
(Jennie Candlish) *in rr: wknd 5f out: t.o* **50/1**

3m 39.9s (-5.10) **Going Correction** -0.20s/f (Good) 9 Ran SP% **114.7**
Speed ratings: **104,102,96,96,88 83,80,66,46**
CSF £34.87 TOTE £11.00: £3.30, £1.50, £4.00; EX 33.70 Trifecta £286.90.
Owner N A Twiston-Davies **Bred** Michael O'Donovan **Trained** Naunton, Gloucs

FOCUS
Run at a surprisingly good gallop for a bumper, this division contained some interesting types with long-term potential. The form should work out.

1646 PAMELA ANN (S) HURDLE (12 hdls) 2m 7f
4:40 (4:40) (Class 5) 4-7-Y-O **£2,274** (£667; £333; £166)

Form RPR
1-4 1 **Grey Monk (IRE)**[41] 1261 7-10-7 120 (t) NathanMoscrop[(5)] 123+
(Sara Ender) *hld up in last pair: hdwy 6th: wnt 2nd next: led after 9th: pushed along fr 2 out: nt fluent last: comf* **11/4**[3]
130 2 4 ½ **Wind Of Hope (IRE)**[75] 959 6-10-12 116 (p) TomScudamore 115
(Lucinda Russell) *hld up in last pair: clsd 6th: outpcd by ldng pair after 9th: rallied 3 out: chsd wnr next: one pce and hld whn nt fluent last* **6/4**[1]
6061 3 14 **Marju's Quest (IRE)**[33] 1346 5-11-5 125 NoelFehily 111
(David Dennis) *t.k.h: j.rt at times: chsd ldr tl led 6th: hdd after 9th: shkn up and fnd little 2 out where lost 2nd: wknd* **9/4**[2]
2PPP 4 32 **Killimordaly (IRE)**[22] 1462 6-10-9 (b) JamesBanks[(3)] 74
(Andy Turnell) *led to 6th: drvn and lost 2nd next: wknd 9th: t.o* **25/1**
556 5 15 **Kyles Faith (IRE)**[20] 1478 7-10-12 95 (b) IanPopham 60
(Martin Keighley) *chsd ldrs tl drvn and dropped to last after 6th: sn bhd: t.o* **11/1**

5m 37.2s (-1.40) **Going Correction** -0.20s/f (Good) 5 Ran SP% **109.6**
Speed ratings: **94,92,87,76,71**
CSF £7.48 TOTE £3.60: £1.50, £1.20; EX 8.20 Trifecta £15.00.The winner was bought in for 14,500gns.
Owner N Ender **Bred** Paddy Meade **Trained** Malton, N Yorks

FOCUS
A seller of fair quality for the grade, but the pace was modest. The winner was the pick at the weights on his best form.

1647 7BETS4FREE.COM SAYS NO.1 WINS H'CAP HURDLE (8 hdls) 2m
5:15 (5:15) (Class 4) (0-110,110) 3-Y-O+ **£3,249** (£954; £477; £238)

Form RPR
1F31 1 **Dream Bolt (IRE)**[7] 1577 7-11-6 104 PaulMoloney 108
(David Rees) *mid-div: hdwy 5th: chal 2 out: led narrowly last: drvn to hold on flat* **9/2**[2]
020- 2 nk **Reyno**[186] 4967 7-10-12 96 (bt[1]) BrendanPowell 101+
(Stuart Edmunds) *led: nt fluent 3 out: rdn next: narrowly hdd last: kpt on u.p: jst hld* **14/1**
40U3 3 4 **Fairy Alisha**[23] 1454 7-10-12 103 JoshWall[(7)] 104
(Trevor Wall) *hld up towards rr: hdwy on outer 3 out: ev ch next: one pce fr last: fin lame* **20/1**
4221 4 2 **Cruise In Style (IRE)**[16] 1525 9-11-4 102 (tp) JamesBest 102
(Kevin Bishop) *hld up in rr: hdwy 3 out: swtchd rt next: nt fluent last: one pce* **14/1**
00-0 5 nk **David John**[147] 56 4-10-6 90 RobertDunne 88
(Dai Burchell) *cl up: ev ch whn stmbld sltly 2 out: sn rdn and nt qckn: grad wknd* **9/1**
/0-P 6 ½ **Alco Sivola (FR)**[72] 999 5-11-12 110 (t[1]) PaddyBrennan 109
(Fergal O'Brien) *hld up in rr: hdwy 3 out: rdn next: r.o flat* **20/1**
0-41 7 3 ¼ **Johnny Og**[20] 1483 6-11-10 108 (b) AndrewTinkler 105
(Martin Keighley) *prom: rdn 3 out where nt fluent: wknd after 2 out* **11/1**
3116 8 hd **Modeligo (IRE)**[34] 1324 6-10-11 102 (t) MrStanSheppard[(7)] 98
(Matt Sheppard) *mid-div: hdwy 5th: rdn 3 out: mstke 2 out: one pce* **12/1**
3334 9 3 ¾ **Anton Dolin (IRE)**[17] 1508 7-10-12 103 MrHFNugent[(7)] 94
(Michael Mullineaux) *chsd ldrs: rdn 3 out: wknd after 2 out* **14/1**
350/ 10 2 **Moscow Me (IRE)**[555] 4899 8-10-12 99 JeremiahMcGrath[(3)] 89
(Henry Oliver) *mid-div: rdn 3 out: wknd 2 out* **6/1**[3]
-030 11 6 **Trojan Star (IRE)**[16] 1518 5-11-12 110 DavidBass 95
(Kim Bailey) *t.k.h: prom: rdn after 5th: wknd 3 out* **14/1**
63-1 12 3 ½ **Pied Du Roi (IRE)**[137] 237 5-11-12 110 DarylJacob 91
(Charlie Longsdon) *mid-div: blnd 3rd: rdn appr 3 out: wknd 2 out* **3/1**[1]
6 13 23 **Double Dan (IRE)**[36] 1295 6-10-0 91 ow1 MikeyHamill[(7)] 51
(Alexandra Dunn) *hld up: drvn 5th: wknd next: t.o* **33/1**

3m 45.8s (-4.80) **Going Correction** -0.20s/f (Good)
WFA 4 from 5yo+ 11lb 13 Ran SP% **122.6**
Speed ratings (Par 105): **104,103,101,100,100 100,98,98,96,95 92,91,79**
CSF £65.42 CT £1170.20 TOTE £4.00: £1.70, £4.60, £5.90; EX 87.80 Trifecta £855.40 Part won..
Owner D A Rees & N Adams **Bred** John Brennan **Trained** Clarbeston, Pembrokes

FOCUS
A routine but competitive handicap hurdle, run at a decent gallop. Soild form, the winner well in on his recent chase win.

1648 GREENLIGHTING.CO.UK FOR A BRIGHTER LIFE NOVICES' HURDLE (10 hdls) 2m 4f
5:50 (5:50) (Class 4) 4-Y-O+ **£3,249** (£954; £477; £238)

Form RPR
214- 1 **Crazy Jack (IRE)**[168] 5261 7-11-0 123 DavidBass 120+
(Kim Bailey) *mid-div: nt fluent 5th: rdn 3 out: swtchd lft 2 out: led appr last: drvn and styd on wl* **9/2**[2]
5-2 2 4 **Mustmeetalady (IRE)**[142] 146 5-11-0 0 BarryGeraghty 115+
(Jonjo O'Neill) *t.k.h: trckd ldrs: rdn and ev ch 2 out: styd on same pce* **6/4**[1]
3 2 ½ **Black Sam The Man**[39] 1283 5-10-11 0 BrianHayes[(3)] 113
(John Joseph Hanlon, Ire) *hld up: rdn and hdwy appr 3 out: styd on fr 2 out: wnt 3rd flat* **20/1**
2- 4 1 ¼ **Kilcullen Flem (IRE)**[183] 4995 5-11-0 0 LeightonAspell 112
(Rebecca Curtis) *racd keenly: led: rdn 2 out: hdd appr last: no ex and lost 3rd flat* **12/1**
5 13 **Super Scorpion (IRE)**[117] 5-11-0 0 TomO'Brien 100
(Debra Hamer) *t.k.h: trckd ldrs: nt fluent 3 out: one pce fr next* **33/1**
6 21 **Ballycross**[153] 4-10-13 0 SamTwiston-Davies 80
(Nigel Twiston-Davies) *prom: mstke 6th: rdn 3 out: wknd 2 out* **6/1**[3]
52-1 7 2 ½ **Clancy's Cross (IRE)**[139] 212 6-11-7 125 BrianHughes 86
(Kevin Frost) *prom tl rdn and wknd appr 3 out* **12/1**
12 8 hd **Sign Manual**[127] 419 6-11-7 119 NoelFehily 86
(Donald McCain) *mid-div: sltly hmpd 1st: hdwy 5th: rdn 3 out: wkng whn mstke next* **6/1**[3]
205- 9 3 ¼ **Murray Mount (IRE)**[161] 5367 5-11-0 0 JamesDavies 76
(Charlie Mann) *t.k.h towards rr: rdn after 7th: sn wknd* **100/1**
00- 10 17 **Aka Doun (FR)**[200] 4679 4-10-13 0 DarylJacob 60
(Emma Lavelle) *hld up: rdn and wknd 3 out* **33/1**
04 11 62 **Generous Pet (IRE)**[23] 1453 6-11-0 0 TomScudamore 5
(Kevin Bishop) *prom: losing pl whn nt fluent 3rd: struggling fr 5th: bhd 7th: t.o* **100/1**
04-6 12 1 ¼ **Rebekah Rabbit (IRE)**[141] 179 5-10-7 0 RobertDunne
(Tom Lacey) *in rr: mstke 1st: wknd after 7th: virtually p.u flat: t.o* **100/1**

4m 49.2s (-4.30) **Going Correction** -0.20s/f (Good)
WFA 4 from 5yo+ 12lb 12 Ran SP% **115.8**
Speed ratings (Par 105): **100,98,97,96,91 83,82,82,80,74 49,48**
CSF £11.25 TOTE £4.60: £1.70, £1.10, £4.60; EX 14.40 Trifecta £80.80.
Owner May We Never Be Found Out Partnership 2 **Bred** M Campbell **Trained** Andoversford, Gloucs

FOCUS
A mid-range novices' race, run at an ordinary pace that didn't play to the strength of several potential improvers. Not form to be confident about.
T/Plt: £27.50 to a £1 stake. Pool: £65,670.33 - 1,742.70 winning tickets T/Qpdt: £8.40 to a £1 stake. Pool: £5,098.70 - 447.40 winning tickets **Richard Lowther**

1649 - 1655a (Foreign Racing) - See Raceform Interactive

1260 MARKET RASEN (R-H)
Saturday, September 26

OFFICIAL GOING: Good (8.2)
Wind: almost nil Weather: bright and sunny then becoming overcast; 16 degrees

1656 RACINGFX.CO.UK JUVENILE HURDLE (8 hdls) 2m 148y
1:40 (1:40) (Class 2) 3-Y-O **£9,747** (£2,862; £1,431; £715)

Form RPR
111 1 **Leoncavallo (IRE)**[37] 1294 3-11-6 126 AidanColeman 134+
(John Ferguson) *small: j. and travelled wl in 2nd pl: led on bit bef 2 out: 5 l clr last: eased flat: impressive* **7/4**[1]

2 14 **Pinkie Brown (FR)**[178] 3-10-12 0.................................. RichardJohnson 113+
(Nick Williams) *plld hrd: led tl hdd and blnd 2 out: rdn and sn outpcd by wnr: edging lft after but kpt on steadily* **9/2**[3]

3 4 **Duke Street (IRE)**[35] 3-10-12 0.. WillKennedy 109
(Dr Richard Newland) *gd-topped: chsd ldrs: rdn after 3 out: wnt 3rd next: kpt on same pce and nvr threatened: bttr for experience* **6/1**

1 4 11 **Cooper**[23] 1456 3-11-3 0.. BrianHughes 105
(Kevin Ryan) *small: v keen and pressed ldrs: lost 3rd and getting outpcd whn pckd 2 out: nt fluent last* **9/2**[3]

5 32 **Cahill (IRE)**[17] 3-10-12 0.. WayneHutchinson 68
(Alan King) *midfield: nt fluent 4th: sn rdn and struggling: t.o bef 2 out* **16/1**

6 16 **Sikandar (IRE)**[35] 3-10-12 0.. DannyCook 64
(Brian Ellison) *blnd 1st and 2nd: nvr got into rhythm: prom tl rdn and wknd after 3 out: t.o whn blnd next* **7/2**[2]

7 73 **No Rum (IRE)**[28] 3-10-12 0.. SeanQuinlan
(Olly Williams) *last whn mstke 3rd: t.o fr 5th* **100/1**

4m 2.2s (-4.50) **Going Correction** -0.05s/f (Good) **7 Ran SP% 116.1**
Speed ratings (Par 107): **108,101,99,94,79 71,37**
CSF £10.61 TOTE £2.20: £1.40, £2.80; EX 9.20 Trifecta £29.30.
Owner Bloomfields **Bred** Darley **Trained** Cowlinge, Suffolk

FOCUS
Rail out 15yds on Wood Bend and 22yds Stands bend. Races 1, 2, 5, 6 & 7 increased by 156yds and races 3 & 4 by 222yds. Arguably the strongest juvenile hurdle race of the season so far. Its impressive roll of honour features subsequent Triumph Hurdle and Champion Hurdle winner Katchit. The winner sets a decent standard.

1657 RACING FX PRELUDE HURDLE H'CAP (LISTED RACE) (8 hdls) 2m 148y
2:15 (2:15) (Class 1) 3-Y-0+
£19,932 (£7,479; £3,745; £1,865; £938; £469)

Form RPR

215- 1 **Cloonacool (IRE)**[231] 4080 6-10-4 **132**.................................. PaddyBrennan 135+
(Stuart Edmunds) *hld up towards rr: effrt gng wl after 3 out: 3rd next: led last: drvn and in command after: r.o gamely* **11/2**

/65- 2 2 **Queen Alphabet (IRE)**[24] 784 6-10-4 **132**..............................(t) JJBurke 135+
(Peter Fahey, Ire) *t.k.h: prom: clipped heels after 3 out: cl 2nd and rdn 2 out: 3rd and nt qckn last: regained 2nd cl home but wnr in command* **13/2**

3 nk **Swansea Mile (IRE)**[72] 1016 5-10-6 **134**.................................. HarrySkelton 135+
(Dan Skelton) *hld up towards rr: effrt and clipped heels after 3 out: styd on fr 2 out: drvn into 2nd at last: kpt on steadily but lost 2nd nr fin* **8/1**

0121 4 nk **Broughton (GER)**[21] 1482 5-10-4 **132**..............................(bt) AidanColeman 132
(John Ferguson) *pressed ldrs: drvn and outpcd bef 2 out where j.big: drvn and kpt on after last but no threat to wnr* **5/1**[3]

3-31 5 hd **Manhattan Swing (IRE)**[42] 1263 5-10-10 **138**..............................(b) DannyCook 138
(Brian Ellison) *midfield: rdn and effrt after 3 out: drvn ahd home turn: hdd last: nt qckn after* **4/1**[1]

32-1 6 6 **Gran Maestro (USA)**[22] 1039 6-10-3 **131**..............................(bt) WillKennedy 126
(Dr Richard Newland) *prom: wnt 2nd at 4th: ev ch bef 2 out: rdn and dropped out tamely bef last* **9/2**[2]

2P42 7 5 **Laudatory**[21] 1482 9-10-12 **140**.................................. NicodeBoinville 132
(Nicky Henderson) *led at str pce: 6 l clr after 3rd: pressed next: rdn and hdd wl bef 2 out: sn lost pl* **9/1**

-102 P **Commissioned (IRE)**[35] 1333 5-11-7 **154**..............................(p) MikeyEnnis(5)
(John Ferguson) *prom tl 4th: rdn and wknd next: t.o and p.u 2 out* **8/1**

114- U **Goodbye Dancer (FR)**[364] 1639 4-10-6 **134**..........[1] SamTwiston-Davies 116
(Nigel Twiston-Davies) *last whn nt fluent 3rd: drvn and brief effrt after 3 out: last and struggling whn landed awkwardly and uns rdr next* **14/1**

4m 0.2s (-6.50) **Going Correction** -0.05s/f (Good)
WFA 4 from 5yo+ 11lb **9 Ran SP% 122.5**
Speed ratings (Par 111): **113,112,111,111,111 108,106, ,**
CSF £43.70 CT £293.30 TOTE £6.80: £2.20, £2.10, £3.00; EX 48.30 Trifecta £529.40.
Owner Nick Brown Racing **Bred** Thomas McParland **Trained** Newport Pagnell, Bucks
■ Stewards' Enquiry : Danny Cook one-day ban; encouraged gelding forward to break into a canter before start (10th Oct)

FOCUS
An excellent turnout for this valuable handicap hurdle. They went off quickly, and it paid to be held up. The winner was on a good mark.

1658 RACING FX PRELUDE CHASE H'CAP (LISTED RACE) (14 fncs) 2m 5f 89y
2:50 (2:50) (Class 1) 4-Y-0+
£28,475 (£10,685; £5,350; £2,665; £1,340; £670)

Form RPR

11F- 1 **Oscar Rock (IRE)**[161] 5389 7-11-4 **147**..............................(b) BrianHughes 155+
(Malcolm Jefferson) *hld up in midfield: effrt 10th: 3rd and travelling strly bef 3 out: sn 2nd: w ldr 2 out tl only had to be pushed out to go clr despite idling sltly after last* **4/1**[1]

-104 2 3 ¼ **Claret Cloak (IRE)**[35] 1322 8-11-12 **155**..............................(p) AidanColeman 158
(Emma Lavelle) *trckd ldrs: wnt 2nd at 8th: led bef 3 out where blnd: sn jnd: drvn and stl ev ch last: sn outpcd flat* **12/1**

11-2 3 5 **Cloud Creeper (IRE)**[140] 198 8-11-9 **152**.................................. RichardJohnson 151
(Philip Hobbs) *mstke 4th: hld up and bhd: rdn and hdwy after 11th: chsd ldng pair bef 3 out: one pce and no imp fr next* **8/1**

1213 4 5 **Gold Futures (IRE)**[35] 1322 6-10-10 **139**.................................. BrianHarding 133
(Nicky Richards) *hld up: qcknd to go 2nd after 7th tl next: rdn after 11th: kpt on same pce and n.d fr 2 out* **11/2**[3]

1-11 5 11 **Gray Hession (IRE)**[41] 1268 8-10-12 **141**.................................. RichieMcLernon 124
(Jonjo O'Neill) *midfield: blnd 6th: shkn up 8th: rdn bef 3 out: sn btn* **9/2**[2]

4132 6 ¾ **Valco De Touzaine (FR)**[35] 1322 6-11-2 **145**........(t) SamTwiston-Davies 130
(Paul Nicholls) *set str pce and sn clr: blnd 5th: 15 l ahd after 7th: nt fluent next: rdn and pressed after 11th: hdd bef next and dropped out tamely* **4/1**[1]

123U 7 21 **Owen Na View (IRE)**[34] 1343 7-10-6 **135**..............................(t[1]) PaddyBrennan 99
(Fergal O'Brien) *hit 4th: hld up last tl 1/2-way: nvr rchd ldrs and drvn and struggling after 11th: t.o* **16/1**

306- 8 1 ½ **Edgardo Sol (FR)**[168] 5274 8-11-2 **145**.................................. DarylJacob 110
(Emma Lavelle) *midfield: t.k.h early: rdn and fdd qckly fr 11th: t.o* **9/1**

10P- 9 9 **Wiesentraum (GER)**[161] 5392 9-11-0 **143**..............................(p) LeightonAspell 102
(Lucy Wadham) *towards rr: rdn 8th: t.o 11th* **28/1**

-043 P **Conquisto**[21] 1481 10-10-8 **137**.................................. DannyCook
(Brian Ellison) *chsd clr ldr tl after 7th: stopped qckly to last next: p.u 9th* **10/1**

5m 22.1s (-23.90) **Going Correction** -0.80s/f (Firm) **10 Ran SP% 120.8**
Speed ratings (Par 111): **113,111,109,107,103 103,95,94,91,**
CSF £51.73 CT £375.65 TOTE £5.10: £2.10, £4.10, £1.90; EX 53.20 Trifecta £325.00.
Owner Mr & Mrs G Calder **Bred** Alice Kehoe **Trained** Norton, N Yorks

FOCUS
This Listed feature was hugely competitive and would not have looked out of place at one of the big festivals later in the season. The winner ran to the level of his best novice form.

1659 @RACINGFX H'CAP CHASE (14 fncs) 2m 5f 89y
3:25 (3:25) (Class 4) (0-115,115) 4-Y-0+ **£3,898** (£1,144; £572; £286)

Form RPR

5P41 1 **Forever My Friend (IRE)**[26] 1418 8-11-9 **115**..............................(p) SeanBowen(3) 122+
(Peter Bowen) *mostly j. soundly: led 2nd tl deliberate 8th: sn led again: drvn and hrd pressed whn hit last: galvanised flat and kpt on strly* **3/1**[2]

P4-4 2 ¾ **Master Neo (FR)**[101] 760 9-11-11 **114**..............................(t) ConorO'Farrell 119
(Nigel Hawke) *last much of way: rdn and outpcd 11th: rallied next: wnt 2nd 2 out: drvn and chal wnr last: nt qckn flat* **13/2**

-464 3 ½ **Lock Towers (IRE)**[87] 873 6-10-13 **102**.................................. DavidBass 107
(Ben Pauling) *cl up in 2nd or 3rd: drvn and ev ch 2 out: nt qckn fr last* **5/1**[3]

-236 4 ¾ **He's A Bully (IRE)**[37] 1298 6-10-13 **102**.................................. RichardJohnson 108
(Philip Hobbs) *hld up and nt a fluent: slow 8th: blnd 11th: effrt gng wl in 2nd 3 out: 4th and rdn next: no rspnse and outbattled after* **5/2**[1]

-554 5 8 **Moyode Wood**[8] 1571 10-10-11 **107**..............................(p) CraigGallagher(7) 106
(Brian Ellison) *hmpd 1st: cl up: rdn bef 3 out: sn btn* **10/1**

3-2P 6 shd **Friendly Society (IRE)**[119] 557 10-11-9 **115**..............................(b) JamesBanks(3) 115
(Noel Williams) *led: v slow 1st: hdd 2nd: lft in ld briefly 8th: 2nd and drvn after 11th: hit 3 out whn losing pl and fnd little after* **12/1**

4246 P **The Society Man (IRE)**[28] 1403 8-9-11 **91**.................................. JoeCornwall(5)
(Michael Chapman) *impeded 1st: chsd ldrs: rdn bef 8th: dropping bk to last whn p.u qckly 10th: lost action* **10/1**

UP P **Sureness (IRE)**[30] 1372 5-11-12 **115**..............................(tp) GavinSheehan
(Charlie Mann) *j.rt 3rd and rdn: nvr travelling in rr: lost tch 11th: t.o and p.u last: dismntd* **12/1**

5m 32.3s (-13.70) **Going Correction** -0.80s/f (Firm) **8 Ran SP% 117.1**
Speed ratings (Par 105): **94,93,93,93,90 90, ,**
CSF £23.52 CT £95.22 TOTE £4.10: £1.50, £2.00, £1.90; EX 25.70 Trifecta £249.90.
Owner Mrs J H Docker **Bred** Eamon Fitzgerald **Trained** Little Newcastle, Pembrokes
■ Stewards' Enquiry : Sean Bowen two-day ban; used whip in the incorrect place (10th-11th Oct)
Joe Cornwall jockey said gelding lost his action
Gavin Sheehan trainers representative said mare had a breathing problem.

FOCUS
An ordinary handicap chase, but it produced a tight and exciting finish.

1660 RACING FX ONLINE NOVICES' HURDLE (8 hdls) 2m 148y
4:00 (4:01) (Class 4) 4-Y-0+ **£3,249** (£954; £477; £238)

Form RPR

2-1 1 **Viens Chercher (IRE)**[30] 1365 4-11-5 135.................................. DannyCook 127+
(Brian Ellison) *led: rdn and jnd and looked v vulnerable 2 out tl last: drvn and gamely fnd ex to edge ahd flat but only jst hld on* **7/4**[2]

1 2 nse **Anomaly**[45] 1234 6-11-5 0.................................. AidanColeman 128+
(John Ferguson) *t.k.h: pressed wnr gng strly: chal 2 out: rdn and upsides whn hit last: briefly outpcd: rallied fnl 100yds: jst hld cl home* **11/10**[1]

230- 3 10 **Double W's (IRE)**[169] 5255 5-10-12 0.................................. BrianHughes 113+
(Malcolm Jefferson) *t.k.h in midfield: effrt 3 out: rdn next: 5 l 3rd and hld whn blnd last* **4/1**[3]

-160 4 7 **Countersign**[36] 1308 6-11-5 117.................................. AdamPogson 113
(Charles Pogson) *plld hrd and cl up tl rdn and wknd 2 out* **20/1**

23F0 5 14 **Tiger Twenty Two**[23] 1459 4-10-12 105.................................. AndrewTinkler 94
(Brian Rothwell) *racd in 5th pl: nt fluent 4th: lost tch u.p next* **25/1**

6 87 **Rosie Hall (IRE)**[154] 5-10-5 0.................................. SeanQuinlan 7
(John Wainwright) *small: wl-mde: j. poorly and qckly lost tch: t.o fr 1/2-way* **100/1**

4m 3.9s (-2.80) **Going Correction** -0.05s/f (Good) **6 Ran SP% 113.6**
Speed ratings (Par 105): **104,103,99,95,89 48**
CSF £4.24 TOTE £2.70: £2.30, £1.10; EX 4.10 Trifecta £9.60.
Owner P J Martin **Bred** P Ryan **Trained** Norton, N Yorks
■ Stewards' Enquiry : Danny Cook two-day ban; used whip above the permitted level (11th-12th Oct)

FOCUS
What this lacked in depth it more than made up for in drama as the favourite was beaten at 1.02 (1-50) in photo finish betting on the exchanges.

1661 RACING FX ELECTRONIC PAYMENTS H'CAP HURDLE (10 hdls) 2m 2f 140y
4:35 (4:37) (Class 4) (0-120,120) 4-Y-0+ **£3,249** (£954; £477; £238)

Form RPR

FP-3 1 **Handsome Dan (IRE)**[42] 1264 9-11-7 **115**.................................. PaulMoloney 122+
(Sarah Hollinshead) *hld up last early: stdy prog 7th: led after 2 out: 2 l clr last: rdn and idled but a looked holding on flat* **11/4**[1]

0-60 2 ¾ **Laser Blazer**[76] 973 7-11-12 **120**..............................(p) WayneHutchinson 124
(Alan King) *settled 3rd or 4th: mstke 7th: wnt 2nd after 3 out: sn rdn: led briefly next: a hld fr last: gng lft u.p flat* **6/1**

210/ 3 1 ½ **Ben Cee Pee M (IRE)**[525] 5384 10-10-12 **113**..............(v) CraigGallagher(7) 115
(Brian Ellison) *t.k.h: pressed ldr tl after 3 out: rdn bef next: nt qckn appr last but plugged on wl flat* **8/1**

00-4 4 ¾ **Dr Irv**[20] 1260 6-10-3 **107**.................................. FinianO'Toole(10) 109+
(Micky Hammond) *t.k.h: midfield: mstke 7th: rdn and effrt bef 2 out: kpt on flat but nvr got in a blow* **9/2**[2]

5 5 7 **Alf Wright (IRE)**[30] 1381 9-11-12 **120**.................................. JamesBest 116
(Philip Hobbs) *t.k.h in midfield: drvn bef 2 out: sn no ex: hit last* **16/1**

44-1 6 ½ **Fair Loch**[42] 1261 7-11-5 **120**.................................. HarryCobden(7) 115
(Brian Ellison) *led at mod pce: hit 7th: rdn and hdd 2 out: lost pl qckly* **5/1**[3]

0- 7 2 ¼ **Asockastar (IRE)**[326] 2274 7-11-4 **112**.................................. AidanColeman 105
(Tim Vaughan) *towards rr: lost tch 7th* **16/1**

52-0 8 7 **Champagne Chaser**[17] 1518 5-10-13 **107**.................................. MichaelByrne 95
(Tim Vaughan) *mstkes in rr: last and struggling 3 out* **16/1**

0-13 9 22 **Fleet Dawn**[107] 691 9-11-12 **120**.................................. AndrewThornton 86
(John Wainwright) *chsd ldrs tl 7th: wknd and mstke next: t.o* **20/1**

-625 F **Don Padeja**[42] 1263 5-11-9 **117**..............................(t) RichardJohnson 119+
(Jonjo O'Neill) *settled 3rd or 4th: cl 3rd and rdn whn fell 2 out* **6/1**

4m 47.3s (7.90) **Going Correction** -0.05s/f (Good) **10 Ran SP% 123.6**
Speed ratings (Par 105): **81,80,80,79,76 76,75,72,63,**
CSF £21.54 CT £123.84 TOTE £4.10: £1.70, £2.00, £3.50; EX 21.10 Trifecta £233.00.
Owner Graham Brothers Racing Partnership **Bred** Diarmuid O' Riordan **Trained** Upper Longdon, Staffs

FOCUS
This looked a relatively weak affair for the grade. The winner ran to his best.

1662 RACINGFX.CO.UK OPEN NATIONAL HUNT FLAT RACE 2m 148y
5:10 (5:12) (Class 6) 4-6-Y-O £1,559 (£457; £228; £114)

Form RPR
31- 1 **Desertmore Hill (IRE)**[156] 5501 5-11-4 0 SeanBowen(3) 113
(Peter Bowen) *str: mde all: set sedate pce: rdn and hrd pressed fr over 1f out: hld on wl fnl 100yds* 7/4[2]
3 2 ¾ **Scorpion Princess (IRE)**[148] 67 4-10-7 0 RichardJohnson 100+
(Charlie Longsdon) *t.k.h in rr: effrt to press ldrs whn hmpd wl over 2f out: rallied and upsides wnr but hanging lft and running green whn j. path 1f out: lost momentum: drvn and tried to chal again fnl 100yds: no imp after* 6/4[1]
3 1 **Point The Way (IRE)**[146] 4-11-0 0 WillKennedy 104
(Brian Ellison) *ly: pressed wnr tl rdn and wnt rt wl over 2f out: outpcd 2f out: styd on again ins fnl f: should do bttr* 10/1
4 3 **The Barbury Queen (IRE)** 5-10-7 0 WayneHutchinson 97+
(Alan King) *small: cl up: rdn over 2f out: no ex over 1f out* 12/1
1 5 2 **Captain Bocelli (IRE)**[141] 187 6-11-7 0 RichieMcLernon 106
(Anabel K Murphy) *tall: gd-topped: chsd ldrs tl rdn over 2f out: one pce and n.d after* 5/1[3]
04 6 15 **Good Rhythm**[37] 1300 5-11-0 0 TrevorWhelan 89
(Neil King) *hanging lft: in rr but in tch: tried to run out on bnd after 7f: rdn 3f out: wknd 2f out: eased and t.o* 22/1

4m 10.2s (9.10) **Going Correction** -0.05s/f (Good)
WFA 4 from 5yo+ 11lb **6 Ran SP% 114.2**
Speed ratings: **76,75,75,73,72 65**
CSF £4.90 TOTE £2.60: £1.50, £1.10; EX 5.00 Trifecta £28.00.
Owner West Coast Haulage Limited **Bred** Charlie Carter **Trained** Little Newcastle, Pembrokes

FOCUS
An informative bumper and a strong suspicion that the best horse finished second. The winner set a fair standard.
T/Plt: £70.30 to a £1 stake. Pool: £64,472.72 - 669.33 winning units. T/Qpdt: £10.40 to a £1 stake. Pool: £4,364.02 - 310.00 winning units. **Iain Mackenzie**

1663 - 1670a (Foreign Racing) - See Raceform Interactive

MERANO
Saturday, September 26

OFFICIAL GOING: Turf: soft

1671a LXI GRAN CORSA SIEPI DI MERANO (HURDLE) (GRADE 1) (5YO+) (TURF) 2m 4f
4:20 (12:00) 5-Y-O+ £24,806 (£9,922; £4,961; £2,976; £1,984)

RPR
1 **Fafintadenient**[133] 8-10-8 0 JVanaJr 7 123
(Josef Vana Jr, Czech Republic) 89/20[2]
2 1 ½ **Sol Invictus (ITY)**[741] 7-10-8 0 JosefBartos 2 122
(P Favero, Italy) 79/10
3 snk **Chiaromonte (FR)** 6-10-8 0 IvanCherchi 6 121
(Ilenia Nero, Italy) 107/20[3]
4 nk **Taupin Rochelais (FR)**[25] 8-10-8 0 (p) ArnoldCisel 3 121
(Patrice Quinton, France) 87/10
5 ¾ **Makler (CZE)** 8-10-8 0 JanFaltejsek 1 120
(Michal Lisek, Czech Republic) 13/2
6 nse **Falconettei (GER)**[148] 6-10-8 0 DFuhrmann 8 120
(P Vovcenko, Germany) 247/10
7 dist **Thousand Stars (FR)**[50] 1163 11-10-8 0 (p) RWalsh 4
(W P Mullins, Ire) *w.w in rr: hit 7th: hit 5 out and next: sn detached: t.o fr 2 out* 3/4[1]

7 Ran SP% 130.0

Owner Statek Chyse-Vana **Bred** Azienda Agricola Francesca **Trained**

[1671] MERANO
Sunday, September 27

OFFICIAL GOING: Turf: soft

1672a LXXVI GRAN PREMIO MERANO (CHASE) (GRADE 1) (4YO+) (TURF) 3m 1f
3:50 (12:00) 4-Y-O+
£100,387 (£36,472; £15,503; £7,751; £5,000; £3,875)

RPR
1 **Kazzio (GER)**[26] 7-10-9 0 CevinChan 11 130
(P Vovcenko, Germany) 74/10
2 1 ¼ **Marinas (GER)**[133] 374 8-10-9 0 ArnaudDuchene 12 128
(G Macaire, France) 83/100[1]
3 ½ **Ole Companero (GER)**[1436] 2117 9-10-9 0 JamesReveley 2 128
(G Macaire, France) 83/100[1]
4 ¾ **Frolon (FR)**[742] 10-10-9 0 DPastuszka 1 127
(P Favero, Italy) 21/1
5 ½ **Nando (FR)**[112] 663 5-10-9 0 DavidCottin 10 126
(Alex Taber, Italy) 15/1
6 6 **Company Of Ring (IRE)** 4-10-1 0 JosefBartos 14 112
(P Favero, Italy) 142/10
7 7 **Demon Magic (CZE)** 9-10-9 0 LukasMatusky 6 113
(Cestmir Olehla, Czech Republic) 38/1
8 dist **Kauto Sweety (FR)**[150] 8-10-9 0 DavideSatalia 8
(Giuseppe Satalia, Italy) 62/1
P **Budapest (IRE)**[714] 1905 10-10-9 0 JVanaJr 5
(Josef Vana, Czech Republic) 208/10
P **Mighty Mambo**[61] 489 8-10-9 0 JohnBrennan 9
(P Favero, Italy) 45/1
F **Perfect Gentleman (IRE)**[27] 1435 10-10-9 0 RWalsh 4
(W P Mullins, Ire) *w.w in fnl 3rd: 9th and in tch whn j. into bk of rival and c down 18th* 13/2[3]
P **Tomcat De Kerser (FR)**[26] 8-10-9 0 ArnoldCisel 3
(Patrice Quinton, France) 126/10
P **Kamelie (FR)**[390] 8-10-9 0 JanFaltejsek 7
(Michal Lisek, Czech Republic) 6/1[2]
P **Ciro Vincenti (IRE)** 7-10-9 0 RaffaeleRomano 13
(R Romano, Italy) 125/10

WFA 4 from 5yo+ 2lb **14 Ran SP% 191.9**

Owner Bernd Huckschlag **Bred** K Kaufmann & H J Wiesner **Trained** Germany

[1574] NEWTON ABBOT (L-H)
Monday, September 28

OFFICIAL GOING: Good (good to firm in places; 7.0)
Wind: quite strong against Weather: sunny with cloudy periods Rails: Rail movements effected distances as follows; Race 1 add 72yds, Race 2 add 19yds, Race 3 add 92yds, Races 4 & 5 add 65yds, Race 6 add 38yds.

1673 ALLAN AND BARBARA'S GOLDEN WEDDING CELEBRATION "NATIONAL HUNT" NOVICES' HURDLE (9 hdls) 2m 2f 110y
2:00 (2:00) (Class 4) 4-Y-O+ £3,898 (£1,144; £572; £286)

Form RPR
3-61 1 **General Ginger**[138] 279 5-11-5 0 (t) NoelFehily 117+
(Harry Fry) *prom: led after 3 out: pushed clr after next: nt fluent last: r.o wl: readily* 11/10[1]
5P- 2 4 ½ **Full Blast (FR)**[293] 2998 4-10-11 0 (t[1]) SamTwiston-Davies 104+
(Paul Nicholls) *racd keenly: hld up in tch: chal after 3 out: ev ch whn mstke 2 out: kpt on but nt gng pce of wnr* 11/10[1]
4 3 9 **Shaky Gift (IRE)**[20] 1505 6-10-5 0 MarkQuinlan 87
(Neil Mulholland) *prom: led 6th tl rdn after 3 out: styd on same pce fr next* 50/1
00F 4 2 ½ **Lilbourne Legacy**[10] 1576 4-10-4 0 DavidNoonan(7) 90
(David Pipe) *trckd ldrs: rdn appr 2 out: kpt on same pce* 12/1[2]
0/5 5 2 ½ **Looking For Mick**[10] 1576 6-10-9 0 GilesHawkins(3) 90
(Chris Down) *led tl 6th: rdn after 3 out: sn one pce* 33/1
6-04 6 3 ¼ **Dashul (IRE)**[132] 387 6-10-5 0 LiamHeard 78
(Jeremy Scott) *hld up: nudged along after 5th: rdn after 3 out: nt gng pce to get on terms* 14/1[3]
7 20 **Tell Tony (IRE)**[155] 5-10-12 0 NickScholfield 65
(Tim Dennis) *hld up: rdn after 6th: nvr threatened: wknd 2 out* 20/1
606/ F **Larks Rising**[620] 3747 7-10-12 0 TomO'Brien
(Caroline Keevil) *in tch: nt fluent 4th: rdn after 3 out: wknd qckly: bhd whn fell next* 25/1

4m 33.7s (3.70) **Going Correction** -0.275s/f (Good)
WFA 4 from 5yo+ 11lb **8 Ran SP% 123.1**
Speed ratings (Par 105): **81,79,75,74,73 71,63,**
CSF £2.69 TOTE £2.00: £1.10, £1.10, £15.50; EX 2.90 Trifecta £87.50.
Owner Hazard Chase Racing **Bred** Miss E J Lucas **Trained** Seaborough, Dorset

FOCUS
Rail movement increased race 1 by 72yds, race 2 by 19yds, race 3 by 92yds, races 4 & 5 by 65yds and race 6 by 38yds. An uncompetitive novice event. The winner has been rated similar to his Kempton win.

1674 FRANCIS CLARK H'CAP CHASE (13 fncs) 2m 75y
2:30 (2:30) (Class 4) (0-115,110) 4-Y-O+ £3,898 (£1,144; £572; £286)

Form RPR
2F-3 1 **Days Ahead (IRE)**[139] 266 8-11-12 110 (p) RichieMcLernon 122+
(Richenda Ford) *trckd ldrs: wnt 2nd after 5th: chal 9th: rdn to ld bef last: r.o wl to assert run-in* 17/2
421F 2 2 ¼ **The Yank**[25] 1460 6-11-3 101 TomScudamore 111
(David Bridgwater) *led: rdn and narrowly hdd appr last: no ex run-in* 5/4[1]
2321 3 8 **The Bay Bandit**[32] 1367 8-11-10 108 (p) NoelFehily 112
(Neil Mulholland) *hld up in last pair but in tch: hdwy into 3rd after 9th: nt best of runs after 3 out: sn rdn: kpt on same pce* 11/4[2]
6 4 6 **Treacy Hotels Boy (IRE)**[28] 1424 8-11-5 103 NickScholfield 99
(Paul Henderson) *trckd ldr tl nudged along hitting 5th: cl up: rdn after 3 out: styd on same pce fr next* 10/1
2325 5 3 ¾ **Sublime Talent (IRE)**[28] 1416 9-11-2 110 (t) LewisGordon(10) 104
(Evan Williams) *trckd ldrs: rdn after 3 out: sn one pce* 7/1[3]
54F5 6 hd **Macarthur**[23] 1483 11-11-6 104 (v) PaulMoloney 100
(David Rees) *hld up last but in tch: rdn after 4 out: nvr any imp* 12/1

4m 0.3s (-6.20) **Going Correction** -0.275s/f (Good) **6 Ran SP% 110.9**
Speed ratings (Par 105): **104,102,98,95,94 93**
CSF £20.22 TOTE £7.70: £3.80, £1.30; EX 21.10 Trifecta £58.50.
Owner Mr & Mrs K B Snook **Bred** Leo Hayes **Trained** Brockhampton Green, Dorset

FOCUS
A moderate handicap dominated by the principals. The second and third have been rated to their marks.

1675 SOUTH WEST RACING CLUB H'CAP HURDLE (10 hdls) 2m 5f 122y
3:00 (3:00) (Class 4) (0-115,114) 4-Y-O+ £3,898 (£1,144; £572; £286)

Form RPR
0464 1 **Jigsaw Financial (IRE)**[10] 1579 9-10-11 99 SamTwiston-Davies 102
(Laura Young) *prom: led 3 out: kpt on wl fr 2 out: rdn out* 5/1[3]
41- 2 1 **Sykes (IRE)**[334] 2137 6-11-12 114 RichardJohnson 117+
(Philip Hobbs) *hld up: smooth hdwy after 7th: chalng whn wnt lft 2 out: sn rdn: kpt on but a being hld run-in* 2/1[1]
-106 3 4 **Taylor (IRE)**[22] 1488 6-11-12 114 DarylJacob 113
(Nicky Henderson) *trckd ldrs: rdn after 3 out: kpt on but nt quite pce to chal* 13/2
F60P 4 12 **Academy General (IRE)**[14] 1547 9-10-4 95 LucyGardner(3) 85
(Patricia Shaw) *led tl 3 out: sn rdn: styd on same pce* 50/1
-115 5 13 **Archie Rice (USA)**[50] 1046 9-10-11 106 MissBFrost(7) 84
(Jimmy Frost) *hld up: pushed along and sme prog after 3 out: no further imp fr next* 15/2
535/ 6 10 **Jack By The Hedge**[605] 4018 6-11-10 112 TomO'Brien 79
(Caroline Keevil) *trckd ldrs: rdn after 3 out: wknd bef next* 11/1
P3-2 7 6 **Chantara Rose**[151] 28 6-11-2 107 SeanBowen(3) 69
(Peter Bowen) *nt a fluent: prom: rdn after 3 out: wknd bef next* 11/4[2]
3/-0 8 13 **Diddypurptoon**[97] 828 9-10-4 92 JamesBest 42
(Jackie Du Plessis) *struggling after 7th: a towards rr* 40/1

5m 16.4s (-3.80) **Going Correction** -0.275s/f (Good)
WFA 4 from 6yo+ 12lb **8 Ran SP% 114.5**
Speed ratings (Par 105): **95,94,93,88,84 80,78,73**
CSF £15.95 CT £64.97 TOTE £7.20: £2.20, £1.10, £2.30; EX 19.60 Trifecta £108.10.

Owner Mrs Laura Young **Bred** Joseph Kent **Trained** Broomfield, Somerset
FOCUS
This ordinary handicap was run at a fair enough gallop. The principals were clear at the finish. A pb from the runner-up.

1676 ILVA AND BRYAN WESTCOTT MEMORIAL NOVICES' H'CAP HURDLE (8 hdls) 2m 167y
3:30 (3:30) (Class 3) (0-125,125) 3-Y-O+ £5,523 (£1,621; £810; £405)

Form RPR
61-1 1 **Kapstadt (FR)**[30] 751 5-11-1 114........ WillKennedy 121+
(Ian Williams) *trckd ldrs: travelling wl whn nt best of runs after 3 out: chal 2 out: sn led: r.o wl: readily* 2/1[2]
2121 2 3 1/4 **Lilac Tree**[32] 1381 5-11-12 125........ AidanColeman 127
(John Ferguson) *led after 2nd: rdn and hdd appr last: no ex run-in* 5/6[1]
00-2 3 17 **Air Of Glory (IRE)**[26] 1453 5-10-5 104........(tp) NicodeBoinville 90
(Martin Bosley) *racd keenly: trckd ldrs: rdn after 3 out: wnt rt last 2: nt gng pce of front pair* 20/1
1365 4 nse **Frozen Over**[60] 1156 7-10-13 112........(t) JamesDavies 98
(Chris Down) *led tl after 2nd: trckd ldr tl rdn after 3 out: one pce fr next* 8/1[3]
335- 5 47 **Triple Chief (IRE)**[179] 4746 4-11-1 114........ PaulMoloney 57
(Chris Down) *hld up bhd ldrs: rdn after 3 out: sn wknd: t.o* 16/1
4m 0.9s (-4.80) **Going Correction** -0.275s/f (Good)
WFA 4 from 5yo+ 11lb 5 Ran SP% **109.6**
Speed ratings (Par 107): **100,98,90,90,68**
CSF £4.18 TOTE £2.80: £1.30, £1.10; EX 5.10 Trifecta £20.30.
Owner Anchor Men **Bred** Charles Barel **Trained** Portway, Worcs
FOCUS
A modest novice handicap and it's straightforward form. The second has been rated to his mark.

1677 SOUTH WEST RACING CLUB NEWTON ABBOT H'CAP HURDLE (8 hdls) 2m 167y
4:00 (4:00) (Class 5) (0-100,100) 3-Y-O+ £3,422 (£997; £499)

Form RPR
5241 1 **Bulletproof (IRE)**[10] 1578 9-11-3 91........(p) TomCannon 105+
(Ken Cunningham-Brown) *hld up: hdwy 3 out: led between last 2: kpt on wl* 9/2[2]
5565 2 2 1/2 **Bumble Bay**[19] 1525 5-11-6 94........(t[1]) TomO'Brien 105+
(Robert Stephens) *hld up: hdwy 5th: led after 3 out: wnt rt 2 out: sn rdn and hdd: kpt on same pce* 10/1
5303 3 6 **Hold The Fort (IRE)**[8] 1604 8-11-6 94........(t) AlainCawley 98
(Johnny Farrelly) *trckd ldrs: rdn after 3 out: styd on same pce* 6/1[3]
2631 4 6 **Vexillum (IRE)**[25] 1461 6-11-4 92........(p) NoelFehily 91
(Neil Mulholland) *mid-div: hdwy 3 out: effrt bef next: nt gng pce to get on terms* 9/4[1]
PPP- 5 11 **Miss Lamorna (IRE)**[159] 5476 6-10-0 74........(b[1]) IanPopham 63
(Sue Gardner) *trckd ldrs: rdn after 3 out: wknd next* 33/1
025- 6 6 **Ordensritter (GER)**[179] 5118 7-11-0 88........(t) JamesDavies 71
(Chris Down) *chsd ldrs: rdn after 3 out: wknd next* 7/1
-160 7 2 3/4 **Bertie Moon**[18] 1324 5-11-12 100........ NickScholfield 82
(Polly Gundry) *pressed ldr: led 3 out: rdn and hdd bef next: grad fdd* 14/1
U-P0 8 2 **Surprise Us**[20] 1509 8-9-11 78........(p) MichaelHeard(7) 57
(Mark Gillard) *led: rdn after 5th: hdd next: wknd bef 2 out* 25/1
6323 9 12 **Mix N Match**[20] 1510 11-10-0 74 oh4........(b[1]) RichieMcLernon 42
(Laura Young) *a towards rr* 12/1
000- P **East Hill**[162] 5412 5-10-4 78........(b[1]) AidanColeman
(Colin Tizzard) *slowly away: sn chsng ldrs: rdn after 5th: wknd next: t.o whn p.u bef 2 out* 7/1
4m 0.2s (-5.50) **Going Correction** -0.275s/f (Good) 10 Ran SP% **118.5**
Speed ratings (Par 103): **101,99,97,94,89 86,84,83,78,**
CSF £49.32 CT £275.69 TOTE £4.60: £1.60, £4.20, £1.90; EX 46.90 Trifecta £230.50.
Owner Danebury Racing Stables **Bred** Miss Laura Duggan **Trained** Danebury, Hants
FOCUS
A weak handicap which saw two come clear in the home straight. A big step up on his current form from the winner, while the fourth helps set the level.

1678 SOUTH WEST RACING CLUB CONDITIONAL JOCKEYS' H'CAP CHASE (20 fncs) 3m 1f 170y
4:30 (4:32) (Class 5) (0-100,100) 4-Y-O+ £3,422 (£997; £499)

Form RPR
4314 1 **Conas Taoi (IRE)**[37] 1326 6-11-3 91........(p) SeanBowen 101+
(Paul Morgan) *led: rdn and narrowly hdd between last 2: rallied to regain ld run-in: styd on wl* 7/4[1]
-234 2 1/2 **Supapowers (IRE)**[32] 1371 9-11-8 99........(t) CiaranGethings(3) 108
(Robert Stephens) *trckd ldrs: chal 4 out: rdn after 3 out: led narrowly between last 2: hdd run-in: kpt on* 5/1[2]
1213 3 25 **Moorlands George**[37] 1326 7-11-9 100........(t) MattGriffiths(3) 91
(Jeremy Scott) *trckd wnr: pressed wnr fr 8th tl rdn after 4 out: outpcd fr next* 7/4[1]
06P0 4 22 **Skating Home (IRE)**[40] 1287 9-10-0 74 oh4........(p) ConorShoemark 41
(Richard Hawker) *cl up: pushed along after 11th: rdn appr 4 out: sn btn: t.o* 66/1
0005 5 1 1/2 **Midnight Whisper**[14] 1546 9-10-8 82........(tp) KieronEdgar 47
(Richard Woollacott) *trckd ldrs: rdn after 4 out: wknd 2 out: t.o* 12/1
5322 P **The Wee Midget**[34] 1355 10-10-6 85........(b) ConorSmith(5)
(Arthur Whiting) *chsd ldrs: rousted along fr 5th: dropped to last after 13th: t.o 15th: p.u next* 6/1[3]
6m 32.5s (-12.10) **Going Correction** -0.275s/f (Good) 6 Ran SP% **112.9**
Speed ratings (Par 103): **107,106,99,92,91**
CSF £11.13 TOTE £2.60: £1.30, £2.40; EX 11.60.
Owner All Stars Sports Racing **Bred** Martin McCaughey **Trained** Ystrad, Rhondda C Taff
FOCUS
A weak staying handicap, confined to conditional riders. The second has been rated to her best.
T/Plt: £14.70 to a £1 stake. Pool: £68,341.71 - 3,380.83 winning tickets T/Qpdt: £7.60 to a £1 stake. Pool: £4,748.43 - 457.69 winning tickets **Tim Mitchell**

1435 ROSCOMMON (R-H)
Monday, September 28
OFFICIAL GOING: Flat course - yielding ; jumps courses - good

1679a IRISH STALLION FARMS EUROPEAN BREEDERS FUND KILBEGNET NOVICE CHASE (GRADE 3) (10 fncs) 2m
4:15 (4:15) 4-Y-O+ £17,635 (£5,155; £2,441; £813)

RPR
1 **The Game Changer (IRE)**[20] 1515 6-11-8 144........(t) BJCooper 148+
(Gordon Elliott, Ire) *settled bhd ldrs in 3rd: nt fluent 4th: tk clsr order in 2nd 3 out: gng best in cl 2nd between last 2 and led fr last where nt fluent: kpt on wl run-in to asset clsng stages* 11/10[2]
2 2 1/2 **Sizing Platinum (IRE)**[60] 1161 7-11-5 0........ JJBurke 142
(Henry De Bromhead, Ire) *led: over 1 l clr at 1/2-way: rdn and strly pressed after 2 out: hdd u.p fr last and no imp on wnr clsng stages: kpt on same pce* 10/11[1]
3 17 **King Of The Picts (IRE)**[37] 1333 6-11-1 0........ APHeskin 123
(John Patrick Shanahan, Ire) *trckd ldr in 2nd: pushed along after 4 out and dropped to 3rd at next: no imp on ldrs after and wknd bef 2 out* 12/1[3]
4 78 **Give Her Bach (IRE)**[25] 1466 6-10-8 0........(t) PierceGallagher 36
(Patrick Cronin, Ire) *in rr thrght and detached early: trailing bef 6th: nvr involved: completely t.o* 28/1
3m 57.2s (237.20) 4 Ran SP% **111.1**
CSF £2.68 TOTE £2.30; DF 2.50 Trifecta £4.00.
Owner Gigginstown House Stud **Bred** Arctic Tack Stud & Crossogue Stud **Trained** Longwood, Co Meath
FOCUS
A disappointing turnout but still a smart little race. The pace was not crazy. The first two have been rated to their marks.

1680 - 1682a (Foreign Racing) - See Raceform Interactive

1456 SEDGEFIELD (L-H)
Tuesday, September 29
OFFICIAL GOING: Good to firm (good in places) changing to good (good to firm in places) after race 1 (2.00)
Wind: light across Weather: Sunny

1683 ONLY PAXTONS FOR GENUINE KVERNELAND PARTS NOVICES' H'CAP HURDLE 2m 3f 188y
2:00 (2:00) (Class 5) (0-100,98) 4-Y-O+ £2,729 (£801; £400; £200)

Form RPR
3201 1 **Perseid (IRE)**[9] 1599 5-11-3 89 7ex........ SeanQuinlan 100+
(Sue Smith) *trckd ldr: led 7th: rdn between last 2: kpt on wl* 5/6[1]
0546 2 6 **Pixiepot**[58] 1178 5-11-1 87........ DenisO'Regan 89+
(Peter Niven) *midfield: pushed along bef 2 out: hdwy appr last: wnt 2nd jst after last: kpt on* 12/1
12P1 3 7 **Craigdancer (IRE)**[33] 1368 6-11-6 92........ DougieCostello 87
(Joanne Foster) *hld up: hit 7th: rdn after 3 out: hit 2 out: styd on fr last: wnt 3rd post* 11/2[2]
04-5 4 hd **Dalby Spook (IRE)**[8] 843 5-10-12 84........ BrianHughes 79
(Dianne Sayer) *midfield: rdn appr 2 out: plugged on* 25/1
0504 5 3/4 **Alys Rock (IRE)**[29] 1427 6-11-12 98........ SamTwiston-Davies 95
(Michael Appleby) *in tch: trckd ldr after 3 out: rdn after 2 out: pckd on landing last and sn lost 2nd: wknd and lost 2 more pls towards fin* 10/1
P-60 6 3/4 **Stormont Bridge**[11] 1568 7-10-4 83........(t) ThomasDowson(7) 79
(Maurice Barnes) *trckd ldrs: rdn bef 2 out: nt fluent last: wknd run-in* 25/1
5664 7 2 3/4 **Naburn**[13] 1552 7-11-12 98........ BrianHarding 90
(Andrew Wilson) *hld up: rdn and sme hdwy after 3 out: wknd appr last* 11/1
06-2 8 22 **Alwaysrecommended (IRE)**[136] 328 6-10-4 76........ PeterBuchanan 47
(Jane Walton) *hld up: rdn after 3 out: sn wknd* 17/2[3]
000- 9 3 3/4 **Palmello**[178] 5129 4-10-7 83........ TonyKelly(3) 50
(Ann Hamilton) *in tch: rdn after 3 out: sn wknd* 33/1
23-P 10 1 **Mister Hendre**[11] 1570 7-10-5 84........ JamesCorbett(7) 51
(Susan Corbett) *midfield: rdn after 3 out: wknd* 40/1
0P40 P **Cash Is King**[13] 1550 5-11-1 92........(tp) CallumBewley(5)
(Kenny Johnson) *led: hdd 7th: sn wknd: t.o whn p.u bef last* 100/1
4m 46.4s (-7.70)
WFA 4 from 5yo+ 12lb 11 Ran SP% **116.8**
CSF £11.33 CT £37.89 TOTE £1.70: £1.10, £3.30, £1.50; EX 13.10 Trifecta £62.00.
Owner Mrs S Smith **Bred** P Connell **Trained** High Eldwick, W Yorks
FOCUS
Divided bends. Chasers on inner line, distances as advertised. Hurdles on outer and races at maximum distance. Brian Hughes reported "It's good ground" after the opener, and the official description was amended before race two. The pace for this modest event lifted on the second circuit. The third and fourth help set the level.

1684 DAVID BAMLET'S BIRTHDAY CELEBRATION MAIDEN HURDLE (BETFRED HURDLE SERIES QUALIFIER) (8 hdls) 2m 178y
2:30 (2:30) (Class 4) 4-Y-O+ £3,768 (£1,106; £553; £276)

Form RPR
043- 1 **Ardmay (IRE)**[12] 3659 6-11-0 108........ BrianHughes 113+
(Kevin Ryan) *in tch: trckd ldr after 3rd: upsides on bit whn lft in front last: rdn and kpt on* 5/2[2]
-442 2 5 **Rocky Two (IRE)**[26] 1457 5-10-11 105........ AdamNicol(3) 106
(Philip Kirby) *midfield: hdwy after 3 out to chse ldng pair 2 out: rdn between last 2: lft 2nd last: kpt on* 20/1
5-4 3 5 **Cosmic Tigress**[38] 1334 4-10-7 0........ DenisO'Regan 97
(John Quinn) *midfield: hdwy 3 out to trck ldng pair 2 out: pushed along between last 2: lft 3rd and hmpd last: one pce* 18/1
F 4 20 **Golden Heritage**[27] 1453 4-10-7 0........ MrAlexFerguson(7) 87
(John Ferguson) *midfield: in tch after 2 out: hdwy to chse ldng pair appr 2 out: rdn after 2 out: sn wknd: hit last* 7/4[1]
224- 5 14 **Beer Goggles (IRE)**[189] 4975 4-10-11 0........ CraigNichol(3) 71
(Micky Hammond) *hld up: nvr threatened* 28/1
6 4 1/2 **Devon River (FR)**[261] 5-10-9 0........ CallumBewley(5) 67
(Simon Waugh) *hld up: nvr threatened* 100/1
00/ 7 3 3/4 **Trooper Royal**[581] 4480 5-11-0 0........ SeanQuinlan 63
(Sue Smith) *mstkes in midfield: wknd after 3 out* 100/1

 The Form Book Jumps 2015-16, Raceform Ltd, Newbury, RG14 5SJ

4-40 **8** *23* **Sackett**[5] 1634 4-10-11 0............................. HarryChalloner(3) 43
(Dianne Sayer) *midfield: wknd after 5th* **200/1**

9 *29* **Fort Belvedere**[55] 7-10-4 0............................. FinianO'Toole(10) 17
(Micky Hammond) *a in rr* **66/1**

42 **F** **Lady Clitico (IRE)**[21] 1499 4-10-4 113............................. TonyKelly(3) 102
(Rebecca Menzies) *racd keenly: trckd ldr: lft in front 3rd: rdn after 2 out: sn jnd: fell last* **7/2**[3]

-332 **R** **Raise A Spark**[33] 1365 5-11-0 110............................. AdrianLane
(Donald McCain) *led: jinked lft and rn out appr 3rd* **15/2**

3m 57.6s (-9.30) **Going Correction** -0.425s/f (Good) **11 Ran SP% 116.4**
Speed ratings (Par 105): **104,101,99,89,83 81,79,68,54,**
CSF £49.90 TOTE £4.60: £1.60, £3.30, £4.90; EX 63.10 Trifecta £590.60.
Owner A C Henson **Bred** Tom Kelly **Trained** Hambleton, N Yorks

FOCUS
Fairly ordinary form. The winner and the faller were clear for a time on the second circuit. A hurdle pb from the winner, and a pb from the second.

1685 WILLS PROPERTY SERVICES H'CAP CHASE (16 fncs) 2m 3f 65y
3:05 (3:05) (Class 4) (0-105,104) 4-Y-0+ **£4,548** (£1,335; £667; £333)

Form RPR

P-01 **1** **The Backup Plan (IRE)**[33] 1370 6-11-12 104............................. BrianHarding 112+
(Donald McCain) *mde all: rdn after 2 out: strly pressed appr last: kpt on run-in* **13/8**[1]

4525 **2** *2 ½* **Sendiym (FR)**[13] 1551 8-10-11 89.............................(p) BrianHughes 95
(Dianne Sayer) *trckd ldr in 2nd: rdn after 3 out: chal strly appr last: one pce run-in* **2/1**[2]

6-26 **3** *12* **Humbel Ben (IRE)**[39] 1306 12-11-2 94............................. (p) NickSchofield 93
(Alan Jones) *in tch in 3rd: mstke 4 out: rdn after 3 out: sn no imp on ldng pair* **10/3**[3]

30P6 **4** *26* **Prince Blackthorn (IRE)**[22] 1492 9-10-0 78 oh10..........(p) HenryBrooke 56
(Barry Murtagh) *hld up: nt fluent 5 out and 4 out: sn wknd* **16/1**

0345 **5** *49* **Roxyfet (FR)**[33] 1367 5-10-12 93.............................(t) JoeColliver(3) 21
(Micky Hammond) *j. slowly in rr: t.o after 5 out* **9/1**

4m 44.2s (-18.80) **Going Correction** -0.875s/f (Firm) course record **5 Ran SP% 110.4**
Speed ratings (Par 105): **104,102,97,86,66**
CSF £5.53 TOTE £2.00: £1.20, £1.50; EX 5.20 Trifecta £8.90.
Owner N.Y.P.D Racing **Bred** Miss Sharon Spillane **Trained** Cholmondeley, Cheshire

FOCUS
There was little depth to this modest handicap, but the form of the first pair looks sound. The second has been rated to his C&D mark.

1686 COUNTRY HARVEST FARM FOODS H'CAP HURDLE 2m 3f 188y
3:40 (3:40) (Class 4) (0-110,110) 4-Y-0+ **£3,768** (£1,106; £553; £276)

Form RPR

3401 **1** **Drifter (IRE)**[22] 1493 4-11-2 108............................. PaulNO'Brien(7) 116+
(Harry Whittington) *trckd ldr: led 3 out: rdn 2 out: kpt on* **4/1**[3]

012 **2** *4 ½* **Ever So Much (IRE)**[9] 1600 6-11-8 106.............................(p) AndrewTinkler 110
(Ben Haslam) *in tch: trckd ldr 3 out: rdn 2 out: hit last: one pce* **9/4**[1]

2364 **3** *1 ½* **Brigadoon**[15] 1549 8-11-12 110............................. SamTwiston-Davies 112
(Michael Appleby) *hld up in tch: hdwy into 3rd after 3 out: rdn appr 2 out: one pce* **10/1**

5U-0 **4** *6* **Talkin Thomas (IRE)**[21] 1508 9-11-4 102............................. SeanQuinlan 100
(Michael Appleby) *hld up: rdn and outpcd after 3 out: plugged on fr between last 2: nvr threatened* **14/1**

5 *1 ¾* **Key Account (IRE)**[57] 1193 7-11-1 102............................. BrianHayes(3) 97
(L Byrne, Ire) *led: clr 3rd tl 5th: hdd 3 out: grad wknd* **28/1**

U24F **6** *1* **Danceintothelight**[33] 1370 8-10-1 95............................. FinianO'Toole(10) 89
(Micky Hammond) *hld up: rdn after 3 out: sn struggling* **10/1**

-531 **7** *53* **Howaboutnever (IRE)**[29] 1427 7-11-8 106.............................(p) DarylJacob 52
(Ian Williams) *trckd ldr: lost pl 5th: dropped to rr after next: t.o after 3 out* **7/2**[2]

3-35 **R** **Downtown Boy (IRE)**[26] 1459 7-11-2 103.............................(p) TonyKelly(3)
(Ray Craggs) *ref to r* **7/1**

4m 40.8s (-13.30)
WFA 4 from 6yo+ 12lb **8 Ran SP% 113.8**
CSF £13.70 CT £81.58 TOTE £4.00: £1.70, £1.40, £2.50; EX 13.70 Trifecta £97.60.
Owner The Boardwalk Partnership **Bred** Churchtown, Lane & Orpendale Bloodstock **Trained** Sparsholt, Oxfordshire

FOCUS
A fair handicap hurdle. A big step up from the winner, with the third and fourth close to their marks.

1687 CHRIS GRANT RACING NOVICES' H'CAP CHASE (13 fncs) 2m 77y
4:15 (4:15) (Class 5) (0-100,94) 4-Y-0+ **£3,249** (£954; £477; £238)

Form RPR

P56 **1** **So Bazaar (IRE)**[26] 1461 8-10-0 68.............................(t) HenryBrooke 77+
(Andrew Wilson) *hld up: hdwy 3 out: rdn after 3 out: chal whn sltly hmpd 2 out: led narrowly appr last: hld on wl* **12/1**

-565 **2** *½* **Aregra (FR)**[44] 1272 5-10-4 72.............................(p) BrianHughes 80+
(Peter Niven) *led: often j. sltly rt: rdn after 3 out: pressed 2 out: hdd narrowly appr last: one pce* **2/1**[1]

-0PP **3** *9* **Bob's Call (IRE)**[44] 1272 6-11-8 90.............................(t) DenisO'Regan 90
(Tony Coyle) *prom: rdn after 3 out: no ex in 3rd between last 2* **7/2**[3]

06F0 **4** *11* **Dover The Moon (IRE)**[26] 1461 4-10-0 79 oh1.............(t) JamesDavies 61
(Tom Gretton) *in tch: blnd 4 out: rdn after 3 out: wknd after 2 out* **16/1**

6364 **5** *24* **Short Takes (USA)**[24] 1478 7-11-12 94.............................(p) BrianHarding 61
(Donald McCain) *trckd ldrs: mstke 4 out: reminders after 7th: wknd after 3 out* **3/1**[2]

PP54 **6** *1 ¾* **Duhallowcountry (IRE)**[11] 1570 9-9-13 74.............(p) SamColtherd(7) 40
(Victor Thompson) *in tch: mstke 4 out: sn wknd* **10/1**

-466 **U** **Private Jones**[20] 1525 6-11-0 82............................. RobertDunne
(Miss Imogen Pickard) *in tch: blnd and uns rdr 5th* **8/1**

3m 57.9s (-16.10) **Going Correction** -0.875s/f (Firm)
WFA 4 from 5yo+ 11lb **7 Ran SP% 114.3**
Speed ratings (Par 103): **105,104,100,94,82 82,**
CSF £37.86 TOTE £12.70: £5.00, £1.50; EX 45.10 Trifecta £230.40.
Owner Andy Wilson **Bred** Mrs Virginia Moeran And Mount Coote Stud **Trained** Orton, Cumbria

FOCUS
A very weak novice handicap chase. The first two pulled clear. The winner has been rated in line with his 2014 hurdle form.

1688 JOHN WADE GROUP MARES' STANDARD OPEN NATIONAL HUNT FLAT RACE 2m 178y
4:50 (4:52) (Class 6) 4-6-Y-0 **£1,949** (£572; £286; £143)

Form RPR

1 **Absolute Angel** 4-10-12 0............................. BrianHughes 86+
(Peter Niven) *hld up in tch: rdn and outpcd over 3f out: stl only 4th ent fnl f: styd on wl: led towards fin* **3/1**[2]

2 *½* **Mount Mizooka** 4-10-12 0............................. SamTwiston-Davies 86
(Brian Ellison) *trckd ldng pair: tended to hang lft: rdn over 3f out: chal over 1f out: led 110yds out: one pce: hdd towards fin* **9/2**[3]

3 *½* **Catch The Magic (IRE)**[29] 1434 6-10-9 0............................. BrianHayes(3) 85
(John Joseph Hanlon, Ire) *w ldr: rdn 3f out: led over 1f out: hdd 110yds out: one pce* **7/1**

0-5 **4** *1* **Due East**[27] 1449 5-10-2 0............................. FinianO'Toole(10) 84
(Micky Hammond) *in tch: rdn and outpcd over 3f out: edgd lft over 1f out: styd on wl fnl f* **9/1**

2 **5** *3 ¾* **Fishy Story**[23] 1491 5-10-12 0............................. ConorO'Farrell 81
(David Pipe) *led narrowly: rdn 3f out: hdd over 1f out: wknd ins fnl f* **5/4**[1]

000- **6** *6* **Kicking Lily**[341] 2014 5-10-5 0.............................(t[1]) JamieHamilton(7) 74
(Ann Hamilton) *hld up in rr: rdn over 3f out: nvr threatened* **40/1**

7 *8* **Knysna Bay** 4-10-7 0............................. DiarmuidO'Regan(5) 66
(Chris Grant) *in tch on outer: rdn over 3f out: sn wknd* **25/1**

0 **8** *12* **Skiddaw Poppy**[38] 1334 4-10-5 0............................. ThomasDowson(7) 54
(Maurice Barnes) *hld up: rdn over 4f out: sn btn* **80/1**

4m 4.5s (3.20) **Going Correction** -0.425s/f (Good) **8 Ran SP% 117.6**
Speed ratings: **75,74,74,74,72 69,65,60**
CSF £17.28 TOTE £4.60: £1.50, £1.60, £2.10; EX 19.10 Trifecta £66.20.
Owner Francis Green Racing Ltd **Bred** Paul D'Amato **Trained** Barton-le-Street, N Yorks

FOCUS
This modest mares' bumper was steadily run, before turning into a sprint up the home straight. It's been rated around the balance of the third and fourth.
T/Plt: £102.60 to a £1 stake. Pool: £65,622.69 - 466.83 winning tickets. T/Qpdt: £19.40 to a £1 stake. Pool: £4,865.45 - 185.3 winning tickets. **Andrew Sheret**

1444 SOUTHWELL (L-H)
Tuesday, September 29

OFFICIAL GOING: Good (7.8)
Wind: light 1/2 against Weather: fine and sunny

1689 LADBROKES H'CAP CHASE (13 fncs) 1m 7f 153y
2:20 (2:20) (Class 5) (0-100,89) 5-Y-0+ **£4,659** (£1,446; £779)

Form RPR

0-04 **1** **Youm Jamil (USA)**[20] 1525 8-9-13 67.............................(t) NickSlatter(5) 79
(Tony Carroll) *hld up in tch: wnt 3rd 10th: lft handy 2nd next: abt 2 l down whn lft clr last* **8/1**

2554 **2** *5* **Larkhall**[9] 1603 8-10-3 73............................. RyanDay(7) 82
(Mike Sowersby) *chsd ldng pair: drvn 9th: lft 3rd 3 out: lft abt 3 l 2nd and hmpd last: one pce* **5/1**[3]

3P43 **3** *20* **Red Rosso**[29] 1422 10-10-11 74.............................(t) TrevorWhelan 68
(Rob Summers) *in rr but in tch: effrt 9th: outpcd next: lft modest 4th 3 out: wknd and hit next: bhd whn lft poor 3rd last* **5/1**[3]

0242 **F** **Chankillo**[9] 1603 6-11-4 81.............................(p) TomScudamore 95
(Sarah-Jayne Davies) *led: j.rt: abt 2 l ahd whn fell last* **9/4**[2]

44F **F** **Shady Glen (IRE)**[7] 1614 6-11-6 83.............................(p) KielanWoods 91
(Graeme McPherson) *chsd ldr: cl 2nd whn fell 3 out* **15/8**[1]

4m 1.6s (-0.40) **Going Correction** +0.025s/f (Yiel) **5 Ran SP% 110.0**
Speed ratings: **102,99,89,,**
CSF £42.62 TOTE £8.30: £2.50, £2.00; EX 36.70 Trifecta £85.70.
Owner Neville Statham & Family **Bred** Ashleigh Stud Farm **Trained** Cropthorne, Worcs

FOCUS
The opening contest was a moderate handicap chase. They went a decent gallop on good ground. The fortunate winner has been rated to his best.

1690 DOWNLOAD THE LADBROKES APP H'CAP CHASE (16 fncs) 2m 4f 62y
2:55 (2:55) (Class 4) (0-120,120) 5-Y-0+ **£5,848** (£1,717; £858; £429)

Form RPR

2323 **1** **Cut The Corner (IRE)**[9] 1601 7-11-12 120............................. WillKennedy 134+
(Dr Richard Newland) *j. soundly: trckd ldr: led 9th: wnt clr appr 3 out: 14 l ahd last: easily* **15/8**[1]

-413 **2** *22* **Ballybogey (IRE)**[76] 1005 9-11-12 120............................. AdamPogson 116
(Charles Pogson) *last whn mstke 2nd: trckd ldrs 6th: wnt 8 l 2nd bef 3 out: kpt on same pce* **6/1**[3]

2P5- **3** *7* **Swing Hard (IRE)**[195] 4848 7-11-2 110............................. DannyCook 97
(Sue Smith) *led: hdd 9th: sn drvn: one pce fr 4 out* **2/1**[2]

-542 **4** *21* **Boss In Boots (IRE)**[27] 1451 7-11-9 117.............................(b) AndrewThornton 86
(Seamus Mullins) *hld up: hit 9th: pushed along next: lost pl 4 out: sn bhd* **7/1**

1124 **5** *8* **Zama Zama**[24] 1483 8-10-4 105.............................(p) MrConorOrr(7) 68
(Evan Williams) *chsd ldng pair: hit 8th: sn pushed along: mstke next: lost pl bef 10th: sn bhd* **7/1**

5m 14.2s (-2.80) **Going Correction** +0.025s/f (Yiel) **5 Ran SP% 107.4**
Speed ratings: **106,97,94,86,82**
CSF £11.91 TOTE £2.60: £1.40, £2.60; EX 11.20 Trifecta £23.70.
Owner Paul L Drinkwater **Bred** P F Corbet **Trained** Claines, Worcs

FOCUS
The feature contest was a fair handicap chase. They went an, at best, respectable gallop. Another step up from the winner, and there's a case for rating the race 7lb higher through the second.

1691 LADBROKES H'CAP HURDLE (11 hdls) 2m 4f 62y
3:30 (3:30) (Class 5) (0-100,106) 3-Y-0+ **£3,249** (£954; £477; £238)

Form RPR

1304 **1** **Tennessee Bird**[9] 1598 7-10-8 82............................. GavinSheehan 90
(Mike Sowersby) *hld up in rr: stdy hdwy 8th: trcking ldrs appr 2 out: led appr last: drvn clr* **13/2**

4 **2** *4 ½* **Shaiyzar (IRE)**[9] 1604 6-11-7 100.............................(p) HarryBannister(5) 105
(David Thompson) *chsd ldrs: led appr 2 out: hdd and hit last: kpt on same pce* **12/1**

4/6- **3** *10* **Theredballoon**[496] 405 9-11-1 89............................. PaulMoloney 84
(Conrad Allen) *chsd ldrs: 3rd appr last: kpt on one pce* **11/2**[2]

-0PF **4** 4½ **Exit To Freedom**[33] 1370 9-9-8 **75** oh1 ow1......................(p) RyanDay(7) 66
(John Wainwright) *in rr: hdwy into midfield 6th: kpt on one pce fr 2 out: tk modest 4th sn after last* **33/1**

5560 **5** ¾ **Mullinavat (IRE)**[33] 1375 6-11-7 **95**..............................(t) RichardJohnson 86
(Jennie Candlish) *trckd ldrs: t.k.h: led after 7th: hdd appr 2 out: wknd last* **9/2**[1]

4540 **6** 2½ **Bob's Legend (IRE)**[11] 1578 9-10-13 **87**......................(tp) BrendanPowell 75
(Jamie Snowden) *in rr: kpt on fr 2 out: nvr a factor* **14/1**

060/ **7** nk **Razzle Dazzle 'Em**[50] 2051 6-10-8 **82**.................................... TrevorWhelan 70
(Shaun Harris) *trckd ldrs: drvn 3 out: one pce* **50/1**

000 **8** 6 **Prince Of Silver**[47] 1240 9-10-11 **88**............................(t) JamesBanks(3) 70
(Andy Turnell) *chsd ldrs: one pce fr 3 out* **25/1**

-P01 **9** 1¼ **Pattara**[29] 1423 6-11-3 **91**..(t) GerardTumelty 76
(Noel Williams) *chsd ldrs: rdn and mstke 2 out: sn wknd* **6/1**[3]

0-64 **10** 1½ **Watchmetail (IRE)**[38] 1323 9-9-7 **74** oh10............ ThomasCheesman(7) 54
(John Panvert) *prom: wknd 3 out* **20/1**

2-00 **11** 28 **Oxalido (FR)**[13] 1552 13-10-13 **90**...................................... GrahamWatters(3) 45
(Hugh Burns) *in rr: hit 5th: bhd and reminders next* **18/1**

0F6P **P** **Prairie Hawk (USA)**[40] 1297 10-9-11 **74** oh4...................(t) BenPoste(3)
(Adrian Wintle) *nt fluent in last: drvn 6th: sn bhd: t.o whn p.u after 3 out* **16/1**

6055 **P** **Hi Tide (IRE)**[27] 1446 11-11-7 **95**.. AidanColeman
(J R Jenkins) *t.k.h in rr: lost pl 3 out: sn bhd: t.o whn p.u bef last* **8/1**

-P0P **P** **Stitched In Time (IRE)**[11] 1573 8-10-8 **87**..............(p) NathanMoscrop(5)
(Sara Ender) *led to 3rd: lost pl after 7th: sn bhd: t.o whn p.u bef 2 out* **16/1**

-P00 **P** **Cool Fusion**[128] 462 6-10-3 **82** ow3..............................(v[1]) JakeHodson(5)
(Anthony Day) *w ldrs: led 3rd: mstke 5th: hdd after 7th: sn lost pl: bhd 3 out: t.o whn p.u bef last* **100/1**

5m 8.0s (-5.00) **Going Correction** -0.325s/f (Good) **15** Ran SP% **118.2**
Speed ratings (Par 103): **97,95,91,89,89 88,87,85,85,84 73, , , ,**
CSF £75.61 CT £461.35 TOTE £7.70: £3.40, £2.80, £2.90; EX 83.90 Trifecta £421.30.
Owner Queens Head Racing Club **Bred** Mrs J Wiltschinsky **Trained** Goodmanham, E Yorks

FOCUS
A modest handicap hurdle. They went a steady gallop. A small pb from the winner, with the second in line with the best of his Irish form.

1692 LADBROKES CONDITIONAL JOCKEYS' TRAINING SERIES H'CAP HURDLE (PART OF RACING EXCEL. INITIATIVE) (13 hdls) 2m 7f 209y
4:05 (4:05) (Class 4) (0-110,110) 4-Y-0+ **£3,898** (£1,144; £572; £286)

Form RPR

63-3 **1** **The Big Dipper**[27] 1453 6-11-4 **102**.. JamieBargary 104
(David Dennis) *hld up in rr: hdwy 8th: handy 4th next: effrt 10th: chsng ldng trio whn swtchd ins sn after next: 2nd between last 2: led last: drvn out* **11/2**

PP-3 **2** 1¼ **Jimmy Shan (IRE)**[27] 1447 7-11-9 **107**.............................. AlanJohns 108
(Tim Vaughan) *j.rt at times: led: drvn 3 out: j.rt: mstke and hdd last: styd on same pce* **7/4**[1]

-230 **3** ½ **Weybridge Light**[25] 839 10-11-1 **102**..............(b) PaddyBradley(3) 102
(David Thompson) *chsd ldrs: handy 3rd bef 9th: 2nd bef 2 out: styd on same pce between last 2* **5/1**[3]

4-P0 **4** 9 **Knocklong (IRE)**[20] 1522 7-11-12 **110**...................(b[1]) FreddieMitchell 103
(Ben Haslam) *chsd ldr: drvn 3 out: fdd fr next* **10/1**

3/66 **5** 29 **Optical High**[33] 1370 6-9-7 **84** oh12.................. StephenMcCarthy(7) 50
(Sue Smith) *chsd ldrs: pushed along 3rd: outpcd bef 9th: wl bhd fr 3 out* **16/1**

P-PP **6** 1 **Bit Of A Jig (IRE)**[90] 869 8-11-9 **110**...................... PatrickCowley(3) 75
(Adrian Wintle) *chsd ldrs: drvn 8th: lost pl bef next: wl bhd fr 3 out* **8/1**

3564 **7** ¾ **Little Windmill (IRE)**[27] 1447 5-11-4 **105**..........(p) ConorSmith(3) 69
(Neil King) *trckd ldrs: lost pl 10th: wl bhd fr next* **9/2**[2]

040P **P** **Monzino (USA)**[44] 1272 7-10-0 **84** oh15.................. ThomasCheesman
(Michael Chapman) *racd in last: drvn along 4th: reminders 7th: sn bhd: t.o whn p.u bef 9th* **80/1**

6m 7.9s (-7.10) **Going Correction** -0.325s/f (Good) **8** Ran SP% **113.9**
Speed ratings (Par 105): **98,97,97,94,84 84,84,**
CSF £15.94 CT £50.62 TOTE £6.70: £2.30, £1.30, £1.30; EX 18.90 Trifecta £70.50.
Owner The Lucky Seven **Bred** Direct Sales (uk) Ltd **Trained** Hanley Swan, Worcestershire

FOCUS
A modest conditional jockeys' staying handicap hurdle. They went an even gallop. The winner has been rated as improving in line with the best of his bumper figures, with the second, third and fourth pretty much to their marks.

1693 LADBROKES NOVICES' HURDLE (9 hdls) 1m 7f 153y
4:40 (4:41) (Class 4) 4-Y-0+ **£3,898** (£1,144; £572; £286)

Form RPR

1 **1** **Francis Of Assisi (IRE)**[24] 1480 5-11-5 0.......................... AidanColeman 132+
(John Ferguson) *trckd ldrs: 2nd 5th: led 2 out: smoothly* **4/7**[1]

2402 **2** 7 **Ballycamp (IRE)**[29] 1425 6-10-12 120.................................(t) AdamPogson 115
(Charles Pogson) *t.k.h: led: j.rt 1st: hdd 2nd: hung rt and led 4th: j.rt 6th: drvn 3 out: hdd next: kpt on: no ch w wnr* **5/2**[2]

33-0 **3** 8 **Rustamabad (FR)**[41] 1289 5-10-12 0.............................. RichardJohnson 108
(Tim Vaughan) *in rr: mstke 1st: hdwy and poor 5th 5th: handy 3rd whn hit 2 out: kpt on one pce* **10/1**

6143 **4** 8 **Jarlath**[33] 1377 4-11-0 110... KevinJones(5) 106
(Seamus Mullins) *t.k.h: trckd ldrs: hung lft and one pce 2 out* **6/1**[3]

4-26 **5** 22 **Lawless Island (IRE)**[118] 595 6-10-12 0.............................. MichaelByrne 79
(Tim Vaughan) *in rr: hdwy and distant 5th bef 2 out: nvr on terms* **16/1**

6 38 **Streele (USA)**[807] 5-9-12 0.. MissTWorsley(7) 38
(Ken Wingrove) *in rr: bhd fr 4th: tailed rt off* **100/1**

50- **7** 14 **Ferngrove (USA)**[15] 5065 4-10-12 0.............................(t) GavinSheehan 32
(Warren Greatrex) *t.k.h: w ldr: led 2nd: hdd 4th: wknd 6th: sn bhd: tailed rt off* **33/1**

0 **8** 10 **Whitstable Native**[15] 1544 7-10-12 0.............................(t) PaulMoloney 23
(Sophie Leech) *hld up in rr: bhd 3rd: tailed rt off whn eased 2 out* **100/1**

5 **P** **Dr Izzymoo (IRE)**[33] 1378 6-10-12 0...................................... PeterCarberry
(Jennie Candlish) *t.k.h: trckd ldrs: j.lft 3rd: sn lost pl: bhd fr 5th: tailed rt off whn p.u bef 2 out* **50/1**

3m 47.8s (-9.20) **Going Correction** -0.325s/f (Good)
WFA 4 from 5yo+ 11lb **9** Ran SP% **128.4**
Speed ratings (Par 105): **110,106,102,98,87 68,61,56,**
CSF £2.84 TOTE £1.50: £1.10, £1.10, £2.30; EX 2.90 Trifecta £10.10.
Owner Bloomfields **Bred** Queen Cleopatra Syndicate **Trained** Cowlinge, Suffolk

FOCUS
A fair novices' hurdle. They went a respectable gallop. There's a case for rating the race 5lb higher through the second and fourth, while the third has been rated in line with his bumper form.

1694 BOOK CHRISTMAS AT SOUTHWELL RACECOURSE MARES' NOVICES' HURDLE (13 hdls) 2m 7f 209y
5:10 (5:11) (Class 4) 4-Y-0+ **£3,898** (£1,144; £572; £286)

Form RPR

4-12 **1** **Kayla**[21] 1506 5-10-11 0..(t) PaddyBrennan 98+
(Stuart Edmunds) *trckd ldng pair: t.k.h: blnd 5th: hit 10th: led on bit appr 2 out: rdn between last 2: styd on wl: eased last 50yds* **11/10**[1]

44F0 **2** 2½ **Tir Dubh (IRE)**[15] 1547 6-10-11 104... TomO'Brien 91
(Robert Stephens) *chsd ldr: pushed along 9th: drvn whn bmpd 2 out: 2nd appr last: styd on same pce* **5/4**[2]

65 **3** 2¾ **Little Dream (IRE)**[21] 1506 8-10-11 0..........................[1] PaulMoloney 89
(Evan Williams) *hld up in rr: chsng ldrs 9th: 3rd appr last: kpt on same pce* **14/1**[3]

630 **4** 2½ **Brenda De Ronceray (FR)**[21] 1506 4-10-9 0.........(t[1]) TomScudamore 87
(David Pipe) *t.k.h: led: j.rt at times: hit 10th: hdd and j.rt 2 out: hung rt appr last: kpt on one pce* **14/1**[3]

00 **5** 10 **Sawwala**[3] 591 5-10-11 0.. AidanColeman 78
(J R Jenkins) *in tch: chsd ldrs 7th: outpcd and reminders 3 out: no ch after* **25/1**

6m 14.3s (-0.70) **Going Correction** -0.325s/f (Good)
WFA 4 from 5yo+ 13lb **5** Ran SP% **109.2**
Speed ratings (Par 105): **88,87,86,85,82**
CSF £2.84 TOTE £1.60; £1.10, £1.10; EX 3.20 Trifecta £6.60.
Owner Exors of the Late Mrs P Robeson **Bred** Mrs P Robeson **Trained** Newport Pagnell, Bucks

FOCUS
The concluding contest was a modest staying mares' novices' hurdle. They went an ordinary gallop, and the comparative winning time was slow. The second has again been rated well below her Market Rasen mark.
T/Plt: £61.90 to a £1 stake. Pool: £62,264.04 - 733.25 winning tickets. T/Qpdt: £3.20 to a £1 stake. Pool: £7,419.04 - 1,686.93 winning tickets. **Walter Glynn**

1695 - 1697a (Foreign Racing) - See Raceform Interactive

CHEPSTOW (L-H)
Wednesday, September 30

OFFICIAL GOING: Good (chs 7.6, hdl 8.3)
Wind: breezy Weather: very bright and sunny; 17 degrees

1698 LONGCROFT BUILDING SERVICES SUPPORTS PAUL'S PLACE MAIDEN HURDLE (11 hdls) 2m 3f 100y
2:00 (2:01) (Class 5) 4-Y-0+ **£2,274** (£667; £333; £166)

Form RPR

13- **1** **Potters Corner (IRE)**[173] 5255 5-11-0 0.................................. TomO'Brien 121+
(Paul Morgan) *pressed ldr tl led bef 5th: clr and gng wl fr 3 out: 4 l ahd last: eased cl home: v readily* **8/11**[1]

2 2¼ **Tried And Tested (IRE)** 4-10-13 0.................................... RichardJohnson 115+
(Jonjo O'Neill) *midfield: effrt 8th: rdn 2 out: drvn into 2nd at last: styd on wl after but no match for wnr: promising* **15/2**[3]

335- **3** 6 **Western Xpress (IRE)**[194] 4887 7-10-11 116.......................... SeanBowen(3) 111
(Peter Bowen) *led at stdy pce tl hdd bef 5th: rdn and hld fr 3 out: lost 2nd at last where edgd lft* **3/1**[2]

042U **4** 1¾ **Buy Me Out**[8] 1618 5-10-7 100... PaulMoloney 102
(Grace Harris) *chsd ldrs: effrt and rdn 8th: styd on same pce fr 2 out: nvr looked a serious threat* **20/1**

05- **5** 1¼ **Arthur's Gift (IRE)**[172] 5285 4-10-13 0..................... SamTwiston-Davies 107+
(Nigel Twiston-Davies) *tall: mstkes: chsd ldng pair tl rdn 2 out: plugged on same pce after* **12/1**

2-66 **6** 15 **Loch Garman (FR)**[125] 528 4-10-13 0................................ ConorO'Farrell 91
(Nigel Hawke) *hld up and wl bhd: lost tch w ldrs 3 out* **25/1**

7 17 **Winterlude (IRE)**[40] 5-11-0 0... HenryBrooke 77
(Jennie Candlish) *t.k.h: hld up in last and often lacked fluency: stdy prog 5th: midfield and in tch home turn: wknd 3 out: eased and t.o* **20/1**

8 12 **Kelsey (IRE)**[213] 5-11-0 0.. RobertDunne 73
(Tom Lacey) *chsd ldrs: mstke 7th: rdn and wknd 3 out: blnd bdly 2 out: eased after mstke last: t.o* **50/1**

00 **9** 14 **The Bank Manager**[123] 558 4-10-13 0...............................(t) TomScudamore 48
(David Pipe) *a towards rr: lost tch bef 3 out: bdly t.o* **33/1**

10 1¾ **Prince Mahler (IRE)**[213] 5-11-0 0.. JamesBest 47
(Caroline Keevil) *plld hrd in rr: lost tch bef 8th: sn bdly t.o: b.b.v* **200/1**

000- **11** 49 **Right On Roy**[329] 2277 5-11-0 0... AndrewTinkler
(Martin Keighley) *bhd: bdly t.o fr 8th* **200/1**

P **Derrymix**[486] 7-10-7 0... MrStanSheppard(7)
(Matt Sheppard) *bhd: bdly t.o 8th: wnt wrong and p.u and dismntd 2 out* **100/1**

F **U** **Seeanythingyoulike (IRE)**[21] 1519 4-10-13 0........................[1] LiamHeard
(Jeremy Scott) *t.k.h in midfield: prog to chse ldrs whn pckd and uns rdr 7th* **100/1**

4m 45.1s (-16.70) **Going Correction** -0.95s/f (Hard)
WFA 4 from 5yo+ 11lb **13** Ran SP% **123.6**
Speed ratings (Par 103): **97,96,93,92,92 85,78,73,67,67 46,**
CSF £7.08 TOTE £1.90: £1.30, £1.40, £1.10; EX 7.70 Trifecta £19.40.
Owner Walters Plant, Maule, Davies, Potter **Bred** Mrs P J O'Connor **Trained** Ystrad, Rhondda C Taff

FOCUS
The return of jumps racing at Chepstow and the watered ground looked in great nick. The far bend was railed out an average of 8yds from the innermost position, adding approximately 24yds to races 1, 3, 5, 6 & 7, and 48yds to races 2 & 4. This was the hottest maiden run so far this season, albeit at a very early stage, and it'll produce future winners. The winner has been rated in line with his good bumper form and should rate higher. The fourth helps set the level.

1699 PP BUSINESS IMPROVEMENTS SUPPORTS PAUL'S PLACE H'CAP HURDLE (12 hdls) 2m 7f 131y
2:30 (2:32) (Class 4) (0-120,120) 4-Y-0+ **£3,249** (£954; £477; £238)

Form RPR

6-11 **1** **Tobefair**[91] 878 5-11-2 **109**... TrevorWhelan 117+
(Debra Hamer) *settled in rr: confidently handled: clsd to 5th and gng wl home turn: stdy run after: jnd ldr gng best and hit last: pushed ahd wout recrse to whip fnl 100yds* **7/1**

061- **2** 1 **Ballyknock Lad (IRE)**[159] 5510 6-11-8 **115**.........................(t) DavidBass 120
(Kim Bailey) *cl up: rdn 9th: led 3 out: hrd drvn and hdd last: outpcd by wnr flat but kpt on gamely* **7/2**[1]

3030 **3** *6* **Storm Alert**[42] 1293 8-9-11 **93** oh1.......................... LucyGardner(3) 92
(Sue Gardner) *mde most tl rdn and hdd 3 out: remained cl up tl bmpd along and no ex bef last* **12/1**

0533 **4** *6* **Airpur Desbois (FR)**[22] 1507 5-11-0 **107**.......... PaddyBrennan 100
(Charlie Mann) *settled towards rr: effrt bef 9th: rdn and no imp fr 2 out* **14/1**

-013 **5** *7* **Adrenalin Flight (IRE)**[94] 855 9-11-8 **115**.......... AndrewThornton 101
(Seamus Mullins) *nt a fluent: prom tl lost pl qckly after 8th: plugged on and n.d fr next* **8/1**

22F- **6** *8* **Regal Flow**[193] 4907 8-11-6 **113**.......................... JamesBest 93
(Caroline Keevil) *prom: hrd rdn 9th: wknd between last two* **20/1**

30- **7** *6* **Drumlee Lad (IRE)**[168] 5343 5-11-10 **117**..........(t) TomScudamore 89
(David Pipe) *trckd ldrs: wnt 3rd briefly home turn: pushed along and wknd 3 out* **5/1[3]**

4154 **8** *nk* **Lava Lamp (GER)**[30] 1419 8-11-2 **119**..........(p) LewisGordon(10) 91
(Evan Williams) *in last pair: sn urged along and nvr travelling: lost tch 8th: mstke 2 out* **10/1**

10P- **9** *73* **Bishop Wulstan (IRE)**[158] 5535 4-11-8 **120**..........(p) SeanBowen(3) 17
(Peter Bowen) *in last pair and nt travelling sweetly: rdn bef 8th: sn t.o* **16/1**

0521 **U** **Church Field (IRE)**[36] 1350 7-11-0 **117**..........(p) JackSavage(10)
(Jonjo O'Neill) *midfield tl uns rdr 2nd* **4/1[2]**

5m 50.3s (-11.90) **Going Correction** -0.95s/f (Hard)
WFA 4 from 5yo+ 13lb **10** Ran SP% **116.6**
Speed ratings (Par 105): **81,80,78,76,74 71,69,69,45,**
CSF £32.41 CT £293.08 TOTE £6.90: £2.80, £1.90, £4.50; EX 34.50 Trifecta £534.00.
Owner Down The Quay Club **Bred** Mickley Stud **Trained** Nantycaws, Carmarthens

FOCUS
This modest staying handicap was run at a steady gallop and it only began to wind up nearing four out. The runner-up is a sound guide. Another step up from the winner, with a pb from the second. The third has been rated to the best of his recent form.

1700 LONGCROFT BUILDING SERVICES SUPPORTS PAUL'S PLACE (S) HURDLE (11 hdls) 2m 3f 100y

3:00 (3:02) (Class 5) 4-7-Y-0 **£2,274** (£667; £333; £166)

Form RPR

2336 **1** **Fuzzy Logic (IRE)**[25] 1479 6-10-9 110..........(b) RobertWilliams(3) 115
(Bernard Llewellyn) *chsd clr ldr: pushed along bef 2 out: led bef last: plugged on and in command flat* **7/1**

53-3 **2** *6* **Tijori (IRE)**[36] 1354 7-10-5 112..........(tp) JordanWilliams(7) 111
(Bernard Llewellyn) *towards rr: pushed along bef 5th: mstkes 5th and 7th: rdn to go 3rd at 8th: no real imp fr next but managed to snatch modest 2nd cl home* **11/4[2]**

0613 **3** *shd* **Marju's Quest (IRE)**[5] 1646 5-10-12 125.......... JamieBargary(7) 119
(David Dennis) *plld hrd: led and sn 6 l clr: j.rt: rdn bef 3 out: hdd u.p bef last: sn paid for earlier exertions and lost 2nd nr fin* **6/5[1]**

4 *72* **Toptempo**[18] 6-10-5 0.......................... GavinSheehan 38
(Ali Stronge) *mstkes in last pair: already struggling whn mstke 8th: sn t.o and eased* **16/1**

5 *99* **Synchronicity (IRE)**[11] 759 6-10-12 114..........(tp) PaulMoloney
(C Byrnes, Ire) *cl up tl rdn bef 7th: sn last and bdly t.o but hacked on: fin lame bhd* **4/1[3]**

4m 40.4s (-21.40) **Going Correction** -0.95s/f (Hard) **5** Ran SP% **110.5**
Speed ratings: **107,104,104,74,32**
CSF £26.26 TOTE £7.80: £3.70, £1.70; EX 25.30 Trifecta £61.90.There was no bid for the winner.
Owner Gethyn Mills **Bred** John Connaughton **Trained** Fochriw, Caerphilly

FOCUS
A very weak affair. The winner has been rated in line with the best of his summer chase runs, and the second to his mark.

1701 DALEPAK LTD SUPPORTS PAUL'S PLACE NOVICES' H'CAP CHASE (18 fncs) 2m 7f 131y

3:35 (3:35) (Class 3) (0-135,129) 4-Y-0+ **£6,498** (£1,908; £954; £477)

Form RPR

-211 **1** **Ballykan**[21] 1520 5-11-12 **129**..........(t) DarylJacob 139+
(Nigel Twiston-Davies) *j. soundly: led tl after 2nd: settled cl up: wnt 2nd at 10th: led 15th: rdn whn j.rt last: kpt on stoutly flat* **10/3[2]**

415- **2** *2 1/4* **Derrintogher Bliss (IRE)**[193] 4911 6-11-5 **125**..........(p) TomBellamy(3) 131+
(Kim Bailey) *hld up in midfield: effrt 14th: wnt 2nd bef 3 out: sn rdn: 2 l 2nd and hld last but kpt on steadily flat* **3/1[1]**

44-1 **3** *3 1/2* **Kilmurvy (IRE)**[151] 86 7-11-7 **124**..........(tp) NickScholfield 126
(Jeremy Scott) *settled in rr: effrt 14th: wnt 4th bef 3 out: rdn and no real imp after tl tk 3rd at last and styd on pleasingly flat* **12/1**

P30- **4** *1/2* **Flying Eagle (IRE)**[166] 5366 7-11-0 **120**.......... SeanBowen(3) 123
(Peter Bowen) *settled towards rr: effrt 14th: wnt 3rd bef 3 out: sn rdn and no imp: lost one pce 3rd at last* **8/1**

2251 **5** *4 1/2* **Set List (IRE)**[22] 1504 6-11-8 **125**.......... AidanColeman 123
(Emma Lavelle) *last trio most of way: sme prog 14th: rdn and nt trble ldrs fr 3 out* **6/1[3]**

5222 **6** *26* **Mac Bertie**[34] 1377 6-10-6 **109**.......... AdamWedge 83
(Evan Williams) *led after 2nd: rdn and hdd 15th: dropped out v tamely: t.o and eased* **16/1**

2321 **7** *3 3/4* **Volcanic (FR)**[32] 1401 6-11-10 **127**..........(t) WayneHutchinson 98
(Donald McCain) *wore earplugs: pressed ldr tl mstke 9th: dropped himself out v qckly: lost tch bef 14th: sn t.o* **14/1**

3140 **P** **Commitment**[45] 1268 6-11-5 **122**.......... NoelFehily
(Neil Mulholland) *j.rt and nvr travelling in last: rdn bef 8th: t.o and p.u 12th* **10/1**

-411 **P** **Mortlestown (IRE)**[77] 1005 7-11-4 **121**..........(p) AndrewTinkler
(Martin Keighley) *settled towards rr: effrt 13th: 3rd briefly home turn: rdn and wknd 15th: t.o and p.u last* **9/1**

601- **U** **Ivy Gate (IRE)**[229] 4214 7-11-4 **121**.......... RichieMcLernon
(Jonjo O'Neill) *pckd 11th: cl up tl blnd and nrly fell and uns rdr 14th* **33/1**

5m 48.3s (-33.70) **Going Correction** -1.20s/f (Hard) **10** Ran SP% **115.7**
Speed ratings (Par 107): **108,107,106,105,104 95,94, ,**
CSF £14.24 CT £105.44 TOTE £3.30: £1.50, £1.60, £2.90; EX 14.60 Trifecta £181.80.
Owner Simon Munir & Isaac Souede **Bred** Donhead Stud **Trained** Naunton, Gloucs

FOCUS
They got sorted out from the fifth-last in this fair novice handicap and the form looks decent. The second has been rated to the best of his hurdle form, while the third helps set the level.

1702 LOCAL PARKING SECURITY LTD SUPPORTS PAUL'S PLACE H'CAP HURDLE (8 hdls) 2m 11y

4:10 (4:10) (Class 5) (0-100,98) 3-Y-0+ **£2,274** (£667; £333; £166)

Form RPR

40-P **1** **Sadma**[142] 241 6-11-2 **95**.......... WilliamFeatherstone(7) 100+
(Nick Lampard) *cl up: wnt 2nd 3 out: abt 2 l bhd and rdn whn lft in ld 2 out: jnd briefly and idling last: sn wnt over one l clr: all out but hld on wl flat* **8/1**

-053 **2** *3/4* **Taste The Wine (IRE)**[10] 1600 9-11-5 **98**..........(t) JordanWilliams(7) 101
(Bernard Llewellyn) *midfield: rdn 4th: sn dropped towards rr: 7th at next: hrd drvn and styd on after melee 2 out: snatched 2nd but no real danger to wnr* **3/1[1]**

-F00 **3** *nk* **Drummond**[12] 1578 6-10-0 **72** oh5 ow3.......... RobertWilliams(3) 79
(Katie Stephens) *last pair tl rdn and prog bef 5th: lft 2nd 2 out: urged upsides wnr whn hit last: no ex flat: lost 2nd cl home* **12/1**

500- **4** *3/4* **Haverstock**[174] 5243 5-11-1 **87**..........(p) IanPopham 90
(Caroline Keevil) *chsd ldrs: rdn 3 out: hmpd next: no imp between last two* **8/1**

-P05 **5** *28* **Laughingalltheway**[41] 1295 4-10-5 **77**..........(b1) AndrewTinkler 54
(Martin Keighley) *t.k.h: 2nd or 3rd tl rdn and fdd bef 5th: wl btn whn hmpd 2 out* **20/1**

0/0- **6** *23* **Peak Storm**[15] 1672 6-11-3 **89**.......... DaveCrosse 45
(John O'Shea) *cl up tl rdn 4th: no rspnse: wl bhd next: blnd 3 out: t.o* **11/2[3]**

B **Percys Choice (IRE)**[117] 629 7-11-1 **94**.......... MrStanSheppard(7) 97
(Matt Sheppard) *t.k.h: led bef 2nd tl rdn and hdd 5th: disputing btn 3rd whn b.d 2 out* **4/1[2]**

0PP3 **F** **Oscar Jane (IRE)**[12] 1578 8-10-0 **72**..........(bt) AlainCawley 77+
(Johnny Farrelly) *led tl bef 2nd: prom tl led again 5th: hit next: abt 2 l clr and probably gng best whn fell 2 out* **6/1**

0-P **P** **Columbanus (IRE)**[66] 1115 4-10-3 **75**..........(b) TomScudamore
(Kevin Bishop) *last pair: blnd 3rd: sn struggling: t.o and p.u 2 out* **14/1**

3m 53.0s (-17.60) **Going Correction** -0.95s/f (Hard)
WFA 4 from 5yo+ 11lb **9** Ran SP% **116.0**
Speed ratings (Par 103): **106,105,105,105,91 79, ,**
CSF £33.18 CT £291.15 TOTE £8.60: £2.90, £1.90, £3.70; EX 46.20 Trifecta £297.90.
Owner Just A Bit Of Fun **Bred** Darley **Trained** Clatford, Wilts

FOCUS
A moderate handicap which saw drama at the second-last and produced a bunched four-way finish. The third and fourth help set the level.

1703 PAUL'S PLACE H'CAP CHASE (12 fncs) 2m 11y

4:40 (4:40) (Class 4) (0-105,105) 4-Y-0+ **£3,768** (£1,106; £553; £276)

Form RPR

6022 **1** **My Nosy Rosy**[16] 1548 7-10-10 **89**..........(tp) DarylJacob 103+
(Ben Case) *qckly wnt 2nd fr 3rd tl 5th and again 7th: led gng wl 9th: mstke next: asserted last: idling and drvn rt out whn clr flat* **10/1**

-323 **2** *6* **Maizy Missile (IRE)**[10] 1603 13-10-5 **84**.......... PaulMoloney 94
(Mary Evans) *prom: j. soundly: pressed wnr fr 9th: drvn and nt qckn bef last: kpt on gamely although wl hld flat* **10/1**

0432 **3** *5* **Battlecat**[16] 1595 8-11-6 **104**.......... ConorRing(5) 110
(Evan Williams) *wnt 2nd at 5th tl blnd next: lost pl and mstke 7th: mod 4th at 9th: nt trble ldrs after but tk 3rd after last* **3/1[2]**

4211 **4** *3/4* **Going Nowhere Fast (IRE)**[10] 1603 10-11-0 **96** 7ex. RobertWilliams(3) 104+
(Bernard Llewellyn) *hld up last: effrt whn blnd 8th: rdr unbalanced briefly and nvr rcvrd: drvn into mod 3rd fr 2 out tl blnd again last* **6/1[3]**

5433 **5** *3 3/4* **Accessallareas (IRE)**[16] 1548 10-10-10 **89**..........(tp) RichardJohnson 90+
(Sarah-Jayne Davies) *led: rdn and hdd and nt fluent 9th: mstke next: 4th and wl btn 2 out* **10/1**

4P55 **6** *47* **Stafford Charlie**[28] 1237 9-10-0 **79** oh12.......... DaveCrosse 36
(John O'Shea) *chsd ldrs tl drvn after 7th: t.o next and jumping v erratically after* **66/1**

4-4 **P** **Giant O Murchu (IRE)**[68] 1099 11-11-12 **105**.......... SamTwiston-Davies
(John Upson) *j. slowly 2nd: nt fluent 5th and sn struggling in rr: bdly t.o after 7th: p.u next* **25/1**

0- **F** **Not For You (IRE)**[473] 695 7-10-11 **90**..........(t) PaddyBrennan
(C Byrnes, Ire) *fell 1st* **11/8[1]**

3m 56.0s (-21.10) **Going Correction** -1.20s/f (Hard) **8** Ran SP% **114.0**
Speed ratings (Par 105): **104,101,98,98,96 72, ,**
CSF £97.92 CT £373.87 TOTE £8.70: £2.70, £2.50, £1.30; EX 74.60 Trifecta £297.90.
Owner Case Racing Partnership **Bred** Ian Low **Trained** Edgcote, Northants

FOCUS
This lost plenty of its interest due to the first-fence faller. A big chase pb from the winner, with the second and third rated close to form.

1704 PAUL'S PLACE STANDARD NATIONAL HUNT FLAT RACE (CONDITIONALS & AMATEURS) 2m 11y

5:10 (5:10) (Class 6) 4-6-Y-0 **£1,559** (£457; £228; £114)

Form RPR

54- **1** **Fact Of The Matter (IRE)**[166] 5373 5-10-13 0..........(t) SeanBowen(3) 113+
(Jamie Snowden) *2nd tl led 1/2-way: clr w rdr taking it v easily over 1f out: shkn up ins fnl f but a wl in command and eased again cl home* **3/1[2]**

2 *1 1/2* **Desert Retreat (IRE)** 4-10-9 0.......... MrSeanHoulihan(7) 111+
(Philip Hobbs) *bhd and running green: rn v wd first turn: 12 l 3rd and rdn and outpcd home turn: stuck to task wl fr over 1f out and wnt 2nd ins fnl f: flattered by proximity to wnr* **5/1[3]**

3 *7* **Petethepear (IRE)**[139] 312 5-10-13 0.......... TomBellamy(3) 105
(Stuart Edmunds) *cl up and t.k.h: wnt 2nd 1/2-way: drew clr w wnr 6f out but on and off bridle: hrd drvn 3f out: outpcd 2f out: lost 2nd ins fnl f* **5/6[1]**

0-5 **4** *4* **Run Bob Run**[25] 1484 4-10-9 0.......... CiaranGethings(7) 100
(John Flint) *midfield: 15 l 4th and rdn home turn: one pce and no threat fnl 3f* **12/1**

5 *22* **Lady Cardinal (IRE)** 4-10-6 0.......... ThomasGarner(3) 73
(Mark Usher) *midfield: rdn and lost tch 6f out: t.o fnl 3f* **25/1**

00 **6** *24* **Gentle Nature**[25] 1484 4-10-13 0.......... ConorShoemark(3) 59
(John Flint) *t.k.h in last pl: lost tch 7f out: bdly t.o fnl 5f* **66/1**

7 *6* **Minmore Grey (IRE)**[158] 6-10-9 0.......... WilliamFeatherstone(7) 53
(Nick Lampard) *tall rngy: led at stdy pce tl 1/2-way: bdly t.o fnl 6f* **25/1**

3m 46.2s (-18.80) **Going Correction** -0.95s/f (Hard) **7** Ran SP% **113.1**
Speed ratings: **109,108,104,102,91 79,76**
CSF £17.56 TOTE £4.00: £1.50, £2.10; EX 12.90 Trifecta £33.00.
Owner The Sandylini Racing Partnership **Bred** Gabriel Fahy **Trained** Lambourn, Berks

FOCUS
A modest little bumper, rated around the winner. A big step up from the winner.
T/Plt: £87.70 to a £1 stake. Pool: £73,274.62 - 609.27 winning tickets T/Qpdt: £29.90 to a £1 stake. Pool: £4,934.81 - 122.00 winning tickets **Iain Mackenzie**

1705 - 1711a (Foreign Racing) - See Raceform Interactive

1305 BANGOR-ON-DEE (L-H)
Thursday, October 1

OFFICIAL GOING: Good (6.8)
Wind: Light, half against Weather: Sunny

1712 RED DOOR BAR CHESTER & LIVERPOOL JUVENILE HURDLE (9 hdls) 2m 145y
2:20 (2:20) (Class 4) 3-Y-O **£3,898** (£1,144; £572; £286)

Form RPR
21 **1** **Paddys Runner**^{11} [1593] 3-11-5 0 WayneHutchinson 108+
(Alan King) *chsd ldrs: shkn up to ld 3 out: rdn appr 2 out and pressed: mstke last: drvn out and kpt on* **8/13**^{1}

4 **2** 1 1/4 **Impulsive American**^{8} [1631] 3-10-12 0 (t) TomScudamore 100+
(David Pipe) *hld up: racd keenly: hdwy appr 3 out where ev ch and nt fluent: wnt 2nd bef 2 out and chalng: nt qckn bef last where nt fluent: a hld run-in* **11/4**^{2}

62 **3** 7 **Chic Name (FR)**^{29} [1452] 3-10-12 105 (p) AlainCawley 93
(Richard Hobson) *chsd ldr: rdn appr 4 out: lost 2nd bef 3 out: btn and wl outpcd sn after flight: tk mod 3rd last: no imp on front two* **16/1**

23 **4** 9 **Our Kylie (IRE)**^{31} [1415] 3-10-5 0 (p) DenisO'Regan 79
(Tony Coyle) *led: blnd and hdd 3 out: wknd appr 2 out: eased whn wl btn towards fin* **12/1**^{3}

P **Aussie Berry (IRE)**^{68} 3-10-12 0 (t) BrianHarding
(Donald McCain) *in rr: reminder after 3rd: rdn after 4th: lost tch 5th: t.o whn p.u after 3 out* **22/1**

4m 6.1s (-4.80) **Going Correction** -0.325s/f (Good) **5 Ran SP% 106.5**
Speed ratings (Par 103): **98,97,94,89,**
CSF £2.41 TOTE £1.40: £1.10, £1.10; EX 2.60 Trifecta £9.00.
Owner Let's Live Racing **Bred** Miss K Rausing **Trained** Barbury Castle, Wilts

FOCUS
Races 1, 3 5, & 6 increased by 44yds, race 2 reduced by 8yds, and race 4 reduced by 5yds. The opening contest was an ordinary juvenile hurdle. They went an even gallop on good ground. The winner set a fair standard and has been rated similar to his previous best, with small steps up from the second and third.

1713 MALISE NICOLSON NOVICES' CHASE (FOR THE CROSS FOXES TROPHY) (18 fncs) 3m 30y
2:50 (2:50) (Class 4) 4-Y-0+ **£5,198** (£1,526; £763)

Form RPR
1241 **1** **Weather Babe**^{69} [1097] 7-10-12 133 (tp) TomScudamore 132+
(David Pipe) *chsd ldr: pushed along appr 13th: last u.p but stl cl up bef 3 out: bmpd 2 out: rallied to ld last: styd on run-in* **11/8**^{1}

-112 **2** 1 1/2 **Silver Man**^{95} [855] 8-11-11 137 (b) NicodeBoinville 145+
(Jo Hughes) *led: mstke 7th: blnd 11th: hrd pressed fr 3 out: rdn appr 2 out: hdd last: no ex fnl 75yds* **7/4**^{2}

1 **3** 20 **Dabinett Moon**^{125} [531] 7-10-5 0 MissCVHart$^{(7)}$ 119
(Charlie Longsdon) *in rr early: mainly disp 2nd fr 4th: chalng fr appr 3 out: bmpd 2 out: dropped to last pl between last 2: wknd after last: sn eased whn wl btn* **11/4**^{3}

6m 3.4s (-16.40) **Going Correction** -0.40s/f (Good) **3 Ran SP% 105.1**
Speed ratings (Par 105): **111,110,103**
CSF £3.90 TOTE £2.00; EX 1.90 Trifecta £2.60.
Owner Wayne Clifford **Bred** Mrs S Clifford **Trained** Nicholashayne, Devon

FOCUS
A fairly decent little novice chase. They went an honest gallop. The winner has been rated to her mark, with the runner-up posting a pb.

1714 DEVA RACING H'CAP HURDLE (9 hdls) 2m 145y
3:25 (3:26) (Class 4) (0-115,115) 3-Y-O+ **£4,223** (£1,240; £620; £310)

Form RPR
40P2 **1** **Stormbay Bomber (IRE)**^{29} [1446] 6-10-5 94 RichieMcLernon 104+
(George Moore) *mde all: drew clr appr last: styd on wl* **6/1**^{3}

0-12 **2** 3 1/4 **Triple Eight (IRE)**^{11} [1604] 7-9-12 90 AdamNicol$^{(3)}$ 97
(Philip Kirby) *midfield: hdwy after 3 out: wnt 2nd 2 out: no imp on wnr* **10/3**^{2}

4441 **3** 9 **Prince Khurram**^{35} [1366] 5-11-5 113 (t) JamesCowley$^{(5)}$ 112
(Donald McCain) *chsd wnr: rdn appr 2 out: sn lost 2nd: kpt on same pce after* **6/1**^{3}

6F61 **4** 4 **Polstar (FR)**^{31} [1421] 6-11-2 112 PaulNO'Brien$^{(7)}$ 107
(Harry Whittington) *chsd ldrs: rdn and wknd 2 out* **3/1**^{1}

5/3- **5** shd **Orthodox Lad**^{508} [213] 7-10-12 108 CiaranGethings$^{(7)}$ 102
(David Rees) *midfield: rdn 2 out: no hdwy* **8/1**

-2P3 **6** nk **Samoset**^{93} [860] 5-11-7 110 (t) KielanWoods 104
(Graeme McPherson) *chsd ldrs: rdn after 2 out: sn btn* **12/1**

-0 **7** 15 **Maoi Chinn Tire (IRE)**^{6} [1170] 8-11-9 112 (p) PeterCarberry 93
(Jennie Candlish) *hld up: struggling bef 3 out: wl btn* **22/1**

-335 **8** 5 **Falcarragh (IRE)**^{31} [1418] 8-11-7 115 AlanJohns$^{(5)}$ 91
(Tim Vaughan) *hld up: struggling 3 out: wl btn* **7/1**

0-U5 **9** 1 1/4 **Camachoice (IRE)**^{147} [176] 5-11-9 112 DougieCostello 87
(Joanne Foster) *in rr: niggled along after 4th: lft wl bhd bef 3 out* **25/1**

4m 3.1s (-7.80) **Going Correction** -0.325s/f (Good) **9 Ran SP% 116.1**
Speed ratings (Par 105): **105,103,99,97,97 97,90,87,87**
CSF £27.07 CT £126.26 TOTE £7.10: £2.70, £1.80, £2.20; EX 26.90 Trifecta £170.10.
Owner J B Wallwin **Bred** Victoria Crawford **Trained** Middleham Moor, N Yorks

FOCUS
An ordinary handicap hurdle. They went a respectable gallop. A big step up from the winner, with the second to his mark.

1715 BARRINGTONS CLEANING LTD H'CAP CHASE (15 fncs) 2m 4f 72y
4:00 (4:00) (Class 3) (0-140,138) 4-Y-0+ **£6,498** (£1,908; £954; £477)

Form RPR
P-00 **1** **Lost Legend (IRE)**^{40} [1322] 8-11-11 137 (p) RichieMcLernon 153+
(Jonjo O'Neill) *hld up: mstke 6th: hdwy 9th: led 2 out: rdn appr last: styd on wl to draw clr run-in* **8/1**^{3}

33P- **2** 10 **Open Hearted**^{237} [4071] 8-11-12 138 (t) HarrySkelton 144
(Dan Skelton) *in tch: niggled along and lost pl appr 11th: effrt after 4 out: led after 3 out: hdd 2 out: kpt on same pce and no imp run-in* **3/1**^{2}

F211 **3** 4 1/2 **Faustina Pius (IRE)**^{42} [1298] 7-9-12 117 (p) MrStanSheppard$^{(7)}$ 120
(Matt Sheppard) *in rr and sltly detached: hdwy bef 3 out: 2nd and chalng appr 2 out: sn lost 2nd: one pce bef last* **11/1**

-310 **4** 6 **Carrigmorna King (IRE)**^{75} [1040] 9-11-12 138 (t) MichealNolan 135
(Philip Hobbs) *chsd ldr fr 2nd tl mstke 9th: remained handy: rdn and lost pl after 3 out: u.p and n.d after* **17/2**

5532 **5** 1 3/4 **Witness In Court (IRE)**^{35} [1382] 8-11-12 138 WayneHutchinson 134
(Donald McCain) *racd keenly: prom: blnd 8th: chsd ldr after 9th tl 11th: wknd after 3 out* **10/1**

21 **6** 7 **Valadom (FR)**^{6} [1641] 6-10-8 120 7ex AlainCawley 110
(Richard Hobson) *led: rdn and hdd after 3 out: wknd appr 2 out* **11/10**^{1}

4m 55.7s (-13.40) **Going Correction** -0.40s/f (Good) **6 Ran SP% 111.7**
Speed ratings (Par 107): **110,106,104,101,101 98**
CSF £32.14 TOTE £9.40: £3.40, £1.70; EX 43.30 Trifecta £246.10.
Owner Mrs Gay Smith **Bred** Highfort Stud **Trained** Cheltenham, Gloucs

FOCUS
The feature contest was a fairly good handicap chase. They went a searching gallop. A big pb from the winner, with the second close to his mark.

1716 LG BLOODSTOCK MARES' NOVICES' HURDLE (11 hdls) 2m 3f 123y
4:30 (4:30) (Class 4) 4-Y-O+ **£3,898** (£1,144; £572; £286)

Form RPR
3 **1** **Miss Tiger Lily**^{23} [1506] 5-10-10 0 BrendanPowell 111+
(Jamie Snowden) *racd keenly: mde all: mstke 1st: rdn appr last: readily drew clr run-in* **10/1**

3413 **2** 8 **Flower Power**^{35} [1374] 4-11-3 115 DenisO'Regan 110
(Tony Coyle) *chsd ldrs: lost pl briefly after 3 out: sn rallied: wnt 2nd bef 2 out: trying to chal whn dived 2 out: nt qckn bef last: no ch run-in* **11/2**^{3}

4F **3** 3 1/2 **Impeccability**^{137} [361] 5-10-10 0 (p) HenryBrooke 98
(John Mackie) *hld up: pushed along after 3 out: swtchd rt and hdwy appr 2 out: wnt 3rd last: kpt on but no real imp* **100/1**

2 **4** 7 **Tahira (GER)**^{67} [1109] 5-10-10 0 BrianHughes 93
(Kevin Frost) *midfield: swtchd rt and hdwy appr 3 out: rdn and no imp on ldrs bef 2 out: wknd bef last: fin 5th: plcd 4th* **7/4**^{1}

-016 **5** 2 1/4 **All Riled Up**^{42} [1297] 7-10-5 81 DanielHiskett$^{(5)}$ 88
(Harry Chisman) *racd in 2nd pl: w wnr 4th and 5th: pushed along appr 4 out: lost 2nd bef 2 out: sn wknd: fin 6th: plcd 5th* **50/1**

52 **6** 12 **Midnight Gem**^{112} [696] 5-10-10 0 WayneHutchinson 76
(Charlie Longsdon) *racd keenly: chsd ldrs: rdn appr 3 out: wknd bef 2 out: fin 7th: plcd 6th* **7/1**

0 **7** 9 **Kilty Caul (IRE)**^{148} [152] 6-10-7 0 TomBellamy$^{(3)}$ 67
(Kim Bailey) *in rr: niggled along appr 4 out: nvr a threat: fin 8th: plcd to 7th* **16/1**

4-5 **8** 56 **Omgnotanother (IRE)**^{148} [152] 4-10-10 0 AdamWedge 11
(Evan Williams) *hld up: niggled along after 6th: struggling whn mstke 4 out: t.o: fin 9th: plcd 8th* **66/1**

3-11 **D** 1 1/4 **Native Princess**^{37} [1352] 5-11-3 0 PaddyBrennan 104
(Stuart Edmunds) *mstkes: midfield: hdwy and effrt appr 2 out: sn chsd ldrs: one pce bef last where lost 3rd: no imp after: fin 4th: disqualified and plcd last: jockey failed to draw correct weight* **9/4**^{2}

4m 50.2s (-1.80) **Going Correction** -0.325s/f (Good) **9 Ran SP% 114.4**
Speed ratings (Par 105): **90,86,85,82,81 76,72,50,84**
CSF £63.17 TOTE £11.90: £2.00, £1.50, £11.90; EX 39.40 Trifecta £930.30.
Owner Mr & Mrs D Hearson **Bred** Granham Farm Partnership **Trained** Lambourn, Berks

FOCUS
A fair mares' novices' hurdle. They went an, at best, respectable gallop. A big step up from the winner, with the second, fifth and sixth setting the level.

1717 STELLA ARTOIS STANDARD NATIONAL HUNT FLAT RACE (CONDITIONALS & AMATEURS) 2m 145y
5:05 (5:06) (Class 6) 4-6-Y-O **£2,395** (£698; £349)

Form RPR
1 **Loch Garman Aris (IRE)**^{139} 5-10-13 0 NickSlatter$^{(5)}$ 95
(Gary Hanmer) *chsd ldrs: rdn over 2f out: big effrt over 1f out: rn green: r.o to ld towards fin* **10/1**

2 1/2 **Tanarpino**^{179} 4-10-13 0 NathanMoscrop$^{(5)}$ 95
(Jennie Candlish) *chsd ldrs: wnt 2nd 9f out: rdn to ld 2f out: hrd pressed fnl f: hdd towards fin* **6/4**^{1}

3 3 1/4 **Nampararoo** 6-10-6 0 JakeHodson$^{(5)}$ 85
(David Bridgwater) *hit rail s and slowly away: in rr: hdwy 4f out: chsd ldrs over 2f out: rdn and stl cl up over 1f out: nt qckn: kpt on same pce after* **16/1**

4 4 **Kilronan Castle**^{158} 4-10-13 0 JamesCowley$^{(5)}$ 88
(Donald McCain) *led: rdn over 3f out: hdd 2f out: wknd 1f out* **3/1**^{3}

-0 **5** 28 **Bestwork (FR)**^{146} [187] 4-11-1 0 SeanBowen$^{(3)}$ 63
(Charlie Longsdon) *hld up: pushed along 5f out: rdn 4f out: dropped away* **11/4**^{2}

6 **F** **Golden Feet**^{78} [1003] 4-10-13 0 (t) AlanJohns$^{(5)}$
(Tim Vaughan) *chsd ldr to 9f out: wknd over 3f out: fell over 2f out* **12/1**

4m 0.8s (-4.50) **Going Correction** -0.325s/f (Good) **6 Ran SP% 114.3**
Speed ratings: **97,96,95,93,80**
CSF £26.32 TOTE £10.00: £5.60, £1.30; EX 35.10 Trifecta £247.10.
Owner George Brookes **Bred** M Bolger & J Lazenby **Trained** Nantwich, Cheshire

FOCUS
The concluding contest was a modest bumper restricted to conditional and amateur riders. They went a respectable gallop. Ordinary form.
T/Plt: £291.70 to a £1 stake. Pool of £43685.10 - 109.31 winning tickets. T/Qpdt: £81.30 to a £1 stake. Pool of £2842.80 - 25.85 winning tickets. **Darren Owen**

1612 WARWICK (L-H)
Thursday, October 1

OFFICIAL GOING: Good
Wind: Light against Weather: Fine

1718 IGNITE INCENTIVES "NATIONAL HUNT" NOVICES' HURDLE (8 hdls) 2m
2:10 (2:12) (Class 4) 4-Y-O+ **£3,249** (£954; £477; £238)

Form RPR
2412 **1** **Canicallyouback**^{9} [1612] 7-11-5 121 PaulMoloney 119+
(Evan Williams) *mde all: shkn up appr last: drvn out: idled towards fin* **11/8**^{1}

2- **2** nk **Abbreviate (GER)**^{178} [5200] 4-10-12 0 DavidBass 112+
(Kim Bailey) *trckd ldrs: hit 1st: nt fluent 3rd: ev ch whn hit 2 out: rdn and edgd rt appr last: fin u.p* **9/4**^{2}

00/ **3** 3 ½ **Valseur Du Granval (FR)**[658] 3034 6-10-12 0.....(t) SamTwiston-Davies 108
(Tom George) *chsd ldrs: rdn appr last: styd on same pce flat* **16/1**

6/25 **4** 1 ½ **Jazz Thyme (IRE)**[35] 1374 6-10-5 0.............................. TomO'Brien 98
(Robert Stephens) *a.p: racd keenly: shkn up after 2 out: hung rt and no ex flat* **13/2**[3]

/60- **5** 14 **Palermo Don**[180] 5143 5-10-12 0.............................(t) NoelFehily 92
(Donald McCain) *hld up: hdwy 3 out: wknd next* **20/1**

50 **6** ¾ **The Mythologist (IRE)**[17] 1544 7-10-12 0.......................... MichaelByrne 90
(Tim Vaughan) *hld up: hdwy after 3rd: rdn and wknd after 3 out* **50/1**

7 2 ¾ **Inchiquin All Star (IRE)**[193] 5-10-12 0.................. RichardJohnson 89
(Tim Vaughan) *w wnr tl rdn after 3 out: wknd bef next* **9/1**

8 19 **Gentle Mel (IRE)**[124] 7-10-5 0.............................. CharliePoste 62
(Anabel K Murphy) *hld up: bhd fr 4th* **66/1**

6 **P** **Christmas Twenty (IRE)**[29] 1449 5-10-12 0.................. JoshuaMoore
(Stuart Edmunds) *unruly to post: mid-div: wknd after 3rd: bhd whn p.u bef next* **20/1**

3m 43.7s (-15.30) **Going Correction** -1.075s/f (Hard)
WFA 4 from 5yo+ 9lb **9** Ran SP% **115.1**
Speed ratings (Par 105): **95,94,93,92,85 84,83,74,**
CSF £4.47 TOTE £2.20: £1.30, £1.50, £3.40; EX 5.40 Trifecta £38.80.
Owner Mrs D E Cheshire **Bred** Charles And David Hodge **Trained** Llancarfan, Vale Of Glamorgan

FOCUS
Some starts have been moved at this track following remeasuring, so some races will not have speed figures until there is sufficient data to calculate updated median times. All hurdle races were run on the inner course. Those who rode in the opener said the ground was riding beautifully. An ordinary novice hurdle that was fought out by the two market leaders. The winner set a fair standard and has been rated close to his mark, while the fourth and sixth help set the level.

1719 2015 DEALER PRINCIPAL EVENT H'CAP HURDLE (8 hdls) 2m
2:40 (2:41) (Class 3) (0-130,127) 3-Y-0+ **£6,498** (£1,908; £954; £477)

Form RPR

05-0 **1** **Satanic Beat (IRE)**[32] 638 6-11-9 **127**.......................... ConorShoemark(3) 132+
(Phil Middleton) *hld up: hdwy 3 out: nt clr run bef next: led last: rdn out* **7/1**

F52 **2** ½ **Watt Broderick (IRE)**[23] 1508 6-10-8 **109**.......................(t) WillKennedy 113
(Ian Williams) *a.p: ev ch fr 2 out: styd on u.p* **11/4**[1]

332 **3** 3 ½ **Hawdyerwheesht**[17] 1549 7-10-12 **120**.....................(tp) JamieBargary(7) 121
(David Dennis) *led: rdn appr 2 out: hdd last: styd on same pce flat* **8/1**

32-2 **4** 8 **Desert Recluse (IRE)**[35] 1381 8-11-8 **123**........................ JamesDavies 118
(Henry Oliver) *chsd ldr tl rdn and hmpd appr 2 out: wknd bef last* **7/2**[2]

32F- **5** ¾ **Dormouse**[164] 5427 10-11-3 **118**..............................(p) CharliePoste 111
(Anabel K Murphy) *hld up: sme hdwy after 3 out: wknd bef next* **20/1**

4F0- **6** hd **Here's Herbie**[229] 4231 7-11-1 **119**.......................... LucyGardner(3) 112
(Sue Gardner) *hld up: pushed along and outpcd after 3 out: n.d after* **14/1**

1140 **7** 1 **Zarzal (IRE)**[75] 1035 7-11-2 **124**.............................. MrConorOrr(7) 116
(Evan Williams) *hld up: mstke 5th: sn pushed along: wknd after 3 out* **5/1**[3]

4-01 **8** 15 **Cusheen Bridge (IRE)**[35] 1377 7-11-7 **122**.....................(t) AdamPogson 100
(Charles Pogson) *chsd ldrs tl wknd appr 2 out* **8/1**

3m 38.6s (-20.40) **Going Correction** -1.075s/f (Hard) **8** Ran SP% **111.7**
Speed ratings (Par 107): **108,107,106,102,101 101,101,93**
CSF £25.97 CT £154.42 TOTE £8.90: £2.30, £1.40, £2.00; EX 35.50 Trifecta £275.20.
Owner P W Middleton **Bred** Patrick Gleeson **Trained** Dorton, Bucks

FOCUS
The front pair came away on the flat in what was a modest handicap. The first two have been rated pretty much to their marks.

1720 HAGUE PRINT MANAGEMENT H'CAP CHASE (17 fncs) 2m 4f
3:15 (3:15) (Class 4) (0-110,110) 5-Y-0+ **£3,898** (£1,144; £572; £286)

Form RPR

/P42 **1** **Badgers Retreat**[9] 1614 9-10-10 **94**.............................. GavinSheehan 103+
(Nick Mitchell) *led to 3rd: chsd ldrs: wnt 2nd 11th: blnd next: led 3 out: sn rdn: hdd briefly gng to the last: edgd rt flat: styd on gamely* **11/8**[1]

4P4- **2** 1 ¾ **Handsome Buddy (IRE)**[230] 4203 8-10-5 **96**..............(v) MikeyHamill(7) 102+
(Michael Gates) *hld up: hmpd 2nd: hdwy bef 11th: chsd wnr appr 2 out: sn ev ch: led briefly gng to the last: styd on same pce flat* **9/2**[3]

4/5F **3** 33 **Koup De Kanon (FR)**[24] 1494 9-11-12 **110**........................ NoelFehily 84
(Donald McCain) *hld up: hdwy 6th: mstke 12th: rdn and wknd appr 2 out* **14/1**

3-41 **4** ½ **Jackthejourneyman (IRE)**[31] 1422 6-11-9 **107**.................(t) JamesDavies 81
(Tom Gretton) *w ldr tl led 3rd: reminder after 10th: hdd 3 out: sn rdn: wknd bef next* **4/1**[2]

4U4- **5** 5 **Kapricorne (FR)**[189] 4992 8-10-5 **92**........................(t) KillianMoore(3) 61
(Sophie Leech) *hld up and bhd: j.lft 2nd: nvr on terms* **6/1**

-624 **6** 1 ½ **Try Catch Me (IRE)**[37] 1353 10-11-5 **103**.....................(b) LeightonAspell 71
(Alison Batchelor) *w ldr: mstke 5th: nt fluent 8th: lost pl 11th: wknd 13th* **14/1**

6UPP **7** 15 **Mostly Bob (IRE)**[17] 1545 12-11-4 **102**.......................(vt) JamesBest 56
(Sophie Leech) *chsd ldrs: lost pl 3rd: sn drvn along: bhd fr 6th: j.rt fr 10th* **33/1**

4m 56.6s (-21.40) **Going Correction** -1.50s/f (Hard) **7** Ran SP% **110.8**
Speed ratings: **82,81,68,67,65 65,59**
CSF £7.81 TOTE £2.40: £1.50, £3.20; EX 10.50 Trifecta £75.40.
Owner Miss R J Thomas & Miss R S Savage **Bred** Wood Farm Stud **Trained** Piddletrenthide, Dorset

FOCUS
Modest chasing form. The front pair came well clear.

1721 KEN MUIR MEMORIAL H'CAP HURDLE (11 hdls) 2m 5f
3:50 (3:50) (Class 4) (0-115,115) 3-Y-0+ **£3,249** (£954; £477; £238)

Form RPR

P-45 **1** **Bayley's Dream**[108] 746 6-10-11 **100**.......................... LiamTreadwell 108
(Paul Webber) *a.p: led after 3 out: rdn out* **6/1**[3]

6P2- **2** nk **Shadarpour (IRE)**[174] 5258 6-11-2 **115**............ WilliamFeatherstone(10) 123
(Alan King) *hld up: hdwy 3 out: rdn to chse ldr appr last: ev ch flat: styd on* **10/3**[2]

2 **3** 10 **Top Spin (IRE)**[47] 1265 8-11-7 **110**..........................(t) RichardJohnson 112
(Jonjo O'Neill) *hld up: hmpd 8th: hdwy 3 out: ev ch bef 2 out: sn rdn: wknd flat* **13/8**[1]

331 **4** 13 **Over The Air**[29] 1455 7-11-9 **112**.............................. JamieMoore 99
(John Spearing) *chsd ldrs tl led 5th: hdd bef next: led again 7th: rdn and hdd after 3 out: wkng whn blnd next* **9/1**

200 **5** 5 **Only Gorgeous (IRE)**[40] 1324 6-10-13 **105**..................... LucyGardner(3) 90
(Sue Gardner) *chsd ldrs: ev ch after 3 out: wkng whn hit next* **12/1**

12F- **6** 5 **Full Ov Beans**[230] 4204 11-10-5 **101**.......................... MikeyHamill(7) 79
(Michael Gates) *hld up: wknd bef 3 out* **12/1**

4432 **F** **Almagest**[42] 1295 7-10-13 **102**................................(tp) RhysFlint
(Robert Stephens) *led to 5th: led again bef next: hdd 7th: w ldr whn fell next* **8/1**

4m 55.8s (-25.20) **Going Correction** -1.075s/f (Hard) **7** Ran SP% **112.0**
Speed ratings (Par 105): **105,104,101,96,94 92,**
CSF £25.51 CT £46.22 TOTE £6.60: £2.00, £2.20; EX 27.30 Trifecta £90.20.
Owner The Sweep Stakes Partnership **Bred** E E Williams **Trained** Mollington, Oxon

FOCUS
Modest form. The third is well treated on the best of his Irish form but has only been rated in line with his recent Market Rasen run.

1722 COLLIERS INTERNATIONAL RATING DIVISION H'CAP CHASE (18 fncs) 3m
4:20 (4:21) (Class 3) (0-135,134) 5-Y-0+ **£6,498** (£1,908; £954; £477)

Form RPR

1212 **1** **Urcalin (FR)**[29] 1445 7-11-3 **125**................................(t) TomCannon 137+
(David Arbuthnot) *chsd ldrs: lost pl after 1st: hdwy 6th: chsd ldr 13th: led appr 2 out: clr bef last: eased nr fin* **9/1**

104- **2** 5 **Horatio Hornblower (IRE)**[195] 4884 7-11-3 **125**.... SamTwiston-Davies 130
(Nick Williams) *hld up: hdwy 9th: rdn whn lft 2nd 2 out: styng on same pce whn nt fluent last* **10/3**[3]

P312 **3** 1 ¼ **American Legend (IRE)**[43] 1288 7-10-12 **120**..........(v) RichardJohnson 125
(Jonjo O'Neill) *hld up: drvn along and hdwy 15th: styd on same pce last* **11/4**[1]

41P6 **4** 34 **Perfect Timing**[40] 1322 7-11-5 **127**..............................(b) NoelFehily 98
(Neil Mulholland) *led to 5th: chsd ldr to 9th: rdn appr 12th: wknd next* **8/1**

25P- **F** **Off The Ground (IRE)**[159] 5536 9-11-12 **134**.................. AidanColeman
(Charlie Longsdon) *trckd ldr after 1st: racd keenly: nt fluent 3rd: led 5th: rdn and jst hdd whn fell 2 out* **3/1**[2]

6-00 **P** **Tales Of Milan (IRE)**[9] 1615 8-10-11 **122**.............(bt) ConorShoemark(3)
(Phil Middleton) *sn prom: chsd ldr 9th: rdn and lost 2nd 13th: wknd 15th: bhd whn p.u bef 2 out* **25/1**

13-0 **P** **Gallery Exhibition (IRE)**[150] 101 8-11-10 **132**..................(t) DavidBass
(Kim Bailey) *trckd ldrs: mstke 6th: lost pl 11th: sn bhd: p.u bef next* **6/1**

5m 52.6s (-41.40) **Going Correction** -1.50s/f (Hard) **7** Ran SP% **114.0**
Speed ratings: **109,107,106,95,**
CSF £39.47 CT £105.20 TOTE £8.70: £3.60, £3.00; EX 41.10 Trifecta £89.90.
Owner A T A Wates & Mrs S Wates **Bred** Bernard-Louis Dutertre **Trained** Beare Green, Surrey

FOCUS
A fair handicap chase with a pair of progressive types coming to the fore. The in-form third has been rated to his mark.

1723 WARWICK RACECOURSE SUPPORTING RACING TO SCHOOL MAIDEN HURDLE (11 hdls) 2m 5f
4:55 (4:55) (Class 4) 4-Y-0+ **£3,249** (£954; £477; £238)

Form RPR

20-2 **1** **Atlantic Gold (IRE)**[146] 185 5-11-0 125.......................... AidanColeman 115+
(Charlie Longsdon) *mde all: pushed clr appr 2 out: comf* **4/9**[1]

1 **2** 5 **Who You For (IRE)**[29] 1449 5-11-0 0.............................. JackQuinlan 109+
(Sarah Humphrey) *chsd wnr: mstke 5th: rdn after 3 out: sn outpcd* **4/1**[2]

2U **3** 1 ¾ **Theatre Goer**[13] 1576 6-10-4 0.............................. JamesBanks(3) 98+
(Noel Williams) *hld up: pushed along and outpcd 7th: hdwy to 3rd appr 2 out: nt trble ldrs* **14/1**

640 **4** 33 **Black Kettle (IRE)**[29] 1449 5-10-11 0.......................... RyanHatch(3) 75
(Ronald Thompson) *hld up: hdwy 8th: rdn and wknd after 3 out* **100/1**

P **Snowmane (IRE)**[44] 4-11-0 0......................................(t) DavidBass
(Kim Bailey) *hld up: tk clsr order 6th: wknd 8th: bhd whn p.u bef 2 out* **13/2**[3]

4m 54.1s (-26.90) **Going Correction** -1.075s/f (Hard)
WFA 4 from 5yo+ 10lb **5** Ran SP% **110.2**
Speed ratings (Par 105): **108,106,105,92,**
CSF £2.75 TOTE £1.50: £1.10, £1.60; EX 2.70 Trifecta £7.30.
Owner C W Booth & Mark E Smith **Bred** Miss Mary Kelly **Trained** Over Norton, Oxon

FOCUS
Little depth to this and the favourite won as expected. The winner set a good standard and has been rated 10lb off his best.
T/Plt: £44.10 to a £1 stake. Pool of £51400.78 - 849.55 winning tickets. T/Qpdt: £19.40 to a £1 stake. Pool of £2847.30 - 108.50 winning tickets. **Colin Roberts**

1724 - 1731a (Foreign Racing) - See Raceform Interactive

1485
FONTWELL (L-H)
Friday, October 2

OFFICIAL GOING: Good (7.0)
Wind: almost nil Weather: hot and sunny; 17 degrees

1732 CHANCELLOR OF THE FORMCHECKER JUVENILE MAIDEN HURDLE (9 hdls) 2m 1f 145y
2:10 (2:10) (Class 4) 3-Y-0 **£3,249** (£954; £477; £238)

Form RPR

1 **Oceane (FR)**[14] 3-10-12 0.............................. WayneHutchinson 108+
(Alan King) *neat: trckd ldng pair gng wl: chal 2 out: sn led: 4 l clr last: pushed out: easily* **4/6**[1]

2 12 **Consortium (IRE)**[8] 3-10-12 0.............................. TrevorWhelan 95
(Neil King) *chsd ldrs: mstke 4th: 5th home turn: rdn and kpt on steadily after: passed two rivals after last to go 2nd fnl 100yds: no ch w wnr* **5/1**[3]

3 3 **Albert Herring**[35] 3-10-12 0.............................. GavinSheehan 91
(Jonathan Portman) *small: cl 2nd tl rdn and upsides ldr 2 out: sn hdd: stl disputing btn 2nd 100yds out: plodded on* **33/1**

3325 **4** nk **Auld Fyffee (IRE)**[35] 1384 3-10-5 97.............................. JamesDavies 84
(Tom Gretton) *slt ld tl rdn and hdd jst after 2 out: stl disputing btn 2nd 100yds out: no ex* **14/1**

2 **5** 8 **Jersey Bull (IRE)**[26] 1486 3-10-12 0.............................. MarcGoldstein 84
(Michael Madgwick) *towards rr: drvn bef 2 out: sn btn* **7/1**

6 27 **Darebin (GER)**[63] 3-10-12 0.............................. JamieMoore 60
(Gary Moore) *tall: str: chsd ldrs tl 4th and drvn home turn: no rspnse and sn dropped out: eased last: t.o* **9/2**[2]

4 **P** **Konnos Bay**[12] 1593 3-10-12 0..............................(p) BrendanPowell
(Brendan Powell) *j.v.slowly 2nd: sn last: drvn bef 6th and continued t.o tl nrly ref next and p.u* **100/1**

P **Our Nipper** 3-10-12 0.............................. TomCannon
(Chris Gordon) *ly: burly: mstke 1st: last whn blnd 2nd and p.u lame* **40/1**

4m 16.1s (-18.20) **Going Correction** -1.25s/f (Hard) **8** Ran SP% **120.4**
Speed ratings (Par 103): **90,84,83,83,79 67,,**
CSF £5.08 TOTE £1.70: £1.10, £1.50, £5.60; EX 6.00 Trifecta £68.20.
Owner McNeill Family **Bred** S C E A Haras De Manneville **Trained** Barbury Castle, Wilts

FOCUS
Good ground, with 5mm of water put on the track on Thursday. Hurdles and fences on the inner line. Rail movements added 24yds to the 2m1f96y chase and 36yds to the 2m5f31yds chase. They went a reasonable gallop in this ordinary juvenile hurdle. Ordinary form rated through the fourth.

1733 WEST SUSSEX VAN CENTRE SUPPLIES WINNER CONDITIONAL JOCKEYS' H'CAP CHASE (19 fncs) 3m 1f 106y
2:40 (2:40) (Class 4) (0-120,120) 4-Y-O+ **£3,768** (£1,106; £553)

Form | | | | RPR
/P-3 **1** **Danimix (IRE)**[32] 1417 10-11-10 **118**....(t) SeanBowen 135+
(Peter Bowen) *nt a fluent: led 6th tl 10th and again 12th: mstke 15th: easily drew clr fr 3 out: eased flat* **1/1**[1]
0422 **2** *7* **Shantou Tiger (IRE)**[23] 1520 6-11-6 **120**.... JamesCowley[(6)] 124
(Donald McCain) *led tl shkn up 6th: led again 10th tl 12th but making several ragged jumps: u.p 16th: 2 l 2nd home turn: sn lft bhd by wnr and all out to hold 2nd* **13/8**[2]
3-U5 **3** *1 ¼* **Ballyvoneen (IRE)**[12] 1592 10-10-7 **104**....(p) LizzieKelly[(3)] 108
(Neil King) *a last: rdn bef 14th: outpcd and mstke next: 4 l 3rd home turn: carried hd awkwardly and plodded on whn no ch w wnr after* **4/1**[3]
6m 49.0s (-12.10) **Going Correction** -0.475s/f (Good) **3** Ran SP% **108.1**
Speed ratings (Par 105): **100,97,97**
CSF £3.00 TOTE £1.90; EX 3.00 Trifecta £1.80.
Owner Steve & Jackie Fleetham **Bred** Brendan Corbett **Trained** Little Newcastle, Pembrokes
FOCUS
A modest handicap for conditionals, run 24sec slower than standard. It's difficult to know what this form is worth but it could be rated up to 3lb higher.

1734 NICOLA COY APPRECIATION SOCIETY BREAKTHROUGH H'CAP HURDLE (9 hdls) 2m 1f 145y
3:15 (3:15) (Class 3) (0-125,119) 3-Y-O **£5,697** (£1,683; £841; £421; £210)

Form | | | | RPR
-411 **1** **Shear Rock (IRE)**[119] 624 5-11-8 **115**.... RichardJohnson 120+
(Charlie Longsdon) *led at decent pce: 12 l clr 3rd: hit 5th: pressed after 3 out: rdn and hdd next: hrd drvn and rallied after last: led fnl 100yds: forged clr* **5/6**[1]
2 *5* **Disputed (IRE)**[45] 1285 5-11-12 **119**.... TomCannon 117
(Chris Gordon) *chsd ldr: clsd after 3 out: led next: sn rdn: over one l clr last: hung rt: hdd 100yds out: sn outpcd* **7/1**[3]
-565 **3** *8* **Lyssio (GER)**[32] 1423 8-9-11 **93** oh10.... SeanBowen[(3)] 85
(Mark Hoad) *taken down early: j. deliberately 2nd: in last pair and hld up tl 1/2-way: on and off bridle after: effrt 3 out: sn rdn w no rspnse: wl hld by ldng pair fr next* **12/1**
4312 **4** *32* **Royal Battalion**[38] 1354 4-11-6 **113**....(p) JamieMoore 75
(Gary Moore) *chsd ldng pair: pushed along 1/2-way: struggling after hitting 3 out: nt run on: t.o whn blnd last* **5/2**[2]
P/P- **5** *6* **Superciliary**[285] 3213 6-11-8 **115**....(t) MarcGoldstein 72
(Chris Gordon) *burly: last pair: t.o after 3 out* **16/1**
4m 13.5s (-20.80) **Going Correction** -1.25s/f (Hard)
WFA 4 from 5yo+ 9lb **5** Ran SP% **109.2**
Speed ratings (Par 107): **96,93,90,76,73**
CSF £6.89 TOTE £1.70: £1.20, £2.20; EX 5.70 Trifecta £25.90.
Owner Jones, Smith & Walsh **Bred** Cyril O'Hara **Trained** Over Norton, Oxon
FOCUS
Not a strong race for the grade. Arguably a small step up from the winner, with the third in line with his recent form.

1735 FULLER'S LONDON PRIDE H'CAP CHASE (13 fncs) 2m 1f 96y
3:50 (3:50) (Class 2) (0-145,145) 4-Y-O+ **£11,818** (£3,567; £1,837; £974)

Form | | | | RPR
3-35 **1** **Workbench (FR)**[41] 1322 7-10-9 **128**....(t) HarrySkelton 142+
(Dan Skelton) *trckd ldng pair: wnt 2nd befor 3 out: led next: sn rdn: 4 l clr last: urged along but in command after* **3/1**[2]
0131 **2** *8* **Purple 'n Gold (IRE)**[7] 1643 6-10-9 **135** 7ex....(p) DavidNoonan[(7)] 142
(David Pipe) *sn cl 2nd: led 10th: rdn and hdd 2 out: outpcd by wnr between last two: plugged on* **7/2**[3]
2112 **3** *25* **Easily Pleased (IRE)**[14] 1577 9-10-0 **122**.... JeremiahMcGrath[(3)] 110
(Martin Hill) *led in s: t.k.h: hld up towards rr: rdn and no rspnse 3 out: poor 3rd fr next* **7/1**
-U24 **4** *16* **Australia Day (IRE)**[48] 1263 12-11-12 **145**.... DenisO'Regan 115
(Paul Webber) *taken down early: led but nt exubernt and kpt jumping markedly rt: hdd 10th: fdd v qckly bef next and sn t.o* **11/1**
1343 **F** **Noble Friend (IRE)**[26] 1488 7-10-3 **122**.... TomCannon
(Chris Gordon) *sn last: lost tch 8th: wl bhd whn fell 3 out* **11/2**
2F4- **U** **Chris Pea Green**[187] 5046 6-11-9 **142**.... JoshuaMoore
(Gary Moore) *cl up: pushed along 7th: nvr looked to be gng wl enough after: nt fluent 8th: disputing btn 4th whn stmbld bdly and uns rdr after 3 out* **11/4**[1]
4m 21.8s (-12.90) **Going Correction** -0.475s/f (Good) **6** Ran SP% **110.1**
Speed ratings (Par 109): **111,107,95,87,**
CSF £13.53 TOTE £3.70: £2.00, £1.90; EX 13.60 Trifecta £66.10.
Owner N W Lake **Bred** M Bernard Le Roux **Trained** Alcester, Warwicks
FOCUS
Quite a valuable handicap chase. The pace was decent and the form should hold up. A pb from the winner, and the form could be rated slightly higher.

1736 JAMES TODD CHARTERED ACCOUNTANTS H'CAP HURDLE (13 hdls) 3m 1f 142y
4:25 (4:25) (Class 3) (0-135,134) 4-Y-O **£5,697** (£1,683; £841; £421; £210)

Form | | | | RPR
0P2- **1** **Sir Mangan (IRE)**[173] 5296 7-11-2 **124**.... HarrySkelton 133+
(Dan Skelton) *pressed ldr in strly run r: led gng best after 3 out: hit next: 7 l clr last: tiring sltly flat but r.o gamely and a looked like holding on* **3/1**[2]
44-F **2** *2 ½* **Cannon Fodder**[12] 1594 8-10-9 **117**.... MarcGoldstein 120
(Sheena West) *pressed ldrs: rdn after 9th: sn outpcd: 20 l 4th home turn: drvn to go 2nd after last and r.o v gamely but wnr a had enough in hand* **10/1**
3011 **3** *2 ½* **Western Way (IRE)**[24] 1503 6-11-1 **123**....(b) DenisO'Regan 126
(Don Cantillon) *t.k.h: wnt 3rd at 6th: lost tch w ldng pair after 10th: 17 l 3rd home turn: drvn and sme prog bef last: hung rt and lft flat and no imp after* **7/2**[3]
6346 **4** *3 ¾* **Morestead Screamer**[26] 1490 6-10-0 **108** oh1.... TomCannon 107
(Chris Gordon) *last pair: nt fluent 9th and rdn: struggling fr next: sme late prog* **14/1**
2-63 **5** *1 ¼* **Champagne Present (IRE)**[23] 1521 5-11-3 **125**....(t) RichardJohnson 123
(Jonjo O'Neill) *racd freely in ld at str gallop: nt a fluent: rdn and hdd after 3 out: lost wl hld 2nd after mstke last and edgd rt* **5/2**[1]
366- **6** *13* **Bally Legend**[160] 5538 10-11-12 **134**.... TomO'Brien 122
(Caroline Keevil) *pressed ldrs tl 10th: sn dropped out* **8/1**
26P- **7** *34* **Royale Knight**[160] 5538 9-10-11 **119**.... WillKennedy 73
(Dr Richard Newland) *hld up in last pair: rdn after 9th: t.o fr next* **7/1**
6m 14.0s (-38.80) **Going Correction** -1.25s/f (Hard) course record **7** Ran SP% **115.2**
Speed ratings (Par 107): **109,108,107,106,105 101,91**
CSF £31.36 TOTE £4.00: £1.90, £3.60; EX 35.80 Trifecta £152.80.
Owner Frank McAleavy **Bred** Patrick F Doyle **Trained** Alcester, Warwicks
FOCUS
A fair handicap hurdle in which they went a good gallop, and the time was four seconds inside the standard. A small pb from the winner, with the third and fourth rated close to form.

1737 SOUTHERN WATER CHARITY RACE DAY TOMORROW NOVICES' CHASE (16 fncs) 2m 5f 31y
5:00 (5:00) (Class 4) 4-Y-O+ **£6,724**

Form | | | | RPR
445- **1** **Henryville**[174] 5273 7-11-4 0.... NoelFehily 130+
(Harry Fry) *lft solo 2nd and lit up by loose horse tl 1/2-way: heavily eased bef 10th and j. efficiently after* **1/9**[1]
U **Mesut (FR)**[113] 4-10-7 110.... JackQuinlan
(Sarah Humphrey) *abt 8 l clr tl awkward 2nd and uns rdr* **6/1**[2]
5m 55.5s (12.50) **Going Correction** -0.475s/f (Good)
WFA 4 from 7yo 10lb **2** Ran SP% **104.3**
Speed ratings (Par 105): **57,**
TOTE £1.10.
Owner R P B Michaelson & E M Thornton **Bred** Karen George **Trained** Seaborough, Dorset
FOCUS
A non-event, with the short-priced favourite left alone as early as the second fence.
T/Plt: £31.90 to a £1 stake. Pool: £46,870.84 - 1072.26 winning units. T/Qpdt: £11.30 to a £1 stake. Pool: £2,432.09 - 158.20 winning units. **Iain Mackenzie**

1568 HEXHAM (L-H)
Friday, October 2

OFFICIAL GOING: Good (7.4)
Wind: Fresh, half against Weather: Sunny, warm

1738 HEXHAM RACECOURSE IDEAL FOR MARRIAGE INTERACTIVE H'CAP CHASE (12 fncs) 1m 7f 133y
2:00 (2:02) (Class 4) (0-115,113) 4-Y-O+ **£3,768** (£1,106; £553; £276)

Form | | | | RPR
2404 **1** **Harrys Whim**[29] 1458 10-11-4 110....(t) DaraghBourke[(5)] 116+
(Maurice Barnes) *led to bef 3rd: chsd clr ldr: hdwy to regain ld between last 2: sn clr: rdn out run-in* **7/1**
-551 **2** *3 ¼* **Heist (IRE)**[29] 1460 5-11-10 111....(t) BrianHughes 114
(Patrick Griffin, Ire) *hld up in tch: pushed along and outpcd 1/2-way: pushed along whn hit 2 out: rallied whn nt fluent last: chsd (clr) wnr run-in: kpt on: no imp* **15/8**[1]
3P-5 **3** *6* **Ballycool (IRE)**[146] 202 8-11-7 111....(t) DerekFox[(3)] 107
(Lucinda Russell) *hld up in tch: outpcd 1/2-way: rallied after 2 out: rdn and wnt 2nd briefly last: no ex run-in* **5/1**[3]
3P32 **4** *7* **Kitchapoly (FR)**[32] 1416 5-11-12 113.... SamTwiston-Davies 102
(Donald McCain) *chsd wnr to 2nd: chsd clr ldrs: rdn along after 3 out: wknd appr last* **9/4**[2]
615F **5** *hd* **Gin Cobbler**[8] 1639 9-10-11 105.... SamColtherd[(7)] 94
(Victor Thompson) *t.k.h: in tch: hdwy to ld bef 3rd: clr next: rdn and hdd between last 2: wknd last* **12/1**
446/ **P** **Rupert Bear**[565] 4836 9-10-9 101.... MissCWalton[(5)]
(James Walton) *nt fluent: in tch tl wknd and p.u after 6th* **16/1**
4m 6.1s (-3.70) **Going Correction** -0.10s/f (Good) **6** Ran SP% **108.3**
Speed ratings (Par 105): **105,103,100,96,96**
CSF £19.89 TOTE £10.30: £3.40, £1.50; EX 33.50 Trifecta £154.00.
Owner John Wills **Bred** J R Wills **Trained** Farlam, Cumbria
FOCUS
All bends on fresh ground. A modest handicap. The second has been rated in line with his best hurdle form, and there's a case for rating the race up to 7lb higher.

1739 RACING WELFARE (S) HURDLE (10 hdls) 2m 4f 28y
2:30 (2:34) (Class 5) 4-Y-O+ **£2,395** (£698; £349)

Form | | | | RPR
150 **1** **What A Steel (IRE)**[48] 1264 11-10-11 107....(v[1]) CraigNichol[(3)] 112
(Alistair Whillans) *prom: hdwy to ld 6th: mde rest: rdn whn idled appr last: drvn and hld on wl run-in* **15/8**[1]
P-65 **2** *¾* **Sean Airgead (IRE)**[44] 1291 10-10-11 109....(tp) DerekFox[(3)] 110
(Mark Michael McNiff, Ire) *led 1st to 4th: cl up: lost pl whn nt fluent 4 out: rallied after next: effrt and chsd wnr last: kpt on u.p: hld nr fin* **9/4**[2]
60-U **3** *nk* **Teochew (IRE)**[10] 1618 7-10-7 110....(t) DavidEngland 103
(Richard Drake) *hld up in tch: hdwy to chse wnr after 6th: rdn bef 2 out: lost 2nd last: rallied: hld towards fin* **8/1**
24F6 **4** *46* **Danceintothelight**[3] 1686 8-10-9 95.... FinianO'Toole[(10)] 74
(Micky Hammond) *prom: drvn and outpcd bef 2 out: wknd between last 2* **7/2**[3]
-606 **5** *8* **Stormont Bridge**[3] 1683 7-10-7 83....(t) ThomasDowson[(7)] 61
(Maurice Barnes) *led to 1st: chsd ldrs: drvn and outpcd bef 2 out: lost tch bef last* **22/1**
P- **P** **Shabach (IRE)**[151] 8-11-0 0....(p) JakeGreenall
(Mark Walford) *cl up: hit 1st: led 4th to 6th: struggling fr 3 out: lost tch and p.u bef last* **16/1**
UP0 **P** **Cobh National (IRE)**[118] 634 7-10-7 0.... SamColtherd[(7)]
(Victor Thompson) *hld up in tch: mstke and struggling 6th: lost tch and p.u bef next* **150/1**
5m 8.0s (-4.50) **Going Correction** -0.10s/f (Good) **7** Ran SP% **109.8**
Speed ratings (Par 103): **105,104,104,86,82**
CSF £5.99 TOTE £3.20: £1.70, £2.10; EX 6.40 Trifecta £23.90.
Owner J D Wright **Bred** D Dean **Trained** Newmill-On-Slitrig, Borders

FOCUS
A poor seller in which the front three finished clear. The first two have been rated pretty much to their marks.

1740 WALKING THE COURSES SUPPORTED BY HEXHAM RACECOURSE MAIDEN HURDLE (8 hdls) 2m 48y
3:05 (3:07) (Class 5) 4-Y-0+ £2,395 (£698; £349)

Form RPR
30-3 1 **Quick Brew**[148] 154 7-10-9 112........................(t) DaraghBourke(5) 112+
(Maurice Barnes) *hld up in midfield: hdwy to chse ldr 4 out: led after 2 out: pushed clr fr last* **5/2**[2]
3-24 2 9 **Nuts Well**[131] 459 4-11-0 0........................ BrianHughes 105
(Ann Hamilton) *nt fluent on occasions: hld up in tch: hdwy to chse wnr between last 2: kpt on run-in: no imp* **15/8**[1]
2-23 3 3¼ **Sacred Square (GER)**[14] 1568 5-11-0 113.........(p) SamTwiston-Davies 102
(Donald McCain) *hld up: hit 4th: hdwy to chse ldrs 2 out: rdn and outpcd bef last* **3/1**[3]
0-3F 4 12 **Bentons Lad**[109] 746 4-11-0 109........................ RichieMcLernon 89
(George Moore) *hld up: pushed along and effrt bef 2 out: outpcd bef last* **7/1**
3 5 7 **Landmeafortune (IRE)**[14] 1570 6-11-0 0........................ HenryBrooke 83
(Martin Todhunter) *chsd ldrs: lost pl after 4th: outpcd 3 out: sn n.d* **100/1**
6 4 **Inchcolm (IRE)**[138] 5-10-11 0........................ JoeColliver(3) 79
(Micky Hammond) *chsd ldrs: wnt 2nd 3rd to bef 3 out: rdn and wknd bef next* **16/1**
540- 7 3½ **Dibble Bridge**[199] 4832 4-10-11 0........................ AdamNicol(3) 76
(Philip Kirby) *chsd ldr to 3rd: lost pl 4 out: struggling after next* **28/1**
UU0P 8 6 **Bertielicious**[36] 1368 7-10-11 61........................(p) HarryChalloner(3) 71
(Jonathan Haynes) *led: clr bef 3 out: hdd after next: wknd bef last* **200/1**
9 71 **Swiftly Beyond** 7-11-0 0........................ BrianHarding 7
(Brian Storey) *unruly in paddock: bhd: lost tch 1/2-way: t.o* **200/1**

4m 14.4s (-3.00) **Going Correction** -0.10s/f (Good)
WFA 4 from 5yo+ 9lb 9 Ran SP% **112.2**
Speed ratings (Par 103): **103,98,96,90,87 85,83,80,45**
CSF £7.52 TOTE £3.50: £1.30, £1.20, £1.30; EX 8.70 Trifecta £21.80.
Owner The Wizards **Bred** D V Gardner Woodhayes Stud **Trained** Farlam, Cumbria
FOCUS
A modest maiden hurdle. Possibly a step up from the winner, and the form could be rated up to 8lb higher through the third and fourth, but it's not one to be confident about.

1741 MARQUIS OF GRANBY & GORDON SCORER NOVICES' LIMITED H'CAP CHASE (15 fncs) 2m 4f 15y
3:40 (3:40) (Class 4) (0-120,120) 4-Y-0+ £5,475 (£1,596; £798)

Form RPR
5321 1 **Skylander (IRE)**[14] 1579 6-11-8 **120**........................ TomScudamore 132+
(David Pipe) *hld up in tch: stdy hdwy 1/2-way: effrt and pressed wnr after 2 out: shkn up to ld whn nt fluent last: styd on strly to go clr run-in* **6/4**[1]
FP41 2 7 **Brother Scott**[14] 1569 8-9-12 **101** oh6........................ DiarmuidO'Regan(5) 106
(Sue Smith) *mostly j.w: led: rdn and hdd bef last: kpt on same pce run-in* **3/1**[2]
F213 3 20 **Mr Burgees (IRE)**[29] 1460 6-11-6 **118**........................ SamTwiston-Davies 105
(Donald McCain) *pressed ldr: rdn 3 out: lost 2nd after next: wkng whn mstke last* **6/1**
044- 4 1½ **Bonzo Bing (IRE)**[295] 3025 7-11-8 **120**........................ HenryBrooke 107
(Martin Todhunter) *prom: lost pl 1/2-way: struggling after 4 out: n.d after* **5/1**[3]
2-44 P **Flash Crash**[23] 1518 6-10-9 **110**........................(t) JamesBanks(3)
(Barry Brennan) *prom: rdn along 10th: wknd after 4 out: t.o whn p.u bef last* **20/1**
064 F **Drop A Gear (IRE)**[24] 1498 5-10-5 **103**........................ PeterBuchanan
(Lucinda Russell) *hld up last but in tch: fell heavily 8th* **9/1**

5m 9.4s (-4.10) **Going Correction** -0.10s/f (Good) 6 Ran SP% **110.7**
Speed ratings (Par 105): **104,101,93,92,**
CSF £6.51 TOTE £2.20: £1.30, £2.20; EX 7.70 Trifecta £18.70.
Owner The Trap Team Partnership **Bred** M Sheehy **Trained** Nicholashayne, Devon
FOCUS
A fair handicap. The second has been rated to his mark.

1742 YOUNGS RPS H'CAP HURDLE (10 hdls) 2m 4f 28y
4:15 (4:15) (Class 3) (0-130,124) 3-Y-0+ £5,393 (£1,583; £791; £395)

Form RPR
2313 1 **Miss Macnamara (IRE)**[17] 1404 6-10-6 **104**........................ HenryBrooke 109
(Martin Todhunter) *trckd ldrs: hdwy to chal 2 out: led last: drvn and edgd lft run-in: kpt on wl* **4/1**[3]
-520 2 ¾ **Willem (FR)**[36] 1035 5-11-12 **124**........................(p) TomScudamore 128
(David Pipe) *chsd ldr to bef 2 out: rdn and outpcd between last 2: rallied run-in: regained 2nd towards fin: kpt on* **5/1**
20-1 3 ½ **Serenity Now (IRE)**[22] 802 7-10-9 **114**........................ CraigGallagher(7) 119+
(Brian Ellison) *t.k.h: in tch: pushed along after 2 out: pushed along and gd hdwy bef last: chsd wnr run-in: no ex and lost 2nd nr fin* **15/8**[1]
2/13 4 1¼ **Celtic Monarch (IRE)**[73] 1074 6-10-10 **108**........................ AidanColeman 110
(Mark Michael McNiff, Ire) *led at stdy pce: rdn and jnd 2 out: hdd last: sn one pce* **3/1**[2]
26P- 5 2¼ **Tantamount**[162] 5491 6-11-0 **115**........................ DerekFox(3) 115
(Lucinda Russell) *t.k.h: hld up in last pl: effrt and pushed along between last 2: rdn and outpcd fr last* **7/1**

5m 20.6s (8.10) **Going Correction** -0.10s/f (Good) 5 Ran SP% **108.9**
Speed ratings (Par 107): **79,78,78,78,77**
CSF £21.91 TOTE £3.50: £1.90, £3.10; EX 22.80 Trifecta £64.20.
Owner Javas Charvers **Bred** Airlie Stud **Trained** Orton, Cumbria
FOCUS
A weak contest for the grade. The first three have been rated to their marks.

1743 CELEBRATE YOUR BIRTHDAY OR ANNIVERSARY AT HEXHAM H'CAP CHASE (15 fncs) 2m 4f 15y
4:50 (4:52) (Class 4) (0-115,112) 4-Y-0+ £3,969 (£1,157; £578)

Form RPR
2413 1 **Mia's Anthem (IRE)**[14] 1573 7-11-5 **108**........................(tp) DerekFox(3) 125+
(Noel C Kelly, Ire) *in tch: lft 3rd 10th: led 3 out shkn up and gng clr whn hit last: easily* **11/8**[1]
-P1P 2 8 **Dystonia's Revenge (IRE)**[41] 1332 10-11-5 **112**........................ JamieHamilton(7) 117
(Sheena Walton) *cl up: led 2nd: hdd and rdn 3 out: rallied: outpcd bef last* **6/1**
62P 3 15 **Manger Hanagment (IRE)**[18] 1548 10-10-12 **101**........(p) JamesBanks(3) 96
(Barry Brennan) *led: hdd whn hit 2nd: cl up tl outpcd 3 out: struggling fr next* **10/3**[3]
1540 F **Kai Broon (IRE)**[41] 1332 8-11-7 **107**........................(p) TomScudamore
(Lucinda Russell) *trckd ldrs: cl 3rd whn fell 10th* **5/2**[2]

5m 10.8s (-2.70) **Going Correction** -0.10s/f (Good) 4 Ran SP% **108.0**
Speed ratings (Par 105): **101,97,91,**
CSF £8.62 TOTE £1.90; EX 8.00 Trifecta £13.50.
Owner Don't Ask Now Syndicate **Bred** Cornelius Walsh **Trained** Draperstown, Co. Derry
FOCUS
A modest handicap run at a fair pace despite the small field. Seemingly a big step up from the winner in the first-time headgear, with the runner-up to his mark.

1744 HEXHAM PAVILION RESTAURANT A CERTAIN WINNER H'CAP HURDLE (12 hdls) 2m 7f 63y
5:20 (5:21) (Class 5) (0-100,100) 4-Y-0+ £2,274 (£667; £333; £166)

Form RPR
P124 1 **Native Optimist (IRE)**[98] 838 8-10-8 **87**........................ MissCWalton(5) 107+
(Sheena Walton) *led to 7th: pressed ldr: drew clr of rest fr 3 out: rdn to ld bef last: drew clr run-in* **5/2**[1]
000 2 dist **Distant Sound (IRE)**[44] 1293 8-10-11 **85**........................(b[1]) PaulMoloney 80
(Grace Harris) *t.k.h: cl up: led 7th: clr w wnr fr 3 out: rdn and hdd bef last: wknd run-in* **11/2**
06-0 3 9 **Late For Supper (IRE)**[16] 1552 6-10-8 **85**........................(t) HarryChalloner(3) 64
(Richard Ford) *prom: drvn and outpcd after 3 out: no imp fr next* **12/1**
-044 4 33 **Alba King (IRE)**[14] 1569 9-9-7 **77**........................ StephenMcCarthy(10) 27
(Sue Smith) *chsd ldrs: nt fluent 2nd: lost pl 4th: drvn along after 5 out: struggling fr 3 out: t.o* **7/2**[2]
056P 5 46 **Mrs Grass**[14] 1573 8-10-0 **74** oh5........................(tp) HenryBrooke
(Jonathan Haynes) *hld up: struggling 4 out: lost tch after next: t.o* **33/1**
0300 P **Stand Clear**[16] 1552 10-9-9 **74** oh3........................(t) DiarmuidO'Regan(5)
(Chris Grant) *bhd: struggling bef 4 out: lost tch after next: t.o whn p.u bef last* **12/1**
3605 F **Another Bygones (IRE)**[25] 1493 6-11-7 **95**........................ TomScudamore
(Karen McLintock) *hld up: fell 4th* **9/2**[3]
33 P **Jumpandtravel (IRE)**[36] 1365 6-11-2 **100**........................ FinianO'Toole(10)
(Micky Hammond) *prom: nt fluent 7th: struggling bef 4 out: lost tch after next: t.o whn p.u bef last* **8/1**

6m 5.3s (-3.70) **Going Correction** -0.10s/f (Good) 8 Ran SP% **113.8**
Speed ratings (Par 103): **102,89,86,75,59 , ,**
CSF £16.76 CT £135.88 TOTE £2.80: £1.30, £2.50, £3.50; EX 17.50 Trifecta £158.00.
Owner R H & S C Walton **Bred** Rodney Deacon **Trained** Hexham, Northumberland
FOCUS
A weak handicap. Possibly a step up from the winner after a break, but not one to be confident about.
T/Plt: £35.50 to a £1 stake. Pool: £52,844.15 - 1086.27 winning units. T/Qpdt: £10.00 to a £1 stake. Pool: £3,285.04 - 242.20 winning units. **Richard Young**

1745 - 1747a (Foreign Racing) - See Raceform Interactive

791 GOWRAN PARK (R-H)
Friday, October 2

OFFICIAL GOING: Good

1748a PAT WALSH MEMORIAL MARES HURDLE (LISTED RACE) (11 hdls) 2m 4f
3:30 (3:31) 4-Y-0+ £12,596 (£3,682; £1,744; £581)

RPR
1 **Daisy's Gift (IRE)**[23] 1527 8-11-3 130........................ PaulTownend 140
(W P Mullins, Ire) *chsd ldrs: 4th 1/2-way: impr on nr side to chal 2 out: rdn to ld between last 2: edgd sltly rt w narrow advantage at last and kpt on wl u.p run-in: all out* **13/2**
2 ½ **Whiteout (GER)**[21] 1385 4-10-12 132........................ RWalsh 134
(W P Mullins, Ire) *chsd ldrs: 5th 1/2-way: tk clsr order far side 2 out: rdn in 2nd between last 2 and kpt on wl u.p fr last in cl 2nd: hld* **5/4**[1]
3 7 **Collen Beag (IRE)**[16] 1558 5-10-13 122........................ MarkWalsh 128
(David M O'Brien, Ire) *settled bhd ldr: led narrowly fr 5th tl hdd narrowly fr next: effrt bef 2 out where slt mstke: sn rdn and no imp on ldrs u.p in 3rd bef last: kpt on one pce* **9/1**
4 ¾ **Emcon (IRE)**[19] 1540 6-10-13 122........................ KevinSexton 127
(W J Austin, Ire) *led: hdd narrowly fr 5th: 3rd 1/2-way: pushed along bef 3 out and wnt 2nd u.p appr st: no ex fr 2 out and nt fluent in 4th at last: kpt on one pce* **10/1**
5 4¼ **Carrigmoorna Rock (IRE)**[180] 5175 7-11-9 135........................ PhillipEnright 134
(Robert Tyner, Ire) *hld up in rr: last at 1/2-way: tk clsr order in 5th after 3 out: n.m.r bhd horses 2 out: sn swtchd lft and no imp on ldrs bef last where nt fluent: one pce run-in* **6/1**[3]
6 2½ **Queen Alphabet (IRE)**[6] 1657 6-11-3 126........................(t) JJBurke 125
(Peter Fahey, Ire) *chsd ldrs: cl 3rd bef 4th: racd keenly and led narrowly fr 6th: rdn and hdd bef 2 out: sn hdd & wknd u.p bef last* **4/1**[2]
7 52 **She's A Leader (IRE)**[351] 1924 8-11-3 118........................ BrianHayes 73
(Robert Honner, Ire) *towards rr: 6th 1/2-way: sme hdwy on outer into cl 5th 3 out: sn rdn and wknd qckly bef next: eased fr 2 out: completely t.o* **66/1**

4m 57.8s (297.80)
WFA 4 from 5yo+ 10lb 7 Ran SP% **112.6**
CSF £15.19 TOTE £6.70: £3.30, £1.02; DF 19.10 Trifecta £60.40.
Owner N G King **Bred** Wainbody Estates And N G King **Trained** Muine Beag, Co Carlow
FOCUS
The first running of this race as a Listed contest and it warranted such a tag with three of the seven runners rated 130 or higher. There was no fear of it turning into a sprint as the gallop was really generous from the start. The first two, both trained by Willie Mullins, pulled nicely clear of the rest up the home straight. The third and fourth help with the standard.

1749 - 1751a (Foreign Racing) - See Raceform Interactive

[1732]FONTWELL (L-H)

Saturday, October 3

OFFICIAL GOING: Good (7.1)

Wind: light breeze Weather: fairly bright; 16 degrees

1752 MTS CLEANSING SERVICES SUPPORTING ROCKINGHORSE NOVICES' HURDLE (10 hdls) 2m 3f 33y

2:10 (2:10) (Class 4) 4-Y-0+ **£3,249** (£954; £477; £238)

Form RPR

4334 **1** **Mercers Court (IRE)**[107] 773 7-11-5 **122**.................. TrevorWhelan 115+
(Neil King) *settled trcking ldrs: wnt 2nd after 3 out: clr of rest whn clipped next: rdn to ld last: sn clr but hung rt to stands' rails after* **7/4**[2]

2 *6* **Le Legro (IRE)**[145] 250 5-10-12 0.................. NoelFehily 101
(Charlie Mann) *stocky: chsd ldrs tl j. slowly 7th: 10 l 3rd and outpcd home turn: plugged on fr bef last: wnt mod 2nd 100yds out* **8/1**[3]

563 **3** *2 ¼* **Native Robin (IRE)**[15] 1576 5-10-12 0.................. NickScholfield 98
(Jeremy Scott) *led at stdy pce tl 6th: lost 2nd after 3 out: 6 l 3rd and rdn and outpcd home turn: kpt gng steadily to take modest 3rd ins fnl 100yds* **16/1**

2-12 **4** *1 ¼* **Benissimo (IRE)**[136] 401 5-11-0 122.................. BridgetAndrews(5) 104
(Dan Skelton) *t.k.h: 2nd tl led 6th: hdd 2 out: rdn and btn in 2nd whn mstke last: tired to lose two pls fnl 100yds* **5/6**[1]

0-46 **5** *23* **Palmaria**[15] 1574 5-10-5 0.................. JamesBest 69
(Caroline Keevil) *tall: in last pair: nt fluent 3rd: struggling fr 3 out* **50/1**

P-0 **P** **Leith Hill (IRE)**[51] 1246 5-10-12 0.................. TomCannon
(Laura Mongan) *mstkes in last pair: drvn 5th: nvr travelling after: blnd 3 out: sn bdly t.o: p.u last* **100/1**

4m 45.2s (-14.20) **Going Correction** -1.05s/f (Hard) **6** Ran SP% **110.9**
Speed ratings (Par 105): **87,84,83,83,73**
CSF £15.00 TOTE £2.50: £1.30, £2.40; EX 12.50 Trifecta £51.90.

Owner David Nott, Ken Lawrence, Tim Messom **Bred** Alistair Thompson **Trained** Barbury Castle, Wiltshire

■ Stewards' Enquiry : Tom Cannon two-day ban: used whip without giving gelding time to respond (Oct 17-18)

FOCUS

Fresh running lines were provided on the bends and the hurdle track following racing at the course the previous day. Fences were on the inner and the hurdles were middle inner. Races 1, 3 & 7 increased by 24yds, race 2 by 48yds, races 4 & 6 by 60yds and race 5 by 36yds. A couple of these had official ratings in the 120s, so this was a fair contest. However the time was slow. The winner is rated below his best.

1753 BTU SUPPORTING THE RAINBOW CENTRE NOVICES' LIMITED H'CAP CHASE (15 fncs) 2m 3f 35y

2:45 (2:45) (Class 4) (0-120,120) 4-Y-0+ **£3,768** (£1,106; £553; £276)

Form RPR

-251 **1** **Vikekhal (FR)**[116] 670 6-11-8 **120**.................. (b) JoshuaMoore 130+
(Gary Moore) *racd freely and mde all at str pce: drew 5 l clr bef 3 out and nvr looked like being ct after: eased flat* **7/2**[2]

1434 **2** *7* **Zarawi (IRE)**[27] 1488 4-10-7 **116**.................. (p) RichardJohnson 108
(Charlie Longsdon) *detached in last pair and t.k.h: nt a fluent: clsd 10th: wnt 2nd 3 out: sn rdn and no rspnse: hld whn hit 2 out and last* **7/2**[2]

6426 **3** *31* **Newton Geronimo**[72] 1083 6-11-2 **114**.................. NicodeBoinville 87
(Ben Pauling) *on his toes and mounted on crse: plld hrd: sn pressing wnr: blnd 11th: lost 2nd briefly 12th and again bef 3 out and sn fdd: poor 3rd whn hit last* **8/1**[3]

21-2 **4** *25* **Very Noble (FR)**[155] 64 6-10-12 **110**.................. (t) TomCannon 60
(Chris Gordon) *detached in last pair: mstke 7th: pushed along 9th: nt travelling: t.o after blundering 11th: eased flat* **2/1**[1]

0-44 **U** **Adam Du Breteau (FR)**[24] 1522 5-10-9 **107**.................. (b[1]) RichieMcLernon
(Jonjo O'Neill) *settled in 3rd pl: wnt 2nd at 9th: looked to be gng v strly whn uns rdr 12th* **7/2**[2]

4m 53.8s (-13.50) **Going Correction** -0.35s/f (Good)
WFA 4 from 5yo+ 9lb **5** Ran SP% **111.1**
Speed ratings (Par 105): **114,111,98,87,**
CSF £15.86 TOTE £3.90: £1.90, £2.20; EX 17.40 Trifecta £39.20.

Owner N J Roach **Bred** E A R L Guittet-Desbois Et Al **Trained** Lower Beeding, W Sussex

FOCUS

Probably just ordinary form but the winner is on an upward curve. The second was 6lb off the best of his hurdles runs.

1754 CLANCY DOCWRA SUPPORTING ROCKINGHORSE CHILDRENS CHARITY H'CAP HURDLE (10 hdls) 2m 3f 33y

3:20 (3:20) (Class 2) (0-145,137) 4-Y-£9,495 (£2,805; £1,402; £702; £351)

Form RPR

301- **1** **After Eight Sivola (FR)**[185] 5101 5-10-4 **120**.................. LizzieKelly(5) 128+
(Nick Williams) *settled in rr: stdy prog on outer fr 7th: wnt 2nd 2 out: pushed into ld bef last: styd on wl and sn asserted flat* **6/1**

545- **2** *4 ½* **Dragon's Den (IRE)**[161] 5541 8-11-2 **127**.................. LeightonAspell 130
(Chris Down) *nt a fluent: towards rr: mstkes 3 out and next: stl 5th at last: tk 2nd fnl 100yds* **25/1**

1322 **3** *2* **Antony (FR)**[27] 1485 5-10-9 **120**.................. JamieMoore 120
(Gary Moore) *led 2nd and set str gallop: rdn bef 2 out: hdd and hit last: kpt on same pce flat: lost 2nd fnl 100yds* **7/1**

3-11 **4** *1* **Promanco**[128] 516 6-10-11 **122**.................. (t) RichardJohnson 122
(Charlie Longsdon) *bhd: rdn and effrt in 6th home turn: styng on same pce whn blnd last* **9/2**[2]

340- **5** *3* **Istimraar (IRE)**[160] 4891 4-10-6 **117**.................. HarrySkelton 114
(Dan Skelton) *plld hrd: cl up: wnt 2nd briefly and rdn bef 2 out: no ex appr last and hit flight* **3/1**[1]

32UF **6** *nse* **Mile House (IRE)**[8] 1642 7-11-5 **130**.................. TomO'Brien 126
(Robert Stephens) *led tl 2nd: rdn bef 7th and sn lost pl: struggling bef 2 out* **14/1**

1P0- **7** *1 ¾* **Foxcub (IRE)**[266] 3609 7-11-12 **137**.................. JamesDavies 133
(Tom Symonds) *cl up tl j. slowly 3rd: in rr and u.p after 6th: nt gng wl enough after but plugged on* **9/1**

2151 **8** *8* **Gioia Di Vita**[27] 1485 5-11-6 **131**.................. WillKennedy 119
(Dr Richard Newland) *midfield: wnt 2nd 3 out: drvn bef next: sn dropped out tamely* **5/1**[3]

2-10 **9** *9* **Benbecula**[43] 556 6-10-6 **117**.................. TomScudamore 96
(Richard Mitchell) *prom: j. slowly 3rd: hit 6th and rdn: dropped bk last after 3 out* **10/1**

4m 34.3s (-25.10) **Going Correction** -1.05s/f (Hard)
WFA 4 from 5yo+ 9lb **9** Ran SP% **116.2**
Speed ratings (Par 109): **110,108,107,106,105 105,104,101,97**
CSF £126.47 CT £1072.90 TOTE £5.90: £1.80, £6.30, £2.50; EX 132.20 Trifecta £1345.80.

Owner Larkhills Racing Partnership III **Bred** Gilles Trapenard **Trained** George Nympton, Devon

FOCUS

A decent handicap, and the winning time wasn't too bad. A pb from the winner with the next four pretty much to their marks.

1755 SOUTHERN WATER WATER EFFICIENCY H'CAP CHASE (16 fncs) 2m 5f 31y

3:50 (3:50) (Class 3) (0-130,127) 4-Y-0+ **£6,498** (£1,908; £954; £477)

Form RPR

243- **1** **Top Cat Henry (IRE)**[166] 5432 7-11-3 **118**.................. (tp) WillKennedy 125+
(Dr Richard Newland) *str-topped: settled gng wl in midfield: effrt in 4th after 13th: led 2 out: 3 l clr last: rdn and kpt on wl flat* **15/8**[1]

216- **2** *2 ¼* **Midnight Lira**[165] 5450 8-11-9 **124**.................. JamesBest 127
(Caroline Keevil) *settled in midfield: wnt 3rd at 9th and 2nd at 12th: led bef 3 out: hrd drvn and hdd next: no imp after but styd on pluckily* **14/1**

522 **3** *1 ¼* **Town Mouse**[44] 1296 5-11-7 **122**.................. (p) TrevorWhelan 124
(Neil King) *taken down v early: plld hrd: led after 1st: hdd 12th: rdn after next: 3rd and no imp fr 2 out: kpt on flat* **10/1**

2254 **4** *3* **Kitegen (IRE)**[15] 1577 9-10-6 **107**.................. RichardJohnson 109+
(Robin Dickin) *hld up towards rr: effrt bef 3 out: 4th and rdn and hld whn blnd next: plugged on* **6/1**[3]

2463 **5** *28* **Porters War (IRE)**[43] 1309 13-10-13 **114**.................. NickScholfield 88
(Jeremy Scott) *mstkes in rr: last after 10th: continued wl bhd* **9/1**

31P- **6** *1* **Comeonginger (IRE)**[182] 5141 8-11-12 **127**.................. (t) TomCannon 100
(Chris Gordon) *led tl after 1st: prom tl led again 12th: rdn and hdd bef 3 out: lost pl rapidly* **4/1**[2]

4-11 **7** *7* **Venetian Lad**[122] 598 10-11-0 **115**.................. MarcGoldstein 82
(Lydia Richards) *chsd ldrs: rdn and lost pl 12th: struggling after* **10/1**

424 **8** *23* **Domtaline (FR)**[44] 1296 8-11-10 **125**.................. PaulMoloney 71
(Evan Williams) *prom: nt fluent 7th: drvn and fading 12th: t.o and eased 2 out: b.b.v* **17/2**

5m 31.8s (-11.20) **Going Correction** -0.35s/f (Good) **8** Ran SP% **114.4**
Speed ratings (Par 107): **107,106,105,104,93 93,90,82**
CSF £26.76 CT £210.46 TOTE £2.60: £1.10, £4.80, £2.90; EX 33.70 Trifecta £237.80.

Owner Off The Clock Partners & Dr RDP Newland **Bred** Mrs Mary Margaret Roche **Trained** Claines, Worcs

FOCUS

This may not produce too many winners in the short-term, but there was a good battle between a few of these down the home straight for the final time. Straightforward form, rated around the second and third.

1756 SOUTHERN WATER BAG IT AND BIN IT H'CAP HURDLE (13 hdls) 3m 1f 142y

4:25 (4:25) (Class 5) (0-100,97) 4-Y-0+ **£3,249** (£954; £477; £238)

Form RPR

6343 **1** **Tokyo Javilex (FR)**[13] 1598 8-10-9 **87**.................. (t) MrLDrowne(7) 97
(Nigel Hawke) *hld up in midfield: effrt after 3 out: 3rd next: wnt 2nd at last: styd on dourly to ld fnl 100yds: edgd clr* **11/4**[1]

6/BP **2** *1 ¼* **Lady From Geneva**[19] 1546 8-11-4 **89**.................. (t) BrendanPowell 98
(Brendan Powell) *sn 2nd or 3rd: led 3 out: rdn bef last: hdd and no ex fnl 100yds* **16/1**

1-05 **3** *5* **Aaly**[83] 966 8-10-4 **75**.................. MarcGoldstein 79
(Lydia Richards) *bhd: effrt 8th: began to stay on between last two: rdn to snatch 3rd but nt trble ldrs* **14/1**

-366 **4** *shd* **Marlpit Oak**[25] 1509 10-10-5 **83**.................. MrDSansom(7) 87
(Seamus Mullins) *t.k.h: midfield: wnt 3rd at 10th and 2nd and rdn bef 2 out: nt qckn appr last: lost 3rd fnl strides* **25/1**

203 **5** *1* **Ennisnag (IRE)**[25] 1509 10-11-5 **97**.................. MrGTreacy(7) 101
(Paul Henderson) *in last trio tl 10th: cl to midfield 3 out: 5th 2 out: rdn and no imp after: blnd last* **14/1**

5465 **6** *1* **Spanish Fork (IRE)**[33] 1426 6-10-11 **82**.................. MattieBatchelor 84
(Sheena West) *cajoled along thrght: led at mod pce after 1st tl 5th: led again 7th: str reminders after 9th: hdd 3 out: plodded on same pce fr next* **8/1**

004- **7** *2 ¼* **Lady A**[223] 4381 5-11-4 **89**.................. TomCannon 90
(Chris Gordon) *burly: cl up: mstkes: rdn after 9th: making no imp whn hit 3 out and next* **16/1**

432- **8** *¾* **Snowball (IRE)**[303] 2900 8-10-11 **82**.................. LeightonAspell 82
(David Arbuthnot) *sweating: chsd ldrs: effrt and disp 3rd 3 out: rdn and fdd between last two* **7/2**[2]

0P35 **9** *52* **Al Guwair (IRE)**[33] 1427 5-9-12 **72**.................. JamesBanks(3) 25
(Mark Hoad) *midfield: rdn and dropped to rr 10th: bdly t.o bef 2 out* **16/1**

P-25 **10** *10* **Peaceful Gardens**[13] 1599 6-9-11 **75**.................. (t[1]) DavidPrichard(7) 19
(Jeremy Scott) *last trio: rdn and struggling bef 10th: bdly t.o bef 2 out* **10/1**

52-0 **11** *12* **Orsm**[48] 1272 8-11-10 **95**.................. (t) RichardJohnson 28
(Laura Mongan) *sweating bdly: t.k.h: led tl after 1st and again 5th tl 7th: mstke 9th and rdn: dropped out tamely: bdly t.o bef 2 out* **6/1**[3]

6m 29.2s (-23.60) **Going Correction** -1.05s/f (Hard) **11** Ran SP% **118.2**
Speed ratings (Par 103): **94,93,92,92,91 91,90,90,74,71 67**
CSF £46.25 TOTE £3.60: £1.50, £6.20, £2.90; EX 45.40 Trifecta £568.90 Part won..

Owner D R Mead **Bred** Scea Ecurie Jc Laisis **Trained** Stoodleigh, Devon

FOCUS

Not much happened in this moderate contest until the final circuit. The first two could still be competitive when reassessed

1757 SOUTHERN WATER CUSTOMER FIRST CONDITIONAL JOCKEYS' H'CAP CHASE (14 fncs 2 omitted) 2m 5f 31y

5:00 (5:00) (Class 5) (0-100,98) 4-Y-0+ **£2,469** (£725; £362; £181)

Form RPR

5354 **1** **Tribal Dance (IRE)**[37] 1380 9-11-1 **87**.................. (v) SeanBowen 91
(John O'Shea) *led: pushed along 11th: nt fluent next and hdd: outpcd normal 3 out: rallied u.p to make 6 l fr last: forced ahd cl home* **4/1**

4621 **2** *½* **Herecomesthetruth (IRE)**[27] 1487 13-11-2 **98**.................. MrWRClarke(10) 104+
(Chris Gordon) *t.k.h: sn 2nd: mstke normal 9th: led after 12th: 6 l clr and rdn 2 out: idled flat: ct fnl 50yds* **9/4**[1]

2-36 **3** *16* **The Cat's Away (IRE)**[42] 1326 7-10-0 **72** oh2.................. (b) ConorShoemark 61
(Richenda Ford) *sn last pair: outpcd and rdn and nt travelling 10th: effrt normal 12th and cl 3rd home turn: sn fnd nil* **10/3**[2]

The Form Book Jumps 2015-16, Raceform Ltd, Newbury, RG14 5SJ

60P5 4 *49* **Appropriate (FR)**[13] 1595 5-10-1 **73**...........................(t) ThomasGarner 18
(Dominic Ffrench Davis) *sn last pair: mstke 7th: outpcd and rdn 10th: t.o bef omitted 3 out* **20/1**
241P U **Sylvan Legend**[37] 1380 7-10-3 **83**.......................(tp) MrMartinMcIntyre(8)
(Neil Mulholland) *pitched sltly and uns rdr 2nd* **7/2**[3]
-UP6 F **Yes I Will**[19] 1546 6-10-13 **85**...........................(tp) JackSherwood
(Linda Jewell) *last whn unstdy 1st: mstke and wnt into bk of rival and fell 2nd* **10/1**
5m 36.1s (-6.90) **Going Correction** -0.35s/f (Good) **6** Ran SP% **109.9**
Speed ratings (Par 103): **99,98,92,74,**
CSF £13.31 TOTE £5.20: £2.50, £1.50; EX 14.40 Trifecta £60.70.
Owner Quality Pipe Supports (Q P S) Ltd **Bred** Liam O'Regan **Trained** Elton, Gloucs

FOCUS
This moderate chase was run at a decent gallop from the start, and two runners came down early at the first fence in the home straight. That obstacle was missed out the next two times they got to it. The winner is rated to his mark.

1758 SOUTHERN WATER SUPPORTING LOCAL CHARITIES STANDARD OPEN NATIONAL HUNT FLAT RACE 2m 1f 145y
5:30 (5:30) (Class 6) 4-6-Y-O **£1,559** (£457; £228; £114)

Form RPR
43- 1 **Jennifer Eccles**[203] 4755 5-10-7 0........................... TomO'Brien 105
(Suzy Smith) *small stocky: pressed ldr: led gng wl over 2f out: sn clr w one rival: rdn and battled on v gamely fnl f* **7/2**[2]
0- 2 *¾* **Vivas (FR)**[175] 5285 4-11-0 0........................... KielanWoods 111
(Charlie Longsdon) *small: cl up: wnt 2nd over 2f out: sn rdn and clr of rest: kpt trying thrght fnl f but a jst hld* **16/1**
06- 3 *17* **Shake Devaney (IRE)**[239] 4072 5-11-0 0........................... PaddyBrennan 96
(Fergal O'Brien) *str: bhd: rdn 6f out: short-lived effrt and on heels of ldrs home turn: rdn and sn lost tch w ldng pair but kpt on steadily for poor 3rd* **8/1**
2- 4 *shd* **Oulamayo (FR)**[185] 5104 4-11-0 0........................... HarrySkelton 96
(Dan Skelton) *cl up: rdn home turn: outpcd by ldng pair over 2f out: plugged on in duel for poor 3rd* **4/1**[3]
3 5 *7* **Pinnacle Panda (IRE)**[141] 320 4-11-0 0........................... RobertDunne 90
(Tom Lacey) *midfield: 7th home turn: sn pushed along and lost tch w ldrs* **5/2**[1]
0- 6 *2¾* **Glance Back**[247] 3944 4-10-11 0........................... JamesBanks(3) 87
(Emma Baker) *led tl rdn and hdd over 2f out: dropped out rapidly: t.o* **33/1**
7 *13* **Knightly Pleasure** 4-10-7 0........................... JoshuaMoore 68
(Gary Moore) *wl bhd at 1/2-way: no ch fnl 6f: t.o* **7/1**
8 *8* **Montecito (FR)**[202] 5-11-0 0........................... TomCannon 68
(Chris Gordon) *chsd ldrs: drvn 5f out: fdd 3f out: bdly t.o* **20/1**
9 *11* **Dame Doris** 5-10-7 0........................... NickScholfield 51
(Lawney Hill) *v small: unruly paddock: prom tl 1/2-way: bdly t.o* **20/1**
10 *16* **Colonel Ali** 4-11-0 0........................... JackQuinlan 44
(Denis Quinn) *chsd ldrs tl rdn 5f out: bdly t.o* **40/1**
11 *26* **Lady Bella**[545] 6-10-3 0 ow1........................... [1] KevinJones(5) 15
(Seamus Mullins) *mounted on crse: overshot s: a last: bdly t.o fnl 3f* **66/1**
4m 11.7s (-17.00) **Going Correction** -1.05s/f (Hard) **11** Ran SP% **116.7**
Speed ratings: **95,94,86,86,83 82,76,72,68,60 49**
CSF £52.24 TOTE £4.30: £1.90, £4.00, £2.80; EX 67.20 Trifecta £1256.00.
Owner P Mercer & K W Allisat **Bred** P J Mercer **Trained** Lewes, E Sussex

FOCUS
Plenty of these had raced before, and two of those with experience came well clear. The winner set a fair standard and is rated to his mark.
T/Plt: £186.00 to a £1 stake. Pool: £59,190.05 - 232.19 winning tickets. T/Qpdt: £22.80 to a £1 stake. Pool: £4,975.31 - 161.10 winning tickets. **Iain Mackenzie**

1759 - 1762a (Foreign Racing) - See Raceform Interactive

1745 GOWRAN PARK (R-H)
Saturday, October 3

OFFICIAL GOING: Good (good to firm in places on chase course)

1763a PWC CHAMPION CHASE (GRADE 2) (14 fncs) 2m 4f
4:35 (4:35) 5-Y-O+ **£21,162** (£6,186; £2,930; £976)

RPR
1 **Cailin Annamh (IRE)**[62] 1185 7-10-13 145.................(bt) BarryGeraghty 143+
(Mrs John Harrington, Ire) *led tl bad mstke 6th and hdd: rcvrd wl to trck ldr: mstke in 3rd 3 out: styd on on strly to press ldr in 2nd run-in: led clsng stages* **9/1**
2 *½* **Alelchi Inois (FR)**[17] 1556 7-11-8 147........................... RWalsh 152
(W P Mullins, Ire) *trckd ldr in 2nd tl led 6th: strly pressed after last: kpt on wl: hdd clsng stages* **9/2**[3]
3 *3¾* **Clarcam (FR)**[177] 5235 5-11-8 159...........................(t) BJCooper 149
(Gordon Elliott, Ire) *hld up: rdn in 6th bef 3 out: prog to dispute 2nd last: sn nt qckn w principals: kpt on same pce* **7/2**[2]
4 *4¾* **Indevan**[17] 1556 7-11-6 142........................... PaulTownend 141
(W P Mullins, Ire) *racd in rr whn mstke 6th: sme hdwy bef 3 out: 6th 2 out: kpt on into 4th clsng stages: nvr nrr* **25/1**
5 *1* **Texas Jack (IRE)**[15] 1580 9-11-3 150...........................(b) SeanFlanagan 137
(Noel Meade, Ire) *chsd ldrs: tk clsr order bef 3 out in 4th: no imp last: dropped to 5th clsng stages* **8/1**
6 *8* **Devils Bride (IRE)**[15] 1580 8-11-6 144...........................(t) DavidMullins 133
(W P Mullins, Ire) *trckd ldrs in 3rd: prog and almost on terms after 4 out: nt fluent 3 out: no ex in 5th at next: wknd* **8/1**
7 *21* **Shanahan's Turn (IRE)**[66] 1152 7-11-8 153........................... JJBurke 120
(Henry De Bromhead, Ire) *hld up tl tk clsr order to trck ldrs in 4th after 4 out: sn rdn and nt qckn bef next: no threat in rr whn mstke 2 out* **7/4**[1]
4m 51.0s (-20.30) **7** Ran SP% **112.8**
CSF £47.58 TOTE £11.00: £3.60, £2.80; DF 59.10 Trifecta £122.20.
Owner Flyers Syndicate **Bred** A J Nevin **Trained** Moone, Co Kildare

FOCUS
An intriguing renewal and a cracking finish. The pace was steady and the first two help with the standard.

1764 - 1765a (Foreign Racing) - See Raceform Interactive

1421 HUNTINGDON (R-H)
Sunday, October 4

OFFICIAL GOING: Good (watered; chs 7.8, hdl 8.1)
Wind: Light; against Weather: Sunny

1766 WINNER APP NOVICES' HURDLE (8 hdls) 1m 7f 171y
1:50 (1:50) (Class 4) 4-Y-O+ **£3,994** (£1,240; £667)

Form RPR
11 1 **Maputo**[20] 1544 5-11-10 138........................... AidanColeman 141+
(John Ferguson) *t.k.h: mde all: nudged along and asserted bef last: comf* **2/11**[1]
1631 2 *1¾* **Regulation (IRE)**[12] 1612 6-11-5 123...........................(p) LizzieKelly(5) 134
(Neil King) *chsd wnr: clsd and upsides 3 out: rdn after next: unable qck w wnr: comf hld and r.o same pce flat* **9/2**[2]
1434 3 *19* **Jarlath**[5] 1693 4-10-13 110........................... KevinJones(5) 111
(Seamus Mullins) *a 3rd: mstke 5th: struggling 3 out: sn lost tch* **33/1**[3]
F **Expensive Taste (IRE)**[10] 4-10-12 0...........................(t) JackQuinlan
(Phil McEntee) *a last: rdn and struggling after 5th: lost tch next: t.o whn fell 2 out* **200/1**
3m 41.85s (-13.05) **Going Correction** -0.725s/f (Firm)
WFA 4 from 5yo+ 9lb **4** Ran SP% **106.2**
Speed ratings (Par 105): **103,102,92,**
CSF £1.41 TOTE £1.10; EX 1.30 Trifecta £1.50.
Owner Bloomfields **Bred** Darley **Trained** Cowlinge, Suffolk

FOCUS
All rails in innermost position and the official going was good (watered). An uncompetitive novices' hurdle to start featuring a very warm unbeaten favourite.

1767 WINNER.CO.UK H'CAP CHASE (16 fncs) 2m 3f 189y
2:25 (2:25) (Class 4) (0-120,120) 4-Y-O+ **£3,898** (£1,144; £572; £286)

Form RPR
-433 1 **Here I Am (IRE)**[117] 672 8-10-6 **100**........................... MarcGoldstein 111+
(Diana Grissell) *j. boldly: mde all: slt mstke 3 out: jnd next: rdn bef last: styd on and forged ahd flat: rdn out* **14/1**
1112 2 *1½* **Tangolan (IRE)**[20] 1544 7-11-12 **120**...........................(t) PaddyBrennan 131+
(Fergal O'Brien) *chsd ldrs: nt fluent 5th: wnt 2nd 10th: chalng whn dived and mstke 2 out: sn rdn: edging rt and styd on same pce flat* **3/1**[2]
56/2 3 *7* **Shockingtimes (IRE)**[34] 1424 8-11-10 **118**........................... BrendanPowell 121
(Jamie Snowden) *in tch in midfield: mstke 8th: effrt in 4th after 3 out: no imp between last 2: wnt 3rd and mstke last: plugged on same pce flat* **9/2**[3]
-3P4 4 *4* **Milgen Bay**[32] 1444 9-10-13 **110**........................... ThomasGarner(3) 110
(Oliver Sherwood) *in tch in midfield: lft 3rd 13th: rdn after next: no imp between last 2: mstke and lost 3rd last: wknd flat* **10/1**
30F 5 *6* **King's Legacy (IRE)**[26] 1500 11-11-6 **114**...........................(t) AidanColeman 107
(Lawney Hill) *hld up in last trio: 5th and clsd after 3 out: pushed along and no imp bef next: wknd last* **12/1**
2-44 6 *6* **Bertie's Desire**[129] 523 7-11-1 **109**........................... LeightonAspell 99
(Oliver Sherwood) *chsd ldr tl 10th: 3rd whn blnd 13th: lost pl and wl hld in 6th after next: wkng whn j.rt last 2* **5/2**[1]
41-4 7 *29* **Golanova**[150] 170 7-10-4 **105**...........................(v) GeorgeGorman(7) 66
(Gary Moore) *hld up: mstke and dropped to last pair 4th: nvr j. or travelling wl enough after: rdn after 9th: lost tch 3 out: t.o* **6/1**
4-4P 8 *½* **Giant O Murchu (IRE)**[4] 1703 11-10-6 **105**........................... ConorRing(5) 66
(John Upson) *a last: sprawled on landing 1st: rdn and struggling 12th: lost tch 3 out: t.o* **66/1**
4m 52.9s (-12.40) **Going Correction** -0.65s/f (Firm) **8** Ran SP% **111.0**
Speed ratings (Par 105): **98,97,94,93,90 88,76,76**
CSF £54.35 CT £215.54 TOTE £10.10: £3.20, £1.50, £1.40; EX 31.50 Trifecta £244.10.
Owner Nigel & Barbara Collison **Bred** M Conaghan **Trained** Brightling, E Sussex

FOCUS
A fair handicap chase run at a good pace thanks to the winner.

1768 WINNER.CO.UK JUVENILE HURDLE (8 hdls) 1m 7f 171y
3:05 (3:11) (Class 4) 3-Y-O **£3,898** (£1,144; £572; £286)

Form RPR
6 1 **Big McIntosh (IRE)**[9] 1452 3-10-12 0...........................(t) MattieBatchelor 109+
(John Ryan) *racd freely: mde all and sn clr: reduced ld fr 5th: rdn and pressed bef 2 out: jst over 1 l ahd and keeping on whn lft 8 l clr last: styd on* **20/1**
2 2 *10* **Consortium (IRE)**[2] 1732 3-10-7 0........................... LizzieKelly(5) 100
(Neil King) *t.k.h: hld up in main gp: rdn after 4th: 6 l 4th whn mstke next: no imp next: lft 8 l 2nd last* **1/1**[1]
5 3 *4½* **Cahill (IRE)**[8] 1656 3-10-12 0...........................(v[1]) WayneHutchinson 95
(Alan King) *chsd clr ldr: clsd 5th: 2 l down 3 out: rdn and lost 2nd bef next: mstke 2 out: sn wknd: lft 3rd last* **9/4**[2]
4 *27* **Aspasius (GER)**[175] 3-10-12 0........................... NoelFehily 71
(Charlie Mann) *t.k.h: hld up in last pair: nvr on terms w ldrs: lost tch bef 3 out: t.o whn lft 4th last* **15/2**[3]
5 *31* **Philba**[47] 3-10-12 0........................... DarylJacob 43
(Michael Appleby) *t.k.h: hld up in last pair: nvr on terms w ldrs: mstke and lost tch 5th: t.o* **10/1**
U U **Whisky Marmalade (IRE)**[61] 778 3-10-0 0........................... NathanMoscrop(5) 99
(Ben Haslam) *chsd ldng pair: clsd 5th: effrt to chse wnr bef 2 out: mstke 2 out: jst over 1 l down and struggling to qckn whn landed awkwardly and uns rdr last* **20/1**
3m 42.0s (-12.90) **Going Correction** -0.725s/f (Firm) **6** Ran SP% **111.1**
Speed ratings (Par 103): **103,98,95,82,66**
CSF £41.79 TOTE £18.20: £5.90, £1.20; EX 55.00 Trifecta £155.20.
Owner Kilco (International) Ltd **Bred** M P & R J Coleman **Trained** Newmarket, Suffolk

FOCUS
Not a strong juvenile hurdle and another all-the-way winner on the card.

1769 DOWNLOAD THE WINNER.CO.UK APP NOW CHASE (A NOVICES' LIMITED H'CAP) (12 fncs) 2m 104y
3:35 (3:37) (Class 4) (0-120,120) 4-Y-O+ **£6,498** (£1,431; £1,431; £477)

Form RPR
11P3 1 **Walden Prince (IRE)**[32] 1451 8-11-2 **119**...........................(v[1]) JakeHodson(5) 129+
(David Bridgwater) *mde all: rdn bef 2 out: in command and ears pricked last: styd on: rdn out* **16/1**
4302 2 *4½* **Halling's Wish**[14] 1591 5-10-13 **111**...........................(bt) JoshuaMoore 117+
(Gary Moore) *chsd ldng pair: drvn after 3 out: no imp on wnr: wnt 2nd sn after last: kpt on same pce after: jnd for 2nd on post* **4/1**[3]

426- **2** *dht* **Le Fin Bois (FR)**[172] 5345 5-11-8 **120**..........(t) PaddyBrennan 125
(Tim Vaughan) *t.k.h: hld up in tch: effrt in 5th after 3 out: no imp: kpt on and battling for 2nd last: no threat to wnr: plugged on to join 2nd on post* **3/1**[1]

2-5P **4** *5* **Yabadabadoo**[120] 643 7-10-12 **110**.......... AidanColeman 109
(Emma Lavelle) *chsd wnr: stl looked to be travelling wl bnd bef 2 out: effrt after 2 out: fnd nil and lost 2nd sn after last: plugged on same pce flat* **5/1**

0300 **5** *3/4* **Trojan Star (IRE)**[9] 1647 5-10-6 **107**..........(t) TomBellamy(3) 106
(Kim Bailey) *t.k.h: hld up in last pair: clsd 8th: cl enough and rdn in 4th after 3 out: no imp: no threat to wnr but pressing for 2nd whn mstke last: outpcd flat* **9/1**

2463 **6** *32* **Breaking The Bank**[34] 1424 6-11-5 **117**..........(p) DarylJacob 87
(Ben Case) *in tch in midfield: mstke 3rd: j. slowly 7th: struggling and mstke next: lost tch after 3 out: t.o* **10/3**[2]

P- **P** **Moonlight Boy (IRE)**[21] 1541 8-11-5 **117**..........(t) AndrewTinkler
(Ben Haslam) *hld up in last pair: struggling 9th: wkng whn mstke next: t.o whn p.u 2 out* **8/1**

3m 57.1s (-13.10) **Going Correction** -0.65s/f (Firm) **7 Ran SP% 111.7**
Speed ratings (Par 105): **106,103,103,101,100 84,**
WIN: 8.90; PL: 4.90, 1.10 Halling's Wish, 1.00 Le Fin Bois; EX: WP/LFB 35.60, WP/HW 12.30; CSF: WP/LFB 31.06, WP/HW 37.70; TF: WP/LFB/HW 154.20, WP/HW/LFB 91.20.
Owner Gary Attwood **Bred** John McEnery **Trained** Icomb, Gloucs

FOCUS
A fair novices' handicap chase and yet another winner to make all.

1770 WINNER.CO.UK CASINO H'CAP HURDLE (10 hdls) 2m 3f 137y
4:05 (4:06) (Class 4) (0-120,118) 3-Y-O+ **£3,249** (£954; £477; £238)

Form RPR

-411 **1** **Occasionally Yours (IRE)**[126] 571 11-10-4 **103**.......... MissTWorsley(7) 107
(Alan Blackmore) *pressed ldr tl led bef 2 out: shkn up between last 2: rdn and styd on wl to readily assert flat: pushed out towards fin* **5/1**[3]

-650 **2** *1 3/4* **Tiradia (FR)**[14] 1591 8-10-10 **102**.......... AidanColeman 104
(J R Jenkins) *hld up in tch in last: nt clr run and swtchd lft bnd bef 2 out: produced to chal 2 out: rdn between last 2: no ex and outstyd fnl 150yds* **5/1**[3]

5505 **3** *1 3/4* **Factor Fifty (IRE)**[49] 1270 6-10-13 **110**..........(tp) NathanMoscrop(5) 111
(Philip Kirby) *cl up in 4th: rdn bef 3 out: pressing ldng pair 2 out: drvn and one pce whn j.rt last: no imp flat* **6/4**[1]

45-P **4** *7* **Flashman**[146] 237 6-10-12 **104**.......... JoshuaMoore 100
(Gary Moore) *chsd ldng pair: effrt after 3 out: outpcd in 4th next: btn whn hung bdly lft flat* **5/2**[2]

0-P6 **5** *14* **Dispour (IRE)**[31] 1459 5-11-12 **118**..........(bt) WayneHutchinson 102
(Donald McCain) *led tl rdn and hdd bef 2 out: sn btn: wknd and bhd last* **8/1**

4m 41.2s (-17.80) **Going Correction** -0.725s/f (Firm) **5 Ran SP% 113.0**
Speed ratings (Par 105): **106,105,104,101,96**
CSF £28.23 TOTE £4.00: £2.00, £2.20; EX 18.70 Trifecta £58.40.
Owner A G Blackmore **Bred** Gerard Connolly **Trained** Little Berkhamsted, Herts

FOCUS
The pace looked ordinary in this fair handicap hurdle.

1771 100% MATCHES BONUS AT WINNER.CO.UK H'CAP HURDLE (12 hdls) 3m 1f 10y
4:40 (4:40) (Class 5) (0-100,98) 4-Y-O+ **£2,599** (£763; £381; £190)

Form RPR

4345 **1** **Amber Flush**[20] 1547 6-11-1 **94**.......... MrJamesSmith(7) 104+
(Martin Smith) *w ldr and sn clr of field: led 4th: mde rest: wnt clr 9th: pressed whn pushed along and asserted bef 2 out: styd on* **11/2**

-2P2 **2** *3* **Hassadin**[38] 1383 9-11-3 **89**..........(p) NoelFehily 94
(Michael Blake) *midfield: chsd ldrs 6th: 4th and rdn after 9th: drvn and looked wl hld bef 2 out: wnt 3rd 2 out: plugged on to go 2nd flat: no threat to wnr* **3/1**[1]

152- **3** *3 1/2* **Boherna Lady (IRE)**[8] 1665 7-11-5 **98**..........(t) KevinDarcy(7) 101
(Denis Gerard Hogan, Ire) *hld up in last pair: chsd clr ldng pair after 7th: steadily clsd: wnt 2nd bef 3 out: rdn and effrt to press wnr bef 2 out: no ex and struggling whn landed awkwardly 2 out: btn last: lost 2nd flat* **10/3**[2]

/051 **4** *34* **Miss Mayfair (IRE)**[34] 1426 8-11-4 **90**..........(p) TomCannon 73
(Lawney Hill) *led and clr w wnr: hdd 4th but remained clr w wnr tl drvn 9th: 3rd and no ex next: wknd bef 2 out: eased flat: t.o* **3/1**[1]

-234 **5** *58* **Stay In My Heart (IRE)**[28] 1490 6-11-9 **95**..........(p) LeightonAspell 14
(Laura Mongan) *chsd clr ldng pair tl lost pl and pushed along 6th: rdn after next and nvr travelling wl after: lost tch and t.o bef 3 out* **9/2**[3]

0PP0 **P** **Oscar Baby (IRE)**[28] 1490 9-10-5 **77**.......... MarcGoldstein
(Diana Grissell) *a towards rr: in tch in 5th whn rdn bef 9th: lost tch bef 3 out: t.o whn p.u 2 out: lame* **22/1**

6m 3.5s (-19.40) **Going Correction** -0.725s/f (Firm) **6 Ran SP% 111.0**
Speed ratings (Par 103): **102,101,99,89,70**
CSF £21.98 TOTE £8.80: £3.70, £1.70; EX 23.20 Trifecta £98.50.
Owner Mrs Rachel Rennie **Bred** Wood Farm Stud **Trained** Newmarket, Suffolk

FOCUS
A modest staying handicap hurdle, but a fair pace with a disputed lead.

1772 BET & WATCH AT WINNER.CO.UK "JUNIOR" STANDARD OPEN NATIONAL HUNT FLAT RACE 1m 5f 148y
5:10 (5:11) (Class 6) 3-Y-O **£1,949** (£572; £286; £143)

Form RPR

1 **Walpole (IRE)** 3-10-12 0.......... AidanColeman 100+
(Hugo Palmer) *chsd ldrs tl led over 2f out: rdn and rn green over 1f out: in command and r.o wl fnl f: rdn out* **9/4**[1]

2 *1 3/4* **Passmore** 3-10-5 0.......... WayneHutchinson 91+
(Alan King) *hld up in tch: clsd to chse ldrs over 2f out: effrt to chse wnr 2f out: styd on same pce ins fnl f* **9/4**[1]

3 *1 1/2* **Anne Of Brittany (FR)** 3-10-5 0.......... JackQuinlan 89
(Henry Spiller) *hld up in tch: effrt bnd over 2f out: wnt 3rd over 1f out: styd on same pce ins fnl f* **12/1**

4 *2 1/2* **Culture De Sivola (FR)** 3-10-1 0 ow1.......... LizzieKelly(5) 87
(Nick Williams) *in tch in midfield: rdn and effrt to chse ldrs over 2f out: outpcd over 1f out: 4th and kpt on same pce fnl f* **12/1**

5 *7* **Miss Feistypants** 3-10-0 0.......... KevinJones(5) 76
(Seamus Mullins) *hld up in tch in last pair: effrt and hdwy into midfield 2f out: sn rdn and no imp: wknd fnl f* **25/1**

6 *3 1/4* **Golden Gate Bridge (GER)** 3-10-12 0.......... DenisO'Regan 80
(Mark Pitman) *led for over 1f: styd handy: rdn 3f out: sn struggling: wknd 2f out* **9/2**[2]

7 *1 3/4* **Oceans Glory** 3-10-12 0.......... MattieBatchelor 77
(John Ryan) *t.k.h: rn green: chsd ldr tl led 7f out: hdd and rdn over 2f out: no ex 2f out: sn wknd* **33/1**

8 *nse* **Very First Time** 3-10-12 0.......... LeightonAspell 77
(Tim Easterby) *t.k.h: in tch: hdwy to ld over 11f out: hdd 7f out: styd prom tl wknd over 2f out* **9/1**[3]

9 *10* **Twycross Warrior** 3-10-5 0.......... ConorSmith(7) 64
(Robin Dickin) *hld up in tch in last pair: rdn over 3f out: struggling and outpcd over 2f out: sn wknd* **33/1**

10 *3 1/4* **Hank Williams** 3-10-5 0.......... MrBenjaminStephens(7) 60
(Kristin Stubbs) *hld up in tch: rdn and hmpd 3f out: sn lost pl: bhd over 1f out* **50/1**

3m 11.9s (-8.10) **10 Ran SP% 116.8**
CSF £6.71 TOTE £3.30: £1.10, £1.60, £4.00; EX 9.00 Trifecta £75.10.
Owner Roldvale Limited **Bred** Roundhill Stud **Trained** Newmarket, Suffolk

FOCUS
No form to go on in this junior bumper and, as is often the case in races like this, the runners were reluctant to jump off. However, the finish was dominated by a couple of nice sorts and the first four pulled well clear.
T/Plt: £57.50 to a £1 stake. Pool: £41,424.42 - 525.61 winning units T/Qpdt: £29.80 to a £1 stake. Pool: £2,540.54 - 62.94 winning units **Steve Payne**

1550 KELSO (L-H)
Sunday, October 4

OFFICIAL GOING: Good to firm (8.2)
Wind: Almost nil Weather: Overcast

1773 NEWCASTLE ARMS COLDSTREAM H'CAP HURDLE (8 hdls) 2m 51y
2:05 (2:05) (Class 4) (0-120,115) 3-Y-O+ **£3,898** (£1,144; £572; £286)

Form RPR

2321 **1** **Dynamic Drive (IRE)**[16] 1572 8-10-12 **108**..........(t) ThomasDowson(7) 118+
(Maurice Barnes) *hld up in tch: stdy hdwy to chse ldr between last 2: rdn to ld run-in: edgd lft: kpt on strly* **13/2**

F5-1 **2** *2* **Mighty Whitey (IRE)**[31] 1459 9-11-3 **109**..........(t) DerekFox(3) 116
(Noel C Kelly, Ire) *j. sltly rt: led: pushed along after 2 out: rdn and hdd run-in: kpt on same pce* **17/2**

4216 **3** *6* **Endeavor**[10] 1639 10-10-4 **96**..........(p) EmmaSayer(3) 98
(Dianne Sayer) *t.k.h: cl up: wnt 2nd bef 2 out to between last 2: sn pushed along and outpcd* **22/1**

20-3 **4** *3/4* **Push Me (IRE)**[31] 1459 8-10-13 **102**.......... AdrianLane 104
(Iain Jardine) *nt fluent on occasions: hld up: pushed along and hdwy bef 2 out: no imp fr last* **5/1**[3]

54-0 **5** *1/2* **Rockabilly Riot (IRE)**[19] 638 5-11-2 **105**.......... HenryBrooke 107
(Martin Todhunter) *hld up: stdy hdwy gng wl bef 2 out: shkn up and effrt whn nt fluent last: fnd little* **40/1**

1-22 **6** *2* **Muwalla**[18] 1553 8-10-10 **104**..........(t) DiarmuidO'Regan(5) 103
(Lisa Harrison) *hld up in tch: rdn along fr 2 out: edgd lft and wknd bef last* **9/2**[2]

0-03 **7** *12* **Calton Entry (IRE)**[26] 1501 6-11-7 **110**.......... BrianHughes 98
(Linda Perratt) *t.k.h: chsd ldr to bef 2 out: rdn and wknd after 2 out* **8/1**

5233 **8** *23* **Sleep In First (FR)**[38] 1367 9-11-7 **115**..........(t) DaleIrving(5) 82
(James Ewart) *cl up: drvn and lost pl 4th: hit and wknd 3 out: t.o* **9/1**

3/0- **9** *1 1/4* **Love Marmalade (IRE)**[7] 5361 5-10-10 **102**.......... CraigNichol(3) 68
(Alistair Whillans) *t.k.h: prom on outside: lost pl bef 4th: struggling fr next: t.o* **10/3**[1]

4-50 **10** *2 3/4* **Mwangaza (FR)**[105] 804 5-10-1 **90**..........[1] BrianHarding 54
(Pauline Robson) *nt fluent on occasions: hld up: outpcd after 3rd: struggling fr next: t.o* **22/1**

3m 40.4s (-21.40) **Going Correction** -1.10s/f (Hard) **10 Ran SP% 114.0**
Speed ratings (Par 105): **109,108,105,104,104 103,97,85,85,83**
CSF £57.11 CT £1138.75 TOTE £6.40: £2.20, £2.80, £4.10; EX 54.80 Trifecta £779.70 Part won..
Owner Ring Of Fire **Bred** Pendley Farm **Trained** Farlam, Cumbria

FOCUS
Chase rail at innermost position and distances as advertised. Hurdle rail out 2yds on all bends and races 1 & 2 increased by 9yds and races 4 & 7 increased by 14yds. A routine handicap hurdle run at a solid pace and in a good time. The third to sixth help set the level.

1774 EDINBURGH'S MATHERS BAR MAIDEN HURDLE (8 hdls) 2m 51y
2:35 (2:37) (Class 4) 3-Y-O+ **£3,898** (£1,144; £572; £286)

Form RPR

F25 **1** **Sindarban (IRE)**[84] 960 4-11-10 104..........(t) BrianHarding 106+
(Donald McCain) *plld hrd: hld up in tch: mstke 1st: smooth hdwy to ld 2 out: sn pushed along: kpt on strly fr last* **4/1**[3]

56-F **2** *2 3/4* **Bowdler's Magic**[7] 661 8-11-10 100.......... BrianHughes 100
(David Thompson) *led to 1st: cl up: led 3 out: blnd and hdd next: sn rcvrd and chsd wnr: rdn and one pce fr last* **7/2**[2]

25-2 **3** *3 1/4* **Summer Storm**[16] 1568 5-11-7 114..........(t) TonyKelly(3) 96
(Rebecca Menzies) *t.k.h: trckd ldrs: hit 3 out: effrt and rdn next: kpt on same pce fr last* **11/8**[1]

3-6 **4** *3/4* **Beechroad Ally (IRE)**[18] 1550 6-11-0 0..........(t[1]) DerekFox(3) 87
(Sandy Thomson) *cl up: led 1st to 3 out: rallied and ev ch next: kpt on same pce appr last* **4/1**[3]

5 *10* **Slide Show**[101] 7-11-0 0.......... AdamNicol(3) 79
(David Thompson) *t.k.h: hld up: hdwy on outside bef 2 out: outpcd whn nt fluent last: sn wknd* **50/1**

05- **6** *3/4* **Ethan (IRE)**[237] 4128 6-11-5 0.......... MissCWalton(5) 84
(Sheena Walton) *t.k.h: in tch on outside: outpcd bef 3 out: struggling whn nt fluent next: n.d after* **50/1**

P-P **7** *3* **Centre Haafhd**[10] 1634 4-11-3 0.......... LorcanMurtagh(7) 81
(Barry Murtagh) *t.k.h: hld up: stdy hdwy after 3 out: rdn and outpcd next: wkng whn hit last* **200/1**

/ **8** *3 1/2* **Parlour Of Dreams (IRE)**[546] 8-11-3 0.......... SamColtherd(7) 77
(Andrew Hamilton) *plld hrd: hld up: hdwy and prom 4 out: rdn and wknd 2 out* **25/1**

60 **R** **Housewives Choice**[19] 1328 4-11-0 0.......... JoeColliver(3)
(James Bethell) *ref to r* **20/1**

3m 52.5s (-9.30) **Going Correction** -1.10s/f (Hard) **9 Ran SP% 117.4**
Speed ratings (Par 105): **79,77,76,75,70 70,68,67,**
CSF £18.14 TOTE £3.80: £1.10, £1.40, £1.20; EX 25.00 Trifecta £63.90.
Owner Paul & Clare Rooney **Bred** His Highness The Aga Khan's Studs S C **Trained** Cholmondeley, Cheshire

FOCUS
The first four all set a fair standard at this level. However the time was relatively slow and the form is rated a lot lower than it might have been.

1775 GEOFF & ELSPETH CELEBRATION NOVICES' H'CAP CHASE (17 fncs) 2m 7f 96y
3:15 (3:15) (Class 4) (0-105,103) 4-Y-O+ **£5,848** (£1,717; £858; £429)

Form RPR
665- **1** **Present Flight (IRE)**[218] 4486 6-11-4 **98**..........(t) DerekFox(3) 121+
(Lucinda Russell) *t.k.h: prom: hdwy to chse ldr after 5 out: led 2 out: drew clr fr last: eased towards fin* **7/1**

2 **2** *11* **Derryfadda (IRE)**[38] 1371 6-11-1 **95**.......... HarryChalloner(3) 106+
(Richard Ford) *led: nt fluent 6th: hit 3 out: hdd next: rdn and outpcd whn nt fluent last: no ch w wnr* **3/1**[2]

535 **3** *10* **Longueville Flier (IRE)**[16] 1571 6-11-2 **93**.......... TomO'Brien 91
(Micky Hammond) *hld up in tch: rdn and outpcd 4 out: rallied to chse clr ldng pair after 2 out: no imp* **5/1**[3]

-P11 **4** *7* **Sgt Bull Berry**[38] 1380 8-9-10 **80**.......... JamieHamilton(7) 71
(Peter Maddison) *chsd ldr: hit 12th: lost 2nd after next: drvn and outpcd bef 3 out: struggling fr next* **15/8**[1]

0516 **5** *16* **Bayfirth (IRE)**[31] 1462 12-9-11 **81**.......... SamColtherd(7) 58
(Andrew Hamilton) *chsd ldrs: drvn and outpcd whn hit 3 out: sn wknd* **22/1**

-036 **6** *6* **District Attorney (IRE)**[18] 1552 6-10-6 **86**.......... JohnKington(3) 63
(Chris Fairhurst) *mstkes in rr: struggling fnl circ: lost tch fr 4 out* **20/1**

-040 **F** **Emkae (IRE)**[120] 637 7-10-11 **88**..........(t) BrianHarding
(Alison Hamilton) *hld up in tch: fell 5th* **6/1**

5m 49.7s (-18.30) **Going Correction** -0.85s/f (Firm) 7 Ran SP% **112.3**
Speed ratings (Par 105): **97,93,89,87,81 79,**
CSF £27.99 CT £113.64 TOTE £4.30: £2.20, £1.60; EX 11.50 Trifecta £77.90.
Owner Kilco (International) Ltd **Bred** Brian Kiely **Trained** Arlary, Perth & Kinross

FOCUS
A modest race of its type, run at a moderate tempo, but the easy winner has some potential. He produced a big step up on his hurdles form.

1776 BORDERS EMPLOYMENT LAW INTERMEDIATE HURDLE (11 hdls) 2m 4f 189y
3:50 (3:50) (Class 4) 4-Y-O+ **£5,198** (£1,526; £763; £381)

Form RPR
402- **1** **Hello George (IRE)**[183] 5142 6-11-5 126..........(p) RichardJohnson 127+
(Philip Hobbs) *mde all: nt fluent 6th: pushed along 2 out: kpt on strly fr last* **4/6**[1]

14-5 **2** *6* **Cooking Fat**[38] 1369 4-11-5 120.......... BrianHughes 119
(Dianne Sayer) *hld up in tch: smooth hdwy 3 out: effrt and chsd wnr next: rdn and kpt on same pce fr last* **12/1**

2301 **3** *6* **Welcome Ben (IRE)**[26] 1498 6-11-2 115.......... TonyKelly(3) 113
(Jackie Stephen) *chsd wnr to 3rd: cl up: hdwy and regained 2nd after 3 out to next: rdn and outpcd between last 2* **14/1**

20-3 **4** *nk* **Thorpe (IRE)**[143] 301 5-11-2 122.......... DerekFox(3) 113
(Lucinda Russell) *in tch: pushed along and hdwy 3 out: drvn and outpcd fr next* **11/2**[3]

4-21 **5** *1 3/4* **Waterclock (IRE)**[18] 1550 6-11-5 122..........(v) BrianHarding 113
(Jedd O'Keeffe) *cl up: wnt 2nd 3rd: nt fluent 6th: rdn and lost 2nd after 3 out: outpcd whn hit next: btn whn flattened last* **5/2**[2]

1F-0 **6** *45* **Slaney Star (IRE)**[18] 1552 7-11-5 91..........(v) HenryBrooke 66
(Jean McGregor) *nt fluent on occasions: hld up: pushed along and outpcd after 4 out: lost tch after next: t.o* **66/1**

0006 **7** *15* **Raifteiri (IRE)**[16] 1573 8-10-12 68..........(tp) MrJDixon(7) 51
(William Young Jnr) *towards rr: pushed along 1/2-way: lost tch fr 4 out: t.o* **100/1**

P **Benvardin (IRE)**[121] 633 5-10-5 0.......... SamColtherd(7)
(Andrew Hamilton) *bhd: struggling bef 7th: lost tch and p.u after next* **100/1**

4m 50.9s (-17.10) **Going Correction** -1.10s/f (Hard) 8 Ran SP% **121.8**
Speed ratings (Par 105): **88,85,83,83,82 65,59,**
CSF £12.15 TOTE £1.70: £1.10, £3.00, £2.60; EX 12.40 Trifecta £66.40.
Owner M St Quinton/ C Hellyer/ M Strong **Bred** George Ward **Trained** Withycombe, Somerset

FOCUS
Some useful hurdlers contested this non-handicap, which was run at a sound pace but a comfortable one for the all-the-way winner. He's rated close to his mark.

1777 NSPCC SCHOOL SERVICE H'CAP CHASE (12 fncs) 2m 1f 14y
4:20 (4:21) (Class 2) 4-Y-O+
£13,986 (£4,137; £2,067; £1,032; £517; £261)

Form RPR
356- **1** **Simply Ned (IRE)**[177] 5252 8-11-12 **157**.......... BrianHarding 164+
(Nicky Richards) *hld up: stdy hdwy 5 out: effrt and led between last 2: sn drvn along: kpt on strly run-in* **6/4**[1]

3311 **2** *3* **Robin's Command (IRE)**[18] 1553 8-9-11 **131**.......... CraigNichol(3) 134
(Rose Dobbin) *cl up: led bef 4 out: drvn and hdd between last 2: kpt on fr last: nt pce of wnr* **7/2**[2]

33P- **3** *1/2* **Croco Bay (IRE)**[177] 5252 8-11-6 **151**.......... KielanWoods 155
(Ben Case) *in tch: stdy hdwy 1/2-way: effrt and ev ch whn hit 2 out: sn drvn along: kpt on same pce fr last* **8/1**[3]

FF-3 **4** *16* **Dunraven Storm (IRE)**[153] 103 10-11-3 **148**.......... RichardJohnson 137
(Philip Hobbs) *j.rt on occasions: t.k.h and sn led: hdd bef 4 out: rdn and wknd bef 2 out* **7/2**[2]

3214 **5** *2* **Lisbon (IRE)**[18] 1554 7-10-0 **131** oh7..........(t) BrianHughes 119
(Patrick Griffin, Ire) *nt fluent on occasions: hld up: pushed along and outpcd 1/2-way: rallied bef 2 out: wknd bef last* **10/1**

-335 **6** *18* **Fair Dilemma (IRE)**[29] 1482 10-10-7 **138**.......... TomO'Brien 108
(Paul Henderson) *t.k.h: early ldr: cl up: lost pl 7th: struggling fr next: t.o* **14/1**

3m 57.8s (-20.20) **Going Correction** -0.85s/f (Firm) 6 Ran SP% **111.3**
Speed ratings (Par 109): **113,111,111,103,102 94**
CSF £7.33 TOTE £3.20: £1.40, £1.80; EX 5.10 Trifecta £23.90.
Owner David & Nicky Robinson **Bred** Miss Irene Hatton **Trained** Greystoke, Cumbria

FOCUS
With the winner rated 157, this was a smart line-up, though the pace was ordinary. Solid form. The winner is verging on top-class and this rates a pb.

1778 WALKING THE COURSES H'CAP CHASE (17 fncs) 2m 7f 96y
4:55 (4:55) (Class 5) (0-100,97) 4-Y-O+ **£3,898** (£1,144; £572; £286)

Form RPR
4P-3 **1** **Donapollo**[26] 1500 7-11-9 **97**..........(t) CraigNichol(3) 106+
(Rose Dobbin) *cl up on outside: hdwy to ld 3 out: rdn and kpt on strly fr next* **7/2**[2]

2342 **2** *6* **Solway Bay**[18] 1551 13-11-2 **94**..........(t) MissRMcDonald(7) 100
(Lisa Harrison) *nt fluent: hld up in tch: rdn and outpcd 5 out: rallied bef 2 out: chsd wnr bef last: no imp* **4/1**[3]

662P **3** *5* **Generous Chief (IRE)**[36] 1403 7-11-9 **94**..........(b) BrianHughes 95
(Chris Grant) *rn in snatches: bhd: outpcd fnl circ: struggling after 5 out: plugged on fr 2 out: nvr able to chal* **7/1**

P-6P **4** *7* **Reverse The Charge (IRE)**[100] 842 8-9-9 **71** oh2.......... DaleIrving(5) 66
(Jane Walton) *cl up: led 5 out: nt fluent next: hdd 3 out: rallied: wknd bef last* **10/1**

2PP2 **5** *2 1/4* **Winter Alchemy (IRE)**[65] 1171 10-11-2 **90**.......... AdamNicol(3) 81
(Nicky Richards) *led to 5 out: cl up: drvn and outpcd 3 out: btn fr next* **11/4**[1]

3361 **6** *5* **Bescot Springs (IRE)**[16] 1573 10-11-7 **95**..........(v) GrahamWatters(3) 84
(Lucinda Russell) *trckd ldrs: drvn and outpcd whn mstke 3 out: sn wknd* **7/2**[2]

5m 50.6s (-17.40) **Going Correction** -0.85s/f (Firm) 6 Ran SP% **112.7**
Speed ratings (Par 103): **96,93,92,89,88 87**
CSF £17.95 TOTE £3.30: £1.20, £2.60; EX 12.10 Trifecta £69.10.
Owner Mrs Rose Dobbin **Bred** J M Bates **Trained** South Hazelrigg, Northumbria
■ Stewards' Enquiry : Dale Irving one-day ban: careless riding

FOCUS
The pace was respectable for the trip in this modest handicap chase. The form is rated around the second to his mark.

1779 RADIO BORDERS NOVICES' H'CAP HURDLE (11 hdls) 2m 6f 151y
5:30 (5:30) (Class 5) (0-100,92) 3-Y-O+ **£2,599** (£763; £381; £190)

Form RPR
0001 **1** **Touch Of Steel (IRE)**[18] 1552 6-11-1 **86**..........(b) DaleIrving(5) 96
(James Ewart) *mde all: idled and jnd bef 2 out: sn rdn: styd on strly to draw clr fr last* **2/1**[2]

2654 **2** *3 1/4* **Destiny Awaits (IRE)**[43] 1329 6-11-5 **90**.......... GrantCockburn(5) 98
(Keith Pollock) *hld up in last pl: hdwy and cl up whn nt fluent 7th: wnt 2nd bef 3 out: rdn and ev ch bef next and between last 2: one pce run-in* **4/1**[3]

U464 **3** *4 1/2* **Miss Joeking (IRE)**[11] 1627 4-10-10 **84**.......... RossChapman(7) 85
(Lucinda Russell) *in tch: lft 3rd 2nd: pushed along and outpcd bef 4 out: tk modest 3rd last: no ch w first two* **12/1**

-000 **4** *2 3/4* **Warksburn Boy**[43] 1328 5-11-5 **92**.......... JamieHamilton(7) 94
(Sheena Walton) *chsd wnr: effrt and ch bef 2 out: sn rdn: disputing 2nd whn mstke 2 out: sn outpcd: btn last* **15/2**

-462 **U** **Marlee Massie (IRE)**[36] 1400 6-10-12 **78**..........(p) LucyAlexander
(N W Alexander) *chsd ldrs: nt fluent and uns rdr 2nd* **15/8**[1]

5m 22.8s (-18.20) **Going Correction** -1.10s/f (Hard)
WFA 4 from 5yo+ 10lb 5 Ran SP% **107.6**
Speed ratings (Par 103): **87,85,84,83,**
CSF £9.72 TOTE £2.10: £1.50, £2.40; EX 7.50 Trifecta £37.70.
Owner Mrs Hugh Fraser **Bred** Frances Galloway **Trained** Langholm, Dumfries & G'way

FOCUS
In a low-grade event, the pace was pedestrian until the real race began at the second-last. Not strong form but the winner is improving.
T/Jkpt: £6,918.20 to a £1 stake. Pool: £29,232.14 - 3.00 winning units T/Plt: £47.40 to a £1 stake. Pool: £63,058.88 - 969.52 winning units T/Qpdt: £11.00 to a £1 stake. Pool: £4,345.43 - 291.49 winning units **Richard Young**

1597 UTTOXETER (L-H)
Sunday, October 4

OFFICIAL GOING: Good (watered; 8.2)
Wind: Light; behind Weather: Fine

1780 A & S ENTERPRISES CONDITIONAL JOCKEYS' MAIDEN HURDLE (10 hdls) 2m 3f 207y
2:15 (2:15) (Class 5) 4-Y-O+ **£2,599** (£763; £381; £190)

Form RPR
1 **Royal Sea (IRE)**[31] 6-11-0 0.......... BenPoste 108+
(Michael Mullineaux) *hld up: j. slowly 2nd: hdwy 7th: led appr last: rdn out* **40/1**

503 **2** *6* **Bare Necessities (IRE)**[34] 1425 5-11-0 0.......... ConorShoemark 104
(Shaun Lycett) *led tl after 2nd: trckd ldrs: led after 3 out: rdn and hdd appr last: styd on same pce flat* **11/10**[1]

3 **3** *14* **Medieval Bishop (IRE)**[14] 1597 6-10-11 0.......... JoshWall(3) 90
(Tony Forbes) *hld up: hdwy 7th: rdn and wknd bef next* **5/1**[3]

/1-5 **4** *nk* **Theatrical Style (IRE)**[18] 1550 6-10-8 0.......... JamesCowley(6) 92
(Donald McCain) *w ldr tl led after 2nd: hdd next: led again appr 7th: rdn and hdd after 3 out: wknd next* **7/4**[2]

F-P6 **5** *64* **Just Lewis**[14] 1597 8-10-9 72.......... WilliamFeatherstone(5) 32
(Nikki Evans) *plld hrd and prom: led 3rd: clr 5th: hdd appr 7th: sn wknd* **150/1**

6 *1/2* **Happy Jack (IRE)**[39] 4-11-0 0.......... RyanHatch 32
(Michael Wigham) *hld up: hdwy 7th: sn rdn and wknd* **16/1**

4m 57.5s (-5.70) **Going Correction** -0.75s/f (Firm)
WFA 4 from 5yo+ 10lb 6 Ran SP% **109.6**
Speed ratings (Par 103): **81,78,73,72,47 47**
CSF £84.64 TOTE £28.00: £11.90, £1.30; EX 104.70 Trifecta £362.00.
Owner Keith Jones & Mrs Pam Sephton **Bred** Rabbah Bloodstock Limited **Trained** Alpraham, Cheshire

FOCUS
Divided bends with Hurdles on inside rail. The going was given as good (GoingStick 8.2). This looked likely to involve the two favourites in the betting, but they began racing down the back and left the door open for one of the outsiders to cause an upset.

1781 A & S (MECHANICAL SERVICES) MAIDEN HURDLE (FOR THE MERCIAN REGIMENT TROPHY) (8 hdls 1 omitted) 1m 7f 168y
2:45 (2:45) (Class 5) 4-Y-O+ £2,599 (£763; £381; £190)

Form RPR
31- 1 **Younevercall (IRE)**[170] 5380 4-11-0 0 DavidBass 117+
(Kim Bailey) *j.rt at times: chsd ldr tl led 3rd: shkn up appr last: styd on wl* 5/4[1]
2020 2 3 **Clock On Tom**[10] 1421 5-11-0 105 WillKennedy 111
(Denis Quinn) *racd keenly and sn prom: chsd wnr 5th: rdn appr last: styd on same pce flat* 15/2
2135 3 5 **Tilinisi (IRE)**[25] 1518 5-10-4 0 ConorShoemark(3) 99
(Phil Middleton) *chsd ldrs: rdn appr last: no ex flat* 11/4[2]
5-26 4 13 **Fields Of Glory (FR)**[20] 1544 5-11-0 0 MichaelByrne 93
(Tim Vaughan) *set stdy pce: j.rt 2nd: hdd next: chsd wnr to 5th: wknd appr 2 out* 10/1
464- 5 7 **City Dreams (IRE)**[237] 3217 5-10-7 0 NickScholfield 79
(Michael Blake) *hld up: mstke 1st: sme hdwy appr 2 out: sn rdn and wknd* 20/1
6 6 **Ellie's Choice (IRE)**[36] 1406 6-10-7 0 PaulMoloney 73
(Des Donovan) *chsd ldr tl mstke and wknd 3 out* 7/1[3]
P606 7 17 **Captain Starlight (IRE)**[44] 1154 5-11-0 73 LeeEdwards 63
(Aytach Sadik) *hld up: rdn and wknd 3 out* 100/1
R **Magnus Romeo**[490] 4-10-9 0 (t) AliceMills(5)
(Gail Haywood) *prom: j. slowly and lost pl 1st: nt fluent 2nd and 3rd: sn bhd: hung rt: rn out and uns rdr 3 out* 25/1

3m 58.1s (0.70) **Going Correction** -0.75s/f (Firm) 8 Ran SP% 114.1
Speed ratings (Par 103): **68,66,64,57,54 51,42,**
CSF £11.33 TOTE £2.20: £1.20, £2.30, £1.10; EX 11.30 Trifecta £32.60.
Owner Younverknow Partnership **Bred** Paddy Kennedy **Trained** Andoversford, Gloucs
FOCUS
Hurdle in the chute omitted. This was run at a crawl and was completely dominated by the pacesetting favourite

1782 KALAHARI KING BEGINNERS' CHASE (15 fncs) 2m 4f
3:25 (3:25) (Class 3) 4-Y-O+ £9,384 (£2,772; £1,386; £693)

Form RPR
32P- 1 **Killala Quay**[208] 4694 8-11-4 139 (p) SamTwiston-Davies 146+
(Charlie Longsdon) *mde all: shkn up and nt fluent 3 out: styd on wl* 5/6[1]
202- 2 4½ **Souriyan (FR)**[172] 5339 4-10-7 0 MichealNolan 131
(Jamie Snowden) *trckd wnr: pushed along after 9th: rdn appr last: styd on same pce flat* 7/2[3]
3PP- 3 17 **Kylemore Lough**[162] 5539 6-11-4 0 JamieMoore 130
(Kerry Lee) *prom: racd keenly: nt fluent 11th: wknd 3 out* 11/4[2]
2162 4 25 **Gurkha Brave (IRE)**[50] 1263 7-11-4 0 NickScholfield 104
(Karen McLintock) *prom tl wknd 4 out* 12/1

4m 55.8s (-14.00) **Going Correction** -0.45s/f (Good)
WFA 4 from 6yo+ 10lb 4 Ran SP% 111.1
Speed ratings (Par 107): **110,108,101,91**
CSF £4.33 TOTE £1.70; EX 3.80 Trifecta £8.70.
Owner Richard & Mrs Susan Perkins **Bred** N Franklin **Trained** Over Norton, Oxon
FOCUS
This looked a decent novice chase, albeit one that had the feel of an early-season contest with the main contenders likely to come on for the run.

1783 A & S (ELECTRICAL SERVICES) H'CAP CHASE (FOR THE QUEEN'S ROYAL LANCERS CHALLENGE CUP) (18 fncs) 3m 2y
3:55 (3:56) (Class 4) (0-120,120) 4-Y-O £6,330 (£1,870; £935; £468; £234)

Form RPR
5006 1 **Feast Of Fire (IRE)**[12] 1615 8-9-8 95 RyanDay(7) 103
(Mike Sowersby) *hld up: hdwy 10th: chsd ldr 3 out: led appr last: rdn out* 8/1
2-34 2 1¾ **Frampton (IRE)**[121] 622 6-11-12 120 (p) SamTwiston-Davies 127
(Charlie Longsdon) *chsd ldr: led 3rd: rdn and hdd appr last: styd on same pce flat* 4/1[2]
0415 3 15 **Presented (IRE)**[11] 1632 8-11-1 114 StephenMulqueen(5) 109
(Lisa Harrison) *lft in ld 1st: hdd 3rd: chsd ldr tl rdn 3 out: wknd next* 12/1
4111 4 1¼ **Clubs Are Trumps (IRE)**[32] 1450 6-11-6 114 (p) WillKennedy 109
(Jonjo O'Neill) *chsd ldr: disputing cl 3rd whn hit 4 out: sn rdn: wknd next* 11/4[1]
6053 5 11 **Big Sound**[16] 1571 8-11-5 113 (p) JakeGreenall 97
(Mark Walford) *prom: lost pl 10th: pushed along 12th: wknd after 14th* 15/2
4-42 F **Master Neo (FR)**[8] 1659 9-11-7 115 (t) ConorO'Farrell
(Nigel Hawke) *hld up: hmpd 1st: fell 8th* 5/1[3]
2602 F **Green Wizard (IRE)**[16] 1571 9-11-2 110 DannyCook
(Sue Smith) *led and fell 1st* 4/1[2]

6m 4.6s (-3.50) **Going Correction** -0.45s/f (Good) 7 Ran SP% 113.9
Speed ratings (Par 105): **87,86,81,81,77 ,**
CSF £39.83 TOTE £12.50: £7.40, £2.30; EX 57.20 Trifecta £629.30.
Owner Mrs E A Verity **Bred** Patrick Joyce **Trained** Goodmanham, E Yorks

1784 DAINS ACCOUNTANTS H'CAP HURDLE (FOR THE ROYAL YEOMANRY STAFFORDSHIRE & SHROPSHIRE CUP) (12 hdls) 2m 7f 70y
4:30 (4:31) (Class 3) (0-130,129) 4-Y-O £6,330 (£1,870; £935; £468; £234)

Form RPR
5112 1 **Princeton Royale (IRE)**[14] 1594 6-11-12 129 (v) TrevorWhelan 136+
(Neil King) *hld up: hdwy 7th: rdn and swtchd rt bef 2 out: led appr last: sn clr* 9/2[3]
5/01 2 7 **Dartford Warbler (IRE)**[14] 1600 8-11-0 117 DannyCook 118
(Sue Smith) *led: rdn bef 3 out: hdd appr last: styd on same pce* 9/2[3]
/15- 3 14 **San Telm (IRE)**[352] 1932 10-11-5 122 (p) SamTwiston-Davies 112
(Stuart Edmunds) *hld up: hdwy after 9th: ev ch fr 3 out tl rdn and wknd appr last* 10/3[1]
-106 4 2¼ **Valleyofmilan (IRE)**[34] 1417 8-10-7 115 JamesCowley(5) 101
(Donald McCain) *hld up: drvn along and outpcd 8th: styd on appr last* 16/1
4002 5 10 **Solway Prince**[10] 1637 6-9-11 105 (p) StephenMulqueen(5) 82
(Lisa Harrison) *chsd ldrs: drvn along 9th: wknd bef next* 7/2[2]
406- 6 14 **Victor Leudorum (IRE)**[403] 1351 8-10-1 114 (t) TommyDowling(10) 82
(Charlie Mann) *chsd ldr to 3 out: wknd bef next* 20/1
P-11 P **Big Generator**[32] 1448 9-11-7 124 (t) HarrySkelton
(Caroline Bailey) *chsd ldrs tl rdn and wknd appr 3 out: bhd whn p.u bef last* 6/1

5m 36.6s (-22.20) **Going Correction** -0.75s/f (Firm) 7 Ran SP% 106.6
Speed ratings (Par 107): **108,105,100,99,96 91,**
CSF £21.64 CT £61.89 TOTE £5.00: £2.20, £2.80; EX 18.70 Trifecta £70.00.
Owner D Nott, P Beadles, R Clarke **Bred** Brett Merry **Trained** Barbury Castle, Wiltshire
■ Lamps was withdrawn. Price at time of withdrawal 12-1. Rule 4 applies to all bets - deduction 5p in the pound.
FOCUS
This was run at a good pace, which eventually found out those, including the favourite, lacking race fitness.

1785 A & S ENTERPRISES H'CAP CHASE (16 fncs) 2m 6f 108y
5:05 (5:05) (Class 5) (0-100,94) 4-Y-O+ £2,859 (£839; £419; £209)

Form RPR
13P0 1 **Mr Robinson (FR)**[44] 1306 8-10-9 77 TrevorWhelan 86
(Rob Summers) *hld up: hdwy appr 4 out: led last: rdn out* 12/1
-560 2 1¾ **Dawnieriver (IRE)**[43] 1326 5-10-10 78 TomScudamore 85
(Michael Scudamore) *hld up: hdwy after 8th: ev ch fr 2 out: sn rdn: no ex towards fin* 8/1
3444 3 1¼ **Lost In Newyork (IRE)**[12] 1614 8-10-6 74 (p) AdamWedge 80
(Nick Kent) *hld up: hdwy 10th: chsd ldr 3 out: led next: rdn and hdd last: styd on same pce flat* 7/1
1360 4 24 **The Purchaser (IRE)**[46] 1287 7-11-12 94 (b) TomMessenger 83
(Chris Bealby) *led: rdn: hdd and mstke 2 out: wknd bef last* 15/2
PU2- 5 38 **Typical Oscar (IRE)**[185] 5117 8-11-9 91 (p) NickScholfield 42
(Michael Blake) *chsd ldr to 6th: reminder after next: wknd appr 4 out* 4/1[1]
1-62 P **Local Present (IRE)**[16] 1569 12-10-13 84 (be) JamesBanks(3)
(Denis Quinn) *prom: rdn after 10th: wknd next: bhd whn p.u bef 3 out* 6/1[3]
133F P **Adios Alonso (IRE)**[45] 1298 9-11-8 93 BenPoste(3)
(Rosemary Gasson) *chsd ldrs: pushed along and lost pl after 8th: wknd 10th: bhd whn p.u bef 12th* 9/2[2]
1202 P **Troubled (IRE)**[36] 1403 8-10-13 81 (p) LeeEdwards
(Aytach Sadik) *prom: chsd ldr 6th tl rdn after 4 out: wknd next: bhd whn p.u and dismntd bef last* 9/2[2]

5m 42.4s (-0.30) **Going Correction** -0.45s/f (Good) 8 Ran SP% 113.7
Speed ratings (Par 103): **82,81,80,72,58 , ,**
CSF £98.85 CT £726.21 TOTE £13.80: £3.50, £3.00, £2.70; EX 136.40 Trifecta £812.80.
Owner Mrs Gill Summers **Bred** Haras De La Faisanderie & C Bouillette **Trained** Tanworth-in-Arden, Warwicks
FOCUS
This produced a good finish between the three at the foot of the weights, who finished well clear of the pacesetting top-weight.

1786 A & S RENTALS H'CAP HURDLE (8 hdls 1 omitted) 1m 7f 168y
5:40 (5:40) (Class 5) (0-100,99) 3-Y-O+ £2,599 (£763; £381; £190)

Form RPR
0-00 1 **Ullswater (IRE)**[9] 1650 7-11-3 90 (tp) TomScudamore 96+
(Gordon Elliott, Ire) *chsd ldrs: led appr last: hrd rdn flat: jst hld on* 11/8[1]
6322 2 ½ **Sweet World**[16] 1578 11-11-1 95 JordanWilliams(7) 100
(Bernard Llewellyn) *hld up: hdwy 5th: rdn and hit 2 out: r.o u.p* 10/1
6636 3 3 **Mr McGuiness (IRE)**[20] 1549 5-11-9 99 BenPoste(3) 101
(Rosemary Gasson) *hld up: rdn appr 2 out: r.o flat: nt rch ldrs* 20/1
P40- 4 1¼ **Bobby Dove**[176] 5280 8-11-0 87 SeanBowen 88
(Bernard Llewellyn) *chsd ldr tl rdn after 2 out: styd on same pce last* 11/1
-P3P 5 ¾ **Nellie The Elegant**[16] 1578 4-10-12 90 (bt[1]) AlanJohns(5) 90
(Tim Vaughan) *led: rdn after 3 out: hdd appr last: no ex flat* 25/1
2246 6 ¾ **Supernoverre (IRE)**[16] 1578 9-10-0 80 (b) DavidNoonan(7) 82
(Alan Jones) *prom: rdn appr 2 out: styng on same pce whn mstke last* 9/1[3]
-621 7 13 **Gin And Tonic**[14] 1604 5-11-10 97 SamTwiston-Davies 88
(Michael Wigham) *hld up: rdn after 5th: wknd appr 2 out* 5/2[2]
2440 U **Wymeswold**[25] 1525 8-10-9 85 JamesBanks(3)
(Michael Mullineaux) *mstke and uns rdr 1st* 25/1
50-P P **Amirli (IRE)**[88] 489 4-11-6 93 (tp) WillKennedy
(Donald McCain) *hld up in tch: rdn after 5th: wknd bef next: bhd whn p.u bef 2 out* 25/1
00-0 P **Bells Of Castor (IRE)**[45] 1299 5-11-5 92 (t) MichaelByrne
(Tim Vaughan) *hld up: rdn and wknd appr 3 out: bhd whn p.u bef last* 50/1

3m 44.9s (-12.50) **Going Correction** -0.75s/f (Firm)
WFA 4 from 5yo+ 9lb 10 Ran SP% 116.4
Speed ratings (Par 103): **101,100,99,98,98 97,91, , ,**
CSF £14.06 CT £195.95 TOTE £2.30: £1.30, £2.50, £4.90; EX 15.40 Trifecta £204.00.
Owner Ten Men Syndicate **Bred** J P Dwan **Trained** Longwood, Co Meath
FOCUS
A moderate handicap with a well-supported favourite landing the spoils.
T/Plt: £170.60 to a £1 stake. Pool: £61,596.63 - 263.55 winning units T/Qpdt: £120.10 to a £1 stake. Pool: £3,458.13 - 21.30 winning units **Colin Roberts**

1058 TIPPERARY (L-H)
Sunday, October 4

OFFICIAL GOING: Flat course - good to yielding (yielding in places); jumps courses - good (good to yielding in places)

1787a ISTABRAQ HURDLE (GRADE 2) (9 hdls) 2m
3:45 (3:45) 4-Y-O+
£25,581 (£8,100; £3,837; £1,279; £852; £426)

RPR
1 **Plinth (IRE)**[15] 1588 5-11-7 138 (bt) MarkWalsh 144
(A P O'Brien, Ire) *pressed ldr in 2nd: rdn fr 2 out: on terms last: rdn to assert ins fnl 100yds: kpt on wl* 6/1[3]
2 1 **Fethard Player (IRE)**[159] 7 8-11-4 137 (t) DavidMullins 140
(W F Treacy, Ire) *led: strly pressed appr last where nt fluent: kpt on wl tl hdd ins fnl 100yds: no ex w wnr cl home* 7/1
3 1¾ **Thomas Edison (IRE)**[66] 1163 8-11-4 150 (t) BarryGeraghty 138
(A J Martin, Ire) *hld up: tk clsr order in 4th after 3 out: wnt 3rd bef next: rdn and no imp appr last: kpt on same pce* 4/6[1]

4 7 **Usa (IRE)**[12] 1621 8-11-4 119 (t) PaulTownend 131
(S J Mahon, Ire) *racd in rr: sme hdwy into 5th after 3 out: kpt on into 4th bef last: nvr on terms* **25/1**

5 1 ½ **Thousand Stars (FR)**[8] 1671 11-11-10 152 (p) RWalsh 136
(W P Mullins, Ire) *trckd ldrs early in 3rd: dropped to 5th 4 out: sn rdn and detached in rr: plenty to do 2 out: styd on again fr last* **9/2**[2]

6 4 **Kalann (IRE)**[23] 1151 8-11-4 123 AELynch 126
(Sabrina J Harty, Ire) *chsd ldrs in 4th: wnt 3rd at 1/2-way: rdn in 4th bef 2 out where nt fluent: sn no ex* **40/1**

3m 49.5s (229.50) **6 Ran SP% 111.2**
CSF £42.88 TOTE £7.00: £1.70, £2.50; DF 40.90 Trifecta £80.20.
Owner John P McManus **Bred** Lynch Bages Ltd & Samac Ltd **Trained** Cashel, Co Tipperary

FOCUS
A pretty controversial renewal and the first and second should not have been up to fighting out a Grade 2 like this. The time doesn't support a higher rating.

1788a DOLORES PURCELL MEMORIAL NOVICE HURDLE (GRADE 3) (9 hdls) 2m
4:15 (4:15) 4-Y-O+ **£15,116** (£4,418; £2,093; £697)

RPR

1 **Bachasson (FR)**[26] 1514 4-11-4 147 RWalsh 148+
(W P Mullins, Ire) *chsd ldrs in 3rd: 4th after 2nd: prog to chse ldr in 2nd bef 2 out: led last: sn rdn clr* **2/5**[1]

2 4 ½ **Three Stars (IRE)**[68] 1140 5-11-1 127 JJBurke 138
(Henry De Bromhead, Ire) *trckd ldr in 2nd: on terms after 4 out: led 3 out: swvd markedly lft between fnl two flights: hdd last where nt fluent and sn no match for wnr* **12/1**

3 15 **Cardinal Palace (IRE)**[21] 1538 5-11-1 132 PaulTownend 125
(J A Nash, Ire) *hld up in rr: nt fluent 4th: rdn into mod 3rd after 2 out: kpt on one pce: nvr on terms* **10/1**[3]

4 2 ¼ **Moonmeister (IRE)**[29] 1408 4-11-1 130 DonaghMeyler 122
(A J Martin, Ire) *hld up in 5th: nt fluent 2 out in 4th: sn rdn and one pce* **20/1**

5 3 ¼ **Rocky Court (IRE)**[26] 1514 6-11-1 114 (t) BJCooper 118
(S J Mahon, Ire) *led: jnd after 4 out and hdd next: wknd bef next* **40/1**

6 19 **Tully East (IRE)**[18] 1557 5-11-1 0 APHeskin 99
(Alan Fleming, Ire) *chsd ldrs in 4th: wnt 3rd after 2nd: nt qckn in 3rd bef 2 out where nt fluent: sn no ex and eased bef last* **5/1**[2]

3m 46.1s (226.10) **6 Ran SP% 112.1**
CSF £6.53 TOTE £1.50: £1.70, £1.50; DF 5.60 Trifecta £17.50.
Owner Edward O'Connell **Bred** P De Quatrebarbes & T De Quatrebarbes **Trained** Muine Beag, Co Carlow

FOCUS
There was a significant non-runner here and it made it a good deal easier for the winner. The first two were clear and recorded fair pbs.

1789a (Foreign Racing) - See Raceform Interactive

1790a LIKE A BUTTERFLY NOVICE CHASE (GRADE 3) (14 fncs) 2m 4f
5:15 (5:15) 4-Y-O+ **£15,116** (£4,418; £2,093; £697)

RPR

1 **The Game Changer (IRE)**[6] 1679 6-11-8 145 (t) RWalsh 152+
(Gordon Elliott, Ire) *racd in 3rd: travelled wl to dispute 2nd 2 out: pressed ldr in 2nd appr last: sn led and pushed clr* **5/2**[3]

2 2 ½ **Rule The World**[18] 1556 8-11-2 150 (p) BJCooper 144
(M F Morris, Ire) *attempted to make all: rdn and pressed appr last: sn hdd: nt qckn w wnr* **6/4**[1]

3 15 **Viconte Du Noyer (FR)**[45] 1302 6-11-5 143 (t) JJBurke 131
(Henry De Bromhead, Ire) *chsd ldr in 2nd: clsr w a circ to r: mstke 4 out: pushed along after 3 out: nt fluent 2 out and sn dropped to 3rd: no ex appr last* **15/8**[2]

4 65 **Bashful Beauty (IRE)**[12] 1624 8-11-2 0 BrianO'Connell 63
(Norman Lee, Ire) *nt fluent 1st: in rr thrght: nvr a factor: t.o* **33/1**

4m 59.8s (299.80) **4 Ran SP% 106.3**
CSF £6.61 TOTE £2.60; DF 4.70 Trifecta £7.20.
Owner Gigginstown House Stud **Bred** Arctic Tack Stud & Crossogue Stud **Trained** Longwood, Co Meath

FOCUS
An intriguing and smart novice event run at a proper gallop. A fair pb from the winner with the second below his best.

1791a (Foreign Racing) - See Raceform Interactive

1656 MARKET RASEN (R-H)
Monday, October 5

OFFICIAL GOING: Good (good to soft places in home straight on both courses)
Wind: light breeze Weather: very overcast and dank and drizzling after race two; 14 degrees

1792 32RED CASINO "NATIONAL HUNT" NOVICES' HURDLE (10 hdls) 2m 2f 140y
2:10 (2:11) (Class 4) 4-Y-O+ **£3,573** (£1,049; £524; £262)

Form RPR

/5-2 1 **Closest Friend**[30] 1480 6-10-12 0 (t) HarrySkelton 119+
(Dan Skelton) *sn lft in front and mde rest at pedestrian pce: gng 5 l clr whn hit 2 out: unchal after and heavily eased flat* **5/4**[1]

4 2 17 **Jethro (IRE)**[19] 1555 4-10-12 0 RichardJohnson 95
(Brian Ellison) *chsd ldr: drvn and outpcd bef 2 out: plodded on and all out to hold poor 2nd* **11/1**

50-F 3 ½ **Fair To Middling**[150] 181 5-10-12 0 SeanBowen 95
(Peter Bowen) *a in 3rd pl: rdn and outpcd bef 2 out: plodded on and nt quite overtake rival after last* **33/1**

4-61 4 ½ **Lincoln County**[78] 1050 4-10-12 0 AidanColeman 99+
(John Ferguson) *v nrly ref 1st: nvr j. w any zest in 4th or 5th pl: shkn up after 3 out: nt keen fr bef next and nvr making any imp after* **2/1**[2]

0F- 5 82 **Gifted Island (IRE)**[248] 3959 5-10-7 0 AlanJohns(5) 12
(Tim Vaughan) *in last pair: rdn and lost tch bef 7th: t.o next* **66/1**

24/F R **Cloudy Joker (IRE)**[17] 1570 7-10-12 0 WayneHutchinson
(Donald McCain) *led for a few strides and then plld himself up* **4/1**[3]

4m 52.0s (12.60) **Going Correction** +0.625s/f (Soft) **6 Ran SP% 110.5**
Speed ratings (Par 105): **98,90,90,90,55**
CSF £14.83 TOTE £2.40: £1.30, £3.60; EX 15.50 Trifecta £123.00.
Owner Lottie Parsons & Sue Raymond **Bred** Upperwood Farm Stud **Trained** Alcester, Warwicks

FOCUS
Rail out 18yds on Wood bend and 24yds on Stands bend. Races 1, 2, 5 and 6 increased by 180yds, while 3 and 4 were increased by 252yds. Conditions had eased slightly throughout the morning and the official going was good, good to soft in places in the home straight. Only an ordinary novice hurdle, which was weakened when Cloudy Joker refused to race. The easy winner has been rated similar to his recent run. There's a case for rating the race higher through the bumper marks of the second and fourth, but it's probably not one to get carried away with.

1793 32RED MARES' H'CAP HURDLE (8 hdls) 2m 148y
2:45 (2:45) (Class 4) (0-120,115) 3-Y-O+ **£3,573** (£1,049; £524; £262)

Form RPR

1253 1 **Russian Royale**[20] 1369 5-10-9 108 FinianO'Toole(10) 114+
(Micky Hammond) *racd keenly: trckd ldrs: 4th and gng best home turn: produced to ld bef last: sn in command: rdn out* **4/1**[3]

3123 2 4 ½ **Miss Sassypants**[50] 1269 6-11-12 115 RyanMahon 116
(Seamus Mullins) *settled towards rr: nt fluent 5th: effrt after next: drvn wl bef 2 out where led: hdd bef last: plugged on and wl hld flat* **3/1**[2]

53-4 3 ¾ **Announcement**[79] 1036 4-11-10 113 RichardJohnson 112
(Brian Ellison) *mounted on crse: last whn nt fluent 3rd: effrt in cl 6th after 3 out: drvn next: tried to chal between last two: no imp bef last* **8/1**

6221 4 ¾ **Wintour Leap**[33] 1454 4-11-8 111 TomO'Brien 111
(Robert Stephens) *cl up: rdn bef 2 out: ev ch of wl hld 3rd whn blnd last* **11/4**[1]

212- 5 6 **Grimley Girl**[197] 4939 9-11-6 109 JamesDavies 102
(Henry Oliver) *hit 4th: led or disp ld tl bef 2 out: hit flight: wknd between last two* **4/1**[3]

045- 6 1 ¾ **Haatefina**[169] 5408 5-11-6 109 DaveCrosse 102
(Mark Usher) *led or disp ld tl hrd drvn and hdd bef 2 out: fdd between last two* **12/1**

5/00 7 15 **Kheskianto (IRE)**[39] 1384 9-9-9 89 oh10 (t) AliceMills(5) 70
(Michael Chapman) *in last pair: mstke 4th: sn rdn: lost tch 3 out: t.o bef next* **100/1**

4m 15.1s (8.40) **Going Correction** +0.625s/f (Soft)
WFA 4 from 5yo+ 9lb **7 Ran SP% 111.5**
Speed ratings (Par 105): **105,102,102,102,99 98,91**
CSF £15.89 TOTE £6.40: £3.40, £2.30; EX 23.00 Trifecta £135.40.
Owner M H O G **Bred** Mrs P A & M J Reditt **Trained** Middleham, N Yorks

FOCUS
A fair mares' handicap hurdle which was run at a sensible gallop. A step up from the winner, with the second, third and fourth rated pretty much to their marks.

1794 £10 FREE AT 32RED.COM H'CAP HURDLE (12 hdls) 2m 7f 16y
3:15 (3:15) (Class 4) (0-120,120) 4-Y-O+ **£3,898** (£1,144; £572; £286)

Form RPR

1-22 1 **Oh Land Abloom (IRE)**[122] 621 5-11-12 120 (t) TrevorWhelan 131+
(Neil King) *settled towards rr: shkn up after 3 out: led bef next: looked like gng clr but idled: almost jnd whn nt fluent last and edgd lft: urged clr again flat* **5/2**[1]

6-34 2 4 ½ **Wily Fox**[115] 705 8-10-13 107 (b) JackQuinlan 111
(James Eustace) *pressed ldr: led 8th: rdn and hdd bef 2 out: rallied as wnr idled and almost upsides at last: sn outpcd flat* **10/3**[3]

14-4 3 8 **Mawaqeet (USA)**[50] 1269 6-11-7 115 (p) RichardJohnson 113
(Michael Appleby) *trckd ldrs: rdn 9th: drvn and outpcd by ldng pair bef 2 out where 10 l 3rd: fnd little after* **11/4**[2]

1050 4 1 ¼ **To Begin**[51] 1260 4-11-1 110 (t) NoelFehily 105
(Charlie Mann) *towards rr: lost tch bef 2 out: plugged on* **25/1**

1-P6 5 nk **Sinbad The Sailor**[26] 1522 10-11-8 116 (vt) AndrewTinkler 111
(George Baker) *hld up in last: rdn and lost tch after 3 out: drvn and styd on fr appr last: nvr able to get in a blow but nrly snatched 4th* **20/1**

12F2 6 ¾ **Bennachie (IRE)**[28] 1493 6-10-10 109 (t) AlanJohns(5) 104
(Tim Vaughan) *chsd clr ldng pair and nt a fluent: rdn and lost pl after 3 out: wl btn next* **9/2**

3-0P 7 23 **Come On Sunshine**[15] 1600 4-10-10 105 (bt[1]) WillKennedy 81
(Brian Ellison) *led at stdy pce: outj. and hdd 8th: 2nd tl hit 3 out and reminders: fdd home turn: t.o and eased* **20/1**

6m 6.2s (15.70) **Going Correction** +0.625s/f (Soft)
WFA 4 from 5yo+ 10lb **7 Ran SP% 109.9**
Speed ratings (Par 105): **97,95,92,92,92 91,83**
CSF £10.38 TOTE £3.20: £1.60, £2.10; EX 11.30 Trifecta £31.70.
Owner Reefer Distribution Services Ltd **Bred** Martin Donovan **Trained** Barbury Castle, Wiltshire

FOCUS
A fair handicap and they were well strung out. A pb from the winner, with the second and third below their best.

1795 32RED.COM H'CAP CHASE (17 fncs) 2m 7f 191y
3:50 (3:50) (Class 4) (0-110,109) 4-Y-O+ **£4,288** (£1,259; £629; £314)

Form RPR

-613 1 **Ready Token (IRE)**[109] 771 7-11-12 109 (t) AidanColeman 124+
(Charlie Longsdon) *led: j. slowly 5th: hdd next: pressed ldr: j. slowly 11th: led again after 14: sn 7 l clr: nvr looked like being ct: pushed out* **9/4**[1]

5412 2 15 **Bouggietopieces**[12] 1629 5-11-8 105 RichardJohnson 109
(Gordon Elliott, Ire) *bhd: nt fluent 3rd: rdn 11th: drvn to chse wnr who was clr 3 out: nvr gng wl enough and nvr looked like chalng* **5/2**[2]

246P 3 1 ½ **The Society Man (IRE)**[9] 1659 8-10-3 91 DannyBurton(5) 89
(Michael Chapman) *chsd ldrs: rdn 12th: outpcd after 14th: plugged on gamely fr next: wnt 3rd bef last and tried hrd for poor 2nd flat* **20/1**

P-32 4 14 **Jimmy Shan (IRE)**[6] 1692 7-11-1 103 AlanJohns(5) 96
(Tim Vaughan) *kpt wl away fr rest at s: led in: smetimes j.rt: mstke 3rd: 2nd tl led 6th: drvn and hdd after 14th: lost 2nd and blnd next: blnd again 2 out: lost poor 3rd bef last and fin v tired* **7/2**[3]

4643 5 39 **Lock Towers (IRE)**[9] 1659 6-11-6 103 DavidBass 67
(Ben Pauling) *chsd ldng pair: drvn 12th: dropped out v tamely after 14th: bdly t.o next* **6/1**

21-P P **Harris (IRE)**[157] 58 8-11-6 103 (v) DavidEngland
(Alan Brown) *blnd 1st: bhd: rdn and nt travelling fr 7th: tailing off whn p.u 11th* **10/1**

6m 22.8s (-8.50) **Going Correction** -0.275s/f (Good) **6 Ran SP% 109.7**
Speed ratings (Par 105): **103,98,97,92,79**
CSF £8.21 TOTE £3.10: £1.90, £1.60; EX 7.10 Trifecta £66.10.
Owner Foxtrot Racing: Ready Token **Bred** Sean Moran **Trained** Over Norton, Oxon

FOCUS
A modest handicap and the form looks ordinary. A small pb from the winner, and there's a case for rating the race up to 5lb higher.

1796 32REDSPORT.COM H'CAP CHASE (14 fncs) 2m 3f 34y
4:25 (4:25) (Class 5) (0-100,100) 4-Y-0+ £2,599 (£763; £381; £190)

Form RPR
242F **1** **Chankillo**[6] 1689 6-10-10 **84**..............................(p) SamTwiston-Davies 99+
(Sarah-Jayne Davies) *j. soundly in 2nd or 3rd: led bef 3 out: 4 l clr next: rdn and styd on steadily flat* **4/1**[2]
55P **2** *5* **Butlergrove King (IRE)**[54] 1235 6-11-5 **100**.............. FreddieMitchell[(7)] 108
(Dai Burchell) *a in 2nd or 3rd: chsd wnr bef 3 out: hrd drvn after: v one pce and nvr making any imp* **15/8**[1]
6062 **3** *6* **The Omen**[37] 1402 9-10-10 **89**.................................... AlanJohns[(5)] 92
(Tim Vaughan) *settled in last pair: rdn 3 out: fnd little: wnt mod 3rd and mstke next* **9/2**[3]
0PP3 **4** *2 1/4* **Bob's Call (IRE)**[6] 1687 6-11-2 **90**............................ DenisO'Regan 90
(Tony Coyle) *in last pair: last and rdn after 11th: struggling bef next* **5/1**
355 **5** *1/2* **Cara Court (IRE)**[37] 1402 9-10-0 **74** oh4.......................(p) HenryBrooke 76
(Joanne Foster) *led at stdy pce: cajoled along 1/2-way: drvn after 11th: hdd bef next: nt run on* **10/1**
4335 **6** *7* **Accessallareas (IRE)**[5] 1703 10-11-1 **89**.................... RichardJohnson 84
(Sarah-Jayne Davies) *chsd ldrs: hit 8th: j. slowly next: pushed along after 11th: sn dropped out* **8/1**

5m 4.9s (-0.80) **Going Correction** -0.275s/f (Good) 6 Ran SP% **109.8**
Speed ratings (Par 103): **90,87,85,84,84 81**
CSF £11.90 TOTE £4.40: £2.00, £1.40; EX 15.20 Trifecta £40.30.
Owner Andrew Gough **Bred** Dullingham Park **Trained** Leominster, H'fords

FOCUS
A moderate handicap and the field was strung out a long way from home. A step up from the winner for the switch to a right-handed track, while the third, fourth and fifth help set the level.

1797 32RED ON THE APP STORE INTERMEDIATE OPEN NATIONAL HUNT FLAT RACE 2m 148y
4:55 (4:56) (Class 6) 4-6-Y-0 £1,559 (£457; £228; £114)

Form RPR
4 **1** **Mahlerdramatic (IRE)**[33] 1449 5-11-0 0.............................. WillKennedy 98+
(Brian Ellison) *ly: cl up in 2nd or 3rd: rdn 4f out: led over 2f out: 3 l clr 1f out: kpt up to work and styd on steadily after* **7/2**[2]
2 *3 1/2* **Canton Prince (IRE)** 4-11-0 0.. RichardJohnson 95
(Tim Vaughan) *workmanlike scope: pressed ldrs and racd freely: rdn 3f out: wnt 2nd wl over 1f out: no imp on wnr after* **9/2**[3]
5 **3** *4* **Alf 'N' Dor (IRE)**[150] 188 4-11-0 0.................................. SeanBowen 92
(Peter Bowen) *str: led: set slow pce: drvn and hdd over 2f out: rn green and edgd lft: lost 2nd wl over 1f out and no ex* **11/10**[1]
0- **4** *1 1/2* **Bling Noir (IRE)**[198] 4901 5-10-7 0................................ DenisO'Regan 82
(Tony Coyle) *small: towards rr: rdn and outpcd 3f out: plugged on wout threatening ins fnl f* **50/1**
0- **5** *4* **Cupachai**[171] 5380 4-11-0 0..(t) HarrySkelton 85
(Dan Skelton) *small: prom tl rdn and lost pl over 2f out* **10/1**
20 **6** *3 1/2* **Golden Thread**[33] 1449 5-11-0 0.................................. TrevorWhelan 82
(Neil King) *towards rr: rdn 6f out: struggling 3f out* **8/1**
7 *36* **Off The Cuff** 4-11-0 0..[1] WayneHutchinson 46
(Donald McCain) *small: t.k.h in last: rdn and lost tch over 4f out: bdly t.o fnl 3f* **16/1**

4m 15.3s (14.20) **Going Correction** +0.625s/f (Soft)
WFA 4 from 5yo 9lb 7 Ran SP% **116.1**
Speed ratings: **91,89,87,86,84 83,66**
CSF £20.15 TOTE £3.10: £1.60, £3.00; EX 15.90 Trifecta £49.90.
Owner P J Martin **Bred** Tony Mullins **Trained** Norton, N Yorks

FOCUS
Probably just a modest bumper. The form is rated around the winner and third.
T/Plt: £53.20 to a £1 stake. Pool of £52711.19 - 722.13 winning tickets. T/Qpdt: £12.10 to a £1 stake. Pool of £4291.14 - 260.80 winning tickets. **Iain Mackenzie**

1798 - 1804a (Foreign Racing) - See Raceform Interactive

214
LUDLOW (R-H)
Wednesday, October 7

OFFICIAL GOING: Good (good to firm in places; 7.6)
Wind: slight half behind Weather: sunny spells

1805 WELCOME BACK TO LUDLOW JUVENILE MAIDEN HURDLE (9 hdls) 1m 7f 169y
2:10 (2:10) (Class 4) 3-Y-0 £3,898 (£1,144; £572; £286)

Form RPR
3 **1** **Duke Street (IRE)**[11] 1656 3-10-12 0.............................. WillKennedy 113+
(Dr Richard Newland) *racd keenly: disp ld tl def advantage 6th: hung rt 3 out: wandered 2 out and last: rdn out flat* **4/11**[1]
2 *2 1/4* **Duke Of Medina (IRE)**[53] 3-10-12 0...........................(b) GavinSheehan 109
(Harry Whittington) *disp ld tl hdd 6th: styd cl up: rdn between last 2: one pce flat* **11/2**[2]
34 **3** *15* **Fast Scat (USA)**[48] 778 3-9-12 0.................................. DavidNoonan[(7)] 88
(Steve Flook) *t.k.h: chsd ldrs: rdn and outpcd by ldng pair appr 3 out: no ch after* **33/1**
44 **4** *20* **Dylan's Storm (IRE)**[31] 1486 3-10-12 0........................(t) AidanColeman 77
(David Dennis) *hld up in 4th: relegated to last after 6th: wknd and lost tch appr 3 out* **10/1**[3]
5 *7* **Or So (USA)**[113] 3-10-12 0.. KielanWoods 70
(Phil Middleton) *hld up in last: briefly impr a pl after 6th: sn rdn and wknd* **10/1**[3]

3m 47.6s (-1.90) **Going Correction** -0.35s/f (Good) 5 Ran SP% **109.8**
Speed ratings (Par 103): **90,88,81,71,67**
CSF £2.94 TOTE £1.30: £1.10, £2.10; EX 3.10 Trifecta £23.40.
Owner Chris Stedman & Mark Albon **Bred** Mrs Joan Keaney **Trained** Claines, Worcs

FOCUS
Inside rail on both shared bends. Despite 20mm of overnight rain the official going remained good, good to firm in places. The opener was an uncompetitive juvenile hurdle and only the front two mattered. The winner set a decent standard and has been rated in line with his debut run.

1806 BETFAIR SUPPORTING GRASS-ROOTS RACING NOVICES' HURDLE (11 hdls) 2m 5f 55y
2:45 (2:45) (Class 4) 4-Y-0+ £3,898 (£1,144; £572; £286)

Form RPR
512P **1** **Uncle Tone (IRE)**[15] 1615 6-11-5 120.............................. MichealNolan 120+
(Tim Vaughan) *led: jinked 2nd: hdd 4th: chsd ldr: 6 l down 8th: clsd appr 3 out: led 2 out: 2 l up and gng the bttr whn pursuer blnd last: styd on wl* **3/1**[2]
1 **2** *12* **Samtu (IRE)**[28] 1518 4-11-5 0.....................................(t) HarrySkelton 111
(Dan Skelton) *racd keenly: trckd wnr: j. slowly 2nd: led 4th and increased pce: 6 l clr 8th: reduced ld appr 3 out: rdn whn hdd 2 out: 2 l down whn blnd last: no ex* **5/4**[1]
-114 **3** *29* **In On The Act**[32] 1482 5-11-12 123................................ PaulMoloney 94
(Evan Williams) *racd in 3rd most of way: rdn after 8th: sn no ch w ldng pair: wl btn whn mstke 2 out* **3/1**[2]
14 **4** *90* **Time Is Money**[105] 831 6-10-5 0.................................. RichieMcLernon
(Emma Lavelle) *mainly in last: nt fluent 7th: sn rdn and lost tch: t.o: b.b.v* **8/1**[3]

5m 11.3s (-3.50) **Going Correction** -0.35s/f (Good)
WFA 4 from 5yo+ 10lb 4 Ran SP% **105.6**
Speed ratings (Par 105): **92,87,76,42**
CSF £7.04 TOTE £3.50; EX 6.30 Trifecta £11.30.
Owner Kings Head Duffield Racing Partnership **Bred** Michael J Bowe **Trained** Aberthin, Vale of Glamorgan

FOCUS
This looked a fair novice hurdle on paper, but they finished well strung out and the form is unreliable. A messy race, rated through the winner back to his best, but it's not one to be confident about.

1807 BETFAIR PRICE RUSH H'CAP CHASE (22 fncs) 3m 1f 125y
3:15 (3:17) (Class 3) (0-130,130) 4-Y-0+ £12,996 (£3,816; £1,908; £954)

Form RPR
2P3- **1** **Azure Fly (IRE)**[179] 5282 7-11-11 **129**............................(tp) AidanColeman 135+
(Charlie Longsdon) *chsd ldng pair: wnt 2nd after 14th: led appr 4 out: rdn 2 out: swvd bdly lft flat: stened up towards fin and hld on wl* **7/2**[1]
P-11 **2** *1 1/4* **Dreamsoftheatre (IRE)**[37] 1417 7-11-10 **128**...............(t) BarryGeraghty 134+
(Jonjo O'Neill) *chsd ldrs: nt fluent 3rd: rdn after 18th: chal 4 out: hit 2 out: 1 l down whn blnd last: kpt on u.p* **7/1**
5P1- **3** *2 1/4* **Rio Milan (IRE)**[188] 5109 9-11-2 **120**...........................(tp) PaddyBrennan 123
(Fergal O'Brien) *chsd ldrs: sltly outpcd 4 out: rdn and styd on fr 2 out: wnt 3rd flat* **14/1**
24-3 **4** *1/2* **King Massini (IRE)**[154] 149 9-10-9 **113**.......................... AdamWedge 116
(Evan Williams) *hld up towards rr: hdwy 9th: nt fluent 16th: chsd ldrs after 18th: hit 3 out: one pce after: lost 3rd flat* **4/1**[2]
1-23 **5** *12* **Best Boy Barney (IRE)**[49] 1288 9-11-9 **130**...............(bt) MattGriffiths[(3)] 122
(Jeremy Scott) *led: j.rt 11th: hdd appr 4 out: rdn and grad wknd* **12/1**
1-4P **6** *4 1/2* **Rockiteer (IRE)**[136] 457 12-11-4 **122**...........................(p) JakeGreenall 109
(Henry Daly) *chsd ldr tl after 14th: styd prom tl wknd after 4 out* **33/1**
-64P **7** *2 1/4* **Highway Code (USA)**[47] 1309 9-10-3 **114**...................(t) MikeyHamill[(7)] 109+
(Kerry Lee) *s.s: in tch in rr fr 3rd: hdwy into mid-div 12th: chsng ldrs whn mstke 4 out: hld whn blnd bdly 2 out* **18/1**
4221 **8** *30* **Lemony Bay**[41] 1372 6-11-3 **121**.................................... LeightonAspell 79
(Oliver Sherwood) *wnt to post early: hld up towards rr: hdwy 9th: chsng ldrs whn rdn 4 out: sn wknd: t.o: b.b.v* **9/1**
06-5 **9** *9* **Sybarite (FR)**[151] 196 9-11-10 **128**............................ SamTwiston-Davies 78
(Nigel Twiston-Davies) *prom tl lost pl 6th: rdn along and nvr gng after: last fr 10th: t.o* **13/2**[3]
U1-5 **10** *1 1/4* **Allthekingshorses (IRE)**[15] 1616 9-11-9 **127**..........(tp) RichardJohnson 75
(Philip Hobbs) *mid-div: dropping towards rr whn mstke 6th: struggling fr 15th: t.o: b.b.v* **14/1**
25P- **P** **Firm Order (IRE)**[192] 5047 10-11-2 **127**....................(p) MrMJPKendrick[(7)]
(Paul Webber) *a towards rr: rdn 16th: sn lost tch: wl bhd whn p.u bef 2 out* **12/1**

6m 27.6s (-7.70) **Going Correction** -0.275s/f (Good) 11 Ran SP% **115.0**
Speed ratings (Par 107): **100,99,98,98,95 93,93,83,81,80**
CSF £28.14 CT £303.74 TOTE £4.70: £1.90, £2.00, £3.50; EX 33.50 Trifecta £139.40.
Owner Girls Allowed **Bred** Noel Fenton **Trained** Over Norton, Oxon

FOCUS
A decent, competitive handicap chase and the form should work out. It's been rated around the balance of the first four.

1808 LUDLOW GOLF CLUB MARES' H'CAP HURDLE (12 hdls) 2m 7f 174y
3:50 (3:50) (Class 3) (0-130,130) 4-Y-0+ £7,797 (£2,289; £1,144; £572)

Form RPR
3243 **1** **Still Believing (IRE)**[45] 1348 7-10-11 **115**........................ AdamWedge 118+
(Evan Williams) *hld up: stdy hdwy 3 out: rdn after 2 out: led jst after last: styd on strly and sn clr* **8/1**
321- **2** *4 1/2* **Jean Fleming (IRE)**[200] 4905 8-10-12 **116**...................... BrendanPowell 115
(Jamie Snowden) *prom: chsd ldr 9th: rdn to ld 3 out: hdd sn after last: kpt on same pce* **9/2**[1]
1115 **3** *2* **Miss Serious (IRE)**[46] 1325 5-11-12 **130**...................... NickScholfield 128
(Jeremy Scott) *hld up in rr: rdn and hdwy appr 3 out: ev ch last: one pce flat* **9/2**[1]
2P-4 **4** *3 3/4* **A Shade Of Bay**[144] 339 7-10-13 **120**.........................(p) TomBellamy[(3)] 114
(Kim Bailey) *trckd ldr tl led 8th: rdn and hdd 3 out: wknd appr last* **7/1**[3]
564- **5** *2 1/2* **Loyaute (FR)**[221] 4493 8-11-10 **128**.............................. JamesDavies 120
(Chris Down) *hld up in mid-div: rdn appr 3 out: styd on same pce fr 2 out* **16/1**
2-0F **6** *12* **Lily Waugh (IRE)**[35] 1445 8-11-4 **122**........................(t) AidanColeman 106
(Anthony Honeyball) *led 1st to 8th: nt fluent next: rdn 3 out: wknd 2 out* **5/1**[2]
24F- **7** *5* **Annaluna (IRE)**[24] 3895 6-10-0 **104** oh1.......................(v) PeterCarberry 84
(David Evans) *hld up towards rr: and hdwy 9th: wknd 3 out* **20/1**
P34- **8** *8* **Woodland Walk**[200] 4905 7-11-3 **121**............................(t) GavinSheehan 100
(Emma Lavelle) *chsd ldrs: rdn whn j.lft 3 out: wkng whn blnd next* **12/1**
5323 **9** *17* **Handmaid**[37] 1419 6-11-0 **118**..(p) SeanBowen 72
(Peter Bowen) *led to 1st: chsd ldrs tl dropped to rr 9th: sn lost tch: t.o* **9/2**[1]

5m 38.9s (-13.40) **Going Correction** -0.35s/f (Good) 9 Ran SP% **113.2**
Speed ratings (Par 107): **108,106,105,104,103 99,98,95,89**
CSF £43.56 CT £181.85 TOTE £9.40: £2.70, £2.20, £1.60; EX 42.60 Trifecta £168.50.
Owner R E R Williams **Bred** Declan Moran **Trained** Llancarfan, Vale Of Glamorgan

The Form Book Jumps 2015-16, Raceform Ltd, Newbury, RG14 5SJ

FOCUS
A competitive handicap hurdle for mares, in which they went a good gallop. The winner has been rated to the level of her best chase form, with the third rated to her mark.

1809 RACING UK NOVICES' LIMITED H'CAP CHASE (16 fncs) 2m 4f 11y
4:25 (4:25) (Class 3) (0-135,130) 4-Y-O+ £8,447 (£2,480; £1,240; £620)

Form — RPR

3312 1 **Jayo Time (IRE)**[17] 1601 6-10-5 120 ....(p) CiaranGethings(7) 136+
(Kerry Lee) *towards rr: bmpd 2nd and 4th: hdwy to chse ldrs 6th: wnt 2nd appr 4 out where mstke: chal 2 out: led narrowly last: styd on u.p* **5/1**

2131 2 1 3/4 **Hepijeu (FR)**[32] 1479 4-10-6 125 ....(tp) AidanColeman 126
(Charlie Longsdon) *led: rdn and jnd 2 out: hdd narrowly last: kpt on tl no ex nr fin* **2/1[1]**

3231 3 15 **Cut The Corner (IRE)**[8] 1690 7-11-7 129 7ex .... WillKennedy 132
(Dr Richard Newland) *chsd ldr: chal 11th to 12th: rdn and lost 2nd appr 4 out: sn hld: mstke last* **7/2[2]**

4340 4 68 **King Alfonso**[12] 1643 6-10-12 120 .... RobertDunne 57
(Dai Burchell) *hld up: lost tch w ldng trio 12th: t.o* **14/1**

120- P **Allez Vic (IRE)**[175] 5342 9-11-3 130 .... ConorRing(5)
(Evan Williams) *chsd ldrs tl dropped to rr 5th: j. slowly 9th (water): struggling next: t.o whn p.u bef 2 out* **4/1[3]**

P-64 P **Foxtail Hill (IRE)**[80] 1047 6-11-3 125 .... SamTwiston-Davies
(Nigel Twiston-Davies) *tended to jump lft: chsd ldrs to 9th: rdn 12th: bhd fr next: disputing poor 4th whn j.lft 3 out: p.u bef next* **7/1**

4m 54.8s (-9.60) **Going Correction** -0.275s/f (Good)
WFA 4 from 6yo+ 10lb 6 Ran SP% 111.4
Speed ratings (Par 107): **108,107,101,74,**
CSF £15.78 TOTE £5.20: £2.90, £1.40; EX 10.20 Trifecta £40.30.
Owner S R Holt & Mrs B M Ayres **Bred** E J P Kane **Trained** Byton, H'fords

FOCUS
An open handicap chase, albeit not the stongest event for the grade. There's a case for rating the race a few pounds higher through the third.

1810 LUDLOW RACING PARTNERSHIP H'CAP HURDLE (9 hdls) 1m 7f 169y
5:00 (5:00) (Class 4) (0-110,108) 3-Y-O+ £5,198 (£1,526; £763; £381)

Form — RPR

P411 1 **Grams And Ounces**[9] 1369 8-11-4 107 ....(t) DavidNoonan(7) 112+
(Grace Harris) *prom: trckd ldr 6th: chal 3 out: sn led narrowly: drvn out to hold on flat* **11/4[1]**

6505 2 3/4 **Rye House (IRE)**[73] 1115 6-11-0 96 ....(t) RichardJohnson 100
(Tim Vaughan) *led tl hdd narrowly appr 2 out: rdn and ev ch tl no ex nr fin* **8/1**

03-4 3 7 **Very Intense (IRE)**[148] 267 4-11-0 96 .... RobertDunne 94
(Tom Lacey) *hld up in tch: hdwy 5th: chsd ldng pair appr 3 out: one pce fr 2 out* **14/1**

0013 4 1 3/4 **Worldor (FR)**[19] 1572 9-11-7 103 ....(t) AdamWedge 100
(Alexandra Dunn) *hld up in last: hdwy after 6th: one pce fr 3 out* **14/1**

1121 5 4 1/2 **Empty The Tank (IRE)**[17] 1596 5-11-10 106 .... LeightonAspell 98
(Jim Boyle) *t.k.h: trckd ldrs: lost pl after 6th: clsd 3 out: sn one pce and no further imp* **7/2[2]**

56-0 6 4 1/2 **Arthamint**[15] 1613 7-11-6 102 ....(t) HarrySkelton 92
(Dan Skelton) *taken steadily to post: t.k.h in rr: sme hdwy appr 3 out: sn one pce* **8/1**

3F0- 7 4 1/2 **Moojaned (IRE)**[30] 5481 4-10-12 94 .... PeterCarberry 78
(David Evans) *chsd ldr tl rdn and lost pl 6th: wknd 3 out* **4/1[3]**

4313 8 14 **Ladies Dancing**[29] 1508 9-11-7 103 ....(b) JamesDavies 75
(Chris Down) *chsd ldrs tl rdn and wknd appr 3 out* **8/1**

3m 43.2s (-6.30) **Going Correction** -0.35s/f (Good)
WFA 4 from 5yo+ 9lb 8 Ran SP% 115.6
Speed ratings (Par 105): **101,100,97,96,94 91,89,82**
CSF £25.11 CT £261.87 TOTE £3.30: £1.30, £2.40, £4.30; EX 25.00 Trifecta £305.30.
Owner Ron C Williams **Bred** Brook Stud Bloodstock Ltd **Trained** Shirenewton, Monmouthshire

FOCUS
A modest handicap hurdle and they finished well strung out. The in-form winner has been rated in line with his recent Flat win, the runner-up as recording a hurdle pb and a small pb from the third.

1811 BOOK EARLY FOR CHRISTMAS MARES' INTERMEDIATE OPEN NATIONAL HUNT FLAT RACE 1m 7f 169y
5:35 (5:35) (Class 4) 4-6-Y-O £3,249 (£954; £477; £238)

Form — RPR

-U0 1 **Alizee Javilex (FR)**[127] 594 5-10-12 0 .... LeightonAspell 111+
(Lucy Wadham) *hld up: hdwy 4f out: led over 1f out: r.o: comf* **50/1**

23- 2 4 **Yes I Did (IRE)**[178] 5299 5-10-12 0 .... HarrySkelton 104
(Dan Skelton) *chsd ldrs: pushed along briefly over 4f out: led 2f out: sn edgd lft and hdd: kpt on but a hld by wnr* **7/4[1]**

040- 3 10 **Fizzy Dancer**[174] 5359 5-10-9 0 .... TomBellamy(3) 95
(Kim Bailey) *trckd ldr tl rdn and lost 2nd over 2f out: kpt on same pce* **6/1[3]**

36- 4 3/4 **Tara's Honour**[212] 4687 5-10-12 0 ....[1] GavinSheehan 94
(Emma Lavelle) *hld up: hdwy 4f out: outpcd by ldrs over 2f out: styd on fnl f* **8/1**

2- 5 3/4 **Lamanver Alchemy**[322] 2594 4-10-12 0 .... RobertDunne 95
(Tom Lacey) *chsd ldrs: hung lft bnd over 2f out: wknd 1f out* **16/1**

2 6 13 **Tullow Tonic (IRE)**[120] 682 4-10-12 0 .... AidanColeman 85
(Charlie Longsdon) *t.k.h: led to 2f out: wknd qckly* **2/1[2]**

0- 7 8 **Miss Mash**[174] 5359 4-10-12 0 .... RichardJohnson 78
(Henry Daly) *hld up: rdn 3f out: sn wknd* **18/1**

0- 8 15 **The Little Red Fox**[170] 5439 5-10-12 0 .... JamesDavies 61
(Chris Down) *mid-div: rdn along after 7f: bhd fnl 4f: t.o* **50/1**

06- 9 31 **Orbit Light (IRE)**[180] 5262 4-10-12 0 .... PeterCarberry 33
(Nicky Henderson) *t.k.h: trckd ldrs: rdn 5f out: wknd 3f out: t.o* **14/1**

3m 34.3s (-9.60) **Going Correction** -0.35s/f (Good) 9 Ran SP% 116.8
Speed ratings: **110,108,103,102,102 95,91,84,68**
CSF £139.52 TOTE £54.00: £9.80, £1.10, £1.60; EX 225.80 Trifecta £1109.10.
Owner J J W Wadham **Bred** Scea Ecurie Jc Laisis **Trained** Newmarket, Suffolk

FOCUS
Just a modest bumper. The second, fourth and sixth set the level.
T/Plt: £138.40 to a £1 stake. Pool: £44,860.64 - 236.49 winning tickets T/Qpdt: £13.80 to a £1 stake. Pool: £4,381.32 - 234.19 winning tickets **Richard Lowther**

377 # TOWCESTER (R-H)
Wednesday, October 7

OFFICIAL GOING: Good to firm (good in places)
Wind: Fresh across Weather: Overcast

1812 BET TOTEPLACEPOT "NATIONAL HUNT" NOVICES' H'CAP HURDLE (11 hdls) 2m 4f 217y
2:20 (2:21) (Class 5) (0-100,100) 3-Y-O+ £3,898 (£1,144; £572; £286)

Form — RPR

0052 1 **Barton Antix**[29] 1510 6-11-10 98 ....(p) NoelFehily 112+
(Neil Mulholland) *hld up: hdwy after 7th: led appr 2 out: rdn bef last: styd on wl* **11/2**

1332 2 3 3/4 **Mr Mafia (IRE)**[29] 1504 6-11-7 95 ....(t) LeeEdwards 106
(Tony Carroll) *hld up: hdwy 3 out: chsd wnr next: rdn appr last: styd on same pce flat* **7/2[2]**

5P-0 3 8 **Ask A Bank (IRE)**[17] 1598 5-10-8 89 .... JamieBargary(7) 93
(David Dennis) *hld up in tch: rdn appr 2 out: styd on same pce* **4/1[3]**

-203 4 9 **Darnitnev**[17] 1599 5-11-11 99 ....(p[1]) AndrewTinkler 97
(Martin Keighley) *hld up: blnd 8th: sn rdn: sme hdwy appr 2 out: n.d* **7/1**

0-3 5 18 **Urban Storm (IRE)**[140] 398 5-11-9 97 .... DavidBass 82
(Ben Pauling) *chsd ldrs: mstke 3 out: sn rdn: wknd next* **11/4[1]**

44-P 6 15 **Just Skittles**[108] 808 7-9-9 74 oh13 .... DannyBurton(5) 40
(Richard Harper) *chsd ldrs to 3 out: in rr whn j.lft next* **66/1**

P5-0 7 2 3/4 **Jackfield**[148] 262 5-10-6 80 .... CharliePoste 44
(Robin Dickin) *hld up: rdn appr 3 out: wknd bef next* **25/1**

F62- 8 19 **Truckers Highway (IRE)**[172] 5398 6-11-1 92 ....(t) HarryChalloner(3) 38
(John Groucott) *led to 4th: chsd ldr: ev ch 3 out: sn rdn and wknd* **14/1**

21-5 P **Lord Landen (IRE)**[153] 174 10-11-5 100 ....(t) MissAEStirling(7) 98
(Fergal O'Brien) *chsd ldr tl led 4th: hdd appr 2 out: wknd bef last: p.u and dismntd flat* **9/1**

5m 8.2s (-19.00) **Going Correction** -1.375s/f (Hard) 9 Ran SP% 118.8
Speed ratings (Par 103): **81,79,76,73,66 60,59,52,**
CSF £26.41 CT £86.98 TOTE £5.90: £2.10, £1.40, £2.30; EX 25.50 Trifecta £155.20.
Owner Exors of the Late Lady Clarke **Bred** Lady H J Clarke **Trained** Limpley Stoke, Wilts
■ Stewards' Enquiry : Charlie Poste one-day ban: failed to ride out for 6th (Oct 21)

FOCUS
Shared bends and race 2 reduced by 120yds and race 4 reduced by 67yds. The ground, not raced on since May, took 16mm of rain overnight, but was still officially given as good to firm, good in places. The jockeys after the first agreed with the description, with Noel Fehily stating it was "beautiful ground". None of these had previously won a hurdle race and it looks like weak form. A big step up from the winner, with the right horses in the frame.

1813 TOTETRIFECTA PICK THE 1,2,3 H'CAP CHASE (17 fncs) 3m 102y
2:55 (2:56) (Class 5) (0-100,100) 4-Y-O+ £3,898 (£1,144; £572; £286)

Form — RPR

3141 1 **Conas Taoi (IRE)**[9] 1678 6-11-3 91 ....(p) TomO'Brien 101+
(Paul Morgan) *a.p: chsd ldr 11th: led 3 out: drvn out* **15/8[1]**

6043 2 2 1/2 **Xenophon**[23] 1546 7-9-9 74 oh5 .... AliceMills(5) 81
(Michael Chapman) *hld up: hmpd 8th: hdwy 10th: chsd wnr 2 out: j.rt last: styd on same pce flat* **25/1**

2400 3 3 3/4 **Interpleader**[93] 926 10-10-7 88 ....(tp) MrMartinMcIntyre(7) 93
(Sheila Lewis) *hld up: hdwy appr 2 out: styd on same pce last* **10/1**

-332 4 17 **Combustible Kate (IRE)**[110] 782 9-10-1 80 .... CharlieDeutsch(5) 72
(Nick Kent) *chsd ldr to 5th: remained handy: wnt 2nd again after 8th: led 10th: hdd 3 out: sn rdn: wknd appr last* **8/1**

05-P 5 7 **Bedrock Fred**[125] 610 9-10-10 84 .... NicodeBoinville 65
(David Weston) *hld up: hdwy 12th: sn pushed along: wknd 2 out* **11/2[3]**

23-4 6 shd **Jolly Boys Outing (IRE)**[149] 239 12-10-8 85 .... BenPoste(3) 66
(Rosemary Gasson) *prom: racd keenly: lost pl after 6th: hdwy appr 3 out: wknd next* **11/1**

54-4 7 10 **Bebinn (IRE)**[151] 211 8-11-4 92 ....(p) DarylJacob 64
(Ben Case) *prom: mstke 1st: lost pl next: in rr and rdn whn mstke 14th: sn wknd* **12/1**

UP-0 8 30 **Monty's Revenge (IRE)**[49] 1293 10-10-7 81 ....(p) IanPopham 26
(Martin Keighley) *prom: chsd ldr 5th: led 7th to 10th: wknd 14th* **16/1**

40-6 P **Top Benefit (IRE)**[160] 44 13-9-10 75 oh9 ow1 .... DannyBurton(5)
(Richard Harper) *mid-div: hdwy 6th: wknd after 10th: bhd whn p.u bef 2 out* **66/1**

6P04 U **Skating Home (IRE)**[9] 1678 9-10-0 74 oh4 ....(p) MarkQuinlan
(Richard Hawker) *hld up: hdwy 6th: 3 l 6th whn blnd and uns rdr 8th* **100/1**

22-2 P **Cosway Spirit (IRE)**[149] 239 8-11-12 100 .... DavidBass
(Ben Pauling) *led to 7th: rdn and wknd 12th: bhd whn p.u bef 2 out* **9/2[2]**

6m 8.2s (-28.70) **Going Correction** -1.125s/f (Hard) 11 Ran SP% 116.8
Speed ratings (Par 103): **102,101,99,94,91 91,88,78, , ,**
CSF £44.88 CT £385.88 TOTE £2.60: £1.20, £5.00, £3.50; EX 43.50 Trifecta £860.40.
Owner All Stars Sports Racing **Bred** Martin McCaughey **Trained** Ystrad, Rhondda C Taff

FOCUS
A moderate handicap chase, taking place over 120 yards less than the official distance. The first two have been rated pretty much to their marks.

1814 HAYGAIN HAY STEAMERS CLEAN HEALTHY FORAGE H'CAP HURDLE (8 hdls) 1m 7f 181y
3:25 (3:26) (Class 3) (0-130,130) 3-Y-O+ £6,498 (£1,908; £954; £477)

Form — RPR

0-13 1 **Serenity Now (IRE)**[5] 1742 7-10-3 114 .... CraigGallagher(7) 120+
(Brian Ellison) *hld up: hdwy 3 out: chsd ldr bef next: led appr last: r.o wl: comf* **15/8[2]**

22-1 2 3 3/4 **Argot**[17] 1590 4-10-11 122 ....(p) GarethMalone(7) 117
(Charlie Longsdon) *chsd ldrs: mstke 3rd: nt fluent 5th: rdn to chse wnr last: no imp on flat* **7/4[1]**

144 3 3 1/2 **Bigindie (IRE)**[17] 1602 5-10-13 117 .... TomScudamore 110
(John Weymes) *trckd ldr: ev ch 3 out: sn rdn: styd on same pce appr last* **9/2[3]**

11-3 4 1 **Quebec**[150] 214 4-11-12 130 .... NoelFehily 122
(Charlie Mann) *led: rdn and hdd appr last: wknd flat* **8/1**

/P06 5 14 **Franciscan**[21] 1554 7-11-7 125 ....(p) DarylJacob 104
(Donald McCain) *hld up: rdn and wknd after 3 out* **10/1**

3m 49.1s (-18.80) **Going Correction** -1.375s/f (Hard) 5 Ran SP% 109.5
Speed ratings (Par 107): **92,90,88,87,80**
CSF £5.68 TOTE £2.90: £2.00, £1.50; EX 6.50 Trifecta £11.90.
Owner J M Basquill **Bred** Citadel Stud **Trained** Norton, N Yorks

FOCUS
Despite the small field this had the look of a fair handicap hurdle. They were well bunched until late on. The second, third and fourth have been rated close to their marks.

1815 DALEPAK LTD NOVICES' CHASE (11 fncs) 2m 70y
4:00 (4:00) (Class 4) 4-Y-0+ **£5,198** (£1,526; £763; £381)

Form RPR
100- **1** **Violet Dancer**[172] 5390 5-11-0 0 ....(p) JoshuaMoore 138+
(Gary Moore) *mde all: sn clr: hit 4th: nt fluent 5th: c bk to the field 6th: bmpd 2 out: shkn up appr last: styd on wl* **9/4**[2]
2-31 **2** *3 ¼* **Minella Present (IRE)**[126] 596 6-11-6 0 .... NoelFehily 139
(Neil Mulholland) *hld up: hdwy 5th: ev ch after 3 out: j.lft next: sn rdn: styd on same pce flat* **4/1**[3]
22-0 **3** *17* **Thomas Crapper**[159] 69 8-11-0 139 .... CharliePoste 122
(Robin Dickin) *chsd clr ldr: tk clsr order 6th: rdn after 3 out: wknd appr last* **5/6**[1]
40PP **4** *50* **Monzino (USA)**[8] 1692 7-10-9 0 .... DannyBurton(5) 72
(Michael Chapman) *sn bhd: nt fluent in rr: j. slowly 7th: blnd last* **150/1**
3m 55.1s (-21.00) **Going Correction** -1.125s/f (Hard) **4** Ran SP% **106.0**
Speed ratings (Par 105): **107,105,96,71**
CSF £10.15 TOTE £3.60; EX 8.30 Trifecta £9.50.
Owner D Bessell & Galloping On The South Downs **Bred** Jeremy Hinds **Trained** Lower Beeding, W Sussex

FOCUS
An intriguing novice chase, which was ran over 67yds less than the official distance. The second has been rated to the best of his hurdle form.

1816 HAYGAIN HAY STEAMERS CLEAN HEALTHY FORAGE H'CAP HURDLE (10 hdls) 2m 3f 34y
4:35 (4:35) (Class 5) (0-100,99) 3-Y-0+ **£3,898** (£1,144; £572; £286)

Form RPR
52-3 **1** **Boherna Lady (IRE)**[3] 1771 7-11-4 98 ....(t) KevinDarcy(7) 115+
(Denis Gerard Hogan, Ire) *hld up: hdwy 6th: led 2 out: clr last: styd on wl* **2/1**[1]
0166 **2** *10* **All Riled Up**[6] 1716 7-10-3 81 .... DanielHiskett(5) 88
(Harry Chisman) *a.p: chsd ldr 4th: led after 3 out: hdd next: styd on same pce appr last* **11/2**[3]
430- **3** *5* **Carhue Princess (IRE)**[174] 5354 9-11-0 90 .... BenPoste(3) 93
(Tom Symonds) *chsd ldrs: rdn after 3 out: no ex fr next* **14/1**
2400 **4** *hd* **Canarbino Girl**[17] 1599 8-10-4 77 ....(t) JamesBest 79
(Caroline Keevil) *hld up: hdwy after 3 out: sn rdn: styd on same pce fr next* **14/1**
4063 **5** *16* **Pretty Rose (IRE)**[15] 1618 5-11-10 97 .... DarylJacob 85
(Ben Case) *mid-div: hdwy 6th: rdn and wknd 2 out* **7/2**[2]
4-P2 **6** *2 ¼* **Izzy Piccolina (IRE)**[41] 1384 7-11-12 99 .... MarkGrant 85
(Geoffrey Deacon) *hld up: rdn appr 3 out: nvr on terms* **12/1**
PP-5 **7** *½* **Miss Lamorna (IRE)**[9] 1677 6-10-1 74 ....(b) IanPopham 59
(Sue Gardner) *mid-div: mstke 5th: hdwy next: rdn and wknd appr 2 out* **14/1**
05U- **8** *25* **Ambre Des Marais (FR)**[227] 4383 5-11-8 95 .... JoshuaMoore 58
(Alison Batchelor) *racd freely: led: clr 2nd to 6th: rdn and hdd after 3 out: sn wknd: bhd whn hit next* **16/1**
P400 **9** *15* **Midnight Memories**[17] 1599 5-11-0 87 .... TrevorWhelan 36
(Steph Hollinshead) *chsd ldr to 4th: remained handy tl rdn and wknd 3 out* **40/1**
6-0F **P** **Olymnia**[23] 1084 4-10-13 86 ....(b) JamieMoore
(Gary Moore) *hld up: towards rr whn p.u bef 3 out* **16/1**
0-P3 **P** **Spurned Girl**[113] 748 5-9-12 78 ow2 ....(t) ConorSmith(7)
(Robin Dickin) *s.s: hld up: rdn and wknd after 7th: bhd whn p.u bef 2 out* **14/1**
4m 40.1s (-29.50) **Going Correction** -1.375s/f (Hard)
WFA 4 from 5yo+ 9lb **11** Ran SP% **119.5**
Speed ratings (Par 103): **107,102,100,100,93 92,92,82,75,**
CSF £14.18 CT £124.88 TOTE £2.80: £1.20, £2.40, £3.10; EX 13.70 Trifecta £109.10.
Owner Premier Racing Club **Bred** R Cotton & S Lannigan O'Keeffe **Trained** Cloughjordan, Co Tipperary

FOCUS
A weak mares handicap hurdle, turned into a procession by the well-backed winner. A step up from the easy winner, with the second, third and fourth rated to form.

1817 COLOSSUS BETS MAIDEN OPEN NATIONAL HUNT FLAT RACE 1m 5f 146y
5:10 (5:10) (Class 6) 4-6-Y-0 **£1,949** (£572; £286; £143)

Form RPR
1 **Samson** 4-11-2 0 .... NicodeBoinville 93+
(Hughie Morrison) *trckd ldrs: rdn over 3f out: n.m.r wl over 1f out: styd on to ld nr fin* **13/8**[1]
0- **2** *½* **Primrose Brown**[244] 4052 4-10-9 0 .... AndrewTinkler 84
(Conrad Allen) *hld up: hdwy over 3f out: led wl over 1f out: rdn ins fnl f: hdd nr fin* **20/1**
20- **3** *¾* **Chief Brody**[179] 5285 4-11-2 0 .... PaulMoloney 91+
(Grace Harris) *hld up: hdwy over 3f out: rdn and ev ch whn hmpd wl over 1f out: sn outpcd: edgd rt and rallied ins fnl f: styd on* **13/2**[3]
4 *15* **Callnineninenine** 4-11-2 0 .... TomScudamore 71
(John Weymes) *prom: rdn over 3f out: sn outpcd: kpt on towards fin* **20/1**
5 *hd* **Ballyandrew (IRE)** 4-10-13 0 .... RyanHatch(3) 70
(Nigel Twiston-Davies) *trckd ldrs: racd keenly: chsd ldr over 3f out: led over 2f out: rdn: hung lft and hdd wl over 1f out: sn wknd* **11/4**[2]
6 *4* **Tara Well (IRE)**[192] 5-10-9 0 .... CharliePoste 58
(Robin Dickin) *led at stdy pce: rdn and hdd over 2f out: wknd over 1f out* **7/1**
40- **7** *½* **Ezetiger**[243] 4072 5-11-2 0 .... NoelFehily 64
(Pat Eddery) *chsd ldr tl rdn over 3f out: wknd over 2f out* **8/1**
3m 16.7s (-23.90) **7** Ran SP% **111.2**
CSF £33.54 TOTE £2.00: £1.30, £9.20; EX 33.20 Trifecta £171.00.
Owner Pangfield Racing IV **Bred** Gemma & Tim Billington **Trained** East Ilsley, Berks

FOCUS
A moderate bumper which, despite the small field, was quite a rough race. A step up from the second, with the third helping to set the level.
T/Plt: £61.90 to a £1 stake. Pool: £61,744.26 - 728.10 winning tickets T/Qpdt: £14.40 to a £1 stake. Pool: £4,164.19 - 213.90 winning tickets **Colin Roberts**

119 EXETER (R-H)
Thursday, October 8

OFFICIAL GOING: Good (6.8)
Wind: almost nil Weather: overcast Rails: All races will be run on Hurdle bends reducing Chase distances by about 45 yards per circuit.

1818 HAGUE PRINT MANAGEMENT H'CAP HURDLE (10 hdls) 2m 2f 111y
2:25 (2:25) (Class 4) (0-120,119) 3-Y-0+ **£3,898** (£1,144; £572; £286)

Form RPR
/30- **1** **Mystifiable**[492] 571 7-10-11 107 ....(t) ConorShoemark(3) 115+
(Fergal O'Brien) *travelled wl most of way: trckd ldr: led 5th: looked wl in command whn nt fluent last: picked up wl whn briefly chal sn after: rdn out* **7/2**[1]
3424 **2** *1 ¾* **Fred Le Macon (FR)**[24] 1545 6-10-0 103 .... JamieInsole(10) 105
(Alan King) *mid-div: hdwy 6th: rdn to chse wnr appr 3 out: briefly flattered after last: kpt on same pce* **5/1**[3]
1140 **3** *5* **The Kvilleken**[29] 1524 7-10-4 97 ....(p) AndrewTinkler 97
(Martin Keighley) *hld up: rdn after 7th: hdwy next: wnt 3rd 2 out: styd on same pce fr last* **14/1**
4535 **4** *20* **Perspicace**[20] 1579 4-11-1 115 ....(bt) MichaelHeard(7) 95
(David Pipe) *hld up: hdwy fr 5th: effrt to chse ldng pair 3 out: wknd next* **4/1**[2]
221- **5** *6* **Milord (GER)**[357] 1922 6-11-12 119 .... DavidBass 95
(Kim Bailey) *mid-div: rdn after 7th: wnt hld 4th next: wknd 2 out* **5/1**[3]
4040 **6** *1 ¾* **Party Palace**[32] 1490 11-10-7 100 .... SeanBowen 73
(Stuart Howe) *chsd ldrs: rdn after 7th: wknd next* **12/1**
5 **7** *9* **Beau Bay (FR)**[18] 1602 4-11-3 110 ....(t) RhysFlint 74
(Alan Jones) *j.lft: led tl 5th: grad lost pl: btn after 7th* **33/1**
00/ **8** *22* **Chakisto (FR)**[90] 951 7-10-12 105 .... NickScholfield 50
(Katie Stephens) *a towards rr* **16/1**
55 **9** *1* **Alf Wright (IRE)**[12] 1661 9-11-11 118 .... JamesBest 62
(Philip Hobbs) *mstke 1st: a towards rr* **11/1**
112/ **F** **Walter White (IRE)**[759] 1536 5-11-8 115 ....(t) TomO'Brien
(Philip Hobbs) *trckd ldrs tl 5th: grad lost pl: in last pair whn fell 3 out* **9/1**
4m 33.1s (-9.60) **Going Correction** -0.475s/f (Good)
WFA 4 from 5yo+ 9lb **10** Ran SP% **117.1**
Speed ratings (Par 105): **101,100,98,89,87 86,82,73,73,**
CSF £21.91 CT £218.96 TOTE £4.20: £1.40, £2.10, £3.00; EX 24.60 Trifecta £344.90.
Owner Graham And Alison Jelley **Bred** Overbury Stallions Ltd **Trained** Naunton, Gloucs

FOCUS
All races were run on the hurdle bends reducing the chase course by about 45 yards per circuit. An open handicap. The winner was well in on old form, while the in-form second has been rated to his mark.

1819 AGGREGATE INDUSTRIES HELP FOR HEROES NOVICES' H'CAP HURDLE (11 hdls) 2m 5f 135y
2:55 (2:58) (Class 4) (0-105,105) 3-Y-0+ **£3,249** (£954; £477; £238)

Form RPR
53-5 **1** **Do We Like Him (IRE)**[160] 61 5-11-9 102 .... TomCannon 109+
(Chris Gordon) *hld up: rdn and hdwy 3 out: slt ld last: drifted lft: r.o: rdn out* **8/1**
00/1 **2** *1 ¾* **Our Folly**[24] 1545 7-11-6 99 ....(t) NickScholfield 103
(Stuart Kittow) *prom: led narrowly 3 out: rdn after next: hdd last: kpt on but no ex* **9/4**[1]
P-11 **3** *12* **Shalianzi (IRE)**[49] 1297 5-11-8 101 ....(b) JamieMoore 96
(Gary Moore) *trckd ldrs: rdn appr 3 out: styd on same pce fr 2 out* **9/2**[3]
350- **4** *4 ½* **Craiganee (IRE)**[171] 5434 8-11-12 105 .... SamTwiston-Davies 95
(Chris Down) *hld up: hdwy to ld 6th: rdn and hdd 3 out: styd chsng ldrs tl no ex appr last* **16/1**
24-0 **5** *nk* **Mist The Boat**[18] 1598 7-11-3 96 .... MichaelByrne 85
(Tim Vaughan) *led at stdy pce tl 6th: rdn in last but in tch after 8th: nt pce to get bk involved* **14/1**
432F **6** *4 ½* **Almagest**[7] 1721 7-11-9 102 ....(tp) RhysFlint 91
(Robert Stephens) *trckd ldrs: rdn appr 3 out: sn hld: wknd 2 out* **7/1**
0-10 **7** *2 ½* **King's Song (FR)**[20] 1573 5-11-3 96 .... AidanColeman 79
(David Dennis) *prom: rdn appr 3 out: wknd 2 out* **10/1**
2-60 **8** *8* **A Hairy Koala (FR)**[54] 1264 5-11-7 103 ....(bt) KieronEdgar(3) 79
(David Pipe) *trckd ldrs: rdn appr 3 out: sn btn: nt fluent 2 out* **3/1**[2]
5m 38.3s (5.30) **Going Correction** -0.475s/f (Good) **8** Ran SP% **119.2**
Speed ratings (Par 105): **71,70,66,64,64 62,61,58**
Polo The Mumm was withdrawn. Price at time of withdrawal 40-1. Rule 4 does not apply. CSF £28.35 CT £94.60 TOTE £10.70: £3.20, £1.10, £2.20; EX 38.80 Trifecta £136.10.
Owner Roger Alwen Mrs Heather Alwen **Bred** Owen Hickey **Trained** Morestead, Hampshire

FOCUS
A modest contest run at a steady gallop. The first two are on the upgrade, while the third has been rated below his recent form over shorter. The fourth helps set the level.

1820 GREAT POINT MEDIA INVESTMENTS H'CAP CHASE (18 fncs) 3m 54y
3:30 (3:30) (Class 4) (0-120,120) 4-Y-0+ **£5,848** (£1,717; £858; £429)

Form RPR
P4-P **1** **Whats Left (IRE)**[42] 1372 7-11-10 118 .... SamTwiston-Davies 134+
(Neil Mulholland) *mounted in pre-parade ring: in tch: shkn up bhd ldng pair after 14th: chal next: led 2 out: kpt on: drvn out* **4/1**[2]
2364 **2** *1* **He's A Bully (IRE)**[12] 1659 6-10-8 102 .... TomO'Brien 118+
(Philip Hobbs) *racd keenly: trckd ldrs: awkward 2nd: rdn in cl 4th 4 out: chal 2 out tl last: kpt on but a being hld run-in* **4/1**[2]
565 **3** *16* **Kyles Faith (IRE)**[13] 1646 7-10-9 103 ....(p) IanPopham 105
(Martin Keighley) *disp ld: rdn after 4 out: hdd 2 out: sn no ex* **16/1**
-5P1 **4** *3* **King Fontaine (IRE)**[18] 1592 12-11-5 113 ....(p) AidanColeman 113
(Lawney Hill) *trckd ldrs tl outpcd after 14th: plugged on fr 3 out but nvr any threat after* **15/2**
6P-4 **5** *6* **Kasbadali (FR)**[123] 660 10-11-12 120 .... LeightonAspell 116
(Oliver Sherwood) *disp ld: rchd for 4th: rdn appr 4 out: hdd bef 3 out: wknd after 2 out* **11/4**[1]
3-12 **6** *2 ¾* **I'm In Charge**[149] 266 9-11-0 108 ....(t) NickScholfield 98
(Grant Cann) *hld up in tch: rdn after 14th: nvr threatened: wknd after 2 out* **6/1**[3]
1P-4 **7** *1 ¼* **Midnight Request**[154] 174 6-11-6 114 .... ConorO'Farrell 104
(Nigel Hawke) *hld up in tch: rdn after 14th: nvr any imp: mstke 2 out: wknd* **6/1**[3]
5m 54.0s (-15.30) **Going Correction** -0.475s/f (Good) **7** Ran SP% **112.9**
Speed ratings (Par 105): **106,105,100,99,97 96,96**
CSF £20.11 TOTE £5.90: £2.20, £1.90; EX 27.70 Trifecta £240.70.
Owner Mrs Angela Hart **Bred** E G Canavan **Trained** Limpley Stoke, Wilts

FOCUS
Not a strong contest for the grade. A big step up from his hurdle form by the winner, and there's a case for rating the race at least 5lb higher.

1821 WATCH ON THE RACING UK APP BEGINNERS' CHASE (18 fncs) 3m 54y
4:05 (4:05) (Class 4) 4-Y-0+ **£4,659** (£1,446; £779)

Form RPR
03P- **1** **How About It (IRE)**[236] 4226 6-11-5 0..........................(p) LeightonAspell 126+
(Rebecca Curtis) *trckd ldrs: rdn whn lft cl 3rd 4 out: led 2 out: clr last: styd on wl* **5/2**[2]
-145 **2** *11* **For 'N' Against (IRE)**[36] 1450 6-11-5 117.....................(tp) ConorO'Farrell 118+
(David Pipe) *trckd ldrs: shkn up and chalng whn blnd 4 out: ev ch next tl after 2 out: drifted lft last: no ex* **11/2**[3]
1P- **3** *49* **Ballycoe**[320] 2651 6-11-5 0..................................(t) SamTwiston-Davies 86
(Paul Nicholls) *pressed ldr: led 12th tl after 14th: drvn whn lft in narrow advantage 4 out: hdd bef 2 out: wknd last: eased* **1/1**[1]
5-04 **F** **Bonne Fee**[33] 1479 8-10-12 0..(p) DavidBass
(Kim Bailey) *led most of way: hdd 12th tl drvn into narrow advantage after 14th: hrd pressed whn fell 4 out* **6/1**

5m 58.9s (-10.40) **Going Correction** -0.475s/f (Good) **4 Ran SP% 108.2**
Speed ratings (Par 105): **98,94,78,**
CSF £13.68 TOTE £4.30; EX 12.90 Trifecta £23.40.
Owner Carl Hinchy **Bred** Geoffrey Thompson **Trained** Newport, Pembrokeshire

FOCUS
A modest chase. The time doesn't justify a rating as high as this, but the winner could be okay.

1822 GREAT POINT MEDIA INVESTMENTS NOVICES' HURDLE (8 hdls) 2m 175y
4:40 (4:40) (Class 4) 4-Y-O+ **£3,249** (£954; £477; £238)

Form RPR
321- **1** **Abidjan (FR)**[171] 5434 5-11-5 123..............................(t) SamTwiston-Davies 134+
(Paul Nicholls) *veered lft whn tapes wnt bk: grnted uncontested ld: drew clr on bridle fr 3 out: unextended* **4/7**[1]
U123 **2** *11* **Angus Glens**[118] 710 5-11-5 121.......................................(p) AidanColeman 121+
(David Dennis) *chsd wnr thrght: rdn appr 3 out: sn no ch* **5/2**[2]
6305 **3** *16* **Menace**[18] 1590 4-10-9 0.. JamesBanks(3) 95
(Noel Williams) *hld up: wnt btn 3rd whn hitting 3 out: nvr any threat to front pair* **14/1**
00- **4** *19* **Culm Counsellor**[329] 2468 6-10-9 0..................................(p) GilesHawkins(3) 78
(Chris Down) *racd keenly: a towards rr* **100/1**
4 **5** *¾* **Silver Dixie (USA)**[16] 1612 5-10-12 0................................. LeightonAspell 77
(Peter Hedger) *hld up: tk clsr order 4th: wnt 3rd next: nvr threatened front pair: wknd 3 out* **8/1**[3]
6P- **P** **Ghost Runner (IRE)**[486] 641 5-10-9 0...............................(t) BrianToomey(3)
(Mark Shears) *chsd ldrs tl 5th: t.o whn p.u bef 3 out* **150/1**
P **New Reaction**[422] 4-10-12 0.. RhysFlint
(Alexandra Dunn) *a towards rr: wknd after 5th: t.o whn p.u after 3 out* **66/1**

4m 7.0s (-8.50) **Going Correction** -0.475s/f (Good)
WFA 4 from 5yo+ 9lb **7 Ran SP% 113.1**
Speed ratings (Par 105): **101,95,88,79,79**
CSF £2.32 TOTE £1.40: £1.10, £1.50; EX 3.00 Trifecta £8.20.
Owner Axom L **Bred** Gabriel Vagne & Michele Vagne **Trained** Ditcheat, Somerset

FOCUS
They went an even gallop for this uncompetitive hurdle. The easy winner could be okay but the time was slow compared to the following handicap, so this is a race to come back to.

1823 BET WITH YOUR RACING UK APP CONDITIONAL JOCKEYS' H'CAP HURDLE (8 hdls) 2m 175y
5:10 (5:12) (Class 4) (0-105,104) 3-Y-O+ **£3,249** (£954; £477; £238)

Form RPR
2411 **1** **Bulletproof (IRE)**[10] 1677 9-11-6 98 7ex...........................(p) SeanBowen 110+
(Ken Cunningham-Brown) *hld up: smooth hdwy after 5th: ldng whn nt fluent 2 out: nudged clr run-in: readily* **7/2**[1]
-435 **2** *5* **Createur (IRE)**[48] 1305 4-11-6 104......................................(t) AlanJohns(6) 107
(Tim Vaughan) *hld up: hdwy after 5th: rdn to chse ldrs after 3 out: styd on into 2nd run-in: no ch w wnr* **6/1**
0564 **3** *2* **Prince Of Poets**[20] 1578 4-11-0 95..................................(tp) KieronEdgar(3) 98+
(David Pipe) *led: mstke 3 out: rdn and hdd next: no ex fr last* **7/2**[1]
0065 **4** *1 ¾* **Tenby Jewel (IRE)**[20] 1578 10-9-13 80..........................(tp) MichaelHeard(3) 81
(Mark Gillard) *trckd ldrs: rdn after 5th: styd on same pce fr next* **12/1**
600- **5** *17* **Kayf Charmer**[187] 5148 5-9-11 78 oh4.......................... ThomasCheesman(3) 62
(Stuart Howe) *mid-div: effrt after 5th: wknd bef 2 out* **14/1**
F56P **6** *¾* **Prettyasapicture**[16] 1618 6-11-5 100..................................(v[1]) TomBellamy(3) 84
(Alan King) *trckd ldrs: rdn appr 3 out: wknd bef 2 out* **11/2**[3]
PP **7** *23* **Tiger D'Oust (FR)**[57] 1237 6-10-12 90................................(p) GilesHawkins 53
(Chris Down) *mid-div: rdn after 4th: wknd after next: t.o* **25/1**
P-U0 **8** *3 ½* **Dance**[97] 892 6-10-6 87.. PaulO'Brien(3) 47
(Rod Millman) *hld up: rdn after 7th: wknd bef next: t.o* **22/1**
46-6 **P** **Mexican Border (GER)**[142] 391 6-11-3 95............................. JeremiahMcGrath
(Martin Hill) *hld up: hdwy 3rd: trckd ldrs 5th: folded tamely 3 out: p.u bef next* **5/1**[2]
POPU **P** **Fashion Icon (FR)**[54] 1261 4-10-2 85.................................(tp) ConorSmith(5)
(Nigel Hawke) *struggling 4th: a towards rr: lost tch after 5th: p.u bef 2 out* **33/1**

4m 4.2s (-11.30) **Going Correction** -0.475s/f (Good) **10 Ran SP% 116.3**
Speed ratings (Par 105): **107,104,103,102,94 94,83,82, ,**
CSF £24.40 CT £78.64 TOTE £3.20: £1.40, £2.40, £1.60; EX 14.10 Trifecta £50.90.
Owner Danebury Racing Stables **Bred** Miss Laura Duggan **Trained** Danebury, Hants

FOCUS
A weak handicap but the winner did it well. The winner has been rated back to the best of his old form, the runner-up as recording a pb and the fourth as running to form.
T/Plt: £49.20 to a £1 stake. Pool: £52,947.22 - 784.24 winning units. T/Qpdt: £17.60 to a £1 stake. Pool: £2,989.11 - 125.25 winning units. **Tim Mitchell**

1641 WORCESTER (L-H)
Thursday, October 8

OFFICIAL GOING: Good (good to soft in places; 7.0)
Wind: Light behind Weather: Cloudy with sunny spells

1824 RICHARD WRIGHT MEMORIAL NOVICES' H'CAP CHASE (13 fncs) 2m 4f
2:00 (2:01) (Class 4) (0-105,105) 4-Y-0+ **£3,898** (£1,144; £572; £286)

Form RPR
55P2 **1** **Butlergrove King (IRE)**[3] 1796 6-11-0 100.................. FreddieMitchell(7) 110+
(Dai Burchell) *chsd ldr tl led after 6th: hdd 8th: led again next: pushed clr appr 4 out: rdn and hung rt flat: styd on* **11/4**[2]
4P0- **2** *4 ½* **Gowanauthat (IRE)**[169] 5467 7-11-0 93..........................(t) GavinSheehan 100+
(Charlie Mann) *chsd ldrs: outpcd 7th: j.rt 9th: hdwy to chse wnr 4 out: rdn whn blnd 2 out: styd on same pce flat* **14/1**
P55- **3** *14* **Copperfacejack (IRE)**[179] 5293 5-11-8 101...................(p) CharliePoste 96
(Paul Webber) *hld up: hit 1st: hmpd sn after: rdn appr 4 out: wnt 3rd towards fin: nvr on terms* **28/1**
536- **4** *1* **Rock Des Champs (IRE)**[205] 4821 5-11-8 101............. BarryGeraghty 93
(Jonjo O'Neill) *mstke 1st: sn prom: outpcd 7th: hdwy appr 4 out: wknd next* **5/2**[1]
24-P **5** *20* **Ride On Time (IRE)**[150] 237 5-11-7 100.......................... NicodeBoinville 79
(Ben Pauling) *led: nt fluent 4th: hit 6th: sn hdd: led again 8th tl next: rdn and lost 2nd 4 out: mstke and wknd next* **25/1**
66U0 **P** **Nicky Nutjob (GER)**[117] 599 9-10-0 79 oh15.................(p) DaveCrosse
(John O'Shea) *hld up: p.u and dismntd bnd after 5th* **100/1**
2-22 **P** **Henry Oliver (IRE)**[134] 515 7-10-13 92............................(tp) NoelFehily
(Neil Mulholland) *hmpd 1st: hld up: bhd fr 8th: p.u bef 4 out* **10/1**
60 **P** **Double Dan (IRE)**[13] 1647 6-10-5 84.................................. AdamWedge
(Alexandra Dunn) *hld up: a in rr: rdn and lost tch bef 6th: bhd whn p.u bef 4 out* **50/1**
4122 **F** **Mighty Leader (IRE)**[29] 1522 7-11-12 105........................ JamesDavies
(Henry Oliver) *fell 1st* **4/1**[3]
560- **U** **Gold Man (IRE)**[182] 5245 6-11-6 102..................................(t) TomBellamy(3)
(Kim Bailey) *hmpd and uns rdr 1st* **8/1**

4m 59.5s (-5.10) **Going Correction** -0.125s/f (Good) **10 Ran SP% 112.4**
Speed ratings (Par 105): **105,103,97,97,89 , , , ,**
CSF £35.30 CT £872.09 TOTE £4.30: £1.50, £4.80, £6.20; EX 47.60 Trifecta £631.50.
Owner Mrs K Lewis **Bred** Butlersgrove Stud **Trained** Briery Hill, Blaenau Gwent

FOCUS
All starts have been moved at this track following remeasuring, so there will be no speed figures here until there is sufficient data to calculate updated median times. The ground had dried out a little from its overnight description. After the first, Barry Geraghty said: "It's lovely, just on the slow side of good", and Gavin Sheehan's take on it was: "It's good, but on the slow side." Both bends were railed out from the innermost position, adding approximately 66yds to races 1, 4 & 6, and 36yds to races 2, 3 and 5. Not many got into this ordinary novice handicap chase, which saw trouble at the first. The third has been rated similar to his hurdle mark.

1825 WORCESTER NEWS AMATEUR RIDERS' H'CAP CHASE (12 fncs) 2m 110y
2:35 (2:35) (Class 5) (0-100,100) 4-Y-O+ **£2,495** (£774; £386; £193)

Form RPR
15-4 **1** **Ashcott Boy**[18] 1595 7-11-3 96.. DavidNoonan(5) 112+
(Neil Mulholland) *a.p: led 3 out: nt fluent next: rdn and hung lft flat: r.o wl: eased nr fin* **10/3**[2]
620- **2** *18* **Mon Chevalier (IRE)**[191] 5084 12-11-7 100..........(b) MrRobertHawker(5) 99
(Carroll Gray) *chsd ldr: mstke 2nd: lost 2nd after 4th: wnt 2nd again after 8th: led 4 out: hdd next: wknd flat* **16/1**
32-0 **3** *1 ¾* **Cool Bob (IRE)**[48] 1306 12-10-0 79..........................(tp) MrStanSheppard(5) 77
(Matt Sheppard) *hld up: hmpd 5th: hdwy appr 4 out: wknd 2 out* **11/1**
31-6 **4** *6* **The Informant**[137] 446 9-10-8 89.....................................(b) MrDSansom(7) 83
(Seamus Mullins) *prom: j.rt at times: chsd ldr after 4th tl after 8th: sn rdn: wknd 2 out* **12/1**
2446 **5** *8* **Mount Vesuvius (IRE)**[18] 1596 7-10-4 85..............(t) MrBParis-Crofts(7) 74
(Paul Henderson) *hld up: mstke 3rd: hdwy appr 4 out: wknd next* **8/1**
P556 **6** *12* **Stafford Charlie**[8] 1703 9-9-7 74 oh7..............................(b) MrTGreatrex(7) 47
(John O'Shea) *hld up: rdn appr 4 out: wknd next* **50/1**
3-2U **U** **Samtheman**[132] 536 10-10-12 93.. MissABroome(7) 87
(Pam Ford) *led: j.rt at times: hdd 4 out: wkng whn mstke and uns rdr 2 out* **6/1**
0221 **F** **My Nosy Rosy**[8] 1703 7-11-1 96 7ex..............................(tp) MrMJPKendrick(7)
(Ben Case) *hld up: fell 2nd* **11/2**[3]
3604 **U** **The Purchaser (IRE)**[4] 1785 7-11-1 94...........(vt[1]) MrTommieMO'Brien(5)
(Chris Bealby) *prom: hmpd 2nd: blnd bdly and uns rdr 5th* **11/4**[1]

4m 8.1s (3.10) **Going Correction** -0.125s/f (Good) **9 Ran SP% 114.4**
Speed ratings (Par 103): **87,78,77,74,71 65, , ,**
CSF £50.80 CT £525.96 TOTE £3.60: £1.70, £4.20, £3.80; EX 77.20 Trifecta £393.60.
Owner John Hobbs **Bred** Mrs J A Gawthorpe **Trained** Limpley Stoke, Wilts

FOCUS
A weak handicap chase for amateur jockeys. The easy winner has been rated to the level of last year's hurdle form, and there's a case for rating the race a few pounds higher through the second and third, but it's probably not form to be getting carried away with.

1826 BRITISH STALLION STUDS EBF "NATIONAL HUNT" NOVICES' HURDLE (QUALIFIER) (8 hdls) 2m
3:05 (3:07) (Class 4) 4-6-Y-O **£3,898** (£1,144; £572; £286)

Form RPR
21- **1** **Wishfull Dreaming**[280] 3447 4-10-12 0......................... RichardJohnson 116+
(Philip Hobbs) *hld up in tch: chsd ldr 3rd: led 3 out: wnt lft last: drvn out* **4/6**[1]
5 **2** *½* **Super Scorpion (IRE)**[13] 1648 5-10-12 0............................ TrevorWhelan 114+
(Debra Hamer) *a.p: lft disputing 2nd 3 out: sn chsng wnr: nt clr run last: rdn flat: styd on* **28/1**
063- **3** *7* **Bekkensfirth**[185] 5198 6-10-12 0.. HarrySkelton 107
(Dan Skelton) *hld up: hdwy appr 3 out: styd on same pce fr next: nt fluent last* **6/1**[2]
1-64 **4** *8* **Florrie Boy (IRE)**[24] 1544 4-10-5 0.............................. JamieBargary(7) 101
(Nigel Twiston-Davies) *hld up: shkn up after 5th: outpcd fr 3 out* **10/1**
42- **5** *9* **Frosty Steel (IRE)**[167] 5520 5-10-12 0.............................. PaddyBrennan 94
(Tom George) *mid-div: hdwy 4th: lft disputing 2nd 3 out: sn rdn: wknd appr last* **14/1**
6 *22* **All In Favour (IRE)** 4-10-12 0.. BarryGeraghty 72
(Jonjo O'Neill) *hld up: blnd 1st: bhd fr 4th: mstke next* **16/1**
40- **7** *1 ¼* **Northandsouth (IRE)**[314] 2776 5-10-9 0............................. RyanHatch(3) 71
(Nigel Twiston-Davies) *hld up: hdwy 4th: wknd 3 out* **33/1**
0-3 **P** **Rushvale (IRE)**[133] 528 6-10-5 0.................................. MrMJPKendrick(7)
(Ben Case) *nt fluent 1st: sddle sn slipped: chsd ldr 2nd tl 3rd: p.u bef next* **12/1**
32U0 **F** **Magna Cartor**[18] 1590 5-10-12 0.. KielanWoods
(Ronald Thompson) *led: jnd and fell 3 out* **50/1**
2- **P** **Basilic D'Alene (FR)**[233] 4283 4-10-7 0.................................. LizzieKelly(5)
(Nick Williams) *prom: lost pl bef 3rd: sn bhd: p.u bef next* **9/1**[3]

3m 46.3s (-4.30) **Going Correction** -0.05s/f (Good) **10 Ran SP% 122.0**
Speed ratings: **108,107,104,100,95 84,84, , ,**
CSF £28.60 TOTE £1.50: £1.10, £6.90, £1.60; EX 24.40 Trifecta £241.80.
Owner Mrs Diana L Whateley **Bred** R F And S D Knipe **Trained** Withycombe, Somerset

FOCUS
An interesting novices' hurdle which should produce winners. The time was 1.3sec quicker than the later handicap. The winner was building on the promise of his bumper form, while the third and fourth help set the level.

1827 BOOK CHRISTMAS PARTIES AT WORCESTER RACECOURSE (S) HURDLE (10 hdls) 2m 4f
3:40 (3:40) (Class 5) 4-7-Y-O **£2,599** (£763; £381; £190)

Form RPR
521U **1** **Church Field (IRE)**[8] 1699 7-11-1 117..........................(b[1]) BarryGeraghty 115
(Jonjo O'Neill) *a.p: chsd ldr bef 3 out: nt fluent next: led appr and nt fluent last: drvn out* **4/5**[1]

4F-P **2** *2 1/4* **Bar A Mine (FR)**[15] 1629 6-10-3 103.......................... MrJJSlevin(7) 108
(Nigel Twiston-Davies) *chsd ldr tl lft in ld 2nd: rdn and hdd appr last: styd on same pce flat* **5/1**[3]

3-32 **3** *11* **Tijori (IRE)**[8] 1700 7-10-7 112..................................(bt) RobertWilliams(3) 101
(Bernard Llewellyn) *prom: rdn appr 3 out: styd on same pce fr next* **9/4**[2]

4 *35* **Maxximus (IRE)** 5-10-10 0.. JackQuinlan 66
(Sarah Humphrey) *hld up: plld hrd: hdwy 6th: rdn and wknd after next* **50/1**

1504 **P** **Y A Bon (IRE)**[40] 1401 7-10-10 90..................................(b) LeeEdwards
(Aytach Sadik) *led: j.big 1st: j. slowly and hdd next: nt fluent 4th: sn jnd ldr tl rdn: lost pl and p.u bef 3 out: dismntd* **66/1**

4m 58.9s (5.40) **Going Correction** -0.05s/f (Good) **5** Ran SP% **106.4**
Speed ratings: **87,86,81,67,**
CSF £5.01 TOTE £1.70: £1.10, £2.70; EX 4.80 Trifecta £7.50.

Owner John P McManus **Bred** Mrs Eleanor Hadden **Trained** Cheltenham, Gloucs

FOCUS
The pace wasn't strong in this modest event. The first two have been rated pretty much to their marks.

1828 7BETS4FREE.COM SAYS NO2 WINS H'CAP HURDLE (8 hdls) 2m
4:15 (4:15) (Class 4) (0-120,117) 3-Y-O+ **£3,898** (£1,144; £572; £286)

Form RPR
440- **1** **Ink Master (IRE)**[257] 3855 5-11-7 **112**.......................... RichardJohnson 123+
(Philip Hobbs) *w ldr: led 2nd shkn up after 2 out: drvn clr flat* **2/1**[1]

/5-1 **2** *11* **What A Laugh**[132] 534 10-11-4 **114**.......................... BridgetAndrews(5) 115
(Gary Hanmer) *hld up: hdwy 3rd: chsd wnr appr 3 out: shkn up appr last: rdn and wknd flat* **5/1**[3]

15-2 **3** *2* **While You Wait (IRE)**[18] 1602 6-11-10 **115**.......................... JamesDavies 113
(Paul Fitzsimons) *prom: lost pl 3rd: hdwy 5th: styd on same pce fr 3 out* **8/1**

2353 **4** *nk* **Gambol (FR)**[29] 1518 5-11-8 **113**..................................(t) WillKennedy 112
(Ian Williams) *prom: chsd wnr after 2nd: mstke 5th: sn rdn: wknd 2 out* **5/1**[3]

45-6 **5** *16* **Zip Wire (IRE)**[30] 1508 6-11-7 **112**.......................... WayneHutchinson 98
(Donald McCain) *hld up: wknd 5th: bhd whn mstke last* **12/1**

040F **P** **Western Diva (IRE)**[46] 1348 6-11-9 **114**..........................(t[1]) TomScudamore
(David Pipe) *led to 2nd: pushed along and nt keen after 3rd: wknd next: bhd whn p.u bef 3 out* **3/1**[2]

3m 47.6s (-3.00) **Going Correction** -0.05s/f (Good) **6** Ran SP% **110.5**
Speed ratings (Par 105): **105,99,98,98,90**
CSF £11.94 CT £59.41 TOTE £2.90: £1.40, £3.10; EX 13.00 Trifecta £68.70.

Owner Alan Peterson **Bred** Michael G Daly **Trained** Withycombe, Somerset

FOCUS
Not a strong handicap for the grade. A big step up from the winner, with the second and fourth rated close to their marks.

1829 SUPPORT RIDING FOR THE DISABLED TODAY MAIDEN HURDLE (12 hdls) 2m 7f
4:50 (4:50) (Class 5) 4-Y-O+ **£2,599** (£763; £381; £190)

Form RPR
1-2 **1** **Fingerontheswitch (IRE)**[22] 1550 5-10-12 0.......................... NoelFehily 128+
(Neil Mulholland) *led to 3rd: chsd ldr tl after 6th: led again 9th: drvn out* **8/11**[1]

5- **2** *1 3/4* **Ballydine (IRE)**[192] 5077 5-10-12 0.......................... RichardJohnson 125
(Charlie Longsdon) *prom: blnd 2nd: chsd ldr after 6th tl lost pl 8th: hdwy appr 3 out: rdn to chse wnr after next: styd on* **4/1**[3]

0- **3** *12* **Florida Calling (IRE)**[192] 5077 6-10-12 0.......................... PaddyBrennan 114
(Tom George) *trckd ldrs: racd keenly: rdn to chse wnr 3 out tl after next: wknd last* **12/1**

3- **4** *20* **Ballybane (IRE)**[213] 4679 5-10-12 0.......................... TomScudamore 99
(Rebecca Curtis) *prom: j.lft 1st and 7th: rdn and wknd after 3 out* **7/2**[2]

5 *8* **Daulys Anthem (IRE)**[165] 7-10-12 0.......................... TrevorWhelan 88
(David Dennis) *hld up: hdwy 9th: rdn and wknd 3 out* **33/1**

6 *25* **Fire (IRE)**[185] 5218 5-10-12 0.......................... TomMessenger 65
(Chris Bealby) *plld hrd: trckd wnr tl led 3rd: hdd 9th: rdn and wknd bef next* **20/1**

04/4 **7** *5* **Boxatrix**[20] 1576 7-10-7 0 ow2.......................... MrDAndrews(7) 63
(Paul Phillips) *hld up: rdn and wknd after 8th: bhd whn hung rt flat* **66/1**

6/60 **8** *20* **Millksheikh**[36] 1447 8-10-9 0 ow2..................................(t) MrPYork(5) 45
(Raymond York) *hld up: rdn and wknd 8th* **150/1**

-U40 **U** **Double Court (IRE)**[126] 613 4-10-8 0.......................... RyanHatch(3)
(Nigel Twiston-Davies) *tried to refuse and uns rdr 1st* **66/1**

5m 43.1s (4.50) **Going Correction** -0.05s/f (Good)
WFA 4 from 5yo+ 10lb **9** Ran SP% **119.2**
Speed ratings (Par 103): **90,89,85,78,75 66,65,58,**
CSF £4.24 TOTE £1.70: £1.10, £1.50, £2.60; EX 4.50 Trifecta £22.30.

Owner Cahill, Atwell & Crofts **Bred** Denis Cleary **Trained** Limpley Stoke, Wilts

FOCUS
There were several chasing types on show in this staying novice hurdle. The winner stood out on his Kelso run and has been rated a bit below that level here. The second and third have been rated as building on their bumper form.

T/Plt: £49.20 to a £1 stake. Pool: £59070.79 - 875.35 winning tickets T/Qpdt: £3.00 to a £1 stake. Pool: £5036.3 - 1234.47 winning tickets **Colin Roberts**

1830 - 1836a (Foreign Racing) - See Raceform Interactive

1673 NEWTON ABBOT (L-H)
Friday, October 9

OFFICIAL GOING: Good to soft (good in places; 6.2)
Wind: almost nil Weather: sunny periods

1837 BRITISH STALLION STUDS EBF "NATIONAL HUNT" NOVICES' HURDLE (QUALIFIER) (9 hdls) 2m 2f 110y
1:55 (1:55) (Class 4) 4-6-Y-O **£5,064** (£1,496; £748; £374; £187)

Form RPR
1/0- **1** **Simon Squirrel (IRE)**[294] 3170 5-10-12 0..........(t) SamTwiston-Davies 124+
(Paul Nicholls) *trckd ldr: led 2 out: sn in command: readily* **5/2**[2]

5- **2** *2* **Barranco Valley**[214] 4679 4-10-12 0.......................... RichardJohnson 120+
(Nick Williams) *hld up: hdwy after 3 out: styd on nicely fr 2 out: wnt 2nd bef last: kpt on wl flat but wnr a in control* **20/1**

21-0 **3** *4* **Wade Harper (IRE)**[163] 23 5-10-12 0.......................... AidanColeman 117+
(David Dennis) *racd keenly: trckd ldr: led after 3 out: hdd next: sn rdn: kpt on same pce* **6/1**

6/ **4** *2 1/4* **Kilkishen (IRE)**[20] 1588 5-11-2 135.......................... BrianHayes(3) 123
(John Joseph Hanlon, Ire) *led: rdn and hdd after 3 out: hmpd bef next: no ex between last 2* **3/1**[3]

15- **5** *6* **Going For Broke (IRE)**[203] 4881 5-10-12 0.......................... PaulTownend 108
(Rebecca Curtis) *mid-div: rdn after 3 out: nvr any imp* **2/1**[1]

233/ **6** *8* **Flamenco Lad**[563] 5021 5-10-9 0.......................... JeremiahMcGrath(3) 101
(Martin Hill) *mid-div: hdwy 5th to trck ldrs: rdn after 3 out: wknd bef next* **33/1**

00-5 **7** *14* **Fountains Blossom**[160] 83 6-10-5 0.......................... ConorO'Farrell 82
(Anthony Honeyball) *trckd ldr: rdn after 3 out: sn wknd* **100/1**

00-5 **8** *7* **Act Now**[153] 207 6-10-5 0.......................... MichealNolan 75
(Anthony Honeyball) *trckd ldrs tl 4th: sn struggling in rr* **50/1**

0/55 **9** *3 3/4* **Looking For Mick**[11] 1673 6-10-9 0.......................... GilesHawkins(3) 79
(Chris Down) *a towards rr* **100/1**

4m 27.4s (-2.60) **Going Correction** +0.175s/f (Yiel)
WFA 4 from 5yo+ 9lb **9** Ran SP% **112.8**
Speed ratings: **112,111,109,108,106 102,96,93,92**
CSF £43.80 TOTE £3.50: £2.20, £2.90, £2.40; EX 36.40 Trifecta £263.20.

Owner Andrea & Graham Wylie **Bred** John O'Dwyer **Trained** Ditcheat, Somerset

FOCUS
Rail movement increased race 1 by 27yds, race 2 by 23yds, race 3 by 42yds, race 4 by 37yds, race 5 34yds, race 6 by 45yds and race 7 by 25yds. An interesting novice hurdle, run at an average gallop, and it should produce winners. Fair form.

1838 "EGGY" NOVICES' CHASE (13 fncs) 2m 75y
2:30 (2:30) (Class 3) 4-Y-O+ **£8,229** (£2,431; £1,215; £608; £304)

Form RPR
1131 **1** **Ittirad (USA)**[31] 1505 7-11-5 0.......................... AidanColeman 146+
(John Ferguson) *trckd ldrs: chal between last 2: led sn after last: r.o wl* **11/8**[1]

12U1 **2** *1 3/4* **Dormello Mo (FR)**[21] 1575 5-11-10 147..........(t) SamTwiston-Davies 150
(Paul Nicholls) *trckd ldr: rdn to ld 2 out: hdd sn after last: nt pce of wnr* **6/4**[2]

22-3 **3** *6* **Nicolas Chauvin (IRE)**[21] 1575 7-11-0 0.......................... NicodeBoinville 136+
(Nicky Henderson) *racd keenly: led: nt fluent 3rd and 4th: hdd whn stmbld 2 out: sn no ex* **5/1**[3]

43P- **4** *3 3/4* **Ted Spread**[209] 4749 8-11-0 129..................................(t) TomO'Brien 129
(Suzy Smith) *hld up bhd ldrs: wnt 4th after 7th: rdn after 3 out: sn one pce* **14/1**

11-5 **5** *33* **Mr Burbidge**[139] 442 7-11-0 0..................................(p) MarkQuinlan 100
(Neil Mulholland) *chsd ldrs tl outpcd 8th: t.o* **25/1**

0-22 **P** **Winged Express (IRE)**[143] 391 6-11-0 0.......................... IanPopham
(Alexandra Dunn) *sn t.o: p.u after 7th* **100/1**

(-6.50) **Going Correction** -0.15s/f (Good) **6** Ran SP% **110.3**
Speed ratings (Par 107): **110,109,106,104,87**
CSF £3.84 TOTE £2.00: £1.60, £1.10; EX 3.20 Trifecta £6.50.

Owner Bloomfields **Bred** Darley **Trained** Cowlinge, Suffolk

FOCUS
A fair little novice chase, run at a decent gallop. The winner is improving in line with his hurdle form.

1839 SIS H'CAP HURDLE (12 hdls) 3m 2f 105y
3:00 (3:00) (Class 2) 4-Y-O+
£15,640 (£4,620; £2,310; £1,155; £577; £290)

Form RPR
10-0 **1** **Milan Bound (IRE)**[153] 196 7-10-13 **130**..........(t) RichardJohnson 128
(Jonjo O'Neill) *trckd ldrs: chal after 3 out: sn rdn: led sn after last: kpt on: all out* **11/4**[1]

/60- **2** *hd* **Rydon Pynes**[230] 4354 7-10-9 **129**.......................... JeremiahMcGrath(3) 129+
(Martin Hill) *hld up in tch: trckd ldrs 3 out: led appr 2 out: rdn between last 2: hit last: sn hdd: kpt on* **6/1**

3105 **3** *1/2* **On The Bridge (IRE)**[19] 1594 10-11-1 **132**..........(tp) NickScholfield 130
(Jeremy Scott) *led: rdn and hdd appr 2 out: stuck to task v gamely: styd on fr last* **7/1**

-113 **4** *1 1/4* **Just A Normal Day (IRE)**[83] 1035 5-10-7 **124**..........(p) HarrySkelton 120
(Dan Skelton) *hld up in tch: trckd ldrs after 3 out: rdn bef next where wnt lft: styd on same pce* **9/2**[3]

06-0 **5** *1 1/2* **Gevrey Chambertin (FR)**[35] 1477 7-11-12 **143**.......................... TomScudamore 138
(David Pipe) *hld up last but in tch: outpcd after 3 out: styd on between last 2 but no threat* **8/1**

1-P3 **6** *nse* **Kalmbeforethestorm**[21] 1579 7-10-0 **117** oh8.......................... PaulMoloney 112
(Helen Nelmes) *hld up in tch: rdn to chse ldrs after 3 out: wnt lft next: no ex fr last* **16/1**

261- **7** *3/4* **Morito Du Berlais (FR)**[194] 5048 6-11-8 **139**.......(t) SamTwiston-Davies 134
(Paul Nicholls) *trckd ldrs: rdn whn sltly short of room after 3 out: kpt chsng ldrs: nt fluent last: no ex* **7/2**[2]

6m 38.3s (-2.70) **Going Correction** +0.175s/f (Yiel) **7** Ran SP% **110.8**
Speed ratings (Par 109): **111,110,110,110,109 109,109**
CSF £18.22 TOTE £3.10: £2.20, £3.60; EX 16.00 Trifecta £128.60.

Owner John P McManus **Bred** T J Nagle **Trained** Cheltenham, Gloucs

FOCUS
A fair staying handicap, run at an ordinary gallop and they finished in a heap.

1840 NEWTONABBOTRACING.COM INTERMEDIATE CHASE (16 fncs) 2m 4f 216y
3:35 (3:35) (Class 2) 5-Y-O+ £18,837 (£5,613; £2,841; £1,455; £762)

Form RPR

F4-2 1 **Irish Cavalier (IRE)**[161] 69 6-11-6 151..........................(p) PaulTownend 161+
(Rebecca Curtis) *trckd ldrs: led appr 2 out: nt fluent last: comf* **9/4[2]**

45-1 2 ½ **Henryville**[7] 1737 7-10-8 0.. NoelFehily 145+
(Harry Fry) *patiently rdn in last: ct flat-footed after 4 out: hdwy after 3 out: wnt 2nd sn after last: fin wl but nvr gng to catch eased down wnr* **15/8[1]**

51-1 3 2½ **Art Mauresque (FR)**[158] 99 5-11-4 144.......................... NickScholfield 151
(Paul Nicholls) *led: rdn whn jnd 4 out: hdd next: sn hld by wnr: kpt on but no ex whn lost 2nd sn after last* **8/1**

1-23 4 2¼ **Cloud Creeper (IRE)**[13] 1658 8-11-6 152..................... RichardJohnson 153
(Philip Hobbs) *hld up: wnt 4th and sltly hmpd 4 out: sn rdn: nt pce to get on terms* **7/2[3]**

P11- 5 12 **Shantou Magic (IRE)**[175] 5375 8-11-0 143......................... WillKennedy 136
(Charlie Longsdon) *trckd ldrs: chal 11th: led 3 out: rdn and hdd bef next where mstke: sn wknd* **14/1**

212- P **Seventh Sky (GER)**[174] 5389 8-11-4 147.....................(tp) GavinSheehan
(Charlie Mann) *trckd ldr: pushed along after 12th: wknd 3 out: p.u bef next* **16/1**

5m 11.2s (-10.20) **Going Correction** -0.15s/f (Good) 6 Ran SP% 111.4
Speed ratings: **113,112,111,111,106**
CSF £7.12 TOTE £3.00: £1.30, £2.70; EX 9.20 Trifecta £40.10.
Owner A McIver **Bred** Limetree Stud **Trained** Newport, Pembrokeshire

FOCUS
The feature chase was run at an average gallop and the smart winner is value for plenty further.

1841 ON COURSE BOOKMAKERS AT NEWTON ABBOT MARES' H'CAP HURDLE (10 hdls) 2m 5f 122y
4:05 (4:05) (Class 4) (0-115,114) 4-Y-O+ £5,064 (£1,496; £748; £374; £187)

Form RPR

-123 1 **Kayf Willow**[86] 1012 6-11-9 111.. RichardJohnson 115+
(Philip Hobbs) *in tch: trckd ldrs 7th: led appr 2 out: kpt on wl: drvn out* **11/4[1]**

2506 2 2¼ **Lady Of Longstone (IRE)**[25] 1547 5-10-0 95........................ MichaelHeard(7) 96
(David Pipe) *led: hdd after 6th: remained pressing ldr: led 3 out: rdn and hdd bef 2 out: rallied last: kpt on same pce flat* **15/2**

1622 3 2½ **Midnight Sapphire**[25] 1545 5-11-4 106........................(t) DenisO'Regan 106
(Victor Dartnall) *in tch: rdn after 3 out: styd on same pce fr next: drifted lft run-in* **4/1[2]**

1441 4 1¾ **Popping Along**[45] 1354 6-11-9 114...........................(tp) MattGriffiths(3) 113+
(Jeremy Scott) *hld up: rdn and hdwy after 3 out: styd on but nt pce to get on terms: hmpd run-in* **11/2[3]**

5221 5 1½ **Amour D'Or**[60] 1231 4-11-1 108.. LizzieKelly(5) 104
(Nick Williams) *trckd ldrs: rdn after 3 out: disp 3rd whn hit 2 out: fdd flat* **4/1[2]**

3125 6 4½ **Titch Strider (IRE)**[33] 1490 10-11-4 106.............................. ConorO'Farrell 98
(John Panvert) *hld up: rdn after 3 out: nvr threatened* **20/1**

-4P6 7 4½ **Hija**[75] 1109 4-10-11 104...(p) AliceMills(5) 92
(Gail Haywood) *hld up: nudged along after 6th: rdn after 3 out: nvr gng pce to get involved* **33/1**

8 7 **Isabellesprincess (IRE)**[64] 1207 7-10-12 110....(t) CharlieHammond(10) 92
(Mike Hammond) *in tch: rdn after 3 out: wknd next* **10/1**

21-6 9 21 **Ice Tres**[155] 162 6-11-2 104...(p) JamesDavies 67
(Chris Down) *trckd ldrs: racing keenly whn ldng after 6th: hdd 3 out: wknd qckly* **20/1**

5m 20.7s (0.50) **Going Correction** +0.175s/f (Yiel)
WFA 4 from 5yo+ 10lb 9 Ran SP% 115.4
Speed ratings (Par 105): **106,105,104,103,103 101,99,97,89**
CSF £22.87 CT £81.70 TOTE £3.40: £2.00, £2.50, £1.50; EX 28.00 Trifecta £144.60.
Owner Newton Abbot Racing Syndicate **Bred** R Johnson **Trained** Withycombe, Somerset
■ Stewards' Enquiry : Denis O'Regan three-day ban; careless riding (23rd-25th Oct)

FOCUS
A moderate mares' handicap, run at an average gallop.

1842 ATTHERACES IN APP BETTING H'CAP CHASE (20 fncs) 3m 1f 170y
4:35 (4:36) (Class 4) (0-110,107) 4-Y-O+ £4,548 (£1,335; £667; £333)

Form RPR

5-3 1 **Distracted (IRE)**[74] 1118 7-10-11 99.............................(p) CiaranGethings(7) 116+
(Robert Stephens) *mde all: clr 9th tl 11th: clr again after 14th: in command fr 3 out: nt fluent 2 out: comf* **15/8[1]**

622 2 4 **Railway Storm (IRE)**[48] 1326 10-10-8 96................................ MissBFrost(7) 103
(Jimmy Frost) *hld up: outpcd after 4 out: styd on after 3 out: chal for 2nd fr last: nvr any ch w wnr* **4/1[2]**

FP-3 3 nse **Johns Luck (IRE)**[45] 1351 6-11-7 102.............................. NoelFehily 108
(Neil Mulholland) *trckd ldrs: rdn to chse wnr after 4 out: nvr quite on terms: tiring between last 2: lost 2nd fnl stride* **9/2[3]**

/2-0 4 13 **Jayandbee (IRE)**[19] 1592 8-11-12 107...........................(p) RichardJohnson 102
(Philip Hobbs) *hmpd 1st: j.rt 1st circ: prom: pressed wnr 9th tl 14th: rdn after 4 out: wknd 2 out* **5/1**

1-20 5 20 **Flugzeug**[128] 599 7-10-4 90.. KevinJones(5) 72
(Seamus Mullins) *disp ld tl 9th: trckd ldrs: rdn appr 4 out: wknd after 3 out: t.o* **9/1**

32U- U **Ethelred (IRE)**[173] 5416 7-11-8 103.................................(t) BrendanPowell
(Jamie Snowden) *trckd ldrs tl wknd 15th: tailing off whn mstke and uns rdr 4 out* **8/1**

6m 46.0s (1.40) **Going Correction** -0.15s/f (Good) 6 Ran SP% 110.7
Speed ratings (Par 105): **91,89,89,85,79**
CSF £9.71 TOTE £2.90: £1.60, £2.30; EX 9.80 Trifecta £54.60.
Owner Alan Roberts **Bred** William Neville **Trained** Penhow, Newport

FOCUS
This ordinary staying handicap was run at a steady gallop and only two mattered turning for home. This was a step up from the winner and there is probably more to come.

1843 LAST RACE THIS SEASON STANDARD OPEN NATIONAL HUNT FLAT RACE 2m 167y
5:05 (5:08) (Class 6) 4-6-Y-O £2,053 (£598; £299)

Form RPR

14- 1 **Copper Kay**[216] 4634 5-11-0 0.. RichardJohnson 112+
(Philip Hobbs) *trckd ldrs: nt clr run on rails fr 3f out tl 2f out: qckdn up wl to ld over 1f out: readily* **1/2[1]**

2 5 **Clondaw Cian (IRE)**[229] 5-11-0 0... TomO'Brien 102
(Suzy Smith) *led: rdn 2f out: hdd over 1f out: kpt on but nt pce of wnr* **12/1**

3 3 **Our Reward (IRE)**[195] 5-11-0 0.. BrendanPowell 100
(Jamie Snowden) *trckd ldrs: rdn over 2f out: styd on same pce* **8/1[3]**

30- 4 1¾ **Biretta**[308] 2922 4-10-7 0...(t) NoelFehily 91
(Harry Fry) *prom: rdn 2f out: kpt on same pce* **11/2[2]**

1 5 2¾ **Arthur Burrell**[74] 1122 6-11-7 0.. JamesBest 103
(Jackie Du Plessis) *mid-div: rdn over 2f out: styd on but nt pce to threaten* **12/1**

3 6 8 **Acajou Des Bieffes (FR)**[128] 601 5-11-0 0...................... AidanColeman 88
(Anthony Honeyball) *hld up: rdn over 2f out: wknd over 1f out* **8/1[3]**

7 27 **Poets Day** 5-10-7 0... NickScholfield 57
(Katie Stephens) *in tch: rdn 4f out: sn btn* **66/1**

8 ½ **Badger Run (IRE)** 4-11-0 0.. LeightonAspell 64
(Pat Murphy) *mid-div tl wknd over 2f out* **33/1**

00 9 1 **Palmers Bridge**[125] 644 6-10-7 0..................................(t) ConorSmith(7) 63
(Linda Blackford) *hld up: rdn over 2f out: sn wknd* **200/1**

3m 58.7s (-1.40) **Going Correction** +0.175s/f (Yiel)
WFA 4 from 5yo+ 9lb 9 Ran SP% 124.6
Speed ratings: **110,107,106,105,104 100,87,87,86**
CSF £9.81 TOTE £1.50: £1.10, £3.20, £2.50; EX 6.50 Trifecta £30.00.
Owner Aiden Murphy & Alan Peterson **Bred** Aiden Murphy & Alan Peterson **Trained** Withycombe, Somerset

FOCUS
Not a bad bumper. The winner didn't need to improve to land the odds.
T/Plt: £51.90 to a £1 stake. Pool: £63,943.06 - 899.13 winning tickets T/Qpdt: £8.40 to a £1 stake. Pool: £5,849.03 - 515.20 winning tickets **Tim Mitchell**

1698 CHEPSTOW (L-H)
Saturday, October 10

OFFICIAL GOING: Good (good to soft in places; 7.6)
Wind: breezy Weather: overcast; 12 degrees

1844 TOTEPLACEPOT RACING'S FAVOURITE BET "NATIONAL HUNT" NOVICES' HURDLE (8 hdls) 2m 11y
2:10 (2:10) (Class 4) 4-Y-O+ £3,898 (£1,144; £572; £286)

Form RPR

13-6 1 **Altior (IRE)**[164] 23 5-10-12 0.. NicodeBoinville 136+
(Nicky Henderson) *tall: racd keenly: cl 2nd mostly tl led gng wl and lft clr 3 out: 15 l ahd next: hacked on: unchal* **5/6[1]**

05-0 2 34 **Murray Mount (IRE)**[15] 1648 5-10-12 0................................. JamesDavies 104
(Charlie Mann) *settled 3rd or 4th: rdn and outpcd bef 5th: lft in hopeless pursuit of wnr after being hmpd 3 out* **66/1**

0-65 3 8 **Marley Joe (IRE)**[18] 1612 4-10-12 0................................. AndrewTinkler 94
(Martin Keighley) *settled wl off the pce in rr: t.o after 4th: inherited remote 3rd 2 out* **50/1**

0 4 12 **Bishops Court**[148] 320 5-10-12 0.. NoelFehily 82
(Neil Mulholland) *big: str: hld up wl off the pce in rr: t.o after 4th* **20/1**

6-0P 5 69 **Kayf Tiger**[44] 1379 6-10-12 0.. CharliePoste 20
(Robin Dickin) *nt jump wl and wl off the pce in rr: t.o after 4th: clambered over last* **100/1**

0F0- U **Grey Messenger (IRE)**[334] 2410 6-10-9 0...................(t) JamesBanks(3)
(Emma Baker) *wl off pce in last pair: nt fluent 1st: uns rdr 2nd* **100/1**

0 F **Inchiquin All Star (IRE)**[9] 1718 5-10-12 0............................ MichaelByrne
(Tim Vaughan) *hld up wl off the pce in rr: t.o after 4th: fell next* **33/1**

31-1 F **Desertmore Hill (IRE)**[14] 1662 5-10-12 0................................ SeanBowen 104+
(Peter Bowen) *led at stdy pce: pushed along and jst hdd whn fell 3 out* **4/1[3]**

B **Brave Jaq (FR)**[305] 4-10-12 0...................................... SamTwiston-Davies 104+
(Paul Nicholls) *small: prom: t.k.h: cl 3rd home turn: b.d 3 out* **3/1[2]**

6- F **Kid Kalanisi (IRE)**[182] 5285 4-10-12 0................................ HarrySkelton 104+
(Dan Skelton) *plld hrd in midfield: hit 1st: sme prog whn bdly hmpd 3 out: rdr lost iron but lft 3rd: 15 l 3rd whn wnt lft and fell next* **12/1**

3m 55.4s (-15.20) **Going Correction** -0.875s/f (Firm) 10 Ran SP% 120.4
Speed ratings (Par 105): **103,86,82,76,41** , , , ,
CSF £86.93 TOTE £1.80: £1.10, £7.30, £6.70; EX 73.20 Trifecta £597.50.
Owner Mrs Patricia Pugh **Bred** Paddy Behan **Trained** Upper Lambourn, Berks

FOCUS
A valuable new two-day fixture, combining cards which were previously held a fortnight apart. The hurdles were positioned on the Flat track in the back straight. Only a handful were involved in this dramatic novice hurdle, which saw mayhem at the third-last. The pace wasn't strong and the time was 8.4sec slower than standard, but the easy winner looks a smart prospect, being rated in line with the best of his bumper form. Winning rider Nico De Boinville described it as "lovely ground, on the easy side of good."

1845 TOTESCOOP6 RESULTS AT TOTEPOOLLIVEINFO.COM MARES' NOVICES' HURDLE (11 hdls) 2m 3f 100y
2:45 (2:45) (Class 4) 4-Y-O+ £3,898 (£1,144; £572; £286)

Form RPR

111- 1 **Hollies Pearl**[182] 5277 5-10-12 0.. SeanBowen 120+
(Peter Bowen) *t.k.h and j. and hung lft: sn 2nd: rdn to ld between last two but stl gng lft: asserted last and kpt on stoutly* **8/11[1]**

033- 2 2 **Brise Vendeenne (FR)**[308] 2930 4-10-12 0........................ RichardJohnson 115+
(Philip Hobbs) *led at mod pce: hit 7th: rdn and impeded 3 out: blnd next: hdd between last two: wl hld but kpt on steadily* **2/1[2]**

64- 3 3 **Rene's Girl (IRE)**[213] 4715 5-10-12 0................................ HarrySkelton 111+
(Dan Skelton) *cl up: last of three gng wl clr home turn: rdn 3 out: continued to press ldrs tl no ex bef last: game effrt* **12/1[3]**

500- 4 19 **Bourdello**[215] 4679 6-10-9 0.. JamesBanks(3) 93
(Emma Baker) *hung lft 1st: novicey in rr: 20 l 6th and wl btn home turn: plugged on* **100/1**

520 5 1½ **Midnight Gem**[9] 1716 5-10-12 0.. AidanColeman 92
(Charlie Longsdon) *midfield: hit 1st: blnd 3rd: 5th and struggling bdly home turn* **16/1**

6 13 **Jester Jet** 5-10-12 0... LeeEdwards 80
(Tony Carroll) *towards rr: lost tch after 7th: t.o whn blnd 3 out* **50/1**

30-0 7 25 **Margaret's Rose (IRE)**[139] 462 5-10-12 0.................. SamTwiston-Davies 57
(Nigel Twiston-Davies) *mstkes: chsd ldrs tl 7th: 15 l 4th and rdn and fading home turn: bdly t.o* **20/1**

06-0 8 30 **Vodka Island (IRE)**[18] 1613 6-10-12 0.............................. MichaelByrne 30
(Tim Vaughan) *str: hld up and wl bhd: novicey: t.o after 7th* **66/1**

P **Delagoa Bay (IRE)**[322] 7-10-12 0.. DaveCrosse
(Sylvester Kirk) *j. v erratically in rr: t.o after 7th: p.u 2 out* **50/1**

4 F **Dear Lottie (FR)**[129] 601 4-10-12 0........................ JamieMoore
(Gary Moore) *chsd ldrs: nt jump wl: drvn and weakend after 7th: 100 l last and exhausted whn crashing fall last* **12/1**[3]

04 P **Sultan's Dancer**[51] 1295 6-10-12 0..............................(t) BrendanPowell
(Brendan Powell) *hld up and wl off pce: t.o after 7th: p.u 2 out* **100/1**

4m 48.1s (-13.70) **Going Correction** -0.875s/f (Firm)
WFA 4 from 5yo+ 9lb **11 Ran SP% 124.7**
Speed ratings (Par 105): **93,92,90,82,82 76,66,53, ,**
CSF £2.55 TOTE £1.70: £1.10, £1.10, £2.90; EX 3.00 Trifecta £15.70.
Owner Roy Swinburne **Bred** Shade Oak Stud And D Jenks **Trained** Little Newcastle, Pembrokes
■ Stewards' Enquiry : Jamie Moore eight-day ban; continued in the race when his horse appeared to be exhausted (24th-31st Oct)

FOCUS
There wasn't a whole lot of depth to this mares' novices' hurdle, but the first three are useful and the wayward winner looks sure to rate higher.

1846 TOTESCOOP6 PLAY FOR BIG MONEY TODAY NOVICES' CHASE (FOR THE ROBERT MOTTRAM MEMORIAL TROPHY) (16 fncs) 2m 3f 98y

3:20 (3:20) (Class 2) 4-Y-0+ **£12,996** (£3,816; £1,908; £954)

Form RPR

401- **1** **Cocktails At Dawn**[168] 5540 7-11-12 145.................. NicodeBoinville 155+
(Nicky Henderson) *mde all: gng bttr than two main pursuers up home st: at least 3 l clr fr 2 out: rdn out flat* **6/1**

116- **2** 3 **As De Mee (FR)**[182] 5271 5-11-4 0.......................... SamTwiston-Davies 144+
(Paul Nicholls) *pressed wnr: rdn 3 out: kpt on but no real imp fr next* **3/1**[2]

F10- **3** ¾ **Native River (IRE)**[211] 4738 5-11-4 0.......................... BrendanPowell 145+
(Colin Tizzard) *settled in 4th pl: pushed along bef 12th: outpcd briefly: rdn and rallied bef 2 out: 3rd and nt qckn whn landed awkwardly last: rallied to snatch 3rd on line* **10/1**

2P4- **4** hd **Blaklion**[183] 5254 6-11-4 0.......................... TomScudamore 144+
(Nigel Twiston-Davies) *pressed ldng pair: nt fluent 12th: sn rdn: kpt on same pce fr 2 out: lost 3rd at last and again fnl stride* **9/4**[1]

104- **5** 10 **Regal Encore (IRE)**[184] 5241 7-11-4 0..................(t) BarryGeraghty 135+
(Anthony Honeyball) *racd keenly in last: nt a fluent: lost tch bef 12th: styd on v strly after last: promising* **7/1**

60-4 **6** ½ **Pearl Swan (FR)**[154] 196 7-11-4 0..........................(p) SeanBowen 134
(Peter Bowen) *settled towards rr: brief effrt after 11th: rdn next: sn btn* **25/1**

326/ **7** 21 **Racing Pulse (IRE)**[554] 5157 6-11-4 0.......................... PaulTownend 126
(Rebecca Curtis) *racd keenly: chsd ldrs tl 12th: sn dropped out: eased last* **5/1**[3]

4m 47.1s (-24.20) **Going Correction** -0.875s/f (Firm) **7 Ran SP% 112.2**
Speed ratings (Par 109): **115,113,113,113,109 108,100**
CSF £24.02 TOTE £4.70: £2.20, £2.20; EX 17.40 Trifecta £122.00.
Owner R J H Geffen & Sir John Ritblat **Bred** Mrs J Way **Trained** Upper Lambourn, Berks

FOCUS
The four previous runnings of this event have been won by Cue Card (with Silviniaco Conti third), Fingal Bay, Balder Succes and Southfield Theatre, so this edition has plenty to live up to. It looked the best novice chase run so far this season. The order didn't change a great deal.

1847 WEATHERBYS HAMILTON HURDLE (A LIMITED H'CAP) (8 hdls) 2m 11y

3:55 (3:59) (Class 2) 4-Y-O **£12,996** (£3,816; £1,908; £954)

Form RPR

-111 **1** **Tea In Transvaal (IRE)**[76] 1109 4-10-9 128.......................... PaulMoloney 134+
(Evan Williams) *led 2nd and racd enthusiastically: rdn bef last and bravely shook off two rivals sn after last: edging clr cl home* **14/1**

203- **2** ¾ **Karezak (IRE)**[195] 5045 4-11-10 143..................(b) WayneHutchinson 147
(Alan King) *cl up: disp 2nd home turn: ev ch fr 3 out tl drvn last: one pce fnl 50yds* **12/1**

042- **3** nse **Dexcite (FR)**[203] 4920 4-10-4 123 oh2.......................... PaddyBrennan 127
(Tom George) *hld up in rr: t.k.h: prog gng wl 5th: chal 2 out: drvn and ev ch and nt fluent last: no ex fnl 75yds* **7/1**[3]

410- **4** 5 **Boss Des Mottes (FR)**[188] 5154 4-10-4 123 oh1.......................... HarrySkelton 123
(Dan Skelton) *midfield: effrt to dispute 2nd home turn: ev ch 2 out: rdn and fdd bef last* **7/1**[3]

100- **5** 3 ¾ **Prairie Town (IRE)**[22] 5045 4-10-4 123 oh3.......................... LeeEdwards 121
(Tony Carroll) *bhd: nt fluent 2nd and 4th: rdn and effrt next: nvr rchd ldrs: mod 7th 2 out: kpt on* **50/1**

003- **6** 2 ½ **Box Office (FR)**[168] 5539 4-11-2 135.......................... BarryGeraghty 129
(Jonjo O'Neill) *dropped out in last pair: nvr gng wl enough fr 5th: sn rdn: plugged on* **9/2**[2]

2-10 **7** shd **Ryeolliean**[127] 556 4-10-5 124..........................(p) JamieMoore 118
(Gary Moore) *settled towards rr: effrt bef 5th: rdn and wknd next* **33/1**

04-4 **8** 1 ¾ **Stars Over The Sea (USA)**[161] 94 4-11-8 141..........(t) TomScudamore 133
(David Pipe) *prom: disp 2nd home turn: sn rdn: wknd 3 out* **12/1**

41-4 **9** 12 **Lucky Jim**[156] 162 4-10-8 127.......................... AidanColeman 108
(David Dennis) *prom: disp 2nd home turn: rdn and wknd 3 out* **25/1**

14-U **10** ½ **Goodbye Dancer (FR)**[14] 1657 4-10-7 129.......................... RyanHatch(3) 111
(Nigel Twiston-Davies) *plld hrd: mde most tl j. slowly 2nd: rallied and mstke 4th: sn lost pl* **33/1**

153- **11** 5 **Bivouac (FR)**[231] 4358 4-11-6 139.......................... NoelFehily 115
(Nicky Henderson) *chsd ldrs: rdn 5th: sn lost pl* **10/1**

1- **P** **Monsieur Gibraltar (FR)**[189] 5146 4-11-5 138.......... SamTwiston-Davies
(Paul Nicholls) *trckd ldrs tl rdn 5th: dropped out v tamely: p.u 2 out* **9/4**[1]

3m 52.4s (-18.20) **Going Correction** -0.875s/f (Firm) **12 Ran SP% 116.8**
Speed ratings: **110,109,109,107,105 103,103,103,97,96 94,**
CSF £159.58 CT £1282.65 TOTE £10.00: £2.30, £2.90, £2.30; EX 115.50 Trifecta £540.30.
Owner M J Haines **Bred** Summerville Bloodstock **Trained** Llancarfan, Vale Of Glamorgan

FOCUS
A good edition of this 4yo handicap. The winner is on a good mark, but this still rates a step up.

1848 TOTEPOOL SILVER TROPHY H'CAP HURDLE (GRADE 3) (11 hdls) 2m 3f 100y

4:30 (4:33) (Class 1) 4-Y-O+

£28,475 (£10,685; £5,350; £2,665; £1,340; £335)

Form RPR

-001 **1** **Court Minstrel (IRE)**[49] 1333 8-11-12 149.......................... PaulMoloney 155+
(Evan Williams) *hld up in last pair and confidently rdn: stdy prog on inner fr bef 8th: 3rd and chalng between last two: rdn to pass ldng pair after last: sn in command: readily: fine ride* **40/1**

21P- **2** 2 **Rock The Kasbah (IRE)**[175] 5393 5-10-8 131.............. RichardJohnson 133
(Philip Hobbs) *prom and t.k.h: cajoled to ld 3 out: hrd pressed after: rdn and hdd after last: outpcd by wnr fnl 50yds* **10/1**[3]

41-0 **3** 2 ¼ **Hurricane Hollow**[84] 1039 5-10-13 136.......................... HarrySkelton 138+
(Dan Skelton) *small: midfield: effrt after 8th: chal gng wl and nt fluent 2 out: upsides and drvn whn hit last: no ex fnl 100yds* **20/1**

113- **4** 4 **Our Kaempfer (IRE)**[183] 5254 6-11-3 140.......................... NoelFehily 137
(Charlie Longsdon) *nt fluent: effrt 8th: rdn next: kpt on same pce fr next and wl-hld 4th at last* **9/1**[2]

654- **5** 2 **Rons Dream**[176] 5365 5-10-7 130.......................... SeanBowen 125
(Peter Bowen) *set fast pce: mde most tl rdn and hdd 3 out: kpt on steadily but hld fr next* **20/1**

12P- **6** shd **Tea For Two**[211] 4738 6-11-0 142.......................... LizzieKelly(5) 137
(Nick Williams) *cl up: rdn 3 out: btn next* **7/2**[1]

14-2 **6** dht **Mantou (IRE)**[34] 1488 4-10-7 130..........................(t) AidanColeman 126
(John Ferguson) *trckd ldrs: gng wl tl bef 2 out: fnd little whn asked and sn hld* **20/1**

251- **8** 2 ½ **Sound Investment (IRE)**[224] 4496 7-11-2 149..........(t) HarryCobden(10) 141
(Paul Nicholls) *midfield: rdn bef 8th: n.d after* **16/1**

413- **9** 2 **Starluck (IRE)**[16] 3316 10-11-2 139.......................... TomCannon 130
(David Arbuthnot) *pressed ldrs tl rdn 3 out: sn btn* **33/1**

304- **10** ½ **Saffron Wells (IRE)**[210] 4750 7-10-11 134.......................... TrevorWhelan 124
(Neil King) *towards rr: nvr threatened ldrs* **20/1**

335- **11** nk **The Tourard Man (IRE)**[184] 5241 9-10-13 139.......................... TomBellamy(3) 129
(Alan King) *w ldr tl rdn 8th: wknd next* **33/1**

504/ **12** 3 ½ **The Liquidator**[529] 9 7-11-0 137.......................... TomScudamore 124
(David Pipe) *trckd ldrs: effrt in 3rd home turn: rdn 3 out: sn fdd* **7/2**[1]

3F0- **13** 23 **L'Unique (FR)**[177] 5355 6-11-6 143.......................... WayneHutchinson 109
(Alan King) *nt fluent 1st: nvr rchd ldrs* **25/1**

1P1- **14** 7 **Carningli (IRE)**[174] 5410 6-11-0 137.......................... PaulTownend 97
(Rebecca Curtis) *cl up: rdn bef 8th: sn lost pl: t.o* **14/1**

1/11 **15** 10 **Cousin Khee**[20] 1602 8-10-7 130..........................(p) TomO'Brien 81
(Hughie Morrison) *bhd: drvn and lost tch bef 8th: sn t.o* **12/1**

315- **P** **Gassin Golf**[175] 5390 6-11-3 140..........................(b[1]) JamieMoore
(Kerry Lee) *t.k.h: wknd 8th: t.o and p.u last: dismntd* **20/1**

P12- **P** **Earthmoves (FR)**[191] 5116 5-10-9 132..................(t) SamTwiston-Davies
(Paul Nicholls) *sn bhd: t.o bef 8th: p.u 2 out* **16/1**

4m 42.4s (-19.40) **Going Correction** -0.875s/f (Firm)
WFA 4 from 5yo+ 9lb **17 Ran SP% 125.6**
Speed ratings (Par 113): **105,104,103,101,100 100,100,99,98,98 98,96,87,84,80 , ,**
CSF £363.77 CT £8063.01 TOTE £30.70: £7.10, £3.10, £4.60, £3.00; EX 517.10 Trifecta £974.40 Part won..
Owner Mrs Janet Davies **Bred** William Flood **Trained** Llancarfan, Vale Of Glamorgan

FOCUS
A strong renewal of this valuable Grade 3 handicap and very solid form, with the winner rated back to his very best. It was run at a strong pace and three of the first four home came from the back of the field.

1849 GET SOCIAL WITH TOTEPOOL ON FACEBOOK H'CAP CHASE (18 fncs) 2m 7f 131y

5:05 (5:06) (Class 2) 4-Y-0+ **£16,245** (£4,770; £2,385; £1,192)

Form RPR

20-4 **1** **Drop Out Joe**[148] 318 7-10-9 133..........................(p) AidanColeman 145+
(Charlie Longsdon) *j. and travelled wl: led 11th: qcknd clr 15th: 6 l ahd last: sn drvn but a doing enough* **5/1**[2]

-321 **2** 1 ¼ **Buachaill Alainn (IRE)**[52] 1288 8-10-6 130..................(vt) SeanBowen 139
(Peter Bowen) *midfield: 6th home turn: sn hrd drvn: wnt 10 l 2nd and nt fluent 2 out: styd on wl and tried to chal and clsd gap appreciably fr last but wnr a holding him* **20/1**

20-0 **3** 3 ½ **Doing Fine (IRE)**[162] 69 7-10-8 132..........................(bt) LeightonAspell 137
(Rebecca Curtis) *towards rr and pushed along bef 8th: sme prog 14th: 4th 3 out: no imp after* **9/1**

231- **4** 11 **Cowards Close (IRE)**[239] 4211 8-10-6 130..........(t) SamTwiston-Davies 125
(Paul Nicholls) *towards rr: outpcd bef 14th: kpt on wout threatening fr 2 out: snatched mod 4th* **13/2**[3]

15P- **5** nk **Sego Success (IRE)**[175] 5392 7-11-1 139.......................... WayneHutchinson 136
(Alan King) *settled towards rr: mstke 12th: effrt after 13th: tk 3rd but outpcd by wnr 15th: plugged on same pce and sn btn: nt fluent last* **14/1**

31-2 **6** 6 **Audacious Plan (IRE)**[161] 92 6-10-6 130..........................(p) PaulTownend 121
(Rebecca Curtis) *trckd ldrs: effrt in 4th whn hit 14th: nt hrd pushed whn no impressin fr 3 out* **8/1**

111- **7** 8 **The Romford Pele (IRE)**[358] 1933 8-11-12 150..........(b) BarryGeraghty 132
(Rebecca Curtis) *midfield: nt fluent 8th: rdn and btn bef 14th* **12/1**

0113 **8** 20 **Standing Ovation (IRE)**[31] 1522 8-10-12 136..........(bt) TomScudamore 100
(David Pipe) *racd keenly: pressed ldng pair: wnt 2nd at 11th tl rdn and fdd qckly bef 14th: t.o* **14/1**

364P **P** **Terminal (FR)**[18] 1616 8-9-10 127..........................(b[1]) JamieBargary(7)
(David Dennis) *mstkes: chsd ldrs: drvn 9th: fnd nil: t.o and p.u 3 out* **66/1**

453- **P** **Handy Andy (IRE)**[176] 5370 9-10-1 125..........................(tp) BrendanPowell
(Colin Tizzard) *led tl hdd and mstke 11th: rdn and wknd bef 14th: t.o and p.u 3 out* **14/1**

U5-3 **P** **Garrahalish (IRE)**[18] 1616 7-10-8 132.......................... CharliePoste
(Robin Dickin) *last pair: rdn and struggling 9th: t.o and p.u 14th* **25/1**

22F- **P** **Sausalito Sunrise (IRE)**[288] 3247 7-11-6 144.......................... RichardJohnson
(Philip Hobbs) *settled towards rr: hdwy to go cl up after 13th: 2nd and pushed along along and outpcd by wnr 15th: qckly eased and p.u next* **11/4**[1]

146- **P** **Oscar Fortune (IRE)**[175] 5388 7-10-8 132..........................(p) AndrewTinkler
(Jonjo O'Neill) *in last pair: struggling 9th: t.o and p.u 14th* **33/1**

5m 52.9s (-29.10) **Going Correction** -0.875s/f (Firm) **13 Ran SP% 118.5**
Speed ratings (Par 109): **113,112,111,107,107 105,102,96, , , ,**
CSF £99.74 CT £883.60 TOTE £6.30: £1.70, £4.90, £2.90; EX 100.30 Trifecta £1165.20 Part won..
Owner The Jesters **Bred** Jethro Bloodstock **Trained** Over Norton, Oxon

FOCUS
A good handicap chase, run 10.7sec quicker than the following Class 4 handicap. A small personal best from the winner and there may be more to come.

1850 TOTEPOOL SUPPORTING THE SPORT YOU LOVE CONDITIONAL JOCKEYS' H'CAP CHASE (16 fncs 2 omitted) 2m 7f 131y

5:40 (5:40) (Class 4) (0-110,110) 4-Y-0+ **£3,898** (£1,144; £572; £286)

Form RPR

P-FP **1** **Pure Poteen (IRE)**[123] 676 7-10-13 105..............(t) MrMartinMcIntyre(8) 117+
(Neil Mulholland) *hld up and bhd: nt fluent 6th and 9th: stl 8th but gng wl bef 14th: clsd smoothly to ld bef 2 out: sn 4 l clr: rdn and styd on steadily flat* **8/1**

U14- **2** 3 ½ **Smart Exit (IRE)**[322] 2669 8-11-9 110.......................... CiaranGethings(3) 116
(Stuart Edmunds) *settled in midfield: effrt in 4th bef 14th: sn rdn: outpcd bef 2 out and hit fence: kpt on for driving to go 2nd after last: nt rch wnr* **13/2**[3]

5345 **3** 2 1/4 **Georgian King**[52] 1288 12-11-6 **109**..............(p) ConorSmith(5) 113
(Martin Keighley) *racd keenly: led at mod pce 3rd tl 10th: lft in ld 13th: hrd rdn next: hdd bef 2 out: fnd little: lost 2nd after last* **10/1**

1/PP **4** 18 **Tom Bach (IRE)**[114] 771 11-9-11 **84**..............(b) AlanJohns(3) 72
(Hywel Evans) *lft 2nd fr 5th tl 8th: remained cl up tl 13th: rdn and plodded on whn wl hld fr next* **33/1**

3541 **5** 1/2 **Tribal Dance (IRE)**[7] 1757 9-10-5 **89**..............(v) SeanBowen 77
(John O'Shea) *rn in snatches: prom tl blnd 4th: outpcd 13th: 3rd and drvn bef next where chal ldr: ev ch passing omitted 3 out: fnd nil and btn bef next* **7/1**

P4-2 **6** 15 **Handsome Buddy (IRE)**[9] 1720 8-10-11 **98**..............(v) MikeyHamill(3) 72
(Michael Gates) *last pair: lost tch 1/2-way: mstke 11th: plugged rnd* **9/2**[2]

32-4 **P** **Musical Wedge**[162] 58 11-10-2 **86**.............. MauriceLinehan
(Claire Dyson) *mstke 3rd: sn bhd: mstke 8th: t.o and p.u 12th* **16/1**

-U53 **U** **Ballyvoneen (IRE)**[8] 1733 10-11-1 **102**..............(v) LizzieKelly(3)
(Neil King) *cl up tl blnd and uns rdr 4th: fatally injured* **11/1**

FPP- **P** **Midnight Charmer**[183] 5259 9-11-2 **105**.............. HarrisonBeswick(5)
(Emma Baker) *rn in snatches: nvr bttr than midfield: drvn and struggling bef 14th: t.o and p.u 2 out* **33/1**

51F- **U** **Market Option (IRE)**[367] 1795 9-11-5 **106**.............. CharlieDeutsch(3)
(Venetia Williams) *led tl 3rd: mstke 4th: cl up whn blnd and uns rdr next* **16/1**

3-1P **P** **Mor Brook**[147] 331 7-11-12 **110**.............. TomBellamy
(Kim Bailey) *hit 4th: trckd ldrs: wnt 2nd at 8th: hit next: led 11th tl blnd 13th: fading whn p.u after next* **11/4**[1]

6m 3.6s (-18.40) **Going Correction** -0.875s/f (Firm) **11** Ran SP% **116.9**
Speed ratings (Par 105): **95,93,93,87,86 81,,,,**
CSF £59.65 CT £525.19 TOTE £8.60: £2.90, £2.60, £3.90; EX 69.80 Trifecta £750.20 Part won..
Owner Nick Robinson **Bred** Miss Joanne Mulcahy **Trained** Limpley Stoke, Wilts

FOCUS
This was run 10.7sec slower than the preceding Grade 2 handicap. The fourth-last and third-last fences were bypassed. A step up from the winner.
T/Plt: £326.20 to a £1 stake. Pool: £84,261.09 - 188.54 winning units. T/Qpdt: £214.70 to a £1 stake. Pool: £5,280.69 - 18.20 winning units. **Iain Mackenzie**

1851 (Void)

1738 HEXHAM (L-H)
Saturday, October 10

OFFICIAL GOING: Good to soft (soft in places; 6.8)
Wind: Almost nil Weather: Overcast

1852 INTU METROCENTRE PLATINUM MALL MAIDEN HURDLE (10 hdls) 2m 4f 28y
1:50 (1:50) (Class 5) 4-Y-O+ **£2,274** (£667; £333; £166)

Form RPR

613- **1** **Oscar Blue (IRE)**[175] 5395 5-11-0 **0**.............. WillKennedy 112+
(Brian Ellison) *trckd ldrs: hit and outpcd 2 out: rallied bef last: led and hrd pressed last 100yds: hld on wl towards fin* **6/4**[1]

6-50 **2** nk **Fairy Theatre (IRE)**[24] 1555 4-10-7 **0**.............. BrianHarding 102
(Iain Jardine) *hld up: hdwy and prom bef 4 out: effrt and chsd ldr between last 2: drvn and ev ch last 100yds: kpt on: hld cl home* **28/1**

2 **3** 1 3/4 **Celtic Flames (IRE)**[16] 1640 5-10-11 **0**.............. GrahamWatters(3) 107
(Lucinda Russell) *t.k.h: cl up: led 4th: rdn between last 2: hung rt and hdd last 100yds: kpt on same pce towards fin* **11/2**[3]

24- **4** 22 **Stilo Blue Native (IRE)**[233] 4326 7-11-0 **115**.............. BrianHughes 90
(John Wade) *t.k.h: led to bef 3rd: w ldr: rdn and outpcd between last 2: wknd fr last* **11/4**[2]

5 4 **Pikes Peak (IRE)**[167] 6-10-9 **0**.............. DiarmuidO'Regan(5) 84
(Chris Grant) *prom: drvn and outpcd bef 2 out: btn bef last* **33/1**

6 3/4 **Whatsthestoryman (IRE)**[146] 7-10-9 **0**..............(t) CallumBewley(5) 83
(Katie Scott) *hld up: stdy hdwy bef 2 out: sn rdn and wknd* **66/1**

P0-0 **7** 33 **Just My Luke**[163] 33 6-10-7 **0**..............(t) JamesCorbett(7) 53
(Susan Corbett) *hld up: pushed along bef 2 out: sn wknd: t.o* **200/1**

8 32 **Mister Don (IRE)**[258] 5-10-11 **0**.............. CraigNichol(3) 25
(Rose Dobbin) *nt fluent: hld up: pushed along whn hit 3 out: wknd bef next: t.o* **10/1**

P/0- **9** 7 **Messina Straights**[520] 157 7-10-9 **0**.............. GaryRutherford(5) 18
(George Bewley) *t.k.h: hld up: outpcd bef 3 out: btn next: t.o* **250/1**

35 **P** **Landmeafortune (IRE)**[8] 1740 6-11-0 **0**.............. HenryBrooke
(Martin Todhunter) *hld up: nt fluent 1st: p.u bef next* **150/1**

0-0 **P** **Pickle And Tickle (IRE)**[24] 1555 5-10-9 **0**.............. JonathonBewley(5)
(George Bewley) *t.k.h: cl up: led bef 3rd to next: lost pl bef 6th: wknd and p.u bef next* **200/1**

22- **P** **Far From Defeat (IRE)**[179] 5331 5-11-0 **0**.............. LiamTreadwell
(Michael Scudamore) *t.k.h: stdd on outside: struggling 5th: lost tch and p.u after next* **13/2**

5m 9.4s (-3.10) **Going Correction** -0.30s/f (Good)
WFA 4 from 5yo+ 10lb **12** Ran SP% **114.4**
Speed ratings (Par 103): **94,93,93,84,82 82,69,56,53,**
CSF £42.95 TOTE £2.90: £1.50, £5.60, £1.60; EX 64.90 Trifecta £485.20.
Owner P J Martin **Bred** Mary Fanning McCormack **Trained** Norton, N Yorks

FOCUS
All bends on fresh ground. An average maiden hurdle, in which only a handful of runners could be seriously fancied. It was race of quickly changing fortunes in the home straight.

1853 INTU METROCENTRE ALWAYS A WINNER NOVICES' H'CAP CHASE (15 fncs) 2m 4f 15y
2:25 (2:26) (Class 4) (0-105,105) 4-Y-O+ **£5,198** (£1,526; £763; £381)

Form RPR

305- **1** **Friendly Royal (IRE)**[180] 5312 6-11-7 **100**.............. SeanQuinlan 114+
(Sue Smith) *mde all: rdn whn lft 2 l clr 2 out: jnd whn lft 15 l in front last: rdn out* **4/1**[2]

65-1 **2** 12 **Present Flight (IRE)**[6] 1775 6-11-9 **105** 7ex..............(t) DerekFox(3) 105+
(Lucinda Russell) *t.k.h early: cl up: outpcd bef 10th: rallied after 4 out: lft cl 3rd and outpcd again 2 out: lft 15 l 2nd last: no ch w wnr* **7/4**[1]

0663 **3** 7 **Amilliontimes (IRE)**[17] 1630 7-11-5 **101**..............(t) TonyKelly(3) 93
(Jackie Stephen) *nt fluent: hld up in midfield: hit and lost pl 6th: drvn along fr 10th: rallied whn lft 27 l 4th last: plugged on: no imp* **10/1**

2-14 **4** 2 1/2 **Scorpions Sting (IRE)**[139] 455 6-11-7 **105**..............(b[1]) DaleIrving(5) 96
(James Ewart) *nt fluent: hld up in tch: rdn and outpcd bef 3 out: no imp whn lft 26 l 3rd last* **15/2**

040F **5** 6 **Emkae (IRE)**[6] 1775 7-10-9 **88**..............(t) BrianHarding 69
(Alison Hamilton) *in tch: drvn and outpcd after 4 out: struggling bef next* **11/1**

F6P/ **6** 8 **Mia Matriarch**[629] 9-9-9 **79** oh8.............. GrantCockburn(5) 53
(Stuart Coltherd) *nt fluent on occasions: hld up: pushed and effrt after 4 out: pckd and wknd next* **80/1**

005U **P** **Agricultural**[17] 1629 9-9-11 **79**.............. AdamNicol(3)
(Lucy Normile) *bhd: outpcd whn p.u bef 9th* **33/1**

0/64 **U** **Kilmainham (IRE)**[33] 1496 7-10-11 **90**..............(p) HenryBrooke 89
(Martin Todhunter) *w wnr: pushed along and ev ch whn pckd and uns rdr 2 out* **28/1**

0-U5 **P** **Top Cat Dj (IRE)**[139] 453 7-9-9 **79** oh3..............(p) DiarmuidO'Regan(5)
(Chris Grant) *in tch: pushed along and struggling after 4 out: wknd bef next: p.u bef 2 out* **16/1**

4414 **F** **Solway Legend**[17] 1629 8-11-4 **97**.............. BrianHughes 110+
(Lisa Harrison) *prom: stdy hdwy bef 10th: lft 2 l 2nd 2 out: chalng gng wl whn fell last* **11/2**[3]

5P-2 **P** **Harleys Max**[154] 201 6-10-0 **86**.............. JamesCorbett(7)
(Susan Corbett) *a bhd: struggling 4 out: t.o whn p.u bef 2 out* **40/1**

5m 17.6s (4.10) **Going Correction** +0.20s/f (Yiel) **11** Ran SP% **116.9**
Speed ratings (Par 105): **99,94,91,90,88 84,,,,**
CSF £11.59 CT £64.90 TOTE £5.20: £2.00, £1.20, £3.10; EX 17.80 Trifecta £125.40.
Owner Formulated Polymer Products Ltd **Bred** Jim Dempsey **Trained** High Eldwick, W Yorks

FOCUS
No shortage of drama. This looked a step up from the winner.

1854 INTU ELDON SQUARE HEART OF THE CITY MARES' NOVICES' HURDLE (8 hdls) 2m 48y
3:00 (3:01) (Class 4) 4-Y-O+ **£3,898** (£1,144; £572; £286)

Form RPR

23-3 **1** **Mardale (IRE)**[24] 1555 5-10-10 **0**..............(t) BrianHarding 120+
(Nicky Richards) *nt fluent on occasions: hld up in midfield: hdwy to chse ldrs bef 2 out: led run-in: rdn and styd on strly* **7/1**[3]

-2 **2** 4 **Smart Talk (IRE)**[154] 206 5-10-10 **0**.............. WillKennedy 115
(Brian Ellison) *tk keen old early: cl up: led 2nd: rdn after 2 out: hdd run-in: kpt on same pce* **15/2**

3 3 3/4 **Lady Yeats**[34] 4-10-7 **0**.............. AdamNicol(3) 111
(George Moore) *prom: hdwy to chse ldr briefly between last 2: sn rdn: one pce fr last* **8/1**

4 4 1/2 **Rivabodiva (IRE)**[202] 5-10-7 **0**.............. DerekFox(3) 107
(Lucinda Russell) *nt fluent on occasions: hld up in midfield: pushed along after 3 out: hdwy after 2 out: pushed along and no imp fr last* **8/1**

253- **5** 2 1/4 **Attention Seaker**[11] 3270 5-10-3 **109**.............. MrWEasterby(7) 105
(Tim Easterby) *in tch: hdwy and cl up 2 out to appr last: sn rdn and outpcd* **3/1**[1]

54-3 **6** 2 1/2 **La Dama De Hierro**[17] 1627 5-10-10 **0**.............. BrianHughes 104
(Malcolm Jefferson) *in tch: pushed along and outpcd bef 2 out: n.d after* **28/1**

7 1 3/4 **Feel The Air (IRE)**[40] 1431 5-11-0 **110**.............. ConorShoemark(3) 108
(Mark Michael McNiff, Ire) *hld up: pushed along after 3 out: plugged on fr next: nvr able to chal* **6/1**[2]

8 18 **The Toft**[168] 6-10-5 **0**.............. GrantCockburn(5) 90
(Lucinda Russell) *hld up: pushed along bef 2 out: sn wknd* **25/1**

36- **9** 11 **Twenty Eight Guns**[181] 5299 5-10-10 **0**.............. LiamTreadwell 75
(Michael Scudamore) *hld up: rdn after 3 out: struggling fr next* **16/1**

20-5 **10** 3 3/4 **Innis Shannon (IRE)**[17] 1627 5-10-5 **0**.............. JonathonBewley(5) 72
(George Bewley) *nt jump wl in rr: sn wl bhd: nvr on terms* **28/1**

4132 **11** 41 **Flower Power**[9] 1716 4-11-3 **115**.............. DenisO'Regan 42
(Tony Coyle) *nt fluent on occasions: led to 2nd: ev ch appr 2 out: rdn and wknd qckly after 2 out: t.o* **8/1**

0- **12** 46 **Spirit Dame (IRE)**[235] 4290 4-10-7 **0**.............. CraigNichol(3)
(Rose Dobbin) *midfield on ins: struggling after 3 out: sn btn: t.o* **100/1**

05-6 **P** **Toarmandowithlove (IRE)**[17] 1627 7-10-3 **0**..............(bt[1]) JamesCorbett(7)
(Susan Corbett) *cl up: wnt 2nd 3rd: blnd 3 out: rdn and wknd qckly next: t.o whn p.u bef last* **100/1**

4m 6.8s (-10.60) **Going Correction** -0.30s/f (Good) **13** Ran SP% **115.5**
Speed ratings (Par 105): **114,112,110,107,106 105,104,95,90,88 67,44,**
CSF £54.53 TOTE £8.80: £3.10, £2.70, £2.80; EX 40.90 Trifecta £74.30.
Owner East To West Racing Club **Bred** Frank Motherway **Trained** Greystoke, Cumbria

FOCUS
This was run at a searching early gallop and represents solid form for the level. The winner is rated similar to the best of her bumper form.

1855 INTU METROCENTRE ALWAYS A GREAT DAY IN H'CAP CHASE (15 fncs) 2m 4f 15y
3:35 (3:35) (Class 4) (0-120,117) 4-Y-O+ **£5,198** (£1,526; £763; £381)

Form RPR

113- **1** **Present Lodger (IRE)**[210] 4757 7-11-1 **109**..............(t) DerekFox(3) 121+
(Lucinda Russell) *t.k.h early: hld up in tch: smooth hdwy to chse ldr appr 3 out: jst led whn hit last: rdn and r.o strly run-in* **10/3**[1]

P412 **2** 4 **Brother Scott**[8] 1741 8-10-8 **99**.............. SeanQuinlan 106
(Sue Smith) *led: rdn and hdd appr last: rallied: kpt on same pce last 150yds* **7/2**[2]

14U- **3** 15 **No Through Road**[194] 5061 8-11-11 **116**.............. LiamTreadwell 111
(Michael Scudamore) *chsd ldr to appr 3 out: rdn and outpcd after next: 12 l down and no imp whn lft 3rd last* **8/1**

P2P- **4** 1/2 **Benefit In Kind (IRE)**[173] 5423 7-9-11 **93**..............(tp) CallumBewley(5) 86
(Katie Scott) *t.k.h: hld up in tch: pushed along and outpcd 3 out: 16 l down and hld whn lft 4th last* **6/1**

1135 **5** 24 **Pekanheim (IRE)**[16] 1639 7-11-7 **112**.............. HenryBrooke 83
(Martin Todhunter) *hld up: hit and pushed along 9th: outpcd 4 out: n.d after* **5/1**[3]

5545 **6** 1 1/4 **Moyode Wood**[14] 1659 10-11-0 **105**..............(p) WillKennedy 75
(Brian Ellison) *cl up tl outpcd after 4 out: rdn and wknd bef next* **14/1**

33-3 **F** **Suprise Vendor (IRE)**[152] 142 9-11-2 **114**.............. SamColtherd(7)
(Stuart Coltherd) *prom: outpcd after 10th: no imp fr 3 out: 30 l 5th and btn whn fell last* **17/2**

-652 **F** **Sean Airgead (IRE)**[8] 1739 10-11-9 **117**..............(tp) ConorShoemark(3) 117+
(Mark Michael McNiff, Ire) *t.k.h: hld up: stdy hdwy 10th: rdn after 3 out: 6 l 3rd and styng on whn fell heavily last* **12/1**

P **Telex Du Berlais (FR)**[354] 6-11-5 **110**.............. BrianHughes
(Simon Waugh) *hld up: pushed along 4 out: outpcd whn hit next: sn btn: t.o whn p.u bef last* **33/1**

5m 14.4s (0.90) **Going Correction** +0.20s/f (Yiel) **9** Ran SP% **115.2**
Speed ratings (Par 105): **106,104,98,98,88 88,,,**
CSF £15.99 CT £85.13 TOTE £4.20: £1.30, £1.40, £2.60; EX 14.80 Trifecta £61.70.
Owner Sandy Seymour **Bred** Mrs M Curran **Trained** Arlary, Perth & Kinross

FOCUS
A strong renewal of this handicap chase. It was won for the second year in succession by Lucinda Russell and a personal best from the winner.

1856 INTU ELDON SQUARE ALIVE AFTER FIVE H'CAP HURDLE (12 hdls) 2m 7f 63y
4:10 (4:12) (Class 3) (0-125,125) 4-Y-0+ **£6,844** (£1,995; £998)

Form RPR
035- **1** **Five In A Row (IRE)**[176] 5366 7-11-12 **125**........................ WillKennedy 128+
(Brian Ellison) *chsd ldrs: effrt and wnt 2nd 2 out: led last 75yds: styd on wl* **15/2**[3]
501 **2** 3/4 **What A Steel (IRE)**[8] 1739 11-10-6 **108**........................(p) CraigNichol(3) 109
(Alistair Whillans) *in tch: pushed along briefly 1/2-way: hdwy to ld 3 out: rdn bef last: hung rt run-in: hdd last 75yds: one pce* **14/1**
2141 **3** 1/2 **Johnny Go**[16] 1637 5-10-9 **108**........................ BrianHughes 109
(Lisa Harrison) *hld up in tch on ins: pushed along and effrt 2 out: kpt on wl u.p fr last* **13/2**[2]
-164 **4** 3 1/2 **Manballandall (IRE)**[17] 1633 7-11-3 **123**........................(t) JamesCorbett(7) 120
(Susan Corbett) *hld up bhd ldng gp: effrt and rdn bef 2 out: kpt on same pce fr last* **20/1**
1-32 **5** nk **Cowslip**[23] 705 6-11-7 **123**........................ AdamNicol(3) 120
(George Moore) *hld up: rdn and effrt after 2 out: styd on fr last: nt pce to chal* **14/1**
U020 **6** nk **Fresh By Nature (IRE)**[18] 1615 8-10-4 **108**........................ HarryBannister(5) 105
(Harriet Bethell) *hld up: rdn bef 2 out: rallied bef last: kpt on run-in: nt pce to chal* **50/1**
1241 **7** 12 **Native Optimist (IRE)**[8] 1744 8-9-10 **100**........................ MissCWalton(5) 86
(Sheena Walton) *cl up: led 4th: hdd 3 out: drvn and outpcd after next: n.d after* **8/1**
2011 **8** 1 1/4 **Perseid (IRE)**[11] 1683 5-10-1 **100**........................ SeanQuinlan 85
(Sue Smith) *chsd ldrs: rdn and outpcd 2 out: btn bef last* **3/1**[1]
3131 **9** 1/2 **Miss Macnamara (IRE)**[8] 1742 6-10-7 **106**........................ HenryBrooke 90
(Martin Todhunter) *hld up: hdwy and prom bef 2 out: rdn and wknd bef last* **10/1**
606- **10** 10 **Total Assets**[180] 5312 7-10-3 **109**........................ MissAWaugh(7) 84
(Simon Waugh) *towards rr: pushed along 1/2-way: hdwy on outside and prom after 3 out: rdn and wknd next* **25/1**
1101 **11** 3 1/2 **Chicago Outfit (IRE)**[22] 1571 10-11-4 **122**........................(p) JonathonBewley(5) 94
(George Bewley) *led to 4th: cl up tl rdn and wknd fr 2 out* **10/1**
1111 **P** **Ruaraidh Hugh (IRE)**[90] 969 6-11-2 **122**........................(b) MrTommieMO'Brien(7)
(Chris Bealby) *midfield: nt fluent 3rd: outpcd 1/2-way: hit and struggling 3 out: p.u bef next* **14/1**
11P- **P** **Streets Of Promise (IRE)**[177] 5355 6-11-12 **125**........................ LiamTreadwell
(Michael Scudamore) *hld up on outside: pushed along fr 8th: wknd and p.u bef next* **14/1**

6m 2.5s (-6.50) **Going Correction** -0.30s/f (Good) **13 Ran SP% 116.6**
Speed ratings (Par 107): **99,98,98,97,97 97,92,92,92,88 87, ,**
CSF £101.55 CT £721.69 TOTE £10.40: £2.80, £4.40, £2.20; EX 123.70 Trifecta £1229.20 Part won..
Owner P J Martin **Bred** Ms M Maher **Trained** Norton, N Yorks

FOCUS
Comfortably the strongest race on the card. Seven of these had won last time out.

1857 INTU ELDON SQUARE WORLD ERVICE H'CAP CHASE (12 fncs) 1m 7f 133y
4:45 (4:47) (Class 5) (0-100,98) 4-Y-0+ **£2,924** (£858; £429; £214)

Form RPR
40-5 **1** **Roc De Prince**[36] 728 6-11-7 **98**........................(bt[1]) DaleIrving(5) 111+
(James Ewart) *w ldr to 3rd: lost pl and reminders 5th: rallied to ld 3 out: drvn and kpt on wl fr last* **7/1**
-343 **2** 2 1/4 **Shine A Diamond (IRE)**[33] 1492 7-10-13 **88**........................(tp) GrahamWatters(3) 97
(Lucinda Russell) *hld up in tch: hdwy to chse wnr after 2 out: kpt on fr last: nt rch wnr* **15/8**[1]
-6P4 **3** 6 **Reverse The Charge (IRE)**[6] 1778 8-9-7 **72** oh3........ CraigGallagher(7) 79
(Jane Walton) *hld up in tch: stdy hdwy bef 4 out: nt fluent and outpcd next: rallied to chse ldrs whn mstke last: sn outpcd* **5/1**[3]
P3-0 **4** 2 1/4 **Azerodegree (IRE)**[42] 1402 6-9-13 **78**........................(p) ThomasDowson(7) 80
(Harriet Graham) *in tch: rdn along 1/2-way: outpcd after 4 out: rallied after next: outpcd fr 2 out* **14/1**
2144 **5** 1 1/4 **Everylasting (IRE)**[24] 1551 8-10-11 **86**........................(b) CraigNichol(3) 86
(Rose Dobbin) *chsd ldrs: nt fluent 4th: hdwy to chal 5th to 6th: ev ch 3 out: rdn and wknd between last 2* **5/2**[2]
P546 **6** 3 1/2 **Duhallowcountry (IRE)**[11] 1687 9-9-7 **72** oh2........(p) SamColtherd(7) 69
(Victor Thompson) *nt fluent in rr: pushed along and effrt after 4 out: wknd after next* **50/1**
0P64 **7** 24 **Prince Blackthorn (IRE)**[11] 1685 9-10-0 **72** oh4........(p) LucyAlexander 48
(Barry Murtagh) *led tl hit and hdd 3 out: wknd fr next* **16/1**
-0PP **8** 99 **Jimmie Brown (USA)**[119] 731 7-9-13 **74** oh8 ow2........ JohnKington(3)
(Andrew Crook) *bhd: struggling 4 out: lost tch fr next: t.o* **22/1**
U0P0 **U** **Bertielicious**[8] 1740 7-9-11 **72** oh16........................(p) HarryChalloner(3)
(Jonathan Haynes) *hld up in midfield: effrt bef 3 out: wknd next: 6th and no ch whn blnd and uns rdr last* **40/1**

4m 9.82s (0.02) **Going Correction** +0.20s/f (Yiel) **9 Ran SP% 113.8**
Speed ratings (Par 103): **107,105,102,101,101 99,87, ,**
CSF £20.91 CT £71.80 TOTE £6.40: £2.00, £1.30, £1.70; EX 17.80 Trifecta £100.60.
Owner Ewart, Humbert, Kesson, Wilson **Bred** Mrs James Wigan & London TB Services Ltd **Trained** Langholm, Dumfries & G'way

FOCUS
Five of the runners were out of the handicap in this weak affair. A small personal best from the winner.

1858 INTU METROCENTRE ALWAYS A SAFE BET INTERMEDIATE NATIONAL HUNT FLAT RACE (CONDITIONALS/AMATEURS) 2m 48y
5:20 (5:25) (Class 6) 4-6-Y-0 **£1,580** (£486; £243)

Form RPR
3 **1** **Point The Way (IRE)**[14] 1662 4-10-11 0........................ CraigGallagher(7) 104+
(Brian Ellison) *mde all at stdy pce: drvn along over 2f out: styd on strly fnl f* **4/9**[1]
2 1 1/2 **Puddle Jumper (IRE)** 4-10-8 0........................ FinianO'Toole(10) 102
(Micky Hammond) *chsd wnr to over 2f out: sn drvn: rallied to chse wnr ins fnl f: kpt on* **5/1**[3]
3 2 **Solway Storm (IRE)** 5-10-13 0........................ CallumBewley(5) 100
(Lisa Harrison) *trckd ldrs: effrt and ev ch briefly over 2f out: kpt on same pce ins fnl f* **16/1**
4 5 **Storm Forecast (IRE)** 4-10-11 0........................ MrBenjaminStephens(7) 95
(Malcolm Jefferson) *in tch: pushed along and outpcd 3f out: rdn and no imp fr over 1f out* **9/2**[2]
5 11 **Thats Digby** 5-11-1 0........................ AdamNicol(3) 84
(David Thompson) *prom: drvn and outpcd over 3f out: sn btn* **33/1**
6 22 **Arco (IRE)** 4-10-4 0........................ RossTurner(7) 55
(Philip Kirby) *hld up in tch: rdn and outpcd over 5f out: sn struggling: t.o* **9/1**
6- **7** 1 1/2 **Ruby Vodka**[273] 3625 4-10-8 0........................ CraigNichol(3) 54
(Sharon Watt) *hld up in tch on outside: stdy hdwy 1/2-way: rdn and wknd over 3f out: t.o* **25/1**
P **Best Of Company** 4-10-6 0........................ DiarmuidO'Regan(5)
(Chris Grant) *bhd: struggling whn broke down over 5f out: fatally injured* **28/1**

4m 13.8s (1.10) **Going Correction** -0.30s/f (Good)
WFA 4 from 5yo 9lb **8 Ran SP% 130.2**
Speed ratings: **85,84,83,80,75 64,63,**
CSF £4.15 TOTE £1.50: £1.10, £2.10, £4.00; EX 4.40 Trifecta £18.20.
Owner P J Martin **Bred** Mrs Kay Cottrell **Trained** Norton, N Yorks
■ Stewards' Enquiry : Finian O'Toole two-day ban; used whip above permitted level (24th-25th Oct)

FOCUS
This took little winning with the winner dictating.
T/Plt: £61.70 to a £1 stake. Pool: £57,882.03 - 684.24 winning units. T/Qpdt: £34.50 to a £1 stake. Pool: £4431.82 - 95.05 winning units. **Richard Young**

1859 - 1865a (Foreign Racing) - See Raceform Interactive

1844 CHEPSTOW (L-H)
Sunday, October 11

OFFICIAL GOING: Good (chs 7.5; hdl 7.8)
Wind: breezy Weather: rather overcast; 14 degrees

1866 CHAMPION HATS JUVENILE HURDLE (8 hdls) 2m 11y
2:15 (2:15) (Class 4) 3-Y-O **£3,898** (£1,144; £572; £286)

Form RPR
1 shd **Adrien Du Pont (FR)**[187] 3-11-5 0........................ SamTwiston-Davies 119+
(Paul Nicholls) *tall: plld hrd towards rr: effrt in 2nd whn hit 3 out: drvn and swtchd rt bef last: hit flight: r.o u.p flat: bmpd cl home: jst failed: fin 2nd: plcd 1st* **4/9**[1]
2 **Sceau Royal (FR)**[198] 3-11-5 0........................ DarylJacob 119+
(Alan King) *small: wnt 2nd at 2nd: led appr 5th: rdn bef last where 2 l clr: kpt on gamely but edgd rt flat: jst hld on: fin 1st: disqualified and plcd 2nd* **11/4**[2]
3 16 **Sky Lino (FR)** 3-10-12 0........................ RichardJohnson 96
(Nick Williams) *cl up: 2nd briefly after 4th: outpcd next and nt given a hrd time after: tk 20 l 3rd at last and styd on in v pleasing fashion after* **12/1**[3]
65 **4** 7 **Layerthorpe (IRE)**[39] 1452 3-10-12 0........................ PaulMoloney 91
(Debra Hamer) *led at mod pce: hdd bef 5th: sn lost tch w ldng pair: hit 2 out* **100/1**
0 **5** 9 **Social Climber (IRE)**[18] 1631 3-10-5 0........................ JamesO'Neill(7) 85
(Fergal O'Brien) *trckd ldrs: chal briefly 5th: sn rdn: no ch w ldng pair fr next* **25/1**
6 9 **Nosper (FR)**[133] 3-10-7 0........................ AliceMills(5) 74
(Martin Hill) *small: j. modly in rr: pushed along and lost tch bef 5th: t.o* **66/1**
P **Capatosta (USA)**[201] 3-10-12 0........................ NoelFehily
(Charlie Mann) *tall: cl up tl drvn and dropped out rapidly after 5th: sn t.o: p.u 2 out* **50/1**

3m 59.4s (-11.20) **Going Correction** -1.075s/f (Hard) **7 Ran SP% 111.9**
Speed ratings (Par 103): **84,85,76,73,68 64,**
CSF £1.90 TOTE £1.50: £1.20, £1.20; EX 2.20 Trifecta £5.60.
Owner Mrs Johnny de la Hey **Bred** Thierry Cypres **Trained** Ditcheat, Somerset
■ Stewards' Enquiry : Daryl Jacob one-day ban: careless riding (Oct 25)

FOCUS
This looks a good piece of juvenile form because the front two, who drew a long way clear, both look pretty smart. Royal Sceau won the race by a short-head but, after reviewing the head on, it transpired he had carried his rival to his right and given him a bump close home, which the stewards decided cost Adrien Du Pont victory, so the result was turned around.

1867 TOTEPOOL RACING'S BIGGEST SUPPORTER NOVICES' CHASE (18 fncs) 2m 7f 131y
2:45 (2:46) (Class 4) 4-Y-0+ **£5,198** (£1,526; £763; £381)

Form RPR
141- **1** **It's A Close Call (IRE)**[209] 4813 6-11-0 0........................(t) SamTwiston-Davies 141+
(Paul Nicholls) *led 6th tl 11th: led again 13th: hit next: sn hdd: dived at 15th: pushed along and stl ev ch but looked getting worst of argument whn lft 15 l clr 2 out: eased fnl 100yds* **5/2**[2]
360- **2** 17 **Abracadabra Sivola (FR)**[239] 4225 5-11-0 0........................ NoelFehily 121+
(Nick Williams) *led tl hdd 6th: led 11th tl 13th: rdn and outpcd by ldng pair after 14th: lft 15 l 2nd 2 out: hit last* **20/1**
/22- **3** 5 **Cloudy Copper (IRE)**[279] 3537 8-11-0 138........................ RichardJohnson 116
(Jonjo O'Neill) *midfield: nt fluent 12th: lost tch whn ldng pair qcknd after 14th* **11/2**[3]
111- **4** shd **Shubaat**[455] 933 8-11-0 0........................ AidanColeman 113
(John Ferguson) *hld up towards rr: lost tch whn ldng pair qcknd clr after 14th* **7/1**
415- **5** 26 **Wizards Bridge**[179] 5343 6-11-0 0........................ DarylJacob 94
(Colin Tizzard) *pressed ldrs tl blnd 9th: lost tch bef 14th: t.o* **25/1**
015/ **6** 8 **Berkeley Barron (IRE)**[542] 5372 7-11-0 0........................(t) IanPopham 83
(Richard Phillips) *sn last: pushed along bef 8th: lost tch bef 14th: t.o* **25/1**
110- **U** **Beast Of Burden (IRE)**[214] 4702 6-11-0 0........................ PaulTownend 146+
(Rebecca Curtis) *tall: imposing: t.k.h and travelled strly: cl up: chal 14th: sn led: looked to be gng best whn blnd bdly and uns rdr 2 out* **11/8**[1]

5m 55.9s (-26.10) **Going Correction** -1.075s/f (Hard) **7 Ran SP% 111.0**
Speed ratings (Par 105): **100,94,92,92,83 81,**
CSF £40.60 TOTE £3.50: £1.90, £7.10; EX 50.80 Trifecta £226.20.
Owner C G Roach **Bred** M Mahon **Trained** Ditcheat, Somerset

FOCUS
This looked a good novice chase and we were in the process of being treated to something a bit special from Beast Of Burden, but he made a mess of the second-last when appearing to have the race at his mercy, and that left It's A Close Call miles clear to win easily.

1868 GET SOCIAL WITH @TOTEPOOL ON TWITTER H'CAP HURDLE (8 hdls) 2m 11y

3:20 (3:20) (Class 2) (0-150,140) 5-Y-O+ **£9,747** (£2,862; £1,431; £715)

Form RPR

1214 **1** **Broughton (GER)**[15] 1657 5-11-4 **132**..........................(b) AidanColeman 137+
(John Ferguson) *settled in midfield: smooth prog 5th to ld bef next: wnt lft 2 out: 3 l clr and gng strly last: pushed out: readily* **9/2**[3]

0411 **2** 1 3/4 **Makethedifference (IRE)**[25] 1554 7-10-1 **115**.................. MichaelByrne 117
(Tim Vaughan) *hld up last tl effrt bef 5th: tk 2nd 2 out where already clr of rest: drvn and no imp on wnr whn nt fluent last* **4/1**[2]

110- **3** 3 1/4 **Cool Sky**[15] 1640 6-10-8 **122**.. RichardJohnson 122
(Ian Williams) *hld up in rr tl effrt 5th: wnt 3rd but rdn and outpcd by ldng pair 2 out: making no imp whn blnd last* **11/4**[1]

1-52 **4** 3 1/2 **Yes Daddy (IRE)**[53] 1083 7-10-1 **115**.............................. HarrySkelton 111
(Robert Stephens) *settled towards rr: rdn and outpcd bef 3 out: sme prog after hitting last to snatch wl hld 4th* **10/1**

P-33 **5** 1/2 **Dresden (IRE)**[16] 1643 7-11-2 **130**.................................. JamesDavies 125
(Henry Oliver) *settled trcking ldrs: rdn 4th: one pce and btn next: nt fluent 4th: lost 4th cl home* **10/1**

0203 **6** 1 **Ballyglasheen (IRE)**[21] 1591 5-11-7 **135**........................(b) PaulMoloney 130
(Evan Williams) *trckd ldrs: shkn up bef 5th: btn next* **7/1**

220- **7** 6 **Rock On Rocky**[184] 5249 7-11-7 **135**..............................(p) CharliePoste 124
(Matt Sheppard) *led after 1st: racd enthusiastically and set fast pce: hit 4th and 5th: rdn and hdd bef 3 out: sn dropped out* **12/1**

110- **8** 5 **Discay**[379] 1640 6-11-2 **130**... WillKennedy 115
(Dr Richard Newland) *t.k.h: led tl after 1st: nt fluent 3rd: chsd ldr tl rdn 5th: no rspnse: dropped to rr and mstke next* **8/1**

3m 47.7s (-22.90) **Going Correction** -1.075s/f (Hard) **8 Ran SP% 114.3**
Speed ratings: **114,113,111,109,109 109,106,103**
CSF £23.21 CT £57.76 TOTE £4.00: £1.70, £1.60, £1.30; EX 23.90 Trifecta £46.80.
Owner Bloomfields **Bred** Gestut Westerberg **Trained** Cowlinge, Suffolk

FOCUS
A competitive handicap which appeared to turn into a bit of a sprint from the third-last.

1869 JOHN AYRES MEMORIAL H'CAP CHASE (16 fncs) 2m 3f 98y

3:55 (3:58) (Class 2) 4-Y-O+ **£15,825** (£4,675; £2,337; £1,170; £585)

Form RPR

00F- **1** **Astracad (FR)**[177] 5363 9-9-7 **132** oh2..........................(t) JamieBargary[(7)] 140
(Nigel Twiston-Davies) *t.k.h: led or disp ld tl 5th: pressed ldr tl led again 12th: sn drvn: hdd next: looked hld fr 3 out but rallied u.str driving fr last and wore down ldr fnl strides* **14/1**

103- **2** nk **Third Intention (IRE)**[169] 5536 8-11-5 **158**........................(t) PaulO'Brien[(7)] 164
(Colin Tizzard) *prom and t.k.h: stmbld bnd after 5th: gng wl in 2nd 12th: led and ears pricked fr next: 3 l clr last: urged along and idled flat: jst ct* **12/1**

32U- **3** 7 **Wilton Milan (IRE)**[192] 5109 7-10-0 **132** oh2........................(t) HarrySkelton 132
(Dan Skelton) *dropped out in rr: effrt 12th: rdn next: making no imp on ldng pair and finding little fr 2 out: 5 l 3rd at last* **13/2**

236- **4** 1 3/4 **Present View**[260] 3852 7-11-0 **146**................................... BrendanPowell 146
(Jamie Snowden) *reluctant to leave paddock: mounted on crse: pressed ldrs in 4th pl mostly: rdn 14th: hld whn jolting error 2 out* **3/1**[1]

512- **5** shd **Howlongisafoot (IRE)**[169] 5540 6-10-3 **135**.........(p) SamTwiston-Davies 133
(Paul Nicholls) *settled in midfield: effrt 12th: rdn next: kpt on same pce wout threatening fr 3 out* **9/2**[2]

46U- **6** 1 1/4 **Ballygarvey (FR)**[184] 5253 9-10-5 **137**.............................. TomO'Brien 134
(Philip Hobbs) *led or disp ld tl led after 5th: hdd 12th: plugged on and wl hld fr 3 out* **6/1**[3]

4PP- **7** nk **Tara Road**[233] 4341 7-10-0 **132** oh4.................................(t) AidanColeman 131
(Rebecca Curtis) *settled towards rr: hit 11th: effrt bef next: rdn 13th: n.d fr bef 3 out* **8/1**

033- **8** 9 **Filbert (IRE)**[171] 5493 9-10-5 **137**..................................(p) RichardJohnson 129+
(Philip Hobbs) *pressed ldrs tl j. slowly 6th: lost pl next: last whn mstke 11th: no ch whn jumping sltly rt up st* **9/1**

251- **P** **Top Gamble (IRE)**[176] 5389 7-11-8 **154**.............................. JamieMoore
(Kerry Lee) *towards rr and nt a fluent: rdn after 11th: sn btn: t.o and p.u 2 out* **15/2**

4m 42.9s (-28.40) **Going Correction** -1.075s/f (Hard) **9 Ran SP% 118.0**
Speed ratings (Par 109): **116,115,112,112,112 111,111,107,**
CSF £162.71 CT £1205.43 TOTE £18.30: £4.00, £3.20, £2.30; EX 204.70 Trifecta £2195.10.
Owner Mrs Caroline Mould **Bred** Charlotte Thoreau **Trained** Naunton, Gloucs

FOCUS
A cracking handicap chase in which all of the runners were having their first run of the season. There were a whole host in with a chance early in the straight, but it looked all over when Third Intention forged clear, only for the top-weight to tie up in the closing stages and allow the winner to nail him late in the day.

1870 TOTEPOOL PERSIAN WAR NOVICES' HURDLE (GRADE 2) (11 hdls) 2m 3f 100y

4:30 (4:31) (Class 1) 4-Y-O+

£17,085 (£6,411; £3,210; £1,599; £804; £402)

Form RPR

111 **1** **Roadie Joe (IRE)**[19] 1613 6-11-4 130................................ PaulMoloney 136
(Evan Williams) *2nd tl led bef 8th: rdn and hdd bef last: battled bk v gamely to regain advantage nr fin* **8/1**[3]

4-13 **2** shd **Cardinal Palace (IRE)**[7] 1788 5-11-4 135.................... RichardJohnson 137
(J A Nash, Ire) *mounted on crse: hld up last tl stdy prog gng wl fr 8th: 4th 2 out: produced to ld bef last and wnt rt: 1/2 l ahd flat: drvn and outbattled nr fin and jst ct* **10/1**

1- **3** 6 **Definite Outcome (IRE)**[211] 4770 6-11-0 0........................ PaulTownend 127
(Rebecca Curtis) *pressed ldng pair: wnt 2nd bef 8th: sn pushed along: ev ch 2 out: wknd bef last* **3/1**[2]

2F2- **4** 1 1/4 **Emerging Talent (IRE)**[245] 4108 6-11-0 136........[1] SamTwiston-Davies 129+
(Paul Nicholls) *plld hrd and hld up: mstke 6th: effrt in 3rd bef 8th: ev ch whn j.rt next: hrd drvn and tried to chal betwseen last two: nt looking keen whn blnd and pckd bdly last: no ch after* **8/11**[1]

1521 **5** 20 **Samedi Soir**[23] 1570 5-10-11 118.. NoelFehily 104
(Keith Reveley) *taken down early: plld hrd in 5th pl: rdn and wknd bef 8th* **14/1**

51 **6** 9 **Gallic Destiny (IRE)**[124] 671 4-11-4 0...............................(t) JamesBanks 105
(Jo Davis) *led at stdy pce: hit 7th: rdn and hdd bef 8th: t.o 2 out* **66/1**

4m 42.3s (-19.50) **Going Correction** -1.075s/f (Hard) **6 Ran SP% 111.3**
Speed ratings (Par 115): **98,97,95,94,86 82**
CSF £71.57 TOTE £6.20: £2.00, £3.10; EX 27.60 Trifecta £129.70.
Owner Billy Bates **Bred** Michael McEvoy **Trained** Llancarfan, Vale Of Glamorgan

FOCUS
This looked no more than a reasonable renewal of this Grade 2 contest and, as the odds-on favourite backed out of the reckoning between the last two flights, the finish was fought out by two horses that had achieved identical RPRs of just 122 on their last start, a figure normally well short of the standard required to win at this level. The front two also had the benefit of being match-fit.

1871 ASCF SUPPORTS BOB CHAMPION CANCER TRUST VETERANS' H'CAP CHASE (QUALIFIER) (18 fncs) 2m 7f 131y

5:00 (5:02) (Class 2) (0-150,144)
10-Y-O+

£18,768 (£5,544; £2,772; £1,386; £693; £348)

Form RPR

P-31 **1** **Danimix (IRE)**[9] 1733 10-10-9 **127**..............................(t) NoelFehily 140+
(Peter Bowen) *j.w in midfield: 4th bef 14th: qcknd to ld after next and sn 4 l clr: galloped on resolutely flat* **11/2**[3]

12P- **2** 10 **Court By Surprise (IRE)**[183] 5275 10-11-8 **140**.................. DarylJacob 145+
(Emma Lavelle) *settled in midfield: effrt 15th: wnt 3rd next: rdn and wl hld by wnr whn clumsy mstkes 2 out and last* **11/2**[3]

2-0P **3** 3 **Your Busy (IRE)**[8] 1764 12-11-3 **135**..........................(t) PaulTownend 135
(J A Nash, Ire) *led: rdn and hdd after hitting 15th: styd on at same pce in 3rd fr next* **10/1**

406- **4** 2 **Alfie Spinner (IRE)**[227] 4447 10-10-5 **123**................ RichardJohnson 121
(Nick Williams) *pressed ldr tl rdn and lost pl bef 14th: plugged on steadily wout threatening fr 3 out* **3/1**[1]

P65- **5** 1 1/2 **Mountainous (IRE)**[182] 5289 10-11-1 **133**..................(p) JakeGreenall 130
(Kerry Lee) *a abt same pl: pushed along 15th: kpt on same pce and n.d after* **8/1**

4436 **6** shd **Houston Dynimo (IRE)**[77] 1112 10-9-9 **120**..........(tp) DavidNoonan[(7)] 117
(David Pipe) *racd in last pl: hit 7th: pushed along bef next: mstke 9th: brief effrt 13th: n.d fr next* **14/1**

0U3- **7** 2 **Benbens (IRE)**[176] 5392 10-11-8 **140**....................... SamTwiston-Davies 137
(Nigel Twiston-Davies) *cl up: wnt 2nd and mstke 14th: drvn and lost pl bef next* **9/2**[2]

000- **8** 2 3/4 **Pineau De Re (FR)**[183] 5275 12-11-12 **144**........................ WillKennedy 136
(Dr Richard Newland) *hld up and bhd: v brief effrt 13th: n.d fr next* **14/1**

1P5- **9** 26 **Representingceltic (IRE)**[174] 5431 10-10-5 **123**.............. JoshuaMoore 101
(Pat Phelan) *last pair: blnd 8th: rdn 14th: sn btn: t.o* **16/1**

5m 51.5s (-30.50) **Going Correction** -1.075s/f (Hard) **9 Ran SP% 113.4**
Speed ratings: **107,103,102,102,101 101,100,99,91**
CSF £35.57 CT £292.35 TOTE £6.70: £2.00, £2.00, £3.30; EX 28.00 Trifecta £200.20.
Owner Steve & Jackie Fleetham **Bred** Brendan Corbett **Trained** Little Newcastle, Pembrokes

FOCUS
A competitive veterans' chase on paper but it was taken apart by the winner.

1872 PICKWICK BOOKMAKERS STANDARD OPEN NATIONAL HUNT FLAT RACE (DIV I) 2m 11y

5:30 (5:31) (Class 6) 4-6-Y-O **£1,949** (£572; £286; £143)

Form RPR

1 **Above Board (IRE)** 4-11-0 0...................................... RichardJohnson 113+
(Jonjo O'Neill) *workmanlike scope: bhd in slowly run r: pushed along 6f out: rdn to go 2nd 3f out: led over 2f out: forged clr ins fnl f* **5/1**[3]

2 6 **Ballyhill (FR)**[132] 4-10-7 0.. JamieBargary[(7)] 108
(Nigel Twiston-Davies) *tall chser type: midfield tl quicked to ld 6f out: rdn and hdd over 2f out: wknd fnl 100yds* **9/1**

3 1 **Spoilt Rotten** 6-11-0 0.. DenisO'Regan 106
(Mark Pitman) *trckd ldrs: wnt 4th and pushed along 3f out: chsd ldng pair vainly fr over 2f out* **12/1**

4 nk **Mountain Eagle (IRE)**[217] 6-11-0 0...............................(t) NoelFehily 106
(Harry Fry) *tall: racd keenly in ld at mod pce: hdd 6f out: lost 2nd and rdn 3f out: kpt on steadily whn wl hld after* **7/2**[2]

2 **5** 3 3/4 **Hello Jazz**[152] 271 5-10-0 0... MrMLegg[(7)] 95
(John Ryall) *t.k.h in 3rd pl: rdn 4f out: plugged on same pce and n.d fnl 3f* **25/1**

24/ **6** 11 **Max The Minister**[548] 5264 5-11-0 0................................ TomO'Brien 91
(Hughie Morrison) *hld up in last pl: wknd home turn: t.o fnl 3f* **14/1**

7 8 **Rouge Devils (IRE)** 4-11-0 0.................................. SamTwiston-Davies 83
(Paul Nicholls) *t.k.h: chsd ldrs tl rdn and dropped to rr home turn: t.o fnl 4f* **3/1**[1]

8 5 **Cucklington** 4-11-0 0.. DarylJacob 78
(Colin Tizzard) *tall: pressed ldr tl 6f out: rdn and rapidly dropped to rr home turn: sn t.o* **7/2**[2]

3m 51.0s (-14.00) **Going Correction** -1.075s/f (Hard) **8 Ran SP% 114.3**
Speed ratings: **92,89,88,88,86 80,76,74**
CSF £48.53 TOTE £6.40: £1.60, £2.60, £3.70; EX 48.90 Trifecta £538.20.
Owner John P McManus **Bred** Kevin Fox **Trained** Cheltenham, Gloucs

FOCUS
This looked a potentially useful bumper on paper, but two of the horses who attracted serious market attention bombed out, so it's hard to know how this will work out.

1873 PICKWICK BOOKMAKERS STANDARD OPEN NATIONAL HUNT FLAT RACE (DIV II) 2m 11y

6:00 (6:00) (Class 6) 4-6-Y-O **£1,949** (£572; £286; £143)

Form RPR

1 **Bentworth Boy** 4-11-0 0... NicodeBoinville 112+
(Patrick Chamings) *gd topped: settled in 4th pl: effrt gng wl 3f out: led over 2f out: readily drew clr* **33/1**

2 5 **Pure Vision (IRE)** 4-11-0 0..(t) AidanColeman 108
(Anthony Honeyball) *str: bhd: pushed along 6f out: rdn to chse wnr over 2f out: nvr making any imp after but clr of rest fnl f* **7/1**

3 11 **Master Ally (IRE)**[168] 5-11-0 0...................................... PaulTownend 98
(Rebecca Curtis) *led at stdy pce: pushed along and jnd over 3f out: hdd over 2f out: plugged on same pce and sn btn* **13/8**[1]

4 **4** 2 **Debece**[148] 341 4-11-0 0.. RichardJohnson 96
(Tim Vaughan) *disp 2nd pl tl rdn and lost pl tamely 4f out: plodded on* **5/2**[2]

5 1 1/2 **Contempt Of Court (IRE)**[146] 384 6-11-0 0.................... DenisO'Regan 94
(Mark Pitman) *cl cpld: disp 2nd pl tl pushed along to join ldr over 3f out: hdd over 2f out: fdd over 1f out* **12/1**

5 **6** *6* **Baron De Ligniere (FR)**[155] 213 4-11-0 0............ SamTwiston-Davies 89
(Paul Nicholls) *hld up last: lost pl v tamely 4f out: t.o* **6/1**[3]
7 *9* **Blue Prairie** 4-11-0 0.. HarrySkelton 81
(Dan Skelton) *small: bhd: rdn 6f out: lost tch 4f out: t.o fnl 3f* **14/1**
P **Carvers Hill** 4-11-0 0.. WayneHutchinson
(Pat Murphy) *midfield: fdd 6f out: sn t.o: p.u and dismntd over 2f out* **50/1**
3m 51.2s (-13.80) **Going Correction** -1.075s/f (Hard) **8** Ran SP% **112.7**
Speed ratings: **91,88,83,82,81 78,73,**
CSF £238.33 TOTE £16.20: £2.10, £2.10, £1.10; EX 126.30 Trifecta £516.80.
Owner Robinson,Wiggin,Hayward-Cole,Roberts **Bred** Miss K Rausing **Trained** Baughurst, Hants
FOCUS
There was a turn-up here.
T/Plt: £360.50 to a £1 stake. Pool: £89,979.65 - 182.19 winning units. T/Qpdt: £137.20 to a £1 stake. Pool: £8085.48 - 43.60 winning units. **Iain Mackenzie**

1874 - (Foreign Racing) - See Raceform Interactive

1087 LIMERICK (R-H)
Sunday, October 11

OFFICIAL GOING: Yielding (good to yielding in places)

1875a SHANNON AIRPORT CHRISTMAS RACING FESTIVAL NOVICE HURDLE (GRADE 3) (12 hdls) 2m 5f
1:35 (1:35) 4-Y-0+ **£15,116** (£4,418; £2,093; £697)

RPR
1 **Long Dog**[25] 1558 5-11-8 144.. RWalsh 144+
(W P Mullins, Ire) *mde all: clr at times: in cl to 7th where untidy: reduced advantage and almost jnd appr 2 out: hld together whn chal between last 2: cruised clr run-in: easily* **1/7**[1]
2 *3 ¾* **Solatentif (FR)**[75] 1140 5-11-2 128.. JJBurke 130
(Henry De Bromhead, Ire) *trckd ldr in 2nd: jnd for 2nd at times: untidy 5th: wnt clr 2nd fr 7th: rdn to chal appr 2 out and tk clsr order: kpt on wl between last 2 but no imp on wnr: no ex run-in* **12/1**[3]
3 *11* **Little Mitch (IRE)**[8] 1762 6-10-9 111.. MarkWalsh 112
(Yvonne Latta, Ire) *chsd ldrs in 3rd mostly: disp 2nd at times: dropped to 3rd at 7th: untidy 3 out: pushed along wl bef next and dropped to 5th: sn no imp on principals in 4th between last 2: lft 3rd run-in* **14/1**
4 *6 ½* **Fu's Island (IRE)**[8] 1761 5-10-9.. AELynch 108
(P Meany, Ire) *hld up towards rr: 4th 1/2-way: wnt 3rd briefly after 3 out: sn rdn and dropped to 4th again: no imp fr next: 5th between last 2: lft 4th run-in* **25/1**
F **Delegate**[172] 5488 5-11-2.. BJCooper 117+
(Gordon Elliott, Ire) *hld up in rr: tk clsr order after 3 out and sn wnt 3rd: rdn to cl bef next but no imp on front pair between last 2: fell last* **10/1**[2]
5m 6.6s (306.60) **5** Ran SP% **114.8**
CSF £3.62 TOTE £1.10: £1.02, £3.60; DF 2.70 Trifecta £9.60.
Owner Mrs S Ricci **Bred** G B Turnbull Ltd **Trained** Muine Beag, Co Carlow
FOCUS
This was a soft touch for the favourite - a winners' race masquerading as a Grade 3. The fourth horse helps set the standard.

1876-1880a (Foreign Racing) - See Raceform Interactive

1731 AUTEUIL (L-H)
Sunday, October 11

OFFICIAL GOING: Turf: very soft

1881a PRIX GEORGES DE TALHOUET-ROY (HURDLE) (GRADE 2) (3YO) (TURF) 2m 2f
1:30 (1:30) 3-Y-0 **£61,046** (£29,844; £17,635; £12,209; £6,782; £4,748)

RPR
1 **Device (FR)**[19] 3-10-12 0.. JamesReveley 147
(G Macaire, France) **2/5**[1]
2 *4 ½* **Chimere Du Berlais (FR)**[15] 3-10-6 0.................. LudovicPhilipperon 136
(Robert Collet, France) **14/1**
3 *nk* **Mocalacato Has (FR)**[19] 3-10-10 0..............................(b) JacquesRicou 140
(J-P Gallorini, France) **16/1**
4 *1 ¾* **Irmao Joao Has (FR)**[19] 3-10-10 0..............................(p) FelixDeGiles 138
(J-P Gallorini, France) **25/1**
5 *15* **Frodon (FR)**[19] 3-10-8 0.. KevinNabet 121
(G Macaire, France) **14/1**
6 *1 ½* **Politikar (FR)**[19] 3-10-10 0.. BertrandLestrade 122
(G Macaire, France) **8/1**[3]
7 *dist* **Pinkie Brown (FR)**[15] 1656 3-10-6 0.. TomScudamore
(Nick Williams) *t.k.h: hld up in rr: awkward 1st and rushed up to ld sn after: j. path after 4th: got in cl 5th: jnd 6th: hdd after 3 out: lost pl and pushed along whn bade mstke 2 out: t.o* **7/1**[2]
4m 18.7s (258.70) **7** Ran SP% **118.1**
PARI-MUTUEL (all including 1 euro stake): WIN 1.50PLACE 1.20, 2.40SF 8.70.
Owner Magalen O Bryant **Bred** Mme B Gabeur **Trained** Les Mathes, France

1882a PRIX ORCADA (CHASE) (GRADE 3) (4YO) (TURF) 2m 5f 110y
3:20 (3:20) 4-Y-0 **£54,069** (£26,434; £15,620; £10,813; £6,007; £4,205)

RPR
1 **Kobrouk (FR)**[25] 1562 4-11-0 0.. KevinNabet 143
(G Macaire, France) **5/4**[1]
2 *3 ½* **Bossa Nova (FR)**[10] 1731 4-10-3 0.. RegisSchmidlin 129
(F-M Cottin, France) **10/1**
3 *snk* **Karelcytic (FR)**[25] 1562 4-10-12 0.. DavidCottin 137
(F-M Cottin, France) **15/2**[3]
4 *5* **Bandito Conti (FR)**[25] 1562 4-10-12 0..............................(p) JamesReveley 132
(G Macaire, France) **11/2**[2]
5 *9* **Achour (FR)**[31] 1536 4-10-6 0.. AlexisAcker 117
(F-M Cottin, France) **33/1**
6 *½* **Groove (FR)**[18] 4-10-10 0.. MlleNathalieDesoutter 121
(Francois Nicolle, France) **8/1**
7 *1 ¾* **Ballotin (FR)**[40] 4-10-8 0..............................(p) BertrandLestrade 117
(G Macaire, France) **8/1**
8 *¾* **Solway (FR)**[25] 1562 4-10-10 0..............................(p) AnthonyLecordier 118
(G Cherel, France) **10/1**

9 *snk* **Djagble (FR)**[132] 586 4-10-10 0.. Marc-AntoineBillard 118
(J Bertran De Balanda, France) **12/1**
5m 32.5s (-14.50) **9** Ran SP% **122.6**
PARI-MUTUEL (all including 1 euro stake): WIN 2.20PLACE 1.20, 2.10, 1.90DF 10.10SF 15.90.
Owner J D Cotton **Bred** Haras Des Coudraies **Trained** Les Mathes, France

1883a PRIX CARMARTHEN (HURDLE) (GRADE 3) (5YO+) (TURF) 2m 3f 110y
3:55 (3:55) 5-Y-0+ **£47,093** (£23,023; £13,604; £9,418; £5,232; £3,662)

RPR
1 **Saint Firmin (FR)**[25] 1563 6-10-10 0.. KevinNabet 148
(Robert Collet, France) **10/1**
2 *1 ¼* **Voiladenuo (FR)**[25] 1563 6-10-10 0..............................(p) WilfridDenuault 147
(Guy Denuault, France) **8/1**
3 *1* **Roll On Has (FR)**[25] 1563 5-10-3 0.. JacquesRicou 139
(J-P Gallorini, France) **4/1**[1]
4 *1 ½* **Hippomene (FR)**[25] 1563 5-10-7 0 ow4..............................(p) DavidCottin 142
(J-P Gallorini, France) **9/2**[2]
5 *3* **Le Chateau (FR)**[25] 1563 6-10-6 0.. ErvanChazelle 138
(C Scandella, France) **14/1**
6 *1 ¼* **Plumeur (FR)**[25] 1563 8-10-8 0.. AlainDeChitray 138
(G Chaignon, France) **28/1**
7 *snk* **Aubusson (FR)**[213] 4719 6-10-6 0.. LizzieKelly 136
(Nick Williams) *cl up: disp ld bef 5th tl hdd 5 out: chsd ldr: 2nd and ev ch whn rdn 2 out: sltt mstke last: wknd run-in* **10/1**
8 *1 ¼* **Dos Santos (FR)**[25] 1563 5-10-6 0..............................(p) FelixDeGiles 135
(Emmanuel Clayeux, France) **13/2**[3]
9 *nk* **Dynaste (FR)**[260] 3850 9-10-6 0.. TomScudamore 135
(David Pipe) *t.k.h early: hld up in midfield: pushed along and no imp fr 3 out: sme mod late prog run-in: nvr in contention* **9/2**[2]
10 *2 ½* **Street Name (FR)**[19] 5-10-1 0.. AnthonyLecordier 127
(G Cherel, France) **12/1**
11 *9* **Lamego (FR)**[25] 1563 8-10-6 0.. Jean-LucBeaunez 123
(Mme P Butel, France) **20/1**
12 *¾* **Dulce Leo (FR)**[148] 349 9-10-8 0..............................(p) FrankieLeroy 124
(J-P Gallorini, France) **33/1**
F **Monsamou (IRE)**[15] 6-10-6 0..............................(p) JoAudon
(P Chevillard, France) **20/1**
4m 43.5s (-11.50) **13** Ran SP% **129.3**
PARI-MUTUEL (all including 1 euro stake): WIN 8.00PLACE 2.50, 3.00, 1.80DF 25.20SF 39.30.
Owner Mlle Micheline Vidal **Bred** J Collet & Mlle M-L Collet **Trained** Chantilly, France

1884a PRIX HEROS XII (CHASE) (GRADE 3) (5YO+) (TURF) 2m 6f
4:25 (4:25) 5-Y-0+ **£55,813** (£27,286; £16,124; £11,162; £6,201; £4,341)

RPR
1 **Vezelay (FR)**[31] 1535 6-10-8 0.. MathieuCarroux 146
(Emmanuel Clayeux, France) **10/1**[3]
2 *nk* **Milord Thomas (FR)**[37] 1477 6-11-5 0.. JacquesRicou 157
(D Bressou, France) **6/4**[1]
3 *1* **Jemy Baie (FR)**[31] 1535 6-10-8 0.. KevinNabet 145
(M Postic, France) **7/2**[2]
4 *3 ½* **Saint Palois (FR)**[31] 1535 7-10-6 0.. JamesReveley 139
(Emmanuel Clayeux, France) **10/1**[3]
5 *5* **Shannon Rock (FR)**[147] 375 9-11-3 0..............................(p) DavidCottin 145
(J-P Gallorini, France) **16/1**
6 *4* **Saint Pistol (FR)**[147] 375 7-10-12 0.. AngeloGasnier 136
(L Viel, France) **11/1**
7 *4 ½* **Pindare (FR)**[126] 664 6-10-8 0..............................(p) FelixDeGiles 128
(J-P Gallorini, France) **20/1**
8 *3 ½* **Rasique (FR)**[31] 1535 5-10-1 0.. PACarberry 117
(C Scandella, France) **18/1**
9 *5* **Royal Astarania (FR)**[147] 375 6-10-10 0.. AlainDeChitray 121
(P Peltier, France) **14/1**
F **Vieux Morvan (FR)**[19] 6-10-8 0..............................(b) JonathanNattiez
(G Cherel, France) **22/1**
P **Vent Sombre (FR)**[126] 664 6-10-10 0..............................(b) BertrandLestrade
(G Cherel, France) **14/1**
P **Iroufìcar Has (FR)**[37] 1477 5-10-1 0.. ThomasBeaurain
(J-P Gallorini, France) **20/1**
5m 32.1s (-11.90) **12** Ran SP% **127.1**
PARI-MUTUEL (all including 1 euro stake): WIN 7.70PLACE 1.70, 1.20, 1.60DF 10.30SF 30.90.
Owner P Joubert & Ecurie Couderc **Bred** Mme M Juhen-Cypres **Trained** France

PARDUBICE (L-H)
Sunday, October 11

OFFICIAL GOING: Turf: good

1885a VELKA PARDUBICKA S CESKOU POJISTOVNOU (CHASE) (LISTED RACE) (6YO+) (TURF) 4m 2f 110y
3:40 (12:00) 6-Y-0+ **£56,148** (£30,881; £19,651; £14,037; £9,825; £5,614)

RPR
1 **Nikas (CZE)**[364] 1881 10-10-10 0.. MarekStromsky 131
(Stanislav Popelka Jr, Czech Republic) **20/1**
2 *3 ¾* **Ribelino (FR)** 7-10-10 0.. PavelKasny 127
(Stanislav Kovar, Czech Republic) **20/1**
3 *3 ½* **Zarif (IRE)**[364] 1881 8-10-10 0.. JosefBartos 124
(Josef Vana Jr, Czech Republic) **3/1**[3]
4 *2 ½* **Universe Of Gracie (GER)**[364] 1881 10-10-10 0.. JanFaltejsek 121
(Jiri Kousek, Czech Republic) **5/2**[2]
5 *5* **Rabbit Well**[1512] 1462 9-10-10 0.. JosefVana 116
(Josef Vana, Czech Republic) **6/4**[1]
6 *6* **Kasim (CZE)**[364] 1881 10-10-10 0.. MarcelNovak 110
(Premek Kejzlar, Czech Republic) **31/1**
7 *1 ½* **Lorain (CZE)**[728] 1904 8-10-10 0.. JaroslavMyska 109
(Stepanka Myskova, Czech Republic) **39/1**
8 *10* **Modena (CZE)** 8-10-6 0.. DusanAndres 95
(Stanislav Popelka Jr, Czech Republic) **10/1**

9 6 **Templar (CZE)** 8-10-3 0 .... KevinGuignon 86
(Antonin Novak, Czech Republic) 69/1
10 3 1/4 **Pasquini Rouge (FR)**[252] 7-10-10 0 .... JordanDuchene 89
(Patrice Quinton, France) 20/1
11 3 **Klaus (POL)**[364] 1881 10-10-10 0 .... RaffaeleRomano 86
(Cestmir Olehla, Czech Republic) 10/1
F **Peintre Abstrait (IRE)**[364] 1881 9-10-10 0 .... CevinChan
(Radek Holcak, Czech Republic) 99/1
F **Sherardo (CZE)**[364] 1881 11-10-10 0 .... LukasSloup
(Lenka Syslova, Czech Republic) 54/1
B **Pareto (CZE)**[364] 1881 8-10-10 0 .... MatejRigo
(Cestmir Olehla, Czech Republic) 99/1
F **Al Jaz (CZE)**[364] 1881 9-10-10 0 .... JosefSovka
(Jan Blecha, Czech Republic) 9/1
U **Ter Mill (CZE)**[364] 1881 9-10-3 0 .... OndrejVelek
(Antonin Novak, Czech Republic) 64/1
F **Amaragon (CZE)**[364] 1881 10-10-10 0 .... MartinLiska
(Pavel Poles, Czech Republic) 99/1
U **Gauner Danon (GER)**[364] 1881 9-10-10 0 .... SertashFerhanov
(Frantisek Holcak, Czech Republic) 87/1
P **Orix (CZE)** 8-10-10 0 .... VlastislavKorytar
(Lenka Horakova, Czech Republic) 119/1
F **Sokol (CAN)** 8-10-10 0 .... ThomasGarner
(Michal Lisek, Czech Republic) 19/1
F **Nebrius (POL)** 7-10-10 0 .... JakubKocman
(Pavlina Surova, Czech Republic) 99/1
P **Hipo Jape (CZE)** 9-10-10 0 .... PetrTuma
(Josef Vana, Czech Republic) 31/1

8m 55.29s (535.29) 22 Ran SP% **160.5**

Owner Castor **Bred** F Vocasek **Trained** Czech Republic

1683 **SEDGEFIELD** (L-H)
Monday, October 12

OFFICIAL GOING: Good (good to soft in places) changing to good to soft after race 3 (3:10)
Wind: fairly strong across Weather: cloudy, shower before 2nd

1886 AMCO ENGINEERING NOVICES' HURDLE (BETFRED HURDLE SERIES QUALIFIER) (8 hdls) 2m 178y
2:10 (2:10) (Class 4) 4-Y-0+ **£3,638** (£1,068; £534; £267)

Form RPR
12 1 **Vancouverite**[18] 1634 5-11-5 132 .... AidanColeman 129+
(John Ferguson) *trckd ldrs: hit 5th: nt fluent 3 out: led jst after 2 out: pushed clr: easily* 2/5[1]
5F1 2 12 **Where's Tiger**[18] 1634 4-11-0 0 .... GrantCockburn(5) 116
(Lucinda Russell) *led: jnd bef 2 out: rdn whn hdd jst after 2 out: one pce and sn no ch w wnr: hit last* 7/2[2]
3 10 **Absolute (IRE)**[423] 4-10-12 0 .... DannyCook 97
(Sue Smith) *in tch: outpcd by ldng trio bef 2 out: rdn after 2 out: plugged on: wnt 3rd towards fin* 25/1
P 4 1 1/2 **Marshgate Lane (USA)**[23] 1117 6-10-12 0 .... MarkQuinlan 97
(Neil Mulholland) *prom: jnd ldr bef 2 out: sn rdn: stl disputing 2nd last: wknd: lost 3rd towards fin: dismntd after line* 12/1
6 5 3 1/4 **Baysbrown (IRE)**[141] 459 5-10-12 0 .... BrianHarding 93
(Nicky Richards) *hld up in midfield: nt fluent 5th: sn pushed along: plugged on: nvr threatened ldrs* 6/1[3]
24-5 6 2 1/4 **Beer Goggles (IRE)**[13] 1684 4-10-9 0 .... CraigNichol(3) 91
(Micky Hammond) *hld up: rdn after 2 out: nvr threatened ldrs* 28/1
0/ 7 2 **Grammar**[42] 3601 6-10-9 0 .... TonyKelly(3) 89
(David Thompson) *in tch: rdn after 3 out: wknd after 2 out* 200/1
03-5 8 15 **Tickanrun (IRE)**[159] 145 5-10-7 0 .... DiarmuidO'Regan(5) 75
(Chris Grant) *midfield: wknd bef 3 out* 66/1
40-0 9 2 1/2 **Dibble Bridge**[10] 1740 4-10-9 0 .... AdamNicol(3) 73
(Philip Kirby) *a towards rr* 100/1
P-P0 10 9 **Centre Haafhd**[8] 1774 4-10-5 0 .... LorcanMurtagh(7) 65
(Barry Murtagh) *a towards rr* 250/1
6 11 39 **Rosie Hall (IRE)**[16] 1660 5-10-5 0 .... SeanQuinlan 23
(John Wainwright) *midfield: wknd bef 3 out* 200/1
0 12 40 **Swiftly Beyond**[10] 1740 7-10-5 0 .... ThomasDowson(7)
(Brian Storey) *midfield: nt fluent 3rd: sn lost pl and bhd fr 5th* 250/1

4m 3.8s (-3.10) **Going Correction** +0.05s/f (Yiel)
WFA 4 from 5yo+ 9lb 12 Ran SP% **127.2**
Speed ratings (Par 105): **109,103,98,97,96 95,94,87,86,81 63,44**
CSF £2.60 TOTE £1.30: £1.02, £1.30, £6.90; EX 3.40 Trifecta £30.10.
Owner Bloomfields **Bred** Darley **Trained** Cowlinge, Suffolk

FOCUS
Divided bends, Hurdles on the outer. After 2mm of rain during the morning the going had eased to good, good to soft in places. The opener was an uncompetitive novice hurdle and the short-priced favourite won as he liked. The winer step up compared to the second on Perth form.

1887 VHE CONSTRUCTION H'CAP HURDLE 2m 3f 188y
2:40 (2:40) (Class 4) (0-105,105) 3-Y-0+ **£3,638** (£1,068; £534; £267)

Form RPR
1432 1 **Amuse Me**[40] 1444 9-10-12 91 .... RichardJohnson 107+
(James Moffatt) *hld up: hdwy fr 6th: rdn bef 2 out: led between last 2: kpt on wl* 9/2[2]
3140 2 13 **Keep To The Beat**[20] 1618 4-11-12 105 .... (p) BrianHughes 111
(Kevin Ryan) *chsd clr ldr: led 6th: rdn and hdd between last 2: one pce* 20/1
63-5 3 14 **Attention Please (IRE)**[26] 1552 5-10-9 91 .... CraigNichol(3) 83
(Rose Dobbin) *in tch: rdn bef 2 out: sn one pce: wnt 3rd appr last* 8/1
034- 4 1 1/4 **Tomorrow's Legend**[181] 5325 5-11-6 102 .... JoeColliver(3) 93
(George Moore) *midfield: rdn and hdwy to chse ldr 3 out: no ex between last 2: lost 3rd appr last* 4/1[1]
-455 5 2 3/4 **Burnt Sienna (IRE)**[24] 1572 5-10-8 90 .... (tp) DerekFox(3) 79
(Noel C Kelly, Ire) *midfield: rdn and outpcd after 6th: plugged on after 2 out* 13/2[3]
03-6 6 3/4 **Hatton Springs (IRE)**[117] 157 4-11-1 101 .... SamColtherd(7) 90
(Stuart Coltherd) *midfield: in tch after 3 out: rdn appr 2 out: wknd between last 2* 25/1
-362 7 9 **King's Chorister**[44] 1405 9-9-11 83 .... (t) LorcanMurtagh(7) 63
(Barry Murtagh) *hld up: nvr threatened* 14/1
-35R 8 1/2 **Downtown Boy (IRE)**[13] 1686 7-11-10 103 .... (b) AndrewThornton 82
(Ray Craggs) *led: clr 3rd tl 5th: reminders and reduced advantage bef 6th: hdd 6th and sn dropped to midfield: wknd bef 2 out* 16/1
543U 9 13 **Louloumills**[26] 1550 5-9-10 82 .... ThomasDowson(7) 49
(Maurice Barnes) *in tch: rdn 3 out: sn wknd* 10/1
0366 10 6 **District Attorney (IRE)**[8] 1775 6-10-4 86 .... JohnKington(3) 48
(Chris Fairhurst) *midfield: reminders after 3rd: wknd bef 3 out* 25/1
6-50 11 2 1/2 **The Western Force (IRE)**[60] 1240 5-11-6 99 .... (t) HarrySkelton 59
(Dan Skelton) *hld up: nvr threatened* 12/1
134- 12 nk **Kashstaree**[38] 4517 4-11-12 105 .... DenisO'Regan 65
(John Quinn) *hld up: nvr threatened* 22/1
4/0- 13 2 1/2 **Patavium (IRE)**[56] 2875 12-10-9 91 .... TonyKelly(3) 48
(Edwin Tuer) *a towards rr* 50/1
6054 14 3 3/4 **Hunters Belt (IRE)**[24] 1572 11-11-6 104 .... (bt) JonathonBewley(5) 58
(George Bewley) *hld up: hdwy 5th: cl up 6th: wknd after 3 out* 11/1

4m 47.6s (-6.50) 14 Ran SP% **119.1**
CSF £95.99 CT £708.87 TOTE £3.90: £2.20, £3.90, £3.10; EX 29.50 Trifecta £161.30.
Owner Vilprano, Bowron & Beaumont **Bred** Whatton Manor Stud **Trained** Cartmel, Cumbria

FOCUS
A modest handicap hurdle, in which they went a good gallop, and they finished well strung out. The winner was well in and there's a case for rating the race a bit higher.

1888 SEYMOUR CIVIL ENGINEERING CONTRACTORS NOVICES' H'CAP CHASE (13 fncs) 2m 77y
3:10 (3:10) (Class 4) (0-105,103) 5-Y-0+ **£4,288** (£1,259; £629; £314)

Form RPR
5-41 1 **Ashcott Boy**[4] 1825 7-11-6 103 7ex .... DavidNoonan(7) 121+
(Neil Mulholland) *in tch: pckd on landing 1st: rdn to chse ldr 2 out: upsides last: kpt on: led towards fin* 10/11[1]
240/ 2 1 **Blades Lad**[45] 3288 6-11-12 102 .... BrianHughes 116
(Peter Niven) *trckd ldr: led 3 out: rdn after 2 out: jnd last: one pce: hdd towards fin* 28/1
5360 3 16 **Morning With Ivan (IRE)**[44] 1400 5-11-8 98 .... HenryBrooke 98
(Martin Todhunter) *in tch: rdn and outpcd 4 out: plugged on fr 2 out: wnt modest 3rd between last 2* 20/1
0-45 4 1 1/4 **The Shropshire Lad**[52] 1306 5-11-5 95 .... HarrySkelton 94
(Dan Skelton) *hld up: hdwy and in tch 4 out: nt fluent 3 out: wknd after 2 out* 7/2[2]
42P- 5 16 **Six One Away (IRE)**[273] 3654 6-10-6 82 .... (p) JakeGreenall 69
(Paul Webber) *led: hdd 3 out: sn wknd* 6/1[3]
F23U 6 13 **Great Demeanor (USA)**[19] 1630 5-10-0 79 .... (p) HarryChalloner(3) 51
(Dianne Sayer) *hld up: pushed along and struggling fr 7th* 16/1
P561 P **So Bazaar (IRE)**[13] 1687 8-10-0 76 oh1 .... (t) BrianHarding
(Andrew Wilson) *hld up: wnt wrong and p.u sharply after 3rd* 16/1
P **Allthedollars (IRE)**[81] 1089 5-11-1 91 .... JamesReveley
(Joanne Foster) *hld up: lost tch after 5th: p.u bef 9th* 18/1

4m 1.3s (-12.70) **Going Correction** -0.975s/f (Hard) 8 Ran SP% **114.1**
Speed ratings: **92,91,83,82,74 68, ,**
CSF £24.19 CT £321.04 TOTE £1.90: £1.10, £3.90, £3.90; EX 20.00 Trifecta £34.80.
Owner John Hobbs **Bred** Mrs J A Gawthorpe **Trained** Limpley Stoke, Wilts

FOCUS
An uncompetitive novices' handicap chase and the two principals pulled a long way clear. A step up from the winner with the second to the level of his best hurdles form.

1889 RENEW HOLDINGS H'CAP CHASE (21 fncs) 3m 2f 59y
3:40 (3:40) (Class 3) (0-125,125) 4-Y-0+ **£6,498** (£1,908; £954; £477)

Form RPR
4131 1 **Mia's Anthem (IRE)**[10] 1743 7-11-4 120 .... (t) DerekFox(3) 134+
(Noel C Kelly, Ire) *hld up in rr: slow 8th: hdwy after 4 out: trckd ldr gng wl bef 2 out: led between last: pushed clr* 7/2[3]
04-0 2 5 **Highland Lodge (IRE)**[20] 1616 9-11-12 125 .... (b[1]) DarylJacob 131
(Emma Lavelle) *led narrowly: reminders after 4th: rdn along fr 14th: hdd between last 2: no ex* 2/1[1]
P5-3 3 10 **Swing Hard (IRE)**[13] 1690 7-10-10 109 .... DannyCook 108
(Sue Smith) *in tch: wnt 2nd after 14th: rdn 4 out: nt fluent 3 out and sn lost 2nd: wknd between last 2* 9/4[2]
66P- 4 5 **Isla Pearl Fisher**[182] 5313 12-11-9 122 .... (t) LucyAlexander 116
(N W Alexander) *hld up: hdwy 5 out: rdn 3 out: wknd 2 out* 14/1
1-PP P **Harris (IRE)**[7] 1795 8-10-4 103 .... (v) GavinSheehan
(Alan Brown) *pressed ldr: slow 14th and lost pl: sn rdn and struggling: hit 4 out: p.u bef next* 5/1

6m 40.7s (-30.30) **Going Correction** -0.975s/f (Hard) 5 Ran SP% **109.7**
Speed ratings (Par 107): **107,105,102,100,**
CSF £11.14 TOTE £3.90: £2.10, £1.40; EX 12.00 Trifecta £16.80.
Owner Don't Ask Now Syndicate **Bred** Cornelius Walsh **Trained** Draperstown, Co. Derry

FOCUS
The going changed to good to soft before this race. A fair handicap but not the strongest event for the grade, and possibly a case of only one horse in form.

1890 RENEW HOLDINGS H'CAP HURDLE (12 hdls 1 omitted) 3m 3f 9y
4:10 (4:10) (Class 5) (0-100,100) 4-Y-0+ **£2,599** (£763; £381; £190)

Form RPR
3-P3 1 **Darsi Dancer (IRE)**[159] 143 7-10-11 92 .... SamColtherd(7) 97+
(Stuart Coltherd) *w ldr: led appr last (normal 2 out): styd on* 25/1
3431 2 3/4 **Tokyo Javilex (FR)**[9] 1756 8-10-13 94 .... (t) MrLDrowne(7) 99+
(Nigel Hawke) *midfield: stl only 6th appr last (normal 2 out): styd on wl extended run-in: wnt 2nd 50yds out* 4/1[2]
4230 3 1 3/4 **Finish The Story (IRE)**[46] 1375 9-11-11 99 .... (bt) BrendanPowell 100
(Johnny Farrelly) *led narrowly: rdn whn hdd appr last (normal 2 out): one pce extended run-in: lost 2nd 50yds out* 9/1
/665 4 nk **Optical High**[13] 1692 6-9-4 74 oh2 .... StephenMcCarthy(10) 75
(Sue Smith) *trckd ldng pair: pushed along fr 9th: plugged on extended run-in* 22/1
5644 5 11 **Minella Bliss (IRE)**[28] 1547 10-11-1 89 .... (b) LiamTreadwell 82
(James Evans) *hld up: hdwy after 10th: disp 3rd last (normal 2 out): wknd fnl f* 10/1
4324 6 3 1/2 **Solway Trigger**[24] 1573 6-9-11 76 .... CallumBewley(5) 64
(Lisa Harrison) *midfield: hdwy to chse ldrs 2 out (normal 3 out): wknd appr last (normal 2 out)* 8/1[3]
3043 7 4 1/2 **Maybe I Wont**[44] 1400 10-11-7 100 .... DiarmuidO'Regan(5) 84
(James Moffatt) *hld up: nvr threatened ldrs* 9/1
4F64 8 2 1/2 **Danceintothelight**[10] 1739 8-10-8 92 .... (t) FinianO'Toole(10) 74
(Micky Hammond) *hld up: hit 6th: nvr threatened* 22/1
143- 9 21 **Apache Pilot**[175] 5423 7-10-7 86 .... (t) DaraghBourke(5) 49
(Maurice Barnes) *trckd ldng pair: lost pl 2 out (normal 3 out): sn wknd* 10/3[1]

5605 **10** 3 ½ **Mullinavat (IRE)**[13] 1691 6-11-5 **93**..........(t) AidanColeman 53
(Jennie Candlish) *hld up: hmpd by faller 10th: nvr threatened* **11/1**
062- **11** 6 **Clenagh Castle (IRE)**[305] 3024 5-11-4 **92**.......... BrianHughes 46
(Chris Grant) *midfield: rdn after 2 out (normal 3 out): sn wknd* **33/1**
4-23 **F** **Duroob**[11] 1727 13-10-13 **87**..........(v) RichardJohnson
(Anthony McCann, Ire) *midfield on outer: fell 10th* **10/1**
6m 50.9s (-1.10) **Going Correction** +0.05s/f (Yiel) **12** Ran SP% **116.2**
Speed ratings (Par 103): **103,102,102,102,98 97,96,95,89,88 86,**
CSF £118.19 CT £994.89 TOTE £22.00: £6.70, £1.90, £2.80; EX 146.90 Trifecta £1079.70.
Owner Coltherd Gillie **Bred** Patrick Carey And J Archdeacon **Trained** Selkirk, Borders
■ The first winner under rules for Sam Coltherd, 16, the son of winning trainer Stuart Coltherd.
FOCUS
A moderate staying handicap. The winner was potentially thrown in on his Kelso hunter chase second.

1891 AMCO RAIL H'CAP CHASE (16 fncs) 2m 3f 65y
4:40 (4:40) (Class 4) (0-105,105) 5-Y-0+ **£4,288** (£1,259; £629; £314)

Form RPR
5545 **1** **Champagne Agent (IRE)**[35] 1492 9-9-11 **78** oh10(bt) CallumWhillans(3) 92+
(Donald Whillans) *pressed ldr: led after 2nd: mde rest: rdn after 3 out: styd on to draw clr after 2 out* **8/1**
0321 **2** 12 **Court Of Law (IRE)**[20] 1614 7-11-7 **99**..........(p) WayneHutchinson 102
(Donald McCain) *trckd ldr: rdn bef 2 out: wknd appr last* **15/8**[1]
15F5 **3** 9 **Gin Cobbler**[10] 1738 9-11-5 **104**.......... SamColtherd(7) 103
(Victor Thompson) *hld up: wnt modest 3rd 4 out: sn rdn: no imp* **22/1**
5252 **4** 21 **Sendiym (FR)**[13] 1685 8-10-11 **89**..........(p) BrianHughes 71
(Dianne Sayer) *in tch: prom 8th: mstke 11th: wknd after 4 out* **5/2**[2]
3455 **5** 20 **Roxyfet (FR)**[13] 1685 5-10-6 **87**.......... JoeColliver(3) 45
(Micky Hammond) *j. none too fluently in rr: a bhd* **12/1**
340P **6** 2 ½ **Pindar (GER)**[92] 964 11-10-0 **78** oh4..........(p) HenryBrooke 34
(Joanne Foster) *led narrowly tl after 2nd: prom: slow and lost pl 9th: sn struggling: t.o 5 out* **14/1**
20-6 **P** **Marlee Mourinho (IRE)**[151] 303 9-9-10 **79**..........(t) StephenMulqueen(5)
(N W Alexander) *in tch: reminders and lost pl 8th: struggling fr 10th: p.u bef 5 out* **9/2**[3]
4m 54.6s (-8.40) **Going Correction** -0.975s/f (Hard) **7** Ran SP% **111.4**
Speed ratings: **78,72,69,60,51 50,**
CSF £23.21 CT £309.23 TOTE £7.90: £3.20, £1.80; EX 24.70 Trifecta £328.30.
Owner Star Racing **Bred** Vincent Holian **Trained** Hawick, Borders
FOCUS
A modest handicap and one-way traffic for the winner, who had slipped to a very good mark.

1892 SHEPLEY ENGINEERS H'CAP HURDLE (3 hdls 5 omitted) 2m 178y
5:10 (5:18) (Class 5) (0-100,98) 3-Y-0+ **£2,599** (£763; £381; £190)

Form RPR
0-05 **1** **David John**[17] 1647 4-11-4 **90**.......... RobertDunne 96+
(Dai Burchell) *midfield: smooth hdwy appr last (normal 2 out): led extended run-in: rdn and kpt on* **3/1**[1]
060/ **2** 4 ½ **Gunner Lindley (IRE)**[73] 4817 8-10-6 **85**.......... SamColtherd(7) 85
(Stuart Coltherd) *midfield: styd on wl extended run-in: wnt 2nd towards fin* **25/1**
654/ **3** ½ **Pinotage**[38] 3830 7-11-1 **94**.......... JamieHamilton(7) 94
(Peter Niven) *midfield: hdwy appr last (normal 2 out): styd on extended run-in* **14/1**
6-35 **4** 1 ¼ **Hi Dancer**[39] 1461 12-11-4 **90**.......... AndrewTinkler 88
(Ben Haslam) *trckd ldr: led 1/2-way: rdn whn hdd jst after last: no ex and lost 2 more pls ins fnl f* **16/1**
4-54 **5** ¾ **Dalby Spook (IRE)**[13] 1683 5-10-12 **84**.......... BrianHughes 82
(Dianne Sayer) *hld up: hdwy appr last: one pce extended run-in* **8/1**[2]
66-6 **6** 14 **Lady Busanda**[125] 679 5-10-9 **84**.......... JoeColliver(3) 70
(George Moore) *midfield: wnt prom 1/2-way: nt fluent last (normal 2 out): wknd extended run-in* **22/1**
5P-0 **7** 3 ½ **Desert Island Dusk**[158] 155 4-11-6 **97**..........(t) DaraghBourke(5) 79
(Maurice Barnes) *midfield: in tch appr last (normal 2 out): wknd extended run-in* **25/1**
/64- **8** 1 ¾ **Woodstock (IRE)**[446] 472 5-11-4 **97**..........(t) MrTHamilton(7) 77
(Ann Hamilton) *nvr bttr than midfield* **16/1**
52P/ **9** 10 **Academy (IRE)**[4] 881 7-11-0 **86**.......... LucyAlexander 57
(N W Alexander) *hld up: nvr threatened* **20/1**
-4P0 **10** *hd* **Beyondtemptation**[24] 1572 7-10-10 **87**..........(t) DiarmuidO'Regan(5) 58
(Jonathan Haynes) *led: hdwy 1/2-way: wknd bef last (normal 2 out)* **20/1**
0-06 **11** 3 ½ **Skyfire**[46] 1377 8-11-7 **98**.......... CharlieDeutsch(5) 66
(Nick Kent) *hld up: nvr threatened* **25/1**
546- **12** 40 **Our Phylli Vera (IRE)**[153] 5060 6-11-10 **96**.......... JamesReveley 28
(Joanne Foster) *prom: wknd after 1/2-way* **9/1**[3]
P40P **13** 3 ½ **Cash Is King**[13] 1683 5-10-10 **87**..........(b) CallumBewley(5) 16
(Kenny Johnson) *a towards rr* **80/1**
4m 1.7s (-5.20) **Going Correction** -0.25s/f (Good)
WFA 4 from 5yo+ 9lb **13** Ran SP% **91.2**
Speed ratings (Par 103): **102,99,99,99,98 92,90,89,84,84 83,64,62**
CSF £47.23 CT £377.11 TOTE £3.30: £1.60, £5.10, £3.80; EX 59.40 Trifecta £362.60.
Owner David J Llewellyn Toni P James **Bred** Toni P James **Trained** Briery Hill, Blaenau Gwent
■ Snowed In was withdrawn. Price at time of withdrawal 5/2f. Rule 4 applies to all bets - deduction 25p in the pound.
FOCUS
A moderate handicap hurdle, in which the favourite Snowed In was withdrawn after being kicked at the start. They only jumped three of the eight hurdles, with both flights down the far side omitted due to low sun, as well one up the home straight due to earlier damage. The winenr is on the upgrade with the second close to his mark.
T/Plt: £12.40 to a £1 stake. Pool: £74,984.42 - 4,383.11 winning tickets T/Qpdt: £9.60 to a £1 stake. Pool: £5,708.27 - 436.50 winning tickets **Andrew Sheret**

1766 HUNTINGDON (R-H)
Tuesday, October 13
OFFICIAL GOING: Good (chs 7.5, hdl 7.4)
Wind: strong across early becoming variable Weather: sunny after race one; 12 degrees

1893 32RED CASINO H'CAP HURDLE (8 hdls) 1m 7f 171y
2:10 (2:10) (Class 4) (0-115,114) 3-Y-0+ **£3,249** (£954; £477; £238)

Form RPR
340- **1** **Isaac Bell (IRE)**[199] 5022 7-11-12 **114**..........(t) NoelFehily 117
(Alex Hales) *prom and t.k.h: nt fluent 5th: rdn to chal and hit 2 out: pressed ldr hrd fr last and wore him down fnl stride: gamely* **7/1**
/6-3 **2** *nse* **Breaking Bits (IRE)**[23] 1602 8-11-10 **112**.......... MichealNolan 115
(Jamie Snowden) *pressed ldr: led bef 2 out: sn rdn: maintained slt advantage fr last tl pipped on post* **4/1**[2]
00P- **3** ¾ **Keppel Isle (IRE)**[190] 5212 6-10-2 **90** oh1 ow2.......... TomCannon 92
(Laura Mongan) *prom: drvn in 3rd bef 2 out: rnged upsides ldng pair last: carried hd awkwardly flat: ev ch tl n.g.t fnl 100yds* **66/1**
2P36 **4** 8 **Samoset**[12] 1714 5-11-6 **108**..........(t) KielanWoods 102
(Graeme McPherson) *led: rdn and hdd bef 2 out: 4th and wkng last* **16/1**
-U30 **5** 9 **Brinestine (USA)**[136] 556 6-11-2 **107**..........(t) JamesBanks(3) 92
(Emma Baker) *chsd ldrs: rdn and outpcd bef 2 out: no ch after* **12/1**
435- **6** 7 **Norse Light**[197] 5070 4-11-8 **110**.......... AidanColeman 90
(David Dennis) *midfield: rdn and wknd after 3 out* **20/1**
02-2 **7** *shd* **Giveagirlachance (IRE)**[159] 179 6-11-8 **110**.......... AndrewThornton 90
(Seamus Mullins) *hld up in last pair: struggling fr 3 out* **20/1**
236- **8** 12 **Shimba Hills**[250] 4057 4-11-10 **112**.......... NickScholfield 85
(Lawney Hill) *cl up tl rdn 3 out: dropped to rr and impeded next* **16/1**
343- **9** 6 **Belize**[197] 5063 4-11-7 **109**.......... RichardJohnson 79
(Tim Vaughan) *towards rr: rdn 3 out: sn lost tch: eased next: t.o* **10/1**
P3/3 **B** **Spa's Dancer (IRE)**[21] 1613 8-11-10 **112**..........[1] JackQuinlan 97
(James Eustace) *t.k.h in rr: effrt after 3 out: sn rdn: btn 6th whn b.d next* **6/1**[3]
42 **F** **Impulsive American**[12] 1712 3-10-7 **112**..........(t) TomScudamore 95
(David Pipe) *t.k.h in midfield: drvn bef 2 out and outpcd in abt 5 l 5th whn fell at flight* **9/4**[1]
3m 43.8s (-11.10) **Going Correction** -0.675s/f (Firm)
WFA 3 from 4yo 17lb 4 from 5yo+ 9lb **11** Ran SP% **117.1**
Speed ratings (Par 105): **100,99,99,95,91 87,87,81,78,**
CSF £34.87 CT £1717.31 TOTE £8.50: £2.20, £1.60, £14.50; EX 43.00 Trifecta £1021.20 Part won. Pool: £1,361.63 - 0.23 winning units..
Owner A E Frost **Bred** M Kennelly **Trained** Edgcote, Northamptonshire
FOCUS
Rail on all bends moved out 1yd, meaning races 1 & 6 were run over approximately 8.68yds further, races 2, 3 & 4 over 10.36yds further and race 5 over 13.36yds further. This proved quite open and the favourite was held when falling late. The winner was similar to the best of his Irish form and his Warwick reappearance last year.

1894 32RED.COM H'CAP CHASE (16 fncs) 2m 3f 189y
2:40 (2:43) (Class 4) (0-105,110) 4-Y-0+ **£3,898** (£1,144; £572; £286)

Form RPR
F456 **1** **Kayfton Pete**[47] 1376 9-11-12 **103**.......... AdamPogson 109
(Charles Pogson) *taken down early: t.k.h: mstke 1st: cl up: nt a fluent: rdn and sltly outpcd bef 2 out: rallied on inner last: styd on gamely to ld fnl 75yds* **13/2**
333 **2** ½ **Blackwood Rover (IRE)**[47] 1373 7-10-12 **89**.......... PaulMoloney 93
(J R Jenkins) *settled trcking ldrs: effrt gng wl bef 2 out: led bef last: looked wnr tl rdn and flagged 1/2-way up run-in: ct fnl 75yds* **10/3**[1]
5322 **3** 2 ¾ **Keychain (IRE)**[49] 1356 5-11-9 **100**..........(v) BrendanPowell 104
(Brendan Powell) *cl up: hit 9th: mstke 13th: drvn 2 out: tried to chal but hung rt flat: snatched 3rd but nt get in a blow at ldrs* **7/2**[2]
/0-P **4** *nk* **Michigan Assassin (IRE)**[54] 1298 13-10-13 **95**..........(p) MrBMoorcroft(5) 98
(Debra Hamer) *racd keenly in ld: j.lft 4th: blnd 13th: rdn 2 out: hdd last: plugged on same pce and jst lost 3rd* **7/1**
-U23 **5** *shd* **Dr Anubis (IRE)**[124] 699 10-9-10 **78** oh11 ow1.......... DannyBurton(5) 81
(Dai Burchell) *reluctant to line up: wl in tch tl hit 3 out and rdn: rallied after next: kpt on wl after last wout quite threatening* **6/1**
6246 **6** 9 **Try Catch Me (IRE)**[12] 1720 10-11-3 **101**..........(b) HarryCobden(7) 97
(Alison Batchelor) *pressed ldr and t.k.h: mstkes: nrly uns at 10th and rdr briefly lost an iron: cajoled along bef 2 out: finding little whn hit last* **14/1**
660- **7** 17 **Vent Nivernais (FR)**[221] 4606 6-11-4 **95**.......... LiamTreadwell 78
(James Evans) *last pair: wl in tch tl hit 3 out and rdn: sn dropped out* **4/1**[3]
5m 3.4s (-1.90) **Going Correction** -0.425s/f (Good) **7** Ran SP% **112.1**
Speed ratings (Par 105): **86,85,84,84,84 80,74**
CSF £27.84 CT £86.98 TOTE £7.00: £4.30, £1.40; EX 35.20 Trifecta £141.30.
Owner Wordingham Plant Hire & Partner **Bred** Hatton **Trained** Farnsfield, Notts
FOCUS
Any one of six still held a chance taking the second-last in what was an open handicap chase. The winner was close to the best of his spring form.

1895 32RED ON THE APP STORE NOVICES' HURDLE (10 hdls) 2m 3f 137y
3:10 (3:12) (Class 4) 4-Y-0+ **£3,898** (£1,144; £572; £286)

Form RPR
21 **1** **Nabucco**[100] 912 6-11-5 128.......... AidanColeman 137+
(John Ferguson) *confidently rdn in rr: wnt 2nd after 7th: cruised into ld bef 2 out: sn clr: hrd hld* **1/5**[1]
2 11 **Ballyarthur (IRE)**[255] 5-10-12 0..........(t) SamTwiston-Davies 116+
(Nigel Twiston-Davies) *t.k.h: hit 1st: disp 2nd tl led 6th: rdn and hdd bef 2 out: no match for wnr after: hit last and nt given hrd time flat* **5/1**[2]
3 13 **Baltic Storm (IRE)**[170] 4-10-12 0.......... GavinSheehan 103
(Charlie Mann) *settled trcking ldrs: effrt in 8 l 3rd whn hit 2 out: no ch w ldrs after* **12/1**
\- **4** 15 **Denboy (IRE)** 5-10-12 0.......... BrendanPowell 84
(Jamie Snowden) *disp 2nd tl 1/2-way: outpcd and mstke 6th: lft bhd bef 3 out: flattened last* **10/1**[3]
P-0P **P** **Leith Hill (IRE)**[10] 1752 5-10-12 0..........(b[1]) TomCannon
(Laura Mongan) *blnd 1st: bhd tl v brief effrt bef 6th: t.o next: p.u 3 out* **150/1**
5P **P** **Dr Izzymoo (IRE)**[14] 1693 6-10-12 0.......... PeterCarberry
(Jennie Candlish) *nt jump wl: led tl hdd and hit 6th: bdly t.o whn p.u after 3 out* **100/1**
4m 41.1s (-17.90) **Going Correction** -0.675s/f (Firm)
WFA 4 from 5yo+ 10lb **6** Ran SP% **118.4**
Speed ratings (Par 105): **108,103,98,92,**
CSF £2.27 TOTE £1.20: £1.10, £2.10; EX 2.00 Trifecta £5.00.
Owner Bloomfields **Bred** Darley **Trained** Cowlinge, Suffolk
FOCUS
Little depth to this novice event and it played out as the market suggested it would. The winner set a decent standard and has the potential to rate a lot higher.

1896 WEATHERBYS HAMILTON CHASE (A NOVICES' LIMITED H'CAP) (16 fncs) 2m 3f 189y
3:40 (3:43) (Class 4) (0-120,119) 4-Y-0+ **£6,498** (£1,908; £954; £477)

Form RPR
F243 **1** **Cayman Islands**[19] 1639 7-10-11 **115**.......... MrAlexFerguson(7) 127+
(John Ferguson) *led fr 4th: rdn 2 out: over 3 l clr last: gazing arnd but nvr had a chalr fr last* **5/1**[3]

-333 **2** *6* **Vinnie The Fish (IRE)**[43] 1416 7-10-11 **108**....................(p) RobertDunne 115
(Dai Burchell) *hld up last: blnd 5th: pushed into 2nd bef 2 out: drvn and wl hld fr last* **8/1**

43-3 **3** *17* **Verano (GER)**[154] 259 6-11-8 **119**....................(t) HarrySkelton 117+
(Dan Skelton) *last pair: blnd 8th: rdn 3 out: lost tch tamely bef next* **7/4**[2]

1P3- **4** *13* **Red Tortue (IRE)**[197] 5066 6-11-6 **117**.................... RichardJohnson 101
(Charlie Longsdon) *led tl mstke 4th: pressed wnr: outj. 12th: ev ch tl lost tch v tamely bef 2 out: sn eased* **5/4**[1]

4m 53.8s (-11.50) **Going Correction** -0.425s/f (Good)
WFA 4 from 6yo+ 10lb **4** Ran SP% **108.6**
Speed ratings (Par 105): **106,103,96,91**
CSF £30.63 TOTE £4.80; EX 12.50 Trifecta £42.40.
Owner Bloomfields **Bred** Granham Farm And P Hearson Bloodstock **Trained** Cowlinge, Suffolk
■ Stewards' Enquiry : Mr Alex Ferguson caution: careless riding

FOCUS
The two at the head of the market failed to jump with any conviction and so this ultimately took little winning. A chase personal best for the winner under a claimer.

1897 £10 FREE AT 32RED.COM H'CAP HURDLE (12 hdls) 3m 1f 10y
4:10 (4:11) (Class 4) (0-110,110) 4-Y-0+ **£3,249** (£954; £477; £238)

Form RPR

P312 **1** **Presence Felt (IRE)**[47] 1375 7-11-6 **104**....................(v) RichardJohnson 116+
(Jonjo O'Neill) *trckd ldrs: 3rd and gng wl 9th: led bef 3 out and qckly wnt clr: in no real danger after: j.rt last: rdn out* **11/4**[1]

0-2U **2** *11* **Vendredi Trois (FR)**[21] 1615 6-11-7 **105**.................... GavinSheehan 108
(Emma Lavelle) *a 2nd or 3rd: rdn to chse wnr who was already gng clr bef 3 out: no imp after: j.rt last* **6/1**[3]

13FP **3** *6* **The Kings Assassin (IRE)**[29] 1547 7-11-2 **100**....................(p) TomCannon 97
(Chris Gordon) *hld up and bhd: effrt 9th: drvn next: no ch w ldng pair fr bef 2 out* **22/1**

3451 **4** *2 ¼* **Amber Flush**[9] 1771 6-10-10 **101** 7ex.................... MrJamesSmith(7) 96
(Martin Smith) *led tl hdd bef 3 out: rdn and outpcd in 15 l 3rd at next: plugged on* **15/2**

2345 **5** *1 ¼* **Stay In My Heart (IRE)**[9] 1771 6-10-4 **95**.................... PaddyBradley(7) 88
(Laura Mongan) *hld up and bhd: plugged past btn horses after 3 out: nvr nr ldrs* **33/1**

6031 **6** *nk* **Spending Time**[29] 1547 6-11-6 **104**....................(tp) BrendanPowell 97
(David Pipe) *hld up: hdwy 8th: wnt 4th and drvn 3 out: little rspnse: wl hld next* **4/1**[2]

2-00 **7** *2 ½* **Orsm**[10] 1756 8-10-6 **90**....................(t) LeightonAspell 81
(Laura Mongan) *chsd ldrs tl rdn 9th: wknd after next* **50/1**

-00P **8** *hd* **Tales Of Milan (IRE)**[12] 1722 8-11-9 **110**....................(p) TomBellamy(3) 101
(Phil Middleton) *pressed ldr tl rdn 9th: lost pl qckly bef next* **16/1**

46-5 **9** *nk* **Bourne**[41] 1455 9-11-9 **107**....................(b) WayneHutchinson 97
(Donald McCain) *midfield: rdn bef 8th where nt fluent: fnd little after and wl btn 3 out* **11/1**

5640 **10** *12* **Little Windmill (IRE)**[14] 1692 5-11-7 **105**....................(t) TrevorWhelan 85
(Neil King) *a bhd: rdn and struggling 9th* **20/1**

300- **11** *15* **Giveitachance (IRE)**[178] 5400 8-11-5 **103**....................(t) NickScholfield 69
(Claire Dyson) *midfield: rdn and lost pl 8th: t.o* **18/1**

2216 **P** **Steel Gold (IRE)**[58] 1273 9-9-13 **88**.................... ConorRing(5)
(John Upson) *j. slowly 3rd: cl up tl lost pl and rdn 7th: t.o bef 3 out: p.u next* **16/1**

116P **P** **Pennant Dancer**[47] 1375 8-11-2 **100**....................(t) PaulMoloney
(Debra Hamer) *last trio: pushed along 8th: t.o bef 3 out: p.u next* **25/1**

33-4 **P** **Dardanella**[123] 711 8-11-9 **107**.................... DaveCrosse
(Hugo Froud) *bhd: mstke 7th: rdn next: t.o 9th: p.u 3 out* **33/1**

6m 3.2s (-19.70) **Going Correction** -0.675s/f (Firm) **14** Ran SP% **118.9**
Speed ratings (Par 105): **104,100,98,97,97 97,96,96,96,92 87,,,**
CSF £17.58 CT £306.64 TOTE £3.20: £2.20, £2.40, £5.10; EX 19.60 Trifecta £1394.50 Part won. Pool: £1,859.41 - 0.97 winning units..
Owner Mrs Peter Bond **Bred** Pete Roche **Trained** Cheltenham, Gloucs

FOCUS
Not as competitive as the field size suggested, with the favourite a clear-cut winner. The winner is rated back to his best.

1898 32REDSPORT.COM MAIDEN HURDLE (8 hdls) 1m 7f 171y
4:40 (4:42) (Class 5) 3-Y-0+ **£2,274** (£667; £333; £166)

Form RPR

1 **Great Hall**[38] 5-11-10 0.................... BrianHughes 111+
(Kevin Frost) *hld up: effrt gng wl 5th: delayed effrt fr 2 out tl led after last: impeded briefly: hung lft and drvn out: all out* **9/2**[2]

4-1 **2** *½* **Ballinure (IRE)**[146] 407 5-11-7 0.................... JeremiahMcGrath(3) 108+
(Nicky Henderson) *prom: led 2 out: pushed along and wnt rt last: hdd and wnt lft flat: no ex fnl 75yds* **2/1**[1]

0 **3** *6* **Bold Henmie (IRE)**[25] 1568 4-11-7 0.................... BrianToomey(3) 102
(Philip Kirby) *prom: slt ld bef 2 ou where hdd: stl ev ch bef last: kpt on same pce flat* **250/1**

4 *2 ½* **Baratineur (FR)**[171] 4-11-10 0.................... HarrySkelton 102+
(Dan Skelton) *plld hrd: nt a fluent: settled towards rr: effrt 3 out: 5th and rdn bef next: no imp after* **9/2**[2]

5 *1 ¼* **Willy Brennan (IRE)**[8] 4-11-7 0....................(t) JamesBanks(3) 100
(Jo Davis) *plld hrd: led at mod pce: rdn and hdd bef 2 out: plugged on and sn btn* **66/1**

11 **6** *½* **Alyasan (IRE)**[54] 1300 4-11-10 0....................(t[1]) NoelFehily 98
(Seamus Durack) *nt fluent: hld up towards rr: effrt after 5th: rdn next: little rspnse: sn btn* **2/1**[1]

5U- **7** *8* **Allnecessaryforce (FR)**[300] 3146 5-11-10 0.................... KielanWoods 90
(Alex Hales) *dropped out in last pair: in tch in tight bunch tl after 5th: sn wknd* **20/1**[3]

8 *7* **Galuppi**[42] 4-11-10 0.................... PaulMoloney 83
(J R Jenkins) *towards rr: hung lft bef 3 out: no ch after* **33/1**

P5- **9** *1* **Perfect Timing (FR)**[296] 3206 5-11-3 0.................... LiamTreadwell 75
(Paul Webber) *towards rr: struggling bef 3 out* **66/1**

P6 **10** *12* **Dragon City**[21] 1613 5-11-10 0....................(t) GavinSheehan 70
(Charlie Mann) *cl up: pushed along after 5th: dropped out tamely* **100/1**

- **11** *3 ¼* **Notebook**[199] 4-11-10 0....................(p) LeightonAspell 68
(Martin Smith) *midfield: hit 3rd: handy tl fdd bef 3 out: t.o* **66/1**

12 *½* **Music Hall (FR)**[21] 5-11-10 0.................... TrevorWhelan 66
(Shaun Harris) *nvr bttr than midfield: struggling whn hit 3 out: t.o* **250/1**

0- **13** *18* **Luna Nuova (IRE)**[238] 4289 5-11-3 0.................... TomMessenger 41
(Chris Bealby) *bhd: rdn and lost tch whn mstke 3 out: t.o* **66/1**

3m 43.9s (-11.00) **Going Correction** -0.675s/f (Firm) **13** Ran SP% **118.5**
Speed ratings (Par 103): **100,99,96,95,94 94,90,87,86,80 79,78,69**
CSF £13.88 TOTE £5.30: £2.00, £1.30, £9.90; EX 19.10 Trifecta £702.30.
Owner Carl Hinchy **Bred** Aston House Stud **Trained** Red Hill, Warwickshire

FOCUS
An interesting maiden hurdle, with a few promising types lining up, and it was a useful ex-Flat racer who came out on top. The gallop was a moderate one. The first are two probably capable of rating a fair bit higher.
T/Plt: £162.70 to a £1 stake. Pool: £50,489.89 - 226.42 winning tickets. T/Qpdt: £26.90 to a £1 stake. Pool: £3,447.74 - 94.50 winning tickets. **Iain Mackenzie**

516 WETHERBY (L-H)
Wednesday, October 14

OFFICIAL GOING: Good to soft (good in places) changing to good (good to soft in places) after race 1 (2:10)
Wind: light 1/2 against Weather: fine

1899 SPINAL RESEARCH RACHEL WRIGHT MEMORIAL JUVENILE MAIDEN HURDLE (9 hdls) 2m
2:10 (2:11) (Class 5) 3-Y-0 **£2,599** (£763; £381; £190)

Form RPR

1 **Our Thomas (IRE)**[18] 3-10-12 0.................... BrianHughes 94+
(Tim Easterby) *hld up in mid-div: hdwy to trck ldrs 3 out: chal and wnt lft last: styd on to ld post* **1/1**[1]

2 *nse* **The Lampo Genie**[46] 3-10-12 0.................... HenryBrooke 93+
(K R Burke) *chsd ldrs: led appr 2 out: jnd last: hdd post* **11/1**

0 **3** *6* **No Rum (IRE)**[18] 1656 3-10-12 0....................(p) AdamWedge 86
(Olly Williams) *led: hdd appr 2 out: kpt on same pce* **66/1**

4 *2 ½* **Quill Art**[257] 3-10-12 0.................... BrianHarding 84
(Richard Fahey) *mid-div: chsd ldrs 5th: one pce appr 2 out: blnd last* **17/2**

5 *2 ¼* **Stormin Tom (IRE)**[13] 3-10-12 0.................... JamesReveley 83
(Tim Easterby) *hld up in rr: nt fluent 5th: hdwy 3 out: hit 2 out: kpt on one pce* **4/1**[2]

6 *hd* **Poet Mark (IRE)**[29] 3-10-12 0.................... JakeGreenall 82
(Tim Easterby) *mid-div: chsd ldrs 3rd: one pce fr 3 out* **33/1**

7 *nk* **Harley Rebel**[163] 3-10-12 0.................... NoelFehily 81
(Neil Mulholland) *hld up in rr: j. slowly 4th: kpt on fr 3 out: nvr a factor* **6/1**[3]

0 **8** *1 ½* **Hey Bob (IRE)**[41] 1456 3-10-9 0.................... TonyKelly(3) 80
(Chris Grant) *t.k.h in rr: sme hdwy after 6th: hung lft and j.lft last 3: nvr a factor* **150/1**

0 **9** *8* **Danny O'Ruairc (IRE)**[21] 1631 3-10-7 0.................... DiarmuidO'Regan(5) 71
(James Moffatt) *mid-div: hit 1st: chsd ldrs 5th: lost pl 3 out* **28/1**

0 **10** *¾* **Bond Starprincess**[21] 1631 3-10-2 0.................... AdamNicol(3) 63
(George Moore) *t.k.h in rr: hdwy 5th: chsng ldrs after next: lost pl appr 3 out* **100/1**

40 **11** *1 ¼* **Sarafina**[21] 1631 3-10-5 0.................... SeanQuinlan 62
(David Thompson) *chsd ldrs: wknd bef 2 out* **100/1**

12 *1* **Lord Of Words (IRE)**[45] 3-10-9 0....................(t) JohnKington(3) 68
(Patrick Holmes) *w ldr: wknd between last 2* **125/1**

F **Angrove Fatrascal**[18] 3-10-9 0.................... JoeColliver(3)
(Micky Hammond) *chsd ldrs: fell 2nd* **250/1**

3m 58.9s (3.10) **Going Correction** -0.925s/f (Hard) **13** Ran SP% **114.9**
Speed ratings (Par 101): **55,54,51,50,49 49,49,48,44,44 43,43,**
CSF £13.00 TOTE £2.00: £1.20, £3.00, £8.50; EX 13.20 Trifecta £641.20.
Owner Trevor Hemmings **Bred** Gleahill House Stud Ltd **Trained** Great Habton, N Yorks

FOCUS
All rails at innermost position and all races run over new official distances. This opening juvenile event was steadily run yet the form is worth viewing positively with the first pair going clear after the last. The time was very slow compared with the later handicap.

1900 WATCH ON THE RACING UK APP NOVICES' CHASE (16 fncs) 2m 3f 85y
2:40 (2:43) (Class 4) 4-Y-0+ **£3,898** (£1,144; £572; £286)

Form RPR

405/ **1** **Twelve Roses**[581] 4750 7-11-4 0.................... DavidBass 140+
(Kim Bailey) *trckd ldrs: upsides 4 out: led next: abt 3 l clr 100yds out: drvn and jst hld on* **4/1**

201- **2** *½* **Southfield Royale**[197] 5085 5-11-4 0.................... NoelFehily 140+
(Neil Mulholland) *blnd 3rd: trckd ldrs 8th: drvn and outpcd 12th: chsng ldrs 3 out: 2nd next: styd on clsng stages: jst hld* **2/1**[1]

P3-3 **3** *5* **Kilgefin Star (IRE)**[151] 329 7-11-4 125.................... BrianHughes 134
(Michael Smith) *w ldr: upsides 10th: hit next: upsides 4 out: outpcd 2 out: kpt on to take 3rd closinng stages* **16/1**

223- **4** *1 ½* **The Grey Taylor (IRE)**[235] 4360 6-11-4 0.................... WillKennedy 134+
(Brian Ellison) *led: hdd 3 out: outpcd between last 2: wknd last 75yds* **7/2**[3]

50P- **5** *33* **Spirit Of Shankly**[188] 5241 7-11-4 0....................(p) RichardJohnson 110
(Charlie Longsdon) *chsd ldrs: blnd 8th: drvn and rallied 12th: lost pl next: sn bhd: t.o* **11/4**[2]

P-P **P** **Shabach (IRE)**[12] 1739 8-11-4 0....................(b[1]) JakeGreenall
(Mark Walford) *detached in last: hit 1st 2: shkn up 7th: t.o 12th: p.u bef 4 out* **300/1**

4m 47.8s (-20.00) **Going Correction** -0.975s/f (Hard) **6** Ran SP% **108.4**
Speed ratings (Par 105): **103,102,100,100,86**
CSF £12.04 TOTE £5.00: £1.90, £2.30; EX 14.00 Trifecta £62.00.
Owner Jones Broughtons Wilson Weaver **Bred** Coln Valley Stud **Trained** Andoversford, Gloucs

FOCUS
A definite sign the novice chase division is hotting up. The first two can rate higher than the bare form.

1901 RACING UK 1 PRICE 3 DEVICES NOVICES' HURDLE 2m 3f 154y
3:15 (3:15) (Class 4) 4-Y-0+ **£3,249** (£954; £477; £238)

Form RPR

5-22 **1** **Mustmeetalady (IRE)**[19] 1648 5-10-12 124.................... NoelFehily 123
(Jonjo O'Neill) *hld up in mid-div: trckd ldrs 5th: upsides 2 out: styd on run-in: led post* **3/1**[2]

0- **2** *nse* **Dalia Pour Moi (FR)**[311] 6-10-12 0.................... RichardJohnson 123+
(Philip Hobbs) *trckd ldrs: t.k.h: led narrowly 2 out: hdd post* **6/1**[3]

13-1 **3** *9* **Potters Corner (IRE)**[14] 1698 5-11-5 0.................... TomO'Brien 125+
(Paul Morgan) *led: nt jump wl: drvn whn blnd 3 out: hdd next: wknd last* **4/6**[1]

4 *nk* **Kid Valentine (IRE)**[199] 5-10-12 0.................... DannyCook 116
(Michael Smith) *trckd ldrs: drvn 3 out: outpcd appr next: kpt on run-in* **25/1**

22-1 **5** *22* **Wolf Sword (IRE)**[160] 155 6-11-5 118.................... HenryBrooke 108
(George Moore) *hld up in rr: nt fluent: hdwy 7th: chsng ldrs next: lost pl appr 2 out* **9/1**

0-2 6 *10* **Hillview Lad (IRE)**[166] 56 7-10-12 0 .... AdamWedge 86
(Nick Kent) *in rr: outpcd and lost pl 8th: bhd next: wl bhd whn hit last* 33/1

00- 7 *42* **Wayward Sun (IRE)**[201] 5020 4-10-2 0 .... FinianO'Toole(10) 48
(Micky Hammond) *in rr: hdwy 7th: lost pl next: sn bhd: t.o 3 out* 100/1

6 8 *4 1/2* **Inchcolm (IRE)**[12] 1740 5-10-9 0 .... JoeColliver(3) 44
(Micky Hammond) *mid-div: pushed along 6th: lost pl 8th: sn bhd: t.o next* 100/1

9 *hd* **Robinshill (IRE)** 4-10-9 0 .... RyanHatch(3) 44
(Nigel Twiston-Davies) *chsd ldrs: hit 8th: sn lost pl: bhd whn blnd next: sn t.o* 28/1

4m 40.9s (-26.10) **Going Correction** -0.925s/f (Hard)
WFA 4 from 5yo+ 10lb **9** Ran SP% **121.5**
Speed ratings (Par 105): **115,114,111,111,102 98,81,79,79**
CSF £21.06 TOTE £4.20: £1.20, £2.10, £1.10; EX 20.60 Trifecta £49.00.
Owner Ms Diane Carr **Bred** Clongiffin Stud **Trained** Cheltenham, Gloucs

FOCUS
An interesting novice event, run at a fair gallop. It was another race where two came well clear. The winner set the level.

1902 BOBBY RENTON H'CAP CHASE (16 fncs) 2m 3f 85y
3:50 (3:50) (Class 3) (0-135,134) 4-Y-O+
£6,256 (£1,848; £924; £462; £231; £116)

Form RPR

12P- 1 **Village Vic (IRE)**[193] 5137 8-11-3 **125** .... RichardJohnson 137+
(Philip Hobbs) *chsd ldrs: lft in ld 3rd: drvn 3 out: hit last: sn jnd: fnd ex nr fin* 11/4[1]

433- 2 *nk* **Upepito (FR)**[222] 4607 7-11-4 **126** .... (t) HarrySkelton 136+
(Dan Skelton) *trckd ldng pair: hit 6th: handy 2nd 12th: upsides 2 out: no ex nr fin* 3/1[2]

623- 3 *3/4* **Final Assault (IRE)**[179] 5388 6-11-4 **129** .... DerekFox(3) 138
(Lucinda Russell) *hld up in rr: stdy hdwy 9th: 4th and styng on whn hit 4 out: 3rd next: styd on to chal last 75yds: kpt on same pce clsng stages* 11/2

0-44 4 *11* **Foundation Man (IRE)**[100] 927 8-11-0 **122** .... (v) NoelFehily 121
(Jonjo O'Neill) *chsd ldrs: lft 2nd 3rd: pushed along 4 out: wknd between last 2* 5/1[3]

44-4 5 *13* **Bonzo Bing (IRE)**[12] 1741 7-10-9 **117** .... HenryBrooke 103
(Martin Todhunter) *in rr: hdwy to chse ldrs 9th: sn lost pl and bhd* 12/1

25-P 6 *hd* **Carrigdhoun (IRE)**[152] 318 10-11-3 **130** .... (t) DaraghBourke(5) 116
(Maurice Barnes) *chsd ldrs: reminders 7th: lost pl 4 out* 14/1

-130 7 *12* **Houndscourt (IRE)**[88] 1032 8-10-2 **110** .... BrianHughes 86
(Joanne Foster) *in rr: bhd fr 10th* 16/1

PF5- 8 *2* **Distime (IRE)**[228] 4484 9-11-3 **125** .... DavidEngland 102
(Richard Drake) *prom: drvn and lost pl 8th: bhd fr 4 out: 7th whn blnd and rdr briefly lost iron last* 40/1

0U6/ U **Kauto Stone (FR)**[536] 5570 9-11-12 **134** .... DavidBass
(Ben Pauling) *led: mstke and uns rdr 3rd* 14/1

P4-P P **Swift Arrow (IRE)**[28] 1553 9-11-0 **127** .... (t) JamesCowley(5)
(Donald McCain) *in rr: bhd and drvn 7th: t.o 4 out: p.u bef 2 out* 66/1

4m 44.8s (-23.00) **Going Correction** -0.975s/f (Hard) **10** Ran SP% **114.6**
Speed ratings (Par 107): **109,108,108,103,98 98,93,92, ,**
CSF £11.72 CT £41.06 TOTE £3.10: £1.50, £1.60, £1.80; EX 11.70 Trifecta £34.00.
Owner Alan Peterson **Bred** Tom Curran **Trained** Withycombe, Somerset

FOCUS
There was no hanging about in this fair handicap and the form is strong. A chase best from the winner.

1903 BET365 CHARLIE HALL MEETING 30/31 OCTOBER H'CAP HURDLE (12 hdls) 2m 5f 56y
4:25 (4:25) (Class 3) (0-140,129) 4-Y-O+ £5,523 (£1,621; £810; £405)

Form RPR

U1-0 1 **Lord Wishes (IRE)**[152] 319 8-11-2 **124** .... (p) DaleIrving(5) 128+
(James Ewart) *chsd ldrs: led appr 3 out: drvn out* 14/1

34P- 2 *1 3/4* **L'Aigle Royal (GER)**[172] 5539 4-11-11 **128** .... RichardJohnson 129
(John Quinn) *hld up in rr: hdwy to trck ldrs 9th: handy 2nd 2 out: styd on same pce run-in* 13/2

14-1 3 *5* **Crazy Jack (IRE)**[19] 1648 7-11-8 **125** .... DavidBass 123+
(Kim Bailey) *chsd ldrs: kpt on one pce fr 2 out: tk 3rd last 50yds* 9/2[2]

423- 4 *1 1/4* **Racing Europe (IRE)**[180] 5362 6-11-11 **128** .... WillKennedy 126
(Brian Ellison) *chsd ldrs: pushed along 9th: one pce fr 2 out* 11/4[1]

602- 5 *10* **Rival D'Estruval (FR)**[221] 4621 10-11-8 **125** .... JamesReveley 112
(Pauline Robson) *in rr-div: hdwy to chse ldrs 9th: one pce fr next: eased between last 2* 20/1

0U2/ 6 *1 1/4* **Now This Is It (IRE)**[42] 1569 11-11-3 **127** .... MrBGCrawford(7) 114
(S R B Crawford, Ire) *t.k.h in rr: hdwy 4th: w ldr next: led 8th: hdd sn after next: wknd and eased between last 2* 16/1

/53- 7 *5* **Walk On Al (IRE)**[322] 2740 7-11-7 **124** .... HarrySkelton 105
(Dan Skelton) *in rr: sme drvn and hdwy 9th: lost pl 2 out* 5/1[3]

34-3 8 *4 1/2* **Lackamon**[142] 471 10-10-7 **117** .... MrRHogg(7) 96
(Sue Smith) *chsd ldrs: lost pl and mstke 7th: sn bhd* 16/1

4-32 9 *hd* **Bowie (IRE)**[131] 624 8-11-8 **125** .... AdamWedge 102
(Nick Kent) *in rr-div: bhd fr 9th* 20/1

220- 10 *4 1/2* **Western Jo (IRE)**[181] 5357 7-11-12 **129** .... DavidEngland 102
(Alan Brown) *in rr: reminders and sme hdwy 9th: sn lost pl* 20/1

0-44 11 *7* **Dr Irv**[18] 1661 6-10-1 **107** .... JoeColliver(3) 78
(Micky Hammond) *led: nt fluent 2nd: hdd 8th: led sn after next: hdd appr 3 out: sn lost pl: lame* 12/1

-130 12 *52* **Fleet Dawn**[18] 1661 9-10-9 **119** .... RyanDay(7) 39
(John Wainwright) *in rr: bhd fr 9th: t.o 2 out: virtually p.u* 100/1

-F0P P **Arctic Court (IRE)**[21] 1628 11-11-0 **117** .... BrianHarding
(Jim Goldie) *chsd ldrs: drvn 7th: sn lost pl: bhd fr 9th: p.u bef next* 100/1

5m 2.8s (-24.00) **Going Correction** -0.925s/f (Hard)
WFA 4 from 6yo+ 10lb **13** Ran SP% **117.2**
Speed ratings (Par 107): **108,107,105,104,101 100,98,97,96,95 92,72,**
CSF £95.54 CT £482.01 TOTE £17.10: £5.60, £2.80, £1.90; EX 150.80 Trifecta £2680.70 Part won..
Owner Leeds Plywood And Doors Ltd **Bred** Mrs M O'Driscoll **Trained** Langholm, Dumfries & G'way

FOCUS
They went a sound gallop in this modest handicap and got sorted out from the third-last. The top weight was rated 11lb below the race ceiling but it's still fair form.

1904 RACING UK ANYWHERE AVAILABLE NOW H'CAP CHASE (13 fncs) 1m 7f 36y
4:55 (4:57) (Class 3) (0-130,130) 4-Y-O+ £6,498 (£1,908; £954; £477)

Form RPR

3325 1 **Oliver's Gold**[28] 1554 7-11-2 **120** .... (p) JakeGreenall 130+
(Mark Walford) *mid-div: hdwy appr 4 out: handy 3rd 3 out: 2nd last: led last 150yds: styd on wl* 12/1

5-14 2 *2 1/4* **Notnowsam**[155] 261 4-10-8 **122** .... (p) HarrySkelton 121+
(Dan Skelton) *led to 3rd: pushed along 6th: led bef 4 out: hdd briefly 3 out: hdd last 150yds: kpt on same pce* 11/4[2]

-226 3 *1* **Muwalla**[10] 1773 8-9-13 **108** .... (t) CallumBewley(5) 115
(Lisa Harrison) *chsd ldrs: led briefly 3 out: kpt on same pce appr last* 17/2[3]

06-2 4 *1 1/2* **Such A Legend**[165] 84 7-11-8 **126** .... DavidBass 132
(Kim Bailey) *chsd ldrs: kpt on same pce fr 2 out* 9/4[1]

2044 5 *nk* **Claragh Native (IRE)**[37] 1494 10-10-6 **110** .... (p) HenryBrooke 115
(Martin Todhunter) *in rr: kpt on fr 3 out: styd on run-in* 16/1

01F4 6 *2 1/4* **Jack The Gent (IRE)**[28] 1553 11-10-7 **111** .... RichieMcLernon 114
(George Moore) *w ldr: led 3rd: hdd bef 4 out: one pce fr 2 out* 20/1

4-PP 7 *11* **Indian Voyage (IRE)**[152] 315 7-11-2 **125** .... (t) DaraghBourke(5) 118
(Maurice Barnes) *mid-div: outpcd 9th: wknd appr 2 out* 20/1

F0-5 8 *hd* **Kilronan High (IRE)**[19] 1642 6-11-2 **123** .... (t) RyanHatch(3) 117
(Nigel Twiston-Davies) *chsd ldrs: drvn 9th: lost pl next: bhd fr 3 out* 25/1

5/13 P **Run With The Wind (IRE)**[36] 1502 9-11-12 **130** .... (t) RichardJohnson
(S R B Crawford, Ire) *in rr: nt fluent: sme hdwy whn blnd 9th: lost pl next: heavily eased 3 out: t.o whn p.u bef next* 12/1

4543 P **Midnight Game**[39] 1479 8-11-2 **120** .... WillKennedy
(Brian Ellison) *in rr: bhd and drvn 8th: t.o whn p.u bef 2 out* 12/1

F-25 F **Vengeur De Guye (FR)**[124] 709 6-11-6 **127** .... (t) DerekFox(3) 127
(Lucinda Russell) *in rr: sme hdwy 4 out: 7th and one pce whn fell 2 out* 16/1

3m 41.6s (-14.20) **Going Correction** -0.975s/f (Hard) **11** Ran SP% **116.2**
Speed ratings (Par 107): **98,96,96,95,95 94,88,88, ,**
CSF £45.00 CT £304.23 TOTE £14.50: £3.10, £1.70, £2.10; EX 57.40 Trifecta £433.20.
Owner CW Racing Club & Partner **Bred** Bearstone Stud Ltd **Trained** Sheriff Hutton, N Yorks

FOCUS
A fair handicap, run at a reasonable gallop. Sound-looking form.

1905 WATCH RACING UK ANYWHERE H'CAP HURDLE (8 hdls 1 omitted) 2m
5:25 (5:27) (Class 3) (0-135,133) 3-Y-O+ £5,523 (£1,621; £810; £405)

Form RPR

444- 1 **Superb Story (IRE)**[188] 5245 4-10-13 **120** .... HarrySkelton 132+
(Dan Skelton) *hld up in rr: stdy hdwy 4 out: cl 2nd next: led 2 out: hit last: styd on wl* 4/1[1]

211- 2 *2 1/4* **Mad Jack Mytton (IRE)**[177] 5428 5-11-11 **132** .... RichardJohnson 138+
(Jonjo O'Neill) *hld up in rr: hdwy whn sltly hmpd 4 out: trcking ldrs next: upsides 2 out: sn drvn: kpt on same pce run-in* 4/1[1]

P6-5 3 *4* **Uriah Heep (FR)**[25] 642 6-10-10 **122** .... CallumBewley(5) 123
(R Mike Smith) *mid-div: sltly hmpd 4 out: chsng ldrs next: 3rd last: kpt on one pce* 28/1

65-0 4 *3 1/4* **Rockawango (FR)**[130] 638 9-10-12 **119** .... (tp) LucyAlexander 117
(James Ewart) *in rr: sltly hmpd 4 out: drvn and outpcd appr next: kpt on between last 2* 40/1

125- 5 *4* **Teo Vivo (FR)**[235] 4365 8-11-3 **124** .... (b) BrianHughes 118
(Pauline Robson) *t.k.h: trckd ldrs: sltly hmpd 4 out: one pce whn hit last* 16/1

25-0 6 *3/4* **Aniknam (FR)**[145] 436 5-10-12 **119** .... JamesReveley 114
(Philip Kirby) *rr-div: hdwy 4 out: chsng ldrs next: fdd last* 6/1

110- 7 *nk* **Beatabout The Bush (IRE)**[15] 4707 4-11-7 **128** .... AdamWedge 123
(Henry Oliver) *mid-div: sltly hmpd 4 out: sn chsng ldrs: fdd last* 8/1

11F- 8 *1/2* **Endless Credit (IRE)**[38] 5250 5-11-1 **132** .... FinianO'Toole(10) 125
(Micky Hammond) *chsd clr ldr: lft in ld 4 out: hdd 2 out: wknd last* 20/1

2-10 9 *64* **Another Journey**[137] 556 6-10-13 **120** .... RobertDunne 55
(Sarah-Jayne Davies) *t.k.h: trckd ldrs: drvn and sltly hmpd 4 out: sn lost pl and bhd: t.o next: eventually completed* 66/1

026- U **Kashmir Peak (IRE)**[25] 4766 6-11-5 **133** .... DeanPratt(7)
(John Quinn) *trckd ldrs: stmbld on landing 2nd and sn uns rdr* 5/1[2]

111- F **Aristo Du Plessis (FR)**[180] 5361 5-11-0 **126** .... DaleIrving(5)
(James Ewart) *led: clr 3rd: 10 l ahd whn fell 4 out* 11/2[3]

3m 43.9s (-11.90) **Going Correction** -0.925s/f (Hard)
WFA 4 from 5yo+ 9lb **11** Ran SP% **115.5**
Speed ratings (Par 107): **92,90,88,87,85 84,84,84,52,**
CSF £19.57 CT £391.23 TOTE £6.60: £1.90, £1.10, £5.40; EX 22.70 Trifecta £701.30.
Owner A Holt, J Robinson, A Taylor & S Miller **Bred** Mrs Gilles Forien **Trained** Alcester, Warwicks

FOCUS
A pair of progressive young performers fought out this competitive-looking handicap, which was well run. Big steps up from the first two.
T/Jkpt: Not won. Consolation Placepot: £118.10 to a £1 stake. Pool: £2,979.00 - 23.90 winning units. T/Plt: £21.00 to a £1 stake. Pool: £55,489.42 - 1,927.43 winning tickets T/Qpdt: £6.30 to a £1 stake. Pool: £4,359.64 - 509.02 winning tickets **Walter Glynn**

1824 WORCESTER (L-H)
Wednesday, October 14

OFFICIAL GOING: Good (6.8)
Wind: moderate half behind Weather: sunny spells

1906 WORCESTER NEWS NOVICES' LIMITED H'CAP CHASE (16 fncs) 2m 7f
2:20 (2:23) (Class 4) (0-120,120) 4-Y-O+ £3,898 (£1,144; £572; £286)

Form RPR

3P-3 1 **Bob Tucker (IRE)**[163] 109 8-11-6 **118** .... AidanColeman 128+
(Charlie Longsdon) *mde virtually all: j.rt 6th: drew clr fr 4 out: in n.d whn j.rt last: eased towards fin* 3/1[1]

060- 2 *13* **Somerset Lias (IRE)**[177] 5437 7-10-9 **107** .... LiamHeard 102+
(Bob Buckler) *hld up wl in tch: bdly hmpd 6th: mstke 9th: rdn after 12th: styd on to go 2nd flat: no ch w wnr* 40/1

65-0 3 *nk* **Trapper Peak (IRE)**[155] 261 6-11-3 **115** .... AndrewThornton 110
(Caroline Bailey) *nvr far away: rdn whn hmpd 4 out: one pce after: disp 2nd flat* 16/1

35-5 4 *3/4* **Brownville**[157] 216 6-11-8 **120** .... (t) SamTwiston-Davies 112
(Nigel Twiston-Davies) *prom: rdn after 12th: kpt on same pce* 9/2[2]

154- **5** *3* **Carn Rock**[354] 2050 7-10-7 **105**.. PeterCarberry 96
(Michael Gates) *in rr: rdn fr 9th: hdwy after 12th: lft 2nd 4 out: hld by wnr whn mstke next: stl in 2nd whn mstke last: wknd* **9/1**

312- **6** *3 1/4* **Dolores Delightful (FR)**[222] 4615 5-11-8 **120**........................ DarylJacob 107
(Nick Williams) *t.k.h: prom: hmpd 4 out: wknd 2 out* **6/1**[3]

36P- **7** *15* **Nimbus Gale (IRE)**[264] 3838 6-9-13 **107**.............. TommyDowling[(10)] 79
(Charlie Mann) *a towards rr: struggling fr 9th* **33/1**

46-5 **8** *2 1/4* **Withoutdefavourite (IRE)**[24] 1601 7-10-8 **106**.................. JamesDavies 76
(Henry Oliver) *mid-div: nt fluent 9th: rdn next: wknd after 12th* **13/2**

00-P **P** **Dream Deal**[162] 122 7-11-8 **120**.. NickScholfield
(Jeremy Scott) *chsd ldrs tl blnd and lost pl 6th: rdn 10th: sn bhd: t.o whn p.u bef 2 out* **12/1**

012- **F** **Free Of Charge (IRE)**[176] 5442 6-10-12 **110**........................ MichealNolan
(Philip Hobbs) *mid-div: hdwy after 8th: j.rt and chsd wnr 12th: 4 l 2nd and rdn whn fell 4 out* **15/2**

5m 38.3s (-11.60) **Going Correction** -0.35s/f (Good) **10** Ran SP% **111.5**
Speed ratings (Par 105): **106,101,101,101,100 98,93,92, ,**
CSF £89.43 CT £1599.83 TOTE £3.50: £1.40, £8.40, £5.20; EX 109.40 Trifecta £2174.30 Part won..
Owner Nigel M Davies **Bred** Mrs Mary Mangan **Trained** Over Norton, Oxon

FOCUS
All starts have been moved at this track following remeasuring, so there will be no speed figures here until there is sufficient data to calculate updated median times. All fences and hurdles were towards the inside, with the home turn bend on the inside line and the cathedral bend approximately 2 yards off the inside, adding about 15 yards to a 2m race. A modest handicap run at a steady gallop. The easy winner was up 10lb on his previous best, with the next five close to their hurdles marks.

1907 LEWIS BADGES H'CAP CHASE (12 fncs) 2m 110y
2:50 (2:50) (Class 4) (0-110,110) 4-Y-0+ **£3,898** (£1,144; £572; £286)

Form RPR

0- **1** **Be On Time (FR)**[167] 4-11-3 **110**.. BrendanPowell 109+
(Jamie Snowden) *trckd ldrs: rdn to chal 3 out: led and j.rt next: drvn and hld on gamely flat* **15/8**[1]

535- **2** *nk* **Helium (FR)**[156] 4731 10-11-11 **108**.. RhysFlint 116
(Alexandra Dunn) *t.k.h: cl up: led 8th: jnd 3 out: hdd next: stl ev ch last: r.o flat: jst hld* **9/1**

3213 **3** *5* **The Bay Bandit**[16] 1674 8-11-11 **108**..............................(p) MarkQuinlan 112
(Neil Mulholland) *hld up wl in tch in last pair: hdwy 4 out: rdn and ch next: styd on same pce fr 2 out* **4/1**[3]

214- **4** *9* **Take The Crown**[186] 5279 6-11-6 **103**............................ JamesDavies 99
(Henry Oliver) *reluctant ldr and set stdy pce: t.k.h: hdd 8th: styd prom and stl ev ch 3 out: wknd appr last* **11/4**[2]

313- **5** *1 1/2* **Midnight Chorister**[198] 5067 7-11-12 **109**.................(t) KielanWoods 107
(Alex Hales) *chsd ldrs: cl 5th whn blnd 4 out: one pce and hld after* **7/1**

466U **6** *28* **Private Jones**[15] 1687 6-9-9 **83** oh1............................ MikeyEnnis[(5)] 61
(Miss Imogen Pickard) *t.k.h in rr: nudged along and lost tch after 8th: no ch after but gng on flat* **16/1**

4m 31.5s (26.50) **Going Correction** -0.35s/f (Good)
WFA 4 from 6yo+ 9lb **6** Ran SP% **109.8**
Speed ratings (Par 105): **23,22,20,16,15 2**
CSF £16.83 TOTE £2.80: £1.30, £3.00; EX 17.80 Trifecta £71.10.
Owner The Folly Partnership **Bred** G Cherel, A Pacault & O Dolemieux **Trained** Lambourn, Berks
■ Stewards' Enquiry : Mikey Ennis 14-day ban: schooling on the racecourse (Oct 28-Nov 10)

FOCUS
Not a strong handicap. The runners stood still for 62 seconds after the starter dropped his flag, and the time was taken from when the leading horse passed the starter. The Stewards held an enquiry into why the riders had waited so long and noted their explanations that they had all been instructed by their trainers to drop their horses in and not to make the running. The winner should still be competitive when reassessed.

1908 WORCESTER NEWS MARES' INTERMEDIATE OPEN NATIONAL HUNT FLAT RACE 2m
3:25 (3:25) (Class 6) 4-6-Y-0 **£1,642** (£478; £239)

Form RPR

24- **1** **Girly Girl (IRE)**[181] 5359 6-10-7 0........................ BridgetAndrews[(5)] 104+
(Dan Skelton) *mde all: rdn over 1f out: r.o and a holding runner-up* **11/8**[1]

0- **2** *3/4* **Pink Play (IRE)**[181] 5359 4-10-12 0................................ GavinSheehan 104+
(Harry Whittington) *chsd ldrs: rdn to go 2nd 2f out: styd on u.p fnl f: a being hld by wnr* **12/1**

46- **3** *3 1/2* **Hoponandsee**[181] 5359 4-10-12 0.. AndrewTinkler 101
(George Baker) *mainly chsd wnr tl lost 2nd 2f out: kpt on same pce after* **11/1**

4 *1 3/4* **Zara Hope (IRE)** 4-10-12 0.. AidanColeman 99
(Charlie Longsdon) *disp 2nd tl rdn 3f out: one pce* **7/2**[2]

5 *2 1/2* **Keep Up Keira (IRE)** 4-10-12 0........................ SamTwiston-Davies 97
(Neil Mulholland) *hld up: sme hdwy 3f out: one pce fnl 2f* **7/1**

4 **6** *3/4* **The Barbury Queen (IRE)**[18] 1662 5-10-12 0.......... WayneHutchinson 96
(Alan King) *chsd ldrs: rdn over 3f out: one pce* **13/2**[3]

40 **7** *3 3/4* **A Touch Of Sass (IRE)**[56] 1289 5-10-12 0........................ JamieMoore 93
(John Spearing) *t.k.h in rr: rdn 3f out: no imp* **25/1**

5- **8** *1 1/4* **Storm Run (IRE)**[323] 2724 4-10-12 0............................ LeightonAspell 92
(Roger Teal) *hld up: rdn over 3f out: hanging rt after and no imp* **33/1**

3m 41.9s (-3.10) **Going Correction** -0.60s/f (Firm) **8** Ran SP% **113.0**
Speed ratings: **83,82,80,80,78 78,76,75**
CSF £19.47 TOTE £2.30: £1.10, £4.80, £2.30; EX 19.70 Trifecta £177.50.
Owner T Crowe **Bred** Sean McNamara **Trained** Alcester, Warwicks

FOCUS
A fair bumper run at an honest gallop. The winner set a fair standard and is probably the best guide to the level.

1909 BOOK CHRISTMAS PARTIES AT WORCESTER RACECOURSE NOVICES' HURDLE (10 hdls) 2m 4f
4:00 (4:00) (Class 4) 4-Y-0+ **£3,249** (£954; £477; £238)

Form RPR

1 **Flying Angel (IRE)** 4-10-12 0........................ SamTwiston-Davies 117+
(Nigel Twiston-Davies) *trckd ldrs: lft 2nd 3 out: led last: sn pushed clr: comf* **8/1**

4/FR **2** *7* **Cloudy Joker (IRE)**[9] 1792 7-10-12 117........................ WayneHutchinson 108+
(Donald McCain) *led: rdn 2 out: hdd last: one pce* **17/2**

1- **3** *6* **After Hours (IRE)**[186] 5285 6-10-12 0............................ JamesDavies 101
(Henry Oliver) *a.p: rdn 3 out: one pce fr 2 out* **5/2**[2]

F-5 **4** *4* **Ashtown (IRE)**[35] 1519 8-10-12 0................................ MarkQuinlan 97
(Malcolm Jones) *hld up towards rr: hdwy 3 out: sn one pce* **14/1**

5 *nk* **Agrapart (FR)**[192] 4-10-12 0.. DarylJacob 101+
(Nick Williams) *t.k.h: chsd ldrs: mstke 3 out: no hdwy and hld after* **5/1**[3]

6 *6* **Quantum Of Solace** 5-10-2 0.. JamesBanks[(3)] 84
(Noel Williams) *mid-div: rdn 3 out: no real imp* **50/1**

F0-U **7** *13* **Grey Messenger (IRE)**[4] 1844 6-10-5 0................(t) HarrisonBeswick[(7)] 80
(Emma Baker) *hld up: rdn and wknd after 7th* **250/1**

000 **8** *13* **The Bank Manager**[14] 1698 4-10-9 0............................(t) KieronEdgar[(3)] 68
(David Pipe) *hld up: pushed along 6th: wknd after next: mstke 3 out: t.o* **66/1**

54-1 **U** **Fact Of The Matter (IRE)**[14] 1704 5-10-12 0...............(t) BrendanPowell 108+
(Jamie Snowden) *mainly trckd ldr: cl 2nd whn stmbld and uns rdr 3 out* **7/4**[1]

4m 45.6s (-7.90) **Going Correction** -0.60s/f (Firm) **9** Ran SP% **113.8**
Speed ratings (Par 105): **91,88,85,84,84 81,76,71,**
CSF £70.51 TOTE £8.80: £2.50, £2.10, £1.40; EX 42.10 Trifecta £154.70.
Owner R J Rexton **Bred** Arctic Tack Stud **Trained** Naunton, Gloucs

FOCUS
The gallop was steady for this fair hurdle. The winner looks a decent prospect.

1910 R & A MASON MARES' H'CAP HURDLE (10 hdls 2 omitted) 2m 7f
4:35 (4:36) (Class 4) (0-105,103) 4-Y-0+ **£3,249** (£954; £477; £238)

Form RPR

5062 **1** **Lady Of Longstone (IRE)**[5] 1841 5-10-11 **95**................ MichaelHeard[(7)] 106+
(David Pipe) *planted herself briefly whn flag dropped: c through to ld 1st and mde rest: rdn appr 2 out: clr last: in command whn idled flat* **9/4**[1]

-121 **2** *3 3/4* **Kayla**[15] 1694 5-11-5 **103**..(t) CiaranGethings[(7)] 108
(Stuart Edmunds) *chsd ldrs: rdn after 8th: disputing 2nd whn bmpd last: kpt on but no ch w wnr* **7/2**[2]

4 **3** *3/4* **Think Of Me (IRE)**[48] 1384 6-10-13 **90**.......................[1] AlainCawley 94
(Fergal O'Brien) *hld up: hdwy 7th: rdn bef 2 out: styd on u.p to dispute 2nd flat* **16/1**

F226 **4** *6* **Midnight Sequel**[48] 1375 6-11-10 **101**........................(bt) MarkQuinlan 101
(Neil Mulholland) *mid-div tl dropped towards rr and rdn 7th: rallied 2 out: styd on* **7/1**

403- **5** *2 1/4* **Tyre Hill Lady**[164] 6-11-12 **103**.. AidanColeman 102
(David Dennis) *chsd ldrs: wnt 2nd appr 2 out tl j.rt and bmpd last: wknd* **25/1**

5622 **6** *3 3/4* **Bus Named Desire**[24] 1599 7-10-1 **85**...............(t) MrStanSheppard[(7)] 78
(Matt Sheppard) *led to 1st: styd prom: rdn bef 2 out: wknd appr last* **11/2**[3]

5-P3 **7** *nse* **Pembridge**[39] 1478 6-9-11 **77** oh7..................................(t) BenPoste[(3)] 71
(Adrian Wintle) *hld up: hdwy after 8th: pckd 2 out: one pce* **20/1**

214- **8** *23* **Tea Caddy**[173] 5510 9-11-5 **103**..............................(bt) MissPFuller[(7)] 75
(Jamie Snowden) *t.k.h: prom: chsd ldr 7th tl rdn and wknd appr 2 out* **11/1**

-046 **9** *10* **Dashul (IRE)**[16] 1673 6-11-1 **92**.. LiamHeard 55
(Jeremy Scott) *hld up in rr: rdn and wknd after 8th* **16/1**

-260 **10** *3* **Honour A Promise**[99] 934 7-11-7 **98**..............................(p) JamesBest 59
(Paul Webber) *mainly trckd wnr to 7th: rdn after next: wknd 2 out* **33/1**

00-S **11** *29* **Walk Of Gleams**[22] 1618 6-11-3 **94**.. RhysFlint 29
(Anna Newton-Smith) *towards rr: wknd 8th: t.o* **100/1**

-500 **P** **Poetic Presence (IRE)**[82] 1098 5-10-0 **77** oh8.................. JamesDavies
(Adrian Wintle) *mid-div: rdn along and reminders after 5th: lost tch 7th: t.o whn p.u bef 2 out* **66/1**

5m 33.1s (-5.50) **Going Correction** -0.60s/f (Firm) **12** Ran SP% **115.0**
Speed ratings (Par 105): **85,83,83,81,80 79,79,71,67,66 56,**
CSF £9.75 CT £98.17 TOTE £3.20: £1.20, £2.50, £4.50; EX 11.10 Trifecta £145.90.
Owner Miss S E Hartnell **Bred** David Crimmins **Trained** Nicholashayne, Devon

FOCUS
A modest contest run at a steady gallop. The winner was back to the best of his summer form.

1911 R & A MASON H'CAP HURDLE (8 hdls 2 omitted) 2m 4f
5:05 (5:05) (Class 4) (0-120,120) 3-Y-0+ **£3,249** (£954; £477; £238)

Form RPR

1212 **1** **Mont Choisy (FR)**[36] 1507 5-11-12 **120**.................. SamTwiston-Davies 134+
(Nigel Twiston-Davies) *chsd ldr tl after 1st: styd prom: rdn bef 2 out: led last: styd on wl to draw clr flat* **11/8**[1]

04-P **2** *7* **Masterplan (IRE)**[149] 378 5-10-12 **106**........................ AidanColeman 114
(Charlie Longsdon) *chsd ldrs: wnt 2nd after 1st: led after 3rd: rdn bef 2 out: hdd last: no ex* **9/2**[2]

3314 **3** *12* **Over The Air**[13] 1721 7-11-4 **112**................................ NicodeBoinville 107
(John Spearing) *hld up: hdwy 6th: sn rdn: wnt 3rd bef 2 out: no imp on ldng pair* **8/1**

1445 **4** *9* **Vaihau (FR)**[24] 1600 6-11-1 **116**................................ PatrickCowley[(7)] 106
(Jonjo O'Neill) *hld up: nt fluent 3rd: rdn and struggling 5th: styd on after next: disputing modest 3rd whn mstke 2 out: no further hdwy* **6/1**[3]

30-0 **5** *13* **Drumlee Lad (IRE)**[14] 1699 5-11-4 **115**....................(t) KieronEdgar[(3)] 90
(David Pipe) *mid-div: chsd ldng pair 6th tl wknd bef 2 out* **10/1**

U6-P **6** *53* **Hallings Comet**[19] 87 6-11-12 **120**................................ JamesDavies 47
(Adrian Wintle) *t.k.h: led: clr after 1st to 3rd: sn hdd: styd cl up: nt fluent 5th: wknd after next: t.o* **40/1**

P252 **7** *47* **Spring Steel (IRE)**[59] 1266 6-11-2 **110**................................(t) RhysFlint
(Alexandra Dunn) *hld up in rr: rdn after 5th: lost tch after next: t.o* **25/1**

030- **8** *53* **American Life (FR)**[222] 4613 8-11-12 **120**.....................(tp) PaulMoloney
(Sophie Leech) *mid-div tl dropped to last 4th: t.o fr next* **25/1**

660- **P** **So Oscar (IRE)**[174] 5496 7-11-2 **113**....................(t) ConorShoemark[(3)]
(Fergal O'Brien) *mid-div: rdn and wknd after 6th: t.o whn p.u bef 2 out* **12/1**

4m 38.5s (-15.00) **Going Correction** -0.60s/f (Firm) **9** Ran SP% **112.6**
Speed ratings (Par 105): **106,103,98,94,89 68,49,28,**
CSF £7.86 CT £34.19 TOTE £2.10: £1.10, £3.00, £1.80; EX 8.30 Trifecta £28.60.
Owner Mrs N Unsworth **Bred** Scea Ecurie Domaine De Baune **Trained** Naunton, Gloucs

FOCUS
A fair handicap in which the front two dominated. This looks a step up from the winner and it will be interesting to see how he is reassessed.

1912 R & A MASON MAIDEN HURDLE (10 hdls 2 omitted) 2m 7f
5:35 (5:35) (Class 5) 4-Y-0+ **£2,599** (£763; £381; £190)

Form RPR

0-P0 **1** **Net Work Rouge (FR)**[19] 1642 6-10-11 120..................(t) TomBellamy[(3)] 130+
(Kim Bailey) *trckd ldng pair tl wnt 2nd at 5th: led 8th: styd on wl to draw clr fr 2 out: kpt up to work flat tl eased towards fin* **7/2**[2]

24 **2** *27* **Dusk Till Dawn (IRE)**[35] 1519 6-11-0 0........................ ConorO'Farrell 101
(David Pipe) *led to 1st: trckd wnr tl lost 2nd at 5th: styd prom: rdn to go 2nd again appr 2 out: one pce and no ch w wnr* **13/2**[3]

1353 **3** *28* **Tilinisi (IRE)**[10] 1781 5-10-7 0.. KielanWoods 76
(Phil Middleton) *chsd ldrs: wnt 2nd after 8th tl rdn and wknd appr 2 out* **8/1**

4 12 **The Lizard King (IRE)**[283] 6-11-0 0........................ AidanColeman 65
(Charlie Longsdon) *a in last pair: rdn and lost tch after 8th: t.o* **25/1**

-44P 5 10 **Flash Crash**[12] [1741] 6-11-0 110........................(vt) SamTwiston-Davies 56
(Barry Brennan) *a in last pair: rdn 7th: lost tch after next: t.o* **14/1**

5-2 U **Morning Symphony (IRE)**[73] [1179] 6-11-0 0................(t) GavinSheehan 80
(Warren Greatrex) *cl up tl led 1st: hdd 8th: sn rdn: 4th and wkng whn blnd and uns rdr 2 out* **10/11**[1]

5m 28.12s (-10.48) **Going Correction** -0.60s/f (Firm) **6** Ran SP% **109.6**
Speed ratings (Par 103): **94,84,74,70,67**
CSF £23.77 TOTE £4.00: £2.30, £1.90; EX 23.20 Trifecta £92.00.
Owner John Wills & David Reid Scott Partnership **Bred** Scea Haras Des Rouges **Trained** Andoversford, Gloucs
■ Stewards' Enquiry : Tom Bellamy two-day ban: used whip when clearly winning (Oct 28-29)

FOCUS
An uncompetitive maiden hurdle but the winner did it well, taking a big step up on his previous form.
T/Plt: £37.60 to a £1 stake. Pool: £63,690.20 - 1,236.09 winning tickets T/Qpdt: £8.00 to a £1 stake. Pool: £5,923.21 - 546.16 winning tickets **Richard Lowther**

1913 - 1919a (Foreign Racing) - See Raceform Interactive

153
CARLISLE (R-H)
Thursday, October 15

OFFICIAL GOING: Good (good to firm in places; chs 7.3, hdl 7.6)
Wind: Light, half behind Weather: Cloudy, bright

1920 APOLLOBET IN PLAY BETTING CONDITIONAL JOCKEYS' H'CAP HURDLE (9 hdls) 2m 1f 33y
2:10 (2:10) (Class 4) (0-110,115) 3-Y-0+ **£3,249** (£954; £477; £238)

Form RPR

2163 1 **Endeavor**[11] [1773] 10-10-10 95........................(p) EmmaSayer(3) 102+
(Dianne Sayer) *hld up on ins: stdy hdwy bef 3 out: effrt next: led last 100yds: kpt on strly* **12/1**

3211 2 3 **Dynamic Drive (IRE)**[11] [1773] 8-11-11 115 7ex.......(t) ThomasDowson(8) 119
(Maurice Barnes) *hld up: stdy hdwy to chse ldrs 4th: led gng wl bef 2 out: 2 l up and rdn last: hung rt and hdd last 100yds: no ex* **9/2**[1]

3343 3 4 ½ **Urban Kode (IRE)**[38] [1493] 7-10-11 96...............(v) GrahamWatters(3) 96
(Lucinda Russell) *led to 4th: cl up: rdn and ev ch bef 2 out: outpcd fr last* **8/1**

0-55 4 4 ½ **Nafaath (IRE)**[45] [1421] 9-11-0 102...................(p) JamesCowley(6) 98
(Donald McCain) *w ldr: led briefly 4th: rdn bef 3 out: outpcd fr next* **8/1**

-122 5 7 **Triple Eight (IRE)**[14] [1714] 7-10-12 94........................ NathanMoscrop 86
(Philip Kirby) *prom: hdwy whn lft in ld 5th: jst hdd and rdn whn mstke 2 out: sn wknd* **5/1**[2]

6-20 6 1 ¾ **Alwaysrecommended (IRE)**[16] [1683] 6-10-0 82 oh8............ DaleIrving 70
(Jane Walton) *nt fluent in rr: pushed along 1/2-way: hdwy bef 3 out: pushed along and no imp fr next* **40/1**

0-40 7 1 ¼ **Playhara (IRE)**[142] [482] 6-11-11 107........................ CraigNichol 94
(Martin Todhunter) *cl up: rdn after 4 out: wknd bef next* **14/1**

-054 8 4 **Toola Boola**[42] [1461] 5-10-0 82 oh13................ ThomasGarner 66
(George Moore) *bhd: drvn and outpcd 4 out: sn btn* **20/1**

420- 9 1 ¾ **Not A Bother Boy (IRE)**[240] [4288] 7-10-9 101....... StephenMcCarthy(10) 83
(Sue Smith) *chsd ldrs on outside: lost pl 4th: struggling fr next* **9/2**[1]

P-66 10 15 **Triumph Davis (IRE)**[45] [1430] 6-10-7 99....... HugoThompsonBrown(10) 68
(Micky Hammond) *in tch on outside: pushed along after 3rd: wknd fr next* **20/1**

54P- 11 14 **Uplifted (IRE)**[234] [4402] 4-10-10 92........................ JoeColliver 48
(Martin Todhunter) *in tch: drvn and outpcd after 4 out: wknd bef next* **33/1**

0-34 P **Push Me (IRE)**[11] [1773] 8-11-1 102........................ BlairCampbell(5)
(Iain Jardine) *t.k.h in rr: sddle slipped forward and gd hdwy to ld after 4th: p.u bef next* **13/2**[3]

4m 8.8s (-18.90) **Going Correction** -1.30s/f (Hard)
WFA 4 from 5yo+ 9lb **12** Ran SP% **117.8**
Speed ratings (Par 105): **92,90,88,86,83 82,81,79,78,71 65,**
CSF £63.10 CT £468.55 TOTE £15.30: £3.60, £2.30, £3.20; EX 39.30 Trifecta £362.90.
Owner Mrs Margaret Coppola **Bred** Bradmill Meat Ltd **Trained** Hackthorpe, Cumbria

FOCUS
Bends moved off inside line. Races 1, 2 & 7 increased by 23yds, race 3 by 17yds, race 4 by 29yds, race 5 by 51yds and race 6 by 69yds. Lively conditions greeted the runners for the first of a seven-race card. This featured some in-form individuals and represents solid form for the grade. A tep up with the winner compared with the second on their Kelso form.

1921 DOWNLOAD YOUR RACING UK APP NOVICES' HURDLE (9 hdls) 2m 1f 33y
2:40 (2:40) (Class 4) 4-Y-0+ **£3,328** (£1,033; £556)

Form RPR

3 1 **Frederic Chopin**[21] [1634] 4-10-12 0........................ BrianHughes 108+
(James Moffatt) *trckd ldrs: shkn up to ld last: rdn and edgd rt run-in: kpt on wl* **11/4**[2]

2 4 ½ **Don'tdropmein (IRE)**[73] [1194] 5-10-12 0........................ NoelFehily 106+
(Neil Mulholland) *t.k.h: cl up: led 3rd: mstke and rdn 2 out: hdd last: kpt on same pce run-in* **4/5**[1]

120 3 23 **Sign Manual**[20] [1648] 6-11-5 119........................ BrianHarding 93
(Donald McCain) *nt fluent: led to 3rd: cl up tl rdn and wknd fr 2 out* **7/2**[3]

5-5 P **Question Of Faith**[161] [159] 4-10-5 0........................ HenryBrooke
(Martin Todhunter) *nt fluent in rr: struggling fr 1/2-way: no ch whn hit 3 out: sn p.u* **22/1**

4m 12.7s (-15.00) **Going Correction** -1.30s/f (Hard)
WFA 4 from 5yo+ 9lb **4** Ran SP% **108.8**
Speed ratings (Par 105): **83,80,70,**
CSF £5.63 TOTE £4.10; EX 6.10 Trifecta £7.60.
Owner Bowes Lodge Stables **Bred** Brook Stud **Trained** Cartmel, Cumbria

FOCUS
They came home at long intervals in this poorly contested contest. The favourite pulled away his winning chance and the form probably doesn't amount to much.

1922 BOOK YOUR CHRISTMAS PARTY HERE NOVICES' LIMITED H'CAP CHASE (12 fncs) 1m 7f 207y
3:15 (3:15) (Class 3) (0-135,134) 4-Y-0+ **£6,498** (£1,908; £954; £477)

Form RPR

0-12 1 **Germany Calling (IRE)**[144] [461] 6-11-8 134........................ AidanColeman 145+
(Charlie Longsdon) *mde virtually all: nt fluent 3rd: j. path bef 5 out: pushed along after 4 out: kpt on strly fr 2 out* **1/1**[1]

232- 2 3 **Relic Rock (IRE)**[221] [4644] 7-10-8 120........................ WillKennedy 124
(Brian Ellison) *lft chsng wnr 1st: effrt and ch 4 out: sn rdn and edgd rt: kpt on fr last: nt rch wnr* **7/2**[2]

U42F 3 12 **Fantasy King**[29] [1553] 9-10-7 124........................ DiarmuidO'Regan(5) 118
(James Moffatt) *hld up in tch: stdy hdwy and pushed along after 4 out: keeping on and 6 l 3rd whn mstke last: sn wknd* **16/1**

24-2 4 14 **Court Dismissed (IRE)**[152] [332] 5-10-7 119........................ BrianHarding 100
(Donald McCain) *prom: drvn and outpcd 5 out: struggling fr next* **7/1**

1021 5 41 **Vodka Wells (FR)**[116] [801] 5-10-13 132........................ JamieBargary(7) 76
(Micky Hammond) *hld up in tch: nt fluent 7th: rdn and outpcd bef 4 out: lost tch fr next* **4/1**[3]

0-06 U **Lucky Bridle (IRE)**[21] [1333] 6-11-1 127........................ BrianHughes
(Chris Grant) *w wnr tl blnd and uns rdr 1st* **80/1**

3m 53.7s (-22.40) **Going Correction** -1.175s/f (Hard) **6** Ran SP% **111.8**
Speed ratings (Par 107): **109,107,101,94,74**
CSF £5.19 TOTE £1.80: £1.10, £2.20; EX 6.30 Trifecta £45.40.
Owner Tyrone Hanlon **Bred** Gabriel Fahy **Trained** Over Norton, Oxon

FOCUS
An informative event, in which four of the six runners had winning claims. The market proved a key guide. A step up from the winner and there should be more to come.

1923 RACING UK ANYWHERE "NATIONAL HUNT" NOVICES' HURDLE (11 hdls) 2m 4f 8y
3:50 (3:50) (Class 4) 4-Y-0+ **£3,249** (£954; £477; £238)

Form RPR

1- 1 **Shantou Village (IRE)**[202] [5020] 5-10-12 0........................ NoelFehily 130+
(Neil Mulholland) *led to 2nd: cl up: led on bit 3 out: drew clr fr next: nt fluent last: easily* **1/4**[1]

2 19 **Delusionofgrandeur (IRE)**[193] 5-10-12 0........................ DannyCook 108
(Sue Smith) *w wnr: led 2nd: rdn and hdd 3 out: plugged on same pce fr next: no ch w easy wnr* **8/1**[3]

-614 3 7 **Lincoln County**[10] [1792] 4-10-12 0........................(p) AidanColeman 105
(John Ferguson) *nt fluent on occasions: prom: effrt and pushed along bef 3 out: mstke next: sn wknd* **3/1**[2]

35P 4 32 **Landmeafortune (IRE)**[5] [1852] 6-10-12 0........................ HenryBrooke 73
(Martin Todhunter) *hld up on outside: stdy hdwy 7th: drvn and struggling after next: btn fnl 3* **50/1**

3-P0 5 54 **Mister Hendre**[16] [1683] 7-10-12 80........................(t) BrianHughes 25
(Susan Corbett) *hld up in tch: mstke and outpcd 7th: lost tch fr next: t.o* **40/1**

00-6 P **Kicking Lily**[16] [1688] 5-9-12 0........................(t) JamieHamilton(7)
(Ann Hamilton) *t.k.h early: hld up: nt fluent 4th: struggling fr 7th: lost tch fr next: t.o whn p.u bef 2 out* **33/1**

4m 50.8s (-32.00) **Going Correction** -1.30s/f (Hard)
WFA 4 from 5yo+ 10lb **6** Ran SP% **123.5**
Speed ratings (Par 105): **112,104,101,88,67**
CSF £4.30 TOTE £1.20: £1.10, £3.40; EX 4.30 Trifecta £6.50.
Owner Mrs Jane Gerard-Pearse **Bred** Mrs Mary F Griffin **Trained** Limpley Stoke, Wilts

FOCUS
This was turned into a procession by the long odds-on favourite. He stood out on his bumper win and should develop into a 135+ hurdler.

1924 RACING UK H'CAP CHASE (18 fncs) 3m 110y
4:25 (4:25) (Class 3) (0-135,135) 4-Y-0+ **£6,657** (£2,067; £1,113)

Form RPR

231F 1 **Enchanted Garden**[37] [1502] 7-11-12 135........................(b) BrianHughes 148+
(Malcolm Jefferson) *trckd ldr: led gng wl 2 out: hit last: sn drvn and edgd rt: styd on wl towards fin* **5/1**[3]

123- 2 1 ¾ **Loose Chips**[183] [5340] 9-11-7 130........................(b) AidanColeman 138
(Charlie Longsdon) *led at ordinary gallop: rdn 3 out: hdd next: rallied: kpt on same pce fnl 150yds* **5/4**[1]

11F1 3 23 **By The Boardwalk (IRE)**[22] [1632] 7-11-5 131..............(t) TomBellamy(3) 124
(Kim Bailey) *t.k.h: prom: hit 6th: nt fluent fnl circ: outpcd whn j. hesitantly 3 out: wknd fr next* **13/8**[2]

3-P0 U **George Fernbeck**[27] [1571] 7-9-12 117 ow2........................ FinianO'Toole(10)
(Micky Hammond) *prom: nt fluent 1st: mstke and uns rdr 3rd* **9/1**

6m 12.5s (-30.10) **Going Correction** -1.175s/f (Hard) **4** Ran SP% **109.2**
Speed ratings (Par 107): **101,100,93,**
CSF £12.08 TOTE £5.10; EX 8.90 Trifecta £17.90.
Owner Mrs D W Davenport **Bred** Mrs S Camacho **Trained** Norton, N Yorks

FOCUS
Only a small field but it was run at a decent gallop and appears fair form. The winner improved in line the best of his hurdles form and can rate higher.

1925 WATCH RACING UK ANYWHERE H'CAP HURDLE (12 hdls) 3m 123y
5:00 (5:00) (Class 4) (0-120,120) 4-Y-0+ **£3,249** (£954; £477; £238)

Form RPR

-020 1 **Maggie Blue (IRE)**[45] [1420] 7-9-8 95 oh1 ow1........... ThomasDowson(7) 105+
(Harriet Graham) *cl up: led 4th: mde rest: qcknd clr after 3 out: eased last 100yds* **11/1**

2-01 2 7 **Omid**[49] [1371] 7-10-8 105........................(tp) JohnKington(3) 105
(Kenneth Slack) *led to 4th: hit next: chsd wnr to 4 out: rallied and regained 2nd after next: plugged on fr last: no imp* **5/1**[3]

P/P- 3 7 **Simarthur**[330] [2582] 8-10-10 107........................(p) GrahamWatters(3) 100
(Lucinda Russell) *chsd ldrs: effrt and wnt 2nd briefly 3 out: drvn and outpcd after next* **16/1**

4153 4 2 ¾ **Presented (IRE)**[11] [1783] 8-10-4 103........................ CallumBewley(5) 93
(Lisa Harrison) *hld up in tch: outpcd 1/2-way: hdwy after 4 out: no imp fr 2 out: nt fluent last* **7/1**

21 5 60 **Cooper's Friend (IRE)**[25] [1597] 6-11-9 117........................ AidanColeman 53
(Charlie Longsdon) *chsd ldrs: wnt 2nd 4 out: hit and outpcd next: wkng whn mstke 2 out: sn lost tch: t.o* **5/2**[1]

0-11 6 38 **Minella Hero (IRE)**[124] [726] 7-11-2 120........................ FinianO'Toole(10) 22
(Micky Hammond) *hld up: drvn and outpcd after 4 out: lost tch fr next: t.o* **10/1**

0-5P P **Master Murphy (IRE)**[142] [486] 10-9-9 94 oh10........................ DaleIrving(5)
(Jane Walton) *bhd: struggling fnl circ: t.o whn p.u 3 out* **80/1**

P1P- P **Madam Lilibet (IRE)**[10] [4965] 6-10-11 110........................ JamesCowley(5)
(Sharon Watt) *sn towards rr and drvn along: struggling whn flashed tail 1/2-way: lost tch and p.u 3 out* **20/1**

01-1 P **Horsted Valley**[144] [445] 5-11-6 114........................ GavinSheehan
(Warren Greatrex) *hld up in tch: effrt whn nt fluent 4 out: rdn and wknd appr next: sixth and hld whn nt fluent 2 out: sn p.u* **3/1**[2]

6m 2.3s (-36.70) **Going Correction** -1.30s/f (Hard) course record **9** Ran SP% **112.0**
Speed ratings (Par 105): **106,103,101,100,81 69,,,**
CSF £63.26 CT £877.03 TOTE £15.00: £3.50, £2.30, £2.90; EX 73.80 Trifecta £924.20.
Owner Exors of the Late Sam Hamilton **Bred** George Ward **Trained** Philip Law, Borders

FOCUS
Some improving hurdlers were on show in this sternly run affair. Those at the head of the market proved bitterly disappointing and the form is not the strongest.

1926 WEDDINGS AT CARLISLE RACECOURSE STANDARD OPEN NATIONAL HUNT FLAT RACE 2m 1f 33y
5:30 (5:30) (Class 6) 4-6-Y-O **£1,559** (£457; £228; £114)

Form RPR
31- **1** **Cloudy Dream (IRE)**[178] 5425 5-11-7 0 BrianHughes 115+
(Malcolm Jefferson) *hld up: smooth hdwy to chal over 2f out: led and rdn over 1f out: edgd rt ins fnl f: kpt on strly* **15/8**[1]
2 1 1/4 **Groundunderrepair (IRE)** 4-11-0 0 GavinSheehan 107+
(Warren Greatrex) *trckd ldrs: pushed along over 3f out: rallied to ld over 2f out: sn hrd pressed: hdd over 1f out: rallied: hld towards fin* **9/4**[2]
3 15 **Final Fling (IRE)** 4-10-11 0 CraigNichol(3) 93
(Rose Dobbin) *hld up in tch: drvn and outpcd over 4f out: rallied 3f out: plugged on same pce fr 2f out* **10/1**
4 7 **Kalondra (IRE)**[151] 4-11-0 0 NoelFehily 87
(Neil Mulholland) *t.k.h: hld up: hdwy and prom over 4f out: drvn and wknd fr 2f out* **4/1**[3]
5 1/2 **Handittolewi** 4-11-0 0 HenryBrooke 87
(Dianne Sayer) *hld up: hdwy on outside over 3f out: sn drvn: wknd over 2f out* **40/1**
6 2 1/4 **Almahoy** 4-10-4 0 JohnKington(3) 78
(Andrew Crook) *hld up in tch: pushed along 1/2-way: struggling 5f out: sn btn* **33/1**
3 **7** 2 3/4 **Still Together (IRE)**[20] 1645 5-10-11 0 BrianToomey(3) 82
(David Pipe) *led: rdn and hdd over 2f out: sn wknd* **15/2**
0 **8** 29 **Just Nobby**[20] 1645 4-11-0 0 (p) PeterCarberry 56
(Jennie Candlish) *w ldr: reminder 1/2-way: drvn and outpcd over 4f out: lost tch fnl 3f: t.o* **100/1**

4m 5.0s (-19.20) **Going Correction** -1.30s/f (Hard)
WFA 4 from 5yo 9lb **8** Ran SP% **112.8**
Speed ratings: **93,92,85,82,81 80,79,65**
CSF £6.08 TOTE £2.60: £1.10, £1.20, £2.70; EX 7.10 Trifecta £39.60.
Owner Trevor Hemmings **Bred** Eimear Purcell **Trained** Norton, N Yorks

FOCUS
The first two home pulled nicely clear of the remainder in what appeared an above-average bumper. The winner looks a fair prospect.
T/Plt: £512.30 to a £1 stake. Pool of £46461.83 - 66.20 winning tickets. T/Qpdt: £67.80 to a £1 stake. Pool of £3399.12 - 37.05 winning tickets. **Richard Young**

1780
UTTOXETER (L-H)
Thursday, October 15

OFFICIAL GOING: Good
Wind: Light behind Weather: Cloudy with sunny spells

1927 CHARLES HOLLIS BIRTHDAY CELEBRATION H'CAP HURDLE (DIV I) (10 hdls) 2m 3f 207y
1:50 (1:50) (Class 5) (0-100,100) 3-Y-O+ **£2,339** (£686; £343; £171)

Form RPR
065- **1** **Bruce Almighty (IRE)**[205] 4970 4-11-0 **91** AdamNicol(3) 102+
(Philip Kirby) *hld up: hdwy appr 3 out: led 2 out: rdn out* **9/2**[2]
3041 **2** 1 1/2 **Tennessee Bird**[16] 1691 7-10-9 **90** RyanDay(7) 99
(Mike Sowersby) *hld up: hdwy 6th: led after 3 out: hdd next: rdn and ev ch whn nt fluent last: styd on same pce flat* **11/4**[1]
0532 **3** 20 **Taste The Wine (IRE)**[15] 1702 9-11-4 **99** (t) JordanWilliams(7) 93
(Bernard Llewellyn) *hld up: hdwy 5th: rdn appr 3 out: wkng whn blnd next: nt fluent last* **9/2**[2]
0002 **4** 8 **Distant Sound (IRE)**[13] 1744 8-10-11 **85** (p) PaulMoloney 69
(Grace Harris) *led: rdn and hdd after 3 out: wknd bef next* **9/2**[2]
P-03 **5** 6 **Mulligan's Man (IRE)**[36] 1525 8-11-7 **95** DavidEngland 73
(Clare Ellam) *hdwy 3rd: rdn and wknd appr 3 out* **8/1**[3]
6-60 **6** 30 **New Tarabela**[28] 354 4-11-7 **95** LeeEdwards 46
(Tony Carroll) *chsd ldr: drvn along 7th: ev ch 3 out: sn wknd* **18/1**
566/ **7** 6 **Minden March**[627] 3924 10-9-9 **74** oh15 DanielHiskett(5) 20
(Peter Maddison) *mid-div: hdwy 6th: rdn and wknd bef 3 out* **66/1**
1-0P **P** **Walkabout Creek (IRE)**[140] 529 8-11-12 **100** LiamTreadwell
(Derek Frankland) *chsd ldrs: mstke and lost pl 5th: sn bhd: p.u bef 2 out* **20/1**
-010 **P** **Thefriendlygremlin**[25] 1598 7-10-1 **80** (p) ConorRing(5)
(John Upson) *prom to 6th: bhd whn p.u bef 3 out* **10/1**

4m 53.4s (-9.80) **Going Correction** -0.425s/f (Good)
WFA 4 from 7yo+ 10lb **9** Ran SP% **112.9**
Speed ratings (Par 103): **102,101,93,90,87 75,73,,**
CSF £17.31 CT £57.37 TOTE £5.50: £2.00, £1.10, £1.80; EX 20.90 Trifecta £134.40.
Owner Andrew Bradshaw **Bred** Cathal Ennis **Trained** East Appleton, N Yorks

FOCUS
Some starts have been moved at this track following remeasuring, so some races will not have speed figures until there is sufficient data to calculate updated median times. The hurdles were moved off the inside rail by 3-4 yards. Divided bends. There was no hurdle in the chute for 2m races as the ground under repair. After riding the first winner Adam Nicol described it as "genuine good ground". The first two drew well clear in this very modest handicap hurdle. It was the quicker division by 2.1sec and there's a case for rating the form 5lb+ higher.

1928 MARSTONS PEDIGREE JUVENILE MAIDEN HURDLE (8 hdls 1 omitted) 1m 7f 168y
2:20 (2:20) (Class 5) 3-Y-O **£2,599** (£763; £381; £190)

Form RPR
1 **Duke Of Sonning**[22] 3-11-0 0 WayneHutchinson 113+
(Alan King) *hld up: hdwy appr 3 out: led 2 out: rdn and edgd lft flat: styd on* **10/3**[1]
623 **2** nk **Chic Name (FR)**[14] 1712 3-11-0 105 (p) AlainCawley 113
(Richard Hobson) *led: nt fluent 3rd: rdn and hdd 2 out: ev ch whn bmpd flat: styd on* **5/1**[2]
3 9 **Borak (IRE)**[19] 3-10-11 0 RobertWilliams(3) 105+
(Bernard Llewellyn) *chsd ldrs: wnt 2nd 3 out: ev ch next: sn rdn: wknd last* **11/2**[3]
4 12 **Celestial Magic**[387] 3-11-0 0 IanPopham 93
(Richard Phillips) *hld up: pckd 4th: pushed along after 3 out: nvr trbld ldrs* **100/1**
5 13 **Diamond Joel**[33] 3-11-0 0 RobertDunne 81
(Tom Lacey) *hld up: nt fluent 1st: hdwy appr 3 out: rdn and wknd bef next* **10/3**[1]
6 7 **Lucie Rie (IRE)**[51] 3-10-7 0 BrendanPowell 68
(K R Burke) *hld up: rdn and wknd appr 3 out* **20/1**
7 6 **Midtech Star (IRE)**[19] 3-11-0 0 (p) TomO'Brien 70
(Ian Williams) *prom tl rdn and wknd bef 3 out* **33/1**
43 **8** 1 **Champagne Ransom (FR)**[28] 1452 3-10-7 0 NicodeBoinville 62
(Nicky Henderson) *prom: chsd ldr after 5th tl 3 out: sn rdn and wknd* **8/1**
9 10 **Mister Dick (FR)**[119] 3-11-0 0 RichardJohnson 60
(Jonjo O'Neill) *hld up: mstkes 1st and 5th: rdn and wknd after 3 out* **9/1**
5 **P** **Philba**[11] 1768 3-11-0 0 (p) SamTwiston-Davies
(Michael Appleby) *chsd ldr tl rdn and wknd after 5th: bhd whn p.u bef next* **18/1**

3m 48.2s (-9.20) **Going Correction** -0.425s/f (Good) **10** Ran SP% **113.3**
Speed ratings (Par 101): **106,105,101,95,88 85,82,81,76,**
CSF £19.29 TOTE £4.60: £1.90, £1.80, £2.10; EX 18.50 Trifecta £115.60.
Owner McNeill Family **Bred** Lordship Stud **Trained** Barbury Castle, Wilts

FOCUS
A juvenile hurdle that should produce winners. The second set a fair standard and is rated to his mark.

1929 EBF STALLIONS "NATIONAL HUNT" NOVICES' HURDLE (QUALIFIER) (8 hdls 1 omitted) 1m 7f 168y
2:55 (2:55) (Class 4) 4-6-Y-O **£3,798** (£1,122; £561; £280; £140)

Form RPR
62 **1** **A Little Magic (IRE)**[23] 1613 4-10-12 0 RichardJohnson 116+
(Jonjo O'Neill) *hld up: plld hrd: hdwy to ld appr 2nd: nt fluent next: hit 5th: pushed clr whn blnd 2 out: comf* **1/3**[1]
5-5 **2** 9 **Aliandy (IRE)**[152] 341 4-10-12 0 DavidBass 102
(Kim Bailey) *plld hrd: led: hdd bef 2nd: trckd wnr: rdn after 3 out: sn outpcd* **4/1**[2]
04-4 **3** 4 1/2 **The Lion Man (IRE)**[159] 207 5-10-12 105 CharliePoste 99
(Robin Dickin) *hld up: hdwy 4th: mstke next: rdn and hung lft fr 3 out: nt trble ldrs* **16/1**
1-3 **4** 13 **Preseli Star (IRE)**[20] 1644 5-10-12 0 AndrewTinkler 91+
(George Baker) *chsd ldrs tl rdn and wknd after 3 out* **8/1**[3]
00/0 **5** 52 **Trooper Royal**[16] 1684 5-10-12 0 SeanQuinlan 40
(Sue Smith) *chsd ldrs: nt fluent 2nd: dropped in rr 4th: bhd fr next* **100/1**

3m 51.8s (-5.60) **Going Correction** -0.425s/f (Good) **5** Ran SP% **113.0**
Speed ratings: **97,92,90,83,57**
CSF £2.35 TOTE £1.20: £1.10, £1.80; EX 2.40 Trifecta £7.10.
Owner John P McManus **Bred** Brian Gleeson **Trained** Cheltenham, Gloucs

FOCUS
No depth to this event. The easy winner set a fair standard and is on the upgrade.

1930 OLD DOG AT THORPE H'CAP CHASE (18 fncs) 3m 2y
3:30 (3:30) (Class 5) (0-100,97) 4-Y-O+ **£2,729** (£801; £400; £200)

Form RPR
PFP- **1** **Double Chocolate**[495] 626 12-10-7 **78** (p) AndrewTinkler 95+
(Martin Keighley) *chsd ldrs: led 3rd: clr 11th: shkn up appr 2 out: comf* **8/1**
0-01 **2** 4 **Alta Rock (IRE)**[42] 1462 10-11-4 **89** SeanQuinlan 101+
(Sue Smith) *a.p: chsd wnr 13th: rdn appr 4 out: styd on same pce fr 2 out* **8/1**
2320 **3** 22 **Kilcascan**[57] 1287 11-11-0 **88** (p) BenPoste(3) 80
(Rosemary Gasson) *led to 3rd: chsd wnr to 13th: rdn and wknd appr 3 out* **14/1**
P114 **4** 3 3/4 **Sgt Bull Berry**[11] 1775 8-10-9 **80** JakeGreenall 67
(Peter Maddison) *hld up: hdwy appr 4 out: rdn and wknd bef next* **8/1**
3422 **5** 1 **Solway Bay**[11] 1778 13-11-2 **94** (tp) MissRMcDonald(7) 80
(Lisa Harrison) *chsd ldrs: lost pl after 3rd: hdwy 7th: pushed along 11th: wknd bef 4 out* **12/1**
2141 **6** hd **Etania**[25] 1598 7-11-12 **97** TomO'Brien 83
(Ian Williams) *hld up: nt fluent 10th: rdn after 13th: nvr on terms* **4/1**[1]
-461 **7** 26 **Urban Gale (IRE)**[47] 1403 10-11-1 **91** DaraghBourke(5) 54
(Joanne Foster) *chsd ldrs tl rdn and wknd 13th* **11/2**[2]
4443 **8** 1 3/4 **Lost In Newyork (IRE)**[11] 1785 8-10-3 **74** (p) AdamWedge 35
(Nick Kent) *hld up: hdwy 13th: rdn and wknd bef 4 out* **9/1**
4003 **9** 12 **Interpleader**[8] 1813 10-10-10 **88** (tp) MrMartinMcIntyre(7) 38
(Sheila Lewis) *hld up: a in rr: bhd whn hit 14th* **7/1**[3]
304- **P** **Bishophill Jack (IRE)**[364] 1912 9-10-12 **83** (p) AndrewThornton
(Caroline Bailey) *chsd ldrs: lost pl 6th: pushed along 8th: wknd 12th: bhd whn p.u bef 4 out* **10/1**

6m 3.5s (-4.60) **Going Correction** -0.125s/f (Good) **10** Ran SP% **114.7**
Speed ratings (Par 103): **102,100,93,92,91 91,83,82,78,**
CSF £69.02 CT £881.28 TOTE £9.60: £3.50, £2.30, £4.10; EX 87.50 Trifecta £1417.70.
Owner Red & Black Racing **Bred** John Jones **Trained** Condicote, Gloucs

FOCUS
The winner set a solid pace in this ordinary handicap chase. The winner is rated to the best of his 2014 runs.

1931 MALKINS BANK GOLF CLUB H'CAP HURDLE (8 hdls 1 omitted) 1m 7f 168y
4:05 (4:05) (Class 5) (0-100,100) 3-Y-O+ **£2,339** (£686; £343; £171)

Form RPR
206- **1** **Back By Midnight**[188] 5260 6-11-4 **95** (t) JamesBanks(3) 107+
(Emma Baker) *mde all: nt fluent 1st: hit next: nt fluent 3rd: hit 5th: rdn clr appr last* **10/1**
5052 **2** 9 **Rye House (IRE)**[8] 1810 6-11-8 **96** (t) RichardJohnson 99
(Tim Vaughan) *a.p: chsd wnr 3rd: rdn after 3 out: styd on same pce appr last* **2/1**[1]
20-2 **3** 1/2 **Reyno**[20] 1647 7-11-12 **100** (bt) BrendanPowell 102
(Stuart Edmunds) *chsd wnr to 3rd: remained handy: rdn appr 2 out: styd on* **9/2**[2]
60/0 **4** 5 **Razzle Dazzle 'Em**[16] 1691 6-10-4 **78** DaveCrosse 77
(Shaun Harris) *chsd ldrs: rdn after 3 out: wknd appr last* **28/1**
3222 **5** 8 **Sweet World**[11] 1786 11-11-0 **95** JordanWilliams(7) 85
(Bernard Llewellyn) *hld up: hdwy and mstke 4th: rdn whn nt fluent 3 out: sn wknd* **11/2**[3]
3250 **6** 8 **Rose Red**[49] 1384 8-10-10 **84** TrevorWhelan 67
(Rob Summers) *hld up: rdn after 5th: wkng whn mstke 3 out* **14/1**
6/F- **7** shd **Monderon (FR)**[532] 43 8-11-7 **95** JamesDavies 78
(Henry Oliver) *mid-div: rdn and wknd appr 3 out* **6/1**
PP-P **8** 1 **Polarbrook (IRE)**[25] 1600 8-11-8 **96** (t) SeanQuinlan 78
(Derek Shaw) *hld up: rdn and wknd after 5th* **100/1**

F00- 9 *43* **Vertueux (FR)**[31] 4862 10-10-4 **78**....................(p) LeeEdwards 21
(Tony Carroll) *chsd ldrs tl rdn and wknd after 5th* **20/1**

63P- 10 *47* **Guanciale**[239] 4300 8-11-11 **99**.................... RobertDunne
(Dai Burchell) *hld up: wknd after 5th* **16/1**

P5P4 P **Cearys (IRE)**[37] 1506 7-11-2 **90**....................(p) AndrewTinkler
(Martin Keighley) *mid-div: rdn and wknd after 5th: bhd whn p.u bef 2 out* **28/1**

3m 49.5s (-7.90) **Going Correction** -0.425s/f (Good) 11 Ran SP% **115.5**
Speed ratings (Par 103): **102,97,97,94,90 86,86,86,64,41**
CSF £29.65 CT £105.75 TOTE £13.00: £3.00, £1.20, £1.70; EX 35.90 Trifecta £249.10.
Owner Mrs M J Arnold **Bred** Mrs J Arnold **Trained** Naunton, Gloucs
FOCUS
Not many got into this modest handicap, which was run at a decent clip. Pretty solid form.

1932 BLACK BOY AT HEAGE NOVICES' LIMITED H'CAP CHASE (16 fncs) 2m 6f 108y
4:40 (4:40) (Class 3) (0-135,135) 4-Y-0 **£6,330** (£1,870; £935; £468; £234)

Form RPR
450- 1 **Junction Fourteen (IRE)**[217] 4717 6-11-8 **135**....................(t) DarylJacob 146+
(Emma Lavelle) *mde all: j.w: rdn appr last: styd on wl* **9/4**[2]

3211 2 *2 ¾* **Skylander (IRE)**[13] 1741 6-10-7 **127**.................... MichaelHeard[(7)] 135
(David Pipe) *a.p: chsd wnr 4 out: ev ch next: rdn after 2 out: styd on same pce flat* **5/2**[3]

21-2 3 *2 ½* **Ebony Empress (IRE)**[152] 339 6-10-10 **123**....................(p) MarkQuinlan 130
(Neil Mulholland) *hld up: hdwy 4 out: rdn after 2 out: styd on same pce* **12/1**

22-2 4 *3 ¼* **Simply The West (IRE)**[150] 382 6-10-10 **123**..........(t) RichardJohnson 128
(Charlie Longsdon) *hld up: hdwy 4 out: rdn after 3 out: styd on same pce fr next* **15/8**[1]

1-44 5 *18* **She's Late**[37] 1507 5-10-8 **121**....................(p) SeanBowen 108
(Jonjo O'Neill) *chsd wnr to 4 out: wknd next* **12/1**

5m 43.1s (0.40) **Going Correction** -0.125s/f (Good) 5 Ran SP% **109.5**
Speed ratings (Par 107): **94,93,92,90,84**
CSF £8.38 TOTE £3.50: £1.80, £1.60; EX 11.30 Trifecta £48.50.
Owner Martin St Quinton & Tim Syder **Bred** John And Iris Lunny **Trained** Hatherden, Hants
FOCUS
An interesting novices' handicap, run at a reasonable pace. The winner was up 7lb on the best of his hurdle figures and is a potential 150+ chaser.

1933 CHARLES HOLLIS BIRTHDAY CELEBRATION H'CAP HURDLE (DIV II) (10 hdls) 2m 3f 207y
5:10 (5:14) (Class 5) (0-100,100) 3-Y-0+ **£2,339** (£686; £343; £171)

Form RPR
0/10 1 **Duke's Affair**[25] 1598 7-10-8 **85**.................... MattGriffiths[(3)] 94+
(Jeremy Scott) *trckd ldrs: wnt 2nd 3rd: led 7th: rdn after 2 out: all out* **9/4**[1]

0456 2 *1 ¾* **Icanmotor**[25] 1598 8-9-11 **74** oh4....................(tp) ConorShoemark[(3)] 78
(Claire Dyson) *a.p: chsd wnr after 7th: sn rdn and ev ch: no ex towards fin* **7/1**[3]

P045 3 *27* **Primo Rossi**[36] 1524 6-10-0 **74** oh2....................(tp) JamesDavies 54
(Tom Gretton) *hld up: mstke 4th: hdwy 7th: rdn and wknd next* **10/1**

33FP 4 *18* **Adios Alonso (IRE)**[11] 1785 9-11-0 **91**....................(p) BenPoste[(3)] 55
(Rosemary Gasson) *chsd ldr to 3rd: remained handy tl rdn and wknd appr 3 out* **10/1**

4/0 5 *1 ½* **Man Of God (IRE)**[56] 1297 7-11-7 **95**.................... MichaelByrne 57
(Tim Vaughan) *hld up: bhd fr 5th* **16/1**

40-4 6 *30* **Bobby Dove**[11] 1786 8-10-10 **87**.................... RobertWilliams[(3)] 22
(Bernard Llewellyn) *hld up: rdn and wknd 7th* **9/2**[2]

P00/ P **Wild Desert (FR)**[17] 1689 10-11-7 **95**.................... RichardJohnson
(Jennie Candlish) *led to 7th: sn rdn and wknd: bhd whn p.u bef next* **7/1**[3]

PP/6 P **He's A Hawker (IRE)**[25] 1602 10-11-2 **100**....................(b) LewisStones[(10)]
(Michael Mullineaux) *in rr: drvn along and rel to r after 2nd: sn wl bhd: p.u after 5th* **20/1**

P **Arquebusier (FR)**[287] 3477 5-11-4 **95**....................(p) JamesBanks[(3)]
(Emma Baker) *hld up: rdn and wknd after 7th: bhd whn p.u bef 3 out* **8/1**

4m 55.5s (-7.70) **Going Correction** -0.425s/f (Good) 9 Ran SP% **113.9**
Speed ratings (Par 103): **98,97,86,79,78 66, , ,**
CSF £18.45 CT £129.38 TOTE £3.10: £1.70, £2.40, £3.50; EX 21.50 Trifecta £257.60.
Owner Mrs Helen L Stoneman **Bred** Mrs J Munnis And Mrs E Hockenhull **Trained** Brompton Regis, Somerset
FOCUS
The slower division by 2.1 sec, and weaker form. As in division one, the first two came a long way clear. The winner is likely to remain well in on his bumper form.
T/Plt: £30.90 to a £1 stake. Pool of £65858.60 - 1551.87 winning tickets. T/Qpdt: £13.90 to a £1 stake. Pool of £4317.54 - 229.50 winning tickets. **Colin Roberts**

1934 - 1936a (Foreign Racing) - See Raceform Interactive

1913 PUNCHESTOWN (R-H)
Thursday, October 15
OFFICIAL GOING: Good (good to firm in places)

1937a BUCK HOUSE NOVICE CHASE (GRADE 3) (13 fncs) 2m 2f
3:55 (3:56) 4-Y-0+ **£15,116** (£4,418; £2,093; £697)

RPR
1 **The Game Changer (IRE)**[11] 1790 6-11-10 151....................(t) BJCooper 153+
(Gordon Elliott, Ire) *w.w bhd ldrs: 3rd 1/2-way: nt fluent 5 out: tk clsr order 2 out and impr travelling wl between horses to ld fr last: qcknd wl to assert run-in: easily* **1/1**[1]

2 *3* **Sizing Platinum (IRE)**[17] 1679 7-11-5 145.................... JJBurke 142
(Henry De Bromhead, Ire) *led: nt fluent 1st: 2 l clr at 1/2-way: slt mstke 4 out: rdn bef 2 out where hdd narrowly: sn on terms tl hdd u.p fr last: no ch w easy wnr run-in: kpt on same pce* **7/4**[2]

3 *2 ¼* **Miss Dinamic (IRE)**[22] 1627 6-10-8 0.................... RWalsh 128
(Gordon Elliott, Ire) *trckd ldr in 2nd: rdn to ld narrowly 2 out where mstke and sn disp: hdd at last and no ex in 3rd run-in* **11/2**[3]

4 *dist* **Rightdownthemiddle (IRE)**[8] 1609 7-11-1 134.................... APHeskin
(Michael Mulvany, Ire) *w.w bhd ldrs: last 1/2-way: stl in tch in rr whn fell 3 out: rmntd to fin completely t.o* **12/1**

4m 35.6s (-5.70) 4 Ran SP% **109.4**
CSF £3.28 TOTE £1.60; DF 3.10 Trifecta £4.20.
Owner Gigginstown House Stud **Bred** Arctic Tack Stud & Crossogue Stud **Trained** Longwood, Co Meath
FOCUS
The usual concern with a small field is that the race could develop into a sprint but Sizing Platinum went a decent clip. The winner did this easily, the next two setting the standard.

1938a IRISH DAILY STAR CHASE (GRADE 3) 2m 7f
4:30 (4:32) 5-Y-0+ **£16,124** (£4,713; £2,232; £744)

RPR
1 **Don Cossack (GER)**[169] 22 8-11-10 175....................(t) BJCooper 178+
(Gordon Elliott, Ire) *hld up: sltly slow 6th: wnt 3rd after 8th: tk clsr order into 2nd travelling wl after 3 out: nt helped by attentions of loose horse: led fr next and eased clr: easily* **1/4**[1]

2 *12* **Roi Du Mee (FR)**[193] 5170 10-11-8 153....................(t) KevinSexton 160
(Gordon Elliott, Ire) *led: edgd lft bef 8th: slt mstke next and hdd: regained advantage at 12th tl hdd again after 5 out: nt helped by attentions of loose horse: led again bef 3 out tl hdd fr next and no ch w easy wnr: kpt on one pce* **14/1**[3]

3 *21* **Cailin Annamh (IRE)**[12] 1763 7-11-1 145....................(tp) BarryGeraghty 130
(Mrs John Harrington, Ire) *settled bhd ldr tl led fr 9th: hdd fr 12th tl regained advantage after 5 out: nt helped by attentions of loose horse: hdd again bef 3 out and wknd into 3rd bef next: eased* **7/1**[2]

4 *59* **Aranhill Chief (IRE)**[19] 1668 8-11-6 125....................(t) PaulTownend 81
(S J Mahon, Ire) *cl up on outer early: sn settled bhd ldrs in 3rd: dropped to rr of remaining quartet after 8th: lost tch after 11th and wknd after 5 out: completely t.o* **66/1**

F **Bright New Dawn (IRE)**[169] 24 8-11-0 148....................(t) RWalsh
(Gordon Elliott, Ire) *hld up: racd keenly and in rr whn fell 2nd* **7/1**[2]

6m 4.2s (6.70) 5 Ran SP% **113.2**
CSF £5.30 TOTE £1.10: £1.02, £3.70; DF 5.70 Trifecta £13.20.
Owner Gigginstown House Stud **Bred** Gestut Etzean **Trained** Longwood, Co Meath
FOCUS
Gigginstown are really keeping this race going. They have now won it for five years in a row. This performance would have given them most pleasure. Roi Du Mee ensured they didn't crawl. The race concerned just three for the final mile. Don Cossack, as expected, was in a different league. He wasn't extended.

1939 - 1940a (Foreign Racing) - See Raceform Interactive

566 FAKENHAM (L-H)
Friday, October 16
OFFICIAL GOING: Good (good to soft in places; 6.5)
Wind: breezy Weather: overcast, 13 degrees

1941 DEREHAM CONDITIONAL JOCKEYS' (S) H'CAP HURDLE (9 hdls) 2m 3y
2:15 (2:15) (Class 5) (0-100,100) 3-Y-0+ **£2,737** (£798; £399)

Form RPR
043F 1 **Maid Of Tuscany (IRE)**[18] 1299 4-11-2 **98**..........(b) MrShaneQuinlan[(8)] 110+
(Neil Mulholland) *settled in midfield: wnt 2nd at 6th: led and only one travelling between last two: pushed along and sn in command* **5/1**[3]

6P-2 2 *4* **Nebula Storm (IRE)**[26] 1596 8-10-8 **90**....................(v) GeorgeGorman[(8)] 98+
(Gary Moore) *settled towards rr: wnt 3rd 3 out: rdn after mstke next: tk 2nd bef last bur no ch w wnr* **2/1**[1]

P3P5 3 *8* **Nellie The Elegant**[12] 1786 4-10-10 **90**....................(bt) AlanJohns[(6)] 90
(Tim Vaughan) *led 2nd and wnt v hrd in 5 l ld: rdn 2 out: hdd between last two: fnd nil and sn 3rd and btn* **8/1**

/000 4 *6* **Kheskianto (IRE)**[11] 1793 9-10-2 **79**....................(t) DavidPrichard[(3)] 72
(Michael Chapman) *last tl 1/2-way: tk 4th 3 out: rdn and nvr nr ldng trio after* **100/1**

10-0 5 *45* **Anginola (IRE)**[162] 167 6-10-3 **80**....................(p) JamieBargary[(3)] 33
(David Dennis) *in rr and nt fluent 2nd: rdn fr next: nvr travelling after: t.o 3 out: lft remote 5th at last* **8/1**

2F-6 6 *3 ¾* **Full Ov Beans**[15] 1721 11-11-9 **100**.................... MikeyHamill[(3)] 50
(Michael Gates) *led at str pce tl 2nd: rdn and dropped himself rt out after 5th: sn t.o: has been retired* **9/2**[2]

50P/ 7 *4* **Valantino Oyster (IRE)**[55] 1419 8-10-8 **82**....................(p) TomBellamy 28
(Ali Stronge) *cl up tl 5th: rdn and lost tch bef next where blnd: continued t.o* **7/1**

2-06 F **Staff Sergeant**[64] 811 8-11-10 **98**....................(v) JackSherwood
(Jim Best) *t.k.h: wnt 2nd fr 4th tl rdn 6th: wkng tamely whn mstke next: 20 l 5th whn crashing fall last* **10/1**

4m 6.6s (-6.40) **Going Correction** -0.275s/f (Good)
WFA 4 from 6yo+ 9lb 8 Ran SP% **113.0**
Speed ratings (Par 103): **105,103,99,96,73 71,69,**
CSF £15.52 CT £76.97 TOTE £4.60: £1.40, £1.10, £2.40; EX 13.50 Trifecta £68.60.The winner was bought in 4,200gns.
Owner Qdos Racing **Bred** Cora Srl **Trained** Limpley Stoke, Wilts
FOCUS
Fakenham's first meeting after a summer break. After the first Jamie Bargary said: "It's lovely ground", while Shane Quinlan said: "There is a lovely covering." This ordinary seller was run at a decent clip. Rail movements added 158yds to the advertised race distance. Steps up from the first two, with the third setting the level.

1942 HELHOUGHTON NOVICES' CHASE (16 fncs) 2m 5f 44y
2:50 (2:50) (Class 3) 4-Y-0+ **£7,797** (£2,289; £1,144; £572)

Form RPR
610- 1 **Katgary (FR)**[190] 5241 5-11-3 0....................(p) NickScholfield 121+
(Paul Nicholls) *pressed ldr tl led 6th: j. soundly: pushed along and clr between last two: comf* **9/4**[2]

421- 2 *7* **Minella Forfitness (IRE)**[209] 4897 8-11-8 133.................... AdamPogson 117
(Charles Pogson) *taken down v early: t.k.h in 3rd tl wnt 2nd at 11th: rdn 2 out: a chsng wnr vainly after* **6/1**[3]

46P3 3 *14* **The Society Man (IRE)**[11] 1795 8-10-12 91.................... DannyBurton[(5)] 97
(Michael Chapman) *v slow jump 1st: led tl 6th: nt fluent 10th: dropped to last at 12th and outpcd after: 20 l last bef 2 out: plugged on into 3rd bef last* **100/1**

U 4 *11* **Mesut (FR)**[14] 1737 4-10-7 110.................... JackQuinlan 79
(Sarah Humphrey) *j. modly: last tl wnt 3rd at 12th: hit next: 5 l 3rd bef 2 out where mstke whn tiring qckly: lost 3rd and mstke last* **50/1**

6-62 F **Hammersly Lake (FR)**[90] 1039 7-11-3 0.................... PeterCarberry
(Nicky Henderson) *hld up 4th tl fell 7th* **4/6**[1]

5m 45.0s (3.20) **Going Correction** +0.05s/f (Yiel)
WFA 4 from 5yo+ 10lb 5 Ran SP% **108.0**
Speed ratings (Par 107): **95,92,87,82,**
CSF £14.18 TOTE £2.90: £1.40, £2.10; EX 13.10 Trifecta £50.50.
Owner Andrea & Graham Wylie **Bred** S C P Haras Des Coudraies **Trained** Ditcheat, Somerset

FOCUS
A decent novice chase which lost some of its interest when the favourite came down. The pace was fairly steady. Rail movements added 215yds to the advertised race distance. The esy winner was a 139 hurdler and there should be more to come.

1943 ROSALIE MONBIOT 80TH BIRTHDAY CELEBRATION NOVICES' HURDLE (11 hdls) 2m 4f 1y
3:25 (3:25) (Class 4) 4-Y-O+ **£4,431** (£1,309; £654; £327; £163)

Form RPR
32- **1** **Wings Attract (IRE)**[176] 5500 6-11-0 120 .... TomMessenger 118+
(Chris Bealby) *trckd ldrs: nt fluent 4th: wnt 3rd and rdn 3 out: led bef last: outbattled rival to forge clr after last* **8/1**
2123 **2** *1 ¼* **Romulus Du Donjon (IRE)**[85] 1082 4-11-7 119 .... DarylJacob 123
(Oliver Sherwood) *led tl led 3rd: set stdy pce: led again 8th: hit 2 out: rdn and hdd bef last where stl almost upsides: immediately fnd nil flat* **6/1**[3]
12 **3** *11* **Who You For (IRE)**[15] 1723 5-11-0 0 .... JackQuinlan 106
(Sarah Humphrey) *towards rr: rdn and outpcd 3 out: plugged on into mod 3rd between last two* **85/40**[2]
11F- **4** *2 ½* **Until Winning (FR)**[175] 5517 7-11-0 0 .... PaddyBrennan 106+
(Tom George) *prom: wnt 2nd at 8th: jnd ldr briefly whn rdn next: fdd between last two* **11/8**[1]
05- **5** *1 ½* **Charlie's Oscar (IRE)**[178] 5454 5-11-0 0 .... HarrySkelton 102
(Dan Skelton) *t.k.h: hld up towards rr: rdn and wknd bef 2 out* **14/1**
6 *34* **Supreme Hope (IRE)**[140] 540 6-10-7 0 .... MarkQuinlan 65
(Neil Mulholland) *led 3rd tl 8th: rdn and dropped out rapidly next: t.o whn mstke 2 out* **50/1**
P **Platinum Proof (USA)**[123] 5-10-7 0 .... MrTimDonworth[(7)]
(John Berry) *j. modly in last pair: lost tch rapidly 7th: t.o and p.u after next: b.b.v* **100/1**

5m 12.4s (-8.00) **Going Correction** -0.275s/f (Good) **7** Ran SP% **109.1**
Speed ratings (Par 105): **105,104,100,99,98 84,**
CSF £48.92 TOTE £4.60: £1.10, £2.60; EX 17.60 Trifecta £101.30.
Owner The Rann Family **Bred** John McAleese **Trained** Barrowby, Lincs

FOCUS
Fair novice hurdle form, the first two on the upgrade and the third setting the level. Rail movements added 197yds to the advertised race distance.

1944 OCTOBER H'CAP CHASE (18 fncs) 3m 38y
4:00 (4:00) (Class 3) (0-140,140) 4-Y-O+ **£7,507** (£2,217; £1,108; £554; £277)

Form RPR
3P-2 **1** **Open Hearted**[15] 1715 8-11-10 138 .... (t) HarrySkelton 147
(Dan Skelton) *j. boldly: mde all: hrd drvn bef 2 out: jnd on home turn: plld out ex to assert fnl 100yds: v game* **9/2**[2]
251- **2** *¾* **Knock House (IRE)**[193] 5199 6-11-10 138 .... BrianHughes 146
(Mick Channon) *pressed ldr: rdn to rnge upsides home turn: tussled for ld and kpt on wl tl jst outpcd fnl 100yds* **10/11**[1]
412/ **3** *18* **Bucking The Trend**[601] 4425 7-10-6 125 .... AlanJohns[(5)] 118
(Tim Vaughan) *trckd ldrs: 2 l 3rd after 3 out: rdn and outpcd by ldng pair next* **8/1**
0P-0 **4** *11* **Wiesentraum (GER)**[20] 1658 9-11-12 140 .... (p) LeightonAspell 126
(Lucy Wadham) *cl up but tended to lack fluency: mstke 13th: 4 l after 3 out: rdn and btn whn mstke next* **5/1**[3]
-124 **5** *47* **Kilbree Kid (IRE)**[24] 1616 8-11-7 135 .... (tp) PaddyBrennan 75
(Tom George) *kpt making errors but cl up tl rdn after 14th: blnd next and no ch after: mstke 3 out and continued t.o* **6/1**

6m 30.6s (-5.10) **Going Correction** +0.05s/f (Yiel) **5** Ran SP% **112.6**
Speed ratings (Par 107): **110,109,103,100,84**
CSF £9.84 TOTE £5.20: £2.20, £1.10; EX 12.10 Trifecta £34.60.
Owner Craig Buckingham **Bred** The Queen **Trained** Alcester, Warwicks
■ Stewards' Enquiry : Harry Skelton two-day ban; used whip without giving his mount time to respond (30th-31st Oct)

FOCUS
A fair handicap chase in which the first two came clear, and the form looks solid. The winner confirmed the merit of his Bangor second. Rail movements added 258yds to the advertised race distance.

1945 FAKENHAM H'CAP HURDLE (9 hdls) 2m 3y
4:35 (4:35) (Class 4) (0-120,120) 3-Y-O+ **£6,498** (£1,908; £954; £477)

Form RPR
6210 **1** **Gin And Tonic**[12] 1786 5-10-3 97 .... JackQuinlan 101+
(Michael Wigham) *settled last as ldng pair cut each other's throats: effrt bef 3 out: chal next: pushed into ld between last two: 3 l clr last: bit in hand* **5/1**
40-5 **2** *1 ½* **Istimraar (IRE)**[13] 1754 4-11-9 117 .... HarrySkelton 119
(Dan Skelton) *t.k.h in 3rd tl wnt 2nd 6th: led 2 out: sn drvn: hdd between last two and sn outpcd by wnr: a hld flat* **13/8**[1]
323 **3** *17* **Hawdyerwheesht**[15] 1719 7-11-5 120 .... (tp) JamieBargary[(7)] 108
(David Dennis) *t.k.h: duelling for ld and 8 l clr of chsng trio tl 4th: led 5th: rdn and hdd 2 out: nt run on and sn mod 3rd* **7/2**[2]
-323 **4** *2* **Changing The Guard**[30] 1554 9-11-7 115 .... (tp) AidanColeman 100
(Barry Brennan) *t.k.h duelling for ld tl 5th: rdn and losing pl whn hit 6th: nt run on and wl bhd fr 3 out* **4/1**[3]
-150 **P** **El Massivo (IRE)**[62] 1261 5-11-7 115 .... PaddyBrennan
(Harriet Bethell) *cl up tl rdn after 5th: drvn and lost tch bef 3 out: t.o and p.u wl bef next: lost action* **6/1**

4m 6.2s (-6.80) **Going Correction** -0.275s/f (Good) **5** Ran SP% **111.3**
Speed ratings (Par 105): **106,105,96,95,**
CSF £14.10 TOTE £5.30: £2.60, £1.30; EX 15.00 Trifecta £96.60.
Owner The Gin & Tonic Partnership **Bred** Winterbeck Manor Stud **Trained** Newmarket, Suffolk
■ Stewards' Enquiry : Paddy Brennan jockey said gelding lost its action

FOCUS
Rail movements added 158yds to the advertised race distance. The third and fourth disputed a brisk gallop in this modest handicap and the winner and second came from a little off the pace. The winner is rated back to form.

1946 NORFOLK NOVICES' HURDLE (9 hdls) 2m 3y
5:10 (5:10) (Class 4) 4-Y-O+ **£4,548** (£1,335; £667)

Form RPR
11 **1** **Francis Of Assisi (IRE)**[17] 1693 5-11-12 135 .... AidanColeman 128+
(John Ferguson) *restrained and virtually a 2nd: mstke 2 out and outpcd and hrd drvn: clsd again bef last where landed upsides: gained command fnl 50yds* **2/9**[1]
2 *nk* **Ch'Tibello (FR)**[174] 4-11-5 0 .... HarrySkelton 121+
(Dan Skelton) *led at pedestrian pce: handed 5 l advantage 2 out: drvn between last two: jnd last: kpt on tl no ex cl home* **10/3**[2]
0 **3** *18* **Galuppi**[3] 1898 4-10-12 0 .... JamesDavies 96
(J R Jenkins) *cl up in last 2nd briefly 3 out: rdn and wknd bef next* **40/1**[3]

4m 15.7s (2.70) **Going Correction** -0.275s/f (Good)
WFA 4 from 5yo 9lb **3** Ran SP% **107.4**
Speed ratings (Par 105): **82,81,72**
CSF £1.42 TOTE £1.20; EX 1.10 Trifecta £1.10.
Owner Bloomfields **Bred** Queen Cleopatra Syndicate **Trained** Cowlinge, Suffolk

FOCUS
Rail movements added 158yds to the advertised race distance. A good finish to this small-field novice hurdle, which was run at a steady gallop. The form could be rated 9lb+ higher through the winner.
T/Plt: £42.30 to a £1 stake. Pool: £42,369.59 - 730.95 winning tickets T/Qpdt: £13.30 to a £1 stake. Pool: £3,047.30 - 169.10 winning tickets **Iain Mackenzie**

265 WINCANTON (R-H)
Friday, October 16

OFFICIAL GOING: Good to firm (good in places; 8.5)
Wind: almost nil Weather: cloudy

1947 BRUTON NOVICES' H'CAP HURDLE (10 hdls) 2m 3f 166y
2:25 (2:25) (Class 4) (0-115,109) 3-Y-O+ **£3,898** (£1,144; £572; £286)

Form RPR
00-P **1** **East Hill**[18] 1677 5-10-0 83 oh11 .... (t) BrendanPowell 86
(Colin Tizzard) *disp ld most of way: rdn and narrowly hdd 2 out: led sn after last: kpt on: drvn out* **20/1**
22-6 **2** *1 ¾* **The Cider Maker**[165] 108 5-11-6 103 .... (t) RichardJohnson 104
(Colin Tizzard) *j. sltly lft at times: disp ld: narrow advantage 2 out: sn drvn: hdd sn after last: no ex fnl 120yds* **1/1**[1]
1403 **3** *1 ¼* **The Kvilleken**[8] 1818 7-10-11 97 .... (p) KillianMoore[(3)] 98
(Martin Keighley) *trckd ldng pair: rdn appr 2 out: sltly outpcd between last 2: styd on run-in* **13/8**[2]
-666 **4** *5* **Loch Garman (FR)**[16] 1698 4-11-12 109 .... ConorO'Farrell 108
(Nigel Hawke) *plld hrd: trckd ldng trio: j.lft at times: chal 2 out: sn rdn: cl 3rd whn blnd last: fdd* **6/1**[3]

4m 47.8s (287.80) **4** Ran SP% **107.1**
CSF £41.40 TOTE £11.60; EX 27.30 Trifecta £67.70.
Owner The Con Club **Bred** Harrison & Groucott **Trained** Milborne Port, Dorset

FOCUS
A moderate novice handicap which saw a 1-2 for trainer Colin Tizzard, but not in the order the market strongly suggested. Suspect form and not a race to take seriously.

1948 WINCANTON H'CAP CHASE (17 fncs) 2m 4f 35y
3:00 (3:00) (Class 3) (0-130,122) 4-Y-O+ **£6,498** (£1,908; £954; £477)

Form RPR
64P- **1** **Gentleman Jon**[179] 5436 7-11-12 122 .... NoelFehily 131+
(Colin Tizzard) *mde all: styd on strly fr 2 out: rdn out* **4/1**
053- **2** *5* **Polisky (FR)**[201] 5044 8-11-12 122 .... (tp) SamTwiston-Davies 128
(Paul Nicholls) *trckd ldrs: trcking ldr whn nt fluent 12th: rdn after 2 out: nt fluent last: kpt on same pce* **7/4**[1]
4366 **3** *13* **Houston Dynimo (IRE)**[5] 1871 10-11-3 120 .... (bt) DavidNoonan[(7)] 117
(David Pipe) *pressed wnr tl 12th: cl 3rd: rdn whn blnd 3 out: one pce and hld after* **7/2**[3]
1122 **4** *46* **Tangolan (IRE)**[12] 1767 7-11-7 120 .... (t) ConorShoemark[(3)] 91
(Fergal O'Brien) *nvr fluent: chsd ldng trio: mstke 3rd and rdr lost iron: reminders after 5th: rdn after 12th: sn btn: t.o* **5/2**[2]

5m 0.1s (-17.40) **Going Correction** -0.675s/f (Firm) **4** Ran SP% **107.2**
Speed ratings (Par 107): **107,105,99,81**
CSF £11.27 TOTE £6.70; EX 8.60 Trifecta £28.30.
Owner J P Romans **Bred** R Kent & Mrs N O'Neil **Trained** Milborne Port, Dorset

FOCUS
A modest little handicap, run at a fair gallop and best rated around the frustrating runner-up. The winner has the potential to rate higher.

1949 HORSINGTON H'CAP HURDLE (8 hdls) 1m 7f 65y
3:35 (3:37) (Class 3) (0-130,127) 3-Y-O+ **£5,523** (£1,621; £810; £405)

Form RPR
6312 **1** **Regulation (IRE)**[12] 1766 6-11-8 123 .... (p) RichardJohnson 134+
(Neil King) *mid-div: tk clsr order 5th: qcknd to ld after 2 out: rdn clr: readily* **9/4**[1]
-602 **2** *10* **Laser Blazer**[20] 1661 7-11-8 123 .... (v[1]) WayneHutchinson 124
(Alan King) *trckd ldrs: rdn after 3 out: styd on into 2nd run-in: no ch w wnr* **7/1**
5321 **3** *1 ½* **Dry Ol'Party**[28] 1574 5-10-12 113 .... TomO'Brien 113
(Philip Hobbs) *trckd ldr: led after 3 out: rdn and hdd after next: sn outpcd by wnr: no ex whn lost 2nd run-in* **13/2**[3]
5P-2 **4** *1 ¼* **Full Blast (FR)**[18] 1673 4-11-0 115 .... (t) SamTwiston-Davies 113
(Paul Nicholls) *hld up: awkward 5th: rdn after 3 out: styd on into 4th run-in: nvr gng pce to get involved* **8/1**
12 **5** *1 ¼* **Mountain Fighter**[26] 1590 4-11-3 125 .... MrAlexFerguson[(7)] 122
(John Ferguson) *trckd ldrs: rdn after 3 out: one pce fr next* **9/2**[2]
5220 **6** *6* **Byron Blue (IRE)**[40] 1488 6-11-12 127 .... (t) TomCannon 120
(Mark Gillard) *j.lft bdly at times: led: rdn and hdd after 3 out: grad fdd fr next* **10/1**
2135 **7** *13* **Stephen Hero (IRE)**[27] 1296 5-11-10 125 .... GavinSheehan 104
(Brian Barr) *mid-div: rdn after 3 out: wknd bef next* **18/1**
P-31 **8** *56* **Handsome Dan (IRE)**[20] 1661 9-11-6 121 .... PaulMoloney 50
(Sarah Hollinshead) *hld up bhd: rdn after 3 out: sn btn: eased fr next* **8/1**

3m 28.1s (-20.80) **Going Correction** -1.175s/f (Hard) **8** Ran SP% **111.4**
Speed ratings (Par 107): **108,102,101,101,100 97,90,60**
CSF £17.48 CT £84.80 TOTE £2.60: £1.10, £2.40, £2.00; EX 17.80 Trifecta £82.60.
Owner Amber Road Partnership **Bred** Barouche Stud (IRE) Ltd **Trained** Barbury Castle, Wiltshire

FOCUS
There was a sound gallop in this competitive-looking handicap, but it was one-way traffic. Solid form for the class with a step up from the useful winner.

1950 SHEPTON MALLET NOVICES' H'CAP CHASE (21 fncs) 3m 1f 30y
4:10 (4:10) (Class 4) (0-105,104) 4-Y-O+ **£3,898** (£1,144; £572; £286)

Form RPR
3642 **1** **He's A Bully (IRE)**[8] 1820 6-11-10 102 .... RichardJohnson 118+
(Philip Hobbs) *j.lft thrght: racd keenly: hld up: hit 8th: hdwy to trck ldr whn hit 10th: led appr 3 out: sn idling and nt fluent after: drvn clr run-in* **5/4**[1]

2342 **2** 9 **Supapowers (IRE)**[18] 1678 9-11-3 102....................(t) CiaranGethings(7) 112
(Robert Stephens) *trckd ldrs: disp 2nd after 13th tl rdn after 17th: regained 2nd after 3 out: 2 l down but styng on whn blnd last: no ch after* **7/2**[3]

53P **3** 29 **Celtic Fella (IRE)**[55] 1326 8-10-0 78 oh11....................(vt) TrevorWhelan 63
(Debra Hamer) *chsd ldrs: hit 1st: rdn after 16th: wknd after 4 out: lft 3rd 2 out* **25/1**

5415 **4** 32 **Tribal Dance (IRE)**[6] 1850 9-10-11 89....................(v) SeanBowen 39
(John O'Shea) *led tl 2nd: chsd clr ldr tl 10th: dropped to 5th 12th: wknd 15th: lft remote 4th 2 out* **8/1**

U4-6 **F** **Well Rewarded (IRE)**[28] 1579 5-11-11 103....................(b[1]) GavinSheehan 105+
(Emma Lavelle) *j.rt thrght: led 2nd: clr 5th: nt fluent 8th: rdn and hdd appr 3 out: hld in clr 3rd whn fell 2 out* **11/4**[2]

0000 **P** **Prince Of Silver**[17] 1691 9-10-4 85....................(t) JamesBanks(3)
(Andy Turnell) *hld up: pckd 3rd: lost tch after 12th: p.u bef 15th* **25/1**

6m 20.6s (-18.90) **Going Correction** -0.675s/f (Firm) **6** Ran SP% **112.1**
Speed ratings (Par 105): **103,100,90,80,**
CSF £6.34 TOTE £2.00: £1.10, £2.50; EX 8.30 Trifecta £46.60.
Owner Owners For Owners: He's A Bully **Bred** John And Ann Goold **Trained** Withycombe, Somerset

FOCUS
It was very evident this was a novice handicap due to some errant jumping off the strong gallop set by Well Rewarded. The winner was similar to his upgraded recent run.

1951 CASTLE CARY H'CAP HURDLE (11 hdls) 2m 5f 82y
4:45 (5:00) (Class 4) (0-105,105) 4-Y-O+ **£3,249** (£954; £477; £238)

Form RPR

0521 **1** **Barton Antix**[9] 1812 6-11-13 105 7ex....................(p) NoelFehily 113+
(Neil Mulholland) *travelled wl in tch: chal 2 out: sn led: styd on wl fr last: rdn out* **11/10**[1]

/BP2 **2** 2 **Lady From Geneva**[13] 1756 8-11-2 94....................(t) BrendanPowell 98
(Brendan Powell) *trckd ldrs: led appr 2 out: rdn and hdd between last 2: styd on gamely to hold on for hld 2nd* **12/1**

1-65 **3** nk **Demographic (USA)**[32] 1545 6-11-12 104....................(v) RichieMcLernon 107
(Emma Lavelle) *trckd ldrs: rdn appr 3 out: styd on to press for 2nd run-in but nt pce to chal wnr* **15/2**[3]

2035 **4** 1/2 **Ennisnag (IRE)**[13] 1756 10-10-12 97.................... MrGTreacy(7) 100
(Paul Henderson) *hld up: hdwy after 3 out: rdn to dispute 2nd after 2 out: styd on but nt pce to threaten wnr* **14/1**

-126 **5** 3 1/4 **I'm In Charge**[8] 1820 9-11-1 100....................(t) CiaranGethings(7) 99
(Grant Cann) *in tch: ev ch appr 2 out tl rdn between last 2: styd on but no ex fr last* **7/1**[2]

1223 **6** 17 **Billy My Boy**[105] 895 6-11-9 104.................... GilesHawkins(3) 90
(Chris Down) *racd keenly: hld up in last pair: tk clsr order after 4th: rdn after 3 out: wknd next* **7/1**[2]

5620 **7** 8 **Warsaw Pact (IRE)**[129] 675 12-9-7 78 oh4.................... DavidNoonan(7) 55
(Steven Dixon) *chsd ldrs: drvn along fr 7th: wknd 2 out* **16/1**

-600 **8** 1/2 **A Hairy Koala (FR)**[8] 1819 5-11-11 103....................(bt) ConorO'Farrell 79
(David Pipe) *drvn to dispute ld early: hdd appr 4th where lft in clr ld sn after: rdn and hdd appr 2 out: sn btn* **14/1**

PP0 **P** **Tiger D'Oust (FR)**[8] 1823 6-10-9 90....................(b) KieronEdgar(3)
(Chris Down) *disp ld: 3 l clr whn slipped on landing 4th and lost pl: drvn along fr 7th: sn last: t.o whn p.u after 3 out* **50/1**

4m 57.2s (-29.30) **Going Correction** -1.175s/f (Hard) **9** Ran SP% **113.3**
Speed ratings (Par 105): **108,107,107,106,105 99,96,95,**
CSF £14.98 CT £68.79 TOTE £1.80: £1.10, £2.60, £2.60; EX 13.50 Trifecta £88.80.
Owner Exors of the Late Lady Clarke **Bred** Lady H J Clarke **Trained** Limpley Stoke, Wilts

FOCUS
There was a 15-minute delay prior to this moderate handicap. The in-form winner is value for further and there should be more to come.

1952 REDLYNCH MAIDEN HURDLE (11 hdls) 2m 5f 82y
5:20 (5:25) (Class 5) 4-Y-O+ **£2,599** (£763; £381; £190)

Form RPR

304- **1** **Fourth Act (IRE)**[199] 5080 6-11-0 115....................(t) NoelFehily 100+
(Colin Tizzard) *trckd ldr: led after 3 out: rdn whn briefly jnd 2 out: jnd again last: r.o to assert run-in: rdn out* **4/6**[1]

3-03 **2** 1 **Rustamabad (FR)**[17] 1693 5-11-0 0.................... RichardJohnson 100+
(Tim Vaughan) *trckd ldrs: wnt cl 2nd after 3 out: chal briefly next: sn hung rt bhd wnr: chal again last: kpt on same pce* **13/8**[2]

0 **3** 23 **Minmore Grey (IRE)**[16] 1704 6-10-7 0.................... WilliamFeatherstone(7) 76
(Nick Lampard) *hld up: effrt after 3 out: wnt hld 4th next: wnt modest 3rd run-in: nvr trbld ldrs* **66/1**

4P5 **4** 3/4 **Trakeur (FR)**[38] 1510 8-10-7 72....................(p) ThomasCheesman(7) 75
(Simon Hodgson) *hld up in last pair: wnt cl 3rd after 3 out: rdn bef next: wknd last* **14/1**[3]

0 **5** 32 **Jopaan (IRE)**[26] 1590 8-10-11 0.................... ThomasGarner(3) 43
(Brian Barr) *trckd ldr tl 5th: rdn bef 3 out: wknd bef 2 out: t.o* **100/1**

-640 **6** 6 **Watchmetail (IRE)**[17] 1691 9-11-0 64.................... ConorO'Farrell 37
(John Panvert) *led tl rdn after 3 out: wknd next: t.o* **50/1**

5m 1.2s (-25.30) **Going Correction** -1.175s/f (Hard) **6** Ran SP% **109.2**
Speed ratings (Par 103): **101,100,91,91,79 77**
CSF £1.95 TOTE £1.50: £1.10, £1.10; EX 2.00 Trifecta £17.90.
Owner C L Tizzard **Bred** Kenilworth House Stud **Trained** Milborne Port, Dorset

FOCUS
This maiden saw the two clear market leaders dominate from the home turn. Weak form.
T/Plt: £635.40 to a £1 stake. Pool: £35,186.38 - 40.42 winning tickets T/Qpdt: £2.00 to a £1 stake. Pool: £4,764.81 - 1,699.76 winning tickets **Tim Mitchell**

1953 - 1959a (Foreign Racing) - See Raceform Interactive

770 FFOS LAS (L-H)
Saturday, October 17

OFFICIAL GOING: Good (good to firm in places on chase course)
Wind: slight against Weather: overcast

1960 TANNERS WINES MARES' "NATIONAL HUNT" MAIDEN HURDLE (8 hdls) 1m 7f 202y
2:00 (2:03) (Class 4) 4-Y-O+ **£3,898** (£1,144; £572; £286)

Form RPR

22-F **1** **Clemency**[25] 1612 4-10-12 0.................... DavidBass 107
(Nicky Henderson) *hld up towards rr: hdwy 3 out: sn rdn and swtchd rt: chal 2 out: led jst after last: rdn out* **2/1**[1]

00 **2** 1 1/4 **Kilty Caul (IRE)**[16] 1716 6-10-9 0.................... TomBellamy(3) 106
(Kim Bailey) *hld up: rdn and hdwy 3 out: led narrowly 2 out tl jst after last: one pce* **33/1**

05-2 **3** shd **Rest And Be (IRE)**[127] 714 8-10-12 105....................(t) NickScholfield 105
(Alan Jones) *hld up in last: stdy hdwy 3 out: swtchd rt appr last: kpt on same pce flat* **7/2**[3]

423- **4** 3/4 **Coco Des Champs (IRE)**[194] 5181 5-10-12 114.................... LeightonAspell 105
(Oliver Sherwood) *t.k.h: trckd ldrs: nt fluent 2nd: wnt 2nd appr 3 out: rdn and ev ch 2 out tl unable qck bef last* **5/2**[2]

351 **5** 8 **Belcanto (IRE)**[41] 1491 5-10-12 0.................... BrendanPowell 99
(Jamie Snowden) *mid-div: hdwy 3 out: rdn whn mstke 2 out: nt rcvr: styd on again flat* **9/1**

/254 **6** 2 **Jazz Thyme (IRE)**[16] 1718 6-10-12 0.................... RobertDunne 98
(Robert Stephens) *t.k.h: led: j.rt at times: rdn 3 out: hdd 2 out: nudged along and wknd appr last* **5/1**

4-50 **7** 25 **Omgnotanother (IRE)**[16] 1716 4-10-12 0.................... AdamWedge 73
(Evan Williams) *prom: trckd ldr fr 3rd tl rdn appr 3 out: sn wknd: t.o* **33/1**

00-0 **8** 7 **Bronwydd**[39] 1506 5-10-12 0.................... TrevorWhelan 66
(Debra Hamer) *cl up: lost 2nd at 3rd: struggling fr 5th: t.o* **100/1**

3m 53.2s (233.20) **Going Correction** +0.475s/f (Soft)
WFA 4 from 5yo+ 9lb **8** Ran SP% **117.7**
Speed ratings (Par 105): **107,106,106,105,101 100,88,84**
CSF £57.92 TOTE £2.40: £1.10, £6.00, £2.70; EX 34.00 Trifecta £599.50 Part won..
Owner Elite Racing Club **Bred** Elite Racing Club **Trained** Upper Lambourn, Berks

FOCUS
Hurdle races on Flat course. Rail movement around the bends increased races 1 & 7 by 69yds, race 2 by 120yds and race 5 by 103yds. Chase distances as advertised.No more than an ordinary mares' maiden hurdle judged by the past exploits of these runners and the early gallop looked pretty steady. The winner, third and fourth help with the level.

1961 BRIDGESTONE CONDITIONAL JOCKEYS' H'CAP HURDLE (12 hdls) 2m 7f 191y
2:35 (2:37) (Class 5) (0-100,95) 4-Y-O+ **£3,249** (£954; £477; £238)

Form RPR

4312 **1** **Tokyo Javilex (FR)**[5] 1890 8-11-11 94....................(t) TomBellamy 102+
(Nigel Hawke) *trckd ldrs: wnt 2nd appr 3 out: sn rdn: led 2 out: styd on wl* **7/4**[1]

-100 **2** 6 **King's Song (FR)**[9] 1819 5-11-12 95.................... KieronEdgar 97
(David Dennis) *t.k.h in mid-div: hdwy 5th: rdn to ld appr 3 out where hit flight: hdd 2 out: kpt on same pce* **8/1**

0PP- **3** 3 **Shanksforamillion**[249] 4147 6-10-5 77.................... CiaranGethings(3) 76
(David Rees) *hld up: hdwy after 9th: chsd ldng pair 3 out: one pce fr next* **20/1**

2P22 **4** 9 **Hassadin**[13] 1771 9-11-2 90....................(p) MrMartinMcIntyre(5) 83
(Michael Blake) *prom: trckd ldr fr 2nd tl appr 3 out: wkng whn mstke 2 out* **5/2**[2]

-250 **5** 1 **Peaceful Gardens**[14] 1756 6-9-13 74....................[1] DavidPrichard(6) 64
(Jeremy Scott) *hld up: rdn and struggling after 9th: no ch after: styd on flat* **12/1**

-P65 **6** 6 **Just Lewis**[13] 1780 8-10-0 74 ow2.................... WilliamFeatherstone(5) 59
(Nikki Evans) *hld up in last: clsd 9th: rdn 3 out: sn wknd* **25/1**

00-5 **7** 1 3/4 **Mister Chairman (IRE)**[158] 262 7-10-12 89.................... ConorBrassil(8) 72
(Rebecca Curtis) *trckd ldrs tl wknd after 9th* **5/1**[3]

041/ **8** 8 **Ohms Law**[951] 4680 10-10-9 78.................... JakeHodson 54
(Anthony Day) *t.k.h and set slow pce: rdn and hdd appr 3 out: sn wknd* **16/1**

6m 17.8s (28.80) **Going Correction** +0.475s/f (Soft) **8** Ran SP% **114.9**
Speed ratings (Par 103): **71,69,68,65,64 62,62,59**
CSF £16.51 CT £208.33 TOTE £2.30: £1.20, £1.70, £5.10; EX 13.70 Trifecta £157.90.
Owner D R Mead **Bred** Scea Ecurie Jc Laisis **Trained** Stoodleigh, Devon

FOCUS
A modest staying hurdle which, as is so often the case here, turned into a real stamina test despite the fact the early pace didn't look particularly strong, and they finished well strung out. The in-form winner is rated in line with his recent best.

1962 SAXTON DRILLING NOVICES' H'CAP CHASE (15 fncs) 2m 3f 83y
3:10 (3:12) (Class 3) (0-135,130) 4-Y-O+ **£9,747** (£2,862; £1,431; £715)

Form RPR

53-2 **1** **Voix D'Eau (FR)**[42] 1479 5-11-4 122....................(t) NoelFehily 139+
(Harry Fry) *hld up in last of 4: impr a pl 9th: led after 4 out: sn in command: easily* **11/8**[2]

5221 **2** 13 **Henllan Harri (IRE)**[66] 1235 7-11-10 128....................(p) SeanBowen 131+
(Peter Bowen) *led at slow pce: j.rt tl ster fr 9th: led briefly appr 4 out: sn one pce and no ch w easy wnr* **1/1**[1]

3404 **3** 1 **King Alfonso**[10] 1809 6-10-13 117.................... RobertDunne 117
(Dai Burchell) *racd in 3rd to 9th: in tch in last after: mstke 11th: j. slowly 3 out: one pce* **7/1**[3]

20P **4** 31 **Ubaldo Des Menhies (FR)**[39] 1508 7-11-0 118........(p) RichieMcLernon 93
(Jonjo O'Neill) *trckd ldr tl rdn and wknd qckly appr 4 out: t.o* **9/1**

4m 59.8s (-1.30) **Going Correction** -0.30s/f (Good) **4** Ran SP% **114.6**
Speed ratings (Par 107): **90,84,84,71**
CSF £3.54 TOTE £2.70; EX 2.90 Trifecta £6.70.
Owner Harry Fry Racing Club **Bred** Christophe Toussaint & Emmanuel Clayeux **Trained** Seaborough, Dorset

FOCUS
A reasonable novice handicap chase. The winner was quite impressive with the second probably the best guide to the form.

1963 BRIDGESTONE H'CAP HURDLE (12 hdls) 2m 7f 191y
3:50 (3:51) (Class 3) (0-140,138) 3-Y-O+ **£9,747** (£2,862; £1,431; £715)

Form RPR

1P/3 **1** **Ongenstown Lad (IRE)**[30] 1566 11-10-11 123....................(t) RobbieColgan 127+
(Mrs Gillian Callaghan, Ire) *hld up in last pair: hdwy 3 out where nt fluent: sn rdn: led between last 2: styd on wl* **7/1**

PPP- **2** 4 1/2 **Minella On Line (IRE)**[205] 4993 6-10-7 119.................... LeightonAspell 120+
(Rebecca Curtis) *trckd ldrs: blnd 9th: rdn and wnt 2nd 3 out: one pce whn hit last: regained 2nd flat* **3/1**[2]

1121 **3** 3/4 **Princeton Royale (IRE)**[13] 1784 6-11-12 138....................(v) TrevorWhelan 136
(Neil King) *racd in 4th: clsd 8th: wnt 2nd after 9th: led appr 3 out: wandered 2 out: sn hdd: no ex and lost 2nd flat* **11/4**[1]

3215 **4** 10 **Epic Warrior (IRE)**[24] 1633 6-10-10 125....................(p) KieronEdgar(3) 116
(David Pipe) *w ldr: nt fluent 4th: led 7th tl rdn and hdd appr 3 out: one pce and hld after* **6/1**

2-15 **5** 9 **Speed Master (IRE)**[111] 855 9-10-11 130....................(vt) MrJJSlevin(7) 113
(Nigel Twiston-Davies) *led to 7th: lost 2nd after 9th: wknd appr 3 out* **4/1**[3]

32-0 **6** 1/2 **Kingsmere**[155] 319 10-11-0 126.................... NoelFehily 106
(Henry Daly) *hld up in last pair: hdwy after 9th: wknd 2 out* **5/1**

6m 6.3s (17.30) **Going Correction** +0.475s/f (Soft) **6** Ran SP% **115.1**
Speed ratings (Par 107): **71,69,69,65,62 62**
CSF £29.30 TOTE £9.70: £1.90, £2.70; EX 57.90 Trifecta £167.40.
Owner Oliver O'Callaghan **Bred** Mrs M Farrell **Trained** Kells, Co Meath

The Form Book Jumps 2015-16, Raceform Ltd, Newbury, RG14 5SJ

FOCUS
A wide-open heat despite the small field. The winner was a 135+ hurdler at his peak and may still be capable of better than this.

1964 INTEGRAL GEOTECHNIQUE H'CAP HURDLE (10 hdls) 2m 4f
4:20 (4:20) (Class 4) (0-110,110) 3-Y-0+ **£3,898** (£1,144; £572; £286)

Form RPR
434- **1** **Wild Rover (IRE)**[211] 4883 6-11-10 **108**........................ LeightonAspell 123+
(Rebecca Curtis) *trckd ldr: carried rt 3rd: led after next: j.rt fr 6th: rdn after 3 out: drawing clr whn hit last: styd on strly* **3/1**[1]

000- **2** *16* **Captainofindustry (IRE)**[275] 3701 6-11-9 **107**........................ SeanBowen 109+
(Mark Pitman) *mid-div tl mstke and dropped to rr 5th: rdn along fr 7th: slt only 7th whn bmpd bef 2 out: 5th over last: styd on u.p to go 2nd flat: no ch w wnr* **11/1**

0523 **3** *1 3/4* **Skint**[44] 1458 9-11-12 **110**........................(p) AdamWedge 107
(Ali Stronge) *hld up: hdwy after 7th: disp 2nd 2 out tl flat but no imp on wnr* **20/1**

3-02 **4** *1 1/2* **The Geegeez Geegee (IRE)**[158] 261 6-11-12 **110**........(t) RyanMahon 106
(Anthony Honeyball) *hld up: rdn after 7th: styd on same pce fr 3 out: bmpd appr 2 out* **5/1**[2]

U0P- **5** *1 3/4* **War And Contrition (IRE)**[200] 5083 6-11-3 **101**........................ NoelFehily 97+
(Charlie Longsdon) *t.k.h: led: j.rt at times: hdd after 4th: wknd and lost 2nd 2 out* **8/1**

23 **6** *shd* **Top Spin (IRE)**[16] 1721 8-11-12 **110**........................(t) RichieMcLernon 104
(Jonjo O'Neill) *t.k.h in mid-div: rdn and clsd 3 out: chsd wnr 2 out but little imp: wknd and lost 2nd flat* **3/1**[1]

7 *3* **Indian Road Runner (IRE)**[25] 1620 7-11-5 **103**......(bt[1]) KeithDonoghue 96
(Shane Crawley, Ire) *hld up: stdy hdwy 6th: chsd ldrs 3 out: wknd next* **6/1**[3]

00F4 **8** *9* **Lilbourne Legacy**[19] 1673 4-10-13 **104**........................(p) DavidNoonan(7) 88
(David Pipe) *chsd ldrs: rdn 7th: wknd appr 3 out* **20/1**

-050 **9** *51* **Sinndar's Man**[62] 1269 4-11-10 **108**........................ NickScholfield 46
(Michael Blake) *mid-div tl wknd 7th: sn t.o* **12/1**

5m 6.2s (306.20)
WFA 4 from 6yo+ 10lb **9 Ran SP% 117.6**
CSF £36.01 CT £551.78 TOTE £4.30: £1.70, £4.60, £2.40; EX 40.10 Trifecta £789.00.
Owner The Wild Rover Partnership **Bred** Old Meadow Stud **Trained** Newport, Pembrokeshire

FOCUS
This looked fairly open on paper but it was taken apart by one of the least exposed runners in the field, who absolutely hacked up. He should have more to offer going right-handed.

1965 JCP SOLICITORS H'CAP CHASE (17 fncs) 2m 4f 199y
4:55 (4:55) (Class 4) (0-120,120) 4-Y-0+ **£5,198** (£1,526; £763; £381)

Form RPR
204- **1** **The Italian Yob (IRE)**[186] 5333 7-11-9 **117**........................(b) LeightonAspell 125+
(Nick Williams) *trckd ldr tl led 5th: drew clr fr 9th: mstke 13th: sn 12 l up: reduced advantage fr 3 out: styd on u.p* **11/4**[1]

3142 **2** *2 3/4* **Ladfromhighworth**[22] 1641 10-11-12 **120**........................ NickScholfield 124
(Jeremy Scott) *led to 5th: chsd wnr after: 12 l down after 13th: plugged on to cl gap fr 3 out but a being hld* **7/1**[3]

1043 **3** *2 1/4* **Isthereadifference (IRE)**[31] 1551 8-10-13 **107**........(bt) NoelFehily 111
(Neil Mulholland) *hld up: mstke 2nd: stl in rr whn rdn 4 out: styd on fr next: wnt 2nd 2 out: no further imp* **5/1**[2]

P411 **4** *12* **Forever My Friend (IRE)**[21] 1659 8-11-10 **118**........(p) SeanBowen 111
(Peter Bowen) *chsd ldrs: mstke 10th: wknd 3 out* **11/4**[1]

/P-3 **5** *9* **Ciceron (IRE)**[151] 390 9-11-11 **119**........................(t) TrevorWhelan 104
(Neil King) *in rr: nt fluent 9th: hdwy after 13th: wnt modest 3rd 4 out tl wknd next* **16/1**

PP-4 **6** *7* **Gus Macrae (IRE)**[22] 1641 11-10-7 **111**........................(tp) ConorBrassil(10) 92
(Rebecca Curtis) *mid-div: reminder 7th: rdn fr 12th: wknd 3 out* **8/1**

2226 **P** **Mac Bertie**[17] 1701 6-10-13 **107**........................ AdamWedge
(Evan Williams) *mid-div tl wknd after 13th: t.o whn p.u bef 3 out* **5/1**[2]

5m 19.1s (-9.50) **Going Correction** -0.30s/f (Good) **7 Ran SP% 116.2**
Speed ratings (Par 105): **106,104,104,99,96 93,**
CSF £22.44 CT £91.89 TOTE £4.00: £2.30, £4.80; EX 26.10 Trifecta £105.40.
Owner The Macaroni Beach Society **Bred** John Sweeney **Trained** George Nympton, Devon

FOCUS
An open handicap chase. The winner could still be competitive when reassessed.

1966 THOMAS CARROLL MAIDEN OPEN NATIONAL HUNT FLAT RACE 1m 7f 202y
5:30 (5:31) (Class 6) 4-6-Y-0 **£2,053** (£598; £299)

Form RPR
1 **Soupy Soups (IRE)**[209] 4-11-0 0........................ MarkQuinlan 114
(Neil Mulholland) *hld up towards rr: hdwy 6f out: rdn 4f out: stl only 4th ent fnl f: r.o to ld nr fin* **16/1**

2 *nk* **Templeross (IRE)**[194] 4-10-11 0........................ RyanHatch(3) 113
(Nigel Twiston-Davies) *cl up: rdn 3f out: sn edgd rt: led 1f out tl nr fin* **8/1**[3]

3 *3/4* **You Say What (IRE)**[214] 5-11-0 0........................ TrevorWhelan 113
(Neil King) *chsd ldrs: rdn over 2f out: led over 1f out: sn hdd: kpt on u.p* **16/1**

2 **4** *5* **Galveston (IRE)**[122] 761 6-10-11 0........................ ConorShoemark(3) 108
(Fergal O'Brien) *led: rdn 2f out: sn hdd: kpt on but outpcd by ldng trio ins fnl f* **5/2**[1]

5 *6* **Song Of The Night (IRE)**[188] 4-11-0 0........................ LeightonAspell 103
(Charlie Longsdon) *mid-div: hdwy 4f out: one pce fnl 2f* **10/1**

6- **6** *4* **Isla Di Milano (IRE)**[237] 4391 4-10-7 0........................ PaulNO'Brien(7) 99
(Harry Whittington) *trckd ldrs: rdn over 3f out: wknd 2f out* **11/1**

2 **7** *7* **Verygoodverygood (FR)**[158] 264 4-11-0 0........................ RhysFlint 93
(Paul Morgan) *trckd ldrs: rdn 3f out: wknd 2f out* **6/1**[2]

0 **8** *46* **Big Touch (FR)**[147] 444 4-11-0 0........................ NickScholfield 52
(Paul Morgan) *t.k.h in rr: nudged along 4f out: sn lost tch: t.o* **25/1**

9 *18* **Blue Is The Colour (IRE)** 5-11-0 0........................ DavidBass 35
(Nicky Henderson) *t.k.h: trckd ldrs tl grad lost pl 1/2-way: bhd fnl 4f: t.o* **5/2**[1]

10 *24* **Red Lectra** 5-11-0 0........................ SeanBowen 14
(Peter Bowen) *hld up in rr: wknd 4f out: t.o* **12/1**

3m 50.4s (7.50) **Going Correction** +0.475s/f (Soft)
WFA 4 from 5yo+ 9lb **10 Ran SP% 119.7**
Speed ratings: **64,63,63,60,57 55,52,29,20,8**
CSF £141.43 TOTE £23.40: £4.40, £3.50, £5.40; EX 176.20 Trifecta £991.20 Part won..
Owner Equi ex Incertis Partners **Bred** Joe Brennan **Trained** Limpley Stoke, Wilts

FOCUS
This didn't look a bad little bumper with Galveston setting a good standard on his run at Uttoxeter in June, but he was swallowed up by less exposed types in the closing stages. The first four could be above average.
T/Plt: £467.90 to a £1 stake. Pool of £50741.39 - 79.15 winning tickets. T/Qpdt: £331.10 to a £1 stake. Pool of £2550.64 - 5.70 winning tickets. **Richard Lowther**

1792 MARKET RASEN (R-H)
Saturday, October 17

OFFICIAL GOING: Good (7.9)
Wind: light 1/2 against Weather: overcast

1967 LISTERS MERCEDES-BENZ A-AIDEN HURDLE (8 hdls) 2m 148y
2:05 (2:07) (Class 4) 4-Y-0+ **£3,898** (£1,144; £572; £286)

Form RPR
525- **1** **Adrakhan (FR)**[289] 3461 4-11-0 112........................ HarrySkelton 108+
(Dan Skelton) *trckd ldrs: 2nd appr 2 out: led appr last: drvn abt 2 l clr: hld on towards fin* **9/4**[2]

325- **2** *1/2* **Film Director (IRE)**[216] 4782 7-11-0 115........................ DarylJacob 108+
(Brian Ellison) *trckd ldrs: cl 3rd whn j.rt last: sn chsng wnr: styd on towards fin* **13/8**[1]

U53- **3** *2 3/4* **Scoppio Del Carro**[32] 4467 4-11-0 116........................(t) DenisO'Regan 104
(John Quinn) *chsd ldrs: cl 4th last: kpt on same pce* **7/1**

26-5 **4** *1 1/4* **Bleu Et Noir**[151] 392 4-11-0 0........................ RichardJohnson 104+
(Tim Vaughan) *t.k.h towards rr: jnd ldrs 3rd: led appr 5th: hdd appr last: fdd clsng stages* **9/1**

5 *11* **Noble Reach**[60] 4-10-7 0........................ BrianHughes 86
(Lawrence Mullaney) *t.k.h: trckd ldrs: lost pl 3 out: poor 5th appr 2 out* **33/1**

3320 **6** *3 3/4* **Raise A Spark**[18] 1684 5-11-0 110........................ WayneHutchinson 89
(Donald McCain) *hld up towards rr: hdwy 3 out: sn chsng ldrs: wknd between last 2* **11/2**[3]

6 **7** *12* **Devon River (FR)**[18] 1684 5-10-9 0........................ CallumBewley(5) 76
(Simon Waugh) *in rr: bhd fr 3 out* **66/1**

8 *11* **Lazarus Bell**[16] 5-10-7 0........................ CraigGallagher(7) 65
(Alan Brown) *chsd ldrs: lost pl 3 out* **28/1**

P **Gabrial The Boss (USA)**[14] 5-10-11 0........................(t) BrianToomey(3)
(Michael Mullineaux) *j. v big in rr: wl bhd fr 4th: t.o whn p.u after 3 out* **50/1**

2U0F **P** **Magna Cartor**[9] 1826 5-11-0 0........................ JamesDavies
(Ronald Thompson) *led: j.rt 1st: nt fluent next 2: hdd appr 5th: sn lost pl and bhd: t.o whn p.u bef 2 out* **25/1**

4m 11.7s (5.00) **Going Correction** +0.45s/f (Soft) **10 Ran SP% 120.4**
Speed ratings (Par 105): **106,105,104,103,98 96,91,86, ,**
CSF £6.52 TOTE £3.80: £1.40, £1.10, £3.00; EX 7.40 Trifecta £26.70.
Owner Raymond Tooth **Bred** E A R L Haras Du Camp Benard **Trained** Alcester, Warwicks

FOCUS
Rail out 16yds on Wood bend and 27yds on Home bend. Races 1, 3, & 7 increased by about 177yds and races 2, 4, 5 & increased by about 258yds. The early pace was soft until the hard-pulling fourth took over at halfway, but the first four home all look capable of winning races. A step up from the winner with the second below his best but a bit unlucky.

1968 RASE EQUINE NOVICES' HURDLE (10 hdls) 2m 4f 139y
2:40 (2:43) (Class 4) 4-Y-0+ **£3,898** (£1,144; £572; £286)

Form RPR
34 **1** **Crimson Ark (IRE)**[22] 1645 5-10-10 0........................ DarylJacob 119+
(Emma Lavelle) *trckd ldr: t.k.h: nt fluent 1st 2: led appr 2 out: sn drvn hld on wl run-in* **13/2**[3]

-221 **2** *1* **Oh Land Abloom (IRE)**[12] 1794 5-11-10 132........................(t) RichardJohnson 133+
(Neil King) *trckd ldng pair: upsides 2 out: sn drvn: stmbld sltly landing last: no ex last 50yds* **2/5**[1]

2 **3** *34* **Le Legro (IRE)**[14] 1752 5-10-10 0........................ JamesDavies 86
(Charlie Mann) *led: qcknd pce 6th: hit 3 out: hdd appr next: sn wknd* **9/2**[2]

0-4 **4** *7* **Bling Noir (IRE)**[12] 1797 5-10-4 0 ow1........................ DenisO'Regan 71
(Tony Coyle) *in rr: chsd ldrs 5th: outpcd next: bhd 3 out: poor 4th next* **33/1**

6 **5** *14* **Lovely Bubbly**[136] 602 4-10-10 0........................ BrianHughes 67
(Tim Vaughan) *t.k.h in rr: chsd ldrs 5th: outpcd next: bhd 3 out: wknd next* **20/1**

5m 20.3s (11.50)
WFA 4 from 5yo 10lb **5 Ran SP% 110.6**
CSF £10.24 TOTE £8.30: £2.60, £1.10; EX 14.90 Trifecta £27.80.
Owner Gemmell, Langton, Ryan & Sieff **Bred** J Morrison **Trained** Hatherden, Hants

FOCUS
Despite the small field and ordinary gallop, the first two looked above average. A big step up from the winner on his bumper form.

1969 DD STABLE LADS CAFE NOVICES' CHASE (12 fncs) 2m 1f 43y
3:15 (3:18) (Class 3) 4-Y-0+ **£7,797** (£2,289; £1,144; £572)

Form RPR
01-1 **1** **Fox Norton (FR)**[144] 492 5-11-7 0........................ DarylJacob 147+
(Neil Mulholland) *mde all: 2 l ahd last: drvn rt out* **5/2**[2]

2F6- **2** *3/4* **Golden Doyen (GER)**[21] 4920 4-10-7 0........................ RichardJohnson 130
(Philip Hobbs) *chsd wnr: clr 2nd appr 3 out: swtchd rt and styd on last 150yds: jst hld* **15/8**[1]

10-5 **3** *15* **Pain Au Chocolat (FR)**[168] 94 4-10-7 0........................(t) HarrySkelton 119
(Dan Skelton) *chsd wnr: outpcd appr 3 out: wknd appr 2 out* **15/8**[1]

12-5 **4** *21* **Raktiman (IRE)**[168] 87 8-11-2 0........................ DannyCook 107
(Richard Drake) *towards rr: outpcd 8th: sn bhd: lft distant 4th 2 out* **20/1**

-06U **P** **Lucky Bridle (IRE)**[2] 1922 6-10-11 127........................ DiarmuidO'Regan(5)
(Chris Grant) *hld up detached in last: bhd fr 6th: t.o 9th: p.u bef next* **100/1**

P50- **F** **Zaidiyn (FR)**[224] 4633 5-11-2 0........................ BrianHughes 116
(Brian Ellison) *chsd ldng trio: blnd 7th: outpcd whn hit 9th: wknd bef next: 12 l 4th whn fell 2 out* **14/1**[3]

4m 17.7s (-17.30) **Going Correction** -0.60s/f (Firm)
WFA 4 from 5yo+ 9lb **6 Ran SP% 110.6**
Speed ratings (Par 107): **116,115,108,98,**
CSF £7.72 TOTE £3.00: £1.30, £1.70; EX 7.90 Trifecta £13.30.
Owner B Dunn **Bred** S A Scuderia Del Bargelo **Trained** Limpley Stoke, Wilts

FOCUS
The first three were all at least Grade 2 level over hurdles, making this a classy affair which should produce winners. The pace was medium at best but the form looks good. Fox Norton looks a smart early-season novice.

1970 LISTERSMERCEDESBENZ.CO.UK H'CAP CHASE (15 fncs 2 omitted) 2m 7f 191y
3:55 (3:55) (Class 3) (0-125,125) 4-Y-0+ £9,747 (£2,862; £1,431; £715)

Form RPR
462- 1 **Viva Steve (IRE)**[194] 5195 7-11-11 124 .... BrianHughes 132+
(Mick Channon) *chsd ldrs: reminders after normal 4 out: led omitted 3 out: hit 2 out: hdd last: swtchd rt 150yds out: styd on to ld towards fin* 11/2[2]
4P-4 2 1 1/4 **Auvergnat (FR)**[161] 199 5-11-9 122 .... RichardJohnson 127
(Jonjo O'Neill) *trckd ldrs: led normal 4 out: hdd omitted 3 out: led last: edgd rt: hdd and no ex towards fin* 11/2[2]
2515 3 1 **Set List (IRE)**[17] 1701 6-11-11 124 .... DarylJacob 129
(Emma Lavelle) *chsd ldrs: drvn normal 4 out: rallied and chsd ldrs omitted 3 out: kpt on run-in: tk 3rd in clsng stages* 8/1
UP-3 4 3/4 **Cloudy Bob (IRE)**[22] 1641 8-11-5 118 .... HarrySkelton 121
(Pat Murphy) *in rr: hdwy 11th: sn chsng ldrs: kpt on same pce fr 2 out* 4/1[1]
216- 5 49 **Gold Ingot**[282] 3587 8-11-8 121 .... AndrewThornton 80
(Caroline Bailey) *led: hdd normal 4 out: wknd appr omitted 3 out: sn bhd: t.o* 14/1
6 7 **Morney Wing (IRE)**[166] 116 6-11-9 122 ....(p) DenisO'Regan 75
(Charlie Mann) *chsd ldrs: lost pl 12th: bhd normal 4 out: t.o* 14/1
0061 7 6 **Feast Of Fire (IRE)**[13] 1783 8-9-11 103 .... RyanDay(7) 51
(Mike Sowersby) *hld up in rr: hmpd 1st: sme hdwy 9th: lost pl 11th: bhd normal 4 out: t.o* 10/1
0535 8 3 1/2 **Big Sound**[13] 1783 8-10-11 110 ....(p) JakeGreenall 54
(Mark Walford) *in rr: bhd fr 11th: t.o normal 4 out* 16/1
213- P **Desert Joe (IRE)**[211] 4884 9-11-12 125 .... WayneHutchinson
(Alan King) *chsd ldrs: reminders 10th: lost pl 13th: sn bhd: t.o whn p.u bef 2 out* 11/2[2]
10-1 F **Benevolent (IRE)**[139] 568 8-11-4 124 .... MrTommieMO'Brien(7)
(Chris Bealby) *mid-div: fell 1st: fatally injured* 7/1[3]

6m 12.2s (-19.10) **Going Correction** -0.60s/f (Firm) **10** Ran SP% **118.1**
Speed ratings (Par 107): **107,106,106,106,89 87,85,84, ,**
CSF £37.00 CT £244.30 TOTE £7.60: £2.00, £2.70, £1.90; EX 39.90 Trifecta £288.70.
Owner T P Radford **Bred** Peter And Patsy Stone **Trained** West Ilsley, Berks

FOCUS
An above-average chase run at a decent gallop for the trip. Many of the runners were in form when last seen, though in some cases that was several months ago. A pb from the winner.

1971 LISTERS MERCEDES-BENZ GLE MARES' H'CAP HURDLE (10 hdls) 2m 4f 139y
4:25 (4:27) (Class 4) (0-120,118) 4-Y-0+ £3,898 (£1,144; £572; £286)

Form RPR
144- 1 **Presenting Lisa (IRE)**[219] 4729 6-10-13 105 .... WayneHutchinson 111+
(Alan King) *best away: mde all: j.rt at time: qcknd pce 6th: hit 3 out: drvn and styd on wl run-in* 13/8[1]
4P2F 2 3 **Lily Little Legs (IRE)**[25] 1618 6-10-7 99 .... BrianHughes 101
(Mike Sowersby) *t.k.h: trckd ldrs: chsd wnr fr 3 out: drvn next: kpt on same pce: no real imp* 11/1
5462 3 1/2 **Pixiepot**[18] 1683 5-9-7 92 oh2 .... JamieHamilton(7) 96+
(Peter Niven) *hld up in tch: blnd 3rd: trcking ldrs next: 4th 2 out: kpt on same pce to take 3rd last 50yds* 9/4[2]
3F4- 4 2 3/4 **Barton Rose**[178] 5464 6-11-12 118 ....(p) RichardJohnson 118
(Neil Mulholland) *trckd ldrs 5th: effrt 3 out: 3rd and one pce whn j.lft last* 4/1[3]
3-3 5 12 **Cul Dealga (IRE)**[161] 212 6-11-4 110 ....(t) TomMessenger 98
(Chris Bealby) *trckd wnr: pushed along 6th: reminders 3 out: lost pl appr next* 10/1
4F3 6 22 **Impeccability**[16] 1716 5-10-9 101 ....(p) HenryBrooke 69
(John Mackie) *hld up in last: j.lft 7th: chsng ldrs next: sn drvn: lost pl bef 2 out: bhd whn eased fnl 150yds* 16/1

5m 28.8s (20.00) **Going Correction** +0.45s/f (Soft) **6** Ran SP% **112.2**
Speed ratings (Par 105): **79,77,77,76,72 63**
CSF £18.11 TOTE £2.70: £1.50, £2.80; EX 16.30 Trifecta £45.00.
Owner Mrs Peter Prowting **Bred** Kevin Galvin **Trained** Barbury Castle, Wilts

FOCUS
A fair race of its type, in which the winner controlled a routine gallop and is worth following. The winner improved to the level of his bumper win.

1972 RACING UK ANYWHERE NOW H'CAP HURDLE (12 hdls) 2m 7f 16y
5:00 (5:02) (Class 5) (0-100,98) 4-Y-0+ £3,249 (£954; £477; £238)

Form RPR
0660 1 **Love The Leader (IRE)**[27] 1599 7-10-12 84 ....(p) AlainCawley 100+
(Johnny Farrelly) *mid-div: chsd ldrs 3 out: sn 3rd: 2nd appr next: led appr last: drvn clr last 100yds* 6/1
6445 2 7 **Minella Bliss (IRE)**[5] 1890 10-10-10 89 ....(b) CharlieHammond(7) 100
(James Evans) *trckd ldrs: t.k.h: 2nd 9th: led appr 2 out: hdd appr last: kpt on same pce* 7/2[2]
3324 3 22 **Combustible Kate (IRE)**[10] 1813 9-10-3 80 .... CharlieDeutsch(5) 74
(Nick Kent) *led: j.big 1st 2: drvn 3 out: hdd appr next: wknd between last 2* 11/2
4-P6 4 2 1/2 **Just Skittles**[10] 1812 7-9-10 73 oh11 ow1 .... DannyBurton(5) 61
(Richard Harper) *hld up in rr: j.lft at time: hdwy 7th: outpcd 3 out: kpt on run-in: tk distant 4th last 100yds* 66/1
PP-P 5 4 **Black Lily (IRE)**[168] 89 7-11-7 93 .... TomMessenger 77
(Chris Bealby) *towards rr: hdwy 8th: sn lost pl: bhd fr 3 out: lft distant 4th last* 20/1
14-6 6 12 **Bridal Suite (IRE)**[160] 222 6-11-9 95 ....(tp) RichardJohnson 69
(Charlie Mann) *mid-div: nt fluent 4th: j.lft: lost pl and reminders 7th: drvn next: bhd fr 3 out* 9/2[3]
3PP 7 20 **Agent Louise**[102] 939 7-10-0 75 ....(p) AdamNicol(3) 31
(Mike Sowersby) *chsd ldrs: lost pl bef 8th: sn bhd: t.o whn blnd 3 out* 9/1
221P F **Steps And Stairs (IRE)**[47] 1426 5-11-12 98 ....(p) DarylJacob 86
(Jonjo O'Neill) *chsd ldr: hit 6th and next: reminders 9th: wknd sn after 3 out: distant 4th whn fell last* 5/2[1]

6m 1.2s (10.70) **Going Correction** +0.45s/f (Soft) **8** Ran SP% **114.9**
Speed ratings (Par 103): **99,96,88,88,86 82,75,**
CSF £27.95 CT £122.28 TOTE £8.90: £2.10, £1.10, £2.00; EX 43.40 Trifecta £158.30.
Owner Johnny Farrelly **Bred** Mrs Margaret Lacy **Trained** Enmore, Somerset

FOCUS
A modest race, run at a respectable pace and won by a well-backed horse with little previous form. A weak handicap with a pb from the winner.

1973 FAREWELL AND THANK YOU ALEX MCMAHON STANDARD OPEN NATIONAL HUNT FLAT RACE 2m 148y
5:35 (5:36) (Class 6) 4-6-Y-0 £1,711 (£498; £249)

Form RPR
2-5 1 **Braavos**[165] 124 4-11-2 0 .... RichardJohnson 112+
(Philip Hobbs) *trckd ldr: upsides 9f out: led over 5f out: drvn over 2f out: styd on wl* 5/4[1]
2 2 2 3/4 **Dubai Angel (IRE)**[31] 1555 4-11-2 0 .... BrianHughes 108+
(Malcolm Jefferson) *hld up in rr: hdwy 6f out: sn trcking ldrs: effrt over 2f out: chsd wnr over 1f out: kpt on: no real imp* 15/8[2]
3 1 3/4 **Adman Sam (IRE)** 4-11-2 0 .... WayneHutchinson 107
(Ian Williams) *mid-div: hdwy to trck ldrs 6f out: 2nd over 3f out: kpt on same pce fnl 2f* 16/1
3/ 4 4 **Subordinate (GER)**[672] 3098 6-11-2 0 ....(t) DarylJacob 103
(Emma Lavelle) *mid-div: hdwy 6f out: sn chsng ldrs: one pce fnl 2f* 9/1
0- 5 3 3/4 **Fin D'Espere (IRE)**[183] 5373 4-11-2 0 ....(t) DenisO'Regan 99
(Suzy Smith) *led: j. path after 6f: sn faltered: hung lft and hdd: one pce fnl 3f* 16/1
40- 6 3 **Movie Legend**[222] 4679 5-11-2 0 .... KielanWoods 96
(Ben Case) *hld up in rr: hdwy 6f out: sn chsng ldrs: drvn 3f out: sn outpcd* 7/1[3]
7 3 1/4 **Swinton Diamond (IRE)** 4-10-6 0 ....[1] TobyWheeler(10) 93
(Ian Williams) *hld up in rr: outpcd and pushed along 7f out: sn bhd: kpt on fnl 2f* 20/1
0 8 78 **Generous Past**[85] 1101 5-10-13 0 .... BrianToomey(3) 15
(Michael Mullineaux) *trckd ldr: lft in ld after 7f: hdd over 5f out: sn lost pl and wl bhd: t.o over 3f out: eventually completed* 100/1

4m 14.5s (13.40) **Going Correction** +0.45s/f (Soft) **8** Ran SP% **119.2**
Speed ratings: **86,84,83,82,80 78,77,40**
CSF £3.97 TOTE £2.20: £1.10, £1.20, £3.60; EX 5.20 Trifecta £32.20.
Owner Mrs Diana L Whateley **Bred** C R Mason **Trained** Withycombe, Somerset

FOCUS
The early pace was poor, but it soon improved. The first four set a fair bumper standard and the race should produce winners.
T/Plt: £31.70 to a £1 stake. Pool of £45863.08 - 1054.10 winning tickets. T/Qpdt: £33.40 to a £1 stake. Pool of £2164.49 - 47.85 winning tickets. **Walter Glynn**

1544 STRATFORD (L-H)
Saturday, October 17

OFFICIAL GOING: Good
Wind: light breeze Weather: overcast; sunny after race two; 12 degrees

1974 TOTEPLACEPOT MARES' H'CAP HURDLE (8 hdls) 2m 70y
1:45 (1:45) (Class 3) (0-130,130) 3-Y-0+ £5,523 (£1,621; £810; £405)

Form RPR
3315 1 **Northern Meeting (IRE)**[25] 1618 5-10-1 105 ....(p) GavinSheehan 110+
(Robert Stephens) *j. slowly 1st: mde all: drew 5 l clr w ears pricked bef last: pushed out flat* 5/1[2]
1412 2 4 1/2 **Bantam (IRE)**[29] 1574 5-11-12 130 .... PaddyBrennan 130
(Henry Daly) *t.k.h: pressed ldrs: appeared gng wl 2 out: sn chsng wnr: 2 l 2nd and rdn home turn: nvr looked troubling wnr after* 15/2
3 3 **Troubled Soul (IRE)**[14] 1760 6-10-8 112 ....(t) TomO'Brien 109
(Denis Gerard Hogan, Ire) *towards rr: effrt 2 out: wnt wl hld 3rd between last two: plugged on* 11/2[3]
34-1 4 2 1/4 **Poetic Verse**[28] 1180 5-11-0 125 .... DeanPratt(7) 120
(John Quinn) *mounted on crse and taken down early: settled in rr: effrt after 2 out: wnt 3rd and flattered briefly home turn: sn rdn and btn* 11/4[1]
45-6 5 1 1/4 **Haatefina**[12] 1793 5-9-8 105 .... PaulNO'Brien(7) 99
(Mark Usher) *prom tl 3rd: lost tch qckly 3 out: plugged on into poor 5th bef last* 11/2[3]
3-43 6 34 **Announcement**[12] 1793 4-10-9 113 .... AidanColeman 76
(Brian Ellison) *mounted on crse and taken down early: settled in rr: last and nt fluent 5th and rdn: struggling between last two: eased flat* 9/1
5045 7 2 **Alys Rock (IRE)**[18] 1683 6-10-0 104 oh4 .... JamieMoore 65
(Michael Appleby) *disp 2nd tl jnd ldr briefly 2 out: drvn and lost pl v qckly between last two: t.o* 25/1
515- P **Quiet Candid (IRE)**[184] 5353 6-11-1 122 .... JeremiahMcGrath(3)
(Nicky Henderson) *racd keenly and cl up tl 3 out: wknd rapidly after next: t.o and p.u last* 13/2

3m 56.1s (0.10) **Going Correction** +0.10s/f (Yiel)
WFA 4 from 5yo+ 9lb **8** Ran SP% **113.0**
Speed ratings (Par 107): **103,100,99,98,97 80,79,**
CSF £40.44 CT £211.39 TOTE £6.30: £2.20, £2.20, £2.60; EX 48.00 Trifecta £232.10.
Owner The Go Slow Club **Bred** Ballymacoll Stud Farm Ltd **Trained** Penhow, Newport

FOCUS
Going good after selective watering. Open ditch just short of 2m start omitted due to surface work. Rails moved out adding the following distances to races: Race 1, 2, 6 and 7: 54 yards; Race 4: 72 yards; Race 5: 36 yards. There were several potential front-runners which suggested this mares' handicap might be run at a sound pace, but the winner was allowed to dictate affairs. The second and third help set the level.

1975 TOTEPOOLLIVEINFO.COM (S) HURDLE (8 hdls) 2m 70y
2:20 (2:20) (Class 5) 4-6-Y-0 £2,274 (£667; £333; £166)

Form RPR
-560 1 **Milan Of Crystal (IRE)**[66] 1236 6-9-12 74 .... MissBFrost(7) 91+
(Jimmy Frost) *sweating bdly: on her toes: t.k.h early: led tl after 1st: lost pl sltly 3rd: wnt 2nd and styng on again between last two: pushed into ld bef last and hit flight: kpt on gamely flat* 17/2
2-5 2 1 1/4 **Island Villa (IRE)**[24] 1630 6-11-2 106 ....(bt) TomO'Brien 100
(Denis Gerard Hogan, Ire) *led after 2nd: wnt 4 l clr 1/2-way: rdn and hdd bef last where stl in w a ch: fnd little and plugged on flat* 11/8[1]
4 3 6 **Toptempo**[17] 1700 6-10-5 0 ....(p) GavinSheehan 83
(Ali Stronge) *in last whn j. slowly 3rd: rdn and outpcd 5th: plodded into wl hld 3rd home turn: no imp after* 14/1
6- 4 13 **Ede's The Business**[76] 5411 4-9-12 0 ....(b) MissPFuller(7) 74
(Ken Wingrove) *hld up: effrt 5th: wnt 2nd bef next: sn rdn: fdd v tamely between last two* 50/1
-00P 5 10 **Memphis Magic (GER)**[11] 1595 5-10-9 97 ....(tp) JamesBanks(3) 70
(Brendan Powell) *led after 1st tl after 2nd: rdn 5th: no rspnse: dropped to rr and struggling sn after 2 out* 11/4[2]

6 6 62 **Streele (USA)**[18] 1693 5-9-12 0...(p[1]) MissTWorsley(7) 7
(Ken Wingrove) *bhd: struggling after 5th: t.o whn j. slowly 2 out* **100/1**

3/ P **Paladin (IRE)**[37] 2252 6-10-5 0...(t) BenFfrenchDavis(7)
(Dominic Ffrench Davis) *plld hrd: hdwy to go cl up 3rd: mstke next: stopped v rapidly after 5th: t.o: p.u after 2 out: b.b.v* **4/1**[3]

3m 59.8s (3.80) **Going Correction** +0.10s/f (Yiel) **7** Ran SP% **108.9**
Speed ratings: **94,93,90,83,78 47,**
CSF £19.41 TOTE £9.80: £4.40, £1.30; EX 36.90 Trifecta £208.70.The winner was bought by R Stephens for 6700gns. Paladin was claimed by M Blake for £7,000.
Owner Tony Saye & Tony Maddison **Bred** Edmond Coleman **Trained** Buckfast, Devon

FOCUS
Much of the spice was taken out of this contest once the forecast favourite Mighty Missile was a non-runner. This was run at a good pace with the favourite desperately trying to fend off the only challenger. Big hurdles bests from the winner and the third, but the form is suspect.

1976 TOTEQUADPOT OPEN H'CAP CHASE (13 fncs 2 omitted) 2m 4f 205y
2:55 (2:55) (Class 2) 4-Y-0+ **£14,242** (£4,207; £2,103; £1,053; £526)

Form RPR

3104 1 **Carrigmorna King (IRE)**[16] 1715 9-11-5 **137**...(t) TomO'Brien 146
(Philip Hobbs) *trckd ldrs in 4th mostly: effrt after 2 out: rdn to ld sn after last: hung on gamely* **15/2**

43-1 2 ¾ **Top Cat Henry (IRE)**[14] 1755 7-10-5 **123**...(tp) WillKennedy 131
(Dr Richard Newland) *settled towards rr: effrt in 3rd but bit to do 2 out: sn hrd drvn: wnt 2nd and gng lft 1/2-way up run-in: nt quite rch wnr* **7/2**[1]

5-12 3 ½ **What A Laugh**[9] 1828 10-9-13 **122**... BridgetAndrews(5) 131
(Gary Hanmer) *settled in rr: effrt gng wl 3 out: j. ahd next and sn 4 l clr: cajoled along and idling bef last: sn hdd flat and then kpt on at same pce* **13/2**

461- 4 9 **Little Jon**[203] 5031 7-10-13 **138**... JamieBargary(7) 141+
(Nigel Twiston-Davies) *pressed ldr: in dispute fr 7th: nt fluent 9th: led after 3 out: hdd and mstke next: sn drvn: wknd bef last and hit fence* **4/1**[2]

-061 5 nk **Kie (IRE)**[42] 1481 7-11-12 **144**...(t) MichaelHeard 144
(David Pipe) *hit 1st: last mostly: lost tch 9th: drvn and btn next* **12/1**

06-0 6 1½ **Edgardo Sol (FR)**[21] 1658 8-11-11 **143**... AidanColeman 141
(Emma Lavelle) *disp 3rd pl: hit 10th: drvn and wkng whn j.lft 2 out* **15/2**

052- P **Fairy Rath (IRE)**[190] 5253 9-11-0 **132**...(t) TomCannon
(Nick Gifford) *hit 3rd: mde most tl drvn and hdd bef 2 out: lost pl v qckly: t.o and p.u last* **14/1**

322- P **Big Water (IRE)**[225] 4602 7-11-8 **140**... PaulMoloney
(Alan Swinbank) *midfield: hit 8th: sn bhd: hit 10th: t.o and p.u 2 out* **16/1**

613- P **Ceasar Milan (IRE)**[253] 4070 7-11-6 **138**...(tp) SamTwiston-Davies
(Paul Nicholls) *j. deliberately and nvr really travelling: midfield: u.p 7th: lost pl and struggling 9th: t.o and p.u last* **6/1**[3]

5m 5.0s (-10.00) **Going Correction** -0.20s/f (Good) **9** Ran SP% **113.6**
Speed ratings (Par 109): **111,110,110,107,106 106, , ,**
CSF £34.43 CT £180.13 TOTE £8.60: £2.90, £1.70, £3.10; EX 52.00 Trifecta £266.10.
Owner Robert & Janet Gibbs **Bred** Tom McCarthy **Trained** Withycombe, Somerset

FOCUS
A decent and competitive handicap producing a tight finish between the first three home. The winner is rated similar to his May course win.

1977 TOTESCOOP6 H'CAP HURDLE (9 hdls) 2m 2f 148y
3:30 (3:30) (Class 3) (0-130,129) 3-Y-0 **£6,330** (£1,870; £935; £468; £234)

Form RPR

006- 1 **Baron Alco (FR)**[175] 5535 4-10-13 **116**... JamieMoore 123+
(Gary Moore) *racd keenly: mde all: hit 6th: drvn fr 2 out: styd on wl and a holding rivals fr home turn* **3/1**[1]

14/2 2 2¼ **Nesterenko (GER)**[55] 1347 6-11-12 **129**... NicodeBoinville 133
(Nicky Henderson) *settled towards rr: effrt in 4th 3 out: drvn after next: no imp between last two: tk 2nd at last but nt rch wnr* **5/1**[3]

F31 3 3¼ **Great Fighter**[29] 1568 5-11-9 **126**... AidanColeman 127
(John Ferguson) *t.k.h in midfield: effrt after 2 out: disp 3rd and u.p home turn: no imp after: sn tk wl hld 3rd flat* **5/1**[3]

5U16 4 1½ **Honey Pound (IRE)**[49] 1404 7-11-7 **124**... AlanJohns 125
(Tim Vaughan) *chsd ldrs: wnt 3rd 3 out and 2nd after next: sn rdn: a hld by wnr after and losing 5 l 2nd whn mstke last* **20/1**

152- 5 2¼ **Rock Of Leon**[202] 4467 4-11-7 **124**...(t) DavidEngland 123
(Dan Skelton) *cl up: drvn after 2 out: nt qckn between last two* **20/1**

356- 6 6 **Daveron (IRE)**[185] 5341 7-11-2 **122**... MattGriffiths(3) 114
(Jeremy Scott) *prom tl rdn after 2 out: wknd wl bef last* **14/1**

434- 7 8 **Hassle (IRE)**[21] 5294 6-10-13 **119**...(p) JeremiahMcGrath(3) 107
(Clive Cox) *midfield: in tch tl drvn and wknd between last two* **7/2**[2]

2F-5 8 19 **Dormouse**[16] 1719 10-10-12 **115**...(p) CharliePoste 83
(Anabel K Murphy) *detached in last pair: rdn and clsd v briefly bef 3 out: t.o between last two: eased* **33/1**

9 7 **Kentucky Star (FR)**[241] 4309 6-11-3 **120**... GavinSheehan 82
(John Quinn) *chsd ldrs tl dropped to rr 3 out: t.o and eased* **10/1**

3643 P **Brigadoon**[18] 1686 8-10-7 **110**... SamTwiston-Davies
(Michael Appleby) *pressed wnr tl 6th: drvn and dropped out rapidly next: blnd 2 out: t.o and p.u last* **16/1**

0-0 P **Asockastar (IRE)**[21] 1661 7-10-4 **107**... MichaelByrne
(Tim Vaughan) *nt fluent and detached in last pair: t.o after 3 out: p.u last* **50/1**

4m 29.5s (-2.00) **Going Correction** +0.10s/f (Yiel)
WFA 4 from 5yo+ 9lb **11** Ran SP% **116.6**
Speed ratings (Par 107): **108,107,105,105,104 101,98,90,87,**
CSF £17.64 CT £72.70 TOTE £4.10: £1.70, £1.80, £2.20; EX 22.20 Trifecta £99.90.
Owner John Stone **Bred** Yves D'Armaille **Trained** Lower Beeding, W Sussex

FOCUS
A dominant display by the winner and few got into this competitive handicap. The winner is rated back to his best with the next two on the upgrade.

1978 TOTEEXACTA H'CAP CHASE (15 fncs 2 omitted) 2m 6f 125y
4:05 (4:05) (Class 5) (0-100,99) 4-Y-0+ **£3,249** (£954; £477; £238)

Form RPR

0/ 1 **Fennis Moll (IRE)**[25] 1626 6-11-4 **98**... RachaelBlackmore(7) 110+
(John Joseph Hanlon, Ire) *cl up in 3rd or 4th: wnt 2nd 3 out: led between last two: sn rdn: racing w awkward hd carriage after: urged along and kpt finding enough flat* **8/1**

2/22 2 2¼ **Bob Lewis**[33] 1546 9-11-6 **93**...(t) TomO'Brien 101
(Stuart Kittow) *midfield: wnt 2nd at 7th: led bef 11th: rdn and hdd between last two: remained on terms tl last: v one pce and a hld after* **10/3**[2]

3P01 3 24 **Mr Robinson (FR)**[13] 1785 8-10-9 **82**... JamesBest 68
(Rob Summers) *bhd: hdwy 9th: wnt 4 l 4th bef 12th: lft 3rd but already outpcd next: plugged on and wl btn after 2 out* **10/1**

-133 4 9 **Croco Mister (IRE)**[79] 1155 8-10-12 **88**...(t) BenPoste(3) 69
(Rosemary Gasson) *dropping towards rr whn mstke 9th (water): rdn and lost tch next: plodded on* **11/2**[3]

U4-5 5 61 **Kapricorne (FR)**[16] 1720 8-11-5 **92**...(t) PaulMoloney 15
(Sophie Leech) *a bhd: lost tch 11th: sn t.o* **16/1**

5566 P **Stafford Charlie**[9] 1825 9-9-11 **73** oh6...(b) JamesBanks(3)
(John O'Shea) *towards rr: lost tch 11th: t.o and p.u 2 out* **50/1**

3P61 P **Rusty Nail (IRE)**[53] 1355 10-10-9 **89**... MissBFrost(7)
(Jimmy Frost) *detached in last much of way: nt fluent 8th: mstke next (water) and lost tch: t.o and p.u 12th* **9/1**

P421 P **Badgers Retreat**[16] 1720 9-11-12 **99**... GavinSheehan
(Nick Mitchell) *pressed ldr tl 9th: slow next and lost pl u.p: nt keen after: tailing off whn mstke 3 out: p.u last* **5/2**[1]

6-35 F **Lord Fox (IRE)**[24] 1629 8-10-11 **84**... DaveCrosse
(Shaun Harris) *led at v mod pce tl hdd bef 11th: sn rdn: 5 l 3rd and fading whn fell 3 out* **10/1**

5m 42.7s (3.50) **Going Correction** -0.20s/f (Good) **9** Ran SP% **114.2**
Speed ratings (Par 103): **85,84,75,72,51**
CSF £35.59 CT £271.03 TOTE £12.00: £2.80, £1.60, £3.90; EX 45.60 Trifecta £448.00.
Owner T Gaughan & Ms Pauline Twiss **Bred** Joseph Smiddy **Trained** Bagenalstown, Co Carlow
■ Rachael Blackmore's first winner in Britain.

FOCUS
A fair handicap for the grade, though few ran to form. A big step up from the winner.

1979 TOTETRIFECTA MAIDEN HURDLE (8 hdls) 2m 70y
4:40 (4:40) (Class 5) 4-Y-0+ **£2,599** (£763; £381; £190)

Form RPR

3-05 1 **Arctic Gold (IRE)**[23] 1634 4-11-0 0... SamTwiston-Davies 115+
(Nigel Twiston-Davies) *midfield: wnt 3rd 2 out but drvn and sn outpcd by ldng pair: clsd gamely u.p bef last to ld and mstke: all out* **11/1**

2 ½ **Star Foot (IRE)**[74] 1201 4-10-11 0... JamesBanks(3) 114
(Jo Davis) *prom: hit 3rd: wnt 2nd 2 out: rdn to ld between last two: hdd last: kpt on but a jst hld after* **20/1**

61-3 3 3½ **War On The Rocks (IRE)**[109] 865 6-11-0 0... PaddyBrennan 110
(Fergal O'Brien) *t.k.h: chsd ldrs: mstke 3rd: 6th 2 out: sn rdn: tried to cl between last two but no ex bef last* **7/2**[3]

P-3 4 2¼ **Crickel Wood (FR)**[25] 1612 5-11-0 0...(t) AidanColeman 111
(Charlie Longsdon) *led: mstke 5th: rdn and hdd between last two: no ex bef last* **15/8**[1]

224- 5 22 **Final Countdown**[30] 2743 4-11-0 110...(p) TomO'Brien 96
(John Quinn) *chsd ldrs tl drvn and wknd sn after 2 out* **3/1**[2]

6 1¼ **Tobacco Road (IRE)**[376] 5-11-0 0... MichaelByrne 87
(Tim Vaughan) *chsd ldrs tl fdd after 3 out* **14/1**

54- 7 4 **Poulanassy (IRE)**[222] 4680 5-11-0 0... PaulMoloney 84
(Evan Williams) *cl up: rdn 2 out: sn wknd* **33/1**

8 3¼ **Ralphy Lad (IRE)**[21] 4-11-0 0... LucyAlexander 81
(Alan Swinbank) *midfield tl 1/2-way: lost tch 3 out* **25/1**

2 9 35 **Normandy King (IRE)**[136] 601 4-11-0 0... AlanJohns 49
(Tim Vaughan) *towards rr: bdly t.o 2 out* **16/1**

U40U 10 1 **Double Court (IRE)**[9] 1829 4-11-0 0...(v[1]) DaveCrosse 49
(Nigel Twiston-Davies) *j. erratically in rr: bdly t.o 2 out* **80/1**

0 11 10 **Gentle Mel (IRE)**[16] 1718 7-10-7 0... CharliePoste 33
(Anabel K Murphy) *hld up in detached last: t.o whn mstke 4th* **100/1**

F **Boogangoo (IRE)**[17] 4-10-7 0... JamieMoore 99
(Grace Harris) *mstke 1st: hld up and bhd: hdwy 2 out: in last of five gng clr on home turn: 5 l 5th and no further imp whn fell heavily last* **22/1**

0- P **Lined With Silver (IRE)**[242] 4283 6-11-0 0... LiamTreadwell
(Dai Burchell) *chsd ldrs tl fdd rapidly 3 out: sn t.o: p.u last* **150/1**

3m 58.1s (2.10) **Going Correction** +0.10s/f (Yiel) **13** Ran SP% **121.7**
Speed ratings (Par 103): **98,97,96,94,83 83,81,79,62,61 56, ,**
CSF £198.78 TOTE £12.00: £3.40, £4.30, £1.20; EX 218.20 Trifecta £702.60.
Owner Geoffrey & Donna Keeys **Bred** Ms Deidre Connolly **Trained** Naunton, Gloucs

FOCUS
A reasonable maiden run at a good pace which the favourite was unable to sustain. There should be more to come from the winner.

1980 TOTEPOOL RACING'S BIGGEST SUPPORTER LADY RIDERS' H'CAP HURDLE (8 hdls) 2m 70y
5:15 (5:15) (Class 5) (0-100,100) 3-Y-0+ **£2,274** (£667; £333; £166)

Form RPR

314 1 **Vexillum (IRE)**[19] 1677 6-10-11 **92**...(p) MissBHampson(7) 106+
(Neil Mulholland) *setled in midfield: smooth prog to ld 3 out: 6 l clr home turn: unchal after* **11/4**[1]

F003 2 9 **Drummond**[17] 1702 6-9-9 **76**... MissPFuller(7) 80
(Katie Stephens) *settled in 3rd or 4th: wnt 2nd 2 out: sn rdn: 7 l clr of rest home turn but no match for wnr* **12/1**

B 3 13 **Percys Choice (IRE)**[17] 1702 7-11-1 **94**... LizzieKelly(5) 85
(Matt Sheppard) *bhd: stl 6th and lot to do after 2 out: styd on stoutly bef last: snatched mod 3rd* **6/1**[3]

1U-P 4 nse **Jumeirah Liberty**[166] 104 7-10-11 **85**...(tp) LucyAlexander 78
(Zoe Davison) *midfield: mstke 4th: effrt 3 out: 3rd whn mstke next: sn lost tch w ldng pair: 13 l 3rd home turn: lost pl on line* **14/1**

-000 5 7 **Sun Quest**[130] 675 11-9-7 **74** oh7... MissKatyLyons(7) 59
(Steven Dixon) *dropped to rr 1/2-way: nvr nr ldrs after* **20/1**

0-PP 6 11 **Columbanus (IRE)**[17] 1702 4-9-7 **74** oh4... MissNatalieParker(7) 49
(Kevin Bishop) *chsd ldr tl mstke 3 out: dropped out v tamely: t.o* **33/1**

-041 7 4 **Youm Jamil (USA)**[18] 1689 8-9-7 **74** oh6...(t) MissJCWilliams(7) 45
(Tony Carroll) *towards rr: struggling 3 out: t.o* **10/1**

-P3P 8 16 **Spurned Girl**[10] 1816 5-9-9 **74** oh5...(t) AliceMills(5) 31
(Robin Dickin) *lost 15 l s: in last pair: t.o fr 5th* **25/1**

6 9 ½ **Here Comes Molly (IRE)**[28] 1586 4-11-5 **100**... RachaelBlackmore(7) 57
(John Joseph Hanlon, Ire) *rdn and struggling after 4th: t.o 2 out* **13/2**

-454 P **The Shropshire Lad**[5] 1888 5-11-2 **95**...(b[1]) BridgetAndrews(5)
(Dan Skelton) *racd freely in ld: v awkward 4th: hdd 3 out: dropped out v rapidly: t.o and p.u after next* **10/3**[2]

650 P **Polo The Mumm (FR)**[56] 1324 5-11-2 **97**... MissHWelch(7)
(Jimmy Frost) *hit 2nd: bhd: t.o 3 out: p.u last* **20/1**

3m 59.6s (3.60) **Going Correction** +0.10s/f (Yiel) **11** Ran SP% **117.1**
Speed ratings (Par 103): **95,90,84,83,80 74,72,64,64,**
CSF £32.91 CT £186.12 TOTE £3.50: £1.30, £3.50, £2.10; EX 36.30 Trifecta £215.10.
Owner John Heaney **Bred** Rathasker Stud **Trained** Limpley Stoke, Wilts

FOCUS
Few came into this moderate race in much form, and the well-supported favourite duly took advantage. The second is rated to his mark.
T/Plt: £134.40 to a £1 stake. Pool of £61552.72 - 334.15 winning tickets. T/Qpdt: £33.30 to a £1 stake. Pool of £4307.57 - 95.65 winning tickets. **Iain Mackenzie**

1981 - 1982a (Foreign Racing) - See Raceform Interactive

FAR HILLS

Saturday, October 17

OFFICIAL GOING: Turf: firm

1983a GRAND NATIONAL HURDLE STKS (GRADE 1) (4YO+) (TURF) 2m 5f

8:00 (8:00) 4-Y-0+

£115,384 (£34,615; £19,230; £9,615; £7,692; £5,769)

			RPR
1		**Dawalan (FR)**[23] 5-11-2 0 ... RGeraghty (Cyril Murphy, U.S.A)	135
2	*1*	**Eshtiaal (USA)**[82] 562 5-11-2 0 ... BarryGeraghty (Gordon Elliott, Ire)	134
3	*nse*	**Rawnaq (IRE)**[79] 1163 8-11-2 0 ... JackDoyle (Cyril Murphy, U.S.A)	134
4	*4*	**All Together (USA)**[23] 10-11-2 0 ... (b) WillieMcCarthy (David Jacobson, U.S.A)	130
5	*nk*	**Decoy Daddy (IRE)**[693] 13-11-2 0 ... (b) MissCarolAnnSloan (Cyril Murphy, U.S.A)	130
6	*2 ½*	**Charminster (IRE)**[23] 9-11-2 0 ... (b) DNagle (Cyril Murphy, U.S.A)	127
7	*13 ½*	**Alajmal (USA)**[23] 7-11-2 0 ... (b) BDalton (Janet E Elliot, U.S.A)	114
8	*8*	**Hunt Ball (IRE)**[39] 1507 10-11-2 0 ... AndrewTinkler (Nicky Henderson)	106
9	*5*	**Demonstrative (USA)**[51] 8-11-2 0 ... PaddyYoung (Richard L Valentine, U.S.A)	101

Owner Irvin S Naylor **Bred** H H The Aga Khan's Studs Sc **Trained** USA

[279] KEMPTON (R-H)

Sunday, October 18

OFFICIAL GOING: Good (watered; chs 7.6, hdl 7.4)

Wind: light breeze Weather: fairly sunny; 16 degrees

1984 WILLIAM HILL - IN THE APP STORE JUVENILE HURDLE (8 hdls) 2m

2:15 (2:15) (Class 3) 3-Y-O **£5,848** (£1,717; £858; £429)

Form				RPR
1	1		**Oceane (FR)**[16] 1732 3-11-4 0 ... WayneHutchinson (Alan King) *chsd clr ldr: lft clsr after 2nd: led gng best 2 out: 5 l clr last: v easily* 2/9[1]	122+
61	2	*8*	**Big McIntosh (IRE)**[14] 1768 3-11-4 0 ... MattieBatchelor (John Ryan) *led and v free: clr tl hung lft bnd after 2nd: stl hanging lft 3rd: hdd 2 out: immediately outpcd by wnr* 14/1[3]	110
	3	*19*	**Goldslinger (FR)**[22] 3-10-12 0 ... PaulMoloney (Dean Ivory) *t.k.h in 3rd pl: hung lft bnd after 2nd: wl in tch tl hit 3 out: rallied briefly but btn whn given an easy time fr bef next: hit last* 5/1[2]	92
	4	*99*	**Come Up And See Me**[303] 3-10-12 0 ... BrendanPowell (J R Jenkins) *mstkes in detached last: blnd 5th and t.o next: stl coming to last after wnr fin* 100/1	

3m 45.6s (-0.40) **Going Correction** -0.075s/f (Good) **4** Ran SP% **106.2**

Speed ratings (Par 105): **98,94,84,35**

CSF £3.93 TOTE £1.20; EX 3.00 Trifecta £3.90.

Owner McNeill Family **Bred** S C E A Haras De Manneville **Trained** Barbury Castle, Wilts

FOCUS

All starts have been moved at this track following remeasuring, so there will be no speed figures here until there is sufficient data to calculate updated median times. Dual bend alignment was in use for this fixture, and the effect on distances were; race 2, an extra 34 yards, race 4 and extra 60 yards and race 6 and extra 34 yards. Even though the opener was a small field, it looked decent, and the gallop set by the leader was good. It was much the slowest of the races over the trip but the winner looks a fairly useful juvenile.

1985 WILLIAM HILL - DOWNLOAD THE APP STORE NOVICES' LIMITED H'CAP CHASE (12 fncs) 2m

2:45 (2:45) (Class 4) (0-120,115) 4-Y-0+ **£4,548** (£1,335; £667; £333)

Form				RPR
-5P4	1		**Yabadabadoo**[14] 1769 7-11-1 **108** ... (t) AidanColeman (Emma Lavelle) *pressed ldr: led 3 out: j.rt next and rival crashed into him: lft clr: 6 l ahd last: eased cl home* 5/2[1]	116+
343-	2	*3*	**The Green Ogre**[181] 5427 5-11-8 **115** ... JoshuaMoore (Gary Moore) *trckd ldng pair: mstke 7th: rdn 3 out: 5 l 3rd and hld whn lft 2nd 2 out: kpt on same pce* 5/1	118
5211	3	*17*	**Lord Lir (IRE)**[82] 1133 9-10-12 **105** ... (b) RichardJohnson (Tim Vaughan) *led: blnd 2nd: tk off far too sn 5th and great rcvry by rdr: jst hdd whn j.lft 3 out: rdn and nrly upsides whn j.lft and cannoned into wnr: rdr almost uns and miraculous rcvry but lost all ch* 11/4[2]	108
603-	4	*5*	**Under The Phone (IRE)**[202] 5068 6-11-5 **112** ... CharliePoste (Robin Dickin) *last pair: rdn 9th: struggling after: nt fluent next* 9/2[3]	97
0363	5	*17*	**Moveable Asset (IRE)**[40] 1505 7-11-1 **108** ... BrendanPowell (Henry Tett) *dropped bk last at 6th: mstke next and rdn: lost tch after 9th: t.o* 8/1	82
5P0-	F		**Mini Muck**[249] 4159 9-11-3 **110** ... SamTwiston-Davies (Nigel Twiston-Davies) *taken down early: plld hrd in rr: sketchy 1st: fell 2nd* 17/2	

3m 55.3s (0.30) **Going Correction** -0.075s/f (Good) **6** Ran SP% **111.7**

Speed ratings (Par 105): **96,94,86,83,75**

CSF £15.03 TOTE £3.60; £2.10, £2.70; EX 16.30 Trifecta £46.10.

Owner Elite Racing Club **Bred** Elite Racing Club **Trained** Hatherden, Hants

FOCUS

A modest contest, which was run at a good gallop. The winner was well in on the best of last sesaon's form and close to that level.

1986 WILLIAM HILL - ON YOUR MOBILE NOVICES' HURDLE (LISTED RACE) (8 hdls) 2m

3:20 (3:20) (Class 1) 4-Y-0+ **£11,390** (£4,274; £2,140; £1,066; £536)

Form				RPR
111	1		**Maputo**[14] 1766 5-11-6 138 ... AidanColeman (John Ferguson) *t.k.h: settled in 3rd pl: lft 2nd 3 out: led gng wl next: pushed 5 l clr last: sn eased flat* 5/6[1]	150+
3	2	*6*	**Swansea Mile (IRE)**[22] 1657 5-11-8 135 ... HarrySkelton (Dan Skelton) *settled in 4th pl: effrt after 3 out: rdn to go 2nd next: no imp on v easy wnr after* 5/1[3]	138
10-1	3	*6*	**San Benedeto (FR)**[154] 360 4-11-6 131 ... (t) SamTwiston-Davies (Paul Nicholls) *plld hrd in 2nd: nt fluent 5th: chal and lft in ld 3 out: rdn and hdd next: fnd little and sn fighting a losing battle in 3rd* 7/1	130
532-	4	*25*	**Paddy The Deejay (IRE)**[203] 5043 6-11-0 121 ... JoshuaMoore (Stuart Edmunds) *hld up abt 10 l last: hit 3rd: rdn and outpcd 3 out: tk poor 4th bef next* 33/1	106
0-11	5	*20*	**Midnight Shot**[151] 396 5-11-6 127 ... RichardJohnson (Charlie Longsdon) *led at decent pce: nt fluent 3rd: jnd whn blnd 3 out and lost all momentum: poor last bef next where mstke: eased and t.o after* 7/2[2]	105

3m 38.8s (-7.20) **Going Correction** -0.075s/f (Good) course record

WFA 4 from 5yo+ 9lb **5** Ran SP% **108.9**

Speed ratings (Par 111): **115,112,109,96,86**

CSF £5.38 TOTE £2.10; £1.10, £1.80; EX 5.10 Trifecta £12.20.

Owner Bloomfields **Bred** Darley **Trained** Cowlinge, Suffolk

FOCUS

A few nice horses have taken this down the years, like Deep Purple (2008), Woolcombe Folly (2009) and Blue Heron last year, so it's best to view the form positively. Maputo rates a smart novice. The field stood still for a couple of seconds when asked to set off.

1987 WILLIAM HILL - BET ON THE MOVE H'CAP CHASE (18 fncs) 3m

3:50 (3:50) (Class 4) (0-115,115) 4-Y-0+ **£4,548** (£1,335; £667; £333)

Form				RPR
-134	1		**Fond Memory (IRE)**[26] 1617 7-11-12 **115** ... (t) SamTwiston-Davies (Nigel Twiston-Davies) *j.lft at times: settled trcking ldrs: rdn and effrt bef 3 out: drvn to dispute ld fr 2 out tl last: forged ahed flat: gamely* 9/2[2]	122+
0F5	2	*4 ½*	**King's Legacy (IRE)**[14] 1767 11-11-8 **111** ... (t) AidanColeman (Lawney Hill) *hld up in last pair: effrt bef 3 out: rdn to chal 2 out: nt qckn bef last* 12/1	110
R66-	3	*17*	**Hatters River (IRE)**[183] 5401 8-11-10 **113** ... GavinSheehan (Ali Stronge) *j.lft: rdn and hdd and j. bdly lft 2 out: tired qckly and wl btn 4th whn j. bdly lft last* 15/2	104
6-4P	D	*1 ¼*	**Midnight Cataria**[129] 693 6-11-2 **105** ... WayneHutchinson (Alan King) *hld up in midfield: mstke 13th: wnt 3rd next: disp 2nd 3 out: drvn and w wnr 2 out tl last: jst outpcd flat* 13/2	110
64P0	P		**Highway Code (USA)**[11] 1807 9-11-4 **114** ... (t) CiaranGethings[(7)] (Kerry Lee) *hld up in last pair: rdn and lost tch 15th: t.o and p.u last* 8/1	
0022	P		**Koultas King (IRE)**[30] 1573 8-11-1 **104** ... (tp) RichardJohnson (Tim Vaughan) *3rd tl wnt 2nd at 11th tl 15th: rdn and fdd bef next: mod 5th whn p.u and dismntd last: lame* 5/1[3]	
15-2	P		**Balinroab (IRE)**[124] 750 8-11-8 **111** ... NicodeBoinville (Mark Bradstock) *pressed ldr tl 11th: rdn and dropped to rr 14th: t.o and p.u last: bled internally* 15/8[1]	

6m 2.9s (-6.10) **Going Correction** -0.075s/f (Good) **7** Ran SP% **113.5**

Speed ratings (Par 105): **107,105,99, , ,106**

CSF £32.17 CT £324.96 TOTE £5.10; £2.50, £3.70; EX 40.10 Trifecta £635.30.

Owner The Stirling Partnership **Bred** C Kenneally **Trained** Naunton, Gloucs

FOCUS

A modest handicap, run at a respectable gallop.

1988 WILLIAMHILL.COM HURDLE (LISTED RACE) (8 hdls) 2m

4:25 (4:25) (Class 1) 4-Y-0+ **£17,085** (£6,411; £3,210; £1,599; £804)

Form				RPR
115-	1		**The New One (IRE)**[222] 4691 7-11-8 162 ... SamTwiston-Davies (Nigel Twiston-Davies) *trckd ldng pair: pushed ahd bef 2 out: rdn and in command bef last: comf* 2/11[1]	151+
11-0	2	*2*	**Stephanie Frances (IRE)**[80] 1163 7-11-1 138 ... HarrySkelton (Dan Skelton) *settled in 4th pl: rdn and effrt 2 out: chsd wnr between last two: kpt on wout making any imp* 5/1[2]	140
20-0	3	*8*	**Rayvin Black**[162] 197 6-11-0 134 ... ThomasGarner (Oliver Sherwood) *led: rdn and hdd 2 out: lost 2nd between last two: sn btn* 10/1[3]	132
46/6	4	*18*	**Red Riverman**[51] 402 7-11-0 115 ... (v) NoelFehily (Nigel Twiston-Davies) *plld hrd in last pair: j. deliberately 2nd: lost tch bef 2 out: eased wl bef last* 50/1	116
1255	5	*32*	**Mr Lando**[91] 1047 6-11-0 122 ... LeightonAspell (Alison Batchelor) *t.k.h in 2nd tl wknd qckly bef 2 out: sn eased and t.o* 25/1	95

3m 40.5s (-5.50) **Going Correction** -0.075s/f (Good) **5** Ran SP% **116.2**

Speed ratings (Par 111): **110,109,105,96,80**

CSF £2.07 TOTE £1.10; £1.10, £1.90; EX 1.80 Trifecta £3.10.

Owner S Such & Cg Paletta **Bred** R Brown & Ballylinch Stud **Trained** Naunton, Gloucs

FOCUS

With due respect to his rivals, this was all about the return of The New One, not seen since his fifth-place finish in last season's Champion Hurdle. The gallop set by the leaders wasn't that strong, so it developed into a bit of a sprint to the line. The winner was well below the level of his last two wins in this event but the race didn't lend itself to producing a big figure.

1989 WILLIAM HILL - EXCLUSIVE MOBILE OFFERS H'CAP CHASE (12 fncs) 2m

5:00 (5:00) (Class 3) (0-135,134) 4-Y-0+ **£7,797** (£2,289; £1,144; £572)

Form				RPR
41-0	1		**Arkaim**[161] 218 7-11-10 **132** ... KielanWoods (Pam Sly) *reminders to begin: led 2nd: j. boldly and keen after: sn 6 l clr: rdn 2 out: hrd pressed but hld on gamely fr last* 11/2	137+
215-	2	*½*	**Cody Wyoming**[232] 4498 9-11-1 **123** ... (t) GavinSheehan (Charlie Mann) *occasionally j.lft: led tl 2nd: chsd wnr after: reminders 8th: pushed along bef 3 out: drvn and tried to chal bef last: a jst hld flat* 4/1[2]	129+
050-	3	*23*	**Gores Island (IRE)**[176] 5540 9-11-10 **132** ... JoshuaMoore (Gary Moore) *last pair and detached: nt fluent 4th and 7th: 20 l 4th at 1/2-way: pushed along and lost tch bef 3 out: lft poor 3rd after next* 5/1[3]	117
4-	4	*9*	**Cernunnos (FR)**[211] 4922 5-11-1 **123** ... PaddyBrennan (Tom George) *chsd ldng pair: 12 l 3rd at 1/2-way: rdn and btn 3 out: tired 3rd whn blnd next* 15/8[1]	104
-444	5	*5*	**Nearest The Pin (IRE)**[23] 1643 10-11-12 **134** ... (tp) RichardJohnson (John Joseph Hanlon, Ire) *detached in last: 30 l fr ldr 1/2-way: t.o bef 3 out: sn eased* 4/1[2]	109

3m 49.9s (-5.10) **Going Correction** -0.075s/f (Good) **5** Ran SP% **106.8**

Speed ratings (Par 107): **109,108,97,92,90**

CSF £24.66 TOTE £8.10; £2.80, £1.90; EX 31.50 Trifecta £112.50.

Owner G A Libson D L Bayliss G Taylor P M Sly **Bred** Harton Limited **Trained** Thorney, Cambs

FOCUS
The winner set off at a decent gallop and was never headed after taking an early lead. He posted a pb in a good time compared with the earlier handicap.

1990 WILLIAM HILL - THE HOME OF BETTING "NATIONAL HUNT" NOVICES' HURDLE (10 hdls) 2m 5f
5:30 (5:30) (Class 4) 4-Y-0+ **£3,898** (£1,144; £572; £286)

Form				RPR
2F0-	1		**Work In Progress (IRE)**184 [5361] 5-10-12 121 HarrySkelton (Dan Skelton) *racd keenly: hit 3rd: led or 2nd tl def advantage 3 out: gng strly fr next: 7 l clr and on bit last: sn eased* **8/11**[1]	131+
0113	2	8	**Western Way (IRE)**16 [1736] 6-11-5 122 (v1) DavidNoonan(7) (Don Cantillon) *j.lft and tending to edge lft: led or 2nd tl hdd 3 out: sn drvn: no match for wnr fr next* **11/2**[3]	130
	3	1 3/4	**Dark Flame (IRE)**217 6-10-12 0 NoelFehily (Richard Rowe) *hld up and in bhd: effrt after 3 out: plugged on into 3rd next and styd on steadily wout threatening* **20/1**	112
33-5	4	17	**Quincy Magoo (IRE)**165 [146] 6-10-12 0 TrevorWhelan (Neil King) *midfield: 3rd and outpcd whn nt fluent 3 out and drvn: sn btn: lost 3rd at next* **25/1**	106
6-	5	23	**Whispering Speed (IRE)**321 [2858] 5-10-12 0 LeightonAspell (Lucy Wadham) *bhd: rdn 1/2-way: struggling fr 3 out: t.o next* **33/1**	76
45/P	6	2	**Alongthewatchtower (IRE)**153 [378] 7-10-9 0 JamesBanks(3) (Barry Brennan) *last trio: last and rdn 3 out: sn t.o: fin lame* **125/1**	75
	7	27	**Definitly Grey (IRE)**169 4-10-12 0 RichardJohnson (Charlie Longsdon) *chsd ldrs: 3rd briefly bef 7th: rdn and wknd v rapidly after next: sn t.o* **3/1**[2]	50

4m 57.8s (-5.20) **Going Correction** -0.075s/f (Good)
WFA 4 from 5yo+ 10lb **7 Ran SP% 110.6**
Speed ratings (Par 105): **106,102,102,95,87 86,76**
CSF £4.80 TOTE £1.70: £1.70, £2.70; EX 5.30 Trifecta £27.90.
Owner Donlon & Doyle **Bred** Mrs M O'Driscoll **Trained** Alcester, Warwicks

FOCUS
This didn't look overly competitive but the winner made it look very easy. The winner was the pick at the weights but this rates a step up.
T/Plt: £35.30 to a £1 stake. Pool: £65,999.38 - 1,364.16 winning tickets. T/Qpdt: £15.20 to a £1 stake. Pool: £3,808.94 - 185.00 winning tickets. **Iain Mackenzie**

1991 - 1997a (Foreign Racing) - See Raceform Interactive

1590 PLUMPTON (L-H)
Monday, October 19

OFFICIAL GOING: Good (chs 7.6, hdl 7.1)
Wind: light, half behind Weather: overcast, dry

1998 GEOFFREY BUDD PARTNERSHIP MAIDEN HURDLE (8 hdls 1 omitted) 1m 7f 195y
2:30 (2:31) (Class 5) 4-Y-0+ **£2,274** (£667; £333; £166)

Form				RPR
154-	1		**Wishing And Hoping (IRE)**198 [5143] 5-11-0 0 WayneHutchinson (Alan King) *t.k.h: hld up in rr: bmpd 1st: clsd to trck ldrs 5th: hmpd 3 out (actual 2 out): chal last: rdn and qcknd to ld flat: r.o wl: in command at fin* **10/11**[1]	110+
5-	2	1	**Theligny (FR)**318 [2922] 4-11-0 0 RichardJohnson (Tim Vaughan) *j. novicey early: midfield tl lft chsng ldrs 3rd: hmpd 6th: led on long run after 3 out: (actual 2 out): wnt lft last: hdd flat: r.o but nt pce of wnr fnl 100yds* **8/1**	105
	3	2 1/2	**Takeitfromalady (IRE)**48 6-10-7 0 (v) PaddyBradley(7) (Lee Carter) *chsd ldrs: led: wandered and blnd 3 out (actual 2 out): sn hdd but stl ev ch: drvn bypassing 2 out: carried lft last: no ex flat* **22/1**	103
43	4	1	**Dynamic Ranger (USA)**29 [1590] 4-11-0 114 JamieMoore (Gary Moore) *chsd ldrs: lft in ld 3rd: hdd 5th: hmpd next and 3 out (actual 2 out): cl 5th and rdn bnd ent st: stl pressing ldrs whn carried lft last: drvn and sn btn flat* **7/1**[3]	102
35-2	5	1 1/4	**Sebs Sensei (IRE)**103 [221] 4-11-0 114 MarcGoldstein (Mark Hoad) *hld up in tch in midfield: effrt to chal on long run after 3 out (actual 2 out): unable qck u.p bypassing 2 out: styd on same pce after* **14/1**	101
P-	6	7	**Allchilledout**203 [5065] 6-11-0 0 DarylJacob (Colin Tizzard) *chsd ldrs: lft 2nd 3rd: led 5th: hmpd next: hdd 3 out: lost pl bnd bef next: wknd bypassing 2 out* **50/1**	94
	F		**Top Set (IRE)**174 5-11-0 0 IanPopham (Richard Phillips) *hld up in last pair: j.lft: cannoned into rival and fell 1st* **66/1**	
01-2	R		**Amber Spyglass**44 [1484] 5-11-0 0 TomCannon (David Bridgwater) *led: clr and wandered 2nd: rn out and uns rdr next* **9/4**[2]	
0	U		**Prince Mahler (IRE)**19 [1698] 5-11-0 0 JamesBest (Caroline Keevil) *chsd clr ldr: lft in ld whn carried rt by loose horse: bdly hmpd and uns rdr 3rd* **150/1**	

3m 52.2s (-8.60) **Going Correction** -0.80s/f (Firm)
WFA 4 from 5yo+ 9lb **9 Ran SP% 121.9**
Speed ratings (Par 103): **89,88,87,86,86 82, , ,**
CSF £10.25 TOTE £1.80: £1.10, £2.70, £2.60; EX 11.40 Trifecta £134.20.
Owner Mrs Peter Andrews **Bred** Brendan Murphy **Trained** Barbury Castle, Wilts

FOCUS
Common bends and Chases increased by 96yds. Hurdle races 1 & 3 reduced by 18yds, race 5 reduced by 30yds and race 7 reduced by 24yds. The two former bumper winners in the field dominated the betting. There was plenty of drama early after Top Set fell at the opening flight, Amber Spyglass swerved going to the first in the home straight first time round and crashed through the rail, causing the loose Top Set to veer sharply right and take out Prince Mahler. There was a bunch finish in a slow time and this isn't form to take seriously.

1999 KYLE FAMILY JOSH GIFFORD MEMORIAL H'CAP CHASE (FOR THE JOSH GIFFORD MEMORIAL TROPHY) (14 fncs) 2m 3f 164y
3:00 (3:00) (Class 5) (0-100,98) 4-Y-0+ **£2,924** (£858; £429; £214)

Form				RPR
	1		**Killabraher Cross (IRE)**92 [1062] 8-11-3 89 MarcGoldstein (Paddy Butler) *led tl after 2nd: chsd ldr after: hit 5th: mstke 9th: rdn after next: led after 3 out: asserted 2 out: styd on wl: rdn out* **25/1**	95+
P401	2	10	**Dancing Dik**29 [1595] 10-11-3 89 (b) PaddyBrennan (Paul Henderson) *chsd wnr tl led after 2nd: sn clr: 8 l clr whn blnd bdly 3 out: sn hdd: 2 l down and drvn bef next: no ex and btn 2 out: wknd bef last: hld on for 2nd flat* **2/1**[1]	94+
46-P	3	1	**Rebel High (IRE)**170 [88] 11-10-0 72 oh5 (v) LiamTreadwell (Derek Frankland) *j.lft: midfield: lft 3rd 7th: cajoled along after 10th: no rspnse and plugged on same pce fr 3 out* **12/1**	66
424-	4	8	**Albatros De Guye (FR)**205 [5024] 5-10-1 73 (p) AdamWedge (Anna Newton-Smith) *nvr jumping or travelling wl enough in last pair: lft 4th 7th: rdn after 9th: no rspnse* **11/4**[2]	61
6212	5	6	**Herecomesthetruth (IRE)**16 [1757] 13-11-12 98 TomCannon (Chris Gordon) *a in rr and nvr travelling: hmpd 7th: n.d after: fin lame* **11/4**[2]	82
-R10	F		**Houseparty**132 [674] 7-10-5 84 MissTWorsley(7) (Diana Grissell) *chsd ldng pair tl fell 7th* **7/1**[3]	

5m 7.7s (0.40) **Going Correction** -0.40s/f (Good) **6 Ran SP% 110.7**
Speed ratings (Par 103): **83,79,78,75,73**
CSF £75.31 TOTE £10.40: £4.50, £1.60; EX 33.90 Trifecta £753.80.
Owner Homewoodgate Racing Club **Bred** Mr And Mrs J O'Sullivan **Trained** East Chiltington, E Sussex

FOCUS
Another eventful race in which jumping errors had a bearing on the outcome. A step up from the winner on his bumper form.

2000 RETIREMENT VILLAGES NOVICES' H'CAP HURDLE (9 hdls) 1m 7f 195y
3:30 (3:30) (Class 5) (0-100,100) 3-Y-0+ **£2,599** (£763; £381; £190)

Form				RPR
-4F4	1		**Native Display (IRE)**27 [1613] 5-11-9 97 1 AndrewTinkler (Nicky Henderson) *hld up in tch: clsd to trck ldng pair bef 3 out: j. into ld 2 out: clr last: idling flat: comf* **7/2**[1]	108+
PP3F	2	3/4	**Oscar Jane (IRE)**19 [1702] 8-10-0 74 (bt) AlainCawley (Johnny Farrelly) *led: rdn after 3 out: hdd next: kpt on same pce u.p after* **6/1**	79
0-P1	3	1 1/2	**Sadma**19 [1702] 6-11-2 97 WilliamFeatherstone(7) (Nick Lampard) *in tch in midfield: chsd ldr after 6th: 3rd and unable qck u.p 2 out: mstke last: kpt on same pce flat* **5/1**[3]	102
426/	4	nk	**Ragdollianna**37 [5] 11-11-7 95 LiamTreadwell (Mark Hoad) *t.k.h: hld up off the pce in last trio: clsd after 6th: outpcd and swtchd rt after 3 out: rallied in 6 l 4th 2 out: kpt on u.p flat* **20/1**	99
00-4	5	3	**Haverstock**19 [1702] 5-10-13 87 (p) IanPopham (Caroline Keevil) *midfield: rdn along 4th: drvn and outpcd after 3 out: kpt on same pce after* **7/1**	88
600-	6	1 3/4	**Majestic Sun (IRE)**6 [3659] 4-11-9 97 LeightonAspell (Jim Boyle) *stdd s: hld up off the pce in rr: clsd after 6th: 6th and no imp whn rdn bef 2 out: plugged on* **14/1**	97
444	7	18	**Dylan's Storm (IRE)**12 [1805] 3-10-3 94 (t) AidanColeman (David Dennis) *in tch in midfield: rdn and btn after 3 out: wknd bef next* **10/1**	60
0634	8	10	**Warrant Officer**29 [1596] 5-11-5 93 MarcGoldstein (Sheena West) *chsd ldr tl 5th: rdn and wknd wl bef 2 out: wl bhd whn blnd 2 out* **9/2**[2]	70
P/50	9	14	**On Your Max**29 [1590] 7-11-7 100 MrPYork(5) (Raymond York) *in tch in midfield: rdn and lost pl after 5th: bhd whn mstke next: sn lost tch: t.o* **25/1**	62
PP5/	P		**Rachael's Ruby**714 [2271] 8-10-11 85 (p) TomCannon (Roger Teal) *chsd ldrs: wnt 2nd 5th tl next: wknd qckly sn after 3 out: wl bhd whn p.u next* **40/1**	
00-0	P		**Achemenes (FR)**171 [65] 6-9-9 74 oh2 FreddieMitchell(5) (Daniel Steele) *hld up in rr: rdn and no rspnse after 5th: lost tch bef 3 out: t.o whn p.u 2 out* **10/1**	

3m 43.0s (-17.80) **Going Correction** -0.80s/f (Firm)
WFA 3 from 4yo 17lb 4 from 5yo+ 9lb **11 Ran SP% 119.8**
Speed ratings (Par 103): **112,111,110,110,109 108,99,94,87,**
CSF £25.10 CT £106.96 TOTE £4.30: £1.90, £2.60, £2.00; EX 22.90 Trifecta £65.00.
Owner J Palmer-Brown **Bred** Mrs Sheila O'Ryan **Trained** Upper Lambourn, Berks

FOCUS
A moderate handicap and a step up from the cosy winner.

2001 GERALD KARN-SMITH MEMORIAL NOVICES' LIMITED H'CAP CHASE (14 fncs) 2m 3f 164y
4:00 (4:00) (Class 3) (0-135,130) 4-Y-0+ **£7,797** (£2,289; £1,144; £572)

Form				RPR
006-	1		**Andy Kelly (IRE)**240 [4362] 6-11-1 123 GavinSheehan (Emma Lavelle) *chsd ldrs and travelled and j.w: jnd ldrs 11th: led next: pushed along and readily wnt clr 2 out: eased flat: v easily* **4/1**[2]	138+
206-	2	6	**Cadoudoff (FR)**207 [4997] 5-11-6 128 AidanColeman (Charlie Longsdon) *hld up in last trio: wl in tch and hmpd 11th: shkn up and effrt after 3 out: wnt 3rd 2 out and 2nd last: kpt on but no ch w wnr* **12/1**	132
301-	3	2	**Buckhorn Timothy**185 [5367] 6-11-7 129 DarylJacob (Colin Tizzard) *pressed ldr tl led 9th: jnd and mstke 11th: hdd next: drvn and btn 2 out: kpt on same pce and lost 2nd last* **13/2**[3]	132
455-	4	4 1/2	**Come On Laurie (IRE)**185 [5362] 7-11-1 123 LeightonAspell (Oliver Sherwood) *hld up in tch in rr: clsd after 9th: shkn up and effrt after 3 out: 4th and no imp 2 out* **8/1**	123
223	5	7	**Town Mouse**16 [1755] 5-11-0 122 (p) TrevorWhelan (Neil King) *taken down early: led tl 8th: 4th and rdn after 9th: wknd bef 2 out* **8/1**	113
541-	6	1 1/4	**Ar Mad (FR)**197 [5151] 5-11-2 124 JamieMoore (Gary Moore) *j.rt: t.k.h: hld up towards rr: hdwy to chse ldrs and mstke 5th: led 8th: j.rt and hdd next: j.rt 3 out: wknd next* **4/1**[2]	116+
-141	7	16	**Gone Too Far**27 [1617] 7-11-8 130 WayneHutchinson (Alan King) *t.k.h: in tch in midfield: reminders after 8th: cl 4th and mstke 10th: btn next: sn bhd* **10/3**[1]	111
310-	P		**Prouts Pub (IRE)**197 [5154] 6-11-2 124 TomCannon (Nick Gifford) *chsd ldrs: lost pl and mstke 7th: dropped to last 9th: lost tch and p.u 11th* **12/1**	

4m 57.2s (-10.10) **Going Correction** -0.40s/f (Good) **8 Ran SP% 114.0**
Speed ratings (Par 107): **104,101,100,99,96 95,89,**
CSF £47.04 CT £304.01 TOTE £5.30: £2.80, £2.20, £2.10; EX 59.70 Trifecta £301.60.
Owner The Optimists **Bred** Grace Leahy **Trained** Hatherden, Hants

FOCUS
A competitive novice handicap with an impressive performance from the winner, who threatened to be this good as a novice hurdler. The race should work out.

2002 SIS SUPPORTS MOORCROFT H'CAP HURDLE (14 hdls) 3m 217y
4:30 (4:30) (Class 3) (0-130,127) 4-Y-0+ **£6,498** (£1,908; £954; £477)

Form RPR
424- **1** **The Boss's Dream (IRE)**[203] 5075 7-11-6 **121**................ TrevorWhelan 125+
(Neil King) *t.k.h: chsd ldr tl 8th: rdn and sltly outpcd sn after 3 out: rallied u.p to chal 2 out: led last: styd on wl: rdn out* **9/4**[1]
0-23 **2** *2 ¼* **Listen And Learn (IRE)**[29] 1594 7-11-10 **125**...........(v) RichardJohnson 127
(Jonjo O'Neill) *wl in tch in midfield: mstke 7th: jnd ldr 11th: pushed into ld after next: hdd last: sn drvn and fnd little: outpcd fnl 150yds* **10/3**[2]
P00- **3** *6* **Invicta Lake (IRE)**[186] 5357 8-11-12 **127**.......................... TomO'Brien 122
(Suzy Smith) *hld up in tch in last pair: effrt sn after 3 out: no imp next: kpt on to go 3rd flat* **4/1**[3]
4-F2 **4** *½* **Cannon Fodder**[17] 1736 8-11-3 **118**.......................... MarcGoldstein 114
(Sheena West) *led and set stdy gallop: jnd and rdn 11th: hdd after next: 3rd and outpcd 2 out: plugged on same pce after: lost 3rd flat* **9/2**
532- **5** *7* **Floral Spinner**[202] 5086 8-10-9 **115**.......................... RyanWhile[(5)] 104
(Bill Turner) *hld up wl in tch in last pair: effrt 3 out: btn bef next: wknd 2 out* **20/1**
3464 **6** *2 ¾* **Morestead Screamer**[17] 1736 6-9-12 **106**.......................... DavidNoonan[(7)] 92
(Chris Gordon) *chsd ldrs: wnt 2nd and hit 8th: lost 2nd but stl pressing ldrs 11th: wknd u.p bef 2 out* **6/1**

6m 16.4s (-8.60) **Going Correction** -0.80s/f (Firm) **6 Ran SP% 111.1**
Speed ratings (Par 107): **81,80,78,78,75 75**
CSF £10.13 TOTE £2.30: £1.50, £1.70; EX 9.60 Trifecta £32.00.
Owner SLIS Ltd, M Gibbons & D Nott **Bred** Paul Barden **Trained** Barbury Castle, Wiltshire

FOCUS
A competitive handicap run at a crawl for the first two miles, which made for an exciting finish in the dash to the second-last. Not form to take too seriously.

2003 BETFAIR PROUD SUPPORTERS OF MOORCROFT NOVICES' H'CAP CHASE (12 fncs) 2m 214y
5:00 (5:01) (Class 4) (0-105,105) 4-Y-0+ **£3,994** (£1,240; £667)

Form RPR
21F2 **1** **The Yank**[21] 1674 6-11-6 **104**..................................(p[1]) JakeHodson[(5)] 111
(David Bridgwater) *j.rt: mde all: clr tl 3rd: wnt clr again after 7th: rdn and reduced advantage bef 2 out: 2 l ld whn j.rt last: a holding rivals flat: drvn out* **13/8**[1]
5U-0 **2** *1 ½* **Stars Royale (IRE)**[171] 61 6-11-12 **105**...................... LeightonAspell 110
(Nick Gifford) *t.k.h: chsd wnr tl 3rd: wnt 2nd again 8th: rdn and lost 2nd but clsd on wnr whn swtchd lft 2 out: drvn between last 2: snatched 2nd last stride* **4/1**
4465 **3** *shd* **Mount Vesuvius (IRE)**[11] 1825 7-10-3 **82** ow1................(t) TomO'Brien 88
(Paul Henderson) *hld up in rr: wnt 3rd and stl plenty to do 3 out: effrt to go 2nd and clsd on wnr bef 2 out: 2 l down whn sltly hmpd and mstke last: styd on same pce u.p flat: lost 2nd last stride* **7/2**[3]
3330 **P** **Danmurphysdoor (IRE)**[51] 1405 6-11-2 **95**..............(t) RichardJohnson
(Tim Vaughan) *t.k.h: racd in 3rd tl j. into 2nd 3rd: mstke: pckd and lost 2nd 8th: blnd and dropped to last 3 out: sn lost tch: t.o whn p.u next* **5/2**[2]

4m 25.2s (2.20) **Going Correction** -0.40s/f (Good) **4 Ran SP% 108.9**
Speed ratings (Par 105): **78,77,77,**
CSF £7.94 TOTE £2.30; EX 5.30 Trifecta £17.10.
Owner Gary Attwood **Bred** Mrs J L Egan **Trained** Icomb, Gloucs

FOCUS
A moderate handicap run at a sound gallop. The winner is rated to his mark.

2004 AP MCCOY 20 TIMES CHAMPION JOCKEY MOORCROFT H'CAP HURDLE (12 hdls) 2m 4f 114y
5:30 (5:30) (Class 5) (0-100,91) 3-Y-0+ **£2,599** (£763; £381; £190)

Form RPR
6601 **1** **Love The Leader (IRE)**[2] 1972 7-11-12 **91** 7ex..............(p) AlainCawley 103+
(Johnny Farrelly) *a travelling wl: trckd ldrs: hit 9th: sn led: pushed along bef last: readily asserted flat: r.o wl: comf* **11/8**[1]
3664 **2** *4* **Marlpit Oak**[16] 1756 10-10-11 **83**.......................... MrDSansom[(7)] 87
(Seamus Mullins) *t.k.h: hld up in tch in midfield: effrt to chse wnr bnd bef 2 out: pressing ldr 2 out: hit last: sn outpcd: kpt on for clr 2nd* **11/1**
2466 **3** *8* **Try Catch Me (IRE)**[6] 1894 10-11-12 **91**......................(t) LeightonAspell 87
(Alison Batchelor) *led tl wl bef 3 out: rdn bef 2 out: 3rd and outpcd 2 out: wl hld but kpt on to hold 3rd flat* **25/1**
U0-3 **4** *nk* **Maccabees**[162] 222 6-10-0 **72**..........................(p) ThomasCheesman[(7)] 68
(Linda Jewell) *hld up towards rr: pushed along bef 3 out: hdwy to pass btn horses bef 2 out: battling for 3rd flat: kpt on: no threat to ldrs* **14/1**
4004 **5** *8* **Canarbino Girl**[12] 1816 8-10-12 **77**..........................(t) JamesBest 67
(Caroline Keevil) *wl in tch in midfield: cl 5th and drvn after 3 out: outpcd bef next: wknd between last 2* **12/1**
51F- **6** *5* **Little Roxy (IRE)**[178] 5525 10-11-4 **83**......................(tp) AdamWedge 68
(Anna Newton-Smith) *chsd ldr tl 9th: sn rdn: wknd u.p bef 2 out* **16/1**
/600 **7** *10* **Milksheikh**[11] 1829 8-11-0 **84**..........................(t) MrPYork[(5)] 62
(Raymond York) *a bhd: shortlived effrt after 3 out: sn wknd* **100/1**
6660 **8** *15* **Hawk Gold (IRE)**[29] 1596 11-10-2 **67**......................(p) MarcGoldstein 33
(Michelle Bryant) *chsd ldrs tl lost pl 9th: rdn and wknd next: t.o* **28/1**
5653 **F** **Lyssio (GER)**[17] 1734 8-10-13 **85**.......................... MrDGBurchell[(7)]
(Mark Hoad) *hld up in midfield tl fell 8th* **12/1**
00P- **P** **Hortense Mancini**[488] 733 6-10-4 **69**......................(t) NicodeBoinville
(Mark Bradstock) *midfield: j.big 2nd: dropped to rr after 5th: rdn and lost tch after 7th: t.o whn p.u bef 9th* **7/1**[3]
PP-5 **P** **Noir Girl**[167] 130 6-10-9 **81**..........................(p) WilliamFeatherstone[(7)]
(Zoe Davison) *hld up towards rr: lost tch u.p after 8th: t.o whn p.u 2 out* **33/1**
000- **F** **Pay Your Way (IRE)**[241] 4339 7-11-9 **88**..........................[1] PaulMoloney 83
(David Rees) *t.k.h: racd wd: hld up in rr: prog 4th: chsd ldrs and mstke 8th: ev ch bef 3 out: btn bef 2 out: hung lft between last 2: 5th and wl hld whn fell last* **6/1**[2]
PP-F **P** **Kerry Maur**[67] 1243 6-11-1 **80**..........................(p) TomCannon
(Chris Gordon) *t.k.h: wl in tch in midfield: j.big 2nd: lost pl after 8th: sn lost tch: t.o whn p.u after 3 out* **22/1**
P60- **P** **Born To Be Free**[182] 5430 6-10-4 **69**.......................... LiamTreadwell
(Diana Grissell) *midfield: rdn and lost pl 5th: dropped to rr and drvn next: lost tch and p.u after 8th* **50/1**

4m 59.9s (-17.10) **Going Correction** -0.80s/f (Firm) **14 Ran SP% 122.7**
Speed ratings (Par 103): **100,98,95,95,92 90,86,80, , , ,**
CSF £16.60 CT £286.34 TOTE £2.60: £1.20, £3.80, £6.20; EX 19.50 Trifecta £348.50.
Owner Johnny Farrelly **Bred** Mrs Margaret Lacy **Trained** Enmore, Somerset

FOCUS
A weak race despite the large field and the only horse with recent winning form was heavily backed to follow up. He build on his recent win.
T/Plt: £37.50 to a £1 stake. Pool: £76,455.06 - 1,486.99 winning tickets T/Qpdt: £11.20 to a £1 stake. Pool: £7,008.01 - 459.75 winning tickets **Steve Payne**

[1818] EXETER (R-H)
Tuesday, October 20

OFFICIAL GOING: Good to firm (good in places; chs 7.9, hdl 7.7)
Wind: Almost nil Weather: Cloudy

2005 RACING UK PROFITS RETURNED TO RACING AMATEUR RIDERS' NOVICES' HURDLE (12 hdls) 2m 7f 25y
2:10 (2:10) (Class 4) 4-Y-0+ **£3,119** (£967; £483; £242)

Form RPR
1F1- **1** **The Eaglehaslanded (IRE)**[204] 5059 5-11-10 0...........(tp) MrWBiddick 123+
(Paul Nicholls) *disp ld: outrt ldr appr 3 out: sn idling and rdn: blnd 2 out and hdd: rallied u.str.p run-in: edgd lft: led nring fin* **4/7**[1]
1452 **2** *nk* **For 'N' Against (IRE)**[12] 1821 6-11-7 117..................(tp) DavidNoonan[(3)] 122
(David Pipe) *trckd ldrs: rdn to ld after 2 out: drifting rt whn hdd towards fin* **2/1**[2]
3 *25* **Minellacelebration (IRE)**[142] 5-10-13 0.......................... MrJNixon[(5)] 95
(Katy Price) *disp ld: hit 9th: rdn and hdd appr 3 out: 3rd and hld whn nt fluent 2 out: wknd* **12/1**[3]
P04U **4** *27* **Skating Home (IRE)**[13] 1813 9-10-13 72............(tp) MrRobertHawker[(5)] 63
(Richard Hawker) *hld up bhd ldrs: rdn after 9th: wknd after 10th: t.o* **250/1**
0F40 **5** *5* **Lilbourne Legacy**[3] 1964 4-10-10 104..........................(b[1]) MrTGreatrex[(7)] 59
(David Pipe) *nvr really travelling but in tch: rdn after 8th: wknd after 10th: t.o* **33/1**
4/40 **6** *86* **Boxatrix**[12] 1829 7-10-11 0..........................[1] MrDAndrews[(7)]
(Paul Phillips) *hld up wl in tch: rdn in 4th after 10th: hld whn hung bdly lft turning in: t.o* **250/1**

5m 41.3s (-17.70) **Going Correction** -1.325s/f (Hard)
WFA 4 from 5yo+ 10lb **6 Ran SP% 108.4**
Speed ratings (Par 105): **77,76,68,58,57 27**
CSF £1.88 TOTE £1.50: £1.10, £1.50; EX 1.90 Trifecta £3.70.
Owner Mrs Angela Tincknell & W Tincknell **Bred** Grange Stud **Trained** Ditcheat, Somerset
■ Paul Nicholls' 2,500th training success. The first was Olveston at Hereford in December 1991.

FOCUS
All races were run on the hurdle bends, reducing the chase course by about 45yds per circuit. Will Biddick said of the ground: "It's good to firm at worst and good for most of the course." Little depth to this novice hurdle and the market leaders drew clear. The winner was a bit better than the bare result.

2006 ILFRACOMBE FOOD SERVICE H'CAP HURDLE (10 hdls) 2m 2f 111y
2:40 (2:40) (Class 4) (0-115,115) 3-Y-0+ **£3,249** (£954; £477; £238)

Form RPR
2214 **1** **Cruise In Style (IRE)**[25] 1647 9-10-13 **102**..................(tp) JamesBest 106+
(Kevin Bishop) *hld up: stdy prog fr 3 out: chal run-in under hands and heels: led fnl strides* **16/1**
005 **2** *nk* **Only Gorgeous (IRE)**[19] 1721 6-10-8 **100**.......................... LucyGardner[(3)] 105
(Sue Gardner) *pressed ldr: led after 3 out: wnt slt lft last: kpt on: hdd fnl strides* **8/1**
4011 **3** *6* **Drifter (IRE)**[21] 1686 4-11-5 **115**.......................... PaulNO'Brien[(7)] 114
(Harry Whittington) *led: rdn and hdd after 3 out: stl ev ch 2 out: kpt on same pce fr last* **11/4**[1]
4111 **4** *1* **Bulletproof (IRE)**[12] 1823 9-11-5 **108**..........................(p) TomCannon 107
(Ken Cunningham-Brown) *hld up: hdwy fr 6th: cl 3rd whn hit 2 out: sn rdn: kpt on same pce* **4/1**[2]
5643 **5** *3 ¼* **Prince Of Poets**[12] 1823 4-10-3 **95**..........................(tp) KieronEdgar[(3)] 91
(David Pipe) *trckd ldrs: rdn after 3 out: hit next: nvr threatened: one pce after* **11/4**[1]
650- **6** *9* **Tingo In The Tale (IRE)**[38] 4057 6-11-4 **107**.......................... NicodeBoinville 92
(David Arbuthnot) *in tch: effrt appr 3 out: sn btn* **13/2**[3]
0406 **7** *4 ½* **Party Palace**[12] 1818 11-10-8 **97**..........................(t) GavinSheehan 81
(Stuart Howe) *in tch: mstke 3rd: in last trio after next: rdn along fr 7th: nt a threat after* **14/1**
00/0 **8** *9* **Chakisto (FR)**[12] 1818 7-11-0 **103**.......................... NickScholfield 74
(Katie Stephens) *hld up in tch: hdwy after 7th: sn rdn: wknd next* **28/1**

4m 26.0s (-16.70) **Going Correction** -1.325s/f (Hard) **8 Ran SP% 113.8**
Speed ratings (Par 105): **82,81,79,78,77 73,71,68**
CSF £131.70 CT £462.07 TOTE £12.30: £4.00, £2.80, £1.40; EX 225.30 Trifecta £884.90.
Owner Steve Atkinson **Bred** Swordlestown Stud **Trained** Spaxton, Somerset

FOCUS
Moderate form. The winner received a really well-judged ride and recorded a career-best figure.

2007 RACING UK ANYWHERE NOVICES' HURDLE (8 hdls) 2m 175y
3:10 (3:10) (Class 4) 4-Y-0+ **£3,249** (£954; £477; £238)

Form RPR
21-1 **1** **Abidjan (FR)**[12] 1822 5-11-12 130..........................(t) SamTwiston-Davies 140+
(Paul Nicholls) *trckd ldr: led 5th: in command fr 3 out: nt fluent last: comf* **2/13**[1]
5 **2** *8* **Linguine (FR)**[36] 1544 5-10-12 0..........................(p) ConorO'Farrell 107+
(Seamus Durack) *led: hit 4th: hdd next: kpt on same pce and hld fr 3 out* **9/1**[2]
4P60 **3** *12* **Hija**[11] 1841 4-10-7 100..........................(p) AliceMills[(5)] 92
(Gail Haywood) *chsd ldrs: reminders after 4th: rdn after next: sn wknd* **50/1**
5 **4** *23* **Imperial Glance**[28] 1613 5-10-12 0.......................... RichardJohnson 82
(Nick Williams) *trckd ldng trio: rdn after 5th: sn wknd: t.o* **14/1**[3]

3m 57.2s (-18.30) **Going Correction** -1.325s/f (Hard)
WFA 4 from 5yo 9lb **4 Ran SP% 105.3**
Speed ratings (Par 105): **90,86,80,69**
CSF £2.02 TOTE £1.10; EX 3.00 Trifecta £10.50.
Owner Axom L **Bred** Gabriel Vagne & Michele Vagne **Trained** Ditcheat, Somerset

FOCUS
A straightforward opportunity for the favourite and he duly obliged. He stood out on his recent win but looks progressive.

2008 BETFRED MOBILE H'CAP CHASE (18 fncs) 3m 54y
3:45 (3:45) (Class 3) (0-130,129) 4-Y-O+ £7,596 (£2,244; £1,122; £561; £280)

Form RPR
-P3P 1 **Caulfields Venture (IRE)**[93] 1053 9-11-10 **127**..........(v[1]) AidanColeman 135+
(Emma Lavelle) *in tch: hdwy 14th: led appr 4 out where nt fluent: styd on wl: rdn out* **5/1**[3]
24-1 2 1 3/4 **Danandy (IRE)**[93] 1053 8-11-10 **127**..........(p) TomO'Brien 132
(Philip Hobbs) *in tch: hdwy appr 4 out: rdn after 3 out: chal for 2nd appr last: styd on but a being hld by wnr* **8/1**
2313 3 1/2 **Border Breaker (IRE)**[27] 1632 6-11-4 **128**..........(tp) MichaelHeard(7) 133
(David Pipe) *hld up: hdwy appr 4 out: rdn to chse wnr after 2 out: styd on but no ex fr last* **4/1**[2]
-446 4 6 **Bertie's Desire**[16] 1767 7-10-6 **109**.......... LeightonAspell 111
(Oliver Sherwood) *led: rdn and hdd appr 4 out: kpt on tl no ex appr last* **6/1**
4031 5 8 **Dursey Sound (IRE)**[28] 1616 7-11-12 **129**.......... RichardJohnson 126+
(Jonjo O'Neill) *hld up: blnd bdly 1st: effrt whn nt fluent 4 out: nvr quite threatened: wknd after 2 out* **11/4**[1]
0135 6 9 **Adrenalin Flight (IRE)**[20] 1699 9-11-12 **129**..........(v) AndrewThornton 117
(Seamus Mullins) *trckd ldrs tl lost pl 14th: struggling and no threat after: wknd bef 2 out: dismntd after fin* **5/1**[3]
4-30 7 1 1/4 **Fruity O'Rooney**[149] 448 12-11-7 **124**..........(v) JamieMoore 109
(Gary Moore) *chsd clr ldr: pressing ldr whn blnd 6th: rdn after 14th: wknd 2 out* **14/1**

5m 45.3s (-24.00) **Going Correction** -0.775s/f (Firm) 7 Ran SP% **112.1**
Speed ratings (Par 107): **109,108,108,106,103 100,100**
CSF £40.17 TOTE £7.00: £3.30, £4.50; EX 43.10 Trifecta £322.50.
Owner C F Colquhoun **Bred** Michael Crean **Trained** Hatherden, Hants

FOCUS
Not a bad little handicap, although jumping let down a couple of the principals. The winner was back to the level of last season's Kempton run.

2009 RACING UK DAY PASS JUST £10 "JUNIOR" STANDARD OPEN NATIONAL HUNT FLAT RACE 1m 5f 38y
4:15 (4:19) (Class 6) 3-Y-O £1,624 (£477; £238; £119)

Form RPR
6 1 **Golden Gate Bridge (GER)**[16] 1772 3-10-12 0.......... DenisO'Regan 105+
(Mark Pitman) *mde all: edgd lft whn rdn ent fnl f: kpt on wl* **5/1**[3]
2 2 1/4 **Water Willow** 3-10-5 0.......... NickScholfield 90
(Harry Fry) *trckd ldrs: pushed along over 2f out: swtchd lft and rdn over 1f out: kpt on but no quite pce to chal wnr* **4/1**[2]
3 1 **Inner Loop** 3-10-5 0.......... TomO'Brien 89
(Robert Stephens) *trckd wnr: rdn over 2f out: lost 2nd ent fnl f: kpt on but no ex* **5/1**[3]
4 4 **Russian Approval** 3-10-5 0.......... RichardJohnson 84
(William Knight) *hld up but in tch: tk clsr order over 3f out: rdn over 2f out: kpt on same pce* **2/1**[1]
5 4 **Purple Genie (GR)** 3-10-5 0.......... NicodeBoinville 78
(Patrick Chamings) *hld up but in tch: effrt over 3f out: sn one pce* **10/1**
6 9 **Castle Cavalier** 3-10-5 0.......... GavinSheehan 67
(Robert Stephens) *chsd ldrs tl 4f out: no threat after* **8/1**
7 19 **Turbo Charged (IRE)** 3-10-7 0.......... RyanWhile(5) 49
(Bill Turner) *trckd ldrs: effrt over 3f out: wknd over 2f out* **25/1**
8 1 1/2 **Janesmerlin** 3-10-12 0.......... JamieMoore 47
(Kevin Bishop) *towards rr but in tch: struggling 4f out: wknd 3f out* **33/1**

2m 59.7s (-17.00) **Going Correction** -1.325s/f (Hard) 8 Ran SP% **113.7**
Speed ratings (Par 99): **99,97,97,94,92 86,74,73**
CSF £24.96 TOTE £4.20: £1.80, £1.60, £1.60; EX 25.50 Trifecta £95.90.
Owner Malcolm C Denmark **Bred** Gestut Hachetal **Trained** Upper Lambourn, Berks
■ Mark Pitman's first winner since resuming his training career.

FOCUS
An ordinary junior bumper that went to the only runner with previous experience. He appeared to step up quite a bit on his debut run.

2010 BETFRED BEST MATE BEGINNERS' CHASE (12 fncs) 2m 1f 109y
4:50 (4:50) (Class 4) 4-Y-O+ £5,198 (£1,526)

Form RPR
45-2 1 **Dragon's Den (IRE)**[17] 1754 8-11-2 0.......... LeightonAspell 132+
(Chris Down) *trckd ldr: pckd 3rd: led 5th: mstke 3 out: r.o strly fr next: comf* **5/4**[2]
-622 2 13 **Chase The Wind (IRE)**[112] 861 6-11-2 0..........(t) GavinSheehan 120
(Warren Greatrex) *led: nt fluent 2nd (water): hdd 5th: pushed along 7th: chal briefly 4 out: sn rdn: styd on same pce fr 2 out* **8/13**[1]

4m 4.5s (-14.50) **Going Correction** -0.775s/f (Firm) 2 Ran SP% **106.4**
Speed ratings (Par 105): **103,96**
TOTE £1.70.
Owner G Waterman **Bred** Thomas Hassett **Trained** Mutterton, Devon

FOCUS
This didn't play out as the market suggested it would, the odds-on favourite being readily brushed aside. The winner is rated in line with his hurdles form.
T/Plt: £38.90 to £1 stake. Pool: £46,835.07 - 876.88 winning units T/Qpdt: £14.90 to a £1 stake. Pool: £2,269.13 - 112.40 winning units **Tim Mitchell**

1752 FONTWELL (L-H)
Wednesday, October 21

OFFICIAL GOING: Good (good to soft in places) changing to good to soft after race 1 (2.25).changing to soft after race 2 (3.00)
Wind: quite strong behind Weather: rain Rails: Rail movement adding; 66 yards to both Chase races. Hurdle: 2m 1f and 2m 3f add 78 yards, 2m 5f add 88 yards. Bottom bend divided. Fences outer, Hurdle middle outer.

2011 ABP SOUTHAMPTON GATEWAY TO WORLD NOVICES' HURDLE (9 hdls) 2m 1f 145y
2:25 (2:25) (Class 4) 4-Y-O+ £5,198 (£1,526; £763; £381)

Form RPR
1 **Bigmartre (FR)**[234] 4-10-12 0.......... GavinSheehan 124+
(Harry Whittington) *mde all: rdn after 2 out: drifted rt run-in: kpt on strly* **20/1**
11- 2 5 **Board Of Trade**[217] 4852 4-10-12 0.......... WayneHutchinson 118+
(Alan King) *in tch: trckd ldrs: 3rd: rdn after 3 out: chsd wnr after next: hld whn mstke last: kpt on same pce* **5/6**[1]
333- 3 2 1/4 **Red Devil Star (IRE)**[209] 4999 5-10-12 124..........(t) TomO'Brien 115
(Suzy Smith) *trckd wnr: rdn appr 2 out: lost 2nd btween last 2: no ex run-in* **3/1**[2]
F-1 4 9 **Take A Break (FR)**[174] 26 4-11-5 0.......... ConorO'Farrell 114
(Nigel Hawke) *mid-div: lost pl after 6th: styd on into hld 4th 2 out: nvr threatened* **16/1**
-611 5 11 **General Ginger**[23] 1673 5-11-12 128..........(t) NoelFehily 113
(Harry Fry) *trckd ldrs: rdn after 3 out: sn hld: wknd last* **4/1**[3]
5- 6 2 1/4 **Threebarmymen (IRE)**[181] 5502 4-10-9 0.......... MattGriffiths(3) 96
(Jeremy Scott) *j.rt at times: hld up: rdn after 3 out: wknd between last 2* **50/1**
44- 7 10 **Iniesta (IRE)**[24] 4271 4-10-12 0.......... JamieMoore 86
(Gary Moore) *hld up: hdwy 3 out: effrt bef next: wknd between last 2* **20/1**
8 20 **Hallingham**[23] 5-10-12 0.......... TomCannon 68
(Chris Gordon) *nvr that fluent: struggling whn awkward 6th: a towards rr* **50/1**

4m 36.3s (2.00) **Going Correction** +0.30s/f (Yiel)
WFA 4 from 5yo 9lb 8 Ran SP% **118.9**
Speed ratings (Par 105): **107,104,103,99,94 93,89,80**
CSF £39.57 TOTE £21.60: £4.90, £1.10, £1.40; EX 60.00 Trifecta £236.10.
Owner P J Dixon **Bred** E Prigent, E Lecoiffier & S Follain **Trained** Sparsholt, Oxfordshire

FOCUS
Rail movement increased both chases by 66yds and increased 2m1f and 2m3f hurdles by 78yds and 2m5f by 88yds. Bottom bend divided, fences on outer hurdles middle/outer. Worsening ground and gloomy conditions greeted the runners for the first of a six-race card. It looked hard work for most of these and produced an upset. Ordinary from, the fourth probably the best guide.

2012 SOUTHAMPTON MAKES MORE SENSE BEGINNERS' CHASE (15 fncs) 2m 3f 35y
3:00 (3:00) (Class 4) 4-Y-O+ £6,498 (£1,908; £954; £477)

Form RPR
4P6- 1 **Calipto (FR)**[186] 5390 5-11-3 0..........(t) SamTwiston-Davies 146+
(Paul Nicholls) *travelled wl: trckd ldrs: chal 4 out gng best: tk narrow advantage last: eased ahd: unextended* **8/15**[1]
303- 2 4 1/2 **Wadswick Court (IRE)**[195] 5246 7-11-3 131.......... NoelFehily 131
(Neil Mulholland) *pressed ldr: disp 9th tl narrow advantage 4 out: rdn after 2 out: narrowly hdd last: kpt on but sn no ch w wnr* **7/2**[2]
03-6 3 20 **Harristown**[159] 319 5-11-3 0..........(p) AidanColeman 117
(Charlie Longsdon) *hld up bhd ldng 4: nudged along after 6th: reminders after 9th: outpcd 3 out: wnt hld 3rd at the last* **8/1**[3]
11P- 4 17 **Money Talks**[179] 5539 5-11-3 0.......... MarcGoldstein 97
(Michael Madgwick) *trckd ldrs: hit 11th: sn rdn: outpcd 3 out: wknd 2 out* **25/1**
3022 U **Halling's Wish**[17] 1769 5-11-3 111..........(bt) JamieMoore 92
(Gary Moore) *led: jnd 9th tl hdd 4 out: rdn in hld 5th whn knuckled on landing and uns rdr 2 out* **16/1**

5m 9.2s (1.90) **Going Correction** +0.275s/f (Yiel) 5 Ran SP% **108.3**
Speed ratings (Par 105): **107,105,96,89,**
CSF £2.82 TOTE £1.50: £1.10, £1.90; EX 3.00 Trifecta £5.70.
Owner Ian Fogg & Chris Giles **Bred** Andre Priolet **Trained** Ditcheat, Somerset

FOCUS
A hugely impressive start over fences for the odds-on Calipto, who provided Paul Nicholls with a third straight win in the race. He looks like being a decent novice.

2013 SOLENT STEVEDORES H'CAP HURDLE (11 hdls) 2m 5f 139y
3:35 (3:35) (Class 3) (0-135,132) 4-Y-O+ £6,498 (£1,908; £954; £477)

Form RPR
522- 1 **Drum Valley**[319] 2945 7-11-2 **132**.......... BenFfrenchDavis(10) 140+
(Oliver Sherwood) *mde all: styd on strly fr 2 out: rdn out* **5/1**[3]
020- 2 9 **Lightentertainment (IRE)**[179] 5539 7-11-10 **130**.......... TomCannon 130
(Chris Gordon) *hld up: rdn and hdwy appr 2 out: styd on into 2nd sn after last: no ex fnl 100yds* **7/2**[1]
02-4 3 3/4 **Laughton Park**[155] 389 10-10-6 **117**.......... FreddieMitchell(5) 115
(Suzy Smith) *trckd wnr: rdn to chal briefly after 3 out: hld next: kpt on same pce* **14/1**
-114 4 1 1/2 **Promanco**[18] 1754 6-10-8 **121**..........(t) MrSamPainting(7) 120
(Charlie Longsdon) *hld up: hit 1st: nt clr run whn tried to slip up inner after 3 out: rdn into 3rd next where stmbld: kpt on same pce* **4/1**[2]
-511 5 6 **Taradrewe**[45] 1490 8-11-7 **127**..........(t) AidanColeman 120
(Anthony Honeyball) *in tch on outer: effrt after 3 out: one pce fr next* **4/1**[2]
3341 6 15 **Mercers Court (IRE)**[18] 1752 7-11-4 **124**.......... TrevorWhelan 100
(Neil King) *trckd ldrs: rdn after 3 out: wknd last* **5/1**[3]
F42- 7 24 **Sandy Beach**[200] 5146 5-10-9 **115**.......... BrendanPowell 67
(Colin Tizzard) *racd keenly: in tch: effrt after 3 out: wknd next: t.o* **8/1**

5m 47.5s (5.00) **Going Correction** +0.30s/f (Yiel) 7 Ran SP% **113.3**
Speed ratings (Par 107): **102,98,98,97,95 90,81**
CSF £22.70 TOTE £6.30: £3.10, £2.10; EX 22.80 Trifecta £257.50.
Owner A Taylor & A Signy **Bred** Limestone And Tara Studs **Trained** Upper Lambourn, Berks

FOCUS
A highly competitive renewal of this handicap hurdle and much to like about the performances of the first two home. Another pb from the winner.

2014 SOCIETY OF ST JAMES H'CAP CHASE (16 fncs) 2m 5f 31y
4:10 (4:10) (Class 4) (0-120,117) 4-Y-O+ £3,994 (£1,240; £667)

Form RPR
332- 1 **Fergal Mael Duin**[234] 4510 7-11-12 **117**.......... TomCannon 130+
(David Bridgwater) *trckd ldrs: lft disputing 2nd at the 9th: rdn to chal after 4 out: hung rt fr next: 1 l up whn veered bdly rt last: styd on wl to assert run-in* **8/11**[1]
335- 2 4 1/2 **Frizzo (FR)**[198] 5203 8-11-2 **114**..........(b) PaulNO'Brien(7) 121
(Harry Whittington) *led: chal after 4 out: rdn after 3 out: hdd bef last where sltly hmpd: no ex run-in* **11/4**[2]
-110 3 19 **Venetian Lad**[18] 1755 10-11-9 **114**.......... MarcGoldstein 105
(Lydia Richards) *trckd ldrs: lft disputing 2nd at the 9th tl rdn after 3 out: wknd bef last* **13/2**[3]
-2P6 U **Friendly Society (IRE)**[25] 1659 10-11-5 **113**..........(b) JamesBanks(3)
(Noel Williams) *pressed ldr tl mstke and uns rdr 9th* **8/1**

5m 45.7s (2.70) **Going Correction** +0.275s/f (Yiel) 4 Ran SP% **109.0**
Speed ratings (Par 105): **105,103,96,**
CSF £3.25 TOTE £1.60; EX 3.40 Trifecta £7.10.
Owner James Messenger Jean-Marie Buob-Aldorf **Bred** J M Messenger **Trained** Icomb, Gloucs

FOCUS
What this lacked for in numbers it made up for in drama. The winner should still be competitive when reassessed.

2015 ABP KEEPING BRITAIN TRADING CONDITIONAL JOCKEYS' NOVICES' H'CAP HURDLE (10 hdls) 2m 3f 33y
4:45 (4:45) (Class 5) (0-100,100) 3-Y-0+ **£2,339** (£686; £343; £171)

Form | | | | RPR
6-5U **1** **Dainty Diva (IRE)**[140] 597 7-11-7 **98**........................ MattGriffiths(3) 103+
(Jeremy Scott) *travelled strly thrght: trckd ldrs: kpt wdst in bk st: led after 3 out: sn in command: v easily* **3/1**[1]
P350 **2** *6* **Al Guwair (IRE)**[18] 1756 5-10-0 **74** oh5........................ KieronEdgar 69
(Mark Hoad) *hld up bhd: hdwy after 7th: rdn to chse wnr after 3 out: hld whn mstke last: kpt on same pce* **20/1**
6406 **3** *10* **Watchmetail (IRE)**[5] 1952 9-9-11 **74** oh10........... ThomasCheesman(3) 58
(John Panvert) *trckd ldrs tl lost pl after 6th: rdn next: styd on between last 2: wnt 3rd run-in* **40/1**
1662 **4** *1 ¾* **All Riled Up**[14] 1816 7-10-11 **85**........................ DanielHiskett 67
(Harry Chisman) *pressed ldr tl 6th: chsd ldrs: rdn after 3 out: styd on same pce fr next* **10/1**
-113 **5** *9* **Shalianzi (IRE)**[13] 1819 5-11-4 **100**........................(b) GeorgeGorman(8) 73
(Gary Moore) *trckd ldrs: struggling after 7th: nvr threatened: wknd bef last* **3/1**[1]
5421 **6** *3 ½* **Owner Occupier**[45] 1489 10-10-0 **74** oh3........................(p) ThomasGarner 44
(Chris Gordon) *led tl 3 out: sn rdn: wknd bef last* **7/1**[3]
535 **7** *¾* **Minority Interest**[112] 878 6-10-13 **87**........................ BenPoste 56
(Daniel O'Brien) *trckd ldrs tl reminders after 5th: sn bhd* **11/1**
505- **8** *1 ¼* **Surging Seas (IRE)**[239] 4413 6-11-11 **99**........................(p[1]) ConorShoemark 67
(Ali Stronge) *trckd ldrs: led 3 out: sn rdn and hdd: wknd after next* **4/1**[2]
46-P **P** **Burgess Dream (IRE)**[173] 62 6-11-5 **93**........................ JeremiahMcGrath
(Anna Newton-Smith) *hld up: nt fluent 3rd: rdn and hdwy after 3 out: cl enough 5th whn hmpd and stmbld bdly 2 out: not rcvr and p.u bef last: dismntd* **14/1**

5m 8.8s (9.40) **Going Correction** +0.30s/f (Yiel) **9** Ran SP% **113.8**
Speed ratings (Par 103): **92,89,85,84,80 79,78,78,**
CSF £55.69 CT £1968.55 TOTE £3.80: £1.40, £3.70, £8.10; EX 67.90 Trifecta £1499.60.
Owner Langleys **Bred** Mrs M O'Neill **Trained** Brompton Regis, Somerset

FOCUS
This featured some mostly disappointing sorts and was turned into a procession by the well supported winner. The placed horses were both racing from out of the handicap. He was winner well in on the best of his Irish form and is rated back to that level.

2016 ABP CRUISE SOUTHAMPTON STKS MARES' INTERMEDIATE OPEN NATIONAL HUNT FLAT RACE 2m 1f 145y
5:15 (5:15) (Class 6) 4-6-Y-O **£1,559** (£457; £228; £114)

Form | | | | RPR
4- **1** **Late Night Lily**[241] 4391 4-10-12 0........................ HarrySkelton 95+
(Dan Skelton) *hld up: hdwy into 4 l 2nd 4f out: led wl over 2f out: sn clr: comf* **7/1**[3]
2 *8* **Midnight Tune** 4-10-12 0........................ AidanColeman 86
(Anthony Honeyball) *hld up: hdwy 5f out: rdn to chse ldrs 3f out: styd on into 2nd fnl f: no ch w wnr* **9/2**[2]
6 **3** *2 ¾* **Pollyogan (IRE)**[155] 392 5-10-12 0........................ NoelFehily 86+
(Harry Fry) *led: hung rt on bnd whn 4 l clr 4f out: hanging rt u.p whn hdd wl over 2f out: sn hld by wnr: no ex whn lost 2nd ins fnl f* **9/2**[2]
4 *5* **Sweet'N'Chic (IRE)** 5-10-12 0........................ SamTwiston-Davies 78
(Richard Rowe) *pressed ldr tl rdn 4f out: one pce fnl 2f* **22/1**
10- **5** *24* **Miss Crick**[193] 5277 4-11-5 0........................ WayneHutchinson 61
(Alan King) *trckd ldrs: struggling over 4f out: wknd over 2f out* **5/6**[1]
0- **6** *22* **Romanee Vivant**[192] 5299 5-10-12 0........................ TrevorWhelan 32
(Neil King) *trckd ldrs: rdn 4f out: wknd over 2f out* **33/1**
7 *99* **Piccomore** 5-10-12 0........................ TomO'Brien
(Polly Gundry) *chsd ldrs tl 1/2-way: sn bhd: virtually p.u (btn 221 l)* **50/1**

4m 34.4s (5.70) **Going Correction** +0.30s/f (Yiel) **7** Ran SP% **112.7**
Speed ratings: **99,95,94,92,81 71,**
CSF £36.38 TOTE £7.70: £2.50, £2.10; EX 43.60 Trifecta £138.00.
Owner Braybrooke Lodge Partnership **Bred** Martin Bates & Neil Jennings **Trained** Alcester, Warwicks

FOCUS
This already moderate bumper was run on ground significantly more testing than was described at the overnight declaration stage. Most failed to handle to conditions, including the heavily supported favourite. A big step up from the winner but not an easy race to put a figure on.
T/Plt: £245.80 to a £1 stake. Pool: £57,594.00 - 171.02 winning tickets. T/Qpdt: £61.50 to a £1 stake. Pool: £3,378.00 - 40.60 winning tickets. **Tim Mitchell**

1906 WORCESTER (L-H)
Wednesday, October 21

OFFICIAL GOING: Good to soft changing to good to soft (soft in places) after race 3 (2.50)
Wind: Light behind Weather: Overcast

2017 MYSON RADIATORS H'CAP CHASE (16 fncs) 2m 7f
1:45 (1:45) (Class 4) (0-110,110) 4-Y-0+ **£3,898** (£1,144; £572; £286)

Form | | | | RPR
0-40 **1** **Muckle Roe (IRE)**[31] 1601 6-11-4 **109**........................ JamieBargary(7) 119+
(Nigel Twiston-Davies) *hld up: hdwy to chse ldr 10th: led after 12th: drvn out* **15/2**
2F2- **2** *2 ¾* **Cobajayisland (IRE)**[266] 3929 7-11-8 **109**........................ DerekFox(3) 116+
(Lucinda Russell) *a.p: n.m.r 6th: chsd wnr 3 out: ev ch last: rdn and edgd lft flat: styd on same pce* **7/2**[2]
6222 **3** *8* **Railway Storm (IRE)**[12] 1842 10-10-5 **96**........................ MissBFrost(7) 93
(Jimmy Frost) *led to 3rd: chsd ldrs: rdn after 3 out: styd on same pce fr next* **8/1**
/11- **4** *1 ¼* **Playing The Field (IRE)**[516] 433 10-11-5 **103**........................ RichardJohnson 99
(Jonjo O'Neill) *hld up: hdwy 4 out: rdn appr last: wknd flat* **3/1**[1]
5323 **5** *2* **Sandynow (IRE)**[31] 1592 10-11-7 **105**........................(vt) SeanBowen 101
(Peter Bowen) *chsd ldrs: j. slowly and lost pl 1st: hdwy 5th: chsd ldr after 8th tl nt fluent and lost pl 10th: hdwy after 12th: rdn and wknd bef last* **6/1**
4635 **6** *67* **Porters War (IRE)**[18] 1755 13-11-12 **110**........................ NickScholfield 74
(Jeremy Scott) *prom: chsd ldr 5th tl after 8th: remained handy tl rdn after 12th: wknd bef next* **11/1**
066/ **F** **Twyford**[557] 8-10-3 **87**........................ RobertDunne
(Laura Young) *chsd ldrs: led 3rd tl after 12th: disputing 2 l 2nd whn fell 4 out* **50/1**
60-U **U** **Gold Man (IRE)**[13] 1824 6-11-1 **102**........................(t) TomBellamy(3)
(Kim Bailey) *trckd ldrs: mstke and uns rdr 2nd* **11/2**[3]

5m 58.2s (8.30) **Going Correction** +0.30s/f (Yiel) **8** Ran SP% **110.1**
Speed ratings (Par 105): **97,96,93,92,92 68, ,**
CSF £32.25 CT £201.54 TOTE £8.00: £2.60, £1.50, £1.60; EX 52.80 Trifecta £495.50.
Owner Mrs Jane Lane **Bred** Mrs Jane Lane And Ms Cecily Purcell **Trained** Naunton, Gloucs

FOCUS
All starts have been moved at this track following remeasuring, so there will be no speed figures here until there is sufficient data to calculate updated median times. All fences and hurdles were moved out approximately 20 feet from the meeting on the 13th October. The home bend was 4 yards off the inner and the Cathedral bend approximately 6 yards off the inside, adding about 30 yards to a 2m race. Worcester's last meeting until the spring took place on Good to soft ground following 11mm of the rain during the night and the morning. This modest handicap chase was 6.9sec slower than the following Class 3 event. The winner improved in line with his hurdles mark.

2018 RICHARD DAVIS MEMORIAL NOVICES' LIMITED H'CAP CHASE (16 fncs) 2m 7f
2:15 (2:15) (Class 3) (0-135,135) 5-Y-0+ **£7,596** (£2,244; £1,122; £561; £280)

Form | | | | RPR
20-2 **1** **Upswing (IRE)**[26] 1642 7-11-1 **128**........................ RichardJohnson 143+
(Jonjo O'Neill) *hld up: hdwy 4 out: led appr last: drvn out* **9/2**[2]
20-0 **2** *6* **Relentless Dreamer (IRE)**[174] 50 6-10-8 **121**........................(p) LeightonAspell 129
(Rebecca Curtis) *disp ld tl wnt on after 12th: hdd 3 out: sn rdn: styd on same pce flat* **6/1**[3]
15P- **3** *3 ¾* **St Johns Point (IRE)**[227] 4651 7-10-3 **116** oh1........................(p) BrianHughes 121
(Charlie Longsdon) *disp ld tl rdn after 12th: led 3 out: hdd appr last: wknd flat* **14/1**
2112 **4** *3 ½* **Skylander (IRE)**[6] 1932 6-10-8 **128**........................ MichaelHeard(7) 130
(David Pipe) *hld up: hdwy after 12th: ev ch fr 3 out tl rdn appr last: wknd flat* **5/2**[1]
-143 **5** *3 ¾* **Bold Conquest (IRE)**[29] 1615 7-10-9 **122**........................ JoshuaMoore 119
(Stuart Edmunds) *chsd ldrs: pushed along 10th: rdn and wknd 3 out* **6/1**[3]
-211 **6** *11* **Call Me Vic (IRE)**[101] 965 8-11-8 **135**........................ PaddyBrennan 126
(Tom George) *chsd ldrs: mstke 3 out: sn wknd* **9/2**[2]
413- **7** *25* **Doctor Phoenix (IRE)**[200] 5142 7-11-7 **134**........................ NickScholfield 111
(David Dennis) *hld up: rdn and wknd appr 4 out* **10/1**

5m 51.3s (1.40) **Going Correction** +0.30s/f (Yiel) **7** Ran SP% **109.3**
Speed ratings: **109,106,105,104,103 99,90**
CSF £28.13 TOTE £4.20: £1.70, £4.20; EX 37.20 Trifecta £340.80.
Owner John P McManus **Bred** Darren Quaid **Trained** Cheltenham, Gloucs

FOCUS
A decent little chase, this was run 6.9sec quicker than the previous Class 4 handicap. The form looks believable despite the big step up from the winner.

2019 FRED RIMELL MEMORIAL H'CAP CHASE (12 fncs) 2m 110y
2:50 (2:50) (Class 4) (0-120,120) 4-Y-0+ **£4,548** (£1,335; £667; £333)

Form | | | | RPR
35-2 **1** **Helium (FR)**[7] 1907 10-11-3 **108**........................ RhysFlint 127+
(Alexandra Dunn) *trckd ldrs: wnt 2nd 4th tl nt fluent 7th: wnt 2nd again after next: mstke and j.rt 3 out: clr bef last: easily* **3/1**[2]
F0P- **2** *18* **Val D'Arc (FR)**[200] 5146 6-11-11 **116**........................ AlainCawley 117
(Richard Hobson) *led: nt fluent 3rd and 4th: hdd after 3 out: wknd appr last* **14/1**
32 **3** *34* **All Together (FR)**[143] 566 4-11-6 **120**........................ RichardJohnson 90
(Johnny Farrelly) *hld up: nt a fluent: hdwy and mstke 4 out: wknd next: bhd whn j.lft 2 out and last* **6/4**[1]
F-31 **4** *50* **Days Ahead (IRE)**[23] 1674 8-11-12 **117**........................(p) RichieMcLernon 42
(Richenda Ford) *chsd ldr to 4th: wnt 2nd again 7th tl rdn after next: wknd bef 4 out* **7/2**[3]
5424 **U** **Boss In Boots (IRE)**[22] 1690 7-11-10 **115**........................(b) AndrewThornton
(Seamus Mullins) *j.rt: slipped and uns rdr 2nd* **6/1**

4m 8.1s (3.10) **Going Correction** +0.30s/f (Yiel)
WFA 4 from 6yo+ 9lb **5** Ran SP% **108.2**
Speed ratings (Par 105): **104,95,79,56,**
CSF £30.20 TOTE £4.30: £1.90, £4.50; EX 37.10 Trifecta £117.10.
Owner West Buckland Bloodstock Ltd **Bred** Adrian Von Gunten **Trained** West Buckland, Somerset

FOCUS
A small field for this ordinary handicap, but the pace was sound. The winner could be rated higher but this is not a race to be at all confident about.

2020 VISIT WORCESTERSHIRE IN AUTUMN & WINTER "NEWCOMERS" STANDARD OPEN NATIONAL HUNT FLAT RACE 2m
3:25 (3:25) (Class 6) 3-5-Y-O **£1,559** (£457; £228; £114)

Form | | | | RPR
1 **Ballyandy** 4-11-7 0........................ RyanHatch(3) 102+
(Nigel Twiston-Davies) *a.p: led over 2f out: rdn clr over 1f out: styd on* **3/1**[1]
2 *2 ¼* **Rodneythetrotter** 3-10-7 0........................ JoshuaMoore 82+
(Pat Phelan) *hld up: hdwy 5f out: rdn to chse wnr over 1f out: hung lft ins fnl f: styd on* **12/1**[3]
3 *9* **Crazy Penguin (IRE)** 4-11-10 0........................ RichardJohnson 90
(Charlie Longsdon) *mid-div: hdwy 1/2-way: rdn over 4f out: sn outpcd: styd on to go 3rd ins fnl f* **3/1**[1]
4 *2* **Indian Brave (IRE)** 4-11-10 0........................ MarkQuinlan 88
(Neil Mulholland) *led: rdn and hdd over 2f out: wknd over 1f out* **16/1**
5 *2 ¼* **Jackblack** 3-10-7 0........................ NicodeBoinville 69
(Patrick Chamings) *prom: chsd ldr over 12f out: rdn and ev ch over 2f out: wknd fnl f* **20/1**
6 *6* **The Linksman (IRE)** 3-10-7 0........................ WillKennedy 64
(Brian Ellison) *hld up: hdwy 5f out: rdn and wknd 2f out: hung rt fr over 1f out* **3/1**[1]
7 *21* **Sacred Summit (IRE)** 4-11-10 0........................ PaddyBrennan 62
(Tim Vaughan) *hld up: hdwy over 6f out: wknd 4f out* **28/1**
8 *50* **Horseguardsparade** 4-11-10 0........................ PaulMoloney 17
(Paul Morgan) *hld up: a in rr: wknd 6f out: eased* **12/1**[3]
9 *18* **Earth Legend** 4-11-10 0........................(t) DarylJacob 1
(Neil Mulholland) *hld up in tch: racd keenly: rdn over 6f out: sn wknd* **9/1**[2]
10 *4 ½* **Mon Garcon Frankie** 3-10-0 0........................ DavidNoonan(7)
(Steve Flook) *chsd ldr tl rdn over 12f out: wknd over 8f out* **50/1**

3m 45.6s (0.60) **Going Correction** +0.30s/f (Yiel)
WFA 3 from 4yo+ 17lb **10** Ran SP% **116.4**
Speed ratings (Par 101): **110,108,104,103,102 99,88,63,54,52**
CSF £42.79 TOTE £4.40: £1.60, £3.00, £1.60; EX 47.80 Trifecta £243.50.
Owner N A Twiston-Davies **Bred** Pleasure Palace Racing **Trained** Naunton, Gloucs

FOCUS
There was a change in the official going prior to this race. None of these had run before, but it could be that it was a decent race of its type.

2021 MIKE ASHTON IS NEARLY 60 MARES' NOVICES' HURDLE (8 hdls) 2m

4:00 (4:00) (Class 4) 4-Y-0+ **£3,898** (£1,144; £572; £286)

Form RPR
-22 **1** **Smart Talk (IRE)**[11] 1854 5-10-10 0 .... WillKennedy 117+
(Brian Ellison) *led tl after 2nd: chsd ldr tl led again 4th: hdd 2 out: sn rdn: led flat: styd on wl* **7/2**[2]
222- **2** *6* **Avispa**[246] 4278 6-10-10 122 .... DenisO'Regan 112
(Alan King) *chsd ldrs: wnt 2nd appr 3 out: led 2 out: shkn up bef last: hdd flat: sn rdn: fnd nil* **4/11**[1]
3 *32* **La Pyle (FR)**[36] 4-10-10 0 ....[1] RichardJohnson 83
(Philip Hobbs) *plld hrd: trckd ldr tl led after 2nd: hdd 4th: wkng whn mstke 3 out* **10/1**[3]
0-3P **4** *7* **Tara's Rainbow**[150] 462 5-10-10 0 ....(t) DavidBass 77
(Kim Bailey) *hld up: a in rr: bhd fr 3rd* **33/1**
5F- **5** *20* **Lady Helissio**[216] 4866 5-10-10 0 .... MarkQuinlan 59
(Neil Mulholland) *hld up: plld hrd: a in rr: bhd fr 3rd: mstke next: blnd 2 out* **66/1**

3m 53.2s (2.60) **Going Correction** +0.30s/f (Yiel)
WFA 4 from 5yo+ 9lb **5** Ran SP% **109.1**
Speed ratings (Par 105): **105,102,86,82,72**
CSF £5.34 TOTE £5.00: £1.40, £1.10; EX 5.00 Trifecta £9.40.
Owner Mrs J A Martin **Bred** Roland Rothwell **Trained** Norton, N Yorks

FOCUS
An uncompetitive event. There's a case for rating the form up to 11lb higher through the second.

2022 7BETS4FREE.COM SAYS NO 1 WINS MARES' H'CAP HURDLE (10 hdls) 2m 4f

4:35 (4:35) (Class 4) (0-110,109) 3-Y-0+ **£3,898** (£1,144; £572; £286)

Form RPR
0621 **1** **Lady Of Longstone (IRE)**[7] 1910 5-11-0 **104** 7ex........ MichaelHeard(7) 118+
(David Pipe) *mde all: clr fr 3 out: nt fluent last: easily* **2/1**[1]
1000 **2** *15* **Queen Spud**[106] 938 6-11-10 **107** ....(p) JakeGreenall 101
(Henry Daly) *chsd wnr to 5th: wnt 2nd again next: rdn appr 3 out: wknd bef next: wnt lft last* **12/1**
2215 **3** *2 1/4* **Amour D'Or**[12] 1841 4-11-9 **106** .... RichardJohnson 99
(Nick Williams) *chsd ldrs: rdn whn mstke 3 out: wknd bef next* **5/2**[2]
33U- **4** *10* **Ballydague Lady (IRE)**[246] 4279 8-11-5 **109**....(p) MrMartinMcIntyre(7) 91
(Neil Mulholland) *hld up: hdwy after 7th: sn rdn: wknd 3 out* **10/1**
0PP- **5** *nk* **Redanna (IRE)**[218] 4825 6-10-0 **83** oh3.................. RichieMcLernon 65
(Robert Walford) *prom tl rdn and wknd after 7th* **25/1**
4-PP **P** **Definitely Better (IRE)**[146] 524 7-11-0 **97** .... PaddyBrennan
(Tom George) *hld up: reminder after 4th: hdwy next: wknd 7th: bhd whn p.u bef 2 out* **10/1**
000- **P** **Last Echo (IRE)**[226] 4674 4-11-0 **97** .... JamesDavies
(Tom Symonds) *hld up: pushed along 6th: mstke next: sn rdn and wknd: bhd whn p.u bef 2 out* **25/1**
066- **P** **The Scarlett Woman**[288] 3562 6-11-1 **98** .... DavidBass
(Kim Bailey) *prom: chsd wnr 5th to next: rdn and wknd after 7th: bhd whn p.u bef 2 out* **6/1**[3]
604- **P** **Pretty Mobile (FR)**[202] 5108 4-10-4 **87** .... LiamTreadwell
(Paul Webber) *hld up: wknd after 7th: bhd whn p.u bef 2 out* **25/1**

5m 1.1s (7.60) **Going Correction** +0.30s/f (Yiel)
WFA 4 from 5yo+ 10lb **9** Ran SP% **113.6**
Speed ratings (Par 105): **96,90,89,85,84 , , ,**
CSF £24.31 CT £60.75 TOTE £2.80: £2.40, £3.30, £1.10; EX 31.20 Trifecta £93.60.
Owner Miss S E Hartnell **Bred** David Crimmins **Trained** Nicholashayne, Devon
■ Stewards' Enquiry : Richie McLernon seven-day ban: use of whip (4-10 Nov)

FOCUS
They finished well spread out in this ordinary mares' handicap. A step up from the winner and the form could be rated up to 6lb higher.

2023 WORCESTER NEWS MAIDEN HURDLE (DIV I) (10 hdls) 2m 4f

5:05 (5:05) (Class 4) 4-Y-0+ **£3,249** (£954; £477; £238)

Form RPR
1 **Roll The Dough (IRE)**[178] 6-11-0 0 .... RichardJohnson 117+
(Philip Hobbs) *chsd ldrs: led 4th: shkn up appr last: rdn out* **10/3**[2]
320- **2** *1 1/4* **Always Lion (IRE)**[224] 4708 5-11-0 .... DavidBass 116+
(Ben Pauling) *led: hdd after 1st: chsd ldr to 4th: remained handy: ev ch appr 3 out: rdn bef next: styd on* **1/1**[1]
3 *4 1/2* **Viaduct Jack (IRE)**[171] 6-10-11 0 .... TomBellamy(3) 113
(Kim Bailey) *chsd ldrs: rdn appr 3 out: wknd towards fin* **7/1**
250- **4** *11* **Corner Creek (IRE)**[285] 3592 5-11-0 0 .... LiamTreadwell 104
(Michael Scudamore) *plld hrd: led after 1st: nt fluent next: hdd 4th: chsd wnr: ev ch appr 3 out: rdn after next: wknd last* **11/2**[3]
5 *14* **Ballyvaughn (IRE)**[179] 5-11-0 0 .... AndrewTinkler 89
(Caroline Bailey) *hld up: hdwy 5th: rdn and wknd appr 2 out* **33/1**
5 **6** *4* **Daulys Anthem (IRE)**[13] 1829 7-10-11 0 .... KillianMoore(3) 86
(David Dennis) *hld up: rdn and wknd appr 3 out* **33/1**
4- **7** *68* **Guiting Power**[279] 3689 4-10-11 0 .... RyanHatch(3) 25
(Nigel Twiston-Davies) *hld up: plld hrd: drvn along 6th: blnd and lost tch next* **10/1**
FU **U** **Seeanythingyoulike (IRE)**[21] 1698 4-11-0 0 .... LiamHeard
(Jeremy Scott) *hld up: plld hrd: hdwy 6th: rdn and wknd appr 3 out: bhd whn blnd and uns rdr last* **33/1**

5m 8.6s (15.10) **Going Correction** +0.30s/f (Yiel) **8** Ran SP% **118.9**
Speed ratings (Par 105): **81,80,78,74,68 67,39,**
CSF £7.57 TOTE £3.90: £1.40, £1.20, £1.80; EX 8.00 Trifecta £26.40.
Owner The Kingpins **Bred** Noel O'Brien **Trained** Withycombe, Somerset

FOCUS
Some chasing types on show in division one of a modest maiden hurdle. It was slower than the second division by around nine seconds but the first three could be fair novices.

2024 WORCESTER NEWS MAIDEN HURDLE (DIV II) (10 hdls) 2m 4f

5:35 (5:37) (Class 4) 4-Y-0+ **£3,249** (£954; £477; £238)

Form RPR
4/6- **1** **Alcala (FR)**[365] 1986 5-11-0 126 ....[1] SeanBowen 127+
(Paul Nicholls) *hld up: hdwy 6th: jnd ldr 3 out: led on bit appr last: c readily clr flat* **1/2**[1]
223- **2** *16* **Captain McGinley (IRE)**[242] 4356 5-11-0 0 .... LeightonAspell 114+
(Rebecca Curtis) *hld up: hdwy to join ldr 5th: led 3 out: rdn and hdd appr last: eased whn btn flat* **3/1**[2]
P- **3** *11* **Brise Coeur (FR)**[192] 101 4-11-0 0 .... RichardJohnson 98
(Nick Williams) *led: rdn and hdd appr 3 out: wknd next* **10/1**
321- **4** *9* **Nutcracker Prince**[19] 4065 4-11-0 0 ....(t) PeterCarberry 91
(Shaun Lycett) *plld hrd and prom: ev ch appr 3 out: sn wknd* **11/2**[3]
/PP- **5** *47* **Verve Argent (FR)**[334] 2632 6-11-0 0 ....(p) LiamTreadwell 48
(Paul Webber) *prom to 6th* **50/1**
0P2- **P** **Suffice (IRE)**[306] 3171 6-11-0 79 .... RobertDunne
(Laura Young) *trckd ldrs: plld hrd: blnd and wknd 6th: bhd whn p.u after next* **33/1**
0 **P** **Gardiners Hill (IRE)**[132] 702 5-11-0 0 .... PaulMoloney
(David Rees) *hld up: nt fluent 3rd: bhd fr 5th: p.u after 7th* **33/1**
50-6 **P** **Dounya's Boy**[157] 353 6-11-0 0 ....(b) DaveCrosse
(Christopher Kellett) *hld up: plld hrd: hdwy to join ldr after 1st tl lost pl bef 5th: sn wknd: bhd whn p.u after 7th* **150/1**

4m 59.4s (5.90) **Going Correction** +0.30s/f (Yiel)
WFA 4 from 5yo+ 10lb **8** Ran SP% **124.6**
Speed ratings (Par 105): **100,93,89,85,66 , ,**
CSF £2.85 TOTE £1.60: £1.02, £1.40, £2.60; EX 3.40 Trifecta £11.50.
Owner Andrea & Graham Wylie **Bred** Francois Rimaud **Trained** Ditcheat, Somerset

FOCUS
No depth to this, but an impressive winner, and the it was the quicker division by around nine seconds. The easy winner set a decent standard but this looks a step up.
T/Plt: £62.60 to a £1 stake. Pool: £54,002.44 - 629.27 winning tickets. T/Qpdt: £6.90 to a £1 stake. Pool: £4,537.44 - 486.5 winning tickets. **Colin Roberts**

1920 CARLISLE (R-H)

Thursday, October 22

OFFICIAL GOING: Good (chs 7.3; hdl 7.7)
Wind: Fresh, half against Weather: Overcast

2025 APOLLOBET ONLINE GAMES AND CASINO NOVICES' HURDLE (11 hdls) 2m 4f 8y

2:20 (2:21) (Class 4) 4-Y-0+ **£3,249** (£954; £477; £238)

Form RPR
2-2 **1** **Western Miller (IRE)**[27] 1645 4-10-12 0 .... RichardJohnson 115+
(Charlie Longsdon) *t.k.h: hld up on ins: hdwy to ld 6th: mstke next: shkn up whn nt fluent 3 out: sn clr: nt fluent last: edgd lft and styd on wl u.p* **4/5**[1]
-316 **2** *6* **Tickenwolf (IRE)**[118] 839 5-11-2 108 .... JoeColliver(3) 112
(George Moore) *in tch: drvn and outpcd after 4 out: rallied to chse (clr) wnr 2 out: edgd rt and kpt on same pce run-in* **5/1**[3]
3 *8* **Jonniesofa (IRE)**[193] 5-10-9 0 .... CraigNichol(3) 98
(Rose Dobbin) *t.k.h: hld up bhd ldng gp: stdy hdwy 1/2-way: chsd wnr 4 out: drvn next: outpcd fr 2 out* **7/1**
3113 **4** *24* **Classic Palace (IRE)**[52] 1414 6-11-5 123 .... BrianHughes 83
(J J Lambe, Ire) *cl up: drvn and outpcd after 4 out: no imp fr next* **3/1**[2]
45- **5** *10* **Massini's Lady**[185] 5426 4-10-0 0 .... StephenMulqueen(5) 60
(N W Alexander) *hld up: pushed along 1/2-way: effrt u.p after 4 out: wknd fr next* **50/1**
6404 **6** *7* **Black Kettle (IRE)**[21] 1723 5-10-12 0 .... DenisO'Regan 61
(Ronald Thompson) *hld up: drvn and outpcd after 4 out: btn next* **80/1**
05-6 **7** *2 1/2* **Ethan (IRE)**[18] 1774 6-10-7 0 .... MissCWalton(5) 60
(Sheena Walton) *t.k.h: cl up: lost pl 4 out: btn next* **33/1**
55 **8** *hd* **Great Anticipation (IRE)**[34] 1570 6-10-12 0 .... HenryBrooke 58
(Lynsey Kendall) *prom: lost pl 1/2-way: lost tch bef 4 out: no ch after* **100/1**
0P-6 **9** *68* **Hope For Glory**[94] 1065 6-10-7 74 ....(t) DaraghBourke(5)
(Maurice Barnes) *led: hit 4th: hdd 6th: rdn and wknd 5 out: t.o* **66/1**
/0 **P** **Parlour Of Dreams (IRE)**[18] 1774 8-10-5 0 .... SamColtherd(7)
(Andrew Hamilton) *nt fluent in rr: struggling fr 1/2-way: t.o whn p.u bef 2 out* **100/1**

4m 59.2s (-23.60) **Going Correction** -1.075s/f (Hard)
WFA 4 from 5yo+ 10lb **10** Ran SP% **119.3**
Speed ratings (Par 105): **104,101,98,88,84 82,81,80,53,**
CSF £5.71 TOTE £1.70: £1.10, £1.80, £2.40; EX 6.30 Trifecta £23.60.
Owner The Pantechnicons IV **Bred** Robert B Hodgins **Trained** Over Norton, Oxon

FOCUS
Hurdle races run on Flat course. Rail realignment increased races 1, 5 & 6 by 72yds, races 2, 3 & 7 by 54yds and race 4 by 108yds. The opener was an uncompetitive novice hurdle, in which the steady early gallop increased after halfway. The winner was better than the bare result.

2026 APOLLOBET BEGINNERS' CHASE (12 fncs) 1m 7f 207y

2:50 (2:51) (Class 4) 4-Y-0+ **£3,898** (£1,144; £572; £286)

Form RPR
23-4 **1** **The Grey Taylor (IRE)**[8] 1900 6-11-2 0 .... RichardJohnson 133+
(Brian Ellison) *mde all: drew clr after 4 out: eased run-in* **4/7**[1]
P202 **2** *10* **Silk Hall (UAE)**[34] 1401 10-11-2 118 ....(p) BrianHughes 121
(J J Lambe, Ire) *chsd wnr thrght: rdn along 4 out: kpt on same pce fr next* **9/1**[3]
220- **3** *3 3/4* **Special Wells**[201] 5139 6-11-2 0 .... DannyCook 119
(Sue Smith) *chsd ldrs: drvn along whn blnd 3 out: sn outpcd* **10/3**[2]
42-1 **4** *12* **Alto Des Mottes (FR)**[166] 201 5-10-13 0 .... TonyKelly(3) 109
(Henry Hogarth) *hld up in tch: effrt after 5 out: rdn and wknd fr 3 out* **9/1**[3]
5466 **5** *29* **Duhallowcountry (IRE)**[12] 1857 9-10-9 63 ....(p) SamColtherd(7) 80
(Victor Thompson) *nt fluent: prom to 2nd: struggling after next: t.o* **200/1**
00- **6** *20* **Barren Brook**[30] 2776 8-11-2 0 .... JakeGreenall 62
(Michael Easterby) *nt fluent on occasions: hld up in tch: hit and outpcd 6th: struggling fr next: t.o* **100/1**
2-F2 **P** **Vayland**[56] 1366 6-10-13 0 .... CraigNichol(3)
(Micky Hammond) *bhd: struggling 1/2-way: sn lost tch: t.o whn p.u bef last* **20/1**

4m 1.4s (-14.70) **Going Correction** -1.025s/f (Hard) **7** Ran SP% **113.0**
Speed ratings (Par 105): **95,90,88,82,67 57,**
CSF £6.55 TOTE £1.60: £1.10, £3.40; EX 6.20 Trifecta £15.60.
Owner P J Martin **Bred** Michael Kirwan **Trained** Norton, N Yorks

FOCUS
Little depth to this beginners' chase and the odds-on favourite dominated from the off. The winner didn't need to reproduce his hurdle mark to win easily.

2027 APOLLOBET BEST ODDS GUARANTEED INTERMEDIATE H'CAP HURDLE (9 hdls) 2m 1f 33y
3:25 (3:25) (Class 3) (0-125,121) 3-Y-0+ **£6,498** (£1,908; £954; £477)

Form RPR
12 **1** **Hadfield (IRE)**[29] 1631 3-10-8 **120**........................ AidanColeman 106+
(John Ferguson) *hld up: nt fluent and reminders 4th: hdwy to chse ldr 3 out: led between last 2: drvn and pricked ears run-in: kpt on strly* **9/4[2]**
4111 **2** *2* **Shear Rock (IRE)**[20] 1734 5-11-12 **121**........................ RichardJohnson 120
(Charlie Longsdon) *led: clr 2nd to 4th: nt fluent 4 out: rdn bef 2 out: hdd between last 2: rallied whn mstke last: kpt on same pce last 100yds* **6/4[1]**
-006 **3** *10* **Boruma (IRE)**[125] 780 5-10-12 **107**........................ HenryBrooke 96
(Dianne Sayer) *hld up: stdy hdwy bef 3 out: shkn up and chsd clr ldng pair between last 2: kpt on: nvr nrr* **20/1**
443 **4** *6* **Bigindie (IRE)**[15] 1814 5-11-8 **117**........................ DenisO'Regan 104
(John Weymes) *chsd ldr to 4th: cl up: drvn and outpcd 3 out: n.d after* **14/1**
0-31 **5** *1* **Quick Brew**[20] 1740 7-11-6 **120**........................(t) DaraghBourke(5) 105
(Maurice Barnes) *t.k.h early: cl up: chsd ldr 4th to 3 out: sn drvn and outpcd: btn after next* **14/1**
4-52 **6** *5* **Cooking Fat**[18] 1776 4-11-11 **120**........................ BrianHughes 100
(Dianne Sayer) *prom: drvn along bef 3 out: wknd fr next* **9/2[3]**
4360 **7** *81* **Lochalsh (IRE)**[71] 1238 4-11-1 **117**........................ MrTHamilton(7) 23
(Katie Scott) *nt fluent in rr: struggling 1/2-way: t.o* **40/1**
4m 11.2s (-16.50) **Going Correction** -1.075s/f (Hard)
WFA 3 from 4yo 17lb 4 from 5yo+ 9lb 7 Ran SP% **109.5**
Speed ratings (Par 107): **95,94,89,86,86 83,45**
CSF £5.66 TOTE £2.70: £1.60, £1.20; EX 5.90 Trifecta £46.90.
Owner Bloomfields **Bred** Mrs Renata Coleman **Trained** Cowlinge, Suffolk

FOCUS
Not the strongest event for the grade and the two market leaders drew clear. The winner is rated to his Perth mark but there should be more to come.

2028 APOLLOBET £50 FREE BETS H'CAP CHASE (19 fncs) 3m 2f 34y
3:55 (3:55) (Class 3) (0-125,122) 4-Y-0+ **£6,498** (£1,908; £954; £477)

Form RPR
5-3U **1** **Settledoutofcourt (IRE)**[34] 1571 9-11-2 **115**........................ DerekFox(3) 124+
(Lucinda Russell) *w ldr: led 6th to 8th: regained ld 4 out: rdn next: styd on gamely fr last* **7/1**
1534 **2** *1 3/4* **Presented (IRE)**[7] 1925 8-10-12 **113**........................ CallumBewley(5) 120
(Lisa Harrison) *chsd ldrs: effrt and rdn bef 3 out: chsd wnr between last 2: ch after last: kpt on same pce last 100yds* **15/2**
P0-2 **3** *4 1/2* **Orange Nassau (FR)**[168] 156 9-11-12 **122**........................ AidanColeman 126
(Charlie Longsdon) *led to 6th: regained ld 8th: hdd 4 out: rallied: lost 2nd and no ex between last 2* **15/8[1]**
3-00 **4** *3/4* **Mo Rouge (IRE)**[68] 1264 7-10-4 **103**........................(p) TonyKelly(3) 107
(Jackie Stephen) *hld up in tch: pushed along and outpcd after 5 out: rallied 3 out: kpt on same pce fr next* **13/2[3]**
5P14 **5** *37* **King Fontaine (IRE)**[14] 1820 12-11-3 **113**........................(p) NickScholfield 82
(Lawney Hill) *chsd ldrs: drvn and outpcd after 5 out: lost tch fr 3 out* **12/1**
-PP6 **P** **Bit Of A Jig (IRE)**[23] 1692 8-11-5 **115**........................(p) BrianHarding
(Adrian Wintle) *hld up: pushed along 1/2-way: struggling 12th: lost tch next: t.o whn p.u bef 4 out* **40/1**
01-1 **P** **Courtown Oscar (IRE)**[169] 150 6-10-13 **109**........................ RichardJohnson
(Philip Kirby) *hld up: pushed along whn mstke 13th: sn outpcd: lost tch and p.u bef 4 out* **5/2[2]**
6m 43.8s (-23.40) **Going Correction** -1.025s/f (Hard) 7 Ran SP% **111.1**
Speed ratings (Par 107): **95,94,93,92,81**
CSF £51.96 TOTE £9.20: £3.40, £2.90; EX 42.60 Trifecta £178.40.
Owner Andrew McAllister **Bred** Sean Naughton **Trained** Arlary, Perth & Kinross

FOCUS
A fair staying chase, and solid-looking form.

2029 APOLLOBET INPLAY H'CAP HURDLE (11 hdls) 2m 4f 8y
4:25 (4:26) (Class 4) (0-110,110) 3-Y-0+ **£3,249** (£954; £477; £238)

Form RPR
4321 **1** **Amuse Me**[10] 1887 9-11-0 **98** 7ex........................ RichardJohnson 116+
(James Moffatt) *hld up: stdy hdwy 1/2-way: checked 4 out: led gng wl 2 out: pushed clr fr last: readily* **2/1[1]**
3-10 **2** *10* **Pied Du Roi (IRE)**[27] 1647 5-11-12 **110**........................(p) BrianHughes 114
(Charlie Longsdon) *chsd ldrs: effrt and ev ch 2 out: sn chsng wnr: kpt on same pce fr last* **12/1**
1302 **3** *9* **Roll Of Thunder**[36] 1552 6-10-6 **95**........................ MissCWalton(5) 92
(James Walton) *led to 2nd: cl up: led 3 out to next: outpcd bef last* **16/1**
6P-P **4** *10* **Turtle Cask (IRE)**[148] 502 6-10-11 **98**........................ ColmMcCormack(3) 86
(Dianne Sayer) *chsd ldrs: mstke and lost grnd 1st: effrt u.p after 4 out: no imp fr next* **40/1**
-054 **5** *5* **Indepub**[148] 502 6-9-9 **84**........................ CallumBewley(5) 68
(Lisa Harrison) *bhd: pushed along whn checked 4 out: hdwy bef next: sn no imp* **8/1[2]**
06-0 **6** *2 1/2* **Mac N Cheese (IRE)**[34] 1572 5-10-7 **91**........................ BrianHarding 71
(Rose Dobbin) *hld up: rdn and effrt after 4 out: sn no imp: btn fnl 2* **18/1**
1233 **7** *6* **Egmont**[49] 1456 3-10-8 **110**........................(p) HenryBrooke 68
(George Moore) *hld up: hung lft bef 6th: drvn and outpcd 4 out: btn next* **14/1**
5621 **8** *19* **Slipper Satin (IRE)**[21] 1066 5-11-7 **105**........................(t) AidanColeman 63
(Simon West) *cl up: led 2nd to 3 out: rdn and wknd fr next* **9/1[3]**
25P- **9** *1 3/4* **Forty Crown (IRE)**[201] 5135 9-11-7 **110**........................ DiarmuidO'Regan(5) 66
(John Wade) *hld up: outpcd 5 out: struggling whn bdly hmpd next* **66/1**
15-4 **10** *22* **Crinkle Crags (IRE)**[151] 456 5-11-1 **102**........................ CraigNichol(3) 38
(Nicky Richards) *midfield: shkn up whn hmpd 4 out: sn wknd* **8/1[2]**
06-0 **U** **Total Assets**[12] 1856 7-11-1 **106**........................ MissAWaugh(7)
(Simon Waugh) *hld up: nt fluent and uns rdr 6th* **33/1**
520- **U** **The Cobbler Swayne (IRE)**[215] 4914 6-11-8 **106**........................ PeterBuchanan
(Lucinda Russell) *hld up: stdy hdwy and in tch 1/2-way: gng wl whn bdly hmpd and uns rdr 4 out* **10/1**
36-6 **F** **Dutch Canyon (IRE)**[169] 139 5-10-9 **93**........................(p) LucyAlexander
(N W Alexander) *chsd ldrs: stl gng wl whn fell 4 out* **16/1**
4-53 **P** **The Late Shift**[159] 337 5-10-0 **91**........................ LorcanMurtagh(7)
(Barry Murtagh) *bhd: struggling 7th: lost tch and p.u bef 3 out* **20/1**
4m 58.9s (-23.90) **Going Correction** -1.075s/f (Hard)
WFA 3 from 5yo+ 18lb 14 Ran SP% **117.7**
Speed ratings (Par 105): **104,100,96,92,90 89,87,79,78,69** , , ,
CSF £25.17 CT £309.17 TOTE £2.50: £1.30, £4.10, £4.70; EX 20.80 Trifecta £189.90.
Owner Vilprano, Bowron & Beaumont **Bred** Whatton Manor Stud **Trained** Cartmel, Cumbria

FOCUS
A modest handicap hurdle and not as competitive as the numbers would suggest. They finished strung out and the well handicapped winner won as he liked. He's closing in on the best of his old form.

2030 APOLLOBET ENHANCED RACING SPECIALS H'CAP CHASE (16 fncs) 2m 4f
4:55 (4:56) (Class 4) (0-120,119) 4-Y-0+ **£3,898** (£1,144; £572; £286)

Form RPR
5352 **1** **Gleann Na Ndochais (IRE)**[28] 1639 9-11-8 **118**........................ CraigNichol(3) 126
(Alistair Whillans) *hld up in tch: smooth hdwy 5 out: led after next: drvn and kpt on wl fr last* **4/1[3]**
1P2 **2** *2* **Dystonia's Revenge (IRE)**[20] 1743 10-10-12 **112**........................ JamieHamilton(7) 117
(Sheena Walton) *cl up: led 2nd to 5th: regained ld 9th: rdn and hdd after 4 out: outpcd 2 out: rallied to chse wnr last 75yds: kpt on* **11/1**
414F **3** *1 1/2* **Solway Legend**[12] 1853 8-10-9 **102**........................ BrianHughes 108
(Lisa Harrison) *trckd ldrs gng wl: hdwy to chse wnr 3 out: shkn up and hung rt bef next: nt fluent last: no ex and lost 2nd last 75yds* **3/1[1]**
-334 **4** *19* **Quito Du Tresor (FR)**[28] 1639 11-11-7 **114**........................(p) PeterBuchanan 103
(Lucinda Russell) *hld up in tch: hdwy to chal 10th: rdn whn nt fluent 3 out: wknd bef next* **9/1**
1355 **5** *5* **Pekanheim (IRE)**[12] 1855 7-11-3 **110**........................ HenryBrooke 95
(Martin Todhunter) *nt fluent on occasions: hld up: mstke 1st: stdy hdwy bef 10th: rdn after 5 out: wknd fr next* **9/1**
5353 **6** *6* **Longueville Flier (IRE)**[18] 1775 6-9-11 **93** oh2........................ JoeColliver(3) 71
(Micky Hammond) *bhd: struggling 1/2-way: nvr on terms* **8/1**
-510 **7** *30* **Tikkandemickey (IRE)**[149] 483 9-11-7 **119**........................ CallumBewley(5) 69
(Raymond Shiels) *taken early to post: hld up: reminders after 7th: struggling fr 9th: nvr on terms* **12/1**
3P-2 **8** *39* **Bennys Well (IRE)**[175] 38 9-11-4 **111**........................ DannyCook 26
(Sue Smith) *led: nt fluent: hdd and reminders 2nd: led again 5th: hdd 9th: outpcd whn hit next: lost tch fr 5 out: t.o* **7/2[2]**
5m 3.8s (-23.60) **Going Correction** -1.025s/f (Hard) 8 Ran SP% **114.4**
Speed ratings (Par 105): **106,105,104,97,95 92,80,65**
CSF £44.40 CT £148.90 TOTE £4.60: £1.50, £3.10, £1.30; EX 49.10 Trifecta £173.70.
Owner W J E Scott & Mrs M A Scott **Bred** Pat Kinsella **Trained** Newmill-On-Slitrig, Borders

FOCUS
A fair, competitive-looking handicap chase, in which the first three pulled a long way clear. A small pb from the winner with the second to his mark.

2031 APOLLOBET FOLLOW ON TWITTER AND FACEBOOK STANDARD OPEN NATIONAL HUNT FLAT RACE 2m 1f 33y
5:30 (5:30) (Class 6) 4-6-Y-0 **£1,559** (£457; £228; £114)

Form RPR
1 **Monbeg Charmer (IRE)**[193] 4-11-0 0........................ RichardJohnson 120+
(Charlie Longsdon) *hld up in last pl: smooth hdwy over 3f out: shkn up to ld over 1f out: rdn clr fnl f* **10/11[1]**
054- **2** *8* **Berkshire Downs**[215] 4915 5-10-7 0........................ DenisO'Regan 107+
(Lucy Normile) *pressed ldr: led after 6f: drvn and hdd over 1f out: kpt on: no ch w wnr* **50/1**
2-2 **3** *6* **Gully's Edge**[169] 144 5-11-0 0........................(t) BrianHughes 107
(Malcolm Jefferson) *prom: pushed along and outpcd over 3f out: plugged on fr over 1f out: nt rch first two* **2/1[2]**
4 *9* **Robbing The Prey (IRE)**[32] 1611 4-11-0 0........................ AdamWedge 99
(Nick Kent) *t.k.h: hld up in tch: hdwy and cl up over 2f out: edgd lft and wknd over 1f out* **8/1[3]**
5- **5** *2* **Focal Point**[530] 208 5-11-0 0........................ DannyCook 98
(Sue Smith) *trckd ldrs: rdn and outpcd 3f out: n.d after* **66/1**
3 **6** *1 1/2* **Ballinvegga (IRE)**[28] 1640 5-10-11 0........................ TonyKelly(3) 96
(Jackie Stephen) *t.k.h: led at stdy pce for 6f: cl up: outpcd over 3f out: btn fnl 2f* **33/1**
7 *1 1/4* **Bako De La Saulaie (FR)**[207] 4-10-11 0........................ CraigNichol(3) 95
(Rose Dobbin) *hld up on outside: hdwy u.p over 4f out: outpcd over 2f out: btn whn hung rt over 1f out* **12/1**
4m 10.2s (-14.00) **Going Correction** -1.075s/f (Hard) 7 Ran SP% **110.9**
Speed ratings: **89,85,82,78,77 76,75**
CSF £52.12 TOTE £1.60: £1.10, £13.90; EX 43.30 Trifecta £113.60.
Owner Lady Dulverton **Bred** Michael Fennessy **Trained** Over Norton, Oxon

FOCUS
They came home at wide intervals in this ordinary bumper. The winner looks decent.
T/Plt: £87.90 to a £1 stake. Pool: £51,312.16 - 426.00 winning units. T/Qpdt: £55.70 to a £1 stake. Pool: £3,713.85 - 49.27 winning units. **Richard Young**

1805 LUDLOW (R-H)
Thursday, October 22

OFFICIAL GOING: Good (7.3)
Wind: Light against Weather: Fine

2032 RACING TO SCHOOL JUVENILE HURDLE (9 hdls) 1m 7f 169y
2:10 (2:10) (Class 4) 3-Y-O **£3,898** (£1,144; £572; £286)

Form RPR
1 **Wolf Of Windlesham (IRE)**[42] 3-10-12 0........................ JoshuaMoore 115+
(Stuart Edmunds) *prom: lost pl after 4th: hdwy bef 3 out: led appr next: clr last: r.o wl* **16/1**
343 **2** *17* **Fast Scat (USA)**[15] 1805 3-9-12 95........................ DavidNoonan(7) 91
(Steve Flook) *hld up: hdwy after 4th: led 6th: rdn: hung lft and hdd appr 2 out: wknd flat* **33/1**
3 *12* **Red Hammer**[116] 3-10-12 0........................ DarylJacob 89+
(Nicky Henderson) *hld up: mstke 3rd: j. slowly next: hdwy appr 3 out: wkng whn hit next* **8/13[1]**
0 **4** *10* **Harley Rebel**[8] 1899 3-10-12 0........................ NoelFehily 76
(Neil Mulholland) *hmpd 1st: chsd ldrs tl wknd 3 out* **9/2[2]**
5 *1/2* **Put The Boot In (IRE)**[51] 3-10-9 0........................ JamesBanks(3) 75
(Barry Brennan) *prom: j.lft 3rd: hmpd 6th: rdn and wknd appr 3 out* **66/1**
2 **6** *11* **Zabeel Star (IRE)**[32] 1593 3-10-12 0........................ KielanWoods 64
(Graeme McPherson) *led and j.rt 1st: hdd appr 4th: chsd ldr: rdn appr 3 out: wknd bef next* **10/1**
5 **7** *21* **Diamond Joel**[7] 1928 3-10-12 0........................ JamieMoore 43
(Tom Lacey) *w ldr: hmpd 1st: mstke next: led appr 4th: j. slowly and hdd 6th: wknd bef 3 out* **13/2[3]**
3m 44.6s (-4.90) **Going Correction** -0.075s/f (Good) 7 Ran SP% **112.8**
Speed ratings (Par 103): **109,100,94,89,89 83,73**
CSF £301.68 TOTE £24.70: £11.40, £5.80; EX 252.80 Trifecta £1238.70.
Owner M W Lawrence **Bred** Joe And Edel Banahan **Trained** Newport Pagnell, Bucks

FOCUS
The Golf Club bend was out 4m, adding 5yds per circuit to the chases. After winning the first Joshua Moore's verdict was "On the whole it is good ground but a bit quicker in a few places", an opinion backed up by the opening time. This looked a very modest juvenile hurdle but the winner did it well. The second sets the level.

2033 THOROUGHBRED BREEDERS ASSOCIATION MARES' NOVICES' HURDLE (11 hdls) 2m 5f 55y
2:40 (2:40) (Class 4) 4-Y-0+ **£5,198** (£1,526; £763; £381)

Form RPR
51P- **1** **Leaderofthedance**[181] 5510 6-11-0 115.................. JeremiahMcGrath(3) 115+
(Nicky Henderson) mde all: shkn up and hung lft flat: flashed tail: styd on **5/2**[2]
5205 **2** *9* **Midnight Gem**[12] 1845 5-10-10 0.................................. DarylJacob 98
(Charlie Longsdon) chsd wnr: rdn whn mstke 3 out: no ex flat **8/1**
2214 **3** *2* **Wintour Leap**[17] 1793 4-10-10 110............................... CiaranGethings(7) 102
(Robert Stephens) prom: rdn appr 3 out: styd on same pce fr next **7/4**[1]
40-3 **4** *15* **Fizzy Dancer**[15] 1811 5-10-10 0.................................. DavidBass 85
(Kim Bailey) hld up: nt a fluent: outpcd 7th: hdwy appr 3 out: sn wknd **6/1**[3]
0-55 **5** *7* **Highland Life**[165] 219 5-10-3 0.................................. DavidNoonan(7) 76
(Steve Flook) hld up: hdwy 7th: rdn and wknd 3 out **25/1**
2-2 **P** **Just A Feeling**[175] 45 5-10-10 0.. TomO'Brien
(Paul Webber) chsd ldrs tl wknd after 8th: bhd whn p.u bef 3 out **6/1**[3]
5m 9.9s (-4.90) **Going Correction** -0.075s/f (Good)
WFA 4 from 5yo+ 10lb **6 Ran SP% 108.5**
Speed ratings (Par 105): **106,102,101,96,93**
CSF £19.75 TOTE £3.00: £1.20, £3.90; EX 19.30 Trifecta £69.40.
Owner T J Whitley **Bred** T J Whitley **Trained** Upper Lambourn, Berks

FOCUS
A fair novice hurdle, confined to fillies and mares. The winner set a fair standard and is rated to her mark.

2034 THOROUGHBRED BREEDERS' ASSOCIATION NOVICES' LIMITED H'CAP CHASE (12 fncs) 1m 7f 212y
3:10 (3:10) (Class 3) (0-135,129) 4-Y-0+ **£8,772** (£2,575; £1,287; £643)

Form RPR
P1-0 **1** **Arzal (FR)**[166] 197 5-11-8 129.. DavidBass 143+
(Harry Whittington) mde all: j.lft at times: mstke 9th: clr fr 4 out: easily **4/9**[1]
011- **2** *6* **Murrayana (IRE)**[203] 5112 5-10-10 124.......................... MrSamPainting(7) 125+
(Colin Tizzard) j.lft: chsd ldrs: outpcd fr 2nd: wnt mod 2nd 3 out: no ch w wnr **8/1**[3]
1245 **3** *3 1/4* **Zama Zama**[23] 1690 8-9-10 110 oh8..............................(b[1]) MrConorOrr(7) 104
(Evan Williams) hld up and bhd: wnt 3rd after 3 out: nvr nrr **14/1**
11-2 **4** *37* **Lyric Street (IRE)**[44] 1505 7-10-12 119.................... SamTwiston-Davies 95
(Donald McCain) chsd wnr: rdn appr 4 out: sn wknd **7/2**[2]
3m 57.6s (-0.90) **Going Correction** +0.15s/f (Yiel) **4 Ran SP% 109.3**
Speed ratings (Par 107): **108,105,103,84**
CSF £4.42 TOTE £1.40; EX 4.30 Trifecta £13.80.
Owner The Hennessy Six **Bred** Dominique Gouin & Mme Anna Racape **Trained** Sparsholt, Oxfordshire

FOCUS
A fair prize for this interesting event. The winner could be decent and should go on to rate higher.

2035 UK FOREST PRODUCTS ASSOCIATION NOVICES' HURDLE (9 hdls) 1m 7f 169y
3:45 (3:45) (Class 4) 4-Y-0+ **£3,898** (£1,144; £572; £286)

Form RPR
1 **1** **Ascotdeux Nellerie (FR)**[165] 220 5-10-12 0........................ DavidBass 124+
(Kim Bailey) prom: pushed along after 6th: led and j.lft last: styd on wl **8/11**[1]
1232 **2** *10* **Angus Glens**[14] 1822 5-11-5 121..................................(p) NoelFehily 121
(David Dennis) led 2nd: hit 2 out: rdn and hdd last: no ex flat **2/1**[2]
F4 **3** *5* **Golden Heritage**[23] 1684 4-10-12 0........................ SamTwiston-Davies 108
(John Ferguson) trckd ldr: ev ch fr 3 out tl rdn appr last: wknd flat **5/1**[3]
00 **4** *23* **Whitstable Native**[23] 1693 7-10-9 0..............................(t) KillianMoore(3) 85
(Sophie Leech) led to 2nd: chsd ldrs: rdn and wknd appr 3 out **150/1**
5 *3/4* **My Son Max**[37] 7-10-5 0.................................. WilliamFeatherstone(7) 84
(Nikki Evans) chsd ldrs tl rdn and wknd appr 3 out **33/1**
055- **6** *41* **Culworth Boy (IRE)**[350] 2296 5-10-12 0.................................[1] JamesBest 43
(Sophie Leech) hld up: plld hrd: wknd after 6th **66/1**
0 **P** **Foursquare Funtime**[6] 528 6-10-5 0...............................(t) JoshWall(7)
(Trevor Wall) hld up: wknd after 6th: bhd whn p.u bef next **150/1**
3m 50.5s (1.00) **Going Correction** -0.075s/f (Good)
WFA 4 from 5yo+ 9lb **7 Ran SP% 113.7**
Speed ratings (Par 105): **94,89,86,75,74 54,**
CSF £2.55 TOTE £1.90: £1.10, £1.50; EX 3.00 Trifecta £4.90.
Owner The Lucky Nelleries **Bred** M Huame, Mme M Huame Et Al **Trained** Andoversford, Gloucs

FOCUS
This ordinary novice hurdle was run around six seconds slower than the opening juvenile event. The form is rated around the second and third.

2036 EPDS RACING PARTNERSHIPS SUPPORTING RACING WELFARE H'CAP CHASE (19 fncs) 2m 7f 171y
4:15 (4:15) (Class 4) (0-120,119) 4-Y-0+ **£7,472** (£2,194; £1,097; £548)

Form RPR
5P21 **1** **Butlergrove King (IRE)**[14] 1824 6-10-9 107.............. FreddieMitchell(5) 120+
(Dai Burchell) mde all: mstke 12th: rdn out **15/8**[1]
26F4 **2** *5* **Buck Mulligan**[32] 1601 10-11-7 119.................................. ConorRing(5) 128
(Evan Williams) hld up: hdwy to chse wnr 14th: shkn up appr last: styd on same pce flat **7/2**[2]
2-04 **3** *19* **Jayandbee (IRE)**[13] 1842 8-10-10 103.............................(p) TomO'Brien 95
(Philip Hobbs) prom: mstke 9th: chsd wnr after 11th tl 14th: rdn and wknd 3 out **4/1**[3]
06-6 **4** *7* **Victor Leudorum (IRE)**[18] 1784 8-11-9 116......................(tp) NoelFehily 102
(Charlie Mann) w wnr tl nt fluent 6th: lost 2nd after 11th: pushed along 14th: wknd 3 out **11/2**
13 **P** **Dabinett Moon**[21] 1713 7-11-4 118.................................. MissCVHart(7)
(Charlie Longsdon) hld up: pushed along after 15th: wknd 4 out: bhd whn p.u bef 2 out **4/1**[3]
6m 4.5s (364.50) **5 Ran SP% 112.4**
CSF £9.09 TOTE £2.30: £1.30, £2.00; EX 8.30 Trifecta £24.20.
Owner Mrs K Lewis **Bred** Butlersgrove Stud **Trained** Briery Hill, Blaenau Gwent

FOCUS
Just fair form for the class. The winner is on the upgrade and the second was close to his best form of the past year.

2037 AMATEUR JOCKEYS' ASSOCIATION AMATEUR RIDERS' H'CAP CHASE (FOR THE COURT OF HILL CHALLENGE CUP) (16 fncs) 2m 4f 11y
4:45 (4:45) (Class 5) (0-100,99) 4-Y-0+ **£3,743** (£1,161; £580; £290)

Form RPR
2-03 **1** **Cool Bob (IRE)**[14] 1825 12-10-0 78.......................(tp) MrStanSheppard(5) 86
(Matt Sheppard) hld up: hdwy and mstke 8th: chsd ldr and j.rt 3 out: led last: wandered flat: styd on **7/1**
03-U **2** *3 1/4* **Carobello (IRE)**[157] 379 8-10-6 84..................................(t) MrJNixon(5) 88
(Martin Bosley) a.p: rdn appr 2 out: ev ch last: styd on same pce flat **6/1**
0-P4 **3** *2* **Michigan Assassin (IRE)**[9] 1894 13-11-8 95..............(p) MrBMoorcroft 98
(Debra Hamer) led: mstke 1st: clr fr 4th to appr 4 out: rdn and hdd last: edgd lft and styd on same pce flat **12/1**
-2UU **4** *hd* **Samtheman**[14] 1825 10-10-13 91................................ MrRobertHawker(5) 93
(Pam Ford) hld up: hdwy appr 4 out: rdn bef 2 out: styd on same pce flat **8/1**
41PU **5** *7* **Sylvan Legend**[19] 1757 7-10-7 83................................(tp) DavidNoonan(3) 81
(Neil Mulholland) prom: lft 2nd 11th: rdn appr 3 out: wknd bef last: hung lft flat **11/2**[3]
U6P- **6** *80* **Johnnys Legacy (IRE)**[199] 5187 8-10-8 88.......................(p) MissTWorsley(7) 11
(Ken Wingrove) hld up: mstke and wknd 10th **50/1**
3212 **U** **Court Of Law (IRE)**[10] 1891 7-11-5 99.................................(p) MrTGillard(7)
(Donald McCain) j.lft: chsd ldr tl uns rdr 11th **5/1**[2]
P0-2 **U** **Gowanauthat (IRE)**[14] 1824 7-11-1 95.................................(t) MrJJSlevin(7)
(Charlie Mann) nt fluent 1st: blnd and uns rdr next **2/1**[1]
5m 8.8s (4.40) **Going Correction** +0.15s/f (Yiel) **8 Ran SP% 112.9**
Speed ratings (Par 103): **97,95,94,94,92 60, ,**
CSF £46.99 CT £492.91 TOTE £7.20: £2.20, £1.90, £3.60; EX 44.30 Trifecta £451.10.
Owner Mrs N Sheppard **Bred** Jim Halley **Trained** Eastnor, H'fords

FOCUS
Very moderate fare, but a heartwarming victory. They finished in a heap and the first three are rated to their marks.

2038 JOHN OWEN 75TH BIRTHDAY H'CAP HURDLE (9 hdls) 1m 7f 169y
5:15 (5:15) (Class 4) (0-115,115) 3-Y-0+ **£5,848** (£1,717; £858; £429)

Form RPR
522 **1** **Watt Broderick (IRE)**[21] 1719 6-11-9 112.............................(t) NoelFehily 113
(Ian Williams) hld up: hdwy 3 out: styd on to ld fnl 110yds **4/1**[2]
42F **2** *2 3/4* **Impulsive American**[9] 1893 3-9-13 112.........................(p) DavidNoonan(7) 104+
(David Pipe) chsd ldr tl led 6th: clr fr 3 out: 8 l ahd whn blnd last: sn rdn: wknd and hdd fnl 110yds **5/1**
4112 **3** *3* **Makethedifference (IRE)**[11] 1868 7-11-12 115.................. MichaelByrne 115+
(Tim Vaughan) hld up: hdwy 4th: chsd ldr appr 3 out: styng on same pce whn j.lft last 2 flights **7/4**[1]
2-40 **4** *2 1/4* **Hill Fort**[95] 1048 5-10-10 99.. CharliePoste 96+
(Matt Sheppard) chsd ldrs: hit 5th: rdn appr 3 out: styng on same pce whn hmpd 2 out and last **18/1**
6-32 **5** *14* **Breaking Bits (IRE)**[9] 1893 8-11-9 112.............................. DarylJacob 94
(Jamie Snowden) led: hit 3rd: hdd 6th: wknd 3 out **9/2**[3]
-140 **6** *12* **Sunblazer (IRE)**[20] 835 5-11-5 108......................................(t) DavidBass 80
(Kim Bailey) prom: j. slowly and lost pl 4th: hdwy after 6th: wknd bef 3 out **8/1**
/00- **7** *30* **Easydoesit (IRE)**[23] 4967 7-10-5 94.. LeeEdwards 37
(Tony Carroll) rel to r: a bhd **25/1**
3m 46.1s (-3.40) **Going Correction** -0.075s/f (Good)
WFA 3 from 5yo+ 17lb **7 Ran SP% 111.4**
Speed ratings (Par 105): **105,103,102,101,94 88,73**
CSF £22.90 CT £44.73 TOTE £4.80: £2.60, £2.80; EX 23.20 Trifecta £62.10.
Owner Patrick Kelly **Bred** Joe Fogarty **Trained** Portway, Worcs

FOCUS
An ordinary handicap hurdle with a dramatic finish. The fortunate winner is rated to his mark.
T/Plt: £2,234.80 to a £1 stake. Pool: £38,420.92 - 12.55 winning units. T/Qpdt: £14.30 to a £1 stake. Pool: £4,093.77 - 211.29 winning units. **Colin Roberts**

1689 SOUTHWELL (L-H)
Thursday, October 22

OFFICIAL GOING: Good (7.8)
Wind: fresh 1/2 behind Weather: fine

2039 MRFREEBET.CO.UK ON YOUR MOBILE NOVICES' H'CAP CHASE (19 fncs) 2m 7f 209y
2:00 (2:00) (Class 4) (0-120,120) 4-Y-0+ **£3,898** (£1,144; £572; £286)

Form RPR
3234 **1** **Shah Of Persia**[27] 1642 8-11-7 115.........................(tp) GavinSheehan 124+
(Warren Greatrex) in rr: hdwy 13th: sn chsng ldrs: led between last 2: drvn clr run-in **11/1**
2PP- **2** *6* **Castle Cheetah (IRE)**[208] 5032 7-11-7 115........................ NicodeBoinville 118+
(Ben Pauling) t.k.h: jnd ldr 2nd: led bef 13th: j.rt 14th: hdd between last 2: hung rt and one pce run-in **10/1**
22 **3** *7* **Derryfadda (IRE)**[18] 1775 6-9-12 95.............................. HarryChalloner(3) 94
(Richard Ford) trckd ldrs: one pce fr 2 out **9/2**[2]
43-1 **4** *3* **Crack Of Thunder (IRE)**[171] 108 6-11-4 112...................(p) AndrewTinkler 107
(Charlie Longsdon) mid-div: drvn and lost pl 9th: sn bhd and reminders: poor 5th 15th: kpt on fr 3 out: nt rch ldrs **9/4**[1]
100- **5** *23* **Red Danaher (IRE)**[201] 5133 8-11-7 115............................ SeanQuinlan 93
(Sue Smith) chsd ldrs: pckd landing 4th: drvn 15th: 3rd whn mstke 3 out: sn wknd **13/2**[3]
335- **F** **Golan Dancer (IRE)**[203] 5113 7-11-4 112............................... TomCannon
(David Bridgwater) in rr: outpcd 12th: fell 14th **16/1**
4222 **P** **Shantou Tiger (IRE)**[20] 1733 6-11-12 120......................... WayneHutchinson
(Donald McCain) led: reminders 5th: drvn and hdd bef 13th: lost pl 14th: sn bhd: t.o whn p.u bef 3 out **7/1**
34- **P** **Letter Exit (IRE)**[205] 5085 5-11-1 109.................................. LeightonAspell
(Lucy Wadham) j.rt 1st: in rr: hdwy to chse ldrs 9th: lost pl 12th: bhd in rr whn hmpd 14th: t.o whn p.u bef 4 out **7/1**
6m 21.6s (-1.40) **Going Correction** +0.075s/f (Yiel) **8 Ran SP% 110.6**
Speed ratings (Par 105): **105,103,100,99,92 , ,**
CSF £101.45 CT £543.33 TOTE £9.30: £3.10, £3.10, £1.20; EX 117.30 Trifecta £1143.50.
Owner A M Gibbons **Bred** O And Mrs Fox-Pitt **Trained** Upper Lambourn, Berks

FOCUS
Fences, hurdles and golf club bend were inside, and home straight outside, the line used on September 29th. All distances as advertised. Not a bad little race, although the favourite disappointed. A big step up from the winner.

2040 BRAMLEY APPLE H'CAP CHASE (13 fncs) 1m 7f 153y
2:30 (2:30) (Class 5) (0-100,93) 5-Y-O+ **£2,599** (£763; £381; £190)

Form RPR
5542 **1** **Larkhall**[23] 1689 8-9-11 **71** RyanDay(7) 83
(Mike Sowersby) *trckd ldng pair: hit 3rd: 2nd 9th: led next: drvn clr appr last* **2/1**[1]

P433 **2** *5* **Red Rosso**[23] 1689 10-10-4 **71** (t) TrevorWhelan 79
(Rob Summers) *hld up in rr: hdwy to trck ldrs 5th: upsides 4 out: hit next: kpt on same pce between last 2* **5/1**[3]

U10- **3** *14* **Cross To Boston (IRE)**[201] 5134 9-11-5 **93** MrRHogg(7) 89
(Sue Smith) *led: drvn 7th: j.lft next: hdd 4 out: one pce* **4/1**[2]

2114 **4** *6* **Going Nowhere Fast (IRE)**[22] 1703 10-11-9 **93** RobertWilliams(3) 85
(Bernard Llewellyn) *nt jump wl in rr: hdwy 7th: lost pl sn after 4 out: sn bhd* **2/1**[1]

-P00 **5** *1* **Surprise Us**[24] 1677 8-10-3 **70** (p) TommyPhelan 59
(Mark Gillard) *t.k.h: trckd ldr: drvn 8th: sn lost pl: bhd 4 out* **16/1**

0PP4 **6** *4 ½* **Monzino (USA)**[15] 1815 7-9-11 **69** DannyBurton(5) 53
(Michael Chapman) *chsd ldrs: lost pl 6th: bhd fr 4 out* **33/1**

4m 5.8s (3.80) **Going Correction** +0.075s/f (Yiel) **6 Ran SP% 112.2**
Speed ratings: **93,90,83,80,80 77**
CSF £12.37 TOTE £2.70: £1.50, £2.30; EX 10.10 Trifecta £29.10.
Owner T J Stubbins **Bred** R D And Mrs J S Chugg **Trained** Goodmanham, E Yorks

FOCUS
The front pair came clear in this lowly handicap. A pb from the winner with the second to his mark.

2041 SOUTHWELL "NATIONAL HUNT" NOVICES' HURDLE (9 hdls) 1m 7f 153y
3:00 (3:00) (Class 4) 4-Y-O+ **£3,573** (£1,049; £524; £262)

Form RPR
2- **1** **Political Quiz**[182] 5502 5-10-12 0 JamesDavies 116+
(Tom Symonds) *trckd ldrs: cl 2nd 3 out: led appr next: edgd rt between last 2: drvn rt out* **10/1**

3 **2** *1 ¼* **Marquis Of Carabas (IRE)**[147] 525 5-10-12 0 TrevorWhelan 114+
(David Dennis) *trckd ldrs: handy 2nd appr 2 out: swtchd lft appr last: kpt on same pce last 75yds* **13/2**

0-3P **3** *16* **Rushvale (IRE)**[14] 1826 6-10-5 0 MrMJPKendrick(7) 100
(Ben Case) *in rr: pushed along and prom 4th: drvn next: outpcd 3 out: tk modest 3rd last* **7/2**[2]

/FR2 **4** *1 ¼* **Cloudy Joker (IRE)**[8] 1909 7-10-12 117 WayneHutchinson 99
(Donald McCain) *led: blnd 6th: hdd appr 2 out: sn btn* **2/1**[1]

5 *3 ¾* **Good Vibration (FR)**[222] 4-10-12 0 SeanQuinlan 96
(Sue Smith) *trckd ldrs: t.k.h: pushed along 5th: drvn and lost pl 3 out* **15/2**

42 **6** *32* **Jethro (IRE)**[17] 1792 4-10-12 0 WillKennedy 67
(Brian Ellison) *t.k.h: trckd ldr: drvn 3 out: sn lost pl: bhd bef next: t.o* **4/1**[3]

3m 52.6s (-4.40) **Going Correction** -0.125s/f (Good) **6 Ran SP% 109.7**
Speed ratings (Par 105): **106,105,97,96,94 78**
CSF £64.80 TOTE £8.40: £4.70, £2.90; EX 65.20 Trifecta £149.10.
Owner I A Low **Bred** Ian Low **Trained** Harewood End, H'fords

FOCUS
A bit of a turn-up with the market leaders disappointing. The form is rated around the third to his mark.

2042 SOUTHWELL-RACECOURSE.CO.UK H'CAP HURDLE (11 hdls) 2m 4f 62y
3:35 (3:35) (Class 4) (0-120,120) 3-Y-O+ **£3,898** (£1,144; £572; £286)

Form RPR
-010 **1** **Cusheen Bridge (IRE)**[21] 1719 7-11-12 **120** (t) AdamPogson 126+
(Charles Pogson) *mid-div: reminders after 8th: styd on fr 2 out: led appr last: drvn out* **11/1**

10/3 **2** *3 ½* **Ben Cee Pee M (IRE)**[26] 1661 10-10-13 **114** (b) CraigGallagher(7) 116+
(Brian Ellison) *hld up in mid-div: hdwy to trck ldrs 6th: handy 2nd appr 2 out: led briefly bef last: styd on same pce* **10/1**

0 **3** *¾* **Nautical Nitwit (IRE)**[81] 1184 6-11-5 **118** NathanMoscrop(5) 120
(Philip Kirby) *hld up in rr: hdwy whn hit 2 out: styd on to take 3rd last 75yds* **16/1**

2-26 **4** *1 ¼* **Kuda Huraa (IRE)**[138] 638 7-11-3 **116** HarryBannister(5) 116
(Harriet Bethell) *in rr: hdwy appr 2 out: 4th last: kpt on same pce* **20/1**

5053 **5** *1* **Factor Fifty (IRE)**[18] 1770 6-10-13 **110** (tp) AdamNicol(3) 109
(Philip Kirby) *chsd ldrs: kpt on same pce between last 2* **11/2**[2]

3143 **6** *1 ½* **Over The Air**[8] 1911 7-11-4 **112** WillKennedy 110
(John Spearing) *mid-div: effrt appr 2 out: kpt on same pce between last 2* **12/1**

6P-P **7** *nse* **Malibu Sun**[160] 315 8-11-7 **115** NicodeBoinville 114
(Ben Pauling) *led: hdd bef last: one pce* **12/1**

625F **8** *¾* **Don Padeja**[26] 1661 5-11-2 **117** (t) PatrickCowley(7) 114
(Jonjo O'Neill) *in rr: hdwy 8th: one pce fr 2 out* **8/1**

F41- **9** *13* **Clan William (IRE)**[306] 3196 7-10-11 **105** SeanQuinlan 90
(Sue Smith) *trckd ldrs: wknd 2 out* **14/1**

4641 **10** *1 ¾* **Jigsaw Financial (IRE)**[24] 1675 9-10-10 **104** AndrewGlassonbury 88
(Laura Young) *trckd ldrs: t.k.h: wknd 2 out: bhd whn eased run-in* **7/1**[3]

-3F4 **11** *9* **Bentons Lad**[20] 1740 4-10-11 **105** (t) RichieMcLernon 81
(George Moore) *chsd ldrs: drvn appr 2 out: sn wknd: eased run-in* **33/1**

100- **12** *15* **Hear The Chimes**[194] 5283 6-11-7 **115** TrevorWhelan 77
(Shaun Harris) *t.k.h in rr: hdwy 8th: lost pl 2 out: bhd whn eased run-in* **16/1**

426- **13** *½* **Ballinalacken (IRE)**[487] 787 7-11-5 **113** (p) DavidEngland 75
(Clare Ellam) *mid-div: drvn 7th: lost pl after next: wl bhd whn mstke 2 out* **25/1**

0-P6 **P** **Alco Sivola (FR)**[27] 1647 5-11-2 **110** (t) PaddyBrennan
(Fergal O'Brien) *in rr: nt fluent 6th: effrt on inner 8th: eased and lost pl bef 2 out: sn p.u: fatally injured* **5/1**[1]

5m 7.2s (-5.80) **Going Correction** -0.125s/f (Good)
WFA 4 from 5yo+ 10lb **14 Ran SP% 118.5**
Speed ratings (Par 105): **106,104,104,103,103 102,102,102,97,96 92,86,86,**
CSF £112.17 CT £1764.33 TOTE £13.40: £3.90, £3.40, £5.20; EX 152.10 Trifecta £2638.50 Part won..
Owner Wordingham Plant Hire **Bred** Gfe Agri Ltd **Trained** Farnsfield, Notts

FOCUS
A modest but competitive handicap, with a step up from the winner.

2043 SOUTHWELL_RACES ON TWITTER H'CAP HURDLE (9 hdls) 1m 7f 153y
4:05 (4:05) (Class 4) (0-105,104) 3-Y-O+ **£3,573** (£1,049; £524; £262)

Form RPR
/6-3 **1** **Theredballoon**[23] 1691 9-10-11 **89** PaulMoloney 99+
(Conrad Allen) *trckd ldrs: t.k.h: cl 2nd appr 2 out: led last: drvn out* **13/2**

43F1 **2** *1 ¾* **Maid Of Tuscany (IRE)**[6] 1941 4-10-13 **98** (b) MrShaneQuinlan(7) 106+
(Neil Mulholland) *trckd ldrs: led appr 2 out: hdd last: styd on same pce* **3/1**[2]

6363 **3** *3 ½* **Mr McGuiness (IRE)**[18] 1786 5-11-5 **100** BenPoste(3) 104
(Rosemary Gasson) *t.k.h in rr: hdwy 3 out: 3rd last: kpt on one pce* **14/1**

42 **4** *2 ½* **Shaiyzar (IRE)**[23] 1691 6-11-3 **100** (p) HarryBannister(5) 102
(David Thompson) *nt fluent in rr: hdwy appr 2 out: styd on run-in* **6/1**[3]

3-43 **5** *¾* **Very Intense (IRE)**[15] 1810 4-11-4 **96** RobertDunne 97
(Tom Lacey) *trckd ldrs: t.k.h: 3rd 2 out: one pce* **12/1**

055P **6** *7* **Hi Tide (IRE)**[23] 1691 11-10-13 **91** BrendanPowell 86
(J R Jenkins) *hld up in rr: hdwy 3 out: wknd between last 2* **16/1**

3340 **7** *1 ½* **Anton Dolin (IRE)**[27] 1647 7-11-1 **100** MrHFNugent(7) 93
(Michael Mullineaux) *towards rr: hdwy to chse ldrs 3 out: wknd between last 2* **14/1**

0P21 **8** *3 ½* **Stormbay Bomber (IRE)**[21] 1714 6-11-11 **103** RichieMcLernon 94
(George Moore) *led: hdd appr 2 out: lost pl between last 2* **5/2**[1]

P-00 **9** *21* **L'Es Fremantle (FR)**[56] 1379 4-9-9 **78** oh14 DannyBurton(5) 49
(Michael Chapman) *chsd ldrs: drvn 3 out: lost pl bef next: sn bhd* **150/1**

0UP- **P** **The Pier (IRE)**[208] 5024 9-11-12 **104** (t) AndrewTinkler
(Martin Keighley) *chsd ldrs: wknd and eased between last 2: wl bhd whn p.u bef last* **12/1**

050 **P** **Gilmer (IRE)**[38] 1544 4-10-5 **83** (t) GavinSheehan
(Laura Young) *chsd ldrs: drvn 6th: sn lost pl and bhd: t.o whn p.u bef last* **25/1**

3m 54.3s (-2.70) **Going Correction** -0.125s/f (Good)
WFA 4 from 5yo+ 9lb **11 Ran SP% 120.3**
Speed ratings (Par 105): **101,100,98,97,96 93,92,90,80,**
CSF £27.56 CT £272.35 TOTE £7.20: £2.40, £1.60, £3.00; EX 31.60 Trifecta £338.80.
Owner Miss Louise Allan **Bred** Elms Stud Co Ltd **Trained** Newmarket, Suffolk
■ Conrad Allen's first jumps winner for eight seasons.

FOCUS
Moderate hurdles form. There's probably more to come from the winner, and the second was close to her recent level.

2044 ROGER AND PAULINE LILLEY GOLDEN WEDDING MAIDEN OPEN NATIONAL HUNT FLAT RACE 1m 7f 153y
4:35 (4:35) (Class 6) 4-6-Y-O **£1,949** (£572; £286; £143)

Form RPR
1 **Western Cape (IRE)**[152] 4-10-13 0 KevinJones(5) 114+
(Seamus Mullins) *hld up in mid-div: hdwy 4f out: led over 1f out: forged clr* **10/1**

3- **2** *8* **Bilzic (FR)**[258] 4072 4-11-4 0 (t) HarrySkelton 104
(Dan Skelton) *hld up in mid-div: hdwy over 7f out: 2nd over 2f out: sn rdn: chsd wnr fnl f: no imp* **6/4**[1]

0/3 **3** *½* **Grand Introduction (IRE)**[163] 264 5-11-4 0 PaddyBrennan 103
(Fergal O'Brien) *trckd ldrs: led 3f out: hdd over 1f out: kpt on same pce* **12/1**

4 *10* **Looksnowtlikebrian (IRE)** 4-10-13 0 AlanJohns(5) 94
(Tim Vaughan) *trckd ldrs: drvn after 6f: lost pl 5f out: styd on over 1f out: tk modest 4th nr fin* **14/1**

5- **5** *1 ¼* **Ted's Lad**[356] 2172 5-11-4 0 WayneHutchinson 93
(Alan King) *mid-div: drvn 6f out: outpcd over 3f out: kpt on fnl 2f* **5/1**[2]

6 *1 ¾* **Amalfi Doug (FR)** 5-11-4 0 MarkGrant 91
(Michael Blanshard) *hld up in rr: hdwy 6f out: chsng ldrs over 2f out: sn wknd* **50/1**

3- **7** *2 ¾* **Weyburn (IRE)**[177] 11 4-11-4 0 AndrewTinkler 89
(Martin Keighley) *in rr-div: hdwy 6f out: chsng ldrs over 2f out: sn wknd* **6/1**[3]

8 *4 ½* **Lord Westy (IRE)** 4-11-4 0 BrendanPowell 85
(Jamie Snowden) *chsd ldrs: wknd fnl 2f* **16/1**

4-0 **9** *1* **Hey Up Ashey**[159] 341 5-11-1 0 BenPoste(3) 84
(Michael Mullineaux) *mid-div: chsng ldrs after 6f: lost pl over 2f out* **33/1**

10 *6* **Gustav (IRE)**[537] 5-11-4 0 NicodeBoinville 79
(Simon Earle) *in rr: drvn 6f out: bhd fnl 3f* **25/1**

0-2 **11** *8* **Primrose Brown**[15] 1817 4-10-11 0 PaulMoloney 64
(Conrad Allen) *hld up in rr: sme hdwy whn wd bnd 3f out: sn lost pl* **16/1**

12 *7* **Lords Park Star (IRE)**[188] 5387 6-11-4 0 TrevorWhelan 65
(Nicholas Pomfret) *w ldr: led 6f out: hdd 3f out: lost pl and eased over 1f out* **14/1**

0-0 **13** *25* **Singing Hinnie**[27] 1645 4-10-8 0 (b[1]) ThomasGarner(3) 36
(Mark H Tompkins) *led: drvn and hdd 6f out: sn lost pl and bhd: t.o whn virtually p.u over 1f out: eventually completed* **100/1**

3m 46.6s (-4.80) **Going Correction** -0.125s/f (Good) **13 Ran SP% 123.6**
Speed ratings: **107,103,102,97,97 96,94,92,92,89 85,81,69**
CSF £25.64 TOTE £12.40: £3.70, £1.40, £3.80; EX 55.20 Trifecta £550.80.
Owner A A Goodman **Bred** Thomas Browne **Trained** Wilsford-Cum-Lake, Wilts

FOCUS
Not a bad little bumper with the winner looking useful and the placed runners clear of the remainder. The fourth sets the level.
T/Plt: £849.70 to a £1 stake. Pool: £58,552.44 - 50.30 winning units. T/Qpdt: £180.90 to a £1 stake. Pool: £5,330.44 - 21.80 winning units. **Walter Glynn**

2045 - 2051a (Foreign Racing) - See Raceform Interactive

[12]CHELTENHAM (L-H)

Friday, October 23

OFFICIAL GOING: Good (7.7)

Wind: light, half against Weather: dry, overcast

2052 NEPTUNE INVESTMENT MANAGEMENT NOVICES' HURDLE (10 hdls) 2m 5f 26y

2:10 (2:11) (Class 2) 4-Y-0+

£10,635 (£3,141; £1,570; £785; £392; £197)

Form RPR

11 **1** **Penglai Pavilion (USA)**[96] 1052 5-11-6 0 .... AidanColeman 146+
(John Ferguson) *str: lw: hld up in 4th: wnt 3rd and clsd 3 out: hit next: produced to chal last: pushed along and qcknd to ld flat: r.o strly: pushed out: comf* **11/4**[3]

1-21 **2** 4 ½ **Laurium**[153] 441 5-11-6 130 .... DavidBass 140
(Nicky Henderson) *q tall: chsd ldrs: wnt 2nd 5th: mstke next: rdn to chal between last 2: led flat: sn hdd and outpcd by wnr: kpt on for clr 2nd* **16/1**

4 **3** 6 **Sandymount Duke (IRE)**[62] 1336 6-11-6 138 .... BarryGeraghty 136
(Mrs John Harrington, Ire) *str: lw: led: rdn and hrd pressed between last 2: hit last: sn hdd: wknd fnl 150yds* **2/1**[1]

4 5 **Robin Of Locksley (IRE)**[236] 4527 5-10-12 0 .... HarrySkelton 122+
(Dan Skelton) *angular: hld up in last pair: clsd and travelling strly after 3 out: rdn wl bef last: sn outpcd and plugged on same pce flat* **22/1**

0/ **5** ½ **Exxaro (IRE)**[62] 1336 5-11-6 135 .... JJBurke 129
(Henry De Bromhead, Ire) *athletic: chsd ldr: nt fluent 5th: lost 2nd next: rdn 3 out: dropped to last next: sn outpcd and wl hld last: plugged on* **9/4**[2]

6 2 **Casual Approach (IRE)**[27] 1666 6-11-6 130 .... (t) RichardJohnson 129
(Gordon Elliott, Ire) *chasg type: t.k.h: hld up in last pair: clsd and wl in tch 2 out: sn rdn and outpcd: wl hld last* **8/1**

5m 3.8s (-9.60) **Going Correction** -0.25s/f (Good) **6** Ran SP% **112.1**
Speed ratings (Par 109): **108,106,104,102,101 101**
CSF £36.74 TOTE £3.30: £1.80, £4.80; EX 33.10 Trifecta £83.60.
Owner Bloomfields **Bred** Darley **Trained** Cowlinge, Suffolk

FOCUS

All races on Old course. Hurdles and Chases increased by 42yds per circuit. The opening race of the new campaign at Cheltenham was run on ground described by Aidan Coleman as "good, slightly on the slower side in places", and by David Bass as "nice good ground." This was a classy novices' hurdle with the four holding BHA marks each rated in the 130s. The pace was fairly steady and the time was 6.8sec outside the standard. The winner is a smart novice but around 10lb shy of a typical Festival-winning novice here.

2053 SQUAREINTHEAIR.COM NOVICES' CHASE (13 fncs) 1m 7f 199y

2:45 (2:47) (Class 2) 4-Y-0+ **£12,512** (£3,696; £1,848)

Form RPR

0-51 **1** **Rock The World (IRE)**[33] 1609 7-11-10 142 .... (t) BarryGeraghty 153+
(Mrs John Harrington, Ire) *mde all: jnd and hit 2 out: forged ahd u.p flat: styd on: rdn out* **1/1**[1]

2U12 **2** 2 **Dormello Mo (FR)**[14] 1838 5-11-10 147 .... (t) SamTwiston-Davies 150
(Paul Nicholls) *lw: chsd wnr: hit 3rd: clsd and upsides bef 2 out: drvn and styd on same pce flat* **7/2**[3]

153- **3** 2 **Qewy (IRE)**[196] 5250 5-11-2 0 .... AidanColeman 141+
(John Ferguson) *hld up in 3rd: hit 3rd: mstke 6th (water) and 10th: effrt to chal and mstke last: wanting to hang lft and outpcd flat* **7/4**[2]

3m 53.0s (-5.00) **Going Correction** 0.0s/f (Good) **3** Ran SP% **108.6**
Speed ratings (Par 109): **112,111,110**
CSF £4.31 TOTE £1.80; EX 4.40 Trifecta £3.40.
Owner Michael Buckley **Bred** D Donegan **Trained** Moone, Co Kildare

FOCUS

Just the three runners, but three good ones and the pace wasn't bad. The winner is a smart early season-novice but 10lb+ shy of a typical Arkle winner.

2054 PERTEMPS NETWORK H'CAP HURDLE (SERIES QUALIFIER) (12 hdls) 2m 7f 208y

3:20 (3:21) (Class 2) 4-Y-0+

£12,512 (£3,696; £1,848; £924; £462; £232)

Form RPR

260- **1** **Dark Spirit (IRE)**[227] 4692 7-10-10 134 .... LewisGordon(10) 144+
(Evan Williams) *hld up off the pce in main gp: clsd 8th: chsng ldrs and nt clr run jst bef last: swtchd lft and str run ld fnl 150yds: r.o wl and sn asserted* **11/1**

-011 **2** 2 ¼ **Mr Shantu (IRE)**[31] 1615 6-10-9 130 .... (t) PatrickCowley(7) 143+
(Jonjo O'Neill) *hld up off the pce in last pair: clsd and wl in tch whn bdly hmpd 9th: rcvrd and in tch 2 out: chal last: sn led and edgd lft u.p: hdd fnl 150yds: r.o but nt gng pce of wnr* **4/1**[1]

005- **3** 12 **Mijhaar**[196] 5249 7-11-9 137 .... AidanColeman 134
(John Ferguson) *prom in main gp: wnt 3rd 8th and clsd on ldrs: wnt 2nd and mstke next: led on inner bef last: rdn and hdd immediately after last: sn outpcd and wknd flat* **7/1**

1P0- **4** 6 **Polamco (IRE)**[191] 5343 6-10-9 123 .... (t) NoelFehily 115
(Harry Fry) *hld up off the pce in main gp: mstke 6th: clsd and wl in tch 9th: clsd to chal bef last: stl ev ch last: sn rdn and immediately btn: wknd* **9/2**[2]

1111 **5** ½ **Kilfinichen Bay (IRE)**[33] 1594 7-11-12 140 .... RichardJohnson 130
(Charlie Longsdon) *lw: hld up off the pce in midfield: clsd and wl in tch 9th: chsd ldrs and stl handy whn rdn bef last: wknd flat* **8/1**

-P42 **6** 8 **Fighter Jet**[100] 1002 7-10-6 120 .... (tp) BrianHughes 104
(John Mackie) *pressed ldrs tl 2nd: settled bk and prom in main gp: clsd and wl in tch 9th: rdn bef next: struggling and mstke 2 out: wknd bef last* **14/1**

1053 **7** 1 **On The Bridge (IRE)**[14] 1839 10-11-5 133 .... (tp) NickScholfield 116
(Jeremy Scott) *w ldrs tl allowed ldng pair to go clr 3rd: lost 3rd pl 7th: rdn and struggling after 9th: bhd 2 out: wknd bef last* **16/1**

F4-P **8** 2 ¼ **My Lad Percy**[28] 1641 7-9-11 114 oh4 .... (p) KillianMoore(3) 94
(Martin Keighley) *led tl 2nd: clr w rival next: led again 6th: wnt clr after 9th: pressed bef 3 out: rdn and hdd bef last: fdd bdly flat: fin lame* **100/1**

5202 **9** 30 **Willem (FR)**[21] 1742 5-10-8 125 .... (p) BrianToomey(3) 78
(David Pipe) *hld up off the pce in midfield: clsd and wl in tch 9th: chsd ldrs next: pushed along and btn 2 out: sn wknd: t.o flat* **33/1**

0-P2 **B** **King Boru (IRE)**[31] 1615 7-10-9 123 .... (t) HarrySkelton
(Dan Skelton) *hld up off the pce in main gp: clsd and wl in tch whn b.d 9th* **5/1**[3]

11F- **F** **Saint John Henry (FR)**[207] 5075 5-10-7 124 .... KieronEdgar(3)
(David Pipe) *w ldr: led and wnt clr w rival 2nd: hit 5th and 7th: rdn and struggling bef next: losing pl whn fell 9th* **8/1**

5m 51.05s (-12.35) **Going Correction** -0.25s/f (Good) **11** Ran SP% **114.4**
Speed ratings (Par 109): **110,109,105,103,103 100,100,99,89,**
CSF £54.17 CT £334.38 TOTE £12.10: £3.10, £1.90, £3.00; EX 48.20 Trifecta £564.50.
Owner Richard Abbott & Mario Stavrou **Bred** Thomas G N Burrage **Trained** Llancarfan, Vale Of Glamorgan

FOCUS

An eventful handicap hurdle. Two of them, the eighth home and the faller, went out clear of the others. The first two came clear and they, plus the next four, qualify for the series final in March. A big pb from the winner under a claimer with the second unlucky.

2055 RYMAN STATIONERY CHELTENHAM BUSINESS CLUB NOVICES' CHASE (20 fncs) 3m 80y

3:55 (3:56) (Class 2) 5-Y-0+

£12,512 (£3,696; £1,848; £924; £462; £232)

Form RPR

240- **1** **Shantou Flyer (IRE)**[23] 1711 5-11-8 133 .... (t) MarkWalsh 144+
(Colin Bowe, Ire) *lw: chsd ldrs: mstke 10th: hmpd and lost pl 3 out: cl enough in 4th and mstke 2 out: rallied u.p flat: led fnl 75yds: styd on* **14/1**

2411 **2** 1 ½ **Weather Babe**[22] 1713 7-11-1 133 .... (tp) ConorO'Farrell 135
(David Pipe) *racd in last trio: 6th and rdn along after 16th: lft chsng ldrs next: responded to press and hdwy to ld 2 out: drvn flat: hdd and no ex fnl 75yds* **25/1**

0-11 **3** shd **Vicente (FR)**[164] 269 6-11-8 0 .... SamTwiston-Davies 142
(Paul Nicholls) *lw: chsd ldrs: lft 2nd and mstke 3 out: ev ch 2 out: 3rd and sltly outpcd last: kpt on u.p fnl 150yds* **9/2**[3]

2111 **4** 5 **Ballykan**[23] 1701 5-11-8 137 .... (t) DarylJacob 138
(Nigel Twiston-Davies) *lw: chsd ldr tl lft in ld 3 out: hit 2 out and hdd: stl pressing ldrs last: no ex flat: wknd fnl 75yds* **11/4**[2]

211- **5** 3 ¼ **A Good Skin (IRE)**[190] 5358 6-11-8 138 .... PaddyBrennan 136+
(Tom George) *bit bkwd: hld up in last trio: 5th and pushed along after 16th: lft chsng ldrs and sltly hmpd next: lost pl bef 2 out: wknd flat* **5/1**

0-46 **6** 20 **Pearl Swan (FR)**[13] 1846 7-11-0 0 .... SeanBowen 107
(Peter Bowen) *a in rr and nvr travelling wl: lost tch after 15th: t.o 3 out* **17/2**

43-1 **F** **Vintage Vinnie (IRE)**[28] 1642 6-11-5 0 .... LeightonAspell 143+
(Rebecca Curtis) *led: mstke 10th: blnd and pckd 12th: stl travelling okay whn fell 3 out* **5/2**[1]

6m 12.8s (-5.50) **Going Correction** 0.0s/f (Good) **7** Ran SP% **111.1**
Speed ratings: **109,108,108,106,105 99,**
CSF £213.04 TOTE £16.40: £4.90, £7.20; EX 174.90 Trifecta £542.80.
Owner S O'Neill **Bred** Tom McCarthy **Trained** Enniscorthy, Co. Wexford

FOCUS

A classy novice chase contested by six last-time-out winners. Shantou Flyer is on the upgrade over fences, with the next two to their marks.

2056 BET AND WATCH AT WINNER.CO.UK MAIDEN HURDLE (8 hdls) 2m 87y

4:30 (4:34) (Class 3) 4-Y-0+ **£6,279** (£1,871; £947; £485; £254)

Form RPR

311- **1** **Mister Miyagi (IRE)**[209] 5028 6-11-0 .... HarrySkelton 126+
(Dan Skelton) *q str: hld up in tch: wnt 3rd 5th: trckd ldr 2 out: chal last: sn drvn to ld: asserting and drifted rt u.p: r.o wl* **7/2**[3]

1- **2** 2 ¼ **Drumlee Sunset (IRE)**[257] 4113 5-11-0 0 .... RichardJohnson 123+
(Philip Hobbs) *lengthy: lw: chsd ldr tl led 3 out: jnd and slt mstke last: sn hdd: no ex and styd on same pce flat* **5/4**[1]

4F0/ **3** 20 **Save The Bees**[23] 3877 7-11-0 0 .... NickScholfield 107
(Declan Carroll) *led: hdd and mstke 3 out: 3rd and btn whn mstke last: wknd flat* **40/1**

1-5 **4** 3 ¼ **Newsworthy (IRE)**[176] 53 5-11-0 0 .... BarryGeraghty 102
(Nicky Henderson) *lw: sltly on toes: chsd ldrs tl 5th: rdn and struggling after next: btn whn j.lft 2 out: wknd bef last* **5/2**[2]

116 **5** 22 **Alyasan (IRE)**[10] 1898 4-11-0 0 .... (t) NoelFehily 81
(Seamus Durack) *t.k.h: hld up in tch: struggling 3 out: sn wknd* **16/1**

34- **U** **Mr Kit Cat**[216] 4921 5-11-0 0 .... PaulMoloney
(Evan Williams) *t.k.h: midfield whn sltly impeded and uns rdr 1st* **10/1**

P **Gallery Artist (IRE)**[166] 5-10-7 0 .... LiamTreadwell
(Dai Burchell) *j.rt 1st: dropped herself out and lot tch rapidly 3rd: sn t.o: p.u bef 3 out* **100/1**

3m 55.5s (-6.50) **Going Correction** -0.25s/f (Good)
WFA 4 from 5yo+ 9lb **7** Ran SP% **113.6**
Speed ratings (Par 107): **106,104,94,93,82 ,**
CSF £8.49 TOTE £4.40: £1.90, £1.50; EX 9.50 Trifecta £168.00.
Owner Ben Turner & Jay Tabb **Bred** Stephen Nolan **Trained** Alcester, Warwicks

FOCUS

A good race of its type. Lac Fontana won this event two years ago before taking the Vincent O'Brien County Hurdle later in the season. The first two confirmed the merit of their bumper wins and both will probably go on to rate higher.

2057 WINNER.CO.UK AMATEUR RIDERS' H'CAP CHASE (20 fncs) 3m 1f

5:05 (5:07) (Class 3) (0-125,125) 4-Y-0+

£7,195 (£2,247; £1,123; £561; £280; £141)

Form RPR

2F-6 **1** **Regal Flow**[23] 1699 8-11-2 118 .... MrMLegg(3) 126+
(Caroline Keevil) *hld up towards rr: mstke 9th: stdy prog 13th: wnt 2nd bef 3 out: rdn to ld bef 2 out: hdd and n.m.r between last 2: led again flat: drvn out* **8/1**[3]

30-2 **2** ½ **Definite Ruby (IRE)**[27] 1668 7-11-11 124 .... (b) MrJJCodd 133+
(Gordon Elliott, Ire) *hld up in last trio: stdy prog 13th: chal bef 2 out: pckd 2 out: sn led and edgd lft: hdd flat: no ex and hld towards fin* **14/1**

3-12 **3** 14 **Top Cat Henry (IRE)**[6] 1976 7-11-7 123 .... (tp) DavidNoonan(3) 117
(Dr Richard Newland) *hld up towards rr: stdy hdwy 13th: chsd ldrs 3 out: 4th and outpcd 2 out: wl hld last: wnt 3rd flat* **3/1**[1]

U235 **4** 6 **Dr Anubis (IRE)**[10] 1894 10-9-7 99 oh33 .... MissKatyLyons(7) 89
(Dai Burchell) *chsd ldrs tl led 14th: rdn and hdd bef 2 out: stl cl 3rd but no ex last: edgd rt and fdd flat* **100/1**

1-5P **5** 1 ½ **Lord Landen (IRE)**[16] 1812 10-10-5 107 .... (t) MissAEStirling(3) 95
(Fergal O'Brien) *taken down early and mounted on crse: hld up in rr: hdwy after 15th: chsd ldrs after 3 out: rdn next: sn btn and wknd bef last* **22/1**

P6-6 **6** *8* **Five Star Wilsham (IRE)**[30] 1632 11-10-12 **118**............. MrJJSlevin(7) 98
(Nigel Twiston-Davies) *in tch in midfield: n.m.r 17th: rdn and struggling next: sn wknd: burst blood vessel* **14/1**

7 *2 3/4* **Katie Do (IRE)**[23] 1709 9-11-3 **116**..............................(p) MrBO'Neill 95
(Colin Bowe, Ire) *chsd ldr tl led 13th: hdd next: styd chsng ldr tl losing pl whn bdly hmpd 3 out: sn wknd* **8/1**[3]

44P- **8** *hd* **Liberty One (IRE)**[252] 4209 9-11-6 **124**.............. MrMatthewHampton(5) 103
(Richard Woollacott) *chsd ldrs tl 5th: lost pl and midfield 9th: dropped to rr and struggling u.p after 16th: n.d after* **14/1**

04-1 **9** *nk* **Broughtons Bandit**[24] 1433 8-11-6 **119**..........................(b[1]) MrWBiddick 97
(Gordon Elliott, Ire) *hld up in tch in midfield: stdy hdwy 15th: chsd ldrs after 3 out: rdn bnd bef next: sn btn: wknd qckly last* **20/1**

5653 **10** *16* **Kyles Faith (IRE)**[15] 1820 7-9-10 **100**..........(p) MrJoshuaNewman(5) 65
(Martin Keighley) *led tl 13th: struggling and lost pl bef 3 out: lost tch bef 2 out: t.o* **22/1**

3663 **11** *17* **Houston Dynimo (IRE)**[7] 1948 10-11-0 **120**.............(bt) MrTGreatrex(7) 68
(David Pipe) *in tch in midfield: losing pl and mstke 13th: wl bhd 16th: t.o 3 out* **25/1**

1P64 **12** *6* **Perfect Timing**[22] 1722 7-11-12 **125**......................(b) MrSWaley-Cohen 67
(Neil Mulholland) *j.rt: chsd ldrs: rdn and lost pl 17th: bhd whn blnd next: t.o* **12/1**

2F5U **U** **Owen Glendower (IRE)**[62] 1332 10-11-4 **117**.............(tp) MrSClements
(Sophie Leech) *hld up in rr: mstke and uns rdr 16th* **25/1**

1411 **U** **Conas Taoi (IRE)**[16] 1813 6-9-7 **99** oh3..............(p) MrSeanHoulihan(7)
(Paul Morgan) *lw: wl in tch in midfield: mstke 10th and 17th: pckd bdly and uns rdr 3 out* **7/2**[2]

6m 24.8s (-1.20) **Going Correction** 0.0s/f (Good) course record **14 Ran SP% 119.3**
Speed ratings (Par 107): **101,100,96,94,93 91,90,90,90,85 79,77, ,**
CSF £98.71 CT £416.05 TOTE £9.00: £2.70, £4.20, £1.80; EX 131.50 Trifecta £596.70.
Owner Mrs C J Dunn **Bred** Mrs H R Dunn **Trained** Motcombe, Dorset

FOCUS
A competitive amateurs' handicap run at a solid gallop. The first two finished clear. A step up from the winner with the second back to her best.

2058 HARRISON JAMES & HARDIE CONDITIONAL JOCKEYS' H'CAP HURDLE (8 hdls) 2m 87y
5:40 (5:42) (Class 3) (0-140,139) 3-Y-0+

£6,256 (£1,848; £924; £462; £231; £116)

Form RPR

203- **1** **Old Guard**[181] 5535 4-11-2 **137**.................................. HarryCobden(8) 146+
(Paul Nicholls) *in tch in midfield: travelling wl and nt clrest of runs after 2 out: hdwy and j. into ld last: sn clr: r.o strly: readily* **8/1**

1534 **2** *6* **Are They Your Own (IRE)**[33] 1590 7-10-8 **121**..........(t) NickSlatter 123
(Fergal O'Brien) *led: rdn 2 out: out j. and hdd last: outpcd by wnr but hld on gamely for 2nd flat* **25/1**

3 **3** *1/2* **Damefirth (IRE)**[19] 1789 6-10-3 **124**........................ DylanRobinson(8) 125
(Henry De Bromhead, Ire) *in tch in midfield: effrt to press ldrs last: edgd lft u.p and styd on same pce flat* **8/1**

P-10 **4** *3/4* **Savello (IRE)**[59] 1361 9-11-9 **139**........................ BridgetAndrews(3) 139
(Dan Skelton) *lw: taken down early and led to post: t.k.h: hld up in tch in rr: clsd after 2 out: drvn and styd on same pce flat* **7/2**[2]

313- **5** *hd* **Ozzy Thomas (IRE)**[191] 5341 5-10-5 **123**.................. LewisGordon(5) 123
(Henry Oliver) *hld up in tch in midfield: nt clr run after 2 out: rdn and hdwy last: styd on same pce flat* **14/1**

343- **6** *2 1/4* **Clondaw Banker (IRE)**[273] 3840 6-10-5 **121**......... JeremiahMcGrath(3) 119
(Nicky Henderson) *lw: chsd ldrs: rdn and pressing ldrs after 2 out: no ex last: btn whn short of room flat: wknd fnl 150yds* **11/4**[1]

4-26 **7** *2 1/4* **Mantou (IRE)**[13] 1848 4-11-3 **130**.............................. TomBellamy 126
(John Ferguson) *in tch in midfield: rdn to chse ldrs between last 2: no ex last: wknd flat* **10/1**

1F-5 **8** *1/2* **Sir Valentino (FR)**[166] 218 6-10-8 **124**......................(t) JamieBargary(3) 119
(Tom George) *chsd ldr: drvn between last 2: lost 2nd last: wknd flat* **25/1**

3121 **9** *1* **Regulation (IRE)**[7] 1949 6-11-0 **130** 7ex..................(p) LizzieKelly(3) 124
(Neil King) *hld up in tch in lat pair: clsd 3 out: drvn and no imp between last 2: hung lft u.p and wknd flat* **9/2**[3]

1-34 **10** *13* **Quebec**[16] 1814 4-11-0 **127**.. HarryBannister 110
(Charlie Mann) *chsd ldrs: rdn and lost pl after 2 out: wknd between last 2* **50/1**

4342 **11** *3 1/4* **Zarawi (IRE)**[20] 1753 4-9-7 **116**..............................(p) TomHumphries(10) 94
(Charlie Longsdon) *in tch in midfield: rdn and lost pl after 3 out: bhd between last 2* **25/1**

3m 54.4s (-7.60) **Going Correction** -0.25s/f (Good)
WFA 4 from 5yo+ 9lb **11 Ran SP% 118.5**
Speed ratings (Par 107): **109,106,105,105,105 104,103,102,102,95 94**
CSF £183.62 CT £1655.04 TOTE £7.50: £2.60, £8.60, £2.40; EX 325.20 Trifecta £1659.70.
Owner The Brooks, Kyle & Stewart Families **Bred** The Rt Hon Lord Rothschild **Trained** Ditcheat, Somerset

FOCUS
They didn't go a great gallop in this decent handicap for conditionals and it developed into a sprint from the home turn. A big step up from the winner and there's probably more to come.
T/Jkpt: Not won. Consolation placepot: £729.50 to a £1 stake. Pool: £2,098.57 - 2.10 winning tickets T/Plt: £1,628.30 to a £1 stake. Pool: £107,646.54 - 48.26 winning tickets T/Qpdt: £169.60 to a £1 stake. Pool: £9,191.97 - 40.10 winning tickets **Steve Payne**

2052 CHELTENHAM (L-H)
Saturday, October 24

OFFICIAL GOING: Good changing to good (good to soft in places) after race 4 (3.55)
Wind: breezy Weather: raining and rather misty; 13 degrees

2059 WINNER.CO.UK H'CAP CHASE (13 fncs) 1m 7f 199y
2:10 (2:12) (Class 2) 4-Y-0+

£31,280 (£9,240; £4,620; £2,310; £1,155; £580)

Form RPR

421- **1** **Boondooma (IRE)**[308] 3186 8-11-8 **147**..................... WillKennedy 156+
(Dr Richard Newland) *lw: led at str pce 2nd tl 6th: prom tl led again gng strly after 3 out: sn 5 l clr: hit 2 out: rdn and gamely fnd plenty flat* **7/1**[3]

-351 **2** *3* **Workbench (FR)**[22] 1735 7-10-12 **137**.......................(t) HarrySkelton 142
(Dan Skelton) *lw: last whn nt fluent 2nd: stl abt 12 l 8th 3 out: drvn and hdwy next: wnt 2nd at last: tried to cl u.p but hld fnl 100yds* **13/2**[2]

F-34 **3** *2 1/4* **Dunraven Storm (IRE)**[20] 1777 10-11-8 **147**............. RichardJohnson 152
(Philip Hobbs) *chsd ldrs: nt a fluent: mstke 5th: rdn after 3 out: styng on same pce whn mstke next: hld after* **12/1**

0F-1 **4** *1 1/2* **Astracad (FR)**[13] 1869 9-10-12 **137**.........................(t) SamTwiston-Davies 139
(Nigel Twiston-Davies) *lw: midfield: rdn after 3 out: hld fr next and nt qckn u.p flat* **15/2**

356- **5** *6* **Turn Over Sivola (FR)**[209] 5046 8-10-12 **137**........... WayneHutchinson 133+
(Alan King) *settled towards rr: hdwy 10th: wnt 2nd after 3 out: rdn and wknd after next: fin tired* **8/1**

F15- **6** *10* **Going Concern (IRE)**[203] 5147 8-10-4 **129**.................... PaulMoloney 116
(Evan Williams) *towards rr: drvn bef 3 out: btn bef next* **14/1**

50-3 **7** *2 3/4* **Sew On Target (IRE)**[160] 357 10-10-13 **138**................ BrendanPowell 124
(Colin Tizzard) *pressed ldrs tl 1/2-way: rdn 3 out: sn btn* **6/1**[1]

23U0 **8** *3 1/4* **Owen Na View (IRE)**[28] 1658 7-10-8 **133**................... PaddyBrennan 115
(Fergal O'Brien) *towards rr: rdn bef 3 out: sn btn* **28/1**

41P- **9** *1/2* **Next Sensation (IRE)**[198] 5240 8-11-12 **151**...............(t) LiamTreadwell 132
(Michael Scudamore) *led tl 2nd in v strly run r: led again 6th tl 10th: rdn and wknd bef 2 out* **12/1**

1312 **10** *5* **Purple 'n Gold (IRE)**[22] 1735 6-10-11 **136**......................(p) NoelFehily 115
(David Pipe) *nt fluent and nvr gng pce in rr: lost tch 1/2-way: plugged rnd after* **7/1**[3]

45-6 **11** *26* **De Faithesdream (IRE)**[173] 103 9-10-0 **125** oh3........... AdamWedge 98
(Evan Williams) *blnd 3rd: t.k.h in 3rd tl gd jump to ld 10th: rdn and hdd after 3 out: fading whn blnd bdly next* **14/1**

32P- **P** **Eastlake (IRE)**[197] 5253 9-11-9 **148**........................... BarryGeraghty
(Jonjo O'Neill) *dropped bk to last but one and nt fluent 7th: p.u next* **15/2**

3m 55.1s (-2.90) **Going Correction** 0.0s/f (Good) **12 Ran SP% 119.4**
Speed ratings (Par 109): **107,105,104,103,100 95,94,92,92,89 76,**
CSF £53.33 CT £546.01 TOTE £7.00: £3.20, £2.40, £4.10; EX 51.90 Trifecta £695.70.
Owner P Jenkins & C E Stedman **Bred** Colm Griffin **Trained** Claines, Worcs

FOCUS
Damp and grey conditions for the second half of Cheltenham's opening two-day autumn fixture. As on day one, rails on both courses were configured seven yards out from the inner, rendering each circuit 42 yards longer. A strong 2m handicap chase to begin with, reuniting the first, second, fifth and eleventh from the previous season's Grand Annual Chase, and the pace was predictably generous. The form looks solid.

2060 MASTERSON HOLDINGS HURDLE (8 hdls) 2m 87y
2:45 (2:47) (Class 2) 4-Y-0

£21,896 (£6,468; £3,234; £1,617; £808; £406)

Form RPR

142- **1** **Devilment**[198] 5236 4-10-12 146.............................. AidanColeman 147+
(John Ferguson) *racd enthusiastically in last pair in slowly run affair: delayed effrt tl chal on outer between last two: led fnl 100yds: kpt on stoutly* **3/1**[2]

03-2 **2** *3/4* **Karezak (IRE)**[14] 1847 4-10-12 147.....................(b) WayneHutchinson 147
(Alan King) *lw: cl up: wnt 2nd wl bef 3 out: led next: rdn and hrd pressed by several whn clipped last: hdd 100yds out: nt qckn after* **11/2**[3]

411- **3** *1 1/2* **Lil Rockerfeller (USA)**[154] 5535 4-10-12 143...............(p) TrevorWhelan 146+
(Neil King) *cl up: hit 3 out: rdn after next: stl wl on terms whn nt fluent last: kpt on pluckily whn hld fnl 100yds: tk 3rd clsng stages* **12/1**

136- **4** *1* **Hargam (FR)**[198] 5236 4-11-6 152.............................. BarryGeraghty 152
(Nicky Henderson) *settled trcking ldrs: pushed along and effrt 3 out: chal and jnd ldr last: rdn and wknd and lost 3rd fnl 100yds* **5/2**[1]

1111 **5** *2 1/4* **Tea In Transvaal (IRE)**[14] 1847 4-10-5 134..................... PaulMoloney 136
(Evan Williams) *lw: racd keenly: w ldr tl led 4th: hit 2 out and hdd: remained cl up tl wknd after last* **10/1**

11-0 **6** *16* **Qualando (FR)**[175] 94 4-11-2 139.................... SamTwiston-Davies 131
(Paul Nicholls) *trckd ldrs: rdn 3 out: btn next* **7/1**

4-40 **7** *hd* **Stars Over The Sea (USA)**[14] 1847 4-10-12 138...............(t) NoelFehily 129
(David Pipe) *t.k.h and disp ld at mod pce: jumping lacked conviction: hdd 4th: mstke next: dropped to rr and struggling 3 out* **20/1**

12- **8** *10* **Fou Et Sage (FR)**[204] 5127 4-11-2 147............................ HarrySkelton 124
(Dan Skelton) *leggy: athletic: t.k.h in last pair: in tch tl rdn and wknd 2 out* **6/1**

3m 51.3s (-10.70) **Going Correction** -0.25s/f (Good) **8 Ran SP% 117.3**
Speed ratings: **116,115,114,114,113 105,105,100**
CSF £20.69 TOTE £4.00: £1.60, £2.20, £2.40; EX 16.90 Trifecta £189.90.
Owner Bloomfields **Bred** Cliveden Stud **Trained** Cowlinge, Suffolk

FOCUS
The six most recent winners of this contest have subsequently finished unplaced in their respective races at the Festival, so it remains to be seen how informative a piece of form this will prove come March. Nonetheless, this looked a good renewal and the first five finished clear. The early pace was moderate. The winner was up 5lb on his best juvenile form, with the second and fifth similar to Chepstow.

2061 WINNER.CO.UK TROPHY (HANDICAP CHASE) (20 fncs) 3m 1f
3:20 (3:21) (Class 2) 4-Y-0+

£31,280 (£9,240; £4,620; £2,310; £1,155; £580)

Form RPR

P31- **1** **Whats Happening (IRE)**[192] 5340 8-10-8 **136**...................(t) NoelFehily 141+
(Tom George) *midfield: stl 6th after 3 out but gng wl enough: rdn bef next: 5 l 6th at last: str run to ld fnl 100yds and sn in command* **10/1**

150- **2** *2* **Perfect Candidate (IRE)**[228] 4693 8-10-3 **131**.............. PaddyBrennan 133
(Fergal O'Brien) *a 2nd or 3rd: rdn after 3 out: led briefly flat: hdd and outpcd fnl 100yds* **11/1**

2U0- **3** *1/2* **Fox Appeal (IRE)**[192] 5342 8-11-9 **151**.......................... AidanColeman 154
(Emma Lavelle) *hld up towards rr: 5th and effrt whn rdn after 3 out: hit next: styd on same pce in 3rd fr last* **7/1**[2]

1-26 **4** *nk* **Audacious Plan (IRE)**[14] 1849 6-10-2 **130**...................(p) LeightonAspell 131
(Rebecca Curtis) *chsd ldrs: 4th and drvn after 3 out: kpt on after last* **7/1**[2]

U22- **5** *1 1/2* **Theatrical Star**[266] 3978 9-10-11 **139**........................... BrendanPowell 139
(Colin Tizzard) *rn in snatches: led 2nd tl 8th: lost pl 11th: rallied bef last: kpt on wl flat: nvr rchd ldrs* **10/1**

1122 **6** *hd* **Silver Man**[23] 1713 8-10-9 **137**..............................(v[1]) NicodeBoinville 137
(Jo Hughes) *chsd ldrs: rdn bef 3 out: outpcd next: styd on after last* **8/1**[3]

P3-1 **7** *1/2* **Azure Fly (IRE)**[17] 1807 7-10-8 **136**..............................(tp) DarylJacob 135
(Charlie Longsdon) *midfield: rdn and outpcd after 3 out: rallying whn nt fluent last: styd on flat wout threatening* **8/1**[3]

111 **8** *hd* **Champion Court (IRE)**[90] 1112 10-11-12 **154**.............(p) AndrewTinkler 153
(Martin Keighley) *lw: cl up: 2nd or 3rd fr 1/2-way: rdn and ev ch fr bef 2 out tl tired qckly up hill after last* **10/1**

53-1 **9** *1* **Big Casino**[168] 198 9-10-4 **132**........................(v) SamTwiston-Davies 130
(Nigel Twiston-Davies) *lw: led at mod pce: hdd 2nd: led again 8th: hit 13th: stl looked to be gng wl after 3 out: rdn and hdd after last: fnd nthing and slowed bdly up hill after* **9/1**

P2P- **10** *23* **Roalco De Farges (FR)**[182] 5538 10-10-10 **138**........... RichardJohnson 116
(Philip Hobbs) *lw: last trio: rdn and btn bef 3 out* **11/2**[1]

0615 **11** *1½* **Kie (IRE)**[7] 1976 7-10-9 **144**.................... MichaelHeard(7) 120
(David Pipe) *last trio mostly: rdn and btn bef 3 out* **33/1**

33/0 **12** *16* **Black Benny (IRE)**[28] 1668 10-10-6 **134**................(t) PaulMoloney 108
(J P Broderick, Ire) *mostly last trio: rdn and struggling whn mstke 4 out* **18/1**

6m 29.1s (3.10) **Going Correction** 0.0s/f (Good) course record **12** Ran SP% **116.4**
Speed ratings (Par 109): **95,94,94,94,93 93,93,93,93,85 85,80**
CSF £112.09 CT £824.87 TOTE £13.80: £3.80, £3.80, £2.80; EX 155.70 Trifecta £1042.00.
Owner David Rea & Express Contract Drying Ltd **Bred** William Hourigan **Trained** Slad, Gloucs

FOCUS
A race farmed by trainer Philip Hobbs and owners The Brushmakers with Balthazar King (three times) and Roalco De Farges landing every renewal from 2011-14, but the latter was not among the nine runners that finished in a heap this year at the end of a moderately run affair. The first four were all pretty close to their marks.

2062 BET AND WATCH AT WINNER.CO.UK NOVICES' HURDLE (12 hdls) 2m 7f 208y
3:55 (3:59) (Class 3) 4-Y-O+
£6,256 (£1,848; £924; £462; £231; £116)

Form RPR

0-21 **1** **Atlantic Gold (IRE)**[23] 1723 5-11-3 125.................. AidanColeman 131+
(Charlie Longsdon) *lw: led fr 2nd: set stdy pce: rdn bef last: a holding rival flat and won w ears pricked* **7/2**[3]

2121 **2** *2¾* **Mont Choisy (FR)**[10] 1911 5-11-3 132.................. SamTwiston-Davies 129
(Nigel Twiston-Davies) *led tl 2nd: chsd wnr rest of way: nt fluent 7th: drvn bef last: outbattled flat* **6/4**[1]

35-1 **3** *3* **Tradewinds (FR)**[30] 1635 7-11-1 127.................. GrantCockburn(5) 127
(Lucinda Russell) *hld up: effrt 1/2-way: wnt 3rd at 7th: rdn and no imp between last two* **6/1**

1153 **4** *16* **Miss Serious (IRE)**[17] 1808 5-10-13 130.................. NickScholfield 108
(Jeremy Scott) *lw: midfield: effrt 3 out: rdn and wknd after next* **10/3**[2]

063- **5** *4* **Zanstra (IRE)**[261] 4055 5-10-12 0.................. BrendanPowell 102
(Colin Tizzard) *disp 3rd or 4th: rdn bef 2 out: sn wknd* **20/1**

6 *15* **Three Of A Kind (IRE)**[183] 6-10-12 0.................. PaddyBrennan 88
(Fergal O'Brien) *w'like: j. deliberately in rr: effrt 8th: rdn and fdd bef 2 out: t.o* **20/1**

0-P **7** *29* **Lined With Silver (IRE)**[7] 1979 6-10-12 0.................. LiamTreadwell 61
(Dai Burchell) *bhd most of way: fdd rapidly bef 3 out: sn bdly t.o* **200/1**

8 *94* **Hinxworth (IRE)**[202] 6-10-5 0.................. MrJNixon(7)
(Katy Price) *angular: chsd ldrs tl 1/2-way: bdly t.o fr 8th* **33/1**

9 *39* **Flamenco Flyer**[540] 6-10-9 0.................. BenPoste(3)
(Tracey Barfoot-Saunt) *mstkes in rr: blnd 3rd: last whn mstke 7th: sn bdly t.o: rdn rt out flat* **200/1**

0/ **P** **Western Dream**[272] 7-10-12 0.................. RobertDunne
(Dai Burchell) *cl up tl 1/2-way: bdly t.o fr 7th: climbed over 3 out and p.u* **200/1**

5m 58.6s (-4.80) **Going Correction** -0.25s/f (Good) **10** Ran SP% **113.5**
Speed ratings (Par 107): **98,97,96,90,89 84,74,43,30,**
CSF £8.86 TOTE £4.40: £1.40, £1.10, £2.00; EX 9.60 Trifecta £38.80.
Owner C W Booth & Mark E Smith **Bred** Miss Mary Kelly **Trained** Over Norton, Oxon

FOCUS
Only four to consider in a modest staying novices' hurdle for the course. The form is rated around the second and third.

2063 ROYAL GLOUCESTERSHIRE HUSSARS NOVICES' CHASE 2m 3f 166y
4:30 (4:32) (Class 2) 4-Y-O+ **£12,627** (£3,811; £1,963; £1,039)

Form RPR

1-13 **1** **Art Mauresque (FR)**[15] 1840 5-11-11 144.................. NickScholfield 154+
(Paul Nicholls) *lw: led tl 4th: content to trck ldr gng wl after tl breezed ahd after 2 out: sn clr: comf* **5/1**[3]

611- **2** *8* **Double Shuffle (IRE)**[212] 4999 5-11-3 0.................. PaddyBrennan 136
(Tom George) *2nd tl led 4th: pushed along bef 2 out and nt fluent: sn hdd and drvn: easily outpcd* **20/1**

122- **3** *½* **Parlour Games**[196] 5271 7-11-3 0.................. AidanColeman 137+
(John Ferguson) *settled off the pce in last pair: j. deliberately 7th: 7 l 3rd at 12th: rdn and effrt bef 2 out: making no imp whn hit last* **7/4**[2]

3P-5 **4** *3¾* **Azorian (IRE)**[13] 1878 7-11-8 137..................(t) BarryGeraghty 138
(Gordon Elliott, Ire) *w'like: rn in snatches: last pair: looked to be struggling 8th: 12 l last at 12th: tried to rally bef next: rdn and lost tch tamely and j. deliberately 3 out* **9/1**

11-1 **U** **Long House Hall (IRE)**[161] 329 7-11-8 144..................(t) HarrySkelton
(Dan Skelton) *lw: 3rd whn blnd and uns rdr 4th: fell heavily whn loose 2 out* **11/8**[1]

4m 54.1s (294.10) **Going Correction** 0.0s/f (Good) **5** Ran SP% **109.9**
Speed ratings (Par 109): **120,116,116,115,**
CSF £57.40 TOTE £5.10: £2.30, £2.80; EX 45.20 Trifecta £82.80.
Owner Mrs Johnny de la Hey **Bred** Michel Parreau-Delhote **Trained** Ditcheat, Somerset

FOCUS
A fair novice contest, albeit one shorn of some of its interest when the well-supported favourite crashed out early. All four remaining runners held a chance of sorts jumping two out after a moderate early gallop. The winner set the standard and produced a small step up.

2064 DOWNLOAD WINNER.CO.UK APP NOW H'CAP HURDLE (9 hdls 1 omitted) 2m 5f 26y
5:05 (5:07) (Class 3) (0-140,139) 3-Y-O+
£7,507 (£2,217; £1,108; £554; £277; £139)

Form RPR

1214 **1** **Towering (IRE)**[70] 1262 6-10-7 **120**.................. NicodeBoinville 125+
(Nicky Henderson) *lw: cl up: looked to be gng wl 3 out but sn rdn: 4th next: wnt 2nd at last: cajoled along and wl-timed run to get up cl home* **10/1**

2UF6 **2** *nk* **Mile House (IRE)**[21] 1754 7-10-9 **129**.................. CiaranGethings(7) 133
(Robert Stephens) *kpt away fr rest at s: led at stdy gallop: 4 l clr 2 out tl last: sn rdn: styd on steadily tl ct cl home* **25/1**

F0-6 **3** *hd* **Here's Herbie**[23] 1719 7-9-13 **115**..................(t) LucyGardner(3) 120+
(Sue Gardner) *lw: midfield: effrt on ins to go 3rd 2 out: chal after last: urged along and ev ch fnl 100yds tl no ex fnl strides* **15/2**[2]

10-2 **4** *shd* **Dancing Meadows (IRE)**[29] 1649 5-10-7 **120**.................. NoelFehily 125+
(Gordon Elliott, Ire) *hld up in rr: hmpd 5th: effrt next: rdn 2 out: disputing 4th whn hit last: styd on u.p fnl 100yds* **4/1**[1]

503/ **5** *hd* **Face Value**[37] 1388 7-10-0 **120**..................(p) DonaghMeyler(7) 124
(Adrian McGuinness, Ire) *prom: wnt 2nd wl bef 3 out: chsd ldr tl 3rd at last: kpt on in driving fin but a jst hld* **15/2**[2]

2-12 **6** *nk* **Sky Khan**[31] 1633 6-10-13 **129**..................(p) GrahamWatters(3) 132
(Lucinda Russell) *bhd: cajoled along and effrt after 2 out: styd on after last but a had too much to do* **16/1**

04-0 **7** *6* **Saffron Wells (IRE)**[14] 1848 7-11-6 **133**.................. TrevorWhelan 131
(Neil King) *midfield: rdn 2 out: sn no ex* **10/1**

132- **8** *2* **Slim Pickens (IRE)**[447] 1156 7-11-0 **127**.................. WillKennedy 125
(Dr Richard Newland) *bhd: stmbld bnd after 3rd: sme prog after 3 out: nvr got in a blow* **8/1**[3]

1P42 **9** *15* **Detroit Blues**[45] 1521 5-10-5 **118**..................(t) SamTwiston-Davies 101
(Jamie Snowden) *midfield: rdn 3 out: sn btn* **25/1**

130- **10** *5* **Seaviper (IRE)**[189] 5394 6-10-9 **127**.................. DanielHiskett(5) 105
(Richard Phillips) *cl up tl rdn and wknd after 3 out* **25/1**

134- **11** *4* **Generous Ransom (IRE)**[182] 5540 7-11-8 **135**..........(p) PaddyBrennan 109
(Nick Gifford) *chsd ldrs tl drvn and fdd wl bef 3 out: t.o next* **16/1**

2-03 **12** *3* **Thomas Crapper**[17] 1815 8-11-12 **139**.................. CharliePoste 112
(Robin Dickin) *lw: hld up and bhd: hmpd 5th: effrt bef 3 out: sn rdn and dropped out qckly: t.o* **10/1**

210- **13** *4½* **Arabian Revolution**[227] 4707 4-11-8 **135**.................. AidanColeman 103
(John Ferguson) *hld up towards rr: effrt 3 out: rdn next: sn btn: t.o* **12/1**

1U4- **14** *3¾* **Ardkilly Witness (IRE)**[245] 4361 9-11-7 **134**..................(t) BrendanPowell 98
(Jamie Snowden) *pressed ldr tl rdn and lost pl wl bef 3 out: t.o* **25/1**

123- **S** **Baku Bay (IRE)**[230] 4648 7-10-10 **123**.................. GavinSheehan
(Ali Stronge) *bhd whn slipped up wl bef 3 out* **14/1**

1P1- **F** **Morello Royale (IRE)**[187] 5430 5-11-8 **135**..................(t) DarylJacob
(Colin Tizzard) *cl up tl fell 5th* **20/1**

5m 13.5s (0.10) **Going Correction** -0.25s/f (Good)
WFA 4 from 5yo+ 10lb **16** Ran SP% **128.2**
Speed ratings (Par 107): **89,88,88,88,88 88,86,85,79,77 76,75,73,72,**
CSF £250.74 CT £1974.84 TOTE £12.10: £3.20, £5.60, £2.80, £2.20; EX 398.60 Trifecta £3420.20 Part won..
Owner Middleham Park Racing LIX **Bred** Liam O'Byrne **Trained** Upper Lambourn, Berks
■ Stewards' Enquiry : Donagh Meyler four-day ban: use of whip (7-10 Nov)

FOCUS
The first in the straight was omitted due to low sun. A moderate early gallop and bunch finish, with barely a couple of lengths separating the first six. A step up from the winner, with the fourth arguably unlucky.\n\x\x The first in the straight was omitted due to low sun. A moderate early gallop and bunch finish, with barely a couple of lengths separating the first six. A step up from the winner, with the fourth arguably unlucky.\n\x\x The first in the straight was omitted due to low sun. A moderate early gallop and bunch finish, with barely a couple of lengths separating the first six. A step up from the winner, with the fourth arguably unlucky.

2065 CHELTENHAM CLUB STANDARD OPEN NATIONAL HUNT FLAT RACE 2m 87y
5:40 (5:42) (Class 3) 4-6-Y-O **£6,498** (£1,908; £954; £477)

Form RPR

4- **1** **Aurillac (FR)**[195] 5292 5-11-0 0.................. LeightonAspell 117
(Rebecca Curtis) *tall: rngy: mde all: set stdy pce: pushed along over 1f out: fnd plenty and a holding chals after* **16/1**

1 **2** *1* **Air Horse One**[172] 124 4-11-7 0.................. NoelFehily 123
(Harry Fry) *small: athletic: prom: chsd wnr fr 1/2-way: rdn wl over 1f out: kpt on gamely but a hld* **11/1**

2- **3** *1¾* **High Bridge**[260] 4073 4-11-0 0.................. AidanColeman 115
(John Ferguson) *tall: lengthy: lw: settled towards rr: n.m.r 6f out: effrt over 2f out: sn rdn and sltly outpcd: styng on steadily ins fnl f* **5/4**[1]

4 **4** *4½* **Colin's Sister**[171] 152 4-10-4 0.................. ConorShoemark(3) 103
(Fergal O'Brien) *rngy: scopy: leggy: bhd: hdwy over 2f out: styd on nicely ins fnl f: promising* **50/1**

5 *3½* **Some Are Lucky (IRE)**[189] 4-11-0 0.................. PaddyBrennan 107
(Tom George) *str: midfield: rdn over 2f out: rn green and sn outpcd: kpt on again ins fnl f* **25/1**

1 **6** *½* **Fountains Windfall**[143] 602 5-11-7 0.................. BarryGeraghty 113
(Anthony Honeyball) *w'like: midfield: rdn and effrt over 2f out: sn styng on at same pce* **7/2**[2]

0-2 **7** *1* **Vivas (FR)**[21] 1758 4-11-0 0.................. KielanWoods 105
(Charlie Longsdon) *w'like: midfield: rdn 2f out: sn btn* **16/1**

61- **8** *2¾* **Chic Theatre (IRE)**[257] 4135 5-11-4 0.................. KieronEdgar(3) 110
(David Pipe) *prom: rdn wl over 1f out: wknd 1f out* **7/1**[3]

9 *3¼* **Hardtorock (IRE)**[99] 1029 6-11-0 0.................. DarylJacob 99
(Liam Corcoran) *w'like: a bhd: pushed along and btn 4f out* **50/1**

1-6 **10** *2¾* **Cougar Kid (IRE)**[143] 601 4-11-7 0.................. SamTwiston-Davies 103
(Philip Hide) *unf: midfield: rdn 3f out: sn wknd* **33/1**

40- **11** *11* **Windy Writer (IRE)**[238] 4485 5-11-0 0.................. PeterCarberry 85
(Shaun Lycett) *w'like: nvr bttr than midfield: rdn 6f out: fdd 3f out: t.o* **100/1**

P **Close Escape (IRE)**[202] 4-11-0 0.................. NicodeBoinville
(Nicky Henderson) *wl made: plld v hrd and racd awkwardly: prom for 10f: lost pl down hill: t.o and p.u ins fnl f* **11/1**

3m 53.9s (-2.50) **Going Correction** -0.25s/f (Good)
WFA 4 from 5yo+ 9lb **12** Ran SP% **119.3**
Speed ratings: **96,95,94,92,90 90,89,88,86,85 80,**
CSF £174.67 TOTE £21.40: £4.40, £2.70, £1.10; EX 216.80 Trifecta £539.30.
Owner D Mossop, P John & R White **Bred** Mme J Besnouin & J Besnouin **Trained** Newport, Pembrokeshire

FOCUS
A race taken by subsequent Champion Bumper hero Moon Racer twelve months previously, and this renewal should again produce winners. The early pace was slow and it's not an easy race to put a figure on.
T/Jkpt: Not won. Consolation placepot £320.60. Pool: £2130.49 - 4.85 winning units. T/Plt: £557.90 to a £1 stake. Pool: £181,136.73 - 236.98 winning units. T/Qpdt: £78.50 to a £1 stake. Pool: £11,348.58 - 106.90 winning units. **Iain Mackenzie**

[1773] KELSO (L-H)
Saturday, October 24

OFFICIAL GOING: Good (good to soft in places; 6.8)
Wind: Breezy, half against Weather: Cloudy

2066 CARNACRACK "NATIONAL HUNT" MAIDEN HURDLE (8 hdls) 2m 51y
1:55 (1:55) (Class 4) 4-Y-O+ **£3,249** (£954; £477; £238)

Form RPR

21- **1** **Big River (IRE)**[217] 4915 5-11-0 0.................. PeterBuchanan 111+
(Lucinda Russell) *trckd ldrs: effrt and wnt 2nd 2 out: led run-in: rdn and styd on strly* **13/8**[1]

2 *2* **Just Georgie**[201] 5218 5-11-0 0.................. DannyCook 108
(Sue Smith) *cl up: led after 4th: rdn 2 out: hdd run-in: kpt on same pce towards fin* **4/1**[2]

5-15 **3** 1½ **Petapenko**[30] [1640] 4-11-0 0..........(b) BrianHughes 107
(Malcolm Jefferson) *prom: wnt 2nd 4 out to 2 out: pushed along whn nt fluent last: kpt on same pce* **14/1**

34P- **4** 2 **Chain Of Beacons**[214] [4970] 6-10-11 0.......... DerekFox(3) 104
(Sandy Thomson) *hld up: stdy hdwy after 4 out: effrt and pushed along 2 out: kpt on same pce fr last* **10/1**

05-0 **5** 1¾ **Herecomesnelson (IRE)**[171] [144] 6-10-9 0.......... CallumBewley(5) 102
(Katie Scott) *t.k.h: hld up: hdwy and prom 1/2-way: rdn and outpcd 2 out: n.d after* **100/1**

5-43 **6** hd **Cosmic Tigress**[25] [1684] 4-10-7 0.......... SeanBowen 96
(John Quinn) *hld up on outside: hmpd 2nd: outpcd bef 3 out: rallied whn j.lft last: kpt on: no imp* **13/2**[3]

54-2 **7** 2½ **Towerburn (IRE)**[175] [79] 6-10-7 0.......... JamieHamilton(7) 100
(Alison Hamilton) *chsd ldrs: outpcd after 3 out: sn rdn: no imp fr next* **9/1**

65 **8** 5 **Baysbrown (IRE)**[12] [1886] 5-11-0 0.......... BrianHarding 95
(Nicky Richards) *hld up: pushed along after 3 out: struggling fr next* **10/1**

6 **9** 1 **Whatsthestoryman (IRE)**[14] [1852] 7-11-0 0..........(t) SeanQuinlan 94
(Katie Scott) *hld up: rdn and outpcd 3 out: btn next* **80/1**

502- **10** 4 **Valnamixe Du Mee (FR)**[193] [5327] 6-10-11 102.......... JohnKington(3) 91
(Kenny Johnson) *led: j.rt and hit 4th: sn hdd: nt fluent next: wknd fr 3 out* **18/1**

3-50 **11** ½ **Tickanrun (IRE)**[12] [1886] 5-10-9 0.......... DiarmuidO'Regan(5) 89
(Chris Grant) *trckd ldrs: lost pl 4th: struggling fr 3 out* **100/1**

60-5 **12** ¾ **Palermo Don**[23] [1718] 5-11-0 0..........(t) HenryBrooke 92
(Donald McCain) *t.k.h: hld up on ins: rdn along bef 2 out: sn wknd* **16/1**

3m 59.9s (-1.90) **Going Correction** -0.40s/f (Good)
WFA 4 from 5yo+ 9lb **12** Ran SP% **120.6**
Speed ratings (Par 105): **88,87,86,85,84 84,83,80,80,78 77,77**
CSF £8.04 TOTE £2.80: £1.50, £1.90, £4.30; EX 7.10 Trifecta £158.10.
Owner Two Black Labs **Bred** J R Curran **Trained** Arlary, Perth & Kinross

FOCUS
All bends moved out a further 2m from inner line. Races 1 & 4 increased by 18yds, races 2 & 3 by 9yds and races 5 & 6 by 28yds. The overall form of this maiden hurdle has the potential to be a little misleading, the pace steady until past halfway, but the leading pair are both nice prospects, particularly as they are unlikely to be seen to maximum effect until going over further. A few of these may be flattered.

2067 CLIFFORD & MARTIN FIRTH MEMORIAL NOVICES' CHASE (17 fncs) 2m 7f 96y
2:30 (2:30) (Class 4) 4-Y-0+ **£4,548** (£1,335; £667; £333)

Form RPR

11P- **1** **One For Arthur (IRE)**[197] [5254] 6-11-0 0.......... PeterBuchanan 142+
(Lucinda Russell) *trckd ldrs: hdwy to ld after 2 out: pushed out fr last* **4/1**[3]

135- **2** 2 **Seldom Inn**[238] [4482] 7-11-0 0.......... BrianHughes 137
(Sandy Thomson) *prom: wnt 2nd after 10th: effrt bef 2 out: chsd wnr last: kpt on: no imp* **9/2**

2/2- **3** 3¾ **Blakemount (IRE)**[357] [2206] 7-11-0 0.......... DannyCook 136
(Sue Smith) *led: nt fluent and pushed along 3 out: j.rt 2 out: sn hdd: lost 2nd and one pce last: bttr for r* **3/1**[2]

11-4 **4** 4½ **Shubaat**[13] [1867] 8-11-0 0.......... TomCannon 130
(John Ferguson) *trckd ldrs on outside: rdn along 4 out: edgd lft and wknd fr 2 out* **9/2**

23-4 **5** 31 **Racing Europe (IRE)**[10] [1903] 6-11-0 0.......... SeanBowen 110
(Brian Ellison) *nt fluent on occasions: hld up: struggling 11th: no ch fr 4 out* **15/8**[1]

P24- **6** 62 **Landecker (IRE)**[184] [5491] 7-10-9 0.......... StephenMulqueen(5) 91
(N W Alexander) *nt jump wl: hld up in tch: hit and rdn 12th: rallied: outpcd whn mstke 3 out: sn wknd: no ch whn blnd last: virtually p.u* **20/1**

P **P** **Coote Street (IRE)**[101] [1011] 7-10-7 0.......... RyanDay(7)
(Iain Jardine) *bhd: struggling fr 10th: lost tch and p.u bef 2 out* **150/1**

322- **U** **U Name It (IRE)**[190] [5362] 7-10-9 0.......... CallumBewley(5)
(R Mike Smith) *trcking ldrs whn blnd and uns rdr 6th* **14/1**

5m 55.6s (-12.40) **Going Correction** -0.30s/f (Good) **8** Ran SP% **128.2**
Speed ratings (Par 105): **109,108,107,105,94 73, ,**
CSF £25.76 TOTE £3.90: £1.40, £2.60, £1.30; EX 23.90 Trifecta £108.50.
Owner Two Golf Widows **Bred** J P Dwan **Trained** Arlary, Perth & Kinross
■ Stewards' Enquiry : Danny Cook two-day ban: careless riding (7-8 Nov)
Sean Bowen jockey said that the gelding jumped deliberately throughout

FOCUS
A useful novice chase from which a few winners are likely to emerge in the coming weeks. The first two stepped up on the best of their hurdles form.

2068 EDF-ER H'CAP CHASE (19 fncs) 3m 2f 39y
3:05 (3:05) (Class 3) (0-140,138) 4-Y-0+ **£11,046** (£3,243; £1,621; £810)

Form RPR

2134 **1** **Gold Futures (IRE)**[28] [1658] 6-11-12 **138**.......... BrianHarding 146+
(Nicky Richards) *hld up: smooth hdwy bef 4 out: shkn up to ld between last 2: hld on wl u.p run-in* **15/8**[1]

3P4- **2** 1 **Straidnahanna (IRE)**[189] [5388] 6-11-1 **127**.......... DannyCook 135+
(Sue Smith) *chsd ldrs: led 4 out: gd jump next: rdn bef 2 out: hdd between last 2: rallied: hld nr fin* **7/2**[3]

-104 **3** 10 **Ballyben (IRE)**[31] [1632] 7-10-5 **120**..........(p) DerekFox(3) 118
(Lucinda Russell) *chsd ldrs: ev ch briefly bef 4 out: rdn and outpcd by first two fr 2 out* **10/3**[2]

1064 **4** 1¾ **Valleyofmilan (IRE)**[20] [1784] 8-10-5 **122**.......... JamesCowley(5) 119
(Donald McCain) *hld up: stdy hdwy bef 4 out: pushed along whn nt fluent and outpcd next: sn n.d* **16/1**

1010 **5** 11 **Chicago Outfit (IRE)**[14] [1856] 10-10-10 **127**..........(p) JonathonBewley(5) 115
(George Bewley) *led to 4 out: rdn along bef next: wknd bef 2 out* **14/1**

1P1- **6** 4½ **William Money (IRE)**[203] [5138] 8-10-13 **130**.......... DiarmuidO'Regan(5) 112
(Chris Grant) *hld up in last pl: outpcd bef 4 out: nvr on terms* **14/1**

220- **F** **Harry The Viking**[189] [5392] 10-11-6 **132**..........(p) BrianHughes
(Sandy Thomson) *w ldr: mstke and lost pl 5 out: 9 l down and struggling whn fell 3 out* **6/1**

6m 40.0s (-7.20) **Going Correction** -0.30s/f (Good) **7** Ran SP% **113.6**
Speed ratings (Par 107): **99,98,95,95,91 90,**
CSF £9.14 TOTE £2.40: £1.60, £3.00; EX 10.00 Trifecta £32.10.
Owner Mrs C A Torkington **Bred** D W Macauley **Trained** Greystoke, Cumbria

FOCUS
A pretty smart effort from the winner to defy top weight, the leading pair coming nicely clear. The race didn't really begin in earnest until the final circuit. There's a case for rating the form a bit higher.

2069 SIR MAXWELL HARPER GOW MEMORIAL H'CAP HURDLE (8 hdls) 2m 51y
3:40 (3:40) (Class 4) (0-115,115) 3-Y-0+ **£3,898** (£1,144; £572; £286)

Form RPR

305- **1** **Alizee De Janeiro (FR)**[232] [4603] 5-10-1 **90**.......... PeterBuchanan 96+
(Lucinda Russell) *hld up in tch: hdwy 2 out: led last: rdn clr* **8/1**

-554 **2** 3¾ **Claude Carter**[58] [1369] 11-10-10 **102**..........(p) CallumWhillans(3) 103
(Alistair Whillans) *prom: rdn and outpcd after 3 out: rallied next: chsd wnr run-in: kpt on: no imp* **10/1**

1123 **3** ½ **Baraboy (IRE)**[104] [962] 5-10-9 **105**.......... LorcanMurtagh(7) 107
(Barry Murtagh) *hld up: smooth hdwy to chse ldrs bef 2 out: led briefly between last 2: one pce run-in* **17/2**

5-12 **4** 4 **Mighty Whitey (IRE)**[20] [1773] 9-11-9 **115**..........(t) DerekFox(3) 113
(Noel C Kelly, Ire) *nt fluent on occasions: led: rdn and hdd between last 2: sn outpcd* **4/1**[1]

3-64 **5** 2½ **Beechroad Ally (IRE)**[20] [1774] 6-10-3 **99**..........(t) MissRMcDonald(7) 94
(Sandy Thomson) *chsd ldrs: lost pl after 3 out: rallied last: kpt on: no imp* **10/1**

2263 **6** 5 **Muwalla**[10] [1904] 8-10-8 **102**..........(t) CallumBewley(5) 92
(Lisa Harrison) *prom: effrt bef 2 out: wknd between last 2* **5/1**[2]

P30- **7** shd **Another Mattie (IRE)**[217] [4914] 8-11-3 **106**..........(t) BrianHarding 96
(N W Alexander) *hld up: pushed along and outpcd after 3 out: wknd bef next* **15/2**[3]

554P **8** 5 **Running Brook (IRE)**[30] [1638] 8-11-1 **107**.......... AdamNicol(3) 93
(R Mike Smith) *hld up in tch on outside: struggling bef 2 out: sn btn* **20/1**

02P/ **9** 4½ **Another For Joe**[26] [2325] 7-10-5 **94**.......... HenryBrooke 76
(Jim Goldie) *chsd ldrs tl wknd appr 2 out* **8/1**

413- **10** 9 **Parc Des Princes (USA)**[418] [1422] 9-10-13 **105**.......... CraigNichol(3) 78
(Nicky Richards) *bhd: struggling after 3rd: nvr on terms* **8/1**

46/P **P** **Rupert Bear**[22] [1738] 9-10-9 **103**.......... MissCWalton(5)
(James Walton) *bhd: struggling 1/2-way: sn lost tch: t.o whn p.u bef 2 out* **40/1**

3m 53.1s (-8.70) **Going Correction** -0.40s/f (Good) **11** Ran SP% **117.7**
Speed ratings (Par 105): **105,103,102,100,99 97,97,94,92,87**
CSF £84.88 CT £703.32 TOTE £8.30: £2.70, £3.80, £2.30; EX 124.40 Trifecta £314.10 Part won..
Owner Ms Deborah Thomson **Bred** J Regereau, L Regereau & S Regereau **Trained** Arlary, Perth & Kinross

FOCUS
A fair handicap which was run at a good pace. A small pb from the winner, the next two to their marks.

2070 ERIC GILLIE TRANSPORTING HORSES 40 YEARS NOVICES' HURDLE (11 hdls) 2m 6f 151y
4:15 (4:15) (Class 4) 4-Y-0+ **£3,898** (£1,144; £572; £286)

Form RPR

13-1 **1** **Oscar Blue (IRE)**[14] [1852] 5-11-5 0.......... SeanBowen 119
(Brian Ellison) *mde all at stdy gallop: rdn and hrd pressed 2 out: rdr dropped whip run-in: hld on gamely nr fin* **10/11**[1]

2 nk **Sunny West (IRE)**[221] [4839] 6-10-12 0.......... DannyCook 113
(Sue Smith) *nt fluent on occasions: hld up in tch: stdy hdwy whn hit 3 out: impr to chal next: edgd lft run-in: kpt on: hld cl home* **25/1**

1-23 **3** 1¾ **Major Ivan (IRE)**[30] [1635] 6-11-5 127.......... BrianHughes 119
(Malcolm Jefferson) *trckd ldrs: wnt 2nd 3 out to bef next: sn pushed along and edgd lft: kpt on same pce bef last* **5/4**[2]

460- **4** 4½ **Ha'penny Woods (IRE)**[211] [5009] 5-10-7 108.......... DiarmuidO'Regan(5) 106
(Chris Grant) *hld up in tch: rdn and outpcd bef 2 out: hld whn nt fluent last* **22/1**

00-3 **5** 40 **John Williams (IRE)**[170] [155] 6-10-9 0.......... DerekFox(3) 70
(Sandy Thomson) *chsd wnr to 3 out: rdn and wknd qckly bef next* **20/1**[3]

506- **6** 43 **Lucydoli**[175] 6-9-12 0.......... SamColtherd(7) 24
(Stuart Coltherd) *mstkes in rr: lost tch fr 1/2-way: t.o* **100/1**

5m 34.9s (-6.10) **Going Correction** -0.40s/f (Good) **6** Ran SP% **110.8**
Speed ratings (Par 105): **94,93,93,91,77 62**
CSF £19.90 TOTE £1.60: £1.30, £6.80; EX 22.30 Trifecta £39.70.
Owner P J Martin **Bred** Mary Fanning McCormack **Trained** Norton, N Yorks

FOCUS
A fairly useful staying novice. The fourth helps set the level.

2071 B.A.R.K. CONDITIONAL JOCKEYS' TRAINING SERIES H'CAP HURDLE (PART OF THE RACING EXCELLENCE) (10 hdls 1 omitted) 2m 6f 151y
4:50 (4:50) (Class 5) (0-100,100) 4-Y-0+ **£3,249** (£954; £477; £238)

Form RPR

06 **1** **Andhaar**[31] [1633] 9-11-7 **100**.......... BlairCampbell(5) 103+
(N W Alexander) *hld up: stdy hdwy after 3 out (usual 4 out): chal bef omitted 2 out: led last: drifted lft run-in: pushed clr* **12/1**

-0P0 **2** 7 **Willie Hall**[151] [484] 11-10-7 **86**.......... FinianO'Toole(5) 83
(Lisa Harrison) *hld up: smooth hdwy to ld bef omitted 2 out: hdd and rdn last: sn no ex* **9/2**[3]

6/4- **3** 3½ **Marrakech Trader (NZ)**[535] [144] 8-11-0 **93**.......... LorcanMurtagh(5) 87
(Rose Dobbin) *t.k.h early: prom: outpcd 4 out (usual 5 out): rallied to chse ldrs bef omitted 2 out: outpcd fr last* **3/1**[1]

PP25 **4** 1¼ **Winter Alchemy (IRE)**[20] [1778] 10-10-9 **90**.......... JackCollins(7) 82
(Nicky Richards) *led to 4 out (usual 5 out): outpcd after next: plugged on fr last: nvr able to chal* **4/1**[2]

4555 **5** ¾ **Burnt Sienna (IRE)**[12] [1887] 5-11-0 **88**..........(tp) FreddieMitchell 81
(Noel C Kelly, Ire) *hld up: mstke 3 out (usual 4 out): outpcd next: sme late hdwy: nvr on terms* **4/1**[2]

0-00 **6** ½ **Just My Luke**[14] [1852] 6-9-11 **74** oh1..........(t) JamesCorbett(3) 66
(Susan Corbett) *t.k.h early: hld up in tch: rdn and outpcd bef omitted 2 out: sn n.d* **16/1**

0F-P **7** 7 **Petre' Island (IRE)**[172] [136] 6-10-2 **79**.......... ThomasDowson(3) 64
(Katie Scott) *w ldr: led 4 out (usual 5 out): hdd bef omitted 2 out: sn wknd* **10/1**

202P **8** *4* **The Ice Factor**[115] 872 7-11-1 89........................(p) JamieHamilton 71
(Alison Hamilton) *trckd ldrs: nt fluent 2nd: struggling bef omitted 2 out: sn wknd* **12/1**

5m 41.4s (0.40) **Going Correction** -0.40s/f (Good) **8** Ran SP% **113.5**
Speed ratings (Par 103): **83,80,79,78,78 78,76,74**
CSF £64.65 CT £205.73 TOTE £14.40: £3.60, £1.90, £1.40; EX 68.60 Trifecta £407.30 Part won..
Owner Bissett Racing **Bred** Shadwell Estate Company Limited **Trained** Kinneston, Perth & Kinross

FOCUS
Very much run-of-the-mill fare. The pace looked pretty sedate for a long way, the tempo not increasing until the final circuit. The winner may still be capable of better.
T/Plt: £72.60 to a £1 stake. Pool: £42,732.76 - 429.47 winning units. T/Qpdt: £32.30 to a £1 stake. Pool: £3,139.30 - 71.90 winning units. **Richard Young**

2072 - 2079a (Foreign Racing) - See Raceform Interactive

705
AINTREE (L-H)
Sunday, October 25

OFFICIAL GOING: Good (good to soft in places on the mildmay course; mildmay 7.1, hdl 7.4)
Wind: Light, across Weather: Overcast

2080 CRABBIE'S GRAND NATIONAL 2016 ON SALE MAIDEN HURDLE (11 hdls) 2m 4f
1:25 (1:25) (Class 4) 4-Y-O+ **£5,198** (£1,526; £763; £381)

Form RPR
5- **1** **Perform (IRE)**[225] 4769 6-11-0 0........................ RichardJohnson 136+
(Philip Hobbs) *hld up: hdwy gng wl appr 2 out: sn chalng: led bef last: rdn out and r.o wl fnl 100yds* **10/3**[2]

2- **2** *2 ¾* **Knockgraffon (IRE)**[221] 4859 5-11-0 0........................ HarrySkelton 132+
(Dan Skelton) *mainly in midfield early: lft 3rd 6th: chalng fr 2 out: nt qckn fnl 100yds: hld towards fin* **7/2**[3]

3 *3* **American (FR)**[330] 5-11-0 0........................ NoelFehily 128
(Harry Fry) *trckd ldrs: lft in 2nd 6th: led 2 out: hdd bef last: outpcd by front two 1f out on run-in: sn edgd rt: styd on same pce* **3/1**[1]

642- **4** *15* **Echo Springs**[190] 5396 5-11-0 110........................ AdrianLane 113
(Danielle McCormick) *racd keenly: lft after 1st: rdn and hdd 2 out: wknd bef last* **17/2**

15-5 **5** *28* **Going For Broke (IRE)**[16] 1837 5-11-0 0........................ BarryGeraghty 87
(Rebecca Curtis) *hld up: niggled along after 4 out: sn outpcd: lft bhd whn hit 2 out* **3/1**[1]

33 **6** *5* **Medieval Bishop (IRE)**[21] 1780 6-10-7 110........................ JoshWall(7) 81
(Tony Forbes) *hld up in rr: hmpd 7th: pushed along after 4 out: sn outpcd: lft bhd whn hit 2 out* **50/1**

F **Swizzler (IRE)**[175] 6-11-0 0........................ WillKennedy
(Ian Williams) *racd keenly: led: hdd after 1st: chsd ldr after: lost 2nd 6th: stl in 3rd pl whn fell 7th* **20/1**

4m 49.6s (-11.10) **Going Correction** -0.45s/f (Good) **7** Ran SP% **112.5**
Speed ratings (Par 105): **104,102,101,95,84 82,**
CSF £15.18 TOTE £3.60: £2.10, £1.90; EX 12.80 Trifecta £39.60.
Owner Merry Old Souls **Bred** Denis Cleary **Trained** Withycombe, Somerset

FOCUS
All bends and hurdles on the inside, and cool, sunny conditions following a dry night. This well-run novices' hurdle saw three potentially very nice recruits jump the last virtually in unison and finish clear. They look decent but this isn't an easy race to put a figure on.

2081 LIVERPOOL HORSE SHOW JANUARY 2016 CONDITIONAL JOCKEYS' H'CAP HURDLE (13 hdls) 3m 149y
1:55 (1:55) (Class 3) (0-125,125) 4-Y-O+ **£4,052** (£4,052; £924; £462; £231; £116)

Form RPR
214- **1** **Optimistic Bias (IRE)**[193] 5343 6-10-12 119........................ PatrickCowley(8) 127+
(Jonjo O'Neill) *hld up in midfield: hdwy 9th: led appr 2 out: rdn whn pressed bef last: hdd narrowly fnl 150yds: rallied nr fin and got up to dispute ld on line* **15/8**[1]

41-2 **1** *dht* **Sykes (IRE)**[27] 1675 6-10-13 118........................ CiaranGethings(6) 126+
(Philip Hobbs) *hld up in midfield: hdwy appr 3 out: gng wl whn chalng 2 out: led narrowly fnl 150yds: jnd on line* **5/2**[2]

6P-5 **3** *2 ¾* **Tantamount**[23] 1742 6-10-11 113........................(t) DerekFox(3) 119
(Lucinda Russell) *hld up in rr: hdwy appr 2 out: chsd front pair appr last: styd on u.p run-in but no real imp* **10/1**

54-5 **4** *16* **Carn Rock**[11] 1906 7-10-6 108........................ MikeyHamill(3) 100
(Michael Gates) *hld up: effrt 3 out: chsng ldrs but one pce after 2 out: sn n.d* **5/1**[3]

22-P **5** *nk* **Gone Forever**[170] 185 5-11-6 125........................ CraigGallagher(6) 116
(Brian Ellison) *midfield: hdwy 9th: rdn after 4 out: ev ch fr 3 out: stl chalng 2 out: no ex after last* **9/1**

234/ **6** *49* **Benefit Of Youth (IRE)**[561] 8-10-8 115........................ GeorgeBlackwell(8) 62
(Tim Vaughan) *prom: led appr 4 out: rdn and hdd bef 2 out: wknd between last 2* **40/1**

-325 **7** *3 ¾* **Cowslip**[15] 1856 6-11-7 123........................ RyanDay(3) 67
(George Moore) *prom: ev ch 3 out: wknd between last 2* **17/2**

4P/ **P** **Come To The Party (IRE)**[162] 12-11-2 115........................(p) DanielHiskett
(Harry Chisman) *led: pushed along and hdd appr 4 out: wknd long bef 3 out: t.o whn p.u bef last* **66/1**

6m 0.2s (-16.10) **Going Correction** -0.45s/f (Good) **8** Ran SP% **113.6**
Speed ratings (Par 107): **107,107,106,101,100 85,84,**
WIN: £1.50 Optimistic Bias, £1.50 Sykes; PL: £1.30 Optimistic Bias, £1.50 Sykes, £2.50 Tantamount; Exacta: OB&S £4.30, S&OB £4.50; CSF: OB&S £3.57, S&OB £3.87 Tricast: OB&S&T £16.97, S&OB&T £18.31.
Owner Bradley Partnership **Bred** Pat Browne **Trained** Withycombe, Somerset
Owner Optimistic Four **Bred** David Foy **Trained** Cheltenham, Gloucs

FOCUS
All bar one of these still held a chance in this tight staying handicap turning in following a steady early gallop, but the two most unexposed competitors finished both clear and inseparable. Both were on the upgrade under claimers and both are open to further improvement.

2082 SIMON AND LOUISE'S SILVER ANNIVERSARY VETERANS' H'CAP CHASE (LEG 7 OF THE VETERANS' CHASE SERIES) (19 fncs) 3m 210y
2:30 (2:31) (Class 2) (0-150,148) 10-Y-O+ **£18,768** (£5,544; £2,772; £1,386; £693; £34815)

U3-0 **1** **Benbens (IRE)**[14] 1871 10-11-0 139........................ RyanHatch(3) 146+
(Nigel Twiston-Davies) *midfield: hdwy 11th: chalng 3 out: led appr 2 out: drvn out and styd on wl to draw clr ins fnl 110yds* **5/1**

2152 **2** *5* **Russian Regent (IRE)**[22] 1764 11-10-10 132........................ RichardJohnson 135
(Gordon Elliott, Ire) *nt a fluent: hld up: hdwy after 15th: big effrt 2 out: wnt 2nd appr last: no imp fnl 110yds* **12/1**

30-1 **3** *4* **Maggio (FR)**[116] 868 10-11-9 145........................(t) BrianHughes 142
(Patrick Griffin, Ire) *a.p: chalng 3 out: stl there 2 out: rdn and nt qckn bef last: no ex run-in* **10/1**

12-3 **4** *10* **Any Currency (IRE)**[164] 313 12-10-10 132........................(p) AidanColeman 120
(Martin Keighley) *prom: lost pl 11th: rdn bef 14th: rallied 15th: plugged on at one pce after 2 out* **13/2**

45-0 **5** *6* **Mwaleshi**[163] 318 10-10-13 135........................ SeanQuinlan 120
(Sue Smith) *j.rt: led: hdd appr 2 out: wl btn bef last* **14/1**

-311 **6** *38* **Danimix (IRE)**[14] 1871 10-11-1 137........................(t) SeanBowen 100
(Peter Bowen) *hld up: nt fluent 4th: in tch whn mstke 13th: rdn and wknd bef 4 out: eased whn wl btn bef last: lost rt hind shoe* **4/1**[2]

110- **P** **Lie Forrit (IRE)**[190] 5392 11-11-12 148........................ PeterBuchanan
(Lucinda Russell) *midfield early: lost pl 4th: detached after 7th: lost tch 10th: t.o whn p.u bef 12th* **9/2**[3]

PFP- **P** **Ely Brown (IRE)**[183] 5538 10-10-13 135........................(tp) NoelFehily
(Charlie Longsdon) *prom: lost pl 12th: bhd whn hit 15th: t.o whn p.u bef 4 out* **7/2**[1]

6m 14.5s (-15.50) **Going Correction** -0.30s/f (Good) **8** Ran SP% **113.9**
Speed ratings: **112,110,109,105,104 91, ,**
CSF £57.76 CT £574.37 TOTE £6.60: £2.00, £2.90, £2.40; EX 84.20 Trifecta £606.10.
Owner S Such & Cg Paletta **Bred** Patrick Collins **Trained** Naunton, Gloucs

FOCUS
Many old favourites in the line-up for the latest race in the veterans' series, but several failed to give their running. The pace was sound and the winner posted a small pb.

2083 MOLSON COORS H'CAP HURDLE (11 hdls) 2m 4f
3:00 (3:00) (Class 2) 4-Y-O+ **£15,640** (£4,620; £2,310; £1,155; £577; £290)

Form RPR
/11- **1** **Hunters Hoof (IRE)**[240] 4467 6-10-8 130........................ NicodeBoinville 139+
(Nicky Henderson) *in tch: hit 3rd: wnt 2nd appr 3 out: led over 1f out on run-in: edgd rt in clsng stages: styd on* **11/2**[3]

F0-1 **2** *1* **Work In Progress (IRE)**[7] 1990 5-10-5 127 6ex........................ HarrySkelton 134
(Dan Skelton) *edgd rt at flights a few times: led: rdn and hdd over 1f out on run-in: kpt on u.p but hld after* **6/4**[1]

03-6 **3** *12* **Box Office (FR)**[15] 1847 4-10-12 134........................(t) BarryGeraghty 130
(Jonjo O'Neill) *hld up: outpcd after 4 out: hdwy appr 3 out: styd on to take 3rd appr 2 out: no imp bef last: one pce after* **9/2**[2]

6-10 **4** *6* **Bear's Affair (IRE)**[119] 855 9-11-7 148........................ FreddieMitchell(5) 139
(Nicky Henderson) *chsd ldr tl rdn after 4 out: outpcd 3 out: n.d after* **12/1**

223- **5** *2 ¾* **A Vos Gardes (FR)**[191] 5360 5-11-1 137........................(t) RichardJohnson 125
(Charlie Longsdon) *in rr: pushed along and outpcd after 4 out: nvr a danger* **11/2**[3]

520- **6** *14* **Pine Creek**[260] 4084 7-11-7 143........................ AidanColeman 122
(John Ferguson) *handy: rdn appr 3 out: wknd 2 out* **13/2**

4m 45.4s (-15.30) **Going Correction** -0.45s/f (Good) **6** Ran SP% **110.0**
Speed ratings (Par 109): **112,111,106,104,103 97**
CSF £14.11 CT £36.13 TOTE £3.80: £2.10, £1.50; EX 13.50 Trifecta £53.60.
Owner London Bridge Racing Partnership **Bred** Jimmy Coffey **Trained** Upper Lambourn, Berks

FOCUS
A stop-start gallop to this good handicap hurdle, entirely by the design of the eventual runner-up. The first two finished clear and are on the upgrade.

2084 MONET'S GARDEN OLD ROAN CHASE (LIMITED H'CAP) (GRADE 2) (16 fncs) 2m 3f 200y
3:30 (3:31) (Class 1) 4-Y-O+ **£33,762** (£12,720; £6,366; £3,180; £1,596; £798)

Form RPR
51-0 **1** **Sound Investment (IRE)**[15] 1848 7-11-3 155........................(t) NickScholfield 161
(Paul Nicholls) *chsd ldrs: effrt after 2 out: led appr last: drvn out and styd on: a doing enough towards fin* **7/1**[3]

PP0- **2** *½* **Wishfull Thinking**[198] 5252 12-11-10 162........................(t) RichardJohnson 168
(Philip Hobbs) *in tch: clsd 4 out: effrt 2 out: gd prog to go 2nd and chal jst bef last: styd on gamely run-in: continued to press towards fin but hld* **7/1**[3]

145- **3** *3 ¼* **Buywise (IRE)**[197] 5274 8-10-9 147........................ PaulMoloney 150
(Evan Williams) *hld up: niggled along briefly after 9th: hdwy appr 2 out: chsd ldrs bef last: styd on to take 3rd fnl 75yds: no imp on front two* **9/2**[2]

3314 **4** *3 ¼* **Brave Spartacus (IRE)**[29] 1448 9-10-7 145........................ JamesReveley 148
(Keith Reveley) *chsd ldr: blnd 4th: led 10th: rdn and hdd appr last: no ex fnl 75yds* **25/1**

21-4 **5** *10* **Duke Of Navan (IRE)**[174] 103 7-10-9 147........................ BrianHarding 140
(Nicky Richards) *hld up: hdwy 10th: hmpd 11th: trckd ldrs gng wl 4 out: rdn and ev ch appr 2 out: wknd bef last* **7/1**[3]

4-21 **6** *3 ½* **Le Bacardy (FR)**[161] 357 9-10-4 142 oh1........................ HarrySkelton 130
(Dan Skelton) *hld up in rr: rdn after 2 out: nt pick-up: sn btn* **12/1**

5- **7** *½* **Lord Ben (IRE)**[37] 1580 10-10-7 145........................ JJBurke 137
(Henry De Bromhead, Ire) *led: blnd and hdd 10th: mstke 12th: remained prom: stl chalng 2 out: rdn and wknd bef last* **16/1**

410 **8** *9* **Surf And Turf (IRE)**[99] 1039 9-10-6 144........................ BrianHughes 126
(Kevin Frost) *hld up: mstke 2nd: hdwy after 12th: rdn appr 2 out: wknd bef last* **25/1**

001- **P** **Rajdhani Express**[198] 5253 8-11-5 160........................ MrSWaley-Cohen(3)
(Nicky Henderson) *chsd ldrs: wnt wrong on landing 11th: fatally injured* **8/1**

653- **P** **Johns Spirit (IRE)**[198] 5252 8-11-5 157........................ RichieMcLernon
(Jonjo O'Neill) *midfield: hdwy bef 9th: blnd 10th and lost pl: bdly hmpd 11th and sn bhd and nt rcvr: t.o whn p.u bef last* **11/4**[1]

4m 52.4s (-11.60) **Going Correction** -0.30s/f (Good) **10** Ran SP% **114.7**
Speed ratings (Par 115): **111,110,109,108,104 102,102,99, ,**
CSF £54.68 CT £242.71 TOTE £9.60: £2.80, £2.50, £1.90; EX 62.60 Trifecta £412.90.
Owner Owners Group 001 **Bred** Mrs Jacinta McGeough **Trained** Ditcheat, Somerset

FOCUS
A pretty similar renewal to last year's Old Roan Chase, in terms of both the size and ratings composition of the field. Lord Ben and Brave Spartacus ensured it was a truly run contest, and the complexion of the race altered markedly as the more patiently ridden competitors advanced at two out. Solid form, Sound Investment up 5lb on his previous best.

2085 HAMPDEN AGENCIES LTD. NOVICES' H'CAP HURDLE (11 hdls) 2m 4f
4:00 (4:00) (Class 4) (0-115,113) 3-Y-O+ **£4,223** (£1,240; £620; £310)

Form RPR
-14F **1** **Abricot De L'Oasis (FR)**[147] 568 5-11-12 113 HarrySkelton 116+
(Dan Skelton) *mde all: mstke 2 out: rdn appr last: styd on u.p: all out toward fin* **7/4**[1]
50-5 **2** ½ **Silver Shuffle (IRE)**[12] 456 8-10-12 99 BrianHughes 100+
(Dianne Sayer) *hld up: hdwy appr 3 out: effrt to chse ldrs bef last: styd on: tk 2nd fnl 110yds: clsd towards fin* **9/1**[3]
3-31 **3** 1¼ **The Big Dipper**[26] 1692 6-11-5 106 NoelFehily 106
(David Dennis) *midfield: rdn after 3 out: hdwy appr 2 out: wnt 2nd run-in: styd on: lost 3rd fnl 110yds: no further prog towards fin* **8/1**[2]
0412 **4** 5 **Tennessee Bird**[10] 1927 7-10-10 97 GavinSheehan 92
(Mike Sowersby) *hld up: hdwy into midfield after 5th: effrt to chse ldrs appr last: kpt on u.p run-in but no real imp on ldrs* **16/1**
001- **5** 2½ **Tidestream**[237] 4542 5-11-5 106 (t) RichardJohnson 104+
(Tim Vaughan) *midfield: hdwy after 4 out: wnt 2nd after 3 out: shake up and nrly 3 l down whn blnd last: lost 2nd run-in: wknd fnl 150yds* **10/1**
4323 **6** 2¼ **Presenting Streak (IRE)**[41] 1545 6-11-4 112 MrRWinks(7) 104
(Peter Winks) *midfield: hdwy 7th: rdn and lost pl appr 3 out: rallied but no imp whn edgd lft bef 2 out: kpt on but n.d run-in* **11/1**
122F **7** ¾ **Mighty Leader (IRE)**[17] 1824 7-11-1 105 JeremiahMcGrath(3) 95
(Henry Oliver) *handy: lost pl 4th: plugged on fr 2 out: n.d* **10/1**
04-4 **8** 6 **Bassarabad (FR)**[53] 1455 4-11-7 108 AidanColeman 93
(Tim Vaughan) *midfield: rdn and lost pl 4 out: n.d after* **33/1**
4413 **9** nk **Prince Khurram**[24] 1714 5-11-7 113 (t) JamesCowley(5) 99
(Donald McCain) *prom: chsd wnr fr bef 3rd: rdn and lost 2nd after 3 out: wknd last* **28/1**
5351 **10** 1¾ **Keep Calm**[46] 1519 5-11-6 107 HenryBrooke 90
(John Mackie) *handy: lost pl 5th: in rr 6th: struggling 4 out* **16/1**
3543 **11** 9 **Jackofhearts**[31] 1637 7-11-2 103 SeanQuinlan 78
(Jean McGregor) *hld up: struggling after 4 out: nvr a danger* **33/1**
5-23 **12** 10 **Summer Storm**[21] 1774 5-11-6 110 (t) TonyKelly(3) 76
(Rebecca Menzies) *midfield: hdwy to chse ldrs 4th: rdn and wknd appr 3 out* **25/1**
44-F **13** 14 **Smoking Jacket (IRE)**[171] 177 5-11-9 110 PaddyBrennan 63
(Tom George) *racd keenly: in tch: clsd appr 3 out: wknd bef 2 out* **11/1**

4m 53.9s (-6.80) **Going Correction** -0.45s/f (Good)
WFA 4 from 5yo+ 10lb **13** Ran SP% **117.3**
Speed ratings (Par 105): **95,94,94,92,91 90,90,87,87,86 83,79,73**
CSF £16.99 CT £100.30 TOTE £2.60: £1.40, £2.70, £1.70; EX 18.70 Trifecta £115.90.
Owner Frank McAleavy **Bred** S Blanchais, N Blanchais Et Al **Trained** Alcester, Warwicks

FOCUS
A one-horse book beforehand, and the confidence was rewarded. This rates a hurdles best from the winner.

2086 BRITISH STALLION STUDS EBF MARES' STANDARD OPEN NATIONAL HUNT FLAT RACE 2m 209y
4:35 (4:35) (Class 4) 4-6-Y-O **£3,249** (£954; £477; £238)

Form RPR
1- **1** **La Bague Au Roi (FR)**[188] 5439 4-11-0 0 HarryBannister(5) 121+
(Warren Greatrex) *prom early: trckd ldrs after: led gng wl 2f out: shkn up to draw clr ins fnl f: easily* **2/1**[1]
4 **2** 7 **Kalaniti (IRE)**[172] 144 4-10-12 0 BrianHughes 105+
(Chris Grant) *hld up: hdwy 3f out: rdn 2f out: styd on to take wnt 2nd 1f out: m green: veered rt 150yds out: no ch w wnr* **66/1**
2- **3** 5 **Midnight Velvet**[220] 4866 5-10-12 0 RichardJohnson 101+
(Philip Hobbs) *ref to settle: chsd ldrs: impr to ld after 3f: hdd 2f out: lost 2nd 1f out: keeping on u.p whn hmpd 150yds out: one pce after* **5/2**[2]
4 4½ **Jessber's Dream (IRE)**[266] 5-10-12 0 (t) NoelFehily 95
(Harry Fry) *led: hdd after 3f: remained prom: wknd over 1f out* **5/1**[3]
2- **5** ¾ **Jessie Webster (IRE)**[361] 2133 6-10-12 0 LeightonAspell 94
(Rebecca Curtis) *midfield: hdwy 1/2-way: chsd ldrs over 3f out: wknd wl over 1f out* **7/1**
4- **6** 4 **Rock Chick Supremo (IRE)**[209] 5071 4-10-12 0 HarrySkelton 90
(Dan Skelton) *hld up: effrt bhd ldrs 2f out: sn no imp: wl btn* **20/1**
7 25 **Classi Massini** 4-10-12 0 SeanBowen 65
(Peter Bowen) *prom: rdn 4f out: wknd over 2f out* **20/1**
8 16 **Lady Of Llanarmon** 4-10-12 0 DavidBass 49
(Kim Bailey) *hld up: pushed along and struggling after 6f: t.o* **16/1**
2 **9** 19 **Handpicked**[168] 220 4-10-12 0 JakeGreenall 30
(Henry Daly) *midfield: lost pl 6f out: bhd 5f out: t.o* **14/1**

3m 59.5s (-7.90) **Going Correction** -0.45s/f (Good) **9** Ran SP% **114.6**
Speed ratings: **100,96,94,92,91 90,78,70,61**
CSF £154.95 TOTE £2.30: £1.10, £11.20, £1.20; EX 145.70 Trifecta £561.60.
Owner Mrs Julien Turner & Andrew Merriam **Bred** Comtesse Bertrand De Tarragon **Trained** Upper Lambourn, Berks

FOCUS
Just a steady pace to this concluding mares' bumper, but they finished at long intervals behind an impressive winner. He looks decent and should win more races.
T/Plt: £69.30 to a £1 stake. Pool of £108816.18 - 1144.68 winning tickets. T/Qpdt: £28.90 to a £1 stake. Pool of £8738.53 - 223.65 winning tickets. **Darren Owen**

1947 WINCANTON (R-H)
Sunday, October 25

OFFICIAL GOING: Good (chs 8.1, hdl 8.4)
Wind: almost nil Weather: sunny with cloudy periods

2087 WINCANTON H'CAP HURDLE (11 hdls) 2m 5f 82y
1:40 (1:40) (Class 4) (0-110,113) 4-Y-O+ **£3,249** (£954; £477; £238)

Form RPR
4215 **1** **Panis Angelicus (FR)**[55] 1419 6-11-7 110 (v[1]) AlanJohns(5) 116
(Tim Vaughan) *trckd ldrs: rdn after 3 out: chal last: sn led: styd on: all out* **13/2**[3]
5211 **2** ¾ **Barton Antix**[9] 1951 6-11-8 113 (p) MrShaneQuinlan(7) 119+
(Neil Mulholland) *hld up towards rr: stdy prog after 3 out: rdn to chse ldrs after 2 out: ev ch last: styd on* **11/10**[1]
24-5 **3** hd **McCabe Creek (IRE)**[165] 281 5-10-10 104 JamieInsole(10) 109
(Alan King) *hld up bhd: gd hdwy to trck ldr 3 out: sn chal: rdn into narrow advantage last: hdd run-in: styd on* **11/2**[2]
0-P1 **4** 4 **East Hill**[9] 1947 5-10-2 86 (t) BrendanPowell 88
(Colin Tizzard) *led: rdn whn chal 2 out: hdd last: kpt on same pce* **12/1**
50-4 **5** 8 **Craiganee (IRE)**[17] 1819 8-11-5 103 SamTwiston-Davies 97
(Chris Down) *hld up towards rr: midfield u.p 2 out: no further imp on ldrs after* **14/1**
1256 **6** ½ **Titch Strider (IRE)**[16] 1841 10-11-7 105 ConorO'Farrell 100
(John Panvert) *mid-div: rdn after 3 out: one pce whn nt fluent 2 out* **20/1**
5633 **7** 1 **Native Robin (IRE)**[22] 1752 5-11-8 109 MattGriffiths(3) 102
(Jeremy Scott) *hld up towards rr: hdwy 3 out: rdn and ev ch sn after 2 out: wkng whn drifted rt last* **14/1**
064- **8** 16 **Knight ofthe Realm**[214] 4985 6-11-9 107 IanPopham 87
(Caroline Keevil) *trckd ldrs: rdn after 3 out: wknd next* **16/1**
1155 **9** 1¼ **Archie Rice (USA)**[27] 1675 9-11-0 105 MissBFrost(7) 83
(Jimmy Frost) *mid-div: rdn after 3 out: wknd bef next* **25/1**
50 **10** hd **Beau Bay (FR)**[17] 1818 4-11-9 107 (t) RhysFlint 84
(Alan Jones) *mid-div: rdn after 3 out: wknd bef next* **66/1**
/550 **11** 36 **Looking For Mick**[16] 1837 6-11-1 102 GilesHawkins(3) 47
(Chris Down) *trckd ldr: rdn after 3 out: sn wknd: t.o* **66/1**

5m 9.4s (-17.10) **Going Correction** -0.90s/f (Hard) **11** Ran SP% **114.8**
Speed ratings (Par 105): **96,95,95,94,91 90,90,84,83,83 70**
CSF £13.70 CT £41.75 TOTE £8.20: £2.00, £1.10, £2.30; EX 17.20 Trifecta £74.00.
Owner Oceans Racing **Bred** Erick Bec De La Motte Et Al **Trained** Aberthin, Vale of Glamorgan

FOCUS
A modest handicap run at a respectable temp.

2088 MONTAGUE INN NOVICES' HURDLE (11 hdls) 2m 5f 82y
2:15 (2:15) (Class 4) 4-Y-O+ **£3,249** (£954; £477; £238)

Form RPR
1 **Max Forte (IRE)**[161] 5-10-12 0 JamesDavies 122+
(Chris Down) *mde all: styd on strly fr 2 out: readily* **25/1**
10- **2** 8 **Present Man (IRE)**[260] 4086 5-10-12 0 SamTwiston-Davies 116+
(Paul Nicholls) *pressed wnr tl rdn after 3 out: hld next: styd on same pce* **4/6**[1]
2U3 **3** 4 **Theatre Goer**[24] 1723 6-10-2 0 JamesBanks(3) 104
(Noel Williams) *in tch: rdn after 3 out: chal for hld 3rd fr last: styd on same pce* **7/1**[3]
12P1 **4** shd **Uncle Tone (IRE)**[18] 1806 6-11-7 123 AlanJohns(5) 125
(Tim Vaughan) *chsd ldng pair: rdn appr 2 out: nt pce to get on terms: lost 3rd on nod* **9/2**[2]
5 10 **Golden Bird (IRE)**[45] 4-10-12 0 BrendanPowell 102
(Brendan Powell) *trckd ldrs: rdn after 3 out: hld next: wknd run-in* **33/1**
04- **6** 44 **Westend Prince (IRE)**[221] 4859 4-10-12 0 DarylJacob 62
(Colin Tizzard) *in tch: pushed along after 7th: rdn after 3 out: wknd bef next: t.o* **12/1**
P **Knight Watchman (IRE)**[539] 5-10-12 0 RyanMahon
(Harry Fry) *j.lft progively worse: hld up last: lost tch fr 7th: t.o whn p.u bef 2 out* **11/1**
-234 **P** **Alottarain (IRE)**[102] 1009 5-10-0 104 KevinJones(5)
(Seamus Mullins) *hld up in last pair: rdn after 3 out: sn wknd: p.u bef 2 out* **14/1**

5m 6.0s (-20.50) **Going Correction** -0.90s/f (Hard)
WFA 4 from 5yo+ 10lb **8** Ran SP% **120.1**
Speed ratings (Par 105): **103,99,98,98,94 77, ,**
CSF £46.66 TOTE £25.20: £5.50, £1.10, £1.90; EX 69.70 Trifecta £520.30.
Owner P Holland,JT Measures,MA Kerr,V Holland **Bred** P & H Byrne **Trained** Mutterton, Devon

FOCUS
The second favourite set the level in this novice hurdle with an official mark of 123, but was comfortably held. Plenty of praise goes to the rider of the winner, who got everything right from the front.

2089 QUILTER CHEVIOT SUPPORTING SPINAL CORD INJURIES H'CAP CHASE (FOR THE DESERT ORCHID SILVER CUP) (22 fncs) 3m 2f 162y
2:45 (2:45) (Class 3) (0-140,137) 4-Y-O+ **£9,495** (£2,805; £1,402; £702; £351)

Form RPR
443- **1** **Forgotten Gold (IRE)**[211] 5026 9-11-2 127 DarylJacob 136+
(Tom George) *j.w: trckd ldr: led 4 out: styd on strly fr next: comf* **11/2**[3]
53-P **2** 5 **Handy Andy (IRE)**[15] 1849 9-11-0 125 (bt[1]) BrendanPowell 128
(Colin Tizzard) *trckd ldrs: rdn to chse wnr appr 3 out: styd on but a being hld* **13/2**
1130 **3** 13 **Standing Ovation (IRE)**[15] 1849 8-11-10 135 (bt) ConorO'Farrell 126
(David Pipe) *hld up: hdwy after 4 out: sn rdn: wnt 3rd bef 2 out: styd on but nt pce to get on terms* **10/1**
F41- **4** 5 **Dont Do Mondays (IRE)**[230] 4676 8-10-11 127 (p) JakeHodson(5) 115
(David Bridgwater) *trckd ldr: nt fluent 3 out: rdn appr 2 out: sn one pce* **11/1**
-235 **5** 18 **Best Boy Barney (IRE)**[18] 1807 9-11-1 129 (bt) MattGriffiths(3) 110
(Jeremy Scott) *led tl 4 out: sn rdn: wknd 2 out* **8/1**
4-00 **P** **Raajih**[64] 1322 7-11-5 137 (bt) MrMatthewHampton(7)
(Richard Woollacott) *j.lft progively worse: in tch: nt fluent 12th: sn struggling in last: losing tch whn p.u bef 18th* **40/1**
P04- **P** **According To Trev (IRE)**[192] 5356 9-11-7 132 TomCannon
(David Bridgwater) *nvr travelling in rr: wknd 18th: sn p.u* **5/1**[2]
31-4 **P** **Cowards Close (IRE)**[15] 1849 8-11-5 130 (t) SamTwiston-Davies
(Paul Nicholls) *trckd ldrs: rdn after 18th: wknd bef 3 out: bhd whn p.u bef 2 out* **7/4**[1]

6m 43.9s (-24.30) **Going Correction** -0.65s/f (Firm) **8** Ran SP% **112.7**
Speed ratings (Par 107): **110,108,104,103,97 , ,**
CSF £39.41 CT £344.64 TOTE £5.80: £1.70, £2.20, £3.10; EX 39.70 Trifecta £548.90.
Owner Mr & Mrs R Cornock **Bred** Patrick Hayes **Trained** Slad, Gloucs

FOCUS
This looked a decent contest before the off, but the first two in the betting ran poorly, which casts a little bit of doubt about the value of the form.

2090 WELCOME TO STREET FOOTBALL CLUB NOVICES' LIMITED H'CAP CHASE (17 fncs) 2m 4f 35y
3:15 (3:15) (Class 4) (0-120,115) 4-Y-O+ **£6,498** (£1,908; £954; £477)

Form RPR
520/ **1** **Squire Trelawney**[557] 5351 9-11-1 108 (tp) RyanMahon 116+
(Dan Skelton) *trckd ldrs: chal 4 out: slt advantage whn hit 2 out: edgd rt run-in: kpt on wl: rdn out* **7/2**[2]
324- **2** 1 **Sonny The One**[188] 5437 5-11-4 111 BrendanPowell 119+
(Colin Tizzard) *trckd ldrs: rchd for 7th: led 13th: rdn and narrowly hdd 2 out: short of room fr last: kpt on* **9/4**[1]

	3	7	**Royal Chief (IRE)**[70] 1277 6-11-1 **108**....(p) AdamWedge	110
			(Alexandra Dunn) *trckd ldrs: ev ch 3 out: sn rdn: styd on same pce fr next* **6/1**	
3332	4	27	**Vinnie The Fish (IRE)**[12] 1896 7-11-1 **108**....(p) RobertDunne	104+
			(Dai Burchell) *hld up in tch: hdwy after 4 out: styng on and disputing cl 3rd whn blnd 2 out and rdr lost iron: nvr rcvrd* **4/1**[3]	
0-60	5	2	**Changeofluck (IRE)**[33] 1615 7-10-10 **103**....(tp) AndrewThornton	79
			(Lawney Hill) *led tl 2nd: trckd ldr: nt fluent 9th (water): hit next: sn struggling: wknd after 4 out* **7/1**	
4636	6	½	**Breaking The Bank**[21] 1769 6-11-8 **115**.... DarylJacob	92
			(Ben Case) *led 2nd: nt fluent 8th: hdd 13th: sn rdn: wknd after 4 out* **6/1**	

5m 4.2s (-13.30) **Going Correction** -0.65s/f (Firm) **6** Ran SP% **114.1**
Speed ratings (Par 105): **100,99,96,86,85 85**
CSF £12.55 TOTE £3.30: £2.40, £1.80; EX 13.60 Trifecta £89.80.
Owner P J Haycock **Bred** Miss K Rausing **Trained** Alcester, Warwicks
■ Stewards' Enquiry : Ryan Mahon two-day ban: careless riding (8-9 Nov)

FOCUS
Just an ordinary race of its type, but it may have a few winners come out of it in the short term.

2091 DOMINIC BAKER MEMORIAL "NATIONAL HUNT" NOVICES' HURDLE (8 hdls) 1m 7f 65y

3:45 (3:46) (Class 4) 4-Y-0+ **£5,198** (£1,526; £763; £381)

Form				RPR
6-	1		**Marracudja (FR)**[316] 3077 4-10-12 0....(t[1]) SamTwiston-Davies	120+
			(Paul Nicholls) *mde all: r.o wl fr last: comf* **6/4**[2]	
1-03	2	8	**Wade Harper (IRE)**[16] 1837 5-10-12 0.... TomO'Brien	113+
			(David Dennis) *trckd wnr thrght: rdn appr 2 out: sn hld: kpt on same pce* **10/11**[1]	
0-	3	½	**Bim Bam Boum (FR)**[239] 4499 4-10-12 0.... RyanMahon	112+
			(Harry Fry) *hld up last: nt fluent 1st: gd hdwy after 3 out: wnt 3rd next: chal fior 2nd fr last: kpt on same pce* **10/1**[3]	
04	4	17	**Bishops Court**[15] 1844 5-10-12 0.... MarkQuinlan	95
			(Neil Mulholland) *trckd ldrs tl outpcd after 3 out: no threat after* **20/1**	
3/4-	5	6	**Ma'ire Rua (IRE)**[269] 3938 8-10-12 96.... TomCannon	90
			(Alan Jones) *trckd ldrs: rdn in 3rd after 3 out: wknd next* **10/1**[3]	
66	6	25	**Ablazing (IRE)**[30] 1644 4-10-12 0.... AlainCawley	77
			(Johnny Farrelly) *hld up in last trio: wknd after 3 out: t.o* **33/1**	
0-5	7	11	**Cupachai**[20] 1797 4-10-12 0....(t) RobertDunne	57
			(Dan Skelton) *hld up in last pair: hdwy whn hit 5th: wknd after 3 out: t.o* **20/1**	
00-4	8	11	**Culm Counsellor**[17] 1822 6-10-9 0....(p) GilesHawkins(3)	48
			(Chris Down) *trckd ldrs tl wknd after 3 out: t.o* **50/1**	

3m 33.8s (-15.10) **Going Correction** -0.90s/f (Hard) **8** Ran SP% **125.0**
Speed ratings (Par 105): **104,99,99,90,87 73,68,62**
CSF £3.61 TOTE £3.20: £1.10, £1.10, £2.50; EX 3.80 Trifecta £14.90.
Owner Potensis Bloodstock Limited **Bred** E A R L De Cordelles Et Al **Trained** Ditcheat, Somerset

FOCUS
This didn't seem a race with any great depth, and it was soon apparent that the front-runner was going to take some pegging back.

2092 GOLF COURSE JUVENILE HURDLE (8 hdls) 1m 7f 65y

4:15 (4:15) (Class 4) 3-Y-0 **£5,198** (£1,526; £763; £381)

Form				RPR
	1		**Romain De Senam (FR)**[193] 3-11-5 130.... SamTwiston-Davies	121+
			(Paul Nicholls) *mde all: clr 1/2-way: unchal* **2/9**[1]	
3	2	15	**Albert Herring**[23] 1732 3-10-12 0.... DarylJacob	94+
			(Jonathan Portman) *chsd wnr: nt fluent 5th: rdn appr 2 out: nvr threatened to get on terms: styd on same pce* **14/1**[3]	
53	3	6	**Cahill (IRE)**[21] 1768 3-10-12 0....(p) WayneHutchinson	87
			(Alan King) *hld up in last pair: pushed along in 4th after 5th: rdn after 3 out: one pce fr next: wnt 3rd run-in* **10/1**[2]	
	4	2¼	**The Coffee Hunter (FR)**[196] 3-10-7 0....(t) LizzieKelly(5)	86
			(Nick Williams) *trckd ldrs: rdn after 3 out: sn one pce: no ex whn lost 3rd run-in* **14/1**[3]	
	5	49	**Woofie (IRE)**[18] 3-10-12 0.... TomCannon	41
			(Laura Mongan) *hld up: rdn after 3 out: sn wknd: t.o* **10/1**[2]	
C5	6	31	**Ventura Castle**[114] 891 3-10-12 0....(t) BrendanPowell	13
			(Jamie Snowden) *trckd ldrs tl 3rd: sn pushed along in last: wknd after 3 out: t.o* **100/1**	

3m 36.4s (-12.50) **Going Correction** -0.90s/f (Hard) **6** Ran SP% **114.3**
Speed ratings (Par 103): **97,89,85,84,58 41**
CSF £5.29 TOTE £1.20: £1.10, £3.80; EX 5.70 Trifecta £15.80.
Owner Chris Giles & Dan Macdonald **Bred** Pierre Senamaud & Dr Jacques Detre **Trained** Ditcheat, Somerset

FOCUS
At no stage of this race did those who invested on the market leader have the slightest concern. The problem with the form is working out whether he won because he's a Graded winner in waiting or those in behind have very limited ability.

2093 BRUTON H'CAP HURDLE (7 hdls 1 omitted) 1m 7f 65y

4:45 (4:45) (Class 4) (0-120,115) 3-Y-0+ **£3,898** (£1,144; £572; £286)

Form				RPR
F614	1		**Polstar (FR)**[24] 1714 6-11-0 **110**.... PaulNO'Brien(7)	120+
			(Harry Whittington) *hld up bhd: pushed along and hdwy after 3 out: wnt 2nd at the last: swtchd lft and str run fnl 100yds: sn led: r.o wl* **7/1**[3]	
42F2	2	1¼	**Impulsive American**[3] 2038 3-9-13 **112**....(p) DavidNoonan(7)	105+
			(David Pipe) *mid-div: hdwy 3 out: led 2 out: sn rdn and idling: wnt sltly lft last: outpcd whn hdd towards fin* **11/8**[1]	
04-1	3	5	**Fourth Act (IRE)**[9] 1952 6-11-5 **115**....(t) PaulO'Brien(7)	118
			(Colin Tizzard) *trckd ldrs tl 2nd: in tch: rdn after 3 out: styd on between last 2: wnt 3rd run-in* **8/1**	
3213	4	7	**Dry Ol'Party**[9] 1949 5-11-10 **113**.... TomO'Brien	111
			(Philip Hobbs) *mid-div: hdwy after 3 out: mounting chal whn hit 2 out: sn rdn: styd on same pce* **6/1**[2]	
-100	5	7	**Benbecula**[22] 1754 6-11-9 **115**....(b) TomBellamy(3)	106
			(Richard Mitchell) *led: rdn and hdd 2 out: sn btn* **8/1**	
2-00	6	10	**Champagne Chaser**[29] 1661 5-10-13 **102**.... MichaelByrne	84
			(Tim Vaughan) *hld up towards rr: sme late prog past btn horses: n.d* **16/1**	
1-60	7	1¼	**Ice Tres**[16] 1841 6-11-0 **103**....(tp[1]) JamesDavies	84
			(Chris Down) *mid-div: rdn after 3 out: wknd between last 2* **22/1**	
5504	8	nk	**Avel Vor (IRE)**[74] 1233 4-11-7 **110**.... ConorO'Farrell	90
			(Nigel Hawke) *hld up towards rr: sme late prog past btn horses: nvr a threat* **50/1**	
636-	9	1	**Eddiemaurice (IRE)**[218] 4896 4-11-10 **113**.... RhysFlint	92
			(John Flint) *trckd ldrs: lost pl 3rd: hdwy after 3 out: rdn after 2 out: wknd* **25/1**	
U305	10	16	**Brinestine (USA)**[12] 1893 6-10-13 **105**....(t) JamesBanks(3)	70
			(Emma Baker) *trckd ldrs: rdn after 3 out: wknd next* **14/1**	
35-5	11	21	**Triple Chief (IRE)**[27] 1676 4-11-6 **109**.... SamTwiston-Davies	55
			(Chris Down) *chsd ldrs tl 3 out: sn wknd: t.o* **16/1**	

3m 33.4s (-15.50) **Going Correction** -0.90s/f (Hard) **11** Ran SP% **119.7**
Speed ratings (Par 105): **105,104,101,97,94 88,88,88,87,78 67**
CSF £17.51 CT £83.26 TOTE £6.80: £2.10, £1.10, £3.00; EX 23.00 Trifecta £143.40.
Owner Dixon,Ellis,Lynds,Travers,Watkins **Bred** Comte Jean-Jacques De La Rochette **Trained** Sparsholt, Oxforshire
■ Stewards' Enquiry : Rhys Flint jockey said that the gelding became very tired after jumping the last hurdle on his first start for 218 days but that he had not at any point stopped riding completely

FOCUS
A modest but competitive race, run at a respectable gallop. Following concerns raised by the riders at the start regarding the low sun obscuring their vision at the third hurdle, the stewards consulted with the clerk of the course and ordered that the obstacle should be by-passed for this race.
T/Jkpt: Not won. Consolation placepot £436.90. Pool: £1,915.00 - 3.2 winning units. T/Plt: £14.50 to a £1 stake. Pool: £69,018.88 - 3,455.32 winning tickets T/Qpdt: £10.90 to a £1 stake. Pool: £4,276.66 - 288.80 winning tickets **Tim Mitchell**

2094 - 2099a (Foreign Racing) - See Raceform Interactive

AYR (L-H)

Monday, October 26

OFFICIAL GOING: Good to soft (good in places) changing to good (good to soft in places) after race 1 (1:10)
Wind: Light against Weather: Overcast

2100 RACING UK MAIDEN HURDLE (12 hdls) 2m 4f 100y

1:10 (1:11) (Class 5) 4-Y-0+ **£2,599** (£763; £381; £190)

Form				RPR
64-2	1		**Calivigny (IRE)**[165] 299 6-10-9 115.... StephenMulqueen(5)	114+
			(N W Alexander) *trckd ldr: led 3 out: rdn between last 2: hit last: kpt on* **4/1**	
305/	2	2¼	**Caledonia**[360] 4272 8-11-0 0.... JamesReveley	111
			(Jim Goldie) *led: hit 8th: hdd 3 out: sn rdn: kpt on but a hld* **3/1**[2]	
2-	3	5	**John Monash**[10] 1953 4-11-0 113....(t) RichardJohnson	108
			(Gordon Elliott, Ire) *midfield: mstke 3rd: hdwy to trck ldr 8th: briefly short of room on bnd appr 3 out: nt fluent 2 out: sn rdn in 3rd: nt fluent again last: one pce* **2/1**[1]	
	4	7	**Takingrisks (IRE)**[204] 6-11-0 0.... BrianHarding	99
			(Nicky Richards) *in tch: hdwy to trck ldr 8th: pushed along appr 3 out: wknd after 2 out* **7/2**[3]	
P-00	5	10	**Desert Island Dusk**[14] 1892 4-10-9 94....(t[1]) DaraghBourke(5)	90
			(Maurice Barnes) *hld up in rr: rdn 3 out: nvr threatened* **50/1**	
	6	9	**Away For Slates (IRE)**[197] 5-10-11 0.... CraigNichol(3)	82
			(Keith Dalgleish) *midfield: pushed along after 8th: wknd after 3 out: hit 2 out* **25/1**	
4	7	5	**Kilronan Castle**[25] 1717 4-10-9 0.... JamesCowley(5)	77
			(Donald McCain) *in tch: lost pl 8th: sn rdn along: wknd 3 out* **16/1**	
P	P		**Benvardin (IRE)**[22] 1776 5-10-7 0.... SamColtherd(7)	
			(Andrew Hamilton) *hld up: rdn 7th: sn wl bhd: p.u bef 3 out* **200/1**	
0-P0	P		**Persian Fashion (IRE)**[135] 727 6-10-4 0.... GrahamWatters(5)	
			(Ian Duncan) *a towards rr: p.u bef 3 out* **250/1**	

4m 54.0s (294.00)
WFA 4 from 5yo+ 10lb **9** Ran SP% **113.1**
CSF £16.30 TOTE £4.50: £1.60, £2.50, £1.02; EX 21.60 Trifecta £51.30.
Owner Hugh Hodge Ltd **Bred** J P Hand **Trained** Kinneston, Perth & Kinross
■ Stewards' Enquiry : Stephen Mulqueen two-day ban: careless riding (Nov 9-10)

FOCUS
Some starts have been moved at this track following remeasuring, so some races will not have speed figures until there is sufficient data to calculate updated median times. A drying day, and after the first race winning rider Stephen Mulqueen claimed it was good all over. It was therefore no surprise that the going was upgraded by course officials afterwards. This was a modest maiden, but the form looks sound with the first three running close to their pre-race marks.

2101 RACING UK/EBF "NATIONAL HUNT" NOVICES' HURDLE (QUALIFIER) (9 hdls) 2m

1:40 (1:43) (Class 4) 4-6-Y-0 **£3,898** (£1,144; £572; £286)

Form				RPR
13-	1		**Imada (IRE)**[219] 4915 5-10-12 0.... BrianHarding	114+
			(Nicky Richards) *trckd ldrs: hdwy to trck ldr gng wl after 6th: qcknd to ld between last 2: rdn run-in: idled towards fin* **8/13**[1]	
30-3	2	1¾	**Double W's (IRE)**[30] 1660 5-10-12 0.... BrianHughes	111+
			(Malcolm Jefferson) *trckd ldr: led 6th: rdn after 3 out: hdd between last 2: kpt on* **15/8**[2]	
305-	3	3¼	**Leading Score (IRE)**[240] 4485 5-10-7 0.... DaleIrving(5)	106+
			(James Ewart) *midfield: hdwy appr 3 out: wnt 3rd 3 out: sn rdn: kpt on* **40/1**	
61-5	4	16	**Benny's Secret (IRE)**[173] 144 5-10-12 0.... RichardJohnson	96
			(N W Alexander) *racd keenly hld up: nt a fluent: hdwy bef 6th: hit 6th: rdn after 3 out: wknd after 2 out* **14/1**[3]	
040-	5	18	**Rocklim (FR)**[235] 4582 5-10-12 0.... JakeGreenall	75
			(James Ewart) *hld up: rdn after 6th: sn btn* **100/1**	
	6	6	**Fire Rock (IRE)** 4-10-5 0.... RyanDay(7)	70
			(Nicky Richards) *hld up: pushed along after 5th: a towards rr* **66/1**	
5-5P	7	30	**Question Of Faith**[11] 1921 4-10-5 0.... HenryBrooke	36
			(Martin Todhunter) *in tch: lost pl 6th: sn wknd and bhd* **200/1**	
0-	F		**Fifteen Kings (IRE)**[185] 5520 5-10-9 0.... GrahamWatters(3)	
			(Lucinda Russell) *led: hdd 6th: sn rdn and wknd: wl btn whn fell 3 out* **22/1**	

3m 43.9s (223.90)
WFA 4 from 5yo 9lb **8** Ran SP% **113.1**
CSF £2.00 TOTE £1.50: £1.10, £1.10, £4.10; EX 2.30 Trifecta £12.60.
Owner Kenny Haughey & Laura Sabiani **Bred** Jimmy Finn **Trained** Greystoke, Cumbria

FOCUS
This was all about the returning winner and he didn't disappoint. The runner-up sets the level.

2102 HAPPY BIRTHDAY ALLIE H'CAP HURDLE (DIV I) (12 hdls) 3m 70y

2:15 (2:15) (Class 5) (0-100,103) 4-Y-0+ **£2,599** (£763; £381; £190)

Form				RPR
6011	1		**Love The Leader (IRE)**[7] 2004 7-11-8 **103** 7ex....(p) DavidNoonan(7)	114+
			(Johnny Farrelly) *trckd ldng pair: rdn appr 3 out: chal strly between last 2: hit last: led run-in: kpt on* **2/1**[1]	

061 2 1 **Andhaar**[2] 2071 9-11-2 **100** BlairCampbell(10) 109+
(N W Alexander) *hld up in tch: hdwy appr 3 out: hit 3 out but led: sn rdn: strly pressed between last 2: nt fluent last: hdd run-in: kpt on* **5/2**[2]
0011 3 10 **Touch Of Steel (IRE)**[22] 1779 6-10-13 **92** (b) DaleIrving(5) 92
(James Ewart) *trckd ldng pair: hit 9th: rdn and bdly outpcd appr 3 out: plugged on after 2 out: wnt modest 3rd run-in* **15/2**
052- 4 2 1/4 **Farragon (IRE)**[237] 4549 5-11-2 **93** (v) DerekFox(3) 89
(Lucinda Russell) *trckd ldng pair: chal 3 out: sn rdn: wknd after 2 out: lost 3rd run-in* **4/1**[3]
-154 5 nk **My Friend George**[122] 841 9-10-8 **85** (p) ColmMcCormack(3) 82
(Kenneth Slack) *led narrowly: hdd 4th but cl up: slow 7th and lost pl: rdn and dropped to rr 9th: no threat after* **9/1**
52-4 6 2 1/2 **Kilquiggan (IRE)**[165] 299 7-11-7 **95** BrianHughes 89
(Sandy Thomson) *w ldr: led narrowly 4th: hdd 3 out: sn wknd* **14/1**
6m 10.0s (-21.80) **Going Correction** -1.175s/f (Hard) 6 Ran SP% **110.3**
Speed ratings (Par 103): **89,88,85,84,84 83**
CSF £7.37 CT £26.14 TOTE £2.40: £1.70, £2.30; EX 7.70 Trifecta £27.30.
Owner Johnny Farrelly **Bred** Mrs Margaret Lacy **Trained** Enmore, Somerset

FOCUS
Decent form for the class with the right horses to the fore.

2103 HAPPY BIRTHDAY ALLIE H'CAP HURDLE (DIV II) (12 hdls) 3m 70y
2:45 (2:45) (Class 5) (0-100,100) 4-Y-0+ **£2,599** (£763; £381; £190)

Form RPR
6542 1 **Destiny Awaits (IRE)**[22] 1779 6-11-4 **92** RichardJohnson 99+
(Keith Pollock) *hld up: tk clsr order bef 9th: led 3 out: rdn after 2 out: kpt on* **11/4**[2]
21P- 2 3 **Bracing**[187] 5473 6-10-5 **86** MrKitAlexander(7) 90
(N W Alexander) *in tch: hdwy to ld appr 3 out: hdd 3 out: sn rdn: one pce and hld in 2nd run-in* **15/2**
PPP- 3 36 **Finaghy Ayr (IRE)**[205] 5135 7-11-9 **100** GrahamWatters(3) 74
(Ian Duncan) *midfield: nt fluent 5th: rdn after 8th: sn struggling: nt fluent 9th: wnt remote 3rd 2 out* **8/1**
5U2/ 4 22 **Heron's Mill (IRE)**[577] 5056 7-11-0 **93** DaleIrving(5) 45
(James Ewart) *led: hit 3rd: jnd appr 9th: hdd appr 3 out: sn wknd* **11/8**[1]
/0-0 5 22 **Messina Straights**[16] 1852 7-10-4 **83** GaryRutherford(5) 15
(George Bewley) *trckd ldr: nt fluent 3rd: jnd ldr bef 9th: rdn appr 3 out: sn wknd* **33/1**
6640 F **Naburn**[27] 1683 7-11-10 **98** BrianHarding
(Andrew Wilson) *hld up in rr: fell 8th* **6/1**[3]
6m 2.0s (-29.80) **Going Correction** -1.175s/f (Hard) 6 Ran SP% **108.9**
Speed ratings (Par 103): **102,101,89,81,74**
CSF £20.76 CT £128.69 TOTE £3.60: £2.00, £3.70; EX 12.10 Trifecta £79.50.
Owner Keith Pollock **Bred** Rabbah Bloodstock Limited **Trained** Carluke, Lanarks

FOCUS
This moderate staying handicap proved another race where two came well clear. The time was 8secs quicker than the first division.

2104 RACING UK ANDROID APP RACINGUK.COM H'CAP CHASE (11 fncs 1 omitted) 1m 7f 112y
3:20 (3:22) (Class 4) (0-120,120) 4-Y-0+ **£4,223** (£1,240; £620; £310)

Form RPR
36-1 1 **Monbeg River (IRE)**[33] 1630 6-11-7 **115** HenryBrooke 130+
(Martin Todhunter) *trckd ldng pair: lft 2nd 7th: led after 3 out: rdn clr between last 2: eased towards fin* **13/8**[1]
P-53 2 8 **Ballycool (IRE)**[24] 1738 8-11-0 **111** (t) DerekFox(3) 115
(Lucinda Russell) *hld up: stdy hdwy fr 5th: lft 3rd and sltly hmpd by faller 7th: wnt 2nd 2 out: sn drvn and no ex* **4/1**[3]
4/3- 3 8 **Castlelawn (IRE)**[506] 619 8-11-2 **110** PeterBuchanan 108
(Lucinda Russell) *led narrowly: hdd after 3rd: remained cl up: led again 7th: rdn whn hdd after 3 out: lost 2nd w blunder 2 out: wknd* **10/3**[2]
416- 4 18 **Too Cool To Fool (IRE)**[192] 5363 12-10-13 **107** JamesReveley 96
(Jim Goldie) *hld up: rdn after 4 out: sn wknd: blnd 2 out* **10/1**
-212 5 8 **Carters Rest**[120] 848 12-9-11 **98** MissJJWalton(7) 69
(George Bewley) *a towards rr* **14/1**
4/U- 6 10 **Formidableopponent (IRE)**[163] 345 8-11-5 **120** MrJDixon(7) 82
(William Young Jnr) *hld up: mstke 2nd: a towards rr* **33/1**
4041 F **Harrys Whim**[24] 1738 10-11-2 **115** (t) DaraghBourke(5)
(Maurice Barnes) *pressed ldr: led narrowly after 3rd: fell 7th* **9/1**
3m 44.1s (-26.60) **Going Correction** -1.50s/f (Hard) 7 Ran SP% **109.9**
Speed ratings (Par 105): **106,102,98,89,85 80,**
CSF £8.17 CT £16.53 TOTE £2.50: £3.40, £2.40; EX 9.60 Trifecta £21.70.
Owner V Vyner-Brookes & Bill Hazeldean **Bred** Ballycrane Stud **Trained** Orton, Cumbria

FOCUS
This modest handicap was run at a solid gallop and looks straightforward rated around the runner-up. The winner is progressive and should win more races.

2105 WATCH ON 3 DEVICES RACINGUK.COM ANYWHERE NOVICES' H'CAP CHASE (17 fncs) 2m 4f 110y
3:55 (3:56) (Class 3) (0-125,124) 4-Y-0+ **£7,797** (£2,289; £1,144; £572)

Form RPR
33-2 1 **Jack Steel (IRE)**[32] 1638 5-10-13 **115** RichardJohnson 129+
(Lucinda Russell) *hld up: stdy hdwy after 9th: sltly hmpd by faller 3 out (usual 4 out) but sn led gng wl: eased clr on extended run to last: nt fluent last: briefly nudged out: v easily* **5/4**[1]
P0-2 2 5 **Retrieve The Stick**[170] 205 6-10-3 **105** oh2 (b) BrianHughes 104
(Malcolm Jefferson) *in tch: trckd ldr whn blnd 10th: lft in front 3 out (usual 4 out) but sn hdd: drvn after 2 out (usual 3 out): kpt on but no ch w easy wnr* **10/1**
015- 3 1 1/4 **Un Noble (FR)**[203] 5202 5-10-10 **115** CraigNichol(3) 113
(Nicky Richards) *hld up in midfield: sltly hmpd by faller 9th and sn pushed along: hit 2 out (usual 3 out): wnt 3rd on extended run to last: kpt on* **5/1**[2]
3210 4 6 **Volcanic (FR)**[26] 1701 6-11-8 **124** (t) BrianHarding 117
(Donald McCain) *trckd ldr: hit 5th: reminder after 6th: rdn after 3 out (usual 4 out): lost 3rd on extended run to last: nt fluent last: wknd* **12/1**
500- 5 16 **The Bishop (IRE)**[187] 5469 7-9-12 **105** oh3 StephenMulqueen(5) 85
(N W Alexander) *hld up: mstke 8th: sn struggling* **20/1**
60-2 6 33 **Dr Moloney (IRE)**[153] 483 8-10-9 **111** PeterBuchanan 57
(S R B Crawford, Ire) *hld up: mstke 11th: sn wknd: t.o* **10/1**
4-13 F **Ueueteotl (FR)**[153] 483 7-10-13 **120** (p) DaleIrving(5)
(James Ewart) *trckd ldr: fell 9th* **11/2**[3]
/FP- F **Woodpole Academy (IRE)**[316] 3095 8-11-0 **116** JamesReveley
(Philip Kirby) *led: fell 3 out (usual 4 out)* **16/1**
5m 6.9s (306.90) 8 Ran SP% **113.0**
CSF £14.12 CT £47.41 TOTE £2.20: £1.10, £2.40, £1.70; EX 14.80 Trifecta £67.40.
Owner John P McManus **Bred** Mrs Ann Eustace **Trained** Arlary, Perth & Kinross

FOCUS
This novice handicap was eventful, but it was still won by a big improver who looked to have plenty in hand.

2106 WESTERN HOUSE HOTEL STANDARD OPEN NATIONAL HUNT FLAT RACE 2m
4:25 (4:26) (Class 6) 4-6-Y-0 **£1,711** (£498; £249)

Form RPR
3-1 1 **Fagan**[32] 1640 5-11-7 0 RichardJohnson 125+
(Gordon Elliott, Ire) *trckd ldr: pushed along to chal over 1f out: rdn to ld jst ins fnl f: hung repeatedly lft: hld on towards fin* **5/6**[1]
1 2 1/2 **Meet The Legend**[40] 1555 4-11-4 0 CraigNichol(3) 124+
(Keith Dalgleish) *led: rdn whn pressed over 1f out: hdd jst ins fnl f: kpt on* **11/8**[2]
3 17 **Spirit Of Kayf** 4-11-0 0 BrianHughes 103
(Sandy Thomson) *hld up in tch: hdwy into 3rd 4f out: rdn over 2f out: one pce and sn no ch w ldng pair* **20/1**[3]
4 14 **Agentleman (IRE)**[221] 4880 5-11-0 0 JamesReveley 89
(Tim Easterby) *in tch: rdn over 3f out: wknd over 2f out* **22/1**
5 7 **September Son (IRE)** 5-10-11 0 GrahamWatters(3) 83
(Ian Duncan) *hld up: rdn over 4f out: nvr threatened* **80/1**
2- 6 nk **My Simon (IRE)**[233] 4622 6-10-11 0 DerekFox(3) 83
(Peter Croke, Ire) *in tch: rdn over 4f out: wknd over 3f out* **25/1**
7 86 **Mcginty's Dream (IRE)** 4-10-7 0 [1] MrKitAlexander(7) 5
(N W Alexander) *racd keenly in tch tl lost pl qckly 1/2-way: sn t.o* **50/1**
8 4 1/2 **Crookofdevon** 6-11-0 0 HenryBrooke 1
(Jean McGregor) *a in rr: t.o 1/2-way* **200/1**
3m 37.4s (217.40)
WFA 4 from 5yo+ 9lb 8 Ran SP% **113.3**
CSF £2.01 TOTE £1.90: £1.10, £1.10, £2.00; EX 2.60 Trifecta £8.70.
Owner R A Bartlett **Bred** J R Weston **Trained** Longwood, Co Meath

FOCUS
Two potentially very useful sorts dominated this concluding bumper with the winner building on the promise of his Perth win.
T/Plt: £9.20 to a £1 stake. Pool: £53,257.60 - 4,209.33 winning tickets T/Qpdt: £8.70 to a £1 stake. Pool: £4,171.05 - 350.77 winning tickets **Andrew Sheret**

2107 - 2120a (Foreign Racing) - See Raceform Interactive

1712 BANGOR-ON-DEE (L-H)
Tuesday, October 27

OFFICIAL GOING: Good (6.6)
Wind: fresh 1/2 behind Weather: overcast, rain race 4 onwards

2121 LINDOP TOYOTA CONDITIONAL JOCKEYS' H'CAP HURDLE (11 hdls) 2m 3f 123y
1:55 (1:56) (Class 4) (0-110,108) 4-Y-0+ **£3,249** (£954; £477; £238)

Form RPR
5-02 1 **Murray Mount (IRE)**[17] 1844 5-11-4 **100** HarryBannister 105+
(Charlie Mann) *trckd ldrs: stmbld bnd after 5th: led 3 out: nt fluent last: rdr sn dropped reins: kpt on: all out* **5/1**[3]
60-P 2 hd **Drumlang (IRE)**[143] 642 9-11-12 **108** JakeHodson 111
(Kevin Frost) *trckd ldrs: cl 2nd appr 2 out: upsides last: no ex nr fin* **7/1**
4242 3 19 **Fred Le Macon (FR)**[19] 1818 6-11-1 **107** KevinDowling(10) 97
(Alan King) *chsd ldrs: blnd and rdr temporarily lost irons 6th: 3rd appr 2 out: one pce* **2/1**[1]
063- 4 34 **Bears Rails**[206] 5146 5-11-1 **103** PaulO'Brien(6) 58
(Colin Tizzard) *trckd ldrs: t.k.h: lost pl after 3 out: sn bhd* **10/3**[2]
P/6P 5 3 3/4 **He's A Hawker (IRE)**[12] 1933 10-10-13 **95** (v) ConorRing 47
(Michael Mullineaux) *led: drvn 6th: hdd 3 out: lost pl and poor 5th whn blnd 2 out* **20/1**
1F-0 6 6 **Catchin Time (IRE)**[180] 43 7-11-8 **104** TomBellamy 50
(Laura Hurley) *in rr: hdwy 6th: sn chsng ldrs: lost pl sn after 3 out: sn bhd* **8/1**
35-6 P **Norse Light**[14] 1893 4-11-11 **107** (p) KieronEdgar
(David Dennis) *trckd ldrs: t.k.h: reminders 7th: sn lost pl and bhd: t.o whn p.u bef 3 out* **10/1**
4m 59.0s (7.00) **Going Correction** +0.45s/f (Soft)
WFA 4 from 5yo+ 10lb 7 Ran SP% **110.5**
Speed ratings (Par 105): **104,103,96,82,81 78,**
CSF £35.77 TOTE £8.30: £2.50, £4.00; EX 34.80 Trifecta £119.40.
Owner Mark Hitchcroft **Bred** George Masterson **Trained** Upper Lambourn, Berks

FOCUS
Actual race distance 2m 3f 167yds. The first two finished well clear in this weak handicap hurdle and the winner was building on his Chepstow run. It was run at a modest tempo and the time was a full 35 seconds slower than standard.

2122 BETDAQ.COM 2% COMMISSION NOVICES' CHASE (15 fncs) 2m 4f 72y
2:30 (2:30) (Class 4) 5-Y-0+ **£5,198** (£1,526; £763; £381)

Form RPR
14P- 1 **Coologue (IRE)**[193] 5362 6-10-12 128 RichardJohnson 140+
(Charlie Longsdon) *mde all: hit 11th: drvn clr between last 2: eased towards fin* **7/1**[3]
P50- 2 9 **Smooth Stepper**[193] 5362 6-10-12 125 DannyCook 130+
(Sue Smith) *chsd ldrs: outpcd and lost pl 12th: modest 3rd appr 2 out: kpt on to take 2nd towards fin* **28/1**
211- 3 3/4 **Theinval (FR)**[200] 5249 5-10-9 0 JeremiahMcGrath(3) 128+
(Nicky Henderson) *trckd ldrs 3rd: chsd wnr 12th: 7 l down last: wknd and lost 2nd clsng stages* **1/1**[1]
410- 4 20 **Nexius (IRE)**[200] 5249 6-10-12 0 SamTwiston-Davies 112
(Paul Nicholls) *hdwy to chse ldrs 7th: hit 10th: wknd appr 3 out* **2/1**[2]
26/0 5 2 1/2 **Racing Pulse (IRE)**[17] 1846 6-10-12 0 LeightonAspell 110
(Rebecca Curtis) *chsd ldrs: j. slowly 1st: pckd landing 2nd: drvn 10th: wknd 3 out* **10/1**
1U3- 6 24 **Kingfisher Creek**[211] 5059 5-10-12 129 BrendanPowell 97
(Colin Tizzard) *in rr but wl in tch: stmbld on landing 8th: lost pl 10th: bhd fr 3 out* **25/1**
P **Royal Captain (IRE)**[163] 6-10-12 0 (t) DarylJacob
(Ben Case) *chsd ldrs: lost pl 9th: bhd whn p.u bef next* **80/1**
5m 2.9s (-6.20) **Going Correction** -0.025s/f (Good) 7 Ran SP% **113.5**
Speed ratings: **111,107,107,99,98 88,**
CSF £119.07 TOTE £7.10: £3.40, £11.60; EX 123.10 Trifecta £228.30.
Owner The New Club Partnership **Bred** S J Treacy **Trained** Over Norton, Oxon

FOCUS
Race distance as advertised, and the ground on the chase course appeared to be riding close to good. This was a decent novice chase with the winner stepping up on his course hurdle win.

2123 SPORTINGBET NOVICES' HURDLE (9 hdls) 2m 145y
3:00 (3:03) (Class 4) 4-Y-0+ £5,198 (£1,526; £763; £381)

Form RPR
3 1 **Lady Yeats**17 1854 4-10-2 0 AdamNicol(3) 104
(George Moore) *reluctant ldr: increased pce after 3rd: narrowly hdd 2 out: led last: jst hld on* 10/1
10- 2 *shd* **Dashing Oscar (IRE)**312 3170 5-10-12 0 (t) NoelFehily 112+
(Harry Fry) *trckd ldr: 4th and drvn whn hit 3 out: outpcd and 5th next: kpt on and 3rd last: styd on wl towards fin: jst failed* 5/1[3]
1- 3 *shd* **Two Taffs (IRE)**219 4941 5-10-12 0 HarrySkelton 113+
(Dan Skelton) *trckd ldrs: led narrowly 2 out: hit last and narrowly hdd: styd on: jst hld* 11/8[1]
1 4 5 **Great Hall**14 1898 5-11-5 0 BrianHughes 114
(Kevin Frost) *trckd ldrs: 2nd 5th: kpt on one pce appr last* 5/1[3]
1- 5 7 **New Street (IRE)**232 4674 4-11-5 0 DarylJacob 107
(Jim Best) *hld up in rr: hdwy to trck ldrs 6th: effrt next: wknd appr last* 9/2[2]
6- 6 1 1/2 **For Good Measure (IRE)**222 4873 4-10-12 0 RichardJohnson 98
(Philip Hobbs) *in rr: sme hdwy 5th: outpcd next: no threat after* 16/1
3 7 1 1/4 **Absolute (IRE)**15 1886 4-10-12 0 DannyCook 97
(Sue Smith) *prom: outpcd 3 out: nt a factor after* 50/1
-264 8 7 **Fields Of Glory (FR)**23 1781 5-10-12 0 MichaelByrne 93
(Tim Vaughan) *in rr: bhd fr 3 out* 100/1
9 53 **Zarliman (IRE)**25 1746 5-10-5 0 KevinDarcy(7) 43
(Denis Gerard Hogan, Ire) *in rr: bhd fr 6th: t.o 2 out* 200/1
3 U **Precision Five**39 1574 6-10-5 0 (p) WayneHutchinson
(Alan King) *hld up towards rr: blnd and uns rdr 2nd* 12/1

4m 17.9s (7.00) **Going Correction** +0.45s/f (Soft) **10** Ran SP% **119.7**
Speed ratings (Par 105): **101,100,100,98,95 94,93,90,65,**
CSF £61.62 TOTE £15.70: £3.60, £1.70, £1.10; EX 99.30 Trifecta £269.90.
Owner A Crute & Partners **Bred** Biddestone Stud Ltd **Trained** Middleham Moor, N Yorks

FOCUS
Actual race distance 2m 189yds. A tight finish to this ordinary novice hurdle, in which they went a very sedate pace early on. Probably not form to take too literally, but the winner was in line with her Hexham run.

2124 BETDAQ.COM #50 FREE BET H'CAP CHASE (12 fncs) 2m 1f 77y
3:30 (3:32) (Class 4) (0-105,105) 4-Y-0+ £5,475 (£1,596; £798)

Form RPR
0/23 1 **Gee Hi (IRE)**61 1372 9-11-12 105 GavinSheehan 125+
(Warren Greatrex) *w ldrs: led 6th: wnt clr between last 2: heavily eased last 75yds* 5/4[1]
42F1 2 24 **Chankillo**22 1796 6-10-13 92 (p) SamTwiston-Davies 95+
(Sarah-Jayne Davies) *led: hdd 6th: drvn 3 out: 12 l down whn mstke last* 9/4[2]
P634 3 18 **Toe To Toe (IRE)**43 1548 7-10-0 79 oh4 (t) WillKennedy 51
(John Flint) *chsd ldrs: pushed along 7th: lost pl 9th* 13/2
3223 4 1 1/4 **Keychain (IRE)**14 1894 5-11-7 100 (v) BrendanPowell 72
(Brendan Powell) *chsd ldrs: drvn and reminders 7th: sn lost pl bhd fr 9th* 6/1[3]
2F60 5 32 **Red Whisper**37 1603 11-10-9 88 (t) JamesBest 42
(Rob Summers) *in rr: outpcd and reminders 6th: wl bhd 3 out* 16/1
6F04 P **Dover The Moon (IRE)**28 1687 4-10-0 88 oh10 (t) JamesDavies
(Tom Gretton) *chsd ldrs 2nd: drvn 8th: lost pl next: sn bhd: t.o 3 out: last whn p.u bef next* 66/1

4m 25.7s (3.60) **Going Correction** -0.025s/f (Good)
WFA 4 from 5yo+ 9lb 6 Ran SP% **110.2**
Speed ratings (Par 105): **90,78,70,69,54**
CSF £4.52 TOTE £1.90: £1.20, £1.60; EX 4.80 Trifecta £15.60.
Owner Equis **Bred** P Hore **Trained** Upper Lambourn, Berks

FOCUS
Race distance as advertised. This was a weak race for the grade and they finished at wide intervals. The winner threatened this sort of rating over hurdles.

2125 FOURSEASONS MARQUEE HIRE H'CAP HURDLE (12 hdls) 2m 7f 32y
4:00 (4:04) (Class 4) (0-120,120) 4-Y-0+ £5,198 (£1,526; £763; £381)

Form RPR
P4F- 1 **Georgie Lad (IRE)**218 4959 7-11-7 115 RichardJohnson 125
(Philip Hobbs) *hld up towards rr: hdwy 8th: cl 2nd 2 out: led briefly and narrowly last: styd on to ld nr fin* 7/2[1]
26P- 2 *hd* **Nightline**220 4926 5-11-7 115 (t) BrianHughes 125
(Charlie Longsdon) *trckd ldr 2nd: led appr 2 out: hdd narrowly and briefly last: no ex and hdd nr fin* 4/1[2]
560- 3 7 **Harry Hunt**204 5183 8-11-4 112 KielanWoods 116
(Graeme McPherson) *mid-div: chsd ldrs 6th: 3rd appr last: one pce* 10/1
-P65 4 2 3/4 **Sinbad The Sailor**22 1794 10-11-5 113 (t) AndrewTinkler 114
(George Baker) *trckd ldrs: kpt on one pce between last 2* 14/1
0303 5 7 **Storm Alert**27 1699 8-9-12 95 LucyGardner(3) 92
(Sue Gardner) *led: hdd appr 2 out: wknd between last 2* 9/2[3]
155- 6 10 **Monetary Fund (USA)**403 1570 9-11-5 113 AidanColeman 101
(Venetia Williams) *in rr: hdwy to chse ldrs 6th: wknd appr 2 out* 7/1
410- 7 75 **Glenwood Star (IRE)**212 5048 7-11-12 120 LeightonAspell 39
(Rebecca Curtis) *chsd ldrs: drvn 9th: lost pl next: t.o bef 2 out* 16/1
/3R- 8 18 **Wellforth (IRE)**339 2659 11-11-2 110 (p) DavidEngland 12
(Clare Ellam) *chsd ldrs: drvn along 5th: lost pl next: sn bhd: t.o 7th* 33/1
30-0 P **American Life (FR)**13 1911 8-11-7 115 (tp) PaulMoloney
(Sophie Leech) *racd wd: bhd fr 8th: t.o whn p.u next* 33/1
-451 P **Bayley's Dream**26 1721 6-10-12 106 LiamTreadwell
(Paul Webber) *mid-div: pushed along to chse ldrs 6th: lost pl after 8th: sn bhd: t.o whn p.u bef 2 out* 11/2

5m 58.1s (7.10) **Going Correction** +0.45s/f (Soft) 10 Ran SP% **115.8**
Speed ratings (Par 105): **105,104,102,101,99 95,69,63, ,**
CSF £18.19 CT £124.37 TOTE £4.70: £2.00, £1.30, £3.70; EX 16.80 Trifecta £137.50.
Owner D R Peppiatt & Partners (Georgie Lad) **Bred** Patrick Furlong **Trained** Withycombe, Somerset

FOCUS
Actual race distance 2m 7f 90y. Just an ordinary handicap hurdle.

2126 STELLA ARTOIS STANDARD OPEN NATIONAL HUNT FLAT RACE 2m 145y
4:30 (4:32) (Class 6) 4-6-Y-0 £2,053 (£598; £299)

Form RPR
6- 1 **Criq Rock (FR)**220 4921 4-11-0 0 WayneHutchinson 112+
(Alan King) *t.k.h in mid-div: hdwy 9f out: 2nd over 3f out: led over 2f out: forged clr over 1f out* 4/1[2]
2 11 **Royalzaro (FR)**184 5-11-0 0 NoelFehily 102
(Harry Fry) *w ldr: led after 2f: hdd over 2f out: kpt on same pce* 7/4[1]
3 3 7 **Chase End Charlie (IRE)**157 444 4-11-0 0 RobertDunne 96
(Tom Lacey) *chsd ldrs: drvn 6f out: edgd lft over 3f out: one pce* 20/1
0- 4 6 **Sartorial Elegance**209 5105 4-11-0 0 DarylJacob 91
(Colin Tizzard) *chsd ldrs: drvn 6f out: one pce fnl 3f: modest 4th 1f out* 11/1
5 3/4 **Trans Express (IRE)**233 5-10-11 0 LucyGardner(3) 90
(Sue Gardner) *in rr: sme hdwy 8f out: outpcd and poor 8th 2f out: swtchd rt over 1f out: styd on* 33/1
2 6 1 1/4 **Tanarpino**26 1717 4-11-0 0 PeterCarberry 89
(Jennie Candlish) *mid-div: hdwy to chse ldrs 6f out: sn drvn: one pce fnl 3f* 13/2[3]
7 2 **Breath Of Blighty (FR)**198 4-11-0 0 LiamTreadwell 87
(Paul Webber) *led 2f: chsd ldrs: drvn and hmpd over 3f out: one pce* 16/1
8 9 **Manton Boy** 6-11-0 0 KielanWoods 79
(Michael Mullineaux) *in rr: drvn and hdwy 7f out: hmpd and lost pl over 3f out* 100/1
43-0 9 22 **Holy Cross (IRE)**32 1644 4-11-0 0 (b[1]) LeightonAspell 59
(Rebecca Curtis) *chsd ldrs: outpcd whn hmpd over 3f out: sn lost pl* 14/1
10 3 **Just So Cool (IRE)**184 4-11-0 0 AidanColeman 56
(David Dennis) *mid-div: drvn 6f out: sn lost pl and bhd* 14/1
00-0 11 1 **Vitarra**100 1057 6-10-7 0 TomO'Brien 49
(Jim Wilson) *in rr: drvn 7f out: sn wl bhd* 150/1
12 6 **Another Frontier (IRE)** 4-11-0 0 SamTwiston-Davies 50
(Nigel Twiston-Davies) *mid-div: reminders 6f out: sn lost pl and bhd* 9/1
13 1/2 **Thyne For Gold (IRE)**184 4-11-0 0[1] AdrianLane 50
(Donald McCain) *in rr: reminders 7f out: sn wl bhd* 25/1
44 14 85 **Battle Master**152 526 5-10-11 0 BenPoste(3)
(Michael Mullineaux) *mid-div: drvn 8f out: sn lost pl: tailed rt off 4f out* 66/1

4m 6.3s (1.00) **Going Correction** +0.45s/f (Soft)
WFA 4 from 5yo+ 9lb **14** Ran SP% **121.9**
Speed ratings: **115,109,106,103,103 102,101,97,87,85 85,82,82,42**
CSF £10.93 TOTE £4.10: £1.90, £1.70, £5.80; EX 17.50 Trifecta £392.10.
Owner The Trouble Partnership **Bred** S C E A Haras Des Monts D'Arree Et Al **Trained** Barbury Castle, Wilts

FOCUS
Actual race distance 2m 189y. This didn't look a bad bumper overall and the winner, who took a big step up from his debut run, is a nice prospect.
T/Plt: £419.70 to a £1 stake. Pool: £51,032.69 - 88.75 winning tickets. T/Qpdt: £4.80 to a £1 stake. Pool: £6,109.03 - 934.06 winning tickets. **Walter Glynn**

2127 - 2134a (Foreign Racing) - See Raceform Interactive

1941 FAKENHAM (L-H)
Wednesday, October 28

OFFICIAL GOING: Good to soft (6.6)
Wind: Light across Weather: Drizzle

2135 INJURED JOCKEYS FUND H'CAP HURDLE (13 hdls) 2m 7f 95y
1:10 (1:11) (Class 4) (0-110,109) 4-Y-0+ £4,790 (£1,396; £698)

Form RPR
3121 1 **Tokyo Javilex (FR)**11 1961 8-10-12 102 (t) MrLDrowne(7) 107+
(Nigel Hawke) *a.p: chsd ldr 8th: pushed along appr 3 out: rdn to ld whn nt fluent last: styd on wl* 2/1[1]
2303 2 3 1/2 **Weybridge Light**11 1692 10-11-4 104 (b) AdamNicol(3) 104
(David Thompson) *chsd ldrs: led after 3 out: rdn and hdd appr last: styd on same pce flat* 10/1
310- 3 12 **Gilzean (IRE)**216 4991 9-11-11 108 DarylJacob 98
(Alex Hales) *hld up: hdwy after 3 out: rdn and wkng whn blnd last* 11/2
4111 4 1 1/2 **Occasionally Yours (IRE)**24 1770 11-11-5 109 MissTWorsley(7) 97
(Alan Blackmore) *set stdy pce tl hdd 7th: chsd ldr to next: pushed along and outpcd appr 3 out: rallied bef next: wknd after 2 out* 8/1
5 9 **Emmy Lou (IRE)**55 1467 7-10-13 103 (p) KevinDarcy(7) 83
(Denis Gerard Hogan, Ire) *hld up: rdn and wknd after 2 out* 5/1[3]
-342 6 1/2 **Wily Fox**23 1794 8-11-12 109 (b) JackQuinlan 88
(James Eustace) *chsd ldr tl led 7th: nt fluent 10th: hdd after 3 out: sn rdn: wknd after next* 3/1[2]

6m 33.0s (11.00) **Going Correction** +0.45s/f (Soft) 6 Ran SP% **110.6**
Speed ratings (Par 105): **98,96,92,92,88 88**
CSF £19.70 TOTE £2.50: £1.10, £5.10; EX 17.90 Trifecta £77.90.
Owner D R Mead **Bred** Scea Ecurie Jc Laisis **Trained** Stoodleigh, Devon

FOCUS
Rail re-alignment affected race distances. Race 1 add 237 yards, race 2 and 3 add 158 yards, race 4 add 172 yards, race 5 add 197 yards, race 6 add 215 yards and race 7 add 158 yards. The opener was a moderate event for stayers in which the early gallop was very slow, but this was another step up from the winner.

2136 FAKENHAM "NATIONAL HUNT" MAIDEN HURDLE (9 hdls) 2m 3y
1:40 (1:41) (Class 5) 4-Y-0+ £3,249 (£954; £477; £238)

Form RPR
04- 1 **Miami Present (IRE)**81 1209 5-11-0 0 DannyCook 110+
(Harriet Bethell) *chsd ldr tl led after 3 out: rdn clr appr last* 6/1[3]
4- 2 7 **Blue April (FR)**210 5104 4-11-0 0 NickScholfield 103
(Jeremy Scott) *hld up: hdwy after 2 out: r.o to go 2nd flat: no ch w wnr* 25/1
/50- 3 2 1/2 **Act Of Supremacy (IRE)**325 2968 5-11-0 0 GavinSheehan 102
(Warren Greatrex) *led: nt fluent 6th: rdn and hdd after 3 out: wknd appr last* 14/1
16- 4 1 1/4 **Legend Lady**200 5277 4-10-7 0 LeightonAspell 95+
(Oliver Sherwood) *hld up: mstke 1st: hdwy 4th: nt fluent 6th: ev ch 2 out: sn rdn: wknd last* 1/1[1]
/20- 5 7 **Heresmynumber (IRE)**205 5200 5-11-0 0 AdamWedge 93
(Ali Stronge) *hld up: nvr on terms* 20/1
361- 6 14 **Outrath (IRE)**311 3217 5-11-0 0 (t) SamTwiston-Davies 86
(Jim Best) *prom: rdn appr 3 out: wknd bef next* 5/1[2]

7 17 **The Pine Martin (IRE)**[22] 1799 5-11-0 0 TomO'Brien 65
(Denis Gerard Hogan, Ire) *hld up: rdn and wknd bef 6th* 66/1
U4 8 8 **Mesut (FR)**[12] 1942 4-11-0 107 JackQuinlan 58
(Sarah Humphrey) *chsd ldrs tl wknd 3 out* 33/1
2-P P **Basilic D'Alene (FR)**[20] 1826 4-11-0 0 RichardJohnson
(Nick Williams) *hld up: mstke 5th: sn rdn and wknd: bhd whn p.u bef 3 out: fatally injured* 7/1
4m 15.9s (2.90) **Going Correction** +0.45s/f (Soft) **9** Ran SP% **113.2**
Speed ratings (Par 103): **110,106,105,104,101 94,85,81,**
CSF £126.37 TOTE £7.90: £1.90, £5.30, £2.90; EX 81.20 Trifecta £834.30.
Owner W A Bethell **Bred** Kevin Galvin **Trained** Arnold, E Yorks

FOCUS
This probably won't prove to be an overly strong race in the short term, but last year's winner (who has yet to get his head to the front subsequently) reached a mark of 132 over hurdles. The winner set a fair standard and is rated in line with the best of his Irish form.

2137 BREEDERS' CUP ON AT THE RACES FILLIES' JUVENILE HURDLE (9 hdls) 2m 3y
2:10 (2:10) (Class 3) 3-Y-O **£5,848** (£1,717; £858; £429)

Form RPR
1 **Mystery Code**[16] 3-10-12 0 WayneHutchinson 95+
(Alan King) *hld up: hdwy 4th: led 2 out: sn rdn clr: nt fluent last: eased nr fin* 1/1[1]
4 2 4 1/2 **Culture De Sivola (FR)**[24] 1772 3-10-7 0 LizzieKelly(5) 88+
(Nick Williams) *chsd ldr: outpcd after 3 out: rallied to go 2nd last: styd on* 5/1[2]
3254 3 2 **Auld Fyffee (IRE)**[26] 1732 3-10-12 97 JamesDavies 84
(Tom Gretton) *led: hdd 2 out: styd on same pce appr last* 14/1
4 9 **Meadow Cross (IRE)**[11] 1759 3-10-12 0 TomO'Brien 77
(Denis Gerard Hogan, Ire) *hld up: hmpd 2nd: styd on appr last: nvr nrr* 28/1
5 11 **Old Fashion**[77] 3-10-12 0 RichardJohnson 66
(Neil King) *chsd ldrs: nt fluent 3rd: mstke 2 out: sn rdn and wknd* 5/1[2]
6 2 3/4 **Rejaah**[114] 3-10-12 0 ConorO'Farrell 64
(Nigel Hawke) *hld up: wknd appr 2 out* 16/1
7 17 **Rest Easy**[109] 3-10-7 0 KevinJones(5) 48
(Seamus Mullins) *plld hrd and prom: lost pl 4th: wknd appr 6th* 66/1
8 34 **The Wee Barra (IRE)**[20] 3-10-12 0 BrianHughes 18
(Kevin Ryan) *prom tl rdn and wknd appr 3 out* 8/1[3]
P **Miss Excellence**[144] 3-10-12 0 (t) JackQuinlan
(Caroline Fryer) *hld up: j.rt 2nd: bhd whn j. slowly 5th: sn p.u* 100/1
4m 20.7s (7.70) **Going Correction** +0.45s/f (Soft) **9** Ran SP% **112.9**
Speed ratings (Par 102): **98,95,94,90,84 83,74,57,**
CSF £6.14 TOTE £2.00: £1.10, £2.00, £2.90; EX 7.80 Trifecta £31.90.
Owner The Barbury Lions **Bred** Barbury Castle Stud **Trained** Barbury Castle, Wilts

FOCUS
Last year's first three in this haven't managed a win between them in eight subsequent starts, so it remains to be seen how strong this race proved to be. The early gallop wasn't quick, but the cosy winner can rate higher..

2138 COOL ROXY OWNERS' & TRAINERS' BAR H'CAP CHASE (12 fncs) 2m 59y
2:40 (2:40) (Class 4) (0-115,115) 4-Y-O+ **£5,198** (£1,526; £763; £381)

Form RPR
13-4 1 **Artifice Sivola (FR)**[177] 107 5-11-12 113 LeightonAspell 130+
(Lucy Wadham) *mde all: racd keenly: clr fr 4th: unchal* 4/1[2]
0-1 2 17 **Be On Time (FR)**[14] 1907 4-11-5 115 BrendanPowell 109+
(Jamie Snowden) *chsd ldrs: wnt 2nd after 3 out: sn rdn: wknd appr last* 2/1[1]
203- 3 5 **Snowell (IRE)**[201] 5261 8-11-3 107 (p) JamesBanks(3) 104
(Emma Baker) *prom: blnd 1st: nt fluent 7th: chsd wnr 9th tl after 3 out: rdn and wknd after 2 out* 10/1
P-35 4 10 **Ciceron (IRE)**[11] 1965 9-11-12 113 (t) MarkGrant 99
(Neil King) *chsd wnr to 9th: wknd bef next* 16/1
25-2 5 3 1/4 **Sportsreport (IRE)**[174] 175 7-11-7 108 (p) AndrewThornton 91
(Seamus Mullins) *hld up: hdwy 9th: wknd after 3 out* 5/1[3]
13-5 6 3 1/4 **Midnight Chorister**[14] 1907 7-11-7 108 (t) KielanWoods 89
(Alex Hales) *hld up: nt fluent 3rd: wknd 9th* 6/1
222- P **Money For Nothing**[226] 4808 6-11-9 110 (t) DannyCook
(Harriet Bethell) *hld up: hdwy 8th: rdn and wknd bef next: bhd whn p.u after 3 out* 6/1
4m 21.5s (4.90) **Going Correction** +0.45s/f (Soft)
WFA 4 from 5yo+ 9lb **7** Ran SP% **113.5**
Speed ratings (Par 105): **105,96,94,89,87 85,**
CSF £12.83 CT £72.07 TOTE £4.00: £2.10, £1.80; EX 16.40 Trifecta £85.10.
Owner R B Holt **Bred** Gilles Trapenard **Trained** Newmarket, Suffolk

FOCUS
The winner put in a fine display of jumping in front, and never came back to his rivals.

2139 CROWN INN CATERING AT FAKENHAM RACECOURSE H'CAP HURDLE (11 hdls) 2m 4f 1y
3:10 (3:10) (Class 4) (0-105,104) 3-Y-O+ **£3,249** (£954; £477; £238)

Form RPR
6-F2 1 **Bowdler's Magic**[24] 1774 8-11-12 104 BrianHughes 118+
(David Thompson) *a.p: chsd ldr 3 out: led after next: rdn clr bef last* 8/1[3]
633- 2 8 **Iron Butterfly**[135] 4857 6-11-11 103 JackQuinlan 108
(James Eustace) *hld up: n.m.r after 7th: hdwy next: rdn after 2 out: styd on same pce: wnt 2nd last* 6/1[2]
62-3 3 4 **Calin Du Brizais (FR)**[173] 181 4-11-10 102 (t) ConorO'Farrell 104
(Nigel Hawke) *chsd ldr tl led 5th: rdn and hdd after 2 out: wknd last* 8/1[3]
0354 4 13 **Ennisnag (IRE)**[12] 1951 10-11-4 96 TomO'Brien 86
(Paul Henderson) *hld up: hdwy appr 3 out: rdn and wknd bef next* 8/1[3]
-5U1 5 26 **Dainty Diva (IRE)**[7] 2015 7-11-6 98 NickScholfield 64
(Jeremy Scott) *chsd ldrs: n.m.r bnd after 5th: wnt 2nd after 7th: rdn 3 out: wknd after next* 1/1[1]
106- P **Running Wolf (IRE)**[234] 4650 4-11-3 98 JamesBanks(3)
(Alex Hales) *hld up: hdwy 4th: wknd after 8th: bhd whn p.u bef last* 14/1
145 P **Black Iceman**[41] 1346 7-11-5 104 DavidNoonan(7)
(Lydia Pearce) *hld up: mstke 8th: sn wknd: bhd whn p.u bef last* 20/1
0PF4 P **Exit To Freedom**[29] 1691 9-9-11 78 oh5 (p) AdamNicol(3)
(John Wainwright) *led to 5th: sn drvn along: wknd 8th: bhd whn p.u bef last* 25/1
5m 26.6s (6.20) **Going Correction** +0.45s/f (Soft)
WFA 4 from 6yo+ 10lb **8** Ran SP% **112.9**
Speed ratings (Par 105): **105,101,100,95,84 , ,**
CSF £53.44 CT £395.60 TOTE £8.70: £1.90, £2.10, £2.10; EX 53.00 Trifecta £180.90.
Owner N Park **Bred** Miss K Rausing **Trained** Bolam, Co Durham

FOCUS
They only went a modest gallop in this moderate handicap. The winner was on a good mark and is rated back to his best.

2140 REINHOLD JOCKEYS' MEDICAL ROOM AT FAKENHAM H'CAP CHASE (16 fncs) 2m 5f 44y
3:40 (3:40) (Class 4) (0-110,110) 4-Y-O+ **£4,659** (£1,446; £779)

Form RPR
3P44 1 **Milgen Bay**[24] 1767 9-11-7 108 ThomasGarner(3) 120
(Oliver Sherwood) *w ldrs: led 12th: rdn after 2 out: all out* 7/1
3-P1 2 hd **Road To Freedom**[161] 397 6-11-12 110 LeightonAspell 124+
(Lucy Wadham) *hld up: hmpd 1st: hdwy 11th: jnd wnr and pckd 4 out: rdn after 2 out: pckd last: styd on u.p* 5/2[1]
0-UU 3 22 **Gold Man (IRE)**[7] 2017 6-11-4 102 (t) DavidBass 94
(Kim Bailey) *hld up: hit 5th: hdwy 11th: hmpd next: sn outpcd: n.d after: wnt 3rd 2 out* 9/2[3]
PP-P P **Midnight Charmer**[18] 1850 9-11-1 102 (p) JamesBanks(3)
(Emma Baker) *led to 4th: led again 6th: to next: w ldr: j. slowly 11th: sn lost pl: in rr whn p.u bef next* 8/1
125P P **Riddlestown (IRE)**[141] 677 8-11-4 102 (b) HarrySkelton
(Caroline Fryer) *hld up: mstke 3rd: bhd fr 7th: p.u bef 10th* 10/1
64 F **Treacy Hotels Boy (IRE)**[30] 1674 8-11-2 100 TomO'Brien
(Paul Henderson) *w ldrs whn fell 1st* 14/1
56-3 P **Vesuvhill (FR)**[164] 355 6-11-7 105 DarylJacob
(Ben Case) *w ldrs: led 4th to 6th: led 7th: hdd whn blnd 12th: sn rdn: wknd 3 out: bhd whn p.u bef last* 3/1[2]
5m 48.1s (6.30) **Going Correction** +0.45s/f (Soft) **7** Ran SP% **111.1**
Speed ratings (Par 105): **106,105,97, ,**
CSF £24.28 TOTE £6.80: £3.10, £1.90; EX 23.40 Trifecta £59.30.
Owner James & Clare Luck **Bred** G R Waters **Trained** Upper Lambourn, Berks

FOCUS
This only concerned the two top weights some way from home. The winner was well in on his spring form.

2141 OXWICK STANDARD NATIONAL HUNT FLAT RACE (CONDITIONAL JOCKEYS' AND AMATEUR RIDERS' RACE) 2m 3y
4:10 (4:11) (Class 6) 4-6-Y-O **£2,053** (£598; £299)

Form RPR
1 **Potters Legend** 5-10-11 0 DavidNoonan(7) 119+
(Lucy Wadham) *chsd ldr who wnt clr 12f out: tk clsr order over 6f out: led 2 out: r.o wl* 8/1[3]
2 8 **Postbridge (IRE)** 4-10-4 0 ConorWalsh(7) 106+
(Warren Greatrex) *led: clr 12f out tl over 6f out: rdn and hdd 2f out: sn outpcd* 7/4[2]
5- 3 7 **Iconic Star**[195] 5359 5-10-4 0 CiaranGethings(7) 99+
(Philip Hobbs) *chsd ldrs: outpcd over 6f out: styd on fr over 1f out* 10/11[1]
4 34 **Mahlers Spirit (IRE)**[521] 5-10-8 0 RomainClavreul(10) 75
(Sarah Humphrey) *hld up: drvn along over 5f out: sn wknd* 16/1
5 7 **Surprise Choice (IRE)** 4-10-8 0 ConorShoemark(3) 62
(William Stone) *hld up: hdwy 7f out: rdn and wknd 4f out* 33/1
5-0 6 5 **Storm Run (IRE)**[14] 1908 4-10-4 0 HarryTeal(7) 57
(Roger Teal) *hld up: pushed along 1/2-way: wknd 5f out* 25/1
7 11 **Kerry's Lord (IRE)**[158] 6-10-11 0 BenFfrenchDavis(7) 54
(Joanne Thomason-Murphy) *prom tl wknd 5f out* 50/1
4m 12.5s (5.10) **Going Correction** +0.45s/f (Soft)
WFA 4 from 5yo+ 9lb **7** Ran SP% **114.5**
Speed ratings: **105,101,97,80,77 74,69**
CSF £22.60 TOTE £9.00: £3.30, £1.80; EX 24.30 Trifecta £43.90.
Owner Mrs J May **Bred** F S And Mrs May **Trained** Newmarket, Suffolk

FOCUS
Just an ordinary bumper, but the winner looks decent and should win more races.
T/Plt: £170.20 to a £1 stake. Pool: £60,023.53 - 257.32 winning tickets T/Qpdt: £17.40 to a £1 stake. Pool: £6,281.93 - 266.08 winning tickets **Colin Roberts**

1886 SEDGEFIELD (L-H)
Thursday, October 29

OFFICIAL GOING: Soft (good to soft in places; 6.6)
Wind: moderate 1/2 behind Weather: overcast, damp

2142 J AMER & M SWEENEY H'CAP HURDLE 2m 3f 188y
1:00 (1:00) (Class 4) (0-115,111) 3-Y-O+ **£3,768** (£1,106; £553; £276)

Form RPR
3211 1 **Amuse Me**[7] 2029 9-12-1 111 7ex BrianHughes 119+
(James Moffatt) *hld up: trckd ldrs 3rd: chsd ldr appr 2 out: led 2 out: drew clr run-in* 2/1[1]
0110 2 6 **Perseid (IRE)**[19] 1856 5-11-4 100 SeanQuinlan 100
(Sue Smith) *w ldr: led 5th: hdd 2 out: kpt on same pce between last 2* 11/4[2]
F640 3 1 **Danceintothelight**[17] 1890 8-10-1 90 (t) MissBeckySmith(7) 88
(Micky Hammond) *hld up: trckd ldrs 3rd: 3rd 2 out: one pce* 20/1
P-P0 4 12 **Polarbrook (IRE)**[14] 1931 8-10-11 93 (p) DannyCook 79
(Derek Shaw) *chsd ldrs: drvn 6th: wknd 2 out* 100/1
4422 5 5 **Rocky Two (IRE)**[30] 1684 5-11-8 107 AdamNicol(3) 88
(Philip Kirby) *w ldr: led 2nd: hdd 5th: wknd between last 2* 9/1
-U50 6 2 1/2 **Camachoice (IRE)**[28] 1714 5-11-6 107 DaraghBourke(5) 86
(Joanne Foster) *chsd ldrs: wknd appr 2 out* 40/1
133- 7 11 **Light The City (IRE)**[200] 5298 8-11-12 108 JakeGreenall 76
(Ruth Carr) *jnd ldrs 3rd: drvn 3 out: lost pl bef next* 12/1
B21/ P **Vodka Red (IRE)**[580] 5052 7-10-11 93 (p) PeterBuchanan
(Kenny Johnson) *in rr: lost pl 3 out: tailed rt off whn p.u bef next* 20/1
-400 P **Playhara (IRE)**[14] 1920 6-11-7 103 (p) HenryBrooke
(Martin Todhunter) *led to 2nd: drvn 7th: lost pl bef next: t.o whn p.u bef 2 out* 11/1
1PP- P **Hail The Brave (IRE)**[195] 5379 6-11-7 103 BrianHarding
(Michael Smith) *in rr: drvn 5th: sn bhd: tailed rt off whn p.u bef 2 out* 6/1[3]
4m 49.3s (-4.80) **10** Ran SP% **113.3**
CSF £7.50 CT £78.39 TOTE £2.80: £1.40, £1.20, £5.40; EX 10.40 Trifecta £105.40.
Owner Vilprano, Bowron & Beaumont **Bred** Whatton Manor Stud **Trained** Cartmel, Cumbria

FOCUS
Common bends and hurdles sited towards centre. Race 1 reduced by 66yds, races 3 and 7 by 54yds, and race 4 by 90yds. Race 2 increased by 12yds, race 5 by 20yds and race 6 by 19yds. .The opening contest was moderate but competitive with the winner back to his very best.

2143 MELDRUM NOVICES' H'CAP CHASE (16 fncs) 2m 3f 65y
1:30 (1:32) (Class 4) (0-105,105) 4-Y-0+ **£3,898** (£1,144; £572; £286)

Form RPR
0111 **1** **Love The Leader (IRE)**[3] 2102 7-11-3 **96**........................(p) AlainCawley 110+
(Johnny Farrelly) *trckd ldrs: led 11th: hdd 2 out: led last: styd on* **5/2**[1]

045- **2** *2* **Nautical Twilight**[207] 5161 5-11-11 **104**........................(b) BrianHughes 116+
(Malcolm Jefferson) *mid-div: chsd ldrs 6th: 2nd appr 3 out: led narrowly 2 out: hdd last: no ex* **11/1**

345- **3** *7* **Fly Home Harry**[206] 5191 6-10-8 **87**........................ PaulMoloney 92
(Alan Swinbank) *hld up in rr: hdwy 13th: 4th and drvn appr 2 out: kpt on one pce to take modest 3rd appr last* **4/1**[2]

3603 **4** *3 1/2* **Morning With Ivan (IRE)**[17] 1888 5-11-5 **98**........................ HenryBrooke 99
(Martin Todhunter) *w ldrs: led 4th to 11th: one pce appr 2 out* **20/1**

603- **5** *14* **Bollin Line**[381] 1888 8-10-8 **87**........................ JakeGreenall 74
(Lucinda Egerton) *mid-div: chsd ldrs 8th: lost pl bef 2 out* **20/1**

560- **6** *4* **Bennylicious (IRE)**[199] 5312 6-11-9 **105**........................ CraigNichol[(3)] 88
(Rose Dobbin) *chsd ldrs: drvn 13th: lost pl bef 2 out* **16/1**

5451 **P** **Champagne Agent (IRE)**[17] 1891 9-10-4 **86**........(bt) CallumWhillans[(3)]
(Donald Whillans) *led to 4th: lost pl 12th: sn bhd: t.o whn p.u bef 2 out* **8/1**

PP46 **P** **Monzino (USA)**[7] 2040 7-9-9 **79** oh10........................ DannyBurton[(5)]
(Michael Chapman) *in rr: j. slowly 2nd: t.o 8th: p.u bef 11th* **100/1**

6PP- **P** **Asuncion (FR)**[281] 3790 5-10-6 **88**........................ TonyKelly[(3)]
(Rebecca Menzies) *chsd ldrs: lost pl 8th: sn bhd: t.o 13th: p.u bef 2 out* **16/1**

45-3 **P** **Thatildee (IRE)**[180] 78 7-9-13 **83**........................ DiarmuidO'Regan[(5)]
(Chris Grant) *in rr-div: drvn and sme hdwy 10th: lost pl after 12th: sn bhd: t.o whn p.u bef last* **11/1**

26-2 **P** **Be A Dreamer**[177] 134 7-10-12 **91**........................ SeanQuinlan
(Sue Smith) *chsd ldrs: lost pl 12th: sn bhd: t.o whn p.u bef last* **7/1**[3]

6-66 **F** **Lady Busanda**[17] 1892 5-10-0 **82**........................(t) JoeColliver[(3)]
(George Moore) *in rr whn fell 1st* **33/1**

5m 0.8s (-2.20) **Going Correction** -0.175s/f (Good) **12** Ran SP% **114.1**
Speed ratings (Par 105): **97,96,93,91,85 84,,,,**
CSF £27.45 CT £106.44 TOTE £3.00: £1.40, £2.80, £1.70; EX 33.30 Trifecta £237.00.
Owner Johnny Farrelly **Bred** Mrs Margaret Lacy **Trained** Enmore, Somerset

FOCUS
Not many of these had chasing experience, so it's difficult to know the strength of the form at this stage. The winner was well in on his recent hurdle form.

2144 TEES LED LIGHTING MARES' H'CAP HURDLE (8 hdls) 2m 178y
2:00 (2:00) (Class 4) (0-120,117) 4-Y-0+ **£3,768** (£1,106; £553; £276)

Form RPR
6-21 **1** **Stoneham**[59] 813 4-10-13 **107**........................[1] KieronEdgar[(3)] 111+
(Iain Jardine) *chsd ldng pair: reminders after 5th: led bef 2 out: drvn clr run-in* **6/1**

2531 **2** *5* **Russian Royale**[24] 1793 5-11-2 **117**........................ FinianO'Toole[(10)] 117
(Micky Hammond) *trckd clr ldr: 2nd appr 2 out: drvn between last 2: 3 l down last: kpt on same pce* **3/1**[2]

3-66 **3** *4 1/2* **Hatton Springs (IRE)**[17] 1887 4-10-1 **99**........................ SamColtherd[(7)] 94
(Stuart Coltherd) *nt fluent in last: mstke 1st: hit 5th: sn drvn and hung lft: tk modest 3rd bef 2 out* **7/2**[3]

46-0 **4** *6* **Our Phylli Vera (IRE)**[17] 1892 6-10-0 **91**........................ HenryBrooke 79
(Joanne Foster) *t.k.h: led and clr to 3 out: hdd bef 2 out: wknd last* **10/1**

21 **U** **Western Breeze (IRE)**[142] 679 6-11-5 **110**........................ JakeGreenall
(Mark Walford) *jinked rt and uns rdr rdr s* **13/8**[1]

4m 7.5s (0.60) **Going Correction** +0.05s/f (Yiel)
WFA 4 from 5yo+ 9lb **5** Ran SP% **108.7**
Speed ratings (Par 105): **100,97,95,92,**
CSF £23.20 TOTE £6.80: £2.70, £1.90; EX 15.80 Trifecta £48.90.
Owner I J Jardine **Bred** Norman Court Stud **Trained** Carrutherstown, D'fries & G'way

FOCUS
Probably just a modest contest, which saw the favourite unship her rider yards after the start.

2145 ROFLOW ENGINEERING CELEBRATING 25 YEARS OF VENTILATION H'CAP HURDLE (13 hdls) 3m 3f 9y
2:30 (2:31) (Class 3) (0-135,128) 4-Y-0 **£6,330** (£1,870; £935; £468; £234)

Form RPR
612- **1** **Jac The Legend**[240] 4552 6-9-10 **105**........................ CraigGallagher[(7)] 111+
(Brian Ellison) *t.k.h: trckd ldrs: led bef 2 out: rdr lost iron last: edgd rt: eased fnl strides* **5/2**[1]

13-2 **2** *1/2* **Snapping Turtle (IRE)**[169] 291 10-10-5 **110**........................ CallumWhillans[(3)] 114+
(Donald Whillans) *led: hdd bef 2 out: rallied and 1 l down last: kpt on same pce* **9/2**[2]

-310 **3** *2 1/4* **Iora Glas (IRE)**[35] 1638 6-10-9 **111**........................ SeanQuinlan 111
(Fergal O'Brien) *hld up in rr: hdwy 10th: chsng ldrs next: kpt on same pce to take 3rd appr last* **13/2**[3]

4454 **4** *22* **Vaihau (FR)**[15] 1911 6-10-12 **114**........................(p) RichieMcLernon 94
(Jonjo O'Neill) *nt fluent: in tch: chsng ldrs 3 out: 3rd whn mstke 2 out: wknd between last 2* **8/1**

1051 **5** *3* **Sealous Scout (IRE)**[36] 1633 7-11-7 **128**........................ JamesCowley[(5)] 103
(Donald McCain) *hld up in mid-div: jnd ldrs 6th: rdn 3 out: sn lost pl and bhd* **9/1**

1-41 **6** *3/4* **Grey Monk (IRE)**[34] 1646 7-11-3 **124**........................(t) NathanMoscrop[(5)] 98
(Sara Ender) *mid-div: pushed along to chse ldrs 10th: lost pl next: sn bhd* **17/2**

330- **7** *11* **Night In Milan (IRE)**[201] 5275 9-11-5 **126**........................ MrJohnDawson[(5)] 89
(Keith Reveley) *w ldrs: lost pl bef 3 out: sn bhd* **7/1**

-P0U **8** *25* **George Fernbeck**[14] 1924 7-10-3 **115**........................ FinianO'Toole[(10)] 53
(Micky Hammond) *drvn along at various stages: reminders after 1st and 7th: chsd ldrs: lost pl and bhd after 8th: t.o 3 out* **25/1**

6m 47.7s (-4.30) **Going Correction** +0.05s/f (Yiel) **8** Ran SP% **108.1**
Speed ratings (Par 107): **108,107,107,100,99 99,96,88**
CSF £12.79 CT £54.13 TOTE £3.90: £1.40, £1.90, £3.20; EX 15.80 Trifecta £69.70.
Owner P J Martin **Bred** Hartshill Stud **Trained** Norton, N Yorks

FOCUS
Not much separated these stayers for a lot of the contest and a small personal best from the winner..

2146 SEAN MAGEE SEDGEFIELDERS DURHAM NATIONAL H'CAP CHASE (24 fncs) 3m 5f 48y
3:00 (3:02) (Class 3) (0-140,140) 5-Y-0+
£12,512 (£3,696; £1,848; £924; £462; £232)

Form RPR
6P-0 **1** **Royale Knight**[27] 1736 9-11-8 **136**........................ WillKennedy 147
(Dr Richard Newland) *hld up: wnt modest 4th 4 out: styd on to chse ldr appr last: led last: kpt on wl* **10/1**

4-30 **2** *2 3/4* **Lackamon**[15] 1903 10-10-7 **121**........................ SeanQuinlan 132
(Sue Smith) *2nd: hit 13th: led after 17th: hdd 20th: led after 4 out: hdd last: no ex* **11/4**[2]

2303 **3** *8* **Finish The Story (IRE)**[17] 1890 9-10-0 **114**........................(bt) AlainCawley 118
(Johnny Farrelly) *led: hdd after 17th: led 20th: hdd after 4 out: kpt on one pce and regained modest 3rd last* **15/2**

41-3 **4** *6* **Sun Cloud (IRE)**[36] 1633 8-11-12 **140**........................ BrianHughes 136
(Malcolm Jefferson) *hld up in rr: outpcd 18th: sn bhd: hdwy appr 2 out: fdd between last 2* **5/1**[3]

6-46 **5** *3 1/4* **Twirling Magnet (IRE)**[123] 855 9-11-7 **135**........................(tp) RichieMcLernon 131
(Jonjo O'Neill) *hld up: 3rd 20th: handy 2nd appr 2 out: 3rd and wkng whn mstke last: b.b.v* **7/1**

330- **6** *34* **Woodford County**[208] 5138 8-10-5 **126**........................(p) CiaranGethings[(7)] 89
(Philip Hobbs) *mstke 1st: chsd ldrs 6th: lost pl 18th: bhd fr 4 out* **5/2**[1]

30-1 **P** **Pinerolo**[180] 81 9-10-11 **125**........................(p) HenryBrooke
(Joanne Foster) *chsd ldr to 4th: drvn 9th: lost pl 12th: sn bhd: t.o 17th: p.u bef 20th* **25/1**

7m 46.5s (-12.50) **Going Correction** -0.175s/f (Good) **7** Ran SP% **109.1**
Speed ratings: **110,109,107,105,104 95,**
CSF £35.31 TOTE £8.30: £3.60, £2.00; EX 21.40 Trifecta £241.00.
Owner C E Stedman & R J Corsan **Bred** R D And Mrs J S Chugg **Trained** Claines, Worcs

FOCUS
A decent field including the first, second and fourth from last year llined up for this marathon handicap. Nothing of any great significance happened on the first few circuits and the leader set a fair gallop.

2147 CUMMINS DIESEL DASH NOVICES' H'CAP CHASE (21 fncs) 3m 2f 59y
3:30 (3:32) (Class 4) (0-105,105) 4-Y-0+ **£4,418** (£1,297; £648; £324)

Form RPR
0-U3 **1** **Teochew (IRE)**[27] 1739 7-11-12 **105**........................(t) DavidEngland 118+
(Richard Drake) *hld up in rr: hdwy to trck ldrs 12th: led 4 out: drew clr fr 2 out* **16/1**

0-2 **2** *14* **Camillas Wish (IRE)**[76] 1254 6-10-10 **89**........................ BrianHughes 90
(J T R Dreaper, Ire) *in rr: mstke 11th: nt fluent 15th: hdwy to chse ldrs 4 out: sn 2nd: kpt on same pce appr 2 out* **6/1**

20-0 **3** *3* **Not A Bother Boy (IRE)**[14] 1920 7-11-5 **98**........................ SeanQuinlan 93
(Sue Smith) *chsd ldrs 5th: one pce fr 4 out: hit 2 out* **5/2**[1]

43-0 **4** *nk* **Apache Pilot**[17] 1890 7-10-7 **91**........................(t) DaraghBourke[(5)] 85
(Maurice Barnes) *trckd ldrs: outpcd 4 out: kpt on one pce fr 2 out* **10/3**[2]

6P33 **5** *18* **The Society Man (IRE)**[13] 1942 8-10-7 **91**........................ DannyBurton[(5)] 67
(Michael Chapman) *led to 3rd: chsd ldrs: outpcd 13th: lost pl bef 3 out: sn bhd* **5/1**[3]

-U5P **6** *9* **Top Cat Dj (IRE)**[19] 1853 7-9-9 **79** oh5........................(v) DiarmuidO'Regan[(5)] 46
(Chris Grant) *chsd ldrs: led 10th: hdd 4 out: lost pl bef next: sn bhd* **9/1**

/2-0 **U** **Alf The Audacious**[63] 1370 9-11-0 **93**........................ DannyCook
(Sue Smith) *w ldrs: led 3rd to 10th: losing pl whn blnd and uns rdr 14th* **7/1**

7m 11.4s (0.40) **Going Correction** -0.175s/f (Good) **7** Ran SP% **111.0**
Speed ratings (Par 105): **92,87,86,86,81 78,**
CSF £98.49 CT £313.73 TOTE £14.70: £5.60, £1.80; EX 34.30 Trifecta £378.30.
Owner Mrs J Drake **Bred** Edmond Kent **Trained** Ilkley, W Yorks

FOCUS
A moderate staying handicap, run at an ordinary gallop. The winner was a 120 hurdler at her peak and looks to have run to that sort of level.

2148 SWIIS FOSTER CARE H'CAP HURDLE (8 hdls) 2m 178y
4:00 (4:02) (Class 5) (0-100,99) 3-Y-0+ **£2,599** (£763; £381; £190)

Form RPR
0540 **1** **Toola Boola**[14] 1920 5-9-11 **73** oh4........................ AdamNicol[(3)] 80
(George Moore) *hld up in rr: hdwy 5th: chsng ldrs next: led bef 2 out: drvn out* **7/1**

60/2 **2** *3/4* **Gunner Lindley (IRE)**[17] 1892 8-10-7 **87**........................ SamColtherd[(7)] 93
(Stuart Coltherd) *mid-div: hdwy to chse ldrs 5th: upsides and drvn appr 2 out: kpt on run-in: jst hld* **3/1**[1]

4330 **3** *6* **My Escapade (IRE)**[43] 1552 4-11-3 **97**........................ MissAWaugh[(7)] 96
(Simon Waugh) *mid-div: hdwy 3 out: sn drvn: kpt on same pce to take modest 3rd sn after last* **16/1**

2524 **4** *2 1/2* **Sendiym (FR)**[17] 1891 8-11-0 **87**........................ BrianHughes 84
(Dianne Sayer) *chsd ldrs: drvn 3 out: sn outpcd styd on run-in* **4/1**[2]

200- **5** *5* **Dark And Dangerous (IRE)**[260] 3621 7-11-7 **99**........................ CallumBewley[(5)] 91
(Simon Waugh) *chsd ldr: drvn 3 out: wknd between last 2* **20/1**

6505 **6** *nse* **Jebulani**[38] 1368 5-10-7 **80**........................ BrianHarding 73
(Barry Murtagh) *hld up in mid-div: hdwy to trck ldrs 3 out: 3rd next: wknd last* **13/2**[3]

435- **7** *nse* **Sirpertan**[242] 4519 4-11-5 **95**........................ JeremiahMcGrath[(3)] 87
(Marjorie Fife) *in rr: hdwy 3 out: kpt on same pce fr next: nvr a threat* **12/1**

4P00 **8** *10* **Beyondtemptation**[17] 1892 7-10-7 **85**........................(t) DiarmuidO'Regan[(5)] 67
(Jonathan Haynes) *led: hdd bef 2 out: wknd between last 2* **16/1**

6-64 **9** *3 1/4* **Miss Conway**[142] 679 4-10-13 **86**........................ JakeGreenall 64
(Mark Walford) *chsd ldrs: drvn 3 out: wknd appr next* **14/1**

6405 **10** *8* **Cherry Princess**[73] 1066 5-10-11 **84**........................(p) SeanQuinlan 54
(Barbara Butterworth) *mid-div: hdwy 5th: drvn to chse ldrs next: wknd between last 2* **25/1**

-660 **11** *8* **Triumph Davis (IRE)**[14] 1920 6-11-1 **98**........ HugoThompsonBrown[(10)] 60
(Micky Hammond) *in rr: bhd fr 5th: t.o 2 out* **28/1**

0-06 **12** *7* **Mitcd (IRE)**[41] 1572 4-10-8 **81**........................ HenryBrooke 36
(Martin Todhunter) *mid-div: hdwy 3 out: lost pl appr next: sn bhd* **16/1**

3-6P **13** *18* **Captain Sharpe**[109] 966 7-11-9 **99**........................(p) BrianToomey[(3)] 36
(Kenny Johnson) *chsd ldrs: drvn 5th: wknd qckly next: sn bhd: t.o whn eased appr 2 out* **40/1**

0P0U **P** **Bertielicious**[19] 1857 7-9-11 **73** oh12..........................(p) HarryChalloner(3)
(Jonathan Haynes) *in rr: bhd fr 5th: t.o whn p.u bef 2 out* **66/1**

4m 9.2s (2.30) **Going Correction** +0.05s/f (Yiel)
WFA 4 from 5yo+ 9lb **14** Ran SP% **118.8**
Speed ratings (Par 103): **96,95,92,91,89 89,89,84,83,79 75,72,63,**
CSF £26.89 CT £332.74 TOTE £9.40: £3.30, £1.20, £7.10; EX 38.60 Trifecta £533.40.
Owner Ingham Racing Syndicate **Bred** G Reed **Trained** Middleham Moor, N Yorks

FOCUS
Even for the class, this was a poor race considering the recent form of the majority of these, but the winner was well on in the best of her 2014 bumper/hurdle figures.
T/Plt: £169.10 to a £1 stake. Pool of £52599.63 - 226.98 winning tickets. T/Qpdt: £92.00 to a £1 stake. Pool of £3904.19 - 31.40 winning tickets. **Walter Glynn**

1974 STRATFORD (L-H)
Thursday, October 29

OFFICIAL GOING: Good to soft changing to soft after race 2 (2.10)
Wind: Light across Weather: Raining

2149 ROA/RACING POST H'CAP CHASE (15 fncs 2 omitted) 2m 6f 125y
1:40 (1:40) (Class 4) (0-120,120) 4-Y-0+ **£4,548** (£1,335; £667; £333)

Form RPR
03P- **1** **Cyrien Star**[235] 4655 8-10-13 **107**.................................. RichardJohnson 112
(Henry Daly) *hld up: hdwy 9th: ev ch after 2 out: sn rdn: styng on same pce whn lft 6 l 2nd last: rallied to ld nr fin* **3/1**[1]

6/23 **2** *nk* **Shockingtimes (IRE)**[25] 1767 8-11-10 **118**..................(t) BrendanPowell 125+
(Jamie Snowden) *hld up: hdwy 9th: led 2 out: rdn: hdd and 4 l down whn lft clr last: no ex and hdd nr fin* **9/1**

2113 **3** *9* **Faustina Pius (IRE)**[28] 1715 7-11-2 **117**...............(p) MrStanSheppard(7) 115
(Matt Sheppard) *hld up and bhd: j. slowly 2nd: hdwy 12th: rdn appr 2 out: styd on same pce: lft 3rd last* **10/1**

P0-P **4** *nk* **Letemgo (IRE)**[167] 319 7-11-12 **120**................................ GavinSheehan 120+
(Giles Smyly) *chsd ldrs: outpcd bef 12th: styd on appr last* **14/1**

1F-U **5** *4½* **Market Option (IRE)**[19] 1850 9-10-12 **106**.................. LiamTreadwell 101
(Venetia Williams) *hld up: rdn after 11th: nvr on terms* **16/1**

2266 **6** *1½* **Strumble Head (IRE)**[41] 1571 10-11-9 **117**..................(b) SeanBowen 108
(Peter Bowen) *chsd ldr: ev ch 3 out: sn rdn: wknd appr last* **14/1**

21P- **7** *4* **Coolking**[197] 5340 8-11-5 **113**... TomCannon 101
(Chris Gordon) *led: nt fluent 3rd: hdd 2 out: sn rdn and wknd* **12/1**

62U- **P** **Roc De Guye (FR)**[307] 3255 10-10-12 **106**...................(p) MarkQuinlan
(James Evans) *prom: lost pl bef 12th: bhd whn p.u bef last* **25/1**

1U6- **F** **What A Good Night (IRE)**[215] 5026 7-11-8 **116**............(t) HarrySkelton 130+
(Dan Skelton) *hld up: hdwy 12th: led appr and 4 l clr whn fell last* **5/1**[3]

-401 **F** **Muckle Roe (IRE)**[8] 2017 6-11-8 **116** 7ex.............. SamTwiston-Davies
(Nigel Twiston-Davies) *hld up: fell 10th* **10/3**[2]

5m 51.8s (12.60) **Going Correction** +0.60s/f (Soft) **10** Ran SP% **114.6**
Speed ratings (Par 105): **102,101,98,98,97 96,95,,,**
CSF £29.77 CT £238.73 TOTE £4.00: £1.70, £2.60, £2.60; EX 42.00 Trifecta £191.60.
Owner Puteus Profundus **Bred** Wood Farm Stud **Trained** Stanton Lacy, Shropshire

FOCUS
Open Ditch by the 2m start was omitted and the final fence had to be omitted in all chases following this opener after it was damaged. Following distances were be added to each race: Race 1 - 12yds, Race 2 - 144yds, Race 3 - 6yds, Race 4 - 168yds and Race 6 - 123yds. There was late drama in this opening chase.

2150 NIGEL REEVE 50TH BIRTHDAY CELEBRATION (S) HURDLE (9 hdls) 2m 2f 148y
2:10 (2:10) (Class 5) 4-7-Y-0 **£2,599** (£763; £381; £190)

Form RPR
-241 **1** **A Little Bit Dusty**[12] 1376 7-11-8 115.........................(b) PaddyBrennan 121
(Conor Dore) *a.p: led 2 out: shkn up appr last: jst hld on* **9/2**[3]

F4-4 **2** *½* **Barton Rose**[12] 1971 6-11-5 118...................................(p) NoelFehily 118
(Neil Mulholland) *hld up: mstke 4th: hdwy after next: chsd wnr after 2 out: rdn appr last: styd on* **7/4**[1]

44P5 **3** *21* **Flash Crash**[15] 1912 6-10-9 105.................................(t) JamesBanks(3) 91
(Barry Brennan) *chsd ldr tl led 4th: hdd 6th: remained handy tl rdn and wknd wl bef last* **10/1**

0-0P **4** *4* **Knight's Parade (IRE)**[15] 1917 5-11-12 128.............(tp) RichardJohnson 101
(Gordon Elliott, Ire) *chsd ldrs: led 6th: hdd 2 out: rdn and wknd wl bef last* **5/2**[2]

5 *83* **Petrify**[23] 5-10-9 0... RobertWilliams(3) 12
(Bernard Llewellyn) *hld up: plld hrd: a in rr: bhd fr 3 out* **33/1**

-323 **S** **Tijori (IRE)**[21] 1827 7-10-11 107............................. JordanWilliams(7)
(Bernard Llewellyn) *chsd ldrs: cl 5th whn slipped up bnd bef 3 out* **7/1**

34P- **P** **Russian Link**[312] 3208 5-10-5 100............................... WayneHutchinson
(John Berry) *hld up in tch: rdn and wknd after 6th: bhd whn hmpd bnd bef next: sn p.u* **14/1**

06 **P** **Desroches (GER)**[63] 1374 7-10-5 0................................ BrendanPowell
(Robin Dickin) *led to 4th: rdn and wknd after next: bhd whn p.u bef 3 out* **66/1**

4 **P** **Maxximus (IRE)**[21] 1827 5-10-12 0................................ JackQuinlan
(Sarah Humphrey) *hld up: j.rt at times: bhd fr 6th: p.u bef next* **100/1**

4m 50.5s (19.00) **Going Correction** +1.05s/f (Soft) **9** Ran SP% **116.8**
Speed ratings: **102,101,92,91,56 ,,,**
CSF £13.35 TOTE £5.80: £1.60, £1.30, £2.60; EX 15.80 Trifecta £102.10.
Owner David Baldwin & Chris Marsh **Bred** T O C S Limited **Trained** Hubbert's Bridge, Lincs

FOCUS
The front pair came a long way clear in this selling hurdle and ran pretty much to their marks.

2151 CHARLIE LONGSDON RACING NOVICES' LIMITED H'CAP CHASE (10 fncs 2 omitted) 2m 213y
2:40 (2:40) (Class 4) (0-120,120) 4-Y-0+ **£4,548** (£1,335; £667; £333)

Form RPR
-410 **1** **Johnny Og**[34] 1647 6-10-12 **110**..................................(b) AndrewTinkler 124+
(Martin Keighley) *mde all: clr after 2 out: styd on wl* **8/1**

4F5- **2** *6* **Colin's Brother**[190] 5469 5-11-5 **117**................... SamTwiston-Davies 124+
(Nigel Twiston-Davies) *hld up: hdwy 6th: hit 3 out: sn outpcd: styd on flat: wnt 2nd nr fin* **4/1**[2]

6PP- **3** *1* **Goohar (IRE)**[250] 4352 6-11-3 **115**.......................... RichardJohnson 121
(Henry Daly) *hld up: hdwy after 7th: chsd wnr appr and nt fluent 2 out: sn rdn: nt fluent last: no ex flat* **5/1**[3]

242- **4** *8* **Crafty Roberto**[224] 4868 7-11-7 **119**............................(t) KielanWoods 115
(Alex Hales) *prom tl rdn and wknd after 2 out* **9/1**

046- **5** *10* **Sea Wall (FR)**[223] 4885 7-11-6 **118**................................ TomCannon 106
(Chris Gordon) *prom: mstke 4th: wknd after 3 out* **6/1**

355- **6** *19* **Cyclop (IRE)**[215] 5032 4-10-11 **118**................................(t) NoelFehily 76
(David Dennis) *chsd ldrs: mstke 3rd: sn lost pl: bhd fr 6th* **7/1**

B3 **P** **Percys Choice (IRE)**[12] 1980 7-10-3 **101** oh8.................... CharliePoste
(Matt Sheppard) *hld up: a in rr: bhd whn p.u bef last* **25/1**

/06- **P** **Chemistry Master**[145] 5079 7-10-10 **108**........................ AdamWedge
(Alexandra Dunn) *prom tl rdn and wknd after 6th: bhd whn p.u bef next* **50/1**

222- **P** **Its A Sting (IRE)**[253] 4291 6-11-8 **120**........................ LeightonAspell
(Oliver Sherwood) *chsd wnr 2nd tl appr 2 out: sn wknd: bhd whn p.u bef last* **3/1**[1]

4m 14.7s (7.60) **Going Correction** +0.60s/f (Soft)
WFA 4 from 5yo+ 9lb **9** Ran SP% **115.4**
Speed ratings (Par 105): **106,103,102,98,94 85,,,**
CSF £41.02 CT £178.09 TOTE £7.90: £1.90, £2.00, £1.90; EX 38.20 Trifecta £205.90.
Owner T Hanlon M Boothright S Hanlon N Martin **Bred** R T Crellin **Trained** Condicote, Gloucs

FOCUS
A fair little chase that should produce winners. A big step up from the impressive winner.

2152 CHARLOTTE COLE MEMORIAL MAIDEN HURDLE (11 hdls) 2m 6f 7y
3:10 (3:10) (Class 5) 4-Y-0+ **£2,599** (£763; £381; £190)

Form RPR
5-2 **1** **Ballydine (IRE)**[21] 1829 5-11-0 .... RichardJohnson 135+
(Charlie Longsdon) *chsd ldr tl led after 5th: clr appr last: comf* **9/2**[3]

2 *10* **Hawkhurst (IRE)**[319] 5-11-0 .... SamTwiston-Davies 124+
(Paul Nicholls) *mid-div: mstke 8th: pushed along next: chsd wnr whn mstke last: no imp* **15/8**[1]

1 **3** *1¼* **Wholestone (IRE)**[34] 1645 4-11-0 .... DarylJacob 121
(Nigel Twiston-Davies) *hld up: hdwy 8th: chsd wnr appr 2 out tl rdn bef last: no ex* **4/1**[2]

F- **4** *13* **Brod Na Heireann (IRE)**[229] 4753 6-11-0 122............... WayneHutchinson 108
(Alan King) *hld up: nt fluent 2nd: hdwy 7th: rdn and wknd after 2 out* **5/1**

/2-3 **5** *1¼* **Master Benjamin**[178] 102 8-11-0 117...............................(p) NickScholfield 106
(Jeremy Scott) *chsd ldrs: rdn and wknd wl bef last* **8/1**

P **Lough Derg Island (IRE)**[179] 7-11-0 .... RhysFlint
(Alexandra Dunn) *a in rr: bhd whn p.u bef 7th* **100/1**

353- **P** **Pyrshan (IRE)**[241] 4541 6-11-0 117..................................(t) KielanWoods
(Graeme McPherson) *chsd ldrs tl wknd after 2 out: bhd whn p.u bef last* **20/1**

0- **P** **Cyrius Moriviere (FR)**[236] 5-11-0 ....(t) NicodeBoinville
(Ben Pauling) *chsd ldrs tl wknd appr 2 out: bhd whn p.u bef last* **33/1**

00-0 **P** **Right On Roy**[29] 1698 5-10-11 .... KillianMoore(3)
(Martin Keighley) *prom: mstke 6th: bhd whn p.u bef next* **200/1**

3-4 **P** **Trespassers Will (IRE)**[35] 1640 4-11-0 .... PaddyBrennan
(Fergal O'Brien) *hld up: drvn along 8th: sn wknd: bhd whn p.u bef last* **66/1**

40- **P** **I'm Oscar (IRE)**[200] 5292 5-10-11 .... MattGriffiths(3)
(Jeremy Scott) *hld up: rdn after 8th: wknd bef next: bhd whn p.u bef last* **66/1**

0-54 **P** **Run Bob Run**[29] 1704 4-11-0 .... AdamWedge
(John Flint) *hld up: a in rr: wknd after 7th: bhd whn p.u bef 3 out* **100/1**

56 **P** **Daulys Anthem (IRE)**[8] 2023 7-11-0 .... NoelFehily
(David Dennis) *hld up: plld hrd: bhd whn p.u bef 7th* **200/1**

3 **P** **Master Ally (IRE)**[18] 1873 5-11-0 .... LeightonAspell
(Rebecca Curtis) *led tl after 5th: wknd 7th: bhd whn p.u bef 3 out* **25/1**

5m 42.4s (14.30) **Going Correction** +1.05s/f (Soft) **14** Ran SP% **118.3**
Speed ratings (Par 103): **116,112,111,107,106 ,,,,,**
CSF £12.92 TOTE £5.90: £2.00, £1.60, £1.70; EX 17.70 Trifecta £43.80.
Owner Mrs S Longsdon **Bred** Fergal O'Mahoney **Trained** Over Norton, Oxon

FOCUS
Only five of the 14 runners completed this maiden hurdle, but it was probably a decent little race and a big step up from the winner..

2153 SUBARU SUPPORTS POINT TO POINT RACING H'CAP CHASE (FOR THE J. H. ROWE MEMORIAL CHALLENGE TROPHY) (11 fncs 3 omitted) 2m 3f 98y
3:40 (3:41) (Class 3) (0-140,134) **£6,408** (£1,908; £954; £477; £15; £Form)

34-0 **1** **Roc D'Apsis (FR)**[139] 710 6-11-0 **122**........................... PaddyBrennan 136+
(Tom George) *a.p: led last: rdn out* **16/1**

P5P- **2** *3¾* **Key To The West (IRE)**[206] 5184 8-10-6 **121**......... MrStanSheppard(7) 130
(Matt Sheppard) *hld up: hdwy 6th: led bef last: hdd last: no ex flat* **25/1**

0-11 **3** *7* **Al Alfa**[41] 1576 8-11-10 **132**...................................... RichardJohnson 132
(Philip Hobbs) *prom: chsd ldr 6th: led 3 out: hdd wl bef last: no ex* **15/2**

21P- **4** *2* **Saint Raph (FR)**[243] 4496 7-11-2 **124**..............................(t) DarylJacob 123
(Robert Walford) *hld up: sme hdwy 3 out: nt fluent last: n.d* **10/1**

010- **5** *1½* **Keel Haul (IRE)**[222] 4917 7-11-6 **128**............................. JamesDavies 125
(Henry Oliver) *mid-div: hdwy 3 out: wknd appr last* **25/1**

3121 **6** *½* **Jayo Time (IRE)**[22] 1809 6-10-12 **127**..................(p) DavidNoonan(7) 124
(Kerry Lee) *mid-div: hdwy 8th: wknd appr last* **10/1**

U6/U **F** **Kauto Stone (FR)**[15] 1902 9-11-12 **134**............................ NoelFehily
(Ben Pauling) *chsd ldrs: wkng whn fell 3 out* **16/1**

15-2 **P** **Cody Wyoming**[11] 1989 9-11-1 **123**...........................(tp) GavinSheehan
(Charlie Mann) *a in rr: reminders after 2nd: bhd fr 4th: p.u bef 8th* **10/1**

1P-6 **P** **Comeonginger (IRE)**[26] 1755 8-11-3 **125**.......................(t) TomCannon
(Chris Gordon) *prom: lost pl 4th: bhd fr 7th: p.u bef 3 out* **20/1**

4FP/ **P** **African Gold (IRE)**[656] 3653 7-11-11 **133**............... SamTwiston-Davies
(Nigel Twiston-Davies) *chsd ldrs: nt fluent 1st: wknd 4 out: bhd whn p.u bef last* **3/1**[1]

2520 **P** **Spring Steel (IRE)**[15] 1911 6-10-7 **115**......................(t) AdamWedge
(Alexandra Dunn) *hld up: bhd fr 7th: p.u bef 2 out* **100/1**

PP-0 **P** **Tara Road**[18] 1869 7-11-6 **128**...................................(t) LeightonAspell
(Rebecca Curtis) *hld up: hmpd 3 out: p.u bef next* **5/1**[2]

1312 **P** **Hepijeu (FR)**[22] 1809 4-10-11 **129**.............................(tp) NickScholfield
(Charlie Longsdon) *led and pckd 1st: hdd 3 out: wknd after next: p.u bef last* **6/1**[3]

4m 59.2s (9.20) **Going Correction** +0.60s/f (Soft)
WFA 4 from 6yo+ 9lb **13** Ran SP% **120.9**
Speed ratings (Par 107): **104,102,99,98,98 97,,,,,**
CSF £351.49 CT £3046.87 TOTE £24.20: £5.70, £8.60, £1.40; EX 386.80 Trifecta £2084.30.
Owner David Rea & Miss Diane Fudge **Bred** N Colliere, C Verry et al **Trained** Slad, Gloucs

FOCUS
A useful chase, with the front pair pulling clear late, and a big step up from the winner.

2154 EBF STALLIONS/WEATHERBYS "NATIONAL HUNT" NOVICES' HURDLE (QUALIFIER) (8 hdls) 2m 70y
4:10 (4:11) (Class 3) 4-6-Y-O **£6,498** (£1,908; £954; £477)

Form RPR
4 **1** **Charbel (IRE)**[183] 23 4-10-12 .... DavidBass 116+
(Kim Bailey) *chsd ldrs: led appr last: rdn out* **11/8**[1]
6P **2** 2 ½ **Christmas Twenty (IRE)**[28] 1718 5-10-12 .... JoshuaMoore 112
(Stuart Edmunds) *a.p: nt fluent 2 out: sn rdn: chsd wnr last: styd on* **50/1**
3 2 ¼ **Mr Mix (FR)**[407] 4-10-12 .... SamTwiston-Davies 110
(Paul Nicholls) *led to 3rd: w ldr: ev ch 2 out: no ex flat* **7/4**[2]
1-33 **4** 4 ½ **War On The Rocks (IRE)**[12] 1979 6-10-12 .... PaddyBrennan 107
(Fergal O'Brien) *chsd ldr: led 3rd: rdn and hdd appr last: wknd flat* **6/1**[3]
PP-6 **5** 10 **Berry De Carjac (FR)**[63] 1379 4-10-12 .... (t) ConorO'Farrell 94
(Nigel Hawke) *hld up: sme hdwy after 2 out: nvr trbld ldrs* **200/1**
5-0 **6** 7 **Better Days (IRE)**[173] 213 4-10-9 .... RyanHatch(3) 87
(Nigel Twiston-Davies) *hld up: hdwy 3 out: wknd after next* **50/1**
5- **7** 3 **Set In My Ways (IRE)**[184] 9 4-10-12 .... RichardJohnson 85
(Jonjo O'Neill) *hld up: mstke 3rd: rdn 3 out: sn wknd* **8/1**
00-0 **8** ½ **Aka Doun (FR)**[34] 1648 4-10-12 ....[1] DarylJacob 84
(Emma Lavelle) *hld up: n.d* **66/1**
403- **9** 1 ½ **Kap Jazz (FR)**[242] 4507 5-10-12 .... LiamTreadwell 83
(Venetia Williams) *hld up: mstke 4th: wknd 3 out* **20/1**
06-0 **P** **Orbit Light (IRE)**[22] 1811 4-10-5 ....[1] PeterCarberry
(Nicky Henderson) *hld up: bhd fr 4th: p.u bef last* **50/1**
3 **P** **Spoilt Rotten**[18] 1872 6-10-12 .... DenisO'Regan
(Mark Pitman) *prom tl wknd 3 out: bhd whn p.u bef last* **20/1**

4m 12.6s (16.60) **Going Correction** +1.05s/f (Soft)
WFA 4 from 5yo+ 9lb **11** Ran SP% **121.3**
Speed ratings: **100,98,97,95,90 86,85,85,84,**
CSF £82.32 TOTE £2.40: £1.20, £14.50, £1.20; EX 102.80 Trifecta £555.90.
Owner Mrs Julie Martin And David R Martin **Bred** Peter & Sandra McCarthy **Trained** Andoversford, Gloucs

FOCUS
A fair little novice hurdle, even if a big outsider split the market leaders in second. The winner should go on to rate higher.
T/Plt: £72.20 to a £1 stake. Pool of £68097.59 - 688.33 winning tickets. T/Qpdt: £22.60 to a £1 stake. Pool of £6085.01 - 198.70 winning tickets. **Colin Roberts**

2155 - 2161a (Foreign Racing) - See Raceform Interactive

[1927] UTTOXETER (L-H)
Friday, October 30

OFFICIAL GOING: Good to soft (good in places on hurdle course) changing to soft (good to soft in places) after race 3 (1:50)
Wind: moderate 1/2 against Weather: fine, light rain after race 5

2162 BREEDERS' CUP EXCLUSIVELY ON ATR H'CAP HURDLE (DIV I) (9 hdls) 1m 7f 168y
12:45 (12:45) (Class 5) (0-100,100) 3-Y-O+ **£2,469** (£725; £362; £181)

Form RPR
40-4 **1** **Vicky's Charm (IRE)**[179] 111 6-11-9 **100** .... JamesBanks(3) 106+
(Barry Brennan) *w ldr: led 3rd: hit 2 out: hld on wl run-in* **11/1**
05P- **2** 1 ½ **Kings River (FR)**[279] 3867 6-11-1 **89** .... LiamTreadwell 92
(Venetia Williams) *trckd ldrs t.k.h: effrt 3 out: hit next: 4th last: kpt on to take 2nd clsng stages* **8/1**
006- **3** ¾ **Neworld (FR)**[190] 5489 6-11-11 **99** .... AlainCawley 101+
(Richard Hobson) *stdd s: hld up in rr: hdwy 3 out: chsng ldng pair whn rdr dropped whip last: kpt on same pce* **5/1**[2]
406/ **4** hd **Hallstatt (IRE)**[14] 1778 9-11-5 **93** .... (t) NoelFehily 96+
(John Mackie) *trckd ldrs: 3rd appr 2 out: upsides last: kpt on same pce* **5/1**[2]
510- **5** 11 **Nolecce**[27] 2763 8-10-6 **87** .... JoshWall(7) 80
(Tony Forbes) *hld up: trckd ldrs 4th: 2nd appr 3 out: wknd appr last* **11/4**[1]
P3P0 **6** 12 **Spurned Girl**[13] 1980 5-9-11 **74** oh5 .... (t) BenPoste(3) 54
(Robin Dickin) *chsd ldrs 4th: stmbld and lost pl bnd appr 3 out* **33/1**
P2-P **7** ¾ **Suffice (IRE)**[9] 2024 6-9-12 **79** .... ThomasCheesman(7) 58
(Laura Young) *hld up in rr: bhd bef 3 out* **6/1**[3]
8 14 **Annakrista (GER)**[163] 413 7-10-12 **93** .... (b) WilliamFeatherstone(7) 60
(Zoe Davison) *chsd ldrs: lost pl appr 2 out: eased whn bhd run-in* **16/1**
140- **9** 37 **Unidexter (IRE)**[358] 2297 5-11-6 **97** .... (t) HarryChalloner(3) 31
(Richard Ford) *led to 3rd: drvn 6th: lost pl bef next: sn bhd: heavily eased whn t.o run-in* **9/1**

4m 8.0s (10.60) **Going Correction** +0.55s/f (Soft) **9** Ran SP% **112.6**
Speed ratings (Par 103): **95,94,93,93,88 82,81,74,56**
CSF £91.82 CT £495.42 TOTE £9.90: £3.60, £2.30, £2.60; EX 52.60 Trifecta £374.70.
Owner Dr Ian Cragg **Bred** Anthony Kelleher **Trained** Upper Lambourn, Berks

FOCUS
Some starts have been moved at this track following remeasuring, so some races will not have speed figures until there is sufficient data to calculate updated median times. The going was good to soft, soft in places on the chase course and good to soft on the hurdles course. Divided bends. Hurdles 9yds off inside line and race 1 increased by 81yds, races 2 & 3 by 54yds and race 6 by 108yds. The opening handicap was uncompetitive and they went a steady gallop. The winner has been rated in line with her course bumper run.

2163 BREEDERS' CUP STARTS TONIGHT ON ATR NOVICES' HURDLE (10 hdls) 2m 3f 207y
1:15 (1:17) (Class 4) 4-Y-O+ **£3,378** (£992; £496; £248)

Form RPR
1- **1** **Onefitzall (IRE)**[315] 3177 5-10-12 0 .... RichardJohnson 131+
(Philip Hobbs) *mid-div: trckd ldrs 6th: upsides bef 3 out: led 3 out: clr whn hit last: heavily eased last 75yds* **6/4**[1]
2 4 **Beware The Bear (IRE)**[188] 5-10-7 0 .... FreddieMitchell(5) 122+
(Nicky Henderson) *hld up in rr-div: hdwy 6th: styd on fr 3 out: wnt 2nd last: no ch w wnr* **7/1**[3]
3-63 **3** 44 **Captain Flash (IRE)**[143] 671 6-10-9 0 .... JamesBanks(3) 84
(Jo Davis) *nt fluent: chsd ldrs: 4th and weakning whn mstke 2 out: lft distant 3rd last* **50/1**
31- **4** 7 **Speredek (FR)**[239] 4582 4-10-12 0 .... ConorO'Farrell 81
(Nigel Hawke) *chsd ldrs: 5th and outpcd whn blnd 3 out: lft distant 4th last* **9/1**
4U5- **5** 32 **Whiskey John**[219] 4985 5-10-9 0 .... MattGriffiths(3) 48
(Laura Young) *in rr: drvn 7th: nvr on terms* **150/1**
4 **6** 5 **Glory For Rory (IRE)**[163] 400 4-10-12 0 .... RichieMcLernon 43
(Jonjo O'Neill) *mid-div: outpcd 6th: nvr on terms* **40/1**
7 4 ½ **Thegreendalerocket (IRE)**[145] 6-10-5 0 .... PaulO'Brien(7) 39
(Jimmy Frost) *in rr: hdwy 6th: lost pl after next* **100/1**
1 **8** 25 **Royal Sea (IRE)**[26] 1780 6-10-9 0 .... BenPoste(3) 17
(Michael Mullineaux) *chsd ldrs: reminders 5th: sn lost pl: wl bhd fr 7th: t.o* **20/1**
P4- **9** 1 **Steuben (GER)**[190] 4274 9-10-12 0 .... PaulMoloney 16
(Des Donovan) *in rr: sme hdwy 5th: lost pl 7th: sn wl bhd: t.o* **100/1**
1- **10** 1 **Suit Yourself (IRE)**[247] 4430 6-10-12 0 .... BarryGeraghty 15
(Jonjo O'Neill) *in rr: sme hdwy 6th: sn wknd: t.o* **9/2**[2]
-653 **11** 20 **Marley Joe (IRE)**[20] 1844 4-10-12 0 .... AndrewTinkler
(Martin Keighley) *in rr: bhd fr 6th: tailed rt off* **66/1**
5-52 **P** **Aliandy (IRE)**[15] 1929 4-10-12 0 .... DavidBass
(Kim Bailey) *gave problems s: led: hdd bef 3 out: j. slowly and sn wknd: distant 6th whn p.u bef 2 out* **12/1**
4 **F** **Paddy's Field (IRE)**[174] 213 5-10-12 0 .... NoelFehily 114+
(Ben Pauling) *chsd ldrs: led briefly bef 3 out: 3rd and wl hld whn fell last* **7/1**[3]
P **Mille Nautique (FR)**[159] 4-10-9 0 .... TomBellamy(3)
(Alan King) *mid-div: hdwy 5th: lost pl 7th: bhd whn p.u bef 2 out* **14/1**

5m 8.7s (5.50) **Going Correction** +0.55s/f (Soft)
WFA 4 from 5yo+ 10lb **14** Ran SP% **120.8**
Speed ratings (Par 105): **111,109,91,89,76 74,72,62,62,61 53,,,**
CSF £12.22 TOTE £2.10: £1.50, £2.80, £11.30; EX 12.60 Trifecta £212.80.
Owner Mick Fitzgerald Racing Club **Bred** Maurice Keane **Trained** Withycombe, Somerset

FOCUS
A moderate novice hurdle won by Coneygree in 2012, and they they went an honest gallop before coming home at wide margin intervals. The impressive winner was confirming the merit of his course bumper win.

2164 ATR GET IN! BREEDERS' CUP SPECIAL TONIGHT MARES' MAIDEN HURDLE (9 hdls) 1m 7f 168y
1:50 (1:52) (Class 5) 3-Y-O+ **£2,469** (£725; £362; £181)

Form RPR
516- **1** **Out Of The Mist (IRE)**[237] 4634 6-11-5 0 .... RichieMcLernon 111+
(Emma Lavelle) *mid-div: hdwy 5th: upsides between last 2: led last 100yds: drvn rt out* **11/4**[1]
333- **2** ½ **Lady Of Lamanver**[241] 4543 5-11-5 0 .... (t) NoelFehily 110
(Harry Fry) *mid-div: trckd ldrs 6th: led appr last: hdd last 100yds: rallied clsng stages* **5/1**
3220 **3** 12 **Irondale Express**[58] 1454 4-11-2 **104** .... JamesBanks(3) 100
(Barry Brennan) *trckd ldrs: led 3 out: hdd appr last: fdd* **33/1**
140- **4** hd **Lady Persephone (FR)**[237] 4634 4-11-5 0 .... DenisO'Regan 99
(Alan King) *mid-div: hdwy to chse ldrs 6th: one pce fr 2 out: modest 4th last* **16/1**
5 7 **Sanaija**[128] 4-11-5 0 .... DarylJacob 94
(Nicky Henderson) *trckd ldrs: hit 5th: 4th 3 out: wknd last* **3/1**[2]
103- **6** 2 **Madame Trigger**[238] 4615 7-11-0 0 .... BridgetAndrews(5) 91
(Dan Skelton) *mid-div: hdwy 6th: lost pl 3 out* **7/2**[3]
46/ **7** 10 **Double Accord**[584] 5026 5-11-5 0 .... RyanMahon 83
(Anthony Honeyball) *in rr-div: hdwy 5th: effrt bef 3 out: sn wknd* **80/1**
0-0 **8** 22 **Miss Mash**[23] 1811 4-11-5 0 .... AndrewTinkler 64
(Henry Daly) *trckd ldrs: t.k.h: lost pl after 6th: sn bhd* **100/1**
9 24 **En Passe (IRE)**[216] 6-11-5 0 .... (t) RichardJohnson 40
(Charlie Longsdon) *led to 2nd: w ldr: led 6th: hdd 3 out: sn lost pl and bhd* **8/1**
10 8 **Gold Bonne Raine (IRE)** 4-11-5 0 .... PaulMoloney 33
(Evan Williams) *in rr: wl bhd fr 6th: t.o 2 out* **50/1**
34 **11** 24 **La Voix (FR)**[69] 1321 3-9-9 0 .... MissBFrost(7)
(Jimmy Frost) *mid-div: lost pl and bhd 6th: t.o 2 out* **150/1**
12 18 **Sweet Midnight**[72] 3-10-2 0 .... CharliePoste
(John Holt) *nt jump wl: in rr whn mstkes 1st 2: t.o 6th* **200/1**
4- **P** **Ninny Noodle**[467] 1022 5-11-5 0 .... LiamTreadwell
(Miss Imogen Pickard) *t.k.h: sn trcking ldrs: led 2nd: hdd 6th: sn lost pl: t.o whn p.u bef 3 out* **150/1**
0- **P** **Velvet Edge**[474] 936 6-10-12 0 .... MrMJPKendrick(7)
(Anthony Day) *in rr: blnd 2nd: wl bhd 4th: t.o whn p.u bef next: sddle slipped* **200/1**

4m 4.9s (7.50) **Going Correction** +0.55s/f (Soft)
WFA 3 from 4yo+ 17lb **14** Ran SP% **117.0**
Speed ratings (Par 103): **103,102,96,96,93 92,87,76,64,60 48,39,,**
CSF £16.69 TOTE £4.10: £1.60, £2.10, £7.70; EX 18.90 Trifecta £317.50.
Owner Swanbridge Bloodstock Limited **Bred** Jethro Bloodstock **Trained** Hatherden, Hants

FOCUS
An ordinary maiden hurdle in which they went a decent gallop, and the first two should go onto better things having pulled clear. The winner has been rated in line with her bumper mark. The third, fourth and seventh help set the level in the fastest of the races over the trip.

2165 BREEDERS' CUP EXCLUSIVELY ON ATR H'CAP HURDLE (DIV II) (9 hdls) 1m 7f 168y
2:25 (2:28) (Class 5) (0-100,100) 3-Y-O+ **£2,469** (£725; £362; £181)

Form RPR
00-F **1** **Pay Your Way (IRE)**[11] 2004 7-11-0 **88** .... PaulMoloney 93+
(David Rees) *chsd ldrs: led 2 out: hung lft: drvn out* **9/2**[3]
6-06 **2** 3 ¾ **Arthamint**[23] 1810 7-11-9 **97** .... (t) RyanMahon 97
(Dan Skelton) *hld up in rr: effrt and chsng ldrs appr 3 out: hit next: 4th last: kpt on to take 2nd last 100yds* **3/1**[1]
-035 **3** shd **Mulligan's Man (IRE)**[15] 1927 8-11-5 **93** .... (p) DavidEngland 95
(Clare Ellam) *trckd ldr: hit 4th: led briefly bef 2 out: kpt on same pce run-in* **6/1**
5-P4 **4** 2 ½ **My Renaissance**[16] 1446 5-10-0 **74** .... (t) TrevorWhelan 72
(Ben Case) *trckd ldrs: upsides whn j.lft 2 out: wknd clsng stages* **8/1**
440U **5** 23 **Wymeswold**[26] 1786 8-10-8 **85** .... BenPoste(3) 59
(Michael Mullineaux) *in rr: drvn 5th: chsd ldrs briefly bef 3 out: sn lost pl and bhd* **16/1**
3/6- **6** 9 **Solidago (IRE)**[499] 732 8-11-4 **95** ....[1] HarryChalloner(3) 60
(Barry Leavy) *trckd ldrs: t.k.h: effrt appr 3 out: sn lost pl and bhd* **12/1**
-554 **7** ¾ **Nafaath (IRE)**[15] 1920 9-11-7 **100** .... (p) JamesCowley(5) 64
(Donald McCain) *led: reminders after 6th: hdd bef 2 out: sn lost pl and bhd* **7/2**[2]

4m 11.0s (13.60) **Going Correction** +0.70s/f (Soft) **7** Ran SP% **104.4**
Speed ratings (Par 103): **94,92,92,90,79 74,74**
CSF £15.61 CT £58.08 TOTE £4.20: £2.80, £2.00; EX 16.80 Trifecta £52.60.
Owner D Rees **Bred** John Quane **Trained** Clarbeston, Pembrokes

■ Positive Vibes was withdrawn. Price at time of withdrawal 15-2. Rule 4 applies to all bets - deduction 10p in the pound.

FOCUS
The ground was changed to soft, good to soft in places for this weak handicap which didn't take much winning. They went a good gallop. The winner was well in on the best of his Irish form and has been rated back to something like that level. The third and fourth are probably the best guide to the level.

2166 ATTHERACES.COM/BREEDERSCUP BEGINNERS CHASE (12 fncs) 1m 7f 214y
3:00 (3:00) (Class 4) 4-Y-O+ **£3,833** (£1,157; £596; £315)

Form RPR
541- **1** **Garde La Victoire (FR)**[272] [3974] 6-11-2 0................ RichardJohnson 157+
(Philip Hobbs) *t.k.h: handy 3rd 2nd: hit 8th: 2nd appr 4 out: led bef 2 out: eased last 75yds* **11/10**[1]
323- **2** *7* **Bristol De Mai (FR)**[204] [5236] 4-10-7 0.................. DarylJacob 140+
(Nigel Twiston-Davies) *t.k.h: w ldr: led after 8th: hdd bef 2 out: 6 l down and wl hld whn hit last* **15/8**[2]
04-5 **3** *21* **Regal Encore (IRE)**[20] [1846] 7-11-2 0.......................(t) BarryGeraghty 125
(Anthony Honeyball) *modest 4th and pushed along 6th: outpcd and lost pl bef 4 out: tk poor 3rd 2 out* **8/1**
110- **4** *19* **Astre De La Cour (FR)**[185] [7] 5-11-2 0................... NickScholfield 112
(Robert Walford) *led: hdd after 8th: 3rd whn hit 4 out: sn wknd* **15/2**[3]
6P2/ **P** **City Slicker (IRE)**[549] [10] 7-11-2 0...................... RichieMcLernon
(Jonjo O'Neill) *3rd whn blnd 1st: bhd 5th: t.o 7th: p.u bef 4 out* **25/1**

3m 59.4s (-2.00) **Going Correction** +0.20s/f (Yiel)
WFA 4 from 5yo+ 9lb **5 Ran SP% 109.1**
Speed ratings (Par 105): **113,109,99,89,**
CSF £3.61 TOTE £1.70: £1.10, £1.60; EX 3.30 Trifecta £8.30.
Owner Mrs Diana L Whateley **Bred** Mlle Laure Godet **Trained** Withycombe, Somerset

FOCUS
Essentially this beginners' chase was a match between two very useful hurdlers from last season and the pair pulled clear having chased a sound gallop. The impressive winner was replicating his smart hurdling form and is a potential 160+ novice chaser.

2167 BREEDERS' CUP LIVE ON ATR MARES' H'CAP HURDLE (12 hdls) 2m 7f 70y
3:35 (3:35) (Class 4) (0-120,119) 4-Y-O+ **£3,378** (£992; £496; £248)

Form RPR
324- **1** **Millicent Silver**[191] [5470] 6-10-9 **105**...................... RyanHatch(3) 118+
(Nigel Twiston-Davies) *chsd ldrs: pushed along 6th: sn outpcd: rallied 9th: 4th 3 out: styd on wl to ld between last 2: drvn clr* **11/2**[3]
6223 **2** *11* **Midnight Sapphire**[21] [1841] 5-10-3 **106**..............(t) MrJakeBament(10) 107
(Victor Dartnall) *hld up in rr: hdwy 4th: sn chsng ldrs: led 3 out: hdd between last 2: kpt on same pce* **5/1**[2]
312- **3** *3 ¾* **Tambura**[218] [4991] 5-11-3 **110**.............................. NickScholfield 107+
(G C Maundrell) *hld up in rr: hdwy 9th: modest 5th next: kpt on run-in: tk modest 3rd last 50yds* **9/1**
1063 **4** *2 ¾* **Taylor (IRE)**[32] [1675] 6-11-7 **114**........................... DarylJacob 110
(Nicky Henderson) *hld up in rr: mstke 5th: hdwy 9th: 3rd next: one pce* **8/1**
34-0 **5** *13* **Woodland Walk**[23] [1808] 7-11-2 **119**..................... RichieO'Dea(10) 106
(Emma Lavelle) *w ldr: led after 5th: hit next: hdd 3 out: wknd after 2 out* **12/1**
320- **6** *48* **Maybe Plenty**[198] [5343] 6-11-7 **114**.......................... TomCannon 47
(Giles Smyly) *chsd ldrs: drvn 7th: lost pl 9th: t.o whn hit 2 out: eventually completed* **10/1**
0-F2 **P** **Magic Money**[38] [1618] 7-11-3 **110**............................ DavidBass
(Kim Bailey) *led tl after 5th: lost pl 9th: t.o whn hit 2 out: p.u bef last* **8/1**
-642 **P** **Surf In September (IRE)**[54] [1490] 6-10-2 **95**.................. MarkGrant
(Dominic Ffrench Davis) *chsd ldrs: drvn and lost pl 7th: rallied next: sn lost pl: t.o 9th: p.u bef next* **16/1**
653 **P** **Little Dream (IRE)**[31] [1694] 8-10-3 **96**...................... PaulMoloney
(Evan Williams) *in rr: lost pl 7th: sn bhd: t.o 9th: p.u bef next* **16/1**
0 **P** **Isabellesprincess (IRE)**[21] [1841] 7-10-7 **110**.....(t) CharlieHammond(10)
(Mike Hammond) *in rr: chsd ldrs 4th: hit 7th: drvn 8th: lost pl next: t.o whn p.u bef 3 out* **33/1**
6211 **P** **Lady Of Longstone (IRE)**[9] [2022] 5-10-10 **110** 7ex...... MichaelHeard(7)
(David Pipe) *chsd ldrs: hit 8th: sn lost pl: eased and bhd whn p.u bef next* **10/3**[1]

6m 10.9s (12.10) **Going Correction** +0.70s/f (Soft) **11 Ran SP% 118.8**
Speed ratings (Par 105): **106,102,100,99,95 78,, , ,**
CSF £34.09 CT £247.71 TOTE £6.30: £2.00, £2.00, £2.60; EX 35.30 Trifecta £307.20.
Owner John Goodman **Bred** Owen Brennan / John Goodman **Trained** Naunton, Gloucs

FOCUS
A competitive enough handicap and the decent pace suited those ridden with restraint. Stamina was very much at a premium. The second has been rated close to her mark.

2168 YOUR BREEDERS' CUP GUIDE AT ATTHERACES.COM/BREEDERSCUP H'CAP CHASE (15 fncs) 2m 4f
4:10 (4:10) (Class 4) (0-120,120) 4-Y-O **£3,798** (£1,122; £561; £280; £140)

Form RPR
646- **1** **Aloomomo (FR)**[196] [5362] 5-11-0 **108**.................. RichardJohnson 133+
(Warren Greatrex) *j. soundly: trckd ldrs gng wl: led 9th: shkn up and clr 2 out: 15 l ahd last: heavily eased* **5/4**[1]
3/3- **2** *12* **Minellaforlunch (IRE)**[534] [288] 8-10-0 **94** oh1............ JamesDavies 97
(Henry Oliver) *led to 2nd: w ldr: drvn 11th: kpt on fr 2 out: no ch w wnr* **4/1**[2]
550 **3** *2 ¾* **Alf Wright (IRE)**[22] [1818] 9-11-5 **120**................. CiaranGethings(7) 121
(Philip Hobbs) *hdwy to chse ldrs 10th: 3rd whn hit 4 out: one pce and modest 3rd 2 out* **14/1**
255- **4** *15* **Major Milborne**[195] [5401] 7-11-7 **115**...............(p) BrendanPowell 100
(Jamie Snowden) *chsd ldrs 8th: drvn 11th: lost pl next* **8/1**
2141 **5** *3 ¼* **Cruise In Style (IRE)**[10] [2006] 9-10-3 **97**...................(tp) JamesBest 82
(Kevin Bishop) *j.lft: drvn to chse ldrs 10th: j.lft 3 out: wknd next* **8/1**
16-5 **6** *18* **Gold Ingot**[13] [1970] 8-11-12 **120**........................ AndrewThornton 84
(Caroline Bailey) *w ldr: led 2nd: hdd 9th: lost pl 11th: sn bhd* **7/1**[3]
2550 **7** *35* **River Purple**[40] [1601] 8-11-4 **112**.........................(t) DarylJacob 41
(John Mackie) *chsd ldrs 8th: drvn 10th: sn lost pl: t.o 4 out* **16/1**

5m 21.2s (11.40) **Going Correction** +0.20s/f (Yiel) **7 Ran SP% 111.7**
Speed ratings (Par 105): **85,80,79,73,71 64,50**
CSF £6.71 TOTE £2.40: £1.80, £2.10; EX 8.10 Trifecta £95.30.
Owner The Large G & T Partnership **Bred** Maurice Goin **Trained** Upper Lambourn, Berks

FOCUS
The concluding handicap revolved around the in-form favourite, who was the most impressive winner on the card. A big sstep up from the impressive winner, and there's a case for rating the race up to 5lb higher through the second and third.
T/Plt: £101.70 to a £1 stake. Pool: £60,962.33 - 437.24 winning tickets T/Qpdt: £16.20 to a £1 stake. Pool: £5,667.90 - 257.60 winning tickets **Walter Glynn**

[1899] WETHERBY (L-H)
Friday, October 30

OFFICIAL GOING: Good to soft changing to soft after race 1 (1:05)
Wind: light across Weather: sunny

2169 WETHERBY WHALER GARRY SCHOFIELD TESTIMONIAL "NATIONAL HUNT" NOVICES' HURDLE 2m 3f 154y
1:05 (1:08) (Class 4) 4-Y-O+ **£3,249** (£954; £477; £238)

Form RPR
232- **1** **Royal Vacation (IRE)**[245] [4473] 5-10-12 130................... PaddyBrennan 123+
(Colin Tizzard) *prom: rdn along and briefly dropped to 3rd after 4 out: lft in front 3 out: styd on* **8/11**[1]
233- **2** *3 ¾* **Bollin Ace**[220] [4975] 4-10-12 0............................ BrianHughes 117+
(Tim Easterby) *midfield: stdy hdwy after 4 out: rdn to go 2nd 2 out: kpt on* **10/1**[3]
3 *17* **I Just Know (IRE)**[181] 5-10-12 0............................ DannyCook 106+
(Sue Smith) *trckd ldng pair: briefly jnd ldr after 4 out: rdn appr 3 out: lft 2nd 3 out: lost 2nd 2 out: wknd* **12/1**
4-56 **4** *8* **Beer Goggles (IRE)**[18] [1886] 4-10-9 0.................. CraigNichol(3) 93
(Micky Hammond) *midfield: plugged on into modest 4th between last 2: nvr threatened* **33/1**
4046 **5** *9* **Black Kettle (IRE)**[8] [2025] 5-10-12 0..................... KielanWoods 85
(Ronald Thompson) *midfield: rdn bef 3 out: wknd after 2 out* **100/1**
6 *15* **Adeenne De Sevres (FR)**[215] 5-10-12 0............... WayneHutchinson 71
(Tom Lacey) *midfield: mstke 3 out: sn wknd* **20/1**
3-4 **7** *6* **Milly Baloo**[178] [132] 4-10-5 0.............................. BrianHarding 59
(Tim Easterby) *midfield: wknd after 4 out* **66/1**
0- **8** *10* **Hattons Hill (IRE)**[364] [2173] 6-10-9 0...................... TonyKelly(3) 57
(Henry Hogarth) *a towards rr* **100/1**
00-0 **9** *shd* **Wayward Sun (IRE)**[16] [1901] 4-10-2 0................. FinianO'Toole(10) 57
(Micky Hammond) *a towards rr* **150/1**
60 **10** *1 ½* **Inchcolm (IRE)**[16] [1901] 5-10-9 0....................... JoeColliver(3) 56
(Micky Hammond) *in tch: wknd after 4 out* **100/1**
0/05 **11** *31* **Trooper Royal**[15] [1929] 5-10-12 0.......................... SeanQuinlan 28
(Sue Smith) *in tch: mstke 6th: wknd after 4 out* **100/1**
6- **12** *11* **Exclusive Tara**[263] [4128] 5-10-12 0........................ JakeGreenall 18
(Tim Easterby) *hld up in midfield: wknd after 4 out* **50/1**
00- **P** **Sirius Star**[166] 6-10-12 0................................. AdamWedge
(Brian Rothwell) *a in rr: p.u bef 3 out* **50/1**
F **Red Hanrahan (IRE)**[216] 4-10-12 0.................. SamTwiston-Davies 125+
(Paul Nicholls) *led: 3 l up and yet to be asked for effrt whn fell 3 out* **9/4**[2]

5m 11.0s (4.00) **Going Correction** +0.40s/f (Soft)
WFA 4 from 5yo+ 10lb **14 Ran SP% 123.2**
Speed ratings (Par 105): **108,106,99,96,92 86,84,80,80,79 67,63, ,**
CSF £10.24 TOTE £1.70: £1.10, £2.20, £2.70; EX 9.20 Trifecta £49.20.
Owner Mrs Jean R Bishop **Bred** Tim Hegarty **Trained** Milborne Port, Dorset

FOCUS
Both bends moved out 3yds. Races 1, 3 & 6 increased by 27yds, races 2 & 4 by 18yds and race 5 by 36yds. The two market leaders made this an exciting event for novices, and there should be several down the field who are capable of winning at a lower level. The second-favourite was going well when falling.

2170 BET365.COM H'CAP HURDLE (9 hdls) 2m
1:40 (1:43) (Class 3) (0-125,127) 3-Y-O+ **£5,393** (£1,583; £791; £395)

Form RPR
14 **1** **Cooper**[34] [1656] 3-10-0 **116**................................ BrianHughes 107+
(Kevin Ryan) *hld up in midfield: smooth hdwy appr 3 out: led 2 out: rdn appr last: kpt on* **8/1**[3]
1-11 **2** *¾* **Kapstadt (FR)**[32] [1676] 5-11-8 **121**......................... WillKennedy 128+
(Ian Williams) *hld up in midfield: hdwy 3 out: wnt 2nd jst after 2 out: pushed along whn nt fluent last: sn rdn: kpt on* **9/2**[2]
22-6 **3** *3* **Kayf Blanco**[168] [317] 6-11-12 **125**........................ KielanWoods 128
(Graeme McPherson) *hld up: pushed along and hdwy between last 2: wnt 3rd last: drvn and kpt on* **9/1**
121 **4** *1 ¾* **Hadfield (IRE)**[8] [2027] 3-10-11 **127** 7ex.....................(p) AidanColeman 112
(John Ferguson) *in tch: rdn 2 out: one pce* **11/4**[1]
2112 **5** *3* **Dynamic Drive (IRE)**[15] [1920] 8-10-13 **119**............(t) ThomasDowson(7) 118
(Maurice Barnes) *midfield: trckd ldrs 4th: rdn 2 out: wknd run-in* **12/1**
4-46 **6** *4 ½* **Sailors Warn (IRE)**[40] [1591] 8-11-2 **120**............(tp) NathanMoscrop(5) 114
(Ronald Thompson) *midfield: rdn bef 2 out: wknd between last 2* **50/1**
430- **7** *shd* **Brigadier Miller**[272] [3979] 8-11-6 **122**............... JeremiahMcGrath(3) 116
(Nicky Henderson) *racd keenly: trckd ldr: led 5th: hdd appr 3 out: led again 3 out: hit 2 out and hdd: sn wknd* **12/1**
10-0 **8** *12* **Beatabout The Bush (IRE)**[16] [1905] 4-11-12 **125**........... AdamWedge 107
(Henry Oliver) *in tch: nt fluent 2 out: sn wknd* **8/1**[3]
3534 **9** *1 ½* **Gambol (FR)**[22] [1828] 5-10-11 **110**.......................... TomO'Brien 90
(Ian Williams) *hld up: nt fluent 2nd and 4th: a in rr* **14/1**
4-20 **10** *2 ½* **Knight In Purple**[136] [751] 11-10-11 **110**....................(vt) PeterCarberry 88
(John Mackie) *led: hdd 5th: rdn to ld again appr 3 out: hdd 3 out: sn wknd* **9/1**
244- **11** *73* **Mystery Drama**[78] [4337] 5-11-1 **121**...................... MikeyHamill(7) 26
(Alexandra Dunn) *midfield: lost pl 6th and sn wl bhd* **33/1**

4m 7.2s (11.40) **Going Correction** +0.925s/f (Soft)
WFA 3 from 4yo 17lb 4 from 5yo+ 9lb **11 Ran SP% 114.0**
Speed ratings (Par 107): **108,107,106,105,103 101,101,95,94,93 56**
CSF £43.24 CT £331.58 TOTE £8.60: £2.20, £1.90, £2.90; EX 33.70 Trifecta £534.80.
Owner Guy Reed Racing **Bred** G Reed **Trained** Hambleton, N Yorks

FOCUS
A well-contested race of its type with a number of the runners in good form beforehand. The form looks pretty solid.

2171 BET365 H'CAP CHASE (LISTED RACE) (16 fncs) 2m 3f 85y
2:15 (2:16) (Class 1) (0-155,145) 4-Y-O+
£15,661 (£5,876; £2,942; £1,465; £737; £368)

Form RPR
124- **1** **Wakanda (IRE)**[203] [5251] 6-11-6 **139**.......................... DannyCook 149+
(Sue Smith) *mde all: rdn after 4 out: jnd after 3 out: styd on run-in* **11/4**[1]
F/P- **2** *4 ½* **Fago (FR)**[307] [3309] 7-11-12 **145**.................. SamTwiston-Davies 153+
(Paul Nicholls) *hld up: smooth hdwy after 5 out: chal on bit after 3 out: rdn between last 2: blnd last: wknd run-in* **17/2**
40R- **3** *6* **Theatre Guide (IRE)**[203] [5253] 8-11-7 **140**..............(tp) PaddyBrennan 140
(Colin Tizzard) *trckd ldr: rdn after 4 out: one pce in 3rd after 3 out* **11/4**[1]

F1-6 **4** *2 ¾* **Mountain King**[175] 184 6-11-6 **139** TomO'Brien 135
(Philip Hobbs) *midfield: rdn after 3 out: no imp* **17/2**
5P-F **5** *6* **Off The Ground (IRE)**[29] 1722 9-11-2 **135** AidanColeman 127
(Charlie Longsdon) *trckd ldr: rdn after 4 out: nt fluent 3 out: wknd after 2 out* **7/1**[3]
502- **6** *10* **Firth Of The Clyde**[196] 5363 10-11-5 **138** BrianHughes 118
(Malcolm Jefferson) *hld up in rr: nvr threatened* **6/1**[2]
630- **7** *14* **Shadows Lengthen**[196] 5363 9-11-0 **133** JakeGreenall 99
(Michael Easterby) *hld up: wknd after 5 out* **25/1**
11-4 **8** *10* **Pumped Up Kicks (IRE)**[104] 1040 8-10-13 **132** IanPopham 88
(Dan Skelton) *in tch: lost pl after 5 out: wknd bef next* **10/1**
5m 10.9s (3.10) **Going Correction** +0.45s/f (Soft) **8** Ran SP% **114.1**
Speed ratings (Par 111): **111,109,106,105,102 98,92,88**
CSF £25.77 CT £68.99 TOTE £3.80: £1.40, £3.00, £1.10; EX 26.10 Trifecta £107.40.
Owner M B Scholey & R H Scholey **Bred** Bluegate Stud **Trained** High Eldwick, W Yorks
FOCUS
Some smart chasers lined up for this, with the first three setting a classy standard. The winner recorded a personal best on his return.

2172 WEATHERBYS HAMILTON WENSLEYDALE JUVENILE HURDLE (LISTED RACE) (9 hdls) 2m
2:50 (2:50) (Class 1) 3-Y-O **£11,390** (£4,274; £2,140; £1,066; £536)

Form RPR
1111 **1** **Leoncavallo (IRE)**[34] 1656 3-11-6 140 AidanColeman 122+
(John Ferguson) *led at slow pce: jnd appr 3 out: nt fluent and hdd 2 out: kpt on run-in: led again post* **4/6**[1]
1 **2** *nse* **Sceau Royal (FR)**[19] 1866 3-11-6 0 WayneHutchinson 121+
(Alan King) *trckd ldr in 2nd: jnd ldr appr 3 out: led narrowly 2 out: briefly ¾ l up jst after last: drvn and one pce fnl 110yds: hdd post* **5/2**[2]
1 **3** *4* **Our Thomas (IRE)**[16] 1899 3-11-2 0 BrianHughes 115+
(Tim Easterby) *in tch in 3rd: pushed along after 2 out: 2 l down whn mstke last: no ex* **6/1**[3]
2 **4** *13* **The Lampo Genie**[16] 1899 3-10-12 0 HenryBrooke 98
(K R Burke) *hld up in 4th: rdn after 3 out: wknd after 2 out* **20/1**
5 *58* **Rio Falls (IRE)**[172] 3-10-12 0 PeterCarberry 38
(Jennie Candlish) *mstkes in rr: wknd and eased after blunder 3 out* **66/1**
4m 25.7s (29.90) **Going Correction** +0.925s/f (Soft) **5** Ran SP% **109.1**
Speed ratings (Par 109): **62,61,59,53,24**
CSF £2.66 TOTE £1.40: £1.10, £2.10; EX 2.30 Trifecta £3.80.
Owner Bloomfields **Bred** Darley **Trained** Cowlinge, Suffolk
FOCUS
Contested by some useful juveniles, this was one of the better races of its type so far this season, but the pace was weak.

2173 WETHERBY WHALER SUPPORTING YORKSHIRE AIR AMBULANCE H'CAP CHASE (19 fncs) 3m 45y
3:25 (3:25) (Class 4) (0-110,109) 4-Y-O+ **£3,768** (£1,106; £553; £276)

Form RPR
4P0- **1** **Blue Kascade (IRE)**[196] 5366 8-11-8 **105** BrianHughes 118+
(Sandy Thomson) *mde all: 5 l clr on bit bef 4 out: rdn 3 out: drvn out run-in* **6/1**
3536 **2** *3 ¼* **Longueville Flier (IRE)**[8] 2030 6-10-5 **91**[1] JoeColliver(3) 100
(Micky Hammond) *hld up: nt a fluent: rdn 6 out: hdwy bef 4 out: plugged on after 2 out: wnt 2nd towards fin* **16/1**
32-2 **3** *1 ½* **Nalim (IRE)**[174] 204 9-9-13 **87** (b) HarryBannister(5) 94
(Harriet Bethell) *midfield: rdn 6 out: sme hdwy bef 4 out: wnt 2nd 2 out: wknd and lost 2nd towards fin* **11/2**[3]
U2U- **4** *7* **Itstimeforapint (IRE)**[209] 5141 7-11-6 **106** DerekFox(3) 108
(Lucinda Russell) *chsd ldr: nt fluent 12th: rdn 6 out: nt fluent 4 out and 3 out: mstke 2 out: grad wknd* **10/3**[1]
3555 **5** *14* **Cara Court (IRE)**[25] 1796 9-10-0 **83** oh13 (v) HenryBrooke 68
(Joanne Foster) *midfield: rdn bef 4 out: sn btn* **50/1**
/5-P **P** **Mansonien L'As (FR)**[66] 1355 9-10-6 **89** (tp) AdrianLane
(Donald McCain) *chsd ldr: reminders after 9th: mstke 13th: wknd appr 4 out: p.u bef 3 out* **22/1**
-012 **P** **Alta Rock (IRE)**[15] 1930 10-10-9 **92** SeanQuinlan
(Sue Smith) *midfield: mstke 12th: blnd next: sn struggling: p.u bef 4 out* **7/2**[2]
214/ **U** **Tiny Dancer (IRE)**[581] 5058 7-11-12 **109** AidanColeman
(Chris Grant) *hld up: nt fluent 7th: rdn after 5 out: wl btn whn mstke and uns rdr 2 out* **16/1**
62P3 **P** **Generous Chief (IRE)**[26] 1778 7-10-5 **93** (b) DiarmuidO'Regan(5)
(Chris Grant) *a in rr: p.u bef 4 out* **12/1**
P-31 **P** **Donapollo**[26] 1778 7-11-4 **104** (t) CraigNichol(3)
(Rose Dobbin) *midfield: nt fluent 11th: sn pushed along: wknd after 5 out: p.u bef 3 out* **13/2**
6m 41.0s (-7.00) **10** Ran SP% **114.1**
CSF £89.34 CT £555.78 TOTE £6.90: £2.10, £5.20, £2.10; EX 105.00 Trifecta £1279.40.
Owner Mrs A M Thomson **Bred** Peter Greene & Joe Fallon **Trained** Lambden, Berwicks
FOCUS
A routine handicap chase, with a mix of in-form and out-of-form runners, but a step up from the winner.

2174 WATCH ON THE RACING UK APP CONDITIONAL JOCKEYS' NOVICES' H'CAP HURDLE (12 hdls) 2m 5f 56y
4:00 (4:00) (Class 4) (0-105,105) 3-Y-O+ **£3,422** (£997; £499)

Form RPR
65-1 **1** **Bruce Almighty (IRE)**[15] 1927 4-11-4 **100** AdamNicol(3) 115+
(Philip Kirby) *hld up: hdwy bef 3 out: hit 3 out but sn led: pushed clr after 2 out: eased fnl 100yds* **11/10**[1]
06-4 **2** *5* **Titans Approach (IRE)**[181] 89 6-10-13 **92** ConorRing 95
(Graeme McPherson) *trckd ldr: nt fluent 7th: hit 3 out: wnt 2nd 2 out: kpt on but no ch easy wnr* **8/1**[3]
064F **3** *3 ¾* **Drop A Gear (IRE)**[28] 1741 5-11-0 **103** RossChapman(10) 101
(Lucinda Russell) *led: nt fluent 7th: hdd jst after 3 out: nt fluent and lost 2nd 2 out: grad wknd run-in* **9/1**
325- **4** *5* **Lowcarr Motion**[200] 5310 5-10-13 **100** FinianO'Toole(8) 93
(Micky Hammond) *hld up: tk clsr order 1/2-way: in tch 3 out: sn rdn: hit last: wknd* **8/1**[3]
3-53 **5** *1 ¼* **Attention Please (IRE)**[18] 1887 5-10-3 **90** LorcanMurtagh(8) 81
(Rose Dobbin) *hld up: hdwy and in tch bef 3 out: sn rdn: wknd last* **5/1**[2]
4524 **6** *36* **The Clonlisk Bug (IRE)**[40] 1597 5-11-12 **105** JakeHodson 60
(Kevin Frost) *trckd ldr: pushed along and lost pl after 7th: wknd and bhd bef 3 out* **10/1**
/30- **7** *22* **Super Lunar (IRE)**[495] 778 6-11-12 **105** GrahamWatters 38
(Henry Hogarth) *in tch: lost pl after 8th: wknd and bhd bef 3 out* **20/1**
5m 43.3s (16.50) **Going Correction** +0.925s/f (Soft)
WFA 4 from 5yo+ 10lb **7** Ran SP% **110.4**
Speed ratings (Par 105): **105,103,101,99,99 85,77**
CSF £9.79 TOTE £1.70: £1.20, £4.00; EX 9.50 Trifecta £65.10.
Owner Andrew Bradshaw **Bred** Cathal Ennis **Trained** East Appleton, N Yorks
FOCUS
A modest race with a convincing winner and probably more to come.
T/Plt: £34.00 to a £1 stake. Pool: £57,742.86 - 1,237.53 winning tickets T/Qpdt: £8.90 to a £1 stake. Pool: £3,740.67 - 308.40 winning tickets **Andrew Sheret**

2175 - (Foreign Racing) - See Raceform Interactive

[1392] DOWN ROYAL (R-H)
Friday, October 30

OFFICIAL GOING: Yielding to soft

2176a EUROPEAN BREEDERS FUND LOUGH CONSTRUCTION LTD. MARES NOVICE HURDLE (GRADE 3) (9 hdls) 2m
1:30 (1:30) 4-Y-O+ **£17,635** (£5,155; £2,441; £813)

RPR
1 **Listen Dear (IRE)**[57] 1463 5-10-10 0 RWalsh 140+
(W P Mullins, Ire) *mde all: clr after 1st: flicked top of several flights: extended advantage fr 3 out and wl clr next where untidy: kpt on strly: eased run-in: unextended* **7/4**[1]
2 *16* **Colla Pier (IRE)**[20] 1864 6-10-10 111 RobertDunne 120
(Patrick Mooney, Ire) *mid-div: 5th 3 out: sn pushed along to go modest 3rd next: wnt 2nd between last 2 but no ch w wnr: one pce* **7/1**
3 *4* **Rathmuck Native (IRE)**[16] 1915 7-10-10 106 JJBurke 116
(Peter Fahey, Ire) *chsd clr ldrs: awkward 3rd: dropped to 7th 4 out: pushed along after next and no imp on wnr in modest 4th 2 out: kpt on steadily to go 3rd last* **20/1**
4 *9* **Dancing Meadows (IRE)**[6] 2064 5-10-10 118 BJCooper 107
(Gordon Elliott, Ire) *sn chsd clr ldrs: modest 3rd at 4th: rdn after 3 out and sn no imp on wnr: dropped to 5th next: one pce* **3/1**[2]
5 *nk* **Dragon Fei (IRE)**[24] 1798 5-10-10 0 ConorMaxwell 107
(Dermot Anthony McLoughlin, Ire) *chsd clr ldr: in turn clr of rest of field: t.k.h early: slt mstke 4 out: pushed along after next but no imp on wnr: untidy 2 out: sn wknd and dropped to 4th between last 2: 5th cl home* **10/3**[3]
6 *21* **Wild Fern (IRE)**[12] 1996 6-11-0 107 ShaneButler 90
(Seamus Fahey, Ire) *mid-div bhd clr ldrs: modest 4th at 4th: rdn after 3 out and sn lost pl: no imp in 7th whn hmpd after next: one pce* **20/1**
7 *32* **Mouskersize (IRE)**[22] 1830 4-10-6 95 MarkBolger 50
(John C McConnell, Ire) *mid-div: dropped to 6th 3 out and sn struggling: no imp whn sltly hmpd next: t.o* **50/1**
F **Rock On Rosie (IRE)**[38] 1621 6-11-0 106 APHeskin
(Adrian Brendan Joyce, Ire) *in rr: 8th whn mstke 4 out: rdn in modest 6th whn mstke and fell 2 out* **12/1**
3m 59.7s (-3.60)
WFA 4 from 5yo+ 9lb **8** Ran SP% **116.1**
CSF £14.77 TOTE £1.90: £1.10, £1.60, £3.90; DF 13.40 Trifecta £153.70.
Owner Supreme Horse Racing Club **Bred** Mr Patrick McCormack **Trained** Muine Beag, Co Carlow
FOCUS
A really impressive display of jumping and galloping here from the winner, somewhat reminiscent of stable companion Morning Run a year previously, even if this year's opposition wasn't quite as strong.

2177a WKD HURDLE (GRADE 2) (9 hdls) 2m
2:05 (2:05) 4-Y-O+
£23,255 (£7,364; £3,488; £1,162; £775; £387)

RPR
1 **Identity Thief (IRE)**[184] 20 5-11-2 137 BJCooper 149
(Henry De Bromhead, Ire) *mde all: pushed along whn chal between last 2: wnt clr last where mstke: rdn run-in and kpt on wl to maintain advantage* **15/8**[1]
2 *3 ½* **Whiteout (GER)**[19] 1748 4-10-8 133 RWalsh 138
(W P Mullins, Ire) *chsd ldrs in 3rd: pushed along fr 2 out and wnt 2nd wl bef last: sn rdn to chal but no imp: kpt on same pce run-in* **5/2**[2]
3 *8 ½* **Modem**[5] 1914 5-11-5 135 (p) RobbiePower 140
(Mrs John Harrington, Ire) *settled in 2nd: mstke 3 out: rdn fr next but no ex and dropped to 3rd between last 2: one pce run-in* **3/1**[3]
4 *2 ¾* **Princely Conn (IRE)**[181] 96 6-11-2 133 MarkWalsh 134
(Thomas Mullins, Ire) *chsd ldrs: 4th 4 out: rdn fr 2 out and sn dropped to 6th u.p: kpt on steadily again fr last to go 4th run-in but nvr a threat* **7/1**
5 *3 ¾* **Officieux (FR)**[264] 4114 4-10-12 130 SeanFlanagan 127
(Noel Meade, Ire) *towards rr: prog to go 5th 4 out: rdn after next: no imp u.p in 5th between last 2: kpt on same pce* **20/1**
6 *1 ¼* **Queen Alphabet (IRE)**[28] 1748 6-10-12 125 (t) JJBurke 125
(Peter Fahey, Ire) *towards rr whn slt mstke 1st: pushed along in 4th fr 2 out but no ex appr last: one pce and dropped to 6th run-in* **12/1**
7 *49* **Finea (IRE)**[138] 737 8-10-12 0 (t) APHeskin 81
(R K Watson, Ire) *towards rr: dropped to 7th 4 out: pushed along and struggling bef next: sn wknd: t.o* **100/1**
4m 4.1s (0.80)
WFA 4 from 5yo+ 9lb **7** Ran SP% **114.3**
CSF £7.05 TOTE £3.20: £1.80, £1.10; DF 7.30 Trifecta £13.90.
Owner Gigginstown House Stud **Bred** Cathal Ennis **Trained** Knockeen, Co Waterford
FOCUS
A really taking performance here from the winner after his novice season ended somewhat disappointingly, and there's no reason why he shouldn't climb the ratings on this evidence.

2178 - 2179a (Foreign Racing) - See Raceform Interactive

ASCOT (R-H)

Saturday, October 31

OFFICIAL GOING: Good (good to soft in places; chs 7.4; hdl 7.9)
Wind: Almost nil Weather: Glorious autumn afternoon

2182 GARDINER & THEOBALD NOVICES' H'CAP HURDLE (10 hdls) 2m 3f 58y
12:40 (12:40) (Class 4) (0-120,120) 3-Y-O+ **£5,848** (£1,717; £858; £429)

Form RPR

4-P2 **1** **Masterplan (IRE)**[17] 1911 5-11-2 **110**.......................... AidanColeman 120+
(Charlie Longsdon) *mde all: nt fluent 5th: hrd pressed fr 2 out: drvn and styd on wl fr last* **13/2**[3]

44-2 **2** *2* **Singlefarmpayment**[177] 177 5-11-10 **118**.......................... RobertDunne 125
(Tom Lacey) *hld up towards rr: prog fr 7th: chsd wnr bef 2 out and sn chalng: nrly upsides last: drifted lft and one pce flat* **16/1**

244- **3** *8* **Bilbrook Blaze**[191] 5500 5-11-7 **115**.......................... TomO'Brien 117
(Philip Hobbs) *prom: chsd wnr after 3 out tl bef next where nt fluent: wl hld in 3rd after* **16/1**

110- **4** *9* **Tanit River (IRE)**[199] 5343 5-10-13 **112**.......................... AlanJohns(5) 104
(Tim Vaughan) *hld up in last pair: hit 6th: rdn and sme prog fr 3 out but stl only midfield bef next and no ch: styd on to take 4th after last: nvr in contention* **9/1**

1232 **5** *nk* **Romulus Du Donjon (IRE)**[15] 1943 4-11-12 **120**.......................... DarylJacob 112
(Oliver Sherwood) *chsd wnr tl after 3 out: steadily fdd bef next* **11/1**

4151 **6** *4* **I'dliketheoption (IRE)**[79] 1240 4-11-12 **120**..........................(t) BarryGeraghty 108
(Jonjo O'Neill) *chsd ldrs: nt fluent 7th: sn rdn: no imp bef 2 out: fdd* **5/1**[2]

30-P **7** *2 ½* **Looks Like Power (IRE)**[177] 177 5-11-2 **110**.......................... PaulMoloney 98
(Debra Hamer) *plld hrd early: hld up in last pair: nt fluent 1st: mstke 7th: prog fr 3 out: rchd midfield and mstke 2 out: no hdwy after* **33/1**

623- **8** *1* **Amidon (FR)**[199] 5343 5-11-12 **120**..........................(p) GavinSheehan 105
(Lucy Wadham) *prom: mstke 7th and lost pl sltly: rdn after 3 out: wknd bef 2 out* **9/2**[1]

63-3 **9** *5* **Bekkensfirth**[23] 1826 6-11-7 **115**.......................... HarrySkelton 95
(Dan Skelton) *nvr bttr than midfield: nt fluent 6th: rdn and no hdwy fr 3 out: wl btn after* **8/1**

220- **10** *2 ¼* **Eminent Poet**[224] 4920 4-11-7 **115**.......................... LiamTreadwell 93
(Venetia Williams) *towards rr: rdn 6th: dropped to last next and sn t.o: plugged on fr 2 out* **25/1**

11 *¾* **Kings Cross (FR)**[60] 5-11-10 **118**.......................... LeeEdwards 96
(Tony Carroll) *hld up in rr: shkn up after 3 out: no real prog and nvr involved* **50/1**

3223 **12** *1* **Antony (FR)**[28] 1754 5-11-5 **120**.......................... GeorgeGorman(7) 97
(Gary Moore) *prom: rdn 3 out: wknd qckly bef 2 out* **12/1**

343F **13** *1 ¾* **Noble Friend (IRE)**[29] 1735 7-11-2 **110**.......................... MarcGoldstein 85
(Chris Gordon) *nvr bttr than midfield: rdn bef 3 out: sn struggling* **22/1**

645- **14** *33* **Charlie Cook (IRE)**[208] 5198 6-11-2 **113**.......................... RyanHatch(3) 59
(Graeme McPherson) *in tch: lost pl fr 7th and mstkes: t.o whn blnd 2 out* **50/1**

3-51 **15** *½* **Do We Like Him (IRE)**[23] 1819 5-11-4 **112**.......................... TomCannon 57
(Chris Gordon) *nvr beyond midfield: rdn after 6th and sn toiling in rr: t.o* **14/1**

4m 40.1s (-4.60) **Going Correction** -0.075s/f (Good) **15** Ran SP% **118.8**
Speed ratings (Par 105): **106,105,101,98,97 96,95,94,92,91 91,90,90,76,76**
CSF £96.50 CT £1592.67 TOTE £7.70: £2.80, £6.20, £7.20; EX 112.30 Trifecta £2302.20.
Owner Gavin MacEchern **Bred** Derek O'Hara **Trained** Over Norton, Oxon

FOCUS
Chase course rail at innermost position and distances as advertised. Hurdle course 9yds off innermost position and race 1 increased by 65yds and races 2, 5 & 7 increased by 53yds. The time of the opener suggested there was still cut in the ground. An ordinary handicap hurdle with the front pair drawing clear. The winner has been rated to his best, with steps up from the second and third.

2183 COLTS & FILLIES CLUB NOVICES' HURDLE (8 hdls) 1m 7f 152y
1:10 (1:12) (Class 3) 4-Y-O+ **£7,797** (£2,289; £1,144; £572)

Form RPR

3-61 **1** **Altior (IRE)**[21] 1844 5-11-4 0.......................... NicodeBoinville 148+
(Nicky Henderson) *t.k.h: hld up in tch: prog to ld after 3 out: hrd pressed 2 out: narrow ld whn flattened last and jnd: fnd ex to assert flat* **4/5**[1]

2 **2** *1 ¼* **Ch'Tibello (FR)**[15] 1946 4-11-4 0.......................... HarrySkelton 143
(Dan Skelton) *hld up in tch: prog to chse wnr wl bef 2 out: sn chalng: lft upsides after last: styd on but hld fnl 150yds* **14/1**

121 **3** *20* **Vancouverite**[19] 1886 5-11-8 132.......................... AidanColeman 129
(John Ferguson) *hld up in tch: clsd on ldrs after 3 out: drvn to take 3rd bef 2 out but ldng pair gng clr: lost further grnd after* **5/1**[3]

4 *5* **Descartes (GER)**[30] 6-11-8 0..........................(t) JamesReveley 123
(G Macaire, France) *trckd ldrs: cl up after 3 out: wknd rather tamely bef 2 out* **7/2**[2]

5 *½* **Chartbreaker (FR)**[473] 4-10-12 0.......................... NickScholfield 112
(Paul Nicholls) *hld up in tch: sharp reminders after 3 out: no prog and wl btn bef next* **10/1**

0- **6** *14* **Centurius**[224] 4916 5-10-12 0.......................... LiamTreadwell 98
(Venetia Williams) *t.k.h: trckd ldr to 3 out: wknd rapidly* **50/1**

7 *6* **Britanio Bello (FR)**[151] 4-10-12 0.......................... JoshuaMoore 92
(Gary Moore) *reluctant ldr and plld hrd: wnt clr after 4th: racd wd and hdd after 3 out: wknd rapidly* **33/1**

2 **8** *7* **Star Foot (IRE)**[14] 1979 4-10-9 0.......................... JamesBanks(3) 85
(Jo Davis) *in tch to 4th: wknd and mstkes next 2: t.o* **33/1**

9 *44* **Master Burbidge**[46] 4-10-12 0.......................... MarkQuinlan 41
(Neil Mulholland) *j. bdly: a in last pair: wl t.o 3 out* **100/1**

3m 43.7s (-3.70) **Going Correction** -0.075s/f (Good)
WFA 4 from 5yo+ 9lb **9** Ran SP% **119.0**
Speed ratings (Par 107): **106,105,95,92,92 85,82,79,57**
CSF £14.53 TOTE £1.70: £1.10, £3.30, £1.70; EX 16.10 Trifecta £75.40.
Owner Mrs Patricia Pugh **Bred** Paddy Behan **Trained** Upper Lambourn, Berks

FOCUS
The front pair came clear in what was a fair novice hurdle. They went just a steady pace. The winner is better than the bare result, and there's a case for rating the race 10lb+ higher through the third and fourth.

2184 ASCOT UNDERWRITING NOVICES' LIMITED H'CAP CHASE (16 fncs) 2m 2f 175y
1:45 (1:45) (Class 3) (0-140,135) 4-Y-O+ **£9,747** (£2,862; £1,431; £715)

Form RPR

312- **1** **Padge (IRE)**[259] 4218 6-11-6 **133**.......................... PaulMoloney 146+
(Evan Williams) *t.k.h early: trckd ldng pair fr 4th: clsd fr 4 out: wnt 2nd 2 out: rdn to ld last: hung bdly lft flat: hld on* **6/1**[3]

3-21 **2** *¾* **Voix D'Eau (FR)**[14] 1962 5-10-10 **130**..........................(t) MrMLegg(7) 142+
(Harry Fry) *tended to jump lft early: settled in midfield: lot to do fr 11th w field strung out: rdn and prog fr 4 out: tk 3rd 2 out: chal last: crossed by wnr flat: kpt on* **9/2**[1]

3 *4* **Anatol (FR)**[588] 5-11-5 **132**.......................... NickScholfield 141+
(Paul Nicholls) *j. w zest and racd keenly: chsd ldr 2nd: led 6th: drew clr 8th: 10 l up 11th: c bk to rivals fr 4 out: hdd and no ex last* **5/1**[2]

226- **4** *5* **Astigos (FR)**[210] 5140 8-10-7 **120**.......................... AidanColeman 122
(Venetia Williams) *chsd ldr to 2nd: sn lost pl and towards rr fr 5th: wl off the pce 11th: kpt on fr 4 out: nvr a threat* **8/1**

2511 **5** *9* **Vikekhal (FR)**[28] 1753 6-11-1 **128**..........................(b) JoshuaMoore 123
(Gary Moore) *led to 6th: chsd ldr after: rdn 3 out: lost 2nd and nt fluent 2 out: wknd* **9/1**

3-15 **6** *5* **Gun Shy (IRE)**[150] 596 7-11-3 **130**.......................... AndrewGlassonbury 119
(Gary Moore) *wl in rr: no ch fr 11th: poor 9th 4 out: kpt on fr 2 out: nvr nrr* **16/1**

4043 **7** *½* **King Alfonso**[14] 1962 6-10-3 **116** oh1.......................... RobertDunne 105
(Dai Burchell) *nvr bttr than midfield: rdn 4 out: disp 5th and no ch bef 2 out: wknd* **25/1**

26-2 **8** *5* **Le Fin Bois (FR)**[27] 1769 5-10-7 **120**..........................(t) NicodeBoinville 104
(Tim Vaughan) *nvr beyond midfield: rdn and no prog fr 12th: wl btn after* **9/1**

110- **9** *54* **Nathans Pride (IRE)**[268] 4048 7-11-0 **132**.......................... AlanJohns(5) 68
(Tim Vaughan) *a in rr and nt fluent: t.o fr 8th* **20/1**

160- **P** **Exitas (IRE)**[336] 2806 7-11-8 **135**..........................(t) DenisO'Regan
(Phil Middleton) *taken down early: hld up in rr: lot to do whn blnd 11th: no ch after: wl bhd whn p.u bef 2 out* **12/1**

2222 **P** **Mont Royale**[39] 1617 7-11-2 **129**..........................(p) BarryGeraghty
(Jonjo O'Neill) *j.lft and wout any fluency: sn toiling: t.o whn p.u bef 8th* **7/1**

4m 37.4s (-9.00) **Going Correction** -0.40s/f (Good) **11** Ran SP% **114.9**
Speed ratings (Par 107): **102,101,100,97,94 92,91,89,66,,**
CSF £33.29 CT £145.07 TOTE £6.00: £2.20, £1.80, £2.20; EX 35.00 Trifecta £103.00.
Owner Mr & Mrs William Rucker **Bred** Mrs Kathleen Lee **Trained** Llancarfan, Vale Of Glamorgan

FOCUS
A decent novice handicap that was run at a really good gallop. A step up from the winner, with the second rated in line with his recent win. There's a case for rating the race up to 7lb higher through the fourth and fifth.

2185 BYRNE GROUP H'CAP CHASE (LISTED RACE) (13 fncs) 2m 192y
2:15 (2:16) (Class 1) (0-150,148) 4-Y-O+
£34,170 (£12,822; £6,420; £3,198; £1,608; £804)

Form RPR

22P- **1** **Cold March (FR)**[235] 4694 5-11-4 **140**.......................... AidanColeman 153+
(Venetia Williams) *sltly impeded in standing s and set off in last pair: stdy prog fr 6th: chsd ldng pair after 3 out: clsd next: led bef last and gd jump: r.o wl and sn clr* **12/1**

113- **2** *7* **Pearls Legend**[205] 5240 8-10-9 **131**.......................... NicodeBoinville 139
(John Spearing) *occasionally j.lft: led after 1st to next: chsd ldr: nt fluent 4th: led 9th: hrd pressed on both sides 2 out: hdd bef last: fdd flat* **10/1**

-222 **3** *3* **Baby Mix (FR)**[105] 1040 7-11-6 **142**..........................(p) NickScholfield 147
(Warren Greatrex) *led briefly 1st: styd prom: pressed ldr fr 10th: chal and upsides 2 out: stl ch bef last: wknd flat: fin lame* **9/2**[1]

43-1 **4** *7* **Bullet Street (IRE)**[174] 218 7-10-10 **132**.......................... PaulMoloney 129
(Evan Williams) *settled in rr: no prog fr 8th and off the pce: kpt on fr 3 out: nvr nrr* **12/1**

3120 **5** *1 ¼* **Purple 'n Gold (IRE)**[7] 2059 6-10-7 **136**..........................(p) DavidNoonan(7) 135
(David Pipe) *wl in tch: prog to trck ldrs 7th: cl 3rd whn blnd 3 out: nt rcvr and btn after* **20/1**

52P- **6** *10* **Royal Regatta (IRE)**[205] 5240 7-11-12 **148**.......................... TomO'Brien 138
(Philip Hobbs) *set off slowly in standing s and swvd lft: a in rr: struggling fr 7th: nvr able to make significant hdwy* **8/1**[3]

561- **7** *17* **Sgt Reckless**[45] 5326 8-11-8 **144**.......................... GavinSheehan 127
(Mick Channon) *prom: mstke 6th: effrt 8th: rt on terms w ldrs whn mstke 4 out: wknd after next: mstke 2 out and blnd last* **9/2**[1]

11U6 **8** *9* **Strongly Suggested**[36] 1643 8-10-10 **132**.......................... BarryGeraghty 95
(Jonjo O'Neill) *chsd ldrs: mstke 6th: lost pl fr 8th: wl btn 4 out: eased after 2 out* **20/1**

100 **P** **Surf And Turf (IRE)**[6] 2084 9-11-8 **144**.......................... DenisO'Regan
(Kevin Frost) *a in rr: struggling fr 6th: sn bhd: t.o in 10th whn p.u bef 2 out* **33/1**

P31- **P** **Ulck Du Lin (FR)**[195] 5413 7-10-13 **142**..........................(bt) HarryCobden(7)
(Paul Nicholls) *led 2nd and set str pce: hdd 9th: wknd qckly: poor 9th whn p.u bef 2 out* **9/1**

04-5 **P** **Bellenos (FR)**[180] 103 7-10-11 **133**..........................(bt) HarrySkelton
(Dan Skelton) *settled in rr: mstke 4th: nvr gng after and dropped to last pl 7th: p.u bef next* **13/2**[2]

134- **P** **Minella Definitely (IRE)**[231] 4752 8-10-8 **130**..........................(p) MarkQuinlan
(Neil Mulholland) *prom to 3rd: sn lost pl: wl in rr and struggling 7th: t.o in 11th whn p.u bef 2 out* **8/1**[3]

4m 2.5s (-12.10) **Going Correction** -0.40s/f (Good) **12** Ran SP% **118.9**
Speed ratings (Par 111): **112,108,107,104,103 98,90,86,,,**
CSF £122.20 CT £630.06 TOTE £13.60: £4.00, £3.50, £2.00; EX 138.70 Trifecta £1134.90.
Owner A Brooks **Bred** Mickael Angee & Alain Angee **Trained** Kings Caple, H'fords

The Form Book Jumps 2015-16, Raceform Ltd, Newbury, RG14 5SJ

FOCUS
A couple of these weren't helped by a standing start in what was a decent handicap chase run at a strong gallop. A step up from the winner, a small pb from the runner-up and the third has been rated close to his mark. Solid form.

2186 WILLIAM HILL H'CAP HURDLE (LISTED RACE) (8 hdls) 1m 7f 152y
2:50 (2:52) (Class 1) 4-Y-0+
£34,170 (£12,822; £6,420; £3,198; £1,608; £804)

Form RPR
211 1 **Nabucco**[18] 1895 6-10-5 **132**........................ AidanColeman 137+
(John Ferguson) *wl plcd: nt fluent 5th: poised to chal after 3 out: led 2 out as others chal: nt fluent last whn a l up: hld on wl* **7/2**[1]
44-5 2 ¾ **Unanimite (FR)**[163] 418 4-10-5 **132**........................ DarylJacob 136+
(David Pipe) *hld up in rr: mstke 3rd: prog on inner bef 2 out: clsng whn mstke last: chsd wnr fnl 100yds: styd on but jst hld* **12/1**
506- 3 nse **Jolly's Cracked It (FR)**[204] 5250 6-10-11 **138**........................ NickScholfield 140
(Harry Fry) *t.k.h: hld up in rr: stl in rr bef 2 out: prog towards outer and hrd rdn bef last: disp 2nd fnl 100yds and clsd on wnr: jst hld* **5/1**[3]
442- 4 2¼ **Sign Of A Victory (IRE)**[196] 5390 6-11-12 **153**........................ AndrewTinkler 154+
(Nicky Henderson) *t.k.h: hld up in rr but wl in tch: prog fr 5th: chal w others 2 out: chsd wnr after: ch after last: lost 2nd and wknd fnl 100yds* **6/1**
15-1 5 2½ **Cloonacool (IRE)**[35] 1657 6-10-9 **136**........................ JoshuaMoore 136+
(Stuart Edmunds) *hld up in rr but in tch: blnd bdly 3 out: prog to chse ldrs 2 out and wl in tch: one pce bef last* **9/2**[2]
110- 6 nk **Wilberdragon**[189] 5539 5-10-3 **130**........................(t) TomCannon 127
(Charlie Longsdon) *prom: pressed hit 4th: pressed ldr 3 out: chal and upsides 2 out: one pce after* **7/1**
126- 7 2¼ **Favorite Girl (GER)**[18] 5205 7-10-1 **127** oh2........................ NicodeBoinville 123
(Michael Appleby) *led at mod pce: tried to kick on fr 3 out: hdd & wknd 2 out* **33/1**
5-01 8 2 **Satanic Beat (IRE)**[7] 1719 6-10-2 **132**........................ ConorShoemark[(3)] 125
(Phil Middleton) *t.k.h: wl in tch in tightly-packed field: rdn and nt qckn bef 2 out: outpcd after* **20/1**
PF4- 9 2¾ **Aerlite Supreme (IRE)**[180] 116 8-10-8 **135**........................ PaulMoloney 126
(Evan Williams) *pressed ldr to 5th: mstke next and lost pl qckly: wl in rr whn mstke 2 out* **33/1**
5-21 10 1¼ **Closest Friend**[26] 1792 6-10-0 **127**........................(t) HarrySkelton 116
(Dan Skelton) *t.k.h: trckd ldrs: rdn to chal and upsides 2 out: wknd qckly bef last* **12/1**
11 1½ **My Manekineko**[29] 1749 6-9-10 **128**........................ JackKennedy[(5)] 115
(J A Nash, Ire) *t.k.h: hld up: trckd ldrs after 4th: lost pl 3 out: wl btn next* **16/1**

3m 45.3s (-2.10) **Going Correction** -0.075s/f (Good)
WFA 4 from 5yo+ 9lb 11 Ran SP% 115.8
Speed ratings (Par 111): **102,101,101,100,99 99,97,96,95,94 94**
CSF £42.87 CT £206.99 TOTE £3.40: £1.80, £3.80, £1.90; EX 50.00 Trifecta £284.50.
Owner Bloomfields **Bred** Darley **Trained** Cowlinge, Suffolk

FOCUS
No great gallop on here and it developed into something of a dash for the line off the final bend. The third to the seventh set the level.

2187 SODEXO GOLD CUP H'CAP CHASE (GRADE 3) (20 fncs) 2m 7f 180y
3:25 (3:25) (Class 1) 4-Y-0+
£56,950 (£21,370; £10,700; £5,330; £2,680; £1,340)

Form RPR
/45- 1 **Pendra (IRE)**[235] 4690 7-10-7 **140**........................(p) BarryGeraghty 149+
(Charlie Longsdon) *mostly trckd ldng pair: wnt 2nd after 3 out: led sn after 2 out and rdn clr: in n.d after last: styd on* **11/2**[1]
R60- 2 3¼ **Double Ross (IRE)**[233] 4718 9-11-0 **150**........................ RyanHatch[(3)] 157+
(Nigel Twiston-Davies) *mstke 1st: in tch in midfield: blnd 10th: struggling fr 14th: 7th and no real prog 3 out: gd hdwy 2 out: tk 2nd last: r.o but no ch to threaten wnr* **16/1**
U0-3 3 3 **Fox Appeal (IRE)**[7] 2061 8-11-5 **152**........................ GavinSheehan 153
(Emma Lavelle) *trckd ldrs: rdn and wl on terms 3 out: cl up next: kpt on same pce after* **9/1**
1P0- 4 ¾ **What A Warrior (IRE)**[235] 4690 8-10-7 **140**........................(t) HarrySkelton 141
(Dan Skelton) *led at gd pce: jnd 6th: kicked on w rival fr 11th: def advantage 14th: hdd after 2 out: one pce* **13/2**[2]
6-0F 5 3¾ **Cantlow (IRE)**[45] 1556 10-10-6 **139**........................(tp) PaulMoloney 139
(Paul Webber) *several mstkes in rr and impeded 8th: struggling fr 15th: modest 8th after 3 out: styd on after: nrst fin* **20/1**
410- 6 nse **Ned Stark (IRE)**[235] 4690 7-10-8 **141**........................ DenisO'Regan 139
(Alan King) *trckd ldrs: rdn in 5th pl 4 out and no imp: tried to cl bef 2 out: one pce after* **7/1**[3]
331- 7 1¾ **Virak (FR)**[210] 5140 6-11-7 **154**........................ NickScholfield 152
(Paul Nicholls) *mstke 1st: mostly in midfield: rdn in 6th 3 out: tried to cl fr next: one pce after* **9/1**
-001 8 5 **Lost Legend (IRE)**[30] 1715 8-10-12 **145**........................(p) AndrewTinkler 137
(Jonjo O'Neill) *trckd ldr: upsides fr 6th: pressed on fr 11th: lost disp ld 14th: lost 2nd after 3 out: fdd fr next* **20/1**
20F- 9 3¼ **Houblon Des Obeaux (FR)**[196] 5392 8-11-12 **159**........................ AidanColeman 148
(Venetia Williams) *mstke 1st and dropped to rr: nvr a factor after: mstke 12th: struggling bdly 15th: kpt on fr 2 out but n.d* **10/1**
42U- P **Bennys Mist (IRE)**[204] 5253 9-10-10 **143**........................ LiamTreadwell
(Venetia Williams) *chsd ldrs: lost pl and in midfield fr 9th: no prog 15th: wl bhd whn p.u bef last* **50/1**
121- P **Leo Luna**[197] 5368 6-10-6 **139**........................(vt) JoshuaMoore
(Gary Moore) *a in last trio: mstke 14th: wl btn after: wl bhd whn p.u bef last* **22/1**
F02- P **No Buts**[215] 5074 7-10-4 **137**........................ TomCannon
(David Bridgwater) *j.lft and nvr gng w much zest in rr: mstke 9th: wl btn 16th: blnd 2 out: wl bhd whn p.u bef last* **16/1**
36-4 P **Present View**[20] 1869 7-10-12 **145**........................ BrendanPowell
(Jamie Snowden) *nvr bttr than midfield: struggling in rr 15th: no real prog after: wl bhd whn p.u bef last* **11/1**
123- P **Le Reve (IRE)**[189] 5538 7-11-2 **149**........................(p) DarylJacob
(Lucy Wadham) *a wl in rr: no prog and struggling 15th: wl bhd in 11th whn p.u bef last* **8/1**
1PP- P **Royal Player**[196] 5392 6-11-0 **147**........................ TomO'Brien
(Philip Hobbs) *towards rr: sme prog into midfield and in tch 13th: lost pl and struggling 16th: 8th and wl btn after 3 out: p.u bef last* **25/1**

5m 51.7s (-11.80) **Going Correction** -0.40s/f (Good) **15** Ran SP% **121.2**
Speed ratings (Par 113): **103,101,100,100,99 99,98,97,96, , , , ,**
CSF £81.05 CT £792.61 TOTE £5.90: £2.40, £6.30, £3.30; EX 110.50 Trifecta £1309.80.
Owner John P McManus **Bred** P Murphy **Trained** Over Norton, Oxon

FOCUS
A truly run staying chase, the form of which looks pretty sound. A big step up from the winner, with the third, fourth and fifth pretty much to their marks.

2188 NEPTUNE INVESTMENT MANAGEMENT STANDARD OPEN NATIONAL HUNT FLAT RACE 1m 7f 152y
3:55 (3:59) (Class 4) 4-6-Y-O
£4,548 (£1,335; £667; £333)

Form RPR
3- 1 **Cultivator**[224] 4921 4-11-0 0........................ BarryGeraghty 109+
(Nicky Henderson) *t.k.h: hld up in tch: trckd ldng pair over 3f out and stl pulling: wnt 2nd 2f out: led 1f out: shkn up and steadily asserted* **10/11**[1]
4- 2 2¼ **He's A Charmer (IRE)**[275] 3944 5-11-0 0........................(t) NickScholfield 105
(Harry Fry) *trckd ldr: led over 2f out: sn rdn: hdd by cruising wnr 1f out: kpt on but no real ch* **4/1**[2]
6- 3 1½ **The Poodle Faker**[245] 4499 4-11-0 0........................ NicodeBoinville 102
(Hughie Morrison) *hld up in last pair: prog 3f out: rdn and kpt on fr 2f out to take 3rd ins fnl f* **8/1**[3]
500/ 4 1 **Henrybrowneyes (IRE)**[574] 5181 6-11-0 0........................ DarylJacob 101
(Ian Williams) *trckd ldrs: rdn to take 3rd over 1f out to ins fnl f: one pce* **33/1**
3/ 5 1¾ **Face To Face**[174] 6-11-0 0........................ DenisO'Regan 99
(Mark Pitman) *led at ordinary pce: rdn and hdd over 2f out: steadily fdd over 1f out* **20/1**
6 7 **Bolister (FR)** 4-11-0 0........................ JoshuaMoore 92
(Gary Moore) *in tch: dropped to last trio 4f out: jst pushed along in 6th and no imp on ldrs 2f out: fdd* **20/1**
7 1 **Opechee (IRE)** 4-10-9 0........................ JakeHodson[(5)] 91
(David Bridgwater) *hld up in last pair: shkn up and no prog over 2f out* **25/1**
8 hd **Brandenburg Gate (IRE)** 4-11-0 0........................ AidanColeman 91
(Charlie Longsdon) *t.k.h: trckd ldrs: drvn and lost pl fr 3f out* **4/1**[2]

3m 44.8s (4.00) **Going Correction** -0.075s/f (Good) **8** Ran SP% **119.8**
Speed ratings: **87,85,85,84,83 80,79,79**
CSF £4.84 TOTE £1.80: £1.10, £1.40, £2.00; EX 5.90 Trifecta £29.90.
Owner Kimmins Family And Friends **Bred** Shade Oak Stud **Trained** Upper Lambourn, Berks

FOCUS
Not the strongest bumper, but it was a taking effort from the winner. A step up from the winner, with the fourth the best guide to the level.
T/Plt: £221.80 to a £1 stake. Pool: £138,230.52 - 454.77 winning units. T/Qpdt: £27.80 to a £1 stake. Pool: £15,179.98 - 402.70 winning units. **Jonathan Neesom**

2100 AYR (L-H)
Saturday, October 31

OFFICIAL GOING: Good to soft (good in places; chs 7.8; hdl 7.5)
Wind: Almost nil Weather: Overcast

2189 FASPRINT MAIDEN HURDLE (9 hdls) 2m
1:15 (1:18) (Class 5) 4-Y-0+
£2,599 (£763; £381; £190)

Form RPR
1 **Cornborough**[24] 4-11-0 0........................ JakeGreenall 116+
(Mark Walford) *in tch: smooth hdwy to chse ldr bef 2 out: led and rdn last: styd on strly* **9/1**[2]
11- 2 2 **Another Bill (IRE)**[302] 3487 5-11-0 0........................ BrianHarding 115+
(Nicky Richards) *nt fluent: chsd ldrs: wnt 2nd bef 4th: led after 4 out: rdn and hdd last: kpt on same pce* **4/9**[1]
46/ 3 1 **Southsea Island (IRE)**[600] 4728 7-10-7 0........................[1] AnthonyFox[(7)] 112+
(S R B Crawford, Ire) *hld up towards rr: hdwy bef 3 out: pushed along bef next: kpt on fr last: nt rch first two* **25/1**
4 13 **Road To Gold (IRE)**[202] 6-11-0 0........................ AndrewThornton 103
(N W Alexander) *t.k.h: chsd ldr to bef 4th: cl up tl rdn and outpcd fr 2 out* **40/1**
5 ½ **Bertalus (IRE)**[188] 6-11-0 0........................ PeterBuchanan 102
(N W Alexander) *hld up in midfield: blnd and pushed along 5th: rallied after next: rdn and wknd fr 2 out* **12/1**[3]
/0P 6 7 **Parlour Of Dreams (IRE)**[9] 2025 8-10-7 81........................ MissRMcDonald[(7)] 91
(Andrew Hamilton) *hld up in tch: rdn bef 3 out: wknd fr next* **100/1**
644- 7 hd **Arantes**[32] 5196 4-10-9 108........................(p) CallumBewley[(5)] 91
(R Mike Smith) *t.k.h: led: nt fluent 2nd: hdd after 4 out: rallied: wknd fr 2 out* **16/1**
4/4- 8 3 **Imperial Prince (IRE)**[276] 3926 6-11-0 0........................ DannyCook 89
(Sandy Thomson) *midfield: pushed along after 4 out: outpcd whn nt fluent next: sn btn* **20/1**
9 6 **Aleksandar**[18] 6-11-0 0........................ HenryBrooke 82
(Jim Goldie) *hld up: pushed along and outpcd bef 3 out: no imp bef next* **18/1**
0 10 nk **Mister Don (IRE)**[21] 1852 5-10-11 0........................ GrahamWatters[(3)] 82
(Rose Dobbin) *hld up towards rr on ins: rdn after 4 out: wknd bef next* **80/1**
11 3¼ **Rioja Day (IRE)**[18] 5-10-9 0........................ StephenMulqueen[(5)] 78
(Jim Goldie) *nt fluent on occasions: hld up: struggling 4 out: nvr on terms* **50/1**
12 2 **Smuggler's Stash (IRE)**[216] 5-10-11 0........................ CraigNichol[(3)] 76
(Rose Dobbin) *hld up in midfield: drvn and outpcd after 4 out: struggling fr next* **14/1**
5-05 13 3 **Herecomesnelson (IRE)**[7] 2066 6-10-7 0........................ JamieHamilton[(7)] 73
(Katie Scott) *hld up towards rr: rdn and struggling bef 4 out: sn btn* **28/1**
P- 14 12 **Norfolk Sound**[284] 3782 4-10-0 0........................ SamColtherd[(7)] 54
(Stuart Coltherd) *mstkes in rr: struggling fr 1/2-way: nvr on terms* **100/1**
66 F **Seven Devils (IRE)**[37] 1634 5-10-11 0........................ DerekFox[(3)] 91
(Lucinda Russell) *hld up in midfield: pushed along and effrt after 4 out: 7 l 7th and outpcd whn fell 2 out* **28/1**

3m 57.3s (237.30)
WFA 4 from 5yo+ 9lb **15** Ran SP% **127.9**
CSF £13.70 TOTE £13.30: £2.60, £1.10, £7.80; EX 24.90 Trifecta £209.00.
Owner Cornborough Racing Club **Bred** Mr & Mrs A E Pakenham **Trained** Sherriff Hutton, N Yorks

FOCUS
Some starts have been moved at this track following remeasuring, so some races will not have speed figures until there is sufficient data to calculate updated median times. Chase course on innermost line and distances as advertised. Hurdle races increased by 6yds. Fair efforts from the leading trio who came clear after the second-last. The time was very slow compared with the later handicap and so this is not form to be confident about.

2190 PLUMBSTORE H'CAP HURDLE (11 hdls 1 omitted) 2m 5f 91y
1:50 (1:51) (Class 4) (0-120,120) 3-Y-0+ £4,223 (£1,240; £620; £310)

Form RPR
21F- **1** **Island Heights (IRE)**[191] 5492 6-11-9 **120**.......................... DerekFox(3) 125+
(Lucinda Russell) *trckd ldrs: hdwy to ld 5th: mde rest at modest gallop: rdn 3 out: styd on gamely fr last* **11/4**[1]
134- **2** *1* **Always Tipsy**[201] 5310 6-11-6 **119**.......................... StephenMulqueen(5) 123+
(N W Alexander) *hld up: stdy hdwy 4 out: effrt and rdn bef 2 out: styd on to take 2nd towards fin: nt rch wnr* **5/1**[2]
/0P- **3** *1 1/4* **Malin Bay (IRE)**[469] 1006 10-11-7 **118**.......................... AdamNicol(3) 120
(Nicky Richards) *hld up on outside: hdwy 1/2-way: effrt and chsng wnr whn hit 2 out: nt fluent last: kpt on same pce and lost 2nd towards fin* **11/2**[3]
536- **4** *8* **Doktor Glaz (FR)**[197] 5366 5-10-13 **110**.......................... CraigNichol(3) 106
(Rose Dobbin) *in tch: hdwy after 4 out: drvn and ev ch next: outpcd fr 2 out* **11/4**[1]
5 *18* **Nakadam (FR)**[211] 5-10-9 **108**.......................... CallumBewley(5) 86
(R Mike Smith) *prom: wnt 2nd 1/2-way to bef 3 out: sn rdn and wknd* **12/1**
0-45 **6** *10* **Pistol (IRE)**[159] 473 6-10-4 **105**.......................... MrJDixon(7) 74
(John Dixon) *cl up: led at stdy pce to 4th: hdd whn hit next: outpcd 7th: wknd fr 4 out* **9/1**
U0-0 **7** *9* **Ballygrooby Bertie (IRE)**[15] 1958 7-10-9 **110**..........(tp) AnthonyFox(7) 71
(S R B Crawford, Ire) *hld up in tch: pushed along after 4 out: wknd bef next* **16/1**
446- **P** **Nashville (IRE)**[15] 4488 6-10-8 **105**..........(b[1]) JohnKington(3)
(Andrew Crook) *led to 4th: lost pl and struggling after 6th: lost tch and p.u 4 out* **33/1**
5m 18.4s (318.40) **8** Ran SP% **111.9**
CSF £16.41 CT £68.06 TOTE £3.00: £1.40, £1.40, £2.10; EX 10.90 Trifecta £22.10.
Owner Gerry McGladery **Bred** Fiona And Michael O'Connor **Trained** Arlary, Perth & Kinross

FOCUS
A fairly useful staying event. Most of the principals are still relatively unexposed and there's no reason why the form won't hold up. The first two have been rated pretty much to their marks.

2191 PARK'S RENAULT KADJAR H'CAP CHASE (15 fncs 2 omitted) 2m 4f 110y
2:20 (2:22) (Class 5) (0-100,94) 4-Y-0+ £3,249 (£954; £477; £238)

Form RPR
226- **1** **What A Dream**[218] 5014 9-10-10 **85**..........(tp) JamieHamilton(7) 99+
(Alison Hamilton) *in tch: pushed along 10th: effrt and rdn bef 3 out: edgd lft: led bef last: drvn clr run-in* **10/1**
264- **2** *10* **Oscar Lateen (IRE)**[210] 5134 7-11-4 **89**..........(p) DerekFox(3) 94
(Sandy Thomson) *cl up: lft 2nd 5th: effrt and led 3 out: edgd lft and hdd bef last: kpt on same pce run-in* **3/1**[1]
/64U **3** *3* **Kilmainham (IRE)**[21] 1853 7-11-8 **90**..........(p) HenryBrooke 95
(Martin Todhunter) *in tch on outside: hdwy to ld bef 9th: nt fluent 4 out: nt fluent and hdd next: rallied and ev ch next: sn outpcd* **9/2**[2]
6P43 **4** *12* **Reverse The Charge (IRE)**[21] 1857 8-9-11 **70**.......... DaleIrving(5) 64
(Jane Walton) *mstkes: hld up in tch: effrt and pushed along after 5 out: hit next and 3 out: wknd* **5/1**[3]
5PP- **5** *4 1/2* **Blueside Boy (IRE)**[233] 4725 7-11-4 **86**.......... BrianHarding 72
(Harriet Graham) *nt fluent in rr: struggling and reminders 1/2-way: shortlived effrt after 6 out: sn btn* **10/1**
0-6P **P** **Marlee Mourinho (IRE)**[19] 1891 9-10-4 **77**.......... StephenMulqueen(5)
(N W Alexander) *prom: lost pl 8th: outpcd whn blnd 10th: lost tch and p.u bef 5 out* **11/1**
-513 **P** **Odds On Dan (IRE)**[166] 379 9-10-13 **81**..........(tp) JakeGreenall
(Lucinda Egerton) *hld up: drvn and outpcd 9th: struggling fr next: p.u bef 2 out* **14/1**
1445 **P** **Everlylasting (IRE)**[21] 1857 8-11-0 **85**..........(bt) CraigNichol(3)
(Rose Dobbin) *cl up: lft in ld 5th: hdd bef 9th: drvn and outpcd whn hit 5 out: sn wknd: lost tch and p.u bef 2 out* **8/1**
PP1- **U** **Hi Bob**[345] 2616 7-11-12 **94**.......... DannyCook
(Lucinda Egerton) *led tl blnd and uns rdr 5th* **13/2**
5m 22.2s (322.20) **9** Ran SP% **117.5**
CSF £42.30 CT £158.40 TOTE £15.40: £3.30, £1.50, £1.40; EX 64.10 Trifecta £360.60.
Owner D & J Byers, The Late R J Kyle **Bred** Mr And Mrs W D Parker **Trained** Denholm, Borders

FOCUS
Some indifferent jumping was a feature of this modest handicap. The third has been rated in line with his recent Hexham run.

2192 LIGHTWAYS CONTRACTORS LTD H'CAP CHASE (15 fncs 2 omitted) 2m 4f 110y
2:55 (2:56) (Class 3) (0-135,128) 4-Y-0+ £9,097 (£2,671; £1,335; £667)

Form RPR
66-4 **1** **Back To Bracka (IRE)**[175] 198 8-11-9 **128**.......... DerekFox(3) 139+
(Lucinda Russell) *hld up: stdy hdwy 1/2-way: effrt and wnt 2nd after 4 out: chal next: mstke 2 out: sn rcvrd: led last: drvn out* **7/2**[2]
112- **2** *1 1/2* **De Vous A Moi (FR)**[218] 5012 7-11-9 **125**.......... DannyCook 133
(Sue Smith) *cl up: led 8th: rdn bef 4 out: rallied: jnd next: hdd last: kpt on same pce run-in: bttr for r* **3/1**[1]
313- **3** *5* **Plus Jamais (FR)**[197] 5364 8-11-1 **117**.......... HenryBrooke 121
(Jim Goldie) *led to 8th: cl up: lost pl 10th: rallied bef 2 out: kpt on fr last: nt rch first two* **6/1**[3]
6P-4 **4** *5* **Isla Pearl Fisher**[19] 1889 12-11-3 **119**..........(t) PeterBuchanan 120
(N W Alexander) *chsd ldrs: wnt 2nd bef 9th to after 4 out: rdn and outpcd fr next* **10/1**
FU1- **5** *7* **Bernardelli (IRE)**[323] 3064 7-11-9 **125**.......... BrianHarding 120
(Nicky Richards) *nt fluent on occasions: hld up: stdy hdwy to trck ldrs bef 4 out: rdn and wknd next* **7/2**[2]
50-0 **6** *13* **More Madness (IRE)**[182] 92 8-10-9 **118**..........(p) MrKitAlexander(7) 102
(N W Alexander) *in tch: nt fluent and lost pl 7th: outpcd fr 9th: hmpd 5 out: sn struggling* **6/1**[3]
-PP0 **U** **Indian Voyage (IRE)**[17] 1904 7-11-1 **122**..........(t) DaraghBourke(5)
(Maurice Barnes) *hld up in tch: blnd 10th: 4 l 6th and pushed along whn mstke and uns rdr 5 out* **11/1**
5m 14.9s (314.90) **7** Ran SP% **115.4**
CSF £15.22 TOTE £5.00: £2.50, £1.70; EX 18.40 Trifecta £60.20.
Owner Peter J S Russell & Mrs Judith Murray **Bred** Mrs Michael Scott **Trained** Arlary, Perth & Kinross

FOCUS
Useful efforts from the leading pair who look set for good seasons. The winner has been rated to his best, with the second pretty much to his mark.

2193 PROCAST BUILDING CONTRACTORS H'CAP CHASE (11 fncs 1 omitted) 1m 7f 112y
3:30 (3:31) (Class 3) (0-140,134) 4-Y-0+ £9,097 (£2,671; £1,335; £667)

Form RPR
3251 **1** **Oliver's Gold**[17] 1904 7-11-4 **126**..........(p) JakeGreenall 140+
(Mark Walford) *hld up: stdy hdwy bef 4 out: effrt bef 2 out: led last: drvn and hld on wl* **10/1**
6-11 **2** *3/4* **Monbeg River (IRE)**[5] 2104 6-11-0 **122** 7ex.......... HenryBrooke 134+
(Martin Todhunter) *t.k.h early: prom: hdwy to ld 3 out: rdn and hdd last: rallied: hld nr fin* **10/11**[1]
112- **3** *23* **Imjoeking (IRE)**[231] 4749 8-11-12 **134**.......... PeterBuchanan 125
(Lucinda Russell) *cl up: led bef 4 out: rdn whn hit and hdd next: wknd fr 2 out* **13/2**[3]
54F- **4** *1 1/4* **Grate Fella (IRE)**[196] 5389 7-11-10 **132**.......... DannyCook 122
(Sue Smith) *cl up: led 5 out to bef next: rdn and wknd bef 3 out* **11/2**[2]
121- **P** **Aye Well**[197] 5364 10-11-5 **127**.......... BrianHarding
(Stuart Coltherd) *hld up on outside: hdwy and prom 1/2-way: rdn and wknd after 4 out: t.o whn p.u bef last* **8/1**
3112 **P** **Robin's Command (IRE)**[27] 1777 8-11-7 **132**.......... CraigNichol(3)
(Rose Dobbin) *led: nt fluent 6 out: hdd whn blnd bdly next: nt rcvr: t.o whn p.u bef last* **10/1**
/U-6 **P** **Formidableopponent (IRE)**[5] 2104 8-10-5 **120**.......... MrJDixon(7)
(William Young Jnr) *mstkes: in tch: struggling 6 out: sn lost tch: p.u bef 2 out* **100/1**
3m 49.1s (-21.60) **Going Correction** -1.125s/f (Hard) **7** Ran SP% **111.4**
Speed ratings (Par 107): **109,108,97,96,** ,
CSF £19.75 TOTE £12.90: £4.30, £1.20; EX 25.10 Trifecta £142.20.
Owner CW Racing Club & Partner **Bred** Bearstone Stud Ltd **Trained** Sherriff Hutton, N Yorks

FOCUS
A useful contest which was soundly run, the finish fought out by a couple of progressive chasers. Another big step up from the winner.

2194 TENNENT'S CUP H'CAP HURDLE (9 hdls) 2m
4:00 (4:03) (Class 2) (0-150,149) 3-Y-0+ £12,996 (£3,816; £1,908; £954)

Form RPR
11-F **1** **Aristo Du Plessis (FR)**[17] 1905 5-9-12 **126**.......... DaleIrving(5) 134+
(James Ewart) *chsd clr ldr: hdwy to ld 5th: hrd pressed fr 3 out: hld on gamely u.p fr last* **5/1**[2]
11-3 **2** *2* **Avidity**[163] 418 6-10-2 **132**.......... MrKitAlexander(7) 136
(James Ewart) *rn wout declared tongue-strap: chsd ldrs: effrt after 3 out: wnt 2nd run-in: kpt on* **11/2**[3]
3 *1 1/2* **Forest Bihan (FR)**[346] 4-10-9 **139**.......... CraigGallagher(7) 143
(Brian Ellison) *hld up in tch: hdwy 1/2-way: disp ld 3 out to last: kpt on same pce u.p run-in* **8/1**
26-U **4** *5* **Kashmir Peak (IRE)**[17] 1905 6-10-10 **133**.......... JakeGreenall 131
(John Quinn) *hld up in midfield: effrt bef 3 out: no imp fr next* **12/1**
66-1 **5** *6* **Jet Master (IRE)**[37] 1638 9-10-4 **127**.......... PeterBuchanan 120
(N W Alexander) *hld up: effrt and hdwy after 4 out: rdn and no imp after next* **12/1**
P30- **6** *1* **Lightening Rod**[203] 5276 10-10-8 **136**.......... HarryBannister(5) 129
(Michael Easterby) *hld up: mstke 5th: hit next: outpcd 4 out: kpt on fr 2 out: nvr rchd ldrs* **16/1**
14-6 **7** *2 3/4* **Circus Star (USA)**[170] 301 7-9-7 **123** oh5.......... MrJDixon(7) 115
(John Dixon) *led and clr to after 4th: hit and hdd next: sn rdn: wknd fr 3 out* **33/1**
25-5 **8** *3 1/2* **Teo Vivo (FR)**[17] 1905 8-10-0 **123**..........(b) HenryBrooke 112
(Pauline Robson) *hld up in tch: nt fluent 4th: struggling after 4 out: btn whn hmpd next* **16/1**
/45- **9** *6* **Cloudy Too (IRE)**[224] 4910 9-10-10 **133**.......... DannyCook 116
(Sue Smith) *hld up: struggling after 4 out: btn next* **11/1**
6-53 **B** **Uriah Heep (FR)**[17] 1905 6-9-9 **123** oh1.......... CallumBewley(5)
(R Mike Smith) *hld up: pushed along after 4 out: nrly 6 l down and styng on steadily whn b.d next* **16/1**
114- **F** **Glingerburn (IRE)**[204] 5250 7-11-12 **149**.......... BrianHarding
(Nicky Richards) *t.k.h early: hld up: stdy hdwy 4 out: 4 l 4th and shkn up whn fell next* **9/4**[1]
3m 49.3s (229.30)
WFA 4 from 5yo+ 9lb **11** Ran SP% **118.2**
CSF £33.37 CT £219.61 TOTE £5.90: £1.80, £2.60, £3.00; EX 35.50 Trifecta £220.80.
Owner Mrs J M Dodd **Bred** J Andriau, O Regley Et Al **Trained** Langholm, Dumfries & G'way

FOCUS
A useful handicap which was soundly run, the form likely to prove solid. The second has been rated to his mark.

2195 SNJ RECRUITMENT "NEWCOMERS" STANDARD OPEN NATIONAL HUNT FLAT RACE 1m 5f 123y
4:30 (4:30) (Class 6) 3-5-Y-0 £1,711 (£498; £249)

Form RPR
1 **Caius Marcius (IRE)** 4-11-7 0.......... CraigNichol(3) 98
(Nicky Richards) *hld up on outside: smooth hdwy to ld over 2f out: sn rdn: hld on gamely fnl f* **4/1**[3]
2 *nk* **Selkirk's Island** 4-11-0 0.......... GrahamWatters(3) 91
(Lucinda Russell) *prom: effrt and rdn over 2f out: ev ch over 1f out: kpt on fnl f: hld nr fin* **8/1**
3 *2 1/4* **Largy Girl (IRE)** 4-10-10 0.......... AnthonyFox(7) 88
(S R B Crawford, Ire) *hld up: smooth hdwy on outside over 2f out: ev ch gng wl over 1f out: sn rdn: kpt on same pce fnl f* **10/3**[2]
4 *1 1/4* **Rosette** 3-9-7 0.......... ThomasCheesman(7) 69
(Alan Swinbank) *hld up: stdy hdwy over 4f out: rdn 3f out: rallied: kpt on same pce fr over 1f out* **5/2**[1]
5 *11* **Toquickly** 3-9-9 0.......... CallumBewley(5) 56
(Harriet Graham) *led to over 2f out: sn rdn and wknd* **33/1**
6 *3 3/4* **Orioninverness (IRE)** 4-11-5 0.......... GrantCockburn(5) 74
(Lucinda Russell) *chsd ldr to 1/2-way: struggling over 5f out: n.d after* **14/1**
7 *1/2* **Oir Ion (IRE)** 3-10-4 0..........(t) DerekFox(3) 56
(Mark Michael McNiff, Ire) *trckd ldrs: rdn over 2f out: wknd wl over 1f out* **14/1**
8 *10* **Painters Lad (IRE)** 4-11-10 0.......... BrianHarding 65
(Alison Hamilton) *hld up in tch: hdwy to chse ldr 1/2-way to over 3f out: sn wknd* **8/1**

9 23 **Hooks Lane** 3-10-7 0.. AndrewThornton 13
(Shaun Harris) *t.k.h: hld up: struggling over 5f out: sn lost tch* **28/1**
3m 16.6s (196.60) **9** Ran SP% **113.6**
CSF £35.25 TOTE £4.50: £1.30, £2.20, £1.80; EX 34.50 Trifecta £127.80.
Owner C P Norbury **Bred** Sean Gorman **Trained** Greystoke, Cumbria
FOCUS
No previous form to go on, but the leading quartet hail from yards with decent records in these events and came nicely clear in the straight.
T/Plt: £30.50 to a £1 stake. Pool: £53,283.62 - 1271.91 winning units. T/Qpdt: £26.00 to a £1 stake. Pool: £2,694.48 - 76.40 winning units. **Richard Young**

[2169]WETHERBY (L-H)
Saturday, October 31

OFFICIAL GOING: Soft (chs 7.0; hdl 6.9)
Wind: light 1/2 against Weather: Overcast

2196 WATCH RACING UK ANYWHERE NOVICES' HURDLE (9 hdls) 2m
12:50 (12:50) (Class 3) 4-Y-0+ **£5,393** (£1,583; £791; £395)

Form RPR
0 1 **Charmix (FR)**[169] 320 5-11-0 0.. NoelFehily 120+
(Harry Fry) *mde all at ordinary gallop: nt fluent 2nd: jnd whn nt fluent and rdn 2 out: styd on gamely fr last* **5/2[2]**
211 2 1 ¼ **Ennistown**[100] 1081 5-11-8 130.. BrianHughes 129+
(John Ferguson) *t.k.h: hld up: hdwy to chse ldrs 1/2-way: chal gng wl bef 2 out: hit and rdn last: kpt on same pce run-in* **11/10[1]**
6- 3 nk **Draytonian (IRE)**[215] 5077 5-11-0 0.. RichardJohnson 119+
(Philip Hobbs) *t.k.h: sn chsng wnr: ev ch 4 out to bef 2 out: pushed along and kpt on fr last* **7/2[3]**
426 4 27 **Jethro (IRE)**[9] 2041 4-11-0 0..[1] WillKennedy 92
(Brian Ellison) *hld up: stdy hdwy on ins after 4 out: shkn up after next: sn outpcd* **12/1**
0/2- 5 8 **Karisma King**[548] 42 6-11-0 0.. SeanQuinlan 84
(Sue Smith) *t.k.h: hld up in tch: outpcd and pushed along 4 out: n.d after* **12/1**
6 4 ½ **Strait Run (IRE)**[14] 4-10-4 0.. FinianO'Toole[(10)] 79
(Micky Hammond) *hld up in tch: nt fluent 1st: outpcd bef 4 out: sn struggling: btn next* **100/1**
5- 7 21 **Par Three (IRE)**[18] 3232 4-10-9 0.. NickSlatter[(5)] 58
(Tony Carroll) *nt fluent on occasions: t.k.h: chsd ldrs: lost pl 1/2-way: btn bef 3 out* **50/1**
U **Alchimix (FR)**[219] 5002 5-10-11 0.. JoeColliver[(3)]
(Micky Hammond) *whipped rnd and uns rdr s* **25/1**
4m 8.4s (12.60) **Going Correction** +0.15s/f (Yiel)
WFA 4 from 5yo+ 9lb **8** Ran SP% **120.6**
Speed ratings (Par 107): **74,73,73,59,55 53,42,**
CSF £6.20 TOTE £3.90: £1.20, £1.10, £1.30; EX 6.50 Trifecta £19.30.
Owner Nicholas Cooper **Bred** Mlle Viviane Pedron & Philippe Mehat **Trained** Seaborough, Dorset
FOCUS
Some starts have been moved at this track following remeasuring, so some races will not have speed figures until there is sufficient data to calculate updated median times. Both bends pushed out 3yds. Races 1, 4 & 6 increased by 18yds, races 2, 3 & 5 by 36yds and race 7 by 27yds. The opening contest was a fairly decent novice hurdle. They went a modest gallop on the soft ground. It's been rated through the winner and fourth.

2197 BET365.COM NOVICES' CHASE (19 fncs) 3m 45y
1:25 (1:25) (Class 4) 4-Y-0+ **£3,861** (£1,198; £645)

Form RPR
01-2 1 **Southfield Royale**[17] 1900 5-11-4 0.. NoelFehily 144+
(Neil Mulholland) *t.k.h: trckd ldr: j.lft at times: hit 11th: led 14th: wnt clr bef 2 out: pushed out* **7/4[2]**
33P- 2 20 **Zeroeshadesofgrey (IRE)**[204] 5254 6-11-4 0.. TrevorWhelan 128+
(Neil King) *chsd ldrs: blnd 15th: drvn to chse wnr appr next: kpt on same pce fr 3 out* **11/8[1]**
111- 3 14 **Beg To Differ (IRE)**[231] 4766 5-11-4 0.. RichardJohnson 115+
(Jonjo O'Neill) *t.k.h: trckd ldrs: nt fluent 3rd: drvn 4 out: sn wknd* **11/4[3]**
04-2 P **Handazan (IRE)**[137] 208 6-11-4 0..(tp) KielanWoods
(Ben Case) *led: hdd 14th: lost pl bef 4 out: t.o whn p.u bef 2 out* **14/1**
P-PP P **Shabach (IRE)**[17] 1900 8-11-1 0..(p) TonyKelly[(3)]
(Mark Walford) *detached in rr: pushed along 10th: wl bhd 14th: t.o next: p.u bef 4 out* **200/1**
P **Under The Red Sky (IRE)**[223] 8-11-1 0.. ColmMcCormack[(3)]
(Kenny Johnson) *detached in rr: bhd whn blnd 12th: sn t.o: p.u bef 15th* **100/1**
6m 29.8s (-18.20) **6** Ran SP% **113.3**
CSF £4.90 TOTE £2.60: £1.40, £1.40; EX 5.90 Trifecta £8.70.
Owner Mrs Angela Yeoman **Bred** Mrs Angela Yeoman **Trained** Limpley Stoke, Wilts
FOCUS
A fairly good staying novice chase. They went a sensible gallop on the soft ground. The winner has been rated as improving in line with his hurdles form.

2198 BET365 WEST YORKSHIRE HURDLE (GRADE 2) (13 hdls) 3m 26y
2:00 (2:00) (Class 1) 4-Y-0+
£22,780 (£8,548; £4,280; £2,132; £1,072; £536)

Form RPR
P10- 1 **Kilcooley (IRE)**[216] 5058 6-11-9 159..(t) RichardJohnson 167+
(Charlie Longsdon) *trckd ldrs: led 8th: wnt clr fr 3 out: v easily* **5/1[3]**
112- 2 13 **Rock On Ruby (IRE)**[205] 5238 10-11-9 160..(t) NoelFehily 149
(Harry Fry) *racd wd: sn trcking ldrs: chsd wnr appr 3 out: drvn 2 out: wl hld whn mstke last* **3/1[1]**
512- 3 ¾ **Aqalim**[189] 5541 5-11-1 152..(v) BrianHughes 140
(John Ferguson) *in rr: pushed along after 6th: hdwy and modest 4th 9th: hit next: kpt on to take modest 3rd last: styng on at fin* **7/2[2]**
13P- 4 16 **Grumeti**[21] 4742 7-11-1 140.. WayneHutchinson 126
(Alan King) *chsd ldrs: drvn 9th: outpcd bef next: modest 3rd and wkng whn mstke last* **7/1**
121- 5 9 **Closing Ceremony (IRE)**[259] 4223 6-11-9 146.. RichieMcLernon 121
(Emma Lavelle) *chsd ldr: led 4th: hdd 8th: sn drvn: lost pl next: sn bhd* **17/2**
51F- 6 85 **The Druids Nephew (IRE)**[203] 5275 8-11-1 139..(p) MichaelByrne 28
(Neil Mulholland) *hld up in rr: nt fluent: hdwy 7th: drvn and lost pl 9th: sn bhd* **10/1**
P0P- 7 2 ¾ **Splash Of Ginge**[204] 5253 7-11-1 146.. JamieBargary 26
(Nigel Twiston-Davies) *in rr-div: nt fluent: hdwy to chse ldrs 5th: lost pl 9th and sn bhd* **14/1**
2-01 P **Goldan Jess (IRE)**[61] 1419 11-11-1 138.. KyleJames
(Philip Kirby) *led: nt fluent 2nd: hdd 4th: drvn 6th: lost pl next: sn bhd: t.o whn p.u bef 3 out* **66/1**
04-1 P **No Planning**[175] 196 8-11-1 143.. SeanQuinlan
(Sue Smith) *nt fluent: chsd ldrs: reminders after 6th: lost pl next: sn bhd: t.o whn p.u bef 3 out* **10/1**
6m 8.0s (-8.50) **Going Correction** +0.15s/f (Yiel) **9** Ran SP% **113.3**
Speed ratings (Par 115): **120,115,115,110,107 78,77, ,**
CSF £20.46 TOTE £6.50: £1.90, £1.50, £1.70; EX 22.00 Trifecta £62.80.
Owner J H & S M Wall **Bred** Fergal O'Mahoney **Trained** Over Norton, Oxon
FOCUS
A competitive renewal of this Grade 2 staying hurdle won last year by subsequent World Hurdle-winner Cole Harden. They went a proper gallop. The winner's Haydock romp could be rated to this sort of level, while the second has been rated 11lb off the best of last year's form on better ground over shorter.

2199 OLBG.COM MARES' HURDLE (LISTED RACE) (9 hdls) 2m
2:30 (2:33) (Class 1) 4-Y-0+
£12,529 (£4,701; £2,354; £1,172; £589; £294)

Form RPR
143- 1 **Blue Buttons (IRE)**[198] 5355 7-10-12 135..(t) NoelFehily 133
(Harry Fry) *mde all: increased pce bef 3 out: wnt clr 2 out: hit last: styd on wl* **2/1[1]**
135- 2 5 **Intense Tango**[42] 5236 4-11-6 135.. BrianHughes 136
(K R Burke) *hld up: trckd ldrs 5th: 4th last: kpt on to take 2nd clsng stages* **5/1[3]**
013- 3 1 **Midnight Jazz**[198] 5353 5-10-12 128.. KielanWoods 127
(Ben Case) *trckd ldrs: kpt on to take 2nd last: styd on same pce* **12/1**
120- 4 1 ¼ **Allez Encore (IRE)**[224] 4918 6-10-12 128.. TomBellamy 126
(Kim Bailey) *trckd ldrs: 2nd 3 out: kpt on same pce* **12/1**
41-U 5 4 ½ **Last Supper**[157] 197 6-10-12 128.. WayneHutchinson 121
(James Bethell) *in tch: chsd ldrs 5th: one pce fr 3 out* **25/1**
226- 6 ½ **Ma Filleule (FR)**[205] 5237 7-10-12 144.. DavidBass 123
(Nicky Henderson) *trckd ldrs: drvn 3 out: wknd sn after 2 out* **9/4[2]**
324 U **Roja Dove (IRE)**[65] 1376 6-10-12 114..(v) JoeColliver
(David Thompson) *in last pair: pushed along and outpcd whn bdly hmpd and uns rdr 3 out* **200/1**
4122 F **Bantam (IRE)**[14] 1974 5-10-12 130.. RichardJohnson
(Henry Daly) *t.k.h in rr: hdwy 6th: drvn and little imp whn fell next* **13/2**
4m 1.5s (5.70) **Going Correction** +0.15s/f (Yiel) **8** Ran SP% **113.8**
Speed ratings (Par 111): **91,88,88,87,85 84, ,**
CSF £12.65 TOTE £3.10: £1.20, £1.80, £3.00; EX 12.20 Trifecta £93.30.
Owner Harry Fry Racing Club **Bred** Miss Annette McMahon **Trained** Seaborough, Dorset
FOCUS
A good quality Listed mares' hurdle. They went a respectable gallop. The winner has been rated to her best, with the third and fourth close to their marks.

2200 BET365 CHARLIE HALL CHASE (GRADE 2) (19 fncs) 3m 45y
3:05 (3:07) (Class 1) 5-Y-0+
£56,950 (£21,370; £10,700; £5,330; £2,680; £1,340)

Form RPR
52-4 1 **Cue Card**[185] 22 9-11-0 160..(t) PaddyBrennan 167+
(Colin Tizzard) *t.k.h: trckd ldng pair: 2nd 15th: led appr next: kpt on wl run-in* **11/4[1]**
23-0 2 3 ¾ **Dynaste (FR)**[20] 1883 9-11-0 166..(p) ConorO'Farrell 161
(David Pipe) *hld up towards rr: hdwy 14th: handy 3rd 3 out: 2nd next: styd on same pce run-in* **3/1[2]**
-F15 3 nk **Ballynagour (IRE)**[146] 663 9-11-0 163..(t) NoelFehily 161
(David Pipe) *hld up detached in last: hdwy to trck ldrs 4 out: 3rd between last 2: styd on same pce run-in* **6/1**
3PP- 4 11 **Sam Winner (FR)**[196] 5392 8-11-10 160..(tp) SeanBowen 163
(Paul Nicholls) *led: qcknd pce after 10th: hdd appr 4 out: wknd bef last* **12/1**
143- 5 8 **Holywell (IRE)**[205] 5237 8-11-6 162..(b) RichieMcLernon 149
(Jonjo O'Neill) *chsd ldrs: drvn 13th: outpcd and lost pl bef 3 out* **10/1**
161- 6 1 ½ **Many Clouds (IRE)**[203] 5275 8-11-10 167.. LeightonAspell 152
(Oliver Sherwood) *hld up: hdwy to chse ldrs 15th: lost pl bef 3 out* **9/2[3]**
051- P **Menorah (IRE)**[189] 5536 10-11-10 167.. RichardJohnson
(Philip Hobbs) *j.lft: hdwy 11th: blnd 14th: bhd next: sn eased and p.u* **7/1**
6m 21.4s (-26.60) **7** Ran SP% **113.4**
CSF £11.57 TOTE £3.20: £1.90, £2.70; EX 10.20 Trifecta £66.80.
Owner Mrs Jean R Bishop **Bred** R T Crellin **Trained** Milborne Port, Dorset
FOCUS
A strong renewal of this Grade 2 staying chase. They went a respectable gallop. This was the winner's best performance since the 2013 King George and there's a case for rating the race up to 7lb higher through the second and third, but the penalised fourth is probably a better guide.

2201 BET365.COM CHASE (A NOVICES' LIMITED H'CAP) (13 fncs) 1m 7f 36y
3:40 (3:41) (Class 3) (0-140,132) 4-Y-0+ **£6,657** (£2,067; £1,113)

Form RPR
/4-2 1 **Katachenko (IRE)**[178] 138 6-11-4 128.. WayneHutchinson 136
(Donald McCain) *led to 4th: led 7th: hdd and outpcd 9th: rallied 3 out: 2nd sn after 2 out: upsides last: sn led: drvn rt out* **11/1**
2 1 **Mon Successeur (FR)**[163] 4-10-9 128.. SeanBowen 128+
(Paul Nicholls) *t.k.h: sn trcking ldrs: 2nd after 4th: led next: hdd 7th: led 9th: shkn up and jnd last: hung rt and sn hdd: kpt on same pce last 50yds* **4/5[1]**
0215 3 9 **Vodka Wells (FR)**[16] 1922 5-11-0 129.. JamieBargary[(5)] 131
(Micky Hammond) *w ldrs: cl 2nd 9th: effrt 3 out: blnd and lost pl next: lame* **20/1**
32-2 P **Relic Rock (IRE)**[16] 1922 7-10-10 120.. WillKennedy
(Brian Ellison) *w ldrs: led 4th: hdd next: sn p.u* **5/2[2]**
1/3- U **Kings Bandit (IRE)**[264] 4131 7-11-8 132..[1] LeightonAspell
(Oliver Sherwood) *hld up in last: in tch whn blnd and uns rdr 5th* **8/1[3]**
3m 58.3s (2.50) **Going Correction** +0.40s/f (Soft) **5** Ran SP% **108.3**
Speed ratings (Par 107): **109,108,103, ,**
CSF £21.08 TOTE £7.60: £3.10, £1.30; EX 17.90 Trifecta £53.10.
Owner Trevor Hemmings **Bred** Charles Harte **Trained** Cholmondeley, Cheshire

FOCUS
A decent novice handicap chase. They went a proper gallop. A small pb from the winner, with the third to form.

2202 RACING UK 1 PRICE 3 DEVICES H'CAP HURDLE 2m 3f 154y
4:10 (4:11) (Class 3) (0-130,127) 3-Y-0+ **£5,393** (£1,583; £791; £395)

Form RPR
143/ 1 **Billy No Name (IRE)**[698] 2859 7-11-0 **115** PaddyBrennan 118+
(Colin Tizzard) *mde most to 7th: rallied 2 out: led sn after last: hld on nr fin* **9/1**
105/ 2 ½ **Muhtaris (IRE)**[25] 4401 5-11-0 **115** LeightonAspell 117
(James Evans) *in rr: hit 4th: nt fluent 6th: hdwy next: chsng ldrs 3 out: upsides last: kpt on wl: no ex nr fin* **25/1**
31P- 3 ¾ **Sir Ivan**[231] 4766 5-11-10 **125** NoelFehily 127+
(Harry Fry) *t.k.h: trckd ldrs: hung rt and led 2 out: hit last and sn hdd: kpt on clsng stages* **13/2[3]**
125- 4 ¾ **Medicine Hat**[26] 4488 4-11-7 **125** JoeColliver(3) 126
(George Moore) *w ldrs: hit 3 out: edgd rt run-in: styd on wl* **5/1[2]**
/20- 5 2 ¼ **Champagne At Tara**[309] 3278 6-11-12 **127** RichardJohnson 125
(Jonjo O'Neill) *t.k.h in rr: hdwy 4th: effrt on inner 3 out: upsides 2 out: kpt on same pce appr last* **4/1[1]**
543P 6 10 **Midnight Game**[17] 1904 8-11-7 **122** WillKennedy 112
(Brian Ellison) *hld up in rr: hdwy 6th: keeping on same pce whn hmpd and lost pl 2 out* **25/1**
4-12 7 3 ½ **Chebsey Beau**[43] 1404 5-11-5 **127** DeanPratt(7) 114
(John Quinn) *mid-div: effrt 3 out: lost pl and hmpd next* **13/2[3]**
33/1 8 16 **Ashbrittle**[175] 210 8-11-8 **123** TrevorWhelan 91
(Neil King) *chsd ldrs: drvn 8th: lost pl next* **5/1[2]**
101/ F **Boogie In The Barn (IRE)**[564] 5343 7-11-12 **127** (t) BrianHughes 121
(Charlie Longsdon) *t.k.h: trckd ldrs: led 7th: hdd and fell 2 out: fatally injured* **5/1[2]**

5m 10.8s (3.80) **Going Correction** +0.15s/f (Yiel)
WFA 4 from 5yo+ 10lb **9** Ran SP% **114.4**
Speed ratings (Par 107): **98,97,97,97,96 92,90,84,**
CSF £181.59 CT £1546.14 TOTE £10.30: £2.90, £5.80, £2.40; EX 243.80 Trifecta £2185.30 Part won..
Owner Mrs Jean R Bishop **Bred** Seamus O'Farrell **Trained** Milborne Port, Dorset

FOCUS
The concluding contest was a fairly decent handicap hurdle. They went a modest gallop. The winner has been rated to the level of his 2013 reappearance, with the second, third and fourth pretty much to their marks.
T/Plt: £7.40 to a £1 stake. Pool: £94,469.69 - 9288.61 winning units. T/Qpdt: £6.20 to a £1 stake. Pool: £5,935.84 - 707.80 winning units. **Walter Glynn**

2203 - 2205a (Foreign Racing) - See Raceform Interactive

2175 DOWN ROYAL (R-H)
Saturday, October 31

OFFICIAL GOING: Yielding to soft

2206a POWERS IRISH WHISKEY CHASE (GRADE 2) (13 fncs) 2m 4f
2:10 (2:11) 5-Y-0+
£23,255 (£7,364; £3,488; £1,162; £775; £387)

RPR
1 **Ptit Zig (FR)**[233] 4716 6-11-10 157 SamTwiston-Davies 161+
(Paul Nicholls) *chsd ldrs in 4th: tk clsr order to trck ldrs bef 4 out: swtchd lft bef 2 out and travelled wl to ld 2 out: clr whn j.rt at last: kpt on wl* **4/5[1]**
2 9 ½ **Clarcam (FR)**[28] 1763 5-11-12 159 (t) BJCooper 151
(Gordon Elliott, Ire) *chsd ldrs in 3rd: tk clsr order to trck ldrs bef 4 out: sn niggled along: rdn and nt qckn w wnr in 2nd appr 2 out: kpt on same pce run-in* **9/4[2]**
3 1 ½ **Shadow Catcher**[13] 1995 7-11-1 133 (tp) KevinSexton 139
(Gordon Elliott, Ire) *led: jnd at 8th: hdd bef 2 out where dropped to 3rd: kpt on same pce run-in* **10/1**
4 7 **Shanahan's Turn (IRE)**[28] 1763 7-11-10 152 JJBurke 143
(Henry De Bromhead, Ire) *trckd ldr in 2nd: bit slow at 7th: on terms next: rdn after 3 out: hdd bef next where dropped to 4th: sn no ex* **5/1[3]**
5 38 **Finea (IRE)**[1] 2177 8-11-1 99 (t) LPDempsey 94
(R K Watson, Ire) *hld up in 5th: detached after 4 out: sn no threat* **100/1**
6 14 **Raydari (FR)**[3] 1279 7-11-1 107 (tp) MPFogarty 80
(R K Watson, Ire) *hld up in 6th: detached fr 8th: t.o* **100/1**
F **Aladdins Cave**[1] 2179 11-11-1 113 (tp) SeanFlanagan
(R K Watson, Ire) *dropped to rr at 5th: fell next* **100/1**
P **Sir Vinnie (IRE)**[192] 5486 6-11-1 81 AELynch
(R K Watson, Ire) *a in rr: nt fluent 5th and sn detached: p.u bef 3 out* **100/1**

4m 53.5s (293.50) **8** Ran SP% **116.0**
CSF £3.21 TOTE £1.70: £1.02, £1.30, £1.70; DF 2.80 Trifecta £10.40.
Owner Barry Fulton, Chris Giles & Richard Webb **Bred** Jean-Francois Vermand **Trained** Ditcheat, Somerset

FOCUS
This renewal was up to scratch, but the easy-to-back second-favourite was probably not quite at his best. One could argue that the winner was also not quite at his best.

2207a JNWINE.COM CHAMPION CHASE (GRADE 1) (15 fncs) 3m
2:40 (2:40) 5-Y-0+ **£65,116** (£20,620; £9,767; £3,255)

RPR
1 **Don Cossack (GER)**[16] 1938 8-11-10 175 (t) BJCooper 178+
(Gordon Elliott, Ire) *settled in 3rd: tk clsr order 5 out and sn trckd ldr in 2nd: travelled wl to ld next: eased clr bef 2 out: nt extended* **2/11[1]**
2 8 **Rocky Creek (IRE)**[189] 5538 9-11-10 160 SamTwiston-Davies 160
(Paul Nicholls) *trckd ldr in 2nd: briefly on terms 4th: pushed along after 5 out and dropped to 3rd: rdn in mod 2nd 2 out: kpt on one pce run-in to jst hold 2nd* **7/1[2]**
3 hd **Roi Du Mee (FR)**[16] 1938 10-11-10 154 (t) RWalsh 160
(Gordon Elliott, Ire) *sn led: briefly jnd 4th: bit slow at 10th: hdd 4 out: no imp on ldr after next: rdn in 3rd 2 out: kpt on one pce run-in: jst hld for 2nd* **11/1[3]**
4 19 **Texas Jack (IRE)**[28] 1763 9-11-10 148 SeanFlanagan 141
(Noel Meade, Ire) *racd in rr: mstke 3rd: tk clsr order 5 out travelling wl: rdn and wknd qckly bef 2 out: no ex* **40/1**

6m 28.0s (9.80) **4** Ran SP% **107.9**
CSF £2.16 TOTE £1.10; DF 1.90 Trifecta £1.70.
Owner Gigginstown House Stud **Bred** Gestut Etzean **Trained** Longwood, Co Meath

FOCUS
Given the remarkable strength in depth in staying chasing in Ireland, this was a disappointing enough renewal, even if today's second is rated 160 and was second in it last year. Even so, and while he did no more than what he was entitled to do on paper, the winner was simply superb again.

2208 - 2209a (Foreign Racing) - See Raceform Interactive

2025 CARLISLE (R-H)
Sunday, November 1

OFFICIAL GOING: Good (good to soft in places down the hill; 7.3) changing to good to soft after race 2 (1.30)
Wind: Almost nil Weather: Overcast

2210 APOLLOBET HOME OF INPLAY BETTING NOVICES' HURDLE (11 hdls) 2m 4f 8y
1:00 (1:00) (Class 4) 4-Y-0+ **£3,249** (£954; £477; £238)

Form RPR
1 **At The Doubble (IRE)**[330] 6-10-12 0 GavinSheehan 120+
(Warren Greatrex) *chsd ldr tl rdn and outpcd after 4 out: rallied and led next: rdn and rn green bef last: edgd lft run-in: styd on strly* **2/1[1]**
215- 2 2 ¼ **Vintage Clouds (IRE)**[253] 4370 5-10-12 0 DannyCook 118+
(Sue Smith) *prom: niggled along 7th: outpcd after next: rdn and rallied 3 out: chsd wnr last: edgd rt: kpt on same pce run-in* **2/1[1]**
6 3 6 **Quinto**[170] 320 5-10-12 0 TomO'Brien 113
(John Quinn) *hld up in midfield: stdy hdwy after 4 out: pushed along and effrt 2 out: outpcd fr last* **6/1[2]**
150- 4 1 ½ **Becauseshesaidso (IRE)**[241] 4578 7-10-12 0 LiamTreadwell 112
(Venetia Williams) *nt fluent: cl up: mstke 1st: hdwy and ev ch whn hit 3 out: rdn and wknd fr last* **17/2**
0-50 5 12 **Innis Shannon (IRE)**[22] 1854 5-10-0 0 JonathonBewley(5) 95
(George Bewley) *hld up: nt fluent 3rd: rdn and hdd 3 out: wknd fr next* **66/1**
31-6 6 40 **Down The Line (IRE)**[179] 145 5-10-12 0 PaulMoloney 64
(Alan Swinbank) *nt fluent on occasions: hld up on ins: pushed along after 4 out: wknd fr next: t.o* **7/1[3]**
60 7 1 ½ **Whatsthestoryman (IRE)**[8] 2066 7-10-12 0 (t) SeanQuinlan 63
(Katie Scott) *bhd: outpcd bef 7th: lost tch fr next: t.o* **66/1**
450- 8 8 **Wee Jock Elliot**[251] 4399 5-10-9 0 CraigNichol(3) 56
(Alistair Whillans) *nt fluent in rr: struggling bef 4 out: t.o* **66/1**
U-0 9 70 **Killiecrankie**[64] 1399 7-10-12 0 HenryBrooke
(Kenneth Slack) *t.k.h: hld up: stdy hdwy whn hit 7th: wknd fr next: t.o* **50/1**
5 P **Pikes Peak (IRE)**[22] 1852 6-10-7 0 DiarmuidO'Regan(5)
(Chris Grant) *midfield: nt fluent and lost pl 5th: lost tch and p.u next* **66/1**

(-22.80) **Going Correction** -0.95s/f (Hard) **10** Ran SP% **111.9**
Speed ratings (Par 105): **107,106,103,103,98 82,81,78,50,**
CSF £5.57 TOTE £2.80: £1.10, £1.10, £3.90; EX 8.00 Trifecta £29.10.
Owner O S Harris **Bred** John Quane **Trained** Upper Lambourn, Berks

FOCUS
Hurdle races on Old course and all distances as advertised. As advertised the going was good, good to soft in places. There was little strength in depth to this novices' hurdle and the two market leaders came to the fore.

2211 APOLLOBET ONLINE GAMES AND CASINO NOVICES' LIMITED H'CAP CHASE (16 fncs) 2m 4f
1:30 (1:30) (Class 3) (0-135,133) 4-Y-0+ **£6,498** (£1,908; £954; £477)

Form RPR
/20- 1 **Shimla Dawn (IRE)**[344] 2662 7-11-7 **132** JakeGreenall 136+
(Mark Walford) *cl up: led after 7th: hrd pressed fr 3 out: styd on gamely u.p fr last* **7/1**
01F- 2 1 **Cultram Abbey**[225] 4911 8-11-0 **125** BrianHarding 127
(Nicky Richards) *cl up: led 3rd to after 7th: ev ch after 5 out: drvn and outpcd after next: rallied 2 out: wnt 2nd last 100yds: kpt on: nt rch wnr* **8/1**
02-2 3 ½ **Souriyan (FR)**[28] 1782 4-10-13 **133** BrendanPowell 127
(Jamie Snowden) *hld up in tch: hdwy and ev ch 2 out: sn chsng wnr: lost 2nd last 100yds: kpt on* **3/1[2]**
0-41 4 6 **Morning Royalty (IRE)**[128] 840 8-10-11 **122** BrianHughes 120
(James Moffatt) *hld up: stdy hdwy bef 3 out: shkn up whn pckd next: edgd rt and kpt on same pce bef last* **7/1**
6/2- 5 6 **For Two (FR)**[536] 290 6-11-3 **128** (t) SamTwiston-Davies 119
(Paul Nicholls) *hld up in tch on outside: smooth hdwy to chal 3 out: rdn after next: wknd fr last* **5/2[1]**
20-3 6 ¾ **Special Wells**[10] 2026 6-10-6 **117** DannyCook 112+
(Sue Smith) *hld up in tch: blnd and sprawled 8th: rdn and outpcd 4 out: sn n.d* **4/1[3]**
314/ 7 5 **The Ramblin Kid**[580] 5103 7-10-8 **119** PaddyBrennan 109
(Micky Hammond) *led to 3rd: cl up: hit 5th: ev ch 4 out: nt fluent and outpcd next: struggling fr 2 out* **25/1**

5m 8.3s (-19.10) **Going Correction** -0.725s/f (Firm)
WFA 4 from 6yo+ 8lb **7** Ran SP% **113.5**
Speed ratings (Par 107): **109,108,108,106,103 103,101**
CSF £56.64 CT £202.85 TOTE £8.70: £3.70, £3.60; EX 50.70 Trifecta £390.50.
Owner Mrs M Cooper **Bred** James Barry **Trained** Sherriff Hutton, N Yorks

FOCUS
This looked a decent novices' handicap chase and the form should work out.

2212 APOLLOBET DAILY RACING SPECIALS NOVICES' H'CAP HURDLE (9 hdls) 2m 1f 33y
2:05 (2:06) (Class 4) (0-110,110) 3-Y-0+ **£3,249** (£954; £477; £238)

Form RPR
64-0 1 **Woodstock (IRE)**[20] 1892 5-10-9 **93** (tp) BrianHughes 97+
(Ann Hamilton) *t.k.h: cl up: smooth hdwy to ld bef 2 out: hrd pressed and drvn last: edgd lft: hld on wl towards fin* **13/2**
3206 2 nk **Raise A Spark**[15] 1967 5-11-9 **107** SamTwiston-Davies 110
(Donald McCain) *hld up: hdwy bef 2 out: rdn and ev ch last: kpt on run-in: hld nr fin* **7/1**
3450 3 3 **Mondlicht (USA)**[121] 895 5-11-7 **105** NoelFehily 106
(James Moffatt) *hld up: effrt bef 2 out: chsd clr ldng pair last 150yds: kpt on: nt pce to chal* **5/1[3]**
33- 4 3 ¼ **Eco Warrior**[225] 4923 5-11-12 **110** LiamTreadwell 107
(Venetia Williams) *t.k.h: early ldr: cl up: hit 4 out: led next to bef 2 out: rdn and wknd after last* **4/1[1]**
24 5 hd **Robben**[27] 1177 3-10-2 **102** (v) PaddyBrennan 83
(John Mackie) *in tch: effrt and pushed along bef 2 out: no imp whn edgd rt after last* **9/2[2]**

-60P **6** *6* **Theflyingportrait (IRE)**[72] 1307 6-11-4 **102**.................(t) HenryBrooke 93
(Jennie Candlish) *hld up: effrt and rdn on outside whn hit 2 out: sn wknd* **16/1**

56-2 **7** *6* **Celestino (FR)**[181] 107 4-11-7 **110**.................. StephenMulqueen(5) 97
(N W Alexander) *chsd ldrs: nt fluent 1st: effrt and ev ch whn nt fluent 3 out: sn rdn: wknd after next* **14/1**

206- **8** *6* **Tomahawk Wood**[246] 4486 6-10-10 **97**.................. CallumWhillans(3) 76
(Donald Whillans) *sn led and set modest gallop: rdn and hdd 3 out: outpcd whn nt fluent next: sn btn* **8/1**

-04P **9** *10* **Wyfield Rose**[126] 845 6-9-11 **84**.................. CraigNichol(3) 53
(Alistair Whillans) *nt fluent on occasions: hld up on outside: drvn bef 3 out: sn wknd* **15/2**

4m 28.6s (0.90) **Going Correction** -0.95s/f (Hard)
WFA 3 from 4yo 15lb 4 from 5yo+ 7lb **9** Ran SP% **116.1**
Speed ratings (Par 105): **59,58,57,55,55 53,50,47,42**
CSF £51.47 CT £247.53 TOTE £8.10: £2.90, £1.90, £1.70; EX 54.90 Trifecta £233.90.
Owner Ian Hamilton **Bred** Butlersgrove Stud **Trained** Great Bavington, Northumbland

FOCUS
A modest but competitive handicap and they finished well strung out.

2213 CUMBERLAND H'CAP CHASE (SPONSORED BY APOLLOBET) (19 fncs) 3m 2f 34y
2:35 (2:37) (Class 3) (0-135,133) 4-Y-O+
£12,512 (£3,696; £1,848; £924; £462; £232)

Form RPR

3PP- **1** **Vintage Star (IRE)**[197] 5392 9-11-12 **133**.................. DannyCook 146+
(Sue Smith) *in tch: hdwy to ld bef 11th: mde rest: rdn and r.o strly fr 3 out* **7/2**[1]

5342 **2** *3 ¾* **Presented (IRE)**[10] 2028 8-10-4 **116**.................. CallumBewley(5) 123
(Lisa Harrison) *hld up in tch: stdy hdwy 13th: effrt and chsd wnr 4 out: rdn next: kpt on same pce fr last* **12/1**

1F-2 **3** *8* **King Of The Wolds (IRE)**[39] 1632 8-11-9 **130**.................. BrianHughes 131
(Malcolm Jefferson) *hld up: stdy hdwy 1/2-way: effrt and cajoled along after 3 out: drvn and no imp fr next* **4/1**[2]

423- **4** *4* **Son Of Suzie**[191] 5519 7-10-13 **120**.................. PaddyBrennan 116
(Fergal O'Brien) *nt fluent on occasions: hld up: stdy hdwy 5 out: drvn and no imp fr next* **4/1**[2]

11-4 **5** *1 ¼* **Basford Ben**[178] 156 7-10-4 **111**.................. (b) HenryBrooke 107
(Jennie Candlish) *cl up: led 2nd to bef 11th: hit next: chsd wnr to 4 out: rdn and outpcd after next* **16/1**

2P-1 **6** *shd* **Tullamore Dew (IRE)**[160] 471 13-11-2 **126**.................. JoeColliver(3) 123
(Micky Hammond) *hld up: outpcd whn blnd 12th: pushed along after 6 out: no imp fr 4 out* **14/1**

-3U1 **7** *11* **Settledoutofcourt (IRE)**[10] 2028 9-10-10 **120**.................. DerekFox(3) 107
(Lucinda Russell) *prom: lost pl 8th: drvn and shortlived effrt after 5 out: wknd fr next* **15/2**[3]

5-P6 **8** *3 ½* **Carrigdhoun (IRE)**[18] 1902 10-11-2 **128**.................(t) DaraghBourke(5) 111
(Maurice Barnes) *cl up: drvn and outpcd 12th: n.d after: btn fr 4 out* **14/1**

360- **9** *2 ½* **Ballyoliver**[234] 4721 11-11-8 **129**.................. LiamTreadwell 113
(Venetia Williams) *nt fluent on occasions: hld up on outside: struggling bef 5 out: btn next* **15/2**[3]

0105 **10** *6* **Chicago Outfit (IRE)**[8] 2068 10-10-13 **125**.........(p) JonathonBewley(5) 99
(George Bewley) *led to 2nd: cl up: outpcd bef 11th: struggling fr 13th: no ch whn hit 4 out* **33/1**

6m 46.0s (-21.20) **Going Correction** -0.725s/f (Firm) **10** Ran SP% **115.6**
Speed ratings (Par 107): **103,101,99,98,97 97,94,93,92,90**
CSF £43.67 CT £175.03 TOTE £4.70: £2.20, £3.40, £1.90; EX 56.00 Trifecta £185.30.
Owner Trevor Hemmings **Bred** Gleadhill House Stud Ltd **Trained** High Eldwick, W Yorks

FOCUS
A useful staying handicap chase.

2214 APOLLOBET BEST ODDS GUARANTEED H'CAP HURDLE (11 hdls) 2m 4f 8y
3:10 (3:11) (Class 2) (0-150,142) 4-Y-O+
£12,512 (£3,696; £1,848; £924; £462; £232)

Form RPR

402- **1** **One For Harry (IRE)**[192] 5491 7-10-13 **129**.................. BrianHarding 137+
(Nicky Richards) *pressed ldr to 6th: rdn to ld 3 out: hit next: hdd last: rallied and regained ld last 75yds: kpt on gamely* **12/1**

034- **2** *½* **Shotavodka (IRE)**[232] 4766 9-10-13 **132**.................(p) KieronEdgar(3) 140+
(David Pipe) *prom: rdn after 4 out: hdwy to ld whn hit last: rdn and edgd rt: hdd last 75yds: hld nr fin* **16/1**

-614 **3** *8* **Octagon**[142] 710 5-10-2 **118**.................. BrianHughes 117
(Dianne Sayer) *hld up: stdy hdwy on ins after 4 out: rdn and effrt bef 2 out: kpt on fr last: nt rch first two* **25/1**

-221 **4** *1 ¼* **Mustmeetalady (IRE)**[18] 1901 5-11-0 **130**.................. NoelFehily 128
(Jonjo O'Neill) *t.k.h in midfield: stdy hdwy and in tch bef 3 out: rdn and edgd lft next: sn one pce* **13/2**[2]

1-01 **5** *½* **Lord Wishes (IRE)**[18] 1903 8-10-9 **130**.................(p) DaleIrving(5) 128
(James Ewart) *hld up in tch: mstke 4th: rdn and outpcd after 4 out: rallied next: no imp fr 2 out* **8/1**

11F- **6** *½* **Out Sam**[233] 4738 6-11-12 **142**.................. GavinSheehan 139
(Warren Greatrex) *trckd ldrs: wnt 2nd 6th: ev ch briefly 3 out: rdn and hung lft after next: sn outpcd* **11/4**[1]

4P-2 **7** *¾* **L'Aigle Royal (GER)**[18] 1903 4-11-2 **132**.................. TomO'Brien 129
(John Quinn) *midfield: rdn and outpcd bef 3 out: rallied bef last: nvr able to chal* **7/1**[3]

0512 **8** *4* **Captain Brown**[46] 1554 7-10-3 **124**.................. DiarmuidO'Regan(5) 117
(James Moffatt) *hld up: stdy hdwy after 4 out: rdn next: outpcd fr 2 out* **22/1**

1U-0 **9** *1 ½* **Milborough (IRE)**[183] 92 9-11-2 **135**.................. GrahamWatters(3) 127
(Ian Duncan) *hld up: stdy hdwy on outside and in tch 1/2-way: rdn and outpcd bef 4 out: sme late hdwy: nvr rchd ldrs* **66/1**

141- **10** *1 ½* **Shades Of Midnight**[211] 5129 5-10-6 **125**.........(t) CallumWhillans(3) 115
(Donald Whillans) *hld up in midfield: outpcd bef 4 out: n.d after* **11/1**

006/ **11** *nk* **Vendor (FR)**[568] 5277 7-11-0 **130**.................. SeanQuinlan 120
(Sue Smith) *t.k.h: led to 3 out: rdn and wknd after next* **22/1**

U00- **12** *8* **Tap Night (USA)**[198] 5363 8-10-11 **127**.................. RichieMcLernon 111
(Lucinda Russell) *hld up: mstke 3rd: struggling 4 out: nvr on terms* **20/1**

22-P **13** *shd* **Big Water (IRE)**[15] 1976 7-11-2 **132**.................. PaulMoloney 115
(Alan Swinbank) *in tch: rdn and outpcd after 4 out: struggling fr next* **33/1**

-23F **14** *1* **Tekthelot (IRE)**[133] 802 9-9-8 **117**.................. RyanDay(7) 99
(Keith Reveley) *hld up on outside: stdy hdwy 1/2-way: rdn and wknd fr 4 out* **14/1**

/0-P **15** *17* **Lexi's Boy (IRE)**[176] 197 7-10-9 **125**.................(t) SamTwiston-Davies 92
(Donald McCain) *hld up: hit and outpcd 7th: struggling fr next: t.o* **22/1**

4m 58.0s (-24.80) **Going Correction** -0.95s/f (Hard)
WFA 4 from 5yo+ 8lb **15** Ran SP% **118.3**
Speed ratings (Par 109): **111,110,107,107,106 106,106,104,104,103 103,100,100,99,93**
CSF £164.04 CT £4644.30 TOTE £16.00: £4.30, £5.30, £4.60; EX 104.30 Trifecta £2468.10.
Owner The Fife Boys + 1 **Bred** Berry Farms **Trained** Greystoke, Cumbria

FOCUS
A competitive handicap hurdle, although not the strongest for the grade, and the first two pulled nicely clear.

2215 COLIN PARKER MEMORIAL INTERMEDIATE CHASE (LISTED RACE) (16 fncs) 2m 4f
3:45 (3:45) (Class 1) 4-Y-O+
£15,661 (£5,876; £2,942)

Form RPR

121- **1** **Saphir Du Rheu (FR)**[205] 5251 6-11-12 **163**.......... SamTwiston-Davies 164+
(Paul Nicholls) *pressed ldr gng wl: led on bit after 3 out: clr whn shkn up briefly run-in: easily* **1/5**[1]

110- **2** *7* **The Young Master**[235] 4703 6-11-8 **150**.................(p) NoelFehily 147+
(Neil Mulholland) *j. sltly lft thrght: led at ordinary gallop: drvn and hdd after 3 out: outpcd fr next* **9/2**[2]

105- **3** *33* **Midnight Belle**[216] 5074 8-10-13 **130**.................. JamesDavies 108
(Tom Symonds) *chsd ldrs: outpcd 10th: drvn along 5 out: lost tch fr next* **25/1**[3]

5m 8.5s (-18.90) **Going Correction** -0.725s/f (Firm) **3** Ran SP% **105.4**
Speed ratings (Par 111): **108,105,92**
CSF £1.52 TOTE £1.20; EX 1.30 Trifecta £1.40.
Owner The Stewart Family **Bred** Claude Duval **Trained** Ditcheat, Somerset

FOCUS
This was all about the favourite and there were no dramas.

2216 APOLLOBET WORLDWIDE LOTTERIES "JUNIOR" STANDARD OPEN NATIONAL HUNT FLAT RACE 1m 6f
4:15 (4:15) (Class 6) 3-Y-O
£1,624 (£477; £238; £119)

Form RPR

1 **Country'N'Western (FR)** 3-10-12 0.................. AndrewTinkler 108+
(David Elsworth) *prom on ins: hdwy to ld over 2f out: rdn clr over 1f out: eased wl ins fnl f* **2/1**[1]

2 *13* **The Phantom (FR)** 3-10-9 0.................. EmmaSayer(3) 89
(Dianne Sayer) *t.k.h: led 2f: pressed ldr: regained ld over 3f out: rdn and hdd over 2f out: plugged on: no ch w wnr* **25/1**

3 *nse* **Applaus (GER)** 3-10-9 0.................. JoeColliver(3) 89
(Micky Hammond) *t.k.h: cl up: led after 2f: rn green and hdd over 3f out: sn outpcd: kpt on fnl f: no imp* **16/1**

4 *11* **Busy Street** 3-10-12 0.................. PaulMoloney 76
(Alan Swinbank) *plld hrd: hld up: drvn and outpcd wl over 3f out: n.d after* **2/1**[1]

5 *1 ¼* **American Gigolo** 3-10-12 0.................. SamTwiston-Davies 75
(Sally Hall) *hld up: drvn and outpcd over 3f out: sn btn* **4/1**[2]

6 *52* **Silver Glaze (IRE)** 3-10-12 0.................. DannyCook 12
(Brian Ellison) *chsd ldrs: drvn and outpcd over 4f out: lost tch fnl 3f: t.o* **10/1**[3]

7 *11* **Kalaharry (IRE)** 3-10-7 0.................. CallumBewley(5)
(Katie Scott) *prom tl rdn and wknd over 4f out: t.o* **14/1**

8 *71* **Thiepval** 3-10-9 0.................. AdamNicol(3)
(Jason Ward) *hld up: drvn and outpcd after 3f: sn lost tch: t.o* **50/1**

3m 26.2s (206.20) **8** Ran SP% **114.1**
CSF £57.94 TOTE £3.40: £1.70, £2.60, £3.20; EX 38.00 Trifecta £303.50.
Owner D R C Elsworth **Bred** Capital Pur Sang **Trained** Newmarket, Suffolk

FOCUS
A junior bumper full of newcomers. The pace was even and the winner was in control from some way out.
T/Plt: £306.90 to a £1 stake. Pool: £76,011.00 - 180.79 winning tickets. T/Qpdt: £66.70 to a £1 stake. Pool: £7,366.00 - 81.62 winning tickets. **Richard Young**

1893 HUNTINGDON (R-H)
Sunday, November 1

OFFICIAL GOING: Good to soft (soft in places)
Wind: Light behind Weather: Fog clearing to leave a sunny day

2217 32RED CASINO CLAIMING HURDLE (DIV I) (8 hdls) 1m 7f 171y
12:45 (12:49) (Class 5) 4-Y-O+
£2,274 (£667; £333; £166)

Form RPR

0202 **1** **Clock On Tom**[16] 1781 5-11-2 109.................. WillKennedy 114
(Denis Quinn) *trckd ldrs: racd keenly: swtchd rt after 2 out: hit last: rdn and r.o to ld post* **6/1**

14-6 **2** *shd* **It's A Mans World**[169] 332 9-10-13 118.................. CraigGallagher(7) 117
(Brian Ellison) *a.p: chsd ldr 5th: rdn to ld last: hdd post* **3/1**[2]

3233 **3** *½* **Hawdyerwheesht**[16] 1945 7-11-5 119.................(tp) JamieBargary(5) 121
(David Dennis) *led: pckd 4th: j.lft next: rdn and hdd last: r.o* **9/4**[1]

P-22 **4** *2* **Nebula Storm (IRE)**[16] 1941 8-9-12 92.................(v) JasonNuttall(10) 102
(Gary Moore) *hld up: hdwy appr 3 out: rdn after next: styd on* **7/2**[3]

666 **5** *15* **Ablazing (IRE)**[7] 2091 4-11-2 0.................. AlainCawley 95
(Johnny Farrelly) *hld up: rdn after 5th: hdwy 3 out: wknd bef next* **25/1**

0004 **6** *3 ¾* **Kheskianto (IRE)**[16] 1941 9-9-10 76.................(t) DannyBurton(5) 76
(Michael Chapman) *chsd ldr after 1st: lost 2nd 5th: rdn and wknd after 3 out: mstke last* **150/1**

1300 **7** *13* **Fleet Dawn**[18] 1903 9-11-2 116.................. AndrewThornton 78
(John Wainwright) *mid-div: nt fluent 2nd: rdn and wknd appr 3 out* **16/1**

6 **8** *1* **Happy Jack (IRE)**[28] 1780 4-11-8 0.................. JackQuinlan 83
(Michael Wigham) *hld up: rdn after 5th: wknd 3 out* **100/1**

66 **9** *6* **Streele (USA)**[15] 1975 5-9-10 0.................. MissTWorsley(7) 58
(Ken Wingrove) *hld up: rdn and wknd appr 3 out* **300/1**

3m 53.1s (-1.80) **Going Correction** -0.125s/f (Good) **9** Ran SP% **104.0**
Speed ratings (Par 103): **99,98,98,97,90 88,81,81,78**
CSF £20.30 TOTE £6.80: £1.60, £1.30, £1.40; EX 20.10 Trifecta £54.90.
Owner John Mangan **Bred** Kingwood Bloodstock **Trained** Newmarket, Suffolk
■ Edlomond (12-1) was withdrawn. Rule 4 applies to all bets. Deduction - 5p in the pound.

FOCUS
All bends out 4yds and races 1, 2 & 3 increased by 34yds, race 4 by 38yds, races 5 & 6 by 41yds and race 7 by 53yds. The market leaders dominated this claiming hurdle.

2218 32RED CASINO CLAIMING HURDLE (DIV II) (8 hdls) 1m 7f 171y
1:15 (1:17) (Class 5) 4-Y-0+ £2,274 (£667; £333; £166)

Form RPR
4-16 1 **Fair Loch**[36] 1661 7-10-13 117 CraigGallagher(7) 115+
(Brian Ellison) *mde all: clr 5th tl rdn appr last: styd on* 11/4[2]
15-6 2 1/2 **Akula (IRE)**[140] 465 8-10-9 106 HarryChalloner(3) 106
(Barry Leavy) *chsd wnr who wnt clr 5th: rdn to take clsr order appr last: r.o* 10/1
6502 3 8 **Tiradia (FR)**[28] 1770 8-11-6 104 AidanColeman 107
(J R Jenkins) *hld up: hdwy appr 3 out: rdn after next: wknd flat* 9/2[3]
53-3 4 1 3/4 **Scoppio Del Carro**[15] 1967 4-11-10 114 (t) DenisO'Regan 109
(John Quinn) *chsd ldrs: rdn after 3 out: wknd appr last* 9/1
2411 5 30 **A Little Bit Dusty**[3] 2150 7-11-2 115 (b) RichardJohnson 82
(Conor Dore) *hld up: hdwy 4th: rdn appr 3 out: sn wknd* 11/8[1]
43 6 8 **Toptempo**[15] 1975 6-10-11 0 MichaelByrne 62
(Ali Stronge) *prom: mstke 1st: lost pl bef 3rd: bhd fr 5th* 33/1
6-4 7 10 **Ede's The Business**[15] 1975 4-9-10 0 (b) MissPFuller(7) 45
(Ken Wingrove) *hld up: hdwy 4th: rdn and wknd appr 3 out* 100/1
0 P **Music Hall (FR)**[19] 1898 5-11-2 0 TrevorWhelan
(Shaun Harris) *hld up: mstke 1st: a in rr: bhd fr 4th: blnd next: p.u bef 3 out* 200/1
P **Gaelic O'Reagan**[31] 4-11-6 0 JamieMoore
(Robert Eddery) *hld up: a in rr: bhd fr 4th: p.u bef 3 out* 100/1

3m 50.3s (-4.60) **Going Correction** -0.125s/f (Good) 9 Ran SP% 111.5
Speed ratings (Par 103): **106,105,101,100,85 81,76,,**
CSF £27.08 TOTE £3.30: £1.10, £2.10, £1.80; EX 29.90 Trifecta £136.90.
Owner Mrs J A Martin **Bred** Steve Hadley **Trained** Norton, N Yorks

FOCUS
A bit less competitive than division one, with the favourite disappointing, and the front pair came clear.

2219 32REDSPORT.COM JUVENILE HURDLE (8 hdls) 1m 7f 171y
1:50 (1:50) (Class 4) 3-Y-0 £3,898 (£1,144; £572; £286)

Form RPR
1 **Jaboltiski (SPA)**[389] 3-10-12 0 RichardJohnson 109+
(Philip Hobbs) *hld up: hdwy appr 3 out: chal next: sn rdn: ev ch whn lft in ld flat: styd on wl* 9/2[3]
1 2 2 **Duke Of Sonning**[17] 1928 3-11-4 0 WayneHutchinson 113
(Alan King) *a.p: chsd ldr appr and hit 3 out: ev ch fr next: rdn and hmpd flat: no ex towards fin* 7/2[2]
31 3 7 **Duke Street (IRE)**[25] 1805 3-11-4 120 WillKennedy 113+
(Dr Richard Newland) *chsd ldr tl led appr and mstke 3 out: jnd next: upsides whn stmbld last: nt rcvr* 4/6[1]
4 13 **Kenobe Star (IRE)**[166] 3-10-12 0 DarylJacob 90
(Jamie Snowden) *hld up: pushed along after 4th: wkng whn blnd 2 out* 66/1
5 4 1/2 **Fizzlestix (FR)** 3-10-12 0 HarrySkelton 85
(Dan Skelton) *hld up: hdwy 4th: rdn and wknd appr 2 out* 16/1
P **Wally's Wisdom**[19] 3-10-5 0 PaddyBradley(7)
(Lee Carter) *led: mstke 1st: hdd & wknd appr 3 out: bhd whn p.u bef next* 25/1
P **Dot Dash Dot**[38] 3-10-0 0 AliceMills(5)
(Christopher Kellett) *plld hrd and sn prom: j.big and lost pl 3rd: sn bhd: nt fluent next: p.u bef 3 out* 250/1

3m 49.1s (-5.80) **Going Correction** -0.125s/f (Good) 7 Ran SP% 112.0
Speed ratings (Par 104): **109,108,104,98,95 ,**
CSF £19.73 TOTE £5.20: £2.40, £1.60; EX 18.20 Trifecta £26.70.
Owner Mrs Sue Lanz **Bred** Cuadra Tiziano Sl **Trained** Withycombe, Somerset

FOCUS
There wasn't much between the front three in what was a fair juvenile contest, the favourite losing all chance late.

2220 MACER GIFFORD H'CAP CHASE (12 fncs) 2m 104y
2:20 (2:21) (Class 4) (0-105,105) 4-Y-0+ £6,498 (£1,908; £954; £477)

Form RPR
P5-3 1 **Vision Des Champs (FR)**[184] 64 6-11-8 101 (t) JamieMoore 121+
(Gary Moore) *chsd ldr tl led 5th: rdn clr flat* 9/4[1]
221F 2 13 **My Nosy Rosy**[24] 1825 7-11-4 97 (tp) DarylJacob 103+
(Ben Case) *chsd ldrs: wnt 2nd 9th: rdn: hung rt and wknd flat* 7/1
2113 3 6 **Lord Lir (IRE)**[14] 1985 9-11-12 105 (b) RichardJohnson 105
(Tim Vaughan) *led to 5th: chsd wnr to 8th: rdn and wknd after 3 out* 5/2[2]
4332 4 6 **Red Rosso**[10] 2040 10-10-0 79 oh9 (p) TrevorWhelan 73
(Rob Summers) *hld up: hdwy 6th: chsd wnr 8th to next: rdn and wknd appr 2 out* 13/2
2234 5 3 **Keychain (IRE)**[5] 2124 5-11-7 100 (b) LeightonAspell 94
(Brendan Powell) *hld up: mstke 5th: pushed along after 8th: wknd 3 out: bhd whn j.lft next* 3/1[3]

4m 10.3s (0.10) **Going Correction** 0.0s/f (Good) 5 Ran SP% 110.2
Speed ratings (Par 105): **99,92,89,86,85**
CSF £16.26 TOTE £3.50: £2.40, £3.10; EX 15.20 Trifecta £54.90.
Owner Polo Racing & Friends **Bred** G A E C Des Champs **Trained** Lower Beeding, W Sussex

FOCUS
This moderate chase didn't take a lot of winning.

2221 32RED ON THE APP STORE NOVICES' HURDLE (10 hdls) 2m 3f 137y
2:55 (2:57) (Class 4) 4-Y-0+ £3,898 (£1,144; £572; £286)

Form RPR
111- 1 **Barters Hill (IRE)**[205] 5255 5-10-12 0 DavidBass 143+
(Ben Pauling) *mde all: nt fluent 2nd: shkn up after 3 out: 3 l ahd whn lft clr after 2 out: styd on strly* 8/13[1]
2 14 **North Hill Harvey**[197] 4-10-12 0 HarrySkelton 129+
(Dan Skelton) *chsd wnr after 2nd: pushed along in 3 l 2nd whn blnd 2 out: eased whn wnr wnt clr sn after* 5/1[3]
5 3 21 **Golden Bird (IRE)**[7] 2088 4-10-12 0 LeightonAspell 107
(Brendan Powell) *chsd wnr tl after 2nd: remained handy tl rdn and wknd 7th* 50/1
12 4 2 1/2 **Anomaly**[36] 1660 6-11-5 135 AidanColeman 113
(John Ferguson) *trckd ldrs tl rdn and wknd after 3 out* 3/1[2]
5 hd **Eastern Magic**[73] 8-10-9 0 RyanHatch(3) 104
(Ben Case) *hld up: nvr on terms* 100/1
34- 6 6 **Petrou (IRE)**[192] 5502 5-10-12 0 DarylJacob 98
(Ben Case) *hld up: nt fluent 1st: bhd fr 6th* 33/1
6 7 29 **Fire (IRE)**[24] 1829 5-10-12 0 TomMessenger 72
(Chris Bealby) *hld up: plld hrd: bhd fr 6th* 80/1
0- 8 nk **Same Ole Trix (IRE)**[224] 4941 5-10-9 0 (t) TomBellamy(3) 72
(Kim Bailey) *hld up: hit 5th: bhd fr next* 50/1
0 9 38 **Blue Prairie**[21] 1873 4-10-7 0 BridgetAndrews(5) 38
(Dan Skelton) *prom: pushed along 4th: reminder after next: wknd 7th* 100/1
P **Allee Bleue (IRE)**[769] 5-10-12 0 RichardJohnson
(Philip Hobbs) *hld up: plld hrd: hdwy 5th: nt fluent next: mstke 3 out: sn wknd and eased: 6th whn p.u bef next* 10/1

4m 48.7s (-10.30) **Going Correction** -0.125s/f (Good)
WFA 4 from 5yo+ 8lb 10 Ran SP% 122.8
Speed ratings (Par 105): **115,109,101,100,99 97,85,85,70,**
CSF £4.83 TOTE £1.40: £1.10, £1.80, £5.80; EX 5.00 Trifecta £78.90.
Owner Circle Of Friends **Bred** Lady J Fowler **Trained** Bourton-On-The-Water, Gloucs

FOCUS
No great depth to this and the second favourite disappointed, but the winner is potentially smart.

2222 32RED NOVICES' CHASE (16 fncs) 2m 3f 189y
3:30 (3:30) (Class 3) 4-Y-0+ £6,498 (£1,908; £954; £477)

Form RPR
350/ 1 **Sametegal (FR)**[599] 4752 6-11-2 0 NickScholfield 138+
(Paul Nicholls) *a.p: led last: rdn out* 3/1[2]
114- 2 1 1/2 **El Namoose**[273] 3994 6-11-2 0 AidanColeman 137
(John Ferguson) *hld up in tch: chsd ldr 3 out: ev ch last: rdn flat: no ex towards fin* 13/2[3]
113- 3 3 **Three Musketeers (IRE)**[204] 5271 5-11-2 0 HarrySkelton 134
(Dan Skelton) *chsd ldr tl led 5th: rdn appr 2 out: hdd last: styd on same pce flat* 1/1[1]
250- 4 16 **Amore Alato**[267] 4084 6-11-2 0 TomCannon 123
(Johnny Farrelly) *led to 5th: chsd ldr: j. slowly 8th: lost 2nd 3 out: rdn and wknd bef next* 17/2
4-00 5 2 1/2 **Saffron Wells (IRE)**[8] 2064 7-11-2 0 TrevorWhelan 119
(Neil King) *hld up: nt a fluent: drvn along after 12th: wknd appr 2 out* 8/1
50/P 6 16 **Venez Horace (FR)**[37] 1642 6-11-2 0 DavidEngland 105
(Giles Smyly) *prom: j. slowly and lost pl 1st: wknd 12th* 150/1
/53- 7 17 **Fight Commander (IRE)**[381] 1922 6-11-2 112 LeightonAspell 94
(Oliver Sherwood) *hld up: mstke 7th: wknd 12th* 25/1
-000 P **L'Es Fremantle (FR)**[10] 2043 4-10-2 0 DannyBurton(5)
(Michael Chapman) *nt jump wl and sn bhd: p.u bef 10th* 250/1

4m 59.8s (-5.50) **Going Correction** 0.0s/f (Good)
WFA 4 from 5yo+ 8lb 8 Ran SP% 114.9
Speed ratings (Par 107): **111,110,109,102,101 95,88,**
CSF £22.45 TOTE £4.10: £1.10, £1.80, £1.30; EX 19.10 Trifecta £50.80.
Owner Mr And Mrs J D Cotton **Bred** Pierre De Maleissye Melun Et Al **Trained** Ditcheat, Somerset

FOCUS
A good-quality novice chase, three very useful types coming clear.

2223 £10 FREE AT 32RED.COM H'CAP HURDLE (12 hdls) 3m 1f 10y
4:00 (4:00) (Class 4) (0-105,109) 4-Y-0+ £3,898 (£1,144; £572; £286)

Form RPR
00-0 1 **Giveitachance (IRE)**[19] 1897 8-11-7 100 (t) NickScholfield 105
(Claire Dyson) *chsd ldrs: led appr 2 out: rdn out* 13/2
135- 2 1 3/4 **Flemi Two Toes (IRE)**[234] 4735 9-10-0 89 RomainClavreul(10) 92
(Sarah Humphrey) *hld up: hdwy 4th: chsd wnr 2 out: styd on* 10/1
5-46 3 5 **Ballochmyle (IRE)**[159] 494 5-10-6 85 JackQuinlan 85
(Caroline Fryer) *hld up: hdwy 8th: led after next: rdn and hdd appr 2 out: nt fluent last: no ex flat* 25/1
1211 4 nk **Tokyo Javilex (FR)**[4] 2135 8-11-9 109 7ex (t) MrLDrowne(7) 109
(Nigel Hawke) *hld up: pushed along and hdwy 5th: rdn after 3 out: styd on same pce appr last* 9/4[1]
64-4 5 1 3/4 **Burgundy Betty (IRE)**[185] 28 5-10-10 89 DavidBass 87
(Ben Pauling) *led to 3rd: chsd ldrs: hit 7th: sn drvn along: outpcd 9th: styd on fr 2 out* 16/1
6400 6 12 **Little Windmill (IRE)**[19] 1897 5-11-7 100 (tp) TrevorWhelan 88
(Neil King) *hld up: hit 2nd: mstke 9th: sn rdn: nvr on terms* 10/1
P-P5 7 22 **Black Lily (IRE)**[15] 1972 7-10-6 85 TomMessenger 51
(Chris Bealby) *w ldr: racd keenly: led 3rd: mstke 6th: hit next: hdd after 9th: sn rdn and wknd* 16/1
F-P2 8 8 **Bar A Mine (FR)**[24] 1827 6-11-7 105 JamieBargary(5) 64
(Nigel Twiston-Davies) *chsd ldrs: rdn and lost pl appr 5th: effrt 8th: rdn and wknd after next* 6/1[3]
U2/5 9 12 **Murchu (IRE)**[53] 1522 9-11-12 105 (t) RichardJohnson 53
(Tim Vaughan) *hld up: hdwy 9th: rdn and wknd after 3 out* 7/2[2]

6m 20.4s (-2.50) **Going Correction** -0.125s/f (Good) 9 Ran SP% 114.4
Speed ratings (Par 105): **99,98,96,96,96 92,85,82,78**
CSF £67.19 CT £1513.40 TOTE £8.20: £2.50, £2.90, £4.00; EX 67.90 Trifecta £2337.50.
Owner Miss Becky Rowland **Bred** Ryan Mc Cusker **Trained** Cleeve Prior, Worcs

FOCUS
Lowly handicap form.
T/Jkpt: Not won. Consolation Placepot: Part won. £2,040.50 to a £1 stake. T/Plt: £26.20 to a £1 stake. Pool: £68,523.00 - 1,906.79 winning tickets. T/Qpdt: £6.80 to a £1 stake. Pool: £5,733.00 - 618.11 winning tickets. **Colin Roberts**

2224 - (Foreign Racing) - See Raceform Interactive

1991 CORK (R-H)
Sunday, November 1

OFFICIAL GOING: Soft (soft to heavy in places on chase course)

2225a PADDY POWER ACCA INSURANCE EUROPEAN BREEDERS FUND NOVICE HURDLE (GRADE 3) (13 hdls) 3m
1:55 (1:55) 4-Y-0+ £18,895 (£5,523; £2,616; £872)

RPR
1 **Moylisha Tim (IRE)**[18] 1915 5-11-0 113 MrJJSlevin 129
(R P Rath, Ire) *trckd ldr in 2nd: led 3rd: strly pressed after 2 out: styd on wl run-in* 6/1[3]
2 3 **Ben Button (IRE)**[173] 272 5-11-0 0 MarkWalsh 126
(P J Rothwell, Ire) *hld up in 4th: nt fluent 1st: tk clsr order 4 out to trck ldrs in 4th: chsd ldr in 2nd 3 out: sn rdn to press wnr: no imp run-in: kpt on same pce* 16/1
3 5 1/2 **Goonyella (IRE)**[197] 5392 8-11-0 0 KeithDonoghue 121
(J T R Dreaper, Ire) *led tl hdd 3rd: chsd ldr in 2nd: almost on terms 4 out: rdn and nt qckn in 3rd bef 3 out: no imp after 2 out in 4th: lft 3rd at last* 6/4[2]

The Form Book Jumps 2015-16, Raceform Ltd, Newbury, RG14 5SJ

4 61 **Altiepix (FR)**[6] 2111 5-11-0 122 .... BJCooper 60
(Gordon Elliott, Ire) *chsd ldrs in 3rd: clsr to press ldrs 4 out: sn rdn and dropped to rr bef next: sn no ex and eased: t.o* **5/4**[1]

F **Cheiliuradh (IRE)**[8] 2072 4-10-2 0 ....(t) PhillipEnright 110
(David Harry Kelly, Ire) *racd in rr: sme prog bef 3 out in 4th: wnt 3rd but no imp on principals bef last where fell* **16/1**

5m 55.2s (-36.90)
WFA 4 from 5yo+ 9lb **5 Ran SP% 110.5**
CSF £64.17 TOTE £8.20: £2.80, £6.20; DF 47.10 Trifecta £97.10.
Owner Timothy Farrell **Bred** Timmy Farrell **Trained** Enniscorthy, Co. Wexford

FOCUS
A sub-standard Grade 3 but nothing can be taken away from the winner, a tough, genuine and very likeable horse. A big pb from the runner-up.

2226a (Foreign Racing) - See Raceform Interactive

2227a PADDY POWER PADDYS NUMBERS WIN A MILLION EUROPEAN BREEDERS FUND NOVICE CHASE (GRADE 3) (14 fncs) 2m 4f
3:05 (3:05) 5-Y-0+ **£18,895** (£5,523; £2,616; £872)

RPR

1 **Lord Scoundrel (IRE)**[7] 2095 6-11-3 138 .... BJCooper 145+
(Gordon Elliott, Ire) *chsd ldr in 2nd: led narrowly bef 3rd: strly pressed bef 2 out: reasserted bef last and drew clr run-in: comf* **4/7**[1]

2 2 3/4 **Rightdownthemiddle (IRE)**[17] 1937 7-11-0 134 .... AELynch 134
(Michael Mulvany, Ire) *racd in 3rd: clsr to chse ldr in 2nd 4 out: pressed wnr next: no imp on wnr bef last: kpt on same pce run-in* **6/1**[3]

3 12 **Padraig's Joy (IRE)**[14] 1995 7-10-7 114 .... PhillipEnright 118
(David Harry Kelly, Ire) *hld up in rr: tk cl order into 3rd bef 3 out: no imp after next where pckd sltly: kpt on one pce* **14/1**

4 39 **Horendus Hulabaloo (IRE)**[46] 1556 6-11-3 135 ....(p) MarkWalsh 98
(M F Morris, Ire) *led: rn wd off bnd after 2nd and hdd: trckd ldr in 2nd: mstke 6 out: nt fluent 4 out in 3rd and dropped to rr next: sn no ex* **3/1**[2]

5m 23.9s (323.90) **4 Ran SP% 109.6**
CSF £4.45 TOTE £1.50; DF 4.00 Trifecta £8.50.
Owner Gigginstown House Stud **Bred** Patrick O'Reilly **Trained** Longwood, Co Meath

FOCUS
A second Grade 3 on the card that lacked strength in depth or any real quality, it was there for a half-decent horse to take advantage of and the winner did just that. The second and third help set the standard.

2228a PADDY POWER CORK GRAND NATIONAL H'CAP CHASE (GRADE B) (19 fncs) 3m 4f
3:35 (3:36) (0-150,138) 4-Y-0+
£23,255 (£7,364; £3,488; £1,162; £775; £387)

RPR

1 **Tulsa Jack (IRE)**[29] 1764 6-9-8 **115** .... JonathanMoore(7) 136+
(Noel Meade, Ire) *hld up towards rr: tk clsr order to chse ldrs on inner 4 out in 3rd: wnt 2nd 3 out: led bef 2 out and sn clr: styd on wl run-in* **5/1**[1]

2 12 **Clar Na Mionn (IRE)**[8] 2077 8-9-9 **112** ow2 .... StephenGray 118
(V T O'Brien, Ire) *chsd ldrs in 3rd: wnt 2nd 7 out: dropped to 3rd bef 3 out: rdn into 2nd bef 2 out: sn no imp on wnr: kpt on same pce run-in* **9/1**[3]

3 9 **Kylecrue (IRE)**[6] 2109 8-10-9 **123** ....(b) DannyMullins 124
(John Patrick Ryan, Ire) *led: nt fluent and strly pressed 3 out: sn hdd: no ex in 3rd 2 out: kpt on one pce* **16/1**

4 10 **Bless The Wings (IRE)**[8] 2077 10-11-4 **132** .... KeithDonoghue 122
(Gordon Elliott, Ire) *racd in rr: prog bef 3 out in 5th: wnt 4th at next: kpt on one pce: nvr on terms* **10/1**

5 1/2 **Riverside City (IRE)**[151] 605 6-9-11 **116** .... JackKennedy(5) 106
(Gordon Elliott, Ire) *hld up towards rr tl tk clsr order 5 out: wnt 4th at next: rdn and nt qckn bef 3 out: dropped to 5th 2 out: no ex* **8/1**[2]

6 14 **Betterthanalright (IRE)**[203] 5304 9-9-7 **110** oh4 .... ConorMaxwell(3) 86
(Liam Casey, Ire) *trckd ldr in 2nd: dropped to 3rd 7 out: wknd 5 out: sn no ex* **11/1**

P **Sword Fish (IRE)**[174] 248 9-10-1 **115** ....(bt) NiallPMadden
(C Roche, Ire) *hld up: dropped to rr and detached 7 out: p.u after next* **10/1**

P **Dushrembrandt (IRE)**[71] 1337 9-10-10 **124** ....(t) PhillipEnright
(Robert Tyner, Ire) *racd in mid-div: tk clsr order to trck ldrs in 3rd bef 5 out: wknd after 4 out: p.u bef 2 out* **14/1**

P **Unoccupied**[364] 2235 9-10-8 **122** .... AELynch
(Eoghan O'Grady, Ire) *racd in mid-div: dropped to rr 5 out: sn detached and p.u* **8/1**[2]

P **Rogue Angel (IRE)**[21] 1879 7-11-10 **138** ....(bt) BJCooper
(M F Morris, Ire) *sn chsd ldrs: rdn and nt qckn bef 4 out: sn dropped to rr and p.u after 3 out* **8/1**[2]

P **A Decent Excuse (IRE)**[14] 1994 8-10-11 **125** .... AlanCrowe
(Eugene M O'Sullivan, Ire) *hld up: rdn bef 5 out: sn dropped to rr and p.u* **10/1**

P **King Leon (IRE)**[17] 1939 6-10-6 **120** ....(p) MarkWalsh
(A P O'Brien, Ire) *racd in rr whn mstke 2nd: mstke 4th and rdn: tk clsr order to chse ldrs on outer after 5 out: rdn and no ex bef 3 out: sn p.u* **8/1**[2]

7m 33.2s (453.20) **12 Ran SP% 119.3**
CSF £50.21 CT £679.26 TOTE £4.40: £1.80, £2.90, £5.00; DF 62.00 Trifecta £899.70.
Owner Grand Alliance Racing Club **Bred** Ms Bernadette McInerney **Trained** Castletown, Co Meath
■ Stewards' Enquiry : Mark Walsh following a veterinary examination, the gelding was reported to be distressed and blowing hard, the gelding had lost its right fore shoe

FOCUS
It didn't look the most competitive renewal of this race, but that was tempered somewhat by the manner of the winner's victory with the prospect of there being more to come. The runner-up, rated to this year's best, helps set the standard.

2229 - 2231a (Foreign Racing) - See Raceform Interactive

NAAS (L-H)
Sunday, November 1

OFFICIAL GOING: Yielding (good to yielding in places)

2232a BRADY FAMILY HAM SUPPORTING KILDARE GAA POPLAR SQUARE CHASE (GRADE 3) (10 fncs) 2m
1:40 (1:40) 5-Y-0+ **£15,116** (£4,418; £2,093; £697)

RPR

1 **Devils Bride (IRE)**[21] 1878 8-11-8 145 ....(t) DavidMullins 150
(W P Mullins, Ire) *chsd ldrs: slt mstke in 4th at 3rd: tk clsr order bhd ldrs 2 out and impr travelling wl into 2nd: rdn to ld after last where slt mstke: edgd lft u.p run-in and all out clsng stages: jst* **5/1**[3]

2 hd **Sizing Granite (IRE)**[204] 5272 7-11-12 154 .... JJBurke 154+
(Henry De Bromhead, Ire) *sn led tl hdd after 2nd: niggled along in cl 2nd bef 2 out where nt fluent: sn rdn and u.p in 3rd bef last: kpt on again run-in where swtchd rt and strly pressed wnr cl home: jst hld* **1/1**[1]

3 1/2 **Azorian (IRE)**[8] 2063 7-11-1 132 ....(t) KevinSexton 142+
(Gordon Elliott, Ire) *w.w in rr: slow 4th: tk clsr order bhd ldrs after 3 out: rdn in 4th after next and kpt on wl u.p nr side fr last into cl 3rd nr fin: hld* **16/1**

4 3/4 **Alelchi Inois (FR)**[29] 1763 7-11-10 149 .... RWalsh 151
(W P Mullins, Ire) *cl up tl led after 2nd: pushed along and pressed clly between last 2: slt mstke last and sn hdd: no ex u.p in 2nd run-in and wknd into 4th clsng stages* **9/4**[2]

5 7 **King Of The Picts (IRE)**[22] 1861 6-10-11 130 .... LPDempsey 131
(John Patrick Shanahan, Ire) *chsd ldrs: 3rd bef 5 out: pushed along bef 2 out and sn no imp on ldrs u.p in rr: wknd* **16/1**

3m 51.0s (-32.30) **5 Ran SP% 109.2**
CSF £10.89 TOTE £5.10: £2.90, £1.02; DF 9.60 Trifecta £54.50.
Owner Gigginstown House Stud **Bred** Charles Persse **Trained** Muine Beag, Co Carlow

FOCUS
This was a smart Grade 3 and truly run, as was expected. The third and fourth help set the standard.

2233-2235a (Foreign Racing) - See Raceform Interactive

2236a TEGRAL SUPPORTING KILDARE GAA BROWN LAD H'CAP HURDLE (GRADE C) (11 hdls) 2m 4f
3:55 (3:55) 4-Y-0+ **£15,116** (£4,418; £2,093; £697)

RPR

1 **Mrs Mac Veale (IRE)**[7] 2098 10-10-10 **127** .... DonaghMeyler(7) 140
(Gavin Dower, Ire) *chsd ldrs: rdn into mod 2nd bef 2 out and clsd u.p to ld fr last: styd on wl to assert run-in: reduced advantage clsng stages* **12/1**

2 1 3/4 **Roll It Out (IRE)**[185] 50 6-10-10 **120** .... BarryGeraghty 131+
(Gordon Elliott, Ire) *mid-div: hdwy fr 3 out: mstke in mod 4th 2 out: no imp on wnr in 3rd bef last: r.o wl into 2nd clsng stages: nrst fin* **9/2**[1]

3 3 3/4 **Buster Dan Dan (IRE)**[29] 1762 7-11-0 **129** .... PaddyKennedy(5) 136+
(Terence O'Brien, Ire) *led and extended advantage bef 2nd: narrow ld at 1/2-way: extended advantage again bef 7th: stl gng wl and wl clr after 3 out: pushed along bef next and reduced ld: hdd fr last and no ex: dropped to 3rd clsng stages* **7/1**[3]

4 3 3/4 **Buck Dancing (IRE)**[281] 3870 6-9-12 **111** .... BenDalton(3) 115
(Edward P Harty, Ire) *mid-div: sme hdwy 3 out: rdn in mod 5th bef next and no imp on ldrs: kpt on u.p fr last: nvr nrr* **12/1**

5 1/2 **Russian Bill (IRE)**[186] 19 5-10-7 **120** .... GerFox(3) 123+
(Noel Meade, Ire) *mid-div early: slt mstke in mod 14th 3 out: hdwy u.p into mod 9th next where slt mstke: r.o wl fr last: nvr nrr* **7/1**[3]

6 3 3/4 **Miley Shah (IRE)**[43] 1588 10-11-6 **130** ....(p) MPFogarty 129
(S J Kenny, Ire) *chsd ldrs: nt fluent in 2nd at 2nd: slt mstke 5th: cl 2nd at 1/2-way: slt mstke 7th: rdn and no imp on ldr in mod 2nd into st: dropped to 3rd bef 2 out and one pce after* **20/1**

7 shd **Massini's Trap (IRE)**[72] 1312 6-11-5 **129** .... KevinSexton 128
(J A Nash, Ire) *in rr of mid-div: prog 3 out to dispute mod 7th next: no imp on ldrs between last 2: kpt on one pce fr last* **20/1**

8 4 **Back Off Mate (IRE)**[44] 500 7-10-1 **111** .... JJBurke 106
(A L T Moore, Ire) *mid-div best: pushed along and no imp in mod 12th 2 out: kpt on fr last* **14/1**

9 3/4 **Federici**[174] 248 6-10-1 **111** .... RobbieColgan 105
(E Bolger, Ire) *in rr of mid-div: pushed along and no imp in mod 10th bef 2 out: kpt on one pce fr last where slt mstke* **12/1**

10 1 **Love Rory (IRE)**[351] 2515 7-10-6 **123** .... MrBMLinehan(7) 116
(E Bolger, Ire) *towards rr for most: rdn and no imp bef 2 out: kpt on one pce fr last* **25/1**

11 1 3/4 **Sammy Black (GER)**[523] 498 7-10-11 **121** .... APHeskin 113
(Alan Fleming, Ire) *mid-div: sme hdwy u.p into mod 6th bef 2 out: rdn and no imp between last 2: wknd run-in* **5/1**[2]

12 1 3/4 **Nickname Exit (FR)**[170] 324 5-10-3 **116** .... LPDempsey(3) 106
(Gordon Elliott, Ire) *chsd ldrs: mod 5th whn hit 4th: pushed along fr 4 out and wknd bef next* **16/1**

13 3 1/2 **Competitive Edge (IRE)**[294] 3643 8-10-4 **117** ....[1] JodyMcGarvey(3) 103
(Conor O'Dwyer, Ire) *in rr: slt mstke 2nd: last at 1/2-way: no imp 3 out: kpt on one pce fr next: nvr involved* **25/1**

14 11 **Phil The Flyer (IRE)**[28] 1789 8-11-5 **134** ....(t) ShaneShortall(5) 109
(Ray Hackett, Ire) *chsd ldr early: slt mstke in 4th at 5th: rdn in mod 3rd after 3 out and sn no ex u.p: wknd bef next* **7/1**[3]

15 4 1/2 **Cairde Aris (IRE)**[168] 368 6-10-8 **118** .... BrianHayes 89
(John E Kiely, Ire) *mid-div early: mod 5th bef 4 out: rdn and wknd after next where slt mstke* **10/1**

4m 48.6s (-12.30) **15 Ran SP% 134.3**
CSF £70.06 CT £430.64 TOTE £13.60: £4.80, £2.20, £3.10; DF 113.10 Trifecta £920.00.
Owner P Corkery **Bred** Tom McCarthy **Trained** Youghal, Co. Waterford

FOCUS
Typically competitive, this was one of those races in which a tough winner goes off hard and quite a few viable contenders end up running out of steam a long way from home. The standard is set around the placed horses.

2237 - (Foreign Racing) - See Raceform Interactive

1984 **KEMPTON** (R-H)

Monday, November 2

OFFICIAL GOING: Good (good to soft in places)

Wind: Almost nil Weather: Overcast but fog lifting just before racing, becoming bright

2238 RACING UK ANYWHERE NOVICES' HURDLE (8 hdls) 2m
1:00 (1:00) (Class 4) 4-Y-O+ **£3,898** (£1,144; £572; £286)

Form RPR

1 **Imperial Presence (IRE)** 4-10-12 0 RichardJohnson 116+
(Philip Hobbs) *trckd ldr: chsing whn wandered into 2 out: sn upsides: narrowly hdd whn lft in ld last: styd on wl* **2/1**[1]

16- 2 1 ¼ **Lettheriverrundry (IRE)**[198] 5395 5-10-12 0 BarryGeraghty 116+
(Brendan Powell) *hld up in tch: cl up 3 out: chal 2 out: narrow ld whn nt fluent last: slithered on landing and hdd: styd on but nt rcvr* **2/1**[1]

24 3 4 ½ **Proofreader**[158] 528 6-10-12 0 NoelFehily 108+
(Neil Mulholland) *plld hrd: hld up: cl up 3 out: chal 2 out and upsides between last 2: nt qckn and fdd flat* **7/2**[2]

4 3 ¾ **My Anchor**[130] 4-10-12 0 GavinSheehan 105
(Charlie Mann) *led after nthing else wanted to: rdn and hdd between last 2: wknd* **20/1**

5 1 **Magic Music Man**[380] 4-10-12 0 WayneHutchinson 103
(Alan King) *trckd ldrs: cl up 3 out: rdn 2 out: wknd bef last* **5/1**[3]

03 6 13 **Galuppi**[17] 1946 4-10-12 0 SamTwiston-Davies 93
(J R Jenkins) *hld up: in tch 3 out: shkn up and fdd 2 out: j.lft last: eased* **40/1**

F 7 20 **Top Set (IRE)**[14] 1998 5-10-7 0 DanielHiskett(5) 70
(Richard Phillips) *a in last pair: lost tch 3 out: sn bhd* **200/1**

3m 53.5s (7.50) **Going Correction** +0.275s/f (Yiel) **7 Ran SP% 113.3**
Speed ratings (Par 105): **92,91,89,87,86 80,70**
CSF £6.24 TOTE £2.60: £1.40, £1.80; EX 6.00 Trifecta £19.50.
Owner Sir Christopher Wates **Bred** Sir Christopher Stephen Wates **Trained** Withycombe, Somerset

FOCUS
All starts have been moved at this track following remeasuring, so there will be no speed figures here until there is sufficient data to calculate updated median times. All bends moved out 2yds and hurdle races on summer course. Race 1 & 7 increased by 11yds, races 2 & 4 by 15yds, race 3 by 81yds, races 5 & 6 by 64yds. The fog lifted around 20 minutes before racing and the ground was fairly decent. The front pair came away on the run-in in what was just an ordinary novice hurdle and would surely have finished in reverse order but for the runner-up's late blunder. It's been given a token rating through the third.

2239 JOIN THE RACING UK CLUB "NATIONAL HUNT" NOVICES' HURDLE (10 hdls) 2m 5f
1:30 (1:30) (Class 4) 4-Y-O+ **£3,898** (£1,144; £572; £286)

Form RPR

522- 1 **Dueling Banjos**[230] 4832 5-10-12 0 DavidBass 128+
(Kim Bailey) *w ldr: led 7th: kicked for home fr 3 out: drvn and hdd after 2 out: rallied after last: kpt on gamely to ld fnl strides* **8/1**

6- 2 hd **Rock On Oscar (IRE)**[269] 4068 5-10-12 0 (t) SamTwiston-Davies 127+
(Paul Nicholls) *t.k.h: hld up: last tl prog fr 5th: stdy hdwy to trck ldr on long run after 3 out: led sn after 2 out and looked sure to win: l ahd last: urged along flat: hdd fnl strides* **10/3**[3]

4-12 3 19 **Ballinure (IRE)**[20] 1898 5-10-9 0 JeremiahMcGrath(3) 112
(Nicky Henderson) *led to 7th: chsd wnr tl long run after 3 out: already wl hld whn j.lft 2 out: wknd last* **3/1**[2]

103- 4 ½ **Fortunate George (IRE)**[233] 4770 5-10-12 0 DarylJacob 112
(Emma Lavelle) *prom: blnd 1st and lost pl: nvr that fluent after: prog 7th: in tch whn mstke 3 out: steadily wknd bef 2 out* **9/4**[1]

4 5 32 **Mountain Eagle (IRE)**[22] 1872 6-10-12 0 (t) NoelFehily 88
(Harry Fry) *t.k.h: mstke 1st and blnd 2nd: wl in tch 7th: wknd after next: t.o* **7/1**

0-5 6 23 **Fin D'Espere (IRE)**[16] 1973 4-10-12 0 (t) GavinSheehan 75
(Suzy Smith) *chsd ldrs: pushed along but stl in tch whn terrible blunder 3 out: no ch after and t.o* **100/1**

65- 7 4 **Auckland De Re (FR)**[225] 4947 5-10-12 0 BarryGeraghty 56
(Neil Mulholland) *t.k.h: hld up in rr: wknd after 7th: t.o* **14/1**

6-5 8 11 **Whispering Speed (IRE)**[15] 1990 5-10-12 0 NickScholfield 47
(Lucy Wadham) *chsd ldrs: lost pl 6th: last and tailing off bef 3 out* **50/1**

030- 9 3 ½ **Mirkat**[339] 2795 5-10-12 0 WayneHutchinson 43
(Alan King) *t.k.h: hld up: in tch 6th: wknd after next: t.o* **50/1**

5m 8.6s (5.60) **Going Correction** +0.275s/f (Yiel) **9 Ran SP% 114.0**
Speed ratings (Par 105): **100,99,92,92,80 71,70,65,64**
CSF £34.99 TOTE £9.20: £1.90, £1.60, £1.30; EX 38.30 Trifecta £149.40.
Owner J Perriss **Bred** Richard Davies **Trained** Andoversford, Gloucs

FOCUS
A fair novice hurdle in which they got racing a fair way out. The front pair came right away over the last two. The third helps set the level.

2240 WEATHERBYS VAT SERVICES NOVICES' LIMITED H'CAP CHASE (18 fncs) 3m
2:00 (2:00) (Class 3) (0-135,134) 4-Y-O+ **£7,797** (£2,289; £1,144; £572)

Form RPR

213- 1 **Port Melon (IRE)**[201] 5339 7-11-6 132 SamTwiston-Davies 140+
(Paul Nicholls) *wl in tch: chsd ldng pair 13th: pushed along after 4 out: no imp tl tk 2nd after 2 out: clsd qckly to ld last: styd on wl* **11/4**[1]

4-13 2 2 **Kilmurvy (IRE)**[33] 1701 7-10-12 124 (tp) NickScholfield 129
(Jeremy Scott) *patiently rdn in rr: stdy prog fr 13th: tk 4th after 4 out but nt on terms: rdn after 3 out: clsd fr next: styd on to take 2nd after last: unable to chal* **8/1**

-342 3 2 ¾ **Frampton (IRE)**[29] 1783 6-10-13 125 (p) RichardJohnson 130
(Charlie Longsdon) *led 3rd to 6th: chsd ldr: led 4 out: drvn 3 l clr 2 out: hdd and mstke last: wknd* **8/1**

P-U3 4 6 **Parish Business (IRE)**[38] 1642 7-11-4 130 (t) DarylJacob 131+
(Emma Lavelle) *led to 3rd: trckd ldr: led 6th: blnd 14th: hdd next: wknd u.p fr 2 out: mstke last* **7/1**[3]

03-4 5 50 **Marden Court (IRE)**[185] 61 5-10-6 118 GavinSheehan 70
(Colin Tizzard) *nt fluent 1st and 2nd: wl in tch: trckd ldng pair 7th to 13th: 4th and sing to struggle whn bad blunder 15th (4 out): nt rcvr and sn t.o* **16/1**

10/U B **Billy Merriott (IRE)**[182] 99 9-11-3 129 (t) NoelFehily
(Harry Fry) *hld up in last: jst sing to make prog and disputing 7th whn b.d 13th* **9/2**[2]

-112 P **Dreamsoftheatre (IRE)**[26] 1807 7-11-8 134 (t) BarryGeraghty
(Jonjo O'Neill) *nt fluent 4th: nvr gng that wl after: wknd after 11th: t.o 14th: p.u bef 3 out* **8/1**

1F13 F **By The Boardwalk (IRE)**[18] 1924 7-11-2 131 (t) TomBellamy(3)
(Kim Bailey) *hld up: trckd ldrs fr 10th: 5th and wl in tch whn fell 13th* **14/1**

2121 F **Urcalin (FR)**[32] 1722 7-11-6 132 (t) TomCannon 132
(David Arbuthnot) *nt a fluent: chsd ldrs: struggling to hold pl fr 12th: rdn 4 out: 10 l bhd in 5th and wl hld whn fell heavily 3 out* **7/1**[3]

6m 8.7s (-0.30) **Going Correction** +0.225s/f (Yiel) **9 Ran SP% 115.7**
Speed ratings (Par 107): **109,108,107,105,88 , , ,**
CSF £25.24 CT £157.37 TOTE £4.10: £1.50, £2.20, £2.60; EX 31.90 Trifecta £278.30.
Owner C G Roach **Bred** Mrs A Darragh **Trained** Ditcheat, Somerset

FOCUS
Ordinary chase form but the race should produce winners at a similar level. The second to fourth set the level.

2241 PERTEMPS NETWORK H'CAP HURDLE (SERIES QUALIFIER) (10 hdls) 2m 5f
2:30 (2:30) (Class 2) 4-Y-O+ **£12,346** (£3,625; £1,812; £906)

Form RPR

421- 1 **Brother Tedd**[191] 5539 6-10-13 144 RichardJohnson 152+
(Philip Hobbs) *hld up bhd ldrs: cl up fr 7th: quick move to ld bef 2 out and sn clr: shkn up and 6 l ahd whn nt fluent last: eased fnl 75yds* **11/8**[1]

101- 2 4 **Silviniaco Conti (FR)**[207] 5237 9-11-12 157 (p) NoelFehily 156
(Paul Nicholls) *led at gd clip but hdd bef 1st: chsd ldr: led 7th: hdd and outpcd bef 2 out: kpt on* **7/2**[2]

-411 3 hd **Low Key (IRE)**[23] 1488 8-10-4 135 ConorO'Farrell 136
(David Pipe) *hld up in detached last: tried to creep clsr fr 7th: nt on terms whn nt fluent 3 out: shkn up bef 2 out: outpcd by wnr but kpt on to press for 2nd nr fin* **5/1**[3]

FUP- 4 3 **Kaysersberg (FR)**[207] 5241 8-10-8 139 GavinSheehan 135
(Warren Greatrex) *led bef 1st and set decent pce: hdd 7th: styd w ldr tl outpcd bef 2 out: one pce after* **7/2**[2]

0-41 5 101 **Mister Fizz**[22] 1325 7-11-0 145 RobertDunne
(Miss Imogen Pickard) *chsd ldrs to 7th: wknd and sn t.o: eased bef 2 out* **12/1**

5m 2.6s (-0.40) **Going Correction** +0.275s/f (Yiel) **5 Ran SP% 110.9**
Speed ratings (Par 109): **111,109,109,108,**
CSF £6.76 TOTE £1.90: £1.10, £1.90; EX 5.70 Trifecta £9.50.
Owner Scrase Farms **Bred** Mrs J E Scrase **Trained** Withycombe, Somerset

FOCUS
Run at a true gallop, much of the focus was on the runner-up pre-race but it went to what looks a fast-improving hurdler. Another step forward from the winner, with the third and fourth rated close to their marks.

2242 WEATHERBYS VAT SERVICES GRADUATION CHASE (16 fncs) 2m 4f 110y
3:05 (3:05) (Class 2) 4-Y-O+ **£12,996** (£3,816; £1,908; £954)

Form RPR

204- 1 **Smad Place (FR)**[207] 5237 8-11-9 155 WayneHutchinson 157+
(Alan King) *cl up: led 4th: mde rest: jnd and shkn up 2 out: forged clr bef last where gd jump: styd on strly* **6/4**[1]

5P3- 2 8 **Fingal Bay (IRE)**[267] 4111 9-11-6 146 RichardJohnson 146
(Philip Hobbs) *led after 1st to 4th: chsd wnr: rdn to chal 3 out: upsides 2 out: no ex bef last: fin tired* **15/8**[2]

P3F- 3 2 ¾ **Kings Lad (IRE)**[201] 5344 8-11-9 145 DarylJacob 147
(Colin Tizzard) *hld up in tch: mstke 11th: cl up fr next: stl wl there whn mstke 3 out: one pce after* **14/1**

4F3- 4 56 **Horizontal Speed (IRE)**[191] 5540 7-11-2 141 NoelFehily 82
(David Dennis) *ldng whn bad mstke 1st and lost pl: mstke 4th: in tch whn mstke 11th: wknd and mstke 4 out: t.o* **7/1**

3FP- P **Easter Day (FR)**[254] 4361 7-11-9 142 SamTwiston-Davies
(Paul Nicholls) *hmpd 1st: mstke 2nd and lost tch: j. 3rd w no confidence: p.u bef next: dismntd* **6/1**[3]

5m 6.5s (-5.50) **Going Correction** +0.225s/f (Yiel) **5 Ran SP% 108.2**
Speed ratings (Par 109): **119,115,114,93,**
CSF £4.70 TOTE £2.20: £1.20, £1.40; EX 4.90 Trifecta £28.10.
Owner Mrs Peter Andrews **Bred** Eric Aubree & Mme Maryse Aubree **Trained** Barbury Castle, Wilts

FOCUS
A small field and the third favourite pulled up early, but none the less the two smart sorts were left to duel it out in the straight, with the market leader pulling clear late. Good form. The winner has been a 163-rated chaser at his peak and didn't neeed to run to that level to win this, although the race could be rated a few pounds higher through the second.

2243 RACING UK 1 PRICE 3 DEVICES H'CAP CHASE (16 fncs) 2m 4f 110y
3:40 (3:40) (Class 4) (0-120,120) 4-Y-O+ **£4,548** (£1,335; £667; £333)

Form RPR

1306 1 **Moorlands Jack**[43] 1601 10-11-7 115 (p) NickScholfield 125+
(Jeremy Scott) *hld up in last pair: mstke 6th: prog fr 11th: stl only 4th 3 out: tk 2nd between last 2 and clsd qckly to ld flat: shkn up and sn in command* **13/2**[3]

6630 2 1 ½ **Houston Dynimo (IRE)**[10] 2057 10-11-0 115 (bt) DavidNoonan(7) 123
(David Pipe) *led: looked to be gng best fr 3 out: 4 l clr after 2 out: slowed sltly into last: qckly hdd and no rspnse flat* **10/1**

-44U 3 5 **Adam Du Breteau (FR)**[30] 1753 5-10-13 107 (b) RichardJohnson 117+
(Jonjo O'Neill) *trckd ldng trio: cl up whn bad blunder 10th: great rcvry but dropped to last: trying to rally in 5th whn mstke 3 out: kpt on to take 3rd last strides but no ch to threaten* **11/8**[1]

412- 4 nk **Somchine**[202] 5336 7-11-12 120 AndrewThornton 124
(Seamus Mullins) *w.w in 5th: prog 10th and trckd ldrs fr next: wnt 2nd 3 out tl between last 2: wknd* **8/1**

1-24 5 22 **Very Noble (FR)**[30] 1753 6-11-2 110 (t) NoelFehily 94
(Chris Gordon) *sloppy jumps in last pair: reminders after 5th: effrt and in tch 11th: wknd after 4 out* **10/1**

66-4 P **Hatters River (IRE)**[15] 1987 8-11-2 110 GavinSheehan
(Ali Stronge) *chsd ldr tl mstke 10th: wknd and blnd next: slow jump 4 out and t.o: p.u bef 3 out* **4/1**[2]

1U6- P **Our Cat (IRE)**[200] 5354 7-11-4 115 (t[1]) ConorShoemark(3) 100
(Fergal O'Brien) *prom: chsd ldr fr 10th: rdn 4 out: lost 2nd and wknd 3 out: 8 l down in 5th whn blnd next: p.u bef last* **8/1**

5m 13.0s (1.00) **Going Correction** +0.225s/f (Yiel) **7 Ran SP% 115.8**
Speed ratings (Par 105): **107,106,104,104,96**
CSF £63.93 TOTE £7.80: £3.10, £4.40; EX 62.30 Trifecta £226.10.
Owner Mrs Lynda M Williams **Bred** Mrs L M Williams **Trained** Brompton Regis, Somerset

FOCUS
Modest chasing form. The winner has been rated to his best.

2244 RACINGUK.COM CONDITIONAL JOCKEYS' H'CAP HURDLE (QUAL FOR CHALLENGER TWO MILE HURDLE SERIES FINAL) (8 hdls) 2m
4:10 (4:10) (Class 4) (0-120,120) 3-Y-0+ £3,249 (£954; £477; £238)

Form RPR
1/0- 1 **Thunder Sheik (IRE)**^{513} [625] 7-11-5 **116**.......................... RyanHatch$^{(3)}$ 124+
(Nigel Twiston-Davies) *trckd ldrs: cl up 3 out: chsd ldr bef 2 out where shkn up to ld: gd battle w runner-up after: jst prevailed* **9/2**^{2}
36-2 2 *hd* **Arty Campbell (IRE)**^{31} [1324] 5-10-5 **102**.......................... RobertWilliams$^{(3)}$ 108
(Bernard Llewellyn) *prom: trckd ldr 5th: led on long run after 3 out gng strly: narrowly hdd and shkn up 2 out: w wnr after and gd battle: nt qckn nr fin* **5/4**^{1}
44-0 3 *19* **Iniesta (IRE)**^{12} [2011] 4-10-13 **115**..........................(v) GeorgeGorman$^{(8)}$ 104
(Gary Moore) *t.k.h: trckd ldrs: cl up 3 out: pushed along and sn lft bhd: tk modest 3rd between last 2* **20/1**
133- 4 *1* **Old Pride (IRE)**^{197} [5404] 7-11-8 **119**.......................... CiaranGethings$^{(3)}$ 107
(David Loder) *trckd ldr: led 4th: hdd on long run after 3 out: wknd* **5/1**^{3}
P5/P 5 *17* **Rachael's Ruby**^{14} [2000] 8-9-9 **94** oh9..........................(p) ConorWalsh$^{(5)}$ 67
(Roger Teal) *hld up: jst in tch after 5th: sn rdn and struggling: no ch after 3 out* **100/1**
/P-5 6 *10* **Superciliary**^{31} [1734] 6-11-2 **110**..........................(t) ThomasGarner 74
(Chris Gordon) *in tch tl rdn and dropped to last after 4th: sn bhd* **16/1**
34P- 7 *41* **Thecorruptor (IRE)**^{217} [5068] 5-11-2 **110**..........................^{1} TomBellamy 37
(Paul Webber) *hld up: prog 5th: trckd ldrs bef 3 out: wknd v rapidly on long run bef 2 out: eased and t.o* **7/1**
2555 P **Mr Lando**^{15} [1988] 6-11-7 **120**.......................... HarryCobden$^{(5)}$
(Alison Batchelor) *led to 4th: lost pl qckly next: sn bhd: t.o whn p.u bef 2 out* **8/1**

3m 49.1s (3.10) **Going Correction** +0.275s/f (Yiel)
WFA 4 from 5yo+ 7lb **8 Ran SP% 114.5**
Speed ratings (Par 105): **103,102,93,92,84 79,58,**
CSF £10.94 CT £99.06 TOTE £5.80: £1.70, £1.20, £3.10; EX 13.20 Trifecta £116.20.
Owner R J Rexton **Bred** Janus Bloodstock Inc **Trained** Naunton, Gloucs

FOCUS
The front pair drew right away in this ordinary handicap. The winner has been rated to his best.
T/Jkpt: Jackpot: £74,743.00 to a £1 stake. Pool: £315,816.00 - 3 winning tickets. Consolation placepot: £34.20 to a £1 stake. Pool: £6,087.00 - 129.90 winning tickets T/Plt: £58.10 to a £1 stake. Pool: £64,754.05 - 813.38 winning tickets T/Qpdt: £32.60 to a £1 stake. Pool: £3,979.78 - 90.20 winning tickets **Jonathan Neesom**

2032 LUDLOW (R-H)
Monday, November 2

OFFICIAL GOING: Good changing to good to soft after race 2 (2.10)
Wind: almost nil Weather: foggy

2245 LUDLOW RACECOURSE BOOKMAKERS CONDITIONAL JOCKEYS' H'CAP HURDLE (12 hdls) 2m 7f 174y
1:40 (1:40) (Class 5) (0-100,96) 4-Y-0+ £2,599 (£763; £381; £190)

Form RPR
4452 1 **Minella Bliss (IRE)**^{16} [1972] 10-11-7 **96**..........................(b) CharlieHammond$^{(5)}$ 102
(James Evans) *in tch in mid-div: chsng ldrs after 9th: led after 2 out: styd on* **10/3**^{2}
4-05 2 *1 1/4* **Mist The Boat**^{25} [1819] 7-11-10 **94**..........................(p) MattGriffiths 99
(Tim Vaughan) *trckd ldr: led 7th tl after 2 out: nt fluent last: one pce* **3/1**^{1}
25-6 3 *3/4* **Ordensritter (GER)**^{35} [1677] 7-10-13 **86**..........................(t) GilesHawkins$^{(3)}$ 90
(Chris Down) *chsd ldrs: rdn 3 out: one pce fr next* **4/1**^{3}
1002 4 *29* **King's Song (FR)**^{16} [1961] 5-11-12 **96**.......................... KieronEdgar 74
(David Dennis) *prom: lost pl by 6th: chsng ldrs again after 9th: rdn and wknd bef next: jst hld poor 4th* **5/1**
-P64 5 *shd* **Just Skittles**^{16} [1972] 7-9-11 **70** oh9.......................... JamieBargary$^{(3)}$ 48
(Richard Harper) *towards rr: in tch and rdn after 9th: sn wknd: plugged on to chal for poor 4th flat* **22/1**
PP-3 6 *9* **Shanksforamillion**^{16} [1961] 6-10-7 **77**.......................... FreddieMitchell 47
(David Rees) *hld up: rdn and wkng after 9th* **6/1**
2505 7 *13* **Peaceful Gardens**^{16} [1961] 6-9-10 **72**.......................... DavidPrichard$^{(6)}$ 30
(Jeremy Scott) *t.k.h in mid-div: rdn and wkng after 9th* **10/1**
P6P- R **Shadesofnavy**^{390} [1800] 9-9-9 **70**..........................(t) ArchieBellamy$^{(5)}$
(Peter Pritchard) *led to 7th: rdn and wknd after 9th: last whn ref and uns rdr 2 out* **66/1**

5m 57.6s (5.30) **Going Correction** +0.25s/f (Yiel) **8 Ran SP% 114.0**
Speed ratings (Par 103): **101,100,100,90,90 87,83,**
CSF £14.05 CT £39.95 TOTE £3.80: £1.20, £1.60, £1.60; EX 13.50 Trifecta £57.80.
Owner Running Dragon Racing 2 **Bred** James Meagher **Trained** Broadwas, Worcs

FOCUS
This opening handicap, confined to conditional riders, was run in poor visibility due to heavy fog. The first three have been rated close to form.

2246 AIUA/BLUEFIN AGRICULTURAL INSURANCE SPECIALISTS H'CAP CHASE (12 fncs) 1m 7f 212y
2:10 (2:10) (Class 4) (0-120,120) 4-Y-0+ £4,548 (£1,335; £667; £333)

Form RPR
5-21 1 **Helium (FR)**^{12} [2019] 10-11-6 **114**.......................... RhysFlint 125+
(Alexandra Dunn) *t.k.h: trckd ldrs: hmpd and lost pl bnd appr 4 out: sn shkn up: clsd 3 out: 4th whn swtchd lft to chal last: sn led: r.o wl* **4/1**^{2}
0/50 2 *4* **Noche De Reyes (FR)**^{38} [1643] 6-11-12 **120**.......................... PaddyBrennan 127
(Tom George) *hld up in 5th: chsng ldrs by 9th: rdn 3 out: kpt on same pce: wnt 2nd flat* **3/1**^{1}
11-0 3 *1* **Kerryhead Storm (IRE)**^{170} [338] 10-11-6 **114**..........................(t) CharliePoste 119
(Matt Sheppard) *trckd ldrs: led after 9th: rdn 3 out: hdd jst after last: no ex* **10/1**
315F 4 *8* **Furrows**^{72} [1327] 10-11-12 **120**.......................... LeightonAspell 120
(Oliver Sherwood) *hld up in last pair: hdwy by 9th: chsd ldr and rdn 4 out: lost 2nd next: no ex appr last* **17/2**
553- 5 *12* **Last Shot (FR)**^{229} [4858] 8-11-6 **114**.......................... LiamTreadwell 101
(Venetia Williams) *trckd wnr to 6th: sn lost pl: last and struggling by 9th* **11/2**^{3}
5P41 P **Yabadabadoo**^{15} [1985] 7-11-6 **114**..........................(t) AidanColeman
(Emma Lavelle) *led tl hdd after 9th: wknd qckly appr next: last whn blnd 3 out: p.u bef 2 out* **3/1**^{1}

4263 F **Newton Geronimo**^{30} [1753] 6-11-4 **112**..........................^{1} NicodeBoinville 114
(Ben Pauling) *hld up in last: hdwy 4 out: rdn next: disputing 3rd whn fell 2 out* **10/1**

4m 2.4s (3.90) **Going Correction** +0.25s/f (Yiel) **7 Ran SP% 114.1**
Speed ratings (Par 105): **106,104,103,99,93**
CSF £16.85 CT £109.84 TOTE £4.20: £1.70, £2.10; EX 14.50 Trifecta £97.00.
Owner West Buckland Bloodstock Ltd **Bred** Adrian Von Gunten **Trained** West Buckland, Somerset

FOCUS
A modest handicap, run at a sound gallop. The winner is closing in on his old mark and might win another.

2247 BREEDON AGGREGATES H'CAP HURDLE (11 hdls) 2m 5f 55y
2:40 (2:40) (Class 3) (0-130,130) 3-Y-0+ £6,498 (£1,908; £954; £477)

Form RPR
661- 1 **Dubawi Island (FR)**^{226} [4906] 6-11-10 **128**.......................... AidanColeman 134+
(Venetia Williams) *midfield: in 2nd by 8th: rdn appr 3 out: led last: drvn out* **7/1**^{3}
0-63 2 *3* **Here's Herbie**^{9} [2064] 7-10-10 **117**..........................(t) LucyGardner$^{(3)}$ 119+
(Sue Gardner) *chsd ldr: stl in 2nd after 6th: lost pl by 8th: rallied 3 out: styd on on flat: wnt 2nd nr fin* **9/4**^{1}
102- 3 *1/2* **Ascendant**^{214} [5110] 9-11-12 **130**..........................(t) AlainCawley 132
(Johnny Farrelly) *midfield: hdwy 5th: wnt 2nd after 8th: led appr 3 out to last: wknd flat: lost 2nd nr fin* **8/1**
10-0 4 *26* **Discay**^{22} [1868] 6-11-7 **125**.......................... WillKennedy 103
(Dr Richard Newland) *wnt to post early: hld up: clsd by 8th: 4th and wkng whn nt fluent 3 out* **7/1**^{3}
F-14 5 *15* **Take A Break (FR)**^{12} [2011] 4-11-6 **124**..........................(p) JamesBest 89
(Nigel Hawke) *hld up: prom by 8th: rdn and wknd bef 3 out: t.o* **16/1**
64-5 6 *7* **Loyaute (FR)**^{26} [1808] 8-11-7 **125**.......................... JamesDavies 84
(Chris Down) *led: clr after 5th: much reduced advantage 8th: sn hdd & wknd: t.o* **10/1**
1224 7 *13* **Tangolan (IRE)**^{17} [1948] 7-10-13 **117**..........................(t) PaddyBrennan 64
(Fergal O'Brien) *chsd ldrs: nt fluent 6th: bhd by 8th: t.o* **11/1**
1P-1 P **Leaderofthedance**^{11} [2033] 6-11-2 **120**.......................... NicodeBoinville
(Nicky Henderson) *hld up: rdn and wknd after 8th: wl bhd whn p.u bef 3 out* **7/2**^{2}

(-314.80) course record
WFA 4 from 6yo+ 8lb **8 Ran SP% 112.4**
CSF £23.00 CT £127.87 TOTE £6.30: £1.90, £1.20, £2.50; EX 27.10 Trifecta £137.80.
Owner Andrew Brooks & Julian Taylor **Bred** Darley Stud Management Co Ltd **Trained** Kings Caple, H'fords

FOCUS
Not a bad handicap and the runner-up helps to set the level. A small pb from the winner, with the third rated close to his mark.

2248 BLUEFIN INSURANCE SOLUTIONS WELSHPOOL H'CAP CHASE (19 fncs) 2m 7f 171y
3:15 (3:15) (Class 4) (0-105,103) 4-Y-0+ £3,768 (£1,106; £553; £276)

Form RPR
UPR- 1 **Upbeat Cobbler (FR)**^{239} [4649] 7-10-12 **89**.......................... JakeGreenall 98
(Henry Daly) *chsd ldrs: led after 15th to 2 out: rallied u.p to ld again fnl 100yds* **4/1**^{2}
4323 2 *1/2* **Battlecat**^{33} [1703] 8-11-7 **103**.......................... ConorRing$^{(5)}$ 113
(Evan Williams) *hld up in last pair: clsd after 10th: in 3rd at 15th: led 2 out tl fnl 100yds: no ex cl home* **11/4**^{1}
1PU5 3 *4 1/2* **Sylvan Legend**^{11} [2037] 7-10-4 **81**..........................(tp) MarkQuinlan 87
(Neil Mulholland) *two handlers in paddock: hld up in last pair: hdwy appr 4 out: wnt 3rd 3 out: ev ch next: no ex appr last: hung lft flat* **5/1**
P43 4 *62* **Michigan Assassin (IRE)**^{11} [2037] 13-10-13 **95**.......(p) MrBMoorcroft$^{(5)}$ 44
(Debra Hamer) *led: in 4th by 15th: sn wknd: t.o* **9/2**^{3}
2UU4 P **Samtheman**^{11} [2037] 10-10-8 **90**.......................... AliceMills$^{(5)}$
(Pam Ford) *chsd ldrs: mstke and lost pl 8th: last and struggling by 10th: bhd whn p.u bef 14th* **5/1**
60-0 P **Vent Nivernais (FR)**^{20} [1894] 6-10-13 **90**..........................(b^{1}) LiamTreadwell
(James Evans) *trckd ldr: in ld 15th: sn hdd: wknd qckly 4 out: mstke next: 4th and no ch whn p.u bef 2 out* **7/1**

6m 11.5s (371.50) **6 Ran SP% 110.7**
CSF £15.32 TOTE £5.10: £2.10, £2.30; EX 14.10 Trifecta £57.50.
Owner Mrs A Timpson **Bred** Daniel & Mme Jeannine Laupretre **Trained** Stanton Lacy, Shropshire

FOCUS
Only the principals mattered from three out in this moderate handicap. The first three have been rated pretty much to their marks.

2249 RACING UK NOVICES' H'CAP CHASE (16 fncs) 2m 4f 11y
3:50 (3:50) (Class 4) (0-105,105) 4-Y-0+ £3,768 (£1,106; £553; £276)

Form RPR
2453 1 **Zama Zama**^{11} [2034] 8-11-9 **102**..........................(b) AdamWedge 110
(Evan Williams) *chsd ldrs: rdn 3 out: led narrowly last: hld on* **5/1**^{3}
3322 2 *1/2* **Mr Mafia (IRE)**^{26} [1812] 6-11-8 **101**..........................(t) LeeEdwards 110
(Tony Carroll) *mid-div: chsng ldrs whn nt fluent 4 out: styd on on flat: wnt 2nd nr fin* **7/2**^{2}
6226 3 *hd* **Bus Named Desire**^{19} [1910] 7-9-13 **85**..........................(tp) MrStanSheppard$^{(7)}$ 94
(Matt Sheppard) *mid-div: hdwy to chse ldrs 4 out: swtchd lft and styd on on flat* **10/1**
200/ 4 *1/2* **Gallic Warrior (FR)**^{566} [5335] 8-11-12 **105**.......................... PaddyBrennan 112
(Fergal O'Brien) *t.k.h: chsd ldr: rdn 4 out: ev ch last: no ex and lost 2 pls towards fin* **9/4**^{1}
2F12 5 *9* **Chankillo**^{6} [2124] 6-10-13 **92**..........................(p) AidanColeman 93
(Sarah-Jayne Davies) *t.k.h: chsd ldng pair: mstke 6th: in 2nd after 13th: wknd bef last* **5/1**^{3}
156- 6 *20* **Try It Sometime (IRE)**^{221} [4991] 7-11-2 **102**.........(t) MrMartinMcIntyre$^{(7)}$ 83
(Sheila Lewis) *hld up in last pair: rdn after 13th: bhd whn pckd 4 out* **16/1**
62-0 F **Truckers Highway (IRE)**^{26} [1812] 6-10-4 **86**.......................... HarryChalloner$^{(3)}$
(John Groucott) *ldng whn runners c into view after 4th: j.rt 4 out: stl in front next: fell 2 out* **9/1**
560- P **What About Molly (IRE)**^{210} [5185] 5-9-13 **85**.......................... FinianO'Toole$^{(7)}$
(Heather Dalton) *hld up in last pair: rdn after 13th: wl bhd whn p.u bef 2 out* **25/1**

(-304.40) course record **8 Ran SP% 115.1**
CSF £23.72 CT £168.13 TOTE £4.70: £1.50, £1.60, £2.90; EX 17.00 Trifecta £75.00.
Owner Tony Cromwell & Partner **Bred** Cheveley Park Stud Ltd **Trained** Llancarfan, Vale Of Glamorgan

FOCUS
There was a very tight four-way finish in this ordinary novice handicap. Again visibility was poor due to the fog. The second has been rated to his mark, with the third in line with her hurdles mark.

2250 RACING UK STANDARD OPEN NATIONAL HUNT FLAT RACE 1m 7f 169y
4:20 (4:20) (Class 5) 4-6-Y-O £2,599 (£763; £381; £190)

Form RPR

1 **Mac Gregory** 4-11-0 0 AdamWedge 101+
(Evan Williams) *hld up: hdwy 3f out: rdn to ld fnl 75yds: styd on wl* **16/1**

2 1 1/4 **Cashanova (IRE)** 4-11-0 0 PaddyBrennan 99
(Henry Daly) *trckd ldrs: rdn 2f out: led 1f out: hdd and no ex fnl 75yds* **13/2**[3]

3 1 **Pickamix** 4-11-0 0 SeanBowen 98
(Rebecca Curtis) *trckd ldrs: led 2f out to 1f out: kpt on u.p* **7/1**

2 4 2 3/4 **Toviere (IRE)**[185] 67 4-11-0 0 LeightonAspell 96
(Oliver Sherwood) *trckd ldrs: rdn 2f out: one pce* **11/8**[1]

3- 5 2 1/4 **Real Gone Kid**[296] 3618 4-11-0 0 AidanColeman 94
(Martin Keighley) *hld up in mid-div: clsd 5f out: rdn 3f out: one pce* **17/2**

5 6 1 1/2 **Trans Express (IRE)**[6] 2126 5-10-11 0 LucyGardner(3) 93
(Sue Gardner) *mid-div: rdn and outpcd by ldrs 3f out: styd on fnl f* **25/1**

322- 7 2 **Oskar's Eva (IRE)**[246] 4520 5-10-7 0 MichaelByrne 85
(Tim Vaughan) *led at stdy pce: rdn and hdd 2f out: sn wknd* **10/3**[2]

8 13 **Buachaill Beag** 4-10-7 0 [1] PhilipDonovan(7) 79
(Fergal O'Brien) *t.k.h in rr: bhd fnl 3f* **33/1**

0 9 98 **Annie'sboydave**[156] 558 5-10-7 0 ArchieBellamy(7)
(Peter Pritchard) *a in rr: sddle slipped by 1/2-way: virtually p.u 4f out: t.o* **100/1**

3m 56.9s (13.00) **Going Correction** +0.25s/f (Yiel) **9** Ran SP% **115.2**
Speed ratings: **77,76,75,74,73 72,71,65,16**
CSF £113.53 TOTE £18.60: £4.10, £2.40, £2.20; EX 109.00 Trifecta £722.20.
Owner Keith And Sue Lowry **Bred** Mrs S Lowry **Trained** Llancarfan, Vale Of Glamorgan

FOCUS
Probably a modest bumper. It's been rated around the balance of the fourth, fifth and sixth.
T/Plt: £116.50 to a £1 stake. Pool: £62,974.37 - 394.29 winning tickets T/Qpdt: £33.90 to a £1 stake. Pool: £4,863.57 - 106.00 winning tickets **Richard Lowther**

1998 PLUMPTON (L-H)
Monday, November 2

OFFICIAL GOING: Chase course - good (good to soft in places; 7.3), hurdles course: good to soft
Wind: virtually nil Weather: bright and sunny

2251 DOWNLOAD THE FREE ATTHERACES APP MAIDEN HURDLE (9 hdls) 1m 7f 195y
1:20 (1:20) (Class 5) 4-Y-O+ £2,274 (£667; £333; £166)

Form RPR

1 **Itsnowcato**[410] 4-10-11 0 MauriceLinehan(3) 113+
(Ben Pauling) *chsd ldr: nt fluent 2nd: upsides ldr sn after 3 out: led 2 out: styd on wl flat: rdn out* **9/1**

3 2 3 **Baltic Storm (IRE)**[20] 1895 4-11-0 0 DenisO'Regan 110
(Charlie Mann) *hld up in tch in midfield: clsd to chse ldrs 5th: trckd ldng pair after 3 out: pressed ldr between last 2: rdn last: no ex and btn fnl 150yds: wknd towards fin* **4/1**[2]

2-4 3 10 **Oulamayo (FR)**[30] 1758 4-11-0 0 HarrySkelton 104
(Dan Skelton) *j.lft at times: led: mstke 2nd: rdn and hdd 2 out: btn 3rd whn mstke last: wknd flat* **9/2**[3]

050- 4 5 **Stonegate**[236] 4715 5-11-0 0 JamieMoore 98
(Gary Moore) *chsd ldrs: nt fluent 3 out: effrt in 4th and little rspnse after 3 out: wl hld 2 out* **6/5**[1]

3 5 8 **Takeitfromalady (IRE)**[14] 1998 6-10-7 0 (v) PaddyBradley(7) 90
(Lee Carter) *midfield: 6th and outpcd after 5th: mstke 3 out: wnt 5th but no imp bef 2 out* **8/1**

6 8 **Fine Tune (IRE)**[39] 4-10-11 0 ThomasGarner(3) 84
(Linda Jewell) *midfield but nvr on terms w ldrs: 8th and wl btn after 6th: mstke 2 out* **200/1**

45 7 1 3/4 **Silver Dixie (USA)**[25] 1822 5-11-0 0 RichieMcLernon 82
(Peter Hedger) *hld up wl off the pce in rr: sme prog after 5th: 7th and no ch bef 3 out: no imp* **16/1**

/ 8 7 **Cantor**[570] 7-11-0 0 MattieBatchelor 74
(Daniel O'Brien) *hld up off the pce in midfield: dropped towards rr and lost tch after 5th: rdn after 3 out: wnt rt next: kpt on flat: t.o* **80/1**

8 dht **Guaracha**[34] 4-10-9 0 RyanWhile(5) 77
(Bill Turner) *mstkes: dropped to rr 2nd: blnd and rdr lost iron briefly 5th: sn lost tch: modest hdwy after 3 out: t.o* **40/1**

-0 10 3 3/4 **Notebook**[20] 1898 4-11-0 0 TrevorWhelan 71
(Martin Smith) *nt fluent in rr: n.d: t.o* **66/1**

0 11 8 **Montecito (FR)**[30] 1758 5-11-0 0 MarcGoldstein 64
(Chris Gordon) *mstke and pckd 1st: chsd ldrs tl dropped out rapidly after 5th: t.o* **50/1**

20 12 3/4 **Normandy King (IRE)**[16] 1979 4-10-9 0 AlanJohns(5) 63
(Tim Vaughan) *in rr: reminders and no hdwy after 6th: n.d: t.o* **66/1**

P- 13 23 **Rectitude**[212] 5144 4-10-2 0 (t) MrFTett(5) 35
(Henry Tett) *in tch in midfield: hdwy to chse ldrs and clr in ldng quintet after 5th: fdd rapidly after 3 out: t.o* **200/1**

3m 53.5s (-7.30) **Going Correction** -0.475s/f (Good) **13** Ran SP% **120.2**
Speed ratings (Par 103): **99,97,92,90,86 82,81,77,77,75 71,71,59**
CSF £45.88 TOTE £14.10: £2.90, £1.90, £1.90; EX 55.70 Trifecta £242.00.
Owner Genesis Racing Partnership II **Bred** Usk Valley Stud **Trained** Bourton-On-The-Water, Gloucs

FOCUS
All bends divided with all races run over minimum advertised trips. The going remained officially good, good to soft in places, though the rider of the runner-up in the first race felt it was soft. This opening maiden hurdle can go to a decent sort with the very useful hurdler/chaser Pendra taking it three years ago and the smart Seedling winning it last season. Following a rather ragged start, not many got into this year's renewal, but the race should produce a few winners. The winner is entitled to rate higher on his Flat form, as is the second, while the third has been rated in line with his bumper form. The race could be rated higher but the sixth finished plenty close enough and the time was modest.

2252 ATTHERACES APP ON IPHONE AND ANDROID MARES' NOVICES' HURDLE (12 hdls) 2m 4f 114y
1:50 (1:50) (Class 4) 4-Y-O+ £3,249 (£954; £477; £238)

Form RPR

24-1 1 **Girly Girl (IRE)**[19] 1908 6-10-10 0 HarrySkelton 111+
(Dan Skelton) *mde all: mstke 2nd: rdn after 3 out: wnt lft next: styd on wl flat: rdn out* **5/2**[2]

/F5- 2 3 1/2 **Catherines Well**[277] 3940 6-10-10 0 TomO'Brien 109+
(Philip Hobbs) *chsd ldrs: wnt 2nd 9th: effrt after next: no imp whn j.lft last: kpt on but no imp flat* **5/2**[2]

10- 3 16 **Angel Face**[205] 5277 4-10-10 0 PaulMoloney 95
(Alan King) *hld up in last pair: hdwy into midfield 5th: wnt 3rd sn after 9th: j. slowly next: sn nudged along and no hdwy: wl btn next* **6/4**[1]

0-0 4 18 **Betsy Boo Boo**[176] 227 6-10-10 0 DavidEngland 80
(Michael Roberts) *mstkes: chsd wnr tl 9th: sn drvn and outpcd: wl btn 4th next: wknd: t.o* **150/1**

5 12 **Attractive Liason (IRE)**[211] 5-10-10 0 BrendanPowell 67
(Neil Mulholland) *chsd ldrs: bmpd 2nd: 5th and pushed along after 9th: sn btn: wknd next: t.o* **8/1**[3]

00 6 11 **Gentle Mel (IRE)**[16] 1979 7-10-10 0 IanPopham 57
(Anabel K Murphy) *midfield: in tch tl 8th: sn rdn and lost tch: t.o whn blnd 3 out* **100/1**

46P- 7 1 **Loves Destination**[215] 5093 4-10-7 0 ThomasGarner(3) 56
(Chris Gordon) *hld up in last pair: j.rt 3rd: rdn and lost tch after 8th: t.o 3 out* **66/1**

005/ P **Generous June (IRE)**[614] 4495 7-10-10 0 MarcGoldstein
(Paddy Butler) *chsd ldrs: j.rt and bmpd rival 2nd: sn dropped to midfield: bhd and reminder 4th: lost tch after 8th: t.o whn p.u after 3 out* **50/1**

4F P **Dear Lottie (FR)**[23] 1845 4-10-10 0 JamieMoore
(Gary Moore) *hld up in tch: in last trio after 5th: lost tch rapidly after 8th: t.o whn dived and blnd next: immediately p.u* **20/1**

5m 7.4s (-9.60) **Going Correction** -0.475s/f (Good) **9** Ran SP% **118.1**
Speed ratings (Par 105): **99,97,91,84,80 75,75, ,**
CSF £9.54 TOTE £3.30: £1.20, £1.10, £1.20; EX 9.10 Trifecta £15.40.
Owner T Crowe **Bred** Sean McNamara **Trained** Alcester, Warwicks

FOCUS
The ground was changed to good to soft on the hurdles track before this race. An interesting mares' novice hurdle and another race that has gone to a useful sort in recent years with the subsequent dual Listed hurdle winner Carole's Spirit successful in 2013. Three dominated the betting this time and they filled the first three places, but despite a modest pace and again few getting into it, the form does look solid. The winner has been rated as building on her bumper form, while the second sets the level.

2253 ATTHERACES IN THE APP STORE H'CAP HURDLE (9 hdls) 1m 7f 195y
2:20 (2:20) (Class 4) (0-105,105) 3-Y-O+ £3,249 (£954; £477; £238)

Form RPR

5-P4 1 **Flashman**[29] 1770 6-11-9 **102** (b) JoshuaMoore 110+
(Gary Moore) *led after 1st: sn clr and mde rest: nt fluent 6th: 5 l clr and rdn bef 2 out: kpt on and nvr seriously chal: rdn out* **11/2**[2]

0P-3 2 6 **Keppel Isle (IRE)**[20] 1893 6-11-0 **93** JamieMoore 96
(Laura Mongan) *in tch in midfield: hdwy to chse ldr 4th: rdn and dropped to 3rd after 3 out: hrd drvn bef 2 out: rallied to chse wnr again flat: kpt on but nvr threatened wnr* **10/1**

4F41 3 4 1/2 **Native Display (IRE)**[14] 2000 5-11-12 **105** AndrewTinkler 105
(Nicky Henderson) *hld up in tch in midfield: hdwy to chse ldrs after 4th: wnt 2nd after 3 out: effrt bnd bef next: no imp and hld last: lost 2nd flat: sn wknd* **2/1**[1]

6600 4 4 **Hawk Gold (IRE)**[14] 2004 11-9-7 **79** oh17 (b) MissBHampson(7) 76
(Michelle Bryant) *hld up in rr: hdwy 4th: 5th and in tch after 5th: effrt after 3 out: 4th and no imp whn mstke and pckd 2 out: kpt on same pce after* **100/1**

/13- 5 7 **Moon Trip**[74] 5189 6-11-9 **102** MarkGrant 91
(Geoffrey Deacon) *in tch: dropped to last pair and pushed along 4th: lost tch after 5th: no ch but styd on to pass btn horses bef 2 out* **9/1**

4352 6 1 1/4 **Createur (IRE)**[25] 1823 4-11-7 **105** (t[1]) AlanJohns(5) 93
(Tim Vaughan) *hld up in last trio: sme hdwy after 5th: clsd qckly on ldrs on downhill run after next: drvn and no prog bef 2 out: wknd between last 2* **11/2**[2]

6340 7 6 **Warrant Officer**[14] 2000 5-10-11 **90** MarcGoldstein 73
(Sheena West) *chsd ldr after 1st tl 4th: struggling u.p after 5th: wknd 3 out* **14/1**

10-P 8 3/4 **King's Road**[49] 354 10-11-10 **103** (t) IanPopham 85
(Anabel K Murphy) *a bhd: mstke 1st: lost tch after 5th* **50/1**

54-0 9 9 **Nouailhas**[175] 240 9-9-8 **80** oh2 ow1 MrJPearce(7) 54
(Daniel O'Brien) *chsd ldrs tl 3rd: lost pl and pushed along after next: bhd after 6th* **25/1**

225/ 10 21 **Diamond Life**[1060] 2896 9-11-12 **105** DenisO'Regan 60
(Mark Pitman) *led tl after 1st: in tch in midfield after: rdn and struggling after 5th: wknd after 3 out: t.o* **11/1**

0-23 P **Air Of Glory (IRE)**[35] 1676 5-11-2 **102** (tp) MrZBaker(7)
(Martin Bosley) *midfield: struggling after 5th: wl btn 3 out: t.o whn p.u bef next: burst blood vessel* **7/1**[3]

3m 49.6s (-11.20) **Going Correction** -0.475s/f (Good)
WFA 4 from 5yo+ 7lb **11** Ran SP% **117.5**
Speed ratings (Par 105): **109,106,103,101,98 97,94,94,89,79**
CSF £58.12 CT £147.51 TOTE £6.70: £2.60, £3.00, £1.50; EX 65.10 Trifecta £231.30.
Owner Andrew Bradmore **Bred** Avenue Farm Stud **Trained** Lower Beeding, W Sussex

FOCUS
A fair handicap hurdle and another race where positive tactics paid off. The pace was decent and the time was almost 4sec quicker than the opener. The second has been rated to his best, and the fourth to his mark.

2254 "STABLE STARS" COMING SOON ON ATTHERACES.COM NOVICES' H'CAP CHASE (18 fncs) 3m 1f 152y
2:55 (2:55) (Class 4) (0-105,103) 4-Y-0+ £3,898 (£1,144; £572; £286)

Form				RPR
P-14	1		**Ya Hafed**124 [600] 7-10-7 84 ... MattieBatchelor (Sheena West) *in tch: hdwy to chse ldrs 12th: wnt 2nd 14th: rdn and clsd after 3 out: 2 l down between last 2: styd on to ld fnl 50yds* 4/1[3]	97+
334	2	1	**Sky Watch (IRE)**43 [1592] 8-11-11 102 ...(t) DaveCrosse (Brian Barr) *j.w but rt at times: w ldr tl led 8th: 5 l clr sn after 3 out: drvn between last 2: kpt on: hdd and no ex fnl 50yds* 9/2	111+
2-62	3	36	**The Cider Maker**17 [1947] 5-11-12 103 ...(t) BrendanPowell (Colin Tizzard) *in tch: j.rt 1st: chsd ldrs 4th: 8 l down and rdn whn mstke 3 out: sn wknd* 3/1[1]	84
53P6	4	6	**Time Is Tickin**43 [1592] 9-11-5 96 ... MarcGoldstein (Diana Grissell) *led tl 8th: chsd ldr: rdn after 12th: lost 2nd 14th: sn wknd: t.o 3 out* 4/1[3]	67
UP6F	F		**Yes I Will**30 [1757] 6-10-8 85 ...(t) KielanWoods (Linda Jewell) *hld up in tch in rr: mstke 9th: fell next* 12/1	
-22P	P		**Winged Express (IRE)**24 [1838] 6-10-12 89 ... IanPopham (Alexandra Dunn) *mstkes: chsd ldrs tl dropped to last pair 6th: rdn after 12th: struggling whn blnd bdly 14th: rdr lost irons: nt rcvr and p.u bef next* 7/2[2]	

6m 40.6s (-10.10) **Going Correction** -0.30s/f (Good) 6 Ran SP% **113.1**
Speed ratings (Par 105): **103,102,91,89,**
CSF £22.17 TOTE £5.50: £2.50, £2.20; EX 21.40 Trifecta £57.20.
Owner Gerald West **Bred** Lady Bland & Miss Anthea Gibson-Fleming **Trained** Falmer, E Sussex

FOCUS
A fair staying novices' handicap and a thrilling finish, though the pace was ordinary and a few of these didn't jump that well. The second has been rated in line with the best of his 2015 hurdle runs.

2255 VISIT OUR JUMPS MICROSITE ATTHERACES.COM/JUMPS H'CAP CHASE (14 fncs) 2m 3f 164y
3:30 (3:30) (Class 5) (0-100,93) 4-Y-0+ £2,729 (£801; £400; £200)

Form				RPR
433-	1		**Ball Hopper (IRE)**204 [5287] 11-10-10 77 ...(p) RichieMcLernon (Richenda Ford) *chsd ldrs: clsd to join ldr and mstke 11th: rdn to ld after next: drew clr between last 2: eased towards fin* 9/2[3]	93+
1	2	14	**Killabraher Cross (IRE)**14 [1999] 8-11-12 93 ... MarcGoldstein (Paddy Butler) *chsd ldr tl led sn after 10th: jnd next: rdn and hdd after 3 out: btn between last 2: mstke last: wknd flat* 13/8[1]	95
FPP/	3	11	**Goring Two (IRE)**602 [4720] 10-10-1 73 ...(p) CharlieDeutsch(5) (Anna Newton-Smith) *in tch: chsd ldrs: 6th: clsd and ev ch 11th: mstke 3 out: btn bef next: wknd between last 2* 6/1	64
4012	4	3/4	**Dancing Dik**14 [1999] 10-11-8 89 ...(b) TomO'Brien (Paul Henderson) *led: hdd sn after 10th: sn drvn and btn: 4th and wl hld 3 out* 2/1[2]	77
0P-P	5	8	**Petit Ecuyer (FR)**177 [211] 9-11-5 86 ... DaveCrosse (Dai Williams) *in tch: mstke 4th: last and blnd 6th: pushed along and struggling after 9th: wl bhd 3 out* 14/1	71

5m 1.25s (-6.05) **Going Correction** -0.30s/f (Good) 5 Ran SP% **110.6**
Speed ratings (Par 103): **100,94,90,89,86**
CSF £12.77 TOTE £5.30: £1.80, £1.30; EX 12.00 Trifecta £39.40.
Owner Mr & Mrs K B Snook **Bred** Mrs E Tector **Trained** Brockhampton Green, Dorset

FOCUS
A modest handicap chase which went to the only one of the five runners that wasn't a previous C&D winner. The easy winner has been rated back to the best of his 2014 figures.

2256 WATCH REPLAYS ON THE ATR APP CONDITIONAL JOCKEYS' H'CAP HURDLE (12 hdls) 2m 4f 114y
4:00 (4:00) (Class 5) (0-100,98) 3-Y-0+ £2,274 (£667; £333; £166)

Form				RPR
P60	1		**Dragon City**20 [1898] 5-10-5 85 ...(t) TommyDowling(8) (Charlie Mann) *mde all: rdn and hit 2 out: r.o flat: rdn out* 9/2[1]	86+
00-0	2	1/2	**Uranox (FR)**146 [675] 7-10-0 72 oh3 ... DanielHiskett (Michael Roberts) *hld up in tch in last pair: clsd into midfield 3 out: effrt bef 2 out: ev ch and nt fluent last: r.o to go 2nd nr fin* 14/1[3]	71
13-3	3	1/2	**Epsom Flyer**135 [449] 5-11-4 98 ... PaddyBradley(8) (Pat Phelan) *chsd wnr tl 2 out: stl pressing wnr and u.p between last 2: lft 2nd again last: styd on: lost 2nd cl home* 9/2[1]	97
0-S0	4	hd	**Walk Of Gleams**19 [1910] 6-10-10 82 ... JeremiahMcGrath (Anna Newton-Smith) *chsd ldrs: effrt bef 2 out: kpt on u.p flat* 100/1	80
6PP	5	3/4	**Prairie Hawk (USA)**34 [1691] 10-10-0 72 oh2 ...(t) BenPoste (Adrian Wintle) *chsd ldrs: effrt and pressing wnr 2 out: unable qck last: styd on same pce flat* 13/2[2]	70
3533	6	3	**Tilinisi (IRE)**19 [1912] 5-11-6 97 ... BenFfrenchDavis(5) (Phil Middleton) *hld up in tch towards rr: effrt on inner 2 out: no imp between last 2* 9/2[1]	93
4063	7	2	**Watchmetail (IRE)**12 [2015] 9-9-11 72 oh8 ... ThomasCheesman(3) (John Panvert) *hld up in tch towards rr: effrt bef 2 out: rdn and wknd flat* 16/1	65
3502	8	3/4	**Al Guwair (IRE)**12 [2015] 5-10-1 73 ... HarryBannister (Mark Hoad) *hld up in tch in rr: mstke 7th: effrt bef 2 out: sn btn* 9/2[1]	65
34-0	R		**Benability (IRE)**185 [65] 5-10-12 92 ... GeorgeBlackwell(8) (Tim Vaughan) *chsd ldrs: lost pl but stl wl in tch 9th: hdwy to press ldr 2 out: ev ch whn rn out and uns rdr last* 9/2[1]	95+

5m 22.4s (5.40) **Going Correction** -0.475s/f (Good) 9 Ran SP% **117.8**
Speed ratings (Par 103): **70,69,69,69,69 68,67,67,**
CSF £63.58 CT £302.41 TOTE £6.30: £1.50, £4.80, £2.50; EX 79.80 Trifecta £667.40.
Owner Earth Wind And Fire **Bred** Sir Eric Parker **Trained** Upper Lambourn, Berks

FOCUS
An open handicap hurdle as five co-favourites would suggest, but a messy content with the pace not picking up until approaching three from home and there was drama at the last. A step up from the winner, while the second and third set the level.
T/Plt: £63.90 to a £1 stake. Pool: £73,600.08 - 840.40 winning tickets T/Qpdt: £20.70 to a £1 stake. Pool: £5,888.99 - 209.55 winning tickets **Steve Payne**

2005 EXETER (R-H)
Tuesday, November 3

OFFICIAL GOING: Good to soft (soft in places) changing to soft (good to soft in places) after race 1 (1.20) changing to soft after race 4 (2.50)
Wind: almost nil Weather: rain/fog (heavy at times) Rails: Chase distances add 15 yards per race. Hurdle distances as advertised. Chase course on fresh ground.

2257 BATHWICK TYRES BIDEFORD "NATIONAL HUNT" NOVICES' HURDLE (11 hdls) 2m 5f 135y
1:20 (1:20) (Class 3) 4-Y-0+ £5,523 (£1,621; £810; £405)

Form				RPR
22-	1		**Yala Enki (FR)**234 [4769] 5-10-12 128 ... AidanColeman (Venetia Williams) *mde all: styd on strly fr 2 out: comf* 4/1[3]	135+
10-	2	16	**Duke Des Champs (IRE)**269 [4086] 5-10-12 0 ... RichardJohnson (Philip Hobbs) *mid-div: hdwy fr 8th: wnt 3rd 3 out: rdn and hld whn wnt 2nd 2 out: styd on same pce* 11/4[2]	122+
	3	13	**Fortunata Fashions**247 5-10-5 0 ... DarylJacob (Ben Case) *trckd wnr: rdn appr 3 out: lost 2nd 2 out: styd on same pce* 33/1	105+
3	4	7	**Minellacelebration (IRE)**14 [2005] 5-10-5 0 ... MrJNixon(7) (Katy Price) *trckd ldrs: rdn and lost pl appr 8th: styd on but no ch fr 2 out: wnt wl-btn 4th nring fin* 100/1	102
1-	5	1 1/2	**Walking In The Air (IRE)**218 [5077] 5-10-12 0 ... HarrySkelton (Dan Skelton) *mid-div: hmpd 1st: hdwy 6th: cl 3rd 8th: rdn appr 3 out: sn btn: lost 4th nring fin* 15/8[1]	104
3-	P		**Boa Island (IRE)**205 5-10-12 0 ...(t) SamTwiston-Davies (Paul Nicholls) *wnt lft 1st: mid-div: rdn after 6th: wknd bef 8th: t.o whn p.u bef 3 out* 8/1	
	P		**Westren Warrior (IRE)**89 [1207] 6-11-8 0 ... WillKennedy (Dr Richard Newland) *hld up towards rr: hdwy into midfield 6th: rdn next: wknd after 8th: p.u bef next* 17/2	
00-	P		**Pawn Star (IRE)**234 [4755] 5-10-12 0 ... RichieMcLernon (Emma Lavelle) *trckd ldrs: rdn after 6th: sn wknd: t.o whn p.u bef 3 out* 25/1	
	P		**Monsieur Murphy (IRE)**191 5-10-12 0 ... NoelFehily (Neil Mulholland) *a bhd: t.o whn p.u bef 3 out* 100/1	
00-3	P		**My Diamond (IRE)**159 [526] 4-10-9 0 ... MattGriffiths(3) (Laura Young) *a towards rr: t.o whn p.u bef 3 out* 200/1	
	F		**Gala Ball (IRE)**205 [5306] 5-10-12 0 ... TomO'Brien (Philip Hobbs) *mid-div: hdwy 6th: wnt cl 3rd briefly u.p appr 3 out: wknd 2 out: tired whn fell last* 25/1	101
3-6	P		**Motts Cross (IRE)**182 [124] 4-10-12 0 ... JamesDavies (Chris Down) *in tch tl wknd 7th: t.o whn p.u bef 3 out* 100/1	
	P		**All Kings (IRE)**206 6-10-12 0 ... ConorO'Farrell (Nigel Hawke) *in tch tl 7th: sn wknd: t.o whn p.u bef 3 out* 100/1	
5	P		**Contempt Of Court (IRE)**23 [1873] 6-10-12 0 ... DenisO'Regan (Mark Pitman) *a towards rr: t.o whn p.u bef 3 out* 100/1	

5m 36.5s (3.50) **Going Correction** +0.375s/f (Yiel)
WFA 4 from 5yo+ 8lb 14 Ran SP% **119.2**
Speed ratings (Par 107): **108,102,97,94,94 ,,,, ,,,**
CSF £15.12 TOTE £5.10: £1.70, £1.60, £7.60; EX 18.70 Trifecta £626.40.
Owner Hills Of Ledbury (Aga) **Bred** Esteve Rouchvarger Et Al **Trained** Kings Caple, H'fords

FOCUS
Hurdle distances as advertised and chases increased by 15yds. Conditions were unpleasant, with further rain making the ground testing - officially changed to soft after the opener - and visibility being limited due to the fog. Just five of the 14 runners were able to complete the course in what looked a fair novice hurdle, emphasising just how how work it was in the conditions. A step up from the winner, with the fourth helping to set the level.

2258 BATHWICK TYRES PLYMOUTH NOVICES' HURDLE (8 hdls) 2m 175y
1:50 (1:50) (Class 3) 4-Y-0+ £5,523 (£1,621; £810; £405)

Form				RPR
124-	1		**Yanworth**237 [4708] 5-10-12 0 ... BarryGeraghty (Alan King) *trckd ldrs: disp ld 3 out: shkn up to take narrow advantage whn mstke last: kpt on and wl on top at fin: cosily* 4/11[1]	138+
1-	2	1 1/4	**Welsh Shadow (IRE)**231 [4832] 5-10-12 0 ... HarrySkelton (Dan Skelton) *mid-div: hdwy after 3rd: disp ld 3 out tl jst bef last where stl ev ch: kpt on but a being readily hld by wnr* 3/1[2]	130+
5	3	4 1/2	**Barney Dwan (IRE)**48 [1555] 5-10-12 0 ... PaddyBrennan (Fergal O'Brien) *mid-div: hdwy after 5th: trckd ldrs 3 out: rdn bef next: wnt 3rd sn after: styd on but nt pce of front pair* 16/1	125+
	4	28	**Antiphony (IRE)** 4-10-12 0 ... RichardJohnson (Philip Hobbs) *racd keenly: trckd ldrs: led after 2nd: hdd 3 out: wknd next: t.o* 10/1[3]	97
/50-	5	12	**Royal Salute**227 [4921] 5-10-12 0 ... RyanMahon (Anthony Honeyball) *disp ld tl after 2nd: trckd ldr: rdn after 3 out: sn wknd: t.o* 25/1	85
5-30	6	2	**Bogoss Du Perret (FR)**133 [823] 4-10-5 0 ... MissBFrost(7) (Jimmy Frost) *trckd ldrs: rdn after 3 out: sn wknd: t.o* 66/1	83
0-0	7	2 1/4	**Up The Junction**39 [1644] 4-10-12 0 ... MichaelByrne (Tim Vaughan) *mid-div: wknd after 3 out: t.o* 100/1	81
0-	8	9	**Apple Pops**323 [3122] 5-10-5 0 ... MarkQuinlan (Neil Mulholland) *disp ld tl after 2nd: trckd ldrs: wknd 3 out: t.o* 100/1	65
0-40	9	41	**Culm Counsellor**9 [2091] 6-10-9 0 ...[1] GilesHawkins(3) (Chris Down) *racd keenly: in tch 2nd: wknd appr 3 out: t.o* 100/1	31
P0-	10	10	**Actonetaketwo**18 [3276] 5-9-12 0 ... HarryCobden(7) (Ron Hodges) *a in rr: t.o 3 out* 100/1	14
	P		**Chantecler**139 4-10-12 0 ... NoelFehily (Neil Mulholland) *a bhd: t.o whn p.u after 5th* 16/1	

(-255.50) course record 11 Ran SP% **128.5**
CSF £2.21 TOTE £1.40: £1.10, £1.20, £2.90; EX 2.00 Trifecta £8.00.
Owner John P McManus **Bred** Wood Farm Stud **Trained** Barbury Castle, Wilts

FOCUS
Visibility had worsened prior to this, with the fog properly setting back in. The market leaders dominated. The winner is a potential 145+ novice hurdler.

2259 SPORTINGBET HALDON GOLD CUP CHASE (A LIMITED H'CAP) (GRADE 2) (12 fncs) 2m 1f 109y
2:20 (2:20) (Class 1) 4-Y-O+ £35,593 (£13,356; £6,687; £3,331; £1,675)

Form RPR
424- **1** **Vibrato Valtat (FR)**[192] 5537 6-11-0 **157**...............(t) SamTwiston-Davies 162+
(Paul Nicholls) *trckd ldrs: chal 4 out: led next: drawing clr and in command whn mstke last: r.o wl* **5/2**[1]
03-2 **2** *4* **Third Intention (IRE)**[23] 1869 8-11-3 **160**........................(t) DarylJacob 158
(Colin Tizzard) *hld up bhd ldrs: tk clsr order 5th: rdn whn sltly outpcd appr 4 out: styd on wl between last 2: wnt 2nd run-in but no ch w wnr* **15/2**
22F- **3** *2 1/4* **God's Own (IRE)**[192] 5537 7-11-3 **160**........................ PaddyBrennan 157
(Tom George) *trckd ldrs: chal 4 out: rdn after 3 out: chsng wnr and hld whn wnt rt last: no ex whn lost 2nd sn after* **7/2**[3]
-343 **4** *5* **Dunraven Storm (IRE)**[10] 2059 10-10-5 **148**.............. RichardJohnson 144
(Philip Hobbs) *led: rdn and hdd whn nt fluent 3 out: kpt on same pce fr next* **7/2**[3]
14F- **5** *28* **Sire De Grugy (FR)**[207] 5252 9-11-10 **167**......................... JamieMoore 150
(Gary Moore) *trckd ldrs: blnd bdly 4th: sn rcvrd: rdn to chal 4 out tl 2 out: sn wknd: eased run-in* **11/4**[2]

4m 26.3s (7.30) **Going Correction** +0.85s/f (Soft) **5 Ran SP% 111.4**
Speed ratings (Par 115): **116,114,113,110,97**
CSF £18.83 TOTE £3.30: £1.70, £2.90; EX 20.20 Trifecta £48.00.
Owner Axom XLIII **Bred** Mme C Duperret & Mlle A-M Duperret **Trained** Ditcheat, Somerset

FOCUS
This wouldn't have been a vintage edition of the race, but it was a good-quality handicap none the less and produced quite a taking winner. The cosy winner has been rated in line with the best of his novice form. The second is probably the best guide to the level, with the ground too soft for the third and fourth.

2260 VIX TECHNOLOGY NOVICES' CHASE (18 fncs) 3m 54y
2:50 (2:50) (Class 2) 4-Y-O+ £12,974 (£4,158; £2,310)

Form RPR
10-3 **1** **Native River (IRE)**[24] 1846 5-11-1 0..................... BrendanPowell 150+
(Colin Tizzard) *trckd ldrs: pushed along after 12th: rdn to chal 4 out: led sn after 3 out: clr whn hit last: styd on wl* **11/8**[1]
60-2 **2** *16* **Abracadabra Sivola (FR)**[23] 1867 5-11-1 130.............. RichardJohnson 134+
(Nick Williams) *led: hit 7th: nt fluent 13th: rdn whn jnd 4 out: hdd sn after 3 out: no ex appr last* **13/2**
35-0 **3** *26* **The Tourard Man (IRE)**[24] 1848 9-11-1 0................ WayneHutchinson 105
(Alan King) *trckd ldrs: lft 2nd after 11th tl 14th: sn rdn: grad fdd fr 4 out: t.o* **9/4**[2]
51P- **P** **Flintham**[207] 5254 6-11-1 0...(p) NicodeBoinville
(Mark Bradstock) *j. sltly lft at times: pressed ldr: nudged along 10th: wknd rapidly and p.u after next* **7/2**[3]
00B- **P** **Art Deco Marsal (FR)**[268] 4107 5-11-1 0.......................... DarylJacob
(Robert Walford) *chsd ldrs: dropped to last and nudged along fr 4th: blnd bdly 10th: sn p.u* **100/1**

6m 22.0s (12.70) **Going Correction** +0.85s/f (Soft) **5 Ran SP% 109.4**
Speed ratings (Par 109): **112,106,98,,**
CSF £10.07 TOTE £1.60: £1.10, £2.80; EX 6.80 Trifecta £20.30.
Owner Brocade Racing **Bred** Fred Mackey **Trained** Milborne Port, Dorset

FOCUS
Three of the five finished in this decent staying novice chase and those who did came home at intervals, the conditions taking a toll. The second has been rated as improving in line with the best of his hurdle form.

2261 SMITH & WILLIAMSON H'CAP CHASE (18 fncs) 3m 54y
3:20 (3:20) (Class 3) (0-130,130) 4-Y-£07,912 (£2,337; £1,168; £585; £292)

Form RPR
F40- **1** **Saroque (IRE)**[223] 4986 8-11-6 **124**........................... AidanColeman 132+
(Venetia Williams) *mde all: styd on strly fr 3 out: hit last: rdn out* **10/1**
32-3 **2** *1 1/4* **Delgany Demon**[163] 461 7-11-7 **125**.............................. TrevorWhelan 129
(Neil King) *hld up towards rr: hdwy after 14th: sn rdn: j.lft last 4: wnt 2nd 2 out: styd on but a being hld fr last* **10/1**
6PU- **3** *3/4* **Umberto D'Olivate (FR)**[211] 5184 7-11-6 **124**.................. TomCannon 126
(Robert Walford) *prom: rdn after 14th: styd on same pce fr 4 out* **14/1**
153- **4** *9* **Sun Wild Life (FR)**[216] 5100 5-11-7 **125**..................(p) NickSchofield 119
(Robert Walford) *hld up towards rr: hdwy after 14th: sn rdn: styd on fr next: wnt 4th bef last* **28/1**
16-2 **5** *3 1/2* **Midnight Lira**[31] 1755 8-11-7 **125**.................................. JamesBest 116
(Caroline Keevil) *mid-div: hdwy after 11th: rdn and ev ch appr 4 out: lost 2nd and sltly hmpd 2 out: wknd last* **20/1**
221- **6** *14* **Russe Blanc (FR)**[233] 4783 8-11-5 **123**.................(p) CharliePoste 99
(Kerry Lee) *chsd ldrs: rdn after 14th: outpcd next: no threat after* **12/1**
-444 **P** **Foundation Man (IRE)**[20] 1902 8-11-4 **122**..............(v) RichardJohnson
(Jonjo O'Neill) *mid-div: struggling 11th: sn bhd: p.u after 14th* **20/1**
25P- **P** **Big Society (IRE)**[193] 5518 9-10-12 **123**..................(b[1]) PaulNO'Brien[(7)]
(Harry Whittington) *slow 1st: sn detached in last: t.o whn p.u bef 10th* **7/1**[3]
240- **P** **Tinker Time (IRE)**[201] 5358 7-11-10 **128**......................... LiamHeard
(Bob Buckler) *trckd ldrs tl 8th: nvr travelling after and sn in rr: p.u after 10th* **8/1**
214- **P** **Quite By Chance**[201] 5358 6-11-4 **122**.......................... DarylJacob
(Colin Tizzard) *a towards rr: rdn after 14th: nvr threatened: wknd after 3 out: p.u after 2 out* **12/1**
4-P1 **P** **Whats Left (IRE)**[26] 1820 7-11-8 **126**............................ NoelFehily
(Neil Mulholland) *mid-div: pushed along after 13th: rdn after next: nvr threatened: wknd after 3 out: p.u bef last* **6/1**[1]
P46- **P** **Ziga Boy (FR)**[213] 5138 6-11-6 **124**........................ WayneHutchinson
(Alan King) *trckd ldrs: rdn after 14th: wknd after 2 out: p.u bef last* **13/2**[2]
3-12 **P** **Belmount (IRE)**[42] 1616 6-11-12 **130**.................. SamTwiston-Davies
(Nigel Twiston-Davies) *trckd ldrs: rdn after 12th: qckly lost pl: tailing off whn p.u bef 4 out* **6/1**[1]

6m 30.2s (20.90) **Going Correction** +0.85s/f (Soft) **13 Ran SP% 118.7**
Speed ratings (Par 107): **99,98,98,95,94 89,,,,,,,**
CSF £102.32 CT £1409.95 TOTE £11.80: £4.10, £3.80, £5.00; EX 136.60 Trifecta £2149.30.
Owner A Brooks **Bred** Miss Mary Condon **Trained** Kings Caple, H'fords

FOCUS
Less than half the field managed to complete in this staying handicap, with the winner making all. The winner has been rated back to the level of last season's Wincanton second.

2262 BATHWICK TYRES H'CAP HURDLE (12 hdls) 2m 7f 25y
3:50 (3:51) (Class 4) (0-115,115) 4-Y-O+ £3,249 (£954; £477; £238)

Form RPR
6-22 **1** **Monbeg Gold (IRE)**[44] 1597 5-11-11 **114**..................... RichardJohnson 131+
(Jonjo O'Neill) *trckd ldrs: led after 3 out: j.lft last 2 but wl in command: easily* **3/1**[1]
43F- **2** *5* **Say My Name (IRE)**[197] 5434 4-11-9 **112**............................ LiamHeard 118
(Bob Buckler) *mid-div: hdwy after 9th: sn rdn to chse ldrs: styd on to snatch 2nd fnl strides but no ch w wnr* **25/1**
500- **3** *shd* **Millanisi Boy**[241] 4625 6-11-12 **115**.................................. DarylJacob 121
(Richard Woollacott) *mid-div: hdwy after 9th: rdn to chse ldrs next: wnt 2nd after 2 out: no ex whn lost 2nd fnl strides* **16/1**
00-2 **4** *9* **Captainofindustry (IRE)**[17] 1964 6-11-4 **107**..............(p) DenisO'Regan 104
(Mark Pitman) *pressed ldr: led after 7th: rdn and hdd 2 out: sn no ex* **8/1**
0 **5** *30* **Captain Canada**[68] 1390 8-11-12 **115**.......................... NickScholfield 81
(Katie Stephens) *hld up towards rr: gd hdwy to press ldr after 9th: rdn bef next: wknd bef 2 out* **80/1**
55- **6** *13* **Bredon Hill Lad**[253] 4409 8-10-5 **97**.......................... LucyGardner[(3)] 50
(Sue Gardner) *mid-div tl lost pl 8th: nvr bk on terms: t.o* **3/1**[1]
42-0 **7** *3 1/2* **Sandy Beach**[13] 2013 5-11-5 **115**...............................(t) PaulO'Brien[(7)] 65
(Colin Tizzard) *mid-div: rdn after 9th: wknd next: t.o* **16/1**
2F-5 **8** *1 1/2* **An Tarbh Og (IRE)**[44] 1597 7-11-2 **105**............................ JamesBest 53
(Caroline Keevil) *mid-div: hdwy after 9th: sn rdn: wknd 3 out: t.o* **15/2**[3]
32-5 **9** *4 1/2* **Floral Spinner**[15] 2002 8-11-7 **115**................................ RyanWhile[(5)] 59
(Bill Turner) *trckd ldrs: rdn after 8th: wknd bef 3 out: t.o* **16/1**
F3-5 **10** *4 1/2* **City Supreme (IRE)**[186] 63 5-11-4 **107**......................(t) AidanColeman 46
(Anthony Honeyball) *mid-div: rdn in rr after 8th: sn wknd: t.o* **6/1**[2]
2P6U **11** *1 3/4* **Friendly Society (IRE)**[13] 2014 10-10-8 **100**..............(b) JamesBanks[(3)] 37
(Noel Williams) *led tl 7th: sn rdn and jumping lft: wknd bef 3 out: t.o* **20/1**
2250 **P** **Rior (IRE)**[50] 1547 8-10-7 **103**.................................. MrGTreacy[(7)]
(Paul Henderson) *towards rr: lost tch 8th: p.u bef 3 out* **16/1**
5-30 **P** **Tuffstuff**[147] 669 7-11-0 **103**..(t) CharliePoste
(Brian Barr) *hld up towards rr: hdwy u.p into midfield after 9th: wknd bef next: p.u bef 2 out* **50/1**
P **Badilou (FR)**[51] 4-11-4 **110**........................... JeremiahMcGrath[(3)]
(Martin Hill) *mid-div tl wknd appr 3 out: sn eased: p.u bef 2 out* **14/1**

6m 17.3s (18.30) **Going Correction** +0.85s/f (Soft)
WFA 4 from 5yo+ 8lb **14 Ran SP% 129.2**
Speed ratings (Par 105): **102,100,100,97,86 82,80,80,78,77 76,,,**
CSF £87.94 CT £1101.60 TOTE £3.40: £2.10, £8.60, £5.50; EX 102.40 Trifecta £955.10.
Owner Martin Broughton Racing Partners 2 **Bred** Frank Marshall **Trained** Cheltenham, Gloucs

FOCUS
A trio of handicap debutants came clear in what was a modest handicap. A big step up from the first two for a stamina test, with the third the best guide to the level.

2263 RACING UK ANYWHERE H'CAP HURDLE (10 hdls) 2m 2f 111y
4:20 (4:20) (Class 5) (0-100,100) 3-Y-O+ £2,599 (£763; £381; £190)

Form RPR
443- **1** **Brave Deed (IRE)**[213] 5148 9-11-4 **92**........................ NickScholfield 105+
(Jeremy Scott) *mid-div on outer: hdwy after 7th: led 2 out: sn clr: styd on wl: comf* **7/1**[2]
6-24 **2** *4* **Doctor Look Here (IRE)**[165] 433 5-11-9 **100**.............. LucyGardner[(3)] 108+
(Sue Gardner) *mid-div on outer: hdwy to chal after 7th: led gng strly bef next: hdd 2 out: sn hld: styd on same pce* **7/1**[2]
036- **3** *8* **Precious Ground**[240] 4651 5-11-1 **89**................................ JamesBest 87
(Kevin Bishop) *mid-div: hdwy appr 3 out: sn rdn: wnt 3rd between last 2: styd on wout threatening front pair* **9/1**
P04- **4** *8* **Buckboru (IRE)**[231] 4825 7-11-3 **91**........................... RobertDunne 84
(Laura Young) *mid-div: hdwy 7th: rdn and ev ch briefly sn after: hld whn mstke 3 out: fdd fr next* **16/1**
6-6P **5** *8* **Mexican Border (GER)**[26] 1823 6-11-4 **95**............ JeremiahMcGrath[(3)] 77
(Martin Hill) *hld up towards rr: sme hdwy after 7th: rdn next: no further imp* **20/1**
-PPP **6** *1 1/2* **Definitely Better (IRE)**[13] 2022 7-11-7 **95**................... PaddyBrennan 76
(Tom George) *hld up towards rr: midfield 6th: rdn after next: wknd after 3 out* **20/1**
P **7** *17* **Arquebusier (FR)**[19] 1933 5-11-1 **92**.......................(p) JamesBanks[(3)] 56
(Emma Baker) *mid-div: rdn after 7th: wknd next* **40/1**
60-6 **8** *1* **Dunmallet Belle**[42] 1618 6-11-1 **89**..............................(p) JamesDavies 52
(Tom Symonds) *led: rdn and hdd appr 3 out: sn wknd* **10/1**
11/- **9** *16* **Sarenice (FR)**[673] 3426 9-11-6 **94**............................. ConorO'Farrell 41
(Jimmy Frost) *racd keenly: towards rr: sme prog after 7th: nvr threatened: wknd next* **20/1**
00P- **10** *23* **What Larks (IRE)**[270] 4069 7-11-12 **100**........................ DaveCrosse 24
(Hugo Froud) *mid-div tl wknd appr 3 out: t.o* **33/1**
-561 **11** *1/2* **Ice Konig (FR)**[64] 824 6-11-5 **100**................................ PaulO'Brien[(7)] 23
(Jimmy Frost) *a towards rr: t.o* **11/1**
03-0 **12** *26* **Petite Fantasie**[177] 222 6-10-12 **86**............................. TomCannon
(Mark Gillard) *trckd ldrs: rdn and ev ch after 7th: wknd bef next: t.o* **33/1**
00-5 **P** **Tomsk (FR)**[167] 396 5-11-1 **89**...................................... MichaelByrne
(Tim Vaughan) *trckd ldrs: rdn after 7th: wknd bef next: p.u bef 2 out* **20/1**
0-3P **P** **Positive Vibes**[160] 514 6-11-3 **91**.................................. TomO'Brien
(Richard Woollacott) *mid-div: struggling 6th: wknd after next: p.u bef 3 out* **25/1**
0-45 **P** **Haverstock**[15] 2000 5-10-13 **87**..................................(p) IanPopham
(Caroline Keevil) *a towards rr: struggling 6th: t.o whn p.u bef 3 out* **8/1**[3]
-543 **P** **Sheer Poetry (IRE)**[144] 712 4-11-12 **100**........................ DarylJacob
(Richard Woollacott) *chsd ldrs tl wknd after 7th: t.o whn p.u bef next* **16/1**
0P-5 **P** **War And Contrition (IRE)**[17] 1964 6-11-11 **99**............ RichardJohnson
(Charlie Longsdon) *mid-div tl wknd 7th: p.u bef next* **9/2**[1]
00-P **P** **Prince Of Thieves (IRE)**[185] 90 5-11-2 **90**...............(t) AidanColeman
(Anthony Honeyball) *mid-div: rdn after 7th: sn wknd and eased: p.u bef 3 out* **16/1**

4m 55.8s (13.10) **Going Correction** +0.85s/f (Soft)
WFA 4 from 5yo+ 7lb **18 Ran SP% 130.6**
Speed ratings (Par 103): **106,104,100,97,94 93,86,86,79,69 69,58,,,,,,**
CSF £52.32 CT £466.89 TOTE £7.40: £1.50, £2.30, £2.80, £5.50; EX 77.50 Trifecta £825.50.
Owner Gale Force Seven **Bred** C W Gash **Trained** Brompton Regis, Somerset

FOCUS
A wide-open handicap, the form of which is moderate. Big steps up from the first two, with the third and fourth setting the level.
T/Plt: £94.40 to a £1 stake. Pool: £78,217.01 - 604.37 winning units. T/Qpdt: £54.90 to a £1 stake. Pool: £5,005.34 - 67.35 winning units. **Tim Mitchell**

The Form Book Jumps 2015-16, Raceform Ltd, Newbury, RG14 5SJ

[1866]CHEPSTOW (L-H)

Wednesday, November 4

OFFICIAL GOING: Soft (6.1)
Wind: almost nil Weather: light rain

2264 GEORGE SMITH HORSEBOXES CONDITIONAL JOCKEYS' H'CAP HURDLE (8 hdls) 2m 11y

1:10 (1:10) (Class 5) (0-100,99) 3-Y-O+ £2,274 (£667; £333; £166)

Form RPR
40 1 **Solstice Star**[101] 1113 5-11-6 **93**..............................(t) KillianMoore 108+
(Martin Keighley) *mde all: pushed clr after 2 out: v easily* **6/1**[3]
0C-6 2 10 **Blue Top**[17] 616 6-10-2 **82**..............................(p) JamieInsole(7) 84
(Dai Burchell) *in tch: rdn to dispute 2nd fr 3 out: no ch w wnr after 2 out: kpt on same pce* **6/1**[3]
-P30 3 ¾ **Pembridge**[21] 1910 6-10-0 **73** oh3..............................(t) BenPoste 74
(Adrian Wintle) *hld up: hdwy 4 out: rdn after next: kpt on same pce* **8/1**
3P-0 4 1¾ **Guanciale**[20] 1931 8-11-7 **94**.............................. FreddieMitchell 94
(Dai Burchell) *in tch: rdn after 3 out: awkward next: kpt on same pce* **14/1**
0654 5 2¼ **Tenby Jewel (IRE)**[27] 1823 10-10-2 **78**..............................(tp) MichaelHeard(3) 76
(Mark Gillard) *chsd ldrs: rdn 4 out: sn one pce* **5/1**[2]
0032 6 ½ **Drummond**[18] 1980 6-10-3 **76**.............................. RobertWilliams 73
(Katie Stephens) *racd keenly: hld up: hdwy into 2nd at the 2nd: rdn after 3 out: kpt on same pce tl no ex appr last* **4/1**[1]
2225 7 2½ **Sweet World**[20] 1931 11-11-6 **98**.............................. GeorgeBlackwell(5) 92
(Bernard Llewellyn) *in tch: rdn after 4 out: sn one pce: hld whn hit 2 out* **10/1**
4F-2 8 nk **Lindsay's Dream**[20] 224 9-10-11 **89**..............................(p) WilliamFeatherstone(5) 83
(Zoe Davison) *hld up: effrt 4 out: one pce fr next* **14/1**
5323 9 13 **Taste The Wine (IRE)**[20] 1927 9-11-7 **99**..............................(p) JordanWilliams(5) 80
(Bernard Llewellyn) *chsd ldrs: effrt 4 out: sn btn* **13/2**

4m 4.3s (-6.30) **Going Correction** -0.35s/f (Good) 9 Ran SP% **112.1**
Speed ratings (Par 103): **101,96,95,94,93 93,92,91,85**
CSF £40.41 CT £286.44 TOTE £5.70: £3.10, £3.00, £2.80; EX 44.80 Trifecta £354.20.
Owner E&G Racing Ltd **Bred** David Allen **Trained** Condicote, Gloucs

FOCUS
There was a sound gallop on in this weak conditional riders's handicap yet nothing could cope with the front-running winner. The winner has been rated back to the level of his bumper form, with the second and third helping to set the level.

2265 TRUVAPE MAIDEN HURDLE (11 hdls) 2m 3f 100y

1:45 (1:46) (Class 5) 4-Y-O+ £2,274 (£667; £333; £166)

Form RPR
3 1 **Tapaculo**[183] 124 4-11-0 0.............................. RichardJohnson 127+
(Philip Hobbs) *nt a fluent: mid-div: hdwy whn hit 4 out: led 2 out: styd on wl: rdn out* **4/1**[1]
3 2 3 **Petethepear (IRE)**[35] 1704 5-11-0 0.............................. JoshuaMoore 122
(Stuart Edmunds) *mid-div: hdwy after 4 out: rdn after next: chsd wnr after 2 out: styd on but a being hld fr last* **20/1**
1-4 3 6 **Ballywilliam (IRE)**[41] 1635 5-10-7 0.............................. DavidNoonan(7) 115
(David Pipe) *in tch: rdn to chse ldrs after 4 out: hung lft and styd on same pce fr 2 out* **12/1**
4 nk **Baoulet Delaroque (FR)**[190] 4-11-0 0.............................. SamTwiston-Davies 116
(Paul Nicholls) *mid-div: hdwy 4 out: cl up whn nt fluent 2 out: sn rdn: styd on same pce* **6/1**[3]
1-3 5 3¼ **After Hours (IRE)**[21] 1909 6-11-0 0.............................. JamesDavies 112
(Henry Oliver) *trckd ldrs: rdn after 4 out: nt fluent 2 out: styd on same pce* **8/1**
3-43 6 2½ **Pilgrims Bay (IRE)**[140] 761 5-10-7 0.............................. MichaelHeard(7) 109
(David Pipe) *trckd ldrs: rdn after 4 out: wknd after 2 out* **20/1**
7 4 **Vic De Touzaine (FR)**[756] 6-11-0 0.............................. LiamTreadwell 107
(Venetia Williams) *racd keenly: trckd ldr: led after 7th: hit 3 out: rdn and hdd bef next: wknd after 2 out: hit last* **7/1**
2 8 1¼ **Don'tdropmein (IRE)**[20] 1921 5-11-0 0.............................. MarkQuinlan 104
(Neil Mulholland) *hld up towards rr: sme late prog past btn horses fr 3 out: nvr a factor* **10/1**
32- 9 nk **Robert's Star (IRE)**[352] 2560 5-11-0 0.............................. NicodeBoinville 103
(Mark Bradstock) *mid-div: rdn after 4 out: btn next* **10/1**
1-1F 10 16 **Desertmore Hill (IRE)**[25] 1844 5-11-0 0..............................[1] SeanBowen 87
(Peter Bowen) *led tl after 7th: rdn after 4 out: wknd appr 2 out* **9/2**[2]
0 11 30 **Kanturk Bank (IRE)**[40] 1645 5-11-0 0.............................. LeightonAspell 57
(Rebecca Curtis) *trckd ldrs: rdn appr 4 out: wknd rapidly: t.o* **80/1**
43- 12 24 **In The Hold (IRE)**[231] 4852 5-11-0 0.............................. PaulMoloney 33
(Evan Williams) *a towards rr: nudged along fr 6th: wknd 4 out: eased fr 2 out: t.o* **20/1**
13 nk **Messery (FR)** 4-10-9 0.............................. AlanJohns(5) 33
(Tim Vaughan) *mid-div tl wknd after 7th: eased fr 2 out: t.o* **100/1**
00- P **Colmers Hill**[206] 5292 5-11-0 0.............................. LiamHeard
(Jeremy Scott) *mstke 7th: a in rr: t.o after 7th: p.u bef 3 out* **100/1**
46 P **Whimsical Notion**[140] 754 5-11-0 0..............................(t) ConorO'Farrell
(Nigel Hawke) *mid-div tl mstke 2nd: sn struggling in last pair: t.o after 7th: p.u bef 3 out* **100/1**

4m 49.6s (-12.20) **Going Correction** -0.35s/f (Good) 15 Ran SP% **120.4**
WFA 4 from 5yo+ 7lb
Speed ratings (Par 103): **111,109,107,107,105 104,102,102,102,95 82,72,72, ,**
CSF £85.17 TOTE £5.20: £2.10, £5.40, £3.30; EX 99.20 Trifecta £1773.70.
Owner Mrs R J Skan **Bred** Aiden Murphy **Trained** Withycombe, Somerset

FOCUS
This was probably a modest maiden hurdle. They got sorted out from the third-last. Big steps up from the first two, with the fifth probably the best guide to the level.

2266 STRATSTONE LAND ROVER SUPPORTS RIDING FOR THE DISABLED NOVICES' LIMITED H'CAP CHASE (12 fncs) 2m 11y

2:15 (2:16) (Class 3) (0-125,124) 4-Y-O+ £6,498 (£1,908; £954; £477)

Form RPR
455- 1 **Javert (IRE)**[269] 4107 6-11-5 **121**..............................[1] SeanBowen 135+
(Emma Lavelle) *j.w: trckd ldr: rn sltly wd on stable bnd after 1st: led after 5 out: r.o wl fr last: rdn out* **15/2**
13-5 2 6 **Ozzy Thomas (IRE)**[12] 2058 5-11-7 **123**.............................. JamesDavies 129
(Henry Oliver) *mid-div: rdn and hdwy appr 5 out: wnt 2nd after 2 out: styd on but readily hld by wnr* **6/1**[3]
/10- 3 4 **Exmoor Mist**[307] 3452 7-10-4 **106** oh3 ow1..............................(t) DenisO'Regan 109
(Victor Dartnall) *hld up: nudged along after 7th: gd hdwy next: ev ch 3 out: sn rdn: kpt on tl no ex appr last* **9/2**[2]
1-55 4 5 **Mr Burbidge**[26] 1838 7-11-5 **121**..............................(p) MarkQuinlan 121
(Neil Mulholland) *led: mstke 5 out and hdd: rdn after next: styd on same pce fr 2 out* **25/1**
32-4 5 1¼ **Paddy The Deejay (IRE)**[17] 1986 6-11-3 **119**.............................. JoshuaMoore 115
(Stuart Edmunds) *hld up in last pair: rdn after 7th: hdwy 4 out: styd on fr 3 out but nt pce to get involved* **6/1**[3]
1-40 6 3¾ **Lucky Jim**[25] 1847 4-11-0 **124**.............................. SamTwiston-Davies 108
(David Dennis) *trckd ldrs: rdn after 5 out: one pce fr next* **12/1**
23-2 7 hd **Blandfords Gunner**[188] 26 6-11-4 **120**.............................. AdamWedge 115
(Evan Williams) *mid-div: hit 1st: hdwy 5 out: blnd bdly 4 out: no ch after but kpt on wl enough* **8/1**
541- 8 6 **Imagine The Chat**[200] 5396 6-11-0 **116**.............................. RichardJohnson 104
(Rebecca Curtis) *mid-div: wnt lft 3rd: hdwy 7th: mstke 4 out: sn rdn: btn next* **4/1**[1]
0430 9 8 **King Alfonso**[4] 2184 6-10-13 **115**.............................. DaveCrosse 93
(Dai Burchell) *mid-div: hdwy 5 out: sn rdn: wknd after next* **9/1**
436- 10 1¾ **Santa's Secret (IRE)**[212] 5180 7-11-1 **117**.............................. LeightonAspell 93
(Oliver Sherwood) *a in rr* **20/1**
10-P 11 5 **Prouts Pub (IRE)**[16] 2001 6-11-8 **124**.............................. TomCannon 95
(Nick Gifford) *chsd ldrs: pushed along after 7th: rdn after 5 out: sn btn* **33/1**

3m 58.9s (-18.20) **Going Correction** -0.95s/f (Hard)
WFA 4 from 5yo+ 7lb 11 Ran SP% **118.9**
Speed ratings (Par 107): **107,104,102,99,98 97,96,93,89,89 86**
CSF £52.08 CT £230.05 TOTE £9.90: £3.10, £2.50, £2.40; EX 53.50 Trifecta £448.80.
Owner Axom Lii **Bred** Cleaboy Stud **Trained** Hatherden, Hants

FOCUS
A modest novice handicap. A big step up from the winner and a smaller one from the runner-up, with the third, fourth and fifth rated in line with their hurdle marks.

2267 TRUVAPE "NATIONAL HUNT" MAIDEN HURDLE (8 hdls) 2m 11y

2:50 (2:50) (Class 4) 4-Y-O+ £3,249 (£954; £477; £238)

Form RPR
22-4 1 **The Gipper (IRE)**[165] 444 5-11-0 0.............................. AdamWedge 116+
(Evan Williams) *j. sltly lft: mde all: jnd briefly last where bttr jump than runner-up: r.o gamely* **3/1**[2]
2/ 2 2¼ **Alibi De Sivola (FR)**[626] 4296 5-11-0 0.............................. SamTwiston-Davies 117+
(Paul Nicholls) *mid-div: nt a fluent: hdwy to trck ldrs after 4th: rdn to chal after 2 out: ev ch whn mstke last: hld after* **13/8**[1]
0U 3 17 **Prince Mahler (IRE)**[16] 1998 5-10-7 0.............................. MrMLegg(7) 97+
(Caroline Keevil) *mid-div: styd on steadily fr 3 out: wnt 3rd run-in: nvr any ch w front pair* **100/1**
42-5 4 2 **Frosty Steel (IRE)**[27] 1826 5-11-0 0.............................. PaddyBrennan 97
(Tom George) *racd keenly: trckd wnr tl after 3 out: wknd bef last: lost 3rd run-in* **3/1**[2]
5 8 **Lord Ballim (FR)**[375] 5-11-0 0..............................(t) ConorO'Farrell 88
(Nigel Hawke) *nvr bttr than mid-div* **20/1**
/0-0 6 ¾ **Padova**[141] 749 9-11-0 0.............................. TommyPhelan 86
(Dr Jeremy Naylor) *hld up: mid-div 4 out: wknd next* **200/1**
31-4 7 hd **Muthabir (IRE)**[140] 761 5-11-0 0.............................. IanPopham 86
(Richard Phillips) *mid-div tl wknd 3 out* **8/1**[3]
5 8 nk **Brown Bear (IRE)**[187] 67 4-11-0 0.............................. TomCannon 86
(Nick Gifford) *hld up: slow 3rd: mid-div 4 out: wknd next* **16/1**
6 9 1¼ **Supreme Hope (IRE)**[19] 1943 6-10-7 0..............................(t) MarkQuinlan 78
(Neil Mulholland) *chsd ldrs: rdn appr 4 out: wknd bef 3 out* **50/1**
0P 10 12 **Gardiners Hill (IRE)**[14] 2024 5-11-0 0.............................. PaulMoloney 73
(David Rees) *chsd ldrs: rdn after 4th: wknd bef next* **80/1**
0/0- 11 16 **Blackdown Babe**[513] 639 7-10-7 0.............................. BrendanPowell 50
(Kevin Bishop) *mid-div tl wknd 4 out: t.o* **100/1**
55-6 12 49 **Culworth Boy (IRE)**[13] 2035 5-11-0 0.............................. SeanQuinlan 8
(Sophie Leech) *racd keenly: hld up: wknd after 4th: t.o* **80/1**
0 13 9 **Renfrew (IRE)**[178] 220 5-11-0 0.............................. MichaelByrne
(Tim Vaughan) *lost tch 4th: t.o* **33/1**

3m 59.8s (-10.80) **Going Correction** -0.35s/f (Good)
WFA 4 from 5yo+ 7lb 13 Ran SP% **119.7**
Speed ratings (Par 105): **113,111,103,102,98 98,97,97,97,91 83,58,54**
CSF £8.31 TOTE £4.60: £1.50, £1.20, £23.60; EX 9.20 Trifecta £707.80.
Owner POS Partnership **Bred** James Nolan **Trained** Llancarfan, Vale Of Glamorgan

FOCUS
This was an uncompetitive maiden hurdle and the first pair finished a long way clear. The first two built on their fair bumper form, and the fourth helps set the level.

2268 OAKGROVE STUD SUPPORTS RIDING FOR THE DISABLED H'CAP HURDLE (QUALIFIER FOR STAYING HURDLE SERIES) (12 hdls) 2m 7f 131y

3:20 (3:21) (Class 3) (0-125,125) 4-Y-O+ £5,393 (£1,583; £791; £395)

Form RPR
1-21 1 **Sykes (IRE)**[10] 2081 6-11-5 **118**.............................. RichardJohnson 128+
(Philip Hobbs) *hld up: hdwy fr 8th: drifting lft whn pushed along to ld appr last: styd on wl run-in: drvn out* **9/4**[1]
F1-1 2 ¾ **The Eaglehaslanded (IRE)**[15] 2005 5-11-8 **121**(tp) SamTwiston-Davies 127
(Paul Nicholls) *trckd ldr: hit 8th: chal 4 out: rdn and ev ch appr last: styd on: hld nring fin* **4/1**[2]
112/ 3 2 **Billy Dutton**[558] 5544 9-11-10 **123**.............................. JamesDavies 128
(Chris Down) *mid-div: hdwy 4 out: chal next: rdn and ev ch 2 out tl no ex run-in* **25/1**
413- 4 2¼ **Altesse De Guye (FR)**[199] 5408 5-10-9 **108**.............................. AndrewTinkler 110
(Martin Keighley) *hld up: hdwy 4 out: edgd lft whn ldng 2 out: rdn and hdd bef last: no ex run-in* **33/1**
54P- 5 1 **Moorlands Mist**[257] 4342 8-11-4 **122**.............................. ConorRing(5) 124
(Evan Williams) *hld up: hdwy after 4 out: nt fluent next: sn rdn: styng on at same pce in hld 5th whn awkward last* **12/1**
1435 6 2¼ **Bold Conquest (IRE)**[14] 2018 7-11-1 **114**.............................. BrendanPowell 113
(Stuart Edmunds) *mid-div: hdwy 4 out: chal next: sn rdn: styd on same pce* **12/1**
132- 7 1 **Princess Tara (IRE)**[212] 5181 5-11-10 **123**.............................. SeanBowen 121
(Peter Bowen) *trckd ldrs: chal 4 out: led 3 out: rdn and hdd next: no ex appr last* **11/1**
412- 8 6 **Dashaway (IRE)**[212] 5183 6-11-12 **125**.............................. NickScholfield 117
(Jeremy Scott) *led: rdn and hdd 3 out: one pce fr next* **7/1**[3]
200- 9 ¾ **Garde Fou (FR)**[257] 4340 9-11-2 **115**..............................(t) PaddyBrennan 106
(Paul Henderson) *a towards rr* **33/1**
216- 10 ½ **Tea Time Fred**[203] 5343 6-10-10 **112**.............................. LucyGardner(3) 105
(Sue Gardner) *mid-div: shortlived effrt 4 out: sn btn* **9/1**
213- 11 17 **Mackerye End (IRE)**[252] 4427 6-11-12 **125**..............................(t) LeightonAspell 99
(Jonjo O'Neill) *trckd ldr: ev ch 4 out: sn rdn: wknd next* **8/1**

P05/ **12** *71* **Ballyrock (IRE)**[901] 358 9-11-7 **125**..........................(t) AlanJohns(5) 28
(Tim Vaughan) *mid-div tl 8th: sn bhd: t.o* **50/1**

6m 3.4s (1.20) **Going Correction** -0.35s/f (Good) 12 Ran SP% **119.8**
Speed ratings (Par 107): **84,83,83,82,82 81,80,78,78,78 72,49**
CSF £11.59 CT £180.80 TOTE £2.80: £1.50, £1.60, £3.90; EX 8.60 Trifecta £183.40.

Owner Bradley Partnership **Bred** Pat Browne **Trained** Withycombe, Somerset

FOCUS
This was very competitive for the grade and the first four were still upsides jumping the final flight. The winner didn't need to improve on his Aintree win, while the third, fourth and fifth have been rated close to their marks.

2269 MCL LOGISTICS SUPPORTS RIDING FOR THE DISABLED H'CAP CHASE (18 fncs) 2m 7f 131y

3:50 (3:52) (Class 4) (0-105,105) 4-Y-0+ **£3,768** (£1,106; £553; £276)

Form RPR

43P- **1** **Leith Hill Legasi**[194] 5512 6-10-0 **79**..................(bt) SamTwiston-Davies 92
(Charlie Longsdon) *mde all: styd on wl: drvn out* **11/4**[1]

4-40 **2** *2 3/4* **Bebinn (IRE)**[28] 1813 8-10-10 **89**..................................(p) KielanWoods 99
(Ben Case) *mid-div: hdwy whn hit 5 out: rdn to chse wnr after next: styd on but nt quite pce to mount chal* **10/1**

65-3 **3** *1 1/2* **Matrow's Lady (IRE)**[100] 1121 8-10-0 **86**..........(bt) MrMartinMcIntyre(7) 95
(Neil Mulholland) *hld up: hdwy 5 out: rdn to dispute 2nd fr 3 out: styd on same pce fr last* **4/1**[2]

P34- **4** *13* **Somerby (IRE)**[206] 5291 12-10-0 **79** oh4..........................(t) AdamWedge 77
(Richenda Ford) *mid-div: rdn and hdwy after 13th: chsd ldrs 4 out: grad fdd fr next* **15/2**

P-33 **5** *23* **Johns Luck (IRE)**[26] 1842 6-11-9 **102**...............................(p) MichaelByrne 80
(Neil Mulholland) *hld up: hdwy fr 11th: cl up but rdn whn hmpd 4 out: wknd next: t.o* **9/2**[3]

UPP0 **6** *nk* **Mostly Bob (IRE)**[34] 1720 12-11-4 **97**..............................(t) SeanQuinlan 69
(Sophie Leech) *j.rt: pressed wnr tl rdn appr 5 out: wknd after 4 out: t.o* **20/1**

142- **F** **Newton Thistle**[237] 4735 8-11-9 **105**..........................(t) MauriceLinehan(3)
(Ben Pauling) *chsd ldrs: mstke 5th: wnt 2nd whn mstke 5 out: rdn whn fell heavily next* **8/1**

/P6- **P** **Bonds Conquest**[334] 2917 6-10-12 **91**.................................... AndrewThornton
(Seamus Mullins) *mid-div: struggling in last trio 12th: wknd bef 5 out: p.u bef next* **33/1**

0-34 **P** **Kinari (IRE)**[63] 1450 5-11-12 **105**.. SeanBowen
(Peter Bowen) *chsd ldrs tl 8th: struggling in last 11th: lost tch after 13th: p.u next* **8/1**

6m 12.3s (-9.70) **Going Correction** -0.95s/f (Hard) 9 Ran SP% **115.6**
Speed ratings (Par 105): **78,77,76,72,64 64,,,**
CSF £30.03 CT £109.58 TOTE £2.70: £1.10, £3.40, £2.50; EX 36.90 Trifecta £170.10.

Owner Neil & Jane Maltby **Bred** Neil And Jane Maltby **Trained** Over Norton, Oxon

FOCUS
A moderate handicap, run at a fair gallop, in which the principals dominated from three out. The second and third have been rated pretty much to their marks.

2270 RIDING FOR THE DISABLED INTERMEDIATE OPEN NATIONAL HUNT FLAT RACE 2m 11y

4:20 (4:22) (Class 6) 4-6-Y-O **£1,559** (£457; £228; £114)

Form RPR

1 **Bun Doran (IRE)**[172] 4-11-0 0.. PaddyBrennan 119+
(Tom George) *travelled strly thrght: trckd ldrs: led 4f out: a in command: quite impressive* **10/3**[2]

2 **2** *2* **Desert Retreat (IRE)**[35] 1704 4-11-0 0........................... RichardJohnson 113+
(Philip Hobbs) *in tch: pushed along 5f out: hdwy over 3f out: styd on strly to go 2nd ins fnl f but no ch w easy wnr* **4/1**[3]

332- **3** *2 1/4* **Preseli Rock (IRE)**[252] 4430 5-11-0 0............................ LeightonAspell 112+
(Rebecca Curtis) *trckd ldrs: trckd wnr fr 4f out: rdn over 2f out: sn hld: no ex whn lost 2nd ins fnl f* **3/1**[1]

4 *7* **Crockery**[234] 5-10-2 0.. BridgetAndrews(5) 97
(Dan Skelton) *in tch: hdwy over 4f out: sn rdn: styd on same pce fnl 2f* **25/1**

0- **5** *3 1/2* **Lime Street (IRE)**[214] 5143 4-11-0 0.............................. JamesDavies 101
(Tom Symonds) *trckd ldrs: rdn over 3f out: one pce fnl 2f* **25/1**

22- **6** *nk* **Sir Will (IRE)**[200] 5395 4-11-7 0.................................... SeanBowen 107
(Peter Bowen) *mid-div: rdn to chse ldrs 4f out: one pce fnl 2f* **4/1**[3]

0- **7** *2* **Monsieur Darsi (IRE)**[269] 4113 5-11-0 0............................ LiamHeard 98
(Martin Hill) *hld up bhd: stdy prog fnl 3f: nvr trbld ldrs* **100/1**

8 *nk* **Island Rendezvous (IRE)** 5-11-0 0.............................. NickScholfield 98
(Jeremy Scott) *nvr bttr than mid-div* **12/1**

0 **9** *7* **Blue Comet**[179] 213 4-11-0 0.. IanPopham 91
(Richard Phillips) *struggling towards rr 1/2-way: nvr any threat* **100/1**

2/ **10** *5* **Scooter Boy**[590] 5014 6-11-0 0.. KielanWoods 86
(Alex Hales) *racd keenly: led tl 4f out: grad fdd* **12/1**

11 *6* **Foxy Act** 4-10-4 0... KieronEdgar(3) 73
(Chris Down) *a towards rr* **100/1**

12 *3 1/4* **Bredon Hill Poppy** 6-10-4 0....................................... LucyGardner(3) 70
(Sue Gardner) *mid-div tl 6f out* **66/1**

13 *3/4* **The Draconian (IRE)** 4-10-7 0..................................... DavidNoonan(7) 76
(David Pipe) *hld up towards rr: rdn in midfield 4f out: wknd 3f out* **12/1**

14 *11* **Bellini Dubreau (FR)** 4-11-0 0...................................... ConorO'Farrell 65
(Nigel Hawke) *a towards rr* **50/1**

3m 57.4s (-7.60) **Going Correction** -0.35s/f (Good) 14 Ran SP% **125.3**
Speed ratings: **105,104,102,99,97 97,96,96,92,90 87,85,85,79**
CSF £17.40 TOTE £4.10: £1.30, £2.40, £1.90; EX 22.70 Trifecta £52.80.

Owner Crossed Fingers Partnership **Bred** Mrs Mary F Griffin **Trained** Slad, Gloucs

FOCUS
This looks fair bumper form. The winner looks well above average and the fourth, fifth and seventh help set the level.

T/Plt: £78.20 to a £1 stake. Pool of £75483.54 - 704.57 winning tickets. T/Qpdt: £11.20 to a £1 stake. Pool of £9396.98 - 616.83 winning tickets. **Tim Mitchell**

[1718] WARWICK (L-H)

Wednesday, November 4

OFFICIAL GOING: Good to soft (soft in places on the hurdle course)
Wind: Light behind Weather: Cloudy

2271 32RED H'CAP HURDLE (8 hdls) 2m

1:00 (1:03) (Class 4) (0-115,115) 3-Y-0+ **£3,898** (£1,144; £572; £286)

Form RPR

P-34 **1** **Crickel Wood (FR)**[18] 1979 5-11-10 **113**.........................(t) AidanColeman 121+
(Charlie Longsdon) *hld up in tch: racd keenly: rdn to ld and edgd rt flat: r.o* **8/1**[2]

/3-5 **2** *2 3/4* **Orthodox Lad**[34] 1714 7-11-0 **106**....................................... JamesBanks(3) 110
(Grace Harris) *chsd ldr tl led after 3rd: rdn and hdd flat: styd on same pce* **20/1**

-051 **3** *2 3/4* **David John**[23] 1892 4-10-12 **101**.. RobertDunne 103
(Dai Burchell) *hld up: hdwy after 3 out: hit next: sn rdn: styd on same pce last* **5/1**[1]

5-23 **4** *2 1/4* **While You Wait (IRE)**[27] 1828 6-11-10 **113**......................... GavinSheehan 113
(Paul Fitzsimons) *mid-div: hdwy appr 4th: rdn after 3 out: styd on same pce fr next* **20/1**

54-6 **5** *2 1/4* **Kamool (GER)**[179] 210 5-11-12 **115**.. NoelFehily 113
(Jonjo O'Neill) *hld up: pushed along 5th: hdwy 3 out: sn rdn: nt fluent next: styd on same pce* **25/1**

3-53 **6** *1/2* **Sword Of The Lord**[41] 1638 5-11-2 **108**............................ RyanHatch(3) 107
(Nigel Twiston-Davies) *hld up: hdwy appr 4th: rdn and hung lft bef 2 out: wknd last* **8/1**[2]

F-50 **7** *1/2* **Dormouse**[18] 1977 10-11-2 **112**.....................................(p) CiaranGethings(7) 110
(Anabel K Murphy) *hld up: styd on appr last: nt clr run flat: nvr nrr* **17/2**[3]

4/21 **8** *1* **Stand To Reason (IRE)**[97] 1156 7-11-10 **113**..................... LeeEdwards 109
(Tony Carroll) *hld up: hdwy after 3 out: mstke next: sn wknd* **8/1**[2]

6-43 **9** *1* **Being Global (FR)**[162] 494 4-11-2 **105**.............................. HarrySkelton 100
(Caroline Bailey) *hld up: effrt appr 2 out: n.d* **16/1**

335- **10** *nse* **Sweeping Rock (IRE)**[221] 5025 5-11-9 **112**....................... JamieMoore 107
(John Spearing) *prom: rdn appr 2 out: wknd last* **11/1**

-056 **11** *1 3/4* **Goal (IRE)**[57] 1501 7-10-12 **108**...............................(t) MissBHampson(7) 102
(Andy Turnell) *hld up: rdn appr last: n.d* **33/1**

0-05 **12** *4 1/2* **Drumlee Lad (IRE)**[21] 1911 5-11-6 **112**.......................(t) KieronEdgar(3) 102
(David Pipe) *led tl after 3rd: remained handy tl rdn and wknd 2 out* **16/1**

4016 **13** *6* **Miss Fortywinks**[108] 1054 6-11-4 **107**................................. RyanMahon 91
(Seamus Mullins) *mid-div: rdn and wknd 3 out* **25/1**

P621 **14** *12* **Powderonthebonnet (IRE)**[29] 1171 7-10-10 **104**.......... DanielHiskett(5) 77
(Richard Phillips) *chsd ldrs tl rdn and wknd after 3 out* **20/1**

56-0 **15** *17* **Rising Breeze (FR)**[160] 98 4-10-9 **103**.......................... JamieBargary(5) 61
(Tom George) *prom: pushed along 5th: wknd after 3 out* **40/1**

330 **16** *12* **Fauve (IRE)**[97] 1153 4-11-4 **114**........................... MrRobertHawker(7) 61
(Richard Hawker) *hld up: rdn and wknd after 3 out* **66/1**

3/0- **F** **Bodega**[440] 1282 7-11-7 **110**.. WillKennedy
(Ian Williams) *hld up: fell 3rd* **14/1**

3m 48.5s (-10.50) **Going Correction** -0.525s/f (Firm)
WFA 4 from 5yo+ 7lb 17 Ran SP% **116.1**
Speed ratings (Par 105): **105,103,102,101,100 99,99,99,98,98 97,95,92,86,77 71,**
CSF £145.83 CT £769.64 TOTE £6.90: £1.80, £5.80, £1.80, £4.20; EX 224.10 Trifecta £1082.30.

Owner Executive Hire News Ltd **Bred** Ecurie Des Monceaux **Trained** Over Norton, Oxon

FOCUS
Hurdle races and bumpers run on inner course and all distances as advertised. The meeting started with an ultra-competitive handicap, but the early gallop wasn't overly strong. The winner is on the upgrade and should rate higher on Flat form. The third has been rated similar to his recent win, with the fourth to his mark.

2272 £10 FREE AT 32RED.COM CONDITIONAL JOCKEYS' H'CAP CHASE (QUALIFIER) (20 fncs) 3m 1f 100y

1:35 (1:36) (Class 4) (0-120,120) 4-Y-0+ **£3,898** (£1,144; £572; £286)

Form RPR

411U **1** **Conas Taoi (IRE)**[12] 2057 6-10-2 **96**.............................(p) ConorShoemark 113+
(Paul Morgan) *chsd ldr to appr 4th: remained handy: wnt 2nd again 11th: led next: rdn out* **10/3**[1]

-FP1 **2** *5* **Pure Poteen (IRE)**[25] 1850 7-10-9 **111**...............(t) MrMartinMcIntyre(8) 122
(Neil Mulholland) *hld up: hdwy appr 14th: outpcd next: rallied after 3 out: chsd wnr bef next: rdn bef last: styd on same pce flat* **7/2**[2]

4522 **3** *17* **For 'N' Against (IRE)**[15] 2005 6-11-4 **115**.................(tp) KieronEdgar(3) 114
(David Pipe) *hld up: hdwy 14th: chsd wnr 16th tl rdn appr 2 out: wknd bef last* **9/2**[3]

S13- **4** *3 3/4* **Barton Gift**[241] 4655 8-11-8 **116**..............................(p) JeremiahMcGrath 111
(John Spearing) *chsd ldrs: hit 2nd: led appr 4th: hdd 12th: chsd wnr tl nt fluent 16th: rdn and wknd bef 2 out* **8/1**

21P- **5** *7* **Paddy The Oscar (IRE)**[223] 4992 12-11-7 **120**................ LewisGordon(5) 105
(Grace Harris) *prom tl rdn and wknd after 3 out* **16/1**

12-F **6** *8* **Free Of Charge (IRE)**[21] 1906 6-10-10 **110**................. CiaranGethings(6) 91
(Philip Hobbs) *hld up: hdwy 4th: rdn and wknd after 3 out* **5/1**

3453 **U** **Georgian King**[25] 1850 12-10-10 **109**...............................(p) ConorSmith(5)
(Martin Keighley) *led: hdd appr 4th: chsd ldr to 11th: cl 3rd whn blnd and uns rdr 13th* **7/1**

6m 34.9s (-24.10) **Going Correction** -0.80s/f (Firm) 7 Ran SP% **109.6**
Speed ratings (Par 105): **106,104,98,97,95 92,**
CSF £14.48 CT £46.61 TOTE £3.00: £1.50, £2.60; EX 15.20 Trifecta £49.10.
Owner All Stars Sports Racing **Bred** Martin McCaughey **Trained** Ystrad, Rhondda C Taff

FOCUS
Just a modest handicap for conditional riders. A step up from the winner, and the race could be rated higher through the third and fourth.

2273 ANIXTER PARTNERS DAY JUVENILE MAIDEN HURDLE (8 hdls) 2m

2:05 (2:06) (Class 4) 3-Y-O **£3,249** (£954; £477; £238)

Form RPR

6232 **1** **Chic Name (FR)**[20] 1928 3-10-12 110..................................(p) AlainCawley 114+
(Richard Hobson) *mde all: wnt clr 4th: mstke 2 out: rdn out* **3/1**[2]

2 *3* **Pemba (FR)**[227] 3-10-5 0.. WayneHutchinson 102
(Alan King) *hld up: hdwy 4th: chsd wnr 3 out: rdn appr last: styd on same pce flat* **6/4**[1]

0- **3** *1 1/4* **Swincombe Toby**[215] 5126 3-10-12 0................................... WillKennedy 108
(Nick Williams) *chsd ldrs: rdn after 3 out: styd on same pce last* **25/1**

32 **4** *25* **Albert Herring**[10] 2092 3-10-12 0.. GavinSheehan 85
(Jonathan Portman) *prom: lost pl and mstke 5th: n.d after* **14/1**

	5	*1*	**Cobra De Mai (FR)**[150] 3-10-12 0 HarrySkelton	84
			(Dan Skelton) *hld up: plld hrd: hdwy 5th: rdn and wknd appr 2 out* **7/2**[3]	
	6	*2 1/4*	**Akavit (IRE)**[53] 3-10-12 0 DavidBass	82
			(Ed de Giles) *chsd wnr: hit 4th: rdn and wknd after 3 out* **14/1**	
	7	*1*	**Vocaliser (IRE)**[102] 3-10-12 0 CharliePoste	82
			(Robin Dickin) *hld up: plld hrd: hdwy 3 out: wknd bef next* **12/1**	
0	**8**	*1/2*	**Midtech Star (IRE)**[20] 1928 3-10-12 0 (p) TomO'Brien	81
			(Ian Williams) *prom tl rdn and wknd after 3 out* **100/1**	
	9	*37*	**Fidelity**[166] 3-10-9 0 ConorShoemark(3)	48
			(Jonathan Geake) *hld up: bhd fr 4th* **100/1**	
	10	*1*	**Red Touch (USA)**[88] 3-10-12 0 LeeEdwards	47
			(Dave Roberts) *hld up: mstke 4th: hdwy appr 3 out: sn rdn and wknd* **100/1**	
	11	*56*	**Prince Of Cardamom (IRE)**[53] 3-10-12 0 MarkGrant	
			(Jonathan Geake) *hld up: wknd 5th* **100/1**	
	12	*21*	**Light Breaks (IRE)**[126] 3-10-9 0 RyanHatch(3)	
			(Nigel Twiston-Davies) *hld up: mstke 3rd: sn rdn: wknd next* **20/1**	

3m 47.3s (-11.70) **Going Correction** -0.525s/f (Firm) **12** Ran SP% **120.8**
Speed ratings (Par 104): **108,106,105,93,92 91,91,91,72,72 44,33**
CSF £8.08 TOTE £5.10: £1.70, £1.10, £7.10; EX 15.10 Trifecta £185.30.
Owner D W Fox **Bred** Pegasus Farms Ltd **Trained** Stow-On-The-Wold, Gloucs

FOCUS
An interesting race for juveniles, in which the first three came well clear. The second has been rated in line with her Auteuil run.

2274 WEATHERBYS DIARY NOVICES' CHASE (12 fncs) 2m
2:40 (2:40) (Class 3) 4-Y-O+ **£7,783** (£2,431; £1,309)

Form				RPR
111/	**1**		**Willow's Saviour**[683] 3200 8-11-1 0 HarrySkelton	139+
			(Dan Skelton) *trckd ldrs: plld hrd: led 7th: rdn flat: all out* **3/1**[3]	
100-	**2**	*nk*	**Aso (FR)**[236] 4737 5-11-1 0 AidanColeman	139+
			(Venetia Williams) *chsd ldr to 7th: chsd wnr thereafter: rdn appr last: r.o u.p* **15/8**[1]	
015-	**3**	*60*	**Ballybolley (IRE)**[207] 5271 6-11-1 0 (t) DarylJacob	85
			(Nigel Twiston-Davies) *led to 7th: wknd appr 3 out: bhd whn nt fluent 2 out* **4/1**	
142/	**U**		**Ballyalton (IRE)**[602] 4750 8-11-1 0 WillKennedy	
			(Ian Williams) *hld up: hdwy 8th: cl 3rd whn knuckled on landing and uns rdr 3 out* **5/2**[2]	

3m 53.2s (-16.80) **Going Correction** -0.80s/f (Firm) **4** Ran SP% **108.4**
Speed ratings (Par 107): **110,109,79,**
CSF £9.02 TOTE £3.30; EX 6.70 Trifecta £22.10.
Owner Triple F Partnership **Bred** Mrs M Cuff **Trained** Alcester, Warwicks

FOCUS
A very classy contest despite the small field. All of these have the possibility of winning at graded level this season. It's been rated around the hurdle marks of the first two.

2275 32RED ON THE APP STORE NOVICES' HURDLE (12 hdls) 3m 2f
3:10 (3:10) (Class 4) 4-Y-O+ **£3,898** (£1,144; £572; £286)

Form				RPR
-P01	**1**		**Net Work Rouge (FR)**[21] 1912 6-11-5 120 (t) DavidBass	134+
			(Kim Bailey) *mde all: rdn appr 2 out: hung lft flat: styd on wl* **5/2**[1]	
325-	**2**	*3 1/2*	**Dan Emmett (USA)**[12] 5422 5-10-12 120 JamieMoore	122
			(Michael Scudamore) *hld up: hdwy 8th: chsd wnr appr 2 out: rdn and ev ch whn hit last: styd on same pce flat* **13/2**	
6	**3**	*3 3/4*	**Ballycross**[40] 1648 4-10-9 0 RyanHatch(3)	118
			(Nigel Twiston-Davies) *hld up: hdwy 7th: rdn after 3 out: styd on same pce fr next* **16/1**	
204-	**4**	*8*	**Gorsky Island**[196] 5472 7-10-7 0 JamieBargary(5)	114
			(Tom George) *chsd ldrs: mstke 4th: rdn appr 2 out: wknd last* **7/2**[3]	
	5	*15*	**A Plein Temps (FR)**[212] 5-10-12 0 NoelFehily	100
			(Harry Fry) *prom: chsd wnr 7th: shkn up and ev ch after 3 out: wknd bef next* **3/1**[2]	
215-	**6**	*10*	**Shouldavboughtgold (IRE)**[354] 2506 8-10-9 0 HarryChalloner(3)	92
			(William Kinsey) *hld up: hdwy 7th: wknd 9th* **14/1**	
23-2	**7**	*42*	**Captain McGinley (IRE)**[14] 2024 5-10-12 0 GavinSheehan	50
			(Rebecca Curtis) *hld up: hdwy after 7th: rdn and wknd bef 3 out* **10/1**	
03	**8**	*27*	**Minmore Grey (IRE)**[19] 1952 6-10-5 0 WilliamFeatherstone(7)	26
			(Nick Lampard) *hld up: bhd fr 8th* **100/1**	
PP-5	**P**		**Verve Argent (FR)**[14] 2024 6-10-12 0 (p) CharliePoste	
			(Paul Webber) *hld up: rdn and wknd after 7th: bhd whn p.u after 3 out* **100/1**	
4	**P**		**The Lizard King (IRE)**[21] 1912 6-10-12 0 AidanColeman	
			(Charlie Longsdon) *w wnr to 6th: lost pl next: rdn and wknd appr 8th: bhd whn p.u bef 9th* **33/1**	
	P		**Le Saumon (IRE)**[234] 5-10-12 0 JackQuinlan	
			(Sarah Humphrey) *prom to 9th: bhd whn p.u after next* **80/1**	

6m 21.2s (-15.80) **Going Correction** -0.525s/f (Firm) **11** Ran SP% **116.9**
WFA 4 from 5yo+ 9lb
Speed ratings (Par 105): **103,101,100,98,93 90,77,69, ,**
CSF £19.40 TOTE £4.50: £1.80, £2.30, £4.00; EX 23.80 Trifecta £180.60.
Owner John Wills & David Reid Scott Partnership **Bred** Scea Haras Des Rouges **Trained** Andoversford, Gloucs

FOCUS
A fair staying event for novices, run at a decent gallop. The winner confirmed the merit of his recent easy win, while the second and fourth help set the level.

2276 32RED.COM H'CAP CHASE (17 fncs) 2m 4f
3:40 (3:41) (Class 4) (0-120,117) 4-Y-O+ **£3,898** (£1,144; £572; £286)

Form				RPR
46-1	**1**		**Aloomomo (FR)**[5] 2168 5-11-10 115 7ex GavinSheehan	133+
			(Warren Greatrex) *a.p: chsd ldr 11th: led next: wnt clr appr 2 out: eased flat* **1/3**[1]	
0P-2	**2**	*2 1/2*	**Val D'Arc (FR)**[14] 2019 6-11-8 113 AlainCawley	120
			(Richard Hobson) *led: clr 3rd tl 8th: hdd 12th: ev ch whn mstke 3 out: outpcd bef next* **16/1**	
4-26	**3**	*20*	**Handsome Buddy (IRE)**[25] 1850 8-10-0 98 CiaranGethings(7)	84
			(Michael Gates) *hld up: wnt 3rd last: nvr on terms* **20/1**	
0-P1	**4**	*13*	**Twojayslad**[138] 782 6-11-9 114 WillKennedy	88
			(Ian Williams) *hld up: hdwy 10th: wknd 13th* **7/1**[2]	
215-	**5**	*20*	**Strawberry Hill (IRE)**[233] 4818 9-11-7 112 (p) JamesBest	68
			(Caroline Keevil) *chsd wnr: nt fluent 5th and next: lost 2nd 11th: wkng whn mstke 14th* **20/1**	
3-22	**P**		**Sergeant Dick (IRE)**[169] 390 10-11-9 117 (t) JamesBanks(3)	
			(Andy Turnell) *prom tl wknd appr 11th: bhd whn p.u bef 13th* **10/1**[3]	

5m 6.5s (-11.50) **Going Correction** -0.80s/f (Firm) **6** Ran SP% **112.0**
Speed ratings (Par 105): **91,90,82,76,68**
CSF £6.94 TOTE £1.20: £1.10, £5.50; EX 8.00 Trifecta £57.80.
Owner The Large G & T Partnership **Bred** Maurice Goin **Trained** Upper Lambourn, Berks

FOCUS
Punters appeared to only want to know about one runner, and those who supported him had few worries after he quickened away heading to the second-last. The second helps with the level, backing up his good Worcester run.

2277 GEORGE MERNAGH MEMORIAL MARES' STANDARD OPEN NATIONAL HUNT FLAT RACE 2m
4:10 (4:11) (Class 6) 4-6-Y-O **£1,624** (£477; £238; £119)

Form				RPR
2-5	**1**		**Lamanver Alchemy**[28] 1811 4-10-12 0 [1] NoelFehily	99+
			(Tom Lacey) *plld hrd and prom: led over 2f out: rdn and edgd rt ins fnl f: styd on* **14/1**	
	2	*3/4*	**My Khaleesi** 4-10-12 0 WayneHutchinson	98+
			(Alan King) *hld up: hdwy over 5f out: chsd wnr over 2f out: rdn: nt clr run and swtchd lft ins fnl f: r.o* **4/1**[2]	
	3	*2*	**Secret Door (IRE)**[248] 4-10-12 0 DarylJacob	96
			(Harry Fry) *a.p: rdn over 2f out: styd on same pce ins fnl f* **3/1**[1]	
4	**4**	*2*	**Zara Hope (IRE)**[21] 1908 4-10-12 0 AidanColeman	94
			(Charlie Longsdon) *prom: racd keenly: rdn over 2f out: styd on same pce fnl f* **9/1**	
6-0	**5**	*2 1/4*	**Stepover**[179] 213 4-10-9 0 JamesBanks(3)	92
			(Alex Hales) *hld up: hdwy over 2f out: nt rch ldrs* **100/1**	
	6	*1 1/2*	**Al Reesha (IRE)** 4-10-12 0 HarrySkelton	91
			(Dan Skelton) *hld up: hdwy 5f out: rdn over 2f out: wknd fnl f* **12/1**	
	7	*1/2*	**Lizzie Langton** 4-10-12 0 JamieMoore	90
			(Robert Walford) *prom: rdn over 3f out: wknd fnl f* **33/1**	
6	**8**	*1 1/4*	**Tara Well (IRE)**[28] 1817 5-10-7 0 ChrisWard(5)	89
			(Robin Dickin) *prom: rdn over 3f out: wknd over 1f out* **100/1**	
	9	*2 3/4*	**Hollow Bay** 5-10-12 0 LiamTreadwell	86
			(Paul Webber) *hld up: hmpd over 9f out: nvr trbld ldrs* **14/1**	
	10	*1 1/2*	**Nancy's Trix (IRE)**[241] 6-10-12 0 NicodeBoinville	85
			(David Loder) *sn led: rdn and hdd over 2f out: wknd over 1f out* **7/1**[3]	
4	**11**	*shd*	**Milan Hart (IRE)**[174] 305 5-10-5 0 CiaranGethings(7)	84
			(Chris Down) *hld up: rdn over 3f out: sn wknd* **33/1**	
	12	*4*	**Waterberry** 4-10-12 0 TomO'Brien	82
			(Lucy Wadham) *hld up: rdn over 3f out: n.d* **20/1**	
3-	**13**	*3 1/4*	**Where's Cherry (IRE)**[214] 5136 4-10-9 0 ConorShoemark(3)	77
			(Fergal O'Brien) *chsd ldr: rdn over 4f out: wknd over 3f out* **16/1**	
	14	*12*	**Lady Markby (IRE)** 4-10-12 0 GavinSheehan	65
			(Emma Lavelle) *w.r.s: hld up: hdwy 1/2-way: wknd over 4f out* **8/1**	
4	**15**	*1 1/2*	**Bitter Virtue**[166] 432 4-10-12 0 TrevorWhelan	64
			(David Dennis) *prom tl wknd over 4f out* **20/1**	
0	**16**	*9*	**Dame Doris**[32] 1758 5-10-12 0 DavidBass	55
			(Lawney Hill) *hld up: hdwy 1/2-way: wknd 4f out* **100/1**	
0	**17**	*21*	**Heighnow**[140] 761 4-10-12 0 TomMessenger	34
			(Conrad Allen) *hld up: hdwy 11f out: wknd over 6f out* **100/1**	

3m 47.1s (1.70) **Going Correction** -0.525s/f (Firm) **17** Ran SP% **124.9**
Speed ratings: **74,73,72,71,70 69,69,68,67,66 66,64,63,57,56 51,41**
CSF £66.80 TOTE £12.60: £3.60, £2.50, £1.90; EX 102.90 Trifecta £826.50.
Owner Dr Donna Christensen **Bred** Dr Donna Christensen **Trained** Ledbury, H'fords

FOCUS
Last year's winner (trained by Paul Nicholls) went on to land a Listed contest on her next start, but prior to that it was very hit or miss whether they went on to be anything more than fair. The form has been rated around the winner and fourth.
T/Plt: £50.00 to a £1 stake. Pool of £50577.81 - 737.99 winning tickets. T/Qpdt: £12.40 to a £1 stake. Pool of £3921.11 - 233.75 winning tickets. **Colin Roberts**

2278-2285a (Foreign Racing) - See Raceform Interactive

[1967] MARKET RASEN (R-H)
Thursday, November 5

OFFICIAL GOING: Soft (6.4)
Wind: moderate 1/2 behind Weather: overcast, damp, rain race 4 onwards

2286 WINNER APP JUVENILE HURDLE (8 hdls) 2m 148y
1:10 (1:12) (Class 4) 3-Y-O **£3,898** (£1,144; £572; £286)

Form				RPR
2	**1**		**Duke Of Medina (IRE)**[29] 1805 3-10-12 0 (b) RichardJohnson	110+
			(Harry Whittington) *led tl after 3rd: led 5th: clr next: heavily eased run-in* **4/7**[1]	
6	**2**	*21*	**Poet Mark (IRE)**[22] 1899 3-10-12 0 JakeGreenall	82
			(Tim Easterby) *trckd ldng pair 3rd: drvn 3 out: mstke last: kpt on to take modest 2nd in clsng stages* **16/1**	
	3	*3/4*	**Denton Carnival (IRE)**[528] 3-10-9 0 JoeColliver(3)	81
			(Michael Dods) *t.k.h: trckd ldr: nt fluent and reminders 3rd: sn led: hdd 5th: one pce fr next* **33/1**	
4	**4**	*19*	**Quill Art**[22] 1899 3-10-5 0 JamieHamilton(7)	61
			(Richard Fahey) *sn pushed along in rr: bhd fr 5th* **11/2**[3]	
5	**5**	*1 1/4*	**Stormin Tom (IRE)**[22] 1899 3-10-12 0 SeanBowen	62
			(Tim Easterby) *chsd ldrs: lost pl 3rd: hit next: bhd whn mstke 5th* **7/2**[2]	

4m 26.9s (20.20) **Going Correction** +1.30s/f (Heav) **5** Ran SP% **110.1**
Speed ratings (Par 104): **104,94,93,84,84**
CSF £10.08 TOTE £1.30: £1.10, £8.80; EX 9.60 Trifecta £75.10.
Owner Exors of the Late H J M Webb **Bred** Old Long Hill Ballinteskin Stud Ltd **Trained** Sparsholt, Oxfordshire

FOCUS
Rail set out 16yds on Wood bend and 30yds on Stands' bend. Races 1, 2, 5 & 6 increased by 186yds and races 3 & 4 by 276yds. This contest has produced some good sorts, most notably Tiger Roll in 2013. The second is probably a better guide to the level than the fourth and fifth.

2287 WINNER.CO.UK MAIDEN HURDLE (10 hdls) 2m 2f 140y
1:45 (1:46) (Class 4) 4-Y-O+ **£3,898** (£1,144; £572; £286)

Form				RPR
6	**1**		**See The Rock (IRE)**[46] 1590 5-10-12 0 [1] RichardJohnson	115+
			(Jonjo O'Neill) *hld up in last: hdwy appr 2 out: 3rd between last 2: 2nd last 150yds: styd on to ld post* **9/2**[2]	
42P-	**2**	*shd*	**Final Nudge (IRE)**[209] 5254 6-10-12 0 AidanColeman	114+
			(David Dennis) *t.k.h: trckd ldrs 3rd: nt fluent 5th: led narrowly appr 2 out: hdd and no ex post* **4/7**[1]	

3 **3** 3 **Dr Cuddles (IRE)**[263] 7-10-12 0 TomO'Brien 111
(David Bridgwater) *hld up towards rr: hdwy to trck ldrs 7th: upsides 2 out and last: kpt on same pce* **9/1**

5U-0 **4** 10 **Allnecessaryforce (FR)**[23] 1898 5-10-12 0 TrevorWhelan 104
(Alex Hales) *in rr: drvn 3 out: chsng ldrs next: 4th and wl hld whn blnd last* **10/1**

06 **5** 11 **Barra Rotha (IRE)**[105] 1082 8-10-6 0 ow1 MikeyHamill(7) 91
(Laura Hurley) *t.k.h: led to 2nd: hit 5th: led briefly bef 2 out: wknd between last 2* **100/1**

4-36 **6** 1¼ **La Dama De Hierro**[26] 1854 5-9-12 0 JamieHamilton(7) 82
(Malcolm Jefferson) *chsd ldrs: drvn whn hit 3 out: lost pl bef next* **8/1**[3]

0-44 **7** 11 **Bling Noir (IRE)**[19] 1968 5-10-5 0 DenisO'Regan 71
(Tony Coyle) *mid-div: chsd ldrs 3rd: hit 7th: lost pl bef 2 out: sn bhd* **50/1**

0-F3 **8** 3 **Fair To Middling**[31] 1792 5-10-12 0 SeanBowen 75
(Peter Bowen) *w ldr: led 2nd: hdd and lost pl appr 2 out: sn bhd* **16/1**

5m 7.0s (27.60) **Going Correction** +1.60s/f (Heavy) **8 Ran SP% 120.9**
Speed ratings (Par 105): **105,104,103,99,94 94,89,88**
CSF £8.21 TOTE £4.50: £1.30, £1.10, £2.40; EX 9.50 Trifecta £29.80.
Owner John P McManus **Bred** Mount Coote Stud & Alan Lillingston **Trained** Cheltenham, Gloucs

FOCUS
This form is far from reliable, as it basically turned into a sprint down the home straight, which suited the winner, who had plenty of winning form on the Flat. The winner is entitled to rate a lot higher on his Flat form.

2288 WINNER.CO.UK H'CAP CHASE (17 fncs) 2m 7f 191y
2:15 (2:17) (Class 4) (0-120,118) 4-Y-O+ **£3,898** (£1,144; £572; £286)

Form RPR

4-54 **1** **Sands Cove (IRE)**[165] 464 8-11-9 115 LiamTreadwell 129+
(James Evans) *t.k.h: hld up in rr: hdwy to trck ldrs 11th: handy 2nd 4 out: led appr next: forged clr 2 out: hit last* **8/1**

6131 **2** 8 **Ready Token (IRE)**[31] 1795 7-11-12 118 (p) AidanColeman 124
(Charlie Longsdon) *led: hdd appr 3 out: wl hld whn stmbld on landing 2 out* **2/1**[1]

5350 **3** 11 **Big Sound**[19] 1970 8-11-2 108 (p) JakeGreenall 103
(Mark Walford) *chsd ldrs: drvn and outpcd 4 out: one pce and modest 3rd appr 2 out* **9/1**

4561 **4** 36 **Kayfton Pete**[23] 1894 9-11-2 108 AdamPogson 67
(Charles Pogson) *chsd ldrs: mstke 4th: lost pl 13th: sn bhd: lft distant 4th between last 2: t.o* **14/1**

-445 **5** 23 **She's Late**[21] 1932 5-11-12 118 (p) SeanBowen 54
(Jonjo O'Neill) *chsd ldrs: lost pl 13th: bhd next: t.o 3 out* **16/1**

-42F **P** **Master Neo (FR)**[32] 1783 9-11-9 115 (tp) ConorO'Farrell
(Nigel Hawke) *in rr: hit 9th: lost pl 11th: bhd 4 out: p.u appr next* **5/2**[2]

-4P2 **P** **Midnight Cataria**[18] 1987 6-11-4 110 DenisO'Regan
(Alan King) *jnd ldrs 5th: modest 3rd and outpcd sn after 4 out: poor 4th whn p.u between last 2* **9/2**[3]

6m 43.3s (12.00) **Going Correction** +0.65s/f (Soft) **7 Ran SP% 113.7**
Speed ratings (Par 105): **106,103,99,87,80**
CSF £25.19 TOTE £10.70: £5.30, £1.80; EX 32.40 Trifecta £131.50.
Owner James Evans Racing **Bred** Colm Griffin **Trained** Broadwas, Worcs

FOCUS
Just a modest handicap for stayers. The winner, who was well in on his best form, has been rated back to that level, with the second rated similar to his recent C&D win.

2289 BET & WATCH AT WINNER.CO.UK NOVICES' LIMITED H'CAP CHASE (14 fncs) 2m 5f 89y
2:45 (2:48) (Class 3) (0-135,132) 4-Y-O+ **£9,747** (£2,862; £1,431; £715)

Form RPR

042- **1** **Kingswell Theatre**[226] 4971 6-11-1 125 LiamTreadwell 130+
(Michael Scudamore) *led to 5th: led bef 8th: styd on wl fr 3 out: eased in clsng stages* **11/4**[2]

1313 **2** 12 **Father Edward (IRE)**[95] 1179 6-11-6 130 AidanColeman 123
(John Ferguson) *trckd ldng pair: trckd wnr 10th: effrt and 3 l down whn hit 3 out: kpt on same pce* **9/2**

2-54 **3** 4 **Raktiman (IRE)**[19] 1969 8-11-1 128 JonathanEngland(3) 118
(Richard Drake) *hld up in last: drvn 8th: modest 3rd 4 out: wknd bef 2 out* **7/2**[3]

102- **4** 47 **No No Mac (IRE)**[196] 5498 6-11-8 132 RichardJohnson 73
(Charlie Longsdon) *trckd ldng pair: nt fluent 9th: lost pl 4 out: sn bhd: t.o next* **6/4**[1]

02P- **P** **Big Jim**[222] 5029 6-10-10 120 TrevorWhelan
(Alex Hales) *w wnr: led 5th: hdd and blnd 8th: drvn and lost pl next: sn bhd: t.o whn p.u bef 4 out* **20/1**

5m 56.5s (10.50) **Going Correction** +0.725s/f (Soft) **5 Ran SP% 111.8**
Speed ratings (Par 107): **109,104,102,85,**
CSF £14.96 TOTE £3.90: £1.90, £1.90; EX 15.60 Trifecta £44.50.
Owner John J Murray **Bred** W C Tincknell **Trained** Bromsash, H'fords

FOCUS
An interesting race of its type, in which the winner jumped much the best of the newcomers to chasing. The second has been rated in line with his hurdle mark.

2290 DOWNLOAD THE WINNER.CO.UK APP NOW H'CAP CHASE (14 fncs) 2m 3f 34y
3:20 (3:22) (Class 5) (0-100,98) 4-Y-O+ **£2,599** (£763; £381; £190)

Form RPR

2125 **1** **Carters Rest**[10] 2104 12-11-5 98 MissJWalton(7) 104
(George Bewley) *w ldr: led bef 2nd: jnd last 200yds: all out* **12/1**

4-P5 **2** shd **Ride On Time (IRE)**[28] 1824 5-11-8 97 MauriceLinehan(3) 104
(Ben Pauling) *led tl bef 2nd: hit 8th: drvn next: rallied and chsd wnr appr 3 out: chalng whn hit last: sn level: jst hld* **9/4**[1]

5421 **3** 20 **Larkhall**[14] 2040 8-9-10 75 RyanDay(7) 62
(Mike Sowersby) *t.k.h: hld up in rr: jnd ldrs 6th: drvn appr 3 out: sn wknd* **9/4**[1]

-466 **4** 20 **Molko Jack (FR)**[46] 1603 11-10-7 79 LeightonAspell 54
(Michael Mullineaux) *hld up towards rr: chsd ldrs 6th: 2nd 9th: lost pl bef 3 out: sn wl bhd* **9/2**[3]

0P0- **R** **Zazamix (FR)**[226] 4978 10-10-1 76 (v) JohnKington(3)
(Andrew Crook) *in rr: pushed along 5th: lost pl and reminders 7th: t.o whn ref next* **20/1**

0 **U** **Goodoldhonkytonk (IRE)**[108] 1067 7-11-8 94 (p) LiamTreadwell
(James Evans) *chsd ldrs: 3rd whn mstke and uns rdr 2nd* **4/1**[2]

5m 24.1s (18.40) **Going Correction** +0.80s/f (Soft) **6 Ran SP% 112.2**
Speed ratings (Par 103): **93,92,84,76,**
CSF £40.24 TOTE £7.90: £3.90, £1.40; EX 30.60 Trifecta £117.90.
Owner Mrs D Walton **Bred** A Dawson **Trained** Bonchester Bridge, Borders

FOCUS
Whatever way you looked at it, this was a weak contest, but it produced an exciting finish. The winner has been rated back to the level of his Cartmel win.

2291 WINNER.CO.UK CASINO "HANDS AND HEELS" H'CAP HURDLE (CONDITIONALS/AMATEURS)(EXCELLENCE INITIATIVE) (10 hdls) 2m 2f 140y
3:55 (3:56) (Class 4) (0-115,115) 3-Y-O+ **£3,249** (£954; £477; £238)

Form RPR

304- **1** **Template (IRE)**[200] 5411 4-11-12 115 LiamMcKenna 120+
(Harry Fry) *lft in ld 1st: hdd next: blnd 3 out: led appr last: drvn out* **8/1**

46/5 **2** 1¾ **Renoyr (FR)**[70] 1376 10-10-13 102 MrStanSheppard 105+
(Malcolm Jefferson) *t.k.h towards rr: trckd ldrs 6th: kpt on fr 2 out: tk 2nd sn after last: styd on same pce* **7/4**[1]

P364 **3** 4 **Samoset**[23] 1893 5-11-2 108 (t) MrTEley(3) 106
(Graeme McPherson) *trckd ldrs: led 5th: sn qcknd pce: hdd appr last: kpt on same pce* **11/2**[3]

334- **4** 2 **Perfect Poison (IRE)**[395] 1780 7-10-7 101 RonanShort(5) 98
(Donald McCain) *towards rr: chsd ldrs 6th: one pce fr 2 out: tk modest 4th last 50yds* **8/1**

54/3 **5** 4 **Pinotage**[24] 1892 7-10-3 95 (p) FinianO'Toole(3) 87
(Peter Niven) *trckd ldrs: effrt between last 2: fdd run-in* **4/1**[2]

0P-0 **6** 1¼ **Bishop Wulstan (IRE)**[36] 1699 4-11-7 115 (b) MrRichardPatrick(5) 107
(Peter Bowen) *led: j. slowly and hdd 1st: led and j. slowly 2nd: t.k.h 4th: hdd and j.lft next: lost pl 2 out* **14/1**

05-0 **7** 22 **Gud Day (IRE)**[181] 186 7-10-13 105 (p) HarryCobden(3) 74
(Conor Dore) *in rr: outpcd and drvn 3 out: bhd fr next* **15/2**

5m 20.8s (41.40) **Going Correction** +1.90s/f (Heavy) **7 Ran SP% 112.4**
Speed ratings (Par 105): **88,87,85,84,83 82,73**
CSF £22.38 TOTE £5.30: £2.90, £1.50; EX 26.50 Trifecta £100.90.
Owner Coral Champions Club **Bred** Deerpark Stud **Trained** Seaborough, Dorset

FOCUS
Nothing more than a modest event, in which whips were not allowed to be used. A big step up on his modest hurdle form from the winner, but in line with his Flat rating.
T/Plt: £40.50 to a £1 stake. Pool of £47736.64 - 859.96 winning tickets. T/Qpdt: £39.20 to a £1 stake. Pool of £2890.54 - 54.55 winning tickets. **Walter Glynn**

MUSSELBURGH (R-H)
Thursday, November 5

OFFICIAL GOING: Good (7.2)
Wind: Almost nil Weather: Overcast, light rain

2292 100% RACING UK PROFITS RETURN TO RACING H'CAP HURDLE (9 hdls) 1m 7f 124y
1:00 (1:02) (Class 4) (0-105,105) 3-Y-O+ **£3,249** (£954; £477; £238)

Form RPR

1225 **1** **Triple Eight (IRE)**[21] 1920 7-11-1 94 (p) AdamNicol(3) 97
(Philip Kirby) *hld up: rdn 3 out: rallied between last 2: led run-in: drvn out* **7/1**

3433 **2** ½ **Urban Kode (IRE)**[21] 1920 7-11-1 96 (v) GrantCockburn(5) 99
(Lucinda Russell) *w ldr to 2nd: chsd ldrs: rdn bef 3 out: rallied to chse ldr after next: ev ch run-in: kpt on: hld nr fin* **6/1**[3]

1631 **3** 1¼ **Endeavor**[21] 1920 10-11-9 102 EmmaSayer(3) 103
(Dianne Sayer) *plld hrd: prom: hdwy on outside to ld after 4 out: rdn next: hdd run-in: kpt on same pce* **12/1**

12 **4** ¾ **Dominada (IRE)**[47] 778 3-10-13 105 WillKennedy 92+
(Brian Ellison) *nt fluent on occasions in midfield: pushed along briefly 4th: hdwy after 4 out: sn pushed along: effrt after next: nt fluent last: kpt on towards fin* **13/8**[1]

000 **5** 13 **Tish Hall (IRE)**[58] 1499 5-10-0 76 oh2 PeterBuchanan 65
(S R B Crawford, Ire) *hld up: rdn bef 3 out: plugged on fr next: nvr able to chal* **28/1**

6 hd **Gabriel Brandy (IRE)**[12] 2074 7-11-10 100 (t) BrianHughes 89
(Robert Alan Hennessy, Ire) *hld up on ins: drvn along 3 out: outpcd fr next* **9/2**[2]

P/0- **7** 1½ **Dhaular Dhar (IRE)**[39] 2297 13-11-5 100 StephenMulqueen(5) 89
(Jim Goldie) *trckd ldrs: effrt and wnt 2nd bef 3 out to after next: wknd qckly fr last* **12/1**

23U6 **8** 20 **Great Demeanor (USA)**[24] 1888 5-10-0 76 oh1 [1] HenryBrooke 53
(Dianne Sayer) *led to after 4 out: rdn and wknd fr next* **40/1**

5F53 **9** 15 **Gin Cobbler**[24] 1891 9-11-4 101 SamColtherd(7) 57
(Victor Thompson) *hld up on outside: struggling 4 out: lost tch fr next* **66/1**

2P/0 **P** **Academy (IRE)**[24] 1892 7-9-13 82 MrKitAlexander(7)
(N W Alexander) *nt fluent on occasions: cl up: chal after 3rd to after 4 out: rdn and wknd next: t.o whn p.u bef last* **18/1**

-P00 **P** **Centre Haafhd**[24] 1886 4-10-2 85 LorcanMurtagh(7)
(Barry Murtagh) *nt fluent on occasions: hld up: hdwy and in tch whn hit 4 out: wknd next: lost tch and p.u bef last* **80/1**

3m 40.5s (-7.90) **Going Correction** -0.40s/f (Good) **11 Ran SP% 112.3**
WFA 3 from 4yo 15lb 4 from 5yo+ 7lb
Speed ratings (Par 105): **103,102,102,101,95 95,94,84,76,**
CSF £45.74 CT £491.76 TOTE £9.30: £2.50, £2.40, £3.20; EX 56.60 Trifecta £298.80.
Owner RedHotGardogs **Bred** Moyglare Stud Farm Ltd **Trained** East Appleton, N Yorks

FOCUS
Bottom bend on hurdles course out 11yds and shared bend with chase course. Chase distances as advertised. Races 1 & 3 increased by 36yds and race 5 by 72yds. Jockeys riding in the first reported the ground as "flicking the top off", "good", and "patchy". Four finished clear in this modest handicap hurdle, which was run at what looked a decent tempo. The first three all met at Carlisle three weeks ago. The first three have been rated pretty much to their marks.

2293 RACING UK AVAILABLE ANYWHERE NOVICES' LIMITED H'CAP CHASE (14 fncs 2 omitted) 2m 3f 193y
1:30 (1:30) (Class 4) (0-120,120) 4-Y-O **£6,330** (£1,870; £935; £468; £234)

Form RPR

20-U **1** **The Cobbler Swayne (IRE)**[14] 2029 6-10-8 106 PeterBuchanan 124+
(Lucinda Russell) *novicey on occasions: hld up in tch: mstke 7th: smooth hdwy to ld 3 out: clr next: easily* **15/8**[1]

4-24 **2** 8 **Court Dismissed (IRE)**[21] 1922 5-11-5 117 BrianHarding 122
(Donald McCain) *led to 6th: chsd clr ldr: effrt and ev ch briefly bef 3 out: one pce whn hit next: no ch w easy wnr* **10/3**[2]

6633 **3** 12 **Amilliontimes (IRE)**[26] 1853 7-10-0 101 oh2 (t) TonyKelly(3) 96
(Jackie Stephen) *hld up: mstke 5th: drvn and outpcd 4 out: rallied whn lft 15 l 3rd last: no ch w first two* **4/1**[3]

123- **4** *3 ¼* **My Betty (IRE)**[14] 2045 7-11-3 118........................ DerekFox(3) 108
(Peter Croke, Ire) *t.k.h early: nt fluent on occasions: hld up: drvn and outpcd after 4 out: no imp fr next* **10/1**
144P **5** *17* **Super Collider**[137] 800 8-10-13 118..............(bt) JamesCorbett(7) 95
(Susan Corbett) *prom: hit and outpcd 4 out: wkng whn nt fluent next* **12/1**
-030 **6** *12* **Calton Entry (IRE)**[32] 1773 6-10-9 107........................ BrianHughes 71
(Linda Perratt) *chsd ldrs: rdn after 4 out: 4th and outpcd whn nt fluent next: sn struggling* **9/1**
-435 **U** **Badged**[126] 885 6-10-2 105........................ GrantCockburn(5)
(Lucy Normile) *nt jump wl in rr: outpcd whn j. awkwardly and uns rdr 7th* **14/1**
06UP **F** **Lucky Bridle (IRE)**[19] 1969 6-11-3 120..................... DiarmuidO'Regan(5)
(Chris Grant) *in tch: hdwy to ld 6th: clr after next to 4 out: hdd bef 3 out: 13 l 3rd and hld whn sprawled and fell last* **33/1**
4m 52.2s (-9.00) **Going Correction** -0.20s/f (Good) **8** Ran SP% **114.3**
Speed ratings (Par 105): **110,106,102,100,93 89, ,**
CSF £9.00 CT £21.38 TOTE £3.60: £1.50, £1.20, £1.70; EX 9.40 Trifecta £28.20.
Owner Mrs R Stobart **Bred** Jerry Russell **Trained** Arlary, Perth & Kinross

FOCUS
The last fence has been omitted from all chases this season, leaving a very long run-in of a furlong and a half. Ordinary form, but a winner who left a decent impression. A big step up on his bumper form from the winner, with the third and fourth rated in line with their recent runs.

2294 PANCREATIC CANCER AWARENESS NOVICES' HURDLE (9 hdls) 1m 7f 124y
2:05 (2:05) (Class 4) 4-Y-0+ **£3,249** (£954; £477; £238)

Form RPR
1 **Innocent Touch (IRE)**[47] 4-10-12 0........................ BrianHughes 110+
(Richard Fahey) *t.k.h early: chsd clr ldr: clsd after 3rd: ev ch gng wl whn nt fluent 2 out: sn rdn: led bef last: drvn and hld on wl run-in* **5/4**[1]
2 *½* **Winter Lion (IRE)**[21] 1934 5-11-5 0..............(t) MarkEnright 115
(Matthew J Smith, Ire) *led: clr to after 3rd: rdn bef 2 out: hdd bef last: rallied and ev ch run-in: kpt on: hld cl home* **11/8**[2]
-233 **3** *16* **Sacred Square (GER)**[34] 1740 5-10-12 108..............(b) BrianHarding 93
(Donald McCain) *hld up on ins: drvn and outpcd after 4 out: rallied and chsng clr ldng pair whn nt fluent last: no imp* **10/1**[3]
60 **4** *5* **Devon River (FR)**[19] 1967 5-10-7 0........................ CallumBewley(5) 87
(Simon Waugh) *hld up: rdn and outpcd bef 3 out: n.d after* **100/1**
5-6P **5** *1 ¼* **Toarmandowithlove (IRE)**[26] 1854 7-9-12 0..........(bt) JamesCorbett(7) 78
(Susan Corbett) *hld up: drvn and outpcd bef 3 out: sn btn* **100/1**
03 **6** *½* **Bold Henmie (IRE)**[23] 1898 4-10-9 110........................ BrianToomey(3) 85
(Philip Kirby) *in tch: hdwy and cl up 4 out: rdn next: wknd after 2 out* **14/1**
43-0 **7** *20* **Buckled**[176] 285 5-10-9 0........................ DerekFox(3) 65
(Sandy Thomson) *chsd ldrs: drvn and outpcd after 4 out: wknd fr next: t.o* **18/1**
3m 39.2s (-9.20) **Going Correction** -0.40s/f (Good)
WFA 4 from 5yo+ 7lb **7** Ran SP% **109.6**
Speed ratings (Par 105): **107,106,98,96,95 95,85**
CSF £3.04 TOTE £2.10: £1.10, £1.10; EX 4.00 Trifecta £9.10.
Owner Nicholas Wrigley & Kevin Hart **Bred** B Kennedy **Trained** Musley Bank, N Yorks

FOCUS
Actual race distance 1m 7f 160yds. A fine tussle between a couple of fairly useful novices, who pulled clear. The time was 1.3sec quicker than the earlier 0-105 handicap. The form has been rated through the second for the time being.

2295 INTERACTIVE H'CAP CHASE (15 fncs 3 omitted) 2m 7f 170y
2:35 (2:35) (Class 3) (0-125,123) 4-Y-0+ **£6,498** (£1,908; £954; £477)

Form RPR
F2-2 **1** **Cobajayisland (IRE)**[15] 2017 7-10-12 112........................ DerekFox(3) 121+
(Lucinda Russell) *led to 9th: w ldr: regained ld and rdn 3 out: lft 3 l clr next: edgd lft u.p run-in: hld on wl cl home* **11/4**[1]
32-6 **2** *hd* **Purcell's Bridge (FR)**[165] 458 8-11-1 115........................ GrahamWatters(3) 122
(Rose Dobbin) *hld up: stdy hdwy to chse ldrs 4 out: rdn whn lft 3 l 2nd 2 out: kpt on wl fr last: jst hld* **5/1**[3]
5-33 **3** *1 ¼* **Swing Hard (IRE)**[24] 1889 7-10-10 107........................ DannyCook 115
(Sue Smith) *chsd ldrs: drvn and outpcd after 4 out: lft 7 l 3rd and hmpd 2 out: rallied and cl 3rd last: one pce last 100yds* **3/1**[2]
0644 **4** *2* **Valleyofmilan (IRE)**[12] 2068 8-11-4 120........................ JamesCowley(5) 125
(Donald McCain) *nt fluent on occasions: hld up: mstke 10th and sn drvn along: outpcd after 4 out: lft 11 l 4th 2 out: plugged on fr last: no imp* **12/1**
-555 **P** **Problema Tic (FR)**[110] 1033 9-11-6 120..............(tp) TonyKelly(3)
(Jackie Stephen) *chsd ldrs: p.u bef 2nd* **5/1**[3]
13-3 **F** **Red Admirable (IRE)**[182] 156 9-11-12 123..............(p) BrianHughes
(Graeme McPherson) *cl up: led 9th: hdd 3 out: ev ch whn fell next* **11/2**
5m 57.0s (-6.40) **Going Correction** -0.20s/f (Good) **6** Ran SP% **108.1**
Speed ratings (Par 107): **102,101,101,100,**
CSF £15.30 TOTE £2.70: £1.30, £3.00; EX 13.80 Trifecta £25.00.
Owner Mrs Lynne Maclennan **Bred** James McGrath **Trained** Arlary, Perth & Kinross
■ Stewards' Enquiry : Graham Watters two-day ban: used whip above the permitted level (19-20 Nov)

FOCUS
Not the strongest event for the grade. The third and fourth have been rated close to their marks.

2296 WATCH ON THE RACING UK APP H'CAP HURDLE (14 hdls) 2m 7f 180y
3:05 (3:05) (Class 4) (0-110,110) 4-Y-0+ **£3,249** (£954; £477; £238)

Form RPR
6115 **1** **Maraweh (IRE)**[42] 1637 5-11-1 102..............(v) DerekFox(3) 104
(Lucinda Russell) *led to 2nd: pressed ldr: rdn and regained ld 3 out: styd on strly fr next* **11/4**[1]
0612 **2** *3* **Andhaar**[10] 2102 9-11-1 109........................ BlairCampbell(10) 109
(N W Alexander) *hld up: rdn bef 3 out: hit next: styd on u.p run-in: tk 2nd cl home* **5/1**[3]
5034 **3** *nk* **St Quintin**[50] 1550 5-11-8 106........................ BrianHughes 105
(David Brown) *trckd ldrs: effrt whn hit 3 out: sn rdn: kpt on u.p fr last* **8/1**
0025 **4** *nse* **Solway Prince**[32] 1784 6-11-2 105........................ CallumBewley(5) 104
(Lisa Harrison) *cl up: led 2nd: rdn and hdd 3 out: drvn and one pce fr last: eased and lost two pls cl home* **7/2**[2]
F0PP **5** *1 ¼* **Arctic Court (IRE)**[22] 1903 11-11-12 110........................ BrianHarding 108
(Jim Goldie) *hld up in tch: outpcd after 4 out: shkn up and kpt on steadily fr 2 out: nvr nrr* **14/1**
0P-6 **6** *5* **No Such Number**[165] 455 7-10-3 94........................ MrTHamilton(7) 87
(Sandy Forster) *trckd ldrs: effrt and rdn after 3 out: edgd rt and wknd bef last* **16/1**
P5U0 **7** *44* **Sharivarry (FR)**[137] 798 9-9-8 85 oh3 ow1........................ SamColtherd(7) 39
(Victor Thompson) *hld up: drvn and struggling bef 3 out: sn lost tch: t.o* **66/1**
F-06 **P** **Slaney Star (IRE)**[32] 1776 7-10-7 91........................ HenryBrooke
(Jean McGregor) *hld up: nt fluent 6th: drvn and struggling bef 3 out: p.u and dismntd after next* **20/1**
2P13 **P** **Craigdancer (IRE)**[37] 1683 6-10-3 92........................ DaraghBourke(5)
(Joanne Foster) *hld up: lost action and p.u bnd bef 8th* **11/2**
6m 6.1s (24.00) **Going Correction** -0.40s/f (Good) **9** Ran SP% **110.9**
Speed ratings (Par 105): **44,43,42,42,42 40,26, ,**
CSF £16.17 CT £90.80 TOTE £2.90: £1.20, £2.00, £3.00; EX 12.10 Trifecta £51.40.
Owner Tay Valley Chasers Racing Club **Bred** Shadwell Estate Company Limited **Trained** Arlary, Perth & Kinross
■ Stewards' Enquiry : Callum Bewley ten-day ban: failed to ride out for third place (19-28 Nov)

FOCUS
Actual race distance 3m 33yds. Just a fair handicap hurdle. A small pb from the winner, with the second, third and fourth pretty much to their marks.

2297 DOWNLOAD RACING UK APP H'CAP CHASE (15 fncs 3 omitted) 2m 7f 170y
3:40 (3:40) (Class 4) (0-105,99) 4-Y-0+ **£3,898** (£1,144; £572; £286)

Form RPR
223 **1** **Derryfadda (IRE)**[14] 2039 6-11-4 94........................ HarryChalloner(3) 112+
(Richard Ford) *t.k.h: mde virtually all: drew clr bef 3 out: eased run-in* **4/1**[1]
2P-4 **2** *9* **Benefit In Kind (IRE)**[26] 1855 7-11-5 92..............(tp) DannyCook 98
(Katie Scott) *prom: hdwy to chse (clr) wnr whn nt fluent 3 out: rdn and no imp fr next* **4/1**[1]
433P **3** *¾* **Shady Sadie (IRE)**[43] 1629 8-9-9 78..............(t) LorcanMurtagh(10) 83
(Rose Dobbin) *hld up: mstke 10th: hdwy after 4 out: drvn and kpt on same pce fr 2 out* **5/1**[2]
4225 **4** *2* **Solway Bay**[21] 1930 13-11-1 93..............(t) CallumBewley(5) 96
(Lisa Harrison) *bhd: outpcd 1/2-way: rdn and hdwy bef 3 out: no imp bef next: hld whn hung lft run-in* **14/1**
212U **5** *8* **Court Of Law (IRE)**[14] 2037 7-11-11 98..............(p) BrianHarding 94
(Donald McCain) *in tch: drvn and outpcd after 4 out: wknd fr next* **9/1**[3]
012P **6** *2 ¼* **Alta Rock (IRE)**[6] 2173 10-11-5 92........................ SeanQuinlan 86
(Sue Smith) *pressed wnr tl rn wd bnd and outpcd bef 3 out: sn struggling* **5/1**[2]
/P-3 **7** *11* **Simarthur**[21] 1925 8-11-12 99..............(p) PeterBuchanan 88
(Lucinda Russell) *nt jump wl: cl up: lost pl whn blnd 11th: sn struggling: t.o* **4/1**[1]
6m 3.2s (-0.20) **Going Correction** -0.20s/f (Good) **7** Ran SP% **110.0**
Speed ratings (Par 105): **92,89,88,88,85 84,81**
CSF £19.06 TOTE £4.30: £1.90, £2.50; EX 16.20 Trifecta £79.40.
Owner Mr & Mrs G E Pickering **Bred** Mrs P Madden **Trained** Garstang, Lancs

FOCUS
Just an ordinary race for the grade. The second has been rated to his mark.
T/Plt: £55.10 to a £1 stake. Pool of £50466.04 - 667.59 winning tickets,. T/Qpdt: £9.30 to a £1 stake. Pool of £3956.38 - 314.10 winning tickets. **Richard Young**

1812 TOWCESTER (R-H)
Thursday, November 5

OFFICIAL GOING: Good (good to soft in places) changing to soft after race 5 (3.30)
Wind: Fresh half-against Weather: Showers

2298 HAYGAIN HAY STEAMERS CLEAN HEALTHY HAY MARES' H'CAP HURDLE (11 hdls) 2m 4f 217y
12:50 (12:51) (Class 5) (0-100,100) 3-Y-0+ **£3,249** (£954; £477; £238)

Form RPR
P3F2 **1** **Oscar Jane (IRE)**[17] 2000 8-10-3 77..............(bt) BrendanPowell 91+
(Johnny Farrelly) *mde all: wnt clr appr 2 out: eased towards fin* **7/1**[2]
P010 **2** *6* **Pattara**[37] 1691 6-11-2 90..............(t) GerardTumelty 94
(Noel Williams) *a.p: rdn to chse wnr appr 2 out: styd on same pce* **11/1**
43 **3** *2 ¾* **Shaky Gift (IRE)**[38] 1673 6-11-12 100........................ NoelFehily 102
(Neil Mulholland) *hld up: hdwy appr 2 out: sn rdn: styng on same pce whn mstke last* **8/1**
06-P **4** *4 ½* **Dolly Diamond**[188] 55 6-10-6 90........................ ArchieBellamy(10) 87
(Graeme McPherson) *hld up: pushed along and hdwy appr 3 out: rdn bef next: wknd bef last* **33/1**
35-F **5** *6* **Pandy Wells**[189] 40 6-10-5 79........................ KielanWoods 71
(Graeme McPherson) *hld up: hdwy 3 out: sn rdn: wknd bef next* **15/2**[3]
43 **6** *10* **Think Of Me (IRE)**[22] 1910 6-11-2 90........................ AlainCawley 73
(Fergal O'Brien) *hld up: hdwy 8th: rdn and wknd appr 2 out* **11/2**[1]
-3P4 **7** *3 ¼* **Tara's Rainbow**[15] 2021 5-11-6 94..............(t) DavidBass 74
(Kim Bailey) *prom: lost pl 4th: rdn and wknd after 8th* **20/1**
0045 **8** *9* **Canarbino Girl**[17] 2004 8-10-2 76..............(t) JamesBest 48
(Caroline Keevil) *hld up: wknd 8th* **12/1**
454- **9** *6* **Glenarm**[280] 3932 6-11-12 100........................ AndrewThornton 66
(Seamus Mullins) *chsd wnr to 2nd: remained handy: wnt 2nd again 6th tl rdn and wknd appr 2 out* **14/1**
43-2 **10** *13* **Sunshine Buddy**[178] 240 8-11-0 88..............(p) JamesDavies 43
(Chris Down) *prom: rdn after 8th: wkng whn hit 3 out* **9/1**
5-30 **P** **Unefille De Guye (FR)**[85] 1236 7-9-10 80..............(bt) MrJakeBament(10)
(Victor Dartnall) *a in rr: bhd fr 7th: p.u bef 3 out* **7/1**[2]
400- **P** **Aroseforoscar**[213] 5185 6-10-9 90..............(b) CiaranGethings(7)
(Chris Down) *hld up in tch: rdn and wknd appr 3 out: bhd whn p.u bef next* **17/2**
0P-P **P** **Hortense Mancini**[17] 2004 6-10-0 74 oh5..............(p) NicodeBoinville
(Mark Bradstock) *chsd wnr 2nd: nt fluent 5th: lost 2nd next: rdn and wknd after 8th: bhd whn p.u bef 2 out* **20/1**
P06- **P** **Showbiz Floozy**[196] 5500 6-10-10 84........................ MarkGrant
(John O'Neill) *hld up: wknd 7th: bhd whn p.u bef 3 out* **66/1**
5m 22.1s (-5.10) **Going Correction** -0.175s/f (Good) **14** Ran SP% **120.4**
Speed ratings (Par 103): **102,99,98,96,94 90,89,86,83,78 , , ,**
CSF £78.09 CT £638.57 TOTE £4.50: £2.00, £4.40, £2.40; EX 85.60 Trifecta £195.90.
Owner P Tosh **Bred** J R Weston **Trained** Enmore, Somerset

FOCUS
Shared bends. Race 3 reduced by 67yds and race 6 reduced by 88yds. They were strung out early on in this weak mares' handicap and those waited with struggled. The winner has been rated back to her best, with the second close to her mark and a step up from the third.

2299 WEATHERBYS NOVICES' HURDLE (11 hdls) 2m 4f 217y
1:20 (1:21) (Class 4) 4-Y-0+ £4,548 (£1,335; £667; £333)

Form RPR
242- **1** **Toby Lerone (IRE)**[248] 4539 8-10-12 123 HarrySkelton 122
(Dan Skelton) *mde all: rdn appr 2 out: all out* **11/4**[1]
/1-2 **2** ½ **For Instance (IRE)**[169] 407 5-10-12 0 NoelFehily 123+
(Jonjo O'Neill) *mid-div: hdwy after 8th: outpcd after 3 out: mstke next: rallied appr and nt fluent last: styd on u.p* **7/2**[3]
143- **3** 1 ¾ **Robinsson (IRE)**[270] 4107 5-10-9 118 ThomasGarner(3) 120
(Oliver Sherwood) *hld up: hdwy 5th: ev ch 3 out: sn rdn: styd on same pce last* **10/3**[2]
0 **4** 39 **Magic Mustard (IRE)**[173] 341 4-10-12 0 KielanWoods 85
(Charlie Longsdon) *chsd ldrs: rdn after 6th: wknd appr 3 out* **25/1**
0-3 **5** 1 ¼ **Florida Calling (IRE)**[28] 1829 6-10-12 0 PaddyBrennan 84
(Tom George) *hld up in tch: mstke 4th: rdn appr 3 out: sn wknd* **6/1**
0-P0 **6** 3 ½ **Lined With Silver (IRE)**[12] 2062 6-10-12 0 MattieBatchelor 83
(Dai Burchell) *hld up: rdn after 6th: sme hdwy appr 3 out: sn wknd* **100/1**
3 **7** 10 **Midnight Folie**[155] 602 5-10-5 0 DavidBass 65
(Ben Pauling) *chsd wnr: hit 5th: rdn and lost 2nd bef 3 out: sn wknd* **25/1**
8 2 ½ **Ceann Sibheal (IRE)**[368] 6-10-12 0 GavinSheehan 69
(Warren Greatrex) *hld up: nvr on terms* **17/2**
00-P **9** 30 **Myroundorurs (IRE)**[185] 105 5-10-12 0 CharliePoste 42
(Robin Dickin) *hld up: hdwy appr 3 out: sn rdn and wknd* **100/1**
05 **10** 47 **Jopaan (IRE)**[20] 1952 8-10-12 0 (t) DaveCrosse
(Brian Barr) *chsd ldrs tl rdn and wknd after 8th* **100/1**
-0P5 **11** 18 **Kayf Tiger**[26] 1844 6-10-7 0 ChrisWard(5)
(Robin Dickin) *a in rr: bhd fr 6th* **100/1**
U **Pantoloni**[502] 4-10-7 0 DannyBurton(5)
(Richard Harper) *hld up: plld hrd: uns rdr after 3rd* **100/1**
0/0- **P** **Banderitos**[207] 6-10-7 0 ConorRing(5)
(Anna Brooks) *mid-div: hdwy 5th: wknd 7th: bhd whn p.u bef 2 out* **100/1**
PP **P** **Thady Quil (IRE)**[156] 590 5-10-12 0 (t) AndrewTinkler
(Martin Keighley) *hld up: sme hdwy 8th: wknd bef next: bhd whn p.u bef 2 out* **66/1**
P **Barenice (FR)**[207] 4-10-12 0 DarylJacob
(Alex Hales) *hld up: hdwy 5th: rdn and wknd 3 out: bhd whn p.u bef 2 out* **10/1**
60 **P** **Lunar Flow**[155] 601 4-10-12 0 BrendanPowell
(Jamie Snowden) *hld up: blnd 7th: sn bhd: p.u bef last* **100/1**

5m 22.0s (-5.20) **Going Correction** -0.175s/f (Good) **16** Ran SP% **122.0**
Speed ratings (Par 105): **102,101,101,86,85 84,80,79,68,50 43, , , ,**
CSF £12.29 TOTE £3.50: £1.60, £2.30, £1.10; EX 12.70 Trifecta £44.20.
Owner Mrs Gill Duckworth & Mrs Pat Dry **Bred** M J Halligan **Trained** Alcester, Warwicks

FOCUS
The principals dominated this novice event from three out and the form is straightforward. The winner and third set the level in a straightforward novice.

2300 WEATHERBYS NOVICES' H'CAP CHASE (11 fncs) 2m 70y
1:55 (1:55) (Class 4) (0-105,112) 4-Y-0+ £4,548 (£1,335; £667; £333)

Form RPR
50/0 **1** **Moscow Me (IRE)**[41] 1647 8-10-12 94 JeremiahMcGrath(3) 110+
(Henry Oliver) *chsd ldr tl led appr 3 out: clr last: rdn out: eased nr fin* **7/1**[2]
313- **2** 13 **Kassis**[197] 5466 6-11-10 103 BrendanPowell 105
(Jamie Snowden) *chsd ldrs: rdn appr 2 out: styd on same pce: wnt 2nd nr fin* **10/1**
3 1 **Sabroclair (FR)**[174] 325 6-11-5 98 DarylJacob 100
(Richard Woollacott) *hld up: racd keenly: mstke 3rd: hdwy 3 out: chsd wnr next: sn rdn: wknd flat* **25/1**
015- **4** 4 ½ **Grand March**[236] 4764 6-11-12 105 (p) DavidBass 105
(Kim Bailey) *hld up in tch: pckd 2nd: mstke 4th: chsd wnr 3 out tl rdn next: wknd last* **8/1**[3]
/231 **5** 30 **Gee Hi (IRE)**[9] 2124 9-12-5 112 7ex GavinSheehan 100
(Warren Greatrex) *chsd ldrs: blnd 3rd: nt fluent and lost pl 5th: nt fluent 7th: rdn and wknd appr 2 out: j. slowly last* **4/7**[1]
324- **P** **Eastern Witness (IRE)**[241] 4675 8-9-13 81 (b) CallumWhillans(3)
(Venetia Williams) *led: rdn and hdd appr 3 out: wknd and p.u bef next* **7/1**[2]
U-02 **P** **Stars Royale (IRE)**[17] 2003 6-11-11 104 TomCannon
(Nick Gifford) *hld up: mstke 3rd: mstke and wknd 6th: bhd whn p.u bef last* **12/1**
4-43 **P** **The Lion Man (IRE)**[21] 1929 5-11-12 105 CharliePoste
(Robin Dickin) *in rr whn blnd 3rd: sn bhd: p.u bef 2 out* **25/1**

4m 4.8s (-11.30) **Going Correction** -0.575s/f (Firm) **8** Ran SP% **124.2**
Speed ratings (Par 105): **105,98,98,95,80 , ,**
CSF £75.42 CT £1669.32 TOTE £14.60: £1.80, £3.30, £3.30; EX 114.10 Trifecta £2243.80 Part won..
Owner Oscar Singh & Miss Priya Purewal **Bred** Egmont Stud **Trained** Abberley, Worcs

FOCUS
This moderate novice handicap fell apart leaving the back straight. The second, third and fourth have been rated in line with their hurdle marks.

2301 AGETUR UK 30TH ANNIVERSARY H'CAP HURDLE (11 hdls) 2m 4f 217y
2:25 (2:25) (Class 3) (0-125,125) 4-Y-0+ £5,848 (£1,717; £858; £429)

Form RPR
21-5 **1** **Milord (GER)**[28] 1818 6-11-4 117 (p) DavidBass 125+
(Kim Bailey) *chsd ldrs: mstke 5th: led appr and pckd 2 out: sn rdn: all out* **9/2**[2]
1350 **2** nk **Stephen Hero (IRE)**[20] 1949 5-11-0 120 (t) MichaelHeard(7) 126
(Brian Barr) *a.p: nt fluent 2nd: rdn appr 3 out: hung rt appr 2 out: ev ch flat: styd on u.p* **16/1**
40-P **3** 1 **Vaillant Creek (FR)**[180] 210 6-10-6 105 KielanWoods 109
(Alex Hales) *chsd ldr to 3rd: remained handy: rdn and ev ch appr 2 out: no ex towards fin* **9/1**
P-P0 **4** 22 **Malibu Sun**[14] 2042 8-11-1 114 NicodeBoinville 98
(Ben Pauling) *led to 7th: led again 3 out: sn rdn hdd & wknd bef next* **5/1**[3]
F0-P **5** ½ **Arthur Mc Bride (IRE)**[187] 86 6-10-5 107 RyanHatch(3) 91
(Nigel Twiston-Davies) *hld up: hdwy appr 3 out: rdn and wknd bef next* **9/2**[2]
516 **6** 4 **Gallic Destiny (IRE)**[25] 1870 4-11-8 124 (t) JamesBanks(3) 104
(Jo Davis) *prom: chsd ldr 3rd: hit next: led 7th: hdd 3 out: sn rdn and wknd* **18/1**
-1U0 **P** **Drombeg West**[153] 625 8-10-9 108 AndrewTinkler
(Anna Brooks) *hld up: rdn and wknd after 7th: bhd whn p.u bef 2 out* **25/1**
333- **P** **Great Choice (IRE)**[247] 4547 6-11-9 125 KieronEdgar(3)
(David Pipe) *hld up: bhd fr 6th: p.u bef 2 out* **5/2**[1]
P3-4 **P** **Red Tortue (IRE)**[23] 1896 6-11-4 117 (t) SamTwiston-Davies
(Charlie Longsdon) *hld up: nt fluent 3rd: rdn and wknd 8th: bhd whn p.u bef 2 out* **8/1**

5m 22.3s (-4.90) **Going Correction** -0.175s/f (Good)
WFA 4 from 5yo+ 8lb **9** Ran SP% **117.7**
Speed ratings (Par 107): **102,101,101,93,92 91, , ,**
CSF £70.46 CT £627.29 TOTE £6.30: £1.90, £2.30, £2.90; EX 72.50 Trifecta £1117.30.
Owner Kim Bailey Racing Partnership VII **Bred** Frau C U R Schatzchen **Trained** Andoversford, Gloucs

FOCUS
A modest handicap, run at a fair gallop, that served up a tight three-way finish. The second and third have been rated pretty much to their marks.

2302 FIREWORKS MARES' "NATIONAL HUNT" MAIDEN HURDLE (8 hdls) 1m 7f 181y
2:55 (2:55) (Class 5) 4-Y-0+ £3,249 (£954; £477; £238)

Form RPR
200- **1** **Ruby Rambler**[220] 5071 5-11-0 0 GavinSheehan 113+
(Lucy Wadham) *mde all: clr after 3 out: eased towards fin* **5/1**[3]
50- **2** 5 **Happy Diva (IRE)**[203] 5359 4-11-0 0 JamieMoore 102
(Kerry Lee) *mid-div: hdwy bef 4th: rdn appr 2 out: wnt 2nd last: no ch w wnr* **20/1**
211- **3** 1 **Midnight Silver**[224] 4995 5-11-0 0 (t) BrendanPowell 102
(Jamie Snowden) *a.p: chsd wnr and j.lft 2 out: sn rdn and lost 2nd: hung rt flat bef last: styd on* **9/2**[2]
002 **4** 1 ¾ **Kilty Caul (IRE)**[19] 1960 6-11-0 0 DavidBass 99
(Kim Bailey) *hld up: hdwy appr 2 out: nt rch ldrs* **10/1**
5 2 ½ **Lakeshore Lady (IRE)**[550] 5-10-9 0 JakeHodson(5) 97
(David Bridgwater) *chsd wnr tl rdn after 3 out: styd on same pce fr next* **25/1**
22-3 **6** 1 **Storming Strumpet**[185] 111 5-11-0 117 PaddyBrennan 97
(Tom George) *hld up: hdwy and mstke 3 out: rdn and wknd appr last* **2/1**[1]
30-4 **7** 1 ½ **Biretta**[27] 1843 4-11-0 0 (t) NoelFehily 94
(Harry Fry) *hld up in tch: pushed along appr 2 out: wkng whn mstke last* **7/1**
30- **8** ½ **Pink Tara**[251] 4478 4-10-11 0 CallumWhillans(3) 94
(Venetia Williams) *mid-div: hdwy bef 3rd: hdwy bef next: wknd 3 out* **25/1**
26 **9** 1 ¾ **Tullow Tonic (IRE)**[29] 1811 4-11-0 0 DarylJacob 92
(Charlie Longsdon) *hld up: nvr on terms* **33/1**
56/ **10** 3 ¾ **Beautiful Gem (FR)**[565] 5388 5-11-0 0 HarrySkelton 88
(Dan Skelton) *hld up: hdwy 3 out: rdn and wknd bef next* **25/1**
46 **11** 1 ¾ **The Barbury Queen (IRE)**[22] 1908 5-10-11 0 TomBellamy(3) 86
(Alan King) *mid-div: rdn after 5th: sn wknd* **33/1**
50- **12** 2 ½ **Another Cobbler (FR)**[207] 5299 5-11-0 0 AndrewTinkler 84
(Henry Daly) *hld up: rdn appr 3 out: sn wknd* **66/1**
205- **13** 6 **Miss Minx**[272] 4065 4-11-0 0 WayneHutchinson 78
(Alan King) *mid-div: hdwy 5th: wknd after 3 out* **14/1**
3- **14** 30 **Cosmic Diamond**[198] 5454 5-11-0 0 PaulMoloney 48
(Paul Webber) *hld up: wknd after 3 out* **25/1**
3/0 **15** ½ **Heartening**[48] 1574 7-11-0 0 DaveCrosse 47
(Paul Phillips) *chsd ldrs tl wknd 3 out* **100/1**
350 **P** **Kaddys Girl**[116] 970 5-10-9 0 ChrisWard(5)
(Robin Dickin) *hld up: rdn and wknd after 5th: bhd whn p.u bef 2 out* **100/1**

4m 0.7s (-7.20) **Going Correction** -0.175s/f (Good) **16** Ran SP% **125.9**
Speed ratings (Par 103): **111,108,108,107,105 105,104,104,103,101 100,99,96,81,81**
CSF £102.57 TOTE £6.50: £2.40, £9.10, £1.50; EX 139.20 Trifecta £776.90.
Owner Sara Dennis,J J W Wadham & J C S Wilson **Bred** Grove Farm Stud **Trained** Newmarket, Suffolk

FOCUS
This is often a fair mares' maiden and the form should work out okay. There's a case for rating the race higher through the fourth and sixth, but they finished in a bit of a heap behind the winner, and this is probably high enough.

2303 AGETUR UK 30TH ANNIVERSARY H'CAP CHASE (15 fncs) 2m 5f 153y
3:30 (3:30) (Class 5) (0-100,88) 4-Y-0+ £3,249 (£954; £477; £238)

Form RPR
P-00 **1** **Monty's Revenge (IRE)**[29] 1813 10-11-0 76 (p) IanPopham 90+
(Martin Keighley) *w ldr tl led 6th: rdn appr 2 out: hdd and 1 l down whn lft in ld last: idled flat: drvn out* **8/1**
2-4P **2** 8 **Musical Wedge**[26] 1850 11-11-7 83 NickScholfield 85
(Claire Dyson) *led to 6th: remained handy tl rdn and wknd after 2 out: lft poor 3rd last: wnt 2nd fnl 100yds* **11/2**[3]
566/ **3** 4 ½ **Salut Honore (FR)**[603] 4759 9-11-9 88 (t) JamesBanks(3) 88
(Alex Hales) *hld up: hdwy 7th: chsd ldr 9th to 11th: rdn whn mstke 2 out: sn wknd: lft 2nd last tl fnl 100yds* **8/1**
6-P3 **4** 13 **Rebel High (IRE)**[17] 1999 11-10-5 67 (v) AdamWedge 52
(Derek Frankland) *prom: chsd ldr wnr 11th tl rdn appr 3 out: wknd bef next* **10/1**
3-46 **5** 6 **Jolly Boys Outing (IRE)**[29] 1813 12-11-4 83 BenPoste(3) 62
(Rosemary Gasson) *hld up: hdwy 6th: wknd 11th* **11/2**[3]
0432 **P** **Xenophon**[29] 1813 7-10-9 76 AliceMills(5)
(Michael Chapman) *a in rr: bhd fr 6th: mstke 8th: bhd whn p.u bef 10th* **5/1**[2]
3243 **P** **Combustible Kate (IRE)**[19] 1972 9-10-12 79 CharlieDeutsch(5)
(Nick Kent) *hld up: drvn along 7th: in rr whn blnd 9th: p.u bef next* **11/2**[3]
0-6P **P** **Toohighforme (IRE)**[155] 600 6-11-6 82 (p) TomCannon
(Nick Gifford) *chsd ldrs tl rdn and wknd 10th: bhd whn p.u bef 3 out* **12/1**
5602 **U** **Dawnieriver (IRE)**[32] 1785 5-11-5 81 JamieMoore 93
(Michael Scudamore) *hld up: hdwy 10th: chsd wnr bef 2 out: rdn to ld and 1 l ahd whn blnd and uns rdr last* **9/2**[1]

5m 47.9s (-5.10) **Going Correction** -0.25s/f (Good) **9** Ran SP% **120.0**
Speed ratings (Par 103): **99,96,94,89,87 , , ,**
CSF £54.02 CT £371.70 TOTE £12.80: £3.50, £2.20, £3.50; EX 80.20 Trifecta £732.90.
Owner The Red Socks & Mrs Belinda Keighley **Bred** Gerald Mitchell **Trained** Condicote, Gloucs

FOCUS
This weak handicap was run at a sound gallop and it saw a slow-motion finish. The second is probably the best guide to the level.

2304 HAYGAIN HAY STEAMERS CLEAN HEALTHY FORAGE FILLIES' "JUNIOR" STANDARD OPEN NATIONAL HUNT FLAT RACE 1m 5f 146y
4:05 (4:05) (Class 6) 3-Y-O £1,949 (£572; £286; £143)

Form RPR
2 **1** **Water Willow**[16] 2009 3-10-10 0 NoelFehily 95+
(Harry Fry) *mde all: rdn over 1f out: styd on* 4/1[2]
2 **2** 1 ¼ **Passmore**[32] 1772 3-10-10 0 WayneHutchinson 94+
(Alan King) *hld up in tch: chsd wnr over 3f out: rdn and hung lft over 1f out: styd on* 1/2[1]
5 **3** 1 ½ **Purple Genie (GR)**[16] 2009 3-10-10 0 NicodeBoinville 90
(Patrick Chamings) *chsd ldr 6f: sn lost pl: outpcd over 2f out: styd on ins fnl f* 25/1
3 **4** 1 ¾ **Anne Of Brittany (FR)**[32] 1772 3-10-10 0 JackQuinlan 88
(Henry Spiller) *a.p: racd keenly: chsd ldr over 7f out tl rdn over 3f out: hung lft and styd on same pce ins fnl f* 7/1[3]
5 **5** 19 **Miss Feistypants**[32] 1772 3-10-5 0 KevinJones(5) 63
(Seamus Mullins) *hld up: rdn over 3f out: wknd over 2f out* 25/1
6 1 ¾ **Coco Flower (FR)** 3-10-7 0 JamesBanks(3) 61
(Alex Hales) *chsd ldrs: rdn over 3f out: wknd over 2f out* 25/1
3m 30.8s (-9.80) 6 Ran SP% 110.7
CSF £6.28 TOTE £4.40: £1.70, £1.10; EX 6.60 Trifecta £40.10.
Owner Avalon Surfacing Ltd **Bred** Avalon Surfacing, R Forgan, L Maudsley **Trained** Seaborough, Dorset

FOCUS
The form of this fillies' bumper is straightforward enough to assess. The runner-up and fourth set the level.
T/Plt: £7,457.60 to a £1 stake. Pool of £78662.48 7.70 winning tickets. T/Qpdt: £686.20 to a £1 stake. Pool of £6862.77 - 7.40 winning tickets. **Colin Roberts**

2305 - 2311a (Foreign Racing) - See Raceform Interactive

2011 **FONTWELL** (L-H)
Friday, November 6

OFFICIAL GOING: Soft (5.5)
Wind: strong half behind Weather: rain Rails: Fences and hurdles outer. Bottom bend divided. Rail movement adding Chase + 70yds, HURDLE 2m 1f and 2m 3f +90yds, 3m 1f +135yds.

2312 WINNER RENTAL SERVICES CONDITIONAL JOCKEYS' NOVICES' HURDLE (10 hdls) 2m 3f 33y
1:40 (1:40) (Class 4) 4-Y-0+ £3,249 (£954; £477; £238)

Form RPR
10- **1** **Bon Enfant (FR)**[192] 9 4-10-9 0 HarryBannister(3) 115+
(Warren Greatrex) *trckd ldrs: chal after 3 out tl bdly hmpd by loose horse appr 2 out: sn rdn: 1 l down whn nt fluent last: styng on whn lft in ld fnl 150yds: rdn out* 5/2[2]
2/3- **2** 6 **Danvinnie**[228] 4969 6-10-9 0 ThomasGarner(3) 111+
(Oliver Sherwood) *kpt quite wd in sts: trckd ldrs: led after 3 out: hmpd by loose horse bef next: 1 l up whn hit last: v bdly hmpd by loose horse by paddock entrnce and hdd fnl 150yds: no ch after* 11/2[3]
44-3 **3** 3 ¼ **Sandygate (IRE)**[189] 61 5-10-6 118 CiaranGethings(6) 105
(Philip Hobbs) *trckd ldrs: rdn after 3 out: styd on same pce fr next* 8/11[1]
5-6 **4** 37 **Threebarmymen (IRE)**[16] 2011 4-10-9 0 MattGriffiths(3) 67
(Jeremy Scott) *hld up in last pair: kpt wd in sts: wknd after 3 out: t.o* 16/1
6 **5** 5 **Repeat The Feat (FR)**[170] 400 4-10-12 0 ConorShoemark 62
(Charlie Longsdon) *cl up: rdn after 3 out: wknd bef next: t.o* 20/1
0-30 **6** 6 **Finnegan's Garden (IRE)**[156] 595 6-10-7 0 WilliamFeatherstone(5) 57
(Zoe Davison) *led tl rdn sn after 3 out: wknd bef next: t.o* 100/1
0 **7** 13 **Victorian Teo (FR)**[83] 5-10-9 0 BenPoste(3) 43
(Tom Symonds) *a in last pair: struggling after 7th: wknd next: t.o* 50/1
F **Doitforthevillage (IRE)**[219] 6-10-12 0 FreddieMitchell
(Paul Henderson) *fell 2nd* 14/1
5m 17.0s (17.60) **Going Correction** +1.00s/f (Soft) 8 Ran SP% 122.1
Speed ratings (Par 105): **102,99,98,82,80 77,72,**
CSF £17.85 TOTE £2.90: £1.10, £1.70, £1.10; EX 16.70 Trifecta £31.60.
Owner Swanee River Partnership **Bred** Haras De Saint-Voir **Trained** Upper Lambourn, Berks

FOCUS
Fences and hurdles on outer line. Rail movement increased races 2 & 4 (chases) by 70yds, races 1, 3 & 6 by 90yds and race 5 by 135yds. There was 8mm of rain overnight and the ground was described as soft. It was run in wet and gloomy conditions which made for poor visibility at times. A loose horse hampered the winner and second up the straight. There's a case for rating the race up to 8lb higher through the third, but not on time compared with the later handicap.

2313 EBF STALLIONS/TBA MARES' BEGINNERS' CHASE (16 fncs) 2m 5f 31y
2:10 (2:10) (Class 4) 4-Y-0+ £5,325 (£1,653; £890)

Form RPR
220- **1** **Emily Gray (IRE)**[241] 4692 7-11-0 143 DavidBass 135+
(Kim Bailey) *disp ld tl clr ldr 9th: wnt sltly rt fr 3 out: hit 2 out and last: styd on wl: rdn out* 5/4[1]
11P- **2** 2 ½ **Cresswell Breeze**[230] 4918 5-11-0 0 (t) AidanColeman 130
(Anthony Honeyball) *trckd ldrs: hit 12th: rdn after 3 out: disputing cl 2nd at the last: styd on but a being hld by wnr fnl 140yds* 4/1[2]
466- **3** 13 **Kayfleur**[204] 5355 6-11-0 0 TomO'Brien 116
(Henry Daly) *hld up 5th: wnt 4th after 12th: rdn after 4 out: styd on fr next but nt pce to get on terms: lft 3rd at the last* 15/2[3]
1-23 **F** **Ebony Empress (IRE)**[22] 1932 6-11-0 123 (p) NoelFehily 130
(Neil Mulholland) *disp ld tl 9th: chsd wnr: rdn after 3 out: styng on in clly disp 2nd whn knuckled on landing and fell last* 4/1[2]
252- **P** **Taniokey (IRE)**[200] 5430 5-11-0 0 LeightonAspell
(Oliver Sherwood) *j.rt at times: chsd ldrs: nt fluent 11th: struggling after next: wknd 4 out: p.u bef next* 8/1
5m 59.7s (16.70) **Going Correction** +1.075s/f (Soft) 5 Ran SP% 107.3
Speed ratings (Par 105): **111,110,105, ,**
CSF £6.31 TOTE £1.90: £1.20, £2.50; EX 4.30 Trifecta £26.30.
Owner J Perriss **Bred** Robert McCarthy **Trained** Andoversford, Gloucs

FOCUS
This was run over 70 yards further than advertised. The gloom had lifted a bit but vision still wasn't great. This was a decent enough race of its type. The winner, who set a decent standard, has been rated 10lb off her Doncaster second. The second has been rated to her hurdle mark.

2314 SOUTHERN CRANES AND ACCESS LTD / TBA MARES' H'CAP HURDLE (10 hdls) 2m 3f 33y
2:40 (2:40) (Class 3) (0-130,126) 3-Y-0+ £5,848 (£1,717; £858; £429)

Form RPR
405- **1** **Flute Bowl**[230] 4905 5-11-2 116 (p) JoshuaMoore 127+
(Gary Moore) *racd inner tl c up stands' side home st: disp ld tl clr ldr 7th: jnd after 3 out tl next: drew clr bef last: styd on strly: pushed out* 6/1
561- **2** 15 **Aces Over Eights (IRE)**[219] 5093 6-10-6 106 CharliePoste 103
(Kerry Lee) *racd wd: trckd ldrs: chal after 3 out tl next: sn rdn: styd on same pce fr last* 13/2
21-2 **3** 1 ¾ **Jean Fleming (IRE)**[30] 1808 8-11-4 118 BrendanPowell 111
(Jamie Snowden) *kpt wd: chsd ldrs: outpcd after 3 out: styd on again between last 2: wnt 3rd run-in* 11/4[2]
012- **4** 1 ¾ **Abundantly**[221] 5060 6-10-6 109 CallumWhillans(3) 101
(Venetia Williams) *racd inner: disp ld most of way tl 7th: sn rdn: hld in 3rd after 3 out: wknd last* 5/2[1]
P1P- **P** **Faerie Reel (FR)**[232] 4872 5-11-12 126 DavidBass
(Kim Bailey) *kpt to inner tl fnl time in bk st: trckd ldrs: pushed along bef 7th: wknd 3 out: t.o whn p.u bef next* 16/1
22-2 **P** **Avispa**[16] 2021 6-11-5 119 [1] DenisO'Regan
(Alan King) *kpt to inner tl fnl time in bk st: hld up wl in tch: wknd 3 out: t.o whn p.u bef next* 7/2[3]
5m 13.7s (14.30) **Going Correction** +1.00s/f (Soft) 6 Ran SP% 111.0
Speed ratings (Par 107): **109,102,101,101,**
CSF £40.54 TOTE £8.30: £3.20, £2.80; EX 48.00 Trifecta £166.80.
Owner C E Stedman **Bred** C E Stedman **Trained** Lower Beeding, W Sussex

FOCUS
This was run over 90 yards further than advertised. It wasn't particularly competitive. The second has been rated close to her mark.

2315 COME TO THE RACES WITH RACING TRAVEL H'CAP CHASE (13 fncs) 2m 1f 96y
3:10 (3:11) (Class 5) (0-100,100) 4-Y-0+ £2,469 (£725; £362; £181)

Form RPR
/00- **1** **Mr Bachster (IRE)**[492] 838 10-10-5 79 JamieMoore 98+
(Kerry Lee) *j.rt: mde all: mstke 2 out: kpt on wl to draw clr: eased towards fin* 5/2[1]
64F **2** 20 **Treacy Hotels Boy (IRE)**[9] 2140 8-11-12 100 NickScholfield 94
(Paul Henderson) *chsd wnr thrght: rdn after 4 out: hld fr next styd on same pce* 3/1[3]
R10F **3** 2 ¼ **Houseparty**[18] 1999 7-10-3 84 MissTWorsley(7) 77
(Diana Grissell) *hld up bhd ldrs: chsd ldng pair after 4 out: sn rdn: styd on same pce fr next* 5/1
1-64 **4** 1 **The Informant**[29] 1825 9-10-13 87 (b) AndrewThornton 85
(Seamus Mullins) *j.rt: trckd ldrs: rdn along after 7th: stl disputing 3rd but u.str.p whn slipped on landing and virtually fell 4 out: no ch after* 11/4[2]
0-6P **P** **Top Benefit (IRE)**[30] 1813 13-9-7 74 oh9 MrMJPKendrick(7)
(Richard Harper) *hld up bhd ldrs: lost tch after 7th: t.o whn p.u after 4 out* 20/1
F605 **P** **Red Whisper**[10] 2124 11-11-0 88 (tp) TrevorWhelan
(Rob Summers) *hld up bhd ldrs: wknd 9th: t.o whn p.u bef 4 out* 10/1
5m 13.8s (39.10) **Going Correction** +1.475s/f (Heav) 6 Ran SP% 110.8
Speed ratings (Par 103): **67,57,56,56,**
CSF £10.42 TOTE £3.00: £1.60, £2.00; EX 9.30 Trifecta £35.80.
Owner Richard Lee **Bred** Mrs Anne Caplice **Trained** Byton, H'fords

FOCUS
This was run over 70 yards further than advertised. The stewards gave permission for this race to be started by flag as the starting tape had become too wet and heavy to be stretched across the course and to be held in place. Another uncompetitive contest. The winner was well in on his 2013 form and has been rated back to that level.

2316 "HONOURABLE, NOBLE LORD LANE OF CRANLEIGH" H'CAP HURDLE (13 hdls) 3m 1f 142y
3:40 (3:41) (Class 5) (0-100,90) 4-Y-0+ £2,339 (£686; £343; £171)

Form RPR
/3-0 **1** **General Girling**[173] 8-10-6 70 (p) JamesBest 95+
(Caroline Keevil) *trckd ldrs: led gng strly after 3 out: drew wl clr after next: v easily* 9/2[2]
0-34 **2** 24 **Maccabees**[18] 2004 6-10-1 72 (p) ThomasCheesman(7) 77
(Linda Jewell) *in tch: mstke 7th: rdn 4th 3 out: hdwy next: wnt 2nd between last 2 but nvr any ch w v easy wnr* 11/4[1]
P224 **3** 10 **Hassadin**[20] 1961 9-11-12 90 (p) NickScholfield 85
(Michael Blake) *trckd ldr: led after 9th: rdn and hdd after 3 out: sn hld: wkng whn lost 2nd bef last* 11/4[1]
146- **4** 22 **Banks Road (IRE)**[249] 4536 10-11-7 85 MarkGrant 53
(Geoffrey Deacon) *hld up in tch: rdn to chse ldng pair 9th: wknd after 3 out: wnt bdly lft and mstke 2 out: t.o* 7/1
350 **P** **Minority Interest**[16] 2015 6-11-4 82 (tp) GavinSheehan
(Daniel O'Brien) *pressed ldr rdn along at times fr 5th: wknd 10th: t.o whn p.u bef 2 out* 11/2[3]
PP-5 **P** **Redanna (IRE)**[16] 2022 6-11-2 80 (p) JamieMoore
(Robert Walford) *led: blnd bdly 9th: sn rdn and hdd: wknd after next: t.o whn p.u bef 2 out* 8/1
7m 29.1s (36.30) **Going Correction** +1.40s/f (Heav) 6 Ran SP% 110.5
Speed ratings (Par 103): **100,92,89,82,**
CSF £16.96 CT £36.88 TOTE £6.30: £3.90, £1.70; EX 19.40 Trifecta £102.50.
Owner Mrs Caroline Keevil **Bred** Amanda Jane Girling **Trained** Motcombe, Dorset

FOCUS
This was run over 135 yards further than advertised. Really moderate form and they were strung out. A big step up from the winner, with the second rated to his mark.

2317 JEB CONSTRUCTION LTD THE BARON OF HOLYBOURNE STANDARD OPEN NATIONAL HUNT FLAT RACE 2m 1f 145y
4:10 (4:11) (Class 6) 4-6-Y-0 £1,559 (£457; £228; £114)

Form RPR
2 **1** **Clondaw Cian (IRE)**[28] 1843 5-11-2 0 TomO'Brien 108
(Suzy Smith) *led for 2f: prom: led over 2f out: styd on strly: rdn out* 9/2[2]
2- **2** 1 **William H Bonney**[242] 4679 4-11-2 0 WayneHutchinson 107
(Alan King) *hld up: hdwy 7f out: ev ch over 2f out: sn rdn: styd on but hld by wnr thrght fnl f* 9/4[1]

2- 3 3 1/2 **Briac (FR)**[199] [5446] 4-11-2 0........ GavinSheehan 103
(Warren Greatrex) *mid-div: hdwy 5f out: rdn over 3f out: ev ch 2f out: styd on same pce fr over 1f out* **9/4**[1]
4 hd **Champagne George (IRE)**[181] 5-11-2 0........ NoelFehily 103
(Neil Mulholland) *trckd ldrs: rdn 3f out: styd on same pce fnl 2f* **22/1**
5-2 5 14 **Bindon Mill**[171] [392] 6-11-2 0........ DenisO'Regan 89
(Victor Dartnall) *sn led: rdn and hdd over 2f out: sn one pce* **8/1**[3]
6 6 3 **Quieto Sol (FR)**[182] [188] 4-11-2 0........ AidanColeman 86
(Charlie Longsdon) *towards rr: sme late prog: nvr trbld ldrs* **14/1**
7 7 **Knight To Open (IRE)** 5-11-2 0........ LeightonAspell 79
(Rebecca Curtis) *mid-div: hdwy over 4f out: trckd ldrs over 3f out: sn rdn: wknd 2f out* **14/1**
8 2 1/2 **Jebs Gamble (IRE)** 4-11-2 0........ JamesDavies 76
(Nick Gifford) *hld up: hdwy 7f out: effrt 3f out: wknd 2f out* **50/1**
5 9 10 **Court King (IRE)**[167] [444] 4-11-2 0........ SeanBowen 66
(Peter Bowen) *a towards rr* **25/1**
6- 10 9 **Sunley Spirit**[203] [5373] 5-10-9 0........ TomCannon 50
(Chris Gordon) *trckd ldrs: rdn over 4f out: wknd over 2f out* **66/1**

4m 51.5s (22.80) **Going Correction** +1.40s/f (Heav) **10 Ran SP% 115.8**
Speed ratings: **105,104,103,102,96 95,92,91,86,82**
CSF £14.46 TOTE £4.90: £1.40, £1.30, £1.30; EX 18.40 Trifecta £44.40.
Owner Wolf Allisat & Chris Ames **Bred** James And Carmel Stephenson **Trained** Lewes, E Sussex

FOCUS
Murky conditions for this ordinary-looking bumper. The second and third have been rated to their marks.
T/Plt: £67.70 to a £1 stake. Pool: £70,665.89 - 761.91 winning tickets T/Qpdt: £54.20 to a £1 stake. Pool: £4,290.56 - 58.50 winning tickets **Tim Mitchell**

1852 HEXHAM (L-H)
Friday, November 6

OFFICIAL GOING: Good to soft (soft in places; 6.8)
Wind: fairly strong across Weather: Overcast, odd shower

2318 THANK YOU LWC "NATIONAL HUNT" MAIDEN HURDLE (8 hdls) 2m 48y
1:20 (1:23) (Class 5) 4-Y-0+ £3,079 (£897; £449)

Form RPR
-242 1 **Nuts Well**[35] [1740] 4-10-11 0........ GrahamWatters(3) 118+
(Ann Hamilton) *trckd ldr: led 3 out: rdn appr last: kpt on* **3/1**[2]
2 1 **Waiting Patiently (IRE)** 4-11-0 0........ JamesReveley 116
(Keith Reveley) *hld up: gd hdwy after 2 out: rdn to go 2nd last: kpt on* **18/1**
31-1 3 1 1/2 **Cloudy Dream (IRE)**[22] [1926] 5-11-0 0........ BrianHughes 115+
(Malcolm Jefferson) *in tch: rdn appr last: sn chsd ldr: one pce run-in* **4/5**[1]
32 4 2 1/4 **Marquis Of Carabas (IRE)**[15] [2041] 5-10-9 0........ JamieBargary(5) 112
(David Dennis) *trckd ldrs: rdn appr last: no ex run-in* **7/2**[3]
6 5 6 **Away For Slates (IRE)**[11] [2100] 5-11-0 0........ HenryBrooke 106
(Keith Dalgleish) *in tch: rdn appr last: grad wknd* **80/1**
06- 6 1 **Dimple (FR)**[282] [3931] 4-11-0 0........[1] AlainCawley 105
(Pauline Robson) *midfield: rdn after 2 out: one pce and nvr threatened* **50/1**
0 7 14 **The Toft**[27] [1854] 6-9-11 0........ RossChapman(10) 84
(Lucinda Russell) *hld up: nvr threatened* **22/1**
0-F 8 1 **Fifteen Kings (IRE)**[11] [2101] 5-10-9 0........(t) GrantCockburn(5) 90
(Lucinda Russell) *midfield: wknd after 2 out* **50/1**
500- 9 1 1/2 **Lucarno Dancer**[200] [5419] 5-10-2 0........(t) CallumBewley(5) 82
(Raymond Shiels) *midfield: rdn after 2 out: wkng whn mstke last* **100/1**
0-00 10 7 **Dibble Bridge**[25] [1886] 4-10-11 0........ AdamNicol(3) 82
(Philip Kirby) *led: hdd 3 out: rdn appr 2 out: wknd after 2 out* **125/1**
6 11 38 **Fire Rock (IRE)**[11] [2101] 4-10-7 0........ RyanDay(7) 44
(Nicky Richards) *a in rr* **100/1**

4m 33.0s (15.60) **Going Correction** +0.65s/f (Soft) **11 Ran SP% 120.3**
Speed ratings (Par 103): **87,86,85,84,81 81,74,73,72,69 50**
CSF £47.58 TOTE £4.30: £1.10, £3.40, £1.10; EX 68.30 Trifecta £166.10.
Owner Ian Hamilton **Bred** Chesters Stud Ltd **Trained** Great Bavington, Northumbland
■ Wayward Jack was withdrawn. Price at time of withdrawal 66-1. Rule 4 does not apply.
■ Stewards' Enquiry : Brian Hughes two-day ban; careless riding (20th,22nd Nov)

FOCUS
Bends moved to fresh ground and hurdles re-sited. Course divided at top of hill and down back straight to provide best available ground. This lacked depth and few got involved. After riding in the race, both James Reveley and Brian Hughes called the ground soft, while Henry Brooke suggested it was good to soft, tacky and dead. The winner is on the upgrade and there's a case for rating him higher through the third and fourth, but the fifth and sixth are obvious concerns.

2319 ROWLANDS "NATIONAL HUNT" NOVICES' HURDLE (10 hdls) 2m 4f 28y
1:50 (1:51) (Class 4) 4-Y-0+ £3,249 (£954; £477; £238)

Form RPR
2 1 **Delusionofgrandeur (IRE)**[22] [1923] 5-10-12 0........ DannyCook 111+
(Sue Smith) *mde all: nt fluent 7th: hit 2 out: sn rdn: strly pressed appr last: hld on gamely* **4/1**[3]
2-1 2 hd **Ryedale Racer**[181] [206] 4-10-12 0........ BrianHughes 110+
(Malcolm Jefferson) *in tch: wnt 2nd appr 2 out: rdn to chal strly appr last: kpt on but a jst hld* **1/1**[1]
1-23 3 19 **Presenting Junior (IRE)**[131] [849] 8-10-12 132........ HenryBrooke 92
(Martin Todhunter) *hld up: rdn appr 2 out: plugged on into remote 3rd appr last* **5/2**[2]
52- 4 32 **Captain Redbeard (IRE)**[214] 6-10-5 0........ SamColtherd(7) 63
(Stuart Coltherd) *hld up: hdwy 3 out: chsd ldrs bef 2 out: wknd appr last* **14/1**
UPOP P **Cobh National (IRE)**[35] [1739] 7-10-5 75........ MrKitAlexander(7)
(Victor Thompson) *midfield: dropped to rr bef 3 out and sn wl bhd: p.u bef 2 out* **150/1**
02-0 P **Valnamixe Du Mee (FR)**[13] [2066] 6-10-5 100........ JamieHamilton(7)
(Kenny Johnson) *chsd ldr: rdn appr 2 out: sn wknd: p.u bef last* **40/1**
03- P **The Conn (IRE)**[219] [5097] 5-10-12 0........ JamesReveley
(Chris Grant) *hld up: j. bdly rt 1st: sme hdwy 3 out: rdn 2 out: sn wknd: p.u bef last* **33/1**

5m 26.0s (13.50) **Going Correction** +0.65s/f (Soft) **7 Ran SP% 111.3**
WFA 4 from 5yo+ 8lb
Speed ratings (Par 105): **99,98,91,78, ,**
CSF £8.29 TOTE £4.60: £2.10, £1.30; EX 9.30 Trifecta £16.40.
Owner McGoldrick Racing Syndicates (3) **Bred** D Cantillon And E Cantillon **Trained** High Eldwick, W Yorks

FOCUS
An informative contest and much to like about the performances of the first two, who pulled well clear. The winner has been building on his recent run and the second should win over hurdles.

2320 WEATHERBYS HAMILTON NOVICES' H'CAP CHASE (19 fncs) 3m 41y
2:20 (2:20) (Class 4) (0-105,103) 4-Y-0+ £4,594 (£1,472; £818)

Form RPR
5-3P 1 **Thatildee (IRE)**[8] [2143] 7-10-1 83........(p) DiarmuidO'Regan(5) 91+
(Chris Grant) *pressed ldr: led 9th: rdn after 2 out: jnd whn lft clr last: kpt on* **15/2**
6-24 2 22 **Kalastar (IRE)**[166] [457] 6-10-11 95........ MrTHamilton(7) 85
(Katie Scott) *hld up in tch: rdn along fr 1/2-way: wnt 3rd 3 out: lft 8 l 2nd last: wknd run-in* **6/4**[1]
P 3 84 **Afterclass (IRE)**[184] [143] 7-10-13 97........ MrKitAlexander(7) 10
(N W Alexander) *chsd ldr: wknd after 3 out* **12/1**
4665 P **Duhallowcountry (IRE)**[15] [2026] 9-9-11 77 oh14........(p) AdamNicol(3)
(Victor Thompson) *led: hdd 9th: lost pl qckly after 14th: t.o whn p.u bef 3 out* **100/1**
5P-0 P **Forty Crown (IRE)**[15] [2029] 9-11-12 103........ BrianHughes
(John Wade) *trckd ldrs: lost pl 18th: sn struggling: nt fluent 12th: p.u after 13th* **5/1**[3]
64U3 U **Kilmainham (IRE)**[6] [2191] 7-10-13 90........(p) HenryBrooke 96+
(Martin Todhunter) *hld up: hdwy into 2nd 15th: rdn after 2 out: chal appr last: disputing ld whn uns last* **13/2**
14F3 P **Solway Legend**[15] [2030] 8-11-7 103........ CallumBewley(5)
(Lisa Harrison) *hld up: rdn after 3 out: sn wknd: in distant 3rd whn p.u bef last* **4/1**[2]

7m 1.4s (29.20) **Going Correction** +1.30s/f (Heav) **7 Ran SP% 110.4**
Speed ratings (Par 105): **103,95,67, , ,**
CSF £18.83 TOTE £9.00: £4.10, £1.40; EX 31.20 Trifecta £141.80.
Owner Peacock Boys Partnership **Bred** Wainbody Estates And N G King **Trained** Newton Bewley, Co Durham

FOCUS
A moderate handicap chase, in which the well supported favourite never looked comfortable. Only three finished. The winner has been rated as improving to his hurdle mark.

2321 WEATHERBYS BANK CONDITIONAL JOCKEYS' H'CAP CHASE (15 fncs) 2m 4f 15y
2:50 (2:51) (Class 5) (0-100,97) 4-Y-0+ £3,246 (£1,180)

Form RPR
2035 1 **Verko (FR)**[49] [1573] 6-10-3 82........ FinianO'Toole(8) 92
(Micky Hammond) *hld up: stdy hdwy fr 11th: rdn to go 2nd appr last: 4 l down last: kpt on: led 110yds out* **9/2**[2]
005- 2 2 1/4 **Trouble In Paris (IRE)**[206] [5329] 8-9-9 71 oh8........(t) LorcanMurtagh(5) 81
(Barry Murtagh) *midfield: hdwy to go 2nd 4 out: led narrowly bef 3 out: rdn and asserted after 2 out: 4 l up last: tied up run-in: hdd 110yds out* **8/1**
0P02 P **Willie Hall**[13] [2071] 11-10-12 86........ CallumBewley(3)
(Lisa Harrison) *trckd ldrs: disp ld bef 3 out: rdn after 2 out: wknd qckly and p.u bef last* **4/1**[1]
464- P **Samson Collonges (FR)**[200] [5423] 9-10-4 75........(tp) AdamNicol
(Rebecca Menzies) *led: hdd 4th: remained cl up: rdn 4 out: wknd bef 3 out: p.u bef 2 out* **9/2**[2]
6P/6 P **Mia Matriarch**[27] [1853] 9-10-0 71........ TomDuffy
(Stuart Coltherd) *trckd ldrs: lost pl after 9th: in rr whn mstke 3 out: p.u bef next* **12/1**
223/ P **Moscow Menace (IRE)**[561] [5536] 8-11-9 97........(t) JamieHamilton(3)
(Katie Scott) *a in rr: p.u after 9th* **9/2**[2]
3-04 P **Azerodegree (IRE)**[27] [1857] 6-9-13 75........(p) ThomasDowson(5)
(Harriet Graham) *trckd ldrs: reminders and lost pl bef 7th: sn struggling: p.u after 9th* **10/1**
PP-2 R **Dundee Blue (IRE)**[185] [135] 7-11-3 88........(bt) GrahamWatters
(Henry Hogarth) *prom: led narrowly 4th: hdd bef 3 out: sn wknd: distant 3rd whn ref last* **7/1**[3]

5m 39.6s (26.10) **Going Correction** +1.35s/f (Heav) **8 Ran SP% 114.9**
Speed ratings (Par 103): **101,100, , , ,**
CSF £39.36 TOTE £6.20: £3.30, £4.40; EX 58.40.
Owner David Green **Bred** E A R L Trinquet, M & O Trinquet **Trained** Middleham, N Yorks

FOCUS
This proved a punishing test with only two of the eight runners finishing. The finishers have been rated to their marks.

2322 TYNESIDE SAMARITANS 50TH ANNIVERSARY H'CAP HURDLE (8 hdls) 2m 48y
3:20 (3:20) (Class 5) (0-100,100) 3-Y-0+ £2,737 (£798; £399)

Form RPR
4643 1 **Miss Joeking (IRE)**[33] [1779] 4-9-13 83........ RossChapman(10) 92+
(Lucinda Russell) *trckd ldrs: led appr 2 out: rdn after 2 out: 3 l up whn mstke last: strly pressed fnl 110yds: hld on wl* **5/1**[2]
0/22 2 1/2 **Gunner Lindley (IRE)**[8] [2148] 8-10-6 87........ SamColtherd(7) 92
(Stuart Coltherd) *midfield: hdwy appr 2 out: rdn to go 2nd appr last: chal strly fnl 110yds: kpt on* **13/8**[1]
02P0 3 5 **The Ice Factor**[13] [2071] 7-10-6 87........(p) JamieHamilton(7) 88
(Alison Hamilton) *in tch: rdn after 2 out: kpt on: wnt 3rd run-in* **17/2**
6-6F 4 1 **Dutch Canyon (IRE)**[15] [2029] 5-11-0 93........(p) StephenMulqueen(5) 94
(N W Alexander) *hld up: rdn after 2 out: styd on fr appr last: wnt 4th run-in* **13/2**[3]
56P5 5 5 **Mrs Grass**[35] [1744] 8-9-9 74 oh5........(vt) DiarmuidO'Regan(5) 70
(Jonathan Haynes) *pressed ldr: led 4th: hdd appr 2 out: sn rdn: lost 2nd appr last: wknd and lost 2 more pls run-in* **16/1**
35P4 6 1 1/4 **Landmeafortune (IRE)**[22] [1923] 6-11-5 93........ HenryBrooke 87
(Martin Todhunter) *hld up: rdn after 2 out: nvr threatened* **25/1**
00-5 7 12 **Dark And Dangerous (IRE)**[8] [2148] 7-11-6 99........ CallumBewley(5) 83
(Simon Waugh) *led narrowly: hdd 4th: remained cl up tl wknd after 2 out* **8/1**
66/0 8 3 1/4 **Minden March**[22] [1927] 10-9-9 74 oh15........ DanielHiskett(5) 55
(Peter Maddison) *a towards rr* **66/1**
-406 9 2 3/4 **Authinger (IRE)**[60] [1493] 7-11-5 100........(t) LorcanMurtagh(7) 78
(Barry Murtagh) *midfield: rdn 2 out: sn wknd* **20/1**
5454 10 140 **Tokyo Brown (USA)**[67] [1414] 6-11-4 92........(p) BrianHughes
(James Moffatt) *pressed ldr: lost pl 5th: bhd after 3 out: eased* **17/2**

4m 26.8s (9.40) **Going Correction** +1.35s/f (Heav) **10 Ran SP% 116.2**
WFA 4 from 5yo+ 7lb
Speed ratings (Par 103): **102,101,99,98,96 95,89,88,86,**
CSF £13.63 CT £67.78 TOTE £6.30: £1.80, £1.40, £2.60; EX 16.80 Trifecta £96.70.
Owner Peter J S Russell **Bred** Patrick Hogan **Trained** Arlary, Perth & Kinross

FOCUS
Few could be seriously fancied for this and the first two in the market that dominated, though, not in the order most would have expected. A step up from the winner, with the second, third and fourth close to their marks.

2323 HEXHAM AUTUMN H'CAP HURDLE (12 hdls) 2m 7f 63y
3:50 (3:51) (Class 5) (0-100,100) 4-Y-0+ £2,737 (£798; £399)

Form RPR
00-4 1 **Dusky Bob (IRE)**[181] 203 10-11-3 91 DannyCook 97
(Brian Ellison) trckd ldr: jnd ldr 4th: led 6th: rdn whn hdd 2 out: remained cl up: led again run-in: kpt on wl 12/1
5-11 2 1 3/4 **Bruce Almighty (IRE)**[7] 2174 4-11-9 100 AdamNicol(3) 105
(Philip Kirby) hld up in midfield: stdy hdwy after 9th: trckd ldng pair gng wl bef 2 out: rdn into narrow ld appr last: hdd run-in: no ex fnl 50yds 4/6[1]
6654 3 3 3/4 **Optical High**[25] 1890 6-9-7 77 StephenMcCarthy(10) 78
(Sue Smith) trckd ldrs: led narrowly 2 out: sn rdn: hdd appr last: edgd lft and no ex run-in 10/1
216P 4 9 **Lilly's Legend**[117] 966 5-9-13 80 (p) JamieHamilton(7) 74
(Mark Walford) midfield: rdn 2 out: no imp 10/1
6-5P 5 3 1/2 **Lady Vivona**[166] 466 7-9-9 74 CallumBewley(5) 64
(Lisa Harrison) midfield: chsd ldrs bef 2 out: wknd appr last 100/1
-P31 6 13 **Darsi Dancer (IRE)**[25] 1890 7-11-3 98 SamColtherd(7) 79
(Stuart Coltherd) led: jnd 4th: hdd 6th: lost pl 9th: wknd after 2 out 5/1[2]
5421 P **Destiny Awaits (IRE)**[11] 2103 6-11-11 99 7ex JamesReveley
(Keith Pollock) hld up in rr: rdn after 3 out: sn btn: p.u bef last 9/1[3]
F-P0 P **Petre' Island (IRE)**[13] 2071 6-9-11 76 GrantCockburn(5)
(Katie Scott) in tch: wknd after 3 out: p.u bef last 50/1
-006 P **Just My Luke**[13] 2071 6-9-7 74 oh1 (t) JamesCorbett(7)
(Susan Corbett) a in rr: p.u bef last 33/1

6m 30.5s (21.50) **Going Correction** +1.35s/f (Heavy)
WFA 4 from 5yo+ 8lb 9 Ran SP% 118.4
Speed ratings (Par 103): **88,87,86,82,81 77, , ,**
CSF £21.86 CT £95.46 TOTE £12.40: £2.20, £1.10, £2.90; EX 31.10 Trifecta £214.20.
Owner Dan Gilbert **Bred** P J O'Connor **Trained** Norton, N Yorks

FOCUS
A weak finale, which revolved heavily around the well treated odds-on favourite. The third helps set the level.
T/Plt: £31.70 to a £1 stake. Pool: £75,713.77 - 1,741.73 winning tickets T/Qpdt: £19.90 to a £1 stake. Pool: £4,785.42 - 177.40 winning tickets **Andrew Sheret**

2292 MUSSELBURGH (R-H)
Friday, November 6

OFFICIAL GOING: Good (good to soft in places; 7.0)
Wind: Fresh, half behind Weather: Overcast

2324 BORDER SAFEGUARD JUVENILE HURDLE (9 hdls) 1m 7f 124y
1:00 (1:00) (Class 4) 3-Y-0 £3,249 (£954; £477; £238)

Form RPR
1 **Sir Chauvelin**[28] 3-10-12 0 [1] BrianHarding 113+
(Jim Goldie) hld up: hdwy and in tch after 4 out: effrt and led after 2 out: edgd lft bef last: rdn clr 6/1
612 2 7 **Big McIntosh (IRE)**[19] 1984 3-11-5 118 (t) MattieBatchelor 114+
(John Ryan) nt fluent: t.k.h: led and sn clr: rdn whn mstke 2 out: sn hdd: rallied whn mstke last: sn no ex 11/2[3]
3 3 8 **The Compeller (IRE)**[44] 1631 3-10-12 0 PeterBuchanan 98
(Lucinda Russell) t.k.h: chsd clr ldr: clsd 4 out: effrt and rdn bef 2 out: outpcd between last 2 2/1[2]
4 2 3/4 **Multi Grain**[67] 3-10-2 0 JoeColliver(3) 88
(Micky Hammond) t.k.h early: hld up in tch: rdn and outpcd 3 out: no imp fr next 40/1
5 5 11 **Moon Arc (IRE)**[44] 1631 3-10-9 0 TonyKelly(3) 85
(Keith Dalgleish) hld up in tch: mstke 4th: drvn and outpcd next: n.d after 66/1
P **Fibre Optic**[83] 3-10-9 0 CraigNichol(3)
(Rose Dobbin) t.k.h: prom tl lost pl qckly and p.u after 3rd 20/1
0 P **Lord Of Words (IRE)**[23] 1899 3-10-9 0 (t) JohnKington(3)
(Patrick Holmes) hld up in tch: outpcd fr 4th: lost tch and p.u bef 3 out 100/1
P **A Lovable Rogue**[29] 3-10-7 0 (p) DaleIrving(5)
(R Mike Smith) mstkes in rr: struggling fr 4th: t.o whn p.u bef 2 out 66/1
P **Vilman (IRE)**[146] 3-10-12 0 RichardJohnson
(Simon West) chsd ldrs: effrt and rdn after 4 out: outpcd whn mstke next: sn btn: p.u bef 2 out 13/8[1]

3m 40.0s (-8.40) **Going Correction** -0.275s/f (Good) 9 Ran SP% 112.3
Speed ratings (Par 104): **110,106,102,101,95 , , ,**
CSF £35.32 TOTE £7.90: £2.00, £1.90, £1.10; EX 36.70 Trifecta £111.90.
Owner J Fyffe **Bred** W M Johnstone **Trained** Uplawmoor, E Renfrews

FOCUS
Bottom bend on hurdles course out 11yds and shared bend with chase course. Chase distances as advertised. Races 1 2, 5 & 7 increased by 36yds and race 3 by 72yds. After 3mm of rain overnight and a few showers in the morning, the going was good, good to soft in places. The winning rider in the first race said: "The ground is just on the slow side of good and it's a bit patchy." An interesting juvenile hurdle to start, albeit not the most competitive of events, and the pace was solid. The runner-up set a fair standard and the winner can rate higher and win more hurdles. The third has been rated in line with his recent debut.

2325 SIMBA CHARITY FILLIES' & MARES' MAIDEN HURDLE (9 hdls) 1m 7f 124y
1:30 (1:30) (Class 5) 3-Y-0+ £3,249 (£954; £477; £238)

Form RPR
3212 1 **Carinena (IRE)**[44] 1627 6-11-2 0 CraigNichol(3) 114
(Nicky Richards) t.k.h: trckd ldrs: led gng wl 2 out: sn shkn up: rdn and kpt on strly fr last 10/3[2]
33-2 2 3 **Brise Vendeenne (FR)**[27] 1845 4-11-5 115 RichardJohnson 112
(Philip Hobbs) nt fluent on occasions: led: rdn 3 out: hdd next: rallied: kpt on same pce fr last 4/11[1]
46-3 3 5 **Blayney Queen (IRE)**[70] 1393 6-10-12 0 (t) AnthonyFox(7) 107
(S R B Crawford, Ire) hld up: smooth hdwy to trck ldrs bef 3 out: rdn and hung rt next: sn outpcd 16/1[3]
5- 4 22 **Near To Tears (IRE)**[518] 606 5-11-5 0 PeterBuchanan 87
(Lucinda Russell) hld up: outpcd 1/2-way: sme late hdwy: nvr rchd ldrs 33/1
5 5 7 **Slide Show**[33] 1774 7-11-2 0 TonyKelly(3) 81
(David Thompson) t.k.h: in tch: outpcd bef 4 out: sn struggling: btn whn hung rt 2 out 100/1
30- 6 6 **Fillydelphia (IRE)**[39] 1896 4-11-2 0 JohnKington(3) 78
(Patrick Holmes) chsd ldr: ev ch after 4 out: rdn and wknd fr next 66/1
0 7 42 **Worcester Pearmain**[76] 1334 5-11-5 0 BrianHarding 38
(Rose Dobbin) nt fluent in rr: struggling 1/2-way: lost tch after 4 out: t.o 100/1

3m 44.4s (-4.00) **Going Correction** -0.275s/f (Good)
WFA 4 from 5yo+ 7lb 7 Ran SP% 108.7
Speed ratings (Par 100): **99,97,95,84,80 77,56**
CSF £4.66 TOTE £2.90: £1.40, £1.10; EX 4.50 Trifecta £16.70.
Owner Mrs C A Torkington **Bred** Cecil And Martin McCracken **Trained** Greystoke, Cumbria

FOCUS
Actual race distance 1m7f160yds. Again not the most competitive mares' maiden hurdle, but another race run at a fair pace and something of a surprise result. A step up from the winner, with the second, third and fifth rated to their marks.

2326 MILLER HOMES SCOTLAND H'CAP HURDLE (10 hdls 2 omitted) 2m 3f 81y
2:00 (2:00) (Class 3) (0-135,127) 4-Y-0+ £8,447 (£2,480; £1,240; £620)

Form RPR
1132 1 **Western Way (IRE)**[19] 1990 6-11-7 122 (v) RichardJohnson 132+
(Don Cantillon) t.k.h: in tch: nt fluent 4 out: rdn and hdwy to ld bef 2 out: clr whn edgd lft bef last: rdn out 13/8[1]
-131 2 6 **Serenity Now (IRE)**[30] 1814 7-11-0 122 CraigGallagher(7) 123
(Brian Ellison) t.k.h: cl up: led bef 3 out: hdd and rdn bef next: no ex fr last 3/1[2]
4135 3 3/4 **Cool Baranca (GER)**[20] 1638 9-10-3 107 EmmaSayer(3) 107
(Dianne Sayer) hld up: stdy hdwy bef 3 out: rdn bef next: kpt on same pce fr last 14/1
5542 4 8 **Claude Carter**[13] 2069 11-10-3 107 (p) CraigNichol(3) 100
(Alistair Whillans) cl up: led bef 4th: rdn and hdd bef 3 out: wknd fr next 9/1
U2/6 5 5 **Now This Is It (IRE)**[23] 1903 11-11-12 127 AELynch 117
(S R B Crawford, Ire) prom on outside: nt fluent 5th: hit 8th: effrt and ev ch briefly bef 3 out: rdn and wknd bef next 9/2[3]
2330 6 72 **Sleep In First (FR)**[33] 1773 9-10-4 110 (t) DaleIrving(5) 34
(James Ewart) led to bef 4th: struggling fr 7th: lost tch bef 3 out: t.o 9/1

4m 44.8s (-6.70) **Going Correction** -0.275s/f (Good) 6 Ran SP% 107.9
Speed ratings (Par 107): **103,100,100,96,94 64**
CSF £6.52 TOTE £2.10: £1.40, £1.80; EX 5.50 Trifecta £34.00.
Owner Don Cantillon **Bred** Don Cantillon **Trained** Newmarket, Suffolk

FOCUS
Actual race distance 2m3f135yds. A fair handicap hurdle run at a good pace thanks to a disputed lead. A step up from the progressive winner, with the second rated to the level of his recent easy win. There's a case for rating the race up to 4lb higher through the third.

2327 THISTLE SYSTEMS MAX CUBE NOVICES' LIMITED H'CAP CHASE (12 fncs 3 omitted) 3m 2f 139y
2:30 (2:30) (Class 4) (0-120,111) 4-Y-0+ £6,486 (£2,026; £1,091)

Form RPR
5-12 1 **Present Flight (IRE)**[27] 1853 6-11-5 111 (t) DerekFox(3) 127+
(Lucinda Russell) t.k.h: cl up: wnt 2nd 6th: lft in ld 11th: shkn up and drew clr fr 3 out: v easily 13/8[1]
0504 2 5 **To Begin**[32] 1794 4-10-9 108 (t) PaulMoloney 99
(Charlie Mann) hld up in tch: wnt 3rd 10th: lft 2nd next: hit 13th: effrt and pushed along 3 out: sn outpcd: no imp whn nt fluent next and last: flattered by proximity to easy wnr 13/2
-004 3 2 1/2 **Mo Rouge (IRE)**[15] 2028 7-10-9 101 (p) TonyKelly(3) 99
(Jackie Stephen) hld up: nt fluent: chsd ldr to 6th: nt fluent and dropped to last 10th: outpcd whn lft 3rd next: mstke 13th: kpt on u.p fr last: no imp 9/4[2]
-011 F **The Backup Plan (IRE)**[38] 1685 6-11-5 108 BrianHarding
(Donald McCain) led: j.w and 5 l in front tl fell 11th 3/1[3]

6m 47.1s (-1.70) **Going Correction** -0.25s/f (Good)
WFA 4 from 6yo+ 9lb 4 Ran SP% 107.2
Speed ratings (Par 105): **92,90,89,**
CSF £10.27 TOTE £2.50; EX 9.30 Trifecta £23.50.
Owner Kilco (International) Ltd **Bred** Brian Kiely **Trained** Arlary, Perth & Kinross

FOCUS
An interesting little novices' handicap chase, though difficult to know what the form is worth. The second and third have been rated in line with their recent runs.

2328 DONALDSON TIMBER ENGINEERING H'CAP HURDLE (9 hdls) 1m 7f 124y
3:00 (3:00) (Class 3) (0-135,132) 4-Y-0+ £8,447 (£2,480; £1,240; £620)

Form RPR
1-F1 1 **Aristo Du Plessis (FR)**[6] 2194 5-11-7 132 6ex DaleIrving(5) 146+
(James Ewart) j.w: mde all: clr to after 4 out: pushed clr fr 2 out: readily 1/1[1]
/04- 2 12 **Space Ship**[6] 2205 5-11-6 126 (t) AELynch 127
(Robert Alan Hennessy, Ire) hld up: hdwy and in tch whn wnt 2nd 5th: clsd on wnr after 4 out: effrt whn nt fluent 2 out: sn one pce: jst hld on for 2nd cl home 5/2[2]
P2-0 3 hd **Meadowcroft Boy**[175] 317 6-11-9 132 CraigNichol(3) 133
(Alistair Whillans) hld up in tch: effrt bef 3 out: pushed along bef next: kpt on run-in: no imp 9/2[3]
31-0 4 15 **Silver Duke (IRE)**[24] 1039 4-11-5 125 BrianHarding 113
(Jim Goldie) hld up in last pl: hit 5th: outpcd whn mstke 3 out: sn wknd 22/1
-340 5 7 **Quebec**[14] 2058 4-11-5 125 PaulMoloney 108
(Charlie Mann) nt fluent on occasions: chsd (clr) wnr to 5th: drvn along 4 out: wknd bef next 12/1

3m 40.2s (-8.20) **Going Correction** -0.275s/f (Good)
WFA 4 from 5yo+ 7lb 5 Ran SP% 108.8
Speed ratings (Par 107): **109,103,102,95,91**
CSF £3.93 TOTE £1.80: £1.10, £1.40; EX 3.60 Trifecta £6.60.
Owner Mrs J M Dodd **Bred** J Andriau, O Regley Et Al **Trained** Langholm, Dumfries & G'way

FOCUS
Actual race distance 1m7f160yds. Quite a good handicap hurdle despite the three non-runners, but ultimately a one-horse race. The winner is on the upgrade and could be rated a bit higher through the second and third, but not on time compared with the the opener.

2329 RACING UK PROFITS RETURNED TO RACING H'CAP CHASE (QUALIFIER) (14 fncs 2 omitted) 2m 3f 193y
3:30 (3:30) (Class 3) (0-135,135) 4-Y-0+ £11,696 (£3,434; £1,717; £858)

Form RPR
2P-1 1 **Village Vic (IRE)**[23] 1902 8-11-6 129 RichardJohnson 141+
(Philip Hobbs) trckd ldrs: led 6th: mde rest: rdn whn hit 2 out: sn clr: kpt on wl fr last 13/8[1]

3344 **2** *3 1/4* **Quito Du Tresor (FR)**[15] 2030 11-10-2 **111**..................(p) PeterBuchanan 118
(Lucinda Russell) *hld up: stdy hdwy to trck ldrs after 4 out: effrt and chsd wnr next: rdn and one pce fr 2 out* **5/1**[3]

/P6- **3** *4 1/2* **Empresario (IRE)**[41] 1668 6-11-5 **128**..................(t) MarkEnright 130
(Matthew J Smith, Ire) *led to 6th: chsd wnr: nt fluent 8th: effrt and pushed along whn lost 2nd 3 out: kpt on same pce fr next* **20/1**

2636 **4** *3 3/4* **Muwalla**[13] 2069 8-10-0 **109**..................(t) BrianHarding 110
(Lisa Harrison) *hld up: hmpd by faller 6th: stdy hdwy and in tch after 4 out: effrt and pushed along next: outpcd fr 2 out* **12/1**

5-05 **5** *47* **Mwaleshi**[12] 2082 10-11-12 **135**.................. SeanQuinlan 92
(Sue Smith) *trckd ldrs: drvn and outpcd bef 4 out: lost tch bef next: t.o* **9/2**[2]

31-5 **6** *31* **Royal Macnab (IRE)**[176] 304 7-10-6 **118**..................(t) TonyKelly[(3)] 47
(Rebecca Menzies) *bhd and detached: mstke 8th: nvr on terms* **16/1**

/13P **P** **Run With The Wind (IRE)**[23] 1904 9-11-3 **129**..........(tp) CraigNichol[(3)]
(S R B Crawford, Ire) *chsd ldrs: outpcd whn nt fluent 9th: sn struggling: t.o whn blnd 2 out: sn p.u* **25/1**

3-41 **F** **Kodicil (IRE)**[26] 1601 7-11-2 **125**..................(p) JakeGreenall
(Mark Walford) *in tch: fell 6th* **5/1**[3]

4m 51.3s (-9.90) **Going Correction** -0.25s/f (Good) **8 Ran SP% 111.8**
Speed ratings (Par 107): **109,107,105,104,85 73, ,**
CSF £10.13 CT £110.59 TOTE £2.50: £1.10, £1.50, £4.90; EX 8.60 Trifecta £83.10.
Owner Alan Peterson **Bred** Tom Curran **Trained** Withycombe, Somerset

FOCUS
A decent handicap chase and with a few in here that like to force it, a good pace was always likely. Another step up from the winner, while the fourth helps set the level.

2330 DOWNLOAD YOUR RACING UK APP STANDARD OPEN NATIONAL HUNT FLAT RACE — 1m 7f 124y

4:00 (4:00) (Class 6) 4-6-Y-0 **£1,949** (£572; £286; £143)

Form RPR

5- **1** **Moonshine Ridge (IRE)**[214] 5193 4-10-9 0.................. PaulMoloney 96
(Alan Swinbank) *pressed ldr: hmpd bnd after 6f: ev ch fr 1f/2-way: rdn and led ins fnl f: styd on wl* **10/1**

22- **2** *1 1/2* **Sand Blast**[251] 4499 4-11-2 0.................. WillKennedy 102
(Brian Ellison) *led at modest gallop: rdn and edgd rt over 1f out: hdd ins fnl f: kpt on same pce* **1/2**[1]

06 **3** *2 3/4* **Druids Lodge**[167] 444 4-11-2 0.................. RichardJohnson 99
(Don Cantillon) *prom: effrt and rdn over 3f out: kpt on same pce fr over 1f out* **7/1**[3]

5 **4** *6* **Handittolewi**[22] 1926 4-10-13 0.................. EmmaSayer[(3)] 93
(Dianne Sayer) *chsd ldrs: drvn and outpcd over 3f out: n.d after* **33/1**

5 *6* **Breakdown Cover (IRE)** 4-10-9 0.................. AnthonyFox[(7)] 87
(S R B Crawford, Ire) *hld up: pushed along and outpcd whn hung lft over 2f out: sn btn* **9/2**[2]

6 *29* **My Vicky (IRE)** 4-10-9 0.................. MarkEnright 51
(Peter Croke, Ire) *hld up: struggling 5f out: lost tch fr over 3f out: t.o* **28/1**

3m 46.0s (3.20) **Going Correction** -0.275s/f (Good) **6 Ran SP% 112.8**
Speed ratings: **81,80,78,75,72 58**
CSF £15.89 TOTE £10.50: £3.00, £1.10; EX 20.10 Trifecta £82.90.
Owner Elm Row Racing Syndicate **Bred** Maddenstown Equine Enterprise Ltd **Trained** Melsonby, N Yorks

FOCUS
This bumper was also run over 1m7f160yds. Like many races of this type, they went no pace early and things didn't quicken up until just before halfway. A step up from the winner, with the race rated around the balance of the second, third and fourth.
T/Plt: £9.70 to a £1 stake. Pool: £53,890.21 - 4,052.39 winning tickets T/Qpdt: £5.40 to a £1 stake. Pool: £3,181.65 - 433.85 winning tickets **Richard Young**

2080 AINTREE (L-H)

Saturday, November 7

OFFICIAL GOING: Soft (chs 7.1; hdl 7.0)
Wind: moderate 1/2 behind Weather: changeable, rain race 3

2331 BETFRED TV EBF STALLIONS "NATIONAL HUNT" NOVICES' HURDLE QUALIFIER (11 hdls) — 2m 4f

12:45 (12:45) (Class 4) 4-6-Y-0 **£5,198** (£1,526; £572; £572)

Form RPR

1-3 **1** **Definite Outcome (IRE)**[27] 1870 6-10-12 0.................. PaulTownend 123
(Rebecca Curtis) *trckd ldr: led 6th: drvn appr last: styd on clsng stages* **8/13**[1]

1 **2** *1 1/4* **Flying Angel (IRE)**[24] 1909 4-11-1 0.................. RyanHatch[(3)] 128
(Nigel Twiston-Davies) *hld up in rr: hdwy 8th: chsd wnr and drvn 2 out: upsides last: kpt on same pce last 75yds* **4/1**[2]

2 **3** *9* **Just Georgie**[14] 2066 5-10-12 0.................. DannyCook 113
(Sue Smith) *chsd ldrs: drvn 3 out: one pce appr next* **7/1**[3]

42-4 **3** *dht* **Echo Springs**[13] 2080 5-10-12 110.................. BrianHughes 113
(Danielle McCormick) *led to 6th: one pce appr 2 out* **25/1**

U-1 **5** *15* **One Cool Scorpion (IRE)**[172] 392 4-10-12 0.................. TomO'Brien 101
(Philip Hobbs) *t.k.h: nt fluent: sn trcking ldrs: drvn 7th: lost pl appr 2 out: bhd whn hit last* **14/1**

6 *19* **Fionn Mac Cul (IRE)**[203] 4-10-12 0.................. LiamTreadwell 83
(Venetia Williams) *chsd ldrs: hit 4th: drvn 8th: lost pl bef next: sn bhd* **20/1**

5m 5.1s (4.40) **Going Correction** +0.45s/f (Soft) **6 Ran SP% 109.7**
Speed ratings: **109,108,104,104,98 91**
CSF £3.14 TOTE £1.50: £1.20, £1.80; EX 3.90 Trifecta £4.10.
Owner Carl Hinchy **Bred** James Wickham **Trained** Newport, Pembrokeshire

FOCUS
Around ten millimetres of rain between 5am and late morning, and riders in the first concurred with the official going description of soft. All bends and hurdles moved out 3yds. Races 1, 4 & 5 increased by 27yds, race 2 by 35yds, race 3 by 37yds, race 6 by 21yds and race 7 by 22yds. Only two hurdles were jumped in the home straight, with a cross hurdle added instead. A race taken by Wichita Lineman and Cue Card in the past decade, and the first two in this year's renewal pulled well clear and look particularly decent prospects. The winner didn't need to match his Chepstow figure to score, while the fifth has been rated similar to his bumper mark.

2332 BETFRED RACING "FOLLOW US ON TWITTER" NOVICES' CHASE (19 fncs) — 3m 210y

1:20 (1:20) (Class 3) 4-Y-0+ **£6,279** (£1,871; £947; £485; £254)

Form RPR

01P- **1** **Bally Beaufort (IRE)**[231] 4911 7-10-11 128.................. RyanHatch[(3)] 141+
(Nigel Twiston-Davies) *led tl after 12th: led 15th: styd on wl run-in* **10/1**

0P-5 **2** *4* **Spirit Of Shankly**[24] 1900 7-11-0 134..................(bt[1]) BrianHughes 138
(Charlie Longsdon) *chsd ldrs: cl 2nd 4 out: 1 l down whn hit last: kpt on same pce* **20/1**

1P2- **3** *14* **Caracci Apache (IRE)**[199] 5471 5-11-0 0.................. NicodeBoinville 124+
(Nicky Henderson) *t.k.h: hld up: cl 3rd 14th: drvn appr 3 out: grad wknd* **2/1**[1]

113- **4** *20* **Spookydooky (IRE)**[231] 4911 7-11-0 0..................(t) BarryGeraghty 104
(Jonjo O'Neill) *t.k.h in rr: hdwy to trck ldrs 12th: drvn 14th: lost pl next: bhd fr 4 out* **2/1**[1]

3P-1 **5** *3* **How About It (IRE)**[30] 1821 6-11-5 0..................(p) PaulTownend 109
(Rebecca Curtis) *nt fluent: chsd wnr: lost pl and hit 13th: sn wl bhd* **5/1**[2]

113- **P** **Rolling Maul (IRE)**[205] 5357 7-11-0 137..................(b) SeanBowen
(Peter Bowen) *hdwy to chse ldrs 5th: led after 12th: hdd 15th: lost pl 4 out: poor 4th whn hit 3 out: bhd whn tired and j.rt next: sn p.u* **6/1**[3]

6m 42.5s (12.50) **Going Correction** +0.60s/f (Soft) **6 Ran SP% 111.5**
Speed ratings (Par 107): **104,102,98,91,90**
CSF £127.42 TOTE £13.90: £4.50, £5.10; EX 164.10 Trifecta £366.80.
Owner R J Rexton **Bred** Isidore And Padraic Murtagh **Trained** Naunton, Gloucs

FOCUS
A decent-looking novice chase, but at least a couple of runners were undone by what appeared no more than a medium gallop until the final mile. The winner has been rated up 10lb on his best hurdle figure, and the second as improving to his hurdle mark.

2333 PERTEMPS NETWORK H'CAP HURDLE (SERIES QUALIFIER) (13 hdls) — 3m 149y

1:55 (1:57) (Class 2) 4-Y-0+ **£11,573** (£3,418; £1,709; £854; £427; £214)

Form RPR

612- **1** **Broxbourne (IRE)**[144] 5355 6-11-0 134.................. DavidBass 140+
(Nicky Henderson) *wnt to the front sn after s after field waited abt 20 2nds to jump off: mde rest: pushed clr after 3 out: styd on wl* **6/1**

13-4 **2** *5* **Our Kaempfer (IRE)**[28] 1848 6-11-6 140.................. BrianHughes 141
(Charlie Longsdon) *hld up in rr: hdwy 10th: chsd wnr bef 2 out: styd on same pce* **9/4**[1]

/15- **3** *3 1/2* **Shutthefrontdoor (IRE)**[210] 5275 8-11-12 146..................(t) BarryGeraghty 144
(Jonjo O'Neill) *j. off in front but didn't want to ld: chsd ldrs: outpcd bef 2 out: modest 3rd between last 2: hung lft and kpt on same pce* **7/2**[2]

1134 **4** *6* **Just A Normal Day (IRE)**[29] 1839 5-9-13 124......(p) BridgetAndrews[(5)] 116
(Dan Skelton) *trckd ldrs: mstke 10th: one pce whn mstke 2 out: sn wknd* **8/1**

100- **5** *2* **Join The Clan (IRE)**[212] 5241 6-10-10 137.................. PatrickCowley[(7)] 129
(Jonjo O'Neill) *mid-div: outpcd 8th: in rr whn mstke 10th: keeping on one pce whn hmpd 2 out* **9/2**[3]

3214 **6** *2 3/4* **Henri Parry Morgan**[48] 1594 7-10-10 130..................(p) SeanBowen 118
(Peter Bowen) *chsd wnr 2nd: drvn 3 out: wkng whn hmpd next* **16/1**

03 **F** **Nautical Nitwit (IRE)**[16] 2042 6-9-11 120.................. KyleJames[(3)] 110
(Philip Kirby) *hld up in rr: hdwy to trck ldrs 7th: 3rd and one pce whn fell 2 out* **12/1**

6m 50.0s (33.70) **Going Correction** +0.45s/f (Soft) **7 Ran SP% 110.1**
Speed ratings (Par 109): **64,62,61,59,58 57,**
CSF £18.94 CT £50.07 TOTE £4.70: £3.40, £1.10; EX 13.40 Trifecta £33.50.
Owner The Gleneagles Partnership **Bred** Mount Coote Stud And M Johnston **Trained** Upper Lambourn, Berks

FOCUS
A decent series qualifier, if a numerically fairly thinly contested one, and the winning time counts for nothing, as the whole field stood still for over 15 seconds and a crawl ensued until past halfway. The second has been rated to his C&D mark, with the third 4lb off his best hurdle figure.

2334 BETFRED HURDLE (11 hdls) — 2m 4f

2:30 (2:30) (Class 2) 4-Y-0+ **£18,941** (£5,717; £2,945; £1,559)

Form RPR

0P0- **1** **Bobs Worth (IRE)**[196] 5538 10-10-12 146.................. NicodeBoinville 153+
(Nicky Henderson) *best away: mde all: pushed along and increased pce 3 out: hit last: styd on wl last 100yds* **11/1**

111/ **2** *1 1/2* **Simonsig**[970] 4720 9-10-12 158.................. BarryGeraghty 151+
(Nicky Henderson) *t.k.h: sltly hmpd and lft 2nd 4th: brought wd bnd bef 2 out: cruising tl shkn up 1f out: rdn and styd on same pce last 75yds* **5/2**[2]

102P **3** *19* **Commissioned (IRE)**[42] 1657 5-10-12 154..................(p) TomCannon 132
(John Ferguson) *s.s: j.lft in rr: bhd and pushed along 7th: tk poor 3rd last 200yds* **9/2**[3]

012- **4** *10* **Purple Bay (IRE)**[316] 3248 6-11-2 161.................. BrianHughes 130
(John Ferguson) *hld up: t.k.h: chsng ldrs whn nt fluent 8th: drvn bef 2 out: wknd and poor 4th whn mstke last* **6/5**[1]

311/ **F** **Royal Boy (FR)**[665] 3644 8-10-12 144.................. PaulTownend
(Rebecca Curtis) *t.k.h: trckd wnr: fell 4th* **12/1**

5m 2.9s (2.20) **Going Correction** +0.45s/f (Soft) **5 Ran SP% 108.2**
Speed ratings (Par 109): **113,112,104,100,**
CSF £37.09 TOTE £9.50: £2.70, £1.60; EX 23.70 Trifecta £116.90.
Owner The Not Afraid Partnership **Bred** Mrs L Eadie **Trained** Upper Lambourn, Berks

FOCUS
A captivating contest, although not one to approach too confidently as a betting medium beforehand given the long absences of four of the field. The winner has been rated in line with his old hurdle form, while the second, who pulled very hard, has been rated 11lb off his old hurdle mark.

2335 BETFRED "SCOOP6SOCCER" H'CAP CHASE (16 fncs) — 2m 3f 200y

3:05 (3:05) (Class 2) (0-150,148) 4-Y-0+ **£24,776** (£7,368; £3,692; £1,848; £936; £480)

Form RPR

264- **1** **Pepite Rose (FR)**[196] 5536 8-11-12 148.................. LiamTreadwell 158+
(Venetia Williams) *mid-div: chsd ldrs 8th: led 3 out: clr between last: styd on strly: v readily* **10/1**

6U-6 **2** *10* **Ballygarvey (FR)**[27] 1869 9-11-0 136.................. TomO'Brien 137
(Philip Hobbs) *w ldr: led after 8th: hit 10th: hdd 3 out: kpt on same pce* **5/1**[2]

51-3 **3** *2* **Bincombe**[182] 199 7-10-0 129..................(bt) ConorSmith[(7)] 127
(Philip Hobbs) *chsd ldrs: drvn appr 3 out: kpt on one pce* **14/1**

P-05 **4** *3* **Baileys Concerto (IRE)**[39] 1417 9-10-11 133.................. BrianHughes 128
(Dianne Sayer) *in rr: outpcd after 4 out: kpt on to take modest 4th last* **12/1**

600- **5** *5* **De Boitron (FR)**[204] 5363 11-10-11 133.................. DannyCook 123
(Sue Smith) *in rr: hdwy 4 out: outpcd appr next: modest 4th between last 2: fdd last* **10/1**

1124 **6** *15* **Alderbrook Lad (IRE)**[68] 1417 9-10-11 143.................. FinianO'Toole[(10)] 117
(Micky Hammond) *led: hdd after 8th: lost pl bef 2 out* **20/1**

21-2 **7** *1* **Minella Forfitness (IRE)**[22] 1942 8-10-11 **133**.................... AdamPogson 107
(Charles Pogson) *t.k.h: trckd ldrs: reminders 4 out: lost pl bef next* **13/2**

33-2 **U** **Upepito (FR)**[24] 1902 7-10-1 **128**.................................(t) BridgetAndrews(5)
(Dan Skelton) *in rr: hit 2nd: hdwy to trck ldrs 9th: slipped landing and uns rdr next* **2/1**[1]

P-0P **P** **Tara Road**[9] 2153 7-10-3 **125**.................................(t) PaulTownend
(Rebecca Curtis) *in rr: no imp whn hmpd 12th: blnd next: sn bhd: eased between last 2: p.u bef last* **6/1**[3]

5m 9.8s (5.80) **Going Correction** +0.60s/f (Soft) **9** Ran SP% **114.9**
Speed ratings (Par 109): **112,108,107,106,104 98,97, ,**
CSF £59.88 CT £705.29 TOTE £10.00: £2.70, £2.20, £3.90; EX 55.50 Trifecta £262.90.
Owner Falcon's Line Ltd **Bred** Pegasus Breeding Ltd **Trained** Kings Caple, H'fords

FOCUS
A competitive event, if a little light on well-handicapped individuals, and little more than 6l covering the field with six to jump. However, it produced a very decisive winner from an in-form operation. The easy winner has been rated up 4lb on her previous best, and there's a case for rating her another 4lb higher through the second and third, but it's inlikely either of those were at their best.

2336 BETFRED LOTTO "£100K CASH GIVEAWAY" H'CAP CHASE (FOR THE JOHN PARRETT MEMORIAL TROPHY) (12 fncs) 1m 7f 176y
3:40 (3:40) (Class 2) (0-145,140) 4-Y-O+ **£12,558** (£3,742; £1,894; £970; £508)

Form RPR

-335 **1** **Dresden (IRE)**[27] 1868 7-11-7 **135**.................... JamesDavies 151+
(Henry Oliver) *trckd ldrs 4th: led 2 out: sn drvn wl clr: v readily* **7/1**

12P- **2** *19* **Tornado In Milan (IRE)**[216] 5154 9-10-13 **127**.................... PaulMoloney 129
(Evan Williams) *t.k.h: led 3rd to 6th: led after 7th: hdd 2 out: 12 l down and wl btn whn blnd last* **12/1**

PP1- **3** *2 1/4* **Russborough (FR)**[221] 5080 6-10-11 **125**.................... LiamTreadwell 123
(Venetia Williams) *nt fluent: t.k.h: stdd to rr 3rd: hit next: bhd 7th: kpt on fr 3 out: tk modest 3rd appr last* **11/2**[3]

-121 **4** *12* **Germany Calling (IRE)**[23] 1922 6-11-12 **140**.................... BrianHughes 124
(Charlie Longsdon) *led to 3rd: chsd ldr: led 6th tl after 7th: 3rd and wkng whn blnd 2 out* **13/8**[1]

232- **5** *3/4* **Yorkist (IRE)**[203] 5391 7-11-8 **139**.................... JoeColliver(3) 123
(Micky Hammond) *chsd ldrs: cl 2nd whn hit 3 out: wknd next* **6/1**

00F- **P** **Festive Affair (IRE)**[211] 5253 7-10-13 **127**.................(t) BarryGeraghty
(Jonjo O'Neill) *hld up in rr: lost pl 6th: sn bhd: t.o 8th: p.u bef next* **7/2**[2]

4m 7.5s (7.50) **Going Correction** +0.60s/f (Soft) **6** Ran SP% **110.2**
Speed ratings (Par 109): **105,95,94,88,88**
CSF £67.75 TOTE £8.30: £3.60, £5.30; EX 76.30 Trifecta £427.80.
Owner Dan Lloyd **Bred** Diana Webley **Trained** Abberley, Worcs

FOCUS
Not the strongest race for the grade, and it was absolutely taken to pieces by the winner between the final two fences. The winner is on the upgrade, the second has been rated to his chase mark, and the third 8lb off on his return from a break.

2337 BETFRED MOBILE STANDARD OPEN NATIONAL HUNT FLAT RACE 2m 209y
4:10 (4:10) (Class 4) 4-6-Y-O **£3,249** (£954; £477; £238)

Form RPR

41 **1** **Mahlerdramatic (IRE)**[33] 1797 5-11-0 0.................... CraigGallagher(7) 116
(Brian Ellison) *chsd ldrs: 2nd 4f out: sn drvn: led over 2f out: styd on* **11/2**[3]

2 *2 1/4* **Golden Investment (IRE)**[230] 6-11-0 0.................... BarryGeraghty 106
(Donald McCain) *hld up in rr: effrt over 3f out: sn chsng ldrs over 2f out: kpt on to take 2nd last 50yds* **13/8**[1]

3 *1/2* **Rebel Beat** 4-11-0 0.................... BrianHughes 106
(David Dennis) *hld up in rr: hdwy 7f out: effrt and chsng ldrs over 3f out: chsd wnr appr fnl f: kpt on same pce* **22/1**

25- **4** *1 3/4* **Return Flight**[207] 5331 4-10-11 0.................... JoeColliver(3) 104
(Micky Hammond) *trckd ldrs: t.k.h: drvn 4f out: hung rt and kpt on fnl f: tk 4th nr line* **15/2**

5 *1/2* **The Fresh Prince (IRE)**[216] 5-11-0 0.................... LeightonAspell 104
(Oliver Sherwood) *led: hdd over 2f out: wknd fnl 75yds* **11/4**[2]

6 *3 3/4* **Premier Rose (IRE)**[160] 6-10-0 0.................... MrJNixon(7) 93
(Katy Price) *hld up in rr: hdwy 6f out: drvn to chse ldrs over 3f out: wknd fnl 2f* **25/1**

3- **7** *19* **Classic Tune**[224] 5028 5-10-11 0.................... MauriceLinehan(3) 81
(Claire Dyson) *t.k.h: trckd ldrs: drvn and outpcd 4f out: lost pl over 3f out: sn bhd* **16/1**

8 *42* **Guadeloupe (IRE)** 6-11-0 0.................... NicodeBoinville 39
(David Loder) *chsd ldrs: drvn 7f out: lost pl over 5f out: sn bhd: eased over 1f out: t.o* **15/2**

4m 20.2s (12.80) **Going Correction** +0.45s/f (Soft)
WFA 4 from 5yo+ 7lb **8** Ran SP% **117.8**
Speed ratings: **87,85,85,84,84 82,73,54**
CSF £15.37 TOTE £5.00: £1.20, £1.40, £5.90; EX 21.50 Trifecta £334.90.
Owner P J Martin **Bred** Tony Mullins **Trained** Norton, N Yorks

FOCUS
No better than a medium sort of gallop to this concluding bumper, but a clear-cut winner. A big step up from the winner, with the fourth the best guide to the level.
T/Jkpt: Not won. JACKPOT PLACEPOT: Part won. £1,840.20 to a £1 stake - 0.4 winning tickets. T/Plt: £2,722.80 to a £1 stake. Pool: £86,011.36 - 23.06 winning tickets. T/Qpdt: £152.10 to a £1 stake. Pool: £7,691.28 - 37.4 winning tickets. **Walter Glynn**

2066 KELSO (L-H)
Saturday, November 7

OFFICIAL GOING: Soft (5.9)
Wind: Almost nil Weather: Overcast, raining

2338 GEORGE HARROW MEMORIAL "NATIONAL HUNT" NOVICES' HURDLE (11 hdls) 2m 6f 151y
12:30 (12:30) (Class 4) 4-Y-O+ **£3,249** (£954; £477; £238)

Form RPR

3 **1** **Jonniesofa (IRE)**[16] 2025 5-10-9 0.................... CraigNichol(3) 121+
(Rose Dobbin) *mde all: pushed along after 2 out: edgd lft and styd on strly fr last* **9/2**[2]

110- **2** *3 1/2* **Western Rules (IRE)**[211] 5255 5-10-12 0.................... BrianHarding 117+
(Nicky Richards) *prom: smooth hdwy to chse wnr bef 3 out: effrt and pushed along appr next: rdn and kpt on same pce fr last* **1/4**[1]

5430 **3** *29* **Jackofhearts**[13] 2085 7-10-12 100.................... SeanQuinlan 88
(Jean McGregor) *chsd wnr to bef 3 out: drvn and outpcd bef next: sn btn* **25/1**

3-0 **4** *53* **Weyburn (IRE)**[16] 2044 4-10-12 0.................... AndrewTinkler 35
(Martin Keighley) *prom: smooth hdwy bef 3 out: rdn and wknd bef next* **9/1**[3]

0/ **P** **Just Annie**[632] 4240 7-10-0 0.................... GrantCockburn(5)
(Lucy Normile) *mstkes in rr: lost tch fr 8th: t.o whn p.u after 2 out* **100/1**

0- **P** **Egon Spenglar**[331] 3030 7-10-9 0.................... CallumWhillans(3)
(Donald Whillans) *t.k.h: mstkes in rr: struggling fr 8th: lost tch and p.u bef 2 out* **100/1**

5m 56.4s (15.40) **Going Correction** +0.725s/f (Soft) **6** Ran SP% **114.0**
Speed ratings (Par 105): **102,100,90,72,**
CSF £6.54 TOTE £5.90: £1.60, £1.10; EX 10.10 Trifecta £27.70.
Owner R & Mrs A Houghton & A Houghton **Bred** T Finn **Trained** South Hazelrigg, Northumbria

FOCUS
All rails on both tracks at innermost position and distances as advertised. Rain throughout the morning eased the going to soft all round. A perfectly judged ride from the front caught out the red-hot favourite in an ordinary novice hurdle.

2339 THE SHIP INN, DALKEITH NOVICES' H'CAP CHASE (12 fncs) 2m 1f 14y
1:05 (1:06) (Class 4) (0-105,105) 4-Y-O+ **£3,898** (£1,144; £572; £286)

Form RPR

00-1 **1** **Throthethatch (IRE)**[178] 286 6-11-10 **103**.................... PeterBuchanan 120+
(Lucinda Russell) *mde all: shkn up and j.rt 2 out: pushed clr* **9/4**[1]

34-4 **2** *8* **Tomorrow's Legend**[26] 1887 5-11-4 **100**.................... AdamNicol(3) 105
(George Moore) *chsd wnr thrght: effrt and ev ch briefly 3 out: sn rdn: edgd lft and kpt on same pce fr next* **5/2**[2]

0412 **3** *5* **Carnaross**[65] 1461 6-11-7 **100**.................................(t) HenryBrooke 102
(Julia Brooke) *midfield: nt fluent 1st: blnd next: stdy hdwy after 4th: effrt whn nt fluent 4 out: rallied u.p 2 out: sn no imp* **5/1**[3]

U20- **4** *9* **Rosquero (FR)**[216] 5163 10-9-13 **81**.................................(p) BrianToomey(3) 72
(Kenny Johnson) *w.r.s and lost many l s: bhd: hdwy and prom 4 out: drvn and outpcd bef 2 out: hung lft and sn btn* **14/1**

430- **5** *13* **Westend Theatre (IRE)**[235] 4827 6-10-11 **90**.................... SeanQuinlan 68
(Jane Walton) *nt fluent on occasions: midfield: pushed along and outpcd after 5 out: btn fnl 3* **22/1**

0-51 **6** *4* **Roc De Prince**[28] 1857 6-11-7 **105**.................................(bt) DaleIrving(5) 79
(James Ewart) *midfield: nt fluent and reminders 3rd: lost pl next: struggling fnl circ: nvr on terms* **17/2**

040- **7** *6* **Jokers And Rogues (IRE)**[216] 5163 7-11-1 **94**.................... AndrewThornton 63
(John Wade) *nt fluent: chsd ldrs: mstke 3rd: rdn and wknd fr 3 out* **14/1**

0124 **8** *14* **Seventeen Black (IRE)**[153] 658 7-10-3 **87**.................... GrantCockburn(5) 41
(Stuart Coltherd) *bhd: outpcd: short-lived effrt 5 out: struggling fr next: t.o* **16/1**

4m 31.3s (13.30) **Going Correction** +0.975s/f (Soft) **8** Ran SP% **112.9**
Speed ratings (Par 105): **107,103,100,96,90 88,85,79**
CSF £8.49 CT £23.55 TOTE £2.90: £1.40, £1.30, £1.40; EX 8.00 Trifecta £27.40.
Owner Mrs Sandra Giles **Bred** Jerry Murphy **Trained** Arlary, Perth & Kinross

FOCUS
Another race dominated from the front. This was run at a good pace and the winner ran this field ragged.

2340 GRAEME TODD & FRIENDS H'CAP HURDLE (13 hdls) 3m 1f 170y
1:40 (1:40) (Class 3) (0-130,130) 4-Y-O+ **£5,848** (£1,717; £858; £429)

Form RPR

6-11 **1** **Isaacstown Lad (IRE)**[178] 291 8-10-11 **115**.................... BrianHarding 127+
(Nicky Richards) *hld up: smooth hdwy 3 out: led gng wl next: shkn up and clr after last: readily* **11/4**[1]

410- **2** *7* **Neptune Equester**[259] 4366 12-10-7 **118**.................(p) MissRMcDonald(7) 122
(Sandy Thomson) *led: rdn and hdd 2 out: kpt on same pce fr last* **12/1**

541- **3** *16* **Donna's Diamond (IRE)**[238] 4759 6-11-7 **130**.................... DiarmuidO'Regan(5) 122
(Chris Grant) *trckd ldrs: hit 5th: ev ch whn mstke 4 out: rdn and wknd 2 out: btn whn mstke last* **7/2**[2]

02-5 **4** *nk* **Rival D'Estruval (FR)**[24] 1903 10-11-4 **125**.................... TonyKelly(3) 113
(Pauline Robson) *hld up: stdy hdwy bef 3 out: rdn and wknd bef next* **6/1**[3]

1413 **5** *10* **Johnny Go**[28] 1856 5-10-2 **111**.................................(p) CallumBewley(5) 89
(Lisa Harrison) *chsd ldrs: rn in snatches: drvn fr 1/2-way: wknd after 3 out* **7/2**[2]

30-0 **6** *46* **Night In Milan (IRE)**[9] 2145 9-11-1 **124**.................... MrJohnDawson(5) 56
(Keith Reveley) *cl up tl rdn and wknd bef 3 out: eased whn no ch fr next* **17/2**

012 **P** **What A Steel (IRE)**[28] 1856 11-10-5 **112**.................(p) CraigNichol(3)
(Alistair Whillans) *chsd ldrs on outside: drvn and struggling bef 3 out: lost tch and p.u next* **17/2**

6m 53.3s (13.30) **Going Correction** +0.725s/f (Soft) **7** Ran SP% **114.1**
Speed ratings (Par 107): **108,105,100,100,97 83,**
CSF £32.53 TOTE £3.50: £1.80, £5.20; EX 33.40 Trifecta £186.70.
Owner M S Borders Racing Club & Partners **Bred** Patrick Cronin **Trained** Greystoke, Cumbria

FOCUS
A competitive handicap run at a good pace, and the favourite pounced late.

2341 FRANK FLANNIGAN SKIPHIRE & BORDER SKIPHIRE H'CAP CHASE (17 fncs) 2m 7f 96y
2:15 (2:15) (Class 3) (0-140,133) 4-Y-O+ **£6,657** (£2,067; £1,113)

Form RPR

3-33 **1** **Kilgefin Star (IRE)**[24] 1900 7-11-8 **129**.................... HenryBrooke 137+
(Michael Smith) *t.k.h early: cl up: mstke 8th: led 5 out: shkn up and styd on strly to draw clr bef last* **7/2**[2]

13-1 **2** *9* **Present Lodger (IRE)**[28] 1855 7-10-7 **117**.................(t) DerekFox(3) 116
(Lucinda Russell) *trckd ldng pair: smooth hdwy to chse wnr 4 out: ev ch whn mstke next: sn rdn: nt fluent 2 out: one pce whn hit last* **7/4**[1]

3521 **3** *25* **Gleann Na Ndochais (IRE)**[16] 2030 9-10-12 **122**.................... CraigNichol(3) 98
(Alistair Whillans) *hld up in tch: pushed along and outpcd 11th: rallied bef 4 out: nt fluent next: wknd bef 2 out* **6/1**

43-3 **P** **Creepy (IRE)**[46] 1617 7-11-12 **133**.................... AndrewTinkler
(Martin Keighley) *nt fluent on occasions: in tch: hit and outpcd 12th: wknd 5 out: p.u after next* **11/2**[3]

44P- **P** **I Need Gold (IRE)**[242] 4693 7-11-6 **127**.................... BrianHarding
(Donald McCain) *led to 5 out: drvn and outpcd 3 out: wknd bef next: p.u between last 2* **7/2**[2]

6m 25.2s (17.20) **Going Correction** +0.975s/f (Soft) **5** Ran SP% **110.5**
Speed ratings (Par 107): **109,105,97, ,**
CSF £10.46 TOTE £5.60: £2.00, £1.60; EX 10.40 Trifecta £33.90.
Owner Mrs Sandra Smith & Ownaracehorse **Bred** John F Gibbons **Trained** Kirkheaton, Northumberland

FOCUS
A fair handicap but conditions took their toll as only three of the five completed.

2342 MAYFIELD RESTAURANT H'CAP CHASE (12 fncs) 2m 1f 14y
2:50 (2:50) (Class 3) (0-125,125) 4-Y-0+ £7,797 (£2,289; £1,144; £572)

Form RPR
PP0U 1 **Indian Voyage (IRE)**[7] 2192 7-11-1 119..........(t) DaraghBourke(5) 131+
(Maurice Barnes) *in tch on outside: hdwy to ld 4 out: pushed along and clr after 2 out: kpt on strly fr last* 12/1

-25F 2 7 **Vengeur De Guye (FR)**[24] 1904 6-11-9 125..........(t) DerekFox(3) 131
(Lucinda Russell) *hld up: hdwy 4 out: effrt and chsd wnr after 2 out: no imp fr last* 10/1

P4-1 3 16 **Quick Decisson (IRE)**[184] 162 7-10-6 110.......... GrantCockburn(5) 101
(Stuart Coltherd) *cl up: ev ch 4 out: sn chsng wnr: drvn and outpcd after 2 out: wknd fr last* 6/1[2]

21-2 4 16 **Amethyst Rose (IRE)**[182] 202 8-10-8 114.......... SamColtherd(7) 87
(Stuart Coltherd) *nt fluent in rr: struggling fnl circ: outpcd whn mstke 3 out: nvr on terms* 20/1

31-3 5 nk **Classinaglass**[191] 35 8-10-6 110.......... HarryBannister(5) 87
(Michael Easterby) *hld up: pushed along 1/2-way: rallied 4 out: rdn and wknd after next: no ch whn lft remote 5th last* 6/1[2]

5-04 F **Rockawango (FR)**[24] 1905 9-11-7 125..........(tp) DaleIrving(5) 101
(James Ewart) *hld up in tch: hdwy to chse ldrs 4 out: effrt after next: 12 l 4th and tired whn fell and down for sme time at last* 8/1[3]

110- P **Scimon Templar (FR)**[207] 5329 7-10-2 104.......... CraigNichol(3)
(Rose Dobbin) *nt fluent: hld up in midfield on ins: struggling 5 out: wknd and p.u bef 2 out* 10/1

312- P **Uno Valoroso (FR)**[231] 4913 7-10-11 113.......... TonyKelly(3)
(Mark Walford) *trckd ldrs: rdn and wknd 4 out: p.u after 2 out* 11/4[1]

FP-F P **Woodpole Academy (IRE)**[12] 2105 8-11-0 116.......... AdamNicol(3)
(Philip Kirby) *led to 4 out: rdn and wknd after next: p.u bef 2 out* 10/1

411P U **Mortlestown (IRE)**[38] 1701 7-11-8 121..........(p) AndrewTinkler
(Martin Keighley) *prom: blnd and uns rdr 7th* 9/1

4m 37.7s (19.70) **Going Correction** +0.975s/f (Soft) 10 Ran SP% **116.1**
Speed ratings (Par 107): **92,88,81,73,73 , , , ,**
CSF £122.61 CT £796.82 TOTE £13.90: £3.50, £3.10, £1.90; EX 154.80 Trifecta £1578.40 Part won..
Owner D Carr & M Carlyle **Bred** Victor Stud Bloodstock Ltd **Trained** Farlam, Cumbria
■ Stewards' Enquiry : Harry Bannister two-day ban: failed to ride out for 4th (22-23 Dec)
Tony Kelly trainer's representative could offer no explanation for the gelding's performance

FOCUS
After a good early pace few were able to keep up the gallop in the conditions.

2343 HAPPY BIRTHDAY SUSAN EVANS NOVICES' H'CAP HURDLE (10 hdls) 2m 2f 25y
3:25 (3:25) (Class 5) (0-100,100) 3-Y-0+ £2,599 (£763; £381; £190)

Form RPR
050- 1 **Clan Legend**[197] 5516 5-10-7 91.......... BlairCampbell(10) 105
(N W Alexander) *mde virtually all: rdn bef 2 out: jnd bef last: edgd lft u.p run-in: hld on wl towards fin* 4/1[2]

05-1 2 hd **Alizee De Janeiro (FR)**[14] 2069 5-11-12 100.......... PeterBuchanan 114
(Lucinda Russell) *hld up: smooth hdwy to press wnr bef 3 out: effrt and chal bef last: kpt on wl run-in: jst hld* 15/8[1]

-005 3 25 **Desert Island Dusk**[12] 2100 4-11-1 94..........[1] DaraghBourke(5) 83
(Maurice Barnes) *hld up: smooth hdwy to chse ldrs appr 3 out: rdn and dropped by first two fr next* 13/2

4-3 4 28 **Paddy's Yarn (IRE)**[71] 1396 5-11-6 94.......... BrianHarding 55
(Valerie Jackson) *prom: lost pl 1/2-way: rallied bef 3 out: rdn: wknd bef next* 11/2[3]

-663 5 3/4 **Hatton Springs (IRE)**[9] 2144 4-11-2 97.......... SamColtherd(7) 57
(Stuart Coltherd) *nt fluent on occasions: prom: hdwy 1/2-way: rdn and wknd bef 2 out* 13/2

4P-0 P **Uplifted (IRE)**[23] 1920 4-10-13 87.......... HenryBrooke
(Martin Todhunter) *hld up: rdn bef 3 out: sn wknd: p.u bef next* 16/1

40-P P **Wildest Dreams (IRE)**[179] 251 6-10-9 88.......... DaleIrving(5)
(Jane Walton) *cl up: rdn and outpcd after 4 out: wknd and p.u next* 10/1

4m 48.2s (21.20) **Going Correction** +0.725s/f (Soft)
WFA 4 from 5yo+ 7lb 7 Ran SP% **111.8**
Speed ratings (Par 103): **81,80,69,57,57 ,**
CSF £11.76 CT £44.91 TOTE £4.70: £2.00, £1.60; EX 12.00 Trifecta £93.40.
Owner Clan Gathering **Bred** Alexander Family **Trained** Kinneston, Perth & Kinross

FOCUS
This produced the closest finish of the afternoon as the favourite battled it out with the long-time leader up the straight.

2344 URWIN FAMILY "NEWCOMERS" STANDARD OPEN NATIONAL HUNT FLAT RACE 2m 51y
4:00 (4:00) (Class 5) 3-5-Y-0 £2,599 (£763; £381; £190)

Form RPR
1 **Bambys Boy** 4-11-4 0.......... MrJohnDawson(5) 110+
(Keith Reveley) *hld up: smooth hdwy to chse ldr over 3f out: effrt and rn green over 2f out: sn led: clr whn hung lft ins fnl f: eased* 3/1[2]

2 13 **Black Ink** 4-11-9 0.......... HenryBrooke 90
(Michael Smith) *in tch: pushed along and outpcd over 5f out: rallied over 3f out: kpt on to chse (clr) wnr towards fin: no imp* 9/4[1]

3 1 3/4 **Captain Mowbray** 4-11-6 0.......... TonyKelly(3) 90+
(Rebecca Menzies) *led: hung rt for much of way: jnd and veered lft over 1f out: sn hdd and outpcd: lost 2nd towards fin* 14/1

4 1/2 **Been Decided (IRE)** 5-10-13 0.......... BlairCampbell(10) 88
(N W Alexander) *hld up in tch: drvn and outpcd over 3f out: kpt on fnl f: nvr rchd ldrs* 4/1[3]

5 15 **Overawed** 4-10-9 0.......... SamColtherd(7) 66
(Stuart Coltherd) *chsd ldr to over 3f out: sn wknd* 14/1

6 18 **Whatatub (IRE)** 4-11-4 0.......... DiarmuidO'Regan(5) 55
(Chris Grant) *trckd ldrs: drvn and struggling over 3f out: sn wknd* 4/1[3]

4m 19.7s (23.50) **Going Correction** +0.725s/f (Soft) 6 Ran SP% **109.1**
Speed ratings (Par 103): **70,63,62,62,54 45**
CSF £9.56 TOTE £2.90: £2.70, £1.60; EX 6.00 Trifecta £26.60.
Owner Mrs Susan Granger **Bred** Mrs Susan Granger **Trained** Lingdale, Redcar & Cleveland

FOCUS
The winner pulled clear in this newcomers' bumper.
T/Plt: £33.60 to a £1 stake. Pool: £44,838.78 - 971.96 winning tickets. T/Qpdt: £34.80 to a £1 stake. Pool: £2,751.21 - 58.4 winning tickets. **Richard Young**

2087 WINCANTON (R-H)
Saturday, November 7

OFFICIAL GOING: Soft (good to soft in places) changing to soft after race 2 (12.55)
Wind: quite strong across Weather: heavy showers with sunny periods

2345 EBF STALLIONS "NATIONAL HUNT" NOVICES' HURDLE (QUALIFIER) (8 hdls) 1m 7f 65y
12:20 (12:21) (Class 3) 4-6-Y-0 £6,498 (£1,908; £954; £477)

Form RPR
6-1 1 **Marracudja (FR)**[13] 2091 4-11-4 138..........(t) SamTwiston-Davies 128+
(Paul Nicholls) *mde all: pushed out: unchal* 6/4[2]

33/6 2 9 **Flamenco Lad**[29] 1837 5-10-9 0.......... JeremiahMcGrath(3) 114
(Martin Hill) *chsd ldrs: wnt 2nd after 3 out: effrt next: sn hld: kpt on same pce* 7/1[3]

21-1 3 19 **Wishfull Dreaming**[30] 1826 4-11-4 0.......... RichardJohnson 100
(Philip Hobbs) *chsd ldrs: rdn after 3 out: wknd next* 4/5[1]

04-6 4 4 **Westend Prince (IRE)**[13] 2088 4-10-12 0.......... AidanColeman 89
(Colin Tizzard) *hld up wl off pce: stdy on appr 2 out: wnt wl hld 4th bef last* 20/1

06- 5 2 3/4 **Get Ready Freddy**[230] 4942 5-10-12 0.......... NickScholfield 86
(Nick Mitchell) *chsd ldrs: rdn after 3 out: wknd next* 100/1

06-3 6 1 3/4 **Shake Devaney (IRE)**[35] 1758 5-10-12 0.......... PaddyBrennan 85
(Fergal O'Brien) *hld up wl off pce: styd on fr 2 out but nvr any threat* 16/1

5F-5 7 21 **Lady Helissio**[17] 2021 5-10-5 0.......... MarkQuinlan 57
(Neil Mulholland) *a bhd: t.o* 100/1

044 8 3 **Bishops Court**[13] 2091 5-10-12 0.......... NoelFehily 61
(Neil Mulholland) *a bhd: t.o* 14/1

3m 46.4s (-2.50) **Going Correction** -0.15s/f (Good) 8 Ran SP% **127.3**
Speed ratings: **100,95,85,82,81 80,69,67**
CSF £14.42 TOTE £2.20: £1.10, £2.00, £1.10; EX 15.30 Trifecta £23.30.
Owner Potensis Bloodstock Limited **Bred** E A R L De Cordelles Et Al **Trained** Ditcheat, Somerset

FOCUS
After being hit by plenty of rain, the going was altered to soft, good to soft in places prior to the opener, which featured a couple of promising types. A step up from the winner, and a bigger one from the runner-up. The third has been rated a stone off his recent win on better ground.

2346 TOBY BALDING MEMORIAL H'CAP CHASE (17 fncs) 2m 4f 35y
12:55 (12:55) (Class 4) (0-120,118) 4-Y-0+ £7,279 (£2,150; £1,075; £538; £269)

Form RPR
6302 1 **Houston Dynimo (IRE)**[5] 2243 10-11-2 115..........(bt) DavidNoonan(7) 123
(David Pipe) *mde virtually all: nt fluent 8th: briefly hdd after 13th: styd on gamely whn chal last: asserted fnl 75yds: drvn out* 4/1[2]

3U-4 2 1 1/4 **Ballydague Lady (IRE)**[17] 2022 8-11-3 109..........(p) NoelFehily 117
(Neil Mulholland) *chsd ldrs: rdn to chse wnr after 4 out: j.lft last 3: mounting chal whn nt fluent last: styd on w ev ch tl no ex fnl 75yds* 9/2[3]

4114 3 23 **Forever My Friend (IRE)**[21] 1965 8-11-12 118..........(p) JamieMoore 102
(Peter Bowen) *chsd wnr: led briefly after 13th: dropped to hld 4th after 4 out: regained modest 3rd cl home* 14/1

223- 4 nk **King Of Glory**[252] 4498 7-11-5 111.......... AidanColeman 96
(Venetia Williams) *chsd ldrs: rdn after 4 out: wknd next* 11/8[1]

2-20 5 1 1/2 **Trillerin Minella (IRE)**[163] 519 7-11-0 106.......... KielanWoods 87
(Graeme McPherson) *chsd ldrs tl wknd 4 out* 6/1

U1-5 P **Lamb's Cross**[191] 31 9-9-7 92 oh5.......... MichaelHeard(7)
(Mark Gillard) *in last pair: struggling 11th: tailing off whn p.u bef 12th* 33/1

0433 P **Isthereadifference (IRE)**[21] 1965 8-11-1 107..........(tp) MarkQuinlan
(Neil Mulholland) *last: nt fluent 2nd: struggling 9th: t.o 13th: p.u next* 10/1

5m 20.1s (2.60) **Going Correction** +0.375s/f (Yiel) 7 Ran SP% **113.3**
Speed ratings (Par 105): **109,108,99,99,98 ,**
CSF £22.01 TOTE £5.20: £2.10, £2.30; EX 25.90 Trifecta £71.60.
Owner Miss S E Hartnell **Bred** Sweetmans Bloodstock **Trained** Nicholashayne, Devon

FOCUS
A modest contest, run in demanding conditions, with raining falling throughout. The second is probably the best guide to the level.

2347 WINCANTON RISING STARS NOVICES' CHASE (GRADE 2) (17 fncs) 2m 4f 35y
1:30 (1:30) (Class 1) 4-Y-0+ £18,309 (£6,924; £3,509; £1,791; £943)

Form RPR
50-1 1 **Junction Fourteen (IRE)**[23] 1932 6-11-8 140..........(t) DarylJacob 150+
(Emma Lavelle) *mde all: nt fluent 7th: styd on strly and in command fr 2 out: stmbld last: rdn out* 9/4[2]

151- 2 4 1/2 **Arpege D'Alene (FR)**[266] 4215 5-11-2 0.......... SamTwiston-Davies 140+
(Paul Nicholls) *trckd ldrs: lft 2nd at the 11th: rdn after 3 out: styd on but a being hld fr next* 13/8[1]

F0-0 3 34 **L'Unique (FR)**[28] 1848 6-10-9 0.......... WayneHutchinson 107+
(Alan King) *prom tl tried to duck out 5th: chsd ldrs: cl 3rd whn hmpd 11th: sn nudged along in 4th: no ch fr 3 out: snatched 3rd fnl strides* 8/1

100- 4 hd **Warrantor (IRE)**[241] 4702 6-11-2 135..........(t) GavinSheehan 105
(Warren Greatrex) *hld up in last pair: lft 3rd after 11th: sn pushed along: wknd 3 out: lost 3rd fnl strides* 7/2[3]

5-21 5 48 **Dragon's Den (IRE)**[18] 2010 8-11-6 129.......... BrendanPowell 74
(Chris Down) *hld up last: stmbld 2nd: hit 7th: rdn after 12th: wknd after next: t.o* 25/1

4P-1 F **Gentleman Jon**[22] 1948 7-11-8 127.......... NoelFehily
(Colin Tizzard) *trckd ldrs: pressed wnr 9th tl fell 11th* 16/1

5m 14.3s (-3.20) **Going Correction** +0.375s/f (Yiel) 6 Ran SP% **111.9**
Speed ratings (Par 115): **121,119,105,105,86**
CSF £6.61 TOTE £3.20: £1.50, £1.40; EX 6.20 Trifecta £33.10.
Owner Martin St Quinton & Tim Syder **Bred** John And Iris Lunny **Trained** Hatherden, Hants

FOCUS
Even though an interesting contender came out earlier in the day, this had the look of a classy contest. Southfield Theatre, Wonderful Charm, Houblon Des Obeaux, Silviniaco Conti and Wishful Thinking were the last five to land this prize, which strongly suggests the winner is one to follow. The going was changed to soft all round prior to the off. The second has been rated in line with his hurdle form.

2348 BADGER ALES TROPHY (HANDICAP CHASE) (LISTED RACE) (21 fncs) 3m 1f 30y
2:05 (2:05) (Class 1) (0-150,149) 4-Y-0+
£34,170 (£12,822; £6,420; £3,198; £1,608; £804)

Form RPR
0-41 **1** **Drop Out Joe**[28] 1849 7-11-6 **143**......................(p) AidanColeman 153
(Charlie Longsdon) *chsd ldrs: rdn after 17th: wnt 2nd after 3 out: led sn after last: styd on wl: drvn out* **11/1**
F4U- **2** ½ **Royal Palladium (FR)**[242] 4693 7-10-0 **123** oh1.................. AlainCawley 132
(Venetia Williams) *in tch: led 7th: rdn after 3 out: styd on gamely whn hdd sn after last: hld nring fin* **20/1**
11-5 **3** 12 **A Good Skin (IRE)**[15] 2055 6-11-0 **137**......................... PaddyBrennan 136+
(Tom George) *hld up towards rr: hmpd 8th: hdwy fr 14th: wnt 2nd 17th: awkward 3 out: sn rdn: styd on same pce* **11/1**
43-1 **4** 7 **Forgotten Gold (IRE)**[13] 2089 9-10-13 **136**..................... DarylJacob 125
(Tom George) *chsd ldrs: rdn after 4 out: styd on same pce fr next* **8/1**[2]
115- **5** 8 **Carole's Destrier**[211] 5251 7-11-12 **149**......................... NoelFehily 131
(Neil Mulholland) *mid-div: trckd ldrs 17th: rdn after 4 out: sn hld: styd on same pce* **8/1**[2]
2U0- **6** 4 **Bertie Boru (IRE)**[238] 4767 8-10-12 **135**..................... RichardJohnson 116
(Philip Hobbs) *hld up last: nvr that fluent: mstke 16th: plugged on but no ch fr after next* **11/1**
22-5 **7** 29 **Theatrical Star**[14] 2061 9-11-2 **139**......................... BrendanPowell 87
(Colin Tizzard) *led tl 3rd: chsd ldrs: rdn after 15th: wknd after next: t.o* **8/1**[2]
06-4 **8** 7 **Alfie Spinner (IRE)**[27] 1871 10-10-0 **123** oh1..................... WillKennedy 64
(Nick Williams) *prom: led 3rd tl 7th: lost pl after 13th: wknd 17th: t.o* **14/1**
52P- **P** **Benvolio (IRE)**[266] 4224 8-11-8 **145**......................(b) NickScholfield
(Paul Nicholls) *in tch: wnt 3rd 14th: wknd 17th: t.o whn p.u bef 2 out* **16/1**
2U-3 **P** **Wilton Milan (IRE)**[27] 1869 7-10-7 **130**......................(t) HarrySkelton
(Dan Skelton) *hld up towards rr: midfield whn mstke 15th: blnd 17th: sn wknd: nt fluent next: p.u bef 3 out* **16/1**
30P- **P** **The Ould Lad (IRE)**[196] 5540 7-10-2 **125**..............(t) SamTwiston-Davies
(Paul Nicholls) *mid-div: pushed along after 16th: rdn after next: nvr any imp: wknd 3 out: p.u bef last* **9/4**[1]
0-03 **P** **Doing Fine (IRE)**[28] 1849 7-10-11 **134**......................(b) WayneHutchinson
(Rebecca Curtis) *mid-div: stmbld and lost pl 6th: hit 16th: wknd next: t.o whn p.u after 4 out* **10/1**[3]

6m 41.2s (1.70) **Going Correction** +0.375s/f (Yiel) 12 Ran SP% **121.4**
Speed ratings (Par 111): **112,111,108,105,103 101,92,90,,**
CSF £203.23 CT £2481.40 TOTE £12.60: £4.20, £5.70, £3.70; EX 275.90 Trifecta £3391.60.
Owner The Jesters **Bred** Jethro Bloodstock **Trained** Over Norton, Oxon

FOCUS
This well-established staying handicap looked competitive as one would expect for the money on offer, and was run at a sound gallop. Another step forward from the winner, with the second rated back to the level of his Market Rasen win.

2349 BRUTON MARES' H'CAP HURDLE (11 hdls) 2m 5f 82y
2:40 (2:41) (Class 2) 4-Y-0+
£15,640 (£4,620; £2,310; £1,155; £577; £290)

Form RPR
-0F6 **1** **Lily Waugh (IRE)**[31] 1808 8-10-3 **119**......................(t) DavidNoonan(7) 140+
(Anthony Honeyball) *mid-div: mstke 6th: hdwy 3 out: led bef 2 out: sn wl in command: comf* **10/1**
211P **2** 13 **Lady Of Longstone (IRE)**[8] 2167 5-10-1 **117**.............. MichaelHeard(7) 126
(David Pipe) *led tl 2nd: chsd ldr: led 7th: rdn and hdd appr 2 out: sn hld by wnr: styd on same pce* **20/1**
241- **3** 10 **Tara Mist**[197] 5514 6-11-0 **123**......................... RichardJohnson 120
(Henry Daly) *in tch: hdwy 5th: rdn after 3 out: one pce fr next* **3/1**[2]
P1-F **4** 1 **Morello Royale (IRE)**[14] 2064 5-11-5 **135**..........(t) PaulO'Brien(7) 130
(Colin Tizzard) *trckd ldrs: rdn after 3 out: one pce fr next* **16/1**
1-1 **5** 24 **Double Silver**[181] 216 8-10-10 **119**......................... PaddyBrennan 90
(Fergal O'Brien) *towards rr: struggling 3 out: plugged on past btn horses fr 2 out: nvr a factor* **14/1**
2566 **6** 3½ **Titch Strider (IRE)**[13] 2087 10-9-7 **109** oh6........... ThomasCheesman(7) 77
(John Panvert) *a in rr* **33/1**
1232 **7** 2¼ **Miss Sassypants**[33] 1793 6-10-7 **116**......................... RyanMahon 81
(Seamus Mullins) *mid-div: rdn after 3 out: nvr threatened: wknd next* **16/1**
35-3 **8** 93 **Bondi Mist (IRE)**[135] 268 6-10-0 **109** oh5......................... MarkGrant
(Jonathan Geake) *in tch: hdwy 5th: rdn after 8th: wknd after next: t.o* **66/1**
11P- **P** **Desert Queen**[216] 5175 7-11-8 **131**......................(t) NoelFehily
(Harry Fry) *racd freely: led 2nd: nt fluent 4th: mstke 5th: hdd 7th: nt fluent 3 out: sn wknd: p.u bef next* **7/2**[3]
31-3 **F** **Kalane (IRE)**[189] 93 6-11-9 **132**......................... AidanColeman
(Charlie Longsdon) *mid-div whn fell 4th* **2/1**[1]

5m 18.2s (-8.30) **Going Correction** -0.15s/f (Good) 10 Ran SP% **117.3**
Speed ratings (Par 109): **109,104,100,99,90 89,88,53,,**
CSF £171.75 CT £749.48 TOTE £14.00: £2.50, £4.10, £1.30; EX 173.10 Trifecta £975.90.
Owner Go To War **Bred** F Boyd **Trained** Mosterton, Dorset

FOCUS
With the market leader coming down early, and the third-favourite pulling far too hard, this form may not be overly reliable for the level. A big hurdle pb from the winner, with the runner-up rated back to the level of her Worcester win.

2350 STANJAMES.COM ELITE HURDLE (A LIMITED H'CAP) (GRADE 2) (8 hdls) 1m 7f 65y
3:15 (3:16) (Class 1) 4-Y-0+
£34,170 (£12,822; £6,420; £3,198; £1,608; £804)

Form RPR
P2P- **1** **Irving**[203] 5390 7-11-10 **154**......................... NickScholfield 158+
(Paul Nicholls) *hld up in tch: hdwy after 3 out: chal 2 out: shkn up to ld bef last: r.o wl: readily* **9/2**[2]
23-5 **2** 7 **Melodic Rendezvous**[191] 51 9-11-7 **151**......................... RichardJohnson 147
(Jeremy Scott) *chsd clr ldr: led appr 2 out: sn hrd pressed and u.p: hdd bef last: kpt on but nt pce of wnr run-in* **11/2**
165- **3** hd **Zarib (IRE)**[223] 5045 4-10-4 **134** oh1......................... HarrySkelton 131
(Dan Skelton) *in tch: hdwy after 3 out: rdn in cl 3rd after 2 out: nt quite pce to chal: kpt on fr last to nrly snatch 2nd fnl strides* **3/1**[1]
111 **4** 1½ **Francis Of Assisi (IRE)**[22] 1946 5-11-0 **144**......................... AidanColeman 140
(John Ferguson) *hld up: hdwy after 3 out: rdn next: styd on fr last but nt pce to get involved* **5/1**[3]
251- **5** 1¼ **All Yours (FR)**[212] 5236 4-11-3 **147**......................(t) SamTwiston-Davies 141
(Paul Nicholls) *hld up: hdwy appr 2 out: rdn to dispute cl 3rd between last 2: nt quite pce to chal: hld in 4th whn awkward last: fdd fnl 140yds* **5/1**[3]
60-0 **6** 10 **Olofi (FR)**[169] 437 9-10-4 **134** oh2......................... PaddyBrennan 118
(Tom George) *chsd clr ldr: rdn and ev ch briefly appr 2 out: wknd bef last* **7/1**
3-10 **7** 5 **Buckwheat**[112] 1039 5-10-6 **143**......................... MrAlexFerguson(7) 122
(John Ferguson) *hld up: outpcd appr 2 out: no threat after* **10/1**
2206 **8** 2 **Byron Blue (IRE)**[22] 1949 6-9-11 **134** oh11..................(t) MichaelHeard(7) 112
(Mark Gillard) *led: sn clr: hdd appr 2 out: sn wknd* **66/1**

3m 38.2s (-10.70) **Going Correction** -0.15s/f (Good) 8 Ran SP% **115.0**
Speed ratings (Par 115): **122,118,118,117,116 111,108,107**
CSF £29.69 CT £85.22 TOTE £6.00: £1.80, £1.60, £1.40; EX 28.00 Trifecta £125.90.
Owner Axom XLIX **Bred** Gestut Schlenderhan **Trained** Ditcheat, Somerset

FOCUS
With no obvious front-runner in attendance among the market principals, it was left to Byron Blue to do that duty, but he was largely ignored as he streaked some 20l clear early. The winner has been rated up 4lb on last year's Fighting Fifth, while the third, fourth and fifth set the level.

2351 JOCKEY CLUB CATERING INTERMEDIATE OPEN NATIONAL HUNT FLAT RACE 1m 7f 65y
3:50 (3:51) (Class 6) 4-6-Y-0 **£1,624** (£477; £238; £119)

Form RPR
322- **1** **Vieux Lille (IRE)**[217] 5143 5-11-4 0......................... RichardJohnson 110+
(Philip Hobbs) *in tch: pressed ldr fr over 4f out: led over 2f out: styd on wl to assert fnl f: drvn out* **5/2**[1]
20- **2** 2¼ **Big Chief Benny (IRE)**[266] 4221 4-11-4 0......................... WayneHutchinson 108+
(Alan King) *hld up towards rr: hdwy fr 5f out: rdn and ev ch over 1f out: styng on but looking hld whn veered lft ins fnl f* **7/2**[2]
3 3¼ **Chelsea Flyer (IRE)** 4-11-4 0......................... AidanColeman 105
(Emma Lavelle) *racd keenly: mid-div: hdwy to trck ldrs over 5f out: rdn in clly disp 2nd over 2f out: styd on same pce fnl f* **5/1**
6-4 **4** 11 **Justatenner**[180] 242 4-10-11 0......................... PaulO'Brien(7) 94
(Colin Tizzard) *prom: led over 7f out: rdn and hdd over 2f out: styd on same pce* **33/1**
5 nk **Bol D'Air (FR)**[188] 4-11-4 0......................... [1] HarryCobden(7) 100
(Paul Nicholls) *mid-div: hdwy 3f out: sn rdn: styd on same pce fnl 2f* **9/1**
6 16 **Bramble Brook** 5-11-4 0......................... BrendanPowell 77
(Colin Tizzard) *mid-div tl lost pl over 6f out: styd on fnl 2f but nvr any threat* **12/1**
7 ½ **Mixelle Days** 4-10-6 0......................... AliceMills(5) 70
(Martin Hill) *hld up towards rr: styd on fnl 2f: nvr any threat* **100/1**
8 15 **Cornish Warrior (IRE)** 4-11-4 0......................... JamieMoore 62
(Rebecca Curtis) *trckd ldrs: pushed along over 5f out: wknd 4f out* **12/1**
9 6 **Galice Du Ciel** 4-10-11 0......................... MrDavidTurner(7) 56
(Giles Smyly) *mid-div on outer: rdn over 4f out: sn wknd* **100/1**
- **10** 7 **Morris The Miner** 5-11-4 0......................... NoelFehily 49
(Neil Mulholland) *trckd ldrs tl 4f out: sn wknd* **33/1**
11 25 **Fazakerley (IRE)** 4-11-4 0......................(t) SamTwiston-Davies 24
(Paul Nicholls) *mid-div: struggling over 6f out: wknd 4f out: eased* **9/2**[3]
12 8 **Shoot Themessenger**[553] 6-10-11 0......................... NickScholfield 9
(Mark Gillard) *led tl rdn over 7f out: wknd 5f out: t.o* **100/1**
000 **13** 17 **Palmers Bridge**[29] 1843 6-10-11 0......................(t) MrSeanHoulihan(7)
(Linda Blackford) *a towards rr: t.o* **100/1**

3m 40.5s (-2.80) **Going Correction** -0.15s/f (Good) 13 Ran SP% **120.9**
Speed ratings: **101,99,98,92,92 83,83,75,72,68 54,50,41**
CSF £11.04 TOTE £3.30: £1.70, £1.50, £1.90; EX 13.70 Trifecta £61.60.
Owner Louisville Syndicate III **Bred** Park Athlete Partnership **Trained** Withycombe, Somerset

FOCUS
Probably just an ordinary bumper. It's been rated around the first two.
T/Plt: £170.20 to a £1 stake. Pool: £79,579.08 - 341.12 winning tickets. T/Qpdt: £64.90 to a £1 stake. Pool: £5,687.43 - 64.8 winning tickets. **Tim Mitchell**

2352 - (Foreign Racing) - See Raceform Interactive

2231 NAAS (L-H)
Saturday, November 7

OFFICIAL GOING: Soft

2353a TEXT YOUR BET TO PADDY POWER ON 51465 FISHERY LANE HURDLE (GRADE 3) (8 hdls) 2m
1:25 (1:25) 4-Y-0 **£16,375** (£4,786; £2,267)

RPR
1 **Gwencily Berbas (FR)**[241] 4707 4-11-8 135......................(t) APHeskin 147+
(Alan Fleming, Ire) *led and disp: lft in front fr 1st and mde rest: 3 l clr at 1/2-way: reduced advantage 3 out: pushed along and pressed bef next: gng best bef last and styd on wl to assert run-in* **6/5**[2]
2 8 **Petite Parisienne (FR)**[153] 665 4-11-3 140......................... BJCooper 133
(W P Mullins, Ire) *hld up bhd ldrs: sltly hmpd by faller at 1st: 2nd 1/2-way: rdn bef 2 out and no imp on wnr u.p bef last where mstke: kpt on one pce* **1/1**[1]
3 ½ **Neverushacon (IRE)**[103] 1123 4-10-13 120......................... RobbiePower 128
(Mrs John Harrington, Ire) *settled bhd ldrs: hmpd by faller at 1st: 2nd bef 3rd where nt fluent: last of remaining trio at 1/2-way: rdn bef 2 out and no imp on wnr u.p bef last: kpt on one pce* **16/1**
F **Hostile Fire (IRE)**[7] 2205 4-10-13 123......................(t) LPDempsey
(Gordon Elliott, Ire) *led and disp: narrow advantage whn fell 1st* **12/1**[3]

3m 58.7s (-4.80) 4 Ran SP% **109.0**
CSF £2.89 TOTE £2.30; DF 2.90 Trifecta £5.20.
Owner Barry Connell **Bred** Mlle Lily-Rose Bernabe **Trained** The Curragh, Co Kildare

FOCUS
This has been won by some top-notch performers. Iktitaf (2005), Catch Me (2006), Jezki (2012), Diakali (2013) and Kitten Rock (2014) are the winners than stand out most in the last decade. This year's renewal was a bit disappointing given the illustrious roll of honour but it did contain a Grade 1 and Grade 2 winner. The winner made all. We lost Hostile Fire at the first. The runner-up was below par in France last time and has been rated off her best again.

2354-2360a (Foreign Racing) - See Raceform Interactive

[2134] AUTEUIL (L-H)

Saturday, November 7

OFFICIAL GOING: Turf: very soft

2361a GRAND PRIX D'AUTOMNE (HURDLE) (GRADE 1) (5YO+) (TURF) 3m

2:45 (12:00) 5-Y-0+

£129,069 (£63,100; £37,286; £25,813; £14,341; £10,038)

RPR

1 **Thousand Stars (FR)**[34] 1787 11-10-10 0..............................(p) RWalsh 150
(W P Mullins, Ire) *w.w in fnl trio: hdwy appr 2 out: abt 5 l bk in 5th jumping last: r.o wl u.p to chal between horses: led fnl stride* **5/1**

2 *nse* **Aubusson (FR)**[27] 1883 6-10-10 0.............................. LizzieKelly 150
(Nick Williams) *chsd ldr: pair clr: led bef 6 out: hrd rdn whn pressed fr 2 out: styd on gamely u.p: hdd narrowly and briefly by eventual 3rd 100yds out: sn led again: hdd fnl stride* **20/1**

3 *hd* **Hippomene (FR)**[27] 1883 5-10-8 0 ow2..............................(p) DavidCottin 148
(J-P Gallorini, France) *w.w towards rr: tk clsr order 4 out: pressed ldr 2 out: styd on u.p to ld narrowly and briefly 100yds out: sn hdd: no ex* **4/1[3]**

4 *2 1/2* **Roll On Has (FR)**[27] 1883 5-10-1 0.............................. JacquesRicou 139
(J-P Gallorini, France) *hld up in midfield: rdn and tk clsr order bef 2 out: chsd ldrs appr last: one pce u.p run-in* **10/3[2]**

5 *2* **Broadway Buffalo (IRE)**[203] 5392 7-10-10 0..............................(b) MsKWalsh 146
(David Pipe) *hld up in fnl trio: last and nudged along bnd after 3 out: styd on and rdn 2 out: kpt on u.p run-in: nt pce to get on terms* **14/1**

6 *1 3/4* **Reve De Sivola (FR)**[240] 4719 10-10-10 0.............................. JamesReveley 144
(Nick Williams) *led: hdd bef 6 out: remained cl up: rdn and outpcd fr 2 out: styd on u.p fr last* **6/1**

7 *nk* **Plumeur (FR)**[27] 1883 8-10-10 0.............................. ThomasBeaurain 143
(G Chaignon, France) *w.w in midfield: rdn and no imp fr 3 out: styd on u.p fr bef last: nvr in contention* **28/1**

8 *6* **Dulce Leo (FR)**[27] 1883 9-10-10 0..............................(b) FelixDeGiles 137
(J-P Gallorini, France) *settled in midfield: chsd ldrs fr 1/2-way: rdn and wknd bef 2 out* **40/1**

9 *dist* **Voiladenuo (FR)**[27] 1883 6-10-10 0..............................(p) WilfridDenuault
(Guy Denuault, France) *led main pack bhd two clr ldrs: lost pl 3 out: sn bhd: t.o* **8/1**

F **Saint Firmin (FR)**[27] 1883 6-10-10 0.............................. KevinNabet
(Robert Collet, France) *slowly away: t.k.h: gd hdwy fr 3 out: cl 3rd whn fell heavily last* **3/1[1]**

5m 56.83s (356.83) **10 Ran SP% 127.5**
PARI-MUTUEL (all including 1 euro stake): WIN 7.40 PLACE 2.60, 7.20, 2.20DF 133.60SF 259.80.

Owner Hammer & Trowel Syndicate **Bred** Mlle Camille & Mlle Ophelie Demercastel **Trained** Muine Beag, Co Carlow

2362a PRIX DU SALON DU CHEVAL DE PARIS 2015 (HURDLE) (CONDITIONS) (4YO) (TURF) 2m 2f

3:55 (12:00) 4-Y-0 **£17,860** (£8,930; £5,209; £3,534; £1,674)

RPR

1 **Burmese Temple (FR)**[52] 4-10-8 0..............................(p) TheoChevillard(4) 112
(Y-M Porzier, France) **41/5[3]**

2 *3 1/2* **Ahzana (FR)**[9] 4-10-12 0.............................. ThomasViel(5) 113
(L Viel, France) **32/1**

3 *4* **Flavin (FR)**[11] 4-11-5 0.............................. AnthonyCardine(4) 115
(Mme P Butel, France) **238/10**

4 *2 1/2* **Bonjour Bonsoir (FR)**[52] 4-10-8 0.............................. FelixDeGiles 98
(Emmanuel Clayeux, France) **92/10**

5 *2 1/2* **Sunday Cerisy (FR)**[14] 4-10-12 0.............................. AnthonyThierry 99
(F Foucher, France) **164/10**

6 *3/4* **Maximo Meridio (FR)**[16] 4-10-10 0.............................. JoAudon 96
(Mme L Audon, France) **141/10**

7 *snk* **Beau Star (FR)**[37] 1731 4-10-12 0.............................. DylanUbeda(5) 103
(M Rolland, France) **186/10**

8 *2 1/2* **Palmerino (FR)**[244] 4-10-12 0.............................. WilfridDenuault 96
(E Leenders, France) **6/1[2]**

9 *nk* **Kapko (FR)** 4-10-8 0.............................. StephanePaillard 91
(J-D Marion, France) **129/1**

10 *1 3/4* **Don Hugues Pipard (FR)** 4-10-8 0.............................. MathieuCarroux 90
(A Chaille-Chaille, France) **23/10[1]**

11 *6* **Brise Coeur (FR)**[17] 2024 4-10-8 0.............................. JamesReveley 84
(Nick Williams) *prom: led after 1st: untidy 4th: hdd 5th: led again 6th: hdd bef 3 out: grad dropped away fr 2 out* **269/10**

12 *2 1/2* **Petilucky (FR)**[532] 4-10-12 0.............................. OlivierAuge 85
(L Viel, France) **79/1**

13 *3/4* **Passing Lore (FR)**[213] 4-10-12 0............(b[1]) Jean-ChristopherGagnon(5) 89
(Yannick Fouin, France) **17/1**

14 *hd* **Trillion Stars (FR)**[366] 2318 4-10-10 0.............................. LudovicPhilipperon 82
(E Moullec, France) **21/1**

P **Pur Sang D'Or (FR)**[22] 4-10-12 0..............................(b) JonathanGiron(5)
(Mlle S Sine, France) **86/1**

P **Kilda Six (FR)**[203] 4-11-0 0.............................. MorganRegairaz
(D Bressou, France) **102/10**

F **Call Hector (FR)**[199] 4-10-12 0.............................. ErvanChazelle
(G Chaignon, France) **47/1**

P **Banco (FR)**[16] 4-10-8 0..............................(p) Marc-AntoineBillard
(R-M Dupuis, France) **160/1**

P **Usher Du Lys (FR)** 4-10-8 0.............................. AlexisPoirier
(J-L Guillochon, France) **117/1**

4m 20.76s (260.76) **19 Ran SP% 119.1**
PARI-MUTUEL (all including 1 euro stake): WIN 9.20 PLACE 3.60, 7.80, 7.30DF 165.90SF 360.00.

Owner Haras De Bernesq **Bred** Ecurie Kura, Mlle A Houssin & S Houssin **Trained** France

[1960] FFOS LAS (L-H)

Sunday, November 8

OFFICIAL GOING: Heavy (4.5)
Wind: strong half across Weather: rain

2363 GAREJ RAYMOND NOVICES' HURDLE (8 hdls) 1m 7f 202y

1:30 (1:32) (Class 4) 4-Y-0+ **£5,198** (£1,526; £763; £381)

Form RPR

/32- 1 **Ma Du Fou (FR)**[321] 3229 5-10-12 0.............................. GavinSheehan 131+
(Warren Greatrex) *trckd ldr tl led after 4th: rdn clr between last 2: styd on wl* **4/6[1]**

5 2 *6* **Agrapart (FR)**[25] 1909 4-10-12 0.............................. DarylJacob 121
(Nick Williams) *chsd ldrs: wnt 2nd after 5th: rdn whn nt fluent 3 out: one pce fr next* **5/1[3]**

110- 3 *8* **Armchair Theatre (IRE)**[212] 5255 5-10-12 0.............................. PaulMoloney 114
(Evan Williams) *hld up in tch: clsd 5th: rdn to chal for 2nd 3 out: wknd next* **9/4[2]**

4 *64* **Never Equalled (IRE)**[210] 6-10-12 0.............................. SeanBowen 49
(Bernard Llewellyn) *hld up in tch: hdwy to chse ldrs 4th: wknd appr 3 out: t.o* **25/1**

5 *27* **Aaman (IRE)**[67] 9-10-12 0.............................. JamesBest 22
(Bernard Llewellyn) *t.k.h early: hld up in last pair: wknd after 5th: t.o* **50/1**

5 6 *7* **Petrify**[10] 2150 5-10-12 0.............................. DaveCrosse 15
(Bernard Llewellyn) *hld up in last pair: wknd after 5th: t.o* **100/1**

3/ P **Fusionforce (IRE)**[1242] 719 8-10-7 0.............................. NickSlatter(5)
(Gary Hanmer) *t.k.h: led: wandered into 1st 2 flights: j.rt and nt fluent 4th: sn hdd: wknd qckly after 5th: t.o whn p.u bef 3 out* **66/1**

4m 12.6s (252.60) **Going Correction** +1.70s/f (Heav)
WFA 4 from 5yo+ 7lb **7 Ran SP% 115.7**
Speed ratings (Par 105): **107,104,100,68,54 51,**
CSF £4.91 TOTE £1.90: £1.50, £2.10; EX 6.00 Trifecta £7.70.
Owner Walters Plant Hire & James & Jean Potter **Bred** Scea Ecurie Jc Laisis **Trained** Upper Lambourn, Berks

FOCUS
All bends dolled out and races 1 & 6 increased by 69yds, race 2 by 14yds, race 3 by 21yds, race 4 by 28yds and race 5 by 121yds. The betting suggested this only concerned three, and so it proved. It's doubtful the form amounts a great deal in this sort of company.

2364 JOHN E JEREMY CHARTERED SURVEYORS H'CAP CHASE (13 fncs) 2m

2:05 (2:05) (Class 4) (0-105,103) 4-Y-0+ **£5,198** (£1,526; £763; £381)

Form RPR

4-43 1 **Bobble Boru (IRE)**[176] 331 7-11-12 103.............................. LiamTreadwell 112+
(Venetia Williams) *racd keenly early: led to 1st: hld up bhd ldrs after: mstke 9th: sn rdn along: led 2 out: drvn out to hold on flat* **5/2[1]**

4P53 2 *1* **Flash Crash**[10] 2150 6-11-8 102..............................(t) JamesBanks(3) 108
(Barry Brennan) *hld up in tch: nt fluent 5th: rdn appr 4 out: lft 3rd 2 out: styd on wl to chse wnr flat: clsng nr fin* **14/1**

00P- 3 *4 1/2* **Capilla (IRE)**[216] 5182 7-11-6 97..............................(t) PaulMoloney 98
(Evan Williams) *t.k.h early: c through to ld 2nd: pushed along 3 out: hdd next: grad wknd: lost 2nd flat* **7/2[3]**

32-5 4 *5* **Magical Man**[169] 438 8-10-5 82..............................(p) PaddyBrennan 78
(Debra Hamer) *prom: chsd ldr 5th: lost 2nd whn mstke 4 out: rdn and grad wknd* **3/1[2]**

-263 5 *hd* **Humbel Ben (IRE)**[40] 1685 12-11-0 91..............................(p) NickScholfield 87
(Alan Jones) *hld up in last: blnd 8th: struggling after next: wknd 3 out* **7/1**

0-2U 6 *2 1/2* **Gowanauthat (IRE)**[17] 2037 7-11-4 95..............................(t) GavinSheehan 96+
(Charlie Mann) *led 1st to 2nd: styd prom: wnt 2nd 4 out: mstke next: chalng whn blnd bdly 2 out: great rcvry by rdr but lost all ch* **4/1**

4m 15.3s (255.30) **6 Ran SP% 115.0**
CSF £31.06 TOTE £3.10: £1.70, £4.10; EX 27.10 Trifecta £70.30.
Owner T Fawcett **Bred** Jimmy Coffey **Trained** Kings Caple, H'fords

FOCUS
A moderate contest but the winner will probably be a solid performer at this sort of level.

2365 HERBERT R THOMAS CHARTERED SURVEYORS NOVICES' LIMITED H'CAP CHASE (15 fncs) 2m 3f 83y

2:40 (2:40) (Class 4) (0-120,118) 4-Y-0+ **£6,657** (£2,067; £1,113)

Form RPR

2P3- 1 **Globalisation (IRE)**[216] 5180 5-11-5 115..............................(t) SeanBowen 125+
(Rebecca Curtis) *hld up in 4th: mstke 5th: rdn 4 out: lft last of 3 stl gng next: mstke 2 out: r.o to ld last: shkn up and qckly clr* **10/3[2]**

12-6 2 *3* **Dolores Delightful (FR)**[25] 1906 5-11-8 118.............................. DarylJacob 123
(Nick Williams) *j.rt at times: led to 2nd: styd cl up: led 8th to 11th: led 3 out to last: one pce* **5/2[1]**

24-4 3 *1 3/4* **Ballyrath (IRE)**[49] 1600 5-10-11 110.............................. RyanHatch(3) 113
(Nigel Twiston-Davies) *cl up: led 2nd to 8th: w ldr after tl led 11th: hdd and mstke 3 out: nt fluent next: no ex flat* **9/2[3]**

145- F **Rouquine Sauvage**[223] 5060 7-11-2 112..............................(t) NoelFehily
(Anthony Honeyball) *t.k.h in last: cl enough and yet to be asked for an effrt whn fell 4 out* **8/1**

262- F **Wild Bill (IRE)**[235] 4851 6-11-6 116.............................. PaulMoloney 119+
(Evan Williams) *chsd ldng pair: gng wl enough in cl 3rd whn fell 3 out* **5/2[1]**

5m 21.7s (20.60) **Going Correction** +0.875s/f (Soft) **5 Ran SP% 109.5**
Speed ratings (Par 105): **91,89,89,,**
CSF £12.09 TOTE £4.20: £2.40, £1.40; EX 13.70 Trifecta £43.30.
Owner John P McManus **Bred** Noel McLaughlin **Trained** Newport, Pembrokeshire

FOCUS
This had looked quite an interesting race of its type, but it developed into a dash to the line heading to four out.

2366 ARUP H'CAP CHASE (18 fncs) 2m 7f 177y

3:15 (3:15) (Class 4) (0-115,115) 4-Y-0+ **£5,848** (£1,717; £858; £429)

Form RPR

11U1 1 **Conas Taoi (IRE)**[4] 2272 6-10-4 96..............................(p) ConorShoemark(3) 117+
(Paul Morgan) *chsd ldr: led 4 out: gng clr whn blnd 2 out: comf* **13/8[1]**

46-5 2 *4* **As De Fer (FR)**[186] 149 9-11-3 106..............................(t) NoelFehily 119
(Anthony Honeyball) *led: j.rt 13th: hdd 4 out: shkn up next: styd on same pce* **3/1[2]**

3-55 3 *15* **Copper Birch (IRE)**[162] 553 7-11-12 115.............................. PaulMoloney 112
(Evan Williams) *hld up in last: hdwy 10th: last again and struggling 4 out: rallied to go modest 3rd after 2 out* **4/1[3]**

4U-3 **4** *2* **No Through Road**[29] 1855 8-11-12 **115**.......................... LiamTreadwell 110
(Michael Scudamore) *hld up bhd ldrs: relegated to cl last 10th: chsd ldng pair again 4 out tl wknd after 2 out* **9/1**

/PP4 **5** *10* **Tom Bach (IRE)**[29] 1850 11-10-0 **89** oh10..........................(b) JamesBest 74
(Hywel Evans) *nt a fluent: chsd ldrs: rdn fr 11th: wknd 4 out* **8/1**

250- **U** **Incentivise (IRE)**[218] 5138 12-11-4 **114**.......................... DavidNoonan[(7)]
(Kerry Lee) *5th whn blnd and uns rdr 2nd* **8/1**

6m 35.2s (17.80) **Going Correction** +0.875s/f (Soft) **6** Ran SP% **115.3**
Speed ratings (Par 105): **105,103,98,98,94**
CSF £7.55 TOTE £2.30: £1.10, £2.50; EX 10.70 Trifecta £28.70.
Owner All Stars Sports Racing **Bred** Martin McCaughey **Trained** Ystrad, Rhondda C Taff

FOCUS
Considering conditions, it wasn't a huge surprise that the two who set the modest early fractions got away from their rivals when they decided to quicken up.

2367 ROB DAVIES CHEMIST H'CAP HURDLE (12 hdls) 2m 7f 191y

3:50 (3:50) (Class 3) (0-135,135) 4-Y-0+ **£7,797** (£2,289; £1,144; £572)

Form RPR

P16- **1** **Molly's A Diva**[210] 5290 8-11-12 **135**..........................(p) DavidBass 140
(Kim Bailey) *chsd clr ldng pair: clsd 7th: wnt 2nd at 9th: rdn 3 out: hit 2 out: styd on u.p to ld fnl 50yds* **6/1**[3]

14U- **2** *1* **Count Guido Deiro (IRE)**[260] 4366 8-10-10 **124**.......... JamieBargary[(5)] 128
(Nigel Twiston-Davies) *trckd ldr and clr of rest by 2nd: led after 3rd: clr on own fr next to 7th: 5 l up 3 out: sn drvn: hdd and no ex fnl 50yds* **7/2**[2]

PP-2 **3** *10* **Minella On Line (IRE)**[22] 1963 6-10-11 **120**.......................... NickScholfield 114
(Rebecca Curtis) *mid-div: clsd 9th: rdn to take 3rd 3 out: no further imp fr next* **7/2**[2]

20-P **4** *nk* **Allez Vic (IRE)**[32] 1809 9-11-7 **130**.......................... PaulMoloney 125
(Evan Williams) *led and clr w one other by 2nd: hdd after 3rd: blnd next: c bk to main body 7th: lost 2nd at 9th: wknd 3 out* **9/1**

40F- **5** *27* **Fishing Bridge (IRE)**[210] 5290 10-10-0 **109** oh2..........(v) PaddyBrennan 76
(David Rees) *hld up: hit 9th: sn wknd: t.o* **10/1**

26/3 **6** *19* **Berea Boru (IRE)**[143] 774 7-11-2 **125**..........................(t) SeanBowen 73
(Peter Bowen) *hld up: clsd 8th: rdn and wknd after next: t.o* **11/4**[1]

0-0P **7** *10* **American Life (FR)**[12] 2125 8-10-3 **112**..........................(tp) JamesBest 50
(Sophie Leech) *a in rr: struggling 8th: t.o* **20/1**

5 **8** *79* **High Counsel (IRE)**[60] 1521 6-10-3 **117**.......................... NickSlatter[(5)]
(Gary Hanmer) *in tch tl wknd after 9th: t.o* **8/1**

6m 52.8s (63.80) **Going Correction** +1.70s/f (Heav) **8** Ran SP% **120.4**
Speed ratings (Par 107): **61,60,57,57,48 41,38,12**
CSF £29.34 CT £87.01 TOTE £7.30: £1.80, £1.50, £1.90; EX 38.10 Trifecta £134.30.
Owner J Perriss **Bred** J F Perriss **Trained** Andoversford, Gloucs
■ Stewards' Enquiry : Sean Bowen jockey said that the gelding was never travelling
David Bass two-day ban: use of whip (22-23 Nov)

FOCUS
Two horses kicked on from their rivals from an early stage, and one of those almost held on.

2368 BLUEBELL RECRUITMENT "JUNIOR" STANDARD OPEN NATIONAL HUNT FLAT RACE 1m 6f

4:20 (4:22) (Class 6) 3-Y-0 **£1,949** (£572; £286; £143)

Form RPR

61 **1** **Golden Gate Bridge (GER)**[19] 2009 3-11-5 0.......................... DenisO'Regan 108+
(Mark Pitman) *mde virtually all: racd wd in bk st: shkn up 3f out: drvn out fnl f and styd on wl* **5/4**[1]

2 *4* **Bilko's Back (IRE)** 3-10-12 0.......................... GavinSheehan 97
(Warren Greatrex) *trckd ldng pair: racd on inner in bk st: chsd wnr 3f out: shkn up 2f out: swtchd rt 1f out: one pce* **6/4**[2]

3 *6* **Allez Sea (IRE)** 3-10-12 0.......................... PaulMoloney 91
(James Leavy, Ire) *hld up in cl last of 4: racd on inner in bk st: rdn to chse ldng pair over 2f out: one pce and no real imp* **7/2**[3]

0 **4** *22* **Janesmerlin**[19] 2009 3-10-12 0.......................... JamesBest 69
(Kevin Bishop) *w ldr: racd wd in bk st: rdn 4f out: wknd over 2f out* **20/1**

3m 55.5s (235.50) **4** Ran SP% **111.4**
CSF £3.59 TOTE £1.80; EX 3.20 Trifecta £4.30.
Owner Malcolm C Denmark **Bred** Gestut Hachetal **Trained** Upper Lambourn, Berks

FOCUS
Owing to the heavy ground the stewards gave permission for the hurdles to be left in situ for this bumper, and for the runners to take a course to the outside in the back straight and the inside of the hurdles in the home straight.
T/Jkpt: Not won. JACKPOT PLACEPOT: £308.80 to a £1 stake. Pool: £4,823.00 - 11.40 winning tickets. T/Plt: £31.20 to a £1 stake. Pool: £75,976.36 - 1,776.82 winning tickets T/Qpdt: £10.30 to a £1 stake. Pool: £5,684.46 - 406.58 winning tickets **Richard Lowther**

SANDOWN (R-H)

Sunday, November 8

OFFICIAL GOING: Chase course - good to soft (good in places); hurdle course - soft

Wind: light, half against Weather: overcast

2369 ASIAN H'CAPS AT 188BET CONDITIONAL JOCKEY'S HANDICAP HURDLE (9 hdls) 2m 3f 173y

12:45 (12:49) (Class 3) (0-130,130) 3-Y-0+ **£6,498** (£1,908; £954; £477)

Form RPR

43-6 **1** **Clondaw Banker (IRE)**[16] 2058 6-10-13 **120**.......... JeremiahMcGrath[(3)] 126+
(Nicky Henderson) *w ldr tl chsd ldr 5th: led bef 2 out: kpt on u.p flat: rdn out* **7/2**[2]

32-0 **2** *2 ½* **Slim Pickens (IRE)**[15] 2064 7-11-1 **127**.......................... CharlieHammond[(8)] 130
(Dr Richard Newland) *hld up in tch in last trio: rdn and effrt after 3 out: lft 4th next: kpt on u.p flat: wnt 2nd last strides* **11/2**

/10- **3** *hd* **Simply A Legend**[519] 625 6-11-1 **122**.......................... TomBellamy[(3)] 126
(Alan King) *t.k.h: hld up in tch: clsd to trck ldrs after 3 out: ev ch next: no ex flat: wknd fnl 75yds: lost 2nd last strides* **12/1**

555- **4** *½* **Little Boy Boru (IRE)**[247] 4613 7-11-5 **123**.......................... HarryBannister 125
(Suzy Smith) *hld up in tch: rdn and effrt after 3 out: lft 3rd next: plugged on u.p flat* **8/1**

413/ **5** *24* **Vicenzo Mio (FR)**[652] 3885 5-11-4 **130**..........................(t) HarryCobden[(8)] 108
(Paul Nicholls) *chsd ldrs tl j. into ld 5th: hdd bef 2 out: sn rdn and btn: wknd between last 2* **9/4**[1]

0/3- **6** *1 ¾* **Stiff Upper Lip (IRE)**[543] 290 5-10-11 **118**.......................... ThomasGarner[(3)] 95
(Oliver Sherwood) *wl in tch in midfield: dropped to rr and rdn after 3 out: wknd next* **16/1**

142- **7** *47* **Filatore (IRE)**[223] 5059 6-10-12 **121**..........................(b) JordanWilliams[(5)] 51
(Bernard Llewellyn) *nt fluent: mde most tl mstke and hdd 5th: rdn and dropped to last after 3 out: sn lost tch: t.o* **20/1**

1211 **U** **Kalifourchon (FR)**[60] 1521 4-11-1 **125**.......................... MichaelHeard[(6)] 122
(David Pipe) *trckd ldrs: cl 3rd whn stmbld on landing and uns rdr 2 out* **5/1**[3]

5m 14.5s (14.90) **Going Correction** +0.30s/f (Yiel)
WFA 4 from 5yo+ 8lb **8** Ran SP% **114.5**
Speed ratings (Par 107): **82,81,80,80,71 70,51,**
CSF £23.27 CT £205.64 TOTE £4.80: £1.60, £2.10, £2.70; EX 24.10 Trifecta £166.90.
Owner A D Spence **Bred** William Flood **Trained** Upper Lambourn, Berks

FOCUS
There had been 15mm of rain since Thursday, but this was a mainly dry day. Chase distances as advertised. Race 1 increased by 48yds and races 3, 5 & 7 by 31yds. This was an interesting, fair conditional jockeys' handicap hurdle.

2370 FREE BET AT 188BET BEGINNERS' CHASE (13 fncs) 1m 7f 119y

1:15 (1:18) (Class 3) 4-Y-0+ **£6,975** (£2,385)

Form RPR

41-6 **1** **Ar Mad (FR)**[20] 2001 5-11-1 124.......................... JoshuaMoore 142+
(Gary Moore) *mde all: j.big and pckd 1st: 3 l clr and hit 3 out: in command and j.rt last: styd on: nvr seriously chal* **16/1**[3]

F6-2 **2** *7* **Golden Doyen (GER)**[22] 1969 4-10-7 0.......................... RichardJohnson 130
(Philip Hobbs) *chsd ldr: jinked at path after 2nd: 3rd next: hit 8th: 3 l down 3 out: sn rdn and no imp whn hit next: plugged on* **4/5**[1]

41- **P** **Sirabad (FR)**[247] 4611 5-11-1 0..........................(t) SamTwiston-Davies
(Paul Nicholls) *t.k.h: hld up in 3rd: wnt 2nd and j. upsides wnr 3rd: dived and blnd 4th: stood a long way off and mstke next: too bold and hit 9th: dropped to last after next: sn lost tch: p.u last* **5/4**[2]

3m 52.7s (-9.10) **Going Correction** 0.0s/f (Good)
WFA 4 from 5yo+ 7lb **3** Ran SP% **105.9**
CSF £28.57 TOTE £8.90; EX 23.00 Trifecta £16.00.
Owner Ashley Head **Bred** Michel Le Meur **Trained** Lower Beeding, W Sussex

FOCUS
A poor turnout numerically and only the front-running winner, who was the outsider of the three, put in a satisfactory round of jumping.

2371 PREMIER LEAGUE BETTING AT 188BET JUVENILE HURDLE (8 hdls) 1m 7f 216y

1:50 (1:51) (Class 4) 3-Y-0 **£3,898** (£1,144; £572; £286)

Form RPR

6 **1** **Darebin (GER)**[37] 1732 3-10-12 0.......................... JamieMoore 110+
(Gary Moore) *trckd ldng pair tl led bef 2 out: sn clr: untidy jump last: drvn and tiring flat: a doing enough but all out* **14/1**

313 **2** *3 ½* **Duke Street (IRE)**[7] 2219 3-11-5 120..........................(p) WillKennedy 113
(Dr Richard Newland) *led tl out j. and hdd 3rd: led again after 3 out: rdn and hdd bef next: sn outpcd by wnr: plugged on u.p flat* **11/8**[2]

22 **3** *2 ½* **Consortium (IRE)**[35] 1768 3-10-12 0.......................... TrevorWhelan 102
(Neil King) *hld up in last pair: effrt in 4th after 3 out: 8 l down and hung rt whn mstke 2 out: swtchd lft between last 2: wnt 3rd last: plugged on flat: no threat to wnr* **8/1**[3]

2321 **4** *5* **Chic Name (FR)**[4] 2273 3-11-5 110..........................(p) AlainCawley 105
(Richard Hobson) *w ldr tl j. into ld 3rd: hdd after 3 out: 3rd and outpcd u.p 2 out: 4th and wl hld last: wknd flat* **5/4**[1]

P **5** *57* **Capatosta (USA)**[28] 1866 3-10-12 0.......................... JamesDavies 40
(Charlie Mann) *in tch in last pair: dropped to last and rdn after 3 out: sn lost tch: t.o next* **50/1**

4m 19.9s (12.70) **Going Correction** +0.30s/f (Yiel) **5** Ran SP% **106.3**
Speed ratings (Par 104): **80,78,77,74,46**
CSF £32.57 TOTE £9.70: £2.80, £1.30; EX 20.90 Trifecta £71.30.
Owner Chris Stedman & Mark Albon **Bred** Stall 5-Stars **Trained** Lower Beeding, W Sussex

FOCUS
An ordinary juvenile hurdle run at a steady early pace and it went to Gary and Jamie Moore for the second straight year.

2372 188BET FUTURE STARS CHASE (INTERMEDIATE RACE) (LISTED RACE) (22 fncs) 3m 37y

2:25 (2:25) (Class 1) 4-Y-0+ **£17,085** (£6,411; £3,210)

Form RPR

111- **1** **Coneygree**[240] 4739 8-11-11 172.......................... NicodeBoinville 175+
(Mark Bradstock) *mde all: extended ld fr 15th: in n.d after 3 out: eased flat: unchal* **1/4**[1]

12-P **2** *25* **Seventh Sky (GER)**[30] 1840 8-11-5 147..........................(tp) AidanColeman 149
(Charlie Mann) *mostly 3rd: struggling and 10 l down 16th: mstke 19th: wnt 2nd bef 2 out: no ch w wnr* **25/1**[3]

212- **3** *19* **Southfield Theatre (IRE)**[242] 4703 7-11-11 154.... SamTwiston-Davies 139
(Paul Nicholls) *mostly chsd clr wnr: mstke 15th: 6 l down next: struggling and btn whn hit 18th: dropped to last bef 2 out: t.o* **7/2**[2]

6m 16.1s (-11.70) **Going Correction** 0.0s/f (Good) **3** Ran SP% **106.1**
Speed ratings (Par 111): **119,110,104**
CSF £4.27 TOTE £1.40; EX 4.70 Trifecta £3.90.
Owner The Max Partnership **Bred** Lord Oaksey **Trained** Letcombe Bassett, Oxon

FOCUS
The winner faced only two inferior rivals and one of them was disappointing, but this was a faultless return to action from last year's Gold Cup hero.

2373 PLAY CASINO AT 188BET H'CAP HURDLE (8 hdls) 1m 7f 216y

3:00 (3:02) (Class 3) (0-130,130) 3-Y-0+ **£12,685** (£3,869; £2,021; £1,097)

Form RPR

00-5 **1** **Prairie Town (IRE)**[29] 1847 4-11-2 **120**.......................... LeeEdwards 125
(Tony Carroll) *hld up in tch: rdn and effrt after 3 out: styng on u.p and lft 2nd 2 out: chal and wandered last: led flat: styd on: rdn out* **5/1**[2]

1-52 **2** *3* **Songsmith**[28] 1448 7-11-7 **125**.......................... LeightonAspell 127
(Lucy Wadham) *in tch in midfield: chsd ldrs 5th: wnt 2nd after next: chal and lft in ld 2 out: drvn and jnd bef last: hdd flat: no ex* **11/4**[1]

503- **3** *2 ¼* **Cape Caster (IRE)**[223] 5070 4-11-2 **120**.......................... AdamWedge 119
(Evan Williams) *in tch in midfield: effrt to chse ldrs bef 2 out: lft 3 l 3rd 2 out: no imp: plugged on same pce flat* **7/1**

1U-0 **4** *25* **Crookstown (IRE)**[184] 184 8-11-9 **127**.......................... KielanWoods 101
(Ben Case) *in tch in last trio: hit 3 out and sn rdn: struggling bef next: lft modest 4th and hmpd 2 out: wknd* **10/1**

-100 **P** **Ryeolliean**[29] 1847 4-11-5 **123**..........................(v[1]) JamieMoore
(Gary Moore) *chsd ldrs: rdn and wknd rapidly bef 2 out: eased and p.u 2 out* **5/1**[2]

33-3 **F** **Red Devil Star (IRE)**[18] 2011 5-11-6 **124**......................(t) TomO'Brien 123
(Suzy Smith) *chsd ldr: mstke 2nd: led after 3 out: jnd and rdn whn fell next* **11/2**[3]

P-24 **P** **Full Blast (FR)**[23] 1949 4-10-11 **115**......................(t) TomCannon
(Chris Gordon) *led tl rdn and hdd after 3 out: dropped out rapidly: t.o whn p.u next* **12/1**

P1P- **P** **Jeanpascal (FR)**[224] 5045 4-11-12 **130**...................... AidanColeman
(Venetia Williams) *hld up in tch in rr: mstke 2nd: rdn after 3 out: sn lost tch: t.o whn p.u next* **12/1**

4m 8.6s (1.40) **Going Correction** +0.30s/f (Yiel) **8** Ran SP% **112.4**
Speed ratings (Par 107): **108,106,105,92,** ,
CSF £18.94 CT £94.15 TOTE £6.60: £2.00, £1.40, £2.30; EX 19.20 Trifecta £221.90.
Owner Cooke & Millen **Bred** S C E A Haras De Manneville **Trained** Cropthorne, Worcs
FOCUS
A fair handicap hurdle.

2374 188BET.CO.UK VETERANS' H'CAP CHASE (QUALIFIER) (LEG 8 OF THE VETERANS' CHASE SERIES) (22 fncs) 3m 37y
3:35 (3:35) (Class 2) (0-150,141)
10-Y-0+
£18,768 (£5,544; £2,772; £1,386; £693; £348)

Form RPR

00-P **1** **Vino Griego (FR)**[188] 101 10-11-3 **132**...................... JamieMoore 141+
(Gary Moore) *chsd ldr: mstke 1st: led 18th: drvn between last 2: styd on strly and drew clr flat: rdn out* **5/1**[2]

00-0 **2** *5* **Pineau De Re (FR)**[28] 1871 12-11-12 **141**...................... WillKennedy 146
(Dr Richard Newland) *hld up wl in tch: clsd to trck ldrs 17th: pressed wnr 3 out: sn rdn: unable qck last: edgd lft and styd on same pce flat* **7/1**

65-5 **3** *3 ¾* **Mountainous (IRE)**[28] 1871 10-11-3 **132**......................(p) JakeGreenall 134
(Kerry Lee) *wl in tch in midfield: clsd to go 3rd 14th: rdn bef 2 out: no ex between last 2: edgd rt and styd on same pce flat* **4/1**[1]

1P4- **4** *12* **Aachen**[224] 5047 11-10-10 **125**...................... AidanColeman 115
(Venetia Williams) *hld up wl in tch: effrt and chsd ldrs after 19th: btn 2 out: wknd bef last* **4/1**[1]

5PP/ **5** *25* **Fine Parchment (IRE)**[588] 5092 12-10-10 **130**.......(tp) HarryBannister[(5)] 98
(Charlie Mann) *led tl 18th: rdn after next: stl pressing ldrs 3 out: wknd qckly bef next: fdd flat* **16/1**

2P-0 **6** *3* **Roalco De Farges (FR)**[15] 2061 10-11-6 **135**.............. RichardJohnson 100
(Philip Hobbs) *chsd ldrs: mstke 1st: lost pl and dropped to rr 14th: losing tch and mstke 18th: t.o* **4/1**[1]

1P2- **P** **Monkerty Tunkerty**[244] 4684 12-10-12 **132**...................... AliceMills[(5)]
(Jess Westwood) *sn bhd and nvr jumping or gng w any relish: lost tch 8th: p.u 10th* **13/2**[3]

6m 21.7s (-6.10) **Going Correction** 0.0s/f (Good) **7** Ran SP% **108.4**
Speed ratings: **110,108,107,103,94 93,**
CSF £34.21 CT £134.46 TOTE £7.20: £3.50, £3.20; EX 46.80 Trifecta £267.70.
Owner C E Stedman **Bred** Francis Montauban **Trained** Lower Beeding, W Sussex
FOCUS
A good veterans' handicap chase.

2375 BIBENDUM WINE STANDARD OPEN NATIONAL HUNT FLAT RACE 1m 7f 216y
4:05 (4:06) (Class 5) 4-6-Y-O **£3,249** (£954; £477; £238)

Form RPR

1 **Full Irish (IRE)** 4-11-0 0...................... AidanColeman 122+
(Emma Lavelle) *hld up in midfield: smooth hdwy to join ldrs 3f out: led 2f out: sn pushed clr: in command and v green ins fnl f: pushed out: comf* **7/1**

2 **2** *5* **Casper King (IRE)**[184] 187 4-11-0 0...................... RichardJohnson 113
(Philip Hobbs) *t.k.h: chsd ldrs: wnt 2nd over 3f out: rdn to ld over 2f out: hdd 2f out and unable qck: kpt on same pce fnl f* **11/2**[2]

3 *½* **Chef D'Oeuvre (FR)**[189] 4-10-9 0...................... HarryBannister[(5)] 113
(Warren Greatrex) *led tl 10f out: chsd ldr tl over 3f out: sn drvn and styd pressing ldrs tl 2f out: kpt on same pce after* **6/4**[1]

26- **4** *4 ½* **Midnight Cowboy**[239] 4755 4-11-0 0...................... WayneHutchinson 108
(Alan King) *in tch in midfield: hdwy to chse ldrs 9f out: rdn and ev ch 3f out tl unable qck 2f out: wknd ent fnl f* **13/2**[3]

5 *¾* **General Bux** 4-11-0 0...................... TomO'Brien 107
(Suzy Smith) *w ldr tl led 10f out: rdn and hdd over 2f out: no ex 2f out: wknd over 1f out* **11/2**[2]

521 **6** *7* **Tour De Ville (IRE)**[77] 1345 5-11-7 0......................(t) ConorO'Farrell 107
(Seamus Durack) *hld up in tch in last trio: rdn 4f out: btn fnl 3f: plugged on* **25/1**

3 **7** *1 ¼* **You Say What (IRE)**[22] 1966 5-11-0 0...................... TrevorWhelan 99
(Neil King) *in tch: rdn and struggling 4f out: wl hld fnl 3f: plugged on* **12/1**

8 *147* **Arroyeau (FR)** 5-11-0 0...................... LeightonAspell
(Nick Gifford) *hld up in tch in last trio: rdn 5f out: sn lost tch: t.o and virtually p.u fnl 3f* **33/1**

0 **9** *4 ½* **Blue Is The Colour (IRE)**[22] 1966 5-11-0 0...................... AndrewTinkler
(Nicky Henderson) *dropped to rr and rdn 11f out: nvr travelling after: lost tch 1/2-way: sn t.o: virtually p.u fnl 3f* **20/1**

4m 7.6s (6.00) **Going Correction** +0.30s/f (Yiel)
WFA 4 from 5yo 7lb **9** Ran SP% **115.8**
Speed ratings: **97,94,94,92,91 88,87,** ,
CSF £44.11 TOTE £9.50: £2.90, £1.90, £1.10; EX 43.70 Trifecta £93.40.
Owner N Mustoe **Bred** Gordon Foster **Trained** Hatherden, Hants
FOCUS
This looked a reasonable enough bumper.
T/Plt: £782.50 to a £1 stake. Pool: £73,000.40 - 68.10 winning tickets T/Qpdt: £21.60 to a £1 stake. Pool: £6,065.37 - 207.60 winning tickets **Steve Payne**

2376 - 2384a (Foreign Racing) - See Raceform Interactive

1663 NAVAN (L-H)
Sunday, November 8
OFFICIAL GOING: Yielding to soft

2385a AT THE RACES AT NAVAN "FOR AUCTION" NOVICE HURDLE (GRADE 3) (10 hdls) 2m
1:10 (1:10) 4-Y-0+ **£15,872** (£4,639; £2,197; £732)

RPR

1 **Three Stars (IRE)**[35] 1788 5-11-1 135...................... JJBurke 140
(Henry De Bromhead, Ire) *trckd ldr in 2nd tl dropped to 3rd bef 4th: tk clsr order far side fr 3 out: rdn to ld narrowly bef next: extended advantage fr last and kpt on wl run-in* **12/1**

2 *2 ¼* **Thomas Hobson**[102] 1149 5-11-1 138...................... RWalsh 139+
(W P Mullins, Ire) *hld up bhd ldrs: racd keenly and wnt 2nd bef 4th: led bef 3 out where slt mstke: hdd narrowly bef 2 out: cl 2nd whn mstke last and no imp on wnr run-in: kpt on same pce* **3/1**[2]

3 *4 ½* **Tycoon Prince (IRE)**[12] 2127 5-11-1 0...................... BJCooper 135
(Gordon Elliott, Ire) *hld up in rr: disp 4th briefly fr 5th: nt fluent 4 out and j. sltly lft: clsr bhd ldrs bef 3 out: rdn in 4th after next and no imp on wnr u.p in 3rd fr last where j. sltly lft: one pce* **4/6**[1]

4 *7* **Archive (FR)**[14] 2094 5-11-1 0...................... DavidMullins 132
(Eoin Griffin, Ire) *hld up bhd ldrs: nt fluent in 4th at 5th: tk clsr order bhd ldrs appr st: rdn in 3rd 2 out and no imp on wnr bef last where dropped to 4th: wknd* **5/1**[3]

5 *36* **Billbushay (IRE)**[29] 1859 6-11-1 123...................... KevinSexton 91
(Sean Byrne, Ire) *led: nt fluent 1st: pushed along and hdd bef 3 out: sn wknd to rr and lost tch: eased run-in* **66/1**

4m 3.2s (-4.80) **5** Ran SP% **110.8**
CSF £46.80 TOTE £5.20: £2.00, £1.80; DF 25.40 Trifecta £38.00.
Owner Robert Finnegan **Bred** A V Bloodstock **Trained** Knockeen, Co Waterford
FOCUS
McKinley won this last year on the way to Grade 1 glory later in the season in the Lawlors Hotel Novice Hurdle at Naas. This looked a really good renewal but it turned into a sprint up the home straight. The runner-up was keen and the odds-on favourite failed to live up to expectations so there has to be question marks hanging over the form.

2386a LISMULLEN HURDLE (GRADE 2) (11 hdls) 2m 4f
1:40 (1:41) 4-Y-0+ **£20,155** (£5,891; £2,790; £930)

RPR

1 **Arctic Fire (GER)**[191] 71 6-11-5 169...................... RWalsh 154+
(W P Mullins, Ire) *wnt rt s and w.w in rr at mod pce: wnt mod 3rd bef 2nd under tk clsr order bhd ldrs next: rdn and struggling in 3rd after 2 out: clsd u.p into 2nd fr last and kpt on best to ld cl home* **4/6**[1]

2 *½* **Monksland (IRE)**[241] 4719 8-11-5 149...................... SeanFlanagan 153
(Noel Meade, Ire) *trckd ldr tl disp after 1st at mod pce: led next: pressed clly appr st: stl gng wl 2 out: pushed along and over 2 l clr whn mstke last: sn rdn and strly pressed run-in: hdd cl home* **11/4**[2]

3 *3 ¾* **Taglietelle**[120] 954 6-11-8 148...................... BJCooper 151
(Gordon Elliott, Ire) *led reluctantly at mod pce tl jnd after 1st: wandered sltly and hdd next: almost on terms appr st: rdn in 2nd after 2 out and no imp on ldr bef last where slt mstke and dropped to 3rd: one pce run-in* **14/1**

4 *dist* **Carlingford Lough (IRE)**[240] 4739 9-11-5 142.............. BarryGeraghty
(John E Kiely, Ire) *chsd ldrs at mod pce: dropped to mod 4th bef 2nd tl tk clsr order bhd ldrs at 3rd: niggled along bef 5th: dropped to rr after 4 out and sn pushed along: no imp bef next where lft remote 4th: t.o* **8/1**[3]

F **Plinth (IRE)**[35] 1787 5-11-10 141......................(bt) MarkWalsh
(A P O'Brien, Ire) *settled in rr at mod pce: impr into 4th after 4 out: niggled along and stl in tch bhd ldrs whn fell 3 out* **10/1**

5m 16.5s (14.70) **5** Ran SP% **113.5**
CSF £3.06 TOTE £1.30: £1.02, £1.30; DF 3.00 Trifecta £12.90.
Owner Wicklow Bloodstock (Ireland) Ltd **Bred** U Gruning **Trained** Muine Beag, Co Carlow
FOCUS
Nothing wanted to make the running and the field stayed motionless for about ten seconds after the tape rose. Once Taglietelle consented to go on, the gallop was reasonably generous. The runner-up probably would have won if he didn't hit the last. The front-running third has been rated to his best.

2387a (Foreign Racing) - See Raceform Interactive

2388a THETOTE.COM FORTRIA CHASE (GRADE 2) (11 fncs) 2m
2:50 (2:50) 5-Y-0+ **£21,414** (£6,259; £2,965; £988)

RPR

1 **Hidden Cyclone (IRE)**[101] 1163 10-11-10 157......................(p) BrianHayes 162
(John Joseph Hanlon, Ire) *settled bhd ldrs: impr bef 6th to trck ldr next where nt helped by attentions of loose horse: disp briefly 4 out: led next and sn clr: j. sltly rt 2 out: slow last and reduced advantage: kpt on again to assert run-in* **3/1**[2]

2 *6 ½* **Days Hotel (IRE)**[280] 4006 10-11-4 150...................... AELynch 149
(Henry De Bromhead, Ire) *in rr early: 4th bef 4th: wnt 3rd bef 4 out: rdn in mod 3rd 3 out and no imp on ldrs: wnt mod 2nd between last 2: no imp on wnr run-in: kpt on one pce* **8/1**

3 *5* **Flemenstar (IRE)**[194] 8 10-11-4 155...................... KeithDonoghue 147
(Anthony Curran, Ire) *settled bhd ldrs tl led after 3rd: jnd next where led and disp after: narrow advantage 3 out whn mstke and hdd: sn rdn in 2nd and no imp on wnr next: dropped to mod 3rd between last 2: one pce* **12/1**

4 *38* **Special Tiara**[197] 5537 8-11-12 168...................... BarryGeraghty 114
(Henry De Bromhead, Ire) *led 1st: narrow advantage whn slt mstke and j. sltly lft 3rd: sn hdd tl disp fr 4th: mstke 5 out and hdd: sn pushed along in 3rd and wknd bef next* **11/4**[1]

P **Twinlight (FR)**[194] 8 8-11-12 158...................... RWalsh
(W P Mullins, Ire) *cl up: j.w rt 3rd and dropped to rr: j.rt 6th: wknd and lost tch fr 5 out: t.o whn p.u bef 3 out* **4/1**

U **Bright New Dawn (IRE)**[24] 1938 8-11-4 148......................(t[1]) BJCooper
(Gordon Elliott, Ire) *towards rr early tl tk clsr order bhd ldrs in 3rd fr 3rd: j. sltly rt and uns rdr 3rd* **10/3**[3]

4m 13.9s (3.40) **6** Ran SP% **113.5**
CSF £25.18 TOTE £3.90: £1.80, £3.30; DF 31.90 Trifecta £696.80.
Owner Mrs A F Mee & David Mee **Bred** Ronald O'Neill **Trained** Bagenalstown, Co Carlow
FOCUS
A race that completely fell apart. First we lost Bright New Dawn at the third. Twinlight then decided to run no sort of race whatsoever and was back-pedaling from early in the back straight. Special Tiara was beaten by the fifth fence. Days Hotel was out the back most of the way and never looked like landing a blow. That left Hidden Cyclone and Flemenstar to fight it out for the final mile. The pace was relentless throughout. The winner and runner-up have been rated to their 2015 best.

2389 - 2395a (Foreign Racing) - See Raceform Interactive

[2210]CARLISLE (R-H)

Monday, November 9

OFFICIAL GOING: Heavy (soft in places) changing to heavy after race 1 (1.15)

Wind: Strong, half against Weather: Overcast, rain

2396 FREE SPINS AT 188BET CASINO NOVICES' H'CAP HURDLE (11 hdls) 2m 4f 8y

1:15 (1:15) (Class 4) (0-110,110) 3-Y-0+ £3,249 (£954; £477; £238)

Form					RPR
065-	1		**Baywing (IRE)**[247] 4618 6-10-5 **89** ... BrianHarding (Nicky Richards) *novicey on occasions: pressed ldr: led gng wl 3 out: hrd pressed and pushed along next: nt fluent last: styd on strly to draw clr run-in: readily* **1/1**[1]	104+
4623	2	10	**Pixiepot**[23] 1971 5-10-10 **94** ... DenisO'Regan (Peter Niven) *hld up in last pl but in tch: pushed along and hdwy bef 3 out: effrt and ev ch next: drvn and outpcd fr last* **7/1**[3]	99
33P	3	2 1/2	**Jumpandtravel (IRE)**[38] 1744 6-10-1 **95** ... FinianO'Toole(10) (Micky Hammond) *trckd ldrs: effrt and chsd wnr 3 out to next: sn rdn and outpcd* **18/1**	96
4503	4	1 1/4	**Mondlicht (USA)**[8] 2212 5-11-7 **105** ... BrianHughes (James Moffatt) *trckd ldrs: effrt and pushed along 3 out: drvn and outpcd fr next* **7/2**[2]	104
002-	P		**Courtlands Prince**[268] 4234 6-11-12 **110** ... NoelFehily (Neil Mulholland) *t.k.h early: led at stdy gallop: rdn and hdd 3 out: sn wknd: lost tch and p.u bef last* **7/2**[2]	

5m 18.3s (-4.50) **Going Correction** 0.0s/f (Good) **5** Ran SP% **112.2**
Speed ratings (Par 105): **109,105,104,103,**
CSF £8.41 TOTE £2.10: £1.10, £2.80; EX 7.30 Trifecta £69.40.
Owner David & Nicky Robinson **Bred** Hugh Suffern Bloodstock **Trained** Greystoke, Cumbria

FOCUS
Bends moved out 2yds and races 1, 2 & 5 increased by 24yds, races 3 & 6 by 18yds and race 4 by 36yds. The opening contest was an ordinary novice handicap hurdle. They went a sensible gallop on heavy ground on a particularly windy afternoon. The winner was taking a big step up on previous hurdle form.

2397 188BET NOVICES' CHASE (16 fncs) 2m 4f

1:45 (1:45) (Class 3) 4-Y-0+ £6,498 (£1,908; £954; £477)

Form					RPR
12-6	1		**Silsol (GER)**[177] 349 6-11-2 0 ... (tp) SamTwiston-Davies (Paul Nicholls) *chsd ldng pair: hit 10th: hdwy after 5 out: effrt and rdn bef 3 out: led run-in: drvn out* **5/2**[2]	150+
11-	2	1/2	**Maximiser (IRE)**[353] 2649 7-10-13 0 ... JoeColliver(3) (Simon West) *j.w: cl up: led 3rd: rdn bef last: hdd run-in: rallied: hld nr fin: bttr for r* **4/1**[3]	147+
/20-	3	6	**Seeyouatmidnight**[242] 4719 7-11-2 0 ... BrianHughes (Sandy Thomson) *led to 3rd: chsd ldr: slipped after 5 out: effrt and pushed along bef 3 out: cl up tl rdn and outpcd fr last: improve* **5/4**[1]	142+
65	4	73	**Veroce (FR)**[169] 461 6-11-2 0 ... JakeGreenall (Mark Walford) *nt fluent in rr: lost tch fr 1/2-way: lft remote 4th 3 out* **200/1**	68
F13-	F		**Kingscourt Native (IRE)**[275] 4093 7-11-2 0 ... (t) NoelFehily (Colin Tizzard) *s.i.s: hld up: nt fluent 4th: shkn up 4 out: 7 l 4th and keeping on steadily whn fell heavily next* **13/2**	
22-U	P		**U Name It (IRE)**[16] 2067 7-11-2 0 ... PeterBuchanan (R Mike Smith) *nt fluent on occasions: towards rr: outpcd and struggling fr 10th: lost tch and p.u bef 4 out* **28/1**	

5m 16.2s (-11.20) **Going Correction** -0.20s/f (Good) **6** Ran SP% **110.3**
Speed ratings (Par 107): **114,113,111,82,**
CSF £12.54 TOTE £3.60: £1.50, £2.10; EX 9.90 Trifecta £18.50.
Owner Michelle And Dan MacDonald **Bred** Gestut Hof Iserneichen **Trained** Ditcheat, Somerset

FOCUS
A good novice chase and smart form. They went an honest gallop.

2398 PREMIER LEAGUE BETTING AT 188BET NOVICES' HURDLE (9 hdls) 2m 1f 33y

2:15 (2:15) (Class 4) 4-Y-0+ £3,249 (£954; £477; £238)

Form					RPR
050-	1		**Virnon**[13] 5255 4-10-12 0 ... LeightonAspell (Alan Swinbank) *prom: stdy hdwy 4 out: pushed along whn hit next: rallied and led between last 2: edgd rt and drvn clr run-in* **7/4**[1]	115+
	2	6	**Freddies Portrait (IRE)**[176] 6-10-12 0 ... SamTwiston-Davies (Donald McCain) *trckd ldrs: wnt 2nd after 3rd: rdn and outpcd between last 2: rallied to chse (clr) wnr run-in: no imp* **9/2**	105
F0/3	3	3	**Save The Bees**[17] 2056 7-10-12 110 ... TomO'Brien (Declan Carroll) *led at stdy pce: rdn along and hdd between last 2: no ex and lost 2nd run-in* **7/2**[3]	102
45-5	4	28	**Massini's Lady**[18] 2025 4-10-0 0 ... StephenMulqueen(5) (N W Alexander) *hld up in last pl: drvn and struggling 1/2-way: lost tch bef 3 out: t.o* **40/1**	67
	P		**Grey Storm (IRE)**[189] 4-10-9 0 ... CraigNichol(3) (Rose Dobbin) *chsd ldr to after 3rd: drvn and outpcd bef 5th: lost tch bef 3 out: t.o whn p.u bef next* **5/2**[2]	

4m 32.3s (4.60) **Going Correction** 0.0s/f (Good) **5** Ran SP% **107.8**
Speed ratings (Par 105): **89,86,84,71,**
CSF £9.44 TOTE £2.20: £1.40, £2.30; EX 10.10 Trifecta £24.60.
Owner Jack Pearce **Bred** World Racing Network **Trained** Melsonby, N Yorks

FOCUS
A fair novice hurdle and the winner could rate higher on his Flat form. They went an ordinary gallop.

2399 WEATHERBYS BANK GRADUATION CHASE (18 fncs) 3m 110y

2:50 (2:51) (Class 2) 4-Y-0+ £12,974 (£4,158; £2,310)

Form					RPR
5/1-	1		**Salubrious (IRE)**[402] 1718 8-11-3 148 ... SamTwiston-Davies (Paul Nicholls) *hld up in last pl: smooth hdwy 5 out: led on bit bef last: drvn and edgd rt run-in: hld on wl nr fin* **11/4**[2]	144+
21U-	2	nk	**Masters Hill (IRE)**[242] 4721 9-11-10 144 ... NoelFehily (Colin Tizzard) *chsd ldrs: led 13th: rdn 3 out: hdd bef last: edgd rt and rallied run-in: kpt on: hld nr fin* **13/2**	149
/2-3	3	31	**Blakemount (IRE)**[16] 2067 7-10-13 133 ... DannyCook (Sue Smith) *nt fluent: led or disp ld to 13th: checked bef next: drvn and wknd fr 3 out* **2/1**[1]	114
612-	P		**Barafundle (IRE)**[219] 5130 11-11-7 143 ... (v) HenryBrooke (Jennie Candlish) *led or disp ld to 13th: rdn whn checked bef next: sn struggling: lost tch whn p.u bef 2 out* **8/1**	
32U-	F		**Deputy Dan (IRE)**[240] 4765 7-11-7 139 ... LeightonAspell (Oliver Sherwood) *trckd ldrs: cl 3rd whn fell 10th* **3/1**[3]	

6m 35.3s (-7.30) **Going Correction** -0.20s/f (Good) **5** Ran SP% **109.4**
Speed ratings (Par 109): **103,102,92, ,**
CSF £18.34 TOTE £3.20: £1.50, £2.80; EX 18.00 Trifecta £48.10.
Owner The Johnson & Stewart Families **Bred** Ciara And Michael Carty **Trained** Ditcheat, Somerset

FOCUS
The feature contest was a good quality staying graduation chase. They went a respectable gallop and the winner was stepping up on his previous chase win.

2400 188BET.CO.UK H'CAP CHASE (16 fncs) 2m 4f

3:25 (3:25) (Class 4) (0-120,120) 4-Y-0+ £3,898 (£1,144; £572; £286)

Form					RPR
4-13	1		**Fourth Act (IRE)**[15] 2093 6-11-6 **114** ... (t) NoelFehily (Colin Tizzard) *hld up on ins: stdy hdwy to chse ldrs 10th: effrt and led between last 2: drew clr run-in: eased down last 100yds* **4/1**[1]	132+
31P/	2	13	**Rocking Blues (FR)**[600] 4898 10-11-1 **112** ... CraigNichol(3) (Rose Dobbin) *led: rdn and hdd between last 2: nt fluent last: sn no ch w easy wnr: improve* **16/1**	115
0-22	3	18	**Retrieve The Stick**[14] 2105 6-10-11 **105** ... (b) BrianHughes (Malcolm Jefferson) *in tch: hdwy to chse ldr 10th: effrt and pushed along whn mstke 2 out: sn rdn and wknd* **4/1**[1]	95
U1P-	4	3	**Little Glenshee (IRE)**[206] 5365 9-11-12 **120** ... BrianHarding (N W Alexander) *pressed ldr to 10th: drvn and outpcd 11th: plugged on fr 2 out: no ch w ldrs* **9/2**[2]	105
2-14	5	nk	**Alto Des Mottes (FR)**[18] 2026 5-11-4 **115** ... TonyKelly(3) (Henry Hogarth) *prom early: sn towards rr: drvn and outpcd 1/2-way: rallied after 3 out: no imp fr next* **9/2**[2]	96
414-	6	10	**Dream Flyer (IRE)**[308] 3546 8-11-9 **117** ... (t) HenryBrooke (Michael Smith) *hld up in tch: stdy hdwy on outside 10th: drvn and outpcd 5 out: struggling fr next* **8/1**	88
11-0	7	28	**Resolute Reformer (IRE)**[187] 141 6-10-8 **105** ... DerekFox(3) (Stuart Coltherd) *in tch: drvn and outpcd bef 8th: sn struggling: t.o* **13/2**[3]	48
32-P	P		**Silverton**[179] 304 8-11-7 **115** ... AdrianLane (Lucy Normile) *nt fluent: in tch on outside: outpcd whn hit 10th: sn struggling: lost tch and p.u after 3 out* **12/1**	
44-P	P		**Auldthunder (IRE)**[193] 35 8-9-13 **96** ... JoeColliver(3) (Micky Hammond) *nt fluent in rr: lost tch 1/2-way: t.o whn p.u after 11th* **22/1**	

5m 24.9s (-2.50) **Going Correction** -0.20s/f (Good) **9** Ran SP% **118.7**
Speed ratings (Par 105): **97,91,84,83,83 79,68, ,**
CSF £62.21 CT £276.09 TOTE £5.30: £1.30, £4.70, £1.90; EX 102.50 Trifecta £576.20.
Owner C L Tizzard **Bred** Kenilworth House Stud **Trained** Milborne Port, Dorset

FOCUS
A fair handicap chase. They went a respectable gallop and the winner took a big step up on his hurdle form.

2401 GRAND SLAM OF DARTS AT 188BET STANDARD OPEN NATIONAL HUNT FLAT RACE 2m 1f 33y

4:00 (4:00) (Class 6) 4-6-Y-0 £1,624 (£477; £238; £119)

Form					RPR
	1		**Three Ways** 4-11-0 0 ... DougieCostello (Ronald O'Leary, Ire) *prom on ins: hdwy to ld over 3f out: edgd lft and hrd pressed over 1f out: kpt on strly last 100yds* **7/4**[1]	115+
	2	2	**Carole's Vigilante (IRE)** 4-11-0 0 ... NoelFehily (Neil Mulholland) *hld up: stdy hdwy 4f out: swtchd rt and chsd wnr 3f out: rdn and ev ch over 1f out: no ex last 100yds* **3/1**[2]	113+
1	3	14	**Dante's Way (IRE)**[187] 145 6-11-7 0 ... BrianHughes (Malcolm Jefferson) *in tch: stdy hdwy and cl up over 4f out: drvn and outpcd by first two fr 2f out* **7/4**[1]	107
	4	22	**Exactly What** 6-11-0 0 ... AdrianLane (Donald McCain) *hld up: hdwy and prom over 4f out: rdn over 3f out: wknd over 2f out* **22/1**	77
5-5	5	16	**Focal Point**[18] 2031 5-11-0 0 ... DannyCook (Sue Smith) *w ldr: led over 5f out: edgd lft and hdd over 3f out: wknd over 2f out* **16/1**[3]	61
	6	8	**Nailer (IRE)** 5-10-9 0 ... (t) DaleIrving(5) (Tristan Davidson) *led to over 5f out: rdn and wknd over 4f out* **33/1**	53
	7	8	**Nine Altars (IRE)**[772] 6-10-7 0 ... JamieHamilton(7) (Ann Hamilton) *t.k.h: in tch: drvn and outpcd 4f out: sn wknd* **25/1**	45

4m 27.3s (3.10) **Going Correction** 0.0s/f (Good)
WFA 4 from 5yo+ 7lb **7** Ran SP% **114.7**
Speed ratings: **92,91,84,74,66 62,59**
CSF £7.34 TOTE £3.20: £1.50, £1.80; EX 8.70 Trifecta £17.10.
Owner Mrs Ronald O'Leary **Bred** S D Hemstock **Trained** Killaloe, Co. Clare

FOCUS
The concluding contest was a fair bumper. They went a sensible gallop and the first two look above average.
T/Plt: £79.40 to a £1 stake. Pool: £57,830.07 - 531.64 winning units. T/Qpdt: £21.90 to a £1 stake. Pool: £4,598.42 - 155.30 winning units. **Richard Young**

[2039]SOUTHWELL (L-H)

Monday, November 9

OFFICIAL GOING: Good to soft (soft in places) changing to soft after race 2 (1.00)

Wind: fresh 1/2 behind Weather: damp, light rain

2402 WINTER GOLF AT SOUTHWELL H'CAP CHASE (19 fncs) 2m 7f 209y

12:30 (12:30) (Class 5) (0-100,100) 4-Y-0+ £3,249 (£954; £477; £238)

Form					RPR
4610	1		**Urban Gale (IRE)**[25] 1930 10-11-3 **91** ... (p) SeanQuinlan (Joanne Foster) *led to 6th: chsd ldrs: reminders 14th: 2nd appr 3 out: led sn after last: drvn rt out* **8/1**	102
3203	2	1	**Kilcascan**[25] 1930 11-10-11 **88** ... (p) BenPoste(3) (Rosemary Gasson) *w ldr: led 6th: drvn 3 out: 1 l ahd whn nt fluent last: sn hdd: kpt on same pce* **6/1**	98
10-3	3	35	**Cross To Boston (IRE)**[18] 2040 9-10-11 **92** ... MrRHogg(7) (Sue Smith) *in rr: nt fluent 4th: sme hdwy 13th: modest 3rd appr 3 out: one pce whn mstke 2 out: sn wknd* **13/2**	76

60P **4** *37* **Double Dan (IRE)**32 1824 6-10-7 **81**....(b1) AdamWedge 26
(Alexandra Dunn) *j.rt: chsd ldrs: mstke 11th: reminders next: wknd bef 3 out: sn bhd: t.o* **25/1**

2003 **U** **Mission Complete (IRE)**72 1403 9-11-2 **100**....(tp) JackSavage(10)
(Jonjo O'Neill) *in tch: drvn along 10th: lost pl 13th: poor 5th whn blnd and uns rdr 4 out* **4/1**2

U2-5 **P** **Typical Oscar (IRE)**36 1785 8-11-3 **91**....(p) NickScholfield
(Michael Blake) *dropped to rr 4th: hit 8th: sn bhd: t.o whn p.u after 12th* **5/1**3

2133 **P** **Moorlands George**42 1678 7-11-12 **100**....(t) NicodeBoinville
(Jeremy Scott) *in rr: bhd and reminders 9th: t.o whn p.u bef next: b.b.v* **5/2**1

000U **P** **League Of His Own (IRE)**68 1445 6-9-11 **74** oh5.(t) ConorShoemark(3)
(Claire Dyson) *t.k.h in rr: hit 2nd: bhd and drvn 12th: t.o whn p.u bef next* **25/1**

6m 45.0s (22.00) **Going Correction** +0.975s/f (Soft) **8** Ran SP% **111.7**
Speed ratings (Par 103): **102,101,90,77, , , ,**
CSF £52.28 CT £325.34 TOTE £9.00: £2.50, £1.90, £2.10; EX 60.30 Trifecta £209.30.
Owner P Foster **Bred** M Wiseman **Trained** Menston, W Yorks

FOCUS
Fences and Golf Club bend inside and bend into home straight outside the line raced on October 22nd and all distances as advertised. The going looked to be more demanding than the official going description in the opener and winning rider Sean Quinlan said "It's soft and it may get heavy as the afternoon goes on." The first two ran to their marks.

2403 FESTIVE FIXTURES MARES' H'CAP CHASE (19 fncs) 2m 7f 209y
1:00 (1:00) (Class 4) (0-120,115) 4-Y-0+ **£4,548** (£1,335; £667; £333)

Form RPR

25-4 **1** **Rosa Fleet (IRE)**175 382 7-11-5 **108**.... LiamTreadwell 122+
(Venetia Williams) *trckd ldr: pushed along 10th: j.rt: led and hit 3 out: rdn 4 l clr whn hit last: styd on wl* **7/2**3

5-31 **2** *3 1/2* **Distracted (IRE)**31 1842 7-10-12 **108**....(p) CiaranGethings(7) 115
(Robert Stephens) *led: hdd 3 out: kpt on same pce between last 2* **13/8**1

2431 **3** *1 1/2* **Still Believing (IRE)**33 1808 7-11-12 **115**.... AdamWedge 120
(Evan Williams) *chsd ldrs: nt fluent 9th: drvn 3 out: kpt on same pce* **11/4**2

14-0 **4** *6* **Tea Caddy**26 1910 9-11-4 **107**....(bt) BrendanPowell 108
(Jamie Snowden) *trckd ldrs: outpcd appr 3 out: one pce* **8/1**

34- **5** *37* **Miss Oscarose (IRE)**224 5059 8-11-0 **103**.... RichardJohnson 65
(Paul Henderson) *chsd ldrs: drvn and lost pl 15th: sn bhd: t.o* **17/2**

6m 59.1s (36.10) **Going Correction** +0.975s/f (Soft) **5** Ran SP% **108.6**
Speed ratings (Par 105): **78,76,76,74,62**
CSF £9.73 TOTE £4.70: £1.90, £1.40; EX 10.70 Trifecta £28.10.
Owner Mezzone Family **Bred** J F C Maxwell **Trained** Kings Caple, H'fords

FOCUS
Not a bad little mares' handicap for the grade and a step up from the winner.

2404 SOUTHWELL JANUARY TO DECEMBER ANNUAL MEMBERSHIP H'CAP CHASE (16 fncs) 2m 4f 62y
1:30 (1:30) (Class 3) (0-130,130) 4-Y-0+ **£6,963** (£2,057; £1,028; £514; £257)

Form RPR

33-P **1** **Simply Wings (IRE)**194 24 11-11-11 **129**.... JamieMoore 135+
(Kerry Lee) *chsd ldrs 5th: led appr 10th: hit 4 out: sn drvn and tended to jump rt-handed: styd on run-in* **9/2**2

1422 **2** *1 1/2* **Ladfromhighworth**23 1965 10-11-4 **122**.... DavidBass 124
(Jeremy Scott) *led to 2nd: chsd ldr: rallied between last 2: kpt pon same pce last 50yds* **8/1**

-6U2 **3** *1 1/2* **Benefit Cut (IRE)**45 1643 9-11-9 **127**.... BrendanPowell 127
(Stuart Edmunds) *led 2nd: hdd appr 10th: outpcd appr 3 out: rallied between last 2: kpt on same pce last 75yds* **9/4**1

41U- **4** *13* **Roberto Pegasus (USA)**236 4850 9-11-7 **125**.... WayneHutchinson 114
(Alan King) *chsd ldrs: one pce fr 4 out* **9/2**2

232- **5** *12* **Lac Sacre (FR)**13 5182 6-11-1 **119**....(bt) RhysFlint 96
(John Flint) *chsd ldrs sn after 2nd: outpcd and lost pl 9th: wknd 4 out* **9/1**

P1P- **6** *13* **Phone Home (IRE)**198 5540 8-11-6 **124**....(p) NickScholfield 86
(Nick Mitchell) *in rr: hit 8th: lost pl 10th: wknd bef 3 out* **6/1**3

3- **P** **Rough Justice (IRE)**127 922 7-11-9 **130**.... JonathanEngland(3)
(Alan Brown) *chsd ldrs: j.lft 6th: drvn and lost pl 8th: sn bhd: t.o whn p.u bef 10th* **33/1**

P640 **P** **Perfect Timing**17 2057 7-11-5 **123**....(p) MarkQuinlan
(Neil Mulholland) *nt jump wl in rr: drvn along 6th: hit 9th: sn bhd: t.o whn j.rt 11th: sn p.u* **14/1**

5m 36.0s (19.00) **Going Correction** +0.975s/f (Soft) **8** Ran SP% **112.1**
Speed ratings (Par 107): **101,100,99,94,89 84, ,**
CSF £37.64 CT £99.55 TOTE £5.40: £1.80, £2.30, £1.30; EX 44.90 Trifecta £180.80.
Owner Sam Thorp & Kerry Lee **Bred** G T Morrow **Trained** Byton, H'fords

FOCUS
There was a sound gallop on in this fair handicap and the form is straightforward enough. The winner has been rated back to his best.

2405 ROYAL AGRICULTURAL BENEVOLENT INSTITUTION CHARITY CLAIMING HURDLE (13 hdls) 2m 7f 209y
2:00 (2:02) (Class 5) 4-Y-0+ **£2,924** (£858; £429; £214)

Form RPR

0206 **1** **Fresh By Nature (IRE)**30 1856 8-10-8 108.... HarryBannister(5) 111
(Harriet Bethell) *mid-div: chsd ldrs 6th: wnt modest 3rd bef 2 out: styd on run-in: led last 50yds* **6/1**3

64PP **2** *1* **Terminal (FR)**30 1849 8-10-9 122....(b) JamieBargary(5) 111
(David Dennis) *chsd ldrs: rdn to ld sn after 3 out: hdd appr next: led narrowly last: hdd and no ex last 50yds* **7/1**

0F-5 **3** *4 1/2* **Touch Back (IRE)**185 185 9-11-3 120.... MrTommieMO'Brien(7) 119
(Chris Bealby) *trckd ldrs: led appr 2 out: hdd and hit last: sn wknd* **10/1**

/53- **4** *20* **Heavenly Brook (IRE)**62 1516 11-10-5 122.... MikeyHamill(7) 85
(Alexandra Dunn) *chsd ldrs 4th: lost pl appr 2 out: sn bhd* **5/1**2

-0PP **5** *30* **Walkabout Creek (IRE)**25 1927 8-10-12 95....(v1) LiamTreadwell 55
(Derek Frankland) *w ldr: led 8th: j.rt 3 out: sn hdd and lost pl: t.o next* **80/1**

-145 **P** **Earcomesthedream (IRE)**145 758 12-10-11 102....(b) TomBellamy(3)
(Peter Pritchard) *detached in last 3rd: drvn 5th: sn t.o: p.u bef 8th* **25/1**

412- **P** **Ministerofinterior**217 5187 10-10-7 109....(b) HarryChalloner(3)
(Barry Leavy) *in rr: drvn 6th: lost pl 8th: bhd 3 out: t.o whn p.u bef next* **9/1**

353- **R** **Lamps**211 5290 8-11-2 129.... NickScholfield
(Michael Blake) *v reluctant to go to s: ref to r* **15/8**1

2P-P **P** **Leath Acra Mor (IRE)**113 1055 9-10-9 110....(v) RobMcCarth(3)
(Ian Williams) *chsd ldrs 3rd: lost pl 9th: sn bhd: t.o whn p.u sn after 3 out* **14/1**

-PPP **P** **Harris (IRE)**28 1889 8-11-3 112....(v) JonathanEngland(3)
(Alan Brown) *led: drvn 3rd: hdd 8th: lost pl next: sn bhd: t.o whn p.u sn after 3 out* **22/1**

6m 33.7s (18.70) **Going Correction** +0.975s/f (Soft) **10** Ran SP% **113.4**
Speed ratings (Par 103): **107,106,105,98,88 , , , ,**
CSF £45.30 TOTE £7.20: £2.50, £1.70, £3.00; EX 46.90 Trifecta £260.10.
Owner W A Bethell **Bred** Bridepark Stud **Trained** Arnold, E Yorks

FOCUS
There was drama from the start in this moderate staying claimer.

2406 SOUTHWELL "NATIONAL HUNT" NOVICES' HURDLE (9 hdls) 1m 7f 153y
2:35 (2:35) (Class 4) 4-Y-0+ **£3,898** (£1,144; £572; £286)

Form RPR

0- **1** **Aqua Dude (IRE)**268 4221 5-10-12 0.... PaulMoloney 122+
(Evan Williams) *mid-div: trckd ldrs 6th: led sn after next: pushed 5 l clr last: eased clsng stages: v comf* **5/2**2

2-P **2** *2 1/2* **Kerisper (FR)**46 1635 6-10-9 0.... RyanHatch(3) 109
(Nigel Twiston-Davies) *chsd ldr: 2nd and drvn 3 out: kpt on same pce between last 2: no imp* **4/1**3

56P **3** *15* **Daulys Anthem (IRE)**11 2152 7-10-9 0.... KillianMoore(3) 94
(David Dennis) *trckd ldrs: one pce appr 2 out: poor 3rd sn after last* **66/1**

5- **4** *nk* **At The Top (FR)**303 3618 5-10-5 0.... HarrySkelton 87
(Dan Skelton) *hld up in rr: drvn and sme hdwy 3 out: one pce* **8/1**

-112 **5** *1/2* **Brave Richard (IRE)**108 1101 4-10-12 0.... RichardJohnson 94
(J R Jenkins) *in rr: hdwy whn hit 5th: hit 3 out: sn drvn: one pce appr next* **6/4**1

6-0 **6** *3/4* **King Simba (IRE)**185 188 4-10-12 0.... DavidBass 93
(Kim Bailey) *chsd ldrs: nt fluent 2nd: 3rd and one pce bef 2 out: 3rd whn hit last: wknd* **25/1**

7 *9* **How's Vienna (IRE)**576 5-10-12 0.... NickScholfield 83
(David Dennis) *hld up in rr: sme hdwy and drvn bef 3 out: lost pl bef 2 out* **16/1**

P **Mr Elevator (IRE)**169 5-10-12 0.... AdamPogson
(Charles Pogson) *t.k.h: led: hdd and lost pl sn after 3 out: sn wl bhd: t.o whn p.u bef next* **25/1**

4m 11.5s (14.50) **Going Correction** +0.975s/f (Soft) **8** Ran SP% **114.7**
Speed ratings (Par 105): **102,100,93,93,92 92,87,**
CSF £13.02 TOTE £4.20: £1.50, £1.60, £4.10; EX 14.00 Trifecta £577.70.
Owner Mr & Mrs William Rucker **Bred** Cathal Ennis **Trained** Llancarfan, Vale Of Glamorgan

FOCUS
A modest novice contest, run at a fair gallop. This winner was value for further.

2407 NOTTINGHAMSHIRE FEDERATION OF YOUNG FARMERS CLUBS NOVICES' HURDLE (11 hdls) 2m 4f 62y
3:10 (3:10) (Class 4) 4-Y-0+ **£3,898** (£1,144; £572; £286)

Form RPR

2-2 **1** **Abbreviate (GER)**39 1718 4-10-12 0.... DavidBass 133+
(Kim Bailey) *trckd ldrs: t.k.h: handy 2nd 8th: led bef 2 out: wnt clr between last 2: heavily eased run-in* **4/1**3

2 *19* **Young Dillon (IRE)**185 189 6-10-12 0.... WillKennedy 114
(Dr Richard Newland) *chsd ldrs: 2nd whn hit 2 out: kpt on one pce* **11/4**2

2-51 **3** *18* **Braavos**23 1973 4-10-12 0.... RichardJohnson 98
(Philip Hobbs) *hld up in rr: hdwy 7th: mstke next: one pce fr 3 out: lft poor 3rd and hmpd next* **15/8**1

32-1 **4** *12* **Wings Attract (IRE)**24 1943 6-11-5 120.... TomMessenger 87
(Chris Bealby) *t.k.h: led to 1st: trckd ldrs: outpcd 3 out: sn bhd: lft distant 4th next* **11/2**

0- **5** *shd* **Spendajennie (IRE)**162 6-10-5 0.... AdamWedge 73
(Nick Kent) *mid-div: chsd ldrs 6th: lost pl 3 out: sn bhd* **150/1**

5 **6** *3 1/2* **Ballyvaughn (IRE)**19 2023 5-10-12 0.... HarrySkelton 76
(Caroline Bailey) *t.k.h: led 1st: hdd 3rd: wknd 3 out* **50/1**

5 **7** *37* **Song Of The Night (IRE)**23 1966 4-10-12 0.... DarylJacob 39
(Charlie Longsdon) *in rr: drvn 7th: sn bhd: t.o 3 out* **20/1**

4- **8** *16* **Little James (IRE)**410 1619 6-10-9 0.... RyanHatch(3) 23
(Nigel Twiston-Davies) *in rr: chsd ldrs 4th: drvn 7th: lost pl next: sn bhd: t.o 2 out* **20/1**

4 **F** **Kalondra (IRE)**25 1926 4-10-12 0.... MarkQuinlan 75
(Neil Mulholland) *t.k.h: trckd ldrs: led and hit 3rd: hdd bef 2 out: modest 3rd and wkng whn fell 2 out* **33/1**

46 **P** **Glory For Rory (IRE)**10 2163 4-10-12 0.... AndrewTinkler
(Jonjo O'Neill) *in rr: hdwy into mid-div whn nt fluent and lost pl 6th: bhd next: t.o whn p.u bef 2 out* **66/1**

5m 28.5s (15.50) **Going Correction** +0.975s/f (Soft)
WFA 4 from 5yo+ 8lb **10** Ran SP% **113.4**
Speed ratings (Par 105): **108,100,93,88,88 86,72,65, ,**
CSF £14.34 TOTE £4.30: £1.60, £1.40, £1.20; EX 14.50 Trifecta £37.10.
Owner Mr & Mrs K R Ellis **Bred** Gestut Gorlsdorf **Trained** Andoversford, Gloucs

FOCUS
This novice event rather fell apart from halfway as most seemed to struggle on the ground, but a big step up from the winner who looks decent.

2408 SOUTHWELL BEER FESTIVAL WEEKEND 12TH DECEMBER H'CAP HURDLE (11 hdls) 2m 4f 62y
3:45 (3:45) (Class 5) (0-100,100) 3-Y-0+ **£2,924** (£858; £429; £214)

Form RPR

-P04 **1** **Polarbrook (IRE)**11 2142 8-11-2 **90**....(tp) JamesDavies 104
(Derek Shaw) *chsd ldrs 3rd: led bef 2 out: drvn 4 l clr last: hld on clsng stages* **12/1**

640- **2** *1* **Carlo Rocks (IRE)**223 5085 5-11-7 **95**.... AndrewThornton 110+
(Caroline Bailey) *trckd ldrs: hit 8th: chsd wnr appr 2 out: hit last: styd on* **7/2**2

25PP **3** *28* **Riddlestown (IRE)**12 2140 8-11-7 **95**.... HarrySkelton 80
(Caroline Fryer) *chsd ldrs: reminders 6th: led briefly 3 out: wknd appr next* **12/1**

505- **4** *1 1/4* **Hurricane Vic**224 5068 5-11-5 **100**.... WilliamFeatherstone(7) 84
(Alan King) *chsd ldrs: drvn after 3 out: wknd appr next* **2/1**1

40U0 **5** *4 1/2* **Double Court (IRE)**23 1979 4-10-7 **81**....(v) DaveCrosse 60
(Nigel Twiston-Davies) *hld up in rr: hdwy to chse ldrs 7th: lost pl 3 out: bhd whn hit next* **25/1**

0-U0 **P** **Grey Messenger (IRE)**26 1909 6-10-12 **89**....(t) JamesBanks(3)
(Emma Baker) *in rr: outpcd 7th: bhd 3 out: t.o whn p.u bef next* **20/1**

0200 **P** **Green And White (ITY)**101 1166 5-11-7 **95**.... LeeEdwards
(Dave Roberts) *mid-div: pushed along to chse ldrs 6th: lost pl next: sn bhd: t.o whn p.u bef 2 out* **22/1**

040- **P** **Memory Of Light (IRE)**[242] 4733 6-11-1 89...............(t) BrendanPowell
(Claire Dyson) *hld up towards rr: lost pl 7th: bhd 3 out: t.o whn p.u bef next* **8/1**

406- **P** **Kavanaghs Corner (IRE)**[229] 4985 6-11-7 95.................... PaddyBrennan
(Simon Earle) *t.k.h: led: j.rt 4th: hdd 3 out: sn lost pl and eased: bhd whn p.u bef 2 out* **9/2**[3]

5m 36.1s (23.10) **Going Correction** +0.975s/f (Soft)
WFA 4 from 5yo+ 8lb **9** Ran SP% **113.2**
Speed ratings (Par 103): **92,91,80,79,78 , , ,**
CSF £52.23 CT £520.46 TOTE £14.90: £3.50, £1.70, £2.80; EX 58.40 Trifecta £916.40.
Owner John R Saville **Bred** Mrs Helen Power Wall **Trained** Sproxton, Leics

FOCUS
They went steadily early on in this weak handicap, but it was still hard work and only two mattered from the penultimate flight. Not an easy race to rate.
T/Plt: £121.20 to a £1 stake. Pool: £65,245.25 - 392.88 winning units. T/Qpdt: £26.30 to a £1 stake. Pool: £7,833.38 - 219.71 winning units. **Walter Glynn**

2217 HUNTINGDON (R-H)
Tuesday, November 10

OFFICIAL GOING: Soft (good to soft in places; chs 5.6; hdl 6.1)
Wind: Fresh across Weather: Overcast

2409 ROA/RACING POST OWNERS JACKPOT NOVICES' HURDLE (8 hdls) 1m 7f 171y
1:10 (1:11) (Class 4) 4-Y-0+ **£3,898** (£1,144; £572; £286)

Form RPR

20-0 **1** **Matorico (IRE)**[192] 94 4-10-12 0.............................. RichardJohnson 121+
(Jonjo O'Neill) *hld up: hdwy 5th: chsd ldr and 2 l down whn lft in ld and hmpd last: shkn up and styd on wl* **11/4**[2]

52 **2** *3¾* **Linguine (FR)**[21] 2007 5-10-12 0...........................(p) ConorO'Farrell 116
(Seamus Durack) *led: wnt clr after 1st: c bk to the field after 3 out: hdd whn blnd 2 out: lft cl 2nd and hmpd last: styd on same pce flat* **8/1**

3 *22* **Camborne**[416] 7-10-12 0.............................. AidanColeman 96
(John Ferguson) *hld up: hdwy appr 3 out: wkng whn blnd next* **15/8**[1]

22- **4** *1* **Draco's Code**[19] 3541 4-10-12 0.............................. AndrewGlassonbury 91
(Gary Moore) *mid-div: blnd 4th: hdwy next: rdn and wknd after 3 out* **20/1**

05/ **5** *4* **Herons Heir (IRE)**[664] 3716 7-10-12 0.............................. HarrySkelton 87
(Dan Skelton) *hld up: sme hdwy appr 3 out: wkng whn blnd next* **6/1**

6-6 **6** *2¼* **For Good Measure (IRE)**[14] 2123 4-10-12 0.............................. JamesBest 85
(Philip Hobbs) *hld up: j.rt 2 out: nvr on terms* **40/1**

7 *12* **Arryzona**[159] 4-10-12 0.............................. TrevorWhelan 73
(Christine Dunnett) *mid-div: wknd 5th: towards rr whn blnd 3 out* **250/1**

P4-0 **8** *3½* **Steuben (GER)**[11] 2163 9-10-12 0.............................. PeterCarberry 69
(Des Donovan) *hld up: bhd fr 5th* **250/1**

600- **9** *22* **On The Road (IRE)**[230] 4984 5-10-12 0.............................. PaulMoloney 47
(Evan Williams) *chsd ldrs: nt fluent 1st and 4th: wknd next* **200/1**

P **Cyril The Squirrel**[1105] 11-10-9 0.............................. ConorShoemark(3)
(Lawney Hill) *chsd ldrs: j.rt 2nd and next: wknd 5th: bhd whn p.u bef 2 out* **150/1**

31-1 **F** **Younevercall (IRE)**[37] 1781 4-11-5 0.............................. DavidBass 128+
(Kim Bailey) *chsd ldr who wnt clr after the 1st: tk clsr order 3 out: led next: 2 l ahd whn fell last* **5/1**[3]

3m 52.1s (-2.80) **Going Correction** +0.175s/f (Yiel) **11** Ran SP% **112.7**
Speed ratings (Par 105): **114,112,101,100,98 97,91,89,78,**
CSF £22.82 TOTE £4.10: £1.80, £2.50, £1.10; EX 32.60 Trifecta £96.60.
Owner John P McManus **Bred** Cadran & Scea Des Bissons **Trained** Cheltenham, Gloucs

FOCUS
Soft but drying ground on a windy afternoon. All bends out 5yds. This was an interesting novice hurdle from which winners should emerge. It was run at a decent gallop once the other riders realised how far clear the runner-up was. Add 43.4yds to advertised race distance.

2410 MOLSON COORS NOVICES' H'CAP CHASE (19 fncs) 2m 7f 129y
1:40 (1:40) (Class 4) (0-105,104) 4-Y-0+ **£4,223** (£1,240; £620; £310)

Form RPR

0316 **1** **Spending Time**[28] 1897 6-11-12 104...........................(tp) ConorO'Farrell 120+
(David Pipe) *prom: lost pl bef 9th: hdwy after 12th: led appr 2 out: sn clr: rdn and hung rt flat: styd on wl* **5/1**[3]

0/6- **2** *13* **Global Domination**[522] 601 7-10-4 82.............................. HarrySkelton 85
(Caroline Bailey) *hld up: hdwy appr 9th: jnd ldr 4 out: rdn appr 2 out: styd on same pce* **9/2**[2]

P61- **3** *14* **I Am Colin**[234] 4928 6-11-12 104.............................. SamTwiston-Davies 96
(Nigel Twiston-Davies) *chsd ldrs: nt fluent 13th: outpcd next: rallied 3 out: rdn and wkng whn mstke 2 out* **9/2**[2]

55-3 **4** *½* **Copperfacejack (IRE)**[33] 1824 5-11-9 101...........................(p) CharliePoste 92
(Paul Webber) *chsd ldrs: pckd 1st: led 2nd to 4th: led again 6th: rdn: hdd & wknd appr 2 out* **8/1**

P05- **P** **El Indio (IRE)**[238] 4825 8-10-9 90...........................(tp) ConorShoemark(3)
(Claire Dyson) *sn pushed along in rr: bhd whn p.u bef 9th* **18/1**

600- **U** **Exmoor Challenge**[238] 4825 6-10-6 84.............................. TrevorWhelan
(Neil King) *led and mstke 1st: hdd next: led again 4th to 6th: chsd ldr to 8th: cl 3rd and pushed along whn blnd and uns rdr next* **14/1**

0-35 **P** **Urban Storm (IRE)**[34] 1812 5-11-3 95...........................(p) DavidBass
(Ben Pauling) *sn pushed along and prom: chsd ldr 8th to 14th: wknd after 3 out: bhd whn p.u bef next* **7/2**[1]

-605 **P** **Changeofluck (IRE)**[16] 2090 7-11-8 100...........................(tp) WayneHutchinson
(Lawney Hill) *hld up: pushed along after 8th: sme hdwy whn mstke 14th: sn wknd: bhd whn p.u bef 2 out* **15/2**

6m 14.3s (4.00) **Going Correction** +0.175s/f (Yiel) **8** Ran SP% **110.1**
Speed ratings (Par 105): **100,95,91,90, , , ,**
CSF £26.08 CT £99.84 TOTE £5.50: £1.90, £2.20, £1.10; EX 29.90 Trifecta £218.50.
Owner Brocade Racing **Bred** Patrick And Roslyn Burling **Trained** Nicholashayne, Devon

FOCUS
A pretty modest novice handicap which was run at a solid gallop and proved quite a test of stamina. There was some hairy jumping on show, but the winner was up 10lb on the best of his hurdling figures. Add 64.08yds to advertised race distance.

2411 OMNI SECURITY MICHAELMAS HURDLE (A H'CAP) (10 hdls) 2m 3f 137y
2:10 (2:12) (Class 2) (0-150,144) 4-Y-0+
£15,640 (£4,620; £2,310; £1,155; £577; £290)

Form RPR

53-0 **1** **Bivouac (FR)**[31] 1847 4-11-2 134.............................. NoelFehily 139+
(Nicky Henderson) *hld up: hdwy 5th: led after 3 out: rdn out* **4/1**[2]

416- **2** *1* **Ruacana**[213] 5276 6-11-10 142.............................. AidanColeman 145
(John Ferguson) *hld up in tch: shkn up after 3 out: rdn flat: styd on* **7/1**

11-3 **3** *1* **Lil Rockerfeller (USA)**[17] 2060 4-11-12 144...........................(p) TrevorWhelan 147
(Neil King) *prom: lost pl 5th: pushed along after 7th: hdwy 3 out: rdn whn mstke next: styd on same pce flat* **13/2**

203- **4** *5* **Run Ructions Run (IRE)**[207] 5365 6-11-5 137....(p) SamTwiston-Davies 134
(Tim Easterby) *chsd ldrs: outpcd after 3 out: styd on flat* **8/1**

23-5 **5** *nk* **A Vos Gardes (FR)**[16] 2083 5-11-3 135...........................(t) DarylJacob 134
(Charlie Longsdon) *prom: chsd ldr and mstke 3rd: ev ch 3 out: sn rdn: styd on same pce fr next* **5/1**[3]

310- **6** *10* **Forthefunofit (IRE)**[242] 4741 6-11-1 133.............................. RichardJohnson 120
(Jonjo O'Neill) *led at stdy pce tl qcknd after 7th: rdn: hdd & wknd after 3 out* **5/2**[1]

032- **7** *9* **Calculated Risk**[56] 3798 6-10-12 130.............................. HarrySkelton 115
(Dan Skelton) *hld up: wknd 3 out* **10/1**

5m 10.6s (11.60) **Going Correction** +0.175s/f (Yiel) **7** Ran SP% **111.3**
Speed ratings (Par 109): **83,82,82,80,80 76,72**
CSF £29.33 TOTE £4.20: £2.00, £3.60; EX 27.40 Trifecta £107.20.
Owner Chris Giles & Potensis Bloodstock Ltd **Bred** Thierry Cypres **Trained** Upper Lambourn, Berks

FOCUS
A good handicap hurdle and the winner was on a decent mark. The runners were reluctant to break into a gallop when the starter dropped his flag, the riders having apparently all been instructed by their trainers to settle in which led to the delay in finding positions, but the pace did eventually become respectable. Add 51.8yds to advertised race distance.

2412 TOM JONES MEMORIAL HTJ CENTRE LTD CHASE (A NOVICES' LIMITED H'CAP) (12 fncs) 2m 104y
2:40 (2:41) (Class 3) (0-135,135) 4-Y-0+ **£6,498** (£1,908; £954; £477)

Form RPR

P-24 **1** **Raven's Tower (USA)**[160] 596 5-11-0 127.............................. DavidBass 138+
(Ben Pauling) *hld up: hdwy 3 out: led last: rdn out* **20/1**

-142 **2** *11* **Notnowsam**[27] 1904 4-10-3 124.............................. HarrySkelton 119
(Dan Skelton) *chsd ldrs: wnt 2nd 3 out: led appr next: rdn and hdd whn mstke last: wknd flat* **7/2**[2]

20F- **3** *7* **Balgarry (FR)**[242] 4741 8-11-8 135..............................1 ConorO'Farrell 131+
(David Pipe) *led and sn clr: c bk to the field after 3 out: rdn and hdd whn mstke next: wknd bef last* **5/2**[1]

00-0 **4** *7* **Sleepy Haven (IRE)**[185] 197 5-11-7 134...........................(t) HenryBrooke 120
(Jennie Candlish) *hld up: wnt 4th flat: nvr nrr* **22/1**

31-1 **5** *½* **Rock N Rhythm (IRE)**[190] 98 5-11-7 134.............................. RichardJohnson 122
(Jonjo O'Neill) *hld up: hdwy 4th: blnd 9th: wknd 3 out* **5/1**[3]

402- **6** *6* **Minellaforleisure (IRE)**[209] 5345 7-11-1 128.............................. DarylJacob 108
(Alex Hales) *hld up: nvr on terms* **10/1**

7 *17* **Monyjean (FR)**[231] 4-10-9 130.............................. PaulMoloney 95
(Evan Williams) *chsd clr ldr: mstke 4th: lost 2nd 3 out: sn wknd: mstke next* **6/1**

23F- **U** **Go West Young Man (IRE)**[213] 5271 7-10-12 125.............................. JakeGreenall
(Henry Daly) *hld up: blnd and uns rdr 3rd* **8/1**

434- **U** **Too Much Too Soon (IRE)**[270] 4214 6-10-4 117.........(t) LiamTreadwell
(Paul Webber) *chsd ldrs tl uns rdr 3rd* **33/1**

4m 8.4s (-1.80) **Going Correction** +0.175s/f (Yiel)
WFA 4 from 5yo+ 7lb **9** Ran SP% **114.0**
Speed ratings (Par 107): **111,105,102,98,98 95,86, ,**
CSF £88.55 CT £241.74 TOTE £14.60: £4.00, £1.60, £1.50; EX 67.80 Trifecta £540.00.
Owner Faithful Friends **Bred** Darley **Trained** Bourton-On-The-Water, Gloucs

FOCUS
They went a good gallop in this decent novice handicap, courtesy of the third. Add 47.04yds to advertised race distance.

2413 HOG ROAST CATERING COMPANY H'CAP HURDLE (10 hdls) 2m 4f 145y
3:10 (3:11) (Class 4) (0-105,105) 3-Y-0+ **£3,249** (£954; £477; £238)

Form RPR

543/ **1** **Flemensmix**[622] 4491 7-11-12 105.............................. DavidBass 117+
(Kim Bailey) *a.p: led 7th: blnd 3 out: clr bef next: hit last: styd on wl* **8/1**

32-0 **2** *5* **Snowball (IRE)**[38] 1756 8-10-3 82.............................. NicodeBoinville 87
(David Arbuthnot) *hld up: hdwy 5th: rdn after 7th: chsd wnr appr 2 out: no imp* **4/1**[1]

5023 **3** *12* **Tiradia (FR)**[9] 2218 8-11-11 104.............................. AidanColeman 99
(J R Jenkins) *hld up: hdwy appr 3 out: sn rdn: wkng whn nt fluent last* **9/2**[2]

1600 **4** *3¼* **In The Crowd (IRE)**[110] 1084 6-11-0 96...........................(p) JamesBanks(3) 86
(Roy Brotherton) *chsd ldr to 4th: remained handy: jnd ldrs 7th: rdn and wknd appr 2 out* **16/1**

F0-4 **5** *7* **Vinegar Hill**[192] 90 6-10-8 92.............................. ConorRing(5) 77
(Anna Brooks) *hld up: mstke 6th: sn rdn and wknd* **6/1**

00-6 **6** *9* **Barneby (FR)**[51] 1599 4-11-0 96.............................. KieronEdgar(3) 70
(David Pipe) *hld up: mstke 4th: wknd 7th* **10/1**

23F/ **P** **Philharmonic Hall**[46] 4398 7-10-11 90.............................. RichardJohnson
(Peter Hiatt) *led to 7th: wknd bef next: bhd whn p.u bef 2 out* **16/1**

053- **P** **Dye Of A Needle (IRE)**[245] 4695 5-11-10 103.............................. PaulMoloney
(Evan Williams) *prom: lost pl and mstke 5th: bhd fr next: p.u bef 3 out* **5/1**[3]

2052 **P** **Midnight Gem**[19] 2033 5-11-12 105.............................. DarylJacob
(Charlie Longsdon) *prom: chsd ldr 4th tl rdn after 7th: wknd bef 3 out: bhd whn p.u bef next* **8/1**

5m 12.5s (1.90) **Going Correction** +0.175s/f (Yiel)
WFA 4 from 5yo+ 8lb **9** Ran SP% **112.2**
Speed ratings (Par 105): **103,101,96,95,92 89, , ,**
CSF £39.26 CT £161.09 TOTE £8.80: £2.70, £1.60, £1.30; EX 44.70 Trifecta £168.00.
Owner The Perfect Mix Racing Club **Bred** E R Hanbury **Trained** Andoversford, Gloucs

FOCUS
Add 51.8yds to advertised race distance. They went an average pace in what was a very ordinary handicap hurdle.

2414 OMNI SECURITY GUARDING "JUNIOR" STANDARD OPEN NATIONAL HUNT FLAT RACE 1m 5f 148y
3:40 (3:42) (Class 6) 3-Y-0 **£1,624** (£477; £238; £119)

Form RPR

2 **1** **Rodneythetrotter**[20] 2020 3-10-5 0.............................. PaddyBradley(7) 92+
(Pat Phelan) *chsd ldrs: led wl over 3f out: shkn up over 1f out: styd on wl* **11/4**[2]

2 *5* **Shining Romeo** 3-10-12 0.............................. TrevorWhelan 86
(Denis Quinn) *a.p: chsd wnr over 2f out: rdn over 1f out: styd on same pce* **20/1**

3 *7* **Quarenta (FR)** 3-10-12 0.............................. RichardJohnson 78
(Jonjo O'Neill) *hld up: hdwy over 3f out: nt trble ldrs* **5/2**[1]

4 1 **Sir Albie** 3-10-9 0 .... JamesBanks(3) 76
(Andy Turnell) *chsd ldr tl rdn wl over 3f out: wknd over 1f out* 66/1

5 4 ½ **Art Of Swing (IRE)** 3-10-12 0 .... JamieMoore 71
(Gary Moore) *hld up: hdwy over 3f out: wknd over 1f out* 6/1

6 4 ½ **William Hunter** 3-10-12 0 .... WayneHutchinson 66
(Alan King) *hld up in tch: chsd wnr over 3f out tl rdn over 2f out: wknd over 1f out* 4/1[3]

5 7 36 **Jackblack**[20] 2020 3-10-12 0 .... NicodeBoinville 22
(Patrick Chamings) *led: rdn: hdd & wknd wl over 3f out* 8/1

8 2 ¼ **Do It Tomorrow (IRE)** 3-10-5 0 .... AidanColeman 13
(J R Jenkins) *hld up: wknd 6f out* 14/1

3m 19.4s (-0.60) 8 Ran SP% 113.6
CSF £53.18 TOTE £3.50: £1.10, £4.80, £1.60; EX 50.50 Trifecta £219.10.
Owner Tony Smith & Allen Pope **Bred** Ermyn Lodge Stud Limited **Trained** Epsom, Surrey

FOCUS
Add 33.4yds to advertised race distance. They went a fair gallop in this ordinary bumper, in which only two had run previously.
T/Plt: £36.50 to a £1 stake. Pool: £45,648.06 - 910.96 winning units. T/Qpdt: £14.60 to a £1 stake. Pool: £3,807.24 - 192.74 winning units. **Colin Roberts**

LINGFIELD (L-H)

Tuesday, November 10

OFFICIAL GOING: Jumps courses - soft (heavy in places); polytrack: standard
Wind: medium, across Weather: overcast

2415 MONEY BACK 2ND AT TITANBET.CO.UK H'CAP HURDLE (10 hdls) 2m 3f 110y
1:00 (1:00) (Class 3) (0-130,130) 3-Y-O+ £5,848 (£1,717; £858; £429)

Form RPR

52-5 1 **Rock Of Leon**[24] 1977 4-11-5 123 .... (t) DavidEngland 126
(Dan Skelton) *wl in tch in midfield: mstke 4th: chsd ldr bef 2 out: rdn and swtchd rt between last 2: led and hanging lft flat: styd on* 7/1

/35- 2 ¾ **Flementime (IRE)**[313] 3453 7-11-5 123 .... AndrewTinkler 125
(Martin Keighley) *chsd ldrs: nt fluent 5th: wnt 2nd next: led wl bef 2 out: rdn between last 2: hdd and sltly crowded flat: styd on same pce* 6/1

001- 3 ¾ **Anteros (IRE)**[200] 5507 7-11-5 130 .... (t) CiaranGethings(7) 132
(Sophie Leech) *t.k.h: hld up in tch in rr: clsd after 3 out: wnt 3rd and mstke 2 out: rdn bef last: no imp tl styd on fnl 100yds: nt rch ldrs* 11/4[1]

000- 4 14 **Like Sully (IRE)**[218] 5210 7-10-6 110 .... AndrewThornton 96
(Richard Rowe) *led tl wl bef 2 out: rdn and lost pl bef next: wl hld between last 2: plugged on flat to go 4th towards fin* 10/1

330- 5 ¾ **Minstrels Gallery (IRE)**[241] 4750 6-11-9 127 .... LeightonAspell 115
(Lucy Wadham) *hld up in tch: hdwy to chse ldrs after 3 out: rdn bef next: 4th and btn between last 2: wknd flat* 3/1[2]

340/ 6 8 **Fitzwilly**[30] 5568 5-11-6 124 .... GavinSheehan 103
(Mick Channon) *chsd ldr tl 6th: rdn next: lost pl u.p bef 2 out: wknd between last 2* 11/2[3]

0U-0 7 10 **First Avenue**[152] 701 10-11-11 129 .... TomCannon 97
(Laura Mongan) *hld up in tch in last trio: rdn and struggling 3 out: lost tch bef next* 11/1

5-25 8 10 **Sebs Sensei (IRE)**[22] 1998 4-10-2 113 .... MarcGoldstein(7) 71
(Mark Hoad) *in tch in midfield: rdn 7th: lost pl after next: bhd 2 out: t.o* 33/1

5m 5.85s (-20.15) **Going Correction** -1.10s/f (Hard)
WFA 4 from 5yo+ 7lb 8 Ran SP% 114.2
Speed ratings (Par 107): **96,95,95,89,89 86,82,78**
CSF £48.05 CT £143.09 TOTE £8.50: £2.30, £2.20, £1.50; EX 35.00 Trifecta £218.50.
Owner Andy Jansons & Dan Skelton **Bred** Worksop Manor Stud **Trained** Alcester, Warwicks
■ Stewards' Enquiry : David England one-day ban: careless riding (24 Nov)

FOCUS
All starts have been moved at this track following remeasuring, so there will be no speed figures here until there is sufficient data to calculate updated median times. All races on inner line. The ground was changed to soft, heavy in places after the opener and Andrew Tinkler described it as "hard work". Three came clear in this ordinary handicap.

2416 MW SOLICITORS H'CAP CHASE (14 fncs) 2m 4f
1:30 (1:30) (Class 5) (0-100,98) 4-Y-O+ £2,729 (£801; £400; £200)

Form RPR

24-4 1 **Albatros De Guye (FR)**[22] 1999 5-9-12 73 oh1 ow1(p) JeremiahMcGrath(3) 85+
(Anna Newton-Smith) *hld up in tch: clsd to trck ldrs 9th: jnd ldrs and gng best 11th: led next: idling in front: rdn and asserted flat: eased towards fin* 7/2[2]

634- 2 6 **Strange Bird (IRE)**[223] 5094 10-10-13 85 .... (t) LeightonAspell 90
(Richard Rowe) *j. low at many fences: chsd ldr tl 7th: hit next: hdd next: 2 l 3rd bef 2 out: chsd wnr after 3 out: plugged on same pce flat* 11/2

0623 3 18 **The Omen**[36] 1796 9-11-2 88 .... MichaelByrne 83
(Tim Vaughan) *led tl mstke and hdd 7th: led again 9th: hdd 3 out: sn rdn and lost 2nd: wknd between last 2: blnd last* 9/2[3]

1-36 4 14 **Red Anchor (IRE)**[184] 223 11-10-8 83 .... (p) ThomasGarner(3) 54
(Linda Jewell) *chsd ldrs: rdn after 5th: styd in tch tl 9th: wl bhd 11th: t.o* 12/1

-23F 5 9 **Head Spin (IRE)**[154] 670 7-11-12 98 .... (p) AndrewThornton 60
(Seamus Mullins) *hld up in tch: chsd ldrs 8th: lost tch qckly after 9th: t.o wl bef 3 out* 5/1

00-1 F **Mr Bachster (IRE)**[4] 2315 10-11-0 86 7ex .... JamieMoore
(Kerry Lee) *j.rt: in tch in rr: rdn 8th: struggling whn virtually ref and fell 10th* 9/4[1]

5m 31.65s (-3.35) **Going Correction** -0.375s/f (Good) 6 Ran SP% 110.9
Speed ratings (Par 103): **91,88,81,75,72**
CSF £21.58 TOTE £4.60: £2.00, £3.30; EX 23.10 Trifecta £108.80.
Owner George Goring **Bred** G A E C Delorme Gerard & Vincent **Trained** Jevington, E Sussex

FOCUS
A couple of the fancied runners disappointed in what was a moderate chase.

2417 EBF STALLIONS "NATIONAL HUNT" NOVICES' HURDLE (QUALIFIER) (10 hdls) 2m 3f 110y
2:00 (2:00) (Class 4) 4-6-Y-0 £5,198 (£1,526; £763; £381)

Form RPR

1/0- 1 **Justanother Muddle**[214] 5255 6-10-12 0 .... MarcGoldstein 126+
(Sheena West) *j.big 1st: chsd ldrs: wnt 2nd 6th: rdn between last: styd on to ld fnl 100yds: forged clr: rdn out* 5/1

2 2 ½ **Tippmanboy (IRE)**[273] 4148 5-10-12 114 .... WillKennedy 123+
(Dr Richard Newland) *t.k.h: hld up in last trio: hdwy to chse ldrs after 4th: led next: rdn bef last: hdd and no ex fnl 100yds* 3/1[2]

236- 3 3 ¾ **Weststreet (IRE)**[220] 5142 5-10-12 121 .... LeightonAspell 120
(Oliver Sherwood) *led tl 5th: chsd ldrs after: rdn between last 2: pckd sltly last: styd on same pce flat* 2/1[1]

1 4 5 **Western Cape (IRE)**[19] 2044 4-10-7 0 .... KevinJones(5) 115
(Seamus Mullins) *chsd ldr tl 5th: chsd ldrs after: 4th and stl in tch after 3 out: swtchd rt and rdn between last 2: no imp and wl hld whn edgd lft flat* 9/2[3]

0 5 40 **Britanio Bello (FR)**[10] 2183 4-10-12 0 .... JoshuaMoore 90
(Gary Moore) *hld up in rr: struggling after 7th: lost tch next: t.o* 12/1

604/ 6 34 **Manhattan Mead**[574] 5341 5-10-12 0 .... MattieBatchelor 40
(Michael Madgwick) *in tch in rr but nvr really travelling: reminders after 4th: struggling 6th: t.o 3 out* 200/1

314- P **Dalaman (IRE)**[313] 3447 4-10-12 0 .... MichaelByrne
(Tim Vaughan) *chsd ldrs tl after 4th: lost pl and bhd 7th: sn lost tch: t.o whn p.u bef 2 out* 20/1

P **Yanmare (IRE)**[191] 5-10-9 0 .... RyanHatch(3)
(Nigel Twiston-Davies) *in tch in midfield: rdn and struggling after 6th: lost tch after next: t.o whn p.u bef 2 out* 14/1

0 P **Kelsey (IRE)**[41] 1698 5-10-12 0 .... (p) RobertDunne
(Tom Lacey) *in tch in midfield: dropped to rr and rdn bef 6th: t.o whn p.u bef 2 out* 100/1

5m 5.45s (-20.55) **Going Correction** -1.10s/f (Hard) 9 Ran SP% 113.8
Speed ratings: **97,96,94,92,76 62, ,**
CSF £20.41 TOTE £6.70: £1.80, £1.30, £1.40; EX 22.60 Trifecta £57.70.
Owner Saloop **Bred** Saloop Ltd **Trained** Falmer, E Sussex

FOCUS
An ordinary novice, but a winner capable of rating higher.

2418 DOWNLOAD TITANBET SPORTS APP "FLAT JOCKEYS" H'CAP HURDLE (TO BE RIDDEN BY PRO FLAT JOCKEYS) (8 hdls) 2m
2:30 (2:30) (Class 4) (0-110,110) 3-Y-O+ £5,848 (£1,717; £858; £429)

Form RPR

01 1 **Solstice Star**[6] 2264 5-10-9 93 .... (t) TomQueally 105+
(Martin Keighley) *mde all: shkn up bef 2 out: styd on flat: rdn out* 4/6[1]

23-1 2 1 ¾ **Mr Fickle (IRE)**[30] 281 6-11-9 107 .... (v) ShaneKelly 115
(Gary Moore) *hld up in last trio: hdwy to chse ldrs 4th: reminder bef next: 3rd and rdn after 3 out: wnt 2nd next: styd on same pce flat* 5/1[2]

2423 3 16 **Fred Le Macon (FR)**[14] 2121 6-11-9 107 .... FergusSweeney 105
(Alan King) *in tch in midfield: chsd ldrs 5th: wnt 2nd 3 out: lost 2nd and mstke next: wknd between last 2* 8/1[3]

-P13 4 19 **Sadma**[22] 2000 6-11-0 98 .... JohnFahy 71
(Nick Lampard) *chsd ldr tl 3rd: styd handy tl 3 out: chsd ldng trio wl bef next: sn btn: wknd 2 out* 8/1[3]

2-20 5 22 **Giveagirlachance (IRE)**[28] 1893 6-11-10 108 .... JustinNewman 59
(Seamus Mullins) *chsd ldrs tl 5th: rdn and lost pl bef next: wknd sn after 3 out: t.o 2 out* 25/1

5-6P 6 39 **Norse Light**[14] 2121 4-11-7 105 .... (b) TimmyMurphy 17
(David Dennis) *t.k.h: chsd ldrs: wnt 3rd tl 3 out: sn rdn and wknd: t.o between last 2* 16/1

/06- P **Spanish Treasure (GER)**[546] 243 9-11-2 100 .... CharlesBishop
(Sophie Leech) *hld up in last pair: struggling 5th: lost tch sn after next: t.o whn mstke 2 out: p.u bef last* 50/1

-245 P **Very Noble (FR)**[8] 2243 6-11-12 110 .... (t) JimCrowley
(Chris Gordon) *in tch: rdn and struggling in last pair whn mstke 5th: losing tch and mstke next: t.o whn p.u 2 out* 14/1

4m 8.65s (-19.35) **Going Correction** -1.10s/f (Hard)
WFA 4 from 5yo+ 7lb 8 Ran SP% 117.2
Speed ratings (Par 105): **104,103,95,85,74 55, ,**
CSF £5.14 CT £15.21 TOTE £1.60: £1.10, £1.70, £2.20; EX 4.80 Trifecta £18.30.
Owner E&G Racing Ltd **Bred** David Allen **Trained** Condicote, Gloucs

FOCUS
A modest handicap, restricted to Flat riders, and it played out the way the market suggested it would. The winner was well in on his recent win.

2419 BET AND WATCH AT TITANBET.CO.UK H'CAP CHASE (12 fncs) 2m
3:00 (3:00) (Class 3) (0-135,132) 4-Y-0£6,963 (£2,057; £1,028; £514; £257)

Form RPR

13-0 1 **Doctor Phoenix (IRE)**[20] 2018 7-11-12 132 .... LeightonAspell 140+
(David Dennis) *j.rt at times: mde all: pushed along and readily asserted 2 out: in command last: eased towards fin: comf* 3/1[2]

2 5 **Walk In The Mill (FR)**[198] 5-11-1 121 .... NickScholfield 119+
(Robert Walford) *chsd ldrs: shkn up after 3 out: outpcd by wnr and pushed along after 2 out: hit last: rdn to go 2nd flat: styd on but no threat to wnr* 5/1[3]

50-3 3 8 **Gores Island (IRE)**[23] 1989 9-11-10 130 .... JoshuaMoore 120
(Gary Moore) *chsd wnr thrght: outpcd 2 out: sn shkn up and btn: rdn and hld whn mstke last: lost 2nd and wknd fnl 150ds* 11/4[1]

133- 4 15 **Morgan's Bay**[225] 5069 10-11-0 120 .... TomCannon 96
(Laura Mongan) *hld up in rr: mstke 1st: wnt 5th and stl jst in tch after 9th: wknd bef next: wnt modest 4th sn after last* 8/1

240- 5 11 **Tresor De Bontee (FR)**[234] 4922 8-10-9 122 .... (p) CiaranGethings(7) 86
(Kerry Lee) *in tch: 4th and cl enough 9th: rdn and btn next: wknd 2 out: lost 4th and wknd flat* 3/1[2]

424U 6 14 **Boss In Boots (IRE)**[20] 2019 7-10-9 115 .... (b) AndrewThornton 65
(Seamus Mullins) *t.k.h: hld up in tch: hit 9th and sn dropped to rr and lost tch after next* 14/1

4m 13.75s (-26.25) **Going Correction** -1.40s/f (Hard) 6 Ran SP% 111.1
Speed ratings (Par 107): **109,106,102,95,89 82**
CSF £17.58 TOTE £3.60: £2.00, £2.10; EX 16.90 Trifecta £60.00.
Owner Favourites Racing Ltd **Bred** John O'Donovan **Trained** Hanley Swan, Worcestershire

FOCUS
Reasonable form, with the front pair looking capable of better.

2420 TITANBET.CO.UK NOVICES' H'CAP CHASE (14 fncs) 2m 4f
3:30 (3:35) (Class 4) (0-105,102) 4-Y-O+ £3,861 (£1,198; £645)

Form RPR

160- 1 2 **Eaton Rock (IRE)**[236] 4861 6-11-12 102 .... JamesDavies 103
(Tom Symonds) *chsd ldr: mstke 5th: j. into ld 8th: shkn up after 2 out: rdn and hdd sn after last: styd on same pce flat: fin 2nd, 2l: awrdd r* 11/2

3/6- 2 1 ¾ **Halo Moon**[356] 2588 7-11-9 99 .... BrendanPowell 100
(Neil Mulholland) *trckd ldng pair: pressed wnr fr 10th: ev ch whn mstke last: rdn and unable qck sn after last: styd on same pce flat: fin 3rd: plcd 2nd* 7/4[1]

362- 3 48 **Onwiththeparty**[218] 5214 6-11-12 102 .... TomCannon 53
(Chris Gordon) *mstkes: led tl mstke and hdd 8th: rdn and after next: dropped to last 10th: lost tch after next: t.o: fin 4th: plcd 3rd* 9/4[2]

-062 **D** **Arthamint**[11] 2165 7-11-9 **99**..............................(t) DavidEngland 105+
(Dan Skelton) *taken down early: t.k.h: hld up in tch in rr: j.rt 9th: pressed ldrs 10th: shkn up to ld and hung sn after last: racing awkwardly and drvn fnl 150yds: kpt on: fin 1st: disqualified: rdr weighed in 1.5lbs light* **4/1**

5m 25.6s (-9.40) **Going Correction** -0.375s/f (Good) 4 Ran SP% **113.8**
Speed ratings (Par 105): **102,101,82,103**
CSF £8.45 TOTE £4.10; EX 9.00 Trifecta £19.80.
Owner Kevin Price **Bred** Jethro Bloodstock **Trained** Harewood End, H'fords
■ Entry To Evrywhere was withdrawn. Price at time of withdrawal 14-1. Rule 4 applies to bets struck prior to withdrawal but not to SP bets. - deduction 5p in the pound. New market formed.

FOCUS
Moderate chasing form and the first past the post was disqualified having weighed in light.

2421 SIS MARES' INTERMEDIATE OPEN NATIONAL HUNT FLAT RACE (TO BE RUN ON THE ALL WEATHER TRACK) 2m

4:00 (4:07) (Class 6) 4-6-Y-O **£1,559** (£457; £228; £114)

Form RPR
010- **1** **Unbuckled (IRE)**[213] 5277 5-11-3 0.............................. JackQuinlan 106+
(Neil King) *t.k.h: hld up in tch in rr: clsd over 2f out: rdn and qcknd to chse ldrs wl over 1f out: led ins fnl f: r.o wl: comf* **6/1**[3]

52- **2** 3 ¾ **Shanandoa**[208] 5359 4-10-10 0.............................. GavinSheehan 95
(Brian Barr) *led: rdn and qcknd ent fnl 2f: hdd and one pce ins fnl f* **2/1**[1]

3 ½ **Queen Odessa (IRE)** 4-10-10 0.............................. NickScholfield 94
(Harry Fry) *chsd ldr tl over 2f out: outpcd over 1f out: rallied ins fnl f: wnt 3rd last strides* **4/1**[2]

361- **4** nk **Mystic Sky**[218] 5193 4-10-10 0.............................. CiaranGethings[(7)] 101
(Lucy Wadham) *hld up in tch in midfield: swtchd rt and hdwy to chse ldrs but wd bnd 2f out: sn outpcd: pushed along and wnt 3rd ins fnl f: kpt on: lost 3rd last strides* **4/1**[2]

0- **5** 1 ¾ **Beautiful People (FR)**[369] 2309 4-10-5 0.............................. DanielHiskett[(5)] 92
(Richard Phillips) *hld up in tch: hdwy on outer 4f out: chsd ldr over 2f out: sn rdn and unable qck wl over 1f out: wknd ins fnl f* **100/1**

6 2 ¾ **Viking Queen** 4-10-10 0.............................. JamesBest 90
(Paul Webber) *hld up in tch in last trio: hdwy on outer over 4f out: rdn and outpcd 2f out: styd on same pce after* **11/1**

0-6 **7** ¾ **Romanee Vivant**[20] 2016 5-10-5 0.............................. LizzieKelly[(5)] 89
(Neil King) *in tch in midfield: rdn and lost pl over 3f out: sme prog 2f out: kpt on same pce after* **100/1**

5- **8** 4 ½ **Raya Hope (IRE)**[225] 5071 4-10-7 0.............................. TomBellamy[(3)] 84
(Alan King) *t.k.h: hld up in tch in rr: hdwy into midfield 1/2-way: pushed rt over 2f out: rdn and outpcd over 2f out: wknd over 1f out* **8/1**

0-20 **9** 3 **Primrose Brown**[19] 2044 4-10-10 0.............................. AndrewTinkler 81
(Conrad Allen) *chsd ldrs: rdn and unable qck jst over 2f out: wknd over 1f out* **33/1**

6 **10** 10 **Breath Of Life**[154] 682 5-10-10 0.............................. MattieBatchelor 71
(Mark Rimell) *t.k.h: wl in tch in midfield: rdn and lost pl 3f out: bhd over 1f out* **66/1**

11 1 ¼ **Owners Day** 5-10-10 0.............................. MarkQuinlan 70
(Neil Mulholland) *t.k.h: chsd ldrs: rdn and struggling whn pushed rt over 2f out: sn lost pl and bhd over 1f out* **33/1**

12 13 **Wun Destination** 6-10-10 0.............................. JamesDavies 57
(John Panvert) *in tch in midfield: dropped to rr and rdn 5f out: lost tch over 3f out: t.o* **66/1**

3m 34.9s (214.90)
WFA 4 from 5yo+ 7lb 12 Ran SP% **117.9**
CSF £17.95 TOTE £7.20: £2.20, £1.30, £1.40; EX 19.70 Trifecta £105.20.
Owner Mrs J K Buckle **Bred** Mrs A S O'Brien **Trained** Barbury Castle, Wiltshire

FOCUS
Typically for these polytrack bumpers there was little pace on.
T/Plt: £147.70 to a £1 stake. Pool: £45,537.03 - 225.06 winning units. T/Qpdt: £17.10 to a £1 stake. Pool: £5,386.67 - 232.50 winning units. **Steve Payne**

2142 SEDGEFIELD (L-H)
Tuesday, November 10

OFFICIAL GOING: Good to soft (6.2)
Wind: strong behind Weather: cloudy

2422 NEWCASTLE FLOORING NOVICES' HURDLE (BETFRED HURDLE SERIES QUALIFIER) 2m 3f 188y

1:20 (1:20) (Class 4) 4-Y-O+ **£3,768** (£1,106; £553; £276)

Form RPR
-221 **1** **Smart Talk (IRE)**[20] 2021 5-10-0 125.............................. CraigGallagher[(7)] 127+
(Brian Ellison) *mde all: pushed clr appr 2 out: kpt on: eased towards fin* **4/9**[1]

2 **2** 12 **Sunny West (IRE)**[17] 2070 6-10-7 0.............................. DannyCook 116
(Sue Smith) *trckd ldr: rdn appr 2 out: one pce and sn hld in 2nd: eased fnl 110yds* **2/1**[2]

-500 **3** 33 **Tickanrun (IRE)**[17] 2066 5-10-2 0.............................. DiarmuidO'Regan[(5)] 82
(Chris Grant) *in tch: rdn and outpcd 6th: sn btn in poor 3rd* **28/1**[3]

6 **4** 30 **Strait Run (IRE)**[10] 2196 4-10-4 0.............................. JoeColliver[(3)] 55
(Micky Hammond) *hld up: bhd fr 1/2-way* **50/1**

0/0 **5** 15 **Grammar**[29] 1886 6-10-4 0.............................. TonyKelly[(3)] 42
(David Thompson) *hld up: nt a fluent: bhd fr 1/2-way* **100/1**

4m 56.9s (2.80)
WFA 4 from 5yo+ 8lb 5 Ran SP% **109.0**
CSF £1.65 TOTE £1.30: £1.10, £1.20; EX 1.70 Trifecta £2.70.
Owner Mrs J A Martin **Bred** Roland Rothwell **Trained** Norton, N Yorks

FOCUS
Some starts have been moved at this track following remeasuring, so some races will not have speed figures until there is sufficient data to calculate updated median times. Hurdles sited towards centre with common bends and rail moved out 2m to provide fresher ground on bends. This looked a match on the book and the market leaders were in control from an early stage. The first two ran pretty much to their marks.

2423 BRITISH STALLION STUDS EBF "NATIONAL HUNT" NOVICES' HURDLE (QUALIFIER) (8 hdls) 2m 178y

1:50 (1:50) (Class 4) 4-6-Y-O **£4,158** (£1,221; £610; £305)

Form RPR
54-0 **1** **Poulanassy (IRE)**[24] 1979 5-10-12 0.............................. AdamWedge 109+
(Evan Williams) *mde all: rdn after 2 out: nt fluent last: edgd ahd fnl 110yds: kpt on* **5/2**[3]

5 **2** 1 ¼ **Good Vibration (FR)**[19] 2041 4-10-12 0.............................. SeanQuinlan 106
(Sue Smith) *in tch: pushed along after 3 out: rdn appr 2 out: disp 2nd last: styd on* **7/4**[1]

-230 **3** 1 ¼ **Summer Storm**[16] 2085 5-10-9 110..............................(t) TonyKelly[(3)] 106
(Rebecca Menzies) *trckd ldr: drvn after 2 out: ¾ l down whn short of room 110yds out: one pce* **2/1**[2]

0- **4** 41 **Benjamin Bogle (IRE)**[210] 5331 4-10-9 0.............................. CraigNichol[(3)] 64
(Rose Dobbin) *hld up: rdn after 3 out: sn wknd* **8/1**

4m 7.1s (0.20) **Going Correction** +0.20s/f (Yiel) 4 Ran SP% **109.4**
Speed ratings: **107,106,105,86**
CSF £7.40 TOTE £3.80; EX 10.00 Trifecta £18.60.
Owner Paul Langford **Bred** J And A Cunningham **Trained** Llancarfan, Vale Of Glamorgan

FOCUS
This was open enough despite the small field. The winner is improving in line with his bumper form.

2424 NORTONTHORPE INDUSTRIAL PARK CHASE (A NOVICES' LIMITED H'CAP) (16 fncs) 2m 3f 65y

2:20 (2:20) (Class 4) (0-120,119) 4-Y-O+ **£4,548** (£1,335; £667; £333)

Form RPR
325- **1** **Hughesie (IRE)**[283] 3971 6-11-8 **119**.............................. AdamWedge 125
(Evan Williams) *trckd ldrs on inner: chal 2 out: pushed along into narrow ld last: rdn and kpt on* **3/1**[2]

222- **2** ½ **Rear Admiral (IRE)**[211] 5309 9-10-11 **108**..............................(t) TomO'Brien 114
(Michael Easterby) *hld up in tch: smooth hdwy after 3 out: pushed along to dispute ld last: drvn and one pce run-in: hld nr fin* **7/1**

6-0U **3** 2 ¾ **Total Assets**[19] 2029 7-10-4 **106**.............................. CallumBewley[(5)] 110
(Simon Waugh) *trckd ldr: led after 4 out: rdn 3 out: hdd appr last: no ex run-in* **22/1**

45-2 **4** 8 **Nautical Twilight**[12] 2143 5-10-13 **110**..............................(b) BrianHughes 107
(Malcolm Jefferson) *hld up in tch: rdn bef 3 out: no imp* **7/2**[3]

05-1 **5** 12 **Friendly Royal (IRE)**[31] 1853 6-10-9 **106**.............................. SeanQuinlan 95
(Sue Smith) *led: jnd 4th: rdn whn hdd after 4 out: wknd after 2 out* **15/8**[1]

1-24 **F** **Lyric Street (IRE)**[19] 2034 7-11-4 **115**.............................. BrianHarding 121+
(Donald McCain) *trckd ldr: jnd ldr 4th: dropped to 3rd after 4 out: nt fluent 3 out and briefly dropped to 4th: rallied and ev ch whn fell 2 out* **9/1**

-116 **P** **Minella Hero (IRE)**[26] 1925 7-10-12 **116**.............................. FinianO'Toole[(7)]
(Micky Hammond) *hld up: slow 3rd: mstke 4th: j. bdly rt next: sn bhd p.u after 9th* **20/1**

5m 4.6s (1.60) **Going Correction** +0.20s/f (Yiel) 7 Ran SP% **113.6**
Speed ratings (Par 105): **104,103,102,99,94**
CSF £23.27 TOTE £3.70: £2.00, £3.20; EX 19.50 Trifecta £205.50.
Owner Andrew Turton & Paul Langford **Bred** Finbar Leahy **Trained** Llancarfan, Vale Of Glamorgan

FOCUS
An open contest which saw an exciting finish. The winner was stepping up on his hurdles form.

2425 HAPPY 70TH BIRTHDAY JENNIE CAFFELL H'CAP CHASE (16 fncs) 2m 3f 65y

2:50 (2:51) (Class 3) (0-140,135) 4-Y-O **£6,330** (£1,870; £935; £468; £234)

Form RPR
F5-0 **1** **Distime (IRE)**[27] 1902 9-10-11 **123**.............................. JonathanEngland[(3)] 133+
(Richard Drake) *mde all: pressed fr early stage: rdn after 3 out: kpt on wl and in command fr after 2 out* **8/1**

4F-4 **2** 3 ¼ **Grate Fella (IRE)**[10] 2193 7-11-7 **130**.............................. DannyCook 135
(Sue Smith) *trckd ldng pair: jnd ldr 11th: rdn 3 out: nt fluent 2 out: one pce and sn hld in 2nd* **5/2**[1]

165- **3** 8 **Saints And Sinners (IRE)**[220] 5141 7-11-12 **135**..............(t) BrianHughes 134
(Michael Easterby) *midfield: hdwy 3 out: rdn between last 2: wnt 3rd last: no threat to ldng pair* **5/1**[2]

122 **4** 1 ½ **Ever So Much (IRE)**[42] 1686 6-10-8 **117**..............................(p) TomO'Brien 114
(Ben Haslam) *midfield: rdn after 4 out: one pce and nvr threatened* **5/1**[2]

0P-0 **5** ½ **Teenage Dream (IRE)**[46] 1643 7-9-10 **112**.............................. CraigGallagher[(7)] 110
(Brian Ellison) *hld up: nt a fluent: pushed along between last 2: sme late hdwy: nvr threatened* **16/1**

FR24 **6** 1 ¼ **Cloudy Joker (IRE)**[19] 2041 7-11-2 **125**.............................. AdamWedge 120
(Donald McCain) *trckd ldng pair: rdn 3 out: outpcd in 3rd after 2 out: lost 3rd last: wknd* **12/1**

7 47 **Tomkevi (FR)**[48] 4-9-11 **118** oh1.............................. TonyKelly[(3)] 62
(Rebecca Menzies) *hld up in rr: blnd 11th: a bhd* **7/1**[3]

P-46 **8** 4 ½ **Master Rajeem (USA)**[158] 625 6-10-13 **122**..............................(p) MarkGrant 71
(Neil King) *pressed ldr: lost pl 11th: mstke next: sn wknd: t.o* **5/1**[2]

5m 2.4s (-0.60) **Going Correction** +0.20s/f (Yiel)
WFA 4 from 6yo+ 7lb 8 Ran SP% **115.8**
Speed ratings (Par 107): **109,107,104,103,103 102,83,81**
CSF £29.86 CT £112.25 TOTE £12.00: £3.60, £1.60, £2.20; EX 42.40 Trifecta £184.60.
Owner Mrs J Drake **Bred** Ms Marisa & Michael Bourke **Trained** Ilkley, W Yorks

FOCUS
The gallop was honest for this fair contest and a small personal best from the winner.

2426 TONY COLLINS SUPPORTING RICHARD FARQUHAR H'CAP HURDLE 2m 3f 188y

3:20 (3:20) (Class 4) (0-120,117) 3-Y-O+ **£3,768** (£1,106; £553; £276)

Form RPR
P03- **1** **Almost Gemini (IRE)**[410] 1626 6-9-11 **91** oh3.............. HarryChalloner[(3)] 95+
(Kenneth Slack) *hld up in rr: pushed along after 7th: hdwy and bk on bit after 3 out: chsd ldng pair 2 out: sn rdn: led last: styd on* **14/1**

5-06 **2** ¾ **Aniknam (FR)**[27] 1905 5-11-9 **117**.............................. AdamNicol[(3)] 120
(Philip Kirby) *midfield: clsr order after 7th: hit 3 out: rdn appr 2 out: nt fluent 2 out: ev ch last: kpt on* **5/4**[1]

P-P4 **3** 6 **Turtle Cask (IRE)**[19] 2029 6-10-5 **96**.............................. BrianHughes 94
(Dianne Sayer) *trckd ldr: rdn to ld appr 2 out: nt fluent and hdd last: wknd* **9/2**[3]

/1F- **4** nk **Pure Science (IRE)**[346] 2820 7-11-11 **116**.............................. DannyCook 113
(Sue Smith) *led: rdn whn hdd appr 2 out: stl ev ch whn nt fluent last: wknd* **3/1**[2]

0/32 **5** 22 **Ben Cee Pee M (IRE)**[19] 2042 10-11-5 **117**..............(b) CraigGallagher[(7)] 95
(Brian Ellison) *midfield: rdn after 3 out: wknd after 2 out* **8/1**

40-4 **6** 4 ½ **Cadore (IRE)**[188] 142 7-10-11 **105**..............(p) JonathanEngland[(3)] 77
(Lucy Normile) *hld up in tch: pushed along after 7th: wknd bef 2 out* **20/1**

4m 54.1s 6 Ran SP% **110.2**
CSF £32.15 TOTE £11.80: £4.50, £2.50; EX 43.10 Trifecta £146.70.
Owner A Slack **Bred** Rockhart Trading Ltd **Trained** Hilton, Cumbria

FOCUS
Not a strong contest for the grade. The winner was well in on last season's Wetherby second.

2427 LAURENCE WILLIAMSON MEMORIAL MARES' H'CAP HURDLE (QUALIFIER FOR CHALLENGER MARES' HURDLE FINAL) (8 hdls) 2m 178y
3:50 (3:50) (Class 5) (0-100,97) 3-Y-0+ £3,768 (£1,106; £553; £276)

Form RPR
660- **1** **Ellistrin Belle**[201] 5490 7-11-1 89...(t) CallumWhillans(3) 91+
(Donald Whillans) *hld up in tch: smooth hdwy after 3 out: led appr 2 out: nt fluent 2 out: sn rdn: strly pressed last: kpt on* 5/1[2]

P000 **2** 1 ½ **Beyondtemptation**[12] 2148 7-10-7 83...(t) DiarmuidO'Regan(5) 82
(Jonathan Haynes) *led: rdn whn hdd appr 2 out: rallied and ev ch last: one pce* 7/1

6/00 **3** 7 **Minden March**[4] 2322 10-9-7 71 oh12... JamieHamilton(7) 63
(Peter Maddison) *hld up in rr: pushed along after 4th: clsr order whn nt fluent 3 out: rdn into 3rd appr 2 out: plugged on* 40/1

3P53 **4** 8 **Nellie The Elegant**[25] 1941 4-10-12 88...(bt) AlanJohns(5) 74
(Tim Vaughan) *trckd ldr: rdn after 3 out: wknd appr 2 out* 6/1[3]

6635 **5** 2 **Hatton Springs (IRE)**[3] 2343 4-11-5 97... SamColtherd(7) 80
(Stuart Coltherd) *in tch: rdn 3 out: sn struggling* 8/1

-545 **6** 12 **Dalby Spook (IRE)**[29] 1892 5-10-13 84... BrianHughes 60
(Dianne Sayer) *hld up in tch: rdn after 3 out: wknd appr 2 out* 15/8[1]

305- **P** **Moon Over Rio (IRE)**[46] 4892 4-11-5 90... TomO'Brien
(Ben Haslam) *in tch: rdn after 3 out: sn wknd: p.u bef last* 5/1[2]

4m 11.9s (5.00) **Going Correction** +0.20s/f (Yiel) **7 Ran SP% 108.5**
Speed ratings (Par 103): **96,95,92,88,87 81,**
CSF £34.44 TOTE £5.40: £3.10, £4.30; EX 41.50 Trifecta £552.80.
Owner Mrs Eileen Smith **Bred** Potassium Partnership II **Trained** Hawick, Borders

FOCUS
A weak handicap run at a decent gallop, but the winner was back to her best.
T/Plt: £303.90 to a £1 stake. Pool: £51,397.31 - 123.46 winning units. T/Qpdt: £46.80 to a £1 stake. Pool: £4,339.05 - 68.50 winning units. **Andrew Sheret**

2189 AYR (L-H)
Wednesday, November 11

OFFICIAL GOING: Soft (hdl 7.2, chs 7.3)
Wind: Breezy, half against Weather: Overcast

2428 RACINGUK.COM/FREETRIAL MAIDEN HURDLE (12 hdls) 2m 4f 100y
1:20 (1:20) (Class 5) 4-Y-0+ £2,924 (£858; £429; £214)

Form RPR
1 **Comragh (IRE)**[75] 1393 5-10-0 0... AdamShort(7) 103+
(S R B Crawford, Ire) *hld up: smooth hdwy 7th: chsd clr ldr 3 out: shkn up after next: 12 l down and no imp whn lft 5 l in front and hmpd jst after last: kpt on wl* 7/1

00 **2** 8 **The Toft**[5] 2318 6-9-11 0... RossChapman(10) 93
(Lucinda Russell) *in tch: and nt fluent 7th: effrt bef 3 out: hung lft next: one pce whn lft 5 l 2nd and nt fluent last: one pce* 40/1

/46- **3** 13 **Duncomplaining (IRE)**[215] 5255 6-11-0 0... PeterBuchanan 90
(William Kinsey) *prom: wnt 2nd 4 out to next: jst outpcd whn nt fluent 2 out: no imp whn lft 10 l 3rd last* 11/4[2]

54-2 **4** 14 **Berkshire Downs**[20] 2031 5-10-4 0... AdamNicol(3) 71
(Lucy Normile) *nt fluent on occasions: chsd ldrs: wnt 2nd bef 7th to next: drvn and outpcd whn mstke 2 out: lft modest 4th last* 14/1

00- **5** 50 **Titian Boy (IRE)**[261] 4399 6-10-11 0... TonyKelly(3) 21
(N W Alexander) *t.k.h: nt fluent in rr: struggling fr 6th: t.o* 300/1

6 2 ½ **Faraway Mountain (IRE)**[26] 1959 7-11-0 0... HenryBrooke 19
(Gordon Elliott, Ire) *nt fluent on occasions: in tch: nt fluent and lost pl 5th: sn pushed along: struggling fr 6th: t.o* 14/1

0 **P** **Aleksandar**[11] 2189 6-10-9 0... DiarmuidO'Regan(5)
(Jim Goldie) *bhd: struggling fr 7th: lost tch next: p.u bef 2 out* 40/1

0 **P** **Rioja Day (IRE)**[11] 2189 5-10-9 0... StephenMulqueen(5)
(Jim Goldie) *bhd: struggling 1/2-way: nvr on terms: t.o whn p.u bef 3 out* 150/1

05/2 **F** **Caledonia**[16] 2100 8-11-0 112... BrianHughes 120+
(Jim Goldie) *led: qcknd 1/2-way: 12 l in front and stl gng wl whn stmbld and fell jst after last* 2/1[1]

P **Fullwak (IRE)**[7] 2282 8-10-7 0... LiamMcKenna(7)
(J J Lambe, Ire) *chsd ldr to bef 7th: sn lost pl and struggling: t.o whn p.u after 4 out* 150/1

P0P- **P** **Victoria Oats**[313] 3481 9-10-4 0... CraigNichol(3)
(Robert Goldie) *bhd: drvn and struggling fnl circ: lost tch and p.u bef 4 out* 300/1

-502 **P** **Fairy Theatre (IRE)**[32] 1852 4-10-7 0... BrianHarding
(Iain Jardine) *prom: hit 4th: wknd after 4 out: t.o whn p.u bef 2 out* 3/1[3]

5m 17.3s (317.30)
WFA 4 from 5yo+ 8lb **12 Ran SP% 117.7**
CSF £209.20 TOTE £7.90: £1.60, £6.60, £1.20; EX 249.10 Trifecta £2351.70 Part won..
Owner Niall Coburn **Bred** Michael Coburn **Trained** Larne, Co Antrim
■ Adam Short's first winner.

FOCUS
Some starts have been moved at this track following remeasuring, so some races will not have speed figures until there is sufficient data to calculate updated median times. Hurdles track out 7yds, adding 21yds per circuit. Chase course on innermost line. Fence 6 (open ditch) omitted in all chases - ground under repair. The official going was soft. Quite an interesting maiden hurdle to start, but a dramatic race.

2429 WATCH RACINGUK WITH FREE TRIAL NOW H'CAP HURDLE (12 hdls) 2m 5f 91y
1:50 (1:56) (Class 4) (0-120,115) 3-Y-0+ £3,898 (£1,144; £572; £286)

Form RPR
30-0 **1** **Another Mattie (IRE)**[18] 2069 8-11-1 104...(t) BrianHarding 118+
(N W Alexander) *in tch on outside: hdwy to ld 4 out: rdn last: styd on strly* 9/1

P-53 **2** 10 **Tantamount**[17] 2081 6-11-9 115...(t) DerekFox(3) 116
(Lucinda Russell) *hld up: pushed along and hdwy after 4 out: chsd wnr after 2 out: kpt on: no imp* 2/1[1]

640- **3** 1 ¼ **Cruachan (IRE)**[201] 5516 6-10-6 98... AdamNicol(3) 97
(Lucy Normile) *hld up: stdy hdwy after 4 out: in tch and rdn after next: edgd lft and kpt on same pce fr last* 11/1

2-3 **4** 6 **John Monash**[16] 2100 4-11-10 113...(t) HenryBrooke 108
(Gordon Elliott, Ire) *trckd ldrs: nt fluent 3rd: effrt and chsd wnr 3 out to after next: outpcd fr last* 8/1

43-2 **5** 7 **Glacial Rock (IRE)**[182] 285 9-11-12 115...(p) BrianHughes 101
(Alistair Whillans) *chsd ldr: ev ch briefly 4 out: drvn and outpcd fr next* 15/2[3]

316- **6** 2 ½ **Cape Arrow**[278] 4074 4-9-11 93... LorcanMurtagh(7) 76
(Barry Murtagh) *hld up: hdwy bef 3 out: no imp whn hit next* 14/1

0254 **7** 4 **Solway Prince**[6] 2296 6-10-11 105... CallumBewley(5) 85
(Lisa Harrison) *led: nt fluent 4th: hdd 4 out: rdn and wknd fr next* 5/1[2]

26-0 **8** 5 **Golans Choice (IRE)**[182] 291 6-11-4 110... CraigNichol(3) 84
(Rose Dobbin) *chsd ldrs tl rdn and wknd fr 3 out* 11/1

0U0- **9** ¾ **Rinnagree Rosie**[256] 4491 9-10-6 95... AdrianLane 69
(Lucy Normile) *nt fluent in rr: struggling 4 out: sn btn* 100/1

43-5 **10** ¾ **Rock Relief (IRE)**[181] 302 9-10-11 105...(p) DiarmuidO'Regan(5) 80
(Chris Grant) *in tch: drvn and outpcd 4 out: wknd bef next* 25/1

16-4 **11** 28 **Too Cool To Fool (IRE)**[16] 2104 12-10-7 101... DaleIrving(5) 46
(Jim Goldie) *towards rr: drvn and struggling fr 1/2-way: t.o* 16/1

P5P- **12** 3 ¾ **Lochnell (IRE)**[249] 4618 6-10-10 102... GrahamWatters(3) 43
(Ian Duncan) *t.k.h in midfield: drvn and outpcd 4 out: wknd bef next: t.o* 25/1

5m 34.5s (334.50)
WFA 4 from 6yo+ 8lb **12 Ran SP% 120.8**
CSF £28.16 CT £211.57 TOTE £9.70: £3.30, £1.30, £3.70; EX 38.70 Trifecta £365.40.
Owner Quandt & Cochrane **Bred** David Kells **Trained** Kinneston, Perth & Kinross

FOCUS
Racing was allowed to continue following an inspection of the ground after the last hurdle where Caledonia came down in the opener. A fair handicap hurdle, but although the pace was ordinary they finished well spread out. The winner was well in on the best of his old form.

2430 WESTERN HOUSE HOTEL NOVICES' H'CAP CHASE (15 fncs 2 omitted) 2m 4f 110y
2:20 (2:21) (Class 4) (0-105,105) 4-Y-0+ £4,548 (£1,335; £667; £333)

Form RPR
26-1 **1** **What A Dream**[11] 2191 9-10-4 90...(tp) JamieHamilton(7) 99
(Alison Hamilton) *prom: effrt bef 3 out: edgd lft: pushed along and keeping on whn lft 2 l 2nd last: led run-in: styd on strly* 3/1[2]

P/2- **2** 3 **Mumgos Debut (IRE)**[242] 4760 7-10-12 91... PeterBuchanan 97
(Lucinda Russell) *led: rdn 4 out: jst hdd and 1 l down whn lft 2 l in front last: hdd and no ex run-in* 4/1

U/6 **3** 3 ½ **Cinder Rua (IRE)**[7] 2284 8-11-3 103... LiamMcKenna(7) 106
(J J Lambe, Ire) *t.k.h: hld up: stdy hdwy bef 3 out: rdn and one pce whn lft 4 l 3rd last: no ex* 25/1

00-5 **4** 11 **The Bishop (IRE)**[16] 2105 7-10-13 97... StephenMulqueen(5) 89
(N W Alexander) *nt fluent on occasions: chsd ldr to 4 out: drvn and outpcd fr next: no imp whn lft modest 4th last* 17/2

/22- **5** 1 **Alfred Oats**[313] 3485 11-10-9 88...(t) BrianHughes 79
(Robert Goldie) *prom: drvn and outpcd after 5 out: no imp fr next: btn fnl 2* 11/4[1]

00P- **U** **Frankie's Promise (IRE)**[232] 4973 7-11-12 105... BrianHarding 114+
(N W Alexander) *nt fluent on occasions: hld up in tch: hit 11th: hdwy to chse ldr 4 out: effrt and edgd lft next: gd hdwy to ld and 1 l in front whn mstke and uns rdr last* 7/2[3]

5m 33.5s (333.50) **6 Ran SP% 108.3**
CSF £14.29 TOTE £3.30: £1.70, £2.50; EX 8.70 Trifecta £74.10.
Owner D & J Byers, The Late R J Kyle **Bred** Mr And Mrs W D Parker **Trained** Denholm, Borders

FOCUS
An ordinary novices' handicap chase, but another race with a dramatic conclusion.

2431 WATCH RACINGUK FREE WITH MONTH TRIAL H'CAP CHASE (QUALIFIER FOR CHALLENGER STAYING CHASE FINAL) (17 fncs 2 omitted) 3m 67y
2:50 (2:50) (Class 3) (0-135,132) 4-Y-0+ £7,797 (£2,289; £1,144; £572)

Form RPR
23-3 **1** **Final Assault (IRE)**[28] 1902 6-11-7 130... DerekFox(3) 149+
(Lucinda Russell) *hld up: smooth hdwy after 5 out: led on bit 3 out: drew clr on bridle after next: v easily* 15/8[1]

13-3 **2** 4 ½ **Plus Jamais (FR)**[11] 2192 8-10-11 117... BrianHughes 121
(Jim Goldie) *led tl rdn and hdd bef 4 out: rallied bef last: wnt 2nd last 75yds: no ch w easy wnr* 11/2

3422 **3** nk **Presented (IRE)**[10] 2213 8-10-5 116... CallumBewley(5) 120
(Lisa Harrison) *pressed ldr: led bef 4 out to next: sn drvn: one pce bef last: lost 2nd last 75yds* 5/1[3]

15-3 **4** 11 **Un Noble (FR)**[16] 2105 5-10-5 114... CraigNichol(3) 110
(Nicky Richards) *nt fluent on occasions: prom: rdn and outpcd 4 out: no imp fr next* 11/4[2]

316- **5** 34 **Chavoy (FR)**[241] 4783 10-11-2 125...(tp) TonyKelly(3) 84
(Rebecca Menzies) *hld up: mstke 11th: sn outpcd: struggling fr 5 out: t.o* 16/1

2PR- **P** **Alpha Victor (IRE)**[219] 5224 10-11-12 132...(t) PeterBuchanan
(William Kinsey) *trckd ldrs: outpcd 11th: struggling 5 out: lost tch and p.u bef next* 8/1

6m 28.8s (-21.10) **6 Ran SP% 110.5**
CSF £12.08 TOTE £2.10: £1.30, £3.00; EX 10.60 Trifecta £33.30.
Owner Mrs S Russell & A M Russell **Bred** Gerard Mullins **Trained** Arlary, Perth & Kinross

FOCUS
A decent staying handicap chase and they went a sensible pace in the conditions.

2432 RACING UK FREE FOR A MONTH H'CAP HURDLE (12 hdls) 3m 70y
3:20 (3:23) (Class 4) (0-115,115) 3-Y-0+ £3,898 (£1,144; £572; £286)

Form RPR
4-21 **1** **Calivigny (IRE)**[16] 2100 6-11-7 115... StephenMulqueen(5) 126+
(N W Alexander) *hld up in tch: smooth hdwy to ld bef 2 out: sn clr on bridle: nt extended* 15/8[1]

0103 **2** 5 **Solway Sam**[72] 1426 12-10-4 98... CallumBewley(5) 94
(Lisa Harrison) *w ldrs: led after 4 out: rdn and hdd bef 2 out: plugged on fr last: no ch w wnr* 6/1[2]

PP-3 **3** 2 **Finaghy Ayr (IRE)**[16] 2103 7-10-3 95...(p) GrahamWatters(3) 89
(Ian Duncan) *chsd ldrs: drvn along 4 out: rallied next: nt fluent 2 out: kpt on same pce* 9/1

3616 **4** 13 **Bescot Springs (IRE)**[38] 1778 10-10-8 102...(p) GrantCockburn(5) 83
(Lucinda Russell) *mde most to 7th: w ldrs: drvn and outpcd bef 3 out: n.d after* 17/2[3]

1P-P **5** 21 **Madam Lilibet (IRE)**[12] 1925 6-10-12 108... FinianO'Toole(7) 68
(Sharon Watt) *in last but in tch early: sn drvn along: lost tch fr 1/2-way: nvr on terms* 9/1

60-4 **6** *2* **Ha'penny Woods (IRE)**[18] [2070] 5-11-2 **110**........... DiarmuidO'Regan(5) 68
(Chris Grant) *trckd ldrs: chal 3rd: led 7th to after 4 out: rdn and wknd next* **17/2**[3]

6m 32.6s (0.80) **Going Correction** +0.175s/f (Yiel) **6** Ran SP% **90.1**
Speed ratings (Par 105): **105,103,102,98,91 90**
CSF £8.33 TOTE £2.00: £1.10, £2.90; EX 7.60 Trifecta £37.30.
Owner Hugh Hodge Ltd **Bred** J P Hand **Trained** Kinneston, Perth & Kinross
■ Quel Elite was withdrawn. Price at time of withdrawal 7-2. Rule 4 applies to all bets - deduction 20p in the pound.

FOCUS
A fair staying handicap hurdle, though weakened slightly when the second-favourite Quel Elite was withdrawn on vet's advice. The pace was only ordinary, but the winner is on the upgrade.

2433 TRIAL RACING UK FOR FREE NOW MARES' STANDARD OPEN NATIONAL HUNT FLAT RACE 2m
3:50 (3:54) (Class 6) 4-6-Y-O **£1,711** (£498; £249)

Form RPR
05- **1** **My Little Cracker (IRE)**[332] [3100] 5-10-12 0...................... BrianHarding 109+
(Iain Jardine) *t.k.h early: led 3f: pressed ldr: led over 6f out to 4f out: rallied and regained ld over 1f out: rdn clr fnl f* **10/1**

431- **2** *12* **Ten Trees**[232] [4975] 5-11-0 0.................................. DaraghBourke(5) 104
(Alan Swinbank) *cl up: led 4f out: drvn and hdd over 1f out: kpt on same pce* **6/4**[1]

3 *½* **Better Back Bracka (IRE)**[122] [984] 4-10-5 0................(t[1]) MrSPKelly(7) 96
(Noel C Kelly, Ire) *chsd ldrs: effrt and pushed along over 2f out: kpt on same pce over 1f out* **9/2**[3]

4 *¾* **Siena Bouquet (FR)** 4-10-12 0................................ MrSCrawford 95
(S R B Crawford, Ire) *hld up: stdy hdwy and in tch over 2f out: sn rdn: 3rd and outpcd whn veered rt ins fnl f* **13/8**[2]

0 **5** *9* **Solway Sunrise**[48] [1640] 4-10-7 0.......................... CallumBewley(5) 86
(Lisa Harrison) *in tch: drvn and outpcd over 4f out: btn over 2f out* **80/1**

4- **6** *1 ¼* **Maura Lily (IRE)**[313] [3487] 6-10-9 0.......................... GrahamWatters(3) 85
(Ian Duncan) *t.k.h early: in tch: drvn and outpcd over 4f out: sn struggling* **25/1**

7 *62* **Rambling Rosie (IRE)** 6-10-5 0........................... AlisonClarke(7) 23
(J J Lambe, Ire) *t.k.h: cl up: hdwy to ld after 3f: hdd over 6f out: sn struggling: eased whn no ch fnl 3f* **25/1**

3m 59.7s (239.70)
WFA 4 from 5yo+ 7lb **7** Ran SP% **114.3**
CSF £25.64 TOTE £13.10: £4.60, £1.30; EX 21.30 Trifecta £133.80.
Owner Paul & Clare Rooney **Bred** Martin Sheridan **Trained** Carrutherstown, D'fries & G'way

FOCUS
An average mares' bumper and a rather messy affair following a ragged start, but the winner was impressive.
T/Plt: £51.80 to a £1 stake. Pool: £49,424.00 - 696 winning tickets T/Qpdt: £4.80 to a £1 stake. Pool: £3,931.00 - 594.72 winning tickets **Richard Young**

2121 BANGOR-ON-DEE (L-H)
Wednesday, November 11

OFFICIAL GOING: Soft (6.1)
Wind: fresh 1/2 behind Weather: overcast

2434 FRIENDS OF THE ANIMAL HEALTH TRUST H'CAP CHASE (FOR THE TARPORLEY HUNT CUP) (QUALIFIER) (15 fncs) 2m 4f 72y
1:00 (1:00) (Class 4) (0-120,120) 4-Y-O+ **£3,898** (£1,144; £572; £286)

Form RPR
3-3P **1** **Uhlan Bute (FR)**[175] [403] 7-11-1 **109**...........................(p) LiamTreadwell 130+
(Venetia Williams) *led 2nd: mde rest: j.rt 2 out: sn wnt clr: heavily eased last 150yds* **11/4**[1]

14-4 **2** *11* **Take The Crown**[28] [1907] 6-10-8 **102**..........................(t) JamesDavies 102
(Henry Oliver) *sn chsng ldrs: drvn 3 out: one pce fr next* **9/2**[3]

55-6 **3** *hd* **Cyclop (IRE)**[13] [2151] 4-11-0 **117**...........................(tp) NoelFehily 108
(David Dennis) *led to 2nd: chsd ldrs: drvn 9th: lost pl next: blnd 3 out: t.o 5th next: styd on and 3rd last: kpt on run-in* **9/1**

6 **4** *9* **Morney Wing (IRE)**[25] [1970] 6-11-12 **120**.........................(p) DarylJacob 113
(Charlie Mann) *chsd ldrs: rdn 3 out: wknd next* **6/1**

5-03 **5** *6* **Trapper Peak (IRE)**[28] [1906] 6-11-7 **115**..................... AndrewThornton 101
(Caroline Bailey) *hld up wl in tch: chsd ldrs 10th: rdn 4 out: lost pl bef next* **3/1**[2]

P-46 **P** **Gus Macrae (IRE)**[25] [1965] 11-10-12 **106**........................(bt[1]) SeanBowen
(Rebecca Curtis) *chsd ldrs: reminders 8th: sn lost pl: t.o 10th: p.u bef next: b.b.v* **15/2**

4154 **P** **Tribal Dance (IRE)**[26] [1950] 9-9-9 **94** oh7......................(b) JamieBargary(5)
(John O'Shea) *chsd ldrs: drvn and dropped to rr 3rd: reluctant and reminders next: t.o 6th: p.u bef next* **22/1**

5m 26.4s (17.30) **Going Correction** +0.575s/f (Soft)
WFA 4 from 6yo+ 8lb **7** Ran SP% **110.2**
Speed ratings (Par 105): **88,83,83,79,77 ,**
CSF £14.61 TOTE £3.90: £1.90, £2.10; EX 18.00 Trifecta £110.60.
Owner R Elliott & N Coe, S Graham & C Watson **Bred** Herve D'Armaille **Trained** Kings Caple, H'fords
■ Stewards' Enquiry : Sean Bowen two-day ban: used whip in incorrect place (Nov 25-26)

FOCUS
Liam Treadwell, who won the first two races, described the ground as "soft, a bit dead", and another senior rider called it "very gluey". The winner set a decent clip in this fair handicap and the form has a sound look to it.

2435 REA VALLEY TRACTORS SIR JOHN HANMER NOVICES' LIMITED H'CAP CHASE (15 fncs) 2m 4f 72y
1:30 (1:31) (Class 4) (0-120,118) 4-Y-O+ **£6,498** (£1,908; £954; £477)

Form RPR
10-6 **1** **John Louis**[47] [1642] 7-11-0 **110**.................................. LiamTreadwell 127+
(Venetia Williams) *chsd ldrs: clr 2nd appr 2 out: led sn after last: drvn out* **6/1**[3]

/012 **2** *2* **Dartford Warbler (IRE)**[38] [1784] 8-11-2 **112**...................... DannyCook 126+
(Sue Smith) *led: jnd whn hit last: sn hdd: edgd lft and kpt on same pce last 50yds* **5/2**[1]

50-3 **3** *26* **Take The Cash (IRE)**[193] [76] 6-11-8 **118**.................. WayneHutchinson 107
(Donald McCain) *trckd ldrs: 2nd 5th: upsides 4 out: wknd appr 2 out: hit last* **5/1**[2]

0002 **4** *3* **Queen Spud**[21] [2022] 6-10-11 **107**................................. JakeGreenall 90
(Henry Daly) *in rr: hdwy 7th: outpcd 11th: wnt poor 4th last* **22/1**

546- **5** *6* **Troika Steppes**[226] [5059] 7-10-10 **106**............................ PaddyBrennan 89
(Fergal O'Brien) *in rr: pckd landing 2nd: hit next and rdr briefly lost iron: mstke 10th: sn lost pl: poor 4th whn mstke last* **12/1**

610- **6** *29* **Gamain (IRE)**[221] [5139] 6-11-4 **114**...............................(p) DarylJacob 62
(Ben Case) *chsd ldrs: lost pl bef 4 out: sn wl bhd: t.o 2 out* **13/2**

020/ **P** **Sir Pitt**[574] [5353] 8-10-11 **107**....................................(tp) TomCannon
(David Bridgwater) *hld up: trckd ldrs 4th: outpcd 4 out: poor 5th whn p.u bef 2 out* **15/2**

1160 **F** **Modeligo (IRE)**[47] [1647] 6-9-11 **100**............................(t) MrStanSheppard(7)
(Matt Sheppard) *hld up towards rr: fell 8th* **6/1**[3]

5m 25.9s (16.80) **Going Correction** +0.575s/f (Soft) **8** Ran SP% **110.9**
Speed ratings (Par 105): **89,88,77,76,74 62, ,**
CSF £20.93 CT £76.39 TOTE £6.80: £1.70, £1.40, £1.60; EX 25.50 Trifecta £69.40.
Owner Miss V M Williams **Bred** Wood Farm Stud (Waresley) **Trained** Kings Caple, H'fords

FOCUS
The first two finished clear in this reasonable novice handicap and the winner is on the upgrade. The time was half a second quicker than that for the opener.

2436 ANNE DUCHESS OF WESTMINSTER MEMORIAL H'CAP CHASE (18 fncs) 3m 30y
2:00 (2:04) (Class 2) (0-150,145) 4-Y-O+ **£16,825** (£4,675; £2,337; £1,170; £585)

Form RPR
U6-F **1** **What A Good Night (IRE)**[13] [2149] 7-10-4 **123**................(t) HarrySkelton 132
(Dan Skelton) *in rr: hdwy 9th: sn chsng ldrs: 2nd appr 2 out: styd on to ld towards fin* **9/1**

R30- **2** *nk* **Algernon Pazham (IRE)**[200] [5538] 6-11-2 **135**........ SamTwiston-Davies 144
(Nigel Twiston-Davies) *trckd ldrs: led 8th: rdn and edgd lft between last 2: hdd and no ex nr fin* **11/4**[1]

/00- **3** *10* **Restless Harry**[361] [2491] 11-11-7 **140**........................... JamesDavies 140
(Henry Oliver) *chsd ldrs: one pce appr 2 out* **9/1**

156- **4** *½* **Achimota (IRE)**[213] [5289] 9-10-4 **123**............................ KielanWoods 123
(Graeme McPherson) *rr-div: hdwy 4 out: kpt on fr 2 out: nvr a factor* **22/1**

424- **5** *8* **Araldur (FR)**[250] [4613] 11-11-0 **133**........................... WayneHutchinson 126
(Alan King) *mid-div: chsd ldrs 6th: hit 12th: drvn 4 out: wknd appr 2 out* **16/1**

32-1 **6** *94* **Fergal Mael Duin**[21] [2014] 7-10-3 **122**............................(p) TomCannon 19
(David Bridgwater) *chsd ldrs: lost pl after 3 out: sn bhd: tailed rt off: eventually completed* **15/2**[2]

/FP- **P** **Dare Me (IRE)**[244] [4720] 11-11-10 **143**............................ LiamTreadwell
(Venetia Williams) *in rr: sme hdwy 12th: lost pl 14th: t.o whn p.u bef 2 out* **14/1**

0F-0 **P** **Portrait King (IRE)**[193] [92] 10-11-4 **137**................................ JJBurke
(Patrick Griffin, Ire) *mid-div: lost pl and drvn 7th: sn bhd: t.o whn p.u after 14th* **33/1**

1U-P **P** **Knock A Hand (IRE)**[193] [95] 10-11-9 **142**...........................(b) JamieMoore
(Kerry Lee) *chsd ldrs: drvn 8th: lost pl 10th: sn bhd: p.u bef 14th* **28/1**

45-0 **P** **Cloudy Too (IRE)**[11] [2194] 9-11-12 **145**............................ DannyCook
(Sue Smith) *in rr: sme hdwy 12th: lost pl after 14th: sn bhd: t.o whn p.u bef 2 out* **11/1**

1PP- **P** **Bob Ford (IRE)**[214] [5275] 8-11-3 **136**................................ SeanBowen
(Rebecca Curtis) *chsd ldrs: lost pl 11th: sn bhd: t.o 3 out: p.u bef next* **14/1**

1F5- **P** **Catching On (IRE)**[207] [5392] 7-11-4 **137**................................ NoelFehily
(Jonjo O'Neill) *in rr: sme hdwy 11th: lost pl 13th: sn bhd: t.o whn p.u bef 3 out* **8/1**[3]

11-5 **P** **Shantou Magic (IRE)**[33] [1840] 8-11-8 **141**........................ WillKennedy
(Charlie Longsdon) *led to 8th: 4th and wkng whn blnd 2 out: sn eased: distant 6th whn p.u between last 2* **9/1**

6m 27.0s (7.20) **Going Correction** +0.575s/f (Soft) **13** Ran SP% **117.8**
Speed ratings (Par 109): **111,110,107,107,104 73, , , , ,**
CSF £33.93 CT £236.18 TOTE £9.70: £3.50, £1.10, £3.60; EX 35.30 Trifecta £455.70.
Owner Mr & Mrs Gordon Pink **Bred** Miss Jane Mangan **Trained** Alcester, Warwicks

FOCUS
A very competitive race for this valuable prize. The winner is on the upgrade and the form looks sound.

2437 BRONCROFT NOVICES' HURDLE (9 hdls) 2m 145y
2:30 (2:37) (Class 4) 4-Y-O+ **£3,249** (£954; £477; £238)

Form RPR
1 **Its'afreebee (IRE)**[55] [1567] 5-10-12 0................................ JJBurke 118+
(Mark Fahey, Ire) *led to 2nd: hit 3rd: led next forged clr between last 2* **15/8**[1]

5-P **2** *8* **Itshard To No (IRE)**[63] [1521] 6-11-5 117......................(t) JamieMoore 116
(Kerry Lee) *hld up towards rr: hdwy 5th: 2nd appr 2 out: kpt on same pce: no imp* **12/1**

3 *5* **Pilgrims Rest (IRE)**[72] 6-10-12 0...................................(t) AndrewTinkler 106+
(George Baker) *hld up in rr: hdwy sn after 3 out: modest 3rd whn blnd 2 out: one pce* **33/1**

06- **4** *11* **Baraza (FR)**[228] [5028] 4-10-12 0................................... PaddyBrennan 93
(Tom George) *hld up in mid-div: chsd ldrs 4th: mstke 3 out: wknd appr next* **25/1**

00/3 **5** *7* **Valseur Du Granval (FR)**[41] [1718] 6-10-12 ....(t) SamTwiston-Davies 86
(Tom George) *hld up in rr: hdwy to chse ldrs 5th: lost pl bef 2 out* **3/1**[2]

0 **6** *1 ¾* **The Artful Cobbler**[186] [213] 4-10-12 0............................ JakeGreenall 85
(Henry Daly) *t.k.h: trckd ldrs 4th: lost pl 3 out* **100/1**

P **Bonne Question (FR)**[898] 6-10-12 0................................ LiamTreadwell
(Venetia Williams) *t.k.h: trckd ldr: led 2nd: hdd 4th: wknd qckly 6th: sn bhd: t.o whn p.u bef last* **17/2**

43-P **P** **Deadly Move (IRE)**[63] [1519] 6-10-12 0.............................. SeanBowen
(Peter Bowen) *chsd ldrs: lost pl after 3 out: sn bhd: t.o whn p.u bef last* **9/1**

P **Bird D'Estruval (FR)**[76] 4-11-5 0...................................... DarylJacob
(David Pipe) *chsd ldrs: outpcd 6th: sn lost pl: t.o whn p.u bef 2 out* **4/1**[3]

4m 28.1s (17.20) **Going Correction** +1.275s/f (Heav) **9** Ran SP% **115.8**
Speed ratings (Par 105): **110,106,103,98,95 94, , ,**
CSF £25.40 TOTE £2.90: £1.20, £2.90, £5.90; EX 25.50 Trifecta £250.40.
Owner Mrs Maureen Fahey **Bred** Edward Sexton **Trained** Cloneygath, Co Kildare

FOCUS
Actual race distance 2m 189yds. This novice hurdle appeared to be steadily run, turning into a sprint from the home turn. As such the form may not be entirely solid.

2438 SPURLING SUPPORTING THE AHT H'CAP HURDLE (11 hdls) 2m 3f 123y
3:00 (3:02) (Class 2) 4-Y-0+ **£14,620** (£4,293; £2,146; £1,073)

Form RPR
P0-0 1 **Foxcub (IRE)**[39] 1754 7-11-2 **134** JamesDavies 143+
(Tom Symonds) *chsd ldrs: led 7th: drvn wl clr between last 2: kpt up to work* **6/1**
01-1 2 *22* **After Eight Sivola (FR)**[39] 1754 5-10-5 **128** LizzieKelly(5) 125
(Nick Williams) *hld up in rr: hdwy 6th: sn chsng ldrs: clr 2nd bef 3 out: wknd bef last: eased run-in* **3/1**[1]
20-0 3 *27* **Rock On Rocky**[31] 1868 7-11-0 **132** (p) CharliePoste 92
(Matt Sheppard) *w ldr: led 6th: hdd next: sn lost pl and bhd* **15/2**
11/F 4 *10* **Royal Boy (FR)**[4] 2334 8-11-12 **144** SeanBowen 94
(Rebecca Curtis) *trckd ldrs: wknd 8th: distant 4th whn hit next* **7/1**
F00- P **Chieftain's Choice (IRE)**[214] 5276 6-10-12 **130** SamTwiston-Davies
(Kevin Frost) *led: hdd 7th: sn lost pl: bhd whn p.u bef next* **5/1**[3]
211- P **Gold Present (IRE)**[219] 5201 5-11-4 **136** AndrewTinkler
(Nicky Henderson) *chsd ldrs 3rd: lost pl after 8th: distant 5th whn p.u bef 2 out* **10/3**[2]
P- P **Azert De Coeur (FR)**[277] 4099 5-10-0 **118** oh4 LiamTreadwell
(Venetia Williams) *nt fluent in last: pushed along 5th: sn bhd: t.o whn p.u bef 7th* **11/1**

5m 14.7s (22.70) **Going Correction** +1.275s/f (Heavy) **7 Ran SP% 111.6**
Speed ratings (Par 109): **105,96,85,81,**
CSF £23.58 CT £133.11 TOTE £6.80: £3.20, £1.40; EX 29.80 Trifecta £172.00.
Owner Celia & Michael Baker **Bred** St Clare Hall Stud **Trained** Harewood End, H'fords

FOCUS
Actual race distance 2m 189yds. The first two had this decent prize between them from the third-last.

2439 ALBERT BARTLETT JUVENILE MAIDEN HURDLE (9 hdls) 2m 145y
3:30 (3:37) (Class 4) 3-Y-0 **£3,249** (£954; £477; £238)

Form RPR
6 1 **Sikandar (IRE)**[46] 1656 3-10-12 0 [1] DannyCook 110+
(Brian Ellison) *hld up in rr: hdwy to trck ldrs 4th: cl 2nd 2 out: sn led: clr last: eased clsng stages* **2/1**[1]
3 2 *6* **Sky Lino (FR)**[31] 1866 3-10-7 0 LizzieKelly(5) 104+
(Nick Williams) *uns rdr and rn loose for abt one m: t.k.h: w ldr: led 4th: hdd sn after 2 out: wknd bef last* **9/4**[2]
3 *14* **Haut Bages (FR)**[148] 3-10-12 0 DarylJacob 92
(Oliver Sherwood) *trckd ldrs: t.k.h: awkward 1st: 2nd 6th: drvn appr 2 out: sn wknd* **9/4**[2]
4 *44* **Baler Boy**[14] 3-10-12 0 MichaelByrne 45
(Des Donovan) *led to 4th: lost pl bef 3 out: sn wl bhd: t.o 2 out: eventually completed* **150/1**
P **Qatea (IRE)**[188] 3-10-12 0 WayneHutchinson
(Donald McCain) *trckd ldrsm: t.k.h: reminders 4th: drvn 6th: sn lost pl and bhd: t.o whn p.u bef 2 out* **15/2**[3]
5 P **Rio Falls (IRE)**[12] 2172 3-10-12 0 PeterCarberry
(Jennie Candlish) *in rr: outpcd and drvn 5th: sn bhd: t.o 3 out: p.u bef next* **20/1**
5 P **Put The Boot In (IRE)**[20] 2032 3-10-12 0 TrevorWhelan
(Barry Brennan) *mid-div: bhd and drvn 5th: sn bhd: t.o whn p.u bef 3 out* **25/1**

4m 38.0s (27.10) **Going Correction** +1.275s/f (Heavy) **7 Ran SP% 115.9**
Speed ratings (Par 104): **87,84,77,56,**
CSF £7.18 TOTE £2.80: £1.40, £2.70; EX 10.30 Trifecta £18.00.
Owner Mrs J A Martin **Bred** His Highness The Aga Khan's Studs S C **Trained** Norton, N Yorks

FOCUS
Actual race distance 2m 189yds. Probably a fair juvenile hurdle, which proved quite a test in the conditions. A big step up from the winner who is entitled to rate higher on Flat form.

2440 TREASURE BEACH HOTEL SUPPORTING THE AHT STANDARD OPEN NATIONAL HUNT FLAT RACE 2m 145y
4:00 (4:03) (Class 6) 4-6-Y-0 **£1,711** (£498; £249)

Form RPR
1 **Compadre (IRE)** 4-11-4 0 NoelFehily 110+
(Jonjo O'Neill) *hld up towards rr: hdwy to trck ldrs 6f out: led over 2f out: edgd lft and drew clr over 1f out: readily* **5/4**[1]
2 *8* **Wild West Wind (IRE)**[605] 6-11-4 0 PaddyBrennan 99
(Tom George) *led: hdd narrowly 8f out: led narrowly over 3f out: hdd over 2f out: kpt on fnl f: tk modest 2nd clsng stages* **15/2**
3 *1* **Mister Kalanisi (IRE)**[955] 6-11-4 0 HarrySkelton 98
(Dan Skelton) *hld up in rr: hdwy to trck ldrs 6f out: chal over 2f out: kpt on same pce: fdd and lost modest 2nd clsng stages* **11/2**[3]
4 *2½* **Hastrubal (FR)** 5-11-4 0 JakeGreenall 96
(Henry Daly) *chsd ldrs: drvn over 3f out: sn outpcd and lost pl: kpt on fnl f* **16/1**
5 *6* **Highway Storm (IRE)**[353] 5-11-4 0 SeanBowen 91
(Rebecca Curtis) *w ldeer: led narrowly 8f out: hdd over 3f out: lost pl and stmbld over 2f out* **9/4**[2]
6 *11* **Artiste Du Gouet (FR)**[214] 5-10-11 0 MissADalton(7) 79
(Heather Dalton) *chsd ldrs: drvn over 3f out: sn lost pl and bhd* **25/1**
0 7 *34* **Manton Boy**[15] 2126 6-11-4 0 KielanWoods 45
(Michael Mullineaux) *trckd ldrs: t.k.h: drvn and outpcd over 5f out: sn bhd: t.o whn eased over 1f out* **66/1**

4m 29.6s (24.30) **Going Correction** +1.275s/f (Heavy)
WFA 4 from 5yo+ 7lb **7 Ran SP% 113.6**
Speed ratings: **93,89,88,87,84 79,63**
CSF £11.55 TOTE £2.00: £1.30, £3.80; EX 11.60 Trifecta £32.50.
Owner Mrs John Magnier, D Smith & M Tabor **Bred** Philip Hore **Trained** Cheltenham, Gloucs

FOCUS
Actual race distance 2m 189yds. They took things steadily in what looked an ordinary bumper.
T/Plt: £31.40 to a £1 stake. Pool: £41,124.67 - 954.87 winning tickets T/Qpdt: £19.00 to a £1 stake. Pool: £4,281.07 - 166.04 winning tickets **Walter Glynn**

2257 EXETER (R-H)
Wednesday, November 11

OFFICIAL GOING: Soft (heavy in places; chs 6.3, hdl 5.9)
Wind: mild breeze behind Weather: overcast Rails: Chase: north bend moved out 6yds. Hurdle bends moved out 2yds. New distances - Races 1 & 3 +22yds, 2, 6 & 7 +15yds, 4 & 5 +21yds.

2441 THANK YOU TO VETERANS AND SERVING MILITARY H'CAP HURDLE (11 hdls 1 omitted) 2m 7f 25y
1:10 (1:10) (Class 4) (0-120,119) 4-Y-0+ **£3,898** (£1,144; £572; £286)

Form RPR
-221 1 **Monbeg Gold (IRE)**[8] 2262 5-12-5 **119** 7ex RichardJohnson 131+
(Jonjo O'Neill) *travelled wl thrght: trckd ldrs: wnt 2nd at the 6th: led briefly appr 3 out: regained ld on bridle whn blnd next: drew clr: v easily* **4/6**[1]
3035 2 *18* **Storm Alert**[15] 2125 8-10-6 **95** LucyGardner(3) 92+
(Sue Gardner) *j.lft at times: chsd ldrs: hit 7th: rdn after next: led appr 3 out: hdd bef 2 out: sn no ch w wnr* **8/1**
55-5 3 *29* **Shoofly Milly (IRE)**[191] 108 6-11-5 **105** LiamHeard 61
(Jeremy Scott) *hld up in last pair: struggling but remained in tch fr 6th: wnt 4th u.p after 8th: wnt btn 3rd bef next: sn wknd: t.o* **33/1**
424- 4 *58* **Bravo Riquet (FR)**[231] 4988 9-10-9 **100** (vt) JakeHodson(5)
(David Bridgwater) *led: clr 3rd tl after 7th: rdn and hdd after 8th: sn wknd: t.o* **16/1**
242 F **Dusk Till Dawn (IRE)**[28] 1912 6-11-2 **102** ConorO'Farrell
(David Pipe) *chsd ldrs: nudged along 6th: wknd after 8th: tailing off whn fell heavily 2 out* **5/1**[2]
2232 P **Midnight Sapphire**[12] 2167 5-10-10 **106** (t) MrJakeBament(10)
(Victor Dartnall) *chsd ldr: struggling after 6th: wknd qckly after next: sn p.u* **6/1**[3]

6m 8.2s (9.20) **Going Correction** +0.55s/f (Soft) **6 Ran SP% 110.9**
Speed ratings (Par 105): **106,99,89,69,**
CSF £6.60 TOTE £1.60: £1.10, £3.30; EX 6.00 Trifecta £64.60.
Owner Martin Broughton Racing Partners 2 **Bred** Frank Marshall **Trained** Cheltenham, Gloucs

FOCUS
Chase north bend moved out 6yds, Hurdle bends moved out 2yds. Race 1 +32yds, Race 2 +15yds, Race 3 +32yds, Race 4 +21yds, Race 5 +21yds, Race 6 +15yds, Race 7 +15yds. The hurdle after the winning post was omitted in all hurdles races. Richard Johnson said of the ground: "It's heavy. It's hard work and very sticky". This took little winning, with the odds-on favourite's two main market rivals failing to fire. The easy winner looks a decent prospect, though.

2442 188BET.CO.UK NOVICES' LIMITED H'CAP CHASE (18 fncs) 3m 54y
1:40 (1:40) (Class 3) (0-135,135) 4-Y-0+ **£6,498** (£1,908; £954; £477)

Form RPR
15-5 1 **Wizards Bridge**[31] 1867 6-10-10 **123** (p) AidanColeman 133+
(Colin Tizzard) *prom: led 4 out: nodded on landing 2 out: hdd sn after last: rallied wl to ld fnl strides: drvn rt out* **9/2**[3]
03-2 2 *hd* **St Dominick (IRE)**[176] 389 8-10-3 **116** oh4 JamesBest 125
(Jackie Du Plessis) *hld up: gd hdwy to chal 4 out: rdn after 2 out: led sn after last: drifted lft: hdd fnl strides* **28/1**
F16- 3 *8* **Heronshaw (IRE)**[226] 5075 8-10-12 **125** TomO'Brien 126
(Henry Daly) *led: rdn and hdd 4 out: kpt pressing ldrs tl no ex appr last* **14/1**
322- 4 *3¾* **Dancing Shadow (IRE)**[203] 5469 6-10-11 **124** DenisO'Regan 121
(Victor Dartnall) *prom: rdn and ev ch appr 4 out: hld fr 3 out: styd on same pce* **11/1**
60-2 5 *7* **Rydon Pynes**[33] 1839 7-11-3 **130** NicodeBoinville 121
(Martin Hill) *in tch: tk clsr order 11th: mounting chal whn short of room 4 out: sn rdn: hld whn hit 2 out: wknd* **4/1**[2]
306- 6 *7* **Onderun (IRE)**[277] 4097 6-10-3 **116** GavinSheehan 100
(Emma Lavelle) *hld up in tch: struggling after 14th: nvr threatened: btn 4 out* **7/2**[1]
22-3 7 *nk* **Cloudy Copper (IRE)**[31] 1867 8-11-8 **135** RichardJohnson 118
(Jonjo O'Neill) *in tch: tk clsr order 6th: short-lived effrt appr 4 out: sn btn* **7/2**[1]
231- 8 *6* **Krackatoa King**[257] 4477 7-10-13 **129** (p) JamesBanks(3) 106
(Noel Williams) *chsd ldrs: pushed along appr 11th: wknd 4 out* **10/1**
11/ P **Mountain Tunes (IRE)**[692] 3177 6-11-2 **129** RichieMcLernon
(Jonjo O'Neill) *hld up: wknd after 13th: t.o whn p.u bef 4 out* **14/1**

6m 36.7s (27.40) **Going Correction** +1.05s/f (Soft) **9 Ran SP% 116.8**
Speed ratings (Par 107): **96,95,93,92,89 87,87,85,**
CSF £100.66 CT £1634.25 TOTE £6.30: £1.80, £4.70, £3.30; EX 41.60 Trifecta £1902.80 Part won..
Owner The Butterwick Syndicate **Bred** Shade Oak Stud **Trained** Milborne Port, Dorset

FOCUS
Ordinary chasing form, but a race that should produce winners at a similar level.

2443 188BET NOVICES' HURDLE (10 hdls 1 omitted) 2m 5f 135y
2:10 (2:11) (Class 4) 4-Y-0+ **£4,548** (£1,335; £667; £333)

Form RPR
1 1 **Roll The Dough (IRE)**[21] 2023 6-11-5 0 RichardJohnson 120+
(Philip Hobbs) *mde all: j.lft: shkn up after 3 out: styd on wl and in command fr next* **10/11**[1]
0 2 *6* **Thegreendalerocket (IRE)**[12] 2163 6-10-5 0 PaulO'Brien(7) 104
(Jimmy Frost) *trckd ldrs: rdn to chse wnr after 3 out: styd on but a being readily hld* **50/1**
0- 3 *3¾* **According To Harry (IRE)**[178] 6-10-12 0 TomO'Brien 99
(Philip Hobbs) *trckd wnr: rdn appr 3 out: styd on same pce fr 2 out* **3/1**[2]
15 4 *2¾* **Arthur Burrell**[33] 1843 6-10-12 0 JamesBest 97
(Jackie Du Plessis) *hld up: hdwy 7th: rdn to chal for 2nd appr 3 out tl appr 2 out: styd on same pce* **5/1**[3]
560- P **Somerset Jem**[249] 4624 6-10-12 0 BrendanPowell
(Kevin Bishop) *chsd ldrs: struggling 6th: wknd after next: t.o whn p.u bef last* **8/1**

5m 53.0s (20.00) **Going Correction** +0.80s/f (Soft) **5 Ran SP% 107.1**
Speed ratings (Par 105): **95,92,91,90,**
CSF £24.29 TOTE £1.50: £1.10, £15.00; EX 30.20 Trifecta £63.50.
Owner The Kingpins **Bred** Noel O'Brien **Trained** Withycombe, Somerset

FOCUS
Little depth to this novice hurdle and the favourite won nicely despite not having to be at his best.

2444 JACK FLETCHER MEMORIAL MARES' NOVICES' HURDLE (9 hdls 1 omitted) 2m 2f 111y
2:40 (2:42) (Class 4) 4-Y-0+ **£3,249** (£954; £477; £238)

Form RPR
4- **1** **Drumviredy (IRE)**[364] [2454] 6-10-10 0........................ AidanColeman 103+
(Venetia Williams) *trckd ldrs: led 3 out gng best: nt fluent next but a in command: eased towards fin* **2/1**[1]
00-4 **2** *1 ½* **Bourdello**[32] [1845] 6-10-7 0........................ JamesBanks(3) 95
(Emma Baker) *in tch: trckd ldrs 4th: ev ch 3 out: sn rdn to chse wnr: kpt on same pce* **16/1**
-465 **3** *nk* **Palmaria**[39] [1752] 5-10-10 0........................ JamesBest 95
(Caroline Keevil) *hld up in tch: hdwy after 6th: sltly outpcd 3 out: styd on again fr last: nrly snatched 2nd nring fin* **40/1**
434- **4** *2* **Jully Les Buxy**[257] [4478] 5-10-10 0........................ NickScholfield 94
(Robert Walford) *trckd ldrs: ev ch 3 out: sn rdn: styd on same pce fr next* **10/3**[3]
3515 **5** *9* **Belcanto (IRE)**[25] [1960] 5-10-10 0........................ BrendanPowell 87
(Jamie Snowden) *trckd ldr: hmpd 4th led next: rdn and hdd 3 out: kpt chsng ldrs tl wknd last* **9/2**
46- **6** *40* **Mrsrobin (IRE)**[237] [4866] 5-10-10 0........................ GavinSheehan 44
(Emma Lavelle) *j.lft bdly at times: led tl jumping bdly lft 4th: wknd bef 3 out: t.o* **3/1**[2]
7 *42* **Arty Bella**[227] 4-10-3 0........................ MissBFrost(7)
(Jimmy Frost) *hld up: lost tch after 6th: t.o* **18/1**
P/ **8** *20* **Midnight Hop**[179] 8-10-3 0........................ ThomasCheesman(7)
(Nick Ayliffe) *trckd ldrs: struggling after 5th: wknd after next: t.o* **66/1**

5m 1.8s (19.10) **Going Correction** +0.80s/f (Soft)
WFA 4 from 5yo+ 7lb **8 Ran SP% 114.7**
Speed ratings (Par 105): **91,90,90,89,85 68,51,42**
CSF £34.75 TOTE £2.80: £1.10, £4.20, £7.40; EX 28.10 Trifecta £286.80.
Owner The M Shones **Bred** S McElroy **Trained** Kings Caple, H'fords

FOCUS
Modest mares' form, but a progressive winner.

2445 RGB BUILDING SUPPLIES H'CAP HURDLE (7 hdls 1 omitted) 2m 175y
3:10 (3:10) (Class 3) (0-135,125) 3-Y-0+ **£6,498** (£1,908; £954; £477)

Form RPR
151- **1** **Pull The Chord (IRE)**[308] [3576] 5-11-12 125........................ RichardJohnson 140+
(Philip Hobbs) *trckd ldrs: rdn to ld 2 out: styd on wl to assert fr last: rdn out* **15/8**[1]
20-0 **2** *4 ½* **Sirop De Menthe (FR)**[54] [1579] 5-10-7 109........................ LucyGardner(3) 118
(Sue Gardner) *led 2nd: rdn whn jnd 3 out: hdd 2 out: hld bef last where wnt lft: kpt on same pce* **9/4**[2]
135- **3** *24* **Clyne**[223] [5112] 5-11-4 117........................ PaulMoloney 106
(Evan Williams) *j.lft at times: racd keenly: led after 1st tl next: trckd ldrs: rdn appr 3 out: sn wknd* **3/1**[3]
00-P **4** *19* **Thundering Home**[81] [1325] 8-11-6 122........................(t) TomBellamy(3) 87
(Richard Mitchell) *j.lft at times: trckd ldrs: effrt after 4th: wknd qckly bef next: blnd last: t.o* **8/1**
141- **5** *1 ¾* **Tamarillo Grove (IRE)**[433] [1441] 8-11-4 122........................(t) DannyBurton(5) 85
(Sophie Leech) *led tl after 1st: trckd ldrs: rdn after 4th: wknd bef next: t.o* **14/1**
44-0 **6** *42* **Mystery Drama**[12] [2170] 5-10-9 115........................ MikeyHamill(7) 36
(Alexandra Dunn) *hld up: struggling after 3rd: wknd after next: t.o* **25/1**

4m 26.0s (10.50) **Going Correction** +0.80s/f (Soft) **6 Ran SP% 112.2**
Speed ratings (Par 107): **107,104,93,84,83 64**
CSF £6.74 TOTE £2.20: £1.60, £1.20; EX 6.50 Trifecta £21.20.
Owner Brocade Racing **Bred** Mrs Rosemary Ross **Trained** Withycombe, Somerset

FOCUS
The front pair came clear in what was an ordinary handicap. A step up from the winner and probably more to come.

2446 PLAY CASINO AT 188BET NOVICES' CHASE (12 fncs) 2m 1f 109y
3:40 (3:43) (Class 4) 4-Y-0+ **£4,548** (£1,335; £667; £333)

Form RPR
100- **1** **On Tour (IRE)**[243] [4741] 7-11-1 137........................ PaulMoloney 145+
(Evan Williams) *trckd ldr: shkn up after 2 out: nodded last: sn led: r.o wl* **9/4**[2]
132- **2** *½* **Otago Trail (IRE)**[231] [4985] 7-11-1 133........................ AidanColeman 143+
(Venetia Williams) *led: rdn after 3 out: hit next: rchd for last: sn hdd: kpt on but nt quite pce of wnr* **8/11**[1]
610- **3** *37* **Heath Hunter (IRE)**[249] [4633] 8-10-12 0........................(bt) KieronEdgar(3) 110
(David Pipe) *trckd ldrs: struggling and j.lft fr 8th: outpcd 4 out: wknd 2 out* **9/2**[3]
5-6 **4** *31* **Bredon Hill Lad**[8] [2262] 8-10-12 97........................ LucyGardner(3) 74
(Sue Gardner) *trckd ldrs: awkward 4th: lost tch after 8th: mstke 2 out: t.o* **66/1**

4m 37.1s (18.10) **Going Correction** +1.05s/f (Soft) **4 Ran SP% 108.3**
Speed ratings (Par 105): **99,98,81,66**
CSF £4.52 TOTE £4.00; EX 4.00 Trifecta £4.60.
Owner T Hywel Jones **Bred** Mrs Meliosa Walshe **Trained** Llancarfan, Vale Of Glamorgan

FOCUS
The two at the head of the market dominated this small-field novice. The pair have been rated in line with their hurdle marks.

2447 WATCH RACINGUK FREE WITH MONTH TRIAL H'CAP CHASE (15 fncs) 2m 3f 48y
4:10 (4:10) (Class 4) (0-110,110) 4-Y-0+ **£3,898** (£1,144; £572; £286)

Form RPR
0666 **1** **Legion D'Honneur (UAE)**[91] [1236] 10-9-12 85........................(tp) KieronEdgar(3) 101+
(Chris Down) *hld up bhd: smooth hdwy to chal 4 out: led next: in command whn rdr lost whip bef last: pushed out* **13/2**
33-1 **2** *2* **Ball Hopper (IRE)**[9] [2255] 11-10-0 84 7ex........................(p) RichieMcLernon 93
(Richenda Ford) *cl up: nudged along 9th: rdn appr 4 out: styd on fr 2 out to chse wnr last: kpt on but a being hld* **3/1**[2]
2223 **3** *8* **Railway Storm (IRE)**[21] [2017] 10-10-5 96........................ MissBFrost(7) 100
(Jimmy Frost) *cl up: rdn to chse wnr 3 out: hit next: no ex fr last* **6/1**[3]
33-4 **4** *6* **Ballyegan (IRE)**[188] [161] 10-10-6 90........................ LiamHeard 85
(Bob Buckler) *led tl 4 out: one pce fr next* **17/2**
3 **5** *1 ¾* **Royal Chief (IRE)**[17] [2090] 6-11-9 107........................(p) RhysFlint 100
(Alexandra Dunn) *trckd ldr: led 4 out tl next: hit 2 out: wknd bef last* **7/1**
153- **6** *74* **Buckhorn Tom**[253] [4546] 7-11-3 108........................(b) PaulO'Brien(7) 27
(Colin Tizzard) *trckd ldrs: j.rt and slow 6th: nvr travelling after: detached in last after 8th: nvr bk on terms: t.o* **9/4**[1]
P0-F **P** **Mini Muck**[24] [1985] 9-11-12 110........................ DaveCrosse
(Nigel Twiston-Davies) *in tch: reminder after 1st: blnd bdly next: nt fluent 3rd: sn p.u* **14/1**

5m 14.9s (17.60) **Going Correction** +1.05s/f (Soft) **7 Ran SP% 113.1**
Speed ratings (Par 105): **104,103,99,97,96 65,**
CSF £26.39 TOTE £8.30: £4.30, £1.70; EX 41.90 Trifecta £252.20.
Owner Mrs M Trueman **Bred** Darley **Trained** Mutterton, Devon

FOCUS
Not bad form for the level with the winner a 117-rated hurdlee at his peak.
T/Plt: £173.90 to a £1 stake. Pool: £37,112.45 - 155.73 winning tickets T/Qpdt: £18.00 to a £1 stake. Pool: £3,249.89 - 133.23 winning tickets **Tim Mitchell**

2245 LUDLOW (R-H)
Thursday, November 12

OFFICIAL GOING: Good to soft (6.7)
Wind: moderate, mainly behind Weather: light rain

2448 RACING UK FREE TRIAL 3 DEVICES JUVENILE HURDLE (9 hdls) 1m 7f 169y
1:30 (1:31) (Class 4) 3-Y-0 **£3,898** (£1,144; £572; £286)

Form RPR
1 **Who Dares Wins (IRE)**[34] 3-10-12 0........................ WayneHutchinson 106+
(Alan King) *trckd ldrs: mstke 6th: chal 3 out: sn rdn: r.o to ld fnl 50yds* **5/6**[1]
2 *¾* **Fouburg (FR)** 3-10-12 0........................ HarrySkelton 105+
(Dan Skelton) *t.k.h towards rr: nt clr run bnd appr 3 out: sn clsd gng wl: led narrowly bef 2 out: shkn up flat: hdd fnl 50yds: jst hld* **15/8**[2]
4 **3** *10* **Celestial Magic**[28] [1928] 3-10-7 0........................ DanielHiskett(5) 94
(Richard Phillips) *t.k.h in last: shkn up after 6th: clsd 3 out: outpcd by ldrs next: r.o to take 3rd flat* **14/1**[3]
4 *½* **Sandgate**[73] 3-10-12 0........................ MarkQuinlan 94
(Neil Mulholland) *chsd ldrs: ev ch 3 out: sn rdn and one pce: lost 3rd flat* **20/1**
00 **5** *13* **Midtech Star (IRE)**[8] [2273] 3-10-12 0........................ WillKennedy 81
(Ian Williams) *trckd ldr: j.lft 3rd: led next: hdd bef 2 out: grad wknd* **33/1**
0 **6** *12* **Light Breaks (IRE)**[8] [2273] 3-10-9 0........................ RyanHatch(3) 72
(Nigel Twiston-Davies) *led tl j. slowly 4th: styd cl up: rdn 3 out: sn wknd* **25/1**
7 *44* **Overlord**[40] 3-10-9 0........................ KillianMoore(3) 25
(Mark Rimell) *t.k.h towards rr: rdn after 6th: wknd 3 out: virtually p.u flat: t.o* **33/1**

3m 55.2s (5.70) **Going Correction** +0.05s/f (Yiel) **7 Ran SP% 110.5**
Speed ratings (Par 104): **87,86,81,81,74 68,46**
CSF £2.40 TOTE £1.50: £1.10, £1.30; EX 2.10 Trifecta £6.90.
Owner W H Ponsonby **Bred** Mount Coote Stud **Trained** Barbury Castle, Wilts

FOCUS
Rails out 6yds on Golf Club bend and 10yds out on Ludlow bend. Races 1 & 5 increased by 44yds, race 2 by 66yds, races 3 & 6 by 79yds and race 4 by 78yds. Little previous hurdles form to go on here, but the front pair came right away from two out and it looked a fair juvenile heat. The first two should rate higher.

2449 SUPPORT THE LUDLOW ON COURSE BOOKMAKERS NOVICES' LIMITED H'CAP CHASE (12 fncs) 1m 7f 212y
2:00 (2:02) (Class 4) (0-120,121) 4-Y-0+ **£7,472** (£2,194; £1,097; £548)

Form RPR
-211 **1** **Helium (FR)**[10] [2246] 10-11-10 121 7ex........................ RhysFlint 135+
(Alexandra Dunn) *chsd ldrs: led 4 out: readily c clr between last 2: easily* **7/2**[1]
45-5 **2** *12* **Queen Olivia**[192] [107] 7-10-3 103........................ ThomasGarner(3) 104
(Oliver Sherwood) *hld up: hdwy 6th: wnt 2nd 3 out: one pce and no ch w easy wnr fr next* **6/1**
12-5 **3** *8* **Grimley Girl**[38] [1793] 9-10-10 107........................ JamesDavies 100
(Henry Oliver) *chsd ldrs: led 2nd to 3rd: nt fluent 6th: ev ch 4 out: lost 2nd next: one pce* **11/2**[3]
03-4 **4** *3* **Under The Phone (IRE)**[25] [1985] 6-10-13 110........................ CharliePoste 100
(Robin Dickin) *cl up: led 3rd: rdn after 9th: hdd 4 out: wknd 2 out* **10/1**
025- **5** *4* **Saffron Prince**[206] [5427] 7-11-8 119........................ HarrySkelton 106
(David Bridgwater) *hld up: clsd 7th: rdn 4 out: grad wknd* **7/1**
3 **6** *8* **Akinspirit (IRE)**[21] [2048] 11-9-13 101........................(t) CharlieDeutsch(5) 80
(Nikki Evans) *mid-div: lost pl 8th: clsd again after next: hld whn sltly hmpd 3 out: sn wknd* **20/1**
2133 **7** *21* **The Bay Bandit**[29] [1907] 8-10-11 108........................(p) MarkQuinlan 71
(Neil Mulholland) *hld up: mstke 2nd: rdn and struggling 8th: clsd after next: wknd 3 out* **10/1**
414 **P** **Jackthejourneyman (IRE)**[42] [1720] 6-10-10 107........................(t) FelixDeGiles
(Tom Gretton) *wore eyeshield in paddock: wnt to post early: led to 2nd: styd prom: rdn 4 out: wknd next: bhd whn p.u bef last* **12/1**
2 **U** **Teviot Prince (IRE)**[64] [1518] 5-10-6 110........................ MrZBaker(7)
(Martin Bosley) *mid-div tl dropped to rr 6th: lost tch after 9th: blnd bdly and uns rdr 3 out* **33/1**
5-40 **U** **Poker School (IRE)**[172] [463] 5-11-3 114........................ WillKennedy
(Ian Williams) *prom: hit 7th: rdn after 9th: wknd 4 out: no ch whn j.big and uns rdr next* **9/2**[2]

4m 1.6s (3.10) **Going Correction** +0.35s/f (Yiel) **10 Ran SP% 116.2**
Speed ratings (Par 105): **106,100,96,94,92 88,78,, ,**
CSF £25.29 CT £113.49 TOTE £2.70: £1.10, £3.50, £2.00; EX 29.00 Trifecta £263.20.
Owner West Buckland Bloodstock Ltd **Bred** Adrian Von Gunten **Trained** West Buckland, Somerset

FOCUS
This looked competitive, but the bang in-form winner took the race apart and they came home behind in Indian file. Helium is rated back to the very best of his old form.

2450 START YOUR RACINGUK FREE TRIAL NOW INTRODUCTORY HURDLE (11 hdls) 2m 5f 55y
2:30 (2:31) (Class 3) 4-Y-0+ **£6,498** (£1,908; £954; £477)

Form RPR
20-2 **1** **Always Lion (IRE)**[22] [2023] 5-11-0 0........................ NicodeBoinville 125+
(Ben Pauling) *cl up tl led 2nd: mde rest: rdn 3 out: edgd lft and hld on wl flat* **7/2**[3]
4 **2** *1 ½* **Robin Of Locksley (IRE)**[20] [2052] 5-11-0 0........................ HarrySkelton 123
(Dan Skelton) *hld up in last: stdy hdwy 8th: wnt 2nd 3 out: ev ch next tl unable qck flat* **11/4**[2]

1 **3** ½ **Max Forte (IRE)**[18] 2088 5-11-5 0 JamesDavies 129
(Chris Down) *led to 2nd: trckd ldr tl lost 2nd and hit 3 out: styd on same pce fr next* **8/1**

032- **4** *nk* **Kerrow (IRE)**[215] 5285 5-11-0 0 WayneHutchinson 122
(Alan King) *hld up: hdwy after 8th: rdn 3 out: styd on same pce: chal for 3rd fr last* **20/1**

0-2 **5** *21* **Dalia Pour Moi (FR)**[29] 1901 6-11-0 0 RichardJohnson 105
(Philip Hobbs) *hld up towards rr: sltly hmpd after 5th: hdwy 7th: chsng ldrs whn rdn 3 out: wknd next* **9/4**[1]

5 **6** *16* **Some Are Lucky (IRE)**[19] 2065 4-11-0 0 PaddyBrennan 89
(Tom George) *j. slowly 1st: chsd ldrs: rdn after 8th: wknd 3 out* **10/1**

3 **7** *14* **Viaduct Jack (IRE)**[22] 2023 6-11-0 0 JamieMoore 76
(Kim Bailey) *chsd ldrs: rdn and hit 7th: wknd after next: t.o* **14/1**

3- **8** *1* **Pressurize (IRE)**[301] 3688 9-11-0 0 LiamTreadwell 75
(Venetia Williams) *t.k.h: chsd ldrs tl grad lost pl fr 5th: in rr by 7th: t.o fr next* **25/1**

53-2 **9** *10* **Bendomingo (IRE)**[168] 525 4-10-9 0 (t) JamieBargary(5) 66
(Nigel Twiston-Davies) *t.k.h in mid-div: rdn and wknd after 8th: t.o* **50/1**

0/33 **10** *8* **Grand Introduction (IRE)**[21] 2044 5-10-11 0 ConorShoemark(3) 59
(Fergal O'Brien) *mid-div: mstke 6th: rdn and wknd after 8th: t.o* **50/1**

0 **11** *66* **Flamenco Flyer**[19] 2062 6-10-11 0 BenPoste(3)
(Tracey Barfoot-Saunt) *hld up: rdn fr 5th: lost tch 7th: t.o* **100/1**

5m 10.9s (-3.90) **Going Correction** +0.05s/f (Yiel)
WFA 4 from 5yo+ 8lb **11 Ran SP% 120.0**
Speed ratings (Par 107): **109,108,108,108,100 94,88,88,84,81 56**
CSF £13.69 TOTE £4.20: £1.30, £1.50, £2.20; EX 18.60 Trifecta £107.10.
Owner Paul & Clare Rooney **Bred** Susan Bredin **Trained** Bourton-On-The-Water, Gloucs

FOCUS
An interesting affair. The first four came clear and it's form to be positive about.

2451 INJURED JOCKEYS FUND H'CAP CHASE (22 fncs) 3m 1f 125y
3:00 (3:01) (Class 3) (0-125,122) 4-Y-0+ **£9,747** (£2,862; £1,431; £715)

Form RPR

4-34 **1** **King Massini (IRE)**[36] 1807 9-11-5 **115** AdamWedge 126+
(Evan Williams) *mid-div: hdwy 12th: wnt 2nd 3 out: led after next: rdn out flat* **3/1**[1]

-4P6 **2** *2½* **Rockiteer (IRE)**[36] 1807 12-11-1 **118** (p) MissJCWilliams(7) 127
(Henry Daly) *cl up: led after 5th: mstke 16th: hdd next: led again after 18th: hit 2 out: sn hdd: kpt on same pce* **12/1**

/214 **3** *2¼* **Cardinal Rose**[111] 1098 8-10-3 **99** KielanWoods 106
(Mark Wall) *j.rt 1st: prom: mainly in 2nd fr 6th tl led 17th: hit next and sn hdd: rdn 4 out: lost 2nd next: one pce* **12/1**

V23- **4** ½ **Hayjack**[499] 827 10-11-7 **117** AndrewTinkler 123
(Martin Keighley) *a.p: hmpd 1st: blnd 11th: rdn 3 out: styd on same pce* **10/1**

245- **5** *22* **Take The Mick**[236] 4925 8-11-7 **117** LiamTreadwell 101
(Venetia Williams) *led tl after 5th: chsd ldrs: rdn 16th: wknd after 18th* **8/1**

16-F **6** *7* **Shy John**[184] 266 9-11-7 **117** JamesDavies 95
(Jennifer Mason) *hld up: hdwy 14th: pushed along 17th: wknd 3 out* **12/1**

-525 **P** **Castle Conflict (IRE)**[147] 774 10-11-2 **112** (b) JakeGreenall
(Henry Daly) *mid-div: rdn along 13th: struggling fr 16th: lost tch after 18th: t.o whn p.u bef 4 out* **20/1**

6-66 **P** **Five Star Wilsham (IRE)**[20] 2057 11-11-3 **116** RyanHatch(3)
(Nigel Twiston-Davies) *hld up: rdn 13th: struggling 15th: t.o whn p.u bef 4 out* **16/1**

1133 **P** **Faustina Pius (IRE)**[14] 2149 7-10-12 **115** (p) MrStanSheppard(7)
(Matt Sheppard) *a in rr: lost tch 15th: t.o whn p.u bef 4 out* **20/1**

1421 **P** **Highpower (IRE)**[73] 1414 6-11-12 **122** (v) RichardJohnson
(Jonjo O'Neill) *towards rr: mstke 7th: rdn along 14th: sme hdwy next: struggling fr 17th: t.o whn p.u bef 4 out* **9/2**[2]

2-24 **P** **Simply The West (IRE)**[28] 1932 6-11-12 **122** (t) HarrySkelton
(Charlie Longsdon) *chsd ldrs: mstke 2nd: rdn whn mstke 4 out: wknd qckly and p.u bef next* **5/1**[3]

6m 45.1s (9.80) **Going Correction** +0.35s/f (Yiel) **11 Ran SP% 118.5**
Speed ratings (Par 107): **98,97,96,96,89 87,,,,**
CSF £39.09 CT £375.37 TOTE £3.90: £1.30, £4.50, £3.90; EX 33.50 Trifecta £389.60.
Owner Border Pointers **Bred** Tim Jones **Trained** Llancarfan, Vale Of Glamorgan

FOCUS
A modest but competitive handicap and fair form for the class. The winner should still be competitive when reassessed.

2452 RACINGUK.COM/FREETRIAL MARES' "NATIONAL HUNT" MAIDEN HURDLE (9 hdls) 1m 7f 169y
3:30 (3:31) (Class 4) 4-Y-0+ **£3,898** (£1,144; £572; £286)

Form RPR

151- **1** **Robins Reef (IRE)**[227] 5071 5-11-0 0 AndrewTinkler 117+
(Nicky Henderson) *trckd ldrs: wnt 2nd after 6th: led gng wl appr 3 out: j.rt 2 out: r.o wl flat* **1/1**[1]

0-2 **2** *4* **Pink Play (IRE)**[29] 1908 4-11-0 0 NicodeBoinville 109
(Harry Whittington) *mid-div: clsd 6th: rdn to chse wnr 3 out: kpt on same pce fr next* **4/1**[3]

10-5 **3** *1¼* **Miss Crick**[22] 2016 4-11-0 0 WayneHutchinson 108
(Alan King) *towards rr: hdwy after 6th: rdn 3 out: styd on to go 3rd flat* **7/1**

0-2 **4** ¾ **Eardisland**[168] 528 5-11-0 0 RichardJohnson 107
(Philip Hobbs) *chsd ldrs: rdn 3 out: sn one pce: lost 3rd flat* **3/1**[2]

-660 **5** *6* **Timon's Tara**[156] 679 6-11-0 0 CharliePoste 104
(Robin Dickin) *hld up: hdwy after 6th: rdn 3 out: one pce fr next* **50/1**

65 **6** *8* **Myrtle Drive (IRE)**[159] 640 4-10-9 0 JamesCowley(5) 95
(Donald McCain) *mid-div: hdwy after 6th: rdn 3 out: wkng whn j.rt next* **50/1**

6 **7** *16* **Jester Jet**[33] 1845 5-11-0 0 LeeEdwards 80
(Tony Carroll) *t.k.h: mid-div: jinked 2nd: clsd after 6th: shkn up and wknd 3 out* **50/1**

P5-0 **8** *6* **Perfect Timing (FR)**[30] 1898 5-11-0 0 LiamTreadwell 75
(Paul Webber) *led: hung lft bnd after 3rd: hdd appr 3 out: sn wknd* **50/1**

6-0P **9** ½ **Orbit Light (IRE)**[14] 2154 4-11-0 0 PeterCarberry 74
(Nicky Henderson) *t.k.h in rr: hit 5th: rdn and wknd after next* **50/1**

0-P **10** *35* **Velvet Edge**[13] 2164 6-10-9 0 JakeHodson(5) 43
(Anthony Day) *a in rr: j.lft and mstke 2nd: wknd appr 3 out: t.o* **100/1**

11 *1¼* **Southfield Fairy**[186] 4-10-9 0 KevinJones(5) 42
(Charles Whittaker) *w ldr tl rdn and wknd after 6th: t.o* **33/1**

3m 52.6s (3.10) **Going Correction** +0.05s/f (Yiel)
WFA 4 from 5yo+ 7lb **11 Ran SP% 121.2**
Speed ratings (Par 105): **94,92,91,91,88 84,76,73,72,55 54**
CSF £5.63 TOTE £2.10: £1.10, £2.00, £2.20; EX 5.50 Trifecta £23.30.
Owner Kelvin-Hughes & Bartlett **Bred** Edward Ryan **Trained** Upper Lambourn, Berks

FOCUS
Not a bad mares' maiden and the first four can all rate higher.

2453 ROBIN MORLAND MEMORIAL AMATEUR RIDERS' H'CAP HURDLE (11 hdls) 2m 5f 55y
4:00 (4:02) (Class 5) (0-100,99) 3-Y-0+ **£4,055** (£1,257; £628; £314)

Form RPR

363- **1** **Scales (IRE)**[204] 5465 9-11-1 **93** MrStanSheppard(5) 110+
(Kerry Lee) *hld up: hdwy after 8th: chal 3 out: rdn next: led flat: r.o wl* **7/2**[1]

6403 **2** *3* **Danceintothelight**[14] 2142 8-10-10 **90** (t) MissAMcCain(7) 101
(Donald McCain) *racd keenly: prom: chsd ldr 5th tl led after 8th: jnd 3 out: rdn next: nt fluent last: hdd and one pce flat* **8/1**[3]

5-00 **3** *24* **Jackfield**[36] 1812 5-10-0 **76** MissHannahWatson(3) 65
(Robin Dickin) *hld up: clsd 7th: rdn after 8th: styd on one pce fr 3 out: tk mod 3rd flat* **16/1**

UU4P **4** *3¼* **Samtheman**[10] 2248 10-10-10 **88** (p) MrRobertHawker(5) 74
(Pam Ford) *hld up: clsd 7th: rdn 3 out: sn no ch w ldrs: wnt mod 3rd last tl flat* **16/1**

6200 **5** *1¾* **Warsaw Pact (IRE)**[27] 1951 12-9-8 **74** MrBParis-Crofts(7) 59
(Steven Dixon) *chsd ldrs: rdn along fr 4th: wknd after 8th* **14/1**

6530 **6** *1* **Kyles Faith (IRE)**[20] 2057 7-10-13 **93** MrHRLCornock(7) 77
(Martin Keighley) *mainly chsd ldr to 5th: wknd after 8th* **8/1**[3]

140- **7** *6* **Bertenbar**[204] 5473 11-10-2 **82** MissCTWyatt(7) 64
(Lawney Hill) *led tl after 8th: lost 2nd appr 3 out: wknd 2 out* **10/1**

5P-2 **8** ¾ **Kings River (FR)**[13] 2162 6-10-11 **91** MissLMTurner(7) 69
(Venetia Williams) *chsd ldrs: jinked lft 4th: rdn along fr 7th: wknd appr 3 out* **7/2**[1]

016 **9** *12* **Colley Row (IRE)**[73] 1426 7-11-5 **99** (b) MrLWilliams(7) 66
(Tim Vaughan) *hld up: hdwy after 8th: wknd 3 out: t.o* **8/1**[3]

-04P **10** *18* **Mazurati (IRE)**[134] 879 6-11-1 **95** MrMJPKendrick(7) 46
(Ben Case) *mid-div: clsd 7th: wknd appr 3 out: t.o* **7/1**[2]

00-0 **11** *36* **Betty Borgia**[185] 240 9-9-8 **74** (t) MrGregoryWalters(7)
(Nicholas Pomfret) *a in rr: struggling fr 6th: t.o* **100/1**

5m 18.5s (3.70) **Going Correction** +0.05s/f (Yiel) **11 Ran SP% 118.8**
Speed ratings (Par 103): **94,92,83,82,81 81,79,78,74,67 53**
CSF £32.43 CT £402.00 TOTE £4.90: £1.40, £2.70, £5.80; EX 43.60 Trifecta £550.20.
Owner A Beard B Beard S Ripley **Bred** Michael Long **Trained** Byton, H'fords

FOCUS
A weak handicap, confined to amateur riders. The first two, who were well in on old form, finished clear.
T/Jkpt: Not won. JACKPOT PLACEPOT: £26.10 to a £1 stake. Pool of £2505.86 - 69.85 winning units. T/Plt: £21.00 to a £1 stake. Pool of £56512.33 - 1960.80 winning tickets. T/Qpdt: £12.60 to a £1 stake. Pool of £4292.81 - 251.95 winning tickets. **Richard Lowther**

TAUNTON (R-H)
Thursday, November 12

OFFICIAL GOING: Good (5.8)
Wind: light breeze across Weather: overcast

2454 TOTEPLACEPOT RACING'S FAVOURITE BET H'CAP HURDLE (12 hdls) 2m 7f 198y
1:10 (1:10) (Class 5) (0-100,100) 4-Y-0+ **£3,249** (£954; £477; £238)

Form RPR

3F21 **1** **Oscar Jane (IRE)**[7] 2298 8-10-10 **84** 7ex (bt) BrendanPowell 91+
(Johnny Farrelly) *mde all: styd on wl: rdn out* **7/2**[1]

-435 **2** ½ **Very Intense (IRE)**[21] 2043 4-11-1 **96** DavidNoonan(7) 102
(Tom Lacey) *mid-div: hdwy after 9th: trckd wnr appr 2 out: rdn between last 2: styd on but no ex nring fin* **6/1**[3]

1265 **3** *8* **I'm In Charge**[27] 1951 9-11-10 **98** (t) NickScholfield 98
(Grant Cann) *trckd ldrs on outer: rdn after 3 out: hit next: styd on same pce: wnt 3rd run-in* **13/2**

4521 **4** *nk* **Minella Bliss (IRE)**[10] 2245 10-11-1 **96** (b) CharlieHammond(7) 96
(James Evans) *t.k.h in midfield: hdwy 7th to trck ldrs: rdn in cl 3rd after 3 out: styd on same pce fr next: lost 3rd run-in* **9/2**[2]

P/15 **5** *8* **Rainbow Haze**[51] 1615 9-11-0 **93** MrBMoorcroft(5) 84
(Phillip Dando) *mid-div: in last pair 7th: styd on fr 2 out but n.d* **15/2**

642P **6** *2¼* **Surf In September (IRE)**[13] 2167 6-10-13 **94** BenFfrenchDavis(7) 84
(Dominic Ffrench Davis) *mid-div: rdn after 3 out: nvr any imp: nt fluent last* **16/1**

2264 **7** *2½* **Midnight Sequel**[29] 1910 6-11-12 **100** NoelFehily 87
(Neil Mulholland) *hld up towards rr: hdwy into midfield 3 out: sn rdn: no further imp fr next* **8/1**

13-P **8** *6* **Follow The Tracks (IRE)**[176] 398 7-11-5 **100** MichaelHeard(7) 83
(Brian Barr) *trckd ldrs: rdn after 9th: wknd bef 2 out* **9/1**

3/0- **9** *hd* **Residence And Spa (IRE)**[229] 5027 7-9-13 **78** GaryDerwin(5) 59
(Helen Rees) *towards rr: pushed along fr 8th: nvr a factor* **33/1**

B45P **10** *14* **Vering (FR)**[67] 1489 9-10-1 **75** (t) JamesBest 44
(Carroll Gray) *trckd ldrs: hit 8th: sn rdn: wknd after 3 out* **66/1**

0-00 **11** *25* **Bronwydd**[26] 1960 5-11-0 **88** TrevorWhelan 34
(Debra Hamer) *trckd ldrs: hit 2nd: rdn after 8th: sn bhd: t.o* **66/1**

61-P **12** *22* **Comical Red**[190] 148 7-11-6 **94** TomCannon 21
(Mark Gillard) *hld up towards rr: midfield 5th: wknd after 9th: t.o* **33/1**

P-PP **P** **Exiles Return (IRE)**[168] 527 13-9-7 **74** oh10 MrMLegg(7)
(Jackie Retter) *a towards rr: struggling 8th: t.o whn p.u bef 2 out* **200/1**

5m 50.8s (-13.20) **Going Correction** -0.575s/f (Firm)
WFA 4 from 5yo+ 9lb **13 Ran SP% 116.1**
Speed ratings (Par 103): **99,98,96,96,93 92,91,89,89,85 76,69,**
CSF £23.77 CT £130.94 TOTE £4.60: £1.30, £2.60, £2.80; EX 30.10 Trifecta £170.80.
Owner P Tosh **Bred** J R Weston **Trained** Enmore, Somerset

FOCUS
Shared bends. Bend out of home straight 13yds off innermost line and bend out of back straight 10yds off innermost line. Races 1, 3, 5, 6 & 7 increased by 138yds and race 2 & 4 increased by 99yds. The time of the opener suggested the ground description of good was accurate. Moderate handicap form, but solid at the level.

2455 MYTOTEPOOL.COM THOROUGHBRED BREEDERS' ASSOCIATION MARES' H'CAP HURDLE (10 hdls) 2m 3f 1y
1:40 (1:40) (Class 4) (0-120,126) 3-Y-0+ **£4,548** (£1,335; £667; £333)

Form RPR

0F61 **1** **Lily Waugh (IRE)**[5] 2349 8-11-11 **126** 7ex (t) DavidNoonan(7) 139+
(Anthony Honeyball) *trckd ldrs: led 2 out: styd on wl fr last: pushed out* **11/4**[1]

4-05 **2** *2* **Woodland Walk**[13] 2167 7-10-12 **116**.......................... RichieO'Dea(10) 125
(Emma Lavelle) *a.p: led 3 out tl next: rdn and ev ch last: kpt on but no ex towards fin* **7/1**

15-P **3** *14* **Quiet Candid (IRE)**[26] 1974 6-11-9 **120**.......................... JeremiahMcGrath(3) 116
(Nicky Henderson) *hld up towards rr: hdwy fr 7th: rdn to chse ldng pair bef 2 out: styd on same pce* **16/1**

-600 **4** *nk* **Ice Tres**[18] 2093 6-10-7 **101**..........................(p[1]) SamTwiston-Davies 97
(Chris Down) *mid-div: rdn after 3 out: styd on fr last: wnt 4th nring fin* **25/1**

33-2 **5** *1* **Lady Of Lamanver**[13] 2164 5-11-8 **116**..........................(t) NoelFehily 112
(Harry Fry) *mid-div: hdwy 3 out: sn one pce: lost 4th nring fin* **7/2**[3]

4414 **6** *1 3/4* **Popping Along**[34] 1841 6-11-2 **113**..........................(tp) MattGriffiths(3) 108
(Jeremy Scott) *hld up towards rr: rdn after 7th: squeezed up on bnd after 3 out: no threat whn blnd 2 out but kpt on past btn horses* **8/1**

P603 **7** *1/2* **Hija**[23] 2007 4-9-12 **97**..........................(p) AliceMills(5) 90
(Gail Haywood) *mid-div on outer: effrt 3 out: sn one pce* **33/1**

1231 **8** *2 3/4* **Kayf Willow**[34] 1841 6-11-1 **116**.......................... CiaranGethings(7) 108
(Philip Hobbs) *mid-div: outpcd after 3 out: nvr any threat* **10/3**[2]

3-4P **9** *33* **Dardanella**[30] 1897 8-10-11 **105**.......................... DaveCrosse 66
(Hugo Froud) *prom: led 5th tl 3 out: sn wknd: t.o* **100/1**

320- **10** *1 1/2* **Rhythm Star**[231] 5001 5-11-7 **115**.......................... BrendanPowell 75
(Jamie Snowden) *led tl 5th: prom: nt fluent 3 out: sn rdn and wknd: t.o* **14/1**

543P **F** **Sheer Poetry (IRE)**[9] 2263 4-10-6 **100**.......................... DarylJacob
(Richard Woollacott) *hld up towards rr: fell 3 out* **50/1**

4m 36.5s (-9.50) **Going Correction** -0.575s/f (Firm)
WFA 4 from 5yo+ 7lb **11** Ran **SP% 117.9**
Speed ratings (Par 105): **97,96,90,90,89 88,88,87,73,73**
CSF £22.14 CT £263.23 TOTE £3.40: £1.70, £2.30, £4.10; EX 21.30 Trifecta £293.50.
Owner Go To War **Bred** F Boyd **Trained** Mosterton, Dorset

FOCUS
The front pair came clear in what was a fair mares' handicap. The winner confirmed the merit of her recent win.

2456 TOTEQUADPOT FOUR PLACES IN FOUR RACES NOVICES' LIMITED H'CAP CHASE (17 fncs) 2m 7f 3y
2:10 (2:10) (Class 4) (0-120,120) 4-Y-0+ **£5,198** (£1,526; £763; £381)

Form RPR
-2U2 **1** **Vendredi Trois (FR)**[30] 1897 6-10-8 **106**.......................... GavinSheehan 115+
(Emma Lavelle) *pressed ldr: rdn after 4 out: led next: kpt on wl: rdn out* **6/1**[3]

6421 **2** *2 1/2* **He's A Bully (IRE)**[27] 1950 6-10-11 **109**.......................... TomO'Brien 118+
(Philip Hobbs) *j.lft: in tch: struggling 12th: styd on steadily fr 3 out: wnt 2nd run-in: nvr any threat to wnr* **4/1**[1]

442- **3** *2* **Horsehill (IRE)**[229] 5029 6-11-3 **115**.......................... LeightonAspell 119
(Oliver Sherwood) *in tch: hit 12th: rdn to chse wnr after 3 out: styd on and a being hld: no ex whn lost 2nd run-in* **9/1**

0052 **4** *30* **Only Gorgeous (IRE)**[23] 2006 6-10-5 **106**.......................... LucyGardner(3) 87+
(Sue Gardner) *hld up: struggling in rr whn mstke 4 out: wnt modest 4th run-in* **16/1**

2-P2 **5** *2 1/2* **Magheral Express (IRE)**[120] 1011 6-11-3 **115**.......................... RichieMcLernon 89
(Jonjo O'Neill) *led: hdd whn v awkward on landing 3 out: wknd qckly* **9/1**

35-F **6** *9* **Golan Dancer (IRE)**[21] 2039 7-11-0 **112**.......................... TomCannon 78
(David Bridgwater) *nudged along after 10th: a towards rr* **25/1**

230- **7** *1/2* **Albert D'Olivate (FR)**[286] 3963 5-10-10 **108**.......................... NickScholfield 73
(Robert Walford) *trckd ldrs: rdn after 11th: pckd bdly 4 out: sn wknd* **4/1**[1]

61-2 **P** **Ballyknock Lad (IRE)**[43] 1699 6-11-8 **120**..........................(t) DavidBass
(Kim Bailey) *trcking ldr whn blnd bdly 2nd and rdr lost iron: nt travelling fr 10th: bhd next: t.o after 4 out: p.u bef last* **6/1**[3]

1111 **F** **Love The Leader (IRE)**[14] 2143 7-10-12 **110**..........................(p) AlainCawley
(Johnny Farrelly) *hld up: nudged along whn mstke 11th: fell next* **5/1**[2]

5m 55.4s (-20.60) **Going Correction** -0.725s/f (Firm) **9** Ran **SP% 115.0**
Speed ratings (Par 105): **106,105,104,94,93 90,89, ,**
CSF £30.92 CT £214.94 TOTE £7.70: £2.20, £1.40, £3.50; EX 26.70 Trifecta £704.90.
Owner Awdry, Gemmell, Pomford & Williams **Bred** Mme Claudine Winkel **Trained** Hatherden, Hants

FOCUS
The form of this modest chase looks sound for the level. The winner was up 7lb on the best of his hurdle figures.

2457 TOTEPOOL RACING'S BIGGEST SUPPORTER NOVICES' HURDLE (10 hdls) 2m 3f 1y
2:40 (2:40) (Class 3) 4-Y-0+ **£5,697** (£1,683; £841; £421; £210)

Form RPR
/2-3 **1** **Modus**[197] 23 5-10-12 0.......................... BarryGeraghty 122+
(Paul Nicholls) *sweating: racd keenly in midfield: smooth hdwy 6th: chal 2 out: shkn up to ld bef last: qcknd clr: readily* **1/3**[1]

6115 **2** *3 3/4* **General Ginger**[22] 2011 5-11-8 128..........................(t) NoelFehily 125
(Harry Fry) *trckd ldr: led after 3 out: rdn and hdd bef last: kpt on but sn outpcd by wnr* **6/1**[2]

3 *6* **Miles To Milan (IRE)** 5-10-12 0.......................... TomO'Brien 109
(Philip Hobbs) *trckd ldrs: rdn after 3 out: kpt on but nt pce of front pair fr next* **14/1**[3]

03-6 **4** *1/2* **Pengo's Boy**[191] 119 6-10-12 0.......................... NickScholfield 108
(Stuart Kittow) *mid-div: prog into hld 3rd 2 out: sn rdn: kpt on same pce* **14/1**[3]

5 *3 3/4* **Iniciar (GER)**[195] 5-10-12 0.......................... DarylJacob 106
(David Pipe) *hld up towards rr: short of room appr 2 out: styd on between last 2 but no threat: nt fluent last* **6/1**[2]

4-1 **6** *10* **Morthanalegend**[129] 928 6-10-12 0..........................(t) BrendanPowell 96
(Brendan Powell) *nvr bttr than mid-div* **14/1**[3]

36 **7** *7* **Acajou Des Bieffes (FR)**[34] 1843 5-10-12 0.......................... RyanMahon 89
(Anthony Honeyball) *trckd ldrs: rdn after 3 out: wknd bef next* **50/1**

00/ **8** *1/2* **Up To Al (IRE)**[165] 7-10-12 0.......................... LiamHeard 89
(Bob Buckler) *hld up towards rr: hdwy into midfield 3 out: wknd next* **50/1**

PP5 **9** *2 1/4* **Highridge Princess (IRE)**[55] 1574 7-9-12 0..........................(t) DavidNoonan(7) 81
(Johnny Farrelly) *mid-div: nt fluent 7th: rdn after 3 out: wkng whn mstke 2 out* **100/1**

0-3P **10** *2* **My Diamond (IRE)**[9] 2257 4-10-9 0.......................... MattGriffiths(3) 86
(Laura Young) *trckd ldrs: rdn after 3 out: wknd bef next* **200/1**

P-65 **11** *14* **Berry De Carjac (FR)**[14] 2154 4-10-12 110..........................(t) ConorO'Farrell 73
(Nigel Hawke) *a towards rr* **50/1**

12 *10* **Dinky Challenger**[592] 7-10-12 0.......................... TomCannon 64
(Mark Gillard) *led tl rdn after 3 out: sn wknd* **200/1**

4m 43.0s (-3.00) **Going Correction** -0.575s/f (Firm)
WFA 4 from 5yo+ 7lb **12** Ran **SP% 131.5**
Speed ratings (Par 107): **83,81,78,78,77 72,69,69,68,67 62,57**
CSF £3.97 TOTE £1.60: £1.10, £1.80, £3.50; EX 4.40 Trifecta £26.70.
Owner John P McManus **Bred** D J And Mrs Deer **Trained** Ditcheat, Somerset

FOCUS
No great depth to this novice hurdle that revolved around the favourite, a potential 140+ hurdler. The time was slow.

2458 TOTEEXACTA PICK THE 1ST AND 2ND H'CAP HURDLE (9 hdls) 2m 104y
3:10 (3:10) (Class 4) (0-115,115) 3-Y-0+ **£4,548** (£1,335; £667; £333)

Form RPR
420- **1** **Qasser (IRE)**[177] 4301 6-10-13 **109**.......................... PaulNO'Brien(7) 119
(Harry Whittington) *mid-div: hdwy 4th lft in ld after 5th: drew clr travelling strly after 3 out: rdn after last: kpt on: rdn out* **8/1**[3]

343- **2** *3/4* **Amanto (GER)**[20] 4454 5-11-5 **115**..........................(b) HarryCobden(7) 124
(Paul Nicholls) *mid-div: squeezed up on bnd after 4th: hdwy after 3 out: wnt 3rd 2 out: sn rdn: chsd wnr fr last: kpt on wl towards fin but a being jst hld* **9/2**[1]

04-1 **3** *4 1/2* **Template (IRE)**[7] 2291 4-11-5 **115**.......................... LiamMcKenna(7) 121
(Harry Fry) *mid-div on outer: hdwy 3 out: trckd wnr appr 2 out: sn rdn: hung lft between last 2: styd on same pce fr last* **9/2**[1]

0560 **4** *9* **Goal (IRE)**[8] 2271 7-10-12 **108**..........................(t) MissBHampson(7) 105
(Andy Turnell) *mid-div tl 5th: towards rr: hdwy appr 2 out: styd on to go 4th run-in* **20/1**

12/F **5** *1 1/2* **Walter White (IRE)**[35] 1818 5-11-7 **110**..........................(t) TomO'Brien 107
(Philip Hobbs) *trckd ldrs: rdn after 3 out: nt pce to chal front 3: no ex whn lost 4th run-in* **16/1**

0000 **6** *1* **Exemplary**[92] 1238 8-10-8 **104**..........................(t) DavidNoonan(7) 99
(Johnny Farrelly) *hld up towards rr: hdwy appr 2 out: styd on but nvr any threat* **11/1**

2-00 **7** *shd* **Sandy Beach**[9] 2262 5-11-10 **113**..........................(t) BrendanPowell 108
(Colin Tizzard) *in tch: trckd ldrs 5th: rdn after 3 out: one pce fr next* **25/1**

5040 **8** *1 1/2* **Avel Vor (IRE)**[18] 2093 4-11-4 **107**.......................... ConorO'Farrell 100
(Nigel Hawke) *hld up towards rr: styd on fr 2 out: nvr trbld ldrs* **33/1**

5354 **9** *4 1/2* **Perspicace**[35] 1818 4-11-10 **113**..........................(p) TomScudamore 102
(David Pipe) *hld up towards rr: hdwy to trck ldrs 5th: rdn after 3 out: wknd next* **7/1**[2]

6250 **10** *17* **Key To Milan**[59] 1545 9-11-1 **107**..........................(tp) GilesHawkins(3) 81
(Chris Down) *trckd ldrs tl 3 out: sn wknd* **18/1**

42- **11** *6* **Abyaat (IRE)**[8] 5489 4-11-11 **114**..........................(t) DenisO'Regan 82
(Victor Dartnall) *mid-div: nt fluent 3 out: sn rdn: wknd bef next* **12/1**

3654 **P** **Frozen Over**[45] 1676 7-11-7 **110**..........................(t) SamTwiston-Davies
(Chris Down) *towards rr: lost tch after 5th: p.u next* **9/1**

160- **P** **Blackwater King (IRE)**[213] 5315 7-11-6 **109**..........................[1] NoelFehily
(Johnny Farrelly) *led tl hung bdly lft towards stable entrnce after 5th: nt rcvr and p.u bef next* **7/1**[2]

UP-P **P** **Dont Call Me Oscar (IRE)**[142] 828 8-10-13 **102**..........................(t) TomCannon
(Mark Gillard) *trckd ldr: hmpd between 5th and 6th: sn rdn: wknd qckly and p.u bef 3 out* **50/1**

3m 56.7s (-11.30) **Going Correction** -0.575s/f (Firm) **14** Ran **SP% 123.2**
Speed ratings (Par 105): **105,104,102,97,97 96,96,95,93,85 82, , ,**
CSF £43.98 CT £188.64 TOTE £10.10: £3.90, £3.30, £1.10; EX 48.00 Trifecta £282.00.
Owner Lead The Way Syndicate **Bred** Me Surrender Syndicate **Trained** Sparsholt, Oxfordshire
■ Stewards' Enquiry : Harry Cobden two-day ban: used whip above permitted level (Nov 26-27)

FOCUS
The front three came clear in this ordinary handicap and the form looks sound. The inner ran to the level of his upgraded Plumpton win

2459 TOTETRIFECTA PICK THE 1, 2, 3 H'CAP CHASE 2m 5f 150y
3:40 (3:40) (Class 3) (0-140,136) 4-Y-0+ **£8,447** (£2,480; £1,240; £620)

Form RPR
12-5 **1** **Howlongisafoot (IRE)**[32] 1869 6-11-10 **134**..........(b) SamTwiston-Davies 141+
(Paul Nicholls) *trckd ldrs: wnt 2nd after 9th: chalng whn nt fluent 2 out: narrow advantage whn hit last: styd on wl: rdn out* **9/2**[2]

65P- **2** *3 3/4* **Shangani (USA)**[247] 4690 9-11-8 **132**..........................(b) AidanColeman 133
(Venetia Williams) *led: rdn appr 3 out: jnd 2 out: hdd whn mstke last: no ex* **6/1**[3]

130- **3** *2 1/2* **Black River (FR)**[292] 3849 6-11-8 **132**..........................(tp) SeanBowen 131
(Paul Nicholls) *rn in snatches: towards rr: mstke 8th: sme prog appr 3 out: chal for hld 3rd bef last: styd on* **4/1**[1]

04-1 **4** *1/2* **The Italian Yob (IRE)**[26] 1965 7-11-0 **124**..........................(b) LeightonAspell 122
(Nick Williams) *pressed ldr tl 9th: sn rdn: kpt chsng ldng pair but hld fr 3 out: no ex whn lost 3rd towards fin* **9/2**[2]

3133 **5** *6* **Border Breaker (IRE)**[23] 2008 6-10-12 **129**..........................(tp) MichaelHeard(7) 122
(David Pipe) *hld up: hdwy 9th: rdn after 11th: nvr threatened: one pce fr 3 out* **7/1**

1F-4 **6** *nk* **Until Winning (FR)**[27] 1943 7-11-8 **132**.......................... NoelFehily 124
(Tom George) *hld up: hdwy into 4th u.p after 4 out: nvr threatened ldrs: wknd last* **14/1**

33-0 **F** **Filbert (IRE)**[32] 1869 9-11-12 **136**..........................(p) TomO'Brien
(Philip Hobbs) *towards rr: hdwy into 4th bef 9th: rdn after 10th: wknd bef 4 out: t.o whn fell 2 out* **11/1**

212- **F** **Tom Neary (IRE)**[205] 5447 8-11-1 **125**..........................(t) NickScholfield
(Robert Walford) *in tch: wkng whn fell heavily 4 out* **14/1**

1-40 **P** **Pumped Up Kicks (IRE)**[13] 2171 8-11-7 **131**.......................... IanPopham
(Dan Skelton) *chsd ldr: drvn along after 7th: wknd after 9th: t.o whn p.u bef 4 out* **10/1**

5m 31.8s (331.80) **9** Ran **SP% 113.9**
CSF £31.52 CT £115.62 TOTE £4.00: £1.50, £2.00, £1.60; EX 14.10 Trifecta £36.10.
Owner P J Vogt **Bred** G Merrigan **Trained** Ditcheat, Somerset

FOCUS
A decent handicap chase and the field was on the stretch from some way out. It looks a race to be pretty positive about.

2460 TOTEPOOL BETTING ON ALL UK RACING MAIDEN OPEN NATIONAL HUNT FLAT RACE 2m 104y
4:10 (4:11) (Class 5) 4-6-Y-0 **£2,737** (£798; £399)

Form RPR
4 **1** **Blu Cavalier**[177] 392 5-11-2 0.......................... ConorO'Farrell 107+
(Alexandra Dunn) *trckd ldrs: qcknd to ld over 2f out: r.o wl: eased towards fin* **10/1**

2 *3 1/4* **Boudry (FR)** 4-11-2 0.......................... GavinSheehan 104+
(Warren Greatrex) *rn green: mid-div: nudged along and hdwy fr over 6f out: rdn to chse wnr over 2f out: kpt on but nt pce to get on terms* **5/2**[1]

6- **3** *3* **Piton Pete (IRE)**[243] 4770 4-11-2 0.......................... LeightonAspell 102
(Oliver Sherwood) *mid-div: rdn over 2f out: styd on wl to go 3rd ins fnl f but nt pce to threaten* **33/1**

4 *nk* **Misterton** 4-11-2 0.......................... NoelFehily 101
(Harry Fry) *led tl rdn over 2f out: kpt on same pce: lost 3rd ins fnl f* **7/1**[3]

0 **5** 1 3/4 **Lets Go Dutchess**[191] [124] 5-10-2 0 .... CiaranGethings(7) 93
(Kevin Bishop) *hld up towards rr: hdwy fr 5f out: rdn to chse ldrs over 2f out: kpt on same pce* **20/1**

50- **6** 1 **Rob Robin (IRE)**[243] [4755] 5-11-2 0 .... SamTwiston-Davies 99
(Paul Nicholls) *mid-div: hdwy over 3f out: rdn to chse ldrs over 2f out: no ex fnl f* **8/1**

2 **7** nk **Walkami (FR)**[180] [341] 4-11-2 0 .... RichieMcLernon 100
(Jonjo O'Neill) *in tch on inner: rdn whn clr run over 2f out: nt pce to get involved* **4/1**[2]

8 3 3/4 **Minella Charmer (IRE)**[211] [5352] 4-10-13 0 ....(t) TomBellamy(3) 95
(Alan King) *mid-div: effrt wl over 2f out: sn outpcd* **7/1**[3]

04 **9** 12 **Cor Wot An Apple**[159] [644] 4-11-2 0 .... BrendanPowell 85
(Colin Tizzard) *chsd ldrs: rdn over 2f out: sn wknd* **25/1**

10 11 **Breeze Along** 5-10-13 0 .... LucyGardner(3) 75
(Sue Gardner) *a towards rr* **100/1**

3/4 **11** 2 3/4 **Subordinate (GER)**[26] [1973] 6-11-2 0 ....(t) DarylJacob 72
(Emma Lavelle) *prom: rdn 3f out: sn wknd* **12/1**

12 7 **Calisto** 5-11-2 0 .... DavidBass 66
(Ben Pauling) *mid-div: pushed along 1/2-way: wknd over 3f out* **16/1**

13 nse **Sahara Haze**[180] 6-10-4 0 .... MrBMoorcroft(5) 59
(Phillip Dando) *mid-div: trckd ldrs 6f out: wknd 4f out* **80/1**

P **The Tall Blonde** 6-10-9 0 .... JamesBest
(Peter Purdy) *a bhd: t.o 1/2-way: p.u 3f out* **200/1**

3m 54.0s (-8.40) **Going Correction** -0.575s/f (Firm)
WFA 4 from 5yo+ 7lb **14 Ran SP% 121.6**
Speed ratings: **98,96,94,94,93 93,93,91,85,79 78,74,74,**
CSF £34.16 TOTE £13.30: £3.30, £1.30, £8.70; EX 93.90 Trifecta £2516.80.
Owner Mrs Angela Tincknell & W Tincknell **Bred** W C Tincknell And Mrs A Tincknell **Trained** West Buckland, Somerset

FOCUS
A classic bumper, with them going a steady pace. A step up from the winner.
T/Plt: £17.80 to a £1 stake. Pool of £70478.32 - 2886.15 winning tickets. T/Qpdt: £4.90 to a £1 stake. Pool of £6210.37 - 930.14 winning tickets. **Tim Mitchell**

2461 - 2463a (Foreign Racing) - See Raceform Interactive

2155

CLONMEL (R-H)
Thursday, November 12

OFFICIAL GOING: Hurdle course - heavy; chase course - soft to heavy

2464a CLONMEL OIL CHASE (GRADE 2) (14 fncs) 2m 4f
2:25 (2:25) 4-Y-O+ **£23,934** (£6,996; £3,313; £1,104)

RPR

1 **Road To Riches (IRE)**[197] [22] 8-11-12 165 .... BJCooper 169+
(Noel Meade, Ire) *mde all: j. sltly lft at times: pressed gng best 2 out: drvn clr bef last and styd on wl to assert run-in: comf* **8/13**[1]

2 6 **Bright New Dawn (IRE)**[4] [2388] 8-11-5 148 ....(t) KeithDonoghue 155
(Gordon Elliott, Ire) *w.w in rr: last at 1/2-way: 4th 3 out and tk clsr order appr st: rdn in 2nd 2 out where pressed wnr: no ex bef last and kpt on same pce run-in* **8/1**[3]

3 1/2 **Felix Yonger (IRE)**[198] [8] 9-11-12 160 .... RWalsh 162
(W P Mullins, Ire) *hld up bhd ldrs: 4th 1/2-way: nt fluent 7th: last 3 out: clsr in 4th bef 2 out: pushed along between last 2 and no imp on wnr: rdn into 3rd after last and kpt on same pce* **11/4**[2]

4 nk **First Lieutenant (IRE)**[194] [95] 10-11-5 147 .... MarkEnright 154
(M F Morris, Ire) *settled bhd ldr in 2nd: slt mstke 3 out and dropped to 3rd briefly: rdn in 2nd into st and no imp on wnr u.p in 3rd bef 2 out: kpt on same pce and dropped to 4th run-in* **25/1**

5 45 **Mallowney (IRE)**[198] [8] 9-11-10 158 .... AELynch 114
(Timothy Doyle, Ire) *hld up bhd ldrs: slt mstke in 4th at 2nd: 3rd 1/2-way: wnt 2nd briefly fr 3 out: sn lost pl and wknd to rr bef 2 out: eased: t.o* **12/1**

5m 16.4s (-1.20) **5 Ran SP% 111.2**
CSF £6.26 TOTE £1.60: £1.02, £2.20; DF 5.30 Trifecta £14.30.
Owner Gigginstown House Stud **Bred** Sunnyhill Stud **Trained** Castletown, Co Meath

FOCUS
This was a proper good renewal and it went the way the market expected. The form is rated around the third, with the time rather slow.

2465a EUROPEAN BREEDERS FUND T.A. MORRIS MEMORIAL MARES CHASE (GRADE 3) (14 fncs) 2m 4f
2:55 (2:55) 4-Y-O+ **£17,635** (£5,155; £2,441; £813)

RPR

1 **Vroum Vroum Mag (FR)**[220] [5225] 6-11-5 153 .... RWalsh 151+
(W P Mullins, Ire) *settled bhd ldrs: nt fluent 7th: wnt 2nd 3 out: led travelling wl 2 out where nt fluent: sn eased clr and styd on wl: easily* **1/4**[1]

2 7 1/2 **Miss Dinamic (IRE)**[21] [2045] 6-10-10 129 .... BJCooper 130
(Gordon Elliott, Ire) *led tl hdd fr 2nd: sn disp: cl 2nd bef 4th: lost pl fr 6th tl regained advantage 5 out: pressed clly appr st: rdn and hdd 2 out: no ch w easy wnr: kpt on one pce* **16/1**

3 43 **Perfect Promise (IRE)**[32] [1879] 7-11-0 130 .... APHeskin 91
(James Joseph Mangan, Ire) *cl up tl led narrowly fr 2nd: sn jnd tl regained advantage bef 4th: hdd 5 out and reminders in 3rd after: no imp on ldrs in rr 3 out: wnt remote 3rd bef next* **8/1**[3]

4 7 1/2 **Emcon (IRE)**[14] [2160] 6-10-7 0 .... KevinSexton 77
(W J Austin, Ire) *bhd ldrs: pckd 1st and dropped to rr: mstke 2nd and rdr lost lft iron briefly: slow 4th: clsr in 2nd fr 6th: mstke and wnt lft 3 out where lost pl: no imp on ldrs after: dropped to remote 4th bef 2 out: mstke last* **6/1**[2]

5m 13.4s (-4.20) **4 Ran SP% 111.3**
CSF £5.02 TOTE £1.10; DF 3.10 Trifecta £6.80.
Owner Mrs S Ricci **Bred** Comte A Maggiar & Mlle A Maggiar **Trained** Muine Beag, Co Carlow

FOCUS
Straightforward stuff for the favourite here, though she had very little to beat as it transpired. The time was qucker than for the Clonmel Oil Chase.

2466 - 2467a (Foreign Racing) - See Raceform Interactive

2059

CHELTENHAM (L-H)
Friday, November 13

OFFICIAL GOING: Good (good to soft in places on chase and hurdle courses, good to firm in places on cross country course; chs & hdl 7.3, cross country 9.0)
mild breeze across**sunny periods with showers**

2468 PADDY POWER H'CAP CHASE (13 fncs) 1m 7f 199y
1:05 (1:06) (Class 2) (0-145,143) 4-Y-O+
£28,152 (£8,316; £4,158; £2,079; £1,039; £522)

Form RPR

10-5 **1** **Keel Haul (IRE)**[15] [2153] 7-10-9 126 ....(p) JamesDavies 136
(Henry Oliver) *in tch: rdn whn sltly hmpd 3 out: hdwy 2 out: kpt on wl to ld fnl 170yds: drvn out* **10/1**

-312 **2** 1 **Minella Present (IRE)**[37] [1815] 6-10-13 130 .... NoelFehily 140+
(Neil Mulholland) *lw: mid-div: rdn and no imp whn hmpd 3 out: running on whn nt clr run bef last: styd on wl to go 2nd run-in: clsng on wnr nring fin* **9/1**

13-2 **3** 2 1/4 **Pearls Legend**[13] [2185] 8-11-1 132 .... JamieMoore 139
(John Spearing) *led: hdd briefly 3 out: rdn whn mstke and hdd briefly 2 out: kpt on gamely but no ex whn hdd fnl 170yds* **8/1**[3]

15-6 **4** nk **Going Concern (IRE)**[20] [2059] 8-10-11 128 .... PaulMoloney 135
(Evan Williams) *lw: mid-div: rdn and hdwy after 3 out: chsd ldrs next: kpt on fr last but nt quite pce to mount chal* **20/1**

F-14 **5** 1 1/2 **Astracad (FR)**[20] [2059] 9-11-6 137 ....(t) SamTwiston-Davies 141
(Nigel Twiston-Davies) *chsd ldrs: rdn after 3 out: ch last: no ex fnl 120yds* **14/1**

2- **6** 3 **La Vaticane (FR)**[244] [4750] 6-11-3 134 ....(t) TomScudamore 137+
(David Pipe) *sn trcking ldrs: led briefly 3 out: rdn bef next where hmpd: kpt on same pce fr last* **10/3**[1]

3-13 **7** 3 3/4 **Lough Kent**[175] [431] 6-11-8 139 .... NicodeBoinville 143+
(Nicky Henderson) *in tch: hdwy after 3 out: slt ld whn mstke and rdr lost irons 2 out (nvr rcvrd irons): sn hdd: stl ev ch last: fdd fnl 120yds* **10/1**

0145 **8** 2 1/2 **Fairyinthewind (IRE)**[26] [1643] 6-9-12 122 ....(t) DavidNoonan(7) 119
(Brendan Powell) *towards rr: rdn after 9th: hdwy fr 3 out: cl up 2 out: wknd appr last* **25/1**

0-30 **9** 3 1/4 **Sew On Target (IRE)**[20] [2059] 10-11-6 137 .... BrendanPowell 131
(Colin Tizzard) *pressed ldr tl rdn after 4 out: in tch but hld whn wnt lft next: wknd bef last* **11/1**

3U00 **10** 9 **Owen Na View (IRE)**[20] [2059] 7-11-0 131 .... PaddyBrennan 116
(Fergal O'Brien) *hmpd 2nd: a towards rr* **33/1**

02-0 **11** 1/2 **Silver Roque (FR)**[189] [184] 9-11-8 142 ....(t) ConorShoemark(3) 127
(Fergal O'Brien) *mid-div: towards rr whn nt fluent 8th: struggling after next: nvr bk on terms* **25/1**

6PP- **12** 15 **Majala (FR)**[204] [5493] 9-11-12 143 ....(t) AlainCawley 117
(Tom George) *mstke 9th: a in rr* **50/1**

-216 **P** **Le Bacardy (FR)**[19] [2084] 9-11-9 140 .... HarrySkelton
(Dan Skelton) *in tch: rdn after 9th: wknd after 4 out: bhd whn p.u after 3 out* **16/1**

5P-2 **F** **Key To The West (IRE)**[15] [2153] 8-10-1 125 .... MrStanSheppard(7)
(Matt Sheppard) *mid-div whn fell 3rd* **14/1**

/16- **P** **The Clock Leary (IRE)**[349] [2804] 7-10-13 130 .... AidanColeman
(Venetia Williams) *in tch whn landed steeply and nrly fell 1st: mid-div: nt travelling in rr fr 7th: p.u bef 4 out* **7/1**[2]

4m 2.5s (4.50) **Going Correction** +0.425s/f (Soft) **15 Ran SP% 119.8**
Speed ratings (Par 109): **105,104,103,103,102 100,99,97,96,91 91,83,,,**
CSF £90.42 CT £766.40 TOTE £10.80: £3.30, £2.90, £2.80; EX 116.40 Trifecta £1195.50.
Owner R G Whitehead **Bred** Aaron Stronge **Trained** Abberley, Worcs

FOCUS
Old Course used. All bends dolled out 9yds and distances increased by 56yds per circuit. Ground on the easy side following 2mm of overnight rain. A classy and competitive handicap chase run at a brisk gallop, and the form has a solid look to it. The winner is back to his Wincanton level.

2469 STEEL PLATE AND SECTIONS NOVICES' CHASE (16 fncs) 2m 4f 78y
1:40 (1:40) (Class 2) 4-Y-O+
£14,388 (£4,250; £2,125; £1,062; £531; £266)

Form RPR

1/3- **1** **More Of That (IRE)**[349] [2807] 7-11-2 0 .... BarryGeraghty 153+
(Jonjo O'Neill) *j.w: cl up: nudged along after 3 out: chal 2 out: led last: pushed clr: comf* **15/8**[1]

16-2 **2** 2 1/2 **As De Mee (FR)**[34] [1846] 5-11-2 0 .... SamTwiston-Davies 146
(Paul Nicholls) *lw: j.w but sltly rt most of way: led: rdn appr 2 out where wnt rt: wnt rt and hdd last: kpt on but sn hld by wnr* **4/1**[2]

0-31 **3** 3 1/2 **Dell' Arca (IRE)**[173] [461] 6-11-7 142 ....(b) TomScudamore 150
(David Pipe) *hld up bhd ldrs: hdwy after 3 out: rdn between last 2: wnt 3rd at the last: kpt on same pce* **15/2**

11-2 **4** 5 **Double Shuffle (IRE)**[20] [2063] 5-11-2 0 .... PaddyBrennan 139
(Tom George) *trckd ldrs: pressed ldr 11th tl rdn after 4 out: lost cl 2nd 2 out: lost 3rd at the last: wknd run-in* **12/1**

311- **5** 2 1/4 **Might Bite (IRE)**[212] [5339] 6-11-2 0 .... NicodeBoinville 139+
(Nicky Henderson) *lw: trckd ldrs: mstke 9th and rdr lost iron briefly: pckd 11th: rdn after 3 out: wknd bef last* **9/2**[3]

42/U **6** 26 **Ballyalton (IRE)**[9] [2274] 8-11-2 0 .... WillKennedy 118
(Ian Williams) *pressed ldr most of way tl 11th: rdn after 4 out: styd chsng ldrs tl wknd bef 2 out* **11/2**

P335 **7** 71 **The Society Man (IRE)**[15] [2147] 8-11-2 88 .... DannyBurton 49
(Michael Chapman) *lost tch after 7th: t.o* **250/1**

5m 12.3s (1.30) **Going Correction** +0.425s/f (Soft) **7 Ran SP% 108.2**
Speed ratings (Par 109): **114,113,111,109,108 98,69**
CSF £8.83 TOTE £2.50: £1.60, £2.30; EX 8.20 Trifecta £32.50.
Owner John P McManus **Bred** Mrs Eleanor Hadden **Trained** Cheltenham, Gloucs

FOCUS
Chasing stars to have won this event in the past decade include Denman, Imperial Commander, Grands Crus, Dynaste and Taquin Du Seuil. This was another high-class renewal, with More Of That an exciting prospect. He should go on to make a 160+ chaser.

2470 NEPTUNE INVESTMENT MANAGEMENT NOVICES' HURDLE (REGISTERED AS THE HYDE NOVICES' HURDLE) (GRADE 2) (10 hdls) — 2m 5f 26y

2:15 (2:18) (Class 1) 4-Y-O+ £17,085 (£6,411; £3,210; £1,599)

Form — RPR

1-1 **1** **Shantou Village (IRE)**[29] 1923 5-11-4 0 NoelFehily 147+
(Neil Mulholland) *str: lw: trckd ldr: chal sn after 8th: led 2 out: rdn clr: styd on strly: quite impressive* 9/2[3]

1 **2** *15* **Champers On Ice (IRE)**[198] 25 5-11-0 0 TomScudamore 130+
(David Pipe) *led: qcknd pce whn jnd sn after 8th: hdd 2 out: sn rdn and hld by wnr: styd on same pce* 11/4[2]

111 **3** *2 3/4* **Penglai Pavilion (USA)**[21] 2052 5-11-7 146 AidanColeman 134
(John Ferguson) *trckd ldrs: effrt 2 out: sn drvn to press for 2nd but nt pce to get on terms w wnr: no ex fnl 150yds: jst hld on for 3rd* 5/6[1]

/6-1 **4** *nk* **Alcala (FR)**[23] 2024 5-11-4 126 SamTwiston-Davies 130
(Paul Nicholls) *trckd ldrs: rdn after 3 out: sltly outpcd after next: styd on fr last: nrly snatched 3rd fnl strides* 12/1

5m 15.3s (1.90) **Going Correction** +0.425s/f (Soft) **4** Ran SP% **107.1**
Speed ratings (Par 115): **113,107,106,106**
CSF £15.93 TOTE £4.90; EX 17.60 Trifecta £26.10.
Owner Mrs Jane Gerard-Pearse **Bred** Mrs Mary F Griffin **Trained** Limpley Stoke, Wilts

FOCUS
This event, a Grade 2 since 2008, has had quite an impact on the staying novice hurdles at the festival. Black Jack Ketchum won this in 2005 and followed up in the Albert Bartlett over 3m, and Massini's Maguire landed what is now the Neptune after taking this. Nenuphar Collonges and Berties Dream won the Albert Bartlett after being placed here, and last year's winner Parlour Games finished second in the Neptune. The best winner is Coneygree, successful in 2012. This edition lacked depth, but delivered an impressive winner who rates a smart novice.

2471 GLENFARCLAS CROSS COUNTRY H'CAP CHASE (32 fncs) — 3m 6f 37y

2:50 (2:50) (Class 2) 5-Y-O+
£15,640 (£4,620; £2,310; £1,155; £577; £290)

Form — RPR

P6-U **1** **Josies Orders (IRE)**[18] 2112 7-10-2 129 MsNCarberry 135+
(E Bolger, Ire) *mid-div: trckd ldrs briefly 21st: lost pl again after next: mstke 28th and slipped sn after: hdwy appr 2 out: chal last: led fnl 120yds: drvn out* 11/4[1]

2-34 **2** *1 1/4* **Any Currency (IRE)**[19] 2082 12-11-11 152 (p) AidanColeman 155
(Martin Keighley) *a.p: led 18th tl next: rdn after 4 out: led after 2 out: hdd fnl 120yds: styd on but no ex* 9/1

3334 **3** *5* **Bless The Wings (IRE)**[12] 2228 10-10-3 133 (p) KevinSexton(3) 133
(Gordon Elliott, Ire) *towards rr of midfield: hdwy fr 27th: chal 2 out: sn rdn: ev ch last: no ex run-in* 12/1

216 **4** *15* **Valadom (FR)**[43] 1715 6-10-0 127 oh2 AlainCawley 113
(Richard Hobson) *led most of way: slow whn hdd 18th: led next: rdn and hdd after 2 out: hld whn lft 4th at the last: no ex* 33/1

0-44 **5** *3* **Rose Of The Moon (IRE)**[172] 471 10-10-0 127 oh1(p) RichieMcLernon 110
(Ben Haslam) *in tch: trckd ldrs 18th: lost pl 20th: hdwy whn rdn after 4 out: styd on but nvr threatened to get on terms w ldrs fr 2 out* 20/1

312- **6** *10* **Saint Are (FR)**[216] 5275 9-11-7 148 (t) PaddyBrennan 120
(Tom George) *in tch: rdn after 24th: styd on same pce fr 3 out* 8/1[3]

110 **7** *24* **Champion Court (IRE)**[20] 2061 10-11-12 153 (p) AndrewTinkler 104
(Martin Keighley) *towards rr: nvr threatened to get involved: t.o* 14/1

1245 **8** *nk* **Kilbree Kid (IRE)**[28] 1944 8-10-7 134 (t) DarylJacob 84
(Tom George) *mid-div: hdwy 25th: blnd bdly 28th and lost pl: sn bhd: t.o* 33/1

10-P **9** *10* **Rivage D'Or (FR)**[197] 48 10-11-0 141 (t) DenisO'Regan 82
(A J Martin, Ire) *mid-div: towards rr fr 20th: nvr bk on terms: t.o* 10/1

1-50 **10** *10* **Allthekingshorses (IRE)**[37] 1807 9-10-0 127 oh3 (tp) JamesBest 59
(Philip Hobbs) *mid-div: nt fluent 1st: mstke 11th: struggling 23rd: wknd 25th: t.o* 25/1

0-1P **11** *11* **Pinerolo**[15] 2146 9-9-9 127 oh4 (p) HarryBannister(5) 50
(Joanne Foster) *struggling 17th a in rr t.o* 66/1

2-06 **U** **Kingsmere**[27] 1963 10-10-3 130 oh5 ow3 TomO'Brien
(Henry Daly) *hld up towards rr: mstke and uns rdr 16th* 20/1

03-1 **S** **Uncle Junior (IRE)**[197] 48 14-11-8 149 (p) MrPWMullins
(W P Mullins, Ire) *hld up bhd: stdy prog fr 25th: upsides wnr travelling wl whn slipped up after 28th* 11/1

62-P **S** **Sire Collonges (FR)**[180] 375 9-11-4 145 (b) SamTwiston-Davies 145
(Paul Nicholls) *trckd ldrs: pushed along in v cl 4th whn slipped up on bnd bef 2 out* 10/1

23-2 **U** **Loose Chips**[29] 1924 9-10-3 130 (b) BrianHughes
(Charlie Longsdon) *trcking ldr whn virtually fell and uns rdr 4th* 10/1

4P-F **F** **Dogora (FR)**[197] 48 6-10-7 134 MsKWalsh 134
(W P Mullins, Ire) *mid-div: mstke 10th: hdwy 20th: rdn to chse ldng pair after 2 out: cl 4th whn v short of room and fell last* 15/2[2]

8m 9.8s (-28.20) **Going Correction** -0.60s/f (Firm) **16** Ran SP% **130.3**
Speed ratings: **113,112,111,107,106 103,97,97,94,92 89, , , ,**
CSF £28.01 CT £278.22 TOTE £3.70: £1.60, £2.10, £3.10, £9.70; EX 24.90 Trifecta £715.30.
Owner John P McManus **Bred** Mrs E Moore **Trained** Bruree, Co Limerick

FOCUS
This race, previously a conditions event, was run as a handicap for the first time, and attracted a competitive field. Six of the first seven home in the cross-country event at the festival crossed swords again, on revised terms. Josies Orders can rate higher.

2472 OPUS ENERGY NOVICES' H'CAP HURDLE (5 hdls 3 omitted) — 2m 87y

3:25 (3:34) (Class 3) (0-125,125) 3-Y-O+
£7,507 (£2,217; £1,108; £554; £277; £139)

Form — RPR

24/ **1** **A Hare Breath (IRE)**[695] 3163 7-11-7 120 NicodeBoinville 128+
(Ben Pauling) *lw: hld up in midfield: prog on outer bef usual 3 out: trckd ldrs next: rdn to ld bef omitted last: drvn out* 6/1[2]

6-21 **2** *2 1/4* **Galizzi (USA)**[124] 960 4-11-12 125 (t) AidanColeman 129
(John Ferguson) *hld up in midfield: prog bef usual 3 out: trckd ldrs next: rdn to chse wnr last 150yds: styd on but unable to chal* 14/1

0-32 **3** *1 1/2* **Double W's (IRE)**[18] 2101 5-11-4 117 BrianHughes 120
(Malcolm Jefferson) *lw: trckd ldrs gng wl: wnt 2nd usual 2 out (actual last): led briefly on long run-in: one pce last 150yds* 14/1

4 **4** *1/2* **Dollar And A Dream (IRE)**[57] 1565 6-11-0 113 (t) RWalsh 115
(A J Martin, Ire) *hld up in last quartet: plenty to do on run bef usual 3 out: gd hdwy bef 2 out: styd on to take 4th last 150yds: nt rch ldrs* 10/3[1]

30-1 **5** *6* **Mystifiable**[36] 1818 7-11-2 115 (t) PaddyBrennan 113
(Fergal O'Brien) *cl up: chsd ldr bef 3 out to 2 out: wknd bef omitted last* 16/1

25-1 **6** *2* **Adrakhan (FR)**[27] 1967 4-11-5 118 HarrySkelton 113
(Dan Skelton) *lw: towards rr: prog bef usual 3 out: rdn and one pce bef omitted last* 20/1

40-1 **7** *1 3/4* **Ink Master (IRE)**[36] 1828 5-11-9 122 RichardJohnson 116
(Philip Hobbs) *lw: trckd ldr: led and mstke 3rd: hdd & wknd bef omitted last* 7/1[3]

24P- **8** *1 3/4* **Briery Belle**[237] 4918 6-11-9 122 JakeGreenall 114
(Henry Daly) *chsd ldrs: rdn wl bef usual 3 out: lost pl usual 2 out: one pce after* 33/1

5342 **9** *shd* **Are They Your Own (IRE)**[21] 2058 7-11-4 122 (t) NickSlatter(5) 114
(Fergal O'Brien) *led to 3rd: rdn and lost pl fr usual 3 out* 33/1

2 **10** *2* **Mon Successeur (FR)**[13] 2201 4-11-5 125 HarryCobden(7) 115
(Paul Nicholls) *hld up in last quartet: tried to make prog bef usual 3 out: no hdwy on long run after usual 2 out* 10/1

125 **11** *1 3/4* **Mountain Fighter**[28] 1949 4-11-4 124 MrAlexFerguson(7) 112
(John Ferguson) *a in rr: shkn up and no real prog after usual 3 out: no ch whn hmpd next* 50/1

33-4 **12** *1 3/4* **Eco Warrior**[12] 2212 5-10-11 110 LiamTreadwell 97
(Venetia Williams) *chsd ldrs: hit 1st: lost pl 3rd: wl bhd usual 3 out* 25/1

2-12 **13** *8* **Argot**[37] 1814 4-11-9 122 (p) NoelFehily 102
(Charlie Longsdon) *chsd ldrs: rdn usual 3 out: wknd qckly after usual 2 out* 25/1

0 **14** *5* **Kings Cross (FR)**[13] 2182 5-11-0 113 LeeEdwards 88
(Tony Carroll) *chsd ldrs to 2nd on outer: lost pl next: wl in rr on long run to usual 3 out* 80/1

-124 **15** *16* **Benissimo (IRE)**[41] 1752 5-11-6 119 RyanMahon 80
(Dan Skelton) *a in rr: t.o whn sltly hmpd usual 2 out* 33/1

30-0 **U** **Brigadier Miller**[14] 2170 8-11-6 119 AndrewTinkler
(Nicky Henderson) *a towards rr: bhd whn hmpd and uns rdr usual 2 out* 25/1

14 **F** **King Muro**[54] 1591 5-10-12 114 (t) ConorShoemark(3) 113
(Fergal O'Brien) *hld up in last quartet: prog bef usual 3 out: stl plenty to do but keeping on whn fell usual 2 out* 50/1

3P6- **S** **Trendsetter (IRE)**[55] 4155 4-11-0 113 TomO'Brien
(John Quinn) *clipped heels and slipped up after 2f* 9/1

-115 **B** **Midnight Shot**[26] 1986 5-11-12 125 SamTwiston-Davies
(Charlie Longsdon) *hld up: b.d after 2f* 20/1

350- **F** **Baraka De Thaix (FR)**[245] 4736 4-11-12 125 DarylJacob
(David Pipe) *blnd 1st: prom: wknd bef usual 3 out: bhd whn fell usual 2 out* 14/1

3m 55.2s (-6.80) **Going Correction** -0.25s/f (Good) **20** Ran SP% **129.9**
Speed ratings (Par 107): **107,105,105,104,101 100,100,99,99,98 97,96,92,89,81 , , , ,**
CSF £78.73 CT £1168.60 TOTE £7.70: £2.60, £2.80, £3.80, £1.60; EX 105.40 Trifecta £2360.50.
Owner Mrs S N J Embiricos **Bred** Martin Byrne **Trained** Bourton-On-The-Water, Gloucs

FOCUS
Obstacles were in short supply in this highly competitive novices' handicap, with an especially long run from the last one they jumped. The race was notable for a gamble on the winner. The first two can rate higher and the form may work out.

2473 CHELTENHAM CLUB AMATEUR RIDERS' H'CAP CHASE (20 fncs) — 3m 1f

4:00 (4:05) (Class 3) (0-140,140) 4-Y-O+
£11,992 (£3,746; £1,872; £936; £468; £236)

Form — RPR

51-2 **1** **Knock House (IRE)**[28] 1944 6-11-12 140 MsNCarberry 151
(Mick Channon) *lw: mid-div: hdwy on outer to trck ldrs 5th: rdn to ld bef last: styd on: rdn out* 9/2[1]

155- **2** *nk* **Foxbridge (IRE)**[211] 5356 9-10-3 124 (t) MrJJSlevin(7) 136+
(Nigel Twiston-Davies) *racd keenly: trckd ldrs: led after 9th: rdn after 3 out: hdd bef last: rallied flat: hld cl home* 9/1

2-22 **3** *5* **Alternatif (FR)**[33] 505 5-11-2 133 DavidNoonan(3) 139
(David Pipe) *hld up: hdwy on outer appr 3 out: rdn bef 2 out: wnt 3rd between last 2: styd on but nt gng pce to threaten front pair* 6/1[2]

0-02 **4** *1 3/4* **Ericht (IRE)**[176] 420 9-11-2 130 MrSWaley-Cohen 134
(Nicky Henderson) *mid-div: hdwy 3 out: sn rdn: styd on same pce fr 2 out* 12/1

500- **5** *8* **Return Spring (IRE)**[202] 5538 8-10-13 134 (b) MrSeanHoulihan(7) 134+
(Philip Hobbs) *lw: in tch: trckd ldrs 7th: rdn after 3 out: 4th but hld whn landed v awkwardly and nrly uns rdr 2 out: regained hld 4th run-in: lost shoe* 7/1[3]

1FP- **6** *4 1/2* **Minellahalfcentury (IRE)**[266] 4341 7-11-6 134 (bt) MrWBiddick 127
(Paul Nicholls) *led tl 7th: prom: rdn after 3 out: hld in 5th whn hmpd 2 out: wknd run-in* 14/1

60P- **7** *3* **Super Duty (IRE)**[216] 5275 9-11-7 135 MrDerekO'Connor 123
(Ian Williams) *trckd ldrs: grad lost pl fr 10th: struggling in last pair after 14th: nvr bk on terms* 9/2[1]

0-22 **8** *3/4* **Definite Ruby (IRE)**[21] 2057 7-11-2 130 (b) MrJJCodd 120
(Gordon Elliott, Ire) *hld up: blnd 4 out: rdn after 3 out: nvr any imp* 12/1

0 **9** *nse* **Our Sox (IRE)**[29] 1939 6-10-4 118 (t) MsKWalsh 108
(A J Martin, Ire) *hld up: pushed along whn hit 3 out: nvr trbld ldrs* 11/1

5P-P **10** *2 1/4* **Firm Order (IRE)**[37] 1807 10-10-5 126 (tp) MrMJPKendrick(7) 111
(Paul Webber) *mid-div: nt fluent 3rd: hdwy 11th: effrt 3 out: wknd next* 50/1

103- **11** *13* **No Duffer**[211] 5356 8-11-4 132 MrBO'Neill 104
(Tom George) *prom: led 7th tl after 9th: rdn after 3 out: wknd bef next* 12/1

1311 **12** *4* **Mia's Anthem (IRE)**[32] 1889 7-10-8 129 (t) MrSPKelly(7) 97
(Noel C Kelly, Ire) *hld up: mstke 10th: hdwy 13th: rdn after 3 out: sn wknd* 18/1

6m 40.7s (14.70) **Going Correction** +0.425s/f (Soft) course record **12** Ran SP% **118.5**
Speed ratings (Par 107): **93,92,91,90,88 86,85,85,85,84 80,79**
CSF £45.10 CT £248.13 TOTE £4.30: £2.40, £4.30, £2.30; EX 50.80 Trifecta £400.40.
Owner T P Radford **Bred** P Cashman **Trained** West Ilsley, Berks
■ Stewards' Enquiry : Mr J J Slevin 15-day ban; used his whip above the permitted level and without giving his horse time to respond (tba)

FOCUS
A decent handicap chase, confined to amateur riders. It was steadily run and the winner produced a step up.
T/Jkpt: Not won. JACKPOT PLACEPOT: £80.50 to a £1 stake. Pool of £2,588.00 - 23.45 winning units. T/Plt: £242.50 to a £1 stake. Pool: £177,222.00 - 533.39 winning tickets T/Qpdt: £27.90 to a £1 stake. Pool: £19,700.00 - 521.75 winning tickets **Tim Mitchell**

2318 HEXHAM (L-H)

Friday, November 13

OFFICIAL GOING: Heavy (3.8)

Wind: Fairly strong, half against Weather: Overcast

2474 FREE SPINS AT 188BET CASINO NOVICES' HURDLE (5 hdls 3 omitted) 2m 48y

12:40 (12:40) (Class 4) 4-Y-0+ **£3,898** (£1,144; £572; £286)

Form RPR

1 **Master Jake (IRE)**215 7-10-12 0 IanPopham 110+
(Dan Skelton) *chsd ldr: led 4th: drew clr fr omitted 2 out: shkn up last: kpt on: unchal* **4/11[1]**

30 2 18 **Absolute (IRE)**17 [2123] 4-10-12 0 DannyCook 90
(Sue Smith) *chsd ldrs: wnt 2nd bef omitted 2 out: sn pushed along and no ch w wnr* **4/1[2]**

00 3 8 **Mister Don (IRE)**13 [2189] 5-10-9 0 GrahamWatters(3) 82
(Rose Dobbin) *hld up: pushed along passing omitted 3 out: plugged on passing omitted 2 out: no ch w first two* **10/1**

POUP 4 6 **Bertielicious**15 [2148] 7-10-5 61 (e[1]) ThomasDowson(7) 76
(Jonathan Haynes) *led to 4th: cl up tl rdn and wknd passing omitted 2 out* **100/1**

0-F0 5 nse **Fifteen Kings (IRE)**7 [2318] 5-10-7 0 (t) GrantCockburn(5) 76
(Lucinda Russell) *hld up in tch: pushed along and outpcd passing omitted 3 out: n.d after* **10/1**

6 33 **Imahustler Baby (IRE)**173 4-10-5 0 MrWHRReed(7) 43
(Andrew Hamilton) *hld up: rdn and struggling passing omitted 3 out: nvr on terms* **40/1**

7 64 **Tommy Dylon (IRE)**180 5-10-12 0 HenryBrooke
(Martin Todhunter) *bhd: struggling fr 3rd: t.o* **40/1**

P **Byronegetonefree**10 4-10-12 0 JamesReveley
(Stuart Coltherd) *nt fluent on occasions in rr: lost tch fr 3rd: t.o whn p.u bef last* **8/1[3]**

4m 44.7s (27.30) **Going Correction** +1.90s/f (Heav)
WFA 4 from 5yo+ 7lb **8 Ran SP% 128.5**
Speed ratings (Par 105): **107,98,94,91,90 74,42,**
CSF £3.08 TOTE £1.30: £1.10, £1.20, £3.60; EX 2.30 Trifecta £12.60.
Owner Craig Buckingham **Bred** Tyrone Molloy **Trained** Alcester, Warwicks

FOCUS
This fixture had been transferred from Newcastle. Hurdles 1 (first in 2m) and 6 omitted, and fence 7 (on top of hill) bypassed in both chases, while fence 9 was also omitted in race 4. Rails and hurdles moved to allow for best possible ground and changes to races distances as follows: 2m hurdle, bumper and 1m7f chase +41yds, 2m4f hurdle and chase +61yds, 2m7f hurdle +82yds. After 6mm of rain overnight and showers through the morning the going remained heavy. This opening novice hurdle was as one-sided as the betting suggested it would be. They went a very steady pace in the conditions, but still finished very tired and the winning time was 49.7sec outside standard. Just five flights were jumped. The easy winner can rate higher.

2475 OPEN MEETING BETTING AT 188BET NOVICES' LIMITED H'CAP CHASE (11 fncs 1 omitted) 1m 7f 133y

1:15 (1:15) (Class 4) (0-120,120) 4-Y-0+ **£5,198** (£1,526; £763; £381)

Form RPR

513- 1 **Mossies Well (IRE)**231 [5009] 6-11-8 120 (t) JamesReveley 121
(Sandy Thomson) *chsd ldr: led 4 out: rdn and jnd run-in: hld on gamely cl home* **6/4[1]**

U63- 2 shd **Forward Flight (IRE)**258 [4487] 9-11-5 117 SeanQuinlan 118
(Sue Smith) *chsd ldrs: effrt and wnt 2nd 2 out: edgd lft and disp ld run-in: kpt on: jst hld* **7/2[2]**

P20- 3 3 1/4 **Gold Opera (IRE)**205 [5469] 6-10-4 107 StephenMulqueen(5) 105
(N W Alexander) *hld up in tch: shkn up and outpcd 4 out: gd hdwy after 2 out: cl 3rd and rdn last: outpcd last 100yds* **6/1**

/0P6 4 47 **Parlour Of Dreams (IRE)**13 [2189] 8-9-12 103 SamColtherd(7) 54
(Andrew Hamilton) *nt fluent on occasions: hld up: outpcd 4 out: lost tch fr next: t.o* **25/1**

134- P **Engrossing**221 [5205] 6-11-6 118 BrianHarding
(Peter Niven) *nt fluent on occasions: hld up in tch: mstke 1st: drvn and outpcd 1/2-way: lost tch 3 out: t.o whn p.u bef last* **5/1[3]**

3555 P **Pekanheim (IRE)**22 [2030] 7-10-9 107 HenryBrooke
(Martin Todhunter) *led to 4 out: drvn and lost 2nd 2 out: wknd quicky and p.u bef last* **5/1[3]**

4m 37.8s (28.00) **Going Correction** +1.90s/f (Heav)
WFA 4 from 6yo+ 7lb **6 Ran SP% 113.7**
Speed ratings (Par 105): **106,105,104,80,**
CSF £7.66 CT £23.11 TOTE £2.20: £1.20, £2.00; EX 6.60 Trifecta £38.80.
Owner Matros Racing **Bred** Andrew Pierce **Trained** Lambden, Berwicks

FOCUS
A fair novices' handicap chase and again this looked gruelling in the conditions, but it produced a thrilling finish. The second sets the level.

2476 188BET.CO.UK MARES' MAIDEN HURDLE (6 hdls 4 omitted) 2m 4f 28y

1:50 (1:50) (Class 5) 4-Y-0+ **£3,898** (£1,144; £572; £286)

Form RPR

-505 1 **Innis Shannon (IRE)**12 [2210] 5-10-7 0 JonathonBewley(5) 98+
(George Bewley) *pressed ldr: led bef last: pushed clr* **5/1**

43U0 2 30 **Louloumills**32 [1887] 5-10-5 80 ThomasDowson(7) 74
(Maurice Barnes) *led at stdy gallop: rdn and hdd bef last: no ch w wnr* **22/1**

03-6 3 12 **Madame Trigger**14 [2164] 7-10-12 112 (t) IanPopham 61
(Dan Skelton) *chsd ldr to bef 2 out (usual 4 out): drvn and outpcd passing omitted 2 out: btn bef last* **5/4[1]**

26- 4 34 **Timeforfirth (IRE)**237 [4901] 5-10-12 0 PeterCarberry 22
(Jennie Candlish) *hld up in tch: stdy hdwy after 2 out (usual 4 out) drvn after omitted 2 out: sn wknd: t.o* **9/2[3]**

03-3 P **Presenting Rose (IRE)**183 [305] 5-10-7 0 StephenMulqueen(5)
(N W Alexander) *t.k.h: prom: drvn and outpcd passing omitted 2 out: lost tch and p.u bef last* **11/4[2]**

6m 0.2s (47.70) **Going Correction** +2.20s/f (Heav) **5 Ran SP% 110.3**
Speed ratings (Par 103): **92,80,75,61,**
CSF £63.01 TOTE £7.40: £2.60, £4.60; EX 43.40 Trifecta £73.80.
Owner Mrs Lesley Bewley & John Gibson **Bred** T Broderick **Trained** Bonchester Bridge, Borders

FOCUS
They went a very steady pace in this mares' maiden hurdle and it became something of a 3f sprint. A few of these patently failed to handle the conditions, so the form may not be reliable. The winner rated in line with best of bumper figures.

2477 188BET H'CAP CHASE (12 fncs 3 omitted) 2m 4f 15y

2:25 (2:25) (Class 4) (0-120,120) 4-Y-0+ **£5,198** (£1,526; £763; £381)

Form RPR

5100 1 **Tikkandemickey (IRE)**22 [2030] 9-11-2 115 CallumBewley(5) 125+
(Raymond Shiels) *cl up: led bef 2nd to 5th (water): pressed ldr: clr of rest fr 8th: led between last 2: clr whn rdn and edgd rt run-in: styd on wl* **11/2[2]**

41-0 2 18 **Clan William (IRE)**22 [2042] 7-11-1 109 SeanQuinlan 104
(Sue Smith) *cl up: led 5th (water): clr w wnr fr 8th: rdn and hdd between last 2: sn no ex* **9/2[1]**

0-06 3 21 **More Madness (IRE)**13 [2192] 8-11-1 116 (p) MrKitAlexander(7) 87
(N W Alexander) *in tch: pushed along and outpcd 1/2-way: rallied to chse clr ldng pair after 2 out: sn no imp* **6/1[3]**

652F 4 2 1/2 **Sean Airgead (IRE)**34 [1855] 10-11-6 117 (t) DerekFox(3) 86
(Mark Michael McNiff, Ire) *hld up in last pl: pushed along after 8th: shortlived effrt bef 3 out: sn no imp* **9/1**

3-3F P **Suprise Vendor (IRE)**34 [1855] 9-10-11 112 SamColtherd(7)
(Stuart Coltherd) *in tch: outpcd fr 8th: wknd fr 3 out: lost tch and p.u after next* **7/1**

6-26 P **Habbie Simpson**159 [657] 10-11-5 120 MrTHamilton(7)
(Pauline Robson) *hld up: pushed along 5th: outpcd whn mstke 7th: sn lost tch: p.u bef 4 out (usual 5 out)* **7/1**

240- P **Trust Thomas**213 [5328] 7-11-2 117 JamieHamilton(7)
(Ann Hamilton) *hld up bhd ldng gp: stdy hdwy to chse clr ldng pair after 5th (water) to after 2 out: sn wknd: p.u bef last* **9/2[1]**

521- P **Boric**314 [3500] 7-10-11 105 HenryBrooke
(Simon Waugh) *chsd ldrs: pckd 5th (water): struggling 7th: lost tch and p.u bef 4 out (usual 5 out)* **11/2[2]**

5m 54.7s (41.20) **Going Correction** +2.20s/f (Heav) **8 Ran SP% 116.4**
Speed ratings (Par 105): **105,97,89,88, , ,**
CSF £31.49 CT £154.48 TOTE £8.00: £2.50, £2.20, £2.60; EX 39.20 Trifecta £229.10.
Owner R Shiels **Bred** Alistair Thompson **Trained** Jedburgh, Roxburgh

FOCUS
A fair handicap chase and quite a test as they started racing from some way out and it only concerned the front pair from that point. Only four managed to complete. The winner is rated in line with the best of her hurdles form round here.

2478 MONEY BACK SPECIAL AT 188BET H'CAP HURDLE (8 hdls 4 omitted) 2m 7f 63y

3:00 (3:00) (Class 5) (0-100,98) 4-Y-0+ **£3,328** (£1,033; £556)

Form RPR

2410 1 **Native Optimist (IRE)**34 [1856] 8-11-7 98 MissCWalton(5) 115+
(Sheena Walton) *hld up in tch: stdy hdwy 1/2-way: led passing omitted 2 out: drew clr bef last* **11/4[2]**

020- 2 22 **Newyearsresolution (IRE)**213 [5329] 11-9-10 75 MissAWaugh(7) 64
(Simon Waugh) *cl up: led 3 out (usual 5 out): hdd passing omitted 2 out: sn outpcd by wnr* **10/1**

055- 3 34 **The Squinty Bridge**276 [4136] 7-11-4 95 GrantCockburn(5) 50
(Lucinda Russell) *t.k.h: hld up in tch: stdy hdwy to chse ldrs bef 2 out (usual 4 out): rdn passing omitted 2 out: wknd bef last: eased run-in* **5/2[1]**

5U00 P **Sharivarry (FR)**8 [2296] 9-10-2 81 SamColtherd(7)
(Victor Thompson) *hld up: drvn after 2 out (usual 4 out): sn outpcd: lost tch bef omitted 2 out: p.u bef last* **40/1**

410- P **Stickleback**165 [4726] 6-11-1 90 JoeColliver(3)
(Micky Hammond) *in tch: sn pushed along: lost tch and p.u bef 2 out (usual 4 out)* **6/1**

0UP- P **Notonebuttwo (IRE)**231 [5014] 8-10-11 88 (tp) DiarmuidO'Regan(5)
(Chris Grant) *cl up: chal 3 out (usual 5 out): wknd bef omitted 2 out: t.o whn p.u bef last* **9/2[3]**

P/P- P **Fozy Moss**166 9-10-5 84 FinianO'Toole(7)
(Sheena Walton) *led at stdy gallop to 3 out (usual 5 out): drvn and outpcd fr next: t.o whn p.u bef last* **8/1**

1300 P **Izbushka (IRE)**54 [1599] 4-10-11 86 (b) AdamNicol(3)
(David Thompson) *cl up: drvn and outpcd after 3 out (usual 5 out): wknd fr next: lost tch and p.u bef last* **12/1**

7m 13.4s (64.40) **Going Correction** +2.50s/f (Heav)
WFA 4 from 6yo+ 8lb **8 Ran SP% 118.0**
Speed ratings (Par 103): **88,80,68, , ,**
CSF £30.60 CT £77.89 TOTE £3.70: £3.20, £3.30, £1.90; EX 31.20 Trifecta £93.60.
Owner R H & S C Walton **Bred** Rodney Deacon **Trained** Hexham, Northumberland

FOCUS
This modest staying handicap hurdle was run in a hailstorm and they understandably went steady, but still only three completed. Another race where previous course form proved key. The form could be at least 7lb out either way.

2479 EURO 2016 BETTING AT 188BET MAIDEN OPEN NATIONAL HUNT FLAT RACE 2m 48y

3:35 (3:39) (Class 6) 4-6-Y-0 **£1,949** (£572; £286; £143)

Form RPR

1 **Lake View Lad (IRE)**195 [97] 5-10-13 0 StephenMulqueen(5) 106+
(N W Alexander) *t.k.h: cl up: led after 5f and maintained stdy pce: pushed along over 2f out: drew clr fr over 1f out* **6/5[1]**

2 6 **Egret (IRE)**180 5-11-1 0 DerekFox(3) 97
(Lucinda Russell) *prom: hdwy to chse wnr over 2f out: sn rdn: one pce fr over 1f out* **2/1[2]**

3 1/2 **Calypso Storm (IRE)** 4-11-1 0 TonyKelly(3) 97
(Rebecca Menzies) *hld up in tch: stdy hdwy 3f out: pushed along and outpcd 2f out: n.d after* **12/1**

4 3 1/2 **Raymond Reddington (IRE)** 4-10-13 0 DiarmuidO'Regan(5) 93
(Chris Grant) *led at slow pce 5f: cl up tl rdn and outpcd fr 2f out* **9/1**

0-54 5 50 **Due East**45 [1688] 5-10-8 0 JoeColliver(3) 36
(Micky Hammond) *cl up tl rdn and struggling fr over 4f out: t.o* **11/2[3]**

5m 15.3s (62.60) **Going Correction** +2.50s/f (Heav) **5 Ran SP% 111.9**
Speed ratings: **43,40,39,38,13**
CSF £3.94 TOTE £1.50: £1.10, £1.30; EX 4.30 Trifecta £18.40.
Owner Alistair Cochrane **Bred** Peter Magnier **Trained** Kinneston, Perth & Kinross

FOCUS
They predictably went steadily in this maiden bumper and cantered around for the first 12 furlongs. The winner set a fair standard but this is not form to take seriously.
T/Plt: £139.70 to a £1 stake. Pool: £48,025.58 - 250.85 winning tickets T/Qpdt: £79.00 to a £1 stake. Pool: £3,525.89 - 33.00 winning tickets **Richard Young**

2468 CHELTENHAM (L-H)

Saturday, November 14

OFFICIAL GOING: Good to soft (good in places) changing to good to soft (soft in places) after race 3 (1.50)

Wind: strong across Weather: rain

2480 JCB TRIUMPH HURDLE TRIAL (REGISTERED AS THE PRESTBURY JUVENILE HURDLE RACE) (GRADE 2) (8 hdls) 2m 87y

12:40 (12:41) (Class 1) 3-Y-O £17,085 (£6,411; £3,210; £1,599; £804)

Form RPR

1 **1** **Wolf Of Windlesham (IRE)**[23] 2032 3-11-2 0 JoshuaMoore 134+
(Stuart Edmunds) *trckd ldrs: nt fluent 4th and briefly nudged along: sn travelling wl again: led after 2 out: kpt on wl: rdn out* **12/1**

60- **2** ½ **Coo Star Sivola (FR)**[210] 5403 3-10-12 0 RichardJohnson 130+
(Nick Williams) *str: q lengthy: trckd ldrs: pushed along appr 2 out: rdn bef last where wnt 2nd and nt fluent: styd on wl and clsng on wnr nring fin but a being hld* **25/1**

1 **3** 4 **Romain De Senam (FR)**[20] 2092 3-11-6 136 SamTwiston-Davies 132
(Paul Nicholls) *str: chasg type: lw: racd freely: led: rdn and hdd after 2 out: sn hld: kpt on same pce run-in* **5/6**[1]

11 **4** 4½ **Oceane (FR)**[27] 1984 3-11-6 132 WayneHutchinson 129
(Alan King) *sltly on toes: lw: trckd ldr: rdn after 2 out: nt pce to chal: no ex run-in* **11/4**[2]

5 28 **Fingertips (FR)**[213] 3-11-6 0 DarylJacob 108
(David Pipe) *angular: swtg: trckd ldr: nudged along bef 3 out: outpcd 2 out* **5/1**[3]

3m 59.3s (-2.70) **Going Correction** +0.15s/f (Yiel) **5 Ran SP% 109.4**

Speed ratings (Par 114): **112,111,109,107,93**

CSF £145.43 TOTE £10.10: £2.60, £5.60; EX 152.20 Trifecta £302.10.

Owner M W Lawrence **Bred** Joe And Edel Banahan **Trained** Newport Pagnell, Bucks

FOCUS

It was dry overnight and light morning drizzle wasn't expected to have affected the going. Old course used. Bends were dolled out 9 yads from the inner, adding 56 yards to each circuit. This is always an informative juvenile contest. They went a fair enough gallop and it looks best rated around the third and fourth. Wolf Of Windlesham is still 20lb+ shy off the level required for a Triumph Hurdle win.

2481 MALLARDJEWELLERS.COM NOVICES' CHASE (20 fncs) 3m 80y

1:15 (1:15) (Class 2) 5-Y-O+ £14,588 (£4,449; £2,324; £1,262)

Form RPR

-113 **1** **Vicente (FR)**[22] 2055 6-11-8 141 SamTwiston-Davies 159+
(Paul Nicholls) *lw: trckd ldrs: mstke 12th: hit 3 out where lft 2nd: rdn to chal 2 out: led bef last: styd on wl: rdn out* **16/1**

63-1 **2** 2¾ **Un Temps Pour Tout (IRE)**[160] 663 6-11-0 0 (t) TomScudamore 146+
(David Pipe) *trckd ldr: led 14th: lft clr 3 out: pushed along whn hit 2 out: rdn and hdd bef last: styd on but no ex run-in* **4/5**[1]

1P-1 **3** 34 **One For Arthur (IRE)**[21] 2067 6-11-5 136 PeterBuchanan 126
(Lucinda Russell) *hld up bhd ldrs: mstke 11th: pushed along whn hit 14th: rdn whn lft hld 3rd 3 out: wknd 2 out* **11/1**

3-1F **4** 86 **Vintage Vinnie (IRE)**[22] 2055 6-11-5 141 PaulTownend 42
(Rebecca Curtis) *led: nt fluent 3rd: 14th: wknd qckly after next: t.o whn lft 4th 3 out* **12/1**

05/1 **P** **Twelve Roses**[31] 1900 7-11-5 143 DavidBass
(Kim Bailey) *trckd ldrs: rchd for 4 out: sn rdn: wknd qckly: p.u bef next* **8/1**[3]

P4-4 **F** **Blaklion**[35] 1846 6-11-0 144 RyanHatch 146+
(Nigel Twiston-Davies) *lw: trckd ldrs: jnd ldr 15th tl next: renewing chal and travelling wl enough whn fell 3 out* **4/1**[2]

6m 16.6s (-1.70) **Going Correction** +0.275s/f (Yiel) **6 Ran SP% 108.6**

Speed ratings: **113,112,100,72,**

CSF £29.47 TOTE £16.90: £4.40, £1.30; EX 39.30 Trifecta £125.90.

Owner Ian Fogg & John Hales **Bred** Thierry Cypres & Jean-Francois Naudin **Trained** Ditcheat, Somerset

FOCUS

Always a decent staying novice chase. There was no hanging about and the first pair were a long way clear at the finish. The 141-rated winner is the best guide. Sam Twiston-Davies said afterwards "It is dead and the rain is really going to start to get into the ground." Ab og step up from the winner, who looks RSA class on this evidence.

2482 MURPHY GROUP H'CAP CHASE (GRADE 3) (22 fncs) 3m 3f 71y

1:50 (1:52) (Class 1) 4-Y-O+

£28,475 (£10,685; £5,350; £2,665; £1,005; £1,005)

Form RPR

2F-P **1** **Sausalito Sunrise (IRE)**[35] 1849 7-11-3 144 RichardJohnson 154+
(Philip Hobbs) *settled in last quartet: mstkes 6th and 8th: prog 16th: blnd 19th (4 out): gd hdwy on wd outside 3 out: rdn to ld 2 out: drvn and styd on wl flat* **7/1**[2]

0-21 **2** 1¼ **Upswing (IRE)**[24] 2018 7-10-9 136 BarryGeraghty 143+
(Jonjo O'Neill) *lw: racd on outer: patiently rdn: prog 15th: chsd ldrs 4 out: hdwy to chal 3 out: sn rdn and nt qckn: styd on again fr last to chse wnr flat: no imp nr fin* **6/1**[1]

214- **3** nk **Knockanrawley (IRE)**[266] 4366 7-10-9 136 (p) DavidBass 143+
(Kim Bailey) *a in ldng gp: led 3 out: hdd and mstke 2 out: nt fluent last: kpt on wl but lost 2nd flat* **14/1**

16F- **4** ¾ **Cogry**[210] 5392 6-10-5 135 RyanHatch[(3)] 139
(Nigel Twiston-Davies) *lw: chsd ldrs: rdn after 4 out: no imp next but stl in tch: styd on wl fr last to take 4th nr fin* **15/2**[3]

3UP- **5** 1½ **Shotgun Paddy (IRE)**[245] 4767 8-11-4 145 DarylJacob 148
(Emma Lavelle) *mostly pressed ldr fr 5th and smetimes j. into the ld: lost 2nd 4 out: styd cl up: kpt on same pce fr 2 out* **10/1**

50-2 **5** dht **Perfect Candidate (IRE)**[21] 2061 8-10-7 134 PaddyBrennan 137
(Fergal O'Brien) *in tch in midfield: prog 15th: clsd to chal and upsides 3 out: nt qckn bef next: one pce after* **20/1**

11-0 **7** 2¼ **The Romford Pele (IRE)**[35] 1849 8-11-7 148 (b) PaulMoloney 149
(Rebecca Curtis) *lw: nt fluent and mostly in last pair: no ch after 4 out: styd on steadily after 3 out: nrst fin* **25/1**

40-0 **8** 2½ **Spring Heeled (IRE)**[34] 1879 8-11-5 149 (p) GerFox[(3)] 150
(J H Culloty, Ire) *racd on outer: in rr: sme prog 15th: lost pl 4 out: renewed effrt 3 out: no imp after* **16/1**

PP0- **9** ¾ **Rigadin De Beauchene (FR)**[245] 4767 10-10-2 129 (b[1]) LiamTreadwell 128
(Venetia Williams) *lw: nt a fluent but mde most: kicked for home after 4 out: hdd & wknd 3 out* **20/1**

23-P **10** 8 **Le Reve (IRE)**[14] 2187 7-11-8 149 (p) LeightonAspell 142
(Lucy Wadham) *wl in tch: mstke 15th: no prog fr next: struggling in rr bef 3 out* **20/1**

3-10 **11** 1¾ **Azure Fly (IRE)**[21] 2061 7-10-9 136 (tp) AidanColeman 125
(Charlie Longsdon) *lw: trckd ldrs: mstke 13th: rdn after 4 out: wknd bef 2 out* **20/1**

150- **12** 1¾ **Black Thunder (FR)**[249] 4690 8-11-12 153 (t) SamTwiston-Davies 153+
(Paul Nicholls) *in rr: prog into midfield 4 out: sn drvn: keeping on in 5th and gd chs of being plcd whn blnd and nrly fell 2 out: nt rcvr* **14/1**

031- **13** 15 **Just A Par (IRE)**[203] 5538 8-11-7 148 (b) SeanBowen 122
(Paul Nicholls) *wl in tch in midfield: blnd 12th and lost pl: tried to make prog 4 out: no hdwy and wl btn 3 out* **16/1**

5P-5 **14** 1½ **Sego Success (IRE)**[35] 1849 7-10-12 139 WayneHutchinson 115
(Alan King) *in tch: blnd bdly 15th: nvr rcvrd: wl in rr bef 3 out* **6/1**[1]

50P- **15** 7 **Godsmejudge (IRE)**[217] 5275 9-10-12 139 BrianHughes 106
(David Dennis) *w ldrs to 4 out: wknd qckly bef next* **28/1**

110- **16** 8 **Soll**[217] 5275 10-11-5 146 (tp) TomScudamore 105
(David Pipe) *a wl in rr: nt fluent 2nd: no prog and struggling 16th: wl bhd bef 3 out* **12/1**

-264 **P** **Audacious Plan (IRE)**[21] 2061 6-10-4 131 (p) PaulTownend
(Rebecca Curtis) *sloppy rnd of jumping and a in last: bhd whn p.u bef 4 out* **10/1**

7m 12.3s (2.90) **Going Correction** +0.45s/f (Soft) **17 Ran SP% 130.2**

Speed ratings (Par 113): **113,112,112,112,111 111,111,110,110,107 107,106,102,101,99 97,**

CSF £47.06 CT £601.30 TOTE £7.50: £2.40, £1.90, £3.50, £2.40; EX 64.80 Trifecta £1553.50.

Owner Mrs Diana L Whateley **Bred** Thomas Corish **Trained** Withycombe, Somerset

■ Stewards' Enquiry : Daryl Jacob two-day ban; used whip above the permitted level (29th-30th Nov)

Ryan Hatch two-day ban; used whip above the permitted level (29th-30th Nov)

FOCUS

A cracking staying handicap. There was a sound gallop on, serving up a stirring finish and it's strong form which should work out.

2483 PADDY POWER GOLD CUP CHASE (A H'CAP) (GRADE 3) (16 fncs) 2m 4f 78y

2:25 (2:31) (Class 1) 4-Y-O+

£91,120 (£34,192; £17,120; £8,528; £4,288; £2,144)

Form RPR

10F- **1** **Annacotty (IRE)**[218] 5253 7-11-0 147 (p) IanPopham 157
(Alan King) *mid-div: mstke 11th: rdn after 4 out: hdwy after 3 out: led sn after last: styd on gamely: all out* **12/1**

45-3 **2** ½ **Buywise (IRE)**[20] 2084 8-11-1 148 PaulMoloney 158+
(Evan Williams) *hld up towards rr: slipped on bnd bef 4th: struggling whn hit 3 out: hdwy next: nt clr run whn swtchd rt after last: r.o wl: wnt 2nd cl home: nt quite rch wnr* **10/1**[3]

1-01 **3** ¾ **Sound Investment (IRE)**[20] 2084 7-11-12 159 (t) SamTwiston-Davies 166
(Paul Nicholls) *towards rr of mid-div: rdn and hdwy after 3 out: styd on wl to chse wnr fnl 160yds: no ex whn lost 2nd cl home* **20/1**

60-2 **4** 3¼ **Double Ross (IRE)**[14] 2187 9-11-3 153 RyanHatch[(3)] 157
(Nigel Twiston-Davies) *lw: trckd ldrs: chal 3 out: rdn to ld appr 2 out: hdd bef last: kpt on but no ex fnl 120yds* **16/1**

4-21 **5** 2 **Irish Cavalier (IRE)**[36] 1840 6-11-9 156 (p) PaulTownend 158
(Rebecca Curtis) *mid-div: smooth hdwy appr 3 out: chal bef 2 out: rdn to ld after 2 out: hdd sn after last: no ex* **8/1**[2]

-131 **6** hd **Art Mauresque (FR)**[21] 2063 5-11-0 147 SeanBowen 150
(Paul Nicholls) *lw: led tl 2nd: trckd ldr: rchd for 4 out: rdn after 3 out: cl 4th jumping last: no ex* **10/1**[3]

0P-0 **7** 5 **Splash Of Ginge**[14] 2198 7-10-11 149 JamieBargary[(5)] 146
(Nigel Twiston-Davies) *trckd ldrs: rdn after 3 out: kpt on same pce fr next* **20/1**

2U-0 **8** 8 **Monetaire (FR)**[196] 96 9-10-8 141 ConorO'Farrell 133
(David Pipe) *hld up towards rr: hit 6th: hdwy 3 out: rdn bef next: wknd between last 2* **12/1**

53-P **9** 7 **Johns Spirit (IRE)**[20] 2084 8-11-10 157 RichieMcLernon 141
(Jonjo O'Neill) *hld up towards rr: sme prog after 3 out: wnt lft next: sn wknd* **10/1**[3]

1P-0 **10** 1 **Next Sensation (IRE)**[21] 2059 8-11-3 150 (t) LiamTreadwell 133
(Michael Scudamore) *led 2nd tl 12th: rdn after 4 out: sn wknd* **50/1**

116- **11** ¾ **Kings Palace (IRE)**[248] 4703 7-11-7 154 (t) TomScudamore 136
(David Pipe) *mid-div: hdwy fr 9th: led after 12th: rdn and hdd bef 2 out: wknd last* **13/2**[1]

1F-1 **12** 6 **Oscar Rock (IRE)**[49] 1658 7-11-8 155 (b) BrianHughes 132
(Malcolm Jefferson) *mid-div: rdn bef 3 out: nvr threatened: wknd bef 2 out* **12/1**

-234 **13** 16 **Cloud Creeper (IRE)**[36] 1840 8-11-3 150 RichardJohnson 113
(Philip Hobbs) *hld up bhd: sme prog u.p after 3 out: nvr threatened to get involved: wknd bef last* **25/1**

01-1 **14** 7 **Cocktails At Dawn**[35] 1846 7-11-6 153 NicodeBoinville 109
(Nicky Henderson) *lw: trckd ldr: ldng whn rchd for 12th: sn hdd: rdn after 3 out: wknd bef next* **16/1**

34-0 **15** 17 **Generous Ransom (IRE)**[21] 2064 7-10-7 140 (p) DarylJacob 81
(Nick Gifford) *mid-div: hit 5th: hdwy after 12th: rdn after 4 out: wknd bef next* **16/1**

01B- **P** **Darna**[218] 5253 9-10-12 145 (t) DavidBass
(Kim Bailey) *lw: trckd ldrs: mstke 5th: losing pl whn mstke 12th: sn wknd: t.o whn p.u bef 3 out* **25/1**

2U-P **P** **Bennys Mist (IRE)**[14] 2187 9-10-7 140 AidanColeman
(Venetia Williams) *mid-div: reminders after 7th: in rr fr 10th: t.o whn p.u bef 4 out* **33/1**

21-1 **P** **Boondooma (IRE)**[21] 2059 8-11-7 154 WillKennedy
(Dr Richard Newland) *in tch: wknd qckly 12th: sn bhd: t.o whn p.u bef 2 out* **10/1**[3]

6-4P **P** **Present View**[14] 2187 7-10-10 143 (b[1]) BrendanPowell
(Jamie Snowden) *dwlt: a bhd and nvr rcvrd: p.u after 8th* **25/1**

6-P5 **P** **Shanpallas (IRE)**[34] 1879 7-10-13 146 BarryGeraghty
(C Byrnes, Ire) *mid-div: nt fluent 4th: towards rr 8th: sn struggling and nvr bk on terms: t.o whn p.u 3 out* **20/1**

5m 12.8s (1.80) **Going Correction** +0.45s/f (Soft) **20 Ran SP% 132.3**

Speed ratings (Par 113): **114,113,113,112,111 111,109,106,103,102 102,100,93,91,84**

CSF £120.63 CT £2436.13 TOTE £19.90: £5.10, £2.70, £3.70, £4.40; EX 229.70 Trifecta £2503.50.

Owner Mrs Peter Prowting **Bred** Patrick Crotty Jnr **Trained** Barbury Castle, Wilts

FOCUS
About as open a running of this prestigious handicap as there's been in recent times and, with the ground becoming fairly testing, it was no surprise to see a horse proven over 3m come to the fore, with them getting racing a long way out. Solid form, Annacotty rated back to his very best.

2484 REGULATORY FINANCE SOLUTIONS H'CAP HURDLE (LISTED RACE) (12 hdls) 3m 1f 67y
3:00 (3:04) (Class 1) 4-Y-O+
£17,085 (£6,411; £3,210; £1,599; £804; £402)

Form RPR

54-5 1 **Rons Dream**[35] 1848 5-10-11 129 SeanBowen 137+
(Peter Bowen) *cl up: mstke 8th: prog to trck ldr after 2 out: rdn to ld sn after last: styd on wl and a holding on* **14/1**

P2-1 2 ½ **Sir Mangan (IRE)**[43] 1736 7-11-0 132 HarrySkelton 138
(Dan Skelton) *lw: led or disp thrght: rdn after 2 out: hdd sn after last: kpt on wl flat: a jst hld* **8/1**[2]

61-0 3 2½ **Morito Du Berlais (FR)**[36] 1839 6-11-0 139 (bt[1]) HarryCobden(7) 144
(Paul Nicholls) *racd on inner: hld up in tch: prog 10th: trckd ldrs gng wl 3 out: shkn up to chse ldng pair after 2 out: styd on same pce and nvr able to chal* **12/1**

012- 4 5 **Un Ace (FR)**[213] 5344 7-11-12 144 (t) DavidBass 145
(Kim Bailey) *lw: racd wd: hld up in rr: stdy prog fr 3 out: tk 4th bef last: sn rdn and no imp: tired nr fin* **16/1**

3F-P 5 ½ **The Job Is Right**[19] 2112 7-11-4 136 (b) PaulTownend 135
(Michael Hourigan, Ire) *prom: mstke 3rd: nt fluent 9th: cl up whn mstke 3 out: hrd rdn 2 out: sn outpcd: kpt on again nr fin* **15/2**[1]

FP-P 6 4 **Easter Day (FR)**[12] 2242 7-11-7 139 (p) SamTwiston-Davies 134
(Paul Nicholls) *racd wd: hld up in tch: tried to cl on ldrs fr 3 out: no imp after 2 out* **14/1**

60-1 7 ¾ **Dark Spirit (IRE)**[22] 2054 7-11-3 142 LewisGordon(7) 137
(Evan Williams) *hld up in last quartet: sme prog fr 3 out and urged along into midfield after 2 out: no real hdwy after* **8/1**[2]

6-05 8 2½ **Gevrey Chambertin (FR)**[36] 1839 7-11-11 143 ConorO'Farrell 136
(David Pipe) *hld up in last pair: lost tch w main gp 10th: sme prog fr 3 out: rchd 11th bef last: rdn and passed a few nr fin: nvr involved* **25/1**

116- 9 nk **Batavir (FR)**[259] 4482 6-11-0 132 (t) TomScudamore 124
(David Pipe) *wl in tch: rt on terms bef 2 out: sn wknd* **8/1**[2]

00-3 10 nk **Invicta Lake (IRE)**[26] 2002 8-10-9 127 PaddyBrennan 119
(Suzy Smith) *mstke 1st: a towards rr: struggling bef 3 out: no ch next: plugged on fr last* **22/1**

P/31 11 nse **Ongenstown Lad (IRE)**[28] 1963 11-10-12 130 (t) PaulMoloney 122
(Mrs Gillian Callaghan, Ire) *hld up in last: lost tch w main gp 10th: sme prog into midfield 2 out: shkn up bef last: nvr involved* **16/1**

-211 12 4 **Atlantic Gold (IRE)**[21] 2062 5-11-1 133 AidanColeman 121
(Charlie Longsdon) *lw: racd on inner: disp ld fr 2nd to 3 out: sn wknd* **10/1**

03/5 13 2¼ **Face Value**[21] 2064 7-9-10 121 (p) JonathanMoore(7) 109
(Adrian McGuinness, Ire) *chsd ldrs: rdn after 10th: struggling whn blnd 3 out: wknd* **20/1**

300/ 14 42 **So Fine (IRE)**[594] 5093 9-10-10 128 RichardJohnson 77
(Philip Hobbs) *racd on inner: in tch tl wknd bef 3 out: eased bef last: t.o* **12/1**

13U- 15 ¾ **Desilvano**[238] 4911 6-11-0 132 LiamTreadwell 80
(James Evans) *racd on inner: in tch: mstke 7th: wknd 3 out: t.o* **10/1**

0-01 P **Milan Bound (IRE)**[36] 1839 7-10-13 131 (t) BarryGeraghty
(Jonjo O'Neill) *hld up in rr: nt fluent 9th and wknd: t.o whn p.u bef next* **9/1**[3]

6m 27.1s (1.00) **Going Correction** +0.325s/f (Yiel) 16 Ran SP% **126.7**
Speed ratings (Par 111): **111,110,110,108,108 107,106,105,105,105 105,104,103,90,90**
CSF £124.16 CT £1419.14 TOTE £16.90: £2.80, £2.20, £3.70, £4.00; EX 248.20 Trifecta £3410.50.
Owner Mrs Tania Stepney **Bred** Peter E Clinton **Trained** Little Newcastle, Pembrokes

FOCUS
A decent staying handicap for the level, no more. The winner stepped up for the longer trip.

2485 MARTIN & CO JEWELLERS INTERMEDIATE H'CAP HURDLE (10 hdls) 2m 5f 26y
3:35 (3:37) (Class 3) (0-140,133) 3-Y-O+
£12,512 (£3,696; £1,848; £924; £462; £232)

Form RPR

1 **Leave At Dawn (IRE)**[19] 2112 5-11-3 124 BarryGeraghty 136+
(C Byrnes, Ire) *hld up: hdwy 2 out: led sn after last: rdn clr: styd on wl* **7/2**[1]

F-4F 2 3¾ **Fort Worth (IRE)**[109] 1138 6-11-4 125 PaddyBrennan 131+
(Jonjo O'Neill) *lw: hld up: hdwy 2 out: led briefly last: sn rdn: kpt on but nt pce of wnr* **8/1**

0101 3 4½ **Cusheen Bridge (IRE)**[23] 2042 7-11-7 128 (t) AdamPogson 130
(Charles Pogson) *mid-div: hdwy 7th: led 3 out: rdn after next: mstke and hdd last: no ex* **20/1**

13- 4 5 **Champagne Express**[239] 4881 5-11-12 133 NicodeBoinville 131
(Nicky Henderson) *mid-div: chsd ldrs 2 out: sn rdn: kpt on same pce* **4/1**[2]

0 5 1 **Erlkonig (GER)**[77] 1337 5-11-12 133 PaulTownend 130
(Anthony Mullins, Ire) *t.k.h: hld up: nt clr run bhd ldrs after 3 out: sn rdn: styd on but nt pce to get on terms* **16/1**

21- 6 1¾ **Hedley Lamarr (IRE)**[251] 4654 5-11-7 128 RichieMcLernon 123
(Jonjo O'Neill) *lw: trckd ldrs: ev ch 3 out: sn rdn: one pce fr after next* **10/1**

1321 7 9 **Western Way (IRE)**[8] 2326 6-11-9 130 (v) LeightonAspell 121
(Don Cantillon) *hld up: hdwy 2 out: rdn bef last: sn one pce* **9/1**

8 30 **Fearachain (IRE)**[30] 1936 7-11-0 128 CiaranGethings(7) 88
(Anthony Mullins, Ire) *trckd ldrs: rdn after 3 out: wknd bef last* **25/1**

223- 9 19 **Coup De Grace (IRE)**[22] 4710 6-10-11 118 JoshuaMoore 61
(Pat Phelan) *pressed ldr: rdn after 3 out: wknd after next* **16/1**

121- U **Herbert Park (IRE)**[229] 5066 5-11-11 132 TomScudamore
(David Pipe) *in tch: effrt after 2 out: sn wknd: in last trio whn nt fluent and uns rdr last* **5/1**[3]

P **Tjongejonge (FR)**[164] 4-11-9 130 RichardJohnson
(Charlie Longsdon) *led: hdd whn p.u appr 3 out (appeared to lose action)* **7/1**

5m 19.9s (6.50) **Going Correction** +0.325s/f (Yiel)
WFA 4 from 5yo+ 8lb 11 Ran SP% **122.0**
Speed ratings (Par 107): **100,98,96,94,94 93,90,79,71,**
CSF £33.41 CT £504.37 TOTE £4.30: £1.90, £2.80, £6.90; EX 35.40 Trifecta £406.00.
Owner John P McManus **Bred** Mrs M Curran **Trained** Ballingarry, Co Limerick

FOCUS
A fair handicap featuring a few promising types. The field bunched right up running down the hill, the pace having increased from halfway, and plenty had their chance, but ultimately the favourite came nicely clear. The first two are on the upgrade.

2486 JOCKEY CLUB VENUES MARES' STANDARD OPEN NATIONAL HUNT FLAT RACE (LISTED RACE) 2m 87y
4:05 (4:09) (Class 1) 4-6-Y-O
£11,390 (£4,274; £2,140; £1,066; £536; £268)

Form RPR

14-1 1 **Copper Kay**[36] 1843 5-11-0 0 RichardJohnson 116+
(Philip Hobbs) *q tall: lengthy: lw: racd wd: wl in tch: trckd ldr over 3f out: led over 1f out and immediately qckd clr: idled sltly ins fnl f and rdn out: impressive* **15/8**[1]

1 2 4½ **Which One Is Which**[156] 696 4-11-0 0 BarryGeraghty 112+
(Jonjo O'Neill) *will make a jumper: hld up wl in rr: prog over 3f out: rdn to chse clr ldng pair 2f out: styd on to take 2nd last 100yds: no ch w wnr* **5/1**[2]

3 2¾ **Theatre Territory (IRE)**[188] 5-10-11 0 MrSWaley-Cohen(3) 110
(Nicky Henderson) *athletic: lw: racd on outer: t.k.h: prom: led over 4f out: shkn up and hdd over 1f out whn stl clr of rest: one pce and lost 2nd last 100yds* **8/1**

4 2¼ **Snag List (IRE)**[43] 1751 4-11-0 0 PaulTownend 108
(W P Mullins, Ire) *hld up in rr: pushed along over 4f out: prog and weaved through 3f out: kpt on to take 4th ins fnl f: n.d* **6/1**[3]

44 5 ½ **Colin's Sister**[21] 2065 4-10-11 0 ConorShoemark(3) 107
(Fergal O'Brien) *hld up in rr: prog on inner 3f out: drvn and kpt on fr over 1f out: n.d* **33/1**

12- 6 ¾ **Miss Mobot**[482] 1028 5-10-7 0 CiaranGethings(7) 106
(Philip Hobbs) *wl in tch: cl up over 2f out: sn rdn: outpcd after* **50/1**

0-22 7 2¾ **Pulling Power**[176] 432 5-11-0 0 (t) DavidBass 104
(Kim Bailey) *q tall: will make a jumper: prom: rdn 3f out: stl disputing 3rd 2f out: wknd* **33/1**

11- 8 1¼ **Tobougaloo**[212] 5359 4-11-0 0 PaddyBrennan 103
(Stuart Kittow) *hld up in rr: prog on wd outside over 4f out: chsd ldrs over 2f out: wknd over 1f out* **6/1**[3]

1 9 5 **Robinesse (IRE)**[182] 341 4-11-0 0 LeightonAspell 98
(Oliver Sherwood) *q str: will make a jumper: rdn after 4f and struggling after in rr: virtually t.o over 3f out: rdr persisted and passed a few late on* **20/1**

25 10 3¾ **Hello Jazz**[34] 1872 5-10-7 0 MrMLegg(7) 95
(John Ryall) *racd on inner: mostly chsd ldr to 5f out: dropped out qckly 3f out* **66/1**

340- 11 1 **Morning Herald**[252] 4634 4-11-0 0 AidanColeman 94
(Martin Keighley) *in tch: rdn over 2f out: sn wknd* **50/1**

10- 12 9 **Sunshine Corner (IRE)**[217] 5277 4-11-0 0 DarylJacob 86
(Lucy Wadham) *hld up in tch: looked to be gng wl whn making effrt towards inner 3f out: sn shkn up and wknd qckly* **16/1**

13 4 **Dreambaby (IRE)**[19] 2113 4-11-0 0 MsKWalsh 82
(W P Mullins, Ire) *q str: will make a jumper: led to over 4f out: sn wknd* **16/1**

4-1 14 3½ **Late Night Lily**[24] 2016 4-11-0 0 HarrySkelton 79
(Dan Skelton) *hld up towards rr: effrt 4f out: no imp on ldrs over 2f out: sn wknd qckly* **14/1**

15 1¼ **The Model County (IRE)**[48] 5-10-7 0 MrAlexEdwards(7) 78
(Alan Phillips) *will make a jumper: in tch: rdn fr 1/2-way: wknd 4f out: sn wl bhd* **50/1**

3-0 16 6 **Where's Cherry (IRE)**[10] 2277 4-10-9 0 NickSlatter(5) 73
(Fergal O'Brien) *racd on inner: struggling by 1/2-way: t.o* **150/1**

3m 58.0s (1.60) **Going Correction** +0.325s/f (Yiel) 16 Ran SP% **128.2**
Speed ratings: **109,106,105,104,104 103,102,101,99,97 96,92,90,88,87 84**
CSF £10.64 TOTE £2.60: £1.40, £2.20, £3.20; EX 13.40 Trifecta £70.30.
Owner Aiden Murphy & Alan Peterson **Bred** Aiden Murphy & Alan Peterson **Trained** Withycombe, Somerset

■ Cajun Fiddle (28-1) was withdrawn. Rule 4 does not apply.

FOCUS
This looked a good mares' bumper and the winner was impressive. She and the runner-up are the first two foals of smart jumper Presenting Copper. The winner was back to the level of her Sandown run.

T/Jkpt: Not won. Jackpot Placepot: £604.10 to a £1 stake. Pool: £3,233.07 - 0.40 winning tickets. T/Plt: £8,525.60 to £1 stake. Pool: £301,316.25 - 25.80 winning tickets. T/Qpdt: £175.30 to £1 stake. Pool: £38,919.36 - 164.25 winning tickets. **Tim Mitchell & Jonathan Neesom**

2162 UTTOXETER (L-H)
Saturday, November 14

OFFICIAL GOING: Soft changing to soft (heavy in places) after race 2 (1.05) changing to heavy after race 4 (2.15)
Wind: moderate 1/2 behind Weather: raining

2487 MARSTON'S PEDIGREE "NATIONAL HUNT" NOVICES' HURDLE (9 hdls) 1m 7f 168y
12:30 (12:31) (Class 4) 4-Y-O+ £3,924 (£1,159; £579; £290; £145)

Form RPR

1- 1 **Captain Chaos (IRE)**[290] 3931 4-10-12 0 HarrySkelton 111+
(Dan Skelton) *mde all: j.rt 1st: green and drvn 6th: hit last: styd on wl* **1/2**[1]

2 1¾ **Athou Du Nord (FR)**[160] 5-10-12 0 AlainCawley 105
(Richard Hobson) *trckd ldrs: chsd wnr appr 2 out: kpt on same pce run-in* **16/1**

3-6 3 1¾ **Will O'The West (IRE)**[189] 213 4-10-12 0 TomO'Brien 105
(Henry Daly) *hld up towards rr: hdwy 6th: outpcd next: hung rt and kpt on fr 2 out: 4th and hit last: tk 3rd towards fin* **8/1**[3]

40-6 4 nk **Movie Legend**[28] 1973 5-10-12 0 GavinSheehan 103
(Ben Case) *sn trcking ldrs: 2nd 7th: kpt on same pce fr 2 out* **14/1**

/2-5 5 7 **Karisma King**[14] 2196 6-10-12 0 SeanQuinlan 96
(Sue Smith) *chsd ldrs: wknd appr last* **10/1**

6 ½ **Supply And Demand (IRE)** 4-10-12 0 NoelFehily 95
(Jonjo O'Neill) *nt fluent in rr: drvn and sme hdwy 3 out: wknd between last 2* **5/1**[2]

60 7 5 **Fire (IRE)**[13] 2221 5-10-12 0 (t) AdamWedge 91
(Chris Bealby) *hld up in rr: j.rt: hdwy and wd bnd appr 3 out: wknd between last 2* **33/1**

8 *25* **Love Anthem (IRE)**[41] 6-10-5 0................................ DGHogan 58
(Denis Gerard Hogan, Ire) *chsd ldrs: lost pl after 6th: sn bhd: t.o* **40/1**

4m 12.8s (15.40) **Going Correction** +1.15s/f (Heav) **8** Ran SP% **121.5**
Speed ratings (Par 105): **107,106,105,105,101 101,98,86**
CSF £12.34 TOTE £1.40: £1.10, £2.90, £1.60; EX 10.00 Trifecta £41.70.
Owner Mike And Eileen Newbould **Bred** Conor Hickey **Trained** Alcester, Warwicks

FOCUS
Some starts have been moved at this track following remeasuring, so some races will not have speed figures until there is sufficient data to calculate updated median times. Divided bends. Races 1, 6 & 7 increased by 73yds and races 2 & 4 by 107yds. Hurdles moved out and adjacent to the chase course on fresher ground. A very ordinary novice hurdle. The winner was allowed to set a sedate pace and most were still involved turning in. The form may not prove copper-bottomed and the winner didn't need to reproduce his bumper figure.

2488 NEW WORLD PALE ALE MAIDEN HURDLE (10 hdls) 2m 3f 207y
1:05 (1:09) (Class 5) 4-Y-O+ **£2,729** (£801; £400; £200)

Form RPR
2U3- **1** **April Dusk (IRE)**[216] 5286 6-11-0 125................ GavinSheehan 127+
(Warren Greatrex) *trckd ldr: led appr 2 out: pushed clr: eased clsng stages* **2/5**[1]

-3P3 **2** *5* **Rushvale (IRE)**[23] 2041 6-10-7 0........................ MrMJPKendrick(7) 112
(Ben Case) *led: hit 4th: hdd appr 2 out: kpt on same pce* **4/1**[2]

P- **3** *23* **Zephyros Bleu (IRE)**[338] 3044 5-10-7 0.................. PaulNO'Brien(7) 90
(Harry Whittington) *chsd ldng pair: outpcd 6th: bhd fr 3 out: mstke next* **6/1**[3]

50-2 **4** *63* **Blue Cove**[193] 136 10-11-0 65.............................. SeanQuinlan 25
(Lynn Siddall) *hld up in rr: hdwy 5th: drvn and lost pl next: sn bhd: t.o 4th after 6th* **18/1**

00/ **P** **Ochiltree Lady**[1476] 2227 9-10-7 0..................[1] AdamWedge
(Nick Kent) *sn bhd: j.lft 1st: reminders 4th: sn t.o: p.u bef 6th* **100/1**

U **F** **Pantoloni**[9] 2299 4-10-9 0.................................. DannyBurton(5)
(Richard Harper) *in rr: hmpd 1st: t.o 5th sn after 7th: fell heavily last* **100/1**

5m 22.4s (19.20) **Going Correction** +1.15s/f (Heav)
WFA 4 from 5yo+ 8lb **6** Ran SP% **113.0**
Speed ratings (Par 103): **107,105,95,70,**
CSF £2.63 TOTE £1.30: £1.10, £1.60; EX 2.60 Trifecta £4.00.
Owner Raymond Tooth **Bred** Paddy O'Leary **Trained** Upper Lambourn, Berks
■ Stewards' Enquiry : Danny Burton 8-day ban; contunued riding when gelding was exhausted (28th-30th Nov, 1st-5th Dec)

FOCUS
A very weak event, run 40.4sec slower than standard. The winner was value for a lot further but didn't need to be at his best.

2489 WYCHWOOD HOBGOBLIN NOVICES' LIMITED H'CAP CHASE (15 fncs) 2m 4f
1:40 (1:43) (Class 3) (0-135,132) 4-Y-O+ **£6,342** (£1,934; £1,010; £548)

Form RPR
PP-3 **1** **Kylemore Lough**[41] 1782 6-11-8 132........................ JamieMoore 150+
(Kerry Lee) *j. soundly: led tl bef 4th: led 5th: wnt clr bef 3 out: 25 l ahd last: sn heavily eased* **5/2**[1]

0P4/ **2** *17* **Oscar Magic (IRE)**[651] 4028 8-10-10 120.................. AdamWedge 114
(Nigel Twiston-Davies) *t.k.h: trckd ldng pair: mstke 4th: hit 7th: 2nd appr 4 out: one pce* **11/2**[3]

5F4- **3** *nk* **Vice Et Vertu (FR)**[224] 5133 6-10-13 123................ AndrewTinkler 113
(Henry Daly) *in rr: modest 3rd 10th: one pce fr 4 out* **9/1**

523- **4** *41* **Go Conquer (IRE)**[238] 4900 6-11-3 127..................... NoelFehily 76
(Jonjo O'Neill) *t.k.h: trckd ldrs: led bef 4th: hdd 5th: wknd qckly appr 4 out: t.o 3 out: eventually completed* **5/2**[1]

42-3 **P** **Themanfrom Minella (IRE)**[180] 382 6-10-8 125...(t) MrMJPKendrick(7)
(Ben Case) *nt fluent: chsd ldrs: lost pl 3rd: drvn 8th: bhd 10th: t.o next: p.u bef 4 out* **12/1**

325- **P** **Blown Cover**[252] 4625 6-10-7 117........................ GavinSheehan
(Emma Lavelle) *chsd ldrs: lost pl 11th: t.o 5th whn p.u bef 4 out* **7/2**[2]

5m 24.5s (14.70) **Going Correction** +0.975s/f (Soft) **6** Ran SP% **112.4**
Speed ratings (Par 107): **109,102,102,85,**
CSF £16.27 TOTE £3.30: £1.90, £2.20; EX 17.10 Trifecta £77.60.
Owner M J McMahon & Denis Gallagher **Bred** M J McMahon **Trained** Byton, H'fords

FOCUS
With rain continuing to come down, the official ground description was changed before this race. This fair novice handicap was run at a decent pace in the conditions. The winner looks a smart mud-loving novice.

2490 BANKS'S SUNBEAM H'CAP HURDLE (10 hdls) 2m 3f 207y
2:15 (2:19) (Class 4) (0-115,115) 3-Y-O+ **£3,924** (£1,159; £579; £290; £145)

Form RPR
220- **1** **Thatchers Gold (IRE)**[501] 825 7-11-2 105................ DenisO'Regan 111+
(Henry Oliver) *chsd ldrs: outpcd after 3 out: rallied and 2nd between last 2: styd on to ld last 40yds* **11/2**[3]

21U **2** *1* **Western Breeze (IRE)**[16] 2144 6-11-7 110................ NoelFehily 115+
(Mark Walford) *t.k.h: led: hit 2 out and last whn 4 l clr: hdd and no ex clsng stages* **10/3**[1]

5310 **3** *3 ½* **Howaboutnever (IRE)**[46] 1686 7-11-5 108.............(p) TomO'Brien 108
(Ian Williams) *sn w ldrs: lost pl bef 3 out: rallied and 3rd appr last: kpt on* **8/1**

1/0- **4** *15* **Ratify**[537] 474 11-11-5 108.................................. RobertDunne 95
(Dai Burchell) *trckd ldrs: 2nd after 7th: wknd qckly last* **14/1**

26-0 **5** *3 ½* **Ballinalacken (IRE)**[23] 2042 7-11-10 113..............(p) DavidEngland 94
(Clare Ellam) *mid-div: outpcd after 7th: no threat after* **20/1**

500- **6** *39* **Beauboreen (IRE)**[224] 5133 8-11-12 115..............(t) PeterCarberry 57
(Jennie Candlish) *hld up in rr: bhd fr 3 out: t.o* **9/1**

-234 **7** *6* **While You Wait (IRE)**[10] 2271 6-11-10 113.............. GavinSheehan 49
(Paul Fitzsimons) *chsd ldrs: lost pl 3 out: sn bhd: t.o* **5/1**[2]

336 **U** **Medieval Bishop (IRE)**[20] 2080 6-10-12 108..............(p) JoshWall(7)
(Tony Forbes) *in rr: hmpd and uns rdr 7th* **33/1**

0-26 **P** **Hillview Lad (IRE)**[31] 1901 7-11-1 104.................... AdamWedge
(Nick Kent) *in rr: bhd fr 7th: t.o whn p.u bef 3 out* **13/2**

F00- **P** **Aristocracy**[32] 5535 4-10-11 107........................ MissBHampson(7)
(Andy Turnell) *chsd ldrs: 2nd whn hit 5th: drvn 7th: wknd next: 6th and bhd whn p.u bef 3 out* **25/1**

3053 **F** **Menace**[37] 1822 4-10-12 104................................ JamesBanks(3)
(Noel Williams) *in rr: hit 2nd: fell 7th* **10/1**

5m 35.1s (31.90) **Going Correction** +1.425s/f (Heav)
WFA 4 from 6yo+ 8lb **11** Ran SP% **116.9**
Speed ratings (Par 105): **93,92,91,85,83 68,65, , ,**
CSF £23.95 CT £147.62 TOTE £6.10: £2.20, £2.00, £2.70; EX 26.10 Trifecta £172.10.
Owner Miss J Green **Bred** Chris Glynn **Trained** Abberley, Worcs

■ Stewards' Enquiry : Denis O'Regan two-day ban; used his whip above the permitted level (29th-30th Nov)

FOCUS
They went a decent gallop in this fair handicap hurdle, and not much became involved from the rear. The third helps set the level.

2491 RINGWOOD OLD THUMPER H'CAP CHASE (16 fncs) 2m 6f 108y
2:50 (2:53) (Class 4) (0-120,112) 4-Y-O+ **£5,382** (£1,725; £958)

Form RPR
12- **1** **Hi Vic (IRE)**[229] 5076 10-11-8 108.............................. NoelFehily 124+
(David Loder) *j.lft: trckd ldrs: 3rd 11th: 2nd 4 out: led next: drvn clr 2 out* **5/4**[1]

64-1 **2** *26* **Loughalder (IRE)**[192] 149 9-11-12 112...............(bt) CharliePoste 109
(Matt Sheppard) *led: hdd 3 out: sn btn* **4/1**[3]

P-20 **3** *24* **Bennys Well (IRE)**[23] 2030 9-11-10 110.................... SeanQuinlan 82
(Sue Smith) *chsd ldr: reminders 8th: lost pl 11th: bhd 4 out: sn trailed off* **8/1**

443- **P** **Whats Up Woody (IRE)**[204] 5518 10-11-4 109......... JonathonBewley(5)
(George Bewley) *sn trcking ldrs: drvn and wknd 4 out: t.o whn p.u bef 2 out* **3/1**[2]

/25- **P** **Ghost Of A Smile (IRE)**[391] 1962 7-11-3 106................ RobMcCarth(3)
(Ian Williams) *nt fluent in rr: hit 1st: reminders 10th: sn bhd: t.o whn p.u bef 4 out* **11/1**

6m 21.0s (38.30) **Going Correction** +1.25s/f (Heav) **5** Ran SP% **108.9**
Speed ratings (Par 105): **80,70,61, ,**
CSF £6.58 TOTE £1.90: £1.50, £2.00; EX 5.10 Trifecta £13.50.
Owner Mrs P G D Sykes **Bred** McCann Bros **Trained** Bishop's Castle, Shropshire

FOCUS
The ground was officially heavy by this stage, placing the emphasis firmly on stamina. Ordinary form.

2492 JENNINGS CUMBERLAND ALE H'CAP HURDLE (9 hdls) 1m 7f 168y
3:25 (3:29) (Class 5) (0-100,100) 3-Y-O+ **£2,729** (£801; £400; £200)

Form RPR
0353 **1** **Mulligan's Man (IRE)**[15] 2165 8-11-7 95................(p) DavidEngland 105+
(Clare Ellam) *chsd ldrs: led 3 out: hit next: drvn clr between last 2* **14/1**

0540 **2** *6* **Hunters Belt (IRE)**[33] 1887 11-11-7 100...........(bt) JonathonBewley(5) 103
(George Bewley) *hld up in rr: sme hdwy 3 out: styd on strly run-in: tk modest 2nd towards fin* **14/1**

-404 **3** *½* **Hill Fort**[23] 2038 5-11-11 99.................................. CharliePoste 103
(Matt Sheppard) *chsd ldrs: clr 2nd whn hit 2 out: kpt on same pce* **14/1**

0-55 **4** *1 ¼* **Lean Burn (USA)**[139] 858 9-10-7 84..................(bt) HarryChalloner(3) 85
(Barry Leavy) *prom: rdn after 3 out: kpt on same pce fr next* **11/1**

6324 **5** *6* **Symphony Of Pearls**[139] 856 4-10-9 83........................ RobertDunne 78
(Dai Burchell) *mid-div: drvn 6th: one pce fr next: fdd run-in* **20/1**

P2P- **6** *¾* **Fiddler's Flight (IRE)**[249] 4695 9-10-5 82............ ColmMcCormack(3) 77
(John Norton) *in rr: sme hdwy 3 out: nvr a factor* **25/1**

4 **7** *2* **Meadow Cross (IRE)**[17] 2137 3-10-0 90 oh1...............(p) DGHogan 68
(Denis Gerard Hogan, Ire) *nt fluent towards rr: effrt 6th: nvr a factor* **7/2**[1]

06-3 **8** *1* **Neworld (FR)**[15] 2162 6-11-12 100............................ AlainCawley 93
(Richard Hobson) *nt fluent in rr: sme hdwy 6th: drvn next: wknd after 2 out* **4/1**[2]

3400 **9** *1 ½* **Anton Dolin (IRE)**[23] 2043 7-11-3 98.................... MrHFNugent(7) 88
(Michael Mullineaux) *chsd ldrs: rdn sn after 3 out: wknd next* **14/1**

0/04 **10** *½* **Razzle Dazzle 'Em**[30] 1931 6-10-4 78........................ DenisO'Regan 68
(Shaun Harris) *led: hdd 3 out: lost pl bef next* **16/1**

10-5 **11** *1 ¼* **Nolecce**[15] 2162 8-10-5 86.................................... JoshWall(7) 74
(Tony Forbes) *hld up in rr: brief effrt 3 out: hit next: sn wknd* **8/1**

020- **12** *11* **Blake Dean**[208] 5422 7-11-2 97.............................. MrHHogg(7) 74
(Sue Smith) *w ldr: hit 6th: sn rdn and lost pl: t.o next* **6/1**[3]

53-2 **13** *44* **First Of Never (IRE)**[193] 137 9-10-0 74 oh3................ SeanQuinlan 7
(Lynn Siddall) *hld up in rr: hdwy 5th: lost pl 3 out: sn bhd: t.o whn virtually p.u clsng stages* **16/1**

4m 23.2s (25.80) **Going Correction** +1.425s/f (Heav)
WFA 3 from 4yo 15lb 4 from 5yo+ 7lb **13** Ran SP% **123.0**
Speed ratings (Par 103): **92,89,88,88,85 84,83,83,82,82 81,76,54**
CSF £199.11 CT £2804.91 TOTE £14.40: £3.50, £4.40, £4.90; EX 230.20 Trifecta £1359.70 Part won..
Owner Harpers Brook Racing **Bred** Andrew Pierce **Trained** Atlow, Derbyshire

FOCUS
Plenty still retained chances turning for home in this modest handicap hurdle, which turned into a slog. The winner's best figure since June 2014.

2493 WAINWRIGHT STANDARD OPEN NATIONAL HUNT FLAT RACE 1m 7f 168y
4:00 (4:00) (Class 6) 4-6-Y-O **£1,949** (£572; £286; £143)

Form RPR
3- **1** **Penn Lane (IRE)**[222] 5200 4-11-0 0........................ GavinSheehan 117
(Warren Greatrex) *trckd ldrs: led 8f out: hrd drvn over 1f out: fnd ex and hld on towards fin* **3/1**[2]

2 **2** *¾* **Call To Order**[189] 213 5-11-0 0................................ NoelFehily 116
(Jonjo O'Neill) *hld up towards rr: hdwy to chse ldrs 6f out: 2nd over 2f out: kpt on: no ex nr fin* **1/1**[1]

3- **3** *9* **Bacchanel (FR)**[227] 5104 4-11-0 0............................ TomO'Brien 107
(Philip Hobbs) *chsd ldrs: 4th over 2f out: 3rd over 1f out: one pce* **8/1**[3]

45- **4** *12* **Ami Desbois (FR)**[210] 5402 5-10-4 0.................. ArchieBellamy(10) 95
(Graeme McPherson) *mid-div: hdwy to chse ldrs 7f out: 2nd over 3f out: wknd over 1f out* **25/1**

0- **5** *24* **Marvellous Monty (IRE)**[260] 4478 5-10-7 0................ AlainCawley 64
(Johnny Farrelly) *bhd: sme hdwy 6f out: wknd over 2f out* **10/1**

0 **6** *¾* **Swinton Diamond (IRE)**[28] 1973 4-10-4 0.............. TobyWheeler(10) 70
(Ian Williams) *in rr: bhd fnl 5f* **50/1**

7 *nk* **Falcons Fall (IRE)** 4-10-11 0................................ BenPoste(3) 70
(Tom Symonds) *chsd ldrs: lost pl over 5f out: sn bhd* **40/1**

8 *46* **Paradis Blanc (FR)** 4-11-0 0.................................. AdamWedge 24
(Nigel Twiston-Davies) *mid-div: bhd fnl 6f: t.o* **16/1**

9 *25* **Surfing The Stars (IRE)** 4-11-0 0............................ RobertDunne
(Laura Young) *chsd ldrs: drvn after 6f: lost pl 7f out: sn bhd: t.o* **100/1**

10 *4 ½* **Megan Mint** 5-10-7 0.. CharliePoste
(Matt Sheppard) *in rr: sme hdwy 7f out: sn lost pl and wl bhd: t.o 4f out* **25/1**

11 *15* **Cordey Warrior** 5-11-0 0.................................... DenisO'Regan
(Victor Dartnall) *in rr: bhd fnl 7f: t.o* **8/1**[3]

12 *7* **Sundance Boy** 6-11-0 0...................................... PeterCarberry
(Giuseppe Fierro) *trckd ldrs: t.k.h: hmpd bnd after 5f: sn drvn: lost pl 6f out: sn bhd: t.o* **100/1**

0 **13** *52* **Guadeloupe (IRE)**[7] 2337 6-10-7 0....................(v[1]) JoshWall[(7)]
(David Loder) *w ldr: led after 4f: hdd 8f out: sn lost pl and wl bhd: tailed rt off: virtually p.u* **33/1**

440 **14** *3 1/4* **Battle Master**[18] 2126 5-10-4 0.................... LewisStones[(10)]
(Michael Mullineaux) *led 4f: lost pl after 6f: sn wl bhd: tailed rt off* **100/1**

4m 12.2s (20.40) **Going Correction** +1.425s/f (Heav) **14** Ran SP% **130.2**
Speed ratings: **106,105,101,95,83 82,82,59,47,44 37,33,7,6**
CSF £6.60 TOTE £3.70: £1.40, £1.10, £2.40; EX 9.00 Trifecta £28.10.
Owner Alan & Andrew Turner **Bred** Ned Morris **Trained** Upper Lambourn, Berks

FOCUS
This was run at a more exacting pace than a lot of bumpers and they finished well strung out. The form horses fought out the finish, and look useful. A big step up from the winner.
T/Plt: £73.60 to £1 stake. Pool: £58,045.25 - 575.25 winning tickets. T/Qpdt: £70.80 to £1 stake. Pool: £3,942.31 - 41.15 winning tickets. **Walter Glynn**

2196 WETHERBY (L-H)

Saturday, November 14

OFFICIAL GOING: Soft (hdl 6.2, chs 6.2)
Wind: light across Weather: overcast

2494 RACINGUK.COM/FREETRIAL MARES' NOVICES' HURDLE (8 hdls 1 omitted) 2m
12:20 (12:20) (Class 4) 4-Y-O+ **£3,573** (£1,049; £524; £262)

Form RPR

32-2 **1** **Actinpieces**[182] 334 4-10-7 0.................... MissGAndrews[(3)] 100+
(Pam Sly) *trckd ldng pair: led appr 3 out: wandered but styd on to go clr after 2 out* **4/1[2]**

2 *17* **Shine Away (IRE)**[209] 5-10-10 0.................... DannyCook 85+
(Sue Smith) *pressed ldr: led 5th: rdn whn hdd appr 3 out: wknd after 2 out* **9/1**

3-40 **3** *4 1/2* **Milly Baloo**[15] 2169 4-10-10 0.................... JakeGreenall 76
(Tim Easterby) *in tch: rdn and outpcd after 5th: plugged on after 2 out: wnt 3rd last* **33/1**

P-0 **4** *13* **Norfolk Sound**[14] 2189 4-10-3 0.................... SamColtherd[(7)] 68
(Stuart Coltherd) *hld up: rdn bef 3 out: plugged on into 3rd jst after 2 out: lost 3rd last: wknd* **150/1**

5 *8* **Lucky Dreamer** 4-10-10 0.................... TomMessenger 61
(Chris Bealby) *hld up in tch: hdwy into 3rd after 5th: rdn 3 out: j.lft 2 out: sn lost 3rd and wknd* **33/1**

2203 **6** *25* **Irondale Express**[15] 2164 4-10-3 104.................... FinianO'Toole[(7)] 30
(Barry Brennan) *led narrowly: hdd 5th: sn wknd* **7/1[3]**

/41- **P** **Bedale Lane (IRE)**[323] 3263 6-10-10 0.................... BrianHarding
(Nicky Richards) *t.k.h: trckd ldng pair: pushed along and lost pl qckly after 5th: sn bhd: p.u bef 3 out* **8/13[1]**

4m 15.1s (19.30) **Going Correction** +0.80s/f (Soft) **7** Ran SP% **111.0**
Speed ratings (Par 105): **83,74,72,65,61 49,**
CSF £33.41 TOTE £4.00: £1.60, £3.10; EX 27.10 Trifecta £296.50.
Owner Mrs P M Sly **Bred** Mrs P Sly **Trained** Thorney, Cambs

FOCUS
Both bends moved out 6yds. Races 1, 2 & 6 increased by 36yds, raced 4 & 5 by 54yds and races 3 & 7 by 72yds. After 4.5mm of overnight rain the official going remained soft. The opener was a mares' novice hurdle with little depth and the odds-on favourite failed to complete. The winner was similar to her bumper mark.

2495 RACING UK FREE FOR A MONTH NOVICES' CHASE (13 fncs) 1m 7f 36y
12:55 (12:55) (Class 4) 4-Y-O+ **£3,898** (£1,144; £572; £286)

Form RPR

11P- **1** **Boru's Brook (IRE)**[213] 5339 7-11-1 0.................... TomCannon 141+
(Jim Best) *mde all: j.w in main: rdn after 3 out: hit last: styd on wl* **6/4[1]**

2 *15* **Dig Deeper**[601] 6-11-1 0.................... AndrewThornton 125+
(Caroline Bailey) *trckd ldr: lost pl and mstke 5 out: bhd in 4th 2 out: styd on fr appr last: wnt 2nd nr fin* **8/1[3]**

2153 **3** *3/4* **Vodka Wells (FR)**[14] 2201 5-11-1 128.................... FinianO'Toole[(7)] 129
(Micky Hammond) *hld up: clsr order 7th: wnt 2nd 4 out: rdn appr 2 out: sn no imp on wnr: wknd run-in: lost 2nd nr fin* **6/4[1]**

215 **4** *18* **Never Up (GER)**[155] 710 4-10-7 113.................... HenryBrooke 101
(George Moore) *hld up: hdwy into 2nd 6th: lost 2nd 4 out: sn rdn: nt fluent 3 out: sn wknd* **6/1[2]**

P **F** **Telex Du Berlais (FR)**[35] 1855 6-10-10 110.................... CallumBewley[(5)]
(Simon Waugh) *in tch: rdn after 5 out: sn struggling in 5th: fell 4 out* **25/1**

4m 3.5s (7.70) **Going Correction** +0.80s/f (Soft) **5** Ran SP% **109.2**
Speed ratings (Par 105): **111,103,102,93,**
CSF £12.51 TOTE £2.30: £1.30, £3.00; EX 10.60 Trifecta £34.80.
Owner Cheltenham Dreamers **Bred** Austin O'Toole **Trained** Lewes, E Sussex

FOCUS
An uncompetitive novice chase in which one of the market leaders was below par. The winner was up 7lb on the best of his hurdle figures and there should be more to come.

2496 DRANSFIELDS CIU CHARITY RACEDAY H'CAP HURDLE (11 hdls 2 omitted) 3m 26y
1:30 (1:30) (Class 4) (0-120,117) 4-Y-O+ **£3,249** (£954; £477; £238)

Form RPR

5/P- **1** **Call It On (IRE)**[35] 3716 9-10-12 106....................(tp) AdamNicol[(3)] 107
(Philip Kirby) *hld up: pushed along 1/2-way: bk on bit and hdwy bef 3 out: rdn to chal 3 out: led 2 out: drvn run-in: pressed fnl 110yds: hld on wl* **7/1**

3-22 **2** *1 1/2* **Snapping Turtle (IRE)**[16] 2145 10-11-6 114.................... CallumWhillans[(3)] 114
(Donald Whillans) *led: pressed fr 6th: rdn bef 3 out: nt fluent 2 out: chal again fnl 110yds: hld towards fin* **9/2[2]**

10-3 **3** *1 3/4* **Gilzean (IRE)**[17] 2135 9-11-2 107.................... TrevorWhelan 104
(Alex Hales) *midfield: rdn to chse ldng pair bef 3 out: plugged on* **10/1**

123 **4** *1/2* **Who You For (IRE)**[29] 1943 5-11-10 115.................... JackQuinlan 113
(Sarah Humphrey) *trckd ldr: rdn and outpcd bef 3 out: nt fluent 3 out: styd on fr last* **4/1[1]**

60-3 **5** *2 1/2* **Harry Hunt**[18] 2125 8-11-7 112.................... KielanWoods 107
(Graeme McPherson) *midfield: rdn bef 3 out: plugged on* **9/2[2]**

3236 **6** *9* **Presenting Streak (IRE)**[20] 2085 6-11-0 112....................(t) MrRWinks[(7)] 101
(Peter Winks) *hld up: hdwy to press ldr 6th: rdn and outpcd bef 3 out: wknd after 2 out* **11/2[3]**

014- **7** *25* **Rayadour (IRE)**[18] 4576 6-10-12 106.................... JoeColliver[(3)] 66
(Micky Hammond) *hld up: rdn and brief bef 3 out: hit 3 out: sn wknd* **16/1**

-3PP **8** *4* **Wolf Shield (IRE)**[111] 1113 8-11-12 117....................(t) HenryBrooke 73
(George Moore) *trckd ldr: lost pl after 6th: wknd bef 3 out* **9/1**

446/ **9** *13* **Joseph Mercer (IRE)**[694] 3191 8-10-4 98.................... JonathanEngland[(3)] 41
(Tina Jackson) *midfield: wknd on extended run to 3 out* **20/1**

6m 35.5s (19.00) **Going Correction** +0.95s/f (Soft) **9** Ran SP% **114.0**
Speed ratings (Par 105): **106,105,104,104,103 100,92,91,86**
CSF £38.53 CT £314.56 TOTE £7.30: £2.30, £1.70, £3.10; EX 45.00 Trifecta £178.00.
Owner P Kirby **Bred** Martyn J McEnery **Trained** East Appleton, N Yorks

FOCUS
A competitive handicap hurdle and they were well bunched on the turn into the home straight. The third is probably the best guide.

2497 TOTESCOOP6 H'CAP CHASE (16 fncs) 2m 3f 85y
2:05 (2:05) (Class 3) (0-130,127) 4-Y-O+ **£8,656** (£3,148)

Form RPR

12-2 **1** **De Vous A Moi (FR)**[14] 2192 7-11-12 127.................... DannyCook 139+
(Sue Smith) *trckd ldng pair: pushed along fr bef 8th: drvn and outpcd in 2nd bef 4 out: clsd after 3 out: jst led whn lft 8 l clr last* **5/2[1]**

2 *6* **Indian Temple (IRE)**[75] 1433 6-10-12 120.................... MrWHRReed[(7)] 125
(W T Reed) *hld up: rdn bef 4 out: one pce: lft 2nd last: hung rt run-in* **12/1**

5-2P **P** **Cody Wyoming**[16] 2153 9-11-11 126....................(tp) JamesDavies
(Charlie Mann) *prom: nt fluent 8th: slow next: sn wl bhd: p.u bef 4 out* **17/2**

300/ **F** **Elenika (FR)**[574] 5385 7-10-13 117.................... CallumWhillans[(3)] 124
(Venetia Williams) *led: hit 5 out: 8 l clr 4 out: sn rdn: reduced advantage bef 2 out: jst hdd whn fell last* **14/5[2]**

255- **P** **Supreme Asset (IRE)**[204] 5515 7-11-7 122.................... BrianHarding
(Donald McCain) *hld up: rdn after 5 out: sn struggling: p.u bef 3 out* **8/1[3]**

41P- **P** **Voyage A New York (FR)**[245] 4765 6-11-4 122.................... DerekFox[(3)]
(Lucinda Russell) *hld up: rdn after 11th: sn bhd: blnd 2 out and p.u* **5/2[1]**

5m 22.4s (14.60) **Going Correction** +0.95s/f (Soft) **6** Ran SP% **112.8**
Speed ratings (Par 107): **107,104, , ,**
CSF £27.67 TOTE £2.70: £2.40, £3.70; EX 17.40.
Owner Mrs J Morgan **Bred** Rene Wattinne **Trained** High Eldwick, W Yorks

FOCUS
Only two finished in an open-looking handicap chase. A pb from the winner.

2498 TRIAL RACING UK FOR FREE NOW NOVICES' HURDLE 2m 3f 154y
2:40 (2:41) (Class 4) 4-Y-O+ **£3,249** (£954; £477; £238)

Form RPR

-F21 **1** **Bowdler's Magic**[17] 2139 8-11-2 114.................... AdamNicol[(3)] 121+
(David Thompson) *led after 1st: mde rest: strly pressed fr 2 out: kpt on wl* **11/4[2]**

33-2 **2** *1/2* **Bollin Ace**[15] 2169 4-10-12 0.................... BrianHarding 114+
(Tim Easterby) *trckd ldng pair: rdn to chal strly 2 out: nt fluent last: one pce fnl 110yds* **11/10[1]**

4 **3** *30* **Agentleman (IRE)**[19] 2106 5-10-12 0.................... DannyCook 89
(Tim Easterby) *hld up in tch: hdwy into 3rd appr 3 out: rdn after 3 out: sn wknd* **4/1[3]**

4 *17* **Holy Dancer** 5-10-5 0.................... TomMessenger 59
(Chris Bealby) *hld up: rdn bef 3 out: sn wknd* **25/1**

5 *3 1/4* **Lacerta**[28] 4-10-5 0.................... FinianO'Toole[(7)] 68
(Micky Hammond) *midfield: nt fluent 3 out: sn rdn and wknd: blnd last* **12/1**

-440 **6** *5* **Bling Noir (IRE)**[9] 2287 5-10-5 0.................... HenryBrooke 51
(Tony Coyle) *led: hdd after 1st: remained prom: rdn appr 3 out: sn wknd* **33/1**

U **7** *20* **Alchimix (FR)**[14] 2196 5-10-9 0.................... JoeColliver[(3)] 38
(Micky Hammond) *trckd ldng pair: wknd on extended run to 3 out* **11/1**

00- **8** *74* **Rebel Roger**[222] 5207 6-10-9 0.................... JonathanEngland[(3)]
(Tina Jackson) *a in rr* **125/1**

5m 28.1s (21.10) **Going Correction** +1.10s/f (Heav)
WFA 4 from 5yo+ 8lb **8** Ran SP% **117.9**
Speed ratings (Par 105): **101,100,88,82,80 78,70,41**
CSF £6.57 TOTE £4.00: £1.10, £1.30, £1.50; EX 7.10 Trifecta £19.50.
Owner N Park **Bred** Miss K Rausing **Trained** Bolam, Co Durham

FOCUS
Not a strong novice hurdle and the two market leaders pulled a long way clear. A hurdles best from the winner.

2499 TOTEPOOLLIVEINFO.COM H'CAP HURDLE (QUALIFIER FOR THE CHALLENGER TWO MILE HURDLE SERIES FINAL) (9 hdls) 2m
3:15 (3:18) (Class 3) (0-130,129) 3-Y-O+ **£7,797** (£2,289; £1,144; £572)

Form RPR

2-63 **1** **Kayf Blanco**[15] 2170 6-11-11 128.................... KielanWoods 140+
(Graeme McPherson) *hld up: smooth hdwy appr 3 out: led jst after 2 out: pushed along appr last: out run-in* **4/1[1]**

06/0 **2** *1 1/4* **Vendor (FR)**[13] 2214 7-11-5 127.................... DiarmuidO'Regan[(5)] 135
(Sue Smith) *pressed ldr: nt fluent 3 out: sn rdn: briefly dropped to 4th appr last: styd on wl run-in* **9/2[2]**

014- **3** *6* **Sir Safir**[232] 5019 5-10-7 107.................... JamieHamilton[(7)] 120
(Peter Niven) *midfield: hdwy to trck ldrs 3 out: rdn 2 out: 2nd last: wandered and wknd fnl 110yds* **15/2**

210- **4** *2 1/2* **Arthurs Secret**[29] 4830 5-11-2 119.................... JakeGreenall 120
(John Quinn) *led narrowly: hit 2 out: sn hdd: wknd run-in* **8/1**

-264 **5** *hd* **Kuda Huraa (IRE)**[23] 2042 7-10-9 117.................... HarryBannister[(5)] 116
(Harriet Bethell) *hld up: hdwy and in tch appr 3 out: sn rdn: no ex run-in* **7/1[3]**

-314 **6** *15* **Hartside (GER)**[187] 237 6-10-4 114.................... MrRWinks[(7)] 101
(Peter Winks) *hld up: rdn appr 3 out: nt fluent 3 out: sn wknd* **9/1**

016- **7** *10* **Hainan (FR)**[270] 4286 4-11-3 120.................... DannyCook 94
(Sue Smith) *trckd ldng pair: rdn and wknd on extended run to 3 out* **14/1**

4-62 **8** *4* **It's A Mans World**[13] 2217 9-10-8 116.................... CraigGallagher[(5)] 86
(Brian Ellison) *trckd ldng pair: nt fluent and lost pl 4th: wknd on extended run to 3 out* **14/1**

0 **9** *1 3/4* **Kentucky Star (FR)**[28] 1977 6-11-0 117.................... BrianHarding 86
(John Quinn) *midfield: rdn appr 3 out: sn wknd* **10/1**

10 *6* **Hollywoodien (FR)**[300] 4-11-12 129.................... JamesDavies 92
(Tom Symonds) *in tch: nt fluent 4th: wknd appr 3 out* **14/1**

205/ **P** **Makbullet**[71] 4549 8-10-10 113.................... HenryBrooke
(Michael Smith) *hld up: rdn appr 3 out: sn wknd: p.u bef last* **33/1**

4m 12.5s (16.70) **Going Correction** +1.25s/f (Heav) **11** Ran SP% **115.6**
Speed ratings (Par 107): **108,107,104,103,103 95,90,88,87,84**
CSF £22.31 CT £129.40 TOTE £4.50: £1.90, £1.70, £2.90; EX 24.70 Trifecta £125.50.
Owner Mrs L Day, H Burdett & G McPherson **Bred** Stewart Pike **Trained** Upper Oddington, Gloucs

FOCUS
A competitive handicap hurdle and they were well strung out. A step up from the winner.

2500 RACINGUK.COM/FREETRIAL H'CAP CHASE (18 fncs 1 omitted) 3m 45y
3:50 (3:50) (Class 4) (0-105,104) 4-Y-0+ **£3,898** (£1,144; £572; £286)

Form RPR
5362 **1** **Longueville Flier (IRE)**[15] 2173 6-10-12 **93**.................... JoeColliver(3) 100+
(Micky Hammond) *hld up: nt fluent 11th and 5 out: rdn bef 4 out: hdwy appr 2 out: led last: styd on* **6/1**[2]
5555 **2** 1 ½ **Cara Court (IRE)**[15] 2173 9-9-9 **78** oh8....................(v) HarryBannister(5) 81
(Joanne Foster) *trckd ldr: lft in front 9th: rdn after 4 out: hdd last: one pce* **20/1**
2U-4 **3** 2 ¾ **Itstimeforapint (IRE)**[15] 2173 7-11-9 **104**.................... DerekFox(3) 106+
(Lucinda Russell) *midfield: pushed along and dropped to rr after 10th: nt fluent 11th and 12th: rallied after 4 out to chse ldr 2 out: nt fluent last: no ex* **2/1**[1]
232- **4** 13 **Silver Dragon**[323] 3271 7-11-4 **96**....................(b) BrianHarding 85
(Tony Coyle) *in tch: nt fluent 7th: wnt prom after 10th: rdn bef 4 out: wknd after 2 out* **15/2**
/44- **5** 14 **Oil Burner**[387] 2011 10-10-13 **96**.................... GrantCockburn(5) 68
(Stuart Coltherd) *hld up: hdwy to trck ldr 5 out: rdn 4 out: wknd 2 out* **7/1**[3]
/1P- **6** ¾ **Brave Buck**[241] 4855 7-11-12 **104**.................... JakeGreenall 76
(Henry Daly) *trckd ldr: rdn bef 4 out: wknd 2 out* **6/1**[2]
34-6 **U** **Brunello**[18] 153 7-11-3 **95**....................(p) HenryBrooke
(Michael Smith) *led: nt fluent 8th: jinked rt and uns rdr jst bef 9th* **25/1**
1144 **P** **Sgt Bull Berry**[30] 1930 8-9-8 **79**.................... JamieHamilton(7)
(Peter Maddison) *hld up in rr: eased and p.u after 10th* **9/1**
6-2P **U** **Be A Dreamer**[16] 2143 7-10-11 **89**.................... DannyCook
(Sue Smith) *prom: mstke 1st: uns rdr 2nd* **10/1**

7m 1.1s (13.10) **9 Ran SP% 113.9**
CSF £102.29 CT £320.84 TOTE £6.10: £2.50, £5.50, £1.20; EX 109.50 Trifecta £823.30.
Owner M D Hammond **Bred** Jim McDonald **Trained** Middleham, N Yorks

FOCUS
A modest handicap chase and it was hard work in the conditions. The first three were pretty much to their marks.
T/Plt: £62.30 to £1 stake. Pool: £57,028.16 - 667.92 winning tickets. T/Qpdt: £5.80 to £1 stake. Pool: £6,160.98 - 779.33 winning tickets. **Andrew Sheret**

2501 - 2508a (Foreign Racing) - See Raceform Interactive

2480
CHELTENHAM (L-H)
Sunday, November 15

OFFICIAL GOING: Good to soft (soft in places; 7.3)
Wind: quite strong across Weather: overcast

2509 SKY BET SUPREME TRIAL NOVICES' HURDLE (REGISTERED AS THE SHARP NOVICES' HURDLE RACE) (GRADE 2) (8 hdls) 2m 87y
1:00 (1:01) (Class 1) 4-Y-0+ **£17,286** (£6,612; £3,411; £1,800)

Form RPR
-611 **1** **Altior (IRE)**[15] 2183 5-11-7 143.................... NicodeBoinville 146+
(Nicky Henderson) *chasing type: lw: trckd ldr: t.k.h after 3rd: ldng whn hmpd by loose horse after 2 out: rdn whn strly chal fr last: kpt on wl to assert cl home* **2/1**[1]
1111 **2** ½ **Maputo**[28] 1986 5-11-7 147.................... AidanColeman 144
(John Ferguson) *trckd ldrs: taking clsr order whn hit 2 out: chal last: ev ch u.str.p run-in: no ex cl home: fin lame* **5/2**[2]
/0-1 **3** 5 **Simon Squirrel (IRE)**[37] 1837 5-11-4 0....................(t) SamTwiston-Davies 136
(Paul Nicholls) *lw: bdly hmpd leaving s: trckd ldrs: rdn to dispute 2nd after 2 out tl appr last: rdn on same pce* **6/1**
2-11 **4** 9 **Viens Chercher (IRE)**[50] 1660 4-11-4 135.................... DannyCook 127
(Brian Ellison) *hmpd s where lft in ld: rdn and hdd after 2 out: sn one pce* **12/1**
1-2 **U** **Drumlee Sunset (IRE)**[23] 2056 5-11-0 0.................... RichardJohnson
(Philip Hobbs) *shied passing through s and uns rdr* **11/4**[3]

4m 7.5s (5.50) **Going Correction** +0.20s/f (Yiel)
WFA 4 from 5yo+ 7lb **5 Ran SP% 110.5**
Speed ratings (Par 115): **94,93,91,86,**
CSF £7.50 TOTE £2.90: £1.60, £1.70; EX 6.40 Trifecta £20.60.
Owner Mrs Patricia Pugh **Bred** Paddy Behan **Trained** Upper Lambourn, Berks

FOCUS
Old Course used. Chase bends dolled out 9yds and chases increased by 56yds per circuit. Hurdle bends out 11yds and hurdle races increased by 68yds per circuit. here was drama at the start in this good-quality novice hurdle as \bDrumlee Sunset\p slipped up as the runners set off. He then galloped around loose and led them to the final hurdle. A steadily run event. The finish was fought out by two decent sorts, with the winner on the upgrade.

2510 RACING POST ARKLE TROPHY TRIAL NOVICES' CHASE (REGISTERED AS THE NOVEMBER NOVICES' CHASE) (GRADE 2) (13 fncs) 1m 7f 199y
1:35 (1:36) (Class 1) 4-Y-0+ **£18,224** (£6,838; £3,424; £1,705)

Form RPR
41-1 **1** **Garde La Victoire (FR)**[16] 2166 6-11-2 0.................... RichardJohnson 152+
(Philip Hobbs) *racd keenly: trckd ldrs: tk clsr order 3 out: rdn appr 2 out: led sn after last: kpt on wl: drvn rt out* **8/15**[1]
1-11 **2** 2 ½ **Fox Norton (FR)**[29] 1969 5-11-6 145.................... NoelFehily 152
(Neil Mulholland) *lw: taken to s early: t.k.h dictating stdy early pce: nt fluent 5th: rdn after 2 out: nt as fluent as wnr last: sn hdd: no ex* **11/2**[3]
P6-1 **3** ½ **Calipto (FR)**[25] 2012 5-11-2 139....................(t) SamTwiston-Davies 149
(Paul Nicholls) *trckd ldrs: nt fluent 3rd: rdn whn sltly outpcd after 3 out: styd on again between last 2: kpt on fr last but nt quite pce to get on terms* **4/1**[2]
U122 **4** 3 ¼ **Dormello Mo (FR)**[23] 2053 5-11-6 147....................(t) SeanBowen 150
(Paul Nicholls) *trckd ldrs: rdn in disp 2nd after 3 out: hld in 4th whn awkward 2 out: kpt on same pce* **14/1**

4m 3.7s (5.70) **Going Correction** +0.60s/f (Soft) **4 Ran SP% 107.3**
Speed ratings (Par 115): **109,107,107,105**
CSF £3.83 TOTE £1.40; EX 3.50 Trifecta £4.90.
Owner Mrs Diana L Whateley **Bred** Mlle Laure Godet **Trained** Withycombe, Somerset

FOCUS
This race is often a leading guide for the 2m novice division and the form is worth treating positively. The winner didn't need to improve.

2511 SHLOER CHASE (REGISTERED AS THE CHELTENHAM CHASE) (GRADE 2) (13 fncs) 1m 7f 199y
2:10 (2:10) (Class 1) 4-Y-0+
£42,712 (£16,027; £8,025; £3,997; £2,010; £1,005)

Form RPR
2P2- **1** **Sprinter Sacre (FR)**[204] 5537 9-11-0 167.................... NicodeBoinville 173+
(Nicky Henderson) *lw: trckd ldrs: led on bit after 4 out: in command fr next: comf* **15/8**[1]
425- **2** 14 **Somersby (IRE)**[204] 5537 11-11-0 164....................(p) BrianHughes 159
(Mick Channon) *taken to s early: trckd ldrs: pressed ldr 8th tl after 4 out: rdn after 3 out: disp hld 2nd appr 2 out: styd on but no ch w wnr* **5/1**[3]
-104 **3** 2 ½ **Savello (IRE)**[23] 2058 9-11-4 154.................... HarrySkelton 161
(Dan Skelton) *taken to s early: hld up: rdn after 3 out: nt pce to get on terms but styd on to go 3rd run-in* **8/1**
56-1 **4** 6 **Simply Ned (IRE)**[42] 1777 8-11-4 161.................... BrianHarding 157
(Nicky Richards) *lw: hld up bhd ldrs: hdwy to dispute 3rd 3 out: sn rdn: disp hld 2nd bef 2 out tl jst bef last: no ex run-in* **3/1**[2]
103- **5** 3 ¼ **Mr Mole (IRE)**[204] 5537 7-11-10 162....................(t) BarryGeraghty 161
(Paul Nicholls) *led: hdd after 4 out: sn rdn: lost hld 2nd bef 2 out: grad fdd* **6/1**
3P-3 **6** 12 **Croco Bay (IRE)**[42] 1777 8-11-4 151.................... KielanWoods 142
(Ben Case) *pressed ldr tl after 9th: rdn after 4 out: sn dropped to rear: wknd 3 out* **12/1**

3m 58.5s (0.50) **Going Correction** +0.60s/f (Soft) **6 Ran SP% 109.5**
Speed ratings (Par 115): **122,115,113,110,109 103**
CSF £11.06 TOTE £2.30: £1.40, £2.60; EX 8.90 Trifecta £37.20.
Owner Mrs Caroline Mould **Bred** Christophe Masle **Trained** Upper Lambourn, Berks

FOCUS
A decent line up got taken apart by the brilliant winner, who was up 3lb on last year's reapperance. The runner-up sets the standard.

2512 STANJAMES.COM GREATWOOD HURDLE (A H'CAP) (GRADE 3) (8 hdls) 2m 87y
2:40 (2:44) (Class 1) 4-Y-0+
£56,950 (£21,370; £10,700; £5,330; £2,680; £1,340)

Form RPR
03-1 **1** **Old Guard**[23] 2058 4-10-10 **145**.................... HarryCobden(7) 159+
(Paul Nicholls) *in tch: smooth hdwy to ld at last: r.o wl: readily* **12/1**
44-1 **2** 2 **Superb Story (IRE)**[32] 1905 4-10-1 **129**.................... HarrySkelton 139+
(Dan Skelton) *lw: mid-div: hdwy whn nt clrest of runs after 2 out: str run on inner appr last: r.o but a being hld by wnr fnl 140yds* **8/1**[3]
00-1 **3** 4 **Waxies Dargle**[189] 231 6-10-10 **138**.................... BarryGeraghty 144
(Noel Meade, Ire) *lw: mid-div: hdwy 3 out: led after 2 out: sn rdn: hdd last: styd on but no ex* **7/1**[2]
2R/ **4** 1 ¼ **Renneti (FR)**[36] 1203 6-11-2 **144**.................... DannyMullins 150+
(W P Mullins, Ire) *slowly away: in rr: hdwy 2 out: sn rdn: styd on to go 4th run-in but no threat to ldrs* **9/1**
P20/ **5** ½ **Totalize**[50] 4147 6-10-4 **132**.................... DannyCook 136
(Brian Ellison) *mid-div: hdwy after 10th: led briefly u.p bef last: no ex run-in* **10/1**
42-1 **6** 1 ¾ **Devilment**[22] 2060 4-11-5 **147**.................... BrianHughes 150
(John Ferguson) *mid-div: rdn and hdwy after 2 out: styd on fr last but nt pce to threaten* **12/1**
000/ **7** hd **Redera (IRE)**[35] 1302 9-9-9 **128**....................(t) ShaneShortall(5) 130
(A J Martin, Ire) *mid-div: hdwy on outer after 2 out: rdn bef last: styd on but nt pce to get on terms* **40/1**
2111 **8** 6 **Nabucco**[15] 2186 6-10-9 **137**.................... AidanColeman 133
(John Ferguson) *lw: mid-div: rdn after 2 out: nvr any imp* **6/1**[1]
PF0- **9** ½ **Goodwood Mirage (IRE)**[121] 4704 5-10-12 **140**.................... WayneHutchinson 136
(Jonjo O'Neill) *racd wd: hld up towards rr: rdn after 2 out: nvr finding pce to get involved* **40/1**
0-06 **10** ¾ **Olofi (FR)**[8] 2350 9-9-13 **132**....................(tp) JamieBargary(5) 127
(Tom George) *towards rr of mid-div: rdn after 2 out: nvr gng pce to get involved* **16/1**
42-3 **11** 1 ¼ **Dexcite (FR)**[36] 1847 4-10-0 **128**.................... PaddyBrennan 122
(Tom George) *hld up bhd: sme late prog: n.d* **16/1**
11P- **12** 2 ¼ **Bidourey (FR)**[253] 4633 4-10-10 **138**.................... TomScudamore 130
(David Pipe) *trckd ldr: disp 2 out: sn rdn and hdd: wknd last* **16/1**
B10- **13** ¾ **Ebony Express**[247] 4737 6-10-9 **137**.................... WillKennedy 128
(Dr Richard Newland) *led: hit 2nd: rdn and hdd after 2 out: sn hld: wknd last* **16/1**
11-2 **14** ¾ **Mad Jack Mytton (IRE)**[32] 1905 5-10-8 **136**.................... RichardJohnson 126
(Jonjo O'Neill) *mid-div: rdn after 2 out: nt pce to threaten: wknd last* **12/1**
420- **15** nk **Bouvreuil (FR)**[220] 5236 4-10-11 **139**....................(t) NoelFehily 129
(Paul Nicholls) *trckd ldrs: rdn after 2 out: wknd bef last* **12/1**
110- **16** ¾ **Days Of Heaven (FR)**[218] 5271 5-11-3 **145**.................... PeterCarberry 134
(Nicky Henderson) *trckd ldrs: rdn after 2 out: sn wknd* **14/1**
32- **P** **Mick Jazz (FR)**[321] 3379 4-10-2 **130**....................(t[1]) SamTwiston-Davies
(Harry Fry) *lw: hld up bhd: struggling bef 3 out: wkng whn p.u bef 2 out* **6/1**[1]

4m 0.1s (-1.90) **Going Correction** +0.20s/f (Yiel)
WFA 4 from 5yo+ 7lb **17 Ran SP% 137.1**
Speed ratings (Par 113): **112,111,109,108,108 107,107,104,103,103 102,101,101,101,100 100,**
CSF £117.63 CT £756.35 TOTE £13.70: £3.60, £2.60, £2.60, £3.10; EX 128.50 Trifecta £1613.20.
Owner The Brooks, Kyle & Stewart Families **Bred** The Rt Hon Lord Rothschild **Trained** Ditcheat, Somerset

FOCUS
As ever this was fiercely competitive and they went a strong gallop. Decent form, the winner on a steep upward curve.

2513 CELEBRATING 20 YEARS OF JETS OPEN CONDITIONAL JOCKEYS' H'CAP HURDLE (Q. FOR CHALLENGER HURDLE) (10 hdls) 2m 5f 26y
3:15 (3:17) (Class 3) (0-125,125) **£7,507** (£2,217; £1,108; £554; £277; £139)

30P- **1** **Unowhatimeanharry**[254] 4613 7-11-2 **123**....................(t) LiamMcKenna(8) 135+
(Harry Fry) *lw: in tch: nt fluent 3 out but sn smooth hdwy: led on bit after 2 out: rdn and kpt on run-in* **7/2**[1]

P2-2 **2** *3* **Shadarpour (IRE)**[28] 1721 6-10-12 **119**...........(p) WilliamFeatherstone(8) 126
(Alan King) *midfield: rdn and hdwy bef 2 out: wnt 2nd last: styd on* **20/1**

214- **3** *2 ¼* **Scoop The Pot (IRE)**[238] 4945 5-11-1 **120**...............(t) CiaranGethings(6) 126
(Philip Hobbs) *hld up in midfield: nt fluent 7th and sn rdn: styd on wl after 2 out: wnt 3rd run-in* **11/2**[3]

1-21 **4** *3 ½* **Fingerontheswitch (IRE)**[38] 1829 5-11-2 **123**.......... MrShaneQuinlan(8) 124
(Neil Mulholland) *lw: midfield: hdwy bef 2 out: rdn to chse ldr appr last: one pce* **4/1**[2]

2141 **5** *hd* **Towering (IRE)**[22] 2064 6-11-6 **122**.................. JeremiahMcGrath(3) 124
(Nicky Henderson) *lw: will make a chaser: in tch: hdwy 2 out: rdn to chal appr last: lost 2nd last: one pce* **9/1**

5/-2 **6** *nk* **Seeyouallincoppers (IRE)**[21] 2098 5-11-9 **125**..........(t) KevinSexton(3) 127
(Gordon Elliott, Ire) *hld up in midfield: gd hdwy whn mstke 2 out: sn rdn and one pce* **40/1**

31F- **7** *¾* **Alzammaar (USA)**[35] 5535 4-11-9 **125**.................(tp) HarryBannister(3) 125
(Warren Greatrex) *prom: rdn and outpcd after 3 out: plugged on run-in* **16/1**

0- **8** *1* **Jansboy**[17] 2158 8-11-2 **120**...............................(p) ConorWalsh(5) 120
(N Dooly, Ire) *prom: led after 6th: rdn after 3 out: hdd after 2 out: grad wknd run-in* **16/1**

4-13 **9** *½* **Crazy Jack (IRE)**[32] 1903 7-11-12 **125**...............(p) ConorShoemark 125
(Kim Bailey) *midfield towards outer: rdn 3 out: one pce* **25/1**

4-U0 **10** *3 ¼* **Goodbye Dancer (FR)**[36] 1847 4-11-6 **125**.......... JamieBargary(6) 122
(Nigel Twiston-Davies) *hld up: mstke 3rd: rdn after 6th: hit last: minor late hdwy: nvr threatened* **50/1**

1124 **11** *nk* **Skylander (IRE)**[25] 2018 6-11-10 **123**...................... GilesHawkins 119
(David Pipe) *midfield: rdn after 3 out: no imp* **33/1**

0-34 **12** *9* **Thorpe (IRE)**[42] 1776 5-11-4 **120**............................ DerekFox(3) 108
(Lucinda Russell) *midfield: rdn after 6th: wknd after 3 out* **16/1**

F-4 **13** *5* **Brod Na Heireann (IRE)**[17] 2152 6-11-4 **120**.......... TomBellamy(3) 103
(Alan King) *midfield: rdn 2 out: sn wknd* **16/1**

341- **14** *11* **Definite Soldier (IRE)**[170] 539 6-11-5 **118**...................(t) ShaneShortall 91
(P J Rothwell, Ire) *led: hdd after 6th: wknd after 3 out* **33/1**

-210 **15** *1* **Brave Helios**[120] 1035 5-11-8 **124**........................ DanielHiskett(3) 96
(Richard Phillips) *chsd ldrs: lost pl 6th: wknd after next* **66/1**

2P14 **16** *16* **Uncle Tone (IRE)**[21] 2088 6-11-2 **123**................. GeorgeBlackwell(8) 81
(Tim Vaughan) *hld up in midfield: rdn after 7th: sn wknd* **40/1**

63-1 **17** *8* **Bohemian Rhapsody (IRE)**[22] 261 6-11-11 **124**......(p) ThomasGarner 75
(Joseph Tuite) *hld up: sltly hmpd by faller 6th: a towards rr* **33/1**

56-6 **18** *18* **Daveron (IRE)**[29] 1977 7-11-4 **120**.......................... MattGriffiths(3) 55
(Jeremy Scott) *chsd ldrs: lost pl after 6th: wknd after next* **33/1**

313- **P** **Valid Point (IRE)**[261] 4475 9-11-4 **120**...................(t) RyanHatch(3)
(Nigel Twiston-Davies) *a in rr: p.u after 2 out* **20/1**

4 **P** **Battling Boru (IRE)**[21] 2096 9-11-4 **122**...............(p) HarryCobden(5)
(Anthony Mullins, Ire) *midfield: rdn after 7th: wknd qckly: wnt wrong and p.u bef next* **28/1**

/03- **P** **Orangeaday**[340] 3023 8-11-9 **122**.............................(t) KillianMoore
(Ben Case) *a towards rr: slow 5th: p.u bef 3 out* **66/1**

4P-0 **P** **Liberty One (IRE)**[23] 2057 9-11-8 **121**........................(p) LizzieKelly
(Richard Woollacott) *hld up: slow 4th and reminders: sn detached: p.u after next* **33/1**

2020 **F** **Willem (FR)**[23] 2054 5-11-6 **125**..........................(p) MichaelHeard(6)
(David Pipe) *hld up: fell 6th* **33/1**

165- **P** **Brook (FR)**[261] 4472 4-11-9 **125**.............................. KieronEdgar(3)
(David Pipe) *in tch: rdn after 6th: sn wknd: p.u bef 3 out* **33/1**

5m 12.9s (-0.50) **Going Correction** +0.20s/f (Yiel)
WFA 4 from 5yo+ 8lb **24** Ran **SP% 136.3**
Speed ratings (Par 107): **108,106,106,104,104 104,104,103,103,102 102,98,96,92,92 86,83,76, , , , ,**
CSF £78.55 CT £409.57 TOTE £4.70: £1.80, £4.60, £2.30, £1.80; EX 113.10 Trifecta £742.90.
Owner Harry Fry Racing Club **Bred** R J Smith **Trained** Seaborough, Dorset

FOCUS
A very strong handicap of its type, and solid form.

2514 "HIGH SHERIFF OF GLOUCESTERSHIRE'S" STANDARD OPEN NATIONAL HUNT FLAT RACE (LISTED RACE) 2m 87y
3:50 (3:50) (Class 1) 4-6-Y-O
£11,390 (£4,274; £2,140; £1,066; £536; £268)

Form RPR

1 **1** **Ballyandy**[25] 2020 4-11-0 0.............................. SamTwiston-Davies 127+
(Nigel Twiston-Davies) *wl made: will make a jumper: mid-div: hdwy over 3f out: chal over 2f out: rdn to ld ent fnl f where strly pressed: kpt on gamely to assert nring fin: drvn rt out* **8/1**

1 **2** *1* **Potters Legend**[18] 2141 5-11-0 0.......................... BarryGeraghty 124
(Lucy Wadham) *str: lw: will make a jumper: in tch: hdwy over 3f out: chal over 2f out: rdn and ev ch ent fnl f: no ex nring fin* **14/1**

4-1 **3** *1* **Aurillac (FR)**[22] 2065 5-11-0 0.............................. LeightonAspell 123
(Rebecca Curtis) *led: rdn and hdd over 2f out: outpcd briefly: styd on again ins fnl f: wnt 3rd fnl 75yds* **14/1**

111 **4** *1 ¼* **Waterlord**[114] 1101 4-11-0 0................................. AidanColeman 122
(John Ferguson) *q lengthy: hld up: hdwy on inner to ld over 2f out: sn rdn: hdd ent fnl f: no ex* **3/1**[1]

1 **5** *9* **Caius Marcius (IRE)**[15] 2195 4-10-11 0.................. CraigNichol(3) 113
(Nicky Richards) *mid-div: hdwy 3f out: sn rdn: outpcd 2f out* **33/1**

31 **6** *3 ¾* **Point The Way (IRE)**[36] 1858 4-10-9 0................ CraigGallagher(5) 109
(Brian Ellison) *trckd ldrs: rdn 3f out: sn outpcd* **66/1**

31- **7** *3 ½* **The Unit (IRE)**[239] 4921 4-11-0 0........................... WayneHutchinson 106
(Alan King) *rdn 3f out: nvr bttr than mid-div* **12/1**

8 *2 ¼* **Lisheen Prince (IRE)**[210] 4-11-0 0........................... RichardJohnson 103
(Philip Hobbs) *q tall: lengthy: lw: will make a jumper: mid-div: pushed along in last trio 1/2-way: hdwy fr 4f out to chse ldrs 3f out: outpcd sn after: wknd over 1f out* **11/2**[3]

1 **9** *8* **Vive Le Roi (IRE)**[51] 1644 4-11-0 0............................. BrianHughes 95
(Charlie Longsdon) *a towards rr* **33/1**

1 **10** *9* **Chap**[184] 320 5-11-0 0.. HarrySkelton 86
(Dan Skelton) *kpt to inner and racd alone coming down the hill fr over 5f out tl 3f out: a towards rr* **7/2**[2]

1- **11** *1 ¼* **Coole Charmer (IRE)**[228] 5097 6-11-0 0......................... NoelFehily 85
(Nicky Henderson) *str: will make a jumper: trckd ldr: rdn over 3f out: sn wknd* **8/1**

1 **12** *30* **Bentworth Boy**[35] 1873 4-11-0 0............................ NicodeBoinville 55
(Patrick Chamings) *trckd ldrs: rdn over 3f out: wknd 4f out* **20/1**

0- **13** *75* **Mighty Mustang**[238] 4941 5-10-7 0............................ MrJMartin(7)
(Andrew J Martin) *chsd ldrs tl 1/2-way: sn bhd: t.o* **250/1**

3m 58.0s (1.60) **Going Correction** +0.20s/f (Yiel) **13** Ran **SP% 118.4**
Speed ratings: **104,103,103,102,97 96,94,93,89,84 84,69,31**
CSF £108.50 TOTE £7.30: £2.20, £3.90, £4.20; EX 124.60 Trifecta £1675.00.
Owner Options O Syndicate **Bred** Pleasure Palace Racing **Trained** Naunton, Gloucs

FOCUS
A hot bumper. The first three are on the upgrade.
T/Jkpt: Jackpot. £71,000 to a £1 stake. Part won. Pool: £100,000 - 0.5 winning units. Jackpot Placepot: £724.90 to a £1 stake. Pool: £3,476.00 - 3.50 winning tickets. T/Plt: £79.90 to a £1 stake. Pool: £249,849.56 - 2280.66 winning units. T/Qpdt: £34.60 to a £1 stake. Pool: £19,971.61 - 426.00 winning units. **Tim Mitchell & Andrew Sheret**

2312 FONTWELL (L-H)
Sunday, November 15

OFFICIAL GOING: Soft (good to soft in places; 5.7)
Wind: strong, across Weather: light rain, windy

2515 TOTEPLACEPOT NOVICES' H'CAP HURDLE (11 hdls) 2m 5f 139y
12:45 (12:45) (Class 5) (0-100,99) 3-Y-O+
£2,339 (£686; £343; £171)

Form RPR

3-01 **1** **General Girling**[9] 2316 8-10-5 **78**..............................(p) JamesBest 95+
(Caroline Keevil) *pressed ldr tl led 3 out: cruised clr bef next: v easily* **8/11**[1]

6-PP **2** *23* **Burgess Dream (IRE)**[25] 2015 6-11-6 **93**..................... AndrewThornton 90
(Anna Newton-Smith) *led tl 3 out: sn outpcd and wl btn whn mstke next: plugged on for clr 2nd* **14/1**

5505 **3** *10* **Element Quartet (IRE)**[68] 1509 6-10-0 **73** oh1...........(t) RichieMcLernon 54
(Brendan Powell) *in tch in rr: mstke 5th: hit 7th and reminders: nt fluent next and sn rdn: lost tch 3 out: t.o next: wnt poor 3rd flat* **5/1**[3]

UB1/ **4** *44* **Highbury High (IRE)**[616] 4696 8-11-12 **99**................(tp) BrendanPowell 34
(Neil Mulholland) *hld up wl in tch: effrt in cl 3rd after 3 out: sn struggling and wl btn whn j. slowly next: fdd and lost poor 3rd flat: t.o* **4/1**[2]

5336 **P** **Tilinisi (IRE)**[13] 2256 5-11-9 **96**..................................(p) JamieMoore
(Phil Middleton) *trckd ldrs: cl 3rd and mstke 3 out: sn rdn and wknd: t.o whn mstke next: p.u last* **8/1**

5m 48.6s (6.10) **Going Correction** +0.325s/f (Yiel) **5** Ran **SP% 112.3**
Speed ratings (Par 103): **101,92,89,73,**
CSF £10.48 TOTE £1.90: £1.10, £4.40; EX 10.90 Trifecta £30.10.
Owner Mrs Caroline Keevil **Bred** Amanda Jane Girling **Trained** Motcombe, Dorset

FOCUS
Bottom bend divided and Hurdle race distances as advertised. Race 4 increased by 12yds and races 3 & 7 increased by 18yds. James Best and Andrew Thornton felt that the ground was no worse than advertised with Best adding: "Not as testing as it was here last Friday." This weak novice handicap was run at a steady pace, and the time was 36.6sec slower than standard. The winner should go in again.

2516 TOTEEXACTA SALMON SPRAY H'CAP HURDLE (FOR THE SALMON SPRAY CHALLENGE TROPHY) (9 hdls) 2m 1f 145y
1:15 (1:15) (Class 3) (0-135,125) 3-Y-O+ **£6,330** (£1,870; £935; £468; £234)

Form RPR

06-1 **1** **Baron Alco (FR)**[29] 1977 4-11-10 **123**.............................. JamieMoore 132+
(Gary Moore) *mde all: jnd 3 out: rdn next: asserted sn after last and drifted rt: styd on wl: rdn out* **5/4**[1]

133- **2** *3 ¼* **Mr Fitzroy (IRE)**[288] 3970 5-10-8 **110**..................... JamesBanks(3) 117
(Jo Davis) *chsd ldr: rdn and stmbld after 3 out: sn dropped to 3rd and u.p: kpt on same pce between last 2: wnt 2nd again last strides* **12/1**

10-4 **3** *nk* **Boss Des Mottes (FR)**[36] 1847 4-11-10 **123**.................. RyanMahon 130
(Dan Skelton) *trckd ldng pair: wnt 2nd after 3 out: mstke next: drvn and ev ch last: sn outpcd: wknd towards fin and lost 2nd last strides* **4/1**[2]

2F22 **4** *3 ½* **Impulsive American**[21] 2093 3-9-11 **119**...................(p) DavidNoonan(7) 106
(David Pipe) *hld up in tch: lft 4th 2nd: clsd 3 out: effrt between last 2: hung lft and wknd flat* **9/2**[3]

0U4- **5** *10* **Kudu Country (IRE)**[241] 4870 9-11-9 **122**.......................(t) PaulMoloney 117
(Evan Williams) *hld up in tch in last: niggled along after 3 out: btn next* **12/1**

1-34 **F** **Faithful Mount**[34] 621 6-11-11 **124**................................ TomO'Brien
(Ian Williams) *t.k.h: hld up in 4th tl fell 2nd* **7/1**

4m 37.85s (3.55) **Going Correction** +0.325s/f (Yiel)
WFA 3 from 4yo+ 15lb **6** Ran **SP% 110.5**
Speed ratings (Par 107): **105,103,103,101,97**
CSF £14.90 CT £44.36 TOTE £2.00: £1.20, £4.60; EX 14.20 Trifecta £58.30.
Owner John Stone **Bred** Yves D'Armaille **Trained** Lower Beeding, W Sussex
■ Stewards' Enquiry : James Banks two-day ban: used whip above permitted level (Nov 29-30)
Jamie Moore two-day ban: used whip above permitted level (Nov 29-30)

FOCUS
A decent handicap hurdle, if not the strongest for the grade. The winner set a fairly steady tempo. The second and third set the level.

2517 TOTEPOOL SOUTHERN NATIONAL H'CAP CHASE (21 fncs) 3m 3f 45y
1:50 (1:50) (Class 3) (0-140,138) 4-Y-O+ **£12,660** (£3,740; £1,870; £936; £468)

Form RPR

044- **1** **Golden Chieftain (IRE)**[214] 5340 10-10-9 **121**.........(tp) BrendanPowell 132+
(Colin Tizzard) *hld up towards rr: stdy prog 13th: rdn to chse clr ldr bef 3 out: led last: styd on wl: rdn out* **8/1**[3]

3033 **2** *2 ¼* **Finish The Story (IRE)**[17] 2146 9-10-0 **112**.................(bt) AlainCawley 121
(Johnny Farrelly) *chsd ldrs: wnt 2nd after 15th: led 18th: clr bef next: rdn after 3 out: hdd last: styd on same pce flat* **12/1**

41-4 **3** *16* **Dont Do Mondays (IRE)**[21] 2089 8-10-10 **127**...........(v) JakeHodson(5) 123
(David Bridgwater) *mstkes: wl in tch in midfield: chsd ldrs 9th: wnt 3rd 3 out: no imp whn mstke and pckd 2 out: wl btn and mstke last: wknd flat* **14/1**

-15P **4** *2 ¾* **Express Du Berlais (FR)**[170] 532 6-10-10 **122**...............(t) TomO'Brien 116
(Dr Richard Newland) *hld up in midfield: hdwy after 15th: 5th and effrt bef 3 out: 4th and no imp whn mstke 2 out: wknd bef last* **6/1**[2]

F-61 **5** *½* **Regal Flow**[23] 2057 8-10-13 **125**.. JamesBest 115
(Caroline Keevil) *hld up towards rr: clsd into midfield 15th: 6th and struggling whn j.rt 18th: sme prog u.p bef next: j. slowly 3 out: wknd bef last* **8/1**[3]

PUF/ **6** *42* **Pete The Feat (IRE)**[610] 4821 11-11-9 **135**..................... GavinSheehan 105
(Charlie Longsdon) *j.rt: led tl 18th: 3rd and struggling bef next: wknd bef 2 out: t.o and virtually p.u fnl 150yds* **20/1**

-300 **P** **Fruity O'Rooney**[26] 2008 12-10-8 **120**.............................. JamieMoore
(Gary Moore) *in tch in midfield: mstke 12th: lost pl and bhd after 15th: t.o whn p.u 18th* **14/1**

P-04 **P** **Qulinton (FR)**[150] 771 11-10-0 **112** oh3......................... RichieMcLernon
(Johnny Farrelly) *pressed ldr tl after 15th: sn rdn and lost pl: losing tch whn p.u 18th* **40/1**

P24- **P** **Reblis (FR)**[205] 5524 10-10-1 **113**................................ JoshuaMoore
(Gary Moore) *nvr travelling: dropped to rr and rdn 7th: lost tch after 9th: wl bhd whn p.u 11th* **11/1**

212/ **P** **Big Occasion (IRE)**[939] 5404 8-11-3 **129**........................(b) ConorO'Farrell
(David Pipe) *a in rr: rdn and no hdwy bef 13th: t.o whn p.u after 15th* **10/1**

1F3- **P** **Shammick Boy (IRE)**[206] 5491 10-11-6 **132**....................(p) DenisO'Regan
(Victor Dartnall) *in tch in midfield: j. slowly 4th: dropped to rr and u.p 16th: blnd next: lost tch and t.o whn p.u 3 out* **10/1**

42P- **P** **Gorgehous Lliege (FR)**[257] 4545 9-10-5 **117**.............. LiamTreadwell
(Venetia Williams) *chsd ldrs tl struggling u.p after 16th: 7th and wkng 18th: t.o whn p.u bef last* **4/1**[1]

15U- **P** **Letbeso (IRE)**[213] 5358 7-10-12 **124**..............................(p) RobertDunne
(Peter Bowen) *midfield: mstke and reminder 8th: mstke 11th and 12th: sn rdn: and dropped to rr: lost tch and t.o whn p.u after 15th* **9/1**

7m 29.4s (2.10) **Going Correction** +0.325s/f (Yiel) **13 Ran SP% 121.2**
Speed ratings (Par 107): **109,108,103,102,102 90,,,,**
CSF £100.97 CT £1338.32 TOTE £10.30: £3.40, £3.50, £4.10; EX 110.70 Trifecta £1987.80.

Owner Brocade Racing **Bred** Robert Donaldson **Trained** Milborne Port, Dorset

■ Stewards' Enquiry : Brendan Powell two-day ban: used whip above permitted level (Nov 29-30)

FOCUS
This competitive handicap chase was run at a solid gallop, and only six completed. The first two came clear and the winner was up a few punds on the best of last season's form.

2518 JOHN ROGERSON MEMORIAL NOVICES' LIMITED H'CAP CHASE (13 fncs) 2m 1f 96y
2:25 (2:26) (Class 3) (0-135,131) 5-Y-0+ **£8,431** (£2,633; £1,418)

Form RPR

01-3 **1** **Buckhorn Timothy**[27] 2001 6-11-6 **129**.................................. DarylJacob 137+
(Colin Tizzard) *j.rt and mstkes: chsd ldr: mstke 9th: led next: j.rt and collided w runner-up 3 out: wnt clr next: eased towards fin* **10/11**[1]

U164 **2** *26* **Honey Pound (IRE)**[29] 1977 7-11-1 **124**........................ MichaelByrne 117
(Tim Vaughan) *led into s: hld up in 4th: clsd and mstke 9th: j. up to press wnr next: ev ch whn j.lft and collided w wnr 3 out: btn next: dived and blnd last: wknd* **6/1**

P31 **3** *47* **Walden Prince (IRE)**[42] 1769 8-10-13 **127**....................(v) JakeHodson[(5)] 75
(David Bridgwater) *led tl hdd: dropped to 4th and mstke 10th: sn wknd and wl btn 4th next: t.o whn lft 3rd last* **9/2**[3]

4121 **R** **Canicallyouback**[45] 1718 7-11-1 **124**............................. PaulMoloney 74
(Evan Williams) *hld up in 3rd: clsd and pressed ldrs whn mstke 10th: immediately struggling and pushed along: wl btn and mstke next: t.o whn ref last* **10/3**[2]

4m 45.3s (10.60) **Going Correction** +0.325s/f (Yiel) **4 Ran SP% 107.9**
Speed ratings: **88,75,53,**
CSF £6.17 TOTE £1.50; EX 6.00 Trifecta £21.60.

Owner The Buckhorn Racing Team **Bred** M M Hooker **Trained** Milborne Port, Dorset

FOCUS
They went a reasonable gallop in this fair novice handicap and it only concerned two from the fourth-last. The winner built on his recent chase debut.

2519 FRUITY O'ROONEY "HEART OF A LION" MAIDEN HURDLE (10 hdls) 2m 3f 33y
2:55 (2:55) (Class 4) 4-Y-0+ **£3,249** (£954; £477; £238)

Form RPR

1 **Emerging Force (IRE)**[203] 5-11-0.......................... GavinSheehan 134+
(Harry Whittington) *led tl after 4th: chsd ldr tl led again 6th: mde rest: wnt clr 2 out: in command and pushed out flat: comf* **9/4**[1]

2 *3* **Hit The Highway (IRE)**[223] 5218 6-11-0.......................... DavidBass 128
(Giles Smyly) *chsd ldrs: wnt clr in ldng sextet after 6th: chsd wnr next: rdn and pressing wnr bef 2 out: outpcd 2 out: kpt on u.p but a hld* **10/1**

1 **3** *27* **Soupy Soups (IRE)**[29] 1966 4-11-0.......................... MarkQuinlan 108
(Neil Mulholland) *chsd ldrs: wnt clr in ldng sextet after 6th: 3rd next: rdn and struggling after 3 out: btn whn mstke next: wknd* **7/2**[2]

03-0 **4** *7* **Kap Jazz (FR)**[17] 2154 5-11-0.......................... LiamTreadwell 94
(Venetia Williams) *chsd ldr tl 3rd: styd handy tl rdn and lost tch w ldng sextet after 6th: n.d after: plugged on into poor 4th after last: t.o* **4/1**[3]

0- **5** *14* **Dragon De La Tour (FR)**[211] 5402 4-11-0.......................... RobertDunne 80
(Dan Skelton) *in tch in midfield: hdwy to chse ldrs after 4th: wnt clr in ldng sextet after 6th: cl 4th and nt fluent 7th: rdn and btn after 3 out: wknd bef next: t.o* **16/1**

F **6** *½* **Doitforthevillage (IRE)**[9] 2312 6-11-0.......................... JamieMoore 82
(Paul Henderson) *hld up in tch: hdwy to chse ldrs and wnt clr in ldng sextet after 6th: hit 3 out: sn rdn and btn: lost tch next: t.o* **20/1**

0-04 **7** *8* **Betsy Boo Boo**[13] 2252 6-10-7.......................... DavidEngland 65
(Michael Roberts) *hld up in last quartet: lost tch after 6th: t.o 3 out* **40/1**

0 **8** *39* **Hardtorock (IRE)**[22] 2065 6-11-0..........................(t) DarylJacob 33
(Liam Corcoran) *in tch in midfield: lost tch w ldng sextet after 6th: lost tch 3 out: t.o* **25/1**

9 *15* **Paris Snow**[76] 5-10-11.......................... RobMcCarth[(3)] 18
(Ian Williams) *t.k.h: chsd ldrs: wnt 2nd 3rd: led after 4th: hdd 6th: dropped to 6th and struggling whn mstke next: wknd next: t.o whn hmpd last* **13/2**

05/P **P** **Generous June (IRE)**[13] 2252 7-10-7.......................... MarcGoldstein
(Paddy Butler) *hld up in midfield: lost pl and reminders after 5th: dropped to rr and lost tch after 6th: t.o whn p.u 3 out* **150/1**

P **Hurricane Volta (IRE)**[78] 4-11-0.......................... JoshuaMoore
(Ralph J Smith) *hld up in rr: lost tch after 6th: wl bhd whn p.u next* **66/1**

0-U5 **P** **Hill Forts Gypse (IRE)**[172] 509 4-10-9.......................... KevinJones[(5)]
(Seamus Mullins) *mstkes: midfield: lost pl and pushed along after 5th: losing tch whn p.u after 6th* **100/1**

0 **F** **Definitly Grey (IRE)**[28] 1990 4-11-0.......................... TomO'Brien 72
(Charlie Longsdon) *hld up towards rr: nvr on terms w ldrs: lost tch after 6th: 7th and no ch whn mstke 2 out: t.o whn fell last* **16/1**

4m 57.7s (-1.70) **Going Correction** +0.325s/f (Yiel) **13 Ran SP% 121.4**
Speed ratings (Par 105): **116,114,103,100,94 94,90,74,68,,,**
CSF £25.66 TOTE £3.10: £1.30, £3.10, £1.70; EX 25.50 Trifecta £79.50.

Owner Webb Holt Carpenter Tucker **Bred** Castletown & Partners **Trained** Sparsholt, Oxfordshire

FOCUS
Plenty of dead wood in this maiden hurdle, in which two finished well clear. The race was was named after Fruity O'Rooney, who was pulled up in the Southern National. This year's World Hurdle hero Cole Harden won this event in 2013. The form could be rated a few pounds higher through the third and fourth.

2520 TOTETRIFECTA H'CAP HURDLE (10 hdls) 2m 3f 33y
3:30 (3:30) (Class 5) (0-100,98) 3-Y-0+ **£2,339** (£686; £343; £171)

Form RPR

F-33 **1** **Anda De Grissay (FR)**[165] 597 5-11-4 **97**..................(t) DavidNoonan[(7)] 105+
(Anthony Honeyball) *trckd ldrs: wnt 2nd 2 out: led and looked wnr whn lft clr last: eased towards fin* **13/8**[1]

-S04 **2** *9* **Walk Of Gleams**[13] 2256 6-10-11 **83**.......................... AdamWedge 81
(Anna Newton-Smith) *trckd ldrs: led on inner after 3 out: hdd and rdn bef next: 3rd and outpcd whn mstke 2 out: wl hld whn lft 2nd last: no imp flat* **12/1**

324- **3** *25* **L Frank Baum (IRE)**[317] 3490 8-11-9 **98**.......................... RobertWilliams[(3)] 71
(Bernard Llewellyn) *w ldr tl mstke 5th: dropped to rr and rdn after next: lost tch 3 out: wnt poor 4th next: lft 3rd last* **8/1**[3]

010P **4** *10* **Thefriendlygremlin**[31] 1927 7-10-2 **79**..........................(p) ConorRing[(5)] 42
(John Upson) *mde most tl 5th: styd w ldr: rdn to ld 3 out: sn hdd and dropped out: t.o whn lft 4th last* **14/1**

250- **P** **Asker (IRE)**[22] 4987 7-10-5 **77**..........................(v[1]) TomO'Brien
(Zoe Davison) *t.k.h: chsd ldrs tl led 5th: mstke next: hdd bef 3 out: dropped out rapidly wl bef 2 out: t.o whn p.u last* **9/1**

6-42 **U** **Titans Approach (IRE)**[16] 2174 6-10-10 **92**.......................... ArchieBellamy[(10)] 98+
(Graeme McPherson) *trckd ldrs: jnd ldrs after 6th: rdn to ld bef 2 out: rn green and wnt lft 2 out: hdd whn slt mstke and uns rdr last* **7/4**[2]

5m 11.9s (12.50) **Going Correction** +0.325s/f (Yiel) **6 Ran SP% 109.9**
Speed ratings (Par 103): **86,82,71,67,**
CSF £18.43 CT £110.69 TOTE £2.80: £1.40, £3.80; EX 20.30 Trifecta £46.50.

Owner The Deauville Connection **Bred** Maurice Batiot & Jacques Cypres **Trained** Mosterton, Dorset

FOCUS
They went a contested gallop in this moderate handicap hurdle, which saw last-flight drama. A step up from the winner.

2521 TOTEPOOL RACING'S BIGGEST SUPPORTER H'CAP CHASE (16 fncs) 2m 5f 31y
4:00 (4:00) (Class 5) (0-100,89) 4-Y-0+ **£2,469** (£725; £362; £181)

Form RPR

BP22 **1** **Lady From Geneva**[30] 1951 8-11-10 **87**..........................(t) BrendanPowell 98+
(Brendan Powell) *w ldr: mstke 7th: sltly outpcd and drvn bef 3 out: rallied to ld and mstke last: styd on: drvn out* **11/4**[1]

4-55 **2** *1½* **Kapricorne (FR)**[29] 1978 8-11-12 **89**..........................(t) PaulMoloney 95
(Sophie Leech) *hld up in tch: dropped to rr 9th: hdwy to trck ldrs 11th: outpcd next: rallied and clsd between last 2: mstke last: drvn to chse wnr flat: no imp towards fin* **11/2**[3]

-363 **3** *1* **The Cat's Away (IRE)**[43] 1757 7-10-6 **69**..........................(b) RichieMcLernon 74
(Richenda Ford) *mde most: forged 2 l clr 3 out: rdn and hdd last: 3rd and styd on same pce u.p flat* **9/2**[2]

PU53 **4** *55* **Sylvan Legend**[13] 2248 7-11-2 **79**..........................(tp) MarkQuinlan 29
(Neil Mulholland) *in tch: mstke 2nd: hmpd 6th: chsd ldrs 11th: wknd u.p bef 3 out: t.o* **11/4**[1]

PP/3 **P** **Goring Two (IRE)**[13] 2255 10-10-9 **72**..........................(p) AndrewThornton
(Anna Newton-Smith) *chsd ldrs tl j. slowly 11th: 5th and struggling whn mstke 13th: lost tch next: p.u 2 out* **10/1**

-205 **P** **Flugzeug**[37] 1842 7-11-4 **86**.......................... KevinJones[(5)]
(Seamus Mullins) *in tch: j. slowly 5th: hmpd next: drvn after 8th: lost tch 11th: t.o 3 out: p.u next* **8/1**

0P54 **F** **Appropriate (FR)**[43] 1757 5-10-7 **70**..........................(t) JamieMoore
(Paul Henderson) *blnd bdly and great rcvry 1st: in rr: hdwy into midfield 4th: 4th whn fell 6th* **16/1**

6m 0.7s (17.70) **Going Correction** +0.325s/f (Yiel) **7 Ran SP% 113.0**
Speed ratings (Par 103): **79,78,78,57,**
CSF £17.81 TOTE £3.60: £1.50, £3.60; EX 19.80 Trifecta £62.00.
Owner L Gilbert **Bred** Rjt290 Ltd **Trained** Upper Lambourn, Berks

FOCUS
Just a modest handicap chase, but the form looks sound enough. The winner is rated to her hurdles mark.
T/Plt: £169.50 to a £1 stake. Pool: £75,175.70 - 323.67 winning units. T/Qpdt: £42.40 to a £1 stake. Pool: 6,683.58 - 116.48 winning units. **Steve Payne**

2522 - 2524a (Foreign Racing) - See Raceform Interactive

2224 CORK (R-H)
Sunday, November 15

OFFICIAL GOING: Heavy

2525a TICKET SALES ONLINE H'CAP HURDLE (GRADE C) (12 hdls) 2m 4f
2:30 (2:30) 4-Y-0+ **£15,116** (£4,418; £2,093; £697)

RPR

1 **Damut (IRE)**[17] 2157 7-10-9 **115**.......................... AELynch 137+
(Joseph Dullea, Ire) *hld up: tk clsr order to chse ldrs 4 out: travelled strly to ld 3 out: clr next: styd on strly run-in: easily* **5/1**[2]

2 *12* **Federici**[14] 2236 6-10-4 **110**.......................... RobbieColgan 120
(E Bolger, Ire) *chsd ldrs on inner: clsr to trck ldrs bef 3 out in 3rd: kpt on same pce into 2nd run-in* **9/1**

3 *¾* **Kerrieonvic (IRE)**[573] 5462 8-11-5 **125**.......................... RogerLoughran 134
(C Byrnes, Ire) *hld up towards rr: tk clsr order 4 out: wnt 4th 3 out: rdn to chse clr ldr in 2nd 2 out: sn no imp: kpt on one pce and dropped to 3rd run-in* **12/1**

4 *2* **Sam Red (FR)**[223] 5220 4-11-6 **130**..........................(t) APHeskin 133
(Alan Fleming, Ire) *hld up: tk clsr order 4 out to chse ldrs: chsd ldr in 2nd 3 out: sn rdn and no imp in 4th whn mstke 2 out: kpt on one pce* **2/1**[1]

5 *24* **Cairde Aris (IRE)**[14] 2236 6-10-10 **116**..........................(t) BrianHayes 99
(John E Kiely, Ire) *chsd ldrs: pressed ldrs on outer 4 out: nt qckn appr 3 out in 6th: no ex whn nt fluent next: wknd* **14/1**

6 *7½* **Miley Shah (IRE)**[14] 2236 10-11-7 **127**..........................(p) MPFogarty 103
(S J Kenny, Ire) *sn led: advantage reduced 4 out: hdd bef 3 out where slow: sn wknd* **20/1**

7 *17* **Keppols Queen (IRE)**[224] 5175 7-11-5 **125**.......................... RobbiePower 84
(Mrs John Harrington, Ire) *hld up: travelled wl to trck ldrs 5 out: wknd qckly appr 3 out* **6/1**[3]

P **Byerley Babe (IRE)**[223] 5225 8-10-10 **116**.......................... PhillipEnright
(Robert Tyner, Ire) *hld up towards rr: sme prog 4 out: sn no imp and detached bef next where p.u* **7/1**

P **Coolmill (IRE)**[42] 1789 8-10-8 **121**.......................... CianCollins[(7)]
(D F O'Shea, Ire) *chsd ldr in 2nd to 5th: wknd qckly an dropped to rr at 7th: p.u after 4 out* **20/1**

P **Pyrus Gold Wind (IRE)**[20] 2112 8-11-1 **121**..................(tp) PaulTownend
(S J Mahon, Ire) *chsd ldrs early: sn mid-div: towards rr at 1/2-way: p.u bef 3 out* **33/1**

P **Rightback Atya (IRE)**[101] 1205 7-9-12 **109**...................... AndrewRing[(5)]
(P J Rothwell, Ire) *chsd ldrs in 3rd tl rdn and dropped to rr 5 out: sn detached: p.u after 4 out* **20/1**

P **Officieux (FR)**[16] 2177 4-11-5 **129**.......................... SeanFlanagan
(Noel Meade, Ire) *racd in mid-div: rdn and dropped towards rr after 4 out: p.u bef next* **16/1**

5m 20.7s (9.50)
WFA 4 from 6yo+ 8lb **12** Ran SP% **124.3**
CSF £48.94 CT £529.17 TOTE £5.30: £1.70, £3.10, £4.40; DF 43.30 Trifecta £704.80.
Owner E P Cogan **Bred** Edmond Cogan **Trained** Bandon, Co Cork

FOCUS
This was a good handicap and it produced a winner of quite astonishing ease.

2526 - 2529a (Foreign Racing) - See Raceform Interactive

2501 PUNCHESTOWN (R-H)
Sunday, November 15

OFFICIAL GOING: Hurdle course - soft (soft to heavy in places); chase course - soft to heavy

2530a RYANS CLEANING CRADDOCKSTOWN NOVICE CHASE (GRADE 2) (11 fncs) 2m
1:05 (1:05) 4-Y-0+ £21,162 (£6,186; £2,930; £976)

RPR

1 **Sizing John**[19] 2130 5-11-4 0.......................... JJBurke 149+
(Henry De Bromhead, Ire) *led and disp: led narrowly fr 7th: extended advantage fr 4 out: pushed along and gng best bef 2 out: drvn clr between last 2 and styd on wl: comf* **4/7**[1]

2 *8* **Lord Scoundrel (IRE)**[14] 2227 6-11-7 144.......................... BJCooper 145
(Gordon Elliott, Ire) *led and disp: slt mstke 7th and hdd: niggled along in 2nd after 4 out: rdn bef 2 out where nt fluent and no imp on wnr: kpt on same pce* **5/2**[2]

3 *28* **My Hometown (IRE)**[14] 2234 5-11-4 0.......................... MarkWalsh 117+
(E Bolger, Ire) *settled bhd ldrs in 3rd: j. sltly lft 2nd: mod 3rd bef 5 out: no imp on ldrs bef 2 out where nt fluent: kpt on one pce* **6/1**[3]

4 *69* **Ballyroe Rambler (IRE)**[11] 2279 8-11-4 0.......................... MarkEnright 56+
(J A Berry, Ire) *detached in rr thrght: mstke 1st: slow next and 3rd: completely t.o 5 out: nvr a factor* **50/1**

4m 12.3s (-6.30) **Going Correction** 0.0s/f (Good) **4** Ran SP% **108.5**
Speed ratings: **115,111,97,62**
CSF £2.49 TOTE £1.50; DF 2.30 Trifecta £2.00.
Owner Ann & Alan Potts Partnership **Bred** Bryan & Sandra Mayoh, Eskdale Stud **Trained** Knockeen, Co Waterford

FOCUS
A rather more revealing performance from the winner who remains unbeaten over fences. He improved in line with his hurdles form.

2531a FLORIDA PEARL NOVICE CHASE (GRADE 2) (15 fncs) 2m 6f
1:40 (1:40) 5-Y-0+ £20,155 (£5,891; £2,790; £930)

RPR

1 **Shantou Flyer (IRE)**[23] 2055 5-11-6 140..................(t) MrBO'Neill 143+
(Colin Bowe, Ire) *chsd ldrs: wnt 2nd bef 3rd and disp briefly 10th: cl 2nd fr 12th and disp again 4 out: cl 2nd after 3 out and rdn to ld next: kpt on wl to assert fr last* **5/1**

2 *1 ¼* **Captain Von Trappe (IRE)**[20] 2108 6-11-3 128.......................... DavidMullins 139+
(Gordon Elliott, Ire) *chsd ldrs: disp fr 10th and sn led narrowly tl hdd fr 12th: disp again after 5 out: narrow advantage 3 out: rdn and hdd next: kpt on wl fr last wout matching wnr* **9/2**[3]

3 *½* **Killer Miller (IRE)**[8] 2355 6-11-3 0.......................... MarkWalsh 139+
(Noel Meade, Ire) *hld up towards rr: nt fluent 2nd: bad mstke 12th: impr into 3rd bef 3 out where mstke: swtchd lft bef 2 out to chal: nt fluent in cl 3rd at last and no imp on wnr: kpt on wl clsng stages: hld* **13/8**[1]

4 *11* **Rightdownthemiddle (IRE)**[14] 2227 7-11-3 134.......................... JJBurke 130
(Michael Mulvany, Ire) *w.w in rr: impr into 4th bef 12th: almost on terms fr 4 out: rdn in 3rd after 3 out and no ex in 4th fr next: one pce after* **9/1**

5 *7* **Unic De Bersy (FR)**[22] 2076 7-11-3 128..................(p) LPDempsey 123
(Gordon Elliott, Ire) *led: j. sltly lft at times: j.lft and mstke 10th where jnd and sn hdd: regained advantage fr 12th: jnd and hdd after 5 out: slt mstke 4 out and sn rdn in 4th: slt mstke next and wknd* **10/1**

6 *12* **Wrath Of Titans (IRE)**[11] 2278 6-11-3 0.......................... BJCooper 111
(Ms Sandra Hughes, Ire) *chsd ldrs: 4th 1/2-way: bad mstke 12th and dropped to rr: tk clsr order bhd ldrs: bef 4 out where nt fluent: sn pushed along in rr and no imp fr 3 out: slt mstke next: eased* **4/1**[2]

6m 17.3s (14.30) **Going Correction** 0.0s/f (Good) **6** Ran SP% **112.0**
Speed ratings: **74,73,73,69,66 62**
CSF £26.88 TOTE £4.20: £2.20, £2.30; DF 23.50 Trifecta £38.40.
Owner S O'Neill **Bred** Tom McCarthy **Trained** Enniscorthy, Co. Wexford

FOCUS
The winner is proving a terrifically tough horse and against horses with far less experience than him he proved too tough a nut to crack.

2532a STANJAMES.COM MORGIANA HURDLE (GRADE 1) (9 hdls) 2m
2:15 (2:16) 4-Y-0+ £39,534 (£12,519; £5,930; £1,976; £1,317)

RPR

1 **Nichols Canyon**[198] 72 5-11-10 155.......................... DavidMullins 165
(W P Mullins, Ire) *mde all: nt fluent 1st and racd keenly: 3 l clr bef 1/2-way: reduced advantage bef 5th: pressed clly between last 2: rdn and extended ld bef last where nt fluent: all out clsng stages where strly pressed: kpt on wl* **7/1**[2]

2 *½* **Faugheen (IRE)**[198] 71 7-11-10 174.......................... RWalsh 164+
(W P Mullins, Ire) *settled bhd ldr in 2nd: nt fluent 4th: hung sltly fr after 5th: slt mstke 2 out and sn niggled along in cl 2nd: rdn and 2 l bhd bef last: clsd again u.p run-in to strly press wnr nr fin: hld* **1/6**[1]

3 *1 ¼* **Wicklow Brave**[29] 1163 6-11-10 152.......................... MrPWMullins 163+
(W P Mullins, Ire) *hld up bhd ldrs in 3rd: nt fluent 3 out: gng wl in cl 3rd after 2 out: rdn bef last and kpt on wl clsng stages: a hld* **8/1**[3]

4 *25* **Thomas Edison (IRE)**[42] 1787 8-11-10 150..................(t) MarkWalsh 138
(A J Martin, Ire) *hld up towards rr: disp 4th at 1/2-way: no imp on clr ldrs bef 2 out: in rr bef last: kpt on one pce into mod 4th fnl stride* **33/1**

5 *hd* **Plinth (IRE)**[7] 2386 5-11-10 141..................(bt) JJBurke 138
(A P O'Brien, Ire) *w.w in rr: disp 4th at 1/2-way: no imp on clr ldrs bef 2 out: mod 4th bef last: one pce run-in and denied mod 4th fnl stride* **40/1**

3m 58.1s (-6.90) **Going Correction** 0.0s/f (Good) **5** Ran SP% **114.7**
Speed ratings: **117,116,116,103,103**
CSF £9.65 TOTE £6.30: £1.80, £1.02; DF 11.20 Trifecta £15.60.
Owner Andrea & Graham Wylie **Bred** Rabbah Bloodstock Limited **Trained** Muine Beag, Co Carlow

FOCUS
Not quite the sound of bubbles bursting as the Champion Hurdle winner lost his unbeaten record, but some question marks were raised by his defeat here as the winner put forward a compelling case for his own Champion Hurdle prospects. The form is rated around the third. Nichols Canyon stepped up 5lb on his best form, but Faugheen was 12lb off.

2533 - 2535a (Foreign Racing) - See Raceform Interactive

SAINT-BRIEUC (R-H)
Wednesday, November 11

OFFICIAL GOING: Turf: good to soft

2536a PRIX ATHEOL (AQPS) (CONDITIONS) (4-5YO NON-THOROUGHBRED FILLIES & MARES) (TURF) 1m 4f
3:00 (12:00) 4-5-Y-0 £3,875 (£1,550; £1,162; £775; £387)

RPR

1 **Bellecoat (FR)** 4-9-13 0.......................... JeromeCabre 13 82
(F Foucher, France) **126/10**

2 *1 ¾* **Alkia D'Oudairies (FR)**[38] 5-10-6 0.......................... RichardJuteau 11 86
(A Le Clerc, France) **4/1**[2]

3 *1* **Ame En Peine (FR)**[143] 5-10-12 0.......................... ChristianLeGalliard 4 91
(Christian Le Galliard, France) **6/1**

4 *1* **Burma (FR)**[50] 1613 4-9-13 0.......................... AntoineWerle 5 76
(Paul Webber) *a.p: led after 1/2-way: rdn and strly pressed into st: hdd ins fnl f: no ex* **10/1**

5 *1 ¼* **Bellemady Monterg (FR)** 4-9-13 0.......................... GuillaumeFourrier 8 74
(Alain Couetil, France) **53/10**[3]

6 *2* **Bella Bourgeoise (FR)** 4-9-13 0.......................... LukasDelozier 1 71
(J-D Marion, France) **14/1**

7 *9* **Belcami (FR)** 4-10-1 0..................(b) AlexandreRoussel 14 58
(C Lotoux, France) **6/1**

8 *4 ½* **Amazone Mome (FR)**[776] 5-9-13 0.......................... ChristopherGrosbois 9 49
(J Delaunay, France) **21/1**

9 *2* **Blondymarie (FR)** 4-9-12 0 ow1.......................... MrRomainBoisnard 2 45
(J-L Delaplace, France) **78/1**

10 *3 ½* **Balkevie (FR)** 4-9-13 0 ow2..................(p) ChristopherCouillaud 6 40
(J Provost, France) **176/1**

11 *14* **Avel Parc Leur (FR)** 5-9-11 0..................(b) StyvenPiton 7 16
(E Mahe, France) **119/1**

12 *3 ½* **Action Du Manoir (FR)**[851] 5-9-11 0.......................... YoannMichaux 10 10
(A Sannier, France) **106/1**

13 *12* **Abba Des Genievres (FR)** 5-9-13 0..................(p) JeromeClaudic 12
(E Vagne, France) **33/10**[1]

\n\x\x PARI-MUTUEL (all including 1 euro stake): WIN 13.60 PLACE 3.10, 2.00, 2.60
Owner David Le Page **Bred** E.A.R.L. De Coet Parquet & D Le Page **Trained** France

LEICESTER (R-H)
Monday, November 16

OFFICIAL GOING: Hurdles - good to soft (soft in places); chase - good to firm (good in places, good to soft on flat course crossings)
Wind: Fresh half-behind Weather: Overcast

2537 ASHBY MAGNA JUVENILE FILLIES' HURDLE (8 hdls) 1m 7f 113y
12:45 (12:45) (Class 4) 3-Y-O £3,898 (£1,144; £572; £286)

Form RPR

42 1 **Culture De Sivola (FR)**[19] 2137 3-10-5 0.......................... LizzieKelly[(5)] 100+
(Nick Williams) *chsd ldrs: rdn after 3 out: led next: styd on wl* **9/4**[2]

2 *1 ¾* **Forgiving Glance**[17] 3-10-10 0.......................... DenisO'Regan 98+
(Alan King) *hld up: hit 1st: hdwy appr 3 out: rdn and ev ch whn mstke last: styd on same pce flat* **15/2**[3]

3 *6* **Bracken Brae**[20] 3-10-10 0.......................... RobertDunne 93
(Mark H Tompkins) *hld up in tch: rdn after 3 out: styd on same pce appr last* **33/1**

4 *3 ¼* **Sky Rose**[30] 3-10-10 0.......................... ConorO'Farrell 89
(Alexandra Dunn) *hld up: blnd 1st: hdwy appr 3 out: styd on same pce fr next* **16/1**

5 *hd* **New Vennture (FR)**[208] 3-10-10 0.......................... NoelFehily 89
(Harry Fry) *chsd ldr tl led 5th: pushed along and hdd 2 out: wknd bef last* **11/8**[1]

6 6 *2 ¾* **Lucie Rie (IRE)**[32] 1928 3-10-10 0..................(v) HenryBrooke 86
(K R Burke) *prom: rdn after 3 out: wknd appr last* **25/1**

7 *23* **Alert**[19] 3-10-10 0.......................... JamieMoore 66
(Jonathan Portman) *hld up: rdn after 5th: wknd 3 out* **33/1**

0 8 *6* **Sweet Midnight**[17] 2164 3-10-10 0.......................... CharliePoste 60
(John Holt) *hld up: rdn and wknd appr 3 out* **100/1**

5 P **Old Fashion**[19] 2137 3-10-10 0.......................... TrevorWhelan
(Neil King) *prom: nt fluent and lost pl 4th: rdn and wknd after next: bhd whn p.u bef 2 out* **12/1**

P- P **Grisedenuit (FR)**[205] 5542 3-10-10 0.......................... AidanColeman
(David Loder) *led to 5th: rdn and wknd bef next: bhd whn p.u bef 2 out* **20/1**

3m 52.4s (-8.60) **10** Ran SP% **113.7**
CSF £17.49 TOTE £3.10: £1.10, £2.10, £6.40; EX 19.60 Trifecta £189.80.
Owner Larkhills Racing Partnership II **Bred** Gilles Trapenard **Trained** George Nympton, Devon

FOCUS
The going on the hurdle course was good to soft, soft in places. Race distance increased by 6 yards. A modest race run at a solid gallop. The winner built on her Fakenham run, and the fifth ran to a similar level as her French form.

2538 EASTWELL (S) HURDLE (8 hdls) 1m 7f 113y
1:15 (1:15) (Class 5) 3-5-Y-O **£2,599** (£763; £381; £190)

Form RPR
2021 **1** **Clock On Tom**[15] 2217 5-11-12 112 WillKennedy 114+
(Denis Quinn) *mstke 1st: chsd ldrs: led 2 out: nt fluent last: rdn clr flat* **13/8**[1]

434 **2** *7* **Dynamic Ranger (USA)**[28] 1998 4-11-8 114 JamieMoore 102
(Gary Moore) *hld up: hdwy 5th: ev ch 2 out: sn rdn: styd on same pce last* **3/1**[3]

5-65 **3** *3 ¾* **Haatefina**[30] 1974 5-11-5 102 DaveCrosse 96
(Mark Usher) *led: mstke 5th: rdn appr 3 out: hdd next: wknd flat* **9/4**[2]

4 *3 ½* **Notts So Blue**[19] 4-10-12 0 JonathanEngland(3) 88
(Shaun Harris) *hld up: pushed along after 4th: hdwy appr 2 out: wkng whn mstke last* **50/1**

4P-P **5** *21* **Russian Link**[18] 2150 5-11-1 95 (t) DarylJacob 70
(John Berry) *chsd ldr rdn after 3 out: wknd bef next* **12/1**

56 **6** *20* **Petrify**[8] 2363 5-11-5 0 (t) RobertWilliams(3) 59
(Bernard Llewellyn) *hld up: hdwy and nt fluent 5th: mstke 3 out: sn rdn and wknd* **100/1**

C56 **7** *22* **Ventura Castle**[22] 2092 3-10-7 0 (bt[1]) SeanBowen 24
(Jamie Snowden) *chsd ldrs: lost pl appr 5th: rdn and wknd bef next* **20/1**

3m 54.6s (-6.40)
WFA 3 from 4yo 15lb 4 from 5yo 7lb **7 Ran SP% 109.3**
CSF £6.32 TOTE £2.40: £1.30, £1.70; EX 5.90 Trifecta £10.80.
Owner John Mangan **Bred** Kingwood Bloodstock **Trained** Newmarket, Suffolk

FOCUS
Race distance increased by 6 yards. A steadily run selling hurdle. This was a small hurdles pb from the winner, with the second again below form but in line with his previous run.

2539 KATHERINE SWYNFORD H'CAP CHASE (18 fncs) 2m 6f 151y
1:45 (1:45) (Class 4) (0-105,104) 4-Y-O+ **£3,898** (£1,144; £572; £286)

Form RPR
1-40 **1** **Golanova**[43] 1767 7-11-12 **104** (b) JamieMoore 115+
(Gary Moore) *hld up: hdwy 7th: chsd ldr 2 out: led last: rdn and styd on wl* **8/1**

FP-1 **2** *9* **Double Chocolate**[32] 1930 12-10-9 **87** (p) AndrewTinkler 90
(Martin Keighley) *led: hdd 4 out: rdn appr last out: styd on same pce: wnt 2nd towards fin* **6/4**[1]

6-3P **3** *1 ¼* **Vesuvhill (FR)**[19] 2140 6-11-11 **103** DarylJacob 106
(Ben Case) *chsd ldr: led 4 out: rdn and hdd last: wknd flat* **16/1**

432P **4** *9* **Xenophon**[11] 2303 7-9-9 **78** oh2 DannyBurton(5) 75
(Michael Chapman) *hld up: blnd 11th: sme hdwy 4 out: wknd appr 2 out* **33/1**

1416 **5** *10* **Etania**[32] 1930 7-11-5 **97** TomO'Brien 82
(Ian Williams) *chsd ldrs: pushed along after 8th: rdn after 14th: wknd appr 2 out* **7/1**[3]

P013 **6** *3 ¼* **Mr Robinson (FR)**[30] 1978 8-10-4 **82** TrevorWhelan 64
(Rob Summers) *hld up: hdwy 13th: rdn and wknd appr 2 out* **12/1**

2263 **7** *1 ¾* **Bus Named Desire**[14] 2249 7-10-0 **85** (tp) MrStanSheppard(7) 65
(Matt Sheppard) *hld up: mstke 2nd: drvn along after 14th: wknd appr 2 out* **7/1**[3]

11-4 **P** **Playing The Field (IRE)**[26] 2017 10-11-10 **102** RichardJohnson
(Jonjo O'Neill) *prom: racd keenly: hung lft: mstke 3rd: nt fluent and lost pl next: bhd fr 5th: j.lft 4 out: sn p.u* **7/2**[2]

5m 48.4s (-15.60) **Going Correction** -0.50s/f (Good) **8 Ran SP% 114.8**
Speed ratings (Par 105): **107,103,103,100,96 95,95,**
CSF £21.63 CT £191.63 TOTE £9.20: £2.50, £1.20, £2.30; EX 38.50 Trifecta £274.20.
Owner Galloping On The South Downs Partnership **Bred** R D And Mrs J S Chugg **Trained** Lower Beeding, W Sussex

FOCUS
The going was good to firm, good in places on the chase course. Not a strong handicap for the grade but it was run at a decent gallop. A small pb from the winner, with the second 5lb off his recent win over further.

2540 H.A.C. PIPELINE SUPPLIES H'CAP HURDLE (8 hdls) 1m 7f 113y
2:15 (2:15) (Class 3) (0-125,122) 3-Y-O+ **£6,498** (£1,908; £954; £477)

Form RPR
F-50 **1** **Sir Valentino (FR)**[24] 2058 6-11-7 **122** (t) JamieBargary(5) 134+
(Tom George) *chsd ldrs: led appr 2 out: clr last: comf* **4/1**[2]

/0-F **2** *3* **Bodega**[12] 2271 7-11-0 **110** WillKennedy 115
(Ian Williams) *hld up: hdwy appr 3 out: chsd wnr next: sn rdn: styd on same pce last* **14/1**

33-3 **3** *4 ½* **Moidore**[188] 263 6-11-5 **115** AdamPogson 117
(Charles Pogson) *hld up: hdwy after 3 out: rdn appr last: styd on same pce* **8/1**

5-62 **4** *7* **Akula (IRE)**[15] 2218 8-10-9 **108** HarryChalloner(3) 103
(Barry Leavy) *w ldr tl led after 2nd: rdn and hdd appr 2 out: wknd bef last* **10/1**

00-0 **5** *6* **Hear The Chimes**[25] 2042 6-11-3 **113** TrevorWhelan 102
(Shaun Harris) *hld up: racd keenly: hdwy 3 out: rdn and wknd next: mstke last* **33/1**

000- **6** *1 ¾* **Canadian Diamond (IRE)**[28] 4301 8-11-3 **113** JamieMoore 101
(Richard Rowe) *hld up: shkn up appr 2 out: nvr on terms* **33/1**

21/ **7** *½* **Mica Mika (IRE)**[23] 3367 7-11-1 **111** BrianHughes 100
(Richard Fahey) *prom: pushed along after 5th: wknd appr 2 out* **7/2**[1]

221 **8** *1 ¼* **Watt Broderick (IRE)**[25] 2038 6-11-4 **117** (t) RobMcCarth(3) 103
(Ian Williams) *hld up: hdwy 5th: rdn and wknd appr 2 out* **10/1**

0-F5 **9** *1 ¾* **It's All An Act (IRE)**[22] 2096 7-11-0 **110** MattieBatchelor 95
(Daniel O'Brien) *hld up: plld hrd: rdn and wknd after 3 out* **66/1**

36-0 **10** *2 ¼* **Eddiemaurice (IRE)**[22] 2093 4-11-3 **113** (p) RhysFlint 96
(John Flint) *prom: mstke 1st: rdn and wknd appr last* **12/1**

124- **11** *1 ½* **Whispering Harry**[254] 4628 6-11-8 **118** JamesDavies 99
(Henry Oliver) *chsd ldrs tl rdn and wknd bef 2 out* **8/1**

424- **12** *hd* **Bladoun (FR)**[219] 5283 7-11-5 **115** (p) TomScudamore 96
(David Pipe) *led tl after 2nd: mstke 4th: sn pushed along: wknd appr 3 out* **7/1**[3]

145F **13** *21* **Captain Swift (IRE)**[20] 1000 4-11-5 **115** HenryBrooke 77
(John Mackie) *hld up: rdn and wknd appr 3 out* **50/1**

3m 48.1s (-12.90)
WFA 4 from 6yo+ 7lb **13 Ran SP% 118.8**
CSF £56.35 CT £434.63 TOTE £5.80: £2.10, £3.00, £3.20; EX 64.30 Trifecta £568.90.

Owner Doone Hulse Susie Saunders & Lady Cobham **Bred** Mlle Camille Serveau & Roger Simon **Trained** Slad, Gloucs

FOCUS
Race distance increased by 6 yards. A competitive handicap run at a sound gallop. The time was good and the form looks solid.

2541 JOHN O'GAUNT BEGINNERS' CHASE (12 fncs) 1m 7f 201y
2:45 (2:45) (Class 3) 4-Y-O+ **£6,486** (£2,026; £1,091)

Form RPR
211- **1** **Red Spinner (IRE)**[240] 4895 5-11-0 0 DavidBass 140+
(Kim Bailey) *w ldr tl led at stdy pce after 1st: qckned appr 3 out: rdn and r.o wl* **7/2**[2]

20-6 **2** *½* **Pine Creek**[22] 2083 7-11-0 0 AidanColeman 140+
(John Ferguson) *trckd ldrs: racd keenly: lft chsng wnr and hmpd bnd after 8th: rdn and ev ch flat: nt qckn towards fin* **4/1**[3]

60-P **3** *47* **Exitas (IRE)**[16] 2184 7-11-0 132 (t) JamieMoore 120+
(Phil Middleton) *hld up in tch: racd keenly: cl up whn bdly hmpd and lost tch bnd after 8th: wknd after 3 out: j.lft next and last* **10/1**

1-02 **F** **Stephanie Frances (IRE)**[29] 1988 7-10-7 0 HarrySkelton
(Dan Skelton) *led at stdy pce tl after 1st: chsd ldr tl clipped heels and fell bnd after 8th* **4/5**[1]

4m 5.8s (-2.40) **Going Correction** -0.50s/f (Good) **4 Ran SP% 106.9**
Speed ratings (Par 107): **86,85,62,**
CSF £15.36 TOTE £3.30; EX 11.50 Trifecta £30.40.
Owner Paul & Clare Rooney **Bred** Horse Breeding Company **Trained** Andoversford, Gloucs

FOCUS
A decent chase. There was drama leaving the back straight when Stephanie Frances clipped the heels of the winner and took a nasty fall.

2542 CASTLE CONDITIONAL JOCKEYS' H'CAP CHASE (15 fncs) 2m 4f 45y
3:15 (3:15) (Class 5) (0-100,98) 4-Y-O+ **£2,599** (£763; £381; £190)

Form RPR
4213 **1** **Larkhall**[11] 2290 8-10-0 **75** RyanDay(3) 82
(Mike Sowersby) *hld up: hdwy 8th: rdn to ld flat: styd on* **9/2**[3]

4430 **2** *¾* **Lost In Newyork (IRE)**[32] 1930 8-10-1 **73** (p) CharlieDeutsch 81+
(Nick Kent) *prom: mstke and lost pl 7th: hdwy appr 4 out: rdn after 2 out: styd on* **3/1**[1]

4F-P **3** *1* **On The Case**[176] 450 7-10-13 **88** (t) JamieBargary(3) 95
(Tom George) *hld up in tch: chsd ldr and mstke 2 out: sn rdn: styng on whn hmpd and swtchd rt towards fin* **5/1**

5306 **4** *nk* **Kyles Faith (IRE)**[4] 2453 7-11-12 **98** (p) KillianMoore 103
(Martin Keighley) *led: rdn appr 4 out: hdd next: styd on u.p* **7/2**[2]

-FPP **5** *2* **June French (FR)**[57] 1595 7-10-3 **83** (p) MrMartinMcIntyre(8) 87
(Neil Mulholland) *chsd ldr to 3rd: remained handy: rdn after 3 out: mstke last: styd on same pce flat* **7/1**

214- **6** *shd* **Bally Lagan (IRE)**[516] 723 7-10-5 **82** (bt[1]) ConorSmith(5) 85
(Robin Dickin) *a.p: chsd ldr 3rd tl led 3 out: rdn appr last: hdd and no ex flat* **6/1**

5m 19.6s (0.70) **Going Correction** -0.50s/f (Good) **6 Ran SP% 108.9**
Speed ratings (Par 103): **78,77,77,77,76 76**
CSF £17.53 TOTE £5.70: £2.50, £2.20; EX 16.20 Trifecta £67.70.
Owner T J Stubbins **Bred** R D And Mrs J S Chugg **Trained** Goodmanham, E Yorks

FOCUS
A modest contest run at a steady gallop and they finished in a heap.

2543 BURTON OVERY NOVICES' HURDLE (8 hdls) 1m 7f 113y
3:45 (3:45) (Class 4) 4-Y-O+ **£3,898** (£1,144; £572; £286)

Form RPR
1 **Iftiraaq (IRE)**[93] 4-10-12 0 (p) ConorO'Farrell 117+
(Seamus Durack) *chsd ldr tl led 4th: hdd next: led again 3 out: nt fluent 2 out and last: shkn up flat: comf* **7/2**[2]

5-2 **2** *¾* **Theligny (FR)**[28] 1998 4-10-12 0 RichardJohnson 112
(Tim Vaughan) *chsd ldrs: rdn appr 2 out: styd on* **3/1**[1]

3 *4* **Arcamante (ITY)**[24] 4-10-12 0 HenryBrooke 109
(K R Burke) *chsd ldrs: rdn after 2 out: styd on same pce last* **12/1**

23/- **4** *5* **Unex Modigliani (IRE)**[13] 5400 6-10-12 110 (t) JamesDavies 104
(Derek Shaw) *hld up: hdwy 5th: rdn appr 2 out: styd on same pce* **20/1**

600- **5** *5* **The Hon Mackinlay (IRE)**[210] 5428 6-10-12 0 DavidBass 100
(Ben Pauling) *hld up: hdwy after 3 out: no imp fr next* **50/1**

2- **6** *½* **Flashjack (IRE)**[260] 4513 5-10-12 0 JakeGreenall 99
(Henry Daly) *mid-div: lost pl bef 3 out: styd on flat* **13/2**

2-43 **7** *3 ¼* **Oulamayo (FR)**[14] 2251 4-10-12 0 HarrySkelton 99
(Dan Skelton) *led to 4th: led again next: hdd 3 out: wknd appr last* **9/2**[3]

5 **8** *nk* **Eastern Magic**[15] 2221 8-10-12 0 DarylJacob 96
(Ben Case) *hld up: hdwy appr 3 out: wknd bef next* **25/1**

9 *3 ½* **Sarpech (IRE)**[132] 4-10-12 0 AidanColeman 93
(Charlie Longsdon) *prom tl wknd appr 2 out* **12/1**

P **10** *28* **Chantecler**[13] 2258 4-10-12 0 MarkQuinlan 68
(Neil Mulholland) *hld up: mstke and hmpd 3rd: mstke 5th: sn wknd* **66/1**

11 *7* **Lady Percy (IRE)**[41] 6-10-5 0 DaveCrosse 54
(Mark Usher) *hld up: hmpd 3rd: sn bhd* **100/1**

0 **12** *nk* **Westerly**[57] 1597 4-10-5 0 (tp) JamieMoore 54
(John Mackie) *hld up: hdwy after 5th: wkng whn mstke next* **50/1**

F **Stout Cortez**[52] 4-10-12 0 BrianHughes
(Malcolm Jefferson) *hld up in tch: plld hrd: fell 3rd* **12/1**

3m 52.1s (-8.90) **13 Ran SP% 116.8**
CSF £13.63 TOTE £4.50: £1.50, £1.60, £3.40; EX 18.90 Trifecta £126.50.
Owner The Acorn Partnership **Bred** Shadwell Estate Company Limited **Trained** Upper Lambourn, Berkshire

FOCUS
Race distance increased by 6 yards. An open novice hurdle. The winner looked to have a bit in hand and should rate higher, and the seventh and eighth help set the level.

T/Plt: £181.30 to a £1 stake. Pool: £61,738.97 - 248.58 winning tickets T/Qpdt: £71.70 to a £1 stake. Pool: £5,340.87 - 55.05 winning tickets **Colin Roberts**

2251 PLUMPTON (L-H)

Monday, November 16

OFFICIAL GOING: Soft (chs 4.9, hdl 4.8)

Wind: Almost nil Weather: Cloudy, mild

2544 JOHN TAMPSETT GALLOPING INTO RETIREMENT NOVICES' HURDLE (9 hdls) 1m 7f 195y
1:00 (1:01) (Class 4) 4-Y-0+ £3,249 (£954; £477; £238)

Form RPR

2-3 1 **Mckenzie's Friend (IRE)**[191] 213 4-10-12 0................ LeightonAspell 116+
(Oliver Sherwood) *t.k.h: trckd ldr to 4th: styd cl up: effrt to ld 2 out: jnd last: rdn and styd on wl flat* **2/1**[2]

2 1 1/4 **Authorized Too**[393] 4-10-9 0................................ JamesBanks(3) 115
(Noel Williams) *trckd ldrs: pushed along 3 out: clsd on clr ldng trio bef next: wnt 2nd after 2 out and jnd wnr last: nt qckn flat* **40/1**

B 3 7 **Brave Jaq (FR)**[37] 1844 4-10-12 0.......................[1] SamTwiston-Davies 110
(Paul Nicholls) *t.k.h: led: slow pce to 4th: gng wl 3 out: rdn and hdd 2 out: wknd last* **5/4**[1]

1 4 3 3/4 **Itsnowcato**[14] 2251 4-11-2 0.............................. MauriceLinehan(3) 113
(Ben Pauling) *t.k.h: prom: trckd ldr 4th to bef 2 out: sn btn* **7/2**[3]

61-6 5 10 **Outrath (IRE)**[19] 2136 5-10-12 0.............................(t) PaulMoloney 94
(Jim Best) *t.k.h: hld up in rr: nt fluent 1st: nudged along and outpcd fr 6th: sme prog to take 5th after 3 out: nvr on terms* **25/1**

04- 6 5 **Ding Ding**[224] 5208 4-10-5 0.............................. MarcGoldstein 83
(Sheena West) *hld up in tch: outpcd by ldrs fr 6th: nudged along in 6th after 3 out: nvr on terms* **50/1**

63- 7 1 3/4 **Bountiful Sin**[460] 1209 4-10-9 0.......................... ThomasGarner(3) 87
(Oliver Sherwood) *in rr: shkn up and outpcd by ldrs 6th: nvr on terms after* **50/1**

0- 8 3 1/2 **Highsalvia Cosmos**[19] 2789 4-10-12 0.....................(bt) LiamTreadwell 85
(Mark Hoad) *mstke 1st: hld up: lost tch w ldrs 6th: nudged along and nvr on terms* **100/1**

/00- 9 4 1/2 **Sir Hubert**[294] 3905 5-10-12 0............................ AndrewThornton 79
(Richard Rowe) *chsd ldrs to 6th: sn outpcd and btn* **100/1**

6 10 1 3/4 **Bolister (FR)**[16] 2188 4-10-12 0.............................. JoshuaMoore 78
(Gary Moore) *hld up in last pair: nvr a factor* **25/1**

35 11 10 **Takeitfromalady (IRE)**[14] 2251 6-10-5 0..................(v) PaddyBradley(7) 68
(Lee Carter) *dropped to last sn after 1/2-way: no ch fr 3 out* **25/1**

4m 2.3s (1.50) **Going Correction** +0.40s/f (Soft) **11 Ran SP% 119.9**
Speed ratings (Par 105): **112,111,107,106,101 98,97,95,93,92 87**
CSF £75.29 TOTE £2.90: £1.10, £9.10, £1.10; EX 97.40 Trifecta £352.70.
Owner Jeremy Dougall & Will Watt **Bred** John Crean **Trained** Upper Lambourn, Berks

FOCUS

Divided bends for all races with the chase course remaining on inner line for minimum trip/race. Hurdle bends moved out 2yds. Race increased by 18yds. Leighton Aspell felt the ground was riding as per the official description. A fair novice hurdle in which the front pair came away late on. It has been rated around the balance of the third to the seventh.

2545 SIS NOVICES' CHASE (14 fncs) 2m 3f 164y
1:30 (1:30) (Class 3) 4-Y-0+ £7,147 (£2,098; £1,049; £524)

Form RPR

030- 1 **Le Mercurey (FR)**[248] 4741 5-11-1 0....................(t) SamTwiston-Davies 145+
(Paul Nicholls) *mostly trckd ldr: rdn after 3 out: chal next: led and bttr jump last: drvn clr* **4/5**[1]

00-1 2 6 **Violet Dancer**[40] 1815 5-11-6 0...............................(p) JoshuaMoore 147+
(Gary Moore) *led: rdn after 3 out: hrd pressed next: hdd and outj. last: no ex and eased whn btn* **5/1**[3]

U3-6 3 25 **Kingfisher Creek**[20] 2122 5-11-1 127.......................(p) BrendanPowell 115
(Colin Tizzard) *mstke 1st: hld up: chsd ldng trio 7th but sn lft bhd: no ch after: tk remote 3rd after last* **28/1**

06-2 4 2 1/4 **Cadoudoff (FR)**[28] 2001 5-11-1 129.............................. TomCannon 115
(Charlie Longsdon) *mostly in last pair: mstke 6th: drvn 8th and no ch after: tk remote 4th after last* **12/1**

/12- 5 2 3/4 **Inner Drive (IRE)**[241] 4881 7-11-1 0.......................... WayneHutchinson 112+
(Alan King) *wl in tch: trckd ldng pair 7th: cl up 4 out: sing to lose grnd whn blnd 3 out: wknd: lost 2 pls fr last* **3/1**[2]

5/4- 6 12 **Kazlian (FR)**[243] 4849 7-11-1 0..........................(t) RichieMcLernon 102
(Johnny Farrelly) *mstkes: prom: chsd ldr 4th to 5th: sn lost pl: last and wl bhd whn blnd 4 out* **50/1**

4m 59.8s (-7.50) **Going Correction** -0.075s/f (Good) **6 Ran SP% 110.3**
Speed ratings (Par 107): **112,109,99,98,97 92**
CSF £5.31 TOTE £1.70: £1.20, £1.90; EX 4.70 Trifecta £43.10.
Owner Colm Donlon & Chris Giles **Bred** S A R L Carion Emm **Trained** Ditcheat, Somerset

FOCUS

A useful novice chase, with the front pair coming a long way clear. The winner made a small step up on his hurdles form and the second built on his recent good win - there's a case for rating this 10lb+ higher through hurdle marks of rest and very good time compared with following race.

2546 188BET.CO.UK H'CAP CHASE (14 fncs) 2m 3f 164y
2:00 (2:00) (Class 4) (0-120,115) 4-Y-0+ £4,548 (£1,335; £667; £333)

Form RPR

-411 1 **Ashcott Boy**[35] 1888 7-11-1 111.............................. DavidNoonan(7) 125+
(Neil Mulholland) *blnd and nrly fell 1st but great rcvry: given time in rr after: prog 9th: tk 3rd and blnd next: rdn to ld after 3 out: jnd last: drvn and jst asserted flat* **11/2**[3]

221- 2 3/4 **Mr Muddle**[224] 5211 8-11-12 115.............................. MarcGoldstein 124
(Sheena West) *pressed ldr: led 8th but only narrowly after: pushed along and hdd after 3 out: rallied to chal bef last: upsides flat: kpt on but jst hld* **8/1**

43-2 3 16 **The Green Ogre**[29] 1985 5-11-12 115.......................... JoshuaMoore 110
(Gary Moore) *settled in last but nt gng that wl: lost tch 5th: rousted fr 9th and staged effrt fr next: cl up 4 out: rdn to go 3rd after next: lost grnd on ldng pair after* **10/3**[1]

24-2 4 5 **Sonny The One**[22] 2090 5-11-12 115.......................... BrendanPowell 105
(Colin Tizzard) *wl in tch: chsd ldng pair 4th tl 10th where hmpd: stl in tch 4 out: wknd after 3 out* **7/2**[2]

1103 5 2 1/4 **Venetian Lad**[26] 2014 10-11-10 113.......................... LeightonAspell 99
(Lydia Richards) *wl in tch: pushed along after 8th: struggling whn sltly impeded 10th: sn bhd* **16/1**

0124 6 3 **Dancing Dik**[14] 2255 10-10-0 89 oh1........................(b) PaddyBrennan 71
(Paul Henderson) *won battle for ld: narrowly hdd 8th: pressed ldr to 3 out: sn wknd* **12/1**

PP2- P **Goring One (IRE)**[307] 3662 10-10-9 98...................... AndrewThornton
(Anna Newton-Smith) *sn dropped to last pair: lost tch 5th: sltly impeded 7th: wl bhd whn p.u bef last* **16/1**

P-22 F **Val D'Arc (FR)**[12] 2276 6-11-12 115.......................... AlainCawley
(Richard Hobson) *unable to ld: chsd ldng pair to 4th: wl in tch whn fell heavily 7th* **7/2**[2]

5m 14.0s (6.70) **Going Correction** -0.075s/f (Good) **8 Ran SP% 113.5**
Speed ratings (Par 105): **83,82,76,74,73 72, ,**
CSF £46.61 CT £167.87 TOTE £5.30: £2.10, £2.10, £1.50; EX 41.00 Trifecta £207.30.
Owner John Hobbs **Bred** Mrs J A Gawthorpe **Trained** Limpley Stoke, Wilts

FOCUS

Reasonable form for the level, the front pair clear. The second is rated to his best with the rest 8lb+ off.

2547 188BET H'CAP HURDLE (10 hdls) 2m 1f 164y
2:35 (2:35) (Class 5) (0-100,100) 3-Y-0+ £2,274 (£667; £333; £166)

Form RPR

620- 1 **Maria's Choice (IRE)**[321] 3407 6-11-9 97........... SamTwiston-Davies 104+
(Jim Best) *hld up in last trio: plenty to do whn prog fr 7th: wnt 3rd 3 out and 2nd next: led last and gng bttr than runner-up: rousted along and drew clr flat* **9/2**[2]

3400 2 4 1/2 **Warrant Officer**[14] 2253 5-10-11 85.......................... MarcGoldstein 87
(Sheena West) *led: shied at boxes bef 6th: clr fr next tl hrd pressed 2 out: hdd last: one pce flat* **7/1**

-450 3 5 **Up Four It (IRE)**[157] 712 7-10-6 80.......................... JeremiahMcGrath 78
(Jamie Poulton) *trckd ldr: clr of rest 7th: blnd 3 out: lost 2nd and one pce fr 2 out* **11/1**

060 4 3 **Moreece (IRE)**[86] 1323 6-11-2 95.............................. AlanJohns(5) 89
(Tim Vaughan) *wl in tch: chsd clr ldng pair 7th tl mstke 3 out: sn btn* **11/4**[1]

26/4 5 1 **Ragdollianna**[28] 2000 11-11-7 95.............................. LiamTreadwell 87
(Mark Hoad) *hld up in last trio: plenty to do whn prog after 7th but alongside wnr: jst in tch 3 out: sn rdn and no hdwy* **11/2**[3]

1F-6 6 14 **Little Roxy (IRE)**[28] 2004 10-10-7 81.......................(tp) AdamWedge 59
(Anna Newton-Smith) *chsd ldng pair to 4th: sn lost pl and rdn: bhd after 6th: t.o* **8/1**

6004 7 19 **Hawk Gold (IRE)**[14] 2253 11-9-7 69......................(b) MissBHampson(7) 33
(Michelle Bryant) *cl up: chsd ldng pair 4th to 7th: wknd qckly: t.o* **12/1**

F-06 8 2 1/2 **Catchin Time (IRE)**[20] 2121 7-11-9 100.......................... KieronEdgar(3) 57
(Laura Hurley) *hld up in last trio: wknd 6th: t.o fr next* **13/2**

4m 37.0s (6.10) **Going Correction** +0.40s/f (Soft) **8 Ran SP% 113.2**
Speed ratings (Par 103): **102,100,97,96,96 89,81,80**
CSF £34.78 CT £322.69 TOTE £3.40: £1.70, £2.20, £3.20; EX 33.30 Trifecta £326.30.
Owner Philip Arrow & Partner **Bred** A Christodoulou **Trained** Lewes, E Sussex

FOCUS

Race increased by 24yds. Moderate handicap form. This was a step up from the winner but he can rate higher still on his Flat form.

2548 SICAME AMATEUR RIDERS' H'CAP HURDLE (12 hdls) 2m 4f 114y
3:05 (3:05) (Class 4) (0-120,119) 3-Y-0+ £3,743 (£1,161; £580; £290)

Form RPR

-024 1 **The Geegeez Geegee (IRE)**[30] 1964 6-11-0 110.....(t) DavidNoonan(3) 114+
(Anthony Honeyball) *a wl plcd: led bef 2 out gng wl and sn 3 l clr: idled last and pressed on all sides: drvn and fended of rivals flat* **7/2**[2]

2-43 2 3/4 **Laughton Park**[26] 2013 10-11-7 117.............................. MrMLegg(3) 117
(Suzy Smith) *wl in tch: rdn and outpcd after 3 out: clsd fr 2 out as wnr idled: styd on to take 2nd flat: clsd nr fin but a hld* **11/2**

3-33 3 1 **Verano (GER)**[34] 1896 6-11-5 119.............................(t) MrEAustin(7) 119
(Dan Skelton) *t.k.h: hld up tl prog to trck ldr 6th: led after 8th: mstke next and hdd: on terms tl nt qckn after 3 out: lft w ch last as wnr idled: kpt on* **4/1**[3]

215 4 1 1/4 **Cooper's Friend (IRE)**[32] 1925 6-11-2 114.............(t) MrSamPainting(5) 113
(Charlie Longsdon) *trckd ldr to 6th: styd prom: led 9th: rdn and hdd bef 2 out: lft cl up again last as wnr idled: fdd flat* **8/1**

3544 5 3 **Ennisnag (IRE)**[19] 2139 10-9-9 95.......................... MrBParis-Crofts(7) 90
(Paul Henderson) *wl in tch: hit 6th and 7th: cl up gng wl 3 out: sn outpcd and pushed along: kpt on and lft w ch last as wnr idled: wknd flat* **25/1**

1114 6 1 **Occasionally Yours (IRE)**[19] 2135 11-10-9 109.......... MissTWorsley(7) 103
(Alan Blackmore) *cl up: rdn and outpcd after 3 out: n.d after: styd on again fr last* **25/1**

12-3 7 1 1/4 **Tambura**[17] 2167 5-10-10 110.............................. MrJJSlevin(7) 107+
(G C Maundrell) *nt fluent: dropped to last pair 4th: lost tch main gp 7th and shoved along: struggling after: tried to cl 3 out but sn outpcd and no ch: styd on again fr last* **3/1**[1]

4P0- 8 17 **Extreme Impact**[206] 5510 9-10-5 105.......................(p) MrMEnnis(7) 81
(Graeme McPherson) *immediately off the bridle in last and nvr gng wl: detached fr 4th: rdr persisted and passed two rivals late on* **14/1**

15-0 9 18 **Kastani Beach (IRE)**[172] 529 9-10-6 106.................. MrDSansom(7) 64
(Seamus Mullins) *in tch: pushed along fr 5th: styd jst in tch despite being under pressed tl wknd 3 out: t.o* **28/1**

-22P 10 29 **Sergeant Dick (IRE)**[12] 2276 10-11-1 115...............(bt) MrSBurton(7) 44
(Andy Turnell) *led at str pce: hdd after 8th: wknd rapidly after next: wl t.o* **25/1**

5m 22.1s (5.10) **Going Correction** +0.40s/f (Soft) **10 Ran SP% 115.4**
Speed ratings (Par 105): **106,105,105,104,103 103,102,96,89,78**
CSF £21.83 CT £79.57 TOTE £4.60: £1.80, £2.40, £1.50; EX 26.60 Trifecta £110.00.
Owner Geegeez.co.uk PA **Bred** Sean Cousins **Trained** Mosterton, Dorset

FOCUS

Race increased by 24yds. Plenty had their chance in this modest handicap. A small pb from the winner, with the second to fourth setting the level.

2549 SW CATERING STANDARD OPEN NATIONAL HUNT FLAT RACE 2m 1f 164y
3:35 (3:35) (Class 6) 4-6-Y-0 £1,624 (£477; £238; £119)

Form RPR

1 **Vinciaettis (FR)**[247] 4776 4-11-9 0.............................. GavinSheehan 123+
(Warren Greatrex) *mde most: set stdy pce tl stretched on fr 6f out: clr w one rival 4f out: drew away sn after: shkn up over 1f out: eased last 75yds* **6/4**[1]

0-4 2 9 **Sartorial Elegance**[20] 2126 4-10-9 0.....................(b[1]) PaulO'Brien(7) 104
(Colin Tizzard) *pressed wnr 5f: styd cl up: shkn up and outpcd by ldng pair 4f out: kpt on to take 2nd fnl f: no ch w wnr* **15/2**

34 3 3/4 **Western Sunrise (IRE)**[158] 696 6-10-9 0.......................... AlainCawley 96
(Johnny Farrelly) *racd wd: cl up: pushed along and outpcd fr 4f out: kpt on fnl 2f to take 3rd fnl f* **10/1**

16 **4** ½ **Fountains Windfall**[23] 2065 5-11-2 0............................ DavidNoonan(7) 110
(Anthony Honeyball) *pressed wnr after 5f: clr of rest 4f out: rdn and outpcd over 3f out: fdd and lost 2 pls 1f out* **2/1**[2]

3 **5** 12 **Lemtara Bay**[158] 696 4-10-9 0............................ LeightonAspell 84
(Oliver Sherwood) *cl up: pushed along 5f out and sn outpcd: no ch after: plugged on* **6/1**[3]

6 ¾ **Brave Cupid** 5-10-9 0............................ DavidEngland 83
(Michael Roberts) *hld up but wl in tch: pushed along 7f out: outpcd 5f out: no ch after: plugged on* **100/1**

4 **7** 18 **Mahlers Spirit (IRE)**[19] 2141 5-11-2 0............................ JackQuinlan 72
(Sarah Humphrey) *pressed ldrs: stl cl up over 4f out: sn rdn and wknd* **66/1**

8 10 **Yenston (IRE)** 4-11-2 0............................ BrendanPowell 62
(Colin Tizzard) *hld up in last pair but wl in tch: pushed along 7f out: sn bhd* **25/1**

9 2¾ **Easyontheeye (IRE)** 4-10-9 0............................ TomCannon 52
(Linda Jewell) *cl up tl wknd rapidly over 4f out* **100/1**

10 35 **Tonythetarmacker (IRE)** 4-11-2 0............................ AdamWedge 24
(Ali Stronge) *in tch in rr to over 6f out: sn wknd: t.o* **33/1**

4m 33.7s (8.40) **Going Correction** +0.40s/f (Soft) **10** Ran SP% **118.7**
Speed ratings: **97,93,92,92,87 86,78,74,73,57**
CSF £13.79 TOTE £2.20: £1.10, £1.90, £2.30; EX 12.70 Trifecta £121.90.
Owner Mrs J & Miss C Shipp **Bred** Michel Leger & F Verger **Trained** Upper Lambourn, Berks

FOCUS
Race increased by 24yds. No great depth to this bumper but a good winner who looks one to follow. The third and fourth are rated close to their marks and this was a fair bumper for the track.
T/Plt: £38.70 to a £1 stake. Pool: £78,584.18 - 1,482.03 winning tickets T/Qpdt: £15.70 to a £1 stake. Pool: £6,075.39 - 284.60 winning tickets **Jonathan Neesom**

2135 FAKENHAM (L-H)
Tuesday, November 17

OFFICIAL GOING: Good to soft changing to soft after race 4 (2.45)
Wind: Fresh against Weather: Showers

2550 FAKENHAM (S) H'CAP HURDLE (11 hdls) 2m 4f 1y
1:05 (1:05) (Class 5) (0-100,100) 3-Y-O+ **£2,737** (£798; £399)

Form RPR

33P3 **1** **Jumpandtravel (IRE)**[8] 2396 6-11-7 **95**............................ SamTwiston-Davies 100
(Micky Hammond) *hld up: hdwy 8th: chsd ldr 3 out: led next: rdn clr appr last: eased towards fin* **11/4**[2]

40-4 **2** 7 **Perennial**[17] 843 6-11-9 **100**............................(b) AdamNicol(3) 98
(Philip Kirby) *hld up: hdwy 7th: sn chsng ldr: led appr 3 out: rdn and hdd next: styd on same pce appr last* **2/1**[1]

436 **3** 18 **Toptempo**[16] 2218 6-11-1 **89**............................(p) MichaelByrne 71
(Ali Stronge) *chsd ldrs tl rdn and wknd after 2 out* **12/1**

0-P0 **4** 2½ **King's Road**[15] 2253 10-11-12 **100**............................(t) IanPopham 79
(Anabel K Murphy) *hld up: blnd 5th: hdwy after 8th: rdn and wknd after 2 out: blnd last* **6/1**[3]

00-P **5** 17 **Lady Knight (IRE)**[50] 530 4-10-11 **88**............................(p) JamesBanks(3) 52
(Andy Turnell) *led: rdn and hdd appr 3 out: sn wknd* **16/1**

00-0 **R** **Easydoesit (IRE)**[7] 2038 7-11-6 **94**............................ LeeEdwards
(Tony Carroll) *ref to r* **6/1**[3]

P46P **P** **Monzino (USA)**[19] 2143 7-9-9 **74** oh12............................ DannyBurton(5)
(Michael Chapman) *chsd ldr: pushed along 5th: lost 2nd after next: wknd 7th: bhd whn p.u bef 3 out* **66/1**

-000 **P** **Dibble Bridge**[11] 2318 4-11-0 **88**............................(p) TomScudamore
(Philip Kirby) *chsd ldrs: pushed along after 6th: wknd 8th: bhd whn p.u bef next* **8/1**

5m 32.7s (12.30) **Going Correction** +0.575s/f (Soft)
WFA 4 from 6yo+ 8lb **8** Ran SP% **114.7**
Speed ratings (Par 103): **98,95,88,87,80**
CSF £9.01 CT £53.56 TOTE £2.10: £1.70, £1.30, £1.60; EX 11.00 Trifecta £26.10.
Owner Val Kelly **Bred** M Kelly **Trained** Middleham, N Yorks

FOCUS
Bends moved to give new ground and distances were increased considerably. Race increased by 198yds. Despite 2mm of overnight rain the official going was changed to good to soft all round. A moderate selling handicap hurdle and they went an even gallop. After winning the opener Sam Twiston-Davies described the ground as "soft".

2551 WEATHERBYS BANK MARES' H'CAP CHASE (16 fncs) 2m 5f 44y
1:40 (1:40) (Class 4) (0-120,115) 4-Y-O+ **£5,325** (£1,653; £890)

Form RPR

35-1 **1** **Emerald Rose**[196] 128 8-11-12 **115**............................(p) MarkGrant 123
(Julian Smith) *chsd ldrs: led after 11th: rdn appr 2 out: styd on wl* **11/4**[2]

U-42 **2** 5 **Ballydague Lady (IRE)**[10] 2346 8-11-9 **112**............................(p) NoelFehily 117
(Neil Mulholland) *hld up: hdwy mstke 5th: hdwy 7th: lft chsng wnr 12th: rdn whn mstke last: fnd nil* **1/1**[1]

30-3 **3** 32 **Carhue Princess (IRE)**[41] 1816 9-10-1 **90**............................ JamesDavies 69
(Tom Symonds) *chsd ldr: j. slowly and lost pl 11th: sn rdn: lft 3rd and hmpd next: sn wknd* **3/1**[3]

0P3- **P** **Miss Dimples (IRE)**[209] 5463 6-9-12 **90** oh10 ow1.....(p) JamesBanks(3)
(Sarah-Jayne Davies) *led and pushed along at various stages: pckd 4th: stmbld 10th: hdd after next: cl 2nd whn blnd 12th: nt rcvr and sn p.u* **10/1**

5m 51.1s (9.30) **Going Correction** +0.575s/f (Soft) **4** Ran SP% **110.8**
Speed ratings (Par 105): **105,103,90,**
CSF £6.33 TOTE £3.30; EX 5.20 Trifecta £7.00.
Owner Grand Jury Partnership **Bred** Grand Jury Partnership **Trained** Tirley, Gloucs

FOCUS
Race increased by 215yds. Only a fair mares' handicap chase and the topweight was 5lb below the ceiling. The winner is on the upgrade and the second is rated to her mark.

2552 COLLECT TOTEPOOL WINNINGS AT BETFRED SHOPS CONDITIONAL JOCKEYS' H'CAP CHASE (12 fncs) 2m 59y
2:10 (2:10) (Class 4) (0-105,103) 4-Y-O+ **£4,548** (£1,335; £667; £333)

Form RPR

-02P **1** **Marky Bob (IRE)**[84] 1353 10-11-9 **100**............................ ConorRing 107
(Hugo Froud) *led and sn clr: nt fluent 3rd: c bk to the field 5th: hdd 8th: sn pushed along: led 2 out: styd on gamely* **9/2**[3]

0410 **2** 1¼ **Youm Jamil (USA)**[31] 1980 8-9-11 **77** oh4............................(t) NickSlatter(3) 82
(Tony Carroll) *hld up: hdwy 3 out: chsd wnr after next: rdn and ev ch last: styd on same pce flat* **12/1**

3635 **3** 7 **Moveable Asset (IRE)**[30] 1985 7-11-12 **103**............................(v) FreddieMitchell 104
(Henry Tett) *chsd clr ldr: tk clsr order 5th: lost pl and pckd next: outpcd 3 out: styd on flat* **10/1**

2-14 **4** shd **All But Grey**[174] 514 9-11-8 **102**............................(t) CiaranGethings(3) 102
(Carroll Gray) *hld up: hdwy and blnd 5th: led 8th: rdn and hdd 2 out: no ex appr last* **9/4**[2]

2-20 **5** hd **Larteta (FR)**[125] 1005 6-11-1 **100**............................ RomainClavreul(8) 100
(Sarah Humphrey) *chsd clr ldrs: tk clsr order 5th: rdn after 3 out: styd on same pce fr next* **5/4**[1]

4m 38.9s (22.30) **Going Correction** +0.575s/f (Soft) **5** Ran SP% **110.2**
Speed ratings (Par 105): **67,66,62,62,62**
CSF £41.17 TOTE £4.30: £1.80, £5.20; EX 31.40 Trifecta £134.70.
Owner The Marky Bob Syndicate **Bred** George Durrheim And Maria Mulcahy Durrhe **Trained** Bruton, Somerset

FOCUS
Race increased by 172yds. Only a modest handicap chase. The second posted a small pb and third ran his best race to date over fences.

2553 WEATHERBYS HAMILTON BEGINNERS' CHASE (18 fncs) 3m 38y
2:45 (2:45) (Class 3) 4-Y-O+ **£7,797** (£2,289; £1,144)

Form RPR

0-35 **1** **Katkeau (FR)**[145] 836 8-11-2 0............................(t[1]) TomScudamore 139+
(David Pipe) *hld up in tch: led 10th: rdn appr last: styd on u.p* **5/2**[2]

113- **2** 1¼ **Southfield Vic (IRE)**[206] 5541 6-11-2 0............................ SamTwiston-Davies 140+
(Paul Nicholls) *nt a fluent: led to 4th: chsd ldr tl chsd wnr after 10th: rdn appr 2 out: ev ch last: styd on same pce flat* **1/3**[1]

3364 **3** 90 **Veauce De Sivola (FR)**[147] 825 6-11-2 95............................(t) TomCannon 57
(Mark Gillard) *chsd ldr tl led 4th: hdd 10th: outpcd fr 14th* **50/1**[3]

6m 54.3s (18.60) **Going Correction** +0.575s/f (Soft) **3** Ran SP% **105.6**
Speed ratings (Par 107): **92,91,61**
CSF £3.88 TOTE £3.40; EX 5.20 Trifecta £4.50.
Owner Prof C Tisdall, J A Gent, R C Wilkin **Bred** P Barthelemy Et Al **Trained** Nicholashayne, Devon

FOCUS
Race increased by 258yds. An interesting beginners' chase featuring a couple of decent hurdlers who were having their first outing over fences. The winner is rated to his hurdles mark.

2554 AT THE RACES MARES' H'CAP HURDLE (13 hdls) 2m 7f 95y
3:15 (3:15) (Class 5) (0-100,100) 4-Y-O+ **£2,737** (£798; £399)

Form RPR

433 **1** **Shaky Gift (IRE)**[12] 2298 6-11-12 **100**............................ NoelFehily 114+
(Neil Mulholland) *hld up: hdwy 5th: chsd ldr 3 out: led appr last: sn clr* **11/4**[2]

0514 **2** 14 **Miss Mayfair (IRE)**[44] 1771 8-11-2 **90**............................(p) TomCannon 94
(Lawney Hill) *chsd ldr tl led 10th: rdn and hdd appr last: sn outpcd* **5/1**

-P50 **3** 5 **Black Lily (IRE)**[16] 2223 7-10-3 **77**............................(p) AdamWedge 71
(Chris Bealby) *hld up: hit 8th: hdwy next: wknd after 3 out* **9/2**[3]

F211 **4** 43 **Oscar Jane (IRE)**[5] 2454 8-11-6 **94** 7ex............................(bt) BrendanPowell 45
(Johnny Farrelly) *led to 10th: wkng whn mstke 3 out* **11/8**[1]

0046 **P** **Kheskianto (IRE)**[16] 2217 9-9-11 **76**............................(t) DannyBurton(5)
(Michael Chapman) *chsd ldrs to 9th: sn bhd: p.u bef 3 out* **33/1**

006 **P** **Gentle Mel (IRE)**[15] 2252 7-10-13 **87**............................(p) TomScudamore
(Anabel K Murphy) *prom: lost pl after 4th: bhd fr 9th: p.u bef next* **14/1**

6m 33.1s (11.10) **Going Correction** +0.575s/f (Soft) **6** Ran SP% **113.2**
Speed ratings (Par 103): **103,98,96,81,**
CSF £16.86 TOTE £3.20: £1.90, £2.40; EX 15.50 Trifecta £46.00.
Owner Mrs P L Bridel **Bred** Clare Kehoe & Bill Byrne **Trained** Limpley Stoke, Wilts

FOCUS
Race increased by 237yds. After further rain the going was changed to soft before this race. A moderate handicap hurdle for mares and they finished well strung out. The winner is on the upgrade and the second is rated to form.

2555 INDEPENDENT RACECOURSES LTD. NOVICES' H'CAP HURDLE (9 hdls) 2m 3y
3:45 (3:45) (Class 4) (0-105,104) 3-Y-O+ **£3,898** (£1,144; £572; £286)

Form RPR

036 **1** **Galuppi**[15] 2238 4-11-8 **100**............................(v[1]) SamTwiston-Davies 110+
(J R Jenkins) *hld up: hdwy 6th: led after 2 out: clr last: pushed out* **7/2**[3]

0-41 **2** 4½ **Vicky's Charm (IRE)**[18] 2162 6-11-9 **104**............................ JamesBanks(3) 106
(Barry Brennan) *a.p: led 6th: nt fluent 2 out: sn rdn and hdd: styd on same pce* **5/2**[2]

-606 **3** 32 **New Tarabela**[33] 1927 4-10-12 **90**............................(b[1]) LeeEdwards 64
(Tony Carroll) *led tl hdd after 2nd: remained handy: hit 5th: sn rdn: wknd appr 2 out* **6/1**

0522 **4** 24 **Rye House (IRE)**[33] 1931 6-11-6 **103**............................(tp) AlanJohns(5) 48
(Tim Vaughan) *chsd ldrs: rdn after 3 out: sn wknd* **9/4**[1]

0- **P** **Smoky Hill (IRE)**[29] 4080 6-11-7 **104**............................ NickSlatter(5)
(Tony Carroll) *a in rr: bhd fr 5th: p.u bef 2 out* **10/1**

5-3P **P** **Victory Rich (IRE)**[189] 263 4-11-3 **100**............................ MrFTett(5)
(Henry Tett) *plld hrd and sn prom: led after 2nd: hdd 6th: rdn and wknd after next: bhd whn p.u bef 2 out* **20/1**

4m 25.8s (12.80) **Going Correction** +0.65s/f (Soft)
WFA 4 from 6yo 7lb **6** Ran SP% **109.7**
Speed ratings (Par 105): **94,91,75,63,**
CSF £12.34 TOTE £4.30: £2.00, £1.70; EX 13.40 Trifecta £51.30.
Owner Miss A Finn **Bred** Tsega Mares Sarl **Trained** Royston, Herts

FOCUS
Race increased by 158yds. Only a moderate handicap and the front two pulled a long way clear. The second is rated to her mark.
T/Plt: £255.90 to a £1 stake. Pool: £56,758.05 - 161.87 winning units. T/Qpdt: £40.60 to a £1 stake. Pool: £4,457.46 - 81.20 winning units. **Colin Roberts**

2402 SOUTHWELL (L-H)
Tuesday, November 17

OFFICIAL GOING: Good to soft (soft in places) changing to soft after race 1 (12.25)
Wind: moderate 1/2 against becoming fresh race 4 Weather: overcast, damp, wet and windy 2.00 and 2.35

2556 BEER FESTIVAL WEEKEND H'CAP CHASE (21 fncs) 3m 1f 129y
12:25 (12:25) (Class 5) (0-100,100) 4-Y-O+ **£3,898** (£1,144; £572; £286)

Form RPR

144P **1** **Sgt Bull Berry**[3] 2500 8-10-0 **79**............................ JamieHamilton(5) 84
(Peter Maddison) *chsd ldr: hmpd 7th: pushed along 16th: led 2 out: kpt on: sddle slipped* **3/1**[2]

5PP3 **2** 1 3/4 **Riddlestown (IRE)**[8] 2408 8-11-12 100 HarrySkelton 104
(Caroline Fryer) *j.rt: led: drvn 4 out: hdd 2 out: kpt on same pce run-in* 9/2[3]

254- **3** 22 **Flichity (IRE)**[219] 5296 10-9-11 74 oh12 BenPoste(3) 58
(John Cornwall) *chsd ldng pair: drvn 4 out: wknd bef 2 out* 14/1

3PP- **4** 26 **Line D'Aois (IRE)**[268] 4385 7-11-9 97 (tp) LiamTreadwell 63
(Michael Scudamore) *chsd ldng pair: nt fluent 4th: shkn up 8th: reminders after 14th: drvn 16th: lost pl bef 3 out: t.o whn eased run-in* 8/11[1]

7m 13.3s (27.30) **Going Correction** +0.725s/f (Soft) **4** Ran SP% **107.8**
Speed ratings (Par 103): **87,86,79,71**
CSF £14.38 TOTE £3.20; EX 14.00 Trifecta £26.10.
Owner Peter Maddison **Bred** P Maddison **Trained** Skewsby, N Yorks

FOCUS
Fences and bends moved from the line raced on November 9th and all distances as advertised. This weak little staying handicap was run at a stop-start gallop and proved tactical. The first two are rated close to their marks.

2557 SOUTHWELL FESTIVE FIXTURES NOVICES' LIMITED H'CAP CHASE (19 fncs) 2m 7f 209y
12:55 (12:55) (Class 3) (0-135,135) 4-Y-0+ £6,330 (£1,870; £935; £468; £234)

Form RPR

131- **1** **Capard King (IRE)**[214] 5362 6-11-8 135 RichardJohnson 139+
(Jonjo O'Neill) *j. soundly: trckd ldr: led 4th: drvn out and hung rt run-in: hld on towards fin* 5/2[1]

35-2 **2** nk **Seldom Inn**[24] 2067 7-11-7 134 BrianHughes 140+
(Sandy Thomson) *chsd ldrs: hit 6th: reminder 9th: hit next: hit 15th: rallied appr 3 out: chsd wnr last: carried rt: kpt on towards fin* 9/2[3]

421- **3** 5 **King's Odyssey (IRE)**[244] 4853 6-11-4 131 PaulMoloney 129
(Evan Williams) *trckd ldrs: drvn appr 3 out: wnt rt appr last: sn wknd: b.b.v* 5/2[1]

1P-P **4** 10 **Streets Of Promise (IRE)**[38] 1856 6-10-10 123 LiamTreadwell 112
(Michael Scudamore) *chsd ldrs: outpcd and lost pl bef 3 out: eased last 100yds* 16/1

2341 **5** 30 **Shah Of Persia**[26] 2039 8-10-8 121 (tp) GavinSheehan 93
(Warren Greatrex) *led to 4th: chsd wnr: 4th and outpcd whn blnd 3 out: sn bhd: t.o whn eased run-in* 11/4[2]

6m 34.8s (11.80) **Going Correction** +0.725s/f (Soft) **5** Ran SP% **107.9**
Speed ratings (Par 107): **109,108,107,103,93**
CSF £12.94 TOTE £2.90: £1.90, £2.30; EX 9.40 Trifecta £22.20.
Owner J B Gilruth & G & P Barker Ltd **Bred** Mrs Annemarie Byrnes **Trained** Cheltenham, Gloucs

FOCUS
A fair novice handicap, run at a reasonable gallop and the form is sound with two coming clear. The winner stepped up on his hurdles form.

2558 WINTER GOLF AT SOUTHWELL NOVICES' HURDLE (13 hdls) 2m 7f 209y
1:30 (1:30) (Class 4) 4-Y-0+ £3,898 (£1,144; £572; £286)

Form RPR

1 **Crosspark**[247] 5-10-12 0 HarrySkelton 120+
(Caroline Bailey) *hld up wl in tch: hdwy to trck ldrs 7th: trckd ldr 4 out: led appr 2 out: 4 l ahd whn hit last: jst hld on* 12/1

2 hd **Battle Dust (IRE)**[296] 6-10-12 0 DavidBass 119+
(Kim Bailey) *chsd ldrs: nt fluent 3rd: pushed along 6th: clr 3rd bef 2 out: 2nd last: styd on strly run-in: jst hld* 9/1[3]

P2-P **3** 3 3/4 **Monkery Tunkerty**[9] 2374 12-10-7 0 AliceMills(5) 115
(Jess Westwood) *led: pushed along fr 2nd: hdd appr 2 out: kpt on one pce between last 2* 16/1

2214 **4** 24 **Mustmeetalady (IRE)**[16] 2214 5-11-5 130 RichardJohnson 101
(Jonjo O'Neill) *t.k.h: trckd ldrs: hit 4th: drvn 9th: mstke next: wknd appr 2 out: sn bhd* 6/4[2]

04P- **5** 8 **Coozan George**[219] 5294 6-10-12 0 BrianHughes 82
(Malcolm Jefferson) *hld up in last: smooth hdwy 10th: lost pl bef 2 out: sn bhd* 22/1

23-0 **P** **Amidon (FR)**[17] 2182 5-10-12 120 LeightonAspell
(Lucy Wadham) *chsd ldrs: hit 8th: lost pl and nt fluent 3 out: sn eased and bhd: t.o whn p.u bef 2 out* 6/5[1]

F **P** **Swizzler (IRE)**[23] 2080 6-10-12 0 WillKennedy
(Ian Williams) *sn trcking ldrs: lost pl bef 3 out: sn wl bhd: tailed rt off whn p.u bef 2 out* 28/1

P **P** **All Kings (IRE)**[14] 2257 6-10-12 0 ConorO'Farrell
(Nigel Hawke) *t.k.h: trckd ldrs: mstke 5th: lost pl 9th: sn bhd: tailed rt off whn p.u bef 2 out* 100/1

6m 17.6s (2.60) **Going Correction** +0.575s/f (Soft) **8** Ran SP% **117.8**
Speed ratings (Par 105): **118,117,116,108,106** , ,
CSF £107.94 TOTE £19.40: £3.10, £2.80, £2.90; EX 128.30 Trifecta £821.40.
Owner C W Booth **Bred** W W & Mrs J E Dennis **Trained** Holdenby, Northants

FOCUS
It proved hard work in this staying novice hurdle, but it could turn out to be a fair race. The third is a 130+ chaser and the fourth is rated 20lb+ off, so this might need to go up.

2559 SOUTHWELL JANUARY TO DECEMBER ANNUAL MEMBERSHIP H'CAP HURDLE (9 hdls) 1m 7f 153y
2:00 (2:00) (Class 5) (0-100,100) 3-Y-0+ £3,249 (£954; £477; £238)

Form RPR

-224 **1** **Nebula Storm (IRE)**[16] 2217 8-11-2 97 (v) HarryCobden(7) 109+
(Michael Blake) *mid-div: hdwy to chse ldrs 3 out: upsides last: sn led: styd on strly: readily* 15/2

6-31 **2** 2 3/4 **Theredballoon**[26] 2043 9-11-4 99 LiamMcKenna(7) 103
(Conrad Allen) *mid-div: hdwy to chse ldrs 3 out: sn edgd lft: led narrowly last: sn hdd and no ex* 2/1[1]

4F36 **3** 2 1/4 **Impeccability**[31] 1971 5-11-11 99 (p) HenryBrooke 101
(John Mackie) *mid-div: hdwy 5th: led sn after 3 out: hdd last: kpt on same pce* 33/1

0450 **4** 3/4 **Alys Rock (IRE)**[31] 1974 6-11-8 99 JonathanEngland(3) 100
(Michael Appleby) *in rr: hdwy 6th: chsng ldrs 2 out: kpt on same pce appr last* 18/1

35 **5** 1/2 **The Bugler (IRE)**[58] 1596 8-11-8 96 (t) PaulMoloney 100+
(Evan Williams) *hld up towards rr: hdwy 6th: trcking ldrs next: n.m.r appr last: swtchd rt: styd on same pl* 6/1[2]

650- **6** 7 **Dandy Duke (IRE)**[234] 5025 4-11-11 99 PaddyBrennan 94
(Tom George) *chsd ldrs: wknd between last 2* 13/2[3]

-P44 **7** 12 **My Renaissance**[18] 2165 5-10-0 74 (t) TrevorWhelan 59
(Ben Case) *chsd ldrs 4th: hmpd sn after 3 out: wkng whn hmpd 2 out: eased run-in* 13/2[3]

004 **8** 19 **Whitstable Native**[26] 2035 7-11-2 90 (t) JamesBest 53
(Sophie Leech) *chsd ldrs: wknd 2 out* 50/1

06-0 **9** 8 **Rockweiller**[100] 180 8-10-0 74 WillKennedy 29
(Shaun Harris) *led: j.rt: hdd appr 3 out: lost pl bef 2 out* 20/1

40P0 **10** 1 **Candelita**[69] 1525 8-10-13 90 (p) KyleJames(3) 44
(Clare Ellam) *w ldrs: lost pland hmpd sn after 3 out: sn bhd* 16/1

-6P0 **11** 10 **Captain Sharpe**[19] 2148 7-11-4 95 (v) BrianToomey(3) 39
(Kenny Johnson) *chsd ldrs: led briefly appr 3 out: lost pl and hmpd sn after 3 out: sn bhd: virtually p.u clsng stages* 66/1

4-34 **F** **Ogaritmo**[155] 744 6-11-9 100 (t) KillianMoore(3) 95
(Alex Hales) *chsd ldrs: drvn 3 out: 7th and wkng whn fell next* 12/1

4m 8.0s (11.00) **Going Correction** +0.725s/f (Soft) **12** Ran SP% **116.0**
Speed ratings (Par 103): **101,99,98,98,97 94,88,78,74,74 69,**
CSF £22.29 CT £475.55 TOTE £9.50: £2.50, £1.60, £10.00; EX 23.80 Trifecta £732.40.
Owner West Wilts Hockey Lads **Bred** Sunderland Holdings Ltd **Trained** Trowbridge, Wilts
■ Stewards' Enquiry : Liam McKenna four-day ban: careless riding (Dec 1-4)

FOCUS
An ordinary handicap. They went a fair gallop and the first five held every chance coming to the last. The easy winner posted a hurdles pb but is entitled to rate higher on Flat form. The second to fourth were close to their marks.

2560 MRFREEBET.CO.UK ON YOUR MOBILE H'CAP HURDLE (11 hdls) 2m 4f 62y
2:35 (2:35) (Class 4) (0-110,110) 3-Y-0+ £3,898 (£1,144; £572; £286)

Form RPR

/24- **1** **Pithivier (FR)**[282] 4108 5-11-12 110 NicodeBoinville 124+
(Ben Pauling) *mde all: t.k.h: increased pce bef 2 out: sn drew clr: 12 l ahd whn mstke last: eased last 50yds* 11/4[1]

P52- **2** 9 **Periquest**[219] 5295 6-11-4 102 (t) PaddyBrennan 102
(Alex Hales) *trckd ldrs: 2nd between last 2: kpt on same pce* 12/1

-644 **3** 4 1/2 **Florrie Boy (IRE)**[40] 1826 4-11-6 107 RyanHatch(3) 101
(Nigel Twiston-Davies) *chsd ldrs: mstke 2nd: chsd wnr 3 out: kpt on same pce appr next* 3/1[2]

331/ **4** 1 1/2 **Daliance (IRE)**[580] 5361 6-10-13 97 WayneHutchinson 90
(Noel Williams) *chsd ldrs: one pce appr 2 out* 14/1

211- **5** 6 **Mondo Cane (IRE)**[231] 5089 8-11-9 107 AdamPogson 94
(Charles Pogson) *hld up towards rr: hdwy 7th: one pce fr 3 out* 15/2[3]

424 **6** 4 **Shaiyzar (IRE)**[26] 2043 6-10-13 100 (p) JoeColliver(3) 85
(David Thompson) *chsd ldrs: blnd 2nd: drvn and outpcd 7th: sn lost pl: kpt on fr 2 out* 9/1

21/P **P** **Vodka Red (IRE)**[19] 2142 7-10-9 93 (p) PeterBuchanan
(Kenny Johnson) *t.k.h in rr: bhd fr 7th: t.o 3 out: p.u after next* 80/1

5-00 **P** **Gud Day (IRE)**[12] 2291 7-11-3 101 (p) TomO'Brien
(Conor Dore) *prom: drvn and lost pl 7th: sn bhd: t.o whn p.u bef 2 out* 40/1

4124 **P** **Tennessee Bird**[23] 2085 7-10-13 97 GavinSheehan
(Mike Sowersby) *in rr: hmpd 1st: nt jump wl after: bhd 7th: sn t.o: p.u bef next* 14/1

1436 **U** **Over The Air**[26] 2042 7-11-5 110 HarryCobden(7) 97
(John Spearing) *mid-div: hdwy to chse ldrs 6th: hit 8th: outpcd bef 2 out: 5th and wl hld whn blnd and uns rdr last* 8/1

5 **F** **Lord Ballim (FR)**[13] 2267 5-11-6 104 (t) ConorO'Farrell
(Nigel Hawke) *t.k.h: trcking ldrs whn fell 1st* 20/1

5m 28.0s (15.00) **Going Correction** +0.725s/f (Soft)
WFA 4 from 5yo+ 8lb **11** Ran SP% **114.0**
Speed ratings (Par 105): **99,95,93,93,90 89**, , ,
CSF £33.75 CT £104.33 TOTE £3.00: £1.60, £3.20, £1.70; EX 38.90 Trifecta £119.50.
Owner Paul & Clare Rooney **Bred** Mme I Corbani & Sarl Jedburgh Stud **Trained** Bourton-On-The-Water, Gloucs

FOCUS
This looked competitive enough on paper but the unexposed winner blew them away from the front. The second and third are probably the best guide to the level.

2561 SOUTHWELL 2016 ON-LINE TICKET DISCOUNT MARES' NOVICES' HURDLE (9 hdls) 1m 7f 153y
3:05 (3:05) (Class 4) 4-Y-0+ £3,249 (£954; £477; £238)

Form RPR

23-2 **1** **Yes I Did (IRE)**[41] 1811 5-10-12 0 HarrySkelton 122+
(Dan Skelton) *trckd ldr: led appr 2 out: 6 l clr whn mstke last: v readily* 2/1[2]

6-22 **2** 7 **Via Volupta**[168] 591 5-10-12 0 GavinSheehan 112
(Warren Greatrex) *led: hdd appr 2 out: kpt on same pce* 11/8[1]

U-21 **3** 3 3/4 **Awesome Rosie**[179] 432 4-10-12 0 WayneHutchinson 108
(Alan King) *chsd ldrs: kpt on same pce appr 2 out* 4/1[3]

014 **4** 9 **Potters Midnight**[154] 748 5-10-12 0 LeightonAspell 99
(Lucy Wadham) *chsd ldrs 4th: wknd between last 2* 10/1

260 **5** 9 **Tullow Tonic (IRE)**[12] 2302 4-10-12 0 AidanColeman 92
(Charlie Longsdon) *in rr: hdwy 6th: wknd appr 2 out* 25/1

6 20 **Princess Tiana (IRE)** 4-10-12 0 RichardJohnson 70
(Jonjo O'Neill) *t.k.h in rr: nt fluent: drvn and sme hdwy 6th: lost pl after next* 25/1

0-0 **7** 53 **Luna Nuova (IRE)**[35] 1898 5-10-12 0 TomMessenger 17
(Chris Bealby) *chsd ldrs: drvn 4th: lost pl next: sn bhd and jumping rt: t.o 3 out* 200/1

P **Testing (FR)**[21] 4-10-9 0 JoeColliver(3)
(David Thompson) *chsd ldrs: lost pl 3rd: bhd and drvn next: tailed rt off whn p.u bef 5th: b.b.v* 150/1

46-3 **P** **Hoponandsee**[34] 1908 4-10-12 0 TrevorWhelan
(George Baker) *chsd ldrs: drvn 6th: sn lost pl and bhd: t.o whn p.u bef 2 out* 14/1

4m 5.7s (8.70) **Going Correction** +0.725s/f (Soft) **9** Ran SP% **120.0**
Speed ratings (Par 105): **107,103,101,97,92 82,56**, ,
CSF £5.51 TOTE £2.90: £1.70, £1.02, £2.10; EX 5.90 Trifecta £13.70.
Owner The Can't Say No Partnership **Bred** Mrs C J Power **Trained** Alcester, Warwicks

FOCUS
A modest mares' novice event. There's a case for rating this 8lb higher through the second, but the third and fourth are in line with their bumper form.

2562 WINTER DEALS AT SOUTHWELL GOLF CLUB INTERMEDIATE OPEN NATIONAL HUNT FLAT RACE 1m 7f 153y
3:35 (3:35) (Class 6) 4-6-Y-0 £1,949 (£572; £286; £143)

Form RPR

3- **1** **Willoughby Court (IRE)**[219] 5292 4-11-0 0 NicodeBoinville 103+
(Ben Pauling) *trckd ldr: led over 2f out: edgd rt and hdd briefly over 1f out: drvn rt out* 1/1[1]

30- 2 1 ¼ **Give Him A Glance**[346] 2956 4-11-0 0........................ WayneHutchinson 99
(Alan King) *t.k.h in rr: effrt over 2f out: chsd wnr appr fnl f: kpt on same pce* 10/1
2- 3 3 **Relight The Fire**[214] 5380 4-11-0 0........................ RichardJohnson 96
(Denis Quinn) *sn chsng ldrs: pushed along over 5f out: hung lft and led briefly over 1f out: one pce fnl f* 9/2[3]
2 4 9 **Ballyhill (FR)**[37] 1872 4-10-11 0........................ RyanHatch[(3)] 87
(Nigel Twiston-Davies) *chsd ldrs: led over 4f out: hdd over 2f out: wknd over 1f out* 5/2[2]
05- 5 shd **Gabriel Oats**[356] 2738 6-11-0 0........................ KielanWoods 87
(Graeme McPherson) *chsd ldrs: effrt 3f out: wknd over 1f out* 50/1
0- 6 2 **Golden Sandstorm (IRE)**[411] 1694 6-11-0 0........................ AlainCawley 85
(Daniel Mark Loughnane) *led: hdd over 4f out: wknd over 1f out* 100/1
0 7 3 ¾ **Apache Pearl (IRE)**[181] 407 4-11-0 0........................ JakeGreenall 81
(Warren Greatrex) *trckd ldrs: drvn 4f out: wknd over 1f out* 25/1
8 16 **Denala** 4-10-4 0........................ JonathanEngland[(3)] 58
(Michael Appleby) *hld up in rr: pushed along 7f out: lost pl over 3f out: sn bhd* 33/1

4m 7.4s (16.00) **Going Correction** +0.725s/f (Soft) **8 Ran SP% 115.6**
Speed ratings: **89,88,86,82,82 81,79,71**
CSF £12.47 TOTE £2.00: £1.30, £2.10, £1.50; EX 10.80 Trifecta £45.40.
Owner Paul & Clare Rooney **Bred** J H Kidd **Trained** Bourton-On-The-Water, Gloucs

FOCUS
The winner set a fair standard and didn't need to be at his best to land steadily run bumper, with the third and fifth probably the best guide to the level.
T/Plt: £496.50 to a £1 stake. Pool: £65,559.72 - 96.38 winning units. T/Qpdt: £44.30 to a £1 stake. Pool: £9,308.81 - 155.29 winning units. **Walter Glynn**

2264 CHEPSTOW (L-H)
Wednesday, November 18

OFFICIAL GOING: Soft (heavy in places) changed to heavy after race 2 (1.20)
Wind: strong half against Weather: rain, sunny spells from race 4

2563 DRIBUILD NOVICES' HURDLE (DIV I) (8 hdls) 2m 11y
12:50 (12:51) (Class 4) 4-Y-0+ £3,898 (£1,144; £572; £286)

Form RPR
10- 1 **Nansaroy**[242] 4921 5-10-12 0........................ PaulMoloney 122+
(Evan Williams) *chsd ldrs: lft in 2nd at 3rd: 5 l down 3 out: styd on to ld appr last where j.rt: rdn out* 1/1[1]
4 2 1 ¼ **Never Equalled (IRE)**[10] 2363 6-10-5 0........................ JordanWilliams[(7)] 120+
(Bernard Llewellyn) *chsd ldr tl lft in ld 2nd: rdn appr 4 out: 5 l clr next: wandered and hdd appr last: kpt on u.p* 33/1
P-6 3 24 **Allchilledout**[30] 1998 6-10-5 0........................ PaulO'Brien[(7)] 96
(Colin Tizzard) *chsd ldrs: rdn to go 3rd 3 out: sn one pce and no ch w ldng pair* 6/1[3]
-P06 4 1 **Lined With Silver (IRE)**[13] 2299 6-10-12 0........................ MattieBatchelor 95
(Dai Burchell) *towards rr: rdn and stdy hdwy 4 out: chal for mod 3rd last but nvr any ch w ldng pair* 20/1
5 5 **Mixchievous** 4-10-12 0........................ AidanColeman 90
(Venetia Williams) *mid-div: clsd appr 4 out: wknd 3 out* 5/1[2]
50-5 6 8 **Royal Salute**[15] 2258 5-10-12 0........................ RyanMahon 82
(Anthony Honeyball) *mid-div: hmpd by loose horse bnd after 1st: hdwy to chse ldng pair 4 out: wknd next* 17/2
7 12 **One Last Dream**[15] 6-10-12 0........................ IanPopham 70
(Ron Hodges) *a in rr: wknd 4 out: t.o* 33/1
0P0 8 15 **Gardiners Hill (IRE)**[14] 2267 5-10-12 0........................ AdamWedge 55
(David Rees) *chsd ldrs tl wknd 4 out: t.o* 66/1
/0-0 F **Blackdown Babe**[14] 2267 7-10-5 0........................ JamesBest
(Kevin Bishop) *in rr: wknd 4 out: fell 3 out* 100/1
20-3 U **Chief Brody**[42] 1817 4-10-12 0........................ JamieMoore
(Grace Harris) *mid-div whn blnd bdly and uns rdr 1st* 17/2
FUU F **Seeanythingyoulike (IRE)**[28] 2023 4-10-12 0........................ LiamHeard
(Jeremy Scott) *racd keenly: led tl stmbld and fell 2nd* 66/1

4m 10.9s (0.30) **Going Correction** +0.175s/f (Yiel) **11 Ran SP% 116.6**
Speed ratings (Par 105): **106,105,93,92,90 86,80,72, ,**
CSF £47.41 TOTE £2.10: £1.30, £5.90, £1.80; EX 26.70 Trifecta £311.70.
Owner T Hywel Jones **Bred** B And Q Syndicate **Trained** Llancarfan, Vale Of Glamorgan

FOCUS
Rail on Stable bend out 6yds and Far bend out 8yds. Race increased by 38yds. Conditions were miserable and the ground looked very testing following excessive rain in the days building up to the meeting. There was little depth to division one of this novice hurdle and the front pair drew well clear. The third, fourth and sixth help set the level.

2564 DRIBUILD NOVICES' HURDLE (DIV II) (8 hdls) 2m 11y
1:20 (1:21) (Class 4) 4-Y-0+ £3,898 (£1,144; £572; £286)

Form RPR
1- 1 **Maxanisi (IRE)**[291] 3972 5-10-12 0........................ AdamWedge 122+
(Evan Williams) *mid-div: hdwy 4 out: shkn up in 4th after next: rdn to chse ldr between last 2: 1 l down last: styd on to ld nr fin* 11/2[3]
20-5 2 nk **Champagne At Tara**[18] 2202 6-10-12 127........................[1] RichardJohnson 122+
(Jonjo O'Neill) *hld up in rr: hdwy after 4th: chsd ldrs 4 out: led 2 out: 1 l up whn blnd last: sn rdn: hdd nr fin* 8/11[1]
0 3 14 **Vic De Touzaine (FR)**[14] 2265 6-10-12 0........................ AidanColeman 110
(Venetia Williams) *chsd ldrs: wnt 2nd appr 4 out: led after 3 out to 2 out: sn wknd* 11/4[2]
0U3 4 9 **Prince Mahler (IRE)**[14] 2267 5-10-5 0........................ MrMLegg[(7)] 98
(Caroline Keevil) *chsd ldrs: rdn 4 out: one pce and no ch after* 20/1
0440 5 1 ½ **Bishops Court**[11] 2345 5-10-12 0........................ MarkQuinlan 98
(Neil Mulholland) *led: 5 l clr 4th: j.lft 4 out: hdd after next: sn wknd* 50/1
6 2 ¾ **Mondello (GER)**[80] 4-10-12 0........................ ConorO'Farrell 94
(Richard Woollacott) *hld up: clsd 4 out: no imp on ldrs fr next: hit 2 out* 20/1
P 7 3 ¼ **Lough Derg Island (IRE)**[20] 2152 7-10-12 0........................ RhysFlint 91
(Alexandra Dunn) *chsd ldr tl wknd appr 4 out* 100/1
600- 8 37 **The Big Mare**[215] 5373 6-10-5 0........................[1] RobertDunne 47
(Laura Young) *j. slowly 1st and in 2nd: a towards rr: wknd 4 out: t.o* 100/1
5 9 1 ½ **Aaman (IRE)**[10] 2363 9-10-9 0........................ RobertWilliams[(3)] 52
(Bernard Llewellyn) *a in rr: mstke 1st: wknd 4 out: t.o* 66/1
4 10 ¾ **Grand Enterprise**[74] 1484 5-10-12 0........................ PaddyBrennan 51
(Tom George) *in rr: struggling 4th: lost tch 4 out: t.o* 12/1

4m 16.5s (5.90) **Going Correction** +0.575s/f (Soft)
WFA 4 from 5yo+ 7lb **10 Ran SP% 122.6**
Speed ratings (Par 105): **108,107,100,96,95 94,92,74,73,72**
CSF £10.61 TOTE £4.90: £1.50, £1.10, £1.40; EX 13.80 Trifecta £27.70.
Owner Mrs Janet Davies **Bred** J McDonald **Trained** Llancarfan, Vale Of Glamorgan

FOCUS
Race increased by 38yds. This looked a little deeper than the first division and again two drew clear. This could be rated a bit higher through the second.

2565 DRIBUILD CONSTRUCTION MARES' H'CAP HURDLE (8 hdls) 2m 11y
1:55 (1:55) (Class 5) (0-100,93) 3-Y-0+ £3,249 (£954; £477; £238)

Form RPR
P5P- 1 **Helamis**[33] 4316 5-10-13 83........................ HarryChalloner[(3)] 90+
(Barry Leavy) *hld up: stdy hdwy 4th: wnt 2nd 4 out: led next: drew clr fr 2 out: comf* 8/1[3]
500P 2 11 **Poetic Presence (IRE)**[35] 1910 5-9-11 69........................(v[1]) JamieBargary[(5)] 61
(Adrian Wintle) *prom tl rdn along and dropped towards rr after 1st: rdn fr 4 out: styd on u.p to go 2nd last: no ch w wnr* 14/1
3-20 3 1 ¾ **Sunshine Buddy**[13] 2298 8-10-13 87........................(p) DavidNoonan[(7)] 77
(Chris Down) *chsd ldrs: rdn along fr 3rd: no ch w wnr fr 3 out: styd on u.p* 7/4[1]
00-P 4 3 **Last Echo (IRE)**[28] 2022 4-11-6 90........................(p) BenPoste[(3)] 78
(Tom Symonds) *prom: chsd ldr 2nd: led appr 4 out: rdn and hdd next: wknd 2 out: lost 2nd last* 16/1
P303 5 11 **Pembridge**[14] 2264 6-10-5 72........................(t) RichardJohnson 50
(Adrian Wintle) *hld up: hdwy after 4th: nt fluent 4 out: sn in 3rd: rdn and wknd 2 out* 5/2[2]
540- P **Bernisdale**[77] 2920 7-11-8 89........................ RhysFlint
(John Flint) *hld up: hdwy 3rd: chsd ldrs after next: wknd 4 out: wl bhd whn p.u bef 2 out* 14/1
0 P **Annakrista (GER)**[19] 2162 7-11-0 88........................(bt) WilliamFeatherstone[(7)]
(Zoe Davison) *w ldr tl led appr 2nd: rdn and hdd appr 4 out: wknd qckly: t.o whn p.u bef 3 out* 16/1
2600 P **Honour A Promise**[35] 1910 7-11-12 93........................(p) JamesBest
(Paul Webber) *mid-div tl dropped to rr 3rd: j. slowly next: sn lost tch: t.o whn p.u bef 2 out* 25/1
31-P P **Passing Fiesta**[184] 383 6-11-6 87........................(tp) TomScudamore
(Sarah-Jayne Davies) *led: hit 1st: hdd appr next: styd prom tl wknd qckly after 4th: t.o whn p.u bef 2 out* 9/1

4m 25.7s (15.10) **Going Correction** +0.975s/f (Soft)
WFA 4 from 5yo+ 7lb **9 Ran SP% 115.0**
Speed ratings (Par 103): **101,95,94,93,87 , , ,**
CSF £106.89 CT £283.28 TOTE £8.90: £2.40, £3.70, £1.10; EX 105.30 Trifecta £345.50.
Owner N Heath **Bred** Shadwell Estate Company Limited **Trained** Forsbrook, Staffs

FOCUS
Race increased by 38yds. Lowly mares' form and it proved hard work for them in the conditions. The winner is rated back to her best, with the second close to form and the third a stone+ off.

2566 DRIBUILD CONSTRUCTION H'CAP CHASE (18 fncs) 2m 7f 131y
2:30 (2:32) (Class 4) (0-120,119) 4-Y-0+ £4,548 (£1,335; £667; £333)

Form RPR
5P-P 1 **Big Society (IRE)**[15] 2261 9-11-9 116........................ GavinSheehan 130+
(Harry Whittington) *hld up in last: hdwy 12th: shkn up 5 out: chsd ldr 3 out: led last: styd on to pull clr towards fin* 7/1
14-2 2 2 ¾ **Smart Exit (IRE)**[39] 1850 8-10-12 112........................ CiaranGethings[(7)] 122
(Stuart Edmunds) *chsd ldrs: wnt 2nd 5 out: led and lft 6 l clr next: rdn 3 out: hdd last: kpt on tl no ex towards fin* 7/2[2]
453U 3 11 **Georgian King**[14] 2272 12-11-2 109........................(p) IanPopham 107
(Martin Keighley) *a.p: bmpd 5th: rdn 5 out: one pce fr 3 out* 33/1
144/ 4 9 **Nail 'M (IRE)**[582] 5334 7-11-2 109........................ ConorO'Farrell 98
(Nigel Hawke) *hld up in rr: rdn after 13th: hdwy 5 out: one pce and no further imp fr next* 25/1
1P-5 5 18 **Paddy The Oscar (IRE)**[14] 2272 12-11-7 114........................ PaulMoloney 85
(Grace Harris) *cl up tl led 3rd: bmpd 5th: hdd after 13th: wknd 4 out: t.o* 22/1
P11- 6 2 **Castarnie**[271] 4342 7-11-4 111........................(p) TomCannon 86
(Robert Walford) *t.k.h: prom: led after 13th: rdn and jnd whn blnd bdly 4 out: mstke and lost 2nd next: sn wknd: t.o* 11/1
63P- U **Safran De Cotte (FR)**[260] 4545 9-11-5 112........................ RichardJohnson
(Henry Daly) *mid-div tl blnd and uns rdr 4th* 11/2[3]
1-45 P **Basford Ben**[17] 2213 7-11-2 109........................(b) HenryBrooke
(Jennie Candlish) *prom: mstke 8th: rdn 10th: wknd rapidly: p.u bef 12th* 20/1
4P0- P **Boyfromnowhere (IRE)**[198] 8-10-9 109........................(t) DavidNoonan[(7)]
(Neil Mulholland) *hld up towards rr: hmpd 4th: rdn 9th: sme hdwy 11th: wknd after 13th: t.o whn p.u bef 5 out* 10/3[1]
5-54 P **Brownville**[35] 1906 6-11-7 119........................(t) JamieBargary[(5)]
(Nigel Twiston-Davies) *led to 3rd: styd prom: mstke 9th and lost pl: rallied after 13th: wkng whn mstke 4 out: p.u bef next* 9/1
3-14 P **Crack Of Thunder (IRE)**[27] 2039 6-11-3 110........................(p) AidanColeman
(Charlie Longsdon) *mid-div: clsd 7th: mstke next: j. slowly 12th: lost tch fr next: t.o whn p.u bef 5 out* 8/1

6m 38.7s (16.70) **Going Correction** +0.825s/f (Soft) **11 Ran SP% 118.5**
Speed ratings (Par 105): **105,104,100,97,91 90, , , ,**
CSF £31.42 CT £771.74 TOTE £8.30: £2.60, £1.80, £9.20; EX 39.40 Trifecta £887.30.
Owner Hill Barn Racing Club **Bred** Mrs Mary O'Connor **Trained** Sparsholt, Oxfordshire
■ Stewards' Enquiry : Tom Cannon one-day ban: failed to ride out for 5th (Dec 2)

FOCUS
Race increased y 62yds. A fair staying handicap that proved a thorough test in the conditions. The winner is rated back to his best and the third close to his mark.

2567 DRIBUILD H'CAP HURDLE (12 hdls) 2m 7f 131y
3:00 (3:05) (Class 5) (0-100,100) 4-Y-0+ £3,249 (£954; £477; £238)

Form RPR
/155 1 **Rainbow Haze**[6] 2454 9-11-0 93........................ MrBMoorcroft[(5)] 102+
(Phillip Dando) *t.k.h: led tl hdd bef 2nd: styd prom: nt fluent 5th: sltly outpcd after 8th: rallied 4 out: led 3 out: drew clr next: mstke last: styd on wl* 3/1[2]
13-5 2 7 **Moon Trip**[16] 2253 6-11-12 100........................ MarkGrant 98
(Geoffrey Deacon) *hld up in tch: hdwy after 8th: wnt 2nd 3 out: nt fluent next: sn one pce and hld by wnr* 8/1
36-3 3 19 **Precious Ground**[15] 2263 5-11-1 89........................ JamesBest 69
(Kevin Bishop) *chsd ldrs: clsd into 2nd at 3rd: led 4 out to next: 3rd and wkng whn blnd 2 out* 15/8[1]
-460 4 nk **West Of The Edge (IRE)**[165] 637 7-11-3 98........................ MrJNixon[(7)] 76
(Dai Williams) *chsd ldrs tl rdn after 8th: lost tch 4 out: plugged on fr 2 out: jst missed 3rd* 9/1
-052 5 43 **Mist The Boat**[16] 2245 7-11-9 97........................(p) RichardJohnson 32
(Tim Vaughan) *prom: led appr 2nd: mstke 4th: j.lft next: hdd 8th: wknd 4 out: t.o* 4/1[3]

3-00 **P** **Petite Fantasie**[15] 2263 6-10-8 **82**........................ TomCannon
(Mark Gillard) *chsd ldrs tl dropped to rr 6th: rdn and struggling next: t.o whn p.u bef 4 out* **28/1**

U5-5 **F** **Whiskey John**[19] 2163 5-11-9 **100**........................ MattGriffiths(3) 78
(Laura Young) *t.k.h towards rr: hdwy 6th: led 8th to 4 out: wknd next: 4th and no ch whn fell last: winded* **12/1**

6m 41.4s (39.20) **Going Correction** +0.975s/f (Soft) **7** Ran SP% **112.0**
Speed ratings (Par 103): **73,70,64,64,49 ,**
CSF £25.10 TOTE £4.70: £2.30, £2.90; EX 27.70 Trifecta £91.70.
Owner Phillip Dando & Dr Michael Armitage **Bred** Phillip C And Mrs Kathryn M Dando **Trained** Peterston-Super-Ely, S Glamorg

FOCUS
Race increased by 62yds. Moderate handicap form. The winner is rated to his old bumper form, with the second a bit below his best.

2568 DRIBUILD H'CAP CHASE (16 fncs) 2m 3f 98y
3:30 (3:35) (Class 4) (0-120,119) 4-Y-0+ **£4,548** (£1,335; £667; £333)

Form RPR

1F4- **1** **Winston Churchill (IRE)**[264] 4475 9-10-6 **102**............(t) KillianMoore(3) 110
(Sophie Leech) *mde all: rdn 4 out: edgd lft flat: styd on wl* **13/2**

14-P **2** *nk* **Quite By Chance**[15] 2261 6-11-12 **119**........................ AidanColeman 125
(Colin Tizzard) *trckd ldr tl relegated a pl 7th: rdn 4 out: keeping on in 3rd whn hmpd and stmbld 100yds out: fin 3rd, 2 3/4l & nk: plcd 2nd* **4/1[2]**

423- **3** *2 3/4* **Tolkeins Tango (IRE)**[271] 4342 7-11-11 **118**............(t) DenisO'Regan 124
(Victor Dartnall) *hld up in mid-div: hdwy to trck wnr 7th: rdn 3 out: nt run on: hung lft flat: fin 2nd, 2 3/4l: disqualified and plcd 3rd* **9/2[3]**

114- **4** *31* **Toowoomba (IRE)**[277] 4230 7-11-4 **111**........................ RichardJohnson 94
(Philip Hobbs) *chsd ldrs: nt fluent 9th: mstke 11th: sn struggling: lost tch bef 5 out: t.o* **1/1[1]**

34-F **5** *20* **Saint Breiz (FR)**[198] 109 9-11-4 **111**........................ IanPopham 65
(Carroll Gray) *t.k.h in mid-div: dropped to rr 11th: lost tch 5 out: t.o* **20/1**

23-4 **P** **Paddy The Stout (IRE)**[195] 163 10-11-3 **110**............(t) PaddyBrennan
(Paul Henderson) *hld up: mstke 1st: clsd into modest 4th after 11th: wknd 5 out: wl bhd whn p.u bef 3 out* **20/1**

520P **P** **Spring Steel (IRE)**[20] 2153 6-11-3 **110**........................(t) RhysFlint
(Alexandra Dunn) *hld up in rr: j. slowly 6th: lost tch after 11th: wl bhd whn p.u bef 5 out* **50/1**

5m 27.2s (15.90) **Going Correction** +1.00s/f (Soft) **7** Ran SP% **113.0**
Speed ratings (Par 105): **106,104,104,91,83 ,**
CSF £31.33 TOTE £7.40: £2.40, £2.00; EX 31.70.
Owner G Thompson **Bred** J R Weston **Trained** Elton, Gloucs
■ Stewards' Enquiry : Denis O'Regan four-day ban: careless riding (Dec 2-4,6)

FOCUS
Race increased by 38yds. Modest chasing form, with the favourite disappointing. The winner is rated to his best, with the second and third close to form.

2569 DRIBUILD CONDITIONAL JOCKEYS' NOVICES' H'CAP HURDLE (11 hdls) 2m 3f 100y
4:00 (4:04) (Class 4) (0-115,115) 3-Y-0+ **£3,249** (£954; £477; £238)

Form RPR

P2P- **1** **Mountain Of Mourne (IRE)**[210] 5467 6-11-3 **111**........................ ConorSmith(5) 118+
(Linda Blackford) *led to 4th: trckd ldr tl disp ld again appr 4 out where nodded: narrowly hdd between last 2: styd on to ld fnl 50yds* **10/1**

4-40 **2** *3/4* **Bassarabad (FR)**[24] 2085 4-10-8 **105**........................ GeorgeBlackwell(8) 110
(Tim Vaughan) *chsd ldrs: disp ld appr 4 out: nt fluent 2 out: sn in narrow ld: hdd 50yds* **16/1**

452- **3** *9* **Spice Fair**[21] 4441 8-11-10 **113**........................ ThomasGarner 110
(Mark Usher) *hld up: hdwy 4 out: wnt 3rd after 2 out: one pce and no imp on ldng pair* **7/1**

63-5 **4** *3 1/4* **Zanstra (IRE)**[25] 2062 5-11-0 **109**........................ PaulO'Brien(6) 102
(Colin Tizzard) *t.k.h: chsd ldrs: rdn 4 out: wknd and lost 3rd after 2 out* **2/1[1]**

33- **5** *16* **Pobbles Bay (IRE)**[281] 4146 5-11-9 **115**........................ ConorRing(3) 92
(Evan Williams) *hld up in tch in last: pushed along 5th: wknd after 4 out* **7/2[2]**

2034 **6** *30* **Darnitnev**[42] 1812 5-10-9 **98**........................(p) KillianMoore 45
(Martin Keighley) *cl up: led 4th tl appr 4 out: sn wknd: t.o* **9/2[3]**

322- **P** **One For The Boss (IRE)**[231] 5100 8-11-0 **103**........................ FreddieMitchell
(Dai Burchell) *mid-div: rdn along 7th: wknd 3 out: bhd whn p.u bef next* **8/1**

5m 17.9s (16.10) **Going Correction** +0.975s/f (Soft)
WFA 4 from 5yo+ 7lb **7** Ran SP% **112.3**
Speed ratings (Par 105): **105,104,100,99,92 80,**
CSF £127.75 TOTE £11.90: £4.00, £5.80; EX 111.00 Trifecta £622.90.
Owner Over The Last Racing **Bred** Lionel Beresford **Trained** Rackenford, Devon

FOCUS
Race increased by 38yds. The front pair came away late on in what was an ordinary hurdle.
T/Plt: £134.40 to a £1 stake. Pool: £78,266.23 - 424.91 winning tickets T/Qpdt: £94.80 to a £1 stake. Pool: £6,564.66 - 51.24 winning tickets **Richard Lowther**

2474 HEXHAM (L-H)
Wednesday, November 18
2570 Meeting Abandoned - waterlogged

2271 WARWICK (L-H)
Wednesday, November 18
OFFICIAL GOING: Good to soft (soft in places on hurdle course; chs 6.4, hdl 6.2)
Wind: Strong behind Weather: Raining

2577 WATCH RACINGUK WITH FREE TRIAL NOW CONDITIONAL JOCKEYS' H'CAP HURDLE (9 hdls) 2m 3f
12:40 (12:40) (Class 4) (0-120,118) 3-Y-0+ **£3,249** (£954; £477; £238)

Form RPR

531- **1** **Dazinski**[462] 1215 9-11-4 **110**........................(t) JeremiahMcGrath 116+
(Henry Oliver) *hld up: hdwy after 3 out: chsd ldr next: led last: rdn out* **14/1**

304- **2** *3/4* **Space Walker (IRE)**[220] 5286 4-11-8 **114**........................ MauriceLinehan 119+
(Ben Pauling) *led: plld hrd: mstke 2nd: hdd 6th: led again 3 out: hdd last: rdn and hdd last: no ex nr fin* **10/1[3]**

55-0 **3** *7* **Guards Chapel**[38] 449 7-10-11 **111**........................(v) GeorgeGorman(8) 109
(Gary Moore) *hld up: pushed along after 3rd: hdwy appr 5th: drvn and outpcd after 3 out: rallied bef last: styd on same pce flat* **100/1**

0-FP **4** *2* **Mini Muck**[7] 2447 9-11-1 **110**........................ RyanHatch(3) 106
(Nigel Twiston-Davies) *chsd ldrs: rdn appr 2 out: no ex last* **33/1**

-102 **5** *3 1/4* **Pied Du Roi (IRE)**[27] 2029 5-11-4 **110**........................(p) ConorShoemark 103
(Charlie Longsdon) *chsd ldrs: rdn appr 2 out: wknd last* **10/1[3]**

-313 **6** *2 1/2* **The Big Dipper**[24] 2085 6-11-4 **110**........................ KieronEdgar 102
(David Dennis) *prom: chsd ldr after 4th: led 6th to next: sn rdn: wknd last* **10/1[3]**

F54- **7** *1 1/4* **Bonobo (IRE)**[244] 4868 8-10-11 **111**........................ LewisGordon(8) 101
(Evan Williams) *hld up: hdwy 6th: rdn after 3 out: wknd appr last* **12/1**

4-53 **8** *2 3/4* **McCabe Creek (IRE)**[24] 2087 5-10-8 **110**........................ JamieInsole(10) 98
(Alan King) *hld up: nt clr run after 3 out: nvr on terms* **10/1[3]**

0-P2 **9** *3 1/4* **Drumlang (IRE)**[22] 2121 9-11-9 **115**........................ JakeHodson 100
(Kevin Frost) *hld up in tch: rdn after 3 out: wknd bef next* **25/1**

255/ **10** *nk* **Varom (FR)**[663] 3872 6-10-9 **109**........................(t) HarryCobden(8) 93
(Paul Nicholls) *chsd ldrs: rdn after 3 out: wkng whn hmpd next* **6/4[1]**

6366 **11** *8* **Breaking The Bank**[24] 2090 6-11-7 **113**........................(t) ThomasGarner 90
(Ben Case) *hld up: wknd 6th* **50/1**

-021 **12** *1 1/2* **Murray Mount (IRE)**[22] 2121 5-11-3 **109**........................ HarryBannister 85
(Charlie Mann) *mid-div: lost pl appr 5th: sn bhd* **9/1[2]**

6210 **13** *56* **Powderonthebonnet (IRE)**[14] 2271 7-10-7 **102**........................ DanielHiskett(3) 27
(Richard Phillips) *chsd ldr tl nt fluent 4th: sn rdn: wknd bef next* **33/1**

-500 **F** **Dormouse**[14] 2271 10-11-4 **110**........................(p) TomBellamy
(Anabel K Murphy) *hld up: fell 4th* **10/1[3]**

-466 **F** **Sailors Warn (IRE)**[19] 2170 8-11-11 **117**........................(tp) NathanMoscrop 107
(Ronald Thompson) *hld up: hdwy 6th: rdn after 3 out: wkng whn fell next* **40/1**

4m 37.7s (-8.30) **Going Correction** -0.475s/f (Good)
WFA 4 from 5yo+ 7lb **15** Ran SP% **124.9**
Speed ratings (Par 105): **98,97,94,93,92 91,90,89,88,88 84,84,60, ,**
CSF £143.84 CT £12829.25 TOTE £19.30: £4.90, £3.40, £18.40; EX 245.80 Trifecta £1101.70.
Owner Dan Lloyd **Bred** Darley **Trained** Abberley, Worcs

FOCUS
All starts have been moved at this track following remeasuring, so there will be no speed figures here until there is sufficient data to calculate updated median times. All Hurdle and NHF Flat races run on Inner Course. Races 1 & 3 increased by 6yds, races 2, 4, 5, & 7 by 4yds and race 6 by 8yds. This competitive conditonal riders' handicap was run at a fair gallop and the first pair came nicely clear from two out. Both of them posted personal bests but they have the potential to rate higher yet on Flat form. The third, fourth and sixth help set an ordinary level.

2578 GUY SALMON LAND ROVER JUVENILE HURDLE (8 hdls) 2m
1:10 (1:11) (Class 4) 3-Y-0 **£3,249** (£954; £477; £238)

Form RPR

12 **1** **Sceau Royal (FR)**[19] 2172 3-11-4 140........................ DarylJacob 133+
(Alan King) *trckd ldr: mstke 2 out: qcknd to ld bef last: r.o wl: comf* **2/5[1]**

2 *9* **Winterfell (FR)**[55] 3-11-4 0........................ HarrySkelton 123
(Dan Skelton) *led: rdn appr 2 out: hdd bef last: eased whn btn flat* **2/1[2]**

0 **3** *94* **Fidelity**[14] 2273 3-10-9 0........................ ConorShoemark(3) 23
(Jonathan Geake) *hld up: wkng whn wnt remote 3rd 5th* **100/1[3]**

0 **4** *86* **Prince Of Cardamom (IRE)**[14] 2273 3-10-12 0........................(vt[1]) DaveCrosse
(Jonathan Geake) *rn wout declared tongue strap: chsd clr ldrs to 4th: sn lost tch: hit 3 out* **100/1[3]**

3m 47.1s (-11.90) **Going Correction** -0.475s/f (Good) **4** Ran SP% **106.7**
Speed ratings (Par 104): **110,105,58,15**
CSF £1.53 TOTE £1.30; EX 1.40 Trifecta £3.40.
Owner Simon Munir & Isaac Souede **Bred** Guy Vimont **Trained** Barbury Castle, Wilts

FOCUS
This was effectively a match and so it played out. The race was run in driving rain as well as a gale, and afterwards winning rider Daryl Jacob said "the wind is making it hard work". The winner progressed again and rates a smart juvenile.

2579 TRIAL RACING UK FOR FREE NOW MARES' NOVICES' HURDLE (11 hdls) 2m 5f
1:45 (1:45) (Class 4) 4-Y-0+ **£3,249** (£954; £477; £238)

Form RPR

64-3 **1** **Rene's Girl (IRE)**[39] 1845 5-10-12 0........................ HarrySkelton 116+
(Dan Skelton) *a.p: chsd ldr appr 2 out: shkn up to ld bef last: rdn out* **7/2**

11-1 **2** *2* **Hollies Pearl**[39] 1845 5-11-5 0........................ SeanBowen 123+
(Peter Bowen) *j.lft at times and nt a fluent: chsd ldr: led appr 2 out: hdd last: rdn and edgd rt flat: styd on same pce* **2/5[1]**

332/ **3** *16* **Coco Shambhala**[580] 5374 7-10-9 0........................ ThomasGarner(3) 102
(Oliver Sherwood) *led: j.rt 4th: pushed along and hdd appr 2 out: sn wknd* **20/1**

5-3 **4** *12* **Iconic Star**[21] 2141 5-10-12 0........................ TomO'Brien 91
(Philip Hobbs) *prom: lost pl appr 7th: hit 3 out: sn wknd* **10/1[3]**

0- **5** *42* **Ruby Yeats**[264] 4478 4-10-12 0........................ NoelFehily 51
(Harry Fry) *hld up: hdwy and mstke 7th: wknd after 3 out* **25/1**

5m 14.5s (-6.50) **Going Correction** -0.475s/f (Good)
WFA 4 from 5yo+ 8lb **5** Ran SP% **111.3**
Speed ratings (Par 105): **93,92,86,81,65**
CSF £5.66 TOTE £4.00: £2.40, £1.10; EX 6.40 Trifecta £21.80.
Owner Andy & Sharon Measham **Bred** Michael Hanrahan **Trained** Alcester, Warwicks

FOCUS
Straightforward form for the division. The first two built on their recent Chepstow form.

2580 HIGHFLYER/MILLION IN MIND 4 & 5YO NOVICES' CHASE (12 fncs) 2m
2:20 (2:20) (Class 3) 4-5-Y-0 **£9,384** (£2,772; £1,386; £693)

Form RPR

23-2 **1** **Bristol De Mai (FR)**[19] 2166 4-10-7 0........................ DarylJacob 148+
(Nigel Twiston-Davies) *mde all: j.w: clr appr 2 out: easily* **8/15[1]**

3-22 **2** *19* **Karezak (IRE)**[25] 2060 4-10-7 0........................(b) WayneHutchinson 131+
(Alan King) *chsd wnr: mstke 8th: pushed along 3 out: wkng whn mstke next* **2/1[2]**

11-2 **3** *13* **Murrayana (IRE)**[27] 2034 5-10-7 124........................(t) MrSamPainting(7) 125
(Colin Tizzard) *sn outpcd: mstke 3rd: hit 6th: n.d* **16/1[3]**

0-04 **4** *26* **Sleepy Haven (IRE)**[8] 2412 5-11-0 134........................(t) PeterCarberry 100
(Jennie Candlish) *sn bhd* **40/1**

3m 55.5s (-14.50) **Going Correction** -0.60s/f (Firm)
WFA 4 from 5yo 7lb **4** Ran SP% **106.9**
Speed ratings: **112,102,96,83**
CSF £1.99 TOTE £1.70; EX 2.40 Trifecta £3.00.

Owner Simon Munir & Isaac Souede **Bred** Jean-Yves Touzaint **Trained** Naunton, Gloucs

FOCUS

This interesting novice event was another match and it saw a highly impressive winner, who built on his recent chase debut and looks smart.

2581 PJ & KR SMITH-MAXWELL HORSE AMBULANCES "NATIONAL HUNT" NOVICES' HURDLE (8 hdls) 2m

2:50 (2:52) (Class 4) 4-Y-0+ **£3,898** (£1,144; £572; £286)

Form RPR

24-1 **1** **Yanworth**[15] [2258] 5-11-5 0... BarryGeraghty 135+
(Alan King) *hld up: hdwy 5th: nt fluent 2 out: led flat: comf* **1/4**[1]

2 *1 ¼* **Le Prezien (FR)**[242] 4-10-12 0...............................(t) SamTwiston-Davies 122+
(Paul Nicholls) *chsd ldrs: led appr 2 out: rdn and hdd flat: styd on same pce* **11/2**[2]

-52P **3** *18* **Aliandy (IRE)**[19] [2163] 4-10-12 0.. DavidBass 105
(Kim Bailey) *hld up: racd keenly: hdwy 3 out: pushed along and pckd next: sn wknd* **25/1**

34-6 **4** *1 ¾* **Petrou (IRE)**[17] [2221] 5-10-12 0... KielanWoods 102
(Ben Case) *plld hrd: led: j.lft 2nd: hdd appr 4th: led again 3 out: rdn and hdd bef next: wknd appr last* **33/1**

0-P0 **5** *19* **Myroundorus (IRE)**[13] [2299] 5-10-12 0................................ CharliePoste 87
(Robin Dickin) *hld up: hdwy after 3 out: wkng whn hmpd next* **100/1**

2-1 **6** *10* **Political Quiz**[27] [2041] 5-11-5 0... JamesDavies 82
(Tom Symonds) *chsd ldrs: ev ch 3 out: sn rdn and wknd* **8/1**[3]

40-0 **7** *9* **Northandsouth (IRE)**[41] [1826] 5-10-9 0............................ RyanHatch[(3)] 64
(Nigel Twiston-Davies) *chsd ldrs: led appr 4th: hdd 3 out: sn rdn and wknd* **50/1**

0 **8** *2* **Just So Cool (IRE)**[22] [2126] 4-10-12 0.............................. TrevorWhelan 62
(David Dennis) *hld up: wknd 5th* **80/1**

9 *1 ½* **Ultimate Dream (FR)** 4-10-12 0... WillKennedy 61
(Jonjo O'Neill) *hld up: reminders bef 4th: hdwy u.p appr 3 out: sn wknd* **33/1**

00 **10** *7* **Blue Prairie**[17] [2221] 4-10-12 0.. HarrySkelton 54
(Dan Skelton) *prom: reminder 4th: wknd after 3 out* **100/1**

00/4 **11** *17* **Henrybrowneyes (IRE)**[18] [2188] 6-10-12 0............................. DarylJacob 37
(Ian Williams) *prom: hit 4th: wknd after 3 out* **33/1**

43/ **12** *11* **Laraghcon Boy (IRE)**[639] [4329] 6-10-12 0............................. LeeEdwards 26
(Tony Carroll) *chsd ldr: nt fluent 2nd: lost 2nd next: wknd 4th* **50/1**

F **Overtown Express (IRE)**[619] 7-10-12 0.................................... NoelFehily 102
(Harry Fry) *hld up: hdwy 4th: ev ch 3 out: 5th and wkng whn fell next* **12/1**

3m 56.4s (-2.60) **Going Correction** -0.475s/f (Good)
WFA 4 from 5yo+ 7lb **13 Ran SP% 134.0**
Speed ratings (Par 105): **87,86,77,76,67 62,57,56,55,52 43,38,**
CSF £2.77 TOTE £1.50: £1.10, £1.70, £3.70; EX 3.30 Trifecta £27.30.

Owner John P McManus **Bred** Wood Farm Stud **Trained** Barbury Castle, Wilts

FOCUS

They got sorted out from the third-last in this modest novice event. The third is rated to his mark.

2582 JEREMY DEEDES TRIBUTE NOVICES' H'CAP CHASE (18 fncs) 3m

3:20 (3:23) (Class 4) (0-105,105) 4-Y-0+ **£3,898** (£1,144; £572; £286)

Form RPR

0621 **1** **Arthamint**[8] [2420] 7-11-6 **99**...(t) HarrySkelton 110+
(Dan Skelton) *hld up: plld hrd: hdwy 4th: chsd ldr and mstke last: rdn flat: r.o to ld post* **13/8**[1]

P50- **2** *shd* **Smartmax (FR)**[293] [3934] 6-11-4 **97**................................... TomMessenger 106
(Caroline Bailey) *sn chsng ldr: led 12th: rdn and edgd rt appr last: hdd post* **12/1**

405- **3** *2 ¼* **Cheat The Cheater (IRE)**[245] [4855] 8-9-11 **79** oh4(tp) ConorShoemark[(3)] 86
(Claire Dyson) *mde most to 12th: drvn along 14th: ev ch 3 out: no ex flat* **4/1**[3]

040 **4** *36* **Generous Pet (IRE)**[54] [1648] 6-10-7 **86**.............................. AlainCawley 69
(Kevin Bishop) *prom: lost pl 4th: wknd 14th: bhd whn hmpd 2 out* **25/1**

00-0 **F** **Tikkapick (IRE)**[191] [240] 5-10-8 **94**................................ MrSamPainting[(7)] 98
(Colin Tizzard) *hdwy 4th: nt fluent 12th: mstke 14th: rdn after 3 out: 4th and looking hld whn fell 2 out* **6/1**

635- **F** **Mother Meldrum (IRE)**[210] [5470] 6-11-12 **105**........ SamTwiston-Davies
(Victor Dartnall) *chsd ldr: upsides whn fell 5th* **11/4**[2]

6m 45.8s (11.80) **Going Correction** -0.60s/f (Firm) **6 Ran SP% 110.6**
Speed ratings (Par 105): **56,55,55,43,**
CSF £18.33 TOTE £2.30: £1.50, £6.70; EX 19.80 Trifecta £71.20.

Owner Mrs A J Higgins **Bred** Mrs A J Higgins **Trained** Alcester, Warwicks

FOCUS

A moderate staying handicap, run at a steady gallop.The winner can rate higher.

2583 DAVID NICHOLSON MEMORIAL FILLIES' "JUNIOR" STANDARD OPEN NATIONAL HUNT FLAT RACE 1m 6f

3:50 (3:53) (Class 6) 3-Y-O **£1,624** (£477; £238; £119)

Form RPR

1 **Miss Fleming** 3-10-12 0... NoelFehily 93+
(David Loder) *hld up in tch: rdn to ld 1f out: r.o* **2/1**[2]

3 **2** *3* **Inner Loop**[29] [2009] 3-10-12 0.. TomO'Brien 89
(Robert Stephens) *w ldr tl wnt on 11f out: rdn and hdd 1f out: styd on same pce* **5/6**[1]

3 *3 ½* **Clanville Lass** 3-10-12 0.. AdamWedge 85
(Ali Stronge) *chsd ldrs: rdn over 2f out: no ex fnl f* **8/1**[3]

6 **4** *7* **Coco Flower (FR)**[13] [2304] 3-10-9 0...................................... JamesBanks[(3)] 76
(Alex Hales) *led 3f: chsd ldr: rdn over 2f out: wknd over 1f out* **25/1**

5 *8* **Combe Breeze** 3-10-5 0... MrMLegg[(7)] 67
(Bob Buckler) *w ldrs 3f: lost pl 9f out: rdn and wknd over 2f out* **14/1**

3m 31.2s (211.20) **5 Ran SP% 109.5**
CSF £3.98 TOTE £2.90: £1.50, £1.10; EX 4.90 Trifecta £8.00.

Owner Quartet **Bred** James & Jean Potter **Trained** Bishop's Castle, Shropshire

FOCUS

This fillies' bumper proved a sufficient test and the runner-up sets the level.

T/Plt: £24.60 to a £1 stake. Pool: £39,567.90 - 1,173.39 winning tickets T/Qpdt: £2.30 to a £1 stake. Pool: £4,931.95 - 1,578.47 winning tickets **Colin Roberts**

2584 - 2590a (Foreign Racing) - See Raceform Interactive

[2286]MARKET RASEN (R-H)

Thursday, November 19

OFFICIAL GOING: Chase course - soft; hurdle course - good to soft (soft in places)

Wind: moderate 1/2 against Weather: overcast but dry

2591 PHS BESAFE BRIGHTGEAR "NATIONAL HUNT" NOVICES' HURDLE (10 hdls) 2m 2f 140y

12:30 (12:31) (Class 4) 4-Y-0+ **£3,898** (£1,144; £572; £286)

Form RPR

53 **1** **Barney Dwan (IRE)**[16] [2258] 5-10-12 0.............................. PaddyBrennan 132+
(Fergal O'Brien) *trckd ldrs: led appr 2 out: hit last: forged clr: eased in clsng stages* **7/2**[3]

2 *10* **Oldgrangewood**[256] 4-10-12 0.. HarrySkelton 123+
(Dan Skelton) *t.k.h in mid-div: trckd ldrs 6th: clr 2nd appr 2 out: kpt on same pce appr last* **10/3**[2]

3 *11* **Amiral Collonges (FR)**[228] 5-10-12 0.................................... LiamTreadwell 108
(James Evans) *in rr: hdwy and poor 6th 3 out: styd on to take modest 3rd last* **20/1**

31-4 **4** *8* **Speredek (FR)**[20] [2163] 4-10-12 0.. TomScudamore 102
(Nigel Hawke) *chsd ldrs: mstke 4th: drvn 3 out: one pce appr next* **10/1**

2-21 **5** *1* **Western Miller (IRE)**[28] [2025] 4-11-5 0............................ RichardJohnson 108
(Charlie Longsdon) *best away: led: mstke 6th: hdd appr 2 out: one pce* **2/1**[1]

4-1U **6** *½* **Fact Of The Matter (IRE)**[36] [1909] 5-10-12 0...........(t) BrendanPowell 99
(Jamie Snowden) *chsd ldr: hit 7th: one pce appr 2 out* **15/2**

31-6 **7** *24* **Kara Tara**[195] [187] 5-10-5 0.. BrianHughes 68
(Lawrence Mullaney) *in rr: sme hdwy 3 out: lost pl bef next: sn wl bhd* **50/1**

6-6 **8** *2 ½* **Isla Di Milano (IRE)**[33] [1966] 4-10-12 0.............................. GavinSheehan 72
(Harry Whittington) *in rr: bhd and pushed along 6th: t.o 3 out* **25/1**

1-66 **9** *75* **Down The Line (IRE)**[18] [2210] 5-10-12 0............................. PaulMoloney
(Alan Swinbank) *chsd ldrs: lost pl 7th: sn bhd: t.o and eased 2 out: eventually completed* **33/1**

/00- **P** **Bold Prince Rupert (IRE)**[237] [5020] 5-10-7 0..........[1] NathanMoscrop[(5)]
(Sara Ender) *sn detached in last: t.o 6th: p.u after 3 out* **250/1**

4m 46.9s (7.50) **Going Correction** +0.55s/f (Soft) **10 Ran SP% 113.4**
Speed ratings (Par 105): **106,101,97,93,93 93,83,82,50,**
CSF £14.69 TOTE £4.00: £1.40, £1.80, £5.80; EX 16.70 Trifecta £167.60.

Owner Paul & Clare Rooney **Bred** Grange Stud **Trained** Naunton, Gloucs

FOCUS

Th rail has been set out 14 yards on Wood Bend and 22 yards on the Stands Bend. Race increased by approximately 150 yards. Assessing the ground, clerk of the course Jane Hedley said "we had 7mm of rain at the weekend and not a lot since. The chase track will ride pretty slow. We opened up a fresh strip of ground on the hurdles and I don't think that will ride any worse than good to soft."The first pair came right away in this novice event and there's a case for rating this a lot higher through the fifth and sixth.

2592 PHS GROUP WASHROOM SOLUTION NOVICES' LIMITED H'CAP CHASE (14 fncs) 2m 5f 89y

1:00 (1:02) (Class 4) (0-120,117) 4-Y-0+ **£5,198** (£1,526; £763; £381)

Form RPR

260- **1** **Chicoria (IRE)**[218] [5343] 6-11-5 **114**.................................. RichardJohnson 128+
(Henry Daly) *t.k.h: mstkes: trckd ldrs 8th: 3rd 4 out: 2nd next: over 1 l down whn hit last: edgd lft and styd on wl to ld last 75yds* **11/2**

5P-3 **2** *2 ¼* **St Johns Point (IRE)**[29] [2018] 7-11-6 **115**.........................(p) BrianHughes 124
(Charlie Longsdon) *trckd ldr 1st: mstke 5th: led sn after 4 out: edgd lft run-in: hdd and no ex last 75yds* **11/4**[2]

4006 **3** *10* **Little Windmill (IRE)**[18] [2223] 5-10-3 **98** oh1.....................(t) TrevorWhelan 99+
(Neil King) *led 1st: j.lft: clr after 4th: hdd sn after 4 out: wknd 2 out* **20/1**

-3P1 **4** *6* **Uhlan Bute (FR)**[8] [2434] 7-11-7 **116** 7ex..........................(p) LiamTreadwell 108
(Venetia Williams) *led to 1st: chsd ldrs: pushed along 8th: hit 10th and reminders: wknd next* **6/4**[1]

-143 **5** *55* **Down Time (USA)**[34] [1956] 5-11-0 **109**.................................(p) DannyCook 46
(Brian Ellison) *nt fluent in rr: bhd whn mstke and reminders 8th: t.o 10th: eventually completed* **9/2**[3]

3230 **P** **Handmaid**[43] [1808] 6-11-8 **117**..(p) SeanBowen
(Peter Bowen) *in rr: reminders 4th: drvn next: bhd 6th: t.o whn p.u bef 8th* **12/1**

5m 53.9s (7.90) **Going Correction** +0.55s/f (Soft) **6 Ran SP% 112.7**
Speed ratings (Par 105): **106,105,101,99,78**
CSF £21.56 TOTE £6.10: £2.50, £1.80; EX 23.90 Trifecta £238.80.

Owner Trevor Hemmings **Bred** Miss Siobhan Madden **Trained** Stanton Lacy, Shropshire

FOCUS

As expected the going was more demanding on the chase course and this modest novice handicap proved a thorough test, as it was run over 216 yard further than the advertised trip.

2593 PHS BESAFE FLAMEGEAR H'CAP CHASE (14 fncs) 2m 5f 89y

1:30 (1:33) (Class 3) (0-125,125) 4-Y-0+ **£9,747** (£2,862; £1,431; £715)

Form RPR

0122 **1** **Dartford Warbler (IRE)**[8] [2435] 8-10-13 **112**................................ DannyCook 127+
(Sue Smith) *mde all: j.lft at time: styd on wl run-in: readily* **9/4**[1]

/232 **2** *5* **Shockingtimes (IRE)**[21] [2149] 8-11-5 **118**...................(bt[1]) BrendanPowell 125
(Jamie Snowden) *trckd ldrs: handy 2nd bef 3 out: sn drvn: kpt on same pce run-in* **12/1**

F5UU **3** *11* **Owen Glendower (IRE)**[27] [2057] 10-11-4 **117**..........(tp) RichieMcLernon 114
(Sophie Leech) *in rr: hdwy to chse ldrs 7th: outpcd 9th: rallied 4 out: 3rd bef 3 out: one pce* **25/1**

U-6P **4** *4* **Up For An Oscar (IRE)**[186] [363] 8-11-7 **120**............................(p) SeanBowen 112
(Peter Bowen) *chsd ldrs: drvn along 7th: hit 4 out: one pce bef next* **8/1**[3]

P1-3 **5** *10* **Rio Milan (IRE)**[43] [1807] 9-11-10 **123**.................................(tp) PaddyBrennan 105
(Fergal O'Brien) *chsd ldrs: pushed along 7th: outpcd 4 out: wknd 2 out* **8/1**[3]

P-34 **6** *1 ½* **Cloudy Bob (IRE)**[33] [1970] 8-11-6 **119**................................. LeightonAspell 101
(Pat Murphy) *mid-div: chsd ldrs 7th: hit 9th: modest 5th whn hit 3 out: hung lft run-in* **5/2**[2]

P1-3 **7** *20* **Russborough (FR)**[12] [2336] 6-11-12 **125**................................ LiamTreadwell 86
(Venetia Williams) *t.k.h: trckd ldrs: lost pl 7th: sn bhd: t.o whn blnd last* **10/1**

2431 **8** *2 ¾* **Cayman Islands**[37] [1896] 7-11-2 **122**................................. MrAlexFerguson[(7)] 80
(John Ferguson) *trckd ldr: lost pl bef 3 out: sn bhd: t.o* **14/1**

4455 **9** *9* **She's Late**14 2288 5-11-0 **113**..........(p) WillKennedy 62
(Jonjo O'Neill) *in rr: reminders after 7th: bhd fr 9th: t.o* **66/1**

3-63 **U** **Harristown**29 2012 5-11-12 **125**..........(p) BrianHughes
(Charlie Longsdon) *mid-div: blnd bdly and uns rdr 2nd* **16/1**

5m 55.3s (9.30) **Going Correction** +0.625s/f (Soft) **10 Ran SP% 116.2**
Speed ratings (Par 107): **107,105,100,99,95 95,87,86,82,**
CSF £29.27 CT £539.36 TOTE £2.90: £1.20, £2.60, £6.80; EX 18.90 Trifecta £661.40.
Owner Mrs S Smith **Bred** John O'Dwyer **Trained** High Eldwick, W Yorks

FOCUS
Race increased by about 216yds. This looked competitive but the going proved too much for the majority and only two mattered from the third-last. The winner was well in on his recent win and has been rated to a similar level, with the second to his mark. There's a case for rating this a few pounds higher through the third.

2594 LORD TENNYSON H'CAP HURDLE (10 hdls) 2m 4f 139y
2:05 (2:05) (Class 2) (0-145,139) 4-Y-0+**£16,245** (£4,770; £2,385; £1,192)

Form RPR

-126 **1** **Sky Khan**26 2064 6-11-3 **130**..........(p) PeterBuchanan 133+
(Lucinda Russell) *in rr: chsd ldrs 5th: outpcd 7th: hdwy and handy 3rd bef 2 out: edgd lft between last 2: led last: edgd lft fnl 75yds: all out* **10/1**

2112 **2** *½* **Ennistown**19 2196 5-11-3 **130**..........BrianHughes 132+
(John Ferguson) *hld up in rr: hdwy bef 8th: handy 4th appr 2 out: hung rt and swtchd lft between last 2: cl 2nd last 75yds: carried lft: reluctant and hmpd nr fin* **14/1**

24-0 **3** *1 ½* **Handiwork**20 197 5-11-12 **139**..........(p) RichardJohnson 139
(Steve Gollings) *trckd ldrs 4th: led bef 2 out: hdd last: styd on same pce last 150yds* **6/1**3

3-61 **4** *11* **Clondaw Banker (IRE)**11 2369 6-10-7 **120**..........JeremiahMcGrath 111
(Nicky Henderson) *disp ld tl def advantage 7th: hdd appr 2 out: wknd fnl 200yds* **2/1**1

2-P5 **5** *10* **Gone Forever**25 2081 5-10-9 **122**..........DannyCook 103
(Brian Ellison) *chsd ldrs: outpcd and hit 7th: lost pl and reminders next: kpt on run-in: tk poor 5th nr fin: fin lame* **15/2**

0-12 **6** *1 ¾* **Work In Progress (IRE)**25 2083 5-11-8 **135**..........HarrySkelton 115
(Dan Skelton) *trckd ldrs: hit 3 out: lost pl bef next* **9/2**2

-543 **7** *40* **Raktiman (IRE)**14 2289 8-10-13 **129**..........JonathanEngland(3) 73
(Richard Drake) *in rr: reminders after 6th: sn bhd: t.o 2 out* **22/1**

3144 **8** *3 ½* **Brave Spartacus (IRE)**25 2084 9-10-13 **126**..........JamesReveley 66
(Keith Reveley) *disp ld to 7th: lost pl appr 2 out: sn bhd* **11/1**

-526 **9** *8* **Cooking Fat**28 2027 4-10-7 **120**..........HenryBrooke 53
(Dianne Sayer) *chsd ldrs: lost pl 5th: bhd fr 7th: t.o last* **66/1**

25-4 **P** **Medicine Hat**19 2202 4-11-0 **127**..........RichieMcLernon
(George Moore) *chsd ldrs: drvn 7th: lost pl bef next: sn bhd: t.o whn p.u bef 2 out* **16/1**

5m 23.0s (14.20) **Going Correction** +0.625s/f (Soft)
WFA 4 from 5yo+ 8lb **10 Ran SP% 113.4**
Speed ratings (Par 109): **97,96,96,92,88 87,72,71,67,**
CSF £132.42 CT £911.26 TOTE £15.20: £2.50, £2.50, £2.10; EX 121.30 Trifecta £482.00.
Owner The Ormello Way **Bred** Heather Raw **Trained** Arlary, Perth & Kinross
■ Stewards' Enquiry : Peter Buchanan two-day ban: careless riding (3-5 Dec)

FOCUS
Race increased by about 216yds. They went a fair gallop in this competitive handicap and the principals fought out a messy finish. Small step ups from the first two, with the third to his best.

2595 PHS BESAFE ARC SOLUTION H'CAP HURDLE (10 hdls) 2m 4f 139y
2:40 (2:42) (Class 4) (0-115,114) 3-Y-0+ **£3,898** (£1,144; £572; £286)

Form RPR

2-33 **1** **Calin Du Brizais (FR)**22 2139 4-10-13 **101**..........(t) TomScudamore 110+
(Nigel Hawke) *trckd ldrs: cl 2nd appr 2 out: led and hit last: drvn out* **11/2**3

0-P3 **2** *2 ¼* **Vaillant Creek (FR)**14 2301 6-11-8 **110**..........KielanWoods 116
(Alex Hales) *led to bef 3rd: hdd bef 3rd: led bef 2 out: hdd narrowly last: styd on same pce last 200yds* **8/1**

3-20 **3** *10* **Chantara Rose**52 1675 6-11-5 **107**..........(p) SeanBowen 104
(Peter Bowen) *t.k.h in rr: hit 3rd: hdwy to trck ldrs 5th: outpcd next: hdwy 3 out: kpt on one pce to take modest 3rd clsng stages* **14/1**

1102 **4** *½* **Perseid (IRE)**21 2142 5-11-0 **102**..........SeanQuinlan 100
(Sue Smith) *chsd ldrs: pushed along 6th: handy 3rd whn hit 2 out: wknd fnl 50yds* **4/1**2

4-65 **5** *4* **Kamool (GER)**15 2271 5-11-12 **114**..........RichardJohnson 108
(Jonjo O'Neill) *chsd ldrs: drvn 3 out: one pce appr next* **17/2**

0-52 **6** *4 ½* **Silver Shuffle (IRE)**25 2085 8-10-13 **104**..........EmmaSayer(3) 96
(Dianne Sayer) *nt fluentm sn detached in last: sme hdwy 2 out: nvr on terms* **8/1**

P2F2 **7** *8* **Lily Little Legs (IRE)**33 1971 6-11-0 **102**..........BrianHughes 84
(Mike Sowersby) *in rr: chsd ldrs 5th: lost pl bef 2 out* **20/1**

6/ **8** *2 ½* **Easter Hunt (IRE)**98 1249 6-11-3 **110**..........(t) NathanMoscrop(5) 91
(Sara Ender) *w ldr: led bef 3rd: hdd bef 2 out: wknd rapidly between last 2* **25/1**

2-2P **9** *7* **Knight Bachelor**170 593 5-11-11 **113**..........GavinSheehan 96
(Warren Greatrex) *chsd ldrs: drvn 7th: outpcd 2 out: sn wknd: eased in clsng stages* **3/1**1

-0P0 **P** **Come On Sunshine**45 1794 4-10-7 **100**..........(tp) CraigGallagher(5)
(Brian Ellison) *chsd ldrs: drvn 4th: sn lost pl: bhd and reminders next next: t.o 7th: p.u bef next* **16/1**

5m 31.0s (22.20) **Going Correction** +0.70s/f (Soft)
WFA 4 from 5yo+ 8lb **10 Ran SP% 114.3**
Speed ratings (Par 105): **85,84,80,80,78 76,73,72,70,**
CSF £47.97 CT £581.96 TOTE £7.10: £2.40, £3.00, £3.60; EX 56.50 Trifecta £514.60.
Owner Pearce Bros Partnership **Bred** E A R L Haras De Magouet **Trained** Stoodleigh, Devon

FOCUS
Race increased by about 216yds. Not many landed a serious blow in this ordinary handicap. There's a case for rating this a few pounds higher through the third and fourth, but not on time compared with the previous handicap.

2596 PHS BESAFE H'CAP CHASE (14 fncs) 2m 3f 34y
3:10 (3:12) (Class 5) (0-100,100) 4-Y-0+ **£2,924** (£858; £429; £214)

Form RPR

45-3 **1** **Fly Home Harry**21 2143 6-11-2 **90**..........PaulMoloney 95
(Alan Swinbank) *trckd ldrs 7th: 2nd 10th: drvn and 6 l down 3 out: styd on run-in: led in clsng stages* **2/1**2

13-5 **2** *½* **Pembroke House**203 43 8-11-9 **100**..........(p) JamesBanks(3) 106+
(Sarah-Jayne Davies) *t.k.h: 2nd 3rd: led bef 9th: hit 2 out: 4 l ahd last: no ex and hdd in clsng stages* **8/1**3

0-0P **3** *3 ¾* **Vent Nivernais (FR)**17 2248 6-10-1 **82**..........(b) CharlieHammond(7) 85
(James Evans) *chsd ldrs: pushed along 8th: reminders 10th: kpt on same pce fr 2 out* **8/1**3

-P52 **4** *18* **Ride On Time (IRE)**14 2290 5-11-9 **100**..........MauriceLinehan(3) 88
(Ben Pauling) *led: reminders bef 8th: hdd bef 9th: lost pl 10th: sn bhd* **11/10**1

-2P0 **U** **Whatsupjack (IRE)**176 502 8-10-2 **79**..........(b) JonathanEngland(3)
(Shaun Harris) *detached in last: pushed along 5th: reminders 7th: mstke and uns rdr next* **16/1**

5m 22.6s (16.90) **Going Correction** +0.70s/f (Soft) **5 Ran SP% 109.1**
Speed ratings (Par 103): **92,91,90,82,**
CSF £15.62 TOTE £2.80: £1.60, £2.10; EX 12.20 Trifecta £44.40.
Owner Mrs J M Penney **Bred** Miss S R Haynes **Trained** Melsonby, N Yorks

FOCUS
Race increased by about 150yds. This weak handicap saw changing fortunes on the run-in. The winner is a 100+ hurdler and there's a case for rating this higher through the third.

2597 PHS BESAFE STANDARD OPEN NATIONAL HUNT FLAT RACE 2m 148y
3:40 (3:43) (Class 6) 4-6-Y-O **£1,642** (£478; £239)

Form RPR

1 **Keeper Hill (IRE)** 4-11-2 0..........AndrewTinkler 115+
(Ronald O'Leary, Ire) *mid-div: trcking ldrs after 6f: led 3f out: rdn over 1f out: styd on wl* **5/4**1

2 *6* **Scarteen (IRE)** 5-11-2 0..........BrianHughes 110+
(John Ferguson) *trckd ldrs: cl 2nd over 2f out: kpt on same pce appr fnl f* **7/2**2

3 *11* **Nobel Leader (IRE)**186 5-11-2 0..........LiamTreadwell 100
(James Evans) *led after 1f: t.k.h: hdd 3f out: fdd over 1f out* **7/1**3

2-2 **4** *8* **Our Three Sons (IRE)**169 602 4-11-2 0..........BrendanPowell 93
(Jamie Snowden) *mid-div: drvn to chse ldrs over 4f out: outpcd over 3f out: lost pl over 2f out* **12/1**

4-00 **5** *6* **Hey Up Ashey**28 2044 5-11-2 0..........KielanWoods 87
(Michael Mullineaux) *led 1f: trckd ldrs: drvn over 3f out: outpcd over 2f out: sn edgd lft and lost pl* **100/1**

45- **6** *12* **Infinityandbeyond (IRE)**210 5501 4-11-2 0..........TrevorWhelan 76
(Neil King) *trckd ldrs on outside: drvn over 4f out: sn lost pl* **8/1**

22-2 **7** *18* **Sand Blast**13 2330 4-10-11 0..........(t) CraigGallagher(5) 60
(Brian Ellison) *trckd ldrs: drvn 5f out: outpcd over 3f out: lost pl over 2f out: sn bhd* **7/1**3

6- **8** *23* **Five For Fifteen (IRE)**351 2881 6-10-11 0..........JamesCowley(5) 39
(Donald McCain) *hld up in rr: drvn 6f out: sn bhd: t.o 4f out* **40/1**

9 *3 ¾* **Airebridge (IRE)** 4-10-11 0..........HarryBannister(5) 36
(Michael Easterby) *in rr: pushed along after 6f: sn bhd: t.o over 4f out* **100/1**

0 **10** *dist* **Badger Run (IRE)**41 1843 4-11-2 0..........LeightonAspell
(Pat Murphy) *in rr: drvn 7f out: sn bhd: t.o 6f out: virtually p.u over 2f out: eventually completed* **100/1**

4m 14.2s (13.10) **Going Correction** +0.775s/f (Soft)
WFA 4 from 5yo+ 7lb **10 Ran SP% 115.9**
Speed ratings: **100,97,92,88,85 79,71,60,58,**
CSF £5.51 TOTE £2.60: £1.10, £1.60, £2.80; EX 7.40 Trifecta £36.40.
Owner Mrs Ronald O'Leary **Bred** Mrs Sharon Ryan **Trained** Killaloe, Co. Clare

FOCUS
Race increased by about 150yds. The winner looks above average and the fourth and fifth help set the level.
T/Plt: £176.30 to a £1 stake. Pool of £62041.81 - 256.76 winning tickets. T/Qpdt: £54.40 to a £1 stake. Pool of £5594.68 - 76.08 winning tickets. **Walter Glynn**

2345 WINCANTON (R-H)
Thursday, November 19

OFFICIAL GOING: Heavy (soft in places: chs; 5.7, hdl; 6.0)
Wind: mild breeze across Weather: light rain, clearing

2598 WINCANTON INTERACTIVE H'CAP CHASE (22 fncs) 3m 2f 162y
12:50 (12:50) (Class 4) (0-110,108) 4-Y-0+ **£3,768** (£1,106; £553; £276)

Form RPR

-312 **1** **Distracted (IRE)**10 2403 7-11-5 108..........(p) CiaranGethings(7) 116+
(Robert Stephens) *j.lft most of way: trckd ldr: led after 9th: mde rest: hit 15th: styd on wl fr 3 out: rdn out* **11/4**2

F-U5 **2** *5* **Market Option (IRE)**21 2149 9-11-5 104..........CallumWhillans(3) 109+
(Venetia Williams) *trckd ldrs: hit 8th: chsd wnr after 16th tl rdn appr 3 out: regained 2nd after 2 out: styd on same pce* **7/1**

60-2 **3** *1 ¼* **Somerset Lias (IRE)**36 1906 7-11-11 107..........LiamHeard 109
(Bob Buckler) *hld up: cl 3rd whn hit 17th: rdn to chse wnr after 4 out tl mstke 2 out: styd on same pce* **5/1**

233- **4** *40* **Armedanddangerous (IRE)**229 5134 10-10-6 88..........(b) NicodeBoinville 47
(Tom Gretton) *led: rchd for 9th: sn hdd: chsd wnr tl 15th: sn wknd: t.o* **9/4**1

2653 **F** **I'm In Charge**7 2454 9-11-12 108..........(t) NickScholfield
(Grant Cann) *hld up: fell 7th* **9/2**3

2U-U **P** **Ethelred (IRE)**41 1842 7-11-5 101..........(tp) DarylJacob
(Jamie Snowden) *trckd ldrs: j.lft 11th: sn struggling and detached: tailing off whn p.u bef 14th* **16/1**

7m 28.3s (20.10) **Going Correction** +0.85s/f (Soft) **6 Ran SP% 110.7**
Speed ratings (Par 105): **104,102,102,90,**
CSF £20.28 TOTE £2.60: £1.70, £3.30; EX 22.20 Trifecta £93.90.
Owner Alan Roberts **Bred** William Neville **Trained** Penhow, Newport

FOCUS
The going was heavy, soft in places. All bends were moved out two yards. The distance of the first race was increased by 27 yards. This opening handicap looked competitive and the winner battled well to hold off the placed horses, who were a long way clear of the fourth. This was a step up from the winner.

2599 RACINGUK.COM FREE TRIAL H'CAP HURDLE (10 hdls) 2m 3f 166y
1:20 (1:20) (Class 5) (0-100,100) 3-Y-0+ **£2,599** (£763; £381; £190)

Form RPR

/101 **1** **Duke's Affair**35 1933 7-11-2 **93**..........MattGriffiths(3) 105+
(Jeremy Scott) *mid-div: hdwy after 6th: chal after 3 out: led 2 out: mstke last: drvn whn idled run-in: styd on to assert again towards fin* **11/2**3

4352 **2** *1* **Very Intense (IRE)**7 2454 4-11-1 **96**..........DavidNoonan(7) 106+
(Tom Lacey) *in tch: tk clsr order 5th: led narrowly after 3 out tl mstke next: sn rdn: flattered briefly whn wnr idled run-in: no ex nring fin* **6/5**1

530 **3** *18* **Thepartysover**[156] 750 10-11-10 **98**................................(t) TomO'Brien 90
(Paul Henderson) *hld up: hdwy fr 6th: rdn to dispute hld 3rd fr next: sn outpcd* **33/1**

0005 **4** *3¼* **Sun Quest**[33] 1980 11-9-10 **77** oh7 ow3.................... MissTWorsley(7) 66
(Steven Dixon) *led tl after 2nd: chsd ldrs: rdn to chse ldng pair after 3 out: one pce fr next* **40/1**

6545 **5** *8* **Tenby Jewel (IRE)**[15] 2264 10-10-3 **77**..........................(tp) TomCannon 58
(Mark Gillard) *trckd ldrs: led after 6th: rdn and hdd after 3 out: wknd bef next* **14/1**

3PP **6** *12* **Positive Vibes**[16] 2263 6-11-0 **88**................................(p) ConorO'Farrell 62
(Richard Woollacott) *hld up: hdwy after 7th: rdn to dispute hld 3rd briefly bef 2 out: wknd bef last* **33/1**

4215 **7** *18* **Shot In The Dark (IRE)**[123] 1055 6-11-12 **100**....................(p) MarkGrant 51
(Jonathan Geake) *chsd ldrs tl after 6th: sn wknd: t.o* **20/1**

460- **P** **Fintan**[424] 1592 12-11-9 **97**.. MarcGoldstein
(Sheena West) *racd keenly: led after 2nd tl rchd for 6th: wknd rapidly: t.o whn p.u after 3 out* **9/4**[2]

3230 **P** **Taste The Wine (IRE)**[15] 2264 9-11-1 **96**..............(tp) JordanWilliams(7)
(Bernard Llewellyn) *hld up: nvr threatened: wknd after 7th: t.o whn p.u bef 2 out* **25/1**

2350 **P** **Spin Cast**[62] 1578 7-10-12 **93**..............................(t) ThomasCheesman(7)
(Laura Young) *a towards rr: struggling after 4th: t.o whn p.u bef 2 out* **33/1**

0630 **P** **Watchmetail (IRE)**[17] 2256 9-10-0 **74** oh10........................ JamieMoore
(John Panvert) *in tch: rdn after 5th: wknd 7th: t.o whn p.u bef 3 out* **66/1**

5m 3.8s (303.80)
WFA 4 from 6yo+ 8lb **11** Ran SP% **119.6**
CSF £12.43 CT £208.11 TOTE £5.20: £1.80, £1.20, £5.60; EX 16.20 Trifecta £217.80.
Owner Mrs Helen L Stoneman **Bred** Mrs J Munnis And Mrs E Hockenhull **Trained** Brompton Regis, Somerset

FOCUS
Race over 18yds further than advertised. The first two pulled clear in this handicap and the big gamble of the race failed to complete. The winner built on his good recent win.

2600 HAGUE PRINT MANAGEMENT H'CAP HURDLE (10 hdls) 2m 3f 166y
1:50 (1:50) (Class 3) (0-135,134) 3-Y-£7,596 (£2,244; £1,122; £561; £280)

Form RPR

0-13 **1** **San Benedeto (FR)**[32] 1986 4-11-8 **130**...............(t) SamTwiston-Davies 140+
(Paul Nicholls) *trckd ldr in chsng gp: hdwy into 2nd appr 2 out: led gng wl bef last where mstke: easily* **7/2**[2]

1005 **2** *5* **Benbecula**[25] 2093 6-10-4 **115**......................................(b) TomBellamy(3) 115
(Richard Mitchell) *trckd ldr clr of rest of field: led appr 2 out: rdn whn hdd bef last: styd on but sn no ch w wnr* **20/1**

205- **3** *5* **Winning Spark (USA)**[248] 4819 8-10-7 **115**........................ JamesBest 110
(Jackie Du Plessis) *hld up: hdwy after 3 out: disp 3rd next: sn rdn: styd on same pce* **14/1**

1-41 **4** *nse* **Shuil Royale (IRE)**[144] 855 10-11-12 **134**...........................(t) NoelFehily 129
(Harry Fry) *led chsng gp: hdwy after 3 out: rdn whn sltly hmpd next: styd on same pce* **6/1**

4UP- **5** *12* **Knight Of Pleasure**[264] 4498 6-11-2 **124**.......................(p) JoshuaMoore 107
(Gary Moore) *hld up: hdwy 3 out: effrt bef next: nvr threatened: wknd bef last* **17/2**

060- **6** *½* **Rebeccas Choice (IRE)**[227] 5184 12-10-10 **118**............. RobertDunne 100
(Dai Burchell) *hld up: sme late prog: nvr trbld ldrs* **40/1**

135- **7** *1* **Miles To Memphis (IRE)**[342] 3058 6-10-12 **120**........ WayneHutchinson 101
(Alan King) *trckd ldrs in chsng gp: tk clsr order after 3 out: effrt next: wknd bef last* **2/1**[1]

2060 **8** *2¾* **Byron Blue (IRE)**[12] 2350 6-11-1 **123**..............................(t) TomCannon 107+
(Mark Gillard) *j. bdly lft thrght: led: clr w one other: nt fluent 7th: blnd next: hdd appr 2 out: wknd bef last* **20/1**

006- **9** *79* **Landscape (FR)**[246] 4849 7-10-6 **114**............................ MattieBatchelor 14
(Sheena West) *a towards rr: wknd after 7th: t.o* **9/2**[3]

5m 2.7s (302.70)
WFA 4 from 6yo+ 8lb **9** Ran SP% **117.2**
CSF £67.25 CT £880.91 TOTE £4.20: £1.80, £3.70, £2.30; EX 44.40 Trifecta £428.10.
Owner P J Vogt **Bred** E A R L Ecurie Haras Du Cadran Et Al **Trained** Ditcheat, Somerset

FOCUS
Race over 18yds further than advertised. They went a decent pace and the winner took a big step forward.

2601 MOSTLY MEDIA H'CAP CHASE (17 fncs) 2m 4f 35y
2:25 (2:25) (Class 4) (0-110,104) 4-Y-0+ £5,991 (£1,860; £1,001)

Form RPR

32-3 **1** **Alder Mairi (IRE)**[199] 107 8-11-12 **104**........................ AndrewThornton 120+
(Seamus Mullins) *trckd ldr: led 7th: stirrup leather broke appr 4 out where awkward: styd on wl and in command fr next* **4/5**[1]

64F2 **2** *17* **Treacy Hotels Boy (IRE)**[13] 2315 8-11-6 **98**........................ TomO'Brien 94
(Paul Henderson) *trckd ldrs: trckd wnr appr 4 out: rdn bef 3 out: sn hld* **7/2**[2]

2P3- **3** *32* **The Sneezer (IRE)**[276] 4276 12-11-6 **103**..................[1] CharlieDeutsch(5) 67
(Nikki Evans) *led tl 7th: rdn after 13th: sn wknd: t.o* **12/1**

1-5P **P** **Lamb's Cross**[12] 2346 9-10-9 **87**..................................(p) TomCannon
(Mark Gillard) *trckd ldrs: mstke 12th: rdn after next: wknd 4 out: t.o whn p.u bef 3 out* **10/1**

66/F **U** **Twyford**[29] 2017 8-10-7 **85**.. RobertDunne
(Laura Young) *hld up: mstke 1st: rdn after 13th: wkng whn blnd and uns rdr next* **6/1**[3]

5m 39.3s (21.80) **Going Correction** +1.175s/f (Heav) **5** Ran SP% **108.8**
Speed ratings (Par 105): **103,96,83, ,**
CSF £4.09 TOTE £1.80: £1.10, £2.30; EX 3.90 Trifecta £12.60.
Owner F G Matthews **Bred** Alan Inglis **Trained** Wilsford-Cum-Lake, Wilts

FOCUS
Race over 18yds further than advertised. The winner had some equipment problems late on but still managed to justify strong support with stacks in hand under a good ride. There's a case for rating this a few pounds higher through the second.

2602 EBF & TBA MARES' NOVICES' CHASE (17 fncs) 2m 4f 35y
3:00 (3:00) (Class 3) 4-Y-0+ £6,975 (£2,385)

Form RPR

1P-2 **1** **Cresswell Breeze**[13] 2313 5-10-7 0...........................(t) DavidNoonan(7) 137+
(Anthony Honeyball) *trckd ldr: j.lft most of way: led after 4th: wl in control fr 4 out: easily* **2/1**[2]

63-0 **2** *19* **Pass The Time**[201] 93 6-11-0 0..............................(p) MarkQuinlan 122+
(Neil Mulholland) *trckd ldrs: j. bdly lft and nvr that fluent: lft 2nd 11th: wl hld fr 4 out: j. v bdly lft last 3* **9/1**[3]

43-1 **U** **Blue Buttons (IRE)**[19] 2199 7-11-0 0..................................(t) NoelFehily
(Harry Fry) *led: veered rt 4th: sn hdd: trcking wnr whn blnd and uns rdr 11th* **8/13**[1]

5m 39.3s (21.80) **Going Correction** +1.175s/f (Heav) **3** Ran SP% **105.3**
Speed ratings (Par 107): **103,95,**
CSF £10.45 TOTE £3.00; EX 7.80 Trifecta £11.50.
Owner Bright N Breezy **Bred** R B McKay **Trained** Mosterton, Dorset

FOCUS
Race over 18yds further than advertised. The winner jumped much better than her two rivals and was in control a long way out in this mares' novice, but this isn't a race to be confident about.

2603 LENNY ROBERTS MEMORIAL TROPHY NOVICES' HURDLE (10 hdls 1 omitted) 2m 5f 82y
3:30 (3:30) (Class 4) 4-Y-0+ £4,548 (£1,335; £667; £333)

Form RPR

2P-2 **1** **Final Nudge (IRE)**[14] 2287 6-10-12 120..................... WayneHutchinson 128+
(David Dennis) *trckd ldrs: led appr 2 out: sn in command: hit last: readily* **7/4**[1]

10-2 **2** *7* **Present Man (IRE)**[25] 2088 5-10-12 0...............(t) SamTwiston-Davies 119
(Paul Nicholls) *trckd ldrs: nt fluent 1st: wnt 2nd after 5th: led briefly appr 2 out: sn rdn and hld: styd on same pce* **15/8**[2]

3 *7* **Whataknight**[172] 6-10-12 0..(t) NoelFehily 113+
(Harry Fry) *mid-div: stdy hdwy after 3 out: rdn bef next: styd on to go 3rd run-in nvr gng pce to rch front pair* **7/2**[3]

65-0 **4** *1½* **Auckland De Re (FR)**[17] 2239 5-10-12 0........................ DarylJacob 110
(Neil Mulholland) *led: racd keenly: rdn and hdd appr 2 out: sn hld: edgd lft bef last: no ex run-in* **33/1**

45 **5** *10* **Mountain Eagle (IRE)**[17] 2239 6-10-5 0..................(t[1]) LiamMcKenna(7) 102+
(Harry Fry) *racd keenly: hld up towards rr: rdn and stdy prog fr after 3 out but no threat to ldrs* **16/1**

F **6** *18* **Gala Ball (IRE)**[16] 2257 5-10-12 0.................................... TomO'Brien 82
(Philip Hobbs) *mid-div: hdwy 3 out: rdn to chse ldrs sn after: wknd 2 out* **10/1**

3-6P **7** *1¼* **Motts Cross (IRE)**[16] 2257 4-10-12 0............................. JamesDavies 81
(Chris Down) *mid-div: rdn after 7th: wknd after next* **66/1**

40-0 **8** *28* **Windy Writer (IRE)**[26] 2065 5-10-12 0........................... PeterCarberry 53
(Shaun Lycett) *trckd ldr tl after 5th: mstke 3 out: sn wknd: t.o* **100/1**

9 *3¼* **Trehan Cross**[193] 6-10-5 0.. JamesBest 43
(Jackie Du Plessis) *a towards rr: t.o after 3 out* **100/1**

3/00 **10** *68* **Heartening**[14] 2302 7-10-5 0... DaveCrosse
(Paul Phillips) *a towards rr: t.o 3 out* **250/1**

P **Shift It Franklin**[613] 6-10-5 0... MrNLawton(7)
(Philip Hobbs) *mid-div: rdn appr 3 out: sn wknd: t.o whn p.u bef 2 out* **66/1**

0 **P** **Gustav (IRE)**[28] 2044 5-10-12 0.. NicodeBoinville
(Simon Earle) *a towards rr: t.o whn p.u after 3 out* **100/1**

5m 29.5s (3.00) **Going Correction** +0.45s/f (Soft) **12** Ran SP% **117.6**
Speed ratings (Par 105): **112,109,106,106,102 95,94,84,83,57 ,**
CSF £5.40 TOTE £2.60: £1.20, £1.20, £1.70; EX 5.50 Trifecta £12.10.
Owner Corbett Stud **Bred** M W And Mrs M Doran **Trained** Hanley Swan, Worcestershire

FOCUS
Race over 18yds further than advertised. There didn't seem to be much strength in depth in this novice hurdle but the two leading contenders filled the first two places. This was a step up from the cosy winner.

2604 WINCANTON RACING EXCELLENCE "HANDS AND HEELS" NOVICES' H'CAP HURDLE (CONDITIONAL/AMATEURS) (8 hdls) 1m 7f 65y
4:00 (4:00) (Class 4) (0-105,103) 3-Y-0+ £3,898 (£1,144; £572; £286)

Form RPR

-301 **1** **Hope's Wishes**[84] 1384 5-11-12 **103**.................................. HarryCobden 103+
(Barry Brennan) *sn trcking ldrs: chal 2 out: led sn after last: kpt on: pushed out* **11/4**[2]

-PP6 **2** *¾* **Columbanus (IRE)**[33] 1980 4-9-11 **77** oh7...........(t) MissNatalieParker(3) 77+
(Kevin Bishop) *hld up: hdwy 4th: led appr 2 out: slt ld whn mstke last: sn hdd: kpt on: hld towards fin* **12/1**

0-0P **3** *12* **John Biscuit (IRE)**[172] 569 7-10-10 **90**........................ ArchieBellamy(3) 79
(Jo Davis) *disp fr after 2nd tl rdn appr 2 out where remained w ev ch: fading in 3rd whn mstke last* **9/2**[3]

234P **4** *10* **Alottarain (IRE)**[25] 2088 5-11-5 **101**.............................. MrDSansom(5) 78
(Seamus Mullins) *hld up: hdwy 4th: effrt appr 2 out: wnt hld 4th between last 2* **12/1**

/4-5 **5** *9* **Ma'ire Rua (IRE)**[25] 2091 8-11-12 **103**.............................. DavidNoonan 71
(Alan Jones) *j.lft: led: jnd after 2nd: rdn and hdd appr 3 out: sn wknd* **9/4**[1]

0P0P **6** *nse* **Merry Mast (USA)**[89] 1323 6-9-11 **79**........................ MrBParis-Crofts(5) 47
(Paul Henderson) *a towards rr* **25/1**

5/P5 **7** *nk* **Rachael's Ruby**[17] 2244 8-10-3 **85**..............................(p) HarryTeal(5) 53
(Roger Teal) *trckd ldrs: rdn appr 2 out: sn wknd* **16/1**

P0-0 **8** *87* **Actonetaketwo**[16] 2258 5-10-4 **81**.............................. LiamMcKenna
(Ron Hodges) *in tch tl 4th: sn struggling in last: t.o after 3 out* **25/1**

03-P **P** **Loukhaar (IRE)**[199] 102 7-11-4 **98**.............................. MissKatyLyons(3)
(Jonathan Geake) *mid-div: nt fluent 3rd: rdn after next: wknd after 3 out: p.u bef next* **9/1**

3m 54.3s (5.40) **Going Correction** +0.45s/f (Soft) **9** Ran SP% **114.6**
Speed ratings (Par 105): **103,102,96,90,86 86,85,39,**
CSF £34.61 CT £141.56 TOTE £3.40: £1.50, £2.90, £1.40; EX 38.50 Trifecta £218.20.
Owner M J Hills **Bred** Edward Spurrier **Trained** Upper Lambourn, Berks

FOCUS
Race over 12yds further than advertised distance. The first two had a good battle and pulled clear in this minor handicap. This was a step up from the winner, with the third close to his mark.
T/Plt: £38.70 to a £1 stake. Pool of £50053.99 - 942.61 winning tickets. T/Qpdt: £14.20 to a £1 stake. Pool of £3819.86 - 198.85 winning tickets. **Tim Mitchell**

2605 - (Foreign Racing) - See Raceform Interactive

2305 THURLES (R-H)

Thursday, November 19

OFFICIAL GOING: Soft (soft to heavy in places)

2606a BOOMERANG ANIMAL BEDDING AND BOOMERANG HORSE & COUNTRY STORE CHASE (LISTED RACE) (15 fncs) 2m 6f

12:55 (12:55) 5-Y-O+ £13,100 (£3,829; £1,813; £604)

RPR

1 **Sir Des Champs (FR)**691 3376 9-11-0 0 BJCooper 158+
(W P Mullins, Ire) *hld up bhd ldrs in 4th: lft mod 3rd at 9th: pushed along and impr into mod 2nd 2 out: hdwy gng best between last 2 to ld travelling wl bef last: eased clr run-in: nt extended* 11/10[1]

2 2 3/4 **Rubi Light (FR)**204 24 10-11-7 145 (t) AELynch 155
(Robert Alan Hennessy, Ire) *attempted to make all: wl clr at 1/2-way: stl wl clr whn bad mstke 5 out: reduced advantage fr 2 out and hdd u.p bef last: no ch w wnr: kpt on same pce run-in* 12/1

3 12 **Lyreen Legend (IRE)**568 25 8-11-0 152 BarryGeraghty 136
(Ms Sandra Hughes, Ire) *towards rr: nt fluent 6th: lft mod 4th at 9th where sltly hmpd by faller: slt mstke 4 out: rdn 2 out and no imp on ldrs: kpt on fr last where slt mstke into mod 3rd run-in: nvr trbld ldrs* 7/1[3]

4 1 1/2 **Letter Of Credit (IRE)**11 2381 10-11-4 139 PhillipEnright 139
(James Joseph Mangan, Ire) *settled in rr: nt fluent 4th: no imp stl in rr bef 2 out: sn rdn and kpt on u.p fr last into mod 4th cl home: nvr trbld ldrs* 25/1

5 1/2 **Maggio (FR)**25 2082 10-11-4 140 (t) JJBurke 139
(Patrick Griffin, Ire) *settled bhd ldr in 2nd: slt mstke in mod 2nd at 9th: pushed along after 3 out and no imp on ldr bef next where dropped to mod 3rd: slt mstke at last and wknd to rr cl home* 12/1

F **Mala Beach (IRE)**325 3391 7-11-4 141 DavyRussell
(Gordon Elliott, Ire) *hld up bhd ldrs in 3rd: mod 3rd whn fell 9th* 9/4[2]

5m 51.2s (4.40) 6 Ran SP% 110.1
CSF £13.43 TOTE £2.10: £1.30, £3.70; DF 8.70 Trifecta £48.30.
Owner Gigginstown House Stud **Bred** Dominique Clayeux **Trained** Muine Beag, Co Carlow

FOCUS
A more than satisfactory return to action for the winner, strengthening the hand of trainer and owner in the staying chase division. None of these are solid on recent form, but the second is rated back to last year's best.

2607-2611a (Foreign Racing) - See Raceform Interactive

2182 ASCOT (R-H)

Friday, November 20

OFFICIAL GOING: Soft (good to soft in places; chs 6.7; hdl 7.0)
Wind: Light, across Weather: Fine

2612 GEOTECH SOIL STABILISATION "NATIONAL HUNT" MAIDEN HURDLE (10 hdls) 2m 3f 58y

1:00 (1:05) (Class 3) 4-Y-O+ £5,848 (£1,717; £858; £429)

Form RPR

1 **Krugermac (IRE)**202 97 4-11-0 0 JamieMoore 123+
(Gary Moore) *str: lw: hld up in tch: trckd ldrs 3 out: clsd gng strly fr 2 out: led last: pushed along and qckly drew clr* 9/4[2]

4-2 2 8 **He's A Charmer (IRE)**20 2188 5-11-0 0 (t) NoelFehily 113
(Harry Fry) *led: set modest pce to 7th: nt fluent 3 out: hrd pressed next: hdd last: kpt on but easily outpcd* 3/1[3]

3 1 **What's The Scoop (IRE)** 5-11-0 0 PeterCarberry 112
(Nicky Henderson) *q tall: cl up: disp 2nd pl fr 3 out: chal 2 out: rdn and outpcd last* 15/8[1]

0-20 4 nk **Vivas (FR)**27 2065 4-11-0 0 AidanColeman 111
(Charlie Longsdon) *cl up: disp 2nd pl fr 3 out: shkn up to chal 2 out: stdd into last and lost grnd: outpcd but kpt on flat* 13/2

24/6 5 15 **Max The Minister**40 1872 5-11-0 0 TomO'Brien 96
(Hughie Morrison) *hld up in tch: sltly outpcd 3 out: tried to cl on ldrs bef 2 out: sn shkn up and wknd* 25/1

20-5 6 3 3/4 **Heresmynumber (IRE)**23 2136 5-11-0 0 GavinSheehan 93
(Ali Stronge) *nt fluent: hld up in tch: mstke 4th: shkn up and wknd 3 out* 16/1

0/0- 7 nk **Pursuitofhappiness (IRE)**249 4813 7-11-0 0 MarkQuinlan 92
(Neil Mulholland) *hld up in tch: outpcd 3 out: shkn up bef 2 out: wknd* 100/1

6 8 1 1/2 **Artiste Du Gouet (FR)**9 2440 5-11-0 0 RichieMcLernon 90
(Heather Dalton) *trckd ldr tl nt fluent 3 out: sn wknd qckly* 100/1

4m 50.2s (5.50) **Going Correction** -0.10s/f (Good)
WFA 4 from 5yo+ 7lb 8 Ran SP% 115.6
Speed ratings (Par 107): **84,80,80,80,73 72,72,71**
CSF £9.82 TOTE £3.30: £1.10, £1.30, £1.20; EX 10.40 Trifecta £16.40.
Owner Mr Hinds & Galloping on the South Downs **Bred** Kenilworth House Stud **Trained** Lower Beeding, W Sussex

FOCUS
After a dry night the going remained soft, good to soft in places. Hurdle distances as advertised. Rail on chase course dolled out approximately 2yds at bends around Swinley Bottom and turning into the home straight. An interesting maiden hurdle to start, which has been won by the Grand National/Hennessy winner Many Clouds and the dual Grade 1 winner Beat That in the previous three years, and this year's winner was very impressive. The winning time was 22.2sec outside standard, suggesting soft ground, though the field did rather potter around for a circuit before the tempo increased. The front four pulled miles clear of the rest but this is probably not that strong form for Ascot.

2613 IRON STAND BEGINNERS' CHASE (AN ASCOT APPEARANCE MONEY SCHEME RACE) (16 fncs) 2m 2f 175y

1:30 (1:38) (Class 3) 4-Y-O+ £7,797 (£2,289; £1,144; £572)

Form RPR

1P6- 1 **Thomas Brown**224 5254 6-11-2 0 NoelFehily 144+
(Harry Fry) *lw: j. proficiently: mde all: jnd after 3 out: shkn up and forged clr after next: eased fnl 75yds* 8/13[1]

311- 2 9 **Bon Chic (IRE)**215 5408 6-10-9 0 RobertDunne 126
(Dan Skelton) *trckd ldng pair tl chsd wnr 12th: chal and upsides 3 out to next: sn brushed aside* 10/1[3]

11-U 3 1 1/4 **Remind Me Later (IRE)**189 317 6-11-2 0 JoshuaMoore 132
(Gary Moore) *hld up in detached last: lft bhd fr 12th: pushed along after 3 out: mstke 2 out: shkn up and styd on fr last to take 3rd flat: shaped w promise* 16/1

14-2 4 2 1/4 **El Namoose**19 2222 6-11-2 143 AidanColeman 131
(John Ferguson) *mostly chsd wnr tl lost 2nd pl and mstke 12th: nt fluent next and outpcd: tried to rally bef 2 out: sn no imp: lost 3rd after last* 9/4[2]

4m 53.1s (6.70) **Going Correction** +0.20s/f (Yiel) 4 Ran SP% 107.7
Speed ratings (Par 107): **93,89,88,87**
CSF £6.27 TOTE £1.60; EX 6.90 Trifecta £25.90.
Owner The Corse Lawners **Bred** Elms Stud Co Ltd **Trained** Seaborough, Dorset

FOCUS
Race distance increased by approximately 10yds. A small field for this beginners' chase and a two-horse race according to the market, but a fascinating contest nonetheless and despite the small field they went a good pace thanks to the impressive winner. He should rate higher over fences.

2614 ROBERT GILES AGENCIES INTRODUCTORY HURDLE (8 hdls) 1m 7f 152y

2:05 (2:11) (Class 3) 4-Y-O+ £7,147 (£2,098; £1,049; £524)

Form RPR

54-1 1 **Wishing And Hoping (IRE)**32 1998 5-11-5 0 WayneHutchinson 120
(Alan King) *trckd ldr: stl to be asked for an effrt and cl up whn lft in ld 2 out: hrd pressed fr last: drvn out and styd on wl* 4/1[2]

2 1/2 **Clayton**553 6-11-0 0 JoshuaMoore 114
(Gary Moore) *plld hrd early: hld up in 4th: trckd ldng pair after 5th: lft 2nd 2 out: rdn to chal last: styd on but hung lft and nt qckn nr fin* 8/1[3]

1125 3 7 **Brave Richard (IRE)**11 2406 4-11-0 0 RichardJohnson 108
(J R Jenkins) *hld up in last: pushed along and prog whn lft 3rd 2 out: hanging rt bef last where j.rt: shkn up and one pce* 14/1

4 4 5 **My Anchor**18 2238 4-11-0 0 GavinSheehan 102
(Charlie Mann) *trckd ldng pair to after 5th: stl wl in tch bef 2 out: shkn up and sn lft bhd* 66/1

5 20 **Tilstarr (IRE)**45 5-10-7 0 LeightonAspell 75
(Roger Teal) *j.rt: hld up in last pair: in tch tl jst bef 2 out: sn lft bhd: nudged along and wknd* 100/1

1- F **Kilcrea Vale (IRE)**309 3690 5-11-5 147 JeremiahMcGrath 120+
(Nicky Henderson) *sltly on toes: a bit free to post: chsg type: led at modest pce but untrbld: stl to be asked for a real effrt and narrow ld whn fell 2 out* 1/3[1]

3m 52.3s (4.90) **Going Correction** -0.10s/f (Good)
WFA 4 from 5yo+ 7lb 6 Ran SP% 115.3
Speed ratings (Par 107): **83,82,79,76,66**
CSF £33.71 TOTE £5.20: £1.90, £3.10; EX 28.20 Trifecta £86.30.
Owner Mrs Peter Andrews **Bred** Brendan Murphy **Trained** Barbury Castle, Wilts

FOCUS
This introductory hurdle has gone to some smart types in the last ten years, including the Grade 1-winning hurdler Irving in 2013. Following a ragged start for this year's renewal, the pace was very slow and the tempo had only just started to increase when the shape of the race changed completely at the second-last flight. The winner improved on his best bumper form.

2615 WINKWORTH H'CAP CHASE (17 fncs) 2m 5f 8y

2:40 (2:45) (Class 3) (0-140,139) 4-Y-O+£16,245 (£4,770; £2,385; £1,192)

Form RPR

604- 1 **Tenor Nivernais (FR)**230 5141 8-11-5 132 AidanColeman 156+
(Venetia Williams) *trckd ldng pair: produced to ld 2 out: immediately drew rt away fr exhausted rivals* 9/4[1]

5-3P 2 27 **Garrahalish (IRE)**41 1849 7-11-0 127 CharliePoste 125
(Robin Dickin) *led: hdd and drvn 4 out: rallied after next and tried to chal 2 out: sn btn and v tired* 7/2[3]

52-P 3 4 1/2 **Fairy Rath (IRE)**34 1976 9-11-5 132 (t) TomCannon 125
(Nick Gifford) *trckd ldr: led 4 out gng wl: rdn and hdd 2 out: immediately btn and v tired: lost remote 2nd last* 11/1

60P- 4 hd **Ballinvarrig (IRE)**237 5026 8-11-2 129 PaddyBrennan 123
(Tom George) *in tch: mstke 11th: rdn 4 out: one pce bef 2 out: tired after but nrly snatched 3rd* 10/3[2]

20/1 5 32 **Squire Trelawney**26 2090 9-10-1 114 (tp) RyanMahon 93
(Dan Skelton) *in tch: mstke 6th: blnd 9th and sn rdn: nt fluent 12th and lost tch: t.o* 7/1

6-41 P **Back To Bracka (IRE)**20 2192 8-11-3 133 DerekFox(3)
(Lucinda Russell) *lw: nvr gng that wl of jumping w any great fluency: a in last: struggling fr 9th: t.o 12th: p.u bef 2 out* 11/2

5m 20.1s (-5.90) **Going Correction** +0.20s/f (Yiel) 6 Ran SP% 112.3
Speed ratings (Par 107): **119,108,107,106,94**
CSF £10.80 TOTE £3.10: £1.80, £2.40; EX 11.10 Trifecta £62.40.
Owner Boultbee Brooks Ltd **Bred** Jean-Francois Iandiorio **Trained** Kings Caple, H'fords

FOCUS
Race distance increased by approximately 14yds. A decent handicap chase run at a good pace and apart from the easy winner they finished very tired. A big step up from the winner and the form could be rated 7lb+ higher.

2616 SPEY FROM SPEYSIDE DISTILLERY WHISKY H'CAP CHASE (20 fncs) 2m 7f 180y

3:15 (3:20) (Class 3) (0-135,132) 4-Y-O+£16,245 (£4,770; £2,385; £1,192)

Form RPR

300P 1 **Fruity O'Rooney**5 2517 12-11-0 120 (b) JamieMoore 126
(Gary Moore) *unable to ld and nt a fluent 1st circ: stl pressed ldr and chal fr 11th: j. bttr after and led 15th: drvn 2 out: hdd last and looked btn flat: given ch by ldr and rallied gamely to ld fnl stride* 14/1

3-2U 2 nse **Loose Chips**7 2471 9-11-10 130 (b) NoelFehily 138+
(Charlie Longsdon) *won battle for ld and set gd pce: pressed fr 11th: hdd 15th: rdn 3 out: rallied fr next to ld last: 2 l clr 75yds out: wavered nr fin and hdd fnl stride* 5/1[1]

-541 3 1 3/4 **Sands Cove (IRE)**15 2288 8-11-5 125 LeightonAspell 130
(James Evans) *patiently rdn in last trio: stdy prog fr 15th: rdn after 3 out: trying to cl whn bmpd 2 out: chsd ldng pair after: kpt on but unable to chal* 6/1[3]

13-P 4 2 **Desert Joe (IRE)**34 1970 9-11-5 125 WayneHutchinson 129
(Alan King) *in rr: mstke 4th and reminder: pushed up to go prom 10th: sn lost pl again: mstke 12th: struggling in last pair after: drvn 16th: styd on fr 2 out to take 4th flat* 11/2[2]

5 1 1/2 **Achille (FR)**148 5-11-8 128 LiamTreadwell 128
(Venetia Williams) *athletic: lw: wl in tch: trckd ldng pair 15th: rdn after 3 out: tried to cl next but lost 3rd and one pce after* 11/2[2]

P-31 6 11 **Bob Tucker (IRE)**37 1906 8-11-10 130 AidanColeman 120
(Charlie Longsdon) *lw: prom: chsd ldng pair 7th to 15th: rdn and in tch after 3 out: wknd next* 5/1[1]

136- **7** *6* **Financial Climate (IRE)**[219] 5340 8-11-3 **126**............ ThomasGarner(3) 113
(Oliver Sherwood) *chsd ldrs: shoved along after 10th: a flat out to keep in tch after: mstke 14th: btn in last pair after next* **10/1**

33-4 **P** **Arbeo (IRE)**[198] 149 9-10-4 **110**................................ MarcGoldstein
(Diana Grissell) *unable to ld: chsd ldng pair: nt fluent 4th: lost pl 7th: dropped to rr 10th and struggling bdly: t.o whn p.u bef 15th* **8/1**

P3P1 **P** **Caulfields Venture (IRE)**[31] 2008 9-11-12 **132**............(v) GavinSheehan
(Emma Lavelle) *j. slowly 6th and reminder in last: nvr gng wl after: lost tch 10th: t.o whn p.u bef 15th* **12/1**

6m 9.4s (5.90) **Going Correction** +0.20s/f (Yiel) **9** Ran SP% **112.9**
Speed ratings (Par 107): **98,97,97,96,96 92,90, ,**
CSF £81.78 CT £469.52 TOTE £15.60: £3.20, £2.00, £2.40; EX 73.40 Trifecta £504.90.
Owner Heart Of The South Racing **Bred** R W Russell **Trained** Lower Beeding, W Sussex

FOCUS
Race distance increased by approximately 14yds. A decent staying handicap chase and as exciting a spectacle as you will ever see. The first two dominated throughout and the result was still in doubt between the pair even after they had crossed the line. Fruity O'Rooney was a 145+ horse at his peak but this is probably as good as he is now.

2617 CANACCORD GENUITY H'CAP HURDLE (8 hdls) 1m 7f 152y
3:50 (3:53) (Class 2) (0-145,145) 4-Y-O+
£12,512 (£3,696; £1,848; £924; £462; £232)

Form RPR

01F- **1** **Winner Massagot (FR)**[225] 5236 4-10-4 **123**............ WayneHutchinson 132+
(Alan King) *lw: t.k.h: hld up and confidently rdn: prog 5th: trckd clr ldr 2 out: sn clsd: led after last: rdn clr fnl 150yds* **7/1**

0-03 **2** *2 ½* **Rayvin Black**[33] 1988 6-10-12 **134**...................... ThomasGarner(3) 138
(Oliver Sherwood) *lw: led at gd pce: pressed 3 out: kicked clr again and 4 l up 2 out: hdd sn after last: styd on but readily outpcd by wnr* **8/1**

40P- **3** *7* **Leviathan**[272] 4354 8-10-7 **126**................................ LiamTreadwell 124
(Venetia Williams) *chsd ldr tl after 4th: styd prom: hit 3 out: outpcd bef next: tk 3rd last: styd on* **16/1**

105- **4** *3 ½* **Three Kingdoms (IRE)**[225] 5235 6-11-12 **145**................. AidanColeman 140
(John Ferguson) *hld up: j. slowly 3rd: urged along after next and struggling: rallied bef 2 out: kpt on u.p flat* **17/2**

13-0 **5** *½* **Starluck (IRE)**[41] 1848 10-11-3 **136**............................ TomCannon 130
(David Arbuthnot) *trckd ldrs: effrt after 3 out: disp 2nd and rdn bef 2 out: fdd* **20/1**

3 **6** *3 ¾* **Forest Bihan (FR)**[20] 2194 4-11-7 **140**...................... RichardJohnson 133+
(Brian Ellison) *hld up in rr: sltly hmpd 4th: rdn bef next: rdn and no prog bef 2 out: one pce after* **13/2**[3]

5-15 **7** *2* **Cloonacool (IRE)**[20] 2186 6-11-3 **136**........................ JoshuaMoore 126
(Stuart Edmunds) *lw: trckd ldrs: wnt prom 3 out: chsd ldr briefly bef 2 out: sn wknd* **11/4**[1]

04-1 **8** *1* **War Singer (USA)**[16] 406 8-11-1 **134**........................(tp) NoelFehily 122
(Johnny Farrelly) *hld up in rr: stl in rr but in tch and gng strly whn short of room bnd bef 2 out: nudged along and no prog after: nvr involved* **25/1**

2-24 **9** *6* **Desert Recluse (IRE)**[50] 1719 8-10-3 **122**.................... JamesDavies 105
(Henry Oliver) *mstke 1st: a in rr: rdn after 4th: t.o 3 out: plugged on fr last* **10/1**

-341 **F** **Crickel Wood (FR)**[16] 2271 5-10-4 **123**......................(t) TomScudamore 106
(Charlie Longsdon) *lw: t.k.h: cl up: trckd ldr after 4th: hit next: lost 2nd bef 2 out and wkng qckly whn fell 2 out* **14/1**

4/22 **U** **Nesterenko (GER)**[34] 1977 6-10-13 **132**........................ NicodeBoinville
(Nicky Henderson) *prom tl mstke and uns rdr 4th* **6/1**[2]

3m 41.4s (-6.00) **Going Correction** -0.10s/f (Good)
WFA 4 from 5yo+ 7lb **11** Ran SP% **118.7**
Speed ratings (Par 109): **111,109,106,104,104 102,101,100,97,**
CSF £62.72 CT £873.78 TOTE £6.40: £2.40, £3.20, £5.20; EX 80.60 Trifecta £1459.20.
Owner Masterson Holdings Limited **Bred** Christian Baillet & Jean-Luc Terrieres **Trained** Barbury Castle, Wilts

FOCUS
A decent handicap hurdle and the pace was strong. The first two pulled well clear and Winner Massagot is on the upgrade.
T/Plt: £394.70 to a £1 stake. Pool: £87,352.18 - 161.55 winning tickets T/Qpdt: £115.20 to a £1 stake. Pool: £7,258.46 - 46.60 winning tickets **Jonathan Neesom**

2363 FFOS LAS (L-H)
Friday, November 20
2618 Meeting Abandoned - Waterlogged

196 HAYDOCK (L-H)
Friday, November 20

OFFICIAL GOING: Soft (heavy in places; 5.3)
Wind: Fairly strong Weather: Cold and Wet

2624 MONEY ADVICE GROUP H'CAP HURDLE (12 hdls) 2m 6f 177y
12:50 (12:51) (Class 3) (0-130,129) 4-Y-O+
£7,797 (£2,289; £1,144; £572)

Form RPR

1F-1 **1** **Island Heights (IRE)**[20] 2190 6-11-3 **125**.................... GrantCockburn(5) 132+
(Lucinda Russell) *mde most: blnd 2 out: drvn out and styd on wl* **9/2**[2]

-233 **2** *2* **Major Ivan (IRE)**[27] 2070 6-11-8 **125**......................(b[1]) BrianHughes 129
(Malcolm Jefferson) *trckd ldrs: mstke 4 out: wnt 2nd 2 out: rdn run-in: no imp on wnr* **12/1**

41-0 **3** *3 ¼* **Shades Of Midnight**[19] 2214 5-11-4 **124**...........(t) CallumWhillans(3) 124
(Donald Whillans) *hld up: mstke 2nd: hdwy into midfield 5th: rdn and outpcd after 4 out: prog after last: wnt 3rd fnl 175yds: styd on: nt trble front two* **7/1**[3]

3-11 **4** *4 ½* **Oscar Blue (IRE)**[27] 2070 5-11-8 **125**.......................... DannyCook 121
(Brian Ellison) *w wnr tl after 6th: continued to r in 2nd pl: rdn whn mstke 3 out: lost 2nd 2 out: no ex run-in: lost 3rd fnl 175yds* **7/1**[3]

45-0 **5** *1 ¾* **Charlie Cook (IRE)**[20] 2182 6-10-5 **108**........................ KielanWoods 102
(Graeme McPherson) *chsd ldrs: rdn and kpt on same pce fr 2 out* **100/1**

2U-2 **6** *nk* **Quel Elite (FR)**[195] 203 11-10-7 **113**........................ TonyKelly(3) 106
(James Moffatt) *hld up in rr: hdwy appr 4 out: rdn bef next: no imp after* **10/1**

14-1 **7** *¾* **Optimistic Bias (IRE)**[26] 2081 6-11-1 **125**.................. PatrickCowley(7) 119
(Jonjo O'Neill) *hld up: hdwy into midfield after 4 out: chsd ldrs appr 3 out: wl hld 2 out* **11/4**[1]

001/ **8** *28* **Hidden Justice (IRE)**[21] 4897 6-11-5 **129**...................... DeanPratt(7) 93
(John Quinn) *hld up in midfield: blnd 3 out: no imp after: wl btn* **15/2**

P426 **9** *13* **Fighter Jet**[28] 2054 7-11-3 **120**...................................(tp) HenryBrooke 71
(John Mackie) *midfield: rdn after 6th: lost pl: n.d after: t.o* **25/1**

-232 **10** *6* **Listen And Learn (IRE)**[32] 2002 7-11-10 **127**...............(v) BarryGeraghty 72
(Jonjo O'Neill) *hld up: rdn and struggling after 6th: t.o* **8/1**

3250 **11** *11* **Cowslip**[26] 2081 6-10-12 **122**.. FinianO'Toole(7) 56
(George Moore) *in tch: wknd 4 out: t.o* **33/1**

5m 48.2s (-11.80) **Going Correction** -0.30s/f (Good) **11** Ran SP% **117.3**
Speed ratings (Par 107): **108,107,106,104,104 103,103,93,89,87 83**
CSF £55.43 CT £376.14 TOTE £5.80: £1.90, £3.20, £2.60; EX 62.60 Trifecta £436.30.
Owner Gerry McGladery **Bred** Fiona And Michael O'Connor **Trained** Arlary, Perth & Kinross
■ Stewards' Enquiry : Grant Cockburn two-day ban; used whip above permitted level (4th, 6th Dec)

FOCUS
Brian Hughes described the ground after the first as: "Consistently soft - not much heavy," and Danny Cook called it "Soft." Conditions were unpleasant, with squally showers. A competitive handicap, in which the pace lifted on the final circuit. Last year's winner Closing Ceremony landed the Grade 2 Rendlesham Hurdle back at Haydock later in the season. THe winner built on his recent victory.

2625 MONEY ADVICE GROUP GRADUATION CHASE (13 fncs) 2m 67y
1:20 (1:20) (Class 2) 4-Y-O+ **£12,996** (£3,816; £1,908)

Form RPR

3-01 **1** **Doctor Phoenix (IRE)**[10] 2419 7-11-0 132.......................... BrianHughes 143+
(David Dennis) *chsd ldr: led 2 out: drvn out and styd on wl run-in: a in command* **10/11**[1]

3F-3 **2** *2* **Kings Lad (IRE)**[18] 2242 8-11-7 145.................................. DarylJacob 147
(Colin Tizzard) *led: hdd 2 out: rdn appr last: kpt on u.p run-in but a hld and no imp* **3/1**[3]

263- **3** *2 ¾* **Solar Impulse (FR)**[216] 5389 5-11-4 149............(tp) SamTwiston-Davies 144+
(Paul Nicholls) *hld up: landed awkwardly and nrly uns rdr 1st: nt fluent 4 out: sn rdn and outpcd: rallied appr 2 out: disputing 2nd whn nt fluent last: kpt on same pce in last pl after* **9/4**[2]

4m 22.3s (3.30) **Going Correction** -0.30s/f (Good) **3** Ran SP% **108.2**
Speed ratings (Par 109): **79,78,76**
CSF £3.71 TOTE £1.80; EX 3.90 Trifecta £4.20.
Owner Favourites Racing Ltd **Bred** John O'Donovan **Trained** Hanley Swan, Worcestershire

FOCUS
Actual race distance 2m 91yds. This was a good graduation chase, despite the small field. The winner comfirmed the merit of his recent win and there should be more to come.

2626 BETFAIR TAP TAP BOOM NOVICES' HURDLE (REGISTERED AS THE NEWTON NOVICES' HURDLE) (LISTED RACE) (9 hdls) 1m 7f 144y
1:55 (1:55) (Class 1) 4-Y-O+ **£11,888** (£4,452; £2,224; £1,110)

Form RPR

1-2 **1** **Welsh Shadow (IRE)**[17] 2258 5-11-0 0.............................. HarrySkelton 130+
(Dan Skelton) *hld up: hdwy gng wl bef 3 out: wnt 2nd on bit 2 out: led narrowly appr last: asserted fnl 175yds: drvn out and styd on wl* **1/1**[1]

-114 **2** *2 ¼* **Viens Chercher (IRE)**[5] 2509 4-11-6 135.......................... DannyCook 132
(Brian Ellison) *led: gd jump 3 out: hdd narrowly appr last: kpt on u.p fnl 175yds but a hld* **3/1**[2]

3-31 **3** *3 ¾* **Mardale (IRE)**[41] 1854 5-10-13 0...................................(t) BrianHarding 120
(Nicky Richards) *chsd ldrs: wnt 2nd after 4 out: lost 2nd 2 out: nt fluent last: kpt on same pce and no imp run-in* **9/2**[3]

11 **4** *shd* **Altruism (IRE)**[63] 1399 5-11-6 133.................................... BrianHughes 128
(James Moffatt) *hld up in rr: bmpd after 4 out: nt pick up and hung lft fr bef 2 out: nt fluent last: kpt on u.p run-in but n.d* **6/1**

31 **5** *43* **Lady Yeats**[24] 2123 4-10-13 120.. AdamNicol 87
(George Moore) *chsd ldr: nt fluent 1st: nt fluent 4 out: sn lost pl and wknd: mstke last: t.o* **25/1**

3m 54.7s (-9.50) **Going Correction** -0.30s/f (Good) **5** Ran SP% **111.3**
Speed ratings (Par 111): **111,109,108,107,86**
CSF £4.49 TOTE £1.80: £1.20, £1.70; EX 4.40 Trifecta £9.10.
Owner Walters Plant Hire Ltd **Bred** Hugh O'Connor **Trained** Alcester, Warwicks

FOCUS
Not a strong edition of this Listed race, especially with two of the main contenders taken out. The form could be rated higher.

2627 BETFAIR HOME OF PRICE RUSH NOVICES' CHASE (18 fncs) 2m 5f 127y
2:30 (2:30) (Class 2) 4-Y-O+ **£16,245** (£4,770; £2,385)

Form RPR

2-61 **1** **Silsol (GER)**[11] 2397 6-11-7 0..............................(tp) SamTwiston-Davies 146+
(Paul Nicholls) *w ldr: mstke 6th: fiddled 7th: led 3 out: hdd last: wnt 1 l down run-in: rallied towards fin: got up to prevail on nod* **7/4**[2]

111- **2** *nse* **Private Malone (IRE)**[309] 3696 6-11-2 0.......................... DarylJacob 138
(Emma Lavelle) *led: hdd 3 out: regained ld last: wnt 1 l up run-in: all out towards fin: ct on the nod* **8/1**[3]

11- **3** *2* **Minella Rocco (IRE)**[266] 4473 5-11-2 0.........................(t) BarryGeraghty 136+
(Jonjo O'Neill) *hld up in rr: pushed along and outpcd after 4 out: styd on run-in: unable to chal front two* **4/6**[1]

5m 54.3s (354.30) **3** Ran SP% **107.5**
CSF £9.18 TOTE £2.40; EX 5.60 Trifecta £6.90.
Owner Michelle And Dan MacDonald **Bred** Gestut Hof Iserneichen **Trained** Ditcheat, Somerset

FOCUS
Actual race distance 2m 5f 163yds. A fascinating novices' chase. Silsol is rated a bit below his recent figure.

2628 WINGATE SIGNS SUPPORTS & SUPERJOSH CHARITY "FIXED BRUSH" "NATIONAL HUNT" NOVICES' HURDLE (10 hdls) 2m 2f 191y
3:05 (3:08) (Class 3) 4-7-Y-O **£6,498** (£1,908; £954; £477)

Form RPR

15-2 **1** **Vintage Clouds (IRE)**[19] 2210 5-10-12 0.......................... BrianHughes 133+
(Sue Smith) *prom: chsd ldr after 4 out: upsides whn lft in ld 3 out: over 2 l up whn mstke 2 out: styd on wl to draw clr run-in* **6/5**[1]

4 **2** *9* **Baratineur (FR)**[38] 1898 4-10-12 0................................. HarrySkelton 121
(Dan Skelton) *hld up: hdwy after 4 out: lft in 2nd 3 out: over 2 l down 2 out: shkn up and ev ch briefly bef last: unable to go w wnr run-in: one pce* **8/1**[3]

3 *27* **Celldomfed (IRE)**[243] 4955 5-10-12 0............................ BarryGeraghty 96
(Jonjo O'Neill) *mainly in midfield: hdwy after 4 out: chsng ldrs whn mstke 3 out: sn btn and wknd* **10/1**

26 **4** *1 ½* **Tanarpino**[24] 2126 4-10-12 0.. HenryBrooke 93
(Jennie Candlish) *in rr: struggling after 4 out: plugged on clsng stages: nvr a danger* **100/1**

2 5 *nse* **Freddies Portrait (IRE)**[11] 2398 6-10-12 0............ SamTwiston-Davies 92
(Donald McCain) *chsd ldrs: prom 6th: wknd 4 out* **20/1**

6 *15* **Moorstown (IRE)**[264] 5-10-12 0.............................. PeterBuchanan 77
(Lucinda Russell) *hld up: struggling bef 3 out: nvr a danger* **28/1**

3 7 *14* **I Just Know (IRE)**[21] 2169 5-10-12 0........................ DannyCook 63
(Sue Smith) *prom: mstke 4 out: sn wknd* **8/1**[3]

-032 F **Wade Harper (IRE)**[26] 2091 5-10-12 129.......................... DarylJacob 123+
(David Dennis) *led: stl gng ok and jnd whn fell 3 out* **11/4**[2]

4m 51.4s (-1.60) **Going Correction** -0.30s/f (Good) 8 Ran SP% **112.6**
Speed ratings: **91,87,75,75,75 68,62,**
CSF £11.33 TOTE £2.20: £1.10, £2.40, £2.40; EX 11.30 Trifecta £83.50.
Owner Trevor Hemmings **Bred** Gleadhill House Stud Ltd **Trained** High Eldwick, W Yorks

FOCUS
This proved a stamina test, and they finished strung out. The first two are on the upgrade.

2629 RACING WELFARE "JUNIOR" STANDARD OPEN NATIONAL HUNT FLAT RACE 1m 7f 144y
3:40 (3:40) (Class 4) 3-Y-O **£3,249** (£954; £477; £238)

Form RPR

1 **Du Soleil (FR)** 3-10-11 0.................................... CallumWhillans(3) 106+
(Venetia Williams) *hld up: hdwy after 4f: wnt 2nd 10f out: led over 3f out: sn clr: styd on wl* **15/8**[1]

2 *6* **Crackdeloust (FR)**[159] 3-11-7 0.................................... DannyCook 103
(Brian Ellison) *chsd ldr to 10f out: remained prom: rdn 3f out: chsd wnr wl over 2f out: no imp* **9/4**[2]

3 *8* **Renaissance Red** 3-11-0 0...................................(t) BrendanPowell 88
(Brendan Powell) *chsd ldrs: rn green on bnd after 4f: lost pl over 7f out: rallied u.p over 2f out: kpt on but n.d* **3/1**[3]

4 4 *7* **Sir Albie**[10] 2414 3-11-0 0.................................... NickScholfield 83
(Sally Randell) *led: rn wd and green on bnd after 4f: hdd over 3f out: sn wknd* **8/1**

0 5 *24* **Twycross Warrior**[47] 1772 3-10-9 0..............................(t) ChrisWard(5) 57
(Robin Dickin) *racd keenly in rr: hdwy 1/2-way: rdn and struggling over 6f out: wl bhd after* **33/1**

6 6 *49* **Castle Cavalier**[31] 2009 3-11-0 0.................................... HarrySkelton 8
(Robert Stephens) *in tch: pushed along and lost pl 1/2-way: struggling and bhd fnl 6f: t.o* **14/1**

3m 58.7s (0.10) **Going Correction** -0.30s/f (Good) 6 Ran SP% **111.3**
Speed ratings (Par 104): **87,84,80,76,64 40**
CSF £6.26 TOTE £2.60: £1.70, £1.40; EX 8.10 Trifecta £13.90.
Owner A Brooks **Bred** Louis Fagalde **Trained** Kings Caple, H'fords

FOCUS
This looked a pretty modest bumper. The winner was value for further and can rate higher.
T/Plt: £64.80 to a £1 stake. Pool: £68,767.94 - 773.74 winning tickets T/Qpdt: £7.80 to a £1 stake. Pool: £5,055.59 - 475.24 winning tickets **Darren Owen**

2612 ASCOT (R-H)
Saturday, November 21

OFFICIAL GOING: Good to soft (soft in places)
Wind: Gusty, half against Weather: Bright, cold

2630 MITIE EVENTS & LEISURE NOVICES' HURDLE (AN ASCOT APPEARANCE MONEY SCHEME) (10 hdls) 2m 5f 141y
12:20 (12:20) (Class 2) 4-Y-O+
£12,512 (£3,696; £1,848; £924; £462; £232)

Form RPR

3 1 **American (FR)**[27] 2080 5-10-12 0.................................... BarryGeraghty 138+
(Harry Fry) *prom: trckd ldr 4th: led after 6th: rdn and hdd sn after 2 out: hit last but led again: drifted lft flat but hld on u.p* **11/4**[2]

2 *3/4* **Label Des Obeaux (FR)**[209] 4-10-12 123........................ WayneHutchinson 137+
(Alan King) *trckd ldrs: prog to chse wnr bef 3 out: clsd 2 out where bttr jump and sn led: narrow advantage whn mstke last and hdd: kpt on wl but jst hld* **8/1**

3 *16* **Ephraim**[77] 4-10-12 0.................................... RichardJohnson 122
(Charlie Mann) *hld up in rr: outpcd fr 7th: prog next: kpt on to take 3rd bef last: no ch w ldng pair* **14/1**

24-1 4 *10* **The Boss's Dream (IRE)**[33] 2002 7-11-3 126........................ TrevorWhelan 118
(Neil King) *led to after 6th: rdn next: sn dropped to 3rd: fdd bef 2 out and lost 3rd bef last* **7/1**[3]

53 5 *7* **Golden Bird (IRE)**[20] 2221 4-10-12 0.................................... LiamTreadwell 107
(Brendan Powell) *racd on outer: in tch in rr: pushed along 6th: struggling fr next: no ch after 3 out* **100/1**

6 *1/2* **Neumond (GER)**[244] 4-10-12 0.................................... JeremiahMcGrath 109
(Nicky Henderson) *hld up in rr: shkn up after 6th: struggling fr next: wl btn 3 out: blnd 2 out* **8/1**

7 *30* **Kalanisi Glen (IRE)**[574] 5-10-12 0.................................... DavidBass 108+
(Kim Bailey) *nt jump wl: pressed ldrs tl wknd rapidly 3 out: t.o* **33/1**

F 8 *2 3/4* **Red Hanrahan (IRE)**[22] 2169 4-10-12 0........................ SamTwiston-Davies 102
(Paul Nicholls) *hld up in rr: prog after 6th: rdn after next and struggling: wknd wl bef 2 out: eased and t.o* **7/4**[1]

0-2 P **Mad About The Boy**[196] 212 5-10-12 0.................................... TomCannon
(Robert Walford) *chsd ldr to 4th: lost pl u.p and last fr next: wl t.o whn p.u bef 7th* **20/1**

5m 15.2s (-10.80) **Going Correction** -0.10s/f (Good)
WFA 4 from 5yo+ 8lb 9 Ran SP% **113.1**
Speed ratings (Par 109): **115,114,108,105,102 102,91,90,**
CSF £23.82 TOTE £3.60: £1.40, £2.20, £3.20; EX 25.90 Trifecta £174.00.
Owner The Jago Family Partnership **Bred** Jean-Pierre Hardy **Trained** Seaborough, Dorset

FOCUS
The rail on the chase course was dolled out approximately 2yds at the ends around Swinley Bottom and turning into the home straight. The front pair came clear in what looked a decent novice hurdle and are on the upgrade.

2631 BAM CONSTRUCT UK NOVICES' LIMITED H'CAP CHASE (AN ASCOT APPEARANCE MONEY SCHEME) (20 fncs) 2m 7f 180y
12:55 (12:55) (Class 3) (0-135,130)
4-Y-O+ **£7,147** (£2,098; £1,049; £524)

Form RPR

102/ 1 **Another Hero (IRE)**[584] 5349 6-11-3 125........................ BarryGeraghty 132+
(Jonjo O'Neill) *hld up: nt fluent 10th: prog fr 15th: chsd ldr bef 3 out: clsng whn carried lft and hmpd 2 out: swtchd ins and rdn to ld last: styd on* **9/2**[3]

2-32 2 *1 1/2* **Delgany Demon**[18] 2261 7-11-8 130.................................... TrevorWhelan 136+
(Neil King) *blnd 1st: led 3rd: j.lft after: stl gng wl whn mstke 3 out: pressed and j. bdly lft 2 out: hdd last: kpt on* **9/2**[3]

26-4 3 *2 1/2* **Astigos (FR)**[21] 2184 8-10-12 120.................................... LiamTreadwell 122
(Venetia Williams) *hld up: nt fluent 9th and 11th: outpcd 15th and modest 5th next: rallied to sme degree bef 2 out: sn in 3rd: kpt on but nvr really threatened to chal* **3/1**[1]

23-S 4 *12* **Baku Bay (IRE)**[28] 2064 7-11-1 123........................ SamTwiston-Davies 116
(Ali Stronge) *hld up in tch: bmpd 4th: j. slowly 7th: wnt prom and mstke 11th: rdn to chse ldng pair 3 out: no imp 2 out: sn lost 3rd: wknd and j. slowly last* **9/1**

0-02 5 *18* **Relentless Dreamer (IRE)**[31] 2018 6-11-1 123........(p) RichardJohnson 101
(Rebecca Curtis) *led to 3rd: prom after: rdn bef 15th: wknd after 4 out: fin tired* **4/1**[2]

-U34 P **Parish Business (IRE)**[19] 2240 7-10-9 127..................(t) RichieO'Dea(10)
(Emma Lavelle) *w ldrs: nt fluent fr 11th and steadily lost pl: rdn in last pl after 14th: wknd next: p.u bef 4 out* **4/1**[2]

6m 14.0s (10.50) **Going Correction** +0.20s/f (Yiel) 6 Ran SP% **111.4**
Speed ratings (Par 107): **90,89,88,84,78**
CSF £24.04 TOTE £4.90: £2.20, £2.40; EX 20.50 Trifecta £73.50.
Owner John P McManus **Bred** Miss Noreen Hayes **Trained** Cheltenham, Gloucs

FOCUS
Race increased by 14yds. Fair chasing form, although had the runner-up have jumped straight he may well have won. The first two are rated better than the bare result.

2632 TRISOFT MARES' H'CAP HURDLE (QUALIFIER FOR THE CHALLENGER MARES' HURDLE SERIES FINAL) (10 hdls) 2m 5f 141y
1:30 (1:30) (Class 3) (0-130,130) 4-Y-O+ **£5,848** (£1,717; £858; £429)

Form RPR

1P-P 1 **Desert Queen**[14] 2349 7-11-5 130..................................(t) MrMLegg(7) 144+
(Harry Fry) *disp ld: nt fluent 3rd: def advantage fr next: mde rest: drew clr bef 2 out: shkn up bef last: styd on wl: readily* **8/1**

13-4 2 *12* **Altesse De Guye (FR)**[17] 2268 5-10-2 109........................ KillianMoore(3) 111
(Martin Keighley) *hld up in last: prog fr 5th: hdwy to chse ldng pair 3 out: sn rdn: kpt on to win battle for 2nd after last but no ch w wnr* **11/2**[3]

2211 3 *hd* **Smart Talk (IRE)**[11] 2422 5-11-9 127........................ SamTwiston-Davies 130
(Brian Ellison) *trckd ldng pair: wnt 2nd bef 7th: cl enough 3 out: sn rdn and lft bhd: kpt on but lost 2nd flat* **3/1**[1]

0024 4 *36* **Kilty Caul (IRE)**[16] 2302 6-10-11 115.................................... DavidBass 83
(Kim Bailey) *in tch: prog to go 4th 3 out: sn rdn: btn and wknd 2 out: eased* **16/1**

026- 5 *1* **Gabriella Rose**[218] 5365 5-11-10 128........................ WayneHutchinson 96
(Alan King) *hld up in rr: pushed along and lft wl bhd fr 7th: no ch after: pressed for remote 4th pl after last but swished tail vigorously u.p* **7/2**[2]

1534 6 *19* **Miss Serious (IRE)**[28] 2062 5-11-3 128........................ DavidPrichard(7) 78
(Jeremy Scott) *chsd ldrs: lost pl 5th: rdn next: sn t.o* **8/1**

1144 7 *3/4* **Promanco**[31] 2013 6-11-3 121..................................(tp) RichardJohnson 71
(Charlie Longsdon) *w wnr tl blnd 4th: lost 2nd pl bef 7th: sn wknd: t.o* **11/2**[3]

05-3 8 *12* **Midnight Belle**[20] 2215 8-11-7 125.................................... JamesDavies 64
(Tom Symonds) *chsd ldrs: wknd after 6th: t.o 3 out* **10/1**

5m 16.1s (-9.90) **Going Correction** -0.10s/f (Good) 8 Ran SP% **115.2**
Speed ratings (Par 107): **114,109,109,96,96 89,88,84**
CSF £51.71 CT £162.71 TOTE £9.50: £2.70, £2.30, £1.50; EX 73.00 Trifecta £339.70.
Owner The Jago Family Partnership **Bred** H T Cole **Trained** Seaborough, Dorset

FOCUS
Run at a decent gallop, in part thanks to the winner, they came home quite well strung out in this fair mares' hurdle. The second sets the level.

2633 STELLA ARTOIS 1965 CHASE (GRADE 2) (17 fncs) 2m 5f 8y
2:05 (2:05) (Class 1) 4-Y-O+ **£40,334** (£15,428; £7,959; £4,200)

Form RPR

211- 1 **Vautour (FR)**[254] 4716 6-11-6 171.................................... RWalsh 164+
(W P Mullins, Ire) *tended to edge lft at fences: mde all: mstke 11th: gng wl bef 2 out: shkn up bef last and pressed: drvn out flat* **2/5**[1]

F5-1 2 *1 3/4* **Ptit Zig (FR)**[21] 2206 6-11-11 159........................ SamTwiston-Davies 168
(Paul Nicholls) *nt a that slick over the fences: cl up: chsd wnr 4 out: rdn after next: clsd to threaten after 2 out: kpt on wl but no imp last 100yds* **7/2**[2]

3-22 3 *32* **Third Intention (IRE)**[18] 2259 8-11-7 160..................(t) RichardJohnson 137
(Colin Tizzard) *chsd wnr to 4 out: in tch in 3rd whn mstke next: sn wknd: fin tired* **10/1**[3]

2-P2 4 *1* **Seventh Sky (GER)**[13] 2372 8-11-5 147..................(tp) DenisO'Regan 132
(Charlie Mann) *j.lft: a in 4th: lost tch 8th: t.o 12th: nrly ct tiring 3rd nr fin* **50/1**

115/ P **O'Faolains Boy (IRE)**[596] 5154 8-11-1 150.......................... BarryGeraghty
(Rebecca Curtis) *mstke 1st: last and nt gng w any zest: p.u after 7th* **16/1**

5m 18.3s (-7.70) **Going Correction** +0.20s/f (Yiel) 5 Ran SP% **110.6**
Speed ratings (Par 115): **122,121,109,108,**
CSF £2.41 TOTE £1.20: £1.10, £1.50; EX 2.00 Trifecta £4.00.
Owner Mrs S Ricci **Bred** Haras De Saint Voir & Patrick Joubert **Trained** Muine Beag, Co Carlow

FOCUS
Race increased by 14yds. The eagerly anticipated return of last season's top-notch novice Vautour and the front pair in the market pulled nicely clear. Vautour is rated 7lb off his festival mark, with Ptit Zig taking a step up.

2634 CORAL HURDLE (REGISTERED AS THE ASCOT HURDLE RACE) (GRADE 2) (10 hdls) 2m 3f 58y
2:40 (2:41) (Class 1) 4-Y-O+
£51,255 (£19,233; £9,630; £4,797; £2,412; £1,206)

Form RPR

12-2 1 **Rock On Ruby (IRE)**[21] 2198 10-11-8 160..................(t) BarryGeraghty 160+
(Harry Fry) *mde virtually all: set mod pce tl sent for home bef 2 out: sn hrd pressed: jnd and lft a l in front last: fnd plenty and rdn out* **15/8**[2]

0011 2 *2 1/2* **Court Minstrel (IRE)**[42] 1848 8-11-4 157.................................... PaulMoloney 153
(Evan Williams) *hld up in last pair: cl up bef 2 out: shkn up and nt qckn after 2 out: styd on wl flat to take 2nd last strides* **11/2**[3]

21-1 3 *shd* **Brother Tedd**[19] 2241 6-11-0 155.................................... RichardJohnson 149
(Philip Hobbs) *trckd wnr fr 2nd to 7th and again bef 2 out: sn chalng: jst bhd ldng pair whn lft in 2nd pl last: kpt on same pce flat: lost 2nd fnl strides* **13/8**[1]

2F10 4 *2 1/2* **Sea Lord (IRE)**[91] 1325 8-11-0 152........................ SamTwiston-Davies 147
(John Ferguson) *kpt wd thrght: trckd wnr tl nt fluent 2nd: wnt 2nd again 7th tl shkn up and nt qckn bef 2 out: styd on again flat* **10/1**

The Form Book Jumps 2015-16, Raceform Ltd, Newbury, RG14 5SJ

3P-4 **5** *7* **Grumeti**[21] 2198 7-11-0 140 WayneHutchinson 149+
(Alan King) *hld up in 4th: clsd bef 2 out and sn chalng: tk off alongside wnr last but blnd and nrly fell: nt rcvr* **9/1**

-311 **6** *19* **River Maigue (IRE)**[153] 808 8-11-0 140 (t) DenisO'Regan 120
(Sophie Leech) *hld up in last: taken wd fr 1/2-way: wl in tch after 3 out: outpcd bef next and sn eased* **33/1**

4m 54.9s (10.20) **Going Correction** -0.10s/f (Good) **6** Ran SP% **110.3**
Speed ratings (Par 115): **74,72,72,71,68 60**
CSF £12.02 TOTE £2.40: £1.50, £2.40; EX 10.10 Trifecta £14.30.
Owner The Festival Goers **Bred** John O'Dwyer **Trained** Seaborough, Dorset

FOCUS
No great gallop on here, with the winner dictating under a good ride, and the field bunched up in the straight. The winner dictated and the second was close to his mark.

2635 SHAWBROOK H'CAP CHASE (13 fncs) 2m 192y
3:15 (3:15) (Class 2) 4-Y-0+
£43,792 (£12,936; £6,468; £3,234; £1,617; £812)

Form RPR

3351 **1** **Dresden (IRE)**[14] 2336 7-11-6 **144** JamesDavies 151+
(Henry Oliver) *trckd clr ldng trio: clsd up 7th: wnt 2nd 3 out: led next: rdn and styd on wl fr last* **7/1**

3434 **2** *3 3/4* **Dunraven Storm (IRE)**[18] 2259 10-11-10 **148** RichardJohnson 152+
(Philip Hobbs) *trckd clr ldng pair: blnd 1st and 3rd: wnt 2nd 6th: led 8th: blnd next: hdd 2 out: kpt on fr last but readily hld* **8/1**

2P-1 **3** *1/2* **Cold March (FR)**[21] 2185 5-11-12 **150** LiamTreadwell 153
(Venetia Williams) *t.k.h early: hld up: mstkes 4th and 7th: prog to trck ldng trio 4 out: nt fluent and lost pl next: sn rdn in 7th pl: styd on again after 2 out to take 3rd nr fin* **5/2**[1]

4- **4** *3/4* **Crown Theatre (IRE)**[34] 1994 6-10-10 **134** (t) BarryGeraghty 134
(Henry De Bromhead, Ire) *hld up in last pair: stdy prog fr 9th gng wl: chsd ldng pair 2 out: rdn and limited rspnse bef last where disp 2nd: one pl flat: lost 3rd nr fin* **5/1**[2]

/P-2 **5** *2 1/2* **Fago (FR)**[22] 2171 7-11-10 **148** SamTwiston-Davies 146
(Paul Nicholls) *hld up in tch: trckd ldrs fr 9th: nt fluent next and lost pl: shkn up and one pce bef 2 out* **11/2**[3]

3512 **6** *6* **Workbench (FR)**[28] 2059 7-11-3 **141** (t) RyanMahon 135
(Dan Skelton) *hld up in rr: prog 8th: rdn to cl on ldrs after 3 out: no imp 2 out: wknd bef last* **10/1**

1-01 **7** *16* **Arkaim**[34] 1989 7-10-7 **136** JamieBargary[(5)] 119
(Pam Sly) *led at str pce: j.rt fr 6th: hdd 8th: lost 2nd 3 out: wknd qckly* **14/1**

4203 **8** *13* **My Brother Sylvest**[90] 1344 9-10-8 **135** (bt) KieronEdgar[(3)] 105
(David Pipe) *unable to ld: pressed ldr and clr of rest tl mstke 3rd: lost 2nd pl 6th: dropped through field and nt fluent fr next: bhd after 3 out* **25/1**

3-14 **9** *4 1/2* **Bullet Street (IRE)**[21] 2185 7-10-7 **131** PaulMoloney 101
(Evan Williams) *chsd clr ldrs: lost pl fr 7th and sn in rr: last but in tch whn blnd 10th (4 out): no ch after* **8/1**

4m 12.2s (-2.40) **Going Correction** +0.20s/f (Yiel) **9** Ran SP% **114.9**
Speed ratings (Par 109): **113,111,111,110,109 106,99,93,90**
CSF £60.57 CT £178.36 TOTE £8.00: £2.20, £2.60, £1.40; EX 51.10 Trifecta £220.70.
Owner Dan Lloyd **Bred** Diana Webley **Trained** Abberley, Worcs

FOCUS
Race increased by 10yds. A competitive chase, run at a strong gallop, and the form looks sound. The winner is on the upgrade.

2636 NEPTUNE INVESTMENT MANAGEMENT STANDARD OPEN NATIONAL HUNT FLAT RACE 1m 7f 152y
3:50 (3:50) (Class 4) 4-6-Y-0 **£4,548** (£1,335; £667; £333)

Form RPR

6-1 **1** **Criq Rock (FR)**[25] 2126 4-11-7 0 WayneHutchinson 123+
(Alan King) *hld up in tch: smooth prog over 4f out: trckd ldr 2f out: rdn to chal over 1f out: led last 150yds: styd on wl* **15/8**[1]

2 *1 1/4* **Bags Groove (IRE)** 4-11-0 0 BarryGeraghty 115+
(Harry Fry) *trckd ldrs: led over 2f out gng wl: rdn and pressed over 1f out: hdd last 150yds: styd on* **8/1**

60- **3** *14* **Minstrel Royal**[218] 5373 5-11-0 0 DavidBass 101
(Nicky Henderson) *hld up in tch: prog over 4f out: rdn over 2f out: tk 3rd wl over 1f out but wandered and sn lft bhd by ldng pair* **12/1**

4 *1 1/4* **Semper Invicta (IRE)**[279] 4-11-0 0 SamTwiston-Davies 100
(Paul Nicholls) *hld up: prog on outer 5f out: pushed along over 3f out: outpcd fr over 2f out: kpt on* **8/1**[3]

5 *3 1/2* **Tipperairy (IRE)** 4-11-0 0 RyanMahon 96
(Dan Skelton) *hld up in rr: shkn up in last 5f out and detached fr rest: no ch after but kpt on fnl 2f* **25/1**

6 *shd* **Behind The Wire (IRE)**[174] 4-10-9 0 JamieBargary[(5)] 96
(Tom George) *led to 7f out: pressed ldr: rdn 5f out: wknd over 2f out* **4/1**[2]

3 **7** *1 1/4* **Crazy Penguin (IRE)**[31] 2020 4-11-0 0 RichardJohnson 95
(Charlie Longsdon) *trckd ldrs: urged along over 5f out: wknd over 2f out* **4/1**[2]

8 *1 1/4* **North Hill (IRE)** 4-11-0 0 LiamTreadwell 94
(Ian Williams) *t.k.h: hld up but prom after 5f: led 7f out: hdd & wknd over 2f out* **33/1**

9 *13* **Actiondancer (IRE)** 4-11-0 0 JamesDavies 81
(Henry Oliver) *hld up in rr: pushed along over 4f out: wknd 3f out* **33/1**

10 *3 1/2* **Mr Medic** 4-11-0 0 TomCannon 77
(Robert Walford) *pressed ldr to 1/2-way: styd prom: rdn 5f out: on terms 3f out: sn wknd qckly* **50/1**

3m 44.5s (3.70) **Going Correction** -0.10s/f (Good) **10** Ran SP% **116.4**
Speed ratings: **86,85,78,77,76 75,75,74,68,66**
CSF £17.29 TOTE £2.90: £1.30, £2.30, £3.80; EX 16.90 Trifecta £111.10.
Owner The Trouble Partnership **Bred** S C E A Haras Des Monts D'Arree Et Al **Trained** Barbury Castle, Wilts

FOCUS
The front pair came right away and it was a useful effort by the winner under his penalty. He's still a long way shy of Champion Bumper standard.

T/Plt: £32.10 to a £1 stake. Pool of £122108.77 - 2776.88 winning tickets. T/Qpdt: £6.00 to a £1 stake. Pool of £12102.73 - 1475.24 winning tickets. **Jonathan Neesom**

2624 HAYDOCK (L-H)
Saturday, November 21

OFFICIAL GOING: Soft (heavy in places) changing to soft after race 2 (12.40)
Wind: Moderate, half against Weather: Fine

2637 READ PAUL NICHOLLS EXCLUSIVELY ON BETFAIR H'CAP HURDLE (9 hdls) 1m 7f 144y
12:10 (12:10) (Class 3) (0-135,133) 3-Y-0+
£12,996 (£3,816; £1,908; £954)

Form RPR

350- **1** **Baby King (IRE)**[213] 5475 6-11-2 **123** (t) PaddyBrennan 129+
(Tom George) *midfield: hdwy 4 out: sn wnt 2nd: led appr 2 out: rdn after last: hrd pressed 75yds out: styd on gamely and fnd ex nr fin* **3/1**[1]

50-F **2** *3/4* **Zaidiyn (FR)**[15] 1969 5-11-9 **130** WillKennedy 134
(Brian Ellison) *hld up: hdwy gng wl appr 2 out: wnt 2nd bef last where nt fluent: sn rdn: styd on to chal 75yds out: no ex nr fin* **7/1**

00-5 **3** *7* **De Boitron (FR)**[14] 2335 11-11-4 **125** DannyCook 121
(Sue Smith) *in tch: pushed along and outpcd appr 3 out: kpt on run-in but n.d to front two* **6/1**[3]

342- **4** *2 1/4* **Long Lunch**[215] 5432 6-11-5 **126** (t) AidanColeman 120
(Charlie Longsdon) *chsd ldrs: rdn appr 2 out: kpt on same pce fr bef last* **7/2**[2]

1-5 **5** *1 3/4* **New Street (IRE)**[25] 2123 4-11-4 **125** TomScudamore 117
(Jim Best) *racd keenly: hld up: rdn appr last: one pce and no imp after* **7/1**

4-13 **6** *3/4* **Quick Decisson (IRE)**[14] 2342 7-10-7 **119** GrantCockburn[(5)] 112
(Stuart Coltherd) *led: mstke 3 out: hdd sn after: wknd after 2 out* **16/1**

131- **7** *1 3/4* **Beau Lake (IRE)**[330] 3234 11-10-8 **120** HarryBannister[(5)] 110
(Suzy Smith) *chsd ldr: faltered on road crossing on bnd bef 4th: lost 2nd after 4 out: wknd 3 out: j.rt fnl 3: hung lft whn wl hld bef last* **8/1**

421- **8** *25* **Balmusette**[189] 4481 6-11-12 **133** JamesReveley 98
(Keith Reveley) *in rr: pushed along and sltly detached after 5th: fin wl bhd* **11/1**

3m 57.7s (-6.50) **Going Correction** -0.225s/f (Good)
WFA 4 from 5yo+ 7lb **8** Ran SP% **111.8**
Speed ratings (Par 107): **107,106,103,102,101 100,99,87**
CSF £23.09 CT £115.06 TOTE £3.70: £1.50, £2.50, £1.70; EX 23.30 Trifecta £123.10.
Owner About Two Weeks **Bred** Gerard Mulligan **Trained** Slad, Gloucs

FOCUS
Hurdle bends out 3yds and Chase bends out 4yds for first chase on card and then removed for other chases. Race increased by 18yds. Dry overnight and a bright, windy morning prior to racing. This was a fair handicap, run at an average gallop and only two mattered at the finish. THere'a probably more to come from the winner.

2638 BETFAIR HOME OF PRICE RUSH H'CAP CHASE 3m 4f 97y
12:40 (12:40) (Class 3) (0-135,135) 4-Y-0+
£16,245 (£4,770; £2,385; £1,192)

Form RPR

241- **1** **Emperor's Choice (IRE)**[329] 3308 8-11-12 **135** AidanColeman 143+
(Venetia Williams) *prom: led bef 2nd: hdd 5th: remained prom: mstke 5 out: sn rdn: outpcd bef 4 out: rallied to regain ld 2 out: edgd rt fnl 100yds: styd on gamely* **9/2**[2]

-302 **2** *1 3/4* **Lackamon**[23] 2146 10-11-0 **123** DannyCook 126
(Sue Smith) *in tch: blnd 5th: lost pl after 15th: rdn and bhd after 5 out and gng nowhere: rallied bef 3 out: wnt 2nd bef last: swtchd lft fnl 100yds: kpt on but no imp on wnr cl home* **13/2**[3]

20-F **3** *4* **Harry The Viking**[28] 2068 10-11-3 **129** (p) DerekFox[(3)] 127
(Sandy Thomson) *led: hdd bef 2nd: chsd ldrs after 4th: rdn and outpcd bef 4 out: rallied and chsng ldrs 2 out: kpt on but n.d run-in* **8/1**

F-23 **4** *nk* **King Of The Wolds (IRE)**[20] 2213 8-11-7 **130** BrianHughes 129
(Malcolm Jefferson) *trckd ldrs: wnt 2nd after 4th: led 5th: abt 4 l clr 4 out: rdn and hdd 2 out: no ex after last* **8/1**

3212 **5** *1/2* **Buachaill Alainn (IRE)**[42] 1849 8-11-12 **135** (bt) SeanBowen 133
(Peter Bowen) *prom: mstke 6th: lost pl 13th: rdn after and sn toiling: bhd 5 out: styd on u.p after last: clsd towards fin but no ch* **10/1**

6-50 **6** *3/4* **Sybarite (FR)**[45] 1807 9-10-13 **125** RyanHatch[(3)] 123
(Nigel Twiston-Davies) *in rr: j. carefully early: bhd 6th: sn detached and struggling: sme prog but nt trble others 5 out: styd on u.p run-in but n.d* **9/1**

-553 **7** *1* **Copper Birch (IRE)**[13] 2366 7-10-3 **112** (v[1]) AdamWedge 109
(Evan Williams) *hld up: hdwy to trck ldrs 13th: wnt 2nd bef 4 out but rdn and no imp: rdn and lost 2nd appr 2 out: wknd bef last* **9/2**[2]

413- **P** **No Deal (IRE)**[231] 5132 9-10-9 **118** PeterBuchanan
(Lucinda Russell) *in tch: losing pl whn blnd 15th: mstke and tired 4 out: bhd whn p.u sn after* **7/2**[1]

7m 50.0s (18.40) **Going Correction** -0.05s/f (Good) **8** Ran SP% **113.2**
Speed ratings (Par 107): **71,70,69,69,69 68,68,**
CSF £32.85 CT £224.72 TOTE £4.50: £1.90, £2.30, £2.70; EX 30.20 Trifecta £457.10.
Owner The Bellamy Partnership **Bred** Pat Browne **Trained** Kings Caple, H'fords

FOCUS
Race increased by 48yds. Predictably this was a slog and it was slow-motion stuff from the second-last, and the form is probably not the strongest for the grade. The winner seemingly ran to his best.

2639 BETTER ODDS WITH BETFAIR EXCHANGE H'CAP HURDLE (10 hdls) 2m 2f 191y
1:15 (1:15) (Class 2) 4-Y-0+
£25,024 (£7,392; £3,696; £1,848; £924; £464)

Form RPR

1P-2 **1** **Rock The Kasbah (IRE)**[42] 1848 5-11-9 **136** TomO'Brien 147+
(Philip Hobbs) *trckd ldrs: effrt to take 2nd 2 out: led appr last: styd on wl to draw clr fnl f on run-in* **9/2**[2]

F4-0 **2** *8* **Aerlite Supreme (IRE)**[21] 2186 8-11-3 **130** AdamWedge 133
(Evan Williams) *hld up: nt fluent 4 out: hdwy appr 3 out: wnt 2nd bef last: one pce and no ch fnl f on run-in* **20/1**

10- **3** *2 1/4* **Stilletto (IRE)**[301] 3852 6-11-5 **132** [1] NickScholfield 132
(Paul Nicholls) *racd keenly: hld up: hdwy appr 3 out: chsd ldrs bef last: kpt on u.p run-in but n.d* **9/1**

/12- **4** *hd* **Oscarteea (IRE)**[365] 2647 6-11-3 **130** SeanBowen 129
(Peter Bowen) *hld up: rdn and wl outpcd appr 3 out: 7th and abt 10 l off pce last: kpt on to pass btn horses run-in* **14/1**

P/1- 5 *nk* **Gunner Fifteen (IRE)**[371] 2496 7-10-8 **121**...............[1] NoelFehily 119
(Harry Fry) *racd keenly: chsd ldr and w pce setter at times: nt fluent 3 out: lost 2nd whn nt fluent 2 out: no ex run-in* **13/8**[1]

6-15 6 *1* **Jet Master (IRE)**[21] 2194 9-10-13 **126**...............(t) LucyAlexander 123
(N W Alexander) *hld up in rr: hdwy 4 out: chsd ldrs after: wknd 2 out* **50/1**

6/02 7 *2 1/4* **Vendor (FR)**[7] 2499 7-11-3 **130**............... SeanQuinlan 125
(Sue Smith) *led: rdn and hdd appr last: fdd run-in* **15/2**

11-1 8 *12* **Hunters Hoof (IRE)**[27] 2083 6-11-12 **139**............... NicodeBoinville 123
(Nicky Henderson) *in tch: wknd appr 3 out* **6/1**[3]

1-32 P **Avidity**[21] 2194 6-11-3 **135**............... DaleIrving[(5)]
(James Ewart) *in tch: nt fluent whn wkng 4 out: p.u sn after* **12/1**

4m 46.9s (-6.10) **Going Correction** -0.05s/f (Good)
WFA 4 from 5yo+ 7lb **9 Ran SP% 113.4**
Speed ratings (Par 109): **110,106,105,105,105 105,104,99,**
CSF £80.60 CT £771.22 TOTE £5.20: £1.70, £4.20, £2.50; EX 64.70 Trifecta £1428.50.
Owner Mrs Diana L Whateley **Bred** Joe Rogers **Trained** Withycombe, Somerset

FOCUS
Race increased by 27yds. The going was updated to soft, heavy in places on the hurdles course after the opener. This looked competitive and there was no hanging about, but the winner took a big step up and proved in a different league.

2640 BETFAIR PRICE RUSH HURDLE 2m 45y
1:50 (1:50) (Class 2) 4-Y-O+ **£61,900** (£18,380; £9,190; £4,580)

Form RPR

2P-1 1 **Irving**[14] 2350 7-11-3 162............... NickScholfield 158+
(Paul Nicholls) *hld up bhd ldrs: ct flat footed briefly after 3 out: effrt to cl 2 out: sn in 2nd: chalng whn nt land running last: r.o to ld fnl 75yds and edgd lft: kpt on wl and in control nr fin* **10/11**[1]

112- 2 *1 1/4* **Top Notch (FR)**[253] 4736 4-11-3 156............... DarylJacob 156+
(Nicky Henderson) *chsd ldr: led 2nd: nt fluent 2 out: pressed last: sn rdn: hdd fnl 75yds: short of room and swtchd rt whn hld nr fin* **7/4**[2]

3-52 3 *8* **Melodic Rendezvous**[14] 2350 9-11-3 151............... TomScudamore 147
(Jeremy Scott) *led to 2nd: chsd ldr: j. carefully 4th: lost 2nd 3 out: rdn appr last: outpcd by front two after last: 3rd fnl 110yds whn n.d* **7/1**[3]

12-0 4 *2 1/4* **Fou Et Sage (FR)**[28] 2060 4-11-1 143...............(t) HarrySkelton 144+
(Dan Skelton) *hld up bhd ldrs: wnt 2nd 3 out: lost 2nd whn mstke 2 out: rdn appr last: outpcd by ldrs run-in* **25/1**

4m 1.6s (241.60) **Going Correction** -0.05s/f (Good)
WFA 4 from 7yo+ 7lb **4 Ran SP% 105.1**
Speed ratings (Par 109): **104,103,99,98**
CSF £2.69 TOTE £1.60; EX 2.20 Trifecta £3.70.
Owner Axom XLIX **Bred** Gestut Schlenderhan **Trained** Ditcheat, Somerset

FOCUS
This was tactical, although the big two in the market fought out a tight finish and the form is straightforward. The first two are rated in line with their Wincanton runs.

2641 BETFAIR "TAP TAP BOOM" "FIXED BRUSH" H'CAP HURDLE (GRADE 3) (12 hdls) 2m 6f 177y
2:25 (2:25) (Class 1) 4-Y-O+
£45,560 (£17,096; £8,560; £4,264; £2,144; £1,072)

Form RPR

100- 1 **Baradari (IRE)**[225] 5249 5-11-2 **136**............... HarrySkelton 152+
(Dan Skelton) *hld up: hdwy 4 out: wnt 2nd appr 3 out where mstke: led 2 out: asserted bef last: styd on wl to draw clr fnl f on run-in* **12/1**

11P- 2 *7* **Definitly Red (IRE)**[253] 4738 6-11-4 **138**............... DannyCook 147
(Brian Ellison) *chsd ldrs: led appr 3 out: hdd 2 out: unable to go w wnr run-in: styd on same pce* **13/2**[3]

16-0 3 *12* **Batavir (FR)**[7] 2484 6-10-12 **132**...............(t) TomScudamore 128
(David Pipe) *midfield: hdwy appr 4 out: chsd ldrs bef 2 out: kpt on same pce fr bef last: no imp after* **16/1**

6-14 4 *1 1/4* **Alcala (FR)**[8] 2470 5-10-6 **126**............... SeanBowen 121
(Paul Nicholls) *hld up: hdwy into midfield after 6th: impr to chse ldrs appr 3 out: rdn bef 2 out: kpt on same pce fr bef last* **10/1**

22-1 5 *6* **Yala Enki (FR)**[18] 2257 5-10-10 **130**............... AlainCawley 120
(Venetia Williams) *w ldr tl rdn appr 3 out: wknd bef 2 out* **5/1**[2]

21-5 6 *3/4* **Closing Ceremony (IRE)**[21] 2198 6-11-12 **146**............... RichieMcLernon 135
(Emma Lavelle) *led: hdd appr 3 out: rdn bef 2 out: wknd appr last* **12/1**

2P-6 7 *3 1/2* **Tea For Two**[42] 1848 6-11-2 **141**............... LizzieKelly[(5)] 128
(Nick Williams) *trckd ldrs: rdn appr 3 out: wknd 2 out* **4/1**[1]

3F2- 8 *25* **Vics Canvas (IRE)**[210] 5538 12-11-4 **138**...............(p) RobertDunne 98
(Dermot Anthony McLoughlin, Ire) *midfield: rdn after 4 out: wknd sn after* **33/1**

/0P- 9 *1/2* **Bold Sir Brian (IRE)**[336] 3188 9-10-10 **130**............... PeterBuchanan 89
(Lucinda Russell) *hld up: struggling after 4 out: nvr a danger* **40/1**

4113 10 *24* **Low Key (IRE)**[19] 2241 8-10-8 **135**............... DavidNoonan[(7)] 70
(David Pipe) *midfield: rdn and struggling to hold pl whn hmpd 8th: sn wknd* **16/1**

12-P P **Barafundle (IRE)**[12] 2399 11-11-6 **140**...............(p) PeterCarberry
(Jennie Candlish) *prom: j. slowly 2nd: rdn fr after 3rd: lost pl 5th: bhd and struggling 6th: t.o whn p.u bef 4 out* **50/1**

05-3 P **Mijhaar**[29] 2054 7-11-3 **137**............... AidanColeman
(John Ferguson) *hld up: rdn and struggling appr 7th: t.o whn p.u bef 2 out* **25/1**

02-1 P **One For Harry (IRE)**[20] 2214 7-11-1 **135**............... BrianHarding
(Nicky Richards) *prom: mstke 3rd: sn dropped to midfield: mstke 4th and lost pl: bhd 5th: t.o whn p.u bef 8th* **22/1**

P1P- F **Wychwoods Brook**[252] 4767 9-10-12 **132**............... AdamWedge
(Evan Williams) *in tch: fell 8th* **25/1**

3-42 B **Our Kaempfer (IRE)**[14] 2333 6-11-6 **140**............... NoelFehily
(Charlie Longsdon) *hld up: stl gng ok whn b.d 8th* **11/1**

236- P **Shantou Bob (IRE)**[253] 4738 7-11-9 **143**...............(t) GavinSheehan
(Warren Greatrex) *midfield: rdn and lost pl bef 8th: t.o whn p.u bef 2 out* **8/1**

5m 42.0s (-18.00) **Going Correction** -0.05s/f (Good) **16 Ran SP% 125.1**
Speed ratings (Par 113): **113,110,106,105,103 103,102,93,93,85 , , , ,**
CSF £84.93 CT £1285.87 TOTE £13.50: £2.50, £2.20, £3.80, £2.50; EX 112.70 Trifecta £2280.50.
Owner A Brooks **Bred** His Highness The Aga Khan's Studs S C **Trained** Alcester, Warwicks

FOCUS
Race increased by 36yds. A high-quality staying handicap. There was a searching gallop on and that did for most as few got involved at the business end. A big step up from the winner.

2642 BETFAIR CHASE (REGISTERED AS THE LANCASHIRE CHASE) (GRADE 1) (18 fncs) 3m 24y
3:00 (3:00) (Class 1) 5-Y-O **£112,540** (£42,400; £21,220; £10,600; £5,320)

Form RPR

2-41 1 **Cue Card**[21] 2200 9-11-7 167...............(t) PaddyBrennan 178+
(Colin Tizzard) *racd w zest mainly in 2nd pl: led appr 3 out: effrtlessly wnt clr bef last: easily* **7/4**[2]

01-2 2 *7* **Silviniaco Conti (FR)**[19] 2241 9-11-7 172...............(p) NoelFehily 168
(Paul Nicholls) *led: hdd appr 3 out: rdn bef 2 out: unable to go w wnr bef last: no ch after* **5/4**[1]

3-02 3 *12* **Dynaste (FR)**[21] 2200 9-11-7 165...............(tp) TomScudamore 158
(David Pipe) *prom: outpcd whn nt fluent 3 out: rdn appr 2 out: lost tch w front two bef last* **11/2**[3]

43-5 4 *14* **Holywell (IRE)**[21] 2200 8-11-7 162...............(b) RichieMcLernon 144
(Jonjo O'Neill) *hld up: nt fluent 6th: mstke 9th: reminder after 10th: struggling after 13th: lost tch after 14th* **16/1**

F153 5 *77* **Ballynagour (IRE)**[21] 2200 9-11-7 163...............(t) ConorO'Farrell 65
(David Pipe) *hld up in rr: nt fluent 11th: mstke 12th: mstke 14th and lost tch: t.o* **10/1**

6m 14.7s (-15.80) **Going Correction** -0.05s/f (Good) **5 Ran SP% 111.2**
Speed ratings: **124,121,117,113,87**
CSF £4.62 TOTE £2.50: £1.30, £1.20; EX 4.80 Trifecta £9.20.
Owner Mrs Jean R Bishop **Bred** R T Crellin **Trained** Milborne Port, Dorset

FOCUS
A compelling edition of this cracking Grade 1 chase and it saw a great spectacle from some old favourites. Cue Card is rated back to his very best and this form could even be rated a few pounds higher. Silviniaco Conti is rated similarly to his Aintree win.

2643 CASH OUT IN RUNNING WITH BETFAIR H'CAP CHASE (18 fncs) 3m 24y
3:35 (3:35) (Class 2) (0-145,145) 4-Y-O+
£21,896 (£6,468; £3,234; £1,617; £808; £406)

Form RPR

0-11 1 **Vieux Lion Rouge (FR)**[155] 779 6-11-6 **139**............... TomScudamore 150+
(David Pipe) *hld up in tch: mstke 4th: trckd ldrs appr 4 out: led after 3 out: pressed 150yds out: styd gamely to draw clr fnl 75yds* **8/1**

1-34 2 *4* **Sun Cloud (IRE)**[23] 2146 8-11-5 **138**............... BrianHughes 142
(Malcolm Jefferson) *hld up in rr: hdwy after 14th: chsng ldrs whn swvd to avoid faller 3 out: sn rdn: styd on to take 2nd appr last: chalng 150yds out: no ex fnl 75yds* **14/1**

4-1P 3 *9* **No Planning**[21] 2198 8-11-6 **139**............... SeanQuinlan 136
(Sue Smith) *led: hdd 5th: remained handy: regained ld appr 12th: rdn and hdd bef 3 out where 1/2 l down whn lft in front: sn hdd: lost 2nd bef last: one pce after* **7/1**[3]

44P- 4 *14* **Indian Castle (IRE)**[217] 5392 7-11-9 **142**............... WillKennedy 121
(Ian Williams) *hld up: niggled along appr 14th: rdn and outpcd after 4 out: plugged on fr bef 2 out: n.d* **9/1**

4U-2 5 *3/4* **Royal Palladium (FR)**[14] 2348 7-10-10 **129**............... AidanColeman 109
(Venetia Williams) *prom: rdn and wknd after 4 out: btn whn swvd to avoid faller 3 out* **9/2**[1]

P0P- 6 *14* **Poole Master**[225] 5253 10-11-12 **145**...............(bt) ConorO'Farrell 111
(David Pipe) *prom: led 5th: hdd appr 12th: nt fluent 14th: wknd 4 out* **33/1**

2-50 7 *8* **Theatrical Star**[14] 2348 9-11-3 **136**...............(tp) BrendanPowell 92
(Colin Tizzard) *prom: mstke 4th: mstke and lost pl 10th: bhd 12th* **8/1**

42-1 P **Toby Lerone (IRE)**[16] 2299 8-10-9 **128**............... HarrySkelton
(Dan Skelton) *midfield: rdn along and lost pl after 9th: wl bhd whn p.u bef 13th* **9/2**[1]

U40- P **Firebird Flyer (IRE)**[231] 5140 8-11-4 **137**............... AdamWedge
(Evan Williams) *hld up: mstke 5th: pushed along bef 4 out: nvr a threat: t.o whn p.u bef 3 out* **12/1**

P4-2 F **Straidnahanna (IRE)**[28] 2068 6-10-12 **131**............... DannyCook 132+
(Sue Smith) *trckd ldrs: upsides 4 out: rdn to ld appr 3 out where 1/2 l up and fell* **11/2**[2]

6m 23.2s (-7.30) **Going Correction** -0.05s/f (Good) **10 Ran SP% 113.8**
Speed ratings (Par 109): **110,108,105,101,100 96,93, , ,**
CSF £105.72 CT £819.43 TOTE £7.40: £2.20, £3.40, £2.60; EX 95.50 Trifecta £511.90.
Owner Prof Caroline Tisdall & John Gent **Bred** F M Cottin **Trained** Nicholashayne, Devon

FOCUS
A good-quality staying handicap. A pb from the winner and the form makes sense on time compared with the Betfair Chase.
T/Jkpt: Not won. JACKPOT PLACEPOT: £522.80 to a £1 stake. Pool of £2,757.53 - 3.85 winning units. T/Plt: £84.40 to a £1 stake. Pool of £143,916.48 - 1,244.66 winning tickets. T/Qpdt: £18.30 to a £1 stake. Pool of £10,922.77 - 440.14 winning tickets. **Darren Owen**

2409 HUNTINGDON (R-H)
Saturday, November 21

OFFICIAL GOING: Good to soft (hdl 6.9, chs 6.7)
Wind: strong, half behind Weather: dry, windy

2644 ROYALEQUESTRIAN.CO.UK MARES' "NATIONAL HUNT" NOVICES' HURDLE (10 hdls) 2m 3f 137y
12:00 (12:02) (Class 4) 4-Y-O+ **£3,898** (£1,144; £572; £286)

Form RPR

1 1 **The Organist (IRE)**[191] 305 4-10-10 0............... LeightonAspell 122+
(Oliver Sherwood) *mde all: def advantage 6th: drew readily clr after 3 out: in command and j.rt next: v easily: impressive* **9/4**[2]

2121 2 *15* **Carinena (IRE)**[15] 2325 6-10-13 118............... CraigNichol[(3)] 110
(Nicky Richards) *chsd ldrs: wnt 2nd 7th: rdn after next: btn whn hit 2 out: no ch w wnr but kpt on to hold 2nd* **5/2**[3]

10-3 3 *2 1/2* **Angel Face**[19] 2252 4-10-10 0............... PaulMoloney 102
(Alan King) *chsd ldrs: effrt in 3rd after 7th: outpcd after next: wl hld 3rd 2 out: kpt on* **2/1**[1]

6-05 4 *3 1/2* **Stepover**[17] 2277 4-10-10 0...............[1] KielanWoods 99
(Alex Hales) *hld up in last trio: prog into 5th after 7th: wnt 4th but no ch w wnr whn mstke last: plugged on same pce and hit last* **33/1**

6 5 *11* **Quantum Of Solace**[38] 1909 5-10-7 0............... JamesBanks[(3)] 88
(Noel Williams) *in tch in midfield: wnt 4th but no imp on ldrs after 7th: 5th and wl btn 2 out: wknd* **28/1**

066- 6 18 **Lilywhite Gesture (IRE)**[487] 1054 6-10-7 0 ConorShoemark(3) 72
(Fergal O'Brien) *hld up in last trio: pushed along and struggling 6th: lost tch next: t.o* **66/1**

4 7 1 ½ **Crockery**[17] 2270 5-10-10 0 DavidEngland 70
(Dan Skelton) *w wnr: mstke 6th: sn rdn along: lost 2nd and nt fluent next: wknd bef 3 out: t.o* **7/1**

60- 8 5 **What A Tempest**[247] 4866 5-10-10 0 IanPopham 66
(Richard Phillips) *t.k.h: hld up in rr: lost tch 7th: t.o* **100/1**

0- P **Bonelli's Warbler**[272] 4391 5-10-10 0 JoshuaMoore
(Stuart Edmunds) *hld up in last trio: struggling 6th: lost tch next: t.o whn p.u 2 out* **80/1**

5m 6.3s (7.30) **Going Correction** +0.10s/f (Yiel)
WFA 4 from 5yo+ 8lb 9 Ran SP% **115.3**
Speed ratings (Par 105): **89,83,82,80,76 69,68,66,**
CSF £8.36 TOTE £3.40: £1.10, £1.10, £1.20; EX 7.70 Trifecta £16.50.

Owner Million In Mind Partnership **Bred** John Browne **Trained** Upper Lambourn, Berks

FOCUS
Stable bend and dog-leg rail out 5yds, home bend rail out 6yds. Race distance alteration for this contest was +57.8yds. Only four of these could be seriously fancied on what they'd done on the track previously, but the winner looks a decent prospect. The field went steady and finished strung out but the jockeys reported the ground no worse than the official good to soft although the strong wind was making it tricky.

2645 1ST SECURITY SOLUTIONS NOVICES' H'CAP CHASE (12 fncs) 2m 104y
12:30 (12:31) (Class 4) (0-120,120) 4-Y-0+ **£3,898** (£1,144; £572; £286)

Form RPR

4/0- 1 **Allow Dallow (IRE)**[565] 114 8-11-5 110 JoshuaMoore 121+
(Jonjo O'Neill) *hld up in tch: trckd ldrs and travelling strly 9th: swtchd lft between last 2: shkn up and qcknd to ld flat: r.o wl: comf* **6/1**

3005 2 2 ½ **Trojan Star (IRE)**[48] 1769 5-10-13 107 (t) TomBellamy(3) 112+
(Kim Bailey) *hld up in tch: clsd to trck ldrs and travelling wl 3 out: pressed ldr next: led and j.rt last: sn hdd and drvn: r.o but outpcd by wnr flat* **8/1**

5 3 12 **Old Storm (IRE)**[38] 1917 6-10-4 100 CraigGallagher(5) 92
(Brian Ellison) *led: hdd 3 out: sn u.p: stl cl enough last: sn outpcd: wknd flat* **7/2**[1]

0-52 4 1 **Istimraar (IRE)**[36] 1945 4-11-8 120 IanPopham 104
(Dan Skelton) *racd keenly: chsd ldrs: mstke 4th: pushed along 2 out: clsd 5th last: sn rdn and btn: wknd flat* **4/1**[2]

34-U 5 3 ¼ **Too Much Too Soon (IRE)**[11] 2412 6-11-12 117 (t) JamesBest 107
(Paul Webber) *chsd ldr: nt fluent 6th and 8th: led 3 out: hdd and hit last: sn wknd* **14/1**

2-15 P **Wolf Sword (IRE)**[38] 1901 6-11-12 117 HenryBrooke
(George Moore) *chsd ldrs: j.lft 2nd: rdn after 3 out: sn btn and wl bhd whn p.u next* **5/1**[3]

0-12 P **Be On Time (FR)**[24] 2138 4-11-4 116 (p) BrendanPowell
(Jamie Snowden) *in tch in midfield: dropped to rr and niggled along 7th: nvr travelling after: blnd 3 out: sn lost tch and p.u next* **4/1**[2]

4m 20.3s (10.10) **Going Correction** +0.65s/f (Soft)
WFA 4 from 5yo+ 7lb 7 Ran SP% **111.0**
Speed ratings (Par 105): **100,98,92,92,90 ,**
CSF £46.84 TOTE £7.30: £3.30, £3.60; EX 62.90 Trifecta £360.40.

Owner Regulatory Finance Solutions Limited **Bred** Simon Fahey **Trained** Cheltenham, Gloucs

FOCUS
Race distance alteration for this contest was +54.4yds. Almost certainly this was a modest event, and again they went steady. The easy winner was value for further and is rated to his hurdles mark.

2646 BOONGATE KIA "NATIONAL HUNT" MAIDEN HURDLE (8 hdls) 1m 7f 171y
1:05 (1:08) (Class 5) 3-Y-0+ **£2,599** (£763; £381; £190)

Form RPR

120- 1 **O O Seven (IRE)**[255] 4708 5-11-8 0 AndrewTinkler 132+
(Nicky Henderson) *chsd ldrs: wnt 2nd after 3 out: j. into ld next: readily wnt clr last: v easily* **4/7**[1]

0-P 2 13 **Cyrius Moriviere (FR)**[23] 2152 5-11-5 0 (t) MauriceLinehan(3) 114+
(Ben Pauling) *chsd ldr tl led after 3 out: hdd next: sn rdn and no ex: btn whn wnt lft last* **20/1**

0 3 11 **Lords Park Star (IRE)**[30] 2044 6-11-8 0 AndrewThornton 100
(Nicholas Pomfret) *chsd ldrs tl after 3rd: in tch in midfield after: pushed along and outpcd by ldrs after 3 out: mstke next: wnt modest 3rd last: plugged on* **66/1**

6-36 4 1 ¼ **Shake Devaney (IRE)**[14] 2345 5-11-5 0 ConorShoemark(3) 99
(Fergal O'Brien) *hld up in last pair: pushed along after 3 out: sn outpcd by ldrs and wl btn next: wnt modest 4th flat* **80/1**

5 5 **Icing On The Cake (IRE)**[234] 5-11-8 0 LeightonAspell 94
(Oliver Sherwood) *racd keenly: led tl after 3 out: sn dropped to 3rd and wl btn whn mstke next: wknd and lost pls fr last* **3/1**[2]

3-2 6 1 **Bilzic (FR)**[30] 2044 4-11-8 0 (t) IanPopham 93
(Dan Skelton) *chsd ldrs: rdn and struggling after 5th: lost tch w ldrs after next: wl btn 2 out: wknd* **11/2**[3]

F **Bingo D'Olivate (FR)**[610] 4-11-5 0 JamesBanks(3)
(Noel Williams) *midfield whn fell 1st* **25/1**

6-54 F **Bleu Et Noir**[35] 1967 4-11-3 0 [1] AlanJohns(5)
(Tim Vaughan) *hld up in tch in midfield tl fell 4th* **12/1**

0-0 B **Same Ole Trix (IRE)**[20] 2221 5-11-5 0 (t) TomBellamy(3)
(Kim Bailey) *in tch in midfield: hmpd 1st: b.d 4th* **66/1**

P **Wurring (IRE)** 7-11-8 0 JackQuinlan
(Michael Wigham) *got loose on bef s: hld up in rr: bdly hmpd 1st: lost tch rapidly after 4th: sn t.o: p.u 3 out* **200/1**

3m 59.3s (4.40) **Going Correction** +0.10s/f (Yiel)
WFA 4 from 5yo+ 7lb 10 Ran SP% **125.1**
Speed ratings (Par 103): **93,86,81,80,77 77, , , ,**
CSF £18.70 TOTE £1.40: £1.10, £5.00, £10.90; EX 21.00 Trifecta £426.00.

Owner Triermore Stud **Bred** Robert McCarthy **Trained** Upper Lambourn, Berks

FOCUS
Race distance alteration for this contest was +48.4yds. The betting suggested that only three of these were of interest, but the market leader won without much fuss. He was value for a lot further in a steadily run race.

2647 CAMBRIDGE MAGAZINE LADY RIDERS' H'CAP HURDLE (QUALIFIER FOR THE CHALLENGER TWO MILE HURDLE) (8 hdls) 1m 7f 171y
1:40 (1:42) (Class 3) (0-125,125) 3-Y-0+ **£6,498** (£1,908; £954; £477)

Form RPR

0-02 1 **Sirop De Menthe (FR)**[10] 2445 5-10-9 111 LucyGardner(3) 123+
(Sue Gardner) *t.k.h: chsd ldrs: j.rt and collided w rival 2nd: wnt 2nd after 5th: led and travelling strly bef 2 out: clr and in command between last 2: easily* **5/2**[1]

2101 2 7 **Gin And Tonic**[36] 1945 5-9-10 102 MissBHampson(7) 106
(Michael Wigham) *hld up off the pce in last: clsd and in tch 4th: effrt in 3rd after 3 out: chsd wnr last: no imp* **5/1**[3]

14F1 3 1 ½ **Abricot De L'Oasis (FR)**[27] 2085 5-11-7 123 MissGAndrews(3) 125
(Dan Skelton) *led tl rdn and hdd bef 2 out: sn outpcd: plugged on same pce after: lost 2nd after last* **5/2**[1]

05-1 4 20 **Flute Bowl**[15] 2314 5-11-5 125 (p) MissHayleyMoore(7) 109
(Gary Moore) *chsd ldrs: collided w rival 2nd: lost pl and nvr travelling wl after: last and rdn after 5th: wl btn after next: wnt poor 4th 2 out* **3/1**[2]

2303 5 9 **Summer Storm**[11] 2423 5-10-6 110 (tp) MissCWalton(5) 83
(Rebecca Menzies) *mostly 2nd tl after 3rd: chsd ldrs after: rdn after 5th: btn next: wknd and bhd 2 out: t.o* **22/1**

436/ 6 26 **Memory Cloth**[22] 3659 8-10-2 108 MissTWorsley(7) 55
(Brian Ellison) *chsd ldrs: wnt 2nd after 3rd tl bef 3 out: sn dropped out: bhd after 3 out: t.o* **10/1**

3m 53.55s (-1.35) **Going Correction** +0.10s/f (Yiel) 6 Ran SP% **112.2**
Speed ratings (Par 107): **107,103,102,92,88 75**
CSF £15.18 CT £32.71 TOTE £3.60: £2.00, £2.10; EX 18.10 Trifecta £50.00.

Owner Clear Racing & Partner **Bred** Francois-Marie Cottin **Trained** Longdown, Devon

FOCUS
Race distance alteration for this contest was +48.4yds. Just an ordinary race but the tempo seemed sound. Probably a step up from the winner.

2648 PRICE BAILEY LLP H'CAP CHASE (16 fncs) 2m 3f 189y
2:15 (2:17) (Class 4) (0-120,120) 4-Y-0+ **£5,198** (£1,526; £763; £381)

Form RPR

P441 1 **Milgen Bay**[24] 2140 9-11-3 114 ThomasGarner(3) 123+
(Oliver Sherwood) *chsd ldr: mstke 13th: led bef 2 out: drew clr between last 2: styd on strly flat: rdn out* **8/1**

363/ 2 7 **Denali Highway (IRE)**[623] 4685 8-11-12 120 AndrewThornton 122+
(Caroline Bailey) *chsd ldrs: rdn after 3 out: swtchd rt bef next: unable qck between last 2: wnt 2nd but no imp on wnr flat* **5/2**[1]

3-56 3 1 ½ **Midnight Chorister**[24] 2138 7-10-9 106 (t) JamesBanks(3) 105
(Alex Hales) *hld up in last trio: stdy hdwy after 9th: trckd ldrs 3 out wnt 2nd bef next: rdn and no ex between last 2: lost 2nd and plugged on same pce flat* **10/1**

42-4 4 ½ **Crafty Roberto**[23] 2151 7-11-9 117 (t) KielanWoods 118
(Alex Hales) *in tch in midfield: cl enough in 5th whn blnd and pckd 3 out: rdn and disputing 3rd whn mstke next: sn outpcd: plugged on same pce flat* **4/1**[2]

1143 5 19 **Forever My Friend (IRE)**[14] 2346 8-11-9 117 (p) JamieMoore 99
(Peter Bowen) *led: mstke 12th: rdn after next: hdd bef next: 5th and btn 2 out: wknd* **12/1**

444P 6 2 ¼ **Foundation Man (IRE)**[18] 2261 8-11-0 115 PatrickCowley(7) 96
(Jonjo O'Neill) *chsd ldrs: 6th and struggling bef 3 out: wknd wl bef 2 out* **9/2**[3]

130/ P **Indian Daudaie (FR)**[616] 4820 8-11-11 119 JackQuinlan
(Sarah Humphrey) *in tch: mstke 3rd: struggling 12th: lost tch after 3 out: t.o whn p.u next* **22/1**

5210 P **Tregaro (FR)**[62] 1601 9-10-12 106 (t) LeightonAspell
(Mike Sowersby) *t.k.h: hld up in last pair: sme hdwy 10th: 7th and struggling 3 out: sn wknd: t.o whn p.u next* **14/1**

1-56 P **Royal Macnab (IRE)**[15] 2329 7-11-5 116 (t) TonyKelly(3)
(Rebecca Menzies) *a in rr: mstke and pckd 9th: sn rdn: lost tch 12th: t.o whn p.u 2 out* **12/1**

5m 15.0s (9.70) **Going Correction** +0.65s/f (Soft) 9 Ran SP% **113.4**
Speed ratings (Par 105): **106,103,102,102,94 93, , ,**
CSF £28.95 CT £202.99 TOTE £8.00: £2.40, £1.60, £2.70; EX 32.80 Trifecta £280.20.

Owner James & Clare Luck **Bred** G R Waters **Trained** Upper Lambourn, Berks

FOCUS
Race distance alteration for this contest was +57.8yds. The approach to the fourth fence (the open ditch) in front of the stands was sanded after race 2. The winner is rated back to his best.

2649 SUPPORTING BRITISH BRED THOROUGHBREDS H'CAP HURDLE (12 hdls) 3m 1f 10y
2:50 (2:52) (Class 5) (0-100,100) 4-Y-0+ **£2,599** (£763; £381; £190)

Form RPR

2-02 1 **Snowball (IRE)**[11] 2413 8-10-11 85 LeightonAspell 92
(David Arbuthnot) *in tch in midfield: hdwy to chse ldrs 9th: chsd wnr and rdn wl bef 2 out: jnd blundering wnr last: sn led and 2 l clr: styd on: rdn out* **3/1**[1]

F44- 2 2 **Global Dream**[229] 5194 5-11-3 91 AdamPogson 98+
(Caroline Bailey) *in tch in midfield: wnt 2nd after 8th: j. into ld next: clr and stl on bit bef 2 out: 2 l clr whn blnd and landed awkwardly last: sn hdd: edgd lft u.p and one pce flat* **3/1**[1]

-053 3 14 **Aaly**[49] 1756 8-10-1 75 (t[1]) MarcGoldstein 68
(Lydia Richards) *in tch towards rr: rdn and struggling after 9th: styd on to pass btn horses after 3 out: no threat to ldng pair* **9/1**

35-2 4 6 **Flemi Two Toes (IRE)**[20] 2223 9-10-8 92 RomainClavreul(10) 79
(Sarah Humphrey) *bmpd s: chsd ldr tl mstke 3rd: styd chsng ldrs: rdn and struggling after 9th: wknd bef 2 out* **5/1**[3]

5-40 5 1 ½ **Crinkle Crags (IRE)**[30] 2029 5-11-9 100 CraigNichol(3) 88
(Nicky Richards) *in tch in midfield: hdwy and 4th whn mstke 3 out: effrt in 3rd bef next: no imp and btn 2 out: wknd* **9/1**

05-P 6 21 **El Indio (IRE)**[11] 2410 8-10-13 90 (vt) ConorShoemark(3) 63
(Claire Dyson) *wnt lft s: sn led: out j. and hdd 9th: sn drvn: lost pl sn after next: sn wknd and last next: t.o* **22/1**

-560 P **Strictly The One (IRE)**[54] 1598 5-10-3 80 AdamNicol(3)
(Mike Sowersby) *in tch towards rr: rdn after 8th: struggling next: lost tch 3 out: wl bhd whn p.u next* **33/1**

-463 P **Ballochmyle (IRE)**[20] 2223 5-10-11 85 JackQuinlan
(Caroline Fryer) *chsd ldr 3rd tl after 8th: lost pl wl bef 3 out: wl bhd whn p.u 2 out* **9/2**[2]

60-P **P** **Born To Be Free**[33] 2004 6-9-7 **74** oh10................ ThomasCheesman(7)
(Diana Grissell) *in tch in midfield: rdn 8th: sn lost pl and losing tch in last 9th: t.o whn p.u 3 out* **150/1**
6m 39.3s (16.40) **Going Correction** +0.10s/f (Yiel) **9** Ran SP% **112.8**
Speed ratings (Par 103): **77,76,71,69,69 62,**, ,
CSF £12.27 CT £69.32 TOTE £3.50: £2.30, £1.10, £2.60; EX 14.60 Trifecta £64.30.
Owner The Daring Partnership **Bred** Sean Hurley **Trained** Beare Green, Surrey
■ Stewards' Enquiry : Thomas Cheesman £140 fine: entered the parade ring late

FOCUS
Race distance alteration for this contest was +72.8yds. A moderate handicap for stayers, and not much happened until the final circuit. The winner built on his recent course run.

2650 MATT HAMPSON FOUNDATION - GET BUSY LIVING MAIDEN OPEN NATIONAL HUNT FLAT RACE 1m 5f 148y
3:25 (3:31) (Class 6) 4-6-Y-O **£1,624** (£477; £238; £119)

Form RPR
2-3 **1** **High Bridge**[28] 2065 4-10-11 0.................................... MrAlexFerguson(7) 125+
(John Ferguson) *w ldr tl led 1/2-way: rdn clr over 2f out: styd on: comf* **8/13**[1]
2 **2** *3¾* **Templeross (IRE)**[35] 1966 4-10-11 0................................... MrJJSlevin(7) 117
(Nigel Twiston-Davies) *in tch: hdwy to chse wnr over 3f out: rdn over 2f out: no imp on wnr but kpt on for clr 2nd* **7/1**[3]
0- **3** *12* **Cotswold Road**[296] 3944 5-10-11 0.................................. PaulO'Brien(7) 102
(Colin Tizzard) *in tch in midfield: rdn and outpcd 5f out: rallied to chse ldng pair 2f out: kpt on but no imp* **20/1**
4 *3¾* **Mr Banks (IRE)** 4-11-4 0.. JamesBest 97
(Paul Webber) *chsd ldrs: wnt 2nd 4f out tl 3f out: sn outpcd: wl hld and kpt on same pce after* **16/1**
26 **5** *12* **Throckley**[66] 1555 4-11-4 0.. LeightonAspell 81
(John Davies) *hld up in tch: hdwy 4f out: effrt in 3rd 3f out: no imp and wknd 2f out* **28/1**
6 *1¼* **The Fugitive (IRE)** 4-11-4 0... AndrewTinkler 79
(Charlie Longsdon) *chsd ldrs: rdn over 3f out: outpcd and btn over 2f out: wknd 2f out* **4/1**[2]
7 *14* **Away In May** 4-10-11 0... JamieMoore 54
(John Spearing) *in tch towards rr: rdn 5f out: lost tch 3f out: t.o* **66/1**
0 **8** *13* **Opechee (IRE)**[21] 2188 4-10-13 0.................................... JakeHodson(5) 44
(David Bridgwater) *led tl 4f out: sn rdn and lost pl: bhd 2f out: t.o* **25/1**
9 *52* **I'm Foxy Too** 4-10-11 0... MarkQuinlan
(Neil Mulholland) *in tch towards rr: rdn 5f out: btn over 3f out: sn wknd: t.o* **14/1**
10 *17* **Armement (FR)** 4-11-4 0.. DavidEngland
(James Grassick) *a in rr: lost tch 8f out: sn t.o* **100/1**
3m 16.2s (-3.80) **10** Ran SP% **121.5**
CSF £5.66 TOTE £1.50: £1.10, £1.50, £3.10; EX 5.80 Trifecta £45.70.
Owner Bloomfields **Bred** Darley **Trained** Cowlinge, Suffolk

FOCUS
Race distance alteration for this contest was +36.4yds. The two runners with the best previous form dominated late on, and both were on the upgrade under claimers.
T/Plt: £82.60 to £1 stake. Pool: £50,329.00 - 444.44 winning tickets T/Qpdt: £17.20 to a £1 stake. Pool: £4,415.37 - 189.35 winning tickets **Steve Payne**

2651 - 2657a (Foreign Racing) - See Raceform Interactive

2441

EXETER (R-H)
Sunday, November 22

OFFICIAL GOING: Heavy (soft in places; chs 5.6, hdl 5.9)
Wind: almost nil Weather: sunny

2658 HIGOS FOR YOUR COMMERCIAL INSURANCE H'CAP HURDLE (11 hdls 1 omitted) 2m 7f 25y
1:00 (1:00) (Class 4) (0-115,114) 4-Y-O+ **£3,249** (£954; £477; £238)

Form RPR
64-0 **1** **Knight ofthe Realm**[28] 2087 6-11-3 **105**.......................... IanPopham 110
(Caroline Keevil) *trckd ldrs: rdn to chal appr 2 out: led last (usual 2 out): styd on: drvn out* **9/1**
U2-5 **2** *¾* **Ugly Bug**[197] 210 9-11-11 **113**... RobertDunne 117
(Tony Carroll) *trckd ldrs: led 8th: rdn after 2 out: hdd last (usual 2 out): styd on wl towards fin but a being jst hld* **7/1**
2U33 **3** *7* **Theatre Goer**[28] 2088 6-10-13 **104**............................... JamesBanks(3) 101
(Noel Williams) *chsd ldrs: pushed along fr 7th: styd on same pce fr 2 out (usual 3 out): nvr threatened* **4/1**[2]
5334 **4** *17* **Airpur Desbois (FR)**[53] 1699 5-11-4 **106**...................... PaddyBrennan 91
(Charlie Mann) *trckd ldrs: rdn appr 2 out (usual 3 out): sn hld: nt fluent last (usual 2 out): wknd* **9/2**[3]
05 **5** *46* **Captain Canada**[19] 2262 8-11-8 **110**............................ NickScholfield 44
(Katie Stephens) *struggling and detached 6th: sn t.o* **25/1**
4P/P **P** **Come To The Party (IRE)**[28] 2081 12-11-1 **110**.........(p) MrHFNugent(7)
(Harry Chisman) *struggling after 4th: a towards rr: lost tch 6th: t.o whn p.u after 8th* **50/1**
2-5P **P** **Tara Tavey (IRE)**[187] 388 10-11-5 **114**...........................(t) ConorSmith(7)
(Kevin Bishop) *trckd ldrs: rdn along fr 6th: sn lost pl: wknd 9th: p.u bef last (usual 2 out)* **16/1**
353- **P** **Absolutely Bygones (IRE)**[232] 5150 7-11-9 **111**..............(t) JamesBest
(Jackie Du Plessis) *led tl 8th: sn rdn: wknd qckly: p.u bef 2 out (usual 3 out)* **2/1**[1]
15-5 **P** **Strawberry Hill (IRE)**[18] 2276 9-11-3 **105**......................(tp) TomO'Brien
(Caroline Keevil) *prom: rdn after 8th: wknd bef next: p.u bef last (usual 2 out)* **10/1**
6m 12.9s (13.90) **Going Correction** +0.55s/f (Soft) **9** Ran SP% **114.8**
Speed ratings (Par 105): **97,96,94,88,72** , , ,
CSF £69.68 CT £293.27 TOTE £10.00: £2.70, £2.30, £1.70; EX 80.60 Trifecta £347.70.
Owner Mrs C J Dunn **Bred** Mrs H R Dunn **Trained** Motcombe, Dorset

FOCUS
The Hurdle past the stands had been moved to the back straight, so four flights back straight, three flights home straight. Bends moved out, race increased by 37yds. A modest staying handicap in which the heavy ground played its part.

2659 HIGOS CELEBRATING 25 YEARS H'CAP CHASE (12 fncs) 2m 1f 109y
1:30 (1:30) (Class 3) (0-125,125) 4-Y-O+ **£9,495** (£2,805; £1,402; £702; £351)

Form RPR
5-60 **1** **De Faithesdream (IRE)**[29] 2059 9-11-9 **122**....................... PaulMoloney 138+
(Evan Williams) *travelled strly thrght: mde all: wl in command fr after 8th: easily* **9/2**[2]
3-45 **2** *10* **Marden Court (IRE)**[20] 2240 5-10-12 **111**.......................(t) BrendanPowell 110
(Colin Tizzard) *chsd ldrs: rdn after 8th: wnt hld 2nd 4 out: styd on same pce* **3/1**[1]
P-2F **3** *6* **Key To The West (IRE)**[9] 2468 8-11-5 **125**.............. MrStanSheppard(7) 120
(Matt Sheppard) *hld up bhd ldrs: struggling after 7th: hdwy 4 out: chal for hld 2nd 3 out tl after 2 out: fading whn mstke last* **3/1**[1]
3021 **4** *6* **Houston Dynimo (IRE)**[15] 2346 10-11-0 **120**............(bt) DavidNoonan(7) 107
(David Pipe) *chsd wnr: rdn after 8th: lost 2nd next: wknd 2 out* **7/1**[3]
03-3 **5** *22* **Snowell (IRE)**[25] 2138 8-10-5 **107**................................(p) JamesBanks(3) 81
(Emma Baker) *chsd ldrs tl blnd bdly 7th: sn struggling and no threat after: wknd 2 out* **11/1**
211- **P** **Bobbits Way**[270] 4426 10-10-0 **99** oh1.........................(p) TomScudamore
(Alan Jones) *in tch: nt fluent 1st: struggling 7th: t.o whn p.u bef 4 out* **10/1**
432- **P** **Ubaltique (FR)**[212] 5517 7-11-9 **122**...........................(b) WayneHutchinson
(Donald McCain) *trckd ldrs: rdn after 8th: sn wknd: p.u bef next* **7/1**[3]
4m 34.0s (15.00) **Going Correction** +1.075s/f (Soft) **7** Ran SP% **110.6**
Speed ratings (Par 107): **107,102,99,96,86** ,
CSF £17.68 TOTE £5.50: £2.50, £2.40; EX 24.80 Trifecta £93.80.
Owner R Abbott & M Stavrou **Bred** Pierce Whyte **Trained** Llancarfan, Vale Of Glamorgan

FOCUS
Race increased by 20yds. Again the heavy ground found out the majority on this first race on the chase course.

2660 HIGOS INSURANCE SERVICES NOVICES' CHASE (18 fncs) 3m 54y
2:00 (2:01) (Class 3) 4-Y-O+ **£9,495** (£2,805; £1,402; £702; £351)

Form RPR
211- **1** **Onenightinvienna (IRE)**[214] 5471 6-11-0 0.......................... TomO'Brien 149+
(Philip Hobbs) *chsd ldr: nudged along fr 10th: nt room to chal on inner fr 4 out tl swtchd lft appr 2 out: upsides last: led sn after: styd on wl: rdn clr* **11/4**[2]
12-P **2** *1¼* **Fletchers Flyer (IRE)**[207] 21 7-11-0 0............................(t) NoelFehily 148+
(Harry Fry) *led: rdn after 2 out: hdd sn after last: kpt on but no ex* **8/11**[1]
122- **3** *54* **Dawson City**[237] 5075 6-11-0 0.. AndrewThornton 101
(Polly Gundry) *chsd ldrs: hit 11th and reminders: rdn in 4th after 14th: wnt 3rd next but no ch w front pair* **33/1**
13-P **4** *12* **Rolling Maul (IRE)**[15] 2332 7-11-0 132.............................(b) SeanBowen 87
(Peter Bowen) *v hesitant 1st 3 and sn detached in last: j. more fluently fr 4th but nvr on terms: wnt modest 4th cl home* **20/1**
24-2 **5** *½* **Kayf Moss**[197] 209 7-11-0 0.......................................(bt) RhysFlint 81
(John Flint) *chsd ldrs: rdn after 14th: sn outpcd by front pair: wknd 2 out* **16/1**
0/P- **P** **Palfrey Boy**[196] 9-10-11 0... GilesHawkins(3)
(Chris Down) *mstke 2nd: bhd fr 8th: t.o whn p.u after 11th* **200/1**
13-F **P** **Kingscourt Native (IRE)**[13] 2397 7-11-0 0.........................(t) BrendanPowell
(Colin Tizzard) *chsd ldrs: rdn after 14th: sn wknd: p.u bef 4 out* **7/1**[3]
6m 25.3s (16.00) **Going Correction** +1.075s/f (Soft) **7** Ran SP% **111.2**
Speed ratings (Par 107): **116,115,97,93,93** ,
CSF £5.10 TOTE £4.00: £2.10, £1.40; EX 6.50 Trifecta £43.70.
Owner Mrs Judith Luff **Bred** Colm Griffin **Trained** Withycombe, Somerset

FOCUS
Race increased by 25yds. Two smart staying prospects totally dominated this novice chase.

2661 HIGOS INSURANCE SERVICES EXETER H'CAP HURDLE (11 hdls) 2m 5f 135y
2:30 (2:31) (Class 5) (0-100,104) 3-Y-O+ **£2,274** (£667; £333; £166)

Form RPR
34 **1** **Minellacelebration (IRE)**[19] 2257 5-11-5 **98**.................... MrJNixon(7) 112+
(Katy Price) *mde all: styd on wl to assert fr last: rdn out* **3/1**[2]
-331 **2** *5* **Anda De Grissay (FR)**[7] 2520 5-11-11 **104** 7ex..........(t) DavidNoonan(7) 114
(Anthony Honeyball) *in tch: trckd wnr after 8th: tried to mount chal 3 out: nvr quite upsides and wnt lft last 3: hld bef last: styd on same pce* **5/4**[1]
0/P- **3** *10* **Admiral Blake**[409] 1813 8-10-13 **85**.................................. RobertDunne 85
(Laura Young) *hld up: rdn and prog appr 3 out: wnt hld 3rd 2 out: styd on same pce* **9/1**
5-1P **4** *1¼* **Hi Bronco**[176] 552 8-10-4 **76**.................................(p) SamTwiston-Davies 74
(John Ryall) *trckd ldrs: wnt 2nd 7th: rdn after next: styd on same pce fr 3 out* **7/1**[3]
6-P4 **5** *15* **Dolly Diamond**[17] 2298 6-10-7 **89**.................................. ArchieBellamy(10) 72
(Graeme McPherson) *in tch: effrt after 8th: wknd after 3 out* **7/1**[3]
45P0 **6** *6* **Vering (FR)**[10] 2454 9-10-0 **72** oh3...................................(t) JamesBest 49
(Carroll Gray) *hld up: hdwy after 8th: short-lived effrt bef 3 out: sn wknd* **50/1**
1/-0 **7** *66* **Sarenice (FR)**[19] 2263 9-11-6 **92**.................................. ConorO'Farrell
(Jimmy Frost) *hld up: short-lived effrt bef 3 out: sn wknd and eased* **14/1**
-PPP **P** **Exiles Return (IRE)**[10] 2454 13-9-7 **72** oh8.................... MrMLegg(7)
(Jackie Retter) *chsd wnr tl wknd 7th: t.o whn p.u 2 out* **100/1**
5m 52.7s (19.70) **Going Correction** +0.55s/f (Soft) **8** Ran SP% **114.1**
Speed ratings (Par 103): **86,84,80,80,74 72,48,**
CSF £7.35 CT £27.49 TOTE £3.80: £1.50, £1.10, £1.90; EX 8.50 Trifecta £57.80.
Owner Nick Elliott **Bred** M Doran **Trained** Hay-On-Wye, Powys
■ The first winner under rules for Katy Price.

FOCUS
An ordinary handicap and another winner from the front.

2662 HIGOS INSURANCE SERVICES PLATINUM JUVENILE HURDLE (8 hdls) 2m 175y
3:00 (3:00) (Class 4) 3-Y-O **£3,328** (£1,033; £556)

Form RPR
1 **1** **Jaboltiski (SPA)**[21] 2219 3-11-5 0................................... RichardJohnson 120+
(Philip Hobbs) *trckd ldr: led after 5th: looked to be idling fr 3 out but a doing enough: rdn out* **11/8**[1]
0-3 **2** *3¾* **Swincombe Toby**[18] 2273 3-10-12 0................................... WillKennedy 108
(Nick Williams) *led: hdd after 5th: rdn bef next: kpt chsng wnr but a being hld* **15/8**[2]
4 **3** *70* **Kenobe Star (IRE)**[21] 2219 3-10-12 0...........................(t) BrendanPowell 36
(Jamie Snowden) *trckd ldrs tl wknd after 5th: t.o whn lft 3rd 2 out* **12/1**
P **Blackadder**[108] 3-10-12 0.. TomO'Brien
(Mark Gillard) *racd keenly: trckd ldrs tl wknd after 5th: t.o whn p.u bef 3 out* **150/1**
U **Ikrapol (FR)**[229] 3-10-12 0...(t[1]) DarylJacob 103
(David Pipe) *racd keenly: trckd ldrs: rdn in cl 3rd appr 3 out: styng on at same pce in hld 3rd whn virtually fell and uns rdr 2 out* **5/2**[3]
4m 26.2s (10.70) **Going Correction** +0.55s/f (Soft) **5** Ran SP% **109.1**
Speed ratings (Par 104): **96,94,61,** ,
CSF £4.36 TOTE £2.00: £1.30, £1.20; EX 6.80 Trifecta £34.40.
Owner Mrs Sue Lanz **Bred** Cuadra Tiziano Sl **Trained** Withycombe, Somerset

FOCUS
Race increased by 26yds. This proved a test for juveniles and it was a slow-motion finish.

2663 HIGOS MOTOR INSURANCE DEAL H'CAP CHASE (14 fncs 4 omitted) 3m 54y
3:30 (3:30) (Class 3) (0-125,123) 4-Y-0+ **£7,666** (£2,314; £1,192; £631)

Form RPR
3-22 **1** **St Dominick (IRE)**[11] 2442 8-11-12 **123**.................... JamesBest 131+
(Jackie Du Plessis) *hld up bhd ldrs: hdwy 9th: disp ld after next: outrt ldr after 3 out: in command whn blnd last: rdn out* **9/2**[3]
533- **2** *10* **Dreams Of Milan (IRE)**[212] 5510 7-11-0 **111**..........(p) SeanBowen 109
(Peter Bowen) *trckd ldrs: disp ld after 10th tl rdn after 3 out: sn hld: j.rt last 2* **2/1**[1]
4F-1 **3** *25* **Georgie Lad (IRE)**[26] 2125 7-11-10 **121**.................. RichardJohnson 92
(Philip Hobbs) *trckd ldrs: nt fluent 6th (water): travelling wl enough and upsides on long run after 10th: rdn bef 4 out: fnd little and qckly btn* **11/4**[2]
P43- **4** *½* **Tarraco (FR)**[246] 4907 8-11-4 **115**..........................(b) LiamTreadwell 88
(Venetia Williams) *led tl 4th: led 8th tl drvn after 10th: 4th and hld 4 out: plugged on* **11/2**
32-5 **P** **Lac Sacre (FR)**[13] 2404 6-11-7 **118**.................................(bt) RhysFlint
(John Flint) *hld up bhd ldrs: pushed along after 8th: rdn on long run after 10th: nvr any imp: wknd bef 4 out: p.u bef 3 out* **16/1**
U-1P **P** **Winged Crusader (IRE)**[193] 289 7-11-9 **120**.....(v) SamTwiston-Davies
(Nigel Twiston-Davies) *prom: led 4th tl after 8th: reminders after next: wknd on long run after 10th: t.o whn p.u bef 4 out* **7/1**

6m 32.5s (23.20) **Going Correction** +1.075s/f (Soft) **6** Ran SP% **111.9**
Speed ratings (Par 107): **104,100,92,92,**
CSF £14.41 TOTE £4.30: £1.90, £1.50; EX 15.10 Trifecta £47.30.
Owner Miss J Du Plessis **Bred** Michael O'Driscoll **Trained** Trehan, Cornwall
■ Stewards' Enquiry : James Best two-day ban: used whip without giving gelding time to respond (Dec 6-7)

FOCUS
Race increased by 25yds. This modest handicap was run at an average gallop and once again the surface proved too much for the majority.

2664 HIGOS THATCH PROPERTY INSURANCE CONDITIONAL JOCKEYS' H'CAP HURDLE (6 hdls 2 omitted) 2m 175y
4:00 (4:00) (Class 4) (0-110,108) 3-Y-0+ **£3,249** (£954; £477; £238)

Form RPR
30/P **1** **Never Says Never**[178] 529 7-11-3 **104**..........(t) HarryCobden[(5)] 115+
(Anthony Honeyball) *hld up bhd ldrs: hdwy on long run after 3rd to trck ldrs: j.lft and nt fluent whn chalng last 3: led sn after last: drifted rt: styd on wl to assert towards fin* **9/4**[1]
0-24 **2** *¾* **Oscar Prairie (IRE)**[162] 726 10-11-1 **105**.............. ConorWalsh[(8)] 112
(Warren Greatrex) *trckd ldr: led appr 3 out: rdn bef 2 out: hdd sn after last: leaned on by wnr w ev ch run-in: hld towards fin* **9/2**[3]
11P- **3** *10* **Its A Long Road**[248] 4861 7-11-11 **107**..................... KieronEdgar 105
(Tim Dennis) *hld up bhd ldrs: rdn bef 3 out: styd on into 3rd whn mstke 2 out: no further imp on front pair* **7/1**
6661 **4** *6* **Legion D'Honneur (UAE)**[11] 2447 10-10-9 **94**.........(tp) GilesHawkins[(3)] 85
(Chris Down) *trckd ldrs: rdn appr 3 out: styd on same pce* **5/2**[2]
132- **5** *24* **Hollywood All Star (IRE)**[280] 4248 6-10-9 **99**.......... ArchieBellamy[(8)] 72
(Graeme McPherson) *led: rdn and hdd appr 3 out: sn wknd* **5/1**
35 **6** *7* **Royal Chief (IRE)**[11] 2447 6-11-6 **108**..................(p) MikeyHamill[(6)] 68
(Alexandra Dunn) *trckd ldrs: rdn appr 3 out: sn wknd* **14/1**

4m 23.3s (7.80) **Going Correction** +0.55s/f (Soft) **6** Ran SP% **113.4**
Speed ratings (Par 105): **103,102,97,95,83 80**
CSF £13.03 TOTE £3.30: £1.90, £2.40; EX 11.50 Trifecta £67.50.
Owner Richard Hall **Bred** Dr S G F & P A Cave **Trained** Mosterton, Dorset
■ Stewards' Enquiry : Harry Cobden three-day ban: careless riding (Dec 6-8)

FOCUS
Race increased by 26yds. A weak handicap, confined to conditional riders.
T/Plt: £52.70 to a £1 stake. Pool: £72,732.16 - 1,005.85 winning tickets T/Qpdt: £3.70 to a £1 stake. Pool: £5,574.29 - 1,092.45 winning tickets **Tim Mitchell**

2487 UTTOXETER (L-H)
Sunday, November 22

OFFICIAL GOING: Soft (heavy in places; 6.5)
Wind: Light, half against Weather: Overcast turning fine.

2665 DRAINAGE AND REPAIR SERVICES MARES' "NATIONAL HUNT" NOVICES' HURDLE (9 hdls) 1m 7f 168y
1:20 (1:20) (Class 4) 4-Y-0+ **£3,898** (£1,144; £572; £286)

Form RPR
20-1 **1** **Surtee Du Berlais (IRE)**[202] 111 5-11-2 0.............. LeightonAspell 116+
(Oliver Sherwood) *trckd ldrs: led appr 2 out: drew clr last: eased cl home* **15/8**[2]
2 *5* **Tara Flow**[259] 4664 5-10-10 0................................ AidanColeman 103
(Venetia Williams) *in tch: wnt 2nd and ev ch appr 2 out: rdn and edgd lft between last 2: no imp on wnr last: one pce* **8/13**[1]
2 **3** *12* **Shine Away (IRE)**[8] 2494 5-10-10 0.............................. DannyCook 91
(Sue Smith) *led: hdd 4th: w ldr: led again 3 out: rdn and hdd bef 2 out: wknd bef last* **9/1**[3]
-500 **4** *3* **Omgnotanother (IRE)**[36] 1960 4-10-5 0......................... ConorRing[(5)] 89
(Evan Williams) *racd keenly: wandered appr 1st: w ldr: led 4th: mstke and hdd 3 out: wknd bef 2 out* **66/1**
5- **5** *8* **Appletree Lane**[280] 4249 5-10-10 0............................... JamesDavies 80
(Tom Gretton) *racd keenly: hld up: j. bdly rt 1st: pushed along and outpcd appr 3 out: nvr a danger* **100/1**
0 **6** *1¼* **Gold Bonne Raine (IRE)**[23] 2164 4-10-10 0....................... AdamWedge 79
(Evan Williams) *hld up in rr: struggling appr 3 out: nvr a danger* **100/1**

4m 8.2s (10.80) **Going Correction** +0.775s/f (Soft)
WFA 4 from 5yo 7lb **6** Ran SP% **110.2**
Speed ratings (Par 105): **104,101,95,94,90 89**
CSF £3.39 TOTE £2.60: £1.10, £1.10; EX 3.20 Trifecta £4.90.
Owner Mrs Sue Griffiths **Bred** Mrs Kathryn Lillis **Trained** Upper Lambourn, Berks

FOCUS
Some starts have been moved at this track following remeasuring, so some races will not have speed figures until there is sufficient data to calculate updated median times. Hurdles sited on inside (ground not used since early October) and chases opened to full width and divided bends. All distances as advertised. After the first, Danny Cook described the ground as "soft" while Aidan Coleman felt it was "tacky and hard work".\n\x\x A small field to start the card with and the pace was moderate for much of the contest.

2666 DRAINCARE (LEICESTER) H'CAP CHASE (15 fncs) 2m 4f
1:50 (1:50) (Class 5) (0-100,95) 4-Y-0+ **£2,859** (£839; £419; £209)

Form RPR
5-64 **1** **Bredon Hill Lad**[11] 2446 8-11-9 **95**........................ LucyGardner[(3)] 106
(Sue Gardner) *hld up in rr: hdwy 7th: wnt 2nd 4 out: rdn appr 2 out: styd on to ld run-in: in command cl home* **9/2**[3]
/3-2 **2** *2* **Minellaforlunch (IRE)**[23] 2168 8-11-9 **92**.................... JamesDavies 100
(Henry Oliver) *trckd ldrs: wnt 2nd appr 7th: led 8th: rdn bef 2 out: hdd run-in: no ex cl home* **4/5**[1]
P-64 **3** *11* **American World (FR)**[164] 698 11-10-1 **77**............... MissLBrooke[(7)] 77
(Lady Susan Brooke) *handy: wnt 2nd appr 11th: upsides briefly bef 4 out: lost 2nd 4 out: one pce after 2 out* **33/1**
P-P5 **4** *28* **Petit Ecuyer (FR)**[20] 2255 9-11-0 **83**........................(p) DaveCrosse 52
(Dai Williams) *w ldr: led 3rd: blnd and hdd 8th: stl there but rdn appr 11th: wknd after 4 out* **20/1**
32-4 **5** *2* **Silver Dragon**[8] 2500 7-11-11 **94**.........................(b) DenisO'Regan 61
(Tony Coyle) *in rr: rn in snatches: detached 9th: lost tch 10th: n.d whn mstke 2 out* **10/3**[2]
/6P5 **P** **He's A Hawker (IRE)**[26] 2121 10-11-2 **90**.......................(b) ConorRing[(5)]
(Michael Mullineaux) *led: hdd 3rd: rdn and lost pl appr 7th: in rr and struggling 8th: lost tch 9th: t.o whn p.u bef 4 out* **28/1**

5m 28.9s (19.10) **Going Correction** +1.00s/f (Soft) **6** Ran SP% **108.0**
Speed ratings (Par 103): **101,100,95,84,83**
CSF £8.36 TOTE £4.80: £4.30, £1.10; EX 8.60 Trifecta £85.20.
Owner R W & Mrs J M Mitchell **Bred** R W And Mrs Mitchell **Trained** Longdown, Devon

FOCUS
A moderate handicap, in which only three made much appeal. The early pace, set by a couple of outsiders, seemed fair given the conditions.

2667 DRAIN REPAIR AND MAINTENANCE CONTRACTORS H'CAP HURDLE (10 hdls) 2m3f 207y
2:20 (2:20) (Class 4) (0-120,116) 4-Y-0+ **£3,898** (£1,144; £572; £286)

Form RPR
3-22 **1** **Cochinillo (IRE)**[139] 930 6-11-4 **108**.......................... KielanWoods 112
(Ben Case) *prom: disp ld fr jst after 3 out: sn pushed along: rdn appr last: hdd narrowly briefly run-in: styd on gamely: on top towards fin* **2/1**[1]
60-P **2** *¾* **Blackwater King (IRE)**[10] 2458 7-11-5 **109**..................... AlainCawley 112
(Johnny Farrelly) *hld up in rr: hdwy 4 out: gng wl to dispute ld jst after 3 out: led narrowly for press briefly run-in: no ex towards fin* **16/1**
23-F **3** *23* **Carry On Sydney**[193] 283 5-11-12 **116**..................... LeightonAspell 96
(Oliver Sherwood) *led: hdd 3 out: wknd u.p 2 out* **7/2**[2]
3531 **4** *9* **Mulligan's Man (IRE)**[8] 2492 8-10-12 **102**...................(p) DavidEngland 73
(Clare Ellam) *chsd ldr: led briefly 3 out: rdn and wknd appr 2 out* **5/1**
0/4- **5** *6* **On The Right Path**[239] 5033 8-10-12 **105**.................. HarryChalloner[(3)] 70
(Barry Leavy) *hld up: rdn after 4 out: nvr a danger* **10/1**
3000 **P** **Fleet Dawn**[21] 2217 9-11-5 **112**.................................. AdamNicol[(3)]
(John Wainwright) *hld up: niggled along after 6th: sn detached: toiling whn mstke 3 out: wl bhd whn p.u bef last* **50/1**
16-0 **P** **Tea Time Fred**[18] 2268 6-11-3 **110**.............................. LucyGardner[(3)]
(Sue Gardner) *in tch: mstke 6th: mstke 4 out: prom whn pushed along bef 3 out: sn outpcd: wknd bef 2 out: wl bhd whn p.u bef last: dismntd* **13/8**[1]

5m 16.4s (13.20) **Going Correction** +0.775s/f (Soft) **7** Ran SP% **112.1**
Speed ratings (Par 105): **104,103,94,90,88**
CSF £60.41 CT £276.58 TOTE £3.10: £2.20, £2.90; EX 31.10 Trifecta £137.60.
Owner Goodman, Case & Case **Bred** Henry Chamney **Trained** Edgcote, Northants

FOCUS
This modest handicap was run at an ordinary early gallop. Two came nicely clear.

2668 DRAINCARE COMMERCIAL SERVICES H'CAP CHASE (16 fncs) 2m 6f 108y
2:50 (2:50) (Class 4) (0-120,118) 4-Y-0 **£6,330** (£1,870; £935; £468; £234)

Form RPR
5-15 **1** **Friendly Royal (IRE)**[12] 2424 6-11-0 **106**........................ DannyCook 124+
(Sue Smith) *chsd ldrs fr bef 2nd: wnt 2nd bef 10th: rdn to ld 4 out: gng clr whn mstke 2 out: nt fluent last and wnt lft: kpt up to work run-in* **9/4**[1]
12-2 **2** *13* **Ultimatum Du Roy (FR)**[200] 149 7-11-12 **118**..........(tp) LeightonAspell 124
(Alex Hales) *chsd ldrs fr bef 3rd: racd wd fnl circ: effrt appr 3 out: chsd wnr u.p bef 2 out: no imp* **7/2**[3]
2P-P **3** *10* **Big Jim**[17] 2289 6-11-11 **117**.................................. KielanWoods 113
(Alex Hales) *led 2nd: blnd 12th: hdd 4 out: lost 2nd bef 2 out where mstke whn tired: wl btn* **14/1**
-203 **4** *14* **Bennys Well (IRE)**[8] 2491 9-11-2 **108**......................... SeanQuinlan 88
(Sue Smith) *led to 2nd: racd in 2nd pl tl appr 10th: wkng whn mstke 11th: bhd after* **10/1**
24-3 **5** *37* **Iona Days (IRE)**[181] 470 10-11-7 **113**.......................... MarkGrant 56
(Julian Smith) *hld up: rdn and detached after 9th: struggling 11th: fin wl bhd* **10/1**
31-6 **P** **Ravens Brook (IRE)**[157] 771 9-10-10 **102**...................(b) TrevorWhelan
(Neil King) *prom early: dropped to rr 3rd: rdn after 4th: t.o whn p.u bef 5th* **7/1**
23-4 **P** **King Of Glory**[15] 2346 7-11-4 **110**............................ AidanColeman
(Venetia Williams) *dropped towards rr 3rd: struggling and bhd bef 5th: t.o whn p.u bef 11th* **3/1**[2]

6m 9.7s (27.00) **Going Correction** +1.00s/f (Soft) **7** Ran SP% **115.3**
Speed ratings (Par 105): **90,85,81,76,63** ,
CSF £11.19 TOTE £3.70: £1.90, £1.40; EX 13.50 Trifecta £99.20.
Owner Formulated Polymer Products Ltd **Bred** Jim Dempsey **Trained** High Eldwick, W Yorks

FOCUS
The leaders made sure the pace was sound for this modest handicap.

2669 DRAINCARE H'CAP HURDLE (QUALIFIER FOR THE CHALLENGER STAYING HURDLE SERIES FINAL) (12 hdls) 2m 7f 70y
3:20 (3:20) (Class 3) (0-135,132) 4-Y-0+ **£7,148** (£2,688)

Form RPR
1F-4 **1** **Pure Science (IRE)**[12] 2426 7-10-8 **114**........................ DannyCook 127+
(Sue Smith) *mde all: drew clr appr 2 out: styd on wl: eased towards fin* **10/3**[2]
3R-0 **2** *42* **Wellforth (IRE)**[26] 2125 11-10-0 **106** oh1...................(p) DavidEngland 77
(Clare Ellam) *prom: wknd 8th: lft poor 2nd last* **33/1**
3/10 **U** **Ashbrittle**[22] 2202 8-11-3 **123**....................................(b) TrevorWhelan
(Neil King) *hld up: pushed along after 8th: struggling 5th and wl bhd whn tried and uns rdr 3 out* **12/1**
0FP- **P** **Ambion Wood (IRE)**[230] 5184 9-11-12 **132**.................... DenisO'Regan
(Victor Dartnall) *handy: wknd 4 out: t.o whn p.u bef 3 out* **14/1**

15-3 **P** **San Telm (IRE)**[49] 1784 10-11-2 **122**..........................(p) JoshuaMoore
(Stuart Edmunds) *hld up: hdwy after 8th: chsd wnr bef 4 out: rdn appr 3 out: lost 2nd bef 2 out and wknd: wl adrift whn p.u bef last* **3/1**[1]

55-4 **F** **Little Boy Boru (IRE)**[14] 2369 7-10-13 **124**.................. HarryBannister(5) 117
(Suzy Smith) *hld up in rr: hdwy after 4 out: wnt 2nd appr 2 out: 16 l down and no ch whn fell last* **7/2**[3]

12-1 **R** **Jac The Legend**[24] 2145 6-10-0 **111**.................. CraigGallagher(5)
(Brian Ellison) *prom: rdn and outpcd bef 3 out: sn btn: wl adrift whn lft 2nd and ref last* **3/1**[1]

6m 11.4s (12.60) **Going Correction** +0.775s/f (Soft) **7 Ran SP% 112.6**
Speed ratings (Par 107): **109,94, , ,**
CSF £73.27 TOTE £4.30: £2.30, £9.50; EX 66.10.
Owner Mrs S Smith **Bred** Castlemartin Stud And Skymarc Farm **Trained** High Eldwick, W Yorks

FOCUS
This proved to be a thorough test in the demanding conditions, and only the winner handled them.

2670 DRAINCARE MAINTENANCE SERVICES MARES' H'CAP HURDLE (10 hdls) 2m 3f 207y
3:50 (3:51) (Class 5) (0-100,107) 4-Y-0+ £2,469 (£725; £362; £181)

Form RPR

00-0 **1** **Chasma**[206] 33 5-9-13 **78**.................. HarryBannister(5) 88+
(Michael Easterby) *chsd ldr to 2nd: remained prom: wnt 2nd after 3 out: chalng next: rdn to ld appr last: styd on and drew away fnl 75yds* **12/1**

4-60 **2** *3* **Rebekah Rabbit (IRE)**[58] 1648 5-10-0 **81**.................. MrJDrinkwater(7) 89
(Tom Lacey) *handy: led 3rd: pressed 2 out: rdn and hdd appr last: no ex fnl 75yds* **7/1**[3]

6431 **3** *10* **Miss Joeking (IRE)**[16] 2322 4-10-9 **93**.................. RossChapman(10) 90
(Lucinda Russell) *chsd ldrs: lost pl 4 out: rdn and outpcd appr 3 out: rallied bef 2 out: sn one pce and no imp* **9/4**[2]

4331 **4** *10* **Shaky Gift (IRE)**[5] 2554 6-11-12 **107** 7ex.................. MrShaneQuinlan(7) 97
(Neil Mulholland) *midfield: hdwy appr 4 out: wnt 2nd after flight: lost 2nd after 3 out: wknd 2 out* **11/8**[1]

5456 **5** *39* **Dalby Spook (IRE)**[12] 2427 5-10-6 **83**.................. HarryChalloner(3) 31
(Dianne Sayer) *hld up: nt fluent 5th: struggling bef 3 out: nvr a danger* **10/1**

P-44 **6** *8* **Harriet's Ark**[176] 552 8-10-6 **80**.................. MarkGrant 20
(Julian Smith) *hld up: hdwy appr 4 out: sn chsd ldrs: wknd 3 out* **12/1**

660 **P** **Streele (USA)**[21] 2217 5-9-10 **77**..........................(b[1]) MissTWorsley(7)
(Ken Wingrove) *hld up: pushed along appr 5th: struggling and bhd bef 6th: t.o whn p.u bef 4 out* **100/1**

P-5P **P** **Redanna (IRE)**[16] 2316 6-10-1 **75**..........................(b[1]) JamieMoore
(Robert Walford) *led: hit and hdd 3rd: remained prom: rdn bef 4 out: wknd bef 3 out: sn p.u* **16/1**

5m 18.3s (15.10) **Going Correction** +0.775s/f (Soft)
WFA 4 from 5yo+ 8lb **8 Ran SP% 116.7**
Speed ratings (Par 103): **100,98,94,90,75 72, ,**
CSF £92.91 CT £260.88 TOTE £10.70: £2.70, £2.00, £1.20; EX 112.30 Trifecta £331.00.
Owner B Padgett & Lord Daresbury **Bred** Sandicroft Stud **Trained** Sheriff Hutton, N Yorks

FOCUS
This had looked a fair race for a 0-100, with two last-time-out winners taking their chance, but it was dominated by two horses with weak form previously, albeit both were making their handicap debuts.
T/Jkpt: Not won. JACKPOT PLACEPOT: £646.30 to a £1 stake. Pool of £2,745.00 - 3.1 winning units. T/Plt: £128.80 to a £1 stake. Pool: £78,233.91 - 443.09 winning tickets T/Qpdt: £72.60 to a £1 stake. Pool: £5,666.96 - 57.70 winning tickets **Darren Owen**

2671 - (Foreign Racing) - See Raceform Interactive

[2384] NAVAN (L-H)
Sunday, November 22

OFFICIAL GOING: Soft

2672a "MONKSFIELD" NOVICE HURDLE (GRADE 2) (11 hdls) 2m 4f
1:10 (1:10) 4-Y-0+ £20,155 (£5,891; £2,790; £930)

RPR

1 **Falcon Crest (IRE)**[18] 2282 5-11-3 0.................. BarryGeraghty 142
(€ Roche, Ire) *hld up in tch: 6th 1/2-way: tk clsr order bhd ldrs in 3rd gng wl 3 out: lft 2nd at next and almost on terms whn pckd sltly at last: sn rdn to ld and drvn clr: comf* **10/3**[2]

2 *6 1/2* **Moylisha Tim (IRE)**[21] 2225 5-11-6 118.................. MrJJSlevin 132
(R P Rath, Ire) *led and disp: settled in 2nd fr 4th: tk clsr order after 4 out and led narrowly next: strly pressed bef last and hdd u.p run-in: sn no imp on wnr and one pce clsng stages* **9/1**

3 *1 3/4* **Last Encounter (IRE)**[129] 1016 5-11-3 123.................. DannyMullins 127
(Ms Margaret Mullins, Ire) *settled bhd ldrs: 5th 1/2-way: nt fluent 6th: rdn in 4th after 3 out and lft 3rd at next where sltly hmpd by faller: no imp on ldrs fr last: kpt on u.p clsng stages* **18/1**

4 *9* **Okotoks (IRE)**[21] 2224 5-11-3 127.................. PaulTownend 118
(A J Martin, Ire) *hld up in rr: 8th 1/2-way: tk clsr order bhd ldrs bef 3 out: pushed along in 5th after 3 out and no imp on ldrs next where lft mod 4th and sltly hmpd by faller: kpt on one pce* **16/1**

5 *1 1/2* **Cogryhill (IRE)**[23] 2175 5-11-3 0.................. BJCooper 117
(Gordon Elliott, Ire) *chsd ldrs: 4th 1/2-way: rdn in 3rd appr st and wknd after 3 out: lft mod 5th 2 out* **10/3**[2]

6 *9 1/2* **Ten Times Better (IRE)**[24] 2155 5-10-10 0.................. RWalsh 100
(P A Fahy, Ire) *towards rr: slt mstke 1st and nt fluent next: 7th 1/2-way: rdn in rr 3 out and no imp: one pce after* **9/4**[1]

7 *8 1/2* **The Westener Boy (IRE)**[330] 3329 8-11-3 123.................. MarkWalsh 99
(C A Murphy, Ire) *chsd ldrs: 3rd 1/2-way: nt fluent 7th: rdn in 7th after 3 out and no imp whn lft mod 6th next: one pce* **14/1**

8 *37* **Heathfield (IRE)**[204] 92 8-11-3 0.................. NiallPMadden 62
(A J Martin, Ire) *hld up: last at 1/2-way: rdn and wknd after 4 out: t.o* **33/1**

F **Dallas Cowboy (IRE)**[27] 2116 5-11-3 120.................. DavyRussell 126
(Gordon Elliott, Ire) *led and disp: narrow advantage fr 4th: j. sltly rt next and at times after: over 2 l clr at 1/2-way: reduced advantage after 4 out and hdd narrowly next: rdn and u.p in 2nd bef 2 out where fell* **8/1**[3]

5m 9.3s (7.50) **9 Ran SP% 118.8**
CSF £34.17 TOTE £4.20: £1.02, £2.30, £3.80; DF 32.20 Trifecta £488.00.
Owner John P McManus **Bred** John J M Power **Trained** Coolaghknock Glebe, Co Kildare

FOCUS
A horse spoken of as a good ground two-miler when winning at Fairyhouse last time, the winner showed his versatility with an impressive performance in a pretty truly run race and looks to have plenty of options open to him now. A pb from the winner.

2673-2674a - (Foreign Racing) - See Raceform Interactive

2675a LADBROKES TROYTOWN H'CAP CHASE (GRADE B) (17 fncs) 3m
2:40 (2:41) (0-150,138) 4-Y-0 £46,511 (£14,728; £6,976; £2,325; £1,550)

RPR

1 **Riverside City (IRE)**[21] 2228 6-9-8 **115**.................. JackKennedy(5) 122
(Gordon Elliott, Ire) *w.w towards rr: slt mstke 1st: sme hdwy bef 12th: wnt 6th bef 4 out: almost on terms 2 out: clsd u.p to chal between horses at last where lft in front and edgd rt briefly: kpt on wl run-in* **8/1**

2 *1 3/4* **Georges Conn (IRE)**[31] 2046 7-10-4 **123**.................. LPDempsey(3) 128
(Gordon Elliott, Ire) *hld up: slt mstke in 9th at 5th: clsr in 6th bef 5 out: impr to chal on outer 2 out: clsd u.p to dispute briefly at last where nt fluent: sltly impeded in 2nd after last: kpt on wl run-in wout matching wnr* **14/1**

3 *14* **Kylecrue (IRE)**[10] 2463 8-10-6 **122**..........................(b) AELynch 114
(John Patrick Ryan, Ire) *led and disp early tl settled bhd ldrs fr 1st: disp again fr 7th tl settled in 2nd after next: led 12th: jnd bef 3 out where lft in front: hdd next and sn no ex in 4th: lft 3rd at last where nt fluent: one pce* **14/1**

4 *6* **Aurora Bell (IRE)**[230] 5226 7-10-0 **123**.................. MartinBurke(7) 109
(John M Burke, Ire) *chsd ldrs: gng wl in 4th bef 4 out: lft 2nd fr next and rdn: no ex u.p in 5th after 2 out: lft mod 4th at last* **10/1**

5 *7* **Dromnea (IRE)**[8] 2504 8-11-2 **132**.................. MarkEnright 112
(M F Morris, Ire) *cl up and led after 1st: j. sltly rt at times: jnd and hdd fr 7th: pushed along in 3rd after 4 out: rdn after 3 out and no ex u.p in 6th fr next: lft mod 5th at last* **8/1**

F **Empire Of Dirt (IRE)**[230] 5224 8-11-2 **132**..........................(t) BJCooper 137+
(C A Murphy, Ire) *chsd ldrs tl disp fr 7th: led narrowly after next tl hdd 12th: disp appr st and ev ch on terms whn fell 3 out* **5/1**[2]

B **Knockanarrigan (IRE)**[22] 2208 7-10-5 **121**..........................(p) BrianHayes
(Ms Sandra Hughes, Ire) *mid-div early: slt mstke in 5th at 10th: nt fluent 5 out: stl in tch bhd ldrs whn b.d 3 out* **11/1**

F **Mullaghanoe River (IRE)**[580] 5474 7-11-4 **134**.................. SeanFlanagan
(Noel Meade, Ire) *hld up in mid-div: disputing 7th whn fell 8th: fatally injured* **8/1**

P **Bashful Beauty (IRE)**[14] 2387 8-10-6 **122**.................. JJBurke
(Norman Lee, Ire) *cl up early and settled bhd ldrs fr 1st: rdn in rr and no imp bef 5 out where slt mstke: wknd and p.u bef next* **25/1**

P **He Rock's (IRE)**[8] 2504 6-9-4 **113** ow1.................. DonaghMeyler(7)
(S J Mahon, Ire) *towards rr: rdn in 9th and no ex after 5 out: no imp whn hmpd by faller 3 out and p.u sn after* **10/1**

P **Tulsa Jack (IRE)**[21] 2228 6-10-1 **124**.................. JonathanMoore(7)
(Noel Meade, Ire) *towards rr: nt fluent 1st: mstke in rr at 11th: pushed along and no imp after 12th: wknd and trailing whn p.u bef 3 out* **9/2**[1]

F **Ballychorus (IRE)**[61] 1625 6-11-5 **135**..........................(t) APHeskin 142
(Ms Margaret Mullins, Ire) *chsd ldrs: pushed along in 6th 4 out and clsd u.p fr next to ld 2 out: strly pressed and jnd u.p at last where fell* **7/1**[3]

6m 29.7s (0.40) **12 Ran SP% 124.4**
CSF £116.80 CT £1568.13 TOTE £8.40: £2.80, £3.80, £4.40; DF 104.50 Trifecta £1878.80.
Owner John P McManus **Bred** Frank McGuinness **Trained** Longwood, Co Meath
■ The first winner over fences for Jack Kennedy, 16.

FOCUS
Not the most competitive Troytown of all time but plenty of drama and jumping was very much the name of the proverbial game. The first two were clear with the winner rated to a pb.

2676a PROUDSTOWN H'CAP HURDLE (GRADE C) (13 hdls) 2m 7f
3:10 (3:10) 4-Y-0+ £15,116 (£4,418; £2,093; £697)

RPR

1 **Prince Of Scars (IRE)**[10] 2463 5-11-5 **139**.................. JackKennedy(5) 154
(Gordon Elliott, Ire) *in tch: 7th 1/2-way: mstke 4 out: nt fluent next where tk clsr order: nt fluent 2 out: rdn to chal at last and kpt on wl u.p far side run-in to ld clsng stages: all out: jst* **9/2**[2]

2 *nse* **Russian Bill (IRE)**[21] 2236 5-10-2 **120**.................. GerFox(3) 135
(Noel Meade, Ire) *hld up: 12th 1/2-way: sme hdwy fr bef 4 out to chal next: rdn to ld after 2 out: strly pressed fr last and hdd narrowly between horses towards fin: rallied cl home: jst hld* **9/2**[2]

3 *shd* **Roll It Out (IRE)**[21] 2236 6-10-8 **123**.................. BarryGeraghty 138+
(Gordon Elliott, Ire) *hld up towards rr: 11th 1/2-way: tk clsr order bef 3 out where slt mstke: rdn to dispute 2nd at last: clsd u.p nr side to dispute briefly run-in: kpt on wl in 3rd clsng stages: jst hld* **7/2**[1]

4 *4* **Childrens List (IRE)**[27] 2111 5-11-0 **129**.................. RWalsh 140
(W P Mullins, Ire) *hld up: 10th 1/2-way: mstke on inner at 7th: pushed along after 3 out and clsd u.p after next where swtchd lft in 5th: kpt on u.p into 4th run-in: nvr trbld ldrs* **8/1**[3]

5 *7* **Railway Tommy (IRE)**[27] 2112 7-10-2 **117**.................. JJBurke 121
(Peter Fahey, Ire) *in tch: 6th 1/2-way: rdn bef 2 out and no imp on ldrs u.p in 6th bef last: kpt on one pce into mod 5th run-in* **50/1**

6 *2* **Misty Lady (IRE)**[22] 2205 6-11-0 **129**.................. SeanFlanagan 131
(John Laurence Cullen, Ire) *led 1st tl jnd after 4th and disp after: narrow advantage after 4 out: rdn and hdd after 2 out: no ex u.p in 4th fr last and wknd run-in* **20/1**

7 *1 3/4* **Baie Des Iles (FR)**[238] 5052 4-10-7 **126**.................. MsKWalsh 122
(Ross O'Sullivan, Ire) *hld up towards rr: rdn in 9th bef 2 out and no imp on ldrs between last 2: kpt on one pce* **16/1**

8 *3/4* **Foxrock (IRE)**[255] 4718 7-10-13 **128**..........................(t) APHeskin 127
(T M Walsh, Ire) *chsd ldrs: 4th 1/2-way: cl 7th appr st: lost tch and one pce fr 3 out* **8/1**[3]

9 *14* **Buck Dancing (IRE)**[21] 2236 6-9-7 **111**.................. BenDalton(3) 96
(Edward P Harty, Ire) *chsd ldrs: 5th 1/2-way: rdn and wknd after 3 out* **11/1**

10 *1 3/4* **Fine Rightly (IRE)**[259] 4660 7-11-1 **130**.................. DavyRussell 114
(S R B Crawford, Ire) *hld up in tch: tk clsr order bhd ldrs in 3rd fr 3rd: racd keenly: cl up bhd ldrs 3 out: rdn and no ex after next: sn wknd* **14/1**

11 *14* **Aengus (IRE)**[206] 50 5-9-13 **121**.................. JonathanMoore(7) 91
(Noel Meade, Ire) *hld up: 8th 1/2-way: rdn in mod 11th bef 3 out and no imp* **28/1**

12 *50* **Pencilhimin (IRE)**[22] 2208 10-9-12 **120**..........................(t) DonaghMeyler(7) 40
(Norman Cassidy, Ire) *cl up in 2nd: slt mstke 1st: impr to dispute after 3rd: pushed along in cl 2nd after 4 out and sn lost pl: wknd qckly bef next* **16/1**

13 *44* **Getoutwhenyoucan (IRE)**[304] 3826 6-10-11 **126**................ MarkWalsh
(Augustine Leahy, Ire) *in rr for most: niggled along after 4th: mstke 6th: rdn 4 out and no imp detached bef 3 out where eased: completely t.o* **66/1**

P **Fine Theatre (IRE)**[269] 4460 5-10-8 **123**.......................... MarkEnright
(Paul Nolan, Ire) *hld up: 9th 1/2-way: niggled along briefly fr 7th: slt mstke next: rdn and no imp detached towards rr after 4 out: trailing whn p.u bef next* **10/1**

5m 59.2s (359.20)
WFA 4 from 5yo+ 8lb **14** Ran SP% **128.3**
CSF £26.62 CT £83.71 TOTE £5.20: £1.80, £2.00, £1.40; DF 26.70 Trifecta £167.60.
Owner Gigginstown House Stud **Bred** Eamon Salmon **Trained** Longwood, Co Meath

FOCUS
An ultra competitive contest and a terrific finish involving some quality performers. The standard is set around the placed horses.

2677a COOLMORE N.H. SIRES EUROPEAN BREEDERS FUND MARES INH FLAT RACE (LISTED RACE) 2m

3:40 (3:41) 4-7-Y-O **£20,155** (£5,891; £2,790; £930)

RPR

1 **Augusta Kate**[64] 1589 4-11-3 0........................... MrPWMullins 125+
(W P Mullins, Ire) *settled bhd ldr in 2nd: tk clsr order bhd ldr bef st: smooth hdwy travelling wl to ld 1 1/2f out: rdn clr ins fnl f: easily* **4/6[1]**

2 *7* **Cashelard Lady (IRE)**[29] 2078 5-11-6 0.................... MsKWalsh 121
(Shane Crawley, Ire) *attempted to make all: extended advantage bef 1/2-way: reduced ld bef st: pushed along over 2f out and hdd u.p 1 1/2f out: no ch w easy wnr: kpt on same pce in 2nd ins fnl f* **33/1**

3 *7* **Billy's Hope (IRE)**[7] 2535 4-11-3 0.............. MissKHarrington 111
(Mrs John Harrington, Ire) *chsd ldrs: 3rd 1/2-way: 5th 4f out: sme hdwy into 3rd 3f out: rdn and no ex under 2f out: kpt on one pce* **11/2[2]**

4 *1* **Myztique (IRE)**[305] 3808 5-11-6 0.................(t) MsNCarberry 113
(Gordon Elliott, Ire) *sn chsd ldrs: 6th 1/2-way: clsr in 4th gng wl under 3f out: sn rdn and no ex u.p in 4th under 2f out: kpt on one pce* **7/1[3]**

5 *6* **Barnahash Rose (IRE)**[21] 2230 7-11-6 0...................(t) MissJMMangan 107
(Jonathan Sweeney, Ire) *towards rr: hdwy in 13th under 4f out: rdn in 8th over 2f out and no imp on ldrs: kpt on u.p ins fnl f* **40/1**

6 *4 1/2* **Kalopsia (IRE)**[85] 1406 4-11-6 0....................... MissSO'Brien 103
(A P O'Brien, Ire) *mid-div: 6th 4f out: rdn in mod 7th over 2f out and no imp on ldrs: kpt on one pce* **8/1**

7 *1* **Pariah (IRE)**[231] 5172 6-11-2 0.......................... MrNJRedmond 98
(M F O'Dowd, Ire) *in rr of mid-div: 9th 1/2-way: rdn in 12th and no imp under 3f out: kpt on one pce fr under 2f out* **100/1**

8 *hd* **Rosshaven Lady (IRE)**[74] 1532 5-11-9 0................... MrJJSlevin 104
(A P O'Brien, Ire) *hld up in tch: racd keenly: 5th 1/2-way: rdn in 5th 3f out and no imp under 2f out where flashed tail briefly: wknd fnl f* **20/1**

9 *nk* **Undisputed (IRE)** 4-10-13 0........................... MrSCrawford 94
(S R B Crawford, Ire) *hld up towards rr: sme hdwy over 3f out: rdn in mod 8th over 2f out and no imp: one pce fnl f* **16/1**

10 *5* **Pride Of The Braid (IRE)**[21] 2230 5-11-6 0................. MrFMaguire 96
(John E Kiely, Ire) *cl up early tl sn settled in mid-div: 8th 1/2-way: rdn and no imp 3f out* **16/1**

11 *1* **Petuna (IRE)**[39] 1919 5-11-6 0............................. MrSClements 95
(M Phelan, Ire) *hld up: clsr in 7th at 1/2-way: rdn and no ex 3f out: sn wknd* **16/1**

12 *1 1/2* **Siberian Vixen (IRE)**[14] 2383 5-11-2 0.................. AmbroseMcCurtin 90
(Edmond Kent, Ire) *chsd ldrs: 4th 1/2-way: reminders in 5th over 5f out: rdn and no ex over 3f out: sn wknd* **66/1**

13 *28* **Risk It All (IRE)** 4-10-13 0....................... MrJPO'Sullivan 59
(Thomas James, Ire) *nvr bttr than mid-div: rdn and no imp 3f out: wknd and eased fnl 2f: t.o* **66/1**

14 *1 1/2* **Ninety Seconds (IRE)** 4-10-13 0....................... MrJPMcKeown 57
(T J Taaffe, Ire) *mid-div: wknd and eased fr 3f out: t.o* **50/1**

15 *2 1/2* **Seeking Susan (IRE)**[14] 2383 7-11-2 0...................... MsLO'Neill 58
(Miss Elizabeth Doyle, Ire) *chsd ldrs early: pushed along in mid-div 5f out: rdn no ex under 3f out: wknd and eased fnl 2f: t.o* **40/1**

4m 5.2s (-1.60)
WFA 4 from 5yo+ 7lb **15** Ran SP% **135.1**
Pick Six: 6,677.10 - Pool: 52,463.62 - 5.5 Winning Units. Tote Aggregate: 2015: 380,938.00 - 2014: 203,346.38. CSF £46.65 TOTE £1.70: £1.02, £7.00, £2.30; DF 34.60 Trifecta £196.70.
Owner The Masters Syndicate **Bred** Chesters Stud Ltd **Trained** Muine Beag, Co Carlow

FOCUS
A supremely impressive performance from the winner who looked very good in taking apart a field of quality mares. The form is rated towards the top of the race standard.
T/Jkpt: @348.30. Pool of @10,948.79 - 22 winning units. T/Plt: @73.30. Pool of @52,463.62 - 713.40 winning units. **Brian Fleming**

2678 - 2682a (Foreign Racing) - See Raceform Interactive

2238 KEMPTON (R-H)

Monday, November 23

OFFICIAL GOING: Good to soft (soft on lakeside bend)
Wind: Almost nil Weather: Fine

2683 COOLMORE EBF STALLIONS "NATIONAL HUNT" NOVICES' HURDLE (QUALIFIER) (8 hdls) 2m

1:05 (1:06) (Class 4) 4-6-Y-O **£3,898** (£1,144; £572; £286)

Form RPR

10- **1** **Brain Power (IRE)**[227] 5255 4-10-12 0..................... PeterCarberry 120+
(Nicky Henderson) *hld up in midfield: prog to trck ldng pair 3 out: led 2 out: nt fluent last and shkn up: styd on and soundly in command nr fin* **7/4[1]**

1-3 **2** *1* **Two Taffs (IRE)**[27] 2123 5-10-12 0....................... HarrySkelton 116
(Dan Skelton) *t.k.h: hld up in rr: prog bef 2 out: tried to chal last: styd on but a outpcd by wnr* **11/2**

130- **3** *2* **Theo's Charm (IRE)**[257] 4708 5-10-12 0.................. TomCannon 114
(Nick Gifford) *prom: trckd ldr 4th: led 3 out: shkn up and hdd 2 out: styd on but outpcd flat* **9/2[3]**

16-2 **4** *6* **Lettheriverrundry (IRE)**[21] 2238 5-10-12 0............... BarryGeraghty 109
(Brendan Powell) *hld up in midfield: mstke 5th: clsd on wd outside 2 out: sn shkn up: outpcd last but kpt on to take 4th flat* **8/1**

163- **5** *1 1/4* **Church Leap (IRE)**[268] 4499 4-10-12 0................. NicodeBoinville 107
(Patrick Chamings) *trckd ldrs: wl in tch whn n.m.r sn after 2 out: pushed along and outpcd after* **33/1**

1-60 **6** *nk* **Cougar Kid (IRE)**[30] 2065 4-10-12 0.................... LeightonAspell 106
(Philip Hide) *w ldr: led 3rd to 3 out: cl up 2 out: outpcd after* **100/1**

12 **7** *1 1/4* **Air Horse One**[30] 2065 4-10-12 0........................... NoelFehily 108+
(Harry Fry) *nt jump wl: led at modest pce to 3rd: styd prom: lost pl and j.rt 2 out: in rr and j.rt last: kpt on* **11/4[2]**

6-66 **8** *shd* **For Good Measure (IRE)**[13] 2409 4-10-12 0................. TomO'Brien 105
(Philip Hobbs) *hld up in last pair: nvr quite on terms w main gp: reminder after 2 out and outpcd: reminder after last: kpt on flat: possible improver* **100/1**

9 *27* **Present Times (IRE)** 4-10-12 0.......................... AdamWedge 78
(Evan Williams) *hld up in last: shkn up and wknd bef 3 out: t.o* **100/1**

4m 6.3s (20.30) **Going Correction** +0.725s/f (Soft) **9** Ran SP% **113.6**
Speed ratings: **78,77,76,73,72 72,72,72,58**
CSF £11.89 TOTE £3.00: £1.10, £1.60, £1.60; EX 13.50 Trifecta £57.90.
Owner Michael Buckley **Bred** David Harvey **Trained** Upper Lambourn, Berks

FOCUS
All starts have been moved at this track following remeasuring, so there will be no speed figures here until there is sufficient data to calculate updated median times. All bends had been moved out 3yds since the last fixture, increasing race distances as follows: R1 & R6 +26yds, R2 +63yds, R3 & R5 +47yds and R4 +87yds. Jockeys confirmed the ground to be riding 'good to soft', although felt it may become a little more testing as it became opened up. This looked a good novice hurdle, although it was muddied somewhat by the fact they went such a steady gallop. The form is not to be taken seriously.

2684 STARLIGHT NOVICES' CHASE (12 fncs) 2m

1:35 (1:36) (Class 4) 4-Y-O+ **£4,659** (£1,446; £779)

Form RPR

205- **1** **Vaniteux (FR)**[228] 5238 6-11-0 0..................... NicodeBoinville 161+
(Nicky Henderson) *j. proficiently: mde all: upped the pce after 4 out: more than 3 l ld and looking in full command whn lft further clr next: easily* **8/11[1]**

53-3 **2** *19* **Qewy (IRE)**[31] 2053 5-11-0 **141**.......................... AidanColeman 141
(John Ferguson) *prom: chsd wnr 6th to 8th: lft 2nd again 3 out: easily lft bhd* **5/1[3]**

/110 **3** *16* **Cousin Khee**[16] 1848 8-11-0 0........................... TomO'Brien 128
(Hughie Morrison) *hld up in last: mstke 5th: nt fluent after: lost tch 7th: lft remote 3rd 3 out* **33/1**

4-53 **F** **Regal Encore (IRE)**[24] 2166 7-11-0 0...............(t) BarryGeraghty
(Anthony Honeyball) *chsd wnr to 6th: nudged along and disputing 3rd whn fell next* **8/1**

02F **F** **Stephanie Frances (IRE)**[7] 2541 7-10-7 0............... HarrySkelton 134+
(Dan Skelton) *hld up: prog to chse wnr 8th: pushed along and more than 3 l down whn fell 3 out* **7/2[2]**

4m 0.2s (240.20) **5** Ran SP% **110.8**
CSF £5.04 TOTE £1.70: £1.10, £2.10; EX 4.50 Trifecta £24.80.
Owner Mr & Mrs R Kelvin-Hughes **Bred** Jacques Cypres **Trained** Upper Lambourn, Berks

FOCUS
A race that revolved around the favourite, a smart hurdler, and he couldn't have made a better start to his chasing career. The second has been rated in line with his recent run.

2685 OLBG MARES' HURDLE (LISTED RACE) (12 hdls) 3m 110y

2:10 (2:10) (Class 1) 4-Y-O+ **£14,237** (£5,342; £2,675; £1,332; £670)

Form RPR

1-F4 **1** **Morello Royale (IRE)**[16] 2349 5-10-12 **132**...............(t) AidanColeman 142+
(Colin Tizzard) *trckd ldr to 5th: styd cl up: rdn to chal after 2 out: led sn after last: readily asserted* **6/1[3]**

P21- **2** *2* **Polly Peachum (IRE)**[212] 5541 7-11-6 **152**................ DavidBass 148+
(Nicky Henderson) *hld up in tch: mstke 5th: jnd ldrs after 9th: led briefly 3 out: led 2 out: sn pressed and rdn: hdd and one pce after last* **1/2[1]**

432- **3** *17* **Fairytale Theatre (IRE)**[261] 4619 8-10-12 **130**..............(t) HarrySkelton 128
(Dan Skelton) *led: set modest pce tl past 1/2-way: mstke 3 out and hdd briefly: hdd 2 out: sn wknd* **5/1[2]**

1114 **4** *7* **Minnie Milan (IRE)**[113] 1181 6-10-12 **125**............... TrevorWhelan 117
(Neil King) *t.k.h: trckd ldr 5th tl mstke 9th: wknd 3 out* **16/1**

66-3 **5** *2 1/4* **Kayfleur**[17] 2313 6-10-12 **125**.............................. JakeGreenall 116
(Henry Daly) *hld up in tch: jnd ldrs 9th: on terms after 3 out: wknd qckly bef next* **20/1**

6m 20.3s (0.30) **5** Ran SP% **108.3**
CSF £9.70 TOTE £6.80: £2.00, £1.10; EX 9.70 Trifecta £17.80.
Owner Ann & Tony Gale **Bred** Peter And Maria Byrne **Trained** Milborne Port, Dorset

FOCUS
The front pair came clear late on in what was a decent mares' hurdle and there was a bit of a turn up. The pace was fairly steady. The second and third have been rated close to their marks.

2686 LARKSHILL ENGINEERING NETWORK H'CAP CHASE (QUALIFIER FOR THE CHALL. MIDDLE DISTANCE CHASE FINAL) (16 fncs) 2m 4f 110y

2:45 (2:45) (Class 3) (0-135,135) 4-Y-O+ **£9,747** (£2,862; £1,431; £715)

Form RPR

3-0P **1** **Gallery Exhibition (IRE)**[53] 1722 8-11-9 **132**.................(t) DavidBass 140+
(Kim Bailey) *in tch: trckd ldng pair 5th and chsd ldr 11th: rdn to ld sn after 3 out: drvn clr after next: pushed out flat* **8/1**

-211 **2** *6* **Risk A Fine (IRE)**[131] 1006 6-11-12 **135**.................. TomO'Brien 139
(Philip Hobbs) *led at gd pce: lit up by loose horse and wnt clr after 9th: hmpd by it next and c bk to rivals: hdd sn after 3 out: one pce* **13/2**

-005 **3** *2 1/2* **Saffron Wells (IRE)**[22] 2222 7-11-7 **130**................. TrevorWhelan 130
(Neil King) *settled in last pair: pushed along 8th: sme prog 11th: wnt 3rd bef 3 out and briefly threatened to cl: mstke 2 out and one pce after* **9/2[2]**

-P12 **4** *1 3/4* **Road To Freedom**[26] 2140 6-10-6 **115**................... LeightonAspell 114
(Lucy Wadham) *hld up in last: stl there 11th: sme prog after: wnt 4th and mstke 3 out: mstke 2 out: pushed along and kpt on: nvr in contention* **5/1[3]**

-300 **5** *23* **Sew On Target (IRE)**[10] 2468 10-11-5 **135**................. PaulO'Brien(7) 111
(Colin Tizzard) *tried to match strides w ldr but couldn't: racd in 2nd pl to 11th: wknd bef 3 out* **8/1**

02-6 **U** **Minellaforleisure (IRE)**[13] 2412 7-11-3 **126**.................. KielanWoods
(Alex Hales) *hld up: bdly hmpd and uns rdr 1st* **12/1**

16-P **F** **The Clock Leary (IRE)**[10] 2468 7-11-5 **128**................. AidanColeman
(Venetia Williams) *nt fluent: chsd ldng pair to 5th: struggling whn mstkes 10th and 12th: wkng whn fell next* **4/1[1]**

1410 **U** **Gone Too Far**[35] 2001 7-11-6 **129**..............................(p) BarryGeraghty
(Alan King) *blnd bdly and uns rdr 1st* **6/1**

5m 14.2s (2.20) **Going Correction** +0.35s/f (Yiel) **8** Ran SP% **112.4**
Speed ratings (Par 107): **109,106,105,105,96 , ,**
CSF £56.16 CT £261.54 TOTE £10.40: £2.70, £2.10, £1.90; EX 65.20 Trifecta £221.80.
Owner The GFH Partnership **Bred** Joe Fogarty **Trained** Andoversford, Gloucs

FOCUS
Run at a good gallop, they were on the stretch from some way out in what was a fair chase. The first two have been rated pretty much to their marks.

2687 BRADLEY PARTNERSHIP H'CAP HURDLE (12 hdls) 3m 110y
3:15 (3:15) (Class 4) (0-120,120) 4-Y-O+ **£3,898** (£1,144; £572; £286)

Form RPR

11P2 **1** **Lady Of Longstone (IRE)**[16] 2349 5-11-4 **117**............ DavidNoonan(5) 125+
(David Pipe) *mde all at gd pce: drew 10 l clr after 8th: rdn and hrd pressed 2 out: fnd more and in command whn lft clr last* **11/1**

3121 **2** *6* **Presence Felt (IRE)**[41] 1897 7-11-8 **116**..................(v) WillKennedy 122+
(Jonjo O'Neill) *trckd ldng pair: clr of rest after 8th: wnt 2nd 3 out: clsd to chal and nrly upsides 2 out: sn drvn: 2 l down and hld whn stmbld on landing last: kpt on* **6/1**[3]

55-6 **3** *3 1/4* **Monetary Fund (USA)**[27] 2125 9-11-5 **113**........... AidanColeman 112
(Venetia Williams) *prom in chsng gp: rdn and clsd 3 out: chsd ldng pair u.p bef next: kpt on same pce* **8/1**

53-P **4** *5* **Pyrshan (IRE)**[25] 2152 6-11-7 **115**.....................(t) KielanWoods 111
(Graeme McPherson) *hld up in rr: stdy prog after 8th: trckd ldng pair after 3 out and looked a threat: rdn bef 2 out: sn wknd* **20/1**

32U- **5** *5* **Aviador (GER)**[266] 4536 9-10-1 **105**..................... LukeIngram(10) 95
(Lucy Wadham) *prom in chsng gp to 6th: dropped to rr next: struggling 9th: urged along and kpt on again bef 2 out* **20/1**

451P **6** *7* **Bayley's Dream**[27] 2125 6-10-11 **105**........................ TomO'Brien 88
(Paul Webber) *hld up towards rr: sme prog fr 9th: rchd 5th after 3 out and tried to cl on clr ldng quartet: no hdwy bef 2 out* **20/1**

53-0 **7** *12* **Walk On Al (IRE)**[40] 1903 7-11-12 **120**.................. HarrySkelton 93
(Dan Skelton) *hld up in last trio: sme prog after 9th but nvr nr ldrs: wknd 2 out* **5/2**[1]

P-60 **8** *1/2* **Action Master**[183] 458 9-10-6 **110**................. TommyDowling(10) 82
(Charlie Mann) *hld up in last: stl there after 9th: modest late prog: nvr involved* **50/1**

44-1 **9** *15* **Presenting Lisa (IRE)**[37] 1971 6-11-4 **112**............ WayneHutchinson 71
(Alan King) *chsd wnr to 3 out: wknd rapidly: t.o* **11/2**[2]

0-01 **10** *1 1/4* **Giveitachance (IRE)**[22] 2223 8-10-11 **105**..................(t) NickScholfield 63
(Claire Dyson) *racd wd: prom in chsng gp to 1/2-way: sn dropped to rr: wl btn after 9th: t.o* **12/1**

2325 **11** *2* **Romulus Du Donjon (IRE)**[23] 2182 4-11-11 **119**........... LeightonAspell 75
(Oliver Sherwood) *hld up in last trio: mstkes 3rd and 9th: shkn up and no prog after: t.o* **12/1**

1-1P **12** *11* **Horsted Valley**[39] 1925 5-11-6 **114**...................(p) GavinSheehan 60
(Warren Greatrex) *hld up in midfield: sme prog and prom in chsng gp 6th: no hdwy 9th: wknd rapidly 3 out: t.o* **10/1**

6m 7.5s (-12.50)
WFA 4 from 5yo+ 9lb **12 Ran SP% 118.4**
CSF £72.36 CT £567.18 TOTE £10.10: £3.60, £2.10, £3.20; EX 45.30 Trifecta £410.80.
Owner Miss S E Hartnell **Bred** David Crimmins **Trained** Nicholashayne, Devon

FOCUS
No hanging around in this modest staying handicap, with the winner maintaining the gallop for an all-the-way success. The winner has been rated similar to her recent second, with the runner-up posting a small pb.

2688 STARLIGHT CHILDREN'S FOUNDATION CONDITIONAL JOCKEYS' H'CAP HURDLE (8 hdls) 2m
3:45 (3:46) (Class 3) (0-130,128) 3-Y-O+ **£5,393** (£1,583; £791; £395)

Form RPR

110- **1** **Presenting Arms (IRE)**[351] 2966 8-11-6 **127**..............(t) HarryCobden(5) 134+
(Harry Fry) *t.k.h: led 2nd: mde rest: nudged along and only one serious rival after 2 out: sn in total command: eased flat* **2/1**[1]

211 **2** *1 1/4* **Paddys Runner**[24] 1712 3-10-7 **127**........................ TomBellamy(3) 114+
(Alan King) *cl up: chsd wnr bef 2 out: tried to chal bef last but nvr any imp: styd on* **6/1**[3]

6141 **3** *4* **Polstar (FR)**[29] 2093 6-10-11 **119**...................... PaulNO'Brien(6) 116+
(Harry Whittington) *hld up in last pair: detached in last after 4th: stl last and v long way off the pce 3 out: pushed along and 10th 2 out: gd hdwy bef last: fin and r.o wl to take 3rd last strides: far too much to do* **7/2**[2]

/210 **4** *3/4* **Stand To Reason (IRE)**[19] 2271 7-10-6 **111**............... NickSlatter(3) 109
(Tony Carroll) *nt fluent 2nd: hld up in rr: stdy prog fr 5th: in tch after 3 out: chsd ldng pair after 2 out: kpt on but no imp: lost 3rd last strides* **16/1**

-210 **5** *4* **Closest Friend**[23] 2186 6-11-9 **125**.....................(t) ThomasGarner 119
(Dan Skelton) *hld up in last trio: stdy prog bef 3 out: in tch in main gp bef 2 out: sn rdn and one pce* **12/1**

-145 **6** *1 3/4* **Take A Break (FR)**[21] 2247 4-11-8 **124**...............(bt[1]) KieronEdgar 116
(Nigel Hawke) *nt a fluent: hld up wl in rr: urged along and no imp on ldng gp after 3 out: kpt on fr next: nvr nrr* **33/1**

1-PP **7** *2 1/4* **Forever Field (IRE)**[177] 554 5-10-13 **118**............. FreddieMitchell(3) 107
(Nicky Henderson) *prom: cl up on long run bef 2 out: fdd after 2 out* **6/1**[3]

1PU- **8** *1 1/2* **Right Step**[238] 5070 8-10-1 **111**....................(t) PaddyBradley(8) 100
(Pat Phelan) *prom: stl wl in tch on long run after 3 out: wknd 2 out* **16/1**

4-03 **9** *3/4* **Iniesta (IRE)**[21] 2244 4-10-3 **113**.....................(v) GeorgeGorman(8) 100
(Gary Moore) *wl in tch: rdn after 5th: struggling fr 3 out: steadily wknd* **16/1**

212- **10** *42* **Global Thrill**[226] 5278 6-11-9 **128**..................... RobertWilliams(3) 78
(Bernard Llewellyn) *prom: chsd wnr 4th: mstke 3 out: lost 2nd and wknd bef 2 out: sn eased: t.o* **25/1**

313- **11** *14* **Boston Blue**[239] 3588 8-11-2 **118**................................. RyanHatch 55
(Tony Carroll) *chsd ldrs to 3rd: sn lost pl and struggling: bhd after 5th: t.o* **66/1**

41-5 **12** *4 1/2* **Tamarillo Grove (IRE)**[12] 2445 8-10-13 **118**..........(t) KillianMoore(3) 51
(Sophie Leech) *led to 2nd: chsd wnr to 4th: wknd rapidly on long run after 3 out: t.o* **33/1**

3m 54.3s (8.30) **Going Correction** +0.725s/f (Soft)
WFA 3 from 4yo 15lb 4 from 5yo+ 7lb **12 Ran SP% 120.7**
Speed ratings (Par 107): **108,107,105,105,103 102,101,100,99,78 71,69**
CSF £14.67 CT £41.41 TOTE £3.30: £1.40, £2.10, £1.70; EX 17.00 Trifecta £48.50.
Owner J M Dare **Bred** Ms Iona Maguire **Trained** Seaborough, Dorset

FOCUS
Fair hurdles form with a trio of progressive types coming to the fore. The fourth and fifth help set the level.
T/Plt: £18.50 to a £1 stake. Pool: £66,906.68 - 2,629.50 winning tickets T/Qpdt: £7.00 to a £1 stake. Pool: £4,741.32 - 498.93 winning tickets **Jonathan Neesom**

2448 LUDLOW (R-H)
Monday, November 23
OFFICIAL GOING: Good to soft (soft in places; 6.2)
Wind: Nil Weather: Overcast

2689 TOTEPLACEPOT RACING'S FAVOURITE BET MAIDEN HURDLE (9 hdls) 1m 7f 169y
1:20 (1:20) (Class 4) 4-Y-O+ **£3,898** (£1,144; £572; £286)

Form RPR

1 **Banyu (FR)**[217] 4-11-0 0.................................... RichardJohnson 111+
(Philip Hobbs) *racd keenly: novicey at times: led tl after 1st: remained prom: chalng fr 3 out where bmpd rival: led after 2 out: hit last: styd on gamely: a doing enough towards fin* **9/2**[2]

5 **2** *1 1/4* **Magic Music Man**[21] 2238 4-11-0 0............................ DenisO'Regan 107
(Alan King) *trckd ldrs: hit 4 out: pushed along and nt qckn appr 3 out: rallied after last: wnt 2nd fnl 110yds: styd on towards fin* **8/1**[3]

10-3 **3** *1 1/4* **Armchair Theatre (IRE)**[15] 2363 5-11-0 0..................... PaulMoloney 106
(Evan Williams) *a.p: rdn and nt qckn appr 2 out: rallied after last and styd on: one pce fnl 75yds* **8/11**[1]

3/3B **4** *2 1/4* **Spa's Dancer (IRE)**[30] 1893 8-11-0 110......................... JackQuinlan 105
(James Eustace) *wnt lft s and slowly away: rcvrd to ld after 1st: pressed and bmpd 3 out: hdd after 2 out: lost 2nd fnl 110yds: no ex* **9/1**

0-00 **5** *5* **Miss Mash**[24] 2164 4-10-7 0...................................... AndrewTinkler 93
(Henry Daly) *trckd ldrs: pushed along and outpcd appr 3 out: kpt on same pce fr 2 out* **100/1**

0 **6** *3 1/2* **Guaracha**[21] 2251 4-10-9 0.. RyanWhile(5) 97
(Bill Turner) *midfield: pushed along 3 out: sn outpcd: plugged on at one pce fr 2 out* **100/1**

30- **7** *nse* **Cassie**[35] 4634 5-10-7 0.......................................(t) JamesDavies 90
(Ben Pauling) *chsd ldrs: pushed along 3 out: no imp whn hit 2 out: n.d after* **20/1**

P-02 **8** *10* **Midtech Valentine**[177] 558 4-10-4 0.......................... RobMcCarth(3) 80
(Ian Williams) *hld up: pushed along and outpcd whn mstke 3 out: nvr a danger* **50/1**

5- **9** *7* **Black Hawk (IRE)**[236] 5097 6-11-0 0........................ JeremiahMcGrath 81
(Henry Oliver) *hld up: mstke 5th: outpcd bef 3 out: nvr a danger* **50/1**

10 *5* **Un Prophete (FR)**[185] 4-11-0 0.................................. LiamTreadwell 77
(Venetia Williams) *midfield: hdwy appr 4 out: pushed along and wknd bef 3 out* **16/1**

3 **11** *3 3/4* **La Pyle (FR)**[33] 2021 4-10-0 0.......................... ThomasCheesman(7) 66
(Philip Hobbs) *in tch: rdn and wknd bef 3 out* **66/1**

P4 **12** *2 1/2* **Marshgate Lane (USA)**[42] 1886 6-11-0 0........................ MarkQuinlan 76
(Neil Mulholland) *midfield: blnd 1st: no imp whn blnd 2 out: sn wknd* **20/1**

5-60 **13** *21* **Culworth Boy (IRE)**[19] 2267 5-11-0 0............................. SeanQuinlan 52
(Sophie Leech) *a bhd: struggling bef 3 out: t.o* **100/1**

P-0 **P** **Rectitude**[21] 2251 4-10-7 0.....................................(t) BrendanPowell
(Henry Tett) *hld up: blnd 4th: struggling after 4 out: t.o whn p.u bef 3 out* **100/1**

3m 55.6s (6.10) **Going Correction** +0.575s/f (Soft)
WFA 4 from 5yo+ 7lb **14 Ran SP% 122.0**
Speed ratings (Par 105): **107,106,105,104,102 100,100,95,91,89 87,86,75,**
CSF £38.09 TOTE £4.60: £1.70, £2.60, £1.10; EX 42.40 Trifecta £65.60.
Owner David Maxwell & Barber Wadlow Ltd **Bred** Snig Elevage **Trained** Withycombe, Somerset

FOCUS
After a dry night the official going remained good to soft, soft in places. Rail on Ludlow and Golf Club bends out by approximately 10yds. Race distance increased 50yds. An ordinary maiden hurdle, despite the numbers, and the pace was solid throughout. The third and fourth have been rated close to their marks.

2690 TOTEPOOL BETTING ON ALL UK RACING EBF STALLIONS "NATIONAL HUNT" NOVICES' HURDLE (QUALIFIER) (11 hdls) 2m 5f 55y
1:50 (1:50) (Class 4) 4-6-Y-O **£4,548** (£1,335; £667; £333)

Form RPR

3-5 **1** **Apple Of Our Eye**[203] 105 5-10-12 0............................ BrianHughes 113+
(Charlie Longsdon) *trckd ldrs: gng wl appr 3 out: led 2 out: looked to be gng best whn lft clr last: styd on wl* **8/1**[3]

3 **2** *37* **Round Robin (IRE)**[197] 220 4-10-12 0......................... RichardJohnson 81
(Henry Daly) *led: hit 6th: hdd 3 out: mstke 2 out: wl btn whn lft 2nd last* **2/1**[2]

6P- **3** *7* **Whitsundays (IRE)**[290] 4061 6-10-12 0................. SamTwiston-Davies 73
(Donald McCain) *hld up: rdn and outpcd appr 3 out: no imp after: lft 3rd at last* **33/1**

0 **4** *21* **Breath Of Blighty (FR)**[27] 2126 4-10-12 0...................... LiamTreadwell 54
(Paul Webber) *prom tl rdn and wknd appr 3 out* **40/1**

2- **R** **Policy Breach (IRE)**[209] 9 4-10-12 0........................ RichieMcLernon 106+
(Kim Bailey) *racd keenly: chsd ldr after 2nd: hit 5th: led 3 out: sn rdn whn hung lft: hdd 2 out: continued to hang lft: at least 1 l down and looked to be coming off 2nd best whn rn out last* **10/11**[1]

30 **P** **Midnight Folie**[18] 2299 5-10-5 0..................................... JamesDavies
(Ben Pauling) *hld up: struggling and detached after 6th: t.o 4 out: p.u after* **12/1**

5m 18.5s (3.70) **Going Correction** +0.575s/f (Soft) **6 Ran SP% 109.9**
Speed ratings: **115,100,98,90,**
CSF £23.99 TOTE £5.60: £2.50, £1.40; EX 16.30 Trifecta £203.00.
Owner The Tweed Clad Fossils **Bred** Mrs F Marriott **Trained** Over Norton, Oxon

FOCUS
Race distance increased by 85yds. Late drama in this uncompetitive novices' hurdle. A big step up from the easy winner.

2691 TOTEQUADPOT H'CAP CHASE (12 fncs) 1m 7f 212y
2:20 (2:20) (Class 3) (0-135,135) 4-Y-O+ **£11,696** (£3,434; £1,717; £858)

Form RPR

1216 **1** **Jayo Time (IRE)**[25] 2153 6-10-10 **126**...................(p) CiaranGethings(7) 140+
(Kerry Lee) *hld up: hdwy 9th: chsd ldrs appr 4 out: wnt 2nd 3 out: led 2 out: drew clr after last: styd on wl* **6/1**[2]

3-41 **2** *4* **Artifice Sivola (FR)**[26] 2138 5-11-0 **123**............... SamTwiston-Davies 133
(Lucy Wadham) *led: rdn and hdd 2 out: unable to go w wnr run-in: eased whn one pce towards fin* **7/1**[3]

2P-2 **3** *15* **Tornado In Milan (IRE)**[16] 2336 9-11-2 **125**..................... PaulMoloney 122
(Evan Williams) *chsd ldr tl mstke 7th: remained handy tl wknd appr 2 out* **6/1**[2]

34-P **4** 3/4 **Minella Definitely (IRE)**[23] 2185 8-11-6 **129**....................(p) MarkQuinlan 123
(Neil Mulholland) *hld up: pushed along appr 4 out: no imp tl plugged on after last* **10/1**
3132 **5** 7 **Father Edward (IRE)**[18] 2289 6-11-7 **130**....................(p) BrianHughes 119
(John Ferguson) *in tch: wnt 2nd after 9th: lost 2nd 3 out: rdn and wknd bef 2 out* **8/1**
1-15 **6** 15 **Rock N Rhythm (IRE)**[13] 2412 5-11-11 **134**.................... RichardJohnson 113
(Jonjo O'Neill) *hld up: nt fluent 4th: blnd 9th and lost pl: struggling to get on terms and no imp whn mstke 4 out and 3 out: wl btn after* **8/1**
15-3 **7** 1 1/2 **Ballybolley (IRE)**[19] 2274 6-11-12 **135**....................(t) DarylJacob 108
(Nigel Twiston-Davies) *prom: chsd ldr 7th tl after 9th: wknd 4 out* **7/1**[3]
1-03 **8** 9 **Kerryhead Storm (IRE)**[21] 2246 10-10-5 **114**....................(t) CharliePoste 87
(Matt Sheppard) *handy early: in rr 5th (water): struggling after 9th* **10/1**
/502 **P** **Noche De Reyes (FR)**[21] 2246 6-10-12 **121**.................... PaddyBrennan
(Tom George) *hld up: blnd bdly 1st: nt rcvr: p.u bef next* **5/1**[1]
4m 4.1s (5.60) **Going Correction** +0.575s/f (Soft) **9** Ran SP% **110.6**
Speed ratings (Par 107): **109,107,99,99,95 88,87,82,**
CSF £44.47 CT £249.22 TOTE £7.10: £2.00, £2.10, £2.10; EX 47.70 Trifecta £333.80.
Owner S R Holt & Mrs B M Ayres **Bred** E J P Kane **Trained** Byton, H'fords

FOCUS
Race distance increased by 70yds. They were well strung out in this competitive-looking handicap chase and only two mattered from some way out. A small pb from the runner-up.

2692 LAST DAY RACING UK FREE TRIAL NOVICES' H'CAP CHASE (19 fncs) 2m 7f 171y
2:55 (2:55) (Class 4) (0-105,105) 4-Y-0+ **£6,498** (£1,908; £954; £477)

Form RPR
0024 **1** **King's Song (FR)**[21] 2245 5-11-2 **95**.................... BrianHughes 112+
(David Dennis) *hld up: sn in midfield: hdwy appr 4 out: led 3 out: clr 2 out: styd on wl and wl in command after: comf* **12/1**
61-3 **2** 12 **I Am Colin**[13] 2410 6-11-11 **104**.................... SamTwiston-Davies 109+
(Nigel Twiston-Davies) *chsd ldrs: rdn bef 4 out: wnt 2nd u.p 2 out: kpt on run-in but no ch w wnr* **4/1**[2]
342 **3** 8 **Sky Watch (IRE)**[21] 2254 8-11-12 **105**....................(t) DaveCrosse 103
(Brian Barr) *prom: reminder after 9th: ev ch appr 4 out: sn rdn and outpcd: disputing 2nd 2 out but no imp on wnr: one pce after* **8/1**
P3-P **4** 5 **Miss Dimples (IRE)**[6] 2551 6-9-12 **80** ow1....................(b[1]) JamesBanks(3) 71
(Sarah-Jayne Davies) *racd keenly: handy: led appr 12th: hdd after 15th: outpcd bef 4 out: plugged on fr bef last but no ch* **16/1**
5042 **5** 1/2 **To Begin**[17] 2327 4-11-2 **104**....................(t) PaulMoloney 89+
(Charlie Mann) *hld up in rr: rdn after 15th: nvr able to get on terms w ldrs* **8/1**
160F **6** 5 **Modeligo (IRE)**[12] 2435 6-11-0 **100**....................(t) MrStanSheppard(7) 90
(Matt Sheppard) *hld up in rr: struggling 14th: effrt to try and get on terms bef 4 out: no imp: wl btn* **16/1**
-335 **7** 4 1/2 **Johns Luck (IRE)**[19] 2269 6-11-9 **102**....................(b[1]) MichaelByrne 90+
(Neil Mulholland) *midfield: hdwy 10th: led after 15th: mstke and hdd 3 out: wknd qckly next* **6/1**[3]
0-60 **8** 20 **Carhue (IRE)**[195] 265 8-10-0 **86**.................... MrMartinMcIntyre(7) 53
(Sheila Lewis) *led: hdd appr 12th where pckd: sn lost pl: wknd 14th: t.o* **10/1**
3232 **9** 3 3/4 **Battlecat**[21] 2248 8-11-7 **105**.................... ConorRing(5) 66
(Evan Williams) *midfield: j. slowly 2nd (water) and 3rd: lost pl 8th: dropped to rr 11th: n.d whn mstke 4 out: t.o* **7/2**[1]
231- **P** **It's Oscar (IRE)**[332] 3252 8-10-11 **90**....................(p) MarkQuinlan
(James Evans) *hld up: hdwy into midfield bef 12th: rdn after 15th: wknd qckly 4 out: p.u bef next* **9/1**
6m 26.3s (386.30)
WFA 4 from 5yo+ 9lb **10** Ran SP% **117.3**
CSF £61.60 CT £416.87 TOTE £9.80: £2.80, £2.50, £2.70; EX 53.10 Trifecta £564.10.
Owner Favourites Racing (Syndication) Ltd 2 **Bred** Keith Bradley **Trained** Hanley Swan, Worcestershire

FOCUS
Race distance increased by 80yds. A modest novices' handicap chase and a wide-margin winner. The easy winner has been rated up a stone plus on his best hurdle form.

2693 TOTEPOOL RACING'S BIGGEST SUPPORTER CONDITIONAL JOCKEYS' H'CAP HURDLE (12 hdls) 2m 7f 174y
3:25 (3:25) (Class 5) (0-100,97) 4-Y-0+ **£3,898** (£1,144; £572; £286)

Form RPR
6-00 **1** **Vodka Island (IRE)**[44] 1845 6-10-3 **82**.................... GeorgeBlackwell(8) 87+
(Tim Vaughan) *midfield: hdwy 6th: wnt 2nd bef 3 out: blnd last: styd on to ld fnl 150yds: won gng away* **16/1**
5-63 **2** 3 1/4 **Ordensritter (GER)**[21] 2245 7-11-0 **88**....................(bt) GilesHawkins(3) 90+
(Chris Down) *trckd ldrs: led appr 7th: rdn bef 2 out: nt fluent last: sn hung rt: hdd fnl 150yds: kpt on same pce and hld after* **9/4**[1]
-003 **3** 11 **Jackfield**[11] 2453 5-10-0 **76**.................... ConorSmith(5) 67
(Robin Dickin) *trckd ldrs: lost pl 4th: pushed along and prog appr 3 out: kpt on but nt trble front two* **4/1**[2]
00-0 **4** 5 **Thehill Ofthe Rock (IRE)**[203] 98 5-10-10 **87**....................(v[1]) PaulJohn(6) 75
(Jim Best) *prom: hit 4 out: rdn appr 3 out: sn btn* **9/2**[3]
0-4P **5** 2 3/4 **Tisfreetdream (IRE)**[159] 757 14-10-7 **83**....................(p) ArchieBellamy(5) 66
(Peter Pritchard) *hld up in rr: hdwy 4 out: rdn and wknd bef 3 out* **12/1**
/06- **6** 29 **Lily Mars (IRE)**[540] 552 8-9-9 **74**....................(t) MrShaneQuinlan(8) 45
(Neil Mulholland) *hld up: hdwy 4 out: sn chsd ldrs: wknd 3 out* **11/2**
2U-P **P** **Roc De Guye (FR)**[25] 2149 10-11-7 **97**....................(p) WilliamFeatherstone(5)
(James Evans) *w ldr: led bef 4th: hdd appr 7th: wknd 8th: t.o whn p.u bef 3 out* **14/1**
6P-R **P** **Shadesofnavy**[21] 2245 9-9-9 **71** oh7....................(t) JordanWilliams(5)
(Peter Pritchard) *led: hdd bef 4th: rdn along 6th: bhd after 7th: t.o whn p.u bef 4 out* **80/1**
P656 **P** **Just Lewis**[37] 1961 8-10-0 **71** oh2.................... CharlieDeutsch
(Nikki Evans) *hld up: hmpd 1st: hdwy 6th: lost pl 7th: t.o whn p.u bef 3 out* **16/1**
00UP **P** **League Of His Own (IRE)**[14] 2402 6-10-0 **71** oh2.....(t) ConorShoemark
(Claire Dyson) *hld up: hdwy 8th: wknd bef 3 out: sn p.u* **20/1**
6m 11.7s (19.40) **Going Correction** +0.575s/f (Soft) **10** Ran SP% **116.5**
Speed ratings (Par 103): **90,88,85,83,82 73,,,,**
CSF £53.53 CT £179.65 TOTE £11.50: £3.20, £1.50, £1.80; EX 56.30 Trifecta £209.20.
Owner Folly Road Racing Partners (1996) **Bred** Fromrussiawithlove Syndicate **Trained** Aberthin, Vale of Glamorgan
■ Stewards' Enquiry : Giles Hawkins two-day ban: used whip above permitted level (Dec 7-8)

FOCUS
Race distance increased by 90yds. A moderate handicap and again not many got into it. A massive step up from the surprise winner, with the second, third and fourth pretty much to their marks.

2694 COLLECT TOTEPOOL WINNINGS AT BETFRED SHOPS H'CAP HURDLE (11 hdls) 2m 5f 55y
3:55 (3:55) (Class 4) (0-115,115) 4-Y-0+ **£5,198** (£1,526; £763; £381)

Form RPR
21-0 **1** **Kublai (FR)**[66] 1579 5-11-5 **115**.................... CiaranGethings(7) 123+
(Philip Hobbs) *hld up: hmpd 1st: hdwy after 4 out: wnt cl 2nd 2 out: chalng whn blnd last: styd on for press to ld towards fin* **7/2**[1]
33-4 **2** hd **Old Pride (IRE)**[21] 2244 7-11-12 **115**.................... SamTwiston-Davies 119+
(David Loder) *led: pressed fr 2 out: rdn after last: sn edgd lft: hdd towards fin* **8/1**
0-P0 **3** 9 **Looks Like Power (IRE)**[23] 2182 5-11-4 **107**.................... PaulMoloney 103
(Debra Hamer) *racd keenly: hld up: hdwy after 4 out: wnt 2nd appr 3 out: lost 2nd 2 out: kpt on same pce run-in* **10/1**
P0P- **4** 2 1/2 **Moss On The Mill**[231] 5183 7-11-5 **113**.................... JamieBargary(5) 109
(Tom George) *in tch: nt fluent 1st: rdn whn chsng ldrs appr 3 out: one pce fr 2 out* **25/1**
32-4 **5** 1 3/4 **Bold Duke**[11] 880 7-11-6 **112**.................... BenPoste(3) 107+
(Edward Bevan) *midfield: hmpd 1st: effrt appr 3 out: kpt on wout troubling ldrs* **20/1**
U-04 **6** 2 3/4 **Allnecessaryforce (FR)**[18] 2287 5-11-5 **111**.................... JamesBanks(3) 102
(Alex Hales) *hld up: effrt and hdwy appr 3 out: no imp* **22/1**
0U **7** 3 1/4 **Goodoldhonkytonk (IRE)**[18] 2290 7-11-2 **105**....................(p) LiamTreadwell 93
(James Evans) *hld up: struggling 7th: plugged on fr 3 out: nvr trbld ldrs* **50/1**
F456 **8** 1 **Definite Future (IRE)**[64] 1600 6-11-3 **106**....................(p) CharliePoste 93
(Kerry Lee) *hld up: hdwy after 4 out: chsd ldrs 3 out: one pce u.p bef last* **10/1**
6-05 **9** 1 3/4 **Ballinalacken (IRE)**[9] 2490 7-11-7 **110**....................(p) DavidEngland 94
(Clare Ellam) *in tch: hdwy 7th: rdn and wknd appr 3 out* **33/1**
10-4 **10** 1/2 **Tanit River (IRE)**[23] 2182 5-11-3 **111**.................... AlanJohns(5) 95
(Tim Vaughan) *prom: rdn and wknd appr 3 out* **5/1**[3]
-0P0 **11** nk **American Life (FR)**[15] 2367 8-11-7 **110**....................(tp) SeanQuinlan 96
(Sophie Leech) *chsd ldrs tl rdn and wknd bef 4 out* **100/1**
P-06 **12** 1/2 **Bishop Wulstan (IRE)**[18] 2291 4-11-9 **112**....................(v[1]) SeanBowen 95
(Peter Bowen) *prom: rdn along briefly 4th: lost pl 7th: wknd after 4 out* **20/1**
222/ **13** 49 **Instinctual**[38] 1934 5-11-5 **108**....................(b) BrianHughes 47
(Charlie Longsdon) *midfield: pushed along appr 3 out: sn wknd* **20/1**
353/ **P** **Raduis Bleu (FR)**[580] 5488 10-9-13 **95**.................... MissLBrooke(7)
(Lady Susan Brooke) *prom tl wknd qckly after 4 out: t.o whn p.u bef 3 out* **20/1**
63-1 **F** **Scales (IRE)**[11] 2453 9-11-2 **105**.................... JamieMoore
(Kerry Lee) *hld up: blnd 2nd: midfield whn fell 7th* **9/2**[2]
5m 23.9s (9.10) **Going Correction** +0.575s/f (Soft)
WFA 4 from 5yo+ 8lb **15** Ran SP% **119.5**
Speed ratings (Par 105): **105,104,101,100,99 98,97,97,96,96 96,96,77,,**
CSF £26.26 CT £261.23 TOTE £4.70: £2.40, £3.10, £2.70; EX 39.40 Trifecta £489.50.
Owner David W Hill **Bred** Snowdrop Stud Co Ltd **Trained** Withycombe, Somerset
■ Stewards' Enquiry : Liam Treadwell jockey said mare hung right-handed on both bends

FOCUS
Race distance increased by 85yds. A competitive handicap for the grade and another race on the card when the front two were clear of the rest. The second has been rated as running a small pb in defeat.
T/Jkpt: Not won. JACKPOT PLACEPOT: £46.00 to a £1 stake. Pool of £2,790.00 - 44.2 winning units. T/Plt: £80.30 to a £1 stake. Pool: £64,822.91 - 589.17 winning tickets T/Qpdt: £19.00 to a £1 stake. Pool: £6,073.31 - 235.95 winning tickets **Darren Owen**

2695 - 2696a (Foreign Racing) - See Raceform Interactive

2415 LINGFIELD (L-H)
Tuesday, November 24

OFFICIAL GOING: Jumps courses - heavy (soft in places; 4.9); polytrack: standard
Wind: light, across Weather: overcast, showers

2697 TBA INSURANCE BENEFITS MARES' MAIDEN HURDLE (10 hdls) 2m 3f 110y
1:00 (1:01) (Class 4) 4-Y-0+ **£3,898** (£1,144; £572; £286)

Form RPR
4 **1** **Jessber's Dream (IRE)**[30] 2086 5-10-12 0....................(t) NoelFehily 116+
(Harry Fry) *chsd ldrs: clsd and upsides ldr 3 out: led and j.rt next: 4 l clr and in command whn lft further clr last: comf* **9/4**[2]
36-0 **2** 11 **Twenty Eight Guns**[45] 1854 5-10-12 0.................... LiamTreadwell 104
(Michael Scudamore) *hld up in last pair: nt fluent 1st: mstke 5th: clsd next: wnt 3rd and nt fluent 2 out: sn outpcd: wl hld whn lft 2nd last* **33/1**
11-3 **3** 6 **Midnight Silver**[19] 2302 5-10-12 0....................(t) BrendanPowell 96
(Jamie Snowden) *chsd ldrs: clsd and trcking ldrs 3 out: 5th and struggling next: wknd between last 2: lft 4th and sltly hmpd last: wnt modest 3rd towards fin* **2/1**[1]
5 **4** 3/4 **Lakeshore Lady (IRE)**[19] 2302 5-10-12 0.................... TomScudamore 95
(David Bridgwater) *chsd ldr tl clsd to ld 7th: hdd 2 out: sn rdn and btn: wl hld whn lft 3rd and hmpd last: lost 3rd towards fin* **20/1**
5 67 **Rosygo (IRE)**[187] 422 7-10-12 0.................... RichardJohnson 28
(Adrian Wintle) *hld up in last pair: clsd after 6th: wknd qckly bef 2 out: t.o* **8/1**
6 47 **Pennywell (IRE)**[204] 5-10-12 0.................... GavinSheehan
(Warren Greatrex) *midfield: clsd and wl in tch 7th: wknd qckly after next: t.o 2 out* **10/1**
00- **P** **Ruby Susie**[250] 4866 4-10-7 0....................[1] KevinJones(5)
(Seamus Mullins) *led and sn clr: hdd and mstke 7th: dropped out qckly next: t.o whn p.u 2 out* **100/1**
50-2 **F** **Happy Diva (IRE)**[19] 2302 4-10-12 0.................... JamieMoore 110
(Kerry Lee) *hld up in midfield: clsd and wl in tch 7th: wnt 2nd 2 out: sn rdn and no imp: 4 l down and hld whn fell last* **9/2**[3]
5m 26.8s (0.80) **Going Correction** +0.025s/f (Yiel) **8** Ran SP% **111.2**
Speed ratings (Par 105): **99,94,92,91,65 46,,**
CSF £61.69 TOTE £3.40: £1.40, £6.70, £1.20; EX 67.40 Trifecta £173.10.
Owner Chris Giles & Potensis Bloodstock Ltd **Bred** Denis Noonan **Trained** Seaborough, Dorset

FOCUS
All starts have been moved at this track following remeasuring, so there will be no speed figures here until there is sufficient data to calculate updated median times. All races on inner line. The ground was very testing. An ordinary mares' hurdle, although the winner did it in good style. The runner-up has been rated to the best of her bumper marks.

2698 TITANBET MONEY BACK FALLER INSURANCE NOVICES' H'CAP CHASE (14 fncs) 2m 4f
1:30 (1:31) (Class 4) (0-105,104) 4-Y-O+ **£5,198** (£1,526; £763; £381)

Form RPR
P-20 **1** **Kings River (FR)**[12] 2453 6-10-12 **90**........................ AidanColeman 102+
(Venetia Williams) *chsd ldrs: lft upsides ldr 11th: shkn up to ld and j.rt last: rdn and readily asserted flat: eased towards fin: comf* **5/1**[3]
/6-3 **2** *3 ¾* **Halo Moon**[14] 2420 7-11-7 **99**........................(p) NoelFehily 104
(Neil Mulholland) *hld up in last pair: stdy hdwy 6th: trckd ldng pair bef 3 out: rdn and styd on same pce fr 2 out: wnt 2nd towards fin* **7/4**[1]
R13- **3** *¾* **Black Narcissus (IRE)**[244] 4989 6-11-1 **93**........................ RhysFlint 96
(Alexandra Dunn) *chsd ldr tl lft in narrow ld 11th: hdd last: styd on same pce flat: lost 2nd towards fin* **10/1**
4-41 **4** *54* **Albatros De Guye (FR)**[14] 2416 5-10-4 **82**............(tp) JeremiahMcGrath 45
(Anna Newton-Smith) *in tch but a towards rr: mstke 6th: struggling after 11th: wnt 4th but btn next: sn wknd: t.o* **3/1**[2]
-054 **P** **School For Scandal (IRE)**[67] 1575 7-10-7 **92**........................ PaulO'Brien[(7)]
(Jimmy Frost) *in tch in midfield: rdn after 8th: j. slowly and struggling 10th: lost tch bef 3 out: wl bhd whn p.u 2 out* **33/1**
P532 **P** **Flash Crash**[16] 2364 6-11-9 **104**........................(t) JamesBanks[(3)]
(Barry Brennan) *in tch in midfield: pushed along 6th: drvn and struggling after 11th: sn wknd: wl bhd whn p.u 2 out* **5/1**[3]
/3P- **P** **Four Shuck Men (IRE)**[429] 1597 7-10-6 **84**....................(p) RobertDunne
(Sarah-Jayne Davies) *led tl blnd and hdd 11th: 4th and btn bef next: 5th and wkng whn p.u 2 out* **20/1**

5m 46.7s (11.70) **Going Correction** +0.025s/f (Yiel) **7 Ran SP% 111.5**
Speed ratings (Par 105): **77,75,75,53, ,**
CSF £14.12 TOTE £5.80: £2.90, £1.40; EX 19.10 Trifecta £95.80.
Owner Mrs Julian Blackwell **Bred** I Hanamy **Trained** Kings Caple, H'fords

FOCUS
Not a bad race for the level, and the unexposed winner could rate a fair bit higher.

2699 MB REFURBISHMENT NOVICES' HURDLE (8 hdls) 2m
2:00 (2:00) (Class 4) 4-Y-O+ **£3,898** (£1,144; £572; £286)

Form RPR
1 **1** **Master Jake (IRE)**[11] 2474 7-11-5 0........................ HarrySkelton 125+
(Dan Skelton) *mde all: j.w: rdn between last 2: kpt on: rdn out* **5/4**[1]
2 *5* **Alberta (IRE)**[265] 4575 6-10-12 0........................ SamTwiston-Davies 113+
(Jim Best) *in tch: chsd ldr 5th: wnt 2nd 2 out: sn rdn: 2 l down and hit last: no ex flat: plugged on* **5/2**[3]
210- **3** *6* **Wabanaki (IRE)**[228] 5255 5-10-12 0........................ PaulMoloney 105+
(Evan Williams) *hld up in rr: clsd to go 4th bef 2 out: hit 2 out: reminders and wnt 3rd between last 2: no imp* **2/1**[2]
4 *10* **On Demand**[289] 4-10-5 0........................ GavinSheehan 88
(Simon Hodgson) *chsd ldrs tl lost pl 4th: wd on downhill run and looked wl hld in 6th bef 2 out: plugged on to go modest 4th flat* **100/1**
5P **5** *1 ¼* **Contempt Of Court (IRE)**[21] 2257 6-10-12 0............(v[1]) DenisO'Regan 97
(Mark Pitman) *chsd wnr: wd on downhill run after 3 out: lost 2nd and hit 2 out: wknd between last 2* **33/1**
60P **6** *13* **Lunar Flow**[19] 2299 4-10-12 0........................ BrendanPowell 81
(Jamie Snowden) *chsd ldrs tl 3 out: sn struggling u.p: wknd bef 2 out* **100/1**
/0 **7** *25* **Cantor**[22] 2251 7-10-12 0........................ MattieBatchelor 56
(Daniel O'Brien) *a towards rr: lost tch after 3 out: t.o* **100/1**

4m 28.45s (0.45) **Going Correction** +0.025s/f (Yiel)
WFA 4 from 5yo+ 7lb **7 Ran SP% 112.3**
Speed ratings (Par 105): **99,96,93,88,87 81,68**
CSF £4.73 TOTE £2.30: £1.20, £1.40; EX 4.10 Trifecta £5.70.
Owner Craig Buckingham **Bred** Tyrone Molloy **Trained** Alcester, Warwicks

FOCUS
Fair novice hurdle form. The third and fifth have been rated similar to their bumper marks.

2700 DOWNLOAD TITANBET SPORTS APP H'CAP HURDLE (10 hdls) 2m 3f 110y
2:30 (2:30) (Class 3) (0-130,129) 3-Y-O+ **£5,749** (£1,735; £894; £473)

Form RPR
-021 **1** **Sirop De Menthe (FR)**[3] 2647 5-10-12 **118** 7ex............ LucyGardner[(3)] 130+
(Sue Gardner) *midfield: chsd clr ldr 4th: grad clsd 7th: led and travelling strly bef 2 out: sn clr: v easily* **5/4**[1]
24-P **2** *12* **Reblis (FR)**[9] 2517 10-10-5 **108**........................(b) JoshuaMoore 102
(Gary Moore) *led: sn clr: hdd bef 2 out: sn brushed aside by wnr: plugged on for clr 2nd* **14/1**
41-5 **3** *15* **Blue Bear (IRE)**[198] 225 6-11-8 **125**........................ MarcGoldstein 104
(Diana Grissell) *hld up in rr: hdwy 6th: wnt 3rd 7th: rdn and no imp after next: wl hld whn mstke 2 out* **25/1**
30-5 **4** *4 ½* **Minstrels Gallery (IRE)**[14] 2415 6-11-8 **125**........................ LeightonAspell 100
(Lucy Wadham) *hld up in last pair: niggled along after 4th: struggling 6th: t.o 3 out* **4/1**[3]
0/1- **P** **Lovcen (GER)**[544] 509 10-11-12 **129**........................(t) PaulMoloney
(Sophie Leech) *chsd clr ldr tl 4th: dropped to last 6th: lost tch after next: t.o whn p.u 2 out* **12/1**
2-51 **P** **Rock Of Leon**[14] 2415 4-11-12 **129**........................(t) HarrySkelton
(Dan Skelton) *chsd ldrs: 4th and struggling 7th: j. slowly 3 out: losing tch and p.u wl bef next* **5/2**[2]

5m 22.75s (-3.25) **Going Correction** +0.025s/f (Yiel) **6 Ran SP% 111.2**
Speed ratings (Par 107): **107,102,96,94, ,**
CSF £16.86 TOTE £2.40: £1.60, £4.40; EX 20.40 Trifecta £181.80.
Owner Clear Racing & Partner **Bred** Francois-Marie Cottin **Trained** Longdown, Devon

FOCUS
This proved straightforward for the favourite, with his two main market rivals failing to shine.

2701 BET AND WATCH AT TITANBET.CO.UK INTERMEDIATE H'CAP CHASE (18 fncs) 2m 7f 110y
3:00 (3:01) (Class 3) (0-130,128) 4-Y-O+ **£6,388** (£1,928; £993; £526)

Form RPR
U-3P **1** **Wilton Milan (IRE)**[17] 2348 7-11-11 **127**........................(t) HarrySkelton 134+
(Dan Skelton) *hld up in last pair: clsd 1/2-way: trckd ldrs 12th: j.rt into ld and pckd 3 out: 1 l ahd last: wandering and drvn flat: hdd and bmpd fnl 100yds: rallied to ld again last strides* **6/1**
1PP- **2** *nk* **Chase The Spud**[300] 3922 7-11-10 **126**........................ PaddyBrennan 132
(Fergal O'Brien) *mde most tl hdd 3 out: ev ch and j.rt next: 1 l down last: rallied u.p to ld fnl 100yds: edgd rt u.p: hdd and no ex last strides* **9/2**[2]
133- **3** *12* **Fourovakind**[234] 5138 10-11-11 **127**........................(b) LeightonAspell 123
(Harry Whittington) *nt fluent and j.rt several times: chsd ldrs: 4th and outpcd after 15th: wl hld 2 out: plugged on to go 3rd flat* **7/4**[1]
-460 **4** *5* **Master Rajeem (USA)**[14] 2425 6-11-3 **119**....................(p) TrevorWhelan 108
(Neil King) *w ldr: mstke 11th: 3rd and struggling 3 out: sn rdn and wknd next: lost 3rd flat* **14/1**
46U- **F** **Rocky Bender (IRE)**[243] 5000 10-10-3 **105**........................ AidanColeman
(Venetia Williams) *j. slowly: in tch in rr tl fell 6th* **5/1**[3]
15/6 **P** **Berkeley Barron (IRE)**[44] 1867 7-11-12 **128**........................(t) IanPopham
(Richard Phillips) *in tch in midfield: blnd 1st: dropped to rr and reminders after 9th: j. slowly 10th: losing tch whn j. 11th: p.u 12th* **8/1**
5115 **P** **Vikekhal (FR)**[24] 2184 6-11-11 **127**........................(b) JoshuaMoore
(Gary Moore) *in tch: cl 5th and rdn 14th: lost tch next: tailing off whn p.u wl bef 3 out* **8/1**

6m 55.0s (-5.00) **Going Correction** +0.025s/f (Yiel) **7 Ran SP% 114.4**
Speed ratings (Par 107): **109,108,104,103, ,**
CSF £33.05 CT £66.34 TOTE £6.30: £2.90, £2.40; EX 33.80 Trifecta £103.30.
Owner Terry Warner **Bred** Michael Leacy **Trained** Alcester, Warwicks

FOCUS
This was always likely to be a gruelling test considering the conditions and two came clear late. The winner has been rated close to his best.

2702 TITANBET.CO.UK STANDARD OPEN NATIONAL HUNT FLAT RACE (TO BE RUN ON ALL-WEATHER TRACK) 2m
3:30 (3:32) (Class 6) 4-6-Y-O **£1,559** (£457; £228; £114)

Form RPR
1 **Westerbee (IRE)** 4-10-2 0........................ KevinJones[(5)] 95+
(Seamus Mullins) *hld up in rr: rapid hdwy to ld 5f out: rdn and fnd ex over 1f out: r.o wl: comf* **25/1**
2 *3 ¼* **Royal Plaza**[179] 544 4-11-0 0........................ WayneHutchinson 98
(Alan King) *t.k.h: hld up in tch: rdn over 2f out: swtchd rt and hdwy wl over 1f out: styd on ins fnl f: wnt 2nd fnl 50yds: no threat to wnr* **6/1**[3]
6-3 **3** *1 ¼* **The Poodle Faker**[24] 2188 4-11-0 0........................ TomO'Brien 97
(Hughie Morrison) *chsd ldr tl led after 2f: hdd 5f out: rdn over 2f out: no imp over 1f out: styd on same pce ins fnl f: lost 2nd fnl 50yds* **8/15**[1]
0-60 **4** *1* **Romanee Vivant**[14] 2421 5-10-7 0........................ TrevorWhelan 89
(Neil King) *chsd ldrs: 3rd and rdn 3f out: unable qck over 1f out: lost 3rd and one pce ins fnl f* **33/1**
56 **5** *3* **Trans Express (IRE)**[22] 2250 5-10-11 0........................ LucyGardner[(3)] 93
(Sue Gardner) *in tch: rdn over 2f out: unable qck 2f out: styd on same pce after* **12/1**
6 *7* **Maid Of Milan (IRE)**[205] 4-10-7 0........................ NoelFehily 79
(Charlie Mann) *led for 2f: chsd ldr tl 5f out: lost pl and rdn over 3f out: wknd over 1f out* **9/2**[2]

3m 46.25s (226.25) **6 Ran SP% 112.2**
CSF £158.74 TOTE £14.00: £11.20, £3.50; EX 97.20 Trifecta £406.00.
Owner Dr R Jowett **Bred** Oliver Loughlin **Trained** Wilsford-Cum-Lake, Wilts

FOCUS
A bit of a turn up here in what was an ordinary bumper. The fourth and fifth have been rated to their marks.
T/Plt: £434.30 to a £1 stake. Pool: £70,431.96 - 118.38 winning units. T/Qpdt: £157.50 to a £1 stake. Pool: £5,344.88 - 25.10 winning units. **Steve Payne**

2422
SEDGEFIELD (L-H)
Tuesday, November 24

OFFICIAL GOING: Soft (5.3)
Wind: moderate, 1/2 behind Weather: fine

2703 BETFRED RACING "LIKE US ON FACEBOOK" H'CAP HURDLE (DIV I) (8 hdls) 2m 178y
12:20 (12:20) (Class 5) (0-100,98) 3-Y-O+ **£2,729** (£801; £400; £200)

Form RPR
5540 **1** **Nafaath (IRE)**[25] 2165 9-11-2 **98**........................(p) RonanShort[(10)] 110+
(Donald McCain) *hld up in rr: hdwy to chse ldrs 4th: 2nd appr 2 out: styd on to ld last 100yds* **5/1**
3F/P **2** *6* **Philharmonic Hall**[14] 2413 7-11-2 **88**........................ DarylJacob 94
(Peter Hiatt) *trckd ldr: led appr 2 out: hit last: hdd and no ex last 100yds* **8/1**
0003 **3** *17* **Snowed In (IRE)**[69] 1552 6-11-8 **94**........................ SeanQuinlan 88
(Barbara Butterworth) *led: drvn 3 out: hdd appr next: wknd and poor 3rd whn hit last* **11/4**[1]
2P03 **4** *11* **The Ice Factor**[18] 2322 7-10-11 **88**........................(p) JamieHamilton[(5)] 66
(Alison Hamilton) *chsd ldrs: lost pl 4th: sn wl bhd: tk distant 4th last* **9/2**[3]
6P55 **5** *10* **Mrs Grass**[18] 2322 8-9-9 **72** oh3........................(vt) DiarmuidO'Regan[(5)] 40
(Jonathan Haynes) *chsd ldr: lost pl after 5th: sn bhd* **9/1**
6P00 **P** **Captain Sharpe**[7] 2559 7-11-6 **95**........................(v) BrianToomey[(3)]
(Kenny Johnson) *in rr: mstke 2nd: chsd ldrs 4th: mstke next: lost pl and p.u bef 3 out* **50/1**
40-0 **P** **Unidexter (IRE)**[25] 2162 5-11-3 **92**........................(t) HarryChalloner[(3)]
(Richard Ford) *in rr: bhd and drvn 4th: sn tailedd off: p.u bef 2 out* **14/1**
4036 **P** **Cumbrian Farmer**[87] 1400 8-10-3 **75**........................(p) HenryBrooke
(Kenneth Slack) *in rr: drvn 2nd: lost pl 4th: sn bhd: t.o whn p.u bef 2 out* **4/1**[2]

4m 19.7s (12.80) **Going Correction** +1.05s/f (Soft) **8 Ran SP% 111.3**
Speed ratings (Par 103): **111,108,100,95,90 , ,**
CSF £41.16 CT £126.57 TOTE £6.40: £1.80, £2.30, £1.50; EX 45.90 Trifecta £253.60.
Owner D McCain Jnr **Bred** Shadwell Estate Company Limited **Trained** Cholmondeley, Cheshire
■ A first winner on just his second ride for Ronan Short.

FOCUS
Divided bends, hurdles sited on outer and distances as advertised. This moderate handicap was run at a fair gallop and it only concerned the principals from three out. The winner has been rated back to form.

2704 BETFRED TV CONDITIONAL JOCKEYS' NOVICES' HURDLE (BETFRED HURDLE SERIES QUALIFIER) 2m 3f 188y

12:50 (12:50) (Class 4) 4-Y-O+ **£3,378** (£992; £496; £248)

Form RPR

131- **1** **Libby Mae (IRE)**[259] 4701 5-9-11 0 JoeColliver(3) 110+
(Micky Hammond) *chsd ldrs: clr 2nd sn after 3 out: styd on to ld last 150yds* **3/1**[2]

2062 **2** *3* **Raise A Spark**[23] 2212 5-10-1 110 JamesCowley(6) 113
(Donald McCain) *hld up in rr: hdwy to trck ldrs 4th: led sn after 3 out: 3 l clr next: sn drvn: hdd and no ex last 150yds* **7/1**

2-12 **3** *12* **Ryedale Racer**[18] 2319 4-10-7 0 JamieHamilton 101
(Malcolm Jefferson) *trckd ldrs: led 3rd: hdd 5th: led briefly 3 out: sn drvn: wknd appr 2 out* **5/6**[1]

3162 **4** *11* **Tickenwolf (IRE)**[33] 2025 5-10-7 115 FinianO'Toole(7) 99
(George Moore) *chsd ldrs: lost pl 3 out: tk poor 4th appr 2 out* **11/2**[3]

50-0 **5** *14* **Wee Jock Elliot**[23] 2210 5-10-7 0 CraigNichol 76
(Alistair Whillans) *chsd ldrs: pushed along 4th: lost pl after next: sn bhd* **66/1**

6065 **6** *2* **Stormont Bridge**[53] 1739 7-9-13 80 (t) ThomasDowson(8) 74
(Maurice Barnes) *led to 3rd: led 5th: hdd sn after 3 out: lost pl bef next* **150/1**

60 **7** *1 1/4* **Fire Rock (IRE)**[18] 2318 4-10-1 0 RyanDay(6) 73
(Nicky Richards) *chsd ldrs: drvn and lost pl bef 3 out: sn bhd* **100/1**

5m 7.8s (13.70) **7 Ran SP% 110.6**
CSF £21.31 TOTE £3.50: £1.40, £2.90; EX 18.50 Trifecta £30.70.
Owner Mr and Mrs Paul Chapman **Bred** Martin Cullinane **Trained** Middleham, N Yorks
■ Stewards' Enquiry : Joe Colliver two-day ban: used whip above permitted level (Dec 8-9)

FOCUS
An ordinary novice event, confined to conditional riders, that was a two-horse race from the home turn. The runner-up is the benchmark. The winner has been rated similar to her bumper form.

2705 BETFRED "BE PART OF THE ACTION" H'CAP CHASE (13 fncs) 2m 77y

1:20 (1:20) (Class 5) (0-100,99) 4-Y-O+ **£3,249** (£954; £477; £238)

Form RPR

4555 **1** **Roxyfet (FR)**[43] 1891 5-10-0 80 FinianO'Toole(7) 94+
(Micky Hammond) *chsd ldrs: styd on to ld between last 2* **10/1**

665P **2** *3 1/4* **Duhallowcountry (IRE)**[18] 2320 9-9-7 73 oh10 (p) MissAWaugh(7) 84
(Victor Thompson) *led 2nd to 4th: led bef 3 out: hdd and no ex between last 2* **40/1**

2-30 **3** *15* **Star Presenter (IRE)**[65] 1596 7-11-9 99 JonathanEngland(3) 98
(Richard Drake) *chsd ldrs: outpcd after 3 out: kpt on to take poor 3rd between last 2* **5/1**[2]

1240 **4** *11* **Seventeen Black (IRE)**[17] 2339 7-10-7 85 GrantCockburn(5) 70
(Stuart Coltherd) *in rr: sme hdwy 8th: tk poor 5th between last 2* **14/1**

20-4 **5** *nse* **Rosquero (FR)**[17] 2339 10-10-4 80 (v) BrianToomey(3) 65
(Kenny Johnson) *chsd ldrs: lost pl 6th: sn bhd* **5/1**[2]

40-0 **6** *3/4* **Jokers And Rogues (IRE)**[17] 2339 7-11-5 92 BrianHughes 76
(John Wade) *j.rt: led to 2nd: led 4th: hdd bef 3 out: wknd qckly between last 2* **13/2**[3]

0/ **7** *18* **Cerca Trova (IRE)**[424] 1637 9-11-7 94 JJBurke 60
(J T R Dreaper, Ire) *in rr: mstke 8th: sn wl bhd: t.o 2 out* **9/2**[1]

16P/ **P** **Bob's Dream (IRE)**[623] 4748 13-10-9 89 (t) MrTHamilton(7)
(Alison Hamilton) *chsd ldrs: lost pl 6th: sn bhd: t.o whn p.u bef 3 out* **8/1**

P-2R **P** **Dundee Blue (IRE)**[18] 2321 7-10-12 88 (bt) TonyKelly(3)
(Henry Hogarth) *in rr: bhd and reminders 6th: t.o 7th whn p.u after 2 out* **5/1**[2]

4m 19.2s (5.20) **Going Correction** +0.45s/f (Soft) **9 Ran SP% 110.8**
Speed ratings (Par 103): **105,103,95,90,90 89,80, ,**
CSF £243.37 CT £2136.91 TOTE £12.10: £2.80, £5.00, £2.00; EX 412.30 Trifecta £3200.50.
Owner R J Ball **Bred** Jacky Thomas **Trained** Middleham, N Yorks

FOCUS
A very weak handicap. A small pb from the second.

2706 BETFRED RACING "LIKE US ON FACEBOOK" H'CAP HURDLE (DIV II) (8 hdls) 2m 178y

1:50 (1:50) (Class 5) (0-100,97) 3-Y-O+ **£2,729** (£801; £400; £200)

Form RPR

5/0- **1** **Beaumont's Party (IRE)**[38] 1547 8-11-10 95 BrianHughes 99
(Chris Grant) *hld up towards rr: hdwy 3 out: 2nd appr 2 out: led sn after last: drvn rt out* **12/1**

/53- **2** *3/4* **Runswick Relax**[248] 9-10-8 82 (t) ColmMcCormack(3) 86
(Kenneth Slack) *mid-div: lost pl 3rd: sn bhd and drvn along: sme hdwy and modest 7th 2 out: styd on wl to take 2nd last 75yds* **7/1**[3]

5P46 **3** *4 1/2* **Landmeafortune (IRE)**[18] 2322 6-11-5 90 [1] HenryBrooke 89
(Martin Todhunter) *mid-div: outpcd 3 out: hdwy to chse ldrs next: tk 3rd post* **7/1**[3]

0002 **4** *nse* **Beyondtemptation**[14] 2427 7-10-10 86 (t) DiarmuidO'Regan(5) 85
(Jonathan Haynes) *led tl after 3 out: led appr next: hdd sn after last: sn wknd* **5/1**[2]

3303 **5** *5* **My Escapade (IRE)**[26] 2148 4-11-5 97 MissAWaugh(7) 91
(Simon Waugh) *w ldr: led after 3 out: hdd appr next: wknd last* **5/1**[2]

5056 **6** *10* **Jebulani**[26] 2148 5-10-8 79 (t) BrianHarding 66
(Barry Murtagh) *mid-div: chsd ldrs 3 out: wknd last* **5/1**[2]

-6P5 **7** *3 1/4* **Toarmandowithlove (IRE)**[19] 2294 7-11-3 95 (bt) JamesCorbett(7) 76
(Susan Corbett) *in rr: drvn and sme hdwy 5th: reminders next: wknd between last 2* **28/1**

1/PP **8** *8* **Vodka Red (IRE)**[7] 2560 7-11-8 93 (p) PeterBuchanan 66
(Kenny Johnson) *racd wd: hld up in rr: hdwy 4th: chsng ldrs next: lost pl sn after 3 out: sn bhd* **33/1**

4-04 **9** *20* **Wot A Shot (IRE)**[85] 1432 6-11-3 95 (t) RyanDay(7) 48
(Nicky Richards) *in rr: hit 4th: sn drvn and bhd: t.o 2 out* **3/1**[1]

-P0P **P** **Petre' Island (IRE)**[18] 2323 6-9-12 72 AdamNicol(3)
(Katie Scott) *chsd ldrs: rdn 3 out: sn wknd: poor 8th whn p.u between last 2* **22/1**

4m 24.3s (17.40) **Going Correction** +1.05s/f (Soft)
WFA 4 from 5yo+ 7lb **10 Ran SP% 118.4**
Speed ratings (Par 103): **101,100,98,98,96 91,89,86,76,**
CSF £92.34 CT £643.54 TOTE £9.20: £2.70, £3.00, £3.40; EX 93.30 Trifecta £671.40.
Owner Elliott Brothers And Peacock **Bred** Mrs Joan Murphy **Trained** Newton Bewley, Co Durham

FOCUS
The second division of the moderate 2m handicap hurdle. There was no hanging about and the fourth helps set the level. The third has been rated to his mark.

2707 BETFRED LOTTO "£100K CASH GIVEAWAY" NOVICES' H'CAP CHASE (16 fncs) 2m 3f 65y

2:20 (2:20) (Class 4) (0-105,105) 4-Y-O+ **£4,548** (£1,335; £667; £333)

Form RPR

-223 **1** **Retrieve The Stick**[15] 2400 6-11-12 105 (b) BrianHughes 113
(Malcolm Jefferson) *mid-div: hdwy to chse ldrs 8th: mstke 11th: 2nd 2 out: led last: drvn out* **7/1**

4-42 **2** *2* **Tomorrow's Legend**[17] 2339 5-11-5 101 AdamNicol(3) 109
(George Moore) *in rr: hdwy to chse ldrs 10th: led 3 out: hdd last no ex* **7/2**[2]

6-4P **3** *1 1/4* **Lord Usher (IRE)**[67] 1572 8-11-3 101 DaleIrving(5) 106
(George Charlton) *in rr: hdwy 4 out: styd on fr 2 out: tk 3rd appr last: kpt on same pce* **18/1**

60P6 **4** *2 1/2* **Theflyingportrait (IRE)**[23] 2212 6-11-7 100 (t) JJBurke 101
(Jennie Candlish) *in rr: hdwy 11th: chsng ldrs 4 out: kpt on one pce fr 2 out* **20/1**

233- **5** *15* **Wakhan (IRE)**[307] 3797 7-10-7 86 DannyCook 75
(Sue Smith) *prom: drvn 10th: wknd 3 out* **5/2**[1]

PP-P **6** *4 1/2* **Asuncion (FR)**[26] 2143 5-10-2 84 (p) TonyKelly(3) 66
(Rebecca Menzies) *chsd ldrs: lost pl bef 3 out* **40/1**

20-2 **7** *17* **Newyearsresolution (IRE)**[11] 2478 11-9-7 79 oh4 MissAWaugh(7) 44
(Simon Waugh) *nt fluent in rr: bhd fr 9th* **22/1**

2-42 **P** **Newspage (IRE)**[183] 472 9-9-12 84 (b) MrWEasterby(7)
(John Wade) *w ldr: led 4th tl after 6th: lft in ld 10th: hdd 3 out: wknd between last 2: poor 6th whn p.u bef last* **6/1**[3]

6PF- **P** **Silver Gent (IRE)**[278] 4321 7-11-11 104 [1] BrianHarding
(Donald McCain) *in rr: drvn 7th: bhd 9th: t.o whn p.u bef 4 out* **11/1**

4P0- **U** **Clan Chief**[215] 5490 6-11-0 93 LucyAlexander
(N W Alexander) *chsd ldrs: led after 6th: mstke and uns rdr 10th* **8/1**

P **P** **Allthedollars (IRE)**[43] 1888 5-10-7 86 (p[1]) SeanQuinlan
(Joanne Foster) *led to 4th: mstke 9th: sn lost pl and bhd: t.o whn p.u bef 12th* **80/1**

5m 11.3s (8.30) **Going Correction** +0.45s/f (Soft) **11 Ran SP% 115.1**
Speed ratings (Par 105): **100,99,98,97,91 89,82, , ,**
CSF £30.87 CT £425.04 TOTE £4.10: £3.00, £1.70, £4.10; EX 27.80 Trifecta £462.80.
Owner Newstead Racing Partnership **Bred** Mrs M Barker **Trained** Norton, N Yorks

FOCUS
Not a bad handicap for the grade and it was another race run at a decent gallop. The third has been rated in line with his hurdle form.

2708 BETFRED RACING "FOLLOW US ON TWITTER" H'CAP CHASE (21 fncs) 3m 2f 59y

2:50 (2:50) (Class 5) (0-100,96) 4-Y-O+ **£3,249** (£954; £477; £238)

Form RPR

0-03 **1** **Not A Bother Boy (IRE)**[26] 2147 7-11-2 96 TrevorRyan(10) 110+
(Sue Smith) *mid-div: hdwy to chse ldrs 10th: 2nd 4 out: led next: styd on wl fr 2 out: drvn out* **3/1**[1]

6- **2** *7* **Native Que (IRE)**[47] 1835 8-11-4 88 (tp) BrianHughes 92
(J T R Dreaper, Ire) *trckd ldrs: 3rd between last 2: kpt on to take 2nd clsng stages* **9/1**

6101 **3** *2* **Urban Gale (IRE)**[15] 2402 10-11-12 96 (p) SeanQuinlan 100
(Joanne Foster) *w ldrs: hit 6th: led 12th to 14th: hit 3 out: 3rd appr 2 out: kpt on same pce* **7/1**

3135 **4** *1 1/2* **Over And Above (IRE)**[82] 1462 9-11-6 90 (tp) HenryBrooke 92
(Henry Hogarth) *mid-div: chsd ldrs 12th: outpcd 16th: kpt on fr 2 out: tk modest 4th appr last* **11/1**

654 **5** *13* **Veroce (FR)**[15] 2397 6-11-11 95 JakeGreenall 86
(Mark Walford) *led to 3rd: led 6th to 12th: led 14th: hdd 3 out: stmbld bef next: wknd between last 2* **6/1**[3]

3-04 **6** *7* **Apache Pilot**[26] 2147 7-11-0 89 (tp) DaraghBourke(5) 75
(Maurice Barnes) *mid-div: chsd ldrs 9th: outpcd 16th: modest 5th whn mstke 3 out: wknd between last 2* **11/2**[2]

2-00 **P** **West Ship Master (IRE)**[47] 1835 11-11-8 95 (v) DerekFox(3)
(Paul Stafford, Ire) *w ldrs: led 3rd to 6th: reminders 13th: sn lost pl and bhd: t.o 15th: p.u bef 3 out* **16/1**

4-6U **P** **Brunello**[10] 2500 7-11-8 95 AdamNicol(3)
(Michael Smith) *in rr: hit 11th: sn bhd: t.o 4 out: p.u bef next* **33/1**

2P3P **P** **Generous Chief (IRE)**[25] 2173 7-11-1 90 (b) DiarmuidO'Regan(5)
(Chris Grant) *in rr: drvn after 4th: t.o 6th: p.u bef next* **10/1**

P-2P **P** **Harleys Max**[45] 1853 6-10-6 83 JamesCorbett(7)
(Susan Corbett) *t.k.h in rr: mstke 5th: hdwy 9th: sn chsng ldrs: lost pl 16th: bhd 3 out: t.o whn p.u bef last* **66/1**

0-22 **P** **Camillas Wish (IRE)**[26] 2147 6-11-4 88 (p) JJBurke
(J T R Dreaper, Ire) *in rr: drvn 8th: sn bhd: t.o 11th: p.u bef 13th* **8/1**

7m 21.7s (10.70) **Going Correction** +0.45s/f (Soft) **11 Ran SP% 116.0**
Speed ratings (Par 103): **101,98,98,97,93 91, , , ,**
CSF £30.17 CT £175.21 TOTE £4.10: £1.60, £3.20, £2.30; EX 36.90 Trifecta £297.10.
Owner Mrs S Smith **Bred** Kenneth William Quinn **Trained** High Eldwick, W Yorks

FOCUS
A moderate staying handicap, run at an average gallop. The form is fair. The third and fourth help set the level.

2709 BETFRED MOBILE STANDARD OPEN NATIONAL HUNT FLAT RACE 2m 178y

3:20 (3:26) (Class 6) 4-6-Y-O **£1,949** (£572; £286; £143)

Form RPR

4 **1** **Storm Forecast (IRE)**[45] 1858 4-11-2 0 BrianHughes 100+
(Malcolm Jefferson) *trckd ldrs: 2nd 5f out: sn led: drvn clr over 1f out* **9/2**

2 *9* **What Happens Now (IRE)**[247] 6-11-2 0 [1] BrianHarding 90
(Donald McCain) *trckd ldrs: led briefly 5f out: rdn 3f out: kpt on one pce* **2/1**[1]

6- **3** *5* **Heilan Rebel (IRE)**[248] 4915 5-11-2 0 LucyAlexander 85
(N W Alexander) *hld up in mid-div: chsd ldrs 7f out: sn drvn: modest 3rd over 4f out: one pce* **14/1**

4 *14* **Flying Jack** 5-10-11 0 DaraghBourke(5) 71
(Maurice Barnes) *unruly and led rdrless to post: racd in last: shkn up 8f out: reminders over 5f out: modest 3rd over 3f out* **33/1**

4 **5** *22* **Robbing The Prey (IRE)**[33] 2031 4-11-2 0 DarylJacob 49
(Nick Kent) *led: t.k.h: hdd 5f out: sn lost pl and bhd* **3/1**[3]

6 3 ¼ **Benjamin Tree (IRE)** 4-10-13 0 CraigNichol(3) 46
(Rose Dobbin) *hld up in mid-div: chsd ldrs 7f out: drvn 5f out: sn lost pl and bhd* 11/4[2]

4m 18.8s (17.50) **Going Correction** +1.05s/f (Soft) 6 Ran SP% **112.8**
Speed ratings: **100,95,93,86,76 74**
CSF £14.10 TOTE £4.20: £1.90, £1.50; EX 12.40 Trifecta £82.40.
Owner J M Jefferson **Bred** Mrs Christine Kelly **Trained** Norton, N Yorks

FOCUS
An ordinary bumper, run at an uneven gallop. It's been rated through the third.
T/Plt: £475.80 to a £1 stake. Pool: £63,166.58 - 96.90 winning units. T/Qpdt: £66.80 to a £1 stake. Pool: £7,650.14 - 84.65 winning units. **Walter Glynn**

2515 FONTWELL (L-H)
Wednesday, November 25

OFFICIAL GOING: Soft (heavy in places; 5.5)
Wind: almost nil Weather: overcast

2710 PATRICK YOUR 2 WEEKS LATE MURPHY NOVICES' HURDLE (10 hdls) 2m 3f 33y
12:40 (12:40) (Class 4) 4-Y-O+ £3,249 (£954; £477; £238)

Form RPR
21 1 **Clondaw Cian (IRE)**[19] 2317 5-10-12 0 TomO'Brien 135+
(Suzy Smith) *trckd ldr: chal gng best 2 out: led last: pushed clr* 5/4[2]

1 2 9 **Bigmartre (FR)**[35] 2011 4-11-5 133 GavinSheehan 130+
(Harry Whittington) *led: rdn after 2 out: hdd last: sn hld by wnr but wl clr of remainder* 1/1[1]

56-5 3 34 **Itsaboutime (IRE)**[185] 447 5-10-7 0 ConorRing(5) 88
(Helen Nelmes) *hld up: detached fr 4th: wnt modest 3rd run-in: nvr any threat to ldrs* 80/1

4 1 ¼ **Dukes Den**[140] 4-10-12 0 NoelFehily 86
(Charlie Mann) *hld up: detached fr 4th: hit 5th: wnt modest 4th run-in: nvr any threat to ldrs* 25/1

4-2 5 8 **Blue April (FR)**[28] 2136 4-10-12 0 NickScholfield 78
(Jeremy Scott) *trckd ldrs tl rdn after 3 out: sn wknd* 5/1[3]

5-64 6 ¾ **Threebarrymen (IRE)**[19] 2312 4-10-9 0 MattGriffiths(3) 77
(Jeremy Scott) *detached fr 4th: a in rr* 33/1

7 54 **Due South (IRE)** 4-10-12 0 TomCannon 23
(Linda Jewell) *in tch tl 4th: sn struggling in detached gp: t.o* 100/1

2/3- 8 3 ¾ **Spring Wolf**[390] 2172 7-10-12 0 DaveCrosse 19
(John Ryall) *trckd ldr tl rdn after 3 out: wknd next: t.o* 16/1

9 8 **Grayhawk (IRE)**[206] 5-10-5 0 OCdtOswaldWedmore(7) 11
(Diana Grissell) *detached fr 4th: a in rr: t.o* 100/1

5m 10.4s (11.00) **Going Correction** +0.925s/f (Soft) 9 Ran SP% **127.0**
Speed ratings (Par 105): **113,109,94,94,91 90,67,66,63**
CSF £3.35 TOTE £2.50: £1.10, £1.10, £19.20; EX 3.50 Trifecta £135.60.
Owner Wolf Allisat & Chris Ames **Bred** James And Carmel Stephenson **Trained** Lewes, E Sussex

FOCUS
Fences were on the inner and hurdles middle inner. Bends were moved out by 3yds on to fresher ground. Race increased by 24yds. Tom O'Brien said of the ground: "it rides worse than it walks. It's quite testing". Little depth to this and the market leaders, both fair types, dominating. A big step up from the winner on his bumper form.

2711 CHANCELLOR OF THE FORMCHECKER H'CAP HURDLE (11 hdls) 2m 5f 139y
1:10 (1:11) (Class 3) (0-130,125) 3-Y-O+ £5,458 (£1,602; £801; £400)

Form RPR
F12- 1 **Bells 'N' Banjos (IRE)**[220] 5410 5-11-8 121 GavinSheehan 137+
(Warren Greatrex) *nt a fluent: prom: led 4th: pushed clr between last 2: heavily eased towards fin* 5/2[2]

F-1P 2 14 **Decimus (IRE)**[86] 1419 8-11-9 125 MattGriffiths(3) 122
(Jeremy Scott) *led tl 4th: prom tl dropped to hld 4th u.p after 3 out: styd on to regain 2nd after last but no ch w easy wnr* 7/1

14-F 3 3 ½ **Degooch (IRE)**[197] 255 6-11-6 119 NoelFehily 111
(Johnny Farrelly) *hld up bhd ldrs: smooth hdwy to dispute 2nd after 3 out: rdn bef next where nt fluent: 4th sn after last: tired but regained 3rd cl home* 7/4[1]

020F 4 ¾ **Willem (FR)**[10] 2513 5-11-12 125 (p) TomScudamore 115
(David Pipe) *trckd ldrs: disp cl 2nd after 3 out: rdn bef next and qckly hld: regained btn 2nd bef last: wknd and dropped to 4th cl home* 3/1[3]

-205 5 67 **Larteta (FR)**[8] 2552 6-9-5 100 RomainClavreul(10) 23
(Sarah Humphrey) *chsd ldrs tl wknd 3 out: t.o* 10/1

6m 7.1s (24.60) **Going Correction** +0.925s/f (Soft) 5 Ran SP% **111.5**
Speed ratings (Par 107): **92,86,85,85,61**
CSF £18.28 TOTE £3.90: £1.60, £2.90; EX 18.70 Trifecta £42.00.
Owner The Maple Hurst Partnership **Bred** Beech Hill Stud **Trained** Upper Lambourn, Berks

FOCUS
Race increased by 30yds. Modest handicap form but a good winner. The second has been rated close to form.

2712 BROOKS MACDONALD NOVICES' H'CAP CHASE (13 fncs) 2m 1f 96y
1:40 (1:40) (Class 4) (0-105,102) 4-Y-O+ £3,861 (£1,198; £645)

Form RPR
04-P 1 **Showboater (IRE)**[209] 30 6-11-5 95 NicodeBoinville 104+
(Ben Pauling) *trckd ldr: led appr 3 out: rdn after 2 out: kpt on wl* 11/8[1]

P6-P 2 13 **Bonds Conquest**[21] 2269 6-10-3 79 JeremiahMcGrath 78
(Seamus Mullins) *chsd ldrs: rdn appr 3 out: styd on to go 2nd run-in but no ch w wnr* 12/1[3]

652- 3 1 ½ **Entry To Evrywhere (IRE)**[461] 1283 7-10-10 86 RhysFlint 80
(Alexandra Dunn) *racd keenly: led: rdn and hdd appr 3 out: styd on same pce fr next: no ex whn lost 2nd run-in* 10/1[2]

10F3 P **Houseparty**[19] 2315 7-9-13 82 MissTWorsley(7)
(Diana Grissell) *mstke 5th: a last: lost tch 7th: p.u bef 4 out* 20/1

006- P **Dellbuoy**[134] 5283 6-11-11 101 JoshuaMoore
(Pat Phelan) *in tch: hit 3rd: cl up whn stmbld on bnd bef 8th: wknd after 4 out: p.u bef 2 out* 16/1

43-1 P **Brave Deed (IRE)**[22] 2263 9-11-12 102 NickScholfield
(Jeremy Scott) *trckd ldrs: wknd rapidly after 7th: t.o whn p.u after 4 out* 11/8[1]

4m 58.4s (23.70) **Going Correction** +1.475s/f (Heav) 6 Ran SP% **111.6**
Speed ratings (Par 105): **103,96,96, ,**
CSF £16.25 TOTE £2.30: £1.30, £4.30; EX 18.20 Trifecta £106.40.
Owner Paul & Clare Rooney **Bred** Thomas Brennan **Trained** Bourton-On-The-Water, Gloucs

FOCUS
Race increased by 36yds. Moderate chasing form but an unexposed, improving winner. The easy winner has been rated in line with the best of his bumper figures, with the second to his hurdle mark.

2713 GEORGE ROGERS MEMORIAL H'CAP HURDLE (10 hdls) 2m 3f 33y
2:10 (2:10) (Class 4) (0-105,105) 4-Y-O+ £3,249 (£954; £477; £238)

Form RPR
P0 1 **Arquebusier (FR)**[22] 2263 5-10-6 88 (p) JamesBanks(3) 105+
(Emma Baker) *mde all: drew wl clr after 3 out: rdn out run-in* 7/1

1135 2 31 **Shalianzi (IRE)**[35] 2015 5-11-5 98 (b) JamieMoore 84
(Gary Moore) *trckd ldrs: nt fluent 6th: rdn into 2nd appr 2 out but nvr any threat to wnr* 4/1[3]

223- 3 1 ½ **Spa Hill (IRE)**[430] 1593 6-11-12 105 DarylJacob 90
(Richard Woollacott) *in tch: trckd ldrs 6th: rdn after 3 out: sn one pce: wnt wl hld 3rd bef last* 5/2[2]

6-46 4 9 **Rolling Dough (IRE)**[182] 507 7-10-10 89 MarcGoldstein 65
(Diana Grissell) *in tch: rdn after 3 out: sn one pce: wnt wl hld 4th at the last* 10/1

3-50 5 2 ¼ **City Supreme (IRE)**[22] 2262 5-11-7 105 (bt) DavidNoonan(5) 81
(Anthony Honeyball) *prom: drvn after 3 out: sn hld by wnr: 3rd jumping next: dropped to 5th after mstke last* 9/4[1]

133- 6 1 **Join The Navy**[240] 5062 10-11-6 102 KieronEdgar(3) 74
(Kate Buckett) *hld up bhd: sme prog whn mstke 2 out: styd on but nvr on terms* 10/1

P54F 7 43 **Appropriate (FR)**[10] 2521 5-10-0 79 oh4 (t) RichieMcLernon
(Paul Henderson) *mstke 7th: a in rr: t.o* 50/1

0-06 8 30 **Padova**[21] 2267 9-11-10 103 TommyPhelan
(Dr Jeremy Naylor) *chsd ldrs: pushed along after 6th: mstke next: wkng whn blnd 3 out: eased fr next: t.o* 33/1

5m 25.0s (25.60) **Going Correction** +0.925s/f (Soft) 8 Ran SP% **114.9**
Speed ratings (Par 105): **83,69,69,65,64 64,46,33**
CSF £35.77 CT £89.47 TOTE £7.60: £1.80, £1.80, £1.30; EX 40.60 Trifecta £131.40.
Owner Miss E J Baker **Bred** Ecurie Maulepaire **Trained** Naunton, Gloucs
■ Stewards' Enquiry : James Banks two-day ban: used whip when clearly winning (Dec 9-10)

FOCUS
Race increased by 24yds. Lowly handicap form, with the winner showing much improved form. A big step up from the winner, and there's a case for rating him 10lb higher through the rest, but the time was slow compared with the earlier novice hurdle.

2714 DAVID HOW MUCH LEVER CONDITIONAL JOCKEYS' TRAINING SERIES H'CAP CHASE (RACING EXCEL. INITIATIVE) (15 fncs) 2m 3f 35y
2:45 (2:45) (Class 5) (0-100,95) 4-Y-O+ £2,529 (£785; £422)

Form RPR
5-33 1 **Matrow's Lady (IRE)**[21] 2269 8-11-0 86 (bt) MrMartinMcIntyre(3) 97+
(Neil Mulholland) *trckd ldrs: led 2 out: qcknd clr: easily* 1/1[1]

60P4 2 9 **Double Dan (IRE)**[16] 2402 6-10-7 76 (b) MikeyHamill 75
(Alexandra Dunn) *j.rt at times: led: mstke 1st: hit 5th: rdn and hdd appr 3 out: sn hld whn stmbld bdly 2 out: regained 2nd sn after last: no ch w wnr* 6/1

-2U6 3 2 ¾ **Gowanauthat (IRE)**[17] 2364 7-11-7 95 (t) TommyDowling(5) 90
(Charlie Mann) *trckd ldrs: pressed ldr after 3rd: led 3 out: rdn and hdd whn stmbld bdly 2 out: sn hld: no ex run-in* 5/2[2]

12 U **Killabraher Cross (IRE)**[23] 2255 8-11-9 92 FreddieMitchell
(Paddy Butler) *trckd ldrs: mstke 5th: nudged along after next: blnd bdly and uns rdr 7th* 5/1[3]

5m 36.9s (29.60) **Going Correction** +1.475s/f (Heav) 4 Ran SP% **109.5**
Speed ratings (Par 103): **96,92,91,**
CSF £6.78 TOTE £1.90; EX 6.90 Trifecta £15.00.
Owner Matrow Properties Ltd **Bred** B Kendellen **Trained** Limpley Stoke, Wilts

FOCUS
Race increased by 36yds. Weak chase form. Arguably a pb from the winner.

2715 KRZYSZTOF LASTMINUTE.COM KLACTK STANDARD OPEN NATIONAL HUNT FLAT RACE 2m 1f 145y
3:20 (3:20) (Class 6) 4-6-Y-O £1,559 (£457; £228; £114)

Form RPR
4 1 **Champagne George (IRE)**[19] 2317 5-11-2 0 NoelFehily 106+
(Neil Mulholland) *disp ld tl clr ldr over 6f out: jnd again over 3f out: hung rt over 2f out: drvn and drifted lft over 1f out: styd on gamely to edge ahd nring fin* 8/11[1]

2 1 **Not Another Muddle** 4-11-2 0 MarcGoldstein 105+
(Sheena West) *trckd ldrs: jnd wnr travelling sltly the bttr over 3f out: hung lft over 2f out: rdn over 1f out: no ex whn hdd nring fin* 7/1[3]

3 15 **Sporting Milan (IRE)**[238] 4-11-2 0 LeightonAspell 90
(Oliver Sherwood) *trckd ldrs: pushed along w a circ to go: rdn over 3f out: chsd ldng pair sn after: wknd over 1f out* 9/4[2]

4 6 **Hooghly River (IRE)** 5-10-9 0[1] LewisGordon(7) 84
(Jennifer Mason) *trckd ldrs: rdn wl over 3f out: wknd over 1f out* 25/1

5 24 **Wildehearted Woman (IRE)** 4-10-9 0 BrendanPowell 53
(Jamie Snowden) *chsd ldrs: rdn over 3f out: sn wknd: t.o* 12/1

0 6 37 **Garryduff Cross (IRE)**[190] 392 5-10-11 0 ConorRing(5) 23
(Helen Nelmes) *disp ld tl over 7f out: wknd over 5f out: t.o* 100/1

4m 47.6s (18.90) **Going Correction** +0.925s/f (Soft) 6 Ran SP% **113.7**
Speed ratings: **95,94,87,85,74 58**
CSF £7.06 TOTE £1.80: £1.10, £3.30; EX 5.40 Trifecta £11.20.
Owner 7Rus **Bred** J O'Donoghue **Trained** Limpley Stoke, Wilts

FOCUS
Race increased by 24yds. This proved a dour test for these young horses, with the front pair slogging it out a long way clear.
T/Plt: £65.20 to a £1 stake. Pool: £55,888.49 - 625.72 winning tickets T/Qpdt: £18.70 to a £1 stake. Pool: £4,644.13 - 182.84 winning tickets **Tim Mitchell**

[2494]WETHERBY (L-H)

Wednesday, November 25

OFFICIAL GOING: Soft (heavy in places) changing to heavy (soft in places) after race 1 (12.50)

Wind: fresh 1/2 behind Weather: fine Rails: final flight in back straight omitted (wet ground)

2716 WETHERBYRACING.CO.UK "NATIONAL HUNT" NOVICES' HURDLE (8 hdls 1 omitted) 2m

12:50 (12:50) (Class 4) 4-Y-O+ £3,573 (£1,049; £524; £262)

Form RPR

6-3 1 **Draytonian (IRE)**[25] 2196 5-10-12 0 RichardJohnson 122+
(Philip Hobbs) *trckd ldrs: 2nd 4th: led bef 4th: j.rt next: j.lft and clr 2 out: v comf* **4/9**[1]

24- 2 11 **Tara The Tiger**[305] 3861 4-10-5 0 BrianHughes 95
(Tim Easterby) *trckd ldrs 2nd: 2nd after 5th: kpt on same pce fr 3 out: no ch w wnr* **8/1**

52-4 3 1 1/4 **Captain Redbeard (IRE)**[19] 2319 6-10-5 0 SamColtherd(7) 101
(Stuart Coltherd) *mid-div: hdwy to chse ldrs 5th: kpt on same pce to take 3rd last 150yds* **16/1**

5 4 6 **Bertalus (IRE)**[25] 2189 6-10-12 0 LucyAlexander 98+
(N W Alexander) *in rr: shkn up 3rd: hdwy 5th: sn chsng ldrs: 3rd whn j.lft and mstke 3 out: wknd last 150yds* **7/1**[3]

0- 5 2 3/4 **Jellied Eel Jack (IRE)**[280] 4296 6-10-12 0 WayneHutchinson 91
(Donald McCain) *mid-div: hdwy 5th: wknd 2 out* **33/1**

0-00 6 24 **Wayward Sun (IRE)**[26] 2169 4-10-5 0 FinianO'Toole(7) 67
(Micky Hammond) *chsd ldrs: outpcd 4th: lost pl bef 3 out: sn bhd* **125/1**

6-0 7 40 **Exclusive Tara**[26] 2169 5-10-12 0 JakeGreenall 27
(Tim Easterby) *in rr: hdwy 4th: lost pl next: sn bhd: t.o 3 out* **100/1**

0UP4 P **Bertielicious**[12] 2474 7-10-5 68 (e) ThomasDowson(7)
(Jonathan Haynes) *led: hdd bef 4th: reminders and lost pl next: sn bhd: t.o whn p.u bef 3 out* **125/1**

25-4 F **Return Flight**[18] 2337 4-10-9 0 JoeColliver(3)
(Micky Hammond) *w ldr: fell 1st* **7/2**[2]

4m 10.7s (14.90) **Going Correction** +0.775s/f (Soft)
WFA 4 from 5yo+ 7lb 9 Ran SP% **126.5**
Speed ratings (Par 105): **93,87,86,83,82 70,50, ,**
CSF £6.44 TOTE £1.40: £1.02, £1.90, £3.70; EX 6.70 Trifecta £42.70.
Owner Mrs Diana L Whateley **Bred** Mrs C J Berry **Trained** Withycombe, Somerset

FOCUS
Rail alignment was the same as the previous meeting this month, thus meaning adding 45 yards to the official race distances of races 1,3,4 and 6, while 90 yards to race 2, and 70 yards to race 6. The last flight in the back straight was omitted for all hurdle races. An already uncompetitive novice event was weakened by the fall of the second favourite at the first, and it's muddling form. The time was good compared with the later juvenile hurdle.

2717 LAST DAY RACING UK FREE TRIAL BEGINNERS' CHASE (19 fncs) 3m 45y

1:20 (1:21) (Class 4) 4-Y-O+ £4,327 (£1,343; £723)

Form RPR

03-4 1 **Run Ructions Run (IRE)**[15] 2411 6-10-9 0 (p) BrianHughes 138+
(Tim Easterby) *trckd ldrs: upsides 2 out: effrt between last 2: pushed to ld last 75yds: readily* **11/4**[3]

322- 2 1 **Kaki De La Pree (FR)**[298] 3984 8-11-2 135 JamesDavies 144
(Tom Symonds) *led to 3rd: drvn 3 out: upsides next: led narrowly and brifekly 100yds out: styd on same pce* **2/1**[2]

231- 3 3/4 **Milansbar (IRE)**[249] 4911 8-11-2 0 TrevorWhelan 143+
(Neil King) *trckd ldr: led 3rd: drvn 3 out: jnd next: mstke last: sn hdd: styd on same pce* **6/5**[1]

333- P **Masirann (IRE)**[243] 5017 7-11-2 108 SamTwiston-Davies
(Micky Hammond) *trckd ldrs: p.u bef 9th: lame* **40/1**

6m 47.6s (-0.40) 4 Ran SP% **107.9**
CSF £8.56 TOTE £3.90; EX 6.40 Trifecta £13.60.
Owner Tom Ford **Bred** Minch Bloodstock & AV Bloodstock **Trained** Great Habton, N Yorks

FOCUS
A select bunch took on this staying beginners' chase and, while tactical, it proved a fair test. The winner and third have been rated in line with their hurdle marks.

2718 WATCH RACING UK FREE LAST CHANCE JUVENILE MAIDEN HURDLE (8 hdls 1 omitted) 2m

1:50 (1:51) (Class 5) 3-Y-O £2,924 (£858; £429; £214)

Form RPR

6 1 **Akavit (IRE)**[21] 2273 3-10-12 0 DavidBass 112+
(Ed de Giles) *w ldr: lft in ld 1st: wandered between last 2: drvn out* **12/1**

2 6 **Cosmic Statesman**[48] 3-10-12 0 BrianHughes 104
(Richard Fahey) *hld up in mid-div: hdwy 5th: handy 4th appr 3 out: kpt on to take 2nd last 100yds* **8/1**[3]

3 3 1/4 **Kisumu**[140] 3-10-12 0 SamTwiston-Davies 102
(Micky Hammond) *mid-div: hdwy 5th: sn chsng ldrs: handy 2nd appr 3 out: one pce fr next* **11/1**

4 2 1/4 **Tudor City (IRE)**[17] 2376 3-10-12 0 (t) DenisO'Regan 98
(A J Martin, Ire) *mid-div: hdwy 5th: handy 3rd appr 3 out: one pce* **9/2**[2]

00 5 27 **Bond Starprincess**[42] 1899 3-10-5 0 HenryBrooke 64
(George Moore) *in rr: sme hdwy 5th: poor 6th 3 out: nvr on terms* **200/1**

62 6 nk **Poet Mark (IRE)**[20] 2286 3-10-12 0 JakeGreenall 70
(Tim Easterby) *mid-div: outpcd 5th: nvr a factor* **14/1**

UU 7 4 1/2 **Whisky Marmalade (IRE)**[52] 1768 3-10-5 0 AndrewTinkler 59
(Ben Haslam) *in rr: bhd fr 5th* **16/1**

3 8 9 **Goldslinger (FR)**[38] 1984 3-10-12 0 PaulMoloney 60
(Dean Ivory) *led: dived lft and hdd 1st: chsd wnr 4th: wknd appr 3 out* **2/1**[1]

3 9 2 **Denton Carnival (IRE)**[20] 2286 3-10-9 0 JoeColliver(3) 55
(Michael Dods) *prom: lost pl 5th: sn bhd* **12/1**

4 10 8 **Baler Boy**[14] 2439 3-10-12 0 MichaelByrne 47
(Des Donovan) *chsd ldrs: reminders 5th: sn lost pl and bhd* **150/1**

F **Keep Up (GER)**[29] 3-10-9 0 AdamNicol(3)
(Philip Kirby) *chsd ldrs: reminders and lost pl 5th: sn bhd: fell 3 out* **25/1**

P **Pumaflor (IRE)**[26] 3-10-12 0 SeanQuinlan
(Richard Guest) *wnt rt s: t.k.h in rr: brief effrt 5th: bhd next: t.o whn p.u bef 2 out* **12/1**

P **Bollihope**[12] 3-10-12 0 JamesDavies
(Richard Guest) *chsd ldrs: mstke 2nd: reminders after 5th: sn lost pl and bhd: t.o whn p.u bef 3 out* **25/1**

6 P **Toboggan's Gift**[115] 1177 3-10-2 0 ColmMcCormack(3)
(Ann Duffield) *in rr: blnd bdly and rdr briefly lost iron 1st: hit 4th: sn wl bhd: t.o whn j.rt 3 out: sn p.u* **100/1**

5P F **Rio Falls (IRE)**[14] 2439 3-10-12 0 PeterCarberry
(Jennie Candlish) *in rr: bhd and reminders 4th: t.o next: fell heavily 2 out* **80/1**

F P **Angrove Fatrascal**[42] 1899 3-10-5 0 FinianO'Toole(7)
(Micky Hammond) *in rr: sn drvn along: lost tch 3rd: t.o whn p.u bef next* **200/1**

4m 16.4s (20.60) **Going Correction** +0.775s/f (Soft) 16 Ran SP% **118.2**
Speed ratings (Par 102): **79,76,74,73,59 59,57,52,51,47 , , , ,**
CSF £100.35 TOTE £13.30: £3.70, £2.70, £3.20; EX 135.10 Trifecta £1812.40.
Owner Simon Treacher **Bred** Tenuta Genzianella Di Manuela Martinelli **Trained** Ledbury, H'fords
■ Stewards' Enquiry : Peter Carberry 12-day ban: continued on gelding when it appeared to be exhausted (Dec 9-20)

FOCUS
An ordinary juvenile maiden, run at a sound gallop and the form is rated around the fourth to his Irish form.

2719 LAST DAY RACINGUK.COM/FREETRIAL H'CAP CHASE (13 fncs) 1m 7f 36y

2:25 (2:26) (Class 3) (0-140,138) 4-Y-O+ £6,498 (£1,908; £954; £477)

Form RPR

P0U1 1 **Indian Voyage (IRE)**[18] 2342 7-10-10 127 (t) DaraghBourke(5) 136+
(Maurice Barnes) *trckd ldrs: led 6th to 9th: led next: styd on wl fr 2 out: drvn out* **3/1**[2]

10-1 2 1 3/4 **Grey Life**[209] 36 9-10-12 124 BrianHughes 129
(Malcolm Jefferson) *led to 5th: led 9th to next: cl 2nd whn hit 3 out: ridser lost whip between last 2: regained 2nd last: styd on same pce* **6/1**

25F2 3 1 1/4 **Vengeur De Guye (FR)**[18] 2342 6-10-12 127 (t) DerekFox(3) 131
(Lucinda Russell) *trckd ldrs: effrt 3 out: kpt on same pce to take 3rd last 50yds* **13/2**

32-5 4 3 1/4 **Yorkist (IRE)**[18] 2336 7-11-12 138 SamTwiston-Davies 139
(Micky Hammond) *w ldrs: led 5th: hdd next: drvn 3 out: 2nd next: wknd last 75yds* **10/3**[3]

21-P 5 12 **Aye Well**[25] 2193 10-10-13 125 BrianHarding 114
(Stuart Coltherd) *prom: reminders after 4th: chsng ldrs 6th: drvn 9th: lost pl appr 3 out* **14/1**

63-2 6 4 **Forward Flight (IRE)**[12] 2475 9-10-7 119 SeanQuinlan 104
(Sue Smith) *chsd ldrs: nt fluent and reminders 9th: lost pl bef 3 out* **11/4**[1]

4m 3.5s (7.70) **Going Correction** +0.775s/f (Soft) 6 Ran SP% **109.0**
Speed ratings (Par 107): **110,109,108,106,100 98**
CSF £19.17 TOTE £3.40: £1.90, £2.40; EX 20.40 Trifecta £73.50.
Owner D Carr & M Carlyle **Bred** Victor Stud Bloodstock Ltd **Trained** Farlam, Cumbria

FOCUS
This was run at a fair gallop and it's solid handicap form. A small pb from the winner, with the second and third rated to their marks.

2720 BOOK TICKETS FOR BOXING DAY H'CAP HURDLE 2m 3f 154y

3:00 (3:00) (Class 4) (0-105,105) 3-Y-O+ £3,249 (£954; £477; £238)

Form RPR

6-06 1 **Mac N Cheese (IRE)**[34] 2029 5-10-10 89 BrianHarding 103+
(Rose Dobbin) *mid-div: hdwy to chse ldrs 5th: 2nd 3 out: led appr last: drvn clr* **15/2**[3]

603- 2 8 **Diamond D'Amour (IRE)**[235] 5131 9-11-5 103 JonathonBewley(5) 107
(George Bewley) *t.k.h: led: hdd appr last: no ex* **9/1**

F30- 3 29 **Peterpanopirateman (IRE)**[233] 5183 6-11-5 105 ...[1] MrMJPKendrick(7) 90+
(Ben Case) *bdly hmpd s: detached in last: hdwy 6th: chsd ldr appr 3 out: wknd 2 out* **17/2**

-6F4 4 3/4 **Dutch Canyon (IRE)**[19] 2322 5-11-0 93 (p) LucyAlexander 67
(N W Alexander) *prom: pushed along and dropped bk 3rd: hdwy to chse ldrs 5th: reminders and lost pl bef 3 out: tk poor 4th nr fin* **15/2**[3]

-P43 5 nse **Turtle Cask (IRE)**[15] 2426 6-10-12 94 (p) HarryChalloner(3) 68
(Dianne Sayer) *chsd ldrs: drvn 6th: lost pl appr 3 out* **7/2**[1]

03-P 6 2 3/4 **W Six Times**[203] 148 9-10-4 86 (p) CraigNichol(3) 57
(Alistair Whillans) *chsd ldrs: drvn and lost pl appr 3 out* **20/1**

-354 7 10 **Hi Dancer**[44] 1892 12-10-11 90 AndrewTinkler 53
(Ben Haslam) *chsd ldrs: drvn 6th: lost pl bef 3 out: sn bhd* **16/1**

14-0 8 1 1/2 **Rayadour (IRE)**[11] 2496 6-11-6 104 MissCWalton(5) 64
(Micky Hammond) *in rr: bhd 5th: brief effrt bef 3 out: sn lost pl and bhd* **9/1**

-456 U **Pistol (IRE)**[25] 2190 6-11-2 102 MrJDixon(7)
(John Dixon) *w.r.s and uns rdr* **10/1**

605/ P **Cleve Cottage**[688] 3569 7-10-8 90 AdamNicol(3)
(Philip Kirby) *mid-div: lost pl 6th: sn bhd: t.o whn p.u bef 3 out* **9/2**[2]

-66F P **Lady Busanda**[27] 2143 5-10-0 82 (t) JoeColliver(3)
(George Moore) *in rr: drvn 3rd: bhd 6th: t.o whn p.u bef next* **50/1**

5m 19.9s (12.90) **Going Correction** +0.775s/f (Soft) 11 Ran SP% **116.2**
Speed ratings (Par 105): **105,101,90,89,89 88,84,84, ,**
CSF £72.24 CT £588.28 TOTE £9.20: £2.50, £3.00, £3.40; EX 92.80 Trifecta £1302.80.
Owner Richard & Katherine Gilbert **Bred** Mrs K White **Trained** South Hazelrigg, Northumbria

FOCUS
This moderate handicap was wide-open but few got seriously involved due to the decent gallop. A big step up from the winner.

2721 EBFSTALLIONS.COM EBF MARES' STANDARD OPEN NATIONAL HUNT FLAT RACE 2m

3:30 (3:30) (Class 6) 4-6-Y-O £2,274 (£667; £333; £166)

Form RPR

1 **Savingforvegas (IRE)**[186] 5-10-12 0 PaddyBrennan 107+
(Stuart Edmunds) *trckd ldrs: drvn 5f out: led over 2f out: styd on* **7/2**[2]

2 1 1/4 **Cajun Fiddle (IRE)** 4-10-12 0 WayneHutchinson 106+
(Alan King) *mid-div: hdwy to chse ldrs 7f out: 2nd over 1f out: styd on same pce* **2/1**[1]

3 13 **Miss Yeats (IRE)** 4-10-12 0 BrianHughes 94+
(Clive Mulhall) *trckd ldrs: upsides over 4f out: led over 3f out: hdd over 2f out: hung lft and wknd over 1f out* **13/2**

2-51 4 3/4 **Lamanver Alchemy**[21] 2277 4-11-5 0 RichardJohnson 99
(Tom Lacey) *led: drvn 4f out: hdd over 3f out: one pce fnl 2f* **9/2**[3]

4- 5 10 **Zeldina**[334] 3263 5-10-12 0 DannyCook 82
(Brian Ellison) *chsd ldrs: drvn 8f out: outpcd and lost pl 6f out* **25/1**

6 15 **Miss Lillian** 5-10-12 0 AndrewTinkler 67
(John Quinn) *sn trcking ldrs: drvn over 4f out: lost pl over 2f out* **8/1**

6- 7 14 **Bigbury Bay (IRE)**[242] 5035 4-10-7 0 HarryBannister(5) 53
(Warren Greatrex) *lost many position on outer: lost pl 6f out: sn bhd* **16/1**

8 *23* **Sybil Grey** 6-10-7 0........................ JonathonBewley(5) 30
(George Bewley) *in last: pushed along after 6f: brief effrt 6f out: sn lost pl and wl bhd: t.o whn hung rt fnl 4f* **80/1**

9 *44* **Fairlee Grace**[269] 4-10-12 0........................ JanFaltejsek
(George Charlton) *mid-div: chsd ldrs after 7f: lost pl 6f out: sn wl bhd: t.o 4f out* **16/1**

10 *dist* **Bethellie Pride** 5-10-7 0........................ GrantCockburn(5)
(Lynn Siddall) *in rr: bhd and drvn after 7f: t.o 7f out: eventually completed* **200/1**

4m 3.4s (13.20) **Going Correction** +0.775s/f (Soft) 10 Ran **SP% 115.5**
Speed ratings: **98,97,90,90,85 78,71,59,37,**
CSF £10.71 TOTE £4.80: £1.40, £1.20, £2.40; EX 15.70 Trifecta £65.90.
Owner Ben Turner **Bred** David Byrne **Trained** Newport Pagnell, Bucks

FOCUS
There is every chance this will work out to be an above-average mares' bumper. The fourth and fifth set the level.
T/Plt: £450.20 to a £1 stake. Pool: £67,367.93 - 109.22 winning tickets T/Qpdt: £53.00 to a £1 stake. Pool: £5,354.02 - 74.65 winning tickets **Walter Glynn**

2722 - (Foreign Racing) - See Raceform Interactive

NEWBURY (L-H)
Thursday, November 26

OFFICIAL GOING: Hurdle course - soft (heavy in places); chase course - good to soft (soft in places) changing to soft after race 4 (2.10)
Wind: Almost nil Weather: Cloudy

2723 BET365 NOVICES' HURDLE (8 hdls) 2m 69y
12:30 (12:30) (Class 3) 4-Y-O+ **£6,279** (£1,871; £947; £485; £254)

Form RPR

2-31 **1** **Modus**[14] 2457 5-11-8 0........................ BarryGeraghty 139+
(Paul Nicholls) *hld up: chsd ldr 3 out: drvn along appr last: styd on to ld nr fin* **1/2**[1]

01 **2** *nk* **Charmix (FR)**[26] 2196 5-11-8 0........................ NoelFehily 136+
(Harry Fry) *led at modest pce: kpt on u.p run-in: hdd nr fin* **9/2**[3]

1- **3** *24* **See The World**[301] 3944 5-11-0 0........................ DarylJacob 106
(Emma Lavelle) *chsd ldr after 1st tl 3 out: wknd next* **7/2**[2]

4 *3 ¾* **Burning Desire (IRE)**[39] 4-11-0 0........................ BrendanPowell 100
(Richard Hughes) *nt fluent: in tch tl wknd 3 out* **150/1**

P **5** *nk* **Allee Bleue (IRE)**[25] 2221 5-11-0 0........................ RichardJohnson 102
(Philip Hobbs) *hld up in rr: effrt after 5th: wknd 2 out* **66/1**

360 **U** **Acajou Des Bieffes (FR)**[14] 2457 5-11-0 0........................ AidanColeman
(Anthony Honeyball) *2nd whn wnt lft and uns rdr 1st* **150/1**

4m 21.5s (11.50) **Going Correction** +0.45s/f (Soft)
WFA 4 from 5yo 7lb 6 Ran **SP% 109.9**
Speed ratings (Par 107): **89,88,76,74,74**
CSF £3.22 TOTE £1.40: £1.10, £2.20; EX 3.40 Trifecta £4.40.
Owner John P McManus **Bred** D J And Mrs Deer **Trained** Ditcheat, Somerset

FOCUS
Rail out on both courses and the race distance for this contest was 136yds further than advertised. Barry Geraghty reported that the ground on the hurdles track was soft. The opening contest of the Hennessy meeting often goes to a well-above average type, but only three of these made any appeal on what had been seen on the track previously. There was a danger for much of the race that the second was going to steal it from the front having been left alone, so this isn't form to rely on. The winner is a potential 140+ novice hurdler.

2724 ALAN MACKINTOSH AMATEUR RIDERS' H'CAP CHASE (21 fncs) 3m 1f 214y
1:00 (1:00) (Class 3) (0-130,130) 4-Y-O+
£5,996 (£1,873; £936; £468; £234; £118)

Form RPR

213- **1** **Harry's Farewell**[220] 5431 8-11-3 **126**........................ MrJoshuaNewman(5) 138+
(Polly Gundry) *mde virtually all: blnd 3 out: rdn and styd on* **9/1**

21-6 **2** *1 ¼* **Russe Blanc (FR)**[23] 2261 8-11-5 **123**........................(p) MrSClements 132
(Kerry Lee) *chsd ldrs: lft cl 2nd at 16th: mstke next: kpt on wl run-in: a hld* **5/1**[2]

-12P **3** *9* **Belmount (IRE)**[23] 2261 6-11-5 **130**........................ MrJJSlevin(7) 134
(Nigel Twiston-Davies) *hld up: blnd 7th: hdwy 17th: one pce fr 3 out* **9/1**

-5P5 **4** *9* **Lord Landen (IRE)**[34] 2057 10-9-12 **105**........................(t) MissCVHart(3) 102
(Fergal O'Brien) *hdwy to chse ldrs 8th: outpcd fr 3 out* **28/1**

32-0 **5** *11* **Wuff (IRE)**[209] 69 7-11-12 **130**........................(t) MrWBiddick 116+
(Paul Nicholls) *chsd ldrs: bdly hmpd 16th: nt rcvr: 5th and no ch whn j.rt 3 out* **6/4**[1]

4-02 **6** *2* **Top Dancer (FR)**[187] 439 8-10-8 **119**........................(p) MrBHicks(7) 100
(Warren Greatrex) *a bhd* **6/1**[3]

161- **7** *50* **Itoldyou (IRE)**[250] 4907 9-10-10 **119**........................(t) MrRobertHawker(5) 79
(Linda Jewell) *a towards rr: struggling fr 13th: bhd whn hmpd 16th* **28/1**

445- **F** **Baby Shine (IRE)**[236] 5140 9-11-11 **129**........................ MissGAndrews
(Lucy Wadham) *hld up towards rr: fell 16th* **8/1**

155- **F** **Kings Apollo**[252] 4863 6-10-0 **109**........................ MrJNixon(5)
(Tom Symonds) *pressed wnr tl fell 16th* **20/1**

7m 6.0s (20.00) **Going Correction** +0.45s/f (Soft) 9 Ran **SP% 113.7**
Speed ratings (Par 107): **87,86,83,81,77 77,61, ,**
CSF £51.81 CT £415.67 TOTE £8.40: £2.50, £2.00, £2.90; EX 55.20 Trifecta £290.00.
Owner J P Selby **Bred** J Selby **Trained** Ottery St Mary, Devon

FOCUS
The actual race distance for this was 116yds further than advertised. Winning jockey Joshua Newman reported the ground as "good to soft" and "if your horse likes good ground he'll find it a bit wet." The winner made sure this staying handicap was run at a respectable gallop. A small pb from the winner, with the third close to his mark.

2725 BET365.COM NOVICES' H'CAP HURDLE (10 hdls) 2m 4f 118y
1:35 (1:36) (Class 4) (0-125,125) 3-Y-O+ **£6,498** (£1,908; £954; £477)

Form RPR

0P-1 **1** **Unowhatimeanharry**[11] 2513 7-11-10 **123**........................(t) NoelFehily 138+
(Harry Fry) *gng wl towards rr: hdwy 5th: led 2 out: shkn up run-in: styd on wl* **1/2**[1]

00-3 **2** *4* **Millanisi Boy**[23] 2262 6-11-4 **117**........................ DarylJacob 126
(Richard Woollacott) *cl up: chsd wnr and j.lft last: styd on: a hld* **14/1**

-P21 **3** *13* **Masterplan (IRE)**[26] 2182 5-11-6 **119**........................ AidanColeman 115
(Charlie Longsdon) *led tl hdd and hit 2 out: wknd appr last* **10/1**[3]

34-1 **4** *2 ½* **Wild Rover (IRE)**[40] 1964 6-11-7 **120**........................ BarryGeraghty 114
(Rebecca Curtis) *chsd ldr tl appr 3 out: sn btn* **7/1**[2]

6605 **5** *9* **Timon's Tara**[14] 2452 6-10-10 **109**........................ JackQuinlan 93
(Robin Dickin) *hld up in rr: effrt 3 out: sn wknd* **50/1**

43-3 **6** *11* **Robinsson (IRE)**[21] 2299 5-11-4 **120**........................ ThomasGarner(3) 93
(Oliver Sherwood) *hld up: rdn 6th: drvn and lost tch 3 out* **7/1**[2]

43-2 **7** *3 ¾* **Amanto (GER)**[14] 2458 5-11-9 **122**........................(b) SamTwiston-Davies 91
(Paul Nicholls) *in tch tl wknd 3 out* **10/1**[3]

P **8** *2 ¼* **Mille Nautique (FR)**[27] 2163 4-10-10 **109**........................ WayneHutchinson 76
(Alan King) *hld up: short-lived effrt appr 3 out: sn bhd* **33/1**

5m 27.2s (8.20) **Going Correction** +0.45s/f (Soft) 8 Ran **SP% 121.4**
Speed ratings (Par 105): **102,100,95,94,91 86,85,84**
CSF £10.30 CT £44.19 TOTE £1.40: £1.10, £3.20, £2.00; EX 9.80 Trifecta £56.70.
Owner Harry Fry Racing Club **Bred** R J Smith **Trained** Seaborough, Dorset

FOCUS
The distance for this race was 172yds further than advertised. The gallop set by Masterplan wasn't overly quick, and the field raced as a pack for quite some time. The winner was well in on his recent win and has been rated to a similar level.

2726 BET365 NOVICES' CHASE (REGISTERED AS THE WORCESTER NOVICES' CHASE) (GRADE 2) (18 fncs) 2m 7f 86y
2:10 (2:10) (Class 1) 4-Y-O+ **£20,284** (£7,831; £4,096; £2,217)

Form RPR

0-31 **1** **Native River (IRE)**[23] 2260 5-11-9 0........................ BrendanPowell 160+
(Colin Tizzard) *hld up: hdwy 11th: wnt 2nd at 14th: led appr last: styd on wl* **8/1**

3-12 **2** *3 ¾* **Un Temps Pour Tout (IRE)**[12] 2481 6-11-2 0........(bt) TomScudamore 149+
(David Pipe) *disp ld: led 7th: rdn and nt fluent 2 out: hdd appr last: kpt on same pce* **6/4**[1]

13-1 **3** *59* **Port Melon (IRE)**[24] 2240 7-11-9 **140**........................(p) SamTwiston-Davies 95
(Paul Nicholls) *hld up towards rr: blnd 12th: rdn 14th: sn struggling* **20/1**

2P-1 **4** *hd* **Killala Quay**[53] 1782 8-11-9 **139**........................(p) RichardJohnson 97
(Charlie Longsdon) *disp ld tl 7th: chsd ldr after: lost 2nd at 14th: 3rd and btn whn blnd 3 out* **20/1**

5/1P **P** **Twelve Roses**[12] 2481 7-11-6 **143**........................(p) DavidBass
(Kim Bailey) *chsd ldrs: blnd 12th: sn wl bhd: p.u bef 2 out* **40/1**

125- **F** **Value At Risk**[258] 4738 6-11-2 0........................ HarrySkelton
(Dan Skelton) *in tch whn fell 2nd* **2/1**[2]

10-U **F** **Beast Of Burden (IRE)**[46] 1867 6-11-2 0........................ PaulTownend
(Rebecca Curtis) *chsd ldrs: mstke 10th: wknd 13th: bhd whn fell next* **9/2**[3]

6m 7.7s (1.70) **Going Correction** +0.45s/f (Soft) 7 Ran **SP% 114.6**
Speed ratings (Par 115): **115,113,93,93, ,**
CSF £21.35 TOTE £11.40: £4.00, £1.30; EX 29.50 Trifecta £279.10.
Owner Brocade Racing **Bred** Fred Mackey **Trained** Milborne Port, Dorset

FOCUS
The distance for this race was 116yds further than advertised. A strong-looking field was assembled for this contest, which can often produce a classy type. The pace seemed decent. The time was good and the winner rates a smart novice, with the second rated similar to his recent Cheltenham run.

2727 BET365 NOVICES' LIMITED H'CAP CHASE (17 fncs) 2m 6f 93y
2:45 (2:46) (Class 3) (0-135,135) 4-Y-O+
£7,507 (£2,217; £1,108; £554; £277; £139)

Form RPR

13-4 **1** **Spookydooky (IRE)**[19] 2332 7-11-7 **134**........................(t) RichardJohnson 143+
(Jonjo O'Neill) *towards rr: hdwy 4 out: wnt 2nd 2 out: str chal run-in: drvn to ld nr fin* **9/1**

112- **2** *hd* **Warriors Tale**[264] 4616 6-11-8 **135**........................ SamTwiston-Davies 143+
(Paul Nicholls) *chsd ldrs: led 2 out: kpt on u.p run-in: hdd nr fin* **13/2**[2]

24- **3** *7* **Nitrogen (IRE)**[311] 3775 8-10-8 **121**........................ NoelFehily 123+
(Harry Fry) *hld up in rr: effrt 4 out: styd on fr 2 out* **6/1**[1]

144- **4** *6* **Chosen Well (IRE)**[223] 5362 6-11-0 **127**........................(t) WayneHutchinson 124
(Alan King) *in tch: led 4 out: hdd and mstke 2 out: wknd appr last* **6/1**[1]

421- **5** *4* **Thedrinkymeister (IRE)**[245] 4990 6-10-9 **122**........................ RichieMcLernon 112
(Kim Bailey) *prom: led 13th tl 4 out: sn wknd* **16/1**

-63U **6** *24* **Harristown**[7] 2593 5-10-12 **125**........................(p) TomCannon 91
(Charlie Longsdon) *bhd: effrt 4 out: sn wknd: no ch whn hmpd and blnd 2 out* **50/1**

214- **7** *9* **Grove Silver (IRE)**[236] 5142 6-11-0 **127**........................ PeterCarberry 84
(Jennie Candlish) *led tl 13th: wknd next* **50/1**

210- **8** *14* **Special Agent**[223] 5362 6-10-12 **125**........................ DavidBass 68
(Nicky Henderson) *pressed ldr tl 13th: wknd 3 out* **14/1**

FP/P **P** **African Gold (IRE)**[28] 2153 7-11-1 **131**........................(t) RyanHatch(3)
(Nigel Twiston-Davies) *in tch: blnd 10th: outpcd in midfield whn hmpd 13th: bhd whn p.u bef 3 out* **7/1**[3]

-131 **F** **Fourth Act (IRE)**[17] 2400 6-10-10 **123**........................(t) BrendanPowell
(Colin Tizzard) *hld up: mstke 12th: wnt prom and fell next* **13/2**[2]

135- **P** **Sidbury Hill**[264] 4631 7-10-0 **118**........................ KevinJones(5)
(Seamus Mullins) *prom tl blnd and slithered bdly 13th: nt rcvr and p.u* **8/1**

P3-1 **P** **Globalisation (IRE)**[18] 2365 5-10-7 **120**........................(t) BarryGeraghty
(Rebecca Curtis) *bhd: blnd 5th: t.o whn p.u bef 4 out* **8/1**

6m 5.0s (18.00) **Going Correction** +0.45s/f (Soft) 12 Ran **SP% 116.4**
Speed ratings (Par 107): **85,84,82,80,78 70,66,61, , ,**
CSF £66.33 CT £380.91 TOTE £10.10: £3.50, £1.70, £3.00; EX 48.60 Trifecta £546.60.
Owner The Piranha Partnership **Bred** Paul McWilliams **Trained** Cheltenham, Gloucs
■ Stewards' Enquiry : Richard Johnson two-day ban: used whip above permitted level (Dec 10-11)

FOCUS
The distance for this race was 116yds further than advertised. The going was altered to soft all over on the chase course prior to the off. The first two looked to have stepped up on the level of their hurdle form, with the third rated similar to his hurdle mark.

2728 BET365 INTERMEDIATE HURDLE (LIMITED H'CAP) (REGISTERED AS THE GERRY FEILDEN HURDLE) (LISTED RACE) (8 hdls) 2m 69y
3:15 (3:18) (Class 1) (0-£25,627)(£9,606; £4,815; £2,398; £1,206; £60315)

22-1 **1** **Sternrubin (GER)**[205] 119 4-11-1 **128**........................ RichardJohnson 136+
(Philip Hobbs) *mde all: sn 10 l clr: c bk and 2 l ahd 3 out: fnd ex and styd on wl fr next* **4/1**[3]

11- **2** *4* **John Constable (IRE)**[234] 5198 4-11-10 **137**........................ PaulMoloney 141
(Evan Williams) *prom in chsng gp: chsd wnr 2 out: no imp* **16/1**

22 **3** *5* **Ch'Tibello (FR)**[26] 2183 4-11-10 **137**........................ HarrySkelton 139
(Dan Skelton) *hld up in 5th: hdwy to dispute 2nd whn nt fluent 2 out: 3rd and btn whn mstke last* **7/2**[2]

10-6 **4** *7* **Wilberdragon**[26] 2186 5-11-3 **130**........................(t) TomCannon 122
(Charlie Longsdon) *chsd wnr tl wknd 2 out* **8/1**

-131 **5** *3* **San Benedeto (FR)**[7] 2600 4-11-9 **136** 6ex........................(t) SamTwiston-Davies 125
(Paul Nicholls) *hld up in 4th: rdn and wknd 2 out* **11/8**[1]

-112 **6** *1 ½* **Kapstadt (FR)**[27] 2170 5-11-2 **129**........................ WillKennedy 117
(Ian Williams) *bhd: rdn 3 out: nvr trbld ldrs* **14/1**

05-3 **7** *9* **Song Light**[110] 197 5-11-1 **133**.............................. KevinJones(5) 112
(Seamus Mullins) *a towards rr: rdn and lost tch 2 out* **14/1**

4m 13.2s (3.20) **Going Correction** +0.45s/f (Soft) **7** Ran SP% **114.7**
Speed ratings (Par 111): **110,108,105,102,100 99,95**
CSF £56.54 TOTE £3.90: £1.90, £3.20; EX 30.80 Trifecta £93.70.
Owner Terry Warner **Bred** Gestut Karlshof **Trained** Withycombe, Somerset

FOCUS
The distance for this race was 136yds further than advertised. Plenty of decent horses have taken this down the years, most notably Rock On Ruby (when in the care of Paul Nicholls) in 2011. The gallop set by the winner appeared quite strong. A pb from the winner, and a big hurdle pb from the second, but in line with his Flat form.

2729 BET365.COM STANDARD OPEN NATIONAL HUNT FLAT RACE 2m 69y
3:50 (3:50) (Class 6) 4-6-Y-0 **£1,689** (£496; £248; £124)

Form RPR
1 **Fly Du Charmil (FR)**[215] 4-11-0 0.............................. GavinSheehan 117
(Warren Greatrex) *pressed ldr and clr of others at gd pce: led 4f out: hld on gamely fnl f* **7/1**[3]

2 **2** *hd* **Pure Vision (IRE)**[46] 1873 4-11-0 0..............................(t) BarryGeraghty 117
(Anthony Honeyball) *hld up towards rr: hdwy 4f out: str chal fnl f: kpt on wl* **10/1**

3 *8* **Kir Royal** 4-10-7 0.............................. WayneHutchinson 102
(Alan King) *hld up towards rr: gd hdwy 4f out: chsd wnr over 2f out tl no ex over 1f out* **25/1**

4 *6* **Onthewesternfront (IRE)** 5-11-0 0.............................. RichardJohnson 104
(Jonjo O'Neill) *hld up in rr: hdwy 4f out: wknd over 1f out* **3/1**[2]

5 *9* **Red Infantry (IRE)** 5-10-11 0.............................. RobMcCarth(3) 94
(Ian Williams) *hld up in rr: hdwy over 3f out: wknd over 2f out* **100/1**

0- **6** *2 ¾* **Druid's Folly (IRE)**[229] 5285 5-11-0 0.............................. PaulTownend 92
(Rebecca Curtis) *led: sn wnt clr w wnr and set gd pce: hdd 4f out: wknd over 2f out* **7/1**[3]

P **7** *34* **Close Escape (IRE)**[33] 2065 4-11-0 0..............................[1] NicodeBoinville 57
(Nicky Henderson) *hld up towards rr: hdwy over 3f out: sn wknd* **11/1**

8 *2 ¼* **Tower Of Allen (IRE)** 4-11-0 0.............................. DavidBass 55
(Nicky Henderson) *n.d* **12/1**

9 *4 ½* **Zero Grand (IRE)** 4-11-0 0.............................. RichieMcLernon 51
(Johnny Farrelly) *handy in chsng gp: wknd 6f out: sn bhd* **66/1**

10 *6* **Baron Du Plessis (FR)**[214] 4-11-0 0.............................. WillKennedy 45
(Ian Williams) *handy in chsng gp tl wknd 4f out* **100/1**

6 **11** *9* **Bramble Brook**[19] 2351 5-11-0 0.............................. BrendanPowell 36
(Colin Tizzard) *handy in chsng gp tl wknd 5f out* **33/1**

0 **12** *3 ¼* **Horseguardsparade**[36] 2020 4-11-0 0.............................. SamTwiston-Davies 32
(Nigel Twiston-Davies) *mid-div tl wknd over 4f out* **33/1**

2 **13** *21* **Royalzaro (FR)**[30] 2126 5-11-0 0.............................. NoelFehily 11
(Harry Fry) *handy in chsng gp: wknd 7f out: sn wl bhd: eased fnl 4f* **9/4**[1]

4m 10.5s (6.20) **Going Correction** +0.45s/f (Soft) **13** Ran SP% **119.1**
Speed ratings: **102,101,97,94,90 89,72,70,68,65 61,59,49**
CSF £71.38 TOTE £8.50: £2.60, £3.20, £4.90; EX 63.70 Trifecta £1067.20.
Owner McNeill Family **Bred** Mme Guilhaine Le Borgne **Trained** Upper Lambourn, Berks
■ Stewards' Enquiry : Wayne Hutchinson caution: careless riding

FOCUS
The race distance was 136yds further than advertised. Eight of these had run before, whether it was in bumpers or points, and it saw a fine performance from the winner, who was always prominent. Pretty ordinary bumper form for the track, but the first two look above average. The sixth helps set the level.
T/Plt: £108.80 to a £1 stake. Pool: £85,665.85 - 574.37 winning units. T/Qpdt: £30.90 to a £1 stake. Pool: £6,409.94 - 153.02 winning units. **Lee McKenzie**

2454 TAUNTON (R-H)
Thursday, November 26

OFFICIAL GOING: Good to soft (good in places; 5.2)
Wind: almost nil Weather: overcast

2730 COUNTY GAZETTE - "THE FAVOURITE FOR NEWS" H'CAP HURDLE (DIV I) (10 hdls) 2m 3f 1y
12:40 (12:40) (Class 5) (0-100,100) 3-Y-0+ **£3,249** (£954; £477; £238)

Form RPR
0006 **1** **Exemplary**[14] 2458 8-11-7 **100**..............................(t) DavidNoonan(5) 107+
(Johnny Farrelly) *hld up towards rr: midfield 3rd: trckd ldrs 3 out: sn pushed along: rdn to ld last: kpt on wl: rdn clr* **4/1**[2]

-6P5 **2** *3 ½* **Mexican Border (GER)**[23] 2263 6-11-4 **92**.............................. JeremiahMcGrath 94
(Martin Hill) *trckd ldrs: led 2 out: rdn and hdd last: kpt on but no ex* **8/1**

0-PP **3** *7* **Prince Of Thieves (IRE)**[23] 2263 5-10-11 **85**..............................(bt[1]) RyanMahon 82
(Anthony Honeyball) *trckd ldrs: led 3 out: nt fluent and hdd 2 out: sn rdn: kpt on same pce* **20/1**

44U- **4** *¾* **Barista (IRE)**[37] 5435 7-11-6 **94**.............................. TomO'Brien 89
(Brian Forsey) *j.lft: hld up towards rr: rdn and hdwy appr 2 out: styd on fr last: wnt 4th cl home* **12/1**

PP62 **5** *½* **Columbanus (IRE)**[7] 2604 4-9-7 **74** oh4..............................(t) MissNatalieParker(7) 68
(Kevin Bishop) *hld up towards rr: hdwy to sit promly after 5th: led 7th tl next: rdn after 2 out: kpt on same pce* **10/3**[1]

6004 **6** *½* **Ice Tres**[14] 2455 6-11-5 **100**.............................. CiaranGethings(7) 94
(Chris Down) *hld up towards rr of mid-div: blnd 5th: hdwy appr 3 out: chsd ldrs 2 out: sn rdn: styd on same pce* **7/1**[3]

0F5- **7** *3 ½* **Acadian (FR)**[229] 5280 5-11-3 **91**..............................(p) ConorO'Farrell 83
(Nigel Hawke) *a mid-div* **10/1**

6004 **8** *hd* **In The Crowd (IRE)**[16] 2413 6-11-4 **95**..............................(p) JamesBanks(3) 86
(Roy Brotherton) *led tl 7th: rdn after 3 out: wknd bef next* **10/1**

0054 **9** *8* **Sun Quest**[7] 2599 11-9-9 **76** oh7 ow2.............................. MissTWorsley(7) 59
(Steven Dixon) *mid-div: rdn after 3 out: sn wknd* **33/1**

4604 **10** *16* **West Of The Edge (IRE)**[8] 2567 7-11-10 **98**.............................. DaveCrosse 67
(Dai Williams) *prom tl 7th: sn wknd: t.o* **25/1**

0P0- **11** *7* **Upham Running (IRE)**[249] 4944 7-10-13 **94**.............................. WilliamFeatherstone(7) 57
(Kate Buckett) *hld up towards rr: hdwy after 5th: prom after next: ev ch 3 out: sn wknd: t.o* **16/1**

00P- **12** *dist* **Anglo Paddy (IRE)**[316] 3675 6-9-7 **74** oh14..............................(p) MrShaneQuinlan(7)
(Neil Mulholland) *mid-div: rdn appr 6th: wknd after 3 out: t.o* **12/1**

43PF **U** **Sheer Poetry (IRE)**[14] 2455 4-11-9 **97**.............................. SeanBowen
(Richard Woollacott) *mid-div whn blnd bdly and uns rdr 7th* **33/1**

/04- **P** **Miss Siskin**[270] 6-10-6 **87**.............................. MissBFrost(7)
(Jimmy Frost) *chsd ldrs tl wknd 6th: t.o whn p.u after 3 out* **66/1**

4m 47.6s (1.60) **Going Correction** -0.175s/f (Good)
WFA 4 from 5yo+ 7lb **14** Ran SP% **122.1**
Speed ratings (Par 103): **89,87,84,84,84 83,82,82,78,72 69, , ,**
CSF £34.82 CT £587.42 TOTE £4.30: £1.90, £2.80, £6.70; EX 41.90 Trifecta £930.00.
Owner Monday Boys Partnership **Bred** Darley **Trained** Enmore, Somerset

FOCUS
Both bends shared and bend out of home straight moved out 16yds for chases and 6yds for hurdles. Bend out of back straight moved out 13yds for chases and 3yds for hurdles. Actual race distance 2m 3f 37yds. David Noonan and Jerry McGrath agreed after the first that the ground was no worse than good to soft, certainly not sticky or holding although a little dead in places. The opening time was 20.6sec slower than standard. Very modest handicap form. The winner has been rated back to something like his best.

2731 SETSQUARE RECRUITMENT "NATIONAL HUNT" NOVICES' HURDLE (9 hdls) 2m 104y
1:10 (1:11) (Class 4) 4-Y-0+ **£4,548** (£1,335; £667; £333)

Form RPR
11-1 **1** **Mister Miyagi (IRE)**[34] 2056 6-11-5 0.............................. IanPopham 128+
(Dan Skelton) *trckd ldrs: led sn after last: drifted lft: drvn out* **8/11**[1]

1- **2** *1 ¾* **Star Trouper (IRE)**[239] 5105 5-10-12 0..............................(t) TomO'Brien 116
(Philip Hobbs) *led: rdn whn jnd between last 2: hdd sn after last: kpt on but no ex* **4/1**[2]

20 **3** *hd* **Star Foot (IRE)**[26] 2183 4-10-9 0..............................(p) JamesBanks(3) 116
(Jo Davis) *trckd ldrs: chal 2 out: sn rdn: kpt on fr last* **33/1**

0-3U **4** *4* **Chief Brody**[8] 2563 4-10-12 0.............................. JamieMoore 113
(Grace Harris) *mid-div: hdwy after 3 out: lft 4th and hmpd 2 out: kpt on but no further imp on ldrs* **50/1**

0-3 **5** *2 ½* **Bim Bam Boum (FR)**[32] 2091 4-10-12 0.............................. RyanMahon 112
(Harry Fry) *hld up towards rr: stdy prog fr 3 out: sltly hmpd 2 out: no further imp* **7/1**

02 **6** *16* **Thegreendalerocket (IRE)**[15] 2443 6-10-7 0.............................. MrBMoorcroft(5) 96
(Jimmy Frost) *chsd ldrs tl rdn after 3 out: wknd bef next* **66/1**

7 *½* **Cottstown Fox (IRE)** 6-10-12 0.............................. MarkQuinlan 95
(Neil Mulholland) *trckd ldrs tl wknd after 3 out* **100/1**

4-64 **8** *1* **Westend Prince (IRE)**[19] 2345 4-10-5 0.............................. PaulO'Brien(7) 94
(Colin Tizzard) *a towards rr* **50/1**

9 *5* **Jack Snipe** 6-10-9 0.............................. MattGriffiths(3) 90
(Jeremy Scott) *a towards rr* **100/1**

10 *¾* **The Minkle (IRE)** 4-10-12 0.............................. ConorO'Farrell 89
(David Pipe) *mid-div tl wknd 3 out* **50/1**

0-55 **11** *47* **Definately Vinnie**[180] 558 5-10-7 0.............................. ConorRing(5) 47
(Jane Mathias) *nt fluent 1st: struggling in rr 5th: t.o* **100/1**

4423 **12** *57* **Junior Package**[85] 1449 4-10-9 0.............................. BrianToomey(3)
(David Pipe) *lost tch 5th: t.o* **33/1**

342- **F** **The Outlaw (IRE)**[248] 4960 5-10-12 0.............................. NickScholfield 115
(Paul Nicholls) *mid-div: hdwy after 3 out: travelling wl enough in cl 4th whn fell 2 out* **5/1**[3]

06- **P** **Ouest Ocean (FR)**[282] 4283 4-10-12 0..............................(t) DenisO'Regan
(Victor Dartnall) *plld hrd: a in rr: t.o whn p.u* **100/1**

4m 6.1s (-1.90) **Going Correction** -0.175s/f (Good)
WFA 4 from 5yo+ 7lb **14** Ran SP% **124.3**
Speed ratings (Par 105): **97,96,96,94,92 84,84,84,81,81 57,29, ,**
CSF £4.04 TOTE £1.90: £1.10, £1.60, £6.50; EX 4.70 Trifecta £65.10.
Owner Ben Turner & Jay Tabb **Bred** Stephen Nolan **Trained** Alcester, Warwicks

FOCUS
Actual race distance 2m 140yds. An interesting novice hurdle run at just a steady initial gallop. The winner set a fair standard and has been rated similar to his Cheltenham win, with the third, fifth, sixth and faller all helping to set the level.

2732 SIS NOVICES' H'CAP HURDLE (12 hdls) 2m 7f 198y
1:45 (1:45) (Class 4) (0-115,112) 4-Y-0+ **£4,548** (£1,335; £667; £333)

Form RPR
0-24 **1** **Captainofindustry (IRE)**[23] 2262 6-11-7 **106**..............................(p) DenisO'Regan 114+
(Mark Pitman) *led tl after 3rd: led after 8th: rdn whn strly pressed after 3 out: hdd briefly last: styd on dourly: drvn out* **4/1**[3]

0-50 **2** *2 ¼* **Fountains Blossom**[48] 1837 6-10-10 **100**..............................(t) DavidNoonan(5) 105+
(Anthony Honeyball) *in tch: trckd ldrs after 7th: chal 3 out: slt advantage whn mstke last: sn hdd and hung rt: hld after* **7/2**[2]

2114 **3** *4 ½* **Tokyo Javilex (FR)**[25] 2223 8-11-5 **111**..............................(t) MrLDrowne(7) 111
(Nigel Hawke) *chsd ldrs: pushed along fr 7th: rdn after 9th: styd on fr 3 out but nt quite pce to chal* **10/1**

4-01 **4** *17* **Knight ofthe Realm**[4] 2658 6-11-6 **112** 7ex.............................. MrMLegg(7) 96
(Caroline Keevil) *hld up: struggling 8th: sme hdwy 3 out: styd on fr next but nvr gng pce to get on terms* **7/4**[1]

4- **5** *4* **Carre Noir (FR)**[444] 1477 6-11-8 **107**.............................. JeremiahMcGrath 87
(Martin Hill) *in tch: rdn after 9th: wnt 4th 3 out: wknd between last 2* **28/1**

0/12 **6** *57* **Our Folly**[49] 1819 7-11-6 **105**..............................(tp) NickScholfield 34
(Stuart Kittow) *hld up: reminders after 7th: nvr threatened: wknd after 3 out: t.o* **7/1**

0-21 **P** **Upton Wood**[191] 391 9-11-8 **107**..............................(p) JamesDavies
(Chris Down) *chsd ldrs tl after 7th: in rr fr next: t.o whn p.u after 3 out* **12/1**

40-P **P** **Memory Of Light (IRE)**[17] 2408 6-9-12 **86**..............................(t) ConorShoemark(3)
(Claire Dyson) *trckd ldr: led after 3rd tl rdn after 8th: wknd bef 3 out: t.o whn p.u bef 2 out* **33/1**

5m 56.4s (-7.60) **Going Correction** -0.175s/f (Good) **8** Ran SP% **114.3**
Speed ratings (Par 105): **105,104,102,97,95 76, ,**
CSF £18.78 CT £128.67 TOTE £6.00: £1.50, £1.80, £2.20; EX 29.70 Trifecta £245.10.
Owner Malcolm C Denmark **Bred** Nick Blanchfield **Trained** Upper Lambourn, Berks

FOCUS
Actual race distance 3m 32yds. They went a reasonable gallop in this fair novice handicap and it became quite a stamina test. Another boost for the winner's Exeter form. The third has been rated to his mark.

2733 WEATHERBYS HAMILTON NOVICES' LIMITED H'CAP CHASE (17 fncs) 2m 7f 3y
2:20 (2:20) (Class 3) (0-135,135) 4-Y-0+ **£8,447** (£2,480; £1,240; £620)

Form RPR
2/F- **1** **Saint Roque (FR)**[570] 111 9-11-8 **135**..............................(t) ConorO'Farrell 141+
(Paul Nicholls) *trckd ldrs: j.w: chal 2 out: led sn after last: kpt on wl* **11/4**[1]

2-12 **2** *2 ½* **Royalraise (IRE)**[176] 595 6-10-9 **122**.............................. LeightonAspell 124
(Oliver Sherwood) *trckd ldrs: led 13th: jnd after 4 out: rdn after 3 out: led briefly last: kpt on but sn hld by wnr* **9/2**[3]

0-25 **3** *2* **Rydon Pynes**[15] 2442 7-10-13 **126**.............................. JeremiahMcGrath 128+
(Martin Hill) *in tch: trckd ldrs: 11th: mstke 13th: jnd ldr after 4 out: rdn whn nt fluent 2 out: slt ld whn blnd bdly last: nt rcvr* **4/1**[2]

P-1F **4** *9* **Gentleman Jon**[19] 2347 7-10-7 **127**..............................(t) PaulO'Brien[(7)] 122
(Colin Tizzard) *v bdly hmpd 1st and rdr lost irons: rcvrd by 3rd: trckd ldrs: rdn in cl 4th after 4 out: hld in 5th whn stmbld 3 out: regained hld 4th after 2 out* **7/1**

-132 **5** *2 1/4* **Kilmurvy (IRE)**[24] 2240 7-11-1 **128**..............................(tp) NickScholfield 118
(Jeremy Scott) *nvr really travelling in last: nvr got involved* **9/2**[3]

F13F **6** *9* **By The Boardwalk (IRE)**[24] 2240 7-11-1 **131**.............(t) TomBellamy[(3)] 114
(Kim Bailey) *in tch: chsd ldrs after 4 out: sn rdn: hld fr next: wkng whn nt fluent 2 out* **12/1**

02-4 **7** *11* **No No Mac (IRE)**[21] 2289 6-11-5 **132**..............................(tp) TomO'Brien 103
(Charlie Longsdon) *trckd ldrs: led 8th tl 13th: wknd after 4 out* **12/1**

140- **P** **Boardwalk Empire (IRE)**[225] 5343 8-10-8 **124**.............. KieronEdgar[(3)]
(Kate Buckett) *collided w anther 1st: led tl 8th: struggling 11th: sn wknd: t.o whn p.u after 4 out* **25/1**

P **Ballyadeen (IRE)**[266] 4591 7-10-3 **116** oh11.............................. DaveCrosse
(Dai Williams) *hld up: in tch whn blnd bdly 13th: p.u bef next* **100/1**

6m 6.1s (-9.90) **Going Correction** -0.175s/f (Good) **9** Ran SP% **115.8**
Speed ratings (Par 107): **110,109,108,105,104 101,97, ,**
CSF £16.17 CT £48.61 TOTE £2.50: £1.30, £1.90, £1.90; EX 19.60 Trifecta £71.80.
Owner Ian J Fogg **Bred** Mme Genevieve Mongin **Trained** Ditcheat, Somerset

FOCUS
Actual race distance 2m 7f 177yds. A decent race of its type, and the form should hold up. The second has been rated to his hurdle mark.

2734 WELL DONE AT CHELTENHAM IAN POPHAM H'CAP HURDLE (9 hdls) 2m 104y
2:55 (2:55) (Class 4) (0-115,115) 3-Y-0+ **£4,548** (£1,335; £667; £333)

Form RPR

243 **1** **Proofreader**[24] 2238 6-11-7 **110**.............................. MarkQuinlan 123+
(Neil Mulholland) *hld up bhd: smooth hdwy fr 5th: wnt cl 3rd 2 out: led last: qcknd clr: readily* **8/1**[3]

522- **2** *9* **Floresco (GER)**[264] 4624 5-11-11 **114**.............................. IanPopham 115
(Richard Woollacott) *mid-div: hdwy sn after 3 out: sltly outpcd bef next: r.o fr last: wnt 2nd fnl strides: no ch w wnr* **7/1**[2]

06-1 **3** *hd* **Back By Midnight**[42] 1931 6-11-1 **107**..............................(t) JamesBanks[(3)] 108
(Emma Baker) *led: rdn after 2 out: hdd last: kpt on but nt pce of wnr: lost 2nd fnl strides* **16/1**

4 *1 3/4* **Shadow Blue (IRE)**[55] 1750 6-10-13 **109**.............................. MrGTreacy[(7)] 109
(Steven Dixon) *chsd ldrs: chal 3 out: rdn and ev ch sn after 2 out: hld last: kpt on same pce* **100/1**

34-6 **5** *3 3/4* **Ourmanmassini (IRE)**[209] 63 7-11-4 **112**.............(t) HarryBannister[(5)] 108
(Suzy Smith) *mid-div: outpcd after 3 out: styd on again fr next* **8/1**[3]

6664 **6** *shd* **Loch Garman (FR)**[41] 1947 4-11-6 **109**.............................. ConorO'Farrell 105
(Nigel Hawke) *towards rr: rdn after 3 out: styd on fr next: nvr threatened* **33/1**

3-52 **7** *1 1/2* **Orthodox Lad**[22] 2271 7-11-1 **111**.............................. CiaranGethings[(7)] 106
(Grace Harris) *taken to s early: chsd ldrs: rdn after 3 out: one pce fr next* **14/1**

5340 **8** *1/2* **Gambol (FR)**[27] 2170 5-11-5 **108**.............................. KielanWoods 104
(Ian Williams) *hld up towards rr: midfield 3 out: rdn bef next: nt pce to get involved* **25/1**

-U60 **9** *1 3/4* **Romeo Americo (IRE)**[148] 876 8-11-7 **110**.............................. AndrewThornton 103
(Seamus Mullins) *towards rr: sme prog after 3 out but nvr any threat* **20/1**

31-1 **10** *1 1/4* **Dazinski**[8] 2577 9-11-7 **110**..............................(t) JamesDavies 107+
(Henry Oliver) *mid-div: trcking ldrs whn virtually fell 6th: nvr rcvrd and sn btn* **2/1**[1]

2/F5 **11** *shd* **Walter White (IRE)**[14] 2458 5-11-4 **107**..............................(t) TomO'Brien 98
(Philip Hobbs) *chsd ldrs: rdn after 3 out: wknd bef last* **14/1**

35-0 **12** *1* **Sweeping Rock (IRE)**[22] 2271 5-11-6 **109**.............................. JamieMoore 100
(John Spearing) *mid-div: mstke 3 out: wknd next* **14/1**

42-0 **13** *13* **Abyaat (IRE)**[14] 2458 4-11-4 **107**..............................(t) DenisO'Regan 86
(Victor Dartnall) *mid-div tl wknd appr 2 out* **33/1**

400- **14** *1 3/4* **Navanman (IRE)**[324] 3555 6-10-13 **107**.............................. DavidNoonan[(5)] 84
(David Pipe) *mid-div: struggling after 5th: btn 3 out* **9/1**

555P **15** *3 1/2* **Mr Lando**[24] 2244 6-11-12 **115**.............................. LeightonAspell 89
(Alison Batchelor) *trckd ldr: struggling 6th: wknd next* **50/1**

4-06 **16** *30* **Mystery Drama**[15] 2445 5-11-5 **108**.............................. RhysFlint 55
(Alexandra Dunn) *mid-div tl wknd 3 out: t.o* **40/1**

1415 **17** *11* **Cruise In Style (IRE)**[27] 2168 9-11-6 **109**..............................(tp) JamesBest 46
(Kevin Bishop) *a towards rr: t.o* **20/1**

4m 4.2s (-3.80) **Going Correction** -0.175s/f (Good)
WFA 4 from 5yo+ 7lb **17** Ran SP% **128.6**
Speed ratings (Par 105): **102,97,97,96,94 94,93,93,92,92 92,91,85,84,82 67,61**
CSF £61.33 CT £908.78 TOTE £8.20: £2.00, £2.20, £3.60, £11.10; EX 50.60 Trifecta £1852.40.
Owner The Boot Inn Partnership **Bred** Darley **Trained** Limpley Stoke, Wilts

FOCUS
Actual race distance 2m 140yds. A wide-margin winner in this ordinary handicap, in which they went a solid gallop. A massive step up from the easy winner for a strongly run race, and he looks a potential 130+ hurdler. The second and third have been rated pretty much to their marks.

2735 FESTIVE FIXTURE 10TH DECEMBER H'CAP CHASE (17 fncs) 2m 7f 3y
3:25 (3:25) (Class 5) (0-100,88) 4-Y-0+ **£3,898** (£1,144; £572; £286)

Form RPR

2630 **1** **Bus Named Desire**[10] 2539 7-11-2 **85**..............................(tp) MrStanSheppard[(7)] 94
(Matt Sheppard) *hld up: hdwy after 4 out: led 2 out: styd on: drvn out* **17/2**

602U **2** *1 1/2* **Dawnieriver (IRE)**[21] 2303 5-11-12 **88**.............................. LiamTreadwell 95
(Michael Scudamore) *hld up: pushed along after 10th: hdwy after 11th: jnd ldr 13th: led 3 out: rdn and hdd 2 out: styd on but a being hld fr last* **4/1**[2]

3-44 **3** *18* **Ballyegan (IRE)**[15] 2447 10-11-12 **88**.............................. LiamHeard 85
(Bob Buckler) *chsd ldrs: lft 2nd and hmpd 11th: led 13th: rdn and hdd 3 out: hld whn rchd for next: fdd* **9/2**[3]

PP06 **4** *6* **Mostly Bob (IRE)**[22] 2269 12-11-11 **87**..............................(tp) JamesBest 74
(Sophie Leech) *led: hdd whn mstke 13th: sn btn* **10/1**

P-12 **U** **Double Chocolate**[10] 2539 12-11-11 **87**..............................(p) AndrewTinkler
(Martin Keighley) *pressing ldr whn blnd and uns rdr 11th* **7/4**[1]

-P54 **P** **Petit Ecuyer (FR)**[4] 2666 9-11-0 **83**.............................. ThomasCheesman[(7)]
(Dai Williams) *in tch: rdn after 12th: wknd 4 out: p.u bef next* **20/1**

0066 **U** **Toast And Jam (IRE)**[126] 1079 6-10-8 **73**.............(t) ConorShoemark[(3)]
(Claire Dyson) *trckd ldrs tl lost pl 6th: in last pair whn blnd and uns rdr 9th* **5/1**

6m 18.3s (2.30) **Going Correction** -0.175s/f (Good) **7** Ran SP% **115.6**
Speed ratings (Par 103): **89,88,82,80,**
CSF £43.47 TOTE £8.40: £3.60, £2.20; EX 54.80 Trifecta £130.70.
Owner E J Ford **Bred** Mrs P Grainger **Trained** Eastnor, H'fords

FOCUS
Actual race distance 2m 7f 177yds. This modest handicap chase was run at a sound pace, and rather fell apart. Probably not form to treat too seriously. The first two have been rated pretty much to their marks.

2736 COUNTY GAZETTE - "THE FAVOURITE FOR NEWS" H'CAP HURDLE (DIV II) (10 hdls) 2m 3f 1y
4:00 (4:00) (Class 5) (0-100,100) 3-Y-0+ **£3,249** (£954; £477; £238)

Form RPR

40P- **1** **Kleitomachos (IRE)**[27] 4651 7-11-7 **100**.............................. (b[1]) DavidNoonan[(5)] 107+
(Stuart Kittow) *racd keenly in tch: trckd ldrs 5th: rdn to chal 2 out: led sn after last: r.o wl: rdn out* **3/1**[1]

46/0 **2** *2* **Double Accord**[27] 2164 5-11-6 **94**.............................. RyanMahon 98
(Anthony Honeyball) *trckd ldrs: chal after 3 out: rdn to ld 2 out: hdd sn after last: hung rt: nt pce of wnr* **10/1**

P-04 **3** *5* **Guanciale**[22] 2264 8-11-6 **94**.............................. RobertDunne 93
(Dai Burchell) *mid-div: rdn after 3 out: hdwy next: styd on run-in: styd on* **9/1**

250P **4** *hd* **Rior (IRE)**[23] 2262 8-11-11 **99**.............................. TomO'Brien 98
(Paul Henderson) *in tch: rdn after 3 out: styd on same pce fr next: chal fr hld 3rd fr last* **14/1**

5P06 **5** *3 1/2* **Vering (FR)**[4] 2661 9-10-0 **74** oh5..............................(tp) JamesBest 71
(Carroll Gray) *led: hit 3 out: sn rdn: hdd next: styd on same pce* **40/1**

630P **6** *11* **Watchmetail (IRE)**[7] 2599 9-10-0 **74** oh10..............................(b) ConorO'Farrell 59
(John Panvert) *mid-div: hdwy 7th: effrt after 3 out: sn one pce* **50/1**

3 **7** *5* **Sabroclair (FR)**[21] 2300 6-11-9 **97**.............................. IanPopham 78
(Richard Woollacott) *hld up towards rr: struggling 3 out: sme late prog: nvr a factor* **5/1**

P-36 **8** *3/4* **Shanksforamillion**[24] 2245 6-9-11 **78** ow3.............................. CiaranGethings[(7)] 58
(David Rees) *hld up towards rr: sme late prog: nvr a factor* **14/1**

11-2 **9** *nse* **Seymour Legend**[193] 364 9-11-1 **89**.............................. LiamTreadwell 69
(Jim Wilson) *towards rr of mid-div on outer: hdwy 7th: rdn after 3 out: sn wknd* **4/1**[2]

-0PP **10** *6* **Wicklewood**[170] 676 9-10-13 **92**..............................(t) JakeHodson[(5)] 67
(Mark Gillard) *chsd ldrs tl 7th: wknd after 3 out* **40/1**

0/00 **11** *24* **Chakisto (FR)**[37] 2006 7-11-7 **95**.............................. JamieMoore 48
(Katie Stephens) *mid-div: hdwy 3 out: sn rdn: wknd next: t.o* **25/1**

12 *6* **Lake Chapala (IRE)**[49] 1831 6-11-5 **93**.............................. MichaelByrne 41
(Tim Vaughan) *hld up towards rr: effrt 3 out: wknd bef next: t.o* **9/2**[3]

4m 51.7s (5.70) **Going Correction** -0.175s/f (Good) **12** Ran SP% **123.0**
Speed ratings (Par 103): **81,80,78,77,76 71,69,69,69,66 56,54**
CSF £33.77 CT £253.10 TOTE £4.80: £1.80, £3.70, £3.50; EX 44.20 Trifecta £360.70.
Owner Eric Gadsden **Bred** Carrigbeg Stud Co Ltd **Trained** Blackborough, Devon

FOCUS
Actual race distance 2m 3f 37yds. Not many got involved in this very ordinary handicap, which was run in a time 4.1sec slower than the first division. The winner has been rated back to the level of last season's Chepstow fourth, while the second has been rated as taking a big step up.
T/Jkpt: JACKPOT not won. JACKPOT PLACEPOT £551.40. Pool: £2417.49 - 3.20 winning units. T/Plt: £63.50 to a £1 stake. Pool: £58,862.68 - 675.94 winning units. T/Qpdt: £27.60 toa £1 stake. Pool: £5,818.49 - 155.89 winning units. **Tim Mitchell**

2737-2743a - (Foreign Racing) - See Raceform Interactive

DONCASTER (L-H)
Friday, November 27

OFFICIAL GOING: Good (chs 8.3, hdl 8.3)
Wind: fresh 1/2 against Weather: fine

2744 WALLS MAGNUM CLASSIC H'CAP HURDLE (QUALIFIER FOR THE CHALLENGER STAYING HURDLE SERIES FINAL) (11 hdls) 3m 96y
12:15 (12:15) (Class 4) (0-120,120) 3-Y-0+ **£3,898** (£1,144; £572; £286)

Form RPR

0-35 **1** **Harry Hunt**[13] 2496 8-11-3 **111**.............................. KielanWoods 119
(Graeme McPherson) *trckd ldrs: 2nd appr 3 out: led bef 2 out: drvn out* **10/1**

4356 **2** *3* **Bold Conquest (IRE)**[23] 2268 7-11-5 **113**.............................. TomO'Brien 117
(Stuart Edmunds) *mid-div: hdwy to chse ldrs 7th: 2nd appr 2 out: styd on same pce appr last* **9/2**[1]

P-PP **3** *8* **Leath Acra Mor (IRE)**[18] 2405 9-10-8 **105**..............................(p) RobMcCarth[(3)] 102
(Ian Williams) *chsd ldrs: one pce bef 2 out* **100/1**

4-43 **4** *1 1/4* **Mawaqeet (USA)**[53] 1794 6-11-3 **114**..............................(p) JonathanEngland[(3)] 110
(Michael Appleby) *in rr: hdwy bef 3 out: one pce fr 2 out* **12/1**

03F **5** *2 1/4* **Nautical Nitwit (IRE)**[20] 2333 6-11-9 **120**.............................. AdamNicol[(3)] 114
(Philip Kirby) *in rr: hdwy 8th: one pce fr 3 out* **14/1**

2-43 **6** *3 1/4* **Echo Springs**[20] 2331 5-11-7 **115**.............................. BrianHughes 107
(Danielle McCormick) *chsd ldrs: wknd appr 2 out* **8/1**

4135 **7** *9* **Johnny Go**[20] 2340 5-10-9 **110**..............................(p) FinianO'Toole[(7)] 93
(Lisa Harrison) *rr-div: hdwy 7th: chsng ldrs 8th: lost pl next* **22/1**

0-06 **8** *3 1/2* **Night In Milan (IRE)**[20] 2340 9-11-12 **120**..............................(b) JamesReveley 112+
(Keith Reveley) *led: hit 3rd: hdd bef 2 out: sn wknd: j.lft last* **11/2**[3]

1-2P **9** *5* **Ballyknock Lad (IRE)**[15] 2456 6-11-12 **120**..............................(t) DavidBass 95
(Kim Bailey) *chsd ldrs: drvn 6th: lost pl bef 3 out* **16/1**

0P-3 **10** *8* **Malin Bay (IRE)**[27] 2190 10-11-9 **120**.............................. CraigNichol[(3)] 88
(Nicky Richards) *chsd ldrs: lost pl 3 out* **10/1**

6-64 **11** *10* **Victor Leudorum (IRE)**[36] 2036 8-11-2 **110**..............................(tp) DarylJacob 69
(Charlie Mann) *prom: lost pl after 8th: sn bhd* **33/1**

2/2- **12** *2 1/4* **Billy Biscuit (IRE)**[562] 278 7-11-3 **114**.............................. TomBellamy[(3)] 71
(Alan King) *mid-div: lost pl 4th: sn bhd: reminders 7th* **5/1**[2]

4260 **13** *3/4* **Fighter Jet**[7] 2624 7-11-12 **120**..............................(p) PaulMoloney 76
(John Mackie) *mid-div: hdwy 4th: lost pl 3 out* **40/1**

116P **14** *39* **Minella Hero (IRE)**[17] 2424 7-11-0 **115**.............................. MissBeckySmith[(7)] 36
(Micky Hammond) *in rr: j.rt 1st: bhd fr 4th: t.o 3 out* **66/1**

0343 **P** **St Quintin**[22] 2296 5-10-12 **106**.............................. NickScholfield
(David Brown) *chsd ldrs: lost pl 4th: bhd 7th: t.o whn p.u bef 3 out* **25/1**

5m 49.9s (-9.10) **Going Correction** -0.35s/f (Good) **15** Ran SP% **115.8**
Speed ratings (Par 105): **101,100,97,96,96 95,92,90,89,86 83,82,82,69,**
CSF £50.04 CT £4225.37 TOTE £12.50: £4.00, £2.00, £22.70; EX 65.10 Trifecta £2448.40 Part won..
Owner The Reserved Judgment Partnership **Bred** Darley **Trained** Upper Oddington, Gloucs

FOCUS
The hurdle bend into the home straight was out seven yards from its innermost line and this opening contest was run over 42 yards further than advertised. The ground was given as 'good' on both the hurdles and chase course. This was a fair handicap to start. The second has been rated to his mark.

2745 CADBURY FLAKE 99 NOVICES' H'CAP HURDLE (10 hdls) 2m 3f 120y
12:45 (12:45) (Class 5) (0-100,100) 3-Y-O+ £3,249 (£954; £477; £238)

Form RPR
40U5 1 **Wymeswold**[28] 2165 8-10-4 **81**........................ BenPoste(3) 85
(Michael Mullineaux) *in rr: chsd ldrs 6th: drvn next: sn outpcd and lost pl: hdwy appr 2 out: modest 5th between last 2: 3rd last 150yds: styd on to ld towards fin* **50/1**
P041 2 *nk* **Polarbrook (IRE)**[18] 2408 8-11-8 **96**........................(tp) SeanQuinlan 101
(Derek Shaw) *in rr: hdwy 6th: chsng ldrs 3 out: cl 4th whn hit 2 out: 2nd between last 2: hit last: led last 120yds: hdd and no ex towards fin* **8/1**
P601 3 *1 1/4* **Dragon City**[25] 2256 5-10-8 **87**........................(t) HarryBannister(5) 92
(Charlie Mann) *led: jst over a l ahd whn blnd last: sn hdd: no ex clsng stages* **11/2**[2]
/003 4 *3* **Minden March**[17] 2427 10-9-9 **74** oh7........................ JamieHamilton(5) 75
(Peter Maddison) *chsd ldrs: 3rd whn hit last: kpt on one pce* **33/1**
34-4 5 *1 1/2* **Perfect Poison (IRE)**[22] 2291 7-11-7 **100**........................ JamesCowley(5) 99+
(Donald McCain) *mid-div: in rr 6th: kpt on fr 2 out: 5th between last 2: styd on same pce* **8/1**
3P40 6 *3* **Tara's Rainbow**[22] 2298 5-11-2 **90**........................(t) DavidBass 88
(Kim Bailey) *chsd ldrs: blnd 3 out: sn outpcd: kpt on run-in* **9/1**
-535 7 *3/4* **Attention Please (IRE)**[28] 2174 5-10-11 **88**........................ CraigNichol(3) 83
(Rose Dobbin) *chsd ldrs: 3rd whn hit 2 out: wknd appr last* **15/2**[3]
25-4 8 *6* **Lowcarr Motion**[28] 2174 5-11-3 **98**........................ FinianO'Toole(7) 88
(Micky Hammond) *mid-div: hdwy to chse ldrs 7th: wknd 2 out* **4/1**[1]
F363 9 *16* **Impeccability**[10] 2559 5-11-11 **99**........................(p) BrianHughes 74
(John Mackie) *in rr: hdwy 6th: sn chsng ldrs: lost pl appr 2 out* **9/1**
3-20 10 *12* **First Of Never (IRE)**[13] 2492 9-10-0 **74** oh3........................ WillKennedy 39
(Lynn Siddall) *hld up in rr: hdwy 6th: lost pl bef 3 out: sn bhd* **12/1**
61U/ P **Ben Akram (IRE)**[598] 5216 7-11-2 **93**........................ DerekFox(3)
(Lucinda Russell) *chsd ldrs: hit 5th: sn drvn: lost pl 3 out: bhd whn p.u after next* **14/1**
04P0 P **Mazurati (IRE)**[15] 2453 6-10-13 **94**........................ MrMJPKendrick(7)
(Ben Case) *in rr: drvn 5th: bhd next: t.o whn p.u bef 3 out* **25/1**
4m 43.6s (-7.70) **Going Correction** -0.35s/f (Good) **12** Ran SP% **112.5**
Speed ratings (Par 103): **101,100,100,99,98 97,97,94,88,83 ,**
CSF £392.31 CT £2562.91 TOTE £51.10: £9.70, £2.80, £2.30; EX 766.30 Trifecta £1360.60 Part won..
Owner The Hon Mrs S Pakenham **Bred** Mrs C S Wilson **Trained** Alpraham, Cheshire

FOCUS
This was run over 21 yards further than advertised. This was a moderate contest. The winner was well in on the best of her summer/spring form and has been rated back to that sort of level.

2746 ICE CREAM DIRECT UK H'CAP CHASE (15 fncs) 2m 3f 44y
1:20 (1:20) (Class 3) (0-140,139) 4-Y-O+ £6,498 (£1,908; £954; £477)

Form RPR
-212 1 **Voix D'Eau (FR)**[27] 2184 5-11-4 **138**........................(t) MrMLegg(7) 146+
(Harry Fry) *hld up towards rr: hdwy 6th: lft 3rd 8th: chsd ldrs appr 4 out: mstke 2 out: led last: drvn out* **7/4**[1]
P-F5 2 *3 1/2* **Off The Ground (IRE)**[28] 2171 9-11-8 **135**........................ TomCannon 138
(Charlie Longsdon) *w ldrs: led 3rd: hdd next: led 11th: hdd last: kpt on same pce* **6/1**[2]
254- 3 *6* **Waltz Darling (IRE)**[24] 5492 7-10-8 **121**........................ JamesReveley 120+
(Keith Reveley) *in rr: modest 4th 11th: 3rd 2 out: kpt on* **12/1**
/3-U 4 *13* **Kings Bandit (IRE)**[27] 2201 7-11-5 **132**........................ LeightonAspell 123
(Oliver Sherwood) *nt jump wl in rr: mstke 3rd: hmpd 8th: bhd fr 11th: poor 4th sn after last* **8/1**
1-20 5 *2 1/4* **Minella Forfitness (IRE)**[20] 2335 8-11-5 **132**........................ AdamPogson 117
(Charles Pogson) *t.k.h: trckd ldrs: led 4th: j.rt and mstke 7th: hdd 11th: sn lost pl: wknd 2 out* **11/1**
1U60 6 *10* **Strongly Suggested**[27] 2185 8-11-3 **130**........................ WillKennedy 108
(Jonjo O'Neill) *mid-div: nt fluent 1st: chsd ldrs 8th: 4th and outpacxed whn blnd 10th: reminders and sn lost pl* **40/1**
6F42 U **Buck Mulligan**[36] 2036 10-10-6 **119**........................ PaulMoloney
(Evan Williams) *hld up towards rr: hdwy and in tch whn bdly hmpd and uns rdr 8th* **7/1**[3]
216P B **Le Bacardy (FR)**[14] 2468 9-11-11 **138**........................ RobertDunne
(Dan Skelton) *trckd ldrs: handy 4th whn b.d 8th* **25/1**
31F1 F **Enchanted Garden**[43] 1924 7-11-12 **139**........................(b) BrianHughes
(Malcolm Jefferson) *led to 3rd: 2nd whn fell 8th: fatally injured* **8/1**
224 F **Ever So Much (IRE)**[17] 2425 6-10-2 **115**........................(p) TomO'Brien
(Ben Haslam) *in rr: outpcd 8th: 6th and in rr whn fell 11th* **18/1**
4m 43.6s (-5.40) **Going Correction** -0.25s/f (Good) **10** Ran SP% **112.9**
Speed ratings (Par 107): **101,99,97,91,90 86, , , ,**
CSF £12.80 CT £93.56 TOTE £2.70: £1.50, £1.80, £3.70; EX 12.90 Trifecta £124.00.
Owner Harry Fry Racing Club **Bred** Christophe Toussaint & Emmanuel Clayeux **Trained** Seaborough, Dorset

FOCUS
A useful handicap chase. The second is on a mark he can win off but has been rated 8lb off last season's best.

2747 MASSARELLAS "MISTER SOFTEE" NOVICES' HURDLE (DIV I) (8 hdls) 2m 140y
1:55 (1:56) (Class 4) 4-Y-O+ £3,898 (£1,144; £572; £286)

Form RPR
1-26 1 **Holly Bush Henry (IRE)**[104] 1260 4-10-12 0........................(t) KielanWoods 116+
(Graeme McPherson) *trckd ldrs: 2nd appr 3 out: led bef last: forged clr* **7/2**[3]
2 *8* **Deadly Approach**[770] 4-10-12 0........................ RobertDunne 108
(Sarah-Jayne Davies) *reluctant ldr: t.k.h: clr tl appr 5th: hdd bef last: kpt on same pce* **100/1**
32 3 *2 1/4* **Baltic Storm (IRE)**[25] 2251 4-10-12 118........................ LeightonAspell 108
(Charlie Mann) *trckd ldrs: 3rd bef 2 out: kpt on one pce: hit last* **13/2**
1 4 *5* **Innocent Touch (IRE)**[22] 2294 4-11-5 0........................ BrianHughes 110
(Richard Fahey) *nt jump wl: trckd ldrs: mstke 3rd: 4th and one pce whn mstke 2 out* **5/2**[1]
5 *7* **Spifer (IRE)**[92] 7-10-9 0........................ JohnKington(3) 94+
(Julia Brooke) *hld up in rr: stdy hdwy appr 3 out: nvr threatened: will do bttr* **66/1**
6-06 6 *1 1/2* **King Simba (IRE)**[18] 2406 4-10-12 0........................ DavidBass 93
(Kim Bailey) *chsd ldrs: drvn 3 out: wknd appr next* **40/1**
5 7 *1 3/4* **Iniciar (GER)**[15] 2457 5-10-12 0........................ DarylJacob 91
(David Pipe) *in rr: hdwy to chse ldrs 3 out: wknd next* **11/2**
34-U 8 *1 1/4* **Mr Kit Cat**[35] 2056 5-10-12 0........................ PaulMoloney 90
(Evan Williams) *chsd clr ldr: drvn 3 out: wknd appr next* **11/4**[2]
P-40 9 *56* **Zakety Zak**[187] 459 4-10-7 0........................ NathanMoscrop(5) 34
(James Turner) *in rr: bhd whn j.lft and blnd 3 out: sn t.o* **100/1**
4m 2.3s (-2.40) **Going Correction** -0.35s/f (Good) **9** Ran SP% **112.1**
Speed ratings (Par 105): **91,87,86,83,80 79,79,78,52**
CSF £228.24 TOTE £4.50: £1.20, £14.80, £2.80; EX 403.00 Trifecta £2294.50.
Owner Lady Bamford & Alice Bamford **Bred** John Connolly **Trained** Upper Oddington, Gloucs
■ Stewards' Enquiry : John Kington 14-day ban: guilty of schooling the horse on the racecourse (11 - 22, 26-27

FOCUS
This was run over 21 yards further than advertised. A muddling contest run in a time much slower than the second division. The runner-up raced in a clear lead, ignored by the others for the most part, and the race was slow to develop in the straight. The third, fourth and sixth have been rated pretty much to their marks.

2748 MASSARELLAS "MISTER SOFTEE" NOVICES' HURDLE (DIV II) (8 hdls) 2m 140y
2:30 (2:30) (Class 4) 4-Y-O+ £3,898 (£1,144; £572; £286)

Form RPR
3- 1 **Go Long (IRE)**[254] 4859 5-10-12 0........................ PaulMoloney 133+
(Evan Williams) *chsd ldrs: hmpd by loose horse 3rd: upsides whn hit 2 out: led last: drvn out* **6/1**
41 2 *3 1/4* **Charbel (IRE)**[29] 2154 4-11-5 0........................ DavidBass 137+
(Kim Bailey) *trckd ldr: j.rt 4th and next: led narrowly 2 out: hdd last: styd on same pce* **1/2**[1]
/2P- 3 *14* **Emperor Commodos**[308] 3840 8-10-12 0........................ TomO'Brien 119+
(David Bridgwater) *j.rt: led: hdd 2 out: wknd bef last* **11/2**[3]
1-40 4 *5* **Muthabir (IRE)**[23] 2267 5-10-12 0........................ IanPopham 112
(Richard Phillips) *mid-div: hit 1st: drvn bef 3 out: one pce* **25/1**
5 *shd* **Boston De La Roche (FR)**[192] 4-10-12 0........................ NickScholfield 111
(David Loder) *mid-div: hdwy appr 3 out: drvn appr 2 out: one pce* **4/1**[2]
6 *43* **Cactus Valley (IRE)**[101] 6-10-12 0........................ BrianHughes 72
(Michael Easterby) *in rr: bhd fr 3 out: t.o* **33/1**
7 *31* **Little Big Town (IRE)**[33] 5-10-9 0........................ KyleJames(3) 44
(Julia Brooke) *mid-div: drvn 5th: bhd bef next: sn t.o* **100/1**
0 U **Sarpech (IRE)**[11] 2543 4-10-12 0........................ TomCannon
(Charlie Longsdon) *mid-div: blnd and uns rdr 2nd* **33/1**
P **That Be Grand**[24] 4-10-5 0........................ WillKennedy
(Shaun Harris) *in rr: bhd fr 4th: t.o next: p.u bef 3 out* **100/1**
3m 53.2s (-11.50) **Going Correction** -0.35s/f (Good) **9** Ran SP% **128.0**
Speed ratings (Par 105): **113,111,104,102,102 82,67, ,**
CSF £10.90 TOTE £9.10: £1.60, £1.10, £1.80; EX 13.10 Trifecta £53.30.
Owner Mr & Mrs William Rucker **Bred** Pat Tobin **Trained** Llancarfan, Vale Of Glamorgan

FOCUS
Like the first division, this was run over 21 yards further than the official distance. The time was significantly quicker than the muddling first leg. A big step up from the winner on his bumper form.

2749 KELLY'S OF CORNWALL NOVICES' LIMITED H'CAP CHASE (18 fncs) 3m 6y
3:05 (3:05) (Class 4) (0-120,120) 4-Y-O+ £3,898 (£1,144; £572; £286)

Form RPR
62-F 1 **Wild Bill (IRE)**[19] 2365 6-11-4 **116**........................ PaulMoloney 129+
(Evan Williams) *trckd ldrs: cl 2nd 3 out: led last: pushed out* **4/1**[1]
-13F 2 *2 1/2* **Ueueteotl (FR)**[32] 2105 7-11-8 **120**........................(p) JamesReveley 125
(James Ewart) *led: reminder after 1st: hdd 2nd: led 7th: to 9th: led bef 12th: jnd 2 out: hdd last: kpt on same pce* **16/1**
4F3P 3 *3 1/4* **Solway Legend**[21] 2320 8-10-5 **103**........................ BrianHughes 105
(Lisa Harrison) *in rr: mstke 12th: hdwy appr 4 out: 3rd 2 out: kpt on one pce* **25/1**
36-4 4 *7* **Doktor Glaz (FR)**[27] 2190 5-10-7 **108**........................ CraigNichol(3) 104
(Rose Dobbin) *chsd ldrs: drvn 4 out: wknd between last 2* **8/1**[2]
13P 5 *8* **Dabinett Moon**[36] 2036 7-10-12 **117**........................ MissCVHart(7) 107
(Charlie Longsdon) *rr-div: hdwy to chse ldrs 12th: wknd between last 2* **40/1**
2-F6 6 *hd* **Free Of Charge (IRE)**[23] 2272 6-10-4 **102**........................ TomO'Brien 92
(Philip Hobbs) *chsd ldrs: led 9th tl hdd befgore 12th: wknd between last 2* **11/1**
P60- 7 *6* **Pay The King (IRE)**[229] 5295 8-10-5 **110**........................ FinianO'Toole(7) 93
(Micky Hammond) *in rr: sme hdwy 12th: lost pl bef 4 out* **25/1**
250/ 8 *3 3/4* **Silver Eagle (IRE)**[607] 5093 7-11-8 **120**........................(t) DavidBass 100
(Kim Bailey) *in rr: sn pushed along: bhd fr 14th* **4/1**[1]
-121 P **Present Flight (IRE)**[21] 2327 6-11-2 **117**........................(t) DerekFox(3)
(Lucinda Russell) *t.k.h: w ldrs: j.rt: led 2nd: hdd and hung rt 7th: lost pl and bhd 11th: t.o whn j. bdly rt 12th: p.u bef next: b.b.v* **4/1**[1]
-P25 P **Magheral Express (IRE)**[15] 2456 6-11-3 **115**........................(p) WillKennedy
(Jonjo O'Neill) *trckd ldrs: mstke 1st: carried rt 6th: lost pl 3 out: bhd whn p.u bef next* **14/1**
-035 P **Trapper Peak (IRE)**[16] 2434 6-11-1 **113**........................(b[1]) AndrewThornton
(Caroline Bailey) *mid-div: sme hdwy whn blnd 11th: chsng ldrs next: lost pl 4 out: bhd whn p.u bef 2 out* **17/2**[3]
3-35 U **Cul Dealga (IRE)**[41] 1971 6-10-9 **107**........................(t) TomMessenger
(Chris Bealby) *mid-div: lost pl 11th: bhd whn blnd and uns rdr 14th* **33/1**
6m 1.9s (-10.10) **Going Correction** -0.25s/f (Good) **12** Ran SP% **115.6**
Speed ratings (Par 105): **106,105,104,101,99 99,97,95, , ,**
CSF £58.66 CT £1409.81 TOTE £4.80: £2.00, £3.80, £5.20; EX 56.40 Trifecta £368.80.
Owner Mr & Mrs William Rucker **Bred** James F Barry **Trained** Llancarfan, Vale Of Glamorgan

FOCUS
A fair novices' handicap chase. The second and third have been rated pretty much to their marks.

2750 EDEN FARM HULLEYS STANDARD NATIONAL HUNT FLAT RACE (CONDITIONAL JOCKEYS' AND AMATEUR RIDERS' RACE) 2m 140y
3:35 (3:35) (Class 6) 4-6-Y-O £1,871 (£580; £290; £145)

Form RPR
1 **Meribel Millie** 4-10-4 0........................(t) MrMLegg(7) 99+
(Harry Fry) *trckd ldrs: t.k.h: led over 2f out: hung lft: drvn out* **3/1**[1]
33 2 *2 1/4* **Chase End Charlie (IRE)**[31] 2126 4-10-13 0........................ DavidNoonan(5) 103
(Tom Lacey) *in rr: hdwy after 6f: drvn over 3f out: hrd rdn and chsd wnr 2f out: kpt on same pce* **5/1**[2]
00- 3 *1 1/4* **The Missus**[283] 4289 4-10-8 0........................[1] MrSWaley-Cohen(3) 95
(Warren Greatrex) *hld up in mid-div: hdwy to trck ldrs after 3f: effrt 3f out: 3rd over 1f out: kpt on one pce* **6/1**[3]

4 1 1/4 **Helmsley Lad** 4-10-13 0........................ JamieHamilton(5) 101
(Malcolm Jefferson) *trckd ldrs: outpcd over 4f out: styd on fnl f* **8/1**
3 5 2 **Grow Nasa Grow (IRE)**181 558 4-10-11 0.................. MrRWinks(7) 99
(Peter Winks) *hld up in rr: drvn and outpcd over 3f out: kpt on fnl f* **10/1**
1 6 1 1/4 **Improved (IRE)**135 1003 5-11-8 0.................. AdamNicol(3) 104
(Philip Kirby) *set stdy pce: increased pce over 4f out: hdd over 2f out: wknd fnl f* **8/1**
6- 7 2 1/4 **Scooby (IRE)**223 5402 4-10-13 0.................. ConorRing(5) 95
(Graeme McPherson) *trckd ldrs: t.k.h: effrt 3f out: wknd over 1f out* **22/1**
8 7 **Walk Waterford**179 4-11-4 0.................. MrDerekO'Connor 88
(Jonjo O'Neill) *hld up in rr: effrt 3f out: wknd 2f out* **13/2**
9 5 **Lynda's Boy** 4-11-1 0.................. MattGriffiths(3) 83
(Dan Skelton) *hld up in rr: hdwy after 6f: drvn and lost pl over 3f out* **9/1**

3m 56.0s (-3.10) **Going Correction** -0.35s/f (Good)
WFA 4 from 5yo 7lb **9** Ran SP% **114.9**
Speed ratings: **93,91,91,90,89 89,88,84,82**
CSF £17.63 TOTE £3.60: £1.70, £1.30, £2.60; EX 15.60 Trifecta £96.20.
Owner Andrew Polson **Bred** Hawks And Doves Racing Syndicate **Trained** Seaborough, Dorset
■ Stewards' Enquiry : David Noonan seven-day ban: use of whip (13, 15, 17, 21 Dec, 1, 8, 13 Jan(

FOCUS
This was run over 21 yards further than advertised. The pace was slow, then steady and they only really raced up the straight for the final time. Just an ordinary-looking bumper. Suspect form, but it's been rated around the second and fifth for the time being.
T/Jkpt: Not won. JACKPOT PLACEPOT £519.20. Pool: £2,347.00 - 3.3 winning units. T/Plt: £525.10 to a £1 stake. Pool: £67,253.54 - 93.48 winning tickets T/Qpdt: £21.20 to a £1 stake. Pool: £9,552.25 - 332.18 winning tickets **Walter Glynn**

2324 MUSSELBURGH (R-H)
Friday, November 27

OFFICIAL GOING: Good (good to soft in places) changing to good to soft after race 2 (1.10)
Wind: Fairly strong, half against Weather: Overcast, raining

2751 ELC - THE SALTIRE CONDITIONAL JOCKEYS' H'CAP HURDLE (14 hdls) 2m 7f 180y
12:35 (12:35) (Class 5) (0-100,100) 4-Y-O+ **£3,249** (£954; £477; £238)

Form RPR
0113 1 **Touch Of Steel (IRE)**32 2102 6-11-1 92..................(b) DaleIrving(3) 102+
(James Ewart) *mde all: clr bef 2 out: sn rdn along: styd on wl fr last* **8/1**
13-0 2 7 **Parc Des Princes (USA)**34 2069 9-11-6 100.................. RyanDay(6) 103
(Nicky Richards) *hld up: pushed along and hdwy 10th: chsd (clr) wnr after last: kpt on: no imp* **9/1**
64F3 3 2 3/4 **Drop A Gear (IRE)**28 2174 5-11-4 100.................. RossChapman(8) 101
(Lucinda Russell) *midfield: effrt bef 3 out: 3rd and rdn whn hit last: kpt on same pce run-in* **4/1**1
1P-2 4 1 **Bracing**32 2103 6-10-6 88.................. BlairCampbell(8) 88
(N W Alexander) *hld up: effrt bef 4 out: shkn up bef next: no imp fr 2 out* **5/1**2
5003 5 2 **Tickanrun (IRE)**17 2422 5-11-3 94.................. DiarmuidO'Regan(3) 92
(Chris Grant) *prom: pushed along after 4 out: kpt on same pce fr next* **16/1**
P254 6 hd **Winter Alchemy (IRE)**34 2071 10-10-6 90.................. JackCollins(10) 88
(Nicky Richards) *prom: rdn and outpcd 4 out: no imp fr next* **11/1**
-53P 7 nk **The Late Shift**36 2029 5-10-9 88.................. LorcanMurtagh(5) 87
(Barry Murtagh) *pressed wnr: pushed along bef 3 out: outpcd whn mstke last: sn wknd* **22/1**
P-66 8 1 **No Such Number**22 2296 7-11-3 91.................. GrantCockburn 88
(Sandy Forster) *hld up in tch: hdwy bef 4 out: effrt next: wknd fr 2 out* **18/1**
PP-0 9 13 **Apache Blue (IRE)**154 842 11-11-0 88..................(b1) ColmMcCormack 73
(Kenneth Slack) *j.lft: cl up to 4 out: sn outpcd: struggling fr next* **16/1**
04P0 10 3 1/2 **Wyfield Rose**26 2212 6-10-2 79..................(p) CiaranGethings(3) 61
(Alistair Whillans) *hld up: rdn along 10th: struggling fr next* **15/2**3
2254 11 1/2 **Solway Bay**22 2297 13-10-13 87..................(t) CraigGallagher 68
(Lisa Harrison) *hld up: outpcd after 9th: sn struggling: n.d after* **16/1**
006P 12 5 **Just My Luke**21 2323 6-9-9 74 oh2..................(t) ThomasDowson(5) 51
(Susan Corbett) *hld up in midfield on outside: struggling fr 10th: btn fnl 3* **80/1**
0545 13 44 **Indepub**36 2029 6-10-8 82.................. StephenMulqueen 19
(Lisa Harrison) *hld up: stdy hdwy 4 out: rdn and wknd next* **17/2**
-000 P **Oxalido (FR)**59 1691 13-10-12 86.................. GrahamWatters
(Hugh Burns) *bhd: struggling 9th: t.o whn p.u bef 3 out* **50/1**
-P05 U **Mister Hendre**43 1923 7-9-12 80..................(t) JamesCorbett(8)
(Susan Corbett) *trckg ldrs whn mstke and uns rdr 8th* **100/1**

6m 9.7s (27.60) **Going Correction** +0.55s/f (Soft) **15** Ran SP% **119.8**
Speed ratings (Par 103): **76,73,72,72,71 71,71,71,66,65 65,63,49, ,**
CSF £76.29 CT £335.92 TOTE £7.70: £3.30, £3.70, £2.00; EX 62.00 Trifecta £118.30.
Owner Mrs Hugh Fraser **Bred** Frances Galloway **Trained** Langholm, Dumfries & G'way

FOCUS
Bottom bend shared and chase out 2yds and hurdles 13yds. Actual race distance 3m 46yds. A big-field handicap hurdle run at a fair gallop in wet and windy conditions. Not many got into it. Another step up from the winner, with the next four close to their marks.

2752 MITSUBISHI ELECTRIC MARES' MAIDEN HURDLE (9 hdls) 1m 7f 124y
1:10 (1:11) (Class 5) 4-Y-O+ **£3,249** (£954; £477; £238)

Form RPR
-436 1 **Cosmic Tigress**34 2066 4-10-12 0.................. DannyCook 97+
(John Quinn) *hld up in tch: hdwy and ev ch whn lft in ld 3 out: hdd next: rallied to ld run-in: drvn and hld on wl* **2/1**2
656 2 hd **Myrtle Drive (IRE)**15 2452 4-10-12 0.................. BrianHarding 96+
(Donald McCain) *hld up in tch: stdy hdwy bef 3 out: led next: pushed along bef last: hdd run-in: kpt on u.p: jst hld* **8/1**3
5-4 3 8 **Near To Tears (IRE)**21 2325 5-10-12 0.................. PeterBuchanan 89
(Lucinda Russell) *in tch: effrt after 4 out: pushed along and outpcd after next: edgd rt and kpt on same pce run-in* **17/2**
210- 4 5 **Verona Opera (IRE)**191 414 4-10-12 0.................. AELynch 87+
(S R B Crawford, Ire) *trckd ldrs: effrt 3 out: ev ch and pushed along whn mstke next: wknd fr last* **11/8**1
4-6 5 8 **Maura Lily (IRE)**16 2433 6-10-9 0.................. GrahamWatters(3) 76
(Ian Duncan) *hld up: pushed along and outpcd after 4 out: n.d after* **100/1**

5-0 6 15 **Miss Mackie (IRE)**197 305 4-10-12 0.................. HenryBrooke 63
(R Mike Smith) *t.k.h early: cl up tl rdn and wknd fr 3 out* **40/1**
0-0 7 49 **Jane's Fantasy (IRE)**197 305 5-10-12 0..................1 LucyAlexander 19
(N W Alexander) *hld up in tch: struggling bef 4 out: lost tch bef next: t.o* **150/1**
8 1 3/4 **Cadmium**114 4-10-7 0.................. MissCWalton(5) 17
(Micky Hammond) *hld up: nt fluent 3rd: outpcd whn tried to refuse next: sn struggling and nt jump wl after: t.o* **16/1**
5 F **Noble Reach**41 1967 4-10-12 0.................. JakeGreenall
(Lawrence Mullaney) *led: jst in front and pushed along whn fell 3 out* **14/1**
P- P **Buckshot Robert (IRE)**32 2113 4-10-9 0.................. CallumWhillans(3)
(Noel C Kelly, Ire) *t.k.h: nt fluent on occasions: hld up: hdwy and prom 3rd: struggling 4 out: lost tch and p.u appr next* **100/1**

3m 57.3s (8.90) **Going Correction** +0.55s/f (Soft) **10** Ran SP% **114.7**
Speed ratings (Par 103): **99,98,94,92,88 80,56,55, ,**
CSF £18.14 TOTE £3.10: £1.20, £2.50, £2.60; EX 16.80 Trifecta £72.10.
Owner The Cosmic Cases **Bred** The Cosmic Cases **Trained** Settrington, N Yorks

FOCUS
Actual race distance 1m 7f 167yds. This modest maiden hurdle was run in difficult, gusty conditions. The winner was pretty much to her mark.

2753 RACINGUK.COM/BLACKFRIDAY SPECIAL PRICE TODAY NOVICES' LIMITED H'CAP CHASE (14 fncs 2 omitted) 2m 3f 193y
1:45 (1:45) (Class 4) (0-120,113) 4-Y-O+
£5,004 (£1,478; £739; £369; £184; £92)

Form RPR
22-2 1 **Rear Admiral (IRE)**17 2424 9-11-6 111..................(t) JakeGreenall 121+
(Michael Easterby) *hld up in tch: stdy hdwy 1/2-way: wnt 2nd and poised to chal 2 out: shkn up to ld run-in: rdn out nr fin* **11/2**
011F 2 2 3/4 **The Backup Plan (IRE)**21 2327 6-11-3 108.................. BrianHarding 113
(Donald McCain) *racd wd: cl up: hit 1st: led 7th: rdn along 2 out: hdd run-in: kpt on same pce* **7/2**2
144 3 7 **Scorpions Sting (IRE)**48 1853 6-10-6 102..................(p) DaleIrving(5) 103
(James Ewart) *cl up: rdn 4 out: rallied and ev ch briefly next: outpcd 2 out: no imp fr last: b.b.v* **5/1**3
-11F 4 1/2 **Chanceofa Lifetime (IRE)**187 457 8-11-1 113.................. SamColtherd(7) 113
(Victor Thompson) *nt fluent: hld up: pushed along 1/2-way: effrt after 4 out: kpt on same pce fr 2 out* **14/1**
0-11 5 shd **Throthethatch (IRE)**20 2339 6-11-7 112.................. PeterBuchanan 112
(Lucinda Russell) *mde most to 7th: cl up: pushed along and outpcd bef 2 out: btn whn hit last* **11/8**1
6-20 6 31 **Celestino (FR)**26 2212 4-10-13 112..................(t) LucyAlexander 81
(N W Alexander) *mstkes: in tch: outpcd 1/2-way: rallied: lost tch fr 3 out: t.o* **16/1**
0P64 F **Parlour Of Dreams (IRE)**14 2475 8-10-2 100.................. MrWHRReed(7)
(Andrew Hamilton) *hld up: fell 1st* **100/1**

5m 6.6s (5.40) **Going Correction** +0.40s/f (Soft)
WFA 4 from 6yo+ 8lb **7** Ran SP% **109.9**
Speed ratings (Par 105): **105,103,101,100,100 88,**
CSF £23.54 TOTE £5.60: £2.40, £2.30; EX 23.40 Trifecta £88.60.
Owner S Hollings, S Hull, A Turton, D Fielding **Bred** J Harding **Trained** Sheriff Hutton, N Yorks

FOCUS
Actual race distance 2m 3f 207 yds. The official going description was changed to Good to soft before this contest, a fair novice handicap. The winner is rated back to his best.

2754 BAM CONSTRUCTION MAIDEN HURDLE (12 hdls) 2m 3f 81y
2:20 (2:20) (Class 5) 4-Y-O+ **£3,249** (£954; £477; £238)

Form RPR
20-1 1 **Chitu (IRE)**28 2181 5-11-0 0.................. AELynch 121+
(S R B Crawford, Ire) *hld up in midfield: stdy hdwy after 4 out: led gng wl bef last: pushed out run-in: comf* **5/2**2
2 4 **Round Tower (IRE)**19 2378 6-10-11 124.................. GrahamWatters(3) 112
(Karl Thornton, Ire) *j.lft: t.k.h early: led and clr to 3rd: rdn and hdd 3 out: rallied and regained ld briefly after next: kpt on same pce fr last* **13/8**1
05-3 3 4 1/2 **Leading Score (IRE)**32 2101 5-10-9 0.................. DaleIrving(5) 109
(James Ewart) *prom: hdwy to ld 3 out to after next: rdn and outpcd whn hit last* **11/2**
0/2- 4 4 **Kings Folly (IRE)**502 923 7-10-9 110..................(t) GrantCockburn(5) 104
(Lucinda Russell) *hld up: stdy hdwy after 4 out: shkn up next: no imp fr 2 out* **16/1**
40 5 1 1/4 **Kilronan Castle**32 2100 4-11-0 0.................. BrianHarding 103
(Donald McCain) *hld up in midfield: stdy hdwy 1/2-way: effrt and cl up bef 3 out: wknd fr next* **40/1**
40-5 6 18 **Rocklim (FR)**32 2101 5-11-0 0.................. LucyAlexander 87
(James Ewart) *nt fluent in rr: pushed along 7th: nvr on terms* **150/1**
0P 7 3/4 **Rioja Day (IRE)**16 2428 5-11-0 0.................. DannyCook 86
(Jim Goldie) *nt fluent in rr: shortlived effrt 4 out: wknd fr next* **100/1**
3 8 1 3/4 **Arcamante (ITY)**11 2543 4-11-0 0.................. HenryBrooke 85
(K R Burke) *cl up: wnt 2nd 1/2-way: to bef 3 out: sn rdn and wknd* **9/2**3
524/ 9 59 **Latin Rebel (IRE)**50 4177 8-10-9 0.................. StephenMulqueen(5) 32
(Jim Goldie) *nt fluent in rr: struggling fnl circ: t.o* **50/1**
2U P **Teviot Prince (IRE)**15 2449 5-10-11 110.................. CallumWhillans(3)
(Martin Bosley) *nt fluent in rr: struggling fnl circ: t.o whn p.u bef 3 out* **40/1**
6 P **Imahustler Baby (IRE)**14 2474 4-10-7 0.................. SamColtherd(7)
(Andrew Hamilton) *chsd ldr to 7th: hit and outpcd 8th: wknd next: lost tch and p.u bef 3 out* **100/1**

4m 57.6s (6.10) **Going Correction** +0.55s/f (Soft) **11** Ran SP% **115.6**
Speed ratings (Par 103): **109,107,105,103,103 95,95,94,69, ,**
CSF £6.98 TOTE £3.50: £1.60, £1.10, £1.60; EX 9.60 Trifecta £30.50.
Owner Graham Slesser **Bred** Michael Coburn **Trained** Larne, Co Antrim

FOCUS
Actual race distance 2m 3f 166yds. This ordinary maiden hurdle saw a 1-2 for Irish stables, both of which had winners on this card last year. The third to fifth are perhaps the best guide.

2755 SEMICHEM H'CAP CHASE (10 fncs 2 omitted) 1m 7f 182y
2:55 (2:55) (Class 4) (0-115,115) 4-Y-O+ **£6,498** (£1,908; £954; £477)

Form RPR
40/2 1 **Blades Lad**15 1888 6-11-5 108..................(p) DannyCook 116+
(Peter Niven) *cl up: led 3 out: rdn next: hung lft run-in: kpt on wl* **9/4**1
1251 2 nk **Carters Rest**22 2290 12-10-5 101.................. MissJWalton(7) 108
(George Bewley) *t.k.h: trckd ldrs: outpcd 3 out: rallied to chse wnr run-in: kpt on fin* **14/1**
/3-3 3 4 1/2 **Castlelawn (IRE)**32 2104 8-11-6 109.................. PeterBuchanan 113
(Lucinda Russell) *led tl 3 out: rdn and one pce fr last* **4/1**2

6313 **4** 3 **Endeavor**[22] 2292 10-10-10 **102** ColmMcCormack(3) 101
(Dianne Sayer) *hld up: hit 4th: effrt bef 3 out: no imp fr next* **9/1**

5244 **5** ¾ **Sendiym (FR)**[29] 2148 8-9-11 **89** oh2 HarryChalloner(3) 89
(Dianne Sayer) *hld up: j. awkwardly and rdr lost iron briefly 2nd: nt fluent and outpcd 4th: kpt on fr 2 out: nvr able to chal* **8/1**

6364 **6** 2¼ **Muwalla**[21] 2329 8-11-1 **109** (t) DiarmuidO'Regan(5) 106
(Lisa Harrison) *hld up: mstke and rdn 4 out: no imp fr next* **6/1**[3]

U-6P **7** 1¼ **Formidableopponent (IRE)**[27] 2193 8-11-7 **115** DaraghBourke(5) 110
(William Young Jnr) *hld up: hdwy and prom 4 out: rdn and wknd after next* **100/1**

0-54 **8** 1¼ **Morning Time (IRE)**[185] 485 9-9-10 **90** (tp) GrantCockburn(5) 85
(Lucinda Russell) *hld up in midfield: mstke 4th: effrt 5 out: wknd fr 3 out* **10/1**

00F- **9** 4½ **Why But Why (USA)**[290] 4139 7-11-7 **113** GrahamWatters(3) 103
(Ian Duncan) *hld up: hdwy and prom 4th: rdn and effrt 3 out: wknd fr next* **28/1**

0445 **P** **Claragh Native (IRE)**[44] 1904 10-11-7 **110** (p) BrianHarding
(Martin Todhunter) *prom: mstke and lost pl 5th: struggling fr next: t.o whn p.u bef 3 out: b.b.v* **12/1**

F530 **R** **Gin Cobbler**[22] 2292 9-10-5 **101** SamColtherd(7)
(Victor Thompson) *t.k.h: hld up: rn out 1st* **50/1**

0306 **P** **Calton Entry (IRE)**[22] 2293 6-11-2 **105** HenryBrooke
(Linda Perratt) *hld up in tch: outpcd 1/2-way: lost tch and p.u bef 3 out* **40/1**

4m 1.6s (9.20) **Going Correction** +0.40s/f (Soft) **12 Ran SP% 118.5**
Speed ratings (Par 105): **93,92,90,89,88 87,86,86,84,**
CSF £32.52 CT £123.36 TOTE £2.80: £1.40, £3.80, £1.70; EX 31.00 Trifecta £121.80.
Owner Crown Select **Bred** David Holgate **Trained** Barton-le-Street, N Yorks

FOCUS
Actual race distance 1m 7f 189yds. Not many got into this ordinary handicap chase, with the first three always prominent. The form looks sound enough.

2756 BELMONT WALLYFORD MAIDEN OPEN NATIONAL HUNT FLAT RACE 1m 7f 124y
3:25 (3:26) (Class 6) 4-6-Y-O **£1,949** (£572; £286; £143)

Form RPR

42 **1** **Kalaniti (IRE)**[33] 2086 4-10-4 0 DiarmuidO'Regan(5) 98+
(Chris Grant) *hld up: gd hdwy 2f out: led and hung rt ins fnl f: kpt on wl towards fin* **9/4**[1]

2 **2** ½ **Black Ink**[20] 2344 4-11-2 0 HenryBrooke 104
(Michael Smith) *led: rdn over 2f out: hdd and carried rt ins fnl f: kpt on: hld cl home* **12/1**

3 2¼ **Paper Roses (IRE)** 4-10-6 0 CallumWhillans(3) 95
(Donald Whillans) *hld up in midfield on outside: hdwy over 5f out: effrt and hung rt 2f out: kpt on ins fnl f* **50/1**

4 1¼ **Grays Choice (IRE)** 4-10-11 0 JonathonBewley(5) 101
(George Bewley) *pressed ldr: rdn and outpcd over 2f out: rallied fnl f: no imp* **18/1**

5 shd **Sammy B** 5-11-2 0 PeterBuchanan 100
(Lucinda Russell) *t.k.h: hld up in tch: pushed along and hdwy 2f out: no imp fnl f* **16/1**

6 1¼ **Outlaw Josey Wales (IRE)** 4-11-2 0 BrianHarding 99
(R Mike Smith) *hld up: hdwy and prom 2f out: no ex ins fnl f* **40/1**

7 ¾ **Mutdula (IRE)** 5-11-2 0 DannyCook 98
(Alan Swinbank) *trckd ldrs: effrt and rdn over 2f out: no ex over 1f out* **11/4**[2]

U **8** 2¾ **Dubai Shen (IRE)**[199] 257 4-10-11 0 GrantCockburn(5) 96
(Alistair Whillans) *hld up: outpcd 5f out: rallied over 2f out: nvr able to chal* **10/1**

9 1 **Brian Boranha (IRE)** 4-11-2 0 JakeGreenall 95
(Peter Niven) *t.k.h: prom: rdn over 2f out: sn outpcd: n.d after* **5/1**[3]

10 ½ **Sweet Holly** 4-10-2 0 MrWHRReed(7) 87
(Lucinda Russell) *in tch: rdn over 4f out: wknd over 2f out* **20/1**

11 nk **Canny Tom (IRE)**[99] 1304 5-11-2 0 AELynch 94
(S Donohoe, Ire) *hld up in midfield: drvn and outpcd over 2f out: sn wknd* **10/1**

0 **12** 17 **Mr Gillespie**[187] 459 5-10-9 0 MissAWaugh(7) 77
(Simon Waugh) *hld up towards rr: hdwy on outside over 4f out: hung rt and wknd over 2f out* **100/1**

3m 57.6s (14.80) **Going Correction** +0.55s/f (Soft) **12 Ran SP% 121.3**
Speed ratings: **85,84,83,83,82 82,81,80,80,79 79,71**
CSF £31.14 TOTE £2.90: £1.20, £3.80, £8.10; EX 23.10 Trifecta £1039.30.
Owner Mrs S Sunter **Bred** Simon Walford **Trained** Newton Bewley, Co Durham

FOCUS
Actual race distance 1m 7f 167yds. The pace in this ordinary bumper was fairly steady and it became a bit of a sprint in the straight, so the form is suppect. The result stood following an enquiry into interference between the first two.
T/Plt: £48.30 to a £1 stake. Pool: £48,755.19 - 736.70 winning tickets T/Qpdt: £8.50 to a £1 stake. Pool: £5,653.86 - 487.73 winning tickets **Richard Young**

2723 NEWBURY (L-H)
Friday, November 27

OFFICIAL GOING: Soft (heavy in places on hurdle course; hdl 3.5, chs 4.4)
Wind: medium to strong, against Weather: overcast, breezy

2757 Q ASSOCIATES JUVENILE HURDLE (8 hdls) 2m 69y
12:25 (12:25) (Class 3) 3-Y-O **£6,498** (£1,908; £954; £477)

Form RPR

1 **Kasakh Noir (FR)**[60] 3-10-12 0 HarrySkelton 123+
(Dan Skelton) *hld up in rr: hdwy on long run after 5th: chsd clr wnr next: clsd and led on bit after 2 out: cruised clr: eased towards fin: v easily: impressive* **4/1**[2]

4 **2** 16 **The Coffee Hunter (FR)**[33] 2092 3-10-12 0 (t) RichardJohnson 100
(Nick Williams) *hld up in last pair: hdwy on long run after 5th: wnt 3rd and j. awkwardly 2 out: sn chsng cantering wnr and u.p: btn last: battled on to hold 2nd flat* **9/1**

3 1¼ **Major Mac**[64] 3-10-12 0 TomScudamore 100
(Hughie Morrison) *t.k.h: led and wnt clr after 1st: j.lft and mstke 5th: 6 l clr next: mstke 2 out: sn hdd and outpcd u.p: no ch w wnr but battling for 2nd flat: plugged on* **7/1**

4 9 **Fitzwilliam**[13] 3-10-12 0 ConorO'Farrell 93
(Mick Channon) *chsd ldrs: nt fluent and lost pl 4th: in rr of main gp but stl in tch on long run after 5th: outpcd and btn next: plugged on to pass btn horse between last 2: wnt modest 4th flat* **40/1**

5 8 **Ardamir (FR)**[203] 3-11-8 0 DenisO'Regan 94
(Alan King) *hld up in tch: mstke 4th: 5th on long run bef 3 out: cl enough in 4th 2 out: sn rdn and btn: wknd last* **7/1**

6 10 **Extreme Appeal (IRE)**[202] 3-10-12 0 (p) GavinSheehan 72
(Warren Greatrex) *chsd ldr: rdn bef 3 out: lost 2nd 3 out: sn btn and bhd next: wknd: t.o flat* **10/1**

61 **P** **Darebin (GER)**[19] 2371 3-11-4 0 JamieMoore
(Gary Moore) *in tch in midfield: hdwy to chse ldrs 4th: lost pl rapidly jst bef 3 out: t.o whn p.u 2 out* **9/2**[3]

P **Kingston Mimosa**[78] 3-10-12 0 BrendanPowell
(Mark Gillard) *midfield: j. slowly and dropped to rr 2nd: j. slowly and lost tch next: t.o 5th: p.u next* **200/1**

F **Copain De Classe (FR)**[206] 3-10-12 0 SamTwiston-Davies 72
(Paul Nicholls) *in tch in midfield: clsd to chse ldrs 4th: rdn after 3 out: sn btn: 6th and wkng whn fell last* **9/4**[1]

4m 19.3s (9.30) **Going Correction** +0.425s/f (Soft) **9 Ran SP% 116.0**
Speed ratings (Par 106): **93,85,84,79,75 70, , ,**
CSF £39.50 TOTE £4.90: £1.10, £3.50, £2.60; EX 45.50 Trifecta £258.10.
Owner T P Radford **Bred** P Jabot, G Harari & H De Watrigant **Trained** Alcester, Warwicks

FOCUS
The going was officially soft, heavy in places on the hurdle course (GoingStick: hurdle 3.5, chase 4.4). Rail still out but moved in from Thursday. Opening race distance increased by 110yds. Richard Johnson said of the ground: "It's hard work, but I wouldn't call it heavy." This juvenile hurdle has been won by some smart sorts in recent years, Turko, Smad Place and Old Guard to name but a few, but this year's winner was as impressive as any of them. However the time was slow and it's not form to be confident about.

2758 BET365 CONDITIONAL JOCKEYS' H'CAP CHASE (15 fncs) 2m 2f 64y
12:55 (12:56) (Class 3) (0-130,128) 4-Y-O+ **£6,498** (£1,908; £954; £477)

Form RPR

0-26 **1** **Rouge Et Blanc (FR)**[186] 470 10-11-4 **122** (p) ThomasGarner(3) 136+
(Oliver Sherwood) *midfield: wnt 3rd 8th: clsd and wnt 2nd 11th: led on bit next: shkn up and wnt jst over 1 l clr sn after last: drvn fnl 150yds: hld on: rdn out* **10/1**

20 **2** ¾ **Mon Successeur (FR)**[14] 2472 4-10-12 **128** HarryCobden(8) 132
(Paul Nicholls) *hld up in midfield: clsd and trcking ldrs bef 12th: jnd wnr 3 out: shkn up bef last: sltly outpcd sn after last: rallied u.p to press wnr fnl 150yds: hld towards fin* **11/4**[1]

F5-2 **3** 17 **Colin's Brother**[29] 2151 5-11-0 **118** RyanHatch(3) 114
(Nigel Twiston-Davies) *last trio: mstke and struggling 7th: prog into 6th after 11th: no imp 12th: no ch w ldng pair but kpt on u.p to go 3rd flat* **5/1**[3]

P64- **4** 1¾ **Drumshambo (USA)**[239] 5107 9-11-6 **124** CharlieDeutsch(3) 118
(Venetia Williams) *led tl 1st: chsd ldr tl 4th: styd chsng ldrs: mstke 8th: reminder after 10th: rdn bef 12th: wknd between last 2* **10/3**[2]

1-33 **5** nk **Bincombe**[20] 2335 7-11-4 **127** (bt) ConorSmith(8) 120
(Philip Hobbs) *chsd ldrs: wnt 2nd 4th tl 12th: drvn and no ex 3 out: wknd between last 2* **13/2**

5-31 **6** 3 **Vision Des Champs (FR)**[26] 2220 6-10-3 **112** (t) GeorgeGorman(8) 102
(Gary Moore) *t.k.h: j. into ld 1st: sn clr: hdd 3 out: sn u.p and btn 3rd next: wknd last* **7/1**

-2PP **P** **Cody Wyoming**[13] 2497 9-11-0 **123** TommyDowling(8)
(Charlie Mann) *a bhd: losing tch and mstke 6th: t.o 8th tl p.u last* **25/1**

55-4 **P** **Major Milborne**[28] 2168 7-10-13 **114** (b[1]) ConorShoemark
(Jamie Snowden) *midfield: nt fluent 3rd: 6th and nt on terms w ldrs whn mstke 9th: lost tch after next: wl bhd whn p.u 12th* **12/1**

4m 50.65s (20.65) **Going Correction** +0.425s/f (Soft)
WFA 4 from 5yo+ 7lb **8 Ran SP% 112.9**
Speed ratings (Par 107): **71,70,63,62,62 60, ,**
CSF £38.06 CT £155.40 TOTE £12.50: £2.90, £1.30, £1.80; EX 46.70 Trifecta £192.80.
Owner O Sherwood & Tim Syder **Bred** Sean Mulryan **Trained** Upper Lambourn, Berks
■ Stewards' Enquiry : George Gorman two-day ban: use of whip (11-23 Dec)

FOCUS
Race distance increased by 60yds. A decent conditional jockey's handicap chase and there was no hanging about. The front pair had the race between themselves over the last two fences. A pb from the winner in first-time headgear, while the second has been rated to form.

2759 PERTEMPS NETWORK H'CAP HURDLE (SERIES QUALIFIER) (12 hdls) 3m 52y
1:30 (1:31) (Class 3) (0-145,142) 4-Y-O+
£9,384 (£2,772; £1,386; £693; £346; £174)

Form RPR

113- **1** **Missed Approach (IRE)**[356] 2950 5-10-7 **123** GavinSheehan 140+
(Warren Greatrex) *chsd ldrs tl led after 5th: mde rest: rdn and asserted jst bef last: styd on strly to draw clr flat: readily* **5/2**[1]

43/1 **2** 12 **Billy No Name (IRE)**[27] 2202 7-10-4 **120** PaddyBrennan 125
(Colin Tizzard) *chsd ldrs: wnt 2nd jst bef 3 out: rdn between last 2 out: no ex last: outpcd by wnr but kpt on to hold 2nd flat* **10/1**[3]

-211 **3** 3½ **Sykes (IRE)**[23] 2268 6-10-9 **125** RichardJohnson 129
(Philip Hobbs) *hld up in last trio: clsd on long run after 9th: effrt to chse ldrs 2 out: drvn and unable qck whn hit last: styd on same pce flat* **10/3**[2]

10-6 **4** 2¼ **Forthefunofit (IRE)**[17] 2411 6-11-2 **132** BarryGeraghty 131
(Jonjo O'Neill) *hld up towards rr: stdy prog 7th: clr in ldng quintet 2 out: sn rdn and outpcd last: no ch w wnr and kpt on same pce flat* **14/1**

2212 **5** 8 **Oh Land Abloom (IRE)**[41] 1968 5-11-2 **132** (t) TrevorWhelan 125
(Neil King) *hld up in midfield: hdwy bef 3 out: chsd ldrs and clr in ldng quintet next: swtchd rt and unable qck between last 2: 5th and hld whn hit last: wknd flat* **33/1**

120- **6** 4 **Unique De Cotte (FR)**[232] 5241 7-11-8 **141** (t) KieronEdgar(3) 129
(David Pipe) *hld up towards rr: rdn after 3 out: sn outpcd and btn next: wnt modest 6th last: plugged on* **10/1**[3]

-050 **7** 3 **Gevrey Chambertin (FR)**[13] 2484 7-11-11 **141** (p) ConorO'Farrell 126
(David Pipe) *in tch towards rr: effrt u.p after 3 out: sn btn and no ch next* **11/1**

1F-F **8** 1¼ **Saint John Henry (FR)**[35] 2054 5-10-8 **124** [1] TomScudamore 108
(David Pipe) *in tch in midfield: mstke 6th: u.p on long run bef 3 out: lost pl and wl btn bef 2 out* **16/1**

P-P6 **9** 3½ **Easter Day (FR)**[13] 2484 7-11-7 **137** (p) SamTwiston-Davies 117
(Paul Nicholls) *chsd ldrs: rdn after 3 out: no rspnse and btn in 6th next: wknd* **10/1**[3]

16-1 **10** 36 **Molly's A Diva**[19] 2367 8-11-11 **141** (p) RichieMcLernon 85
(Kim Bailey) *chsd ldr tl 5th: styd prom: wnt 2nd again 8th tl lost 2nd and struggling u.p 3 out: sn btn: wknd qckly bef 2 out: t.o* **20/1**

P-21 **11** *13* **Open Hearted**[42] [1944] 8-11-12 **142**..............................(t) HarrySkelton 73
(Dan Skelton) *hld up towards rr: hdwy into midfield after 5th: lost pl on long run after 9th: bhd next: t.o 2 out* **14/1**

14-1 **P** **Grape Tree Flame**[191] [404] 7-11-5 **135**..............................(p) SeanBowen
(Peter Bowen) *led tl after 5th: chsd ldr tl rdn and lost pl 8th: dropped to rr next: losing tch and p.u wl bef 3 out: burst blood vessel* **33/1**

6m 26.0s (386.00) **12** Ran SP% **117.1**
CSF £27.12 CT £83.80 TOTE £3.50: £1.40, £3.20, £1.60; EX 33.70 Trifecta £121.70.

Owner Alan & Andrew Turner **Bred** John Ryan **Trained** Upper Lambourn, Berks

FOCUS
Race distance increased by 196yds. A decent staying handicap hurdle, but only a two-horse race according to the market. The early pace was steady and not that many got into it from behind. The third and fourth have been rated close to their marks.

2760 FULLER'S LONDON PRIDE NOVICES' CHASE (REGISTERED AS THE BERKSHIRE NOVICES' CHASE) (GRADE 2) (16 fncs) 2m 3f 187y
2:05 (2:06) (Class 1) 4-Y-0+ **£20,026** (£7,573; £3,838; £1,959; £1,031)

Form RPR

13-3 **1** **Three Musketeers (IRE)**[26] [2222] 5-11-1 0.............................. HarrySkelton 156+
(Dan Skelton) *hld up in tch: lft cl up and hmpd 11th: led and travelling strly 13th: shkn up and in command between last 2: r.o strly: rdn out* **7/2**[3]

35-0 **2** *4½* **Activial (FR)**[173] [663] 5-11-1 0.............................. NoelFehily 150+
(Harry Fry) *chsd ldrs: j.big and collided w rival 2nd: lft in ld 11th: blnd and hdd next: chsd ldr 13th: j.big and rdn 2 out: no imp: kpt on* **11/8**[1]

0-03 **3** *7* **L'Unique (FR)**[20] [2347] 6-10-8 137.............................. WayneHutchinson 135
(Alan King) *chsd ldrs: j. slowly 12th: rdn and outpcd after next: btn 4th 2 out: wnt 3rd last: no imp* **20/1**

012/ **4** *6* **Ubak (FR)**[945] [5562] 7-11-1 0.............................. JoshuaMoore 137+
(Gary Moore) *t.k.h: hld up in tch: clsd to chse ldrs 10th: j. into ld 12th: hdd and mstke next: lost 2nd and mstke 3 out: 4th and wl hld whn mstke last* **33/1**

-313 **5** *27* **Dell' Arca (IRE)**[14] [2469] 6-11-8 142..............................(b) TomScudamore 127
(David Pipe) *hld up in tch: nt fluent 5th: lft cl up and hmpd 11th: struggling and rdn 3 out: sn wknd: virtually p.u towards fin* **11/1**

50/1 **U** **Sametegal (FR)**[26] [2222] 6-11-8 145.............................. SamTwiston-Davies
(Paul Nicholls) *chsd ldr: lft in ld whn bdly hmpd and uns rdr 11th* **10/1**

11-2 **F** **Maximiser (IRE)**[18] [2397] 7-11-1 0..............................(t) JoeColliver
(Simon West) *led: stood off too far and mstke 8th: crumpled on landing and fell 11th* **3/1**[2]

5m 9.6s (6.60) **Going Correction** +0.425s/f (Soft) **7** Ran SP% **114.5**
Speed ratings (Par 115): **103,101,98,96,85** ,
CSF £9.24 TOTE £4.60: £2.30, £1.50; EX 10.00 Trifecta £90.80.

Owner Mrs G Widdowson & Mrs R Kelvin-Hughes **Bred** W B Mactaggart **Trained** Alcester, Warwicks

FOCUS
Race distance increased by 74yds. Three of the previous nine runnings of this had gone to subsequent Gold Cup winners in Denman, Bobs Worth and Coneygree last year. This year's winner looks a smart prospect in his own right, though the shape of the race changed quite a bit jumping the final fence in the back straight. A big step up from the winner on his recent chase debut, with the second and third rated close to the level of last season's hurdle form.

2761 BET365 OPEN H'CAP CHASE (16 fncs) 2m 3f 187y
2:40 (2:41) (Class 2) 4-Y-0+
£31,280 (£9,240; £4,620; £2,310; £1,155; £580)

Form RPR

61-4 **1** **Little Jon**[41] [1976] 7-10-5 **137**.............................. JamieBargary(5) 147+
(Nigel Twiston-Davies) *chsd ldr tl led 9th: mde rest: rdn 2 out: kpt on u.p and out battled runner-up flat: styd on: rdn out* **6/1**[3]

3-2U **2** *2* **Upepito (FR)**[20] [2335] 7-10-1 **128**..............................(t) HarrySkelton 135+
(Dan Skelton) *hld up in tch towards rr: stdy hdwy fr 6th: trckd ldrs after 12th: jnd ldr 2 out: hld onto tl asked for effrt after last: fnd nil whn drvn: btn 150yds out* **5/1**[1]

51-P **3** *3¾* **Top Gamble (IRE)**[47] [1869] 7-11-12 **153**.............................. JamieMoore 157
(Kerry Lee) *chsd ldrs: wnt 2nd 13th: 3rd and unable qck u.p 2 out: styd on same pce after* **14/1**

0010 **4** *17* **Lost Legend (IRE)**[27] [2187] 8-11-4 **145**..............................(v) BarryGeraghty 133
(Jonjo O'Neill) *in tch in midfield: hdwy to chse ldrs after 6th: wnt 2nd 11th: 4th and struggling u.p 3 out: btn next: wknd last* **14/1**

2P-6 **5** *6* **Royal Regatta (IRE)**[27] [2185] 7-11-6 **147**..............................(p) RichardJohnson 127
(Philip Hobbs) *hld up in tch towards rr: effrt after 12th: 6th and no imp whn j.rt 3 out: wl btn next: plugged on* **8/1**

U-00 **6** *5* **Monetaire (FR)**[13] [2483] 9-10-13 **140**.............................. TomScudamore 119
(David Pipe) *dropped to rr after mstke 1st: rdn after 12th: no rspnse and wl btn after next: no ch whn swtchd rt and kpt on to pass btn horses flat* **11/2**[2]

F-32 **7** *7* **Kings Lad (IRE)**[7] [2625] 8-11-4 **145**.............................. BrendanPowell 115
(Colin Tizzard) *in tch in midfield: dropped towards rr after 6th: effrt 13th: sn btn and wknd 3 out: t.o* **12/1**

P-00 **8** *3¾* **Next Sensation (IRE)**[13] [2483] 8-11-8 **149**..............................(t) LiamTreadwell 113
(Michael Scudamore) *led tl 9th: steadily lost pl: bhd 13th: lost tch next: t.o* **33/1**

223- **9** *3½* **Upsilon Bleu (FR)**[223] [5393] 7-11-6 **147**.............................. NoelFehily 110
(Pauline Robson) *chsd ldrs: 5th and struggling 12th: wl btn next: sn wknd: t.o* **12/1**

110- **P** **Niceonefrankie**[314] [3727] 9-11-4 **145**.............................. AidanColeman
(Venetia Williams) *chsd ldrs: losing pl whn bdly hmpd and dropped to rr 10th: losing tch whn p.u 12th* **8/1**

4-01 **P** **Roc D'Apsis (FR)**[29] [2153] 6-10-5 **132**.............................. PaddyBrennan
(Tom George) *in tch in midfield: mstke 12th: struggling next: sn btn: bhd whn p.u 2 out* **14/1**

2-51 **F** **Howlongisafoot (IRE)**[15] [2459] 6-11-0 **141**..............................(b) SamTwiston-Davies
(Paul Nicholls) *in tch in midfield tl fell 10th* **15/2**

5m 10.5s (7.50) **Going Correction** +0.425s/f (Soft) **12** Ran SP% **118.6**
Speed ratings (Par 109): **102,101,99,92,90 88,85,84,82,**
CSF £37.07 CT £408.91 TOTE £7.50: £2.30, £2.20, £4.40; EX 42.30 Trifecta £703.50.

Owner R Frosell & Mrs L Taylor **Bred** Michael Griese And Mrs Mary Griese **Trained** Naunton, Gloucs

FOCUS
Race distance increased by 74yds. A decent handicap chase and a valuable prize. The winning time was just under a second slower than the preceding Grade 2. The second and third have been rated pretty much to their marks.

2762 INKERMAN LONDON NOVICES' HURDLE (10 hdls) 2m 4f 118y
3:15 (3:15) (Class 3) 4-Y-0+ **£6,498** (£1,908; £954; £477)

Form RPR

12 **1** **Champers On Ice (IRE)**[14] [2470] 5-10-12 0.............................. TomScudamore 137+
(David Pipe) *mde all: nt a fluent: mstke 3 out: rdn and dived last: styd on: rdn out* **2/1**[1]

2 *¾* **Minella Awards (IRE)**[292] 4-10-12 0.............................. NoelFehily 135
(Nicky Henderson) *hld up in tch: hdwy to chse ldrs after 3 out: wnt 2nd and swtchd rt to press ldr sn after last: styd on but a hld after* **8/1**

11-2 **3** *2½* **Board Of Trade**[37] [2011] 4-10-12 0.............................. WayneHutchinson 132
(Alan King) *chsd ldrs: wnt 2nd 3 out: rdn between last 2: dropped to 3rd sn after last: r.o same pce after* **8/1**

32-1 **4** *15* **Royal Vacation (IRE)**[28] [2169] 5-11-3 130.............................. PaddyBrennan 123
(Colin Tizzard) *chsd ldrs: 4th and rdn 3 out: struggling next: wknd bef last* **7/1**

2- **5** *2½* **Ten Sixty (IRE)**[229] [5292] 5-10-12 0.............................. RichardJohnson 117
(Philip Hobbs) *hld up in tch in rr: effrt bef 3 out: 5th and no imp 2 out: wl hld whn blnd last* **13/2**[3]

11- **6** *15* **Ballyhenry (IRE)**[271] [4513] 5-10-12 0.............................. JamesDavies 101
(Ben Pauling) *chsd ldr tl 3 out: sn rdn and lost pl: wknd next* **3/1**[2]

5 **7** *½* **Chartbreaker (FR)**[27] [2183] 4-10-12 0.............................. SamTwiston-Davies 100
(Paul Nicholls) *hld up in tch: effrt 3 out: sn btn and wknd next* **16/1**

05-5 **8** *27* **Arthur's Gift (IRE)**[58] [1698] 4-10-9 0.............................. RyanHatch(3) 72
(Nigel Twiston-Davies) *dropped to rr after 2nd: rdn along on long run bef 3 out: wknd wl bef 2 out: t.o* **66/1**

0 **9** *6* **Ceann Sibheal (IRE)**[22] [2299] 6-10-12 0.............................. GavinSheehan 66
(Warren Greatrex) *in tch in rr: rdn on long run bef 3 out: wknd wl bef 2 out: t.o* **100/1**

10 *17* **Bigbadjohn (IRE)**[179] [585] 6-10-12 0.............................. PaulTownend 49
(Rebecca Curtis) *t.k.h: hld up in tch: lost pl and bhd 3 out: sn lost tch: t.o* **22/1**

5m 19.7s (0.70) **Going Correction** +0.425s/f (Soft)
WFA 4 from 5yo+ 8lb **10** Ran SP% **119.1**
Speed ratings (Par 107): **115,114,113,108,107 101,101,90,88,82**
CSF £19.46 TOTE £2.80: £1.30, £2.80, £2.60; EX 20.60 Trifecta £105.30.

Owner Professor Caroline Tisdall & Bryan Drew **Bred** Mrs Gail C List **Trained** Nicholashayne, Devon

FOCUS
Race distance increased by 142yds. An interesting novice hurdle with some promising sorts lining up, but not many got into it. A small step up from the winner, with a biggish step up from the third.

2763 BET365 "NATIONAL HUNT" MAIDEN HURDLE (8 hdls) 2m 69y
3:45 (3:46) (Class 3) 4-Y-0+ **£6,498** (£1,908; £954; £477)

Form RPR

24- **1** **Buveur D'Air (FR)**[231] [5255] 4-11-0 0.............................. NoelFehily 152+
(Nicky Henderson) *hld up in tch: chsd ldrs and clsd bef 3 out: wnt 2nd 2 out: j. into ld last: pushed along and readily qcknd clr: impressive* **3/1**[2]

13- **2** *11* **Wait For Me (FR)**[261] [4708] 5-11-0 0.............................. RichardJohnson 139+
(Philip Hobbs) *mstkes: led: rdn after 2 out: hdd last: sn brushed aside by wnr: kpt on for clr 2nd* **10/11**[1]

20-2 **3** *6* **Big Chief Benny (IRE)**[20] [2351] 4-11-0 0.............................. WayneHutchinson 132+
(Alan King) *in tch in midfield: hdwy to chse ldrs 3 out: 4th and cl enough whn blnd 2 out: wnt 3rd bef last: kpt on same pce after* **20/1**

1 **4** *19* **Bun Doran (IRE)**[23] [2270] 4-11-0 0.............................. PaddyBrennan 111
(Tom George) *chsd ldrs: wnt 2nd on long run after 5th: pushed along and btn after 2 out: wknd flat* **6/1**[3]

1-35 **5** *4½* **After Hours (IRE)**[23] [2265] 6-11-0 0.............................. JamesDavies 106
(Henry Oliver) *in tch in midfield: rdn after 3 out: sn outpcd and wl btn next: plugged on to go poor 5th last: t.o* **33/1**

20 **6** *3½* **Don'tdropmein (IRE)**[23] [2265] 5-11-0 0.............................. MarkQuinlan 104
(Neil Mulholland) *hld up in last pair: sme hdwy 3 out: 5th and no imp whn mstke next: sn wknd: t.o* **100/1**

-436 **7** *2¾* **Pilgrims Bay (IRE)**[23] [2265] 5-11-0 0.............................. TomScudamore 100
(David Pipe) *hld up in tch towards rr: rdn after 3 out: sn btn and wknd bef next: t.o* **100/1**

8 *2½* **Behind Time (IRE)** 4-11-0 0.............................. BarryGeraghty 97
(Harry Fry) *dropped to rr after slow jump 2nd: lost tch bef 3 out: no ch but plugged on to pass btn horses flat: t.o* **25/1**

14- **9** *5* **West Approach**[286] [4221] 5-11-0 0.............................. AidanColeman 94
(Colin Tizzard) *chsd ldrs tl 3 out: sn btn and wknd bef next: t.o* **8/1**

6-F **10** *1* **Kid Kalanisi (IRE)**[48] [1844] 4-11-0 0.............................. HarrySkelton 91
(Dan Skelton) *hld up in rr: sme hdwy 5th: btn next and sn wknd: t.o* **66/1**

11 *18* **Some Finish (IRE)**[327] 6-11-0 0.............................. CharliePoste 73
(Robin Dickin) *chsd ldr tl wl bef 3 out: steadily lost pl: bhd 2 out: t.o* **100/1**

0-56 **12** *36* **Royal Salute**[9] [2563] 5-11-0 0.............................. RyanMahon 37
(Anthony Honeyball) *in tch tl dropped to rr wl bef 3 out: sn lost tch: t.o* **100/1**

4m 12.8s (2.80) **Going Correction** +0.425s/f (Soft) **12** Ran SP% **119.8**
Speed ratings (Par 107): **110,104,101,92,89 88,86,85,82,82 73,55**
CSF £6.13 TOTE £4.20: £1.40, £1.10, £3.30; EX 7.40 Trifecta £82.80.

Owner Potensis Bloodstock Ltd & Chris Giles **Bred** Gerard Ferte **Trained** Upper Lambourn, Berks

FOCUS
Race distance increased by 110yds. A fascinating maiden hurdle which has been won by some smart sorts over the years, including Sizing Europe in 2006, and this year's winner looks a very nice prospect. Another race that not many got into and they finished very well spread out. A big step up on his bumper form from the third.

T/Plt: £71.90 to a £1 stake. Pool: £89,693.91 - 909.71 winning tickets T/Qpdt: £10.10 to a £1 stake. Pool: £9,544.12 - 695.43 winning tickets **Steve Payne**

2434 **BANGOR-ON-DEE** (L-H)
Saturday, November 28

OFFICIAL GOING: Heavy (4.8)
Wind: Moderate, half against Weather: Heavy Rain

2764 GINGER MCCAIN MEMORIAL NOVICES' CHASE (18 fncs) 3m 30y
12:35 (12:37) (Class 3) 4-Y-0+ **£6,498** (£1,908; £954; £477)

Form RPR
212- **1** **Blameitalonmyroots (IRE)**^{250} 4965 5-10-6 122 ThomasGarner(3) 125+
(Oliver Sherwood) *w ldr: led 5th: mde rest: rdn whn pressed after last: kpt on and a doing enough towards fin* **13/8**^{1}

1F2- **2** *1* **Teddy Tee (IRE)**^{267} 4601 6-10-9 123 RyanDay(7) 130+
(Nicky Richards) *hld up trcking ldrs: effrt 2 out: wnt 2nd appr last: tried to chal whn wanted to lug lft run-in: hld towards fin* **11/2**

213- **3** *15* **Subtle Grey (IRE)**^{266} 4616 6-11-2 0 WillKennedy 118+
(Donald McCain) *led: hdd 5th: remained w wnr: rdn after 2 out and lost 2nd: btn bef last* **7/4**^{2}

2146 **4** *19* **Henri Parry Morgan**^{21} 2333 7-11-2 0 (p) JoshuaMoore 108
(Peter Bowen) *hld up trcking ldrs: last 4 out: j. slowly 3 out: rdn and outpcd after: wnt lft 2 out: wl bhd whn j.lft again last* **9/2**^{3}

7m 9.8s (50.00) **Going Correction** +2.025s/f (Heav) **4 Ran SP% 108.0**
Speed ratings (Par 107): **97,96,91,85**
CSF £9.45 TOTE £2.50; EX 7.30 Trifecta £21.80.
Owner Tim Syder **Bred** Thomas Stacey **Trained** Upper Lambourn, Berks

FOCUS
Clerk of the course Andrew Morris reported before racing that the track had taken a sustained period of rain well and that they were racing on relatively fresh ground for the time of year. However, this opener was run in a rainstorm and jockeys riding in it firmly agreed that the ground was heavy - comments on the nature of the going ranged from 'sloppy' to 'very hard work'. The form is rated ariund the winner and second's hurdles marks.

2765 BETTER ODDS WITH BETFAIR H'CAP CHASE (12 fncs) 2m 1f 77y
1:05 (1:07) (Class 4) (0-120,120) 4-Y-0+ **£4,548** (£1,335; £667; £333)

Form RPR
323 **1** **All Together (FR)**^{38} 2019 4-11-1 116 JamesBest 130+
(Johnny Farrelly) *hld up in tch: clsd 5th: led appr 4 out: drew clr 2 out: styd on wl: eased down towards fin* **7/2**^{2}

PP-3 **2** *32* **Goohar (IRE)**^{30} 2151 6-11-7 115 TomCannon 104
(Henry Daly) *racd keenly early on: prom: mstke 7th: lost pl and outpcd 4 out: rallied to go 2nd appr 3 out: u.p and no imp on wnr bef 2 out: no ch after* **7/4**^{1}

22-P **3** *32* **Money For Nothing**^{31} 2138 6-11-1 109 (t) AdamWedge 73
(Harriet Bethell) *hld up in rr: hdwy 8th: rdn whn chsng ldrs bef 2 out: no imp after: wl btn* **8/1**

2-56 **4** *38* **Chestnut Ben (IRE)**^{187} 469 10-11-5 120 MrRWinks(7) 39
(Peter Winks) *hld up: mstke 5th: struggling after: detached 7th: t.o* **8/1**

/P5- **P** **Satu (IRE)**^{357} 2939 11-9-10 97 ow1 MissLBrooke(7)
(Lady Susan Brooke) *racd keenly: hld up: hdwy after 3rd: led 4th: hdd appr 4 out: wknd bef next: t.o whn p.u bef last* **100/1**

-3FP **P** **Suprise Vendor (IRE)**^{15} 2477 9-10-6 107 SamColtherd(7)
(Stuart Coltherd) *led: hdd 4th: remained handy: rdn and wknd 4 out: bhd whn p.u bef 3 out* **8/1**

-24F **P** **Lyric Street (IRE)**^{18} 2424 7-11-7 115 (p) WillKennedy
(Donald McCain) *prom: mstke 4th: hit 5th: hit 7th: rdn and wknd 4 out: t.o whn p.u bef 2 out* **4/1**^{3}

4m 53.7s (31.60) **Going Correction** +2.025s/f (Heav)
WFA 4 from 6yo+ 7lb **7 Ran SP% 112.9**
Speed ratings (Par 105): **106,90,75,58, , ,**
CSF £10.29 TOTE £3.00: £2.10, £1.30; EX 10.50 Trifecta £66.10.
Owner Mrs Z Wentworth **Bred** Maurice Hassan **Trained** Enmore, Somerset

FOCUS
They came home at long intervals as many failed to handle conditions. The form could be rated a fair bit higher through the second.

2766 BETFAIR SUPPORTS WALKING COURSES H'CAP CHASE (QUALIFIER FOR THE CHALLENGER STAYING CHASE FINAL) (18 fncs) 3m 30y
1:35 (1:38) (Class 3) (0-125,124) 5-Y-0+ £6,498 (£1,845; £928; £469; £242; £130)

5PP- **1** **Union Jack D'Ycy (FR)**^{238} 5138 7-11-4 119 CallumWhillans(3) 130+
(Venetia Williams) *j.rt: chsd ldrs: mstke 13th: led 14th: drew clr after 3 out: styd on wl* **8/1**

U1-5 **2** *7* **Bernardelli (IRE)**^{28} 2192 7-11-9 124 CraigNichol(3) 127+
(Nicky Richards) *nt a fluent: in rr: hdwy appr 14th: wnt 2nd after 3 out: styd on after 2 out: mstke last: one pce fnl 75yds* **9/1**

52P- **3** *14* **Hellorboston (IRE)**^{219} 5492 7-11-0 112 (p) AdrianLane 100
(Donald McCain) *hld up: hdwy 13th: rdn after 3 out: one pce and no imp after: n.d whn j.lft last* **7/1**

15P4 **4** *19* **Express Du Berlais (FR)**^{13} 2517 6-11-9 121 (t) WillKennedy 89
(Dr Richard Newland) *in tch: lost pl 6th: rdn appr 4 out: wkng whn mstke 3 out* **9/4**^{1}

1312 **5** *shd* **Ready Token (IRE)**^{23} 2288 7-11-6 118 (tp) TomCannon 87
(Charlie Longsdon) *led: nt fluent 9th: hdd 14th: rdn and wknd after 3 out: blnd whn struggling 2 out: wl btn* **9/2**^{3}

PP/5 **6** *47* **Fine Parchment (IRE)**^{20} 2374 12-11-5 122 (tp) HarryBannister(5) 42
(Charlie Mann) *chsd ldr to 14th: wknd after 4 out: t.o* **14/1**

3P-U **P** **Safran De Cotte (FR)**^{10} 2566 9-10-11 112 ThomasGarner(3)
(Henry Daly) *hld up in tch: lost pl 9th: struggling bef 11th: t.o whn p.u bef 13th* **7/2**^{2}

-1P0 **P** **Pinerolo**^{15} 2471 9-11-4 123 (b) RyanDay(7)
(Joanne Foster) *a bhd and nvr travelling: t.o whn p.u bef 10th* **25/1**

7m 4.2s (44.40) **Going Correction** +2.025s/f (Heav) **8 Ran SP% 115.3**
Speed ratings (Par 107): **107,104,100,93,93 77, ,**
CSF £74.32 CT £530.33 TOTE £9.20: £2.70, £1.60, £2.70; EX 106.50 Trifecta £340.10.
Owner Ian Josephs **Bred** Mme Anne Vallee & Claude Gouin **Trained** Kings Caple, H'fords

FOCUS
This was run at a fair pace in the stamina-sapping conditions and took plenty of getting. The winner is rated to his best.

2767 BETFAIR PRICE RUSH H'CAP HURDLE (12 hdls) 2m 7f 32y
2:10 (2:13) (Class 3) (0-135,135) 4-Y-0+ **£6,498** (£1,908; £954; £477)

Form RPR
111- **1** **Top Billing**^{392} 2195 6-10-7 123 RyanDay(7) 133+
(Nicky Richards) *mde all: effrtlessly drew clr appr last: styd on wl: comf* **9/1**

3-55 **2** *10* **A Vos Gardes (FR)**^{18} 2411 5-11-10 133 (t) TomCannon 131
(Charlie Longsdon) *chsd wnr: rdn after 3 out: one pce and no imp bef last: no ch after* **9/2**^{3}

51P- **3** *1 1/2* **Sir Vinski (IRE)**^{225} 5362 6-10-10 122 CraigNichol(3) 119
(Nicky Richards) *trckd ldrs: rdn after 3 out: one pce fr next* **3/1**^{2}

14-P **4** *11* **Up And Go (FR)**^{203} 208 7-10-11 125 JamesCowley(5) 110
(Donald McCain) *hld up: effrt appr 2 out: sn no imp* **28/1**

0112 **5** *2* **Mr Shantu (IRE)**^{36} 2054 6-11-5 135 (t) PatrickCowley(7) 120
(Jonjo O'Neill) *hld up: blnd 3 out: sn rdn: btn bef next* **9/4**^{1}

2-02 **6** *12* **Slim Pickens (IRE)**^{20} 2369 7-11-6 129 WillKennedy 100
(Dr Richard Newland) *trckd ldrs: rdn after 3 out: sn wknd* **3/1**^{2}

6m 52.5s (61.50) **Going Correction** +1.475s/f (Heav) **6 Ran SP% 112.4**
Speed ratings (Par 107): **52,48,48,44,43 39**
CSF £47.64 TOTE £8.40: £3.20, £3.10; EX 30.60 Trifecta £139.80.
Owner Doreen McGawn & Stewart Tate **Bred** Newsells Park Stud **Trained** Greystoke, Cumbria

FOCUS
This looked competitive, despite the small field and was turned into a procession by the fast-improving winner. The second and third are rated close to their marks.

2768 BETFAIR TAP TAP BOOM BOOM NOVICES' HURDLE (11 hdls) 2m 3f 123y
2:45 (2:47) (Class 4) 4-Y-0+ **£3,249** (£954; £477; £238)

Form RPR
-051 **1** **Arctic Gold (IRE)**^{42} 1979 4-11-2 0 ConorShoemark(3) 120+
(Nigel Twiston-Davies) *chsd ldr: led appr 2nd: mde rest: pressed last: sn rdn: kpt on gamely* **13/8**^{1}

4F **2** *3/4* **Kalondra (IRE)**^{19} 2407 4-11-2 0 WillKennedy 112+
(Neil Mulholland) *hld up in rr: hdwy after 3 out: chsd wnr appr 2 out: chalng last: kpt on u.p run-in but hld* **12/1**

1-54 **3** *25* **Theatrical Style (IRE)**^{55} 1780 6-10-7 0 JamesCowley(5) 87
(Donald McCain) *hld up: hdwy after 3 out: one pce and no imp fr 2 out* **7/2**^{3}

06-3 **4** *3/4* **Uncle Monty (IRE)**^{211} 56 6-10-12 0 (p) AdrianLane 86
(Donald McCain) *led: hdd appr 2nd: chsd ldrs after: rdn after 3 out: wknd bef 2 out* **18/1**

5 *11* **Goldboy (IRE)**^{769} 2001 7-10-12 0 JoshuaMoore 78
(Jonjo O'Neill) *racd keenly: trckd ldrs: chsd ldr appr 2nd: rdn and wknd bef 2 out* **2/1**^{2}

0 **6** *23* **Master Burbidge**^{28} 2183 4-10-5 0 MrMartinMcIntyre(7) 52
(Neil Mulholland) *hld up: rdn after 3 out: sn btn: t.o* **100/1**

5m 43.9s (51.90) **Going Correction** +1.475s/f (Heav) **6 Ran SP% 107.6**
Speed ratings (Par 105): **55,54,44,44,40 30**
CSF £18.32 TOTE £3.00: £1.60, £4.30; EX 19.30 Trifecta £48.60.
Owner Geoffrey & Donna Keeys **Bred** Ms Deidre Connolly **Trained** Naunton, Gloucs

FOCUS
This was weak and with the strongly backed second favourite running well below expectations, it's hard to get overly excited. The first two home pulled well clear, however. The winner set a fair standard but this looks a step up under a claimer.

2769 CASH OUT IN RUNNING WITH BETFAIR "NATIONAL HUNT" NOVICES' HURDLE (9 hdls) 2m 145y
3:20 (3:25) (Class 4) 4-Y-0+ **£3,249** (£954; £477; £238)

Form RPR
P-21 **1** **Final Nudge (IRE)**^{9} 2603 6-11-5 124 TomCannon 132
(David Dennis) *chsd clr ldr: clsd 5th: rdn after 3 out: led 2 out: mstke last: continually pressed: gamely kpt finding for press* **5/4**^{2}

2 **2** *1/2* **Tippmanboy (IRE)**^{18} 2417 5-10-12 117 WillKennedy 124
(Dr Richard Newland) *led: clr after 1st tl 5th: rdn and hdd 2 out: continued to chal: kpt on u.p* **1/1**^{1}

43-0 **3** *75* **In The Hold (IRE)**^{24} 2265 5-10-12 0 AdamWedge 49
(Evan Williams) *hld up: plugged on to take 3rd appr 2 out: no ch w front two* **20/1**^{3}

30-0 **4** *12* **Pink Tara**^{23} 2302 4-10-2 0 CallumWhillans(3) 30
(Venetia Williams) *sn chsd ldrs: wl adrift 3 out: lost 3rd and btn appr 2 out: tired whn blnd last* **25/1**

650 **5** *4 1/2* **Baysbrown (IRE)**^{35} 2066 5-10-9 0 CraigNichol(3) 33
(Nicky Richards) *a bhd: nvr gng wl: hit 4th: mstke 4 out: t.o* **40/1**

P **Feather Lane (IRE)**^{595} 5-10-7 0 JamesCowley(5)
(Donald McCain) *chsd ldrs: rdn and wknd bef 4 out: t.o whn p.u bef 3 out* **33/1**

4m 32.9s (22.00) **Going Correction** +1.475s/f (Heav)
WFA 4 from 5yo+ 7lb **6 Ran SP% 108.4**
Speed ratings (Par 105): **107,106,71,65,63**
CSF £2.67 TOTE £2.00: £1.30, £1.10; EX 2.70 Trifecta £9.40.
Owner Corbett Stud **Bred** M W And Mrs M Doran **Trained** Hanley Swan, Worcestershire

FOCUS
This developed into a duel from a very early stage and produced a thrilling finish. A good effort from the winner to give weight to the second.

2770 BERNARD CORBETT & CO MARES' STANDARD OPEN NATIONAL HUNT FLAT RACE 2m 145y
3:50 (3:52) (Class 6) 4-6-Y-0 **£2,053** (£598; £299)

Form RPR
1 **1** **The Nipper (IRE)**^{196} 334 4-11-0 0 HarryBannister(5) 125+
(Warren Greatrex) *racd in cl 2nd pl tl led after 4f: drew clr over 3f out: easily* **1/5**^{1}

2 *9* **Miss Giselle** 6-10-5 0 HarrisonBeswick(7) 98
(Sam Thomas) *hld up: hdwy 4f out: wnt 2nd over 2f out: no ch w wnr* **20/1**

343 **3** *11* **Western Sunrise (IRE)**^{12} 2549 6-10-12 0 LiamHeard 89
(Johnny Farrelly) *chsd ldrs: rdn 4f out: wnt 2nd briefly over 2f out: one pce after* **6/1**^{2}

00-0 **4** *19* **Mari Me Oscar (IRE)**^{190} 432 5-10-7 0 ChrisWard(5) 68
(Nikki Evans) *led: hdd after 4f: racd in 2nd pl: rdn and unable to go w wnr over 3f out: wknd and lost 2nd over 2f out* **100/1**

53- 5 11 **Superfection (IRE)**^{245} 5035 6-10-12 0........................ AdrianLane 57
(Donald McCain) *racd keenly: hld up: rdn and wknd over 3f out: wl btn* **14/1^{3}**

6 93 **West Hill Legend** 4-10-12 0........................ AdamWedge
(Richard Woollacott) *hld up: struggling 1/2-way: t.o* **20/1**

4m 41.6s (36.30) **Going Correction** +1.475s/f (Heav) **6 Ran SP% 114.8**
Speed ratings: **73,68,63,54,49 5**
CSF £8.47 TOTE £1.10: £1.10, £7.20; EX 8.70 Trifecta £21.60.
Owner Smith, Ratcliffe & Bowring **Bred** W L Smith & Partners **Trained** Upper Lambourn, Berks

FOCUS
This bumper was run in near darkness. It revolved around the long odds-on favourite, who confirmed herself a very useful bumper mare.
T/Plt: £156.00 to a £1 stake. Pool: £45,230.40 - 211.63 winning units. T/Qpdt: £35.80 to a £1 stake. Pool: £3,080.72 - 63.56 winning units. **Darren Owen**

2744 DONCASTER (L-H)
Saturday, November 28

OFFICIAL GOING: Good (chs 8.0, hdl 7.7)
Wind: fresh 1/2 behind Weather: overcast, breezy, cold, light rain race 3 onwards

2771 BETDAQ.COM - SERIOUS ABOUT HORSES CONDITIONAL JOCKEYS' H'CAP CHASE (18 fncs) 3m 6y
12:20 (12:20) (Class 5) (0-100,98) 4-Y-0+ **£3,573** (£1,049; £524; £262)

Form RPR

32P4 1 **Xenophon**^{12} 2539 7-9-13 **74**........................ ThomasCheesman$^{(3)}$ 85
(Michael Chapman) *chsd ldrs: 2nd 5th: hit 15th: led 3 out: drew clr bef last* **8/1**

44P1 2 15 **Sgt Bull Berry**^{11} 2556 8-10-9 **81**........................ JamieHamilton 79
(Peter Maddison) *in rr: shkn up 6th: trcking ldrs 8th: 2nd 2 out: kpt on same pce* **3/1^{2}**

00-U 3 3 **Exmoor Challenge**^{18} 2410 6-10-9 **84**........................(p) LizzieKelly$^{(3)}$ 81
(Neil King) *chsd ldrs: mstke 3rd: outpcd 8th: reminders 11th: chsd ldrs 14th: 3rd and one pce fr 2 out* **5/1^{3}**

5552 4 16 **Cara Court (IRE)**^{14} 2500 9-10-9 **81**........................(v) ColmMcCormack 60
(Joanne Foster) *chsd ldrs: drvn 12th: sn bhd: blnd 3 out: tk distant 4th clsng stages* **8/1**

U5P6 5 7 **Top Cat Dj (IRE)**^{30} 2147 7-9-11 **74**........................(v) ThomasDowson$^{(5)}$ 57
(Chris Grant) *j.rt: led: hit 14th: mstke 4 out: hdd next: wknd between last 2: poor 4th whn blnd last* **6/1**

P/6P 6 ½ **Mia Matriarch**^{22} 2321 9-10-0 **72** oh6........................(t) JonathanEngland 45
(Stuart Coltherd) *in rr: chsd ldrs 4th: lost pl 14th: sn bhd: b.b.v* **12/1**

003U F **Mission Complete (IRE)**^{19} 2402 9-11-0 **94**........................(tp) JackSavage$^{(8)}$
(Jonjo O'Neill) *chsd ldr: bdly hmpd and fell 1st* **11/4^{1}**

6m 9.5s (-2.50) **Going Correction** -0.10s/f (Good) **7 Ran SP% 112.5**
Speed ratings (Par 103): **100,95,94,88,86 86,**
CSF £31.97 CT £132.15 TOTE £8.50: £3.60, £1.80; EX 36.80 Trifecta £180.20.
Owner Milson Robinson **Bred** Winterbeck Manor Stud **Trained** Market Rasen, Lincs

FOCUS
Hurdle bends into home straight railed out 7yds from innermost line. The opening contest was a modest conditional jockeys' staying handicap chase. They went a decent gallop on good ground. The winner is rated back to the level of his 2013 form.

2772 EBF STALLIONS BETDAQ.COM 2% COMMISSION "NATIONAL HUNT" NOVICES' HURDLE (QUALIFIER) (10 hdls) 2m 3f 120y
12:50 (12:51) (Class 4) 4-6-Y-O **£3,898** (£1,144; £572; £286)

Form RPR

1-13 1 **Cloudy Dream (IRE)**^{22} 2318 5-10-12 0........................ BrianHughes 126+
(Malcolm Jefferson) *trckd ldrs: t.k.h: hmpd 5th: led appr 3 out: wandered and hung rt between last 2: edgd lft and styd on last 100yds* **9/4^{2}**

2 2 1¼ **Waiting Patiently (IRE)**^{22} 2318 4-10-12 0........................ JamesReveley 123+
(Keith Reveley) *hld up towards rr: smooth hdwy appr 3 out: cl 2nd 2 out: hung rt run-in: checked and swtchd lft 75yds out: styd on same pce* **9/2**

3 13 **Stage One (IRE)**^{251} 4-10-12 0........................ HarrySkelton 111
(Dan Skelton) *hld up towards rr: hdwy and handy 3rd 3 out: wknd between last 2* **4/1^{3}**

4 9 **Some Kinda Lama (IRE)**^{237} 4-10-12 0........................ MarkGrant 103
(Charlie Mann) *chsd ldrs: wknd 2 out* **33/1**

65 5 8 **Quantum Of Solace**^{7} 2644 5-10-2 0........................ JamesBanks$^{(3)}$ 88
(Noel Williams) *t.k.h in mid-div: hdwy to chse ldrs 3 out: wknd bef next* **66/1**

00-P 6 22 **Sirius Star**^{29} 2169 6-10-7 0........................ JamieHamilton$^{(5)}$ 75
(Brian Rothwell) *in rr: bhd and drvn 6th: tk distant 6th last* **150/1**

11 7 1 **Ascotdeux Nellerie (FR)**^{37} 2035 5-11-1 0........................ TomBellamy$^{(3)}$ 80
(Kim Bailey) *chsd ldrs 3rd: lost pl bef 2 out: sn bhd: b.b.v* **6/4^{1}**

6-50 8 15 **Whispering Speed (IRE)**^{26} 2239 5-10-12 0........................ TrevorWhelan 61
(Lucy Wadham) *chsd ldrs: hmpd 5th: lost pl sn after 3 out: sn bhd* **100/1**

43/0 9 10 **Laraghcon Boy (IRE)**^{10} 2581 6-10-12 0........................ LeeEdwards 52
(Tony Carroll) *chsd ldrs: outpcd after 7th: lost pl bef next: sn bhd* **100/1**

200 10 8 **Normandy King (IRE)**^{26} 2251 4-10-12 0........................ MichaelByrne 45
(Tim Vaughan) *led: j.lft 5th: hdd appr 3 out: sn lost pl and bhd* **100/1**

65 11 12 **Repeat The Feat (FR)**^{22} 2312 4-10-12 0........................ AndrewTinkler 34
(Charlie Longsdon) *chsd ldrs: reminders after 6th: lost pl next: sn bhd* **66/1**

4m 43.2s (-8.10) **Going Correction** -0.20s/f (Good)
WFA 4 from 5yo+ 8lb **11 Ran SP% 118.5**
Speed ratings: **108,107,102,98,95 86,86,80,76,73 68**
CSF £13.14 TOTE £3.40: £1.10, £1.60; EX 8.30 Trifecta £75.10.
Owner Trevor Hemmings **Bred** Eimear Purcell **Trained** Norton, N Yorks

FOCUS
Race increased from advertised distance by 21yds. A fair novice hurdle run at an even gallop. The first two are on the upgrade.

2773 BETDAQ.COM £50 IN FREE BETS "NATIONAL HUNT" INTERMEDIATE H'CAP HURDLE (8 hdls) 2m 140y
1:20 (1:23) (Class 3) (0-135,128) 4-Y-0+ **£5,430** (£1,639; £844; £447)

Form RPR

1516 1 **I'dliketheoption (IRE)**^{28} 2182 4-11-4 **120**........................(t) RichieMcLernon 125+
(Jonjo O'Neill) *hld up wl in tch: trckd ldrs 5th: handy 3rd 2 out: upsides whn lft clr last: eased towards fin* **10/1**

-323 2 12 **Double W's (IRE)**^{15} 2472 5-11-7 **123**........................ BrianHughes 120+
(Malcolm Jefferson) *trckd ldr: upsides 3 out: blnd next: lft 6 l 2nd and sltly hmpd last: fdd* **5/2^{2}**

3136 3 1½ **The Big Dipper**^{10} 2577 6-10-5 **107**........................ TrevorWhelan 98
(David Dennis) *chsd ldrs: drvn 3 out: lost pl bef next: lft modest 3rd last: kpt on* **9/1**

5-16 4 nk **Adrakhan (FR)**^{15} 2472 4-11-2 **118**........................ HarrySkelton 110
(Dan Skelton) *hld up in tch: hdwy 4th: sn trcking ldrs: drvn 3 out: sn lost pl: blnd next: lft modest 4th last: kpt on* **6/1^{3}**

11P- P **Bobs Lady Tamure**^{252} 4918 8-11-6 **127**........................(t) DaraghBourke$^{(5)}$
(Maurice Barnes) *chsd ldrs: lost pl after 5th: p.u bef next* **25/1**

/U1- F **Zulu Oscar**^{380} 2465 6-11-5 **128**........................(t) MrMLegg$^{(7)}$ 132+
(Harry Fry) *led: jnd 3 out: drvn appr next: narrow advantage whn fell heavily last* **11/10^{1}**

4m 0.3s (-4.40) **Going Correction** -0.20s/f (Good)
WFA 4 from 5yo+ 7lb **6 Ran SP% 113.4**
Speed ratings (Par 107): **102,96,95,95,**
CSF £36.32 TOTE £7.20: £3.10, £1.60; EX 36.20 Trifecta £130.90.
Owner John P McManus **Bred** Stephen O'Flynn **Trained** Cheltenham, Gloucs

FOCUS
Race increased from advertised distance by 21yds. A fair handicap hurdle. It had begun raining and the ground was cutting up. The winner is on the upgrade.

2774 BETDAQ.COM 50% COMMISSION REFUND NOVICES' LIMITED H'CAP CHASE (15 fncs) 2m 3f 44y
1:55 (1:56) (Class 3) (0-135,135) 4-Y-0+ **£6,498** (£1,908; £954; £477)

Form RPR

2-14 1 **Wings Attract (IRE)**^{19} 2407 6-10-6 **119**........................ TomMessenger 130+
(Chris Bealby) *trckd ldrs: handy 3rd 4 out: upsides and sltly hmpd appr last: sn led: drvn out* **33/1**

4-21 2 2¼ **Katachenko (IRE)**^{28} 2201 6-11-2 **129**........................ HarrySkelton 136
(Donald McCain) *w ldr: led 11th: hdd 4 out: led sn after 3 out: hung lft appr last: hdd last 175yds: no ex* **15/2**

4P-1 3 hd **Coologue (IRE)**^{32} 2122 6-11-8 **135**........................ BrianHughes 143
(Charlie Longsdon) *led: hit 10th: hdd next: led 4 out tl hdd sn after 3 out: styd on same pce last 150yds* **7/2^{1}**

/41- 4 9 **Elmore Back (IRE)**^{552} 467 6-10-10 **123**........................ MarkGrant 123
(Charlie Mann) *in rr: hdwy to chse ldrs 10th: hit 11th: wknd appr last* **16/1**

-545 5 13 **Lord Grantham (IRE)**^{133} 1042 8-10-7 **120**........................ AndrewThornton 109
(Henry Daly) *chsd ldrs: wknd appr 2 out* **12/1**

2511 6 16 **Oliver's Gold**^{28} 2193 7-11-0 **132**........................(p) JamieHamilton$^{(5)}$ 105
(Mark Walford) *in rr: bhd fr 10th* **9/1**

3-21 7 54 **Jack Steel (IRE)**^{33} 2105 5-11-0 **127**........................ RichieMcLernon 51
(Lucinda Russell) *nt fluent in rr: bhd fr 8th: t.o 3 out: eventually completed* **11/2^{3}**

0/UB U **Billy Merriott (IRE)**^{26} 2240 9-10-9 **129**........................(t) MrMLegg$^{(7)}$
(Harry Fry) *in rr: hdwy 10th: 5th and keeping on whn blnd and uns rdr 4 out* **9/2^{2}**

130/ P **Special Catch (IRE)**^{623} 4805 8-11-3 **130**........................ JamesReveley
(Keith Reveley) *mid-div: chsd ldrs 10th: j. slowly and lost pl 3 out: eased and 6th whn p.u bef next* **15/2**

26-0 U **Favorite Girl (GER)**^{28} 2186 7-10-9 **125**........................ JonathanEngland$^{(3)}$
(Michael Appleby) *in rr: hdwy 4th: lost pl 12th: bhd whn blnd and uns rdr 12th* **20/1**

222P F **Mont Royale**^{28} 2184 7-11-1 **128**........................ AndrewTinkler
(Jonjo O'Neill) *in rr: hit 10th: bhd fr 12th: t.o whn fell last* **18/1**

4m 42.5s (-6.50) **Going Correction** -0.10s/f (Good) **11 Ran SP% 115.9**
Speed ratings (Par 107): **109,108,107,104,98 91,69, ,**
CSF £261.14 CT £1101.79 TOTE £42.90: £8.70, £2.40, £1.80; EX 345.40 Trifecta £565.30 Part won..
Owner The Rann Family **Bred** John McAleese **Trained** Barrowby, Lincs

■ Stewards' Enquiry : Tom Messenger two-day ban; used his whip above the permitted level (12th-13th Dec)

FOCUS
The feature contest was a fairly decent novices' handicap chase. They went an honest gallop and the second and third give the form a solid look.

2775 BETDAQ.COM £100 CASINO BONUS H'CAP HURDLE (10 hdls) 2m 3f 120y
2:30 (2:33) (Class 3) (0-130,126) 3-Y-0+ **£6,256** (£1,848; £924; £462; £231; £116)

Form RPR

F24- 1 **Red Devil Boys (IRE)**^{292} 4126 8-11-11 **125**........................(p) BrianHughes 132
(John Ferguson) *trckd ldrs: hit 1st: led 3 out: hdd appr next: led last 100yds: drvn out* **5/2^{1}**

U-04 2 1½ **Crookstown (IRE)**^{20} 2373 8-11-4 **118**........................ KielanWoods 124
(Ben Case) *trckd ldrs: led appr 2 out: hdd and no ex last 100yds* **14/1**

0063 3 1 **Boruma (IRE)**^{37} 2027 5-10-4 **107**........................ HarryChalloner$^{(3)}$ 112
(Dianne Sayer) *led: hdd 3 out: rallied and 3rd last: styd on clsng stages* **8/1^{3}**

12-6 4 9 **Hannah's Princess (IRE)**^{212} 52 6-11-12 **126**........................ AndrewTinkler 122
(Warren Greatrex) *hld up in rr: hdwy 6th: sn chsng ldrs: wknd last* **11/4^{2}**

3416 5 4 **Mercers Court (IRE)**^{38} 2013 7-11-9 **123**........................ TrevorWhelan 115
(Neil King) *trckd ldrs: wknd between last 2* **9/1**

0-51 6 ½ **Prairie Town (IRE)**^{20} 2373 4-11-11 **125**........................ LeeEdwards 118
(Tony Carroll) *in rr: drvn 6th: rallied next: sn chsng ldrs: wknd between last 2* **8/1^{3}**

-11P 7 32 **Big Generator**^{55} 1784 9-11-10 **124**........................ HarrySkelton 87
(Caroline Bailey) *trckd ldrs: lost pl and nt fluent 2 out: sn wl bhd: t.o* **10/1**

2334 8 1½ **Harvey's Hope**^{25} 1270 9-10-12 **112**........................ JamesReveley 73
(Keith Reveley) *chsd ldrs: lost pl 7th: in rr whn eased bef 2 out: t.o* **8/1^{3}**

265/ 9 15 **Mixologist**^{650} 4300 8-10-12 **112**........................ MarkQuinlan 60
(James Evans) *t.k.h in rr: trckd ldrs 5th: drvn bef 3 out: nt run on and sn lost pland bhd: t.o* **40/1**

4m 43.8s (-7.50) **Going Correction** -0.20s/f (Good)
WFA 4 from 5yo+ 8lb **9 Ran SP% 116.8**
Speed ratings (Par 107): **107,106,106,102,100 100,87,87,81**
CSF £36.67 CT £248.97 TOTE £3.30: £1.50, £3.90, £3.10; EX 41.00 Trifecta £352.50.
Owner Bloomfields **Bred** Carl Beame **Trained** Cowlinge, Suffolk

FOCUS
Race increased from advertised distance by 21yds. A fair handicap hurdle run at a respectable gallop. The form looks pretty solid.

2776 BETDAQ.COM £50 GAMES BONUS MARES' "NATIONAL HUNT" NOVICES' HURDLE (10 hdls) 2m 3f 120y
3:05 (3:10) (Class 4) 4-Y-O+ **£3,898** (£1,144; £572; £286)

Form RPR
220- **1** **Briery Queen**[231] 5277 6-10-7 0........................ JamesBanks(3) 125+
(Noel Williams) *sn w reluctant ldr: led 3rd: qcknd pce next: styd on wl run-in* **3/1**[2]
51-1 **2** *4* **Robins Reef (IRE)**[16] 2452 5-11-2 0........................ AndrewTinkler 128+
(Nicky Henderson) *trckd ldrs: handy 2nd appr 3 out: styd on same pce run-in* **8/11**[1]
61-4 **3** *15* **Mystic Sky**[18] 2421 4-10-10 0........................ TrevorWhelan 109+
(Lucy Wadham) *hld up in rr: hdwy to trck ldrs 6th: handy 3rd appr 3 out: wknd between last 2* **16/1**
0 **4** *11* **Nancy's Trix (IRE)**[24] 2277 6-10-3 0........................ CiaranGethings(7) 95
(David Loder) *chsd ldrs: drvn 7th: outpcd appr 3 out: tk poor 4th clsng stages* **40/1**
44 **5** *3/4* **Zara Hope (IRE)**[24] 2277 4-10-10 0........................ RichieMcLernon 94
(Charlie Longsdon) *reluctant ldr: t.k.h: hdd 3rd: chsd ldrs tl lost pl bef 2 out* **25/1**
3- **6** *3 1/4* **The Last Bar**[272] 4513 5-10-10 0........................ HarrySkelton 91
(Dan Skelton) *in rr: sme hdwy 7th: sn drvn lost pl next* **7/1**[3]
3-0 **7** *14* **Cosmic Diamond**[23] 2302 5-10-7 0........................ TomBellamy(3) 77
(Paul Webber) *trckd ldrs: 2nd 6th tl appr 3 out: wknd bef 2 out* **66/1**
1320 **8** *21* **Flower Power**[49] 1854 4-11-2 113........................ JamesReveley 62
(Tony Coyle) *trckd ldrs: lost pl bef 2 out: eased between last 2: t.o whn j.lft last* **14/1**
-34F **9** *2* **Ethelwyn**[81] 1499 5-10-10 0........................ BrianHughes 54
(Malcolm Jefferson) *in rr: sme hdwy 6th: lost pl bef 3 out: sn bhd: t.o* **12/1**
22-0 **P** **Oskar's Eva (IRE)**[26] 2250 5-10-10 0........................ MichaelByrne
(Tim Vaughan) *chsd ldrs: drvn and lost pl 5th: sn bhd: t.o whn p.u bef 3 out* **40/1**

4m 58.3s (7.00) **Going Correction** -0.20s/f (Good)
WFA 4 from 5yo+ 8lb **10 Ran SP% 125.9**
Speed ratings (Par 105): **78,76,70,66,65 64,58,50,49,**
CSF £6.13 TOTE £4.50: £1.60, £1.02, £4.50; EX 6.00 Trifecta £83.70.
Owner Helen Plumbly & Kathryn Leadbeater **Bred** Simon And Helen Plumbly **Trained** Blewbury, Oxon

FOCUS
Race increased from advertised distance by 21yds. An ordinary mares' novice hurdle. Nobody wanted to go on resulting in a slow gallop. The winner should go on to rate higher.

2777 FREE BETDAQ TRADING SOFTWARE ON BETDAQTRADERS.COM "JUNIOR" STANDARD OPEN NATIONAL HUNT FLAT RACE 1m 5f
3:40 (3:42) (Class 6) 3-Y-O **£1,949** (£572; £286; £143)

Form RPR
1 **Jam Session (IRE)** 3-10-9 0........................ RobMcCarth(3) 105+
(Ian Williams) *trckd ldrs: 2nd over 1f out: styd on to ld nr fin* **10/1**
2 *nse* **Captain Sam** 3-10-12 0........................ BrianHughes 105+
(Malcolm Jefferson) *trckd ldrs: led over 3f out: hung rt and wandered over 1f out: hdd nr fin* **4/1**[2]
3 *3/4* **Kafella** 3-10-12 0........................ HarrySkelton 104+
(Dan Skelton) *trckd ldrs hung lft and 3rd over 1f out: kpt on same pce fnl 75yds* **11/8**[1]
4 *5* **Moon Jet (IRE)** 3-10-12 0........................ AlainCawley 98
(John Mackie) *hld up in rr: hdwy on outside over 4f out: one pce fnl 2f* **50/1**
5 *7* **Multipede** 3-10-7 0........................ DaleIrving(5) 89
(James Ewart) *trckd ldrs: upsides over 3f out: wknd over 1f out* **33/1**
0 **6** *3 1/2* **Very First Time**[55] 1772 3-10-12 0........................ JamesReveley 84
(Tim Easterby) *in rr: kpt on fnl 3f: nvr a factor* **25/1**
7 *1* **Greenworldsolution** 3-10-5 0........................ ConorWalsh(7) 83
(Jennie Candlish) *hld up in rr: lost pl over 5f out: kpt on fnl 2f* **40/1**
4 **8** *3/4* **Russian Approval**[39] 2009 3-10-5 0........................ AndrewTinkler 75
(William Knight) *led: hdd over 3f out: wknd fnl 2f* **10/1**
9 *1 1/2* **Desert Sensation (IRE)** 3-10-9 0........................ AdamNicol(3) 80
(Tracy Waggott) *mid-div: hdwy 7f out: sn chsng ldrs: wknd over 2f out* **40/1**
2 **10** *3* **Shining Romeo**[18] 2414 3-10-12 0........................ TrevorWhelan 76
(Denis Quinn) *chsd ldrs: drvn over 3f out: lost pl 2f out* **10/1**
11 *nk* **Shabraque (IRE)** 3-10-5 0........................ CiaranGethings(7) 75
(David Loder) *hld up in mid-div: drvn 4f out: nvr a factor* **13/2**[3]
12 *6* **Earth Shaker** 3-10-12 0........................ JakeGreenall 68
(Michael Easterby) *mid-div: lost pl 3f out* **25/1**
13 *5* **Nightswift** 3-10-12 0........................ MarkQuinlan 61
(James Evans) *in rr: drvn 3f out: nvr on terms* **33/1**
14 *6* **Secretsista** 3-10-5 0........................ PeterCarberry 46
(Jennie Candlish) *in rr-div: drvn over 5f out: sn bhd* **28/1**

3m 4.4s (1.50) **14 Ran SP% 126.6**
CSF £48.68 TOTE £13.70: £3.50, £1.70, £1.50; EX 65.10 Trifecta £165.30.
Owner Michael H Watt **Bred** Haras De l'Hirondelle **Trained** Portway, Worcs

FOCUS
Race increased from advertised distance by 21yds. The concluding contest was probably a modest 'junior' bumper. They went a respectable gallop at best.
T/Plt: £99.00 to a £1 stake. Pool: £66,828.55 - 492.29 winning units. T/Qpdt: £16.50 to a £1 stake. Pool: £6,346.11 - 283.27 winning units. **Walter Glynn**

2757 NEWBURY (L-H)
Saturday, November 28
OFFICIAL GOING: Soft (heavy in places on hurdle course; 4.2)
Wind: medium, half against Weather: overcast, rain Race 2-4

2778 THOROUGHBRED BREEDERS' ASSOCIATION MARES' NOVICES' HURDLE (LISTED RACE) (8 hdls) 2m 69y
12:15 (12:15) (Class 1) 4-Y-O+ **£13,968** (£5,231; £2,613; £1,304)

Form RPR
1115 **1** **Tea In Transvaal (IRE)**[35] 2060 4-11-0 134........................ PaulMoloney 138+
(Evan Williams) *mde all: rdn sn after last: styd on wl and a in command: rdn out* **11/8**[1]
52 **2** *6* **Colla Pier (IRE)**[13] 2529 6-11-0 122........................ RobertDunne 128
(Patrick Mooney, Ire) *hld up in tch: clsd to trck ldr and swtchd rt 2 out: shkn up bef last: kpt on same pce and a hld flat* **7/2**[2]
00-1 **3** *15* **Ruby Rambler**[23] 2302 5-11-0 0........................ LeightonAspell 115
(Lucy Wadham) *chsd ldr tl 3rd and struggling whn mstke 2 out: wknd and wl hld whn j.rt last: plugged on* **11/2**[3]
4 *5* **Very Extravagant (IRE)**[182] 565 6-11-0 0........................ NoelFehily 107
(Neil Mulholland) *bhd: nt fluent 2nd and nvr travelling in detached last after: styd on to pass btn horses after 3 out: nvr trbld ldrs* **20/1**
40-4 **5** *17* **Lady Persephone (FR)**[29] 2164 4-11-0 0........................ WayneHutchinson 90
(Alan King) *in tch in midfield: rdn after 3 out: sn btn: wknd bef 2 out: t.o* **12/1**
3 **6** *6* **Fortunata Fashions**[25] 2257 5-11-0 0........................ GavinSheehan 86
(Ben Case) *chsd ldrs: mstke 3rd and steadily lost pl: dropped to last on long run after 5th: t.o after 3 out* **8/1**
3011 **7** *1 1/2* **Hope's Wishes**[9] 2604 5-11-0 110........................ SamTwiston-Davies 83
(Barry Brennan) *wl in tch in midfield: chsd ldrs 3rd tl struggling 3 out: wknd bef 2 out: t.o* **11/1**

4m 9.05s (-0.95) **Going Correction** +0.35s/f (Yiel)
WFA 4 from 5yo+ 7lb **7 Ran SP% 111.6**
Speed ratings (Par 111): **116,113,105,103,94 91,90**
CSF £6.09 TOTE £2.30: £1.60, £2.40; EX 6.20 Trifecta £14.40.
Owner M J Haines **Bred** Summerville Bloodstock **Trained** Llancarfan, Vale Of Glamorgan

FOCUS
The going remained officially soft, heavy in places on the hurdle track (GoingStick 4.2 on both courses), but there were varying views on the ground from the riders after the first race. Noel Fehily said: "It's harder work than yesterday." Leighton Aspell said: "It's heavy", while winning jockey Paul Moloney said: "It's not too bad. They've given us fresh ground and it's not desperate". The easy winner set a decent dtandard and is rated to her mark.\n\x\x The rail was set out on both courses, though it had been moved in overnight. The actual distance of the opener was 2m 138yds.\n\x\x They went a fair pace in this mares' Listed novices' hurdle and the two market leaders dominated.

2779 BET365.COM NOVICES' LIMITED H'CAP CHASE (FOR THE FULKE WALWYN TROPHY) (13 fncs) 2m 92y
12:45 (12:45) (Class 3) (0-140,137) 4-Y-O+ **£12,512** (£3,696; £1,848; £924; £462; £232)

Form RPR
1-01 **1** **Arzal (FR)**[37] 2034 5-11-7 **136**........................ GavinSheehan 158+
(Harry Whittington) *mde virtually: drew clr after 10th: in n.d 2 out: eased towards fin* **9/2**[3]
00-2 **2** *13* **Aso (FR)**[24] 2274 5-11-8 **137**........................ AidanColeman 142+
(Venetia Williams) *chsd ldrs: pckd 8th: 3rd whn blnd 10th: no ch w wnr whn j.lft next: wnt 2nd last: kpt on* **4/1**[2]
361- **3** *5* **Laser Hawk (IRE)**[346] 3146 8-11-4 **133**........................ PaulMoloney 129
(Evan Williams) *t.k.h: hld up in tch: outpcd 10th: 5th and wl hld whn mstke 2 out: styd on wl flat to go 3rd fnl 50yds: no ch w wnr* **14/1**
0F-3 **4** *1 1/2* **Balgarry (FR)**[18] 2412 8-11-6 **135**........................ TomScudamore 130
(David Pipe) *chsd ldrs: lft 2nd 9th: outpcd after next: wl btn whn lost 2nd last: plugged on same pce flat: lost 2nd fnl 50yds* **15/2**
4101 **5** *9* **Johnny Og**[30] 2151 6-10-3 **118**........................(b) IanPopham 104
(Martin Keighley) *pressed wnr tl mstke and lost pl 9th: 4th and btn after next: wkng whn mstke last* **25/1**
/2-5 **6** *12* **For Two (FR)**[27] 2211 6-10-11 **126**........................(t) SamTwiston-Davies 100
(Paul Nicholls) *hld up in tch: mstke 4th: struggling after 9th: wl btn whn mstke 3 out: wknd: t.o* **11/1**
0-03 **7** *3 1/4* **Rock On Rocky**[17] 2438 7-11-0 **129**........................(p) CharliePoste 99
(Matt Sheppard) *midfield tl dropped to rr 7th: lost tch after 9th: t.o 3 out: blnd last* **40/1**
/0-0 **8** *14* **Full Shift (FR)**[210] 96 6-11-1 **130**........................ BarryGeraghty 86
(Nicky Henderson) *a in rr: lost tch 9th: t.o 3 out* **7/2**[1]
03-2 **F** **Wadswick Court (IRE)**[38] 2012 7-11-2 **131**........................ NoelFehily
(Neil Mulholland) *hld up in midfield: dropped to rr 5th: last whn fell next* **10/1**
55-1 **U** **Javert (IRE)**[24] 2266 6-11-1 **130**........................ SeanBowen
(Emma Lavelle) *w ldrs tl 3rd: in tch in midfield after: 5th whn blnd and uns rdr 9th* **7/1**

4m 9.9s (1.90) **Going Correction** +0.35s/f (Yiel) **10 Ran SP% 115.0**
Speed ratings (Par 107): **109,102,100,99,94 88,87,80, ,**
CSF £23.27 CT £231.85 TOTE £4.90: £1.90, £1.90, £3.20; EX 22.00 Trifecta £325.50.
Owner The Hennessy Six **Bred** Dominique Gouin & Mme Anna Racape **Trained** Sparsholt, Oxforshire

FOCUS
Actual race distance 2m 135yds. A competitive novice handicap which will produce winners. With several front runners in the field, it was always going to be run at a brisk pace. The time was 6.9sec outside standard, very respectable in the conditions. Arzal looks a high-class novice.

2780 SIR PETER O'SULLEVAN MEMORIAL H'CAP CHASE (17 fncs) 2m 6f 93y
1:15 (1:17) (Class 3) (0-140,140) 4-Y-O+ **£25,024** (£7,392; £3,696; £1,848; £924; £464)

Form RPR
6-11 **1** **Aloomomo (FR)**[24] 2276 5-11-1 **129**........................ GavinSheehan 144+
(Warren Greatrex) *in tch and travelled strly: clsd to trck ldrs 13th: led after next: in command between last 2: styd on strly flat: readily* **5/1**[2]
P1P- **2** *9* **O Maonlai (IRE)**[252] 4917 7-11-9 **137**........................(t) PaddyBrennan 143
(Tom George) *hld up in rr: hmpd 1st: mstke 9th: clsd and wl in tch 13th: wnt 3rd 2 out: kpt on flat to snatch 2nd cl home: no ch w wnr* **25/1**
2-6 **3** *1/2* **La Vaticane (FR)**[15] 2468 6-11-6 **134**........................(t) TomScudamore 139
(David Pipe) *in tch: chsd wnr 3 out: rdn and no ex between last 2: kpt on same pce flat: lost 2nd cl home* **7/1**[3]
1/0- **4** *10* **Midnight Prayer**[364] 2808 10-11-9 **137**........................ WayneHutchinson 135
(Alan King) *hld up towards rr: mstke 4th: reminder after 7th: clsd and wl in tch 13th: outpcd 3 out: plugged on to go modest 3rd flat* **20/1**
562- **5** *1 3/4* **Mosspark (IRE)**[266] 4632 7-11-1 **129**........................(p) SeanBowen 121
(Emma Lavelle) *midfield: reminder after 7th: mstke next: reminders and clsd after 12th: outpcd 3 out: battling for modest 4th whn blnd last: plugged on same pce after* **10/1**
3-10 **6** *2 3/4* **Big Casino**[35] 2061 9-10-11 **130**........................(v) JamieBargary(5) 120
(Nigel Twiston-Davies) *chsd ldr: lft in ld 2nd: hdd 3rd: chsd ldrs tl led again 10th: hdd after 14th and struggling next: wl btn between last 2: wknd and lost 2 pls flat* **14/1**
0-22 **7** *3 1/2* **Abracadabra Sivola (FR)**[25] 2260 5-11-0 **128**........................ RichardJohnson 119
(Nick Williams) *j.rt and many mstkes: led tl blnd and hdd 2nd: chsd ldrs: led 9th tl 10th: struggling and blnd 14th: wknd next* **9/2**[1]

1PP- **8** *14* **Loch Ba (IRE)**287 4224 9-11-0 **128**.................. ConorO'Farrell 100
(Mick Channon) *a bhd: j.big 4th: lost tch 13th: t.o* **33/1**

13-P **9** *20* **Ceasar Milan (IRE)**42 1976 7-11-10 **138**...........(tp) SamTwiston-Davies 90
(Paul Nicholls) *wl in tch in midfield: blnd 10th: chsd ldrs after 11th: wknd qckly 3 out: t.o* **14/1**

3-P1 **F** **Simply Wings (IRE)**19 2404 11-11-5 **133**.......................... JamieMoore
(Kerry Lee) *hld up in tch in midfield tl fell 11th* **20/1**

5P-2 **U** **Shangani (USA)**16 2459 9-11-4 **132**......................(b) AidanColeman
(Venetia Williams) *chsd ldrs: led 3rd tl hdd and blnd 9th: lost pl and struggling whn bdly hmpd and uns rdr 11th* **8/1**

304/ **P** **Si C'Etait Vrai (FR)**644 4436 9-11-4 **132**...........................(t) NoelFehily
(Neil Mulholland) *chsd ldrs: blnd 2nd: steadily lost pl: bhd whn p.u 11th* **8/1**

-024 **U** **Ericht (IRE)**15 2473 9-11-1 **129**...................................... NicodeBoinville
(Nicky Henderson) *midfield whn slithered on landing and uns rdr 1st* **14/1**

PP-0 **P** **Majala (FR)**15 2468 9-11-12 **140**.......................(t) DenisO'Regan
(Tom George) *a bhd: j.rt 1st: losing tch whn p.u 12th: lame* **66/1**

1P-6 **F** **Phone Home (IRE)**19 2404 8-10-9 **123**.......................(v) IanPopham
(Nick Mitchell) *chsd ldrs: rdn 14th: wkng whn fell next: fatally injured* **33/1**

12-2 **U** **Morning Reggie**207 128 6-10-8 **122**............................ LeightonAspell
(Oliver Sherwood) *hld up in midfield: blnd bdly and uns rdr 3rd* **14/1**

5m 53.0s (6.00) **Going Correction** +0.35s/f (Yiel) **16** Ran SP% **126.1**
Speed ratings (Par 107): **103,99,99,95,95 94,93,87,80, , , , ,**
CSF £133.84 CT £902.99 TOTE £5.40: £1.70, £6.60, £2.10, £6.00; EX 191.30 Trifecta £1614.20 Part won..

Owner The Large G & T Partnership **Bred** Maurice Goin **Trained** Upper Lambourn, Berks

FOCUS
Actual race distance 2m 6f 150yds. A very competitive handicap chase and something of a war of attrition. The jumping of quite a few of these left plenty to be desired, but there is no arguing with how impressive the winner was. He's a potential 150+ chaser.

2781 BET365 H'CAP HURDLE (10 hdls) 2m 2f 183y
1:50 (1:54) (Class 2) (0-150,138) 4-Y-O+**£22,743** (£6,678; £3,339; £1,669)

Form RPR

10-P **1** **Royal Guardsman (IRE)**203 197 8-11-1 **127**.................. GavinSheehan 131+
(Ali Stronge) *led: rdn and mstke 2 out: hdd between last 2: battled bk u.p to ld again 1f out: hld on cl home: all out* **14/1**

64- **2** *hd* **Ibis Du Rheu (FR)**284 4280 4-11-5 **131**..............(t1) SamTwiston-Davies 134
(Paul Nicholls) *hld up in tch in last pair: effrt to chse ldrs and lft 4th 2 out: drvn last: chsd wnr fnl 100yds: styd on and grad clsd: hld cl home* **4/1**2

26-6 **3** *2 1/4* **Ma Filleule (FR)**28 2199 7-11-8 **134**............................... NicodeBoinville 136
(Nicky Henderson) *chsd ldrs: wnt 2nd bef 3 out: rdn to ld between last 2: hdd 1f out: no ex and lost 2nd fnl 100yds: wknd towards fin* **3/1**1

10-3 **4** *8* **Heath Hunter (IRE)**17 2446 8-11-8 **134**..................(bt) TomScudamore 128
(David Pipe) *in tch: effrt to chse ldrs after 3 out: 4th and no ex last: wknd fnl 150yds* **8/1**

1P-3 **5** *15* **Sir Ivan**28 2202 5-11-2 **128**..1 NoelFehily 106
(Harry Fry) *t.k.h: hld up in last pair: lost tch and j.rt 3 out: no ch but plugged on to pass btn horses flat* **5/1**3

40/6 **6** *4* **Fitzwilly**18 2415 5-10-8 **120**.................................(p) ConorO'Farrell 95
(Mick Channon) *chsd wnr tl bef 3 out: j. slowly and lost pl 3 out: wl btn whn lft modest 6th 2 out* **25/1**

7 *1* **Auenwirbel (GER)**32 4-11-6 **132**............................ RobertDunne 105
(Laura Young) *hld up in tch in last pair: hit 5th: shortlived effrt after 3 out: btn whn lft 5th next: sn wknd* **33/1**

61-1 **8** *2 3/4* **Dubawi Island (FR)**26 2247 6-11-9 **135**........................ AidanColeman 105
(Venetia Williams) *in tch in midfield: lost pl and dropped to rr on long run after 7th: lost tch 3 out* **5/1**3

-212 **U** **Laurium**36 2052 5-11-7 **138**........................... FreddieMitchell(5) 127
(Nicky Henderson) *chsd ldrs: effrt after 3 out: 4th and struggling whn mstke and uns rdr 2 out* **6/1**

4m 52.85s (4.85) **Going Correction** +0.35s/f (Yiel)
WFA 4 from 5yo+ 7lb **9** Ran SP% **117.2**
Speed ratings (Par 109): **103,102,101,98,92 90,90,89,**
CSF £71.38 CT £218.39 TOTE £19.50: £4.20, £2.20, £1.60; EX 95.80 Trifecta £1481.90.

Owner Camilla & Rosie Nock **Bred** Gerard Nock **Trained** Eastbury, Berks

FOCUS
Actual race distance 2m 3f 50yds. This wasn't especially strong for the money on offer, and the pace was fairly steady. The winner is rated to his mark.

2782 BET365 LONG DISTANCE HURDLE (GRADE 2) (12 hdls) 3m 52y
2:25 (2:26) (Class 1) 4-Y-O+ **£25,627** (£9,616; £4,815; £2,398; £1,206)

Form RPR

51-2 **1** **Thistlecrack**213 21 7-11-4 150............................ TomScudamore 161+
(Colin Tizzard) *hld up in tch: trckd ldrs on long run after 9th: chsd ldr bef 2 out: rdn and clsd between last 2: j. into ld last: styd on: rdn out* **7/2**3

2U-F **2** *6* **Deputy Dan (IRE)**19 2399 7-11-0 144.................(b) LeightonAspell 151
(Oliver Sherwood) *chsd ldrs: wnt 2nd 5th tl led bef 3 out: rdn between last 2: hdd and blnd last: no ex: tired but hld on to 2nd cl home* **16/1**

412- **3** *1/2* **Cole Harden (IRE)**231 5273 6-11-8 164.......................(t) GavinSheehan 158
(Warren Greatrex) *led: rdn and hdd bef 3 out: 3rd and wl outpcd bef 2 out: rallied u.p flat: kpt on and pressing for 2nd towards fin* **2/1**2

12-3 **4** *1/2* **Aqalim**28 2198 5-11-0 152...........................(b1) AidanColeman 149
(John Ferguson) *in tch: dropped to rr 4th: pushed along 8th: reminders and struggling 9th: kpt on u.p between last 2: pressing for 2nd towards fin: no ch for wnr* **9/1**

251- **5** *24* **Whisper (FR)**231 5273 7-11-8 167............................ NicodeBoinville 144
(Nicky Henderson) *chsd ldr tl 4th: 3rd and rdn on long run after 9th: 4th and wl hld between last 2: btn whn lost action fnl 150yds: dismntd sn after fin* **6/4**1

6m 18.25s (378.25) **5** Ran SP% **111.4**
CSF £39.83 TOTE £4.30: £1.90, £3.10; EX 39.30 Trifecta £106.30.

Owner John and Heather Snook **Bred** R F And S D Knipe **Trained** Milborne Port, Dorset

FOCUS
Actual race distance 3m 214yds. This Grade 2 contest has been won by some of the greats, with Baracouda (twice), Inglis Drever (three times) and Big Buck's (four times) all successful since 2003. The winners of the Grade 1 staying hurdles at both the Cheltenham and Aintree festivals back in the spring were present this year, so despite the small field the race didn't lack quality. They didn't seem to go a great pace until the tempo quickened after halfway, but even so they appeared to finish very tired in the conditions. Something of a surprise result with the big two beaten, though one of them could be forgiven to a degree. Thistlecrack is closing in on the level of a World Hurdle contender. Cole Harden ran to the level of his run in this last year.

2783 HENNESSY GOLD CUP CHASE (H'CAP) (GRADE 3) (21 fncs) 3m 1f 214y
3:00 (3:02) (Class 1) 4-Y-O+
£113,900 (£42,740; £21,400; £10,660; £5,360; £2,680)

Form RPR

04-1 **1** **Smad Place (FR)**26 2242 8-11-4 **155**..................... WayneHutchinson 173+
(Alan King) *j.rt: chsd ldrs: wnt 2nd after 5th tl led 10th: mde rest: drew clr 3 out: styd on strly: rdn out: impressive* **7/1**3

0R-3 **2** *12* **Theatre Guide (IRE)**29 2171 8-10-2 **139**...................(t) PaddyBrennan 148+
(Colin Tizzard) *hld up in rr: hdwy after 11th: mstke 15th: 7th and wl in tch 17th: rdn after 3 out: wnt 3rd sn after last: kpt on u.p to go 2nd nr fin: no threat to wnr* **12/1**

0-04 **3** *nk* **First Lieutenant (IRE)**16 2464 10-10-10 **147**..................(p) MarkEnright 152
(M F Morris, Ire) *in tch in midfield: hdwy 12th: chsd ldrs 17th: rdn after 3 out: outpcd by wnr but wnt 2nd between last 2: no imp and one pce after: lost 2nd nr fin* **20/1**

P3-2 **4** *9* **Fingal Bay (IRE)**26 2242 9-10-7 **144**........................ RichardJohnson 142
(Philip Hobbs) *chsd ldr tl led 3rd: hmpd by loose horse: hdd 10th: chsd wnr after: hit 15th: outpcd after 3 out: hit 2 out and lost 2nd between last 2: mstke last: wknd but hld on to 4th flat* **12/1**

21-1 **5** *1/2* **Saphir Du Rheu (FR)**27 2215 6-11-12 **163**........... SamTwiston-Davies 160
(Paul Nicholls) *chsd ldrs: cl 3rd and blnd 15th: rdn and outpcd after 3 out: wl hld between last: battling for 4th and wknd flat* **9/2**1

P0-1 **6** *3 3/4* **Bobs Worth (IRE)**21 2334 10-11-2 **153**........................ NicodeBoinville 145
(Nicky Henderson) *hld up in rr: nvr on terms: struggling and mstke 16th: styd on to pass btn horses fr 2 out: nvr trbld ldrs* **11/2**2

4P-F **7** *4* **The Giant Bolster**213 22 10-11-5 **156**........................ TomScudamore 145
(David Bridgwater) *led tl 3rd: chsd ldrs after: mstke 16th: struggling 18th: 6th and wknd after 3 out* **33/1**

10-6 **8** *8* **Ned Stark (IRE)**28 2187 7-10-3 **140**............................ DenisO'Regan 121
(Alan King) *chsd ldrs tl 18th: sn rdn and struggling: wknd after 3 out: t.o* **8/1**

0F-0 **9** *9* **Houblon Des Obeaux (FR)**28 2187 8-11-5 **156**........... AidanColeman 127
(Venetia Williams) *a towards rr: rdn 13th: lost tch after 17th: t.o* **8/1**

3-01 **10** *1* **Benbens (IRE)**34 2082 10-10-4 **144**.............................. RyanHatch(3) 113
(Nigel Twiston-Davies) *midfield: rdn after 16th: stl cl but no imp u.p bef 18th: wknd 3 out: t.o* **33/1**

4-42 **11** *3 1/2* **Urano (FR)**33 2118 7-10-3 **140**... DannyMullins 108
(W P Mullins, Ire) *hld up towards rr: hdwy and hit 13th: midfield and mstke 15th: j.rt 16th: clsd enough 18th: rdn and btn next: wknd: bhd and eased flat: t.o* **22/1**

3U0- **P** **Al Co (FR)**224 5392 10-10-4 **141**.. SeanBowen
(Peter Bowen) *a towards rr: lost tch after 11th: t.o whn blnd 18th: p.u next* **66/1**

10-2 **U** **The Young Master**27 2215 6-10-10 **150**..............(p) MrSWaley-Cohen(3)
(Neil Mulholland) *midfield whn mstke and uns rdr 1st* **10/1**

P-00 **U** **Splash Of Ginge**14 2483 7-10-7 **149**.......................... JamieBargary(5)
(Nigel Twiston-Davies) *midfield: nt fluent 14th: losing pl whn mstke and uns rdr 17th* **25/1**

15P- **P** **If In Doubt (IRE)**236 5224 7-10-12 **149**......................... BarryGeraghty
(Philip Hobbs) *mstkes: hld up in rr: losing tch whn p.u 17th* **8/1**

6m 45.3s (-0.70) **Going Correction** +0.35s/f (Yiel) **15** Ran SP% **124.2**
Speed ratings (Par 113): **115,111,111,108,108 107,105,103,100,100 99, , ,**
CSF £81.76 CT £1631.56 TOTE £8.90: £2.90, £4.20, £6.40; EX 116.10 Trifecta £2301.70.

Owner Mrs Peter Andrews **Bred** Eric Aubree & Mme Maryse Aubree **Trained** Barbury Castle, Wilts

FOCUS
Actual race distance 3m 2f 62yds. A high-quality edition even without Coneygree, whose absence with a foot problem meant that the weights were raised by 9lb and left all the field in the handicap proper. They went a proper gallop and this is very solid form. Smad Place rates a realistic Gold Cup contender on this evidence.

2784 BET365 H'CAP CHASE (FOR THE JIM JOEL MEMORIAL TROPHY) (13 fncs) 2m 92y
3:35 (3:36) (Class 2) (0-150,147) 4-Y-O+
£21,896 (£6,468; £3,234; £1,617; £808; £406)

Form RPR

24-P **1** **Grey Gold (IRE)**212 47 10-11-12 **147**........................ JamieMoore 155
(Kerry Lee) *hld up in tch: clsd to trck ldrs 9th: led next: drvn between last 2: hdd flat: battled bk gamely to ld again fnl 100yds: drvn out* **10/1**

24-0 **2** *1* **Whispering Harry**12 2540 6-10-2 **123**........................ JamesDavies 129
(Henry Oliver) *chsd ldr tl 3rd: chsd ldr tl led next: hdd 9th: chsd wnr 2 out: drvn and led sn after last: hdd fnl 100yds: no ex* **10/1**

3-23 **3** *8* **Pearls Legend**15 2468 8-10-13 **134**........................ TomScudamore 132
(John Spearing) *led tl 3rd: chsd ldrs after: wnt 2nd 6th tl led 9th: hdd next: rallied between last 2 and pressed ldrs again last: no ex and wknd fnl 100yds* **7/1**

1-64 **4** *2 3/4* **Mountain King**29 2171 6-11-3 **138**........................ RichardJohnson 136
(Philip Hobbs) *mstkes: hld up in rr: hdwy 3 out: cl 4th and hit last: no ex and wknd flat* **8/1**

2P-P **5** *3 1/2* **Eastlake (IRE)**35 2059 9-11-12 **147**........................ BarryGeraghty 139
(Jonjo O'Neill) *hld up in tch towards rr: clsd 9th: chsd ldrs next: rdn and no ex after 2 out: wknd flat* **16/1**

U000 **6** *2 1/2* **Owen Na View (IRE)**15 2468 7-10-6 **127**..............(t) DavidEngland 117
(Fergal O'Brien) *hld up in tch in rr: clsd after 8th: rdn and no imp after 3 out: 6th and plugged on same pce between last 2* **50/1**

1450 **7** *6* **Fairyinthewind (IRE)**15 2468 6-9-9 **121** oh1..........(t) DavidNoonan(5) 104
(Brendan Powell) *in tch in midfield: chsd ldrs 8th: rdn and no ex 10th: wknd between last 2: fin lame* **33/1**

00-0 **P** **Parsnip Pete**208 103 9-11-4 **139**...........................(t) PaddyBrennan
(Tom George) *hld up in tch in rr: pushed along bef 9th: rdn and wknd bef 3 out: bhd whn p.u 2 out* **16/1**

-130 **P** **Lough Kent**15 2468 6-11-4 **139**...................................... NicodeBoinville
(Nicky Henderson) *in tch in midfield: chsd ldrs after 9th: rdn after next: no ex and btn 2 out: wl hld whn p.u last* **11/2**2

100- **P** **Stellar Notion (IRE)**[263] 4694 7-11-2 **137**.............(t) SamTwiston-Davies
(Paul Nicholls) *t.k.h: chsd ldr: led 3rd tl next: pushed along and lost pl after 8th: wknd after 3 out: wl hld whn eased and p.u last* **9/4**[1]

/13- **P** **Gardefort (FR)**[322] 3622 6-10-12 **133**.............................. AidanColeman
(Venetia Williams) *t.k.h: hld up in tch in midfield: mstke 9th: btn next: losing tch whn p.u 3 out* **6/1**[3]

4m 17.1s (9.10) **Going Correction** +0.35s/f (Yiel) **11** Ran SP% **118.9**
Speed ratings (Par 109): **91,90,86,85,83 82,79,, ,**
CSF £105.76 CT £754.76 TOTE £12.00: £3.50, £2.60, £2.10; EX 125.20 Trifecta £1012.90.
Owner Mrs M A Boden **Bred** James Keegan And Jeff Hamilton **Trained** Byton, H'fords

FOCUS
Actual race distance 2m 135yds. A competitive handicap chase to close the card and they went a solid pace. The winner was on a decent mark despite top weight and is rated to his best.
T/Plt: £375.60 to a £1 stake. Pool: £175,272.89 - 340.57 winning units. T/Qpdt: £112.80 to a £1 stake. Pool: £15,058.31 - 98.70 winning units. **Steve Payne**

NEWCASTLE (L-H)
Saturday, November 28

OFFICIAL GOING: Soft (5.4)
Wind: Fairly strong, half against Weather: Overcast

2785 WEATHERBYS BANK NOVICES' LIMITED H'CAP CHASE (19 fncs) 2m 7f 91y
12:00 (12:00) (Class 3) (0-135,134)
4-Y-0+ **£7,797** (£2,289; £1,144; £572)

Form RPR

50-2 **1** **Smooth Stepper**[32] 2122 6-11-1 **127**.. DannyCook 134+
(Sue Smith) *prom: hdwy to ld 3 out: sn pushed along: edgd lft and hld on wl fr last* **7/2**[1]

5-51 **2** ¾ **Wizards Bridge**[17] 2442 6-11-5 **131**...............................(p) BrendanPowell 136
(Colin Tizzard) *trckd ldrs: blkd 11th: rdn and outpcd bef 3 out: rallied bef last: kpt on u.p to take 2nd cl home* **7/2**[1]

10-3 **3** *hd* **Lucematic**[205] 158 9-9-12 **115** oh1.......................... DiarmuidO'Regan(5) 120
(Chris Grant) *hld up bhd ldng gp: stdy hdwy 4 out: effrt and cl 3rd whn hit and outpcd 2 out: kpt on fr last* **40/1**

14/0 **4** *hd* **The Ramblin Kid**[27] 2211 7-10-5 **117**........................ DarylJacob 123
(Micky Hammond) *led to 2nd: pressed ldr: led 6 out to 3 out: sn rdn along: cl up tl no ex and lost two pls cl home* **12/1**

P-52 **5** 7 **Spirit Of Shankly**[21] 2332 7-11-6 **132**..............................(bt) TomO'Brien 131
(Charlie Longsdon) *hld up in tch: stdy hdwy whn j.rt 11th: rdn and outpcd 5 out: no imp fr next* **13/2**[3]

20-1 **6** 2¾ **Shimla Dawn (IRE)**[27] 2211 7-11-8 **134**.............................. JakeGreenall 130
(Mark Walford) *cl up: led 2nd to 6 out: rdn and wknd fr 3 out* **5/1**[2]

1F-2 **7** 41 **Cultram Abbey**[27] 2211 8-11-1 **127**.. BrianHarding 81
(Nicky Richards) *nt fluent on occasions: prom: lost pl 9th: rdn fr next: lost tch fr 5 out* **5/1**[2]

3103 **P** **Iora Glas (IRE)**[30] 2145 6-10-3 **115**... AlainCawley
(Fergal O'Brien) *nt fluent in rr: struggling fnl circ: lost tch and p.u 6 out* **12/1**

2-UP **P** **U Name It (IRE)**[19] 2397 7-11-3 **129**.. PeterBuchanan
(R Mike Smith) *nt fluent in rr: lost tch fr 1/2-way: t.o whn p.u bef 12th* **25/1**

6m 14.0s (-8.50) **Going Correction** -0.05s/f (Good) **9** Ran SP% **112.8**
Speed ratings (Par 107): **112,111,111,111,109 108,93, ,**
CSF £16.32 CT £403.41 TOTE £5.00: £2.60, £1.50, £7.00; EX 17.70 Trifecta £588.60.
Owner Mrs Aafke Clarke **Bred** Paul Zetter **Trained** High Eldwick, W Yorks

FOCUS
All rail in normal position on fresh ground. The going was Soft after overnight rain and the wind made it more difficult. A competitive looking novices' handicap chase as evidenced by the market. The pace was steady but it looked hard work and the principals finished in a heap. Small steps up from the first two.

2786 STP CONSTRUCTION H'CAP CHASE (13 fncs) 2m 75y
12:30 (12:30) (Class 5) (0-100,93)
4-Y-0+ **£3,508** (£1,030; £515; £257)

Form RPR

0300 **1** **Caraline (FR)**[160] 805 4-10-3 **80**.. JoeColliver(3) 89+
(Micky Hammond) *hld up in tch: smooth hdwy to ld bef 3 out: sn clr on bridle: easily* **8/1**[3]

/2-2 **2** 12 **Mumgos Debut (IRE)**[17] 2430 7-11-11 **92**..............................(t) PeterBuchanan 93
(Lucinda Russell) *led to bef 4th: w ldr: regained ld 5 out: nt fluent next: hdd and rdn bef 3 out: plugged on: no ch w wnr* **5/2**[1]

6/PP **3** 1½ **Rupert Bear**[35] 2069 9-11-7 **93**... MissCWalton(5) 93
(James Walton) *w ldr: led bef 4th: hit and pckd next: hdd 5 out: rdn bef next: kpt on same pce fr 3 out* **14/1**

2404 **4** 2 **Seventeen Black (IRE)**[4] 2705 7-11-4 **85**........................... DannyCook 85
(Stuart Coltherd) *hld up in tch: hdwy to chse ldrs 4th: blnd and rdn 5 out: outpcd fr 3 out* **9/1**

05-2 **5** 1¼ **Trouble In Paris (IRE)**[22] 2321 8-9-11 **71**.................(t) LorcanMurtagh(7) 67
(Barry Murtagh) *hld up: niggled along 4th: effrt 5 out: rdn and outpcd fr next* **5/2**[1]

22-5 **6** 1½ **Alfred Oats**[17] 2430 11-11-5 **86**...............................(t) HenryBrooke 80
(Robert Goldie) *prom: lost pl 5 out: struggling fr next* **8/1**[3]

513P **7** 2½ **Odds On Dan (IRE)**[28] 2191 9-10-6 **80**..............................(tp) DeanPratt(7) 73
(Lucinda Egerton) *bhd: drvn and outpcd after 6 out: struggling fr next* **7/1**[2]

3 **8** 25 **Afterclass (IRE)**[22] 2320 7-11-3 **91**.................................(p) MrKitAlexander(7) 57
(N W Alexander) *prom: drvn and struggling 5 out: lost tch bef next: t.o* **20/1**

4m 21.4s (0.30) **Going Correction** -0.05s/f (Good)
WFA 4 from 7yo+ 7lb **8** Ran SP% **113.3**
Speed ratings (Par 103): **97,91,90,89,88 87,86,74**
CSF £28.92 CT £276.64 TOTE £10.50: £2.40, £1.20, £2.80; EX 35.70 Trifecta £827.00.
Owner Give Every Man His Due **Bred** Mme Caroline Elizabeth Huni **Trained** Middleham, N Yorks

FOCUS
The pace was steady in this low-grade handicap chase but it produced an easy winner. H was well in on the best of his French form and can probably win again.

2787 WEATHERBYS BANK "THE FRENCH FURZE" NOVICES' HURDLE (13 hdls) 2m 6f
1:00 (1:00) (Class 2) 4-Y-0+
£11,260 (£3,326; £1,663; £831; £415; £208)

Form RPR

5-21 **1** **Ballydine (IRE)**[30] 2152 5-11-3 **132**.. TomO'Brien 136+
(Charlie Longsdon) *trckd ldrs: mstke 3rd: effrt and pressing ldr whn hit 2 out: sn rdn: led run-in: kpt on wl* **2/1**[1]

31 **2** ¾ **Jonniesofa (IRE)**[21] 2338 5-11-3 **119**.. RWalsh 132
(Rose Dobbin) *led to 2nd: w ldr: regained ld 3 out: rdn after next: hdd run-in: kpt on same pce u.p* **6/1**[3]

21 **3** 7 **Delusionofgrandeur (IRE)**[22] 2319 5-11-3 **115**.................. DannyCook 125
(Sue Smith) *cl up: led 2nd: hit 5th: rdn and hdd 3 out: outpcd by first two fr next* **14/1**

11-2 **4** ¾ **Another Bill (IRE)**[28] 2189 5-10-12 **0**................................ BrianHarding 121
(Nicky Richards) *nt fluent on occasions: hld up in midfield: rdn and outpcd after 4 out: plugged on fr 2 out: nt pce to chal* **6/1**[3]

22-1 **5** ½ **Dueling Banjos**[26] 2239 5-11-3 **0**.. DavidBass 124
(Kim Bailey) *prom tl rdn and outpcd after 3 out: n.d after* **5/1**[2]

4 **6** 15 **Rivabodiva (IRE)**[49] 1854 5-10-5 **0**...................................... DerekFox 102
(Lucinda Russell) *hld up: bdly hmpd 4 out: sn rdn along: wknd fr next* **25/1**

-211 **7** 15 **Calivigny (IRE)**[17] 2432 6-11-6 **125**.................................. LucyAlexander 107
(N W Alexander) *t.k.h in midfield: drvn and outpcd after 4 out: struggling fr next* **12/1**

-233 **8** 12 **Presenting Junior (IRE)**[22] 2319 8-10-12 **124**................... HenryBrooke 77
(Martin Todhunter) *bhd: drvn along bef 4 out: wknd bef next* **40/1**

13 **F** **Wholestone (IRE)**[30] 2152 4-10-12 **0**.................................... DarylJacob
(Nigel Twiston-Davies) *nt fluent on occasions: in tch on outside: 3 l down and niggled along whn fell 4 out* **6/1**[3]

5m 39.6s (3.60) **Going Correction** -0.325s/f (Good)
WFA 4 from 5yo+ 8lb **9** Ran SP% **113.5**
Speed ratings (Par 109): **80,79,77,76,76 71,65,61,**
CSF £14.08 TOTE £2.70: £1.20, £2.20, £3.00; EX 12.20 Trifecta £95.00.
Owner Alan Halsall **Bred** Fergal O'Mahoney **Trained** Over Norton, Oxon

FOCUS
A race that has thrown up some smart sorts in it relatively short history, including the graded winners Tazbar and Bygones Of Brid, plus another placed at the top level. The field included five last-time out winners and a couple of bumper scorers and produced a close finish, but was probably an ordinary renewal. The winner set a decent standard.

2788 MARRIOTT GOSFORTH PARK H'CAP CHASE (16 fncs) 2m 4f 19y
1:30 (1:32) (Class 4) (0-115,115) 4-Y-0+ **£3,768** (£1,106; £553; £276)

Form RPR

21-P **1** **Boric**[15] 2477 7-10-11 **105**...............................(p) GrantCockburn(5) 113
(Simon Waugh) *cl up: pushed along whn lft 2nd after 4 out: rdn next: led last: styd on wl* **12/1**

230- **2** ½ **The Orange Rogue (IRE)**[238] 5134 8-10-8 **102**..... StephenMulqueen(5) 111
(N W Alexander) *nt fluent on occasions: led: rdn whn hit 2 out: hdd last: rallied: hld nr fin* **7/1**

0-26 **3** 13 **Dr Moloney (IRE)**[33] 2105 8-11-1 **111**.......................... AnthonyFox(7) 106
(S R B Crawford, Ire) *hld up: stdy hdwy and in tch bef 4 out: rdn bef next: sn outpcd by front two* **16/1**

0P-U **4** 8 **Frankie's Promise (IRE)**[17] 2430 7-11-7 **110**.................. LucyAlexander 96
(N W Alexander) *hld up: rdn along after 5 out: no imp fr next* **6/1**[3]

65-3 **5** 1½ **Pamak D'Airy (FR)**[212] 36 12-11-1 **107**...........................(p) TonyKelly(3) 92
(Henry Hogarth) *t.k.h: hld up in tch: nt fluent 1st: effrt whn lft 4th 4 out: wknd fr next* **16/1**

4-45 **6** 18 **Bonzo Bing (IRE)**[45] 1902 7-11-12 **115**..............................(p) HenryBrooke 82
(Martin Todhunter) *chsd ldr to 9th: cl up tl outpcd 5 out: struggling fr next* **9/2**[2]

P-33 **7** 7 **Safari Journey (USA)**[194] 381 11-10-13 **109**.................(p) DeanPratt(7) 71
(Lucinda Egerton) *hld up on ins: outpcd 8th: mstke 11th: nt fluent next: sn btn* **25/1**

1-00 **8** *shd* **Resolute Reformer (IRE)**[19] 2400 6-10-12 **104**.................. DerekFox(3) 64
(Stuart Coltherd) *hld up in tch: hit 5th: sn lost pl and rdn along: struggling fr 10th* **9/1**

10-P **9** 7 **Scimon Templar (FR)**[21] 2342 7-10-10 **102**..................... GrahamWatters(3) 57
(Rose Dobbin) *mstkes: hld up: drvn and outpcd 5 out: sn wknd* **9/1**

-333 **U** **Swing Hard (IRE)**[23] 2295 7-11-4 **107**..................................... DannyCook
(Sue Smith) *trckd ldrs: wnt 2nd 9th: 3 l 2nd and rdn whn sprawled bdly 4 out: sn uns rdr* **5/2**[1]

5m 24.0s (-3.20) **Going Correction** -0.05s/f (Good) **10** Ran SP% **116.8**
Speed ratings (Par 105): **104,103,98,95,94 87,84,84,81,**
CSF £93.75 CT £1357.76 TOTE £16.10: £4.00, £2.90, £3.30; EX 199.80 Trifecta £1646.80 Part won..
Owner Mrs E C York **Bred** Mrs E C York **Trained** Mitford, Northumberland

FOCUS
An ordinary handicap chase which featured two previous winners of the race. Not strong form but a step up from the winner.

2789 STANJAMES.COM FIGHTING FIFTH HURDLE (GRADE 1) (9 hdls) 2m 98y
2:05 (2:05) (Class 1) 4-Y-0+
£63,585 (£23,956; £11,989; £5,989; £3,005; £1,502)

Form RPR

P2-1 **1** **Identity Thief (IRE)**[29] 2177 5-11-7 **154**................................... BJCooper 164+
(Henry De Bromhead, Ire) *led to 4th: chsd ldr: nt fluent 3 out: rdn to ld next: nt fluent and hdd last: rallied u.p to regain ld towards fin* **6/1**[3]

12-2 **2** *nk* **Top Notch (FR)**[7] 2640 4-11-7 **158**.. DarylJacob 162
(Nicky Henderson) *pressed wnr: led 4th: hdd and rdn 2 out: rallied and regained ld last: kpt on u.p run-in: hdd towards fin* **9/2**[2]

1-03 **3** 10 **Wicklow Brave**[13] 2532 6-11-7 **166**.. RWalsh 153
(W P Mullins, Ire) *nt fluent on occasions: chsd ldrs: stdy hdwy and cl up bef 3 out: rdn whn nt fluent next: sn outpcd by first two* **2/1**[1]

12-4 **4** 16 **Purple Bay (IRE)**[21] 2334 6-11-7 **159**.................................(b[1]) DavidBass 138
(John Ferguson) *hld up: pushed along and outpcd bef 4 out: hung lft next: plugged on fr 2 out: no imp* **14/1**

35-2 **5** 6 **Intense Tango**[28] 2199 4-11-0 **138**.................................... HenryBrooke 122
(K R Burke) *t.k.h early: hld up: effrt after 4 out: rdn and wknd fr next* **50/1**

P-11 **6** 8 **Irving**[7] 2640 7-11-7 **162**... NickScholfield 126
(Paul Nicholls) *hld up on outside: niggled along whn mstke and outpcd 4 out: struggling fr next* **2/1**[1]

116- **7** 15 **Beltor**[260] 4736 4-11-7 **143**... TomO'Brien 106
(Robert Stephens) *t.k.h: in tch: drvn after 4 out: wkng whn hit next: sn btn* **22/1**

3m 57.8s (-12.20) **Going Correction** -0.325s/f (Good)
WFA 4 from 5yo+ 7lb **7** Ran SP% **112.1**
Speed ratings (Par 117): **117,116,111,103,100 96,89**
CSF £31.68 TOTE £6.70: £2.80, £2.10; EX 23.70 Trifecta £87.90.
Owner Gigginstown House Stud **Bred** Cathal Ennis **Trained** Knockeen, Co Waterford

FOCUS
One of the top races for 2m hurdlers and, although the last winner of this to take the Champion Hurdle was Punjabi in 2009, four subsequent winners had gone on to be placed at Cheltenham. Two came clear in the straight here and both look progressive. Identity Thief is worth a place in the Champion Hurdle line-up on this form.

2790 AT THE RACES REHEARSAL CHASE H'CAP (LISTED RACE) (19 fncs) 2m 7f 91y

2:40 (2:40) (Class 1) 4-Y-0+

£34,170 (£12,822; £6,420; £3,198; £1,608; £804)

Form RPR

24-1 **1** **Wakanda (IRE)**[29] 2171 6-11-4 **145**.................... DannyCook 157
(Sue Smith) *w ldr: led after 5 out: rdn 3 out: edgd lft after next: hrd pressed and hld on gamely fr last* **6/1**[3]

31-0 **2** *½* **Virak (FR)**[28] 2187 6-11-5 **153**.................... HarryCobden(7) 164
(Paul Nicholls) *hld up in midfield: hdwy to chse wnr 4 out: effrt and 1 l down last: kpt on: hld towards fin* **11/2**[2]

U12- **3** *7* **The Last Samuri (IRE)**[224] 5388 7-10-13 **140**.................... DavidBass 144
(Kim Bailey) *hld up bhd ldng gp: stdy hdwy 11th: drvn and outpcd after 5 out: rallied and cl 3rd bef 2 out: drvn and outpcd fr last* **5/1**[1]

3-31 **4** *½* **Final Assault (IRE)**[17] 2431 6-10-9 **139**.................... DerekFox(3) 145
(Lucinda Russell) *hld up: smooth hdwy and in tch bef 4 out: rdn next: outpcd fr 2 out* **8/1**

40-1 **5** *3* **Saroque (IRE)**[25] 2261 8-10-5 **132**.................... LiamTreadwell 134
(Venetia Williams) *mde most to after 5 out: rallied: rdn and wknd fr 2 out* **10/1**

34-2 **6** *1 ¼* **Shotavodka (IRE)**[27] 2214 9-10-7 **137**....................(p) KieronEdgar(3) 136
(David Pipe) *hld up: drvn along after 5 out: no imp fr next* **14/1**

U-00 **7** *6* **Milborough (IRE)**[27] 2214 9-10-13 **143**.................... GrahamWatters(3) 136
(Ian Duncan) *chsd ldrs: rdn 5 out: rallied: wknd fr 3 out* **20/1**

5-0P **8** *1* **Cloudy Too (IRE)**[17] 2436 9-11-1 **142**.................... SeanQuinlan 136
(Sue Smith) *hld up on outside: hdwy to chse ldrs whn hit 4 out: rdn and wknd next* **10/1**

1U-2 **P** **Masters Hill (IRE)**[19] 2399 9-11-3 **144**....................(p) BrendanPowell
(Colin Tizzard) *midfield: nt fluent 11th: blnd 13th: rdn and outpcd whn hit 4 out: sn btn: lost tch and p.u bef last* **5/1**[1]

P1-6 **F** **William Money (IRE)**[35] 2068 8-9-10 **128**.................... DiarmuidO'Regan(5)
(Chris Grant) *hld up: nt fluent 1st: fell next* **20/1**

4P-6 **P** **Man With Van (IRE)**[7] 9-10-8 **135**....................(vt) PeterBuchanan
(S R B Crawford, Ire) *nt fluent in rr: struggling fr 11th: lost tch and p.u bef 4 out* **33/1**

1114 **P** **Ballykan**[36] 2055 5-10-9 **136**....................(t) DarylJacob
(Nigel Twiston-Davies) *prom: checked 11th: lost pl bef 13th: sn struggling: t.o whn p.u bef 4 out* **9/1**

6m 13.7s (-8.80) **Going Correction** -0.05s/f (Good) **12 Ran SP% 117.1**
Speed ratings (Par 111): **113,112,110,110,109 108,106,106, ,**
CSF £36.97 CT £178.85 TOTE £7.30: £2.50, £2.10, £2.00; EX 44.80 Trifecta £177.50.
Owner M B Scholey & R H Scholey **Bred** Bluegate Stud **Trained** High Eldwick, W Yorks

FOCUS
A valuable prize produced a decent field for this Listed handicap chase and the two top weights, both just 6yos, had it between them from two out. Rock-solid form. The winner is on the upgrade and rates a smart handicapper.

2791 EBF STALLIONS "NATIONAL HUNT" MAIDEN HURDLE (QUALIFIER) (9 hdls) 2m 98y

3:15 (3:19) (Class 5) 4-6-Y-0 **£3,898** (£1,144; £572; £286)

Form RPR

144- **1** **Baby Bach (IRE)**[220] 5469 5-10-7 0.................... AnthonyFox(7) 124+
(S R B Crawford, Ire) *hld up on outside: smooth hdwy bef 3 out: led appr next: sn clr: rdn run-in: unchal* **3/1**[2]

52 **2** *13* **Good Vibration (FR)**[18] 2423 4-11-0 0.................... SeanQuinlan 109+
(Sue Smith) *cl up: led bef 3 out to appr next: plugged on fr last: no ch w wnr* **5/1**[3]

66F **3** *2 ¾* **Seven Devils (IRE)**[28] 2189 5-10-11 0.................... DerekFox(3) 105
(Lucinda Russell) *hld up: shkn up and hdwy whn hit 3 out: kpt on fr next: nvr able to chal* **40/1**

1-54 **4** *½* **Benny's Secret (IRE)**[33] 2101 5-11-0 0.................... LucyAlexander 104
(N W Alexander) *hld up on ins: stdy hdwy bef 4 out: rdn next: kpt on fr 2 out: no imp* **12/1**

3-00 **5** *3* **Buckled**[23] 2294 5-10-8 0 ow1.................... StevenFox(7) 102
(Sandy Thomson) *hld up: pushed along and outpcd whn nt mstke 3 out: kpt on fr next: nvr a factor* **33/1**

2 **6** *hd* **Golden Investment (IRE)**[21] 2337 6-11-0 0.................... BrianHarding 101
(Donald McCain) *t.k.h: cl up: effrt and ev ch 3 out: hit next: sn rdn and outpcd* **7/4**[1]

0 **7** *2 ¼* **Never Learn (IRE)**[193] 392 4-11-0 0.................... BrendanPowell 99
(Colin Tizzard) *in tch: drvn and outpcd after 4 out: rallied and hung lft next: no imp fr 2 out* **10/1**

06-6 **8** *4 ½* **Dimple (FR)**[22] 2318 4-10-11 0.................... GrahamWatters(3) 94
(Pauline Robson) *t.k.h: hld up: stdy hdwy 4 out: pushed along and wknd after next* **40/1**

/4-0 **9** *2 ½* **Imperial Prince (IRE)**[28] 2189 6-11-0 0.................... DannyCook 91
(Sandy Thomson) *midfield: drvn and outpcd bef 4 out: btn next* **16/1**

5-60 **10** *3* **Ethan (IRE)**[37] 2025 6-10-9 0.................... MissCWalton(5) 88
(Sheena Walton) *t.k.h: led to bef 3rd: chsd ldrs tl wknd bef 3 out* **100/1**

1/ **11** *1* **Heritage Way**[655] 4205 6-10-11 0.................... TonyKelly(3) 87
(Henry Hogarth) *hld up in tch: stdy hdwy after 4 out: shkn up and hung lft after next: wknd fr 2 out* **14/1**

66 **12** *12* **Quieto Sol (FR)**[22] 2317 4-11-0 0.................... TomO'Brien 75
(Charlie Longsdon) *cl up: led bef 3rd: hdd bef 3 out: wknd qckly bef next* **22/1**

2-0P **13** *18* **Valnamixe Du Mee (FR)**[22] 2319 6-11-0 97.................... PeterBuchanan 57
(Kenny Johnson) *nt fluent in rr: struggling 4 out: sn btn* **100/1**

00-0 **P** **Rebel Roger**[14] 2498 6-10-9 0.................... StephenMulqueen(5)
(Tina Jackson) *hld up: struggling after 4 out: wknd and p.u next* **200/1**

4m 11.2s (1.20) **Going Correction** -0.325s/f (Good) **14 Ran SP% 122.0**
Speed ratings: **84,77,76,75,74 74,73,70,69,68 67,61,52,**
CSF £18.44 TOTE £3.50: £1.40, £1.80, £11.00; EX 20.60 Trifecta £722.20.
Owner Pircan Partnership **Bred** Miss Ann Twomey **Trained** Larne, Co Antrim

FOCUS
A modest maiden hurdle on paper, featuring plenty of inexperienced horses and the pace was very steady in the early stages. The winner came right away and the form is rated around the first four.
T/Jkpt: Not won. JACKPOT PLACEPOT £920.10. Pool £2,773.10 - 2.2 winning units. T/Plt: £869.60 to a £1 stake. Pool of £84389.43 - 70.84 winning tickets. T/Qpdt: £189.10 to a £1 stake. Pool of £7439.75 - 29.10 winning tickets/ **Richard Young**

2792 - 2799a (Foreign Racing) - See Raceform Interactive

2396 CARLISLE (R-H)

Sunday, November 29

OFFICIAL GOING: Heavy (chs 6.0, hdl 6.2)
Wind: Races 1-3 strong, half against, races 4 onwards fresh, half against
Weather: Overcast, showers

2800 APOLLOBET IN PLAY BETTING AMATEUR RIDERS' H'CAP HURDLE (DIV I) (14 hdls) 3m 1f

12:20 (12:25) (Class 4) (0-105,105) 4-Y-0+ **£3,119** (£967; £483; £242)

Form RPR

1-1P **1** **Courtown Oscar (IRE)**[38] 2028 6-11-6 **104**........ MrMatthewHampton(5) 119+
(Philip Kirby) *trckd ldrs: led gng wl bef 2 out: sn clr on bridle: eased down run-in* **5/2**[1]

6164 **2** *4* **Bescot Springs (IRE)**[18] 2432 10-11-0 **100**................(p) MrDDelahunt(7) 97
(Lucinda Russell) *cl up: led bef 8th: rdn and hdd bef 2 out: plugged on fr last: flattered by proximity to eased-down wnr* **9/1**

1/0- **3** *12* **Rocky Stone (IRE)**[575] 89 7-10-13 **99**.................... MrMEnnis(7) 84
(Donald McCain) *t.k.h: prom on outside: stdy hdwy bef 4 out: drvn and outpcd after next: no imp fr 2 out* **12/1**

05P/ **4** *19* **Kind Of Easy (IRE)**[260] 9-11-3 **103**.................... MrGaryBeaumont(7) 69
(Alistair Whillans) *nt fluent on occasions: hld up: pushed along and outpcd after 4 out: rallied after next: sn n.d* **66/1**

600 **5** *½* **Triumph Davis (IRE)**[31] 2148 6-10-7 **93**.................... MrJoeWright(7) 59
(Micky Hammond) *hld up bhd ldng gp: stdy hdwy bef 8th: drvn and outpcd 3 out: btn bef next* **14/1**

1PP- **6** *12* **Snuker**[254] 4893 8-10-9 **91**....................(p) MrKitAlexander(3) 45
(James Ewart) *mde most to bef 8th: drvn along next: wknd fr 3 out* **7/2**[3]

0-41 **7** *10* **Dusky Bob (IRE)**[23] 2323 10-11-2 **100**.................... MrKWood(5) 44
(Brian Ellison) *in tch: drvn along after 4 out: wknd fr next* **3/1**[2]

P-P5 **R** **Madam Lilibet (IRE)**[18] 2432 6-11-9 **105**.................... MrTHamilton(3)
(Sharon Watt) *in tch: drvn and lost pl after 2nd: lost tch fnl circ: no ch whn ref last* **7/1**

/P-P **P** **Fozy Moss**[16] 2478 9-10-0 **79**.................... MissCWalton
(Sheena Walton) *chsd ldrs: lost pl 8th: struggling fr next: t.o whn p.u 2 out* **16/1**

6m 49.7s (10.70) **Going Correction** -0.05s/f (Good) **9 Ran SP% 120.0**
Speed ratings (Par 105): **80,78,74,68,68 64,61, ,**
CSF £26.53 CT £235.08 TOTE £3.10: £1.20, £3.40, £3.70; EX 28.00 Trifecta £162.60.
Owner Nobaj Ltd **Bred** Lorcan Allen **Trained** East Appleton, N Yorks

FOCUS
Hurdles races on Inner track and rail at innermost position and distances as advertised. Chase rail out 6yds. Strong winds and heavy ground made for extremely gruelling conditions. The time for this very modest amateurs' handicap was almost a minute slower than standard.

2801 APOLLOBET EBF BRITISH STALLION STUDS "NATIONAL HUNT" NOVICES' HURDLE (QUALIFIER) (11 hdls) 2m 3f 61y

12:50 (12:52) (Class 4) 4-6-Y-0 **£3,898** (£1,144; £572; £286)

Form RPR

2/2 **1** **Alibi De Sivola (FR)**[25] 2267 5-10-12 0.................... SamTwiston-Davies 122+
(Paul Nicholls) *hld up on outside: mstke 1st: hdwy and cl up 4th: led 6th: hit 3 out: rdn last: kpt on strly: fin lame* **5/2**[2]

4 **2** *2 ½* **Takingrisks (IRE)**[34] 2100 6-10-12 0.................... BrianHarding 116
(Nicky Richards) *hld up bhd ldng gp: stdy hdwy 1/2-way: effrt and chsd wnr after 2 out: kpt on same pce fr last* **12/1**

3-22 **3** *13* **Bollin Ace**[15] 2498 4-10-12 120.................... BrianHughes 103
(Tim Easterby) *cl up: ev ch 3 out: drvn and outpcd by first two bef last* **3/1**[3]

2 **4** *6* **Egret (IRE)**[16] 2479 5-10-9 0.................... DerekFox(3) 97
(Lucinda Russell) *hld up in tch: rdn along bef 2 out: plugged on fr last: no imp* **20/1**

63 **5** *2 ¾* **Quinto**[28] 2210 5-10-12 0.................... TomO'Brien 94
(John Quinn) *t.k.h early: chsd ldrs: drvn and outpcd 2 out: btn last* **7/1**

0 **6** *2 ¼* **Veinard (FR)**[200] 285 6-10-7 0....................[1] CallumBewley(5) 95
(Robert Bewley) *hld up: hdwy on outside after 3 out: pushed along whn hit next: 4th and hld whn blnd last: wknd* **100/1**

31-2 **7** *31* **Ten Trees**[18] 2433 5-10-5 0.................... DavidBass 54
(Alan Swinbank) *in tch on ins: mstke 4th: drvn after 3 out: wknd bef next: t.o* **12/1**

8 *19* **De Bene Esse (IRE)**[273] 5-10-12 0.................... PaulMoloney 42
(Evan Williams) *prom tl rdn and wknd bef 2 out: t.o* **9/4**[1]

U0 **9** *19* **Alchimix (FR)**[15] 2498 5-10-9 0.................... JoeColliver(3) 23
(Micky Hammond) *led: nt fluent 5th: hdd next: wknd 4 out: lost tch fr next: t.o* **100/1**

5 **10** *½* **September Son (IRE)**[34] 2106 5-10-9 0.................... GrahamWatters(3) 23
(Ian Duncan) *hld up: struggling 4 out: lost tch after next: t.o* **100/1**

5m 3.6s (-5.20) **Going Correction** -0.05s/f (Good)
WFA 4 from 5yo+ 7lb **10 Ran SP% 120.0**
Speed ratings: **108,106,101,98,97 96,83,75,67,67**
CSF £31.86 TOTE £3.20: £1.40, £3.60, £1.30; EX 32.00 Trifecta £145.50.
Owner Ian Fogg & Chris Giles **Bred** Gilles Trapenard **Trained** Ditcheat, Somerset

FOCUS
Fair novice hurdle form.

2802 APOLLOBET BEST ODDS GUARANTEED H'CAP HURDLE (11 hdls) 2m 3f 61y

1:20 (1:20) (Class 4) (0-120,120) 3-Y-0+ **£3,249** (£954; £477; £238)

Form RPR

136- **1** **Divine Port (USA)**[338] 3257 5-10-13 **107**.................... PaulMoloney 110
(Alan Swinbank) *hld up: stdy hdwy on outside after 3 out: shkn up to ld last: rdn and idled run-in: drvn out towards fin* **2/1**[1]

456U **2** *nk* **Pistol (IRE)**[4] 2720 6-10-1 **102**.................... MrJDixon(7) 104
(John Dixon) *cl up: led bef 4 out: rdn and hdd last: rallied: kpt on u.p: hld nr fin* **8/1**

14-3 **3** *4 ½* **Hartforth**[204] 203 7-11-9 **120**.................... CallumWhillans(3) 118
(Donald Whillans) *led to bef 4 out: cl up: rdn next: kpt on same pce fr last* **12/1**

0 **4** *1 ½* **Tomkevi (FR)**[19] 2425 4-11-1 **112**.................... TonyKelly(3) 109
(Rebecca Menzies) *hld up: stdy hdwy and prom 2 out: sn rdn: kpt on same pce fr last* **33/1**

P/P- **5** *3* **Wintered Well (IRE)**[573] 114 7-11-4 **112**.................... PeterCarberry 106
(Jennie Candlish) *hld up: nt fluent 3rd: rdn along and outpcd after 4 out: kpt on fr 2 out: nt pce to chal* **16/1**

0634 **6** *8* **Taylor (IRE)**[30] 2167 6-11-3 **114** JoeColliver(3) 99
(Micky Hammond) *trckd ldrs tl rdn and wknd fr 2 out* 14/1

5F-5 **7** *5* **Hada Men (USA)**[204] 198 10-11-12 **120** HenryBrooke 100
(Rebecca Menzies) *bhd: drvn and struggling 1/2-way: no imp fr 3 out* 25/1

262- **8** *32* **Allez Cool (IRE)**[278] 4418 6-11-2 **110** BrianHarding 58
(John Wade) *chsd ldrs: lost pl bef 4 out: lost tch after next: t.o* 14/1

23F0 **P** **Tekthelot (IRE)**[28] 2214 9-11-0 **115** RyanDay(7)
(Keith Reveley) *in tch: rdn and outpcd after 3 out: wkng whn nt fluent next: sn p.u* 15/2[3]

6143 **B** **Octagon**[28] 2214 5-11-10 **118** BrianHughes
(Dianne Sayer) *hld up bhd ldng gp: gng wl whn b.d 3 out* 11/4[2]

0004 **F** **Warksburn Boy**[56] 1779 5-9-9 **94** oh5 JamieHamilton(5)
(Sheena Walton) *trckd ldrs: cl 3rd and gng wl whn fell 3 out* 25/1

5m 12.1s (3.30) **Going Correction** -0.05s/f (Good)
WFA 4 from 5yo+ 7lb **11** Ran SP% **120.4**
Speed ratings (Par 105): **91,90,88,88,87 83,81,68, ,**
CSF £19.04 CT £160.06 TOTE £3.20: £1.40, £2.70, £2.70; EX 22.20 Trifecta £201.40.
Owner C G Harrison **Bred** Juddmonte Farms Inc **Trained** Melsonby, N Yorks

FOCUS
An ordinary handicap hurdle run in a time 8.5sec slower than the preceding novice event.

2803 APOLLOBET HOME OF CASHBACK SPECIALS NOVICES' CHASE (12 fncs) 1m 7f 207y
1:50 (1:51) (Class 3) 4-Y-0+ **£6,498** (£1,908; £954; £477)

Form RPR

00-1 **1** **On Tour (IRE)**[18] 2446 7-11-5 137 PaulMoloney 138+
(Evan Williams) *chsd clr ldr: clsd 3 out: led next: rdn whn nt fluent last: edgd rt run-in: styd on strly* 4/6[1]

41-P **2** *3/4* **Sirabad (FR)**[21] 2370 5-11-0 0 (t[1]) SamTwiston-Davies 130+
(Paul Nicholls) *hld up in tch: smooth hdwy bef 3 out: effrt and ev ch last: sn rdn: kpt on run-in: hld nr fin* 2/1[2]

2022 **3** *8* **Silk Hall (UAE)**[11] 2588 10-11-0 120 (vt) BrianHughes 123
(J J Lambe, Ire) *led and clr to 3 out: sn rdn: hdd next: outpcd fr last* 25/1

11-0 **4** *1 1/2* **Looking Well (IRE)**[198] 319 6-11-0 125 BrianHarding 122
(Nicky Richards) *in tch: pushed along and outpcd 4 out: no imp fr next* 7/1[3]

4m 14.2s (-1.90) **Going Correction** -0.05s/f (Good) **4** Ran SP% **109.7**
Speed ratings (Par 107): **102,101,97,96**
CSF £2.52 TOTE £1.50; EX 2.20 Trifecta £8.00.
Owner T Hywel Jones **Bred** Mrs Meliosa Walshe **Trained** Llancarfan, Vale Of Glamorgan

FOCUS
Actual race distance 2m 35yds. An interesting novice chase which produced a good finish between a couple of promising chasers. The wind had dropped by this stage and they went a fair gallop.

2804 APOLLOBET ENHANCED RACING SPECIALS NOVICES' HURDLE (10 hdls) 2m 1f
2:20 (2:22) (Class 4) 4-Y-0+ **£3,249** (£954; £477; £238)

Form RPR

50-1 **1** **Virnon**[20] 2398 4-11-5 0 PaulMoloney 118+
(Alan Swinbank) *chsd ldrs: stdy hdwy gng wl bef 2 out: poised to chal last: sn rdn: led run-in: styd on wl* 5/4[1]

-050 **2** *3/4* **Herecomesnelson (IRE)**[29] 2189 6-10-7 0 CallumBewley(5) 108
(Katie Scott) *hld up: stdy hdwy after 3 out: led briefly last: kpt on: hld nr fin* 33/1

25 **3** *6* **Freddies Portrait (IRE)**[9] 2628 6-10-12 0 SamTwiston-Davies 102
(Donald McCain) *cl up: led 3rd: rdn bef 2 out: hdd last: sn outpcd* 4/1[3]

5 **4** *35* **Lacerta**[15] 2498 4-10-5 0 FinianO'Toole(7) 67
(Micky Hammond) *hld up: shkn up after 3 out: pushed along and outpcd next: btn last* 33/1

5 *15* **Tommy The Rascal**[238] 5-10-12 0 PeterCarberry 52
(Jennie Candlish) *nt fluent in rr: drvn and struggling after 4 out: nvr on terms* 33/1

0-35 **6** *5* **John Williams (IRE)**[36] 2070 6-10-5 0 StevenFox(7) 47
(Sandy Thomson) *led to 3rd: cl up tl drvn and wknd fr 2 out* 12/1

64 **7** *16* **Strait Run (IRE)**[19] 2422 4-10-9 0 JoeColliver(3) 31
(Micky Hammond) *bhd: struggling bef 4th: t.o* 50/1

0 **P** **Play Practice**[207] 144 5-10-0 0 MissCWalton(5)
(James Walton) *bhd: struggling bef 1/2-way: lost tch and p.u 2 out* 100/1

1 **F** **Lake View Lad (IRE)**[16] 2479 5-10-7 0 StephenMulqueen(5)
(N W Alexander) *prom: cl 4th whn fell 4th* 7/4[2]

4m 31.7s (2.50) **Going Correction** -0.05s/f (Good) **9** Ran SP% **120.3**
Speed ratings (Par 105): **92,91,88,72,65 62,55, ,**
CSF £46.02 TOTE £2.20: £1.10, £5.70, £1.30; EX 33.20 Trifecta £166.10.
Owner Jack Pearce **Bred** World Racing Network **Trained** Melsonby, N Yorks

FOCUS
They were soon spread out in this modest novice hurdle.

2805 APOLLOBET MARES' CHASE (LISTED RACE) (16 fncs) 2m 4f
2:50 (2:50) (Class 1) 4-Y-0+ **£17,165** (£6,491; £3,290; £1,679; £884)

Form RPR

20-1 **1** **Emily Gray (IRE)**[23] 2313 7-11-0 143 DavidBass 150
(Kim Bailey) *cl up: jnd ldr 3rd and sn wl clr of rest: rdn whn nt fluent 3 out: led next: hrd rdn and styd on gamely run-in* 11/4[2]

14-0 **2** *1 3/4* **Gitane Du Berlais (FR)**[15] 2502 5-11-5 154 DarylJacob 153
(W P Mullins, Ire) *t.k.h: led and clr w wnr fr 3rd: hit 3 out: hdd and rdn next: kpt on same pce u.p run-in* 1/2[1]

10-3 **3** *30* **Jennys Surprise (IRE)**[193] 404 7-11-0 127 AlainCawley 118
(Fergal O'Brien) *nt fluent: cl up: lost grnd on first two fr 3rd: hit and outpcd 8th: no imp fr 4 out* 14/1

-23F **4** *3 3/4* **Ebony Empress (IRE)**[23] 2313 6-11-0 123 (p) NoelFehily 118
(Neil Mulholland) *hld up: nt fluent 1st: blnd 11th: sn outpcd: n.d after* 9/1[3]

1134 **5** *18* **Classic Palace (IRE)**[38] 2025 6-11-0 120 BrianHughes 100
(J J Lambe, Ire) *hld up: shkn up and outpcd bef 5 out: sn btn* 40/1

1-24 **P** **Amethyst Rose (IRE)**[22] 2342 8-11-0 112 SamColtherd
(Stuart Coltherd) *nt fluent in rr: struggling fr 1/2-way: t.o whn p.u 4 out* 66/1

5m 19.6s (-7.80) **Going Correction** -0.05s/f (Good) **6** Ran SP% **113.9**
Speed ratings (Par 111): **113,112,100,98,91**
CSF £4.89 TOTE £3.40: £1.70, £1.10; EX 7.20 Trifecta £23.40.
Owner J Perriss **Bred** Robert McCarthy **Trained** Andoversford, Gloucs
■ Stewards' Enquiry : David Bass two-day ban; used whip above permitted level (13th,14th Dec)

FOCUS
Actual race distance 2m 4f 45yds. The first running of this event produced a fine tussle between two tough and smart mares, who were clear from an early stage.

2806 APOLLOBET IN PLAY BETTING AMATEUR RIDERS' H'CAP HURDLE (DIV II) (14 hdls) 3m 1f
3:20 (3:20) (Class 4) (0-105,105) 4-Y-0+ **£3,119** (£967; £483; £242)

Form RPR

P-33 **1** **Finaghy Ayr (IRE)**[18] 2432 7-10-11 **95** (p) MrJoshuaNewman(5) 102+
(Ian Duncan) *hld up: hdwy to join ldrs after 2nd: led 8th: mde rest: drew clr bef 2 out: rdn and kpt on strly fr last* 5/1[3]

10-P **2** *4 1/2* **Stickleback**[16] 2478 6-10-4 **88** (p) MissBeckySmith(5) 90
(Micky Hammond) *in tch: effrt after 3 out: chsd (clr) wnr after next: kpt on run-in: nt gng pce to chal* 9/1

13P- **3** *12* **Jonny Eager (IRE)**[286] 4266 6-11-4 **100** MrTHamilton(3) 89
(Alistair Whillans) *w ldrs to 3 out: sn pushed along: rallied and disp 2nd pl briefly after next: sn outpcd* 7/2[2]

/01- **4** *1 1/2* **Prairie Lad**[357] 2977 7-11-3 **101** MissRMcDonald(5) 89
(Sandy Thomson) *prom: lost pl bef 3rd: effrt and pushed along after 3 out: no imp fr next* 11/4[1]

P316 **5** *17* **Darsi Dancer (IRE)**[23] 2323 7-10-12 **98** SamColtherd(7) 69
(Stuart Coltherd) *mde most to 8th: drvn along next: wknd after 3 out* 8/1

5 **6** *3 1/2* **Nakadam (FR)**[29] 2190 5-11-12 **105** MrSClements 72
(R Mike Smith) *prom: chal 4 out to bef 2 out: rdn and wknd between last 2* 7/1

P-30 **7** *21* **Simarthur**[24] 2297 8-11-4 **104** (v) MrWHRReed(7) 50
(Lucinda Russell) *prom on ins: drvn along 8th: wknd after 3 out: t.o* 7/1

00-0 **R** **Palmello**[61] 1683 4-9-7 **79** oh1 MrMEnnis(7)
(Ann Hamilton) *t.k.h early: hld up: rdn and outpcd 4 out: lost tch after next: no ch whn ref last* 14/1

6m 53.3s (14.30) **Going Correction** -0.05s/f (Good)
WFA 4 from 5yo+ 9lb **8** Ran SP% **118.3**
Speed ratings (Par 105): **75,73,69,69,63 62,55,**
CSF £49.29 CT £179.58 TOTE £6.50: £2.80, £3.30, £1.40; EX 35.30 Trifecta £237.60.
Owner Ronald Lilley **Bred** A Steele **Trained** Coylton, Ayrshire
■ Stewards' Enquiry : Mr M Ennis five-day ban; continued on a horse, contrary to its welfare (tba)

FOCUS
A weak handicap hurdle, run in very testing conditions in a time over a minute outside standard.
T/Plt: £25.10 to a £1 stake. Pool: £70,524.05 - 2,048.89 winning tickets. T/Qpdt: £5.00 to a £1 stake. Pool: £5,159.42 - 760.72 winning tickets. **Richard Young**

2537 LEICESTER (R-H)
Sunday, November 29

OFFICIAL GOING: Hurdle course - good to soft (soft in places); chase course - good (good to firm in places, good to soft on flat course crossings)
Wind: Strong behind Weather: Raining

2807 FERNIE NOVICES' HURDLE (10 hdls) 2m 4f 110y
1:00 (1:00) (Class 4) 4-Y-0+ **£5,198** (£1,526; £763; £381)

Form RPR

2-2 **1** **Knockgraffon (IRE)**[35] 2080 5-10-12 0 HarrySkelton 119+
(Dan Skelton) *hld up: racd keenly: hdwy after 3 out: led next: drvn out* 9/4[2]

251- **2** *3/4* **King Kayf**[221] 5468 6-10-9 0 (t) JamesBanks(3) 119+
(Noel Williams) *a.p: racd keenly: chsd ldr 7th: led 3 out: hdd next: rdn and flashed tail flat: styd on* 6/1[3]

1-1 **3** *3 1/2* **Onefitzall (IRE)**[30] 2163 5-11-5 0 RichardJohnson 121+
(Philip Hobbs) *trckd ldrs: racd keenly: wnt 2nd 4th tl nt fluent 7th: ev ch after 3 out: sn rdn: styd on same pce appr last* 1/2[1]

35 **4** *10* **Pinnacle Panda (IRE)**[57] 1758 4-10-12 0 RobertDunne 104
(Tom Lacey) *trckd ldr to 4th: remained handy: rdn after 3 out: wknd next* 14/1

50- **5** *2 3/4* **Expedite (IRE)**[274] 4499 4-10-12 0 GavinSheehan 101
(Charlie Mann) *hld up: rdn after 3 out: nt fluent last: nvr trble ldrs* 25/1

0 **6** *6* **Another Frontier (IRE)**[33] 2126 4-10-7 0 JamieBargary(5) 95
(Nigel Twiston-Davies) *hld up: nt fluent 6th: hdwy appr 3 out: rdn and wknd next* 50/1

56 **7** *59* **Ballyvaughn (IRE)**[20] 2407 5-10-12 0 (t) AidanColeman 36
(Caroline Bailey) *led at stdy pce tl hdd 3 out: sn wknd* 50/1

64- **8** *6* **Nomadic Lad**[277] 4430 5-10-12 0 AndrewTinkler 30
(Sarah Hollinshead) *hld up: rdn and wknd after 7th* 100/1

5m 18.1s (-6.60)
WFA 4 from 5yo+ 8lb **8** Ran SP% **127.1**
CSF £17.53 TOTE £2.90: £1.10, £1.70, £1.10; EX 14.80 Trifecta £34.20.
Owner Mrs Barbara Hester **Bred** R McCarthy **Trained** Alcester, Warwicks

FOCUS
All race distances as advertised. A wet and very blustery day with the wind at their backs up the straight. The going was good to soft, soft in places on the hurdles course and good, good to firm in places (good to soft on Flat course crossings) on the chase track (Goingstick: Hurdle 5.5, chase 7.4). This looked a two-horse race according to the market, but it was still something of a surprising result. They went no pace early.

2808 EAST FARNDON (S) HURDLE (8 hdls) 1m 7f 113y
1:30 (1:30) (Class 5) 4-7-Y-0 **£2,599** (£763; £381; £190)

Form RPR

1 **Edward Elgar**[26] 4-10-11 0 JamesBanks(3) 113
(Natalie Lloyd-Beavis) *chsd ldrs: rdn after 5th: hung rt u.p flat: styd on to ld nr fin* 40/1

150P **2** *nk* **El Massivo (IRE)**[44] 1945 5-11-0 115 HarryBannister(5) 118
(Harriet Bethell) *hld up: hdwy appr 3 out: led bef next: sn rdn: hdd and n.m.r nr fin* 9/2[3]

32-0 **3** *30* **Calculated Risk**[19] 2411 6-11-0 126 (p) HarrySkelton 91
(Dan Skelton) *led to 4th: led again next: rdn and hdd appr 2 out: sn wknd* 8/13[1]

4115 **4** *9* **A Little Bit Dusty**[28] 2218 7-11-8 122 (b) PaddyBrennan 86
(Conor Dore) *hld up: rdn appr 3 out: sn wknd* 7/2[2]

4 **5** *48* **Notts So Blue**[13] 2538 4-10-4 0 (b) JonathanEngland(3) 28
(Shaun Harris) *chsd ldr tl led 4th: hdd next: rdn and wknd 3 out* 25/1

0-0 **P** **Adadream**[197] 341 6-10-11 0 (t) ConorShoemark(3)
(Claire Dyson) *hld up: pushed along 3rd: bhd fr next: p.u bef 3 out* 200/1

3m 59.5s (-1.50)
WFA 4 from 5yo+ 7lb **6** Ran SP% **109.1**
CSF £191.96 TOTE £17.80: £8.00, £2.30; EX 243.00 Trifecta £603.00. The winner was sold to G. Bailey for 5,000gns.

Owner R Eagle **Bred** Hellwood Stud Farm & Paul Davies (h'Gate) **Trained** East Garston, Berks
■ Stewards' Enquiry : James Banks one-day ban; careless riding (13th Dec)

FOCUS
A shocking event, especially with the two market leaders blowing out so badly.

2809 WYMESWOLD VETERANS' H'CAP CHASE (QUALIFIER) (LEG 9 OF THE VETERANS' CHASE SERIES) (18 fncs) 2m 6f 151y

2:00 (2:00) (Class 2) (0-150,148)
10-Y-0+ **£18,768** (£5,544; £2,772; £1,386; £693)

Form RPR

0214 **1** **Houston Dynimo (IRE)**[7] 2659 10-9-9 **122** oh2........(bt) DavidNoonan(5) 130
(David Pipe) *chsd clr ldr: tk clsr order 9th: led 3 out: drvn out* **6/1**

02-6 **2** *2¼* **French Opera**[179] 603 12-11-12 **148**.......................... AndrewTinkler 155
(Nicky Henderson) *hld up: hmpd 7th: hdwy 11th: chsd wnr after 3 out: rdn appr last: styd on same pce flat* **9/2**[3]

24-5 **3** *18* **Araldur (FR)**[18] 2436 11-10-9 **131**.......................... WayneHutchinson 127
(Alan King) *hld up: nt fluent 6th: hdwy 9th: rdn and hit 3 out: wknd next* **15/8**[1]

414- **4** *35* **Creevytennant (IRE)**[220] 5493 11-11-7 **146**.............. ConorShoemark(3) 104
(Fergal O'Brien) *led and sn clr: c bk to the field 9th: hdd 3 out: wknd next* **3/1**[2]

3F4- **5** *nk* **Hansupfordetroit (IRE)**[248] 4993 10-10-5 **130**........(p) RobertWilliams(3) 88
(Bernard Llewellyn) *hld up: nt a fluent: mstke 6th: j.rt next: pushed along 14th: wknd bef next* **5/1**

5m 52.2s (-11.80) **Going Correction** -0.20s/f (Good) **5** Ran SP% **108.9**
Speed ratings: **112,111,104,92,92**
CSF £29.86 TOTE £5.50: £3.10, £2.40; EX 26.00 Trifecta £70.60.
Owner Miss S E Hartnell **Bred** Sweetmans Bloodstock **Trained** Nicholashayne, Devon
■ Stewards' Enquiry : David Noonan two-day ban; used whip above permitted level (tba)

FOCUS
A valuable prize for this veterans' handicap chase, but something of a disappointing turnout especially with the two non-runners. It was run at a decent gallop, though.

2810 JAYNE FERGUSON MEMORIAL H'CAP HURDLE (8 hdls) 1m 7f 113y

2:30 (2:30) (Class 4) (0-120,118) 3-Y-0 **£6,330** (£1,870; £935; £468; £234)

Form RPR

40-1 **1** **Isaac Bell (IRE)**[47] 1893 7-11-12 **118**..........................(t) KielanWoods 122+
(Alex Hales) *a.p: led appr 2 out: rdn flat: all out* **7/2**[1]

-536 **2** *nk* **Sword Of The Lord**[25] 2271 5-10-10 **107**..........(vt[1]) JamieBargary(5) 113+
(Nigel Twiston-Davies) *trckd ldrs: racd keenly: ev ch 2 out: nt fluent last: styd on u.p* **4/1**[2]

32-2 **3** *8* **Malanos (IRE)**[209] 104 7-10-12 **109**.......................... NickSlatter(5) 105
(Tony Carroll) *chsd ldr: mstke 3rd: ev ch 2 out: sn rdn: j.rt last: hung rt and wknd flat* **8/1**

3146 **4** *¾* **Hartside (GER)**[15] 2499 6-11-0 **113**.......................... MrRWinks(7) 108
(Peter Winks) *hld up: pushed along 5th: styd on u.p after 2 out: nt rch ldrs* **6/1**[3]

124- **5** *19* **May Hay**[265] 4669 5-11-2 **108**.......................... JackQuinlan 86
(Anthony Carson) *chsd ldrs: led 3 out: rdn and hdd bef next: sn wknd* **10/1**

0/33 **6** *9* **Save The Bees**[20] 2398 7-11-4 **110**.......................... NickScholfield 80
(Declan Carroll) *led to 3 out: rdn and wknd next* **7/1**

62-4 **7** *20* **Smart Catch (IRE)**[208] 134 9-11-2 **108**.......................... LeeEdwards 60
(Tony Carroll) *hld up: shkn up after 3 out: wknd and hung rt next* **12/1**

0-05 **P** **Hear The Chimes**[13] 2540 6-11-4 **110**.......................... TrevorWhelan
(Shaun Harris) *hld up: hdwy appr 3 out: rdn and wknd bef next: bhd whn p.u bef last* **7/1**

6530 **P** **Marley Joe (IRE)**[30] 2163 4-10-8 **100**.......................... AndrewTinkler
(Martin Keighley) *hld up: rdn after 5th: wknd bef next: bhd whn p.u bef last* **20/1**

3m 58.1s (-2.90)
WFA 4 from 5yo+ 7lb **9** Ran SP% **114.2**
CSF £18.09 CT £102.74 TOTE £4.10: £1.20, £2.10, £2.00; EX 21.70 Trifecta £216.30.
Owner A E Frost **Bred** M Kennelly **Trained** Edgcote, Northamptonshire
■ Stewards' Enquiry : Mr R Winks seven-day ban; used whip above permitted level (tba)

FOCUS
A fair handicap hurdle, but it looked hard work.

2811 CLIPSTON H'CAP CHASE (15 fncs) 2m 4f 45y

3:00 (3:00) (Class 5) (0-100,96) 4-Y-0+ **£3,898** (£1,144; £572; £286)

Form RPR

46-5 **1** **Derryogue (IRE)**[208] 126 10-10-11 **88**..........(t) WilliamFeatherstone(7) 96+
(Zoe Davison) *hld up: hdwy 5th: chsd ldr 8th: led 4 out: rdn out* **20/1**

14-6 **2** *2* **Bally Lagan (IRE)**[13] 2542 7-10-11 **81**..........................(bt) CharliePoste 86
(Robin Dickin) *a.p: chsd wnr after 4 out: ev ch last: rdn and swtchd rt flat: styd on same pce* **11/2**[3]

133- **3** *15* **Expanding Universe (IRE)**[231] 5291 8-11-12 **96**.............. LeeEdwards 90
(Tony Carroll) *chsd ldr to 8th: remained handy: rdn after 11th: j.lft and wknd last* **5/1**[2]

F-4P **4** *6* **Wish In A Well (IRE)**[185] 524 6-11-9 **93**..........................(t) KielanWoods 79
(Ben Case) *hld up: hdwy 4 out: rdn and wknd appr last* **7/2**[1]

32-6 **5** *7* **Tinelyra (IRE)**[214] 18 9-11-6 **93**..........................(t) ConorShoemark(3) 72
(Fergal O'Brien) *prom: lost pl after 5th: hdwy 9th: rdn and wknd 2 out* **5/1**[2]

-001 **6** *33* **Monty's Revenge (IRE)**[24] 2303 10-10-12 **82**..........................(p) IanPopham 31
(Martin Keighley) *led: hdd 4 out: wknd next* **6/1**

243P **P** **Combustible Kate (IRE)**[24] 2303 9-10-7 **77**.......................... AdamWedge
(Nick Kent) *chsd ldrs: pushed along 9th: wknd 11th: bhd whn p.u bef 4 out* **10/1**

-213 **F** **Moonlight Maggie**[150] 884 8-11-4 **88**..........................(t) PaddyBrennan
(Tom George) *hld up: hdwy and disputing 3 l 5th whn fell 3 out: fatally injured* **5/1**[2]

5m 22.5s (3.60) **Going Correction** -0.20s/f (Good) **8** Ran SP% **115.7**
Speed ratings (Par 103): **84,83,77,74,72 58,**
CSF £126.38 CT £646.96 TOTE £23.60: £6.50, £2.10, £1.20; EX 183.90 Trifecta £690.10.
Owner Andy Irvine **Bred** Mrs Margaret E Graham **Trained** Hammerwood, E Sussex

FOCUS
A moderate handicap chase.

2812 STONESBY MARES' H'CAP HURDLE (10 hdls) 2m 4f 110y

3:30 (3:30) (Class 4) (0-110,110) 3-Y-0 **£6,330** (£1,870; £935; £468; £234)

Form RPR

234/ **1** **Bonnet's Vino**[624] 4816 7-11-2 **100**.......................... KielanWoods 112+
(Pam Sly) *trckd ldrs: led appr 2 out: rdn out* **12/1**

F5-2 **2** *6* **Catherines Well**[27] 2252 6-11-12 **110**.......................... RichardJohnson 117
(Philip Hobbs) *hld up in tch: rdn after 3 out: ev ch appr last: wknd flat* **9/4**[1]

-FP4 **3** *4* **Mini Muck**[11] 2577 9-11-7 **108**.......................... RyanHatch(3) 112
(Nigel Twiston-Davies) *prom: ev ch 2 out: sn rdn: wknd last* **6/1**[3]

-F2P **4** *2* **Magic Money**[30] 2167 7-11-7 **108**.......................... TomBellamy(3) 111
(Kim Bailey) *led to 5th: led again after 3 out: rdn and hdd whn hit next: wknd bef last* **8/1**

PPP6 **5** *4* **Definitely Better (IRE)**[26] 2263 7-10-5 **92**.............. ConorShoemark(3) 92
(Tom George) *prom: rdn appr 2 out: wknd bef last* **14/1**

5P-1 **6** *9* **Helamis**[11] 2565 5-10-5 **92**.......................... HarryChalloner(3) 82
(Barry Leavy) *hld up: pushed along whn hmpd 3 out: sn wknd* **10/1**

61-2 **7** *16* **Aces Over Eights (IRE)**[23] 2314 6-11-8 **106**.......................... CharliePoste 82
(Kerry Lee) *sn w ldr: led 5th: hdd after 3 out: sn rdn: wknd bef next* **4/1**[2]

4653 **8** *1¼* **Palmaria**[18] 2444 5-11-7 **105**.......................... JamesBest 79
(Caroline Keevil) *hld up: rdn appr 3 out: sn wknd* **25/1**

P62- **P** **Seas Of Green**[266] 4651 8-11-12 **110**.......................... WayneHutchinson
(Paul Cowley) *hld up: hmpd 3 out: sn wknd: bhd whn p.u bef next* **16/1**

3P31 **F** **Jumpandtravel (IRE)**[12] 2550 6-10-13 **102**.......................... JamieBargary(5)
(Micky Hammond) *hld up: rdn whn fell 3 out* **14/1**

5m 29.4s (4.70) **10** Ran SP% **116.0**
CSF £40.12 CT £184.48 TOTE £13.20: £3.50, £1.10, £2.70; EX 47.20 Trifecta £288.80.
Owner G A Libson D L Bayliss G Taylor P M Sly **Bred** Mrs P Sly **Trained** Thorney, Cambs

FOCUS
A fair mares' handicap hurdle and again it took some getting in the conditions.
T/Jkpt: Not won. Jackpot Placepot: £210.40 to a £1 stake. Pool £2,883.00 - 10 winning tickets.
T/Plt: £441.50 to a £1 stake. Pool: £83,691.29 - 138.37 winning tickets. T/Qpdt: £34.70 to a £1 stake. Pool: £9,187.50 - 195.8 winning tickets. **Colin Roberts**

2792 FAIRYHOUSE (R-H)

Sunday, November 29

OFFICIAL GOING: Hurdle course - soft; chase course - soft to heavy

2813a BAR ONE RACING JUVENILE HURDLE (GRADE 3) (10 hdls) 2m

12:40 (12:40) 3-Y-0 **£15,116** (£4,418; £2,093; £697)

RPR

1 **Rashaan (IRE)**[77] 1537 3-10-13 0.......................... MPFogarty 133+
(Colin Kidd, Ire) *hld up in mid-div: 5th 1/2-way: tk clsr order bhd ldrs fr 4 out: cl 4th after next: travelling wl in 2nd bef 2 out: rdn to ld bef last and sn clr: styd on strly run-in: easily* **5/1**[2]

2 *13* **Missy Tata (FR)**[29] 2203 3-10-2 0.......................... RWalsh 108
(Gordon Elliott, Ire) *hld up in tch: 4th 1/2-way: hdwy 4 out into cl 3rd: disp on outer next and led travelling wl bef 2 out: rdn and hdd bef last and sn no imp on easy wnr: one pce run-in where flashed tail* **1/2**[1]

3 *3¼* **Le Vagabond (FR)**[38] 2047 3-10-9 0.......................... AELynch 112
(E J O'Grady, Ire) *hld up: 6th 1/2-way: tk clsr order bhd ldrs in 3rd gng wl fr 3 out: rdn and no ex fr next where slt mstke: one pce after: nt fluent last* **10/1**[3]

4 *15* **Tiliver (FR)**[29] 2203 3-10-9 0.......................... APHeskin 97
(Alan Fleming, Ire) *w.w towards rr: 7th 1/2-way: tk clsr order fr 4 out: rdn in 5th after 3 out and no imp on ldrs u.p bef next: kpt on one pce* **10/1**[3]

5 *3½* **Thywillbedone (IRE)**[15] 2501 3-10-2 0.......................... DannyMullins 86
(Paul Hennessy, Ire) *led: extended advantage fr 2nd: mstke 4th and reduced ld: 4 l clr at 1/2-way: reduced ld 4 out: jnd bef next and hdd u.p into st: wknd* **25/1**

6 *17* **Rocket Punch (IRE)**[50] 3-10-9 0.......................... BJCooper 76
(Gordon Elliott, Ire) *hld up in rr: nt fluent 1st and next: slow 3rd and niggled along detached in rr: slt mstke 4th: tk clsr order after 4 out: pushed along in mod 7th after 3 out and no imp on ldrs bef next: wnt mod 6th fr last* **14/1**

7 *24* **Sports Barrow (IRE)**[15] 2501 3-10-9 0..........................(p) RogerLoughran 52
(Ms Sandra Hughes, Ire) *chsd ldrs: mstke 1st: 3rd 1/2-way: tk clsr order bhd ldrs fr 4 out: hit next: sn rdn and no ex u.p in 6th appr st: wknd and eased* **66/1**

8 *9½* **Newberry New (IRE)**[15] 2501 3-10-9 0.......................... RobbiePower 43
(Mrs John Harrington, Ire) *cl up early: sn settled bhd ldrs: j. sltly lft and nt fluent w jumping at times: 2nd 1/2-way clsr in 2nd 4 out: rdn and wknd fr next where slt mstke: sn eased* **14/1**

4m 9.5s (-2.50) **Going Correction** -0.175s/f (Good) **8** Ran SP% **120.2**
Speed ratings: **99,92,90,83,81 73,61,56**
CSF £8.63 TOTE £5.30: £1.60, £1.02, £1.70; DF 8.60 Trifecta £33.90.
Owner Mrs T J Kidd & Mrs R Treacy **Bred** His Highness The Aga Khan's Studs S C **Trained** Bagenalastown, Co Carlow

FOCUS
This looked a fairly ordinary renewal, with no Closutton representative, but one had to revise that opinion after the winner's demolition job. The form is rated around the winner and third.

2814a BAR ONE RACING ROYAL BOND NOVICE HURDLE (GRADE 1) (10 hdls) 2m

1:10 (1:10) 4-Y-0+ **£39,534** (£12,519; £5,930; £1,976; £1,317)

RPR

1 **Long Dog**[49] 1875 5-11-10 144.......................... RWalsh 151+
(W P Mullins, Ire) *settled in 2nd: slt mstke 4 out: disp after 3 out and led bef next where nt fluent: rdn and strly pressed bef last: rallied and extended advantage run-in: reduced ld and all out cl home: jst hld on* **1/2**[1]

2 *nk* **Bachasson (FR)**[56] 1788 4-11-7 147.......................... PaulTownend 148+
(W P Mullins, Ire) *hld up in rr: slt mstke 5th: prog on outer fr 3 out to chal in 2nd next: gng wl and effrt between last 2: sn rdn in 2nd and kpt on wl clsng stages to strly press wnr fnl strides: jst hld* **11/4**[2]

3 *14* **Gunnery Sergeant (IRE)**[8] 2652 4-11-7 0.......................... BJCooper 135
(Noel Meade, Ire) *chsd ldrs: nt fluent 1st: 4th 1/2-way: rdn bef 2 out where swtchd lft and sn no imp on ldrs: wnt mod 3rd after 2 out: kpt on one pce* **8/1**[3]

4 *9* **Baily Cloud (IRE)**[34] 2111 5-11-10 125.......................... MarkEnright 129
(M F Morris, Ire) *led: 2 l clr at 1/2-way: jnd after 3 out and hdd u.p bef next where dropped to 3rd: wknd into 4th after 2 out* **25/1**

5 *2* **Archive (FR)**[21] 2385 5-11-10 131.......................... DavidMullins 126
(Eoin Griffin, Ire) *chsd ldrs: 3rd 1/2-way: rdn appr st and sn no imp in rr of quintet: wknd* **16/1**

4m 3.6s (-8.40) **Going Correction** -0.175s/f (Good)
WFA 4 from 5yo 7lb **5** Ran SP% **114.2**
Speed ratings: **114,113,106,102,101**
CSF £2.47 TOTE £1.70: £1.02, £1.50; DF 1.90 Trifecta £4.40.
Owner Mrs S Ricci **Bred** G B Turnbull Ltd **Trained** Muine Beag, Co Carlow

FOCUS
A fascinating contest between two almost unbeaten Willie Mullins novices with the ratings suggesting there was very little between them. The race showed there wasn't and that on another day perhaps the form would be reversed. The time compared well with that for the juvenile event.

2815a BAR ONE RACING HATTON'S GRACE HURDLE (GRADE 1) (12 hdls) 2m 4f
1:40 (1:43) 4-Y-O+

£39,534 (£12,519; £5,930; £1,976; £1,317; £658)

RPR

1 **Arctic Fire (GER)**[21] 2386 6-11-10 169 RWalsh 159+
(W P Mullins, Ire) *hld up towards rr: 5th 1/2-way: smooth hdwy into cl 3rd 2 out and led travelling wl between last 2: eased clr and stdd at last: drvn out run-in: comf* **4/5**[1]

2 *4* **Alpha Des Obeaux (FR)**[212] 72 5-11-10 147 BJCooper 152
(M F Morris, Ire) *settled bhd ldr in 2nd: led appr st: rdn and hdd after 2 out where dropped to 3rd briefly: rallied far side into 2nd u.p bef last where no ch w easy wnr: kpt on same pce* **11/2**[3]

3 *3/4* **Gwencily Berbas (FR)**[22] 2353 4-11-6 139 (t) APHeskin 147
(Alan Fleming, Ire) *chsd ldrs: 4th 1/2-way: impr into cl 2nd appr st: rdn to ld briefly after 2 out: sn strly pressed and hdd: no ch w easy wnr u.p in 3rd bef last: kpt on same pce run-in* **9/2**[2]

4 *1 3/4* **Taglietelle**[9] 2386 6-11-10 148 (b) DavyRussell 149
(Gordon Elliott, Ire) *hld up: 6th 1/2-way: pushed along bef 2 out and no imp on ldrs in 5th between last 2: kpt on one pce in 4th run-in: nvr trbld ldrs* **16/1**

5 *1 1/2* **Snow Falcon (IRE)**[28] 2233 5-11-10 140 SeanFlanagan 148
(Noel Meade, Ire) *chsd ldrs: slt mstke in 3rd at 4th: 3rd 1/2-way: nt fluent 7th: pushed along after 3 out and sn no ex u.p in 4th: kpt on one pce in 5th run-in* **16/1**

6 *30* **Clondaw Court (IRE)**[367] 2770 8-11-10 142 PaulTownend 118
(W P Mullins, Ire) *led: pressed clly 3 out: pushed along and hdd bef st: wknd qckly* **13/2**

7 *hd* **Thomas Edison (IRE)**[14] 2532 8-11-10 150 (t) BarryGeraghty 118
(A J Martin, Ire) *w.w in rr: nt fluent 3rd: slt mstkes 4th and next: last 1/2-way: pushed along after 3 out and no imp into st: wknd* **33/1**

5m 11.4s (-11.60) **Going Correction** -0.175s/f (Good)
WFA 4 from 5yo+ 8lb 7 Ran SP% **117.2**
Speed ratings: **116,114,114,113,112 100,100**
CSF £6.26 TOTE £1.70: £1.30, £2.40; DF 6.00 Trifecta £16.40.
Owner Wicklow Bloodstock (Ireland) Ltd **Bred** U Gruning **Trained** Muine Beag, Co Carlow

FOCUS
They went a fair gallop given the conditions and the form looks reliable. It was no vintage renewal by any means - with one horse rated over 149 (who flopped) apart from the favourite. The second to fifth help with the standard.

2816a (Foreign Racing) - See Raceform Interactive

2817a BAR ONE RACING DRINMORE NOVICE CHASE (GRADE 1) (16 fncs) 2m 4f
2:40 (2:43) 4-Y-O+ **£39,534** (£12,519; £5,930; £1,976; £1,317; £658)

RPR

1 **No More Heroes (IRE)**[33] 2131 6-11-10 0 BJCooper 158+
(Gordon Elliott, Ire) *cl up and racd keenly early: 3rd 1/2-way: cl 3rd 5 out: led travelling wl appr st: pressed and gng best bef last: kpt on wl run-in: eased cl home: comf* **13/8**[1]

2 *2 1/2* **Monksland (IRE)**[8] 2656 8-11-10 0 SeanFlanagan 152+
(Noel Meade, Ire) *w.w: slt mstke in 6th at 7th: hdwy on outer after 3 out to chal in cl 2nd at next where nt fluent: rdn after 2 out and no imp on wnr u.p fr last: kpt on same pce* **7/2**[3]

3 *8 1/2* **Free Expression (IRE)**[15] 2503 6-11-10 0 BarryGeraghty 146+
(Gordon Elliott, Ire) *nt fluent 5th: 5th 1/2-way: tk clsr order bhd ldrs into st: rdn in 3rd fr 2 out where slt mstke and no imp on ldrs bef last where slt mstke: one pce run-in* **7/4**[2]

4 *1/2* **Sub Lieutenant (IRE)**[22] 2355 6-11-10 0 (p) DavidMullins 143
(Ms Sandra Hughes, Ire) *chsd ldrs: 4th 1/2-way: slt mstke 3 out and rdn: no imp on wnr whn slt mstke 2 out: kpt on u.p into mod 4th at last* **25/1**

5 *19* **Shantou Flyer (IRE)**[14] 2531 5-11-10 144 (t) MrBO'Neill 124
(Colin Bowe, Ire) *cl up and disp briefly fr 2nd: sn settled bhd ldr: mstke 8th and nt fluent next: disp fr 5 out: hdd 3 out where slt mstke and no ex u.p bef 2 out: sn wknd* **12/1**

6 *7* **Captain Von Trappe (IRE)**[14] 2531 6-11-10 138 DavyRussell 117
(Gordon Elliott, Ire) *led: jnd briefly fr 2nd: jnd fr 5 out tl regained narrow advantage briefly fr 3 out: pushed along and hdd appr st: wknd qckly bef 2 out* **20/1**

P **Rightdownthemiddle (IRE)**[14] 2531 7-11-10 134 JJBurke
(Michael Mulvany, Ire) *settled in rr: slt mstke 3rd: detached at 1/2-way: lost tch fr 5 out: sn wknd and t.o whn p.u bef 2 out* **100/1**

5m 22.5s (-1.50) **Going Correction** +0.25s/f (Yiel) 7 Ran SP% **114.0**
Speed ratings: **113,112,108,108,100 98,**
CSF £7.93 TOTE £1.80: £1.60, £1.80; DF 6.90 Trifecta £11.90.
Owner Gigginstown House Stud **Bred** Peter And Ann Downes **Trained** Longwood, Co Meath

FOCUS
A top class race even in the absence of Outlander with plenty to be interested in for future reference. The first two are smart recruits.

2818 - 2819a (Foreign Racing) - See Raceform Interactive

2722 AUTEUIL (L-H)
Sunday, November 29

OFFICIAL GOING: Turf: heavy

2820a PRIX MORGEX (CHASE) (GRADE 3) (4YO) (TURF) 2m 5f 110y
1:00 (12:00) 4-Y-O

£54,069 (£26,434; £15,620; £10,813; £6,007; £4,205)

RPR

1 **So French (FR)**[21] 2393 4-11-0 0 JamesReveley 143
(G Macaire, France) **11/5**[2]

2 *10* **Djagble (FR)**[21] 2393 4-10-10 0 Marc-AntoineBillard 129
(J Bertran De Balanda, France) **48/1**

3 *1* **Groove (FR)**[21] 2393 4-10-12 0 MlleNathalieDesoutter 130
(Francois Nicolle, France) **131/10**

4 *1 1/4* **Bipolaire (FR)**[33] 2134 4-10-10 0 AlainDeChitray 127
(Francois Nicolle, France) **29/10**[3]

5 *nk* **Kobrouk (FR)**[21] 2393 4-11-0 0 KevinNabet 130
(G Macaire, France) **17/10**[1]

6 *2 1/2* **Diamant Catalan (FR)**[38] 4-10-12 0 (p) MathieuCarroux 126
(P Peltier, France) **132/10**

7 *3/4* **Pinson Du Rheu (FR)**[21] 2393 4-10-10 0 GeoffreyRe 123
(G Cherel, France) **47/1**

P **Grand Moss (FR)**[86] 4-10-6 0 (b) KevinGuignon
(J-P Bernhardt, France) **110/1**

F **Karelcytic (FR)**[21] 2393 4-11-0 0 RegisSchmidlin
(F-M Cottin, France) **121/10**

5m 48.74s (1.74) 9 Ran SP% **120.7**
PARI-MUTUEL (all including 1 euro stake): WIN 3.00 (coupled with Pinson du Rheu); PLACE 1.80, 8.00, 3.30; DF 75.00; SF 109.90.
Owner Magalen O Bryant **Bred** Mme B Gabeur **Trained** Les Mathes, France

2821a PRIX ANDRE MICHEL (HURDLE) (GRADE 3) (4-5YO FILLIES & MARES) (TURF) 2m 2f
1:30 (12:00) 4-5-Y-O

£47,093 (£23,023; £13,604; £9,418; £5,232; £3,662)

RPR

1 **Martalette (FR)**[38] 5-10-12 0 (b) GeoffreyRe 133
(Yannick Fouin, France) **61/10**

2 *6* **Polygona (FR)**[80] 5-10-12 0 KevinNabet 127
(J-Y Artu, France) **6/1**[3]

3 *2 1/2* **Benie Des Dieux (FR)**[31] 4-10-6 0 LudovicPhilipperon 118
(Mlle I Gallorini, France) **9/1**

4 *10* **Bete A Bon Dieu (FR)**[36] 4-10-10 0 BertrandLestrade 112
(A Lacombe, France) **10/1**

5 *1* **Atuvuedenuo (FR)**[61] 1695 5-11-3 0 WilfridDenuault 118
(Guy Denuault, France) **3/1**[1]

6 *1* **Sierra Nevada (FR)**[38] 5-10-12 0 Marc-AntoineBillard 112
(Mlle S Delaroche, France) **86/1**

7 *2* **Comas Sola (FR)**[6] 4-10-3 0 ThomasMessina 101
(J-P Gallorini, France) **10/1**

8 *6* **Energica (FR)**[4] 4-10-6 0 (b) AnthonyLecordier 98
(D Windrif, France) **23/1**

9 *3 1/2* **Rain Artist's (FR)**[25] 4-10-6 0 MathieuCarroux 95
(G Taupin, France) **42/1**

10 *3 1/2* **Kap Call (USA)**[33] 5-10-10 0 MlleNathalieDesoutter 95
(Francois Nicolle, France) **4/1**[2]

P **Arch Duchess (FR)**[64] 5-10-10 0 JamesReveley
(M Rolland, France) **16/1**

P **Une Lapin Rouge (IRE)**[11] 5-10-8 0 (p) StevenColas
(Emmanuel Clayeux, France) **30/1**

P **Boscraie (FR)**[21] 4-10-3 0 RegisSchmidlin
(Emmanuel Clayeux, France) **38/1**

4m 28.25s (268.25)
WFA 4 from 5yo 7lb 13 Ran SP% **120.9**
PARI-MUTUEL (all including 1 euro stake): WIN 7.10; PLACE 2.20, 2.40, 2.70; DF 21.20; SF 34.90.
Owner N Madamet & I Kellitt **Bred** N Madamet, I Kellitt & Mlle B Madamet **Trained** France

2822a PRIX GEORGES COURTOIS (CHASE) (GRADE 2) (5YO+) (TURF) 2m 6f
2:40 (12:00) 5-Y-O+

£83,720 (£40,930; £24,186; £16,744; £9,302; £6,511)

RPR

1 **Pythagore**[36] 2079 10-10-8 0 StevenColas 146+
(Emmanuel Clayeux, France) **143/10**

2 *2 1/2* **Jemy Baie (FR)**[21] 2395 6-10-10 0 Jean-ChristopherGagnon 145
(M Postic, France) **19/5**[2]

3 *2 1/2* **Saint Palois (FR)**[21] 2395 7-10-10 0 JamesReveley 143
(Emmanuel Clayeux, France) **9/10**[1]

4 *4 1/2* **Tito Dela Barriere (FR)**[33] 8-10-6 0 AlexisAcker 134
(E Lecoiffier, France) **218/10**

5 *1/2* **Vent Sombre (FR)**[36] 2079 6-10-12 0 (b) RegisSchmidlin 140
(G Cherel, France) **6/1**[3]

6 *12* **Pindare (FR)**[21] 2395 6-10-8 0 (b) BertrandLestrade 124
(J-P Gallorini, France) **89/10**

R **Lachlan Bridge (GER)**[36] 2079 7-10-8 0 MathieuCarroux
(A Chaille-Chaille, France) **124/10**

F **Aroma Baie (FR)**[43] 1982 5-9-11 0 StevanBourgois
(M Postic, France) **16/1**

5m 49.75s (5.75) 8 Ran SP% **122.1**
PARI-MUTUEL (all including 1 euro stake): WIN 15.30; PLACE 2.20, 1.60, 1.20; DF 35.00; SF 116.80.
Owner Jean-Pierre Colombu **Bred** Jean-Pierre Colombu **Trained** France

2544 PLUMPTON (L-H)
Monday, November 30

OFFICIAL GOING: Soft (hdl 5.2, chs 5.5)
Wind: Strong, half against Weather: Overcast, raining from race 3 onwards

2823 188BET.CO.UK NOVICES' HURDLE (9 hdls) 1m 7f 195y
1:10 (1:10) (Class 4) 4-Y-O+ **£3,249** (£954; £477; £238)

Form RPR

2-2 1 **William H Bonney**[24] 2317 4-10-12 0 WayneHutchinson 117+
(Alan King) *hld up in midfield: trckd ldrs fr 5th: clsd to ld bef 2 out: nt fluent last: shkn up and readily asserted flat* **4/6**[1]

04/6 2 *2* **Manhattan Mead**[20] 2417 5-10-12 0 MarcGoldstein 111
(Michael Madgwick) *chsd ldr: led 3 out: rdn and hdd bef next: hld after: edgd lft but kpt on wl fr last* **200/1**

1-65 3 *1 1/2* **Outrath (IRE)**[14] 2544 5-10-5 0 (t) PaulJohn(7) 109
(Jim Best) *hld up and bhd: gd prog 3 out: chal and mstke 2 out: stl on terms whn nt fluent last: one pce flat* **33/1**

0-0 4 *1/2* **Highsalvia Cosmos**[14] 2544 4-10-12 0 (t) LiamTreadwell 109
(Mark Hoad) *hld up and bhd: gd prog after 3 out: rdn after 2 out: kpt on wl flat* **150/1**

3 5 *4 1/2* **Pilgrims Rest (IRE)**[19] 2437 6-10-12 0 (t) AndrewTinkler 106
(George Baker) *t.k.h: hld up in midfield: prog to trck ldrs 3 out: chal bef 2 out: nt qckn bef last: fdd flat* **5/1**[2]

2605 **6** 6 **Tullow Tonic (IRE)**[13] 2561 4-10-5 0 AidanColeman 92
(Charlie Longsdon) *hld up and bhd: gd prog 3 out: chsd ldrs and in tch bef 2 out: wknd bef last* **33/1**

50-3 **7** 13 **Act Of Supremacy (IRE)**[33] 2136 5-10-12 0 GavinSheehan 93
(Warren Greatrex) *nt a fluent: led to 3 out: pressed ldr tl bef 2 out: wknd rapidly and j.v.slowly last* **6/1**[3]

401- **8** 5 **Missile Man (IRE)**[308] 3905 6-10-12 0 JamieMoore 80
(Jim Best) *nt fluent: chsd ldng pair tl bef 3 out: sn lost pl: eased whn btn 2 out* **8/1**

/00 **9** ¾ **Cantor**[6] 2699 7-10-12 0 MattieBatchelor 79
(Daniel O'Brien) *chsd ldrs to 4th: losing pl whn mstke next and rdn: sn bhd* **200/1**

0361 **10** ½ **Galuppi**[13] 2555 4-11-5 108 (v) SamTwiston-Davies 86
(J R Jenkins) *rousted to get gng and sn in midfield: shkn up and wknd after 3 out* **9/1**

0U **11** 4 **Sarpech (IRE)**[3] 2748 4-10-12 0 TomO'Brien 75
(Charlie Longsdon) *hld up and bhd: shoved along fr 6th: jst in tch bef 3 out: sn wknd* **50/1**

00 **12** 4½ **Montecito (FR)**[28] 2251 5-10-12 0 TomCannon 70
(Chris Gordon) *chsd ldrs to 5th: wknd rapidly: t.o after next* **150/1**

4m 5.0s (4.20) **Going Correction** +0.425s/f (Soft) **12** Ran SP% **122.2**
Speed ratings (Par 105): **106,105,104,104,101 98,92,89,89,89 87,84**
CSF £267.91 TOTE £1.80: £1.10, £28.40, £4.90; EX 201.40 Trifecta £4117.00 Part won..
Owner Mr & Mrs R Scott **Bred** Pitchall Stud **Trained** Barbury Castle, Wilts

FOCUS
Hurdle rail moved out 5yds from inner line, chase rail out 2yds. Races 1 & 4 increased by 45yds, races 2 & 6 by 24yds, race 3 by 75yds and race 5 by 36yds. There was a solid early gallop on in this ordinary novice hurdle, but the field bunched up at the top of the home straight and there was a muddling finish. The winner is rated in line with his bumper form.

2824 188BET NOVICES' CHASE (12 fncs) 2m 214y
1:40 (1:40) (Class 3) 4-Y-O+ £7,147 (£2,098; £1,049)

Form RPR

0-12 **1** **Violet Dancer**[14] 2545 5-11-5 140 (p) JoshuaMoore 147+
(Gary Moore) *mde all and often j. fluently: hit 7th: drew clr bef 2 out: eased flat* **1/5**[1]

0-P3 **2** 22 **Exitas (IRE)**[14] 2541 7-11-0 132 (t) JamieMoore 130+
(Phil Middleton) *trckd wnr: mstke 8th: j.lft after: shkn up and btn after 3 out: eased bef last* **4/1**[2]

3 98 **Myoran Oscar (IRE)**[576] 7-10-7 0 (p) WilliamFeatherstone[(7)] 22
(Zoe Davison) *a last: lost tch 5th: jst jumping 2 out as wnr fin* **33/1**[3]

4m 18.1s (-4.90) **Going Correction** -0.025s/f (Good) **3** Ran SP% **106.3**
Speed ratings (Par 107): **110,99,53**
CSF £1.45 TOTE £1.10; EX 1.40 Trifecta £1.40.
Owner D Bessell & Galloping On The South Downs **Bred** Jeremy Hinds **Trained** Lower Beeding, W Sussex

FOCUS
Race distance increased by 24yds. The going was a lot sounder on the chase course. For the second year running this saw a poor numerical turn out, with a 60,000GBP bonus on offer should the winner go on to success at the Cheltenham Festival. The winner set a decent standard.

2825 HEART MARES' H'CAP HURDLE (14 hdls) 3m 217y
2:10 (2:10) (Class 3) (0-125,122) 4-Y-O+ £6,498 (£1,908; £954; £477)

Form RPR

2-30 **1** **Tambura**[14] 2548 5-10-5 108 MrZBaker[(7)] 123+
(G C Maundrell) *in rr: struggling to keep up whn mstke 6th: bk on terms 10th but urged along: wnt 2nd 3 out: drvn to chal next: wandered but led after last: kpt on really dourly and gamely* **11/4**[1]

-F24 **2** ½ **Cannon Fodder**[42] 2002 8-11-8 118 MarcGoldstein 131
(Sheena West) *trckd ldr: led 11th (4 out): rdn and hrd pressed 2 out: hdd after last: kpt on gamely but jst hld* **5/1**[3]

24-1 **3** 21 **Millicent Silver**[31] 2167 6-11-3 113 SamTwiston-Davies 108
(Nigel Twiston-Davies) *led at decent pce: hdd 11th (4 out): sn rdn: lost 2nd 3 out: steadily wknd* **11/4**[1]

5-12 **4** 41 **Kentford Myth**[187] 513 5-10-9 105 AndrewThornton 56
(Seamus Mullins) *wl in tch: rdn in 4th pl after 11th (4 out): wknd next: fin tired and t.o* **22/1**

32-0 **5** 3¼ **Princess Tara (IRE)**[26] 2268 5-11-12 122 SeanBowen 70
(Peter Bowen) *cl up: rdn 10th: lost pl and wl btn next: t.o* **10/3**[2]

34-2 **P** **Strange Bird (IRE)**[20] 2416 10-10-0 96 oh11 (t) PaddyBrennan
(Richard Rowe) *mstke 3rd and dropped to last: reminder after next and sn lost tch: t.o whn p.u bef 8th* **25/1**

P-P4 **P** **Streets Of Promise (IRE)**[13] 2557 6-11-12 122 (p) TomScudamore
(Michael Scudamore) *pressed ldrs tl lost pl and rdn 9th: sn wknd: p.u bef 11th (4 out)* **9/1**

6m 31.0s (6.00) **Going Correction** +0.425s/f (Soft) **7** Ran SP% **111.3**
Speed ratings (Par 107): **107,106,100,87,85**
CSF £16.02 TOTE £3.30: £1.70, £2.90; EX 16.00 Trifecta £45.10.
Owner G C Maundrell **Bred** Mrs G G A Gregson **Trained** Ogbourne St Andrew, Wilts

FOCUS
Race distance increased by 75yds. There was no hanging about in this competitive mares' handicap and the first pair, who were both well handicapped, dominated from three out.

2826 BUY YOUR ANNUAL MEMBERSHIP TODAY H'CAP HURDLE (9 hdls) 1m 7f 195y
2:40 (2:41) (Class 5) (0-100,100) 3-Y-O+ £2,274 (£667; £333; £166)

Form RPR

335- **1** **Zero Visibility (IRE)**[238] 5189 8-10-5 79 AdamWedge 90+
(Alexandra Dunn) *mde all at decent pce: pressed and rdn 2 out: styd on wl fr last* **9/2**[3]

504- **2** 6 **My Lord**[283] 4339 7-11-11 99 (v[1]) SamTwiston-Davies 106+
(Jim Best) *hld up in last: stdy prog fr 6th: trckd wnr after 3 out: rdn bef next: cl enough last: one pce flat* **5/2**[2]

345- **3** 4½ **Proud Times (USA)**[238] 5194 9-11-5 100 (p) MrJoshuaNewman[(7)] 101
(Ali Stronge) *prom: chsd wnr 3rd to 6th: sn lost pl: pushed along in 5th pl 3 out: chsd ldng pair bef next: kpt on same pce* **6/1**

5PU- **4** 23 **Dude Alert (IRE)**[266] 4671 5-10-3 77 (v) JamieMoore 60
(Gary Moore) *t.k.h early: hld up: pushed along fr 3rd: j.lft 5th: drvn to stay in tch after: wknd 3 out: j. bdly lft last* **2/1**[1]

4-00 **P** **Nouailhas**[28] 2253 9-9-11 74 oh3 BenPoste[(3)]
(Daniel O'Brien) *chsd wnr to 3rd: sn dropped to last: t.o fr 6th: p.u bef 2 out* **15/2**

115/ **P** **Clonusker (IRE)**[630] 4721 7-11-0 88 (t) LeightonAspell
(Linda Jewell) *wl in tch: chsd wnr fr 6th tl after 3 out: wknd rapidly and poor 5th whn p.u bef 2 out* **14/1**

4m 8.0s (7.20) **Going Correction** +0.425s/f (Soft) **6** Ran SP% **112.8**
Speed ratings (Par 103): **99,96,93,82,**
CSF £16.64 TOTE £6.10: £2.90, £1.70; EX 20.30 Trifecta £69.90.
Owner West Buckland Bloodstock & D Fitzgerald **Bred** Ms Bernadette McInerney **Trained** West Buckland, Somerset

FOCUS
Race distance increased by 45yds. A weak handicap, run at an average gallop and rated around the balance of the first three.

2827 TYSERS H'CAP CHASE (18 fncs) 3m 1f 152y
3:10 (3:10) (Class 5) (0-100,99) 4-Y-O+ £2,729 (£801; £400; £200)

Form RPR

3P-1 **1** **Leith Hill Legasi**[26] 2269 6-10-13 86 (bt) SamTwiston-Davies 100+
(Charlie Longsdon) *mde virtually all: j. bttr than nrest rival whn pressed: rdn clr 2 out: styd on wl* **2/1**[1]

-PP2 **2** 10 **Burgess Dream (IRE)**[15] 2515 6-11-0 87 AndrewThornton 93
(Anna Newton-Smith) *trckd ldng pair: looked poised to chal 4 out: mstke next and rdn: n.m.r on inner bef 2 out: tk 2nd after 2 out but wnr clr: no imp* **6/1**

22P- **3** nk **Mr McGregor (IRE)**[238] 5186 7-11-8 95 (b) RichieMcLernon 99
(Heather Dalton) *pressed wnr: frequently tried to dispute ld but outj.: hrd rdn 3 out: outpcd 2 out and sn lost 2nd: one pce* **10/3**[2]

24-P **4** 11 **Eastern Witness (IRE)**[25] 2300 8-10-6 79 LiamTreadwell 76
(Venetia Williams) *hld up in last: chsd ldng trio 13th but sn pushed along: rdn and clsd fr 3 out: disp 2nd bef 2 out: sn wknd* **7/2**[3]

-34P **5** 49 **Kinari (IRE)**[26] 2269 5-11-12 99 SeanBowen 43
(Peter Bowen) *hld up in last pair: struggling after 12th: lost tch next: t.o* **8/1**

-364 **P** **Red Anchor (IRE)**[20] 2416 11-10-5 81 (b) ThomasGarner[(3)]
(Linda Jewell) *nt a fluent: chsd ldrs: dropped to rr after 12th: t.o whn p.u after 14th* **11/1**

6m 57.7s (7.00) **Going Correction** -0.025s/f (Good) **6** Ran SP% **112.4**
Speed ratings (Par 103): **88,84,84,81,66**
CSF £14.11 TOTE £2.60: £1.90, £3.20; EX 12.20 Trifecta £46.90.
Owner Neil & Jane Maltby **Bred** Neil And Jane Maltby **Trained** Over Norton, Oxon

FOCUS
Race distance increased by 36yds. A moderate staying handicap that proved a fair test of the distance. The winner was on a good mark and in line with her previous best.

2828 PLUMPTONRACECOURSE.CO.UK INTERMEDIATE OPEN NATIONAL HUNT FLAT RACE 2m 1f 164y
3:40 (3:41) (Class 6) 4-5-Y-O £1,624 (£477; £238; £119)

Form RPR

2 **1** **Midnight Tune**[40] 2016 4-10-9 0 (t) AidanColeman 92+
(Anthony Honeyball) *racd wd: hld up in last pair but cl up: prog 6f out: led over 4f out: rdn and hrd pressed fr 2 out: kpt on wl* **7/4**[2]

2 ¾ **Who's Micky Brown (IRE)**[211] 5-11-2 0 NoelFehily 98+
(Neil Mulholland) *racd wd: t.k.h: cl up: trckd wnr 3f out: str chal fr 2 out: kpt on but nt qckn ins fnl f* **6/4**[1]

2-3 **3** 7 **Relight The Fire**[13] 2562 4-11-2 0 WillKennedy 91
(Denis Quinn) *led at mod pce to over 4f out: outpcd by ldng pair over 2f out: kpt on* **4/1**[3]

0 **4** 4 **Jebs Gamble (IRE)**[24] 2317 4-11-2 0 JamesDavies 87
(Nick Gifford) *cl up: rdn and outpcd by ldrs over 2f out: one pce u.p after* **25/1**

60 **5** 1½ **Earthwindorfire**[198] 341 4-11-2 0 MarkGrant 86
(Geoffrey Deacon) *hld up in last pair but wl in tch: cl up over 3f out: shkn up and outpcd over 2f out: n.d after* **33/1**

4 **6** 21 **Sweet'N'Chic (IRE)**[40] 2016 5-10-9 0 LeightonAspell 65
(Richard Rowe) *trckd ldr to 6f out: dropped to last wl over 3f out: wknd over 2f out* **14/1**

4m 47.0s (21.70) **Going Correction** +0.425s/f (Soft) **6** Ran SP% **109.8**
Speed ratings: **68,67,64,62,62 52**
CSF £4.50 TOTE £2.70: £1.60, £1.20; EX 5.10 Trifecta £9.30.
Owner The Park Homes Syndicate **Bred** Paul Brewer **Trained** Mosterton, Dorset

FOCUS
Race distance increased by 24yds. A modest little bumper where two came nicely clear in the home straight.
T/Plt: £43.90 to a £1 stake. Pool: £70,116.91 - 1,165.15 winning tickets T/Qpdt: £35.00 to a £1 stake. Pool: £6,300.62 - 133.02 winning tickets **Jonathan Neesom**

2697 LINGFIELD (L-H)
Tuesday, December 1

OFFICIAL GOING: Jumps course - heavy (soft in places); all-weather - polytrack: standard
Wind: Moderate, half behind Weather: Cloudy, mild

2829 HAPPY 2ND BIRTHDAY JENSON ROE MARES' NOVICES' HURDLE (8 hdls) 2m
12:30 (12:30) (Class 4) 3-Y-O+ £3,898 (£1,144; £572; £286)

Form RPR

10-0 **1** **Sunshine Corner (IRE)**[17] 2486 4-11-2 0 LeightonAspell 111+
(Lucy Wadham) *mde virtually all: def advantage after 5th: gng much bttr than only serious rival after 2 out: eased flat* **5/4**[2]

1 **2** 2¼ **Mozo**[209] 152 4-11-2 0 TomScudamore 104+
(David Pipe) *trckd ldrs: wnt 2nd 3 out: shkn up and no imp on wnr after 2 out: kpt on* **1/1**[1]

4-F **3** 12 **Willshebetrying**[181] 595 4-11-2 0 JamieMoore 90
(Jim Best) *t.k.h early: hld up in last trio: prog after 3 out: chsd ldng pair 2 out: pushed along and one pce after* **20/1**

4 3¼ **Zarosa (IRE)**[28] 6-11-2 0 JackQuinlan 87
(John Berry) *nt fluent 2nd: wl in tch: chsd ldng pair 3 out to 2 out: one pce after* **33/1**

04-6 **5** 4½ **Ding Ding**[15] 2544 4-11-2 0 MarcGoldstein 83
(Sheena West) *hld up in last trio: prog whn mstke 5th: lost pl and reminder after next: hdwy again and 4th sn after 2 out: pushed along and fdd* **20/1**

6 **6** 9 **Brave Cupid**[15] 2549 5-11-2 0 AndrewThornton 73
(Michael Roberts) *w wnr to 5th: lost pl qckly next: bhd bef 2 out* **50/1**

The Form Book Jumps 2015-16, Raceform Ltd, Newbury, RG14 5SJ

6-0 **7** *1 ¾* **Sunley Spirit**[25] 2317 5-11-2 0................................ TomCannon 71
(Chris Gordon) *trckd ldrs: wl in tch on long run to 2 out: sn shkn up and wknd* **50/1**

4FP **8** *35* **Dear Lottie (FR)**[29] 2252 4-11-2 0...............................[1] JoshuaMoore 36
(Gary Moore) *in tch to 3 out: wknd and bhd bef next: t.o* **12/1**[3]

P **Dutchesofrathmolyn (IRE)**[115] 1212 6-10-13 0........ ConorShoemark[(3)]
(Alison Batchelor) *in tch to 3 out: wknd rapidly: t.o whn p.u bef next* **66/1**

4m 35.3s (7.30) **Going Correction** -0.725s/f (Firm)
WFA 4 from 5yo+ 5lb **9** Ran SP% **120.0**
Speed ratings (Par 105): **52,50,44,43,41 36,35,18,**
CSF £2.90 TOTE £2.50: £1.10, £1.02, £4.60; EX 3.80 Trifecta £17.00.
Owner P A Philipps & Mrs G J Redman **Bred** John Crean **Trained** Newmarket, Suffolk

FOCUS
All starts have been moved at this track following remeasuring, so there will be no speed figures here until there is sufficient data to calculate updated median times. All bends were moved to provide fresh ground. Leighton Aspell said of the ground: "It's heavy. You don't see it like that very often in the south." The big two in the market dominated a mares' hurdle lacking depth and the pair have been rated broadly in line with their bumper form. The actual race distance was 2m 21yds.

2830 AMBANT NOVICES' H'CAP CHASE (18 fncs) 2m 7f 110y
1:00 (1:00) (Class 4) (0-105,102) 4-Y-0+ **£4,548** (£1,335; £667; £333)

Form RPR
05-3 **1** **Cheat The Cheater (IRE)**[13] 2582 8-10-6 **79**..........(tp) BrendanPowell 97+
(Claire Dyson) *mde all: chivvied along bnd gng on to fnl circ: j. best after: pushed along and drew clr 3 out: in n.d whn hit last* **3/1**[2]

-641 **2** *17* **Bredon Hill Lad**[9] 2666 8-11-12 **102** 7ex........................ LucyGardner[(3)] 98
(Sue Gardner) *hld up in tch: wnt 2nd after 14th: cl enough on long run after next: rdn and no imp on wnr bef 3 out: wl btn after* **1/1**[1]

PP-4 **3** *4 ½* **Line D'Aois (IRE)**[14] 2556 7-11-4 **91**............................ TomScudamore 84
(Michael Scudamore) *chsd wnr: j. slowly 5th and 6th: j. slowly 14th and lost 2nd: slow again next and btn: plugged on* **7/2**[3]

/4-4 **4** *40* **Roparta Avenue**[205] 223 8-10-7 **80**............................... MarcGoldstein 41
(Diana Grissell) *rousted along to s: sn in tch: pushed along whn mstke 12th: sn btn: t.o* **10/1**

6m 59.97s (-0.03) **Going Correction** -0.125s/f (Good) **4** Ran SP% **106.3**
Speed ratings (Par 105): **95,89,87,74**
CSF £6.52 TOTE £4.00; EX 7.20 Trifecta £14.20.
Owner Pink Fizz Fillies **Bred** Mrs Elizabeth Grant **Trained** Cleeve Prior, Worcs

FOCUS
Actual race distance 2m7f 146yds. Lowly chase form but an improved effort from the winner.

2831 DOWNLOAD TITANBET SPORTS APP H'CAP HURDLE (QUALIFIER FOR THE CHALLENGER TWO MILE HURDLE SERIES) (8 hdls) 2m
1:30 (1:30) (Class 3) (0-125,125) 3-Y-0**£5,697** (£1,683; £841; £421; £210)

Form RPR
0/P1 **1** **Never Says Never**[9] 2664 7-10-0 **104**.......................(t) HarryCobden[(7)] 120+
(Anthony Honeyball) *hld up: prog to trck ldng pair 5th: wnt 2nd bef 2 out where mstke and shkn up: led bef last: rdn clr fnl 100yds* **11/10**[1]

0211 **2** *6* **Sirop De Menthe (FR)**[7] 2700 5-11-11 **125** 7ex.............. LucyGardner[(3)] 133
(Sue Gardner) *kpt on inner thrght: cl up: trckd ldr 5th: upsides next: led bef 2 out: rdn and hdd bef last: one pce flat* **5/2**[2]

100/ **3** *24* **Just When**[34] 3169 6-10-11 **108**.......................(v) NicodeBoinville 92
(Patrick Chamings) *led at gd pce: jnd 3 out: drvn and hdd bef 2 out: sn in 3rd and wknd* **25/1**

24-0 **4** *3 ¼* **Bladoun (FR)**[15] 2540 7-11-1 **112**...............................(p) TomScudamore 93
(David Pipe) *nt fluent: trckd ldr: shkn up after 4th: lost 2nd pl next: struggling fr 3 out: sn btn: jst won battle for modest 4th* **16/1**

33-2 **5** *shd* **Mr Fitzroy (IRE)**[16] 2516 5-10-10 **110**............................... JamesBanks[(3)] 91
(Jo Davis) *hld up: rdn and dropped to last after 5th: sn no ch* **6/1**[3]

/0-1 **6** *¾* **Thunder Sheik (IRE)**[29] 2244 7-11-7 **121**...................(t) RyanHatch[(3)] 101
(Nigel Twiston-Davies) *in tch: rdn after 3 out: wknd bef next* **16/1**

1-55 **P** **New Street (IRE)**[10] 2637 4-11-12 **123**.................................. JamieMoore
(Jim Best) *hld up: rdn and wknd qckly after 3 out: t.o whn p.u bef last* **16/1**

4m 13.3s (-14.70) **Going Correction** -0.725s/f (Firm) **7** Ran SP% **112.0**
Speed ratings (Par 107): **107,104,92,90,90 89,**
CSF £4.25 TOTE £2.00: £1.20, £1.80; EX 3.90 Trifecta £33.90.
Owner Richard Hall **Bred** Dr S G F & P A Cave **Trained** Mosterton, Dorset

FOCUS
Actual race distance 2m 21yds. No great depth to this handicap that was run at a good gallop and the big two in the market, who stood out on recent wins, dominated.

2832 TITANBET MONEY BACK FALLER INSURANCE H'CAP CHASE (14 fncs) 2m 4f
2:00 (2:00) (Class 3) (0-125,125) 4-Y-0**£6,330** (£1,870; £935; £468; £234)

Form RPR
00 **1** **Kings Cross (FR)**[18] 2472 5-10-9 **108**.................................. LeeEdwards 114+
(Tony Carroll) *hld up in last: awkward 5th: prog to join ldrs 4 out gng strly: led next: drvn out fr last* **8/1**

1P-4 **2** *3 ¾* **Saint Raph (FR)**[33] 2153 7-11-10 **123**...........................(t) NickScholfield 126
(Robert Walford) *prom: led 4th: hdd and mstke 6th: blnd next: led again 4 out to 3 out: one pce u.p* **11/4**[2]

1F2- **3** *½* **Listen Boy (IRE)**[353] 3081 9-11-7 **123**............................... RyanHatch[(3)] 123
(Nigel Twiston-Davies) *trckd ldrs: cl 4th after 4 out but pushed along: one pce u.p fr 3 out* **9/4**[1]

/P3- **4** *37* **Westward Point**[250] 4998 8-11-12 **125**............................. GavinSheehan 100
(Warren Greatrex) *led after 2nd to 4th: led again 6th to 4 out: w ldrs tl wknd after 3 out: mstke last: fin v tired* **7/2**[3]

2P-P **5** *29* **Noble Legend**[206] 199 8-11-10 **123**............................. AndrewThornton 56
(Caroline Bailey) *led to after 2nd: rdn and struggling 8th: t.o after 10th* **10/1**

P-22 **P** **Atlantic Roller (IRE)**[172] 715 8-11-12 **125**............................. TomCannon
(Chris Gordon) *in tch tl wknd bef 4 out: sn t.o: p.u bef 2 out* **8/1**

5m 35.0s **Going Correction** -0.125s/f (Good) **6** Ran SP% **111.0**
Speed ratings (Par 107): **95,93,93,78,66**
CSF £30.04 TOTE £9.90: £3.90, £1.40; EX 32.80 Trifecta £69.70.
Owner A W Carroll **Bred** Madame Antonia Devin **Trained** Cropthorne, Worcs

FOCUS
Actual race distance 2m4f 33yds. Not a bad little race with the winner fairly treated on his Flat form.

2833 FOWLER SWIMMING POOLS H'CAP HURDLE (10 hdls) 2m 3f 110y
2:30 (2:30) (Class 4) (0-115,110) 3-Y-0+ **£3,994** (£1,240; £667)

Form RPR
011 **1** **Solstice Star**[21] 2418 5-11-5 **106**...............................(t) KillianMoore[(3)] 116+
(Martin Keighley) *mde all: gng best whn mstke 2 out and sn clr: hit last: pushed out* **7/4**[2]

0-P5 **2** *9* **Arthur Mc Bride (IRE)**[26] 2301 6-11-4 **105**......................... RyanHatch[(3)] 103
(Nigel Twiston-Davies) *cl up: chsd wnr 5th: rdn and no imp bef 2 out: n.d after* **6/1**

0400 **3** *37* **Avel Vor (IRE)**[19] 2458 4-11-4 **102**...............................(t) ConorO'Farrell 63
(Nigel Hawke) *cl up: mstke 4th: urged along 3 out: wknd bef 2 out: lft remote 3rd last* **5/1**[3]

P/PP **P** **Come To The Party (IRE)**[9] 2658 12-11-7 **110**..........(p) DanielHiskett[(5)]
(Harry Chisman) *chsd wnr to 5th: sn rdn and dropped to last: wknd 7th: t.o whn p.u after 3 out* **66/1**

0-P2 **F** **Blackwater King (IRE)**[9] 2667 7-11-11 **109**............................ NoelFehily 103
(Johnny Farrelly) *hld up: trckd ldng pair after 3 out gng strly: rdn bef 2 out and no imp: 10 l bhd wnr in 3rd and wl hld whn crumpled on landing last* **6/4**[1]

5m 21.3s (-4.70) **Going Correction** -0.725s/f (Firm)
WFA 4 from 5yo+ 5lb **5** Ran SP% **108.8**
Speed ratings (Par 105): **80,76,61, ,**
CSF £11.59 TOTE £2.20: £1.70, £3.00; EX 8.80 Trifecta £27.40.
Owner E&G Racing Ltd **Bred** David Allen **Trained** Condicote, Gloucs

FOCUS
Actual race distance 2m3f 143yds. Not overly competitive, especially with the favourite running below form, but the winner is on the upgrade.

2834 BET AND WATCH AT TITANBET.CO.UK H'CAP CHASE (12 fncs) 2m
3:00 (3:00) (Class 5) (0-100,99) 4-Y-0+ **£2,599** (£763; £381; £190)

Form RPR
0P-3 **1** **Capilla (IRE)**[23] 2364 7-11-9 **96**...................................(t[1]) PaulMoloney 119+
(Evan Williams) *mde all and set gd pce: drew clr after 9th: blnd 2 out and mstke last: easily* **6/4**[1]

-5PP **2** *25* **Lamb's Cross**[12] 2601 9-10-9 **85**.................................... JamesBanks[(3)] 77
(Mark Gillard) *chsd wnr: mstke 3rd: rdn after 9th and sn dropped to 3rd: n.d after: plugged on fr last to regain remote 2nd fnl strides* **14/1**

511- **3** *½* **Little Jimmy**[248] 5024 8-11-8 **95**..........................(tp) JamesDavies 86
(Tom Gretton) *trckd ldng pair 4th: chsd wnr after 9th: tried to cl bef 3 out but sn no imp and btn: wknd last and lost remote 2nd fnl strides* **6/1**[3]

114/ **4** *6* **Seventh Hussar**[705] 3246 9-11-5 **92**..........................(t) LeightonAspell 77
(Alison Batchelor) *hld up: mstke 6th: chsd ldng trio next: lost tch after 9th and eased: no ch after* **12/1**

-644 **5** *2 ¾* **The Informant**[25] 2315 9-10-12 **85**...........................(b) AndrewThornton 68
(Seamus Mullins) *sn pushed along: nt fluent 4th and struggling after: wknd 8th: t.o after next* **8/1**

3633 **6** *8* **The Cat's Away (IRE)**[16] 2521 7-10-0 **73** oh4...........(b) RichieMcLernon 47
(Richenda Ford) *chsd ldng pair to 4th: sn dropped to rr and rdn: t.o fr 8th* **4/1**[2]

6353 **P** **Moveable Asset (IRE)**[14] 2552 7-11-7 **99**..........(v) CharlieDeutsch[(5)]
(Henry Tett) *nvr gng wl in last: mstke 2nd: lost tch and blnd 6th: t.o whn clambered over next and p.u* **6/1**[3]

4m 32.3s (-7.70) **Going Correction** -0.125s/f (Good) **7** Ran SP% **114.0**
Speed ratings (Par 103): **114,101,101,98,96 92,**
CSF £20.91 CT £100.66 TOTE £1.90: £1.40, £6.90; EX 24.10 Trifecta £260.30.
Owner Mrs Janet Davies **Bred** Sean Kinsella **Trained** Llancarfan, Vale Of Glamorgan

FOCUS
Actual race distance 2m 15yds. Moderate chasing form and another all-the-way winner on the card. It was a massive chase personal best from him.

2835 TITANBET.CO.UK STANDARD OPEN NATIONAL HUNT FLAT RACE 2m
3:30 (3:30) (Class 6) 4-6-Y-0 **£1,559** (£457; £228; £114)

Form RPR
52-2 **1** **Shanandoa**[21] 2421 4-10-11 0...................................... GavinSheehan 95+
(Brian Barr) *hld up in last: clsd on outer over 3f out: led over 1f out gng easily: nudged along and a holding runner-up after: cleverly* **5/6**[1]

2 *½* **Walt (IRE)** 4-11-4 0.. NoelFehily 100+
(Nicky Henderson) *t.k.h: hld up in 4th: clsd over 3f out: rdn to ld wl over 1f out but wnr sn tk over gng easily: kpt on wl but readily hld after* **11/10**[2]

5 **3** *15* **Surprise Choice (IRE)**[34] 2141 4-10-8 0.................. ConorShoemark[(3)] 78
(William Stone) *led at mod pce: hdd over 3f out and sn wl btn in 4th: regained modest 3rd last strides* **66/1**

4 *1 ½* **Mybrotherjohnny** 4-11-4 0...................................... LeightonAspell 83
(John E Long) *t.k.h: cl up: trckd ldr over 4f out: led over 3f out: hdd & wknd wl over 1f out* **33/1**

5 *63* **Racy Lady** 5-10-11 0.. AndrewThornton 13
(Caroline Bailey) *t.k.h after 4f: chsd ldr to over 4f out: wknd and sn t.o* **20/1**[3]

3m 43.2s (223.20) **5** Ran SP% **111.4**
CSF £2.02 TOTE £2.00: £1.10, £1.10; EX 1.90 Trifecta £12.20.
Owner Excel Racing **Bred** Silfield Bloodstock **Trained** Longburton, Dorset

FOCUS
Actual race distance 2m 15yds. No depth to this bumper, which was run at a steady gallop, and the clear market leaders came well clear.
T/Plt: £68.40 to a £1 stake. Pool: £56,198.58 - 599.48 winning tickets. T/Qpdt: £13.70 to a £1 stake. Pool: £4,448.22 - 239.79 winning tickets. **Jonathan Neesom**

2556 SOUTHWELL (L-H)
Tuesday, December 1

OFFICIAL GOING: Soft changing to soft (heavy in places) after race 1 (12.15)
Wind: moderate 1/2 behind Weather: overcast becoming fine

2836 ATTHERACES.COM H'CAP CHASE (19 fncs) 2m 7f 209y
12:15 (12:15) (Class 5) (0-100,89) 4-Y-0+ **£3,898** (£1,144; £572; £286)

Form RPR
/6-2 **1** **Global Domination**[21] 2410 7-11-5 **82**................................ HarrySkelton 99+
(Caroline Bailey) *j.rt: chsd ldrs 5th: mstke 8th: led 4 out: j.rt 2 out: hit last: drvn out* **11/4**[1]

2-54 **2** *4* **Magical Man**[23] 2364 8-11-5 **82**.....................(p) PaddyBrennan 95
(Debra Hamer) *chsd ldrs: hmpd 2nd: mstke 2nd and 13th: 2nd appr 2 out: kpt on same pce* **13/2**

2032 **3** *8* **Kilcascan**[22] 2402 11-11-9 **89**.....................(p) BenPoste(3) 93
(Rosemary Gasson) *led: hdd 4 out: 3rd appr 2 out: wknd and hit last* **9/2**

54-3 **4** *32* **Flichity (IRE)**[14] 2556 10-10-0 **73** oh11..................... AdamWedge 34
(John Cornwall) *in rr: bhd fr 11th: t.o 3 out: lft distant 4th appr last* **28/1**

2-23 **P** **Nalim (IRE)**[32] 2173 9-11-5 **87**.....................(b) HarryBannister(5)
(Harriet Bethell) *chsd ldrs: drvn 10th: sn lost pl: bhd 4 out: 5th whn p.u appr last* **3/1**[2]

4F4- **P** **High Aspirations (IRE)**[377] 2593 7-11-7 **84**........... SamTwiston-Davies
(Michael Blake) *hmpd 2nd: chsd ldrs 5th: wnt 2nd bef 3 out: wknd between last 2: 4th whn p.u appr last* **7/2**[3]

7m 2.1s (39.10) **Going Correction** +1.375s/f (Heavy) **6** Ran SP% **108.9**
Speed ratings (Par 103): **89,87,85,74,**
CSF £18.63 TOTE £4.10: £2.20, £2.40; EX 20.50 Trifecta £84.00.
Owner G T H Bailey **Bred** Mrs Lucia Farmer **Trained** Holdenby, Northants

FOCUS
Both bends moved fences on outside rail and no change to advertised distances. There was 8mm of rain over the 24hrs leading up to racing and it certainly looked hard work in the opening handicap, which is best rated around the third. The winner is on the upgrade.

2837 REUBEN FOUNDATION SUPPORTS JACK BERRY HOUSE H'CAP CHASE (16 fncs) 2m 4f 62y
12:45 (12:45) (Class 4) (0-120,120) 4-Y-0+ **£5,848** (£1,717; £858; £429)

Form RPR

0-50 **1** **Kilronan High (IRE)**[48] 1904 6-11-12 **120**.............(t) SamTwiston-Davies 130+
(Nigel Twiston-Davies) *chsd ldrs: 2nd 9th: led 12th: drew clr fr 3 out: eased clsng stages* **15/2**

11-5 **2** *11* **Mondo Cane (IRE)**[14] 2560 8-10-13 **107**.....................(b) AdamPogson 107+
(Charles Pogson) *hld up: hdwy to chse ldrs 5th: 2nd appr 3 out: kpt on same pce* **7/2**[2]

35-2 **3** *10* **Frizzo (FR)**[41] 2014 8-10-13 **114**.....................(b) PaulNO'Brien(7) 101
(Harry Whittington) *in rr: outpcd 4 out: modest 3rd sn after 2 out: one pce* **5/2**[1]

446- **4** *16* **Ballymoat**[273] 4554 8-11-6 **114**..................... DannyCook 84
(Sue Smith) *trckd ldrs: 2nd sn after 4 out: wknd appr next* **9/2**[3]

24P- **P** **Free World (FR)**[255] 4897 11-9-12 **99**..................... MissLBrooke(7)
(Lady Susan Brooke) *t.k.h: led: hdd 12th: lost pl next: sn wl bhd: t.o whn p.u bef 3 out* **14/1**

-431 **P** **Bobble Boru (IRE)**[23] 2364 7-10-13 **107**..................... LiamTreadwell
(Venetia Williams) *chsd ldrs: outpcd 4 out: modest 3rd whn blnd 3 out: 4th whn hit next: wl bhd whn p.u bef last* **13/2**

36-0 **P** **Santa's Secret (IRE)**[27] 2266 7-11-3 **114**..................... ThomasGarner(3)
(Oliver Sherwood) *chsd ldr: hit 8th: reminders bef 9th: lost pl sn after 4 out: mstke next and sn bhd: p.u bef 2 out* **8/1**

5m 41.5s (24.50) **Going Correction** +1.375s/f (Heavy) **7** Ran SP% **111.9**
Speed ratings (Par 105): **106,101,97,91, , ,**
CSF £32.93 TOTE £11.00: £4.00, £2.30; EX 34.70 Trifecta £153.30.
Owner Mrs J K Powell **Bred** Mrs Elizabeth Grant **Trained** Naunton, Gloucs

FOCUS
A modest handicap and a big step up from the winner.

2838 ARC SUPPORTING THE 2015 ROA AWARDS NOVICES' HURDLE (13 hdls) 2m 7f 209y
1:15 (1:15) (Class 4) 4-Y-0+ **£3,898** (£1,144; £572; £286)

Form RPR

4-22 **1** **Singlefarmpayment**[31] 2182 5-10-12 125..................... RichardJohnson 129+
(Tom Lacey) *hld up: trckd ldrs 6th: 2nd gng wl 2 out: led between last 2: nt fluent last: v comf* **5/4**[1]

P **2** *7* **Westren Warrior (IRE)**[28] 2257 6-11-5 0..................... WillKennedy 127
(Dr Richard Newland) *hld up in mid-div: trckd ldrs 7th: narrow ld sn after 3 out: hdd between last 2: kpt on same pce* **6/1**[3]

1 **3** *3 ¾* **Crosspark**[14] 2558 5-11-5 0..................... HarrySkelton 123
(Caroline Bailey) *trckd ldrs: cl 3rd and drvn 2 out: one pce between last 2* **2/1**[2]

2-P3 **4** *4 ½* **Monkerty Tunkerty**[14] 2558 12-10-7 0..................... AliceMills(5) 112
(Jess Westwood) *led: clr to 5th: hdd sn after 3 out: outpcd appr next: kpt on one pce to take modest 4th nr fin* **7/1**

/330 **5** *hd* **Grand Introduction (IRE)**[19] 2450 5-10-12 0.............. PaddyBrennan 110
(Fergal O'Brien) *dropped in rr 2nd: hdwy 8th: sn chsng ldrs: fdd appr last* **66/1**

4-0 **6** *32* **Little James (IRE)**[22] 2407 6-10-12 0.............. SamTwiston-Davies 83
(Nigel Twiston-Davies) *chsd ldng pair: 2nd 9th: drvn 3 out: lost pl bef next: sn bhd: t.o* **33/1**

0-5 **7** *18* **Spendajennie (IRE)**[22] 2407 6-10-5 0..................... AdamWedge 53
(Nick Kent) *chsd ldrs 6th: drvn 10th: lost pl next: sn bhd: t.o* **100/1**

6-F4 **P** **Rock Of Ages**[15] 460 6-10-5 107.....................(b) CiaranGethings(7)
(Steve Flook) *sn chsng ldr: drvn 8th: lost pl next: bhd whn p.u bef 10th* **66/1**

6P- **P** **Fromdusktilldawn (IRE)**[252] 4971 5-10-12 0..................... KielanWoods
(Graeme McPherson) *mid-div: lost pl and reminders bef 9th: bhd and reminders 10th: t.o whn p.u bef 2 out* **20/1**

6m 41.5s (26.50) **Going Correction** +1.375s/f (Heavy) **9** Ran SP% **116.2**
Speed ratings (Par 105): **110,107,106,104,104 94,88,, ,**
CSF £9.32 TOTE £2.30: £1.10, £1.20, £1.10; EX 7.70 Trifecta £19.90.
Owner Heather Haddock **Bred** Distillery Stud **Trained** Ledbury, H'fords

FOCUS
A modest staying novice hurdle, which was run at a sound gallop. The winner set a decent standard, but this rated a small personal best.

2839 MRFREEBET.CO.UK ON YOUR MOBILE H'CAP HURDLE (13 hdls) 2m 7f 209y
1:45 (1:45) (Class 4) (0-120,115) 4-Y-0+ **£4,548** (£1,335; £667; £333)

Form RPR

40-2 **1** **Carlo Rocks (IRE)**[22] 2408 5-10-12 **101**..................... HarrySkelton 112+
(Caroline Bailey) *hld up towards rr: t.k.h: hdwy to trck ldrs 9th: 2nd next: led bef 2 out: drvn out* **2/1**[1]

2061 **2** *3* **Fresh By Nature (IRE)**[22] 2405 8-11-2 **110**.............. HarryBannister(5) 111
(Harriet Bethell) *hld up towards rr: hdwy to trck ldrs 3 out: 2nd between last 2: no real imp* **7/1**[3]

133/ **3** *13* **Father Probus**[639] 9-10-13 **105**..................... JonathanEngland(3) 93
(Michael Appleby) *w ldr: led briefly 3rd: dropped bk 6th: chsng ldrs next: led bef 9th: hdd 10th: 3rd bef 2 out: one pce* **7/1**[3]

P121 **4** *½* **Blackwell Synergy (FR)**[128] 1113 9-11-2 **110**.............. ConorRing(5) 98
(John Upson) *chsd ldrs: one pce fr 3 out* **12/1**

3-P4 **5** *22* **Get Involved (IRE)**[195] 397 6-11-7 **110**..................... CharliePoste 86
(Robin Dickin) *chsd ldrs: hit 7th: shkn up next: led 10th: hdd bef 2 out: wknd qckly between last 2* **20/1**

525P **P** **Castle Conflict (IRE)**[19] 2451 10-11-4 **107**.....................(b) TomO'Brien
(Henry Daly) *t.k.h: led: hdd briefly 3rd: hdd 7th: lost pl after next: bhd 3 out: t.o whn p.u bef next: lame* **14/1**

33P/ **P** **Moscow Presents (IRE)**[626] 4814 7-11-6 **112**.............. AdamNicol(3)
(Philip Kirby) *chsd ldrs: pushed along 3rd: lost pl 6th: sn bhd: t.o whn p.u bef 9th* **16/1**

-050 **P** **Ballinalacken (IRE)**[8] 2694 7-11-7 **110**.....................(p) DavidEngland
(Clare Ellam) *hld up towards rr: hdwy 6th: sn trcking ldrs: wknd qckly: eased and 6th whn p.u bef 2 out* **20/1**

1234 **P** **Who You For (IRE)**[17] 2496 5-11-12 **115**..................... RichardJohnson
(Sarah Humphrey) *trckd ldrs: led 7th: hdd bef 9th: lost pl after 10th: sn wl bhd: t.o whn p.u bef 2 out* **10/3**[2]

6m 50.2s (35.20) **Going Correction** +1.375s/f (Heavy) **9** Ran SP% **111.2**
Speed ratings (Par 105): **96,95,90,90,83 , , ,**
CSF £15.77 CT £77.26 TOTE £2.60: £1.30, £1.20, £2.60; EX 12.10 Trifecta £88.80.
Owner Mrs Sheree Tucker **Bred** Edmund Vaughan **Trained** Holdenby, Northants

FOCUS
This took plenty of getting, but the form still looks straightforward.

2840 ARC SUPPORTING THE 2015 LESTERS MAIDEN HURDLE (9 hdls) 1m 7f 153y
2:20 (2:20) (Class 5) 4-Y-0+ **£3,249** (£954; £477; £238)

Form RPR

4- **1** **All Set To Go (IRE)**[213] 1961 4-11-0 0.............(t) SamTwiston-Davies 115+
(Paul Nicholls) *hld up towards rr: hdwy to trck ldrs 5th: 3rd 2 out: led on bit between last 2: easily* **5/2**[2]

P- **2** *6* **Boolavard King (IRE)**[359] 2968 6-11-0 0..................... DavidBass 102
(Kim Bailey) *t.k.h: trckd ldr: led after 4th: hdd between last 2: styd on same pce* **14/1**

20 **3** *1 ¼* **Walkami (FR)**[19] 2460 4-11-0 0..................... RichardJohnson 101
(Jonjo O'Neill) *mid-div: trcking ldrs 5th: 3rd between last 2: kpt on same pce* **11/2**[3]

5-4 **4** *5* **At The Top (FR)**[22] 2406 5-10-7 0..................... HarrySkelton 89
(Dan Skelton) *rr-div: hdwy 3 out: one pce and tk modest 4th last* **14/1**

5 *2 ½* **Nam Hai (IRE)**[46] 4-10-11 0..................... TomBellamy(3) 95
(Kim Bailey) *trckd ldrs: handy 4th 2 out: wknd appr last* **10/1**

213- **6** *6* **One More Go (IRE)**[52] 4715 4-11-0 0..................... WillKennedy 90
(Dr Richard Newland) *trckd ldrs: effrt appr 2 out: wknd appr last* **15/8**[1]

/60- **7** *2* **Red Hott Robbie**[354] 3048 6-11-0 0..................... PeterCarberry 87
(Giuseppe Fierro) *led after 1st: hdd after 4th: wknd between last 2* **250/1**

3- **8** *1 ¼* **Bibi D'Eole (FR)**[261] 4780 4-11-0 0..................... KielanWoods 84
(Graeme McPherson) *in rr: hdwy 3 out: wknd after next: j.lft last* **12/1**

02/ **9** *7* **Roycano**[219] 5-10-9 0..................... HarryBannister(5) 77
(Michael Easterby) *in rr: detached and drvn 4th: hung lft: nvr on terms* **14/1**

6 **10** *3 ½* **Adeenne De Sevres (FR)**[32] 2169 5-11-0 0.......... WayneHutchinson 74
(Tom Lacey) *t.k.h: led tl after 1st: chsd ldrs: wknd sn after 2 out* **25/1**

/40- **11** *hd* **Bountiful Bess**[381] 2503 5-10-2 0..................... JamieBargary(5) 69
(Pam Sly) *chsd ldrs: reminders sn after 3 out: lost pl bef next* **33/1**

46- **P** **Steady Eddie**[256] 4894 5-10-7 0..................... CiaranGethings(7)
(Steve Flook) *detached in rr: hung bdly rt fr 5th: bhd whn p.u bef 3 out* **200/1**

P **Sakhalin Star (IRE)**[27] 4-11-0 0.....................(e) JakeGreenall
(Richard Guest) *in rr: hdwy 3 out: sn chsng ldrs: lost pl: eased and bhd whn p.u bef next* **50/1**

F4-0 **P** **Star Benefit (IRE)**[214] 56 5-10-11 0..................... BenPoste(3)
(Adrian Wintle) *mid-div: lost pl 6th: sn bhd: t.o whn p.u bef 2 out* **200/1**

4m 16.4s (19.40) **Going Correction** +1.375s/f (Heavy) **14** Ran SP% **125.7**
Speed ratings (Par 103): **106,103,102,99,98 95,94,94,90,88 88,, ,**
CSF £38.11 TOTE £4.70: £2.20, £3.70, £2.50; EX 72.20 Trifecta £309.90.
Owner C G Roach **Bred** Mrs S M Rogers & Sir Thomas Pilkington **Trained** Ditcheat, Somerset

FOCUS
An above-average maiden by course standards and the easy winner can rate a lot higher on the best of his turf form.

2841 VISIT SOUTHWELL H'CAP HURDLE (11 hdls) 2m 4f 62y
2:50 (2:50) (Class 5) (0-100,100) 3-Y-0+ **£3,249** (£954; £477; £238)

Form RPR

PP32 **1** **Riddlestown (IRE)**[14] 2556 8-11-2 **90**.....................(b) HarrySkelton 98
(Caroline Fryer) *racd wd: trckd ldrs: led 2nd to 4th: led bef 2 out: styd on wl appr last* **6/1**[3]

4/P- **2** *4* **Money Maid (IRE)**[384] 2454 7-11-10 **98**..................... KielanWoods 101
(Graeme McPherson) *hld up towards rr: hdwy 8th: sn trcking ldrs: 3rd after 3 out: chal between last 2: kpt on same pce* **5/1**[2]

4P-5 **3** *6* **Coozan George**[14] 2558 6-11-12 **100**..................... BrianHughes 99
(Malcolm Jefferson) *hld up towards rr: hdwy 8th: handy 3rd appr 2 out: kpt on one pce* **5/2**[1]

30P **4** *12* **Tuffstuff**[28] 2262 7-11-12 **100**.....................(p) CharliePoste 85
(Brian Barr) *rn wout declared tongue strap: led to 2nd: led 4th: wknd bef 2 out* **20/1**

06-0 **5** *½* **Tanner Hill (IRE)**[206] 207 7-10-10 **84**.....................(p) MarkQuinlan 69
(James Evans) *chsd ldrs: drvn 3 out: wknd bef next* **20/1**

-00P **6** *3 ½* **Gud Day (IRE)**[14] 2560 7-11-7 **95**.....................(p) PaddyBrennan 76
(Conor Dore) *racd wd: hld up towards rr: hdwy 6th: wknd bef 2 out* **20/1**

3-54 **7** *10* **Irish Octave (IRE)**[124] 1158 5-10-6 **83**..................... BenPoste(3) 56
(Rosemary Gasson) *chsd ldrs: drvn 6th: lost pl 8th: sn bhd* **8/1**

504P **8** *7* **The Jugopolist (IRE)**[124] 1155 8-10-0 **74** oh6.............(b) AdamWedge 38
(John Cornwall) *racd on inner: chsd ldrs: lost pl appr 2 out* **66/1**

5/4- **P** **Vintage Vixon (IRE)**[324] 8-10-5 **79**..................... RichardJohnson
(Adrian Wintle) *in rr: drvn and sme hdwy 4th: lost pl 6th: sn bhd: t.o whn p.u bef 2 out* **16/1**

1-50 **P** **Pennies And Pounds**[184] 569 8-10-12 **86**..................... MarkGrant
(Julian Smith) *in rr: hdwy 5th: drvn to chse ldrs next: lost pl 8th: sn bhd: t.o whn p.u bef 2 out* **20/1**

P064 **P** **Lined With Silver (IRE)**[13] 2563 6-11-8 **96**.............. MattieBatchelor
(Dai Burchell) *mid-div: wkng whn stmbld bnd bef 2 out: sn eased and p.u sn after 2 out* **13/2**

5-00 **P** **Perfect Timing (FR)**[19] 2452 5-10-13 **87**.....................(p) LiamTreadwell
(Paul Webber) *mid-div: lost pl 8th: sn bhd: t.o whn p.u bef 2 out* **25/1**

5m 44.2s (31.20) **Going Correction** +1.375s/f (Heavy) **12** Ran SP% **114.2**
Speed ratings (Par 103): **92,90,88,83,83 81,77,74,, ,**
CSF £31.01 CT £93.74 TOTE £6.00: £2.70, £1.80, £1.40; EX 41.70 Trifecta £92.20.
Owner J Ward **Bred** Jeremiah O'Brien **Trained** Wymondham, Norfolk

FOCUS
The majority raced wide in this moderate handicap and the first pair dominated the finish. The winner is a better chaser, but a 105 hurdler in the past.

2842 SOUTHWELL GOLF CLUB WINTER OFFER STANDARD OPEN NATIONAL HUNT FLAT RACE 1m 7f 153y
3:20 (3:20) (Class 6) 4-6-Y-O £1,949 (£572; £286; £143)

Form RPR
1 **Lithic (IRE)** 4-11-0 0 RichardJohnson 116+
(Jonjo O'Neill) *hld up towards rr: hdwy 6f out: sn trcking ldrs: led over 2f out: forged clr fnl f* 11/4 1
2 5 **Tommy Rapper (IRE)** 4-11-0 0 HarrySkelton 111+
(Dan Skelton) *in rr: hdwy 8f out: sn chsng ldrs: led briefly 3 out: styd on same pce appr fnl f* 11/2 3
3 12 **Prince Of Steal (IRE)**233 5-11-0 0 LiamTreadwell 99
(James Evans) *t.k.h: towards rr: hdwy on inner to trck ldrs after 5f: 4th over 2f out: kpt on one pce: tk 3rd last 100yds* 14/1
4 2¾ **Alexander The Grey** 4-11-0 0 KielanWoods 96
(Graeme McPherson) *hld up in rr: hdwy 7f out: sn trcking ldrs: handy 3rd over 2f out: fdd fnl f* 14/1
5 5 **Lough Salt (IRE)** 4-11-0 0 JakeGreenall 91
(Mark Walford) *mid-div: chsng ldrs 6f out: one pce over 2f out* 18/1
2 6 10 **Fisherman Frank**104 1289 4-10-9 0 (t) FreddieMitchell(5) 81
(Natalie Lloyd-Beavis) *hld up: hdwy to trck ldrs after 6f: drvn over 7f out: wknd over 3f out* 8/1
5 7 4 **Shan't Agree (IRE)**195 407 4-11-0 0 TomO'Brien 77
(Henry Daly) *chsd ldrs: pushed along 7f out: lost pl over 3f out* 12/1
8 ½ **Ballypoint (IRE)** 4-11-0 0 SamTwiston-Davies 77
(Nigel Twiston-Davies) *led: hdd 3f out: sn wknd* 4/1 2
9 2½ **Hag Stone** 4-11-0 0 WayneHutchinson 74
(Tom Lacey) *hld up in rr: sme hdwy 5f out: sn lost pl and bhd* 9/1
66- 10 69 **Maybe Enough**349 3150 4-10-0 0 (p) MrMartinMcIntyre(7)
(Phil McEntee) *w ldr: t.k.h: drvn 6f out: lost pl 5f out: sn wl bhd: t.o over 2f out: virtually p.u* 33/1
0 11 3 **Sundance Boy**17 2493 6-11-0 0 PeterCarberry 2
(Giuseppe Fierro) *trckd ldrs: lost pl over 4f out: sn bhd: t.o over 2f out: virtually p.u* 200/1
P **Tango Unchained (IRE)** 6-10-9 0 HarryBannister(5)
(Charlie Mann) *chsd ldrs: drvn over 4f out: sn lost pl: eased and bhd whn p.u over 2f out* 25/1

4m 9.5s (18.10) **Going Correction** +1.375s/f (Heav) 12 Ran SP% 116.7
Speed ratings: **109,106,100,99,96 91,89,89,88,53 52,**
CSF £17.04 TOTE £3.40: £1.30, £2.80, £6.00; EX 19.40 Trifecta £258.40.
Owner Jon and Julia Aisbitt **Bred** Declan Dorgan **Trained** Cheltenham, Gloucs

FOCUS
Not a bad bumper and the first two look above average.
T/Plt: £55.60 to a £1 stake. Pool: £65,047.89 - 853.53 winning tickets. T/Qpdt: £5.50 to a £1 stake. Pool: £7,998.93 - 1,072.46 winning tickets. **Walter Glynn**

CATTERICK (L-H)
Wednesday, December 2

OFFICIAL GOING: Good to soft (soft in places; 7.9)
Wind: fresh 1/2 behind Weather: overcast and breezy, rain race 3 onwards

2843 JUMP SEASON STARTS TODAY CONDITIONAL JOCKEYS' H'CAP HURDLE (10 hdls) 2m 3f 66y
12:20 (12:20) (Class 4) (0-110,109) 3-Y-O+ £3,249 (£954; £477; £238)

Form RPR
06-P 1 **Running Wolf (IRE)**35 2139 4-10-13 96 (t) KillianMoore 96
(Alex Hales) *hld up in rr: hdwy 6th: chsng ldrs 3 out: led narrowly last: all out* 12/1
5424 2 hd **Claude Carter**26 2326 11-11-10 107 (p) KieronEdgar 107
(Alistair Whillans) *w ldr: drvn to ld narrowly appr 2 out: hdd last: rallied in clsng stages: jst hld* 10/1
5034 3 nk **Mondlicht (USA)**23 2396 5-11-8 105 DiarmuidO'Regan 105
(James Moffatt) *reluctant early and bhd: drvn 4th: hdwy 3 out: modest 5th next: handy 3rd and hit last: upsides last 75yds: no ex in clsng stages* 13/2 3
P-20 4 14 **Astrum**190 481 5-11-1 106 (b) RonanShort(8) 94
(Donald McCain) *trckd ldrs: upsides and drvn 2 out: wknd appr last* 5/1 2
321/ 5 1¾ **Should I Stay (FR)**590 5441 7-11-8 108 (p) GLavery(3) 94
(Alan Brown) *w ldrs: led after 5th: j.lft next: hdd appr 2 out: wknd between last 2* 14/1
4/35 6 21 **Pinotage**27 2291 7-10-12 95 (p) JamieHamilton 62
(Peter Niven) *mid-div: chsd ldrs 3rd: lost pl sn after 3 out* 13/2 3
-564 7 15 **Beer Goggles (IRE)**33 2169 4-11-10 107 CraigNichol 60
(Micky Hammond) *bhd and nt fluent: drvn 6th: nvr on terms* 4/1 1
000/ 8 17 **Celtic Abbey**360 2985 8-11-8 105 ColmMcCormack 43
(Joanne Foster) *hld up towards rr: bhd fr 3 out* 16/1
00-5 P **Silmi**191 470 11-11-4 101 MauriceLinehan
(Sophie Leech) *t.k.h: trckd ldrs: lost pl and reminders after 5th: sn bhd: t.o whn p.u bef last* 14/1
200- P **Mubrook (USA)**316 3788 10-10-8 96 (b) LorcanMurtagh(5)
(John David Riches) *led tl after 5th: lost pl bef 6th: sn bhd: t.o whn p.u bef last* 50/1
056/ P **Bradbury (IRE)**32 4526 7-11-7 109 (p) FinianO'Toole(5)
(Julia Brooke) *chsd ldrs: lost pl sn after 3 out: poor 7th whn blnd 2 out: p.u between last 2: lame* 9/1

4m 40.5s (4.40) **Going Correction** -0.25s/f (Good) 11 Ran SP% 111.3
Speed ratings (Par 105): **80,79,79,73,73 64,58,50, ,**
CSF £118.96 CT £829.04 TOTE £16.30: £4.40, £2.60, £1.90; EX 138.50 Trifecta £1068.50.
Owner The Wolfgangers **Bred** Ben Browne **Trained** Edgcote, Northamptonshire

FOCUS
All distances as advertised. Some starts have been moved at this track following remeasuring, this so some races will not have speed figures until there is sufficient data to calculate updated median times. A typically modest conditional jockeys' event to open the card, with a tight three-way finish. A big step up from the winner in a tongue-tie.

2844 BHEST RACING TO SCHOOL H'CAP CHASE (16 fncs) 2m 3f 51y
12:50 (12:50) (Class 5) (0-100,100) 4-Y-O+ £3,249 (£954; £477; £238)

Form RPR
5652 1 **Aregra (FR)**64 1687 5-10-3 77 (p) BrianHughes 91+
(Peter Niven) *w ldr: led last: forged clr* 8/1 3
03-5 2 4 **Bollin Line**34 2143 8-10-11 85 DannyCook 94+
(Lucinda Egerton) *in rr whn mstke 1st: chsd ldrs 5th: led narrowly 2 out: hdd last: kpt on same pce* 7/1 2
2U5 3 3¼ **Court Of Law (IRE)**27 2297 7-11-10 98 (p) SamTwiston-Davies 102
(Donald McCain) *led: hdd 2 out: one pce* 9/1
5551 4 4 **Roxyfet (FR)**8 2705 5-10-6 87 7ex FinianO'Toole(7) 88
(Micky Hammond) *in rr: sme hdwy 11th: modest 5th 2 out: 4th and hit last: kpt on one pce* 9/1
60-6 5 11 **Bennylicious (IRE)**34 2143 6-11-9 100 (t) GrahamWatters(3) 91
(Rose Dobbin) *chsd ldrs: drvn appr 3 out: wknd bef 2 out* 7/1 2
P-46 6 1¼ **Foot The Bill**188 519 10-10-13 90 JohnKington(3) 80
(Patrick Holmes) *chsd ldrs: outpcd 9th: drvn and lost pl 11th* 14/1
0-50 7 12 **Dark And Dangerous (IRE)**26 2322 7-11-5 98 CallumBewley(5) 76
(Simon Waugh) *mid-div: j.lft 3rd: lost pl 10th: sn bhd* 20/1
-04P 8 13 **Azerodegree (IRE)**26 2321 6-9-7 74 oh1 (b) ThomasDowson(7) 40
(Harriet Graham) *in rr: bhd fr 10th: blnd bdly last* 40/1
4-PP 9 5 **Auldthunder (IRE)**23 2400 8-11-3 94 JoeColliver(3) 56
(Micky Hammond) *j.rt in rr: reminder 10th: bhd fr 9th* 20/1
33-5 U **Wakhan (IRE)**8 2707 7-10-5 86 (p) TrevorRyan(7)
(Sue Smith) *chsd ldrs: blnd and uns rdr 4th* 9/2 1
53-2 F **Runswick Relax**8 2706 9-10-0 74 oh7 (tp) HenryBrooke
(Kenneth Slack) *towards rr: hmpd and fell 3rd* 9/2 1

4m 54.4s (294.40) 11 Ran SP% 111.1
CSF £58.26 CT £497.17 TOTE £5.40: £2.50, £3.00, £3.20; EX 60.70 Trifecta £800.80.
Owner G C Wragg **Bred** Jean Brest **Trained** Barton-le-Street, N Yorks

FOCUS
A moderate handicap chase in which the joint-favourites both departed the race early. This was a step up from the first two.

2845 SUPPORT THE HOUSE THAT JACK BUILT JUVENILE HURDLE (8 hdls) 1m 7f 156y
1:20 (1:20) (Class 4) 3-Y-O £3,898 (£1,144; £572; £286)

Form RPR
1 **Jaleo (GER)**199 3-10-12 0 AidanColeman 126+
(John Ferguson) *trckd ldrs: modest 2nd appr 4th: nt fluent 2 out: swtchd lft appr last: styd on in clsng stages: led post* 4/1 2
13 2 shd **Romain De Senam (FR)**18 2480 3-11-5 136 (t1) HarryCobden(7) 139+
(Paul Nicholls) *t.k.h: led: 1 l ahd last: sn rdn: hdd post* 1/4 1
4 3 41 **Multi Grain**26 2324 3-10-5 0 SamTwiston-Davies 81
(Micky Hammond) *hld up in mid-div: modest 3rd 5th: no ch w 1st 2* 12/1 3
00 4 1¼ **Hey Bob (IRE)**49 1899 3-10-9 0 TonyKelly(3) 87
(Chris Grant) *hld up in last: hdwy after 3 out: modest 4th next: blnd last* 150/1
5 5 6 **Fizzlestix (FR)**31 2219 3-10-12 0 HarrySkelton 82
(Dan Skelton) *t.k.h in rr: sme hdwy 3 out: wknd next* 14/1
3 6 6 **The Name's Bond**179 636 3-10-12 0 JamesReveley 76
(Keith Reveley) *in rr: hdwy 5th: wknd appr 2 out* 14/1
55 7 3 **Moon Arc (IRE)**26 2324 3-10-9 0 CraigNichol(3) 74
(Keith Dalgleish) *trckd ldr 2nd tl bef 4th: blnd 3 out: wknd bef next* 40/1
00 8 20 **Danny O'Ruairc (IRE)**29 1899 3-10-7 0 DiarmuidO'Regan(5) 56
(James Moffatt) *in rr: nt fluent 3rd: sme hdwy next: lost pl bef 3 out: sn wl bhd: t.o next* 100/1
9 19 **Mercury**20 3-10-12 0 BrianHughes 38
(Kevin Ryan) *chsd ldr to 2nd: pushed along 4th: lost pl 3 out: sn wl bhd: t.o next* 25/1

3m 43.8s (-8.70) **Going Correction** -0.25s/f (Good) 9 Ran SP% 129.0
Speed ratings (Par 104): **111,110,90,89,86 83,82,72,62**
CSF £6.26 TOTE £6.70: £1.10, £1.10, £1.90; EX 8.40 Trifecta £33.70.
Owner Bloomfields **Bred** Gestut Karlshof **Trained** Cowlinge, Suffolk

FOCUS
A weak juvenile hurdle that revolved around the heavy odds-on favourite attempting to negate a double penalty.

2846 COME RACING NEW YEAR'S DAY BEGINNERS' CHASE (16 fncs) 2m 3f 51y
1:50 (1:50) (Class 4) 4-Y-O+ £4,548 (£1,335; £667; £333)

Form RPR
10-3 1 **Stilletto (IRE)**11 2639 6-11-0 0 SamTwiston-Davies 126+
(Paul Nicholls) *t.k.h in rr: hdwy to trck ldrs 7th: led sn after 3 out: rdn and edgd lft run-in kpt on* 6/4 1
50-4 2 1¼ **Amore Alato**31 2222 6-11-0 0 RichardJohnson 123+
(Johnny Farrelly) *in rr: hdwy 8th: sn chsng ldrs: drvn 13th: cl 2nd 2 out: kpt on same pce run-in: regained 2nd nr fin* 15/8 2
5430 3 hd **Raktiman (IRE)**13 2594 8-10-11 123 JonathanEngland(3) 122
(Richard Drake) *led to 3rd: chsd ldrs: outpcd 13th: modest 6th 3 out: 3rd last: chsd wnr last 75yds: lost 2nd nr fin* 18/1
2-24 4 3¼ **Ballyvoque (IRE)**135 1068 9-11-0 0 JanFaltejsek 119
(George Charlton) *w ldrs: led 3rd: hit 3 out: sn hdd: fdd last* 28/1
6222 5 10 **Chase The Wind (IRE)**43 2010 6-11-0 124 HenryBrooke 109
(Joanne Foster) *trckd ldrs: 2nd 8th tl 3 out: wknd last* 25/1
-F2P 6 6 **Vayland**41 2026 6-10-11 119 CraigNichol(3) 106
(Micky Hammond) *in rr: outpcd whn mstke 12th: sme hdwy appr 3 out: sn wknd* 100/1
34-P 7 15 **Engrossing**19 2475 6-11-0 116 BrianHughes 90
(Peter Niven) *chsd ldrs: lost pl 2 out: sn bhd* 50/1
P 8 26 **Under The Red Sky (IRE)**32 2197 8-11-0 0 PeterBuchanan 67
(Kenny Johnson) *in rr: bhd fr 11th: t.o 3 out* 250/1
115/ U **Only Orsenfoolsies**25 4518 6-10-11 0 JoeColliver(3)
(Micky Hammond) *chsd ldrs: lost pl 9th: bhd after 13th: t.o whn mstke and uns rdr 2 out* 15/2 3
2-6U F **Minellaforleisure (IRE)**9 2686 7-11-0 126 KielanWoods
(Alex Hales) *mid-div: fell 4th* 17/2

4m 50.1s (290.10) 10 Ran SP% 113.0
CSF £4.44 TOTE £2.40: £1.40, £1.10, £2.20; EX 6.10 Trifecta £33.60.
Owner R S Brookhouse **Bred** W Powell-Harris **Trained** Ditcheat, Somerset

FOCUS
Just a fair beginners' chase, but the winner was a 132-rated hurdler and should go on to rate higher over fences. They went four seconds faster than the earlier 0-100.

2847 EPDS SUPPORTS RACING WELFARE MARES' NOVICES' HURDLE (10 hdls) 2m 3f 66y
2:20 (2:21) (Class 4) 4-Y-0+ **£3,898** (£1,144; £572; £286)

Form RPR
2-21 **1** **Actinpieces**[18] 2494 4-11-0 0 MissGAndrews(3) 116+
(Pam Sly) *t.k.h: trckd ldrs in 3rd fr 3rd: hit 6th: hmpd bnd after 3 out: 2nd appr 2 out: hit 2 out: swtchd lft between last 2: hung lft and led last: fnd ex last 75yds* **8/11**[1]

23 **2** *3 ¼* **Shine Away (IRE)**[10] 2665 5-10-10 0 DannyCook 101
(Sue Smith) *trckd clr ldr: led sn after 3 out: hdd last: kpt on same pce last 50yds* **7/1**[3]

4-6 **3** *31* **Rock Chick Supremo (IRE)**[38] 2086 4-10-10 0 HarrySkelton 72
(Dan Skelton) *mid-div: hdwy 7th: handy 3rd appr 2 out: wknd qckly between last 2* **9/4**[2]

55 **4** *16* **Slide Show**[26] 2325 7-10-7 0 AdamNicol(3) 58
(David Thompson) *led: j.rt 2nd: clr next tl after 7th: hdd sn after 3 out: 4th and wkng whn hit 2 out: sn bhd* **66/1**

-403 **5** *2 ½* **Milly Baloo**[18] 2494 4-10-10 0 BrianHarding 55
(Tim Easterby) *mid-div: drvn 5th: sn lost pl and bhd: t.o 3 out* **20/1**

00-0 **6** *7* **Lucarno Dancer**[26] 2318 5-10-5 0 (t[1]) CallumBewley(5) 49
(Raymond Shiels) *in rr: drvn 6th: sn bhd: t.o 3 out* **100/1**

00- **U** **Zruda**[29] 2956 4-10-3 0 ThomasDowson(7)
(David Thompson) *3rd whn mstke and uns rdr 1st* **200/1**

4m 42.5s (6.40) **Going Correction** -0.25s/f (Good) **7 Ran SP% 108.9**
Speed ratings (Par 105): **76,74,61,54,53 50,**
CSF £5.85 TOTE £1.80: £1.30, £2.30; EX 5.50 Trifecta £8.80.
Owner Mrs P M Sly **Bred** Mrs P Sly **Trained** Thorney, Cambs
■ Stewards' Enquiry : Danny Cook three-day ban: careless riding (Dec 16-18)

FOCUS
Little depth to this mares' novice hurdle, but the winner is value for further.

2848 BOOK NOW FOR 28TH DECEMBER H'CAP CHASE (19 fncs) 3m 1f 54y
2:50 (2:50) (Class 4) (0-120,118) 4-Y-0+ **£5,198** (£1,526; £763; £381)

Form RPR
3P-1 **1** **Cyrien Star**[34] 2149 8-11-4 **110** RichardJohnson 123+
(Henry Daly) *w ldrs: led 4th: blnd 13th: styd on fr 2 out: edgd rt run-in: drvn rt out* **2/1**[1]

6444 **2** *1 ¾* **Valleyofmilan (IRE)**[27] 2295 8-11-7 **118** JamesCowley(5) 127
(Donald McCain) *trckd ldrs 5th: 3rd and drvn sn after 4 out: chsd wnr sn after last: kpt on same pce* **17/2**

-145 **3** *2 ¾* **Alto Des Mottes (FR)**[23] 2400 5-11-3 **112** TonyKelly(3) 122+
(Henry Hogarth) *chsd wnr: hit 9th: drvn bef 3 out: kpt on one pce run-in* **9/2**[2]

14/U **4** *12* **Tiny Dancer (IRE)**[33] 2173 7-11-0 **106** BrianHughes 102
(Chris Grant) *hld up in rr: hdwy and 4th 4 out: effrt whn mstke 3 out: sn wknd* **15/2**[3]

-45P **5** *46* **Basford Ben**[14] 2566 7-11-0 **106** (v) PeterCarberry 60
(Jennie Candlish) *led to 4th: hit 12th: sn lost pl and bhd: lft distant 4th bef last: t.o* **8/1**

1-4P **P** **Playing The Field (IRE)**[16] 2539 10-10-10 **102** JoshuaMoore
(Jonjo O'Neill) *chsd ldrs 5th: hit 7th: drvn 14th: sn lost pl: t.o 5th whn blnd 2 out: p.u bef last* **15/2**[3]

13P- **P** **Shinooki (IRE)**[259] 4848 8-11-8 **114** (p) KielanWoods
(Alex Hales) *chsd ldrs 4th: wkng whn mstke 15th: sn bhd: t.o whn p.u 3 out* **8/1**

6m 31.5s (-10.50) **Going Correction** -0.25s/f (Good) **7 Ran SP% 107.8**
Speed ratings (Par 105): **106,105,104,100,86 ,**
CSF £16.55 TOTE £2.40: £1.60, £4.60; EX 20.20 Trifecta £72.20.
Owner Puteus Profundus **Bred** Wood Farm Stud **Trained** Stanton Lacy, Shropshire

FOCUS
An ordinary handicap chase, and a chance could be given to all of them. A step up from the winner, but he was a 128-rated hurdler so there may still be more to come.

2849 WATCH RACING UK ANYWHERE INTERMEDIATE OPEN NATIONAL HUNT FLAT RACE 1m 7f 156y
3:20 (3:20) (Class 6) 4-6-Y-0 **£1,949** (£572; £286; £143)

Form RPR
5- **1** **The Tailgater (IRE)**[259] 4852 4-11-4 0 RichardJohnson 103+
(Jonjo O'Neill) *hld up in mid-div: hdwy after 6f: sn trcking ldrs: 2nd over 2f out: led appr fnl f: edgd lft: drvn rt out* **5/1**[3]

2 *1* **Mo Chailin (IRE)**[222] 4-10-11 0 SamTwiston-Davies 95+
(Donald McCain) *trckd ldrs: led 3f out: hdd appr fnl f: kpt on same pce last 50yds* **13/2**

3 *6* **River Dun**[38] 2099 5-10-4 0 AnthonyFox(7) 90
(S R B Crawford, Ire) *hld up in rr: hdwy after 6f: sn trcking ldrs: 4th over 2f out: kpt on one pce to take modest 3rd last 100yds* **9/4**[1]

3- **4** *3 ¼* **Dothraki Raider**[251] 4995 4-11-4 0 AidanColeman 94
(Sophie Leech) *mid-div: hdwy after 6f: sn trcking ldrs: 3rd over 2f out: wknd fnl f* **5/1**[3]

00- **5** *31* **More Play**[261] 4812 4-10-8 0 JoeColliver(3) 59
(George Moore) *led: drvn over 3f out: sn hdd: wknd over 2f out: sn bhd: t.o* **22/1**

6 *2 ¼* **Bon Genre (IRE)**[206] 235 4-10-11 0 HarryCobden(7) 64
(Robert Stephens) *w ldr: drvn over 3f out: lost pl over 2f out: sn bhd: t.o* **5/2**[2]

7 *dist* **Last Pick (IRE)**[192] 5-10-11 0 LorcanMurtagh(7)
(Barry Murtagh) *in rr: drvn after 5f: lost tch 7f out: sn tailed rt off: eventually completed* **150/1**

3m 43.0s (-3.90) **Going Correction** -0.25s/f (Good) **7 Ran SP% 111.0**
Speed ratings: **99,98,95,93,78 77,**
CSF £34.48 TOTE £7.00: £2.90, £3.00; EX 29.90 Trifecta £103.00.
Owner Paul & Clare Rooney **Bred** Sean And Orla Gannon **Trained** Cheltenham, Gloucs

FOCUS
A weak bumper in which only one had the benefit of a recent run. They went a fair pace.
T/Plt: £23.70 to a £1 stake. Pool of £54073.34 0- 1661.07 winning tickets. T/Qpdt: £2.30 to a £1 stake. Pool of £5507.51 - 1722.49 winning tickets. **Walter Glynn**

[2689] LUDLOW (R-H)
Wednesday, December 2

OFFICIAL GOING: Soft (good to soft in places)
Wind: Light behind Weather: Overcast

2850 JENKINSONS CATERING NOVICES' CLAIMING HURDLE (9 hdls) 1m 7f 169y
12:40 (12:40) (Class 4) 4-Y-0+ **£3,898** (£1,144; £572; £286)

Form RPR
3-34 **1** **Scoppio Del Carro**[13] 2218 4-10-1 112 (t) DeanPratt(7) 105+
(John Quinn) *hld up: hdwy 5th: led last: styd on wl* **7/4**[1]

06 **2** *4* **Guaracha**[9] 2689 4-10-9 0 RyanWhile(5) 106
(Bill Turner) *prom: chsd ldr 5th: mstke next: led appr 3 out: rdn and hdd last: styd on same pce flat* **10/1**

2333 **3** *1 ¼* **Sacred Square (GER)**[27] 2294 5-11-0 108 (p) WayneHutchinson 103
(Donald McCain) *hld up: hdwy after 6th: rdn and ev ch appr last: styd on same pce flat* **4/1**[2]

6-30 **4** *¾* **Neworld (FR)**[18] 2492 6-11-0 99 [1] AlainCawley 102
(Richard Hobson) *hld up: hdwy appr 3 out: styd on same pce flat* **5/1**[3]

/6-6 **5** *11* **Solidago (IRE)**[33] 2165 8-10-7 91 HarryChalloner(3) 87
(Barry Leavy) *hld up: hdwy 3 out: nt trble ldrs* **25/1**

1550 **6** *9* **Archie Rice (USA)**[38] 2087 9-10-3 103 MissBFrost(7) 80
(Jimmy Frost) *prom: blnd 3rd: wknd 3 out* **8/1**

3245 **7** *2* **Symphony Of Pearls**[18] 2492 4-10-3 81 RobertDunne 70
(Dai Burchell) *chsd ldrs tl wknd 2 out* **12/1**

50 **8** *hd* **Aaman (IRE)**[14] 2564 9-10-5 0 RobertWilliams(3) 78
(Bernard Llewellyn) *prom: blnd 5th: mstke next: sn rdn: wknd 3 out* **100/1**

0 **9** *7* **One Last Dream**[14] 2563 6-10-10 0 IanPopham 70
(Ron Hodges) *hld up: hdwy 5th: wknd 3 out* **50/1**

06P **10** *16* **Desroches (GER)**[34] 2150 7-9-12 88 BenPoste(3) 44
(Robin Dickin) *chsd ldr tl led after 4th: hdd & wknd appr 3 out* **50/1**

11 *14* **Mr Jalfrazy (IRE)**[220] 6-11-4 0 AdamWedge 47
(Tom Weston) *a in rr: bhd fr 3rd* **22/1**

4-P **12** *20* **Ninny Noodle**[33] 2164 5-10-5 0 [1] LiamTreadwell 14
(Miss Imogen Pickard) *hld up: plld hrd: a in rr: wknd after 6th* **150/1**

0- **P** **Big Smile (IRE)**[321] 3688 7-10-8 0 LiamHeard
(John Groucott) *prom to 5th: bhd whn p.u bef 3 out* **250/1**

P- **P** **Premier Jack's**[294] 1793 4-10-5 0 ChrisWard(5)
(Nikki Evans) *led: mstke 4th: sn hdd: mstke and wknd 6th: bhd whn p.u bef 3 out* **150/1**

-605 **U** **Sadiks Boy (IRE)**[174] 700 6-10-8 0 [1] LeeEdwards
(Aytach Sadik) *tried to refuse and uns rdr 1st* **200/1**

3m 56.1s (6.60) **Going Correction** +0.55s/f (Soft)
WFA 4 from 5yo+ 5lb **15 Ran SP% 116.3**
Speed ratings (Par 105): **105,103,102,102,96 92,91,90,87,79 72,62, , ,**
CSF £19.26 TOTE £2.50: £1.40, £3.30, £1.70; EX 22.60 Trifecta £64.60.Sacred Square was claimed by C Dore for £8000. Scoppio Del Carro was claimed by C T Pogson for £5000.
Owner Ross Harmon **Bred** Sir Eric Parker **Trained** Settrington, N Yorks

FOCUS
Golf House Bend out 8yds, Ludlow Bend out 3yds making the actual distance of the opener 1m7f 191.5yds. Alain Cawley described the ground as "dead, tacky and hard work in places". The right horses came to the fore in this claimer and the winner didn't need to be near his best.

2851 SHUKERS LANDROVER OF LUDLOW NOVICES' H'CAP CHASE (16 fncs) 2m 4f 11y
1:10 (1:10) (Class 4) (0-105,105) 4-Y-0+ **£5,848** (£1,717; £858; £429)

Form RPR
2-0F **1** **Truckers Highway (IRE)**[30] 2249 6-10-4 **86** [1] HarryChalloner(3) 106+
(John Groucott) *mde all: j.lft at times: clr to 5th: wnt clr again 2 out: wnt bdly lft last: styd on wl* **11/2**[3]

00/4 **2** *8* **Gallic Warrior (FR)**[30] 2249 8-11-12 **105** PaddyBrennan 115
(Fergal O'Brien) *a.p: nt fluent 10th: chsd wnr 12th: rdn after 2 out: styd on same pce* **2/1**[1]

36 **3** *27* **Akinspirit (IRE)**[20] 2449 11-11-1 **99** [1] CharlieDeutsch(5) 82
(Nikki Evans) *hld up: hdwy appr 4 out: wknd next* **20/1**

5- **4** *2 ¾* **Railway Benefit (IRE)**[222] 5511 7-10-10 **89** (t) JamesDavies 71
(Adrian Wintle) *chsd wnr to 12th: rdn after next: wkng whn hit 3 out* **7/1**

-0P3 **F** **John Biscuit (IRE)**[13] 2604 7-10-8 **90** JamesBanks(3)
(Jo Davis) *hld up: j.lft: mstke 6th: fell next* **9/1**

03P- **P** **Up Your Game (IRE)**[255] 4937 7-10-0 **82** oh2 ow3 (t) RyanHatch(3)
(Roy Brotherton) *hld up: rdn and wknd 13th: bhd whn p.u bef 3 out* **16/1**

355 **P** **The Bugler (IRE)**[15] 2559 8-11-2 **95** (t) PaulMoloney
(Evan Williams) *hld up and a in rr: bhd fr 9th: p.u bef 14th* **7/2**[2]

4-00 **P** **Benability (IRE)**[30] 2256 5-11-2 **95** MichaelByrne
(Tim Vaughan) *hld up: rdn and wknd after 13th: bhd whn p.u bef 4 out* **10/1**

5m 21.5s (17.10) **Going Correction** +0.85s/f (Soft) **8 Ran SP% 113.2**
Speed ratings (Par 105): **99,95,85,83, , ,**
CSF £17.35 CT £201.40 TOTE £7.90: £2.20, £1.10, £4.70; EX 18.80 Trifecta £236.50.
Owner C J Tipton **Bred** David Pim **Trained** Bourton, Shropshire

FOCUS
Actual distance 2m4f 37yds. Half of the field failed to complete and the front pair drew a long way clear in this moderate chase. The winner was a poor hurdler, but has been rated in line with his bumper mark.

2852 ALFA AGGREGATES PRODUCTS MARES' H'CAP HURDLE (9 hdls) 1m 7f 169y
1:40 (1:40) (Class 2) 3-Y-0+ **£12,346** (£3,625; £1,812; £906)

Form RPR
-15P **1** **Bella (FR)**[148] 938 4-10-11 **113** (t) TomScudamore 117+
(David Pipe) *a.p: shkn up to ld appr last: styd on wl* **25/1**

222- **2** *3 ¾* **Dusky Legend**[307] 3932 5-11-6 **122** WayneHutchinson 124+
(Alan King) *hld up: hdwy appr 3 out: sn ev ch hit 2 out: rdn and hit last: styd on same pce flat* **11/8**[1]

20-4 **3** *2 ½* **Allez Encore (IRE)**[32] 2199 6-11-12 **128** DavidBass 126
(Kim Bailey) *chsd ldrs: led appr 3 out: rdn and hdd appr last: no ex flat* **4/1**[3]

41-3 **4** *10* **Tara Mist**[25] 2349 6-11-7 **123** PaddyBrennan 113
(Henry Daly) *chsd ldr tl rdn appr 3 out: wkg whn hit next* **11/4**[2]

3-21 **5** *10* **Pandorica**[173] 714 7-10-4 **109** (p) RobertWilliams(3) 91
(Bernard Llewellyn) *hld up: rdn appr 3 out: sn wknd* **16/1**

3151 **6** *5* **Northern Meeting (IRE)**[46] 1974 5-10-9 **111**....................(p) TomO'Brien 84
(Robert Stephens) *led: mstke 3rd: hdd appr 3 out: sn wknd* **8/1**
3m 55.1s (5.60) **Going Correction** +0.55s/f (Soft)
WFA 4 from 5yo+ 5lb **6 Ran SP% 109.6**
Speed ratings (Par 109): **108,106,104,99,94 92**
CSF £59.38 TOTE £16.80: £5.20, £1.40; EX 92.70 Trifecta £419.50.
Owner Prof Caroline Tisdall **Bred** Dr Vet R Y Simon & N Simon **Trained** Nicholashayne, Devon
FOCUS
Actual distance 1m7f 191.5yds. A fair mares' handicap, but it produced something of a shock winner.

2853 BOYNE CUP (A H'CAP CHASE) (QUALIFIER FOR THE CHALLENGER STAYING CHASE SERIES FINAL) (22 fncs) 3m 1f 125y

2:10 (2:10) (Class 3) (0-130,130) 4-Y-0+ **£12,996** (£3,816; £1,908; £954)

Form RPR
40-P **1** **Tinker Time (IRE)**[29] 2261 7-11-5 **123**.................................. LiamHeard 136+
(Bob Buckler) *chsd ldrs: led appr last: styd on wl* **7/1**
2P0- **2** *7* **Goodtoknow**[240] 5184 7-11-4 **122**..............................(p) JakeGreenall 127
(Kerry Lee) *chsd ldrs: led after 14th: hdd next: led again 18th: rdn and hdd appr last: wknd towards fin* **7/1**
1240 **3** *1* **Skylander (IRE)**[17] 2513 6-11-5 **128**.......................... DavidNoonan(5) 133
(David Pipe) *hld up: hdwy 15th: rdn appr last: styd on same pce* **6/1**[3]
-341 **4** *3/4* **King Massini (IRE)**[20] 2451 9-11-5 **123**......................... AdamWedge 127
(Evan Williams) *prom: mstke 11th: led after 16th: hdd 18th: outpcd after 4 out: styd on flat* **7/2**[1]
0U-U **5** *7* **Deciding Moment (IRE)**[173] 707 9-11-10 **128**.......(t) WayneHutchinson 127+
(Ben De Haan) *hld up: hdwy appr 4 out: wknd 2 out* **20/1**
55-4 **6** *10* **Come On Laurie (IRE)**[44] 2001 7-11-5 **123**................ LeightonAspell 109
(Oliver Sherwood) *prom: led 15th: blnd next: sn hdd: wknd 3 out* **11/2**[2]
F-46 **7** *5* **Until Winning (FR)**[20] 2459 7-11-7 **130**...................... JamieBargary(5) 111
(Tom George) *mde most tl after 14th: remained handy tl wknd after 4 out* **25/1**
1-35 **8** *7* **Rio Milan (IRE)**[13] 2593 9-11-4 **122**...........................(tp) PaddyBrennan 99
(Fergal O'Brien) *chsd ldrs: nt fluent 14th: wknd 3 out* **8/1**
426- **9** *11* **Howard's Legacy (IRE)**[289] 4269 9-11-11 **129**................ LiamTreadwell 100
(Venetia Williams) *hld up: reminder after 13th: sme hdwy appr 4 out: wknd next* **6/1**[3]
0315 **P** **Dursey Sound (IRE)**[43] 2008 7-11-11 **129**...................... RichieMcLernon
(Jonjo O'Neill) *hld up: lost tch 18th: bhd whn p.u bef 3 out* **20/1**
7m 0.4s (25.10) **Going Correction** +0.85s/f (Soft) **10 Ran SP% 115.7**
Speed ratings (Par 107): **95,92,92,92,90 87,85,83,80,**
CSF £53.05 CT £312.84 TOTE £9.10: £2.70, £2.50, £2.50; EX 61.00 Trifecta £447.80.
Owner Golden Cap **Bred** Patrick Moore **Trained** Henley, Somerset
FOCUS
Actual distance 3m1f 159yds. A decent chase that looked quite open, but was won in good style by the back-to-form winner who was well in the best of last season's form.

2854 TONY RICKARDS BIRTHDAY H'CAP CHASE (11 fncs 1 omitted) 1m 7f 212y

2:40 (2:40) (Class 3) (0-135,135) 4-Y-0+ **£9,747** (£2,862; £1,431; £715)

Form RPR
-501 **1** **Sir Valentino (FR)**[16] 2540 6-11-9 **132**...........................(t) PaddyBrennan 143+
(Tom George) *a.p: chsd ldr 4th: led appr 3 out: hit last: styd on* **9/2**[2]
3-52 **2** *1 3/4* **Ozzy Thomas (IRE)**[28] 2266 5-11-0 **123**........................ JamesDavies 130
(Henry Oliver) *chsd ldrs: lft in ld 3rd: hdd 3 out: styd on same pce flat* **3/1**[1]
2111 **3** *8* **Helium (FR)**[20] 2449 10-11-12 **135**................................... RhysFlint 135
(Alexandra Dunn) *chsd ldrs: hmpd 3rd: rdn appr 3 out: sn outpcd* **8/1**[3]
30-6 **4** *10* **Lightening Rod**[32] 2194 10-11-4 **132**......................... HarryBannister(5) 120
(Michael Easterby) *hld up: a in rr* **10/1**
F-03 **5** *18* **Sonofagun (FR)**[192] 464 9-10-3 **112**.............................. WillKennedy 87
(Ian Williams) *hld up: pushed along after 4th: hdwy 8th: wknd appr 3 out* **20/1**
U4-5 **F** **Kudu Country (IRE)**[17] 2516 9-11-5 **128**..........................(t) PaulMoloney
(Evan Williams) *fell 1st* **14/1**
2030 **F** **My Brother Sylvest**[11] 2635 9-11-10 **133**....................(bt) TomScudamore
(David Pipe) *led tl fell 3rd* **12/1**
30P- **U** **Vivaccio (FR)**[242] 5137 6-11-9 **132**.............................. LiamTreadwell
(Venetia Williams) *chsd ldr tl blnd and uns rdr 2nd* **9/1**
2161 **U** **Jayo Time (IRE)**[9] 2691 6-11-3 **133** 7ex.......................(p) CiaranGethings(7)
(Kerry Lee) *hld up: hmpd and uns rdr 1st* **3/1**[1]
4m 8.2s (9.70) **Going Correction** +0.85s/f (Soft) **9 Ran SP% 117.5**
Speed ratings (Par 107): **109,108,104,99,90 , , ,**
CSF £19.50 CT £105.82 TOTE £5.90: £1.60, £1.40, £2.40; EX 20.80 Trifecta £76.00.
Owner Doone Hulse Susie Saunders & Lady Cobham **Bred** Mlle Camille Serveau & Roger Simon **Trained** Slad, Gloucs
FOCUS
Actual distance 1m7f 36yds. Early drama aplenty, with four of the runners departing over the first three fences, and the first fence in the straight had to be omitted on the final circuit. The winner was building on his recent hurdle win.

2855 GEOFF DUTTON CELEBRATORY CONDITIONAL JOCKEYS' NOVICES' H'CAP HURDLE (11 hdls) 2m 5f 55y

3:10 (3:11) (Class 4) (0-105,105) 3-Y-0+ **£3,898** (£1,144; £572; £286)

Form RPR
341 **1** **Minellacelebration (IRE)**[10] 2661 5-11-12 **105** 7ex.............. BenPoste 111+
(Katy Price) *led to 3rd: chsd ldr tl led again after 8th: rdn after 3 out: hung rt flat: styd on wl* **5/2**[2]
1011 **2** *3 1/2* **Duke's Affair**[13] 2599 7-11-5 **101**............................ MattGriffiths(3) 105
(Jeremy Scott) *trckd ldrs: racd keenly: ev ch fr 3 out: mstke next: rdn flat: styd on same pce* **2/1**[1]
-P20 **3** *4 1/2* **Bar A Mine (FR)**[31] 2223 6-11-9 **105**........................(v[1]) JamieBargary(3) 104
(Nigel Twiston-Davies) *chsd ldr to 3rd: remained handy: mstke 8th: rdn appr 3 out: styd on same pce fr next* **10/1**
4233 **4** *5* **Fred Le Macon (FR)**[22] 2418 6-11-2 **105**................... KevinDowling(10) 97
(Alan King) *hld up: pushed along 6th: hdwy appr 3 out: rdn after next: wknd last* **6/1**[3]
5-F5 **5** *27* **Pandy Wells**[27] 2298 6-10-0 **79** oh1................................ RyanHatch 51
(Graeme McPherson) *hld up: hdwy appr 3 out: rdn and wknd next* **8/1**
0-1F **P** **Mr Bachster (IRE)**[22] 2416 10-10-2 **84**...................(p) CiaranGethings(3)
(Kerry Lee) *trckd ldrs: racd keenly: led 3rd tl after 8th: rdn: wknd and p.u bef next* **17/2**
-43P **P** **The Lion Man (IRE)**[27] 2300 5-11-7 **105**........................ ConorSmith(5)
(Robin Dickin) *hld up: pushed along 4th: wknd 8th: bhd whn p.u bef next* **16/1**
5m 26.9s (12.10) **Going Correction** +0.55s/f (Soft) **7 Ran SP% 112.8**
Speed ratings (Par 105): **98,96,94,93,82**
CSF £7.97 TOTE £3.30: £1.70, £1.60; EX 6.70 Trifecta £52.40.
Owner Nick Elliott **Bred** M Doran **Trained** Hay-On-Wye, Powys
FOCUS
Actual distance 2m5f 88yds. A moderate handicap run at a steady gallop. Another step up from the winner.

2856 EBF STALLIONS MARES' STANDARD OPEN NATIONAL HUNT FLAT RACE 1m 7f 169y

3:40 (3:40) (Class 4) 4-6-Y-O **£3,249** (£954; £477; £238)

Form RPR
1 **Poppy Kay** 5-10-12 0.. TomO'Brien 112+
(Philip Hobbs) *a.p: chsd ldr over 3f out: led over 2f out: styd on wl* **15/2**
0 **2** *8* **Lady Of Llanarmon**[38] 2086 4-10-12 0.............................(p) DavidBass 102
(Kim Bailey) *a.p: racd keenly: chsd wnr over 2f out: styd on same pce fnl f* **10/1**
4 **3** *7* **Stickee Fingers**[183] 594 4-10-12 0................................ GavinSheehan 95
(Warren Greatrex) *prom: rdn over 3f out: wknd fnl f* **9/2**[2]
5 **4** *2 3/4* **Keep Up Keira (IRE)**[49] 1908 4-10-12 0............................ NoelFehily 92
(Neil Mulholland) *chsd ldrs: rdn over 3f out: hung lft and wknd over 1f out* **8/1**
0 **5** *3 1/2* **Midnight Target**[200] 334 5-10-5 0............................... JamieInsole(7) 89
(John Groucott) *hld up: styd on fnl 2f: nt trble ldrs* **100/1**
6 *1/2* **Ballybrowneybridge (IRE)**[148] 945 5-10-12 0................ SamThomas 88
(Sam Thomas) *disp ld tl wnt on 12f out: rdn and hdd over 2f out: wknd over 1f out* **5/2**[1]
7 *2 1/4* **Another Sunshine** 4-10-12 0.. AndrewTinkler 86
(Warren Greatrex) *hld up in tch: rdn over 5f out: wknd over 2f out* **6/1**[3]
0 **8** *6* **Sahara Haze**[20] 2460 6-10-7 0.................................... MrBMoorcroft(5) 80
(Phillip Dando) *chsd ldrs tl rdn and wknd over 4f out* **100/1**
9 *1/2* **Focusing** 5-10-12 0...(t) PaddyBrennan 79
(Stuart Edmunds) *hld up: hdwy over 4f out: wknd over 2f out* **12/1**
6 **10** *8* **Rhianna**[205] 242 4-10-9 0.. TomBellamy(3) 71
(Kim Bailey) *disp ld 4f: chsd ldr: rdn over 3f out: sn wknd* **16/1**
11 *12* **Ourniamheen (IRE)** 5-10-12 0...................................... TrevorWhelan 59
(Matt Sheppard) *hld up: rdn and wknd over 5f out* **50/1**
12 *10* **Midnight Jade (IRE)**[627] 6-10-9 0............................. HarryChalloner(3) 49
(John Groucott) *hld up: wknd over 6f out* **25/1**
4/0- **13** *6* **Port And Ward (IRE)**[382] 2495 6-10-5 0.................... GrahamCarson(7) 43
(John O'Shea) *hld up in tch: wknd over 5f out* **100/1**
14 *hd* **Sage Grouse** 6-10-12 0.. BrendanPowell 43
(Stuart Edmunds) *disp ld 4f: remained handy tl rdn and wknd 4f out* **25/1**
15 *29* **Miss U Peanuts** 6-10-5 0....................................... CharlieHammond(7) 14
(Mike Hammond) *hld up: pushed along 12f out: bhd fr 1/2-way* **100/1**
16 *17* **Babylone Colombe (FR)** 4-10-12 0................................. JamesDavies
(Tom Symonds) *hld up: wknd over 5f out* **40/1**
3m 50.9s (7.00) **Going Correction** +0.55s/f (Soft) **16 Ran SP% 122.6**
Speed ratings: **104,100,96,95,93 93,92,89,88,84 78,73,70,70,56 47**
CSF £77.69 TOTE £9.40: £3.10, £3.90, £2.10; EX 138.70 Trifecta £671.50.
Owner Aiden Murphy **Bred** Aiden Murphy **Trained** Withycombe, Somerset
FOCUS
Actual distance 1m7f 191.5yds. This had looked an open mares' bumper and it was typically run at a steady gallop, but it produced quite a taking winner.
T/Plt: £48.80 to a £1 stake. Pool of £58348.45- 872.79 winning tickets. T/Qpdt: £20.20 to a £1 stake. Pool of £5622.33 - 205.15 winning tickets. **Colin Roberts**

2807 LEICESTER (R-H)

Thursday, December 3

OFFICIAL GOING: Chase course - good (soft on flat course crossings; 6.7); hurdle course - heavy (soft in places; 4.8)
Wind: Strong behind Weather: Overcast

2857 LUBENHAM NOVICES' LIMITED H'CAP CHASE (12 fncs) 1m 7f 201y

12:25 (12:25) (Class 4) (0-120,118) 4-Y-0+ **£6,256** (£1,848; £924; £462; £231; £116)

Form RPR
3-20 **1** **Blandfords Gunner**[29] 2266 6-11-8 **118**............................. AdamWedge 129+
(Evan Williams) *a.p: chsd ldr 3 out: led appr last: styd on wl: comf* **7/2**[2]
0/01 **2** *1 1/4* **Moscow Me (IRE)**[28] 2300 8-10-10 **106**................. JeremiahMcGrath 113
(Henry Oliver) *chsd ldrs: led after 3rd: hdd and hit 6th: led again 8th: rdn and hdd appr last: styd on same pce flat* **9/4**[1]
3-23 **3** *14* **The Green Ogre**[17] 2546 5-11-4 **114**..........................(b[1]) JoshuaMoore 111
(Gary Moore) *w ldr tl led after 2nd: hdd after next: led again 6th: hdd 8th: ev ch whn hit 4 out: sn rdn: wknd 2 out* **5/1**
4-F0 **4** *nk* **Smoking Jacket (IRE)**[39] 2085 5-11-0 **110**.................. PaddyBrennan 105
(Tom George) *hld up: hdwy 4 out: rdn and wknd appr last* **11/1**
-242 **5** *30* **Court Dismissed (IRE)**[28] 2293 5-11-7 **117**.................. BrianHarding 84
(Donald McCain) *led tl after 2nd: chsd ldrs tl rdn and wknd 4 out* **4/1**[3]
-100 **6** *10* **Another Journey**[50] 1905 6-11-6 **116**........................... RobertDunne 74
(Sarah-Jayne Davies) *prom tl rdn and wknd appr 4 out* **33/1**
0/P- **F** **Devil To Pay**[264] 4766 9-11-1 **111**........................... WayneHutchinson 114
(Alan King) *hld up: hdwy 5th: disputing cl 2nd whn fell 2 out* **8/1**
4m 4.6s (-3.60) **Going Correction** -0.075s/f (Good) **7 Ran SP% 112.0**
Speed ratings (Par 105): **106,105,98,98,83 78,**
CSF £11.82 TOTE £4.50: £2.10, £1.80; EX 11.00 Trifecta £49.40.
Owner Kevin & Anne Glastonbury **Bred** David Brace **Trained** Llancarfan, Vale Of Glamorgan
FOCUS
All race distances were as advertised. There were differing opinions of the state of the ground on the chase track after the opener. Josh Moore said: "It's good but easier than that in places", while Paddy Brennan said: "It's soft." The first two finished clear in this ordinary event and the winner can go on to rate higher.

2858 BARKBY CONDITIONAL JOCKEYS' (S) HURDLE (10 hdls) 2m 4f 110y

1:00 (1:01) (Class 5) 4-Y-0+ **£2,599** (£763; £381; £190)

Form RPR
12-P **1** **Ministerofinterior**[24] 2405 10-11-1 106.....................(b) CiaranGethings(3) 112
(Barry Leavy) *hld up: hdwy 4th: led appr 2 out: rdn out* **11/1**
13-0 **2** *3 1/2* **Boston Blue**[10] 2688 8-11-1 118.................................. NickSlatter(3) 107
(Tony Carroll) *hld up: mstke 5th: drvn along after 7th: hit 3 out: hdwy bef next: styd on to go 2nd flat: nt rch wnr* **8/1**
323S **3** *2 1/2* **Tijori (IRE)**[35] 2150 7-10-12 107.......................................(b) RyanHatch 98
(Bernard Llewellyn) *a.p: ev ch 3 out: sn rdn: no ex last* **7/1**
361 **4** *5* **Fuzzy Logic (IRE)**[64] 1700 6-11-5 113.....................(b) RobertWilliams(3) 104
(Bernard Llewellyn) *hld up: hdwy appr 3 out: sn rdn: styd on same pce fr next* **6/1**[3]

2-5P **5** *1 1/4* **Lac Sacre (FR)**[11] 2663 6-11-4 124........(tp) KieronEdgar 98
(John Flint) *led: hdd after 1st: chsd ldr: led 4th to 6th: led again 3 out: rdn and hdd bef next: wknd appr last* **7/2**[2]
0PP5 **6** *39* **Walkabout Creek (IRE)**[24] 2405 8-11-4 93........(v) LizzieKelly 59
(Derek Frankland) *reluctant to s: rcvrd to go prom after 1st: led 6th: hdd 3 out: rdn and wknd bef next* **50/1**
-4P5 **7** *4* **Tisfreetdream (IRE)**[10] 2693 14-11-4 83........(p) TomBellamy 55
(Peter Pritchard) *prom: rdn after 7th: wknd 3 out* **66/1**
-U31 **P** **Teochew (IRE)**[35] 2147 7-10-5 109........(t) JonathanEngland
(Richard Drake) *led after 1st: hdd 4th: dropped to rr bef next: pushed along 6th: rdn and wknd after next: bhd whn p.u bef last* **6/4**[1]

5m 30.8s (6.10) **Going Correction** +0.20s/f (Yiel) **8 Ran SP% 111.9**
Speed ratings (Par 103): **96,94,93,91,91 76,74,**
CSF £88.91 TOTE £12.40: £3.10, £2.00, £2.20; EX 111.30 Trifecta £521.40.
Owner Mrs Laura Leavy **Bred** Deerfield Farm **Trained** Forsbrook, Staffs
■ Stewards' Enquiry : Jonathan England one-day ban: disobeyed starter (Dec 17)

FOCUS
Pretty testing ground on the hurdles track. Not a bad seller, this was run at an initially steady gallop and the time was very slow. The winner earned his best RPR since 2012.

2859 CLIPSTON H'CAP CHASE (12 fncs) 1m 7f 201y
1:35 (1:35) (Class 4) (0-110,110) 4-Y-0+ **£5,198** (£1,526; £763; £381)

Form RPR
10-3 **1** **Exmoor Mist**[29] 2266 7-11-5 103........(t) IanPopham 116+
(Victor Dartnall) *chsd ldrs: led 4 out: rdn out* **7/4**[1]
4-42 **2** *3* **Take The Crown**[22] 2434 6-11-3 101........(t) JamesDavies 109
(Henry Oliver) *hld up in tch: chsd wnr 2 out: sn rdn: styd on same pce flat* **9/2**[2]
0052 **3** *1 1/4* **Trojan Star (IRE)**[12] 2645 5-11-12 110........(t) DavidBass 118
(Kim Bailey) *chsd ldrs: pushed along appr 4 out: rdn and outpcd after next: rallied appr last: styd on* **11/2**[3]
-563 **4** *1 1/2* **Midnight Chorister**[12] 2648 7-11-7 105........(t) KielanWoods 111
(Alex Hales) *prom: rdn appr 2 out: no ex flat* **7/1**
3-52 **5** *5* **Pembroke House**[14] 2596 8-10-13 100........(p) JamesBanks(3) 102
(Sarah-Jayne Davies) *hld up: hdwy 5th: ev ch fr 4 out tl mstke next: sn rdn: wknd last* **11/2**[3]
5-25 **6** *25* **Sportsreport (IRE)**[36] 2138 7-11-9 107........(p) AndrewThornton 86
(Seamus Mullins) *hld up: hdwy appr 4 out: rdn and wknd bef 2 out* **20/1**
52-P **7** *23* **George Nympton (IRE)**[205] 256 9-9-12 89.....(t) WilliamFeatherstone(7) 47
(Zoe Davison) *chsd ldr after 2nd tl rdn appr 4 out: sn wknd* **20/1**
10-P **P** **Topthorn**[210] 175 9-10-12 103........(p) MrZBaker(7)
(Martin Bosley) *led: hdd appr 4 out: sn wknd: bhd whn nt fluent next: sn p.u* **22/1**

4m 7.9s (-0.30) **Going Correction** -0.075s/f (Good) **8 Ran SP% 111.7**
Speed ratings (Par 105): **97,95,94,94,91 79,67,**
CSF £9.72 CT £33.64 TOTE £2.10: £1.30, £1.70, £2.10; EX 11.00 Trifecta £39.80.
Owner Exmoor Mist Partnership **Bred** I M Ham **Trained** Brayford, Devon

FOCUS
A fair handicap and the form should prove sound with the winner on the upgrade.

2860 KNIGHTON NOVICES' HURDLE (8 hdls) 1m 7f 113y
2:10 (2:10) (Class 4) 4-Y-0+ **£5,198** (£1,526; £763; £381)

Form RPR
2-6 **1** **Flashjack (IRE)**[17] 2543 5-10-12 0........JakeGreenall 130+
(Henry Daly) *hld up in tch: rdn bef 3 out: led appr last: styd on wl* **9/1**
4/ **2** *5* **Allysson Monterg (FR)**[593] 5388 5-10-12 0........AlainCawley 123+
(Richard Hobson) *plld hrd: trckd ldr to 5th: wnt 2nd again and mstke 3 out: rdn and ev ch whn nt fluent next: styd on same pce flat* **16/1**
1 **3** *8* **Iftiraaq (IRE)**[17] 2543 4-11-5 0........(p) ConorO'Farrell 120
(Seamus Durack) *led: rdn and hdd appr last: wknd flat* **2/1**[2]
61 **4** *7* **See The Rock (IRE)**[28] 2287 5-11-5 0........WillKennedy 114
(Jonjo O'Neill) *hld up: hdwy u.p appr 2 out: wknd last* **11/8**[1]
2-54 **5** *9* **Frosty Steel (IRE)**[29] 2267 5-10-12 0........PaddyBrennan 97
(Tom George) *hld up: hdwy appr 3 out: wknd next* **6/1**[3]
/55- **6** *18* **Mr Beatle**[260] 4851 6-10-12 0........DavidBass 79
(Kim Bailey) *hld up in tch: rdn after 3 out: wknd bef next* **25/1**
7 *5* **Sting Jet (IRE)**[139] 1029 6-10-12 0........AndrewThornton 74
(Seamus Mullins) *hld up: rdn and wknd appr 3 out* **150/1**
0 **8** *7* **Ultimate Dream (FR)**[15] 2581 4-10-12 0........JoshuaMoore 67
(Jonjo O'Neill) *prom tl rdn and wknd appr 3 out* **100/1**
264 **9** *3/4* **Tanarpino**[13] 2628 4-10-12 0........PeterCarberry 66
(Jennie Candlish) *hld up: rdn and wknd appr 3 out* **50/1**
10 *16* **Pennine Panther**[127] 4-10-9 0........(t) JamesBanks(3) 50
(Sam Thomas) *hld up: rdn and wknd bef 3 out* **66/1**
50 **11** *18* **Song Of The Night (IRE)**[24] 2407 4-10-12 0........LeightonAspell 32
(Charlie Longsdon) *prom tl rdn and wknd bef 3 out* **100/1**
14/ **12** *3 3/4* **Starving Marvin**[1377] 4515 7-10-12 0........JamesDavies 29
(Rod Millman) *chsd ldrs: wnt 2nd 5th tl hit next: sn rdn and wknd* **33/1**
0 **13** *8* **Paris Snow**[18] 2519 5-10-9 0........RobMcCarth(3) 21
(Ian Williams) *hld up: rdn and wknd bef 3 out* **50/1**

3m 58.7s (-2.30) **Going Correction** +0.20s/f (Yiel) **13 Ran SP% 120.5**
Speed ratings (Par 105): **113,110,106,103,98 89,87,83,83,75 66,64,60**
CSF £126.18 TOTE £12.90: £3.50, £2.60, £1.30; EX 276.50 Trifecta £1552.90.
Owner Charles Whittaker & Belinda Clarke **Bred** Seamus Murphy **Trained** Stanton Lacy, Shropshire

FOCUS
Blue Bajan and Three Kingdoms were two smart winners of this event in previous years. They finished well strung out in this edition and the winner looks a decent sort who should rate higher.

2861 MOUNTSORREL NOVICES' H'CAP CHASE (18 fncs) 2m 6f 151y
2:45 (2:45) (Class 4) (0-105,103) 4-Y-0 **£6,330** (£1,870; £935; £468; £234)

Form RPR
46-5 **1** **Troika Steppes**[22] 2435 7-11-9 103........(t) ConorShoemark(3) 118+
(Fergal O'Brien) *mde all: clr 3 out: drvn out* **12/1**
/F-0 **2** *1 1/2* **Monderon (FR)**[49] 1931 8-11-2 93........JamesDavies 108+
(Henry Oliver) *chsd wnr to 10th: remained handy: mstke 14th: wnt 2nd again 4 out: styd on u.p* **4/1**[2]
04-P **3** *30* **Very Live (FR)**[215] 89 6-10-12 89........(p) RichieMcLernon 76
(Paul Webber) *prom: reminder after 6th: chsd wnr 10th to 4 out: sn rdn: wknd next* **40/1**
0241 **4** *7* **King's Song (FR)**[10] 2692 5-11-11 102 7ex........LeightonAspell 80
(David Dennis) *hld up: hdwy 12th: rdn appr 14th: sn wknd* **13/8**[1]
05-4 **5** *6* **Hurricane Vic**[24] 2408 5-11-4 95........WayneHutchinson 68
(Alan King) *hld up: hdwy 8th: rdn and wknd appr 4 out* **4/1**[2]
FPP5 **6** *84* **June French (FR)**[17] 2542 7-9-12 82........(p) MrMartinMcIntyre(7)
(Neil Mulholland) *hld up: sme hdwy appr 4 out: sn wknd* **14/1**

P-RP **P** **Shadesofnavy**[10] 2693 9-9-7 77 oh13........(p) ArchieBellamy(7)
(Peter Pritchard) *prom: lost pl and pushed along 4th: bhd whn p.u bef 7th* **200/1**
065 **P** **Barra Rotha (IRE)**[28] 2287 8-11-8 99........DaveCrosse
(Laura Hurley) *hld up in tch: rdn and wknd 12th: bhd whn p.u bef 4 out* **50/1**
5-34 **P** **Copperfacejack (IRE)**[23] 2410 5-11-8 99........(p) CharliePoste
(Paul Webber) *hld up in tch: wknd 11th: bhd whn p.u bef 4 out* **8/1**[3]
P50 **U** **Bach To Before (IRE)**[189] 527 7-10-13 90........(t) KielanWoods
(Graeme McPherson) *hld up: plld hrd: hdwy whn blnd and uns rdr 5th* **20/1**

5m 58.4s (-5.60) **Going Correction** -0.075s/f (Good) **10 Ran SP% 113.2**
Speed ratings (Par 105): **106,105,95,92,90 61,,,,**
CSF £57.86 CT £1861.91 TOTE £14.30: £2.70, £2.20, £7.80; EX 88.40 Trifecta £1595.40.
Owner William Williamson **Bred** William And Mrs Susan Williamson **Trained** Naunton, Gloucs

FOCUS
A very modest event in which the first two finished a long way clear. The principals were always prominent and the winner took a big step up in the tongue-tie under positive tactics.

2862 WALTHAM ON THE WOLDS H'CAP HURDLE (8 hdls) 1m 7f 113y
3:20 (3:20) (Class 5) (0-100,107) 3-Y-0+ **£3,249** (£954; £477; £238)

Form RPR
P01 **1** **Arquebusier (FR)**[8] 2713 5-11-4 95 7ex........(p) JamesBanks(3) 100
(Emma Baker) *mde all: wandered arnd gng into 2 out: sn rdn: hit last: hung rt towards fin: all out* **6/4**[1]
355- **2** *hd* **Georgieshore (IRE)**[247] 5083 7-11-1 96........WilliamFeatherstone(7) 100
(Zoe Davison) *w wnr tl rdn after 3 out: rallied and ev ch flat: styd on: carried rt nr fin* **8/1**
-554 **3** *3 1/4* **Lean Burn (USA)**[12] 2492 9-10-7 84........(b) HarryChalloner(3) 85
(Barry Leavy) *hld up: rdn appr 3 out: styd on to go 3rd towards fin: nt trble ldrs* **7/1**[3]
0061 **4** *2 1/2* **Exemplary**[7] 2730 8-11-12 107 7ex........(t) CiaranGethings(7) 105
(Johnny Farrelly) *hld up: nt fluent 4th: hdwy appr 3 out: rdn bef last: wknd towards fin* **7/2**[2]
4302 **5** *4 1/2* **Lost In Newyork (IRE)**[17] 2542 8-9-8 75........(p) PaulNO'Brien(7) 69
(Nick Kent) *hld up: hdwy 5th: rdn after 3 out: wknd flat* **7/1**[3]
P-5P **6** *3* **War And Contrition (IRE)**[30] 2263 6-11-8 96........AlainCawley 87
(Charlie Longsdon) *hld up: rdn after 5th: nvr on terms* **8/1**
04-P **7** *nk* **Pretty Mobile (FR)**[43] 2022 4-10-13 87........JakeGreenall 77
(Paul Webber) *chsd ldrs tl rdn and wknd appr last* **50/1**

4m 8.5s (7.50) **Going Correction** +0.20s/f (Yiel)
WFA 4 from 5yo+ 5lb **7 Ran SP% 111.4**
Speed ratings (Par 103): **89,88,87,86,83 82,82**
CSF £13.18 CT £61.44 TOTE £2.30: £1.20, £4.10; EX 12.90 Trifecta £78.40.
Owner Miss E J Baker **Bred** Ecurie Maulepaire **Trained** Naunton, Gloucs

FOCUS
Modest handicap form.
T/Plt: £742.40 to a £1 stake. Pool: £68,555.28 - 67.40 winning units. T/Qpdt: £68.30 to a £1 stake. Pool: £7,430.13 - 80.5 winning units. **Colin Roberts**

2591 MARKET RASEN (R-H)
Thursday, December 3

OFFICIAL GOING: Heavy (soft in places; chs 5.7; hdl 5.6)
Wind: fresh 1/2 behind Weather: overcast, damp, rain race 4

2863 RACING FX JUVENILE HURDLE (8 hdls) 2m 148y
12:05 (12:05) (Class 4) 3-Y-0 **£3,898** (£1,144; £572; £286)

Form RPR
1 **Wolfcatcher (IRE)**[130] 3-10-12 0........AidanColeman 120+
(John Ferguson) *j.lft: trckd ldrs: hit 3rd: led appr 2 out: clr bef last: eased fnl 150yds* **5/6**[1]
2 *6* **Perceus**[53] 3-10-12 0........JackQuinlan 107+
(James Eustace) *t.k.h: trckd ldrs 4th: 2nd 2 out: no ch w wnr* **4/1**[3]
61 **3** *14* **Sikandar (IRE)**[22] 2439 3-11-5 0........DannyCook 101
(Brian Ellison) *hld up in rr: hdwy 3 out: sn pushed along: 4th appr 2 out: kpt on one pce to take poor 3rd run-in* **11/4**[2]
51 **4** *3/4* **Boldbob (IRE)**[94] 1415 3-10-12 0........FinianO'Toole(7) 99
(Micky Hammond) *led: hdd appr 2 out: kpt on one pce: lost 3rd fnl 150yds* **12/1**
00 **5** *3 1/2* **Sweet Midnight**[17] 2537 3-10-5 0........CharliePoste 82
(John Holt) *hld up in rr: hdwy after 3rd: chsng ldrs 3 out: one pce appr next* **200/1**
44 **6** *1* **Quill Art**[28] 2286 3-10-12 106........BrianHughes 88
(Richard Fahey) *chsd ldrs: drvn 3 out: lost pl and poor 6th whn mstke 2 out* **25/1**
7 *19* **Duc De Seville (IRE)**[66] 3-10-12 0........DaveCrosse 69
(Michael Chapman) *in rr: lost pl 4th: bhd and reminders next: t.o 2 out* **50/1**
8 *nk* **Burner (IRE)**[9] 3-10-12 0........(p) TomCannon 68
(Olly Williams) *t.k.h: trckd ldr: mstke 3 out: lost pl bef next: sn wl bhd* **40/1**
P **P** **Dot Dash Dot**[32] 2219 3-10-5 0........[1] TomMessenger
(Christopher Kellett) *in last: drvn 3rd: sn bhd and j. slowly next: t.o whn p.u bef 5th* **200/1**

4m 37.9s (31.20) **Going Correction** +1.50s/f (Heav) **9 Ran SP% 118.2**
Speed ratings (Par 104): **86,83,76,76,74 74,65,65,**
CSF £4.88 TOTE £1.70: £1.10, £1.50, £1.10; EX 4.40 Trifecta £10.60.
Owner Bloomfields **Bred** Darley **Trained** Cowlinge, Suffolk

FOCUS
Rail set out 20yds on both bends. Races 1, 2, 4 & 7 increased by about 180yds and races 3, 5 & 6 by 240yds. The ground conditions were testing and clerk of the course Jane Hedley said "there are still plenty of soft places on the hurdles course but it is going to be hard work, there are no two ways about it." After riding in the opener Aidan Coleman remarked "the ground is pretty soft but they are getting through it". This often proves to be a fair juvenile contest and the winner looks a decent prospect. The penalised third helps set the level.

2864 RACING FX NOVICES' HURDLE (10 hdls) 2m 2f 140y
12:35 (12:36) (Class 4) 4-Y-0+ **£3,898** (£1,144; £572)

Form RPR
10-2 **1** **Duke Des Champs (IRE)**[30] 2257 5-10-12 0........RichardJohnson 127+
(Philip Hobbs) *w ldr: hit 3rd: drvn to ld 3 out: jnd next: hit last: styd on gamely* **4/9**[1]

0-01 2 1 1/4 **Matorico (IRE)**[23] 2409 4-11-5 137 BarryGeraghty 133
(Jonjo O'Neill) *hld up in last: hdwy to trck other 2 4th: cl 2nd bef 2 out: sn upsides: effrt last: sn drvn and hung rt: kpt on same pce last 100yds* **15/8**[2]

F 3 36 **Stout Cortez**[17] 2543 4-10-12 0 BrianHughes 93
(Malcolm Jefferson) *led: j. slowly 1st: hdd 3 out: wknd and 10 l bhd whn blnd bdly 2 out: eventually fin: t.o* **33/1**[3]

5m 2.6s (23.20) **Going Correction** +1.50s/f (Heav) **3** Ran SP% **107.0**
Speed ratings (Par 105): **111,110,95**
CSF £1.65 TOTE £1.40; EX 1.50 Trifecta £1.70.
Owner Diana Whateley & Tim Syder **Bred** David & Leonard O'Brennan **Trained** Withycombe, Somerset

FOCUS
Race distance increased by about 180yds. A disappointing turn out and it proved tactical, although the form is straightforward enough.

2865 LINCS LOOS NOVICES' LIMITED H'CAP CHASE (17 fncs) 2m 7f 191y
1:10 (1:10) (Class 4) (0-120,115) 4-Y-0+ £7,213 (£2,623)

Form RPR
23-4 1 **Askamore Darsi (IRE)**[200] 355 6-11-8 112 (p) HenryBrooke 120
(Donald McCain) *chsd ldr: drvn 4 out: lft virtually alone 2 out: heavily eased run-in* **5/1**

00-5 2 87 **Red Danaher (IRE)**[42] 2039 8-11-8 112 SeanQuinlan 32
(Sue Smith) *chsd ldrs: reminders 10th: outpcd 12th: wknd 4 out: poor 3rd appr next: distant 2nd whn blnd 2 out: fin tired* **4/1**[2]

2-45 P **Silver Dragon**[11] 2666 7-10-4 94 (v[1]) BrianHughes
(Tony Coyle) *nt fluent: chsd ldrs: reminders 7th: lost pl and hit 11th: t.o whn p.u bef 4 out* **9/2**[3]

4P0- P **Oficial Ben (IRE)**[235] 5295 6-11-1 112 (t[1]) PatrickCowley[(7)]
(Jonjo O'Neill) *t.k.h in rr: trckd ldrs 7th: blnd 10th: lost pl: reminders and bhd 11th: t.o whn p.u bef next* **13/2**

20-6 P **Maybe Plenty**[34] 2167 6-11-6 110 TomCannon
(Giles Smyly) *led: blnd 12th: hdd 13th: wknd and poor 4th appr 3 out: p.u after 3 out* **9/1**

5-63 F **Cyclop (IRE)**[22] 2434 4-11-3 115 (tp) AidanColeman 127+
(David Dennis) *trckd ldrs: pckd on landing 8th: 2nd 12th: led next: 13 l ahd and in total command whn fell 2 out* **9/4**[1]

7m 2.4s (31.10) **Going Correction** +1.425s/f (Heav)
WFA 4 from 6yo+ 7lb **6** Ran SP% **109.0**
Speed ratings (Par 105): **105,76, , ,**
CSF £23.51 TOTE £5.70: £1.60, £2.90; EX 30.00.
Owner Deva Racing Darsi Partnership **Bred** William McGladdery **Trained** Cholmondeley, Cheshire

FOCUS
Race distance increased by about 240yds. A weak novice handicap for the class and, after a decent gallop, only two completed as there was late drama.

2866 RACING FX ONLINE H'CAP CHASE (14 fncs) 2m 3f 34y
1:45 (1:46) (Class 4) (0-105,94) 4-Y-0+ £5,325 (£1,653; £890)

Form RPR
-U33 1 **Ivans Back (IRE)**[151] 914 10-11-8 90 GavinSheehan 101+
(Nick Kent) *led after 1st: j. soundly: shkn up last: styd on: eased nr fin* **11/4**[2]

P02P 2 3 1/4 **Willie Hall**[27] 2321 11-10-13 86 CallumBewley[(5)] 91
(Lisa Harrison) *hld up in last: lft 4 l 2nd 3 out: hung lft and no real imp run-in* **11/2**[3]

6521 3 26 **Aregra (FR)**[1] 2844 5-11-2 84 7ex (p) BrianHughes 74
(Peter Niven) *trckd ldrs: 2nd 8th: pushed along 11th: 4 l down and reminder whn blnd 3 out: sn lost pl and bhd* **13/8**[1]

P1-U P **Hi Bob**[33] 2191 7-11-12 94 DannyCook
(Lucinda Egerton) *led tl after 1st: chsd ldrs: dropped bk 7th: chsd ldrs next: drvn next: modest 3rd whn hit 10th: sn bhd: p.u bef next* **11/4**[2]

5m 33.4s (27.70) **Going Correction** +1.425s/f (Heav) **4** Ran SP% **106.8**
Speed ratings (Par 105): **98,96,85,**
CSF £14.66 TOTE £2.70; EX 14.90 Trifecta £30.40.
Owner Ms Victoria Cottingham **Bred** Stephen Lanigan O'Keeffe And Frank Clark **Trained** Brigg, Lincs

FOCUS
Race distance increased by about 180yds. A moderate little handicap. The winner was on a fair mark and back to his best.

2867 LINCS LOOS H'CAP HURDLE (10 hdls) 2m 4f 139y
2:20 (2:20) (Class 4) (0-115,115) 3-Y-0+ £3,898 (£1,144; £572; £286)

Form RPR
15-6 1 **Palm Grey (IRE)**[200] 356 7-11-9 112 DannyCook 117+
(Sue Smith) *trckd ldr: led after 6th: j.lft last 2: kpt on wl* **10/3**[3]

6232 2 1 3/4 **Pixiepot**[24] 2396 5-10-5 94 BrianHughes 97
(Peter Niven) *trckd ldrs: upsides sn after 3 out: swtchd lft appr 2 out: hit 2 out: hung rt and swtchd lft after last: kpt on same pce* **5/2**[2]

3350 3 10 **Falcarragh (IRE)**[63] 1714 8-11-9 112 RichardJohnson 103
(Tim Vaughan) *t.k.h in last: plld v wd 6th: pushed along 3 out: 3rd and swtchd rt sn after 2 out: wknd fnl 50yds* **10/1**

0241 4 1/2 **The Geegeez Geegee (IRE)**[17] 2548 6-11-7 115 (t) DavidNoonan[(5)] 108
(Anthony Honeyball) *trckd ldrs: t.k.h: hit 6th: pushed along 3 out: outpcd appr next* **5/4**[1]

1U0P U **Drombeg West**[28] 2301 8-11-2 105 AndrewTinkler
(Anna Brooks) *t.k.h: led: hdd after 6th: wkng and last whn blnd and uns rdr 8th* **25/1**

5m 50.8s (42.00) **Going Correction** +2.125s/f (Heav) **5** Ran SP% **109.0**
Speed ratings (Par 105): **105,104,100,100,**
CSF £11.91 TOTE £4.10: £2.20, £1.50; EX 15.20 Trifecta £40.30.
Owner Mrs S Smith **Bred** Patrick Doyle **Trained** High Eldwick, W Yorks

FOCUS
Race distance increased by about 240yds. They went steadily in this modest handicap and two came clear from the second-last flight with the winner recording a personal best.

2868 RACING FX ONLINE H'CAP HURDLE (12 hdls) 2m 7f 16y
2:55 (2:56) (Class 5) (0-100,89) 3-Y-0+ £2,599 (£763; £381; £190)

Form RPR
6543 1 **Optical High**[27] 2323 6-10-7 80 StephenMcCarthy[(10)] 93+
(Sue Smith) *w ldr: led 8th: pushed clr bef 2 out: wandered appr last: drvn out* **10/3**[2]

P503 2 13 **Black Lily (IRE)**[16] 2554 7-10-10 73 (p) TomMessenger 72
(Chris Bealby) *hld up in rr: hdwy 8th: outpcd and lost pl 3 out: poor 4th appr next: modest 3rd between last 2: styd on to take 2nd last 150yds* **7/1**[3]

0-45 3 3 3/4 **Vinegar Hill**[23] 2413 6-11-11 88 AndrewTinkler 83
(Anna Brooks) *chsd ldrs: hit 2nd: reminders 5th: drvn next: modest 2nd appr 2 out: wknd run-in* **7/1**[3]

-5P5 4 21 **Lady Vivona**[27] 2323 7-10-2 70 CallumBewley[(5)] 44
(Lisa Harrison) *trckd ldrs: drvn 7th: wknd appr 2 out: sn bhd* **11/1**

325- 5 14 **Deportation**[341] 3323 8-11-1 81 (v) ColmMcCormack[(3)] 41
(John Norton) *in rr: drvn 7th: bhd fr 9th* **16/1**

2P0U P **Whatsupjack (IRE)**[14] 2596 8-10-13 76 TrevorWhelan
(Shaun Harris) *led: hdd and nt fluent 8th: hit 3 out: sn lost pl: wl bhd whn p.u bef 2 out* **14/1**

-001 P **Vodka Island (IRE)**[10] 2693 6-11-5 82 RichardJohnson
(Tim Vaughan) *nt fluent: racd wd: in rr: pushed along after 7th: sme hdwy 9th: sn lost pl and bhd: t.o whn p.u bef 2 out* **11/8**[1]

6m 38.6s (48.10) **Going Correction** +2.125s/f (Heav) **7** Ran SP% **111.1**
Speed ratings (Par 103): **101,96,95,87,83 ,**
CSF £24.60 CT £145.55 TOTE £4.00: £2.10, £3.60; EX 21.60 Trifecta £69.50.
Owner Mrs S Smith **Bred** P E Rodgers **Trained** High Eldwick, W Yorks

FOCUS
Race distance increased by about 240yds. An ordinary handicap, run at an uneven gallop and seemingly a big step up from the winner.

2869 RACING FX CONDITIONAL JOCKEYS' H'CAP HURDLE (8 hdls) 2m 148y
3:30 (3:30) (Class 4) (0-110,108) 3-Y-0+ £3,898 (£1,144; £572; £286)

Form RPR
6/52 1 **Renoyr (FR)**[28] 2291 10-11-10 106 JamieHamilton 110+
(Malcolm Jefferson) *trckd ldrs: hit 3 out: led appr next: styd on wl run-in* **11/4**[1]

2241 2 3 3/4 **Nebula Storm (IRE)**[16] 2559 8-11-6 107 (v) MrShaneQuinlan[(5)] 106
(Michael Blake) *hld up in rr: hit 5th: hdwy after 3 out: handy 3rd appr next: 2nd last: styd on same pce* **4/1**[2]

3050 3 5 **Brinestine (USA)**[39] 2093 6-10-13 100 (t) HarrisonBeswick[(5)] 95
(Emma Baker) *hld up in rr: hdwy 3 out: chsd wnr appr next: one pce run-in* **6/1**[3]

3035 4 6 **Summer Storm**[12] 2647 5-11-4 105 (t) FinianO'Toole[(5)] 93
(Rebecca Menzies) *led: hdd appr 2 out: wknd bef last* **10/1**

-060 5 4 1/2 **Skyfire**[52] 1892 8-10-12 94 MauriceLinehan 77
(Nick Kent) *in rr: hdwy to chse ldrs 3rd: outpcd whn hit 3 out: sn lost pl: kpt on run-in* **16/1**

245 6 hd **Robben**[32] 2212 3-10-6 102 (v) GrahamWatters 70
(John Mackie) *chsd ldrs: drvn 3 out: sn lost pl* **6/1**[3]

56P3 7 1 3/4 **Daulys Anthem (IRE)**[24] 2406 7-11-12 108 KillianMoore 89
(David Dennis) *chsd ldrs: wknd 2 out* **10/1**

-623 8 10 **Mandy's Boy (IRE)**[72] 1524 5-11-6 102 (p) BenPoste 76
(Sally Randell) *chsd ldrs: lost pl bef 2 out: sn bhd* **7/1**

4m 46.8s (40.10) **Going Correction** +2.125s/f (Heav)
WFA 3 from 5yo+ 13lb **8** Ran SP% **111.8**
Speed ratings (Par 105): **90,88,85,83,80 80,80,75**
CSF £13.83 CT £57.91 TOTE £3.20: £1.60, £1.20, £2.10; EX 12.60 Trifecta £70.20.
Owner J M Jefferson **Bred** Mickael Roy & Nicolas De Lageneste **Trained** Norton, N Yorks

FOCUS
Race distance increased by about 180yds. A moderate handicap, confined to conditional riders and again there was an uneven gallop on. The winner has been a 119-rated hurdler in the past and is progressing with each run this season.
T/Plt: £81.50 to a £1 stake. Pool: £34,158.27 - 305.89 winning units. T/Qpdt: £36.20 to a £1 stake. Pool: £2,853.75 - 58.30 winning units. **Walter Glynn**

2598 WINCANTON (R-H)
Thursday, December 3

OFFICIAL GOING: Soft (heavy in places; chs: 5.7; hdl 5.6)
Wind: quite strong against Weather: overcast

2870 RAY THOMAS PROPERTY SERVICES LTD MARES' MAIDEN HURDLE (11 hdls) 2m 5f 82y
12:50 (12:50) (Class 4) 4-Y-0+ £3,249 (£954; £477; £238)

Form RPR
130- 1 **Lifeboat Mona**[236] 5277 5-10-12 0 (t) SamTwiston-Davies 116+
(Paul Nicholls) *travelled wl: in tch: hit 6th: trckd ldrs 3 out: led 2 out: v easily* **1/4**[1]

34-4 2 5 **Jully Les Buxy**[22] 2444 5-10-12 0 NickScholfield 104+
(Robert Walford) *trckd ldrs: chalng whn wandered jst bef 2 out: sn no ch w wnr: styd on same pce* **4/1**[2]

46-6 3 11 **Mrsrobin (IRE)**[22] 2444 5-10-12 0 DarylJacob 90
(Emma Lavelle) *hld up in last pair: tk clsr order 3 out: sn outpcd: styd on into 3rd run-in but nvr any threat* **11/1**[3]

45 4 1 1/2 **Oneforthenure (IRE)**[137] 1057 6-10-12 0 TomO'Brien 87
(Richard Woollacott) *prom: trckd ldrs: led 3 out: rdn and hdd bef next: grad fdd: lost 3rd run-in* **66/1**

5 8 **Rubys Star (IRE)**[202] 8-10-9 0[1] MattGriffiths[(3)] 81
(Jeremy Scott) *j.lft: led tl 3rd: prom tl rdn after 3 out: wknd next* **50/1**

6 20 **Monet Moor**[207] 6-10-5 0 MissBFrost[(7)] 59
(Jimmy Frost) *trckd ldrs: led 3rd tl appr 3 out: sn wknd: t.o* **50/1**

0 7 3/4 **Trehan Cross**[14] 2603 6-10-12 0 JamesBest 58
(Jackie Du Plessis) *struggling 8th: a in last pair: lost tch after 3 out: t.o* **100/1**

5m 41.0s (14.50) **Going Correction** +0.075s/f (Yiel) **7** Ran SP% **114.7**
Speed ratings (Par 105): **75,73,68,68,65 57,57**
CSF £1.82 TOTE £1.20: £1.10, £1.70; EX 1.80 Trifecta £3.00.
Owner Axom LV **Bred** Bryan & Sandra Mayoh, Eskdale Stud **Trained** Ditcheat, Somerset

FOCUS
Rail movement increased races 1, 2 & 5 by 18yds, race 4 & 6 by 12yds and race 3 by 24yds. This contest was over an additional 18yds. Last year's winner Bitofapuzzle went on to land a Grade 1 contest and Mayfair Music, successful in 2014, won a Listed race when she was next seen, suggesting this winner could be well above average if history is repeated. The time was 16sec slower than the race that followed it over the same distance and the winner has been rated similar to her bumper form.

2871 RUPERT McCARTHY MEMORIAL "NATIONAL HUNT" NOVICES' H'CAP HURDLE (11 hdls) 2m 5f 82y
1:25 (1:25) (Class 4) (0-115,114) 3-Y-0+ £3,898 (£1,144; £572; £286)

Form RPR
3-04 1 **Kap Jazz (FR)**[18] 2519 5-11-6 108 LiamTreadwell 107+
(Venetia Williams) *trckd ldrs: rdn after 3 out: chal last: led run-in: styd on: edgd lft nring fin: drvn out* **9/2**[3]

55/0 2 1 **Varom (FR)**[15] 2577 6-11-5 **107**...............................(t) SamTwiston-Davies 103
(Paul Nicholls) *hld up: hdwy 7th: rdn to chse ldr appr 2 out: nt pce to chal: styd on to snatch 2nd fnl strides* **9/4**[1]

3P32 3 hd **Rushvale (IRE)**[19] 2488 6-11-5 **114**............................ MrMJPKendrick[(7)] 112
(Ben Case) *led: nt fluent 4th: rdn and hanging lft whn mstke 2 out: hit last: hdd run-in: edgd lft and lost 2nd fnl strides* **6/1**

34-5 4 23 **Miss Oscarose (IRE)**[24] 2403 8-10-11 **99**.......................... TomO'Brien 72
(Paul Henderson) *trckd ldrs: rdn after 3 out: wknd bef next* **25/1**

0-45 5 3 **Craiganee (IRE)**[39] 2087 8-10-13 **101**.......................... TomScudamore 71
(Chris Down) *trckd ldrs: hit 5th: rdn after 3 out: wknd bef next* **3/1**[2]

-306 P **Bogoss Du Perret (FR)**[30] 2258 4-11-0 **109**.................. MissBFrost[(7)]
(Jimmy Frost) *a in rr: struggling 5th: t.o whn p.u bef 3 out* **33/1**

P-63 P **Allchilledout**[15] 2563 6-10-7 **102**..........................(t) PaulO'Brien[(7)]
(Colin Tizzard) *chsd ldrs: j.lft: struggling 6th: sn bhd: p.u bef 3 out* **5/1**

5m 25.0s (-1.50) **Going Correction** +0.075s/f (Yiel)
WFA 4 from 5yo+ 6lb **7 Ran SP% 111.7**
Speed ratings (Par 105): **105,104,104,95,94** ,
CSF £14.75 TOTE £6.30: £2.80, £1.40; EX 16.30 Trifecta £49.30.
Owner Brooks,Vando,Pummell,Martin & Armstrong **Bred** Pascal Noue **Trained** Kings Caple, H'fords

FOCUS
This contest was over an additional 18yds. Although this was a moderate race, it contained some interesting newcomers to handicapping, one of which proved too good for his rivals.

2872 WEATHERBYS HAMILTON SILVER BUCK H'CAP CHASE (18 fncs 3 omitted) 3m 1f 30y

2:00 (2:00) (Class 3) (0-125,124) 4-Y-0+
£9,384 (£2,772; £1,386; £693; £346; £174)

Form RPR

P4-4 1 **Aachen**[25] 2374 11-11-11 **123**....................................... LiamTreadwell 133+
(Venetia Williams) *mde all: pushed clr 2 out: in command after: styd on strly* **7/1**

3161 2 6 **Spending Time**[23] 2410 6-11-0 **112**..............................(tp) TomScudamore 116
(David Pipe) *sn trcking wnr: rdn after 3 out (usual 4 out): styd on fr last but a being readily hld by wnr* **6/5**[1]

1341 3 4 **Fond Memory (IRE)**[46] 1987 7-11-9 **121**...............(t) SamTwiston-Davies 122
(Nigel Twiston-Davies) *in tch: hdwy fr 12th: rdn to dispute 2nd whn pckd 2 out (usual 3 out): styd on same pce fr last* **5/1**[2]

035- 4 19 **Upham Atom**[232] 5340 12-11-6 **118**.............................. BrendanPowell 98
(Kate Buckett) *prom: rdn appr 3 out (usual 4 out): wknd next* **14/1**

1P-3 5 2 1/4 **Ballycoe**[56] 1821 6-11-5 **117**..................................(t) NickSchofield 97
(Chris Gordon) *nt fluent: hld up last: stmbld v bdly 2nd: hdwy into 4th 3 out (usual 4 out): sn rdn: wknd next (b.b.v)* **25/1**

55-F 6 12 **Kings Apollo**[7] 2724 6-10-4 **109**.................................... MrJNixon[(7)] 75
(Tom Symonds) *in tch: nudged along after 13th: wknd after 3 out (usual 4 out)* **8/1**

6-F6 U **Shy John**[21] 2451 9-10-9 **114**....................................... LewisGordon[(7)]
(Jennifer Mason) *cl up: virtually fell whn unseating rdr 14th* **6/1**[3]

6m 49.1s (9.60) **Going Correction** +0.475s/f (Soft) **7 Ran SP% 110.5**
Speed ratings (Par 107): **103,101,99,93,93 89,**
CSF £15.64 CT £42.82 TOTE £6.90: £2.50, £1.40; EX 16.60 Trifecta £70.10.
Owner Tony Bloom **Bred** Darley **Trained** Kings Caple, H'fords

FOCUS
This contest was over an additional 24yds due to rail movements. The last fence was omitted in all chases due to a false patch of ground. Probably just a modest race for stayers and a chase personal best from the winner, though he was rated 140+ over hurdles..

2873 WEATHERBYS HAMILTON H'CAP HURDLE (8 hdls) 1m 7f 65y

2:35 (2:35) (Class 3) (0-130,128) 3-Y-0+ **£8,229** (£2,431; £1,215; £608; £304)

Form RPR

10-1 1 **Presenting Arms (IRE)**[10] 2688 8-11-4 **127**.....................(t) MrMLegg[(7)] 132+
(Harry Fry) *racd keenly: trckd ldrs: upsides whn hit 3 out: led appr last where wnt lft and pckd: in command but tiring towards fin: pushed out* **1/2**[1]

100P 2 1 1/4 **Ryeolliean**[25] 2373 4-11-4 **120**...(p) JamieMoore 119
(Gary Moore) *trckd ldr: led after 3rd: jnd 3 out: rdn bef 2 out: hdd appr last: sn hld but kpt on gamely to cl on wnr towards fin* **12/1**

0P-3 3 7 **Leviathan**[13] 2617 8-11-10 **126**....................................... LiamTreadwell 120
(Venetia Williams) *racd keenly: trckd ldrs: led 2nd tl after 3rd: rdn to chse ldng pair after 3 out: kpt on same pce fr next* **4/1**[2]

15F- 4 2 **Gabrial The Great (IRE)**[397] 2200 6-11-12 **128**............. TomScudamore 118
(David Pipe) *hld up: hdwy 3 out: rdn to chse ldng pair appr 2 out: nt pce to get on terms: no ex run-in* **8/1**[3]

42-0 5 37 **Filatore (IRE)**[25] 2369 6-10-9 **118**..........................(b) JordanWilliams[(7)] 71
(Bernard Llewellyn) *led tl 2nd: prom tl struggling in last 5th: t.o* **20/1**

3m 51.4s (2.50) **Going Correction** +0.075s/f (Yiel) **5 Ran SP% 110.2**
Speed ratings (Par 107): **96,95,91,90,70**
CSF £6.97 TOTE £1.50: £1.10, £3.60; EX 6.30 Trifecta £14.40.
Owner J M Dare **Bred** Ms Iona Maguire **Trained** Seaborough, Dorset

FOCUS
This contest was over an additional 12yds. A small field, but the market leader was really well in and solidly backed.

2874 #BELIKEDAN DANIEL RHODES MEMORIAL AMATEUR RIDERS' H'CAP CHASE (15 fncs 2 omitted) 2m 4f 35y

3:10 (3:10) (Class 4) (0-115,113) 4-Y-0+ **£4,991** (£1,548; £773; £387)

Form RPR

P-31 1 **Capilla (IRE)**[2] 2834 7-10-9 **103** 7ex.................................(t) MrConorOrr[(7)] 119+
(Evan Williams) *mde virtually all: hdd briefly bef 2 out: sn bk in clr advantage: r.o: rdn out* **7/4**[1]

4-F5 2 5 **Saint Breiz (FR)**[15] 2568 9-10-13 **105**..................(t) MrRobertHawker[(5)] 110
(Carroll Gray) *chsd ldrs: blnd 1st: wnt 2nd 12th tl rdn after next: regained 2nd bef last (usual 2 out): styd on but a being comf hld* **14/1**

-452 3 nk **Marden Court (IRE)**[11] 2659 5-11-7 **111**........................(t) MrMLegg[(3)] 117
(Colin Tizzard) *hld up: hit 9th: struggling 11th: hdwy 2 out (usual 3 out): styd on on long run-in fr last (usual 2 out): chal for hld 2nd fnl 100yds* **3/1**[3]

-331 4 5 **Matrow's Lady (IRE)**[8] 2714 8-10-0 **87** oh1............(bt) MrSWaley-Cohen 91+
(Neil Mulholland) *j.lft and nvr that fluent: chsd ldr: pushed along at times: rdn after 12th: hdwy to ld v briefly bef gng bdly lft 2 out: sn hld: fdd run-in* **2/1**[2]

23F5 5 7 **Head Spin (IRE)**[23] 2416 7-10-2 **96**..............................(b[1]) MrDSansom[(7)] 90
(Seamus Mullins) *trckd ldr tl 12th: sn rdn: wknd after 3 out (usual 4 out)* **14/1**

5m 24.2s (6.70) **Going Correction** +0.475s/f (Soft) **5 Ran SP% 108.0**
Speed ratings (Par 105): **105,103,102,100,98**
CSF £19.06 TOTE £2.80: £2.10, £3.70; EX 17.80 Trifecta £44.60.
Owner Mrs Janet Davies **Bred** Sean Kinsella **Trained** Llancarfan, Vale Of Glamorgan

FOCUS
This contest was over an additional 18yds. The last fence was omitted in all chases due to a false patch of ground. A competitive-looking race for the level with the winner well in on his recent win.

2875 DOUGIE TOOTELL 60TH BIRTHDAY MAIDEN OPEN NATIONAL HUNT FLAT RACE 1m 7f 65y

3:45 (3:45) (Class 6) 4-6-Y-0 **£1,624** (£477; £238; £119)

Form RPR

1 **Rolling Dylan (IRE)**[264] 4-11-4 0....................................... TomO'Brien 110+
(Philip Hobbs) *mde all: clr over 2f out: hung lft fnl f but enough in hand and a holding on* **3/1**[3]

6- 2 1 1/4 **Antartica De Thaix (FR)**[300] 4073 5-10-4 0.................(t[1]) HarryCobden[(7)] 102+
(Paul Nicholls) *hld up: hdwy 5f out: rdn to chse wnr 2f out: styd on but a being hld ins fnl f* **9/4**[2]

3 9 **Hard As A Rock (FR)** 4-11-4 0.. NoelFehily 99
(Emma Lavelle) *trckd ldrs: rdn to chse wnr 3f out tl 2f out: styd on same pce* **13/8**[1]

4 27 **Cove Lodge**[213] 5-11-4 0... DarylJacob 72
(Richard Woollacott) *mid-div: hdwy over 3f out: rdn to chse ldrs over 2f out: sn outpcd: wknd over 1f out* **20/1**

5 9 **Hawaian Rose** 5-10-4 0.. PaulO'Brien[(7)] 56
(Colin Tizzard) *a towards rr* **8/1**

0 6 14 **Wun Destination**[23] 2421 6-10-4 0........................ ThomasCheesman[(7)] 42
(John Panvert) *chsd ldrs tl over 4f out: t.o* **100/1**

7 11 **Primary Suspect (IRE)** 5-10-11 0...................................... ConorSmith[(7)] 38
(Linda Blackford) *trckd ldr tl rdn 4f out: wknd over 3f out: t.o* **25/1**

8 3 **Shady Grey** 5-10-11 0.. JamesBest 28
(Kevin Bishop) *chsd ldrs tl wknd over 3f out: t.o* **50/1**

P **Saruni (IRE)**[243] 4-10-11 0... LewisGordon[(7)]
(Jennifer Mason) *mid-div: hdwy 4f out: cl 3rd whn hung off crse ent st: nt rcvr and sn p.u* **66/1**

3m 46.9s (3.60) **Going Correction** +0.075s/f (Yiel) **9 Ran SP% 118.0**
Speed ratings: **93,92,87,73,68 60,55,53,**
CSF £10.08 TOTE £3.90: £1.20, £1.30, £1.20; EX 12.10 Trifecta £22.10.
Owner Miss I D Du Pre **Bred** Mrs Mary Tynan Phelan **Trained** Withycombe, Somerset

FOCUS
This contest was over an additional 12yds. The three market leaders proved easily the best of these.
T/Plt: £8.60 to a £1 stake. Pool: £54,481.04 - 4607.17 winning units. T/Qpdt: £5.50 to a £1 stake. Pool: £4,095.38 - 546.56 winning units. **Tim Mitchell**

2658 EXETER (R-H)

Friday, December 4

OFFICIAL GOING: Heavy (soft in places, chs; 6.0, hdl; 6.2)
Wind: mild behind Weather: sunny periods Rails: Races 1, 4, 5, & 7 add 26yds; Races 2 & 6 add 25yds; Race 3 add 50yds.

2876 188BET.CO.UK CONDITIONAL JOCKEYS' NOVICES' H'CAP HURDLE (10 hdls) 2m 2f 111y

12:40 (12:40) (Class 5) (0-100,99) 3-Y-0+ **£2,274** (£667; £333; £166)

Form RPR

54-0 1 **Glenarm**[29] 2298 6-11-9 **96**...................................... JeremiahMcGrath 109+
(Seamus Mullins) *prom: led 4th: drew clr after 2 out: eased towards fin* **7/1**

00-5 2 10 **Kayf Charmer**[57] 1823 5-9-12 **76** ow2.............................. ConorSmith[(5)] 78
(Linda Blackford) *trckd ldrs: rdn to chse wnr after 3 out: hld whn nt fluent 2 out: styd on same pce* **9/2**[3]

04-4 3 7 **Buckboru (IRE)**[31] 2263 7-10-13 **89**........................ ThomasCheesman[(3)] 83
(Laura Young) *trckd ldrs: rdn appr 3 out: sn one pce* **3/1**[2]

06U0 4 6 **Arthur's Queen (FR)**[99] 1384 4-11-3 **90**.......................... MattGriffiths 77
(Carroll Gray) *hld up: struggling 6th: wnt hld 4th 3 out: nvr a danger* **16/1**

4043 5 26 **Hill Fort**[20] 2492 5-11-9 **99**.. CiaranGethings[(3)] 60
(Matt Sheppard) *trckd ldrs: prom 4th tl rdn appr 3 out: qckly btn* **9/4**[1]

00P2 P **Poetic Presence (IRE)**[16] 2565 5-10-0 **73** oh4..............(v) JamieBargary
(Adrian Wintle) *led tl 4th: sn struggling in rr: t.o whn p.u bef 3 out* **7/1**

PP50 P **Highridge Princess (IRE)**[22] 2457 7-10-9 **82**............(t) ConorShoemark
(Johnny Farrelly) *hld up: wknd 5th: t.o whn p.u 7th* **16/1**

5m 1.7s (19.00) **Going Correction** +0.575s/f (Soft)
WFA 4 from 5yo+ 5lb **7 Ran SP% 110.7**
Speed ratings (Par 103): **83,78,75,73,62** ,
CSF £35.86 CT £108.99 TOTE £8.40: £3.70, £2.90; EX 41.80 Trifecta £106.60.
Owner The Up The Glens Partnership **Bred** D J Erwin Bloodstock **Trained** Wilsford-Cum-Lake, Wilts

FOCUS
Rail movement increased races 1, 4, 5 & 7 by 26yds, races 2 & 6 by 25yds and race 3 by 50yds. Jeremiah McGrath described the ground as "very dead and holding - hard work". Lowly handicap form but a comprehensive winner. A step forward from the winner, with the second rated pretty much to her mark.

2877 FOOT ANSTEY H'CAP CHASE (15 fncs) 2m 3f 48y

1:10 (1:10) (Class 3) (0-140,133) 4-Y-0+ **£15,698** (£4,678; £2,368; £1,213; £635)

Form RPR

32-2 1 **Otago Trail (IRE)**[23] 2446 7-11-12 **133**.......................... LiamTreadwell 151+
(Venetia Williams) *a.p: led 5th: hit 9th: nt fluent and hdd 3 out: rallied gamely after last: led towards fin* **2/1**[1]

202 2 1/2 **Mon Successeur (FR)**[7] 2758 4-10-7 **128**........................ HarryCobden[(7)] 136+
(Paul Nicholls) *trckd ldrs: chal 4 out: led 3 out: rdn after next: rdr dropped whip on landing last: no ex whn hdd towards fin* **11/4**[2]

4-P3 3 22 **Quite By Chance**[16] 2568 6-10-12 **119**.................................... NoelFehily 114
(Colin Tizzard) *trckd ldrs: rdn appr 4 out: sn outpcd* **7/1**

6-25 4 9 **Midnight Lira**[31] 2261 8-11-3 **124**... JamesBest 108
(Caroline Keevil) *disp tl 5th: prom: rdn appr 4 out: sn hld: wknd 2 out* **14/1**

-261 5 14 **Rouge Et Blanc (FR)**[7] 2758 10-10-12 **122**...............(p) ThomasGarner[(3)] 92
(Oliver Sherwood) *hld up bhd ldrs: cl 4th appr 4 out: rdn bef 3 out: wknd bef 2 out* **9/2**[3]

F3-P **P** **Shammick Boy (IRE)**[19] 2517 10-10-10 **127**..........(p) MrJakeBament(10)
(Victor Dartnall) *nvr travelling: wnt rt at times: struggling in last after 7th: t.o whn p.u bef 3 out* **14/1**

-113 **P** **Al Alfa**[36] 2153 8-11-10 **131**.. RichardJohnson
(Philip Hobbs) *prom tl 10th: rdn after next: wknd after 11th: t.o whn p.u bef 4 out* **9/1**

5m 8.4s (11.10) **Going Correction** +0.825s/f (Soft)
WFA 4 from 6yo+ 5lb **7 Ran SP% 114.0**
Speed ratings (Par 107): **109,108,99,95,89 ,**
CSF £8.28 TOTE £2.00: £1.90, £2.10; EX 10.30 Trifecta £50.50.
Owner Mrs Marie Shone **Bred** Dan O'Brien **Trained** Kings Caple, H'fords

FOCUS
The front pair came clear in what was a fair handicap chase. The winner rates a smart novice, and the second, who was well in on his recent run, has been rated to a similar level.

2878 BREWIN DOLPHIN MARATHON H'CAP CHASE (21 fncs) 3m 6f 153y
1:40 (1:40) (Class 3) (0-125,130) 4-Y-O+ **£12,558** (£3,742; £1,894; £970; £508)

Form RPR

30-6 **1** **Woodford County**[36] 2146 8-11-5 **125**..........(p) CiaranGethings(7) 134
(Philip Hobbs) *mid-div: hdwy 14th: chal 4 out: sn rdn: led 2 out: styd on dourly: drvn rt out* **8/1**

44/4 **2** 1 1/4 **Nail 'M (IRE)**[16] 2566 7-10-10 **109**.................................. TomScudamore 116
(Nigel Hawke) *trckd ldrs: rdn appr 4 out: kpt on into 2nd after last: styd on but nvr quite rching wnr* **13/2**[3]

2233 **3** 2 3/4 **Railway Storm (IRE)**[23] 2447 10-9-7 **99** oh4.................. MissBFrost(7) 103
(Jimmy Frost) *prom: led 3rd tl after 10th: led appr 4 out where sn strly pressed: rdn and hdd 2 out: styd on but no ex whn lost 2nd run-in* **28/1**

4-12 **4** 11 **Loughalder (IRE)**[20] 2491 9-10-13 **112**..........................(bt) CharliePoste 105
(Matt Sheppard) *led tl 3rd: prom: mstke 9th: led after 10th: rdn and hdd appr 4 out: styd on same pce* **20/1**

-221 **5** 21 **St Dominick (IRE)**[12] 2663 8-11-12 **130** 7ex.................. DavidNoonan(5) 112
(Jackie Du Plessis) *hld up bhd: hdwy after 17th: rdn to chse ldrs appr 4 out: wknd 2 out: virtually plld u run-in* **7/1**

-506 **P** **Sybarite (FR)**[13] 2638 9-11-12 **125**..............(v) SamTwiston-Davies
(Nigel Twiston-Davies) *nvr gng: drvn fr the s: becoming detached whn p.u after 3rd* **10/1**

2P-P **P** **Gorgehous Liege (FR)**[19] 2517 9-11-0 **113**.................. LiamTreadwell
(Venetia Williams) *trckd ldrs tl 14th: rdn after next: sn wknd: t.o whn p.u bef 4 out* **12/1**

6-52 **P** **As De Fer (FR)**[26] 2366 9-10-7 **106**..(t) NoelFehily
(Anthony Honeyball) *mid-div: effrt appr 4 out: wknd bef 3 out: p.u bef 2 out* **11/2**[1]

4PP2 **P** **Terminal (FR)**[25] 2405 8-10-11 **115**..........................(v1) JamieBargary(5)
(David Dennis) *towards rr: pushed along fr 6th: losing tch whn p.u after 11th* **25/1**

13-4 **P** **Barton Gift**[30] 2272 8-11-0 **113**...............................(p) JeremiahMcGrath
(John Spearing) *mid-div: rdn appr 14th: sn in last pair: t.o whn p.u bef 4 out* **9/1**

16-3 **P** **Heronshaw (IRE)**[23] 2442 8-11-12 **125**.............................. RichardJohnson
(Henry Daly) *hld up: blnd 5th: struggling after 13th: sn in last pair: tailing off whn p.u bef 4 out* **6/1**[2]

P-42 **U** **Auvergnat (FR)**[48] 1970 5-11-11 **124**.................................... BarryGeraghty
(Jonjo O'Neill) *hld up: mstke and uns rdr 2nd* **7/1**

8m 32.5s (43.90) **Going Correction** +0.825s/f (Soft) **12 Ran SP% 118.0**
Speed ratings (Par 107): **76,75,74,72,66 , , , ,**
CSF £58.27 CT £1396.81 TOTE £10.70: £2.80, £2.60, £8.40; EX 90.80 Trifecta £1635.70 Part won..
Owner The Englands And Heywoods **Bred** Wendy Robinson **Trained** Withycombe, Somerset
■ Stewards' Enquiry : Ciaran Gethings seven-day ban; used whip above the permitted level (18-22nd, 26th-27th Dec)

FOCUS
Only five of the 12 managed to complete in this marathon chase, which served up a gruelling test. The first three have been rated pretty much to their marks.

2879 EBF STALLIONS "NATIONAL HUNT" NOVICES' HURDLE (QUALIFIER) (8 hdls) 2m 175y
2:15 (2:15) (Class 4) 4-6-Y-O **£3,573** (£1,049; £524; £262)

Form RPR

22-1 **1** **Vieux Lille (IRE)**[27] 2351 5-10-12 0.................................. RichardJohnson 132+
(Philip Hobbs) *mid-div on outer: hdwy 2nd: led after 5th: pushed clr fr 3 out: styd on strly: easily* **6/4**[1]

4-16 **2** 14 **Morthanalegend**[22] 2457 6-10-12 0..............................(t) BrendanPowell 116+
(Brendan Powell) *trckd ldr: led briefly after 5th: rdn to chse wnr fr next: styd on but a being comf hld* **16/1**

3 **3** 8 **Mr Mix (FR)**[36] 2154 4-10-12 0.............................. SamTwiston-Davies 107
(Paul Nicholls) *mid-div: hdwy after 4th: rdn to chse ldrs appr 3 out: styd on but nt pce to chal* **13/8**[2]

4 5 **Solomn Grundy (IRE)**[578] 5-10-12 0.............................. TomScudamore 101
(David Pipe) *hld up bhd: midfield 3rd: rdn and styd on fr 3 out: wnt hld 4th at the last* **12/1**[3]

40-P **5** 3 **I'm Oscar (IRE)**[36] 2152 5-10-9 0.................................. MattGriffiths(3) 99
(Jeremy Scott) *trckd ldrs tl lost pl u.p after 3rd: styd on fr 3 out but no threat to ldrs* **66/1**

1 **6** 1 1/4 **Grandmaster George (IRE)**[206] 264 6-10-12 0........ JeremiahMcGrath 99
(Seamus Mullins) *mid-div: hdwy 4th: trckd ldrs next: rdn in hld 3rd whn nt fluent 3 out: no ex appr last* **20/1**

0-42 **7** 3 1/4 **Sartorial Elegance**[18] 2549 4-10-5 0..........................(b) PaulO'Brien(7) 94
(Colin Tizzard) *mid-div: hdwy 4th: rdn to chse ldrs appr 3 out: sn one pce* **14/1**

06 **8** 3 1/2 **The Artful Cobbler**[23] 2437 4-10-12 0.................................. JakeGreenall 90
(Henry Daly) *nvr bttr than mid-div* **100/1**

0 **9** 15 **Arty Bella**[23] 2444 4-9-12 0.. MissBFrost(7) 68
(Jimmy Frost) *a towards rr* **150/1**

0 **10** 1/2 **Bellini Dubreau (FR)**[30] 2270 4-10-9 0.......................... TomBellamy(3) 75
(Nigel Hawke) *mid-div: rdn appr 3 out: sn wknd* **200/1**

60-P **11** 42 **Somerset Jem**[23] 2443 6-10-12 0.. JamesBest 33
(Kevin Bishop) *a bhd: t.o* **80/1**

P- **P** **Lord Of The Hosts**[407] 2044 4-10-7 0.............................. LizzieKelly(5)
(Nick Williams) *mid-div: hdwy 2nd: rdn after 5th: wknd bef next: bhd whn p.u after 2 out* **20/1**

00 **P** **Hardtorock (IRE)**[19] 2519 6-10-12 0..............................(t) RichieMcLernon
(Liam Corcoran) *mid-div: rdn after 4th: wknd after next: bhd whn p.u after 2 out* **100/1**

6 **P** **Three Of A Kind (IRE)**[41] 2062 6-10-9 0.................... ConorShoemark(3)
(Fergal O'Brien) *chsd ldrs tl 2nd: wknd qckly: p.u bef 4th* **40/1**

0 **P** **Poets Day**[56] 1843 5-10-5 0.. JamesDavies
(Katie Stephens) *a towards rr: t.o whn p.u bef 5th* **200/1**

4 **F** **Antiphony (IRE)**[31] 2258 4-10-5 0.................................. ConorSmith(7)
(Philip Hobbs) *led tl rdn after 5th: wknd next: fell 2 out* **16/1**

4 **P** **Indian Brave (IRE)**[44] 2020 4-10-12 0.............................. NoelFehily
(Neil Mulholland) *towards rr of midfield: nt fluent 2nd: wknd 4th: t.o whn p.u bef last* **33/1**

4m 20.6s (5.10) **Going Correction** +0.575s/f (Soft) **17 Ran SP% 125.5**
Speed ratings: **111,104,100,98,96 96,94,93,86,85 66, , , , ,**
CSF £26.31 TOTE £2.60: £1.20, £4.50, £1.10; EX 39.20 Trifecta £97.00.
Owner Louisville Syndicate III **Bred** Park Athlete Partnership **Trained** Withycombe, Somerset

FOCUS
Little depth to this, with it looking a match on paper, but the duel didn't materialise, with the favourite bolting up. The winner looks a smart recruit, with the fifth rated in line with his bumper form.

2880 188BET H'CAP HURDLE (8 hdls) 2m 175y
2:50 (2:50) (Class 4) (0-105,111) 3-Y-O+ **£3,249** (£954; £477; £238)

Form RPR

0/4P **1** **Darwins Theory (IRE)**[191] 510 7-11-5 **105**..................(t) MrMLegg(7) 114+
(Fiona Shaw) *mid-div: pushed along and hdwy after 5th: led next: 1 l up whn lft clr 2 out: styd on wl* **33/1**

-532 **2** 11 **Beat The Tide**[107] 1290 5-11-12 **105**.............................. RichardJohnson 106+
(Tim Vaughan) *nvr that fluent: trckd ldrs: ev ch 3 out: sn rdn and hld: lft 2nd at the next: styd on same pce* **7/1**[2]

0-10 **3** 7 **Tara Mac**[169] 775 6-11-10 **103**.. MichaelByrne 93
(Tim Vaughan) *hld up: stdy prog fr 3 out: styd on to go 4th cl home: nvr a threat* **14/1**

P **4** 3/4 **Badilou (FR)**[31] 2262 4-11-12 **105**.............................. JeremiahMcGrath 96
(Martin Hill) *in tch: hdwy 4th: led after 5th tl rdn next: wkng whn lft 3rd and bdly hmpd 2 out: lost 3rd cl home* **8/1**[3]

PPPP **5** 21 **Exiles Return (IRE)**[12] 2661 13-9-7 **79** oh15......... ThomasCheesman(7) 47
(Jackie Retter) *hld up: hdwy on outer after 1st: pressed ldr next tl rdn appr 3 out: wknd 2 out* **200/1**

00-P **6** 12 **Aristocracy**[20] 2490 4-11-8 **104**.. JamesBanks(3) 60
(Sally Randell) *led tl rdn after 5th: wknd bef next: t.o* **20/1**

-150 **7** 5 **Karl Marx (IRE)**[134] 1085 5-10-13 **92**..................................(p) SeanBowen 43
(Mark Gillard) *mid-div tl 2nd: sn struggling and bhd: t.o* **16/1**

030- **8** 3 1/2 **Norphin**[9] 1211 5-10-11 **90**.. NickScholfield 38
(Simon Hodgson) *racd keenly: pressed ldr tl after 2nd: chsd ldrs: rdn after 5th: sn wknd: t.o* **33/1**

4P0/ **9** 40 **Shivsingh**[722] 3043 6-11-3 **96**.. RobertDunne 4
(Laura Young) *mid-div tl 5th: wknd bef next: t.o* **33/1**

/-00 **P** **Sarenice (FR)**[12] 2661 9-10-13 **92**.................................. TomScudamore
(Jimmy Frost) *chsd ldrs tl 2nd: losing pl whn p.u after 4th* **12/1**

/P11 **F** **Never Says Never**[3] 2831 7-11-11 **111** 7ex..................(t) HarryCobden(7) 112
(Anthony Honeyball) *j.lft at times: hld up: smooth hdwy fr 3rd: chal 3 out: pushed along and 1 l down whn fell 2 out* **4/9**[1]

4m 30.8s (15.30) **Going Correction** +0.575s/f (Soft) **11 Ran SP% 127.2**
Speed ratings (Par 105): **87,81,78,78,68 62,60,58,39,**
CSF £256.56 CT £3438.43 TOTE £52.50: £8.00, £2.00, £3.10; EX 242.30 Trifecta £590.30.
Owner Mrs Fiona Shaw **Bred** M Ryan **Trained** Bradford Peverell, Dorset

FOCUS
A bit of a turn up in this modest handicap. The winner has been rated in line with his 2014 Irish chase form, and the second to his mark.

2881 HARRY DUTFIELD MEMORIAL NOVICES' CHASE (15 fncs) 2m 3f 48y
3:20 (3:20) (Class 2) 4-Y-O+ **£12,685** (£3,869; £2,021; £1,097)

Form RPR

P-60 **1** **Tea For Two**[13] 2641 6-11-0 0.. LizzieKelly 155+
(Nick Williams) *j. and travelled wl: trckd ldrs: led 3 out: pushed clr: eased run-in: impressive* **2/1**[2]

1P1- **2** 10 **Oscar Sunset (IRE)**[236] 5290 8-11-0 0.................................. ConorRing 142
(Evan Williams) *trckd ldrs: rdn after 4 out: styd on to go 2nd cl home but nvr any threat to easy wnr* **8/1**

6-13 **3** shd **Calipto (FR)**[19] 2510 5-11-5 **143**..................(t) SamTwiston-Davies 146
(Paul Nicholls) *disp ld tl clr ldr 8th: hdd 3 out: sn rdn and hld: nt fluent last: no ex whn lost 2nd fnl strides* **11/8**[1]

6-22 **4** 28 **Golden Doyen (GER)**[26] 2370 4-10-7 **138**.......................... RichardJohnson 115
(Philip Hobbs) *disp ld: hit 2nd: hdd 8th: rdn and hld 4 out: mstke next: wknd after hitting 2 out* **9/2**[3]

/0-0 **P** **Pursuitofhappiness (IRE)**[14] 2612 7-11-0 0.............................. NoelFehily
(Neil Mulholland) *nt fluent 7th: sn lost tch: t.o whn p.u bef 4 out* **100/1**

20P- **U** **Monbeg Theatre (IRE)**[238] 5254 6-11-0 0....................(t) BrendanPowell
(Jamie Snowden) *v awkward whn unseating rdr 2nd* **14/1**

-U5P **P** **Hill Forts Gypse (IRE)**[19] 2519 4-10-7 0.................. JeremiahMcGrath
(Seamus Mullins) *lost tch 7th: t.o whn p.u bef 2 out* **200/1**

5m 11.3s (14.00) **Going Correction** +0.825s/f (Soft)
WFA 4 from 5yo+ 5lb **7 Ran SP% 112.9**
Speed ratings (Par 109): **103,98,98,86, ,**
CSF £17.50 TOTE £3.70: £1.60, £3.20; EX 21.90 Trifecta £45.10.
Owner Mrs Jane Williams & Len Jakeman **Bred** Mrs P G Lewin **Trained** George Nympton, Devon

FOCUS
A good novice chase that saw a really impressive debut success from the winner. The second has been rated to his hurdle mark, and the third similar to his recent chase runs.

2882 PREMIER LEAGUE BETTING AT 188BET "JUNIOR" STANDARD OPEN NATIONAL HUNT FLAT RACE 1m 5f 38y
3:50 (3:50) (Class 6) 3-Y-O **£1,624** (£477; £238; £119)

Form RPR

1 **Steel Express (IRE)** 3-10-5 0.. ConorSmith(7) 97
(Linda Blackford) *unruly paddock: trckd ldrs: rdn to chal over 2f out: led over 1f out: rn green whn strly chal ins fnl f: kpt on: drvn out* **9/1**

2 3/4 **Antonio Joli (IRE)** 3-10-12 0.............................. SamTwiston-Davies 96
(Jo Hughes) *hld up bhd ldrs: rdn for str chal over 1f out: ev ch thrght fnl f: hld cl home* **11/4**[2]

3 3 3/4 **El Tiburon (IRE)** 3-10-9 0.. JamesBanks(3) 92+
(Sam Thomas) *trckd ldrs: led over 2f out: hdd wl over 1f out: hld in 4th whn veered lft jst over 1f out: styd on to regain 3rd ins fnl f* **3/1**[3]

4 2 1/2 **Brother Norphin** 3-10-12 0.. NickScholfield 88
(Simon Hodgson) *trckd ldr: led over 1f out: sn rdn and hdd: no ex fnl f* **8/1**

3 **5** 2 1/2 **Renaissance Red**[14] 2629 3-10-12 0..............................(t) BrendanPowell 85
(Brendan Powell) *led: rdn and hdd over 2f out: sn one pce* **6/4**[1]

3m 26.6s (9.90) **5 Ran SP% 112.8**
CSF £34.03 TOTE £9.30: £3.30, £1.50; EX 54.20 Trifecta £153.80.
Owner Mrs Sue Quick **Bred** M Doran **Trained** Rackenford, Devon

FOCUS
Quite a modest bumper and it went to the outsider of the field.
T/Plt: £2,134.30 to a £1 stake. Pool: £49,626.09 - 16.97 winning tickets T/Qpdt: £122.80 to a £1 stake. Pool: £7,286.72 - 43.9 winning tickets **Tim Mitchell**

2369 SANDOWN (R-H)
Friday, December 4

OFFICIAL GOING: Hurdle course - soft (good to soft in places back straight; 5.3); chase course - good to soft (5.8)
Wind: light, against Weather: dry, bright spells

2883 ASPEN INSURANCE JUVENILE HURDLE (8 hdls) 1m 7f 216y
1:00 (1:00) (Class 3) 3-Y-O £6,657 (£2,067; £1,113)

Form RPR
5 **1** **Fingertips (FR)**[20] 2480 3-11-8 129........................(t) DarylJacob 125+
(David Pipe) *mde all jnd and out j. runner-up 2 out: clr and gng bttr after: styd on: rdn out* **5/2**[2]
2 *3 ¾* **Polarisation**[84] 3-10-12 0........................(p) AidanColeman 114+
(John Ferguson) *j.rt and nt fluent: lft 2nd 3rd: clsd to join wnr and out j. 2 out: sn rdn and nvr looked like getting bk on terms after: j.rt last: kpt on same pce: eased towards fin* **8/15**[1]
3 *19* **Jinsha Lake (IRE)**[75] 3-10-12 0........................(t) AdamWedge 93
(Evan Williams) *hld up in rr: lft 3rd 3rd: shkn up bef 2 out: sn btn: wknd between last 2* **7/1**[3]
0 **U** **Rest Easy**[37] 2137 3-10-0 0........................ KevinJones(5)
(Seamus Mullins) *chsd wnr tl mstke and uns rdr 3rd* **100/1**

4m 8.2s (1.00) **Going Correction** +0.275s/f (Yiel) **4** Ran SP% **107.3**
Speed ratings (Par 106): **108,106,96,**
CSF £4.39 TOTE £3.80; EX 4.40 Trifecta £4.70.
Owner Simon Munir & Isaac Souede **Bred** Mme Laurence Gagneux & Ecurie Des Clos **Trained** Nicholashayne, Devon

FOCUS
After 2.5mm of rain overnight the going remained good to soft, good in places on the chase course and soft, good to soft in places on the back straight on the hurdles course. The winning time of the opener was 23.2sec outside standard, suggesting testing conditions on the hurdles track. Rail movement on the hurdles course added 12yds to the distance of race 4. Chase distances as advertised. A small field, but a fascinating juvenile contest won by the subsequent Betfair Hurdle winner Violet Dancer two years ago. This year's race was all about who jumped well and who didn't. A big step up from his poor Cheltenham run by the winner.

2884 ZURICH INSURANCE PLC H'CAP CHASE (12 fncs 1 omitted) 1m 7f 119y
1:30 (1:32) (Class 3) (0-125,129) 4-Y-O+
£9,384 (£2,772; £1,386; £693; £346; £174)

Form RPR
-316 **1** **Vision Des Champs (FR)**[7] 2758 6-11-0 112........................(t) JamieMoore 124+
(Gary Moore) *midfield: swtchd lft 2nd: hdwy to chse ldrs next: chal 2 out: sustained battle w runner-up fr between last 2: kpt on u.p: led last stride* **7/1**[3]
-P04 **2** *shd* **Malibu Sun**[29] 2301 8-11-10 122........................ NicodeBoinville 133
(Ben Pauling) *midfield: outpcd 5th: 10 l 7th 10th: pushed along and gd hdwy bypassing 3 out to ld on inner bef 2 out: sustained battle w wnr fr between last 2: rdn and kpt on: hdd last stride* **8/1**
-412 **3** *13* **Artifice Sivola (FR)**[11] 2691 5-11-11 123........................ LeightonAspell 124
(Lucy Wadham) *chsd ldrs: mstke and pckd 1st: outpcd by ldng trio and mstke 4th: nt fluent next: clsd on long run after 10th and wl in tch bypassing 3 out: 4th and outpcd 2 out: wnt 3rd sn after last: plugged on* **7/2**[1]
0F-P **4** *4 ½* **Festive Affair (IRE)**[27] 2336 7-11-12 124........................(p) JoshuaMoore 120
(Jonjo O'Neill) *chsd ldr: clr in ldng trio 4th: ev ch bypassing 3 out: sn rdn and no ex between last 2: wknd flat* **10/1**
R246 **5** *1 ½* **Cloudy Joker (IRE)**[24] 2425 7-11-8 120........................ WayneHutchinson 115
(Donald McCain) *hld up in last trio: mstke 3rd: clsd on long run after 10th and wl in tch bypassing 3 out: no ex and j.rt next: wknd last* **16/1**
33-4 **6** *1 ½* **Morgan's Bay**[24] 2419 10-11-6 118........................ TomCannon 112
(Laura Mongan) *midfield tl outpcd 4th: dropped to rr and wl off the pce 7th: styd on bypassing 3 out: j.rt 2 out: wnt past btn horses between last 2: j.rt last: plugged on: nvr trbld ldrs* **12/1**
3-4P **7** *5* **Paddy The Stout (IRE)**[16] 2568 10-10-10 108........................(t) TomO'Brien 96
(Paul Henderson) *bhd: lost tch w ldrs 4th: mstkes 8th and 9th: n.d* **14/1**
502P **8** *1* **Noche De Reyes (FR)**[11] 2691 6-11-9 121........................ PaddyBrennan 108
(Tom George) *midfield: hdwy to chse ldng trio 6th: blnd 9th: clsd and wl in tch bypassing 3 out: sn u.p and no ex: skipped out 2 out* **13/2**[2]
-601 **9** *15* **De Faoithesdream (IRE)**[12] 2659 9-12-3 129 7ex........................ AdamWedge 109
(Evan Williams) *led: blnd 2nd: mstke 9th: rdn and hdd bef 2 out: sn btn: fdd between last 2: t.o* **7/2**[1]
24U6 **10** *21* **Boss In Boots (IRE)**[24] 2419 7-11-1 113........................(b) AndrewThornton 68
(Seamus Mullins) *midfield: lost pl 5th: bhd and reminder after 7th: lost tch 10th: t.o* **33/1**

3m 59.1s (-2.70) **Going Correction** +0.05s/f (Yiel) **10** Ran SP% **113.7**
Speed ratings (Par 107): **108,107,101,99,98 97,95,94,87,76**
CSF £60.16 CT £228.29 TOTE £9.30: £2.40, £3.00, £1.70; EX 80.80 Trifecta £421.00.
Owner Polo Racing & Friends **Bred** G A E C Des Champs **Trained** Lower Beeding, W Sussex

FOCUS
Due to the bright sunshine the Pond Fence was omitted in this race. With a few in here that like to force it, a strong pace was inevitable with a three horses skipping well clear by halfway. The winner has been rated back to form, and the second to his best.

2885 AMLIN INSURANCE NOVICES' LIMITED H'CAP CHASE (15 fncs 2 omitted) 2m 4f 10y
2:05 (2:05) (Class 3) (0-125,125) 4-Y-O+
£7,507 (£2,217; £1,108; £554; £277; £139)

Form RPR
2230 **1** **Antony (FR)**[34] 2182 5-11-3 120........................ JamieMoore 130+
(Gary Moore) *hld up in tch: trckd ldng pair after 10th: wnt 2nd bypassing 3 out: led bef last and sn asserted: rdn and readily wnt clr flat: easily* **10/1**
22-4 **2** *8* **Dancing Shadow (IRE)**[23] 2442 6-11-5 122........................ IanPopham 124
(Victor Dartnall) *t.k.h: early: midfield whn mstke and bmpd 1st: lost pl 4th: last and rdn after: hdwy u.p on long run after 13th: wnt 4th 2 out: styd on to go fnl 75yds: no ch w wnr* **7/2**[1]
150- **3** *1 ¾* **Dusky Lark**[265] 4750 5-11-8 125........................ DarylJacob 125
(Colin Tizzard) *hld up in rr: hmpd 1st: mstke 7th: hdwy 10th: 4th and clr in ldng quintet after 13th: rdn and unable qck 2 out: chsd clr wnr flat: no imp and lost 2nd fnl 75yds* **9/1**
42-4 **4** *4 ½* **Long Lunch**[13] 2637 6-11-8 125........................(t) HarrySkelton 121
(Charlie Longsdon) *chsd ldrs: j.w to join ldrs 6th: led next: rdn and hdd after 2 out: btn whn j. and nt fluent last: wknd and lost 2 pls flat* **11/2**[3]
00-4 **5** *15* **Like Sully (IRE)**[24] 2415 7-10-4 107........................ LeightonAspell 88
(Richard Rowe) *chsd ldrs: lost pl after 10th: nt fluent next: wl btn on long run after 13th: plugged on* **11/1**
410- **6** *18* **Cloudy Beach (IRE)**[385] 2481 8-10-8 111........................ AidanColeman 76
(Venetia Williams) *t.k.h: hld up towards rr: bmpd 1st: hdwy 10th: 5th and in tch whn mstke 13th: sn rdn and btn: wknd: t.o* **9/2**[2]
1P-4 **7** *9* **Money Talks**[44] 2012 5-11-5 122........................(t) MarcGoldstein 87
(Michael Madgwick) *chsd ldrs: jnd ldr after 5th: j. into ld next: hdd 7th but styd upsides ldr tl lost pl u.p bypassing 3 out: fdd next: t.o* **16/1**
4-2P **8** *17* **Handazan (IRE)**[34] 2197 6-11-7 124........................(tp) KielanWoods 65
(Ben Case) *mde most tl out j. and hdd 6th: lost pl and rdn after 10th: lost tch 13th: t.o* **14/1**
44-3 **F** **Bilbrook Blaze**[34] 2182 5-10-12 115........................ TomO'Brien
(Philip Hobbs) *fell 1st* **9/2**[2]

5m 12.5s (-5.90) **Going Correction** +0.05s/f (Yiel) **9** Ran SP% **113.9**
Speed ratings (Par 107): **113,109,109,107,101 94,90,83,**
CSF £45.74 CT £329.93 TOTE £10.80: £2.70, £1.60, £3.00; EX 57.30 Trifecta £334.40.
Owner The Winning Hand **Bred** Madame Marie-Laure Besnouin **Trained** Lower Beeding, W Sussex

FOCUS
Again the Pond Fence was omitted for this race. This novices' handicap has been won by some nice chasers, including the subsequent Paddy Power Gold Cup winner Johns Spirit three years ago, and this year's winner did it very nicely. The winner has been rated up 10lb on his best hurdles form.

2886 NEPTUNE INVESTMENT MANAGEMENT NOVICES' HURDLE (REGISTERED AS WINTER NOVICES' HURDLE RACE) (GRADE 2) (8 hdls 1 omitted) 2m 3f 173y
2:40 (2:41) (Class 1) 4-Y-O+ **£17,085** (£6,411; £3,210; £1,599; £804; £15)

2 **1** **Label Des Obeaux (FR)**[13] 2630 4-11-0 129........................ WayneHutchinson 138+
(Alan King) *chsd ldrs: effrt to chse ldr 2 out: rdn to ld between last 2: styd on wl flat: rdn out* **10/3**[2]
1-1 **2** *1 ½* **Captain Chaos (IRE)**[20] 2487 4-11-4 0........................ HarrySkelton 141
(Dan Skelton) *hld up in last pair: effrt jst bef 2 out: hdwy between last 2: styd on u.p to chse wnr fnl 75yds: kpt on but nvr enough pce to chal* **8/1**
1114 **3** *1 ¾* **Francis Of Assisi (IRE)**[27] 2350 5-11-4 144........................ AidanColeman 140
(John Ferguson) *hld up in midfield: cl 4th whn sltly hmpd 2 out: effrt and j. into 2nd last: sn no imp and styd on same pce flat: lost 2nd fnl 75yds* **4/1**[3]
211 **4** *6* **Clondaw Cian (IRE)**[9] 2710 5-11-4 0........................ TomO'Brien 134
(Suzy Smith) *in tch in midfield: effrt in cl 3rd 2 out: outpcd u.p between last 2: wl hld and styd on same pce flat* **13/8**[1]
1111 **5** *¾* **Roadie Joe (IRE)**[54] 1870 6-11-7 141........................ AdamWedge 136
(Evan Williams) *chsd ldr tl led bef 2 out: j.rt 2 out: rdn and hdd between last 2: j. bdly rt again and lost 2nd last: wknd flat* **6/1**
3 **6** *nk* **Dark Flame (IRE)**[47] 1990 6-11-0 0........................ LeightonAspell 129
(Richard Rowe) *hld up in tch in midfield: shkn up and outpcd 2 out: wl hld and plugged on same pce between last 2* **100/1**
P **7** *22* **Tjongejonge (FR)**[20] 2485 4-11-7 130........................ DarylJacob 117
(Charlie Longsdon) *led tl hdd and rdn jst bef 2 out: sn lost pl and wl btn between last 2: wknd last* **20/1**
8 *26* **Talk Of The South (IRE)**[264] 6-11-0 0........................ JamieMoore 80
(Paul Henderson) *hld up in tch in rr: shkn up bef 2 out: sn btn and wknd: t.o* **100/1**

5m 11.0s (11.40) **Going Correction** +0.275s/f (Yiel) **8** Ran SP% **113.3**
Speed ratings (Par 115): **88,87,86,84,84 83,75,64**
CSF £28.33 TOTE £4.40: £1.50, £2.40, £1.40; EX 22.10 Trifecta £133.80.
Owner David Sewell & Terry Warner **Bred** N Devilder, H, Delloye & S Fasquelle **Trained** Barbury Castle, Wilts

FOCUS
Actual race distance 2m3f 185yds. The final hurdle in the back straight was omitted on the final circuit. This Grade 2 novices' hurdle has been won by some high-class jumpers over the years with Fingal Bay taking it four years ago, while further back it has been won by the likes of See More Business, Barton, Inglis Drever and Neptune Collonges. This year's race featured a bigger field than usual, but the pace looked modest and all eight runners were still in with something of a chance starting up the home straight. It's been rated around the third, fourth and fifth for the time being.

2887 COLDUNELL AMATEUR RIDERS' H'CAP CHASE (FOR THE JOHN DUNSDON MEMORIAL CUP) (22 fncs) 3m 37y
3:10 (3:11) (Class 3) (0-130,129) 4-Y-£9,029 (£2,844; £1,439; £737; £386)

Form RPR
1U11 **1** **Conas Taoi (IRE)**[26] 2366 6-10-3 106........................(p) MsKWalsh 121
(Paul Morgan) *hld up in tch: chsd ldrs 12th: chsd ldr 17th: rdn next: almost 2 l down whn lft wl clr flat: eased towards fin* **7/4**[1]
U-15 **2** *16* **Quinz (FR)**[189] 535 11-11-8 125........................ MissGAndrews 127
(Lawney Hill) *j. off handy but sn dropped to rr: struggling whn mstke 17th: styd on u.p to pass btn horses fr 3 out: wnt 3rd and hit last: lft modest 2nd flat: kpt on* **10/1**
P-P0 **3** *2 ¼* **Firm Order (IRE)**[21] 2473 10-10-9 119........................(tp) MrMJPKendrick(7) 118
(Paul Webber) *in tch: nt fluent 5th: chsd ldrs 13th: cl 3rd 3 out: sn u.p and btn: lft modest 3rd flat* **8/1**
PU-3 **4** *20* **Umberto D'Olivate (FR)**[31] 2261 7-11-5 127.....(p) MrJoshuaNewman(5) 107
(Robert Walford) *chsd ldrs lost pl 12th: bhd and struggling 16th: no ch whn hmpd and mstke 2 out: lft poor 4th flat: t.o* **7/2**[2]
/1-P **5** *38* **Lovcen (GER)**[10] 2700 10-11-7 129........................(t) MrRobertHawker(5) 74
(Sophie Leech) *chsd ldr tl 17th: wknd after 19th: t.o* **25/1**
03-0 **P** **No Duffer**[21] 2473 8-11-11 128........................ MrWBiddick
(Tom George) *in tch in midfield: outpcd 15th: rallied 17th: 5th and wkng whn p.u qckly 2 out* **8/1**
2P2- **U** **Silvergrove**[244] 5141 7-11-0 117........................(t) MrTomDavid 135+
(Ben Pauling) *j.w: led: tack problems and stirrups unstable fr 2 out: almost 2 l ahd whn wnt lft u.p sn after last: rdr lost iron and uns 150yds out* **9/2**[3]

6m 24.3s (-3.50) **Going Correction** +0.05s/f (Yiel) **7** Ran SP% **111.9**
Speed ratings (Par 107): **107,101,100,94,81 ,**
CSF £17.98 TOTE £2.30: £1.40, £3.50; EX 20.90 Trifecta £120.40.
Owner All Stars Sports Racing **Bred** Martin McCaughey **Trained** Ystrad, Rhondda C Taff

FOCUS
They jumped the Pond Fence this time. A decent amateur riders' chase and a dramatic conclusion. The unseater was heading for a small pb, whille the winner remains on the upgrade.

2888 JLT GROUP NOVICES' H'CAP HURDLE (8 hdls) 1m 7f 216y

3:40 (3:44) (Class 4) (0-120,120) 3-Y-0+ **£6,498** (£1,908; £954; £477)

Form RPR

3-12 **1** **Mr Fickle (IRE)**[24] 2418 6-11-7 **115**..............................(v) JoshuaMoore 122+
(Gary Moore) *hld up in tch: rdn and effrt bef 2 out: led between last 2: r.o wl and drew clr flat: rdn out* **6/1**[3]

52-3 **2** *2 1/4* **Spice Fair**[16] 2569 8-11-4 **112**.............................. WayneHutchinson 116
(Mark Usher) *hld up in tch: rdn and hdwy between last 2: chsd wnr flat: kpt on* **5/1**[2]

2431 **3** *3* **Proofreader**[8] 2734 6-11-9 **117** 7ex.............................. MarkQuinlan 120+
(Neil Mulholland) *t.k.h: hld up in rr: gng for run on inner and hmpd bnd bef 2 out: hdwy to chse ldrs 2 out: styd on same pce u.p flat* **7/4**[1]

3-40 **4** *1/2* **Eco Warrior**[21] 2472 5-10-13 **107**.............................. AidanColeman 111+
(Venetia Williams) *chsd ldrs: mstke 5th: sltly outpcd and mstke 2 out: rallied to dispute 2nd whn dived and on nose last: nt rcvr and kpt on same pce after* **7/1**

5 **5** *1 3/4* **Agha Des Mottes (FR)**[196] 433 5-10-4 **98**.............................. TomO'Brien 97
(Ian Williams) *hld up in tch in last pair: effrt between last 2: sn outpcd: wl hld and kpt on same pce flat* **8/1**

0160 **6** *3/4* **Miss Fortywinks**[30] 2271 6-10-11 **105**.............................. RyanMahon 103
(Seamus Mullins) *chsd ldr tl rdn to ld bef 2 out: hdd between last 2: no ex and lost 2nd flat: wknd fnl 100yds* **40/1**

522 **7** *1 3/4* **Linguine (FR)**[24] 2409 5-11-12 **120**..............................(p) ConorO'Farrell 116
(Seamus Durack) *led tl bef 2 out: rdn and no ex between last 2: wknd flat* **6/1**[3]

-120 **8** *7* **Argot**[21] 2472 4-11-8 **119**..............................(p) GrahamWatters(3) 108
(Charlie Longsdon) *chsd ldrs: rdn bef 2 out: lost pl between last 2: wknd last* **16/1**

4m 14.3s (7.10) **Going Correction** +0.275s/f (Yiel)
WFA 4 from 5yo+ 5lb **8 Ran SP% 113.5**
Speed ratings (Par 105): **93,91,90,90,89 88,88,84**
CSF £35.65 CT £73.43 TOTE £4.90: £1.80, £1.70, £1.50; EX 33.20 Trifecta £82.00.
Owner Gary Moore Racing **Bred** M Duffy **Trained** Lower Beeding, W Sussex

FOCUS
A fair novices' handicap hurdle, but they didn't go a great pace and it developed into something of a sprint for home. A step up from the winner, with the second rated to his mark.
T/Jkpt: Not won. £83.30 to a £1 stake. Pool: £3,226.00 - 28.25 winning tickets T/Plt: £77.80 to a £1 stake. Pool: £71,944.95 - 674.45 winning tickets T/Qpdt: £10.00 to a £1 stake. Pool: £7,834.57 - 576.88 winning tickets **Steve Payne**

2703 SEDGEFIELD (L-H)

Friday, December 4

OFFICIAL GOING: Heavy (4.9)
Wind: Fairly strong behind Weather: Cloudy

2889 SIS DYLAN MEALE MEMORIAL "HANDS AND HEELS" "NATIONAL HUNT" NOVICES' HURDLE (CONDITIONAL/AMATEURS) 2m 3f 188y

12:20 (12:20) (Class 4) 4-Y-0+ **£3,898** (£1,144; £572)

Form RPR

0622 **1** **Raise A Spark**[10] 2704 5-10-9 110.............................. RonanShort(3) 108+
(Donald McCain) *racd keenly: hld up: plld to way to front bef 3rd: mde rest: pushed clr fr appr 2 out* **1/4**[1]

-2PU **2** *23* **Be A Dreamer**[20] 2500 7-10-9 0.............................. MrRHogg(3) 88
(Sue Smith) *led: hdd bef 3rd: chsd ldr: rdn after 3 out: no imp and hld fr appr 2 out* **7/2**[2]

0-0 **3** *28* **Hattons Hill (IRE)**[35] 2169 6-10-12 0.............................. MrMartinMcIntyre 57
(Henry Hogarth) *trckd ldr: dropped to 3rd at 3rd: bhd fr 7th* **33/1**[3]

5m 21.6s (27.50) **3 Ran SP% 105.2**
CSF £1.47 TOTE £1.20; EX 1.30 Trifecta £1.60.
Owner R Pattison & R Kent **Bred** D Ellis & R Pattison **Trained** Cholmondeley, Cheshire

FOCUS
Hurdles sited on outer with divided bends. The meeting went ahead after a planned morning inspection was cancelled. An uncompetitive novices' hurdle run at an even gallop in the testing conditions. The second sets the level.

2890 SEYMOUR CIVIL ENGINEERING CONTRACTORS MAIDEN HURDLE (10 hdls) 2m 5f 34y

12:50 (12:50) (Class 5) 4-Y-0+ **£2,989** (£877; £438; £219)

Form RPR

6P-3 **1** **Whitsundays (IRE)**[11] 2690 6-11-0 0.............................. WillKennedy 98
(Donald McCain) *in tch: rdn appr 2 out: bit short of room and nt fluent 2 out: styd on run-in: led towards fin* **10/1**

01- **2** *1 1/4* **Huehuecoytle**[278] 4520 5-11-0 0.............................. BrianHarding 97+
(Keith Dalgleish) *pressed ldr: led narrowly 7th: rdn after 2 out: idled but stl 2 l up last: drvn and one pce run-in: hdd towards fin* **6/4**[1]

2-55 **3** *2* **Karisma King**[20] 2487 6-11-0 0.............................. SeanQuinlan 95
(Sue Smith) *trckd ldng pair: nt fluent 7th: rdn to chal after 3 out: one pce fr between last 2* **11/2**[3]

43 **4** *9* **Agentleman (IRE)**[20] 2498 5-11-0 0.............................. JamesReveley 88
(Tim Easterby) *hld up in tch: pushed along to chse ldng pair appr 2 out: wknd between last 2: wknd run-in* **9/1**

2 **5** *31* **Athou Du Nord (FR)**[20] 2487 5-11-0 114.............................. AlainCawley 68
(Richard Hobson) *hld up in tch: rdn appr 2 out: wknd and eased* **2/1**[2]

P **P** **Raknruin (IRE)**[190] 518 5-11-0 0.............................. HenryBrooke
(Joanne Foster) *led narrowly: hdd 7th: sn wknd: t.o whn p.u bef 2 out* **150/1**

5m 49.0s (34.40) **Going Correction** +1.325s/f (Heav) **6 Ran SP% 108.5**
Speed ratings (Par 103): **87,86,85,82,70**
CSF £24.64 TOTE £16.00: £4.40, £1.40; EX 32.50 Trifecta £110.10.
Owner Deva Racing Whitsundays Partnership **Bred** Clongiffin Stud **Trained** Cholmondeley, Cheshire

FOCUS
Not a strong contest run at a steady gallop. The third and fourth help set the level.

2891 STRAY AID COXHOE NOVICES' H'CAP HURDLE (8 hdls) 2m 178y

1:20 (1:20) (Class 5) (0-100,93) 3-Y-0+ **£2,989** (£877; £438)

Form RPR

3001 **1** **Caraline (FR)**[6] 2786 4-10-4 **74**.............................. JoeColliver(3) 88+
(Micky Hammond) *hld up in 3rd: trckd ldr 5th: led appr 2 out: nudged clr* **4/9**[1]

/222 **2** *14* **Gunner Lindley (IRE)**[28] 2322 8-11-5 **93**.............................. SamColtherd(7) 93
(Stuart Coltherd) *trckd ldr: led 5th: rdn whn hdd appr 2 out: sn no ch w wnr* **2/1**[2]

UP4P **3** *3 3/4* **Bertielicious**[9] 2716 7-9-8 **68**..............................(p[1]) ThomasDowson(7) 63
(Jonathan Haynes) *led: hdd 5th: sn dropped to 3rd: bdly outpcd after 3 out: plugged on after 2 out* **20/1**[3]

4m 28.7s (21.80) **Going Correction** +1.325s/f (Heav)
WFA 4 from 7yo+ 5lb **3 Ran SP% 107.3**
Speed ratings (Par 103): **101,94,92**
CSF £1.74 TOTE £1.50; EX 2.30 Trifecta £7.60.
Owner Give Every Man His Due **Bred** Mme Caroline Elizabeth Huni **Trained** Middleham, N Yorks

FOCUS
Another small field but the gallop was honest and the winner did it well. The second sets the level.

2892 HAPPY BIRTHDAY JOHN PAXTON NOVICES' H'CAP CHASE (18 fncs 3 omitted) 3m 2f 59y

1:55 (1:55) (Class 4) (0-105,103) 4-Y-0+ **£4,548** (£1,335; £667; £333)

Form RPR

-031 **1** **Not A Bother Boy (IRE)**[10] 2708 7-11-12 **103** 7ex.......... TrevorRyan(7) 112+
(Sue Smith) *w ldr: rdn to ld narrowly appr last (usual 2 out): styd on and sn in command extended run-in* **10/11**[1]

-3P1 **2** *3 1/2* **Thatildee (IRE)**[28] 2320 7-11-2 **91**..............................(p) DiarmuidO'Regan(5) 92
(Chris Grant) *led narrowly: rdn whn hdd appr last (usual 2 out): one pce extended run-in* **9/4**[2]

-45P **3** *nk* **Silver Dragon**[1] 2865 7-11-10 **94**..............................(v) BrianHughes 96
(Tony Coyle) *trckd ldng pair: nt fluent 12th and 13th: rdn and outpcd 3 out (usual 4 out): styd on extended run-in* **6/1**[3]

U2/4 **4** *46* **Heron's Mill (IRE)**[39] 2103 7-11-4 **93**.............................. DaleIrving(5) 48
(James Ewart) *trckd ldng pair: slow 10th: rdn 3 out (usual 4 out): sn wknd: mstkes fnl 2* **9/1**

7m 32.6s (21.60) **Going Correction** +0.925s/f (Soft) **4 Ran SP% 107.4**
Speed ratings (Par 105): **103,101,101,87**
CSF £3.40 TOTE £1.70; EX 3.70 Trifecta £7.60.
Owner Mrs S Smith **Bred** Kenneth William Quinn **Trained** High Eldwick, W Yorks

FOCUS
A modest handicap run at a fair gallop. The second has been rated to his mark.

2893 ROFLOW SUPPORTING GREAT NORTH AIR AMBULANCE H'CAP HURDLE (8 hdls) 2m 178y

2:30 (2:30) (Class 4) (0-120,116) 3-Y-0+ **£4,028** (£1,182; £591; £295)

Form RPR

024- **1** **Mixboy (FR)**[355] 3096 5-11-11 **115**.............................. BrianHarding 122+
(Keith Dalgleish) *trckd ldr: led gng wl appr 2 out: rdn out run-in* **9/2**[3]

466F **2** *4 1/2* **Sailors Warn (IRE)**[16] 2577 8-11-6 **115**..............................(t) NathanMoscrop(5) 116
(Ronald Thompson) *midfield: hdwy after 3 out: rdn to go 2nd 2 out: styd on but no threat wnr* **9/1**

20-0 **3** *12* **Blake Dean**[20] 2492 7-10-5 **95**.............................. DannyCook 85
(Sue Smith) *trckd ldr: rdn and bdly outpcd 3 out: styd on again after 2 out: wnt 3rd towards fin* **3/1**[1]

1233 **4** *3 1/2* **Baraboy (IRE)**[41] 2069 5-10-12 **109**.............................. LorcanMurtagh(7) 94
(Barry Murtagh) *hld up: wnt 4th after 3 out: rdn and in tch appr 2 out: wknd appr last* **15/2**

505- **5** *1* **Orchard Road (USA)**[296] 4166 8-10-12 **105**..........(t) JonathanEngland(3) 89
(Tristan Davidson) *trckd ldr: led bef 3 out: rdn whn hdd appr 2 out: wknd appr last* **7/1**

-124 **6** *24* **Mighty Whitey (IRE)**[41] 2069 9-11-8 **115**..............................(t) DerekFox(3) 75
(Noel C Kelly, Ire) *led: hdd bef 3 out: sn wknd* **8/1**

-636 **P** **Shrapnel (IRE)**[159] 848 9-11-12 **116**.............................. WillKennedy
(Brian Ellison) *hld up: slow 4th: sn rdn and lost tch: p.u after 3 out* **20/1**

43-1 **P** **Ardmay (IRE)**[31] 1684 6-11-9 **113**.............................. BrianHughes
(Kevin Ryan) *hld up: eased after 3 out and p.u* **4/1**[2]

4m 26.9s (20.00) **Going Correction** +1.325s/f (Heav) **8 Ran SP% 113.3**
Speed ratings (Par 105): **105,102,97,95,95 83, ,**
CSF £42.33 CT £138.71 TOTE £5.40: £1.90, £3.20, £1.50; EX 71.40 Trifecta £244.00.
Owner Paul & Clare Rooney **Bred** E A R L Jourdier **Trained** Carluke, S Lanarks

FOCUS
A fair handicap run at a sound pace in the conditions. A pb from the winner, and there's a case for rating the race 5lb+ higher, but not on time compared with the earlier handicap.

2894 KAREN STAPLETON MEMORIAL H'CAP CHASE (14 fncs 3 omitted) 2m 5f 28y

3:00 (3:00) (Class 4) (0-110,106) 4-Y-0+ **£4,028** (£1,182; £591; £295)

Form RPR

0351 **1** **Verko (FR)**[28] 2321 6-10-1 **84**.............................. CraigNichol(3) 107+
(Micky Hammond) *trckd ldng pair: bit slow 2 out (usual 3 out) and briefly outpcd in 3rd: led extended run-in: styd on wl* **5/2**[2]

-0U3 **2** *8* **Total Assets**[24] 2424 7-11-7 **106**.............................. CallumBewley(5) 117
(Simon Waugh) *pressed ldr: led 9th: rdn appr last (usual 2 out): hdd extended run-in: no ex* **3/1**[3]

5514 **3** *9* **Roxyfet (FR)**[2] 2844 5-10-0 **87** 7ex.............................. FinianO'Toole(7) 92
(Micky Hammond) *trckd ldng pair: chal after 3 out (usual 4 out): nt fluent last (usual 2 out): wknd extended run-in* **3/1**[3]

U13- **4** *34* **Whiskey Chaser (IRE)**[234] 5329 7-11-6 **100**.............................. WillKennedy 68
(Donald McCain) *led narrowly: nt fluent 9th and hdd: wknd qckly after 3 out (usual 4 out)* **9/4**[1]

5m 54.6s (21.60) **Going Correction** +0.925s/f (Soft) **4 Ran SP% 109.3**
Speed ratings (Par 105): **95,91,88,75**
CSF £9.90 TOTE £3.70; EX 9.00 Trifecta £26.70.
Owner David Green **Bred** E A R L Trinquet, M & O Trinquet **Trained** Middleham, N Yorks

FOCUS
An open contest despite the small field. The winner is on the upgrade for his in-form yard, and there's a case for rating him 4lb higher through the second's recent course run.

2895 TEES LED LIGHTING STANDARD OPEN NATIONAL HUNT FLAT RACE 2m 178y
3:30 (3:30) (Class 6) 4-6-Y-O **£1,819** (£534; £267; £133)

Form RPR
1 **Mcgregor's Cottage (IRE)** 4-10-9 0 .... BrianHughes 98+
(Malcolm Jefferson) *hld up: hdwy to trck ldng gng wl over 4f out: led over 1f out: pushed clr* **6/4**[1]
5-1 **2** *10* **Moonshine Ridge (IRE)**[28] 2330 4-11-2 0 .... JamesReveley 95
(Alan Swinbank) *led: rdn whn hdd over 1f out: one pce and no ch w wnr* **11/4**[2]
3 **3** *9* **Final Fling (IRE)**[50] 1926 4-10-13 0 .... CraigNichol(3) 86
(Rose Dobbin) *midfield: rdn into 3rd over 2f out: plugged on* **7/2**[3]
4 **4** *9* **Exactly What**[25] 2401 6-11-2 0 .... AdrianLane 77
(Donald McCain) *in tch: rdn and outpcd over 3f out: grad wknd fnl 2f* **16/1**
5 *5* **Cadellin** 4-11-2 0 .... HenryBrooke 72
(George Moore) *hld up: rdn over 7f out: nvr threatened* **12/1**
6 *½* **Oak Vintage (IRE)**[19] 5-10-11 0 .... JamieHamilton(5) 72
(Ann Hamilton) *hld up: nvr threatened* **17/2**
6- **7** *23* **Beyond The Glen**[290] 4289 5-10-4 0 .... DiarmuidO'Regan(5) 42
(Chris Grant) *trckd ldr: lost pl qckly 5f out: sn bhd* **100/1**
4m 26.0s (24.70) **Going Correction** +1.325s/f (Heav) **7 Ran SP% 114.0**
Speed ratings: **94,89,85,80,78 78,67**
CSF £5.77 TOTE £2.30: £1.80, £1.10; EX 7.40 Trifecta £17.90.
Owner Mrs D W Davenport **Bred** Miss Mary O'Sullivan **Trained** Norton, N Yorks
FOCUS
A fair bumper. The second and fourth set the level.
T/Plt: £115.30 to a £1 stake. Pool: £40,595.32 - 256.99 winning tickets T/Qpdt: £28.40 to a £1 stake. Pool: £3,255.94 - 84.81 winning tickets **Andrew Sheret**

2331 **AINTREE** (L-H)
Saturday, December 5

OFFICIAL GOING: Mildmay course - good to soft (soft in places); grand national & hurdles courses - soft (good to soft in places); all courses changing to soft after race 3 (1.05)
Wind: strong 1/2 against Weather: overcast, very breezy, light rain

2896 BETFRED REMEMBERS HOWARD KENDALL FILLIES' JUVENILE HURDLE (LISTED RACE) (9 hdls) 2m 209y
12:00 (12:02) (Class 1) 3-Y-O
£12,529 (£4,701; £2,354; £1,172; £589; £294)

Form RPR
1 **Jer's Girl (IRE)**[27] 2376 3-10-12 0 .... RichardJohnson 118+
(Gavin Cromwell, Ire) *led after 1st: mde rest: hit last: drvn clr: eased clsng stages* **2/1**[1]
2 **2** *10* **Forgiving Glance**[19] 2537 3-10-12 0 .... DenisO'Regan 107
(Alan King) *hld up in rr: t.k.h: hdwy to trck ldrs 5th: swtchd rt and 3rd whn mstke last: styd on to take modest 2nd post* **16/1**
1 **3** *shd* **Mystery Code**[38] 2137 3-10-12 0 .... WayneHutchinson 106
(Alan King) *t.k.h in mid-div: hdwy to chse ldrs 4th: 2nd after 2 out: kpt on same pce run-in* **5/2**[2]
421 **4** *8* **Culture De Sivola (FR)**[19] 2537 3-10-12 120 .... LizzieKelly 98
(Nick Williams) *mid-div: chsd ldrs 3rd: rdn and outpcd 6th: rallied to chse ldrs 2 out: wknd last 150yds* **8/1**
5 *shd* **Kamaloka (IRE)**[28] 2359 3-10-12 0 ....(t) MathieuDelage 98
(Patrice Quinton, France) *chsd ldrs: 2nd 3 out: wknd last* **3/1**[3]
5 **6** *7* **New Vennture (FR)**[19] 2537 3-10-12 115 .... NickScholfield 93
(Harry Fry) *hld up in rr: hdwy 3 out: chsng ldrs next: wknd and hit last* **16/1**
3 **7** *dist* **Bracken Brae**[19] 2537 3-10-12 0 .... RobertDunne
(Mark H Tompkins) *chsd ldrs: mstke 3rd: drvn 6th: lost pl 3 out: t.o next: sn eased: virtually p.u: eventually fin* **33/1**
234 **P** **Our Kylie (IRE)**[65] 1712 3-10-12 98 .... BrianHarding
(Tony Coyle) *led tl after 1st: chsd ldrs: lost pl 5th: sn bhd: t.o bef 2 out: sn p.u* **100/1**
4m 31.4s (17.70) **Going Correction** +1.45s/f (Heav) **8 Ran SP% 113.7**
Speed ratings (Par 107): **116,111,111,107,107 104, ,**
CSF £33.45 TOTE £2.40: £1.20, £2.30, £1.20; EX 25.20 Trifecta £97.00.
Owner Eugene A Bourke **Bred** E A Bourke M R C V S **Trained** Navan, Co. Meath
FOCUS
Mildmay and Hurdle bends on outer line with hurdles on outside. Inside rail on National course moved out at 2m5f start. Race distance was 109yds further than advertised. A day of high winds and the going was officially upgraded to good to soft, soft in places on the Mildmay course; soft, good to soft in places elsewhere. However, after the first the riders generally reported it was soft. This was a modest juvenile mares' event by Listed standards, but it threw up an impressive winner. The fourth and sixth help set the level.

2897 BETFRED GOALS GALORE H'CAP CHASE (QUALIFIER FOR CHALLENGER MIDDLE DISTANCE CHASE SERIES) (16 fncs) 2m 3f 200y
12:30 (12:34) (Class 3) (0-135,135) 4-Y-O+ **£9,418** (£2,806; £1,420; £727; £381)

Form RPR
1P-1 **1** **Bally Beaufort (IRE)**[28] 2332 7-11-9 135 .... RyanHatch(3) 146+
(Nigel Twiston-Davies) *led tl after 1st: chsd ldrs: reminders 11th: lost pl briefly: chsng ldrs next: upsides whn lft in ld 2 out: forged clr appr last: styd on wl* **3/1**[2]
U5-1 **2** *8* **Great Link**[183] 623 6-10-13 122 .... RobertDunne 126
(Dan Skelton) *trckd ldrs: hit 9th: drvn 3 out: lft cl 2nd last: fdd appr last* **11/2**
2-2U **3** *31* **Morning Reggie**[7] 2780 6-10-13 122 .... LeightonAspell 101
(Oliver Sherwood) *t.k.h: trckd ldrs: j.lft: lft 3rd and wknd 2 out: tired whn blnd last* **13/2**
106- **4** *½* **Aigle De La See (FR)**[254] 4993 5-11-3 126 .... DavidBass 105
(Nicky Henderson) *chsd ldrs: drvn and outpcd 12th: rallied next: j.lft and wknd 3 out* **11/4**[1]
6-20 **5** *30* **Le Fin Bois (FR)**[35] 2184 5-10-11 120 ....[1] AlainCawley 79
(Richard Hobson) *j. bdly rt in last: sme hdwy 8th: lost pl next: sn bhd: t.o 3 out* **13/2**
6U23 **F** **Benefit Cut (IRE)**[26] 2404 9-11-4 127 .... PaddyBrennan 130
(Stuart Edmunds) *led after 1st: hit 4 out: jnd whn fell 2 out: fatally injured* **9/2**[3]
5m 21.7s (17.70) **Going Correction** +1.125s/f (Heav) **6 Ran SP% 111.9**
Speed ratings (Par 107): **109,105,93,93,81**
CSF £19.04 TOTE £3.80: £2.20, £3.00; EX 18.80 Trifecta £64.00.
Owner R J Rexton **Bred** Isidore And Padraic Murtagh **Trained** Naunton, Gloucs
FOCUS
This was a fair little handicap, run at a decent gallop, and it rather fell apart in the home straight. Race distance was 90yds further than advertised. The second and faller have been rated close to their marks.

2898 BETFRED "SCOOP6SOCCER" NOVICES' HURDLE (9 hdls) 2m 209y
1:05 (1:12) (Class 3) 4-Y-O+ **£6,279** (£1,871; £947; £485; £254)

Form RPR
52 **1** **Agrapart (FR)**[27] 2363 4-10-7 0 .... LizzieKelly(5) 143+
(Nick Williams) *t.k.h: led: qcknd pce bef 4th: clr fr 3 out: heavily eased run-in: coasted home* **11/4**[2]
-513 **2** *20* **Braavos**[26] 2407 4-10-12 0 .... RichardJohnson 114
(Philip Hobbs) *nt fluent: chsd ldrs: drvn and outpcd bef 2 out: styd on to take remote 2nd last 200yds* **6/1**
12 **3** *5* **Flying Angel (IRE)**[28] 2331 4-11-1 0 .... RyanHatch(3) 114
(Nigel Twiston-Davies) *hld up in rr: t.k.h: hdwy to trck ldng pair 5th: 2nd 3 out: drvn bef next: wknd run-in* **1/1**[1]
56/0 **4** *9* **Beautiful Gem (FR)**[30] 2302 5-10-5 0 .... IanPopham 92
(Dan Skelton) *hld up in rr: hdwy 5th: modest 3rd 3 out: wknd last* **50/1**
0 **5** *78* **Hallingham**[45] 2011 5-10-12 0 .... MarcGoldstein 21
(Chris Gordon) *chsd ldrs: nt fluent 5th: drvn next: sn lost pl and bhd: t.o 2 out* **100/1**
1- **P** **Duke Arcadio (IRE)**[298] 4141 6-10-12 0 .... LeightonAspell
(Oliver Sherwood) *chsd wnr 2nd: pushed along 4th: wknd 3 out: sn bhd: eased and t.o whn p.u bef next* **9/2**[3]
4m 30.1s (16.40) **Going Correction** +1.45s/f (Heav) **6 Ran SP% 112.1**
Speed ratings (Par 107): **119,109,107,103,66**
CSF £18.81 TOTE £4.30: £1.90, £1.90; EX 21.40 Trifecta £33.10.
Owner The Gascoigne Brookes Partnership Iii **Bred** Jean-Marc Lucas **Trained** George Nympton, Devon
FOCUS
Most failed to handle the demanding conditions in this novice event and the form should be treated with some caution. Race distance was 109yds further than advertised. A big step up from the winner, with the second improving in line with his bumper form.

2899 BETFRED BECHER H'CAP CHASE (GRADE 3) (21 fncs) 3m 1f 188y
1:40 (1:43) (Class 1) 6-Y-O+
£78,597 (£29,569; £14,785; £7,393; £3,725; £1,863)

Form RPR
4-02 **1** **Highland Lodge (IRE)**[54] 1889 9-10-0 132 oh7 ....(p) HenryBrooke 140+
(James Moffatt) *w ldr: led narrowly bef 9th: rdn after 2 out: 2 l up last: styd on wl: wandered fnl 110yds* **20/1**
2P-6 **2** *2¼* **Dare To Endeavour**[55] 1879 8-10-2 134 .... LiamTreadwell 140
(E McNamara, Ire) *prom: lost pl 11th: midfield 13th (Becher's): rallied after 3 out: rdn 2 out: wnt 2nd appr elbow: styd on* **33/1**
000- **3** *¾* **Dolatulo (FR)**[238] 5275 8-11-0 146 ....(tp) GavinSheehan 150
(Warren Greatrex) *in tch on inner: rdn after 2 out: bit tight for room appr elbow: styd on: wnt 3rd post* **10/1**
10-0 **4** *nk* **Soll**[21] 2482 10-10-13 145 ....(bt) TomScudamore 151
(David Pipe) *hld up in midfield: mstke 7th (water): hdwy to go prom on outer next: mstke 13th (Becher's): rdn bef 2 out: one pce fr elbow: lost 3rd post* **9/1**[3]
F2-0 **5** *½* **Vics Canvas (IRE)**[14] 2641 12-11-2 148 ....(p) RobertDunne 151
(Dermot Anthony McLoughlin, Ire) *trckd ldrs: jnd ldr after 4 out: rdn after 2 out: outpcd and dropped to 5th appr elbow: plugged on fnl 110yds* **16/1**
36-0 **6** *1¼* **Financial Climate (IRE)**[15] 2616 8-9-11 132 oh8....(p) ThomasGarner(3) 137+
(Oliver Sherwood) *trckd ldrs: pressed ldr 14th (Foinavon): nt fluent 3 out: rdn and outpcd appr 2 out: plugging on whn hmpd and collided w rail elbow: no imp after* **33/1**
12-6 **7** *27* **Saint Are (FR)**[22] 2471 9-11-2 148 ....(tp) PaddyBrennan 128
(Tom George) *led narrowly: jst hdd whn nt fluent ninth: in tch whn blnd 4 out: wknd after 2 out* **8/1**[2]
3F0- **8** *11* **Unioniste (FR)**[224] 5538 7-11-12 158 ....(t) NickScholfield 122
(Paul Nicholls) *hld up: blnd 11th: a towards rr* **9/1**[3]
12-3 **9** *1½* **Goonyella (IRE)**[34] 2225 8-11-4 150 ....(t) JJBurke 113
(J T R Dreaper, Ire) *in tch on outer: lost pl after 8th: bhd after 16th (Valentine's)* **8/1**[2]
0-02 **F** **Pineau De Re (FR)**[27] 2374 12-10-9 141 .... WillKennedy
(Dr Richard Newland) *hld up: fell 2nd* **10/1**
F-0P **F** **Portrait King (IRE)**[24] 2436 10-9-11 132 ....(p) DerekFox(3) 117
(Patrick Griffin, Ire) *midfield: mstke 9th: styng on in dispute of 5th whn fell 2 out* **14/1**
U4-0 **P** **Ardkilly Witness (IRE)**[42] 2064 9-10-7 139 ....(tp) DenisO'Regan
(Jamie Snowden) *hld up: mstkes 8th and 10th: hit 13th (Becher's): wl bhd whn sltly impeded by loose horse 4 out: p.u bef 2 out* **25/1**
2125 **P** **Buachaill Alainn (IRE)**[14] 2638 8-10-3 135 ....(bt) MichaelByrne
(Peter Bowen) *hld up: sltly hmpd by faller 6th (Chair): reminders after 7th (water): sn bhd: p.u bef 2 out* **25/1**
-1P3 **U** **No Planning**[14] 2643 8-10-5 137 .... SeanQuinlan
(Sue Smith) *midfield: mstke 4th: blnd and uns rdr 6th (Chair)* **8/1**[2]
3U1- **P** **Thunder And Roses (IRE)**[23] 2463 7-11-1 147 ....(p) BJCooper
(Ms Sandra Hughes, Ire) *prom: blnd and nrly uns 9th: hit next: sn bhd: p.u bef 2 out* **10/1**
1-4P **P** **Cowards Close (IRE)**[41] 2089 8-10-0 132 oh3 ....(t) MarcGoldstein
(Chris Gordon) *hld up: mstke 6th (Chair): hit 13th (Becher's): a in rr: p.u bef 15th (Canal Turn)* **33/1**
30-2 **U** **Algernon Pazham (IRE)**[24] 2436 6-10-7 142 .... RyanHatch(3)
(Nigel Twiston-Davies) *mstkes in midfield: blnd and uns rdr 14th (Foinavon)* **7/1**[1]
7m 9.2s (22.20) **Going Correction** +0.975s/f (Soft) **17 Ran SP% 126.9**
Speed ratings: **104,103,103,102,102 102,94,90,90, , , , ,**
CSF £540.46 CT £6813.96 TOTE £27.30: £6.00, £8.40, £3.00, £2.40; EX 1046.30 Trifecta £22430.40.
Owner Bowes Lodge Stables **Bred** Ms Margaret Treacy **Trained** Cartmel, Cumbria

FOCUS
Race distance increased by 18yds. This was a strong Becher, featuring the 2014 Grand National winner and last season's runner-up, along with the latest Irish National winner. There was a solid gallop on and it threw up a cracking finish. It's been rated around the balance of the second to the fifth.

2900 BETFRED LOTTO "£100K CASH GIVEAWAY" CHASE (LISTED RACE) (19 fncs) 3m 210y
2:15 (2:19) (Class 1) 4-Y-O+ **£22,780** (£8,548; £4,280; £2,132)

Form RPR
115- **1** **Don Poli (IRE)**[221] 10 6-11-5 163 BJCooper 166+
(W P Mullins, Ire) *trckd ldng pair: sddle sn slipped fnl circ: pushed along to chse ldrs 15th: upsides 3 out: led last 200yds: forged clr* **6/5**[1]
61-6 **2** *4* **Many Clouds (IRE)**[35] 2200 8-11-10 167 LeightonAspell 168
(Oliver Sherwood) *w ldr: led 12th: pushed along and jnd 3 out: hdd and no ex last 200yds* **13/8**[2]
51-P **3** *13* **Menorah (IRE)**[35] 2200 10-11-10 167 RichardJohnson 162
(Philip Hobbs) *trckd ldrs: hit 15th: outpcd appr 3 out: edgd rt between last 2: sn fdd* **7/1**
12-3 **4** *39* **Southfield Theatre (IRE)**[27] 2372 7-11-5 154 (t) NickScholfield 115
(Paul Nicholls) *led: hdd and hit 12th: mstke next: drvn and lost pl whn hit 15th: sn bhd: t.o 3 out* **11/2**[3]

6m 51.2s (21.20) **Going Correction** +1.125s/f (Heav) **4** Ran SP% **111.4**
Speed ratings (Par 111): **111,109,105,93**
CSF £3.80 TOTE £1.80; EX 3.30 Trifecta £6.90.
Owner Gigginstown House Stud **Bred** Brian J Griffiths And John Nicholson **Trained** Muine Beag, Co Carlow

FOCUS
A fascinating affair and strong staying form. Race distance was 122yds further than advertised. The winner was favoured by the weights and has been rated back to the level of his RSA win. The second has been rated close to his best.

2901 BETFRED "BE PART OF THE ACTION" H'CAP HURDLE (11 hdls) 2m 4f
2:45 (2:50) (Class 2) 4-Y-O+
£13,763 (£4,065; £2,032; £1,016; £508; £255)

Form RPR
11 **1** **Virgilio (FR)**[204] 317 6-11-6 138 (t) IanPopham 148+
(Dan Skelton) *trckd ldrs: t.k.h: 2nd 4th: led appr last: rdn clr: v readily* **5/2**[1]
12-4 **2** *8* **Un Ace (FR)**[21] 2484 7-11-12 144 (t) DavidBass 142
(Kim Bailey) *chsd ldrs 5th: hit 7th: upsides 2 out: hung lft and kpt on same pce run-in* **5/1**[3]
50-3 **3** *3 ¼* **Fort Smith (IRE)**[107] 1302 6-10-0 125 (t) HarrisonBeswick(7) 120
(Sam Thomas) *mid-div: hdwy to chse ldrs 3 out: 4th whn hit last: kpt on same pce* **20/1**
1-U5 **4** *5* **Last Supper**[35] 2199 6-10-7 125 WayneHutchinson 115
(James Bethell) *led: jnd 2 out: hdd appr last: wknd last 150yds* **25/1**
F211 **5** *3 ½* **Bowdler's Magic**[21] 2498 8-10-2 127 MrZBaker(7) 112
(David Thompson) *w ldr: drvn appr 2 out: fdd appr last* **14/1**
4-03 **6** *12* **Handiwork**[16] 2594 5-11-10 142 (p) RichardJohnson 118
(Steve Gollings) *mid-div: hit 3rd: lost pl 6th: drvn 8th: brief effrt 2 out: sn wknd* **5/1**[3]
-4F2 **7** *3* **Fort Worth (IRE)**[21] 2485 6-10-12 130 PaddyBrennan 101
(Jonjo O'Neill) *hld up in rr: hdwy 7th: chsng ldrs next: drvn whn hit 3 out: sn lost pl* **9/2**[2]
1-06 **8** *29* **Qualando (FR)**[42] 2060 4-11-7 139 NickScholfield 80
(Paul Nicholls) *mid-div: chsd ldrs whn hit 5th: lost pl next: drvn 8th: bhd appr next* **8/1**
33P- **9** *½* **Karinga Dancer**[240] 5240 9-10-12 137 (t) LiamMcKenna(7) 78
(Harry Fry) *hld up in rr: j. slowly 7th: hdwy appr 3 out: lost pl bef 2 out* **8/1**

5m 24.1s (23.40) **Going Correction** +1.45s/f (Heav)
WFA 4 from 5yo+ 6lb **9** Ran SP% **117.6**
Speed ratings (Par 109): **111,107,106,104,103 98,97,85,85**
CSF £16.20 CT £205.26 TOTE £3.20: £1.40, £2.00, £5.00; EX 17.80 Trifecta £253.20.
Owner C J Edwards, D Futter, A H Rushworth **Bred** Francois-Marie Cottin **Trained** Alcester, Warwicks

FOCUS
Race distance increased by 139yds. This looked competitive and they went a sound gallop, but the progressive winner was in a different league. The second has been rated to his mark.

2902 BETFRED GRAND SEFTON H'CAP CHASE (18 fncs) 2m 5f 19y
3:20 (3:20) (Class 2) 6-Y-O+
£43,330 (£12,866; £6,433; £3,206; £1,610; £812)

Form RPR
U-PP **1** **Bennys Mist (IRE)**[21] 2483 9-10-4 138 LiamTreadwell 152+
(Venetia Williams) *pressed ldr: led bef 5th: hdd 12th (Canal Turn): remained cl up: hit 14th: rdn to ld again bef 2 out: styd on wl to draw clr fr appr last* **8/1**
-P24 **2** *9* **Seventh Sky (GER)**[14] 2633 8-10-12 146 (tp) GavinSheehan 148
(Charlie Mann) *in tch on inner: hit 8th: wnt 3rd bef 12th (Canal Turn) but 10 l bhd ldng pair: rdn after 2 out: wnt 2nd last: styd on but no ch w wnr* **14/1**
5-01 **3** *2 ¼* **Distime (IRE)**[25] 2425 9-9-11 134 oh5 JonathanEngland(3) 133
(Richard Drake) *hld up in midfield: rdn and styd on wl after 2 out: wnt 3rd run-in* **20/1**
P-25 **4** *25* **Fago (FR)**[14] 2635 7-10-13 147 PaddyBrennan 124
(Paul Nicholls) *hld up: hdwy whn mstke 11th (Foinavon): wnt 4th after 14th: blnd 4 out: slow 2 out: rdn and wknd* **9/1**
0-24 **5** *7* **Double Ross (IRE)**[21] 2483 9-11-2 153 RyanHatch(3) 120
(Nigel Twiston-Davies) *trckd ldr: dropped to midfield bef 5th: mstke 11th (Foinavon): rdn after 4 out: plugged on run-in: nvr threatened* **7/2**[1]
-123 **6** *3 ¼* **Top Cat Henry (IRE)**[43] 2057 7-10-0 134 oh9 (tp) WillKennedy 100
(Dr Richard Newland) *led narrowly: hdd bef 5th: remained prom: led narrowly again 12th (Canal Turn): hit 13th (Valentine's): rdn whn hdd bef 2 out: slow last and lost 2nd: wknd* **10/1**
0P-6 **7** *11* **Poole Master**[14] 2643 10-10-10 144 (bt) TomScudamore 97
(David Pipe) *midfield: trckd ldrs bef 5th: lost pl after 12th (Canal Turn): wknd after 3 out* **15/2**[3]
3-60 **8** *2 ¼* **Rathlin**[129] 1152 10-10-9 143 (t) WayneHutchinson 93
(Micky Hammond) *hld up: hdwy bef 10th (Becher's): disputing 4th 3 out: wknd appr 2 out* **12/1**
-055 **F** **Mwaleshi**[29] 2329 10-10-0 134 oh3 SeanQuinlan
(Sue Smith) *trckd ldrs: hit 3rd (Chair): fell 9th* **14/1**
2-00 **U** **Silver Roque (FR)**[22] 2468 9-10-6 140 (t) AlainCawley
(Fergal O'Brien) *hld up in rr: mstke and uns rdr 12th (Canal Turn)* **33/1**
0P-2 **P** **Rocky Creek (IRE)**[35] 2207 9-11-12 160 (p) NickScholfield
(Paul Nicholls) *prom: hmpd by faller 9th: sn lost pl: bhd fr 12th (Canal Turn): p.u bef 2 out* **11/2**[2]
5325 **U** **Witness In Court (IRE)**[65] 1715 8-10-3 137 BrianHarding
(Donald McCain) *hld up: blnd and uns rdr 6th* **16/1**
6-03 **U** **Art Of Logistics (IRE)**[55] 1879 7-10-6 140 (p) BJCooper
(Ms Sandra Hughes, Ire) *hld up in midfield: blnd 11th (Foinavon): mstke and uns rdr 12th (Canal Turn)* **9/1**

5m 49.8s (12.80) **Going Correction** +0.975s/f (Soft) **13** Ran SP% **124.2**
Speed ratings: **114,110,109,100,97 96,92,91, , , ,**
CSF £117.06 CT £2187.22 TOTE £11.00: £3.60, £5.20, £7.80; EX 179.40 Trifecta £2384.20.
Owner Mezzone Family **Bred** Flan O'Neill **Trained** Kings Caple, H'fords

FOCUS
Race distance increased by 9yds. There was no hiding place in this year's Grand Sefton and the gallop found most out a long way from home. A pb from the winner, with the third rated in line with his recent win.
T/Jkpt: Not won. JACKPOT PLACEPOT £1247.10. Pool: £2904.38 - 1.70 winning units. T/Plt: £333.00 to a £1 stake. Pool: £104,695.02 - 229.48 winning units. T/Qpdt: £92.30 to a £1 stake. Pool: £10,405.88 - 83.42 winning units. **Walter Glynn & Andrew Sheret**

2563 CHEPSTOW (L-H)
Saturday, December 5

OFFICIAL GOING: Heavy (chs 4.8; hdl 4.9)
Wind: strong half against Weather: overcast

2903 MARGARET FLETCHER 75TH BIRTHDAY CONDITIONAL JOCKEYS' NOVICES' HURDLE (10 hdls 2 omitted) 2m 7f 131y
12:20 (12:21) (Class 4) 4-Y-O+ **£3,249** (£954; £477; £238)

Form RPR
2 **1** **Battle Dust (IRE)**[18] 2558 6-10-12 0 ConorShoemark 122+
(Kim Bailey) *cl up: rdn along fr 4th: drvn fr 3 out: one pce whn hmpd and lft 5 l 2nd last: r.o u.p to ld post* **5/2**[2]
1-43 **2** *shd* **Ballywilliam (IRE)**[31] 2265 5-10-9 0 KieronEdgar(3) 122+
(David Pipe) *trckd ldrs: led appr 4th: jnd and rdn 2 out: lft 5 l clr last: idled flat: hdd post* **11/4**[3]
F6 **3** *11* **Doitforthevillage (IRE)**[20] 2519 6-10-12 0 MattGriffiths 110
(Paul Henderson) *hld up in last: hdwy 3 out: rdn next: kpt on same pce* **50/1**
1212 **4** *54* **Mont Choisy (FR)**[42] 2062 5-11-9 132 JamieBargary(3) 68
(Nigel Twiston-Davies) *led: hdd appr 4th where nt fluent: styd prom: rdn after 7th: wknd 2 out: t.o* **6/4**[1]
P **Just Bill (IRE)**[573] 7-10-9 0 ConorRing(3)
(Evan Williams) *hld up in 5th: cl enough whn rdn 3 out: sn wknd: p.u bef next* **14/1**
2 **F** **Wild West Wind (IRE)**[24] 2440 6-10-9 0 CiaranGethings(3) 122+
(Tom George) *trckd ldrs: wnt 2nd 3 out: chal and rdn next: upsides and ev ch whn dived at last and fell* **12/1**

6m 23.9s (21.70) **Going Correction** +0.55s/f (Soft) **6** Ran SP% **111.6**
Speed ratings (Par 105): **85,84,81,63,**
CSF £9.90 TOTE £3.40: £2.10, £1.60; EX 9.10 Trifecta £465.10.
Owner Mr & Mrs Mark Laws **Bred** William Larkin **Trained** Andoversford, Gloucs
■ Stewards' Enquiry : Kieron Edgar three-day ban; careless riding (20th-22nd Dec)

FOCUS
Both bends were railed out adding fresh ground. Those rail movements meant this race was run over approximately 96yds further than advertised. There were three hurdles in the home straight instead of the usual four. Plenty of drama occurred in the final stages of this novice event. The winner has been rated to his mark, with the second in line with his course bumper win.

2904 M S VENT LTD "NATIONAL HUNT" NOVICES' HURDLE (9 hdls 2 omitted) 2m 3f 100y
12:50 (12:54) (Class 4) 4-Y-O+ **£3,249** (£954; £477; £238)

Form RPR
31 **1** **Tapaculo**[31] 2265 4-11-5 0 JamesBest 130+
(Philip Hobbs) *t.k.h: prom: mainly trckd ldr fr 6th: drvn 2 out: keeping on and half a l down whn lft wl clr last* **6/4**[1]
2- **2** *23* **Deputy Commander (IRE)**[330] 3604 6-10-7 0 JamieBargary(5) 103
(Nigel Twiston-Davies) *a.p: mainly trckd ldr fr 3rd to 6th: outpcd by ldng pair fr 2 out: lft mod 2nd last* **6/1**
3 *13* **Jajamcool (IRE)**[552] 5-10-5 0 MrMLegg(7) 90
(Caroline Keevil) *hld up towards rr: stdy hdwy fr 5th: wknd appr 2 out: lft 3rd last* **40/1**
0P **4** *4* **Kelsey (IRE)**[25] 2417 5-10-12 0 AndrewThornton 84
(Tom Lacey) *prom: j. slowly 2nd: rdn fr 6th: wknd 3 out* **100/1**
2P-1 **5** *10* **Mountain Of Mourne (IRE)**[17] 2569 6-10-5 117 ConorSmith(7) 72
(Linda Blackford) *chsd ldrs tl lost pl 5th: drvn along and no ch fr next: plugged on past btn rivals fr 3 out* **11/4**[2]
50 **6** *24* **Court King (IRE)**[29] 2317 4-10-5 0 CiaranGethings(7) 48
(Peter Bowen) *hld up: hdwy 6th: wknd bef 3 out: t.o: fin lame* **50/1**
/62- **7** *2 ½* **Primo Blue**[373] 2766 5-10-9 0 JamesBanks(3) 46
(Noel Williams) *in rr whn stmbld 1st: detached tl hdwy into mid-div 4th: mstke 6th: wknd bef 3 out: t.o* **33/1**
4-0 **8** *4* **Guiting Power**[45] 2023 4-10-5 0 MrJJSlevin(7) 42
(Nigel Twiston-Davies) *mid-div: lost pl and struggling 5th: t.o* **66/1**
P0 **9** *2 ½* **Lough Derg Island (IRE)**[17] 2564 7-10-12 0 MarkQuinlan 39
(Alexandra Dunn) *mid-div: hdwy 4th: rdn and wknd bef 3 out: t.o* **100/1**
6-44 **10** *5* **Justatenner**[28] 2351 4-10-9 0 MauriceLinehan(3) 34
(Colin Tizzard) *mid-div: hdwy 5th: wknd appr 3 out: t.o* **50/1**
0 **P** **Honourable Exit (IRE)**[164] 832 8-10-12 0 RhysFlint
(Alexandra Dunn) *mid-div tl dropped to rr and drvn 4th: lost tch 3 out: t.o* **100/1**
P **Relkwood (IRE)**[56] 5-10-9 0 ConorShoemark(3)
(Paul Morgan) *prom to 3rd: struggling fr next: no ch fr 6th: t.o whn p.u bef 3 out* **66/1**
2-41 **F** **The Gipper (IRE)**[31] 2267 5-11-5 0 AdamWedge 130+
(Evan Williams) *led: rdn after 2 out: half a l up whn fell last* **7/2**[3]
565 **P** **Trans Express (IRE)**[11] 2702 5-10-9 0 LucyGardner(3)
(Sue Gardner) *a in rr: struggling 5th: t.o whn p.u bef 3 out* **100/1**

5m 6.3s (4.50) **Going Correction** +0.55s/f (Soft)
WFA 4 from 5yo+ 5lb **14** Ran SP% **119.4**
Speed ratings (Par 105): **112,102,96,95,90 80,79,78,77,74 , , ,**
CSF £11.25 TOTE £2.30: £1.20, £2.40, £6.60; EX 12.80 Trifecta £243.20.
Owner Mrs R J Skan **Bred** Aiden Murphy **Trained** Withycombe, Somerset

FOCUS
Both bends were railed out adding fresh ground. Those rail movements meant this race was run over approximately 60yds further than advertised. There were three hurdles in the home straight instead of the usual four. Plenty lined up for this novice contest, but not many made strong appeal. Again, there was drama at the final hurdle. The winner may have been lucky but is still on the upgrade, along with the faller.

2905 ANGELA NETTLEFOLD MEMORIAL IN AID OF SSAFA NOVICES' LIMITED H'CAP CHASE (18 fncs) 2m 7f 131y
1:25 (1:27) (Class 3) (0-135,132) 4-Y-0+ **£6,498** (£1,908; £954; £477)

Form RPR
42-1 **1** **Kingswell Theatre**[30] 2289 6-11-8 **132**............................. AdamWedge 137+
(Michael Scudamore) *in tch bhd ldrs: nt fluent 9th: hdwy 5 out: cl 4th whn bmpd in chain reaction 3 out: sn led: drew clr appr last: pushed out* **7/2**[1]
1-31 **2** *9* **Buckhorn Timothy**[20] 2518 6-11-8 **132**............................. BrendanPowell 129
(Colin Tizzard) *hld up in tch: hdwy 11th: chal 5 out: bmpd 3 out: stl ev ch 2 out: no ex appr last* **9/2**[3]
F4-3 **3** *23* **Vice Et Vertu (FR)**[21] 2489 6-10-11 **121**............................. JamesBest 101
(Henry Daly) *t.k.h: trckd ldrs: chal 11th: led appr 5 out to 4 out: drvn whn hmpd next: 3 l 3rd whn blnd bdly 2 out: wknd* **4/1**[2]
6/36 **4** *5* **Berea Boru (IRE)**[27] 2367 7-10-8 **125**.......................(t) CiaranGethings(7) 92
(Peter Bowen) *prom tl rdn and wknd appr 5 out* **25/1**
112P **5** *27* **Dreamsoftheatre (IRE)**[33] 2240 7-11-8 **132**...............(t) RichieMcLernon 72
(Jonjo O'Neill) *hld up in rr: clsng whn mstke 8th: wknd appr 5 out: t.o* **20/1**
353/ **U** **Tidal Dance (IRE)**[629] 4839 8-10-11 **124**............................. CallumWhillans(3)
(Venetia Williams) *hld up: last whn j.big 5th: mstke 12th: wknd appr 5 out: wl bhd whn hmpd and uns rdr 3 out* **11/2**
4P6- **U** **Imperial Leader (IRE)**[272] 4648 7-10-5 **120**...............(t) JamieBargary(5)
(Nigel Twiston-Davies) *blnd and uns rdr 1st* **5/1**
22-3 **U** **Dawson City**[13] 2660 6-11-1 **125**............................. AndrewThornton 130+
(Polly Gundry) *led: jnd 11th: hdd appr 5 out: led again 4 out tl hmpd by loose horse and uns rdr next* **13/2**

6m 31.2s (9.20) **Going Correction** +0.55s/f (Soft) **8** Ran SP% **114.4**
Speed ratings (Par 107): **106,103,95,93,84** , ,
CSF £20.10 CT £64.48 TOTE £3.30: £1.50, £1.90, £1.70; EX 11.20 Trifecta £80.20.
Owner John J Murray **Bred** W C Tincknell **Trained** Bromsash, H'fords

FOCUS
Both bends were railed out adding fresh ground. Those rail movements meant this race was run over approximately 96yds further than advertised. A solid race for the level, in which two came nicely away in the final stages. It's been rated around the first two.

2906 GLAMORGAN LAW H'CAP HURDLE (10 hdls 2 omitted) 2m 7f 131y
2:00 (2:03) (Class 3) (0-130,130) 4-Y-0+ **£5,393** (£1,583; £791; £395)

Form RPR
25-2 **1** **Dan Emmett (USA)**[31] 2275 5-11-0 **118**............................. BrendanPowell 127+
(Michael Scudamore) *mid-div: hdwy and j.rt 5th: led 2 out: drvn out to hold on flat* **9/2**[2]
4P-5 **2** *¾* **Moorlands Mist**[31] 2268 8-10-13 **122**............................. ConorRing(5) 129
(Evan Williams) *hld up: clsd after 7th: rdn 3 out: chsd wnr appr last: styd on u.p flat* **9/4**[1]
2154 **3** *6* **Epic Warrior (IRE)**[49] 1963 6-11-1 **122**.......................(p) KieronEdgar(3) 123
(David Pipe) *trckd ldr to 2nd: styd prom: wnt 2nd again after 7th: led 3 out to 2 out: no ex appr last* **6/1**[3]
600- **4** *6* **Sebastian Beach (IRE)**[175] 5535 4-11-2 **120**...............(t) RichieMcLernon 116
(Jonjo O'Neill) *mid-div: clsd after 7th: rdn appr 2 out: one pce* **14/1**
00-0 **5** *7* **Garde Fou (FR)**[31] 2268 9-10-6 **110**...............(t) JamesBest 102
(Paul Henderson) *hld up: hdwy 7th: ev ch whn mstke 3 out: wknd 2 out* **8/1**
1- **6** *45* **Ocean Venture (IRE)**[235] 5332 7-11-9 **127**............................. KielanWoods 70
(Graeme McPherson) *hld up in rr: struggling 6th: lost tch bef 3 out: t.o* **7/1**
P66- **7** *18* **Awaywiththegreys (IRE)**[91] 4354 8-11-5 **130**...............(b) CiaranGethings(7) 55
(Peter Bowen) *led to 3rd: led 5th to 3 out: sn wknd: t.o* **7/1**
F4P- **8** *4½* **Agreement (IRE)**[107] 3119 5-10-5 **114**...............(p) ChrisWard(5) 35
(Nikki Evans) *chsd ldrs tl wknd after 7th: t.o* **25/1**
P **Lord Adare (IRE)**[165] 653 7-10-13 **120**............................. ConorShoemark(3)
(Nikki Evans) *t.k.h: hld up: hdwy after 1st: led 3rd to 5th: wknd qckly after 7th: t.o whn p.u bef 3 out* **66/1**

6m 34.3s (32.10) **Going Correction** +0.55s/f (Soft)
WFA 4 from 5yo+ 7lb **9** Ran SP% **111.4**
Speed ratings (Par 107): **68,67,65,63,61 46,40,38,**
CSF £14.64 CT £57.65 TOTE £5.30: £1.80, £1.30, £2.10; EX 17.40 Trifecta £61.90.
Owner Mrs Lynne Maclennan **Bred** Swifty Farms Inc Et Al **Trained** Bromsash, H'fords

FOCUS
Both bends were railed out adding fresh ground. Those rail movements meant this race was run over approximately 96yds further than advertised. There were three hurdles in the home straight instead of the usual four. This seemed a competitive race for the level. A small step up from the winner, with the second close to his best.

2907 CORAL WELSH GRAND NATIONAL TRIAL (A H'CAP CHASE) (18 fncs) 2m 7f 131y
2:30 (2:34) (Class 2) (0-145,142) 4-Y£12,660 (£3,740; £1,870; £936; £468)

Form RPR
P35/ **1** **Tour Des Champs (FR)**[634] 4738 8-10-5 **126**............................. JamieBargary(5) 138
(Nigel Twiston-Davies) *chsd ldr to 7th: in 3rd after: 10 l off ldng pair after 13th: clsd 4 out: chsd wnr next: styd on u.p to ld fnl 50yds* **7/2**[1]
324- **2** *1½* **Top Wood (FR)**[237] 5289 8-10-13 **132**...............(bt) KieronEdgar(3) 143
(David Pipe) *j.rt at times: chsd ldrs: wnt 2nd at 7th: led 4 out: 4 l up whn mstke last: sn drvn: hdd and one pce fnl 50yds* **7/2**[1]
40-P **3** *2¼* **Firebird Flyer (IRE)**[14] 2643 8-11-3 **133**............................. AdamWedge 140
(Evan Williams) *hld up towards rr: stdy hdwy after 11th: drvn and wnt 3rd 2 out: styd on flat* **9/1**
P0-0 **4** *4½* **Rigadin De Beauchene (FR)**[21] 2482 10-10-8 **127**(b) CallumWhillans(3) 131
(Venetia Williams) *led: clr to 5th: nodded 5 out: hdd next: lost 2nd 3 out: one pce and no ex* **6/1**[3]
2P-P **5** *26* **Benvolio (IRE)**[28] 2348 8-11-5 **142**...............(b) MrStanSheppard(7) 119
(Paul Nicholls) *chsd ldrs: rdn bef 8th: modest 5th and rdn 10th: no ch fr 13th* **11/2**[2]
60-6 **6** *nse* **Rebeccas Choice (IRE)**[16] 2600 12-10-12 **128**........(p) AndrewThornton 104
(Dai Burchell) *a towards rr: niggled along after 7th: lost tch 13th* **14/1**
PP0- **7** *30* **Victors Serenade (IRE)**[243] 5184 10-11-4 **134**............................. RyanMahon 80
(Anthony Honeyball) *towards rr: hdwy 6th: wknd and lost modest 4th appr 5 out: t.o* **9/1**
3116 **P** **Danimix (IRE)**[41] 2082 10-11-0 **137**...............(t) CiaranGethings(7)
(Peter Bowen) *a in rr: lost tch after 13th: t.o whn p.u bef 2 out* **28/1**

-500 **P** **Theatrical Star**[14] 2643 9-11-5 **135**............................. [1] BrendanPowell
(Colin Tizzard) *chsd ldrs: grad lost pl fr 4th: in rr by 8th: lost tch 13th: t.o whn p.u bef 5 out* **8/1**

6m 31.5s (9.50) **Going Correction** +0.55s/f (Soft) **9** Ran SP% **115.3**
Speed ratings (Par 109): **106,105,104,103,94 94,84,** ,
CSF £16.78 CT £100.46 TOTE £5.20: £1.90, £1.60, £3.30; EX 20.70 Trifecta £156.80.
Owner Mrs Caroline Mould **Bred** Bruno Vagne **Trained** Naunton, Gloucs

FOCUS
Both bends were railed out adding fresh ground. Those rail movements meant this race was run over approximately 96yds further than advertised. This had all the hallmarks of a slog prior to the start, and so it proved after the leader went off at a good gallop. The second and third are the best guides to the form.

2908 RHYS HOWELLS MEMORIAL H'CAP CHASE (16 fncs) 2m 3f 98y
3:05 (3:07) (Class 3) (0-130,128) 4-Y-0+ **£6,657** (£2,067; £1,113)

Form RPR
00/F **1** **Elenika (FR)**[21] 2497 7-10-12 **117**............................. CallumWhillans(3) 127+
(Venetia Williams) *trckd ldrs tl relegated to cl last after 5th: clsd 11th: sn trcking ldng pair: wnt 2nd 3 out: rdn and upsides whn lft wl clr next* **5/1**
2 **2** *34* **Walk In The Mill (FR)**[25] 2419 5-11-5 **121**............................. AndrewThornton 116
(Robert Walford) *hld up in tch: clsd 6th: jnd ldrs 9th: rdn 5 out: chal next tl wknd after 3 out: lft 2nd 2 out: no ch whn blnd last* **3/1**[3]
0-P4 **3** *10* **Allez Vic (IRE)**[27] 2367 9-11-12 **128**............................. AdamWedge 94
(Evan Williams) *cl up tl led 5th: mstke and hdd 11th: sn wknd: t.o* **5/2**[2]
P3-3 **P** **The Sneezer (IRE)**[16] 2601 12-9-11 **102** oh2............................. ConorShoemark(3)
(Nikki Evans) *led narrowly tl hdd 5th: styd cl up to 10th: in last by next: sn lost tch: t.o whn p.u bef 5 out* **33/1**
1-23 **F** **Murrayana (IRE)**[17] 2580 5-11-5 **121**.......................(t) BrendanPowell 128
(Colin Tizzard) *trckd ldrs: j.lft 7th: led 11th: jnd 3 out: rdn whn fell heavily 2 out* **13/8**[1]

5m 17.9s (6.60) **Going Correction** +0.55s/f (Soft) **5** Ran SP% **111.3**
Speed ratings (Par 107): **108,93,89,** ,
CSF £20.21 TOTE £5.20: £2.10, £2.40; EX 18.20 Trifecta £60.60.
Owner Janet Bromet & Andrew Brooks **Bred** Mme G Forien & G Forien **Trained** Kings Caple, H'fords

FOCUS
Both bends were railed out adding fresh ground. Those rail movements meant this race was run over approximately 60yds further than advertised. The small field for this handicap raced in a pack for the majority of the contest. The winner has been rated in line with his old form, with the second close to his mark.

2909 TRUVAPE STANDARD OPEN NATIONAL HUNT FLAT RACE 2m 11y
3:40 (3:41) (Class 6) 4-6-Y-0 **£1,559** (£457; £228; £114)

Form RPR
1 **Positively Dylan**[244] 4-10-7 0............................. LewisGordon(7) 110+
(Evan Williams) *t.k.h in rr: stdy hdwy 5f out: shkn up to ld appr fnl f: hung lft: r.o wl* **10/3**[2]
2 *2½* **Pride Of Lecale**[272] 4-10-11 0.......................(t) ConorShoemark(3) 106
(Fergal O'Brien) *mid-div: gd hdwy 3f out: led gng wl 2f out: rdn and hdd appr fnl f: styd on same pce* **3/1**[1]
0 **3** *4* **The Model County (IRE)**[21] 2486 5-10-0 0............................. MrAlexEdwards(7) 95
(Alan Phillips) *led: jnd 6f out: rdn 3f out: hdd 2f out: hung lft and one pce fnl f* **25/1**
4 *1¾* **Mr Fenton (IRE)** 4-11-0 0............................. RichieMcLernon 100
(Emma Lavelle) *t.k.h in rr: rdn and hdwy over 3f out: styd on steadily fnl 2f* **7/1**
5 *17* **Good Man Hughie (IRE)**[48] 6-10-7 0.......................(p) MissBHampson(7) 83
(Sally Randell) *t.k.h towards rr: rdn over 3f out: grad wknd* **7/1**
6 *nk* **Head To The Stars** 4-11-0 0............................. AndrewTinkler 82
(Henry Daly) *prom: wnt 2nd after 5f: w ldr 6f out tl hung lft 3f out: sn wknd* **9/2**[3]
7 *1½* **Jack Henri (FR)** 4-11-0 0............................. LeeEdwards 81
(Ian Williams) *chsd ldrs: rdn along fr 1/2-way: grad wknd fnl 2f* **12/1**
6- **8** *2¾* **Teachmetobouggie**[237] 5292 5-11-0 0............................. AdamWedge 78
(Alexandra Dunn) *chsd ldr 5f: styd prom: rdn over 3f out: wknd over 2f out* **8/1**
/6- **9** *47* **Stafford Jo**[555] 517 6-11-0 0............................. DaveCrosse 31
(John O'Shea) *chsd ldrs: rdn 5f out: sn wknd: t.o* **50/1**
00/ **10** *76* **Over The Bridge**[592] 5492 5-10-7 0............................. CiaranGethings(7)
(Steve Flook) *t.k.h in rr: wknd over 5f out: t.o* **100/1**

4m 14.3s (9.30) **Going Correction** +0.55s/f (Soft) **10** Ran SP% **116.9**
Speed ratings: **98,96,94,93,85 85,84,83,59,21**
CSF £13.68 TOTE £4.60: £1.70, £1.20, £7.20; EX 10.40 Trifecta £476.00.
Owner Mrs Janet Davies **Bred** P Hughes & A Stennett **Trained** Llancarfan, Vale Of Glamorgan

FOCUS
Both bends were railed out adding fresh ground. Those rail movements meant this race was run over approximately 60yds further than advertised. This race was won by O'Faolains Boy in 2012.
T/Plt: £30.10 to a £1 stake. Pool: £58,389.30 - 1415.93 winning units. T/Qpdt: £6.70 to a £1 stake. Pool: £6,024.76 - 661.14 winning units. **Richard Lowther**

2883 SANDOWN (R-H)
Saturday, December 5

OFFICIAL GOING: Chase course - good to soft (5.7); hurdle course - soft (good to soft in places on back straight; 5.2)
Wind: Strong, against Weather: Overcast

2910 BECKY CUNNINGHAM "NATIONAL HUNT" NOVICES' HURDLE (8 hdls) 1m 7f 216y
12:15 (12:16) (Class 3) 4-Y-0+ **£6,498** (£1,908; £954; £477)

Form RPR
20-1 **1** **O O Seven (IRE)**[14] 2646 5-11-4 0............................. AndrewTinkler 137+
(Nicky Henderson) *trckd ldng pair: drvn to cl on long run after 3 out: led 2 out and sn 3 l clr: kpt on fr last* **11/8**[1]
331- **2** *1¼* **Premier Bond**[237] 5292 5-10-12 0............................. NicodeBoinville 128+
(Nicky Henderson) *inclined to wander into hurdles: chsd ldr: drvn to chal 2 out: chsd wnr after: 3 l down last: kpt on and tried to cl flat: a hld* **9/2**[3]
223- **3** *6* **Ballagh (IRE)**[294] 4226 6-10-5 135............................. MrMJPKendrick(7) 122
(Ben Case) *led: set modest pce to 3rd: drvn and hdd 2 out: sn dropped to 3rd and btn* **2/1**[2]
14- **4** *3¼* **What A Moment (IRE)**[266] 4770 5-10-12 0............................. ConorO'Farrell 118
(David Pipe) *hld up in last: lft bhd on long run after 3 out: shkn up to take modest 4th bef 2 out: kpt on steadily: shaped w promise* **12/1**

1253 **5** *15* **Brave Richard (IRE)**[15] 2614 4-10-12 0.................. SamTwiston-Davies 108
(J R Jenkins) *hld up disputing 4th: mstke 2nd: rdn and wknd bef 2 out where mstke* **16/1**

53-1 **6** *67* **Welluptoscratch (FR)**[209] 227 4-10-12 0.................. TomCannon 36
(David Arbuthnot) *hld up disputing 4th: wknd wl bef 2 out: v tired bef last: t.o* **33/1**

4m 4.7s (-2.50) **Going Correction** +0.175s/f (Yiel)
WFA 4 from 5yo+ 5lb **6** Ran SP% **110.1**
Speed ratings (Par 107): **113,112,109,107,100 66**
CSF £7.85 TOTE £2.20: £1.50, £2.10; EX 5.60 Trifecta £13.10.
Owner Triermore Stud **Bred** Robert McCarthy **Trained** Upper Lambourn, Berks

FOCUS
Chase distances as advertised and races 2 & 3 increased by 12yds. Andrew Tinkler reported the ground to be drying out but tacky. Quite a decent novice hurdle, with Nicky Henderson winning it for a seventh straight year, and training the second for good measure. The winner was building on his recent hurdling debut win, the third has been rated a stone plus off his best, while the fifth has been rated in line with his recent Ascot run.

2911 THEBOOKIESOFFERS.CO.UK MARES' H'CAP HURDLE (QUALIFIER FOR THE CHALLENGER MARES' HURDLE SERIES) (9 hdls) 2m 3f 173y

12:45 (12:47) (Class 3) (0-125,126) 3-Y-O+
£9,384 (£2,772; £1,386; £693; £346; £174)

5-14 **1** **Flute Bowl**[14] 2647 5-11-11 **124**..........................(p) JoshuaMoore 135+
(Gary Moore) *chsd ldr to 2nd: pushed along briefly after 3rd: gng bttr fr next: led bef 2 out and sn dashed clr: nrly 10 l ahd last: drvn out* **5/1**[2]

23-4 **2** *6* **Coco Des Champs (IRE)**[49] 1960 5-10-13 **112**.................... NoelFehily 116
(Oliver Sherwood) *hld up in midfield: rdn bef 2 out: prog to go 2nd bef last: kpt on but no ch w wnr* **11/1**

3-22 **3** *3 ½* **Brise Vendeenne (FR)**[29] 2325 4-11-2 **115**.................... TomO'Brien 115
(Philip Hobbs) *trckd ldrs: rdn and outpcd bef 2 out: kpt on one pce after* **9/2**[1]

4-42 **4** *8* **Barton Rose**[37] 2150 6-10-12 **118**...................... HarryCobden(7) 109
(Michael Blake) *hld up in last pair: drvn sn after 3 out and struggling: passed wkng rivals fr 2 out* **6/1**[3]

-052 **5** *1* **Woodland Walk**[23] 2455 7-10-11 **120**.................. RichieO'Dea(10) 112
(Emma Lavelle) *trckd ldr fr 2nd: led wl bef 2 out and looked to be gng wl: hdd bef 2 out where mstke: wknd and lost 2nd bef last: fin v tired* **9/2**[1]

1P21 **6** *10* **Lady Of Longstone (IRE)**[12] 2687 5-11-8 **126**............. DavidNoonan(5) 106
(David Pipe) *led at gd pce: clr fr 3rd: urged along at various times on fnl circ: hdd & wknd wl bef 2 out* **5/1**[2]

5-30 **7** *9* **Midnight Belle**[14] 2632 8-11-9 **122**...................... ConorO'Farrell 93
(Tom Symonds) *in tch: pushed along fr 4th: rdn and struggling bef 2 out: sn bhd* **20/1**

2121 **P** **At First Light**[108] 1290 6-10-13 **112**.............................. NicodeBoinville
(David Weston) *in tch: rdn bef 2 out where mstke in 4th pl: 5th and btn whn p.u sharply bef last* **8/1**

F-4P **P** **Glenariff**[167] 813 6-10-4 **108**.............................. KevinJones(5)
(Seamus Mullins) *hld up in last: rdn and lost tch 5th: mstke next: sn t.o: p.u bef 2 out* **14/1**

5m 3.6s (4.00) **Going Correction** +0.175s/f (Yiel)
WFA 4 from 5yo+ 6lb **9** Ran SP% **114.9**
Speed ratings (Par 107): **99,96,95,92,91 87,84, ,**
CSF £56.66 CT £264.60 TOTE £6.50: £2.10, £2.70, £2.00; EX 59.50 Trifecta £1231.90.
Owner C E Stedman **Bred** C E Stedman **Trained** Lower Beeding, W Sussex

FOCUS
Race distance increased by 12yds. No hanging around in what was a fair mares' handicap. A step up from the second, while the third helps set the level.

2912 PERTEMPS NETWORK H'CAP HURDLE (SERIES QUALIFIER) (11 hdls) 2m 5f 110y

1:20 (1:21) (Class 2) 4-Y-O+
£12,512 (£3,696; £1,848; £924; £462; £232)

Form RPR

10-3 **1** **Simply A Legend**[27] 2369 6-10-2 **123**.................... TomBellamy(3) 127
(Alan King) *hld up in last pair: prog bef 2 out: drvn to chal and upsides last: kpt on gamely u.p to ld nr fin* **6/1**[3]

0-01 **2** *nk* **Foxcub (IRE)**[24] 2438 7-11-9 **141**........................ JamesDavies 144
(Tom Symonds) *trckd ldng pair: lost pl briefly bef 2 out but sn on terms: drvn to ld narrowly last: kpt on wl but hdd nr fin* **12/1**

16-2 **3** *1 ¼* **Ruacana**[25] 2411 6-11-12 **144**............................ AidanColeman 147
(John Ferguson) *hld up in 6th: prog bef 2 out: led sn after 2 out: hdd last: nt qckn flat but kpt on* **9/1**

3-63 **4** *nse* **Box Office (FR)**[41] 2083 4-11-1 **133**...................(t) BarryGeraghty 137+
(Jonjo O'Neill) *hld up in last quartet: prog bef 2 out: drvn and clsng on ldrs but n.m.r bef last: renewed effrt flat: kpt on but nvr quite able to chal* **9/2**[2]

2-12 **5** *4 ½* **Sir Mangan (IRE)**[21] 2484 7-11-7 **139**.................... HarrySkelton 136
(Dan Skelton) *trckd ldr tl bef 2 out: styd cl up tl fdd jst bef last* **7/1**

2F5- **6** *1 ¾* **Keltus (FR)**[234] 5341 5-11-0 **132**..............(t) SamTwiston-Davies 127
(Paul Nicholls) *trckd ldng trio: effrt to go 2nd bef 2 out: nt qckn and lost pl after 2 out: fdd* **10/1**

144- **7** *7* **Taj Badalandabad (IRE)**[308] 3968 5-10-10 **128**..........(v[1]) ConorO'Farrell 118
(David Pipe) *mde most: poached useful ld after 3 out: hdd & wknd sn after 2 out* **10/1**

-036 **8** *8* **Phare Isle (IRE)**[153] 916 10-9-12 **123**..............(tp) MrMJPKendrick(7) 103
(Ben Case) *chsd ldrs in 5th: rdn sn after 3 out: sn btn: bhd bef 2 out* **66/1**

131/ **9** *¾* **Doctor Harper (IRE)**[611] 5138 7-11-2 **139**............... DavidNoonan(5) 120
(David Pipe) *nt fluent 1st: hld up in last pair: drvn after 3 out: no prog and bhd bef next* **3/1**[1]

20-2 **10** *10* **Lightentertainment (IRE)**[45] 2013 7-10-12 **130**............. TomCannon 103
(Chris Gordon) *hld up in last quartet: rdn and wknd sn after 3 out: bhd bef next* **12/1**

5m 35.4s (12.90)
WFA 4 from 5yo+ 6lb **10** Ran SP% **115.0**
CSF £72.91 CT £642.98 TOTE £6.50: £2.10, £2.90, £2.90; EX 81.40 Trifecta £471.00.
Owner Mrs Peter Prowting **Bred** G Staniek **Trained** Barbury Castle, Wilts

FOCUS
Race distance increased by 12yds. Useful handicap form and several held their chance over the last couple. The first three have been rated pretty much to their marks.

2913 RACING POST HENRY VIII NOVICES' CHASE (GRADE 1) (13 fncs) 1m 7f 119y

1:55 (1:55) (Class 1) 4-Y-O+ **£25,748** (£9,737; £4,935; £2,519; £1,326)

Form RPR

1-61 **1** **Ar Mad (FR)**[27] 2370 5-11-2 130.............................. JoshuaMoore 164+
(Gary Moore) *mde all and sn clr: abt 10 l ahd fr 4th tl breather bef 3 out and c bk to rivals: kicked on again bef 2 out: sn clr again: styd on wl* **14/1**

3-21 **2** *10* **Bristol De Mai (FR)**[17] 2580 4-10-10 146........................ DarylJacob 149
(Nigel Twiston-Davies) *chsd clr wnr: clsd and rt on terms 3 out: rdn and nt qckn next: sn one pce and no imp* **1/1**[1]

6-22 **3** *11* **As De Mee (FR)**[22] 2469 5-11-2 140.................. SamTwiston-Davies 146
(Paul Nicholls) *chsd ldng trio: impeded 3rd: rdn bef 3 out and struggling to get on terms: n.d after: tk modest 3rd last* **4/1**[2]

11/1 **4** *4* **Willow's Saviour**[31] 2274 8-11-2 140........................ HarrySkelton 144
(Dan Skelton) *tended to shift lft at fences: chsd ldng pair: awkward 3rd: clsd and on terms 3 out: rdn and outpcd whn mstke 2 out: lost 3rd pl last: wknd* **11/2**[3]

20-0 **5** *6* **Bouvreuil (FR)**[20] 2512 4-10-10 137...........................(t) NoelFehily 130
(Paul Nicholls) *a last: detached whn nt fluent 9th: no prog after next* **14/1**

335- **U** **Sizing Codelco (IRE)**[77] 1583 6-11-2 142........................ BarryGeraghty
(Henry De Bromhead, Ire) *stmbld and uns rdr 1st* **7/1**

3m 48.6s (-13.20) **Going Correction** -0.30s/f (Good)
WFA 4 from 5yo+ 5lb **6** Ran SP% **111.2**
Speed ratings (Par 117): **121,116,110,108,105**
CSF £29.84 TOTE £14.60: £3.70, £1.30; EX 26.20 Trifecta £111.90.
Owner Ashley Head **Bred** Michel Le Meur **Trained** Lower Beeding, W Sussex

FOCUS
Often a really informative novice chase that has gone to some top chasers over the years. A few of these liked to front-run, so a good pace was assured, and the surprise but emphatic winner made all. The winner rates a top-class novice, with the second, third and fourth rated pretty much to their pre-race marks.

2914 JUMEIRAH HOTELS AND RESORTS DECEMBER H'CAP HURDLE (LISTED RACE) (8 hdls) 1m 7f 216y

2:25 (2:28) (Class 1) 4-Y-O+
£34,170 (£12,822; £6,420; £3,198; £1,608; £804)

Form RPR

1-33 **1** **Lil Rockerfeller (USA)**[25] 2411 4-11-11 **146**..................(p) TrevorWhelan 149
(Neil King) *prom: urged along after 3 out: clsd to chal and edgd lft bef 2 out: led sn after 2 out: rdn and kpt on strly flat* **8/1**

2-16 **2** *2* **Devilment**[20] 2512 4-11-12 **147**............................ AidanColeman 148
(John Ferguson) *hld up in tch: prog to chal 2 out: drvn and nrly upsides wnr last: styd on same pce flat* **13/2**

13/5 **3** *1* **Vicenzo Mio (FR)**[27] 2369 5-10-1 **129**................(t) HarryCobden(7) 130
(Paul Nicholls) *hld up in tch: prog to press ldrs whn carried lft bef 2 out: swtchd lft after 2 out: drvn and kpt on: nt quite able to chal* **5/1**[3]

1043 **4** *4 ½* **Savello (IRE)**[20] 2511 9-11-4 **139**......................... HarrySkelton 135
(Dan Skelton) *quick move to ld bef 1st but maintained ordinary pce: hdd bef 3rd: led again 3 out: drvn for home bef 2 out: hdd after 2 out: fdd flat* **7/1**

210- **5** *1 ¾* **Some Plan (IRE)**[270] 4688 7-11-7 **142**..............(t[1]) SamTwiston-Davies 138+
(Paul Nicholls) *hld up in last trio: smooth prog on long run bef 2 out: cl up whn hit 2 out: sn rdn and fnd nil* **10/3**[1]

/22U **6** *13* **Nesterenko (GER)**[15] 2617 6-10-11 **132**.................. NicodeBoinville 113
(Nicky Henderson) *prom: rdn after 3 out: lost pl and btn bef 2 out: wknd* **8/1**

10-0 **7** *1 ½* **Ebony Express**[20] 2512 6-10-5 **136**................... CharlieHammond(10) 115
(Dr Richard Newland) *led but set modest pce and hdd bef 1st: prom tl drvn and wknd bef 2 out* **9/2**[2]

-010 **8** *6* **Satanic Beat (IRE)**[35] 2186 6-10-4 **130**................ FreddieMitchell(5) 103
(Phil Middleton) *a in last pair: struggling sn after 3 out: sn bhd* **25/1**

9 *12* **Wells De Lune (FR)**[545] 4-10-4 **125**...................... TomO'Brien 86
(Charlie Longsdon) *t.k.h: hld up tl plld way through to ld bef 3 out: j.lft 5th: j.lft 3 out and hdd: wknd qckly bef 2 out* **25/1**

3PF- **P** **Deep Trouble (IRE)**[343] 3312 8-11-9 **144**.......................... DarylJacob
(Ben Case) *a in last pair: wknd sn after 3 out: t.o whn p.u bef 2 out* **25/1**

4m 7.5s (0.30) **Going Correction** +0.175s/f (Yiel) **10** Ran SP% **117.5**
Speed ratings (Par 111): **106,105,104,102,101 94,94,91,85,**
CSF £58.22 CT £284.91 TOTE £6.70: £2.40, £2.40, £2.00; EX 29.10 Trifecta £205.50.
Owner Davies Smith Govier & Brown **Bred** Brushwood Stable **Trained** Barbury Castle, Wiltshire

FOCUS
They dawdled early, with nothing wanting to go on, and then even once the pace increased it was still just an ordinary gallop set. A small pb from the winner, with the second to his mark.

2915 BETFAIR TINGLE CREEK CHASE (GRADE 1) (13 fncs) 1m 7f 119y

3:00 (3:02) (Class 1) 4-Y-O+
£85,425 (£32,055; £16,050; £7,995; £4,020; £2,010)

Form RPR

4F-5 **1** **Sire De Grugy (FR)**[32] 2259 9-11-7 166........................ JamieMoore 171+
(Gary Moore) *chsd ldr: chal fr 6th: led 9th: at least 2 l up whn j.lft 2 out: 1 l up whn j.lft last: bmpd rival and also lost momentum: drvn and hld on gamely flat* **10/3**[3]

31-4 **2** *¾* **Special Tiara**[27] 2388 8-11-7 168............................ NoelFehily 170+
(Henry De Bromhead, Ire) *led at gd pce: pressed fr 6th: hdd 9th: rallied and 1 l down whn hmpd last: kpt on wl but a hld last 75yds* **3/1**[2]

24-1 **3** *7* **Vibrato Valtat (FR)**[32] 2259 6-11-7 162............(t) SamTwiston-Davies 162
(Paul Nicholls) *trckd ldng pair fr 4th: rdn 3 out and sn disp 2nd: no ex and wl hld after 2 out* **11/4**[1]

25-2 **4** *6* **Somersby (IRE)**[20] 2511 11-11-7 164........................(p) MsNCarberry 159
(Mick Channon) *hit 1st and pckd: chsd ldng trio fr 4th: in tch 4 out: drvn and no imp 3 out: fdd* **9/1**

03-5 **5** *7* **Mr Mole (IRE)**[20] 2511 7-11-7 161..............................(t) BarryGeraghty 153
(Paul Nicholls) *hld up in 5th: hmpd 4th and lost tch: t.o 4 out: produced flourish fr last whn r was all over* **8/1**

-223 **6** *shd* **Third Intention (IRE)**[14] 2633 8-11-7 160.....................(t) DarylJacob 150
(Colin Tizzard) *a in last pair: sltly impeded 4th: lost tch 6th: t.o 4 out: plugged on fr 2 out as ldrs tired but nvr a factor and lost poor 5th nr fin* **16/1**

234- **F** **Josses Hill (IRE)**[240] 5235 7-11-7 158........................ NicodeBoinville
(Nicky Henderson) *disp 2nd pl tl fell heavily 4th* **7/1**

3m 53.9s (-7.90) **Going Correction** -0.30s/f (Good) **7** Ran SP% **114.2**
Speed ratings (Par 117): **107,106,103,100,96 96,**
CSF £14.21 CT £30.04 TOTE £3.60: £2.00, £2.30; EX 14.50 Trifecta £36.40.

Owner The Preston Family & Friends Ltd **Bred** La Grugerie **Trained** Lower Beeding, W Sussex
■ Stewards' Enquiry : Jamie Moore two-day ban; used whip above the permitted level (20th-21st Dec)

FOCUS
Losing Simonsig from the race was a blow but it still looked an up-to-scratch edition. They didn't go a mad gallop, although the pace was decent, and the first two home, who were in the first three throughout, pulled away late on, with the winner rightly surviving a Stewards' inquiry. The winner has been rated 3lb off last season's best, while the second has been rated to his best.

2916 BETFAIR LONDON NATIONAL (A H'CAP CHASE) (24 fncs) 3m 4f 166y
3:35 (3:39) (Class 2) (0-150,148) 5-Y-O+
£25,024 (£7,392; £3,696; £1,848; £924; £464)

Form RPR
15-5 1 **Carole's Destrier**[28] [2348] 7-11-10 **146**............ NoelFehily 152+
(Neil Mulholland) *hld up in tch: prog fr 15th: jnd ldrs on outer 3 out: wnt 2nd sn after: drvn to ld after last: styd on wl* **5/1**[2]
2UU- 2 ¾ **Summery Justice (IRE)**[231] [5392] 11-10-8 **135**.......(p) CharlieDeutsch(5) 140
(Venetia Williams) *towards rr: pushed along in last pair briefly after 13th: prog fr 15th: clsd on ldrs 3 out: wnt 3rd next: nt clr run between rivals and swtchd rt bef last: drvn to chal flat: styd on but jst hld* **33/1**
313- 3 2 ¾ **Ballyheigue Bay (IRE)**[273] [4632] 8-10-9 **131**..................(t) TomCannon 134
(Chris Gordon) *led to 7th: pressed ldr tl ld again 14th: hrd pressed after 3 out: hdd and one pce after last* **20/1**
U0-6 4 1 ½ **Bertie Boru (IRE)**[28] [2348] 8-10-10 **132**............ TomO'Brien 135+
(Philip Hobbs) *settled wl in rr: prog into midfield whn blnd 16th: also hmpd and dropped to rr again: hdwy and mstke 19th: rchd 6th and mstke 2 out: styd on fr last: nt rch ldrs* **16/1**
0P-0 5 1 ¼ **Super Duty (IRE)**[22] [2473] 9-10-3 **130**..........................(p) DavidNoonan(5) 130
(Ian Williams) *mostly pressed ldng pair: wnt 2nd after 4 out tl after 3 out: fdd bef last* **12/1**
5-53 6 ¾ **Mountainous (IRE)**[27] [2374] 10-10-10 **132**.......................(p) JakeGreenall 131
(Kerry Lee) *settled towards rr: prog into midfield 17th: mstke 4 out: tried to cl on ldrs 3 out: one pce bef next* **8/1**[3]
00P0 7 23 **Tales Of Milan (IRE)**[53] [1897] 8-9-7 **122** oh2..............(bt) HarryCobden(7) 100
(Phil Middleton) *chsd ldrs: lost pl 15th and struggling in last pl 17th: stl in last pair bef 3 out: kpt on past wkng rivals after* **20/1**
00-3 8 ½ **Restless Harry**[24] [2436] 11-11-4 **140**............ JamesDavies 118
(Henry Oliver) *prom early: sn lost pl and wl in rr 1/2-way: urged along fr 15th: no imp on ldrs 4 out: wknd* **4/1**[1]
31-0 9 2 ½ **Just A Par (IRE)**[21] [2482] 8-11-12 **148**...........................(b) SeanBowen 126
(Paul Nicholls) *hld up in last pair: trying to make prog whn mstke 14th: jumping nvr gd enough to make grnd after: sme hdwy into 7th 2 out but no ch: wknd sn after* **14/1**
21-P 10 5 **Leo Luna**[35] [2187] 6-11-0 **136**...(vt) JamieMoore 106
(Gary Moore) *racd on outer in rr: rdn 4 out: tried to make prog bef 3 out but sn wknd* **4/1**[1]
02P- 11 1 **Relax (FR)**[251] [5047] 10-11-1 **137**............ AidanColeman 110
(Venetia Williams) *pressed ldr: led 7th to 14th: mstkes next 2: lost 2nd 4 out: wknd qckly bef next* **12/1**
0P0- 12 ½ **Grandads Horse**[224] [5538] 9-11-4 **140**...............................(p) DarylJacob 109
(Charlie Longsdon) *wl in rr: urged along after 13th: trying to make prog whn nt fluent next: rdn and stl in rr 4 out: no prog next* **25/1**
0P-0 13 9 **Godsmejudge (IRE)**[21] [2482] 9-10-13 **135**............ TrevorWhelan 96
(David Dennis) *lost gd early pl and sn in midfield: prog and prom 1/2-way: wknd qckly after 4 out* **20/1**
4U-2 P **Count Guido Deiro (IRE)**[27] [2367] 8-10-7 **129**....... SamTwiston-Davies
(Nigel Twiston-Davies) *prom: rdn 13th: sn dropped to rr: last and tailing off whn p.u bef 15th* **9/1**
1226 F **Silver Man**[42] [2061] 8-11-1 **137**...(v) ConorO'Farrell
(Jo Hughes) *chsd ldrs: unsighted and fell 9th* **14/1**

7m 35.9s (-8.10) **Going Correction** -0.30s/f (Good) **15 Ran SP% 130.5**
Speed ratings: **99,98,98,97,97 97,90,90,89,88 88,88,85, ,**
CSF £174.74 CT £3122.93 TOTE £5.90: £2.10, £8.80, £5.70; EX 164.50 Trifecta £3267.60.
Owner Mrs C Skipworth **Bred** Larkinglass Ltd **Trained** Limpley Stoke, Wilts

FOCUS
A good, competitive staying chase that was won by the runner with most upside to him. The winner was well in on last season's Ascot win, while the third has been rated to his mark.
T/Plt: £88.00 to a £1 stake. Pool: £113,922.91 - 944.17 winning units. T/Qpdt: £19.70 to a £1 stake. Pool: £10,665.93 - 398.93 winning units. **Jonathan Neesom**

2716 WETHERBY (L-H)
Saturday, December 5

OFFICIAL GOING: Soft (heavy in places; chs 5.0, hdl 5.3)
Wind: Strong behind Weather: Overcast

2917 TOTESCOOP6 RACING'S MILLIONAIRE MAKER NOVICES' HURDLE (10 hdls 2 omitted) 2m 5f 56y
11:55 (11:55) (Class 4) 4-Y-O+ £3,573 (£1,049; £524; £262)

Form RPR
10-1 1 **Bon Enfant (FR)**[29] [2312] 4-10-7 0............ HarryBannister(5) 126+
(Warren Greatrex) *mde all: shkn up appr 2 out: nt fluent last: rdn out* **1/4**[1]
0- 2 1 ¼ **Dakota Grey**[244] [5179] 4-10-9 0............ JoeColliver(3) 122
(Micky Hammond) *racd keenly: trckd wnr after 2nd: mstke 5th: ev ch 2 out: rdn whn pckd last: styd on* **33/1**
4-11 3 12 **Leanna Ban**[195] [454] 8-10-9 111...............................(t) JonathanEngland(3) 111
(Tristan Davidson) *hld up: hdwy appr and nt fluent 3 out: rdn and wknd bef last* **4/1**[2]
4 14 **What A Game (IRE)**[223] 4-10-12 0............ BrianHughes 96
(Tim Easterby) *prom tl rdn and wknd appr 3 out* **9/1**[3]
0 P **Airebridge (IRE)**[16] [2597] 4-10-12 0............ JamesReveley
(Michael Easterby) *chsd wnr tl nt fluent 2nd: remained handy tl rdn and flashed tail bef 3 out: sn wknd: bhd whn p.u bef next* **100/1**

5m 58.3s (31.50) **Going Correction** +1.30s/f (Heavy) **5 Ran SP% 113.9**
Speed ratings (Par 105): **92,91,86,81,**
CSF £10.61 TOTE £1.20: £1.10, £8.40; EX 11.70 Trifecta £25.30.
Owner Swanee River Partnership **Bred** Haras De Saint-Voir **Trained** Upper Lambourn, Berks

FOCUS
The going was soft, heavy in places (GoingStick: Chase 5.0, Hurdle 5.3) with those in the opening race confirming that conditions were very testing, while the wind was also very strong. The last hurdle and fence in the back straight were omitted throughout the meeting. Hurdles moved in back straight onto fresh ground. Shared A1 bend moved out 12yds from innermost line, as for the last two meetings, while the away hurdle bend was 9yds out from innermost line. The actual distance of the opening race was 2m5f 155yds. An ordinary novices' hurdle to start, though last year it was won by Three Musketeers with the odds-on favourite Missed Approach back in third, and both of those were impressive winners at Newbury last week. They understandably went a steady pace in the conditions here and the tempo didn't increase until turning for home. The winner and third set the level.

2918 CONSTANT SECURITY CHASE (A NOVICES' LIMITED H'CAP) (14 fncs 2 omitted) 2m 3f 85y
12:25 (12:27) (Class 3) (0-125,123) 4-Y-O+
£6,256 (£1,848)

Form RPR
310/ 1 **Mysteree (IRE)**[615] [5093] 7-11-2 **117**............ PeterBuchanan 127+
(Lucinda Russell) *trckd ldr: racd keenly: led 2nd: hdd bef next: wnt upsides 4th tl after 6th: led 9th: wnt lft 3 out: clr whn wnt lft again next: easily* **11/8**[2]
13-1 2 32 **Mossies Well (IRE)**[22] [2475] 6-11-8 **123**...........................(t) JamesReveley 121
(Sandy Thomson) *led to 2nd: led again whn hit next: hdd and blnd 9th: nt fluent next: rdn appr 4 out: wknd bef 2 out* **4/7**[1]

5m 41.3s (33.50) **Going Correction** +1.05s/f (Soft) **2 Ran SP% 105.8**
Speed ratings (Par 107): **71,57**
TOTE £2.10.
Owner Mrs Lynne Maclennan **Bred** Lar & Fiona Cloke **Trained** Arlary, Perth & Kinross

FOCUS
Actual distance 2m3f 175yds. This was reduced to a match following the withdrawal of Dartford Warbler and a predictable game of cat and mouse ensued, but it was the quality of jumping that made the difference. The winner has been given a token rating to his hurdle mark.

2919 SCOOP6SOCCER THE £1 MILLION FOOTBALL BET H'CAP HURDLE (11 hdls 2 omitted) 3m 26y
12:55 (12:57) (Class 4) (0-120,118) 3-Y-O+
£3,764 (£1,097; £548)

Form RPR
4101 1 **Native Optimist (IRE)**[22] [2478] 8-10-13 **110**............ MissCWalton(5) 118+
(Sheena Walton) *hld up: hdwy 4th: led 6th: hdd and hit 3 out: led again bef next: mstke last: styd on* **4/1**[3]
3103 2 2 ¼ **Howaboutnever (IRE)**[21] [2490] 7-11-0 **109**..................(p) RobMcCarth(3) 114
(Ian Williams) *prom: rdn appr 3 out: chsd wnr bef next: kpt on* **7/2**[2]
0-33 3 18 **Gilzean (IRE)**[21] [2496] 9-10-12 **107**............ KillianMoore(3) 94
(Alex Hales) *prom: racd keenly: rdn after 7th: wknd appr last* **5/2**[1]
P55- 4 2 ¾ **Who Owns Me (IRE)**[299] [4124] 9-11-7 **118**............ HarryBannister(5) 100
(Michael Easterby) *led to 6th: rdn and wknd appr 3 out* **6/1**
P-0P 5 hd **Forty Crown (IRE)**[29] [2320] 9-10-13 **105**.....................(b[1]) BrianHughes 87
(John Wade) *chsd ldrs: wnt 2nd after 5th: led appr 3 out: hdd bef next: sn wknd* **12/1**
00-6 6 15 **Beauboreen (IRE)**[21] [2490] 8-11-5 **111**...........................(tp) PeterCarberry 78
(Jennie Candlish) *hld up: hdwy after 7th: rdn appr 3 out: wkng whn hit next* **17/2**
PPPP P **Harris (IRE)**[26] [2405] 8-10-7 **106**............ GLavery(7)
(Alan Brown) *chsd ldr: mstke 3rd: drvn along and lost 2nd after 5th: wknd after 7th: bhd whn p.u bef next* **12/1**

6m 44.3s (27.80) **Going Correction** +1.30s/f (Heavy) **7 Ran SP% 111.0**
Speed ratings (Par 105): **105,104,98,97,97 92,**
CSF £17.54 TOTE £5.00: £1.60, £2.80; EX 19.30 Trifecta £20.60.
Owner R H & S C Walton **Bred** Rodney Deacon **Trained** Hexham, Northumberland

FOCUS
Actual distance 3m 152yds. This was quite a test in the conditions and again they went a sensible pace, but they still finished well spread out. It's been rated around the second.

2920 GET SOCIAL WITH TOTEPOOL ON FACEBOOK H'CAP CHASE (12 fncs 1 omitted) 1m 7f 36y
1:30 (1:33) (Class 3) (0-140,136) 4-Y-O+ £6,498 (£1,908; £954; £477)

Form RPR
1-02 1 **Clan William (IRE)**[22] [2477] 7-10-0 **110** oh1............ DannyCook 121+
(Sue Smith) *mde all: mstke 1st: rdn appr 4 out: styd u.p* **9/4**[1]
0U11 2 3 ¼ **Indian Voyage (IRE)**[10] [2719] 7-11-4 **133**...................(t) DaraghBourke(5) 138
(Maurice Barnes) *a.p: chsd wnr 4 out: rdn appr last: styd on same pce flat* **9/2**[2]
-044 3 10 **Sleepy Haven (IRE)**[17] [2580] 5-11-5 **129**......................(t) PeterCarberry 126
(Jennie Candlish) *hld up: hdwy and j.lft 4 out: rdn whn mstke 2 out: j. slowly and wknd last* **7/1**
2-54 4 1 ¼ **Yorkist (IRE)**[10] [2719] 7-11-5 **136**............ FinianO'Toole(7) 130
(Micky Hammond) *chsd ldrs: wnt 2nd 7th tl rdn appr 4 out: wknd 2 out* **5/1**[3]
12-P 5 4 **Uno Valoroso (FR)**[28] [2342] 7-10-0 **113**............ TonyKelly(3) 105
(Mark Walford) *hld up: hdwy 8th: rdn and wknd next: mstke last* **7/1**
0-12 6 6 **Grey Life**[10] [2719] 9-11-2 **126**............ BrianHughes 112
(Malcolm Jefferson) *w wnr: nt fluent 2nd: settled into 2nd after 4th: lost 2nd 7th: wknd 4 out* **9/2**[2]

4m 8.0s (12.20) **Going Correction** +1.05s/f (Soft) **6 Ran SP% 108.8**
Speed ratings (Par 107): **109,107,101,101,99 95**
CSF £11.98 TOTE £2.90: £1.60, £2.80; EX 11.90 Trifecta £101.60.
Owner Andrew Phillips **Bred** Patrick Cummins **Trained** High Eldwick, W Yorks

FOCUS
Actual distance 1m7f 90yds. A decent handicap chase in which half the field had met over C&D ten days earlier and the 1-2-4 there finished 2-6-4 here. A pb from the second.

2921 TOTEPOOL RACING'S BIGGEST SUPPORTER H'CAP HURDLE (8 hdls 1 omitted) 2m
2:05 (2:09) (Class 3) (0-140,139) 3-Y-O+ £5,523 (£1,621; £810; £405)

Form RPR
/020 1 **Vendor (FR)**[14] [2639] 7-11-3 **130**............ DannyCook 139+
(Sue Smith) *a.p: chsd ldr 3rd tl led appr 3 out: sn clr: easily* **6/4**[1]
1464 2 9 **Hartside (GER)**[6] [2810] 6-9-7 **113**............ MrRWinks(7) 111
(Peter Winks) *prom: pushed along and outpcd after 5th: rallied to chse wnr appr last: no imp flat* **5/1**[3]
4-60 3 ¾ **Circus Star (USA)**[35] [2194] 7-9-12 **118**...........................(t) MrJDixon(7) 115
(John Dixon) *hld up: hdwy bef 3 out: sn rdn: styd on same pce appr last* **12/1**

1U1- **4** *1 1/4* **Sa Suffit (FR)**[273] 4621 12-11-6 **138**....(p) DaleIrving(5) 134
(James Ewart) *chsd ldr to 3rd: remained handy: rdn appr 3 out: sn outpcd* **12/1**

615- **5** *21* **Stopped Out**[210] 4912 10-11-12 **139**....(p) JamesReveley 114
(Philip Kirby) *hld up: hdwy 3rd: chsd wnr appr 3 out: lost 2nd after 3 out: sn rdn and wknd* **22/1**

1P-P **6** *9* **Bobs Lady Tamure**[7] 2773 8-10-9 **127**....(t) DaraghBourke(5) 93
(Maurice Barnes) *hld up: hdwy after 5th: rdn and wknd 3 out* **14/1**

000- **7** *19* **Fourth Estate (IRE)**[232] 5366 9-10-1 **117**.... JohnKington(3) 64
(John Wade) *prom: rdn after 5th: wknd bef next* **33/1**

P-FP **P** **Woodpole Academy (IRE)**[28] 2342 8-10-1 **117**....(tp) AdamNicol(3)
(Philip Kirby) *led: hit 3rd: hdd & wknd appr 3 out: bhd whn p.u bef next* **20/1**

141 **U** **Cooper**[36] 2170 3-10-0 **127** oh1.... BrianHughes 105
(Kevin Ryan) *hld up: hdwy after 5th: chsd wnr after 3 out: sn rdn: wkng whn mstke and uns rdr last* **7/2**[2]

4m 12.3s (16.50) **Going Correction** +1.30s/f (Heav)
WFA 3 from 6yo+ 13lb **9 Ran SP% 113.0**
Speed ratings (Par 107): **110,105,105,104,94 89,80, ,**
CSF £9.21 CT £62.78 TOTE £2.40: £1.10, £1.80, £3.00; EX 10.30 Trifecta £68.20.
Owner Mrs A Ellis **Bred** Mme Marie-Therese Caron **Trained** High Eldwick, W Yorks

FOCUS
Actual distance 2m 63yds. A decent handicap hurdle and they went a solid pace in the ground. Arguably a pb from the winner, with the second, third and fourth all close to their marks.

2922 REBECCA RICHARDSON 21ST BIRTHDAY CHASE (A NOVICES' LIMITED H'CAP) (17 fncs 2 omitted) 3m 45y
2:40 (2:41) (Class 4) (0-120,117) 4-Y-0+ **£3,994** (£1,240; £667)

Form RPR

-1P1 **1** **Courtown Oscar (IRE)**[6] 2800 6-11-0 **109**.... JamesReveley 125+
(Philip Kirby) *chsd ldr after 2nd: led 6th to 8th: led after 11th: nt fluent 13th: clr fr 2 out: comf* **5/6**[1]

46/0 **2** *8* **Joseph Mercer (IRE)**[21] 2496 8-10-3 **98**.... BrianHughes 102
(Tina Jackson) *chsd ldrs: outpcd 10th: rallied after 13th: chsd wnr appr 4 out: styd on same pce fr 2 out* **33/1**

P4-5 **3** *33* **Nosey Box (IRE)**[35] 2208 9-10-11 **113**....(bt) StevenFox(7) 87
(Noel C Kelly, Ire) *led: nt fluent 5th: hdd next: led again 8th: hdd after 11th: chsd wnr tl rdn appr 4 out: sn wknd: j. slowly last* **10/1**

13-0 **P** **Howaboutnow (IRE)**[209] 215 8-11-5 **117**.... RobMcCarth(3)
(Ian Williams) *hld up: mstke 4th: rdn after 9th: wknd bef next: bhd whn blnd 13th: sn p.u* **11/2**[3]

0-36 **P** **Special Wells**[34] 2211 6-11-7 **116**.... DannyCook
(Sue Smith) *chsd ldr tl blnd 2nd: remained handy tl outpcd 10th: rallied after 13th: sn wknd and p.u* **4/1**[2]

002 **P** **The Toft**[24] 2428 6-9-12 **98** oh5.... GrantCockburn(5)
(Lucinda Russell) *hld up: nt fluent 5th: rdn and wknd 10th: bhd whn p.u bef 4 out* **12/1**

7m 0.8s (12.80) **6 Ran SP% 109.7**
CSF £19.84 TOTE £1.80: £1.10, £5.90; EX 30.70 Trifecta £130.40.
Owner Nobaj Ltd **Bred** Lorcan Allen **Trained** East Appleton, N Yorks

FOCUS
Actual distance 3m 153yds. Not the most competitive of novice handicap chases, but the pace was a good one in the conditions and only half the field managed to complete. A step up from the winner.

2923 SUE RYDER WHEATFIELDS HOSPICE "JUNIOR" STANDARD OPEN NATIONAL HUNT FLAT RACE 1m 4f 77y
3:15 (3:16) (Class 6) 3-Y-0 **£1,711** (£498; £249)

Form RPR

3 **1** **Applaus (GER)**[34] 2216 3-10-9 0.... JoeColliver(3) 99+
(Micky Hammond) *mde all: pushed clr fr over 2f out: styd on wl* **2/1**[1]

2 *13* **Loch Linnhe** 3-10-7 0.... JamieHamilton(5) 79
(Mark Walford) *prom: rdn to chse wnr over 2f out: wknd over 1f out* **12/1**

3 *8* **Jack Lamb** 3-10-12 0.... DougieCostello 68
(Sally Hall) *hld up: hdwy over 4f out: rdn over 2f out: sn wknd* **9/4**[2]

4 *3* **Regent's Rock** 3-10-5 0....[1] BrianHughes 56
(Peter Niven) *hld up: pushed along over 3f out: wknd 2f out* **10/3**[3]

5 *2 1/4* **Another (IRE)** 3-10-5 0.... PeterCarberry 53
(David C Griffiths) *hld up in tch: rdn over 3f out: wknd wl over 1f out* **14/1**

6 *6* **Alwareed** 3-10-12.... JamesReveley 54
(John Wade) *chsd wnr after 2f tl rdn and wknd over 2f out* **16/1**

7 *5* **Scootaloo (IRE)** 3-10-9 0....(t) CraigNichol(3) 45
(Alistair Whillans) *chsd ldrs: rdn over 4f out: wknd over 3f out* **20/1**

8 *3/4* **The Masters Choice (IRE)** 3-10-5 0.... MrBenjaminStephens(7) 44
(Mark Campion) *hld up: pushed along over 5f out: wknd over 4f out* **33/1**

3m 15.7s (195.70) **8 Ran SP% 115.1**
CSF £27.34 TOTE £2.60: £1.10, £3.60, £1.10; EX 21.80 Trifecta £80.70.
Owner Joe Buzzeo **Bred** Gestut Hof Ittlingen **Trained** Middleham, N Yorks

FOCUS
Actual distance 1m4f 140yds. A modest junior bumper in which previous experience proved the key. Once the field eventually jumped off they went a fair pace.
T/Plt: £141.90 to a £1 stake. Pool: £34,066.73 - 175.24 winning tickets T/Qpdt: £29.70 to a £1 stake. Pool: £2,525.07 - 62.80 winning tickets **Colin Roberts**

2644 HUNTINGDON (R-H)
Sunday, December 6

OFFICIAL GOING: Good to soft (soft in places) (chs 7.0, hdl 6.5)
Wind: strong, across Weather: dry, breezy

2924 BETFRED "SCOOP6SOCCER" H'CAP HURDLE (10 hdls) 2m 4f 145y
12:15 (12:15) (Class 4) (0-110,110) 3-Y-0+ **£3,898** (£1,144; £572; £286)

Form RPR

52-2 **1** **Periquest**[19] 2560 6-11-4 **102**....(t) PaddyBrennan 103
(Alex Hales) *wl in tch in midfield: trckd ldrs bef 3 out: chal next: led and j.rt last: kpt on u.p flat: jst hld on* **11/4**[1]

5-03 **2** *shd* **Guards Chapel**[18] 2577 7-11-5 **110**....(v) GeorgeGorman(7) 113+
(Gary Moore) *in tch in last trio: blnd 2nd: rdn 7th: drvn after 3 out: stl only 6th last: styd on strly flat: jst failed* **13/2**

5233 **3** *1* **Skint**[50] 1964 9-11-11 **109**....(p) GavinSheehan 109
(Ali Stronge) *led: rdn bef 2 out: hdd last: styd on same pce u.p flat* **11/1**

1146 **4** *hd* **Occasionally Yours (IRE)**[20] 2548 11-11-2 **107**.... MissTWorsley(7) 107
(Alan Blackmore) *in tch in midfield: hdwy to join ldr after 5th: rdn and unable qck between last 2: styd on same pce flat* **14/1**

5614 **5** *1 1/2* **Kayfton Pete**[31] 2288 9-11-5 **103**.... AdamPogson 103
(Charles Pogson) *taken down early: chsd ldrs: rdn and outpcd whn mstke 2 out: mstke last: rallied and styd on again fnl 75yds* **20/1**

-430 **6** *1* **Being Global (FR)**[32] 2271 4-11-7 **105**.... HarrySkelton 103
(Caroline Bailey) *hld up wl in tch in rr: clsd after 7th: effrt bef 2 out: unable qck u.p between last 2: one pce flat* **4/1**[3]

0P00 **7** *45* **American Life (FR)**[13] 2694 8-11-8 **106**....(tp) JamesBest 63
(Sophie Leech) *wl in tch in midfield: dropped to rr 7th and sn rdn: lost tch 3 out: t.o* **25/1**

0513 **8** *48* **David John**[32] 2271 4-11-5 **103**.... RobertDunne 17
(Dai Burchell) *wl in tch in midfield: pushed along after 3 out: sn btn and lost tch bef next: t.o* **10/3**[2]

3U **P** **Jeans Lady**[75] 1618 6-11-0 **98**....(p) AndrewTinkler
(Martin Keighley) *chsd ldrs: mstke 5th: losing pl and j. slowly 3 out: wl bhd whn p.u next* **18/1**

4m 57.55s (-13.05) **Going Correction** -0.45s/f (Good)
WFA 4 from 6yo+ 6lb **9 Ran SP% 111.9**
Speed ratings (Par 105): **106,105,105,105,104 104,87,69,**
CSF £20.35 CT £164.92 TOTE £3.50: £1.10, £2.50, £3.70; EX 22.40 Trifecta £182.10.
Owner The Fortune Hunters **Bred** Miss Kerry Lane **Trained** Edgcote, Northamptonshire

FOCUS
All distances as advertised. Blustery conditions for Peterborough Chase day but that meant the ground was drying out quicker than normal and the time of the handicap hurdle (given they didn't go that hard early on) suggests there wasn't too much soft left in the ground. This looked a pretty ordinary race for the grade on paper given not many of these had much scope for improvement. It's been rated around the balance of the first six.

2925 BETFRED TV EBF/TBA MARES' NOVICES' CHASE (16 fncs) 2m 3f 189y
12:50 (12:50) (Class 4) 4-Y-0+ **£5,325** (£1,653; £890)

Form RPR

1-3F **1** **Kalane (IRE)**[29] 2349 6-11-0 0.... NoelFehily 144+
(Charlie Longsdon) *j.w: mde all: drew wl clr between last 2: unchal: impressive* **1/1**[1]

11-2 **2** *31* **Bon Chic (IRE)**[16] 2613 6-11-0 0.... HarrySkelton 126
(Dan Skelton) *chsd wnr 8th: 4 l down and mstke 13th: shkn up 2 out: sn wl btn eased flat* **11/8**[2]

20-0 **3** *31* **Rhythm Star**[24] 2455 5-11-0 0....(b[1]) BrendanPowell 98
(Jamie Snowden) *chsd wnr tl 8th: struggling whn mstke 10th: nt fluent 12th and sn lost tch: t.o* **25/1**

/50- **P** **Koolala (IRE)**[316] 3858 7-11-0 0.... LiamTreadwell
(Paul Webber) *wnt lft as tapes wnt up: a last: lost tch 12th: t.o whn p.u 2 out* **9/1**[3]

4m 58.6s (-6.70) **Going Correction** -0.45s/f (Good) **4 Ran SP% 106.0**
Speed ratings (Par 105): **95,82,70,**
CSF £2.72 TOTE £2.00; EX 2.20 Trifecta £5.70.
Owner Paul Murphy **Bred** Sunnyhill Stud Ltd **Trained** Over Norton, Oxon

FOCUS
Another disappointing turnout for a mares' novice chase but it served up a treat of a performance from the winner. The second has been rated as running to a similar level as at Ascot.

2926 BETFRED LOTTO "£100K CASH GIVEAWAY" H'CAP HURDLE (8 hdls) 1m 7f 171y
1:25 (1:26) (Class 3) (0-130,130) 3-Y-0+
£8,758 (£2,587; £1,293; £646; £323; £162)

Form RPR

4-13 **1** **Template (IRE)**[24] 2458 4-10-10 **121**.... LiamMcKenna(7) 124
(Harry Fry) *led tl after 3rd: chsd ldr tl led again after 3 out: hrd pressed next: hit last: hld on wl flat: rdn out* **5/1**[3]

F313 **2** *hd* **Great Fighter**[50] 1977 5-11-8 **126**.... AidanColeman 128
(John Ferguson) *chsd ldrs: effrt to chal 2 out: sn drvn: r.o u.p flat: a jst hld* **4/1**[1]

30/6 **3** *2* **Kings Bayonet**[107] 917 8-10-11 **115**.... WayneHutchinson 115
(Alan King) *hld up in last pair: clsd on inner bef 2 out: effrt to chse ldng pair between last 2: r.o but no imp flat* **11/1**

4-10 **4** *7* **War Singer (USA)**[16] 2617 8-11-12 **130**....(tp) NoelFehily 124
(Johnny Farrelly) *hld up in rr: clsd and in tch after 3rd: effrt bef 2 out: 4th and no ex whn mstke last: wknd flat* **7/1**

3-3F **5** *3/4* **Red Devil Star (IRE)**[28] 2373 5-11-7 **125**....(t) PaddyBrennan 117
(Suzy Smith) *chsd ldr tl led after 3rd: hdd after 3 out: no ex and btn between last 2: wknd flat* **6/1**

200/ **6** *3/4* **Swnymor (IRE)**[55] 5349 6-11-11 **129**....(t) MarkGrant 121
(Kevin Frost) *hld up wl in tch in midfield: lost pl and rdn bef 2 out: no imp and kpt on same pce between last 2* **25/1**

1013 **7** *1/2* **Cusheen Bridge (IRE)**[22] 2485 7-11-11 **129**....(t) AdamPogson 120
(Charles Pogson) *in tch in midfield: dropped to rr after 5th: no imp u.p bef 2 out* **11/2**

400/ **8** *hd* **Deepsand (IRE)**[40] 4426 6-11-2 **120**....(p) DaveCrosse 111
(Ali Stronge) *chsd ldrs: rdn after 3 out: lost pl bef next: wknd between last 2* **33/1**

0-00 **9** *28* **Beatabout The Bush (IRE)**[37] 2170 4-11-4 **122**.... AdamWedge 97
(Henry Oliver) *in tch: dropped to rr after 3 out: wl btn and eased next: t.o* **9/2**[2]

3m 52.5s (-2.40) **Going Correction** -0.45s/f (Good)
WFA 4 from 5yo+ 5lb **9 Ran SP% 112.1**
Speed ratings (Par 107): **88,87,86,83,83 82,82,82,68**
CSF £24.80 CT £206.14 TOTE £7.10: £2.40, £1.30, £3.80; EX 19.30 Trifecta £189.40.
Owner Coral Champions Club **Bred** Deerpark Stud **Trained** Seaborough, Dorset
■ Stewards' Enquiry : Mark Grant two-day ban; used whip above permitted level (20th-21st Dec)

FOCUS
A competitive handicap hurdle on paper but the early gallop looked pretty steady and the winner was in the first two throughout. The first three have been rated pretty much to their marks.

2927 BETFRED PETERBOROUGH CHASE (GRADE 2) (16 fncs) 2m 3f 189y
2:00 (2:01) (Class 1) 4-Y-0+ **£38,753** (£15,626; £8,690)

Form RPR

352- **1** **Al Ferof (FR)**[225] 5536 10-11-10 165.... HarrySkelton 171+
(Dan Skelton) *chsd clr ldr 2nd: clsd after 9th: led and travelling best after 3 out: rdn between last 2: over 2 l clr whn lft wl clr last: rdn out* **9/4**[2]

64-1 **2** *40* **Pepite Rose (FR)**[29] 2335 8-10-11 157.... LiamTreadwell 122
(Venetia Williams) *a in rr: lft 4th 12th: pushed along after 3 out: sn lost tch: wnt poor 3rd between last 2: lft 2nd last: t.o* **8/1**

P0-2 **3** *7* **Wishfull Thinking**[42] 2084 12-11-10 167........................(t) RichardJohnson 129
(Philip Hobbs) *j. boldly: led and wnt clr after 1st: c bk to field 10th: hdd after 3 out: sn btn lost 3rd between last 2: lft poor 3rd last: t.o* **11/2**[3]

5-12 **F** **Ptit Zig (FR)**[15] 2633 6-11-10 162.............................. SamTwiston-Davies 168
(Paul Nicholls) *chsd ldr tl nt fluent and dropped to 4th 2nd: nt a fluent after: lft 3rd 12th: chsd wnr bef next and sn rdn: over 2 l down and looked btn whn fell last* **13/8**[1]

14- **U** **Camping Ground (FR)**[274] 4633 5-11-4 153........................(t) DarylJacob
(Robert Walford) *chsd ldng pair 2nd: hit 10th: in tch blnd bdly and uns rdr 12th* **13/2**

4m 48.8s (-16.50) **Going Correction** -0.45s/f (Good) **5** Ran SP% **108.7**
Speed ratings (Par 115): **115,99,96, ,**
CSF £17.21 TOTE £3.00: £1.50, £3.60; EX 16.50 Trifecta £49.00.
Owner J Hales **Bred** J Rauch & G Chenu **Trained** Alcester, Warwicks

FOCUS
A fascinating renewal of this Grade 2 prize. The notable feature of the contest was the furious early gallop set by the third, who went blazing off from the tapes. The winner has been rated to his best.

2928 BETFRED "FRED'S FESTIVE GIVEAWAY" NOVICES' HURDLE (8 hdls) 1m 7f 171y
2:35 (2:35) (Class 4) 4-Y-O+ **£3,898** (£1,144; £572; £286)

Form RPR

0-P2 **1** **Cyrius Moriviere (FR)**[15] 2646 5-10-9 0........................(t) MauriceLinehan(3) 123+
(Ben Pauling) *chsd ldrs: wnt 2nd bef 4th: led after 5th: j.lft 2 out: kpt on wl flat: rdn out* **20/1**

1114 **2** *1 ½* **Waterlord**[21] 2514 4-10-12 0.. AidanColeman 121+
(John Ferguson) *hld up in tch in midfield: clsd to chse ldrs 4th: rdn to chse wnr bef 2 out: kpt on u.p but a hld flat* **11/8**[1]

26-4 **3** *10* **Midnight Cowboy**[28] 2375 4-10-12 0.............................. WayneHutchinson 115+
(Alan King) *t.k.h: in tch in midfield: effrt after 3 out: 4th and no threat to ldng pair whn mstke last: kpt on to go 3rd last stride* **14/1**

4 *shd* **Ebadani (IRE)**[58] 5-10-12 0.. BrendanPowell 112
(Jamie Snowden) *in tch in midfield: clsd to chse ldrs 4th: rdn bef 2 out: outpcd between last 2: lost 3rd last stride* **20/1**

4- **5** *7* **Lac Leman (GER)**[313] 3915 4-10-12 0..................(t[1]) SamTwiston-Davies 108+
(Paul Nicholls) *t.k.h: hld up in rr: mstke 5th: hdwy bef next: 5th and no imp 2 out: wknd last* **9/1**[3]

6P2 **6** *12* **Christmas Twenty (IRE)**[38] 2154 5-10-12 0.................. PaddyBrennan 95
(Stuart Edmunds) *in tch in midfield: nt fluent 4th: rdn after 3 out: sn outpcd: wknd next* **20/1**

7 *1 ¼* **Instant Karma (IRE)**[47] 4-10-12 0.......................... RichardJohnson 96
(Michael Bell) *mstkes: chsd ldr tl led 3rd: hdd after 5th: hit next: wknd 2 out* **10/1**

0-64 **8** *3 ¼* **Movie Legend**[22] 2487 5-10-12 0.................................... DarylJacob 91
(Ben Case) *hld up in tch: towards rr of main gp and stl in tch whn mstke 3 out: wknd bef next* **40/1**

2 **9** *3 ¼* **Clayton**[16] 2614 6-10-12 0... JoshuaMoore 91
(Gary Moore) *t.k.h: hld up towards rr: hdwy after 3rd: wnt 5th 3 out: rdn and btn bef next: sn wknd* **2/1**[2]

U-15 **10** *6* **One Cool Scorpion (IRE)**[29] 2331 4-10-12 0.................... JamesBest 83
(Philip Hobbs) *hld up in rr: pushed along after 5th: sn btn and lost tch after 3 out: t.o* **66/1**

5-06 **11** *1* **Better Days (IRE)**[38] 2154 4-10-9 0.............................. RyanHatch(3) 82
(Nigel Twiston-Davies) *in tch in midfield: rdn and struggling whn hit 5th: lost tch next: t.o* **100/1**

6 **12** *1* **Fine Tune (IRE)**[34] 2251 4-10-9 0..........................(t) ThomasGarner(3) 81
(Linda Jewell) *hld up in rr: struggling 5th: lost tch next: t.o* **250/1**

60 **13** *12* **Artiste Du Gouet (FR)**[16] 2612 5-10-12 0...................... RichieMcLernon 70
(Heather Dalton) *led tl 3rd: steadily lost pl: bhd 3 out: t.o* **150/1**

U **Cobham's Circus (IRE)**[75] 4-10-12 0............................... NoelFehily
(Marcus Tregoning) *midfield: j. slowly and lost pl 1st: towards rr whn j. bdly lft and uns rdr 2nd* **66/1**

3-5 **P** **Real Gone Kid**[34] 2250 4-10-12 0.................................... AndrewTinkler
(Martin Keighley) *a in rr: struggling and mstke 4th: lost tch after next: t.o whn p.u 2 out* **150/1**

3m 48.3s (-6.60) **Going Correction** -0.45s/f (Good) **15** Ran SP% **123.6**
Speed ratings (Par 105): **98,97,92,92,88 82,82,80,78,75 75,74,68, ,**
CSF £48.77 TOTE £26.20: £4.80, £1.30, £3.10; EX 79.80 Trifecta £721.50.
Owner The Pillar P Partnership **Bred** Patrick Harroin **Trained** Bourton-On-The-Water, Gloucs

FOCUS
A wide open novices' hurdle featuring a whole host of promising types, some of whom had shown good form in bumpers, but they were well strung out from an early stage and very little got into it. A step up on his bumper form from the third.

2929 BETFRED MOBILE HENRIETTA KNIGHT MARES' STANDARD OPEN NATIONAL HUNT FLAT RACE (LISTED RACE) 1m 7f 171y
3:05 (3:06) (Class 1) 4-6-Y-O
£11,390 (£4,274; £2,140; £1,066; £536; £268)

Form RPR

1-1 **1** **La Bague Au Roi (FR)**[42] 2086 4-11-0 0.......................... GavinSheehan 126+
(Warren Greatrex) *mde all: rdn and readily fnd ex 2f out: in command fnl f: pushed out: comf* **5/6**[1]

2 *5* **Mia's Storm (IRE)**[244] 5-11-0 0................................... WayneHutchinson 118+
(Alan King) *hld up wl in tch in midfield: clsd to trck ldrs 3f out: effrt 2f out: chsd wnr over 1f out: r.o for clr 2nd but no imp on wnr* **18/1**

-U01 **3** *6* **Alizee Javilex (FR)**[60] 1811 5-11-0 0.............................. LeightonAspell 112
(Lucy Wadham) *t.k.h: hld up in tch: effrt in cl 6th over 2f out: no imp over 1f out: wnt 3rd and one pce ins fnl f* **10/1**[3]

4 *1* **Screaming Rose (IRE)**[35] 2230 4-10-11 0.......................... DavidMullins(3) 111
(W P Mullins, Ire) *chsd wnr: rdn and unable qck w wnr 2f out: 3rd and outpcd over 1f out: kpt on same pce after* **3/1**[2]

445 **5** *2 ¼* **Colin's Sister**[22] 2486 4-10-11 0.................................. ConorShoemark(3) 109
(Fergal O'Brien) *in tch in midfield: rdn 4f out: outpcd and lost pl over 2f out: rallied and swtchd lft ins fnl f: styd on: no threat to ldrs* **33/1**

4 **6** *½* **Snag List (IRE)**[22] 2486 4-11-0 0...................................... MsKWalsh 108
(W P Mullins, Ire) *t.k.h: hld up in tch in last quartet: effrt over 2f out: no imp over 1f out: no threat to ldrs but kpt on ins fnl f* **10/1**[3]

0 **7** *2* **Beyond Measure (IRE)**[213] 159 4-11-0 0...................... SamTwiston-Davies 106
(Don Cantillon) *hld up in tch towards rr: effrt ent fnl 2f: sn outpcd: wl hld but kpt on steadily ins fnl f* **80/1**

12-6 **8** *2 ¼* **Miss Mobot**[22] 2486 5-10-7 0....................................... CiaranGethings(7) 104
(Philip Hobbs) *t.k.h: chsd ldrs: rdn and unable qck over 2f out: wknd over 1f out* **33/1**

32 **9** *½* **Scorpion Princess (IRE)**[71] 1662 4-11-0 0........................ RichardJohnson 105
(Charlie Longsdon) *hld up towards rr: hdwy on inner 3f out: rdn and no ex jst over 2f out: sn btn: wknd fnl f* **18/1**

-0 **10** *1* **Amber Alert**[214] 152 5-11-0 0.......................................(t) AidanColeman 103
(Anthony Honeyball) *hld up in tch in rr: effrt 3f out: sn btn: wknd 2f out* **150/1**

1- **11** *1 ½* **Midnight Tour**[277] 4562 5-11-0 0.. NoelFehily 101
(David Loder) *t.k.h: chsd ldrs: rdn and btn over 2f out: bhd fnl f* **22/1**

3m 50.3s (1.20) **Going Correction** -0.45s/f (Good) **11** Ran SP% **120.4**
Speed ratings: **79,76,73,73,71 71,70,69,69,68 68**
CSF £20.16 TOTE £1.70: £1.10, £3.80, £2.30; EX 18.40 Trifecta £89.30.
Owner Mrs Julien Turner & Andrew Merriam **Bred** Comtesse Bertrand De Tarragon **Trained** Upper Lambourn, Berks

FOCUS
A red hot mares' bumper featuring seven winners, but the outstanding bumper mare of the season so far was once again most impressive in maintaining her unbeaten record. The third to the sixth set the level.

2930 BETFRED RACING "LIKE US ON FACEBOOK" NOVICES' H'CAP CHASE (19 fncs) 2m 7f 129y
3:35 (3:35) (Class 4) (0-105,103) 4-Y-O+ **£4,548** (£1,335; £667; £333)

Form RPR

2143 **1** **Cardinal Rose**[24] 2451 8-11-6 100.................................... KillianMoore(3) 106
(Mark Wall) *chsd ldr: led after 3rd: mde most after: rdn between last 2: hld on wl u.p flat: gamely* **5/1**[3]

3222 **2** *nk* **Mr Mafia (IRE)**[34] 2249 6-11-10 101.................................(t) LeeEdwards 111+
(Tony Carroll) *hld up in tch in rr: clsd 3 out: cl 5th and mstke next: wnt 3rd last: swtchd rt flat: styd on u.p and ev ch fnl 150yds: hld towards fin* **8/1**

6-32 **3** *½* **Halo Moon**[12] 2698 7-11-8 99..(p) NoelFehily 106+
(Neil Mulholland) *hld up in tch: clsd and travelled wl after 3 out wnt 2nd 2 out: ev ch last: sn rdn and unable qck: kpt on u.p towards fin* **9/4**[1]

-42U **4** *5* **Titans Approach (IRE)**[21] 2520 6-11-4 95........................ KielanWoods 97
(Graeme McPherson) *chsd ldrs: cl 5th last: no ex u.p flat: wknd fnl 150yds* **9/1**

335- **5** *2 ¾* **Call The Detective (IRE)**[263] 4856 6-11-12 103................ GavinSheehan 101
(Ali Stronge) *chsd ldrs: wnt 2nd after 3 out tl 2 out: stl cl 4th last: no ex and wknd flat* **6/1**

PR-1 **6** *15* **Upbeat Cobbler (FR)**[34] 2248 7-11-3 94........................ RichardJohnson 82
(Henry Daly) *j. erratically: led tl after 3rd: styd pressing wnr tl hit 13th: lost 2nd sn after 3 out: wknd next* **11/2**

4-6F **7** *nk* **Well Rewarded (IRE)**[51] 1950 5-11-10 101.........................(p) DarylJacob 87
(Emma Lavelle) *in tch: mstke 2nd: rdn after 3 out: sn struggling: wknd next* **9/2**[2]

6m 10.75s (0.45) **Going Correction** -0.45s/f (Good) **7** Ran SP% **116.4**
Speed ratings (Par 105): **81,80,80,79,78 73,73**
CSF £43.02 TOTE £7.70: £2.70, £3.10; EX 43.60 Trifecta £161.20.
Owner M J Wall **Bred** Coln Valley Stud **Trained** Cheltenham, Gloucs

FOCUS
An open looking handicap chase landed in really gutsy style by the winner. The winner sets the level.
T/Plt: £39.20 to a £1 stake. Pool: £84,088.18 - 1,563.27 winning tickets. T/Qpdt: £12.20 to a £1 stake. Pool: £8,302.66 - 501.00 winning tickets. **Steve Payne**

2338 KELSO (L-H)
Sunday, December 6

OFFICIAL GOING: Heavy (5.1)
Wind: Fresh across Weather: Sunny

2931 BLACK SWAN KELSO NOVICES' HURDLE (8 hdls) 2m 51y
12:00 (12:00) (Class 4) 4-Y-O+ **£3,249** (£954; £477; £238)

Form RPR

4 **1** **Road To Gold (IRE)**[36] 2189 6-10-12 0.............................. LucyAlexander 123+
(N W Alexander) *led: nt fluent 3 out: rdn whn hdd between last 2: l down last: styd on to ld again towards fin* **6/1**[3]

2421 **2** *¾* **Nuts Well**[30] 2318 4-11-5 122.. BrianHughes 128
(Ann Hamilton) *trckd ldr in 2nd: rdn to ld between last 2: l up last: edgd lft and one pce run-in: hdd towards fin* **5/4**[1]

1 **3** *22* **Cornborough**[36] 2189 4-11-0 0.................................... JamieHamilton(5) 108
(Mark Walford) *in tch in 3rd: nt fluent 4th and 5th: pushed along appr 2 out: mstke 2 out: rdn and wknd* **6/4**[2]

0 **4** *26* **Red Story**[214] 144 4-10-12 0....................................... PeterBuchanan 73
(Alistair Whillans) *hld up: hit 1st: nt fluent last: nvr threatened* **16/1**

5 **5** *2 ¼* **Bearskin (IRE)**[126] 1178 4-10-9 0................................ CallumWhillans(3) 71
(Donald Whillans) *midfield: pushed along appr 2 out: wknd appr last* **33/1**

503 **6** *nk* **Court Baloo (IRE)**[173] 753 4-10-9 0................................ CraigNichol(3) 70
(Alistair Whillans) *a towards rr* **66/1**

0 **7** *20* **Smuggler's Stash (IRE)**[36] 2189 5-10-12 0.......................... BrianHarding 50
(Rose Dobbin) *a towards rr* **33/1**

P **Secret Act (IRE)** 6-10-7 0....................................... StephenMulqueen(5)
(N W Alexander) *midfield: mstke 5th: sn wknd: p.u bef last* **25/1**

4m 18.5s (16.70) **Going Correction** +1.15s/f (Heav) **8** Ran SP% **115.8**
Speed ratings (Par 105): **104,103,92,79,78 78,68,**
CSF £14.41 TOTE £7.30: £1.50, £1.10, £1.10; EX 16.50 Trifecta £34.80.
Owner Mrs J Douglas Miller **Bred** Kevin Whelan **Trained** Kinneston, Perth & Kinross

FOCUS
All rails moved out on to fresh ground. The distance of this race increased by 60yds as a result. The six non-runners in the opener probably didn't weaken it by much, as the three most obvious candidates for success lined up and completely dominated.

2932 ROXBURGHE HOTEL & GOLF COURSE PARIS PIKE NOVICES' CHASE (17 fncs) 2m 7f 96y
12:30 (12:30) (Class 3) 4-Y-O+ **£10,221** (£3,085; £1,589; £842)

Form RPR

20-3 **1** **Seeyouatmidnight**[27] 2397 7-10-13 151.............................. BrianHughes 158+
(Sandy Thomson) *mde all: pushed clr between last 2: rdn out run-in* **5/6**[1]

-611 **2** *13* **Silsol (GER)**[16] 2627 6-11-9 0.................................(tp) NickScholfield 154
(Paul Nicholls) *trckd ldng pair: nt fluent 12th: lft 2nd 5 out: nt fluent 4 out: sn rdn: readily outpcd by wnr after 2 out: plugged on run-in* **11/4**[2]

P-13 **3** *8* **One For Arthur (IRE)**[22] 2481 6-11-4 136........................ PeterBuchanan 142
(Lucinda Russell) *trckd ldng pair: nt fluent 11th: outpcd in 3rd bef 4 out: nt fluent 4 out: wknd run-in* **8/1**[3]

1644 **4** *54* **Manballandall (IRE)**[57] 1856 7-10-6 0........................(t) JamesCorbett(7) 80
(Susan Corbett) *hld up in rr: t.o after 5 out* **100/1**

-331 F **Kilgefin Star (IRE)**[29] 2341 7-11-4 137 HenryBrooke
(Michael Smith) *in tch: pressed ldr fr 5th: fell 5 out* 9/1
21-0 P **Wicked Spice (IRE)**[220] 50 6-10-13 0 BrianHarding
(Nicky Richards) *hld up: slow 7th: reminder after 8th: bhd fr 11th: p.u bef 2 out* 14/1
6m 25.4s (17.40) **Going Correction** +1.15s/f (Heav) 6 Ran SP% **110.0**
Speed ratings (Par 107): **115,110,107,88,**
CSF £3.47 TOTE £1.70: £1.20, £1.40; EX 3.60 Trifecta £11.10.
Owner Mrs A M Thomson **Bred** Fiona Avice Evans **Trained** Lambden, Berwicks
FOCUS
All rails moved out on to fresh ground. The distance of this race increased by 75yds as a result. This looked a decent contest, and should produce some useful handicappers at the very least.

2933 D.G. PRYDE LTD H'CAP HURDLE (QUALIFIER FOR THE CHALLENGER TWO MILE HURDLE SERIES FINAL) (8 hdls) 2m 51y
1:05 (1:06) (Class 4) (0-120,120) 3-Y-O+ **£3,249** (£954; £477; £238)

Form RPR
5-12 1 **Alizee De Janeiro (FR)**[29] 2343 5-10-12 **106** PeterBuchanan 114+
(Lucinda Russell) *in tch: trckd ldr gng wl after 3 out: led 2 out: sn pushed along: wandered appr last: rdn and kpt on run-in* 7/2[2]
56P- 2 2½ **Smadynium (FR)**[321] 3771 7-11-7 **115** HenryBrooke 119
(Julia Brooke) *hld up: hdwy after 3 out: rdn to chse wnr ldr appr last: kpt on* 28/1
5402 3 4½ **Hunters Belt (IRE)**[22] 2492 11-10-3 **102** (bt) JonathonBewley(5) 102
(George Bewley) *hld up in rr: pushed along after 3rd: rdn and hdwy on outer after 3 out: wnt 3rd appr last: no ex run-in* 3/1[1]
33-0 4 ½ **Maxie T**[197] 87 4-11-8 **119** JoeColliver(3) 119
(Micky Hammond) *midfield: nt fluent 4th: hdwy after 3 out: rdn after 2 out: one pce* 14/1
113- 5 14 **Deep Resolve (IRE)**[12] 3638 4-11-12 **120** TomScudamore 105
(Alan Swinbank) *led: rdn whn hdd 2 out: wknd appr last* 9/2[3]
0-46 6 1¾ **Cadore (IRE)**[26] 2426 7-10-5 **102** (p) JonathanEngland(3) 86
(Lucy Normile) *hld up: drvn after 5th: nvr threatened* 10/1
/21- 7 14 **Bop Along (IRE)**[540] 697 8-11-7 **115** DannyCook 84
(Alistair Whillans) *hld up: rdn bef 3 out: sn wknd* 8/1
036 8 6 **Bold Henmie (IRE)**[31] 2294 4-10-5 **102** AdamNicol(3) 65
(Philip Kirby) *in tch: hit 5th: rdn 3 out: wknd appr 2 out* 9/1
-206 9 4 **Celestino (FR)**[9] 2753 4-10-11 **105** (tp) LucyAlexander 64
(N W Alexander) *trckd ldr: rdn after 3 out: wknd* 16/1
4m 17.5s (15.70) **Going Correction** +1.15s/f (Heav) 9 Ran SP% **111.6**
Speed ratings (Par 105): **106,104,102,102,95 94,87,84,82**
CSF £79.84 CT £318.18 TOTE £3.20: £1.80, £4.90, £1.10; EX 69.90 Trifecta £570.60.
Owner Ms Deborah Thomson **Bred** J Regereau, L Regereau & S Regereau **Trained** Arlary, Perth & Kinross
FOCUS
All rails moved out on to fresh ground. The distance of this race increased by 60yds as a result. A competitive race for the level, run at a decent pace.

2934 PERSIMMON HOMES SCOTTISH BORDERS NATIONAL (A H'CAP CHASE) (24 fncs) 4m 90y
1:40 (1:40) (Class 3) (0-140,128) 5-Y-O+ **£19,577** (£6,353; £3,581)

Form RPR
10-2 1 **Neptune Equester**[29] 2340 12-11-4 **123** (p) DerekFox(3) 135
(Sandy Thomson) *midfield: nt fluent 11th: sn lost pl and dropped to rr: pushed along after 17th: rdn and drvn: rallied and bk in contention 3 out: led appr last: styd on* 11/4[1]
4223 2 16 **Presented (IRE)**[25] 2431 8-10-12 **119** CallumBewley(5) 115
(Lisa Harrison) *trckd ldr: hit 4 out: drvn to ld after 2 out: hdd appr last: wknd run-in* 15/2[3]
1001 3 25 **Tikkandemickey (IRE)**[23] 2477 9-11-4 **125** DaraghBourke(5) 96
(Raymond Shiels) *midfield: mstke 14th: jnd ldr 17th: led 19th: rdn after 3 out: hdd after 2 out: sn wknd* 11/2[2]
16-5 U **Chavoy (FR)**[25] 2431 10-11-3 **122** (vt[1]) TonyKelly(3)
(Rebecca Menzies) *hld up: nt fluent 13th and 14th: in tch whn mstke 17th: rdn and 5 l down in 4th whn blnd and uns rdr 2 out* 11/1
1050 P **Chicago Outfit (IRE)**[35] 2213 10-11-0 **121** (p) JonathonBewley(5)
(George Bewley) *trckd ldr: mstke 15th: lost pl qckly and sn struggling in rr: p.u bef 5 out* 16/1
0332 P **Finish The Story (IRE)**[21] 2517 9-10-9 **116** (bt) DavidNoonan(5)
(Johnny Farrelly) *led: mstke 16th: jnd 17th: hdd 19th: mstke 4 out: wknd: p.u bef 2 out* 11/4[1]
1-6F P **William Money (IRE)**[8] 2790 8-11-7 **128** DiarmuidO'Regan(5)
(Chris Grant) *hld up: mstke 13th: wknd after 3 out: p.u bef next* 11/1
-063 U **More Madness (IRE)**[23] 2477 8-10-10 **112** (p) LucyAlexander
(N W Alexander) *hld up: blnd and uns 7th* 10/1
9m 33.6s (45.60) **Going Correction** +1.625s/f (Heav) 8 Ran SP% **112.1**
Speed ratings: **108,104,97,, ,,**
CSF £22.57 CT £103.75 TOTE £3.60: £1.50, £1.50, £2.20; EX 22.60 Trifecta £142.10.
Owner Jim Beaumont **Bred** Mrs Joanna Daniell **Trained** Lambden, Berwicks
FOCUS
All rails moved out on to fresh ground. The distance of this race increased by 90yds as a result. Despite the ground and distance, the early leader made sure this was a proper slog.

2935 SCOTTY BRAND CHAMPION CHASE (HANDICAP CHASE) (17 fncs) 2m 7f 96y
2:15 (2:15) (Class 2) 4-Y-O+ **£15,012** (£4,531; £2,334; £1,237)

Form RPR
42P- 1 **Vivaldi Collonges (FR)**[271] 4693 6-11-0 **134** (t) NickScholfield 147+
(Paul Nicholls) *trckd ldr: jnd ldr 9th: led 5 out: c clr on bit after 4 out: rdn after 2 out: 9 l up last: eased towards fin* 15/8[1]
02-6 2 4 **Firth Of The Clyde**[37] 2171 10-11-3 **137** BrianHughes 140
(Malcolm Jefferson) *hld up in tch: trckd ldrs 9th: rdn after 3 out: wnt 2nd 2 out: plugged on* 10/3[2]
P-U0 3 ½ **Silver Tassie (IRE)**[119] 1217 7-10-5 **130** MissCWalton(5) 134
(Micky Hammond) *hld up in rr: mstkes 5 out and 4 out: hdwy after 3 out: rdn 2 out: plugged on* 17/2
1P-4 4 19 **Little Glenshee (IRE)**[27] 2400 9-10-0 **120** oh2 LucyAlexander 110
(N W Alexander) *prom: led 5th: jnd 9th: hdd 5 out: rdn 3 out: lost 2nd 2 out: wknd* 9/2[3]
2-P0 P **Big Water (IRE)**[35] 2214 7-11-5 **139** TomScudamore
(Alan Swinbank) *in tch: nt a fluent: rdn and wknd qckly after 12th: p.u bef next* 5/1
1246 P **Alderbrook Lad (IRE)**[29] 2335 9-11-1 **142** FinianO'Toole(7)
(Micky Hammond) *led: hdd 5th: pushed along and lost pl after 10th: struggling whn mstke 12th: p.u bef next* 14/1
6m 44.0s (36.00) **Going Correction** +1.625s/f (Heav) 6 Ran SP% **109.9**
Speed ratings (Par 109): **102,100,100,93,**
CSF £8.42 CT £36.19 TOTE £2.60: £1.60, £1.50; EX 8.10 Trifecta £46.30.
Owner The Gi Gi Syndicate **Bred** G A E C Delorme Freres **Trained** Ditcheat, Somerset
FOCUS
All rails moved out on to fresh ground. The distance of this race increased by 75yds as a result. Quite a range of abilities on show for this staying handicap, in which the early pace wasn't strong.

2936 A M GILHOME JOINERY & BUILDING MARES' NOVICES' HURDLE (11 hdls) 2m 4f 189y
2:45 (2:45) (Class 4) 4-Y-O+ **£3,249** (£954; £477; £238)

Form RPR
-366 1 **La Dama De Hierro**[31] 2287 5-10-10 105 BrianHughes 105+
(Malcolm Jefferson) *in tch: mde several mstkes: wnt 2nd 8th: rdn to ld jst bef last: styd on* 6/1[3]
6- 2 5 **Miss Tiggy (IRE)**[257] 4976 5-10-10 0 PeterBuchanan 99+
(Lucinda Russell) *midfield: mstke 8th: gd hdwy after 3 out: led 2 out: rdn and edgd rt: jst hdd whn hit last: no ex* 12/1
3-3P 3 10 **Presenting Rose (IRE)**[23] 2476 5-10-5 0 StephenMulqueen(5) 89
(N W Alexander) *led: tended to jump sltly lft: hit 8th: mstke 3 out: hdd 2 out: wkng and hld in 3rd whn mstke last* 10/1
5051 4 40 **Innis Shannon (IRE)**[23] 2476 5-10-12 107 JonathonBewley(5) 54
(George Bewley) *hld up in midfield: mstke and pckd on landing 5th: nt fluent 7th: hdwy 8th: nt fluent 3 out: sn rdn: mstke 2 out: wknd* 2/1[2]
0/P P **Just Annie**[29] 2338 7-10-5 0 GrantCockburn(5)
(Lucy Normile) *a towards rr: p.u bef 2 out* 200/1
05-1 P **My Little Cracker (IRE)**[25] 2433 5-10-10 0 BrianHarding
(Iain Jardine) *midfield: stmbld on landing 3rd and rdr lost iron: nt fluent 7th: sn pushed along and lost pl: nt fluent again 3 out: sn wknd: p.u bef next* 15/8[1]
5-54 P **Massini's Lady**[27] 2398 4-10-10 0 LucyAlexander
(N W Alexander) *a towards rr: rdn fr 1/2-way: p.u bef last* 33/1
P **Milan Lady (IRE)**[42] 4-10-5 0 DiarmuidO'Regan(5)
(Chris Grant) *prom: mstke 7th: wknd after next: p.u bef 2 out* 10/1
5m 40.9s (32.90) **Going Correction** +1.625s/f (Heav)
WFA 4 from 5yo+ 6lb 8 Ran SP% **111.7**
Speed ratings (Par 105): **102,100,96,81, ,,**
CSF £67.35 TOTE £4.90: £1.50, £2.90, £2.50; EX 79.50 Trifecta £686.50.
Owner J M Jefferson **Bred** J M Jefferson **Trained** Norton, N Yorks
FOCUS
All rails moved out on to fresh ground. The distance of this race increased by 75yds as a result. Only two of these made much appeal in what was a weak contest, so the fact that they never really featured highlights the level of the race.

2937 KRISTOFFERSEN CARPETS NOVICES' H'CAP HURDLE (11 hdls) 2m 6f 151y
3:15 (3:15) (Class 5) (0-100,100) 3-Y-O+ **£3,249** (£954; £477; £238)

Form RPR
62U 1 **Marlee Massie (IRE)**[63] 1779 6-10-4 **78** LucyAlexander 94+
(N W Alexander) *in tch on outer: wnt cl 2nd bef 3 out: rdn to ld jst after 2 out: forged clr: eased nr fin* 10/1
320- 2 25 **Oscar O'Scar (IRE)**[265] 4810 7-11-5 **100** FinianO'Toole(7) 91
(Micky Hammond) *prom: led narrowly bef 3 out: rdn whn hdd jst after 2 out: wknd appr last: hit last* 4/1[1]
2-46 3 2 **Kilquiggan (IRE)**[41] 2102 7-10-12 **93** StevenFox(7) 79
(Sandy Thomson) *hld up in midfield: rdn and hdwy into 3rd appr 2 out: wknd after 2 out* 11/2[2]
546- 4 19 **Treliver Manor (IRE)**[236] 5325 7-10-8 **92** (t) LorcanMurtagh(10) 59
(Rose Dobbin) *midfield: hdwy bef 8th: 3rd whn nt fluent 3 out: sn rdn: lost 3rd appr 2 out: wknd* 17/2
P05U P **Mister Hendre**[9] 2751 7-10-6 **80** (t) DannyCook
(Susan Corbett) *led: nt fluent 8th: hdd bef 3 out: mstke 3 out: wknd and p.u bef next* 40/1
05/P P **Cleve Cottage**[11] 2720 7-10-10 **87** AdamNicol(3)
(Philip Kirby) *hld up: rdn after 8th: wknd after 2 out: p.u bef last* 14/1
06-0 P **Tomahawk Wood**[35] 2212 6-11-3 **94** CallumWhillans(3)
(Donald Whillans) *midfield: hdwy to trck ldr after 7th: wknd bef 3 out: p.u bef 2 out* 14/1
/53- P **Tambour Major (FR)**[236] 5327 8-11-4 **99** MrTHamilton(7)
(Alison Hamilton) *in tch: rdn and lost pl bef 8th: sn wknd: p.u bef 2 out* 8/1
55-3 P **The Squinty Bridge**[23] 2478 7-11-0 **93** GrantCockburn(5)
(Lucinda Russell) *midfield: wknd qckly after 9th: p.u bef 3 out* 15/2[3]
-206 P **Alwaysrecommended (IRE)**[52] 1920 6-9-9 **74** DaleIrving(5)
(Jane Walton) *nt fluent: a towards rr: p.u bef 2 out* 12/1
62-0 P **Clenagh Castle (IRE)**[55] 1890 5-11-2 **90** (p) BrianHughes
(Chris Grant) *midfield: rdn and lost pl after 7th: sn bhd: p.u bef 3 out* 16/1
0-05 P **Wee Jock Elliot**[12] 2704 5-10-12 **89** (p) CraigNichol(3)
(Alistair Whillans) *prom: rdn and lost pl after 7th: sn struggling: p.u bef 3 out* 12/1
06P0 P **Just My Luke**[9] 2751 6-9-7 **74** oh2 (tp) JamesCorbett(7)
(Susan Corbett) *a in rr: t.o after 7th: p.u bef 3 out* 66/1
6m 18.4s (37.40) **Going Correction** +1.625s/f (Heav) 13 Ran SP% **116.4**
Speed ratings (Par 103): **99,90,89,83, ,,,,**
CSF £49.29 CT £247.00 TOTE £9.10: £2.70, £2.10, £2.50; EX 49.80 Trifecta £270.90.
Owner Nicholas Alexander **Bred** Tom Baker **Trained** Kinneston, Perth & Kinross
FOCUS
All rails moved out on to fresh ground. The distance of this race increased by 75yds as a result. A moderate contest run at a fair gallop, with just four of the 13 finishing, the remainder pulling up.
T/Jkpt: £2,840.00 to a £1 stake. Pool: £50,000 - 12.5 winning tickets. Jackpot Placepot: £9.50 to a £1 stake. Pool: £2,286.00 - 174.3 winning tickets T/Plt: £41.10 to a £1 stake. Pool: £66,848.76 - 1,185.20 winning tickets T/Qpdt: £34.90 to a £1 stake. Pool: £5,805.11 - 123.08 winning tickets
Andrew Sheret

2938 - 2940a (Foreign Racing) - See Raceform Interactive

2529 PUNCHESTOWN (R-H)
Sunday, December 6

OFFICIAL GOING: Heavy

2941a JOHN DURKAN MEMORIAL PUNCHESTOWN CHASE (GRADE 1) (14 fncs) 2m 4f
1:50 (1:50) 5-Y-0+
£39,534 (£12,519; £5,930; £1,976; £1,317; £658)

RPR

1 **Djakadam (FR)**221 22 6-11-10 168 RWalsh 175+
(W P Mullins, Ire) *settled bhd ldr in 2nd tl led bef 2nd and mde rest: nt helped by attentions of loose horse briefly fr 3 out: stl travelling wl bef next: rdn between last 2 and styd on strly* **7/4**1

2 12 **Valseur Lido (FR)**222 10 6-11-10 156 BJCooper 163
(W P Mullins, Ire) *chsd ldrs: swtchd lft in 5th bef 3 out and sn tk clsr order: impr into 2nd bef next: rdn and no imp on wnr between last 2: kpt on same pce* **7/2**2

3 1 ¼ **Gilgamboa (IRE)**245 5177 7-11-10 150 BarryGeraghty 161
(E Bolger, Ire) *chsd ldrs: niggled along briefly fr 7th where slt mstke: pushed along bef 3 out and no imp in 5th bef next: kpt on u.p into mod 3rd fr last: nvr trbld ldrs* **7/2**2

4 1 ½ **Flemenstar (IRE)**28 2388 10-11-10 150 KeithDonoghue 159
(Anthony Curran, Ire) *led tl hdd bef 2nd and settled bhd ldr: rdn and no imp on wnr after 3 out and dropped to 3rd bef next where nt fluent: j. sltly rt at last: lost pl: kpt on one pce in 4th run-in* **25/1**

5 9 ½ **Clarcam (FR)**36 2206 5-11-10 156 (tp) DavyRussell 155
(Gordon Elliott, Ire) *hld up bhd ldrs: mstke 5 out: rdn in 3rd after 3 out and sn lost pl: no ex u.p in 4th bef 2 out: one pce after and dropped to 5th bef last where mstke and wknd* **12/1**

6 17 **Foxrock (IRE)**14 2676 7-11-10 162 (t) APHeskin 135
(T M Walsh, Ire) *hld up bhd ldrs: nt fluent 5th: dropped to rr and reminder fr 6th: reminder again after 5 out and no imp fr next: wknd and eased fr bef 3 out* **8/1**3

U **Hidden Cyclone (IRE)**28 2388 10-11-10 157 (p) BrianHayes
(John Joseph Hanlon, Ire) *w.w in rr: slt mstke 4th: wnt 6th bef 6th: towards rr whn blnd and uns rdr 9th* **10/1**

5m 14.9s (-9.10) **Going Correction** 0.0s/f (Good) 7 Ran SP% 112.5
Speed ratings: **118,113,112,112,108 101,**
CSF £8.21 TOTE £1.90: £2.00, £1.70; DF 9.00 Trifecta £13.10.
Owner Mrs S Ricci **Bred** Richard Corveller **Trained** Muine Beag, Co Carlow

FOCUS
A cracking renewal and a stunning display from Djakadam, even if his immediate victirms were rated sufficiently inferior to him as to suggest he should have been capable of a smooth win. The second and third have been rated to the better view of their form, with the cosy winner also close to his best.

2942 - 2944a (Foreign Racing) - See Raceform Interactive

2751 MUSSELBURGH (R-H)
Monday, December 7

OFFICIAL GOING: Soft (5.7)
Wind: light 1/2 behind Weather: fine

2945 BRITISH STALLION STUDS EBF "NATIONAL HUNT" NOVICES' HURDLE (QUALIFIER) (9 hdls) 1m 7f 124y
12:15 (12:15) (Class 4) 4-6-Y-0 **£3,898** (£1,144; £572; £286)

Form RPR

3-11 1 **Fagan**42 2106 5-11-0 0 RichardJohnson 131+
(Gordon Elliott, Ire) *trckd ldrs: 2nd appr 3 out: led and j.lft 2 out: pushed clr sn after last: eased in clsng stages* **1/7**1

65 2 6 **Away For Slates (IRE)**31 2318 5-10-11 0 CraigNichol(3) 118
(Keith Dalgleish) *t.k.h: trckd ldrs: 2nd 2 out: kpt on: no ch w wnr* **22/1**

2-43 3 12 **Captain Redbeard (IRE)**12 2716 6-11-0 108 JamesReveley 107
(Stuart Coltherd) *led: hdd bef 2nd: led sn after 3rd: hdd narrowly 5th: led appr 3 out: hdd 2 out: sn fdd* **12/1**3

2 4 3 ½ **What Happens Now (IRE)**13 2709 6-11-0 0 BrianHarding 103
(Donald McCain) *trckd ldr: led bef 2nd: nt fluent and hdd sn after 3rd: led narrowly 6th: hdd appr 3 out: edgd rt and lost pl bef 2 out* **8/1**2

5-6 5 11 **Sky Full Of Stars (IRE)**197 452 5-11-0 0 LucyAlexander 92
(James Ewart) *a in last: pushed laog 3rd: reminders next: bhd fr 6th* **80/1**

3m 54.6s (6.20) **Going Correction** +0.55s/f (Soft) 5 Ran SP% 111.9
Speed ratings: **106,103,97,95,89**
CSF £5.56 TOTE £1.10: £1.10, £4.50; EX 5.40 Trifecta £16.60.
Owner R A Bartlett **Bred** J R Weston **Trained** Longwood, Co Meath

FOCUS
Despite 5mm of overnight rain the official going remained soft. Allowing for rail movements the race distance was 59yds further than advertised. The opener was an uncompetitive novice hurdle. The winner was a 125 bumper horse and should at least match that over hurdles.

2946 RACING UK ANYWHERE AVAILABLE NOW H'CAP HURDLE (9 hdls) 1m 7f 124y
12:45 (12:45) (Class 5) (0-100,99) 3-Y-0+ **£3,249** (£954; £477; £238)

Form RPR

U4F- 1 **Moonlone Lane (IRE)**19 2589 8-11-1 95 (p) MissLBrooke(7) 108+
(Paul Stafford, Ire) *w ldrs: led 4th: drvn 3 out: fnd ex and forged clr fnl 75yds* **11/2**

35-0 2 3 **Sirpertan**39 2148 4-11-8 95 JeremiahMcGrath 103
(Marjorie Fife) *trckd ldrs: 2nd gng wl appr 3 out: upsides whn hit 2 out: drvn last: kpt on same pce last 100yds* **4/1**3

2445 3 9 **Sendiym (FR)**10 2755 8-11-0 0 (p) BrianHughes 86
(Dianne Sayer) *w ldrs: drvn 5th: one pce fr 3 out: modest 3rd appr last* **7/2**2

2222 4 6 **Gunner Lindley (IRE)**3 2891 8-11-1 93 GrantCockburn(5) 86
(Stuart Coltherd) *led to 4th: drvn 6th: wknd appr last* **5/1**

0P0 5 9 **Rioja Day (IRE)**10 2754 5-11-12 99 DannyCook 83
(Jim Goldie) *chsd ldrs: drvn 6th: sn lost pl and bhd* **14/1**

4060 6 3 ¼ **Authinger (IRE)**31 2322 7-11-1 95 LorcanMurtagh(7) 77
(Barry Murtagh) *trckd ldrs: drvn 6th: lost pl after next: lame* **25/1**

2251 7 6 **Triple Eight (IRE)**32 2292 7-11-7 97 (p) AdamNicol(3) 75
(Philip Kirby) *hld up in last: blnd bdly 4th: nt rcvr: bhd bef 3 out* **11/4**1

3m 56.3s (7.90) **Going Correction** +0.55s/f (Soft)
WFA 4 from 5yo+ 5lb 7 Ran SP% 111.5
Speed ratings (Par 103): **102,100,96,93,88 86,83**
CSF £26.44 TOTE £5.60: £2.90, £3.30; EX 28.70 Trifecta £109.30.
Owner M Keegan **Bred** John Blake **Trained** Oldtown, Co. Dublin

FOCUS
The race distance was 59yds further than advertised. A moderate handicap hurdle, in which the front two pulled clear. They're on the upgrade.

2947 WATCH ON 3 DEVICES RACINGUK.COM H'CAP CHASE (14 fncs 2 omitted) 2m 3f 193y
1:15 (1:15) (Class 4) (0-120,119) 4-Y-0+ **£5,198** (£1,526; £763; £381)

Form RPR

-56P 1 **Royal Macnab (IRE)**16 2648 7-11-4 114 (t) TonyKelly(3) 126+
(Rebecca Menzies) *mde all: j. soundly: drew clr 3 out: 6 l ahd last: styd on* **12/1**

2 2 3 ½ **Indian Temple (IRE)**23 2497 6-11-5 119 MrWHRReed(7) 123
(W T Reed) *hld up towards rr: hdwy on outside to chse ldrs 8th: hit 2 out: kpt on to take 2nd last 150yds* **11/2**3

0/ 3 1 ¼ **Art Lord (IRE)**30 9-10-10 106 DerekFox(3) 109
(Karl Thornton, Ire) *chsd ldrs: reminders and lost pl after 11th: styd on fr 2 out: tk 3rd last 75yds* **2/1**1

3442 4 1 ¾ **Quito Du Tresor (FR)**31 2329 11-11-9 116 (p) PeterBuchanan 118
(Lucinda Russell) *chsd ldrs: pushed along 10th: 2nd next: wknd last 50yds* **7/2**2

1-34 5 20 **Better B Quick (IRE)**19 2589 9-10-4 104 (p) JonathanMoore(7) 88
(Paul Stafford, Ire) *chsd ldrs: mstke 11th: hit next: wknd appr 2 out* **6/1**

3134 6 1 ¾ **Endeavor**10 2755 10-10-8 101 BrianHughes 80
(Dianne Sayer) *chsd ldrs: dropped bk 8th: rallied to chse ldrs 11th: lost pl sn after 3 out* **15/2**

-6P0 7 11 **Formidableopponent (IRE)**10 2755 8-10-12 110 DaraghBourke(5) 78
(William Young Jnr) *in rr: hdwy 8th: outpcd whn hit 11th: sn bhd: blnd 2 out* **16/1**

P64F P **Parlour Of Dreams (IRE)**10 2753 8-10-7 100 DannyCook
(Andrew Hamilton) *chsd ldrs: mstke 7th: lost pl 11th: wl bhd whn p.u bef next* **50/1**

5m 10.6s (9.40) **Going Correction** +0.625s/f (Soft) 8 Ran SP% 112.5
Speed ratings (Par 105): **106,104,104,103,95 94,90,**
CSF £73.78 CT £187.64 TOTE £10.10: £1.80, £2.60, £1.30; EX 70.40 Trifecta £259.80.
Owner The Extra Time Partnership **Bred** M F Condon **Trained** Stearsby, N Yorks

FOCUS
The race distance was 28yds further than advertised. A modest handicap chase in which the second to fourth set the level.

2948 RACING UK ANDROID APP RACINGUK.COM H'CAP HURDLE (14 hdls) 2m 7f 180y
1:45 (1:45) (Class 4) (0-115,112) 4-Y-0+ **£3,898** (£1,144; £572; £286)

Form RPR

1151 1 **Maraweh (IRE)**32 2296 5-11-2 105 (v) DerekFox(3) 118+
(Lucinda Russell) *chsd ldrs: pushed along 5th: rallied and 3rd 10th: led next: drew clr between last 2* **11/4**1

2106 2 10 **Jack Albert (IRE)**171 781 8-11-8 108 BrianHughes 110
(Dianne Sayer) *led: hdd bef 2nd: led after 10th: hdd next: kpt on same pce fr 2 out: lame* **10/1**

1032 3 5 **Solway Sam**26 2432 12-10-7 98 CallumBewley(5) 94
(Lisa Harrison) *in rr: bmpd 1st: hdwy to chse ldrs 9th: modest 4th between last 2: 3rd nr fin* **7/1**3

0-42 4 hd **Perennial**20 2550 6-10-11 100 (p) AdamNicol(3) 96
(Philip Kirby) *in rr: drvn 8th: hdwy to chse ldrs 3 out: modest 3rd 2 out: one pce* **9/1**

4246 5 3 ½ **One For Hocky (IRE)**127 1181 7-11-12 112 BrianHarding 104
(Nicky Richards) *wore hood in paddock: hld up in rr: hit 8th: hdwy 3 out: nvr a threat* **9/2**2

0PP5 6 5 **Arctic Court (IRE)**32 2296 11-11-10 110 JamesReveley 100
(Jim Goldie) *prom: mstke 6th: lost pl 10th* **7/1**3

12P 7 2 ¾ **What A Steel (IRE)**30 2340 11-11-8 111 (b1) CraigNichol(3) 96
(Alistair Whillans) *chsd ldrs: upsides appr 3 out: lost pl bef 2 out* **20/1**

605F 8 nse **Another Bygones (IRE)**66 1744 6-10-9 95 TomScudamore 81
(Karen McLintock) *hld up in rr: hdwy after 10th: chsng ldrs 2 out: wknd qckly appr last* **8/1**

PP-P 9 17 **Hail The Brave (IRE)**39 2142 6-11-0 100 (p) HenryBrooke 68
(Michael Smith) *t.k.h: w ldr: led bef 2nd: hdd after 10th: sn lost pl: bhd fr 2 out: t.o* **33/1**

516 10 33 **Roc De Prince**30 2339 6-10-13 104 (bt) DaleIrving(5) 39
(James Ewart) *in rr: j.lft 1st: hdwy to chse ldrs 5th: lost pl next: rallied to chse ldrs 8th: lost pl 10th: sn bhd: t.o whn eased between last 2* **20/1**

6m 17.1s (35.00) **Going Correction** +0.55s/f (Soft) 10 Ran SP% 115.5
Speed ratings (Par 105): **63,59,58,57,56 55,54,54,48,37**
CSF £30.23 CT £171.06 TOTE £3.40: £1.40, £2.80, £2.20; EX 30.40 Trifecta £203.70.
Owner Tay Valley Chasers Racing Club **Bred** Shadwell Estate Company Limited **Trained** Arlary, Perth & Kinross

FOCUS
The race distance was 118yds further than advertised. A modest but competitive-looking handicap hurdle and it was turned into a procession by the improving winner. He's rated in line with his best Flat figures.

2949 DOWNLOAD YOUR RACING UK APP H'CAP HURDLE (12 hdls) 2m 3f 81y
2:20 (2:20) (Class 3) (0-125,124) 3-Y-0+
£6,256 (£1,848; £924; £462; £231; £116)

Form RPR

00-0 1 **Tap Night (USA)**36 2214 8-11-12 124 (p) TomScudamore 129+
(Lucinda Russell) *w ldrs: led 9th: hdd narrowly 2 out: led last: styd on wl* **11/2**3

1250 2 2 ¼ **Mountain Fighter**24 2472 4-11-10 122 AidanColeman 123
(John Ferguson) *chsd ldrs: led narrowly 2 out: hdd last: styd on same pce* **4/1**2

102- 3 1 **Donna's Pride**227 5514 6-10-10 108 JamesReveley 109+
(Keith Reveley) *hld up in rr: hdwy 3 out: disputing 3rd whn blnd last: styd on to take 3rd last 75yds* **10/1**

05/P 4 3 ¾ **Makbullet**23 2499 8-10-10 108 HenryBrooke 104
(Michael Smith) *hld up in rr: hdwy to chse ldrs appr 3 out: 3rd 2 out: one pce* **50/1**

-526 **5** 2½ **Silver Shuffle (IRE)**[18] 2595 8-10-3 **101**..........(p) BrianHughes 95
(Dianne Sayer) *towards rr: hdwy 9th: chsng ldrs next: one pce* **15/2**
5260 **6** 3½ **Cooking Fat**[18] 2594 4-11-0 **115**.......... ColmMcCormack(3) 104
(Dianne Sayer) *towards rr: drvn 8th: sn outpcd: kpt on fr 2 out* **22/1**
24-6 **7** 1 **Landecker (IRE)**[44] 2067 7-11-10 **122**..........(v¹) LucyAlexander 110
(N W Alexander) *racd wd: reminder after 1st: sn w ldrs: led 6th to 9th: wknd next* **12/1**
11-1 **8** ¾ **Gingili**[209] 254 5-11-5 **120**.......... CraigNichol(3) 110
(Rose Dobbin) *chsd ldrs: drvn 3 out: wknd between last 2* **7/2**[1]
9 5 **Bright Prospect (IRE)**[121] 1209 6-11-5 **120**.......... TonyKelly(3) 103
(Jackie Stephen) *t.k.h: trckd ldrs: drvn appr 3 out: sn wknd* **17/2**
132/ **10** 7 **Jonny Delta**[94] 344 8-11-3 **115**.......... DannyCook 93
(Jim Goldie) *hld up towards rr: sme hdwy 7th: chsng ldrs appr 3 out: sn lost pl* **10/1**
26F4 **11** 11 **Apachee Prince (IRE)**[107] 1331 6-11-6 **118**..........(t) BrianHarding 83
(Alistair Whillans) *led to 6th: lost pl sn after 3 out: bhd whn eased between last 2* **18/1**

5m 5.5s (14.00) **Going Correction** +0.55s/f (Soft)
WFA 4 from 5yo+ 5lb **11 Ran SP% 117.3**
Speed ratings (Par 107): **92,91,90,89,88 86,86,85,83,80 76**
CSF £28.27 CT £216.79 TOTE £7.20: £2.30, £2.10, £2.90; EX 28.60 Trifecta £341.30.
Owner John P McManus **Bred** Edward P Evans **Trained** Arlary, Perth & Kinross

FOCUS
The race distance was 118yds further than advertised. A fair handicap hurdle and the form should work out. The winner was a 140+ hurdler at his peak and may still be better than this.

2950 100% RACINGUK PROFITS RETURN TO RACING H'CAP CHASE 2m 7f 170y
(15 fncs 3 omitted)
2:50 (2:50) (Class 4) (0-105,104) 4-Y-0+ **£3,898** (£1,144; £572; £286)

Form RPR
U-43 **1** **Itstimeforapint (IRE)**[23] 2500 7-11-9 **104**.......... DerekFox(3) 114+
(Lucinda Russell) *chsd ldrs: hit 12th: led bef 3 out: hdd 2 out: led appr last: drvn out* **11/4**[1]
5-23 **2** 2¼ **Drumlister (IRE)**[162] 847 9-11-10 **102**.......... BrianHughes 108
(Dianne Sayer) *led tl after 1st: w ldrs: led briefly 8th: led narrowly 2 out: hdd appr last: kpt on same pce* **11/1**
33P3 **3** 32 **Shady Sadie (IRE)**[32] 2297 8-9-11 **78** oh2..........(t) HarryChalloner(3) 52
(Rose Dobbin) *in rr: outpcd 9th: bhd 12th: kpt on to take distant 3rd sn after last* **10/1**
15-4 **4** 2½ **Gibbstown (IRE)**[76] 1626 9-11-3 **102**..........(p) JonathanMoore(7) 74
(Paul Stafford, Ire) *in rr: mstke 2nd: hdwy 5th: outpcd 9th: distant 3rd whn j.lft 2 out: wknd last* **20/1**
P-42 **5** ½ **Benefit In Kind (IRE)**[32] 2297 7-10-13 **91**..........(tp) DannyCook 62
(Katie Scott) *sn chsng ldrs: led after 8th: hdd bef 3 out: sn wknd* **3/1**[2]
451P **P** **Champagne Agent (IRE)**[39] 2143 9-10-5 **86**..........(bt) CallumWhillans(3)
(Donald Whillans) *led after 1st: hdd 8th: lost pl 12th: bhd next: t.o whn p.u bef 2 out* **16/1**
UP-P **U** **Notonebuttwo (IRE)**[24] 2478 8-10-0 **83**..........(tp) DiarmuidO'Regan(5)
(Chris Grant) *chsd ldrs: blnd and uns rdr 4th* **6/1**[3]
-31P **P** **Donapollo**[38] 2173 7-11-1 **103**..........(t) LorcanMurtagh(10)
(Rose Dobbin) *in rr: drvn 5th: bhd fr 9th: p.u bef 3 out* **12/1**
0-54 **P** **The Bishop (IRE)**[26] 2430 7-11-2 **94**..........(p) LucyAlexander
(N W Alexander) *chsd ldrs: lost pl and reminders 3rd: bhd and reminders 5th: hdwy 7th: lost pl and bhd 9th: t.o whn p.u bef 3 out* **8/1**

6m 17.0s (13.60) **Going Correction** +0.625s/f (Soft) **9 Ran SP% 112.8**
Speed ratings (Par 105): **102,101,90,89,89 , , ,**
CSF £31.44 CT £260.51 TOTE £3.80: £1.40, £2.10, £2.60; EX 22.00 Trifecta £162.20.
Owner IMEJ Racing **Bred** Ms T Doran **Trained** Arlary, Perth & Kinross

FOCUS
The race distance was 28yds further than advertised. A moderate handicap chase and only two mattered in the home straight. A small pb from the winner.

2951 BET WITH YOUR RACING UK APP STANDARD OPEN NATIONAL HUNT FLAT RACE 1m 7f 124y
3:20 (3:20) (Class 6) 4-6-Y-0 **£1,949** (£572; £286; £143)

Form RPR
4 **1** **Myztique (IRE)**[15] 2677 5-11-2 0..........(t) RichardJohnson 113+
(Gordon Elliott, Ire) *trckd ldrs: 2nd over 3f out: swtchd lft and led over 2f out: pushed clr over 1f out* **1/4**[1]
44-3 **2** 6 **Mr Witmore (IRE)**[221] 39 5-11-2 0.......... HenryBrooke 105
(Michael Smith) *chsd ldrs: led 5f out: hdd over 2f out: kpt on same pce* **6/1**[2]
3 3¼ **Dubai Devils (IRE)**[22] 4-10-9 0.......... JonathanMoore(7) 102
(Paul Stafford, Ire) *racd wd: chsd ldrs after 4f: 2nd over 4f out: one pce* **20/1**
3 **4** 42 **Captain Mowbray**[30] 2344 4-10-13 0.......... TonyKelly(3) 60
(Rebecca Menzies) *t.k.h: trckd ldrs: lost pl after 7f: bhd fnl 4f: t.o 2f out* **9/1**[3]
4 **5** 14 **Raymond Reddington (IRE)**[24] 2479 4-10-11 0.......... DiarmuidO'Regan(5) 46
(Chris Grant) *led: hdd 5f out: sn lost pl and bhd: t.o 2f out* **20/1**

3m 48.0s (5.20) **Going Correction** +0.55s/f (Soft)
WFA 4 from 5yo 5lb **5 Ran SP% 113.8**
Speed ratings: **109,106,104,83,76**
CSF £2.55 TOTE £1.20: £1.10, £2.20; EX 2.90 Trifecta £11.10.
Owner Ms M McKenna **Bred** P McNally **Trained** Longwood, Co Meath

FOCUS
The race distance was 59yds further than advertised. An uncompetitive bumper and the short-priced favourite made no mistake. The second sets the level.
T/Plt: £73.90 to a £1 stake. Pool of £55597.13 - 548.89 winning tickets. T/Qpdt: £18.50 to a £1 stake. Pool of £6855.12 - 273.51 winning tickets. **Walter Glynn**

2710 FONTWELL (L-H)
Tuesday, December 8

OFFICIAL GOING: Soft (heavy in places; 5.8)
Wind: almost nil Weather: showers with sunny periods Rails: Rail movement adding; Race 1, 3, 5 & 7 add 162yds; Race 2 add 114yds; Race 4 add 168yds; Race 6 add 132yds.

2952 SMARTCOMPUTERSBRISTOL.COM MARES' NOVICES' HURDLE 2m 3f 33y
(10 hdls)
12:40 (12:40) (Class 4) 4-Y-0+ **£3,249** (£954; £477; £238)

Form RPR
10- **1** **Katie Too (IRE)**[241] 5277 4-10-10 0.......... WayneHutchinson 123+
(Alan King) *trckd ldrs: mstke 6th: led 2 out: drawing clr whn edging rt between last 2: styd on strly: easily* **4/5**[1]
6-02 **2** 20 **Twenty Eight Guns**[14] 2697 5-10-10 0.......... TomScudamore 102
(Michael Scudamore) *in tch: hdwy 3 out: chal 2 out: rdn and hld between last 2: styd on same pce* **11/2**[3]
4-1 **3** 3¼ **Drumviredy (IRE)**[27] 2444 6-11-3 118.......... LiamTreadwell 107
(Venetia Williams) *disp ld tl rdn appr 2 out where nt fluent: one pce after* **3/1**[2]
32/3 **4** 1¾ **Coco Shambhala**[20] 2579 7-10-10 0.......... LeightonAspell 96
(Oliver Sherwood) *disp ld tl rdn appr 2 out: sn one pce* **7/1**
440- **5** 1 **Ginny's Tonic (IRE)**[246] 5181 6-10-10 0..........(t) TomO'Brien 95
(Suzy Smith) *chsd ldrs: rdn whn outpcd after 3 out: styd on again fr last* **25/1**
460 **6** 1 **The Barbury Queen (IRE)**[33] 2302 5-10-7 0.......... TomBellamy(3) 94
(Alan King) *in tch: rdn after gng rt 6th: outpcd after 3 out: styd on again fr last* **50/1**
24- **P** **Jambul Tree**[232] 5439 5-10-10 0.......... NickScholfield
(Robert Walford) *nvr fluent: detached and slow 3rd: nvr bk on terms: t.o 7th: p.u after 3 out* **25/1**
-040 **P** **Betsy Boo Boo**[23] 2519 6-10-10 0.......... DavidEngland
(Michael Roberts) *in tch: nt fluent 1st: struggling bef 7th: sn bhd: p.u bef last* **100/1**

5m 22.9s (23.50) **Going Correction** +1.35s/f (Heav)
WFA 4 from 5yo+ 5lb **8 Ran SP% 119.1**
Speed ratings (Par 105): **104,95,94,93,93 92, ,**
CSF £6.21 TOTE £1.60: £1.10, £1.80, £1.20; EX 5.20 Trifecta £14.80.
Owner Mr & Mrs Christopher Harris **Bred** Regina Anne Hennessy **Trained** Barbury Castle, Wilts

FOCUS
Fences sited on outer and hurdles on inner. Races 1, 3, 5 & 7 increased by 162yds, race 2 by 114yds, race 4 by 168yds, and race 6 by 132yds. The ground looked hard work and Wayne Hutchinson described it as "heavy, gruelling, hard work". Not a bad mares' hurdle and the winner could be quite useful. The form is rated around the second to sixth.

2953 T I ENGINEERING STRUCTURAL LTD H'CAP CHASE (15 fncs) 2m 3f 35y
1:10 (1:10) (Class 5) (0-100,100) 4-Y-0+ **£2,885** (£1,049)

Form RPR
-6PP **1** **Toohighforme (IRE)**[33] 2303 6-10-4 **78**..........(bt¹) TomCannon 74
(Nick Gifford) *j. sltly rt: trckd wnr: rdn after 4 out: hld whn mstke 2 out: wnt bdly rt whn lft in ld last* **10/1**
B1/4 **2** 26 **Highbury High (IRE)**[23] 2515 8-11-12 **100**..........(tp) NoelFehily 86
(Neil Mulholland) *hld up 4th: wnt 3rd 10th: blnd next: rdn after 4 out: hld fr next: pckd 2 out: tired whn lft 2nd and hmpd last* **11/2**[3]
35-1 **F** **Zero Visibility (IRE)**[8] 2826 8-10-5 **79**.......... AdamWedge 90+
(Alexandra Dunn) *j. sltly rt: led: travelling strly whn landed steeply 2 out: drawing clr and wl in command whn fell last* **13/8**[1]
/1F- **P** **Ilewin For Hannah**[552] 581 8-11-1 **89**.......... JamieMoore
(Gary Moore) *nvr really travelling in last but in tch: grad lost tch: fr 10th: t.o whn p.u bef 3 out* **2/1**[2]
2U63 **P** **Gowanauthat (IRE)**[13] 2714 7-10-9 **93**..........(tp) TommyDowling(10)
(Charlie Mann) *trckd ldrs tl 10th: wknd after next: t.o whn p.u bef 3 out* **7/1**

5m 43.0s (35.70) **Going Correction** +1.525s/f (Heav) **5 Ran SP% 108.4**
Speed ratings (Par 103): **85,74, , ,**
CSF £54.43 TOTE £10.90: £3.30, £1.50; EX 60.60 Trifecta £66.00.
Owner Nick Gifford Racing Club **Bred** Tom Devereux **Trained** Findon, W Sussex

FOCUS
Race distance increased by 114yds. Late drama with the favourite, who had things well under control, coming down at the last. The lucky winner is up 10lb on the best of his hurdle figures.

2954 AXIO SPECIAL WORKS CHRISTMAS RACEDAY JUVENILE HURDLE (9 hdls) 2m 1f 145y
1:40 (1:40) (Class 4) 3-Y-0 **£3,249** (£954; £477; £238)

Form RPR
61P **1** **Darebin (GER)**[11] 2757 3-11-5 0.......... JamieMoore 110+
(Gary Moore) *hld up bhd ldrs: hdwy after 3 out: led sn after next: shkn up after last: kpt on wl: eased cl home* **7/4**[1]
6 **2** 11 **Extreme Appeal (IRE)**[11] 2757 3-10-12 0..........(b¹) TomScudamore 92
(Warren Greatrex) *led: nt fluent 3 out: hit 2 out: sn hdd: styd on same pce fr last* **5/1**
324 **3** 26 **Albert Herring**[34] 2273 3-10-12 105.......... DarylJacob 64
(Jonathan Portman) *trckd ldrs: disputing cl 2nd whn rdn after 3 out: wknd next: wnt modest 3rd cl home* **11/4**[2]
4 **4** 3 **Sandgate**[26] 2448 3-10-12 0.......... NoelFehily 66
(Neil Mulholland) *trckd ldrs: travelling wl in clly disp 2nd after 3 out: fnd little whn asked appr next and qckly btn: v tired whn lost modest 3rd cl home* **10/3**[3]
P **5** 11 **Kingston Mimosa**[11] 2757 3-10-12 0..........(p) TomCannon 50
(Mark Gillard) *chsd ldrs: mstke 6th: rdn after 3 out: sn btn* **100/1**
6 53 **Satin And Lace (IRE)**[13] 3-10-5 0.......... MarcGoldstein
(Michael Madgwick) *hld up bhd ldrs: hit 2nd: nt fluent 5th: wknd after 3 out: t.o* **33/1**

4m 58.3s (24.00) **Going Correction** +1.35s/f (Heav) **6 Ran SP% 106.7**
Speed ratings (Par 104): **100,95,83,82,77 53**
CSF £9.90 TOTE £2.30: £1.40, £2.50; EX 10.10 Trifecta £19.80.
Owner Chris Stedman & Mark Albon **Bred** Stall 5-Stars **Trained** Lower Beeding, W Sussex

FOCUS
Race distance increased by 162yds. This didn't take much winning and they finished well strung out.The winner is rated back to form.

2955 NJS H'CAP CHASE (19 fncs) 3m 1f 106y
2:10 (2:10) (Class 3) (0-135,133) 4-Y-0+ £6,564 (£2,104; £1,169)

Form RPR
-223 1 **Alternatif (FR)**[25] 2473 5-11-12 **133**....................(p) TomScudamore 145+
(David Pipe) *trckd ldrs: upsides 2 out: nt fluent last: pushed ahd towards fin: cosily* 3/1[1]
UF/6 2 1 **Pete The Feat (IRE)**[23] 2517 11-11-1 **132**..........(t) TomHumphries(10) 140
(Charlie Longsdon) *j.rt most of way: disp ld tl 5th: hmpd 8th and 9th: led 12th: rdn appr 3 out: wnt rt and nt fluent whn jnd 2 out: wnt rt and hit last: no ex whn hdd towards fin* 9/1
46-P 3 34 **Ziga Boy (FR)**[35] 2261 6-10-13 **120**.................... WayneHutchinson 106
(Alan King) *trckd ldrs: led 9th tl 10th: ev ch 3 out: sn rdn: mstke and sltly hmpd next: wknd* 10/3[2]
3-P2 P **Handy Andy (IRE)**[44] 2089 9-11-4 **125**....................(t) BrendanPowell
(Colin Tizzard) *trckd ldrs: rdn after 15th: wknd after next: t.o whn p.u bef 2 out* 7/2[3]
1P-0 P **Coolking**[40] 2149 8-10-4 **111**.................... TomCannon
(Chris Gordon) *disp ld tl clr ldr 5th: j.lft 8th: hdd next tl 10th: hdd 12th: prom tl rdn after 14th: wknd bef 4 out: p.u bef 3 out* 14/1
PP-1 P **Union Jack D'Ycy (FR)**[10] 2766 7-11-7 **128**.................... LiamTreadwell
(Venetia Williams) *hld up in tch: j.rt 6th and 12th: reminders: mstke 14th: blnd bdly next: sn p.u* 13/2
53-4 P **Sun Wild Life (FR)**[35] 2261 5-11-3 **124**....................(p) NickScholfield
(Robert Walford) *a last but in tch tl after 13th: p.u next* 8/1
7m 30.3s (29.20) **Going Correction** +1.525s/f (Heav) 7 Ran SP% 111.4
Speed ratings (Par 107): **107,106,95,** ,
CSF £26.82 TOTE £2.70: £1.60, £5.40; EX 34.30 Trifecta £105.50.
Owner Prof Caroline Tisdall **Bred** Cte A Maggiar, A Maggiar & A Maggiar **Trained** Nicholashayne, Devon
FOCUS
Race distance increased by 168yds. Only three managed to complete in this fair staying handicap, with a few of the runners being beaten from quite some way out. The winner is on the upgrade over fences.

2956 JOHN AND MARYANNE BIRCH MEMORIAL H'CAP HURDLE (9 hdls) 2m 1f 145y
2:40 (2:40) (Class 4) (0-110,110) 3-Y-0+ £3,249 (£954; £477; £238)

Form RPR
P-56 1 **Superciliary**[36] 2244 6-11-10 **108**....................(t) MarcGoldstein 118+
(Chris Gordon) *hld up: hdwy 6th: chalng on bit whn mstke 2 out: sn led: pushed clr: comf* 25/1
PU-0 2 10 **Right Step**[15] 2688 8-11-3 **108**....................(t) PaddyBradley(7) 107
(Pat Phelan) *disp ld: clr ldr appr 6th: rdn and hdd after 2 out: sn hld: kpt on same pce* 4/1[3]
241/ 3 3/4 **Tickity Bleue**[707] 3438 7-11-10 **108**.................... WayneHutchinson 106
(Alan King) *hld up: hdwy 6th: rdn after 3 out: wnt 3rd bef last: styd on same pce* 2/1[1]
-242 4 5 **Oscar Prairie (IRE)**[16] 2664 10-11-5 **110**.................... ConorWalsh(7) 102
(Warren Greatrex) *chsd ldrs: rdn in last pair after 5th: plenty to do 3 out: sme imp in 6th but no ch jumping last: fin wl* 3/1[2]
5U15 5 6 **Dainty Diva (IRE)**[41] 2139 7-11-10 **108**.................... NickScholfield 94
(Jeremy Scott) *in tch: trckd ldrs after 3rd: wnt 2nd 3 out tl rdn appr 2 out: nt pce to chal: wknd last* 7/1
5-00 6 2 **Kastani Beach (IRE)**[22] 2548 9-11-1 **104**.................... KevinJones(5) 88
(Seamus Mullins) *chsd ldrs: rdn along fr after 5th: wknd between last 2* 16/1
-060 7 43 **Mystery Drama**[12] 2734 5-11-4 **102**.................... AdamWedge 43
(Alexandra Dunn) *a in rr: wknd after 3 out: t.o* 20/1
0444 8 26 **Ashkoun (FR)**[142] 1054 4-11-4 **102**....................[1] TomCannon 17
(Tim Vaughan) *disp ld tl 6th: sn rdn: wknd after 3 out: t.o* 17/2
4m 56.0s (21.70) **Going Correction** +1.35s/f (Heav) 8 Ran SP% 115.9
Speed ratings (Par 105): **105,100,100,98,95 94,75,63**
CSF £124.96 CT £299.18 TOTE £23.30: £4.00, £1.80, £1.30; EX 178.90 Trifecta £1694.00.
Owner C Gordon **Bred** Prince Of Wales And Duchess Of Cornwall **Trained** Morestead, Hampshire
FOCUS
Race distance increased by 162yds. Modest handicap form with the complete outsider running out a good winner. This rates a pb.

2957 T I ENGINEERING NOVICES' LIMITED H'CAP CHASE (16 fncs) 2m 5f 31y
3:10 (3:11) (Class 4) (0-120,117) 4-Y-0+ £3,898 (£1,144; £572; £286)

Form RPR
3-0P 1 **Amidon (FR)**[21] 2558 5-11-8 **117**.................... LeightonAspell 122+
(Lucy Wadham) *j.rt thrght: disp ld: led 4 out tl narrowly hdd next: sn rdn: wnt rt and bmpd last: led run-in: drvn out* 4/1[3]
03 2 1 **Vic De Touzaine (FR)**[20] 2564 6-11-8 **117**.................... LiamTreadwell 120+
(Venetia Williams) *hld up: hdwy after 4 out: led appr last where mstke and bmpd: sn rdn and hdd: no ex towards fin* 7/2[2]
35/6 3 20 **Jack By The Hedge**[71] 1675 6-11-3 **112**.................... JamesBest 94
(Caroline Keevil) *disp ld most of way tl rdn after 4 out: led next: rdn and hdd appr last: wknd run-in* 7/1
F/4- 4 6 **Agincourt Reef (IRE)**[585] 66 6-11-3 **112**.................... JoshuaMoore 88
(Gary Moore) *hld up: pushed along in 4th after 11th: rdn and disputing cl enough 3rd whn nt fluent 3 out: wknd next* 5/1
104- P **Hold The Bucks (USA)**[288] 4407 9-10-7 **107**.......... FreddieMitchell(5)
(Sheena West) *chsd ldrs: struggling in last after 9th: wknd 4 out: t.o whn p.u bef next* 25/1
343/ F **The Mumper (IRE)**[612] 5176 8-10-7 **102**.................... WayneHutchinson
(Alan King) *trckd ldrs: pushed along and disputing cl enough 3rd whn fell heavily 3 out* 2/1[1]
6m 23.3s (40.30) **Going Correction** +1.525s/f (Heav) 6 Ran SP% 108.6
Speed ratings (Par 105): **84,83,76,73,**
CSF £17.25 TOTE £4.50: £2.70, £1.50; EX 16.30 Trifecta £73.30.
Owner P H Betts **Bred** E A R L Trinquet Et Al **Trained** Newmarket, Suffolk
FOCUS
Race distance increased by 132yds. They dawdled round for much of this modest chase in which two pulled clear in late. The form could be 5lb+ out either way.

2958 ROA/RACING POST H'CAP HURDLE (10 hdls) 2m 3f 33y
3:40 (3:40) (Class 5) (0-100,100) 3-Y-0+ £2,339 (£686; £343; £171)

Form RPR
5303 1 **Thepartysover**[19] 2599 10-11-8 **96**....................(t) TomO'Brien 110+
(Paul Henderson) *trckd ldrs: led appr 2 out: clr last: styd on strly* 4/1[3]
P221 2 16 **Lady From Geneva**[23] 2521 8-11-6 **94**....................(t) BrendanPowell 95
(Brendan Powell) *led: rdn whn hdd appr 2 out: sn hld by wnr but clr of remainder: nt fluent last: tiring and only jst hld on for 2nd* 7/2[2]
50-P 3 hd **Asker (IRE)**[6] 2520 7-9-10 **77** ow3....................(p) WilliamFeatherstone(7) 75
(Zoe Davison) *in last pair: struggling and detached after 7th: no ch in 6th jumping 2 out: styd on strly fr last: nrly snatched 2nd fnl stride* 10/1
6P-0 4 3 **Loves Destination**[36] 2252 4-10-12 **86**.................... TomCannon 82
(Chris Gordon) *trckd ldrs: wnt rt at times: rdn after 3 out: one pce fr next* 16/1
1352 5 2 3/4 **Shalianzi (IRE)**[13] 2713 5-11-9 **97**....................(b) JamieMoore 90
(Gary Moore) *trckd ldrs: rdn after 3 out: one pce fr next* 3/1[1]
0-02 6 2 1/2 **Uranox (FR)**[36] 2256 7-10-0 **74** oh1.................... DavidEngland 64
(Michael Roberts) *in last pair: struggling bef 3 out: nvr gng pce to get on terms* 5/1
25/0 7 24 **Diamond Life**[36] 2253 9-11-12 **100**....................(p) DenisO'Regan 66
(Mark Pitman) *trckd ldr: hit 5th: u.p whn forced wd on home bnd: wknd bef 2 out* 13/2
5m 30.7s (31.30) **Going Correction** +1.35s/f (Heav)
WFA 4 from 5yo+ 5lb 7 Ran SP% 112.2
Speed ratings (Par 103): **88,81,81,79,78 77,67**
CSF £17.94 TOTE £4.20: £2.00, £1.80; EX 15.70 Trifecta £155.30.
Owner R J Galpin **Bred** Simon P Martin **Trained** Whitsbury, Hants
FOCUS
Race distance increased by 162yds. This had looked quite a competitive little handicap, but the winner had other ideas. He's rated in line with the best of his 2014 hurdles runs.
T/Plt: £92.90 to a £1 stake. Pool: £63,901.76 - 501.71 winning units. T/Qpdt: £16.80 to a £1 stake. Pool: £5,638.75 - 247.75 winning units. **Tim Mitchell**

2665 UTTOXETER (L-H)
Tuesday, December 8

OFFICIAL GOING: Soft (heavy in places) changing to heavy after race 1 (12.20)
Wind: moderate 1/2 against Weather: changeable, heavy shower race 5

2959 TBA MARES' MAIDEN HURDLE (9 hdls) 1m 7f 168y
12:20 (12:21) (Class 5) 3-Y-0+ £2,859 (£839; £419; £209)

Form RPR
2 1 **Tara Flow**[16] 2665 5-11-4 0.................... AidanColeman 115+
(Venetia Williams) *trckd ldrs: 2nd 3rd: led after 5th: hit 3 out: wnt clr after 2 out: v easily* 1/6[1]
60 2 13 **Jester Jet**[26] 2452 5-11-4 0.................... LeeEdwards 93
(Tony Carroll) *hld up in last: effrt appr 3 out: 3rd 2 out: lft 2nd last: no ch w wnr* 40/1
3 1 3/4 **Deja Bougg**[475] 4-11-4 0.................... MarkQuinlan 92
(Neil Mulholland) *t.k.h: nt fluent: trckd ldrs: clr 2nd appr 2 out: stmbld on landing last: sn wknd* 25/1
5F 4 12 **Noble Reach**[11] 2752 4-11-4 0....................(p) BrianHughes 79
(Lawrence Mullaney) *led: hdd after 5th: wknd and hit 2 out* 9/2[2]
30 5 7 **La Pyle (FR)**[15] 2689 4-10-11 0.................... ThomasCheesman(7) 71
(Philip Hobbs) *chsd ldrs: lost pl and nt fluent 2 out* 14/1[3]
4m 19.9s (22.50) **Going Correction** +1.25s/f (Heav)
WFA 4 from 5yo 5lb 5 Ran SP% 116.8
Speed ratings (Par 103): **93,86,85,79,76**
CSF £10.46 TOTE £1.10: £1.10, £10.60; EX 14.60 Trifecta £93.70.
Owner Kate & Andrew Brooks **Bred** Miss A Gibson Fleming **Trained** Kings Caple, H'fords
FOCUS
Some starts have been moved at this track following remeasuring, so some races will not have speed figures until there is sufficient data to calculate updated median times. Hurdles moved off inside rail by 4-5 yards. Divided Bends moved on to fresher ground. The rail on the hurdle course was moved out 3 yards on the winning post bend and 4 yards on the far bend, adding approx 21 yards to races 1, 3 & 7 and approx. 30 yards to races 4 and 6. Chase distances were standard.
The easy winner is sure to rate higher.

2960 DOUGLAS FAMILY NOVICES' CHASE (18 fncs) 3m 2y
12:50 (12:50) (Class 4) 4-Y-0+ £4,088 (£1,234; £635; £336)

Form RPR
0-02 1 **Aubusson (FR)**[31] 2361 6-10-10 0.................... LizzieKelly(5) 145+
(Nick Williams) *trckd ldrs: 2nd 10th: led and blnd next: wnt 10 l clr last: heavily eased* 4/5[1]
2 2 4 1/2 **Dig Deeper**[24] 2495 6-11-1 0.................... AndrewThornton 132+
(Caroline Bailey) *sn chsng ldrs: 2nd 3rd: hit 8th: led briefly 10th: drvn bef 4 out: chsd wnr 3 out: no imp* 33/1
11-3 3 2 3/4 **Beg To Differ (IRE)**[38] 2197 5-11-1 0.................... RichardJohnson 127
(Jonjo O'Neill) *led to 2nd: chsd ldrs: 3rd bef 4 out: one pce fr next* 15/2[3]
31-3 4 10 **Milansbar (IRE)**[13] 2717 8-11-1 0.................... TrevorWhelan 124
(Neil King) *led 2nd: drvn 9th: hdd next: sn drvn and outpcd: rallied 4 out: wknd and hit last* 2/1[2]
3-P4 P **Rolling Maul (IRE)**[16] 2660 7-11-1 129....................(v) SeanBowen
(Peter Bowen) *mstkes in last: drvn 5th: lost tch and blnd 11th: t.o 13th: p.u bef 4 out* 28/1
6m 45.7s (37.60) **Going Correction** +1.30s/f (Heav) 5 Ran SP% 107.0
Speed ratings (Par 105): **89,87,86,83,**
CSF £16.56 TOTE £1.60: £1.10, £3.60; EX 22.20 Trifecta £63.90.
Owner Mrs Jane Williams **Bred** Serge Dubois **Trained** George Nympton, Devon
FOCUS
Race distance as advertised. A good-quality little novice chase which took some getting. The easy winner was a 155 hurdler and can match that over fences.

2961 SIS H'CAP HURDLE (9 hdls) 1m 7f 168y
1:20 (1:21) (Class 4) (0-120,120) 3-Y-0+ £3,508 (£1,030; £515; £257)

Form RPR
-660 1 **For Good Measure (IRE)**[15] 2683 4-11-5 **113**.......... RichardJohnson 130+
(Philip Hobbs) *hld up in mid-div: hdwy and 3rd bef 3 out: led sn after 2 out: wnt clr: easily* 5/1[3]
-624 2 8 **Akula (IRE)**[22] 2540 8-10-9 **106**.................... HarryChalloner(3) 108
(Barry Leavy) *led: mstke 3 out: hdd sn after 2 out: kpt on: no ch w wnr* 7/1
500 3 4 1/2 **Beau Bay (FR)**[44] 2087 4-10-13 **107**....................(t) RhysFlint 102
(Alan Jones) *in rr: drvn 6th: styd on fr 3 out: tk modest 3rd appr last* 18/1
-333 4 6 **Verano (GER)**[22] 2548 6-11-12 **120**....................(t) HarrySkelton 110
(Dan Skelton) *trckd ldr: upsides appr 3 out: sn rdn edgd rt between last 2: sn wknd* 5/2[1]
5-P2 5 1/2 **Itshard To No (IRE)**[27] 2437 6-11-4 **117**....................(t) DavidNoonan(5) 105
(Kerry Lee) *mid-div: drvn and outpcd bef 3 out: hdwy and modest 3rd bef 2 out: wknd appr last* 5/1[3]

31-0 **6** *2* **Beau Lake (IRE)**[17] 2637 11-11-5 **118**........................ HarryBannister(5) 106
(Suzy Smith) *chsd ldrs: drvn and outpcd bef 3 out: wknd appr 2 out: hit last* **11/1**

3-33 **7** *1 3/4* **Moidore**[22] 2540 6-11-7 **115**........................ AdamPogson 101
(Charles Pogson) *chsd ldrs: drvn and outpcd after 6th: wknd appr 2 out* **7/2**[2]

13- **8** *33* **Vedani (IRE)**[492] 649 6-10-11 **105**........................ LeeEdwards 56
(Tony Carroll) *a last: j. slowly 5th: sn bhd: t.o 3 out* **40/1**

4m 14.4s (17.00) **Going Correction** +1.25s/f (Heav)
WFA 4 from 6yo+ 5lb **8 Ran SP% 112.7**
Speed ratings (Par 105): **107,103,100,97,97 96,95,79**
CSF £38.08 CT £574.61 TOTE £5.20: £1.80, £2.70, £6.00; EX 46.50 Trifecta £894.50.
Owner John P McManus **Bred** Sunnyhill Stud **Trained** Withycombe, Somerset

FOCUS
Race disstance increased by about 21yds. A modest handicap, run at a fair gallop. A big step up from the winner on his handicap debut.

2962 DOUGLAS FAMILY H'CAP HURDLE (10 hdls) 2m 3f 207y
1:50 (1:50) (Class 4) (0-120,119) 3-Y-O+ **£3,508** (£1,030; £515; £257)

Form RPR

65-1 **1** **Baywing (IRE)**[29] 2396 6-10-11 **104**........................ BrianHarding 123+
(Nicky Richards) *trckd ldrs: 3rd 7th: 2nd bef 2 out: led between last 2: pushed clr run-in: v readily* **7/4**[1]

F-53 **2** *10* **Touch Back (IRE)**[29] 2405 9-11-11 **118**........................ HarrySkelton 128+
(Chris Bealby) *hld up in mid-div: hdwy 6th: 4th bef 3 out: led bef 2 out: hdd between last 2: no ch w wnr* **7/1**

2-P1 **3** *8* **Ministerofinterior**[5] 2858 10-10-8 **106**........................(b) CiaranGethings(5) 103
(Barry Leavy) *mid-div: hdwy 7th: one pce fr next: modest 3rd last* **9/2**[3]

16-0 **4** *1/2* **Hainan (FR)**[24] 2499 4-11-8 **115**........................ DannyCook 112
(Sue Smith) *chsd ldr: upside 7th: sn drvn: led next: hdd bef 2 out: one pce* **15/2**

1P-3 **5** *13* **Its A Long Road**[16] 2664 7-10-11 **107**........................ KieronEdgar(3) 91
(Tim Dennis) *j.rt: mid-div: drvn and lost pl 5th: bhd fr 3 out* **7/2**[2]

302- **6** *16* **Wake Your Dreams (IRE)**[501] 1082 7-11-12 **119**........................ PeterCarberry 86
(Jennie Candlish) *in rr: hdwy 7th: chsng ldrs appr next: sn wknd* **28/1**

262- **P** **Pret A Thou (FR)**[255] 5034 12-10-8 **104**........................ HarryChalloner(3)
(John Groucott) *led: hdd 3 out: lost pl bef 2 out: wl bhd whn p.u bef last* **20/1**

336U **P** **Medieval Bishop (IRE)**[24] 2490 6-10-8 **108**........................(p) JoshWall(7)
(Tony Forbes) *chsd ldrs: drvn 7th: lost pl bef next: bhd whn p.u bef 2 out* **80/1**

5m 25.0s (21.80) **Going Correction** +1.25s/f (Heav)
WFA 4 from 6yo+ 6lb **8 Ran SP% 110.5**
Speed ratings (Par 105): **106,102,98,98,93 87, ,**
CSF £13.26 CT £43.44 TOTE £2.30: £1.10, £2.80, £1.60; EX 11.30 Trifecta £41.10.
Owner David & Nicky Robinson **Bred** Hugh Suffern Bloodstock **Trained** Greystoke, Cumbria

FOCUS
Race disstance increased by about 30yds. Not a bad handicap for the class and the first pair dominated the finish. Another step forward from the easy winner.

2963 DOUGLAS FAMILY NOVICES' LIMITED H'CAP CHASE (15 fncs) 2m 4f
2:20 (2:20) (Class 3) (0-135,132) 4-Y-O+
£6,256 (£1,848; £924; £462; £231; £116)

Form RPR

U3-1 **1** **April Dusk (IRE)**[24] 2488 6-11-1 125........................ GavinSheehan 138+
(Warren Greatrex) *hld up in mid-div: hdwy 11th: effrt bef next: handy 2nd appr 2 out: upsides last: rdr dropped whip: pushed along to ld nr fin* **2/1**[1]

-151 **2** *1/2* **Friendly Royal (IRE)**[16] 2668 6-10-7 117........................ DannyCook 128
(Sue Smith) *w ldrs: led 8th: drvn next: jnd and hung lft last: hdd and no ex nr fin* **9/2**[3]

-220 **3** *28* **Abracadabra Sivola (FR)**[10] 2780 5-11-4 128........ SamTwiston-Davies 113
(Nick Williams) *w ldr: wknd appr 2 out: mstke last* **9/4**[2]

01-3 **4** *9* **Anteros (IRE)**[28] 2415 7-11-8 132........................(t) AidanColeman 108
(Sophie Leech) *in rr: sme hdwy appr 4 out: modest 4th 2 out: nvr on terms* **17/2**

-01P **5** *13* **Milan Bound (IRE)**[24] 2484 7-11-7 131........................(t) RichardJohnson 92
(Jonjo O'Neill) *nt fluent in rr: outpcd and bhd 11th: distant 5th appr last* **11/1**

14-0 **6** *27* **Grove Silver (IRE)**[12] 2727 6-11-1 125........................ PeterCarberry 59
(Jennie Candlish) *chsd ldrs: lost pl and blnd 3 out: sn bhd: t.o last: eased* **16/1**

5P2- **7** *12* **Lewis**[240] 5290 6-10-10 120........................ JamesDavies 42
(Tom Symonds) *chsd ldrs: lost pl bef 3 out: sn bhd: t.o last: eased* **14/1**

5m 31.3s (21.50) **Going Correction** +1.30s/f (Heav) **7 Ran SP% 113.7**
Speed ratings (Par 107): **109,108,97,94,88 78,73**
CSF £11.64 TOTE £2.80: £1.80, £2.70; EX 13.50 Trifecta £31.20.
Owner Raymond Tooth **Bred** Paddy O'Leary **Trained** Upper Lambourn, Berks

FOCUS
Race distance as advertised. A fair novice handicap and another race where two pulled clear.

2964 SIS NOVICES' H'CAP HURDLE (10 hdls) 2m 3f 207y
2:50 (2:50) (Class 5) (0-100,99) 3-Y-O+ **£2,599** (£763; £381; £190)

Form RPR

P06- **1** **Transient Bay (IRE)**[271] 4726 5-9-11 **73** oh2........................(p) AdamNicol(3) 91+
(Philip Kirby) *w ldr: led after 3rd: hrd drvn and styd on run-in* **5/2**[2]

50-6 **2** *2 1/4* **Dandy Duke (IRE)**[21] 2559 4-11-9 **96**........................ PaddyBrennan 108
(Tom George) *chsd ldrs: nt fluent 7th: sn drvn and outpcd: chsd wnr bef 2 out: 1 l down last: kpt on same pce* **9/1**

6-0U **3** *24* **When In Roam (IRE)**[192] 552 6-11-0 **87**........................ DaveCrosse 75
(John O'Shea) *in rr: drvn to chse ldrs 7th: modest 3rd between last 2* **40/1**

44-2 **4** *10* **Global Dream**[17] 2649 5-11-8 **95**........................ HarrySkelton 73
(Caroline Bailey) *led tl after 3rd: chsd wnr: drvn 3 out: wknd between last 2* **13/8**[1]

2506 **P** **Rose Red**[54] 1931 8-10-2 **82**........................ CharlieHammond(7)
(Rob Summers) *in rr: hdwy to chse ldrs 7th: 3rd whn blnd 3 out: sn wknd: t.o 5th whn p.u bef last* **16/1**

3/6- **P** **Gorey Lane (IRE)**[416] 1958 9-11-3 **93**........................(v) ColmMcCormack(3)
(John Norton) *chsd ldrs: reminders and lost pl 6th: sn bhd: t.o 3 out: p.u bef last* **25/1**

4-45 **P** **Perfect Poison (IRE)**[11] 2745 7-11-2 **99**........................ RonanShort(10)
(Donald McCain) *chsd ldrs: drvn 7th: lost pl bef next: sn bhd: t.o whn p.u bef last* **9/2**[3]

5-5F **P** **Whiskey John**[20] 2567 5-11-8 **95**........................ RobertDunne
(Laura Young) *chsd ldrs: drvn and lost pl 3 out: distant 6th whn blnd next: t.o whn p.u bef last* **16/1**

5m 29.9s (26.70) **Going Correction** +1.25s/f (Heav) **8 Ran SP% 112.9**
Speed ratings (Par 103): **96,95,85,81, , ,**
CSF £24.23 CT £703.86 TOTE £3.80: £2.10, £2.00, £8.80; EX 22.80 Trifecta £612.10.
Owner The Waking Ned Partnership **Bred** Kenneth Parkhill **Trained** East Appleton, N Yorks
■ Stewards' Enquiry : Adam Nicol two-day ban: used whip in incorrect place (Dec 22,28)

FOCUS
Race disstance increased by about 30yds. A weak handicap, but the form looks fair with two finishing a long way clear. They recorded big hurdles bests.

2965 PIRELLI BLUE SHIFT STANDARD OPEN NATIONAL HUNT FLAT RACE 1m 7f 168y
3:20 (3:20) (Class 6) 4-6-Y-O **£1,559** (£457; £228; £114)

Form RPR

1 **Utility (GER)** 4-11-0 0........................ RichardJohnson 121+
(Jonjo O'Neill) *trckd ldrs: 2nd over 3f out: led over 2f out: pushed clr over 1f out: v readily* **1/1**[1]

2 *11* **Boatswain (IRE)** 4-11-0 0........................ JakeGreenall 106
(Henry Daly) *t.k.h in rr: hdwy after 6f: pushed along 6f out: sn chsng ldrs: 3rd over 3f out: kpt on to take 2nd last 150yds: no ch w wnr* **10/1**

30 **3** *4 1/2* **You Say What (IRE)**[30] 2375 5-11-0 0........................ TrevorWhelan 102
(Neil King) *led: hdd over 2f out: wknd fnl f* **6/1**[3]

5 **4** *9* **Beggar's Wishes (IRE)**[74] 1645 4-11-0 0........................ SeanBowen 93
(Peter Bowen) *in rr: drvn 7f out: modest 4th over 3f out: wknd over 1f out* **25/1**

52- **5** *13* **Road To Rome (IRE)**[234] 5402 5-10-11 0........................[1] ThomasGarner(3) 80
(William Kinsey) *sn chsng ldrs: drvn over 4f out: lost pl over 2f out* **14/1**

6 *66* **Big Bad Dude (IRE)**[584] 6-11-0 0........................ PaddyBrennan 14
(Tom George) *t.k.h: sn trcking ldrs: 2nd after 3f: drvn 4f out: sn lost pl: bhd whn eased over 2f out: eventually fin: tailed rt off* **5/2**[2]

0- **7** *2 1/4* **Right Royals Day**[255] 5028 6-10-7 0........................ PeterCarberry 4
(John Needham) *hld up in rr: lost pl over 3f out: sn bhd: eventually completed: tailed rt off* **100/1**

4m 10.4s (18.60) **Going Correction** +1.25s/f (Heav) **7 Ran SP% 113.5**
Speed ratings: **103,97,95,90,84 51,50**
CSF £12.47 TOTE £1.70: £1.20, £3.80; EX 9.70 Trifecta £50.60.
Owner Mrs John Magnier, D Smith & M Tabor **Bred** Gestut Rottgen **Trained** Cheltenham, Gloucs

FOCUS
Race disstance increased by about 21yds. They went an average gallop in this interesting bumper. The winner looks a smart prospect.
T/Plt: £64.50 to a £1 stake. Pool: £54,806.18 - 737.17 winning units. T/Qpdt: £55.30 to a £1 stake. Pool: £5,218.05 - 300.35 winning units. **Walter Glynn**

2474 HEXHAM (L-H)
Wednesday, December 9
2966 Meeting Abandoned - Waterlogged

2857 LEICESTER (R-H)
Wednesday, December 9

OFFICIAL GOING: Hurdle course - heavy (soft in places; 5.2); chase course - good to soft (good in places; 7.0) changing to good to soft (soft in places) after race 2 (1.35)
Wind: Light; half-behind Weather: Fine

2972 RACING EXCELLENCE CONDITIONAL JOCKEYS' TRAINING SERIES NOVICES' HURDLE (10 hdls) 2m 4f 110y
1:05 (1:07) (Class 4) 4-Y-O+ **£3,249** (£954; £477; £238)

Form RPR

1 **Handsome Sam**[192] 4-10-9 0........................ WilliamFeatherstone(3) 110+
(Alan King) *hld up: hdwy 4th: rdn to ld appr 2 out: hit last: styd on* **9/1**[3]

45 **2** *1 1/4* **Petite Power (IRE)**[186] 644 6-10-9 0........................ ConorWalsh(3) 108
(Ali Stronge) *chsd ldrs: stmbld 6th: rdn appr 3 out: ev ch next: styd on same pce flat* **33/1**

2-21 **3** *6* **Abbreviate (GER)**[30] 2407 4-11-2 130........................ MrMartinMcIntyre(3) 112
(Kim Bailey) *plld hrd: led after 1st: hdd after 3rd: led again after 5th: rdn and hdd appr 2 out: styng on same pce whn hmpd last* **4/11**[1]

61-0 **4** *21* **Chic Theatre (IRE)**[46] 2065 5-10-12 0........................ DavidNoonan 80
(David Pipe) *hld up: hdwy appr 5th: rdn after 3 out: wknd bef last* **7/2**[2]

F0- **P** **Ellusivance (IRE)**[205] 2553 5-10-12 0........................ PaulNO'Brien
(Nick Kent) *got loose on the way to post: chsd ldr after 1st: led after 3rd: hdd after 5th: mstke and wknd 7th: bhd whn p.u bef next* **250/1**

P **Dos'Ntsuitme (IRE)**[214] 6-10-9 0........................ LiamMcKenna(3)
(Tom Weston) *led tl after 1st: lost pl bef next: pushed along 4th: bhd fr next: p.u after 6th* **150/1**

0- **F** **Pine Warbler**[291] 4356 6-10-12 0........................ CiaranGethings 104
(Stuart Edmunds) *hdwy to chse ldrs 2nd: rdn and ev ch 2 out: cl 3rd but looking hld whn fell last* **66/1**

5m 26.2s (1.50) **Going Correction** 0.0s/f (Good) **7 Ran SP% 111.0**
Speed ratings (Par 105): **97,96,94,86, ,**
CSF £112.90 TOTE £8.30: £2.70, £9.40; EX 103.80 Trifecta £192.90.
Owner Andrew Gemmell & Ron Sullivan **Bred** Shade Oak Stud **Trained** Barbury Castle, Wilts

FOCUS
All races as advertised. They only got racing seriously from three out in this modest novice event for conditional riders, but it still proved a long way home from there on the testing surface. Not an easy race to put a figure on.

2973 YULETIDE NOVICES' LIMITED H'CAP CHASE (15 fncs) 2m 4f 45y
1:35 (1:35) (Class 4) (0-120,120) 4-Y-O+ **£6,498** (£1,908; £954; £477)

Form RPR

3-30 **1** **Bekkensfirth**[39] 2182 6-11-0 **112**........................ HarrySkelton 132+
(Dan Skelton) *a.p: led 8th: nt fluent 4 out: rdn clr flat* **12/1**

13P- **2** *13* **Lovely Job (IRE)**[249] 5142 5-11-4 **116**........................ PaddyBrennan 125
(Fergal O'Brien) *a.p: chsd wnr 10th: mstke next: ev ch fr 4 out tl rdn after 2 out: wknd flat* **8/1**

/3-P **3** *14* **Benenden (IRE)**[216] 177 7-11-4 **116**........................ TomScudamore 112
(Michael Scudamore) *hld up: hdwy 9th: rdn and wknd 2 out* **10/1**

3-44 **4** *2* **Under The Phone (IRE)**[27] 2449 6-10-10 **108**........................ CharliePoste 105
(Robin Dickin) *chsd ldr tl blnd 7th: rdn after 11th: wknd 4 out* **6/1**[2]

2-45 **5** *15* **Paddy The Deejay (IRE)**[35] 2266 6-11-5 **117**.................. JoshuaMoore 98
(Stuart Edmunds) *hld up: hdwy appr 6th: rdn 4 out: wknd bef 2 out* **7/2**[1]
225- **6** *1 ½* **Hindon Road (IRE)**[249] 5139 8-11-2 **114**.................. WayneHutchinson 96
(Alan King) *hld up: blnd 2nd hdwy 6th: rdn and wknd appr 3 out* **7/1**[3]
25P- **7** *3 ½* **Oliver's Hill (IRE)**[263] 4926 6-11-0 **112**..................(t) NickScholfield 88
(Lawney Hill) *led to 8th: remained handy tl rdn and wknd after 4 out* **33/1**
03-P **8** *hd* **Orangeaday**[24] 2513 8-11-8 **120**..................(t) DarylJacob 96
(Ben Case) *hld up: a in rr: wknd bef 4 out* **25/1**
22-P **P** **Its A Sting (IRE)**[41] 2151 6-11-8 **120**.................. LeightonAspell
(Oliver Sherwood) *prom: nt fluent 3rd: rdn and wknd appr 4 out: bhd whn p.u bef next* **9/1**
4550 **P** **She's Late**[20] 2593 5-10-13 **111**..................(p) SeanBowen
(Jonjo O'Neill) *hld up: bhd fr 8th: p.u bef 4 out* **66/1**
60-1 **P** **Chicoria (IRE)**[20] 2592 6-11-8 **120**.................. RichardJohnson
(Henry Daly) *chsd ldrs: lost pl 4th: in rr and pushed along after next: sn bhd: nt fluent 7th: p.u bef 4 out* **7/2**[1]

5m 11.3s (-7.60) **Going Correction** -0.075s/f (Good) **11** Ran SP% **117.4**
Speed ratings (Par 105): **112,106,101,100,94 93,92,92,** ,
CSF £102.37 CT £1005.51 TOTE £14.30: £1.80, £2.70, £3.90; EX 138.00 Trifecta £1048.70.
Owner Mrs Pam Scott **Bred** Mrs P Scott **Trained** Alcester, Warwicks

FOCUS
This novice handicap looked competitive. It fell apart from the home turn and the form needs treating with some caution, but the winner looks useful.

2974 MISTLETOE (S) HURDLE (8 hdls) 1m 7f 113y
2:05 (2:05) (Class 5) 4-7-Y-0 **£2,599** (£763; £381; £190)

Form RPR
1 **1** **Edward Elgar**[10] 2808 4-11-6 0.................. HarrySkelton 113
(Caroline Bailey) *hld up: hdwy 5th: sn led: rdn whn blnd 2 out: nt fluent last: edgd rt flat: styd on* **7/2**[2]
-520 **2** *4 ½* **Orthodox Lad**[13] 2734 7-10-9 110.................. CiaranGethings(5) 101
(Grace Harris) *a.p: ev ch 3 out: sn rdn: no ex flat* **6/4**[1]
3-60 **3** *8* **Daring Indian**[14] 864 7-11-0 90..................(p) JoshuaMoore 93
(Roger Teal) *hld up: hdwy 5th: rdn after 3 out: wknd last* **11/1**
0 **4** *55* **Mr Jalfrazy (IRE)**[7] 2850 6-11-0 0.................. AdamWedge 38
(Tom Weston) *chsd ldrs to 5th* **16/1**
-436 **P** **Announcement**[14] 1974 4-10-13 113.................. GavinSheehan
(Ronald Thompson) *led tl after 1st: chsd ldr to 5th: rdn and wknd after 3 out: bhd whn p.u bef next* **7/2**[2]
-653 **F** **Haatefina**[8] 2538 5-10-13 100..................(v) DaveCrosse
(Mark Usher) *s.i.s: rcvrd to ld after 1st: hit 5th: sn rdn and hdd: wkng whn fell 3 out* **15/2**[3]

4m 5.5s (4.50) **Going Correction** 0.0s/f (Good) **6** Ran SP% **110.4**
Speed ratings: **88,85,81,54,**
CSF £9.19 TOTE £3.30: £1.70, £1.70; EX 11.90 Trifecta £57.40.There was no bid for the winner.
Owner G T H Bailey **Bred** Hellwood Stud Farm & Paul Davies (h'Gate) **Trained** Holdenby, Northants

FOCUS
A very weak contest and it was a real slow-motion finish. The winner built on his recent C&D win.

2975 SIS H'CAP CHASE (18 fncs) 2m 6f 151y
2:35 (2:35) (Class 4) (0-120,120) 4-Y-0+ **£5,198** (£1,526; £763; £381)

Form RPR
13-P **1** **Valid Point (IRE)**[24] 2513 9-11-8 **116**..................(t) MarkGrant 130+
(Nigel Twiston-Davies) *a.p: rdn whn hung rt after 4 out: led next: drvn clr whn j.lft and nt fluent last: styd on wl* **8/1**
401F **2** *14* **Muckle Roe (IRE)**[41] 2149 6-11-7 **115**.................. SamTwiston-Davies 112
(Nigel Twiston-Davies) *hld up: hdwy and mstke 11th: rdn appr 3 out: styd on same pce: wnt 2nd flat* **7/1**[3]
-346 **3** *8* **Cloudy Bob (IRE)**[20] 2593 8-11-9 **117**.................. HarrySkelton 105
(Pat Murphy) *chsd ldrs: mstke 3rd: led 14th: hdd whn lft in ld again 4 out: rdn and hdd next: wknd appr last* **9/2**[1]
2322 **4** *3 ¼* **Shockingtimes (IRE)**[20] 2593 8-11-12 **120**..................(bt) BrendanPowell 107
(Jamie Snowden) *hld up: hdwy 6th: rdn after 14th: hmpd and wknd 4 out* **8/1**
6-56 **5** *10* **Gold Ingot**[40] 2168 8-11-9 **117**.................. AndrewThornton 92
(Caroline Bailey) *hld up: hdwy 11th: rdn and wknd 4 out* **14/1**
1300 **P** **Houndscourt (IRE)**[56] 1902 8-11-0 **108**.................. BrianHughes
(Joanne Foster) *prom to 10th: bhd whn p.u bef 4 out* **28/1**
32-3 **P** **Keltic Rhythm (IRE)**[210] 283 8-11-7 **115**.................. TrevorWhelan
(Neil King) *led to 12th: rdn appr 4 out: sn wknd: bhd whn p.u bef next* **6/1**[2]
4P2P **P** **Midnight Cataria**[34] 2288 6-11-0 **108**.................. WayneHutchinson
(Alan King) *hld up: nt fluent 6th: hdwy 11th: rdn and wknd 14th: bhd whn p.u bef next* **10/1**
-205 **U** **Trillerin Minella (IRE)**[32] 2346 7-10-10 **104**.................. KielanWoods
(Graeme McPherson) *prom: chsd ldr 7th: led 12th: hdd 14th: 4 l 3rd and rdn whn blnd and uns rdr 3 out* **20/1**
P **Didntitellya (IRE)**[672] 4095 6-11-12 **120**.................. DavidBass
(Kim Bailey) *chsd ldrs: j.rt 2nd: lost pl after 8th: bhd fr 9th: p.u bef 14th* **8/1**
P124 **F** **Road To Freedom**[16] 2686 6-11-7 **115**.................. LeightonAspell
(Lucy Wadham) *hld up: hdwy 13th: led and fell 4 out* **7/1**[3]

5m 57.7s (-6.30) **Going Correction** -0.075s/f (Good) **11** Ran SP% **114.8**
Speed ratings (Par 105): **107,102,99,98,94** , , , ,
CSF £62.13 CT £283.79 TOTE £9.10: £2.80, £2.60, £2.10; EX 47.20 Trifecta £531.30.
Owner W E Sturt **Bred** Pier House Stud **Trained** Naunton, Gloucs

FOCUS
This was wide open. It was run at a sound gallop and saw drama in the home straight. The second is probably the best guide.

2976 IVY NOVICES' H'CAP CHASE (12 fncs) 1m 7f 201y
3:05 (3:05) (Class 4) (0-105,105) 4-Y-0+ **£5,198** (£1,526; £763; £381)

Form RPR
-0F1 **1** **Truckers Highway (IRE)**[7] 2851 6-10-11 **93** 7ex.......... HarryChalloner(3) 110+
(John Groucott) *mde all: j.lft at times: pushed clr appr last: eased towards fin* **3/1**[1]
2 *6* **Thoonavolla (IRE)**[198] 7-10-13 **92**.................. AdamWedge 98+
(Tom Weston) *hld up: hdwy 8th: chsd wnr 2 out: no ex last* **6/1**[2]
0P64 **3** *1* **Theflyingportrait (IRE)**[15] 2707 6-11-5 **98**..................(t) HenryBrooke 104
(Jennie Candlish) *hld up: hdwy 8th: rdn after 3 out: styd on same pce appr last* **10/1**
15-4 **4** *7* **Grand March**[34] 2300 6-11-12 **105**..................(p) DavidBass 107
(Kim Bailey) *chsd ldrs: hit 5th: hmpd 7th: rdn appr 3 out: wknd next* **6/1**[2]
P210 **5** *2* **Stormbay Bomber (IRE)**[48] 2043 6-11-10 **103**.......... RichieMcLernon 100
(George Moore) *chsd wnr to 8th: rdn appr 4 out: wknd 2 out* **8/1**[3]

2131 **6** *3 ¼* **Larkhall**[23] 2542 8-10-0 **79** oh2.................. BrianHughes 73
(Mike Sowersby) *mid-div: hdwy 6th: chsd wnr 8th tl rdn appr 2 out: wknd appr last* **9/1**
31-P **7** *2 ¾* **It's Oscar (IRE)**[16] 2692 8-10-6 **85**..................(p) MarkQuinlan 77
(James Evans) *mid-div: hdwy 7th: rdn and wknd 2 out* **12/1**
00-4 **8** *6* **Big Night Out**[171] 813 9-11-2 **95**..................(t) DenisO'Regan 81
(Laura Hurley) *hld up: a towards rr: wknd 4 out* **40/1**
4102 **9** *13* **Youm Jamil (USA)**[22] 2552 8-9-9 **79** oh1..................(t) NickSlatter(5) 54
(Tony Carroll) *hld up: mstke 2nd: a towards rr: wknd 4 out* **16/1**
054P **10** *5* **School For Scandal (IRE)**[15] 2698 7-10-1 **87**.......... PaulO'Brien(7) 57
(Jimmy Frost) *hld up: mstke 5th: reminder after next: rdn and wknd appr 4 out* **66/1**
3P-P **11** *12* **Four Shuck Men (IRE)**[15] 2698 7-9-7 **79**..........(p) CharlieHammond(7) 38
(Sarah-Jayne Davies) *prom: hung lft after 5th: j.lft next and 7th: rdn and wknd after 4 out* **14/1**
22/0 **U** **Instinctual**[16] 2694 5-11-12 **105**..................(bt) AidanColeman
(Charlie Longsdon) *chsd ldrs: lost pl after 2nd: bhd and rdn next: uns rdr 4th* **12/1**

4m 5.5s (-2.70) **Going Correction** -0.075s/f (Good) **12** Ran SP% **115.6**
Speed ratings (Par 105): **103,100,99,96,95 93,92,89,82,80 74,**
CSF £21.46 CT £159.31 TOTE £3.80: £1.50, £2.10, £4.20; EX 22.60 Trifecta £113.30.
Owner C J Tipton **Bred** David Pim **Trained** Bourton, Shropshire

FOCUS
A moderate handicap. The winner was well in but this rates another step up.

2977 ADVENT H'CAP HURDLE (10 hdls) 2m 4f 110y
3:35 (3:35) (Class 3) (0-130,130) 3-Y-0 **£6,330** (£1,870; £935; £468; £234)

Form RPR
-U00 **1** **Goodbye Dancer (FR)**[24] 2513 4-11-4 **122**.......... SamTwiston-Davies 132+
(Nigel Twiston-Davies) *hld up: hdwy 3 out: led after next: easily* **8/1**
1-51 **2** *5* **Milord (GER)**[34] 2301 6-11-7 **125**..................(p) DavidBass 125
(Kim Bailey) *chsd ldr tl led after 3 out: rdn and hdd after next: styd on same pce last* **9/1**
21-6 **3** *11* **Hedley Lamarr (IRE)**[25] 2485 5-11-10 **128**.................. RichardJohnson 115
(Jonjo O'Neill) *hld up: hdwy appr 3 out: rdn and hung rt bef next: wknd appr last* **2/1**[1]
20-1 **4** *¾* **Thatchers Gold (IRE)**[25] 2490 7-10-7 **111**.................. DenisO'Regan 98
(Henry Oliver) *chsd ldrs: rdn after 3 out: wknd bef next* **5/1**[3]
1P3- **5** *hd* **Salmanazar**[247] 5199 7-11-12 **130**.................. WayneHutchinson 116
(Alan King) *hld up: rdn and wknd after 3 out* **10/1**
0-04 **6** *9* **Discay**[37] 2247 6-11-5 **123**..................(tp) WillKennedy 100
(Dr Richard Newland) *hld up: plld hrd: rdn after 3 out: hit next: sn wknd blnd last* **14/1**
P/P- **P** **Native Gallery (IRE)**[241] 5290 10-11-9 **127**.................. DarylJacob
(Ben De Haan) *hld up: hdwy 4th: wknd 7th: bhd whn p.u bef next* **16/1**
04-2 **P** **Space Walker (IRE)**[21] 2577 4-11-2 **120**.................. NicodeBoinville
(Ben Pauling) *led: rdn and hdd after 3 out: sn wknd: bhd whn p.u bef last* **4/1**[2]

5m 25.2s (0.50) **Going Correction** 0.0s/f (Good)
WFA 4 from 5yo+ 6lb **8** Ran SP% **112.8**
Speed ratings (Par 107): **99,97,92,92,92 89,** ,
CSF £72.57 CT £197.71 TOTE £10.00: £3.10, £1.10, £1.40; EX 72.10 Trifecta £179.50.
Owner The Yes No Wait Sorries **Bred** Christophe Pourteau & Claire Neveux **Trained** Naunton, Gloucs

FOCUS
They went steadily in this modest handicap and few handled the heavy surface. A step up from the winner.
T/Jkpt: Not won. JACKPOT PLACEPOT: £109.30. Pool: £2,832.37 - 18.90 winning units. T/Plt: £614.40 to a £1 stake. Pool: £75,515.17 - 89.71 winning units T/Qpdt: £8.60 to a £1 stake. Pool: £10,844.26 - 930.40 winning units **Colin Roberts**

2785 NEWCASTLE (L-H)
Thursday, December 10

OFFICIAL GOING: Heavy (soft in places; 5.2)
Wind: Fresh, half against Weather: Fine, dry

2978 MONEY BACK SPECIAL AT 188BET NOVICES' HURDLE (12 hdls 1 omitted) 2m 6f
12:20 (12:23) (Class 4) 4-Y-0+ **£3,249** (£954; £477; £238)

Form RPR
36- **1** **Mahler And Me (IRE)**[280] 4582 5-10-12 0.................. HenryBrooke 112+
(Alistair Whillans) *trckd ldrs: shkn up bef 3 out: rallied and led last: styd on wl* **33/1**
0-01 **2** *2 ¼* **Another Mattie (IRE)**[29] 2429 8-11-5 115..................(t) LucyAlexander 118
(N W Alexander) *led at stdy pce to 3rd: pressed ldr: rdn: hung lft and led 3 out: hdd last: kpt on same pce run-in* **15/8**[2]
3 *¾* **Cracked Rear View (IRE)**[568] 412 5-10-12 0.................. BrianHarding 109
(Kim Bailey) *nt fluent on occasions: cl up: led and maintained stdy pce fr 3rd: hit 8th: hdd 3 out: sn rdn: styd upsides tl kpt on same pce fr last* **4/7**[1]
004F **4** *18* **Warksburn Boy**[11] 2802 5-10-7 92.................. JamieHamilton(5) 94
(Sheena Walton) *prom: pushed along and outpcd bef 4 out: no imp fr next* **28/1**[3]

6m 11.9s (35.90) **Going Correction** +0.30s/f (Yiel) **4** Ran SP% **104.8**
Speed ratings (Par 105): **46,45,44,38**
CSF £86.58 TOTE £10.60; EX 29.20 Trifecta £51.50.
Owner Paul & Clare Rooney **Bred** E O'Connell **Trained** Newmill-On-Slitrig, Borders

FOCUS
All bends moved out 3yds. Race 1 increased by 35yds, races 2, 4, 5 & 7 increased by 20yds and races 3 & 6 by 30yds. After 25mm overnight rain conditions were testing. The flight going away from the stands was omitted due to the low sun. A very steadily run novices' hurdle and an upset, but it looked no fluke. A step up from the winner on his modest bumper runs.

2979 PLAY CASINO AT 188BET H'CAP CHASE (10 fncs 3 omitted) 2m 75y
12:50 (12:50) (Class 4) (0-120,120) 4-Y-0+ **£3,768** (£1,106; £553; £276)

Form RPR
5-24 **1** **Nautical Twilight**[30] 2424 5-11-0 **108**..................(b) BrianHughes 119+
(Malcolm Jefferson) *trckd ldrs: effrt whn hit 2 out (usual 3 out): led passing omitted last: pushed out* **3/1**[2]
5-35 **2** *2* **Pamak D'Airy (FR)**[12] 2788 12-10-7 **104**..................(p) TonyKelly(3) 110
(Henry Hogarth) *t.k.h: chsd ldr: led 2 out (usual 3 out): rdn and hdd passing omitted last: kpt on same pce* **8/1**

The Form Book Jumps 2015-16, Raceform Ltd, Newbury, RG14 5SJ

40-P **3** 2 3/4 **Trust Thomas**[27] 2477 7-11-2 **115** .... JamieHamilton(5) 118
(Ann Hamilton) *prom: pushed along and outpcd 2 out (usual 3 out): rallied bef omitted last: kpt on: nt rch first two* **11/4[1]**

5300 **4** 4 1/2 **Gin Cobbler**[13] 2755 9-10-0 **101** .... ThomasDowson(7) 101
(Victor Thompson) *t.k.h: led: rdn and hdd 2 out (usual 3 out): ev ch last: sn rdn and outpcd* **22/1**

-532 **5** 2 3/4 **Ballycool (IRE)**[45] 2104 8-10-13 **110** ....(t) DerekFox(3) 108
(Lucinda Russell) *nt fluent on occasions: hld up in tch: pushed along and outpcd 3 (usual 4 out): no imp fr next* **11/4[1]**

32-P **6** 1 1/2 **Ubaltique (FR)**[18] 2659 7-11-12 **120** ....(b) BrianHarding 117
(Donald McCain) *hld up in last pl: nt fluent 4th: rdn whn nt fluent 3 out (usual 4 out): edgd lft and struggling fr next: n.d after* **5/1[3]**

4m 21.5s (0.40) **Going Correction** +0.10s/f (Yiel) **6 Ran SP% 110.5**
Speed ratings (Par 105): **103,102,100,98,97 96**
CSF £23.96 TOTE £4.10: £2.20, £4.20; EX 23.20 Trifecta £84.40.
Owner Capt M S Bagley **Bred** J M Jefferson **Trained** Norton, N Yorks

FOCUS
Race distance increased by 20yds. The final fence was omitted due to bad ground and the first fence going away from the stands omitted due to the low sun. A modest handicap chase run at a sensible pace in the ground. The winner had threatened this sort of rating over hurdles.

2980 188BET H'CAP HURDLE (11 hdls) 2m 4f 133y
1:20 (1:22) (Class 5) (0-100,100) 3-Y-0+ **£2,274** (£667; £333; £166)

Form RPR

2U1 **1** **Marlee Massie (IRE)**[4] 2937 6-10-11 **85** 7ex...................... LucyAlexander 95+
(N W Alexander) *racd wd: hld up: stdy hdwy 1/2-way: effrt and shkn up whn nt fluent and outpcd 3 out: rallied run-in: led run-in: pushed along and hld on wl run-in* **1/1[1]**

0430 **2** 3/4 **Maybe I Wont**[59] 1890 10-11-11 **99** ....(p) HenryBrooke 107
(James Moffatt) *cl up: chal 3 out to run-in: sn chsng wnr: kpt on towards fin* **11/1**

3-50 **3** 3/4 **Rock Relief (IRE)**[29] 2429 9-11-7 **100** ....(v[1]) DiarmuidO'Regan(5) 107
(Chris Grant) *chsd clr ldr to 1/2-way: sn lost pl: rallied 4 out: led next to run-in: kpt on: hld towards fin* **14/1**

0024 **4** 10 **Beyondtemptation**[16] 2706 7-10-5 **86** ....(t) ThomasDowson(7) 83
(Jonathan Haynes) *led and clr to 1/2-way: rdn and hdd 3 out: outpcd fr next* **20/1**

500- **5** 1 3/4 **Redkalani (IRE)**[258] 5011 7-11-9 **97** .... JamesReveley 93
(Keith Reveley) *hld up: stdy hdwy 4 out: rdn and outpcd next: sn btn* **5/1[2]**

U0-0 **6** 5 **Rinnagree Rosie**[29] 2429 9-11-2 **90** .... AdrianLane 81
(Lucy Normile) *hld up: pushed along 7th: rallied after 4 out: rdn and wknd bef 2 out* **40/1**

40-3 **7** 1 **Cruachan (IRE)**[29] 2429 6-11-7 **98** .... AdamNicol(3) 88
(Lucy Normile) *hld up: pushed along after 4 out: effrt u.p bef 2 out: sn wknd* **6/1[3]**

0-20 **8** 29 **Newyearsresolution (IRE)**[16] 2707 11-9-7 **74** .... MissAWaugh(7) 35
(Simon Waugh) *hld up towards rr: hdwy to chse ldr 1/2-way: lost pl 4 out: sn struggling* **16/1**

-6UP **P** **Brunello**[16] 2708 7-11-2 **90** .... BrianHughes
(Michael Smith) *prom: lost pl whn hit 4 out: sn rdn and lost tch: p.u bef next* **33/1**

5m 23.2s (2.10) **Going Correction** +0.30s/f (Yiel) **9 Ran SP% 112.0**
Speed ratings (Par 103): **108,107,107,103,102 101,100,89,**
CSF £11.98 CT £95.37 TOTE £1.90: £1.10, £2.60, £2.50; EX 13.10 Trifecta £86.00.
Owner Nicholas Alexander **Bred** Tom Baker **Trained** Kinneston, Perth & Kinross

FOCUS
Race distance increased by 30yds. The cross hurdle was jumped this time. A modest handicap hurdle with just the first three seriously involved in the closing stages. The winner was well in on his recent run over further.

2981 188BET.CO.UK NOVICES' CHASE (11 fncs 2 omitted) 2m 75y
1:50 (1:50) (Class 4) 4-Y-0+ **£3,768** (£1,106; £553; £276)

Form RPR

422- **1** **Got The Nac (IRE)**[257] 5031 6-10-13 **123** .... BrianHarding 120+
(Keith Dalgleish) *plld hrd early: chsd ldrs: led 2nd: mde rest: rdn and r.o strly fr last (usual 2 out)* **4/1[2]**

30/P **2** 6 **Special Catch (IRE)**[12] 2774 8-10-13 **129** .... JamesReveley 108
(Keith Reveley) *prom: chsd wnr 4 out (usual 5 out): effrt next: kpt on same pce fr last (usual 2 out)* **11/8[1]**

262- **3** 10 **Kiama Bay (IRE)**[285] 4495 9-10-13 **135** .... JamieMoore 101
(Jim Best) *led to 2nd: chsd wnr to 4 out (usual 5 out): outpcd whn nt fluent next: btn fnl 2* **11/8[1]**

65P2 **4** 12 **Duhallowcountry (IRE)**[16] 2705 9-10-6 **75** ....(p) ThomasDowson(7) 85
(Victor Thompson) *prom: outpcd bef 4 out (usual 5 out): struggling fr next* **100/1[3]**

P0 **5** 3 1/4 **Under The Red Sky (IRE)**[8] 2846 8-10-13 **0** .... PeterBuchanan 83
(Kenny Johnson) *nt fluent on occasions: bhd: outpcd 3rd: rallied 5 out (usual 6 out): struggling bef 3 out (usual 4 out)* **100/1[3]**

0-45 **6** 10 **Rosquero (FR)**[16] 2705 10-10-13 **77** ....(v) BrianHughes 75
(Kenny Johnson) *nt fluent in rr: struggling 1/2-way: lost tch fr 4 out (usual 5 out)* **100/1[3]**

4m 17.6s (-3.50) **Going Correction** +0.10s/f (Yiel) **6 Ran SP% 107.2**
Speed ratings (Par 105): **112,109,104,98,96 91**
CSF £9.47 TOTE £4.30: £2.10, £1.30; EX 10.00 Trifecta £13.50.
Owner Richard & Katherine Gilbert **Bred** Pat Elmore **Trained** Carluke, S Lanarks

FOCUS
Race distance increased by 20yds. The cross fence was jumped this time. A decent novices' chase with just the first three home holding a realistic chance beforehand. There's a case for rating the form a lot higher through the second and third.

2982 MACNAUGHTON MCGREGOR H'CAP HURDLE (8 hdls 1 omitted) 2m 98y
2:20 (2:20) (Class 5) (0-100,100) 3-Y-0+ **£2,274** (£667; £333; £166)

Form RPR

50-1 **1** **Clan Legend**[33] 2343 5-11-10 **98** .... LucyAlexander 108+
(N W Alexander) *w ldr: stdd into 8 l 2nd bef 3rd: hdwy to ld 3 out: nt fluent and pushed along next: kpt on wl run-in* **5/2[1]**

/PP0 **2** 1 3/4 **Vodka Red (IRE)**[16] 2706 7-10-10 **84** ....(b) PeterBuchanan 91
(Kenny Johnson) *hld up: stdy hdwy and in tch 4 out: effrt bef 2 out: chsd wnr last: kpt on: nt pce to chal* **33/1**

/35- **3** 4 1/2 **Old Magic (IRE)**[273] 4733 10-9-10 **75** .... DannyBurton(5) 77
(Sophie Leech) *t.k.h: led: 8 l clr bef 3rd: rdn and hdd 3 out: rallied: outpcd fr last* **11/1**

3620 **4** 6 **King's Chorister**[59] 1887 9-10-1 **82** ....(t) LorcanMurtagh(7) 78
(Barry Murtagh) *hld up in tch: stdy hdwy to chse ldrs bef 4 out: rdn after next: outpcd fr 2 out* **9/2[2]**

2P-6 **5** nk **Fiddler's Flight (IRE)**[26] 2492 9-10-4 **81** ow1...... ColmMcCormack(3) 77
(John Norton) *hld up: pushed along and outpcd 4 out: plugged on fr 2 out: nvr able to chal* **12/1**

/0-1 **6** 4 **Beaumont's Party (IRE)**[16] 2706 8-11-12 **100** .... BrianHughes 92
(Chris Grant) *hld up: pushed along and effrt whn mstke and outpcd 3 out: n.d after* **9/2[2]**

PFP3 **7** 1 1/2 **Redpender (IRE)**[103] 1405 9-11-1 **96** .... MissRMcDonald(7) 88
(James Moffatt) *hld up in tch: gng wl whn mstke 3 out: sn rdn and outpcd: btn fr next* **11/1**

4044 **8** 1 3/4 **Seventeen Black (IRE)**[12] 2786 7-10-2 **81** .... GrantCockburn(5) 70
(Stuart Coltherd) *in tch: hdwy bef 3rd: lost pl whn nt fluent next: struggling 4 out: n.d after* **9/1[3]**

P00P **9** 7 **Captain Sharpe**[16] 2703 7-10-11 **92** ....(v) ThomasDowson(7) 73
(Kenny Johnson) *hld up: nt fluent 1st: stdy hdwy after 4 out: rdn and wknd fr next* **40/1**

205- **10** 19 **Copt Hill**[250] 5131 7-11-0 **88** .... BrianHarding 50
(Tracy Waggott) *chsd ldrs: nt fluent 1st: struggling bef 4 out: btn bef next* **14/1**

5310 **11** 5 **Ardesia (IRE)**[103] 1405 11-9-13 **76** ....(p) JonathanEngland(3) 33
(Tina Jackson) *chsd clr ldng pair: struggling bef 4 out: sn wknd* **16/1**

4m 13.2s (3.20) **Going Correction** +0.10s/f (Yiel) **11 Ran SP% 117.2**
Speed ratings (Par 103): **104,103,100,97,97 95,94,94,90,81 78**
CSF £76.70 CT £787.22 TOTE £3.10: £1.50, £7.20, £3.70; EX 82.40 Trifecta £1109.40.
Owner Clan Gathering **Bred** Alexander Family **Trained** Kinneston, Perth & Kinross

FOCUS
Race distance increased by 20yds. The cross hurdle was again omitted due to the low sun. A sound pace and the winner always in the first two. The winner is on the upgrade and there should be more to come.

2983 FREE BET AT 188BET NOVICES' H'CAP CHASE (14 fncs 2 omitted) 2m 4f 19y
2:50 (2:51) (Class 4) (0-105,102) 4-Y-0+ **£3,768** (£1,106; £553; £276)

Form RPR

64-2 **1** **Oscar Lateen (IRE)**[40] 2191 7-10-13 **89** ....(p) JamesReveley 104+
(Sandy Thomson) *cl up: mstke 6th: led 8th: nt fluent 4 out (usual 5 out): drvn clr fr 2 out (usual 3 out)* **10/11[1]**

-2PP **2** 9 **Harleys Max**[16] 2708 6-9-7 **76** oh1...................... JamesCorbett(7) 79
(Susan Corbett) *hld up in tch on outside: hdwy to chal 8th: rdn bef 3 out (usual 4 out): kpt on same pce fr next* **10/1**

/PP3 **3** 16 **Rupert Bear**[12] 2786 9-10-10 **91** .... MissCWalton(5) 78
(James Walton) *led to 4th: cl up: rallied and led bef 7th to next: drvn and outpcd 4 out (usual 5 out): n.d after* **9/2[2]**

230- **4** 1 1/4 **Higgs Boson**[264] 4914 10-10-6 **87** .... StephenMulqueen(5) 72
(Jim Goldie) *hld up in tch: outpcd whn nt fluent 9th: no imp fr 4 out (usual 5 out)* **14/1**

30 **5** 58 **Afterclass (IRE)**[12] 2786 7-10-1 **84** ....(vt[1]) MrKitAlexander(7) 10
(N W Alexander) *cl up: led 4th to bef 7th: outpcd whn blnd 5 out (usual 6 out): wknd fr next* **9/1**

234- **P** **Major Ridge (IRE)**[261] 4971 6-11-0 **95** .... CallumBewley(5)
(Robert Bewley) *nt fluent on occasions: hld up in tch: mstke 2nd: outpcd fr 7th: lost tch and p.u bef 3 out (usual 4 out)* **13/2[3]**

5m 33.3s (6.10) **Going Correction** +0.10s/f (Yiel) **6 Ran SP% 109.7**
Speed ratings (Par 105): **91,87,81,80,57**
CSF £9.74 CT £24.88 TOTE £1.80: £1.10, £5.60; EX 10.10 Trifecta £45.10.
Owner Sprayclad UK **Bred** John Mulcahy **Trained** Lambden, Berwicks

FOCUS
Race distance increased by 30yds. The cross fence was jumped this time. A weak novices' handicap chase and just two seriously involved from just before the final turn. The winner looks to be on the upgrade.

2984 LIVE BETTING AT 188BET.CO.UK STANDARD OPEN NATIONAL HUNT FLAT RACE 2m 98y
3:20 (3:20) (Class 6) 4-6-Y-0 **£1,559** (£457; £228; £114)

Form RPR

1 **Betameche (FR)** 4-11-0 **0** .... BrianHarding 112+
(Nicky Richards) *hld up on outside: stdy hdwy over 5f out: led over 2f out: shkn up and rn green ent fnl f: pushed clr* **13/8[1]**

2 **2** 5 **Puddle Jumper (IRE)**[61] 1858 4-11-0 **0** .... JamieMoore 105
(Micky Hammond) *t.k.h: mde most to over 2f out: rallied: kpt on same pce fnl f* **4/1[3]**

1 **3** 8 **Bambys Boy**[33] 2344 4-11-2 **0** .... MrJohnDawson(5) 105
(Keith Reveley) *hld up in tch: stdy hdwy over 4f out: pushed along over 2f out: no imp fr over 1f out* **15/8[2]**

4 3 **Eastview Boy** 4-10-11 **0** .... AdamNicol(3) 93
(Philip Kirby) *cl up: pushed along whn edgd lft and checked over 2f out: wknd over 1f out* **50/1**

5 3 **Patience Tony (IRE)** 4-11-0 **0** .... JamesReveley 90
(Alan Swinbank) *prom: effrt and pushed along 3f out: wknd over 1f out* **8/1**

6 2 1/2 **Donna's Delight (IRE)** 4-10-9 **0** .... DiarmuidO'Regan(5) 88
(Chris Grant) *hld up: pushed along and outpcd 4f out: sme late hdwy: nvr on terms* **33/1**

4 **7** 38 **Been Decided (IRE)**[33] 2344 5-10-7 **0** .... MrKitAlexander(7) 50
(N W Alexander) *w ldr to over 5f out: rdn and wknd over 1f out* **25/1**

0 **8** 3/4 **Mcginty's Dream (IRE)**[45] 2106 4-11-0 **0** .... LucyAlexander 49
(N W Alexander) *plld hrd in rr: struggling fr 5f out: sn lost tch* **100/1**

4m 11.7s (7.30) **Going Correction** +0.30s/f (Yiel) **8 Ran SP% 113.7**
Speed ratings: **93,90,86,85,83 82,63,62**
CSF £8.33 TOTE £2.30: £1.10, £1.50, £1.10; EX 12.80 Trifecta £25.90.
Owner Langdale Bloodstock **Bred** Pascal Noue **Trained** Greystoke, Cumbria

FOCUS
Race distance increased by 20yds. Probably a fair bumper and as usual the early pace was very sedate. The winner looks above average.

T/Plt: £451.30 to a £1 stake. Pool: £42,297.01 - 68.41 winning tickets. T/Qpdt: £10.40 to a £1 stake. Pool: £5,647.95 - 400.23 winning tickets. **Richard Young**

[2730]TAUNTON (R-H)

Thursday, December 10

OFFICIAL GOING: Good to soft (soft in places; 5.3)

Wind: mild across Weather: showers Rails: Divided bends. Chase bends at innermost position, distances; races 1 & 2 add 66yds, races 3, 5, & 7 add 45yds.

2985 KINGS COLLEGE TAUNTON H'CAP HURDLE (12 hdls) 2m 7f 198y

12:40 (12:40) (Class 4) (0-110,110) 4-Y-O+ £4,548 (£1,335; £667; £333)

Form RPR

U333 1 **Theatre Goer**[18] 2658 6-11-3 **104**........................ JamesBanks(3) 112+
(Noel Williams) *trckd ldr: led appr 2 out: styd on wl: rdn out* **7/1**[3]

356 2 ½ **Royal Chief (IRE)**[18] 2664 6-11-2 **100**..................(p) AdamWedge 106+
(Alexandra Dunn) *hld up towards rr: hdwy fr 8th: rdn to chse ldrs appr 2 out: styd on to go 2nd run-in: clsng qckly on wnr at fin* **22/1**

0P-1 3 1¾ **Kleitomachos (IRE)**[14] 2736 7-11-3 **106**..................(b) DavidNoonan(5) 112
(Stuart Kittow) *trckd ldrs: rdn to chse wnr appr 2 out: styd on but no ex whn lost 2nd run-in* **4/1**[1]

026 4 4½ **Thegreendalerocket (IRE)**[14] 2731 6-11-5 **110**.............. MissBFrost(7) 111
(Jimmy Frost) *trckd ldrs: hit 3 out: rdn bef next: styd on same pce* **20/1**

3-54 5 3¼ **Zanstra (IRE)**[22] 2569 5-11-9 **107**........................ BrendanPowell 104
(Colin Tizzard) *trckd ldrs: rdn after 3 out: styd on but nt pce to chal* **6/1**[2]

1551 6 shd **Rainbow Haze**[22] 2567 9-11-2 **105**........................ MrBMoorcroft(5) 104
(Phillip Dando) *mid-div: rdn to chse ldrs after 3 out: one pce fr next* **8/1**

35-F 7 3 **Mother Meldrum (IRE)**[22] 2582 6-11-7 **105**.................. DenisO'Regan 99
(Victor Dartnall) *mid-div: trckd ldrs after 5th: nt fluent 9th: rdn after 3 out: one pce fr next* **12/1**

3-P0 8 4½ **Follow The Tracks (IRE)**[28] 2454 7-11-1 **99**.............. DaveCrosse 90
(Brian Barr) *led: rdn and hdd appr 2 out: grad fdd* **12/1**

4/5- 9 20 **Darkestbeforedawn (IRE)**[564] 449 8-11-4 **109**.............. MrMLegg(7) 81
(Caroline Keevil) *mid-div: rdn after 3 out: sn wknd* **9/1**

/15- 10 8 **Knockalongi**[371] 2897 9-11-2 **107**........................ BenFfrenchDavis(7) 72
(Dominic Ffrench Davis) *mid-div on outer: lost pl on bnd after 7th: hdwy after next: sn rdn: wknd after 3 out* **9/1**

5-53 11 1¾ **Shoofly Milly (IRE)**[29] 2441 6-11-4 **102**.................. LiamHeard 65
(Jeremy Scott) *drvn along fr 7th: a towards rr* **25/1**

055 12 5 **Captain Canada**[18] 2658 8-11-7 **105**........................(t) RichieMcLernon 64
(Katie Stephens) *hld up towards rr: midfield 8th: rdn next: wknd after 3 out* **40/1**

-600 13 ¾ **Action Master**[17] 2687 9-10-11 **105**........................(t) TommyDowling(10) 63
(Charlie Mann) *a towards rr* **22/1**

5 P **Rosygo (IRE)**[16] 2697 7-11-5 **103**........................ NoelFehily
(Adrian Wintle) *a towards rr: lost tch 8th: p.u bef next* **20/1**

60P P **Bobble Emerald (IRE)**[92] 1520 7-11-12 **110**.................. IanPopham
(Martin Keighley) *in tch tl 9th: sn in rr: t.o whn p.u bef 2 out* **25/1**

6m 4.8s (0.80) **Going Correction** +0.075s/f (Yiel) **15 Ran SP% 121.6**
Speed ratings (Par 105): **101,100,100,98,97 97,96,95,88,85 85,83,83, ,**
CSF £152.85 CT £708.98 TOTE £6.30: £1.70, £5.60, £1.80; EX 204.50 Trifecta £655.50.
Owner Noel Williams **Bred** David Allen **Trained** Blewbury, Oxon

FOCUS
Chase rail on inner line. Hurdle bends moved out and races 1 & 2 increased by 66yds, races 3, 5 & 7 by 45yds. This moderate handicap was wide open and they went a fair gallop. The form looks solid enough. Race distance 66 yards further than advertised.

2986 JANET DENNING FIFEHEAD FARMS MEMORIAL NOVICES' HURDLE (12 hdls) 2m 7f 198y

1:10 (1:10) (Class 4) 4-Y-O+ £4,548 (£1,335; £667; £333)

Form RPR

3 1 **Whataknight**[21] 2603 6-10-12 0........................(t) NoelFehily 122+
(Harry Fry) *mde all: strly pressed last: drifted rt u.p run-in: styd on wl: rdn out* **2/1**[2]

6-2 2 2 **Rock On Oscar (IRE)**[38] 2239 5-10-12 0..................(t[1]) SamTwiston-Davies 119+
(Paul Nicholls) *racd keenly: mid-div: hdwy after 3 out: mounting chal whn mstke last: sn rdn: nt qckn* **5/6**[1]

0-3 3 11 **Cotswold Road**[19] 2650 5-10-12 0........................ TomScudamore 108
(Colin Tizzard) *mid-div: trckd ldrs 3 out: rdn bef next where lft 3rd: styd on same pce* **16/1**

0-35 4 1½ **Florida Calling (IRE)**[35] 2299 6-10-12 0.................. PaddyBrennan 106
(Tom George) *trckd ldrs: pressed ldr fr 8th tl rdn appr 2 out where lft 4th: styd on same pce* **12/1**

0/ 5 13 **Bel Ami Rich**[694] 3719 5-10-9 0........................ JamesBanks(3) 93
(Sally Randell) *hld up towards rr: stdy prog u.p after 3 out but nvr any threat to ldrs* **150/1**

00/0 6 2 **Up To Al (IRE)**[28] 2457 7-10-12 0........................ LiamHeard 91
(Bob Buckler) *mid-div: wnt lft 3 out: sn rdn: nvr any imp* **66/1**

00-P 7 4½ **Colmers Hill**[36] 2265 5-10-9 0........................ MattGriffiths(3) 89
(Jeremy Scott) *a towards rr* **150/1**

1- 8 19 **Fivefortyfive**[540] 735 7-10-12 0........................(t) NickScholfield 68
(Polly Gundry) *pressed ldr tl 8th: sn rdn: wknd after 3 out* **8/1**[3]

-3P0 9 2¼ **My Diamond (IRE)**[28] 2457 4-10-12 0........................ JamesDavies 65
(Laura Young) *mid-div: hdwy 8th: rdn after 3 out: sn wknd* **150/1**

00 10 37 **One Last Dream**[8] 2850 6-10-12 0........................(t) IanPopham 28
(Ron Hodges) *mid-div tl wknd after 8th: t.o* **150/1**

0 P **Dinky Challenger**[28] 2457 7-10-12 0........................ TommyPhelan
(Mark Gillard) *a towards rr: nt fluent 3rd: t.o whn p.u after 3 out* **150/1**

0-3 F **According To Harry (IRE)**[29] 2443 6-10-12 0.................. JamesBest 111
(Philip Hobbs) *trckd ldrs: rdn after 3 out: styng on at same pce in 2 l 3rd whn fell 2 out* **20/1**

06 P **Garryduff Cross (IRE)**[15] 2715 5-10-12 0.................. RichieMcLernon
(Helen Nelmes) *a towards rr: nt fluent 5th: t.o whn p.u after 3 out* **200/1**

0 P **Calisto**[28] 2460 5-10-9 0........................ MauriceLinehan(3)
(Ben Pauling) *trckd ldrs tl 8th: sn rdn: wknd next: t.o whn p.u after 3 out* **80/1**

6m 5.3s (1.30) **Going Correction** +0.075s/f (Yiel) **14 Ran SP% 123.9**
WFA 4 from 5yo+ 7lb
Speed ratings (Par 105): **100,99,95,95,90 90,88,82,81,69 , , ,**
CSF £4.28 TOTE £3.30: £1.20, £1.02, £4.60; EX 3.90 Trifecta £27.70.
Owner J M Dare, T Hamlin, J W Snook **Bred** J M Dare, T Hamlin, J W Snook **Trained** Seaborough, Dorset

FOCUS
Race distance increased by 66yds. This modest staying novice event saw the first pair dominate the home straight. The winner is on the upgrade and there should be more to come.

2987 DAVE CRIDDLE TRAVEL & KUONI H'CAP HURDLE (9 hdls) 2m 104y

1:40 (1:40) (Class 4) (0-110,110) 3-Y-O+ £4,548 (£1,335; £667; £333)

Form RPR

00-6 1 **Canadian Diamond (IRE)**[24] 2540 8-11-5 **110**.............. MikeyHamill(7) 117
(Richard Rowe) *mid-div: hdwy after 3 out: wnt 2nd next: styd on u.p fr last to ld fnl 100yds: drvn out* **7/1**[3]

4 2 ¾ **Shadow Blue (IRE)**[14] 2734 6-11-4 **109**.................. MrGTreacy(7) 115
(Steven Dixon) *prom: led 3rd: rdn appr 2 out: drifted rt after last: hdd fnl 100yds: no ex* **20/1**

2-00 3 4½ **Abyaat (IRE)**[14] 2734 4-11-4 **102**........................(t) DenisO'Regan 106
(Victor Dartnall) *mid-div: nt fluent 5th: hdwy 3 out: sn rdn: wnt 3rd next: nt fluent last: kpt on same pce* **28/1**

5604 4 4½ **Goal (IRE)**[16] 2458 7-11-0 **105**........................(t) MissBHampson(7) 103
(Sally Randell) *trckd ldrs: rdn after 3 out: styd on same pce fr next* **16/1**

126- 5 2½ **Edlomond (IRE)**[460] 1456 9-11-7 **110**..................(t[1]) RyanWhile(5) 106
(Bill Turner) *hld up towards rr: hdwy into midfield 3 out: sn rdn: styd on fr next but nt pce to get on terms* **40/1**

0046 6 1½ **Ice Tres**[14] 2730 6-11-0 **98**........................(p) JamesDavies 92
(Chris Down) *trckd ldrs: wnt 2nd 6th tl rdn appr 2 out: no ex fr last* **20/1**

5-50 7 1½ **Triple Chief (IRE)**[46] 2093 4-11-7 **105**..................(p) NoelFehily 98
(Chris Down) *mid-div: rdn after 3 out: styd on same pce fr next* **22/1**

4-65 8 3 **Ourmanmassini (IRE)**[14] 2734 7-11-5 **110**..................(t) MrMLegg(7) 101
(Suzy Smith) *mid-div tl rdn after 3 out: n.d after* **7/1**[3]

5362 9 ½ **Sword Of The Lord**[11] 2810 5-11-9 **107**..................(vt) SamTwiston-Davies 97
(Nigel Twiston-Davies) *hld up towards rr: rdn after 3 out: stdy prog fr next but nvr gng pce to get on terms* **10/3**[1]

-650 10 nk **Berry De Carjac (FR)**[28] 2457 4-11-7 **105**..................(tp) TomScudamore 95
(Nigel Hawke) *towards rr of midfield: in tch 3 out: sn rdn: nvr threatened: wkng whn hit last* **25/1**

55-3 11 2¾ **Elkstone**[220] 98 4-11-9 **107**........................ WayneHutchinson 94
(Alan King) *hld up towards rr: rdn after 3 out: nvr finding pce to get involved* **6/1**[2]

0-F1 12 4½ **Pay Your Way (IRE)**[41] 2165 7-10-13 **97**.................. LiamTreadwell 80
(David Rees) *a towards rr* **17/2**

6-13 13 25 **Back By Midnight**[14] 2734 6-11-7 **108**..................(t) JamesBanks(3) 69
(Emma Baker) *led tl 3rd: prom tl rdn after 6th: wknd next: t.o* **8/1**

5P12 14 2¾ **Seacon Beg (IRE)**[96] 1478 6-11-1 **104**..................(t) ChrisWard(5) 62
(Nikki Evans) *mid-div tl wknd after 3 out: t.o* **33/1**

-4P0 15 2 **Dardanella**[28] 2455 8-11-4 **102**........................ DaveCrosse 58
(Hugo Froud) *pushed along fr 4th: a towards rr: t.o* **66/1**

6330 16 14 **Native Robin (IRE)**[46] 2087 5-11-9 **107**.................. NickScholfield 51
(Jeremy Scott) *struggling 5th: a in rr: t.o* **14/1**

P-PP P **Dont Call Me Oscar (IRE)**[28] 2458 8-11-2 **100**..........(tp) TommyPhelan
(Mark Gillard) *trckd ldrs: rdn after 5th: sn wknd: t.o whn p.u after 3 out* **40/1**

4m 6.4s (-1.60) **Going Correction** +0.075s/f (Yiel) **17 Ran SP% 127.0**
Speed ratings (Par 105): **107,106,104,102,100 100,99,97,97,97 96,93,81,79,78 71,**
CSF £144.66 CT £3720.59 TOTE £9.20: £2.40, £4.80, £8.70, £5.10; EX 210.90 Trifecta £2142.60 Part won..
Owner Nicholls Family **Bred** J S Bolger **Trained** Sullington, W Sussex

FOCUS
Race distance increased by 45yds. There was no hanging about in this ordinary handicap. The winner should still be competitive when reassessed.

2988 DAVE CRIDDLE TRAVEL & BRISTOL AIRPORT NOVICES' LIMITED H'CAP CHASE (17 fncs) 2m 7f 3y

2:10 (2:11) (Class 4) (0-120,119) 4-Y-O+ £5,198 (£1,526; £763; £381)

Form RPR

-000 1 **Sandy Beach**[28] 2458 5-10-12 **109**........................ BrendanPowell 130+
(Colin Tizzard) *trckd ldrs: pressed ldr fr 13th: rdn to ld appr 2 out: clr last: eased towards fin* **16/1**

0P-0 2 9 **What Larks (IRE)**[37] 2263 7-10-3 **100** oh5.................. DaveCrosse 108+
(Hugo Froud) *hld up: hdwy 3 out: rdn into 5th 2 out: styd on wl to go 2nd run-in but no ch w wnr* **66/1**

-24P 3 1¼ **Simply The West (IRE)**[28] 2451 6-11-8 **119**..................(t) NoelFehily 128
(Charlie Longsdon) *mid-div: hdwy fr 12th: rdn to dispute 3rd after 4 out: pckd next: nt fluent 2 out: styd on same pce* **17/2**

P211 4 ¾ **Butlergrove King (IRE)**[49] 2036 6-10-13 **113**.............. RobertWilliams(3) 121
(Tony Newcombe) *led: rdn whn pressed after 4 out: hdd 2 out: no ex fr last* **6/1**[2]

0-33 5 hd **Rebel Benefit (IRE)**[169] 834 7-10-9 **106**.................. SamTwiston-Davies 112
(David Dennis) *trckd ldrs: hit 13th: rdn to dispute 3rd after 4 out: styd on same pce fr next* **10/1**

0-23 6 5 **Somerset Lias (IRE)**[21] 2598 7-10-9 **106**.................. LiamHeard 108
(Bob Buckler) *mid-div: trckd ldrs 6th: rdn after 13th: one pce fr 3 out* **7/1**[3]

/30- P **Cool George**[467] 1398 7-11-1 **112**........................ JamesBest
(Jackie Du Plessis) *hld up: effrt after 4 out: wknd next: hmpd 2 out: p.u bef last* **10/1**

1612 P **Spending Time**[7] 2872 6-11-1 **112**........................(tp) TomScudamore
(David Pipe) *in tch: blnd bdly 5th: nvr travelling after: reminders after 7th: losing tch whn p.u bef 4 out* **3/1**[1]

31-0 P **Forgivienne**[222] 85 8-10-12 **109**........................ AdamWedge
(Evan Williams) *hld up: virtually fell 10th after slipping: sn p.u* **20/1**

35-P F **Sidbury Hill**[14] 2727 7-11-2 **118**........................ KevinJones(5) 115
(Seamus Mullins) *trckd ldr tl 13th: sn rdn: btn 6th whn fell 2 out* **3/1**[1]

6m 3.1s (-12.90) **Going Correction** -0.30s/f (Good) **10 Ran SP% 117.6**
Speed ratings (Par 105): **110,106,106,106,106 104, , , ,**
CSF £533.40 CT £9193.25 TOTE £20.80: £4.30, £11.70, £2.30; EX 1977.10 Trifecta £3342.60 Part won..
Owner Brocade Racing **Bred** Alan Gibson **Trained** Milborne Port, Dorset

FOCUS
A modest novice handicap. The winner was up nearly a stone on the best of his hurdle figures.

2989 DAVE CRIDDLE TRAVEL & FLYBE H'CAP HURDLE (10 hdls) 2m 3f 1y

2:40 (2:40) (Class 3) (0-125,125) 3-Y-O+ £6,498 (£1,908; £954; £477)

Form RPR

242 1 **Doctor Look Here (IRE)**[37] 2263 5-10-3 **105**.............. LucyGardner(3) 117+
(Sue Gardner) *mid-div: hdwy after 3 out: lft in ld after 2 out: qcknd clr run-in: readily* **9/2**[1]

-530 2 4½ **McCabe Creek (IRE)**[22] 2577 5-10-1 **110**.................. JamieInsole(10) 115
(Alan King) *mid-div: hdwy 4th: str chal after 2 out: ev ch last: outpcd by wnr run-in* **10/1**

05-3 **3** 1 1/4 **Winning Spark (USA)**[21] 2600 8-11-1 **114**............ JamesBest 121+
(Jackie Du Plessis) *hld up: hdwy after 6th: trckd ldrs 3 out: in ld whn awkward and rdr bec unbalanced and lost irons 2 out: sn hdd: kpt on but nvr rcvrd* **8/1**

-331 **4** 7 **Calin Du Brizais (FR)**[21] 2595 4-10-10 **109**............(t) ConorO'Farrell 107
(Nigel Hawke) *trckd ldrs: led after 3 out: rdn and hdd bef next: lft w ev ch between last 2: styd on same pce run-in* **11/1**

3502 **5** 2 1/2 **Stephen Hero (IRE)**[35] 2301 5-11-7 **125**............(t) DavidNoonan(5) 120
(Brian Barr) *trckd ldrs: rdn and ev ch appr 2 out: hld between last 2: keeping on at same pce whn drifting rt run-in (dismntd)* **12/1**

4146 **6** 5 **Popping Along**[28] 2455 6-10-11 **113**............(tp) MattGriffiths(3) 106
(Jeremy Scott) *mid-div: rdn to chse ldrs appr 2 out: sn one pce* **9/1**

3-64 **7** 3 1/4 **Pengo's Boy**[28] 2457 6-11-2 **115**............ NickScholfield 103
(Stuart Kittow) *hld up towards rr: rdn after 3 out: nt pce to get involved* **6/1**[3]

-24P **8** 3 1/4 **Full Blast (FR)**[32] 2373 4-11-0 **113**............(t) MarcGoldstein 98
(Chris Gordon) *hld up towards rr: rdn after 3 out: nvr threatened* **33/1**

65-P **9** 47 **Brook (FR)**[25] 2513 4-11-10 **123**............(p) TomScudamore 66
(David Pipe) *trckd ldr: lft in ld 4th tl hdd after 3 out: wknd bef next: t.o* **16/1**

5316 **10** 20 **Milestone (IRE)**[81] 1594 5-10-12 **111**............(t) AdamWedge 36
(Evan Williams) *hld up last: struggling 7th: nvr any danger: t.o* **11/1**

P4 **11** 15 **Alefou D'Airy (FR)**[205] 390 5-11-6 **119**............ JamesDavies 30
(Jimmy Frost) *trckd ldrs tl 6th: struggling after next: wknd after 3 out: t.o* **66/1**

6/64 **U** **Red Riverman**[53] 1988 7-11-0 **113**............(v) SamTwiston-Davies
(Nigel Twiston-Davies) *mid-div tl blnd bdly and uns rdr 3rd* **16/1**

14 **C** **Itsnowcato**[24] 2544 4-11-1 **117**............ MauriceLinehan(3)
(Ben Pauling) *led tl carried out by loose horse 4th* **11/2**[2]

4m 50.3s (4.30) **Going Correction** +0.075s/f (Yiel) **13 Ran SP% 118.6**
Speed ratings (Par 107): **93,91,90,87,86 84,83,81,61,53 47, ,**
CSF £49.06 CT £354.52 TOTE £4.40: £1.70, £4.30, £2.70; EX 50.20 Trifecta £438.10.
Owner G N Noye **Bred** James A Slattery **Trained** Longdown, Devon

FOCUS
Race distance increased by 45yds. A moderate handicap that proved dramatic, but the form still looks fair for the class. The second and third set the level.

2990 STABLES BUSINESS PARK CLIENTS DAY OUT H'CAP CHASE (14 fncs) 2m 2f 40y
3:10 (3:10) (Class 3) (0-135,135) 4-Y-O+ **£8,447** (£2,480; £1,240; £620)

Form RPR

F-34 **1** **Balgarry (FR)**[12] 2779 8-11-10 **133**............ TomScudamore 142+
(David Pipe) *mde all: j.w whn strly pressed last 3: r.o wl: rdn out* **9/4**[1]

320- **2** 2 3/4 **Barrakilla (IRE)**[279] 4690 8-11-12 **135**............ AdamWedge 140
(Evan Williams) *trckd ldrs: chal 2 out: sn rdn: kpt on but nt pce of wnr fr last* **11/4**[2]

0-33 **3** 3 3/4 **Gores Island (IRE)**[30] 2419 9-11-4 **127**............ JoshuaMoore 133+
(Gary Moore) *hld up: hdwy after 8th: rdn after 4 out: ev ch 2 out tl last: kpt on same pce* **7/1**

362- **4** 7 **Ut Majeur Aulmes (FR)**[230] 5515 7-11-3 **126**............(t) DenisO'Regan 123
(Victor Dartnall) *trckd ldrs: rdn after 3 out: kpt on same pce fr next* **7/1**

3-P0 **5** 7 **Ceasar Milan (IRE)**[12] 2780 7-11-12 **135**............(tp) SamTwiston-Davies 126
(Paul Nicholls) *hld up: hdwy after 8th: cl 4th after 4 out: rdn after next: wknd 2 out* **5/1**[3]

P445 **6** 2 3/4 **Too Scoops (IRE)**[83] 1577 8-10-9 **118**............(tp) ConorO'Farrell 105
(Richard Woollacott) *prom tl rdn after 4 out: wknd next* **20/1**

12-F **7** 14 **Tom Neary (IRE)**[28] 2459 8-11-0 **123**............(t) NickScholfield 97
(Robert Walford) *hld up: rdn after 4 out: outpcd after next* **20/1**

5-00 **8** 47 **Hurricane Ridge (IRE)**[126] 1185 6-10-0 **109**............ JamesDavies 41
(Jimmy Frost) *chsd ldrs: pushed along fr 7th: hit next: wknd 10th: t.o* **28/1**

4m 45.1s (-6.90) **Going Correction** -0.30s/f (Good) **8 Ran SP% 116.2**
Speed ratings (Par 107): **103,101,100,97,93 92,86,65**
CSF £9.18 CT £27.20 TOTE £3.10: £1.40, £1.20, £2.10; EX 9.00 Trifecta £52.40.
Owner Brocade Racing **Bred** S C E A Haras Des Monts D'Arree Et Al **Trained** Nicholashayne, Devon

FOCUS
A fair handicap. They went an average gallop and the third sets the level. A big chase pb from the winner.

2991 SOMERSET COUNTY GAZETTE "NEWCOMERS" STANDARD OPEN NATIONAL HUNT FLAT RACE 2m 104y
3:40 (3:40) (Class 4) 3-5-Y-O **£3,422** (£997; £499)

Form RPR

1 **Drumcliff (IRE)** 4-11-7 0............ NoelFehily 118+
(Harry Fry) *trckd ldrs: led 2f out: drifted rt u.p sn after: running green but kpt on wl and in command fnl f* **7/4**[2]

2 5 **Capitaine (FR)** 3-10-7 0............ SamTwiston-Davies 96+
(Paul Nicholls) *in tch: hdwy 3f out: rdn to chse ldng pair over 2f out: styd on into 2nd ins fnl f but no threat to wnr* **13/8**[1]

3 2 **Ozzie The Oscar (IRE)** 4-11-7 0............ JamesBest 108+
(Philip Hobbs) *disp ld for 6f: led over 4f out: rdn and hdd 2f out: styd on same pce* **7/1**

4 8 **Orchard Park (IRE)** 4-10-11 0............ GrahamCarson(10) 101
(Jamie Snowden) *trckd ldrs: outpcd over 2f out: styd on into 4th fnl f but no threat to ldrs* **20/1**

5 1 3/4 **Anythingmayhappen (IRE)** 4-11-4 0............ MattGriffiths(3) 99
(Jeremy Scott) *disp ld: clr ldr after 6f tl over 4f out: sn rdn: one pce fnl 2f* **22/1**

6 16 **Sungai Long** 3-10-7 0............ LiamTreadwell 71
(Michael Scudamore) *a towards rr* **20/1**

7 5 **Brin D'Avoine (FR)** 4-11-7 0............ TomScudamore 80
(Neil Mulholland) *racd keenly: trckd ldrs: disp ld after 2f tl over 10f out: trckd ldrs: rdn over 3f out: sn wknd* **13/2**[3]

8 12 **Balmoral Prince** 4-11-7 0............ BrendanPowell 69
(Shaun Lycett) *trckd ldrs: rdn over 4f out: sn wknd* **50/1**

9 2 1/2 **Denny Kerrell** 4-11-7 0............ IanPopham 67
(Caroline Keevil) *in tch tl wknd over 4f out* **33/1**

10 9 **Times Of Trouble** 5-11-0 0............ MrMLegg(7) 59
(Fiona Shaw) *in tch tl wknd over 4f out* **40/1**

4m 5.4s (3.00) **Going Correction** +0.075s/f (Yiel)
WFA 3 from 4yo+ 13lb **10 Ran SP% 121.5**
Speed ratings (Par 105): **95,92,91,87,86 78,76,70,68,64**
CSF £4.73 TOTE £2.70: £1.30, £1.30, £2.10; EX 5.40 Trifecta £21.20.
Owner John P McManus **Bred** Simon Tindall **Trained** Seaborough, Dorset

FOCUS
Race distance increased by 45yds. With no previous form to go one here this bumper is clearly tricky to assess, but the principals were clear at the finish. The winner is probably well above average.
T/Jkpt: Not won. Jackpot Placepot: Part won. £1,653.90 to a £1 stake. Pool: £2,265.72 - 0.2 winning units. T/Plt: £1,364.70 to a £1 stake. Pool: £81,679.34 - 43.69 winning tickets. T/Qpdt: £432.10 to a £1 stake. Pool: £6,177.91 - 10.58 winning tickets. **Tim Mitchell**

2577 WARWICK (L-H)
Thursday, December 10

OFFICIAL GOING: Hurdle course - soft (heavy in places); chase course - soft (good to soft in places)
Wind: Strong behind Weather: Raining

2992 EVENTMASTERS CELEBRATES ITS 30TH ANNIVERSARY JUVENILE HURDLE (8 hdls) 2m
12:30 (12:31) (Class 4) 3-Y-O **£3,249** (£954; £477; £238)

Form RPR

1 **Ashoka (IRE)**[109] 3-10-12 0............ HarrySkelton 115+
(Dan Skelton) *chsd ldrs: wnt 2nd after 3 out: nt fluent next: hmpd appr last: hmpd again after last: shkn up to ld 110yds out: r.o wl: comf* **11/10**[1]

2 2 3/4 **For Goodness Sake (IRE)**[51] 3-10-5 0............ GavinSheehan 101+
(Warren Greatrex) *led: pckd 2 out: sn rdn and hung rt: hung rt again after last: hdd 110yds out: styd on same pce* **8/1**

43 **3** 10 **Celestial Magic**[28] 2448 3-10-7 110............ DanielHiskett(5) 97
(Richard Phillips) *hld up: hdwy 5th: rdn after 3 out: wknd 2 out* **13/2**[3]

0 **4** shd **Mister Dick (FR)**[56] 1928 3-10-5 0............ PatrickCowley(7) 97
(Jonjo O'Neill) *hld up: pushed along bef 4th: hdwy next: rdn appr 2 out: wknd last* **25/1**

5 1 3/4 **Magic Dancer**[45] 3-10-12 0............ AidanColeman 97
(Charlie Longsdon) *prom: chsd ldr 5th tl rdn after 3 out: wknd next* **11/4**[2]

6 8 **Early Retirement (IRE)** 3-10-12 0............ SeanBowen 87
(Caroline Bailey) *in rr and pushed along after 2nd: outpcd appr 4th: nvr on terms after* **20/1**

7 1 **Alhamareer (IRE)**[395] 3-10-12 0............ JakeGreenall 86
(Paul Webber) *hld up: hdwy 3 out: wknd bef next* **100/1**

8 1 **Sneaking Budge**[14] 3-10-12 0............ JoshuaMoore 89
(Stuart Edmunds) *trckd ldrs: racd keenly: rdn and wknd after 3 out* **14/1**

03 **9** 50 **Fidelity**[22] 2578 3-10-9 0............ ConorShoemark(3) 35
(Jonathan Geake) *hld up in tch: nt fluent 5th: rdn and wknd bef next* **100/1**

06 **P** **Light Breaks (IRE)**[28] 2448 3-10-9 0............ RyanHatch(3)
(Nigel Twiston-Davies) *chsd ldr tl mstke 5th: sn rdn and wknd: bhd whn p.u bef last* **50/1**

4m 1.7s (10.70) **Going Correction** +0.175s/f (Yiel) **10 Ran SP% 117.9**
Speed ratings (Par 104): **80,78,73,73,72 68,68,67,42,**
CSF £10.82 TOTE £1.90: £1.10, £2.70, £2.60; EX 10.50 Trifecta £47.60.
Owner Frank McAleavy **Bred** Mrs B Gardiner **Trained** Alcester, Warwicks

FOCUS
All starts have been moved at this track following remeasuring, so there will be no speed figures here until there is sufficient data to calculate updated median times. Hurdles and NHF on Outer course with rail on inner line and distances as advertised. Chase rail moved out and race 2 increased by 59yds, race 3 by 64yds and race 5 by 118yds. Run at an ordinary pace, this was a routine event of its type but the first two were a cut above the rest. The third helps set the level.

2993 EVENTMASTERS 6 NATIONS RUGBY HOSPITALITY PACKAGES NOVICES' LIMITED H'CAP CHASE (12 fncs) 2m
1:00 (1:03) (Class 3) (0-135,135) 4-Y-O+ **£6,498** (£1,908; £954)

Form RPR

11-1 **1** **Red Spinner (IRE)**[24] 2541 5-11-8 **135**............ DavidBass 148+
(Kim Bailey) *mde all: pushed clr appr 2 out: easily* **9/4**[2]

1422 **2** 25 **Notnowsam**[30] 2412 4-10-5 **124**............(p) HarrySkelton 113
(Dan Skelton) *chsd wnr: pushed along 7th: rdn after 3 out: wkng whn nt fluent last* **13/8**[1]

514- **3** 21 **Lanceur (FR)**[152] 5022 6-10-9 **122**............ LeightonAspell 117+
(Lucy Wadham) *hld up: rdn after 3 out: disputing 6 l 2nd and hld whn blnd bdly 2 out: eased* **13/8**[1]

4m 9.7s (-0.30) **Going Correction** +0.225s/f (Yiel)
WFA 4 from 5yo+ 5lb **3 Ran SP% 107.0**
Speed ratings (Par 107): **109,96,86**
CSF £5.88 TOTE £2.70; EX 3.90 Trifecta £3.20.
Owner Paul & Clare Rooney **Bred** Horse Breeding Company **Trained** Andoversford, Gloucs

FOCUS
The chase rail was out 12yds up the hill, 24yds on the reservoir bend and 2yds on the stable bend, adding 59yds to the race distance. The field was disappointingly small for this good prize, but it produced a worthy winner. He looks a decent novice, but the runner-up is rated 8lb off.

2994 RACINGUK.COM H'CAP CHASE (17 fncs) 2m 4f
1:30 (1:31) (Class 4) (0-110,110) 4-Y-O+ **£3,994** (£1,240; £667)

Form RPR

14-4 **1** **Toowoomba (IRE)**[22] 2568 7-11-12 **110**............ TomO'Brien 123+
(Philip Hobbs) *a.p: chsd ldr bef 11th: rdn appr 2 out: mstke last: styd on u.p to ld fnl 75yds* **11/4**[2]

-311 **2** 1 1/4 **Capilla (IRE)**[7] 2874 7-11-5 **110** 14ex............(t) MrConorOrr(7) 119+
(Evan Williams) *led: rdn flat: hdd fnl 75yds* **2/1**[1]

6-51 **3** 86 **Derryogue (IRE)**[11] 2811 10-10-4 **95** 7ex............(t) WilliamFeatherstone(7) 18
(Zoe Davison) *hld up: hdwy 8th: chsd ldr next tl appr 11th: sn drvn along: wknd 14th* **7/1**[3]

-354 **P** **Ciceron (IRE)**[43] 2138 9-11-9 **107**............(tp) TrevorWhelan
(Neil King) *prom: lost pl 8th: tk clsr order bef 11th: sn wknd: bhd whn j. slowly 13th: p.u bef next* **8/1**

-1PP **P** **Mor Brook**[61] 1850 7-11-9 **107**............(tp) DavidBass
(Kim Bailey) *chsd ldr: mstke 5th: nt fluent 7th: mstke and lost 2nd 9th: rdn and wknd qckly after next: bhd whn p.u bef 11th* **11/4**[2]

5m 21.4s (3.40) **Going Correction** +0.275s/f (Yiel) **5 Ran SP% 110.3**
Speed ratings (Par 105): **104,103,69, ,**
CSF £8.97 TOTE £3.00: £1.80, £1.20; EX 8.30 Trifecta £35.40.
Owner Taylormaid **Bred** Colm Griffin **Trained** Withycombe, Somerset

FOCUS
The chase rail remained out 12yds up the hill, 24yds on the reservoir bend and 2yds on the stable bend, adding 64yds to the race distance. The pace was good, making it a good test. The runner-up looks to have run close to his recent level.

2995 EVENTMASTERS TWICKENHAM HOSPITALITY PACKAGES MAIDEN HURDLE (11 hdls) 2m 5f
2:00 (2:02) (Class 4) 4-Y-0+ £3,249 (£954; £477; £238)

Form RPR
1 **Born Survivor (IRE)**[236] 4-11-0 0 HarrySkelton 140+
(Dan Skelton) *a.p: led 3 out: shkn up and edgd lft flat: r.o: readily* 5/6[1]
0 2 2 **Minella Charmer (IRE)**[28] 2460 4-10-11 0 (t) TomBellamy(3) 133+
(Alan King) *hld up: hdwy 6th: chsd wnr 2 out: sn rdn: styd on same pce flat* 20/1
2-P2 3 9 **Kerisper (FR)**[31] 2406 6-10-11 0 RyanHatch(3) 123
(Nigel Twiston-Davies) *chsd ldr tl led 7th: hdd 3 out: sn rdn: wknd last* 5/1[3]
2 4 7 **Beware The Bear (IRE)**[41] 2163 5-10-9 0 FreddieMitchell(5) 117
(Nicky Henderson) *chsd ldrs: pushed along after 7th: wknd appr 2 out* 11/4[2]
0 5 7 **Leith Hill Lad**[209] 320 5-11-0 0 AidanColeman 109
(Charlie Longsdon) *chsd ldrs: mstke 5th: rdn and wknd after 3 out* 20/1
6 5 **Whos De Baby (IRE)**[194] 7-11-0 0 RobertDunne 103
(Sarah-Jayne Davies) *chsd ldrs: wnt upsides 7th tl rdn appr 3 out: wknd sn after* 100/1
7 6 **Bandon Roc** 4-11-0 0 DavidBass 100
(Kim Bailey) *hld up: hdwy 6th: rdn bef next: wknd 3 out* 50/1
0-00 8 4 **Aka Doun (FR)**[42] 2154 4-11-0 0 DarylJacob 93
(Emma Lavelle) *hld up: reminder after 5th: effrt 8th: sn wknd* 100/1
0-56 9 4 **Heresmynumber (IRE)**[20] 2612 5-11-0 0 GavinSheehan 90
(Ali Stronge) *prom: lost pl after 3rd: sme hdwy 7th: rdn and wknd appr 3 out* 66/1
00 10 24 **Paris Snow**[7] 2860 5-10-11 0 RobMcCarth(3) 65
(Ian Williams) *hld up: effrt 7th: rdn and wknd next: mstke 3 out* 100/1
0 11 3 ¾ **Some Finish (IRE)**[13] 2763 6-11-0 0 CharliePoste 61
(Robin Dickin) *prom to 6th* 100/1
6/ P **Lord Valentine**[599] 5417 7-11-0 0 NicodeBoinville
(Mark Bradstock) *led: mstke 4th: j.lft 6th: hdd next: sn wknd: bhd whn p.u bef 3 out* 16/1
22-P P **Far From Defeat (IRE)**[61] 1852 5-11-0 0 TomCannon
(Michael Scudamore) *hld up: rdn and wknd 8th: bhd whn p.u bef 2 out* 50/1
5P5 P **Contempt Of Court (IRE)**[16] 2699 6-11-0 0 (v) SeanBowen
(Mark Pitman) *hld up: wknd 7th: bhd whn p.u bef last* 100/1
5m 23.9s (2.90) **Going Correction** +0.325s/f (Yiel) 14 Ran SP% 123.7
Speed ratings (Par 105): **107,106,102,100,97 95,93,91,90,81 79, , ,**
CSF £23.69 TOTE £1.90: £1.10, £3.80, £2.00; EX 24.10 Trifecta £93.20.
Owner Mrs G Widdowson & Mrs R Kelvin-Hughes **Bred** Liam Brady **Trained** Alcester, Warwicks

FOCUS
Run on the outer track at a sound gallop, the form looks solid. The winner has plenty of potential but the next three home can all win over hurdles too. The time was very fast compared with the later handicap.

2996 WARWICK RACECOURSE H'CAP CHASE (18 fncs) 3m
2:30 (2:32) (Class 4) (0-120,120) 4-Y-0+ £3,898 (£1,144; £572; £286)

Form RPR
-63F 1 **Cyclop (IRE)**[7] 2865 4-10-13 **115** (tp) AidanColeman 133+
(David Dennis) *a.p: chsd ldr 15th: led appr 2 out: sn clr: easily* 2/1[1]
P-55 2 14 **Paddy The Oscar (IRE)**[22] 2566 12-10-13 **112** ConorRing(5) 120
(Grace Harris) *led: nt a fluent: hdd 9th: led again 12th: rdn and hdd appr 2 out: sn btn* 20/1
63/2 3 7 **Denali Highway (IRE)**[19] 2648 8-11-12 **120** AndrewThornton 122
(Caroline Bailey) *chsd ldr tl led 9th: hdd 12th: chsd ldr to 14th: wknd appr 2 out: blnd last* 5/1[2]
2-3P 4 3 **Themanfrom Minella (IRE)**[26] 2489 6-11-5 **120** (t) MrMJPKendrick(7) 115
(Ben Case) *hld up: hdwy 12th: wknd after 3 out* 12/1
4-43 5 2 ½ **Ballyrath (IRE)**[32] 2365 5-10-11 **108** (v[1]) RyanHatch(3) 104
(Nigel Twiston-Davies) *chsd ldrs: mstkes 4th and 6th: rdn appr 12th: wknd 15th* 13/2[3]
50-U 6 1 ½ **Incentivise (IRE)**[32] 2366 12-11-6 **114** JakeGreenall 105
(Kerry Lee) *prom: lost pl 7th: drvn along after 11th: wknd 14th* 16/1
P36- 7 nk **Strollawaynow (IRE)**[265] 4884 8-11-10 **118** (p) TomCannon 111
(David Arbuthnot) *hld up: mstke 3rd: hdwy 8th: rdn appr 12th: wknd 14th* 10/1
F-13 8 6 **Georgie Lad (IRE)**[18] 2663 7-11-10 **118** TomO'Brien 105
(Philip Hobbs) *prom: rdn after 11th: wknd appr 3 out* 10/1
-263 P **Handsome Buddy (IRE)**[36] 2276 8-9-13 **96** KieronEdgar(3)
(Michael Gates) *sn bhd: p.u bef 14th* 33/1
1-6P P **Ravens Brook (IRE)**[18] 2668 9-10-8 **102** TrevorWhelan
(Neil King) *chsd ldrs: lost pl 5th: bhd fr 9th: p.u bef 12th* 66/1
-6P4 P **Up For An Oscar (IRE)**[21] 2593 8-11-10 **118** (p) SeanBowen
(Peter Bowen) *hld up: a in rr: rdn and wknd after 11th: bhd whn p.u bef 2 out* 14/1
25-P P **Blown Cover**[26] 2489 6-11-7 **115** DarylJacob
(Emma Lavelle) *hld up: hdwy 7th: wknd 14th: bhd whn p.u bef 2 out* 16/1
6m 38.8s (4.80) **Going Correction** +0.375s/f (Yiel)
WFA 4 from 5yo+ 7lb 12 Ran SP% 116.8
Speed ratings (Par 105): **107,102,100,99,98 97,97,95, , ,**
CSF £42.20 CT £181.97 TOTE £2.70: £1.70, £6.20, £1.30; EX 43.20 Trifecta £142.40.
Owner DD Racing & Professor L P Hardwick **Bred** John Fallon **Trained** Hanley Swan, Worcestershire

FOCUS
The chase rail continued to be out 12yds up the hill, 24yds on the reservoir bend and 2yds on the stable bend, adding 118yds to the race distance. With two front-runners taking one another on, the pace was testing for the trip and ground, and nothing got into it from far back. Another step forward from the winner.

2997 EVENTMASTERS RUGBY HOSPITALITY PACKAGES H'CAP HURDLE (11 hdls) 2m 5f
3:00 (3:02) (Class 4) (0-105,105) 3-Y-0+ £3,249 (£954; £477; £238)

Form RPR
P0-0 1 **Extreme Impact**[24] 2548 9-11-10 **103** (v) KielanWoods 107
(Graeme McPherson) *led to 7th: drvn along appr 3 out: outpcd whn hit 2 out: rallied and mstke last: styd on u.p to ld nr fin* 12/1
3-1F 2 ¾ **Scales (IRE)**[17] 2694 9-11-9 **105** ConorShoemark(3) 108+
(Kerry Lee) *hld up: hdwy 6th: led next: rdn clr and hung lft appr 2 out: hdd nr fin* 7/1[3]
55P- 3 3 ½ **Springhill Lad**[250] 5150 8-11-11 **104** MarkGrant 104
(Geoffrey Deacon) *hld up: mstke 5th: hdwy 3 out: rdn and nt fluent next: hit last: styd on: nt rch ldrs* 33/1
31/4 4 4 ½ **Daliance (IRE)**[23] 2560 6-11-4 **97** (b[1]) AndrewThornton 92
(Noel Williams) *prom: drvn along 8th: sn outpcd: rallied after 3 out: wknd appr last* 9/2[2]
050P 5 8 **Ballinalacken (IRE)**[9] 2839 7-11-12 **105** (v[1]) DavidEngland 91
(Clare Ellam) *hld up: hdwy 7th: rdn and wknd appr 2 out* 20/1
P-30 6 nk **Brise Coeur (FR)**[33] 2362 4-11-4 **102** LizzieKelly(5) 88
(Nick Williams) *chsd ldrs: rdn appr 3 out: wknd next* 5/2[1]
53/P 7 21 **Raduis Bleu (FR)**[17] 2694 10-10-9 **95** MissLBrooke(7) 60
(Lady Susan Brooke) *mid-div: hdwy 5th: wknd 7th* 20/1
-160 8 ½ **Youngdocgallagher (IRE)**[156] 939 6-11-6 **102** BenPoste(3) 66
(Michael Mullineaux) *chsd ldr: mstke 6th: sn lost 2nd rdn and wknd after 7th* 7/1[3]
-5P6 9 24 **War And Contrition (IRE)**[7] 2862 6-11-3 **96** AlainCawley 36
(Charlie Longsdon) *hld up: nvr on terms* 10/1
2100 10 22 **Powderonthebonnet (IRE)**[22] 2577 7-11-2 **100** DanielHiskett(5) 18
(Richard Phillips) *prom: mstke 4th: wknd 7th* 20/1
34P- P **Triggers Ginger**[349] 3268 10-10-10 **94** CiaranGethings(5)
(Paul Cowley) *mid-div: wknd 7th: bhd whn p.u bef 2 out* 50/1
0346 P **Darnitnev**[22] 2569 5-11-2 **95** (v[1]) AndrewTinkler
(Martin Keighley) *hld up: mstke 5th: wknd 7th: bhd whn p.u bef 2 out* 17/2
P6P- P **Unify**[254] 5078 5-10-6 **85** (t) TomO'Brien
(Grant Cann) *prom to 8th: bhd whn p.u bef 2 out* 33/1
5m 37.7s (16.70) **Going Correction** +0.425s/f (Soft)
WFA 4 from 5yo+ 6lb 13 Ran SP% 121.2
Speed ratings (Par 105): **85,84,83,81,78 78,70,70,61,52 , ,**
CSF £86.52 CT £2722.96 TOTE £14.20: £5.00, £3.30, £9.10; EX 119.00 Trifecta £365.60.
Owner Graeme P McPherson **Bred** Juddmonte Farms Ltd **Trained** Upper Oddington, Gloucs

FOCUS
Run on the outer course, this was a routine handicap hurdle run at a medium gallop. The first two were on reasonable marks.

2998 EVENTMASTERS CELEBRATES ITS 30TH ANNIVERSARY STANDARD OPEN NATIONAL HUNT FLAT RACE 2m
3:30 (3:32) (Class 6) 4-6-Y-O £1,624 (£477; £238; £119)

Form RPR
3-1 1 **Willoughby Court (IRE)**[23] 2562 4-11-7 0 DavidBass 115+
(Ben Pauling) *mde all: rdn over 1f out: styd on wl: eased nr fin* 6/4[1]
45-6 2 8 **Infinityandbeyond (IRE)**[21] 2597 4-11-0 0 TrevorWhelan 98
(Neil King) *a.p: chsd wnr over 6f out: rdn over 2f out: styd on same pce fr over 1f out* 20/1
3 3 ¼ **Minella Daddy (IRE)**[257] 5-11-0 0 SeanBowen 94
(Peter Bowen) *chsd wnr over 9f: rdn over 3f out: sn outpcd* 11/4[2]
4 6 **My Cousin Rachel (IRE)** 4-10-4 0 TomBellamy(3) 81
(Kim Bailey) *hld up: hdwy over 7f out: rdn and wknd 2f out* 8/1
P 5 38 **Saruni (IRE)**[7] 2875 4-10-11 0[1] ConorShoemark(3) 50
(Jennifer Mason) *hld up: rdn and wknd over 5f out* 66/1
0 6 13 **Poetry Emotion (IRE)**[215] 213 4-11-0 0 NicodeBoinville 37
(Nicky Henderson) *plld hrd and prom: rdn and wknd 4f out* 11/2[3]
3 7 2 ¼ **Rebel Beat**[33] 2337 4-11-0 0 AidanColeman 35
(David Dennis) *trckd ldrs: plld hrd: wknd 5f out* 7/1
4m 6.5s (21.10) **Going Correction** +0.475s/f (Soft) 7 Ran SP% 111.9
Speed ratings: **66,62,60,57,38 31,30**
CSF £32.15 TOTE £2.20: £1.60, £7.50; EX 28.60 Trifecta £84.00.
Owner Paul & Clare Rooney **Bred** J H Kidd **Trained** Bourton-On-The-Water, Gloucs

FOCUS
Like the hurdle races, this was run on the outer course. The pace was steady. The winner is still on the upgrade and there should be more to come.
T/Plt: £31.30 to a £1 stake. Pool: £40,489.82 - 942.19 winning tickets. T/Qpdt: £10.10 to a £1 stake. Pool: £3,341.75 - 243.32 winning tickets. **Colin Roberts**

2999 - 3005a (Foreign Racing) - See Raceform Interactive

2764
BANGOR-ON-DEE (L-H)
Friday, December 11

OFFICIAL GOING: Hurdle course - soft (heavy in places); chase course - heavy
Wind: moderate 1/2 behind Weather: fine and sunny but breezy

3006 STELLA ARTOIS NOVICES' CHASE (11 fncs 1 omitted) 2m 1f 77y
12:20 (12:20) (Class 4) 4-Y-0+ £4,659 (£1,446; £779)

Form RPR
242- 1 **Vyta Du Roc (FR)**[245] 5254 6-10-13 0 DarylJacob 146+
(Nicky Henderson) *mde all: drvn and jnd 2 out: j.lft last: fnd ex nr fin* 4/9[1]
32-0 2 ½ **The Saint James (FR)**[223] 96 4-10-7 0 (t) JoshuaMoore 138
(Jonjo O'Neill) *trckd ldrs: clr 2nd 7th: nt fluent next: pushed along and upsides 2 out: level run-in: no ex nr fin* 2/1[2]
3-0 3 33 **Pressurize (IRE)**[29] 2450 9-10-13 0 LiamTreadwell 115
(Venetia Williams) *t.k.h: trckd wnr: nt fluent 2nd: lost pl 5th: reminders next: modest 3rd 9th: sn bhd: t.o* 66/1
1- F **Cloughernagh Boy (IRE)**[578] 232 7-10-10 0 KieronEdgar(3)
(David Pipe) *trckd ldrs: j.lft 6th: j.lft and lost pl next: poor 4th at 9th: t.o next: stmbld on landing and fell heavily last* 20/1[3]
4m 39.2s (17.10) **Going Correction** +1.325s/f (Heav)
WFA 4 from 6yo+ 5lb 4 Ran SP% 108.8
Speed ratings (Par 105): **112,111,96,**
CSF £1.80 TOTE £1.30; EX 1.90 Trifecta £7.90.
Owner Simon Munir & Isaac Souede **Bred** Andre Le Gall **Trained** Upper Lambourn, Berks

FOCUS
The entire length of the hurdle course had been moved onto fresh ground. Hurdle race distances were as advertised, but chase races were subject to the following distance changes: Race 1- 2m 1f 100y (+23y), Race 2- 2m 4f 95y (+23y), Race 3- 3m 61y (+31y). An informative opener, which produced a good finish between two exciting chase recruits. The winner has been rated similar to his hurdle mark but should develop into a 150+ novice chaser. The second has been rated to his French chase mark.

3007 STELLA CIDRE MARES' H'CAP CHASE (14 fncs 1 omitted) 2m 4f 72y
12:55 (12:55) (Class 4) (0-120,116) 4-Y-0+ **£5,198** (£1,526; £763; £381)

Form RPR
13-2 **1** **Kassis**[36] 2300 6-10-13 **103**.......................... BrendanPowell 105
(Jamie Snowden) *w ldr 2nd: led 9th: fnd ex in clsng stages* **13/8**[1]
002/ **2** 1/2 **September Blaze**[631] 4918 8-11-2 **106**.......................... CharliePoste 108
(Paul Webber) *hld up: trckd ldrs 3rd: 2nd 11th: chal 2 out: upsides run-in: no ex nr fin* **22/1**
5-41 **3** 3/4 **Rosa Fleet (IRE)**[32] 2403 7-11-12 **116**.......................... LiamTreadwell 119
(Venetia Williams) *nt fluent: chsd ldrs: lost pl briefly 3rd: drvn 9th: outpcd and hit 11th: rallied and 3rd 2 out: 2 l down last: hung lft: kpt on towards fin* **2/1**[2]
-422 **4** 8 **Ballydague Lady (IRE)**[24] 2551 8-11-8 **112**..........(p) MarkQuinlan 108
(Neil Mulholland) *chsd ldrs: hit 10th: outpcd next: rallied 2 out: wknd last* **10/3**[3]
3-P4 **5** 39 **Miss Dimples (IRE)**[18] 2692 6-9-11 **90** oh14..........(b) JamesBanks(3) 44
(Sarah-Jayne Davies) *led: hdd 9th: lost pl sn after 12th: sn bhd: t.o* **9/1**

5m 51.2s (42.10) **Going Correction** +1.325s/f (Heav) **5 Ran SP% 108.9**
Speed ratings (Par 105): **68,67,67,64,48**
CSF £22.98 TOTE £2.70: £1.60, £9.90; EX 31.60 Trifecta £66.30.
Owner Mrs J A Thomas **Bred** Upton Viva Stud **Trained** Lambourn, Berks

FOCUS
The race distance had been increased by 23yds. The market proved a key guide in this moderate mares' only contest. Small steps up from the first two.

3008 PROACTIVE PERSONNEL H'CAP CHASE (16 fncs 2 omitted) 3m 30y
1:30 (1:30) (Class 3) (0-135,132) 4-Y-0+ **£7,797** (£2,289; £1,144; £572)

Form RPR
20-5 **1** **Ballyculla (IRE)**[223] 95 8-11-12 **132**..........(p) DenisO'Regan 141+
(Warren Greatrex) *led: hdd 14th: led between last 2: j.lft last: styd on* **7/2**[2]
45-5 **2** 2 **Take The Mick**[29] 2451 8-10-8 **114**.......................... LiamTreadwell 120
(Venetia Williams) *chsd wnr: lost pl and hit 10th: sn bhd: hit 2 out: stl 5th last: styd on wl clsng stages: tk 2nd nr fin* **7/2**[2]
12-1 **3** 1/2 **Hi Vic (IRE)**[27] 2491 10-10-11 **122**.......................... CiaranGethings(5) 127
(David Loder) *trckd ldrs: mstke and lost pl 7th: bhd 9th: wnt poor 4th 12th: modest 3rd appr 2 out: 2nd last 75yds: kpt on same pce* **3/1**[1]
-42U **4** 7 **Auvergnat (FR)**[7] 2878 5-11-4 **124**..........(p) JoshuaMoore 125+
(Jonjo O'Neill) *rn in snatches: trcking ldrs whn j.lft 9th: upsides whn hit 13th: led next: hdd between last 2: wknd last* **9/2**[3]
1-62 **5** 1 1/2 **Russe Blanc (FR)**[15] 2724 8-11-7 **127**..........(p) CharliePoste 123
(Kerry Lee) *chsd ldrs: reminder 8th: drvn 13th: wknd 2 out* **3/1**[1]

6m 50.7s (30.90) **Going Correction** +1.325s/f (Heav) **5 Ran SP% 112.6**
Speed ratings (Par 107): **101,100,100,97,97**
CSF £16.07 TOTE £3.30: £2.20, £2.50; EX 18.10 Trifecta £85.70.
Owner No Dramas & Robert Aplin **Bred** J Mangan **Trained** Upper Lambourn, Berks

FOCUS
The race distance had been increased by 31yds. This took plenty of getting in the testing conditions. A small pb from the winner.

3009 MIKE PRYDE ELECTRICAL SERVICES LTD "NATIONAL HUNT" NOVICES' HURDLE (9 hdls) 2m 145y
2:05 (2:05) (Class 4) 4-Y-0+ **£4,548** (£1,335; £667; £333)

Form RPR
32-1 **1** **Ma Du Fou (FR)**[33] 2363 5-11-5 127.......................... DenisO'Regan 135+
(Warren Greatrex) *mde all: clr fr 6th: v easily* **30/100**[1]
4-64 **2** 10 **Petrou (IRE)**[23] 2581 5-10-12 0.......................... CharliePoste 109
(Ben Case) *chsd wnr tl appr 2 out: regained modest 2nd and mstke last: no ch w wnr* **17/2**[3]
05/5 **3** 3 1/2 **Herons Heir (IRE)**[31] 2409 7-10-12 0.......................... IanPopham 106
(Dan Skelton) *trckd ldrs: t.k.h: modest 2nd 3 out: wknd last* **4/1**[2]
405 **4** 6 **Kilronan Castle**[14] 2754 4-10-12 0.......................... AdrianLane 99
(Donald McCain) *towards rr: hdwy to chse ldrs 4th: outpcd 6th* **14/1**
0-5 **5** 4 **Lime Street (IRE)**[37] 2270 4-10-12 0.......................... JeremiahMcGrath 95
(Tom Symonds) *t.k.h: sn trcking ldrs: lost pl 6th* **20/1**
0-5 **6** 3 1/2 **Jellied Eel Jack (IRE)**[16] 2716 6-10-12 0.......................... DarylJacob 91
(Donald McCain) *in rr: hdwy 3rdf: outpcd and lost pl 6th* **20/1**
7 8 **Leaving Las Vegas**[172] 820 4-10-9 0.......................... JamesBanks(3) 83
(William Kinsey) *in rr: pushed along 5th: bhd next* **40/1**
00-0 **8** 14 **On The Road (IRE)**[31] 2409 5-10-7 0.......................... ConorRing(5) 69
(Evan Williams) *chsd ldrs: drvn and lost pl 6th: sn wl bhd* **100/1**

4m 11.0s (0.10) **Going Correction** +0.225s/f (Yiel)
WFA 4 from 5yo+ 5lb **8 Ran SP% 127.1**
Speed ratings (Par 105): **108,103,101,98,96 95,91,84**
CSF £4.90 TOTE £1.20: £1.02, £2.00, £2.10; EX 6.40 Trifecta £18.70.
Owner Walters Plant Hire & James & Jean Potter **Bred** Scea Ecurie Jc Laisis **Trained** Upper Lambourn, Berks

FOCUS
The entire length of the hurdle course had been moved onto fresh ground. Hurdle race distances were as advertised, but chase races were subject to the following distance changes: Race 1- 2m 1f 100y(+23y), Race 2- 2m 4f 95y(+23y), Race 3- 3m 61y(+31y). This was uncompetitive and was won in a canter by the long odds-on favourite. The easy winner was value for a lot further and has been rated in line with his recent win. The fourth and sixth help set the level.

3010 ALFA AGGREGATES GOLDEN SPURS H'CAP HURDLE (QUALIFIER FOR THE CHALLENGER STAYING HURDLE SERIES) (12 hdls) 2m 7f 32y
2:40 (2:41) (Class 3) (0-135,129) 4-Y-0+ **£6,657** (£2,067; £1,113)

Form RPR
2104 **1** **Volcanic (FR)**[46] 2105 6-11-11 **122**..........(t) DarylJacob 128+
(Donald McCain) *mde all: pushed along 2 out: sn clr: eased clsng stages* **4/1**[3]
51P- **2** 9 **Golden Milan (IRE)**[243] 5290 7-11-12 **123**.......................... JamieMoore 119
(Rebecca Curtis) *chsd ldrs: 3rd whn blnd 9th: chsd wnr appr 2 out: no imp* **10/1**
3 2 **The Mad Well (IRE)**[26] 2524 6-11-0 **111**.......................... BrendanPowell 104
(Edmond Daniel Linehan, Ire) *trckd wnr: blnd and rdr briefly lost iron 3rd: effrt 3 out: wknd next* **9/4**[2]
U001 **F** **Goodbye Dancer (FR)**[2] 2977 4-11-13 **129** 7ex.......................... JamieBargary(5)
(Nigel Twiston-Davies) *hld up in last but wl in tch: j.rt at times: trcking other 3 whn fell 8th* **1/1**[1]

6m 9.5s (18.50) **Going Correction** +0.225s/f (Yiel) **4 Ran SP% 109.9**
Speed ratings (Par 107): **76,72,72,**
CSF £28.52 TOTE £5.10; EX 10.40 Trifecta £53.30.
Owner Elite Racing Club **Bred** Guy Cherel And Emmanuel Cherel **Trained** Cholmondeley, Cheshire

FOCUS
The entire length of the hurdle course had been moved onto fresh ground. Hurdle race distances were as advertised, but chase races were subject to the following distance changes: Race 1- 2m 1f 100y(+23y), Race 2- 2m 4f 95y(+23y), Race 3- 3m 61y(+31y). A weak race for the level and with the favourite falling and Irish raider The Mad Well running well below expectations, it took little winning. The winner has been rated to his mark, with the third around 5lb off his Irish mark.

3011 STELLA ARTOIS CONDITIONAL JOCKEYS' H'CAP HURDLE (6 hdls 3 omitted) 2m 145y
3:10 (3:12) (Class 4) (0-105,104) 3-Y-0+ **£3,249** (£954; £477; £238)

Form RPR
32-5 **1** **Hollywood All Star (IRE)**[19] 2664 6-10-9 **95**.......................... ArchieBellamy(8) 113+
(Graeme McPherson) *trckd ldrs: led appr 2 out: wnt wl clr between last 2: heavily eased fnl 100yds* **15/2**
-543 **2** 12 **Theatrical Style (IRE)**[13] 2768 6-11-6 **104**.......................... JamesCowley(6) 102
(Donald McCain) *chsd ldrs: reminders omitted 3 out: kpt on between last 2: tk remote 2nd clsng stages* **9/2**[2]
-060 **3** 1 1/4 **Catchin Time (IRE)**[25] 2547 7-11-5 **97**..........(t) JeremiahMcGrath 96
(Laura Hurley) *t.k.h: trckd ldrs: chsd wnr appr last: kpt on same pce* **16/1**
P-16 **4** nse **Helamis**[12] 2812 5-11-0 **92**.......................... CiaranGethings 88
(Barry Leavy) *mid-div: outpcd normal 3 out: kpt on between last 2: tk 4th clsng stages* **9/1**
640- **5** nk **Jaunty Inflight**[240] 5343 6-11-4 **101**.......................... WilliamFeatherstone(5) 96
(Brian Eckley) *in rr: hdwy normal 5th: drvn normal 3 out: kpt on between last 2* **9/2**[2]
5004 **6** 3/4 **Omgnotanother (IRE)**[19] 2665 4-10-11 **92**.......................... ConorRing(3) 89
(Evan Williams) *led: hdd appr 2 out: 3rd whn blnd last: fdd* **18/1**
00-0 **7** 19 **Navanman (IRE)**[15] 2734 6-11-8 **103**.......................... KieronEdgar(3) 79
(David Pipe) *in rr: chsd ldrs normal 4 out: lost pl after normal 3 out: sn bhd* **6/1**[3]
20-1 **P** **Maria's Choice (IRE)**[25] 2547 6-11-6 **104**.......................... PaulJohn(6)
(Jim Best) *hld up in rr: hdwy normal 5th: drvn next: lost pl bef 2 out: sn bhd: p.u bef last* **9/4**[1]

4m 16.9s (6.00) **Going Correction** +0.225s/f (Yiel)
WFA 4 from 5yo+ 5lb **8 Ran SP% 114.3**
Speed ratings (Par 105): **94,88,87,87,87 87,78,**
CSF £41.47 CT £525.13 TOTE £9.00: £2.70, £1.40, £3.70; EX 50.20 Trifecta £681.80.
Owner The McPherson Racing Partnership **Bred** James Waldron **Trained** Upper Oddington, Gloucs

FOCUS
The entire length of the hurdle course had been moved onto fresh ground. Hurdle race distances were as advertised, but chase races were subject to the following distance changes: Race 1- 2m 1f 100y (+23y), Race 2- 2m 4f 95y (+23y), Race 3- 3m 61y (+31y). This was run an early crawl and benefited those ridden up with the pace. A step up from the easy winner, with the second, fourth and sixth setting the level.

3012 DU CONSTRUCTION LTD INTERMEDIATE OPEN NATIONAL HUNT FLAT RACE 2m 145y
3:40 (3:41) (Class 5) 4-6-Y-O **£1,949** (£572; £286; £143)

Form RPR
/ **1** **Matchaway (IRE)**[137] 1125 6-11-2 0.......................... JakeGreenall 104+
(Kerry Lee) *trckd ldr: drvn over 3f out: led 2f out: drvn out* **13/8**[1]
2 2 3/4 **Apache Outlaw (IRE)**[327] 6-11-2 0.......................... JamieMoore 102
(Rebecca Curtis) *t.k.h: led: hdd 2f out: kpt on same pce appr fnl f* **3/1**[3]
3-0 **3** 1 1/2 **Classic Tune**[34] 2337 5-11-2 0.......................... JoshuaMoore 100
(Claire Dyson) *in rr: hdwy 6f out: 3rd and drvn over 3f out: kpt on same pce fnl 2f* **20/1**
4 25 **Jacksey's Well (IRE)**[54] 1997 4-10-13 0.......................... KieronEdgar(3) 75
(Edmond Daniel Linehan, Ire) *trckd ldrs: modest 4th and drvn over 3f out: lost pl over 2f out* **18/1**
5 2 1/2 **Spirit Of Hale (IRE)** 4-10-9 0.......................... ConorWalsh(7) 73
(Jennie Candlish) *in rr: sn pushed along: bhd and drvn after 6f: nvr on terms* **33/1**
3 **6** 5 **Our Reward (IRE)**[63] 1843 5-11-2 0.......................... BrendanPowell 68
(Jamie Snowden) *racd wd towards rr: hdwy 7f out: sn drvn: lost pl over 5f out: sn wl bhd* **2/1**[2]
7 dist **Despearado** 4-11-2 0.......................... IanPopham
(Richard Phillips) *rr-divisiion: hdwy after 4f: pushed along 9f out: bhd and reminders 6f out: sn t.o: virtually p.u over 1f out: eventually completed* **20/1**

4m 4.8s (-0.50) **Going Correction** +0.225s/f (Yiel) **7 Ran SP% 114.2**
Speed ratings: **110,108,108,96,95 92,**
CSF £6.75 TOTE £2.70: £1.50, £1.80; EX 6.70 Trifecta £42.30.
Owner Mr & Mrs C R Elliott & Will Roseff **Bred** D O'Sullivan & Dr Margaret O'Sullivan **Trained** Byton, H'fords

FOCUS
The entire length of the hurdle course had been moved onto fresh ground. Hurdle race distances were as advertised, but chase races were subject to the following distance changes: Race 1- 2m 1f 100y(+23y), Race 2- 2m 4f 95y(+23y), Race 3- 3m 61y(+31y). The market spoke volumes in this concluding bumper, the winner backed into 13-8 from an opening 11-4. The first three home pulled well clear. The winner was the pick on his Irish form and has been rated to a similar level.
T/Plt: £152.40 to a £1 stake. Pool: £37,982.36 - 181.86 winning tickets T/Qpdt: £38.10 to a £1 stake. Pool: £2,862.71 - 55.6 winning tickets **Walter Glynn**

2509 CHELTENHAM (L-H)
Friday, December 11
OFFICIAL GOING: Chase & hurdle course - soft (good to soft in places; 6.9); cross-country course - good to soft (7.4)
Wind: mild across Weather: light rain

3013 HARRISON JAMES AND HARDIE NOVICES' CHASE (21 fncs) 3m 1f 56y
12:00 (12:01) (Class 2) 4-Y-0+ **£14,442** (£4,303; £2,178; £1,115; £584)

Form RPR
4-4F **1** **Blaklion**[27] 2481 6-11-1 144.......................... RyanHatch 156+
(Nigel Twiston-Davies) *trckd ldrs: chal 2 out: led bef last: styd on wl: rdn out* **3/1**[2]

11-1 **2** *2 1/2* **Onenightinvienna (IRE)**[19] 2660 6-11-6 0........................ TomO'Brien 157
(Philip Hobbs) *trckd ldr: chal 2 out: sn rdn: ev ch last: styd on but no ex* **11/2[3]**

2-P2 **3** *6* **Fletchers Flyer (IRE)**[19] 2660 7-11-1 0..............................(t) NoelFehily 148
(Harry Fry) *led: rdn and hdd after 2 out: styd on same pce fr last* **3/1[2]**

1131 **4** *9* **Vicente (FR)**[27] 2481 6-11-9 153........................... SamTwiston-Davies 154+
(Paul Nicholls) *nvr that fluent: trckd ldrs: hit 11th and 4 out: outpcd after next: wnt wl hld 4th run-in* **13/2**

11-2 **5** *6* **Private Malone (IRE)**[21] 2627 6-11-1 0.......................... GavinSheehan 133
(Emma Lavelle) *trckd ldrs: rdn after 3 out: hld next: wknd last* **16/1**

11-3 **P** **Minella Rocco (IRE)**[21] 2627 5-11-1 0.........................(t) BarryGeraghty
(Jonjo O'Neill) *trcking ldrs whn blnd bdly 4th: nvr rcvrd and p.u after 6th: dismntd* **5/2[1]**

6m 36.2s (-2.00) **Going Correction** +0.225s/f (Yiel) **6** Ran SP% **113.2**
Speed ratings (Par 109): **112,111,109,106,104**
CSF £19.46 TOTE £4.20: £2.00, £2.60; EX 19.60 Trifecta £64.10.
Owner S Such & Cg Paletta **Bred** Mrs M D W Morrison **Trained** Naunton, Gloucs

FOCUS
Some starts have been moved at this track following remeasuring, so some races will not have speed figures until there is sufficient data to calculate updated median times. Chase bends were dolled out 12yds adding 72yds per circuit; Hurdle bends were dolled out 10yds adding 60yds per circuit. The distance of this race was increased by 144yds. Noel Fehily described the ground as "soft". A good-quality novice chase with the emphasis on stamina. Blaklion is on the upgrade and raround 10lb off a typical RSA Chase winner.

3014 THERACINGUNION.CO.UK EXCLUSIVELY FOR STUDENTS CONDITIONAL JOCKEYS' H'CAP CHASE (17 fncs) 2m 4f 166y

12:35 (12:35) (Class 3) (0-125,127)
4-Y-O+
£7,507 (£2,217; £1,108; £554; £277; £139)

Form RPR

5P54 **1** **Lord Landen (IRE)**[15] 2724 10-10-3 102........................(t) NickSlatter 110
(Fergal O'Brien) *hld up: sme hdwy whn lft 4th 4 out: rdn after 3 out: wnt 3rd between last 2: 5 1/2 l down last: hanging lft but styd on wl to ld fnl stride* **16/1**

P-6P **2** *shd* **Comeonginger (IRE)**[43] 2153 8-11-10 123..................(t) ThomasGarner 130+
(Chris Gordon) *trckd ldr: lft in ld 6th: rdn after 3 out: 3 l clr last where rdr briefly lost iron: edgd lft: hdd fnl stride* **25/1**

0-U1 **3** *3 1/4* **The Cobbler Swayne (IRE)**[36] 2293 6-11-6 122........ GrantCockburn(3) 129+
(Lucinda Russell) *hld up: hmpd 6th: hdwy 11th: lft 2nd 4 out: rdn after next: hit 2 out: hld in 3 l 2nd whn mstke last: no ex* **9/1[3]**

-335 **4** *10* **Bincombe**[14] 2758 7-11-6 125.......................................(bt) ConorSmith(6) 122
(Philip Hobbs) *mid-div: pushed along fr 11th: lft 3rd whn hmpd 4 out: styd on same pce fr next: lost 3rd between last 2* **12/1**

23-4 **5** *20* **Son Of Suzie**[40] 2213 7-11-3 119.............................. ConorShoemark(3) 98
(Fergal O'Brien) *mid-div: rdn along fr 10th: hmpd 4 out: wknd after next* **6/1[1]**

1P/2 **6** *7* **Rocking Blues (FR)**[32] 2400 10-10-13 112.......................... CraigNichol 84
(Rose Dobbin) *mid-div: hit 4th: in last pair whn mstke 12th: wknd after 3 out: t.o* **10/1**

1U-4 **7** *18* **Roberto Pegasus (USA)**[32] 2404 9-11-9 125................ TomBellamy(3) 77
(Alan King) *mid-div: rdn after 10th: in last pair whn mstke 13th: wknd after 3 out: t.o* **14/1**

23-4 **F** **Hayjack**[29] 2451 10-11-4 117.. KillianMoore
(Martin Keighley) *led tl fell 6th: fatally injured* **6/1[1]**

-3P2 **U** **Garrahalish (IRE)**[21] 2615 7-11-12 125.......................... CharlieDeutsch
(Robin Dickin) *trckd ldrs: gng wl enough whn sltly hmpd and uns rdr 4 out* **7/1[2]**

446- **F** **Ultragold (FR)**[260] 4998 7-11-5 124.............................(t) PaulO'Brien(6)
(Colin Tizzard) *trckd ldr: travelling wl whn fell 4 out* **6/1[1]**

-501 **F** **Kilronan High (IRE)**[10] 2837 6-11-11 127 7ex................(t) RyanHatch(3)
(Nigel Twiston-Davies) *nt that fluent in last pair: pushed along fr 10th: hdwy after next: rdn after 13th: chsng ldrs whn fell 4 out* **6/1[1]**

5m 28.3s (12.60) **Going Correction** +0.225s/f (Yiel) **11** Ran SP% **112.8**
Speed ratings (Par 107): **85,84,83,79,72 69,62, , ,**
CSF £313.29 CT £3761.26 TOTE £19.30: £5.50, £5.00, £2.60; EX 272.70 Trifecta £3875.90 Part won..
Owner The B Lucky Partnership **Bred** Richard And Marie Hennessy **Trained** Naunton, Gloucs
■ Stewards' Enquiry : Nick Slatter four-day ban: use of whip (28, 30, 31 Dec and 1 Jan)

FOCUS
The distance of this race was increased by 72yds. No hanging around here in what was an eventful handicap chase, with the two outsiders ultimately coming to the fore. The key moment came at the fourth from home when three of the runners, all of whom were in with a chance, exited the race. The winner is rated back to form.

3015 CF ROBERTS ELECTRICAL + MECHANICAL SERVICES H'CAP HURDLE (8 hdls) 2m 179y

1:10 (1:14) (Class 3) (0-140,135) 3-Y-O+
£7,507 (£2,217; £1,108; £554; £277; £139)

Form RPR

0111 **1** **Solstice Star**[10] 2833 5-10-1 113 7ex........................(t) KillianMoore(3) 122+
(Martin Keighley) *a.p: led after 5th: rdn after 2 out: jnd whn hit last: r.o v gamely to assert fnl 120yds: drvn out* **8/1[3]**

1-20 **2** *2 1/2* **Mad Jack Mytton (IRE)**[26] 2512 5-11-12 135............... RichardJohnson 139
(Jonjo O'Neill) *mid-div: hdwy after 2 out: chal last: sn rdn and edging lft: no ex fnl 120yds* **14/1**

-631 **3** *1/2* **Kayf Blanco**[27] 2499 6-11-12 135.................................... KielanWoods 141+
(Graeme McPherson) *hld up towards rr: hdwy 2 out: nt clrest of runs but wnt 5th jumping last: rdn and r.o wl run-in: clsng qckly on 2nd at fin* **9/1**

24/1 **4** *1 1/2* **A Hare Breath (IRE)**[28] 2472 7-11-9 132...................... BarryGeraghty 135+
(Ben Pauling) *mid-div: nt clrest of runs after 2 out: wnt cl 3rd at the last: sn rdn: nt gng pce to chal: no ex fnl 120yds* **11/8[1]**

03-3 **5** *1/2* **Cape Caster (IRE)**[33] 2373 4-10-11 120........................ AdamWedge 122
(Evan Williams) *trckd ldrs: disp 2nd after 2 out: rdn bef last: kpt on but nt pce to chal* **16/1**

560- **6** *4* **Some Buckle (IRE)**[245] 5249 6-11-12 135.........(t) SamTwiston-Davies 134
(Paul Nicholls) *in tch: disp 2nd after 2 out: rdn whn briefly short of room appr last: no ex run-in* **13/2[2]**

2 **7** *1 1/4* **Disputed (IRE)**[70] 1734 5-10-10 119.............................. TomCannon 115
(Chris Gordon) *hld up: outpcd after 2 out: styd on run-in* **33/1**

4F **8** *2* **King Muro**[28] 2472 5-10-2 114..............................(t) ConorShoemark(3) 108
(Fergal O'Brien) *hld up towards rr: hdwy 2 out: rdn to dispute 2nd briefly appr last: one pce run-in* **25/1**

-060 **9** *2 1/4* **Olofi (FR)**[26] 2512 9-11-4 127......................................(tp) PaddyBrennan 120
(Tom George) *mid-div: hdwy 3 out: rdn to chse ldrs after 2 out: fdd run-in* **8/1[3]**

U13- **10** *1/2* **Cappielow Park**[9] 4819 6-10-9 118................................(p) GavinSheehan 111
(Ali Stronge) *prom: led 3rd tl after 5th: chsd wnr tl rdn after 2 out: fading whn rdr dropped whip run-in* **25/1**

0 **11** *6* **Auenwirbel (GER)**[13] 2781 4-11-5 128............................(t) RobertDunne 115
(Laura Young) *mid-div: rdn after 2 out: nvr any imp* **66/1**

02-3 **12** *15* **Ascendant**[39] 2247 9-11-10 133...................................(t) NoelFehily 104
(Johnny Farrelly) *chsd ldrs: pushed along fr 3 out: rdn after 2 out: sn wknd* **25/1**

-325 **13** *1/2* **Breaking Bits (IRE)**[50] 2038 8-9-13 115.............................. MissPFuller(7) 85
(Jamie Snowden) *led tl 3rd: chsd ldrs tl wknd after 3 out* **33/1**

0P-2 **14** *13* **Secret Dancer (IRE)**[112] 1310 10-10-0 109 oh11................. JamesBest 66
(Alan Jones) *struggling fr 5th: a towards rr* **33/1**

4m 7.7s (-3.60) **Going Correction** +0.025s/f (Yiel)
WFA 4 from 5yo+ 5lb **14** Ran SP% **122.1**
Speed ratings (Par 107): **109,107,107,106,106 104,104,103,102,101 99,92,91,85**
CSF £104.58 CT £1043.24 TOTE £7.60: £2.00, £3.20, £2.80; EX 126.20 Trifecta £970.80.
Owner E&G Racing Ltd **Bred** David Allen **Trained** Condicote, Gloucs

FOCUS
The distance of this race was increased by 60yds. They got under way at the second attempt, with the tape failing to go up first time, and two of the runners, including the winner, jumped the first hurdle. Useful form with them going a good gallop, and a race that should produce winners.

3016 RYMAN STATIONERY H'CAP CHASE (GRADE 3) (21 fncs) 3m 2f

1:45 (1:47) (Class 1) 4-Y-O+
£25,627 (£9,616; £4,815; £2,398; £1,206; £603)

Form RPR

4-41 **1** **Aachen**[8] 2872 11-9-9 133 5ex.. CharlieDeutsch(5) 153+
(Venetia Williams) *mde all: clr tl 11th: clr again 13th: nt fluent next: pckd 4 out: unchal* **12/1**

03P- **2** *17* **Wonderful Charm (FR)**[230] 5538 7-11-12 159...(tp) SamTwiston-Davies 161
(Paul Nicholls) *patiently rdn in chsng gp: disp 2nd fr 18th tl clr 12 l 2nd 3 out: rdn bef next but nvr any imp on wnr: tired run-in* **15/2[3]**

150- **3** *1 3/4* **Mon Parrain (FR)**[244] 5275 9-11-0 147..............................(bt) SeanBowen 145
(Paul Nicholls) *disp 2nd most of way tl rdn after 4 out: lft 4th next: wnt hld 3rd 2 out: styd on same pce* **14/1**

1-21 **4** *8* **Knock House (IRE)**[28] 2473 6-10-12 145............................ BrianHughes 138
(Mick Channon) *disp 2nd most of way tl after 4 out: stmbld bdly disputing 3rd 3 out: btn 4th whn hit 2 out* **4/1[2]**

-414 **5** *14* **Shuil Royale (IRE)**[22] 2600 10-10-6 139.............................(t) NoelFehily 117
(Harry Fry) *hld up: struggling after 17th: nvr any threat* **8/1**

1F-6 **6** *1/2* **The Druids Nephew (IRE)**[41] 2198 8-11-9 156............(p) BarryGeraghty 138
(Neil Mulholland) *trckd ldrs in chsng gp: nudged along after 11th: 5th and stl in tch in chsng gp whn nrly fell 3 out: sn wknd* **4/1[2]**

1-00 **F** **The Romford Pele (IRE)**[27] 2482 8-11-0 147......................(b) PaulTownend
(Rebecca Curtis) *hld up in chsng gp: struggling 14th: hit next: fell 16th* **8/1**

-111 **U** **Vieux Lion Rouge (FR)**[20] 2643 6-10-13 146................ TomScudamore
(David Pipe) *trckd ldrs in chsng gp: pushed along disputing 3rd whn knuckled on landing and uns rdr 3 out* **10/3[1]**

6m 49.2s (3.20) **Going Correction** +0.225s/f (Yiel) **8** Ran SP% **111.4**
Speed ratings (Par 113): **104,98,98,95,91 91, ,**
CSF £90.81 CT £1247.32 TOTE £10.70: £2.40, £2.00, £4.20; EX 104.20 Trifecta £1275.50.
Owner Tony Bloom **Bred** Darley **Trained** Kings Caple, H'fords

FOCUS
The distance of this race was increased by 144yds. A decent staying handicap that was dominated by the front-running winner, who quickly opened up a lead and stayed away from them off a light weight. A big step up from the winner.

3017 GLENFARCLAS CROSS COUNTRY CHASE (32 fncs) 3m 6f 37y

2:20 (2:21) (Class 2) 5-Y-O+
£21,896 (£6,468; £3,234; £1,617; £808; £406)

Form RPR

6-U1 **1** **Josies Orders (IRE)**[28] 2471 7-11-8 142............................ MsNCarberry 153+
(E Bolger, Ire) *mid-div: hdwy 29th: wnt 3rd after 2 out: mounting chal whncarried lft last: led run-in: styd on wl: drvn out* **11/4[2]**

2-PS **2** *2* **Sire Collonges (FR)**[28] 2471 9-11-8 145..........(b) SamTwiston-Davies 149
(Paul Nicholls) *trckd ldrs: rdn to ld after 2 out: drifted lft at the last: hdd run-in: styd on but no ex* **7/1[3]**

F **3** *12* **Ballyboker Bridge (IRE)**[27] 2506 8-11-2 139..........................(p) AELynch 132
(Peter Maher, Ire) *trckd ldrs: mstke 28th: led briefly after 2 out: sn rdn: styd on same pce fr last* **28/1**

3343 **4** *12* **Bless The Wings (IRE)**[12] 2818 10-11-8 141......................(p) MrJJCodd 127
(Gordon Elliott, Ire) *hld up bhd: sme prog 28th: rdn and hdwy after 2 out: wnt 4th at the last: nvr trbld ldrs* **14/1**

2164 **5** *6* **Valadom (FR)**[28] 2471 6-11-2 125...................................(t) AlainCawley 114
(Richard Hobson) *led at gd pce: nt fluent 2 out: sn rdn and hdd: fading whn nt fluent last* **50/1**

1/ **6** *1/2* **Martalin (FR)**[76] 9-11-8 0...(tp) ArnoldCisel 119
(Patrice Quinton, France) *in tch: hit 4th: rdn after 30th: wknd bef last* **33/1**

7 *13* **Mtada Supreme (IRE)**[27] 2506 10-11-2 125........................ MrBOWalsh 100
(Peter Maher, Ire) *mid-div: 5th and in tch 15th: disputing 4th w wnr 28th: rdn after 3 out: wknd bef last* **100/1**

-342 **8** *35* **Any Currency (IRE)**[28] 2471 12-11-8 157..................(p) RichardJohnson 71
(Martin Keighley) *chsd ldrs: drvn along fr 17th: wknd 23rd: t.o* **5/2[1]**

0-P0 **9** *30* **Rivage D'Or (FR)**[28] 2471 10-11-8 141..................................(t) DavyRussell 41
(A J Martin, Ire) *mid-div tl wknd 29th: t.o* **16/1**

3-1S **P** **Uncle Junior (IRE)**[28] 2471 14-11-8 149...........................(p) MrPWMullins
(W P Mullins, Ire) *a last: wl bhd whn hmpd 28th: p.u last* **10/1**

-P00 **U** **On His Own (IRE)**[27] 2506 11-11-8 160............................. PaulTownend
(W P Mullins, Ire) *hld up bhd: blnd and uns rdr 20th* **8/1**

2450 **P** **Kilbree Kid (IRE)**[28] 2471 8-11-8 134............................(t) CharlieDeutsch
(Tom George) *mid-div tl wknd 23rd: t.o whn p.u 26th* **50/1**

F **First To Boogie (IRE)**[27] 2506 7-10-10 132........................ MrJPMcKeown
(Aidan Anthony Howard, Ire) *towards rr of midfield: mstke 26th: in last pair and btn whn fell 28th* **50/1**

00/0 **U** **Love Rory (IRE)**[27] 2506 7-11-5 141.................................... APHeskin
(E Bolger, Ire) *mid-div: mstke 4th: blnd and uns rdr 11th* **16/1**

8m 14.0s (-24.00) **Going Correction** -0.475s/f (Good) **14** Ran SP% **119.6**
Speed ratings: **113,112,109,106,104 104,100,91,83, , ,**
CSF £21.73 TOTE £4.10: £1.80, £2.40, £8.20; EX 23.90 Trifecta £581.80.
Owner John P McManus **Bred** Mrs E Moore **Trained** Bruree, Co Limerick

FOCUS
Run at a good gallop, the standard-setting favourite disappointed, but the form still looks solid, with a progressive winner accounting for the 2013 winner of the race. There's surely more to come from Josies Orders.

3018 CITIPOST H'CAP HURDLE (12 hdls) 2m 7f 213y
2:55 (2:56) (Class 2) 4-Y-0+
£13,763 (£4,065; £2,032; £1,016; £508; £255)

Form				RPR
00/0	1		**So Fine (IRE)**[27] 2484 9-10-7 **126**.......................... JamesBest (Philip Hobbs) *mid-div tl lost pl after being hmpd on bnd bef 7th: in last trio 3 out: rdn after 2 out: gd hdwy to ld on landing last: styd on strly: rdn out* **33/1**	131+
04-P	2	1 3/4	**According To Trev (IRE)**[47] 2089 9-10-6 **130**............(p) JakeHodson[(5)] (David Bridgwater) *a.p: rdn after 2 out: ev ch last: styd on but sn hld by wnr* **66/1**	130
12/3	3	3/4	**Billy Dutton**[37] 2268 9-10-6 **125**.......................... JamesDavies (Chris Down) *trckd ldrs: rdn after 2 out: ev ch after last: no ex fnl 120yds* **16/1**	124
1-12	4	1/2	**The Eaglehaslanded (IRE)**[37] 2268 5-10-6 **125**(tp) SamTwiston-Davies (Paul Nicholls) *hld up on outer: hdwy 2 out: rdn whn outpcd sn after: styd on fr last: snatched 4th cl home* **13/2**	125
U41-	5	1/2	**One Track Mind (IRE)**[297] 4286 5-11-6 **139**.......................... GavinSheehan (Warren Greatrex) *mid-div: hdwy 2 out: rdn to chse ldrs appr last: kpt on same pce run-in: lost 4th cl home* **11/4**[1]	137
22-1	6	2 1/4	**Drum Valley**[51] 2013 7-11-7 **140**.......................... LeightonAspell (Oliver Sherwood) *led: rdn after 2 out: hdd sn after last: no ex* **25/1**	137
3P-2	7	2 3/4	**Zeroeshadesofgrey (IRE)**[41] 2197 6-11-7 **140**.......................... TrevorWhelan (Neil King) *mid-div: hdwy 3 out: rdn to chse ldrs after next: kpt on same pce fr last* **10/1**	133
2211	8	nk	**Monbeg Gold (IRE)**[30] 2441 5-10-11 **130**.......................... RichardJohnson (Jonjo O'Neill) *hld up towards rr: hdwy 2 out: sn rdn to chse ldrs: nt fluent last: kpt on same pce* **9/2**[2]	125+
-214	9	10	**Fingerontheswitch (IRE)**[26] 2513 5-10-4 **123**.......................... TomScudamore (Neil Mulholland) *hld up towards rr: hdwy 7th: effrt after 2 out: sn wknd* **5/1**[3]	106
12-4	10	7	**Oscarteea (IRE)**[20] 2639 6-10-10 **129**.......................... SeanBowen (Peter Bowen) *struggling 7th: a towards rr* **12/1**	107
1P-P	11	2	**Flintham**[38] 2260 6-11-2 **142**..........................(p) LiamMcKenna[(7)] (Mark Bradstock) *pressed ldr: rdn after 2 out: sn wknd* **25/1**	116
-104	12	12	**Bear's Affair (IRE)**[47] 2083 9-11-7 **145**.......................... FreddieMitchell[(5)] (Nicky Henderson) *mid-div: hdwy 9th: effrt after 2 out: sn wknd* **25/1**	107
34-2	P		**Always Tipsy**[41] 2190 6-9-12 **122**.......................... StephenMulqueen[(5)] (N W Alexander) *towards rr of midfield: hdwy after 3 out: rdn after next: sn wknd: p.u last* **25/1**	

6m 2.0s (1.00) **Going Correction** +0.025s/f (Yiel) 13 Ran SP% **117.3**
Speed ratings (Par 109): **99,98,98,98,97 97,96,96,92,90 89,85,**
CSF £1300.68 CT £30416.07 TOTE £51.80: £9.50, £8.90, £4.60; EX 1452.40 Trifecta £3555.60 Part won..
Owner Mrs L R Lovell **Bred** Patrick And John O'Connor **Trained** Withycombe, Somerset

FOCUS
The distance of this race was increased by 100yds. Any number held a chance in the straight in what was a fair handicap run at an ordinary gallop and, as in the 12.35 race, the two complete outsiders came to the fore. The winner is rated in line with his old form.

3019 BRITISH STALLION STUDS EBF "NATIONAL HUNT" NOVICES' HURDLE (QUALIFIER) (8 hdls) 2m 179y
3:25 (3:30) (Class 3) 4-6-Y-0
£7,507 (£2,217; £1,108; £554; £277; £139)

Form				RPR
2	1		**North Hill Harvey**[40] 2221 4-10-12 0.......................... HarrySkelton (Dan Skelton) *travelled wl in tch: hdwy after 2 out: led sn after last: qcknd clr: readily* **4/1**[2]	139+
	2	4 1/2	**Baden (FR)**[208] 4-10-12 0.......................... AndrewTinkler (Nicky Henderson) *trckd ldrs: shkn up after 2 out: ev ch last: sn rdn and hung lft: kpt on but nt pce of wnr* **5/1**[3]	134+
1-2U	3	1/2	**Drumlee Sunset (IRE)**[26] 2509 5-10-12 0.......................... RichardJohnson (Philip Hobbs) *trckd ldr: led 2 out: rdn and jnd bef last: hdd run-in: kpt on same pce* **5/4**[1]	132
2-30	4	6	**Dexcite (FR)**[26] 2512 4-10-12 127..........................[1] PaddyBrennan (Tom George) *hld up: hdwy 2 out: rdn into 4th bef last: styd on same pce* **9/1**	127
11	5	2 3/4	**Nicely Indeed (IRE)**[97] 1484 5-10-5 0.......................... MikeyHamill[(7)] (Seamus Durack) *mid-div: tk clsr order 2 out: lft 4th briefly whn hmpd bef last where wnt bdly lft: styd on same pce* **16/1**	125
5	6	21	**Boston De La Roche (FR)**[14] 2748 4-10-12 0.......................... NoelFehily (David Loder) *led tl 2 out: sn rdn: wknd bef last* **50/1**	105
1165	7	8	**Alyasan (IRE)**[49] 2056 4-10-12 0..........................(t) BrianHughes (Seamus Durack) *racd keenly: hld up: wknd after 2 out* **100/1**	94
-066	8	37	**King Simba (IRE)**[14] 2747 4-10-9 0.......................... TomBellamy[(3)] (Kim Bailey) *hung rt thrght: in tch tl dropped to rr 5th: t.o* **100/1**	57
	U		**Politologue (FR)**[172] 4-11-8 0.......................... SamTwiston-Davies (Paul Nicholls) *in tch: tk clsr order 2 out: nudged along to mount chal whn ducked rt and uns rdr bef last* **6/1**	137

4m 10.8s (-0.50) **Going Correction** +0.025s/f (Yiel) 9 Ran SP% **115.2**
Speed ratings: **102,99,99,96,95 85,81,64,**
CSF £24.48 TOTE £4.90: £1.40, £1.80, £1.30; EX 21.70 Trifecta £54.70.
Owner Mrs G Widdowson & Mrs R Kelvin-Hughes **Bred** E Cantillon **Trained** Alcester, Warwicks

FOCUS
The distance of this race was increased by 60yds. No more than a decent novice hurdle but there were a couple of noteworthy performances. A step up from the winner.

T/Jkpt: Not won. Placepot Jackpot: Not won. T/Plt: £91,774.50 to a £1 stake. Pool: £157,148.16 - 1.25 winning tickets T/Qpdt: £1,218.30 to a £1 stake. Pool: £20,909.41 - 12.7 winning tickets
Tim Mitchell

2771 DONCASTER (L-H)
Friday, December 11

OFFICIAL GOING: Good to soft (good in places; chs 7.4, hdl 7.6)
Wind: Fresh against Weather: Fine

3020 BETDAQ - SERIOUS ABOUT SPORT H'CAP CHASE (15 fncs) 2m 3f 44y
11:40 (11:40) (Class 4) (0-120,120) 4-Y-0+
£3,994 (£1,240; £667)

Form				RPR
54-3	1		**Waltz Darling (IRE)**[14] 2746 7-11-12 **120**.......................... JamesReveley (Keith Reveley) *hld up: mstke 5 out but lft 3rd: nt fluent 3 out: sn rdn: styd on run-in: led post* **3/1**[2]	126
4-4	2	nse	**Cernunnos (FR)**[54] 1989 5-11-12 **120**..........................(t) WayneHutchinson (Tom George) *hld up in tch: hdwy to go prom after 8th: led narrowly 10th: rdn after 3 out: 2 l up last: drvn and one pce: hdd post* **6/1**	125
1/5-	3	7	**Young Palm (IRE)**[42] 2179 8-10-5 **106**..........................(t) AnthonyFox[(7)] (S R B Crawford, Ire) *racd keenly: trckd ldr: led 3rd: hdd 10th: rdn after 3 out: wknd run-in* **9/2**[3]	106
-015	F		**Lord Wishes (IRE)**[40] 2214 8-11-7 **120**..........................(p) DaleIrving[(5)] (James Ewart) *in tch: reminders and dropped to rr after 7th: rallied after 4 out: 2 l down in dispute of 2nd whn fell last* **15/8**[1]	121
0063	U		**Little Windmill (IRE)**[22] 2592 5-9-13 **95** ow3..........................(t) LizzieKelly[(5)] (Neil King) *led: hdd 3rd: trckd ldr: 3 l down in 3rd whn blnd and uns rdr 5 out* **5/1**	

4m 56.1s (7.10) **Going Correction** 0.0s/f (Good) 5 Ran SP% **108.9**
Speed ratings (Par 105): **85,84,82, ,**
CSF £18.70 TOTE £2.90: £1.60, £2.60; EX 14.10 Trifecta £37.70.
Owner Mrs M B Thwaites & M E Foxton **Bred** Ms Natalie Cleary **Trained** Lingdale, Redcar & Cleveland

FOCUS
Hurdle dividing rail on bend into home straight 5yds off inner line. Races 2, 3, 4 & 7 increased by 18yds and race 6 by 36yds. Following only 1mm of overnight rain and a dry morning the ground remained good to soft, good in places. A useful and fairly open handicap but one in which the gallop was an ordinary one. The winner sets the level, with the third rated similar to his hurdle mark.

3021 BETDAQ.COM £25 FREE BET MAIDEN HURDLE (DIV I) (8 hdls) 2m 140y
12:10 (12:11) (Class 5) 4-Y-0+ **£2,924** (£858; £429; £214)

Form				RPR
	1		**Winter Escape (IRE)** 4-11-0 0.......................... WayneHutchinson (Alan King) *in tch: trckd ldng pair gng wl after 3 out: led last: kpt on wl pushed out* **15/8**[1]	123+
	2	3 3/4	**Deauville Dancer (IRE)**[47] 4-11-0 0.......................... AidanColeman (David Dennis) *racd keenly: trckd ldrs: led narrowly 3 out: rdn 2 out: hdd last: kpt on but sn no ch w wnr* **7/2**[3]	113+
22	3	1 1/2	**Call To Order**[27] 2493 5-11-0 0.......................... RichieMcLernon (Jonjo O'Neill) *trckd ldrs: jnd ldr jst after 3 out: rdn 2 out: 3rd whn nt fluent last: kpt on same pce* **11/4**[2]	111+
10-	4	7	**Pomme**[244] 5277 4-10-7 0.......................... ConorO'Farrell (Nigel Hawke) *midfield: mstke and stmbld on landing 2nd: dropped towards rr: hdwy after 3 out: rdn to go 4th jst bef last: kpt on* **50/1**	102+
3	5	3 1/2	**Mister Kalanisi (IRE)**[30] 2440 6-11-0 0.......................... DavidEngland (Dan Skelton) *in tch: rdn after 3 out: nt fluent 2 out: grad wknd* **14/1**	102
30	6	9	**I Just Know (IRE)**[21] 2628 5-11-0 0.......................... DannyCook (Sue Smith) *led: rdn whn hdd 3 out: wknd after 2 out* **14/1**	91
-020	7	2	**Midtech Valentine**[18] 2689 4-10-4 0.......................... RobMcCarth[(3)] (Ian Williams) *midfield: sme hdwy appr 3 out: wknd after 2 out* **100/1**	83
06-4	8	nk	**Baraza (FR)**[30] 2437 4-11-0 0.......................... WillKennedy (Tom George) *prom: rdn 3 out: wknd 2 out* **33/1**	90
0F	9	2 1/4	**Definitly Grey (IRE)**[26] 2519 4-10-11 0.......................... GrahamWatters[(3)] (Charlie Longsdon) *trckd ldrs: rdn appr 3 out: sn wknd* **100/1**	86
F0	10	6	**Top Set (IRE)**[39] 2238 5-10-9 0.......................... DanielHiskett[(5)] (Richard Phillips) *midfield: rdn appr 3 out: wknd bef 2 out* **150/1**	81
0-0B	11	2	**Same Ole Trix (IRE)**[20] 2646 5-11-0 0..........................(t) DavidBass (Kim Bailey) *hld up in midfield: rdn appr 3 out: nvr threatened* **200/1**	78
	12	nk	**Al Fatih (IRE)**[21] 4-10-9 0.......................... DavidNoonan[(5)] (Steve Flook) *midfield: rdn appr 3 out: wknd bef 2 out* **100/1**	79
65-4	13	nk	**Temple Tiger**[216] 206 5-11-0 0.......................... PeterBuchanan (James Turner) *hld up: nvr threatened* **100/1**	79
220-	14	1/2	**Shotofwine**[265] 4915 6-11-0 0.......................... BrianHarding (Nicky Richards) *midfield: rdn appr 3 out: sn wknd* **12/1**	79
	15	1 1/2	**Dalaki (IRE)**[22] 4-11-0 0.......................... MichaelByrne (Des Donovan) *midfield: mstke 1st: sn dropped to rr: bhd fr 5th* **100/1**	76
0-	16	2 3/4	**Fighting Back**[349] 3321 4-10-11 0.......................... TonyKelly[(3)] (Henry Hogarth) *a in rr* **100/1**	73
	17	22	**Tom Hall**[57] 5-11-0 0.......................... MarkGrant (Neil King) *a in rr* **150/1**	51

4m 4.3s (-0.40) **Going Correction** +0.05s/f (Yiel) 17 Ran SP% **117.4**
Speed ratings (Par 103): **102,100,99,96,94 90,89,89,88,85 84,84,84,83,83 81,71**
CSF £8.16 TOTE £3.00: £2.00, £1.60, £1.20; EX 10.60 Trifecta £27.40.
Owner John P McManus **Bred** Oliver And Salome Brennan **Trained** Barbury Castle, Wilts

FOCUS
Race distance increased by 18yds. Several interesting runners but a ready winner in the first division of this maiden hurdle. The gallop was reasonable and the first three pulled clear in the closing stages. Rail movements increased the race distance by 18yards. The winner could be decent, with the seventh and eighth helping to set the level.

3022 BETDAQ.COM £25 FREE BET MAIDEN HURDLE (DIV II) (8 hdls) 2m 140y
12:45 (12:48) (Class 5) 4-Y-0+ **£2,924** (£858; £429; £214)

Form				RPR
10-1	1		**Unbuckled (IRE)**[31] 2421 5-10-7 0.......................... JackQuinlan (Neil King) *midfield: rdn and sme hdwy appr 3 out: wnt 3rd 2 out: clsd on ldng pair between last 2: chsd ldr jst after last: styd on to ld 50yds out* **5/2**[2]	103+
600/	2	2 3/4	**Aldeburgh**[8] 2802 6-11-0 0.......................... MarkGrant (Nigel Twiston-Davies) *trckd ldrs: chsd ldr bef 3 out and clr of remainder: led 2 out: rdn last: sn one pce: hdd 50yds out: wknd* **12/1**	108+
6-60	3	2 1/4	**Dimple (FR)**[13] 2791 4-10-11 0.......................... GrahamWatters[(3)] (Pauline Robson) *hld up in midfield: rdn appr 3 out: stl only 9th after 2 out: styd on: wnt 3rd towards fin* **40/1**	105
6-	4	2 1/4	**Park Place**[28] 679 5-11-0 0.......................... JamesReveley (John Quinn) *trckd ldr: led 2nd: pressed on bef 3 out: hdd 2 out: sn rdn: wknd run-in* **7/1**[3]	103+

660 **5** *1* **Quieto Sol (FR)**[13] 2791 4-11-0 0 AidanColeman 102
(Charlie Longsdon) *in tch: chsd clr ldng pair bef 3 out: rdn after 3 out: plugged on* **100/1**
00-5 **6** *5* **The Hon Mackinlay (IRE)**[25] 2543 6-11-0 0 NicodeBoinville 98
(Ben Pauling) *midfield: sltly hmpd 5th: pushed along bef 3 out: nvr threatened* **11/1**
30 **7** *1 ½* **Still Together (IRE)**[57] 1926 5-10-11 0 BrianToomey(3) 97
(David Pipe) *hld up in midfield: rdn and hdwy bef 3 out: mstke 2 out: wknd* **66/1**
4-1 **8** *hd* **Top Priority (FR)**[208] 366 4-11-0 0 RichieMcLernon 99+
(Jonjo O'Neill) *in tch: mstke 5th: rdn 3 out: nt fluent 2 out: wknd* **8/1**
1-60 **9** *1* **Kara Tara**[22] 2591 5-10-7 0 DannyCook 89
(Lawrence Mullaney) *trckd ldrs: rdn appr 3 out: wknd bef 2 out* **80/1**
6 **10** *20* **Cactus Valley (IRE)**[14] 2748 6-11-0 0 (t) BrianHarding 77
(Michael Easterby) *a towards rr* **66/1**
60-0 **11** *1* **What A Tempest**[20] 2644 5-10-7 0 SeanQuinlan 69
(Richard Phillips) *a bhd* **100/1**
-400 **12** *hd* **Zakety Zak**[14] 2747 4-11-0 0 PeterBuchanan 76
(James Turner) *a in rr* **200/1**
13 *10* **Applejack Lad**[122] 4-11-0 0 (t) HenryBrooke 70
(Michael Smith) *j. slowly in rr: a bhd* **50/1**
03 **14** *24* **Lords Park Star (IRE)**[20] 2646 6-11-0 0 AndrewThornton 45
(Nicholas Pomfret) *led 1st: hdd 2nd: trckd ldrs: wknd after 5th* **33/1**
46-P **U** **Steady Eddie**[10] 2840 5-10-9 0 DavidNoonan(5)
(Steve Flook) *led: jinked and uns rdr 1st* **200/1**
P **Forgotten Hero (IRE)**[48] 6-11-0 0 (t) DavidBass
(Kim Bailey) *racd keenly in tch: rdn bef 3 out: sn wknd and eased: p.u bef last* **2/1**[1]
4-P **R** **Ashes Corner (IRE)**[204] 419 5-10-11 0 TonyKelly(3)
(Julia Brooke) *ref to r* **66/1**

4m 8.8s (4.10) **Going Correction** +0.05s/f (Yiel) **17** Ran SP% **117.6**
Speed ratings (Par 103): **92,90,89,88,88 85,85,84,84,75 74,74,69,58,**
CSF £29.96 TOTE £3.80: £1.60, £3.50, £12.80; EX 32.70 Trifecta £1308.70.
Owner Mrs J K Buckle **Bred** Mrs A S O'Brien **Trained** Barbury Castle, Wiltshire

FOCUS
The lesser of the two divisions quality wise and, although the gallop was fair, not many got involved. Rail movements increased the distance by 18yds. The winner, third, fourth and fifth set the level.

3023 BETDAQ.COM 50% COMMISSION REFUND NOVICES' H'CAP HURDLE (10 hdls) 2m 3f 120y
1:20 (1:52) (Class 4) (0-115,115) 3-Y-0+ **£3,249** (£954; £477; £238)

Form RPR
43/1 **1** **Flemensmix**[31] 2413 7-11-12 **115** DavidBass 121+
(Kim Bailey) *trckd ldr: nt fluent 3 out but led: sn rdn: a strly pressed but hld on wl* **15/8**[1]
0412 **2** *hd* **Polarbrook (IRE)**[14] 2745 8-10-11 **100** (v[1]) SeanQuinlan 106
(Derek Shaw) *hld up in midfield: hdwy bef 3 out: nt fluent 2 out: rdn to chal strly last: kpt on* **10/1**
-005 **3** *7* **Buckled**[13] 2791 5-10-8 **104** StevenFox(7) 104
(Sandy Thomson) *hld up: rdn and gd hdwy to chal 3 out: no ex and hld in 3rd fr appr last* **10/1**
02P- **4** *6* **Summer Sounds (IRE)**[243] 5286 6-11-0 **106** BenPoste(3) 99
(Tom Symonds) *trckd ldr: rdn bef 3 out: wknd after 2 outer 3 out: plugged on* **28/1**
3510 **5** *nk* **Keep Calm**[47] 2085 5-11-2 **105** HenryBrooke 98
(John Mackie) *hld up: hit 4th: reminders in rr after 6th: plugged on after 2 out: nvr threatened* **25/1**
1-44 **6** *1 ¾* **Speredek (FR)**[22] 2591 4-11-7 **110** (tp) ConorO'Farrell 102
(Nigel Hawke) *trckd ldr: rdn 3 out: wknd 2 out* **7/1**[2]
005 **7** *1* **Midtech Star (IRE)**[29] 2448 3-10-0 **104** oh4 (p) WillKennedy 79
(Ian Williams) *midfield: rdn 3 out: wknd after 2 out* **66/1**
1240 **8** *5* **Benissimo (IRE)**[28] 2472 5-11-11 **114** RyanMahon 100
(Dan Skelton) *led: hit 7th: hdd 3 out: sn wknd* **11/1**
124P **9** *4 ½* **Tennessee Bird**[24] 2560 7-10-5 **97** AdamNicol(3) 82
(Mike Sowersby) *hld up: slow 1st: hdwy on outer bef 6th: rdn after 3 out: wknd after 2 out* **28/1**
P-34 **10** *4 ½* **Spitz (FR)**[133] 1170 7-10-6 **105** LorcanMurtagh(10) 85
(Rose Dobbin) *hld up in midfield: pushed along bef 7th: wknd after 3 out* **17/2**[3]
3F40 **11** *26* **Bentons Lad**[50] 2042 4-10-11 **100** (t) RichieMcLernon 54
(George Moore) *hld up: mstke 4th: a towards rr* **50/1**
44 **12** *17* **My Anchor**[21] 2614 4-11-7 **110** WayneHutchinson 49
(Charlie Mann) *midfield: rdn appr 3 out: sn wknd* **20/1**
4P0- **P** **Merchant Of Dubai**[90] 5394 10-11-8 **111** JamesReveley
(Jim Goldie) *hld up: rdn bhd fr 7th: p.u bef 3 out* **28/1**
02-P **P** **Courtlands Prince**[32] 2396 6-11-6 **109** (t) AidanColeman
(Neil Mulholland) *midfield: wknd after 3 out: p.u bef last* **17/2**[3]

4m 48.8s (-2.50) **Going Correction** +0.05s/f (Yiel) **14** Ran SP% **117.3**
WFA 3 from 4yo 14lb 4 from 5yo+ 6lb
Speed ratings (Par 105): **107,106,104,101,101 100,100,98,96,94 84,77, ,**
CSF £18.64 CT £153.06 TOTE £2.80: £1.60, £2.70, £3.60; EX 23.20 Trifecta £227.60.
Owner The Perfect Mix Racing Club **Bred** E R Hanbury **Trained** Andoversford, Gloucs

FOCUS
Race distance increased by 18yds. A fair handicap in which the gallop was a fair one. The winner was building on his good recent win, while the in-form second has been rated 114 at his best and there's a case for rating the race a few pounds higher.

3024 BETDAQ.COM 2% COMMISSION H'CAP CHASE (19 fncs) 3m 2f 14y
1:55 (2:20) (Class 3) (0-130,127) 4-Y-0+ **£6,498** (£1,908; £954; £477)

Form RPR
366- **1** **Ikorodu Road**[239] 5356 12-11-11 **126** (p) DavidBass 136
(Graeme McPherson) *trckd ldrs: wnt 2nd 11th: rdn 4 out: led 110yds out: drvn out* **8/1**
2-36 **2** *¾* **Beeves (IRE)**[173] 800 8-11-8 **123** (v[1]) HenryBrooke 133+
(Jennie Candlish) *sn led: mstke 5 out: rdn after 3 out: hdd 110yds out: one pce* **12/1**
4604 **3** *13* **Master Rajeem (USA)**[17] 2701 6-11-0 **115** MarkGrant 115
(Neil King) *midfield: wnt 3rd 14th: rdn bef 4 out: wknd run-in* **22/1**
3022 **4** *21* **Lackamon**[20] 2638 10-11-11 **126** DannyCook 108
(Sue Smith) *prom: pressed ldr whn blnd 10th: sn lost pl and dropped towards rr: hit 14th: plugged on again after 3 out* **13/2**[2]
1043 **5** *1 ½* **Ballyben (IRE)**[48] 2068 7-11-0 **118** (p) DerekFox(3) 102
(Lucinda Russell) *led 1st: trckd ldr: rdn in dispute of 3rd whn blnd 3 out: wknd* **7/1**[3]
13F2 **6** *15* **Ueueteotl (FR)**[14] 2749 7-11-8 **123** (p) LucyAlexander 87
(James Ewart) *midfield: rdn after 5 out: sn wknd* **12/1**
3-P4 **7** *22* **Desert Joe (IRE)**[21] 2616 9-11-10 **125** (p) WayneHutchinson 69
(Alan King) *midfield: rdn whn blnd 5 out: sn wknd* **10/3**[1]
0610 **8** *8* **Feast Of Fire (IRE)**[55] 1970 8-10-1 **102** BrianHarding 39
(Mike Sowersby) *hld up: reminders after 8th: a in rr* **25/1**
1325 **9** *5* **Father Edward (IRE)**[18] 2691 6-11-12 **127** (p) AidanColeman 59
(John Ferguson) *hld up: nt fluent 7th: sme hdwy 12th: mstke 5 out: blnd 4 out: sn wknd* **8/1**
0-23 **P** **Orange Nassau (FR)**[50] 2028 9-10-10 **121** TomHumphries(10)
(Charlie Longsdon) *hld up in midfield: rdn 12th: sn struggling: p.u bef 4 out* **13/2**[2]
UP-1 **P** **Ruapehu (IRE)**[213] 266 9-10-13 **119** (t) KevinJones(5)
(Charles Whittaker) *in tch: wkng whn blnd 14th: p.u bef 4 out* **10/1**

6m 37.4s (-5.60) **Going Correction** 0.0s/f (Good) **11** Ran SP% **117.1**
Speed ratings (Par 107): **108,107,103,97,96 92,85,83,81,**
CSF £97.27 CT £2025.28 TOTE £12.00: £4.10, £6.20, £8.30; EX 102.90 Trifecta £1329.30.
Owner W J Odell **Bred** R W Huggins **Trained** Upper Oddington, Gloucs

FOCUS
A useful handicap and one in which the gallop was fair. The first two pulled clear over the last two fences. Rail movements added 36yds to the original distance of this race. The winner had slipped to a good mark and has been rated to the best of last season's figures.

3025 DOWNLOAD THE BETDAQ APP MARES' H'CAP HURDLE (11 hdls) 3m 96y
2:30 (2:50) (Class 4) (0-120,120) 4-Y-0+ **£3,573** (£1,049; £524; £262)

Form RPR
33-2 **1** **Iron Butterfly**[44] 2139 6-10-11 **105** JackQuinlan 118+
(James Eustace) *trckd ldng pair: led gng wl 3 out: pushed clr after 2 out: eased towards fin* **9/2**[3]
-203 **2** *5* **Chantara Rose**[22] 2595 6-10-13 **107** (p) AidanColeman 109
(Peter Bowen) *hld up in tch: rdn to go 2nd 2 out: kpt on but no ch w wnr* **8/1**
-301 **3** *2 ½* **Tambura**[11] 2825 5-11-0 **115** 7ex MrZBaker(7) 118+
(G C Maundrell) *in tch: lost pl bef 3 out: rdn 2 out: styd on to go 3rd appr last* **9/4**[1]
0201 **4** *6* **Maggie Blue (IRE)**[57] 1925 7-10-6 **105** CallumBewley(5) 99
(Harriet Graham) *led narrowly: rdn whn hdd 3 out: wknd after 2 out* **12/1**
1616 **5** *8* **Flemensbay**[157] 939 7-10-13 **107** (p) SeanQuinlan 94
(Richard Phillips) *pressed ldr: rdn 8th: wknd 2 out* **16/1**
1-23 **6** *38* **Jean Fleming (IRE)**[35] 2314 8-11-9 **117** (p) NickScholfield 70
(Jamie Snowden) *trckd ldng pair: nt fluent 4th: pushed along and lost pl 7th: bhd fr bef 3 out* **4/1**[2]
-15 **P** **Double Silver**[34] 2349 8-11-10 **118** WayneHutchinson
(Fergal O'Brien) *hld up: hit 6th: a in rr: p.u bef 3 out* **7/1**
2500 **P** **Cowslip**[21] 2624 6-11-5 **120** FinianO'Toole(7)
(George Moore) *hld up: rdn after 7th: sn bhd: p.u bef 3 out* **20/1**
2F20 **P** **Lily Little Legs (IRE)**[22] 2595 6-10-3 **100** AdamNicol(3)
(Mike Sowersby) *in tch: rdn bef 3 out: sn wknd and eased: p.u bef 2 out* **20/1**

6m 4.8s (5.80) **Going Correction** +0.05s/f (Yiel) **9** Ran SP% **115.7**
Speed ratings (Par 105): **92,90,89,87,84 72, , ,**
CSF £40.09 CT £99.49 TOTE £5.20: £1.80, £2.40, £1.50; EX 42.90 Trifecta £190.40.
Owner Harold Nass **Bred** Rockville Pike Partnership **Trained** Newmarket, Suffolk

FOCUS
Race distance increased by 36yds. A fair handicap, in which the gallop was reasonable. The winner won with plenty in hand. The cosy winner was on a fair mark and has been rated back to her best, with the second close to her mark.

3026 DOWNLOAD BETDAQ TRADING SOFTWARE ON BETDAQTRADERS.COM NOVICES' CHASE (15 fncs) 2m 3f 44y
3:00 (3:14) (Class 4) 4-Y-0+ **£3,753** (£1,108; £554)

Form RPR
253- **1** **Volnay De Thaix (FR)**[246] 5238 6-11-0 0 NicodeBoinville 138+
(Nicky Henderson) *trckd ldr in 2nd: nt fluent 4 out and pushed along: nt fluent again 3 out: rdn to ld narrowly appr last: gd jump last: kpt on* **4/11**[1]
0-62 **2** *2* **Pine Creek**[25] 2541 7-11-0 0 (p) AidanColeman 135
(John Ferguson) *in tch in 3rd: smooth hdwy to chal 2 out: disputing ld whn nt fluent last: kpt on* **11/2**[3]
10-1 **3** *6* **Katgary (FR)**[56] 1942 5-11-7 137 (p) NickScholfield 139
(Paul Nicholls) *led: rdn whn hdd appr last: no ex run-in: eased towards fin* **5/1**[2]

4m 51.1s (2.10) **Going Correction** 0.0s/f (Good) **3** Ran SP% **105.4**
Speed ratings (Par 105): **95,94,91**
CSF £2.54 TOTE £1.30; EX 2.20 Trifecta £2.60.
Owner Mrs Judy Wilson **Bred** Michel Bourgneuf **Trained** Upper Lambourn, Berks

FOCUS
Only three runners in this decent novice event but, although the muddling gallop means the bare form isn't entirely reliable, the winner remains a good chasing prospect. Rail movements meant the race was run over 18yds longer than advertised. The winner was a 155+ hurdler and may match that over fences. The second has been rated similar to his recent run.

3027 CASH OUT WITH BETDAQ H'CAP HURDLE (10 hdls) 2m 3f 120y
3:30 (3:39) (Class 3) (0-135,135) 3-Y-0+ **£5,848** (£1,717; £858; £429)

Form RPR
24-1 **1** **Red Devil Boys (IRE)**[13] 2775 8-11-8 **131** (p) AidanColeman 138+
(John Ferguson) *midfield on outer: hdwy to chse ldr bef 3 out: led jst bef 2 out: rdn 6 l clr appr last: idled and reduced advantage towards fin* **10/3**[2]
0633 **2** *¾* **Boruma (IRE)**[13] 2775 5-9-12 **110** HarryChalloner(3) 115
(Dianne Sayer) *led tl after 2nd: trckd ldr: rdn and outpcd appr 3 out: rallied to go 2nd 2 out: styd on wl* **8/1**
1F-0 **3** *6* **Alzammaar (USA)**[26] 2513 4-10-13 **125** (tp) HarryBannister(3) 124
(Warren Greatrex) *hld up: rdn bef 3 out: stl only 6th last: styd on* **11/2**[3]
21-0 **4** *1 ¼* **Balmusette**[20] 2637 6-11-10 **133** JamesReveley 131
(Keith Reveley) *hld up: hdwy to go 4th after 3 out: sn rdn: one pce* **33/1**
1-11 **5** *¾* **Abidjan (FR)**[52] 2007 5-11-5 **135** (t) HarryCobden(7) 134+
(Paul Nicholls) *in tch: hdwy to chse ldr bef 3 out: rdn to chal appr 2 out: wknd run-in* **5/2**[1]
01/0 **6** *3 ¼* **Hidden Justice (IRE)**[21] 2624 6-10-11 **125** DeanPratt(5) 119
(John Quinn) *hld up: nt fluent 5th and 6th: rdn after 3 out: nvr threatened* **10/1**
211U **7** *¾* **Kalifourchon (FR)**[33] 2369 4-10-11 **125** DavidNoonan(5) 119
(David Pipe) *prom: led after 2nd: nt fluent 3 out: rdn whn hdd jst bef 2 out: wknd run-in* **10/1**
5-4P **8** *13* **Medicine Hat**[22] 2594 4-11-4 **127** RichieMcLernon 111
(George Moore) *trckd ldr: nt fluent 3rd: hit 7th: wknd after 3 out* **40/1**

The Form Book Jumps 2015-16, Raceform Ltd, Newbury, RG14 5SJ

30-0 **9** *6* **Seaviper (IRE)**[48] 2064 6-10-11 **125**................................ DanielHiskett(5) 102
(Richard Phillips) *midfield: hmpd by faller 3 out: sn rdn and wknd* **20/1**

215- **10** *26* **Jacks Last Hope**[360] 3133 6-10-9 **123**................................ DiarmuidO'Regan(5) 76
(Chris Grant) *in tch: mstke 7th: wknd and bhd bef 3 out* **33/1**

6-U4 **F** **Kashmir Peak (IRE)**[41] 2194 6-11-10 **133**................................ NickScholfield
(John Quinn) *midfield: fell 3 out* **12/1**

4m 47.7s (-3.60) **Going Correction** +0.05s/f (Yiel)
WFA 3 from 4yo 14lb 4 from 5yo+ 6lb **11 Ran SP% 117.1**
Speed ratings (Par 107): **109,108,106,105,105 104,103,98,96,85**
CSF £28.79 CT £144.05 TOTE £4.10: £1.70, £2.50, £2.70; EX 33.70 Trifecta £312.10.
Owner Bloomfields **Bred** Carl Beame **Trained** Cowlinge, Suffolk

FOCUS
A very useful handicap and one in which an ordinary gallop increased on the approach to the home turn. The first two finished clear. A pb from the winner, with the third and fourth setting the level.
T/Plt: £247.30 to a £1 stake. Pool: £54,594.89 - 161.15 winning tickets T/Qpdt: £162.80 to a £1 stake. Pool: £5,695.64 - 25.88 winning tickets **Andrew Sheret**

3013 CHELTENHAM (L-H)
Saturday, December 12

OFFICIAL GOING: Soft (good to soft in places; 6.9)
Wind: quite strong half across Weather: overcast Rails: Chase bends dolled out 12 yards adding 72 yards to races 2, 3 and 4. Hurdle bends dolled out 10 yards adding 60 yards to races 1, 6 and 7 and 100 yards to race 5.

3028 JCB TRIUMPH HURDLE TRIAL (A JUVENILE HURDLE) (8 hdls) 2m 179y
12:05 (12:07) (Class 2) 3-Y-O **£12,627** (£3,811; £1,963; £1,039)

Form RPR

121 **1** **Sceau Royal (FR)**[24] 2578 3-11-7 140................................ DarylJacob 137+
(Alan King) *trckd ldrs: chal last: sn led: kpt on wl: rdn out* **7/4**[2]

2 **2** *1 3/4* **Adrien Du Pont (FR)**[62] 1866 3-11-7 0................................ SamTwiston-Davies 135
(Paul Nicholls) *trckd ldr: led appr last where jnd: rdn and hdd run-in: kpt on but hld fnl 120yds* **13/8**[1]

3214 **3** *10* **Chic Name (FR)**[34] 2371 3-11-3 127................................(v[1]) AlainCawley 120
(Richard Hobson) *led: j. v sltly rt: rdn and hdd after 2 out: keeping on at same pce in hld 4th whn lft 3rd at the last* **66/1**

32 **4** *75* **Sky Lino (FR)**[31] 2439 3-11-0 113................................ RichardJohnson 42
(Nick Williams) *last but in tch tl outpcd after 3 out: t.o* **12/1**

1111 **U** **Leoncavallo (IRE)**[43] 2172 3-11-7 140................................ AidanColeman 135
(John Ferguson) *trckd ldrs: nudged along to mount chal whn blnd bdly and uns rdr last* **3/1**[3]

4m 12.1s (0.80) **Going Correction** +0.45s/f (Soft) **5 Ran SP% 108.6**
Speed ratings (Par 108): **116,115,110,75,**
CSF £5.02 TOTE £2.60: £1.40, £1.40; EX 6.10 Trifecta £59.10.
Owner Simon Munir & Isaac Souede **Bred** Guy Vimont **Trained** Barbury Castle, Wilts

FOCUS
The course was set up the same as the previous day. The hurdle bends were dolled out 10yds and the race distance of the opener was increased by 60yds. Despite 4-5mm of rain prior to racing the official going remained good, good to soft in places. An interesting juvenile hurdle, although a weak betting heat, and they went an even gallop. The winner has been rated 10lb+ shy of a typical Triumph Hurdle winner.

3029 RAYMOND MOULD MEMORIAL NOVICES' CHASE (17 fncs) 2m 4f 166y
12:40 (12:41) (Class 2) 4-Y-O+ **£15,451** (£5,313)

Form RPR

/3-1 **1** **More Of That (IRE)**[29] 2469 7-11-8 0................................ BarryGeraghty 162+
(Jonjo O'Neill) *disp ld tl clr ldr 4th: jnd again 8th: clever whn getting in tight to 13th: rdn clr between last 2: kpt up to work run-in: comf* **1/3**[1]

0/1U **2** *13* **Sametegal (FR)**[15] 2760 6-11-5 145................................ SamTwiston-Davies 149
(Paul Nicholls) *disp tl 4th: pressed wnr fr 8th: hit 3 out: rdn bef next: hld between last 2: styd on same pce* **5/1**[2]

12-1 **U** **Padge (IRE)**[42] 2184 6-11-5 143................................ NoelFehily
(Evan Williams) *trckd ldng pair: nt fluent 2nd: pckd 3rd: outpcd in 7 l 3rd whn slipped on landing and uns rdr 3 out* **5/1**[2]

5m 28.8s (13.10) **Going Correction** +0.60s/f (Soft) **3 Ran SP% 108.4**
Speed ratings (Par 109): **99,94,**
CSF £2.41 TOTE £1.20; EX 2.20.
Owner John P McManus **Bred** Mrs Eleanor Hadden **Trained** Cheltenham, Gloucs

FOCUS
The chase bends were dolled out 12yds and the race distance was increased by 72yds per circuit. Just three runners turned out from an initial entry of 17, but this race usually goes to a smart novice and this year is no exception. They went an ordinary gallop. The second has been rated to his hurdle mark.

3030 UNICOIN GROUP H'CAP CHASE (14 fncs) 2m 62y
1:15 (1:18) (Class 2) 4-Y-O+
£18,768 (£5,544; £2,772; £1,386; £693; £348)

Form RPR

-233 **1** **Pearls Legend**[14] 2784 8-10-7 **133**................................ NicodeBoinville 142
(John Spearing) *chsd ldr: led after 10th: strly pressed after 3 out: rdn between last 2: styd on v gamely to assert towards fin* **15/2**[3]

5-64 **2** *1* **Going Concern (IRE)**[29] 2468 8-10-3 **129**................................ AdamWedge 137
(Evan Williams) *in tch: trckd ldrs 8th: chal 2 out: ev ch last: sn rdn: kpt on but no ex towards fin* **12/1**

5126 **3** *9* **Workbench (FR)**[21] 2635 7-11-1 **141**................................(t) RyanMahon 140
(Dan Skelton) *hld up towards rr: hdwy after 3 out: rdn next: wnt 3rd at the last: styd on but no further imp on front pair* **25/1**

0-51 **4** *11* **Keel Haul (IRE)**[29] 2468 7-10-5 **131**................................(p) JamesDavies 120
(Henry Oliver) *chsd ldrs: rdn to chse ldng pair after 3 out: nt pce to get on terms: no ex whn lost 3rd at the last* **9/2**[1]

0006 **5** *1 1/2* **Owen Na View (IRE)**[14] 2784 7-9-11 **126** oh3..........(t) ConorShoemark(3) 113
(Fergal O'Brien) *mid-div: rdn after 3 out: styd on fr next but nt gng pce to get on terms* **66/1**

P-13 **6** *nk* **Cold March (FR)**[21] 2635 5-11-10 **150**................................ AidanColeman 136
(Venetia Williams) *mid-div tl dropped in rr u.p 7th: wl bhd and no ch 3 out: styd on wl fr 2 out: snatched 6th cl home* **9/2**[1]

-145 **7** *1/2* **Astracad (FR)**[29] 2468 9-10-10 **136**................................(t) SamTwiston-Davies 123
(Nigel Twiston-Davies) *chsd ldrs: rdn after 10th: outpcd after 3 out: no threat after* **9/1**

P0-0 **8** *1/2* **Bold Henry**[226] 47 9-10-8 **134**................................ RichardJohnson 121
(Philip Hobbs) *hld up towards rr: hdwy whn mstke 10th: rdn into 4th 2 out: fading whn wnt lft last* **11/2**[2]

31-P **9** *5* **Ulck Du Lin (FR)**[42] 2185 7-10-8 **141**................................(tp) HarryCobden(7) 123
(Paul Nicholls) *mid-div: hdwy 3 out: sn rdn: nt pce to threaten: wknd bef last* **20/1**

-000 **10** *6* **Next Sensation (IRE)**[15] 2761 8-11-7 **147**................................(t) BrendanPowell 123
(Michael Scudamore) *led: nt fluent 1st: hit 3rd whn clr: hdd after 10th: wknd after 2 out* **10/1**

504- **11** *2 1/4* **Desert Cry (IRE)**[259] 5040 9-11-12 **152**................................ WillKennedy 125
(Donald McCain) *struggling after 4 out: a towards rr* **33/1**

0-0P **12** *1* **Parsnip Pete**[14] 2784 9-10-11 **137**................................(t) NoelFehily 108
(Tom George) *mid-div on outer: stdy prog to trck ldrs 5th: rdn after 3 out: wknd after next* **33/1**

P-P5 **P** **Eastlake (IRE)**[14] 2784 9-11-5 **145**................................ BarryGeraghty
(Jonjo O'Neill) *mid-div: blnd bdly 9th and lost pl: nvr travelling after: bhd whn p.u after 3 out* **8/1**

4m 11.0s (4.30) **Going Correction** +0.60s/f (Soft) **13 Ran SP% 117.4**
Speed ratings (Par 109): **113,112,108,102,101 101,101,101,98,95 94,93,**
CSF £84.55 CT £2134.95 TOTE £8.10: £2.20, £3.90, £7.20; EX 102.30 Trifecta £1385.40.
Owner The Corsairs **Bred** Choice Set **Trained** Kinnersley, Worcs

FOCUS
Due to rail movements the race distance was 2m134yds. A good-quality handicap chase, in which they went a decent gallop, with the first two pulling clear. The first two are on the upgrade, while the third has been rated to his mark. There's a case for rating the race a lot higher through the rest.

3031 CASPIAN CAVIAR GOLD CUP (A H'CAP CHASE) (GRADE 3) (17 fncs) 2m 4f 166y
1:50 (1:51) (Class 1) 4-Y-O+
£56,950 (£21,370; £10,700; £5,330; £2,680; £1,340)

Form RPR

P-11 **1** **Village Vic (IRE)**[36] 2329 8-10-0 **136**................................ RichardJohnson 152+
(Philip Hobbs) *mde all: rdn after 2 out: r.o strly: unchal* **8/1**[2]

12F- **2** *4 1/2* **Champagne West (IRE)**[315] 3976 7-11-0 **150**................................ TomO'Brien 162+
(Philip Hobbs) *chsd wnr thrght: blnd 7th: rdn after 3 out: styd on but a being hld fr next* **8/1**[2]

04-1 **3** *1* **Tenor Nivernais (FR)**[22] 2615 8-10-8 **144**................................ AidanColeman 154
(Venetia Williams) *in tch: lft disputing 2nd whn sltly hmpd 7th: rdn after 3 out: kpt on same pce fr next* **10/1**[3]

5-32 **4** *3 3/4* **Buywise (IRE)**[28] 2483 8-11-2 **152**................................ AdamWedge 158
(Evan Williams) *mid-div: hit 3 out: rdn bef 2 out: hdwy between last 2: wnt 4th sn after last but nt pce to get on terms* **8/1**[2]

-013 **5** *6* **Sound Investment (IRE)**[28] 2483 7-11-12 **162**....(t) SamTwiston-Davies 162
(Paul Nicholls) *in tch: disp 3rd 3 out: rdn bef next: lost 4th sn after the last: wknd* **14/1**

0F-1 **6** *8* **Annacotty (IRE)**[28] 2483 7-11-2 **152**................................(p) IanPopham 144
(Alan King) *mid-div tl struggling towards rr 12th: styd on past btn horses fr 2 out: nvr a threat* **13/2**[1]

1316 **7** *nk* **Art Mauresque (FR)**[28] 2483 5-10-11 **147**................................ NickScholfield 138
(Paul Nicholls) *trckd ldrs: sltly hmpd 7th: rdn after 3 out: nt pce to chal: fdd run-in* **12/1**

-011 **8** *shd* **Doctor Phoenix (IRE)**[22] 2625 7-10-5 **141**................................ DarylJacob 132
(David Dennis) *hld up towards rr: midfield after 3 out: sn rdn: nvr gng pce to get involved* **14/1**

3-P0 **9** *3 1/2* **Johns Spirit (IRE)**[28] 2483 8-11-5 **155**................................ NoelFehily 143
(Jonjo O'Neill) *hld up towards rr of midfield: rdn after 3 out: nvr any imp* **12/1**

1-41 **10** *3 3/4* **Little Jon**[15] 2761 7-10-2 **143**................................ JamieBargary(5) 139+
(Nigel Twiston-Davies) *trcking ldr whn mstke and slipped bdly 7th: mid-div: hit 4 out: no threat fr 3 out: nvr really rcvrd* **8/1**[2]

1-5P **11** *21* **Shantou Magic (IRE)**[31] 2436 8-10-1 **137**................................ WillKennedy 100
(Charlie Longsdon) *struggling 12th: a towards rr* **40/1**

56-5 **12** *2 3/4* **Turn Over Sivola (FR)**[49] 2059 8-10-1 **137**................................ BrendanPowell 98
(Alan King) *mid-div: in tch 3 out: sn rdn: wknd between last 2* **25/1**

FU5/ **P** **Mozoltov**[592] 13 9-10-12 **148**................................ RWalsh
(W P Mullins, Ire) *nvr travelling or jumping: a in detched last: t.o whn p.u bef 12th* **8/1**[2]

-054 **P** **Texas Jack (IRE)**[42] 2207 9-11-0 **150**................................(b) BarryGeraghty
(Noel Meade, Ire) *nvr really travelling: a in last pair: t.o whn p.u bef 12th* **20/1**

5m 20.1s (4.40) **Going Correction** +0.60s/f (Soft) **14 Ran SP% 117.7**
Speed ratings (Par 113): **115,113,112,111,109 106,106,105,104,103 95,94,,**
CSF £68.33 CT £652.78 TOTE £6.90: £2.80, £3.10, £4.20; EX 49.10 Trifecta £1397.20.
Owner Alan Peterson **Bred** Tom Curran **Trained** Withycombe, Somerset

FOCUS
Race distance increased by 72yds per circuit. A competitive edition of this long-established and classy handicap, although leading ante-post fancy Irish Cavalier was ruled out. The pace held up, with the winner making all and the next two home always prominent too. The time was 8.7sec quicker than that recorded by More Of That in the three-runner novice chase. Rock-solid handicap form, with the winner taking another step up for a return to a left-handed track, the third rated similar to his recent runaway win, and the fourth rated to his mark.

3032 ALBERT BARTLETT NOVICES' HURDLE (REGISTERED AS THE BRISTOL NOVICES' HURDLE RACE) (GRADE 2) (12 hdls) 2m 7f 213y
2:25 (2:25) (Class 1) 4-Y-O+ **£17,165** (£6,491; £3,290; £1,679; £884)

Form RPR

P-11 **1** **Unowhatimeanharry**[16] 2725 7-11-4 137................................(t) NoelFehily 141+
(Harry Fry) *in tch: tk clsr order after 5th: led after 2 out: styd on wl fr last: drvn rt out* **11/10**[1]

-211 **2** *1 1/2* **Final Nudge (IRE)**[14] 2769 6-11-4 125................................ DarylJacob 138
(David Dennis) *trckd ldrs: wnt 2nd bef last: sn rdn: ch run-in: styd on but a being hld fnl 120yds* **6/1**[3]

14-0 **3** *9* **West Approach**[15] 2763 5-11-0 0................................ RichardJohnson 125
(Colin Tizzard) *hld up in tch: hdwy after 3 out: disp 2nd after 2 out: sn rdn: styd on same pce fr last* **12/1**

1122 **4** *4 1/2* **Ennistown**[23] 2594 5-11-4 134................................ AidanColeman 126
(John Ferguson) *nvr fluent: last but in tch: hit 2 out: rdn sn after: styd on into 4th cl home but nt pce to trble ldrs* **10/1**

63 **5** *nk* **Ballycross**[38] 2275 4-11-0 0................................ SamTwiston-Davies 119
(Nigel Twiston-Davies) *trckd ldrs: jnd ldr 8th: led briefly after 2 out: sn rdn and hld: styd on tl no ex and lost 4th cl home* **20/1**

P011 **P** **Net Work Rouge (FR)**[38] 2275 6-11-4 135................................(t) DavidBass
(Kim Bailey) *led: hit 8th: sn pushed along: rdn and hdd after 2 out: wknd qckly: p.u bef next* **5/1**[2]

/0-1 P **Justanother Muddle**[32] 2417 6-11-4 0............................ MarcGoldstein
(Sheena West) *pressed ldr: mstkes 7 and 9th: rdn after 3 out: sn wknd: p.u after next* **9/1**

6m 4.4s (3.40) **Going Correction** +0.45s/f (Soft)
WFA 4 from 5yo+ 7lb **7** Ran SP% **110.1**
Speed ratings (Par 115): **112,111,108,107,106** ,
CSF £7.52 TOTE £1.90: £1.30, £2.70; EX 6.20 Trifecta £61.70.

Owner Harry Fry Racing Club **Bred** R J Smith **Trained** Seaborough, Dorset

FOCUS
The actual race distance was 3m93yds. This did not look the strongest renewal of this Grade 2, but it was run at a good gallop and proved to be a true test in the conditions. The winner set a decent standard and has been rated similar to his recent wins. He's still a stone plus off a typical Festival winning novice, though.

3033 STANJAMES.COM INTERNATIONAL HURDLE (GRADE 2) (8 hdls) 2m 179y
3:00 (3:00) (Class 1) 4-Y-0+
£74,035 (£27,781; £13,910; £6,929; £3,484; £1,742)

Form RPR
3-11 1 **Old Guard**[27] 2512 4-11-4 157............................ SamTwiston-Davies 157
(Paul Nicholls) *trckd ldrs: chal after 2 out: rdn after last: led fnl 175yds: kpt on wl: drvn out* **7/1[3]**

61-4 2 *1* **Sempre Medici (FR)**[169] 72 5-11-4 148............................ RWalsh 156
(W P Mullins, Ire) *trckd ldrs: chal last: sn drvn: ev ch fnl 175yds: no ex cl home* **5/1[2]**

36-4 3 *nk* **Hargam (FR)**[49] 2060 4-11-4 154............................ BarryGeraghty 156
(Nicky Henderson) *hld up bhd ldrs: hdwy to ld after 2 out: rdn after last: hdd fnl 175yds: no ex nring fin* **8/1**

-523 4 *4½* **Melodic Rendezvous**[21] 2640 9-11-0 150............................ NickScholfield 147
(Jeremy Scott) *trckd ldr tl after 3rd: detached in last 5th: hdwy appr last where wnt 4th: styd on run-in: no threat but clsng on ldrs towards fin* **20/1**

01-6 5 *7* **Cheltenian (FR)**[217] 197 9-11-4 153............................ RichardJohnson 145
(Philip Hobbs) *led at stdy pce tl hdd after 3rd: trckd ldr: rdn after 2 out: sn outpcd* **10/1**

111- 6 *8* **Peace And Co (FR)**[274] 4736 4-11-4 159............................ DarylJacob 139
(Nicky Henderson) *racd too freely: plld way into ld after 3rd: hdd after 2 out: wknd tamely* **4/5[1]**

4m 12.8s (1.50) **Going Correction** +0.45s/f (Soft) **6** Ran SP% **109.7**
Speed ratings (Par 115): **114,113,113,111,107 104**
CSF £38.34 TOTE £6.50: £2.50, £2.30; EX 44.00 Trifecta £103.30.

Owner The Brooks, Kyle & Stewart Families **Bred** The Rt Hon Lord Rothschild **Trained** Ditcheat, Somerset

FOCUS
Actual race distance 2m 1f 19yds. A stirring finish to this Grade 2, but it wasn't a strong edition on paper and, with the favourite bombing out, this is some way removed from Champion Hurdle form. The pace was a little muddling. The winner remains on the upgrade but is still 10lb shy of a typical Champion Hurdle winner. The fourth helps with setting an ordinary level.

3034 OLBG MARES' H'CAP HURDLE (10 hdls) 2m 4f 56y
3:35 (3:35) (Class 2) 4-Y-0+
£18,768 (£5,544; £2,772; £1,386; £693; £348)

Form RPR
F611 1 **Lily Waugh (IRE)**[30] 2455 8-10-11 134............................(t) DavidNoonan(5) 142+
(Anthony Honeyball) *hld up bhd: hdwy after 7th: rdn after 2 out: str run bef last: led but wandering u.p run-in: styd on wl: pushed out* **6/1[3]**

4-51 2 *1¾* **Rons Dream**[28] 2484 5-11-5 137............................ RichardJohnson 141
(Peter Bowen) *hld up on outer: hdwy after 4th: led 2 out: rdn appr last: hdd run-in: edgd lft: styd on but no ex* **6/1[3]**

4P-0 3 *2¼* **Briery Belle**[29] 2472 6-10-2 120............................ TomO'Brien 121
(Henry Daly) *led tl 7th: sn pushed along: sltly outpcd in 4th after 2 out: styd on again fr last to snatch 3rd cl home* **13/2**

13-3 4 *½* **Midnight Jazz**[42] 2199 5-10-11 129............................ DarylJacob 130
(Ben Case) *in tch: hdwy whn nt fluent 2 out: str chal last: sn rdn and bmpd: no ex fnl 175yds: lost 3rd cl home* **9/1**

3-1U 5 *12* **Blue Buttons (IRE)**[23] 2602 7-11-5 137............................(t) NoelFehily 131
(Harry Fry) *trcking ldrs whn stmbld on bnd after 4th: lost pl and struggling after 3 out: nvr bk on terms* **5/1[1]**

12-1 6 *4½* **Broxbourne (IRE)**[35] 2333 6-11-7 139............................ NicodeBoinville 125
(Nicky Henderson) *mid-div whn hmpd on bnd after 4th: nvr travelling in rr after: nvr bk on terms* **5/1[1]**

35-2 7 *23* **Flementime (IRE)**[32] 2415 7-10-8 126............................(p) AndrewTinkler 87
(Martin Keighley) *prom: led 7th tl 2 out: wknd bef last* **16/1**

-211 8 *32* **Stoneham**[44] 2144 4-9-11 118 oh4............................ KieronEdgar(3) 47
(Iain Jardine) *bdly hmpd 5th: a towards rr: wknd after 2 out: t.o* **25/1**

3-02 P **Pass The Time**[23] 2602 6-11-7 139............................(p) BarryGeraghty
(Neil Mulholland) *trckd ldrs tl hmpd on bnd after 4th: grad lost pl: t.o 7th: p.u bef next* **16/1**

11-3 F **The Govaness**[217] 196 6-11-12 144............................ WillKennedy
(Dr Richard Newland) *hld up: hdwy after 4th: trcking ldrs whn fell next* **11/2[2]**

5m 12.2s (14.80) **Going Correction** +0.45s/f (Soft)
WFA 4 from 5yo+ 6lb **10** Ran SP% **116.2**
Speed ratings (Par 109): **88,87,86,86,81 79,70,57,** ,
CSF £42.13 CT £242.88 TOTE £6.00: £2.20, £2.20, £2.40; EX 37.40 Trifecta £670.00.

Owner Go To War **Bred** F Boyd **Trained** Mosterton, Dorset

■ Stewards' Enquiry : Daryl Jacob four-day ban; used whip above the permitted level (28th,30th Dec-1st Jan)

Tom O'Brien two-day ban; careless riding (28th,30th Dec)

FOCUS
The actual race distance was 2m4f 116yds. A competitive mares' handicap and solid form for the division. The first two are progressive, while the third and fourth help set the level.

T/Jkpt: £35,500.00 to a £1 stake. Jackpot Placepot: £2,739.20 to a £1 stake. Pool: £13,509.00 - 3.6 winning tickets T/Plt: £151.80 to a £1 stake. Pool: £179,297.56 - 861.81 winning tickets T/Qpdt: £61.90 to a £1 stake. Pool: £14,599.06 - 174.48 winning tickets **Tim Mitchell**

3020 DONCASTER (L-H)
Saturday, December 12

OFFICIAL GOING: Soft (good to soft in places) changing to soft after race 1 (11.50) changing to heavy after race 4 (1.30)
Wind: moderate 1/2 against Weather: raining

3035 BET365.COM H'CAP HURDLE (8 hdls) 2m 140y
11:50 (11:50) (Class 4) (0-120,120)
3-Y-0+ **£3,898** (£1,144; £572; £286)

Form RPR
-261 1 **Holly Bush Henry (IRE)**[15] 2747 4-11-12 120............................(t) KielanWoods 138+
(Graeme McPherson) *trckd ldrs tl led narrowly 3 out: drew clr fnl 150yds* **5/2[1]**

20-1 2 *6* **Qasser (IRE)**[30] 2458 6-11-2 117............................ PaulNO'Brien(7) 128
(Harry Whittington) *trckd ldrs: upsides 2 out: fdd fnl 200yds* **4/1[2]**

2645 3 *16* **Kuda Huraa (IRE)**[28] 2499 7-11-5 116............................ HarryBannister(3) 111
(Harriet Bethell) *in rr: hdwy appr 3 out: kpt on and 5th last: tk 3rd fnl 50yds* **10/1**

/35- 4 *2½* **Marcus Antonius**[556] 579 8-10-8 105............................ DerekFox(3) 98
(Lucinda Russell) *chsd ldrs: upsides 3 out: one pce appr next* **20/1**

/336 5 *3* **Save The Bees**[13] 2810 7-10-11 105............................ PaddyBrennan 95
(Declan Carroll) *led 2nd: hdd 3 out: wknd last* **14/1**

-04F 6 *5* **Rockawango (FR)**[35] 2342 9-11-7 115............................(tp) LucyAlexander 100
(James Ewart) *in rr: bhd and reminders 4th: kpt on fr 3 out: nvr on terms* **25/1**

4642 7 *7* **Hartside (GER)**[7] 2921 6-10-12 113............................ MrRWinks(7) 91
(Peter Winks) *in rr: bhd 3rd: sme hdwy 3 out: nvr on terms* **15/2[3]**

1-50 8 *6* **Tamarillo Grove (IRE)**[19] 2688 8-11-1 114............................(t) DannyBurton(5) 86
(Sophie Leech) *chsd ldrs: lost pl appr 2 out* **100/1**

3340 9 *24* **Harvey's Hope**[14] 2775 9-11-2 110............................(b) JamesReveley 58
(Keith Reveley) *in rr: hdwy 3rd: chsng ldrs 5th: lost pl next: sn bhd: t.o whn blnd bdly last: eased* **12/1**

-050 10 *3¾* **Drumlee Lad (IRE)**[38] 2271 5-10-12 109............................(bt[1]) KieronEdgar(3) 53
(David Pipe) *led to 2nd: chsd ldrs: rdn and lost pl bef 3 out: sn bhd: t.o last: eased* **8/1**

5F12 11 *8* **Where's Tiger**[61] 1886 4-11-6 119............................(t) GrantCockburn(5) 55
(Lucinda Russell) *in rr: bhd fr 3 out: t.o last: eased* **10/1**

4m 5.4s (0.70) **Going Correction** +0.20s/f (Yiel) **11** Ran SP% **113.6**
Speed ratings (Par 105): **106,103,95,94,93 90,87,84,73,71 67**
CSF £12.36 CT £82.45 TOTE £2.90: £1.40, £1.80, £4.80; EX 12.40 Trifecta £72.20.
Owner Lady Bamford & Alice Bamford **Bred** John Connolly **Trained** Upper Oddington, Gloucs

FOCUS
Filthy wet conditions before and during racing, with the going changed from good to soft all round just after 11am. The divided bend into the straight had been moved out 5yds since the previous day's action, adding extra distance to all hurdles events - 15yds in the case of this opener. This concerned just the two last-time winners over the final pair of flights and the form makes sense. A big step up from the impressive winner.

3036 BET365 H'CAP CHASE (15 fncs) 2m 3f 44y
12:20 (12:20) (Class 3) (0-140,137)
4-Y-0+ **£6,498** (£1,908; £954; £477)

Form RPR
5-1U 1 **Javert (IRE)**[14] 2779 6-11-5 130............................ SeanBowen 145+
(Emma Lavelle) *w ldr: led 4th: lft 5 l clr 2 out: drvn out* **9/2[1]**

2-P3 2 *12* **Fairy Rath (IRE)**[22] 2615 9-11-5 130............................(t) PaddyBrennan 135
(Nick Gifford) *w ldrs tl hdd 4th: lft 2nd 2 out: wl hld whn hit last* **7/1**

65-3 3 *1½* **Saints And Sinners (IRE)**[32] 2425 7-11-9 134............................(t) BrianHughes 139
(Michael Easterby) *chsd ldrs: outpcd appr 4 out: lft modest 4th 2 out: tk 3rd clsng stages* **5/1[2]**

0-16 4 *1½* **Shimla Dawn (IRE)**[14] 2785 7-11-9 134............................ JakeGreenall 134
(Mark Walford) *chsd ldrs: hit 5th: outpcd appr 4 out: lft modest 3rd 2 out: one pce* **6/1[3]**

21P/ 5 *10* **Victor Hewgo**[616] 5170 10-11-8 133............................ JamesReveley 123
(Keith Reveley) *hld up in rr: hdwy 8th: modest 4th 3 out: wknd next* **5/1[2]**

2-54 6 *25* **Rival D'Estruval (FR)**[35] 2340 10-11-5 130............................ BrianHarding 95
(Pauline Robson) *chsd ldrs: drvn and lost pl after 8th: bhd 4 out: t.o whn hmpd 2 out* **16/1**

16PB 7 *11* **Le Bacardy (FR)**[15] 2746 9-11-11 136............................ HarrySkelton 90
(Dan Skelton) *hld up in rr: hdwy 6th: chsng ldrs 9th: lost pl and hit 4 out: sn bhd: t.o* **14/1**

3-33 B **Strongpoint (IRE)**[14] 2794 11-11-7 132............................ PeterBuchanan
(S R B Crawford, Ire) *hld up in rr: b.d 1st* **14/1**

-F52 F **Off The Ground (IRE)**[15] 2746 9-11-9 137............................ GrahamWatters(3) 138
(Charlie Longsdon) *chsd ldrs: 2 l 2nd whn fell 2 out* **15/2**

235 F **Town Mouse**[54] 2001 5-10-10 121............................ TrevorWhelan
(Neil King) *mid-div: fell 1st* **20/1**

4m 54.2s (5.20) **Going Correction** +0.25s/f (Yiel) **10** Ran SP% **114.0**
Speed ratings (Par 107): **99,93,93,92,88 77,73,** ,
CSF £35.55 CT £162.12 TOTE £5.10: £2.10, £2.60, £1.80; EX 31.80 Trifecta £306.80.
Owner Axom Lii **Bred** Cleaboy Stud **Trained** Hatherden, Hants

FOCUS
Really competitive-looking for the grade with the entire field covered by 8lb on adjusted RPRs, but few handled the deteriorating conditions. The early pace appeared modest. A step up from the impressive winner, with the second and second-last faller helping to set the level.

3037 BET365 NOVICES' HURDLE (11 hdls) 3m 96y
12:55 (12:55) (Class 4) 4-Y-0+ **£3,898** (£1,144; £572; £286)

Form RPR
3 1 **Ephraim**[21] 2630 4-10-12 0............................ PaddyBrennan 125+
(Charlie Mann) *trckd ldr: led and mstke 3 out: styd on run-in* **9/4[2]**

45-4 2 *1½* **Ami Desbois (FR)**[28] 2493 5-10-12 0............................ KielanWoods 122
(Graeme McPherson) *t.k.h in rr: hdwy 7th: trcking ldrs next: 4th last: chsd wnr fnl 200yds: no real imp* **25/1**

3 *3* **Bugsie Malone (IRE)**[209] 5-10-12 0............................ SeanBowen 119
(Paul Nicholls) *trckd ldrs: upsides 3 out: kpt on same pce run-in* **5/2[3]**

3-0 4 *6* **High Hopper (IRE)**[218] 187 5-10-12 0............................ BrianHughes 115
(Malcolm Jefferson) *trckd ldrs: disputing 2nd whn hit last: grad wknd* **12/1**

2110 5 *13* **Atlantic Gold (IRE)**[28] 2484 5-11-0 131............................ TomHumphries(10) 114
(Charlie Longsdon) *led: hdd 3 out: wknd between last 2* **2/1[1]**

30 6 *4* **Viaduct Jack (IRE)**[30] 2450 6-10-9 0............................ TomBellamy(3) 96
(Kim Bailey) *chsd ldrs: effrt 3 out: wkng whn mstke next* **9/1**

P 7 53 **Mr Elevator (IRE)**[33] 2406 5-10-12 0 AdamPogson 43
(Charles Pogson) *t.k.h in rr: lost pl 8th: bhd fr next: t.o* **66/1**

0- P **Flora Aurora**[394] 2468 7-10-12 0 ConorO'Farrell
(Nigel Hawke) *t.k.h: trckd ldrs: nt fluent 2nd: lost pl bef 8th: sn bhd: t.o whn p.u bef 3 out* **66/1**

6m 24.5s (25.50) **Going Correction** +0.20s/f (Yiel)
WFA 4 from 5yo+ 7lb **8** Ran SP% **117.2**
Speed ratings (Par 105): **65,64,63,61,57 55,38,**
CSF £46.23 TOTE £3.50: £1.20, £5.90, £1.20; EX 63.90 Trifecta £181.20.
Owner Power Panels Electrical Systems Ltd **Bred** Gestut Rottgen **Trained** Upper Lambourn, Berks

FOCUS
Rail realignments added 30yds to this race. A fair staying novice hurdle but not much of a gallop on early, and all runners raced in the centre of the course initially. Not form to be confident about, but the winner has been rated as stepping up on his recent run, with the second and fourth taking big steps up from their bumper form.

3038 BET365.COM H'CAP CHASE (18 fncs) 3m 6y
1:30 (1:30) (Class 2) (0-150,150) 4-Y-0+
£12,512 (£3,696; £1,848; £924; £462; £232)

Form RPR

P-50 1 **Sego Success (IRE)**[28] 2482 7-11-1 **139** (p) WayneHutchinson 147+
(Alan King) *mde all: edgd rt appr 3 out: styd on wl run-in* **4/1**[2]

412- 2 5 **Reaping The Reward (IRE)**[297] 4293 11-10-8 **132** (t) PeterBuchanan 136
(Lucinda Russell) *hld up in rr: hdwy 12th: sn trcking ldrs: 2nd bef 3 out: hung rt and kpt on same pce run-in* **20/1**

56-4 3 12 **Achimota (IRE)**[31] 2436 9-10-0 **124** oh1 KielanWoods 115
(Graeme McPherson) *chsd ldrs: 3rd sn after 2 out: one pce* **7/1**

4-2F 4 2 3/4 **Straidnahanna (IRE)**[21] 2643 6-10-7 **131** DannyCook 122
(Sue Smith) *chsd wnr: 3rd and hld whn blnd 2 out* **10/3**[1]

4-00 5 1/2 **Generous Ransom (IRE)**[28] 2483 7-11-0 **138** (p) HarrySkelton 126
(Nick Gifford) *mid-div: chsd ldrs 11th: wknd between last 2* **9/1**

3-14 6 12 **Forgotten Gold (IRE)**[35] 2348 9-10-10 **134** PaddyBrennan 109
(Tom George) *chsd ldrs: outpcd whn mstke 14th: sn wknd* **17/2**

-060 7 1 1/4 **Night In Milan (IRE)**[15] 2744 9-11-4 **142** (b) JamesReveley 116
(Keith Reveley) *hld up in rr: hdwy 11th: lost pl 14th: sn bhd* **9/1**

-054 P **Baileys Concerto (IRE)**[35] 2335 9-10-7 **131** BrianHughes
(Dianne Sayer) *in rr: hit 12th: sn bhd: t.o whn p.u bef 3 out* **12/1**

4P-4 P **Indian Castle (IRE)**[21] 2643 7-11-1 **139** SeanBowen
(Ian Williams) *chsd ldrs: j.rt and reminders 5th: 4th whn blnd 10th: sn drvn: lost pl 12th: sn bhd: t.o whn p.u bef 3 out* **6/1**[3]

226F F **Silver Man**[7] 2916 8-10-13 **137** (v) BrianHarding
(Jo Hughes) *hld up towards rr: hdwy 8th: drvn and outpcd whn fell 12th* **20/1**

6m 11.1s (-0.90) **Going Correction** +0.25s/f (Yiel) **10** Ran SP% **117.6**
Speed ratings (Par 109): **111,109,105,104,104 100,99, , ,**
CSF £74.55 CT £538.37 TOTE £5.10: £2.10, £3.80, £2.50; EX 78.40 Trifecta £1073.20.
Owner Tim Leadbeater **Bred** Brendan Noone **Trained** Barbury Castle, Wilts

FOCUS
A decent contest and really hard work for many on ground officially changed to heavy straight after. The winner was belatedly building on his Warwick win and there's a case for rating him 5lb+ higher through the third downwards.

3039 BET365 SUMMIT JUVENILE HURDLE (GRADE 2) (8 hdls) 2m 140y
2:05 (2:05) (Class 1) 3-Y-0 **£17,165** (£6,491; £3,290; £1,679; £884)

Form RPR

1 1 **Who Dares Wins (IRE)**[30] 2448 3-11-2 0 WayneHutchinson 135+
(Alan King) *trckd ldr: led bef 5th: hit 2 out: drvn clr between last 2: eased clsng stages* **3/1**[3]

2 20 **Robertstown (IRE)**[55] 3-10-12 0 BrianHughes 113+
(John Ferguson) *j.lft: trck ldrs: hit 5th: 2nd appr next: 7 l down and wl hld whn tired jump last: wknd* **11/8**[1]

1 3 12 **Sir Chauvelin**[36] 2324 3-11-2 0 BrianHarding 101
(Jim Goldie) *t.k.h in rr: hdwy 4th: sn trcking ldrs: outpcd 3 out: tk distant 3rd last 50yds* **8/1**

2 4 6 **Fouburg (FR)**[30] 2448 3-10-12 0 HarrySkelton 95
(Dan Skelton) *hld up in rr: t.k.h: hdwy to trck ldrs 5th: handy 3rd 3 out: fnd little: wl btn 3rd whn blnd last* **5/2**[2]

223 5 28 **Consortium (IRE)**[34] 2371 3-10-12 119 (p) TrevorWhelan 63
(Neil King) *led: hdd bef 5th: reminders appr 3 out: sn lost pl and wl bhd* **20/1**

5P P **Old Fashion**[26] 2537 3-10-5 0 SeanBowen
(Neil King) *in rr: hdwy 4th: pushed along and lost pl next: sn wl bhd: t.o whn p.u bef 3 out* **100/1**

4m 8.2s (3.50) **Going Correction** +0.50s/f (Soft) **6** Ran SP% **112.5**
Speed ratings (Par 114): **111,101,95,93,79**
CSF £7.88 TOTE £3.00: £1.70, £1.40; EX 6.60 Trifecta £24.40.
Owner W H Ponsonby **Bred** Mount Coote Stud **Trained** Barbury Castle, Wilts

FOCUS
Rail realignments added 15yds to this race. The fifth renewal of this contest since its relocation from Lingfield and, twelve months on from subsequent Triumph Hurdle hero Peace And Co's emphatic success, another very clear-cut scorer on this occasion. The tempo seemed reasonable enough in the conditions. The impressive winner has been rated in line with the best of his Flat form, but may need to go up with the third and fourth both rated 10lb+ off.

3040 BET365 DECEMBER NOVICES' CHASE (GRADE 2) (18 fncs) 3m 6y
2:40 (2:40) (Class 1) 4-Y-0+ **£19,221** (£7,835; £4,421)

Form RPR

1-21 1 **Southfield Royale**[42] 2197 5-11-5 0 (p) WayneHutchinson 156+
(Neil Mulholland) *trckd ldr sn after 1st: drvn and upsides 3 out: led next: clr last: drvn out* **2/1**[2]

P-13 2 13 **Coologue (IRE)**[14] 2774 6-11-5 139 BrianHughes 145
(Charlie Longsdon) *led: jnd and drvn 3 out: hdd whn stmbld bdly next: 6 l down last: wknd* **9/2**[3]

4112 3 7 **Weather Babe**[50] 2055 7-10-12 134 (tp) ConorO'Farrell 130
(David Pipe) *chsd ldr: stmbld bdly landing and lost pl 1st: lft modest 3rd 3rd: effrt and in tch 11th: hit next and lost pl: sn drvn: nvr a factor* **15/2**

3116 P **River Maigue (IRE)**[21] 2634 8-11-5 135 (t) DenisO'Regan
(Sophie Leech) *in rr: lft poor 4th and hmpd 3rd: pushed along 10th: t.o and drvn 12th: p.u bef 14th: lame* **25/1**

0-21 F **Smooth Stepper**[14] 2785 6-11-8 130 DannyCook
(Sue Smith) *chsd ldrs 1st: in rr whn fell 3rd* **9/1**

41-1 F **It's A Close Call (IRE)**[62] 1867 6-11-5 0 (t) SeanBowen
(Paul Nicholls) *trckd ldng pair: fell 3rd* **15/8**[1]

6m 15.7s (3.70) **Going Correction** +0.55s/f (Soft) **6** Ran SP% **111.9**
Speed ratings (Par 115): **115,110,108, ,**
CSF £11.44 TOTE £2.70: £1.60, £2.50; EX 9.60 Trifecta £57.40.
Owner Mrs Angela Yeoman **Bred** Mrs Angela Yeoman **Trained** Limpley Stoke, Wilts

FOCUS
The second running here of another race to have been relocated from Lingfield in the recent past, and a sextet all able to boast novice chase successes already as part of a collective record of eight wins from 13 chase starts. Despite that, however, errors were conspicuous early and the first three fences thinned out the field. The winner's Wetherby win could be rated to this sort of level. The runner-up has been rated 3lb off his best.

3041 BET365 H'CAP HURDLE (8 hdls) 2m 140y
3:15 (3:18) (Class 2) 3-Y-0+
£11,886 (£3,511; £1,755; £877; £438; £220)

Form RPR

0-54 1 **Minstrels Gallery (IRE)**[18] 2700 6-10-3 **122** WayneHutchinson 123+
(Lucy Wadham) *racd on inner: in rr: hdwy to chse ldrs 3 out: sn outpcd: modest 4th and styd on between last 2: chsd ldr last 150yds: kpt on to ld nr fin* **4/1**[3]

3-32 2 1/2 **Qewy (IRE)**[19] 2684 5-11-8 **141** BrianHughes 141
(John Ferguson) *mid-div: trckd ldrs 4th: 2nd 3 out: led last: sn drvn: hdd and no ex nr fin* **13/8**[1]

00-P 3 2 **Chieftain's Choice (IRE)**[31] 2438 6-10-9 **128** JamesReveley 126
(Kevin Frost) *best away: led: jnd 2 out: hdd last: kpt on same pce* **5/1**

36 4 3/4 **Forest Bihan (FR)**[22] 2617 4-11-7 **140** [1] DannyCook 137
(Brian Ellison) *chsd ldrs: kpt on one pce between last 2* **7/2**[2]

1-04 5 37 **Silver Duke (IRE)**[36] 2328 4-9-12 **120** [1] DerekFox(3) 80
(Jim Goldie) *t.k.h: racd on inner: trckd ldrs: lost pl and hit 3 out: sn bhd: t.o* **20/1**

1210 6 4 **Regulation (IRE)**[9] 2058 6-11-1 **134** TrevorWhelan 90
(Neil King) *hld up in mid-div: trckd ldrs 5th: 2nd briefly appr 3 out: 5th and wkng whn mstke 2 out: sn bhd: t.o* **20/1**

223- P **Ifandbutwhynot (IRE)**[238] 5390 9-11-8 **141** PaddyBrennan
(Tim Easterby) *in rr: pushed along 5th: sn drvn and bhd: t.o whn p.u bef 3 out* **9/1**

4m 12.5s (7.80) **Going Correction** +0.55s/f (Soft)
WFA 4 from 5yo+ 5lb **7** Ran SP% **116.5**
Speed ratings (Par 109): **109,108,107,107,90 88,**
CSF £11.72 CT £31.13 TOTE £6.10: £2.50, £1.70; EX 13.40 Trifecta £57.70.
Owner G Pascoe & S Brewer **Bred** Morecool Stud **Trained** Newmarket, Suffolk

FOCUS
Rail realignments added 15yds to this race. Not as competitive a class 2 as it might have been without the non-runners, and a difference of opinion ground-wise for much of the contest, with runners charting several different paths around the course. The second, third and fourth have been rated pretty much to their marks.
T/Plt: £34.80 to a £1 stake. Pool: £86,137.36 - 1,803.82 winning tickets T/Qpdt: £16.10 to a £1 stake. Pool: £6,706.94 - 307.26 winning tickets **Walter Glynn**

2829 LINGFIELD (L-H)
Saturday, December 12

OFFICIAL GOING: Turf course - heavy; aw - polytrack: standard
Wind: strong, half behind Weather: overcast

3042 8TH CELEBRATE A LIFE SHAREN BLAQUIERE NOVICES' H'CAP CHASE (12 fncs) 2m
12:00 (12:00) (Class 4) (0-120,116)
4-Y-0+ **£5,198** (£1,526; £763; £381)

Form RPR

46-5 1 **Sea Wall (FR)**[44] 2151 7-11-12 **116** TomCannon 129+
(Chris Gordon) *led tl after 3rd: pressed ldr tl led again 8th: clr 3 out and in command after: rdn out* **11/4**[1]

45-F 2 8 **Rouquine Sauvage**[34] 2365 7-11-3 **112** (t[1]) DavidNoonan(5) 115
(Anthony Honeyball) *chsd ldrs: wnt 2nd bef 3 out: no imp and btn whn nt fluent 2 out: plugged on to hold 2nd flat* **7/1**[3]

2-44 3 2 **Crafty Roberto**[21] 2648 7-11-9 **116** (tp) JamesBanks(3) 117
(Alex Hales) *chsd ldr tl led after 3rd: hdd 8th: 3rd and btn 3 out: plugged on* **3/1**[2]

-023 4 27 **Third Act (IRE)**[162] 896 6-11-6 **110** (t) TomScudamore 84
(Colin Tizzard) *midfield: outpcd by ldng trio 7th: effrt after 9th: no imp: wknd after 3 out: t.o* **7/1**[3]

23-0 5 41 **Coup De Grace (IRE)**[28] 2485 6-11-12 **116** JoshuaMoore 49
(Pat Phelan) *a in rr: lost tch w ldrs 7th: t.o after 9th* **7/1**[3]

/44- P **Major Martin (IRE)**[564] 491 6-10-6 **96** JamieMoore
(Gary Moore) *midfield: j.lft 6th and 7th: sn struggling and losing tch w ldrs: j. slowly and lft 9th: t.o whn p.u next* **8/1**

4/3- U **Generous Helpings (IRE)**[586] 112 6-11-3 **107** AndrewGlassonbury
(Gary Moore) *midfield: dropped to rr and losing tch w ldrs whn bmpd 6th and 7th: dropped to last whn hmpd and uns rdr 9th* **9/1**

4m 29.1s (-10.90) **Going Correction** -0.55s/f (Firm) **7** Ran SP% **110.3**
Speed ratings (Par 105): **105,101,100,86,66**
CSF £20.18 TOTE £3.70: £2.00, £2.90; EX 17.80 Trifecta £112.80.
Owner Draper Edmonds Draper **Bred** Ian Hanamy **Trained** Morestead, Hampshire

FOCUS
Hurdles moved over 6yds and sited on fresh ground and bends same as for last meeting. Races 2 & 4 increased by 33yds and race 6 by 21yds. Conditions were testing and the routine pace was sensible in the circumstances. A big step up on his previous chase form from the winner, and there's a case for rating him a bit higher through the third, but the second has been rated similar to her hurdle mark.

3043 BESTBINGOSITES.CO.UK THE ONLINE BINGO SITE NOVICES' HURDLE (10 hdls) 2m 3f 110y
12:35 (12:35) (Class 4) 4-Y-0+ **£4,548** (£1,335; £667; £333)

Form RPR

3 1 **Chef D'Oeuvre (FR)**[34] 2375 4-10-12 0 GavinSheehan 143+
(Warren Greatrex) *mde all: drew wl clr 2 out: heavily eased flat: unchal* **5/2**[2]

1 2 28 **Krugermac (IRE)**[22] 2612 4-11-5 0 JamieMoore 120+
(Gary Moore) *in tch: wnt 2nd after 4th: rdn after 3 out: 5 l down and no imp on bnd bef 2 out: wl btn and eased flat* **1/4**[1]

20-0 3 15 **Norman The Red**[215] 242 5-10-12 0 [1] MattieBatchelor 83
(Jamie Poulton) *chsd wnr tl after 4th: 3rd and lost tch w ldng pair 6th: t.o 3 out* **50/1**[3]

66 4 40 **Brave Cupid**[11] 2829 5-10-5 0 DavidEngland 36
(Michael Roberts) *dropped to rr and j. slowly 4th: sn struggling: mstke 5th: t.o next* **50/1**[3]

030 5 9 **Minmore Grey (IRE)**[38] 2275 6-10-5 0 (p) WilliamFeatherstone(7) 34
(Nick Lampard) *5th and lost tch after 4th: t.o fr 6th* **50/1**[3]

-00 P **Notebook**[40] 2251 4-10-12 0 LeightonAspell
(Martin Smith) *hld up in rr: wnt modest 4th after 4th: lost tch next: t.o 6th tl p.u after 3 out* 50/1[3]
5m 26.5s (0.50) **Going Correction** +0.05s/f (Yiel) 6 Ran SP% 116.4
Speed ratings (Par 105): **101,89,83,67,64**
CSF £3.89 TOTE £4.30: £1.20, £1.10; EX 2.90 Trifecta £13.60.
Owner McNeill Family **Bred** Ecurie Winning **Trained** Upper Lambourn, Berks

FOCUS
Rail adjustments added 33yds to the distance of this race, which was run at a reasonable pace in the conditions. The winner defied the market and looks useful. The easy winner rates a smart novice.

3044 JULIE GREHAN BIRTHDAY SURPRISE H'CAP CHASE (14 fncs) 2m 4f
1:10 (1:10) (Class 4) (0-120,118) 4-Y-0+ **£5,198** (£1,526; £763; £381)

Form RPR
2-31 1 **Alder Mairi (IRE)**[23] 2601 8-11-8 114 AndrewThornton 128+
(Seamus Mullins) *mde all: clr and only runner on the bridle after 11th: 7 l clr 2 out: pushed out flat* 5/1
001 2 12 **Kings Cross (FR)**[11] 2832 5-11-7 113 LeeEdwards 114
(Tony Carroll) *hld up in tch in rr: hdwy 7th: rdn 10th: chsd wnr 3 out: 7 l down whn j.lft and mstke 2 out: no prog after* 7/4[1]
14/4 3 19 **Seventh Hussar**[11] 2834 9-10-0 92 oh4 (t) JamieMoore 72
(Alison Batchelor) *in tch: mstke 7th: u.p after 10th: chsd clr wnr after next tl 3 out: sn wknd* 16/1
F4-1 4 3 1/4 **Winston Churchill (IRE)**[24] 2568 9-10-10 105 (t) KillianMoore(3) 82
(Sophie Leech) *chsd wnr: rdn after 10th: lost pl wl bef 3 out: wknd 3 out* 3/1[3]
P4/2 5 10 **Oscar Magic (IRE)**[28] 2489 8-11-9 118 (t) RyanHatch(3) 85
(Nigel Twiston-Davies) *chsd ldrs: mstke and lost pl 8th: sn rdn: rallied after 11th but no threat to wnr: wknd 3 out: t.o* 5/2[2]
5m 45.5s (10.50) **Going Correction** +0.05s/f (Yiel) 5 Ran SP% 112.5
Speed ratings (Par 105): **81,76,68,67,63**
CSF £14.97 TOTE £4.30: £2.10, £1.70; EX 12.30 Trifecta £41.50.
Owner F G Matthews **Bred** Alan Inglis **Trained** Wilsford-Cum-Lake, Wilts

FOCUS
The first four home are all proven on heavy ground but the winner had it wrapped up a long way out, suggesting that she was more favourably handicapped than her rivals. The easy winner was on a very good mark and has been rated as improving in line with the best of her heavy ground hurdle form. The second has been rated to his C&D winning mark.

3045 RED SCAFFOLDING & SITE SECURITY SERVICES H'CAP HURDLE (10 hdls) 2m 3f 110y
1:45 (1:45) (Class 3) (0-140,136) 3-Y-0 **£6,330** (£1,870; £935; £468; £234)

Form RPR
0500 1 **Gevrey Chambertin (FR)**[15] 2759 7-11-12 136 (p) TomScudamore 144+
(David Pipe) *in tch: chsd ldrs after 4th: led 2 out: sn in command: easily* 13/8[1]
U-00 2 11 **First Avenue**[32] 2415 10-10-7 124 PaddyBradley(7) 118
(Laura Mongan) *in tch: 4th and outpcd sn after 3 out: rallied to chse clr wnr between last 2: hit last: no imp flat* 10/1
22P- 3 3 1/4 **Norse Legend**[266] 4920 4-11-3 127 TomCannon 119
(Chris Gordon) *w ldr tl 4th: chsd ldr after: rdn sn after 3 out: led on inner bnd bef 2 out: sn hdd and btn 3rd 2 out: nt fluent last: plugged on* 12/1
-042 4 1 **Crookstown (IRE)**[14] 2775 8-10-12 122 GavinSheehan 112
(Ben Case) *chsd ldrs tl led 4th: moved rt and hdd bnd bef 2 out: sn led again: hdd and mstke 2 out: sn btn: 3rd and wl hld whn nt fluent last* 9/4[2]
/3-6 5 19 **Stiff Upper Lip (IRE)**[34] 2369 5-10-6 116 LeightonAspell 85
(Oliver Sherwood) *mde most tl 4th: dropped to last and rdn after next: lost tch sn after 3 out: t.o* 5/1[3]
443- 6 5 **Top Man Marty (IRE)**[286] 4512 6-10-3 113 JackQuinlan 77
(Sarah Humphrey) *hld up in tch: cl 5th 3 out: sn rdn and wknd wl bef next: t.o* 8/1
5m 25.7s (-0.30) **Going Correction** +0.05s/f (Yiel)
WFA 4 from 5yo+ 5lb 6 Ran SP% 113.4
Speed ratings (Par 107): **102,97,96,95,88 86**
CSF £17.29 TOTE £2.40: £2.20, £5.30; EX 16.70 Trifecta £139.80.
Owner Roger Stanley & Yvonne Reynolds III **Bred** M Jean-Marie Prost Alamartine **Trained** Nicholashayne, Devon

FOCUS
Rail adjustments added 33yds to the distance of this race, which was well contested despite the smallish field. The pace was nothing special but the class horse won easily. The winner was on a very good mark and has been rated to the best of last season's chase runs. The third helps set the level.

3046 J.A. RATTIGAN PLANT HIRE H'CAP CHASE (QUALIFIER FOR THE CHALLENGER STAYING CHASE SERIES FINAL) (18 fncs) 2m 7f 110y
2:20 (2:20) (Class 3) (0-130,130) 4-Y-0 **£9,495** (£2,805; £1,402; £702; £351)

45-F 1 **Baby Shine (IRE)**[16] 2724 9-11-11 129 LeightonAspell 139+
(Lucy Wadham) *chsd ldrs tl led 14th: gng best after: drew clr and in command fr 3 out: rdn out flat* 6/1
06-6 2 9 **Onderun (IRE)**[31] 2442 6-10-11 115 GavinSheehan 117+
(Emma Lavelle) *bhd: hdwy 7th: chsd ldrs 9th: rdn after 14th: sn struggling and wl hld on downhill run bef 3 out: rallied 2 out: kpt on u.p to go 2nd towards fin: no ch w wnr* 7/1
00P1 3 1/2 **Fruity O'Rooney**[22] 2616 12-11-7 125 (b) JamieMoore 123
(Gary Moore) *led tl 14th: sn rdn: no ex bef 3 out: 3rd and no threat to wnr 3 out: plugged on to go 2nd fnl 100yds: lost 2nd towards fin* 7/1
6-24 4 3 3/4 **Cadoudoff (FR)**[26] 2545 5-11-11 129 RichieMcLernon 124
(Charlie Longsdon) *midfield: clsd and wl in tch 10th: rdn after: outpcd wl bef 3 out: no ch w wnr after: wnt 4th nr fin* 12/1
P-42 5 1/2 **Saint Raph (FR)**[11] 2832 7-11-5 123 (t) TomCannon 118
(Robert Walford) *in last pair: j. slowly and rdn 4th: hdwy to chse ldr and travelling bttr 9th: 3rd and rdn 15th: chsd clr wnr bef next: no imp: wknd and lost 3 pls fnl 100yds* 3/1[1]
P1P- P **Farbreaga (IRE)**[244] 5289 9-11-12 130 (p) MattieBatchelor
(Jamie Poulton) *chsd ldr: j. bdly lft and lost pl: rdn and sn rcvrd to chse ldr again: lost 2nd 9th and sn dropped to rr u.p: losing tch and p.u 13th* 20/1
30/P P **Indian Daudaie (FR)**[21] 2648 8-10-10 114 JackQuinlan
(Sarah Humphrey) *in tch towards rr: mstke 1st: mstke 11th: sn struggling: tailing off whn p.u 14th* 50/1
43-4 P **Tarraco (FR)**[20] 2663 8-10-8 112 (b) LiamTreadwell
(Venetia Williams) *chsd ldrs tl dropped out and no rspnse to press after 9th: losing tch whn p.u 13th* 5/1[3]
12/3 P **Bucking The Trend**[57] 1944 7-11-2 125 AlanJohns(5)
(Tim Vaughan) *in tch in midfield: 6th and struggling u.p 14th: sn lost tch: t.o and p.u bef 3 out* 4/1[2]
6m 55.9s (-4.10) **Going Correction** +0.05s/f (Yiel) 9 Ran SP% 115.4
Speed ratings (Par 107): **108,105,104,103,103 , ,**
CSF £47.34 CT £301.04 TOTE £8.00: £2.40, £2.60, £1.60; EX 48.70 Trifecta £288.10.
Owner P A Philipps,T S Redman & Mrs L Redman **Bred** Kevin Francis O'Donnell **Trained** Newmarket, Suffolk

FOCUS
This was run at a solid gallop in the heavy ground, making it a good test. The winner was on a good mark and has been rated to her best, while the second has been rated in line with his hurdle form.

3047 NSSLGLOBAL H'CAP HURDLE (8 hdls) 2m
2:55 (2:55) (Class 4) (0-120,120) 3-Y-0+ **£3,898** (£1,144; £572; £286)

Form RPR
500F 1 **Dormouse**[24] 2577 10-11-2 110 (p) TomScudamore 113
(Anabel K Murphy) *hld up in tch: hdwy to chse ldr 3 out: 2 l down and styng on last: led fnl 100yds: pushed out* 3/1[2]
/43- 2 2 3/4 **Tara Bridge**[303] 4176 7-11-12 120 TomCannon 120
(Chris Gordon) *chsd ldrs tl led bef 3 out: clr 2 out: rdn between last: drvn and hdd fnl 100yds: no ex* 7/1[3]
20-0 3 10 **Eminent Poet**[42] 2182 4-11-2 110 LiamTreadwell 100
(Venetia Williams) *in tch in midfield: effrt bef 2 out: 3rd and no imp 2 out: plugged on* 6/4[1]
424- 4 15 **Brother Bennett (FR)**[257] 5065 5-10-12 113 (vt[1]) PaulJohn(7) 88
(Jim Best) *in tch in last pair: hdwy to chse ldrs after 5th: 3rd and hung rt bnd bef 2 out: 4th and wknd 2 out* 3/1[2]
63-0 5 42 **Bountiful Sin**[26] 2544 4-11-7 115 LeightonAspell 48
(Oliver Sherwood) *chsd ldr tl led 5th: sn hdd and dropped out: t.o bef 2 out* 14/1
P **Chambord Du Loir (FR)**[201] 5-11-7 115[1] JackQuinlan
(Sarah Humphrey) *led tl 5th: sn rdn and immediately dropped out: t.o and p.u wl bef 2 out* 16/1
4m 26.1s (-1.90) **Going Correction** +0.05s/f (Yiel)
WFA 4 from 5yo+ 5lb 6 Ran SP% 115.0
Speed ratings (Par 105): **106,104,99,92,71**
CSF £23.55 CT £42.20 TOTE £4.20: £2.20, £3.20; EX 14.70 Trifecta £79.00.
Owner Aiden Murphy **Bred** Deerfield Farm **Trained** Wilmcote, Warwicks

FOCUS
Rail adjustments added 21yds to the distance of this race. The early leader set a good pace but the others ignored him and that was a wise move in the conditions. It's been rated around the first two.

3048 RACING WELFARE "JUNIOR" STANDARD OPEN NATIONAL HUNT FLAT RACE (THIS RACE WILL BE RUN ON THE AW) 2m
3:30 (3:30) (Class 6) 3-Y-0 **£1,559** (£457; £228; £114)

Form RPR
3 1 nse **Quarenta (FR)**[32] 2414 3-11-0 0 JoshuaMoore 97
(Jonjo O'Neill) *in tch in midfield: rdn and hdwy to chse wnr 2f out: styd on wl u.p ins fnl f: jst failed* 4/1[2]
2 **The Blue Bomber** 3-11-0 0 GavinSheehan 97
(Mick Channon) *mde all: 2 l clr and rdn 2f out: drvn ins fnl f: jst hld on* 5/2[1]
3 6 **Fella** 3-11-0 0 AndrewGlassonbury 91
(Gary Moore) *chsd ldrs: wnt 2nd 6f out tl 2f out: styd on same pce u.p after* 20/1
4 1 1/4 **The Racing Duke (IRE)** 3-11-0 0 TomScudamore 90
(Graeme McPherson) *chsd wnr tl 6f out: rdn and unable qck in 4th 2f out: styd on same pce* 4/1[2]
34 5 3 1/2 **Anne Of Brittany (FR)**[37] 2304 3-10-7 0 JackQuinlan 79
(Henry Spiller) *hld up in tch in midfield: 5th and unable qck u.p 2f out: wl hld and one pce after* 8/1
6 4 **Deauville Dame** 3-10-7 0 JamesBest 75
(Sir Mark Prescott Bt) *hld up in tch in last trio: rdn over 3f out: struggling and drvn 2f out: no ch after* 8/1
5 7 1 **Art Of Swing (IRE)**[32] 2414 3-11-0 0 JamieMoore 81
(Gary Moore) *hld up in tch in last trio: shkn up ent fnl 2f: rdn and no hdwy over 1f out: sn wknd* 12/1
0 8 3 **Do It Tomorrow (IRE)**[32] 2414 3-10-2 0 MikeyEnnis(5) 71
(J R Jenkins) *in tch in midfield: rdn over 4f out: lost pl and wkng whn hung lft over 1f out* 50/1
9 5 **Farrells Destiny** 3-10-7 0 MrTommieMO'Brien(7) 73
(Chris Bealby) *hld up in tch in last trio: rdn 3f out: sn struggling: bhd over 1f out* 7/1[3]
3m 33.8s (213.80) 9 Ran SP% 117.7
CSF £12.73 TOTE £4.50: £1.60, £1.70, £3.00; EX 18.90 Trifecta £186.20.
Owner Martin, Jocelyn & Steve Broughton **Bred** Robin Van Haaren & Evelyne Van Haaren **Trained** Cheltenham, Gloucs
■ Stewards' Enquiry : Gavin Sheehan two-day ban; used his whip above the permitted level (28th,30th Dec)

FOCUS
A routine event of its type, but the pace wasn't bad for a bumper. Seemingly a big step up from the winner, but not form to be confident about. On the day, the winner was declared as The Blue Bomber, and that remains the result for betting purposes unless a bookmaker specifies otherwise. However, the quality of the photo-finish was affected by poor light and Quarenta was given the race five days later.
T/Plt: £64.70 to a £1 stake. Pool of £52124.28 - 587.88 winning tickets. T/Qpdt: £20.70 to a £1 stake. Pool of £4066.94 - 144.88 winning tickets. **Steve Payne**

3049 - 3053a (Foreign Racing) - See Raceform Interactive

2800 CARLISLE (R-H)
Sunday, December 13

OFFICIAL GOING: Heavy (chs 5.6; hdl 4.9)
Wind: Almost nil Weather: Overcast, cold

3054 CASINO AND GAMES AT 188BET NOVICES' HURDLE (10 hdls) 2m 1f
12:05 (12:10) (Class 4) 4-Y-0+ **£3,249** (£954; £477; £238)

Form RPR
1-0 1 **Suit Yourself (IRE)**[44] 2163 6-10-12 0 (t) RichardJohnson 122+
(Jonjo O'Neill) *hld up: smooth hdwy bef 2 out: led gng wl bef last: qcknd clr on bridle run-in: readily* 10/3[2]
4-24 2 3 **Berkshire Downs**[32] 2428 5-10-2 0 AdamNicol(3) 103
(Lucy Normile) *led to after 1st: lft in ld after 3rd: rdn bef 2 out: hdd bef last: kpt on: nt pce of ready wnr* 11/1

3 4 **Mango Cap (FR)**[39] 4-11-5 0 .... (t) TomScudamore 113
(David Pipe) *prom: nt fluent 3 out: sn chsng ldr: drvn bef next: kpt on same pce fr last* **10/11**[1]

4 4 **Sean Ban (IRE)**[70] 5-10-12 0 .... WayneHutchinson 102
(Donald McCain) *nt fluent on occasions: hld up: rdn and hdwy bef 2 out: outpcd between last 2* **11/1**

046- 5 9 **Red Mystique (IRE)**[528] [846] 6-10-7 79 .... DaraghBourke(5) 92
(Maurice Barnes) *cl up: lft 2nd after 3rd: rdn bef 2 out: sn wknd* **100/1**

24-2 6 4 **Tara The Tiger**[18] [2716] 4-10-5 0 .... BrianHughes 81
(Tim Easterby) *nt fluent: trckd ldrs tl rdn and wknd bef 2 out* **9/2**[3]

54 P **Lacerta**[14] [2804] 4-10-9 0 .... JoeColliver(3)
(Micky Hammond) *hld up: nt fluent 4th: lost tch 3 out: broke down bdly appr next: fatally injured* **40/1**

00-U P **Zruda**[11] [2847] 4-10-5 0 .... HenryBrooke
(David Thompson) *t.k.h: midfield on outside: struggling 4 out: lost tch next: p.u bef 2 out* **200/1**

00-0 P **Turtleplex**[78] [144] 4-9-12 0 .... ThomasDowson(7)
(Maurice Barnes) *hld up: plld hrd and sddle sn slipped: led after 1st: j.lft next two and sn p.u* **200/1**

4m 31.9s (2.70) **Going Correction** +0.375s/f (Yiel) **9 Ran SP% 114.7**
Speed ratings (Par 105): **108,106,104,102,98 96,,,**
CSF £36.56 TOTE £4.00: £1.30, £3.30, £1.10; EX 34.70 Trifecta £99.40.
Owner John P McManus **Bred** Michael G Daly **Trained** Cheltenham, Gloucs

FOCUS
Hurdle races on Inner hurdles track. Races 1 & 7 increased by 35yds, race 2 by 63yds, race 3 by 38yds, race 4 by 86yds, race 5 by 50yds and race 6 by 60yds. Testing ground but they seemed to be going through it okay. This opening novices' hurdle lacked depth and the winner proved a class apart. The third and fifth help set the level.

3055 188BET NOVICES' LIMITED H'CAP CHASE (14 fncs 4 omitted) 2m 4f 198y
12:35 (12:40) (Class 3) (0-135,128) 4-Y-0+ **£6,498** (£1,908; £954; £477)

Form RPR

13-3 1 **Subtle Grey (IRE)**[15] [2764] 6-11-4 **124** .... WayneHutchinson 134+
(Donald McCain) *mde all: rdn bypassing omitted 4 out: drvn and edgd lft run-in: holding on wl whn edgd rt towards fin* **7/4**[2]

-414 2 1 ½ **Morning Royalty (IRE)**[42] [2211] 8-11-0 **120** .... BrianHughes 128+
(James Moffatt) *t.k.h: prom gng wl: shkn up after 3 out: rdn to chse wnr bef last: drvn and edgd rt run-in: hld towards fin* **11/8**[1]

15/U 3 18 **Only Orsenfoolsies**[11] [2846] 6-11-1 **128** .... FinianO'Toole(7) 124
(Micky Hammond) *nt fluent on occasions: in tch: hit and outpcd 4 out (usual 5 out): rallied gng wl bef next: effrt and ev ch 2 out: drvn and wknd bef last* **9/1**

3-25 4 16 **Glacial Rock (IRE)**[32] [2429] 9-10-8 **114** .... (p) HenryBrooke 97
(Alistair Whillans) *pressed ldr: nt fluent 8th: rdn whn nt fluent 3 out: wknd fr next* **4/1**[3]

5m 49.3s (12.30) **Going Correction** +0.15s/f (Yiel) **4 Ran SP% 108.5**
Speed ratings (Par 107): **82,81,74,68**
CSF £4.72 TOTE £2.40; EX 3.90 Trifecta £10.80.
Owner Deva Racing Subtle Grey Partnership **Bred** James A Slattery **Trained** Cholmondeley, Cheshire

FOCUS
Races distance increased by 63yds. Fences 4 and 9 were omitted from the chase races throughout the afternoon. A tight little handicap chase which was run at what looked a reasonable gallop in the conditions, and the form looks solid enough. The winner has been rated as improving to his hurdle mark.

3056 BET NOW AT 188BET "NATIONAL HUNT" NOVICES' HURDLE (11 hdls) 2m 3f 61y
1:05 (1:10) (Class 4) 4-Y-0+ **£3,249** (£954; £477; £238)

Form RPR

10-2 1 **Western Rules (IRE)**[36] [2338] 5-10-12 0 .... BrianHarding 113+
(Nicky Richards) *trckd ldrs: led 3 out: rdn bef last: edgd rt and kpt on wl towards fin* **4/9**[1]

21- 2 1 ½ **Bronco Billy (IRE)**[398] [2405] 5-10-12 0 .... RichardJohnson 112
(Jonjo O'Neill) *hld up in tch: smooth hdwy to chse wnr after 3 out: effrt and 1 l down next: drvn and edgd rt whn nt fluent last: kpt on: hld towards fin* **15/8**[2]

/63- 3 16 **Along Came Theo (IRE)**[362] [3136] 5-10-12 0 .... BrianHughes 98
(Andrew Crook) *in tch: hmpd 3 out: sn rcvrd and trcking ldrs: rdn and wknd bef last* **22/1**[3]

02P- 4 50 **Bolton Blue (IRE)**[237] [5420] 6-10-7 0 .... CallumBewley(5) 45
(Katie Scott) *cl up: sprawled 3 out: sn rdn: wknd bef next: t.o* **66/1**

0/ 5 8 **Forty Something (IRE)**[1869] [2102] 10-10-12 0 .... JamesReveley 37
(Stuart Coltherd) *led to 3 out: rdn and wknd bef next: t.o* **150/1**

5m 15.1s (6.30) **Going Correction** +0.375s/f (Yiel) **5 Ran SP% 110.5**
Speed ratings (Par 105): **101,100,93,72,69**
CSF £1.66 TOTE £1.60: £1.10, £1.10; EX 1.50 Trifecta £3.20.
Owner Bob Bennett & Jimmy Dudgeon **Bred** John Joe Shaughnessy **Trained** Greystoke, Cumbria

FOCUS
Races distance increased by 38yds. This looked a match on paper and, although the early gallop was only steady, the big two drew clear in the closing stages. The winner set a fair standard and has been rated close to his mark. The second and third have been rated similar to the best of their bumper figures.

3057 188BET VETERANS' H'CAP CHASE (QUALIFIER) (LAST QUALIFIER OF THE 2015 VETERANS' CHASE SERIES) (14 fncs 4 omitted) 3m 110y
1:40 (1:45) (Class 2) (0-150,139) 10-Y-0+ **£18,768** (£5,544; £2,772; £1,386; £15; £Form)

P-16 1 **Tullamore Dew (IRE)**[42] [2213] 13-10-8 **124** .... JoeColliver(3) 140+
(Micky Hammond) *hld up in tch: smooth hdwy to take 2nd 9th: led after 3 out: drew clr fr next: shkn up after last: easily* **9/1**

44-1 2 12 **Golden Chieftain (IRE)**[28] [2517] 10-11-2 **129** .... (tp) BrendanPowell 127
(Colin Tizzard) *in tch: nt fluent and outpcd 8th: plenty to do 4 out (usual 5 out): rallied after 2 out: styd on wl to take 2nd cl home: no ch w wnr* **11/4**[2]

0-F3 3 nk **Harry The Viking**[22] [2638] 10-10-13 **129** .... (p) DerekFox(3) 125
(Sandy Thomson) *chsd ldrs: drvn and outpcd 5th: rallied to chse ldng pair 4 out (usual 5 out): outpcd next: rallied and chsd (clr) wnr after last: one pce: lost 2nd nr fin* **9/2**

U-PP 4 nk **Knock A Hand (IRE)**[32] [2436] 10-11-12 **139** .... (b) RichardJohnson 135
(Kerry Lee) *cl up: led 1st to 4th: reminders after 7th: nt fluent 4 out (usual 5 out): sn outpcd: rallied 2 out: kpt on same pce fr last* **3/1**[3]

24P- 5 11 **Renard (FR)**[295] [4361] 10-11-10 **137** .... AidanColeman 128
(Venetia Williams) *led to 1st: led 4th: jnd 9th: hdd after 3 out: drvn and outpcd next: wknd after last* **5/2**[1]

6m 39.5s (-3.10) **Going Correction** +0.15s/f (Yiel) **5 Ran SP% 108.4**
Speed ratings: **110,106,106,105,102**
CSF £32.45 TOTE £7.80: £3.90, £1.70; EX 23.50 Trifecta £99.10.
Owner Give Every Man His Due **Bred** Michael Daly **Trained** Middleham, N Yorks

FOCUS
Races distance increased by 86yds. A valuable veterans' chase and it looked a competitive heat on paper despite the small field, but a few of these didn't run to the level we know they are capable of. The easy winner has been rated as running his best race since 2012, with the third close to his recent Haydock mark.

3058 PERTEMPS NETWORK H'CAP HURDLE (SERIES QUALIFIER) (14 hdls) 3m 1f
2:10 (2:15) (Class 2) 4-Y-0+ **£12,021** (£3,529; £1,764; £882)

Form RPR

-02F 1 **Pineau De Re (FR)**[8] [2899] 12-11-8 **136** .... RichardJohnson 142+
(Dr Richard Newland) *in tch: smooth hdwy to ld 2 out: rdn clr fr last* **7/1**[3]

U-26 2 4 **Quel Elite (FR)**[23] [2624] 11-9-11 **114** oh3 .... TonyKelly(3) 117+
(James Moffatt) *hld up: hmpd 5th: rdn after 3 out: rallied and chsd wnr appr last: edgd rt run-in: no ex last 75yds* **10/1**

41-3 3 1 **Donna's Diamond (IRE)**[36] [2340] 6-10-11 **130** .... DiarmuidO'Regan(5) 131
(Chris Grant) *chsd ldrs: outpcd whn hit 3 out: rallied next: nt fluent last: kpt on u.p towards fin* **9/1**

1011 4 12 **Native Optimist (IRE)**[8] [2919] 8-10-2 **121** .... MissCWalton(5) 111
(Sheena Walton) *in tch: lost pl bef 3rd: hdwy on outside to ld 8th: rdn and hdd 2 out: wknd after last* **14/1**

F-11 5 ¾ **Island Heights (IRE)**[23] [2624] 6-10-13 **130** .... DerekFox(3) 118
(Lucinda Russell) *led tl bmpd and hdd 2nd: lost pl 5th: rallied whn nt fluent 4 out: hit next: rdn and outpcd 2 out: wkng whn mstke last* **9/4**[2]

2-PP 6 4 ½ **Barafundle (IRE)**[22] [2641] 11-11-9 **137** .... (b[1]) HenryBrooke 120
(Jennie Candlish) *cl up: led 2nd to 8th: rdn and outpcd after 3 out: no imp fr next* **25/1**

4-33 7 1 ¼ **Hartforth**[14] [2802] 7-10-3 **120** .... CallumWhillans(3) 101
(Donald Whillans) *chsd ldrs tl rdn and wknd after 3 out* **12/1**

-111 F **Isaacstown Lad (IRE)**[36] [2340] 8-10-11 **125** .... BrianHarding
(Nicky Richards) *hld up: fell 5th* **85/40**[1]

6m 42.0s (3.00) **Going Correction** +0.375s/f (Yiel) **8 Ran SP% 112.6**
Speed ratings (Par 109): **110,108,108,104,104 102,102,**
CSF £68.95 CT £630.62 TOTE £8.10: £2.30, £3.10, £2.60; EX 77.30 Trifecta £703.20.
Owner J A Provan **Bred** Michel Hardy **Trained** Claines, Worcs

FOCUS
Races distance increased by 50yds. A good quality handicap hurdle, run at what looked a sound gallop, so this should be form that stands up. The second and third help set the level in a straightforward handicap.

3059 ASIAN H'CAPS AT 188BET HANDICAP CHASE (13 fncs 3 omitted) 2m 4f
2:40 (2:45) (Class 4) (0-105,105) 4-Y-0+ **£3,898** (£1,144; £572; £286)

Form RPR

3511 1 **Verko (FR)**[9] [2894] 6-10-8 **94** .... FinianO'Toole(7) 110+
(Micky Hammond) *hld up: outpcd 5th: rallied 8th: hdwy to ld 2 out: clr bef last: shkn up briefly run-in: kpt on strly* **9/4**[2]

5-PP 2 5 **Mansonien L'As (FR)**[44] [2173] 9-10-6 **85** .... (tp) BrianHarding 91
(Donald McCain) *mde most tl rdn and hdd 2 out: kpt on same pce fr last* **9/2**[3]

6545 3 hd **Veroce (FR)**[19] [2708] 6-10-7 **91** .... JamieHamilton(5) 97
(Mark Walford) *cl up: effrt and ev ch 3 out: rdn and kpt on same pce fr next* **5/4**[1]

P-P6 4 20 **Asuncion (FR)**[19] [2707] 5-9-11 **79** .... (p) TonyKelly(3) 67
(Rebecca Menzies) *chsd ldrs: outpcd bef 9th: drvn and struggling fr next* **17/2**

64-P U **Samson Collonges (FR)**[37] [2321] 9-10-0 **79** oh6 .... (tp) HenryBrooke
(Rebecca Menzies) *hld up in tch: outpcd after 8th: struggling fr 4 out (usual 5 out): 30 l last and no ch whn uns rdr last* **14/1**

5m 29.9s (2.50) **Going Correction** +0.15s/f (Yiel) **5 Ran SP% 110.6**
Speed ratings (Par 105): **101,99,98,90,**
CSF £12.33 TOTE £2.90: £1.60, £2.90; EX 12.40 Trifecta £25.90.
Owner David Green **Bred** E A R L Trinquet, M & O Trinquet **Trained** Middleham, N Yorks

FOCUS
Races distance increased by 60yds. A modest handicap chase in which only a couple brought credible recent form to the table. The winner is on the upgrade, while the second was a 100+ horse in 2013-14, so the ratings may need to be adjusted upwards.

3060 PREMIER LEAGUE BETTING AT 188BET MARES' STANDARD OPEN NATIONAL HUNT FLAT RACE 2m 1f
3:10 (3:15) (Class 6) 4-6-Y-0 **£1,559** (£457; £228; £114)

Form RPR

1 **Billy Billy (IRE)**[36] 5-10-12 0 .... RichardJohnson 108+
(S R B Crawford, Ire) *mde all at stdy gallop: shkn up and qcknd clr 2f out: kpt on strly: eased nr fin* **11/10**[1]

2 8 **Conquer Gold (IRE)**[287] 5-10-12 0 .... BrianHarding 98
(Nicky Richards) *prom on outside: pushed along and hdwy to chse (clr) wnr wl over 1f out: no imp fnl f* **7/4**[2]

2 3 3 ¾ **Selkirk's Island**[43] [2195] 4-10-2 0 .... RossChapman(10) 94
(Lucinda Russell) *w wnr: rdn over 3f out: no ex over 1f out* **7/2**[3]

4 4 ½ **Baby Ticker** 6-10-9 0 .... CallumWhillans(3) 90
(Donald Whillans) *trckd ldrs: pushed along and outpcd 4f out: rallied over 2f out: wknd over 1f out* **33/1**

0 5 99 **Flowalong (IRE)**[220] [159] 5-10-12 0 .... BrianHughes
(Bruce Mactaggart) *chsd ldrs: struggling 5f out: sn wknd: t.o* **150/1**

4m 40.6s (17.00) **Going Correction** +0.375s/f (Yiel)
WFA 4 from 5yo+ 5lb **5 Ran SP% 109.8**
Speed ratings: **75,71,69,67,20**
CSF £3.29 TOTE £2.10: £1.30, £1.50; EX 2.90 Trifecta £4.60.
Owner W Cromie **Bred** William McGladdery **Trained** Larne, Co Antrim

FOCUS
Races distance increased by 35yds. A small field for this bumper but there was market confidence behind the runner-up and there must be a good chance that the winner is above average. A token rating has been given through the third.
T/Plt: £90.10 to a £1 stake. Pool: £60,395.40 - 488.82 winning units. T/Qpdt: £19.80 to a £1 stake. Pool: £5,122.03 - 191.27 winning units. **Richard Young**

2836 SOUTHWELL (L-H)
Sunday, December 13

OFFICIAL GOING: Soft (heavy in places) changing to heavy after race 1 (12.20)
Wind: virtually nil Weather: cold and damp, light rain race 4 onwards

3061 VERTU VW MANSFIELD H'CAP CHASE (14 fncs 2 omitted) 2m 4f 62y
12:20 (12:20) (Class 4) (0-115,115) 4-Y-0+ £5,325 (£1,653; £890)

Form RPR
5-34 1 **Un Noble (FR)**[32] 2431 5-11-12 **113** CraigNichol 123
(Nicky Richards) *chsd ldrs: outpcd 8th: drvn next: wnt 4 l 2nd bef 3 out: styd on to ld sn after last: drvn out* **2/1**[2]
4-35 2 2 1/4 **Iona Days (IRE)**[21] 2668 10-11-9 **110** (p) MarkGrant 118
(Julian Smith) *hld up: wnt 2nd 7th: led next: sn briefly hdd: 3 l clr and rdn appr 2 out: hdd and no ex last 75yds* **7/1**
50-2 3 47 **Smartmax (FR)**[25] 2582 6-10-11 **98** TomMessenger 66
(Caroline Bailey) *trckd ldrs: drvn 10th: wknd 3 out: sn bhd: t.o* **7/4**[1]
-6PP P **Ravens Brook (IRE)**[3] 2996 9-11-1 **102** (v[1]) TrevorWhelan
(Neil King) *led: drvn 7th: hdd next bef sn briefly regaining ld: lost pl 10th: sn bhd: t.o 4th whn p.u bef 3 out* **10/1**
-12P P **Be On Time (FR)**[22] 2645 4-11-7 **115** (b) SamTwiston-Davies
(Jamie Snowden) *j.rt: chsd ldrs: reminders 6th: lost pl next: j. slowly 8th: sn bhd: t.o whn p.u bef 4 out* **5/1**[3]

5m 39.8s (22.80) **Going Correction** +1.275s/f (Heav)
WFA 4 from 5yo+ 6lb **5 Ran SP% 108.0**
Speed ratings (Par 105): **105,104,85, ,**
CSF £14.08 TOTE £2.90: £1.20, £3.30; EX 12.90 Trifecta £33.10.
Owner Mrs C A Torkington **Bred** Richard Godefroy **Trained** Greystoke, Cumbria

FOCUS
All distances as advertised. 15mm of rain overnight had changed the going from good to soft with soft places to heavy. Changing fortunes after the clear leader began to weary, opening the door for the winner, who had been under pressure until finding a second wind turning for home.

3062 LIKE MW ENTERTAINMENTS LTD ON FACEBOOK H'CAP CHASE (18 fncs 3 omitted) 3m 1f 129y
12:50 (12:50) (Class 5) (0-100,96) 4-Y-0+ £3,249 (£954; £477; £238)

Form RPR
0323 1 **Kilcascan**[12] 2836 11-11-1 **88** (p) BenPoste(3) 96
(Rosemary Gasson) *led to 2nd: w ldr: led 8th: hrd drvn 3 out: edgd rt run-in: kpt on: all out* **5/1**[2]
5-31 2 1 **Cheat The Cheater (IRE)**[12] 2830 8-11-2 **89** (tp) ConorShoemark(3) 96
(Claire Dyson) *chsd ldrs: drvn 14th: upsides 3 out: cl 2nd last: carried rt: no ex clsng stages* **9/2**[1]
66/3 3 4 **Salut Honore (FR)**[38] 2303 9-11-2 **86** (t) KielanWoods 91
(Alex Hales) *trckd ldrs: upsides 3 out: wknd clsng stages* **9/2**[1]
03UF 4 11 **Mission Complete (IRE)**[15] 2771 9-11-0 **94** (tp) JackSavage(10) 88
(Jonjo O'Neill) *chsd ldrs: hmpd 7th: drvn and outpcd 17th: lost pl bef 3 out* **7/1**
P50U 5 13 **Bach To Before (IRE)**[10] 2861 7-11-3 **90** (t) JonathanEngland(3) 74
(Graeme McPherson) *hld up in rr: hdwy 14th: effrt and upsides 3 out: wknd appr 2 out: mstke last* **10/1**
5524 6 28 **Cara Court (IRE)**[15] 2771 9-10-6 **79** (v) ColmMcCormack(3) 30
(Joanne Foster) *j.rt: led 2nd: hdd 8th: drvn 12th: lost pl and hit 13th: sn bhd: t.o 4 out* **16/1**
330- P **Dixie Bull (IRE)**[270] 4855 10-11-4 **88** (p) JamesDavies
(Tom Symonds) *chsd ldrs: mstke 6th: lost pl and hit 9th: sn bhd: reminders 12th: p.u after 14th* **9/2**[1]
0-U3 P **Exmoor Challenge**[15] 2771 6-10-11 **81** TrevorWhelan
(Neil King) *chsd ldrs: pushed along 8th: lost pl next: bhd fr 11th: t.o whn p.u after 13th* **6/1**[3]

7m 25.4s (39.40) **Going Correction** +1.275s/f (Heav) **8 Ran SP% 113.0**
Speed ratings (Par 103): **90,89,88,85,81 72, ,**
CSF £27.51 CT £106.96 TOTE £5.90: £1.80, £1.70, £2.50; EX 44.10 Trifecta £111.30.
Owner Mrs Rosemary Gasson **Bred** Lady Sutton **Trained** Balscote, Oxon

FOCUS
An open-looking moderate handicap with four still challenging going to the first in the home straight.

3063 TICKETS AT SOUTHWELL-RACECOURSE.CO.UK MAIDEN HURDLE (9 hdls 2 omitted) 2m 4f 62y
1:20 (1:21) (Class 5) 4-Y-0+ £3,249 (£954; £477; £238)

Form RPR
42 1 **Robin Of Locksley (IRE)**[31] 2450 5-11-0 123 HarrySkelton 129+
(Dan Skelton) *trckd ldrs: 2nd appr 2 out: led between last 2: forged clr run-in* **5/4**[1]
455 2 5 **Mountain Eagle (IRE)**[24] 2603 6-11-0 0 (t) NoelFehily 122
(Harry Fry) *t.k.h: hld up towards rr: handy 4th 3rd: effrt sn after 3 out: sn outpcd: rallied between last 2: 3 l 2nd whn blnd last* **12/1**
3-1 3 3 **Penn Lane (IRE)**[29] 2493 4-11-0 0 GavinSheehan 120
(Warren Greatrex) *nt fluent: led: blnd 5th: sn increased pce: hdd between last 2: 3rd and one pce whn blnd last* **7/4**[2]
2-0 4 1 1/2 **Policy Breach (IRE)**[20] 2690 4-10-11 0 TomBellamy(3) 118
(Kim Bailey) *chsd ldr: drvn and hung lft appr 2 out: 4th and outpcd appr last: keeping on at fin* **11/2**[3]
5 5 39 **Goldboy (IRE)**[15] 2768 7-11-0 0 JoshuaMoore 78
(Jonjo O'Neill) *t.k.h in rr: modest 5th and pushed along 6th: wkng whn hit 3 out: sn bhd: t.o* **20/1**
0 6 9 **Kerry's Lord (IRE)**[46] 2141 6-10-7 0 RomainClavreul(7) 69
(Joanne Thomason-Murphy) *in rr: drvn 6th: bhd fr 3 out: t.o* **250/1**
0P 7 13 **Airebridge (IRE)**[8] 2917 4-10-11 0 (t) HarryBannister(3) 56
(Michael Easterby) *chsd ldrs: mstke 1st: dropped bk to rr 2nd: reminders 6th: sn bhd: t.o* **250/1**

5m 38.8s (25.80) **Going Correction** +1.275s/f (Heav) **7 Ran SP% 109.4**
Speed ratings (Par 103): **99,97,95,95,79 76,70**
CSF £14.81 TOTE £2.20: £1.20, £3.70; EX 11.70 Trifecta £28.60.
Owner Simon Caunce & J Tierney **Bred** Ms Erica Dalton **Trained** Alcester, Warwicks

FOCUS
A reasonable maiden hurdle with the two market leaders dominating the betting.

3064 FLAMES OF NEWARK NOVICES' HURDLE (11 hdls 2 omitted) 2m 7f 209y
1:55 (1:55) (Class 4) 4-Y-0+ £4,328 (£1,574)

Form RPR
36-3 1 **Weststreet (IRE)**[33] 2417 5-10-12 119 LeightonAspell 120
(Oliver Sherwood) *led: pushed along 7th: hit 3 out: hdd appr next: wl hld whn lft dist clr abt 100yds out* **7/4**[2]
/F3- 2 28 **Ganbei**[225] 9-10-9 0 HarryBannister(3) 92
(Michael Easterby) *chsd ldng pair: sn remote: drvn and sme hdwy 3 out: wknd next: lft distant 2nd sn after last* **25/1**[3]
2 U **Hawkhurst (IRE)**[45] 2152 5-10-12 0 SamTwiston-Davies 130+
(Paul Nicholls) *trckd ldr: t.k.h: led on bit appr 2 out: 8 l clr whn bucked twice and jinked bdly rt and uns rdr abt 100yds out* **8/15**[1]
0-0P P **Adadream**[14] 2808 6-10-9 0 (t) ConorShoemark(3)
(Claire Dyson) *remote in last: pushed along 5th: t.o next: p.u bef 8th* **250/1**

6m 43.0s (28.00) **Going Correction** +1.275s/f (Heav) **4 Ran SP% 105.8**
Speed ratings (Par 105): **104,94, ,**
CSF £20.02 TOTE £2.40; EX 20.40 Trifecta £13.90.
Owner Weststreet Partnership **Bred** Michael C Griffin **Trained** Upper Lambourn, Berks

FOCUS
An unexpected result as the odds-on favourite had the race at his mercy when jinking and unseating his jockey on the run-in.

3065 THOROUGHBRED BREEDERS ASSOCIATION MARES' H'CAP HURDLE (QUALIFIER FOR THE MARES' SERIES FINAL) (8 hdls 1 omitted) 1m 7f 153y
2:25 (2:25) (Class 3) (0-125,125) 3-Y-0+ £6,498 (£1,908; £954; £477; £15)

0-13 1 **Ruby Rambler**[15] 2778 5-11-12 **125** LeightonAspell 135+
(Lucy Wadham) *j. soundly: trckd ldrs: led appr 2 out: wnt clr between last 2: eased last 100yds* **11/4**[2]
21U2 2 9 **Western Breeze (IRE)**[29] 2490 6-11-2 **115** JakeGreenall 113
(Mark Walford) *led: drvn and hdd appr 2 out: kpt on: no ch w wnr* **15/8**[1]
6055 3 3 **Timon's Tara**[17] 2725 6-10-8 **107** JackQuinlan 102
(Robin Dickin) *hld up towards rr: effrt 6th: chsng ldrs and drvn next: 3rd and one pce appr last* **7/1**
1212 4 1 1/4 **Carinena (IRE)**[22] 2644 6-11-5 **118** CraigNichol 111
(Nicky Richards) *j.lft 1st: chsd ldrs: drvn sn after 3 out: one pce between last 2* **9/2**[3]
6-46 5 4 **Gold Chain (IRE)**[127] 1036 5-10-0 **102** ColmMcCormack(3) 91
(Dianne Sayer) *in rr: hmpd 1st: outpcd and lost pl 3 out: kpt on run-in: tk modest 5th nr fin* **14/1**
1353 6 nk **Cool Baranca (GER)**[37] 2326 9-10-4 **106** HarryChalloner(3) 94
(Dianne Sayer) *mid-div: hdwy 5th: drvn next: outpcd appr 2 out* **9/1**

4m 21.4s (24.40) **Going Correction** +1.275s/f (Heav) **6 Ran SP% 108.8**
Speed ratings (Par 107): **90,85,84,83,81 81**
CSF £8.04 TOTE £3.30: £1.60, £1.30; EX 9.50 Trifecta £51.60.
Owner Sara Dennis,J J W Wadham & J C S Wilson **Bred** Grove Farm Stud **Trained** Newmarket, Suffolk

FOCUS
The inexperienced horses dominated this mares' handicap, which was run at a steady early pace.

3066 SOUTHWELL GOLF CLUB MARES' MAIDEN HURDLE (8 hdls 1 omitted) 1m 7f 153y
2:55 (2:55) (Class 4) 4-Y-0+ £3,898 (£1,144; £572; £286)

Form RPR
0-22 1 **Pink Play (IRE)**[31] 2452 4-11-0 0 GavinSheehan 121+
(Harry Whittington) *chsd ldr: led 4th: drvn appr 2 out: forged clr bef last: 7 l ahd whn eased last 50yds* **11/10**[1]
3 2 3 3/4 **Secret Door (IRE)**[39] 2277 4-11-0 0 DarylJacob 113+
(Harry Fry) *trckd ldrs: chsd wnr sn after 3 out: sn drvn: kpt on same pce between last 2* **15/8**[2]
42-3 3 12 **What A Scorcher**[220] 179 4-11-0 107 LeightonAspell 102
(Oliver Sherwood) *trckd ldrs: t.k.h: 3rd and drvn appr 2 out: one pce* **11/2**[3]
1-04 4 11 **Burma (FR)**[32] 2536 4-11-0 0 [1] JamesBest 89
(Paul Webber) *hld up in rr: hdwy to chse ldrs 3 out: wknd next: bhd whn j.rt last* **20/1**
445 5 10 **Zara Hope (IRE)**[15] 2776 4-11-0 0 RichieMcLernon 79
(Charlie Longsdon) *led to 4th: sn pushed along: lost pl sn after 3 out: sn bhd* **16/1**
3-00 6 15 **Cosmic Diamond**[15] 2776 5-11-0 0 LiamTreadwell 64
(Paul Webber) *hld up towards rr: hdwy 5th 5th: effrt next: sn lost pl and bhd* **50/1**
0-0 P **Samarinta**[218] 213 6-11-0 0 TrevorWhelan
(Nicholas Pomfret) *hld up towards rr: t.k.h: drvn and lost pl 5th: sn bhd: t.o 3 out: p.u bef next* **250/1**

4m 18.7s (21.70) **Going Correction** +1.275s/f (Heav) **7 Ran SP% 110.8**
Speed ratings (Par 105): **96,94,88,82,77 70,**
CSF £3.25 TOTE £1.90: £1.30, £1.50; EX 4.10 Trifecta £7.40.
Owner Paul G Jacobs **Bred** Berry Farms **Trained** Sparsholt, Oxfordshire

FOCUS
With the 117-rated \bVia Volupta\p a non-runner, this did not take that much winning.

3067 JENNY WALLACE MEMORIAL AMATEUR RIDERS' H'CAP HURDLE (11 hdls 2 omitted) 2m 7f 209y
3:25 (3:25) (Class 4) (0-105,103) 4-Y-0+ £3,743 (£1,161; £580; £290)

Form RPR
0311 1 **Not A Bother Boy (IRE)**[9] 2892 7-11-5 **103** MrRHogg(7) 109+
(Sue Smith) *chsd ldr: hit 6th: upsides 8th: led 2 out: forged clr run-in* **7/4**[1]
6/2- 2 3 1/4 **Over My Head**[397] 2414 7-10-1 **83** (t) MrTGreatrex(5) 85
(Claire Dyson) *led: jnd 8th: hdd 2 out: kpt on same pce run-in* **8/1**
0U0 3 1 1/2 **Goodoldhonkytonk (IRE)**[20] 2694 7-11-2 **100** (b) MrJMorris(7) 100
(James Evans) *hld up towards rr: hdwy appr 2 out: 3rd last: styd on* **12/1**
000- 4 2 1/4 **Glendermot (IRE)**[299] 4281 6-10-10 **94** MrJAndrews(7) 92
(Paul Cowley) *racd on inner: t.k.h: hdwy to trck ldrs 3rd: 3rd and drvn appr 2 out: kpt on same pce* **7/1**[3]
45P3 5 nk **Silver Dragon**[9] 2892 7-11-3 **99** MrKWood(5) 96
(Tony Coyle) *chsd ldrs: drvn 3 out: one pce appr next* **7/1**[3]
4-66 6 hd **Bridal Suite (IRE)**[57] 1972 6-10-10 **94** (tp) MrSAHarte(7) 91
(Charlie Mann) *trckd ldrs: swtchd rt sn after 3 out: one pce* **9/1**
003 7 4 **Mister Don (IRE)**[30] 2474 5-11-6 **102** MrTommieMO'Brien(5) 95
(Rose Dobbin) *chsd ldrs: drvn bef 2 out: fdd appr last* **13/2**[2]

PP0 8 1 1/4 **Agent Louise**[57] 1972 7-9-7 77 oh5......................(p) MrHHunt(7) 69
(Mike Sowersby) *chsd ldrs: 3rd and drvn appr 2 out: hung rt and wknd bef last* **25/1**

0-00 9 53 **Betty Borgia**[31] 2453 9-9-7 77 oh8......................(t) MrGregoryWalters(7) 16
(Nicholas Pomfret) *t.k.h: trckd ldrs: hit 7th: lost pl next: sn bhd: t.o bef 2 out* **200/1**

P3/- 10 3/4 **Call At Midnight**[567] 10-9-11 81...................... MrBEClark(7) 19
(Sarah Humphrey) *in rr: hdwy 5th: lost pl bef 8th: sn bhd: t.o bef 2 out* **33/1**

6-00 11 2 **Rockweiler**[15] 2559 8-9-7 77 oh7...................... MrAidenBlakemore(7) 13
(Shaun Harris) *in last: sme hdwy 8th: sn lost pl and bhd: t.o bef 2 out* **33/1**

7m 8.7s (53.70) **Going Correction** +1.275s/f (Heavy) **11 Ran SP% 113.7**
Speed ratings (Par 105): **61,59,59,58,58 58,57,56,39,38 38**
CSF £15.33 CT £127.46 TOTE £2.40: £1.20, £2.30, £3.50; EX 13.70 Trifecta £135.60.
Owner Mrs S Smith **Bred** Kenneth William Quinn **Trained** High Eldwick, W Yorks

FOCUS
A number of inexperienced amateur jockeys in the line-up, and this was run at a slow pace, producing yet another winner on the card to be ridden prominently.
T/Jkpt: £1,775.00. Pool: £10,000.00 - 4.0 wining units. JACKPOT PLACEPOT £25.30. Pool: £2221.16 - 63.90 winning units. T/Plt: £53.90 to a £1 stake. Pool: £71,682.87 - 970.67 winning units. T/Qpdt: £14.90 to a £1 stake. Pool: £7,185.17 - 356.42 winning units. **Walter Glynn**

3068 - (Foreign Racing) - See Raceform Interactive

2671 NAVAN (L-H)
Sunday, December 13

OFFICIAL GOING: Heavy

3069a IRISH STALLION FARMS EUROPEAN BREEDERS FUND KLAIRON DAVIS NOVICE CHASE (GRADE 3) (12 fncs) 2m 1f
12:30 (12:30) 4-Y-0+ £17,635 (£5,155; £2,441)

RPR

1 **Ttebbob (IRE)**[24] 2605 6-11-0 0...................... RobbiePower 151+
(Mrs John Harrington, Ire) *led fr 1st and mde rest: over 8 l clr at 1/2-way: in command stl wl clr bef 3 out: eased clsng stages: v easily* **2/5**1

2 41 **Lord Scoundrel (IRE)**[28] 2530 6-11-6 144...................... BJCooper 122+
(Gordon Elliott, Ire) *prom tl settled bhd ldr fr 1st: slt mstke 4th: pushed along in mod 2nd bef 3 out and no imp on easy wnr: eased fr bef last* **5/2**2

3 53 **Shadow Catcher**[43] 2206 7-11-3 139......................(tp) BarryGeraghty 63
(Gordon Elliott, Ire) *hld up bhd ldrs: niggled along after 4th and lost tch whn slt mstke next: completely t.o* **9/1**3

4m 35.0s (1.70) **3 Ran SP% 110.0**
CSF £1.92 TOTE £1.20; DF 1.20 Trifecta £1.50.
Owner David Bobbett **Bred** Neil Tyrrell **Trained** Moone, Co Kildare

FOCUS
This Grade 3 was supposed to be run eight days previously but that fixture was lost to high winds. The field was reduced to three as a result of the delay. The winner made all and produced an exhilarating display of jumping. The fact that he could dispose of a 144-rated rival with such ease means that it is now time for him to dip his toes into Grade 1s.

3070a NAVAN NOVICE HURDLE (GRADE 2) (11 hdls) 2m 4f
1:00 (1:01) 4-Y-0+ £20,155 (£5,891; £2,790)

RPR

1 **Bellshill (IRE)**[28] 2523 5-11-3 0...................... RWalsh 149+
(W P Mullins, Ire) *settled bhd ldr in 2nd tl lft in front at 7th: gng wl 3 out where slt mstke: extended advantage after next and pushed out run-in: easily* **4/6**1

2 12 **Tycoon Prince (IRE)**[35] 2385 5-11-3 0......................(t) BJCooper 135
(Gordon Elliott, Ire) *hld up bhd ldrs tl lft 2nd at 7th: gng wl in cl 2nd bef 2 out where slt mstke: sn rdn and no imp on easy wnr bef last: kpt on one pce* **3/1**2

3 22 **Chesterfieldavenue (IRE)**[42] 2231 4-10-13 0...................... BarryGeraghty 111
(C Roche, Ire) *w.w in rr of quartet: sltly hmpd whn lft 3rd at 7th: slt mstke 4 out: niggled along bef 3 out: sn rdn and lost tch bef next: wknd* **14/1**

U **Stone Hard (IRE)**[22] 2653 5-11-3 0...................... PaulTownend
(W P Mullins, Ire) *led: nt fluent 1st and at times after: slt mstke 4th: 3 l clr whn slt mstke 6th: extended advantage bef next where blnd and uns rdr* **7/2**3

5m 12.0s (10.20)
WFA 4 from 5yo 6lb **4 Ran SP% 113.9**
CSF £3.38 TOTE £1.40; DF 4.20 Trifecta £10.70.
Owner Andrea & Graham Wylie **Bred** Frank Motherway **Trained** Muine Beag, Co Carlow

FOCUS
Willie Mullins tends to aim his best novice hurdlers at this, with Boston Bob (2011), Pont Alexandre (2013) and Briar Hill (2013) winning it when it was a Grade 1. In keeping with recent trends, this year's renewal attracted a small, but select, gathering. Stone Hard ensured the first half of the race was run at a decent clip but he departed at the seventh. The winner could not have been more impressive. The standard is set by the runner-up.

3071a TARA H'CAP HURDLE (GRADE B) (11 hdls) 2m 4f
1:30 (1:31) 4-Y-0+
£23,255 (£7,364; £3,488; £1,162; £775; £387)

RPR

1 **Rossvoss**[29] 2504 7-9-10 112 oh3......................(bt) MsKWalsh 137+
(T M Walsh, Ire) *settled bhd ldrs: 4th bef 6th: led travelling wl after 3 out: extended advantage fr next and wnt wl clr bef last: styd on strly: easily* **14/1**

2 18 **Bentelimar (IRE)**[28] 2529 6-11-3 140...................... DonaghMeyler(7) 147
(J R Barry, Ire) *hld up in rr: hdwy to chse ldrs after 7th: gng wl in 5th bef 3 out: rdn after 3 out and no imp on easy wnr u.p in mod 2nd bef last: kpt on one pce* **13/2**3

3 5 1/2 **Jimmy Two Times (IRE)**[225] 96 6-10-13 134...................... MrDGLavery(5) 136
(B R Hamilton, Ire) *in tch: j. sltly rt at times: j.w rt at 7th and reminder: tk clsr order bhd ldrs 3 out: rdn into 2nd after next and no imp on easy wnr: dropped to 3rd bef last and one pce run-in: hld on for 3rd* **14/1**

4 1/2 **Russian Bill (IRE)**[21] 2676 5-10-8 124...................... SeanFlanagan 125
(Noel Meade, Ire) *hld up in rr of mid-div: pushed along bef 3 out: rdn in 9th after 3 out and no imp on easy wnr u.p in 7th between last 2: slt mstke last and kpt on into mod 4th run-in: hld for 3rd* **10/3**1

5 1 1/4 **All You Need (FR)**[42] 2235 5-10-4 127...................... JohnFitzpatrick(7) 127
(Alan Fleming, Ire) *chsd ldrs on outer and wnt 2nd after 1st: j.big 3 out and sn rdn: no imp on easy wnr u.p in 5th after next: one pce after* **4/1**2

6 7 **Misty Lady (IRE)**[21] 2676 6-10-12 128...................... RobbieColgan 121
(John Laurence Cullen, Ire) *led narrowly: j. sltly rt 1st and at times after: slt mstke 2nd: pressed clly whn mstke 3 out and sn hdd: no imp on easy wnr in 2nd next: wknd bef last* **20/1**

7 1/2 **Go Paddy Go (IRE)**[42] 2235 9-9-5 112 oh3...................... JackKennedy(5) 104
(James Grace, Ire) *in tch: rdn in 7th after 3 out and no imp on ldrs fr next: kpt on one pce* **16/1**

8 1 **Aminabad (FR)**[91] 1538 5-10-12 135...................... NiallKelly(7) 126
(W P Mullins, Ire) *mid-div: wnt 6th after 3 out: rdn and no imp on easy wnr u.p in 5th bef last: wknd run-in* **16/1**

9 5 **Harvey Logan (IRE)**[14] 2816 6-10-5 121...................... BarryGeraghty 107
(Noel Meade, Ire) *in rr of mid-div: slt mstke 6th and dropped to 13th: rdn in 10th after 3 out and no imp: one pce after and slt mstke last* **4/1**2

10 shd **Mine Now (IRE)**[48] 2112 7-10-0 119...................... LPDempsey(3) 105
(Peter Fahey, Ire) *mid-div: rdn and no ex 3 out: sn wknd* **20/1**

11 3 **Glenquest (IRE)**[240] 5363 12-10-9 125...................... AELynch 108
(S R B Crawford, Ire) *chsd ldrs: clsr in 3rd bef 6th: rdn and wknd 3 out* **33/1**

12 1 **The Crafty Butcher (IRE)**[17] 2742 8-11-0 130...................... RWalsh 112
(Michael Hourigan, Ire) *hld up: reminders in rr after 5th: pushed along after 4 out and no imp bef mod 12th bef 2 out* **16/1**

13 68 **Mrs Mac Veale (IRE)**[29] 2502 10-10-7 130...................... JonathanMoore(7) 44
(Gavin Dower, Ire) *in tch: 5th bef 6th: pushed along bef 3 out and sn wknd u.p: completely t.o* **22/1**

14 8 1/2 **Princely Conn (IRE)**[44] 2177 6-11-3 133...................... MarkWalsh 39
(Thomas Mullins, Ire) *towards rr: pushed along after 4 out and no imp whn mstke next: wknd: completely t.o* **20/1**

5m 14.3s (12.50) **14 Ran SP% 129.0**
CSF £102.30 CT £1342.81 TOTE £19.50: £4.90, £2.40, £5.00; DF 137.00 Trifecta £1512.50.
Owner D F Desmond **Bred** Charlie Wyatt **Trained** Kill, Co Kildare

FOCUS
An incredible result here in some respects. They went a proper gallop on the ground, many horses clearly in trouble a long way out. The winner has been rated to another pb, with the placed horses helping to set the standard.

3072a (Foreign Racing) - See Raceform Interactive

3073a FOXROCK H'CAP CHASE (GRADE C) (14 fncs) 2m 4f
2:35 (2:36) 4-Y-0+ £15,116 (£4,418; £2,093; £697)

RPR

1 **Fine Rightly (IRE)**[21] 2676 7-11-7 140...................... AELynch 150+
(S R B Crawford, Ire) *chsd ldrs: 3rd 1/2-way: slt mstke 9th and lost pl: impr to dispute between horses 2 out and sn led: kpt on wl u.p fr last where pressed clly* **3/1**1

2 1 3/4 **Fever Pitch (IRE)**[45] 2159 9-9-11 121......................(t) JackKennedy(5) 129
(A L T Moore, Ire) *cl up in 2nd: cl 3rd bef 4 out: led next: jnd u.p next and sn hdd: kpt on wl in 2nd fr last wout matching wnr* **11/2**

3 7 **My Murphy (IRE)**[251] 5224 9-11-7 140...................... RobbiePower 141
(W J Burke, Ire) *chsd ldrs: 4th 1/2-way: almost on terms after 5 out: ev ch nr side bef 2 out: sn rdn and no imp on ldrs u.p bef last: kpt on in 4th run-in and wnt 3rd on line* **9/2**3

4 nse **Leavethelighton (IRE)**[135] 1173 8-11-1 134...................... MPButler 135
(Eoin Doyle, Ire) *hld up in tch: 6th bef 4 out: mstke next and rdn in rr: kpt on again u.p to chse ldrs in 4th after next: no imp on ldrs in 3rd run-in: denied 3rd on line* **16/1**

5 1/2 **Buckers Bridge (IRE)**[617] 5171 9-11-7 140...................... JJBurke 141
(Henry De Bromhead, Ire) *mid-div: 1/2-way: 5th bef 4 out: rdn and no imp on ldrs after 2 out: slt mstke last and kpt on one pce run-in* **9/1**

6 6 1/2 **Ucello Conti (FR)**[389] 7-11-4 137...................... BarryGeraghty 131
(Gordon Elliott, Ire) *hld up: 7th 1/2-way: pushed along after 3 out and no imp on ldrs after next: kpt on one pce* **4/1**2

7 1 **Dressedtothenines (IRE)**[735] 2986 8-10-6 125...................... MarkWalsh 118
(Edward P Harty, Ire) *w.w: mstke in rr at 1st: j. sltly rt 6th: last 1/2-way: nt fluent 9th: tk clsr order on outer after 4 out: pushed along and no ex next: kpt on one pce run-in* **10/1**

8 1 **Irish Thistle (IRE)**[195] 583 8-10-12 131......................(t) MarkBolger 123
(H Rogers, Ire) *hld up: 8th 1/2-way: rdn in 7th after 2 out and no imp on ldrs bef last* **14/1**

9 8 **Smokey Joe Joe (IRE)**[28] 2527 9-10-7 129......................(t) LPDempsey(3) 113
(S J Mahon, Ire) *led narrowly: mstke 9th: pressed clly 4 out and hdd next: no ex u.p in 4th after 2 out: sn wknd* **8/1**

5m 54.3s (14.00) **9 Ran SP% 121.3**
CSF £21.57 CT £75.72 TOTE £3.80: £1.80, £1.90, £1.70; DF 20.90 Trifecta £122.20.
Owner Miss Patricia Duffin **Bred** Miss Patricia Duffin **Trained** Larne, Co Antrim

FOCUS
A competitive maiden and class came to the fore. It's been rated around the runner-up, with the winner running a fair pb.

3074 - 3075a (Foreign Racing) - See Raceform Interactive

2363 FFOS LAS (L-H)
Monday, December 14

OFFICIAL GOING: Heavy (soft in places; chs 4.7; hdl 5.2)
Wind: strong half behind Weather: rain

3076 CELTIC ENERGY JUVENILE MAIDEN HURDLE (8 hdls) 1m 7f 202y
12:25 (12:26) (Class 4) 3-Y-0 £3,898 (£1,144; £572; £286)

Form RPR

3 1 **Borak (IRE)**[60] 1928 3-10-9 0...................... RobertWilliams(3) 115+
(Bernard Llewellyn) *hld up: sltly hmpd 2nd: disp 2nd fr 4th: wnt def 2nd after 5th: led gng wl after 3 out: easily* **4/9**1

2 8 **Nabhan**[400] 3-10-12 0...................... MichaelByrne 97+
(Bernard Llewellyn) *hld up in last: clsd after 5th: shkn up 3 out: wnt 2nd and mstke next: kpt on steadily but nvr threatened wnr* **6/1**3

0 3 31 **Shabraque (IRE)**[16] 2777 3-10-7 0...................... CiaranGethings(5) 66
(David Loder) *hld up: hmpd and lft chsng ldr 2nd: lost 2nd after 5th: outpcd by ldng pair 3 out: wknd after next* **5/1**2

P 4 21 **Blackadder**[22] 2662 3-10-9 0...................... TomBellamy(3) 45
(Mark Gillard) *t.k.h: j.rt at times: trckd ldr tl hmpd and lft in ld 2nd: clr next: reduced ld after 5th: hdd after 3 out: wkng whn mstke next: t.o* **33/1**

F **Darkening Night**[171] 3-10-12 0......................[1] RobertDunne
(Sarah-Jayne Davies) *t.k.h: led tl fell 2nd* **20/1**

4m 24.3s (35.80) **Going Correction** +1.575s/f (Heavy) **5 Ran SP% 107.9**
Speed ratings (Par 104): **73,69,53,43,**
CSF £3.52 TOTE £1.20: £1.10, £2.40; EX 2.60 Trifecta £4.10.
Owner D A Smerdon **Bred** Tom Kelly **Trained** Fochriw, Caerphilly

FOCUS
The ground was heavy, soft in places. Bends were dolled out, adding approximately 34yds for the opener, a weak maiden hurdle dominated by the odds-on favourite.

3077 THOMAS CARROLL NOVICES' HURDLE (8 hdls) 1m 7f 202y
1:00 (1:01) (Class 4) 4-Y-0+ £3,898 (£1,144; £572; £286)

Form RPR
42 1 **Never Equalled (IRE)**26 2563 6-10-5 0 JordanWilliams(7) 128+
(Bernard Llewellyn) *w ldr tl led 2nd: nt fluent 3 out: sn rdn: 3 l up whn mstke last: jst hld on* 9/2³
32-3 2 *shd* **Preseli Rock (IRE)**40 2270 5-10-12 0 SeanBowen 127+
(Rebecca Curtis) *chsd ldrs: wnt 2nd after 3 out: 3 l down whn nt fluent last: hung rt and styd on u.p flat: jst failed* 3/1²
50-F 3 *17* **Baraka De Thaix (FR)**31 2472 4-10-12 123 DarylJacob 112
(David Pipe) *led to 2nd: trckd wnr tl lost 2nd after 3 out: rdn and grad wknd* 5/2¹
35 4 *6* **Pilgrims Rest (IRE)**14 2823 6-10-12 0 (t) AndrewTinkler 104
(George Baker) *mid-div: hit 3rd: hdwy next: wnt 4th 2 out: one pce and no further imp: mstke last* 12/1
506 5 *7* **Court King (IRE)**9 2904 4-10-7 0 CiaranGethings(5) 97
(Peter Bowen) *chsd ldrs: rdn 3 out: wknd 2 out* 66/1
6 *7* **Grandasowt (IRE)**617 6-10-12 0 AdamWedge 89
(Evan Williams) *mid-div: hdwy to chse ldrs after 2nd: wknd 3 out* 7/1
06 7 *¾* **Master Burbidge**16 2768 4-10-12 0 NoelFehily 88
(Neil Mulholland) *mid-div tl wknd after 5th* 100/1
8 *2* **Ayla's Emperor**33 6-10-5 0 (p) RobertDunne 79
(John Flint) *hld up towards rr: sme hdwy appr 3 out: no further imp* 33/1
-3U4 9 *hd* **Chief Brody**18 2731 4-10-12 0 JamieMoore 86
(Grace Harris) *chsd ldrs: rdn after 5th: wknd appr 3 out* 11/2
60P6 10 *12* **Lunar Flow**20 2699 4-10-12 0 BrendanPowell 74
(Jamie Snowden) *mid-div: wknd appr 3 out* 100/1
11 *3 ¼* **Shouting Hill (IRE)**50 5-10-12 0 LiamHeard 71
(Johnny Farrelly) *t.k.h: a towards rr: wknd after 5th: t.o* 33/1
-54P 12 *13* **Run Bob Run**46 2152 4-10-12 0 WillKennedy 58
(John Flint) *a in rr: wknd after 5th: t.o* 50/1
P0 P **Chantecler**28 2543 4-10-12 0 MarkQuinlan
(Neil Mulholland) *a towards rr: mstke 5th: sn rdn and wknd: t.o whn p.u bef 3 out* 66/1
06-5 P **Get Ready Freddy**37 2345 5-10-12 0 NickScholfield
(Nick Mitchell) *prom tl p.u after 2nd: sddle slipped* 100/1
4m 7.0s (18.50) **Going Correction** +1.575s/f (Heav) 14 Ran SP% 121.1
Speed ratings (Par 105): **116,115,107,104,100 97,97,96,95,89 88,81,,**
CSF £18.55 TOTE £6.30: £2.00, £1.50, £1.20; EX 18.90 Trifecta £77.10.
Owner Miss I G Tompsett **Bred** Mrs Mary Dicker **Trained** Fochriw, Caerphilly

FOCUS
Bends were dolled out, adding approximately 34yds for this modest event in which they went a sensible gallop in the ground. Mucj the fastest of the races over the trip with the winner building on his good Chepstow run.

3078 FUCHS H'CAP HURDLE (10 hdls) 2m 4f
1:35 (1:35) (Class 3) (0-125,122) 3-Y-0+ £5,848 (£1,717; £858; £429)

Form RPR
33-5 1 **Pobbles Bay (IRE)**26 2569 5-11-3 113 AdamWedge 117
(Evan Williams) *hld up towards rr: hdwy 7th: chsd ldr 3 out: sn rdn: chal last: styd on u.p to ld last strides* 8/1
-241 2 *hd* **Captainofindustry (IRE)**18 2732 6-11-2 112 (p) DenisO'Regan 116
(Mark Pitman) *chsd ldr: ld after 2nd: ruidden appr 2 out: jnd whn nt fluent last: kpt on: hdd last strides* 9/4¹
F-F0 3 *15* **Saint John Henry (FR)**17 2759 5-11-12 122 TomScudamore 112
(David Pipe) *chsd ldrs: nt fluent 4 out: wknd 2 out: plugged on to go 3rd post* 11/4²
-P03 4 *shd* **Looks Like Power (IRE)**21 2694 5-10-11 107 ¹ TrevorWhelan 95
(Debra Hamer) *t.k.h in rr: hdwy 3rd: rdn and one pce 3 out: wnt mod 3rd last tl post* 5/1³
0F-5 5 *1* **Fishing Bridge (IRE)**36 2367 10-10-11 107 (v) NickScholfield 95
(David Rees) *hld up in last: hit 7th: sn clsd: rdn 3 out: wnt mod 3rd 2 out tl mstke last* 14/1
2-05 6 *17* **Filatore (IRE)**11 2873 6-10-10 113 (p) JordanWilliams(7) 83
(Bernard Llewellyn) *chsd ldrs: mstke 7th: sn hrd rdn: wknd 2 out* 12/1
0600 7 *34* **Byron Blue (IRE)**25 2600 6-11-7 120 (t) TomBellamy(3) 56
(Mark Gillard) *led and racd keenly: j.lft: hdd & wknd after 7th: t.o* 12/1
23S3 8 *37* **Tijori (IRE)**11 2858 7-10-5 104 (b) RobertWilliams(3)
(Bernard Llewellyn) *hld up: mstke 6th: wknd next: t.o* 10/1
5m 31.5s (331.50) 8 Ran SP% 116.4
CSF £27.65 CT £63.49 TOTE £8.30: £2.30, £1.50, £1.10; EX 26.40 Trifecta £49.50.
Owner David M Williams **Bred** James T Williams **Trained** Llancarfan, Vale Of Glamorgan

FOCUS
Bends dolled out, adding approximately 51yds. An ordinary handicap in which they went a decent pace and the first two finishers, who are both on the upgrade, came clear.

3079 "WE MISS YOU CLAIMS" H'CAP CHASE (19 fncs) 3m 1f 60y
2:10 (2:10) (Class 3) (0-135,133) 4-Y-0+ £7,797 (£2,289; £1,144; £572)

Form RPR
PP-P 1 **Bob Ford (IRE)**33 2436 8-11-12 133 SeanBowen 148+
(Rebecca Curtis) *led tl mstke 3rd: cl up: led 3 out: drew clr fr next: styd on strly* 8/1
2-30 2 *11* **Cloudy Copper (IRE)**33 2442 8-11-9 130 (p) RichardJohnson 133+
(Jonjo O'Neill) *hld up: hdwy to chse ldrs 11th: mstke and rdn 4 out: styd on to go 2nd last: no ch w wnr* 4/1³
1P-F 3 *2 ¼* **Wychwoods Brook**23 2641 9-11-11 132 AdamWedge 129
(Evan Williams) *chsd ldrs: nt fluent 3rd: pckd 3 out: chsd wnr 2 out: no imp and lost 2nd last* 6/1
21-5 4 *53* **Thedrinkymeister (IRE)**18 2727 6-11-1 122 DavidBass 89
(Kim Bailey) *w ldr tl led 3rd: rdn 4 out: hdd next: blnd and lost 2nd 2 out: last whn j. bdly rt last: virtually p.u* 9/4¹
P-P0 P **Dark Glacier (IRE)**185 707 10-11-3 124 (bt) JamieMoore
(Peter Bowen) *hld up: nt fluent 2nd: rdn bef 11th: sn struggling: lost tch 15th: t.o whn p.u bef 3 out* 25/1
P/PP P **African Gold (IRE)**18 2727 7-11-7 128 (vt¹) NoelFehily
(Nigel Twiston-Davies) *hld up: hdwy 3rd: mstke 11th: sn struggling: t.o whn p.u after 15th* 12/1
U-25 P **Royal Palladium (FR)**23 2643 7-11-8 129 LiamTreadwell
(Venetia Williams) *chsd ldrs to 4th: in last by 6th: mstke 7th: blnd bdly 9th: rdn along after next: struggling 12th: t.o whn p.u bef 4 out* 3/1²
7m 8.3s (27.30) **Going Correction** +1.325s/f (Heav) 7 Ran SP% 112.7
Speed ratings (Par 107): **109,105,104,87,**
CSF £39.02 TOTE £8.20: £4.10, £1.80; EX 38.40 Trifecta £191.60.
Owner The JJ Partnership **Bred** Lorcan Allen **Trained** Newport, Pembrokeshire

FOCUS
Bends dolled out, adding approximately 54yds for the feature contest, a fair staying handicap chase in which they went an even gallop.

3080 HUGH JAMES SOLICITORS H'CAP HURDLE (QUALIFIER FOR THE CHALLENGER TWO MILE HURDLE SERIES FINAL) (8 hdls) 1m 7f 202y
2:40 (2:41) (Class 3) (0-135,132) 3-Y-0+ £6,498 (£1,908; £954; £477)

Form RPR
35-3 1 **Clyne**33 2445 5-10-9 115 AdamWedge 121+
(Evan Williams) *trckd ldrs: wnt 2nd after 5th: shkn up 2 out: led appr last where j.lft: comf* 2/1²
0-34 2 *2 ¾* **Heath Hunter (IRE)**16 2781 8-11-12 132 (bt) TomScudamore 132
(David Pipe) *chsd ldrs: hit 1st: rdn 3 out: styd on to chse wnr flat but a being hld* 5/4¹
-060 3 *2* **Bishop Wulstan (IRE)**21 2694 4-10-2 108 (p) SeanBowen 105
(Peter Bowen) *led: rdn 2 out: hdd appr last where sltly hmpd: one pce and lost 2nd flat* 12/1
-5P5 4 *1* **Lac Sacre (FR)**11 2858 6-10-9 115 (tp) JamieMoore 111
(John Flint) *hld up in tch in last pair: rdn 3 out: clsd 2 out: kpt on same pce flat* 8/1³
-215 5 *38* **Pandorica**12 2852 7-9-8 107 (p) JordanWilliams(7) 65
(Bernard Llewellyn) *trckd ldr tl lost 2nd after 5th: wknd 3 out: last whn hmpd next: t.o* 10/1
12-0 F **Global Thrill**21 2688 6-11-1 124 RobertWilliams(3)
(Bernard Llewellyn) *hld up in tch in last pair: rdn 3 out: hld in 5th whn fell next* 14/1
4m 10.5s (22.00) **Going Correction** +1.575s/f (Heav)
WFA 4 from 5yo+ 5lb 6 Ran SP% 112.3
Speed ratings (Par 107): **108,106,105,105,86**
CSF £5.09 TOTE £2.90: £1.40, £1.40; EX 4.70 Trifecta £30.50.
Owner David M Williams **Bred** The Kathryn Stud **Trained** Llancarfan, Vale Of Glamorgan

FOCUS
Bends dolled out, adding approximately 34yds. An ordinary handicap hurdle in which they raced close up, each of the runners holding some sort of chance heading into the home straight when the pace picked up. The winner was finally building on his course debut win.

3081 FELINFOEL BREWERY NOVICES' H'CAP CHASE (17 fncs) 2m 4f 199y
3:15 (3:15) (Class 4) (0-105,105) 4-Y-0+ £5,198 (£1,526; £763; £381)

Form RPR
U32- 1 **Supreme Bob (IRE)**364 3118 9-11-2 95 TrevorWhelan 103+
(Debra Hamer) *hld up towards rr: hdwy 3 out: chsd ldr 2 out: led last: edgd lft u.p flat: r.o* 11/4¹
532P 2 *nk* **Flash Crash**20 2698 6-11-4 104 (t) MrZBaker(7) 112
(Barry Brennan) *prom: led appr 3 out: hdd last: carried lft flat: kpt on u.p: jst hld* 7/1
3643 3 *2* **Veauce De Sivola (FR)**27 2553 6-10-13 95 (t) TomBellamy(3) 102
(Mark Gillard) *hld up: stl last but in tch whn mstke 4 out: sn rdn and clsd: ev ch whn nt fluent last: one pce* 10/1
-600 4 *18* **Carhue (IRE)**21 2692 8-9-7 79 oh2 MrMartinMcIntyre(7) 69
(Sheila Lewis) *t.k.h in rr: hdwy to chse ldrs 3rd: rdn 4 out: ev ch whn mstke next: wknd appr last* 20/1
-552 5 *4 ½* **Kapricorne (FR)**29 2521 8-10-11 90 (t) JamesBest 77
(Sophie Leech) *prom: hit 10th: mstke 13th: sn led: mstke and hdd 4 out: wknd 2 out* 7/2²
P F **Ballyadeen (IRE)**18 2733 7-11-12 105 DaveCrosse
(Dai Williams) *hld up: mstkes 5th and 7th: hdwy 12th: disputing 3rd whn fell 4 out* 14/1
56-6 U **Try It Sometime (IRE)**42 2249 7-11-5 101 (t) BenPoste(3)
(Sheila Lewis) *hld up: rdn after 13th: hdwy 4 out: 5th and wkng whn blnd and uns rdr 2 out* 10/1
3350 S **Johns Luck (IRE)**21 2692 6-11-7 100 (b) NoelFehily
(Neil Mulholland) *t.k.h in mid-div: mstke 12th: chsng ldrs whn stmbld and fell on flat appr 3 out* 4/1³
U00- F **Steel A Tune**282 4624 6-10-0 79 oh4 ConorO'Farrell
(Nick Mitchell) *led tl hdd after 13th: led again 4 out: sn hdd: disputing 3rd whn fell 3 out* 50/1
05P- P **Riversbridge**312 4059 6-10-1 80 (bt¹) AlainCawley
(Johnny Farrelly) *chsd ldrs: blnd 11th: wknd appr 4 out: wl bhd whn p.u bef 2 out* 11/1
6m 7.9s (39.30) **Going Correction** +1.325s/f (Heav) 10 Ran SP% 121.3
Speed ratings (Par 105): **78,77,77,70,68 ,,,,**
CSF £23.97 CT £174.21 TOTE £3.80: £1.70, £1.10, £3.60; EX 23.90 Trifecta £151.90.
Owner Mrs J M Edmonds **Bred** Tom Murray **Trained** Nantycaws, Carmarthens

FOCUS
Bends dolled out, adding approximately 41yds for this fair handicap chase in which they went an even gallop, although the well-backed favourite managed to come from behind.

3082 MARUBENI-KOMATSU "NEWCOMERS" STANDARD OPEN NATIONAL HUNT FLAT RACE 1m 7f 202y
3:45 (3:52) (Class 6) 3-5-Y-0 £1,949 (£572; £286; £143)

Form RPR
1 *shd* **Prime Venture (IRE)** 4-11-2 0 ConorRing(5) 113+
(Evan Williams) *hld up: gd hdwy 4f out: chsd ldr over 2f out: chal 1f out: ev ch whn bmpd and carried rt towards fin: jst hld: fin 2nd: plcd 1st* 4/1³
2 **Gayebury** 5-11-7 0 JamesDavies 113+
(Tom Symonds) *cl up tl lost pl 5f out: rallied 3f out: led over 2f out: jnd 1f out: edgd rt u.p towards fin: jst hld on: fin 1st: disqualified and plcd 2nd* 14/1
3 *24* **What A Diva** 4-11-0 0 SeanBowen 82
(Peter Bowen) *t.k.h in rr: hdwy after 4f: rdn 4f out: sn outpcd by ldrs: kpt on to go modest 3rd 1f out* 2/1²
4 *3 ¼* **Zadok** 5-11-7 0 BrendanPowell 86
(Jamie Snowden) *led tl rdn and hdd over 2f out: grad wknd* 8/1
5 *3 ¾* **Bien Well (IRE)** 4-10-7 0 JohnMulvihill(7) 75
(Edmond Daniel Linehan, Ire) *t.k.h: prom tl wknd 3f out* 16/1
6 *1 ¾* **Westbrooke Warrior (IRE)** 4-11-7 0 (t) TomScudamore 80
(David Pipe) *mid-div: hdwy 5f out: wknd 3f out* 15/8¹
7 *52* **Daddy's Favourite** 3-10-2 0 RyanWhile(5) 14
(Bill Turner) *cl up: rdn 6f out: wknd 4f out: t.o* 25/1
8 *dist* **Sevenoaks** 4-11-2 0 JakeHodson(5)
(Bill Turner) *mid-div tl dropped to rr 1/2-way: t.o: fnl 6f: virtually p.u* 20/1
4m 11.9s (29.00) **Going Correction** +1.575s/f (Heav)
WFA 3 from 4yo+ 13lb 8 Ran SP% 120.4
Speed ratings (Par 101): **89,90,77,76,74 73,47,**
CSF £59.99 TOTE £4.80: £1.60, £3.20, £1.20; EX 41.40 Trifecta £163.60.
Owner Mrs Janet Davies **Bred** Mrs Mary Doyle **Trained** Llancarfan, Vale Of Glamorgan

■ Stewards' Enquiry : James Davies two-day ban: careless riding (Dec 28,30)

FOCUS
The bends were dolled out, adding approximately 34yds for the finale, a "newcomers" bumper run at a sedate pace. There was late drama and a tight finish in which the first two finished a long way clear. After a stewards' enquiry the result was reversed.
T/Plt: £13.30 to a £1 stake. Pool of £53658.57 - 2925.83 winning tickets. T/Qpdt: £10.30 to a £1 stake. Pool of £4483.35 - 320.23 winning tickets. **Richard Lowther**

2823 PLUMPTON (L-H)

Monday, December 14

OFFICIAL GOING: Soft (good to soft in places)
Wind: Almost nil Weather: Overcast

3083 J H BUILDERS NOVICES' HURDLE (9 hdls) 1m 7f 195y
12:10 (12:10) (Class 4) 3-Y-O+ **£3,249** (£954; £477; £238)

Form RPR
30-3 **1** **Theo's Charm (IRE)**[21] 2683 5-11-7 0 TomCannon 123+
(Nick Gifford) *disp ld: set mod pce tl 6th: led 3 out: shkn up and asserted 2 out: rdn out* **4/5**[1]
22-4 **2** 7 **Draco's Code**[34] 2409 4-11-7 0 JoshuaMoore 118+
(Gary Moore) *disp ld: set mod pce to 6th: stl w wnr 3 out and clr of rest: rdn and one pce bef 2 out* **8/1**
6 **3** 12 **The Fugitive (IRE)**[23] 2650 4-11-7 0 AidanColeman 104
(Charlie Longsdon) *hld up in midfield: outpcd after 6th: pushed along and styd on steadily fr 3 out to take 3rd after last: shaped w promise* **50/1**
4-5 **4** 3 ½ **Lac Leman (GER)**[8] 2928 4-11-7 0 (t) SamTwiston-Davies 100
(Paul Nicholls) *hld up in midfield: prog and lft in 3rd pl 6th: sn outpcd by ldng pair: no imp bef 2 out: fdd fr last* **13/2**[3]
5 1 **Echo Brava**[105] 5-11-0 0 PaulJohn(7) 99
(Jim Best) *wl in tch: steadily lost pl after 5th and in rr next: styd on in quite taking style bef 2 out: likely improver* **22/1**
60- **6** 5 **Mount Shamsan**[41] 5155 5-11-7 0 AndrewGlassonbury 96+
(Gary Moore) *hld up in last pair: last whn blnd 3rd: lft bhd fr 6th: kpt on steadily bef 2 out: likely improver* **33/1**
7 7 **Red Orator**[887] 6-11-7 0 AndrewThornton 91
(Jim Best) *hld up in last pair: gd prog fr 6th to dispute 3rd 3 out: wl hld but stl in 4th whn blnd 2 out: wknd and eased* **25/1**
-606 **8** 4 ½ **Cougar Kid (IRE)**[21] 2683 4-11-7 0 LeightonAspell 85
(Philip Hide) *chsd ldrs: outpcd fr 6th: struggling fr 3 out* **16/1**
04-4 **9** 14 **Crashing Thew Life**[181] 749 5-11-7 0 MarcGoldstein 69
(Sheena West) *wl in tch on outer: outpcd fr 6th: pushed along 3 out: sn wknd* **100/1**
10 9 **Ruzeiz (USA)**[14] 6-11-7 0 RichieMcLernon 60
(Peter Hedger) *hld up in rr: bhd after 6th: no ch after* **100/1**
11 3 **Tee It Up Tommo (IRE)**[25] 6-11-7 0 MattieBatchelor 57
(Sheena West) *hld up in rr: prog into midfield 6th: wknd qckly sn after 3 out* **66/1**
000 **12** 3 ¾ **Montecito (FR)**[14] 2823 5-11-7 0 GavinSheehan 53
(Chris Gordon) *prom to 4th: wknd rapidly after next: t.o after 6th* **100/1**
2 **F** **Authorized Too**[28] 2544 4-11-4 0 JamesBanks(3)
(Noel Williams) *prom: 3rd and wl in tch whn fell heavily 6th* **7/2**[2]

4m 5.1s (4.30) **Going Correction** +0.50s/f (Soft) **13 Ran SP% 125.7**
Speed ratings (Par 105): **109,105,99,97,97 94,91,89,82,77 76,74,**
CSF £8.68 TOTE £1.50: £1.10, £3.30, £9.80; EX 9.20 Trifecta £36.40.
Owner Michael O'Shea **Bred** Mrs Brid McCrea **Trained** Findon, W Sussex
■ Stewards' Enquiry : Paul John 14-day ban: failed to take all reasonable and permissable measures to obtain best possibly placing (Dec 28-Jan 10, 2016)

FOCUS
The bend rails were out 7yds, adding 63yds to the distance of this race. The pace was ordinary and the shape of the race changed when one of the two principal contestants fell four from home. The winner is improving towards his smart bumper form.

3084 SIS NOVICES' CHASE (12 fncs) 2m 214y
12:45 (12:46) (Class 3) 4-Y-O+ **£6,498** (£1,908; £954; £477)

Form RPR
-53F **1** **Regal Encore (IRE)**[21] 2684 7-10-13 0 (t) BarryGeraghty 123+
(Anthony Honeyball) *cl up: jnd ldr 4th: led after 3 out: pushed clr last: comf* **5/2**[2]
-150 **2** 5 **Cloonacool (IRE)**[24] 2617 6-10-13 0 JoshuaMoore 117+
(Stuart Edmunds) *trckd ldng pair: mstke 3 out: wnt cl 2nd next: sn rdn: one pce and no threat to wnr whn nt fluent last* **7/2**[3]
/25- **3** 2 **Zamdy Man**[366] 3071 6-10-13 0 AidanColeman 115+
(Venetia Williams) *tended to jump rt: mde most: rdn and hdd after 3 out: dropped to 3rd next: wl hld whn mstke last* **5/6**[1]
140- **4** 2 ¼ **Officer Drivel (IRE)**[276] 4736 4-10-7 126 SamTwiston-Davies 106
(Jim Best) *hld up in last pair: pushed along fr 8th: nvr quite on terms w ldrs after but kpt on: nt disgraced* **20/1**
U-P4 **5** 20 **Jumeirah Liberty**[58] 1980 7-10-6 84 (tp) WilliamFeatherstone(7) 93
(Zoe Davison) *hld up in last pair: struggling whn mstke 4 out: sn btn* **200/1**

4m 20.8s (-2.20) **Going Correction** +0.175s/f (Yiel)
WFA 4 from 6yo+ 5lb **5 Ran SP% 110.6**
Speed ratings (Par 107): **112,109,108,107,98**
CSF £11.57 TOTE £3.40: £1.40, £1.60; EX 11.00 Trifecta £13.10.
Owner John P McManus **Bred** John Browne **Trained** Mosterton, Dorset

FOCUS
The bend rails were out 2yds, adding 24yds to the distance of this above-average novices' chase, in which the first three home were all decent hurdlers. The pace was medium.

3085 J H BUILDERS "NATIONAL HUNT" NOVICES' HURDLE (12 hdls) 2m 4f 114y
1:20 (1:20) (Class 4) 4-Y-O+ **£3,249** (£954; £477; £238)

Form RPR
2-31 **1** **Mckenzie's Friend (IRE)**[28] 2544 4-11-5 0 LeightonAspell 122+
(Oliver Sherwood) *mde most to 5th: led again 7th: shkn up and drew clr after 3 out: in n.d fr next: pushed out* **1/2**[1]
0-56 **2** 12 **Fin D'Espere (IRE)**[42] 2239 4-10-12 0 (t) GavinSheehan 99
(Suzy Smith) *trckd ldrs: mstke 3rd: lost pl 8th and in rr bef next: renewed effrt and prog to chse wnr bef 3 out: rdn and lft bhd bef 2 out* **12/1**
3-4P **3** 4 ½ **Trespassers Will (IRE)**[46] 2152 4-10-12 0 PaddyBrennan 95
(Fergal O'Brien) *nt fluent: hld up: prog after 8th: chsd ldng pair 3 out: urged along and lft bhd bef next* **20/1**
00- **4** 9 **Dun Bay Creek**[282] 4622 4-10-12 0 WayneHutchinson 87
(Alan King) *hld up in tch: prog to go 4th 3 out and gng bttr than many: shkn up and fdd bef 2 out: nt fluent last* **12/1**
5 33 **Rocknrobin (IRE)**[204] 4-10-12 0 TomCannon 52
(Chris Gordon) *w wnr to 5th: urged along after 8th: wnt 2nd again next tl bef 3 out: wknd qckly: t.o* **10/1**[3]
P **P** **Le Saumon (IRE)**[40] 2275 5-10-12 0 (t) JackQuinlan
(Sarah Humphrey) *cl up to 8th: sn wknd: t.o whn p.u bef last* **66/1**
040 **P** **Cor Wot An Apple**[32] 2460 4-10-12 0 TomO'Brien
(Colin Tizzard) *t.k.h: in tch: nt fluent 3rd: wknd qckly after 8th: t.o in last whn p.u bef 2 out* **20/1**
56 **P** **Baron De Ligniere (FR)**[64] 1873 4-10-12 0 SamTwiston-Davies
(Paul Nicholls) *hld up: t.k.h and prog to ld 5th to 7th: wknd qckly bef 3 out: poor 6th whn p.u bef 2 out* **7/2**[2]

5m 28.0s (11.00) **Going Correction** +0.50s/f (Soft) **8 Ran SP% 124.4**
Speed ratings (Par 105): **99,94,92,89,76 , ,**
CSF £9.45 TOTE £1.40: £1.02, £2.50, £4.00; EX 9.10 Trifecta £59.30.
Owner Jeremy Dougall & Will Watt **Bred** John Crean **Trained** Upper Lambourn, Berks

FOCUS
The bend rails were out 7yds, adding 84yds to the distance of the race. The winner is interesting but there was little depth to the race, which was run at a slack pace until the final circuit.

3086 BOOK NOW FOR THE ATR SUSSEX NATIONAL H'CAP CHASE (18 fncs) 3m 1f 152y
1:50 (1:50) (Class 4) (0-115,114) 4-Y-O+ **£3,898** (£1,144; £572; £286)

Form RPR
P2-P **1** **Leg Iron (IRE)**[188] 670 10-11-12 **114** (p) MarcGoldstein 121+
(Sheena West) *led to 5th: urged along fr 9th but pressed ldr: led 4 out: drvn clr bef 2 out: mstke last: kpt on* **8/1**
53-6 **2** 3 ¾ **Buckhorn Tom**[33] 2447 7-11-5 **107** (b) PaddyBrennan 107
(Colin Tizzard) *chsd ldrs: rdn bef 13th: no imp in 3rd after next: tk 2nd after 3 out and tried to cl on wnr: kpt on same pce* **5/1**[3]
4-P2 **3** 20 **Reblis (FR)**[20] 2700 10-11-9 **111** (b) JoshuaMoore 96
(Gary Moore) *chsd ldrs: urged along fr 7th: kpt in tch tl after 13th: sn bhd: drvn into modest 3rd last* **9/4**[1]
-F6U **4** 13 **Shy John**[11] 2872 9-11-9 **114** ConorShoemark(3) 84
(Jennifer Mason) *hld up in last early: gng wl enough whn blnd 12th: sn rdn: wl btn in 4th pl fr 14th* **11/2**
0F-3 **P** **On Trend (IRE)**[217] 239 9-11-11 **113** (bt) TomCannon
(Nick Gifford) *chsd ldr to 4th: drvn and wknd qckly after 6th: sn t.o: p.u bef 12th* **4/1**[2]
U-34 **P** **No Through Road**[36] 2366 8-11-9 **111** LeightonAspell
(Michael Scudamore) *prom: led 5th: pckd bdly 8th: only one gng wl fr 13th: hdd 4 out: mstke next and wknd rapidly: dropped to last whn p.u bef last* **5/1**[3]

6m 56.5s (5.80) **Going Correction** +0.175s/f (Yiel) **6 Ran SP% 110.6**
Speed ratings (Par 105): **98,96,90,86,**
CSF £44.11 TOTE £8.90: £3.40, £2.60; EX 49.50 Trifecta £88.90.
Owner Michael Moriarty **Bred** Miss Jane Mangan **Trained** Falmer, E Sussex

FOCUS
The bend rails were out 2yds, adding 36yds to the distance of this race, run at a modest gallop and largely featuring a collection of characters whose performances are almost impossible to predict. The winner may be a bit better than the bare result.

3087 DEREK HUNNISETT MEMORIAL H'CAP HURDLE (14 hdls) 3m 217y
2:20 (2:23) (Class 5) (0-100,100) 4-Y-O+ **£2,274** (£667; £333; £166)

Form RPR
-342 **1** **Maccabees**[38] 2316 6-9-7 **74** oh2 ThomasCheesman(7) 81+
(Linda Jewell) *hld up towards rr: t.k.h and quick prog to press ldrs 7th: led 9th and bounded clr: stdd and jnd 4 out: drvn and looked to have asserted 2 out: jnd again last: all out but hld on* **8/1**
5142 **2** 1 ¼ **Miss Mayfair (IRE)**[27] 2554 8-11-2 **90** (p) TomCannon 94
(Lawney Hill) *led to 9th: jnd wnr 4 out: drvn after next: rallied and upsides last: tired and jst hld flat* **6/1**[3]
6040 **3** 6 **West Of The Edge (IRE)**[18] 2730 7-10-12 **93** MrJNixon(7) 91
(Dai Williams) *hld up in rr: stdy prog bef 4 out and gng bttr than many: shkn up bef 3 out: chsd clr ldng pair bef 2 out: kpt on and clsd gap as they tired but nvr able to chal* **14/1**
3-52 **4** 4 ½ **Moon Trip**[26] 2567 6-11-12 **100** MarkGrant 94
(Geoffrey Deacon) *hld up: drvn in last pl after 10th: struggling rest of way but kpt on and mde inroads fr 2 out as ldrs tired* **7/2**[1]
5-24 **5** 11 **Flemi Two Toes**[23] 2649 9-10-6 **90** (b) RomainClavreul(10) 73
(Sarah Humphrey) *chsd ldrs: urged along fr 9th: struggling to stay in tch 4 out: no hdwy after next* **6/1**[3]
PP22 **6** 28 **Burgess Dream (IRE)**[14] 2827 6-11-2 **90** AndrewThornton 45
(Anna Newton-Smith) *chsd ldrs: rdn in 3rd pl and nt fluent 4 out: wknd qckly after 3 out: virtually p.u nr fin* **7/1**
205P **P** **Flugzeug**[29] 2521 7-10-12 **91** KevinJones(5)
(Seamus Mullins) *racd on inner: chsd ldrs: urged along fr 6th: wknd 10th: wl bhd whn p.u bef 2 out* **9/1**
0-04 **P** **Thehill Ofthe Rock (IRE)**[21] 2693 5-10-11 **85** (v) SamTwiston-Davies
(Jim Best) *hld up in rr: tried to make prog after 10th but rdn next (4 out): no hdwy 3 out: bhd whn p.u bef 2 out* **5/1**[2]
5053 **F** **Element Quartet (IRE)**[29] 2515 6-10-0 **74** oh5 (tp) RichieMcLernon
(Brendan Powell) *pressed ldr tl fell 8th* **11/1**

6m 44.8s (19.80) **Going Correction** +0.50s/f (Soft) **9 Ran SP% 116.1**
Speed ratings (Par 103): **88,87,85,84,80 71, , ,**
CSF £55.74 CT £665.70 TOTE £9.70: £2.60, £1.80, £2.70; EX 55.20 Trifecta £1646.00.
Owner K Johnson, K Jessup 1 **Bred** Mrs J A Cornwell **Trained** Sutton Valence, Kent

FOCUS
The bend rails were out 7yds, adding 105yds to the distance of the race. The pace was respectable, making this staying hurdle a good test of stamina. The winner was building on his good Fontwell run.

3088 G.E. WHITE & SONS AGRICULTURAL BUILDINGS H'CAP CHASE (14 fncs) 2m 3f 164y
2:55 (2:56) (Class 5) (0-100,94) 4-Y-O+ **£2,662** (£826; £445)

Form RPR
13-3 **1** **Black Narcissus (IRE)**[20] 2698 6-11-11 **93** RhysFlint 96
(Alexandra Dunn) *s.s: tended to jump rt: chsd ldng trio 5th: pushed along and outpcd in 3rd pl bef 10th: rdn to chse clr ldr 4 out: 20 l down and no ch whn lft 6 l 2nd last: drvn out* **9/4**[1]
P54P **2** 1 ¼ **Petit Ecuyer (FR)**[18] 2735 9-10-5 **80** (v[1]) MrJNixon(7) 80
(Dai Williams) *hld up in rr: lost tch 8th: pushed along to chse ldng trio after next: mstke 10th and wl bhd: tk modest 3rd whn lft 2nd last: clsd on wnr but unable to chal* **10/1**
3F55 **3** 3 ¾ **Head Spin (IRE)**[11] 2874 7-11-12 **94** (bt) AndrewThornton 91
(Seamus Mullins) *racd in 3rd: nt fluent 6th: chsd ldr 8th: outpcd fr next: lost 2nd 4 out: no ch whn lft in 3rd pl again last: one pce* **9/2**[3]

1246 P **Dancing Dik**[28] 2546 10-11-5 **87**....................................(b) PaddyBrennan
(Paul Henderson) *led to 7th: sn dropped away qckly: t.o in last whn p.u bef 10th* **7/1**

2635 P **Humbel Ben (IRE)**[36] 2364 12-11-6 **88**..........................(tp) TomCannon
(Alan Jones) *s.s: a in rr: urged along and lost tch 8th: poor 5th whn p.u bef 4 out* **7/1**

3-12 P **Ball Hopper (IRE)**[33] 2447 11-11-5 **87**.......................(p) RichieMcLernon
(Richenda Ford) *chsd ldng trio to 5th: sn struggling: t.o in 6th whn p.u after 10th* **4/1**[2]

P/3P U **Goring Two (IRE)**[29] 2521 10-9-10 **69**......................... CharlieDeutsch(5) 96+
(Anna Newton-Smith) *trckd ldr: led 7th: drew clr fr 9th: 20 l ahd and stl gng strly whn big jump last: untidy landing and uns rdr* **8/1**

5m 20.1s (12.80) **Going Correction** +0.175s/f (Yiel) **7** Ran SP% **114.2**
Speed ratings (Par 103): **81,80,79, , ,**
CSF £23.43 TOTE £2.90: £1.50, £4.80; EX 29.10 Trifecta £157.50.
Owner Team Dunn **Bred** Patrick Davern **Trained** West Buckland, Somerset

FOCUS
The bend rails were out 2yds, adding 24yds to the distance of this race, which was run at a good gallop considering the conditions. The lucky winner ran similar to her Lingfield run.

3089 BLUERIBANDBET 1/4 ODDS EACH WAY EVERY RACE H'CAP HURDLE (9 hdls) 1m 7f 195y
3:25 (3:26) (Class 5) (0-100,100) 3-Y-O+ **£2,274** (£667; £333; £166)

Form RPR

6PP- 1 **Torero**[301] 4273 6-10-6 **80**.................................(p) JoshuaMoore 90+
(Gary Moore) *racd on outer: in tch: prog to chse ldr whn hit 3 out: rdn to chal 2 out: drvn to ld flat: idled but hld on* **2/1**[1]

4002 2 *nk* **Warrant Officer**[28] 2547 5-10-12 **86**......................... MarcGoldstein 95
(Sheena West) *trckd ldr: led 6th: rdn and hrd pressed 2 out: hdd flat: kpt on wl: jst hld* **7/2**[3]

04-2 3 *½* **My Lord**[14] 2826 7-11-12 **100**.....................................(v) SamTwiston-Davies 109
(Jim Best) *racd on outer: hld up in rr: prog to trck ldng pair after 3 out: cl up whn nt fluent 2 out: rdn and tried to chal last: nt find enough but kpt on* **3/1**[2]

52-3 4 *15* **Entry To Evrywhere (IRE)**[19] 2712 7-10-2 **83**............ MikeyHamill(7) 77
(Alexandra Dunn) *t.k.h: led: mstke and hdd 6th: fdd into 4th after 3 out and wl btn after* **9/2**

/000 5 *9* **Cantor**[14] 2823 7-11-6 **94**.. MattieBatchelor 79
(Daniel O'Brien) *nt fluent: hld up in last: reminders after 5th: lost tch bef 3 out: modest late hdwy* **33/1**

34P4 6 *1* **Alottarain (IRE)**[25] 2604 5-11-6 **99**.............................. KevinJones(5) 83
(Seamus Mullins) *racd on inner: chsd ldrs tl wknd 3 out* **16/1**

P0P6 7 *½* **Merry Mast (USA)**[25] 2604 6-10-2 **76**........................(b) PaddyBrennan 59
(Paul Henderson) *wl in tch tl rdn and wknd 3 out* **20/1**

-464 8 *44* **Rolling Dough (IRE)**[19] 2713 7-10-13 **87**.................... AndrewThornton 26
(Diana Grissell) *racd on inner: cl up tl wknd rapidly bef 3 out: t.o* **14/1**

4m 7.7s (6.90) **Going Correction** +0.50s/f (Soft) **8** Ran SP% **119.0**
Speed ratings (Par 103): **102,101,101,94,89 89,88,66**
CSF £10.31 CT £20.72 TOTE £2.60: £1.20, £1.70, £1.70; EX 10.40 Trifecta £35.60.
Owner Ashley Head **Bred** G Reed **Trained** Lower Beeding, W Sussex
■ Stewards' Enquiry : Joshua Moore two-day ban: used whip above permitted level (Dec 28,30)

FOCUS
The bend rails were out 7yds, adding 63yds to the distance of this race, which was run at a ordinary pace. The winner has been a 105+ hurdler at his best.
T/Jkpt: Not won. JACKPOT PLACEPOT: £166.90 to a £1 stake. Pool of £2069.32 - 9.05 winning units. T/Plt: £179.60 to Pool of £62145.68, 252.49 winning tickets T/Qpdt: £47.70 to a £1 stake. Pool of £5489.19 - 85.00 winning units. **Jonathan Neesom**

3090 - 3091a (Foreign Racing) - See Raceform Interactive

3068 NAVAN (L-H)
Monday, December 14
OFFICIAL GOING: Heavy

3092a KERRY GROUP HILLY WAY CHASE (GRADE 2) (12 fncs) 2m 1f
12:35 (12:35) 5-Y-O+ **£23,934** (£6,996; £3,313; £1,104)

RPR

1 **Felix Yonger (IRE)**[32] 2464 9-11-12 **160**.................................... RWalsh 165
(W P Mullins, Ire) *w.w: 4th 1/2-way: disp 3rd briefly bef 5th: wnt 3rd next: rdn in 4th after 2 out and swtchd rt: clsd u.p to ld bef last: kpt on wl run-in* **11/10**[1]

2 *2½* **Bright New Dawn (IRE)**[32] 2464 8-11-4 **148**.......................(t) BJCooper 153
(Gordon Elliott, Ire) *hld up in rr: slt mstke 2nd: wnt 4th after 4 out and impr to chal in 3rd 2 out: ev ch between horses between last 2: kpt on same pce in 2nd run-in: nt matching wnr* **4/1**[3]

3 *¾* **Hidden Cyclone (IRE)**[8] 2941 10-11-10 **157**.........................(p) BrianHayes 158+
(John Joseph Hanlon, Ire) *settled bhd ldrs: nt fluent 1st: j.rt at times: mstke 3rd: sn disp and led bef next: slow 7th and reduced ld: rdn and hdd bef last where dropped to 3rd: kpt on again run-in: a hld* **7/2**[2]

4 *2¼* **Days Hotel (IRE)**[36] 2388 10-11-4 **150**................................ AELynch 150
(Henry De Bromhead, Ire) *trckd ldrs: sltly hmpd 3rd and impr to dispute briefly bef next: 2nd 1/2-way: effrt far side between last 2: no ex bef last where dropped to 4th: kpt on one pce run-in* **9/1**

P **Twinlight (FR)**[36] 2388 8-11-12 **158**....................................... DannyMullins
(W P Mullins, Ire) *led: j. sltly rt at times: hdd after 3rd and dropped to 3rd bef next: dropped to rr of quintet after 4 out and wknd qckly next: trailing whn p.u after 2 out* **8/1**

4m 51.4s (18.10) **5** Ran SP% **111.0**
CSF £6.09 TOTE £1.70: £1.60, £1.60; DF 4.80 Trifecta £8.30.
Owner Andrea & Graham Wylie **Bred** J Brophy **Trained** Muine Beag, Co Carlow

FOCUS
Cork and Navan are two very different tracks but it made no difference to the winner who won decisively in the end and followed up his win in last year's race when it was run at its traditional Cork home. The runner-up and fourth help set the standard.

3093a KERRY GROUP EUROPEAN BREEDERS FUND MARES NOVICE CHASE (GRADE 3) (12 fncs) 2m 1f
1:10 (1:10) 4-Y-O+ **£18,643** (£5,449; £2,581; £860)

RPR

1 **Queens Wild (IRE)**[37] 2355 5-10-11 0.................................... APHeskin 126+
(Edward P Harty, Ire) *settled bhd ldrs: 3rd 1/2-way: cl 3rd 4 out: disp next and sn led narrowly tl hdd bef 2 out: cl 2nd whn mstke last and sn dropped to 3rd: kpt on again nr side run-in to ld on line* **11/1**

2 *shd* **Perfect Woman (IRE)**[39] 2308 7-10-11 0...........................(p) MarkWalsh 126+
(Michael Winters, Ire) *led and disp: on terms at 1/2-way: rdn and hdd after 3 out: u.p and struggling in 3rd bef last: rallied run-in to ld in clsng stages tl hdd on line* **9/2**[3]

3 *¾* **Emcon (IRE)**[32] 2465 6-10-11 0.. KevinSexton 125+
(W J Austin, Ire) *hld up in tch: 5th 1/2-way: reminders after 7th: disp cl 4th bef 4 out: rdn in 5th bef 2 out and u.p in 4th bef last where slow: rallied and kpt on wl into 3rd in clsng stages: hld* **6/1**

4 *¾* **Miss Dinamic (IRE)**[16] 2793 6-11-4 **135**................................ RWalsh 131
(Gordon Elliott, Ire) *chsd ldrs: 4th 1/2-way: disp cl 4th 4 out: effrt far side after next and led narrowly bef 2 out: rdn clr tl slow at last and sn strly pressed: hdd run-in and wknd into 4th clsng stages* **11/4**[1]

5 *4½* **Melbourne Lady**[199] 542 7-10-11 0.............................. MatthewBowes 122
(P Fegan, Ire) *led and disp: slt mstke 1st: on terms at 1/2-way: hdd after 3 out and no ex u.p in 4th after next: one pce after* **25/1**

6 *2¾* **Curragh Na Gold (IRE)**[23] 2656 6-10-11 0..................(p) SeanFlanagan 119
(David Harry Kelly, Ire) *hld up: 7th 1/2-way: pushed along in rr after 5 out and impr into 6th fr next: rdn in rr after 3 out and u.p whn bad mstke 2 out where wnt lft: kpt on one pce in 6th after last* **20/1**

P **Solita (IRE)**[16] 2793 6-10-11 **124**..(t) BJCooper
(Paul Nolan, Ire) *settled in rr: nt fluent 1st and reminder: trailing whn p.u after 6th* **5/1**

P **I'm All You Need (IRE)**[26] 2588 5-10-11 **123**.................... RobbiePower
(Paul Nolan, Ire) *hld up in tch: 6th 1/2-way: k clsr order 3 out: rdn next and sn no ex u.p in rr: wknd and p.u bef last* **7/2**[2]

4m 54.6s (21.30) **8** Ran SP% **115.0**
CSF £60.81 TOTE £19.20: £3.40, £1.50, £2.20; DF 73.40 Trifecta £518.00.
Owner Robert Guiry **Bred** R Guiry **Trained** Curragh, Co Kildare

FOCUS
This was transferred from Sunday's Cork fixture which was lost to waterlogging. Very little separated the first four home and six of the eight runners were in with a shout jumping the second-last. The runner-up and sixth help set the standard.

3094 - 3097a (Foreign Racing) - See Raceform Interactive

2843 CATTERICK (L-H)
Tuesday, December 15
OFFICIAL GOING: Soft (6.7)
Wind: light 1/2 behind Weather: damp and misty, light rain and foggy last 2

3098 RACINGUK.COM AMATEUR RIDERS' H'CAP HURDLE (10 hdls) 2m 3f 66y
12:15 (12:16) (Class 5) (0-100,100) 3-Y-O+ **£2,495** (£774; £386; £193)

Form RPR

4032 1 **Danceintothelight**[33] 2453 8-11-0 **95**......................(t) MissAMcCain(7) 110+
(Donald McCain) *t.k.h: trckd ldr: led 3rd: sn wl clr: pushed along between last 2: stmbld on landing last* **11/8**[1]

6-P1 2 *27* **Running Wolf (IRE)**[13] 2843 4-11-9 **100**......................(t) MrMLegg(3) 88
(Alex Hales) *chsd ldng pair 4th: pushed along next: remote 2nd 6th: no ch w wnr whn hit last* **7/4**[2]

0PP0 3 *18* **Jimmie Brown (USA)**[66] 1857 7-10-0 **74**........................ MissCWalton 44
(Andrew Crook) *in rr: bhd 3rd: drvn 6th: distant 4th 3 out: poor 3rd whn hit 2 out* **66/1**

0-P6 4 *4* **Aristocracy**[11] 2880 4-11-8 **99**.................................(tp) MissBHampson(3) 65
(Sally Randell) *led to 3rd: chsd clr ldr: wknd bef 2 out: j.lft last 2* **11/1**

640 5 *2* **Strait Run (IRE)**[16] 2804 4-10-6 **87**........................ MrJoeWright(7) 51
(Micky Hammond) *in rr: bhd 3rd: blnd and rdr temporarily lost iron 7th: sn t.o* **16/1**

04P- 6 *20* **Troubled Waters**[239] 5420 6-10-5 **84**....................(t) MrTommieMO'Brien(5) 28
(Chris Fairhurst) *in rr: bhd 3rd: t.o bef 2 out* **28/1**

-640 U **Miss Conway**[47] 2148 4-10-3 **82**.. MissETodd(5)
(Mark Walford) *hld up in rr: stmbld and uns rdr sn after 1st* **17/2**[3]

4m 49.4s (13.30) **Going Correction** +0.425s/f (Soft) **7** Ran SP% **108.2**
Speed ratings (Par 103): **89,77,70,68,67 59,**
CSF £3.78 CT £66.03 TOTE £2.10: £1.70, £1.20; EX 4.30 Trifecta £65.40.
Owner Mrs Sian McCain **Bred** Mrs David Low **Trained** Cholmondeley, Cheshire
■ The first winner for Abby McCain, 16, daughter of Donald.

FOCUS
Soft conditions and all race distances as advertised. A weak handicap in which the favourite, who has been a 118-rated hurdler at his best, was a long way ahead from an early stage.

3099 BOOK NOW FOR 28TH DECEMBER JUVENILE HURDLE (8 hdls) 1m 7f 156y
12:45 (12:45) (Class 4) 3-Y-O **£3,573** (£1,049; £524; £262)

Form RPR

1 **Berland (IRE)**[46] 3-10-12 0.. AidanColeman 110+
(John Ferguson) *t.k.h: trckd ldrs: upsides whn nt fluent 4th: led after 3 out: pushed out: readily* **11/10**[1]

2 *1* **Miss Ranger (IRE)**[68] 3-10-5 0..[1] DannyCook 95+
(Brian Ellison) *trckd ldrs: 4th 2 out: styd on to take 2nd last 75yds: no real imp* **7/1**

2 3 *3½* **Cosmic Statesman**[20] 2718 3-10-12 0.............................. BrianHughes 100
(Richard Fahey) *w ldrs: 1 l 2nd whn hit last: one pce* **11/4**[2]

F 4 *2¼* **Keep Up (GER)**[20] 2718 3-10-9 0................................ AdamNicol(3) 96
(Philip Kirby) *in rr: hdwy 3 out: 5th last: kpt on* **200/1**

5 *6* **Hubal (POL)**[80] 3-10-12 0.. JanFaltejsek 91
(George Charlton) *chsd ldrs: drvn 2 out: 4th whn hit last: sn fdd* **66/1**

3 6 *2½* **Kisumu**[20] 2718 3-10-12 0.................................... SamTwiston-Davies 87
(Micky Hammond) *trckd ldrs: rdn 2 out: wknd appr last* **11/2**[3]

004 7 *nk* **Hey Bob (IRE)**[13] 2845 3-10-9 0.................................. TonyKelly(3) 87
(Chris Grant) *t.k.h in rr: sme hdwy 3 out: fdd last* **125/1**

P 8 *6* **Qatea (IRE)**[34] 2439 3-10-12 0......................................(t) AdrianLane 81
(Donald McCain) *mid-div: chsng ldrs 3 out: sn drvn and lost pl* **33/1**

626 9 *1½* **Poet Mark (IRE)**[20] 2718 3-10-12 **106**............................ JakeGreenall 79
(Tim Easterby) *led: hdd after 3 out: sn lost pl* **33/1**

10 *3* **Mr Morocco**[17] 3-10-12 0..(t) JackQuinlan 77
(Giles Bravery) *t.k.h in mid-div: hdwy 5th: mstke next: lost pl bef 2 out* **66/1**

36 11 *15* **The Name's Bond**[13] 2845 3-10-9 0......................... HarryChalloner(3) 61
(Keith Reveley) *in rr: bhd fr 3 out: eased run-in* **40/1**

12 *20* **Lipstickandpowder (IRE)**[315] 3-10-5 0.............................. HenryBrooke 34
(Dianne Sayer) *t.k.h in rr: bhd 3 out: t.o whn eased last* **250/1**

P **Hugh's Secret (IRE)** 3-10-7 0.................................. NathanMoscrop(5)
(Philip Kirby) *in rr: blnd 1st: mstke next: bhd 3 out: t.o whn p.u bef next* **80/1**

3m 57.7s (5.20) **Going Correction** +0.425s/f (Soft) **13** Ran SP% **116.4**
Speed ratings (Par 104): **104,103,101,100,97 96,96,93,92,90 83,73,**
CSF £9.42 TOTE £1.90: £1.10, £2.20, £1.70; EX 8.80 Trifecta £24.70.

Owner Bloomfields **Bred** Darley **Trained** Cowlinge, Suffolk
FOCUS
A modest juvenile hurdle run at a steady initial gallop. The winner was impressive, but not strong form behind and some of these may be flattered.

3100 COME RACING NEW YEAR'S DAY BEGINNERS' CHASE (19 fncs) 3m 1f 54y
1:15 (1:15) (Class 3) 4-Y-O+ £7,135 (£2,286; £1,270)

Form RPR
11- 1 **Hester Flemen (IRE)**346 3495 7-10-8 0........................ BrianHarding 137+
(Nicky Richards) *j. soundly: mde all: wnt clr 2 out: shkn up after last: eased clsng stages* 11/2[3]
3-45 2 6 **Racing Europe (IRE)**52 2067 6-11-1 128........................ DannyCook 134
(Brian Ellison) *chsd wnr: mstke 7th: drvn 15th: one pce fr 3 out* 10/1
5-22 3 20 **Seldom Inn**28 2557 7-11-1 135........................ BrianHughes 117
(Sandy Thomson) *nt fluent in modest 4th: bhd fr 6th: brief effrt 11th: sn lost tch: lft poor 3rd last* 7/2[2]
111- P **Central Flame**239 5422 7-10-10 133........................ MissCWalton(5)
(James Walton) *dropped in last: bhd and nt fluent 3rd: sn tailed rt off: p.u bef 12th* 10/1
12-2 P **Warriors Tale**19 2727 6-11-1 142........................ SamTwiston-Davies 117
(Paul Nicholls) *j. v big in 3rd: hdwy 11th: disputing 2nd 4 out: rn wd bnd: lost pl and hit 3 out: sn bhd: poor 3rd whn p.u appr last* 10/11[1]
6m 30.8s (-11.20) **Going Correction** -0.175s/f (Good) 5 Ran SP% 108.2
Speed ratings (Par 107): **110,108,101, ,**
CSF £43.51 TOTE £5.70: £2.50, £4.00; EX 47.20 Trifecta £143.50.
Owner Paul & Clare Rooney **Bred** Miss Ann Twomey **Trained** Greystoke, Cumbria
FOCUS
If In Doubt won this event last year before taking the Skybet Chase at Doncaster. This edition looked a cracking little race, and produced a very promising winner.

3101 GO RACING IN YORKSHIRE WINTER FESTIVAL NOVICES' HURDLE (10 hdls) 2m 3f 66y
1:45 (1:47) (Class 4) 4-Y-O+ £3,573 (£1,049; £524; £262)

Form RPR
4-01 1 **Poulanassy (IRE)**35 2423 5-11-5 0........................ AdamWedge 119+
(Evan Williams) *led to 6th: chsd ldrs: styd on between last 2: 1 l down last: led last 150yds: fnd ex nr fin* 9/2[2]
15 2 1 1/4 **Captain Bocelli (IRE)**80 1662 6-10-12 0........................ RichardJohnson 111+
(Philip Hobbs) *t.k.h: trckd ldrs 2nd: led 6th: drvn between last 2: hit last: sn hdd: no ex clsng stages* 5/6[1]
1203 3 14 **Sign Manual**61 1921 6-11-5 115........................ WillKennedy 104
(Donald McCain) *in rr: modest 5th 3 out: 3rd sn after 2 out: one pce* 12/1
5-4F 4 4 1/2 **Return Flight**20 2716 4-10-12 0........................ DarylJacob 94
(Micky Hammond) *nt fluent 1st: sn in rr: poor 6th sn after 3 out: modest 4th last* 13/2[3]
5 13 **Carthage (IRE)**17 4-10-12 0........................ DannyCook 86
(Brian Ellison) *mid-div: chsd ldrs 6th: hit next: wknd sn after 2 out* 16/1
6 22 **Nortonthorpelegend (IRE)**213 5-10-12 0........................ BrianHughes 56
(John Wade) *chsd ldrs: lost pl 6th: t.o 2 out* 125/1
00- 7 9 **Magnolia Ridge (IRE)**24 3060 5-10-12 0........................ JakeGreenall 47
(Mark Walford) *chsd ldrs: lost pl 6th: t.o 2 out* 200/1
50-6 8 10 **Rob Robin (IRE)**33 2460 5-10-12 0........................ SamTwiston-Davies 37
(Paul Nicholls) *in rr: hdwy 5th: lost pl bef 2 out: hit 2 out: sn bhd: t.o* 13/2[3]
0P 9 26 **Play Practice**16 2804 5-10-0 0........................ MissCWalton(5) 4
(James Walton) *t.k.h: trckd ldrs: lost pl after 5th: sn bhd: t.o 3 out* 250/1
4m 52.1s (16.00) **Going Correction** +0.425s/f (Soft)
WFA 4 from 5yo+ 5lb 9 Ran SP% 114.7
Speed ratings (Par 105): **83,82,76,74,69 59,56,51,41**
CSF £8.95 TOTE £5.40: £1.40, £1.10, £2.60; EX 10.50 Trifecta £48.90.
Owner Paul Langford **Bred** J And A Cunningham **Trained** Llancarfan, Vale Of Glamorgan
FOCUS
Ordinary novice hurdle form, but the winner is on the upgrade.

3102 RACING UK PROFITS RETURNED TO RACING H'CAP HURDLE (12 hdls) 3m 1f 71y
2:20 (2:20) (Class 4) (0-110,110) 4-Y-O+ £3,573 (£1,049; £524; £262)

Form RPR
P435 1 **Turtle Cask (IRE)**20 2720 6-10-9 93........................(p) BrianHughes 100+
(Dianne Sayer) *mde all: styd on wl between last 2: 6 l ahd last: forged away* 3/1[3]
0-03 2 13 **Blake Dean**11 2893 7-10-9 93........................ DannyCook 85
(Sue Smith) *trckd ldrs: 2nd after 8th: effrt 3 out: wknd appr last* 5/2[2]
253 3 3 **Freddies Portrait (IRE)**16 2804 6-11-10 108........ SamTwiston-Davies 97
(Donald McCain) *trckd ldrs: 3rd after 8th: effrt 3 out: wknd appr last* 2/1[1]
-466 4 18 **Foot The Bill**13 2844 10-10-5 89........................ BrianHarding 60
(Patrick Holmes) *w ldrs: pushed along 7th: lost pl and reminders 9th: rallied appr 2 out: hung lft and wknd between last 2: b.b.v* 9/2
16P0 5 dist **Minella Hero (IRE)**18 2744 7-11-2 110........ HugoThompsonBrown(10)
(Micky Hammond) *w ldrs: shkn up 5th: drvn 7th: sn lost pl and bhd: t.o 3 out: eventually completed* 16/1
6m 35.4s (7.80) **Going Correction** +0.425s/f (Soft) 5 Ran SP% 111.0
Speed ratings (Par 105): **104,99,98,93,**
CSF £11.11 TOTE £4.40: £2.30, £1.60; EX 11.80 Trifecta £25.30.
Owner Mellissa Lamb & Andrew Sayer **Bred** Andrew & Garry Brazil **Trained** Hackthorpe, Cumbria
FOCUS
Not a strong handicap. The winner made it a decent test of stamina and is rated back to his best.

3103 BUY YOUR 2016 ANNUAL BADGE TODAY H'CAP CHASE (12 fncs) 1m 7f 145y
2:50 (2:50) (Class 4) (0-105,102) 4-Y-O+ £4,223 (£1,240; £620; £310)

Form RPR
-303 1 **Star Presenter (IRE)**21 2705 7-11-5 98........................ JonathanEngland(3) 112+
(Richard Drake) *hld up in mid-div: trckd ldrs 7th: 2nd 9th: led 2 out: clr whn hit last: eased towards fin* 13/2[3]
3-52 2 7 **Bollin Line**13 2844 8-10-11 87........................ DannyCook 94+
(Lucinda Egerton) *in rr: hdwy to chse ldrs whn j.rt 8th: 3rd next: outpcd 3 out: kpt on to take modest 2nd last 150yds* 11/4[2]
13P0 3 3 1/4 **Odds On Dan (IRE)**17 2786 9-9-11 78........................(tp) DeanPratt(5) 78
(Lucinda Egerton) *in rr: outpcd and drvn 7th: hdwy appr 3 out: kpt on to take modest 3rd towards fin* 14/1
6230 4 1 **Mandy's Boy (IRE)**12 2869 5-11-7 100........................(tp) JamesBanks(3) 100
(Sally Randell) *led: hdd 2 out: wknd fnl 200yds* 33/1
6034 5 9 **Morning With Ivan (IRE)**47 2143 5-11-7 97........................ HenryBrooke 90
(Martin Todhunter) *chsd ldrs: 4th 9th: wknd bef 2 out* 7/1
-422 6 9 **Tomorrow's Legend**21 2707 5-11-9 102........................ JoeColliver(3) 84
(George Moore) *chsd ldrs 4th: hit 7th: lost pl next* 7/4[1]
P0-R 7 1 3/4 **Zazamix (FR)**40 2290 10-9-10 77 oh2 ow1........................(v) JamieBargary(5) 57
(Andrew Crook) *chsd ldrs: j.lft 3rd: drvn 5th: sn lost pl* 40/1
-2RP 8 23 **Dundee Blue (IRE)**21 2705 7-10-5 84........................(bt) TonyKelly(3) 40
(Henry Hogarth) *in rr: chsd ldrs 5th: lost pl 7th: blnd 9th: sn bhd: t.o* 12/1
4m 5.6s (5.50) **Going Correction** -0.175s/f (Good) 8 Ran SP% 108.6
Speed ratings (Par 105): **79,75,73,73,68 64,63,52**
CSF £23.09 CT £213.00 TOTE £8.10: £2.30, £1.60, £2.50; EX 29.40 Trifecta £259.10.
Owner Mrs J Drake **Bred** J R Weston **Trained** Ilkley, W Yorks
FOCUS
This modest handicap chase was run in gloomy conditions. A personal best from the winner.

3104 CATTERICKBRIDGE.CO.UK INTERMEDIATE OPEN NATIONAL HUNT FLAT RACE 1m 7f 156y
3:20 (3:20) (Class 6) 4-6-Y-O £1,949 (£572; £286; £143)

Form RPR
2-31 1 **High Bridge**24 2650 4-11-7 0........................ AidanColeman 130+
(John Ferguson) *trckd ldr: led 3f out: wnt clr over 1f out: v easily* 10/11[1]
2 13 **Atomix (GER)** 4-11-0 0........................ BrianHughes 107
(Peter Niven) *hld up in mid-div: effrt and outpcd over 4f out: styd on to take 2nd over 1f out: no ch w wnr* 7/1[3]
3 3 1/4 **Shambougg**268 4-11-0 0........................ RichardJohnson 104
(Philip Hobbs) *trckd ldrs: pushed along 6f out: kpt on to take modest 3rd over 1f out* 4/1[2]
2- 4 8 **Be Daring (FR)**258 5105 4-11-0 0........................ SamTwiston-Davies 97
(Paul Nicholls) *led: hdd 3f out: wknd over 1f out* 4/1[2]
5 4 1/2 **Paddling (FR)** 4-10-11 0........................ JoeColliver(3) 92
(Micky Hammond) *mid-div: pushed along 7f out: sn chsng ldrs: lost pl over 2f out* 25/1
6 7 **Mahler Bay (IRE)**205 5-11-0 0........................ HenryBrooke 85
(Michael Smith) *in rr: drvn 6f out: nvr a factor* 80/1
0 7 1 **Mutdula (IRE)**18 2756 5-11-0 0........................ PaddyBrennan 84
(Alan Swinbank) *hld up in rr: effrt 6f out: lost pl over 4f out* 22/1
8 15 **Pottinger (IRE)** 4-11-0 0........................(t) PeterBuchanan 69
(Lucinda Russell) *hld up in last: drvn 6f out: sn wl bhd* 16/1
3m 47.9s (1.00) **Going Correction** +0.425s/f (Soft) 8 Ran SP% 120.2
Speed ratings: **114,107,105,101,99 96,95,88**
CSF £8.75 TOTE £1.90: £1.10, £2.40, £1.50; EX 8.50 Trifecta £32.90.
Owner Bloomfields **Bred** Darley **Trained** Cowlinge, Suffolk
FOCUS
It was pretty dark for this bumper, but it produced a bright performance from the winner.
T/Plt: £43.40 to a £1 stake. Pool: £47,112.37 - 792.17 winning units. T/Qpdt: £39.70 to a £1 stake. Pool: £3,498.33 - 65.20 winning units. **Walter Glynn**

2850 LUDLOW (R-H)
Wednesday, December 16

OFFICIAL GOING: Soft
Wind: almost nil Weather: sunny spells

3105 TANNERS CAVA "NATIONAL HUNT" MAIDEN HURDLE (9 hdls) 1m 7f 169y
12:20 (12:20) (Class 4) 4-Y-O+ £3,898 (£1,144; £572; £286)

Form RPR
2 1 **Le Prezien (FR)**28 2581 4-11-0 125........................(t) NickScholfield 126+
(Paul Nicholls) *t.k.h: trckd ldrs: hit 3 out: chal next: sn led and qcknd clr: nt fluent last: comf* 13/8[1]
22 2 6 **Casper King (IRE)**38 2375 4-11-0 0........................ TomO'Brien 115+
(Philip Hobbs) *a.p: mstke 3 out: ev ch next: sn outpcd by wnr: kpt on* 4/1[2]
21- 3 6 **Monkhouse (IRE)**242 5402 5-11-0 0........................ DavidBass 109
(Kim Bailey) *chsd ldrs: wnt 2nd after 6th: rdn 3 out where j.rt: sn led narrowly: hdd after 2 out: no ex flat* 8/1
52 4 2 **Super Scorpion (IRE)**69 1826 5-11-0 0........................ PaddyBrennan 106
(Debra Hamer) *cl up: lft in ld after 2nd: hit next: rdn 3 out: hdd bef next: one pce* 11/2[3]
3-63 5 1/2 **Will O'The West (IRE)**32 2487 4-11-0 0........................ JakeGreenall 106
(Henry Daly) *chsd ldrs: rdn appr 3 out: one pce* 11/1
60 6 5 **Bramble Brook**20 2729 5-11-0 0........................ BrendanPowell 100
(Colin Tizzard) *chsd ldrs: rdn appr 3 out: kpt on same pce* 66/1
40 7 hd **Grand Enterprise**28 2564 5-10-9 0........................ JamieBargary(5) 100
(Tom George) *mid-div: rdn and sme hdwy after 6th: no imp fr 3 out* 100/1
0 8 6 **Bonvilston Boy**222 188 4-11-0 0........................ MichaelByrne 95
(Tim Vaughan) *mid-div: nt fluent and reminder 4th: rdn and no hdwy after 6th: no ch whn mstke 2 out* 250/1
0 9 3/4 **Thyne For Gold (IRE)**50 2126 4-11-0 0........................ WillKennedy 93
(Donald McCain) *towards rr: rdn appr 3 out: styd on: nvr threatened ldrs* 150/1
00 10 6 **Just So Cool (IRE)**28 2581 4-10-7 0........................ GarethMalone(7) 89+
(David Dennis) *j.lft: lft trcking ldr after 2nd: lost 2nd after 6th: wknd 3 out* 200/1
-550 11 26 **Definately Vinnie**20 2731 5-11-0 0........................ AdamWedge 61
(Jane Mathias) *a towards rr: lost tch after 6th: t.o* 200/1
4230 12 6 **Junior Package**20 2731 4-10-11 0........................ BrianToomey(3) 55
(David Pipe) *mid-div: hdwy 3rd: rdn and wknd after 6th: t.o* 200/1
-0F3 13 5 **Quench Tara**178 813 8-10-7 0........................ TomScudamore 43
(Michael Scudamore) *a in rr: lost tch after 6th: t.o* 40/1
0 14 8 **Babylone Colombe (FR)**14 2856 4-10-4 0........................ BenPoste(3) 35
(Tom Symonds) *a in rr: stmbld 2nd: lost tch 6th: t.o* 250/1
45- 15 27 **Sandford Castle (IRE)**261 5063 5-11-0 0........................ LiamHeard 15
(Johnny Farrelly) *a in rr: struggling 4th: wl bhd fr 6th: t.o* 100/1
3/62 P **Flamenco Lad**39 2345 5-11-0 0........................ JeremiahMcGrath
(Martin Hill) *led tl wnt wrong landing over 2nd and qckly p.u: fatally injured* 11/2[3]
4m 2.8s (13.30) **Going Correction** +1.075s/f (Soft) 16 Ran SP% 117.2
Speed ratings (Par 105): **109,106,103,102,101 99,99,96,95,92 79,76,74,70,56**
CSF £7.80 TOTE £2.40: £1.20, £1.70, £2.30; EX 10.50 Trifecta £31.50.
Owner Million In Mind Partnership **Bred** Jean-Raymond Breton & Thomas Trapenard **Trained** Ditcheat, Somerset

FOCUS
All distances as advertised. A maiden hurdle run at a sound pace in the testing conditions. Any price bar six and one of those was sadly out of the contest at an early stage. The remaining five dominated the finish after four were in line at the second last. The winner set a decent standard.

3106 ALFA AGGREGATE PRODUCTS NOVICES' LIMITED H'CAP CHASE (16 fncs) 2m 4f 11y
12:55 (12:55) (Class 3) (0-135,134) 4-Y-0+ £11,371 (£3,339; £1,669; £834)

Form RPR
1-24 1 **Double Shuffle (IRE)**[33] 2469 5-11-8 **134**........ PaddyBrennan 142+
(Tom George) *t.k.h: trckd ldrs: led appr 4 out: hit 2 out: sn shkn up: drvn out flat* 4/1[2]
131F 2 ¾ **Fourth Act (IRE)**[20] 2727 6-10-11 **123**........(t) BrendanPowell 131+
(Colin Tizzard) *hld up: mstke 6th: hdwy 10th: mstke 4 out: chsd wnr next: pckd 2 out: kpt on wl* 10/3[1]
P-15 3 nk **How About It (IRE)**[39] 2332 6-10-12 **124**........(p) SeanBowen 131
(Rebecca Curtis) *chsd ldrs: wnt 2nd 7th tl mstke 12th: rdn 4 out: rallied 2 out: r.o u.p flat* 6/1
2403 4 17 **Skylander (IRE)**[14] 2853 6-10-11 **128**........(p) DavidNoonan(5) 118
(David Pipe) *w wnr to 5th: lost 2nd 7th: rdn fr 9th: struggling after 13th: styd on fr 2 out: wnt modest 4th flat* 11/2[3]
2-56 5 ¾ **For Two (FR)**[18] 2779 6-10-10 **122**........(tp) NickScholfield 110
(Paul Nicholls) *hld up: nt fluent 2nd: hdwy 9th: mstke 12th: bmpd and rdn 4 out: disputing 2nd whn mstke next: wknd appr last* 8/1
3-2F 6 14 **Wadswick Court (IRE)**[18] 2779 7-11-5 **131**........ TomScudamore 105
(Neil Mulholland) *chsd ldrs: j.lft 4 out tl wknd 3 out* 15/2
/03- 7 1¼ **Portway Flyer (IRE)**[418] 2038 7-10-12 **124**........(t) WillKennedy 101
(Ian Williams) *towards rr: blnd and dropped to last 3rd: stl cl enough after 13th: no imp fr 4 out* 20/1
44-0 8 1 **Huff And Puff**[221] 196 8-10-8 **120**........ LiamTreadwell 96
(Venetia Williams) *hld up: blnd bdly 12th: shkn up and no imp 4 out: no ch whn mstke 2 out* 15/2
121R 9 17 **Canicallyouback**[31] 2518 7-10-10 **122**........ AdamWedge 87
(Evan Williams) *mde most tl hdd appr 4 out: j.rt next: wkng whn mstke 2 out: t.o* 25/1

5m 21.6s (17.20) **Going Correction** +0.825s/f (Soft) **9** Ran SP% **116.0**
Speed ratings (Par 107): **98,97,97,90,90 84,84,83,77**
CSF £18.51 CT £78.89 TOTE £5.10: £1.80, £1.90, £2.50; EX 15.10 Trifecta £150.80.
Owner Crossed Fingers Partnership **Bred** A W Young **Trained** Slad, Gloucs

FOCUS
Quite a competitive novices' limited handicap chase. The pace was sound and the first three finished some way clear. the winner is steadily progressive.

3107 TANNERS WINES H'CAP CHASE (12 fncs) 1m 7f 212y
1:30 (1:30) (Class 2) (0-145,139) 4-Y-0+ £17,869 (£5,247; £2,623; £1,311)

Form RPR
5011 1 **Sir Valentino (FR)**[14] 2854 6-11-12 **139**........(t) PaddyBrennan 148+
(Tom George) *chsd clr ldr: clsd 5th: chal 6th tl led 9th: rdn 2 out: kpt on wl* 9/4[1]
161U 2 1¾ **Jayo Time (IRE)**[14] 2854 6-11-3 **135**........(p) CiaranGethings(5) 142
(Kerry Lee) *hld up: hdwy 3rd: wnt 2nd after 9th: rdn whn hit 2 out: kpt on same pce* 3/1[2]
0P-U 3 24 **Vivaccio (FR)**[14] 2854 6-11-5 **132**........ LiamTreadwell 116
(Venetia Williams) *mid-div tl dropped to last 4th: outpcd 7th: rdn after 9th: no ch after: 4th whn blnd 3 out: sn wnt mod 3rd* 5/1[3]
0-64 4 3¾ **Lightening Rod**[14] 2854 10-10-13 **129**........ HarryBannister(3) 113
(Michael Easterby) *towards rr: outpcd by ldrs 8th: wnt mod 3rd appr 4 out: blnd 3 out and lost 3rd* 8/1
030F 5 28 **My Brother Sylvest**[14] 2854 9-11-6 **133**........(bt) TomScudamore 100
(David Pipe) *racd keenly: led: mstke 1st: clr to 5th: jnd next: rdn 7th: mstke next: hdd 9th: sn wknd* 12/1
4-5F F **Kudu Country (IRE)**[14] 2854 9-11-1 **128**........(t) AdamWedge
(Evan Williams) *chsd ldng pair: mstke 5th (water): rdn 8th: wknd appr 4 out: last whn fell 3 out* 11/1
-010 F **Arkaim**[25] 2635 7-11-8 **135**........ KielanWoods
(Pam Sly) *s.i.s and in rr: racd keenly and hdwy 2nd: mstke 3rd: fell next* 13/2

4m 7.7s (9.20) **Going Correction** +0.825s/f (Soft) **7** Ran SP% **112.9**
Speed ratings (Par 109): **110,109,97,95,81**
CSF £9.59 TOTE £2.90: £1.50, £1.90; EX 8.00 Trifecta £45.50.
Owner Doone Hulse Susie Saunders & Lady Cobham **Bred** Mlle Camille Serveau & Roger Simon **Trained** Slad, Gloucs

FOCUS
Six of the seven ran over the C&D two weeks earlier. Four were out of the contest at an early stage. Sir Valentino followed up that success in this valuable 128-139 handicap chase and is on the upgrade.

3108 TANNERS PROSECCO LADY AMATEUR RIDERS' H'CAP HURDLE (9 hdls) 1m 7f 169y
2:05 (2:05) (Class 4) (0-105,105) 3-Y-0+ £5,615 (£1,741; £870; £435)

Form RPR
0435 1 **Hill Fort**[12] 2876 5-11-3 **99**........(t) MissCVHart(3) 118+
(Matt Sheppard) *chsd ldrs: led appr 3 out: gng clr whn hit 2 out: sn shkn up: easily* 7/1
0 2 15 **Lake Chapala (IRE)**[20] 2736 6-10-4 **90**........ MissRPLeyshon(7) 92
(Tim Vaughan) *mid-div tl dropped to rr and rdn 5th: hdwy after next: wnt 2nd appr last: styd on but no ch w easy wnr* 14/1
363 3 2¼ **Akinspirit (IRE)**[14] 2851 11-11-5 **105**........(t) MissRDagge(7) 103
(Nikki Evans) *hld up in rr: hdwy after 6th: rdn 3 out: styd on u.p to go 3rd flat* 50/1
6044 4 2¾ **Goal (IRE)**[6] 2987 7-11-9 **105**........(t) MissBHampson(3) 101
(Sally Randell) *cl up: led after 6th tl appr 3 out where lft 2nd: mstke 2 out: sn lost 2nd and no ex* 8/1
5401 5 3½ **Nafaath (IRE)**[22] 2703 9-11-5 **105**........(b) MissAMcCain(7) 97
(Donald McCain) *t.k.h: prom tl led after 3rd: hdd after 6th: wknd 3 out* 5/1[2]
-1F2 6 1 **Scales (IRE)**[6] 2997 9-11-5 **105**........ MissTWorsley(7) 105+
(Kerry Lee) *hld up: hdwy 5th where nt fluent: wnt 2nd 2 out where blnd bdly and lost all ch: styd on flat* 10/3[1]
526- 7 ¾ **Yasir (USA)**[254] 5187 7-11-3 **103**........ MissPFuller(7) 93
(Sophie Leech) *mid-div: hdwy 6th: rdn 3 out: grad wknd* 20/1
P4 8 1¼ **Badilou (FR)**[12] 2880 4-11-7 **105**........ MissBFrost(5) 94
(Martin Hill) *a towards rr: no ch fr 6th: modest hdwy fr 3 out* 6/1[3]
062 9 hd **Guaracha**[14] 2850 4-11-2 **102**........ MissPSkipper(7) 90
(Bill Turner) *chsd ldrs: rdn after 6th: sn wknd* 13/2
0P00 10 3½ **Candelita**[20] 2559 8-10-3 **87**........(v[1]) MissJWalton(5) 72
(Clare Ellam) *a towards rr: rdn and lost tch after 6th* 40/1
P5-P 11 20 **Satu (IRE)**[18] 2765 11-11-3 **101**........ MissLBrooke(5) 66
(Lady Susan Brooke) *mid-div: dropped to rr 6th: sn wl bhd: virtually p.u flat* 66/1
4/05 P **Man Of God (IRE)**[62] 1933 7-10-6 **90**........ MissHLewis(5)
(Tim Vaughan) *t.k.h: prom to 4th: bhd fr 6th: t.o whn p.u bef 3 out* 25/1
5-30 P **Bondi Mist (IRE)**[39] 2349 6-11-4 **104**........(v) MissKatyLyons(7)
(Jonathan Geake) *led tl hdd after 3rd: lost 2nd appr 6th where mstke: wknd qckly: wl bhd whn p.u bef 3 out* 40/1
654 P **Layerthorpe (IRE)**[66] 1866 3-10-6 **103**........ MissJodieHughes(5)
(Debra Hamer) *mid-div: hdwy 6th: sn wknd: wl bhd whn p.u bef 3 out* 25/1

4m 5.2s (15.70) **Going Correction** +1.075s/f (Soft)
WFA 3 from 4yo 13lb 4 from 5yo+ 5lb **14** Ran SP% **118.4**
Speed ratings (Par 105): **103,95,94,93,91 90,90,89,89,87 77,,,**
CSF £89.57 CT £4487.91 TOTE £7.00: £2.50, £4.60, £9.30; EX 90.30 Trifecta £3327.60.
Owner Tony Scrivin **Bred** Darley **Trained** Eastnor, H'fords

FOCUS
A modest lady amateur riders' handicap hurdle but a facile winner

3109 TANNERS CHAMPAGNE H'CAP CHASE (19 fncs) 2m 7f 171y
2:40 (2:41) (Class 3) (0-140,139) 4-Y-0+ £16,245 (£4,770; £2,385; £1,192)

Form RPR
-351 1 **Katkeau (FR)**[29] 2553 8-11-12 **139**........(t) TomScudamore 149+
(David Pipe) *towards rr tl hdwy 2nd: chsd ldr after 11th: led 3 out: j.lft last 2: styd on wl* 6/1[2]
111- 2 5 **Red Devil Lads (IRE)**[248] 5289 6-11-9 **136**........ SeanBowen 143+
(Rebecca Curtis) *tended to jump lft: pckd 1st: cl up tl led after 2nd: hdd 3 out: mstke next: no ex flat* 10/1
04-4 3 13 **Gorsky Island**[42] 2275 7-11-7 **134**........ PaddyBrennan 125
(Tom George) *t.k.h towards rr: hdwy 4th: rdn appr 4 out: sn one pce: tk modest 3rd after 2 out* 6/1[2]
5-03 4 2¼ **The Tourard Man (IRE)**[43] 2260 9-11-8 **138**........ TomBellamy(3) 130+
(Alan King) *mid-div: hdwy to chse ldrs 7th: mstke 3 out: wkng in 3rd whn blnd next* 12/1
P52- 5 4½ **It's A Steal (IRE)**[258] 5109 8-11-3 **130**........(t) AdamWedge 113
(Evan Williams) *s.i.s: in rr: stdy hdwy after 11th: rdn and wknd 4 out* 15/2[3]
64-4 6 2 **Drumshambo (USA)**[19] 2758 9-10-4 **122**........ CharlieDeutsch(5) 103
(Venetia Williams) *prom: mstke 8th: rdn 12th: rdn and wknd appr 4 out* 17/2
P0-4 7 63 **What A Warrior (IRE)**[46] 2187 8-11-12 **139**........(t) HarrySkelton 57
(Dan Skelton) *led tl after 2nd: chsd ldrs tl hmpd and lost pl after 5th: clsd again 10th: struggling fr 12th: lost tch 15th: t.o* 9/2[1]
-P2P P **Handy Andy (IRE)**[8] 2955 9-10-12 **125**........(bt) BrendanPowell
(Colin Tizzard) *chsd ldrs tl lost pl fr 5th: in rr 7th: lost tch 13th: t.o whn p.u bef 4 out* 14/1
-100 P **Azure Fly (IRE)**[32] 2482 7-11-5 **135**........(tp) GrahamWatters(3)
(Charlie Longsdon) *prom: nt fluent 5th and grad lost pl: in rr by 10th: no ch fr 12th: wl bhd whn p.u bef 4 out* 25/1
P0-2 P **Goodtoknow**[14] 2853 7-10-9 **122**........(p) JakeGreenall
(Kerry Lee) *in rr: rdn 12th: mstkes next 2: sn lost tch: wl bhd whn p.u bef 4 out* 15/2[3]
-0P1 P **Gallery Exhibition (IRE)**[23] 2686 8-11-12 **139**........(t) DavidBass
(Kim Bailey) *towards rr: sme hdwy 11th: rdn next: lost tch 14th: t.o whn p.u bef 4 out* 14/1

6m 25.4s (385.40) **11** Ran SP% **114.8**
CSF £62.64 CT £375.25 TOTE £5.80: £2.30, £2.50, £2.10; EX 46.50 Trifecta £170.50.
Owner Prof C Tisdall, J A Gent, R C Wilkin **Bred** P Barthelemy Et Al **Trained** Nicholashayne, Devon

FOCUS
Quite a valuable 122-139 stayers' handicap run at a sound pace. Just five in contention turning for home, but soon just a match. The winner is on the upgrade over fences.

3110 TONY RICKARDS / BRITISH STALLION STUDS EBF MARES' "NATIONAL HUNT" NOVICES' HURDLE (11 hdls) 2m 5f 55y
3:10 (3:10) (Class 4) 4-Y-0+ £5,848 (£1,717; £858; £429)

Form RPR
4-31 1 **Rene's Girl (IRE)**[28] 2579 5-11-3 119........ HarrySkelton 122+
(Dan Skelton) *t.k.h towards rr: hdwy after 8th: chalng whn lft in command 3 out: drew clr fr next: hit last: styd on wl* 9/4[1]
-220 2 6 **Pulling Power**[32] 2486 5-10-10 0........(t) DavidBass 109+
(Kim Bailey) *chsd ldrs tl led 8th: rdn and jnd whn blnd bdly 3 out: no ch w wnr after but kpt on to hold 2nd* 6/1
5-34 3 8 **Iconic Star**[28] 2579 5-10-10 0........ TomO'Brien 99
(Philip Hobbs) *chsd ldrs: hit 8th: sn rdn and lost pl: styd on u.p fr 2 out: wnt 3rd flat* 11/1
40-0 4 ¾ **Morning Herald**[32] 2486 4-10-10 0........ AndrewTinkler 97
(Martin Keighley) *chsd ldrs: nt fluent 7th: rdn appr 3 out: one pce* 12/1
0-53 5 3½ **Miss Crick**[34] 2452 4-10-7 0........ TomBellamy(3) 93
(Alan King) *mid-div: hit 4th: hdwy after 8th: rdn 3 out: sn one pce: wknd and lost 2 pls flat* 11/4[2]
04 6 shd **Nancy's Trix (IRE)**[18] 2776 6-10-5 0........ CiaranGethings(5) 93
(David Loder) *mainly trckd ldr tl rdn and lost a few pls after 8th: one pce fr 3 out* 25/1
350P 7 16 **Kaddys Girl**[41] 2302 5-10-5 0........ ChrisWard(5) 77
(Robin Dickin) *hld up: hdwy after 8th: rdn bef 3 out: grad wknd* 200/1
12 8 17 **Mozo**[15] 2829 4-10-10 0........ TomScudamore 60
(David Pipe) *mid-div: hdwy 7th: in 2nd after 8th tl wknd qckly appr 3 out* 7/2[3]
26-4 9 66 **Timeforfirth (IRE)**[33] 2476 5-10-10 0........ SeanQuinlan
(Jennie Candlish) *a in rr: lost tch 8th: t.o* 66/1
0-04 10 68 **Mari Me Oscar (IRE)**[18] 2770 5-10-5 0........ CharlieDeutsch(5)
(Nikki Evans) *t.k.h early: led tl hdd 8th: sn wknd: t.o* 200/1

5m 36.6s (21.80) **Going Correction** +1.075s/f (Soft)
WFA 4 from 5yo+ 6lb **10** Ran SP% **116.3**
Speed ratings (Par 105): **101,98,95,95,94 94,87,81,56,30**
CSF £16.47 TOTE £3.00: £1.20, £2.40, £3.10; EX 19.30 Trifecta £132.90.
Owner Andy & Sharon Measham **Bred** Michael Hanrahan **Trained** Alcester, Warwicks

FOCUS
A mares' 'NH' novices' hurdle and a useful wide-margin winner.

3111 TANNERS CLARET STANDARD OPEN NATIONAL HUNT FLAT RACE 1m 6f 7y
3:40 (3:40) (Class 4) 4-5-Y-O £3,898 (£1,144; £572; £286)

Form RPR
U 1 **Rather Be (IRE)**[220] [220] 4-11-2 0........................[1] AndrewTinkler 120+
(Nicky Henderson) *hld up: hdwy 4f out: pushed along to chal 2f out: rdn and led 1f out: r.o wl* 6/4[1]
2 3 ¼ **No Comment** 4-11-2 0........................ TomO'Brien 116+
(Philip Hobbs) *hld up in mid-div: hdwy 4f out: led narrowly 2f out: rdn and hdd 1f out: outpcd by wnr but kpt on* 5/2[2]
4-4 3 19 **Officer Hoolihan**[202] [525] 5-11-2 0........................(t) MichaelByrne 93
(Tim Vaughan) *chsd ldrs: rdn over 2f out and outpcd by ldrs: styd on to go 3rd mod 3rd fnl 50yds* 14/1
4 1 ¼ **Big Windmill (IRE)**[206] 4-10-11 0........................ JamieBargary(5) 92
(Tom George) *led: rdn and hdd 2f out: sn outpcd by ldng pair: lost 3rd fnl 50yds* 11/4[3]
0 5 16 **Cordey Warrior**[32] [2493] 5-11-2 0........................ NickScholfield 72
(Victor Dartnall) *t.k.h: trckd ldr tl rdn and wknd 3f out* 50/1
5-0 6 1 ½ **Quarryman**[225] [124] 4-10-9 0........................ HarryCobden(7) 71
(Ron Hodges) *racd keenly: trckd ldrs tl lost pl 5f out: bhd fnl 3f* 33/1
7 ¾ **Kaddys Dream** 4-10-4 0........................ ChrisWard(5) 63
(Robin Dickin) *hld up: hdwy on outside 5f out: wknd 3f out* 18/1
S **Ladybird Blue** 4-10-4 0........................ AliceMills(5)
(Martin Hill) *t.k.h towards rr: rdn 3f out: 5th and no ch whn stmbld and fell jst over 1f out* 33/1

3m 28.7s (15.70) 8 Ran SP% 116.9
CSF £5.49 TOTE £2.20: £1.20, £1.20, £2.80; EX 4.70 Trifecta £33.90.
Owner Matt & Lauren Morgan **Bred** John Hore **Trained** Upper Lambourn, Berks

FOCUS
Probably a fair bumper with the first two home a cut above.
T/Plt: £123.00 to a £1 stake. Pool of £69464.36 - 412.20 winning tickets. T/Qpdt: £61.40 to a £1 stake. Pool of £5278.53 - 63.60 winning tickets. **Richard Lowther**

2778 NEWBURY (L-H)
Wednesday, December 16

OFFICIAL GOING: Soft
Wind: Moderate, across towards stands Weather: Cloudy

3112 BLACKMORE BUILDING JUVENILE HURDLE (8 hdls) 2m 69y
12:10 (12:11) (Class 4) 3-Y-O £3,249 (£954; £477; £238)

Form RPR
1 **Clan Des Obeaux (FR)**[248] 3-10-12 0........................ SamTwiston-Davies 137+
(Paul Nicholls) *t.k.h in 3rd: wnt 2nd at 5th: led 3 out: cruising whn hit last: sn rdn wl clr: impressive* 2/1[2]
1 2 21 **Jaleo (GER)**[14] [2845] 3-11-5 0........................ AidanColeman 122
(John Ferguson) *hld up: hdwy fr 5th: chsd wnr 2 out: easily outpcd run-in* 7/4[1]
5 3 10 **Cobra De Mai (FR)**[42] [2273] 3-10-12 0........................ IanPopham 103
(Dan Skelton) *hld up in rr: hdwy and in tch 3 out: one pce appr last* 14/1
4 4 10 **Fitzwilliam**[19] [2757] 3-10-12 0........................ ConorO'Farrell 95
(Mick Channon) *led: j.lft and hit 1st: sn 5 l clr: hdd 3 out: wknd after next* 20/1
5 28 **Shintori (FR)**[78] 3-10-12 0........................ DarylJacob 65
(Richard Woollacott) *chsd ldr tl 5th: wknd qckly 2 out* 33/1
6 5 **Baraymi (FR)**[174] 3-10-12 0........................ GavinSheehan 60
(Jamie Snowden) *a bhd: no ch fr 5th* 7/1[3]
7 6 **Closer To Home (IRE)**[116] 3-10-9 0........................ KieronEdgar(3) 54
(David Pipe) *nt jump wl: lost tch 5th* 10/1
5 P **Ardamir (FR)**[19] [2757] 3-11-5 0........................ DenisO'Regan
(Alan King) *a towards rr: wl bhd appr 3 out: p.u bef 2 out* 8/1

4m 20.0s (10.00) **Going Correction** +0.80s/f (Soft) 8 Ran SP% 116.8
Speed ratings (Par 104): **107,96,91,86,72 70,67,**
CSF £6.29 TOTE £3.50: £1.20, £1.10, £3.60; EX 6.20 Trifecta £39.80.
Owner Mr & Mrs P K Barber & Potensis Bloodstock Ltd **Bred** Mme Marie Devilder **Trained** Ditcheat, Somerset

FOCUS
Following over 7mm of overnight rain the ground was described as soft, heavy in places on the hurdle course. Rail movements meant this race was 109yds further than advertised. Sam Twiston-Davies reported: "It's soft. The bit of rain has left it loose and it's hard work." Not too much in the way of strength in depth, but a taking performance from the winner who won with a good deal in hand. The gallop was reasonable in the conditions.

3113 CSP NOVICES' LIMITED H'CAP CHASE (18 fncs) 2m 7f 86y
12:40 (12:40) (Class 3) (0-135,133) 4-Y-O+ £6,498 (£1,908; £954; £477)

Form RPR
312- 1 **Local Show (IRE)**[288] [4547] 7-11-0 125........................ NicodeBoinville 144+
(Ben Pauling) *j.rt: mde all: in control fr 2 out: styd on wl* 7/2[2]
2-05 2 13 **Wuff (IRE)**[20] [2724] 7-11-2 127........................(tp) SamTwiston-Davies 133
(Paul Nicholls) *prom: 2nd and hld whn mstke 2 out and j.rt last* 5/2[1]
P-23 3 7 **Minella On Line (IRE)**[38] [2367] 6-11-2 127........................ WayneHutchinson 126
(Rebecca Curtis) *hld up: mstke 12th: shkn up and wnt prom 14th: one pce 2 out: 3rd and btn whn mstke last* 7/1
-1F4 4 6 **Gentleman Jon**[20] [2733] 7-11-1 126........................(t) DarylJacob 115
(Colin Tizzard) *hld up in tch: rdn 5th: tl outpcd fr 3 out* 16/1
12-1 5 2 **Blameitalonmyroots (IRE)**[18] [2764] 5-10-11 122........................ LeightonAspell 109
(Oliver Sherwood) *a abt same pl: outpcd and btn 3 out* 9/2[3]
0-30 6 8 **Invicta Lake (IRE)**[32] [2484] 8-10-13 124........................ DenisO'Regan 103
(Suzy Smith) *t.k.h in rr: struggling fr 13th* 20/1
3415 7 76 **Shah Of Persia**[29] [2557] 8-10-10 121........................(tp) GavinSheehan 24
(Warren Greatrex) *in rr: j. slowly 3rd: wl bhd fr 9th* 25/1
-22P P **Atlantic Roller (IRE)**[15] [2832] 8-10-12 123........................ TomCannon
(Chris Gordon) *in tch tl wknd 13th: wl bhd whn p.u bef next* 20/1
-322 U **Delgany Demon**[25] [2631] 7-11-8 133........................ TrevorWhelan
(Neil King) *prom tl j.lft and wknd 13th: 7th and no ch whn blnd and uns rdr next* 8/1
-P1P P **Whats Left (IRE)**[43] [2261] 7-11-1 126........................ NoelFehily
(Neil Mulholland) *a bhd: t.o whn p.u bef 14th* 14/1

6m 18.7s (12.70) **Going Correction** +0.80s/f (Soft) 10 Ran SP% 118.5
Speed ratings (Par 107): **109,104,102,99,99 96,70,,,**
CSF £13.09 CT £58.48 TOTE £4.30: £1.60, £1.50, £2.60; EX 14.90 Trifecta £96.60.
Owner Nicholas Piper & Claire E Piper **Bred** J J Harty **Trained** Bourton-On-The-Water, Gloucs

FOCUS
A useful handicap in which the gallop was sound throughout. The race was run 72yds further than advertised.

3114 EVENTS BAR MANAGEMENT MAIDEN HURDLE (8 hdls) 2m 69y
1:15 (1:15) (Class 4) 4-Y-O+ £3,249 (£954; £477; £238)

Form RPR
13-2 1 **Wait For Me (FR)**[19] [2763] 5-11-0 0........................ RichardJohnson 139+
(Philip Hobbs) *t.k.h: in tch: chal and blnd 3 out: led 2 out: j.lft last: drvn clr* 30/100[1]
12 2 7 **Potters Legend**[31] [2514] 5-11-0 0........................ LeightonAspell 131+
(Lucy Wadham) *t.k.h: prom: slt ld 3 out tl j.lft 2 out: one pce run-in* 3/1[2]
6-F0 3 24 **Kid Kalanisi (IRE)**[19] [2763] 4-11-0 0........................ RobertDunne 104
(Dan Skelton) *hld up in rr: stdy late hdwy whn mstke last: styd on to take 3rd run-in: nvr rchd chalng position* 100/1
63-5 4 5 **Church Leap (IRE)**[23] [2683] 4-11-0 0........................ NicodeBoinville 99
(Patrick Chamings) *mid-div: effrt 5th: no imp 3 out* 12/1[3]
5 2 ¾ **Fire Ship**[42] 6-11-0 0........................ RichieMcLernon 95
(Brendan Powell) *t.k.h in rr: stdy hdwy into midfield 3 out: shkn up next: no further prog* 12/1[3]
P5 6 hd **Allee Bleue (IRE)**[20] [2723] 5-11-0 0........................ JamesBest 97
(Philip Hobbs) *led tl 3 out: 3rd and btn whn blnd next: wknd* 100/1
4-25 7 7 **Blue April (FR)**[21] [2710] 4-10-11 0........................ MattGriffiths(3) 88
(Jeremy Scott) *prom tl wknd appr 3 out* 33/1
2640 8 1 ¼ **Tanarpino**[13] [2860] 4-11-0 0........................ HenryBrooke 87
(Jennie Candlish) *towards rr: mod effrt and rdn 3 out: nvr trbld ldrs* 100/1
50 9 6 **Brown Bear (IRE)**[42] [2267] 4-11-0 0........................ TomCannon 81
(Nick Gifford) *mid-div: wknd 5th: sn bhd* 66/1
0 10 4 ½ **The Minkle (IRE)**[20] [2731] 4-11-0 0........................ ConorO'Farrell 76
(David Pipe) *a towards rr: last and rdn 5th: n.d after* 100/1
66P/ 11 3 **Primo Milano**[600] [5548] 6-10-9 0........................ ConorRing(5) 73
(Evan Williams) *chsd ldr tl wknd 3rd: wknd 5th* 100/1
05 12 6 **Hallingham**[11] [2898] 5-11-0 0........................ MarcGoldstein 67
(Chris Gordon) *nvr nr ldrs: mstke 5th: sn bhd* 100/1
4 13 20 **On Demand**[22] [2699] 4-10-7 0........................ JamesDavies 40
(Simon Hodgson) *t.k.h: in tch tl wknd appr 3 out: wl bhd whn blnd next* 100/1
14 8 **Camakasi (IRE)**[111] 4-11-0 0........................ GavinSheehan 39
(Ali Stronge) *chsd ldrs: mstkes 1st and 2nd: wknd 3 out* 33/1
P **Emilio Largo**[53] 7-11-0 0........................ DenisO'Regan
(Mark Pitman) *a bhd: t.o whn p.u bef last* 50/1

4m 23.1s (13.10) **Going Correction** +0.80s/f (Soft) 15 Ran SP% 133.6
Speed ratings (Par 105): **99,95,83,81,79 79,76,75,72,70 68,65,55,51,**
CSF £1.92 TOTE £1.20: £1.10, £1.20, £16.30; EX 2.10 Trifecta £63.50.
Owner Andrew L Cohen **Bred** Haras D'Etreham **Trained** Withycombe, Somerset

FOCUS
The betting suggested this was a two-horse race and that's how it turned out with the two market leaders pulling well clear in last quarter-mile. The gallop was a reasonable one and the winner was building on his hurdle debut run. The race was 109yds further than advertised.

3115 POWERSOLVE ELECTRONICS GREATWOOD CHARITY H'CAP CHASE (13 fncs) 2m 92y
1:50 (1:53) (Class 4) (0-120,120) 4-Y-O+ £4,548 (£1,335; £667; £333)

Form RPR
0-31 1 **Exmoor Mist**[13] [2859] 7-11-2 110........................(t) DenisO'Regan 126+
(Victor Dartnall) *in tch: pressed ldrs 6th: carried rt and bmpd after last: sn led: drvn out* 9/4[1]
-554 2 1 **Mr Burbidge**[42] [2266] 7-11-10 118........................(p) MarkQuinlan 131
(Neil Mulholland) *led tl 4th: mstke and led 9th: hrd rdn 2 out: edgd rt and bmpd after last: sn hdd: hit on* 8/1
-22F 3 18 **Val D'Arc (FR)**[30] [2546] 6-11-7 115........................ AlainCawley 111
(Richard Hobson) *pressed ldr: led 4th tl 9th: wknd 2 out* 9/2[3]
1035 4 6 **Venetian Lad**[30] [2546] 10-11-2 110........................ MarcGoldstein 99
(Lydia Richards) *chsd ldrs: outpcd and dropped to last after 8th: n.d after: wnt modest 4th run-in* 25/1
/0-1 5 1 ¾ **Allow Dallow (IRE)**[25] [2645] 8-11-11 119........................ JoshuaMoore 106
(Jonjo O'Neill) *hld up in 6th: hdwy to chse ldrs 4 out: wknd 2 out* 3/1[2]
245P 6 ¾ **Very Noble (FR)**[36] [2418] 6-11-0 108........................(t) TomCannon 96
(Chris Gordon) *chsd ldrs: rdn 9th: wknd 2 out* 16/1
40-5 P **Tresor De Bontee (FR)**[36] [2419] 8-11-12 120........................(p) RichardJohnson
(Kerry Lee) *j. modestly in rr: blnd bdly 2nd: wl bhd fr 4 out: p.u bef 2 out* 9/2[3]

4m 23.0s (15.00) **Going Correction** +0.80s/f (Soft) 7 Ran SP% 113.0
Speed ratings (Par 105): **94,93,84,81,80 80,**
CSF £19.49 TOTE £2.80: £1.80, £4.00; EX 17.90 Trifecta £60.50.
Owner Exmoor Mist Partnership **Bred** I M Ham **Trained** Brayford, Devon

FOCUS
A fair handicap in which the first two, who are both on the upgrade, deserve credit for pulling clear over the last two fences. A reasonable gallop steadied starting the final circuit. Rail movements meant this race was run 47yds further than advertised.

3116 DAVID MARTIN GRADUATION CHASE (18 fncs) 2m 7f 86y
2:25 (2:26) (Class 2) 4-Y-O+ £14,427 (£5,247)

Form RPR
15/P 1 **O'Faolains Boy (IRE)**[25] [2633] 8-11-7 150........................ NoelFehily 163+
(Rebecca Curtis) *j.w: t.k.h: led 2nd: tiring appr last: styd on gamely and drew clr run-in* 10/3[3]
F-P1 2 15 **Sausalito Sunrise (IRE)**[32] [2482] 7-11-7 150........................ RichardJohnson 151
(Philip Hobbs) *t.k.h in rr: chsd wnr 7th: 4 l 2nd and rdn whn mstke 3 out: one pce* 11/8[1]
UP-4 P **Kaysersberg (FR)**[44] [2241] 8-11-0 143........................ GavinSheehan
(Warren Greatrex) *led tl 2nd: dropped to last at 7th: no ch whn blnd 12th: p.u bef 14th* 8/1
51-2 P **Arpege D'Alene (FR)**[39] [2347] 5-10-10 0........................(t) SamTwiston-Davies
(Paul Nicholls) *cl up: mstke and hrd rdn 11th: wknd 14th: 3rd and wkng whn j. slowly and p.u 4 out* 2/1[2]

6m 17.31s (11.31) **Going Correction** +0.80s/f (Soft) 4 Ran SP% 109.6
Speed ratings (Par 109): **112,106,,**
CSF £8.64 TOTE £4.10; EX 6.90.
Owner Trembath, Hyde, Outhart & Hill **Bred** Tom And P Phelan **Trained** Newport, Pembrokeshire

FOCUS
Past winners include good-quality performers Carruthers, Restless Harry and Time For Rupert and, although only two finished, this year's victor looks well up to scratch. He has been rated back to his RSA mark. The gallop was an ordinary one and the race was run 72yds further than advertised.

3117 BRITISH STALLION STUDS EBF "NATIONAL HUNT" NOVICES' HURDLE (QUALIFIER) (10 hdls) 2m 2f 183y
3:00 (3:01) (Class 4) 4-6-Y-O **£3,898** (£1,144; £572; £286)

Form RPR
012 1 **Charmix (FR)**[20] 2723 5-11-5 0 NoelFehily 144+
(Harry Fry) *racd on inner: pressed ldr: led 3rd: clr 2 out: comf* 5/2[2]
0-23 2 17 **Big Chief Benny (IRE)**[19] 2763 4-10-12 0 WayneHutchinson 119
(Alan King) *chsd ldrs: mstke 3 out: wnt 2nd appr next: rdn and no imp* 7/4[1]
1 3 21 **Emerging Force (IRE)**[31] 2519 5-11-5 0 GavinSheehan 106
(Harry Whittington) *racd wd: led tl 3rd: pressed wnr tl 3 out: 3rd and btn whn mstke next: tired run-in: jst hld 3rd* 7/4[1]
0 4 ½ **Cottstown Fox (IRE)**[20] 2731 6-10-12 0 MarkQuinlan 96
(Neil Mulholland) *t.k.h in 5th: mstke 5th: btn 3 out: 4th and no ch whn j.lft last* 100/1
252- P **Rude And Crude (IRE)**[303] 4271 6-10-12 0 TomCannon
(Chris Gordon) *in tch tl wknd 3 out: 5th and no ch whn p.u after next* 10/1[3]
4/65 P **Max The Minister**[26] 2612 5-10-12 0 NicodeBoinville
(Hughie Morrison) *towards rr: mstke 7th: 6th and no ch whn p.u bef 3 out* 33/1
2-16 F **Political Quiz**[28] 2581 5-11-5 0 JamesDavies
(Tom Symonds) *mid-div whn fell 2nd* 33/1
00 P **Never Learn (IRE)**[18] 2791 4-10-12 0 SamTwiston-Davies
(Colin Tizzard) *a bhd: t.o fr 7th: p.u bef last* 66/1
44 P **Nordical (IRE)**[117] 1305 5-10-7 0 (t) ConorRing(5)
(Evan Williams) *a bhd: t.o fr 6th: p.u bef last* 100/1
360U P **Acajou Des Bieffes (FR)**[20] 2723 5-10-12 0 RyanMahon
(Anthony Honeyball) *in tch tl 4th: wl bhd fr 7th: t.o whn p.u bef last* 100/1
3P P **Spoilt Rotten**[48] 2154 6-10-12 0 DenisO'Regan
(Mark Pitman) *a wl bhd: t.o whn blnd 6th: p.u bef last* 100/1

4m 59.9s (11.90) **Going Correction** +0.80s/f (Soft)
WFA 4 from 5yo+ 5lb **11** Ran SP% **121.7**
Speed ratings: **106,98,90,89, , , , ,**
CSF £7.80 TOTE £3.50: £1.10, £1.20, £1.10; EX 8.60 Trifecta £16.30.
Owner Nicholas Cooper **Bred** Mlle Viviane Pedron & Philippe Mehat **Trained** Seaborough, Dorset

FOCUS
Not the most competitive of novice hurdles for the course, but a very useful performance from the wide-margin winner. The gallop was fair. Rail movements meant 109yds were added to the length of this contest.

3118 NEWBURYRACECOURSE.CO.UK FILLIES' "JUNIOR" STANDARD OPEN NATIONAL HUNT FLAT RACE 1m 4f 143y
3:30 (3:31) (Class 6) 3-Y-O **£1,711** (£498; £249)

Form RPR
1 **Woolstone One** 3-10-12 0 GavinSheehan 117+
(Harry Whittington) *t.k.h: in tch: led on bit over 3f out: shkn up over 1f out: edgd lft: r.o wl* 11/4[2]
2 3¼ **Little Miss Poet** 3-10-12 0 RichardJohnson 110
(Philip Hobbs) *hld up towards rr: hdwy 4f out: drvn to chse wnr over 2f out: kpt on wl: a hld* 13/8[1]
3 30 **Crazy Queen** 3-10-5 0 GrahamCarson(7) 68
(Anthony Carson) *led tl over 3f out: sn outpcd* 25/1
4 1½ **Potters Lady Jane** 3-10-12 0 LeightonAspell 66
(Lucy Wadham) *in tch: effrt and disp 2nd 3f out: sn outpcd* 4/1[3]
3 5 8 **Clanville Lass**[28] 2583 3-10-12 0 NoelFehily 55
(Ali Stronge) *chsd ldr tl 4f out: wknd 3f out* 12/1
6 26 **Parisian Star** 3-10-12 0 AidanColeman 19
(J R Jenkins) *a bhd: no ch fnl 3f* 12/1
7 1 **Choochoobugaloo** 3-10-12 0 JamesDavies 17
(Tom Symonds) *chsd ldrs tl hrd rdn and wknd 3f out* 25/1
53 8 2¾ **Purple Genie (GR)**[41] 2304 3-10-12 0 NicodeBoinville 14
(Patrick Chamings) *prom tl wknd over 4f out* 9/1
9 6 **Grumpy Jackie** 3-10-9 0 KieronEdgar(3)
(Chris Down) *a bhd: no ch fnl 4f* 33/1
0 10 77 **Secretsista**[18] 2777 3-10-12 0 HenryBrooke
(Jennie Candlish) *dropped to last after 5f: sn t.o* 100/1

3m 12.0s (6.20) **10** Ran SP% **121.8**
CSF £7.77 TOTE £3.90: £1.50, £1.10, £6.50; EX 9.10 Trifecta £123.80.
Owner Paul G Jacobs **Bred** D R Tucker **Trained** Sparsholt, Oxfordshire

FOCUS
A race lacking in strength but the first two, who pulled a long way clear, look useful prospects. The gallop was an ordinary one and this race was run 109yds further than advertised.
T/Plt: £24.10 to a £1 stake. Pool of £73260.01 - 2217.91 winning units. T/Qpdt: £12.00 to a £1 stake. Pool of £4620.30 - 284.75 - winning units. **Lee McKenzie**

2876 EXETER (R-H)
Thursday, December 17
OFFICIAL GOING: Heavy (chs 6.2; hdl; 6.1)
Wind: fair breeze half across Weather: light rain with heavy fog at times

3119 FREE SPINS AT 188BET CASINO MARES' NOVICES' HURDLE (10 hdls) 2m 2f 111y
12:50 (12:50) (Class 4) 4-Y-0+ **£3,249** (£954; £477; £238)

Form RPR
41 1 **Jessber's Dream (IRE)**[23] 2697 5-11-2 0 (t) NoelFehily 124+
(Harry Fry) *trckd ldrs: chal 7th: led 2 out: shkn up to assert run-in: styd on wl* 8/11[1]
10 2 1¼ **Robinesse (IRE)**[33] 2486 4-10-10 0 LeightonAspell 114
(Oliver Sherwood) *trckd ldr: led 6th: hdd 2 out: sn rdn: styd on but a being hld run-in* 5/1[3]
3 23 **Cailleach Annie (IRE)**[221] 6-10-10 0 (t) JamesBest 94
(Jackie Du Plessis) *hld up: prog u.p after 7th: wnt 3rd next: wkng whn nt fluent 2 out* 25/1
250 4 12 **Hello Jazz**[33] 2486 5-10-3 0 MrMLegg(7) 83
(John Ryall) *trckd ldrs: reminders after 6th: cl 3rd appr 3 out: sn rdn: wknd bef 2 out* 25/1
0-24 5 32 **Eardisland**[35] 2452 5-10-10 115 (t) RichardJohnson 47
(Philip Hobbs) *trckd ldrs: rdn appr 3 out: sn wknd: t.o* 3/1[2]
F-50 6 7 **Lady Helissio**[40] 2345 5-10-10 0 MarkQuinlan 40
(Neil Mulholland) *led: wandered bdly at her hurdles at times: stmbld bdly 4th: hdd 6th: wknd after next: tailing off whn blnd 3 out* 200/1
00 7 2¼ **Arty Bella**[13] 2879 4-10-3 0 PaulO'Brien(7) 38
(Jimmy Frost) *a towards rr: wknd after 7th: t.o* 200/1
06 8 ½ **Gold Bonne Raine (IRE)**[25] 2665 4-10-10 0 AdamWedge 37
(Evan Williams) *a towards rr: wknd 7th: t.o* 50/1
0 P **Berwin (IRE)**[170] 860 6-10-10 0 DenisO'Regan
(Sarah Robinson) *j. bdly lft and nvr that fluent: a bhd: t.o after 5th: p.u after 7th* 250/1
4 P **Baby Bee Jay**[215] 334 4-10-10 0 SamTwiston-Davies
(Nigel Twiston-Davies) *in tch tl wknd after 6th: t.o whn p.u bef 3 out* 8/1

5m 0.3s (17.60) **Going Correction** +1.075s/f (Soft)
WFA 4 from 5yo+ 5lb **10** Ran SP% **121.7**
Speed ratings (Par 105): **105,104,94,89,76 73,72,72, ,**
CSF £5.39 TOTE £1.60: £1.02, £1.60, £9.60; EX 5.00 Trifecta £80.10.
Owner Chris Giles & Potensis Bloodstock Ltd **Bred** Denis Noonan **Trained** Seaborough, Dorset

FOCUS
All races were run on the chase course bend turning into the home straight, with the distance of the opener increased by 65yds. Noel Fehily described the ground as "heavy and hard work". No great depth to this mares' hurdle and the front pair came clear. The winner was building on her recent win

3120 WATCH RACINGUK WITH FREE TRIAL NOW H'CAP HURDLE (8 hdls) 2m 175y
1:20 (1:20) (Class 3) (0-130,130) 3-Y-O+ **£5,991** (£1,860; £1,001)

Form RPR
6601 1 **For Good Measure (IRE)**[9] 2961 4-11-2 120 7ex RichardJohnson 127+
(Philip Hobbs) *trckd ldrs: led in home st: v easily* 4/11[1]
0052 2 3¼ **Benbecula**[28] 2600 6-10-11 118 (b) TomBellamy(3) 115
(Richard Mitchell) *led: rdn and hdd in home st: no ch w wnr but rallied bk into 2nd cl home* 11/2[3]
646- 3 ¾ **Jumps Road**[240] 5441 8-11-12 130 (t) NoelFehily 126
(Colin Tizzard) *trckd ldrs: jnd ldr 3rd tl 5th: rdn to chse wnr in home st: no ex whn lost 2nd cl home* 5/1[2]
PPP5 P **Exiles Return (IRE)**[13] 2880 13-9-7 104 oh40 ThomasCheesman(7)
(Jackie Retter) *racd keenly: trckd ldr: jnd ldr 3rd tl 5th: sn wknd: p.u 3 out* 200/1

(-255.50) course record
WFA 4 from 6yo+ 5lb **4** Ran SP% **105.9**
CSF £2.74 TOTE £1.20; EX 2.80 Trifecta £3.50.
Owner John P McManus **Bred** Sunnyhill Stud **Trained** Withycombe, Somerset

FOCUS
Race distance increased by 65yds. Visibility for this race was poor, with the runners disappearing from sight as they turned in and only coming back into view on the run-in, by which time the favourite, who was well in on his recent win, had things well under control.

3121 188BET GRADUATION CHASE (12 fncs) 2m 1f 109y
1:50 (1:50) (Class 2) 4-Y-0+ **£12,820** (£4,004; £2,156)

Form RPR
P-31 1 **Kylemore Lough**[33] 2489 6-11-0 145 JamieMoore 149+
(Kerry Lee) *trckd ldrs: wnt 2nd after 4th: chal after 8th: led 4 out: clr whn rdn after 3 out: runner-up clsng but enough in hand and a holding on fr last: drvn out* 5/4[1]
4342 2 2½ **Dunraven Storm (IRE)**[26] 2635 10-11-7 149 RichardJohnson 150
(Philip Hobbs) *led: rdn: hdd and hit 4 out where wnt rt: looking hld whn wnt rt and nt that fluent 3 out: rallied after 2 out but a being hld fr last* 15/8[2]
1U-2 3 69 **Cash And Go (IRE)**[227] 99 8-11-7 145 LiamTreadwell 81
(Venetia Williams) *trckd ldrs: blnd 1st: wnt 3rd but losing tch after 8th: j.rt and n.d fr 4 out: t.o* 8/1
63-3 P **Solar Impulse (FR)**[27] 2625 5-11-4 146 (tp) SamTwiston-Davies
(Paul Nicholls) *trckd ldr tl after 3rd: drvn after 5th: wknd after 8th: t.o whn p.u bef 4 out* 5/1[3]

4m 46.4s (27.40) **Going Correction** +1.525s/f (Heav) **4** Ran SP% **107.0**
Speed ratings (Par 109): **96,94,62,**
CSF £4.00 TOTE £2.40; EX 3.30 Trifecta £12.80.
Owner M J McMahon & Denis Gallagher **Bred** M J McMahon **Trained** Byton, H'fords

FOCUS
Race distance increased by 29yds. A decent graduation chase. The market got it right and the front pair came a long way clear. The winner is a bit better than the bare result.

3122 EBF/TBA MARES' NOVICES' CHASE (15 fncs) 2m 3f 48y
2:20 (2:20) (Class 3) 4-Y-0+ **£6,498** (£1,908; £954; £477)

Form RPR
131- 1 **Bitofapuzzle**[256] 5175 7-11-0 0 (t) NoelFehily 147+
(Harry Fry) *j.w: mde all: clr fr 8th: unchal* 1/2[1]
6-35 2 11 **Kayfleur**[24] 2685 6-11-0 0 RichardJohnson 127
(Henry Daly) *hld up: hdwy into 2nd 11th: rdn bef next: nvr on terms w wnr: styd on same pce* 20/1
P-21 3 10 **Cresswell Breeze**[28] 2602 5-11-6 130 (t) AidanColeman 127
(Anthony Honeyball) *trckd wnr: mstke 4th: rdn in 3rd after 11th: styd on same pce fr 4 out* 4/1[2]
0-10 4 7 **Dark Spirit (IRE)**[33] 2484 7-11-0 0 AdamWedge 110
(Evan Williams) *trckd ldrs: rdn after 11th: wknd bef next* 6/1[3]
324- P **Red Penny (IRE)**[260] 5098 8-10-7 0 MissBFrost(7)
(Jimmy Frost) *trckd ldrs tl wknd after 11th: t.o whn p.u bef next* 100/1
2-62 P **Dolores Delightful (FR)**[39] 2365 5-11-0 118 LeightonAspell
(Nick Williams) *trckd ldrs tl wknd 11th: t.o whn wnt rt and hit 4 out: sn p.u* 20/1

5m 17.9s (20.60) **Going Correction** +1.525s/f (Heav) **6** Ran SP% **111.5**
Speed ratings (Par 107): **117,112,108,105,**
CSF £11.26 TOTE £1.30: £1.10, £4.10; EX 8.00 Trifecta £37.00.
Owner Potensis Bloodstock Ltd & Chris Giles **Bred** R J & S A Carter **Trained** Seaborough, Dorset

FOCUS
Race distance increased by 29yds. A good mares' chase and a really impressive performance from the returning favourite, who has been rated in line with the best of her hurdles form.

3123 188BET.CO.UK H'CAP CHASE (QUALIFIER FOR THE CHALLENGER MIDDLE DISTANCE CHASE SERIES FINAL) (15 fncs) 2m 3f 48y
2:50 (2:50) (Class 4) (0-120,118) 4-Y-O+ **£3,994** (£1,240; £667)

Form RPR

25-0 **1** **Long John**[204] 514 8-10-11 **103**............................... JamesBest 113+
(Jackie Du Plessis) *cl up: wnt 3rd 11th: led travelling best 4 out: in command fr next: easily* **10/1**

/64U **2** *12* **Red Riverman**[7] 2989 7-11-11 **117**.....................(v) SamTwiston-Davies 112
(Nigel Twiston-Davies) *cl up: led after 11th: hdd next: sn rdn and hld: styd on same pce* **15/2**

253- **3** *57* **Sunny Ledgend**[250] 5279 10-10-12 **111**.............................. MrJMartin(7) 49
(Andrew J Martin) *sn trcking ldrs: hit 6th: wknd after 11th: t.o* **8/1**

23-2 **P** **Tolkeins Tango (IRE)**[29] 2568 7-11-12 **118**.....................(t) DenisO'Regan
(Victor Dartnall) *cl up: niggled along fr 8th: rdn after 11th: sn btn: t.o whn p.u 3 out* **5/2**[2]

U6-P **P** **Our Cat (IRE)**[45] 2243 7-11-4 **113**...........................(t) ConorShoemark(3)
(Fergal O'Brien) *led: rdn and hdd after 11th: sn wknd: p.u after next* **11/2**[3]

4-3F **P** **Bilbrook Blaze**[13] 2885 5-11-9 **115**.............................. RichardJohnson
(Philip Hobbs) *prom tl lost pl qckly after 8th: t.o whn p.u after 11th* **2/1**[1]

5m 30.7s (33.40) **Going Correction** +1.525s/f (Heav) **6** Ran SP% **109.3**
Speed ratings (Par 105): **90,84,60,** ,
CSF £69.77 TOTE £12.40: £5.10, £2.50; EX 70.00 Trifecta £325.20.
Owner R J Reip, M Stevenson **Bred** Parman Group Ltd **Trained** Trehan, Cornwall

FOCUS
Race distance increased by 29yds. Only three managed to complete in what was a modest chase, with the outsiders dominating.

3124 FREE BET AT 188BET MAIDEN HURDLE (12 hdls) 2m 7f 25y
3:20 (3:20) (Class 4) 4-Y-O+ **£3,249** (£954; £477; £238)

Form RPR

303 **1** **You Say What (IRE)**[9] 2965 5-11-0 0........................ TrevorWhelan 118+
(Neil King) *cl up: hdwy 3 out: led 2 out: sn clr: comf* **9/1**

5 **2** *9* **A Plein Temps (FR)**[43] 2275 5-11-0 0............................... NoelFehily 106
(Harry Fry) *prom: led appr 3 out: u.p whn hdd and hit 2 out: sn hld: styd on same pce* **13/8**[1]

5 **3** *8* **Highway Storm (IRE)**[36] 2440 5-11-0 0....................... LeightonAspell 100
(Rebecca Curtis) *led: nt fluent 7th: rdn and hdd appr 3 out: sn one pce* **4/1**[3]

0-3F **4** *9* **According To Harry (IRE)**[7] 2986 6-11-0 0................ RichardJohnson 90
(Philip Hobbs) *trckd ldrs: rdn appr 3 out: nt pce to threaten: fdd after 2 out* **5/2**[2]

-6P0 **5** *1 1/2* **Motts Cross (IRE)**[28] 2603 4-10-11 0........................ GilesHawkins(3) 88
(Chris Down) *in tch: rdn after 8th: wknd after next* **33/1**

6 *42* **Sweettoothtommy (IRE)**[256] 5-10-11 0......................... KieronEdgar(3) 46
(David Pipe) *trckd ldrs: rdn appr 3 out: wknd qckly: t.o* **11/2**

00 **7** *12* **Trehan Cross**[14] 2870 6-10-7 0................................... JamesBest 27
(Jackie Du Plessis) *struggling in rr fr 6th: t.o* **100/1**

P/0 **P** **Midnight Hop**[36] 2444 8-10-0 0......................... ThomasCheesman(7)
(Nick Ayliffe) *cl up tl struggling 7th: sn wknd: t.o whn p.u bef 3 out* **200/1**

6m 39.3s (40.30) **Going Correction** +1.825s/f (Heav)
WFA 4 from 5yo+ 6lb **8** Ran SP% **116.5**
Speed ratings (Par 105): **102,98,96,92,92 77,73,**
CSF £25.45 TOTE £10.20: £3.00, £1.10, £2.00; EX 30.90 Trifecta £150.30.
Owner Turner Webb **Bred** W Dillon **Trained** Barbury Castle, Wiltshire

FOCUS
Race distance increased by 120yds. Ordinary maiden hurdle form and they finished quite strung out. The winner has been rated similar to his Ffos Las bumper run.

3125 25% OFF NYD TICKETS UNTIL CHRISTMAS EVE AMATEUR RIDERS' H'CAP HURDLE (10 hdls 1 omitted) 2m 5f 135y
3:50 (3:50) (Class 5) (0-100,103) 3-Y-O+ **£2,183** (£677; £338; £169)

Form RPR

004- **1** **Mogestic (IRE)**[257] 5148 6-10-13 **92**...................... MrStanSheppard(5) 99
(Seamus Mullins) *mid-div in chsng gp tl dropped to rr after 4th: hdwy after 8th: chsd ldr after last (usual 2 out): 4 l down by-passing omitted last: str run fnl 140yds to ld towards fin* **7/1**[3]

2005 **2** *1 1/4* **Warsaw Pact (IRE)**[35] 2453 12-9-7 **74** oh2.................. MrBParis-Crofts(7) 79
(Steven Dixon) *clr w one other setting decent pce: rdn appr 2 out (usual 3 out): 4 l clr by-passing omitted last: no ex whn hdd towards fin* **16/1**

-1P4 **3** *12* **Hi Bronco**[25] 2661 8-9-11 **74**...........................(p) MrMLegg(3) 67
(John Ryall) *led chsng gp tl rdn after 6th: styd on at same pce wout ever threatening fr 2 out (usual 3 out): wnt 3rd towards fin* **9/2**[2]

3031 **4** *1* **Thepartysover**[9] 2958 10-11-8 **103** 7ex......................(t) MrGTreacy(7) 100+
(Paul Henderson) *w.r.s: bhd: gd hdwy fr 5th: trckd ldr 2 out: blnd last: sn rdn and hld: no ex whn lost 3rd towards fin* **3/1**[1]

1500 **5** *15* **Karl Marx (IRE)**[13] 2880 5-10-8 **89**.......................(b) MrTGillard(7) 66
(Mark Gillard) *trckd ldrs in chsng gp: rdn after 8th: wknd next* **16/1**

45-3 **6** *24* **Proud Times (USA)**[17] 2826 9-11-4 **97**...............(p) MrJoshuaNewman(5) 50
(Ali Stronge) *chsd ldr clr of remainder tl rdn after 8th: sn wknd: t.o* **7/1**[3]

06-6 **7** *hd* **Lily Mars (IRE)**[24] 2693 8-9-7 **74** oh3...................(tp) MrRexDingle(7) 27
(Neil Mulholland) *hmpd s: sn mid-div: wknd bef 2 out: t.o* **22/1**

6460 **8** *1* **I'llhavealook (IRE)**[90] 1579 10-11-4 **99**....................(p) MissPFuller(7) 51
(Katie Stephens) *led chsng gp tl after 7th: sn rdn: wknd after next: t.o* **16/1**

5506 **P** **Archie Rice (USA)**[15] 2850 9-11-7 **100**........................ MissBFrost(5)
(Jimmy Frost) *mid-div tl wknd 7th: t.o whn p.u after 2 out (usual 3 out)* **16/1**

-30P **P** **Unefille De Guye (FR)**[42] 2298 7-9-12 **79**..............(t) MrSeanHoulihan(7)
(Victor Dartnall) *mid-div in chsng gp: drvn after 8th: sn wknd: t.o whn p.u bef next* **8/1**

0P4 **F** **Tuffstuff**[16] 2841 7-11-3 **98**.................................(t) MrEDoggrell(7)
(Brian Barr) *chsd ldrs in chsng gp: rdn after 8th: wknd next: btn 6th whn fell heavily last (usually 2 out)* **12/1**

6U04 **P** **Arthur's Queen (FR)**[13] 2876 4-10-7 **86**................. MrRobertHawker(5)
(Carroll Gray) *mstkes and nvr fluent: a in rr: t.o whn p.u after 2 out (usual 3 out)* **20/1**

0-0F **P** **Blackdown Babe**[29] 2563 7-9-9 **74**.......................... MrMartinMcIntyre(5)
(Kevin Bishop) *hmpd s: a in rr: t.o whn p.u after 2 out (usual 3 out)* **50/1**

6m 11.4s (38.40) **Going Correction** +1.825s/f (Heav)
WFA 4 from 5yo+ 6lb **13** Ran SP% **121.6**
Speed ratings (Par 103): **103,102,98,97,92 83,83,83,** ,
CSF £110.58 CT £568.26 TOTE £7.50: £2.70, £3.50, £2.00; EX 125.60 Trifecta £986.60.
Owner Andrew Cocks And Tara Johnson **Bred** Mick Berry **Trained** Wilsford-Cum-Lake, Wilts

FOCUS
Race distance increased by 120yds. The final hurdle had to be omitted second time around for what was a moderate handicap hurdle.
T/Plt: £107.70 to a £1 stake. Pool: £49,990.19 - 338.56 winning units. T/Qpdt: £107.50 to a £1 stake. Pool: £3,225.96 - 22.20 winning units. **Tim Mitchell**

2298 TOWCESTER (R-H)
Thursday, December 17

OFFICIAL GOING: Soft (7.9)
Wind: Fresh across Weather: Overcast

3126 BET TOTEPLACEPOT NOVICES' HURDLE (11 hdls) 2m 4f 217y
12:40 (12:40) (Class 4) 4-Y-O+ **£3,898** (£1,144; £572; £286)

Form RPR

F-40 **1** **Brod Na Heireann (IRE)**[32] 2513 6-10-12 115......... WayneHutchinson 121+
(Alan King) *trckd ldrs: shkn up to ld after 2 out: styd on wl* **7/4**[1]

54 **2** *10* **Lakeshore Lady (IRE)**[23] 2697 5-10-0 0........................ JakeHodson(5) 104
(David Bridgwater) *chsd ldr tl led appr 2 out: hdd after 2 out: no ex last* **10/1**

P-3 **3** *10* **Zephyros Bleu (IRE)**[33] 2488 5-10-12 0......................... NicodeBoinville 101
(Harry Whittington) *chsd ldrs: outpcd appr 7th: styd on to go 3rd last* **10/1**

2-1P **4** *8* **Toby Lerone (IRE)**[26] 2643 8-11-0 123......................... BridgetAndrews(5) 100
(Dan Skelton) *led: nt fluent 6th: rdn and hdd appr 2 out: wknd bef last* **15/8**[2]

400 **5** *6* **A Touch Of Sass (IRE)**[64] 1908 5-10-0 0....................... CharlieDeutsch(5) 82
(John Spearing) *hld up: hdwy bef 7th: rdn and wknd appr 2 out* **66/1**

00 **6** *16* **Ceann Sibheal (IRE)**[20] 2762 6-10-12 0............................ GavinSheehan 71
(Warren Greatrex) *hld up: pushed along after 6th: wknd bef next* **20/1**

0-P **P** **Big Smile (IRE)**[15] 2850 7-10-12 0.. LiamHeard
(John Groucott) *hld up: wknd after 6th: bhd whn p.u bef 3 out* **150/1**

3 **P** **Celldomfed (IRE)**[27] 2628 5-10-12 0..................................... JoshuaMoore
(Jonjo O'Neill) *hld up: plld hrd: hdwy 4th: mstke next: wknd 3 out: bhd whn p.u bef next* **5/1**[3]

5m 28.8s (1.60) **Going Correction** +0.275s/f (Yiel) **8** Ran SP% **112.9**
Speed ratings (Par 105): **107,103,99,96,94 87,** ,
CSF £18.82 TOTE £3.20: £1.10, £2.60, £2.80; EX 20.80 Trifecta £110.00.
Owner David Sewell **Bred** John J Brennan **Trained** Barbury Castle, Wilts

FOCUS
A blustery day. The chase and hurdle courses were on shared bends with the hurdle course dolled out to the middle position. The favourite won this opening novice in decent style and they finished quite well strung out.

3127 BET TOTEEXACTA H'CAP CHASE (17 fncs) 3m 102y
1:10 (1:10) (Class 4) (0-120,120) 4-Y-O+ **£4,548** (£1,335; £667; £333)

Form RPR

42-F **1** **Newton Thistle**[43] 2269 8-10-11 **105**.................................(t) DavidBass 117+
(Ben Pauling) *chsd ldr: mstke 4th: tk clsr order 10th: led 11th: clr fr 14th: j. slowly last: eased flat* **5/2**[1]

10-6 **2** *14* **Gamain (IRE)**[36] 2435 6-11-6 **114**..................................(b) DarylJacob 108
(Ben Case) *hld up: hdwy 5th: chsd wnr 14th: styd on same pce fr 3 out* **7/1**[3]

4-22 **3** *11* **Smart Exit (IRE)**[29] 2566 8-11-3 **116**............................ CiaranGethings(5) 99
(Stuart Edmunds) *hld up: outpcd 10th: nvr on terms afterwards* **5/2**[1]

53U3 **4** *28* **Georgian King**[29] 2566 12-10-13 **107**.................................(p) IanPopham 62
(Martin Keighley) *chsd ldrs: hmpd 2nd: nt fluent and lost pl 5th: bhd fr 7th* **7/1**[3]

1P0P **5** *6* **Pinerolo**[19] 2766 9-11-12 **120**......................................(p) SeanQuinlan 69
(Joanne Foster) *led: clr 5th to 10th: hdd next: wknd appr 3 out* **33/1**

4-04 **F** **Tea Caddy**[38] 2403 9-10-10 **104**......................................(tp) BrendanPowell
(Jamie Snowden) *hld up: hdwy 10th: 4th whn fell 12th* **12/1**

-U52 **U** **Market Option (IRE)**[26] 2598 9-10-7 **104**........................ CallumWhillans(3)
(Venetia Williams) *prom: j.rt 2nd: blnd and uns rdr 6th* **9/2**[2]

6m 30.8s (-6.10) **Going Correction** -0.15s/f (Good) **7** Ran SP% **111.0**
Speed ratings (Par 105): **104,99,95,86,84** ,
CSF £18.72 TOTE £2.90: £1.80, £3.70; EX 16.60 Trifecta £66.60.
Owner J H And N J Foxon **Bred** J H And N J Foxon **Trained** Bourton-On-The-Water, Gloucs

FOCUS
A fair handicap, which was won in emphatic style by one of the market leaders who has a good record around here.

3128 CAROLINE BEESLEY MEMORIAL H'CAP HURDLE (12 hdls) 2m 7f 211y
1:40 (1:41) (Class 5) (0-100,100) 4-Y-O+ **£3,249** (£954; £477; £238)

Form RPR

145P **1** **Earcomesthedream (IRE)**[38] 2405 12-11-5 **100**......(b) ArchieBellamy(7) 104
(Peter Pritchard) *chsd ldr after 1st: pushed along and lost 2nd after 6th: regained 2nd again 8th: drvn to ld appr 3 out: kpt on* **16/1**

463P **2** *2 1/4* **Ballochmyle (IRE)**[26] 2649 5-10-9 **83**.................................. JackQuinlan 84
(Caroline Fryer) *prom: chsd ldr after 6th tl 8th: outpcd bef 2 out: rallied to chse wnr last: styd on u.p* **7/1**[3]

06-P **3** *12* **Kavanaghs Corner (IRE)**[38] 2408 6-10-10 **89**.................. KevinJones(5) 81
(Simon Earle) *hld up: hdwy 6th: chsd wnr appr 2 out: sn rdn: wknd last* **15/2**

-500 **4** *15* **Whispering Speed (IRE)**[19] 2772 5-10-13 **87**...........(p) GavinSheehan 61
(Lucy Wadham) *led: hdd appr 3 out: rdn and wknd bef next* **4/1**[2]

04U4 **5** *4 1/2* **Skating Home (IRE)**[58] 2005 9-10-0 **74** oh2........................ JamesDavies 44
(Richard Hawker) *chsd ldrs: rdn appr 3 out: wknd bef next* **33/1**

25-5 **6** *7* **Deportation**[14] 2868 8-10-0 **77**...................................(v) ColmMcCormack(3) 40
(John Norton) *hld up: bhd fr 5th* **16/1**

46-4 **7** *33* **Banks Road (IRE)**[41] 2316 10-10-6 **80**................................ MarkGrant 10
(Geoffrey Deacon) *hld up: racd keenly: hdwy after 7th: rdn and wknd 3 out* **7/1**[3]

4-45 **P** **Burgundy Betty (IRE)**[46] 2223 5-11-1 **89**...................(p) NicodeBoinville
(Ben Pauling) *prom: mstke 4th: pushed along 6th: wknd 9th: bhd whn p.u bef 2 out* **2/1**[1]

0U05 **P** **Double Court (IRE)**[38] 2408 4-10-1 **75**..........................(v) DaveCrosse
(Nigel Twiston-Davies) *hld up: nt fluent 1st: rdn and wknd appr 3 out: bhd whn p.u bef next* **10/1**

6m 27.6s (12.60) **Going Correction** +0.275s/f (Yiel)
WFA 4 from 5yo+ 7lb **9** Ran SP% **113.9**
Speed ratings (Par 103): **90,89,85,80,78 76,65,** ,
CSF £120.83 CT £915.83 TOTE £9.10: £2.50, £2.40, £2.70; EX 101.60 Trifecta £649.60.
Owner Woodlands Generators **Bred** Cornelius O'Riordan **Trained** Whatcote, Warwicks

FOCUS
Most of the runners had struggled on their last start and a veteran, who was well in on last season's Uttoxeter win, bounced back to land this modest handicap.

3129 BET TOTETRIFECTA NOVICES' LIMITED H'CAP CHASE (15 fncs) 2m 5f 153y
2:10 (2:10) (Class 4) (0-120,120) 4-Y-0+ £4,548 (£1,335; £667; £333)

Form RPR
364- 1 **Waldorf Salad**[273] 4863 7-10-11 **112**.......................... CallumWhillans(3) 129+
(Venetia Williams) *led to 11th: led again 3 out: j. slowly and hit last: hdd flat: rallied to ld again sn after: edgd lft: styd on gamely* **5/1**[3]
P-32 2 1 3/4 **St Johns Point (IRE)**[28] 2592 7-11-5 **117**......................(tp) BrianHughes 127
(Charlie Longsdon) *chsd wnr to 4th: remained handy: rdn to go 2nd again appr 2 out: led flat: sn hdd: no ex towards fin* **11/4**[1]
0-45 3 22 **Like Sully (IRE)**[13] 2885 7-10-7 **105**.................... AndrewGlassonbury 95
(Richard Rowe) *prom: chsd wnr 4th tl led 11th: hdd 3 out: mstke and wknd next* **7/1**
0-1P 4 18 **Chicoria (IRE)**[8] 2973 6-11-8 **120**...........................(p) JakeGreenall 90
(Henry Daly) *prom: blnd 5th: mstke 7th: hit next: sn rdn and wknd* **10/1**
103P 5 1 1/2 **Iora Glas (IRE)**[19] 2785 6-11-3 **115**......................... PaddyBrennan 84
(Fergal O'Brien) *hld up: wknd 10th* **15/2**
5-F6 6 1 1/2 **Golan Dancer (IRE)**[35] 2456 7-10-7 **110**...................... JakeHodson(5) 77
(David Bridgwater) *hmpd 1st: prom: rdn and wknd after 3 out* **40/1**
F-02 U **Monderon (FR)**[14] 2861 8-10-3 **101** oh1......................... JamesDavies
(Henry Oliver) *hld up in tch: blnd and uns rdr 9th* **7/2**[2]
10-0 F **Glenwood Star (IRE)**[51] 2125 7-11-5 **117**......................... SeanBowen
(Rebecca Curtis) *hld up: hit 8th: wknd 10th: bhd whn fell 2 out* **8/1**

5m 45.9s (-7.10) **Going Correction** -0.15s/f (Good) **8** Ran SP% **112.5**
Speed ratings (Par 105): **106,105,97,90,89, ,**
CSF £19.22 CT £94.22 TOTE £7.00: £2.20, £1.10, £3.00; EX 25.60 Trifecta £193.60.
Owner Alan Parker **Bred** A Parker **Trained** Kings Caple, H'fords

FOCUS
They went a stop-start gallop and the first two pulled clear in this handicap. The winner was well in on the best of his hurdles form.

3130 TOTEPOOL BETTING ON ALL UK RACING MAIDEN HURDLE (8 hdls) 1m 7f 181y
2:40 (2:41) (Class 5) 4-Y-0+ £2,599 (£763; £381; £190)

Form RPR
1 **Que Sera (IRE)**[585] 356 5-11-0 0......................... TomO'Brien 106+
(Philip Hobbs) *chsd ldr: wandered into 3 out: led after 3 out: j.rt last: rdn out* **11/4**[1]
0 2 2 1/2 **Ballypoint (IRE)**[16] 2842 4-10-11 0......................... RyanHatch(3) 100
(Nigel Twiston-Davies) *hld up: hdwy 3 out: chsd wnr bef next: styd on* **14/1**
122- 3 3 **Generous Jack (IRE)**[297] 4411 6-11-0 0......................... DarylJacob 97
(Jim Best) *a.p: shkn up appr last: styd on same pce flat* **5/1**
14- 4 1 **Kingussie**[380] 2874 7-11-0 0......................... NicodeBoinville 96
(Ben Pauling) *chsd ldrs: rdn after 3 out: styd on same pce appr last* **7/2**[3]
00- 5 4 **Busy Baro (IRE)**[238] 5502 5-11-0 0......................... CharliePoste 93
(Paul Cowley) *led: j.lft at times: hdd after 3 out: wknd appr last* **200/1**
2/0 6 5 **Scooter Boy**[43] 2270 6-11-0 0..........................[1] KielanWoods 88
(Alex Hales) *hld up: hdwy after 3 out: wknd next* **11/1**
30-2 7 3 1/2 **Give Him A Glance**[30] 2562 4-11-0 0......................... WayneHutchinson 85
(Alan King) *hld up: racd keenly: hdwy 5th: rdn and wknd appr 2 out* **3/1**[2]
04 8 2 3/4 **Mr Jalfrazy (IRE)**[8] 2974 6-10-11 0......................... KillianMoore(3) 81
(Tom Weston) *hld up: effrt 3 out: sn wknd* **150/1**
000 9 2 1/2 **Blue Prairie**[29] 2581 4-11-0 0......................... HarrySkelton 78
(Dan Skelton) *hld up: rdn after 5th: wknd after next* **40/1**
00 10 1/2 **Ultimate Dream (FR)**[14] 2860 4-11-0 0......................... JoshuaMoore 78
(Jonjo O'Neill) *hld up: rdn and wknd after 3 out* **100/1**
5 11 1/2 **Tommy The Rascal**[18] 2804 5-11-0 0......................... SeanQuinlan 77
(Jennie Candlish) *hld up: plld hrd: wknd after 5th* **100/1**
00 12 2 3/4 **Opechee (IRE)**[26] 2650 4-10-9 0......................... JakeHodson(5) 75
(David Bridgwater) *hld up: mstke 1st: wknd 3 out* **50/1**
01-0 13 1 **Missile Man (IRE)**[17] 2823 6-10-7 0......................... PaulJohn(7) 74+
(Jim Best) *prom: lost pl 5th: stdd bef 2 out* **14/1**
5 14 4 1/2 **Tilstarr (IRE)**[27] 2614 5-10-7 0..........................(p) TomCannon 62
(Roger Teal) *prom: j.rt 2nd: rdn and wknd appr 2 out* **33/1**

4m 11.6s (3.70) **Going Correction** +0.275s/f (Yiel) **14** Ran SP% **122.7**
Speed ratings (Par 103): **101,99,98,97,95 93,91,90,88,88 88,87,86,84**
CSF £42.62 TOTE £3.70: £1.70, £5.60, £1.20; EX 55.20 Trifecta £333.60.
Owner Miss I D Du Pre **Bred** Tinnakill Bloodstock Ltd **Trained** Withycombe, Somerset

FOCUS
The favourite delivered in this interesting maiden hurdle, but there was scary moment for her backers three out.

3131 TOTEPOOL WISHING RACEGOERS A MERRY CHRISTMAS H'CAP CHASE (13 fncs) 2m 3f 179y
3:10 (3:10) (Class 5) (0-100,97) 4-Y-0+ £3,249 (£954; £477; £238)

Form RPR
-443 1 **Ballyegan (IRE)**[21] 2735 10-11-1 **86**......................... LiamHeard 100+
(Bob Buckler) *chsd ldr tl led 8th: rdn clr appr last: styd on* **6/1**[3]
P321 2 5 **Riddlestown (IRE)**[16] 2841 8-11-12 **97**......................(b) HarrySkelton 104
(Caroline Fryer) *a.p: chsd wnr 3 out: rdn bef next: styd on same pce last* **11/4**[1]
0-33 3 11 **Carhue Princess (IRE)**[30] 2551 9-11-0 **88**......................... BenPoste(3) 83
(Tom Symonds) *chsd ldrs: outpcd 3 out: styd on to go 3rd flat* **7/1**
54P2 4 2 **Petit Ecuyer (FR)**[3] 3088 9-10-2 **80**......................(v) MrJNixon(7) 74
(Dai Williams) *hld up: hdwy to go 3rd 2 out: wknd last* **8/1**
0016 5 11 **Monty's Revenge (IRE)**[18] 2811 10-10-11 **82**......................(p) IanPopham 66
(Martin Keighley) *led: hit 7th: hdd next: chsd ldr to 3 out: rdn and wknd bef next* **8/1**
-465 6 10 **Jolly Boys Outing (IRE)**[42] 2303 12-10-6 **80**......................... KillianMoore(3) 52
(Rosemary Gasson) *hld up in tch: dropped to rr after 5th: bhd fr 7th* **8/1**
2-65 P **Tinelyra (IRE)**[18] 2811 9-11-6 **91**......................(t) PaddyBrennan
(Fergal O'Brien) *hld up: hdwy 9th: wknd after 3 out: bhd whn p.u bef next* **9/2**[2]
065P P **Barra Rotha (IRE)**[14] 2861 8-11-5 **97**......................... MikeyHamill(7)
(Laura Hurley) *hld up: hdwy 6th: bhd fr next: p.u bef 2 out* **33/1**
3550 P **Dougalstar (FR)**[163] 934 6-9-7 **71** oh1......................(p) ConorWalsh(7)
(Jennie Candlish) *prom to 9th: in rr whn blnd 3 out: bhd whn p.u bef next* **11/1**

5m 20.2s (2.00) **Going Correction** -0.15s/f (Good) **9** Ran SP% **116.2**
Speed ratings (Par 103): **90,88,83,82,78 74, , ,**
CSF £23.95 CT £119.26 TOTE £5.30: £1.90, £1.20, £2.60; EX 18.40 Trifecta £85.40.
Owner R H Buckler **Bred** Dan O'Regan **Trained** Henley, Somerset

FOCUS
The winner, who is good around here and was on a good mark, put in a dominant display in this low-grade handicap.

3132 TOTEPOOLLIVEINFO.COM MARES' STANDARD OPEN NATIONAL HUNT FLAT RACE 1m 7f 181y
3:40 (3:40) (Class 6) 4-6-Y-0 £1,949 (£572; £286; £143)

Form RPR
1 **Sister Sibyl (IRE)** 4-10-12 0......................... TomO'Brien 103+
(Hughie Morrison) *hld up: hdwy 9f out: lost pl over 6f out: hdwy over 2f out: r.o to ld wl ins fnl f* **15/2**[3]
2 1 1/2 **Graceful Legend** 4-10-12 0......................... KielanWoods 101
(Ben Case) *hld up in tch: lost pl 9f out: hdwy over 6f out: rdn over 1f out: r.o* **28/1**
3 hd **Chilli Romance (IRE)** 4-10-7 0......................... NickSlatter(5) 101
(Fergal O'Brien) *hld up: hdwy over 2f out: rdn to ld 1f out: hdd wl ins fnl f* **16/1**
2 4 nk **Cajun Fiddle (IRE)**[22] 2721 4-10-12 0......................... WayneHutchinson 102+
(Alan King) *hld up in tch: nt clr run over 3f out: rdn over 1f out: styd on same pce ins fnl f* **4/5**[1]
5 nk **Atlanta Ablaze** 4-10-12 0......................... JakeGreenall 100
(Henry Daly) *hld up: rdn over 4f out: hdwy over 1f out: r.o* **25/1**
6 3/4 **Llantara** 4-10-12 0......................... JamesDavies 100
(Tom Symonds) *chsd ldrs: led over 1f out: sn rdn and hdd: styd on same pce* **20/1**
03 7 4 1/2 **The Model County (IRE)**[12] 2909 5-10-5 0......................... MrAlexEdwards(7) 95
(Alan Phillips) *led: rdn over 2f out: hdd over 1f out: wknd fnl f* **18/1**
0 8 nk **Lady Markby (IRE)**[43] 2277 4-10-12 0..........................[1] DarylJacob 95
(Emma Lavelle) *hld up: rdn over 2f out: nt trble ldrs* **20/1**
9 1 3/4 **Harvey (IRE)** 4-10-12 0......................... TomCannon 93
(Laura Mongan) *prom: rdn over 3f out: wknd over 1f out* **50/1**
10 7 **Stoical Patient (IRE)** 6-10-9 0......................... KillianMoore(3) 86
(Mark Wall) *hld up: rdn over 2f out: n.d* **50/1**
11 17 **Sweetlittlekitty (IRE)**[277] 5-10-12 0......................... SeanBowen 69
(Rebecca Curtis) *chsd ldrs: rdn over 2f out: wknd over 1f out* **7/2**[2]
0 12 27 **Away In May**[26] 2650 4-10-12 0..........................(p) NicodeBoinville 42
(John Spearing) *chsd ldrs: ev ch 3f out: wknd over 1f out* **66/1**

4m 8.7s (6.40) **Going Correction** +0.275s/f (Yiel) **12** Ran SP% **122.9**
Speed ratings: **95,94,94,94,93 93,91,91,90,86 78,64**
CSF £202.69 TOTE £7.60: £2.10, £6.90, £3.90; EX 267.40 Trifecta £3977.20.
Owner L A Garfield **Bred** Hugh Fitzpatrick **Trained** East Ilsley, Berks

FOCUS
They went a steady pace and there was not much separating the first six in this mares' bumper.
T/Plt: £167.90 to a £1 stake. Pool: £88,368.65 - 384.20 winning units. T/Qpdt: £15.80 to a £1 stake. Pool: £7,379.76 - 344.84 winning units. **Colin Roberts**

2630 ASCOT (R-H)
Friday, December 18

OFFICIAL GOING: Soft (good to soft in places; chs 6.3, hdl 6.2)
Wind: Light, across Weather: Cloudy, mild

3133 FOLLOW @ASCOT ON TWITTER "NATIONAL HUNT" MAIDEN HURDLE (10 hdls) 2m 5f 141y
12:50 (12:52) (Class 3) 4-Y-0+ £7,797 (£2,289; £1,144; £572)

Form RPR
14 1 **Western Cape (IRE)**[38] 2417 4-10-9 0......................... KevinJones(5) 123+
(Seamus Mullins) *angular: hld up in rr: gd prog fr 7th and sn prom: trckd ldr after 3 out: rdn to ld sn after 2 out: styd on wl fr last* **33/1**
51-2 2 3 3/4 **King Kayf**[19] 2807 6-10-11 0......................(t) JamesBanks(3) 119
(Noel Williams) *w ldrs: led after 3 out: rdn and hdd sn after 2 out: one pce* **8/1**
60-3 3 1 1/2 **Minstrel Royal**[27] 2636 5-11-0 0......................... DavidBass 118
(Nicky Henderson) *hld up in rr: prog 7th: mstke 3 out: rdn and cl up 2 out: tk 3rd last: kpt on same pce* **20/1**
32-4 4 1 3/4 **Kerrow (IRE)**[36] 2450 5-11-0 0......................... WayneHutchinson 116
(Alan King) *wl in tch: clsd on ldrs and rdn bef 2 out: one pce bef last* **7/2**[2]
32 5 hd **Petethepear (IRE)**[44] 2265 5-11-0 0......................... JoshuaMoore 117
(Stuart Edmunds) *t.k.h: hld up in rr: mstke 6th: prog 3 out: chsd ldrs and shkn up 2 out: one pce bef last* **10/1**
4 6 4 **Semper Invicta (IRE)**[27] 2636 4-11-0 0......................... SamTwiston-Davies 113
(Paul Nicholls) *lw: in tch: rdn after 3 out: effrt u.p whn forced wd bnd bef 2 out: lost grnd and n.d after* **25/1**
4/62 7 hd **Manhattan Mead**[18] 2823 5-11-0 117......................... MarcGoldstein 112
(Michael Madgwick) *mde most to 3rd and fr 5th tl after 3 out: stl cl up and drvn 2 out: wknd bef last* **100/1**
8 8 **Valhalla (IRE)**[82] 5-11-0 0......................... RichardJohnson 108+
(Colin Tizzard) *angular: mstkes: hld up in rr: prog 6th: cl up whn mstkes next 2: rdn and wknd bef 2 out: eased* **8/1**
0-2P 9 6 **Mad About The Boy**[27] 2630 5-11-0 0......................... AidanColeman 98
(Robert Walford) *chsd ldrs: mstke and wknd 7th: sn wl btn* **66/1**
1 10 34 **Fly Du Charmil (FR)**[22] 2729 4-11-0 0......................... GavinSheehan 64
(Warren Greatrex) *swtg: w ldrs: led 3rd to 5th: rdn and lost pl after next: toiling in rr 3 out: t.o* **15/8**[1]
6-53 11 6 **Itsaboutime (IRE)**[23] 2710 5-10-9 0......................... ConorRing(5) 58
(Helen Nelmes) *nt jump wl: mostly in last: struggling after 6th: t.o* **200/1**
4-22 P **He's A Charmer (IRE)**[28] 2612 5-11-0 0......................(t) NoelFehily
(Harry Fry) *lw: wl in tch tl wknd after 7th: wl bhd whn p.u bef 2 out* **7/1**[3]
6-0 P **Silver Ticket (IRE)**[222] 227 4-11-0 0......................... TomCannon
(Laura Mongan) *mstke 3rd: prom to 6th: wkng rapidly whn mstke 3 out: sn p.u* **200/1**

5m 33.3s (7.30) **Going Correction** +0.375s/f (Yiel)
WFA 4 from 5yo+ 6lb **13** Ran SP% **115.8**
Speed ratings (Par 107): **101,99,99,98,98 96,96,93,91,79 77, ,**
CSF £264.22 TOTE £40.10: £7.60, £2.80, £5.60; EX 372.60 Trifecta £4694.20 Part won..
Owner A A Goodman **Bred** Thomas Browne **Trained** Wilsford-Cum-Lake, Wilts

FOCUS
Allowing for rail movements the distance of the opener was increased by 29yds. A bit of a turn up in what had looked a fair maiden hurdle full of future staying chasers, but the first two are on the upgrade. They went a steady gallop through the early stages.

3134 HAPPY RETIREMENT CHAMPION COURT NOVICES' LIMITED H'CAP CHASE (13 fncs) 2m 192y
1:20 (1:21) (Class 3) (0-135,132) 4-Y-0+ £9,747 (£2,862; £1,431; £715)

Form				RPR
0	1		**Hollywoodien (FR)**[34] 2499 4-10-7 **122** ... AidanColeman (Tom Symonds) *str: trckd ldrs: mstke 6th: rdn to cl after 3 out: led and blnd 2 out: styd on wl fr last* **20/1**	132+
3231	2	2 1/4	**All Together (FR)**[20] 2765 4-10-13 **128** ... JamesBest (Johnny Farrelly) *chsd ldr to 2nd: styd prom: hit 8th: wnt 2nd again 4 out: led briefly bef 2 out: stl w wnr last: one pce* **5/1**	132
0-F2	3	4 1/2	**Bodega**[32] 2540 7-10-4 **114** ... (p) WillKennedy (Ian Williams) *hld up in last trio and wl off the pce: pushed along and prog fr 9th: 5th whn blnd 3 out: hanging fr 2 out but tk 3rd bef last: kpt on* **10/1**	120
5-30	4	12	**Ballybolley (IRE)**[25] 2691 6-11-8 **132** ... (t) SamTwiston-Davies (Nigel Twiston-Davies) *led to 4th: chsd ldr to 4 out: wknd bef 2 out* **9/1**	127
-522	5	6	**Ozzy Thomas (IRE)**[16] 2854 5-11-2 **126** ... JamesDavies (Henry Oliver) *nvr bttr than midfield and nt on terms w ldrs: shkn up and no imp fr 8th* **3/1**[1]	115
0-10	6	3 1/4	**Ink Master (IRE)**[35] 2472 5-10-12 **122** ... RichardJohnson (Philip Hobbs) *lw: chsd ldr and blnd 2nd: led 4th: hdd & wknd rapidly bef 2 out* **4/1**[2]	107
4-U5	7	23	**Too Much Too Soon (IRE)**[27] 2645 6-10-5 **115** ... (t) DenisO'Regan (Paul Webber) *nvr fluent: a in last trio: struggling fr 7th: t.o* **33/1**	75
0/21	8	21	**Blades Lad**[21] 2755 6-10-4 **114** ... (p) BrianHughes (Peter Niven) *prom: mstke 4th: wknd 6th: t.o whn mstke 4 out* **14/1**	53
50-3	P		**Dusky Lark**[14] 2885 5-11-1 **125** ... (t) NoelFehily (Colin Tizzard) *blnd 1st: a last: wl bhd whn p.u bef 10th* **9/2**[3]	

4m 14.1s (-0.50) **Going Correction** +0.375s/f (Yiel)
WFA 4 from 5yo+ 5lb **9 Ran SP% 113.3**
Speed ratings (Par 107): **116,114,112,107,104 102,92,82,**
CSF £116.26 CT £1071.88 TOTE £26.70: £5.60, £2.00, £3.20; EX 160.00 Trifecta £1022.90.
Owner Sir Peter & Lady Gibbings **Bred** Mme Aliette Forien & Gilles Forien **Trained** Harewood End, H'fords

FOCUS
Race distance increased by 34yds. No hanging around here in what was a fair handicap chase and the winner looks better than the bare result.

3135 SKY BET SUPREME TRIAL NOVICES' HURDLE (REGISTERED AS KENNEL GATE NOVICES' HURDLE) (GRADE 2) (8 hdls) 1m 7f 152y
1:55 (1:56) (Class 1) 4-Y-0+ £17,085 (£6,411; £3,210; £1,599; £804)

Form				RPR
4-11	1		**Yanworth**[30] 2581 5-11-7 145 ... BarryGeraghty (Alan King) *lw: mde all: nt fluent 3rd: wl in command and stl on the bridle 2 out: eased flat* **1/3**[1]	151+
412	2	2 3/4	**Charbel (IRE)**[21] 2748 4-11-7 132 ... DavidBass (Kim Bailey) *t.k.h: chsd wnr fr 3rd: rdn and no imp bef 2 out: kpt on but nvr able to chal* **7/1**[3]	139
0-1	3	12	**Aqua Dude (IRE)**[39] 2406 5-11-4 0 ... AdamWedge (Evan Williams) *hld up in tch: pushed along bef 2 out: steadily lft bhd* **9/1**	124
4-1	4	1 1/2	**All Set To Go (IRE)**[17] 2840 4-11-0 0 ... (t) SamTwiston-Davies (Paul Nicholls) *lw: hld up in tch: disp 3rd pl fr 5th: pushed along and lft bhd bef 2 out* **6/1**[2]	118
565P	5	22	**Trans Express (IRE)**[13] 2904 5-11-0 0 ... LucyGardner (Sue Gardner) *chsd wnr tl mstke 3rd: lost tch in last pl 5th: sn bhd* **100/1**	98

3m 51.8s (4.40) **Going Correction** +0.375s/f (Yiel) **5 Ran SP% 112.8**
Speed ratings (Par 115): **104,102,96,95,84**
CSF £3.69 TOTE £1.20: £1.10, £2.20; EX 2.80 Trifecta £7.50.
Owner John P McManus **Bred** Wood Farm Stud **Trained** Barbury Castle, Wilts

FOCUS
Race distance increased by 18yds. A decent novice hurdle, although lacking depth somewhat for the grade, and the red-hot favourite enhanced his reputation with a dominant display, being value for further.

3136 MITIE NOVICES' CHASE (REGISTERED AS NOEL NOVICES' CHASE) (GRADE 2) (17 fncs) 2m 5f 8y
2:30 (2:30) (Class 1) 4-Y-0+ £18,309 (£6,924; £3,509; £1,791; £943)

Form				RPR
30-1	1		**Le Mercurey (FR)**[32] 2545 5-11-4 142 ... (t) SamTwiston-Davies (Paul Nicholls) *lw: hld up in cl tch: nt fluent 11th: prog to chse ldr next: rdn after 3 out: keeping on but stl 2 l down whn lft in ld last: drvn out* **2/1**[2]	152
P6-1	2	6	**Thomas Brown**[28] 2613 6-11-4 0 ... NoelFehily (Harry Fry) *lw: cl up: mde most fr 4th to 8th: chsd ldr to 11th: dropped to 5th and rdn next: rallied u.p to go 3rd bef 2 out: lft 2nd last: no imp on wnr* **7/4**[1]	146
1F-6	3	6	**Out Sam**[47] 2214 6-11-0 0 ... GavinSheehan (Warren Greatrex) *nt as slick as rivals over the fences: settled in last: effrt to chse ldrs 12th but sn rdn: one pce fr 3 out: lft 3rd last* **11/2**	136
P-14	4	7	**Killala Quay**[22] 2726 8-11-4 139 ... (p) RichardJohnson (Charlie Longsdon) *led: outj. and hdd 4th: styd cl up: chsd ldr 11th to next: sn rdn: fdd after 3 out: lft 4th last* **20/1**	136
0-11	5	12	**Junction Fourteen (IRE)**[41] 2347 6-11-6 142 ... (t) AidanColeman (Emma Lavelle) *chsd ldrs: rdn after 10th and sn struggling: last fr 12th: n.d after: lft remote 5th last* **9/2**[3]	125
0-42	U		**Amore Alato**[16] 2846 6-11-0 0 ... HarrySkelton (Johnny Farrelly) *pressed ldr: led 8th: stretched field fr 12th: nt fluent 4 out: rdn 2 out: stl 2 l up and looked likely to hold on whn blnd bdly and uns rdr last* **40/1**	150

5m 27.0s (1.00) **Going Correction** +0.375s/f (Yiel) **6 Ran SP% 110.5**
Speed ratings (Par 115): **113,110,108,105,101**
CSF £6.00 TOTE £3.50: £1.60, £1.50; EX 7.50 Trifecta £22.80.
Owner Colm Donlon & Chris Giles **Bred** S A R L Carion Emm **Trained** Ditcheat, Somerset

FOCUS
Race distance increased by 46yds. A good-quality novice chase but there was late drama when the complete outsider Amore Alato, who appeared much the likeliest winner, parted ways with his rider after a bad blunder at the last.

3137 MITIE CONDITIONAL JOCKEYS' H'CAP HURDLE (10 hdls) 2m 5f 141y
3:05 (3:05) (Class 3) (0-130,129) 4-Y-0+ £6,498 (£1,908; £954; £477)

Form				RPR
P213	1		**Masterplan (IRE)**[22] 2725 5-11-0 **119** ... GrahamWatters[3] (Charlie Longsdon) *mde all: kicked on fr 3 out: drvn after 2 out: jst hld on* **16/1**	123
0-21	2	shd	**Duke Des Champs (IRE)**[15] 2864 5-11-6 **128** ... ConorSmith[6] (Philip Hobbs) *wl in tch: prog to chse wnr after 3 out: trying to mount a chal whn blnd 2 out: rallied after last: styd on nr fin: jst failed* **5/1**[2]	133+
	3	1	**Woodford Island (IRE)**[12] 2940 4-11-0 **119** ... (t) JackKennedy[3] (Gordon Elliott, Ire) *w'like: hld up in midfield: prog bef 3 out: chsd ldng pair bef 2 out: rdn to dispute 2nd and ch whn blnd last: nt qckn flat: kpt on* **3/1**[1]	123+
001F	4	11	**Goodbye Dancer (FR)**[7] 3010 4-11-10 **129** 7ex ... JamieBargary[3] (Nigel Twiston-Davies) *wl in rr: rdn after 7th: only modest prog tl kpt on fr 2 out to take 4th last: no ch* **12/1**	121
2-22	5	1 3/4	**Shadarpour (IRE)**[33] 2513 6-11-1 **125** ... (p) WilliamFeatherstone[8] (Alan King) *towards rr: effrt 7th: drvn in 8th pl after 3 out: kpt on to take modest 4th 2 out to last: one pce* **9/1**	115
5-3P	6	shd	**San Telm (IRE)**[26] 2669 10-11-4 **120** ... (p) CharlieDeutsch (Stuart Edmunds) *wl in tch: effrt to chse ldrs 3 out: sn rdn: lft bhd by ldrs bef 2 out: stl battling for 4th pl last: one pce* **33/1**	110
1540	7	1	**Lava Lamp (GER)**[79] 1699 8-10-5 **117** ... CianMaher[10] (Evan Williams) *lw: hld up in rr: last after 6th: pushed along after 3 out: stl only 12th 2 out: shkn up and kpt on: nvr involved* **50/1**	106
-P36	8	hd	**Kalmbeforethestorm**[70] 1839 7-10-8 **110** ... (t) ConorRing (Helen Nelmes) *s.s: wl in rr: mstke 3rd: rdn and struggling after 7th: modest late prog* **25/1**	99
24-1	9	10	**Pithivier (FR)**[31] 2560 5-11-7 **123** ... MauriceLinehan (Ben Pauling) *lw: chsd wnr: rdn 3 out: lost 2nd after 3 out: wknd 2 out* **5/1**[2]	102
-130	10	1 1/4	**Crazy Jack (IRE)**[33] 2513 7-11-7 **123** ... (p) TomBellamy (Kim Bailey) *trckd ldng pair: rdn to dispute 2nd after 3 out: wknd qckly bef 2 out* **12/1**	101
00-4	11	7	**Sebastian Beach (IRE)**[13] 2906 4-10-8 **118** ... (t) PatrickCowley[8] (Jonjo O'Neill) *wl in tch: effrt to chse ldrs 7th: rdn 3 out: wknd wl bef next* **8/1**[3]	89
4165	12	shd	**Mercers Court (IRE)**[20] 2775 7-11-2 **121** ... LizzieKelly[3] (Neil King) *hld up wl in rr: shkn up 3 out: no prog and wl btn bef next* **33/1**	92
62-4	13	1	**Onwiththeparty**[38] 2420 6-10-0 **102** ... ThomasGarner (Chris Gordon) *prom whn mstke 1st: dropped to rr 4th: blnd next and rdn: brief rally 7th: sn wknd and bhd* **33/1**	72

5m 29.7s (3.70) **Going Correction** +0.375s/f (Yiel) **13 Ran SP% 115.3**
Speed ratings (Par 107): **108,107,107,103,102 102,102,102,98,98 95,95,95**
CSF £88.09 CT £311.17 TOTE £17.30: £4.50, £2.10, £1.70; EX 119.00 Trifecta £1175.00.
Owner Gavin MacEchern **Bred** Derek O'Hara **Trained** Over Norton, Oxon

■ Stewards' Enquiry : Conor Smith four-day ban; used whip above the permitted level (1st-5th Jan)

FOCUS
Race distance increased by 29yds. Useful handicap form, the first three coming clear.

3138 NEPTUNE INVESTMENT MANAGEMENT CHAMPIONSHIP STANDARD OPEN NATIONAL HUNT FLAT RACE (LISTED RACE) 1m 7f 152y
3:40 (3:41) (Class 1) 4-6-Y-O
£17,085 (£6,411; £3,210; £1,599; £804; £402)

Form				RPR
2-	1		**Coeur Blimey (IRE)**[279] 4770 4-11-1 0 ... LucyGardner[3] (Sue Gardner) *rangy: hld up in tch: prog to trck ldr over 2f out: led 2f out: urged along and hld on wl fnl f* **16/1**	131
11	2	1	**Ballyandy**[33] 2514 4-11-8 0 ... SamTwiston-Davies (Nigel Twiston-Davies) *trckd clr ldr: clsd fr 1/2-way: led 3f out: sn rdn: hdd 2f out: fought on wl but a jst hld* **7/2**[2]	134
1	3	8	**Full Irish (IRE)**[40] 2375 4-11-4 0 ... AidanColeman (Emma Lavelle) *w'like: hld up in tch: cl up over 3f out: rdn to chse ldng pair 2f out: readily lft bhd by them after* **5/1**	122
	4	3 3/4	**De Plotting Shed (IRE)**[20] 2799 5-11-4 0 ... BarryGeraghty (Gordon Elliott, Ire) *athletic: lw: wl in tch: shkn up and on term 3f out: sn outpcd: wl hld in 4th over 1f out* **6/4**[1]	118
1	5	8	**Burlington Bert (FR)**[223] 213 4-11-4 0 ... (t) GavinSheehan (Warren Greatrex) *str: trckd clr ldr: rdn 3f out: fdd fnl 2f* **9/2**[3]	111
1	6	13	**Westerbee (IRE)**[24] 2702 4-10-6 0 ... KevinJones[5] (Seamus Mullins) *leggy: led after nthing else wanted to and clr: c bk to rivals fr 1/2-way: hdd 3f out: sn wknd* **33/1**	90
1	7	11	**Monbeg Charmer (IRE)**[57] 2031 4-11-4 0 ... RichardJohnson (Charlie Longsdon) *athletic: hld up in last pair: pushed along 5f out: sn struggling: wl btn fnl 3f* **8/1**	86
10	8	3	**Bentworth Boy**[33] 2514 4-11-4 0 ... NicodeBoinville (Patrick Chamings) *hld up in last pair: pushed along 5f out: sn struggling: wl btn fnl 3f* **50/1**	83

3m 48.6s (7.80) **Going Correction** +0.375s/f (Yiel) **8 Ran SP% 119.0**
Speed ratings: **95,94,90,88,84 78,72,71**
CSF £74.26 TOTE £24.90: £4.80, £1.50, £1.70; EX 124.90 Trifecta £520.60.
Owner Keith Harris **Bred** J P King **Trained** Longdown, Devon

FOCUS
Race distance increased by 18yds. This looked a decent bumper and, unusually for these contests, the pace was an honest one. The front pair came clear late on.

T/Plt: £420.20 to a £1 stake. Pool: £127,926.45 - 222.24 winning tickets T/Qpdt: £7.30 to a £1 stake. Pool: £12,604.89 - 1,275.94 winning tickets **Jonathan Neesom**

2959 UTTOXETER (L-H)

Friday, December 18

OFFICIAL GOING: Heavy (5.9)
Wind: moderate 1/2 behind Weather: overcast

3139 BETFRED "RACING'S BIGGEST SUPPORTER" JUVENILE MAIDEN HURDLE (10 hdls) 2m 3f 207y

12:10 (12:10) (Class 5) 3-Y-O **£2,511** (£858)

Form				RPR
2	1		**Perceus**^{15} 2863 3-10-12 0 JackQuinlan (James Eustace) *t.k.h: mde all: dist clr fr 7th: hit last: canter* **1/8**^{1}	115+
0	2	91	**Duc De Seville (IRE)**^{15} 2863 3-10-7 0 (p) GaryDerwin$^{(5)}$ (Michael Chapman) *detached in last: pushed along 3rd: hit 4th: tk distant 2nd 7th* **25/1**^{3}
03	P		**Shabraque (IRE)**^{4} 3076 3-10-12 0 JamieMoore (David Loder) *trckd wnr: nt fluent 1st 2: wknd qckly 7th: slowed rt up and sn tailed rt off: p.u bef 3 out* **7/1**^{2}

5m 39.4s (36.20) **Going Correction** +1.70s/f (Heav) **3** Ran SP% **105.2**
Speed ratings (Par 102): **95,58,**
CSF £3.28 TOTE £1.10; EX 3.70 Trifecta £4.10.
Owner Ian Rushby & T H Barma **Bred** Mr & Mrs A E Pakenham **Trained** Newmarket, Suffolk

FOCUS
Some starts have been moved at this track following remeasuring, so some races will not have speed figures until there is sufficient data to calculate updated median times. The official going was heavy and, after winning the opener, Jack Quinlan described the ground as "only just heavy and soft in places". The actual race distance for this uncompetitive juvenile maiden hurdle was 2m4f 68yds.

3140 BETFRED "FRED'S FESTIVE GIVEAWAY" "HANDS & HEELS" H'CAP HURDLE (FOR COND. JOCKEYS & AMATEURS) (10 hdls) 2m 3f 207y

12:40 (12:43) (Class 5) (0-100,102) 3-Y-0+ **£2,339** (£686; £343; £171)

Form				RPR
2-51	1		**Hollywood All Star (IRE)**^{7} 3011 6-11-11 102 7ex ArchieBellamy$^{(3)}$ (Graeme McPherson) *trckd ldrs: pushed along 7th: 2nd sn after next: led 2 out: clr last: sn heavily eased* **11/4**^{2}	112+
-6P6	2	10	**Norse Light**^{38} 2418 4-11-12 100 (p) GarethMalone (David Dennis) *hld up in last: t.k.h: hdwy to trck ldrs 7th: drvn to ld bef 3 out: rdn and hdd 2 out: no ch w wnr* **20/1**	95
00P6	3	2	**Gud Day (IRE)**^{17} 2841 7-11-2 90 (p) HarryCobden (Conor Dore) *w ldr: narrow ld 3rd: hdd after 6th: lost pl next: last at last: kpt on to take modest 3rd nr fin* **20/1**	80
06-1	4	1	**Transient Bay (IRE)**^{10} 2964 5-10-4 78 7ex (p) DavidNoonan (Philip Kirby) *narrow ldr: hdd 3rd: drvn and outpcd bef 3 out: one pce and modest 4th bef 2 out* **8/13**^{1}	67
-22P	5	2	**Henry Oliver (IRE)**^{71} 1824 7-10-13 92 (tp) MrDSymes-Meineck$^{(5)}$ (John O'Shea) *trckd ldrs: upsides after 5th: led after next: hdd bef 3 out: lost pl bef 2 out* **33/1**	79
2U53	6	hd	**Court Of Law (IRE)**^{16} 2844 7-11-4 97 (p) CaiWilliams$^{(5)}$ (Donald McCain) *trckd ldrs: outpcd appr 3 out: sn lost pl* **8/1**^{3}	84

6m 8.6s (65.40) **Going Correction** +1.70s/f (Heav) **6** Ran SP% **112.2**
Speed ratings (Par 103): **37,33,32,31,31 30**
CSF £40.94 CT £904.15 TOTE £4.60: £1.80, £2.70; EX 43.30 Trifecta £280.00.
Owner The McPherson Racing Partnership **Bred** James Waldron **Trained** Upper Oddington, Gloucs
■ Stewards' Enquiry : Gareth Malone seven-day ban: used his whip (tba)

FOCUS
They went a steady gallop for this moderate handicap hurdle and it developed into a sprint up the home straight. The winner was well in on his recent win. The actual race distance was 2m4f 68yds.

3141 BETFRED "BE PART OF THE ACTION" H'CAP CHASE (15 fncs) 2m 4f

1:10 (1:14) (Class 4) (0-115,113) 4-Y-0+ **£4,069** (£1,304; £724)

Form				RPR
0F11	1		**Truckers Highway (IRE)**^{9} 2976 6-10-13 103 7ex HarryChalloner$^{(3)}$ (John Groucott) *mde all: drew clr fr 3 out: 12 l ahd whn hit last: sn eased* **13/8**^{1}	121+
P-P3	2	15	**Big Jim**^{26} 2668 6-11-12 113 KielanWoods (Alex Hales) *chsd wnr: drvn 11th: hit next: wknd after 3 out: fin tired* **15/8**^{2}	116
60F6	3	13	**Modeligo (IRE)**^{25} 2692 6-10-0 94 (t) MrStanSheppard$^{(7)}$ (Matt Sheppard) *bhd: hdwy 8th: mstke 10th: sn outpcd: remote 3rd appr 4 out: j.rt last 2* **5/1**^{3}	81
431P	F		**Bobble Boru (IRE)**^{17} 2837 7-11-6 107 LiamTreadwell (Venetia Williams) *chsd ldng pair: nt fluent 5th: shkn up 8th: drvn and outpcd 10th: wknd appr 4 out: detached last whn fell last* **5/1**^{3}	89
20PP	P		**Spring Steel (IRE)**^{30} 2568 6-11-3 104 (t) RhysFlint (Alexandra Dunn) *in rr: sme hdwy 8th: drvn 10th: lost pl and bhd whn reminders next: sn t.o: p.u bef 4 out* **22/1**

5m 43.1s (33.30) **Going Correction** +1.80s/f (Heav) **5** Ran SP% **110.6**
Speed ratings (Par 105): **105,99,93, ,**
CSF £5.34 TOTE £2.60: £1.40, £1.30; EX 4.80 Trifecta £13.90.
Owner C J Tipton **Bred** David Pim **Trained** Bourton, Shropshire

FOCUS
Race distance increased by 23yds. Only a modest handicap chase and not the strongest for the grade, but the improving winner, who was suited by the switch to a left-handed track, did it nicely.

3142 BETFRED LOTTO "£100K CASH GIVEAWAY" H'CAP HURDLE (12 hdls) 2m 7f 70y

1:45 (1:45) (Class 4) (0-120,117) 4-Y-0+ **£3,508** (£1,030; £515; £257)

Form				RPR
5-11	1		**Baywing (IRE)**^{10} 2962 6-11-7 112 7ex BrianHarding (Nicky Richards) *trckd ldrs: 2nd bef 3 out: upsides next: pushed along to ld between last 2: forged clr run-in* **4/9**^{1}	129+
242-	2	14	**Bangkok Pete (IRE)**^{381} 2871 10-11-0 105 MattieBatchelor (Jamie Poulton) *trckd ldrs: hit 7th: led bef 3 out: hdd between last 2: kpt on same pce* **14/1**^{3}	111
0-01	3	28	**Extreme Impact**^{8} 2997 9-11-5 110 7ex (v) KielanWoods (Graeme McPherson) *drvn away fr s: sn chsng ldr: led briefly 3rd: reminders 5th and 7th: lost pl 9th: sn bhd: hit 2 out: tk remote 3rd last* **7/2**^{2}	85
3235	4	32	**Sandynow (IRE)**^{58} 2017 10-11-3 108 (b^{1}) SeanBowen (Peter Bowen) *led: hdd briefly 3rd: hdd bef 3 out: lost pl and remote 3rd bef 2 out: eased and t.o sn after last* **16/1**	51
3P/P	P		**Moscow Presents (IRE)**^{17} 2839 7-11-4 112 (p) AdamNicol$^{(3)}$ (Philip Kirby) *chsd ldrs: pushed along 8th: lost pl next: sn bhd: t.o whn p.u bef 3 out* **14/1**^{3}

6m 34.8s (36.00) **Going Correction** +1.70s/f (Heav) **5** Ran SP% **110.7**
Speed ratings (Par 105): **105,100,90,79,**
CSF £7.20 TOTE £1.40: £1.10, £2.60; EX 7.70 Trifecta £9.80.
Owner David & Nicky Robinson **Bred** Hugh Suffern Bloodstock **Trained** Greystoke, Cumbria

FOCUS
An uncompetitive event and the well-handicapped winner made no mistake. The actual race distance was 2m7f 176yds.

3143 BETFRED "SCOOP6SOCCER" NOVICES' H'CAP HURDLE (8 hdls 1 omitted) 1m 7f 168y

2:20 (2:20) (Class 5) (0-100,100) 3-Y-0+ **£2,339** (£686; £343; £171)

Form				RPR
4U-4	1		**Barista (IRE)**^{22} 2730 7-11-5 93 TomO'Brien (Brian Forsey) *t.k.h: trckd ldrs: pushed along 4th: outpcd bef 3 out: chsng ldrs next: led between last 2: 4 l clr sn after last: fdd and hld on nr fin* **11/4**^{2}	96
55-2	2	3/4	**Georgieshore (IRE)**^{15} 2862 7-11-12 100 PaddyBrennan (Zoe Davison) *led: hdd 4th: rallied and 2nd sn after 2 out: styd on towards fin: jst hld* **6/4**^{1}	102
6-65	3	5	**Solidago (IRE)**^{16} 2850 8-11-0 91 HarryChalloner$^{(3)}$ (Barry Leavy) *in rr: hdwy to chse ldrs 3rd: outpcd 2 out: kpt on to take modest 3rd appr last* **9/2**^{3}	88
	4	4 1/2	**Sussex Road (IRE)**^{43} 2309 5-11-0 88 (p) LeeEdwards (Aytach Sadik) *w ldrs: led narrowly 4th: pushed along and hdd next: upsides 2 out: wknd appr last* **16/1**	81
506P	5	4 1/2	**Rose Red**^{10} 2964 8-10-1 82 CharlieHammond$^{(7)}$ (Rob Summers) *chsd ldrs: drvn 5th: outpcd and lost pl next* **10/1**	70
PP5	6	2	**Prairie Hawk (USA)**^{27} 2256 10-9-11 74 oh2 (t) BenPoste$^{(3)}$ (Adrian Wintle) *w ldr: led 5th: hdd between last 2: sn wknd* **11/1**	62
005	7	9	**Sweet Midnight**^{15} 2863 3-10-13 100 CharliePoste (John Holt) *chsd ldrs: reminders and lost pl 5th: sn bhd* **33/1**	64

4m 23.4s (26.00) **Going Correction** +1.70s/f (Heav)
WFA 3 from 5yo+ 13lb **7** Ran SP% **111.1**
Speed ratings (Par 103): **103,102,100,97,95 94,90**
CSF £7.09 TOTE £3.70: £1.90, £1.60; EX 8.80 Trifecta £36.30.
Owner Three Oaks Racing & Mrs P Bosley **Bred** Rathasker Stud **Trained** Ash Priors, Somerset

FOCUS
Race distance increased by 59yds. Only a moderate novices' handicap hurdle with the first two running to their marks.

3144 BETFRED "WISHES YOU A MERRY CHRISTMAS" H'CAP CHASE (18 fncs) 3m 2y

2:55 (2:55) (Class 4) (0-110,105) 4-Y-0+ **£3,924** (£1,159; £579; £290; £145)

Form				RPR
33-4	1		**Armedanddangerous (IRE)**^{29} 2598 10-10-9 88 (b) JamesReveley (Tom Gretton) *chsd ldrs: reminders after 7th: 2nd next: led after 10th: styd on wl fr run-in: drvn out* **10/3**^{1}	99+
6301	2	3 1/2	**Bus Named Desire**^{22} 2735 7-10-4 90 (tp) MrStanSheppard$^{(7)}$ (Matt Sheppard) *hld up in rr: hdwy to trck ldrs 11th: chsd wnr 2 out: chal last: kpt on same pce* **8/1**	94
2P-3	3	50	**Mr McGregor (IRE)**^{18} 2827 7-11-2 95 (b) RichieMcLernon (Heather Dalton) *w ldr: led 3rd tl after 10th: sn drvn: lost pl 14th: t.o 3 out: tk distant 3rd run-in* **7/2**^{2}	49
02/1	4	10	**Don't Hang About**^{231} 60 10-11-4 102 NickSlatter$^{(5)}$ (Gary Hanmer) *chsd ldrs: 2nd 14th: wknd 3 out: sn bhd: t.o* **5/1**^{3}	46
PP-6	5	2	**Snuker**^{19} 2800 8-11-3 96 (p) LucyAlexander (James Ewart) *rn in snatches: in rr: drvn 8th: hdwy to chse ldrs 12th: sn lost pl and bhd: blnd 3 out: t.o* **10/1**	38
45P5	P		**Basford Ben**^{16} 2848 7-11-5 105 (p) ConorWalsh$^{(7)}$ (Jennie Candlish) *led to 3rd: pushed along 8th: reminders and lost pl 6th: sn bhd: t.o whn p.u bef 11th* **10/1**
1P-6	P		**Brave Buck**^{34} 2500 7-11-7 100 JakeGreenall (Henry Daly) *chsd ldrs: 2nd 12th: lost pl bef 4 out: sn bhd: t.o whn p.u bef 2 out* **10/3**^{1}

7m 7.3s (59.20) **Going Correction** +1.80s/f (Heav) **7** Ran SP% **114.3**
Speed ratings (Par 105): **73,71,55,51,51 ,**
CSF £28.61 TOTE £4.30: £2.10, £2.90; EX 32.10 Trifecta £97.40.
Owner Not The Peloton Partnership **Bred** Tony McKiernan **Trained** Holberrow Green, Worcs

FOCUS
Race distance increased by 31yds. A modest handicap chase in which the front two pulled miles clear of the rest. The winner has been a 110+ chaser at his best.

3145 BETFRED TV STANDARD OPEN NATIONAL HUNT FLAT RACE 1m 7f 168y

3:30 (3:30) (Class 6) 4-6-Y-0 **£1,559** (£457; £228; £114)

Form				RPR
22	1		**Templeross (IRE)**^{27} 2650 4-10-11 0 RyanHatch$^{(3)}$ (Nigel Twiston-Davies) *led: hdd after 5f: pushed along 7f out: drvn over 4f out: 2nd over 3f out: led over 2f out: wandered and forged clr over 1f out: eased towards fin* **11/10**^{1}	119+
1	2	10	**Loch Garman Aris (IRE)**^{78} 1717 5-11-2 0 NickSlatter$^{(5)}$ (Gary Hanmer) *hld up in last: hdwy 8f out: 3rd over 2f out: modest 2nd over 1f out* **14/1**	114
1	3	1	**Three Ways**^{39} 2401 4-11-7 0 (t) BrendanPowell (Jamie Snowden) *trckd ldrs: drvn over 4f out: led over 3f out: hdd over 2f out: fdd over 1f out* **6/4**^{2}	113
4	4	5	**Hastrubal (FR)**^{37} 2440 5-11-0 0 TomO'Brien (Henry Daly) *trckd ldrs: pushed along 6f out: wknd over 2f out* **13/2**^{3}	101
00	5	42	**Sundance Boy**^{17} 2842 6-11-0 0 AndrewThornton (Giuseppe Fierro) *racd wd: hld up in rr: hdwy to ld after 5f: hdd over 3f out: wknd and eased over 2f out: sn wl bhd: tailed rt off* **100/1**	59
4	6	82	**Hooghly River (IRE)**^{23} 2715 5-10-7 0 LewisGordon$^{(7)}$ (Jennifer Mason) *t.k.h: w ldrs: pushed along 8f out: reminders and lost pl over 6f: sn wl bhd: tailed rt off 4f out: eventually completed* **40/1**

4m 13.0s (21.20) **Going Correction** +1.70s/f (Heav) **6** Ran SP% **111.0**
Speed ratings: **115,110,109,107,86 45**
CSF £17.11 TOTE £2.10: £1.10, £4.70; EX 10.20 Trifecta £22.00.
Owner N A Twiston-Davies **Bred** Maurice Smiddy **Trained** Naunton, Gloucs

FOCUS
Race distance increased by 59yds. A couple had already showed fair bumper form, including the winner, and they finished well strung out.
T/Plt: £21.50 to a £1 stake. Pool: £43,343.26 - 1,469.38 winning tickets T/Qpdt: £8.40 to a £1 stake. Pool: £4,767.49 - 419.36 winning tickets **Walter Glynn**

3133 ASCOT (R-H)

Saturday, December 19

OFFICIAL GOING: Good to soft (soft in places; 6.4)

Wind: Fresh, across Weather: Fine but cloudy, very mild

3146 FOUNDATION DEVELOPMENTS LTD NOVICES' H'CAP HURDLE (11 hdls) 2m 7f 118y

12:40 (12:40) (Class 4) (0-120,121)
4-Y-0+ **£6,498** (£1,908; £954; £477)

Form				RPR
3	1		**Amiral Collonges (FR)**[30] 2591 5-11-6 **114**............ LeightonAspell (James Evans) *trckd ldrs: quick move to ld 3 out and sn clr gng wl: shkn up after 2 out: pushed out flat* **12/1**	126+
-014	2	9	**Knight ofthe Realm**[23] 2732 6-11-2 **110**............ IanPopham (Caroline Keevil) *nt a fluent: pressed ldrs: chal 3 out: sn outpcd by wnr and no ch w him after: kpt on* **14/1**	112
3411	3	1 ½	**Minellacelebration (IRE)**[17] 2855 5-10-12 **113**............ MrJNixon(7) (Katy Price) *pressed ldr: led 8th to next (3 out): outpcd by ldng pair sn after: kpt on* **11/2**[2]	112
3-P4	4	10	**Pyrshan (IRE)**[26] 2687 6-11-5 **113**............(t) KielanWoods (Graeme McPherson) *hld up in rr: sme prog whn nt fluent 8th: sn outpcd: rdn in 5th after next: no imp after: tk modest 4th bef last* **10/1**	104
5/02	5	9	**Varom (FR)**[16] 2871 6-11-2 **110**............(t) SamTwiston-Davies (Paul Nicholls) *wl in tch: chsd ldng trio 3 out but immediately outpcd by them: n.d after: lost modest 4th bef last* **8/1**	90
0-21	6	1	**Carlo Rocks (IRE)**[18] 2839 5-11-5 **113**............ RichardJohnson (Caroline Bailey) *trckd ldrs: wl there 8th: outpcd fr next: fdd* **5/1**[1]	92
-041	7	12	**Kap Jazz (FR)**[16] 2871 5-11-5 **113**............ AidanColeman (Venetia Williams) *chsd ldrs: rdn fr 7th: struggling fr next: mstke 3 out: wknd* **8/1**	80
314-	8	11	**Alanjou (FR)**[281] 4747 5-10-9 **108**............(p) FreddieMitchell(5) (Henry Tett) *led to 8th: losing pl whn mstke next (3 out): wknd qckly* **50/1**	64
3F-2	9	3 ½	**Say My Name (IRE)**[46] 2262 4-11-7 **115**............ LiamHeard (Bob Buckler) *nt jump wl: last and lost tch 6th: wl bhd after: plugged on* **7/1**[3]	70
3400	10	7	**Gambol (FR)**[23] 2734 5-10-13 **107**............(t) WillKennedy (Ian Williams) *taken down early: hld up in rr: nvr a factor: t.o whn blnd 2 out* **25/1**	53
F63	11	½	**Doitforthevillage (IRE)**[14] 2903 6-11-2 **110**............ NickScholfield (Paul Henderson) *hld up in rr: effrt bef 8th but sn no prog: wknd after 3 out* **25/1**	55
-P45	P		**Get Involved (IRE)**[18] 2839 6-10-12 **106**............(t) CharliePoste (Robin Dickin) *chsd ldrs: wknd rapidly after 7th: bhd whn p.u bef next* **33/1**	
P33-	P		**The Wexfordian (IRE)**[292] 4539 6-11-7 **115**............ AndrewTinkler (Martin Keighley) *hld up in rr: brief effrt 7th: no prog after next: wl bhd whn p.u bef last* **25/1**	
2165	P		**Wait A Second (IRE)**[125] 1269 5-11-8 **116**............(p) BarryGeraghty (Jonjo O'Neill) *lw: nt fluent 1st: hld up in rr: brief effrt 7th: sn wknd rapidly: p.u bef next* **12/1**	
2154	P		**Cooper's Friend (IRE)**[33] 2548 6-11-3 **114**............(t) GrahamWatters(3) (Charlie Longsdon) *trckd ldrs: losing pl whn bad mstke 3 out: wl bhd whn p.u bef 2 out* **20/1**	

5m 58.5s (2.50) **Going Correction** +0.275s/f (Yiel) **15** Ran SP% **119.1**
Speed ratings (Par 105): **108,105,104,101,98 97,93,90,89,86 86, , , ,**
CSF £149.43 CT £1037.89 TOTE £16.80: £5.20, £3.20, £2.20; EX 219.30 Trifecta £1472.50.
Owner S D Faiers **Bred** G A E C Delorme Freres **Trained** Broadwas, Worcs

FOCUS

Due to rail movement this race distance was increased by 46yds. Richard Johnson said of the ground: "It is much better ground on the chase course as it is good to soft while the hurdles track is very sticky and hard work." A good test at the distance and the form looks sound for the level. A big step up from the easy winner, with the fourth rated to his latest run.

3147 GL EVENTS OWEN BROWN GRADUATION CHASE (17 fncs) 2m 5f 8y

1:15 (1:15) (Class 2) 4-Y-0+ **£15,856** (£4,836; £2,526; £1,371)

Form				RPR
P-65	1		**Royal Regatta (IRE)**[22] 2761 7-11-7 145............(bt[1]) RichardJohnson (Philip Hobbs) *racd w enthusiasm: trckd ldr: led 7th: in command 3 out: drew rt away next: 15 l ahd last: eased* **8/1**[3]	161+
/4-F	2	11	**Mala Beach (IRE)**[30] 2606 7-11-4 142............ DavyRussell (Gordon Elliott, Ire) *lw: mstke 1st: in tch: effrt and lft chsng wnr after 12th: no imp fr 3 out: lft wl bhd fr next* **9/4**[1]	143
2121	3	1	**Voix D'Eau (FR)**[22] 2746 5-11-3 144............(t) NoelFehily (Harry Fry) *racd wd: hld up but sn in tch: disp 2nd pl 13th but then outpcd: kpt on to chal for 2nd again last but no ch w wnr* **5/2**[2]	140
-320	4	26	**Kings Lad (IRE)**[22] 2761 8-11-7 145............ TomScudamore (Colin Tizzard) *in tch: urged along fr 8th: struggling fr 11th: poor 4th after 4 out* **16/1**	124
F3-4	F		**Horizontal Speed (IRE)**[47] 2242 7-11-0 139............ AidanColeman (David Dennis) *led to 7th: mstkes next 2: chsd wnr tl stmbld bdly 12th and lost all ch: mstke next: fell heavily 4 out* **14/1**	
20P-	P		**Blue Fashion (IRE)**[252] 5273 6-10-10 147............ DavidBass (Nicky Henderson) *in tch: mstke 12th and wknd qckly: bhd whn p.u bef 14th* **5/2**[2]	

5m 22.6s (-3.40) **Going Correction** +0.275s/f (Yiel) **6** Ran SP% **111.6**
Speed ratings (Par 109): **117,112,112,102,**
CSF £26.80 TOTE £8.70: £2.90, £1.60; EX 29.70 Trifecta £81.50.
Owner Mrs Lesley Field & Mrs Eileen Murphy **Bred** W B Mactaggart **Trained** Withycombe, Somerset

FOCUS

Race distance increased by 46yds. A good-quality graduation event that was won in dominant fashion. A big step up from the impressive winner in first-time headgear, with the second and third rated close to their marks.

3148 BGC PARTNERS H'CAP CHASE (16 fncs) 2m 2f 175y

1:50 (1:50) (Class 3) (0-140,135) 4-Y-0+ **£16,245** (£4,770; £2,385; £1,192)

Form				RPR
2022	1		**Mon Successeur (FR)**[15] 2877 4-11-6 **135**............ SamTwiston-Davies (Paul Nicholls) *lw: patiently rdn in rr: stdy prog fr 12th: stl waiting to be asked bef 2 out: smooth prog to ld bef last: gd jump and sn clr: rdn out* **6/1**[2]	142+
-644	2	7	**Mountain King**[21] 2784 6-11-12 **135**............ RichardJohnson (Philip Hobbs) *often nt fluent: hld up in last pair: mstke 8th: quick prog on outer fr 12th to ld after 3 out: drvn for home bef next: hdd bef last and sn no ch w wnr: tired but hld on for 2nd* **8/1**	142
-333	3	nk	**Gores Island (IRE)**[9] 2990 9-11-3 **126**............ JamieMoore (Gary Moore) *hld up in rr but wl in tch: awkward 1st: prog fr 11th: cl up 3 out: rdn to chse ldr bef 2 out: tl after 2 out: kpt on fr last* **9/1**	132
46-F	4	¾	**Ultragold (FR)**[8] 3014 7-11-1 **124**............(t) NoelFehily (Colin Tizzard) *wl in tch: prog on outer to ld 4 out gng strly: hdd after next and fnd nil: kpt on again fr last* **15/2**[3]	130
2-63	5	nk	**La Vaticane (FR)**[21] 2780 6-11-11 **134**............(t) TomScudamore (David Pipe) *wl in tch: trckd ldrs 3 out gng wl: shkn up and fnd nil 2 out: kpt on fr last* **4/1**[1]	139
1015	6	3	**Johnny Og**[21] 2779 6-10-8 **117**............(b) AndrewTinkler (Martin Keighley) *trckd ldrs: mstke 4th: lost pl and struggling fr 12th: no ch after 3 out: kpt on* **20/1**	119
1221	7	13	**Dartford Warbler (IRE)**[30] 2593 8-10-13 **122**............ DannyCook (Sue Smith) *j.lft: led: mstke and hdd 8th: styd w ldr to 4 out: wkng whn mstke next* **8/1**	115+
-106	8	5	**Big Casino**[21] 2780 9-11-6 **129**............(v) WayneHutchinson (Nigel Twiston-Davies) *pressed ldr: led 8th: hdd 4 out: wknd and mstke next* **8/1**	113
212/	9	3 ¼	**Marcilhac (FR)**[644] 4805 6-11-12 **135**............ AidanColeman (Venetia Williams) *prom: mstke 3rd: mstke 9th and dropped to last: a struggling after* **6/1**[2]	121+
P042	P		**Malibu Sun**[15] 2884 8-11-6 **129**............ NicodeBoinville (Ben Pauling) *prom: lost pl 9th: struggling in rr next: mstke 11th: t.o whn p.u bef 2 out* **14/1**	

4m 50.0s (3.60) **Going Correction** +0.275s/f (Yiel)
WFA 4 from 6yo+ 5lb **10** Ran SP% **115.1**
Speed ratings (Par 107): **103,100,99,99,99 98,92,90,89,**
CSF £52.53 CT £429.31 TOTE £5.90: £2.30, £2.70, £2.80; EX 56.20 Trifecta £309.70.
Owner Mr And Mrs J D Cotton **Bred** P Decouz & P De Maleissye Melun **Trained** Ditcheat, Somerset

FOCUS

Race distance increased by 34yds. No hanging around here in what was a fair handicap, with the winner coming from off the pace. Solid form, with the second to the fifth rated close to their marks.

3149 JLT LONG WALK HURDLE (GRADE 1) (12 hdls) 3m 97y

2:25 (2:27) (Class 1) 4-Y-0+
£56,950 (£21,370; £10,700; £5,330; £2,680; £1,340)

Form				RPR
1-21	1		**Thistlecrack**[21] 2782 7-11-7 161............ TomScudamore (Colin Tizzard) *lw: trckd ldrs: wnt 2nd bef 9th: led 2 out gng strly: sn clr: impressive* **2/1**[1]	171+
20-6	2	8	**Reve De Sivola (FR)**[42] 2361 10-11-7 160............ RichardJohnson (Nick Williams) *swtg: led at gd pce: mstke 8th: urged along after nt fluent 9th: hdd 2 out: kpt on wl but no match for wnr* **11/4**[2]	162
U-F2	3	12	**Deputy Dan (IRE)**[21] 2782 7-11-7 151............(b) LeightonAspell (Oliver Sherwood) *hld up in last pair: nt fluent 4th: mstke 7th: prog fr 9th: drvn to dispute 3rd bef 2 out: one pce after: v awkward jump last* **14/1**	151
-222	4	8	**Karezak (IRE)**[31] 2580 4-11-7 150............(b) WayneHutchinson (Alan King) *hld up in tch: hit 7th and nt fluent next: wl on terms after 3 out: disputing 3rd bef 2 out where mstke: wknd* **33/1**	142
1-15	5	2 ½	**Saphir Du Rheu (FR)**[21] 2783 6-11-7 161............ SamTwiston-Davies (Paul Nicholls) *lw: chsd ldr tl bef 9th: styd cl up tl drvn and dropped to 5th on long run bef 2 out: wl btn after* **11/4**[2]	139
2-34	6	2 ¾	**Aqalim**[21] 2782 5-11-7 150............(v) AidanColeman (John Ferguson) *in tch: urged along fr 1/2-way: dropped to last and lost tch after 8th: no ch after: plugged on fr 2 out* **20/1**	135
-434	7	9	**Taglietelle**[20] 2815 6-11-7 154............(bt) DavyRussell (Gordon Elliott, Ire) *hld up in last pair: nt on terms w ldrs after 3 out and nudged along: wknd bef 2 out* **16/1**	128
-023	8	63	**Dynaste (FR)**[28] 2642 9-11-7 153............(p) ConorO'Farrell (David Pipe) *trckd ldrs: lost pl 7th: struggling in rr bef 9th: t.o and virtually p.u after last* **12/1**[3]	63

6m 5.3s (-5.70) **Going Correction** +0.275s/f (Yiel) **8** Ran SP% **114.6**
Speed ratings (Par 117): **120,117,113,110,109 108,105,84**
CSF £7.94 CT £57.01 TOTE £2.60: £1.30, £1.40, £2.30; EX 7.80 Trifecta £66.10.
Owner John and Heather Snook **Bred** R F And S D Knipe **Trained** Milborne Port, Dorset

FOCUS

Race distance increased by 49yds. A good edition of the race and the form can be rated around the runner-up, who ensured there was a good gallop and ran to something like his best. A big step up from the impressive winner, and he's now at the level of a World Hurdle winner. The second has been rated 5lb off last season's best.

3150 SODEXO SILVER CUP H'CAP CHASE (LISTED RACE) (20 fncs) 2m 7f 180y

3:00 (3:00) (Class 1) 4-Y-0+
£56,950 (£21,370; £10,700; £5,330; £2,680; £1,340)

Form				RPR
4-11	1		**Wakanda (IRE)**[21] 2790 6-11-5 **151**............ DannyCook (Sue Smith) *lw: w ldr: led 3rd to 6th: led again 13th: hdd and drvn 2 out: led again last: hld on most gamely* **8/1**	157
1-02	2	1	**Virak (FR)**[21] 2790 6-11-5 **158**............ HarryCobden(7) (Paul Nicholls) *pressed ldrs thrght: rdn to chal 2 out: tried to edge between ldng pair bef last but n.m.r: swtchd rt after last: styd on to take 2nd nr fin* **14/1**	163
3-24	3	¾	**Fingal Bay (IRE)**[21] 2783 9-10-10 **142**............ RichardJohnson (Philip Hobbs) *prom: lost pl and in midfield 1/2-way: mstke 14th: prog again next to press wnr 16th: rdn to ld 2 out: hdd and one pce last* **6/1**[2]	147
0-2U	4	1 ½	**The Young Master**[21] 2783 6-11-1 **150**............(p) MrSWaley-Cohen(3) (Neil Mulholland) *hld up in rr: prog fr 15th: chsd ldrs 4 out: rdn 2 out: cl 5th last: styd on flat but unable to chal* **8/1**	152
45-1	5	7	**Pendra (IRE)**[49] 2187 7-11-1 **147**............(p) BarryGeraghty (Charlie Longsdon) *lw: trckd ldrs: waiting in bhd them fr 15th: rdn to chal fr 2 out: nrly upsides and nt fluent last: wknd qckly flat* **9/2**[1]	144
/1-1	6	2 ¾	**Salubrious (IRE)**[40] 2399 8-11-2 **148**............ SamTwiston-Davies (Paul Nicholls) *lw: racd on outer: towards rr: prog fr 14th: on terms 4 out: stl cl up and rdn whn nt fluent 2 out: wknd* **13/2**[3]	140
332/	7	5	**Gullinbursti (IRE)**[602] 5569 9-10-5 **137**............ LeightonAspell (Emma Lavelle) *hld up toward rr: mstke 5th: limited prog fr 15th: rdn in 8th after 3 out and no imp on ldrs* **14/1**	126
F-00	8	½	**Houblon Des Obeaux (FR)**[21] 2783 8-10-13 **150**............ CharlieDeutsch(5) (Venetia Williams) *led: nt fluent and hdd 3rd: led 6th tl mstke and hdd 13th: lost pl 16th: sn btn* **8/1**	140

P-F0 **9** *2* **The Giant Bolster**[21] 2783 10-11-3 **149**.......................... TomScudamore 135
(David Bridgwater) *nt fluent 1st: cl up: mstke 11th: sn lost pl: toiling in rr after 14th: n.d after* **16/1**

6-63 **10** *11* **Ma Filleule (FR)**[21] 2781 7-11-11 **157**.......................... NicodeBoinville 131
(Nicky Henderson) *hld up in rr: prog to trck ldrs 14th: cl up 4 out: wknd qckly after next* **16/1**

0-33 **11** *1* **Fox Appeal (IRE)**[49] 2187 8-11-6 **152**..........................[1] SeanBowen 125
(Emma Lavelle) *towards rr: shkn up and no real prog fr 15th: wl btn after* **14/1**

F0-0 **12** *8* **Unioniste (FR)**[14] 2899 7-11-9 **155**..........................(p) NickScholfield 126
(Paul Nicholls) *sloppy rnd of jumping and a in last pair: lost tch fr 15th* **20/1**

0/P- **P** **Katenko (FR)**[413] 2191 9-11-1 **147**.......................... AidanColeman
(Venetia Williams) *wl in tch: chsng ldrs and gng wl whn blnd bdly 12th: nt rcvr and p.u bef next* **20/1**

6m 7.7s (4.20) **Going Correction** +0.275s/f (Yiel) **13** Ran SP% **120.4**
Speed ratings (Par 111): **104,103,103,102,100 99,98,97,97,93 93,90,**
CSF £113.72 CT £720.74 TOTE £9.30: £2.70, £4.30, £2.20; EX 136.00 Trifecta £1295.00.
Owner M B Scholey & R H Scholey **Bred** Bluegate Stud **Trained** High Eldwick, W Yorks

FOCUS
Race distance increased by 46yds. They didn't go overly fast in what was a well-contested handicap chase and plenty had their chance. Solid form, though. The third and fourth given the form a solid look.

3151 THE LADBROKE (HANDICAP HURDLE) (GRADE 3) (8 hdls) 1m 7f 152y
3:35 (3:35) (Class 1) 4-Y-0+
£58,740 (£58,740; £16,050; £7,995; £4,020; £2,010)

Form RPR

06-3 **1** **Jolly's Cracked It (FR)**[49] 2186 6-11-3 **141**.......................... NoelFehily 147
(Harry Fry) *in tch: mstke 3rd: prog in chsng gp after 3 out: chsd ldr 2 out: drvn to cl last: led flat and sn half a l up: jnd last stride* **7/1**[1]

2-11 **1** *dht* **Sternrubin (GER)**[23] 2728 4-10-10 **134**.......................... RichardJohnson 140
(Philip Hobbs) *led at str pce: breather 1/2-way: stretched field out again fr 5th: drvn 2 out: hdd after last: rallied to force dead-heat last stride: fine ride* **9/1**[3]

2R/4 **3** *2 ¼* **Renneti (FR)**[34] 2512 6-11-9 **147**.......................... DannyMullins 151
(W P Mullins, Ire) *humoured along in last pair: stl same pl whn mstke 3 out: rapid prog bef 2 out: drvn and r.o to take 3rd nr fin: gave himself too much to do* **14/1**

10-5 **4** *½* **Some Plan (IRE)**[14] 2914 7-11-2 **140**..........................(t) SamTwiston-Davies 144
(Paul Nicholls) *hld up in midfield: stdy prog on inner after 3 out: clsng on ldrs and looked a threat whn nt fluent 2 out: sn rdn and kpt on same pce* **14/1**

5-30 **5** *3 ¼* **Song Light**[23] 2728 5-10-2 **131**.......................... KevinJones[(5)] 131
(Seamus Mullins) *hld up wl in rr: prog into midfield after 3 out: rdn and hdwy again 2 out: styd on fr last: nrst fin but nvr able to threaten* **25/1**

65-3 **6** *¾* **Zarib (IRE)**[42] 2350 4-10-9 **133**.......................... HarrySkelton 132
(Dan Skelton) *towards rr: shkn up 3 out: prog bef 2 out: rdn and kpt on after: nrst fin but n.d* **8/1**[2]

63- **7** *6* **Vercingetorix (IRE)**[21] 2797 4-10-6 **135**..........................(bt) JackKennedy[(5)] 128
(Gordon Elliott, Ire) *mostly in midfield: rdn and prog on long run bef 2 out but nvr on terms w ldrs: no imp after 2 out* **20/1**

-162 **8** *¾* **Devilment**[14] 2914 4-11-5 **150**.......................... MrAlexFerguson[(7)] 143
(John Ferguson) *prom in chsng gp: mstke 3 out: lost pl 2 out: wknd bef last* **25/1**

1-03 **9** *1* **Hurricane Hollow**[70] 1848 5-10-10 **139**..........................(p) BridgetAndrews[(5)] 131
(Dan Skelton) *mstke 1st: wl in rr: nt fluent 5th: stl wl in rr after 3 out: kpt on bef 2 out: n.d* **16/1**

4-52 **10** *1* **Unanimite (FR)**[49] 2186 4-10-12 **136**.......................... ConorO'Farrell 126
(David Pipe) *mstke 1st: hld up wl in rr: stl there after 3 out: kpt on inner and styd on fr 2 out: no ch* **20/1**

-212 **11** *½* **Galizzi (USA)**[36] 2472 4-10-9 **133**..........................(t) AidanColeman 123
(John Ferguson) *trckd clr ldrs: wnt cl 3rd after 3 out: rdn and nt fluent 2 out: sn btn: mstke last and wknd* **25/1**

3/53 **12** *nk* **Vicenzo Mio (FR)**[14] 2914 5-10-0 **131**..........................(t) HarryCobden[(7)] 120
(Paul Nicholls) *lw: in tch: wl plcd in chsng gp and seemed to be gng wl 3 out: sn rdn: no imp 2 out: fdd* **11/1**

05-4 **13** *3 ½* **Three Kingdoms (IRE)**[29] 2617 6-11-2 **145**..........................(p) MikeyEnnis[(5)] 133
(John Ferguson) *chsd ldng pair and clr of rest to 4th: wnt 2nd next tl 2 out: wknd* **33/1**

02-1 **14** *14* **Sort It Out (IRE)**[231] 96 6-11-6 **144**.......................... MarkWalsh 116
(Edward P Harty, Ire) *lw: wl in tch in chsng gp: drvn after 5th: wknd fr 3 out* **8/1**[2]

1F-1 **15** *4 ½* **Winner Massagot (FR)**[29] 2617 4-10-11 **135**.......................... WayneHutchinson 102
(Alan King) *hld up in rr: prog into midfield 1/2-way: shkn up and tried to cl on ldrs bef 2 out: hld whn mstke 2 out: wknd* **7/1**[1]

-032 **16** *2* **Rayvin Black**[29] 2617 6-10-13 **140**.......................... ThomasGarner[(3)] 105
(Oliver Sherwood) *chsd ldr to 5th: sn rdn: wknd bef 2 out* **25/1**

61-0 **17** *5* **Sgt Reckless**[49] 2185 8-11-6 **144**.......................... WillKennedy 104
(Mick Channon) *nvr bttr than midfield: lost pl and struggling bef 5th: n.d after* **33/1**

0/0- **18** *½* **Noble Inn (FR)**[37] 2467 5-11-0 **141**.......................... DavidMullins[(3)] 101
(W P Mullins, Ire) *in tch in midfield: rdn and losing pl whn hit 3 out: sn bhd* **14/1**

0-11 **19** *2 ¼* **Presenting Arms (IRE)**[16] 2873 8-10-6 **137**..........................(t) LiamMcKenna[(7)] 95
(Harry Fry) *a wl in rr: shkn up and no prog after 3 out: nvr a factor* **25/1**

0-13 **P** **Waxies Dargle**[34] 2512 6-11-4 **142**.......................... BarryGeraghty
(Noel Meade, Ire) *taken wd thrght: nvr bttr than midfield: struggling fr 5th: wl bhd whn p.u bef 2 out* **12/1**

1P-0 **P** **Bidourey (FR)**[34] 2512 4-10-11 **135**.......................... TomScudamore
(David Pipe) *in tch in midfield tl dropped to last after 4th and sn p.u* **25/1**

3m 47.0s (-0.40) **Going Correction** +0.275s/f (Yiel)
WFA 4 from 5yo+ 5lb **21** Ran SP% **137.6**
Speed ratings (Par 113): **112,112,110,110,109 108,105,105,104,104 104,103,102,95,92 91,89,89,87,**
WIN: 4.10 Jolly's Cracked It, 4.80 Sternrubin; PL: 2.40 Jolly's Cracked It, 4.30 Renneti, 3.00 Sternrubin, 4.40 Some Plan; EX: 43.40, 47.00; CSF: 32.50, 34.07; TC: 451.21, 460.40; TF: 811.10, 841.20;.
Owner Gdm Partnership **Bred** Henrietta Charlet & Daniel Charlesworth **Trained** Seaborough, Dorset
Owner Terry Warner **Bred** Gestut Karlshof **Trained** Withycombe, Somerset

FOCUS
Race distance increased by 28yds. A smart handicap in which they were soon strung out courtesy of Sternrubin, who rallied in incredibly game fashion to force a dead-heat. Rock-solid form. The first four are on the upgrade, while the fifth and sixth are probably the best guide to the level.
T/Jkpt: Not won. Jackpot Placepot: £2,844.50 to a £1 stake. Pool: £6,234.67 - 1.60 winning tickets. T/Plt: £498.00 to a £1 stake. Pool: £235,744.31 - 345.56 winning tickets. T/Qpdt: £24.70 to a £1 stake. Pool: £25,574.86 - 765.04 winning tickets. **Jonathan Neesom**

2637 HAYDOCK (L-H)
Saturday, December 19

OFFICIAL GOING: Heavy (chs 4.3 hdl 5.2)
Wind: Moderate, variable Weather: Drizzle

3152 DOWNLOAD YOUR RACING UK APP H'CAP HURDLE (9 hdls) 1m 7f 144y
11:55 (11:55) (Class 3) (0-125,123)
3-Y-0+ **£7,797** (£2,289; £1,144; £572)

Form RPR

-355 **1** **After Hours (IRE)**[22] 2763 6-10-13 **110**.......................... JamesDavies 119+
(Henry Oliver) *chsd ldr: led jst bef 3 out: rdn and hdd appr last: tried to renew effrt over 1f out: sn nrly 3 l down: rallied towards fin: led on post* **6/1**

42 **2** *shd* **Baratineur (FR)**[29] 2628 4-11-5 **116**.......................... HarrySkelton 125+
(Dan Skelton) *hld up: hdwy after 4 out: wnt 2nd bef 2 out: led appr last: edgd lft and nrly 3 l up 1f out: all out towards fin: hdd post* **11/4**[1]

-433 **3** *12* **Captain Redbeard (IRE)**[12] 2945 6-10-4 **108**.......................... SamColtherd[(7)] 105
(Stuart Coltherd) *hld up: hdwy 4 out: chsng ldrs whn mstke 3 out: sn rdn: wnt 3rd bef last: no imp on front pair* **25/1**

0-11 **4** *3 ¼* **Virnon**[20] 2804 4-11-11 **122**.......................... PaddyBrennan 116
(Alan Swinbank) *midfield: mstke 5th: hdwy appr 4 out: rdn whn chsng ldrs 2 out: one pce and no imp after* **5/1**[2]

0/F- **5** *½* **Fatcatinthehat**[266] 5022 6-11-12 **123**.......................... GavinSheehan 117
(Harry Whittington) *led: hdd jst bef 3 out: wknd after 2 out* **11/2**[3]

0 **6** *8* **Wells De Lune (FR)**[14] 2914 4-11-11 **122**..........................[1] BrianHughes 110
(Charlie Longsdon) *hld up in rr: sme hdwy appr 3 out: hit 2 out: u.p and wl btn after* **16/1**

5312 **7** *10* **Russian Royale**[51] 2144 5-11-1 **117**.......................... JamieBargary[(5)] 95
(Micky Hammond) *midfield: hdwy 5th: sn chsd ldrs: rdn after 4 out: losing pl whn blnd 3 out: wl btn* **33/1**

2210 **8** *1 ¾* **Watt Broderick (IRE)**[33] 2540 6-11-6 **117**..........................(p) DenisO'Regan 91
(Ian Williams) *hld up: struggling after 4 out: nvr a threat* **28/1**

4-33 **9** *1 ¼* **Sandygate (IRE)**[43] 2312 5-11-5 **116**.......................... TomO'Brien 88
(Philip Hobbs) *chsd ldrs tl rdn and wknd after 4 out* **7/1**

01- **10** *14* **Two B'S**[396] 2562 4-11-4 **115**.......................... BrianHarding 73
(Tim Easterby) *chsd ldrs tl wknd 4 out: t.o* **25/1**

-603 **11** *2 ½* **Circus Star (USA)**[14] 2921 7-10-13 **117**..........................(t) MrJDixon[(7)] 73
(John Dixon) *hld up: struggling 5th: t.o* **9/1**

3m 59.3s (-4.90) **Going Correction** -0.125s/f (Good)
WFA 4 from 5yo+ 5lb **11** Ran SP% **115.5**
Speed ratings (Par 107): **107,106,100,99,99 95,90,89,88,81 80**
CSF £22.00 CT £385.42 TOTE £6.70: £3.20, £1.30, £6.10; EX 23.20 Trifecta £490.90.
Owner R G Whitehead **Bred** Michael Heskin **Trained** Abberley, Worcs

FOCUS
Chases and hurdles sharing a single bend at both ends of the course. The bend into the home straight was 4yds out and the bend after winning post was 6yds out. This race distance was increased by 30yds. A competitive handicap started the meeting off. The first two are on the upgrade. The third is on a toughish mark but helps set the level.

3153 RACING UK ANYWHERE NOVICES' CHASE (13 fncs) 1m 7f 157y
12:25 (12:25) (Class 2) 4-Y-0+ **£12,627** (£3,811; £1,963; £1,039)

Form RPR

0-53 **1** **Pain Au Chocolat (FR)**[63] 1969 4-10-7 0.......................... HarrySkelton 138+
(Dan Skelton) *prom: mstke 2nd: led 7th: blnd 2 out: rdn appr last: edgd lft fnl 75yds: drvn out* **15/8**[2]

0-22 **2** *1 ¼* **Aso (FR)**[21] 2779 5-10-12 137.......................... LiamTreadwell 142+
(Venetia Williams) *led appr 2nd: j.lft several times: j. slowly and hdd 7th: nt fluent 4 out: sn rdn: rallied last: swtchd rt as wnr c across fnl 75yds: kpt on but hld nr fin* **8/13**[1]

121- **3** *12* **Captain Hox (IRE)**[9] 2999 6-10-12 125..........................(t) BrianHughes 127
(Patrick Griffin, Ire) *hld up in rr: hdwy bef 7th: no imp fr 3 out* **20/1**

1113 **4** *72* **Helium (FR)**[17] 2854 10-11-6 133.......................... RhysFlint 63
(Alexandra Dunn) *handy: lost pl 6th: j. slowly 7th: struggling bef 8th: t.o* **14/1**[3]

P **Killone (IRE)**[272] 6-10-12 0.......................... DerekFox
(Stuart Coltherd) *racd keenly early: led: hdd appr 2nd: lost pl 6th: struggling whn mstke 9th: t.o whn p.u bef 3 out* **100/1**

4m 10.2s (-0.80) **Going Correction** +0.40s/f (Soft)
WFA 4 from 5yo+ 5lb **5** Ran SP% **109.1**
Speed ratings (Par 109): **118,117,111,75,**
CSF £3.51 TOTE £2.70: £1.10, £1.10; EX 4.00 Trifecta £10.30.
Owner Mike And Eileen Newbould **Bred** Mme Karine Du Pont De Romemont **Trained** Alcester, Warwicks
■ Stewards' Enquiry : Harry Skelton caution; careless riding

FOCUS
Chases and hurdles sharing a single bend at both ends of the course. The bend into the home straight was 4yds out and the bend after winning post was 6yds out. This race distance was increased by 30yds. The betting suggested only two counted here and that pair pulled clear. A step up from the winner on the best of his hurdle figures. The second set a decent standard and the third has been rated in line with his hurdle mark.

3154 WATCH RACING UK ON THREE DEVICES MARES' NOVICES' HURDLE (REG' AS ABRAM MARES' NOV HDL) (LISTED RACE) (10 hdls) 2m 2f 191y
12:55 (12:56) (Class 1) 4-Y-0+ **£11,591** (£4,475; £2,341; £1,267)

Form RPR

2113 **1** **Smart Talk (IRE)**[28] 2632 5-11-0 127.......................... PaddyBrennan 138+
(Brian Ellison) *mde all: drew clr 3 out: styd on wl: a in command* **3/1**[1]

0-01 **2** *8* **Sunshine Corner (IRE)**[18] 2829 4-11-0 0.......................... GavinSheehan 130
(Lucy Wadham) *chsd wnr to 1st and lft 2nd at 5th: no imp fr 3 out* **7/1**

3-21 **3** *16* **Yes I Did (IRE)**[32] 2561 5-11-0 0.......................... HarrySkelton 117
(Dan Skelton) *hld up in tch: swvd to avoid faller 5th: cl up after 4 out: outpcd bef 3 out: rdn and hung lft fr bef 2 out: wl btn* **7/2**[2]

16-1 **4** *14* **Out Of The Mist (IRE)**[50] 2164 6-11-0 0.......................... RichieMcLernon 103
(Emma Lavelle) *in tch: mstke 3rd: struggling bef 3 out: wl btn* **13/2**

20-1 **F** **Briery Queen**[21] 2776 6-11-0 0.......................... JamesBanks
(Noel Williams) *chsd wnr fr 1st tl fell 5th* **7/2**[2]

-313 **P** **Mardale (IRE)**[29] 2626 5-11-0 128..........................(t) BrianHarding
(Nicky Richards) *a bhd: pushed along bef 5th: p.u bef 4 out* **11/2**[3]

4m 48.8s (-4.20) **Going Correction** -0.125s/f (Good) **6** Ran SP% **110.7**
Speed ratings (Par 111): **103,99,92,87,**
CSF £22.46 TOTE £3.20: £1.50, £3.20; EX 19.80 Trifecta £72.00.
Owner Mrs J A Martin **Bred** Roland Rothwell **Trained** Norton, N Yorks

FOCUS
Chases and hurdles sharing a single bend at both ends of the course. The bend into the home straight was 4yds out and the bend after winning post was 6yds out. This race distance was increased by 42yds. Just an ordinary looking race for the level, which was won by a mare who made every yard. The winner set a decent standard on her Ascot run and has been rated to that level.

3155 D H WELTON 40TH ANNIVERSARY H'CAP CHASE (13 fncs) 1m 7f 157y
1:30 (1:30) (Class 3) (0-135,134) 4-Y-0+ **£9,747** (£2,862; £1,431; £715)

Form RPR
431- **1** **Arthur's Oak**[257] 5195 7-11-2 **124**........ LiamTreadwell 147+
(Venetia Williams) *mde all: drew clr appr 4 out: a in command: easily* **11/4**[1]
-41P **2** *17* **Back To Bracka (IRE)**[29] 2615 8-11-9 **134**........ DerekFox(3) 135
(Lucinda Russell) *hld up in tch: hit 2nd: in rr after 4th: pushed along appr 4 out: styd on u.p 3 out: lft 2nd 2 out: j.lft last: no ch w wnr* **8/1**
30-5 **3** *8* **Abigail Lynch (IRE)**[221] 259 7-10-9 **122**........(t) JamieBargary(5) 113
(Nigel Twiston-Davies) *in tch: struggling after 9th: plugged on u.p to take 3rd nr fin* **12/1**
1533 **4** *1* **Vodka Wells (FR)**[35] 2495 5-11-5 **127**........ BrianHughes 117
(Micky Hammond) *hld up: hdwy bef 5th: no imp 2 out: wl btn* **5/1**
U606 **5** *67* **Strongly Suggested**[22] 2746 8-11-5 **127**........ RichieMcLernon 50
(Jonjo O'Neill) *hld up: hdwy after 4th: sltly hmpd 5th: sn bhd: t.o* **25/1**
-021 **P** **Clan William (IRE)**[14] 2920 7-10-8 **116**........ SeanQuinlan
(Sue Smith) *chsd wnr: u.p and no imp whn wnt wrong and p.u jst bef 2 out: fatally injured* **3/1**[2]
4-02 **F** **Whispering Harry**[21] 2784 6-11-7 **129**........ JamesDavies
(Henry Oliver) *chsd ldrs tl fell 5th* **7/2**[3]
4m 13.7s (2.70) **Going Correction** +0.40s/f (Soft) **7 Ran SP% 113.2**
Speed ratings (Par 107): **109,100,96,96,62**
CSF £23.50 CT £223.30 TOTE £3.40: £2.10, £3.30; EX 26.60 Trifecta £201.40.
Owner Mrs J K Burt **Bred** J L Burt **Trained** Kings Caple, H'fords

FOCUS
Chases and hurdles sharing a single bend at both ends of the course. The bend into the home straight was 4yds out and the bend after winning post was 6yds out. This race distance was increased by 30yds. A few of these had run well when last seen, but the winner was much the best after a lengthy absence. A big step up from the impressive winner, while the second helps set the level.

3156 NATIONWIDEVEHICLECONTRACTS.CO.UK H'CAP HURDLE (10 hdls) 2m 2f 191y
2:05 (2:05) (Class 2) 3-Y-0+
£13,763 (£4,065; £2,032; £1,016; £508; £255)

Form RPR
0-1 **1** **Montdragon (FR)**[229] 105 5-11-10 **128**........(t) JoshuaMoore 132
(Jonjo O'Neill) *in tch: rdn along and sltly outpcd bef 3 out: sn rallied to go 2nd: rdn and upsides last: styd on to ld 1f out: kpt on* **9/2**[2]
44-1 **2** *2 ¼* **Baby Bach (IRE)**[21] 2791 5-11-7 **125**........ BrianHughes 127
(S R B Crawford, Ire) *hld up in rr: hdwy bef 3 out: rdn and hung appr last: continued to hang lft run-in: wnt 2nd fnl 100yds: no real imp on wnr* **11/2**[3]
111- **3** *4 ½* **Three Faces West (IRE)**[276] 4851 7-11-12 **130**........ TomO'Brien 128
(Philip Hobbs) *led: hit 3rd: shkn up on bnd after 4th: rdn whn jnd last: hdd 1f out: no ex fnl 100yds* **2/1**[1]
50-1 **4** *6* **Baby King (IRE)**[28] 2637 6-11-11 **129**........(t) PaddyBrennan 123
(Tom George) *chsd ldrs: rdn and ch 2 out: one pce after last* **9/2**[2]
0-53 **5** *6* **De Boitron (FR)**[28] 2637 11-11-7 **125**........ SeanQuinlan 110
(Sue Smith) *chsd ldr to 3 out: rdn and wknd after 2 out* **14/1**
-524 **6** *26* **Istimraar (IRE)**[28] 2645 4-11-2 **120**........(t) RyanMahon 79
(Dan Skelton) *hld up: hdwy appr 5th: hit 6th: wknd bef 3 out* **12/1**
4-02 **7** *18* **Aerlite Supreme (IRE)**[28] 2639 8-11-12 **130**........ AdamWedge 106
(Evan Williams) *hld up: chsd ldrs bef 2 out: rdn and nt pick up bef last: sn wknd* **6/1**
5m 0.6s (7.60) **Going Correction** -0.125s/f (Good)
WFA 4 from 5yo+ 5lb **7 Ran SP% 113.7**
Speed ratings (Par 109): **79,78,76,73,71 60,52**
CSF £28.66 TOTE £5.20: £2.80, £2.40; EX 31.60 Trifecta £62.20.
Owner John P McManus **Bred** Csse Bertrand De Tarragon **Trained** Cheltenham, Gloucs

FOCUS
Chases and hurdles sharing a single bend at both ends of the course. The bend into the home straight was 4yds out and the bend after winning post was 6yds out. This race distance was increased by 42yds for this race. This featured some promising types but the pace didn't seem overly strong and at least five of the field held some sort of chance going to the second-last. The winner was on a decent mark and has been rated in line with his Warwick win.

3157 TOMMY WHITTLE H'CAP CHASE (SPONSORED BY NATIONWIDE VEHICLE CONTRACTS) (18 fncs) 2m 6f 204y
2:40 (2:40) (Class 2) (0-145,145) 4-Y-0+
£18,768 (£5,544; £2,772; £1,386; £693; £348)

Form RPR
P242 **1** **Seventh Sky (GER)**[14] 2902 8-11-12 **145**........(tp) GavinSheehan 156+
(Charlie Mann) *mde all: styd on wl* **10/1**
3-41 **2** *7* **Spookydooky (IRE)**[23] 2727 7-11-9 **142**........(t) JoshuaMoore 143
(Jonjo O'Neill) *in tch: effrt 4 out: wnt 2nd 3 out: j.lft last: no imp on wnr* **5/1**[1]
-0P0 **3** *6* **Cloudy Too (IRE)**[21] 2790 9-11-5 **138**........ SeanQuinlan 133
(Sue Smith) *prom 3rd: wnt 2nd 12th: blnd 4 out: lost 2nd 3 out: one pce after* **8/1**[3]
3-32 **4** *8* **Plus Jamais (FR)**[38] 2431 8-10-0 **119** oh2........ BrendanPowell 109
(Jim Goldie) *chsd wnr tl hit 12th: wknd 3 out: j.lft and mstke last whn wl btn* **11/1**
1-PP **5** *nk* **Hollow Blue Sky (FR)**[174] 855 8-9-12 **122**........(tp) JamieBargary(5) 110
(Nigel Twiston-Davies) *in tch: rdn whn chsng ldrs appr 4 out: fdd fr 3 out* **11/1**
-3P1 **6** *17* **Wilton Milan (IRE)**[25] 2701 7-11-0 **133**........(t) RyanMahon 102
(Dan Skelton) *hld up: rdn after 14th: nvr a threat* **12/1**
-342 **P** **Sun Cloud (IRE)**[28] 2643 8-11-7 **140**........ BrianHughes
(Malcolm Jefferson) *hld up: struggling 14th: t.o whn p.u bef 4 out* **6/1**[2]
-525 **P** **Spirit Of Shankly**[21] 2785 7-10-13 **132**........(bt) TomO'Brien
(Charlie Longsdon) *mstke 1st: chsd ldrs to 3rd: in rr bef 10th: bhd whn p.u bef 14th* **8/1**[3]
1P-2 **P** **O Maonlai (IRE)**[21] 2780 7-11-4 **137**........(t) PaddyBrennan
(Tom George) *hld up in rr: nt fluent 5th: mstke 6th: hdwy 10th: rdn and wknd bef 4 out: bhd whn p.u bef 2 out* **5/1**[1]
-314 **U** **Final Assault (IRE)**[21] 2790 6-11-3 **139**........ DerekFox(3)
(Lucinda Russell) *midfield tl blnd and uns rdr 10th* **6/1**[2]
6m 19.5s (5.50) **Going Correction** +0.40s/f (Soft) **10 Ran SP% 117.6**
Speed ratings (Par 109): **106,103,101,98,98 92,,,,**
CSF £61.07 CT £427.27 TOTE £13.70: £3.80, £2.10, £2.80; EX 81.90 Trifecta £1034.60.
Owner John Heron **Bred** Gestut Karlshof **Trained** Upper Lambourn, Berks

FOCUS
Chases and hurdles sharing a single bend at both ends of the course. The bend into the home straight was 4yds out and the bend after winning post was 6yds out. This race distance was increased by 60yds for this race. The winner set decent fractions from the outset, meaning plenty got really tired. The winner was nicely in on the best of his novice form, but this rates a step up. The third has been rated similar to his recent Newcastle run. Chases and hurdles sharing a single bend at both ends of the course. The bend into the home straight was 4yds out and the bend after winning post was 6yds out. This race distance was increased by 60yds for this race. The winner set decent fractions from the outset, meaning plenty got really tired. The winner was nicely in on the best of his novice form, but this rates a step up. The third has been rated similar to his recent Newcastle run.

3158 BET WITH YOUR RACING UK APP H'CAP HURDLE (12 hdls) 2m 6f 177y
3:15 (3:15) (Class 3) (0-135,129) 4-Y-0+ **£7,797** (£2,289; £1,144; £572)

Form RPR
111F **1** **Isaacstown Lad (IRE)**[6] 3058 8-11-8 **125**........ BrianHarding 129+
(Nicky Richards) *hld up: hdwy appr 3 out: wnt 2nd 2 out: styd on to ld ins fnl f: in command towards fin* **5/2**[1]
-114 **2** *4* **Oscar Blue (IRE)**[29] 2624 5-11-7 **124**........ PaddyBrennan 125
(Brian Ellison) *hld up: hdwy 4th: mstke 4 out: effrt to chal 3 out: led appr 2 out: hdd ins fnl f: no ex towards fin* **9/2**[3]
506P **3** *10* **Sybarite (FR)**[15] 2878 9-11-7 **129**........ JamieBargary(5) 121
(Nigel Twiston-Davies) *prom: sn rdn along: nvr travelled: lost pl 4th: detached after 4 out: plugged on to take 3rd run-in: no imp on front two* **12/1**
2332 **4** *16* **Major Ivan (IRE)**[29] 2624 6-11-11 **128**........(b) BrianHughes 106
(Malcolm Jefferson) *led bef 2nd: hdd appr 2 out where nt fluent: wknd bef last* **11/4**[2]
2-52 **F** **Ugly Bug**[27] 2658 9-11-0 **117**........ RobertDunne
(Tony Carroll) *sn led: hdd bef 2nd: remained prom: rdn appr 3 out: sn wknd: bhd whn fell last* **11/4**[2]
2320 **P** **Listen And Learn (IRE)**[29] 2624 7-11-9 **126**........(v) JoshuaMoore
(Jonjo O'Neill) *chsd ldrs: nt fluent 6th: lost pl 7th: t.o whn p.u bef 3 out* **20/1**
6m 4.6s (4.60) **Going Correction** -0.125s/f (Good) **6 Ran SP% 112.5**
Speed ratings (Par 107): **87,85,82,76,**
CSF £14.17 TOTE £3.50: £1.70, £2.50; EX 12.20 Trifecta £156.80.
Owner M S Borders Racing Club & Partners **Bred** Patrick Cronin **Trained** Greystoke, Cumbria

FOCUS
Chases and hurdles sharing a single bend at both ends of the course. The bend into the home straight was 4yds out and the bend after winning post was 6yds out. This race distance was increased by 60yds for this race. Not many runners lined up but this was a competitive contest, with only a couple difficult to fancy. Another step forward from the progressive winner.
T/Plt: £170.40 to a £1 stake. Pool: £77,088.18 - 330.22 winning tickets. T/Qpdt: £70.30 to a £1 stake. Pool: £5,179.55 - 54.46 winning tickets. **Darren Owen**

2978 NEWCASTLE (L-H)
Saturday, December 19
OFFICIAL GOING: Heavy (soft in places; 5.1)
Wind: Strong, half against Weather: Overcast

3159 MONEY BACK SPECIAL AT 188BET NOVICES' HURDLE (11 hdls 2 omitted) 2m 6f
11:45 (11:45) (Class 4) 4-Y-0+ **£3,249** (£954; £477; £238)

Form RPR
312 **1** **Jonniesofa (IRE)**[21] 2787 5-11-5 126........ CraigNichol 132+
(Rose Dobbin) *mde all: shkn up and drew clr bef omitted 3 out: easily* **4/9**[1]
2-2 **2** *41* **Deputy Commander (IRE)**[14] 2904 6-10-9 0........ RyanHatch(3) 84
(Nigel Twiston-Davies) *nt fluent: in tch: hdwy whn hit 8th: sn chsng wnr: rdn and outpcd passing omitted 3 out: fin tired* **11/4**[2]
4F36 **3** *24* **King Of The Dark (IRE)**[6] 8-10-5 100........ ThomasDowson(7) 60
(Victor Thompson) *chsd ldrs: wnt 2nd whn hit 7th: rdn and struggling 3 out (usual 4 out): sn lost tch* **50/1**
22-2 **4** *46* **Australasia (IRE)**[189] 732 5-10-12 0........ JamesReveley 14
(Karen McLintock) *mstkes: in tch: drvn and struggling 7th: lost tch fr next: t.o* **8/1**[3]
45 **P** **Raymond Reddington (IRE)**[12] 2951 4-10-7 0........ DiarmuidO'Regan(5)
(Chris Grant) *chsd wnr tl lost pl 7th: sn lost tch: t.o whn p.u 3 out (usual 4 out)* **100/1**
5m 52.6s (16.60) **Going Correction** +0.60s/f (Soft)
WFA 4 from 5yo+ 6lb **5 Ran SP% 110.0**
Speed ratings (Par 105): **93,78,69,52,**
CSF £2.09 TOTE £1.30: £1.10, £1.50; EX 1.60 Trifecta £14.40.
Owner R & Mrs A Houghton & A Houghton **Bred** T Finn **Trained** South Hazelrigg, Northumbria

FOCUS
The last fence was omitted in all chases and the first flight in the home straight was removed for all hurdle races. This opening novice lacked depth and it was easy for the useful winner. Due to rail movements the actual race distance was 2m6f 35yds.

3160 FREE BET AT 188BET NOVICES' LIMITED H'CAP CHASE (17 fncs 2 omitted) 2m 7f 91y
12:15 (12:15) (Class 4) (0-120,120) 4-Y-0+ **£3,987** (£1,178; £589; £294; £147)

Form RPR
1453 **1** **Alto Des Mottes (FR)**[17] 2848 5-10-11 **112**........ TonyKelly(3) 134+
(Henry Hogarth) *cl up: led 4 out (usual 5 out): drew clr fr 2 out: rdn out* **3/1**[1]
3-41 **2** *13* **Askamore Darsi (IRE)**[16] 2865 6-10-13 **111**........(p) HenryBrooke 120
(Donald McCain) *chsd ldr to 12th: drvn and outpcd 4 out (usual 5 out): rallied next: chsd (clr) wnr passing omitted last: no imp* **3/1**[1]
30-2 **3** *3 ¼* **The Orange Rogue (IRE)**[21] 2788 8-10-5 **108**........ StephenMulqueen(5) 115
(N W Alexander) *led to 4 out (usual 5 out): ev ch next: sn pushed along: one pce fr 2 out: lost 2nd passing omitted last* **4/1**[3]
11F4 **4** *7* **Chanceofa Lifetime (IRE)**[22] 2753 8-10-8 **113**........ ThomasDowson(7) 113
(Victor Thompson) *prom: hit 9th: rdn and outpcd 3 out: struggling fr next* **9/1**

U31P **5** 1 ½ **Teochew (IRE)**[16] 2858 7-11-2 **114**..............................(t) DavidEngland 111
(Richard Drake) *hld up: outpcd 10th: rallied to chse ldrs 5 out (usual 6 out): rdn bef 3 out: wknd bef next* **16/1**

P6-U **P** **Imperial Leader (IRE)**[14] 2905 7-11-5 **120**..............................(t) RyanHatch(3)
(Nigel Twiston-Davies) *nt fluent: in tch: pckd and outpcd 10th: struggling 4 out (usual 5 out): lost tch and p.u bef next* **10/3**[2]

6m 31.5s (9.00) **Going Correction** +0.35s/f (Yiel) **6** Ran SP% **109.0**
Speed ratings (Par 105): **98,93,92,89,89**
CSF £11.94 TOTE £3.40: £1.80, £2.10; EX 9.10 Trifecta £33.70.
Owner Hogarth Racing **Bred** E A R L Ecurie Des Mottes **Trained** Stillington, N Yorks

FOCUS
A fairly useful effort from the winner, who was well suited by the emphasis on stamina. Due to rail movements the actual race distance was 2m7f 126yds.

3161 PLAY CASINO AT 188BET NOVICES' H'CAP HURDLE (8 hdls 1 omitted) 2m 98y
12:50 (12:50) (Class 5) (0-100,100) 3-Y-0+ £2,274 (£667; £333; £166)

Form RPR

P0-U **1** **Clan Chief**[25] 2707 6-11-5 **93**.............................. LucyAlexander 99+
(N W Alexander) *cl up: led 3rd: mde rest: pushed along and edgd lft 2 out: kpt on wl fr last* **6/4**[1]

05UP **2** 4 **Mister Hendre**[13] 2937 7-9-8 **75**..............................(t) JamesCorbett(7) 76
(Susan Corbett) *prom: wnt 2nd bef 4 out (usual 4 out): effrt and ch next: hung rt and one pce fr last* **10/1**

P0-P **3** 12 **Agesilas (FR)**[226] 153 7-10-0 **74** oh5..............................(p) JonathanEngland 64
(Andrew Crook) *hld up: pushed along and outpcd 3 out (usual 4 out): kpt on fr 2 out: nvr able to chal* **20/1**

/3F- **4** 4 ½ **New Academy**[388] 2741 7-11-12 **100**.............................. HenryBrooke 85
(John Wade) *chsd ldrs: outpcd bef 3 out (usual 4 out): n.d after* **8/1**

005 **5** 4 ½ **Triumph Davis (IRE)**[20] 2800 6-10-13 **90**..............................(p) JoeColliver(3) 70
(Micky Hammond) *nt fluent on occasions: hld up: outpcd 4th: sn struggling: n.d after* **7/1**[3]

P4P3 **6** 30 **Bertielicious**[15] 2891 7-9-7 **74** oh13..............................(p) ThomasDowson(7) 24
(Jonathan Haynes) *led to 3rd: cl up: rdn and wknd bef omitted 3 out: t.o* **20/1**

F20- **P** **River Bollin**[303] 4324 5-11-12 **100**.............................. JamesReveley
(Tim Easterby) *nt fluent on occasions: hld up in tch: hdwy after 3 out (usual 4 out): wknd and p.u bef 2 out* **5/2**[2]

4m 21.1s (11.10) **Going Correction** +0.60s/f (Soft) **7** Ran SP% **110.8**
Speed ratings (Par 103): **96,94,88,85,83 68,**
CSF £15.46 CT £198.85 TOTE £2.50: £1.90, £4.10; EX 20.30 Trifecta £189.00.
Owner Clan Gathering **Bred** Alexander Family **Trained** Kinneston, Perth & Kinross

FOCUS
A weak handicap, the leading pair coping with conditions a lot better than the rest. Due to rail movements the actual race distance was 2m 118yds.

3162 188BET NORTHUMBERLAND CHASE (A H'CAP CHASE) (QUAL' FOR CHALLENGER MIDDLE DISTANCE CHASE FINAL) (14 fncs 2 omitted) 2m 4f 19y
1:20 (1:21) (Class 3) (0-135,125) 4-Y£0,472 (£2,194; £1,097; £548; £Form)

1-52 **1** **Bernardelli (IRE)**[21] 2766 7-11-12 **125**.............................. CraigNichol 141+
(Nicky Richards) *hld up: hdwy to chse ldrs 5th: chal 8th: led gng wl bef 3 out (usual 4 out): styd on strly fr last* **4/1**[2]

-P60 **2** 5 **Carrigdhoun (IRE)**[48] 2213 10-11-7 **125**..............................(tp) DaraghBourke(5) 133
(Maurice Barnes) *cl up: chal 4th: led 6th: hdd bef 3 out (usual 4 out): sn rdn: kpt on fr last to take 2nd nr fin: no ch w wnr* **9/1**

0-P3 **3** ½ **Trust Thomas**[9] 2979 7-10-9 **113**.............................. JamieHamilton(5) 120
(Ann Hamilton) *in tch: stdy hdwy bef 3 out (usual 4 out): effrt next: chsd wnr and rdn last: no ex and lost 2nd nr fin* **5/1**[3]

6444 **4** 17 **Manballandall (IRE)**[13] 2932 7-11-3 **123**..............................(t) JamesCorbett(7) 113
(Susan Corbett) *hld up in tch: hdwy to chse ldrs 5 out (usual 6 out): rdn and wknd fr 3 out* **20/1**

13-P **F** **No Deal (IRE)**[28] 2638 9-11-5 **118**..............................(t) PeterBuchanan
(Lucinda Russell) *hld up: fell 1st* **5/1**[3]

4/04 **F** **The Ramblin Kid**[21] 2785 7-10-11 **117**.............................. FinianO'Toole(7)
(Micky Hammond) *cl up on outside: rdr lost iron briefly 2nd: sn rcvrd and led bef next: nt fluent and hdd 6th: ev ch whn fell 9th* **5/2**[1]

1-P1 **B** **Boric**[21] 2788 7-10-8 **112**..............................(p) GrantCockburn(5)
(Simon Waugh) *led to bef 3rd: chsd ldrs: pushed along whn b.d 9th* **6/1**

5m 35.2s (8.00) **Going Correction** +0.35s/f (Yiel) **7** Ran SP% **111.0**
Speed ratings (Par 107): **98,96,95,89,**
CSF £34.74 TOTE £4.90: £2.70, £4.30; EX 31.00 Trifecta £151.00.
Owner Henriques & LLoyd-Bakers **Bred** Minch Bloodstock **Trained** Greystoke, Cumbria

FOCUS
With three of the seven departing this wasn't as competitive as it might have been, though the winner has still produced a pretty useful effort to defy joint top weight. With rail movements the actual race distance was 2m4f 49yds.

3163 PREMIER LEAGUE BETTING AT 188BET MARES' H'CAP HURDLE (8 hdls 1 omitted) 2m 98y
1:55 (1:55) (Class 4) (0-110,104) 3-Y-0+ £3,249 (£954; £477; £238)

Form RPR

24-5 **1** **May Hay**[20] 2810 5-11-12 **104**.............................. JackQuinlan 113+
(Anthony Carson) *chsd ldr: clsd bef 4th: led gng wl bef omitted 3 out: sn clr: easily* **2/1**[1]

0244 **2** 12 **Beyondtemptation**[9] 2980 7-10-3 **86**..............................(t) DiarmuidO'Regan(5) 80
(Jonathan Haynes) *led: nt fluent 5th: hdd bef omitted 3 out: sn rdn: no ch w wnr* **9/4**[2]

5P-0 **3** 26 **Lochnell (IRE)**[38] 2429 6-11-3 **95**.............................. LucyAlexander 63
(Ian Duncan) *hld up: stdy hdwy 4th: outpcd whn nt fluent 3 out (usual 4 out): sn btn* **5/1**

5-43 **4** 82 **Near To Tears (IRE)**[22] 2752 5-11-1 **93**.............................. PeterBuchanan
(Lucinda Russell) *nt fluent: chsd clr ldng pair: clsd bef 4th: wknd 3 out (usual 4 out): t.o* **5/2**[3]

4m 17.7s (7.70) **Going Correction** +0.60s/f (Soft) **4** Ran SP% **109.3**
Speed ratings (Par 105): **104,98,85,44**
CSF £6.91 TOTE £2.60; EX 5.70 Trifecta £17.40.
Owner W H Carson **Bred** Minster Enterprises Ltd **Trained** Newmarket, Suffolk

FOCUS
A very one-sided contest. After rail movements the actual race distance was 2m 118yds.

3164 188BET.CO.UK NOVICES' LIMITED H'CAP CHASE (11 fncs 2 omitted) 2m 75y
2:30 (2:33) (Class 4) (0-120,116) 4-Y-0+ £4,024 (£1,214; £625; £331)

Form RPR

20-3 **1** **Gold Opera (IRE)**[36] 2475 6-10-12 **106**.............................. LucyAlexander 109+
(N W Alexander) *chsd ldrs: lost pl 3rd: outpcd next: rallied bef 3 out (usual 4 out): sn pushed along: chsd wnr last: hung lft: corrected and led run-in: kpt on wl* **2/1**[1]

263- **2** 1 ½ **Island Confusion (IRE)**[299] 4400 7-11-8 **116**.............................. PeterBuchanan 119+
(Lucinda Russell) *nt fluent on occasions: hld up: hdwy to chse ldrs 3rd: led bef 3 out (usual 4 out): clr whn nt fluent last: hdd run-in: kpt on towards fin* **2/1**[1]

2154 **3** 18 **Never Up (GER)**[35] 2495 4-11-0 **113**.............................. HenryBrooke 91
(George Moore) *t.k.h early: cl up: led 4 out (usual 5 out) to next: rallied: outpcd next: rdn and wknd fr last* **8/1**[3]

5P24 **4** 1 ¼ **Duhallowcountry (IRE)**[9] 2981 9-9-10 **97** oh24....(p) ThomasDowson(7) 78
(Victor Thompson) *mde most to 4 out (usual 5 out): rdn and outpcd next: wknd fr 2 out* **33/1**

P **Raise Hell (IRE)**[266] 8-10-10 **111**.............................. StevenFox(7)
(Sandy Thomson) *nt fluent: in tch: struggling 4th: lost tch bef 4 out (usual 5 out): p.u bef next* **8/1**[3]

P **Officer Cadet**[148] 1105 6-11-4 **112**..............................[1] JamesReveley
(Karen McLintock) *in tch: hdwy to chal 3rd to 6th: struggling 4 out (usual 5 out): lost tch and p.u bef next* **9/2**[2]

4m 24.0s (2.90) **Going Correction** +0.35s/f (Yiel)
WFA 4 from 6yo+ 5lb **6** Ran SP% **110.0**
Speed ratings (Par 105): **106,105,96,95,**
CSF £6.44 TOTE £2.80: £1.70, £1.50; EX 6.10 Trifecta £36.80.
Owner Macdonalds, Cardwell, Castle & Davies **Bred** J W George **Trained** Kinneston, Perth & Kinross

FOCUS
A fair novice handicap, the two market leaders dominating. After rail movements the actual race distance was 2m 95yds.

3165 FREE SPINS AT 188BET CASINO "JUNIOR" STANDARD OPEN NATIONAL HUNT FLAT RACE 1m 6f 139y
3:05 (3:07) (Class 6) 3-Y-O £1,559 (£457; £228; £114)

Form RPR

1 **Red Indian** 3-10-12 0.............................. JakeGreenall 107
(Chris Bealby) *hld up in tch: stdy hdwy 6f out: rdn to ld over 1f out: sn hrd pressed: hld on wl towards fin* **9/1**[3]

06 **2** nk **Very First Time**[21] 2777 3-10-12 0.............................. JamesReveley 106
(Tim Easterby) *hld up on outside: stdy hdwy 1/2-way: led over 2f out to over 1f out: ev ch ins fnl f: hld nr fin* **10/1**

31 **3** 15 **Applaus (GER)**[14] 2923 3-11-2 0.............................. JoeColliver(3) 99
(Micky Hammond) *t.k.h: led: rdn and hdd over 2f out: edgd lft and wknd over 1f out* **1/2**[1]

5 **4** 21 **American Gigolo**[48] 2216 3-10-7 0.............................. JamesCowley(5) 67
(Sally Hall) *prom: rdn over 3f out: wknd over 2f out* **7/1**[2]

0 **5** ¾ **Desert Sensation (IRE)**[21] 2777 3-10-9 0.............................. AdamNicol(3) 66
(Tracy Waggott) *t.k.h: prom: rdn over 5f out: wknd fr 3f out* **33/1**

0 **6** 36 **Greenworldsolution**[21] 2777 3-10-5 0.............................. ConorWalsh(7) 26
(Jennie Candlish) *trckd ldrs: drvn and outpcd over 6f out: lost tch fr over 4f out: t.o* **12/1**

4 **7** 16 **Regent's Rock**[14] 2923 3-10-0 0.............................. JamieHamilton(5) 2
(Peter Niven) *hld up: pushed along and shortlived effrt over 5f out: wknd fr 4f out: t.o* **12/1**

8 dist **Mini Frank** 3-10-7 0.............................. DiarmuidO'Regan(5)
(Chris Grant) *bhd: struggling 1/2-way: t.o* **20/1**

6 **P** **Alwareed**[14] 2923 3-10-12 0.............................. HenryBrooke
(John Wade) *t.k.h early: cl up tl lost pl 6f out: sn struggling: p.u 4f out* **100/1**

3m 35.3s (215.30) **9** Ran SP% **122.3**
CSF £97.40 TOTE £10.40: £2.20, £2.60, £1.10; EX 85.10 Trifecta £275.60.
Owner J R Weatherby **Bred** Preston Lodge Stud **Trained** Barrowby, Lincs

FOCUS
Hard to be certain what this form worth, the short-priced favourite likely not close to his Wetherby form in third, though the runner-up has clearly improved on previous efforts and the winner knuckled down really well considering his inexperience. After rail movements the actual race distance was 1m6f 159yds.
T/Plt: £60.80 to a £1 stake. Pool: £47,867.45 - 573.85 winning tickets. T/Qpdt: £43.20 to a £1 stake. Pool: £3,044.32 - 52.10 winning tickets **Richard Young**

3166 - 3168a (Foreign Racing) - See Raceform Interactive

2813

FAIRYHOUSE (R-H)
Saturday, December 19

OFFICIAL GOING: Heavy

3169a KERRY GROUP STAYERS NOVICE HURDLE (REGISTERED AS THE CORK STAYERS NOVICE HURDLE) (GRADE 3) (13 hdls) 3m
1:00 (1:00) 4-Y-0+ £16,375 (£4,786; £2,267; £755)

RPR

1 **Gangster (FR)**[91] 1587 5-11-3 138.............................. BJCooper 147+
(W P Mullins, Ire) *settled bhd ldrs and wnt 2nd bef 3rd: j. sltly lft 6th and next: disp briefly 4 out: led narrowly 2 out and drvn clr: sn in command: easily* **5/6**[1]

2 10 **Last Encounter (IRE)**[27] 2672 5-11-0 125.............................. RWalsh 130
(Ms Margaret Mullins, Ire) *led narrowly: slt mstke 3rd: jnd briefly 4 out: rdn and hdd 2 out and sn no imp on easy wnr: kpt on same pce* **7/1**

3 11 **Cogryhill (IRE)**[27] 2672 5-11-0 0.............................. LPDempsey 123
(Gordon Elliott, Ire) *cl up in 2nd tl dropped to 3rd bef 3rd: dropped to cl 4th bef 4 out: wnt 3rd again into st: no imp on ldrs 2 out: one pce after and slt mstke last* **4/1**[3]

4 18 **Damut (IRE)**[34] 2525 7-11-6 131.............................. AELynch 107
(Joseph Dullea, Ire) *hld up bhd ldrs: impr into cl 3rd 4 out: gng wl bhd ldrs fr next: sn rdn and no ex u.p in 4th into st: wknd* **7/2**[2]

5 15 **Cheiliuradh (IRE)**48 2225 4-10-3 0 ow1 (t) SeanFlanagan 75
(David Harry Kelly, Ire) *in rr thrght: detached bef 5 out: pushed along and no ex after 3 out: brought wd and trailing into st: t.o* 25/1

6m 51.7s (23.70) **Going Correction** +1.15s/f (Heav)
WFA 4 from 5yo+ 7lb 5 Ran SP% 113.1
Speed ratings: **106,102,99,93,88**
CSF £7.58 TOTE £1.60: £1.02, £4.30; DF 9.30 Trifecta £22.70.
Owner Gigginstown House Stud **Bred** Newsells Park Stud Ltd **Trained** Muine Beag, Co Carlow

FOCUS
The winner was unproven over this trip but he was very impressive and is possibly the best staying novice we've seen so far this season.

3170 - 3173a (Foreign Racing) - See Raceform Interactive

2550 **FAKENHAM** (L-H)
Sunday, December 20

OFFICIAL GOING: (good to soft)
Wind: light, against Weather: dry, bright spells

3174 CHRISTMAS H'CAP HURDLE (13 hdls) 2m 7f 95y
12:50 (12:50) (Class 4) (0-115,115) 4-Y-0+ £4,548 (£1,335; £667; £333)

Form RPR
3314 1 **Shaky Gift (IRE)**28 2670 6-11-9 112 NoelFehily 116
(Neil Mulholland) *hld up in tch: hdwy to chse ldrs 10th: wnt 2nd bef 2 out: rdn and swtchd lft bef last: led fnl 100yds: styd on* 7/1
34/1 2 ¾ **Bonnet's Vino**21 2812 7-11-5 108 KielanWoods 112
(Pam Sly) *hld up in tch in midfield: chsd ldr after 9th: led3 out: mstke next: drvn between last 2: mstke last: hdd 100yds out: no ex and hung rt cl home* 3/1¹
0352 3 29 **Storm Alert**39 2441 8-10-3 95 LucyGardner(3) 72
(Sue Gardner) *chsd ldr tl after 9th: mstke and lost pl next: sn u.p: 5th and wl btn 3 out: plugged on to go modest 3rd flat* 3/1¹
PP2P 4 5 **Terminal (FR)**16 2878 8-11-4 112 JakeHodson(5) 84
(Anthony Day) *nt a fluent: chsd ldrs tl 3rd: steadily lost pl: rdn after 5th: dropped to last 9th: t.o 3 out: plugged on to go modest 4th flat: fin lame* 16/1
2141 5 ¾ **Houston Dynimo (IRE)**21 2809 10-11-7 115 (bt) DavidNoonan(5) 87
(David Pipe) *led: mstke 7th: hdd 3 out: sn rdn: 3rd and btn next: fdd last* 9/2²
3344 6 7 **Airpur Desbois (FR)**28 2658 5-11-2 105 GavinSheehan 73
(Charlie Mann) *hld up in tch: hdwy into midfield and mstke 9th: 4th and cl enough 3 out: btn next: wnt 3rd but no ch between last 2: mstke last: fdd and eased flat* 5/1³
-640 P **Westend Prince (IRE)**24 2731 4-11-2 105 TomScudamore
(Colin Tizzard) *chsd ldrs: mstke 5th: rdn and wknd qckly after 9th: t.o whn p.u 3 out* 9/1

6m 19.3s (-2.70) **Going Correction** +0.025s/f (Yiel)
WFA 4 from 5yo+ 6lb 7 Ran SP% 113.2
Speed ratings (Par 105): **105,104,94,92,92 90,**
CSF £28.19 CT £76.14 TOTE £7.10: £2.70, £2.50; EX 26.10 Trifecta £82.60.
Owner Mrs P L Bridel **Bred** Clare Kehoe & Bill Byrne **Trained** Limpley Stoke, Wilts

FOCUS
Both courses were on fresh ground the whole way around. There was an extra 213yds on top of the stated race distance. The opener looked reasonably competitive for the level. Steps up from the first two, who were clear.

3175 THOROUGHBRED BREEDERS' ASSOCIATION MARES' NOVICES' HURDLE (9 hdls) 2m 3y
1:20 (1:22) (Class 4) 4-Y-0+ £3,898 (£1,144; £572; £286)

Form RPR
1-43 1 **Mystic Sky**22 2776 4-10-10 0 RichardJohnson 114+
(Lucy Wadham) *chsd ldr: upsides and travelling bttr 3 out: led between last: steadily asserted: in command last: styd on* 15/8²
1 2 7 **Savingforvegas (IRE)**25 2721 5-10-10 0 PaddyBrennan 107
(Stuart Edmunds) *led: jnd and rdn 3 out: hdd and no ex between last 2: kpt on same pce after* 11/8¹
-054 3 9 **Stepover**29 2644 4-10-10 0 KielanWoods 99
(Alex Hales) *chsd ldng pair: 4th and outpcd after 3 out: chsd ldng pair again between last 2: plugged on but no imp* 8/1
2-21 4 21 **Shanandoa**19 2835 4-10-10 0 GavinSheehan 83
(Brian Barr) *hld up in tch in 4th: wnt 3rd 3 out: sn outpcd and rdn: btn next: lost 3rd and wknd between last 2: tired and mstke last: t.o* 4/1³
P **Water For Life**411 4-10-10 0 TrevorWhelan
(Martin Smith) *t.k.h: hld up in tch in rr: mstke 6th: sn btn: t.o whn p.u last* 66/1

4m 16.9s (3.90) **Going Correction** +0.025s/f (Yiel) 5 Ran SP% 109.5
Speed ratings (Par 105): **91,87,83,72,**
CSF £4.97 TOTE £2.50: £1.10, £1.20; EX 4.60 Trifecta £13.90.
Owner Tim Wood **Bred** T Wood **Trained** Newmarket, Suffolk

FOCUS
Both courses were on fresh ground the whole way around. There was an extra 136yds on top of the stated race distance. Three horses that were likely to be well-fancied for this came out overnight/during the morning (five didn't take part in total), so this was far weaker than it had promised to be when the final declarations came out. The third helps set the level.

3176 AT THE RACES H'CAP CHASE (16 fncs) 2m 5f 44y
1:50 (1:51) (Class 3) (0-130,130) 4-Y-0+ £7,147 (£2,098; £1,049; £524)

Form RPR
P-P5 1 **Noble Legend**19 2832 8-11-2 120 (p) HarrySkelton 136+
(Caroline Bailey) *mde all: drew clr after 12th: pushed along between last 2: pushed out: unchal* 5/1³
5-11 2 11 **Emerald Rose**33 2551 8-11-1 119 (p) MarkGrant 123
(Julian Smith) *chsd ldrs: 4th and outpcd after 12th: wl btn after 3 out: rallied and swtchd rt bnd bef last: wnt 2nd last: styd on flat: no ch w wnr* 5/1³
-141 3 10 **Wings Attract (IRE)**22 2774 6-11-9 127 TomMessenger 123
(Chris Bealby) *chsd ldrs: mstke 11th: rdn bef next: chsd clr wnr 2 out: no imp: lost 2nd last: wknd flat* 9/4¹
4310 4 7 **Cayman Islands**31 2593 7-10-11 122 MrAlexFerguson(7) 112
(John Ferguson) *chsd wnr: rdn and outpcd after 11th: wl btn whn lost 2nd and j. slowly 2 out: wknd bef last* 11/1
0/ 5 10 **Sizing Sahara**157 1020 7-10-6 110 TomO'Brien 90
(Paul Henderson) *a in rr: j.rt and bmpd 1st: mstke 11th: sn rdn and lost tch: t.o 3 out* 25/1
61-0 6 49 **Itoldyou (IRE)**24 2724 9-11-1 119 (t) TomCannon 55
(Linda Jewell) *last pair after 2nd: last and struggling 8th: lost tch 11th: t.o 13th: bdly hmpd by loose horse flat and c to a halt: continued* 20/1
-205 F **Minella Forfitness (IRE)**23 2746 8-11-12 130 AdamPogson 108
(Charles Pogson) *in tch in midfield: blnd 6th: struggling u.p after 11th: lost tch 3 out: t.o whn fell last* 7/1
-632 F **Here's Herbie**48 2247 7-10-13 120 LucyGardner(3)
(Sue Gardner) *hld up in last pair: j.lft: bmpd and fell 1st* 7/2²

5m 43.6s (1.80) **Going Correction** +0.30s/f (Yiel) 8 Ran SP% 115.8
Speed ratings (Par 107): **108,103,100,97,93 74, ,**
CSF £30.88 CT £71.30 TOTE £5.80: £1.90, £1.70, £1.10; EX 31.10 Trifecta £40.00.
Owner P Dixon Smith **Bred** P Dixon Smith **Trained** Holdenby, Northants

FOCUS
Both courses were on fresh ground the whole way around. There was an extra 258yds on top of the stated race distance. This was run at a decent gallop, one that the winner kept up to the line. Not many featured with a chance. There's a case for rating the form a few pounds higher.

3177 RACING AT FAKENHAM NEW YEAR'S DAY H'CAP HURDLE (9 hdls) 2m 3y
2:20 (2:20) (Class 4) (0-105,111) 3-Y-0+ £4,548 (£1,335; £667; £333)

Form RPR
-304 1 **Neworld (FR)**18 2850 6-11-7 99 AlainCawley 102+
(Richard Hobson) *hld up in tch: effrt to chse ldrs after 3 out: mstke 2 out: chal bnd bef last: j. into ld last: rdn out* 9/2²
-34F 2 ½ **Ogaritmo**33 2559 6-11-3 98 (t) JamesBanks(3) 99
(Alex Hales) *hld up in tch in rr: rdn and hdwy after 3 out: wnt 3rd bnd bef last: ev ch last: pressed wnr flat: kpt on* 6/1
1012 3 2¾ **Gin And Tonic**29 2647 5-11-10 102 JackQuinlan 102
(Michael Wigham) *hld up in tch: hdwy on inner 6th: trckd ldrs next: rdn to ld between last 2: hdd and mstke last: sn btn: wknd u.p flat* 5/4¹
0034 4 3½ **Minden March**23 2745 10-9-9 78 oh4 JamieHamilton(5) 74
(Peter Maddison) *pressed ldr: rdn and ev ch after 3 out: 4th and outpcd bnd bef last: plugged on same pce flat* 16/1
40-0 5 3½ **Bountiful Bess**19 2840 5-11-0 92 (t) KielanWoods 85
(Pam Sly) *in tch in midfield: rdn bef 3 out: drvn and outpcd bef 2 out: wl hld and plugged on same pce between last 2* 10/1
3333 6 9 **Sacred Square (GER)**5 2850 5-11-10 102 (p) PaddyBrennan 89
(Conor Dore) *chsd ldrs tl led after 6th: hdd between last 2: sn btn and fdd bef last* 11/2³
4-60 7 8 **Kingscombe (USA)**210 451 6-10-0 78 oh9 MarcGoldstein 55
(Linda Jewell) *led tl after 6th: sn rdn and lost pl bef next: 7th and wkng whn mstke 2 out* 20/1
0P 8 11 **Annakrista (GER)**32 2565 7-10-0 85 (tp) WilliamFeatherstone(7) 53
(Zoe Davison) *t.k.h: hld up in tch in midfield: dropped to rr and u.p after 6th: lost tch 2 out: t.o* 33/1

4m 19.8s (6.80) **Going Correction** +0.025s/f (Yiel) 8 Ran SP% 115.0
Speed ratings (Par 105): **84,83,82,80,78 74,70,64**
CSF £31.73 CT £52.33 TOTE £5.00: £1.90, £1.70, £1.40; EX 28.60 Trifecta £100.00.
Owner Richard Hobson **Bred** Andre Larrieu & Jean-Paul Larrieu **Trained** Stow-On-The-Wold, Gloucs

FOCUS
Both courses were on fresh ground the whole way around. There was an extra 136yds on top of the stated race distance. A moderate but competitive contest. The form is rated around the second to sixth.

3178 FAKENHAM 2016 ANNUAL MEMBERSHIP NOVICES' H'CAP CHASE (18 fncs) 3m 38y
2:50 (2:50) (Class 4) (0-105,102) 4-Y-0+ £4,548 (£1,335; £667; £333)

Form RPR
63-4 1 **Bears Rails**54 2121 5-11-11 101 NoelFehily 115+
(Colin Tizzard) *led: mstke 6th: mstke and hdd 12th: led again and nt fluent 3 out: gng best and nt fluent next: rdn between last 2: gd jump last: styd on: rdn out* 9/4¹
6-05 2 2 **Tanner Hill (IRE)**19 2841 7-10-5 81 (p) MarkQuinlan 91+
(James Evans) *pressed wnr tl j. into ld 12th: hdd 3 out: u.p but stl ev ch next: no ex last: one pce flat* 9/2
P31F 3 48 **Jumpandtravel (IRE)**21 2812 6-11-9 102 JoeColliver(3) 67
(Micky Hammond) *j.rt: chsd ldrs tl struggling 9th: nvr on terms w ldrs after: 4th and wl hld whn nt fluent 3 out: wnt poor 3rd between last 2: t.o* 7/2²
-306 4 23 **Finnegan's Garden (IRE)**44 2312 6-10-0 83 WilliamFeatherstone(7) 27
(Zoe Davison) *in tch: trckd ldng pair after 11th: rdn and btn 15th: lost tch next: dropped to last and t.o between last 2: rdr weighed in at 10st 2lbs* 25/1
-P00 P **Follow The Tracks (IRE)**10 2985 7-11-7 97 DaveCrosse
(Brian Barr) *pressed ldrs tl 11th: losing pl and mstke 12th: last and lost tch after next: t.o whn p.u 15th* 4/1³
50P4 P **Rior (IRE)**24 2736 8-11-8 98 TomO'Brien
(Paul Henderson) *a in rr: hit 1st: mstke and pckd 6th: lost tch 10th: t.o whn p.u after 11th* 11/2

6m 46.1s (10.40) **Going Correction** +0.30s/f (Yiel) 6 Ran SP% 110.4
Speed ratings (Par 105): **94,93,77,69,**
CSF £12.36 CT £30.93 TOTE £2.80: £1.60, £2.50; EX 14.50 Trifecta £34.00.
Owner P M Warren **Bred** Brian And Gwen Griffiths **Trained** Milborne Port, Dorset
■ Stewards' Enquiry : William Featherstone three-day ban; weighed in 2lb heavy (3rd-5th Jan)

FOCUS
Both courses were on fresh ground the whole way around. There was an extra 221yds on top of the stated race distance. Only two of the declared runners had chasing experience under rules but both of those came out during the morning, so it's difficult to know what this form is worth at this stage. The winner is better than the bare result.

3179 INDEPENDENT RACECOURSES LTD MAIDEN HURDLE (11 hdls) 2m 4f 1y
3:20 (3:20) (Class 5) 4-Y-0+ £3,573 (£1,049; £524; £262)

Form RPR
3 1 **Prince Of Steal (IRE)**19 2842 5-11-0 0 LiamTreadwell 117
(James Evans) *chsd ldr: rdn and ev ch between last 2: flashed tail u.p: led last: styd on: rdn out* 16/1
14-4 2 nk **What A Moment (IRE)**15 2910 5-11-0 0 TomScudamore 118+
(David Pipe) *led: rdn bef 2 out: rdn and hrd pressed between last 2: hdd and mstke last: drvn and unable qck flat* 4/5¹
2 3 2 **Young Dillon (IRE)**41 2407 6-11-0 120 WillKennedy 116+
(Dr Richard Newland) *chsd ldrs: 3rd and rdn bef 3 out: styd on same pce last* 7/2²
4F2 4 shd **Kalondra (IRE)**22 2768 4-11-0 0 NoelFehily 115
(Neil Mulholland) *t.k.h: hld up in tch: clsd bef 3 out: effrt after 2 out: kpt on same pce flat* 5/1³

0144 **5** *nk* **Potters Midnight**[33] 2561 5-10-7 0.......................... RichardJohnson 108
(Lucy Wadham) *hld up in tch in rr: rdn and hdwy after 3 out: kpt on same pce between last 2* **10/1**

0-00 **6** *73* **Windy Writer (IRE)**[31] 2603 5-10-11 0.......................... RyanHatch(3) 49
(Shaun Lycett) *in tch in midfield: 4th and rdn whn mstke 3 out: wknd rapidly next: tired and t.o whn mstke last* **80/1**

P0 **7** *52* **Mr Elevator (IRE)**[8] 3037 5-11-0 0.......................... AdamPogson
(Charles Pogson) *t.k.h: chsd ldrs tl 7th: sn lost pl: t.o bef 3 out* **200/1**

5m 24.1s (3.70) **Going Correction** +0.025s/f (Yiel)
WFA 4 from 5yo+ 6lb **7 Ran SP% 111.1**
Speed ratings (Par 103): **93,92,92,92,91 62,41**
CSF £29.08 TOTE £14.60: £3.00, £1.20; EX 38.50 Trifecta £121.90.
Owner The Cheltenham Flyers **Bred** A Ryan **Trained** Broadwas, Worcs

FOCUS
Both courses were on fresh ground the whole way around. There was an extra 170yds on top of the stated race distance. Probably just an ordinary contest, with a bunch finish, but the form makes sense.
T/Plt: £9.80 to a £1 stake. Pool: £103,809.15 - 7,691.73 winning tickets. T/Qpdt: £3.40 to a £1 stake. Pool: £7,732.98 - 1,646.56 winning tickets. **Steve Payne**

3180 - 3186a (Foreign Racing) - See Raceform Interactive

2428 AYR (L-H)

Monday, December 21

3187 Meeting Abandoned - Waterlogged

3042 LINGFIELD (L-H)

Monday, December 21

OFFICIAL GOING: Jumps course: heavy (4.4); awt - polytrack: standard
Wind: Strong, behind Weather: Overcast with rain

3194 MONEY BACK 2ND AT TITANBET.CO.UK NOVICES' HURDLE (9 hdls 1 omitted) 2m 3f 110y
12:40 (12:40) (Class 4) 4-Y-O+ **£3,994** (£1,240; £667)

Form RPR

P2 **1** **Westren Warrior (IRE)**[20] 2838 6-11-4 122.......................... WillKennedy 132+
(Dr Richard Newland) *prom: trckd ldr passing omitted 5th: led 3 out: drew clr bef next: easily* **11/10**[1]

6-5P **2** *30* **Get Ready Freddy**[7] 3077 5-10-12 0.......................... NickScholfield 86
(Nick Mitchell) *led at gd pce for the conditions: hdd 3 out: lft bhd by wnr bef next but plugged on for remote 2nd* **66/1**

2 **3** *12* **Who's Micky Brown (IRE)**[21] 2828 5-10-12 0.......................... NoelFehily 74
(Neil Mulholland) *racd wd: in tch: rdn 3 out: sn struggling: wl btn bef next: fin tired* **3/1**[3]

P **Kent Ragstone (USA)**[9] 6-10-12 0.......................... MattieBatchelor
(Sheena West) *in tch to 6th: wknd rapidly: t.o whn p.u bef 3 out* **50/1**

/3-2 **P** **Danvinnie**[45] 2312 6-10-12 0.......................... LeightonAspell
(Oliver Sherwood) *hmpd 1st: racd wd: in tch: rdn 3 out: wknd qckly: t.o in 4th whn p.u bef 2 out* **9/4**[2]

0- **P** **Inch Wing (IRE)**[494] 1222 7-9-12 0.......................... PaulJohn(7)
(Jim Best) *chsd ldr tl passing omitted 5th: wknd rapidly: t.o whn p.u bef 4 out* **66/1**

33- **P** **Saucysioux**[301] 4411 5-10-5 0.......................... [1] DavidEngland
(Michael Roberts) *in tch to 6th: sn bhd: t.o 3 out: p.u wl bef 2 out* **20/1**

5m 37.2s (11.20) **Going Correction** +0.625s/f (Soft) **7 Ran SP% 113.1**
Speed ratings (Par 105): **102,90,85, , ,**
CSF £68.91 TOTE £2.30: £1.50, £10.80; EX 75.30 Trifecta £208.70.
Owner C E Stedman & P Jenkins **Bred** Miss Susan Hogan **Trained** Claines, Worcs

FOCUS
All starts have been moved at this track following remeasuring, so there will be no speed figures here until there is sufficient data to calculate updated median times. The first hurdle in the back straight was omitted and the ground was extremely testing. Only the winner really coped with the conditions and this was arguably a step up from him.

3195 DOWNLOAD THE TITANBET SPORTS APP NOVICES' H'CAP CHASE (12 fncs) 2m
1:10 (1:10) (Class 4) (0-105,100) 5-Y-O+ **£4,548** (£1,335; £667; £333)

Form RPR

-525 **1** **Pembroke House**[18] 2859 8-11-9 100.......................... (p) JamesBanks(3) 109+
(Sarah-Jayne Davies) *prom: chsd ldr 5th to 8th: styd cl up: led 3 out gng best: drvn out fr last whn pressed* **6/1**[3]

/01- **2** *1 ¾* **Bawden Rocks**[582] 368 6-11-12 100.......................... TomScudamore 108+
(David Bridgwater) *trckd ldr 2nd to 5th and again 8th: led after next: hdd and rdn 3 out: kpt on wl but a hld by wnr* **6/1**[3]

5-1F **3** *28* **Zero Visibility (IRE)**[13] 2953 8-10-11 85.......................... AdamWedge 72
(Alexandra Dunn) *led: hdd sn after 4 out: dropped to 3rd and btn bef 3 out: wknd* **11/8**[1]

6-P2 **4** *12* **Bonds Conquest**[26] 2712 6-10-2 76.......................... JeremiahMcGrath 43
(Seamus Mullins) *trckd ldrs: struggling to stay in tch fr 8th: wknd after 4 out: bhd bef next* **3/1**[2]

5455 **5** *11* **Tenby Jewel (IRE)**[32] 2599 10-10-2 76.......................... (tp) ConorO'Farrell 32
(Mark Gillard) *chsd ldr to 2nd: sn in rr: lost tch and nudged along fr 5th: nvr on terms after and steadily lost grnd* **20/1**

3314 **6** *30* **Matrow's Lady (IRE)**[18] 2874 8-10-11 92.......... (bt) MrMartinMcIntyre(7) 18
(Neil Mulholland) *a in rr: urged along and lost tch fr 6th: nvr on terms after: clambered over last: t.o* **13/2**

4m 40.3s (0.30) **Going Correction** +0.075s/f (Yiel) **6 Ran SP% 113.8**
Speed ratings: **102,101,87,81,75 60**
CSF £39.64 TOTE £7.30: £2.70, £2.70; EX 40.60 Trifecta £104.40.
Owner Andrew Mortimer **Bred** G H Jones **Trained** Leominster, H'fords

FOCUS
A moderate novices' handicap chase. The first two are rated in line with best of their hurdles form, with those else within 20lb of their marks.

3196 RACING WELFARE H'CAP HURDLE (7 hdls 1 omitted) 2m
1:40 (1:40) (Class 3) (0-135,135) 4-Y-O+ **£5,848** (£1,717; £858; £429)

Form RPR

00F1 **1** **Dormouse**[9] 3047 10-10-5 114.......................... (p) TomScudamore 118
(Anabel K Murphy) *prom: trckd ldr 5th: led 2 out: 3 l clr last: all out to hold on nr fin* **11/4**[1]

-516 **2** *nk* **Prairie Town (IRE)**[23] 2775 4-11-2 125.......................... LeeEdwards 129
(Tony Carroll) *in tch: rdn bef 2 out: responded wl to chse wnr bef last where 3 l down: clsd steadily towards fin: jst hld* **6/1**[3]

-561 **3** *14* **Superciliary**[13] 2956 6-10-1 117.......................... (t) HarryCobden(7) 108
(Chris Gordon) *wl in tch: rdn and outpcd by ldrs 2 out: kpt on to take 3rd after last* **4/1**[2]

-131 **4** *3 ¼* **Template (IRE)**[15] 2926 4-10-10 126.......................... LiamMcKenna(7) 112
(Harry Fry) *led: rdn and hdd 2 out: wknd bef last* **4/1**[2]

04-P **P** **Hold The Bucks (USA)**[13] 2957 9-9-9 109 oh2.......... FreddieMitchell(5)
(Sheena West) *chsd ldr tl passing omitted 3rd: sn wknd: t.o whn p.u bef usual 5th* **33/1**

06-0 **P** **Landscape (FR)**[32] 2600 7-10-2 111.......................... MattieBatchelor
(Sheena West) *in tch to 4th: sn toiling: t.o and p.u bef 2 out* **16/1**

2/3- **P** **Light Well (IRE)**[415] 2187 7-10-7 116.......................... JamieMoore
(Gary Moore) *prom: trckd ldr passing omitted 3rd tl nt fluent 5th: cl up after 3 out: wknd qckly and p.u bef 2 out* **4/1**[2]

00 **P** **Auenwirbel (GER)**[10] 3015 4-11-1 124.......................... (t) RobertDunne
(Laura Young) *trckd ldrs: pushed along 3 out: wknd suddenly and p.u bef 2 out* **12/1**

4m 35.2s (7.20) **Going Correction** +0.625s/f (Soft)
WFA 4 from 6yo+ 5lb **8 Ran SP% 117.5**
Speed ratings (Par 107): **107,106,99,98, , ,**
CSF £20.45 CT £66.07 TOTE £3.40: £1.70, £1.90, £1.90; EX 20.40 Trifecta £64.50.
Owner Aiden Murphy **Bred** Deerfield Farm **Trained** Wilmcote, Warwicks

FOCUS
The first hurdle in the back straight was omitted. This was a fair contest. The winner is rated to his mark.

3197 HOLZHEIM FASCHING MIENZIES ROCK MUNICH BEGINNERS' CHASE (18 fncs) 2m 7f 110y
2:10 (2:10) (Class 4) 5-Y-O+ **£4,548** (£1,335; £667; £333)

Form RPR

00-4 **1** **Warrantor (IRE)**[44] 2347 6-11-0 132.......................... (t) GavinSheehan 139+
(Warren Greatrex) *cl up and racd on inner: chsd ldr 6th: chal and upsides fr 3 out: hrd rdn and kpt on to ld flat* **9/4**[1]

0-33 **2** *1 ½* **Jennys Surprise (IRE)**[22] 2805 7-10-7 127.......................... PaddyBrennan 129
(Fergal O'Brien) *led and j. proficiently: jnd 3 out: kpt on wl and narrow ld tl hdd and no ex flat* **4/1**[3]

2/2- **3** *44* **Kris Spin (IRE)**[590] 198 7-11-0 0.......................... JamieMoore 96
(Kerry Lee) *trckd ldrs: stmbld bdly 6th: disp 2nd pl fr 10th tl wknd rapidly bef 3 out: fin tired* **5/2**[2]

4-25 **4** *2 ¼* **Kayf Moss**[29] 2660 7-11-0 0.......................... (tp) RhysFlint 90
(John Flint) *cl up: mstke 11th and lost tch w ldrs: no imp 4 out: wknd 3 out* **10/1**

40-P **P** **Boardwalk Empire (IRE)**[25] 2733 8-10-11 122.......................... KieronEdgar(3)
(Kate Buckett) *chsd ldr tl mstke 6th: last after next: lost tch and p.u bef 12th* **16/1**

6-10 **P** **Molly's A Diva**[24] 2759 8-10-7 0.......................... (p) DavidBass
(Kim Bailey) *cl up: mstke 6th: wknd 12th: p.u bef 14th* **4/1**[3]

7m 4.7s (4.70) **Going Correction** +0.025s/f (Yiel) **6 Ran SP% 114.3**
Speed ratings: **93,92,77,77,**
CSF £12.15 TOTE £3.00: £1.40, £2.40; EX 10.70 Trifecta £33.50.
Owner Mrs Sarah Drysdale **Bred** Jim Lanigan **Trained** Upper Lambourn, Berks
■ Stewards' Enquiry : Gavin Sheehan two-day ban: use of whip (4-5 Jan)

FOCUS
A useful enough beginners' chase. The winner is a 139 hurdler and can match that over fences.

3198 INJURED JOCKEYS FUND MARES' H'CAP HURDLE (9 hdls 1 omitted) 2m 3f 110y
2:40 (2:40) (Class 4) (0-115,111) 3-Y-O+ **£3,898** (£1,144; £572; £286)

Form RPR

3312 **1** **Anda De Grissay (FR)**[29] 2661 5-11-5 111.......................... (t) HarryCobden(7) 123+
(Anthony Honeyball) *cl up: trckd ldr 3 out: led bef 2 out: sn clr: easily* **5/2**[1]

-022 **2** *22* **Twenty Eight Guns**[13] 2952 5-11-9 108.......................... (p) TomScudamore 85
(Michael Scudamore) *racd on outer: wl in tch: rdn on long run bef 2 out: tk 2nd bef last but no ch w wnr* **7/2**[3]

4P00 **3** *9* **Dardanella**[11] 2987 8-11-0 99.......................... DaveCrosse 67
(Hugo Froud) *hit 2nd: trckd ldr and hit 4th: led 4 out tl bef 2 out: sn btn* **50/1**

FP43 **4** *1 ½* **Mini Muck**[22] 2812 9-11-9 108.......................... SamTwiston-Davies 75
(Nigel Twiston-Davies) *racd on outer: cl up: rdn 3 out: sn struggling: no ch fr 2 out: plugged on* **4/1**

4-2P **P** **Strange Bird (IRE)**[21] 2825 10-10-0 85.......................... (t) PaddyBrennan
(Richard Rowe) *led to 3rd: sn struggling: wl bhd whn p.u bef usual 6th* **6/1**

0011 **P** **Kentford Heiress**[131] 1236 5-10-11 101.......................... KevinJones(5)
(Seamus Mullins) *kpt to inner: led 3rd to 4 out: wknd qckly: t.o whn p.u bef 2 out* **3/1**[2]

5m 47.8s (21.80) **Going Correction** +0.625s/f (Soft) **6 Ran SP% 112.0**
Speed ratings (Par 105): **81,72,68,68,**
CSF £11.77 TOTE £3.30: £1.50, £1.80; EX 11.90 Trifecta £198.10.
Owner The Deauville Connection **Bred** Maurice Batiot & Jacques Cypres **Trained** Mosterton, Dorset

FOCUS
The first hurdle in the back straight was omitted. Nothing could live with the progressive winner. There's a case for rating the form much higher.

3199 BET AND WATCH AT TITANBET.CO.UK H'CAP CHASE (12 fncs) 2m
3:10 (3:10) (Class 5) (0-100,100) 5-Y-O+ **£2,662** (£826; £445)

Form RPR

4-P3 **1** **Very Live (FR)**[18] 2861 6-11-1 89.......................... (p) RichieMcLernon 106
(Paul Webber) *cl up: trckd ldr 7th: led after 4 out: rdn and jnd 3 out: hdd after last: rallied gamely u.p to ld fnl strides* **7/1**

2 *hd* **Bold Bachelor (IRE)**[22] 6-11-12 100.......................... WillKennedy 117
(Dr Richard Newland) *settled bhd ldrs but wl in tch: prog to go 2nd after 4 out: jnd wnr 3 out gng wl: rdn after 2 out: led after last: edgd lft flat: hdd fnl strides* **11/10**[1]

4P24 **3** *49* **Petit Ecuyer (FR)**[4] 3131 9-9-13 80.......................... MrJNixon(7) 48
(Dai Williams) *set off in detached last and sticky jumps early: lost no more grnd tl wknd on long run bef 3 out: lft remote 3rd 2 out* **8/1**

5PP2 **U** **Lamb's Cross**[20] 2834 9-10-5 82.......................... JamesBanks(3)
(Mark Gillard) *chsd ldr 3rd to 7th: 4th and wkng whn blnd and uns rdr 4 out* **6/1**[3]

33-3 **F** **Expanding Universe (IRE)**[22] 2811 8-11-8 96.......................... LeeEdwards
(Tony Carroll) *chsd ldr to 3rd: lost pl qckly and toiling fr next: last whn fell 6th* **7/2**[2]

P-P0 **P** **Four Shuck Men (IRE)**[12] 2976 7-9-7 **74**..........(b[1]) CharlieHammond[(7)]
(Sarah-Jayne Davies) led: rdn and hdd after 4 out: stl in 3rd but wkng and tired whn p.u bef 2 out **12/1**

4m 46.8s (6.80) **Going Correction** +0.025s/f (Yiel) **6** Ran **SP% 115.4**
Speed ratings: **84,83,59,** ,
CSF £16.67 TOTE £8.30: £2.70, £1.30; EX 17.30 Trifecta £85.40.
Owner R V Shaw **Bred** Patrick Ansault And Claudine Ansault **Trained** Mollington, Oxon

FOCUS
Only three completed in this moderate contest, but there was a good battle between the front two. Guessy form, the winner stepping up on Leicester.

3200 TITANBET.CO.UK STANDARD OPEN NATIONAL HUNT FLAT RACE (THIS RACE WILL BE RUN ON THE AW TRACK) 2m

3:40 (3:40) (Class 6) 4-6-Y-O **£1,559** (£457; £228; £114)

Form RPR

1 **Manhattan Spring** 4-11-2 0.......................... AndrewThornton 101
(Seamus Mullins) hld up in rr: stl there 2f out: rdn and gd prog over 1f out to chse ldr fnl f: clsd qckly to ld last 100yds: sn clr **16/1**

4- **2** 1 1/4 **Mr Mountain (IRE)**[303] 4363 5-11-2 0..........[1] AidanColeman 100
(Emma Lavelle) hld up in last: stl there and pushed along 2f out: rdn and gd prog fnl f: r.o to take 2nd nr fin: too much to do **3/1**[2]

2-3 **3** 3/4 **Briac (FR)**[45] 2317 4-11-2 0.......................... SamTwiston-Davies 99
(Jim Best) trckd ldrs: led over 2f out and sent for home: 3 l clr 1f out: hdd and outpcd last 100yds: lost 2nd nr fin **4/6**[1]

4 3 3/4 **Kelpie Blaze (IRE)** 4-11-2 0.......................... ConorO'Farrell 95
(Seamus Durack) t.k.h: led at modest pce: hung rt and hdd bnd 9f out and dropped to rr: effrt 2f out: disp 2nd 1f out: sn outpcd **6/1**[3]

6 **5** hd **Amalfi Doug (FR)**[60] 2044 5-11-2 0.......................... NickScholfield 95
(Michael Blanshard) t.k.h: hld up: in tch 2f out: outpcd over 1f out **16/1**

6 nk **Mab Dab (IRE)** 4-11-2 0.......................... TomCannon 95
(Linda Jewell) trckd ldr: lft in ld 9f out: hdd over 2f out: lost 2nd and outpcd fnl f **33/1**

5-06 **7** 6 **Storm Run (IRE)**[54] 2141 4-10-2 0.......................... HarryTeal[(7)] 82
(Roger Teal) t.k.h: cl up: trckd ldr 9f out to wl over 2f out: wknd wl over 1f out **50/1**

3m 44.5s (224.50) **7** Ran **SP% 115.9**
CSF £65.28 TOTE £14.50: £5.00, £2.60; EX 60.50 Trifecta £189.50.
Owner Woodford Valley Racing **Bred** Wriggle Valley Thoroughbreds **Trained** Wilsford-Cum-Lake, Wilts

FOCUS
Gloomy conditions for this concluding bumper, so viewing wasn't great. Probably just an ordinary race, rated around the third and fifth.
T/Plt: £96.80 to a £1 stake. Pool: £70,743.27 - 533.13 winning tickets T/Qpdt: £9.50 to a £1 stake. Pool: £8,708.43 - 678.33 winning tickets **Jonathan Neesom**

3006 BANGOR-ON-DEE (L-H)
Tuesday, December 22
3201 Meeting Abandoned - Waterlogged

3208 - 3212a (Foreign Racing) - See Raceform Interactive

2952 FONTWELL (L-H)
Saturday, December 26

OFFICIAL GOING: Heavy (soft in places; 5.3)
Wind: Fresh, behind Weather: Sunny spells

3213 SOUTHERN CRANES AND ACCESS LTD JUVENILE HURDLE (9 hdls) 2m 1f 145y

12:20 (12:20) (Class 4) 3-Y-O **£3,249** (£954; £477; £238)

Form RPR

04 **1** **Harley Rebel**[65] 2032 3-10-5 0.......................... MrShaneQuinlan[(7)] 115+
(Neil Mulholland) chsd ldrs: led 2 out: hit last: clr run-in: styd on wl **8/1**

2 9 **Searching (IRE)**[112] 3-10-12 0.......................... JoshuaMoore 105
(Gary Moore) chsd ldr: led briefly appr 2 out: no ex run-in **11/4**[2]

44 **3** 12 **Fitzwilliam**[10] 3112 3-10-12 108.......................... LeightonAspell 95
(Mick Channon) led: j.lft 4th: hdd & wknd appr 2 out **11/4**[2]

4 23 **Mr Caffrey**[80] 3-10-12 0.......................... DavidBass 70
(Robert Stephens) chsd ldrs tl wknd 3 out **9/4**[1]

6 **5** 8 **Satin And Lace (IRE)**[18] 2954 3-10-5 0..........(t) MarcGoldstein 55
(Michael Madgwick) a bhd: no ch fr 3 out **33/1**

0U **F** **Rest Easy**[22] 2883 3-10-0 0.......................... KevinJones[(5)]
(Seamus Mullins) a bhd: t.o whn mstke 6th: fell 3 out **25/1**

55 **P** **Fizzlestix (FR)**[24] 2845 3-10-7 0.......................... BridgetAndrews[(5)]
(Dan Skelton) prom tl wknd 6th: t.o whn p.u after 3 out **15/2**[3]

5m 3.1s (28.80) **Going Correction** +1.55s/f (Heav) **7** Ran **SP% 113.8**
Speed ratings (Par 104): **98,94,88,78,74** ,
CSF £30.56 TOTE £8.50: £3.60, £2.00; EX 29.70 Trifecta £191.30.
Owner Mrs Gloria Seymour **Bred** Stephen & Gloria Seymour **Trained** Limpley Stoke, Wilts

FOCUS
Fresh ground on bends. Race distance increased by 208yds. The opening contest was an ordinary juvenile hurdle. They went a sensible gallop on ground officially described as heavy, soft in places.

3214 SELFTRADE SMARTER INVESTING H'CAP CHASE (13 fncs) 2m 1f 96y

12:55 (12:55) (Class 4) (0-105,104) 4-Y-O+ **£5,902**

Form RPR

4-P1 **1** **Showboater (IRE)**[31] 2712 6-11-9 **101**.......................... DavidBass 114+
(Ben Pauling) often j.rt: chsd ldr: led after 7th: 2 l ahd and in control whn lft alone 2 out **4/6**[1]

1020 **U** **Youm Jamil (USA)**[17] 2976 8-9-9 **78** oh1..........(t) NickSlatter[(5)]
(Tony Carroll) hld up in rr: outpcd 9th: btn whn blnd and uns rdr 4 out **16/1**

-04F **F** **Tea Caddy**[9] 3127 9-11-5 **104**..........(tp) MissPFuller[(7)] 113
(Jamie Snowden) cl up: w wnr whn bdly hmpd by loose horse 4 out: 2 l 2nd and hld whn fell 2 out **11/1**

1/42 **U** **Highbury High (IRE)**[18] 2953 8-10-11 **96**..........(tp) MrShaneQuinlan[(7)]
(Neil Mulholland) carried rt and uns rdr 1st **8/1**[3]

6PP1 **P** **Toohighforme (IRE)**[18] 2953 6-9-7 **78** oh2..........(bt) HarryCobden[(7)]
(Nick Gifford) led: hmpd by loose horse after 3rd: hdd after 7th: wknd appr 3 out: 3rd and wl btn whn p.u bef next **11/4**[2]

5m 26.5s (51.80) **Going Correction** +2.375s/f (Heav) **5** Ran **SP% 112.0**
Speed ratings (Par 105): **73,** , , ,
TOTE £1.60: £2.20; EX 1.40 Trifecta £1.30.
Owner Paul & Clare Rooney **Bred** Thomas Brennan **Trained** Bourton-On-The-Water, Gloucs

FOCUS
Race distance increased by 156yds. A modest handicap chase in gruelling conditions.

3215 SELFTRADE STOCK AND SHARES ISA MARES' NOVICES' HURDLE (10 hdls) 2m 3f 33y

1:30 (1:30) (Class 4) 4-Y-O+ **£3,249** (£954; £477; £238)

Form RPR

11 **1** **The Organist (IRE)**[35] 2644 4-11-3 0.......................... LeightonAspell 125+
(Oliver Sherwood) mde all: clr 2 out: eased run-in **1/7**[1]

30-0 **2** 28 **Cassie**[33] 2689 5-10-10 0..........(t) DavidBass 93
(Ben Pauling) chsd wnr tl 6th: mstke next: regained 2nd 3 out: btn next **6/1**[2]

0-0 **3** 45 **Georgies Pip**[206] 602 4-10-10 0.......................... MichaelByrne 45
(Brendan Powell) dropped to last at 6th: lost tch 3 out: wnt remote 3rd run-in **33/1**

305 **4** 1/2 **La Pyle (FR)**[18] 2959 4-10-3 0..........(b) ThomasCheesman[(7)] 45
(Philip Hobbs) hld up: chsd wnr 6th tl hrd rdn and wknd 3 out **20/1**[3]

5m 26.6s (27.20) **Going Correction** +1.55s/f (Heav) **4** Ran **SP% 109.5**
Speed ratings (Par 105): **104,92,73,73**
CSF £1.70 TOTE £1.10; EX 1.20 Trifecta £4.00.
Owner Million In Mind Partnership **Bred** John Browne **Trained** Upper Lambourn, Berks

FOCUS
Race distance increased by 208yds. A fair mares' novice hurdle and they went a respectable gallop on the testing ground.

3216 WINTERFIELDS FARM H'CAP HURDLE (9 hdls) 2m 1f 145y

2:05 (2:05) (Class 3) (0-130,128) 3-Y-O+ **£6,498** (£1,908; £954; £477)

Form RPR

0-P0 **1** **Prouts Pub (IRE)**[52] 2266 6-11-7 **123**.......................... LeightonAspell 131+
(Nick Gifford) hld up: hdwy 5th: led appr 2 out: sn clr **10/1**

241- **2** 17 **Needless Shouting (IRE)**[102] 5208 4-11-4 **120**.......... MattieBatchelor 109
(Mick Channon) chsd ldr: led 5th tl appr 2 out: sn btn **10/1**

0-04 **3** 6 **Highsalvia Cosmos**[26] 2823 4-10-12 **114**..........(t) DavidBass 97
(Mark Hoad) hld up towards rr: promising hdwy 3 out: rdn appr next: sn outpcd **25/1**

1-06 **4** 3 **Beau Lake (IRE)**[18] 2961 11-10-5 **114**.......................... MrMLegg[(7)] 95
(Suzy Smith) chsd ldrs: rdn 4th: outpcd and btn appr 2 out **7/1**

2-23 **5** 12 **Malanos (IRE)**[27] 2810 7-10-2 **109**.......................... NickSlatter[(5)] 79
(Tony Carroll) led at gd pce tl 5th: wknd 3 out: 5th and no ch whn blnd last **6/1**[3]

20 **6** 19 **Disputed (IRE)**[15] 3015 5-11-2 **118**.......................... MarcGoldstein 66
(Chris Gordon) a in rr: rdn 3 out: sn wl bhd **6/1**[3]

-121 **P** **Mr Fickle (IRE)**[22] 2888 6-10-8 **120**..........(v) JasonNuttall[(10)]
(Gary Moore) in tch: rdn and wknd 5th: sn bhd: p.u after next **3/1**[1]

1123 **F** **Makethedifference (IRE)**[65] 2038 7-11-3 **119**.......... MichaelByrne
(Tim Vaughan) hld up towards rr: fell 2nd **11/2**[2]

-51P **P** **Rock Of Leon**[32] 2700 4-11-7 **128**..........(t) BridgetAndrews[(5)]
(Dan Skelton) in tch: rdn 4th: wknd qckly next: t.o whn p.u bef 6th **13/2**

4m 58.6s (24.30) **Going Correction** +1.55s/f (Heav) **9** Ran **SP% 116.8**
Speed ratings (Par 107): **108,100,97,96,91 82,** , ,
CSF £103.51 CT £2421.51 TOTE £13.50: £3.30, £2.10, £8.40; EX 82.50 TRIFECTA Not won..
Owner Nick Gifford Racing Club **Bred** Edward Gleeson **Trained** Findon, W Sussex

FOCUS
Race distance increased by 208yds. The feature contest was a fairly decent handicap hurdle and they went a respectable gallop.

3217 SELFTRADE MOBILE INVESTING MARES' H'CAP HURDLE (QUALIFIER FOR CHALLENGER MARES' SERIES FINAL) (11 hdls) 2m 5f 139y

2:40 (2:40) (Class 4) (0-120,118) 3-Y-O+ **£3,508** (£1,030; £515; £257)

Form RPR

121P **1** **At First Light**[21] 2911 6-11-8 **112**.......................... DavidBass 117
(David Weston) mde most tl 3 out: rallied gamely to ld again run-in: all out **10/1**

3013 **2** 3/4 **Tambura**[15] 3025 5-11-11 **115**.......................... LeightonAspell 119
(G C Maundrell) w wnr tl 3 out: outpcd appr next: styd on wl run-in **10/3**[2]

3121 **3** 2 1/4 **Anda De Grissay (FR)**[5] 3198 5-11-7 **118** 7ex..........(t) HarryCobden[(7)] 119
(Anthony Honeyball) in tch: led 2 out tl run-in: one pce **10/11**[1]

1-33 **4** 7 **Midnight Silver**[32] 2697 5-11-3 **114**..........(t) MissPFuller[(7)] 108
(Jamie Snowden) chsd ldrs: mstke 4th: dropped to rr at 6th: 5th and hld whn hit 3 out **8/1**[3]

-424 **5** 12 **Barton Rose**[21] 2911 6-11-5 **116**.......................... MrShaneQuinlan[(7)] 102
(Michael Blake) in tch: led 3 out tl wknd next **10/1**

-103 **P** **Tara Mac**[22] 2880 6-10-13 **103**.......................... MichaelByrne
(Tim Vaughan) hld up in rr: rdn 7th: sn wl bhd: p.u bef 3 out **8/1**[3]

6m 18.6s (36.10) **Going Correction** +1.55s/f (Heav) **6** Ran **SP% 115.9**
Speed ratings (Par 105): **96,95,94,92,88**
CSF £44.62 CT £60.57 TOTE £10.10: £3.50, £1.90; EX 43.90 Trifecta £97.20.
Owner Miss E J Tanner **Bred** D J Weston **Trained** Marlborough, Wilts

FOCUS
Race distance increased by 264yds. An ordinary mares' handicap hurdle and they went a sensible gallop.

3218 SOUTHERN CRANES ACCESS H'CAP CHASE (19 fncs) 3m 1f 106y

3:15 (3:17) (Class 5) (0-100,100) 4-Y-O+ **£2,921** (£1,062)

Form RPR

35-5 **1** **Call The Detective (IRE)**[20] 2930 6-11-12 **100**.......................... FelixDeGiles 113
(Ali Stronge) patiently rdn in rr: hdwy 13th: bmpd and led 2 out: sn clr **2/1**[1]

2212 **2** 27 **Lady From Geneva**[18] 2958 8-11-2 **90**..........(t) LeightonAspell 88
(Brendan Powell) chsd ldr: mstkes 2nd and 9th: led 14th tl hdd and bmpd 2 out: sn btn **3/1**[2]

364P **P** **Red Anchor (IRE)**[26] 2827 11-10-7 **81**..........(b) MarcGoldstein
(Linda Jewell) led: mstke 9th: hdd 14th: wknd 4 out: 3rd and wl btn whn blnd and p.u 2 out **12/1**

-141 **U** **Ya Hafed**[54] 2254 7-11-1 **89**.......................... MattieBatchelor
(Sheena West) hld up in 5th: wl bhd fr 14th: 4th and no ch whn j. slowly and uns rdr 3 out **9/2**[3]

4/5P **P** **Molly Oscar (IRE)**[205] 610 9-10-10 **84**..........(vt[1]) MichaelByrne
(Johnny Farrelly) chsd ldrs: wknd 12th: bhd whn p.u after next **7/1**

3-3F **P** **Expanding Universe (IRE)**[5] 3199 8-11-3 **96**.......................... NickSlatter[(5)]
(Tony Carroll) dropped to rr and blnd 9th: t.o whn p.u after 13th **9/2**[3]

7m 58.7s (57.60) **Going Correction** +2.375s/f (Heav) **6** Ran **SP% 114.9**
Speed ratings (Par 103): **102,93,** , , ,
CSF £9.06 TOTE £2.90: £1.70, £1.80; EX 11.50 Trifecta £13.70.
Owner J J King **Bred** Rockvale Stud **Trained** Eastbury, Berks

FOCUS
Race distance increased by 234yds. A modest staying handicap chase run in particularly testing conditions.

3219 THANK YOU WINNER FOR YOUR SUPPORT CONDITIONAL JOCKEYS' H'CAP HURDLE (10 hdls) 2m 3f 33y
3:45 (3:45) (Class 5) (0-100,89) 3-Y-O+ £2,599 (£763; £381; £190)

Form RPR

2243 1 **Hassadin**[50] 2316 9-11-9 **89**........................(p) HarryCobden(3) 102
(Michael Blake) *mde all: rdn and styd on wl fr 2 out* **5/1**[2]

P-04 2 6 **Loves Destination**[18] 2958 4-11-1 **83**........................ LewisGordon(5) 91
(Chris Gordon) *hld up: hdwy appr 2 out: drvn to chse wnr appr last: styd on same pce* **12/1**

PP-1 3 15 **Torero**[12] 3089 6-11-2 **87**........................(p) GeorgeGorman(8) 82
(Gary Moore) *cl up: chsd wnr 3 out: mstke next: lost 2nd and wknd appr last* **6/4**[1]

35-3 4 14 **Old Magic (IRE)**[16] 2982 10-10-10 **76**........................ ThomasCheesman(3) 54
(Sophie Leech) *chsd wnr tl 3 out: sn wknd* **7/1**[3]

0-P3 5 24 **Asker (IRE)**[18] 2958 7-10-6 **74**........................(tp) WilliamFeatherstone(5) 28
(Zoe Davison) *hld up: hdwy 6th: rdn next: sn struggling* **10/1**

4503 6 22 **Up Four It (IRE)**[40] 2547 7-11-1 **78**........................ JackSherwood 10
(Jamie Poulton) *in tch: mstke 7th: sn wknd* **8/1**

0-5P P **Tomsk (FR)**[53] 2263 5-10-13 **84**........................(t) GeorgeBlackwell(8)
(Tim Vaughan) *chsd ldrs tl 6th: sn wl bhd: p.u bef last* **8/1**

P-00 P **Moving Waves (IRE)**[108] 1524 4-11-7 **84**........................ MattGriffiths
(Johnny Farrelly) *a towards rr: lost tch 3 out: p.u bef next* **16/1**

5m 33.0s (33.60) **Going Correction** +1.55s/f (Heav)
WFA 4 from 5yo+ 5lb **8 Ran SP% 114.1**
Speed ratings (Par 103): **91,88,82,76,66 56, ,**
CSF £59.01 CT £130.90 TOTE £6.10: £1.80, £3.20, £1.10; EX 68.30 Trifecta £149.60.
Owner Wayne Clifford **Bred** Mrs S Clifford **Trained** Trowbridge, Wilts

FOCUS
Race distance increased by 208yds. The concluding contest was a moderate conditional jockeys' handicap hurdle.
T/Plt: £438.20 to a £1 stake. Pool: £29,428.77 - 49.02 winning units. T/Qpdt: £132.70 to a £1 stake. Pool: £2,349.63 - 13.10 winning units. **Lee McKenzie**

2924 HUNTINGDON (R-H)
Saturday, December 26

OFFICIAL GOING: Soft (good to soft in places; hdl 6.7, chs 6.2)
Wind: strong, across Weather: dry, blustery

3220 ROYALEQUESTRIAN.CO.UK CONDITIONAL JOCKEYS' H'CAP HURDLE (12 hdls) 3m 1f 10y
12:15 (12:15) (Class 4) (0-110,110) 4-Y-O+ £3,508 (£1,030; £515; £257)

Form RPR

-245 1 **Flemi Two Toes (IRE)**[12] 3087 9-9-9 **89**........................(p) RomainClavreul(10) 95+
(Sarah Humphrey) *in tch in midfield: hdwy after 7th: led next: rdn clr bef 3 out: nvr threatened after: styd on: rdn out* **16/1**

-PP3 2 4 ½ **Leath Acra Mor (IRE)**[29] 2744 9-10-11 **105**........................(v) TobyWheeler(10) 104
(Ian Williams) *pressed ldrs: led 7th: sn hdd: rdn bef 3 out: wnt 9 l 2nd 2 out: pushed rt last: kpt on u.p flat* **12/1**

-333 3 shd **Gilzean (IRE)**[21] 2919 9-11-9 **107**........................ KillianMoore 106
(Alex Hales) *hld up in tch in rr: rdn 8th: hdwy into 6th bef 3 out: swtchd lft between last 2: j.rt last: kpt on u.p flat* **9/1**

2546 4 9 **Winter Alchemy (IRE)**[29] 2751 10-9-13 **89**........................ RyanDay(6) 79
(Nicky Richards) *w ldrs tl led after 7th: hdd next: rdn and outpcd bef 3 out: wl hld and plugged on same pce fr 2 out* **10/1**

2U-5 5 nk **Aviador (GER)**[33] 2687 9-10-12 **103**........................ BenFfrenchDavis(7) 96+
(Lucy Wadham) *in tch in midfield: effrt to chse clr wnr 9th: no imp: lost 2nd and mstke 2 out: wknd last* **7/1**[2]

/5-0 6 4 ½ **Darkestbeforedawn (IRE)**[16] 2985 8-11-11 **109**........................ JackSherwood 94
(Caroline Keevil) *in tch in midfield: effrt u.p in 5th bef 3 out: sn no imp: wl hld 2 out* **16/1**

-666 7 1 ¾ **Bridal Suite (IRE)**[13] 3067 6-10-0 **94**........................(tp) TommyDowling(10) 78
(Charlie Mann) *in tch towards rr: rdn 8th: struggling after next: wknd after 3 out* **11/1**

5-P6 8 1 **El Indio (IRE)**[35] 2649 8-10-1 **85**........................(vt) DanielHiskett 67
(Claire Dyson) *w ldrs tl led after 4th: hdd and rdn 7th: lost pl after 8th: wl btn 3 out* **40/1**

535 9 5 **Golden Bird (IRE)**[35] 2630 4-11-7 **110**........................(p) WilliamFeatherstone(5) 88
(Brendan Powell) *in tch in midfield: stmbld bnd after 7th: mstke and rdn 9th: wknd next* **9/1**

5214 10 34 **Minella Bliss (IRE)**[44] 2454 10-10-9 **100**........................(b) CharlieHammond(7) 43
(James Evans) *chsd ldrs tl rdn and lost pl 8th: sn bhd: t.o after 3 out* **9/2**[1]

P-UP 11 31 **Safran De Cotte (FR)**[28] 2766 9-11-7 **105**........................ MattGriffiths 17
(Henry Daly) *chsd ldrs: rdn after 6th: lost pl after next: bhd and t.o 3 out* **10/1**

45P1 P **Earcomesthedream (IRE)**[9] 3128 12-11-0 **105**........................(b) ArchieBellamy(7)
(Peter Pritchard) *nvr gng wl: dropped to rr 3rd: tailing off whn p.u 6th* **14/1**

3634 P **Maypole Lass**[148] 1165 5-11-2 **100**........................ FreddieMitchell
(Clare Hobson) *led tl after 4th: losing pl and mstke 6th: losing tch whn p.u after 7th* **25/1**

-14P P **Crack Of Thunder (IRE)**[38] 2566 6-11-9 **110**........................(p) GrahamWatters(3)
(Charlie Longsdon) *nvr travelling wl in rr: detached last 6th: losing tch whn p.u 8th* **8/1**[3]

6m 32.3s (9.40) **Going Correction** +0.50s/f (Soft)
WFA 4 from 5yo+ 7lb **14 Ran SP% 120.7**
Speed ratings (Par 105): **104,102,102,99,99 98,97,97,95,84 74, , ,**
CSF £195.66 CT £1849.15 TOTE £16.70: £4.00, £3.30, £2.70; EX 303.20 Trifecta £725.40 Part won..
Owner Entente Cordiale **Bred** C Kenneally **Trained** West Wratting, Cambs

FOCUS
Chase rail out 1yd. Hurdle rail out 1yd on stable bend and dog-leg, and 2yds out on home bend, making the actual distance of the opener 3m 1f 29yds. The ground had dried out a little from previously forecast and was now soft, good to soft in places, but this opening conditional jockeys' event was still quite a test of stamina. The winner is rated in line with his best form in the last year.

3221 RACING FX NOVICES' HURDLE (10 hdls) 2m 3f 137y
12:45 (12:46) (Class 4) 4-Y-O+ £3,898 (£1,144; £572; £286)

Form RPR

50-5 1 **Expedite (IRE)**[27] 2807 4-10-2 0........................ TommyDowling(10) 111+
(Charlie Mann) *chsd ldrs: led sn after 3 out: hdd but clr w runner-up bnd bef 2 out: led again 2 out: blown lft by wind between last 2: mstke last: styd on: rdn out* **25/1**

4-10 2 3 **Late Night Lily**[42] 2486 4-10-5 0........................ RobertDunne 102
(Dan Skelton) *in tch in midfield: hdwy after 7th: wnt clr w wnr and led on bnd bef 2 out: hdd and sltly impeded between last 2: ev ch and mstke last: blown lft and no ex flat* **10/1**

3 11 **Sonneofpresenting (IRE)** 5-10-12 0........................ RyanMahon 98
(Kim Bailey) *hld up in midfield: 8th and j. slowly 3 out: kpt on to go 3rd last: styd on flat but no threat to ldng pair* **25/1**

13-1 4 3 ¼ **Imada (IRE)**[61] 2101 5-11-5 0........................ BrianHarding 101
(Nicky Richards) *t.k.h: chsd ldrs: wnt 3rd after 3 out but sn outpcd by ldrs: wl hld 4th between last 2: plugged on* **5/4**[1]

5-1 5 2 ¼ **The Tailgater (IRE)**[24] 2849 4-10-12 0........................ RichardJohnson 92
(Jonjo O'Neill) *in tch in midfield: effrt bef 3 out: 4th and no imp on ldng pair bef 2 out: wnt 3rd 2 out tl last: plugged on* **7/2**[3]

-16F 6 9 **Political Quiz**[10] 3117 5-11-5 0........................ JamesDavies 90
(Tom Symonds) *hld up in tch in midfield: effrt after 7th: no ex sn after next and wknd bef 2 out* **25/1**

7 15 **Hopefordebest (IRE)**[258] 5-10-9 0........................ RobMcCarth(3) 68
(Ian Williams) *in tch in midfield: struggling and mstke 7th: rdn and btn bef next: wknd bef 2 out: t.o* **40/1**

4-00 8 1 **Guiting Power**[21] 2904 4-10-5 0........................ MrJJSlevin(7) 67
(Nigel Twiston-Davies) *in tch in midfield: mstke 3rd: reminders 5th: rdn and mstke 7th: drvn and wknd bef 3 out: t.o* **80/1**

030 9 2 ½ **Lords Park Star (IRE)**[15] 3022 6-10-12 0........................ TrevorWhelan 64
(Nicholas Pomfret) *mstkes: led tl mstke and hdd 3 out: sn wknd: t.o* **66/1**

40 10 ½ **Mahlers Spirit (IRE)**[40] 2549 5-10-12 0........................ JackQuinlan 64
(Sarah Humphrey) *chsd ldr tl led 3 out: sn hdd and btn: fdd bef next: t.o* **80/1**

500 11 ½ **Song Of The Night (IRE)**[23] 2860 4-10-9 0........................ GrahamWatters(3) 63
(Charlie Longsdon) *in tch towards rr: rdn 6th: wknd bef 3 out: t.o* **66/1**

6 12 ¾ **Head To The Stars**[21] 2909 4-10-12 0........................ JamesBest 62
(Henry Daly) *in tch towards rr: dropped to last 6th: rdn next: sn wknd: t.o* **33/1**

F00 13 1 ¼ **Top Set (IRE)**[15] 3021 5-10-7 0........................ DanielHiskett(5) 61
(Richard Phillips) *hld up in last trio: hdwy after 5th: rdn and btn after 7th: sn wknd: t.o* **100/1**

4 P **Zarosa (IRE)**[25] 2829 6-10-5 0........................ DavidEngland
(John Berry) *mstkes: a in rr: lost tch after 7th: t.o whn p.u 2 out* **50/1**

P **Groundbreaking**[189] 5-10-12 0........................ AidanColeman
(John Ferguson) *chsd ldrs: wknd after 7th: mstke next: wl bhd whn p.u 2 out* **3/1**[2]

-600 P **Culworth Boy (IRE)**[33] 2689 5-10-9 0........................(t) KillianMoore(3)
(Sophie Leech) *hld up in rr: shortlived effrt 7th: lost tch next: t.o whn p.u 2 out* **100/1**

5m 2.75s (3.75) **Going Correction** +0.50s/f (Soft)
WFA 4 from 5yo+ 6lb **16 Ran SP% 127.1**
Speed ratings (Par 105): **112,110,106,105,104 100,94,94,93,93 92,92,92, ,**
CSF £246.91 TOTE £31.00: £6.60, £2.60, £5.60; EX 167.60 Trifecta £733.70 Part won..
Owner Simon Kimber **Bred** R McCarthy **Trained** Upper Lambourn, Berks

FOCUS
Actual race distance 2m 3f 153yds. They bet 25-1 bar four in this novices' hurdle, but something of a surprise result with the market leaders disappointing.

3222 RACING FX ONLINE H'CAP CHASE (19 fncs) 2m 7f 129y
1:20 (1:20) (Class 5) (0-100,94) 4-Y-O+ £2,924 (£858; £429; £214)

Form RPR

2P41 1 **Xenophon**[28] 2771 7-10-7 **82** ow1........................ BenFfrenchDavis(7) 100+
(Olly Williams) *in tch in rr: outpcd 13th: rdn after next: wnt 3rd after 3 out: clsd and led on inner 2 out: clr last: styd on: eased towards fin* **7/1**[3]

5525 2 6 **Kapricorne (FR)**[12] 3081 8-11-3 **90**........................(tp) DannyBurton(5) 100
(Sophie Leech) *j.lft: chsd ldr: rdn after 14th: led 3 out: hdd next: no ex last: plugged on same pce flat* **16/1**

-402 3 6 **Bebinn (IRE)**[52] 2269 8-11-10 **92**........................(p) AidanColeman 97
(Ben Case) *in tch in midfield tl j. slowly and outpcd 13th: 7 l 4th 2 out: plugged on to 3rd nr fin: no ch w wnr* **4/1**[1]

02U2 4 1 **Dawnieriver (IRE)**[30] 2735 5-11-11 **93**........................(p) RobertDunne 95
(Michael Scudamore) *chsd ldrs: chsd ldr sn after 3 out: clsd and pressing ldr whn bmpd 2 out: 3rd and btn whn j.rt last: wknd flat: lost 3rd nr fin* **8/1**

R-16 5 31 **Upbeat Cobbler (FR)**[20] 2930 7-11-12 **94**........................ RichardJohnson 65
(Henry Daly) *racd wd: chsd ldrs tl outpcd 13th: 6th and lost tch 16th: t.o 2 out* **6/1**[2]

1-P0 6 ½ **It's Oscar (IRE)**[17] 2976 8-11-0 **82**........................(b) RyanMahon 60
(James Evans) *led: wnt clr after 12th: hdd 3 out: sn u.p and dropped out: wl btn next: wknd: t.o* **7/1**[3]

3231 P **Kilcascan**[13] 3062 11-11-6 **91**........................(p) BenPoste(3)
(Rosemary Gasson) *in tch in midfield: dropped to rr and struggling u.p 12th: t.o whn p.u 16th* **7/1**[3]

/P-1 P **Banksandditches (IRE)**[214] 488 9-11-7 **94**........................ FreddieMitchell(5)
(Clare Hobson) *bhd and nvr travelling: j. slowly 4th and 6th: wl bhd whn p.u 8th* **10/1**

-PP2 P **Mansonien L'As (FR)**[13] 3059 9-11-2 **84**........................(tp) BrianHarding
(Donald McCain) *chsd ldrs: losing pl and mstke 8th: bhd next: losing tch whn p.u 11th* **7/1**[3]

0/2- P **Electric Mayhem**[251] 5416 8-11-6 **88**........................ JamesDavies
(Nick Mitchell) *chsd ldrs: blnd 11th: lost action jst bef next: immediately p.u after jumping 12th and dismntd: fatally injured* **14/1**

6m 18.8s (8.50) **Going Correction** +0.40s/f (Soft) **10 Ran SP% 117.0**
Speed ratings (Par 103): **101,99,97,96,86 86, , ,**
CSF £105.69 CT £510.95 TOTE £8.00: £2.20, £4.40, £2.10; EX 105.50 Trifecta £404.70 Part won..
Owner Milson Robinson **Bred** Winterbeck Manor Stud **Trained** Market Rasen, Lincs

FOCUS
Actual race distance 2m 7f 142yds. A moderate handicap chase and this took some getting with the pace a decent one. The winner was a 108-rated hurdler at his best and there may still be a bit more to come.

3223 RACING FX ONLINE H'CAP HURDLE (10 hdls) 2m 4f 145y
1:50 (1:52) (Class 4) (0-110,110) 3-Y-0+ £3,573 (£1,049; £524; £262)

Form RPR
50P5 1 **Ballinalacken (IRE)**[16] 2997 7-11-5 103..........(v) DavidEngland 106
(Clare Ellam) *hld up in tch in last trio: hdwy after 7th: chsd clr ldng pair 2 out: 6 l down last: styd on u.p to ld cl home* **16/1**
U0PU 2 ½ **Drombeg West**[23] 2867 8-11-2 100.......... TrevorWhelan 103+
(Anna Brooks) *hld up in last pair: hdwy after 6th: led 2 out: mstke last: hung / blown lft flat: kpt on: hdd and no ex cl home* **20/1**
4306 3 1¾ **Being Global (FR)**[20] 2924 4-11-7 105.......... RichardJohnson 104
(Caroline Bailey) *hld up in tch in midfield: hdwy 6th: jnd ldrs next: led 3 out: rdn and hdd next: wnt lft and mstke last: swtchd rt flat: styd on same pce fnl 100yds* **2/1[1]**
0110 4 17 **Hope's Wishes**[28] 2778 5-11-1 106.......... MrZBaker[(7)] 88
(Barry Brennan) *in tch in midfield: hdwy to chse ldrs 3rd: cl 3rd and rdn 3 out: btn and mstke next: wknd between last 2* **8/1[3]**
/0-4 5 8 **Ratify**[42] 2490 11-11-7 105.......... RobertDunne 79
(Dai Burchell) *chsd ldrs: led 2nd: hdd 3 out: rdn and btn bef next: wknd between last 2* **8/1[3]**
0233 6 1¾ **Tiradia (FR)**[46] 2413 8-11-8 106.......... AidanColeman 79
(J R Jenkins) *hld up in tch: hdwy on inner 6th: rdn 3 out: sn btn and wknd bef next* **9/1**
3-02 7 5 **Parc Des Princes (USA)**[29] 2751 9-10-11 102.......... RyanDay[(7)] 70
(Nicky Richards) *in tch in last pair: rdn after 5th: wknd bef 3 out* **7/1[2]**
0U34 8 3 **Prince Mahler (IRE)**[38] 2564 5-11-10 108.......... JamesBest 73
(Caroline Keevil) *chsd ldrs tl 3rd: dropped to midfield but stl wl in tch: effrt u.p after 7th: wknd qckly after 3 out: t.o* **16/1**
1000 9 2 **Powderonthebonnet (IRE)**[16] 2997 7-10-10 99.......... DanielHiskett[(5)] 62
(Richard Phillips) *hld up in tch in rr: struggling and rdn after 6th: lost tch bef 3 out: t.o* **33/1**
-204 10 30 **Astrum**[24] 2843 5-11-6 104..........(b) AdrianLane 37
(Donald McCain) *chsd ldrs: 2nd 6th: ev ch and rdn after next: btn 3 out: sn wknd: eased flat: t.o* **16/1**
211/ P **Polo Springs**[616] 5395 8-10-1 95..........(t) ArchieBellamy[(10)]
(Graeme McPherson) *chsd ldrs 3rd tl rdn and btn bef 3 out: wl btn whn eased and p.u 2 out* **8/1[3]**
2150 P **Shot In The Dark (IRE)**[37] 2599 6-11-0 98..........(p) GerardTumelty
(Jonathan Geake) *led tl 2nd: chsd ldr tl 6th: wknd next: t.o whn p.u 2 out* **22/1**

5m 26.5s (15.90) **Going Correction** +0.50s/f (Soft)
WFA 4 from 5yo+ 6lb **12 Ran SP% 118.9**
Speed ratings (Par 105): **89,88,88,81,78 77,76,74,74,62 ,**
CSF £290.61 CT £923.63 TOTE £18.10: £4.30, £7.00, £1.40; EX 468.30 Trifecta £339.60 Part won..
Owner Chrissy's Passion Racing **Bred** Mrs Bridget Delaney **Trained** Atlow, Derbyshire

FOCUS
Actual race distance 2m 4f 161yds. A fair handicap hurdle, but a slow-motion finish with a couple of the principals hanging badly in the strong wind up the home straight. The winner was a 110+ hurdler in 2014 and has been rated back to something similar.

3224 RACING FX NOVICES' H'CAP CHASE (16 fncs) 2m 3f 189y
2:25 (2:26) (Class 4) (0-110,109) 4-Y-0+ £3,898 (£1,144; £572; £286)

Form RPR
-F55 1 **Pandy Wells**[24] 2855 6-9-4 83 oh6.......... ArchieBellamy[(10)] 92+
(Graeme McPherson) *chsd ldrs: upsides ldr 10th led 12th: 4 l clr last: idling and reminder flat: rdn out hands and heels and doing enough fnl 100yds* **12/1**
-043 2 1¾ **Guanciale**[30] 2736 8-11-2 99.......... RobertDunne 104
(Dai Burchell) *hld up in tch in last pair: hdwy to chse wnr 3 out: mstke 2 out: rallied u.p flat: kpt on but a hld* **8/1**
2P-3 3 4½ **Hellorboston (IRE)**[28] 2766 7-11-12 109..........(p) AdrianLane 110
(Donald McCain) *led tl 4th: w ldrs after tl outpcd u.p after 3 out: j.ftt next: plugged on same pce flat* **4/1[3]**
6211 4 4 **Arthamint**[38] 2582 7-11-5 102..........(t) DavidEngland 98
(Dan Skelton) *t.k.h: hld up in tch in rr: cl 5th and effrt after 3 out: no rspnse and wl hld next: plugged on into 4th flat* **3/1[2]**
3-22 5 7 **Minellaforlunch (IRE)**[34] 2666 8-10-11 94..........(p) JamesDavies 88
(Henry Oliver) *chsd ldrs: 4th and outpcd u.p after 3 out: hld and mstke next: wknd last* **7/4[1]**
5/63 6 60 **Jack By The Hedge**[18] 2957 6-11-12 109..........(t) JamesBest 38
(Caroline Keevil) *w ldr tl led 4th: hdd and pckd 12th: dropped to last 3 out: sn lost tch: t.o 2 out* **13/2**

5m 20.1s (14.80) **Going Correction** +0.40s/f (Soft) **6 Ran SP% 113.5**
Speed ratings (Par 105): **86,85,83,81,79 55**
CSF £92.18 TOTE £11.20: £3.60, £3.30; EX 105.50 Trifecta £415.90 Part won..
Owner Mike & Linda Paul **Bred** M R Paul **Trained** Upper Oddington, Gloucs

FOCUS
Actual race distance 2m 3f 199yds. Not the deepest of races of its type and a big step up from the winner on her hurdles form.

3225 RACING FX H'CAP CHASE (12 fncs) 2m 104y
3:00 (3:02) (Class 4) (0-110,109) 4-Y-0+ £3,898 (£1,144; £572; £286)

Form RPR
-035 1 **Sonofagun (FR)**[24] 2854 9-11-12 109..........(p) RichardJohnson 120+
(Ian Williams) *chsd ldr: led 3 out: clr and wnt lft next: in command whn wnt bdly lft last: sn stened and rdn clr: comf* **9/4[1]**
-330 2 9 **Safari Journey (USA)**[28] 2788 11-11-9 106..........(p) BrianHarding 104
(Lucinda Egerton) *hld up in tch: outpcd by ldng pair 7th: 3rd and no imp after 3 out: chsd clr wnr next: kpt on same pce* **14/1**
063U 3 9 **Little Windmill (IRE)**[15] 3020 5-10-10 93..........(tp) TrevorWhelan 86+
(Neil King) *j.lft: led: clr w wnr 7th: hdd 3 out: btn whn wnt bdly lft and lost 2nd next: plugged on* **9/2[3]**
-422 4 21 **Take The Crown**[23] 2859 6-11-6 103..........(t) JamesDavies 71
(Henry Oliver) *chsd ldrs: outpcd 7th: rdn next: wknd bef 2 out: t.o* **11/4[2]**
0-PP 5 8 **Topthorn**[23] 2859 9-10-11 101..........(p) MrZBaker[(7)] 63
(Martin Bosley) *chsd ldrs: mstke and lost pl 2nd: outpcd 7th: sme hdwy 9th: wknd after next: t.o* **11/1**
354P P **Ciceron (IRE)**[16] 2994 9-11-7 104..........(t) AidanColeman
(Neil King) *hld up in rr: effrt sn after 3 out: no rspnse and wl btn bef: t.o whn p.u last* **7/1**

4m 19.25s (9.05) **Going Correction** +0.40s/f (Soft) **6 Ran SP% 103.1**
Speed ratings (Par 105): **93,88,84,73,69**
CSF £23.39 CT £93.12 TOTE £3.10: £1.60, £4.80; EX 25.10 Trifecta £134.60.
Owner The Piranha Partnership **Bred** Dora Bloodstock Ltd **Trained** Portway, Worcs
■ Boss In Boots was withdrawn. Price at time of withdrawal 9/1. Rule 4 applies to all bets - deduction 10p in the pound.

FOCUS
Actual race distance 2m 114yds. A fair handicap chase, but it proved hard work and was notable for some wayward jumping. The winner has been rated in line with the best of his form on right-handed tracks.

3226 RACING UK £10 DAY PASS INTERMEDIATE OPEN NATIONAL HUNT FLAT RACE 1m 7f 171y
3:35 (3:35) (Class 6) 4-6-Y-O £1,624 (£477; £238; £119)

Form RPR
1 **Westend Story (IRE)**[258] 4-11-0 0.......... RichardJohnson 120+
(Philip Hobbs) *hld up in tch in midfield: smooth hdwy to ld 3f out: sn clr: hung lft and rn green over 1f out: r.o wl: readily* **10/11[1]**
2 6 **Better Getalong (IRE)** 4-11-0 0.......... BrianHarding 111
(Nicky Richards) *hld up in tch in last trio: hdwy over 4f out: chsd clr wnr over 2f out: no threat to wnr but kpt on wl for clr 2nd* **3/1[2]**
4 3 11 **Mr Banks (IRE)**[35] 2650 4-11-0 0.......... JamesBest 100
(Paul Webber) *chsd ldrs: rdn and ev ch 4f out tl outpcd over 2f out: 3rd and wknd over 1f out* **14/1**
3 4 7 **Adman Sam (IRE)**[70] 1973 4-11-0 0.......... AidanColeman 93
(Ian Williams) *hld up in tch in last quartet: effrt in 6th 3f out: no imp and no ch w ldrs after: wnt modest 4th 1f out* **10/1[3]**
5 1¼ **Torhousemuir** 4-10-7 0.......... [1] HarrisonBeswick[(7)] 92
(Sam Thomas) *t.k.h: hld up in rr: effrt over 3f out: no real imp: plugged on to pass btn horses fnl 2f: nvr trbld ldrs* **33/1**
3 6 6 **Nobel Leader (IRE)**[37] 2597 5-11-0 0.......... RyanMahon 86
(James Evans) *t.k.h: chsd ldrs: lft in ld after 3f: rdn and hrd pressed over 3f out: hdd 3f out: sn outpcd: wknd 2f out* **12/1**
3-4 7 8 **Dothraki Raider**[24] 2849 4-10-11 0.......... KillianMoore[(3)] 78
(Sophie Leech) *chsd ldrs: rdn and ev ch 4f out: wknd wl over 2f out: t.o* **25/1**
331- 8 10 **Cresswell Prince (IRE)**[528] 981 5-11-7 0..........(t) TrevorWhelan 75
(Claire Dyson) *t.k.h: chsd ldrs: rdn 4f out: sn btn and wknd 3f out: t.o* **20/1**
9 1 **Little Vic** 4-11-0 0.......... JackQuinlan 67
(Eugene Stanford) *in tch in midfield: rdn and lost pl over 3f out: wknd 3f out: t.o* **20/1**
P **Goldie Lynch (IRE)** 6-10-9 0.......... [1] DanielHiskett[(5)]
(Richard Phillips) *t.k.h: led: hung bdly lft bnd after 2f: unsteerable and p.u arnd next wing* **33/1**
P **Marey (IRE)** 6-10-7 0.......... RobertDunne
(Ms N M Hugo) *in tch in midfield tl lost pl 6f out: sn lost tch: t.o whn p.u 4f out* **40/1**
P **The New Trick (IRE)** 5-10-9 0..........(t) DannyBurton[(5)]
(Sophie Leech) *hld up in tch in last quartet: lost action over 4f out: p.u and dismntd 4f out: fatally injured* **50/1**

3m 57.5s (8.40) **Going Correction** +0.50s/f (Soft)
WFA 4 from 5yo+ 5lb **12 Ran SP% 124.5**
Speed ratings: **99,96,90,87,86 83,79,74,73, ,**
CSF £3.34 TOTE £1.70: £1.10, £1.50, £2.50; EX 4.80 Trifecta £38.60.
Owner Mick Fitzgerald Racing Club **Bred** James F Barry **Trained** Withycombe, Somerset

FOCUS
Actual race distance 1m 7f 185yds. This bumper was won by this season's smart novice hurdler O O Seven last year. They bet 10-1 bar two this time and the market got it right with the big two in the betting pulling well clear of the others. The winner looks decent and should win more races.
T/Plt: £4,925.70 to a £1 stake. Pool: £34750.13 - 5.15 winning tickets T/Qpdt: £173.40 to a £1 stake. Pool: £2753.98 - 11.75 winning tickets **Steve Payne**

[2683]KEMPTON (R-H)
Saturday, December 26

OFFICIAL GOING: Good to soft (soft in places; chs 5.5; hdl 5.3)
Wind: Fresh, across Weather: Cloudy, mild

3227 WILLIAM HILL ON YOUR MOBILE NOVICES' HURDLE (8 hdls) 2m
12:50 (12:50) (Class 2) 4-Y-0+ £11,696 (£3,434; £1,717; £858)

Form RPR
6111 1 **Altior (IRE)**[41] 2509 5-11-8 147.......... NicodeBoinville 157+
(Nicky Henderson) *lw: t.k.h: prom: trckd ldr 3rd to 5th: shkn up bef 2 out where clsd to ld: sn romped clr: impressive* **11/8[1]**
2 13 **Open Eagle (IRE)**[38] 2584 6-11-8 0.......... RWalsh 142
(W P Mullins, Ire) *prom: trckd ldr 5th: gng strly whn chalng bef 2 out: sn outpcd by wnr: kpt on but no ch* **3/1[2]**
6-11 3 7 **Marracudja (FR)**[49] 2345 4-11-8 138..........(t) SamTwiston-Davies 134
(Paul Nicholls) *led at decent pce: hdd and btn 2 out: wknd flat but hld on for 3rd* **11/2**
0-13 4 ½ **Simon Squirrel (IRE)**[41] 2509 5-11-5 140..........(t) SeanBowen 132
(Paul Nicholls) *trckd ldrs: t.k.h after 5th: cl up after 3 out: outpcd and btn in 4th whn blnd 2 out: kpt on* **8/1**
12 5 ¾ **Meet The Legend**[61] 2106 4-11-0 0.......... [1] HarrySkelton 124
(Dan Skelton) *lengthy: lw: plld hrd: hld up in rr: clsd on ldrs and in tch in 6th after 3 out: shkn up and lft bhd bef 2 out: kpt on* **5/1[3]**
6 6 **Gwafa (IRE)**[476] 4-11-0 0.......... RichieMcLernon 119
(Paul Webber) *hld up in midfield: in tch in 5th after 3 out: outpcd bef next: steadily fdd: nt fluent last* **33/1**
04 7 12 **Breath Of Blighty (FR)**[33] 2690 4-11-0 0.......... TomScudamore 107
(Paul Webber) *chsd ldr to 3rd: sn in midfield: rdn and in tch whn hit 3 out: wknd* **100/1**
2 8 1¼ **Cashanova (IRE)**[54] 2250 4-11-0 0.......... PaddyBrennan 105
(Nick Gifford) *hld up in rr: wknd sn after 3 out: sn bhd* **40/1**
0 9 8 **Red Orator**[12] 3083 6-11-0 0.......... BrendanPowell 97
(Jim Best) *sn in rr: pushed along and lost tch sn after 3 out: bhd bef next* **150/1**
UF P **Pantoloni**[42] 2488 4-11-0 0.......... MikeyHamill
(Richard Harper) *a in rr: wknd 4th: t.o next: p.u bef 3 out* **150/1**

3m 50.1s (-7.90) **Going Correction** +0.025s/f (Yiel)
WFA 4 from 5yo+ 5lb **10 Ran SP% 118.0**
Speed ratings (Par 109): **120,113,110,109,109 106,100,99,95,**
CSF £5.86 TOTE £2.10: £1.10, £1.40, £2.00; EX 6.50 Trifecta £18.90.

Owner Mrs Patricia Pugh **Bred** Paddy Behan **Trained** Upper Lambourn, Berks

FOCUS
All starts have been moved at this track following remeasuring, so there will be no speed figures here until there is sufficient data to calculate updated median times. Chase course at innermost configuration and distances as advertised. Winter Hurdle course used and rail 4yds out from inner configuration, increasing the distance of the opener by 22yds. This is traditionally a good-quality novice event and the form looks rock-solid, with the winner taking a step up.

3228 WILLIAM HILL WINTER FESTIVAL NOVICES' LIMITED H'CAP CHASE (16 fncs) 2m 4f 110y

1:25 (1:27) (Class 3) (0-140,140) 4-Y-0+ **£12,996** (£3,816; £1,908; £954)

Form RPR

0-00 **1** **Full Shift (FR)**[28] 2779 6-10-9 **127**........ BarryGeraghty 139+
(Nicky Henderson) *cl up on outer: chsd ldr 11th: rdn after 4 out: lft in ld after next: hrd pressed again 2 out: drvn to assert fr last* **5/1**[2]

-301 **2** *3/4* **Bekkensfirth**[17] 2973 6-10-4 **122**........ HarrySkelton 135+
(Dan Skelton) *lw: trckd ldr: led 10th: 3 l up 4 out: stl nrly 2 l ahd whn blnd 3 out and hdd: rallied 2 out: w wnr last: styd on but jst hld* **9/2**[1]

1-P2 **3** *12* **Sirabad (FR)**[27] 2803 5-10-13 **131**........(t) SamTwiston-Davies 131
(Paul Nicholls) *patiently rdn in rr: prog fr 10th: chsd ldng pair after 4 out: lft w gd ch 3 out: nt fluent 2 out and wknd* **6/1**

-156 **4** *29* **Rock N Rhythm (IRE)**[33] 2691 5-10-13 **131**........(t) RichieMcLernon 100
(Jonjo O'Neill) *led to 10th: wknd 4 out: bmpd next: t.o* **16/1**

20-6 **U** **Unique De Cotte (FR)**[29] 2759 7-11-8 **140**........(t) TomScudamore
(David Pipe) *hld up in rr: 8th but in tch whn uns rdr 9th* **8/1**

2P-1 **F** **West Wizard (FR)**[236] 100 6-10-8 **129**........ RyanHatch(3) 90
(Nigel Twiston-Davies) *lw: in tch on outer: rdn and btn after 4 out: wl bhd whn fell last: winded* **7/1**

-312 **F** **Buckhorn Timothy**[21] 2905 6-11-0 **132**........ PaddyBrennan
(Colin Tizzard) *chsd ldrs: mstke 5th: in tch in 5th whn fell 11th* **8/1**

-153 **P** **How About It (IRE)**[10] 3106 6-10-10 **128**........(p) SeanBowen
(Rebecca Curtis) *set off promly but j. sloppily and sn in rr: last fr 6th: losing tch whn sltly hmpd 9th: t.o after: p.u bef 4 out* **8/1**

2301 **P** **Antony (FR)**[22] 2885 5-10-12 **130**........ JamieMoore
(Gary Moore) *nt fluent 3rd: chsd ldng pair to 10th: rdn and wknd after 4 out: no ch whn bmpd 3 out: p.u bef last* **11/2**[3]

5m 9.6s (-2.40) **Going Correction** +0.15s/f (Yiel) **9** Ran SP% **116.2**
Speed ratings (Par 107): **110,109,105,94, , , ,**
CSF £28.63 CT £138.49 TOTE £6.40: £2.00, £1.90, £2.20; EX 32.90 Trifecta £241.00.

Owner John P McManus **Bred** Mme Catherine Niederhauser Dietrich **Trained** Upper Lambourn, Berks

FOCUS
This was a decent novice handicap and they went a solid gallop. Only the principals mattered from three out. The winner has been rated in line with the best of his hurdles form.

3229 KAUTO STAR NOVICES' CHASE (IN MEMORY OF NIGEL CLARK) (FORMERLY THE FELTHAM NOVICES CHASE) (GRADE 1) (18 fncs) 3m

2:00 (2:00) (Class 1) 4-Y-0+

£39,865 (£14,959; £7,490; £3,731; £1,876; £938)

Form RPR

-601 **1** **Tea For Two**[22] 2881 6-11-7 146........ LizzieKelly 161+
(Nick Williams) *lw: racd wd: wl in tch: trckd ldrs fr 12th: wnt 2nd bef 3 out: clsd to ld immediately after 2 out: pushed out and r.o wl flat* **9/4**[2]

-211 **2** *4* **Southfield Royale**[14] 3040 5-11-7 147........(p) NoelFehily 158+
(Neil Mulholland) *j.lft: nt fluent 1st: led 2nd to 4th: led again 10th: sent for home after 4 out: ouj. 2 out and sn hdd: outpcd after* **11/2**[3]

-311 **3** *3 3/4* **Native River (IRE)**[30] 2726 5-11-7 153........ BrendanPowell 155+
(Colin Tizzard) *lw: trckd ldrs: sed jumping lft fr 8th: nt fluent 10th and 11th and sn dropped to last: rallied 13th: nt fluent 4 out and drvn: outpcd bef next where modest 3rd: styd on but no ch to threaten* **6/4**[1]

-033 **4** *10* **L'Unique (FR)**[29] 2760 6-11-0 137........ WayneHutchinson 135
(Alan King) *hld up in last pair but wl in tch: drvn 4 out: outpcd bef next where disp modest 3rd: wknd 2 out* **25/1**

6- **5** *8* **Net D'Ecosse (FR)**[16] 2999 5-11-7 131........ BJCooper 135
(W P Mullins, Ire) *led 4th to 10th: mstkes 12th and next: chsd ldr tl bef 3 out: wknd* **16/1**

P-11 **6** *29* **Bally Beaufort (IRE)**[21] 2897 7-11-7 144........ RyanHatch 113
(Nigel Twiston-Davies) *led to 2nd: nt as fluent as rivals and unable to hold pl: rdn to stay in tch 13th: wknd 4 out: t.o* **10/1**

-223 **F** **As De Mee (FR)**[21] 2913 5-11-7 140........ SamTwiston-Davies
(Paul Nicholls) *hld up in last pair but wl in tch: prog fr 12th: cl up 4 out: wknd and 6th whn fell 3 out: winded* **10/1**

6m 10.0s (1.00) **Going Correction** +0.15s/f (Yiel) **7** Ran SP% **114.1**
Speed ratings (Par 117): **104,102,101,98,95 85,**
CSF £15.11 TOTE £3.40: £2.00, £2.60; EX 19.30 Trifecta £33.10.

Owner Mrs Jane Williams & Len Jakeman **Bred** Mrs P G Lewin **Trained** George Nympton, Devon

FOCUS
A Grade 1 novice chase that has gone to some top-notchers down the years, most recently subsequent Gold Cup winner Coneygree last term. It was run at a decent tempo and, rated around the third, rates another decent renewal.

3230 WILLIAMHILL.COM CHRISTMAS HURDLE (GRADE 1) (8 hdls) 2m

2:35 (2:35) (Class 1) 4-Y-0+ **£56,950** (£21,370; £10,700; £5,330; £2,680)

Form RPR

1-12 **1** **Faugheen (IRE)**[41] 2532 7-11-7 171........ RWalsh 170+
(W P Mullins, Ire) *mde all: drew clr bef 2 out: j.rt last 2: easily* **1/4**[1]

15-1 **2** *7* **The New One (IRE)**[69] 1988 7-11-7 162........ NoelFehily 161
(Nigel Twiston-Davies) *chsd wnr: already outpcd whn mstke 2 out: no ch after: nt fluent last* **6/1**[2]

6-43 **3** *3/4* **Hargam (FR)**[14] 3033 4-11-7 155........ BarryGeraghty 159
(Nicky Henderson) *hld up in 4th: chsd ldng pair after 3 out: rdn and outpcd whn mstke 2 out: kpt on* **16/1**

-111 **4** *4 1/2* **Old Guard**[14] 3033 4-11-7 157........ SamTwiston-Davies 155
(Paul Nicholls) *chsd ldng pair tl after 3 out: sn rdn: btn bef 2 out* **8/1**[3]

42-4 **5** *25* **Sign Of A Victory (IRE)**[21] 2186 6-11-7 154........ AndrewTinkler 137
(Nicky Henderson) *hld up in last: nt fluent 3 out: gng bttr than sme bef 2 out but no prog and wknd sn after it: mstke last: eased* **25/1**

3m 47.7s (-10.30) **Going Correction** +0.025s/f (Yiel) **5** Ran SP% **115.1**
Speed ratings (Par 117): **126,122,122,119,107**
CSF £2.80 TOTE £1.10: £1.10, £1.50; EX 2.60 Trifecta £7.20.

Owner Mrs S Ricci **Bred** Dr John Waldron **Trained** Muine Beag, Co Carlow

FOCUS
Race distance increased by 22yds. This year's Christmas Hurdle was run at a sound gallop and looks best rated around the runner-up. The winner has been rated similar to last year's win.

3231 WILLIAM HILL KING GEORGE VI CHASE (GRADE 1) (18 fncs) 3m

3:10 (3:10) (Class 1) 4-Y-0 **£114,436** (£43,276; £21,936; £11,196; £5,896)

Form RPR

-411 **1** **Cue Card**[35] 2642 9-11-10 172........(t) PaddyBrennan 180
(Colin Tizzard) *trckd ldrs: prog 10th: chsd ldr 12th: shkn up bef 3 out: no imp and jst hdd for 2nd whn lft in it again 2 out: hrd rdn and clsd last: styd on gamely u.p to ld post* **9/2**[3]

11-1 **2** *hd* **Vautour (FR)**[35] 2633 6-11-10 171........ RWalsh 180
(W P Mullins, Ire) *trckd ldr: led 11th: gng best fr 4 out: 2 l up 2 out: rdn bef last: pressed and drvn flat: hdd post* **3/1**[2]

52-1 **3** *13* **Al Ferof (FR)**[20] 2927 10-11-10 165........ HarrySkelton 166
(Dan Skelton) *lw: settled in rr: effrt fr 12th: tk 4th bef 3 out but nt on terms w ldrs: lft 3rd 2 out: n.d* **16/1**

4-11 **4** *3 1/4* **Smad Place (FR)**[28] 2783 8-11-10 168........ WayneHutchinson 163
(Alan King) *lw: trckd ldrs: wl on terms 4 out: rdn and one pce bef next: wl hld after* **8/1**

-215 **5** *23* **Irish Cavalier (IRE)**[42] 2483 6-11-10 156........(p) BarryGeraghty 145
(Rebecca Curtis) *hld up in last trio and nt a fluent: struggling fr 14th: wknd after 4 out* **40/1**

1535 **P** **Ballynagour (IRE)**[35] 2642 9-11-10 162........(t) TomScudamore
(David Pipe) *set off in last: nt fluent: lost tch after 9th: t.o whn p.u bef 12th* **66/1**

1-22 **P** **Silviniaco Conti (FR)**[35] 2642 9-11-10 168........(p) NoelFehily
(Paul Nicholls) *led and j.w: hdd 11th: steadily lost pl fr next: wknd 4 out: last whn p.u bef 3 out* **9/1**

-111 **F** **Don Cossack (GER)**[56] 2207 8-11-10 175........(t) BJCooper 180
(Gordon Elliott, Ire) *lw: chsd ldrs: effrt to go 3rd 4 out: sn rdn: tk 2nd 2 out and 2 l down but styng on whn fell 2 out* **15/8**[1]

61-2 **F** **Valseur Lido (FR)**[20] 2941 6-11-10 157........ JacquesRicou 161
(W P Mullins, Ire) *chsd ldrs: lost pl fr 1/2-way: in tch but rdn 4 out: wl btn in 5th whn fell last* **25/1**

6m 3.5s (-5.50) **Going Correction** +0.15s/f (Yiel) **9** Ran SP% **112.7**
Speed ratings (Par 117): **115,114,110,109,101 , , ,**
CSF £18.36 CT £193.41 TOTE £4.60: £1.40, £1.60, £4.30; EX 18.50 Trifecta £238.10.

Owner Mrs Jean R Bishop **Bred** R T Crellin **Trained** Milborne Port, Dorset

■ Stewards' Enquiry : Paddy Brennan 11-day ban; used his whip above the permitted level (9th-19th Jan). £4,200 fine: used his whip above the permitted level.
R Walsh two-day ban; used his whip above the permitted level (9th-10th Jan)

FOCUS
A mouth watering King George on paper and, predictably run at a hard gallop, it certainly didn't disappoint. A small personal best from the winner and the best RPR for the winner of this race since Kauto Star in 2011.

3232 WILLIAM HILL WORLD DARTS CHAMPIONSHIP H'CAP HURDLE (10 hdls) 2m 5f

3:45 (3:45) (Class 3) (0-140,135) 3-Y-0+ **£9,747** (£2,862; £1,431; £715)

Form RPR

6-11 **1** **Baron Alco (FR)**[41] 2516 4-11-4 **127**........ JamieMoore 132+
(Gary Moore) *racd freely: mde all: set mod pce: mstke 7th: hrd pressed fr 2 out: jnd last: drvn and kpt on wl flat* **7/1**[3]

0-31 **2** *3/4* **Simply A Legend**[21] 2912 6-11-5 **128**........ WayneHutchinson 131
(Alan King) *lw: hld up towards rr: prog on inner bef 3 out: chsd wnr bef 2 out: drvn to chal and nrly upsides last: kpt on but a jst hld* **8/1**

F5-6 **3** *1 3/4* **Keltus (FR)**[21] 2912 5-11-7 **130**........(t) SamTwiston-Davies 132
(Paul Nicholls) *trckd ldrs: rdn bef 2 out: cl up after: ch between last 2: styd on same pce and nvr quite able to chal* **9/1**

-012 **4** *3/4* **Matorico (IRE)**[23] 2864 4-11-10 **133**........ BarryGeraghty 135
(Jonjo O'Neill) *hld up towards rr: nt clrest of runs after 3 out: rdn and prog bef 2 out: tk 3rd and looked a threat whn hit last: one pce flat* **9/1**

123 **5** *9* **Flying Angel (IRE)**[21] 2898 4-11-4 **130**........ RyanHatch(3) 123
(Nigel Twiston-Davies) *wl in tch: prog to take 4th on long run after 3 out: no imp 2 out: fdd after: mstke last* **20/1**

114- **6** *nk* **Sugar Baron (IRE)**[287] 4753 5-11-8 **131**........ NicodeBoinville 124
(Nicky Henderson) *lw: towards rr: rdn and struggling sn after 3 out: tried to rally bef 2 out: plugged on but nvr able to threaten* **9/2**[2]

3/12 **7** *4* **Billy No Name (IRE)**[29] 2759 7-10-13 **122**........ PaddyBrennan 113
(Colin Tizzard) *hld up in last trio: tried to make prog after 3 out but out v wd and lost grnd bnd bef 2 out: nvr able to threaten after* **10/1**

13 **8** *3* **Max Forte (IRE)**[44] 2450 5-11-5 **128**........ TomScudamore 114
(Chris Down) *lw: prom: chsd wnr 3 out tl wknd bef 2 out* **11/1**

00/6 **9** *5* **Swnymor (IRE)**[20] 2926 6-11-4 **127**........(t) HarrySkelton 109
(Kevin Frost) *hld up in last trio and nt fluent early: pushed along after 3 out: plugged on but nvr any ch of being involved* **33/1**

/1-5 **10** *3 1/4* **Gunner Fifteen (IRE)**[35] 2639 7-10-12 **121**........ NoelFehily 101
(Harry Fry) *hld up in last pair: stl last whn mstke 3 out: rdn and no great prog bef 2 out: no ch* **4/1**[1]

12-1 **11** *35* **Bells 'N' Banjos (IRE)**[31] 2711 5-11-12 **135**........ GavinSheehan 82
(Warren Greatrex) *chsd wnr to 3 out: wknd rapidly: t.o* **10/1**

1130 **12** *9* **Dubh Eile (IRE)**[161] 1038 7-10-9 **118**........ SeanBowen 57
(Tim Vaughan) *wl in tch tl wknd rapidly on long run after 3 out: t.o* **66/1**

1/1- **P** **Seebright**[580] 452 8-11-8 **131**........ AndrewTinkler
(Victor Dartnall) *prom tl wknd rapidly 3 out: t.o whn p.u bef last* **25/1**

-6UF **P** **Minellaforleisure (IRE)**[24] 2846 7-11-3 **126**........ BrendanPowell
(Alex Hales) *wl in tch: wknd rapidly on long run after 3 out: t.o whn p.u bef last* **40/1**

5m 17.6s (-3.40) **Going Correction** +0.025s/f (Yiel)
WFA 4 from 5yo+ 6lb **14** Ran SP% **123.8**
Speed ratings (Par 107): **107,106,106,105,102 102,100,99,97,96 83,79, ,**
CSF £60.87 CT £522.60 TOTE £7.90: £2.80, £3.00, £3.10; EX 73.40 Trifecta £853.10.

Owner John Stone **Bred** Yves D'Armaille **Trained** Lower Beeding, W Sussex

FOCUS
Race distance increased by 32yds. A fair and competitive handicap. The first four were clear at the finish and a small personal best from both the front two.

T/Jkpt: £4,437.50. Pool: £17,750 - 4 winning units. JACKPOT PLACEPOT £92.70. Pool: £1,488 - 16.05 winning units. T/Plt: £35.40 to a £1 stake. Pool: £208,856.53 - 4303.24 winning units. T/Qpdt: £14.30 to a £1 stake. Pool: £13,553.91 - 700.93 winning units. **Jonathan Neesom**

2863 **MARKET RASEN** (R-H)

Saturday, December 26

OFFICIAL GOING: Soft (heavy in places on chase course; good to soft in places on hurdle course; chs 5.6, hdl 6.0)

Wind: fresh 1/2 against Weather: fine but very breezy

3233 MOUNT & MINSTER CHARTERED SURVEYORS & LAND AGENTS (S) H'CAP HURDLE (8 hdls) 2m 148y

12:25 (12:26) (Class 5) (0-100,104) 3-Y-0+ £2,599 (£763; £381; £190)

Form RPR

00-0 1 **Vertueux (FR)**[72] 1931 10-10-0 **74**....(p) LeeEdwards 80+
(Tony Carroll) *mde all: hit 3 out: drvn clr appr last: hit last: hld on clsng stages* **16/1**

0-05 2 1 1/4 **Anginola (IRE)**[5] 1941 6-9-12 **75**....(v) JamesBanks(3) 78
(David Dennis) *chsd ldrs: 2nd appr 2 out: styd on run-in* **7/1**

0P63 3 9 **Gud Day (IRE)**[8] 3140 7-11-0 **88**....(bt) AlainCawley 82
(Conor Dore) *chsd ldrs: 2nd 5th: one pce appr 2 out* **7/1**

5543 4 1/2 **Lean Burn (USA)**[23] 2862 9-10-8 **85**....(t) HarryChalloner(3) 79
(Barry Leavy) *in rr: pushed along and hdwy to chse ldrs 4th: outpcd 3 out: kpt on run-in* **10/3**[2]

0605 5 3 1/2 **Skyfire**[23] 2869 8-10-10 **89**.... CharlieDeutsch(5) 79
(Nick Kent) *chsd wnr: drvn 5th: reminders next: wknd appr 2 out* **8/1**

4-23 6 4 **My Lord**[12] 3089 7-11-11 **104**....(v) DeanPratt(5) 94
(Jim Best) *hld up in rr: hdwy 5th: hung rt and wknd after 2 out: hit last* **3/1**[1]

-P04 7 6 **King's Road**[39] 2550 10-11-9 **97**....(t) TomMessenger 78
(Anabel K Murphy) *hld up in rr: hdwy 5th: lost pl after next* **5/1**[3]

34-0 8 8 **Kashstaree**[75] 1887 4-11-7 **100**.... CallumBewley(5) 72
(Lisa Harrison) *in rr: sme hdwy 5th: sn lost pl and bhd* **10/1**

46PP 9 36 **Monzino (USA)**[39] 2550 7-9-9 **74** oh12.... GaryDerwin(5) 10
(Michael Chapman) *chsd ldrs: pushed along 3rd: sn lost pl and bhd: t.o 3 out* **40/1**

4m 15.9s (9.20) **Going Correction** +0.325s/f (Yiel)
WFA 4 from 5yo+ 5lb **9** Ran SP% **118.3**
Speed ratings (Par 103): **91,90,86,85,84 82,79,75,58**
CSF £125.07 CT £869.87 TOTE £20.60: £3.90, £2.70, £2.10; EX 242.30 Trifecta £811.30 Part won..no bid for the winner
Owner A W Carroll **Bred** Roger Baudouin **Trained** Cropthorne, Worcs

FOCUS
Hurdles and fences moved onto fresh ground. Standard distances. The going on the chase course was soft, heavy in places, while the hurdle course was soft, good to soft in places. The opener was a typically moderate selling hurdle and the front two pulled clear. The winner was a 105 hurdler at his peak and put in his best run for over a year.

3234 LEES OF GRIMSBY FURNISHERS NOVICES' H'CAP HURDLE (10 hdls) 2m 4f 139y

1:00 (1:02) (Class 5) (0-100,100) 3-Y-0+ £2,599 (£763; £381; £190)

Form RPR

4035 1 **Milly Baloo**[24] 2847 4-10-12 **89**.... DerekFox(3) 101+
(Tim Easterby) *trckd ldrs: 2nd sn after 3 out: led appr next: drvn clr between last 2: eased clsng stages* **6/1**[3]

/P-2 2 6 **Money Maid (IRE)**[25] 2841 7-11-12 **100**.... KielanWoods 104
(Graeme McPherson) *chsd ldrs: drvn after 5th: 2nd appr 2 out: kpt on: no imp* **5/2**[1]

4313 3 15 **Miss Joeking (IRE)**[34] 2670 4-10-9 **93**.... RossChapman(10) 82
(Lucinda Russell) *w ldr: wknd appr last* **9/2**[2]

0UPP 4 7 **League Of His Own (IRE)**[33] 2693 6-10-0 **74** oh10....(t) LeeEdwards 56
(Claire Dyson) *t.k.h: trckd ldrs: led 2nd: clr next: hit 5th: hdd appr 2 out: sn wknd* **28/1**

5P54 5 14 **Lady Vivona**[23] 2868 7-9-9 **74** oh7.... CallumBewley(5) 42
(Lisa Harrison) *chsd ldrs: outpcd and lost pl bef 3 out* **14/1**

-446 6 6 **Harriet's Ark**[34] 2670 8-10-2 **76**.... MarkGrant 38
(Julian Smith) *trckd ldrs: 4th whn hit 3 out: sn lost pl* **11/1**

66-6 7 7 **Lilywhite Gesture (IRE)**[35] 2644 6-11-5 **93**.... AlainCawley 48
(Fergal O'Brien) *in rr: bhd fr 7th* **9/1**

600 8 14 **Fire (IRE)**[42] 2487 5-11-11 **99**....(t) TomMessenger 40
(Chris Bealby) *t.k.h in rr: bhd fr 7th: eased run-in* **6/1**[3]

0050 9 29 **Midtech Star (IRE)**[15] 3023 3-10-12 **100**....(p) WillKennedy
(Ian Williams) *led to 2nd: chsd ldrs: lost pl 3 out: sn wl bhd: virtually p.u run-in: t.o* **8/1**

5m 23.8s (15.00) **Going Correction** +0.325s/f (Yiel)
WFA 3 from 4yo 14lb 4 from 5yo+ 6lb **9** Ran SP% **114.9**
Speed ratings (Par 103): **84,81,76,73,68 65,63,57,46**
CSF £21.85 CT £73.96 TOTE £6.00: £1.90, £1.40, £1.70; EX 21.70 Trifecta £51.80.
Owner R W Metcalfe **Bred** R W Metcalfe **Trained** Great Habton, N Yorks

FOCUS
A moderate handicap hurdle and they finished well strung out. A big step up from the winner with the second setting the level.

3235 GARTHWEST NOVICES' LIMITED H'CAP CHASE (14 fncs) 2m 5f 89y

1:35 (1:35) (Class 3) (0-125,125) 4-Y-0+ £7,988 (£2,480; £1,335)

Form RPR

PF 1 **Ballyadeen (IRE)**[12] 3081 7-10-0 **106** oh1.... JamesBanks(3) 132+
(Dai Williams) *j.lft: sn trcking ldrs: led 4th: clr 11th: heavily eased run-in* **16/1**

2425 2 28 **Court Dismissed (IRE)**[23] 2857 5-10-8 **116**.... JamesCowley(5) 107
(Donald McCain) *chsd ldr: reminders 7th: outpcd 9th: chsd wnr between last 2* **9/1**

5-61 3 15 **Palm Grey (IRE)**[23] 2867 7-10-5 **115**.... TrevorRyan(7) 98
(Sue Smith) *towards rr: modest 4th whn hit 9th: wknd 3 out: bdly hmpd and lft distant 3rd last* **5/1**

2-16 F **Fergal Mael Duin**[45] 2436 7-11-0 **122**....(bt[1]) JakeHodson(5) 105
(David Bridgwater) *led: hdd 4th: reminders bef 7th: wknd between last 2: poor 3rd whn fell heavily last* **8/1**

33-2 F **Dreams Of Milan (IRE)**[34] 2663 7-10-3 **111**....(tp) CharlieDeutsch(5)
(Peter Bowen) *trckd ldrs: pushed along whn fell 5th* **4/1**[2]

F3P3 P **Solway Legend**[29] 2749 8-9-12 **106** oh2.... CallumBewley(5)
(Lisa Harrison) *in rr: hmpd 6th: sn bhd: lft distant 5th bef 8th: sn t.o: p.u after 4 out* **12/1**

1236 P **Top Cat Henry (IRE)**[21] 2902 7-11-8 **125**....(tp) WillKennedy
(Dr Richard Newland) *in rr: pushed along 4th: hmpd 5th: reminders and lost tch after 7th: t.o whn p.u bef next* **11/4**[1]

41-4 P **Elmore Back (IRE)**[28] 2774 6-11-5 **122**.... MarkGrant
(Charlie Mann) *towards rr: hmpd 6th: blnd and lost pl next: sn bhd: distant 5th whn p.u bef 8th* **9/2**[3]

6m 0.1s (14.10) **Going Correction** +0.85s/f (Soft) **8** Ran SP% **116.2**
Speed ratings (Par 107): **107,96,90, , ,**
CSF £145.23 CT £833.10 TOTE £17.90: £4.60, £2.30, £2.00; EX 249.00 Trifecta £682.30.
Owner F Michael **Bred** Michael Woodlock & Seamus Kennedy **Trained** Broad Hinton, Wilts

FOCUS
A fair and competitive handicap chase, in which only three finished and the winner was out on his own. He has the potential to rate higher.

3236 CLUGSTON LINCOLNSHIRE NATIONAL (A H'CAP CHASE) (19 fncs) 3m 3f 123y

2:10 (2:10) (Class 4) (0-120,120) 4-Y-0+ £7,472 (£2,194; £1,097; £548)

Form RPR

0403 1 **West Of The Edge (IRE)**[12] 3087 7-9-11 **94** oh3.... JamesBanks(3) 109+
(Dai Williams) *hld up in mid-div: hdwy to trck ldrs 9th: 2nd 3 out: led next: forged clr last 150yds* **14/1**

3111 2 6 **Not A Bother Boy (IRE)**[13] 3067 7-10-11 **112**.... TrevorRyan(7) 123
(Sue Smith) *chsd ldrs: hit 3rd and 11th: upsides 4 out: led bef next: hdd narrowly 2 out: hung rt and kpt on same pce run-in* **9/2**[1]

3-4P 3 6 **Barton Gift**[22] 2878 8-11-3 **111**....(b) JeremiahMcGrath 114
(John Spearing) *w ldrs: led after 2nd: hdd 6th: led 10th to 12th: led 14th: hdd bef 3 out: one pce fr 2 out* **11/1**

-312 4 11 **Cheat The Cheater (IRE)**[13] 3062 8-10-0 **94** oh4....(tp) LeeEdwards 88
(Claire Dyson) *in rr and sn drvn along: lost rt-hand cheekpiece after 5th: hdwy 12th: modest 4th 4 out: wknd appr last* **8/1**

3U10 5 15 **Settledoutofcourt (IRE)**[55] 2213 9-11-9 **120**.... DerekFox(3) 96
(Lucinda Russell) *led tl after 2nd: lost pl 13th: brief effrt 4 out: sn wknd* **14/1**

-3P4 6 1/2 **Themanfrom Minella (IRE)**[16] 2996 6-11-3 **118**....(t) MrMJPKendrick(7) 94
(Ben Case) *in rr: hdwy to chse ldrs 12th: mstke and lost pl 14th: sn bhd* **14/1**

2-22 7 26 **Ultimatum Du Roy (FR)**[34] 2668 7-11-10 **118**....(tp) KielanWoods 68
(Alex Hales) *hld up towards rr: hdwy to chse ldrs 12th: lost pl next: sn bhd* **7/1**

2U4- P **Soudain (FR)**[294] 4620 9-11-6 **119**....(p) CraigGallagher(5)
(Brian Ellison) *w ldrs: led 6th to 10th: led and nt fluent 12th: hdd 14th: lost pl next: sn bhd: t.o whn p.u sn after 4 out: b.b.v* **5/1**[2]

3350 P **The Society Man (IRE)**[4] 2469 8-9-9 **94** oh6.... GaryDerwin(5)
(Michael Chapman) *in rr: bhd fr 9th: t.o whn p.u bef 13th* **25/1**

1-52 P **Mondo Cane (IRE)**[25] 2837 8-10-13 **107**....(b) AdamPogson
(Charles Pogson) *t.k.h: sn trcking ldrs: lost pl 13th: bhd whn p.u bef 15th* **12/1**

6P4P P **Up For An Oscar (IRE)**[16] 2996 8-11-0 **113**....(bt[1]) CharlieDeutsch(5)
(Peter Bowen) *mid-div: drvn along 7th: chsd ldrs 9th: lost pl 13th: sn bhd: p.u bef 15th* **12/1**

5P44 P **Express Du Berlais (FR)**[28] 2766 6-11-9 **117**....(b[1]) WillKennedy
(Dr Richard Newland) *nt jump wl: chsd ldrs: mstke 10th: reminders 11th: lost pl 14th: t.o whn p.u bef 4 out* **11/2**[3]

7m 52.0s (18.00) **Going Correction** +0.85s/f (Soft) **12** Ran SP% **121.4**
Speed ratings (Par 105): **108,106,104,101,97 97,89, , ,**
CSF £79.85 CT £741.71 TOTE £23.30: £4.50, £2.40, £4.70; EX 131.00 Trifecta £853.20 Part won..
Owner F Michael **Bred** Michael Lee **Trained** Broad Hinton, Wilts

FOCUS
An open-looking renewal of this marathon staying chase and they went a good gallop in the conditions. The winner was well in on his Irish form and has been rated back to that sort of level.

3237 MOUNT & MINSTER RESIDENTIAL PROPERTY EXPERTS H'CAP CHASE (12 fncs) 2m 1f 43y

2:45 (2:46) (Class 4) (0-120,117) 4-Y-0+ £3,898 (£1,144; £572; £286)

Form RPR

F125 1 **Chankillo**[54] 2249 6-9-11 **91**....(p) JamesBanks(3) 107+
(Sarah-Jayne Davies) *swvd rt s: chsd clr ldr: hit 3rd: led 2 out: drvn clr run-in* **5/2**[1]

02P2 2 14 **Willie Hall**[23] 2866 11-9-9 **91** oh5.... CallumBewley(5) 95
(Lisa Harrison) *led: clr 2nd to 4th: hdd 2 out: jst over 1 l down last: kpt on same pce* **9/2**

2-P6 3 13 **Ubaltique (FR)**[16] 2979 7-11-12 **117**....(b) WillKennedy 108
(Donald McCain) *hld up in rr: hdwy to chse ldrs 9th: handy 3rd but outpcd whn mstke 3 out: modest 3rd whn hit last* **11/4**[2]

-564 4 2 3/4 **Chestnut Ben (IRE)**[28] 2765 10-11-5 **117**.... MrRWinks(7) 104
(Peter Winks) *trckd ldrs: outpcd appr 3 out: sn lost pl* **5/1**

2-P3 P **Money For Nothing**[28] 2765 6-11-2 **107**....(t) AlainCawley
(Harriet Bethell) *t.k.h: trcking ldrs whn mstke 5th: pushed along 8th: lost pl next: t.o 3 out: p.u bef 2 out* **7/2**[3]

4m 46.2s (11.20) **Going Correction** +0.85s/f (Soft) **5** Ran SP% **112.3**
Speed ratings (Par 105): **107,100,94,93,**
CSF £13.79 TOTE £3.20: £1.50, £2.30; EX 11.10 Trifecta £30.60.
Owner Andrew Gough **Bred** Dullingham Park **Trained** Leominster, H'fords

FOCUS
Not the strongest handicap for the grade and they went an ordinary gallop. The winner has been rated similar to his previous course win.

3238 HANSORD & HELLEY H'CAP HURDLE (QUALIFIER FOR CHALLENGER TWO MILE SERIES FINAL) (10 hdls) 2m 2f 140y

3:20 (3:22) (Class 4) (0-120,120) 3-Y-0+ £3,249 (£954; £477; £238)

Form RPR

2-32 1 **Spice Fair**[22] 2888 8-11-6 **114**.... JeremiahMcGrath 128+
(Mark Usher) *hld up in rr: stdy hdwy 5th: sn trcking ldrs: led appr 2 out: wnt clr sn after last: v readily* **7/1**[3]

240 2 6 **Domtaline (FR)**[84] 1755 8-11-5 **120**.... MrRWinks(7) 125
(Peter Winks) *chsd ldrs 4th: 3rd whn hit last: sn 2nd: no ch w wnr* **25/1**

5-05 3 hd **Charlie Cook (IRE)**[36] 2624 6-10-12 **106**.... KielanWoods 110
(Graeme McPherson) *mid-div: chsd ldrs 5th: 2nd 3 out: kpt on same pce fr next* **7/1**[3]

P323 4 14 **Rushvale (IRE)**[23] 2871 6-11-3 **118**.... MrMJPKendrick(7) 112
(Ben Case) *chsd ldrs 4th: led sn after 3 out: hdd and nt fluent next: modest 2nd whn hit last: sn wknd* **14/1**

-532 5 3/4 **Touch Back (IRE)**[18] 2962 9-11-3 **118**....(p) MrTommieMO'Brien(7) 107
(Chris Bealby) *in rr: pushed along 5th: sn bhd: t.o after 3 out: styd on fr next: tk modest 5th last 75yds* **9/2**[1]

6453 **6** *3* **Kuda Huraa (IRE)**[14] 3035 7-11-3 **116**........................ CharlieDeutsch(5) 102
(Harriet Bethell) *in rr: sme hdwy 6th: fdd appr 2 out* **14/1**

6242 **7** *1 ½* **Akula (IRE)**[18] 2961 8-10-9 **106**........................ HarryChalloner(3) 91
(Barry Leavy) *chsd ldrs: lost pl 3 out* **11/1**

/325 **8** *41* **Ben Cee Pee M (IRE)**[46] 2426 10-11-3 **116**..............(v) CraigGallagher(5) 60
(Brian Ellison) *mid-div: chsng ldrs 4th: lost pl bef 6th: sn bhd: t.o 3 out* **16/1**

-341 **9** *19* **Scoppio Del Carro**[24] 2850 4-11-2 **110**..............(t) AdamPogson 35
(Charles Pogson) *mid-div: chsd ldrs 4th: lost pl after 6th: sn bhd: t.o 3 out: heavily eased run-in* **14/1**

1200 **10** *4 ½* **Argot**[22] 2888 4-10-11 **115**..............(p) TomHumphries(10) 35
(Charlie Longsdon) *mid-div: blnd bdly and lost pl 2nd: sn reminders: hdwy into mid-div 4th: lost pl next: sn bhd: t.o 3 out* **14/1**

2104 **F** **Stand To Reason (IRE)**[33] 2688 7-11-2 **110**........................ LeeEdwards
(Tony Carroll) *in rr: sme hdwy 7th: hit next: lost pl bef 2 out: poor 6th whn fell last* **10/1**

3405 **P** **Quebec**[50] 2328 4-11-11 **119**........................ MarkGrant
(Charlie Mann) *chsd ldr: drvn 5th: lost pl after 6th: sn bhd: t.o 3 out: p.u bef next* **16/1**

14C **P** **Itsnowcato**[16] 2989 4-11-6 **117**........................ MauriceLinehan(3)
(Ben Pauling) *led: hdd sn after 3 out: sn lost pl and bhd: t.o whn p.u bef next* **5/1**[2]

4m 42.3s (2.90) **Going Correction** +0.325s/f (Yiel) **13** Ran SP% **119.6**
Speed ratings (Par 105): **106,103,103,97,97 95,95,78,70,68 ,,**
CSF £161.94 CT £1278.82 TOTE £6.90: £2.70, £5.30, £3.10; EX 182.10 Trifecta £1239.50 Part won..
Owner Saxon House Racing **Bred** Mrs D Hughes **Trained** Upper Lambourn, Berks

FOCUS
A fair and competitive handicap in which they went a strong gallop. The winner is on the upgrade, but has the potential to rate higher on his Flat form.
T/Plt: £836.70 to a £1 stake. Pool: £32028.28 - 27.94 winning tickets T/Qpdt: £70.70 to a £1 stake. Pool: £2990.8 - 31.3 winning tickets **Walter Glynn**

2889 SEDGEFIELD (L-H)
Saturday, December 26

OFFICIAL GOING: Heavy (5.0)
Wind: Almost nil Weather: Overcast, raining

3239 HR FABRICATION LTD "NATIONAL HUNT" NOVICES' HURDLE (BETFRED HURDLE SERIES QUALIFIER) (8 hdls) 2m 178y
12:10 (12:10) (Class 4) 4-Y-0+ **£3,768** (£1,106; £553; £276)

Form RPR

531 **1** **Barney Dwan (IRE)**[37] 2591 5-11-2 **130**........................ ConorShoemark(3) 126+
(Fergal O'Brien) *hld up in tch: hdwy bef 4 out: led after next: pushed clr fr 2 out* **1/2**[1]

23 **2** *8* **Just Georgie**[49] 2331 5-10-12 115........................ DannyCook 111
(Sue Smith) *chsd ldrs: ev ch after 4 out: drvn and outpcd next: rallied to chse (clr) wnr between last 2: kpt on: no imp* **11/4**[2]

24 **3** *5* **What Happens Now (IRE)**[19] 2945 6-10-2 0.............. RonanShort(10) 106
(Donald McCain) *t.k.h: in tch: hdwy to ld after 4 out: hit next: sn hdd: rallied: nt fluent 2 out: no ex and lost 2nd between last 2* **7/1**[3]

00 **4** *27* **Smuggler's Stash (IRE)**[20] 2931 5-10-12 0........................ CraigNichol 79
(Rose Dobbin) *hld up: drvn and outpcd after 3rd: rallied bef 2 out: plugged on fr last: nvr able to chal* **50/1**

U-00 **5** *½* **Killiecrankie**[55] 2210 7-10-9 0..............[1] ColmMcCormack(3) 79
(Kenneth Slack) *led and sn clr: hdd after 4 out: rdn and wknd bef 2 out* **66/1**

400 **6** *2* **Grand Enterprise**[10] 3105 5-10-12 0........................ AndrewThornton 77
(Tom George) *prom: drvn and outpcd after 3 out: wknd bef next* **16/1**

-5P0 **7** *16* **Question Of Faith**[61] 2101 4-10-5 0........................ HenryBrooke 54
(Martin Todhunter) *hld up: drvn and outpcd after 4th: nvr on terms after* **100/1**

6 **8** *3* **Nortonthorpelegend (IRE)**[11] 3101 5-10-12 0.............. BrianHughes 58
(John Wade) *prom: lost pl 2nd: struggling 4th: sn btn* **100/1**

1/0 **9** *19* **Heritage Way**[28] 2791 6-10-9 0........................ TonyKelly(3) 39
(Henry Hogarth) *prom: outpcd after 4 out: struggling fr next* **14/1**

50 **P** **Tommy The Rascal**[9] 3130 5-10-12 0........................ PeterCarberry
(Jennie Candlish) *nt fluent in rr: struggling after 3rd: lost tch and p.u after 3 out* **100/1**

4m 19.4s (12.50) **Going Correction** +0.95s/f (Soft)
WFA 4 from 5yo+ 5lb **10** Ran SP% **124.8**
Speed ratings (Par 105): **108,104,101,89,88 88,80,79,70,**
CSF £2.56 TOTE £1.30: £1.10, £1.10, £1.80; EX 2.20 Trifecta £5.10.
Owner Paul & Clare Rooney **Bred** Grange Stud **Trained** Naunton, Gloucs

FOCUS
Roadside bend dolled out 4yds on stand-side bend 8yds. Actual race distance 2m 163yds. This was a relatively uncompetitive novice hurdle and the first three, who were the first three in the market, finished well clear.

3240 CASTLE CONSTRUCTION NORTH EAST LTD. NOVICES' HURDLE (BETFRED HURDLE SERIES QUALIFIER) 2m 3f 188y
12:40 (12:40) (Class 4) 4-Y-0+ **£3,768** (£1,106; £553; £276)

Form RPR

316 **1** **Point The Way (IRE)**[41] 2514 4-10-12 0........................ JamesReveley 123+
(Brian Ellison) *novicey on occasions: mde virtually all: pushed along and drew clr fr 2 out* **3/1**[2]

522 **2** *10* **Good Vibration (FR)**[28] 2791 4-10-12 110........................ SeanQuinlan 113
(Sue Smith) *w wnr: rdn and outpcd bef 2 out: rallied last: plugged on: nt pce to chal* **6/1**

-223 **3** *9* **Bollin Ace**[27] 2801 4-10-12 118........................ LucyAlexander 104
(Tim Easterby) *t.k.h: hld up in tch: pushed along bef 4 out: outpcd next: plugged on fr 2 out: no imp* **3/1**[2]

4212 **4** *6* **Nuts Well**[20] 2931 4-11-5 122........................ BrianHughes 106
(Ann Hamilton) *trckd ldrs: effrt and rdn 2 out: outpcd whn nt fluent last: sn btn* **5/2**[1]

5 *16* **Ash Park (IRE)**[244] 7-10-5 0........................ SamColtherd(7) 81
(Stuart Coltherd) *in tch: pushed along bef 4 out: outpcd next: btn whn lft modest 4th bnd bef 2 out* **100/1**

6221 **F** **Raise A Spark**[22] 2889 5-10-12 114........................ HenryBrooke 113
(Donald McCain) *t.k.h: hld up in tch: stdy hdwy to trck ldrs bef 3 out: cl 4th and gng wl whn clipped heels and fell bnd bef next* **5/1**[3]

5m 15.8s (21.70) **6** Ran SP% **110.5**
CSF £19.80 TOTE £3.90: £1.90, £2.20; EX 16.50 Trifecta £97.50.
Owner P J Martin **Bred** Mrs Kay Cottrell **Trained** Norton, N Yorks

FOCUS
Actual race distance 2m 3f 144yds. The pace wasn't strong, but they were well strung out in the ground and the winner is an interesting prospect.

3241 CHRIS MUSGRAVE IS 42+VAT TODAY H'CAP CHASE (11 fncs 2 omitted) 2m 77y
1:15 (1:15) (Class 5) (0-100,98) 4-Y-0+ **£2,989** (£877; £438; £219)

Form RPR

5143 **1** **Roxyfet (FR)**[22] 2894 5-10-6 **85**........................ FinianO'Toole(7) 100+
(Micky Hammond) *hld up in tch: stdy hdwy bef 6th: effrt and led last (usual 2 out): pushed clr* **13/8**[1]

P643 **2** *8* **Theflyingportrait (IRE)**[17] 2976 6-11-12 **98**..............(t) HenryBrooke 104
(Jennie Candlish) *t.k.h: in tch: hdwy to chse ldr 2nd: led bef 6th: rdn and hdd last (usual 2 out): kpt on same pce* **9/4**[2]

F-P3 **3** *3 ¼* **On The Case**[40] 2542 7-11-3 **89**..............(t) AndrewThornton 93
(Tom George) *led to bef 6th: cl up tl rdn and outpcd fr last (usual 2 out)* **3/1**[3]

00P0 **4** *33* **Captain Sharpe**[16] 2982 7-10-8 **87**..............(b) ThomasDowson(7) 57
(Kenny Johnson) *prom: pushed along and outpcd 8th: rallied after next: rdn and wknd bef last (usual 2 out)* **22/1**

4664 **5** *6* **Molko Jack (FR)**[51] 2290 11-10-4 **76**........................ LucyAlexander 40
(Michael Mullineaux) *nt fluent on occasions: chsd ldr to 2nd: prom tl outpcd bef 7th: struggling fr 3 out (usual 4 out)* **7/1**

4m 33.8s (19.80) **Going Correction** +1.30s/f (Heav) **5** Ran SP% **110.7**
Speed ratings (Par 103): **102,98,96,79,76**
CSF £5.96 TOTE £2.20: £1.40, £1.70; EX 5.60 Trifecta £3.80.
Owner R J Ball **Bred** Jacky Thomas **Trained** Middleham, N Yorks

FOCUS
Actual race distance 2m 107yds. A low-grade handicap chase in which the pace was fair.

3242 WILLS PROPERTY SERVICES H'CAP HURDLE 2m 3f 188y
1:55 (1:56) (Class 4) (0-115,115) 3-Y-0+ **£3,638** (£1,068; £534; £267)

Form RPR

36-1 **1** **Divine Port (USA)**[27] 2802 5-11-10 **113**........................ JakeGreenall 119+
(Alan Swinbank) *led at stdy pce: hdd 5th: w ldr: pushed along and led 2 out: sn edgd rt: nt fluent last: drvn and kpt on wl* **4/1**[1]

4130 **2** *3* **Prince Khurram**[62] 2085 5-10-12 **111**..............(t) RonanShort(10) 113
(Donald McCain) *in tch: wnt 2nd 3rd: led 5th: rdn and hdd 3 out: rallied and ev ch last: kpt on same pce run-in* **9/1**

5265 **3** *1 ¾* **Silver Shuffle (IRE)**[19] 2949 8-10-11 **100**........................ HenryBrooke 100
(Dianne Sayer) *chsd ldrs: drvn and outpcd bef 2 out: kpt on fr last: nt rch first two* **10/1**

652 **4** *2* **Away For Slates (IRE)**[19] 2945 5-11-12 **115**........................ CraigNichol 112
(Keith Dalgleish) *hld up: hdwy to chse ldrs 3 out: effrt and rdn next: kpt on same pce bef last* **8/1**[3]

-433 **5** *10* **Card Game (IRE)**[200] 679 6-11-0 **103**........................ BrianHughes 93
(Malcolm Jefferson) *hld up: stdy hdwy and in tch after 3 out: drvn and outpcd appr next: sn wknd* **7/1**[2]

0/0 **6** *17* **Roman Numeral (IRE)**[93] 1638 7-11-6 **112**........................ TonyKelly(3) 82
(David Thompson) *bhd: drvn and struggling 6th: n.d after* **33/1**

/P-5 **7** *½* **Wintered Well (IRE)**[27] 2802 7-11-7 **110**........................ PeterCarberry 80
(Jennie Candlish) *hld up on outside: niggled along bef 4 out: hdwy and cl up bef 2 out: sn outpcd: wkng whn j.lft last* **8/1**[3]

-553 **8** *5* **Karisma King**[22] 2890 6-11-3 **106**........................ SeanQuinlan 71
(Sue Smith) *chsd wnr to 3rd: cl up: drvn and outpcd after 3 out: wknd bef next* **9/1**

0444 **P** **Goal (IRE)**[10] 3108 7-10-6 **102**..............(t) MissBHampson(7)
(Sally Randell) *in tch: lost pl and outpcd whn hit 6th: struggling fr next: t.o whn p.u bef 2 out* **16/1**

P3-5 **P** **Azure Glamour (IRE)**[219] 421 6-10-1 **90**..............(p) LucyAlexander
(Kenneth Slack) *prom: drvn and outpcd bef 3 out: sn btn: p.u bef last* **8/1**[3]

4264 **P** **Jethro (IRE)**[56] 2196 4-11-5 **108**........................ JamesReveley
(Brian Ellison) *hld up: stdy hdwy on outside 6th: nt fluent next: rdn and wknd bef 3 out: p.u bef next* **8/1**[3]

5m 22.9s (28.80)
WFA 4 from 5yo+ 6lb **11** Ran SP% **114.9**
CSF £39.07 CT £335.16 TOTE £4.20: £1.50, £3.80, £3.50; EX 43.60 Trifecta £219.10.
Owner C G Harrison **Bred** Juddmonte Farms Inc **Trained** Melsonby, N Yorks

FOCUS
Actual race distance 2m 3f 144yds. Although the early pace was slow, they finished tired.

3243 HAPPY CHRISTMAS FROM PAXTONS H'CAP CHASE (14 fncs 2 omitted) 2m 3f 65y
2:30 (2:31) (Class 4) (0-110,110) 4-Y-0+ **£4,548** (£1,335; £667; £333)

Form RPR

1545 **1** **My Friend George**[61] 2102 9-10-6 **90**..............(p) HenryBrooke 103+
(Kenneth Slack) *chsd ldrs: wnt 2nd 6th: effrt and led 2 out (usual 3 out): clr bef last: pricked ears run-in: kpt on* **4/1**[3]

0-52 **2** *10* **Red Danaher (IRE)**[23] 2865 8-11-9 **107**........................ SeanQuinlan 107
(Sue Smith) *chsd ldrs: outpcd 10th: rallied to chse (clr) wnr last: kpt on: no imp* **6/1**

1435 **3** *5* **Down Time (USA)**[37] 2592 5-11-11 **109**..............(v) JamesReveley 104
(Brian Ellison) *chsd ldr to 6th: cl up: outpcd 4 out (usual 5 out): rallied bef last: sn no imp* **7/1**

4/U4 **4** *14* **Tiny Dancer (IRE)**[24] 2848 7-11-4 **102**........................ BrianHughes 83
(Chris Grant) *nt fluent on occasions: hld up: stdy hdwy bef 9th: outpcd 11th: shortlived effrt after 3 out (usual 4 out): sn wknd* **9/4**[1]

P244 **5** *2 ¼* **Duhallowcountry (IRE)**[7] 3164 9-9-7 **84** oh3........(p) ThomasDowson(7) 65
(Victor Thompson) *led: mstke 8th: rdn and hdd 2 out (usual 3 out): wknd fr last* **16/1**

636P **P** **Shrapnel (IRE)**[22] 2893 9-11-11 **109**..............(tp) DannyCook
(Brian Ellison) *nt fluent on occasions prom tl lost pl 5th: struggling fnl circ: lost tch and p.u bef 11th* **10/1**

-4P3 **F** **Lord Usher (IRE)**[32] 2707 8-11-3 **101**........................ JanFaltejsek
(George Charlton) *in tch: fell 2nd* **7/2**[2]

5m 38.1s (35.10) **Going Correction** +1.95s/f (Heav) **7** Ran SP% **114.8**
Speed ratings (Par 105): **104,99,97,91,90 ,**
CSF £27.77 CT £162.03 TOTE £4.80: £2.20, £3.10; EX 31.50 Trifecta £154.20.
Owner A Slack **Bred** G A Slack And H D Sayer **Trained** Hilton, Cumbria

The Form Book Jumps 2015-16, Raceform Ltd, Newbury, RG14 5SJ

FOCUS
Actual race distance 2m 3f 99yds. This handicap chase was run at a fair gallop considering the conditions.

3244 MINISTERS INDIAN RESTAURANT SEDGEFIELD H'CAP HURDLE (8 hdls) 2m 178y
3:00 (3:01) (Class 5) (0-100,95) 3-Y-O+ **£2,729** (£801; £400; £200)

Form RPR
P-65 **1** **Fiddler's Flight (IRE)**[16] 2982 9-10-8 **80**........ ColmMcCormack(3) 86+
(John Norton) *hld up: nt fluent 4 out: hdwy after next: rdn bef 2 out: led whn mstke last: drvn out* **13/2**
PP05 **2** 1 3/4 **Discoverie**[159] 1067 7-10-12 **81**........(p) HenryBrooke 84
(Kenneth Slack) *led to bef 4th: w ldr: regained ld bef 3 out: hdd bef last: rallied u.p: kpt on: hld towards fin* **11/4**[1]
05-0 **3** 1/2 **Copt Hill**[16] 2982 7-10-12 **81**........ BrianHughes 85+
(Tracy Waggott) *cl up: ev ch bef 2 out: sn rdn: outpcd bef last: rallied run-in: hld nr fin* **6/1**
2224 **4** nk **Gunner Lindley (IRE)**[19] 2946 8-11-0 **90**........ SamColtherd(7) 92
(Stuart Coltherd) *hld up in tch: drvn and outpcd after 3 out: rallied next: kpt on same pce run-in* **4/1**[3]
6204 **5** 15 **King's Chorister**[16] 2982 9-10-6 **82**........(t) LorcanMurtagh(7) 69
(Barry Murtagh) *in tch: nt fluent and outpcd 4th: rallied next: rdn and wknd fr 2 out* **15/2**
554 **P** **Slide Show**[24] 2847 7-11-0 **86**........ AdamNicol(3)
(David Thompson) *cl up: reminders after 3rd: led bef next: hdd bef 3 out: sn struggling: lost tch and p.u bef next* **20/1**
0033 **P** **Snowed In (IRE)**[32] 2703 6-11-11 **94**........(p) SeanQuinlan
(Barry Murtagh) *hld up in tch: struggling bef 3 out: lost tch and p.u next* **7/2**[2]

4m 36.9s (30.00) **Going Correction** +1.80s/f (Heav)
WFA 4 from 5yo+ 5lb 7 Ran SP% **113.0**
Speed ratings (Par 103): **101,100,99,99,92** ,
CSF £24.64 CT £112.16 TOTE £8.60: £2.90, £2.20; EX 27.80 Trifecta £173.80 Part won..
Owner Fellowship Of The Rose Partnership **Bred** Joe Magee **Trained** High Hoyland, S Yorks

FOCUS
Actual race distance 2m 163yds. With the rain continuing unabated conditions had worsened for this handicap hurdle in which less than 3l covered the first four home and all four finished tired.

3245 HARDWICK ARMS HOTEL SEDGEFIELD STANDARD OPEN NATIONAL HUNT FLAT RACE 2m 178y
3:30 (3:35) (Class 6) 4-6-Y-O **£1,559** (£457; £228; £114)

Form RPR
1 **Tomngerry (IRE)**[62] 5-10-13 0........ MeganCarberry(5) 115+
(Brian Ellison) *pressed ldr: led gng wl over 1f out: pushed clr fnl f* **6/4**[1]
2 14 **Rolling Thunder (IRE)**[293] 5-11-4 0........ HenryBrooke 100
(Donald McCain) *led at ordinary gallop: rdn and hdd over 1f out: no ch w wnr* **3/1**[3]
4 **3** 15 **Eastview Boy**[16] 2984 4-11-1 0........ KyleJames(3) 85
(Philip Kirby) *hld up in tch: drvn and outpcd 4f out: sn n.d: btn fnl 2f* **11/1**
41 **4** 11 **Storm Forecast (IRE)**[32] 2709 4-11-11 0........ BrianHughes 89
(Malcolm Jefferson) *trckd ldrs: pushed along over 3f out: wknd over 2f out: eased whn btn fnl f* **7/4**[2]

4m 30.7s (29.40) **Going Correction** +1.80s/f (Heav) 4 Ran SP% **109.7**
Speed ratings: **102,95,88,83**
CSF £6.31 TOTE £2.50; EX 6.20 Trifecta £26.20.
Owner Mrs J A Martin **Bred** Mrs E Tector **Trained** Norton, N Yorks

FOCUS
Actual race distance 2m 163yds. This was reduced to just four runners.
T/Plt: £213.30 to a £1 stake. Pool: £36851.79 - 126.08 winning tickets T/Qpdt: £58.40 to a £1 stake. Pool: £2883.05 - 36.5 winning tickets **Richard Young**

2917 WETHERBY (L-H)
Saturday, December 26
3246 Meeting Abandoned - Back straight flooded

2870 WINCANTON (R-H)
Saturday, December 26
OFFICIAL GOING: Soft (heavy in places; 6.9)
Wind: strong against Weather: overcast

3252 BOXING DAY MARES' NOVICES' HURDLE (7 hdls 1 omitted) 1m 7f 65y
12:30 (12:30) (Class 4) 4-Y-O+ **£3,249** (£954; £477; £238)

Form RPR
-213 **1** **Awesome Rosie**[39] 2561 4-10-7 0........ TomBellamy(3) 112+
(Alan King) *in tch: hdwy 3 out: led 2 out: in command last: readily* **15/8**[1]
3 **2** 6 **Deja Bougg**[18] 2959 4-10-10 0........ MarkQuinlan 105
(Neil Mulholland) *trckd ldrs: disputing cl 2nd whn blnd 2 out: kpt on but nt pce of wnr fr last* **14/1**
4-13 **3** 2 1/2 **Drumviredy (IRE)**[18] 2952 6-11-3 113........ LiamTreadwell 108
(Venetia Williams) *prom: lft in ld on bnd bef 3rd: hdd 2 out: sn rdn: styd on same pce* **9/2**[3]
4 **4** 7 **Very Extravagant (IRE)**[28] 2778 6-10-3 0........ MrMartinMcIntyre(7) 94+
(Neil Mulholland) *hld up: outpcd 3 out: styd on to go 4th at the last but no threat to ldrs* **9/2**[3]
5-5 **5** 2 1/2 **Appletree Lane**[34] 2665 5-10-10 0........ TommyPhelan 91
(Tom Gretton) *trckd ldrs: rdn appr 2 out: sn one pce* **33/1**
40 **6** 6 **On Demand**[10] 3114 4-10-10 0........ DenisO'Regan 86
(Simon Hodgson) *hld up: hdwy 3 out: effrt next: wknd last* **33/1**
6-2 **U** **Antartica De Thaix (FR)**[23] 2875 5-10-10 0........(t) NickScholfield
(Paul Nicholls) *hld up in tch: trckd ldrs 3rd: eventually unseating rdr* **9/4**[2]
6-00 **P** **Sunley Spirit**[25] 2829 5-10-10 0........ TomCannon
(Chris Gordon) *led tl rn wd on stable bnd bef 3rd: chsd ldrs: rdn after 3 out: sn wknd: p.u bef next* **50/1**

3m 59.2s (10.30) **Going Correction** +0.80s/f (Soft) 8 Ran SP% **116.4**
Speed ratings (Par 105): **104,100,99,95,94 91**, ,
CSF £27.54 TOTE £2.90: £1.20, £3.40, £1.70; EX 33.70 Trifecta £186.90.
Owner Mrs Meacham, Withyslade & Mrs A L Davies **Bred** Meacham, King And Withyslade **Trained** Barbury Castle, Wilts

FOCUS
Both courses moved out on to fresh ground. The hurdle on the stables bend was omitted all meeting. There was extra yardage in this race, adding about 12yds to the advertised distance. Probably just an ordinary race of its type and the early gallop wasn't strong. The winner was building on her Southwell run.

3253 BATHWICK TYRES LORD STALBRIDGE MEMORIAL CUP (A H'CAP CHASE) (21 fncs) 3m 1f 30y
1:05 (1:07) (Class 3) (0-125,125) 4-Y-O+ **£7,985** (£2,410; £1,241; £658)

Form RPR
3224 **1** **Shockingtimes (IRE)**[17] 2975 8-11-6 **119**........(bt) TomO'Brien 128+
(Jamie Snowden) *hld up: hmpd 1st: trckd ldrs 5th: wnt 2nd 10th: led after 4 out: sn clr: rdn between last 2: in command whn mstke last: rdn out* **6/1**[3]
6-43 **2** 7 **Astigos (FR)**[35] 2631 8-11-7 **120**........ LiamTreadwell 122+
(Venetia Williams) *j.lft bdly at times: led 4th: 8 l clr 9th: hit next: blnd 16th: hdd sn after 4 out: styd on same pce fr next* **3/1**[1]
4523 **3** 8 **Marden Court (IRE)**[23] 2874 5-10-4 **110**........(t) PaulO'Brien(7) 100
(Colin Tizzard) *in tch tl struggling on last trio 14th: nvr threatened ldrs: one pce and hld fr 4 out* **3/1**[1]
U-34 **4** shd **Umberto D'Olivate (FR)**[22] 2887 7-11-12 **125**........(p) FelixDeGiles 114
(Robert Walford) *led tl 4th: trckd ldr tl mstke 10th: hit next and reminders: rdn fr 15th: one pce and hld fr 4 out* **5/1**[2]
42FP **P** **Master Neo (FR)**[51] 2288 9-10-8 **114**........(t) MrLDrowne(7)
(Nigel Hawke) *chsd ldrs: pushed along fr 9th: dropped to last after 13th: tailing off whn p.u bef 17th* **17/2**
0-P4 **F** **Letemgo (IRE)**[58] 2149 7-11-6 **119**........ DenisO'Regan
(Giles Smyly) *fell 1st* **5/1**[2]
P-35 **P** **Ballycoe**[23] 2872 6-10-12 **111**........(t) TomCannon
(Chris Gordon) *hld up last: wknd after 15th: tailing off whn p.u bef 4 out* **10/1**

7m 1.3s (21.80) **Going Correction** +0.95s/f (Soft) 7 Ran SP% **117.2**
Speed ratings (Par 107): **103,100,98,98**, ,
CSF £25.96 CT £65.38 TOTE £6.80: £2.60, £2.10; EX 32.30 Trifecta £74.80.
Owner S Beccle,Lady Hart,Boscobel Estates Ltd **Bred** Brendan Healy **Trained** Lambourn, Berks

FOCUS
There was extra yardage in this race to the advertised distance of about 24yds. A strange race with regards to form analysis, as the leader set a good gallop but hampered his progress by jumping left throughout, and two other fancied runners were soon held. A small personal best from the winner, but not the strongest form.

3254 PERTEMPS NETWORK H'CAP HURDLE (SERIES QUALIFIER) (10 hdls 1 omitted) 2m 5f 82y
1:40 (1:42) (Class 2) 4-Y-O+
£11,573 (£3,418; £1,709; £854; £427; £214)

Form RPR
5P-P **1** **If In Doubt (IRE)**[28] 2783 7-11-6 **140**........ TomO'Brien 143+
(Philip Hobbs) *hld up: rdn and hdwy between last 2: led run-in: r.o strly: readily* **9/2**[2]
1-10 **2** 2 1/4 **Dubawi Island (FR)**[28] 2781 6-11-0 **134**........ LiamTreadwell 135
(Venetia Williams) *in tch: hit 5th: rdn to chse ldrs 2 out: styd on run-in to go 2nd nring fin* **14/1**
P-35 **3** shd **Sir Ivan**[28] 2781 5-10-1 **128**........ LiamMcKenna(7) 130
(Harry Fry) *set stdy pce: qcknd appr 2 out: drifting lft and hdd u.p after last: hld disputing 2nd whn jockey stopped riding briefly nring fin* **8/1**
6-23 **4** 1 1/2 **Ruacana**[21] 2912 6-11-5 **146**........ MrAlexFerguson(7) 145
(John Ferguson) *trckd ldrs: rdn appr 2 out: kpt on but nvr quite pce to chal* **7/1**
P11/ **5** 3/4 **Saddlers Encore (IRE)**[620] 5332 6-10-2 **129**........ ConorSmith(7) 129
(Philip Hobbs) *pressed ldr most of way: rdn and ev ch appr 2 out tl wnt lft and slow last: no ex run-in* **16/1**
-144 **6** 3/4 **Alcala (FR)**[35] 2641 5-10-5 **125**........ NickScholfield 124
(Paul Nicholls) *in tch: trckd ldrs 6th: rdn bef 2 out: nt quite pce to get on terms: no ex run-in* **9/4**[1]
-020 **7** 2 3/4 **Aerlite Supreme (IRE)**[7] 3156 8-10-5 **130**........(t) ConorRing(5) 125
(Evan Williams) *hld up towards rr: sme hdwy whn hit 2 out: no further imp* **14/1**
5-4F **8** shd **Little Boy Boru (IRE)**[34] 2669 7-9-12 **123**........ DavidNoonan(5) 118
(Suzy Smith) *mid-div: rdn appr 2 out: nt pce to get involved* **10/1**
21-U **9** 1/2 **Herbert Park (IRE)**[42] 2485 5-10-12 **132**........(p) ConorO'Farrell 127
(David Pipe) *mid-div: hit 6th and sn struggling in last pair: drvn 3 out: sme hdwy bef next but nvr gng pce to get involved* **6/1**[3]
FP-P **10** 9 **Ambion Wood (IRE)**[34] 2669 9-10-5 **125**........ DenisO'Regan 111
(Victor Dartnall) *mid-div: effrt bef 2 out: wknd bef last* **33/1**

5m 37.4s (10.90) **Going Correction** +0.80s/f (Soft)
WFA 4 from 5yo+ 6lb 10 Ran SP% **118.1**
Speed ratings (Par 109): **111,110,110,109,109 108,107,107,107,104**
CSF £64.59 CT £495.00 TOTE £4.90: £2.00, £3.90, £3.00; EX 61.80 Trifecta £911.40.
Owner John P McManus **Bred** James Browne **Trained** Withycombe, Somerset

FOCUS
There was extra yardage in this race to the advertised distance of about 18yds. Plenty of interest was removed from this Pertemps qualifier when talented chaser Buywise came out, and it developed into a sprint down the home straight, rendering the form untrustworthy. The winner is on a good mark over hurdles.

3255 ARMISHAWS REMOVALS HARRY DUFOSEE NOVICES' CHASE (17 fncs) 2m 4f 35y
2:15 (2:15) (Class 3) 4-Y-O+ **£6,657** (£2,067; £1,113)

Form RPR
21-3 **1** **King's Odyssey (IRE)**[39] 2557 6-11-0 130........ AdamWedge 147+
(Evan Williams) *occasionally drifted lft: trckd ldrs: disp ld 7th: stmbld next: outrt ldr 9th: travelling best whn hit 3 out: wl in command fr next: comf* **10/3**[2]
13-2 **2** 3 1/4 **Southfield Vic (IRE)**[39] 2553 6-11-0 0........(p) NickScholfield 140
(Paul Nicholls) *disp ld tl 9th: trckd wnr: niggled along after next: rdn appr 3 out: kpt on but a being comf hld* **4/6**[1]
0-0P **3** 75 **Pursuitofhappiness (IRE)**[22] 2881 7-11-0 0........ MarkQuinlan 64
(Neil Mulholland) *led tl 7th: grad lost tch fr 11th: t.o* **20/1**
2-23 **F** **Souriyan (FR)**[55] 2211 4-10-8 132........ TomO'Brien
(Jamie Snowden) *trcking ldrs whn fell heavily 3rd* **7/2**[3]

5m 35.5s (18.00) **Going Correction** +0.95s/f (Soft)
WFA 4 from 6yo+ 6lb 4 Ran SP% **110.1**
Speed ratings (Par 107): **102,100,70**,
CSF £6.45 TOTE £4.60; EX 6.90 Trifecta £24.10.
Owner Mr & Mrs William Rucker **Bred** The Hon Mrs V M A Tower **Trained** Llancarfan, Vale Of Glamorgan

FOCUS
There was extra yardage in this race to the advertised distance of about 18yds. This only featured two from some way out and the winner, who was taking a big step up, proved much the best.

3256 BATHWICK TYRES NOVICES' H'CAP HURDLE (7 hdls 1 omitted) 1m 7f 65y
2:50 (2:51) (Class 5) (0-100,98) 3-Y-0+ **£2,599** (£763; £381; £190)

Form RPR
P134 **1** **Sadma**[46] 2418 6-11-9 **98** ThomasGarner(3) 110+
(Nick Lampard) *travelled wl: mid-div: hdwy 3 out: led 2 out: clr whn hit last: eased nring fin* **15/2**
P065 **2** *4* **Vering (FR)**[30] 2736 9-9-7 **72** oh2 (t) MrSeanHoulihan(7) 77
(Carroll Gray) *mid-div: hdwy 3 out: rdn bef 2 out: styd on to chse wnr bef last but a being hld* **20/1**
605- **3** *7* **Badger Wood**[436] 1917 6-11-12 **98** TomCannon 96
(Giles Smyly) *trckd ldrs: led briefly appr 2 out: sn rdn: styd on but no ex fr last* **11/1**
4-34 **4** *11* **Lions Charge (USA)**[24] 616 8-11-6 **92** (tp) MarkQuinlan 80
(Neil Mulholland) *trckd ldrs: ch appr 2 out: sn rdn and hld: grad fdd* **13/2**[3]
54F0 **5** *13* **Appropriate (FR)**[31] 2713 5-9-7 **72** (t) MrMartinMcIntyre(7) 46
(Paul Henderson) *towards rr: struggling w plenty to do after 3 out: styd on past btn horses fr after 2 out: nvr any danger* **33/1**
2114 **6** *nk* **Oscar Jane (IRE)**[39] 2554 8-11-5 **91** (bt) LiamHeard 65
(Johnny Farrelly) *pressed ldr tl after 4th: wknd after next* **10/1**
3PFU **7** *3 ¼* **Sheer Poetry (IRE)**[30] 2730 4-11-4 **97** MrMatthewHampton(7) 67
(Richard Woollacott) *mid-div: rdn and sme prog after 3 out: wknd next* **28/1**
-P14 **8** *½* **East Hill**[62] 2087 5-10-9 **88** (t) PaulO'Brien(7) 58
(Colin Tizzard) *led: nt fluent 3rd: rdn and hdd appr 2 out: sn wknd* **5/1**[2]
-060 **9** *10* **Padova**[31] 2713 9-11-11 **97** TommyPhelan 57
(Dr Jeremy Naylor) *a towards rr* **33/1**
0-00 **10** *32* **On The Road (IRE)**[15] 3009 5-10-8 **80** AdamWedge 8
(Evan Williams) *a towards rr: t.o* **8/1**
30-0 **11** *12* **Norphin**[22] 2880 5-10-12 **84** NickScholfield
(Simon Hodgson) *nt fluent 1st: a in rr: t.o* **33/1**
-3PP **P** **Victory Rich (IRE)**[39] 2555 4-11-9 **95** (t) LiamTreadwell
(Henry Tett) *racd keenly: midfield: rdn after 3 out: sn wknd: p.u bef next* **25/1**
P625 **P** **Columbanus (IRE)**[30] 2730 4-10-0 **79** (t) MissNatalieParker(7)
(Kevin Bishop) *hld up towards rr: nt fluent 4th: sn struggling: t.o whn p.u after 3 out* **9/2**[1]
F5-0 **P** **Acadian (FR)**[30] 2730 5-11-2 **88** (b[1]) ConorO'Farrell
(Nigel Hawke) *mid-div tl wknd after 3 out: p.u after next* **13/2**[3]

4m 1.4s (12.50) **Going Correction** +0.80s/f (Soft) **14 Ran SP% 122.7**
Speed ratings (Par 103): **98,95,92,86,79 79,77,77,71,54 48, , ,**
CSF £152.80 CT £1641.26 TOTE £8.90: £3.20, £5.90, £3.40; EX 211.10 Trifecta £757.20 Part won..
Owner Just A Bit Of Fun **Bred** Darley **Trained** Clatford, Wilts

FOCUS
There was extra yardage in this race to the advertised distance of about 12yds. A moderate but competitive contest and a step up from the winner..

3257 BATHWICK TYRES MID SEASON CHASE (A H'CAP CHASE) (13 fncs) 1m 7f 149y
3:25 (3:27) (Class 3) (0-130,129) 4-Y-0+ **£7,985** (£2,410; £1,241; £658)

Form RPR
-P33 **1** **Quite By Chance**[22] 2877 6-10-9 **119** PaulO'Brien(7) 129+
(Colin Tizzard) *trckd ldrs: led 7th: rdn and hdd appr last: rallied run-in to regain ld towards fin* **10/3**[1]
62-4 **2** *nk* **Ut Majeur Aulmes (FR)**[16] 2990 7-11-7 **124** (t) DenisO'Regan 132
(Victor Dartnall) *awkward 1st: hld up: smooth hdwy after 9th: led appr last: rdn run-in: no ex whn hdd towards fin* **5/1**[3]
-2U3 **3** *12* **Morning Reggie**[21] 2897 6-11-0 **120** ThomasGarner(3) 122+
(Oliver Sherwood) *j. bdly lft thrght: led tl 7th: pressed wnr: rdn and ev ch appr 3 out tl bef 2 out: kpt on same pce* **9/2**[2]
4-P4 **4** *8* **Minella Definitely (IRE)**[33] 2691 8-11-10 **127** (p) MarkQuinlan 116
(Neil Mulholland) *chsd ldr tl dropped to cl 3rd 6th: rdn after 4 out: hld fr next: wknd bef last* **5/1**[3]
-4P0 **U** **Paddy The Stout (IRE)**[22] 2884 10-10-2 **105** (t) LiamTreadwell
(Paul Henderson) *hld up: jinked rt after 2nd and uns rdr* **16/1**
-2F3 **F** **Key To The West (IRE)**[34] 2659 8-11-0 **124** MrStanSheppard(7)
(Matt Sheppard) *fell heavily 2nd* **6/1**
-140 **U** **Bullet Street (IRE)**[35] 2635 7-11-12 **129** AdamWedge
(Evan Williams) *hld up: v bdly hmpd and uns rdr 2nd* **9/1**
45P6 **P** **Very Noble (FR)**[10] 3115 6-10-2 **105** ow1 (t) TomCannon
(Chris Gordon) *chsd ldrs tl after 5th: lost tch qckly: v slow 7th: p.u after 9th* **14/1**
-144 **P** **All But Grey**[39] 2552 9-9-7 **103** oh1 (t) MrSeanHoulihan(7)
(Carroll Gray) *chsd ldrs: stmbld 8th: wknd after 9th: t.o whn mstke 3 out: sn p.u* **16/1**

4m 11.9s (12.00) **Going Correction** +0.95s/f (Soft) **9 Ran SP% 117.3**
Speed ratings (Par 107): **108,107,101,97, , , ,**
CSF £21.30 CT £75.94 TOTE £4.00: £1.70, £1.80, £1.80; EX 20.30 Trifecta £104.90.
Owner T Hamlin,J M Dare,J W Snook,J T Warner **Bred** Mrs S M Newell **Trained** Milborne Port, Dorset

FOCUS
There was extra yardage to the advertised distance of this race of about 12yds. Quite a few of these had jumping mishaps, three coming down early, but the two that came clear were comfortably the best. The winner was on a very good mark and should still be competitive when reassessed.

3258 WINCANTON STANDARD OPEN NATIONAL HUNT FLAT RACE 1m 7f 65y
3:55 (3:56) (Class 6) 4-6-Y-0 **£1,624** (£477; £238; £119)

Form RPR
1 **My Liege (IRE)** 4-11-2 0 AdamWedge 106+
(Evan Williams) *hld up: hdwy over 2f out: rdn to ld over 1f out: styd on wl fnl f* **5/1**[3]
3 **2** *1 ¼* **Chelsea Flyer (IRE)**[49] 2351 4-10-6 0 RichieO'Dea(10) 105+
(Emma Lavelle) *trckd ldrs: led over 2f out: rdn and hdd over 1f out: styd on but a being hld fnl f* **2/1**[2]
3 *11* **Ambion Lane (IRE)** 5-11-2 0 IanPopham 94
(Victor Dartnall) *trckd ldrs tl outpcd over 2f out: styd on again fr over 1f out: wnt 3rd nring fin* **20/1**
0 **4** *hd* **North Hill (IRE)**[35] 2636 4-11-2 0 LiamTreadwell 94
(Ian Williams) *hld up but in tch: rdn over 2f out: styd on fr over 1f out but nt pce to get on terms w ldrs* **16/1**
5 **5** *2 ½* **Stop The Press**[202] 6-11-2 0 DenisO'Regan 91
(Mark Pitman) *trckd ldrs: rdn over 3f out: styd on same pce fnl 2f* **14/1**
6 *12* **Double Treasure** 4-11-2 0 ConorO'Farrell 79
(Jamie Snowden) *trckd ldr: rdn over 2f out: wknd over 1f out* **8/1**
7 *4 ½* **Bagad Bihoue (FR)**[265] 4-11-9 0 NickScholfield 82
(Paul Nicholls) *led tl over 2f out: sn btn* **13/8**[1]
5 **U** **Hawaian Rose**[23] 2875 5-10-2 0 PaulO'Brien(7)
(Colin Tizzard) *v unruly gng to s and at s unseating rdr twice: bucked and uns rdr as tapes wnt bk* **25/1**

3m 57.4s (14.10) **Going Correction** +0.80s/f (Soft) **8 Ran SP% 120.4**
Speed ratings: **94,93,87,87,86 79,77,**
CSF £16.36 TOTE £6.50: £1.70, £1.20, £4.70; EX 20.50 Trifecta £171.40.
Owner Mr & Mrs William Rucker **Bred** T Horgan **Trained** Llancarfan, Vale Of Glamorgan

FOCUS
There was extra yardage to the advertised distance of this race of about 12yds. Two came clear of the remainder in this ordinary bumper.
T/Plt: £1239.90 to a £1 stake. Pool: £39,066.92 - 23.00 winning units. T/Qpdt: £182.70 to a £1 stake. Pool: £2,951.11 - 11.95 winning units. **Tim Mitchell**

3259 - 3267a (Foreign Racing) - See Raceform Interactive

LEOPARDSTOWN (L-H)
Saturday, December 26

OFFICIAL GOING: Heavy

3268a KNIGHT FRANK JUVENILE HURDLE (GRADE 2) (8 hdls) 2m
1:20 (1:20) 3-Y-0 **£21,414** (£6,259; £2,965; £988)

RPR
1 **Apple's Jade (FR)**[235] 3-10-5 0 JJBurke 135+
(W P Mullins, Ire) *hld up in 6th: tk clsr order bef 2 out: rdn in 4th appr last: wnt 2nd at last: styd on wl on inner to ld cl home* **12/1**
2 *hd* **Jer's Girl (IRE)**[21] 2896 3-10-5 0 RobbiePower 133
(Gavin Cromwell, Ire) *attempted to make all: advantage reduced after 2 out: styd on wl bef last where nt fluent: kpt on gamely: hdd cl home* **9/2**[3]
3 *8* **Footpad (FR)**[35] 2651 3-10-12 0 DavidMullins 133
(W P Mullins, Ire) *chsd ldr in 2nd: dropped to 3rd after 3rd: rdn and no imp appr last: no ex run-in* **5/2**[1]
4 *2* **Campeador (FR)**[179] 3-10-12 0 MarkWalsh 130
(Gordon Elliott, Ire) *chsd ldrs in 3rd: wnt 2nd after 3rd: rdn to press ldr after 2 out: no imp appr last in 4th: kpt on one pce* **3/1**[2]
5 *nk* **Rashaan (IRE)**[27] 2813 3-11-1 0 MPFogarty 133
(Colin Kidd, Ire) *hld up in 4th: rdn along in 5th after 2 out: sn no imp: kpt on one pce* **5/2**[1]
6 *26* **Le Vagabond (FR)**[27] 2813 3-10-12 0 AELynch 104
(E J O'Grady, Ire) *hld up in 5th: dropped to 6th 3 out: nt qckn after 2 out and sn no ex* **33/1**
7 *20* **Officer Sydney (IRE)**[110] 1495 3-10-12 0 DavyRussell 84
(Gordon Elliott, Ire) *hld up towards rr: mstke 2nd: no threat fr 3 out* **25/1**
8 *15* **Nice Vintage (IRE)**[7] 3168 3-10-5 0 LPDempsey 62
(Adrian Paul Keatley, Ire) *in rr thrght: nvr a factor: t.o* **80/1**

4m 13.1s (5.60) **Going Correction** +0.725s/f (Soft) **8 Ran SP% 116.0**
Speed ratings: **115,114,110,109,109 96,86,79**
CSF £64.99 TOTE £12.40: £2.50, £1.50, £1.10; DF 75.40 Trifecta £190.30.
Owner Gigginstown House Stud **Bred** Ronny Coveliers **Trained** Muine Beag, Co Carlow **FOCUS**
This has not been a good trial for the Triumph Hurdle in recent years. It has also been the source of shocks with Blood Cotil (2012) the sole winning favourite in the last eight years. Last year's winner Fiscal Focus went off at 33-1, while Carlito Brigante did the business in 2009 at 20-1. That trend continued here. The gallop was dictated throughout by the runner-up who was only collared in the final few strides. The winning time was 6.1 seconds quicker than the opening maiden hurdle.

3269 - 3270a (Foreign Racing) - See Raceform Interactive

3271a RACING POST NOVICE CHASE (GRADE 1) (11 fncs) 2m 1f
2:55 (2:55) 4-Y-0+ **£42,558** (£13,953; £6,976)

RPR
1 **Douvan (FR)**[34] 2674 5-11-12 MrPWMullins 170+
(W P Mullins, Ire) *led narrowly tl hdd bef 2nd: kpt wd and led again after 4th: nt fluent 2 out: stl travelled wl appr last where mstke: rcvrd wl: v easily* **4/7**[1]
2 *18* **Sizing John**[41] 2530 5-11-12 151 JJBurke 149
(Henry De Bromhead, Ire) *pressed ldr early in 2nd: sn settled in 3rd: chsd wnr in 2nd after 4 out: rdn to briefly press wnr after 2 out: no imp appr last: kpt on same pce* **5/1**[3]
3 *46* **Velvet Maker (FR)**[55] 2234 6-11-12 APHeskin 100
(Alan Fleming, Ire) *racd in rr tl tk clsr order in 3rd bef 3 out: no imp after next and eased bef last* **16/1**
P **Ttebbob (IRE)**[13] 3069 6-11-12 154 RobbiePower
(Mrs John Harrington, Ire) *trckd ldrs early in 3rd: led bef 2nd tl hdd after 4th: dropped to rr bef 3 out and sn p.u* **3/1**[2]

4m 29.1s (7.10) **Going Correction** +0.95s/f (Soft) **4 Ran SP% 111.2**
Speed ratings: **121,112,90,**
CSF £4.06 TOTE £1.60; DF 2.80 Trifecta £21.80.
Owner Mrs S Ricci **Bred** S A R L Haras De La Faisanderie **Trained** Muine Beag, Co Carlow

FOCUS
The winner looks a genuine star novice in the making, though some of the gloss is taken from the bare form by the flop of the previously impressive second favourite.

3272 - 3278a (Foreign Racing) - See Raceform Interactive

3227 KEMPTON (R-H)
Sunday, December 27

OFFICIAL GOING: Good to soft (soft in places)
Wind: Fresh, across Weather: Murky

3279 WILLIAM HILL WINTER FESTIVAL JUVENILE HURDLE (8 hdls) 2m
12:50 (12:50) (Class 3) 3-Y-0 **£6,498** (£1,908; £954; £477)

Form RPR
1 **Gibralfaro (IRE)**[72] 3-10-12 0 WayneHutchinson 121+
(Alan King) *str: hld up: prog after 5th: waiting for room after 3 out: hdwy to chse clr ldr bef 2 out: rdn bef last: r.o wl flat to ld fnl strides* **9/1**
21 **2** *½* **Duke Of Medina (IRE)**[52] 2286 3-11-4 124 (b) GavinSheehan 124
(Harry Whittington) *led: nt fluent 3rd and 4th: kicked clr after 3 out: 5 l up and nt fluent 2 out: stl looked in charge last: kpt on but hdd fnl strides* **8/1**
1 **3** *13* **Berland (IRE)**[12] 3099 3-11-4 0 AidanColeman 110
(John Ferguson) *hld up in tch: rdn on long run after 3 out: tk 3rd 2 out but no imp on ldng pair after* **7/1**[3]

1 **4** *8* **Ashoka (IRE)**[17] 2992 3-11-4 0 HarrySkelton 103
(Dan Skelton) *hld up in tch: nt fluent 2nd: prog to chse clr ldr briefly on long run bef 2 out: sn wknd and wl hld in 4th* **9/4[2]**

61P1 **5** *14* **Darebin (GER)**[19] 2954 3-11-8 127 JamieMoore 94
(Gary Moore) *hld up in last: shkn up after 3 out: no imp on ldrs: nvr involved* **20/1**

P **Favorito Buck's (FR)**[102] 1560 3-11-8 0 SamTwiston-Davies
(Paul Nicholls) *tall: lengthy: lw: trckd ldr: shkn up after 3 out: no imp and lost 2nd sn after: wknd qckly and p.u bef 2 out* **11/8[1]**

P **Cabernet D'Alene (FR)** 3-10-7 0 LizzieKelly[(5)]
(Nick Williams) *chsd ldng pair tl mstke 5th: wknd and mstke 3 out: wl bhd whn p.u bef 2 out* **33/1**

3m 57.5s (-0.50) **Going Correction** +0.05s/f (Yiel) **7** Ran SP% **114.2**
Speed ratings (Par 106): **103,102,96,92,85**
CSF £73.69 TOTE £11.30: £4.90, £3.50; EX 72.20 Trifecta £465.90.
Owner McNeill Family **Bred** Sarl Darpat France **Trained** Barbury Castle, Wilts

FOCUS
All starts have been moved at this track following remeasuring, so there will be no speed figures here until there is sufficient data to calculate updated median times. All rails had been moved 2yds from the previous day's configuration. The Winter Hurdle course was 6yds out from its innermost configuration, increasing the distance of the opener by 33yds. There was no hanging around in this fair juvenile event and it saw changing fortunes on the run-in as two finished well clear. The winner could be a bit better than the bare result.

3280 WILLIAMHILL.COM NOVICES' CHASE (REGISTERED AS THE WAYWARD LAD NOVICES' CHASE) (GRADE 2) (12 fncs) 2m
1:25 (1:27) (Class 1) 4-Y-0+ **£19,932** (£7,479; £3,745; £1,865; £938)

Form RPR

-611 **1** **Ar Mad (FR)**[22] 2913 5-11-8 155 JoshuaMoore 161+
(Gary Moore) *lw: led at str pce and mostly j.w: rdn and pressed 3 out: hdd 2 out: rallied and great jump last: sn led again: drvn out* **5/2[2]**

05-1 **2** *nk* **Vaniteux (FR)**[34] 2684 6-11-6 150 NicodeBoinville 160+
(Nicky Henderson) *lw: blnd 1st: chsd ldng pair: wnt 2nd after 6th: rdn to chal 3 out: led 2 out and sn at least a l ahd: drvn and hdd sn after last: styd on* **10/11[1]**

-011 **3** *5* **Arzal (FR)**[29] 2779 5-11-8 149 GavinSheehan 158
(Harry Whittington) *swtg: pressed wnr: nt fluent 5th: blnd next and lost 2nd: renewed effrt bef 3 out: no imp on ldng pair 2 out: mstke last: kpt on* **5/1[3]**

1311 **4** *4 ½* **Ittirad (USA)**[79] 1838 7-11-8 0 AidanColeman 152
(John Ferguson) *hld up in last: nt fluent 2nd and 3rd: effrt after 4 out and in tch bef next: no imp 2 out: nt fluent last and fdd* **25/1**

2-02 **5** *16* **The Saint James (FR)**[16] 3006 4-10-11 144 (t) RichardJohnson 130
(Jonjo O'Neill) *racd in 4th: chsd ldng pair 7th tl blnd 8th: dropped to last and sn btn* **12/1**

3m 53.1s (-1.90) **Going Correction** +0.30s/f (Yiel)
WFA 4 from 5yo+ 5lb **5** Ran SP% **109.2**
Speed ratings (Par 115): **116,115,113,111,103**
CSF £5.38 TOTE £3.20: £1.40, £1.20; EX 5.70 Trifecta £9.80.
Owner Ashley Head **Bred** Michel Le Meur **Trained** Lower Beeding, W Sussex

FOCUS
Race distance increased by 12yds. Predictably this long-established Grade 2 novice chase was run at a frantic gallop and it provided a dramatic finish. The form is straightforward enough with the winner confirming the merit of his recent win.

3281 WILLIAMHILL.COM DESERT ORCHID CHASE (GRADE 2) (12 fncs) 2m
2:00 (2:00) (Class 1) 4-Y-0+ **£45,560** (£17,096; £8,560; £4,264; £2,144)

Form RPR

P2-1 **1** **Sprinter Sacre (FR)**[42] 2511 9-11-10 173 NicodeBoinville 171
(Nicky Henderson) *hld up in 4th: moved up to join ldng pair on outer 8th: shkn up 3 out: rdn to chal 2 out: led and bttr jump last: rdn out* **8/11[1]**

F-51 **2** *¾* **Sire De Grugy (FR)**[22] 2915 9-11-10 169 JamieMoore 171
(Gary Moore) *lw: cl up: trckd ldr 5th: led 7th: jnd after next: hrd pressed fr 3 out: hdd and mstke last: kpt on wl but jst hld* **11/4[2]**

4-13 **3** *3 ¾* **Vibrato Valtat (FR)**[22] 2915 6-11-6 162 (t) SamTwiston-Davies 162
(Paul Nicholls) *trckd ldr to 5th: styd cl up: w ldr fr 8th to 3 out: rdn and one pce after* **6/1[3]**

5-24 **4** *10* **Somersby (IRE)**[22] 2915 11-11-0 162 (p) BrianHughes 148
(Mick Channon) *led to 7th: outpcd in 4th after next: one pce and no imp on ldrs fr 3 out* **12/1**

0111 **5** *12* **Sir Valentino (FR)**[11] 3107 6-11-4 143 (t) PaddyBrennan 144
(Tom George) *hld up in last: unable to keep on terms w rest fr 6th: nursed home fr 3 out* **33/1**

3m 55.8s (0.80) **Going Correction** +0.30s/f (Yiel) **5** Ran SP% **109.5**
Speed ratings (Par 115): **110,109,107,102,96**
CSF £3.22 TOTE £1.60: £1.10, £1.70; EX 2.80 Trifecta £5.00.
Owner Mrs Caroline Mould **Bred** Christophe Masle **Trained** Upper Lambourn, Berks

FOCUS
Race distance increased by 12yds. A fascinating affair. There was a strong gallop set and two top-class chasers locked horns in the home straight. The winner has been rated in line with his Cheltenham run.

3282 WILLIAM HILL H'CAP CHASE (18 fncs) 3m
2:35 (2:35) (Class 2) (0-145,145) 4-Y-0+**£25,992** (£7,632; £3,816; £1,908)

Form RPR

12-3 **1** **The Last Samuri (IRE)**[29] 2790 7-11-7 140 DavidBass 152
(Kim Bailey) *trckd ldrs: rdn after 4 out: wnt 3rd next: clsd to take 2nd bef last: gd burst to ld fnl 100yds: r.o wl* **9/2[1]**

62-1 **2** *1 ¼* **Viva Steve (IRE)**[71] 1970 7-10-8 127 BrianHughes 139
(Mick Channon) *prom: trckd ldr 11th: led next: blnd and jnd 3 out: drvn and def advantage after 2 out: hdd and outpcd last 100yds* **10/1**

5413 **3** *14* **Sands Cove (IRE)**[37] 2616 8-10-8 127 LiamTreadwell 129
(James Evans) *nvr that fluent: mostly in last to 10th: sme prog fr 12th: last of nine w a ch whn hmpd bnd bef 3 out: rdn and kpt on wl fr 2 out to take 3rd nr fin* **20/1**

55-2 **4** *½* **Foxbridge (IRE)**[44] 2473 9-10-3 127 (t) JamieBargary[(5)] 127
(Nigel Twiston-Davies) *lw: trckd ldrs: mstke 14th: sn rdn: no imp on ldrs 3 out: kpt on to chse ldng pair after last: lost 3rd nr fin* **8/1[2]**

211- **5** *2 ½* **Opening Batsman (IRE)**[77] 1879 9-11-10 143 (bt) NoelFehily 140
(Harry Fry) *in tch on outer: prog 12th: trckd ldr 14th: upsides fr 3 out gng strly: rdn after 2 out and fnd nil: wknd rapidly bef last* **14/1**

-2U2 **6** *11* **Loose Chips**[37] 2616 9-10-12 134 (b) GrahamWatters[(3)] 121
(Charlie Longsdon) *mde most tl hdd and nt fluent 12th: steadily wknd bef 3 out* **16/1**

02-P **7** *2 ¼* **No Buts**[57] 2187 7-11-3 136 TomScudamore 123
(David Bridgwater) *in tch: dropped to rr 10th: blnd bdly 12th: no ch after: plugged on* **20/1**

13-3 **8** *¾* **Ballyheigue Bay (IRE)**[22] 2916 8-10-13 132 (t) TomCannon 117
(Chris Gordon) *pressed ldr to 11th: nt fluent 13th: stl rt on terms 14th: wknd after mstke next* **10/1**

0P-4 **9** *14* **Ballinvarrig (IRE)**[37] 2615 8-10-8 127 (p) PaddyBrennan 101
(Tom George) *trckd ldrs gng wl: mstke 11th: rdn 4 out: wl hld whn blnd 3 out: wknd* **9/1[3]**

4-0P **10** *14* **Ardkilly Witness (IRE)**[22] 2899 9-11-3 136 (p) BrendanPowell 94
(Jamie Snowden) *trckd ldrs: lost pl fr 12th: wl in rr 4 out: wknd next* **33/1**

P-2U **S** **Shangani (USA)**[29] 2780 9-10-13 132 (b) AidanColeman
(Venetia Williams) *reminders to s: wl in rr: prog on outer fr 13th: drvn and in tch in 7th whn slipped up on bnd bef 3 out* **12/1**

-210 **P** **Open Hearted**[30] 2759 8-11-7 145 (t) BridgetAndrews[(5)]
(Dan Skelton) *hmpd 1st: a in rr: lost tch w main gp 11th: t.o whn p.u bef 3 out* **25/1**

13-1 **F** **Harry's Farewell**[31] 2724 8-11-0 133 NickScholfield
(Polly Gundry) *w ldrs whn fell 1st* **14/1**

0-60 **P** **Ned Stark (IRE)**[29] 2783 7-11-4 137 DenisO'Regan
(Alan King) *lw: hmpd 1st: nvr gng that wl after: dropped off main gp bef 12th: wl bhd in 11th whn p.u bef last* **9/2[1]**

-51F **P** **Howlongisafoot (IRE)**[30] 2761 6-11-8 141 (b) SamTwiston-Davies
(Paul Nicholls) *in tch on inner: mstke 9th: dropped to rr 13th: mstke next and t.o after: p.u bef 3 out* **14/1**

6m 9.5s (0.50) **Going Correction** +0.30s/f (Yiel) **15** Ran SP% **125.5**
Speed ratings (Par 109): **111,110,105,105,104 101,100,100,95,90 , , , ,**
CSF £48.72 CT £847.10 TOTE £5.70: £2.10, £3.90, £7.00; EX 68.70 Trifecta £1468.70.
Owner Paul & Clare Rooney **Bred** Edmond Coleman **Trained** Andoversford, Gloucs

FOCUS
Race distance increased by 20yds. A fair staying handicap that looked wide open. They got sorted out in the home straight and it's solid form with the winner providing another boost for the Rehearsal Chase form.

3283 WILLIAM HILL EXCLUSIVE MOBILE OFFERS MARES' H'CAP HURDLE (12 hdls) 3m 121y
3:10 (3:10) (Class 2) 4-Y-0+ **£12,996** (£3,816; £1,908; £954)

Form RPR

F242 **1** **Cannon Fodder**[27] 2825 8-10-7 123 MarcGoldstein 128
(Sheena West) *chsd ldr: nt fluent 6th: rdn 3 out and looked to be getting the worst of it: kpt on tenaciously after: wore down ldr and led last: styd on wl* **7/1**

P-P1 **2** *1 ¾* **Desert Queen**[36] 2632 7-11-5 142 (t) MrMLegg[(7)] 146
(Harry Fry) *lw: racd freely: led and often j.w: mstkes 9th and 3 out: stl gng wl after: rdn after j.lft 2 out: hdd last: kpt on but no ex* **2/1[1]**

2-16 **3** *17* **Broxbourne (IRE)**[15] 3034 6-11-9 139 DavidBass 127
(Nicky Henderson) *chsd ldrs: urged along fr 8th: dropped to rr next and sn struggling: kpt on fr 3 out to take modest 3rd last* **9/2[3]**

1-34 **4** *5* **Tara Mist**[25] 2852 6-10-6 122 RichardJohnson 104
(Henry Daly) *hld up in last trio: prog 9th: chsd ldng pair 3 out and only threat to them: rdn on long run bef next and sn wknd: lost 3rd last* **11/4[2]**

1144 **5** *12* **Minnie Milan (IRE)**[34] 2685 6-10-9 125 TrevorWhelan 96
(Neil King) *swtg: trckd ldng pair: rdn after 9th: struggling and lost pl 3 out: mstke 2 out* **16/1**

/06- **6** *15* **Tagrita (IRE)**[394] 2791 7-10-10 126 (t) SamTwiston-Davies 83
(Paul Nicholls) *hld up in last trio: in tch 9th: rdn and wknd 3 out* **6/1**

666 **7** *15* **Titch Strider (IRE)**[50] 2349 10-9-7 116 oh13 ThomasCheesman[(7)] 60
(John Panvert) *hld up in last trio: struggling fr 9th: wknd 3 out: t.o* **66/1**

6m 15.9s (-4.10) **Going Correction** +0.05s/f (Yiel) **7** Ran SP% **112.3**
Speed ratings (Par 109): **108,107,102,100,96 91,86**
CSF £21.28 TOTE £7.80: £3.40, £1.60; EX 23.90 Trifecta £142.40.
Owner The Cheapskates **Bred** Andrew And Mrs S R B Davis **Trained** Falmer, E Sussex

FOCUS
Race distance increased by 71yds. This mares' handicap was run at a demanding gallop and the first two home dominated from the offset. The winner has long been on a good mark and has been rated back to her very best.

3284 WILLIAM HILL WORLD DARTS CHAMPIONSHIP H'CAP HURDLE (8 hdls) 2m
3:40 (3:40) (Class 3) (0-140,138) 3-Y-0+ **£12,996** (£3,816; £1,908; £954)

Form RPR

U1-F **1** **Zulu Oscar**[29] 2773 6-11-4 130 (t) NoelFehily 138+
(Harry Fry) *a in ldng trio: led 3 out gng strly: more than 2 l clr 2 out: rdn bef last: kpt on wl and a holding on* **5/1[3]**

2 *1* **Affaire D'Honneur (FR)**[53] 4-10-12 124 GavinSheehan 131+
(Harry Whittington) *athletic: lw: wl in tch in midfield: prog after 3 out: rdn to chse wnr 2 out: kpt on wl fr last: a hld* **11/2**

1-32 **3** *7* **Two Taffs (IRE)**[34] 2683 5-10-13 125 HarrySkelton 125+
(Dan Skelton) *lw: patiently rdn in last pair: sme prog after 3 out gng wl enough: shkn up bef 2 out: styd on to take 3rd after last: too much to do* **7/2[1]**

0-61 **4** *3 ½* **Canadian Diamond (IRE)**[17] 2987 8-9-12 117 MikeyHamill[(7)] 116
(Richard Rowe) *prom: chsd wnr on long run after 3 out to 2 out: steadily fdd* **16/1**

1-12 **5** *5* **After Eight Sivola (FR)**[46] 2438 5-10-11 128 LizzieKelly[(5)] 120
(Nick Williams) *t.k.h early: hld up in rr: shkn up after 3 out: kpt on one pce fr 2 out: nvr able to threaten* **11/1**

1-P **6** *1 ¼* **Monsieur Gibraltar (FR)**[78] 1847 4-11-12 138 (t) SamTwiston-Davies 130
(Paul Nicholls) *hld up in rr: prog on inner bef 3 out: rdn to chse ldrs bef 2 out: wknd bef last* **12/1**

3-05 **7** *6* **Starluck (IRE)**[37] 2617 10-11-8 134 (p) NicodeBoinville 120
(David Arbuthnot) *trckd ldrs: rdn on long run after 3 out: steadily fdd fr 2 out* **14/1**

00P2 **8** *1 ¼* **Ryeolliean**[24] 2873 4-10-8 120 (p) JamieMoore 106
(Gary Moore) *mde most to 3 out: sn rdn: wknd 2 out* **12/1**

2-20 **9** *1* **Un Beau Roman (FR)**[70] 1994 7-11-10 136 PaddyBrennan 121
(Paul Henderson) *hld up in last: passed a few 2 out: reminders bef last: nvr involved* **100/1**

5161 **10** *7* **I'dliketheoption (IRE)**[29] 2773 4-10-13 125 (t) RichieMcLernon 103
(Jonjo O'Neill) *settled in midfield: urged along sn after 3 out: steadily wknd bef 2 out* **14/1**

-P32 **11** *10* **Exitas (IRE)**[27] 2824 7-11-5 134 (t) ConorShoemark[(3)] 103
(Phil Middleton) *settled towards rr: drvn sn after 3 out: wknd wl bef 2 out* **33/1**

6-31 **12** *6* **Draytonian (IRE)**[32] 2716 5-11-0 **126**.......................... RichardJohnson 95
(Philip Hobbs) *trckd ldrs: nt fluent 5th: wl in tch whn blnd bdly 3 out: sn dropped to last then hmpd bnd bef 2 out: bhd after* **9/2**[2]

2P-3 **P** **Emperor Commodos**[30] 2748 8-10-10 **122**...............(p) TomScudamore
(David Bridgwater) *pressed ldr to 5th: wknd qckly 3 out: wl bhd whn p.u bef next* **25/1**

3m 54.6s (-3.40) **Going Correction** +0.05s/f (Yiel) **13** Ran SP% **123.2**
Speed ratings (Par 107): **110,109,106,104,101 101,98,97,97,93 88,85,**
CSF £33.88 CT £112.22 TOTE £6.50: £2.30, £2.50, £1.40; EX 43.20 Trifecta £258.10.
Owner Caroline Fry & Susie Dilhorne **Bred** R Robinson **Trained** Seaborough, Dorset

FOCUS
Race distance increased by 33yds. It paid to race handily in this competitive handicap and the first two are on the uprade..
T/Jkpt: not won. JACKPOT PLACEPOT £1,077.60. Pool: £2,371 - 2.20 winning units. T/Plt: £200.50 to a £1 stake. Pool: £150,763.20 - 548.75 winning units. T/Qpdt: £12.10 to a £1 stake. Pool: £18,863.35 - 1153.15 winning units. **Jonathan Neesom**

2917
WETHERBY (L-H)
Sunday, December 27

3285 Meeting Abandoned - Back straight flooded

CHEPSTOW (L-H)
Sunday, December 27

3273 Meeting Abandoned - Waterlogged

3266
LEOPARDSTOWN (L-H)
Sunday, December 27

OFFICIAL GOING: Heavy

3293a PADDY POWER "SO QUICK, SO EASY IPHONE APP" CHASE (GRADE 1) (11 fncs) 2m 1f
1:15 (1:15) 5-Y-0+ **£46,511** (£14,728; £6,976; £2,325; £1,550)

RPR

1 **Flemenstar (IRE)**[21] 2941 10-11-12 150.............................. AELynch 162+
(Anthony Curran, Ire) *chsd ldrs tl wnt 2nd bef 2nd: cl 2nd bef 2 out where hmpd by faller: sn rdn in 2nd and no imp on ldr: styd on wl u.p on outer fr last to ld clsng stages: all out* **16/1**

2 *1* **Simply Ned (IRE)**[42] 2511 8-11-12 159.............................. BrianHarding 160
(Nicky Richards) *settled towards rr after 1st where nt fluent: impr into 3rd after 6th: lft in front fr 2 out where sltly hmpd by faller: drvn clr bef last where stdd: all out far side run-in where reduced advantage and hdd clsng stages* **14/1**[3]

3 *20* **Hidden Cyclone (IRE)**[13] 3092 10-11-12 156..................(p) BrianHayes 143
(John Joseph Hanlon, Ire) *hld up towards rr: slt mstke in 5th at 3rd: slow 7th: rdn in 4th after 3 out and no imp on ldrs bef next where mstke and sltly hmpd by faller: sn rdn in mod 4th: kpt on one pce in 3rd fr bef last* **16/1**

4 *5* **Clarcam (FR)**[21] 2941 5-11-12 153........................(tp) BJCooper 135
(Gordon Elliott, Ire) *w.w in rr: nt fluent 2nd and niggled along briefly: wnt 5th bef 3 out: no imp on ldrs next where lft mod 3rd briefly: kpt on one pce in mod 4th fr bef last: sddle slipped* **14/1**[3]

5 *19* **Sizing Granite (IRE)**[56] 2232 7-11-12 154.............................. JJBurke 116
(Henry De Bromhead, Ire) *chsd ldr early: 4th 1/2-way: rdn towards rr and struggling after 4 out: slt mstke in rr next and no imp after* **8/1**[2]

F **Un De Sceaux (FR)**[241] 51 7-11-12 168.............................. RWalsh
(W P Mullins, Ire) *led: racd keenly: over 8 l clr at 1/2-way: reduced advantage bef 7th where j. sltly lft: 2 l clr stl gng wl bef 2 out where fell* **1/4**[1]

4m 21.2s (-0.80) **Going Correction** +0.375s/f (Yiel) **6** Ran SP% **116.2**
Speed ratings: **116,115,106,103,94**
CSF £170.68 TOTE £23.60: £5.40, £2.60; DF 305.70 Trifecta £205.60.
Owner Stephen Curran **Bred** Donal Barnwell **Trained** Tara, Co. Meath

FOCUS
This was all about Un De Sceaux who made his belated return to action a few weeks later than planned. He missed the Tingle Creek because Willie Mullins was not entirely happy with him in the days leading up to the race and freshness seemed to be his undoing here. His clear lead had been dwindled down to about 2l at the time of his departure, but you sensed that Ruby Walsh was only giving him a breather. His exit left Simply Ned and Flemenstar to fight it out and it was the last-named who was most willing on the gruelling climb to the line. This was the winner's best performance since 2013.

3294a PADDY POWER FUTURE CHAMPIONS NOVICE HURDLE (GRADE 1) (8 hdls) 2m
1:45 (1:45) 4-Y-0+ **£39,534** (£12,519; £5,930; £1,976; £1,317; £658)

RPR

1 **Long Dog**[28] 2814 5-11-10 147.............................. RWalsh 146
(W P Mullins, Ire) *mde virtually all: narrow advantage at 1/2-way: jnd briefly bef 2 out: pushed along w narrow advantage after 2 out and extended ld into st: rdn bef last and kpt on wl u.p run-in where reduced ld: all out* **9/4**[1]

2 *3/4* **Tombstone (IRE)**[29] 2795 5-11-10.............................. BJCooper 146+
(Gordon Elliott, Ire) *chsd ldrs: racd keenly: 6th after 1/2-way: cl 5th bef 2 out where nt fluent: n.m.r between horses appr st: rdn into 2nd bef last and kpt on wl run-in to press wnr: hld* **3/1**[2]

3 *3/4* **Petit Mouchoir (FR)**[31] 2739 4-11-7.............................. JacquesRicou 142+
(W P Mullins, Ire) *hld up in tch: clsr in 4th at 1/2-way: slt mstke 4 out and next: rdn on inner after 2 out and wnt 2nd briefly bef last: no imp on wnr after last: kpt on wl u.p in 3rd run-in: nvr on terms* **10/1**

4 *3 1/2* **Bleu Et Rouge (FR)**[42] 2522 4-11-7.............................. MarkWalsh 141+
(W P Mullins, Ire) *hld up: racd keenly: last at 1/2-way: nt fluent 4 out: cl 8th after 2 out and gd hdwy on outer to chse ldrs in 4th at last: no imp on ldrs run-in and kpt on one pce* **18/1**

5 *2 1/4* **Falcon Crest (IRE)**[35] 2672 5-11-10 136.............................. BarryGeraghty 139
(C Roche, Ire) *hld up in tch: 5th 1/2-way: cl 4th bef 2 out: gng wl appr st disputing 3rd: sn rdn and no ex u.p bef last: dropped to 7th at last: kpt on again run-in* **7/1**

6 *1/2* **Tully East (IRE)**[43] 2505 5-11-10 132.............................. APHeskin 139
(Alan Fleming, Ire) *hld up: 8th 1/2-way: stl gng wl in rr after 2 out: hdwy bef last into 5th: no ex u.p after last and one pce run-in* **33/1**

7 *2 1/4* **Baily Cloud (IRE)**[28] 2814 5-11-10 128.............................. MarkEnright 136
(M F Morris, Ire) *on toes befhand: in rr: clsr in 7th bef 1/2-way: rdn in 6th between last 2 and no ex u.p in 8th bef last: kpt on one pce run-in* **66/1**

8 *nk* **Bachasson (FR)**[28] 2814 4-11-7 146.............................. MrPWMullins 133
(W P Mullins, Ire) *settled bhd ldr in 2nd: cl 2nd bef 1/2-way: disp briefly bef 2 out: cl 2nd after 2 out gng wl: sn rdn in 2nd and wknd bef last where nt fluent* **9/2**[3]

9 *19* **Woodland Opera (IRE)**[35] 2671 5-11-10.............................. RobbiePower 117
(Mrs John Harrington, Ire) *chsd ldrs: 3rd 1/2-way: cl 3rd bef 2 out: rdn and wknd to rr after 2 out: eased bef last* **6/1**

4m 8.4s (0.90) **Going Correction** +0.375s/f (Yiel)
WFA 4 from 5yo 5lb **9** Ran SP% **119.5**
Speed ratings: **112,111,111,109,108 108,107,106,97**
CSF £9.75 TOTE £2.70: £1.10, £1.70, £2.50; DF 11.60 Trifecta £76.90.
Owner Mrs S Ricci **Bred** G B Turnbull Ltd **Trained** Muine Beag, Co Carlow

FOCUS
Whether there was a star here is questionable, but we had several unexposed types, and it was pretty fascinating. The best horse did not win the race. Plenty of improvers in a tight finish and the winner ran roughly to form.

3296a PADDY POWER CHASE (H'CAP) (GRADE B) (17 fncs) 3m 100y
2:55 (2:56) (0-150,150) 5-Y-0+
£82,790 (£28,294; £13,565; £4,728; £3,255; £1,782)

RPR

1 **Minella Foru (IRE)**[29] 2794 6-10-8 **134**.............................. BarryGeraghty 145+
(Edward P Harty, Ire) *mid-div: hdwy in 10th after 3 out: clsd u.p after next to chse ldrs in 5th bef last where pckd sltly: styd on wl to ld clsng stages where wandered sltly* **7/1**[2]

2 *1 1/2* **Ucello Conti (FR)**[14] 3073 7-10-11 **137**..........................(t) JacquesRicou 146
(Gordon Elliott, Ire) *in tch: mstke 10th: impr in 7th 2 out to ld fr last: strly pressed u.p run-in and hdd clsng stages* **25/1**

3 *3 1/4* **Folsom Blue (IRE)**[385] 2990 8-9-13 **130**..................(p) ShaneShortall[(5)] 135
(M F Morris, Ire) *towards rr early: disp 4th bef 11th: rdn after 2 out and led narrowly briefly bef last: sn hdd and sltly hmpd after last where dropped to 5th: kpt on u.p run-in into 3rd clsng stages* **20/1**

4 *1/2* **Gilgamboa (IRE)**[21] 2941 7-11-5 **150**.............................. JackKennedy[(5)] 155
(E Bolger, Ire) *mid-div: 8th after 9th: clsr in 5th bef 11th: tk clsr order bhd ldrs after 4 out travelling wl: led after 2 out: rdn into st and hdd bef last where slt mstke and wnt sltly rt: wknd clsng stages* **4/1**[1]

5 *2* **The Job Is Right**[43] 2484 7-10-13 **139** ow2....................(b) DavyRussell 140
(Michael Hourigan, Ire) *mid-div: lft mod 12th and rdn after 2 out: no imp on ldrs u.p bef last: r.o wl run-in: nvr nrr* **16/1**

6 *nk* **Riverside City (IRE)**[35] 2675 6-9-10 **122**.............................. MsNCarberry 124
(Gordon Elliott, Ire) *in rr of mid-div: rdn in 10th after 2 out where slt mstke and clsd u.p bef last where swtchd lft: kpt on one pce run-in: nvr trbld ldrs* **16/1**

7 *1 3/4* **Dromnea (IRE)**[35] 2675 8-10-6 **132**.............................. MarkEnright 133
(M F Morris, Ire) *in tch: rdn after 2 out and no imp on ldrs u.p in 8th bef last where lft 7th: kpt on one pce run-in* **25/1**

8 *1 3/4* **Futuramic (IRE)**[43] 2503 8-9-11 **123**.............................. RobbieColgan 122
(Andrew Lynch, Ire) *chsd ldrs early: lft mod 15th 2 out: kpt on u.p into mod 8th run-in: nvr nrr* **50/1**

9 *6* **Heathfield (IRE)**[35] 2672 8-10-7 **133**.............................. MarkWalsh 126
(A J Martin, Ire) *hld up: pckd sltly 1st: tk clsr order after 3 out: lft mod 11th next: kpt on one pce* **14/1**

10 *2 1/2* **Los Amigos (IRE)**[265] 5224 8-10-12 **138**..........................(b[1]) AELynch 128
(Dermot Anthony McLoughlin, Ire) *in tch: gng wl in cl 5th bef 2 out: rdn and no imp on ldrs into st: dropped to mod 10th bef last where hmpd by faller: one pce run-in* **20/1**

11 *2* **Knockanarrigan (IRE)**[35] 2675 7-10-0 **126** oh1 ow4.......... IanMcCarthy 113
(Ms Sandra Hughes, Ire) *led tl hdd fr 2nd: sn disp: narrow advantage whn slt mstke 7th and jnd again: in front fr 10th: nt fluent next: j.rt 4 out: rdn and hdd after 2 out: wknd bef last* **25/1**

12 *15* **Cause Of Causes (USA)**[260] 5275 7-11-3 **143**..................(tp) AlanCrowe 116
(Gordon Elliott, Ire) *hld up: trailing towards rr after 4 out: kpt on one pce fr after 2 out* **20/1**

13 *6 1/2* **Spring Heeled (IRE)**[43] 2482 8-11-2 **145**..................(p) GerFox[(3)] 112
(J H Culloty, Ire) *hld up towards rr: slt mstke 1st: mstke 5th: reminders after 7th: pushed along after 10th and no imp in 16th bef 2 out: kpt on one pce* **33/1**

14 *8 1/2* **Urano (FR)**[29] 2783 7-10-11 **137**.............................. NiallKelly[(7)] 95
(W P Mullins, Ire) *in rr of mid-div: pushed along after 4 out and no imp fr next* **25/1**

15 *1/2* **Rossvoss**[14] 3071 7-10-6 **132**..........................(bt) MsKWalsh 90
(T M Walsh, Ire) *in tch: slt mstke 9th: clsr in 8th bef 3 out where mstke and lost pl: bad mstke next and no imp after* **11/1**

16 *14* **Dushrembrandt (IRE)**[31] 2742 9-9-4 **123**..............(tp) JonathanMoore[(7)] 67
(Robert Tyner, Ire) *chsd ldrs: pushed along after 12th and wknd 4 out* **50/1**

U **Gallant Oscar (IRE)**[239] 95 9-11-1 **148**.............................. DonaghMeyler[(7)]
(A J Martin, Ire) *in rr of mid-div: tk clsr order 4 out: impr into 9th after 3 out: styng on whn blnd and uns rdr 2 out* **20/1**

R **Cantlow (IRE)**[57] 2187 10-10-6 **135**..........................(t) JodyMcGarvey[(3)]
(Paul Webber) *ref to r* **25/1**

P **My Murphy (IRE)**[14] 3073 9-11-0 **140**..........................(b) RobbiePower
(W J Burke, Ire) *in rr of mid-div: mstke 7th and pushed along: rdn and no imp after 4 out: trailing whn p.u bef last* **16/1**

P **Empire Of Dirt (IRE)**[21] 2943 8-10-6 **132**............(t) MrJohnJFitzpatrick[(7)]
(C A Murphy, Ire) *hld up in rr: trailing whn p.u bef 11th* **14/1**

P **Operating (IRE)**[36] 2655 8-10-11 **140**..........................(p) LPDempsey[(3)]
(Gordon Elliott, Ire) *in rr of mid-div: rdn towards rr after 5 out and no imp bef next: trailing whn p.u bef last* **50/1**

R **Grand Jesture (IRE)**[246] 5538 7-11-5 **145**..........................(b[1]) JJBurke
(Henry De Bromhead, Ire) *ref to r* **25/1**

P **Dogora (FR)**[44] 2471 6-10-7 **133**..........................(p) RWalsh
(W P Mullins, Ire) *chsd ldrs: pckd sltly 1st: led fr next tl sn jnd: 2nd whn bad mstke and pckd 11th where lost pl: eased bef 5 out and trailing towards rr whn p.u after 4 out where slt mstke* **12/1**

B **Sumos Novios (IRE)**[21] 2943 7-10-6 **132** 9ex.............................. BrianHayes 134+
(W J Burke, Ire) *chsd ldrs: rdn in 3rd 2 out and no imp on ldrs u.p in 6th whn b.d at last* **8/1**[3]

P **Perfect Promise (IRE)**[45] 2465 7-10-4 **130**.............................. SeanFlanagan
(James Joseph Mangan, Ire) *chsd ldrs early: rdn towards rr after 12th and no imp: sn wknd and p.u bef 3 out* **33/1**

U **Carriganog (IRE)**[29] 2794 6-10-0 **129**..........................(tp) BenDalton[(3)]
(A P O'Brien, Ire) *in rr of mid-div: blnd and uns rdr 10th* **33/1**

F **Ballychorus (IRE)**[35] 2675 6-10-12 **138**..........................(t) APHeskin 143+
(Ms Margaret Mullins, Ire) *chsd ldrs: pushed along in 5th into st and impr far side to chal w ev ch bef last where fell* **16/1**

P Captain Von Trappe (IRE)[28] 2817 6-10-11 137.................. BJCooper
(Gordon Elliott, Ire) mid-div early: rdn towards rr after 5 out and no imp bef next: trailing whn p.u bef last 20/1

6m 40.9s (1.90) Going Correction +0.375s/f (Yiel) 28 Ran SP% 158.1
Speed ratings: 111,110,109,109,108 108,107,107,105,104 103,98,96,93,93 88, , , ,
CSF £188.36 CT £3504.61 TOTE £9.00: £2.70, £10.50, £6.50, £1.40; DF 450.30 Trifecta £16838.50.
Owner John P McManus **Bred** Louis G Vambeck **Trained** Curragh, Co Kildare

FOCUS
The winner had been rated 142 over hurdles and improved again for the big step up in trip.

3295 - 3300a (Foreign Racing) - See Raceform Interactive

2376 **LIMERICK** (R-H)
Sunday, December 27

OFFICIAL GOING: Heavy

3301a SHANNON AIRPORT NOVICE CHASE (GRADE 2) (14 fncs) 2m 3f 120y
1:35 (1:35) 4-Y-0+ £21,162 (£6,186; £2,930; £976)

RPR
1 Outlander (IRE)[43] 2503 7-11-4 0.................. DavidMullins 154+
(W P Mullins, Ire) chsd ldr in 2nd: clsr w a circ to r: pressed ldr 2 out: led last and styd on wl to assert clsng stages 1/2[1]
2 1 3/4 Avant Tout (FR)[211] 563 5-11-4 0.................. DannyMullins 151
(W P Mullins, Ire) led: advantage reduced w a circ to r: strly pressed 2 out: hdd last: no ex w wnr clsng stages 6/1[3]
3 7 Free Expression (IRE)[28] 2817 6-11-4 144.................. KevinSexton 144
(Gordon Elliott, Ire) hld up in 3rd: clsr at 6th: nt fluent 3 out: sn disp 2nd: rdn and nt qckn bef 2 out: sn no imp 11/4[2]
4 38 King Of The Picts (IRE)[29] 2794 6-11-4 128.................. BrianO'Connell 106
(John Patrick Shanahan, Ire) racd in rr: clsr at 6th: rdn and detached bef 3 out 25/1

5m 43.6s (343.60) 4 Ran SP% 111.5
CSF £4.17 TOTE £1.50; DF 3.40 Trifecta £4.50.
Owner Gigginstown House Stud **Bred** Ronnie O'Neill **Trained** Muine Beag, Co Carlow

FOCUS
A Mullins-dominated contest with the winner proving himself a high-class performer and the runner-up surprising one or two people. The pair ran in line with their hurdle marks.

3302a TIM DUGGAN MEMORIAL H'CAP CHASE (GRADE B) (14 fncs) 2m 3f 120y
2:10 (2:10) (0-145,140) 5-Y-0+
£23,255 (£7,364; £3,488; £1,162; £775; £387)

RPR
1 Pairofbrowneyes (IRE)[42] 2527 6-10-6 122..................(p) MPFogarty 134+
(Barry John Murphy, Ire) chsd ldrs in 3rd: led 8th and clr bef 3 out: advantage reduced bef next: styd on wl run-in 11/2[2]
2 4 1/4 Killer Crow (IRE)[14] 3074 6-10-11 127..................(t) KevinSexton 136
(Gordon Elliott, Ire) hld up: clsr towards inner at 6th: nt fluent 9th: prog again on inner after 3 out: chsd ldr in 2nd bef next: no imp run-in: kpt on same pce 4/1[1]
3 3 1/2 Leavethelighton (IRE)[14] 3073 8-11-4 134..................(p) MPButler 138
(Eoin Doyle, Ire) racd in mid-div: prog bef 2 out in 5th: kpt on wl into 3rd after last: nt rch principals 16/1
4 2 3/4 Leap Dearg (IRE)[29] 2794 7-11-2 132.................. PhillipEnright 134
(Robert Tyner, Ire) hld up: prog 3 out: rdn in 3rd bef next: no imp and dropped to 4th after last: kpt on one pce 9/1
5 6 Black Zero (IRE)[7] 3180 7-9-7 112..................(b) ConorMaxwell[(3)] 110
(Michael J McDonagh, Ire) chsd ldr in 2nd: rdn and nt qckn in 4th bef 2 out: no ex in 5th whn nt fluent last 14/1
6 9 Rightville Boy (IRE)[31] 2738 7-9-11 113.................. DGHogan 100
(Patrick Neville, Ire) racd in rr tl prog 5 out where hmpd: wnt remote 6th 2 out: nvr on terms 8/1
7 8 Unzing (FR)[21] 2943 7-9-10 117.................. AndrewRing[(5)] 96
(Mrs S A Bramall, Ire) racd in mid-div: rdn and nt qckn after 3 out: sn no ex 7/1[3]
P Page Turner (IRE)[273] 5055 10-11-4 139..................(b) AmbroseMcCurtin[(5)]
(John J Walsh, Ire) led: hdd 8th: sn wknd: p.u bef 2 out 10/1
P Sonny B (IRE)[17] 3002 8-10-12 128..................(t) BrianO'Connell
(John J Walsh, Ire) chsd ldrs in 4th tl mstke 5 out: sn wknd: p.u bef 2 out 9/1
P Kylecrue (IRE)[35] 2675 8-10-5 121..................(b) DannyMullins
(John Patrick Ryan, Ire) hld up: dropped to rr after 5th: p.u after 3 out 8/1
F Noble Emperor (IRE)[36] 2655 7-11-10 140.................. NiallPMadden
(A J Martin, Ire) racd in mid-div tl fell 5 out 8/1

5m 44.7s (344.70) 11 Ran SP% 122.9
CSF £30.04 CT £343.63 TOTE £5.90: £2.00, £1.90, £4.40; DF 26.10 Trifecta £485.50.
Owner Fibbage Syndicate **Bred** Raymond McDonnell **Trained** Enniscorthy, Co Wexford

FOCUS
A very solid performance of galloping and particularly jumping by the winner and there could be another big day in him. A small personal best from each of the first two.

3303 - 3305a (Foreign Racing) - See Raceform Interactive

3098 **CATTERICK** (L-H)
Monday, December 28

OFFICIAL GOING: Soft (chs 6.6; hdl 6.9)
Wind: fresh 1/2 behind Weather: overcast

3306 WATCH ON 3 DEVICES RACINGUK.COM/ANYWHERE MAIDEN HURDLE (DIV I) (8 hdls) 1m 7f 156y
11:55 (11:55) (Class 4) 3-Y-0+ £3,898 (£1,144; £572; £286)

Form RPR
0-52 1 Champagne At Tara[40] 2564 6-11-6 127.................. RichieMcLernon 130+
(Jonjo O'Neill) trckd ldrs: 2nd 2 out: drvn upsides between last 2: hit last: led last 75yds: kpt on 4/1[3]
22 2 1 3/4 Tippmanboy (IRE)[30] 2769 5-11-6 117.................. WillKennedy 127
(Dr Richard Newland) led: jnd between last 2: hdd and no ex last 75yds 9/4[1]
3 6 Blue Rambler[264] 5-11-6 0.................. AidanColeman 122+
(John Ferguson) trckd ldrs: effrt 2 out: one pce between last 2 4/1[3]
4 11 William Of Orange[66] 4-11-6 0.................. HenryBrooke 111
(Donald McCain) sn chsng ldrs: drvn 5th: outpcd sn after next: tk modest 4th between last 2 8/1
2 5 26 Deauville Dancer (IRE)[17] 3021 4-11-6 0.................. BrianHughes 87
(David Dennis) chsd ldr: wkng whn mstke 2 out: sn bhd: b.b.v 11/4[2]
4000 6 12 Zakety Zak[17] 3022 4-11-6 0.................. PeterBuchanan 72
(James Turner) in rr: tk distant 6th appr last 250/1
6 7 4 Seraffimo[104] 1415 3-10-0 0.................. FinianO'Toole[(7)] 55
(Sharon Watt) prom: lost pl bef 3 out: sn bhd 250/1
60- 8 13 Snow Prince[53] 4941 4-11-6 0.................. TomScudamore 55
(Steve Gollings) in rr-div: hdwy 5th: lost pl next: sn bhd 50/1
9 4 1/2 Iman (GER)[256] 5-11-6 0..................[1] JakeGreenall 51
(Sophie Leech) stdd s: hld up in rr: hdwy 5th: lost pl next: sn bhd: hung rt and eased between last 2 66/1
0 10 39 Lipstickandpowder (IRE)[13] 3099 3-9-11 0.................. HarryChalloner[(3)]
(Dianne Sayer) in rr: bhd fr 5th: t.o 2 out 250/1
P 11 53 Hugh's Secret (IRE)[13] 3099 3-10-2 0.................. NathanMoscrop[(5)]
(Philip Kirby) nt fluent in rr: bhd fr 3rd: t.o next: eventually completed 250/1
0/ P Mary May[15] 7-10-6 0.................. JamesCorbett[(7)]
(Susan Corbett) in rr: j.lft 1st: bhd whn hung bdly rt bnd after 3rd and p.u 250/1
0-0P P Rebel Roger[30] 2791 6-11-6 0..................[1] JonathanEngland
(Tina Jackson) in rr: bhd and drvn 3rd: tailed rt off whn p.u bef next 250/1

3m 49.9s (-2.60) Going Correction +0.05s/f (Yiel)
WFA 3 from 4yo+ 13lb 13 Ran SP% 114.4
Speed ratings (Par 105): 108,107,104,98,85 79,77,71,68,49 22, ,
CSF £13.51 TOTE £4.90: £1.70, £1.10, £1.80; EX 12.20 Trifecta £42.50.
Owner John P McManus **Bred** A M Armitage **Trained** Cheltenham, Gloucs

FOCUS
After only 1mm of overnight rain the official going remained soft. Bends moved out 3yds and races 1, 2, 4 & 6 increased by 18yds, race 3 by 27yds and race 5 & 7 by 36yds. The opener was an interesting maiden hurdle, in which they went a good gallop, and the two with the most solid form claims fought out the finish. A pb from the winner.

3307 YORKSHIRE-OUTDOORS.CO.UK (S) H'CAP HURDLE (8 hdls) 1m 7f 156y
12:25 (12:25) (Class 5) (0-100,100) 3-Y-0+ £2,599 (£763; £381; £190)

Form RPR
-00P 1 Notebook[16] 3043 4-10-2 83..................(p) ThomasCheesman[(7)] 84
(Martin Smith) t.k.h: hdwy to ld bef 2nd: kpt on fr 2 out: hld on clsng stages 16/1
6405 2 1 1/2 Strait Run (IRE)[13] 3098 4-10-5 82..................(tp) JoeColliver[(3)] 82
(Micky Hammond) in rr: nt fluent 4th: hdwy 3 out: upsides next: hung rt run-in: kpt on towards fin 12/1
05-5 3 1 1/4 Orchard Road (USA)[24] 2893 8-11-12 100..................(t) JonathanEngland 98
(Tristan Davidson) chsd ldrs: upsides 3 out: kpt on same pce last 100yds 10/3[2]
4453 4 5 Sendiym (FR)[21] 2946 8-10-12 86..................(p) BrianHughes 79
(Dianne Sayer) chsd ldrs: outpcd and modest 4th appr 2 out 11/4[1]
0-05 5 7 Bountiful Bess[8] 3177 5-11-4 92..................(tp) BrianHarding 78
(Pam Sly) towards rr: pushed along after 3rd: hdwy to chse ldrs 3 out: lost pl bef next 17/2
6P50 6 7 Toarmandowithlove (IRE)[34] 2706 7-10-11 92..........(t) JamesCorbett[(7)] 71
(Susan Corbett) in rr: drvn 4th: hdwy to chse ldrs 3 out: lost pl bef next 33/1
-052 7 5 Anginola (IRE)[2] 3233 6-10-1 75..................(v) TomScudamore 49
(David Dennis) chsd ldrs: reminders 3 out: lost pl bef next: sn bhd 7/2[3]
3630 8 8 Impeccability[31] 2745 5-11-11 99..................(p) HenryBrooke 65
(John Mackie) in rr: bhd fr 3 out 16/1
4P36 9 10 Bertielicious[9] 3161 7-9-7 74 oh13..................(p) ThomasDowson[(7)] 30
(Jonathan Haynes) in rr: drvn 4th: nt fluent and lost pl 3 out: sn wl bhd 100/1
00-P 10 48 Mubrook (USA)[26] 2843 10-10-12 93..................(b) LorcanMurtagh[(7)] 1
(John David Riches) led: hdd bef 2nd: drvn bef 4th: lost pl 3 out: sn wl bhd: t.o next: eventually completed 28/1
046- P Air Chief[299] 4556 10-11-3 94.................. JohnKington[(3)]
(Andrew Crook) in rr: drvn 3rd: sn bhd: tailed rt off 3 out: p.u bef next 18/1

3m 55.3s (2.80) Going Correction +0.05s/f (Yiel)
WFA 4 from 5yo+ 5lb 11 Ran SP% 114.6
Speed ratings (Par 103): 95,94,93,91,87 84,81,77,72,48
CSF £182.63 CT £798.39 TOTE £19.00: £5.40, £3.80, £1.60; EX 252.20 Trifecta £2338.20.
Owner Little Princess Racing **Bred** Mr & Mrs G Middlebrook **Trained** Newmarket, Suffolk

FOCUS
Race distance increased by 18yds. A typically modest selling handicap. The winner is entitled to rate higher on Flat form.

3308 TERRY VEPERS H'CAP CHASE (16 fncs) 2m 3f 51y
1:00 (1:00) (Class 5) (0-100,94) 4-Y-0+ £3,249 (£954; £477; £238)

Form RPR
3-2F 1 Runswick Relax[26] 2844 9-9-11 68 oh1..................(tp) HarryChalloner[(3)] 90+
(Kenneth Slack) chsd ldrs: drvn appr 3 out: upsides 2 out: led last 150yds: drvn rt out 11/4[1]
-456 2 1 1/4 Rosquero (FR)[18] 2981 10-9-12 73..................(b[1]) ThomasDowson[(7)] 93
(Kenny Johnson) chsd ldrs: 2nd 11th: led 2 out: hdd last 150yds: no ex 12/1
5-25 3 18 Trouble In Paris (IRE)[30] 2786 8-9-9 70..................(tp) LorcanMurtagh[(7)] 73
(Barry Murtagh) in tch: chsd ldrs 6th: outpcd whn hit 10th and next: modest 4th 4 out: kpt on run-in to take modest 3rd last 150yds 11/1
-522 4 1 3/4 Bollin Line[13] 3103 8-11-5 87.................. DannyCook 87
(Lucinda Egerton) in rr: hdwy to chse ldrs 6th: drvn 9th: outpcd whn hit 12th: kpt on fr 3 out: tk modest 4th last 100yds 7/2[2]
-42P 5 1 3/4 Newspage (IRE)[34] 2707 9-11-2 84..................(b) BrianHughes 83
(John Wade) led to 3rd: led bef 8th: hdd 2 out: modest 3rd last: sn wknd 17/2
0345 6 22 Morning With Ivan (IRE)[13] 3103 5-11-12 94.................. HenryBrooke 71
(Martin Todhunter) in rr: bhd fr 11th: t.o 3 out 16/1
3P03 7 1/2 Odds On Dan (IRE)[13] 3103 9-10-3 76..................(tp) DeanPratt[(5)] 52
(Lucinda Egerton) in rr: hdd and drvn 10th: t.o 3 out 8/1
0-R0 P Zazamix (FR)[13] 3103 10-10-1 72..................(v) JohnKington[(3)]
(Andrew Crook) chsd ldrs: drvn 8th: sn lost pl and bhd: t.o 11th: p.u bef 2 out 28/1
U331 P Ivans Back (IRE)[25] 2866 10-11-12 94.................. AdamWedge
(Nick Kent) trckd ldrs: led 5th: hdd bef 8th: wknd qckly 4 out: sn bhd: t.o whn p.u bef 2 out: b.b.v 13/2[3]

P-PP **P** **Fozy Moss**[29] 2800 9-10-13 **81** BrianHarding
(Sheena Walton) *hld up in rr: bhd and drvn sn after 8th: t.o 10th: p.u bef 3 out* **33/1**

5m 0.3s (300.30) **10** Ran SP% **112.2**
CSF £33.55 CT £303.90 TOTE £3.60: £1.60, £2.80, £3.40; EX 34.90 Trifecta £296.90.
Owner A Slack **Bred** Mrs S Barraclough **Trained** Hilton, Cumbria

■ Stewards' Enquiry : Harry Challoner two-day ban; used his whip above the permitted level (11th-12th Jan)

FOCUS
Race distance increased by 27yds. Even for the grade this was a very moderate handicap chase. The first two were very well in on the best of their form.

3309 WATCH ON 3 DEVICES RACINGUK.COM/ANYWHERE MAIDEN HURDLE (DIV II) (8 hdls) 1m 7f 156y

1:35 (1:35) (Class 4) 3-Y-0+ **£3,898** (£1,144; £572; £286)

Form | | | RPR

1 **Always Resolute**[73] 4-11-6 0 DannyCook 127+
(Brian Ellison) *trckd ldrs: led 5th: wandered appr 2 out: 10 l ahd whn j.lft last: easily* **10/3**[3]

2 *13* **Caged Lightning (IRE)**[61] 5-11-6 0 TomScudamore 109
(Steve Gollings) *chsd ldrs: clr 2nd bef 3 out: one pce 2 out* **9/4**[1]

F4 **3** *14* **Keep Up (GER)**[13] 3099 3-10-4 0 AdamNicol(3) 82
(Philip Kirby) *hld up towards rr: hdwy 4th: modest 3rd 3 out: mstke next: nvr a threat* **10/1**

43 **4** *12* **Multi Grain**[26] 2845 3-10-0 102 BrianHughes 64
(Micky Hammond) *mid-div: chsd ldrs: modest 4th 3 out: nvr a factor* **14/1**

5 *8* **Lord Golan**[232] 7-11-6 0 AdamWedge 76
(Nick Kent) *mid-div: hdwy 4th: outpcd next: wknd bef 2 out* **28/1**

60 **6** *5* **Cactus Valley (IRE)**[17] 3022 6-11-6 0 (t) JakeGreenall 70
(Michael Easterby) *hld up towards rr: hdwy 4th: lost pl bef 3 out* **66/1**

4 **7** *6* **Will Take Charge (IRE)**[94] 1644 4-11-6 0 RichieMcLernon 64
(Jonjo O'Neill) *chsd ldrs: hung lft and lost pl 5th: bhd fr next* **8/1**

6/P **8** *2 1/4* **Sory**[233] 200 8-11-6 0 JonathanEngland 62
(Tina Jackson) *hld up in rr: bhd fr 4th: sme late hdwy* **100/1**

5-40 **9** *3/4* **Temple Tiger**[17] 3021 5-11-6 0 PeterBuchanan 61
(James Turner) *in rr: bhd fr 4th* **100/1**

P0 **10** *7* **Qatea (IRE)**[13] 3099 3-10-2 0 (t) JamesCowley(5) 41
(Donald McCain) *mid-div: nt fluent 5th: reminders and sn lost pl: bhd fr 2 out* **66/1**

11 *15* **Just Like Dylan (IRE)**[79] 1865 4-11-6 0 LucyAlexander 39
(Barry Murtagh) *in rr: hit 2nd: bhd fr 4th* **25/1**

6-4 **P** **Park Place**[17] 3022 5-11-6 0 JamesReveley
(John Quinn) *t.k.h: led: hdd 5th: lost pl next: sn eased and bhd: p.u bef 2 out: b.b.v* **3/1**[2]

3m 52.3s (-0.20) **Going Correction** +0.05s/f (Yiel)
WFA 3 from 4yo 13lb 4 from 5yo+ 5lb **12** Ran SP% **118.0**
Speed ratings (Par 105): **102,95,88,82,78 76,73,71,71,68 60,**
CSF £11.17 TOTE £4.60: £1.70, £1.50, £3.50; EX 12.60 Trifecta £78.30.
Owner Market Avenue Racing Club Ltd **Bred** Jarvis Associates **Trained** Norton, N Yorks

FOCUS
Race distance increased by 18yds. Little depth to division two of the maiden hurdle and they finished well strung out. The easy winner is rated in line with his best Flat form.

3310 RAYDALE PRESERVES H'CAP CHASE (19 fncs) 3m 1f 54y

2:10 (2:10) (Class 4) (0-110,110) 4-Y-0+
£6,881 (£2,032; £1,016; £508; £254; £127)

Form | | | RPR

25/P **1** **Gonalston Cloud (IRE)**[232] 8-10-8 **92** AdamWedge 112+
(Nick Kent) *trckd ldrs: 2nd appr 3 out: led appr last: drvn and styd on* **8/1**

2-1R **2** *2 1/4* **Jac The Legend**[36] 2669 6-11-12 **110** (p) WillKennedy 124
(Brian Ellison) *mid-div: chsd ldrs 11th: 3rd last: chsd wnr fnl 200yds: no real imp* **13/2**[2]

333U **3** *3 1/4* **Swing Hard (IRE)**[30] 2788 7-11-9 **107** DannyCook 118
(Sue Smith) *w ldrs: led 5th: hdd appr last: kpt on one pce* **6/1**[1]

5111 **4** *1 3/4* **Verko (FR)**[15] 3059 6-10-13 **104** FinianO'Toole(7) 114
(Micky Hammond) *in rr: sme hdwy and poor 7th 4 out: 4th 2 out: kpt on same pce* **9/1**

-046 **5** *36* **Apache Pilot**[34] 2708 7-9-8 **85** (tp) ThomasDowson(7) 58
(Maurice Barnes) *chsd ldrs 3rd: hit 11th: lost pl 15th: sn bhd: t.o* **11/1**

43-P **6** *2 1/4* **Whats Up Woody (IRE)**[44] 2491 10-11-2 **105** JonathonBewley(5) 76
(George Bewley) *w ldrs: wknd qckly between last 2: bhd whn j.rt last: sn t.o* **8/1**

P-00 **P** **Apache Blue (IRE)**[31] 2751 11-10-2 **86** (bt) HenryBrooke
(Kenneth Slack) *mid-div: chsd ldrs 8th: hit 11th: lost pl 13th: sn bhd: t.o whn p.u bef 2 out* **14/1**

1013 **P** **Urban Gale (IRE)**[34] 2708 10-10-7 **96** (p) DaraghBourke(5)
(Joanne Foster) *chsd ldrs: reminders 6th: lost pl and bhd 11th: t.o whn p.u bef 4 out* **12/1**

-232 **P** **Drumlister (IRE)**[21] 2950 9-11-7 **105** (p) BrianHughes
(Dianne Sayer) *led to 5th: drvn 11th: sn lost pl and bhd: t.o whn p.u bef next* **8/1**

/4P- **P** **Frank The Slink**[421] 2220 9-11-8 **109** JoeColliver(3)
(Micky Hammond) *mid-div: lost pl and p.u bef 9th* **50/1**

3P-P **P** **Shinooki (IRE)**[26] 2848 8-11-9 **107** (p) JamesReveley
(Alex Hales) *nt fluent towards rr: hit 10th: sn bhd: t.o whn p.u bef 14th* **18/1**

6100 **P** **Feast Of Fire (IRE)**[17] 3024 8-10-10 **101** RyanDay(7)
(Mike Sowersby) *in rr: nt fluent: blnd bdly and rdr briefly lost iron 4th: sn bhd: t.o 12th: p.u bef 14th* **33/1**

-335 **P** **Rebel Benefit (IRE)**[18] 2988 7-11-8 **106** TomScudamore
(David Dennis) *chsd ldrs: mstke 4th: wkng whn blnd 15th: bhd whn p.u bef 3 out* **7/1**[3]

6m 44.3s (2.30) **Going Correction** +0.20s/f (Yiel) **13** Ran SP% **116.3**
Speed ratings (Par 105): **104,103,102,101,90 89, , , , ,**
CSF £58.73 CT £337.10 TOTE £9.00: £3.50, £2.10, £2.10; EX 70.10 Trifecta £546.10.
Owner R J Jackson **Bred** Conna Stud **Trained** Brigg, Lincs

FOCUS
Race distance increased by 36yds. A modest and open-looking staying chase but it was competitive for the grade. The winner should go in again.

3311 COME RACING AGAIN NEW YEAR'S DAY CHASE (A NOVICES' LIMITED H'CAP) (12 fncs) 1m 7f 145y

2:45 (2:45) (Class 4) (0-120,120) 4-Y-0+
£6,881 (£2,032; £1,016; £508; £254; £127)

Form | | | RPR

-241 **1** **Nautical Twilight**[18] 2979 5-11-0 **112** (b) BrianHughes 126+
(Malcolm Jefferson) *hld up off pce: hdwy 6th: trcking ldrs 8th: cl 2nd 2 out: led on bit last: shkn up and wnt clr: eased last 75yds* **3/1**[2]

P0-P **2** *10* **Oficial Ben (IRE)**[25] 2865 6-10-1 **106** (t) PatrickCowley(7) 107
(Jonjo O'Neill) *sn trcking ldrs: led 5th: hdd last: no ch w wnr* **17/2**

F111 **3** *10* **Truckers Highway (IRE)**[10] 3141 6-11-1 **116** HarryChalloner(3) 107
(John Groucott) *led to 2nd: outpcd and lost pl 4th: kpt on fr 3 out: tk modest 3rd sn after last* **7/4**[1]

-046 **4** *1* **Discay**[19] 2977 6-11-8 **120** (tp) WillKennedy 112
(Dr Richard Newland) *mstkes: w ldrs: led 2nd tl after 4th: reminders 6th: outpcd appr 2 out: hit last 2: tk modest 4th sn after last* **13/2**[3]

-15P **5** *3/4* **Wolf Sword (IRE)**[37] 2645 6-11-3 **115** HenryBrooke 103
(George Moore) *nt jump wl: sn detached and bhd: kpt on fr 3 out: tk modest 4th last 150yds* **13/2**[3]

4-P0 **6** *7* **Engrossing**[26] 2846 6-10-10 **113** JamieHamilton(5) 109+
(Peter Niven) *trckd ldrs: led after 4th: hdd next: 3rd and wl hld whn blnd bdly last: sn lost pl and eased* **10/1**

6-04 **7** *11* **Our Phylli Vera (IRE)**[60] 2144 6-10-0 **101** oh16.....[1] ColmMcCormack(3) 71
(Joanne Foster) *sn detached in rr: t.o 5th: nvr on terms* **50/1**

4m 3.2s (3.10) **Going Correction** +0.20s/f (Yiel) **7** Ran SP% **109.6**
Speed ratings (Par 105): **100,95,90,89,89 85,80**
CSF £24.90 TOTE £3.40: £1.50, £4.00; EX 23.90 Trifecta £69.20.
Owner Capt M S Bagley **Bred** J M Jefferson **Trained** Norton, N Yorks

FOCUS
Race distance increased by 18yds. A fair handicap chase for novices and the gallop was sound throughout. The cosy winner is on the upgrade.

3312 GO RACING IN YORKSHIRE WINTER FESTIVAL CONDITIONAL JOCKEYS' H'CAP HURDLE (12 hdls) 3m 1f 71y

3:15 (3:15) (Class 4) (0-110,110) 4-Y-0+ **£3,898** (£1,144; £572; £286)

Form | | | RPR

4442 **1** **Valleyofmilan (IRE)**[26] 2848 8-11-6 **110** JamesCowley(6) 121+
(Donald McCain) *hld up: hdwy to trck ldrs 4th: led sn after 3 out: drew clr fr 2 out: hit last: eased clsng stages* **4/1**[2]

31F3 **2** *12* **Jumpandtravel (IRE)**[8] 3178 6-11-1 **102** JoeColliver(3) 101
(Micky Hammond) *in rr: hdwy 6th: chsng ldrs 3 out: 2nd bef 2 out: sn no ch w wnr* **16/1**

4351 **3** *33* **Turtle Cask (IRE)**[13] 3102 6-11-3 **101** (p) JamieHamilton 66
(Dianne Sayer) *led: hit 2nd: hdd bef next: drvn 7th: outpcd after 3 out: distant 3rd next* **10/3**[1]

3UF4 **4** *1 1/4* **Mission Complete (IRE)**[15] 3062 9-10-7 **99** (tp) JackSavage(8) 60
(Jonjo O'Neill) *chsd ldrs: drvn 8th: lost pl bef 2 out: distant 4th last* **11/1**

2PU2 **5** *43* **Be A Dreamer**[24] 2889 7-9-10 **88** StephenMcCarthy(8) 6
(Sue Smith) *w ldrs: led bef 3rd: hdd sn after 3 out: wknd last: heavily eased: t.o* **6/1**

-410 **P** **Dusky Bob (IRE)**[29] 2800 10-10-13 **100** CraigGallagher(3)
(Brian Ellison) *chsd ldrs: drvn and lost pl 7th: bhd fr 3 out: t.o whn p.u bef next* **8/1**

0U03 **P** **Goodoldhonkytonk (IRE)**[15] 3067 7-10-13 **102**(b) WilliamFeatherstone(5)
(James Evans) *in rr: hdwy 4th: reminders and lost pl next: sme hdwy 8th: lost pl next: sn bhd: t.o whn p.u bef 2 out* **5/1**[3]

4060 **P** **Lawsons Thorns (IRE)**[134] 1273 6-10-8 **95** RyanDay(3)
(Mike Sowersby) *t.k.h in last: bhd 3rd: drvn 6th: t.o whn p.u after next* **14/1**

-05P **P** **Wee Jock Elliot**[22] 2937 5-10-5 **89** (tp) CraigNichol
(Alistair Whillans) *chsd ldrs: drvn and lost pl 7th: brief effrt 3 out: sn lost pl and bhd: t.o whn p.u bef next* **16/1**

6m 36.6s (9.00) **Going Correction** +0.05s/f (Yiel) **9** Ran SP% **111.9**
Speed ratings (Par 105): **87,83,72,72,58 , , ,**
CSF £59.52 CT £231.78 TOTE £4.30: £2.10, £3.10, £1.60; EX 51.70 Trifecta £257.60.
Owner Tim & Miranda Johnson **Bred** Kenneth William Quinn **Trained** Cholmondeley, Cheshire

■ Stewards' Enquiry : James Cowley two-day ban; used his whip whilst clearly winning (11th-12th Jan)

FOCUS
Race distance increased by 36yds. Only a modest handicap and another easy winner on the card. He's rated in line with his old hurdles mark.
T/Plt: £175.20 to a £1 stake. Pool: £32,235.86 - 230.74 winning units. T/Qpdt: £22.60 to a £1 stake. Pool: £6,546.31 - 213.70 winning units. **Walter Glynn**

2972 LEICESTER (R-H)

Monday, December 28

OFFICIAL GOING: Chase course - soft (heavy in places; 6.2); hurdles course - heavy (4.0)
Wind: Light behind Weather: Fine

3313 STILTON H'CAP CHASE (12 fncs) 1m 7f 201y

12:50 (12:52) (Class 3) (0-125,120)
4-Y-0+ **£6,498** (£1,908; £954; £477)

Form | | | RPR

/012 **1** **Moscow Me (IRE)**[25] 2857 8-11-0 **108** JeremiahMcGrath 117+
(Henry Oliver) *chsd ldr: led 4th to 6th: led again 8th: hdd bef next: led appr last: rdn out* **9/4**[1]

-565 **2** *3 1/4* **Gold Ingot**[19] 2975 8-11-7 **115** AndrewThornton 120
(Caroline Bailey) *racd wd: chsd ldrs: led 6th to 8th: led again 4 out: rdn and hdd appr last: styd on same pce flat* **5/1**

55-P **3** *3* **Supreme Asset (IRE)**[44] 2497 7-11-9 **117** WayneHutchinson 121
(Donald McCain) *hld up: nt fluent 5th: hdwy 8th: ev ch 2 out: no ex flat* **9/2**[3]

-030 **4** *1 1/4* **Kerryhead Storm (IRE)**[35] 2691 10-11-5 **113** (t) CharliePoste 116
(Matt Sheppard) *led to 4th: chsd ldrs: rdn whn mstke 2 out: styd on same pce* **7/2**[2]

-P34 **5** *41* **Rebel High (IRE)**[53] 2303 11-10-0 94 oh29.....................(v) LiamTreadwell 54
(Derek Frankland) *hld up: pushed along 7th: wknd after next: bhd whn j.lft last* 80/1

-205 **U** **Le Fin Bois (FR)**[23] 2897 5-11-12 120.............................. AlainCawley
(Richard Hobson) *prom tl wnt wrong appr and uns rdr 3rd* 7/2[2]

4m 12.2s (4.00) **Going Correction** +0.40s/f (Soft) **6** Ran SP% **111.3**
Speed ratings (Par 107): **106,104,102,102,81**
CSF £13.54 TOTE £2.70: £1.40, £3.40; EX 12.90 Trifecta £47.80.
Owner Oscar Singh & Miss Priya Purewal **Bred** Egmont Stud **Trained** Abberley, Worcs

FOCUS
The bends had been moved out adding 6yds to the race distance. A modest handicap chase run on testing ground but a win for the favourite, who's on the upgrade.

3314 PARSLEY (S) HURDLE (10 hdls) 2m 4f 110y
1:25 (1:26) (Class 5) 4-Y-0+ £3,249 (£954; £477; £238)

Form RPR

120/ **1** **Cotillion**[12] 4851 9-10-12 124..............................(t) RichardJohnson 125+
(Ian Williams) *hld up: hdwy to chse ldr bef 3 out: led appr next: sn clr: easily* 5/4[1]

P203 **2** *12* **Bar A Mine (FR)**[26] 2855 6-10-12 105..................(v) SamTwiston-Davies 105
(Nigel Twiston-Davies) *mde most tl rdn and hdd appr 2 out: sn btn* 11/4[2]

/4-5 **3** *16* **On The Right Path**[36] 2667 8-10-7 102........................ CiaranGethings(5) 89
(Barry Leavy) *hld up: hdwy 3 out: sn wknd: wnt 3rd flat* 9/1

3-02 **4** *5* **Boston Blue**[25] 2858 8-11-4 112.............................. LeeEdwards 95
(Tony Carroll) *prom: lost pl after 1st: wnt prom 3rd: rdn appr 3 out: wknd next: blnd last* 7/1[3]

PP56 **5** *24* **Walkabout Creek (IRE)**[25] 2858 8-11-4 88..................(vt) LiamTreadwell 66
(Derek Frankland) *chsd ldr: led briefly 4th: rdn whn hit 3 out: sn wknd* 66/1

635P **6** *7* **Humbel Ben (IRE)**[14] 3088 12-10-12 84.........................(p) NickScholfield 53
(Alan Jones) *hld up: bhd fr 5th* 100/1

P-20 **P** **Secret Dancer (IRE)**[17] 3015 10-10-12 98..........................(p) RhysFlint
(Alan Jones) *chsd ldrs: lost pl 6th: wnt prom again next: rdn and wknd appr 3 out: bhd whn p.u bef next* 16/1

26-5 **P** **Edlomond (IRE)**[18] 2987 9-10-13 109..............................(t) RyanWhile(5)
(Bill Turner) *prom tl rdn and wknd appr 3 out: bhd whn p.u bef next* 16/1

P-P **P** **Lord Of The Hosts**[24] 2879 4-10-7 0..............................(b[1]) LizzieKelly(5)
(Nick Williams) *plld hrd and prom: mstke 7th: sn rdn and wknd: bhd whn p.u after 3 out* 10/1

5m 36.8s (12.10) **Going Correction** +0.575s/f (Soft)
WFA 4 from 6yo+ 6lb **9** Ran SP% **116.9**
Speed ratings (Par 103): **99,94,88,86,77 74,,,**
CSF £4.93 TOTE £2.10: £1.10, £1.50, £2.50; EX 5.00 Trifecta £30.90.
Owner Jamie Robert Roberts **Bred** Mr & Mrs G Middlebrook **Trained** Portway, Worcs

FOCUS
Rail movement added 24yds to the race distance. An uncompetitive seller and a very easy winner. The second is probably the best guide.

3315 LEICESTERSHIRE SILVER FOX H'CAP CHASE (QUALIFIER FOR THE CHALLENGER MIDDLE DISTANCE CHASE FINAL) (15 fncs) 2m 4f 45y
2:00 (2:03) (Class 3) (0-125,127) 4-Y-0+ £9,495 (£2,805; £1,402; £702; £351)

0-15 **1** **Mystifiable**[45] 2472 7-10-13 112..............................(t) PaddyBrennan 128+
(Fergal O'Brien) *hld up: hdwy 6th: led appr 3 out: clr last: styd on wl* 11/2

1645 **2** *7* **Valadom (FR)**[17] 3017 6-11-12 125..............................(t) AlainCawley 132
(Richard Hobson) *led: rdn and hdd bef 3 out: styd on same pce appr last* 8/1

4-14 **3** *1 ¼* **The Italian Yob (IRE)**[46] 2459 7-11-6 124..................(b) LizzieKelly(5) 130
(Nick Williams) *prom: chsd ldr 5th tl rdn appr 4 out: wnt 2nd again bef last tl wknd flat* 5/1

5-12 **4** *8* **Great Link**[23] 2897 6-11-9 122.............................. HarrySkelton 121
(Dan Skelton) *prom: rdn appr 4 out: wknd after 2 out* 11/4[1]

-P51 **5** *99* **Noble Legend**[8] 3176 8-12-0 127 7ex..........................(p) AndrewThornton 26
(Caroline Bailey) *w ldr to 3rd: lost 2nd 5th: sn rdn: wknd 7th* 9/2[3]

3061 **P** **Moorlands Jack**[56] 2243 10-11-8 121..........................(p) NickScholfield
(Jeremy Scott) *hld up: a in rr: bhd fr 6th: p.u bef 11th* 20/1

3463 **F** **Cloudy Bob (IRE)**[19] 2975 8-11-1 114.............................. LeightonAspell
(Pat Murphy) *hld up: fell 4th* 7/2[2]

5m 22.8s (3.90) **Going Correction** +0.40s/f (Soft) **7** Ran SP% **115.0**
Speed ratings (Par 107): **108,105,104,101,61 ,**
CSF £46.18 CT £233.79 TOTE £7.20: £3.10, £3.80; EX 59.60 Trifecta £421.10.
Owner Graham And Alison Jelley **Bred** Overbury Stallions Ltd **Trained** Naunton, Gloucs

FOCUS
The bends had been moved, adding 10yds to the race distance. The feature race and a fairly competitive handicap chase. The gallop appeared sound and only the winner was travelling in the straight. He was up 10lb on his best hurdles figures.

3316 OLD YEAR NOVICES' HURDLE (10 hdls) 2m 4f 110y
2:35 (2:36) (Class 4) 4-Y-0+ £4,548 (£1,335; £667; £333)

Form RPR

2 **1** **Hit The Highway (IRE)**[43] 2519 6-10-12 0.............................. TomCannon 132+
(Giles Smyly) *led tl after 2nd: lft in ld 4th: rdn clr fr 2 out: wnt lft last: styd on wl* 7/1

635 **2** *13* **Ballycross**[16] 3032 4-10-12 121.............................. SamTwiston-Davies 119
(Nigel Twiston-Davies) *chsd ldrs: hmpd 4th: ev ch and nt fluent 3 out: styd on same pce fr next* 3/1[2]

0-F **3** *1 ¼* **Pine Warbler**[19] 2972 6-10-7 0.............................. CiaranGethings(5) 118
(Stuart Edmunds) *hld up: hdwy appr 3 out: sn rdn: blnd 2 out: styd on same pce* 33/1

1 **4** *8* **Handsome Sam**[19] 2972 4-10-12 0.............................. WayneHutchinson 110
(Alan King) *prom: hit 3 out: sn rdn: wknd last* 7/2[3]

000 **5** *45* **Paris Snow**[18] 2995 5-10-9 0..............................(p) RobMcCarth(3) 63
(Ian Williams) *hld up: wknd after 7th* 100/1

00 **6** *3 ½* **Some Finish (IRE)**[18] 2995 6-10-12 0.............................. CharliePoste 59
(Robin Dickin) *w ldr tl after 2nd: lft disputing ld 4th tl next: wknd after 7th* 200/1

21-2 **7** *9* **Bronco Billy (IRE)**[15] 3056 5-10-12 0.............................. RichardJohnson 50
(Jonjo O'Neill) *hld up: hdwy and hmpd 4th: rdn to chse wnr appr 2 out: sn wknd: j. slowly last* 15/8[1]

8 *14* **Onurbike** 7-10-12 0.............................. MarkGrant 36
(John O'Neill) *hld up: effrt and mstke 7th: sn wknd* 250/1

3/00 **9** *1* **Laraghcon Boy (IRE)**[30] 2772 6-10-12 0.............................. LeeEdwards 35
(Tony Carroll) *hld up: a in rr: wknd after 7th* 300/1

44- **P** **Jamrham (IRE)**[233] 8-10-5 0.............................. HarrisonBeswick(7)
(Sam Thomas) *hld up: hdwy 4th: ev ch 3 out: sn rdn: wknd next: p.u bef last* 250/1

0 **P** **Paradis Blanc (FR)**[44] 2493 4-10-9 0.............................. RyanHatch(3)
(Nigel Twiston-Davies) *hld up: mstke 1st: rdn and wknd after 7th: bhd whn p.u bef last* 100/1

F **Churchtown Champ (IRE)**[79] 1860 5-10-12 0.............................. HarrySkelton
(Dan Skelton) *chsd ldrs: led after 2nd tl fell 4th* 13/2

62- **P** **Mr K (IRE)**[280] 4969 4-10-12 0.............................. LiamTreadwell
(Paul Webber) *plld hrd and prom: lost pl 5th: wknd after 7th: bhd whn p.u bef last* 50/1

0-56 **P** **Jellied Eel Jack (IRE)**[17] 3009 6-10-12 0.............................. AdrianLane
(Donald McCain) *hld up: j.lft 1st: wknd after 7th: bhd whn p.u bef last* 100/1

5m 34.9s (10.20) **Going Correction** +0.575s/f (Soft)
WFA 4 from 5yo+ 6lb **14** Ran SP% **117.3**
Speed ratings (Par 105): **103,98,97,94,77 76,72,67,66, , , ,**
CSF £28.54 TOTE £8.40: £2.20, £1.30, £7.00; EX 32.90 Trifecta £680.50.
Owner Anthony Ward-Thomas **Bred** Ballymorris Stables **Trained** Wormington, Worcs

FOCUS
Rail movements added 24yds to the race distance. This novices' hurdle was run in a time 1.9sec faster than the earlier seller. Fair form, with a step up from the winner.

3317 GREAT GLEN NOVICES' CHASE (15 fncs) 2m 4f 45y
3:10 (3:12) (Class 3) 4-Y-0+ £6,330 (£1,870; £935)

Form RPR

-212 **1** **Bristol De Mai (FR)**[23] 2913 4-10-13 146.............................. SamTwiston-Davies 147+
(Nigel Twiston-Davies) *mde all: j.w: clr fr 2nd: canter* 1/3[1]

1-22 **2** *7* **Bon Chic (IRE)**[22] 2925 6-10-7 127.............................. HarrySkelton 126
(Dan Skelton) *chsd wnr: shkn up appr 3 out: styd on same pce: hit last* 7/1[3]

00-5 **3** *1 ¼* **Join The Clan (IRE)**[51] 2333 6-11-0 136.............................. RichardJohnson 134
(Jonjo O'Neill) *hld up: mstke 2nd: nt fluent next and 7th: shkn up appr last: nvr nr to chal* 4/1[2]

5m 28.0s (9.10) **Going Correction** +0.40s/f (Soft)
WFA 4 from 6yo 6lb **3** Ran SP% **107.5**
Speed ratings (Par 107): **97,94,93**
CSF £2.85 TOTE £1.30; EX 3.10 Trifecta £2.60.
Owner Simon Munir & Isaac Souede **Bred** Jean-Yves Touzaint **Trained** Naunton, Gloucs

FOCUS
The bends had been moved adding 10yds to the race distance. A small but interesting field for this novices' chase, although it turned into something of a procession, and the time was 5.25sec slower than the earlier feature race. Bristol De Mai was value for further and close to his mark.

3318 LEICESTERSHIRE BRONZE FOX H'CAP HURDLE (8 hdls) 1m 7f 113y
3:40 (3:40) (Class 3) (0-125,125) 3-Y-0+ £6,498 (£1,908; £954; £477)

Form RPR

21 **1** **Tara Flow**[20] 2959 5-11-1 114.............................. AidanColeman 130+
(Venetia Williams) *chsd ldrs: wnt 2nd after 5th: led on bit appr 2 out: rdn bef last: styd on: eased nr fin* 9/4[1]

6-00 **2** *12* **Eddiemaurice (IRE)**[42] 2540 4-10-9 108.............................. RhysFlint 111
(John Flint) *hld up: hdwy after 5th: hit 3 out: rdn to chse wnr appr last: styd on same pce* 18/1

2100 **3** *2 ½* **Brave Helios**[43] 2513 5-11-4 122.............................. DanielHiskett(5) 122
(Richard Phillips) *prom: lost pl after 5th: rallied appr last: styd on* 25/1

4351 **4** *6* **Hill Fort**[12] 3108 5-11-2 115..............................(t) CharliePoste 110
(Matt Sheppard) *hld up: hdwy appr 5th: rdn and nt fluent 2 out: wkng whn mstke last* 12/1

-161 **5** *3 ½* **Fair Loch**[57] 2218 7-10-13 117.............................. MeganCarberry(5) 109
(Brian Ellison) *led: rdn and hdd bef 2 out: sn hung lft: wknd last* 16/1

50P2 **6** *13* **El Massivo (IRE)**[29] 2808 5-11-6 122.............................. HarryBannister(3) 99
(Harriet Bethell) *hld up: sme hdwy 3 out: sn wknd* 25/1

5162 **7** *12* **Prairie Town (IRE)**[7] 3196 4-11-12 125.............................. LeeEdwards 90
(Tony Carroll) *pushed along in rr: rdn and wknd appr 3 out* 3/1[2]

3620 **8** *1 ½* **Sword Of The Lord**[18] 2987 5-11-0 113..................(vt) SamTwiston-Davies 77
(Nigel Twiston-Davies) *hld up: rdn and wknd after 5th* 15/2[3]

9 *48* **Blackfire (FR)**[67] 3-10-13 125.............................. RichardJohnson 28
(Jonjo O'Neill) *hld up: hdwy 4th: wknd after next* 15/2[3]

333/ **P** **Looking On**[640] 5061 7-10-8 110.............................. BenPoste(3)
(Edward Bevan) *prom: lost pl after 3rd: wknd 5th: bhd whn p.u bef last* 50/1

010F **P** **Arkaim**[12] 3107 7-11-9 122.............................. KielanWoods
(Pam Sly) *chsd ldr after 2nd tl rdn after 5th: wknd 3 out: bhd whn p.u bef next* 10/1

4m 7.1s (6.10) **Going Correction** +0.575s/f (Soft)
WFA 3 from 4yo+ 13lb **11** Ran SP% **116.9**
Speed ratings (Par 107): **107,101,99,96,95 88,82,81,57,,**
CSF £40.44 CT £815.62 TOTE £3.10: £1.30, £5.40, £4.10; EX 40.60 Trifecta £1072.30.
Owner Kate & Andrew Brooks **Bred** Miss A Gibson Fleming **Trained** Kings Caple, H'fords

FOCUS
Rail movements added 14yds to the race distance. An interesting handicap hurdle featuring some relatively unexposed types, and it produced a clearcut winner. There's probably more to come from her.

T/Jkpt: not won. JACKPOT PLACEPOT: £476.30. Pool: £3360.78 - 5.15 winning units. T/Plt: £291.00 to a £1 stake. Pool: £78,841.10 - 197.75 winning units. T/Qpdt: £110.90 to a £1 stake. Pool: £6,132.44 - 40.90 winning units. **Colin Roberts**

3319 - 3321a (Foreign Racing) - See Raceform Interactive

3291
LEOPARDSTOWN (L-H)
Monday, December 28

OFFICIAL GOING: Hurdle course - soft to heavy changing to heavy after race 1 (12.10); chase course - heavy

3322a SQUARED FINANCIAL CHRISTMAS HURDLE (GRADE 1) (12 hdls) 3m
1:55 (1:55) 4-Y-0+ £39,534 (£12,519; £5,930; £1,976)

RPR

1 **Prince Of Scars (IRE)**[36] 2676 5-11-10 145.............................. DavyRussell 163+
(Gordon Elliott, Ire) *hld up bhd ldrs tl lft 3rd fr 4th: nt fluent 2 out: impr on outer travelling wl to ld bef last: rdn out run-in and kpt on wl* 10/1

2 *4* **Alpha Des Obeaux (FR)**[29] 2815 5-11-10 152.............................. BJCooper 159
(M F Morris, Ire) *chsd ldr tl lft in front fr 4th: pressed clly after 3 out: rdn into st and hdd u.p bef last: no ch w wnr run-in: kpt on same pce* 2/1[2]

3 *5 ½* **Martello Tower (IRE)**[290] 4738 7-11-10 149.............................. APHeskin 154
(Ms Margaret Mullins, Ire) *chsd ldrs tl lft 2nd fr 4th: niggled along briefly after 3 out and sn tl sn wnt 2nd and no imp on easy wnr u.p in 3rd bef last where j. sltly rt: one pce run-in* 7/2[3]

4 2 **Arctic Fire (GER)**29 2815 6-11-10 169 RWalsh 152
(W P Mullins, Ire) *t.k.h to post: w.w in rr: pushed along stl in rr after 2 out and no imp on ldrs into st: one pce after* 5/4[1]
F **Snow Falcon (IRE)**29 2815 5-11-10 145 (b[1]) SeanFlanagan
(Noel Meade, Ire) *led: over 3 l clr whn fell 4th* 22/1
6m 22.2s (2.20) **Going Correction** +0.40s/f (Soft) 5 Ran SP% 113.4
Speed ratings: **112,110,108,108,**
CSF £31.53 TOTE £9.60: £2.80, £1.50; DF 21.40 Trifecta £89.70.
Owner Gigginstown House Stud **Bred** Eamon Salmon **Trained** Longwood, Co Meath
FOCUS
With the favourite clearly not getting home, this was a race in which the average rating of the first three was under 149, so it is hard to see it as proper Grade 1 form in theory, but these are still smart and promising stayers in the main. There may be more to come from Prince Of Scars.

3323a IRISH DAILY STAR CHRISTMAS NOVICE H'CAP HURDLE (8 hdls) 2m
2:30 (2:30) 4-Y-0+ £9,360 (£2,170; £949; £542)

RPR
1 **Whatsforuwontgobyu (IRE)**44 2505 5-11-4 117 BarryGeraghty 132+
(A J Martin, Ire) *hld up: 9th 1/2-way: hdwy on outer bef 2 out to chse ldrs: travelling wl bhd ldrs in 3rd bef last: pushed out to ld after last and kpt on wl under hands and heels: nt extended* 9/2[2]
2 1 3/4 **Mighty Concorde (IRE)**50 2387 5-10-7 106 JackDoyle 118+
(J H Culloty, Ire) *hld up in tch: 6th 1/2-way: tk clsr order bhd ldrs gng wl bef last where slt mstke: rdn into 2nd clsng stages and kpt on wl: nrst fin: nt trble easy wnr* 7/1
3 2 1/2 **Theturnofthesun (IRE)**18 3005 6-9-9 101 (t) KevinSmith(7) 111
(Matthew J Smith, Ire) *chsd ldr: impr to dispute 4 out and led after next: strly pressed u.p bef last: sn hdd and no ch w wnr run-in: one pce clsng stages where dropped to 3rd* 11/1
4 1 3/4 **Elusive Ivy (IRE)**54 2284 5-10-9 108 RobbiePower 116
(Gavin Cromwell, Ire) *chsd ldrs: 4th 1/2-way: gng wl into st: sn rdn and no imp on ldrs u.p in 5th bef last: kpt on one pce run-in* 3/1[1]
5 nk **Camlann (IRE)**14 3090 4-9-12 100 [1] AlanCrowe 105+
(John Joseph Hanlon, Ire) *towards rr: slt mstke 4th: pushed along after 3 out and no imp on ldrs in 9th bef last: kpt on again run-in: nrst fin* 33/1
6 nk **Herminator (FR)**565 5-11-10 123 MrDHDunsdon 130
(W P Mullins, Ire) *mid-div: 8th 1/2-way: hdwy 3 out to chse ldrs in 4th: n.m.r between horses bef last where lost pl and dropped to 7th: kpt on u.p run-in* 11/2[3]
7 shd **Prince Kup (IRE)**44 2505 4-10-10 112 BJCooper 116
(E J O'Grady, Ire) *mid-div: 7th 1/2-way: pushed along on outer after 2 out and impr u.p to chse ldrs in 4th bef last: sn no ex and wknd clsng stages* 7/1
8 11 **First Post (IRE)**40 2584 8-10-6 112 JonathanMoore(7) 108
(Adrian McGuinness, Ire) *chsd ldrs: 3rd 1/2-way: impr to chal gng wl in 3rd into st: rdn and no ex at last where slt mstke: wknd qckly run-in* 33/1
9 8 1/2 **Definite Earl (IRE)**30 2798 7-11-0 113 (t) RobbieColgan 101
(D Broad, Ire) *towards rr: 10th 1/2-way: pushed along in 9th after 2 out and no imp into st: kpt on one pce* 14/1
10 1 1/4 **Deputy Marshall (IRE)**36 2673 6-10-4 108 JackKennedy(5) 95
(Peter Fahey, Ire) *hld up: sltly hmpd after 2 out and sn rdn in rr: no imp into st: kpt on one pce* 16/1
11 nk **Winter Lion (IRE)**30 2798 5-11-2 115 (t) MarkEnright 101
(Matthew J Smith, Ire) *led and clr: jnd 4 out and hdd after next: rdn in 3rd and wknd after 2 out: eased bef last* 10/1
12 27 **Anoosou (FR)**50 2389 11-10-3 102 APHeskin 61
(Barry John Murphy, Ire) *towards rr: rdn after 2 out and no imp u.p in 11th into st: sn wknd and eased* 25/1
U **Next Bend (IRE)**14 3090 4-9-12 100 JJBurke
(Thomas Gibney, Ire) *hld up in tch: 5th 1/2-way: pushed along in 6th bef 2 out: stl in tch whn sddle slipped jst after 2 out and uns rdr* 14/1
4m 15.8s (8.30) **Going Correction** +0.70s/f (Soft) 13 Ran SP% 129.9
WFA 4 from 5yo+ 5lb
Speed ratings: **107,106,104,104,103 103,103,98,93,93 93,79,**
CSF £39.37 CT £342.59 TOTE £4.60: £1.70, £2.40, £3.10; DF 50.60 Trifecta £408.10.
Owner John P McManus **Bred** Tom Baker **Trained** Summerhill, Co. Meath
FOCUS
This was run at a generous pace in the conditions.

3324a LEXUS CHASE (GRADE 1) (17 fncs) 3m
3:05 (3:05) 5-Y-0+
£69,767 (£22,093; £10,465; £3,488; £2,325; £1,162)

RPR
1 **Don Poli (IRE)**23 2900 6-11-10 167 BJCooper 162
(W P Mullins, Ire) *chsd ldrs in 3rd: tk clsr order after 3 out and impr between horses to chal into st: rdn bef last and sn led: kpt on wl u.p w narrow advantage run-in where edgd sltly lft: all out* 4/6[1]
2 1/2 **First Lieutenant (IRE)**30 2783 10-11-10 147 (p) DavyRussell 161
(M F Morris, Ire) *hld up bhd ldrs in 4th: stl gng wl in 4th appr st: clsd u.p into 3rd run-in and r.o wl clsng stages to press wnr in 2nd: hld* 16/1
3 1/2 **Foxrock (IRE)**22 2941 7-11-10 160 (bt[1]) APHeskin 162
(T M Walsh, Ire) *settled in 2nd: disp briefly 7th and again 5 out: nt fluent in 2nd next: rdn after 2 out and lost pl briefly: clsd u.p far side to dispute at last: n.m.r on inner in cl 2nd run-in and dropped to 3rd: kpt on wl* 10/1
4 2 1/4 **On His Own (IRE)**17 3017 11-11-10 157 (b) MrPWMullins 158
(W P Mullins, Ire) *led on outer: jnd briefly at 7th: j. sltly rt at times: jnd briefly again 5 out: in front next and extended ld bef 3 out: rdn and jnd into st: hdd bef last and sn no imp nr side in 4th: kpt on same pce* 25/1
5 18 **Sir Des Champs (FR)**39 2606 9-11-10 160 RWalsh 141
(W P Mullins, Ire) *w.w towards rr: nt fluent 7th: mstke in 5th at 12th: niggled along after 5 out and no imp on ldrs bef 2 out: one pce after* 10/3[2]
6 13 **Carlingford Lough (IRE)**50 2386 9-11-10 163 BarryGeraghty 129
(John E Kiely, Ire) *hld up in rr: niggled along briefly after 9th: pushed along after 7th and no imp struggling bef 4 out: eased run-in* 9/1[3]
6m 35.9s (4.90) **Going Correction** +0.625s/f (Soft) 6 Ran SP% 111.9
Speed ratings: **116,115,115,114,108 104**
CSF £11.62 TOTE £1.50: £1.20, £3.80; DF 10.00 Trifecta £59.60.
Owner Gigginstown House Stud **Bred** Brian J Griffiths And John Nicholson **Trained** Muine Beag, Co Carlow
■ Stewards' Enquiry : Davy Russell one-day ban: used whip with excessive frequency (tbn)
B J Cooper caution: careless riding
FOCUS
A thrilling Grade 1 race certainly, but the ground was too testing for it to provide any new information in the context of the 2016 Cheltenham Gold Cup. THe form is rated around First Lieutenant to last year's form in this race. Don Poli was 6lb off his best.

3325 - 3332a (Foreign Racing) - See Raceform Interactive

3035 DONCASTER (L-H)
Tuesday, December 29

OFFICIAL GOING: Good to soft (soft in places; chs 7.1, hdl 7.2)
Wind: light 1/2 against Weather: fine and sunny

3333 BETDAQ.COM THOROUGHBRED BREEDERS' ASSOCIATION MARES' H'CAP HURDLE (10 hdls) 2m 3f 120y
12:00 (12:00) (Class 4) (0-120,118)
3-Y-0+ £3,898 (£1,144; £572; £286)

Form RPR
5-22 1 **Catherines Well**30 2812 6-11-7 113 RichardJohnson 127+
(Philip Hobbs) *mde all: j.lft 3rd: c clr fr 3 out: eased last 100yds* 2/1[1]
02-3 2 12 **Donna's Pride**22 2949 6-11-4 110 JamesReveley 106
(Keith Reveley) *sn chsng wnr: kpt on same pce fr 3 out* 10/3[2]
0244 3 4 1/2 **Kilty Caul (IRE)**38 2632 6-11-5 114 (t) ConorShoemark(3) 106
(Kim Bailey) *chsd ldrs: drvn 7th: one pce fr next* 16/1
2322 4 49 **Pixiepot**26 2867 5-10-3 95 TomScudamore 43
(Peter Niven) *chsd wnr: j. bdly lft and mstke 1st: lost pl and j.lft 4th: drvn 7th: 4th and no ch whn bdly hmpd and carried bdly lft off trck 3 out: retracd steps: continued tailed rt off* 7/2[3]
2-66 P **Whatdoesthefoxsay (IRE)**200 711 6-11-7 118 JamesCowley(5)
(Donald McCain) *hld up: hdwy to trck ldrs 3rd: blnd and lost pl 7th: sn eased: wl bhd whn p.u bef next* 12/1
0-33 F **Angel Face**38 2644 4-11-1 110 TomBellamy(3)
(Alan King) *chsd ldrs: drvn 7th: modest 4th and wl hld whn fell next* 4/1
4m 48.7s (-2.60) **Going Correction** 0.0s/f (Good)
WFA 4 from 5yo+ 6lb 6 Ran SP% 112.2
Speed ratings (Par 105): **105,100,98,78,**
CSF £9.29 TOTE £2.40: £1.60, £2.20; EX 6.60 Trifecta £148.60.
Owner M W Pendarves **Bred** Mrs E A Pendarves **Trained** Withycombe, Somerset
FOCUS
After a dry night the official going remained good to soft, soft in places. Races 1, 2 & 6 increased by about 15yds, races 3, 5 & 7 by 6yds and race 4 by 24yds. The opener was a fair handicap hurdle for mares, but it was turned into a procession by the front-running winner. She's on the upgrade.

3334 BETDAQ.COM 50% COMMISSION REFUND "NATIONAL HUNT" NOVICES' HURDLE (10 hdls) 2m 3f 120y
12:35 (12:35) (Class 4) 4-Y-0+ £3,249 (£954; £477; £238)

Form RPR
032F 1 **Wade Harper (IRE)**39 2628 5-10-12 127 NoelFehily 120+
(David Dennis) *trckd ldr: led 7th: styd on wl fr 3 out: drvn out* 7/2[2]
3-1 2 3 1/2 **Go Long (IRE)**32 2748 5-11-5 0 AdamWedge 124+
(Evan Williams) *trckd ldrs: 2nd 2 out: 3 l down last: kpt on same pce* 13/8[1]
3 3 3/4 **Royal Milan (IRE)**247 5-10-12 0 (t) RichardJohnson 114+
(Philip Hobbs) *in rr-div: hdwy appr 3 out: sn 4th: nt fluent 2 out: modest 3rd and mstke last* 16/1
3-51 4 8 **Apple Of Our Eye**36 2690 5-11-5 0 AidanColeman 114
(Charlie Longsdon) *trckd ldrs: outpcd 3 out: wknd appr last* 9/1
0-50 5 12 **Spendajennie (IRE)**28 2838 6-10-2 0 MauriceLinehan(3) 88
(Nick Kent) *chsd ldrs: outpcd 3 out: sn wknd* 200/1
5- 6 6 **Beneficial Joe (IRE)**284 4894 5-10-12 0 KielanWoods 90
(Graeme McPherson) *hld up in rr: hdwy appr 3 out: sn outpcd: wknd 2 out* 66/1
5-0 7 3 1/4 **Set In My Ways (IRE)**61 2154 4-10-12 0 TomScudamore 87
(Jonjo O'Neill) *mid-div: hdwy 5th: nt fluent 7th: lost pl bef next* 33/1
6- 8 3 3/4 **Wild Ginger**267 5200 4-10-12 0 RichieMcLernon 84
(Jonjo O'Neill) *in rr-div: sme hdwy 7th: lost pl bef next* 100/1
10 9 6 **Chap**44 2514 5-10-12 0 RyanMahon 78
(Dan Skelton) *mid-div: lost pl 6th* 9/2[3]
00-3 10 6 **The Missus**32 2750 4-10-2 0 HarryBannister(3) 66
(Warren Greatrex) *hld up in mid-div: hdwy to chse ldrs 3rd: pushed along 7th: lost pl bef next* 20/1
1- 11 1/2 **Beggars Cross (IRE)**293 4715 5-10-12 0 WillKennedy 73
(Jonjo O'Neill) *chsd ldrs: stmbld bdly landing 2nd: drvn sn after 7th: lost pl and hit next* 8/1
-604 12 1 **Romanee Vivant**35 2702 5-10-5 0 JackQuinlan 64
(Neil King) *mid-div: drvn after 7th: lost pl bef next* 100/1
5-62 13 19 **Infinityandbeyond (IRE)**19 2998 4-10-12 0 TrevorWhelan 54
(Neil King) *mid-div: hdwy to chse ldrs 3rd: drvn 7th: sn lost pl and bhd* 33/1
55-6 P **Mr Beatle**26 2860 6-10-9 0 TomBellamy(3)
(Kim Bailey) *in rr: reminders after 6th: sn bhd: t.o whn p.u bef next* 100/1
00-P P **Pass On The Mantle**243 26 7-10-12 0 (p) MarkGrant
(Julian Smith) *in rr: mstke 1st: bhd fr 7th: t.o whn hung rt fr 3 out: p.u bef last* 200/1
20-0 P **Shotofwine**18 3021 6-10-12 0 PaddyBrennan
(Nicky Richards) *in rr: bhd and reminders after 6th: p.u bef 2 out* 50/1
-05 P **Bestwork (FR)**89 1717 4-10-12 0 (t) JamesReveley
(Charlie Longsdon) *led: mstke 1st: hdd 6th: bhd next: t.o whn p.u bef 3 out* 100/1
4m 46.9s (-4.40) **Going Correction** 0.0s/f (Good)
WFA 4 from 5yo+ 6lb 17 Ran SP% 124.5
Speed ratings (Par 105): **108,106,105,101,97 94,93,91,89,87 86,86,78, ,**
CSF £9.59 TOTE £4.50: £1.70, £1.40, £3.40; EX 11.90 Trifecta £116.40.
Owner Favourites Racing (Syndication) Ltd 4 **Bred** Mrs J O'Callaghan **Trained** Hanley Swan, Worcestershire
FOCUS
Races distance increased by about 15yds. Plenty of dead wood in this novices' hurdle and the two market leaders came to the fore. The form looks solid.

3335 BETDAQ.COM £25 FREE BET NOVICES' LIMITED H'CAP CHASE (12 fncs) 2m 90y
1:10 (1:10) (Class 3) (0-140,139) 4-Y-0 £6,279 (£1,871; £947; £485; £254)

Form RPR
004- 1 **Baltimore Rock (IRE)**262 5276 6-11-8 139 (t) TomScudamore 143+
(David Pipe) *hld up wl in tch: trckd ldrs 7th: 2nd sn after 4 out: upsides 2 out: shkn up to ld appr last: drvn rt out: edgd lft clsng stages* 3/1[2]
-212 2 1/2 **Katachenko (IRE)**31 2774 6-11-2 133 NoelFehily 136
(Donald McCain) *trckd ldrs 3rd: 2nd 6th: rdn and hung lft bef 2 out: rallied last: kpt on to take 2nd clsng stages* 10/3[3]

3-41 **3** ¾ **The Grey Taylor (IRE)**[68] 2026 6-11-5 **136**.................. RichardJohnson 138
(Brian Ellison) *led: hdd whn hit last: kpt on same pce last 100yds: short of room nr fin* **2/1**[1]

0 **4** 54 **Monyjean (FR)**[49] 2412 4-10-5 **127**.................. AdamWedge 74
(Evan Williams) *in rr: outpcd and bhd fr 7th: lft distant 4th 3 out: t.o* **14/1**

6-0U **5** 35 **Favorite Girl (GER)**[31] 2774 7-10-5 **122**.................. JonathanEngland 43
(Michael Appleby) *chsd ldr: lost pl 6th: t.o 8th: lft distant 5th 3 out* **25/1**

2-44 **F** **Long Lunch**[25] 2885 6-10-8 **125**..................(t) AidanColeman
(Charlie Longsdon) *trckd ldrs: hit 4 out: modest 4th and wl hld whn fell next* **4/1**

4m 0.8s (-4.20) **Going Correction** 0.0s/f (Good)
WFA 4 from 6yo+ 5lb **6** Ran SP% **111.9**
Speed ratings (Par 107): **110,109,109,82,64**
CSF £13.55 TOTE £4.30: £2.00, £2.10; EX 12.70 Trifecta £34.20.
Owner R S Brookhouse **Bred** Lynn Lodge Stud And Foxtale Farm **Trained** Nicholashayne, Devon

FOCUS
Races distance increased by 6yds. An interesting novices' handicap chase and they went an even gallop. Solid form, with more to come from the winner.

3336 DOWNLOAD THE BETDAQ APP H'CAP HURDLE (11 hdls) 3m 96y
1:45 (1:45) (Class 3) (0-140,138) 4-Y-0+ **£6,498** (£1,908; £954; £477)

Form RPR

P-20 **1** **Zeroeshadesofgrey (IRE)**[18] 3018 6-11-12 **138**.................. TrevorWhelan 142+
(Neil King) *nt fluent: mid-div: trcking ldrs 3rd: upsides 2 out: led between last 2: edgd rt appr last: all out* **11/4**[1]

11-1 **2** nk **Top Billing**[31] 2767 6-11-2 **135**.................. RyanDay(7) 136
(Nicky Richards) *led 1st: hdd 2 out: swtchd lft appr last: edgd lft and styd on run-in: no ex nr fin* **7/1**

-P23 **3** 1 **Kerisper (FR)**[19] 2995 6-10-8 **123**.................. RyanHatch(3) 123
(Nigel Twiston-Davies) *mid-div: trckd ldrs 4th: rdr dropped whip sn after 2 out: styd on and 3rd last: keeping on wl whn carried lft clsng stages* **16/1**

3562 **4** 3 ¼ **Bold Conquest (IRE)**[32] 2744 7-10-6 **118**.................. PaddyBrennan 115
(Stuart Edmunds) *mid-div: chsd ldrs 5th: fdd last 75yds* **5/1**[3]

-512 **5** 4 **Milord (GER)**[20] 2977 6-10-10 **125**..................(p) TomBellamy(3) 119
(Kim Bailey) *trckd ldrs: t.k.h: led 2 out: edgd rt and hdd between last 2: fdd last 150yds* **11/1**

1-04 **6** 5 **Balmusette**[18] 3027 6-11-5 **131**.................. JamesReveley 120
(Keith Reveley) *trckd ldrs: effrt appr 2 out: wknd appr last* **8/1**

F0-0 **7** 3 **Goodwood Mirage (IRE)**[44] 2512 5-11-12 **138**.................. RichardJohnson 124
(Jonjo O'Neill) *hld up in rr: t.k.h: hdwy appr 3 out: hung lft and wknd 2 out* **12/1**

4-11 **8** 3 **Red Devil Boys (IRE)**[18] 3027 8-11-12 **138**..................(p) AidanColeman 124
(John Ferguson) *trckd ldrs: blnd 3 out: wknd between last 2* **9/2**[2]

-445 **9** 27 **Rose Of The Moon (IRE)**[46] 2471 10-10-7 **119**..................(tp) JakeGreenall 78
(Ben Haslam) *w ldr: blnd 4th: lost pl bef 3 out: sn bhd: t.o* **33/1**

1/0- **P** **Trackmate**[598] 198 9-11-4 **130**.................. LiamTreadwell
(James Evans) *in rr: drvn 7th: bhd next: t.o whn p.u bef 3 out* **25/1**

4-1P **P** **Grape Tree Flame**[32] 2759 7-11-9 **135**..................(p) JamieMoore
(Peter Bowen) *led to 1st: w ldrs: drvn 7th: lost pl bef next: sn bhd: p.u bef 3 out* **40/1**

6m 6.5s (7.50) **Going Correction** 0.0s/f (Good) **11** Ran SP% **116.3**
Speed ratings (Par 107): **87,86,86,85,84 82,81,80,71,**
CSF £21.98 CT £260.38 TOTE £3.60: £1.50, £2.50, £4.90; EX 25.20 Trifecta £379.00.
Owner Mrs J K Buckle **Bred** Joe Fogarty **Trained** Barbury Castle, Wiltshire
■ Stewards' Enquiry : Ryan Day caution: careless riding

FOCUS
Races distance increased by 24yds. A decent staying handicap hurdle and solid form, rated through the second.

3337 BETDAQ.COM 2% COMMISSION MARES' CHASE (LISTED RACE) (16 fncs) 2m 4f 126y
2:20 (2:20) (Class 1) 4-Y-0+ **£17,386** (£6,712; £3,511; £1,900)

Form RPR

-630 **1** **Ma Filleule (FR)**[10] 3150 7-10-12 **152**.................. NicodeBoinville 143+
(Nicky Henderson) *trckd ldrs: hit 10th: led narrowly 3 out: styd on towards fin* **9/4**[2]

0-11 **2** 1 ¾ **Emily Gray (IRE)**[30] 2805 7-11-8 **145**.................. RichardJohnson 150
(Kim Bailey) *led: drvn 4 out: hung rt: hdd narrowly next: no ex last 75yds* **11/2**

3-41 **3** 2 ¼ **Run Ructions Run (IRE)**[34] 2717 6-10-12 **135**..................(p) JamesReveley 139
(Tim Easterby) *in rr: in tch: effrt 10th: lft 3rd 4 out: 4 l down whn hit last: kpt on fnl 100yds* **9/1**

31PF **4** 48 **Bobble Boru (IRE)**[11] 3141 7-10-12 **107**.................. CallumWhillans 95
(Venetia Williams) *t.k.h in last: nt fluent 1st: hmpd 8th: outpcd and lost pl 11th: lft distant 4th 4 out* **100/1**

4-12 **F** **Pepite Rose (FR)**[23] 2927 8-11-2 **155**.................. LiamTreadwell
(Venetia Williams) *trckd ldrs: t.k.h: hit 3rd: handy 4th whn fell 8th* **7/2**[3]

-3F1 **F** **Kalane (IRE)**[23] 2925 6-10-12 **0**.................. NoelFehily
(Charlie Longsdon) *t.k.h: trckd ldrs: drvn and disputing 3rd whn fell 4 out* **2/1**[1]

5m 10.8s (-1.20) **Going Correction** 0.0s/f (Good) **6** Ran SP% **112.7**
Speed ratings (Par 111): **102,101,100,82,**
CSF £14.86 TOTE £3.20: £1.80, £2.50; EX 12.60 Trifecta £69.70.
Owner Simon Munir & Isaac Souede **Bred** Serge Dubois **Trained** Upper Lambourn, Berks

FOCUS
Races distance increased by 6yds. An exciting finish to this good-quality mares' Listed chase. Ma Filleule was a stone+ off last year's Ryanair mark.

3338 CASH OUT ON BETDAQ FILLIES' JUVENILE MAIDEN HURDLE (8 hdls) 2m 140y
2:55 (2:55) (Class 4) 3-Y-O **£3,606** (£1,311)

Form RPR

2 **1** **Pemba (FR)**[55] 2273 3-10-9 **0**.................. TomBellamy(3) 110+
(Alan King) *w ldr: led 3rd: clr next: shkn up 3 out: pushed along between last 2: nt fluent last: coasted home* **1/5**[1]

P-P **2** 82 **Grisedenuit (FR)**[43] 2537 3-10-5 **0**.................. JoshWall(7) 36
(Trevor Wall) *t.k.h: trckd ldng pair: poor 2nd after 4th: t.o bef 3 out* **33/1**

5PP **U** **Old Fashion**[17] 3039 3-10-12 **0**..................(b) TrevorWhelan
(Neil King) *rn wout declared tongue strap: t.k.h: led to 3rd: sn drvn: lost pl after 4th: t.o 3rd next: distant 3rd whn slt mstke and uns rdr last* **12/1**[3]

P **Krafty One**[25] 3-10-12 **0**.................. TomScudamore
(Michael Scudamore) *nt fluent 1st: sn last: tailed rt off 4th: hit next: p.u bef 3 out* **13/2**[2]

4m 8.0s (3.30) **Going Correction** 0.0s/f (Good) **4** Ran SP% **107.3**
Speed ratings (Par 101): **92,53,,**
CSF £6.66 TOTE £1.10; EX 8.20.
Owner Million In Mind Partnership **Bred** M L Bloodstock Ltd **Trained** Barbury Castle, Wilts

FOCUS
Races distance increased by about 15yds. Easy pickings for the long-odds-on favourite but not form to be confident about.

3339 BETDAQ - SERIOUS ABOUT SPORT H'CAP CHASE (18 fncs) 3m 6y
3:25 (3:02) (Class 3) (0-135,133) 4-Y-0+ **£6,498** (£1,908; £954; £477)

Form RPR

6-P3 **1** **Ziga Boy (FR)**[21] 2955 6-10-7 **117**.................. TomBellamy(3) 139+
(Alan King) *trckd ldrs: led sn after 11th: wnt clr bef 4 out: 15 l ahd last: eased last 150yds* **9/2**[2]

P-00 **2** 7 **Godsmejudge (IRE)**[24] 2916 9-11-8 **129**..................(t) NoelFehily 139
(David Dennis) *chsd ldrs: lft modest 3rd 4 out: chsd wnr next: kpt on: no ch w wnr* **10/1**

2-F1 **3** 13 **Wild Bill (IRE)**[32] 2749 6-11-3 **124**.................. AdamWedge 124
(Evan Williams) *mid-div: lft modest 4th 4 out: 3rd 2 out: one pce* **11/4**[1]

3-3F **4** 11 **Red Admirable (IRE)**[54] 2295 9-11-2 **123**..................(p) KielanWoods 119+
(Graeme McPherson) *hit 2nd: hdwy to chse ldrs 7th: 2nd 14th: mstke next: wknd bef 2 out* **14/1**

6043 **5** 49 **Master Rajeem (USA)**[18] 3024 6-10-7 **114**..................(p) RichieMcLernon 58
(Neil King) *chsd ldrs: reminders 6th: drvn 11th: sn lost pl and bhd: t.o whn hmpd 2 out: eventually completed* **16/1**

3-P1 **U** **Valid Point (IRE)**[20] 2975 9-11-4 **125**..................(t) MarkGrant
(Nigel Twiston-Davies) *chsd ldrs: drvn 11th: 3rd and one pce whn bdly hmpd and uns rdr 4 out* **14/1**

-P1F **P** **Simply Wings (IRE)**[31] 2780 11-11-12 **133**.................. JamieMoore
(Kerry Lee) *in rr: sme hdwy 11th: sn lost pl: wl bhd whn mstke 14th: t.o whn p.u bef next* **20/1**

11U- **F** **Double Whammy**[437] 1954 9-10-12 **119**..................(b) LiamTreadwell
(Iain Jardine) *led: j.rt: hdd sn after 11th: wknd after 14th: poor 5th whn fell 2 out* **20/1**

1P/5 **F** **Victor Hewgo**[17] 3036 10-11-10 **131**.................. JamesReveley
(Keith Reveley) *in rr: outpcd 11th: bhd whn fell 13th* **9/2**[2]

2-3P **P** **Keltic Rhythm (IRE)**[20] 2975 8-10-7 **114**..................(tp) TrevorWhelan
(Neil King) *in rr: drvn 9th: sn bhd: t.o whn p.u bef 12th* **25/1**

3-P **P** **Rough Justice (IRE)**[50] 2404 7-11-6 **127**..................(tp) JonathanEngland
(Alan Brown) *racd in last: detached 7th: t.o whn p.u bef 9th: b.b.v* **80/1**

3123 **U** **American Legend (IRE)**[89] 1722 7-10-12 **119**..................(v) RichardJohnson
(Jonjo O'Neill) *in rr: drvn 9th: bhd whn hmpd and uns rdr 13th* **15/2**[3]

P3-4 **P** **Westward Point**[28] 2832 8-10-12 **122**.................. HarryBannister(3)
(Warren Greatrex) *prom: chsd ldrs 6th: outpcd 12th: wknd 4 out: wl bhd whn p.u bef last* **16/1**

6m 5.7s (-6.30) **Going Correction** 0.0s/f (Good) **13** Ran SP% **123.6**
Speed ratings (Par 107): **110,107,103,99,83 ,,,,,,,,**
CSF £48.44 CT £150.72 TOTE £8.00: £3.20, £3.90, £1.60; EX 26.70 Trifecta £287.90.
Owner Axom Ll **Bred** Guy Cherel **Trained** Barbury Castle, Wilts

FOCUS
Races distance increased by 6yds. A useful handicap chase, but not many finished and the winner was on his own from some way out. He was very well in on the best of last year's form and is rated back to that level.
T/Jkpt: £7,100.00. Pool: £17,750.00 - 2.5 winning units. JACKPOT PLACEPOT £114.60. Pool: £2,843.00 - 18.10 winning units. T/Plt: £18.60 to a £1 stake. Pool: £60684.47 - 2369.11 winning tickets T/Qpdt: £9.90 to a £1 stake Pool: £4880.66 - 363.2 winning tickets **Walter Glynn**

2931 KELSO (L-H)
Tuesday, December 29

OFFICIAL GOING: Heavy
Wind: Fresh, half against Weather: Cloudy, bright

3340 MCGRATH 1000 BAGS OF CARROTS "NATIONAL HUNT" MAIDEN HURDLE (11 hdls) 2m 6f 151y
12:05 (12:05) (Class 5) 4-Y-0+ **£2,599** (£763; £381; £190)

Form RPR

42 **1** **Takingrisks (IRE)**[30] 2801 6-11-0 **122**.................. BrianHarding 125+
(Nicky Richards) *hld up: stdy hdwy bef 3 out: chsd clr ldr and effrt bef next: 4 l down and styng on whn lft 10 l clr last: kpt on* **10/11**[1]

5- **2** 13 **Sevenballs Of Fire (IRE)**[428] 2102 6-11-0 **0**.................. BrianHughes 114
(Iain Jardine) *cl up: rdn along after 3 out: 3rd and hld whn lft 10 l 2nd and blnd last: no ch w wnr* **12/1**

0-2 **3** 29 **Dakota Grey**[24] 2917 4-10-11 **0**.................. JoeColliver(3) 89
(Micky Hammond) *prom: hdwy to chse ldr 4th: rdn and lost 2nd bef 2 out: hld whn lft 25 l 3rd last* **3/1**[2]

24 **4** 27 **Egret (IRE)**[30] 2801 5-10-11 **0**.................. DerekFox(3) 61
(Lucinda Russell) *cl up: disputing 3rd pl whn stmbld bdly and nrly uns rdr 4 out: nt rcvr and sn lost tch: lft poor 4th last* **11/1**

4-PR **5** dist **Ashes Corner (IRE)**[18] 3022 5-10-11 **0**.................. JohnKington(3)
(Julia Brooke) *hld up: pushed along fr 1/2-way: struggling fnl circ: t.o whn j.v.slowly last: virtually p.u* **100/1**

0/5 **P** **Forty Something (IRE)**[16] 3056 10-10-7 **0**.................. SamColtherd(7)
(Stuart Coltherd) *cl up: lost pl 5th: reminders and struggling next: lost tch and p.u after 7th* **150/1**

F **Flemensfirthleader**[667] 6-10-7 **0**.................. CraigNichol 118+
(Keith Dalgleish) *cl up: nt fluent 2nd: sn led: shkn up bef 2 out: 4 l in front and keeping on whn fell and down for sme time at last* **33/1**

3- **P** **Mahler Lad (IRE)**[335] 3931 5-11-0 **0**.................. HenryBrooke
(Donald McCain) *hld up: drvn and struggling bef 7th: sn lost tch: t.o whn p.u 2 out* **4/1**[3]

2P-4 **P** **Bolton Blue (IRE)**[16] 3056 6-10-9 **0**.................. CallumBewley(5)
(Katie Scott) *hld up: drvn and struggling 1/2-way: no ch whn p.u bef 2 out* **100/1**

6m 7.3s (26.30) **Going Correction** +1.325s/f (Heav) **9** Ran SP% **119.0**
WFA 4 from 5yo+ 6lb
Speed ratings (Par 103): **107,102,92,83, , , ,**
CSF £14.66 TOTE £1.60: £1.02, £2.90, £1.40; EX 9.60 Trifecta £34.20.
Owner Frank Bird **Bred** James Murray **Trained** Greystoke, Cumbria

FOCUS
All bends out from innermost line and races 1 & 5 increased by 44yds, race 2 & 6 by 80yds, race 4 by 64yds and races 3 & 7 by 36yds. The actual race distance was 2m 6f 195yds. A dramatic conclusion to this opener, with the odds-on favourite still four lengths down when gifted the race at the final flight. The time was reasonable.

3341 JOE SULLIVAN MEMORIAL H'CAP CHASE (QUALIFIER FOR THE CHALLENGER STAYING CHASE SERIES FINAL) (19 fncs) 3m 2f 39y

12:40 (12:40) (Class 4) (0-120,120) 4-Y-O+ £6,498 (£1,908; £954; £477)

Form | | | | RPR
0U32 **1** **Total Assets**[25] 2894 7-10-7 **106**........................ CallumBewley[(5)] 117+
(Simon Waugh) *prom: wnt 2nd 5 out: led after 3 out: rdn next: kpt on wl fr last* **4/1**[2]
121P **2** *2 ½* **Present Flight (IRE)**[32] 2749 6-11-6 **117**..................(t) DerekFox[(3)] 125
(Lucinda Russell) *hld up: nt fluent 12th: hdwy to press wnr after 3 out: rdn and edgd lft next: kpt on same pce fr last* **10/3**[1]
6-5U **3** *1 ½* **Chavoy (FR)**[23] 2934 10-11-9 **120**..................(tp) TonyKelly[(3)] 126
(Rebecca Menzies) *w ldr: led 12th: rdn whn nt fluent 3 out: sn hdd and outpcd: rallied bef last: kpt on run-in* **9/2**[3]
1F44 **4** *½* **Chanceofa Lifetime (IRE)**[10] 3160 8-10-10 **111**...... ThomasDowson[(7)] 116
(Victor Thompson) *nt fluent on occasions: t.k.h: prom: rdn after 3 out: outpcd next: plugged on fr last* **8/1**
063U **5** *36* **More Madness (IRE)**[23] 2934 8-11-4 **112**..................(p) LucyAlexander 80
(N W Alexander) *in tch: hit 6th: drvn and outpcd after 13th: lost tch 5 out: t.o* **11/2**
PP6/ **P** **Tipsy Dara (IRE)**[276] 11-10-4 **103**........................ StephenMulqueen[(5)]
(N W Alexander) *led to 12th: cl up tl drvn and outpcd after 5 out: struggling fr next: t.o whn p.u bef last* **28/1**
14-6 **P** **Dream Flyer (IRE)**[50] 2400 8-11-7 **115**..................(t) HenryBrooke
(Michael Smith) *cl up on outside: outpcd 13th: struggling fr next: lost tch whn p.u bef 4 out* **4/1**[2]

7m 44.4s (57.20) **Going Correction** +1.875s/f (Heavy) **7** Ran SP% **111.2**
Speed ratings (Par 105): **87,86,85,85,74 ,**
CSF £17.16 TOTE £4.30: £2.30, £2.10; EX 19.10 Trifecta £89.20.
Owner Northumberland Racing Club **Bred** H L Kirpalani & Shade Oak Stud **Trained** Mitford, Northumberland

FOCUS
A gruelling stamina test. After rail movements the actual race distance was 3m 2f 119yds. The third and fourth set the level.

3342 G. MARSHALL TRACTORS CASE IH MARES' NOVICES' HURDLE (8 hdls) 2m 51y

1:15 (1:15) (Class 4) 4-Y-O+ £3,898 (£1,144; £572; £286)

Form | | | | RPR
-3P3 **1** **Presenting Rose (IRE)**[23] 2936 5-10-7 0.............. StephenMulqueen[(5)] 110+
(N W Alexander) *j.lft on occasions: mde all: hrd pressed and pushed along fr 2 out: hung rt u.p run-in: kpt on wl* **7/1**
-242 **2** *½* **Berkshire Downs**[16] 3054 5-10-9 106........................ AdamNicol[(3)] 108
(Lucy Normile) *chsd ldr: clsng whn nt fluent 2 out: sn rdn: effrt and ev ch whn carried rt run-in: kpt on: hld nr fin* **7/2**[3]
53-5 **3** *4* **Attention Seaker**[80] 1854 5-10-12 109........................ BrianHughes 102
(Tim Easterby) *chsd ldrs on outside: effrt bef 2 out: rdn and outpcd fr last* **9/4**[2]
46 **4** *7* **Rivabodiva (IRE)**[31] 2787 5-10-9 0........................ DerekFox[(3)] 96
(Lucinda Russell) *hld up: stdy hdwy 3 out: effrt and cl up whn rdn next: outpcd bef last* **6/4**[1]
0P0 **5** *28* **Play Practice**[14] 3101 5-10-7 0........................ MissCWalton[(5)] 67
(James Walton) *hld up: struggling 4 out: lost tch fr next* **250/1**
P-04 **6** *25* **Norfolk Sound**[45] 2494 4-10-5 0........................ SamColtherd[(7)] 42
(Stuart Coltherd) *nt fluent on occasions: hld up: stdy hdwy bef 3 out: rdn and outpcd whn mstke next: sn btn* **50/1**
0-00 **P** **Jane's Fantasy (IRE)**[32] 2752 5-10-12 0........................ LucyAlexander
(N W Alexander) *taken early to post: hld up: struggling bef 4 out: sn btn: lost tch and p.u after 3 out* **200/1**

4m 27.7s (25.90) **Going Correction** +1.775s/f (Heavy)
WFA 4 from 5yo 5lb **7** Ran SP% **108.3**
Speed ratings (Par 105): **106,105,103,100,86 73,**
CSF £28.29 TOTE £8.10: £3.40, £2.30; EX 29.50 Trifecta £102.60.
Owner Alistair Cochrane **Bred** Patrick Cullinan And Sandra Bromley **Trained** Kinneston, Perth & Kinross

■ Stewards' Enquiry : Adam Nicol two day ban: careless riding (12-13 Jan)

FOCUS
An ordinary mares' novice. After rail movements the actual race distance was 2m 87yds. A big step up from the winner, but probably not form to get carried away with.

3343 MONTEITH MEMORIAL H'CAP CHASE (12 fncs) 2m 1f 14y

1:50 (1:52) (Class 4) (0-120,112) 4-Y-O+ £6,498 (£1,908; £954; £477)

Form | | | | RPR
0011 **1** **Caraline (FR)**[25] 2891 4-10-3 **97**........................ JoeColliver[(3)] 115+
(Micky Hammond) *hld up on outside: hdwy 7th: led 4 out to next: regained ld gng wl 2 out: rdn clr fr last* **11/4**[1]
-P33 **2** *15* **Trust Thomas**[10] 3162 7-11-7 **112**........................ JamieHamilton[(5)] 120
(Ann Hamilton) *hld up: rdn and hdwy 3 out: chsd wnr bef last: outpcd run-in* **9/2**[3]
PP33 **3** *3 ¾* **Rupert Bear**[19] 2983 9-9-12 **89**..................(p) MissCWalton[(5)] 92
(James Walton) *chsd ldrs: nt fluent and lost grnd 5th: rallied bef 4 out: led next to 2 out: drvn and outpcd bef last* **12/1**
436- **4** *10* **Vinny Gambini (IRE)**[277] 5018 8-11-8 **108**........................ CraigNichol 99
(Rose Dobbin) *prom: rdn bef 4 out: outpcd next: btn fnl 2* **6/1**
2231 **5** *17* **Retrieve The Stick**[35] 2707 6-11-8 **108**..................(b) BrianHughes 82
(Malcolm Jefferson) *hld up: hdwy to chse ldrs after 4th: rdn 3 out: sn wknd* **3/1**[2]
-24P **6** *18* **Amethyst Rose (IRE)**[30] 2805 8-11-7 **112**........................ GrantCockburn[(5)] 68
(Stuart Coltherd) *cl up: drvn whn nt fluent 3 out: rdn and wknd fr next* **20/1**
1346 **P** **Endeavor**[22] 2947 10-10-11 **100**........................ HarryChalloner[(3)]
(Dianne Sayer) *prom: lost pl 7th: struggling fr 4 out: wknd and p.u bef 2 out* **25/1**
6P00 **P** **Formidableopponent (IRE)**[22] 2947 8-11-3 **108**........................ DaraghBourke[(5)]
(William Young Jnr) *bhd: struggling after 5 out: lost tch and p.u bef 2 out* **40/1**
3-33 **P** **Castlelawn (IRE)**[32] 2755 8-11-10 **110**........................ PeterBuchanan
(Lucinda Russell) *mde most to 4 out: rdn and wknd fr next: lost tch and p.u bef 2 out* **6/1**

4m 47.4s (29.40) **Going Correction** +1.875s/f (Heavy)
WFA 4 from 6yo+ 5lb **9** Ran SP% **117.2**
Speed ratings (Par 105): **105,97,96,91,83 75, , ,**
CSF £15.90 CT £127.77 TOTE £4.00: £1.60, £1.70, £3.00; EX 16.70 Trifecta £115.20.
Owner Give Every Man His Due **Bred** Mme Caroline Elizabeth Huni **Trained** Middleham, N Yorks

FOCUS
A one-sided contest, the winner clearly still well ahead of her mark. After rail movements the actual race distance was 2m1f 78yds. The winner is on the upgrade.

3344 SPG FIRE & SECURITY LTD H'CAP HURDLE (11 hdls) 2m 6f 151y

2:25 (2:27) (Class 4) (0-115,115) 4-Y-O+ £3,898 (£1,144; £572; £286)

Form | | | | RPR
-012 **1** **Another Mattie (IRE)**[19] 2978 8-11-12 **115**..................(t) LucyAlexander 123+
(N W Alexander) *cl up on outside: led 3 out: rdn next: kpt on wl fr last* **9/1**
1642 **2** *3* **Bescot Springs (IRE)**[30] 2800 10-10-6 **100**..................(p) GrantCockburn[(5)] 104
(Lucinda Russell) *led: rdn and hdd 3 out: rallied: kpt on fr last to take 2nd nr fin: nt rch wnr* **9/1**
5P/4 **3** *½* **Kind Of Easy (IRE)**[30] 2800 9-10-9 **103**........................ DaraghBourke[(5)] 107
(Alistair Whillans) *prom: effrt and ev ch after 3 out: sn chsng wnr: kpt on fr last tl no ex and lost 2nd nr fin* **28/1**
03-1 **4** *4* **Almost Gemini (IRE)**[49] 2426 6-10-5 **97**..................(p) HarryChalloner[(3)] 99
(Kenneth Slack) *hld up: hdwy to chse ldrs after 4 out: drvn and outpcd after next: no imp fr 2 out* **15/8**[1]
6-00 **5** *9* **Golans Choice (IRE)**[48] 2429 6-11-5 **108**........................ CraigNichol 101
(Rose Dobbin) *hld up bhd ldng gp: drvn along and outpcd bef 3 out: plugged on fr last: no imp* **10/1**
-436 **6** *2 ¾* **Echo Springs**[32] 2744 5-11-12 **115**........................ BrianHarding 103
(Danielle McCormick) *prom tl rdn and wknd bef 2 out* **5/1**[3]
3661 **7** *6* **La Dama De Hierro**[23] 2936 5-11-10 **113**........................ BrianHughes 95
(Malcolm Jefferson) *cl up: nt fluent and lost pl 8th: struggling fr next: n.d after* **8/1**
-0P5 **8** *28* **Forty Crown (IRE)**[24] 2919 9-11-2 **105**..................(b) PeterBuchanan 59
(John Wade) *cl up: nt fluent and lost pl 8th: wknd fr next: t.o* **20/1**
6332 **P** **Boruma (IRE)**[18] 3027 5-11-10 **113**........................ HenryBrooke
(Dianne Sayer) *hld up: pushed along and outpcd after 4 out: struggling next: lost tch and p.u 2 out* **9/2**[2]

6m 18.9s (37.90) **Going Correction** +1.775s/f (Heavy) **9** Ran SP% **118.0**
Speed ratings (Par 105): **105,103,103,102,99 98,96,86,**
CSF £87.06 CT £2181.86 TOTE £6.90: £2.50, £3.10, £7.40; EX 42.10 Trifecta £2538.20.
Owner Quandt & Cochrane **Bred** David Kells **Trained** Kinneston, Perth & Kinross

■ Stewards' Enquiry : Henry Brooke jockey said that the gelding was unsuited by the heavy going

FOCUS
A fairly useful effort from the winner to defy top weight. After rail movements the actual race distance was 2m 6f 195yds. A step up from the winner.

3345 CHILDREN'S IMMUNOLOGY TRUST NOVICES' LIMITED H'CAP CHASE (16 fncs) 2m 5f 133y

3:00 (3:00) (Class 4) (0-120,120) 4-Y-O+ £7,147 (£2,098; £1,049; £524)

Form | | | | RPR
015F **1** **Lord Wishes (IRE)**[18] 3020 8-11-8 **120**..................(p) BrianHarding 132+
(James Ewart) *j.w: mde all: rdn clr fr 2 out: readily* **9/2**[3]
336/ **2** *11* **Kilbree Chief (IRE)**[627] 5252 7-11-7 **119**........................ PeterBuchanan 118
(Lucinda Russell) *hld up: pushed along and outpcd 9th: rallied after 3 out: rdn and chsd (clr) wnr bef last: drifted rt run-in: kpt on: no imp* **4/1**[2]
6-11 **3** *7* **What A Dream**[48] 2430 9-9-12 **101** oh6..................(tp) JamieHamilton[(5)] 93
(Alison Hamilton) *t.k.h: prom: lost grnd bef 10th: drvn and outpcd bef 4 out: rallied 2 out: no imp fr last* **9/2**[3]
254 **4** *½* **Glacial Rock (IRE)**[16] 3055 9-10-11 **109**..................(p) HenryBrooke 101
(Alistair Whillans) *cl up: effrt and chsd wnr after 4 out: rdn next: outpcd and lost 2nd bef last: sn btn* **8/1**
F2P6 **5** *44* **Vayland**[27] 2846 6-11-2 **114**........................ CraigNichol 76
(Micky Hammond) *hld up in tch: stdy hdwy 10th: effrt and disp 2nd pl after 4 out: sn rdn: wknd 2 out: fin tired* **16/1**
P-U4 **P** **Frankie's Promise (IRE)**[31] 2788 7-10-11 **109**........................ LucyAlexander
(N W Alexander) *nt fluent: hld up: blnd and outpcd 9th: nt jump wl after: rallied bef 4 out: struggling next: lost tch and p.u bef last* **3/1**[1]
434 **P** **Agentleman (IRE)**[25] 2890 5-10-3 **101** oh1........................ BrianHughes
(Tim Easterby) *cl up: rdn whn nt fluent 4 out: nt fluent and wknd next: lost tch and p.u bef 2 out* **11/2**

6m 17.4s (48.20) **Going Correction** +1.875s/f (Heavy) **7** Ran SP% **113.7**
Speed ratings (Par 105): **87,83,80,80,64 ,**
CSF £22.85 TOTE £5.00: £2.20, £2.50; EX 20.80 Trifecta £97.10.
Owner Leeds Plywood And Doors Ltd **Bred** Mrs M O'Driscoll **Trained** Langholm, Dumfries & G'way

■ Stewards' Enquiry : Brian Hughes jockey said that the gelding stopped quickly

FOCUS
The second one-sided handicap chase on the card. The winner hadn't exactly looked a natural over fences previously but was totally transformed here. He was a 136 hurdler at his peak and might match that over fences. After rail movements the actual race distance was 2m 5f 213yds.

3346 TAKE IT EASY TIGER H'CAP HURDLE (10 hdls) 2m 2f 25y

3:30 (3:32) (Class 4) (0-120,119) 3-Y-O+ £4,548 (£1,335; £667; £333)

Form | | | | RPR
3-04 **1** **Maxie T**[23] 2933 4-11-5 **119**........................ FinianO'Toole[(7)] 136+
(Micky Hammond) *hld up: smooth hdwy 3 out: led between last 2: sn clr: easily* **9/1**
-121 **2** *18* **Alizee De Janeiro (FR)**[23] 2933 5-11-6 **113**........................ PeterBuchanan 110
(Lucinda Russell) *hld up in tch: hdwy to ld 3 out: rdn and hdd between last 2: no ch w wnr* **7/2**[1]
/521 **3** *11* **Renoyr (FR)**[26] 2869 10-11-6 **113**........................ BrianHughes 99
(Malcolm Jefferson) *trckd ldrs: effrt and ev ch after 3 out: rdn and outpcd fr next* **11/2**[2]
4023 **4** *6* **Hunters Belt (IRE)**[23] 2933 11-10-4 **102**..................(vt) JonathonBewley[(5)] 83
(George Bewley) *rn in snatches: in tch: lost pl 1/2-way: rallied and chal after 3 out: rdn whn mstke next: sn wknd* **15/2**
56U2 **5** *nse* **Pistol (IRE)**[30] 2802 6-10-6 **106**........................ MrJDixon[(7)] 87
(John Dixon) *pressed ldr to 1/2-way: sn drvn along: outpcd after 4 out: n.d after* **6/1**[3]
P-P0 **6** *5* **Hail The Brave (IRE)**[22] 2948 6-10-5 **98**..................(p) HenryBrooke 71
(Michael Smith) *prom on outside: led after 4 out to next: drvn and wknd bef 2 out* **18/1**
0502 **7** *7* **Herecomesnelson (IRE)**[30] 2804 6-10-13 **111**........................ CallumBewley[(5)] 77
(Katie Scott) *hld up in tch: smooth hdwy to ld briefly 4 out: rdn and wknd bef 2 out* **8/1**

3FPP **8** *1* **Suprise Vendor (IRE)**[31] 2765 9-10-7 **107**..................... SamColtherd(7) 74
(Stuart Coltherd) *led to 4 out: sn drvn along: wknd after next* **25/1**
3536 **9** *24* **Cool Baranca (GER)**[16] 3065 9-10-9 **105**..................... HarryChalloner(3) 46
(Dianne Sayer) *hld up: drvn and struggling bef 4 out: nvr on terms* **33/1**
24FP **P** **Lyric Street (IRE)**[31] 2765 7-11-6 **113**.....................(p) BrianHarding
(Donald McCain) *prom tl rdn and wknd 3 out: p.u next* **12/1**
21-0 **P** **Bop Along (IRE)**[23] 2933 8-11-5 **112**..................... CraigNichol
(Alistair Whillans) *bhd: struggling fnl circ: no ch whn p.u bef 2 out* **28/1**
-544 **F** **Benny's Secret (IRE)**[31] 2791 5-10-13 **106**..................... LucyAlexander 91
(N W Alexander) *hld up in tch: nt fluent 4 out: effrt and cl up next: drvn and outpcd bef 2 out: 16 l 4th and hld whn fell last* **15/2**

4m 55.1s (28.10) **Going Correction** +1.775s/f (Heav)
WFA 4 from 5yo+ 5lb **12** Ran SP% **119.7**
Speed ratings (Par 105): **108,100,95,92,92 90,87,86,75, ,**
CSF £41.02 CT £195.78 TOTE £11.10: £4.10, £1.50, £2.20; EX 70.20 Trifecta £321.00.
Owner Newroc & Co **Bred** Meon Valley Stud **Trained** Middleham, N Yorks

FOCUS
This looked quite competitive beforehand but turned out to be anything but, the wide-margin most impressive. The second sets the level. After rail movements the actual race distance was 2m 2f 61yds.
T/Plt: £128.50 to a £1 stake. Pool: £37,976.38 - 215.68 winning units. T/Qpdt: £36.80 to a £1 stake. Pool: £3,582.32 - 71.90 winning units. **Richard Young**

3112 NEWBURY (L-H)
Tuesday, December 29

OFFICIAL GOING: Soft (heavy in places on hurdle course; 3.5)
Wind: Moderate, against; becoming moderate, across towards stands Weather: Sunny and mild

3347 BETFRED MOBILE JUVENILE HURDLE (8 hdls) 2m 69y
12:15 (12:20) (Class 3) 3-Y-O **£6,498** (£1,908; £954; £477)

Form RPR
1 **Fixe Le Kap (FR)**[236] 3-10-12 0..................... JeremiahMcGrath 125+
(Nicky Henderson) *led tl narrowly hdd 2 out: drvn to regain ld fnl 75yds* **6/5**[1]
2 *1* **Tommy Silver (FR)**[187] 3-10-12 0..................... SamTwiston-Davies 123+
(Paul Nicholls) *prom: wnt 2nd at 5th: slt ld 2 out: kpt on u.p run-in: hdd fnl 75yds* **7/1**[3]
1 **3** *11* **Kasakh Noir (FR)**[32] 2757 3-11-8 0..................... HarrySkelton 123
(Dan Skelton) *hld up: hdwy to chal 2 out: 3rd and hld whn blnd last* **5/4**[2]
4 *19* **Me Voila (FR)** 3-10-7 0..................... LizzieKelly(5) 96
(Nick Williams) *chsd ldrs tl wknd appr 2 out* **25/1**
5 *6* **Sea Serpent (FR)** 3-10-12 0..................... JoshuaMoore 90
(Gary Moore) *towards rr: mstke 5th: lost tch 3 out: 6th and no ch whn blnd last* **33/1**
P5 **6** *4* **Kingston Mimosa**[21] 2954 3-10-12 0.....................(p) TomCannon 84
(Mark Gillard) *chsd wnr tl 5th: wknd appr 2 out* **250/1**
7 *48* **Monsieur Valentine**[29] 3-10-12 0..................... LeeEdwards 35
(Tony Carroll) *a last: mstkes 1st and 3rd: lost tch 3 out: wl bhd whn j.lft last* **150/1**

4m 20.2s (10.20) **Going Correction** +0.35s/f (Yiel) **7** Ran SP% **110.2**
Speed ratings (Par 106): **88,87,82,72,69 67,43**
CSF £8.88 TOTE £2.20: £1.30, £2.20; EX 9.50 Trifecta £16.00.
Owner Simon Munir & Isaac Souede **Bred** Olivier Tricot & Max Hennau **Trained** Upper Lambourn, Berks

FOCUS
Rail has been moved in on both courses, adding 91yds to the opening juvenile hurdle. The going looked genuinely soft as advertised, and winning rider Jeremiah McGrath said it was "heavy in places". Although the penalised third was below par and it being a tactical gallop, this looks a decent affair with two coming well clear. The winner looks a smart long-term prospect.

3348 BETFRED TV NOVICES' LIMITED H'CAP CHASE (17 fncs) 2m 6f 93y
12:50 (12:55) (Class 3) (0-125,125) 4-Y-0+ **£6,498** (£1,908; £954; £477)

Form RPR
41-0 **1** **Imagine The Chat**[55] 2266 6-10-12 **115**..................... SeanBowen 133+
(Rebecca Curtis) *hld up in midfield: hdwy 9th: led appr last: rdn clr* **8/1**
0001 **2** *7* **Sandy Beach**[19] 2988 5-11-5 **122**..................... BrendanPowell 130
(Colin Tizzard) *mid-div: hmpd 11th: hdwy 12th: led 4 out tl appr last: one pce* **6/1**[1]
1543 **3** *9* **Epic Warrior (IRE)**[24] 2906 6-11-2 **122**.....................(b[1]) KieronEdgar(3) 123
(David Pipe) *led: blnd 11th: hdd 4 out: wknd after 2 out* **14/1**
5/6P **4** *15* **Berkeley Barron (IRE)**[35] 2701 7-11-7 **124**.....................(tp) IanPopham 116+
(Richard Phillips) *sn niggled along towards rr: hmpd 11th: mstke 13th: rallied and in tch 4 out: sn wknd* **33/1**
351- **5** *11* **Ashford Wood (IRE)**[276] 5033 7-11-8 **125**.....................(p) MichaelByrne 98
(Tim Vaughan) *in tch: hmpd 11th: wknd 4 out* **40/1**
11/P **6** *nk* **Mountain Tunes (IRE)**[48] 2442 6-11-8 **125**..................... JoshuaMoore 98
(Jonjo O'Neill) *hld up towards rr: hmpd 11th: hdwy 12th: wknd 3 out* **16/1**
53/U **7** *19* **Tidal Dance (IRE)**[24] 2905 8-11-0 **122**..................... CharlieDeutsch(5) 76
(Venetia Williams) *in tch: wknd 8th: sn bhd* **16/1**
411/ **F** **Willoughby Hedge**[783] 2296 8-11-3 **120**..................... WayneHutchinson
(Alan King) *hld up in rr: stdy hdwy fr 10th: disputing 2nd whn fell 13th* **8/1**
1464 **U** **Henri Parry Morgan**[31] 2764 7-11-5 **122**.....................(p) TomO'Brien
(Peter Bowen) *hld up in midfield: promising hdwy 11th: prom whn blnd and virtually fell next: uns rdr* **40/1**
4-33 **F** **Vice Et Vertu (FR)**[24] 2905 6-11-1 **118**..................... AndrewTinkler
(Henry Daly) *chsd ldr tl fell 11th* **13/2**[2]
24P3 **P** **Simply The West (IRE)**[19] 2988 6-11-2 **119**.....................(t) HarrySkelton
(Charlie Longsdon) *prom tl 10th: losing pl whn sltly hmpd next: sn bhd: t.o whn p.u bef 4 out: lame* **8/1**
4-13 **P** **Millicent Silver**[29] 2825 6-10-10 **113**.....................(p) SamTwiston-Davies
(Nigel Twiston-Davies) *several mstkes: towards rr: rdn along fr 5th: wl bhd fr 11th: p.u bef 4 out* **10/1**
124F **U** **Road To Freedom**[20] 2975 6-10-12 **115**..................... LeightonAspell
(Lucy Wadham) *bhd: blnd bdly 1st: last and struggling whn blnd and uns rdr 11th* **8/1**
06-4 **B** **Aigle De La See (FR)**[24] 2897 5-11-8 **125**..................... JeremiahMcGrath
(Nicky Henderson) *t.k.h: trckd ldrs tl b.d 11th* **7/1**[3]

6m 3.9s (16.90) **Going Correction** +0.95s/f (Soft) **14** Ran SP% **119.9**
Speed ratings (Par 107): **107,104,101,95,91 91,84, , , , ,**
CSF £55.68 CT £668.71 TOTE £8.00: £2.90, £2.60, £4.90; EX 45.70 Trifecta £847.60.
Owner John P McManus **Bred** Northcombe Stud **Trained** Newport, Pembrokeshire

FOCUS
Even by novice standards this was a highly eventful handicap. The runner-up sets the level. Race distance 62yds further than advertised. The winner was up a stone on the best of his hurdle figures.

3349 BETFRED MANDARIN H'CAP CHASE (21 fncs) 3m 1f 214y
1:25 (1:31) (Class 3) (0-130,129) 4-Y-0+ **£7,797** (£2,289; £1,144; £572)

Form RPR
P2-U **1** **Silvergrove**[25] 2887 7-11-7 **124**.....................(t) DavidBass 132+
(Ben Pauling) *pressed ldr: led 7th: hld on gamely fr 2 out: all out* **5/2**[1]
-0P1 **2** *3/4* **Amidon (FR)**[21] 2957 5-11-4 **121**..................... LeightonAspell 125
(Lucy Wadham) *prom: w wnr fr 9th tl sltly outpcd 4 out: rallied and regained 2nd run-in: styd on* **15/2**
P-P1 **3** *1 1/4* **Big Society (IRE)**[41] 2566 9-11-7 **124**..................... GavinSheehan 132+
(Harry Whittington) *nt jump wl and several bad mstkes: bhd: rdn and hdwy 4 out: wnt 2nd and clsng whn blnd last: styd on* **7/2**[2]
3-4P **4** *11* **Arbeo (IRE)**[39] 2616 9-10-4 **107**..................... MarcGoldstein 103
(Diana Grissell) *led tl 7th: blnd 16th: hrd rdn 4 out: in contention tl wknd last* **16/1**
-302 **5** *22* **Cloudy Copper (IRE)**[15] 3079 8-11-12 **129**.....................(p) JoshuaMoore 107
(Jonjo O'Neill) *hld up: mstke 11th (water): hdwy 15th: j. slowly and rdn 17th: wnt 2nd 3 out tl wknd appr last* **13/2**
P-0P **P** **Coolking**[21] 2955 8-10-5 **108**..................... TomCannon
(Chris Gordon) *prom tl lost pl 10th: sn bhd: p.u bef 16th* **20/1**
12P3 **P** **Belmount (IRE)**[33] 2724 6-11-11 **128**..................... SamTwiston-Davies
(Nigel Twiston-Davies) *in tch: mstke 13th: blnd next: wknd 4 out: bhd whn p.u after next* **4/1**[3]
2212 **P** **Henllan Harri (IRE)**[73] 1962 7-11-9 **126**.....................(p) SeanBowen
(Peter Bowen) *sn towards rr: effrt 4 out: 6th and n.d whn p.u bef 2 out* **12/1**

7m 11.1s (25.10) **Going Correction** +0.95s/f (Soft) **8** Ran SP% **114.2**
Speed ratings (Par 107): **99,98,98,95,88 , ,**
CSF £21.51 CT £64.93 TOTE £3.20: £1.60, £2.00, £1.50; EX 18.50 Trifecta £68.40.
Owner Nicholas Piper & Claire E Piper **Bred** Elms Stud Co Ltd & Miss J Winter **Trained** Bourton-On-The-Water, Gloucs
■ Stewards' Enquiry : Leighton Aspell four-day ban: use of whip (12-15 Jan)

FOCUS
Race distance increased by 62yds. This fair staying handicap proved a thorough test. The form is rated around the second to his hurdles mark.

3350 BETFRED "GOALS GALORE" CHALLOW NOVICES' HURDLE (GRADE 1) (10 hdls) 2m 4f 118y
2:00 (2:06) (Class 1) 4-Y-0+ **£22,780** (£8,548; £4,280)

Form RPR
11-1 **1** **Barters Hill (IRE)**[58] 2221 5-11-7 0..................... DavidBass 153+
(Ben Pauling) *mde all: green on paddock bnd: rdn clr appr last: comf* **4/11**[1]
U **2** *12* **Politologue (FR)**[18] 3019 4-11-7 0..................... SamTwiston-Davies 138
(Paul Nicholls) *hld up and gng wl in 3rd: shkn up appr last: one pce: wnt 2nd fnl 100yds* **6/1**[3]
21 **3** *3/4* **Label Des Obeaux (FR)**[25] 2886 4-11-7 141..................... WayneHutchinson 138
(Alan King) *chsd wnr: edgd rt after 2 out: sn rdn and btn: lost 2nd fnl 100yds* **4/1**[2]

5m 20.1s (1.10) **Going Correction** +0.35s/f (Yiel) **3** Ran SP% **107.6**
Speed ratings (Par 117): **111,106,106**
CSF £2.81 TOTE £1.30; EX 2.30 Trifecta £2.50.
Owner Circle Of Friends **Bred** Lady J Fowler **Trained** Bourton-On-The-Water, Gloucs
■ The first Grade 1 winner for both Ben Pauling and David Bass.

FOCUS
Race distance increased by 118yds. This Grade 1 novice event often sees a small field, but from an original 16 entries (seven of them trained by Willie Mullins) it was surprising to see only a trio turn up. Despite that there was a fair gallop on and it the winner is potentially top notch. He's at a level similar to the average required to win at Cheltenham.

3351 BETFRED "BE PART OF THE ACTION" NOVICES' LIMITED H'CAP CHASE (FOR THE HALLOWE'EN TROPHY) (13 fncs) 2m 92y
2:35 (2:40) (Class 3) 4-Y-0+ **£8,656** (£3,148)

Form RPR
-121 **1** **Violet Dancer**[29] 2824 5-11-8 **140**.....................(p) JoshuaMoore 150+
(Gary Moore) *several mstkes and nt a fluent: mde most tl 3 out: drvn to regain ld after last: gamely* **15/8**[1]
0-31 **2** *4* **Stilletto (IRE)**[27] 2846 6-11-0 **132**..................... SamTwiston-Davies 135+
(Paul Nicholls) *plld hrd: lft 2nd at 4th: led on bit 3 out: shkn up and hdd after last: no ex* **9/4**[2]
-341 **U** **Balgarry (FR)**[19] 2990 8-11-5 **137**..................... ConorO'Farrell
(David Pipe) *pressed ldr: disputing ld whn stmbld and virtually fell 3rd (water): uns rdr* **4/1**[3]
1642 **U** **Honey Pound (IRE)**[44] 2518 7-9-13 **122**..................... AlanJohns(5)
(Tim Vaughan) *t.k.h: disputing 4th whn hmpd and uns rdr 3rd (water)* **20/1**
6-51 **F** **Sea Wall (FR)**[17] 3042 7-10-4 **122**..................... TomCannon
(Chris Gordon) *chsd ldrs: lft 2nd at 3rd: pressing wnr whn fell next* **4/1**[3]

4m 18.6s (10.60) **Going Correction** +0.95s/f (Soft) **5** Ran SP% **110.3**
Speed ratings (Par 107): **111,109, , ,**
CSF £6.75 TOTE £2.60: £1.60, £1.60; EX 6.80 Trifecta £7.70.
Owner D Bessell & Galloping On The South Downs **Bred** Jeremy Hinds **Trained** Lower Beeding, W Sussex

FOCUS
Race distance increased by 37yds. This was an interesting novice handicap on paper, but it fell apart early with only two getting home. It's debatable as to whether this was a step up from the winner.

3352 BETFRED WISHES YOU A HAPPY NEW YEAR H'CAP HURDLE (10 hdls) 2m 4f 118y
3:10 (3:15) (Class 2) 4-Y-0+ **£11,573** (£3,418; £1,709; £854; £427; £214)

Form RPR
41-5 **1** **One Track Mind (IRE)**[18] 3018 5-11-12 **140**..................... GavinSheehan 152+
(Warren Greatrex) *hld up in 5th: reminders 6th: hdwy 3 out: led 2 out: drvn out* **11/8**[1]
1315 **2** *1 1/2* **San Benedeto (FR)**[33] 2728 4-11-5 **140**.....................(t) HarryCobden(7) 147
(Paul Nicholls) *in tch: led briefly appr 2 out: hrd rdn appr last: styd on same pce* **9/2**[3]

1/F- **3** *28* **Lower Hope Dandy**[395] 2800 8-10-6 **125**.................... CharlieDeutsch(5) 104
(Venetia Williams) *t.k.h: trckd ldr: led 4th: mstke 3 out: sn hdd & wknd* **4/1**[2]
0-11 **4** *20* **Isaac Bell (IRE)**[30] 2810 7-10-11 **125**............................(t) LeightonAspell 84
(Alex Hales) *hld up in rr: effrt and wnt 4th 3 out: sn wknd* **9/1**
4-26 **5** *11* **Shotavodka (IRE)**[31] 2790 9-11-4 **135**.......................(p) KieronEdgar(3) 83
(David Pipe) *dropped to rr after 3rd: rdn and hung lft after 7th: sn bhd* **7/1**
0-P3 **6** *19* **Chieftain's Choice (IRE)**[17] 3041 6-11-1 **129**..................... SeanBowen 58
(Kevin Frost) *led tl 4th: wknd appr 3 out: 6th and no ch whn j. slowly next* **11/1**

5m 21.0s (2.00) **Going Correction** +0.35s/f (Yiel)
WFA 4 from 5yo+ 6lb **6** Ran SP% **111.1**
Speed ratings (Par 109): **110,109,98,91,86 79**
CSF £8.00 TOTE £2.30: £1.80, £2.30; EX 8.70 Trifecta £22.40.
Owner Andy Weller **Bred** Tony Mullins **Trained** Upper Lambourn, Berks

FOCUS
Race distance increased by 118yds. Only two counted from the penultimate flight in this fair handicap and the runner-up sets the standard.

3353 BETFRED 1400 SHOPS NATIONWIDE CHARITY INTRODUCTORY HURDLE (8 hdls) 2m 69y
3:45 (3:46) (Class 4) 4-Y-0+

£3,128 (£924; £462; £231; £115; £58)

Form RPR
31-2 **1** **Premier Bond**[24] 2910 5-11-0 0.................................... DavidBass 133+
(Nicky Henderson) *prom: mstke 3 out: disp ld appr 2 out: drvn ahd run-in: styd on wl* **10/11**[1]
2-21 **2** *4 ½* **William H Bonney**[29] 2823 4-11-5 0.......................... WayneHutchinson 131
(Alan King) *hld up: smooth hdwy to dispute ld appr 2 out: no ex fnl 150yds* **4/1**[3]
5 **3** *9* **Icing On The Cake (IRE)**[38] 2646 5-11-0 0.................... LeightonAspell 118
(Oliver Sherwood) *t.k.h towards rr: promising hdwy to press ldrs 2 out: wknd appr last* **16/1**
2 **4** *5* **Oldgrangewood**[40] 2591 4-11-0 0.................................... HarrySkelton 112
(Dan Skelton) *hld up in rr: hdwy after 5th: rdn to chal whn j.rt 2 out: wknd appr last* **3/1**[2]
3 **5** *8* **Jajamcool (IRE)**[24] 2904 5-11-0 0.................................... JamesBest 105
(Caroline Keevil) *led tl 3rd: led after 5th tl appr 2 out: sn wknd* **100/1**
6 *11* **Stonecutter (IRE)**[67] 4-11-0 0.................................... BrendanPowell 93
(Brendan Powell) *in tch: clsd on ldrs 3 out: sn wknd* **20/1**
0 **7** *10* **Talk Of The South (IRE)**[25] 2886 6-11-0 0.................... NickScholfield 83
(Paul Henderson) *a bhd: no ch fr 5th* **100/1**
16 **8** *3 ½* **Grandmaster George (IRE)**[25] 2879 6-11-0 0.......... JeremiahMcGrath 79
(Seamus Mullins) *chsd ldrs tl wknd appr 3 out* **33/1**
445 **9** *31* **Oh So Gigolo (IRE)**[95] 1644 5-11-0 0.................................... PeterCarberry 48
(Nicky Henderson) *mid-div tl wknd 5th: sn bhd* **50/1**
1 **P** **Banyu (FR)**[36] 2689 4-11-5 0.................................... TomO'Brien
(Philip Hobbs) *plld hrd: sn prom: led 3rd: blnd next: hdd after 5th: 7th and btn whn blnd 3 out: t.o whn p.u bef last* **12/1**

4m 18.2s (8.20) **Going Correction** +0.35s/f (Yiel) **10** Ran SP% **122.6**
Speed ratings (Par 105): **93,90,86,83,79 74,69,67,52,**
CSF £5.29 TOTE £2.30: £1.50, £1.50, £2.10; EX 6.10 Trifecta £60.30.
Owner Middleham Park Racing Xi **Bred** Mickley Stud & Mr & Mrs P Emery **Trained** Upper Lambourn, Berks

FOCUS
Race distance increased by 62yds. Once again this interesting introductory hurdle went the way of Nicky Henderson and the first pair pulled nicely clear. The winner set a decent standard and is rated similar to his Sandown mark.
T/Plt: £29.10 to a £1 stake. Pool: £76600.02 - 1918.82 winning tickets T/Qpdt: £6.30 to a £1 stake. Pool: £5689.05 - 658.08 winning tickets **Lee McKenzie**

3354 - 3355a (Foreign Racing) - See Raceform Interactive

3319 LEOPARDSTOWN (L-H)
Tuesday, December 29

OFFICIAL GOING: Heavy

3356a WILLIS EUROPEAN BREEDERS FUND MARES HURDLE (GRADE 3) (10 hdls) 2m 4f
1:20 (1:21) 4-Y-0+ **£18,895** (£5,523; £2,616; £872)

RPR
1 **Keppols Queen (IRE)**[31] 2797 7-11-5 124.......................... MarkBolger 140+
(Mrs John Harrington, Ire) *chsd ldrs tl wnt 2nd after 1st: impr to dispute gng wl bef 2 out: led fr 2 out and wnt clr into st: rdn bef last and styd on wl run-in: comf* **14/1**
2 *11* **Rock On The Moor (IRE)**[241] 93 7-11-2 138.................... RobbiePower 127
(Mrs John Harrington, Ire) *hld up bhd ldrs in 4th: clsr in 3rd 3 out: nt fluent next and rdn: clsd u.p into mod 2nd into st: no imp on wnr bef last where slow: one pce run-in* **5/1**[3]
3 *13* **Morning Run (IRE)**[332] 3989 6-11-7 145.......................... RWalsh 121+
(W P Mullins, Ire) *led and clr: racd keenly: slt mstke 3 out: jnd bef next: hdd fr 2 out and sn no imp on wnr: dropped to mod 3rd into st and no ex: mstke last* **9/10**[1]
4 *4 ¼* **Whiteout (GER)**[45] 2502 4-11-1 136.......................... JacquesRicou 108
(W P Mullins, Ire) *hld up in 5th: pushed along into 4th bef 2 out and no imp on ldrs u.p appr st: one pce after* **3/1**[2]
5 *8 ½* **The Brock Inn (IRE)**[19] 3004 4-10-9 113.......................... DavidMullins 93
(John W Nicholson, Ire) *chsd ldr tl dropped to 3rd after 1st: dropped to 4th 3 out and lost pl bef next: pushed along and no imp in mod 5th after 2 out* **25/1**
6 *4* **Miss Dinamic (IRE)**[15] 3093 6-11-5 123.......................... BJCooper 99
(Gordon Elliott, Ire) *in rr: slt mstke 1st: slt mstke on outer at 6th: niggled along in 6th after 4 out and no imp on ldrs bef 2 out* **14/1**
P **Thanks For Tea (IRE)**[7] 3209 6-11-2 116......................(t) MarkEnright
(Edmond Kent, Ire) *hld up towards rr: slt mstke 3rd: pushed along in rr after 3 out and wknd bef next: t.o whn p.u bef last* **50/1**

5m 28.2s (21.80) **Going Correction** +0.85s/f (Soft)
WFA 4 from 6yo+ 6lb **7** Ran SP% **113.4**
Speed ratings: **90,85,80,78,75 73,**
CSF £79.54 TOTE £17.60: £5.30, £2.30; DF 99.90 Trifecta £203.90.
Owner Ms C O'Loughlin **Bred** Mrs Mona O'Loughlin **Trained** Moone, Co Kildare

FOCUS
The market hinted strongly at a possible one-two for Willie Mullins, but instead it was Jessica Harrington who achieved that feat with her two runners. The margins reflected the testing nature of conditions for these mares. The time was slow, and the winner is rated in line with her best 2m form.

3357a NEVILLE HOTELS NOVICE CHASE (GRADE 1) (17 fncs) 3m
1:55 (1:55) 4-Y-0+ **£39,534** (£12,519; £5,930; £1,976)

RPR
1 **No More Heroes (IRE)**[30] 2817 6-11-10 154.......................... BJCooper 163+
(Gordon Elliott, Ire) *settled bhd ldr in 2nd tl led narrowly fr 12th: stl gng wl and extended advantage bef last: rdn clr and styd on wl run-in: eased cl home: easily* **4/9**[1]
2 *9* **Rule The World**[86] 1790 8-11-10 148.......................... DavyRussell 153
(M F Morris, Ire) *sweated up befhand: hld up bhd ldrs: tk clsr order briefly at 11th: dropped to rr after 5 out tl disp 2nd 2 out: rdn in 2nd bef last and no imp on easy wnr: kpt on same pce: eased clsng stages* **7/1**[3]
3 *18* **Monksland (IRE)**[30] 2817 8-11-10 149.......................... SeanFlanagan 141+
(Noel Meade, Ire) *hld up bhd ldrs: slt mstke 6th: mstke in rr at 11th: clsr bhd ldrs fr 12th: mstke in 3rd 5 out: disp 2nd bef 2 out where mstke: sn rdn and no imp on wnr in 3rd bef last where mstke: wknd* **10/3**[2]
4 *½* **Wrath Of Titans (IRE)**[44] 2531 6-11-10 0.......................... JJBurke 134
(Ms Sandra Hughes, Ire) *led: j. sltly rt 8th and next: hdd narrowly fr 12th: remained prom tl rdn and lost tch after 2 out: sn wknd* **25/1**

6m 45.1s (14.10) **Going Correction** +0.85s/f (Soft) **4** Ran SP% **108.7**
Speed ratings: **110,107,101,100**
CSF £4.03 TOTE £1.40; DF 3.30 Trifecta £4.70.
Owner Gigginstown House Stud **Bred** Peter And Ann Downes **Trained** Longwood, Co Meath

FOCUS
The in-depth strength of the Gigginstown team in this category was reflected by the composition of this field. A poor turn-out for a race of this nature, but it produced a top-class winner who is a strong candidate for the RSA Chase. The form is rated around the second.

3358a RYANAIR HURDLE (GRADE 1) (8 hdls) 2m
2:30 (2:30) 4-Y-0+ **£46,511** (£14,728; £6,976; £2,325)

RPR
1 **Nichols Canyon**[44] 2532 5-11-10 160.......................... RWalsh 167+
(W P Mullins, Ire) *prom: settled in 2nd after 1st: disp and led bef 4th: jnd bef 2 out where mstke and hdd: sn rdn and u.p in cl 2nd bef last: kpt on wl on inner to ld fnl 100yds and asserted cl home* **2/5**[1]
2 *2* **Identity Thief (IRE)**[31] 2789 5-11-10 158.......................... BJCooper 164
(Henry De Bromhead, Ire) *prom and led after 1st: jnd and hdd bef 4th: disp bef 2 out where led: rdn and strly pressed w narrow advantage bef last: hdd fnl 100yds and kpt on wl wout matching wnr cl home* **11/4**[2]
3 *16* **Plinth (IRE)**[44] 2532 5-11-10 141..........................(bt) BarryGeraghty 148
(A P O'Brien, Ire) *hld up bhd ldrs: last bef 4th: nt fluent 3 out: rdn in 3rd bef 2 out and no imp on clr ldrs whn sn dropped to rr: kpt on one pce after 2 out into mod 3rd* **40/1**
4 *4* **Windsor Park (IRE)**[108] 4702 6-11-10 153.......................... DavyRussell 145
(D K Weld, Ire) *hld up bhd ldrs: slt mstke 1st: 3rd bef 4th: wnt mod 3rd 2 out and no imp on clr ldrs appr st: one pce after and dropped to rr of quartet* **7/1**[3]

4m 13.2s (5.70) **Going Correction** +0.85s/f (Soft) **4** Ran SP% **113.0**
Speed ratings: **119,118,110,108**
CSF £2.13 TOTE £1.30; DF 2.00 Trifecta £11.60.
Owner Andrea & Graham Wylie **Bred** Rabbah Bloodstock Limited **Trained** Muine Beag, Co Carlow

FOCUS
Only four runners, and only two of them counted, but this produced a titanic finish, unexpectedly making it one of the most enthralling races of the four-day festival. Sound form.

3359 - 3360a (Foreign Racing) - See Raceform Interactive

3152 HAYDOCK (L-H)
Wednesday, December 30

OFFICIAL GOING: Heavy (chs 4.4; hdl 4.2)
Wind: Strong, half against Weather: Rain

3361 FREE BET AT 188BET CONDITIONAL JOCKEYS' H'CAP HURDLE (12 hdls) 2m 6f 177y
12:20 (12:20) (Class 4) (0-120,120) 4-Y-0+ **£3,898** (£1,144; £572; £286)

Form RPR
P000 **1** **American Life (FR)**[24] 2924 8-10-8 **105**..........................(vt) KillianMoore(3) 118+
(Sophie Leech) *hld up: hdwy 6th: led jst bef 3 out: drew clr fr 2 out: easily* **13/2**[3]
-503 **2** *13* **Rock Relief (IRE)**[20] 2980 9-10-7 **104**....................(v) DiarmuidO'Regan(3) 98
(Chris Grant) *chsd ldrs: nt fluent 3rd: pushed along appr 5th: mainly u.p after: dropped to rr 8th: mstke 4 out: wl outpcd tl kpt on fr bef last: wnt 2nd jst over 1f out on run-in: no ch w wnr* **15/2**
-432 **3** *9* **Ballywilliam (IRE)**[25] 2903 5-11-9 **120**..........................(p) KieronEdgar(3) 109
(David Pipe) *led: chsd into most flights: rdn after 8th: hdd jst bef 3 out: sn hung lft u.p and no ch w wnr: lost 2nd and wknd run-in* **5/4**[1]
4-P4 **4** *2 ¼* **Up And Go (FR)**[32] 2767 7-11-6 **120**.......................... JamesCowley(6) 104
(Donald McCain) *chsd ldr to 8th: sn rdn: mstke 4 out: sn wknd* **13/2**[3]
60-6 **5** *1 ½* **Bell Weir**[81] 1419 7-11-6 **114**.......................... JamieHamilton 94
(Dianne Sayer) *hld up: niggled along bef 7th: rdn appr 3 out: no imp: wknd last* **11/1**
-112 **6** *59* **Bruce Almighty (IRE)**[54] 2323 4-11-7 **115**.......................... JonathanEngland 75
(Philip Kirby) *chsd ldrs: wnt 2nd 8th: rdn and lost 2nd appr 3 out: sn wknd: t.o* **9/2**[2]

6m 15.7s (15.70) **Going Correction** +0.50s/f (Soft)
WFA 4 from 5yo+ 6lb **6** Ran SP% **109.4**
Speed ratings (Par 105): **92,87,84,83,83 62**
CSF £46.99 TOTE £8.00: £3.30, £3.50; EX 49.70 Trifecta £188.80.
Owner American Life Partnership **Bred** J Y Payet-Descombes **Trained** Elton, Gloucs

FOCUS
The meeting survived two inspections and it provided extreme going, as was advertised in the moderate opening handicap for conditional riders. Shared bends and the bend after the winning post moved out 10yds. Races 1 & 4 increased by 60yds and race 2, 3, 5, 6, & 7 increased by 30yds. The form could be rated a bit higher through the second.

3362 188BET.CO.UK NOVICES' LIMITED H'CAP CHASE (15 fncs) 2m 2f 211y
12:50 (12:50) (Class 3) (0-125,122)
4-Y-0+ **£6,388** (£1,928; £993; £526)

Form RPR
-115 **1** **Throthethatch (IRE)**[33] 2753 6-10-12 **112**........................ PeterBuchanan 120+
(Lucinda Russell) *led: mstke 2nd: hdd 10th: rdn and outpcd bef 3 out: rallied 2 out: sn regained ld: drvn out and styd on wl to go clr fnl 100yds* **10/3**[2]

4142 **2** *5* **Morning Royalty (IRE)**[17] 3055 8-11-6 **120**........................ BrianHughes 123
(James Moffatt) *in tch: wnt 2nd after 11th: swtchd lft and ch 4 out: lft in ld 3 out: hdd jst after 2 out: kpt on same pce run-in* **3/1**[1]

-36P **3** *3 ½* **Special Wells**[25] 2922 6-10-13 **113**........................ DannyCook 114
(Sue Smith) *chsd ldr fr 2nd: led 10th: sltly hmpd by loose horse appr 11th: blnd 3 out: sn hdd: one pce bef last* **7/2**[3]

4-06 **4** *7* **Grove Silver (IRE)**[22] 2963 6-11-8 **122**........................ AidanColeman 115
(Jennie Candlish) *in tch: hmpd by loose horse 8th: rdn bef 3 out: sn wknd* **8/1**

32P2 **P** **Flash Crash**[16] 3081 6-10-2 **109** ow3........................(t) MrZBaker[(7)]
(Barry Brennan) *j. slowly 1st: in rr: rdn along after 6th: tk clsr order 7th: rdn after 9th: toiling after 11th: bhd whn p.u bef 4 out* **8/1**

1006 **U** **Another Journey**[27] 2857 6-10-13 **113**........................ RobertDunne
(Sarah-Jayne Davies) *chsd ldr: blnd and uns rdr 2nd* **66/1**

-404 **P** **Eco Warrior**[26] 2888 5-10-7 **107**........................ AlainCawley
(Venetia Williams) *in tch: lost pl 7th: hmpd by loose horse 8th: in rr after: bhd whn mstke 11th: t.o whn p.u bef 3 out* **5/1**

5m 20.6s (10.60) **Going Correction** +0.75s/f (Soft) **7 Ran SP% 110.7**
Speed ratings (Par 107): **107,104,103,100, ,**
CSF £13.28 TOTE £4.10: £2.20, £1.80; EX 11.40 Trifecta £59.60.
Owner Mrs Sandra Giles **Bred** Jerry Murphy **Trained** Arlary, Perth & Kinross

FOCUS
Race distance increased by 30yds. This modest novice handicap was a messy affair due to the loose Another Journey, but the finishing order still makes sense. The winner should go on to rate higher.

3363 EBF STALLIONS 188BET "NATIONAL HUNT" NOVICES' HURDLE (QUALIFIER) (9 hdls) 1m 7f 144y
1:25 (1:25) (Class 4) 4-6-Y-0 **£3,898** (£1,144; £572; £286)

Form RPR
12 **1** **Bigmartre (FR)**[35] 2710 4-11-5 133........................ NicodeBoinville 134+
(Harry Whittington) *mde all: mstke 5th: rdn between last 2: gd jump and outj. rival last: sn over 2 l clr: kpt on gamely and a doing enough towards fin* **9/4**[2]

5-21 **2** *1 ¼* **Vintage Clouds (IRE)**[40] 2628 5-11-5 130........................ DannyCook 133+
(Sue Smith) *chsd wnr: rdn and ev ch last where outj. by wnr: sn over 2 l down: rallied towards fin but hld* **6/5**[1]

2-61 **3** *10* **Flashjack (IRE)**[27] 2860 5-11-5 0........................ JakeGreenall 125
(Henry Daly) *in tch: hdwy appr 4 out where mstke: effrt whn cl 3rd 2 out: no ex fnl 150yds* **4/1**[3]

4 **4** *11* **Sean Ban (IRE)**[17] 3054 5-10-12 0........................ WillKennedy 106+
(Donald McCain) *hld up in rr: hdwy after 4 out: mstke 3 out: sn no imp* **25/1**

10-3 **5** *7* **Wabanaki (IRE)**[36] 2699 5-10-12 0........................ AdamWedge 98
(Evan Williams) *racd keenly: chsd ldrs: wknd appr 3 out* **8/1**

4 **6** *shd* **Kauto Riko (FR)**[219] 467 4-10-12 0........................ JamesDavies 97
(Tom Gretton) *racd keenly: sn prom: lost pl after 4 out: struggling after* **100/1**

50-0 **7** *14* **Another Cobbler (FR)**[55] 2302 5-10-5 0........................ JamieMoore 76
(Henry Daly) *midfield: wknd bef 3 out* **100/1**

0 **8** *1 ½* **Leaving Las Vegas**[19] 3009 4-10-12 0........................ DenisO'Regan 82
(William Kinsey) *hld up: in midfield bef 4th: wknd bef 3 out* **100/1**

9 *1 ½* **Sarazen Bridge** 4-10-12 0........................ JoshuaMoore 80
(Jonjo O'Neill) *hld up: struggling after 4 out: nvr a threat* **25/1**

60-0 **10** *2* **Red Hott Robbie**[29] 2840 6-10-12 0........................ AndrewThornton 78
(Giuseppe Fierro) *hld up: rdn after 4 out: nvr a threat* **200/1**

4m 8.5s (4.30) **Going Correction** +0.50s/f (Soft) **10 Ran SP% 118.5**
Speed ratings: **109,108,103,97,94 94,87,86,85,84**
CSF £5.56 TOTE £2.70: £1.60, £1.10, £1.30; EX 8.10 Trifecta £13.00.
Owner P J Dixon **Bred** E Prigent, E Lecoiffier & S Follain **Trained** Sparsholt, Oxfordshire

FOCUS
Race distance increased by 30yds. A fair novice event and straightforward form, the first two pretty much to their marks.

3364 THE LAST FLING CHASE (HANDICAP SPONSORED BY CLASSIC LODGES LTD) (22 fncs) 3m 3f 57y
2:00 (2:00) (Class 2) (0-145,142) 4-Y-0+
£13,763 (£4,065; £2,032; £1,016; £508; £255)

Form RPR
0-04 **1** **Rigadin De Beauchene (FR)**[25] 2907 10-10-11 **127**....(b) RobertDunne 139+
(Venetia Williams) *mde all: mstke 3 out: rdn bef 2 out: kpt on run-in* **4/1**[3]

-F33 **2** *3* **Harry The Viking**[17] 3057 10-10-12 **128**....................(p) BrianHughes 134
(Sandy Thomson) *prom: chsd wnr 3 out: rdn and hung lft appr last: no real imp run-in* **11/1**

F2-3 **3** *12* **Listen Boy (IRE)**[29] 2832 9-10-4 **123**........................ RyanHatch[(3)] 118
(Nigel Twiston-Davies) *handy: chsd wnr 15th: rdn and lost 2nd 3 out: one pce bef last* **11/2**

63F1 **4** *8* **Cyclop (IRE)**[20] 2996 4-10-9 **132**....................(tp) AidanColeman 117+
(David Dennis) *midfield: blnd 16th: rdn and outpcd after 18th: blnd 4 out: no imp after* **6/1**

0-30 **5** *3* **Restless Harry**[25] 2916 11-11-7 **137**........................ JamesDavies 120
(Henry Oliver) *prom: rdn and lost pl 16th: wknd 3 out* **7/2**[2]

2-11 **6** *10* **Kingswell Theatre**[25] 2905 6-11-12 **142**........................ TomScudamore 118
(Michael Scudamore) *prom: lost pl 7th: reminder after 13th: nt fluent 14th whn struggling: wl btn* **3/1**[1]

-6FP **7** *6* **William Money (IRE)**[24] 2934 8-10-4 **125**........................ DiarmuidO'Regan[(5)] 95
(Chris Grant) *in rr: mstke 13th: rdn after 18th: n.d* **22/1**

1P-P **8** *25* **Voyage A New York (FR)**[46] 2497 6-10-4 **120**........................ DerekFox 62
(Lucinda Russell) *hld up: struggling whn blnd 17th: t.o* **16/1**

7m 51.5s (35.50) **Going Correction** +0.75s/f (Soft)
WFA 4 from 6yo+ 7lb **8 Ran SP% 115.5**
Speed ratings (Par 109): **77,76,72,70,69 66,64,57**
CSF £44.83 CT £243.10 TOTE £5.70: £1.80, £2.10, £1.80; EX 54.30 Trifecta £257.20.
Owner Andrew Wiles **Bred** Raymond Bellanger **Trained** Kings Caple, H'fords

FOCUS
Race distance increased by 60yds. A fair staying handicap which saw few get seriously involved on the attritional going. The winner was on a very good mark and is rated back to form.

3365 LIVE CASINO AT 188BET.CO.UK H'CAP CHASE (17 fncs) 2m 4f 135y
2:30 (2:31) (Class 3) (0-130,130) 4-Y-0+ **£9,097** (£2,671; £1,335; £667)

Form RPR
64 **1** **Morney Wing (IRE)**[49] 2434 6-10-13 **117**....................(tp) DenisO'Regan 127+
(Charlie Mann) *mde all: lft abt 3 l clr 3 out: hrd pressed 110yds out: fnd ex and styd on gamely towards fin* **7/1**[2]

1512 **2** *1 ¾* **Friendly Royal (IRE)**[22] 2963 6-11-2 **120**........................ DannyCook 128
(Sue Smith) *prom: rdn and outpcd after 4 out: lft abt 3 l 2nd whn j.lft 3 out: rallied u.p last: chalng 110yds out: no ex towards fin* **7/4**[1]

0/F1 **3** *32* **Elenika (FR)**[25] 2908 7-11-2 **120**........................ AidanColeman 101
(Venetia Williams) *in tch: rdn appr 4 out: lft 3rd u.p whn trying to keep on 3 out: tired last: wl btn* **7/4**[1]

0443 **4** *8* **Sleepy Haven (IRE)**[25] 2920 5-11-8 **126**........................(t) PeterCarberry 92
(Jennie Candlish) *in rr: j.lft 10th: struggling 13th: wl btn bef 2 out* **10/1**

241- **F** **Minella Reception (IRE)**[496] 1275 9-11-9 **130**....................(t) RyanHatch[(3)]
(Nigel Twiston-Davies) *hld up: hdwy to chse wnr 12th: stl travelling wl enough and ev ch whn fell 3 out* **9/1**[3]

-300 **P** **Midnight Belle**[25] 2911 8-11-8 **126**........................ JamesDavies
(Tom Symonds) *prom: mstke 8th: lost pl 12th: struggling and bhd after 13th: p.u bef 4 out* **14/1**

5m 54.4s (354.40) **6 Ran SP% 111.0**
CSF £20.08 TOTE £10.20: £3.60, £1.50; EX 25.40 Trifecta £46.30.
Owner The Steeple Chasers **Bred** G Bell **Trained** Upper Lambourn, Berks

FOCUS
Race distance increased by 30yds. This was not a bad handicap and yet again the going played a big part. Arguably steps up from the first two.

3366 PREMIER LEAGUE BETTING AT 188BET.CO.UK "FIXED BRUSH" NOVICES' HURDLE (10 hdls) 2m 2f 191y
3:05 (3:05) (Class 4) 4-7-Y-0 **£3,898** (£1,144; £572; £286)

Form RPR
1 **1** **Its'afreebee (IRE)**[49] 2437 5-11-0 0........................ BridgetAndrews[(5)] 133+
(Dan Skelton) *mde all: drew clr fr 2 out: 8 l ahd whn lft further clr last: styd on wl: unchal* **6/4**[2]

0 **2** *24* **Robinshill (IRE)**[77] 1901 4-10-9 0........................ RyanHatch[(3)] 104
(Nigel Twiston-Davies) *chsd ldrs: rdn appr 2 out: one pce whn lft 2nd last: no ch w wnr* **33/1**

306 **3** *4 ½* **I Just Know (IRE)**[19] 3021 5-10-12 112........................ DannyCook 98
(Sue Smith) *chsd wnr to 6th: lost pl and rdn after 4 out: plugged on in clsng stages* **13/2**[3]

06 **4** *13* **Veinard (FR)**[31] 2801 6-10-7 0........................ CallumBewley[(5)] 85
(Robert Bewley) *hld up: stmbld 6th: hdwy after: wkng whn mstke 3 out* **25/1**

55 **5** *60* **Goldboy (IRE)**[17] 3063 7-10-12 0........................ JoshuaMoore 25
(Jonjo O'Neill) *in rr: struggling after 6th: j.lft 4 out: t.o: b.b.v* **10/1**

5/4- **6** *7* **Just Like Beth**[398] 2766 7-10-8 0 ow3........................ AndrewThornton 14
(Giuseppe Fierro) *hld up in tch: lost pl and rdn after 5th: struggling after: t.o* **200/1**

10-1 **U** **Nansaroy**[42] 2563 5-11-5 0........................ AdamWedge 115
(Evan Williams) *chsd ldrs: wnt 2nd 6th: rdn appr 2 out: abt 8 l down and no imp on wnr whn stmbld and uns rdr last* **11/8**[1]

5m 6.5s (13.50) **Going Correction** +0.85s/f (Soft)
WFA 4 from 5yo+ 5lb **7 Ran SP% 111.8**
Speed ratings: **105,94,93,87,62 59,**
CSF £37.70 TOTE £2.10: £1.30, £8.70; EX 45.60 Trifecta £190.30.
Owner Rebel Jumping **Bred** Edward Sexton **Trained** Alcester, Warwicks

FOCUS
Race distance increased by 30yds. An uncompetitive novice contest. A step up from winner for his new yard and there's probably more to come.

3367 ASIAN H'CAPS AT 188BET.CO.UK "FIXED BRUSH" HANDICAP HURDLE (10 hdls) 2m 2f 191y
3:35 (3:35) (Class 4) (0-120,118) 3-Y-0+ **£3,898** (£1,144; £572; £286)

Form RPR
04 **1** **Tomkevi (FR)**[31] 2802 4-11-2 **111**........................ TonyKelly[(3)] 120
(Rebecca Menzies) *in tch: upsides 4 out: sn led on inner: rdn appr last: abt 3 l clr 1f out on run-in: hung lft: reduced margin towards fin: hld on gamely* **7/1**

6-04 **2** *nk* **Hainan (FR)**[22] 2962 4-11-6 **112**........................ DannyCook 120
(Sue Smith) *chsd ldr: upsides 4 out: rdn appr 3 out: ev ch u.p 2 out: abt 3 l down 1f out run-in: hung lft: styd on to cl towards fin* **3/1**[2]

143B **3** *5* **Octagon**[31] 2802 5-11-12 **118**........................ BrianHughes 121
(Dianne Sayer) *hld up: hdwy after 4 out: gng wl appr 3 out: ev ch on bit 2 out: rdn bef last: nt pick up run-in: no ex ins fnl f* **13/8**[1]

2/1P **4** *13* **Glen Countess (IRE)**[219] 470 8-11-0 **113**........................ MrRHogg[(7)] 103
(Sue Smith) *led: jnd 4 out: sn hdd: nt fluent 3 out: rdn and wanted to lug lft whn wknd bef 2 out* **15/2**

66F3 **5** *23* **Seven Devils (IRE)**[32] 2791 5-11-1 **107**........................ DerekFox 74
(Lucinda Russell) *hld up: rdn and outpcd appr 3 out: n.d whn blnd 2 out* **11/2**[3]

0-5P **6** *1 ¾* **Tresor De Bontee (FR)**[14] 3115 8-11-11 **117**....................(p) JamieMoore 82
(Kerry Lee) *chsd ldrs: lost pl appr 3 out: wknd bef 2 out* **11/1**

5m 16.7s (23.70) **Going Correction** +0.85s/f (Soft)
WFA 4 from 5yo+ 5lb **6 Ran SP% 111.1**
Speed ratings (Par 105): **84,83,81,76,66 65**
CSF £27.80 CT £48.17 TOTE £6.40: £2.60, £1.90; EX 24.90 Trifecta £74.20.
Owner P J Howe & R G Oliver **Bred** Y Molliere **Trained** Stearsby, N Yorks

FOCUS
Race distance increased by 30yds. An ordinary handicap fought out by the first pair from the last and again it was hard work. The winner is rated in line with his French mark.
T/Plt: £174.30 to a £1 stake. Pool of £55496.29 - 232.32 winning tickets. T/Qpdt: £9.40 to a £1 stake. Pool of £6676.68 - 523.05 winning tickets. **Darren Owen**

[2985]TAUNTON (R-H)

Wednesday, December 30

OFFICIAL GOING: Heavy

Wind: almost nil by the time of racing Weather: rain, heavy at times

3368 BET TOTEPLACEPOT H'CAP HURDLE (9 hdls) 2m 104y

12:40 (12:41) (Class 5) (0-100,100) 3-Y-O+ £3,898 (£1,144; £572; £286)

Form RPR

22PP 1 **Winged Express (IRE)**[58] 2254 6-11-1 89........................[1] IanPopham 105+
(Alexandra Dunn) *trckd ldr: lft 2nd 3 out: chal next: led bef last: drifted lft whn rdn clr: readily* 8/1

6P62 2 11 **Norse Light**[12] 3140 4-11-4 99........................(p) GarethMalone(7) 102
(David Dennis) *hld up towards rr: pushed along and hdwy fr 3 out: rdn to chse ldrs next: styd on into 2nd run-in: no ch w wnr* 7/1[3]

-500 3 6 **Triple Chief (IRE)**[20] 2987 4-11-7 100........................(tp) CiaranGethings(5) 97
(Chris Down) *led 3rd: rdn and hdd appr last: no ex run-in* 7/1[3]

500 4 7 **Aaman (IRE)**[28] 2850 9-10-8 85........................ RobertWilliams(3) 77
(Bernard Llewellyn) *mid-div: hdwy after 6th: rdn to chse ldrs appr 2 out: sn one pce* 33/1

0-52 5 2 **Kayf Charmer**[26] 2876 5-9-8 75........................ ConorSmith(7) 63
(Linda Blackford) *trckd ldrs: rdn after 3 out: nt pce to chal: fdd appr last* 4/1[1]

0503 6 8 **Brinestine (USA)**[27] 2869 6-11-5 100........................(t) HarrisonBeswick(7) 80
(Emma Baker) *hld up towards rr: hdwy into midfield 3 out: sn rdn: no further imp fr next* 8/1

2000 7 12 **Normandy King (IRE)**[32] 2772 4-11-6 94........................ MichaelByrne 62
(Tim Vaughan) *towards rr: hmpd 3 out: sme minor late prog past btn horses: nvr a factor* 20/1

P00 8 ½ **Lough Derg Island (IRE)**[25] 2904 7-11-8 96........................ RhysFlint 64
(Alexandra Dunn) *led tl 3rd: midfield after next: wknd after 3 out* 25/1

04-P 9 3 **Miss Siskin**[34] 2730 6-10-2 83........................ PaulO'Brien(7) 48
(Jimmy Frost) *a bhd* 100/1

30 10 nk **Sabroclair (FR)**[34] 2736 6-11-7 95........................ PaddyBrennan 61
(Richard Woollacott) *trckd ldrs: losing pl whn hmpd 3 out: sn rdn: wknd bef next* 10/1

-603 11 1¾ **Daring Indian**[21] 2974 7-10-9 90........................(p) HarryTeal(7) 52
(Roger Teal) *trckd ldrs tl wknd after 3 out* 16/1

4003 12 26 **Avel Vor (IRE)**[29] 2833 4-11-10 98........................(t) ConorO'Farrell 34
(Nigel Hawke) *chsd ldrs tl 5th: struggling in rr: t.o after 3 out* 11/1

000- 13 22 **Petergate**[128] 4465 4-11-1 89........................ JamesBest 3
(Nigel Hawke) *struggling after 5th: a towards rr: t.o after 3 out* 33/1

2-P0 P **Suffice (IRE)**[61] 2162 6-9-8 75........................(b[1]) ThomasCheesman(7)
(Laura Young) *hld up towards rr: hdwy fr 5th: trcking ldrs whn bdly hmpd 3 out: no ch after whn p.u bef next* 5/1[2]

625P F **Columbanus (IRE)**[4] 3256 4-9-12 79........................(tp) MissNatalieParker(7)
(Kevin Bishop) *in tch: hdwy 6th: trcking ldr whn fell 3 out* 14/1

4m 27.4s (19.40) **Going Correction** +1.275s/f (Heav) 15 Ran SP% 129.3
Speed ratings (Par 103): **102,96,93,90,89 85,79,78,77,77 76,63,52,,**
CSF £64.85 CT £429.54 TOTE £10.60: £3.50, £2.80, £3.70; EX 79.50 Trifecta £970.00.
Owner J Burley & The Bucklanders **Bred** Sean And Orla Gannon **Trained** West Buckland, Somerset

FOCUS
Chase bend on inner line and hurdle bend out of home straight moved out 9yds and out of back straight by 6yds. Race distance increased by 63yds. Persistent rain in the lead up to the meeting meant the ground was changed to heavy about an hour before the first race and the track had to survive a late inspection due to high winds. A very ordinary handicap hurdle to open the card. A big pb from the winner.

3369 GET SOCIAL WITH TOTEPOOL ON FACEBOOK H'CAP HURDLE (12 hdls) 2m 7f 198y

1:10 (1:10) (Class 5) (0-100,100) 4-Y-O+ £3,898 (£1,144; £572; £286)

Form RPR

-021 1 **Snowball (IRE)**[39] 2649 8-11-3 91........................ LeightonAspell 92
(David Arbuthnot) *mid-div: hdwy 8th: led after 3 out: styd on: drvn out* 9/2[2]

2-40 2 1 **Onwiththeparty**[12] 3137 6-11-12 100........................(p) TomCannon 101
(Chris Gordon) *prom tl 4th: in tch: rdn after 8th: hdwy into 3rd whn stmbld bdly on bnd after 3 out: wnt 2nd bef last: styd on but a being hld* 10/1

-34 3 6 **The Last Bridge**[210] 599 8-10-7 81........................ RichardJohnson 74
(Susan Johnson) *trckd ldrs tl lost pl and pushed along towards rr of midfield after 4th: styd on u.p fr 3 out: wnt 3rd bef 2 out: clsd on ldrs fr last but a being hld* 5/1[3]

4U45 4 9 **Skating Home (IRE)**[13] 3128 9-9-11 74 oh3........................(b) ConorShoemark(3) 59
(Richard Hawker) *in tch: led after 3rd: rdn and hdd after 3 out: styd on same pce fr next* 66/1

/10- 5 20 **Phar Away Island (IRE)**[297] 7-10-0 81........................ HarryTeal(7) 45
(John Berwick) *hld up towards rr: rdn and sme prog after 8th: nvr trbld ldrs: wknd 2 out* 25/1

1-P0 6 1¾ **Comical Red**[48] 2454 7-11-1 92........................(b) TomBellamy(3) 54
(Mark Gillard) *mid-div: rdn after 9th: wnt hld 4th after 3 out tl next: wknd* 14/1

0-PP 7 19 **Memory Of Light (IRE)**[34] 2732 6-10-6 80........................(t) BrendanPowell 23
(Claire Dyson) *led tl 5th: chsd ldrs tl wknd 9th: t.o* 33/1

223- P **Green Du Ciel (FR)**[204] 5247 10-10-6 87........................(t) ThomasCheesman(7)
(Carroll Gray) *towards rr: pushed along in midfield 7th: wknd next: p.u bef 9th* 20/1

405/ P **Subtle Approach (IRE)**[1624] 1168 10-9-11 74........................ JamesBanks(3)
(Emma Baker) *a towards rr: t.o whn p.u bef 2 out* 50/1

-632 P **Ordensritter (GER)**[37] 2693 7-11-2 93........................(bt) GilesHawkins(3)
(Chris Down) *towards rr of midfield: struggling 8th: p.u after 3 out* 9/1

4-54 P **Miss Oscarose (IRE)**[27] 2871 8-11-7 95........................ TomO'Brien
(Paul Henderson) *nvr gng in rr: p.u bef 7th* 16/1

6/02 P **Double Accord**[34] 2736 5-11-5 98........................ DavidNoonan(5)
(Anthony Honeyball) *in tch: struggling after 8th: wknd bef 3 out: t.o whn p.u bef 2 out* 7/2[1]

24-4 P **Kahdian (IRE)**[237] 164 5-11-6 99........................ GaryDerwin(5)
(Helen Rees) *a towards rr: t.o whn p.u bef 2 out* 20/1

0-50 P **Mister Chairman (IRE)**[74] 1961 7-10-11 85........................(t) SeanBowen
(Rebecca Curtis) *trcking ldrs whn mstke and stmbld bdly 8th: nvr rcvrd and p.u bef 9th* 7/1

001P P **Vodka Island (IRE)**[27] 2868 6-10-12 91........................ AlanJohns(5)
(Tim Vaughan) *mid-div tl appr 8th: t.o whn p.u bef 9th* 14/1

6m 54.5s (50.50) **Going Correction** +1.75s/f (Heav) 15 Ran SP% 127.6
Speed ratings (Par 103): **85,84,82,79,73 72,66,,,,**
CSF £47.90 CT £244.53 TOTE £5.50: £1.80, £3.60, £2.20; EX 55.40 Trifecta £282.40.
Owner The Daring Partnership **Bred** Sean Hurley **Trained** Beare Green, Surrey

FOCUS
Race distance increased by 90yds. A moderate handicap hurdle. It was predictably tough going, they were strung out from an early stage and those that did manage to complete finished very tired. Another step forward from the winner.

3370 BET TOTEQUADPOT NOVICES' HURDLE (10 hdls) 2m 3f 1y

1:45 (1:45) (Class 4) 4-Y-O+ £4,548 (£1,335; £667; £333)

Form RPR

3 1 **Miles To Milan (IRE)**[48] 2457 5-10-12 0........................ RichardJohnson 127+
(Philip Hobbs) *trckd ldrs on outer: chalng whn hit 2 out: stl upsides whn nt fluent last: led flat: r.o wl: rdn out* 6/1[3]

0-35 2 2½ **Bim Bam Boum (FR)**[34] 2731 4-10-12 0........................ NoelFehily 124
(Harry Fry) *hld up towards rr on outer: hdwy fr 6th: rdn to ld appr last: hdd run-in: kpt on but no ex* 8/1

-311 3 3 **Modus**[34] 2723 5-11-8 139........................ BarryGeraghty 131
(Paul Nicholls) *racd inner: mid-div: hdwy 7th: cl 3rd whn rdn between last 2: kpt on same pce fr last* 1/1[1]

1-23 4 7 **Board Of Trade**[33] 2762 4-10-12 132........................ WayneHutchinson 114
(Alan King) *racd inner: mid-div: hdwy 7th: led after 3 out: sn rdn: hdd bef last: no ex* 2/1[2]

5 5 5 **The Fresh Prince (IRE)**[53] 2337 5-10-12 0........................ LeightonAspell 108
(Oliver Sherwood) *racd keenly on inner most of way: pressed ldr: rdn after 3 out: hld next: no ex fr last* 12/1

6 19 **Coeur Tantre (IRE)**[139] 1250 4-10-12 0........................ GavinSheehan 89
(Hugo Froud) *racd outer: mid-div: rdn after 3 out: nvr any threat: wknd between last 2* 50/1

5-U2 7 2¾ **Viva Rafa (IRE)**[183] 865 5-10-12 0........................ IanPopham 86
(Richard Phillips) *racd keenly on inner: led tl after 3 out: wknd bef next* 50/1

0/06 8 ¾ **Up To Al (IRE)**[20] 2986 7-10-12 0........................ LiamHeard 85
(Bob Buckler) *racd inner: mid-div tl wknd 3 out* 100/1

6 9 shd **Mondello (GER)**[42] 2564 4-10-12 0........................ ConorO'Farrell 85
(Richard Woollacott) *racd outer: mid-div: hdwy 3 out: sn rdn: wknd bef next* 50/1

0 10 ½ **Mr Medic**[39] 2636 4-10-12 0........................ FelixDeGiles 84
(Robert Walford) *racd inner: a bhd: t.o* 100/1

0-00 P **Up The Junction**[57] 2258 4-10-12 0........................ MichaelByrne
(Tim Vaughan) *racd outer: a towards rr: losing tch whn p.u after 6th* 100/1

650 P **Repeat The Feat (FR)**[32] 2772 4-10-12 0........................ SamTwiston-Davies
(Charlie Longsdon) *racd outer: trckd ldrs tl wknd after 7th: t.o whn p.u bef 2 out* 100/1

0 P **Jack Snipe**[34] 2731 6-10-12 0........................ NickScholfield
(Jeremy Scott) *racd outer: a bhd: t.o fr 5th: p.u after 3 out* 100/1

5m 17.5s (31.50) **Going Correction** +1.75s/f (Heav)
WFA 4 from 5yo+ 5lb 13 Ran SP% 127.3
Speed ratings (Par 105): **103,101,100,97,95 87,86,86,86,85 ,,**
CSF £55.12 TOTE £8.80: £2.20, £3.00, £1.02; EX 62.70 Trifecta £144.30.
Owner Mrs Lesley Field & Mrs Caren Walsh **Bred** Michael O'Neill **Trained** Withycombe, Somerset

FOCUS
Race distance increased by 63yds. All eyes were focused on the favourite bidding for a hat-trick of hurdle wins, but he couldn't defy a penalty in the conditions. They raced right across the track, with jockeys attempting to steer clear of churned up ground and this is not form to take at face value. A big step up from the winner compared with the third on course form.

3371 SETSQUARE RECRUITMENT NOVICES' LIMITED H'CAP CHASE (15 fncs 2 omitted) 2m 7f 3y

2:20 (2:20) (Class 4) (0-120,120) 4-Y-O+ £5,198 (£1,526; £763; £381)

Form RPR

64-1 1 **Waldorf Salad**[13] 3129 7-11-2 119........................ CharlieDeutsch(5) 134+
(Venetia Williams) *led after 3rd: mde rest: jockeys foot slipped out of iron between 11th and 12th: sn rcvrd: styd on dourly and in command fr fr 3 out* 7/2[1]

4-24 2 5 **Sonny The One**[44] 2546 5-11-2 114........................(p) BrendanPowell 119
(Colin Tizzard) *trckd ldrs: wnt 2nd after 12th: rdn appr 3 out: styd on but nt pce to chal* 10/1

4-14 3 20 **Wild Rover (IRE)**[34] 2725 6-11-8 120........................ SeanBowen 107
(Rebecca Curtis) *hld up in tch: wnt 3rd after 12th: rdn bef 3 out: nvr threatened: wknd 2 out* 9/2[2]

3125 4 6 **Ready Token (IRE)**[32] 2766 7-11-6 118........................(tp) SamTwiston-Davies 97
(Charlie Longsdon) *led tl 3rd: chsd wnr: rdn after 12th: wknd 3 out* 6/1

-F52 P **Saint Breiz (FR)**[27] 2874 9-10-7 105........................(t) IanPopham
(Carroll Gray) *hld up in tch: wknd after 12th: p.u bef 3 out* 10/1

460- F **Geton Xmoor (IRE)**[349] 3696 8-10-13 118........................ MrMatthewHampton(7)
(Richard Woollacott) *hit 1st: fell next* 50/1

P-0P P **Liberty One (IRE)**[45] 2513 9-11-6 118........................(p) NoelFehily
(Richard Woollacott) *trckd ldrs: rdn after 12th: wknd on long run bef 3 out where p.u* 11/2[3]

42-3 P **Horsehill (IRE)**[48] 2456 6-11-5 117........................ LeightonAspell
(Oliver Sherwood) *hld up: hmpd 7th: awkward 10th: sn lost tch: p.u bef 12th* 7/2[1]

0264 F **Thegreendalerocket (IRE)**[20] 2985 6-10-5 110........................ PaulO'Brien(7)
(Jimmy Frost) *hld up: fell 7th* 8/1

6m 29.8s (13.80) **Going Correction** +0.75s/f (Soft) 9 Ran SP% 118.4
Speed ratings (Par 105): **106,104,97,95,,,,**
CSF £38.46 CT £162.54 TOTE £4.30: £1.50, £3.30, £2.00; EX 48.20 Trifecta £247.00.
Owner Alan Parker **Bred** A Parker **Trained** Kings Caple, H'fords

FOCUS
The open ditch in the back straight was omitted. Not much got involved in what looked a fair handicap chase. The winner should go in again.

3372 HAPPY NEW YEAR FROM TOTEPOOL MARES' NOVICES' HURDLE (LISTED RACE) (9 hdls) 2m 104y

2:50 (2:50) (Class 1) 3-Y-O+ £11,546 (£4,334; £2,170; £1,082; £542)

Form RPR

1 **Myska (IRE)**[41] 2608 5-11-2 0........................ RWalsh 136+
(W P Mullins, Ire) *racd on outer: hld up bhd ldrs: tk clsr order 3 out: chal 2 out: ldng whn mstke last: styd on: rdn out* 10/11[1]

411 **2** 2 1/2 **Jessber's Dream (IRE)**[13] 3119 5-11-2 122..........(t) NoelFehily 130
(Harry Fry) *racd outer: trckd ldrs: drifted rt whn ldng 2 out: sn rdn: edgd lft and hdd bef last: styd on but no ex run-in* **5/1**[2]

0-11 **3** 5 **Surtee Du Berlais (IRE)**[38] 2665 5-11-2 122.......... LeightonAspell 125
(Oliver Sherwood) *racd outer: hld up bhd ldrs: nudged along but too cl order 3 out: ev ch 2 out: sn rdn: kpt on same pce fr last* **14/1**

-131 **4** 10 **Ruby Rambler**[17] 3065 5-11-2 135.......... GavinSheehan 115
(Lucy Wadham) *racd inner: led tl 5th: led after 3 out: rdn and hdd bef next: one pce after* **5/1**[2]

4-11 **5** 3/4 **Girly Girl (IRE)**[58] 2252 6-11-2 0.......... HarrySkelton 114
(Dan Skelton) *racd inner: prom: swtchd to outer to ld 5th tl after 3 out: sn rdn: kpt to inner and one pce fr next* **16/1**

30-1 **P** **Lifeboat Mona**[27] 2870 5-11-2 0..........(t) SamTwiston-Davies
(Paul Nicholls) *racd outer: trckd ldrs: rdn after 3 out: wknd qckly: p.u bef next* **11/2**[3]

4m 32.2s (24.20) **Going Correction** +1.75s/f (Heav)
WFA 4 from 5yo+ 5lb **6 Ran SP% 113.7**
Speed ratings (Par 111): **109,107,105,100,99**
CSF £6.19 TOTE £1.80: £1.10, £2.40; EX 8.50 Trifecta £48.80.

Owner Supreme Horse Racing Club **Bred** Kenneth Parkhill **Trained** Muine Beag, Co Carlow

FOCUS
Race distance increased by 63yds. A good quality Listed event for mares, with the whole field coming into this race off a win and some top stables represented. The form of this race could prove to have a bearing on the new mares' novice event at the Cheltenham Festival with the winner posting an impressive effort. The jockeys once again were spread across the course looking for fresh ground. Myska is on the upgrade.

3373 TOTESCOOP6 PLAY NEW YEAR'S DAY H'CAP CHASE (15 fncs 2 omitted) 2m 7f 3y
3:25 (3:25) (Class 3) (0-130,130) 4-Y-0+ £8,654 (£2,687; £1,446)

Form RPR
5-F6 **1** **Kings Apollo**[27] 2872 6-9-11 104 oh1.......... BenPoste(3) 112
(Tom Symonds) *w ldr tl after 6th: trckd ldr: disp after 12th tl clr ldr 3 out: styd on and in command fr next* **6/1**

P-1P **2** 6 **Union Jack D'Ycy (FR)**[22] 2955 7-11-5 128.......... CharlieDeutsch(5) 130
(Venetia Williams) *trckd ldrs: disp ld after 12th tl bef 3 out where blnd: hld after* **5/1**[3]

P/56 **3** 34 **Fine Parchment (IRE)**[32] 2766 12-10-9 116..........(tp) HarryBannister(3) 90
(Charlie Mann) *led tl after 12th: sn rdn in hld 3rd: wknd last* **8/1**

1P-P **P** **Farbreaga (IRE)**[18] 3046 9-11-11 129..........(p) MattieBatchelor
(Jamie Poulton) *nvr fluent in rr: losing tch whn blnd 10th: p.u bef 11th* **14/1**

P5P/ **P** **Same Difference (IRE)**[613] 5571 9-11-12 130..........(p) GavinSheehan
(Warren Greatrex) *trckd ldrs: nudged along after 9th: losing pl whn p.u bef 12th* **2/1**[1]

12P5 **P** **Dreamsoftheatre (IRE)**[25] 2905 7-11-12 130..........(t) RichieMcLernon
(Jonjo O'Neill) *cl up: struggling 10th: wknd 12th: t.o whn p.u bef 3 out* **12/1**

23F4 **P** **Ebony Empress (IRE)**[31] 2805 6-11-5 123..........(p) NoelFehily
(Neil Mulholland) *hld up: j.lft: pushed along after 9th: hdwy next: wkng whn hit 11th: t.o whn p.u bef 3 out* **3/1**[2]

6m 45.2s (29.20) **Going Correction** +1.475s/f (Heav) **7 Ran SP% 114.8**
Speed ratings (Par 107): **108,105,94,** , ,
CSF £35.82 CT £241.47 TOTE £7.00: £3.10, £3.10; EX 37.60 Trifecta £213.30.

Owner G&M Roberts Churchward Frost Green W-Williams **Bred** M Watt & Exors Of The Late Miss J John **Trained** Harewood End, H'fords

FOCUS
This proved to be a stamina-sapping test for mainly decent performers, and only three finished, so the form may not be overly reliable. The open ditch in the back straight was omitted. The winner was back to the level of the best of last season's form, the second to his mark.

3374 TOTEPOOL BETTING ON ALL UK RACING CONDITIONAL JOCKEYS' H'CAP HURDLE (10 hdls) 2m 3f 1y
3:55 (3:55) (Class 4) (0-110,110) 3-Y-0+ £4,548 (£1,335; £667; £333)

Form RPR
0-03 **1** **Eminent Poet**[18] 3047 4-11-8 109.......... CharlieDeutsch(3) 128+
(Venetia Williams) *a.p: led 7th: drew clr fr 2 out: comf* **2/1**[1]

33-6 **2** 15 **Join The Navy**[35] 2713 10-11-0 101.......... ThomasCheesman(3) 105
(Kate Buckett) *hld up bhd: hdwy fr after 6th: wnt 2nd whn blnd bdly and rdr lost iron 2 out: styd on but no ch after* **8/1**

2-45 **3** 3 **Bold Duke**[37] 2694 7-11-12 110.......... TomBellamy 109
(Edward Bevan) *in tch: trckd ldr 3 out tl rdn bef next: styd on same pce* **6/1**[3]

-4PP **4** 20 **Glenariff**[25] 2911 6-11-8 106.......... JeremiahMcGrath 85
(Seamus Mullins) *trckd ldrs: rdn appr 2 out: sn wknd* **10/1**

0614 **5** 3 1/2 **Exemplary**[27] 2862 8-11-9 107..........(t) DavidNoonan 83
(Johnny Farrelly) *in tch: rdn after 3 out: sn wknd* **5/1**[2]

24-3 **6** 27 **L Frank Baum (IRE)**[45] 2520 8-10-9 96..........(p) RobertWilliams(3) 45
(Bernard Llewellyn) *trckd ldrs tl dropped in rr u.p after 6th: n.d after: t.o* **7/1**

01-5 **7** 12 **Tidestream**[66] 2085 5-11-4 110..........(t) GeorgeBlackwell(8) 47
(Tim Vaughan) *trckd ldrs: rdn after 3 out: sn wknd: t.o* **5/1**[2]

6P30 **8** 27 **Daulys Anthem (IRE)**[27] 2869 7-10-13 105.......... GarethMalone(8) 15
(David Dennis) *led: wnt lft 2nd: hdd 7th: chsd wnr tl rdn after 3 out: sn wknd: t.o* **14/1**

5m 21.6s (35.60) **Going Correction** +1.75s/f (Heav) **8 Ran SP% 120.3**
Speed ratings (Par 105): **95,88,87,79,77 66,61,49**
CSF £19.72 CT £86.14 TOTE £2.60: £1.10, £2.40, £2.40; EX 18.90 Trifecta £115.30.

Owner B C Dice **Bred** George Strawbridge **Trained** Kings Caple, H'fords

FOCUS
Race distance increased by 63yds. A modest handicap to close the card, the bsecond probably the best guide.

T/Jkpt: Not won. JACKPOT PLACEPOT: £1066.10 to a £1 stake. Pool of £2628.90 - 1.80 winning units. T/Plt: £222.20 to a £1 stake. Pool of £101064.56 - 331.90 winning tickets. T/Qpdt: £36.00 to a £1 stake. Pool of £7500.15 - 154.0 winning tickets. **Tim Mitchell**

3139 UTTOXETER (L-H)
Thursday, December 31

OFFICIAL GOING: Heavy (hdl 5.6; chs 5.2)
Wind: light 1/2 behind Weather: fine and sunny becoming overcast and heavy shower race 7 (3.20)

3375 ABACUS DECORATORS MAIDEN HURDLE (7 hdls 2 omitted) 1m 7f 168y
12:20 (12:20) (Class 4) 4-Y-0+ £3,249 (£954; £477; £238)

Form RPR
354 **1** **Pinnacle Panda (IRE)**[32] 2807 4-11-0 0.......... RobertDunne 121
(Tom Lacey) *mid-div: hdwy to chse ldrs bef 4 out: upsides whn hmpd 2 out: led and j.rt last: edgd lft and bmpd last 100yds: hld on nr fin* **9/2**[3]

2F **2** 1/2 **Authorized Too**[17] 3083 4-10-11 0.......... JamesBanks(3) 121+
(Noel Williams) *trckd ldrs: effrt on inner and hmpd last 75yds: no ex nr fin* **3/1**[1]

342- **3** 3 1/2 **Verni (FR)**[357] 3585 6-11-0 0.......... RichardJohnson 118
(Philip Hobbs) *chsd ldrs: led bef 3 out: hit 2 out: hung lft between last 2: hdd and hmpd last: kpt on one pce* **7/2**[2]

4 **4** 10 **Solomn Grundy (IRE)**[27] 2879 5-11-0 0.......... TomScudamore 108
(David Pipe) *hld up towards rr: hdwy 4 out: wknd bef 2 out* **9/2**[3]

633- **5** 15 **Jaunty Thor**[309] 4430 5-10-7 0.......... WilliamFeatherstone(7) 94
(Brian Eckley) *chsd ldrs: lost pl bef 2 out* **33/1**

-646 **6** 9 **Threebarmymen (IRE)**[36] 2710 4-10-11 0.......... MattGriffiths(3) 83
(Jeremy Scott) *racd wd: chsd ldrs: lost pl bef 3 out* **80/1**

7 1 3/4 **Gone Viral (IRE)**[57] 4-11-0 0..........(t) TrevorWhelan 81
(George Baker) *hld up in rr: brief effrt bef 3 out: sn wknd* **11/1**

122/ **8** 1 1/4 **Georgian Firebird**[443] 4944 5-10-4 0.......... HarryChalloner(3) 73
(Barry Leavy) *in rr: bhd fr 3 out* **33/1**

6-40 **9** 29 **Baraza (FR)**[20] 3021 4-11-0 0.......... PaddyBrennan 51
(Tom George) *in rr: pushed along 4th: wl bhd bef 3 out: tailed rt off* **25/1**

P **Violoniste (FR)**[579] 6-11-0 0.......... JonathanEngland
(Richard Drake) *in rr: bhd fr 4th: t.o whn p.u bef 3 out* **66/1**

4-P0 **P** **Ninny Noodle**[29] 2850 5-10-7 0.......... LiamTreadwell
(Miss Imogen Pickard) *led to 3rd: lost pl 4 out: sn wl bhd: t.o whn p.u bef 3 out* **200/1**

25 **P** **Athou Du Nord (FR)**[27] 2890 5-11-0 114.......... AlainCawley
(Richard Hobson) *w ldr: led 3rd: hdd bef 3 out: sn lost pl and eased: p.u bef 2 out* **15/2**

4m 20.9s (23.50) **Going Correction** +1.60s/f (Heav)
WFA 4 from 5yo+ 5lb **12 Ran SP% 116.6**
Speed ratings (Par 105): **105,104,103,98,90 86,85,84,70,** ,
CSF £17.86 TOTE £6.10: £1.90, £1.50, £1.70; EX 24.80 Trifecta £93.80.
Owner Mr Hinds & Galloping on the South Downs **Bred** Daniel Furini **Trained** Ledbury, H'fords
■ Stewards' Enquiry : Robert Dunne two-day ban: careless riding (14-16 Jan)

FOCUS
Some starts have been moved at this track following remeasuring, so some races will not have speed figures until there is sufficient data to calculate updated median times. The first hurdle in the 2m races and the first hurdle in the back straight were omitted. Due to rail movement the race distance was increased by 67yds. The track passed a morning inspection and, having ridden in the opener, Richard Johnson said of the ground: "It's wet but they are getting through it". Modest maiden hurdle form and the winner had to survive a stewards' inquiry. The second and fourth set the level.

3376 WHITLEY GROUNDWORKS H'CAP HURDLE (7 hdls 2 omitted) 1m 7f 168y
12:50 (12:53) (Class 5) (0-100,100) 3-Y-0+ £2,339 (£686; £343; £171)

Form RPR
0603 **1** **Catchin Time (IRE)**[20] 3011 7-11-6 97..........(t) KieronEdgar(3) 106+
(Laura Hurley) *hld up: hdwy after 4 out: upsides 2 out: sn led: drew clr run-in* **13/2**

62-P **2** 8 **Pret A Thou (FR)**[23] 2962 12-11-9 100..........(p) HarryChalloner(3) 102
(John Groucott) *trckd ldrs: t.k.h: chsd wnr after 2 out: no imp* **8/1**

6645 **3** 4 **Molko Jack (FR)**[5] 3241 11-9-11 81..........(p) LewisStones(10) 78
(Michael Mullineaux) *mid-div: lost pl 4 out: hit next: kpt on fr 2 out: modest 3rd last* **33/1**

5434 **4** 14 **Lean Burn (USA)**[5] 3233 9-10-11 85..........(bt) RichardJohnson 72
(Barry Leavy) *hld up in rr: hit 4 out: sme hdwy next: wkng whn hit last* **11/4**[1]

26-0 **5** 3 1/2 **Yasir (USA)**[15] 3108 7-11-11 99.......... PaddyBrennan 79
(Sophie Leech) *in rr: hdwy 4 out: wknd between last 2* **10/1**

04P0 **6** 11 **The Jugopolist (IRE)**[30] 2841 8-10-0 74 oh6..........(b) AdamWedge 43
(John Cornwall) *chsd ldrs: lost pl after 4 out: sn bhd* **50/1**

0P0 **7** 22 **Annakrista (GER)**[11] 3177 7-10-4 85..........(bt) WilliamFeatherstone(7) 32
(Zoe Davison) *chsd clr ldr: led bef 2 out: hit 2 out: sn hdd & wknd: heavily eased run-in* **66/1**

5-36 **8** 3/4 **Proud Times (USA)**[14] 3125 9-11-8 96..........(p) GavinSheehan 42
(Ali Stronge) *chsd ldrs: drvn and lost pl after 3rd: reminders next: sn wl bhd* **6/1**[3]

4440 **9** 17 **Ashkoun (FR)**[23] 2956 4-11-7 100.......... AlanJohns(5) 29
(Tim Vaughan) *sn trcking ldrs: lost pl after 4 out: sn wl bhd* **25/1**

U-41 **P** **Barista (IRE)**[13] 3143 7-11-10 98.......... TomO'Brien
(Brian Forsey) *in rr: drvn 4 out: sn wl bhd: t.o whn p.u bef 2 out* **4/1**[2]

-6F0 **F** **Gorman (FR)**[196] 776 4-10-11 95..........(t) CianMaher(10) 82
(Evan Williams) *t.k.h: led: clr 2nd: huit 3 out: hdd bef next: fell heavily 2 out* **8/1**

4m 29.5s (32.10) **Going Correction** +2.10s/f (Heav)
WFA 4 from 7yo+ 5lb **11 Ran SP% 115.8**
Speed ratings (Par 103): **103,99,97,90,88 82,71,71,62,** ,
CSF £54.76 CT £1591.02 TOTE £7.60: £2.10, £2.20, £6.30; EX 52.90 Trifecta £1334.50.
Owner Mrs R Hurley **Bred** J G F Fox **Trained** Kineton, Warwicks
■ Stewards' Enquiry : Gavin Sheehan jockey said that the gelding was never travelling
Tom O'Brien jockey said that the gelding ran flat

FOCUS
Due to rail movement the race distance was increased by 67yds. This turned into a good test, with them getting racing a long way from the finish, and the winner came from off the pace. He is rated back to the best of last year's form.

3377 DEREK FOWER TRANSPORT H'CAP HURDLE (8 hdls 2 omitted) 2m 3f 207y
1:20 (1:20) (Class 4) (0-115,118) 3-Y-0+ £3,249 (£954; £477; £238)

Form RPR
522- **1** **Thats My Rabbit (IRE)**[251] 5521 6-11-12 115.......... JamieMoore 121
(Jim Best) *trckd ldrs: led bef 3 out: hit next: hdd briefly last: styd on to forge clr run-in* **4/1**[1]

-412 **2** 4 **Vicky's Charm (IRE)**[44] 2555 6-10-9 **105**.......... MrZBaker(7) 108
(Barry Brennan) *w ldr: led after 4th: hdd and blnd 3 out: led briefly and nt fluent last: kpt on same pce* **4/1**[1]

0553 **3** 1 ½ **Timon's Tara**[18] 3065 6-11-2 **105**.......... JackQuinlan 104
(Robin Dickin) *hld up in rr: hdwy to trck ldrs 4 out: mstke 3 out: kpt on same pce run-in* **8/1**

0-40 **4** 2 ½ **Tanit River (IRE)**[38] 2694 5-11-2 **110**.......... AlanJohns(5) 107
(Tim Vaughan) *chsd ldrs: one pce fr 3 out* **11/2**[2]

633 **5** 7 **Captain Flash (IRE)**[62] 2163 6-10-9 **101**.......... JamesBanks(3) 94
(Jo Davis) *hld up in tch: chsd ldrs 4 out: mstke next: lost pl bef next: hit last* **7/1**

P-31 **6** 30 **Whitsundays (IRE)**[27] 2890 6-11-7 **110**.......... WillKennedy 70
(Donald McCain) *trckd ldrs: t.k.h: lost pl bef 3 out: sn wl bhd: t.o* **4/1**[1]

0/0- **P** **Seymour Eric**[439] 1948 10-11-11 **114**..........(p) IanPopham
(Martin Keighley) *led: hdd after 4th: lost pl next: sn bhd: t.o whn p.u bef 2 out* **6/1**[3]

5m 52.4s (49.20) **Going Correction** +2.60s/f (Heav) **7** Ran SP% **113.3**
Speed ratings (Par 105): **105,103,102,101,99 87,**
CSF £20.14 CT £119.81 TOTE £4.00: £2.00, £2.00; EX 15.60 Trifecta £70.10.
Owner The Best Elite Partnership **Bred** Martin Durack **Trained** Lewes, E Sussex
■ Stewards' Enquiry : Will Kennedy trainer's representative had no explanation for the gelding's poor run

FOCUS
Due to rail moevement the race distance was increased by 104yds. Modest handicap form, with a step up from the winner.

3378 ASHLEIGH BUILDERS AND WHITLEY GROUNDWORKS H'CAP HURDLE (10 hdls 2 omitted) 2m 7f 70y

1:50 (1:50) (Class 5) (0-100,100) 4-Y-0+ **£2,339** (£686; £343; £171)

Form RPR

/6-P **1** **Gorey Lane (IRE)**[23] 2964 9-10-12 **89**..........(vt) ColmMcCormack(3) 96
(John Norton) *hld up: hmpd 1st: hdwy to trck ldrs 4 out: led 2 out: 2 l ahd last: all out nr fin* **14/1**

P00 **2** ½ **Agent Louise**[18] 3067 7-9-11 **74** oh2..........(p) AdamNicol(3) 79
(Mike Sowersby) *in rr: hdwy to chse ldrs 5th: reminders after next: chal appr 2 out: styd on run-in: jst hld* **10/1**

/2-2 **3** 7 **Over My Head**[18] 3067 7-10-11 **85**..........(t) BrendanPowell 83
(Claire Dyson) *mde most: hdd 2 out: wknd last 50yds* **6/4**[1]

R-02 **4** 26 **Wellforth (IRE)**[39] 2669 11-11-12 **100**..........(p) DavidEngland 72
(Clare Ellam) *trckd ldrs: lost pl bef 3 out: sn bhd* **7/1**

0P4 **5** 39 **Kelsey (IRE)**[26] 2904 5-11-4 **92**.......... AndrewThornton 25
(Tom Lacey) *j.lft: trckd ldr: drvn 5th: led briefly appr 3 out: lost pl bef 2 out: sn wl bhd: t.o whn virtually p.u run-in* **11/4**[2]

/4-P **P** **Vintage Vixon (IRE)**[30] 2841 8-10-5 **79**..........(p) RichardJohnson
(Adrian Wintle) *j.lft 1st: trckd ldrs: pushed along 6th: lost pl next: sn bhd: t.o whn p.u bef 3 out* **20/1**

6P **P** **Strictly Glitz (IRE)**[19] 856 4-10-5 **79**.......... BrianHughes
(Mike Sowersby) *in rr: hdwy 5th: drvn and lost pl next: sn wl bhd: t.o whn p.u bef 4 out* **66/1**

6-34 **P** **Uncle Monty (IRE)**[33] 2768 6-11-11 **99**..........(p) WillKennedy
(Donald McCain) *chsd ldrs 3rd: mstke 4th: drvn 4 out: sn lost pl: wl bhd whn p.u bef 2 out* **11/2**[3]

7m 5.6s (66.80) **Going Correction** +2.60s/f (Heav)
WFA 4 from 5yo+ 6lb **8** Ran SP% **116.6**
Speed ratings (Par 103): **87,86,84,75,61 , ,**
CSF £140.26 CT £335.99 TOTE £19.60: £4.90, £3.10, £1.02; EX 296.80 Trifecta £582.30.
Owner Jaffa Racing Syndicate **Bred** Louis Vambeck **Trained** High Hoyland, S Yorks
■ Stewards' Enquiry : Colm McCormack trainer said , regarding the apparent improvement of form, the the gelding had come on for the Uttoxeter run having had a fourteen month lay-off and seemed to be suited by the longer trip of three miles

FOCUS
Due to rail moevement the race distance was increased by 104yds. Lowly handicap form, with the front pair coming away from the tired favourite late on. The winner was well in on the best of his 2014 form and back to that sort of level.

3379 TOWN ELECTRICAL NOVICES' LIMITED H'CAP CHASE (12 fncs) 1m 7f 214y

2:20 (2:20) (Class 4) (0-120,118) 4-Y-0+ **£3,898** (£1,144; £572; £286)

Form RPR

13-0 **1** **Cappielow Park**[20] 3015 6-11-7 **117**..........(tp) GavinSheehan 120
(Ali Stronge) *led 2nd: hdd 6th: upsides last: edgd rt and led last 150yds: drvn out* **6/1**[3]

40-5 **2** 1 ¼ **Jaunty Inflight**[20] 3011 6-10-4 **100**.......... RobertDunne 102
(Brian Eckley) *trckd ldrs: led 4 out: edgd lft and hdd last 150yds: no ex* **8/1**

6-60 **3** 4 **Daveron (IRE)**[46] 2513 7-11-5 **118**.......... MattGriffiths(3) 115
(Jeremy Scott) *j.lft: chsd ldrs: reminders and lost pl 8th: sn bhd: styd on fr 2 out: modest 3rd last: gng on at fin* **6/1**[3]

33P- **4** 4 **Parting Way (IRE)**[282] 4979 7-10-9 **105**.......... RichardJohnson 104+
(Tim Vaughan) *chsd ldrs: outpcd 8th: hit next: kpt on run-in* **16/1**

6P0- **5** 5 **Virtuose Du Chenet (FR)**[275] 5082 6-10-3 **99** oh2.......... LiamTreadwell 89
(Venetia Williams) *led to 2nd: led 8th: hdd 4 out: wknd appr 2 out* **7/2**[2]

5-F2 **6** 22 **Rouquine Sauvage**[19] 3042 7-10-10 **111**..........(t) DavidNoonan(5) 91
(Anthony Honeyball) *w ldrs: led 6th to 8th: wkng whn hmpd 3 out: bhd whn heavily eased run-in: virtually p.u: t.o* **10/3**[1]

-545 **U** **Frosty Steel (IRE)**[28] 2860 5-10-10 **106**..........(t[1]) PaddyBrennan
(Tom George) *t.k.h in last: nt fluent: mstke 6th: trcking ldrs 7th: outpcd 4 out: modest 4th and wl hld whn mstke and uns rdr next* **7/2**[2]

4m 43.0s (41.60) **Going Correction** +2.675s/f (Heav) **7** Ran SP% **113.1**
Speed ratings (Par 105): **103,102,100,98,95 84,**
CSF £48.57 TOTE £7.60: £3.40, £5.20; EX 50.30 Trifecta £205.50.
Owner Tim Dykes & Miss Anna Yorke **Bred** Mary-Ann Penfold **Trained** Eastbury, Berks

FOCUS
Due to rail moevement the race distance was increased by 34yds. Hard work in the conditions for what was an ordinary chase. Not a race to be confident about.

3380 DEREK FOWER TRANSPORT H'CAP CHASE (12 fncs) 1m 7f 214y

2:50 (2:50) (Class 4) (0-115,113) 4-Y-0+ **£3,768** (£1,106; £553; £276)

Form RPR

11-3 **1** **Little Jimmy**[30] 2834 8-10-8 **95**..........(tp) FelixDeGiles 110+
(Tom Gretton) *t.k.h in last pair: hdwy to trck ldng pair 7th: c through on bridle to jump last upsides: drvn to ld last 100yds: forged clr* **4/1**[3]

3112 **2** 3 ¾ **Capilla (IRE)**[21] 2994 7-11-5 **113**..........(t) MrConorOrr(7) 123
(Evan Williams) *led: drvn 2 out: hdd and no ex last 100yds* **6/5**[1]

22F3 **3** 3 ¼ **Val D'Arc (FR)**[15] 3115 6-11-11 **112**.......... AlainCawley 119
(Richard Hobson) *chsd ldr: pushed along 8th: rdn next: kpt on same pce run-in* **2/1**[2]

P1-4 **4** 14 **Tiquer (FR)**[209] 623 7-11-7 **108**.......... RhysFlint 101
(Alan Jones) *in last pair detached: pushed along 6th: drvn and outpcd next: bhd 4 out* **8/1**

4m 42.1s (40.70) **Going Correction** +2.675s/f (Heav) **4** Ran SP% **109.9**
Speed ratings (Par 105): **105,103,101,94**
CSF £9.66 TOTE £3.90; EX 8.60 Trifecta £12.40.
Owner Tom Gretton Racing & Ownaracehorse Ltd **Bred** Mrs Marigold West **Trained** Holberrow Green, Worcs

FOCUS
Due to rail moevement the race distance was increased by 34yds. Not form to get excited about, with a big step up from the winner.

3381 ASHLEIGH BUILDERS MARES' MAIDEN OPEN NATIONAL HUNT FLAT RACE 1m 7f 168y

3:20 (3:20) (Class 6) 4-6-Y-0 **£1,559** (£457; £228; £114)

Form RPR

1 **Tearsofclewbay** 4-11-2 0.......... RichardJohnson 110+
(Philip Hobbs) *hld up in rr: hdwy to trck ldrs 7f out: 2nd over 4f out: led over 1f out: pushed wl clr over 1f out: eased clsng stages* **11/8**[1]

60 **2** 16 **Tara Well (IRE)**[57] 2277 5-10-9 0.......... ConorSmith(7) 94
(Robin Dickin) *mde most: hdd over 2f out: kpt on: no ch w wnr* **8/1**

2 **3** 17 **Graceful Legend**[14] 3132 4-10-13 0.......... RyanHatch(3) 77
(Ben Case) *sn trcking ldrs: drvn over 5f out: modest 3rd over 3f out: one pce* **5/2**[2]

05 **4** nk **Midnight Target**[29] 2856 5-10-13 0.......... KyleJames(3) 77
(John Groucott) *chsd ldrs: drvn 6f out: modest 4th over 3f out: one pce* **14/1**

5 21 **Whenskiesareblue (IRE)** 4-10-13 0.......... HarryChalloner(3) 56
(William Kinsey) *mid-div: sme hdwy 7f out: outpcd and poor 5th 4f out* **16/1**

2 **6** 36 **Miss Giselle**[33] 2770 6-10-9 0.......... HarrisonBeswick(7) 20
(Sam Thomas) *hld up in rr: hdwy 7f out: lost pl over 5f out* **7/1**[3]

7 ¾ **Pettal**[264] 4-10-9 0.......... CharlieHammond(7) 19
(Sarah-Jayne Davies) *t.k.h in rr: hdwy to trck ldrs after 6f: lost pl 5f out* **40/1**

0/ **8** nk **Sprogzilla**[389] 6-10-11 0.......... DavidNoonan(5) 19
(Hannah James) *t.k.h: sn trcking ldrs: lost pl 6f out: sn bhd* **100/1**

9 4 ½ **Annie Hughes (IRE)** 6-10-13 0.......... BenPoste(3) 14
(Adrian Wintle) *w ldrs: drvn after 6f: sn lost pl: wl bhd fnl 7f* **33/1**

0-5 **10** 10 **Beautiful People (FR)**[51] 2421 4-10-11 0.......... DanielHiskett(5) 4
(Richard Phillips) *mid-div: lost pl 6f out: sn wl bhd* **16/1**

60- **11** 85 **Romann Angel**[400] 2745 6-10-9 0.......... MrHFNugent(7)
(Michael Mullineaux) *sn trcking ldrs: t.k.h: lost pl over 6f out: sn wl bhd: t.o 4f out: virtually p.u: eventually completed* **25/1**

4m 31.8s (40.00) **Going Correction** +2.60s/f (Heav) **11** Ran SP% **122.9**
Speed ratings: **104,96,87,87,76 58,58,58,56,51 8**
CSF £14.09 TOTE £2.20: £1.10, £2.60, £1.40; EX 20.90 Trifecta £54.50.
Owner Mrs Caren Walsh & Mrs Kathleen Quinn **Bred** W P Jenks **Trained** Withycombe, Somerset

FOCUS
Due to rail moevement the race distance was increased by 67yds. They came home at long intervals in this mares' bumper, with the clear-cut winner looking useful. The second helps set the level.
T/Plt: £544.80 to a £1 stake. Pool: £73515.68 - 98.48 winning tickets T/Qpdt: £54.30 to a £1 stake. Pool: £7025.04 - 95.66 winning tickets **Walter Glynn**

[2992] WARWICK (L-H)

Thursday, December 31

OFFICIAL GOING: Heavy (chs 4.1; hdl 4.2)
Wind: Light behind Weather: Fine

3382 LOCAL PARKING SECURITY LTD NOVICES' H'CAP HURDLE (8 hdls 1 omitted) 2m 3f

12:40 (12:40) (Class 5) (0-100,100) 3-Y-0+ **£2,339** (£686; £343; £171)

Form RPR

-653 **1** **Solidago (IRE)**[13] 3143 8-10-12 **91**.......... CiaranGethings(5) 97+
(Barry Leavy) *hld up: hdwy appr 5th: chsd ldr 3 out: led bef next: rdn appr last: styd on* **3/1**[1]

-602 **2** 3 ½ **Rebekah Rabbit (IRE)**[39] 2670 5-10-4 **85**.......... MrTommieMO'Brien(7) 84
(Tom Lacey) *chsd ldr tl led after 4th: rdn and hdd appr 2 out: hung rt flat: styd on same pce* **3/1**[1]

-530 **3** 1 **Young Lou**[197] 757 6-10-0 **74** oh5 ow3..........(p) ConorShoemark(3) 76
(Robin Dickin) *hld up: nt fluent 2nd: hdwy after 4th: rdn whn mstkes 2 out and last: styd on same pce flat* **20/1**

-540 **4** 19 **Irish Octave (IRE)**[30] 2841 5-10-3 **80**.......... BenPoste(3) 59
(Rosemary Gasson) *prom: lost pl after 4th: rdn and wknd appr 3 out* **6/1**[3]

4-06 **5** nk **Little James (IRE)**[30] 2838 6-11-6 **94**.......... SamTwiston-Davies 73
(Nigel Twiston-Davies) *chsd ldrs tl rdn and wknd after 3 out* **7/2**[2]

00U- **P** **Crazy Jane (IRE)**[279] 5021 6-10-0 **74** oh10..........(t) JamesDavies
(Tom Gretton) *prom: rdn after 5th: wknd bef next: bhd whn p.u bef 2 out* **28/1**

-P05 **P** **Myroundorurs (IRE)**[43] 2581 5-11-12 **100**.......... CharliePoste
(Robin Dickin) *hld up: hdwy appr 5th: rdn and wknd wl bef next: bhd whn p.u bef 2 out* **10/1**

-506 **P** **Lady Helissio**[14] 3119 5-11-4 **92**..........[1] MarkQuinlan
(Neil Mulholland) *led: rdn and hdd after 4th: wknd qckly: bhd whn p.u bef next* **12/1**

5m 10.4s (24.40) **Going Correction** +1.35s/f (Heav) **8** Ran SP% **111.5**
Speed ratings (Par 103): **102,100,100,92,91 , ,**
CSF £12.11 CT £141.81 TOTE £4.00: £1.30, £2.00, £3.40; EX 14.00 Trifecta £101.00.
Owner Mrs S D Ashford & D B Holmes **Bred** Patrick Heffernan **Trained** Forsbrook, Staffs

FOCUS
All starts have been moved at this track following remeasuring, so there will be no speed figures here until there is sufficient data to calculate updated median times. The hurdle and bumper races were run on the outer track. Due to rail movement this race distance was reduced by 6yds. The middle hurdle in the back straight was omitted. A low-grade novices' handicap hurdle and hard work despite a steady gallop. The winner was well in on the best of his 2014 form and is rated back to that sort of level.

3383 LOCAL PARKING SECURITY LTD CONDITIONAL JOCKEYS' H'CAP HURDLE (CHALLENGER STAYING HURDLE QUAL') (10 hdls 2 omitted) 3m 2f
1:10 (1:12) (Class 4) (0-120,120) 4-Y-0+ £3,249 (£954; £477; £238)

Form RPR
1032 1 **Howaboutnever (IRE)**[26] 2919 7-10-13 **115**..............(p) TobyWheeler(8) 119+
(Ian Williams) *led tl after 1st: chsd ldrs tl led again 7th: hdd appr 2 out: sn rdn: rallied to ld flat: styd on u.p* 9/2[3]

21 2 ½ **Battle Dust (IRE)**[26] 2903 6-11-12 **120**..............(p) ConorShoemark 122
(Kim Bailey) *disp ld after 1st: hdd 7th: sn rdn: drvn to ld appr 2 out: hung rt bef last: hdd flat: styd on u.p* 2/1[2]

0001 3 11 **American Life (FR)**[1] 3361 8-11-1 **112** 7ex..............(vt) KillianMoore(3) 105
(Sophie Leech) *hld up in tch: rdn appr 2 out: wknd bef last* 13/8[1]

0-05 4 23 **Garde Fou (FR)**[26] 2906 9-10-13 **107**..............(t) ThomasGarner 75
(Paul Henderson) *hld up in tch: rdn and wknd appr 2 out* 7/1

0P-4 5 15 **Moss On The Mill**[38] 2694 7-11-4 **112**.............. JamieBargary 65
(Tom George) *disp ld after 1st tl after 6th: rdn and wknd 3 out* 12/1

7m 15.1s (38.10) **Going Correction** +1.55s/f (Heav) 5 Ran SP% **109.8**
Speed ratings (Par 105): **103,102,99,92,87**
CSF £14.08 TOTE £4.80: £2.00, £1.30; EX 10.60 Trifecta £30.30.

Owner Brannon, Dick, Hernon & Holden **Bred** Mrs A Connolly **Trained** Portway, Worcs

FOCUS
The race distance was reduced by 12yds. This modest conditionals' staying handicap hurdle produced a close finish between a pair who had been close up throughout. The winner is on the upgrade.

3384 LOCAL PARKING SECURITY LTD NOVICES' LIMITED H'CAP CHASE (15 fncs 2 omitted) 2m 4f
1:40 (1:42) (Class 4) (0-120,120) 4-Y-0+ £3,898 (£1,144; £572; £286)

Form RPR
3-4P 1 **King Of Glory**[39] 2668 7-10-10 **108**.............. AidanColeman 118+
(Venetia Williams) *led 2nd to 6th: chsd ldr tl led appr 2 out: drvn out* 6/1[3]

01F2 2 5 **Muckle Roe (IRE)**[22] 2975 6-11-2 **114**.............. SamTwiston-Davies 118
(Nigel Twiston-Davies) *a.p: rdn after 3 out: chsng wnr whn mstke last: styd on same pce flat* 11/2[2]

-F23 3 12 **Bodega**[13] 3134 7-11-2 **114**..............(p) NoelFehily 104
(Ian Williams) *hld up: pushed along after 6th: hdwy 11th: rdn and wknd appr 2 out* 5/2[1]

4122 4 2½ **Always On The Run (IRE)**[166] 1030 5-11-8 **120**....... WayneHutchinson 110
(Tom George) *hld up: plld hrd: hdwy 4th: led 6th: rdn and hdd whn mstke 2 out: sn wknd* 12/1

0-14 P **Thatchers Gold (IRE)**[22] 2977 7-10-13 **111**.............. DenisO'Regan
(Henry Oliver) *chsd ldrs: rdn appr 7th: wknd bef 10th: bhd whn p.u bef next* 8/1

032- P **Alberto's Dream**[315] 4316 6-10-4 **102**.............. JamesDavies
(Tom Symonds) *prom: nt fluent 3rd: sn lost pl: hdwy appr 10th: wknd bef 3 out: bhd whn p.u bef next* 14/1

1-54 P **Thedrinkymeister (IRE)**[17] 3079 6-11-5 **117**.............. DavidBass
(Kim Bailey) *led to 2nd: chsd ldrs tl rdn appr 10th: sn wknd: bhd whn p.u bef 2 out* 5/2[1]

5m 32.1s (14.10) **Going Correction** +0.875s/f (Soft) 7 Ran SP% **112.3**
Speed ratings (Par 105): **106,104,99,98,**
CSF £36.72 CT £102.23 TOTE £6.60: £2.60, £2.60; EX 33.50 Trifecta £75.80.

Owner Mrs Marion Willcocks **Bred** Peter Willcocks **Trained** Kings Caple, H'fords

FOCUS
Rail movements increased the race distance by 60yds, and the open ditch in the back straight was omitted. A competitive looking novices' handicap chase but an attritional contest. The winner was well in on form from this time last year.

3385 LOCAL PARKING SECURITY LTD H'CAP CHASE (16 fncs 2 omitted) 3m
2:10 (2:12) (Class 4) (0-120,124) 4-Y-0+ £5,198 (£1,526; £763; £381)

Form RPR
-552 1 **Paddy The Oscar (IRE)**[21] 2996 12-11-2 **112**.............. ConorRing(5) 121+
(Grace Harris) *led after 1st: nt fluent next: clr appr 11th: shkn up flat: styd on* 4/1[3]

0-U6 2 3 **Incentivise (IRE)**[21] 2996 12-11-2 **112**.............. CiaranGethings(5) 115
(Kerry Lee) *sn prom: rdn after 7th: outpcd 11th: rallied to chse wnr appr 2 out: styd on gamely* 7/1

0-62 3 22 **Gamain (IRE)**[14] 3127 6-11-9 **114**..............(b) KielanWoods 95
(Ben Case) *hld up: hdwy 4th: chsd wnr 8th: rdn and outpcd 11th: wknd after 3 out* 7/2[2]

3/P0 4 23 **Raduis Bleu (FR)**[21] 2997 10-9-11 **95**.............. MissLBrooke(7) 61
(Lady Susan Brooke) *hld up: hdwy appr 11th: wknd bef next* 20/1

351- P **Emma Soda**[288] 4855 10-10-13 **104**..............(b) PeterCarberry
(Paul Davies) *prom: lost pl after 1st: bhd fr 5th: p.u bef 12th* 10/1

-124 P **Loughalder (IRE)**[27] 2878 9-11-4 **109**..............(bt) CharliePoste
(Matt Sheppard) *chsd ldrs: slipped bnd appr 8th: rdn and wknd 11th: bhd whn p.u bef last* 3/1[1]

P-11 P **Leith Hill Legasi**[31] 2827 6-10-9 **100**..............(bt) SamTwiston-Davies
(Charlie Longsdon) *led tl after 1st: chsd ldrs tl rdn and wknd after 10th: bhd whn p.u bef 2 out* 5/1

6m 51.4s (17.40) **Going Correction** +0.875s/f (Soft) 7 Ran SP% **110.2**
Speed ratings (Par 105): **106,105,97,90,** ,
CSF £28.64 CT £99.06 TOTE £5.10: £2.10, £3.40; EX 35.90 Trifecta £136.50.

Owner Michelle Harris & Deberah Lawton **Bred** Kevin Ahern **Trained** Shirenewton, Monmouthshire

FOCUS
Rail movements increased the race distance by 109yds, and the open ditch in the back straight was omitted. The feature race but a modest handicap chase in which the finish was dominated by the veterans. The winner is rated 4lb off last season's best.

3386 BREEDERS BACKING RACING/LOCAL PARKING SECURITY LTD EBF MARES' "NATIONAL HUNT" NOVICES' HURDLE (9 hdls 2 omitted) 2m 5f
2:40 (2:42) (Class 4) 4-Y-0+ £3,898 (£1,144; £572; £286)

Form RPR
10-1 1 **Katie Too (IRE)**[23] 2952 4-11-5 0.............. WayneHutchinson 130+
(Alan King) *chsd ldrs: led appr 2 out: sn clr: nt fluent last: sn edgd rt: easily* 1/2[1]

-514 2 24 **Lamanver Alchemy**[36] 2721 4-10-12 0.............. NoelFehily 98+
(Tom Lacey) *plld hrd: led after 2nd: hdd & wknd appr 2 out: mstke last: hung rt flat* 5/1[3]

6-63 3 hd **Mrsrobin (IRE)**[28] 2870 5-10-12 0.............. LeightonAspell 95
(Emma Lavelle) *hld up: outpcd after 6th: styd on flat* 16/1

02-4 4 4 **Miss Tongabezi**[238] 179 6-10-12 0.............. JamesBest 91
(Paul Webber) *hld up: hdwy appr 6th: ev ch 3 out: sn rdn and wknd* 20/1

060/ 5 41 **Viking Mistress**[627] 5300 7-10-12 0.............. AndrewTinkler 61
(Martin Keighley) *prom tl wknd qckly after 3 out* 66/1

36-4 F **Tara's Honour**[85] 1811 5-10-12 0.............. AidanColeman
(Emma Lavelle) *hld up: wknd 6th: bhd whn fell 3 out: fatally injured* 12/1

06-P P **Showbiz Floozy**[56] 2298 6-10-12 77.............. MarkGrant
(John O'Neill) *hld up: wknd after 5th: bhd whn p.u bef 3 out* 100/1

0 P **Sage Grouse**[29] 2856 6-10-12 0.............. JoshuaMoore
(Stuart Edmunds) *chsd ldrs tl rdn and wknd appr 6th: bhd whn p.u bef 3 out* 50/1

2-2P P **Just A Feeling**[70] 2033 5-10-12 0.............. RichieMcLernon
(Paul Webber) *chsd ldrs tl wknd appr 3 out: bhd whn p.u bef next* 20/1

36 P **Fortunata Fashions**[33] 2778 5-10-12 0.............. KielanWoods
(Ben Case) *led: hdd after 2nd: chsd ldr: blnd 6th: lost 2nd 3 out: sn wknd: bhd whn p.u bef next* 9/2[2]

50P0 P **Kaddys Girl**[15] 3110 5-10-7 0.............. ChrisWard(5)
(Robin Dickin) *racd wd: mid-div: mstke 5th: wknd next: bhd whn hmpd 3 out: sn p.u* 100/1

5m 52.6s (31.60) **Going Correction** +1.75s/f (Heav) 11 Ran SP% **130.0**
Speed ratings (Par 105): **109,99,99,98,82** , , , ,
CSF £4.14 TOTE £1.40: £1.10, £1.80, £4.90; EX 4.00 Trifecta £34.10.

Owner Mr & Mrs Christopher Harris **Bred** Regina Anne Hennessy **Trained** Barbury Castle, Wilts

FOCUS
The race was run on the outer track and due to rail movement the race distance was reduced by 6yds. Alan King had won this mares' novices' hurdle twice in recent years and produced the winner again. The winner is a decent mare.

3387 LPS LTD H'CAP CHASE (15 fncs 2 omitted) 2m 4f
3:10 (3:19) (Class 4) (0-105,104) 4-Y-0+ £3,898 (£1,144; £572; £286)

Form RPR
42P- 1 **Merchant Of Milan**[329] 4056 7-11-2 **94**..............(p) TomO'Brien 102
(John Flint) *a.p: chsd ldr 10th: led after 2 out: rdn and hung rt flat: all out* 11/2[3]

1-32 2 shd **I Am Colin**[38] 2692 6-11-7 **104**.............. JamieBargary(5) 117+
(Nigel Twiston-Davies) *nt a fluent: chsd ldrs: mstke 8th: outpcd 12th: rallied to ld appr whn blnd and rdr lost iron briefly 2 out: sn hdd: stl ev ch whn carried rt flat: styd on* 7/2[2]

-4P4 3 24 **Wish In A Well (IRE)**[32] 2811 6-10-12 **90**..............(t) KielanWoods 74
(Ben Case) *hld up: hdwy 9th: rdn and wknd appr 2 out* 6/1

60-2 4 13 **Eaton Rock (IRE)**[51] 2420 6-11-11 **103**.............. JamesDavies 74
(Tom Symonds) *led: rdn and hdd appr 2 out: wknd qckly* 3/1[1]

P064 5 13 **Mostly Bob (IRE)**[35] 2735 12-10-4 **82**..............(vt) JamesBest 40
(Sophie Leech) *hld up: pushed along 6th: rdn and wknd appr 10th* 11/1

4/43 6 21 **Seventh Hussar**[19] 3044 9-10-7 **85**.............. LeightonAspell 22
(Alison Batchelor) *prom to 10th* 8/1

231- P **Princesse Fleur**[529] 1027 7-11-6 **98**.............. TomScudamore
(Michael Scudamore) *hld up: hdwy 10th: wknd after 3 out: bhd whn p.u bef next* 11/2[3]

5P-P P **Riversbridge**[17] 3081 6-10-0 **78** oh3..............(bt) RichieMcLernon
(Johnny Farrelly) *chsd ldr to appr 10th: mstke and wknd next: bhd whn p.u bef 3 out* 20/1

5m 43.6s (25.60) **Going Correction** +1.375s/f (Heav) 8 Ran SP% **116.5**
Speed ratings (Par 105): **103,102,93,88,82 74,** ,
CSF £26.31 CT £120.29 TOTE £7.00: £2.20, £1.60, £1.90; EX 30.50 Trifecta £150.10.

Owner Mr & Mrs A J Mutch **Bred** M Watt & The Late Miss Jemima Johnson **Trained** Kenfig Hill, Bridgend

■ Stewards' Enquiry : Tom O'Brien caution: careless riding

FOCUS
Rail movements increased the race distance by 60yds, and the open ditch in the back straight was omitted. This moderate handicap chase was run in pouring rain and produced a desperate finish. The form could be rated higher, but not on time.

3388 LOCAL PARKING SECURITY LTD STANDARD OPEN NATIONAL HUNT FLAT RACE 2m
3:40 (3:47) (Class 6) 4-6-Y-O £1,559 (£457; £228; £114)

Form RPR
1 **Mystical Knight**[319] 6-11-0 0.............. SeanBowen 121+
(Rebecca Curtis) *chsd ldrs: led on bit over 2f out: shkn up and c clr fnl f: easily* 11/8[1]

03- 2 21 **Holbrook Park**[252] 5502 5-11-0 0.............. TrevorWhelan 96
(Neil King) *disp ld tl wnt on 6f out: rdn and hdd over 2f out: wknd over 1f out* 14/1

3 4½ **Informationisking (IRE)** 4-11-0 0.............. WayneHutchinson 91
(Alan King) *hld up: hdwy 1/2-way: rdn and wknd over 2f out* 11/4[3]

0 4 59 **Lord Westy (IRE)**[70] 2044 4-10-4 0.............. GrahamCarson(10) 32
(Jamie Snowden) *hld up in tch: rdn and wknd over 3f out* 33/1

0-0 5 6 **Sugar Mix**[236] 213 4-11-0 0.............. AndrewTinkler 26
(Martin Keighley) *prom: pushed along over 9f out: rdn and wknd over 5f out* 80/1

6 6 hd **Premier Rose (IRE)**[54] 2337 6-10-0 0.............. MrJNixon(7) 18
(Katy Price) *disp ld 10f: rdn and wknd over 4f out* 14/1

7 24 **Executive Order** 6-10-7 0.............. ThomasCheesman(7) 1
(Martin Smith) *hld up: hdwy 11f out: rdn and wknd over 4f out* 28/1

401/ 8 11 **Little Dotty**[938] 647 6-10-9 0.............. KevinJones(5)
(Giuseppe Fierro) *hld up: wknd 7f out* 33/1

2 9 34 **Boatswain (IRE)**[23] 2965 4-11-0 0.............. JakeGreenall
(Henry Daly) *prom: lost pl over 8f out: bhd fnl 7f* 9/4[2]

P **Oscar Robin (IRE)** 6-10-0 0 MrSeanHoulihan(7)
(Ken Wingrove) *unruly to post: s.s: sn wl bhd: p.u 10f out* **100/1**
P **Coppice Lad** 6-10-7 0 (t) MissPFuller(7)
(Ken Wingrove) *sn pushed along in rr: lost tch after 3f: bhd whn p.u bef 1/2-way* **100/1**
4m 13.4s (28.00) **Going Correction** +1.95s/f (Heav) **11** Ran SP% **125.4**
Speed ratings: **108,97,95,65,62 62,50,45,28,**
CSF £24.96 TOTE £2.40: £1.10, £3.00, £2.90; EX 23.40 Trifecta £74.60.
Owner G Costelloe **Bred** The Jacobean Group **Trained** Newport, Pembrokeshire
FOCUS
The race was run on the outer track and due to rail movement the race distance was reduced by 6yds. A bumper run in very wet conditions following the heavy rain, and only three were involved in the latter stages. The impressive winner looks a smart prospect.
T/Plt: £58.40 to a £1 stake. Pool: £61858.73 - 772.23 winning tickets T/Qpdt: £16.10 to a £1 stake. Pool: £5418.76 - 247.74 winning tickets **Colin Roberts**

3389 - 3392a (Foreign Racing) - See Raceform Interactive

2999 PUNCHESTOWN (R-H)
Thursday, December 31
OFFICIAL GOING: Heavy

3393a DORANS PRIDE NOVICE HURDLE (GRADE 2) (14 hdls) 3m
2:05 (2:05) 4-Y-0+ **£21,162** (£6,186; £2,930; £976)

RPR
1 **Up For Review (IRE)**43 2585 6-11-3 0 RWalsh 151+
(W P Mullins, Ire) *trckd ldr tl led after 1st and mde rest: over 1 l clr bef 3 out where slt mstke: extended advantage travelling wl after next and in command bef last: easily* **4/5**1
2 13 **Jetstream Jack (IRE)**21 3002 5-11-3 131 DavyRussell 136
(Gordon Elliott, Ire) *chsd ldrs: slt mstke in 3rd at 5th: wnt 2nd 3 out: rdn and no imp on easy wnr after next: kpt on one pce* **6/1**3
3 13 **Nambour (GER)**33 2796 5-11-3 0 BJCooper 123
(W P Mullins, Ire) *chsd ldrs: wnt 2nd briefly at 9th: pushed along in 3rd after 3 out and sn no imp on easy wnr: one pce after* **9/4**2
4 37 **Ben Button (IRE)**42 2607 5-11-3 113 MarkWalsh 86
(P J Rothwell, Ire) *hld up in rr: wnt 5th fr 6th: pushed along in 5th after 4 out and no imp bef next: kpt on one pce fr last into remote 4th run-in* **66/1**
5 2 **Moylisha Tim (IRE)**39 2672 5-11-6 129 MrJJSlevin 87
(R P Rath, Ire) *led narrowly tl hdd after 1st and settled in 2nd: mstke 3rd: nt fluent and lost pl briefly at 9th: lost pl after 4 out: rdn and no imp in 4th after next: one pce after and dropped to remote 5th run-in* **14/1**
6 42 **Cogryhill (IRE)**12 3169 5-11-3 123 (p) BarryGeraghty 42
(Gordon Elliott, Ire) *hld up: niggled along briefly in 5th fr 3rd: pushed along in rr fr 6th and struggling detached fr 8th: no imp and wknd 4 out: completely t.o* **20/1**
6m 13.4s (6.40) **6** Ran SP% **113.5**
CSF £6.69 TOTE £1.90: £1.30, £2.20; DF 7.40 Trifecta £12.10.
Owner Andrea & Graham Wylie **Bred** Ms Colette O'Driscoll **Trained** Muine Beag, Co Carlow
FOCUS
Hard to argue with the authority of the winner's victory, he has an impressive engine and there's every chance that he will be equally effective on better ground. The second and third help with the standard.

3394 - 3396a (Foreign Racing) - See Raceform Interactive

3306 CATTERICK (L-H)
Friday, January 1
OFFICIAL GOING: Soft (chs 6.3, hdl 6.6)
Wind: light 1/2 behind Weather: overcast, cold

3397 HAPPY NEW YEAR NOVICES' HURDLE (10 hdls) 2m 3f 66y
12:30 (12:30) (Class 4) 4-Y-0+ **£5,198** (£1,526; £763; £381)

Form RPR
315 1 **Lady Yeats**42 2626 5-10-13 120 JoeColliver(3) 103
(George Moore) *led: reminder bnd after 5th: hdd narrowly sn after last: rallied to regain ld nr fin* **9/2**3
5 2 hd **Nam Hai (IRE)**31 2840 5-10-13 0 TomBellamy(3) 103
(Kim Bailey) *trckd ldrs: upsides last: tk cl 2nd and no ex nr fin* **4/1**2
0-33 3 nk **Fort Smith (IRE)**27 2901 7-10-9 124 (t) HarrisonBeswick(7) 102
(Sam Thomas) *trckd ldrs: hmpd by loose horse 3rd: upsides last: sn led narrowly: hdd and no exnr fin* **11/10**1
5 4 1 1/4 **Lough Salt (IRE)**31 2842 5-10-11 0 JamieHamilton(5) 101
(Mark Walford) *trckd ldrs: kpt on same pce run-in* **14/1**
606 5 10 **Cactus Valley (IRE)**4 3309 7-10-13 0 (t) HarryBannister(3) 91
(Michael Easterby) *hld up in rr: sme hdwy appr 2 out: wknd between last 2* **66/1**
4 6 3 1/2 **What A Game (IRE)**27 2917 5-11-2 0 DannyCook 88
(Tim Easterby) *in rr: hdwy to chse ldrs 5th: wknd 2 out* **40/1**
7 3 1/4 **Rhythm Of Sound (IRE)**41 6-10-9 0 MissBeckySmith(7) 84
(Micky Hammond) *hld up towards rr: brief effrt appr 2 out: sn lost pl* **22/1**
1-20 8 3/4 **Ten Trees**33 2801 6-10-9 0 JakeGreenall 77
(Alan Swinbank) *in rr: sme hdwy 3 out: lost pl bef next* **12/1**
005- F **Apples And Trees (IRE)**342 3862 7-10-6 0 RonanShort(10)
(Donald McCain) *in rr: hdwy 6th: chsng ldrs 2 out: wkng whn fell between last 2: fatally injured* **66/1**
-660 P **Down The Line (IRE)**43 2591 6-10-11 0 DaraghBourke(5)
(Alan Swinbank) *chsd ldrs: lost pl 7th: sn wl bhd: t.o whn p.u bef 2 out* **40/1**
F **Pretty Miss Mahler (IRE)**40 5-10-9 0 HenryBrooke 91
(Martin Todhunter) *mid-div: j.rt 2nd: chsd ldrs 5th: 5th and wl hld whn fell last* **50/1**
44 U **Exactly What**28 2895 7-10-11 0 JamesCowley(5)
(Donald McCain) *w ldr: mstke and uns rdr 1st* **66/1**
5m 5.1s (29.00) **Going Correction** +0.375s/f (Yiel) **12** Ran SP% **121.1**
Speed ratings (Par 105): **53,52,52,52,48 46,45,44, , ,**
CSF £22.95 TOTE £5.60: £2.30, £1.70, £1.10; EX 26.00 Trifecta £44.30.
Owner A Crute & Partners **Bred** Biddestone Stud Ltd **Trained** Middleham Moor, N Yorks

FOCUS
The ground was officially soft and clerk of the course Fiona Needham said: "We have had 13mm of rain since we raced on Monday but we have had wind as well. Both bends were out three yards so the distance of 2m races is increased by 18 yards, that of 2m3f races is up 27 yards and 3m1f races are over 36 yards further. A dramatic opener, in which the first three home were separated by only 1/2l. The form is suspect with the winner rated 8lb off. Conditions were described as tacky, hard work, dead and gluey by the riders of the principals.

3398 BUY YOUR 2016 ANNUAL BADGE TODAY H'CAP HURDLE (8 hdls) 1m 7f 156y
1:05 (1:05) (Class 4) (0-110,109) 4-Y-0+ **£5,848** (£1,717; £858; £429)

Form RPR
34 1 **Hitman Hearns (IRE)**105 1568 7-11-10 107 CraigNichol 116+
(Keith Dalgleish) *mde all: blnd 1st: styd on wl fr 2 out: unchal* **9/2**2
P052 2 3 1/2 **Discoverie**6 3244 8-10-0 83 oh2 (p) HenryBrooke 88+
(Kenneth Slack) *chsd ldrs: sddle slipped briefly bnd after 3rd: 2nd appr 2 out: no imp whn mstke last* **7/2**1
52P3 3 6 **Aliandy (IRE)**44 2581 5-11-9 109 TomBellamy(3) 108
(Kim Bailey) *stdd s: in rr: hdwy 5th: modest 4th appr 2 out: kpt on one pce* **9/2**2
-05P 4 1/2 **Hear The Chimes**33 2810 7-11-9 109 MauriceLinehan(3) 107
(Shaun Harris) *t.k.h: hld up: hdwy 5th: chsng ldrs next: modest 3rd appr 2 out: kpt on one pce* **10/1**
4054 5 2 3/4 **Kilronan Castle**21 3009 5-11-7 109 JamesCowley(5) 104
(Donald McCain) *chsd ldrs: drvn and outpcd 3 out: kpt on between last 2* **16/1**
4333 6 19 **Captain Redbeard (IRE)**13 3152 7-11-4 108 SamColtherd(7) 84
(Stuart Coltherd) *chsd ldrs: drvn 3 out: lost pl appr next* **15/2**3
2334 7 1 1/2 **Baraboy (IRE)**28 2893 6-11-3 107 LorcanMurtagh(7) 81
(Barry Murtagh) *mid-div: chsng ldrs 4th: outpcd appr 2 out: wknd between last 2* **16/1**
0-16 8 10 **Beaumont's Party (IRE)**22 2982 9-11-3 100 JakeGreenall 64
(Chris Grant) *in rr: bhd fr 3 out* **16/1**
9 19 **Shalamzar (FR)**18 899 7-11-0 107 HugoThompsonBrown(10) 52
(Micky Hammond) *mid-div: nt fluent 4th: bhd fr 3 out* **33/1**
U00 10 34 **Alchimix (FR)**33 2801 6-11-2 102 JoeColliver(3) 13
(Micky Hammond) *in rr: drvn 3rd: bhd fr 3 out: t.o next* **50/1**
35R0 P **Downtown Boy (IRE)**81 1887 8-11-3 103 (p) HarryChalloner(3)
(Ray Craggs) *hdwy to join ldrs 3rd: sn given reminders and reluctant: lost pl next: t.o 3 out: p.u bef next* **20/1**
363- P **Triumvirate**274 5108 6-11-10 107 LiamTreadwell
(Venetia Williams) *chsd ldrs: lost pl 5th: sn bhd: t.o whn p.u bef 2 out* **9/1**
3m 56.7s (4.20) **Going Correction** +0.375s/f (Yiel) **12** Ran SP% **116.8**
Speed ratings (Par 105): **104,102,99,99,97 88,87,82,72,55 ,**
CSF £20.31 CT £75.14 TOTE £6.60: £2.40, £1.30, £2.10; EX 23.60 Trifecta £152.20.
Owner Richard & Katherine Gilbert **Bred** Tom O'Doherty **Trained** Carluke, S Lanarks
FOCUS
Few got involved in what had looked a competitive handicap hurdle race on paper. The winner is on the upgrade.

3399 DINE AND VIEW AT CATTERICK RACES NOVICES' CHASE (19 fncs) 3m 1f 54y
1:40 (1:41) (Class 4) 5-Y-0+ **£7,147** (£2,098; £1,049; £524)

Form RPR
1P-2 1 **Definitly Red (IRE)**41 2641 7-11-0 0 DannyCook 140+
(Brian Ellison) *chsd ldr: led 12th: blnd 14th: sn drvn: styd on to forge clr appr last: eased clsng stages* **1/5**1
1-04 2 5 **Looking Well (IRE)**33 2803 7-11-0 123 CraigNichol 130+
(Nicky Richards) *trckd ldng pair: cl up 12th: hit 14th: 2nd appr 3 out: chal 2 out: 4 l down and hld whn hit last* **5/1**2
222P 3 39 **Shantou Tiger (IRE)**71 2039 7-11-0 118 (p) HenryBrooke 100
(Donald McCain) *led: hit 4th and 8th: hdd 12th: blnd and reminders next: 3rd and outpcd whn mstke 3 out: sn lost pl and bhd: t.o* **10/1**3
P05 4 78 **Under The Red Sky (IRE)**22 2981 9-10-7 73 ThomasDowson(7) 12
(Kenny Johnson) *nt fluent: hdwy to chse ldrs 4th: outpcd 12th: sn lost pl and bhd: t.o 4 out* **80/1**
6m 37.8s (-4.20) **Going Correction** +0.075s/f (Yiel) **4** Ran SP% **110.3**
Speed ratings: **109,107,94,69**
CSF £1.95 TOTE £1.10; EX 1.80 Trifecta £1.70.
Owner P J Martin **Bred** James Keegan **Trained** Norton, N Yorks
FOCUS
This was much harder work for the long odds-on favourite than many would have anticipated. The winner is a 147 hurdler and can probably match that over fences.

3400 RACING UK PROFITS RETURNED TO RACING NOVICES' HURDLE (11 hdls 1 omitted) 3m 1f 71y
2:15 (2:15) (Class 4) 4-Y-0+ **£5,198** (£1,526; £763; £381)

Form RPR
213 1 **Delusionofgrandeur (IRE)**34 2787 6-11-8 120 DannyCook 140+
(Sue Smith) *mde all: nt fluent 3rd: drvn 3 out: stmbld on landing 2 out: styd on: hit last: drvn clr* **5/2**2
3121 2 6 **Jonniesofa (IRE)**13 3159 6-12-0 130 CraigNichol 138
(Rose Dobbin) *chsd wnr to 8th: 2nd 3 out: kpt on same pce fr 2 out* **15/8**1
2F 3 12 **Wild West Wind (IRE)**27 2903 7-11-2 0 LiamTreadwell 114
(Tom George) *trckd ldrs: t.k.h: 2nd 8th tl 3 out: wknd appr last* **9/2**3
03F5 4 1 3/4 **Nautical Nitwit (IRE)**35 2744 7-11-3 119 NathanMoscrop(5) 117
(Philip Kirby) *in rr: chsd ldrs 8th: outpcd and lost pl 3 out* **12/1**
3031 5 30 **You Say What (IRE)**15 3124 6-11-5 0 HarryBannister(3) 87
(Neil King) *chsd ldrs 5th: nt fluent next: sn pushed along: lost pl after 8th: sn bhd: t.o 2 out* **5/1**
36-1 P **Mahler And Me (IRE)**22 2978 6-11-8 0 HenryBrooke
(Alistair Whillans) *hit 4th: sn chsng ldrs: lost pl 3 out: sn eased and p.u* **22/1**
1624 P **Tickenwolf (IRE)**38 2704 6-11-5 112 JoeColliver(3)
(George Moore) *in last: pushed along after 2nd: reminders 4th: sn bhd: t.o whn p.u bef 8th* **25/1**
6m 32.7s (5.10) **Going Correction** +0.375s/f (Yiel) **7** Ran SP% **114.1**
Speed ratings (Par 105): **106,104,100,99,90 ,**
CSF £7.85 TOTE £2.90: £1.40, £1.40; EX 9.60 Trifecta £38.40.
Owner McGoldrick Racing Syndicates (3) **Bred** D Cantillon And E Cantillon **Trained** High Eldwick, W Yorks

FOCUS
An informative staying novice hurdle, which featured three last-time-out winners, and good novice form for the track.

3401 WATCH ON 3 DEVICES RACINGUK.COM/ANYWHERE H'CAP CHASE (16 fncs) 2m 3f 51y
2:50 (2:51) (Class 4) (0-120,117) 5-Y-O+ **£7,147** (£2,098; £1,049; £524)

Form RPR
2465 **1** **Cloudy Joker (IRE)**[28] 2884 8-11-12 **117**................ HenryBrooke 127+
(Donald McCain) *mde all: drvn 3 out: kpt on: all out* **3/1**[2]
2-P5 **2** 1 ¾ **Uno Valoroso (FR)**[27] 2920 8-11-0 **110**............ JamieHamilton(5) 117
(Mark Walford) *t.k.h: sn trcking ldng pair: hit 4th: 2nd 10th: drvn 13th: hit 2 out and last: kpt on to take 2nd clsng stages* **9/2**[3]
2-21 **3** nk **Rear Admiral (IRE)**[35] 2753 10-11-12 **117**..............(t) JakeGreenall 124
(Michael Easterby) *t.k.h: handy 3rd 11th: chsd wnr sn after 2 out: kpt on same pce run-in* **3/1**[2]
1431 **4** 3 ¾ **Roxyfet (FR)**[6] 3241 6-9-12 **92** 7ex.................. JoeColliver(3) 97
(Micky Hammond) *detached in last: bhd and pushed along 8th: hdwy 11th: outpcd 13th: hit next: kpt on fr last* **2/1**[1]
300P **5** 14 **Houndscourt (IRE)**[23] 2975 9-11-0 **105**..................(t) SeanQuinlan 96
(Joanne Foster) *chsd wnr: drvn and lost pl 11th: bhd fr 13th* **10/1**
5m 7.0s (307.00) **5** Ran SP% **110.6**
CSF £16.02 TOTE £4.20: £1.70, £2.90; EX 15.50 Trifecta £51.70.
Owner On Cloud Eight **Bred** Miss Penny Downes **Trained** Cholmondeley, Cheshire
■ Stewards' Enquiry : Henry Brooke two-day ban: use of whip (15-16 Jan)

FOCUS
This lacked depth but was an exciting watch as Cloudy Joker put on a jumping clinic. The second and third are rated to their marks.

3402 RACING AGAIN 14TH JANUARY H'CAP HURDLE (12 hdls) 3m 1f 71y
3:25 (3:25) (Class 5) (0-100,99) 4-Y-O+ **£3,249** (£954; £477; £238)

Form RPR
036P **1** **Cumbrian Farmer**[38] 2703 9-9-11 **73** oh3..............(bt[1]) HarryChalloner(3) 76
(Kenneth Slack) *led 1st: hdd next: w ldr: led 8th: hdd narrowly and hit last: styd on to ld last 50yds* **12/1**
055 **2** ¾ **Triumph Davis (IRE)**[13] 3161 7-10-8 **84**...................... JoeColliver(3) 85
(Micky Hammond) *hld up in rr: gd hdwy sn after 3 out: cl 2nd next: led narrowly last: hdd and no ex last 50yds* **16/1**
/0-3 **3** 8 **Rocky Stone (IRE)**[33] 2800 8-11-0 **97**...................... RonanShort(10) 90
(Donald McCain) *chsd ldrs: drvn 3 out: wknd appr last* **10/3**[1]
-032 **4** 1 ¼ **Blake Dean**[17] 3102 8-11-5 **92**...................................... DannyCook 85
(Sue Smith) *in rr: hdwy 3 out: swtchd lft appr next: modest 4th last: one pce* **7/2**[2]
0-01 **5** 3 ½ **Chasma**[40] 2670 6-10-13 **86**.. JakeGreenall 76
(Michael Easterby) *chsd ldrs: one pce appr 2 out* **9/2**[3]
3P-3 **6** 36 **Jonny Eager (IRE)**[33] 2806 7-11-12 **99**..................(p) HenryBrooke 52
(Alistair Whillans) *nt fluent: led 2nd: j. slowly 6th: hdd and drvn 8th: lost pl 2 out: bhd whn eased between last 2: t.o* **13/2**
/4-3 **7** shd **Marrakech Trader (NZ)**[69] 2071 8-10-10 **93**............ LorcanMurtagh(10) 45
(Rose Dobbin) *hdwy to chse ldrs 5th: wkng whn hit 2 out: sn bhd: t.o* **8/1**
3165 **P** **Darsi Dancer (IRE)**[33] 2806 8-11-3 **97**...................... SamColtherd(7)
(Stuart Coltherd) *led to 1st: lost pl 5th: reminders next: sn bhd: t.o 8th: p.u bef 2 out* **18/1**
53P0 **P** **The Late Shift**[35] 2751 6-11-0 **87**.............................. CraigNichol
(Barry Murtagh) *mid-div: hdwy 5th: lost pl 3 out: wl bhd whn p.u bef next* **12/1**
6m 40.9s (13.30) **Going Correction** +0.375s/f (Yiel) **9** Ran SP% **114.5**
Speed ratings (Par 103): **93,92,90,89,88 77,77, ,**
CSF £172.78 CT £784.95 TOTE £15.10: £4.00, £3.70, £1.30; EX 182.60 Trifecta £725.30 Part won..
Owner A Slack **Bred** E R Hanbury **Trained** Hilton, Cumbria
■ Stewards' Enquiry : Harry Challoner trainer said, regarding the apparent improvement of form, that the gelding had benefited from the reapplication of a tongue strap and wearing blinkers for the first time

FOCUS
Recent winning form was very thin on the ground in this moderate finale. The winner is rated in line with the best of his 2015 form.
T/Plt: £37.10 to a £1 stake. Pool: £29,807.81 - 586.03 winning tickets T/Qpdt: £17.70 to a £1 stake. Pool: £2,072.32 - 86.6 winning tickets **Walter Glynn**

3028 CHELTENHAM (L-H)
Friday, January 1

OFFICIAL GOING: Heavy (soft in places; 5.4)
Wind: Strong across Weather: Overcast

3403 NEPTUNE INVESTMENT MANAGEMENT NOVICES' HURDLE (10 hdls) 2m 4f 56y
12:10 (12:11) (Class 3) 4-Y-O+

£6,256 (£1,848; £924; £462; £231; £116)

Form RPR
121 **1** **Champers On Ice (IRE)**[35] 2762 6-11-12 139............ TomScudamore 145
(David Pipe) *mde all: shkn up appr last: hung rt flat: drvn out* **7/2**[1]
4/2 **2** nk **Allysson Monterg (FR)**[29] 2860 6-11-2 0...................... AlainCawley 135
(Richard Hobson) *chsd wnr tl after 1st: remained handy: wnt 2nd again 7th: ev ch fr 2 out: sn rdn: nt clr run and swtchd lft flat: styd on wl* **33/1**
2-32 **3** 8 **Preseli Rock (IRE)**[18] 3077 6-11-2 0............................ SeanBowen 127
(Rebecca Curtis) *chsd wnr after 1st tl 7th: rdn bef 2 out: styd on same pce last* **12/1**
-2U3 **4** 12 **Drumlee Sunset (IRE)**[21] 3019 6-11-2 133.............. RichardJohnson 115
(Philip Hobbs) *chsd ldrs tl rdn and wknd appr last* **4/1**[2]
4-03 **5** 7 **West Approach**[20] 3032 6-11-2 0.............................. PaddyBrennan 107
(Colin Tizzard) *prom: rdn after 2 out: wknd bef last* **13/2**
2U **6** 2 ¾ **Hawkhurst (IRE)**[19] 3064 6-11-2 0.......................... BarryGeraghty 105
(Paul Nicholls) *hld up: pushed along 7th: wknd after 2 out* **5/1**[3]
1-12 **7** 1 ¾ **Captain Chaos (IRE)**[28] 2886 5-11-8 143.................. HarrySkelton 109
(Dan Skelton) *hld up: racd wd: hdwy 7th: wknd after 2 out* **7/2**[1]
-215 **8** 10 **Western Miller (IRE)**[43] 2591 5-11-8 0...................... AidanColeman 99
(Charlie Longsdon) *hld up: wknd appr 2 out* **50/1**
1-0 **9** 43 **Coole Charmer (IRE)**[47] 2514 7-11-2 0.......................... NoelFehily 75
(Nicky Henderson) *hld up: wknd after 2 out* **16/1**
-P3P **P** **Wildmoor Boy**[206] 680 5-11-2 0.................................. CharliePoste
(Robin Dickin) *hld up: bhd fr 7th: p.u bef last* **200/1**
5m 16.6s (19.20) **Going Correction** +1.125s/f (Heav) **10** Ran SP% **113.4**
Speed ratings (Par 107): **106,105,102,97,95 93,93,89,72,**
CSF £96.67 TOTE £4.50: £1.60, £7.90, £3.20; EX 121.00 Trifecta £584.10.
Owner Professor Caroline Tisdall & Bryan Drew **Bred** Mrs Gail C List **Trained** Nicholashayne, Devon
■ Stewards' Enquiry : Tom Scudamore one-day ban: careless riding (15 Jan)

FOCUS
Hurdles bends dolled out 12yds and Chase bends 14yds. The ground was testing but they got through it well enough. There was a wind to cope with too. This was a decent novice hurdle, dominated by those who raced up with the gallop. The first two are on the upgrade. The actual race distance was 2m 4f 128yds.

3404 WATCH LIVE RACING ON BETBRIGHT.COM H'CAP CHASE (19 fncs 3 omitted) 3m 2f 70y
12:45 (12:46) (Class 2) (0-145,139)
5-Y-O+

£12,512 (£3,696; £1,848; £924; £462; £232)

Form RPR
0-25 **1** **Perfect Candidate (IRE)**[48] 2482 9-11-7 **134**..............(t) PaddyBrennan 149+
(Fergal O'Brien) *hld up: hdwy 14th: chsd ldr 16th: lft in ld 3 out: shkn up flat: styd on wl* **4/1**[2]
1-33 **2** 8 **Beg To Differ (IRE)**[24] 2960 6-11-6 **133**.................... RichardJohnson 142+
(Jonjo O'Neill) *hld up: mstke 11th: hdwy 16th: rdn appr last: styd on same pce: wnt 2nd flat* **5/1**[3]
6-06 **3** 11 **Financial Climate (IRE)**[27] 2899 9-11-2 **132**..........(p) ThomasGarner(3) 127
(Oliver Sherwood) *chsd ldr tl rdn 16th: wknd appr last* **12/1**
2231 **4** 1 ¼ **Alternatif (FR)**[24] 2955 6-11-10 **137**........................(p) TomScudamore 133
(David Pipe) *hld up in tch: lft 2nd 3 out: ev ch whn nt fluent last: wknd flat* **9/4**[1]
P-4P **5** 12 **Indian Castle (IRE)**[20] 3038 8-11-12 **139**...................... AidanColeman 121
(Ian Williams) *prom: lost pl after 14th: sn rdn: wknd 2 out* **5/1**[3]
-PP5 **6** 4 ½ **Hollow Blue Sky (FR)**[13] 3157 9-10-1 **119**..........(tp) JamieBargary(5) 98
(Nigel Twiston-Davies) *hld up: hdwy 16th: hit 2 out: sn rdn and wknd* **14/1**
U0-P **7** 16 **Al Co (FR)**[34] 2783 11-11-12 **139**................................ SeanBowen 104
(Peter Bowen) *prom to 16th* **20/1**
111- **U** **De Kerry Man (IRE)**[305] 4533 8-10-7 **125**.................... JakeHodson(5)
(David Bridgwater) *led tl slipped on landing and uns rdr 3 out* **8/1**
7m 22.4s (28.60) **Going Correction** +1.125s/f (Heav) **8** Ran SP% **114.3**
Speed ratings: **101,98,95,94,91 89,84,**
CSF £24.63 CT £218.42 TOTE £5.30: £1.70, £1.60, £3.00; EX 27.10 Trifecta £159.70.
Owner ISL Recruitment **Bred** Hugh Suffern Bloodstock Ltd **Trained** Naunton, Gloucs

FOCUS
The second-last fence was omitted in all chases. This wasn't a strong handicap chase for the grade, but it was run at what looked a fair pace and proved a stern test of stamina. A step up from the winner. Actual race distance 3m 3f 18yds.

3405 BETBRIGHT #REALFANSONLY NOVICES' CHASE (REGISTERED AS THE DIPPER NOVICES' STEEPLE CHASE) (GRADE 2) (15 fncs 2 omitted) 2m 4f 166y
1:20 (1:20) (Class 1) 5-Y-O+ **£18,224** (£6,838; £3,424; £1,705; £8515; £Form)

0-31 **1** **Seeyouatmidnight**[26] 2932 8-11-4 151........................ BrianHughes 161+
(Sandy Thomson) *mde all: rdn appr and nt fluent last: hung lft flat: styd on wl* **7/2**[2]
-4F1 **2** 3 ¼ **Blaklion**[21] 3013 7-11-7 149.................................... RyanHatch 160
(Nigel Twiston-Davies) *a.p: chsd wnr 8th: rdn appr last: styd on same pce flat* **7/1**
0-11 **3** 20 **Le Mercurey (FR)**[14] 3136 6-11-7 142..................(t) SamTwiston-Davies 141
(Paul Nicholls) *chsd wnr to 5th: remained handy tl rdn and wknd appr last* **12/1**
53-1 **4** 7 **Volnay De Thaix (FR)**[21] 3026 7-11-0 0...................... NicodeBoinville 129
(Nicky Henderson) *hld up: mstke 9th: wkng whn mstke 3 out* **9/2**[3]
3-31 **5** 1 ¾ **Three Musketeers (IRE)**[35] 2760 6-11-7 155.................. HarrySkelton 133
(Dan Skelton) *hld up: hdwy 3 out: rdn and wknd appr last* **3/1**[1]
1-3P **6** 43 **Minella Rocco (IRE)**[21] 3013 6-11-0 0.......................(t) BarryGeraghty 81
(Jonjo O'Neill) *chsd ldrs tl mstke and wknd 11th* **10/1**
-021 **P** **Aubusson (FR)**[24] 2960 7-11-0 0.................................... LizzieKelly
(Nick Williams) *prom: mstke 2nd: chsd wnr 5th to 8th: rdn and wknd after 3 out: bhd whn p.u bef last* **9/2**[3]
5m 31.1s (15.40) **Going Correction** +1.125s/f (Heav) **7** Ran SP% **112.9**
Speed ratings: **115,113,106,103,102 86,**
CSF £26.49 TOTE £4.00: £2.00, £3.20; EX 23.40 Trifecta £167.70.
Owner Mrs A M Thomson **Bred** Fiona Avice Evans **Trained** Lambden, Berwicks

FOCUS
A high-class edition of this event, and strong novice form from the first two, who finished clear. The winner builto on his good recent win and is obvious RSA Chase material.

3406 BETBRIGHT BEST FOR FESTIVAL BETTING H'CAP CHASE (GRADE 3) (15 fncs 2 omitted) 2m 4f 166y
1:55 (1:55) (Class 1) 5-Y-O+

£34,170 (£12,822; £6,420; £3,198; £1,608; £804)

Form RPR
-111 **1** **Village Vic (IRE)**[20] 3031 9-10-10 **144**...................... RichardJohnson 160+
(Philip Hobbs) *mde all: mstke 2nd: nt fluent 12th: drvn out* **7/2**[1]
4-13 **2** 3 **Tenor Nivernais (FR)**[20] 3031 9-10-11 **145**.................... AidanColeman 156
(Venetia Williams) *chsd wnr to 3 out: rdn after 2 out: styd on same pce appr last: wnt 2nd again towards fin* **11/2**[2]
1-P3 **3** ¾ **Top Gamble (IRE)**[35] 2761 8-11-5 **153**............................ JamieMoore 163
(Kerry Lee) *hld up: hdwy 6th: chsd wnr 3 out: rdn appr last: no ex flat* **8/1**
0104 **4** 19 **Lost Legend (IRE)**[35] 2761 9-10-3 **144**..................(v) PatrickCowley(7) 135
(Jonjo O'Neill) *hld up: in tch: rdn and wknd after 12th* **33/1**
2421 **5** ½ **Seventh Sky (GER)**[13] 3157 9-11-6 **154**........................(tp) GavinSheehan 146
(Charlie Mann) *chsd ldrs: lost pl 6th: n.d after* **14/1**
-P00 **6** hd **Johns Spirit (IRE)**[20] 3031 9-11-3 **151**............................ JoshuaMoore 142
(Jonjo O'Neill) *hld up: hdwy 12th: rdn and wknd appr last: hmpd flat* **11/1**
0221 **7** 1 ¾ **Mon Successeur (FR)**[13] 3148 5-10-6 **145**.................... SamTwiston-Davies 130
(Paul Nicholls) *hld up: hdwy 8th: rdn and wknd appr last* **13/2**
-030 **8** 3 ¼ **Thomas Crapper**[69] 2064 9-10-4 **138**............................ CharliePoste 126
(Robin Dickin) *prom: mstke and lost pl 4th: hdwy 8th: wknd appr 12th* **14/1**
1-53 **9** 2 ½ **A Good Skin (IRE)**[55] 2348 7-10-2 **136**...................... PaddyBrennan 119
(Tom George) *hld up: a in rr: bhd fr 12th* **6/1**[3]

3-55 **10** *¾* **Mr Mole (IRE)**[27] 2915 8-11-12 **160**..............................(t) BarryGeraghty 145
(Paul Nicholls) *hld up: nt fluent 10th: sn wknd* **16/1**

-410 **11** *6* **Little Jon**[20] 3031 8-10-4 **143**.............................. JamieBargary(5) 125
(Nigel Twiston-Davies) *prom: nt fluent 7th: hit 9th: rdn and wknd after 3 out* **8/1**

5m 31.5s (15.80) **Going Correction** +1.125s/f (Heav)
WFA 5 from 7yo+ 4lb **11** Ran SP% **117.9**
Speed ratings: **114,112,112,105,105 105,104,103,102,101 99**
CSF £23.88 CT £145.45 TOTE £4.20: £1.80, £2.20, £2.70; EX 14.60 Trifecta £143.20.

Owner Alan Peterson **Bred** Tom Curran **Trained** Withycombe, Somerset

FOCUS
A valuable and competitive event, and strong handicap form, with the first three well clear. The time was 0.4sec slower than that for the Dipper. Another step forward from the winner. Actual race distance 2m 5f 30yds.

3407 BETBRIGHT CASINO H'CAP HURDLE (12 hdls) 2m 7f 213y
2:30 (2:31) (Class 2) 4-Y-0+
£12,512 (£3,696; £1,848; £924; £462; £232)

Form RPR

-221 **1** **Singlefarmpayment**[31] 2838 6-10-7 **125**.............................. NicodeBoinville 129+
(Tom Lacey) *hld up: hdwy after 3 out: led flat: drvn out* **9/2**[1]

00P- **2** *3½* **Knockara Beau (IRE)**[286] 4910 13-11-8 **140**.............................. JanFaltejsek 140
(George Charlton) *led to 9th: led again next: rdn and hdd appr last: styd on same pce flat* **25/1**

1-34 **3** *hd* **Anteros (IRE)**[24] 2963 8-10-13 **131**..............................(t) PaddyBrennan 131
(Sophie Leech) *hld up: hdwy after 3 out: ev ch whn n.m.r appr last: rdn and hung lft flat: styd on same pce* **25/1**

3-4F **4** *½* **Horizontal Speed (IRE)**[13] 3147 8-11-5 **137**.............................. BrianHughes 136
(David Dennis) *chsd ldrs: led 9th to next: led again appr last: rdn and hdd flat: no ex towards fin* **25/1**

-512 **5** *8* **Rons Dream**[20] 3034 6-11-8 **140**.............................. SeanBowen 132
(Peter Bowen) *prom: rdn after 2 out: wknd flat* **6/1**[2]

0/01 **6** *14* **So Fine (IRE)**[21] 3018 10-10-13 **131**.............................. RichardJohnson 110
(Philip Hobbs) *mid-div: blnd 9th: hdwy 3 out: rdn and wknd appr last* **6/1**[2]

5-21 **7** *2* **Dan Emmett (USA)**[27] 2906 6-10-7 **125**.............................. JamieMoore 100
(Michael Scudamore) *hld up: hdwy after 3 out: rdn and wknd after next* **10/1**

2110 **8** *8* **Monbeg Gold (IRE)**[21] 3018 6-10-12 **130**.............................. JoshuaMoore 100
(Jonjo O'Neill) *mid-div: hdwy 7th: rdn and wknd appr last* **8/1**[3]

2/33 **9** *8* **Billy Dutton**[21] 3018 10-10-9 **127**.............................. JamesDavies 87
(Chris Down) *prom: mstke 2nd: rdn and wknd after 2 out* **12/1**

06P3 **10** *2¾* **Sybarite (FR)**[13] 3158 10-10-9 **127**..............................(t) SamTwiston-Davies 84
(Nigel Twiston-Davies) *prom: lost pl 3rd: sn drvn along: bhd fr 5th* **16/1**

-012 **11** *½* **Foxcub (IRE)**[27] 2912 8-11-5 **144**.............................. MrJNixon(7) 100
(Tom Symonds) *mid-div: drvn along after 9th: wknd 3 out* **14/1**

4-P2 **12** *5* **According To Trev (IRE)**[21] 3018 10-10-11 **134**.........(p) JakeHodson(5) 85
(David Bridgwater) *chsd ldrs tl rdn and wknd 3 out* **16/1**

15-5 **P** **Stopped Out**[27] 2921 11-11-0 **135**..............................(p) AdamNicol(3)
(Philip Kirby) *chsd ldr to 9th: rdn and wknd after 2 out: bhd whn p.u bef last* **50/1**

-030 **P** **Rock On Rocky**[34] 2779 8-10-10 **128**.............................. CharliePoste
(Matt Sheppard) *hld up: in rr and hit 7th: sn wknd: bhd whn p.u bef last* **40/1**

-552 **P** **A Vos Gardes (FR)**[34] 2767 6-11-1 **133**..............................(t) AidanColeman
(Charlie Longsdon) *hld up: bhd fr 5th: p.u bef 7th* **14/1**

6-03 **P** **Batavir (FR)**[41] 2641 7-10-12 **130**..............................(tp) TomScudamore
(David Pipe) *mid-div: hdwy 7th: rdn and wknd after 3 out: bhd whn p.u bef last* **8/1**[3]

6m 20.6s (19.60) **Going Correction** +1.125s/f (Heav) **16** Ran SP% **126.8**
Speed ratings (Par 109): **112,110,110,110,107 103,102,99,97,96 96,94, , ,**
CSF £124.95 CT £2597.07 TOTE £4.80: £1.70, £6.40, £5.60, £5.70; EX 122.20 Trifecta £4477.30 Part won..

Owner Heather Haddock **Bred** Distillery Stud **Trained** Ledbury, H'fords

FOCUS
A competitive handicap hurdle in which the gallop appeared only ordinary. Soild form. Actual race distance 3m 17yds.

3408 DORNAN ENGINEERING RELKEEL HURDLE (GRADE 2) (10 hdls) 2m 4f 56y
3:05 (3:06) (Class 1) 5-Y-0+
£22,780 (£8,548; £4,280; £2,132; £1,072; £536)

Form RPR

14-U **1** **Camping Ground (FR)**[26] 2927 6-11-0 152..............................(t) LeightonAspell 163+
(Robert Walford) *a.p: chsd ldr 5th: led 3 out: clr last: styd on strly* **10/1**

-331 **2** *11* **Lil Rockerfeller (USA)**[27] 2914 5-11-4 151..............................(p) TrevorWhelan 156
(Neil King) *prom: pushed along after 3 out: chsd wnr next: rdn appr last: wknd flat* **20/1**

12-3 **3** *9* **Cole Harden (IRE)**[34] 2782 7-11-8 164..............................(t) GavinSheehan 150
(Warren Greatrex) *led to 3 out: rdn bef next: wknd appr last* **4/1**[2]

121- **4** *1¼* **Aurore D'Estruval (FR)**[363] 3503 6-11-1 144.............................. SeanBowen 143
(Rebecca Curtis) *hld up: hdwy 5th: rdn and wknd appr last* **20/1**

2-22 **5** *nse* **Top Notch (FR)**[34] 2789 5-11-2 158.............................. DavidBass 144
(Nicky Henderson) *chsd ldr 2nd tl mstke 5th: remained handy tl rdn and wknd appr last* **13/8**[1]

0-16 **6** *28* **Bobs Worth (IRE)**[34] 2783 11-11-4 152.............................. BarryGeraghty 130
(Nicky Henderson) *racd wd: chsd ldr to 2nd: lost pl next: hdwy 5th: wknd appr 2 out* **14/1**

51-5 **P** **Whisper (FR)**[34] 2782 8-11-8 167.............................. NicodeBoinville
(Nicky Henderson) *hld up: mstke 5th: rdn and wknd after 3 out: bhd whn p.u bef last* **6/1**

111 **P** **Virgilio (FR)**[27] 2901 7-11-0 149..............................(t) HarrySkelton
(Dan Skelton) *hld up: rdn and wknd qckly appr 3 out: sn p.u* **5/1**[3]

5m 15.7s (18.30) **Going Correction** +1.125s/f (Heav) **8** Ran SP% **114.3**
Speed ratings: **108,103,100,99,99 88, ,**
CSF £164.02 TOTE £13.10: £3.50, £4.00, £1.60; EX 185.90 Trifecta £457.20.

Owner G L Porter **Bred** Gerard Samama **Trained** Child Okeford, Dorset

FOCUS
Previously run at the December meeting, the Relkeel replaces a non-Graded conditions hurdle that used to be run over the same trip on this card. The time was nearly a second quicker than that for the opening novice hurdle, which took place on the best of the ground. Some of the main contenders weren't at their best, but the winner impressed. He's still around 10lb shy of what would be required in the World Hurdle. Actual race distance 2m 4f 128yds.

3409 EBF STALLIONS & CHELTENHAM PONY CLUB STANDARD OPEN NATIONAL HUNT FLAT RACE (LISTED RACE) 1m 5f 209y
3:40 (3:41) (Class 1) 4-Y-O
£11,888 (£4,452; £2,224; £1,110)

Form RPR

1 **Capeland (FR)**[245] 4-10-12 0.............................. SamTwiston-Davies 105+
(Paul Nicholls) *hld up: hdwy over 2f out: r.o u.p to ld towards fin* **7/4**[1]

1 **2** *½* **Jam Session (IRE)**[34] 2777 4-10-12 0.............................. BrianHughes 104+
(Ian Williams) *a.p: chsd ldr over 1f out: rdn to ld and wandered ins fnl f: hdd towards fin* **8/1**

1 **3** *1* **The Blue Bomber**[20] 3048 4-10-12 0.............................. GavinSheehan 103
(Mick Channon) *led: rdn over 1f out: hdd and hmpd ins fnl f: kpt on* **12/1**

4 *2* **One Of Us** 4-10-12 0.............................. RichardJohnson 101+
(Nick Williams) *chsd ldrs: outpcd over 1f out: r.o towards fin* **8/1**

5 *10* **Le Coeur Net (FR)** 4-10-12 0.............................. BarryGeraghty 89
(Anthony Honeyball) *hld up: shkn up over 2f out: wknd fnl f* **9/2**[2]

6 *1½* **Soulsaver** 4-10-12 0.............................. AidanColeman 87
(Anthony Honeyball) *hld up: pushed along over 5f out: effrt over 1f out: wknd fnl f* **25/1**

611 **7** *1¼* **Golden Gate Bridge (GER)**[54] 2368 4-10-12 0.............................. DenisO'Regan 86
(Mark Pitman) *chsd ldr: ev ch over 2f out: wknd fnl f* **15/2**[3]

8 *7* **Cable** 4-10-12 0.............................. TomScudamore 77
(John Joseph Hanlon, Ire) *hld up: rdn over 3f out: wknd over 2f out* **25/1**

1 **9** *nk* **Miss Fleming**[44] 2583 4-10-5 0.............................. HarrySkelton 70
(David Loder) *hld up: hdwy over 4f out: wknd over 2f out* **9/1**

3m 36.4s (216.40) **9** Ran SP% **113.9**
CSF £16.18 TOTE £2.70: £1.20, £2.50, £2.50; EX 19.80 Trifecta £174.80.

Owner Mrs Kathy Stuart **Bred** Alain Couetil **Trained** Ditcheat, Somerset

FOCUS
A Listed bumper confined to four-year-olds, this event was won by The New One four years ago. The first four are probably decent. Actual race distance 1m 6f 61yds.
T/Plt: £851.30 to a £1 stake. Pool: £208,881.31 - 179.11 winning tickets T/Qpdt: £97.80 to a £1 stake. Pool: £25,029.79 - 189.2 winning tickets **Colin Roberts**

3119 EXETER (R-H)
Friday, January 1

OFFICIAL GOING: Heavy (5.2)
Wind: very strong half across Weather: heavy rain clearing from 2.00pm

3410 PASSAGE HOUSE INN TOPSHAM NOVICES' H'CAP HURDLE (10 hdls 2 omitted) 2m 7f 25y
12:35 (12:35) (Class 5) (0-100,100) 4-Y-0+
£2,599 (£763; £381; £190)

Form RPR

6-33 **1** **Precious Ground**[44] 2567 6-11-0 **88**.............................. JamesBest 93+
(Kevin Bishop) *trckd ldrs: wnt 2nd after 7th: led 2 out: styd on dourly: rdn out* **3/1**[1]

-00P **2** *7* **Petite Fantasie**[44] 2567 7-9-12 **77**.............................. CharlieDeutsch(5) 75
(Mark Gillard) *led: rdn and hdd after 3 out: wnt bdly lft and hld fr next: styd on same pce* **16/1**

05P- **3** *1½* **Mount Prospex (IRE)**[285] 7-11-6 **94**.............................. NickScholfield 90
(Tim Dennis) *hld up in tch: rdn and detached on long run bef 3 out: hdwy 2 out: styd on fr last: wnt 3rd nring fin* **5/1**[3]

56-P **4** *nk* **Kudu Shine**[242] 108 10-11-5 **100**.............................. MrMatthewHampton(7) 95
(Richard Woollacott) *trckd ldr tl after 7th: rdn to chse ldng pair 3 out: no ex fr last whn losing 3rd nring fin* **7/2**[2]

-530 **5** *shd* **Shoofly Milly (IRE)**[22] 2985 7-11-7 **95**..............................(p) LiamHeard 90
(Jeremy Scott) *hld up in tch: effrt appr 3 out: sn one pce* **7/1**

4-43 **6** *22* **Buckboru (IRE)**[28] 2876 8-10-5 **86**..............................(p) ThomasCheesman(7) 66
(Laura Young) *hld up in tch: effrt appr 3 out: wknd bef 2 out* **3/1**[1]

000 **P** **Arty Bella**[15] 3119 5-10-10 **91**.............................. MissBFrost(7)
(Jimmy Frost) *trckd ldrs tl dropped to last appr 5th: sn struggling: t.o whn p.u after 3 out* **9/1**

7m 7.3s (68.30) **Going Correction** +1.975s/f (Heav) **7** Ran SP% **117.3**
Speed ratings (Par 103): **60,57,57,56,56 49,**
CSF £44.98 CT £236.29 TOTE £3.60: £1.60, £7.20; EX 48.40 Trifecta £157.30.

Owner Jim Kilduff & Ken Jones **Bred** Jim & Dan Kilduff & Ken Jones **Trained** Spaxton, Somerset

FOCUS
All races run on hurdle bend turning into the home straight. Last hurdle in back straight omitted. The actual race distance of the opener was 2m 7f 70yds. The meeting had to pass two inspections, one the previous day and another in the morning. The going was predictably heavy, so it was no surprise that they went a steady pace in this modest staying novices' handicap hurdle, with the tempo not picking up until the long run to three from home. The time was a whopping 98.3sec outside standard and the winning rider said about the ground: "It's very heavy, but they are slopping through it and it seems safe at present". The winner was entitled to improve on previous course form over shorter.

3411 BATHWICK TYRES BRIDGWATER MAIDEN HURDLE (7 hdls 1 omitted) 2m 175y
1:10 (1:10) (Class 5) 4-Y-0+
£2,599 (£763; £381; £190)

Form RPR

F2-4 **1** **Emerging Talent (IRE)**[82] 1870 7-11-5 135..............................(t) NickScholfield 127+
(Paul Nicholls) *trckd ldrs: led after 4th: in command fr 3 out: readily* **4/6**[1]

F6 **2** *8* **Gala Ball (IRE)**[43] 2603 6-11-5 0.............................. TomO'Brien 115
(Philip Hobbs) *trckd ldrs: nt fluent 3rd: rdn appr 3 out: styd on into 2nd at the last: no ch w wnr* **12/1**

45-0 **3** *3* **Sandford Castle (IRE)**[16] 3105 6-11-5 0.............................. LiamHeard 114
(Johnny Farrelly) *mid-div: hdwy 4th: wnt 2nd appr 3 out where nt fluent: sn rdn and hld: nt fluent next: no ex and lost 2nd at the last* **9/1**

-150 **4** *32* **One Cool Scorpion (IRE)**[26] 2928 5-11-5 0.............................. JamesBest 80
(Philip Hobbs) *hld up towards rr: stdy prog after 4th: wnt modest 4th after 3 out: nvr threatened ldrs* **50/1**

4360 **5** *5* **Pilgrims Bay (IRE)**[35] 2763 6-11-5 0.............................. ConorO'Farrell 75
(David Pipe) *mid-div: hdwy after 4th: rdn bef 3 out: sn wknd* **33/1**

F **6** *8* **Bingo D'Olivate (FR)**[41] 2646 5-11-2 0..............................[1] JamesBanks(3) 67
(Noel Williams) *hld up towards rr: sme prog into midfield after 4th: wknd bef next* **33/1**

The Form Book Jumps 2015-16, Raceform Ltd, Newbury, RG14 5SJ

65P5 7 1 3/4 **Trans Express (IRE)**[14] 3135 6-11-2 0 LucyGardner(3) 65
(Sue Gardner) *in tch: rdn appr 3 out: sn wknd* **66/1**

0 8 22 **De Bene Esse (IRE)**[33] 2801 6-11-5 0 [1] AdamWedge 43
(Evan Williams) *led tl 4th: wknd bef next: t.o* **15/2**[3]

4 9 5 **Ebadani (IRE)**[26] 2928 6-11-5 0 BrendanPowell 38
(Jamie Snowden) *trckd ldrs: rdn appr 3 out: wknd qckly: t.o* **5/1**[2]

10 3 **Smart Thinking (IRE)** 5-11-5 0 RichieMcLernon 35
(Jonjo O'Neill) *mid-div: wknd on long run bef 3 out: t.o* **18/1**

50 11 31 **Iniciar (GER)**[35] 2747 6-11-2 0 KieronEdgar(3)
(David Pipe) *towards rr of midfield: wknd after 4th: t.o* **50/1**

300 12 3 1/2 **Still Together (IRE)**[21] 3022 6-11-2 0 BrianToomey(3)
(David Pipe) *mid-div tl wknd after 4th: t.o* **50/1**

00 13 3/4 **The Minkle (IRE)**[16] 3114 5-11-5 0 IanPopham
(David Pipe) *a bhd: t.o* **80/1**

0 14 6 **Brin D'Avoine (FR)**[22] 2991 5-10-12 0 MrShaneQuinlan(7)
(Neil Mulholland) *hit 1st: a in rr: t.o* **50/1**

4-3 15 49 **Lift The Lid (IRE)**[229] 359 6-11-5 0 WayneHutchinson
(Neil Mulholland) *in tch: hit 4th: sn wknd: t.o* **20/1**

0P P **Dinky Challenger**[22] 2986 8-11-0 0 (t) CharlieDeutsch(5)
(Mark Gillard) *prom tl 2nd: dropped to rr qckly: t.o whn p.u after 4th* **150/1**

0-55 P **Lime Street (IRE)**[21] 3009 5-11-2 0 BenPoste(3)
(Tom Symonds) *racd keenly: mid-div: hit 4th: sn wknd: t.o whn p.u bef 3 out* **33/1**

0660 P **King Simba (IRE)**[21] 3019 5-11-2 0 ConorShoemark(3)
(Kim Bailey) *a towards rr: t.o whn p.u bef 3 out* **80/1**

4m 45.2s (29.70) **Going Correction** +1.975s/f (Heavy) **18** Ran SP% **137.4**
Speed ratings (Par 103): **109,105,103,88,86 82,81,71,69,67 53,51,51,48,25 , ,**
CSF £11.60 TOTE £1.60: £1.10, £3.50, £4.60; EX 14.70 Trifecta £128.50.
Owner Mr & Mrs Paul Barber **Bred** T J Nagle **Trained** Ditcheat, Somerset

FOCUS
Last hurdle in back straight omitted. Actual race distance 2m 205yds. An uncompetitive maiden hurdle despite the size of the field. They went a sensible pace in the conditions, but the first three still pulled a long way clear of the others. Much the fastest race on the card and the form is given the benefit of the doubt.

3412 BATHWICK TYRES H'CAP CHASE (12 fncs 6 omitted) 3m 54y
1:45 (1:47) (Class 4) (0-110,110) 5-Y-O+ **£6,498** (£1,908; £954; £477)

Form RPR

6U-F 1 **Rocky Bender (IRE)**[38] 2701 11-11-7 **105** TomO'Brien 120+
(Venetia Williams) *trckd ldrs: chal 3 out: led after 2 out: styd on wl: rdn out* **14/1**

-236 2 13 **Somerset Lias (IRE)**[22] 2988 8-11-6 **104** LiamHeard 109
(Bob Buckler) *prom: led by-passing omitted 4 out: sn rdn: hdd after 2 out: styd on but no ex fr last* **13/2**

5-01 3 10 **Long John**[15] 3123 9-11-12 **110** JamesBest 102
(Jackie Du Plessis) *hld up bhd: smooth hdwy bef omitted 4 out: wnt cl 4th 3 out: sn rdn: styd on at same pce fr next: wnt 3rd towards fin* **15/2**

6412 4 1 1/2 **Bredon Hill Lad**[31] 2830 9-11-0 **101** LucyGardner(3) 93
(Sue Gardner) *hld up bhd ldrs: nt fluent 7th: disp cl 3rd by-passing omitted 4 out: sn rdn: hld fr next: no ex fr last* **6/1**[3]

3-62 5 3 3/4 **Buckhorn Tom**[18] 3086 8-11-3 **108** (b) PaulO'Brien(7) 96
(Colin Tizzard) *disp ld tl after 3rd: prom: rdn to hold pl bhd ldrs after 9th: hld fr 3 out: styd on but no ch fr last* **6/1**[3]

34-4 6 29 **Somerby (IRE)**[58] 2269 13-10-0 **84** oh9 (t) RichieMcLernon 42
(Richenda Ford) *trckd ldrs: led 4th tl after 9th: rdn bef omitted 4 out: sn wknd: t.o* **25/1**

2333 P **Railway Storm (IRE)**[28] 2878 11-10-8 **99** MissBFrost(7)
(Jimmy Frost) *disp ld tl 3rd: trckd ldrs tl 8th: sn pushed along in last pair: wknd bef 3 out: t.o whn p.u bef last* **8/1**

0/42 U **Gallic Warrior (FR)**[30] 2851 9-11-4 **105** ConorShoemark(3) 96
(Fergal O'Brien) *hld up but in tch: rdn to chse ldrs appr 3 out: wkng in 5th whn slipped and uns rdr after 2 out* **5/1**[2]

-201 P **Kings River (FR)**[38] 2698 7-10-7 **96** CharlieDeutsch(5)
(Venetia Williams) *trckd ldrs: prom 8th: hit next: sn led: rdn and hdd by-passing omitted 4 out: sn wknd: t.o whn p.u bef last* **3/1**[1]

7m 10.3s (61.00) **Going Correction** +2.275s/f (Heavy) **9** Ran SP% **117.0**
Speed ratings: **89,84,81,80,79 69, , ,**
CSF £102.69 CT £745.17 TOTE £16.10: £4.10, £2.30, £2.30; EX 141.10 Trifecta £1814.80.
Owner Miss V M Williams **Bred** B Deane **Trained** Kings Caple, H'fords

FOCUS
Last two fences in back straight and first fence in home straight omitted. Actual race distance 2m 7f 214yds. Despite the reduced number of fences and the fact that they went a steady pace, this was still a war of attrition in the conditions. The winner was well in on the best of last season's form and is rated back to that level.

3413 ROYAL CASTLE HOTEL "NATIONAL HUNT" NOVICES' HURDLE (9 hdls 1 omitted) 2m 2f 111y
2:20 (2:20) (Class 4) 5-Y-O+ **£3,249** (£954; £477; £238)

Form RPR

2-11 1 **Vieux Lille (IRE)**[28] 2879 6-11-5 0 TomO'Brien 131+
(Philip Hobbs) *mde virtually all: in command fr 3 out: blnd last: comf* **1/4**[1]

3 2 9 **Cailleach Annie (IRE)**[15] 3119 7-10-5 0 (t) JamesBest 103
(Jackie Du Plessis) *trckd ldrs: rdn appr 3 out: styd on into 2nd 2 out: kpt on but no ch w wnr* **16/1**[3]

5-25 3 4 **Bindon Mill**[56] 2317 7-10-12 0 IanPopham 105
(Victor Dartnall) *hld up: rdn and styd on fr 2 out: wnt 3rd towards fin: nvr threatened ldng pair* **33/1**

0-33 4 3 3/4 **Cotswold Road**[22] 2986 6-10-12 0 BrendanPowell 102
(Colin Tizzard) *trckd ldrs: rdn to chse wnr appr 3 out tl 2 out: no ex fr last* **7/1**[2]

5 83 **Easy Street (IRE)**[371] 3296 6-10-12 0 RichieMcLernon 18
(Jonjo O'Neill) *hld up: hdwy after 6th: wknd qckly bef 3 out: virtually p.u run-in* **7/1**[2]

0-P0 P **Somerset Jem**[28] 2879 7-10-12 0 MichealNolan
(Kevin Bishop) *hld up: lost tch after 5th: t.o whn p.u bef 3 out* **66/1**

0-P5 P **I'm Oscar (IRE)**[28] 2879 6-10-9 0 MattGriffiths(3)
(Jeremy Scott) *pressed wnr tl rdn after 6th: wknd bef 3 out: t.o whn p.u bef last* **33/1**

5m 32.3s (49.60) **Going Correction** +2.45s/f (Heavy) **7** Ran SP% **118.3**
Speed ratings: **93,89,87,85,51 ,**
CSF £6.81 TOTE £1.10: £1.10, £5.70; EX 6.70 Trifecta £52.30.
Owner Louisville Syndicate III **Bred** Park Athlete Partnership **Trained** Withycombe, Somerset

FOCUS
Last hurdle in back straight omitted. Actual race distance 2m 2f 141yds. A very uncompetitive novices' hurdle and few worries for the long-odds-on favourite, who's rated below his best.

3414 THURLESTONE HOTEL H'CAP HURDLE (9 hdls 1 omitted) 2m 2f 111y
2:55 (2:55) (Class 4) (0-115,115) 4-Y-O+ **£3,328** (£1,033; £556)

Form RPR

5132 1 **Braavos**[27] 2898 5-11-3 **113** ThomasCheesman(7) 124+
(Philip Hobbs) *racd keenly: in tch: hdwy 4th: rdn to chal 3 out: led 2 out: styd on to assert nring fin: drvn out* **11/4**[1]

-455 2 1 **Craiganee (IRE)**[29] 2871 9-10-6 **98** (t[1]) KieronEdgar(3) 106
(Chris Down) *prom: led after 5th: rdn whn jnd 3 out: hdd 2 out: rallied gamely and ev ch after last: no ex towards fin* **16/1**

-545 3 7 **Zanstra (IRE)**[22] 2985 6-11-2 **105** BrendanPowell 106
(Colin Tizzard) *trckd ldrs: rdn and ev ch appr 3 out: sn hld: styd on same pce* **5/1**

5-33 F **Winning Spark (USA)**[22] 2989 9-11-12 **115** JamesBest 118+
(Jackie Du Plessis) *hld up bhd: smooth hdwy into 2 l 3rd whn fell 3 out* **9/2**[3]

U600 P **Romeo Americo (IRE)**[36] 2734 9-11-5 **108** AndrewThornton
(Seamus Mullins) *mid-div tl struggling in rr 5th: t.o whn p.u bef 3 out* **12/1**

0524 P **Only Gorgeous (IRE)**[50] 2456 7-10-11 **103** LucyGardner(3)
(Sue Gardner) *trckd ldrs: wknd on long run after 6th: t.o whn p.u bef 3 out* **9/1**

5-04 P **Auckland De Re (FR)**[43] 2603 6-11-7 **110** NoelFehily
(Neil Mulholland) *led tl nt fluent 5th: chsd ldr tl wknd qckly and p.u bef 3 out* **7/2**[2]

306P P **Bogoss Du Perret (FR)**[29] 2871 5-10-9 **105** MissBFrost(7)
(Jimmy Frost) *chsd ldr: struggling after in rr after 5th: t.o whn p.u bef 3 out* **40/1**

5-F0 P **Mother Meldrum (IRE)**[22] 2985 7-11-0 **103** IanPopham
(Victor Dartnall) *mid-div tl wknd on long run after 6th: t.o whn p.u bef 3 out* **9/1**

5m 26.6s (43.90) **Going Correction** +2.45s/f (Heavy) **9** Ran SP% **119.8**
Speed ratings (Par 105): **105,104,101, , , , ,**
CSF £45.66 CT £216.34 TOTE £3.20: £1.40, £6.40, £2.20; EX 60.40 Trifecta £600.20.
Owner Mrs Diana L Whateley **Bred** C R Mason **Trained** Withycombe, Somerset

FOCUS
Last hurdle in back straight omitted. Actual race distance 2m 2f 141yds. This was extremely hard work with only three of the nine remaining runners managing to complete. The second and third set the level.

3415 BATHWICK TYRES TAUNTON BEGINNERS' CHASE (11 fncs 4 omitted) 2m 3f 48y
3:30 (3:30) (Class 4) 5-Y-O+ **£3,898** (£1,144; £572; £286)

Form RPR

5-02 1 **Activial (FR)**[35] 2760 6-11-0 149 NoelFehily 154+
(Harry Fry) *trckd ldrs: hmpd 3rd: led by-passing omitted 4 out: j. bdly lft next 2: shkn up to draw clr last: readily* **2/7**[1]

P1-2 2 16 **Oscar Sunset (IRE)**[28] 2881 9-11-0 140 AdamWedge 139+
(Evan Williams) *led: hdd by-passing omitted 4 out: sltly hmpd next 2: outpcd bef last* **3/1**[2]

41/- 3 29 **Fear Glic (IRE)**[620] 5429 10-11-0 123 JamesBest 107
(Jackie Du Plessis) *trckd ldr: pckd bdly 2nd: rdn bef omitted 4 out: sn outpcd: wknd 2 out: t.o* **20/1**

P2-2 4 14 **Union Saint (FR)**[219] 512 8-10-7 128 MissBFrost(7) 92
(Jimmy Frost) *chsd ldrs tl outpcd bef omitted 4 out: t.o whn stmbld bdly 2 out* **12/1**[3]

20P/ P **Kilrush (IRE)**[237] 10-10-7 0 HarryTeal(7)
(John Berwick) *chsd ldrs tl rdn after 8th: sn lost tch: t.o whn p.u bef omitted 4 out* **100/1**

5m 34.7s (37.40) **Going Correction** +2.275s/f (Heavy)
WFA 5 from 6yo+ 3lb **5** Ran SP% **116.2**
Speed ratings: **112,105,93,87,**
CSF £1.95 TOTE £1.30: £1.10, £1.20; EX 2.00 Trifecta £5.20.
Owner Potensis Bloodstock Limited **Bred** Francis Maze **Trained** Seaborough, Dorset

FOCUS
Last two fences in back straight and first fence in home straight omitted. Actual race distance 2m 3f 8yds. A fascinating beginners' chase featuring two horses that had finished second behind smart sorts on their respective chase debuts. There's a case for rating the form a few pounds higher through the second.

3416 BILLY WILLIAMS MEMORIAL MAIDEN OPEN NATIONAL HUNT FLAT RACE 2m 175y
4:00 (4:00) (Class 6) 4-6-Y-O **£1,624** (£477; £238; £119)

Form RPR

1 1 **Gayebury**[18] 3082 6-11-5 0 AndrewThornton 113+
(Tom Symonds) *mde all: jnd briefly over 3f out: edgd lft but in command fnl f: styd on* **2/1**[1]

3-3 2 6 **Bacchanel (FR)**[48] 2493 5-11-5 0 TomO'Brien 107+
(Philip Hobbs) *racd keenly: sn trcking wnr: upsides over 3f out: sn hung lft and dropped to 3 l 2nd: rallied briefly ent fnl f: sn no ex* **2/1**[1]

3 36 **Zammia (FR)** 4-10-7 0 WayneHutchinson 59
(David Dennis) *hld up: rdn along and hdwy 6f out: sn wnt wl hld 3rd: nvr threatened to get on terms w ldrs: wknd 2f out: t.o* **7/1**[3]

4 89 **Burton Boru (IRE)** 4-10-7 0 NoelFehily
(Colin Tizzard) *struggling in rr 1/2-way: sn t.o* **4/1**[2]

0 5 1/2 **Breeze Along**[50] 2460 6-11-2 0 LucyGardner(3)
(Sue Gardner) *chsd ldrs tl wknd 5f out: t.o* **33/1**

0 6 39 **Denny Kerrell**[22] 2991 5-11-5 0 IanPopham
(Caroline Keevil) *chsd ldrs tl wknd 5f out: t.o* **50/1**

3 7 9 **El Tiburon (IRE)**[28] 2882 4-10-4 0 JamesBanks(3)
(Sam Thomas) *hld up in tch: struggling 6f out: sn wknd: t.o* **8/1**

0 8 51 **Primary Suspect (IRE)**[29] 2875 6-11-5 0 MichealNolan
(Linda Blackford) *lost tch 1/2-way: t.o* **33/1**

4m 54.2s (45.40) **Going Correction** +2.45s/f (Heavy)
WFA 4 from 5yo+ 11lb **8** Ran SP% **118.1**
Speed ratings: **91,88,71,29,29 10,6,**
CSF £6.14 TOTE £2.60: £1.10, £1.10, £2.10; EX 8.20 Trifecta £31.60.
Owner Mrs R F Knipe **Bred** R F And S D Knipe **Trained** Harewood End, H'fords
■ Stewards' Enquiry : Noel Fehily £80 fine: passport irregularity

FOCUS
Actual race distance 2m 205yds. This bumper only concerned the joint-favourites from a very long way out and the form is rated around them.
T/Plt: £36.80 to a £1 stake. Pool: £31,953.69 - 633.47 winning tickets T/Qpdt: £10.20 to a £1 stake. Pool: £3,377.64 - 243.38 winning tickets **Tim Mitchell**

3174

FAKENHAM (L-H)

Friday, January 1

OFFICIAL GOING: Soft (5.5)

Wind: light, half against Weather: overcast

3417 COOL ROXY BAR FOR PRIVATE FUNCTIONS (S) HURDLE (11 hdls) 2m 4f 1y

12:40 (12:41) (Class 5) 4-Y-0+ £2,737 (£798; £399)

Form RPR

20/1 **1** **Cotillion**[4] 3314 10-11-6 124..........................(t) RobMcCarth(3) 131+
(Ian Williams) *hld up in tch: nt fluent 4th: clsd to trck ldrs and mstke 8th: led on bit and mstke 2 out: sn cruised clr: v easily* **4/6**[1]

035P **2** *19* **Trapper Peak (IRE)**[35] 2749 7-11-6 113.......................... AdamPogson 103
(Caroline Bailey) *led: drvn and jnd after 3 out: hdd next and sn btn: plugged on* **11/4**[2]

0620 **3** *2* **Guaracha**[16] 3108 5-10-13 102..........................(p) MikeyHamill(7) 103
(Bill Turner) *t.k.h: hld up in rr: clsd 7th: effrt after 3 out: 3rd and btn next: disputing modest 2nd whn blnd last* **20/1**

1464 **4** *9* **Occasionally Yours (IRE)**[26] 2924 12-11-5 108.......... MissTWorsley(7) 99
(Alan Blackmore) *chsd ldr tl 5th: styd prom: rdn 8th: sn outpcd: lost tch bef 2 out* **8/1**[3]

1154 **P** **A Little Bit Dusty**[33] 2808 8-11-12 120..........................(b) TomCannon
(Conor Dore) *hld up in tch: chsd ldrs 3rd: chsd ldr 5th: ev ch 3 out: sn rdn and btn: fdd next: t.o whn p.u last* **16/1**

P0P- **P** **Craftybird**[313] 4390 5-10-13 92.......................... MichaelByrne
(Denis Quinn) *chsd ldrs tl 3rd: steadily lost pl: bhd and mstke 7th: sn lost tch u.p: t.o whn p.u 3 out* **50/1**

5m 32.85s (12.45) **Going Correction** +0.70s/f (Soft) **6** Ran SP% **110.4**

Speed ratings (Par 103): **103,95,94,91,**

.There was no bid for the winner. Guaracha was claimed by Mrs A. Dunn for £5000. \n\x\x Trapper Peak was claimed by Mrs A. Dunn for £5000.

Owner Jamie Robert Roberts **Bred** Mr & Mrs G Middlebrook **Trained** Portway, Worcs

FOCUS

A one-sided seller, the winner in a different league. He's rated in line with the best of his hurdle figures. After rail movements the actual race distance was 2m 4f 171yds.

3418 FAKENHAM RACECOURSE ANNUAL MEMBERS MAIDEN HURDLE (9 hdls) 2m 3y

1:15 (1:15) (Class 5) 4-Y-0+ £3,422 (£997; £499)

Form RPR

0 **1** **Dalaki (IRE)**[21] 3021 5-11-5 0.......................... PeterCarberry 125+
(Des Donovan) *chsd ldrs: wnt 2nd after 5th: ev ch after 3 out: led wl bef last: sn drvn clr: styd on strly* **50/1**

2 **2** *18* **Alberta (IRE)**[38] 2699 7-11-5 0.......................... AndrewTinkler 107
(Jim Best) *chsd ldrs: led on inner bnd bef 2 out: rdn and mstke 2 out: sn hdd and btn: no ch w wnr but plugged on for 2nd* **10/11**[1]

0 **3** *5* **Instant Karma (IRE)**[26] 2928 5-11-5 0.......................... TomCannon 101
(Michael Bell) *t.k.h: hld up in tch: clsd after 5th: cl enough in 3rd 2 out: sn u.p and no ex* **11/4**[2]

4 *12* **Counterfeiter**[680] 6-10-12 0.......................... MrZBaker(7) 89
(Martin Bosley) *hld up in midfield: 6th but nt on terms after 6th: no imp: wnt 4th between last 2: n.d* **14/1**

0200 **5** *16* **Midtech Valentine**[21] 3021 5-10-9 0.......................... RobMcCarth(3) 70
(Ian Williams) *led: hit 6th: rdn and hdd bnd bef 2 out: sn btn and fdd between last 2: t.o* **10/1**[3]

6 *4* **Bobby Benton (IRE)**[248] 5-11-5 0.......................... AndrewGlassonbury 69
(Jim Best) *hld up off the pce in rr: sme prog 6th: modest 6th and no imp 3 out: t.o whn blnd last* **14/1**

7 *12* **Cocker**[135] 4-10-7 0.......................... JackQuinlan 45
(Alan Blackmore) *chsd ldr tl after 5th: 4th and struggling next: wknd 3 out: t.o* **33/1**

0-5 **8** *5* **Sir Bentley**[230] 335 6-11-5 0.......................... AdamPogson 52
(Caroline Bailey) *nvr on terms in midfield: lost tch 6th: t.o* **33/1**

0 **9** *hd* **Arryzona**[52] 2409 5-11-5 0.......................... MattieBatchelor 52
(Christine Dunnett) *mstkes: off the pce in rr: hdwy into midfield but no ch after 6th: wkng whn mstke 2 out: t.o* **125/1**

10 *3 ¾* **Ulanda (IRE)**[13] 3168 4-10-3 0 ow3.......................... RobertDunne 32
(Paul John Gilligan, Ire) *hld up in rr: sme hdwy 5th but nt on terms w ldrs: wknd 3 out: blnd next: t.o* **33/1**

11 *2 ¾* **Allegri (IRE)**[25] 7-10-12 0.......................... MrTommieMO'Brien(7) 45
(Alan Coogan) *hld up towards rr: nvr on terms: blnd 2 out: t.o* **100/1**

12 *7* **Beau Knight**[98] 4-10-7 0.......................... MichaelByrne 26
(Alexandra Dunn) *a last and nvr on terms: t.o* **14/1**

P **Oakbank (USA)**[30] 5-11-5 0.......................... MarcGoldstein
(Brett Johnson) *chsd ldrs tl rdn and lost pl qckly after 4th: j. slowly next: bhd and losing tch whn p.u 6th* **66/1**

4m 22.65s (9.65) **Going Correction** +0.70s/f (Soft) **13** Ran SP% **122.2**

WFA 4 from 5yo+ 11lb

Speed ratings (Par 103): **103,94,91,85,77 75,69,67,66,65 63,60,**

CSF £101.45 TOTE £109.80: £19.30, £1.10, £1.20; EX 591.50 Trifecta £810.10 Part won..

Owner W P Flynn **Bred** Rabbah Bloodstock Limited **Trained** Newmarket, Suffolk

FOCUS

The ground was changed to soft after the first and they ended up well strung out in this maiden, the winner springing a surprise, though there was no fluke about it. The winner is entitled to be this good on Flat form. After rail movements the actual race distance was 2m 139yds.

3419 FAKENHAM AMATEUR RIDERS' H'CAP CHASE (16 fncs) 2m 5f 44y

1:50 (1:50) (Class 5) (0-100,100) 5-Y-0+ £4,367 (£1,354; £676; £338)

Form RPR

2 **1** **Bold Bachelor (IRE)**[11] 3199 7-11-12 100.......................... MissGAndrews 120+
(Dr Richard Newland) *led tl 3rd: chsd ldrs: lft 2nd and hmpd 5th: led 10th: clr 13th: rdn bef 2 out: in command between last 2: eased flat* **10/11**[1]

350S **2** *13* **Johns Luck (IRE)**[18] 3081 7-11-7 100..........................(b) MrMartinMcIntyre(5) 105
(Neil Mulholland) *hld up in tch: chsd wnr 11th: rdn bef 2 out: no imp: wl btn and plugged on same pce between last 2* **11/2**[2]

0F3P **3** *31* **Houseparty**[37] 2712 8-9-13 80.......................... MissTWorsley(7) 54
(Diana Grissell) *in tch: chsd ldng pair after 11th: stl cl enough whn mstke and pckd 3 out: sn wknd: t.o* **28/1**

6PPP **4** *3 ¼* **Ravens Brook (IRE)**[19] 3061 10-11-3 98..........................(p) MissKGowing(7) 67
(Neil King) *chsd ldr tl 2nd: wnt 2nd again 4th: lft in ld 5th: hit 10th: blnd and lost pl 11th: lost tch after next: poor 4th 3 out: t.o* **16/1**

6-34 **P** **No Principles**[200] 743 13-11-0 93..........................(b) MrTommieMO'Brien(5)
(Julian Smith) *in tch in midfield: hmpd 5th: mstke 9th: lost pl and rdn next: last and losing tch whn p.u 13th* **7/1**[3]

3025 **U** **Lost In Newyork (IRE)**[29] 2862 9-9-8 75..........................(p) MrTPBroughton(7)
(Nick Kent) *hld up in rr: mstke and pckd 1st: stl last but in tch whn blnd and uns rdr 11th* **9/1**

5-2 **F** **Slidecheck (IRE)**[232] 293 9-10-11 92..........................(tp) MrWGordon(7)
(Alexandra Dunn) *pressed ldr 2nd: led next tl fell 5th* **7/1**[3]

1-UP **R** **Hi Bob**[29] 2866 8-11-4 92.......................... MrJohnDawson
(Lucinda Egerton) *hld in tch: hdwy and lft chsng ldrs 11th: rdn and wknd after next: losing tch and j. slowly 3 out: t.o whn ref and uns rdr last* **16/1**

6m 4.5s (22.70) **Going Correction** +0.875s/f (Soft) **8** Ran SP% **118.0**

Speed ratings: **91,86,74,73, , ,**

CSF £7.29 CT £85.14 TOTE £1.70: £1.10, £2.20, £4.40; EX 8.70 Trifecta £89.20.

Owner The Berrow Hill Partnership **Bred** J McLoughlin & Bachelor Duke Syn **Trained** Claines, Worcs

FOCUS

A weak race overall but the easy winner is one to keep on side. He improved in line with his best Irish hurdle form. After rail movements the actual race distance was 2m 6f 9yds.

3420 DAVE HARRISON MEMORIAL H'CAP HURDLE (11 hdls) 2m 4f 1y

2:25 (2:25) (Class 3) (0-125,125) 4-Y-0+ £6,657 (£2,067; £1,113)

Form RPR

-211 **1** **Actinpieces**[30] 2847 5-11-1 117.......................... MissGAndrews(3) 135+
(Pam Sly) *a gng wl: hld up in tch: hdwy to trck ldrs 3rd: led 7th: gng clr and untidy jump next: in n.d after: eased fr bef last* **5/2**[2]

2115 **2** *28* **Bowdler's Magic**[27] 2901 9-11-5 125.......................... MrZBaker(7) 108
(David Thompson) *chsd ldrs: 3rd 8th and sn rdn: no ch w wnr but wnt 2nd 3 out: plugged on* **12/1**

0/PP **3** *39* **Indian Daudaie (FR)**[20] 3046 9-10-0 109..........................(p) RomainClavreul(10) 53
(Sarah Humphrey) *pressed ldr 2nd tl after 7th: rdn and wl btn after 8th: lost 2nd next and sn t.o* **50/1**

1/06 **P** **Hidden Justice (IRE)**[21] 3027 7-11-9 122.......................... AndrewTinkler
(John Quinn) *in tch: dropped to rr and rdn after 4th: lost tch 6th: t.o whn p.u after 7th* **7/1**

3-42 **P** **Old Pride (IRE)**[39] 2694 8-11-2 120.......................... CiaranGethings(5)
(David Loder) *led tl 7th: 4th and btn next: sn wknd: t.o whn p.u 2 out* **11/2**[3]

-123 **P** **Ballinure (IRE)**[60] 2239 6-10-13 112.......................... JeremiahMcGrath
(Nicky Henderson) *in tch: 5th and rdn after 7th: sn btn: t.o whn p.u 2 out* **7/4**[1]

6P26 **P** **Christmas Twenty (IRE)**[26] 2928 6-11-2 115.......................... TomCannon
(Stuart Edmunds) *chsd ldr tl 2nd: rdn after 5th and sn lost pl: lost tch and p.u after 7th* **14/1**

5m 32.6s (12.20) **Going Correction** +0.70s/f (Soft) **7** Ran SP% **109.1**

Speed ratings (Par 107): **103,91,76, ,**

CSF £27.21 TOTE £3.20: £1.90, £3.90; EX 20.30 Trifecta £693.70 Part won..

Owner Mrs P M Sly **Bred** Mrs P Sly **Trained** Thorney, Cambs

FOCUS

A race which fell apart but that shouldn't detract from the winner who is clearly very useful. This win could be rated higher. After rail movements the actual race distance was 2m 4f 171yds.

3421 INDEPENDENT RACECOURSES LTD. NOVICES' H'CAP CHASE (16 fncs) 2m 5f 44y

3:00 (3:00) (Class 5) (0-100,99) 5-Y-0+ £5,049 (£1,836)

Form RPR

6-21 **1** **Global Domination**[31] 2836 8-11-2 89.......................... AdamPogson 99+
(Caroline Bailey) *hld up in tch: chsd ldrs and lft 2nd 10th: lft in ld but hmpd and hdd 12th: styd upsides rival and gng bttr fr 3 out: led bef last: drvn and styd on flat* **5/2**[1]

630- **2** *½* **Spartilla**[252] 5527 7-10-11 84.......................... MattieBatchelor 91
(Daniel O'Brien) *in tch: lft chsng ldrs 10th: lft in ld 12th: clr w wnr and rdn 3 out: hdd bef last: battled on but hld fnl 100yds* **28/1**

-323 **B** **Halo Moon**[26] 2930 8-11-12 99..........................(p) MarkQuinlan
(Neil Mulholland) *hld up in tch tl b.d 10th* **5/2**[1]

F4-P **P** **High Aspirations (IRE)**[31] 2836 8-10-5 78.......................... TomCannon
(Michael Blake) *hld up in tch: j. slowly 1st and 3rd: chsd ldrs 5th: lft 3rd 12th: rdn and btn 3 out: sn wknd: t.o whn p.u last* **3/1**[2]

-50P **U** **Pennies And Pounds**[31] 2841 9-10-11 84.......................... MarkGrant
(Julian Smith) *in tch towards rr: dropped to last and pushed along after 9th: bdly hmpd next: losing tch and lft 4th 12th: t.o next: j.v.slowly and uns rdr 2 out* **25/1**

3 **F** **Glenwood For Ever (IRE)**[13] 3167 8-11-9 96..........................(bt[1]) RobertDunne
(Paul John Gilligan, Ire) *chsd ldr: j.rt 5th: lft in ld 10th tl fell 12th* **9/1**

63U3 **F** **Little Windmill (IRE)**[6] 3225 6-11-6 93..........................(tp) JackQuinlan
(Neil King) *led: mstke 7th: fell 10th* **5/1**[3]

5m 58.8s (17.00) **Going Correction** +0.875s/f (Soft) **7** Ran SP% **116.1**

Speed ratings: **102,101, , , ,**

CSF £51.75 TOTE £3.10: £2.00, £7.20; EX 78.20 Trifecta £60.20.

Owner G T H Bailey **Bred** Mrs Lucia Farmer **Trained** Holdenby, Northants

FOCUS

A race which was decimated by fallers. The form is rated around the second to huis hurdles mark. After rail movements the actual race distance was 2m 6f 9yds.

3422 HAPPY NEW YEAR H'CAP HURDLE (11 hdls 2 omitted) 2m 7f 95y

3:35 (3:37) (Class 4) (0-110,110) 4-Y-0+ £4,548 (£1,335; £667; £333)

Form RPR

300P **1** **Izbushka (IRE)**[49] 2478 5-10-1 85 oh1 ow1..........................(b) PeterCarberry 90+
(David Thompson) *mde all: hit 5th: rdn after 3 out (actual 2 out): forged clr ent st: styd on strly* **16/1**

3522 **2** *9* **Very Intense (IRE)**[43] 2599 5-10-11 102.......................... MrTommieMO'Brien(7) 99
(Tom Lacey) *t.k.h: trckd ldrs: wnt 2nd 3 out: effrt u.p between last 2: little rspnse and btn ent st: wknd bypassing last* **6/4**[1]

4-24 **3** *18* **Global Dream**[24] 2964 6-10-11 95..........................(p) AdamPogson 76
(Caroline Bailey) *chsd ldrs: effrt after 3 out (actual 2 out): btn whn blnd next (last): wknd* **9/4**[2]

2055 **4** *14* **Larteta (FR)**[37] 2711 7-10-11 95.......................... JackQuinlan 59
(Sarah Humphrey) *hld up in last pair: rdn and btn bef 3 out (actual 2 out): wnt poor 4th nr fin: t.o* **12/1**

3032 **5** *¾* **Weybridge Light**[20] 2135 11-11-2 107..........................(b) PaddyBradley(7) 70
(David Thompson) *mostly chsd wnr tl 3 out (actual 2 out): wknd bef next (last): t.o* **8/1**

43-6 **6** *26* **Top Man Marty (IRE)**[20] 3045 7-11-2 **110**................ RomainClavreul(10) 47
(Sarah Humphrey) *hld up in last pair: rdn 10th (actual 3 out): sn lost tch: t.o* **9/2**[3]

6m 35.73s (13.73) **Going Correction** +0.70s/f (Soft) **6** Ran SP% **113.6**
Speed ratings (Par 105): **104,100,94,89,89 80**
CSF £42.70 TOTE £15.40: £5.80, £1.10; EX 49.90 Trifecta £237.20.
Owner J A Moore **Bred** Mrs J Norris **Trained** Bolam, Co Durham

FOCUS
A modest contest. The form could be 5lb out either way. After rail movements the actual race distance was 3m 88yds.
T/Plt: £17.60 to a £1 stake. Pool: £37,150.63 - 1,535.1 winning tickets T/Qpdt: £24.90 to a £1 stake. Pool: £3,048.66 - 90.57 winning tickets **Steve Payne**

2945 MUSSELBURGH (R-H)
Friday, January 1

OFFICIAL GOING: Good to soft (soft in places; 6.0)
Wind: Almost nil Weather: Overcast, dry

3423 TOTEPLACEPOT FIRST FOOT JUVENILE HURDLE (9 hdls) 1m 7f 124y
12:25 (12:25) (Class 2) 4-Y-O **£12,996** (£3,816; £1,908; £954)

Form RPR
13 **1** **Sir Chauvelin**[20] 3039 4-11-3 0.................................. JamesReveley 120+
(Jim Goldie) *trckd ldrs: stdy hdwy to chse ldr after 4 out: shkn up bef next: led 2 out: pushed clr fr last: readily* **10/11**[1]
5 **2** *12* **Magic Dancer**[22] 2992 4-10-12 0..........................(tp) GrahamWatters 106
(Charlie Longsdon) *t.k.h: pressed ldr: nt fluent 3rd: led and j.lft fr 5th: j. bdly lft and rdn 3 out: hdd whn nt fluent next: outpcd whn hit last* **7/2**[2]
613 **3** *3* **Sikandar (IRE)**[29] 2863 4-11-3 120.................................... WillKennedy 106
(Brian Ellison) *nt fluent: in tch: rdn and outpcd 3 out: no imp fr next* **7/2**[2]
514 **4** *25* **Boldbob (IRE)**[29] 2863 4-11-3 110.............................. FinianO'Toole 87
(Micky Hammond) *led to 5th: rdn and wkng whn hit 3 out: sn btn* **16/1**
5 *22* **Pointillism**[396] 4-10-12 0.. BrianHarding 57
(J J Lambe, Ire) *hld up: struggling bef 5th: lost tch after next: t.o* **12/1**[3]

3m 46.6s (-1.80) **Going Correction** -0.15s/f (Good) **5** Ran SP% **110.4**
Speed ratings: **98,92,90,78,67**
CSF £4.56 TOTE £1.60: £1.10, £2.00; EX 4.90 Trifecta £8.70.
Owner J Fyffe **Bred** W M Johnstone **Trained** Uplawmoor, E Renfrews

FOCUS
Hurdle distances as advertised. After a dry night the going remained good to soft with soft places. A fair juvenile hurdle run at a good pace thanks to Magic Dancer and Boldbob duelling for the early lead. The winner stepped up on his previous C&D win.

3424 TOTEPOOL HAPPY NEW YEAR H'CAP HURDLE (12 hdls) 2m 3f 81y
1:00 (1:00) (Class 4) (0-120,120) 4-Y-O+ **£6,498** (£1,908; £954; £477)

Form RPR
6524 **1** **Away For Slates (IRE)**[6] 3242 6-11-0 **115**........................ RyanDay(7) 125+
(Keith Dalgleish) *hld up in midfield: hdwy bef 3 out: led bef last: edgd rt run-in: kpt on strly* **3/1**[1]
5-50 **2** *3 ¼* **Teo Vivo (FR)**[62] 2194 9-11-9 **120**...........................(b) GrahamWatters(3) 127
(Pauline Robson) *hld up on outside: stdy hdwy 1/2-way: led 3 out to after next: kpt on same pce fr last* **14/1**
-455 **3** *3 ½* **So Satisfied**[183] 881 5-10-6 **105** ow2.......................... StevenFox(7) 111
(Sandy Thomson) *led to bef 4th: prom: outpcd 4 out: rallied bef 2 out: plugged on fr last: nt rch first two* **12/1**
0 **4** *¾* **Bright Prospect (IRE)**[25] 2949 7-11-6 **117**...................... TonyKelly(3) 120
(Jackie Stephen) *hld up: hdwy and prom after 4 out: rdn and hung rt next: kpt on same pce fr 2 out* **20/1**
3F0P **5** *8* **Tekthelot (IRE)**[33] 2802 10-11-4 **112**............................. JamesReveley 109
(Keith Reveley) *hld up: hdwy to ld 5th: hdd whn nt fluent 3 out: sn outpcd* **10/1**
4242 **6** *6* **Claude Carter**[30] 2843 12-10-13 **110**........................(p) CallumWhillans(3) 101
(Alistair Whillans) *chsd ldrs: wnt 2nd 7th to after 4 out: rdn and wknd fr next* **9/1**
32/0 **7** *1* **Jonny Delta**[25] 2949 9-10-12 **111**.......................... StephenMulqueen(5) 101
(Jim Goldie) *hld up: stdy hdwy after 4 out: shkn up and wknd after next* **25/1**
P25- **8** *nk* **Never Never (IRE)**[360] 3561 6-11-4 **119**......................... FinianO'Toole(7) 108
(Iain Jardine) *hld up: stdy hdwy after 4 out: rdn and wknd fr next* **16/1**
F120 **9** *18* **Where's Tiger**[20] 3035 5-11-4 **117**.......................(t) GrantCockburn(5) 98
(Lucinda Russell) *t.k.h: trckd ldrs: rdn whn hit 3 out: sn wknd* **16/1**
1-10 **10** *15* **Gingili**[25] 2949 6-11-11 **119**.. BrianHarding 79
(Rose Dobbin) *hld up: drvn and outpcd after 4 out: struggling fr next* **7/2**[2]
-465 **R** **Gold Chain (IRE)**[19] 3065 6-10-2 **99**........................ ColmMcCormack(3)
(Dianne Sayer) *bhd and nvr gng wl: losing tch whn ref 7th* **11/1**
/2-4 **P** **Kings Folly (IRE)**[35] 2754 8-11-2 **110**.........................(t) PeterBuchanan
(Lucinda Russell) *cl up: led bef 4th to next: lost pl 7th: struggling fr next: t.o whn p.u bef 2 out* **8/1**[3]

4m 43.3s (-8.20) **Going Correction** -0.15s/f (Good) **12** Ran SP% **120.5**
Speed ratings (Par 105): **111,109,108,107,104 101,101,101,93,87 , ,**
CSF £45.79 CT £454.86 TOTE £3.70: £1.50, £4.00, £3.40; EX 49.70 Trifecta £397.20.
Owner Equus Syndicate **Bred** Mrs Kay Curtis **Trained** Carluke, S Lanarks

FOCUS
Rail movements added 35yds to the overall distance, taking it to 2m4f 8yds. Plenty vying for the lead but the pace was not that strong, so there were still a handful with chances turning for home, before the first two pulled clear. A step up from the winner under a claimer.

3425 TOTEQUADPOT SCOTTISH PREMIER CHASE (H'CAP) (14 fncs 2 omitted) 2m 3f 193y
1:35 (1:35) (Class 3) (0-140,140) 5-Y-O+**£19,494** (£5,724; £2,862; £1,431)

Form RPR
22 **1** **Indian Temple (IRE)**[25] 2947 7-9-13 **120**....................... MrWHRReed(7) 132+
(W T Reed) *in tch: hdwy to ld 4th: mde rest: rdn and clr whn nt fluent last: kpt on strly* **17/2**
56P1 **2** *7* **Royal Macnab (IRE)**[25] 2947 8-10-5 **122**......................(t) TonyKelly(3) 126
(Rebecca Menzies) *led to 4th: w wnr: rdn and led briefly after 4 out: outpcd after next: rallied to chse (clr) wnr run-in: no imp* **12/1**
4424 **3** *1 ½* **Quito Du Tresor (FR)**[25] 2947 12-10-1 **115**..................(p) PeterBuchanan 118
(Lucinda Russell) *hld up: stdy hdwy after 4 out: chsd wnr after 2 out to run-in: kpt on same pce* **10/1**
152/ **4** *½* **Humbie (IRE)**[791] 2199 12-10-6 **120**.............................. JamesReveley 125+
(Pauline Robson) *a cl up: effrt and chsng wnr whn blnd 2 out: sn outpcd* **8/1**
0110 **5** *11* **Doctor Phoenix (IRE)**[20] 3031 8-11-12 **140**............................(t) BrianHarding 134
(David Dennis) *hld up: pushed along after 4 out: drvn and outpcd bef next* **6/1**[2]
-013 **6** *3 ¼* **Distime (IRE)**[27] 2902 10-11-1 **129**............................... JonathanEngland 119
(Richard Drake) *prom: lost pl 9th: struggling fr 4 out* **15/2**
-600 **7** *6* **Rathlin**[27] 2902 11-11-5 **140**...(t) FinianO'Toole(7) 124
(Micky Hammond) *hld up: drvn after 4 out: wknd bef next* **9/1**
133- **F** **Rowdy Rocher (IRE)**[252] 5517 10-10-6 **120**..............................(p) DerekFox
(Lucinda Russell) *hld up bhd ldng gp: fell 1st* **12/1**
5-33 **U** **Saints And Sinners (IRE)**[20] 3036 8-11-4 **132**...........................(t) WillKennedy
(Michael Easterby) *hld up: hmpd 4th: blnd and uns rdr 8th* **5/1**[1]
246P **F** **Alderbrook Lad (IRE)**[26] 2935 10-11-7 **140**.................. MissCWalton(5)
(Micky Hammond) *trckd ldrs: lost pl whn nt fluent 10th: struggling whn fell next* **22/1**
26- **F** **Colms Dream (IRE)**[62] 2208 7-11-3 **136**............................(t) MrJCBarry(5)
(Karl Thornton, Ire) *t.k.h: prom whn fell 4th* **7/1**[3]

5m 6.4s (5.20) **Going Correction** +0.525s/f (Soft) **11** Ran SP% **115.7**
Speed ratings: **110,107,106,106,102 100,98, , ,**
CSF £101.87 CT £1035.63 TOTE £9.10: £2.70, £4.20, £3.70; EX 102.70 Trifecta £1387.00.
Owner Ken Huddleston **Bred** Liam Flannery **Trained** Haydon Bridge, Northumberland

FOCUS
Race distance increased by 35yds. Last fence omitted in all chases, leaving a run-in of around 1.5 furlongs. An open-looking contest for this valuable handicap, with the fences proving too tricky for a third of the field. A step up from the winner compared with the second on recent C&D form.

3426 TOTEPOOLLIVEINFO.COM HOGMANEIGH HURDLE (H'CAP) (9 hdls) 1m 7f 124y
2:10 (2:10) (Class 2) 4-Y-O+ **£25,992** (£7,632; £3,816; £1,908)

Form RPR
-F11 **1** **Aristo Du Plessis (FR)**[56] 2328 6-11-7 **145**........... DiarmuidO'Regan(5) 148+
(James Ewart) *mde all: clr tl given breather bef 3 out: rdn next: kpt on strly fr last* **5/2**[1]
640- **2** *2 ¼* **Pearl Castle (IRE)**[13] 5390 6-10-11 **137**...................... FinianO'Toole(7) 138
(K R Burke) *chsd ldrs: hdwy to press wnr 2 out: effrt and rdn whn hit last: kpt on: nt pce to chal* **4/1**[2]
0-F2 **3** *1 ½* **Zaidiyn (FR)**[41] 2637 6-11-1 **134**.................................... WillKennedy 134
(Brian Ellison) *hld up: stdy hdwy bef 3 out: effrt after next: 3rd and keeping on whn blnd last: r.o* **9/2**[3]
-045 **4** *2* **Silver Duke (IRE)**[20] 3041 5-10-0 **119** oh2......................... LucyAlexander 117
(Jim Goldie) *hld up: stdy hdwy whn hit 2 out: sn rdn: no imp fr last* **25/1**
-33B **5** *1 ¾* **Strongpoint (IRE)**[20] 3036 12-11-7 **140**............................ PeterBuchanan 136
(S R B Crawford, Ire) *chsd wnr tl outpcd 2 out: n.d after* **15/2**
23-0 **6** *1 ¼* **Upsilon Bleu (FR)**[35] 2761 8-11-5 **138**............................ JamesReveley 132
(Pauline Robson) *prom: rdn 3 out: wknd fr next* **6/1**
160- **7** *nk* **Frederic**[288] 4867 5-10-0 **119** oh1...................................... BrianHarding 113
(Micky Hammond) *hld up: rdn and outpcd 3 out: btn next* **10/1**
5120 **8** *nse* **Captain Brown**[61] 2214 8-10-1 **123**.................................. TonyKelly(3) 117
(James Moffatt) *hld up: rdn bef 3 out: shortlived effrt next: sn btn* **9/1**

3m 41.6s (-6.80) **Going Correction** -0.15s/f (Good) **8** Ran SP% **115.7**
Speed ratings (Par 109): **111,109,109,108,107 106,106,106**
CSF £13.50 CT £42.06 TOTE £2.50: £1.60, £2.00, £1.80; EX 12.90 Trifecta £28.70.
Owner Mrs J M Dodd **Bred** J Andriau, O Regley Et Al **Trained** Langholm, Dumfries & G'way

FOCUS
A bold front-running performance from an improving 6yo left a frantic field behind as he took the feature race. Good handicap form.

3427 SCOOP6SOCCER THE £1 MILLION FOOTBALL BET NOVICES' H'CAP CHASE (15 fncs 3 omitted) 2m 7f 170y
2:45 (2:45) (Class 4) (0-105,102) 5-Y-O+ **£5,198** (£1,526; £763; £381)

Form RPR
3-5U **1** **Wakhan (IRE)**[30] 2844 8-10-9 **85**.. DerekFox 96
(Sandy Thomson) *chsd ldrs: lost pl briefly bef 9th: effrt and ev ch 3 out: led run-in: styd on wl* **11/4**[1]
5P65 **2** *3 ¾* **Top Cat Dj (IRE)**[34] 2771 8-9-9 **76** oh8.................(v) DiarmuidO'Regan(5) 84
(Chris Grant) *led: rdn and hrd pressed fr 3 out: hdd run-in: kpt on same pce* **20/1**
0-26 **3** *5* **Vision De La Vie (FR)**[209] 637 6-11-4 **94**.........................(b[1]) JamesReveley 97
(Pauline Robson) *cl up: pushed along and outpcd appr 3 out: rallied run-in: nt rch first two* **7/2**[2]
104- **4** *1* **Spring Over (IRE)**[318] 4285 10-10-11 **90**...................(t) GrahamWatters(3) 92
(Ian Duncan) *hld up: hmpd 2nd: hdwy and prom 1/2-way: drvn and outpcd bef 3 out: kpt on fr last: no imp* **10/1**
46-4 **5** *4 ½* **Treliver Manor (IRE)**[26] 2937 8-10-13 **89**.........................(t) BrianHarding 87
(Rose Dobbin) *hld up: drvn and outpcd fr 10th: no imp fr 3 out* **13/2**
60-0 **6** *9* **Pay The King (IRE)**[35] 2749 9-11-5 **102**.......................... FinianO'Toole(7) 92
(Micky Hammond) *hld up: nt fluent 10th: drvn and outpcd next: btn fnl 3* **9/2**[3]
4P00 **7** *53* **Wyfield Rose**[35] 2751 7-9-11 **76** oh1.......................(p) CallumWhillans(3) 18
(Alistair Whillans) *hld up: outpcd 10th: struggling fr 4 out: t.o* **12/1**
30-4 **P** **Higgs Boson**[22] 2983 11-10-1 **84**.. RyanDay(7)
(Jim Goldie) *nt fluent: hld up: hmpd 2nd: struggling 8th: wknd and p.u bef next* **12/1**
50-0 **F** **Proud Gamble (IRE)**[240] 139 7-10-5 **84**...........................(t) TonyKelly(3)
(Rose Dobbin) *t.k.h: prom: fell 2nd* **12/1**

6m 21.8s (18.40) **Going Correction** +0.525s/f (Soft) **9** Ran SP% **117.3**
Speed ratings: **90,88,87,86,85 82,64, ,**
CSF £51.58 CT £200.36 TOTE £3.50: £1.40, £4.90, £1.40; EX 60.80 Trifecta £208.50.
Owner Jim Beaumont & Douglas Pryde **Bred** Anthony Rafferty **Trained** Lambden, Berwicks

FOCUS
Rail movements added 35yds to the overall distance, taking it to 2m7f 205yds. An ordinary novice handicap with the first two battling it out in the home straight. A small pb from the winner.

3428 WIN A FOOTBALL FORTUNE WITH SCOOP6SOCCER H'CAP HURDLE (QUAL. FOR THE CHALLENGER STAYING HURDLE) (15 hdls) 3m 2f 26y
3:20 (3:20) (Class 3) (0-130,130) 4-Y-O+ **£7,797** (£2,289; £1,144; £572)

Form RPR
1-33 **1** **Donna's Diamond (IRE)**[19] 3058 7-11-7 **130**.......... DiarmuidO'Regan(5) 133+
(Chris Grant) *cl up: led 9th: mde rest: pushed along whn hit 2 out: edgd rt run-in: kpt on gamely* **6/1**[2]
-351 **2** *¾* **Harry Hunt**[35] 2744 9-11-1 **119**.. KielanWoods 120
(Graeme McPherson) *in tch: stdy hdwy after 4 out: wnt 2nd bef 2 out: effrt between last 2: edgd rt run-in: kpt on* **7/1**[3]

0600 **3** 4 1/2 **Night In Milan (IRE)**[20] 3038 10-11-0 **118**....................(b) JamesReveley 115
(Keith Reveley) *trckd ldrs: effrt and rdn after 3 out: kpt on same pce between last 2* **10/1**

4-60 **4** 1/2 **Landecker (IRE)**[25] 2949 8-11-1 **119**............................(v) LucyAlexander 116
(N W Alexander) *hld up in midfield: effrt bef 3 out: kpt on fr next: nt pce to chal* **25/1**

1PU/ **5** 3/4 **Kris Cross (IRE)**[625] 5348 9-10-13 **122**.....................(t) GrantCockburn(5) 118
(Lucinda Russell) *hld up: stdy hdwy after 4 out: rdn next: kpt on fr last: nvr able to chal* **25/1**

PP56 **6** 4 1/2 **Arctic Court (IRE)**[25] 2948 12-9-11 **108**........................ RyanDay(7) 100
(Jim Goldie) *hld up: stdy hdwy after 4 out: rdn next: outpcd fnl 2* **16/1**

1P-3 **7** 5 **Sir Vinski (IRE)**[34] 2767 7-11-4 **122**................................. BrianHarding 110
(Nicky Richards) *hld up in midfield: drvn after 4 out: no imp bef 2 out* **3/1**[1]

-546 **8** 3 **Rival D'Estruval (FR)**[20] 3036 11-10-13 **120**............ GrahamWatters(3) 105
(Pauline Robson) *prom tl rdn and wknd bef 3 out* **22/1**

4-2P **9** hd **Always Tipsy**[21] 3018 7-10-13 **122**........................ StephenMulqueen(5) 106
(N W Alexander) *hld up: hdwy after 4 out: rdn and wknd fr next* **18/1**

30-0 **10** 3/4 **Glenquest (IRE)**[19] 3071 13-11-5 **130**......................... AnthonyFox(7) 115
(S R B Crawford, Ire) *midfield: drvn and outpcd after 4 out: wknd fr next* **28/1**

-222 **11** 2 1/2 **Snapping Turtle (IRE)**[48] 2496 11-10-10 **117**............ CallumWhillans(3) 98
(Donald Whillans) *cl up: led 6th to 9th: ev ch tl wknd fr 2 out* **10/1**

2540 **12** 2 **Solway Prince**[51] 2429 7-9-10 **105**...................... CallumBewley(5) 85
(Lisa Harrison) *hld up: drvn along fr 11th: sn struggling* **16/1**

35-1 **13** 1 **Five In A Row (IRE)**[83] 1856 8-11-11 **129**..................... WillKennedy 108
(Brian Ellison) *hld up: drvn and struggling after 4 out: nvr on terms* **15/2**

F-50 **14** nse **Hada Men (USA)**[33] 2802 11-10-6 **117**..................(p) FinianO'Toole(7) 96
(Rebecca Menzies) *hld up: pushed along and struggling 11th: btn bef 3 out* **40/1**

1511 **15** 71 **Maraweh (IRE)**[25] 2948 6-11-0 **118**..............................(v) DerekFox 33
(Lucinda Russell) *midfield: lost pl bef 1/2-way: lost tch fnl circ: t.o* **8/1**

6m 30.4s (15.30) **15** Ran **SP% 127.8**
CSF £47.78 CT £431.61 TOTE £7.30: £3.10, £2.40, £3.90; EX 51.00 Trifecta £352.70.
Owner D&D Armstrong Ltd **Bred** C Kenneally **Trained** Newton Bewley, Co Durham

FOCUS
Another finely judged ride from Diarmuid O'Regan to give the jockey a pacesetting double on the day. The first two were pretty much to their marks in this fair handicap.
T/Jkpt: Not won. JACKPOT PLACEPOT £1,129.90 to a £1 stake. Pool: £3,482.75 - 2.25 winning tickets T/Plt: £72.40 to a £1 stake. Pool: £48,528.59 - 489.03 winning tickets T/Qpdt: £22.60 to a £1 stake. Pool: £5,076.52 - 165.8 winning tickets **Richard Young**

3429 - 3435a (Foreign Racing) - See Raceform Interactive

2428
AYR (L-H)
Saturday, January 2

OFFICIAL GOING: Heavy (soft in places on chase course; chs 6.5, hdl 5.7)
Wind: Fresh, half behind Weather: Overcast

3436 32RED CASINO MAIDEN HURDLE (12 hdls) 2m 4f 100y
12:20 (12:20) (Class 5) 4-Y-O+ £2,599 (£763; £381; £190)

Form RPR

1 **Bigirononhiship (IRE)**[238] 5-11-2 0.............................. CraigNichol 122+
(Rose Dobbin) *hld up bhd ldng gp: hdwy bef 3 out: styng on whn lft 2 l 2nd last: led run-in: drvn and styd on wl* **18/1**

2 1 1/4 **The Dutchman (IRE)**[314] 6-11-2 0.............................. DannyCook 121
(Sandy Thomson) *cl up: chal fnl circ: 1 l down and keeping on whn lft 2 l in front last: hdd run-in: kpt on same pce* **3/1**[2]

30- **3** 20 **Mount Beckham (IRE)**[35] 2795 7-11-2 0.............................(t) AELynch 104
(Miss Clare Louise Cannon, Ire) *t.k.h: prom: effrt and rdn 3 out: outpcd next: lft 10 l 3rd last: wknd* **3/1**[2]

6 **4** 24 **Moorstown (IRE)**[43] 2628 6-11-2 0.............................. DerekFox 77
(Lucinda Russell) *led to 2nd: cl up: drvn and outpcd after 4 out: no ch whn lft poor 4th last* **12/1**

5 16 **Red Piano**[987] 7-10-9 0.............................. MrWHRReed(7) 61
(Andrew Hamilton) *hld up bhd ldng gp: drvn and outpcd bef 4 out: btn next: t.o* **80/1**

5036 **6** 5 **Court Baloo (IRE)**[27] 2931 5-11-2 0.............................. HenryBrooke 56
(Alistair Whillans) *hld up: outpcd 8th: struggling fr 4 out: t.o* **125/1**

0 **F** **Craiganboy (IRE)**[20] 3068 7-10-9 0.............................. AnthonyFox(7) 92
(S R B Crawford, Ire) *t.k.h: hld up in tch: nt fluent 8th: drvn and outpcd bef 4: rallied next: sn pushed along and no imp lft 18 l 4th whn fell and down for sme time at last* **100/1**

01-2 **P** **Huehuecoytle**[29] 2890 6-11-2 0.............................. BrianHarding
(Keith Dalgleish) *nt fluent: hld up in midfield: effrt 4 out: wkng bef next: p.u after 2 out* **14/5**[1]

1F **F** **Lake View Lad (IRE)**[34] 2804 6-10-11 0.................. StephenMulqueen(5) 122+
(N W Alexander) *cl up: led 2nd: 1 l in front and gng wl whn fell last* **7/2**[3]

50 **P** **September Son (IRE)**[34] 2801 6-10-13 0.................. GrahamWatters(3)
(Ian Duncan) *hld up: nt fluent 6th: struggling fnl circ: t.o whn p.u bef 3 out* **200/1**

5m 28.2s (328.20) **10** Ran **SP% 115.0**
CSF £72.96 TOTE £16.10: £3.40, £1.20, £1.30; EX 50.20 Trifecta £597.50.
Owner Mr & Mrs Duncan Davidson **Bred** Mrs Philomena Crampton **Trained** South Hazelrigg, Northumbria

FOCUS
The course had taken 44mm of rain since Boxing Day but none in the 24 hours preceding raceday, and action took place in warm and mostly dry conditions. Hurdles were sited 6yds further out than usual, adding 36yds per circuit. A modest opener run at a steady early pace, with a dramatic conclusion. The first two and the final-flight faller are all fair nothern novices. The fourth has been rated close to his mark.

3437 32REDSPORT.COM H'CAP HURDLE (12 hdls) 3m 70y
12:55 (12:55) (Class 4) (0-115,115) 4-Y-O+ £3,898 (£1,144; £572; £286)

Form RPR

P-03 **1** **Lochnell (IRE)**[14] 3163 7-10-0 **89**.............................. LucyAlexander 96+
(Ian Duncan) *hld up: stdy hdwy bef 4 out: chsd ldr and gng wl bef next: shkn up to ld last: edgd rt: kpt on strly* **12/1**

2014 **2** 3 **Maggie Blue (IRE)**[22] 3025 8-10-10 **104**.................. CallumBewley(5) 107
(Harriet Graham) *led: rdn along 2 out: hdd last: rallied: kpt on same pce last 100yds* **4/1**[3]

-22P **3** 13 **Camillas Wish (IRE)**[39] 2708 7-10-0 **89**.............................. AELynch 79
(J T R Dreaper, Ire) *chsd ldr to bef 3 out: sn rdn and outpcd: no imp fr next* **13/2**

56 **4** 1 1/4 **Nakadam (FR)**[34] 2806 6-10-11 **100**..............................(t) BrianHarding 89
(R Mike Smith) *chsd ldrs: effrt and rdn bef 3 out: outpcd bef next: sn btn* **3/1**[2]

-532 **F** **Tantamount**[52] 2429 7-11-12 **115**..............................(t) DerekFox
(Lucinda Russell) *nt fluent: hld up: hung rt fnl circ: struggling 4 out: lost tch next: nrly 50 l 5th whn fell and down for sme time at last* **11/8**[1]

6m 42.4s (10.60) **Going Correction** +0.575s/f (Soft) **5** Ran **SP% 108.1**
Speed ratings (Par 105): **105,104,99,99,**
CSF £53.67 TOTE £16.50: £4.10, £1.80; EX 70.40 Trifecta £148.10.
Owner Alan & Barry MacDonald **Bred** J F C Maxwell **Trained** Coylton, Ayrshire

FOCUS
This looked weak for the grade, and they didn't appear to go that searching a pace. Actual race distance 72yds longer than usual. The second sets the level.

3438 32RED.COM H'CAP HURDLE (9 hdls) 2m
1:30 (1:31) (Class 4) (0-105,105) 4-Y-O+ £3,898 (£1,144; £572; £286)

Form RPR

0-11 **1** **Clan Legend**[23] 2982 6-11-12 **105**.............................. LucyAlexander 117+
(N W Alexander) *led to 2nd: pressed ldr: nt fluent 4 out: regained ld 2 out: edgd rt and styd on wl u.p fr last* **3/1**[2]

030- **2** 1 1/4 **Molly Milan**[548] 847 8-10-4 **83**.............................. BrianHughes 94
(Jim Goldie) *hld up in tch: stdy hdwy bef 3 out: edgd lft and outpcd appr next: rallied to chse wnr run-in: kpt on: hld nr fin* **12/1**

03-2 **3** 8 **Diamond D'Amour (IRE)**[38] 2720 10-11-6 **104**......... JonathonBewley(5) 106
(George Bewley) *cl up: led 2nd: rdn and hdd 2 out: rallied: outpcd fr last* **7/2**[3]

5-53 **4** 3 1/4 **Orchard Road (USA)**[5] 3307 9-11-2 **100**..................(t) CallumBewley(5) 100
(Tristan Davidson) *hld up in tch: stdy hdwy to chse ldrs 1/2-way: rdn 3 out: wknd after last* **9/2**

0440 **5** 8 **Seventeen Black (IRE)**[23] 2982 8-9-7 **79**.................. SamColtherd(7) 71
(Stuart Coltherd) *hld up: stdy hdwy and prom 1/2-way: rdn and wknd after 3 out* **16/1**

0053 **6** 33 **Buckled**[22] 3023 6-11-4 **104**.............................. StevenFox(7) 71
(Sandy Thomson) *prom: drvn and outpcd 4 out: wknd next: btn whn hmpd 2 out* **11/4**[1]

0F-0 **F** **Why But Why (USA)**[36] 2755 8-11-7 **103**..................(p) GrahamWatters(3)
(Ian Duncan) *hld up: pushed along bef 3 out: 13 l down and no imp whn fell next* **33/1**

2-PP **P** **Silverton**[54] 2400 9-11-12 **105**.............................. AdrianLane
(Lucy Normile) *trckd ldrs: outpcd whn nt fluent 5th: struggling fr next: lost tch and p.u bef 2 out* **16/1**

4m 10.7s (250.70) **8** Ran **SP% 114.5**
CSF £36.92 CT £130.61 TOTE £4.00: £1.50, £2.20, £1.60; EX 19.70 Trifecta £103.50.
Owner Clan Gathering **Bred** Alexander Family **Trained** Kinneston, Perth & Kinross

FOCUS
Competitive for the grade, although in practice few got involved. Actual race distance 36yds longer than usual. Another step up from the progressive winner, with the second rated to the level of her previous course best.

3439 32RED £10 FREE H'CAP CHASE (15 fncs 4 omitted) 3m 67y
2:05 (2:05) (Class 3) (0-140,139) 5-Y-O+ £9,747 (£2,862; £1,431; £715)

Form RPR

2232 **1** **Presented (IRE)**[27] 2934 9-9-12 **116**.............................. CallumBewley(5) 123+
(Lisa Harrison) *cl up: led 10th: rdr dropped whip bef 2 out: jst hdd whn lft 2 l in front last: hld on wl* **9/2**[3]

F-20 **2** 1/2 **Cultram Abbey**[35] 2785 9-10-13 **126**.............................. BrianHarding 130
(Nicky Richards) *trckd ldrs: nt fluent 6th: effrt whn mstke 3 out: sn outpcd: j.lft next: rallied and lft 3 l 2nd last: kpt on run-in* **4/1**[2]

2330 **3** 8 **Presenting Junior (IRE)**[35] 2787 9-11-10 **137**.................. HenryBrooke 132
(Martin Todhunter) *hld up: nt fluent 5 out: outpcd after next: plugged on fr last: nt rch first two* **10/1**

P-6P **4** 1 1/4 **Man With Van (IRE)**[35] 2790 10-11-6 **133**..............................(tp) AELynch 128
(S R B Crawford, Ire) *trckd ldrs: mstke 5 out: rdn and outpcd 3 out: no imp fr next* **13/2**

31-1 **5** 7 **Capard King (IRE)**[46] 2557 7-11-12 **139**.................. RichieMcLernon 130
(Jonjo O'Neill) *led: faltered and nrly uns rdr bnd after 8th: hdd 10th: nt fluent 4 out: rdn rallied and ev ch next: edgd rt and wknd bef last* **15/8**[1]

-U03 **U** **Silver Tassie (IRE)**[27] 2935 8-10-10 **130**.................. FinianO'Toole(7) 136+
(Micky Hammond) *hld up in tch: stdy hdwy 3 out: slt ld whn blnd and uns rdr last* **11/2**

6m 54.5s (4.60) **Going Correction** -0.075s/f (Good) **6** Ran **SP% 110.8**
Speed ratings: **89,88,86,85,83**
CSF £21.98 TOTE £5.30: £2.40, £2.20; EX 18.80 Trifecta £124.80.
Owner Abbadis Racing Club & Partner **Bred** Miss Catherine M Walsh **Trained** Aldoth, Cumbria

FOCUS
The chase course was railed out 2yds further than usual, extending race distances by 12yds per circuit. Fences 6 and 9 were omitted and not even in situ. A fair handicap chase run at a steady tempo, and as in the opening event plenty of late drama. Actual race distance 24yds longer than usual. The first two have been rated pretty much to their marks.

3440 32RED CASINO H'CAP HURDLE (12 hdls) 2m 5f 91y
2:40 (2:40) (Class 2) (0-150,140) 4-Y-O+ £12,996 (£3,816; £1,908; £954)

Form RPR

0-PP **1** **Yes Tom (IRE)**[209] 660 11-10-7 **121**..............................(p) AELynch 129+
(S R B Crawford, Ire) *nt fluent on occasions: hld up: smooth hdwy to ld after 4 out: pushed along and clr 2 out: kpt on wl* **9/1**

5/2F **2** 9 **Caledonia**[52] 2428 9-10-3 **117**.............................. BrianHughes 117
(Jim Goldie) *cl up: led 7th to after 4 out: chsd wnr to next: sn rdn: 6 l down and styng on same pce whn lft 2nd last: no imp* **11/8**[1]

U1-4 **3** 22 **Sa Suffit (FR)**[28] 2921 13-11-8 **136**..................(p) LucyAlexander 113
(James Ewart) *nt fluent on occasions: chsd ldrs: rdn and outpcd after 4 out: j.lft 2 out: plugged on to take modest 3rd run-in: no ch w first two* **7/1**[3]

04-0 **4** 4 1/2 **Desert Cry (IRE)**[21] 3030 10-11-10 **138**.............................. HenryBrooke 113
(Donald McCain) *hld up: stdy hdwy to chse ldrs 4 out: outpcd whn hit next: nt fluent 2 out: btn whn lft modest 3rd last* **10/1**

-UPP **5** 16 **U Name It (IRE)**[35] 2785 8-11-1 **129**.............................. BrianHarding 87
(R Mike Smith) *hld up on outside: stdy hdwy 1/2-way: rdn and outpcd after 4 out: wknd bef next* **12/1**

0-01 **6** 9 **Tap Night (USA)**[26] 2949 9-11-2 **130**..................(p) RichieMcLernon 80
(Lucinda Russell) *pressed ldr: nt fluent 7th: drvn and outpcd after 4 out: wknd bef next* **4/1**[2]

21P- **7** 5 **Scotswell**[315] 4366 10-10-5 **126**.............................. ThomasDowson(7) 69
(Harriet Graham) *led to 7th: cl up tl outpcd 4 out: sn btn* **25/1**

P-P6 **F** **Bobs Lady Tamure**[28] 2921 9-10-4 **123**......................(t) DaraghBourke(5) 123+
(Maurice Barnes) *hld up in tch: stdy hdwy 1/2-way: chsd wnr bef 3 out: rdn next: 5 l down and one pce whn fell heavily last* **14/1**

5m 45.0s (345.00) **8 Ran SP% 111.9**
CSF £21.64 CT £92.19 TOTE £8.00: £2.10, £1.10, £1.70; EX 21.10 Trifecta £92.80.
Owner T J Topping **Bred** B A Hamilton **Trained** Larne, Co Antrim

FOCUS
A decent handicap hurdle, albeit one with nothing rated within 11lb of the ceiling in the top-weight's absence. Something of a sprint ensued up the straight, for all that they hadn't dawdled up to that point. Actual race distance 72yds longer than usual. The winner is a better chaser but this rates a hurdle pb, with the second rated similar to his recent course fall.

3441 32RED ON THE APP STORE H'CAP CHASE (10 fncs 2 omitted) 1m 7f 112y
3:15 (3:15) (Class 4) (0-110,110) 5-Y-0+ **£4,223** (£1,240; £620; £310)

Form RPR

2P22 **1** **Willie Hall**[7] 3237 12-9-11 **86**.................................. CallumBewley(5) 95
(Lisa Harrison) *hld up in rr: stdy hdwy 1/2-way: effrt after 2 out: led last 50yds: pushed out* **11/2**

-136 **2** ½ **Quick Decisson (IRE)**[42] 2637 8-11-7 **110**.................. GrantCockburn(5) 118
(Stuart Coltherd) *pressed ldr and clr of rest to 4th: hdd bef last: rallied and regained ld briefly last 75yds: hld cl home* **4/1**[2]

2-22 **3** 1¼ **Mumgos Debut (IRE)**[35] 2786 8-10-8 **92**......................(t) DerekFox 99
(Lucinda Russell) *led and clr w one other to 4th: rdn bef 3 out: rallied and regained ld whn mstke last: hdd and no ex last 75yds* **11/4**[1]

0-P0 **4** 4 **Scimon Templar (FR)**[35] 2788 8-11-2 **100**.................. CraigNichol 105+
(Rose Dobbin) *nt fluent on occasions: chsd clr ldrs: hdwy bef 4th: chal bef 3 out to after next: edgd lft: outpcd fr last* **15/2**

-352 **5** 15 **Pamak D'Airy (FR)**[23] 2979 13-11-3 **104**..................(p) GrahamWatters(3) 93
(Henry Hogarth) *hld up in tch: stdy hdwy 1/2-way: rdn along 3 out: wknd bef next* **8/1**

6-40 **6** 9 **Too Cool To Fool (IRE)**[52] 2429 13-11-7 **105**................... BrianHughes 83
(Jim Goldie) *hld up: pushed along and outpcd 1/2-way: rallied 4 out: wknd bef next* **9/1**

1443 **P** **Scorpions Sting (IRE)**[36] 2753 7-11-4 **102**.................(tp) LucyAlexander
(James Ewart) *in tch to 1/2-way: sn outpcd: lost tch 4 out: p.u bef 3 out* **9/2**[3]

4m 7.6s (-3.10) **Going Correction** -0.075s/f (Good) **7 Ran SP% 113.1**
Speed ratings: **104,103,103,101,93 89,**
CSF £27.37 TOTE £6.10: £3.50, £2.60; EX 32.70 Trifecta £190.10.
Owner R H Hall **Bred** G E Leech **Trained** Aldoth, Cumbria

FOCUS
A generously run event in the conditions, and the winner came late. A small step up from the winner, with the third rated to his mark.

3442 32RED.COM STANDARD OPEN NATIONAL HUNT FLAT RACE 2m
3:45 (3:46) (Class 6) 4-6-Y-0 **£1,711** (£498; £249)

Form RPR

3 **1** **Spirit Of Kayf**[68] 2106 5-11-5 0.................................... DannyCook 108+
(Sandy Thomson) *mde all: rdn over 2f out: pressed whn hung rt over 1f out: kpt on strly fnl f* **3/1**[2]

2 4½ **Reivers Lad** 5-11-5 0.. BrianHarding 106+
(Nicky Richards) *hld up: smooth hdwy on outside to chse wnr 4f out: effrt and rn green over 2f out: jst over 1 l down whn checked and stmbld over 1f out: kpt on same pce* **9/1**

6-3 **3** 10 **Heilan Rebel (IRE)**[39] 2709 6-10-12 0.......................... MrKitAlexander(7) 90
(N W Alexander) *hld up: pushed along over 4f out: kpt on fr 2f out: nvr able to chal: fin 4th: plcd 3rd* **20/1**

4 3¾ **Our Morris (IRE)** 5-11-0 0............................... JonathonBewley(5) 88
(George Bewley) *hld up: stdy hdwy on outside and in tch 1/2-way: rdn and outpcd over 3f out: n.d after: fin 5th: plcd 4th* **25/1**

3 **5** 7 **Calypso Storm (IRE)**[50] 2479 5-11-5 0.............................. BrianHughes 81
(Rebecca Menzies) *prom: hdwy to chse wnr over 6f out to 4f out: sn drvn and outpcd: btn fnl 2f: fin 6th: plcd 5th* **14/1**

6 12 **Shanroe Street (IRE)**[90] 6-10-9 0.......................... RossChapman(10) 69
(Lucinda Russell) *trckd ldrs: drvn and outpcd 6f out: wknd 4f out: fin 7th: plcd 6th* **10/3**[3]

6 **7** shd **Orioninverness (IRE)**[63] 2195 5-11-0 0.................. GrantCockburn(5) 69
(Lucinda Russell) *bhd: pushed along and struggling 1/2-way: nvr on terms: fin 8th: plcd 7th* **33/1**

8 26 **Broad Spectrum (IRE)**[273] 5-11-5 0................................ HenryBrooke 43
(Donald McCain) *t.k.h: prom: rdn and struggling over 5f out: sn btn: fin 9th: plcd 8th* **14/1**

9 36 **Smooth River (IRE)** 6-10-5 0...................................... AnthonyFox(7)
(S R B Crawford, Ire) *plld hrd: hld up: sddle slipped and hdwy to chse wnr after 6f: struggling fr 4f out: t.o: fin 10th: plcd 9th* **17/2**

6 **10** 10 **Outlaw Josey Wales (IRE)**[36] 2756 5-11-0 0.............. CallumBewley(5)
(R Mike Smith) *t.k.h in midfield: drvn and struggling over 5f: sn btn: lost tch fnl 3f: fin 11th: plcd 10th* **20/1**

D 6 **Progress Drive (IRE)** 5-11-0 0.............................. StephenMulqueen(5) 98+
(Nicky Richards) *hld up: pushed along and hdwy over 4f out: kpt on fr 2f out: nt pce of first two: fin 3rd: disqualified and plcd last: jockey weighed in 2lb light* **5/2**[1]

4m 4.5s (244.50) **11 Ran SP% 126.8**
CSF £31.30 TOTE £4.70: £1.80, £3.50, £5.70; EX 35.40.
Owner Sprayclad UK **Bred** Old Rectory Stud **Trained** Lambden, Berwicks

FOCUS
Not a great deal of pace on early in this bumper, but the winner was committed a fair way out and they finished well stretched out. The winner set a fair standard but this still rates a step up. The fourth helps set the level.
T/Plt: £253.40 to a £1 stake. Pool: £67,228.52 - 193.65 winning tickets T/Qpdt: £18.80 to a £1 stake. Pool: £8,203.55 - 322.50 winning tickets **Richard Young**

2910 SANDOWN (R-H)
Saturday, January 2

OFFICIAL GOING: Heavy (soft in places on chase course; chs 4.4, hdl 4.0)
Wind: Moderate, half behind Weather: Dank, raining until race 5

3443 32RED CASINO JUVENILE HURDLE (8 hdls) 1m 7f 216y
12:05 (12:05) (Class 3) 4-Y-0 **£6,498** (£1,908; £954; £477)

Form RPR

0 **1** **Sneaking Budge**[23] 2992 4-10-12 0.............................. JoshuaMoore 111+
(Stuart Edmunds) *chasing type: t.k.h early: hld up in 3rd: effrt to go 2nd 2 out and sn w ldr: led and quicker jump last: rdn clr* **10/1**[3]

2 5 **Pillard (FR)**[113] 4-11-8 129...........................[1] RichardJohnson 116
(Jonjo O'Neill) *athletic: slightly on toes: led: pushed along whn awkward 2 out and sn jnd: hdd and outj. last: one pce* **6/5**[2]

3 16 **Master Of Speed (IRE)**[119] 4-10-12 0................................ JamieMoore 92
(Gary Moore) *chsd ldr: mstke 2nd: j.lft 3 out: sn rdn: lost 2nd 2 out: wknd* **11/10**[1]

0 **4** 39 **Burner (IRE)**[30] 2863 4-10-12 0.................................... TomCannon 60
(Olly Williams) *a in last: mstkes 4th and 3 out: wknd bef 2 out: j.lft last 2: t.o* **25/1**

4m 19.0s (11.80) **Going Correction** +0.65s/f (Soft) **4 Ran SP% 106.0**
Speed ratings: **96,93,85,66**
CSF £22.22 TOTE £8.30; EX 20.90 Trifecta £28.10.
Owner Nick Brown Racing **Bred** Niarchos Family **Trained** Newport Pagnell, Bucks

FOCUS
Testing ground on a dank day, and all distances as advertised. Josh Moore said of the ground: "It's heavy but they are slopping through it", while Richard Johnson's verdict was "heavy and fairly hard work." There was a surprise outcome to this weak juvenile hurdle, which was steadily run in a time 34sec slower than standard. The winner has been rated as taking a big step up on his debut run, but it's in line with his Flat form. The second has been rated to his French mark.

3444 32RED.COM MARES' HURDLE (LISTED RACE) (9 hdls) 2m 3f 173y
12:40 (12:40) (Class 1) 4-Y-0+
£12,529 (£4,701; £2,354; £1,172; £589; £294)

Form RPR

21-2 **1** **Polly Peachum (IRE)**[40] 2685 8-11-8 150.............................. DavidBass 148
(Nicky Henderson) *in tch: prog to trck ldng pair 5th: shkn up and clsd to ld 2 out: hrd pressed fr last: drvn and hld on* **9/2**[3]

1-3F **2** hd **The Govaness**[21] 3034 7-11-4 144................................ WillKennedy 145
(Dr Richard Newland) *sltly on toes: settled in rr: pushed along and prog to chal 2 out: chsd wnr after: kpt on gamely and grad clsd nr fin: jst hld* **7/1**

32-3 **3** 3¾ **Fairytale Theatre (IRE)**[40] 2685 9-11-0 130......................(t) HarrySkelton 136
(Dan Skelton) *disp ld: std upsides 2 out: chsd ldng pair after: kpt on same pce* **33/1**

4-02 **4** 5 **Gitane Du Berlais (FR)**[34] 2805 6-11-8 145............................ RWalsh 140
(W P Mullins, Ire) *disp ld: sn hdd and hdd 2 out: sn btn: mstke last* **6/4**[1]

230- **5** 5 **Queen Of The Stage (IRE)**[287] 4918 6-11-0 126................. LizzieKelly 126
(Nick Williams) *lw: in tch: pushed along sn after 3 out: stl jst in tch bef 2 out: steadily fdd* **50/1**

-141 **6** 17 **Flute Bowl**[28] 2911 6-11-0 132....................................(p) JoshuaMoore 111
(Gary Moore) *prom to 4th: sn rdn: dropped to last 3 out: wknd wl bef 2 out* **10/1**

-102 **7** 4½ **Petite Parisienne (FR)**[56] 2353 5-11-8 144............................ BJCooper 115
(W P Mullins, Ire) *wl in tch: shkn up and wknd qckly bef 2 out* **3/1**[2]

-F41 **8** 17 **Morello Royale (IRE)**[40] 2685 6-11-8 140......................(t) AidanColeman 98
(Colin Tizzard) *in tch: wknd rapidly wl bef 2 out: t.o* **20/1**

5m 18.5s (18.90) **Going Correction** +0.65s/f (Soft) **8 Ran SP% 114.4**
Speed ratings (Par 111): **88,87,86,84,82 75,73,67**
CSF £34.19 TOTE £4.10: £1.60, £1.90, £4.80; EX 28.70 Trifecta £250.30.
Owner Lady Tennant & Robert Waley-Cohen **Bred** Colman O'Flynn **Trained** Upper Lambourn, Berks

FOCUS
A competitive and classy mares' race. The first two have been rated pretty much to their marks.

3445 32RED H'CAP CHASE (17 fncs) 2m 4f 10y
1:15 (1:15) (Class 3) (0-130,130) 5-Y-0+
£9,384 (£2,772; £1,386; £693; £346; £174)

Form RPR

3-00 **1** **Bishops Road (IRE)**[139] 1278 8-11-12 **130**......................... JamieMoore 152+
(Kerry Lee) *j.big: led to 4th: led again 10th: drew clr fr 3 out: easily* **8/1**

21-2 **2** 17 **Mr Muddle**[47] 2546 9-11-2 **120**.................................. MarcGoldstein 124
(Sheena West) *prom: led 6th to 10th: drvn and dropped to 3rd 4 out: kpt on to regain modest 2nd last: all out nr fin* **16/1**

032 **3** ½ **Vic De Touzaine (FR)**[25] 2957 7-11-2 **120**...................... AidanColeman 127
(Venetia Williams) *lw: patiently rdn in last pair: stl to be asked for an effrt whn mstke 4 out: prog bef next: rdn after 3 out: styd on fr last* **5/1**[3]

3P2U **4** 1 **Garrahalish (IRE)**[22] 3014 8-11-7 **125**............................ CharliePoste 129
(Robin Dickin) *lw: prom whn j. wildly 1st: chsd ldrs after: rdn 4 out: no imp next: kpt on* **8/1**

-615 **5** 1¼ **Regal Flow**[48] 2517 9-11-0 **125**...................................... MrMLegg(7) 129
(Caroline Keevil) *mstke 3rd and dropped to last: mstke 6th: reminder next: nvr gng wl after and nt fluent: stl last appr fnl fence: fin strly* **14/1**

01-U **6** 5 **Ivy Gate (IRE)**[94] 1701 8-11-3 **121**..........................(p) WillKennedy 117
(Jonjo O'Neill) *in tch: mstkes 7th and 8th: sn shkn up: no imp on ldrs bef 3 out* **16/1**

-P32 **7** hd **Fairy Rath (IRE)**[21] 3036 10-11-11 **129**.........................(t) TomCannon 125
(Nick Gifford) *w ldrs: led 4th to 6th: styd prom: chsd wnr 4 out: no imp fr next: lost 2nd last and wknd qckly* **13/2**

6-F4 **8** 3 **Ultragold (FR)**[14] 3148 8-11-4 **122**..............................(t) NoelFehily 115
(Colin Tizzard) *lw: w.w in midfield: gng bttr than many after 4 out: shkn up 3 out and fnd nil: sn wknd* **9/2**[2]

4-41 **9** 3¾ **Toowoomba (IRE)**[23] 2994 8-10-12 **116**........................... TomO'Brien 105
(Philip Hobbs) *in tch: 5th whn blnd 11th (water): nvr gng wl after: struggling bef 3 out* **11/4**[1]

5m 33.4s (15.00) **Going Correction** +0.95s/f (Soft) **9 Ran SP% 115.5**
Speed ratings: **108,101,101,100,100 98,98,96,95**
CSF £115.71 CT £705.58 TOTE £8.80: £2.90, £3.10, £2.10; EX 138.50 Trifecta £1149.40.
Owner Alan Halsall **Bred** P J Morrissey **Trained** Byton, H'fords

FOCUS
A fair handicap chase run in driving rain, and dominated by those who raced up with the pace. The second to the fourth have all been rated pretty much to their marks.

3446 32RED CASINO H'CAP CHASE (13 fncs) 1m 7f 119y
1:50 (1:50) (Class 2) 5-Y-0+
£15,640 (£4,620; £2,310; £1,155; £577; £290)

Form RPR

0-00 **1** **Bold Henry**[21] 3030 10-10-7 **134**................................ BarryGeraghty 143+
(Philip Hobbs) *hld up but sn in 5th: prog to trck ldr 3 out: led after 2 out: pushed out: comf* **15/2**

31-1 **2** 2¼ **Arthur's Oak**[14] 3155 8-10-12 **139**............................. AidanColeman 147+
(Venetia Williams) *lw: mde most: rdn whn nt fluent 2 out: sn hdd: kpt on wl but easily hld by wnr* **10/3**[1]

U-23 **3** 13 **Cash And Go (IRE)**[16] 3121 9-10-13 **140**....................... LiamTreadwell 134
(Venetia Williams) *wl in rr: pushed along in 7th 4 out and wl out of tch: effrt fr 3 out: stl only 6th last: styd on to snatch 3rd nr fin* **14/1**

20-2 **4** *nk* **Barrakilla (IRE)**[23] 2990 9-10-9 **136**.............................. AdamWedge 130
(Evan Williams) *trckd ldng trio: wl in tch 4 out: rdn bef next: outpcd after: kpt on in battle for 3rd after last* **11/2**[3]
2331 **5** *shd* **Pearls Legend**[21] 3030 9-10-12 **139**.............................. NicodeBoinville 133
(John Spearing) *lw: pressed ldr to 6th: styd prom: rdn bef 3 out: wl hld in 3rd 2 out: kpt on but lost pls nr fin* **5/1**[2]
11-2 **6** *12* **Just Cameron**[247] 51 9-11-5 **149**.............................. JoeColliver(3) 132
(Micky Hammond) *prom: chsd ldr 6th to 3 out: wknd qckly* **15/2**
35-0 **7** *21* **Enjoy Responsibly (IRE)**[130] 1361 7-10-7 **141**.....(t) HarrisonBeswick(7) 101
(Sam Thomas) *awkward jump 1st and v awkward 2nd: a towards rr: lost tch in 6th 4 out: wknd next: t.o* **25/1**
-514 **8** *12* **Keel Haul (IRE)**[21] 3030 8-10-4 **131**..............................(p) JamesDavies 79
(Henry Oliver) *chsd ldrs in 6th: rdn 7th: sn struggling: wknd 4 out: t.o* **10/1**
4-P1 **P** **Grey Gold (IRE)**[35] 2784 11-11-12 **153**.............................. JamieMoore
(Kerry Lee) *last whn j. slowly 3rd: sn lost tch and nt gng wl after: wknd 8th: t.o whn p.u bef 3 out* **6/1**

4m 12.2s (10.40) **Going Correction** +0.95s/f (Soft) **9** Ran SP% **112.5**
Speed ratings: **112,110,104,104,104 98,87,81,**
CSF £32.80 CT £341.17 TOTE £8.60: £2.60, £1.40, £3.50; EX 29.40 Trifecta £470.00.
Owner John P McManus **Bred** Mrs S M Reeks **Trained** Withycombe, Somerset

FOCUS
A good handicap chase, run at what appeared to be a decent gallop. Master Minded won this event in 2008 on his way to Champion Chase glory. The winner has been rated back to the level of last season's Cheltenham reappearance win.

3447 32RED TOLWORTH NOVICES' HURDLE (GRADE 1) (8 hdls) 1m 7f 216y
2:25 (2:25) (Class 1) 4-Y-O+ **£23,048** (£8,816; £4,548; £2,400)

Form RPR
1 **1** **Yorkhill (IRE)**[27] 2939 6-11-7 0.............................. RWalsh 152+
(W P Mullins, Ire) *lengthy: will make a chaser: lw: occasionally j.lft: hld up in 4th: prog to chal 2 out and stl gng easily: led last: rdn out and kpt on* **4/9**[1]
0-11 **2** *2 1/4* **O O Seven (IRE)**[28] 2910 6-11-7 145.............................. AndrewTinkler 148
(Nicky Henderson) *lw: chasing type: trckd ldng pair: wnt 2nd after 3 out: rdn to ld 2 out: hdd and mstke last: styd on but readily hld* **5/1**[2]
521 **3** *8* **Agrapart (FR)**[28] 2898 5-11-7 134.............................. LizzieKelly 139
(Nick Williams) *led: rdn and hdd 2 out: sn in 3rd: steadily fdd* **10/1**
1-21 **4** *39* **Welsh Shadow (IRE)**[43] 2626 6-11-7 137.............................. HarrySkelton 114
(Dan Skelton) *nt a fluent: hld up in last: rdn and no imp on ldrs bef 2 out: wknd bef last: virtually p.u flat* **7/1**[3]
-P21 **P** **Cyrius Moriviere (FR)**[27] 2928 6-11-7 132.....................(t) NicodeBoinville
(Ben Pauling) *pressed ldr: rdn after 3 out: sn lost 2nd and wknd rapidly: t.o whn p.u bef 2 out* **33/1**

4m 11.4s (4.20) **Going Correction** +0.65s/f (Soft) **5** Ran SP% **110.5**
Speed ratings (Par 117): **115,113,109,90,**
CSF £3.26 TOTE £1.60: £1.10, £2.00; EX 3.00 Trifecta £8.80.
Owner Andrea & Graham Wylie **Bred** Patrick Keating **Trained** Muine Beag, Co Carlow

FOCUS
An up-to-scratch edition of this Grade 1 event, if lacking in depth. The time was 7.6sec quicker than the opening juvenile hurdle, run when the ground wasn't as poached. The winner looks a top-class novice and is obvious Festival material, while the third has been rated similar to his Aintree mark.

3448 32REDSPORT.COM VETERANS' H'CAP CHASE FINAL (THE FINAL OF THE 2015 VETERANS' CHASE SERIES) (22 fncs) 3m 37y
3:00 (3:00) (Class 2) 10-Y-O+
£61,900 (£18,380; £9,190; £4,580; £2,300; £1,160)

Form RPR
0-04 **1** **Soll**[28] 2899 11-11-9 **145**..............................(bt) TomScudamore 152
(David Pipe) *prom: rdn in 3rd 4 out: looked hld tl rallied after 2 out: tk 2nd last: styd on dourly to ld nr fin* **7/1**[1]
-411 **2** *nk* **Aachen**[22] 3016 12-11-5 **146**.............................. CharlieDeutsch(5) 153
(Venetia Williams) *prom: trckd ldr 9th: led 3 out and wnt for home: 3 l up last: drvn and hdd nr fin* **11/1**
12-2 **3** *6* **Reaping The Reward (IRE)**[21] 3038 12-10-12 **134**...(t) RichardJohnson 136
(Lucinda Russell) *lw: w.w towards rr: nt fluent 12th: stdy prog fr next: trckd ldrs 4 out gng wl: wnt 2nd 3 out: rdn 2 out: no imp on ldr last: lost 2nd and no ex* **8/1**[2]
4-12 **4** *22* **Golden Chieftain (IRE)**[20] 3057 11-10-7 **129**..............(bt) BrendanPowell 108
(Colin Tizzard) *unable to ld: chsd ldrs: no imp fr 15th: struggling whn mstke 18th: wl btn 6th after next (4 out)* **12/1**
-010 **5** *shd* **Benbens (IRE)**[35] 2783 11-11-7 **143**.............................. SamTwiston-Davies 124
(Nigel Twiston-Davies) *lw: nvr bttr than midfield: rdn 16th: nvr on terms after: wl btn 7th after 4 out* **9/1**[3]
-161 **6** *1 3/4* **Tullamore Dew (IRE)**[20] 3057 14-10-10 **135**.............................. JoeColliver(3) 112
(Micky Hammond) *a towards rr: lost tch bef 12th: t.o 4 out: plodded on* **8/1**[2]
10-P **7** *16* **Lie Forrit (IRE)**[69] 2082 12-11-9 **145**.............................. PeterBuchanan 106
(Lucinda Russell) *taken off his feet and struggling in rr: wl bhd fr 12th: t.o 4 out: plodded on* **14/1**
4-53 **8** *3/4* **Araldur (FR)**[34] 2809 12-10-7 **129**.............................. WayneHutchinson 92
(Alan King) *trckd ldrs: gng wl 17th: rdn in 4th after 4 out: wknd next: disputing modest 4th whn blnd 2 out: fin v tired* **8/1**[2]
2-62 **P** **French Opera**[34] 2809 13-11-12 **148**.............................. AndrewTinkler
(Nicky Henderson) *in midfield whn blnd 6th: dropped to rr: lost tch 12th: p.u bef next* **20/1**
1415 **P** **Houston Dynimo (IRE)**[13] 3174 11-9-12 **125**............(bt) DavidNoonan(5)
(David Pipe) *unable to ld: chsd ldrs: lost pl and struggling whn mstke 15th: sn no ch: wl bhd 3 out: p.u bef last* **33/1**
14-4 **P** **Creevytennant (IRE)**[34] 2809 12-11-5 **144**.............(t) ConorShoemark(3)
(Fergal O'Brien) *led and set str pce: hdd 3 out: wknd bef next: p.u bef last* **25/1**
-0P3 **P** **Your Busy (IRE)**[83] 1871 13-10-12 **134**..............................(t) RWalsh
(J A Nash, Ire) *a wl in rr: lost tch bef 1/2-way: last and t.o whn p.u bef 17th* **16/1**
4P-5 **P** **Renard (FR)**[20] 3057 11-10-11 **133**.............................. LiamTreadwell
(Venetia Williams) *in tch in midfield: rdn 16th and no prog: wl btn 8th after 4 out: t.o whn p.u bef 3 out* **12/1**
2P-0 **P** **Relax (FR)**[28] 2916 11-10-13 **135**.............................. AidanColeman
(Venetia Williams) *chsd ldr to 9th: mstke 11th: wknd and mstke 15th: wl btn 9th after to whn p.u bef 3 out* **7/1**[1]
-PP4 **P** **Knock A Hand (IRE)**[20] 3057 11-11-0 **136**..............(b) JamieMoore
(Kerry Lee) *sn in last and jumping slowly: t.o whn p.u 1/2-way* **16/1**

6m 49.9s (22.10) **Going Correction** +0.95s/f (Soft) **15** Ran SP% **122.0**
Speed ratings: **101,100,98,91,91 90,85,85, , , , ,**
CSF £80.64 CT £641.25 TOTE £8.70: £2.80, £3.30, £2.70; EX 89.80 Trifecta £870.10.
Owner Derrick Mossop **Bred** D Mossop **Trained** Nicholashayne, Devon
■ Stewards' Enquiry : Tom Scudamore seven-day ban: use of whip (16-22 Jan); £1,150 fine

FOCUS
A very valuable prize for this inaugural series final and a terrific field. The pace was solid and they were soon spread out. The first three finished well clear. The winner has been rated to the level of last season's Newbury win.

3449 32RED.COM H'CAP HURDLE (8 hdls) 1m 7f 216y
3:35 (3:36) (Class 2) (0-150,150) 4-Y-O+
£15,640 (£4,620; £2,310; £1,155; £577; £290)

Form RPR
0320 **1** **Rayvin Black**[14] 3151 7-10-10 **137**.............................. ThomasGarner(3) 150
(Oliver Sherwood) *led at gd pce: hdd after 3 out and shkn up but clr of rest: renewed effrt to ld 2 out: forged clr fr last* **10/1**
2112 **2** *5* **Sirop De Menthe (FR)**[32] 2831 6-10-1 **128**.............................. LucyGardner(3) 136
(Sue Gardner) *lw: trckd ldr: led after 3 out and sent for home: rdn and hdd 2 out: clr of rest but one pce after* **13/2**[3]
5234 **3** *12* **Melodic Rendezvous**[21] 3033 10-11-12 **150**.............................. NickScholfield 147
(Jeremy Scott) *lw: prom: lost pl after 5th: effrt to go 3rd bef 2 out but ldng pair clr: no imp after* **5/1**[1]
-541 **4** *1 1/4* **Minstrels Gallery (IRE)**[21] 3041 7-10-2 **126**.............................. LeightonAspell 122
(Lucy Wadham) *prom on outer: cl 3rd 3 out: sn rdn and outpcd: no imp fr 2 out* **10/1**
132 **5** *hd* **Romain De Senam (FR)**[31] 2845 4-10-0 **136**.......(t) SamTwiston-Davies 119
(Paul Nicholls) *t.k.h: hld up in rr: prog 5th: outpcd after 3 out: rdn bef 2 out: pressed for 3rd pl last: no ex* **6/1**[2]
0-00 **6** *7* **Ebony Express**[28] 2914 7-10-11 **135**.............................. WillKennedy 123
(Dr Richard Newland) *hld up in rr: pushed along in 7th bef 2 out and no real prog: rdn bef last: nvr involved* **12/1**
P-33 **7** *2 3/4* **Leviathan**[30] 2873 9-10-1 **125**.............................. AidanColeman 110
(Venetia Williams) *chsd ldrs: dropped towards rr 5th: nvr on terms after: rdn and no prog bef 2 out* **16/1**
6313 **8** *hd* **Kayf Blanco**[22] 3015 7-11-2 **140**.............................. KielanWoods 125
(Graeme McPherson) *t.k.h: hld up towards rr: prog to trck ldrs 3 out: sn outpcd: rdn and wknd bef 2 out* **6/1**[2]
614 **9** *3/4* **See The Rock (IRE)**[30] 2860 6-10-0 **124** oh2.............................. RichardJohnson 108
(Jonjo O'Neill) *lw: hld up in rr: modest prog bef 3 out: sn outpcd by ldrs: shkn up and no hdwy bef 2 out: nvr involved* **13/2**[3]
-132 **10** *4 1/2* **Cardinal Palace (IRE)**[83] 1870 6-11-2 **140**.............................. RWalsh 119
(J A Nash, Ire) *hld up in last pair: lost tch in last pl after 4th: nvr a factor* **9/1**
51U- **11** *29* **Lochnagar (GER)**[380] 3152 7-10-0 **124** oh2.............................. LiamTreadwell 74
(Venetia Williams) *chsd ldrs: lost pl qckly 3rd and sn in last pair: lost tch 3 out: wknd 2 out: blnd last and t.o* **33/1**

4m 17.1s (9.90) **Going Correction** +0.65s/f (Soft)
WFA 4 from 6yo+ 11lb **11** Ran SP% **116.6**
Speed ratings (Par 109): **101,98,92,91,91 88,86,86,86,84 69**
CSF £73.58 CT £368.11 TOTE £10.50: £2.90, £2.60, £2.40; EX 71.40 Trifecta £382.70.
Owner R White & V J Walsh **Bred** Mystic Meg Limited **Trained** Upper Lambourn, Berks

FOCUS
A good handicap run on the worst of the ground. Not many got into it and the first two finished a long way clear. A step up from the winner, with the second helping to set the level.
T/Plt: £952.20 to a £1 stake. Pool: £149,218.14 - 114.39 winning tickets T/Qpdt: £19.60 to a £1 stake. Pool: £23,538.38 - 887.08 winning tickets **Jonathan Neesom**

3083 PLUMPTON (L-H)
Sunday, January 3

OFFICIAL GOING: Heavy (hdl 4.0, chs 4.5) abandoned after race 3 (1.40); waterlogged course
Wind: Strong, against Weather: heavy rain (atrocious conditions)

3450 DOWNLOAD THE AT THE RACES APP NOVICES' HURDLE (9 hdls) 1m 7f 195y
12:40 (12:40) (Class 4) 4-Y-O+ **£3,898** (£1,144; £572; £286)

Form RPR
0-31 **1** **Theo's Charm (IRE)**[20] 3083 6-11-12 128.............................. TomCannon 133+
(Nick Gifford) *w ldr: mstke 3rd: led 6th: asserted 2 out: in command and mstke last: rdn out: easily* **4/11**[1]
20 **2** *23* **Clayton**[28] 2928 7-11-5 0.............................. JoshuaMoore 104
(Gary Moore) *t.k.h: chsd ldrs: wnt 3rd and mstke 5th: mstke 3 out: sn chsng wnr and rdn: btn next: wkng whn hit last* **3/1**[2]
60 **3** *6* **Fine Tune (IRE)**[28] 2928 5-11-2 0..............................(t) ThomasGarner(3) 95
(Linda Jewell) *in tch in midfield: 4th and outpcd u.p after 5th: wl btn 3 out: plugged on to go modest 3rd flat* **100/1**
00-0 **4** *8* **Sir Hubert**[48] 2544 6-11-5 0.............................. LeightonAspell 87
(Richard Rowe) *in tch in midfield: outpcd after 5th: no ch 3 out: plugged on to go modest 4th nr fin* **100/1**
6605 **5** *nk* **Quieto Sol (FR)**[23] 3022 5-11-5 0.............................. AidanColeman 87
(Charlie Longsdon) *hld up in tch in last trio: stdy hdwy into 4th after 6th but nt on terms w ldrs: no imp* **10/1**[3]
60 **6** *3/4* **Bolister (FR)**[48] 2544 5-11-5 0.............................. JamieMoore 86
(Gary Moore) *led tl 6th: rdn and btn 3rd wl bef 2 out: wknd steadily: lost 3 pls flat* **18/1**
P **Little Buxted (USA)**[410] 6-11-5 0.............................. AndrewGlassonbury
(Jim Best) *chsd ldrs tl 5th: sn rdn and lost pl: t.o 3 out tl p.u next* **12/1**
6665 **P** **Ablazing (IRE)**[63] 2217 5-11-5 0.............................. AlainCawley
(Johnny Farrelly) *hld up in rr: j. slowly 1st: rdn after 4th: lost tch 6th: t.o whn p.u 2 out* **25/1**
040P **P** **Cor Wot An Apple**[20] 3085 5-10-12 0.............................. PaulO'Brien(7)
(Colin Tizzard) *in tch in midfield: 5th and beginning to struggle whn blnd 6th: wl bhd next: t.o whn p.u 2 out* **50/1**
000 **P** **Opechee (IRE)**[17] 3130 5-11-0 0.............................. JakeHodson(5)
(David Bridgwater) *hld up in tch in rr: struggling after 5th: t.o 3 out tl p.u next* **66/1**

4m 27.7s (26.90) **Going Correction** +1.90s/f (Heav)
WFA 4 from 5yo+ 11lb **10** Ran SP% **129.6**
Speed ratings (Par 105): **108,96,93,89,89 88, , , ,**
CSF £2.30 TOTE £1.20: £1.10, £1.10, £20.50; EX 2.20 Trifecta £124.60.
Owner Michael O'Shea **Bred** Mrs Brid McCrea **Trained** Findon, W Sussex

FOCUS
After a lengthy deliberation by the stewards the meeting passed a late morning inspection, but the going was understandably attritional. Only six got home in this uncompetitive novice hurdle. Race distance 144yds further than advertised. The winner set a good standard and has been rated pretty much to his mark, along with the third, fourth and sixth.

3451 AT THE RACES APP ON IPHONE NOVICES' CHASE (8 fncs 4 omitted) **2m 214y**
1:10 (1:11) (Class 3) 5-Y-O+ £6,498 (£1,908; £954)

Form RPR
114- 1 **L'Ami Serge (IRE)**[299] 4688 6-11-0 0 NicodeBoinville 153+
(Nicky Henderson) *mde all: readily wnt clr bef 2 out: unchal* 2/11[1]
31/0 2 27 **Doctor Harper (IRE)**[29] 2912 8-11-0 0 TomScudamore 133+
(David Pipe) *chsd wnr thrght: 3 l down bypassing 3 out: sn pushed along and btn next: eased flat* 9/2[2]
/22- 3 27 **Dollar Bill**[541] 649 7-11-0 110 LeightonAspell 98
(Nick Gifford) *a last: mstke 5th: lost tch on long run to next: blnd 6th: t.o* 25/1[3]
4m 52.4s (29.40) **Going Correction** +2.075s/f (Heav) **3** Ran SP% **106.6**
Speed ratings: **113,100,87**
CSF £1.49 TOTE £1.20; EX 1.20 Trifecta £1.30.
Owner Simon Munir & Isaac Souede **Bred** P Ryan **Trained** Upper Lambourn, Berks
FOCUS
Race distance increased by 24yds. This was predictably one-way traffic. Two fences, one at the top of the hill and the open ditch, were omitted. The winner is a potential 160+ novice.

3452 AT THE RACES APP ON ANDROID/EBF STALLIONS "NATIONAL HUNT" NOVICES' HURDLE (QUALIFIER) (9 hdls 3 omitted) **2m 4f 114y**
1:40 (1:41) (Class 3) 4-7-Y-O £5,393 (£1,583; £791; £395)

Form RPR
02 1 **Minella Charmer (IRE)**[24] 2995 5-11-2 0 (t) WayneHutchinson 141+
(Alan King) *trckd ldrs: led on bit bef 2 out (actual last): readily drew clr on long run-in: easily* 4/5[1]
36 2 15 **Dark Flame (IRE)**[30] 2886 7-11-2 0 LeightonAspell 129
(Richard Rowe) *hld up in tch in last pair: clsd to trck ldrs 7th: rdn and led on bnd bef 2 out (actual last): sn hdd and btn: no ch w wnr on long run-in* 3/1[2]
/620 3 15 **Manhattan Mead**[16] 3133 6-11-2 117 MarcGoldstein 111
(Michael Madgwick) *rn in snatches: w ldrs tl: lost pl u.p after 6th: 5th and stl in tch 3 out (actual 2 out): wl btn next: plugged on into modest 3rd on long run-in* 9/1
3-20 4 6 **Captain McGinley (IRE)**[60] 2275 6-11-2 0 (p) SeanBowen 106
(Rebecca Curtis) *mde most tl 5th: styd upsides ldrs tl rdn to ld again after 3 out (actual 2 out): hdd bnd bef last: immediately btn and wknd on long run-in* 5/1[3]
5 5 14 **Rocknrobin (IRE)**[20] 3085 5-11-2 0 TomCannon 91
(Chris Gordon) *t.k.h: jnd ldrs after 1st: led 5th tl after 3 out (actual 2 out): sn rdn: wkng whn mstke 2 out (actual last): fdd* 66/1
P **Karens Lad (IRE)**[622] 6-11-2 0 JoshuaMoore
(Nick Gifford) *hld up in tch in last pair: rdn and mstke 7th: wknd next: t.o whn p.u 2 out (actual last)* 16/1
6m 6.4s (49.40) **Going Correction** +2.575s/f (Heav) **6** Ran SP% **114.6**
Speed ratings: **108,102,96,94,88**
CSF £3.78 TOTE £1.80: £1.20, £2.00; EX 4.50 Trifecta £10.80.
Owner David Sewell **Bred** Michael Carroll **Trained** Barbury Castle, Wilts
FOCUS
Race distance increased by 192yds. This fair novice hurdle proved extremely hard work and course officials called the meeting off afterwards. The second and third have been rated to their pre-race marks.

3453 AT THE RACES SKY 415 H'CAP HURDLE (12 hdls) **2m 4f 114y**
() (Class 5) (0-100,) 4-Y-O+ £

3454 AT THE RACES SUSSEX NATIONAL (A H'CAP CHASE) (20 fncs) **3m 4f 102y**
() (Class 3) (0-130,) 5-Y-O+ £

3455 VISIT ATTHERACES.COM H'CAP CHASE (14 fncs) **2m 3f 164y**
() (Class 4) (0-105,) 5-Y-O+ £

3456 AT THE RACES VIRGIN 535 H'CAP HURDLE (9 hdls) **1m 7f 195y**
() (Class 4) (0-110,) 4-Y-O+ £

T/Jkpt: £938.30 to a £1 stake. £24,451- 18.5 winning units. Placepot Jackpot: £6.40 to a £1 stake. £3,227.00 - 366.07 winning units T/Plt: 1.10 to a £1 stake. £82,014 - 55008.26 winning units T/Qpdt: 1.10 to a £1 stake. £7,453 - 6460.55 winning units **Steve Payne**

3457 - 3458a (Foreign Racing) - See Raceform Interactive

2352 NAAS (L-H)
Sunday, January 3

OFFICIAL GOING: Heavy

3459a LAWLOR'S HOTEL NOVICE HURDLE (GRADE 1) (11 hdls) **2m 4f**
1:50 (1:50) 5-Y-O+ £39,705 (£12,573; £5,955; £1,985)

RPR
1 **Bellshill (IRE)**[21] 3070 6-11-10 150 RWalsh 143+
(W P Mullins, Ire) *chsd ldrs in 3rd: tk clsr order fr 7th and wnt 2nd on outer fr 3 out: cl 2nd 2 out where slt mstke: led travelling wl and wnt clr bef last where slt mstke: rdn out run-in: comf* 2/5[1]
2 5 **Last Encounter (IRE)**[15] 3169 6-11-10 127 DannyMullins 137
(Ms Margaret Mullins, Ire) *led: j. sltly lft 1st: narrow advantage 4 out: pushed along and pressed clly bef 2 out: hdd u.p and no ch w wnr in 2nd bef last where slt mstke: kpt on same pce run-in* 66/1
3 1 1/4 **Anibale Fly (FR)**[21] 3068 6-11-10 0 BarryGeraghty 136+
(A J Martin, Ire) *hld up bhd ldrs in 4th: tk clsr order after 3 out: rdn in 3rd 2 out and sn no imp on ldrs: kpt on u.p run-in: hld for 2nd* 7/1[3]
4 19 **Marakoush (IRE)**[50] 2507 5-11-7 0 APHeskin 117
(Alan Fleming, Ire) *settled in rr: wnt 4th gng wl into st: sn rdn in 4th and no ex fr 2 out: one pce after and mod 4th whn slt mstke last* 9/1
P **Stone Hard (IRE)**[21] 3070 6-11-10 0 BJCooper
(W P Mullins, Ire) *settled bhd ldr in 2nd: cl 2nd 4 out: dropped to 3rd 3 out and pushed along: no ex u.p in 4th appr st and sn wknd to rr: eased bef 2 out and t.o whn p.u after 2 out* 5/1[2]
5m 5.9s (5.00) **5** Ran SP% **112.1**
CSF £18.15 TOTE £1.30: £1.02, £5.10; DF 23.30 Trifecta £72.70.
Owner Andrea & Graham Wylie **Bred** Frank Motherway **Trained** Muine Beag, Co Carlow
FOCUS
Mistakes at the last two hurdles besides, this was a perfectly satisfactory outing from the winner. The front-running outsider an the runner-up set the level for now.

3460 - 3463a (Foreign Racing) - See Raceform Interactive

3105 LUDLOW (R-H)
Monday, January 4

OFFICIAL GOING: Heavy (soft in places; 4.9)
Wind: Fresh against Weather: Raining

3464 BEST WISHES FOR 2016 JUVENILE MAIDEN HURDLE (8 hdls 1 omitted) **1m 7f 169y**
1:00 (1:00) (Class 5) 4-Y-O £2,599 (£763; £381; £190)

Form RPR
1 **St Saviour**[84] 4-10-12 0 RichardJohnson 125+
(Philip Hobbs) *a.p: mstke 1st: nt fluent next: hit 3rd: led 2 out: clr last: styd on strly* 1/1[1]
42 2 21 **The Coffee Hunter (FR)**[38] 2757 4-10-12 0 (t) TomScudamore 100
(Nick Williams) *prom: chsd ldr after 5th: led 3 out: hdd next: sn rdn and btn* 5/2[2]
433 3 1 **Celestial Magic**[25] 2992 4-10-7 110 DanielHiskett[(5)] 100
(Richard Phillips) *chsd ldr tl led 4th: hdd 3 out: rdn and hit next: wknd bef last: hung lft flat* 9/2[3]
43 4 36 **Kenobe Star (IRE)**[43] 2662 4-10-12 0 BrendanPowell 63
(Jamie Snowden) *led to 4th: wkng whn mstke 3 out* 20/1
5 5 21 **Shintori (FR)**[19] 3112 4-10-12 0 PaddyBrennan 48
(Richard Woollacott) *prom tl rdn and wknd appr 3 out* 8/1
6 17 **Star Ascending (IRE)**[80] 4-10-12 0 SeanQuinlan 25
(Jennie Candlish) *hld up: rdn and wknd appr 3 out* 50/1
06P P **Light Breaks (IRE)**[25] 2992 4-10-9 0 RyanHatch[(3)]
(Nigel Twiston-Davies) *hld up: rdn and wknd appr 4th: bhd whn p.u bef 3 out* 50/1
P **Keep 'r Lit**[5] 4-10-5 0 (t[1]) RobertDunne
(Miss Imogen Pickard) *hld up: rdn and wknd 4th: bhd whn p.u bef 3 out* 200/1
P **As A Dream (IRE)**[192] 4-10-0 0 ChrisWard[(5)]
(Nikki Evans) *hld up: plld hrd early: j.rt 1st: nt fluent next: losing tch whn j. slowly 3rd: sn wl bhd: p.u bef 3 out* 100/1
4m 6.6s (17.10) **Going Correction** +1.375s/f (Heav) **9** Ran SP% **118.0**
Speed ratings: **112,101,101,83,72 64,,,**
CSF £3.88 TOTE £1.90: £1.10, £1.20, £1.10; EX 4.50 Trifecta £9.70.
Owner Highclere Thoroughbred Racing-St Saviour **Bred** Floors Farming **Trained** Withycombe, Somerset
FOCUS
Rail movements added 10.5yds to the race distance. The hurdle past the stands was omitted; the winning rider said it was as soft as he had known it here. A moderate maiden hurdle in which only three mattered in the straight, but quite an impressive winner. The second and third give the form a solid enough look.

3465 1871 H'CAP HURDLE (10 hdls 2 omitted) **2m 7f 174y**
1:35 (1:35) (Class 3) (0-130,130) 4-Y-O+ £5,848 (£1,717; £858; £429)

Form RPR
0511 1 **Arctic Gold (IRE)**[37] 2768 5-11-4 122 SamTwiston-Davies 132+
(Nigel Twiston-Davies) *mde all: clr fr 2 out: hit last: styd on* 11/4[2]
1300 2 5 **Crazy Jack (IRE)**[17] 3137 8-11-4 122 (p) DavidBass 125
(Kim Bailey) *chsd wnr: rdn appr 3 out: styd on same pce fr next* 7/2[3]
2-50 3 9 **Floral Spinner**[62] 2262 9-10-2 111 JakeHodson[(5)] 106
(Bill Turner) *chsd ldrs: rdn appr 3 out: sn outpcd: hmpd last: wnt 3rd flat* 20/1
P-20 4 6 **L'Aigle Royal (GER)**[64] 2214 5-11-12 130 RichardJohnson 120
(John Quinn) *hld up: hdwy after 7th: rdn and wknd 3 out* 13/8[1]
1U1 5 1 3/4 **Church Field (IRE)**[88] 1827 8-10-10 117 ConorShoemark[(3)] 103
(Phil Middleton) *prom: rdn appr 3 out: wknd next* 12/1
12-P P **Billfromthebar (IRE)**[103] 1632 9-11-5 123 WayneHutchinson
(Donald McCain) *hld up: rdn and wknd after 7th: bhd whn p.u bef 3 out* 9/1
6m 30.8s (38.50) **Going Correction** +1.45s/f (Heav) **6** Ran SP% **109.4**
Speed ratings (Par 107): **93,91,88,86,85**
CSF £12.23 TOTE £3.50: £1.70, £2.10; EX 13.60 Trifecta £72.10.
Owner Geoffrey & Donna Keeys **Bred** Ms Deirdre Connolly **Trained** Naunton, Gloucs
FOCUS
Rail movements added 21yds to the race distance. The hurdle past the stands was omitted. A fair staying handicap hurdle that was run in steady rain on already testing ground and proved an attritional test. This was another step forward from the winner.

3466 LUDLOW CLUB NOVICES' LIMITED H'CAP CHASE (12 fncs) **1m 7f 212y**
2:10 (2:10) (Class 3) (0-135,135) 5-Y-O+ £6,498 (£1,908; £954; £477)

Form RPR
1502 1 **Cloonacool (IRE)**[21] 3084 7-11-8 135 JoshuaMoore 147+
(Stuart Edmunds) *a.p: mstke 4th: led 3 out: clr whn wnt lft last: rdn out* 5/2[2]
P-32 2 3 3/4 **Goohar (IRE)**[37] 2765 7-10-3 116 oh2 TomO'Brien 124
(Henry Daly) *hld up: hdwy 8th: chsd wnr last: no imp flat* 11/2[3]
40-4 3 4 1/2 **Officer Drivel (IRE)**[21] 3084 5-10-8 125 SamTwiston-Davies 123
(Jim Best) *chsd ldr: ev ch 3 out: sn rdn: wknd flat* 11/2[3]
P-P 4 10 **Azert De Coeur (FR)**[54] 2438 6-10-3 116 oh2 LiamTreadwell 107
(Venetia Williams) *prom: rdn appr 4 out: sn wknd* 14/1
-106 5 17 **Ink Master (IRE)**[17] 3134 6-10-7 120 RichardJohnson 99
(Philip Hobbs) *led: clr 4th tl 7th: hdd 3 out: wknd after next* 85/40[1]
03-0 P **Portway Flyer (IRE)**[19] 3106 8-10-7 120 (t) WillKennedy
(Ian Williams) *hld up: reminders after 5th: bhd fr next: p.u bef 4 out* 8/1
006U P **Another Journey**[5] 3362 7-10-0 116 oh3 JamesBanks[(3)]
(Sarah-Jayne Davies) *mid-div: nt fluent 5th: rdn and wknd after 9th: bhd whn p.u bef 2 out* 40/1
P40 P **Alefou D'Airy (FR)**[25] 2989 6-10-3 116 oh6 JamesDavies
(Jimmy Frost) *in rr and pushed along after 1st: bhd whn mstke 5th: sn p.u* 100/1
4m 16.8s (18.30) **Going Correction** +1.375s/f (Heav)
WFA 5 from 6yo+ 3lb **8** Ran SP% **112.5**
Speed ratings: **109,107,104,99,91 ,,**
CSF £16.44 CT £67.23 TOTE £3.30: £1.30, £1.80, £1.60; EX 14.00 Trifecta £35.00.
Owner Nick Brown Racing **Bred** Thomas McParland **Trained** Newport Pagnell, Bucks

FOCUS
The rails were moved out, adding 18yds to the race distance. The feature race and a fairly interesting novices' handicap chase, although half the field were out of the weights. A big step up from the winner from his chase debut.

3467 JUBILEE RESTAURANT MAIDEN HURDLE (10 hdls 1 omitted) 2m 5f 55y
2:45 (2:45) (Class 5) 4-Y-O+ £2,599 (£763; £381; £190)

Form				RPR
430-	1		**Mount Haven (IRE)**[303] 4631 6-11-6 122........ TomScudamore (David Pipe) *hld up in tch: chsd ldr 3 out: rdn to ld flat: r.o* **5/2**[1]	118+
005-	2	1 ½	**Saint Lino (FR)**[271] 5323 5-11-1 118........ LizzieKelly(5) (Nick Williams) *a.p: chsd ldr 4th to 7th: led appr 3 out: hit next: mstke last: hdd flat: styd on same pce* **7/2**[3]	116+
000	3	11	**Just So Cool (IRE)**[19] 3105 5-11-6 0........ AidanColeman (David Dennis) *hld up: hdwy appr 3 out: styd on same pce fr next* **66/1**	104
4	4	½	**Dukes Den**[40] 2710 5-11-6 0........ GavinSheehan (Charlie Mann) *hld up: pushed along 6th: hdwy appr 3 out: sn rdn: styd on same pce fr next* **16/1**	104
0	5	29	**Midnight Jade (IRE)**[33] 2856 7-10-10 0........ HarryChalloner(3) (John Groucott) *hld up: bhd fr 6th* **100/1**	68
	6	shd	**Kit Casey (IRE)**[330] 6-11-6 0........ SeanBowen (Rebecca Curtis) *chsd ldrs: rdn after 7th: wknd bef next* **4/1**	74
4/4-	7	18	**Crowd Control (IRE)**[268] 7-10-13 0........ MissLBrooke(7) (Lady Susan Brooke) *led: j.rt 1st: hdd 7th: wknd bef next* **200/1**	68
6	P		**Whos De Baby (IRE)**[25] 2995 8-11-3 0........ JamesBanks(3) (Sarah-Jayne Davies) *prom tl rdn: wknd qckly and p.u wl bef 3 out* **14/1**	
	P		**Texas Forever (IRE)**[57] 7-11-6 0........ DavidBass (Kim Bailey) *chsd ldr: hmpd 1st: nt fluent and rdr lost iron briefly next: swvd rt and lost 2nd 4th: remained handy: led 7th: rdn: hdd & wknd appr 3 out: p.u bef next* **11/4**[2]	

5m 42.9s (28.10) **Going Correction** +1.525s/f (Heav) **9 Ran SP% 113.0**
Speed ratings (Par 103): **107,106,102,102,91 90,84,,**
CSF £11.60 TOTE £3.40: £1.20, £1.40, £8.30; EX 11.20 Trifecta £264.60.
Owner The Angove Family **Bred** Eamonn And Liam O'Donovan **Trained** Nicholashayne, Devon

FOCUS
Rail movements added 21yds to the race distance. The hurdle past the stands was omitted. An ordinary maiden hurdle which two appeared to dominate on the ratings, and they had it between them in the straight.

3468 ANNUAL MEMBERS RACING EXCELLENCE "HANDS AND HEELS" H'CAP CHASE (CONDITIONALS/AMATEURS) (19 fncs) 2m 7f 171y
3:20 (3:20) (Class 5) (0-100,88) 5-Y-O+ £3,249 (£954; £477; £238)

Form				RPR
U63P	1		**Gowanauthat (IRE)**[27] 2953 8-11-9 **88**........(tp) TommyDowling(3) (Charlie Mann) *mde all: shkn up appr 4 out: hung lft flat: jst hld on* **7/1**[3]	101+
-542	2	nk	**Magical Man**[34] 2836 9-11-6 **82**........(p) HarryCobden (Debra Hamer) *chsd ldrs: nt fluent 4th: ev ch fr 4 out: shkn up after 2 out: nt clr run flat: styd on* **11/8**[1]	95+
6/33	3	12	**Salut Honore (FR)**[22] 3062 10-11-3 **84**........(t) LukeWatson(5) (Alex Hales) *chsd wnr: ev ch 4 out: shkn up after 2 out: wknd flat* **7/2**[2]	84
-65P	4	9	**Tinelyra (IRE)**[18] 3131 10-11-9 **88**........(t) PhilipDonovan(3) (Fergal O'Brien) *prom: pushed along 10th: wknd appr 4 out* **10/1**	81
P243	5	2	**Petit Ecuyer (FR)**[14] 3199 10-11-2 **78**........ MrJNixon (Dai Williams) *chsd ldrs: lost pl 2nd: hdwy 7th: ev ch 4 out: wknd 2 out* **8/1**	67
P61P	P		**Rusty Nail (IRE)**[79] 1978 11-11-11 **87**........ MissBFrost (Jimmy Frost) *hld up: in rr whn hit 8th: mstke next: bhd fr 12th: p.u bef 14th* **20/1**	
U534	P		**Sylvan Legend**[50] 2521 8-11-3 **79**........(t) MrStanSheppard (Matt Sheppard) *hld up: bhd fr 12th: blnd 3 out: sn p.u* **9/1**	

6m 57.8s (417.80) **7 Ran SP% 111.8**
CSF £17.20 TOTE £8.80: £2.70, £1.30; EX 19.80 Trifecta £55.10.
Owner Bryan Beacham and Mrs J M Mayo **Bred** Raymond McCurtain **Trained** Upper Lambourn, Berks

FOCUS
The rails were moved out, adding 18yds to the race distance. A low-grade hands and heels handicap chase for conditional and amateur riders that produced a close finish. The winner is rated back to the level of his Worcester second.

3469 £210 ANNUAL MEMBERSHIP MARES' STANDARD OPEN NATIONAL HUNT FLAT RACE 1m 6f 7y
3:50 (3:50) (Class 5) 4-6-Y-O £2,599 (£763; £381; £190)

Form				RPR
	1		**Royal Debutante (IRE)** 5-11-4 0........ LiamTreadwell (Paul Webber) *chsd clr ldrs: tk clsr order 7f out: led over 2f out: rdn out* **20/1**	109+
	2	6	**Miss Spent (IRE)** 6-11-4 0........ LeightonAspell (Lucy Wadham) *chsd clr ldrs: tk clsr order over 7f out: rdn to chse wnr over 1f out: styd on same pce fnl f* **10/3**[2]	102+
6	3	6	**Deauville Dame**[23] 3048 4-10-6 0........ MichealNolan (Sir Mark Prescott Bt) *w ldr 4f: remained handy: rdn and ev ch over 2f out: wknd ins fnl f* **14/1**	82
2	4	½	**Mo Chailin (IRE)**[33] 2849 5-11-4 0........ SamTwiston-Davies (Donald McCain) *led: rdn and hdd over 2f out: styd on same pce* **4/1**[3]	93
	5	18	**Glevum Acrobatis** 5-11-4 0........(t) DaveCrosse (Hugo Froud) *hld up: rdn and wknd over 2f out* **33/1**	71
	6	5	**Kahaleesi** 4-10-6 0........ RichardJohnson (Philip Hobbs) *hld up: hdwy over 5f out: rdn and wknd over 2f out* **10/11**[1]	53
	7	11	**Over To Midnight** 6-10-11 0........ MissLBrooke(7) (Lady Susan Brooke) *hld up: plld hrd: wknd 1/2-way* **100/1**	52

3m 37.6s (24.60) **7 Ran SP% 110.8**
CSF £80.16 TOTE £19.70: £6.90, £2.50; EX 79.20 Trifecta £738.60.
Owner The Ping Partnership **Bred** William McCarthy **Trained** Mollington, Oxon

FOCUS
Rail movements added 10.5yds to the race distance. Limited experience amongst the runners in this mares' bumper and the finish was dominated by the two daughters of Presenting.
T/Plt: £44.30 to a £1 stake. Pool: £53,128.14 - 874.86 winning units. T/Qpdt: £14.70 to a £1 stake. Pool: £5,252.17 - 263.40 winning units. **Colin Roberts**

3423 MUSSELBURGH (R-H)
Monday, January 4

OFFICIAL GOING: Good to soft (soft in places)
Wind: Fresh, half behind Weather: Overcast

3470 RACING UK DAY PASS JUST £10 MAIDEN HURDLE (DIV I) (9 hdls) 1m 7f 124y
12:20 (12:20) (Class 5) 4-Y-O+ £3,249 (£954; £477; £238)

Form				RPR
4-54	1		**Lac Leman (GER)**[21] 3083 5-11-7 116........(t) BrianHughes (Pauline Robson) *pressed ldr: led 4 out: drew clr fr next: easily* **4/1**[2]	120+
-P	2	17	**Archipeligo**[34] 960 5-11-7 0........ HenryBrooke (Iain Jardine) *hld up in midfield: stdy hdwy after 4 out: chsd (clr) wnr after next: kpt on: no imp* **14/1**	102
0-56	3	10	**Rocklim (FR)**[38] 2754 6-11-7 0........ LucyAlexander (James Ewart) *bhd: pushed along 1/2-way: plugged on fr 3 out: nvr able to chal* **66/1**	93
20	4	4 ½	**Chaz Michaels (IRE)**[135] 1328 6-11-7 0........ DerekFox (Lucinda Russell) *hld up: rdn along and outpcd 5th: plugged on fr 2 out: nvr on terms* **12/1**	89
	5	1 ¾	**Strait Of Magellan (IRE)**[79] 4-10-9 0........ BrianHarding (Nicky Richards) *nt fluent: in tch: pushed along and effrt whn j.lft 3 out: wknd fr next* **5/6**[1]	75
	6	6	**Hunters Vision (IRE)**[13] 3208 7-11-7 0........ DGHogan (Denis Gerard Hogan, Ire) *hld up: pushed along and outpcd 1/2-way: nvr on terms* **33/1**	82
5-06	7	11	**Miss Mackie (IRE)**[38] 2752 5-10-9 0........ CallumBewley(5) (R Mike Smith) *nt jump wl in rr: struggling fnl circ: nvr on terms* **100/1**	65
	8	4	**Oregon Gift**[90] 4-10-9 0........ DannyCook (Brian Ellison) *t.k.h early: led to 4 out: lost 2nd after next: wknd fr 2 out* **10/1**	60
133-	9	7	**Crockett**[41] 4168 5-11-7 0........ JamesReveley (Noel Wilson) *prom: blnd 4 out: rdn and wknd fr next: b.b.v* **9/1**[3]	62
6P	10	10	**Imahustler Baby (IRE)**[38] 2754 5-11-0 0........ MrWHRReed(7) (Andrew Hamilton) *hld up in midfield: outpcd after 4 out: wknd bef next* **250/1**	53

3m 45.0s (-3.40) **Going Correction** -0.05s/f (Good)
WFA 4 from 5yo+ 11lb **10 Ran SP% 113.8**
Speed ratings (Par 103): **106,97,92,90,89 86,80,78,75,70**
CSF £52.73 TOTE £4.20: £1.20, £3.40, £10.90; EX 63.10 Trifecta £1027.10.
Owner D&D Armstrong Ltd **Bred** Gestut Auenquelle **Trained** Kirkharle, Northumberland

FOCUS
As advertised the official going was good to soft, soft in places. They went an even gallop in the first division of an ordinary maiden hurdle and they finished well strung out. The winner took another step forward.

3471 RACING UK DAY PASS JUST £10 MAIDEN HURDLE (DIV II) (9 hdls) 1m 7f 124y
12:50 (12:50) (Class 5) 4-Y-O+ £3,249 (£954; £477; £238)

Form				RPR
	1		**My Painter (IRE)**[79] 5-11-0 0........(t[1]) DGHogan (Denis Gerard Hogan, Ire) *t.k.h: prom: smooth hdwy to ld between last 2: rdn and hung rt run-in: hld on wl* **13/2**[3]	101
5	2	nk	**Carthage (IRE)**[20] 3101 5-11-7 0........ DannyCook (Brian Ellison) *hld up in tch: pushed along and outpcd 4 out: rallied 2 out: chsd wnr run-in: kpt on u.p: hld nr fin* **7/2**[2]	108
0/4-	3	3 ½	**Superior Command (IRE)**[599] 300 7-11-7 0........ PeterBuchanan (Lucinda Russell) *hld up in midfield on ins: stdy hdwy after 4 out: effrt and rdn 2 out: kpt on same pce fr last* **9/1**	104
426-	4	2	**Definitely Glad (IRE)**[402] 2783 9-10-7 90........(t) JamesCorbett(7) (Susan Corbett) *mde most to between last 2: drvn and outpcd fr last* **25/1**	95
5-33	5	2	**Leading Score (IRE)**[38] 2754 6-11-7 117........ LucyAlexander (James Ewart) *trckd ldrs: wnt 2nd 4 out: rdn and outpcd bef 2 out: plugged on run-in: no imp* **10/11**[1]	101
0	6	1	**Applejack Lad**[24] 3022 5-11-7 0........(t) HenryBrooke (Michael Smith) *hld up on ins: rdn and hdwy after 4 out: rdn and outpcd fr 2 out* **50/1**	99
5-65	7	7	**Sky Full Of Stars (IRE)**[28] 2945 6-11-7 0........ JakeGreenall (James Ewart) *hld up: drvn and outpcd after 4 out: no imp fr next* **18/1**	92
55	8	¾	**Bearskin (IRE)**[29] 2931 5-11-4 0........ CallumWhillans(3) (Donald Whillans) *hld up: pushed along after 4 out: wknd bef next* **25/1**	91
24/0	9	3 ¾	**Latin Rebel (IRE)**[38] 2754 9-11-2 0........ StephenMulqueen(5) (Jim Goldie) *nt fluent in rr: mstke 4th: struggling 4 out: nvr on terms* **100/1**	88
/FP-	10	38	**Flying Native (IRE)**[254] 7-11-2 0........ JonathonBewley(5) (George Bewley) *chsd ldr to 4 out: rdn and wknd bef next: t.o* **125/1**	50

3m 51.4s (3.00) **Going Correction** -0.05s/f (Good) **10 Ran SP% 114.6**
Speed ratings (Par 103): **90,89,88,87,86 85,82,81,79,60**
CSF £28.58 TOTE £8.80: £2.30, £1.30, £2.60; EX 30.80 Trifecta £152.60.
Owner Premier Racing Club **Bred** Keatly Overseas Ltd **Trained** Cloughjordan, Co Tipperary

FOCUS
The second division of the maiden hurdle was run in a time 6.4secs slower than the first leg. They finished in a bit of a heap off the steady pace.

3472 ALEX DONALDSON HANDSOME H'CAP CHASE (15 fncs 3 omitted) 2m 7f 170y
1:20 (1:20) (Class 4) (0-115,115) 5-Y-O+ £5,198 (£1,526; £763; £381)

Form				RPR
3-P3	1		**Benenden (IRE)**[26] 2973 8-11-12 **115**........ RichieMcLernon (Michael Scudamore) *hld up: mstke 6th: stdy hdwy and cl up whn hit 4 out: sn chsng ldr: drvn whn lft in ld next: drew clr fr 2 out* **5/1**[3]	130+
	2	11	**Eiri Na Casca (IRE)**[8] 3305 7-10-5 **94**........(p) DGHogan (Denis Gerard Hogan, Ire) *nt fluent: hld up: hdwy after 11th: rdn whn lft disputing ld and j.lft 3 out: outpcd fr next* **9/2**[2]	98+
-425	3	17	**Benefit In Kind (IRE)**[28] 2950 8-9-12 **90**........(tp) AdamNicol(3) (Katie Scott) *cl up: rdn 9th: struggling 4 out: no imp whn lft 15 l 3rd 3 out* **11/1**	76
-000	4	4	**Resolute Reformer (IRE)**[37] 2788 7-10-5 **101**........ SamColtherd(7) (Stuart Coltherd) *hld up in tch: blnd 5th: pushed along and hdwy 1/2-way: outpcd 11th: btn whn lft modest 4th 3 out* **16/1**	82
2540	U		**Solway Bay**[38] 2751 14-9-11 **91**........(t) CallumBewley(5) (Lisa Harrison) *hld up in midfield: outpcd 1/2-way: struggling whn uns rdr 10th* **33/1**	

311/ **F** **Mr Supreme (IRE)**[622] 5481 11-11-9 **112**.......................... JamesReveley
(Keith Reveley) *cl up: led 5th: jst in front and pushed along whn fell 3 out: fatally injured* **12/1**

3P0/ **P** **Tears From Heaven (USA)**[628] 5358 10-9-9 **89** oh10(p) DiarmuidO'Regan[(5)]
(Chris Grant) *in tch: reminders after 8th: outpcd next: wknd and p.u 3 out* **100/1**

0/3 **F** **Art Lord (IRE)**[21] 3096 10-11-0 **106**.............................(t) GrahamWatters[(3)]
(Karl Thornton, Ire) *prom: disputing 2nd pl whn fell 9th* **6/1**

0435 **P** **Ballyben (IRE)**[24] 3024 8-11-12 **115**...................................(p) BrianHughes
(Lucinda Russell) *led to 5th: chsd ldr to 4 out: wknd bef next: p.u 3 out: b.b.v* **4/1**[1]

-431 **P** **Itstimeforapint (IRE)**[28] 2950 8-11-7 **110**................................ DerekFox
(Lucinda Russell) *nt fluent: sn towards rr: lost tch fnl circ: p.u after 4 out* **4/1**[1]

6m 1.8s (-1.60) **Going Correction** +0.075s/f (Yiel) **10** Ran SP% **115.0**
Speed ratings: **105,101,95,94, , , , ,**
CSF £28.14 CT £235.77 TOTE £5.90: £2.00, £2.10, £2.20; EX 31.00 Trifecta £320.10.
Owner Mark Blandford **Bred** J Hennessy **Trained** Bromsash, H'fords

FOCUS
A fair and competitive-looking handicap, but the four that finished came home at big intervals. The winner is on the upgrade with probably more to come. Actual race distance was 2m 7f 80yds.

3473 RACING UK PROFITS RETURNED TO RACING H'CAP HURDLE (9 hdls) 1m 7f 124y

1:50 (1:50) (Class 4) (0-105,105) 4-Y-0+ £3,249 (£954; £477; £238)

Form RPR

550- **1** **Shrewd**[24] 826 6-11-5 **105**.. RyanDay[(7)] 124+
(Iain Jardine) *hld up on ins: hdwy bef 3 out: shkn up to ld next: qcknd clr fr last: readily* **85/40**[1]

4F-1 **2** *6* **Moonlone Lane (IRE)**[9] 3260 9-11-3 **103**...............(p) JonathanMoore[(7)] 112+
(Paul Stafford, Ire) *prom: led after 4 out: rdn and hdd 2 out: plugged on: no ch w ready wnr* **6/1**[3]

446 **3** *10* **Quill Art**[32] 2863 4-10-8 **99**.. BrianHughes 87
(Richard Fahey) *prom: drvn and outpcd bef 3 out: plugged on fr last: no ch w first two* **9/1**

35-4 **4** *hd* **Marcus Antonius**[23] 3035 9-11-11 **104**.............................. DerekFox 102
(Lucinda Russell) *in tch: rdn along bef 3 out: hung rt and outpcd fr next* **15/2**

5UP2 **5** *¾* **Mister Hendre**[16] 3161 8-9-7 **79** oh1..................(t) JamesCorbett[(7)] 76
(Susan Corbett) *t.k.h: hld up on outside: hdwy bef 3 out: hung rt and wknd fr next* **22/1**

6- **6** *5* **Mystic Princess (IRE)**[9] 3264 5-11-4 **104**................... StevenFox[(7)] 96
(Mark Michael McNiff, Ire) *t.k.h early: prom: drvn and outpcd bef 3 out: btn next* **28/1**

0P05 **7** *3* **Rioja Day (IRE)**[28] 2946 6-11-1 **94**................................ DannyCook 84
(Jim Goldie) *bhd: outpcd after 3rd: rdn and hdwy bef 3 out: sn n.d* **25/1**

3041 **8** *4* **Neworld (FR)**[15] 3177 7-11-10 **103**................................ AlainCawley 90
(Richard Hobson) *hld up: hdwy on outside to chse ldr whn hit 3 out: rdn and wknd next* **11/2**[2]

60-1 **9** *2 ¼* **Ellistrin Belle**[55] 2427 8-10-12 **94**.....................(t) CallumWhillans[(3)] 77
(Donald Whillans) *t.k.h early: hld up: rdn after 4 out: wknd after next* **12/1**

540 **10** *7* **Morning Time (IRE)**[38] 2755 10-10-8 **92**...........(tp) GrantCockburn[(5)] 70
(Lucinda Russell) *hld up: drvn and outpcd bef 3 out: sn btn* **28/1**

P- **11** *16* **Bolero Collonges (FR)**[309] 5-11-5 **103**......................... CallumBewley[(5)] 63
(Simon Waugh) *w ldr: rdn after 4 out: wknd fr next* **50/1**

0/ **12** *10* **Vinniespride (IRE)**[61] 2284 9-11-12 **105**....................(t) RichieMcLernon 55
(Mark Michael McNiff, Ire) *led to after 4 out: rdn and wknd qckly bef next* **50/1**

5/P4 **13** *13* **Makbullet**[28] 2949 9-11-12 **105**.................................... HenryBrooke 42
(Michael Smith) *chsd ldrs: lost pl 1/2-way: sn struggling: btn and eased fnl 3* **8/1**

3m 45.2s (-3.20) **Going Correction** -0.05s/f (Good)
WFA 4 from 5yo+ 11lb **13** Ran SP% **121.3**
Speed ratings (Par 105): **106,103,98,97,97 95,93,91,90,86 78,73,67**
CSF £14.41 CT £97.93 TOTE £2.40: £1.20, £2.40, £3.20; EX 16.80 Trifecta £205.00.
Owner Tapas Partnership **Bred** Darley **Trained** Carrutherstown, D'fries & G'way

FOCUS
A well-contested handicap for the grade but the winner, who was putting up a big personal-best over hurdles, proved far too good.

3474 RACINGUK.COM/ANYWHERE H'CAP HURDLE (14 hdls) 2m 7f 180y

2:25 (2:25) (Class 4) (0-105,104) 4-Y-0+ £3,249 (£954; £477; £238)

Form RPR

-300 **1** **Simarthur**[36] 2806 9-11-4 **96**.............................(v) PeterBuchanan 105+
(Lucinda Russell) *cl up: led after 4 out: rdn clr 2 out: unchal* **14/1**

P-24 **2** *6* **Bracing**[38] 2751 7-10-3 **88**.. MrKitAlexander[(7)] 89
(N W Alexander) *midfield on ins: drvn and outpcd bef 3 out: rallied and chsd (clr) wnr last: kpt on: no imp* **15/2**

0323 **3** *nk* **Solway Sam**[28] 2948 13-11-1 **98**................................ CallumBewley[(5)] 100
(Lisa Harrison) *hld up in midfield: stdy hdwy bef 3 out: rdn next: kpt on fr last* **12/1**

4 *nk* **Easy To Find (IRE)**[13] 3212 6-11-2 **94**......................(tp) DGHogan 96
(Denis Gerard Hogan, Ire) *hld up: stdy hdwy after 4 out: rdn and outpcd after next: rallied last: kpt on: no imp* **4/1**[1]

4246 **5** *2 ¼* **Shaiyzar (IRE)**[48] 2560 7-11-5 **100**............................(p) AdamNicol[(3)] 99
(David Thompson) *hld up: outpcd 1/2-way: rallied bef 3 out: kpt on fr next: nvr able to chal* **16/1**

1131 **6** *2* **Touch Of Steel (IRE)**[38] 2751 7-11-8 **100**..................(b) LucyAlexander 100
(James Ewart) *led to after 4 out: chsd wnr: drvn bef next: edgd lft and wknd after last* **11/2**[2]

P-PU **7** *8* **Notonebuttwo (IRE)**[28] 2950 9-10-7 **85**........................(tp) BrianHughes 76
(Chris Grant) *trckd ldrs tl drvn and outpcd after 3 out: wknd fr next* **18/1**

6-0P **8** *4* **Tomahawk Wood**[29] 2937 7-10-6 **87**.............................. CallumWhillans[(3)] 73
(Donald Whillans) *nt fluent on occasions: hld up: hdwy and prom bef 3 out: rdn whn mstke next: sn btn* **18/1**

-600 **9** *nk* **Ethan (IRE)**[37] 2791 7-11-0 **97**................................ MissCWalton[(5)] 85
(Sheena Walton) *hld up: rdn bef 4 out: nvr on terms* **66/1**

-356 **10** *7* **John Williams (IRE)**[36] 2804 7-11-3 **102**.................... StevenFox[(7)] 82
(Sandy Thomson) *prom: drvn after 4 out: wknd fr next* **20/1**

-405 **11** *8* **Crinkle Crags (IRE)**[44] 2649 6-10-13 **98**........................ RyanDay[(7)] 70
(Nicky Richards) *hld up in midfield on ins: lost pl and outpcd whn mstke 9th: sn struggling: n.d after* **4/1**[1]

CP4- **12** *1 ¼* **Simply Lucky (IRE)**[303] 4616 7-9-7 **78** oh9..................... MrWHRReed[(7)] 49
(W T Reed) *hld up: rdn along after 9th: struggling fr 4 out* **100/1**

5640 **13** *2 ¼* **Beer Goggles (IRE)**[33] 2843 5-11-12 **104**........................ CraigNichol 73
(Micky Hammond) *cl up: lost grnd 1/2-way: drvn and struggling fr 4 out* **7/1**[3]

-345 **14** *1* **Better B Quick (IRE)**[28] 2947 10-11-3 **102**...............(p) JonathanMoore[(7)] 70
(Paul Stafford, Ire) *hld up: stdy hdwy after 4 out: rdn and hung rt next: sn wknd* **33/1**

5m 58.6s (16.50) **Going Correction** -0.05s/f (Good) **14** Ran SP% **120.6**
Speed ratings (Par 105): **70,68,67,67,67 66,63,62,62,59 57,56,56,55**
CSF £113.67 CT £1318.31 TOTE £13.20: £3.50, £2.60, £3.30; EX 149.40 Trifecta £1298.80.
Owner Dig In Racing **Bred** Simon Tindall **Trained** Arlary, Perth & Kinross
■ Stewards' Enquiry : D G Hogan two-day ban; used his whip above the permitted level and without giving his mount time to respond (20th-21st Jan)

FOCUS
A modest handicap and not many got in it. The winner has been rated 117 over hurdles at his best.

3475 KILMANY CUP (A H'CAP CHASE) (10 fncs 2 omitted) 1m 7f 182y

3:00 (3:00) (Class 3) (0-130,127) 5-Y-0+ £7,797 (£2,289; £1,144; £572)

Form RPR

5644 **1** **Chestnut Ben (IRE)**[9] 3237 11-10-6 **114**........................ MrRWinks[(7)] 119
(Peter Winks) *hld up in tch: stdy hdwy after 4 out: chsd ldr and j.lft fr next: led run-in: styd on wl* **14/1**

1-P5 **2** *½* **Aye Well**[40] 2719 11-11-8 **123**...................................... JamesReveley 128
(Stuart Coltherd) *j.w: led at ordinary gallop: qcknd bef 3 out: hdd run-in: rallied: hld nr fin* **6/1**

-644 **3** *hd* **Lightening Rod**[19] 3107 11-11-7 **125**........................ HarryBannister[(3)] 130
(Michael Easterby) *hld up: blkd 6th: effrt on outside 3 out: rdn bef next: kpt on u.p fr last* **13/2**

P0OP **4** *2 ¾* **Formidableopponent (IRE)**[6] 3343 9-10-7 **108**................ DerekFox 110
(William Young Jnr) *chsd ldr to 4 out: drvn and outpcd next: rallied 2 out: kpt on same pce fr last* **40/1**

5334 **5** *10* **Vodka Wells (FR)**[16] 3155 6-11-2 **124**........................ FinianO'Toole[(7)] 120
(Micky Hammond) *nt fluent: hld up in tch: effrt whn hit and outpcd 3 out: struggling fr next* **10/3**[1]

/210 **6** *1 ½* **Blades Lad**[17] 3134 7-10-13 **114**...............................(p) BrianHughes 108
(Peter Niven) *t.k.h early: cl up: chsng ldr whn hit and pckd 4 out: outpcd after next: wkng whn nt fluent last* **9/2**[3]

-210 **7** *19* **Jack Steel (IRE)**[37] 2774 6-11-12 **127**........................ RichieMcLernon 107
(Lucinda Russell) *hld up: outpcd whn mstke 6th: bmpd and sprawled next: lost tch after 4 out* **7/2**[2]

04F6 **P** **Rockawango (FR)**[23] 3035 10-11-5 **120**.........................(tp) LucyAlexander
(James Ewart) *bhd: struggling fnl circ: t.o whn p.u bef 3 out* **17/2**

3m 57.2s (4.80) **Going Correction** +0.075s/f (Yiel) **8** Ran SP% **110.7**
Speed ratings: **91,90,90,89,84 83,74,**
CSF £88.57 CT £578.60 TOTE £15.30: £3.50, £2.00, £1.90; EX 97.70 Trifecta £644.50.
Owner P Winks **Bred** Sean Deu Burca **Trained** Little Houghton, S Yorks

FOCUS
A competitive handicap chase, albeit not the strongest for the grade. The winner had slipped to a good mark and is rated 5lb off his best. Actual race distance was 1m 7f 142yds.

3476 WATCH RACING UK ON 3 DEVICES STANDARD OPEN NATIONAL HUNT FLAT RACE 1m 7f 124y

3:30 (3:30) (Class 6) 4-6-Y-O £1,949 (£572; £286; £143)

Form RPR

5 **1** **Sammy B**[38] 2756 6-11-5 0.. PeterBuchanan 106+
(Lucinda Russell) *hld up: smooth hdwy 4f out: led over 1f out: shkn up and drew clr: readily* **10/1**

2 *8* **Fenlon's Hill (IRE)**[247] 5-10-12 0.............................. JonathanMoore[(7)] 97
(Paul Stafford, Ire) *prom: hdwy to ld over 3f out: hdd over 1f out: no ch w wnr* **25/1**

3 *2 ¼* **Misfits (IRE)**[92] 5-10-9 0.. RossChapman[(10)] 95
(Lucinda Russell) *hld up: pushed along and hdwy 4f out: styd on fr 2f out: nt pce to chal* **12/1**

00- **4** *8* **Derrydoon**[420] 2405 6-11-5 0...................................... RichieMcLernon 88
(Karen McLintock) *hld up in midfield on outside: pushed along and hdwy over 3f out: edgd rt and no imp fr 2f out* **66/1**

5 *2 ½* **General Mahler (IRE)**[71] 6-11-5 0................................ DannyCook 86
(Brian Ellison) *slt ld to over 3f out: rdn and wknd fr 2f out* **15/8**[1]

6 *2 ½* **Sam Fairyann** 5-11-5 0.. BrianHughes 84
(Peter Niven) *hld up: stdy hdwy 4f out: rdn and wknd fr 2f out* **9/2**[3]

0- **7** *2 ¼* **Vic's Last Stand (IRE)**[345] 3861 6-10-12 0........................ JamesReveley 74
(Keith Reveley) *hld up on ins: rdn along 5f out: outpcd over 3f out: n.d after* **14/1**

22 **8** *4 ½* **Black Ink**[38] 2756 5-11-5 0...................................... HenryBrooke 77
(Michael Smith) *w ldr to 1/2-way: cl up tl outpcd over 3f out: btn fnl 2f* **5/2**[2]

9 *7* **Silver Trix (IRE)** 6-10-7 0.. JonathonBewley[(5)] 64
(George Bewley) *w ldr tl rdn and wknd over 3f out* **33/1**

0 **10** *1 ¾* **Fairlee Grace**[40] 2721 5-10-12 0.................................. JanFaltejsek 63
(George Charlton) *in tch to 1/2-way: drvn and wknd over 4f out* **20/1**

5 **11** *13* **Overawed**[58] 2344 5-10-5 0.. SamColtherd[(7)] 51
(Stuart Coltherd) *hld up in midfield: drvn and outpcd over 5f out: sn btn* **80/1**

0-6 **12** *99* **Dream Place**[237] 257 5-10-5 0.................................... LorcanMurtagh[(7)]
(Barry Murtagh) *bhd: lost tch fr 1/2-way: virtually p.u fnl 3f* **250/1**

3m 41.2s (-1.60) **Going Correction** -0.05s/f (Good) **12** Ran SP% **119.7**
Speed ratings: **102,98,96,92,91 90,89,87,83,82 76,26**
CSF £237.97 TOTE £10.90: £2.70, £3.90, £4.10; EX 110.90 Trifecta £840.50.
Owner G S Brown **Bred** G Brown **Trained** Arlary, Perth & Kinross

FOCUS
Little depth to this maiden and another facile winner on the card.
T/Plt: £533.90 to a £1 stake. Pool: £63,280.22 - 86.52 winning units. T/Qpdt: £79.80 to a £1 stake. Pool: £9,420.59 - 87.35 winning units. **Richard Young**

3006 BANGOR-ON-DEE (L-H)

Tuesday, January 5

3477 Meeting Abandoned - waterlogged

3220 HUNTINGDON (R-H)

Wednesday, January 6

OFFICIAL GOING: Soft (heavy in places; chs 5.8, hdl 6.2)

Wind: Light across Weather: Overcast

3483 RACINGUK.COM/WINTERSEASONTICKET MAIDEN HURDLE (DIV I) (8 hdls) 1m 7f 171y

12:40 (12:40) (Class 5) 5-Y-O+ £2,274 (£667; £333; £166)

Form RPR

122 1 **Potters Legend**[21] 3114 6-11-2 0 LeightonAspell 122+
(Lucy Wadham) *chsd ldr after 1st tl led appr 4th: shkn up flat: styd on: comf* **2/13**[1]

-404 2 2 ¾ **Muthabir (IRE)**[40] 2748 6-11-2 0 IanPopham 116+
(Richard Phillips) *a.p: chsd wnr 2 out: rdn appr last: styd on same pce flat* **16/1**

-4P3 3 17 **Trespassers Will (IRE)**[23] 3085 5-11-2 0 (t) PaddyBrennan 101
(Fergal O'Brien) *prom: chsd wnr 3 out tl rdn next: wkng whn nt fluent last* **16/1**

5 4 7 **Mixchievous**[49] 2563 5-11-2 0 AidanColeman 93
(Venetia Williams) *hld up: hdwy after 5th: rdn and wknd 2 out* **10/1**[3]

4455 5 8 **Zara Hope (IRE)**[24] 3066 5-10-9 0 RichieMcLernon 77
(Charlie Longsdon) *led: nt fluent 3rd: hdd bef next: chsd wnr to 3 out: rdn and wknd sn after* **66/1**

3000 6 ½ **Still Together (IRE)**[5] 3411 6-10-13 0 BrianToomey(3) 84
(David Pipe) *hld up: hdwy 5th: rdn and wknd after 3 out* **100/1**

21-4 7 ½ **Nutcracker Prince**[77] 2024 5-11-2 0 (t) PeterCarberry 83
(Shaun Lycett) *hld up: rdn and wknd appr 3 out* **12/1**

4F 8 2 ¾ **Antiphony (IRE)**[33] 2879 5-11-2 0[1] RichardJohnson 81
(Philip Hobbs) *hld up: plld hrd: hdwy 5th: wknd after 3 out* **9/1**[2]

500 9 2 **Brown Bear (IRE)**[21] 3114 5-11-2 0 BarryGeraghty 78
(Nick Gifford) *prom tl wknd 3 out* **25/1**

05-5 10 3 **Gabriel Oats**[50] 2562 7-11-2 0 KielanWoods 75
(Graeme McPherson) *hld up: hdwy appr 3 out: sn wknd* **66/1**

P 11 2 **Kent Ragstone (USA)**[16] 3194 7-10-11 0 FreddieMitchell(5) 76
(Sheena West) *hld up: racd keenly: bhd fr 4th: blnd 2 out* **150/1**

3-3P P **Anti Cool (IRE)**[218] 590 7-10-11 0 ChrisWard(5)
(Robin Dickin) *chsd ldr tl after 1st: remained handy tl rdn and wknd after 5th: bhd whn p.u bef next* **100/1**

4m 7.3s (12.40) **Going Correction** +0.80s/f (Soft) 12 Ran SP% 134.7
Speed ratings: **101,99,91,87,83 83,83,81,80,79 78,**
CSF £7.30 TOTE £1.10: £1.10, £3.80, £2.80; EX 9.10 Trifecta £63.90.
Owner Mrs J May **Bred** F S And Mrs May **Trained** Newmarket, Suffolk

FOCUS
The going was soft, heavy in places. A maiden hurdle that was weakened by two withdrawals. The clear form pick had to knuckle down in the closing stages, but he managed to cash in on this golden opportunity. He didn't need to run to his mark.

3484 RACINGUK.COM/WINTERSEASONTICKET MAIDEN HURDLE (DIV II) (8 hdls) 1m 7f 171y

1:10 (1:10) (Class 5) 5-Y-O+ £2,274 (£667; £333; £166)

Form RPR

P56 1 **Allee Bleue (IRE)**[21] 3114 6-11-2 0 RichardJohnson 127+
(Philip Hobbs) *mde all: mstke 2 out: clr last: comf* **4/1**[2]

2 12 **Travertine (IRE)**[144] 6-11-2 0 BarryGeraghty 109
(Alan King) *hld up in tch: chsd wnr 2 out: sn rdn: styd on same pce appr last* **8/11**[1]

14/0 3 nk **Starving Marvin**[34] 2860 8-11-2 0 JamesDavies 110
(Rod Millman) *chsd wnr to 2 out: styd on same pce appr last* **33/1**

060 4 14 **The Artful Cobbler**[33] 2879 5-11-2 0 JakeGreenall 95
(Henry Daly) *prom: rdn after 5th: wknd appr 3 out* **100/1**

3-0 5 6 **Bibi D'Eole (FR)**[36] 2840 5-11-2 0 KielanWoods 89
(Graeme McPherson) *hld up: hdwy 5th: rdn and wkng whn blnd 2 out* **16/1**

0-00 6 2 ¼ **What A Tempest**[26] 3022 6-10-9 0[1] IanPopham 80
(Richard Phillips) *hld up: nvr nrr* **150/1**

500 7 ½ **Iniciar (GER)**[5] 3411 6-11-2 0 TomScudamore 86
(David Pipe) *hld up: nt fluent 2nd: rdn after 5th: wknd bef next* **20/1**

8 hd **Guantoshol (IRE)**[68] 5-11-2 0 AidanColeman 86
(Venetia Williams) *hld up: sme hdwy appr 3 out: wknd bef next* **25/1**

5 9 16 **Fire Ship**[21] 3114 7-11-2 0 BrendanPowell 70
(Brendan Powell) *hld up: rdn after 5th: sn wknd* **7/1**[3]

-0B0 10 22 **Same Ole Trix (IRE)**[26] 3021 6-11-2 0 (t) DavidBass 48
(Kim Bailey) *hld up: bhd fr 4th* **100/1**

0-6P 11 2 ¼ **Dounya's Boy**[77] 2024 7-11-2 0 DaveCrosse 46
(Christopher Kellett) *hld up: bhd fr 4th* **200/1**

12 8 **Give Him Time**[247] 5-11-2 0 LeightonAspell 38
(Nick Gifford) *chsd ldrs: j.rt at times: wknd after 3 out* **10/1**

0P 13 4 **Art Libre (FR)**[227] 447 5-11-2 0 (t) JamieMoore 34
(Gary Moore) *hld up: plld hrd: bhd fr 4th* **100/1**

0U0 14 1 ½ **Sarpech (IRE)**[37] 2823 5-11-2 0 TomO'Brien 32
(Charlie Longsdon) *plld hrd and prom: rdn and wknd appr 3 out* **100/1**

4m 5.1s (10.20) **Going Correction** +0.80s/f (Soft) 14 Ran SP% 122.0
Speed ratings: **106,100,99,92,89 88,88,88,80,69 68,64,62,61**
CSF £7.37 TOTE £4.90: £1.80, £1.10, £6.40; EX 8.00 Trifecta £123.00.
Owner Andrew L Cohen **Bred** Wood Hall Stud **Trained** Withycombe, Somerset

FOCUS
The second division of this maiden hurdle. They went a good pace, but only a few runners got involved and the winner, who was value for further, dominated under a front-running ride.

3485 TURFTV MARES' NOVICES' HURDLE (10 hdls) 2m 4f 145y

1:40 (1:42) (Class 4) 4-Y-O+ £3,249 (£954; £477; £238)

Form RPR

2-F1 1 **Clemency**[81] 1960 5-11-7 0 AndrewTinkler 111+
(Nicky Henderson) *led at stdy pce tl qcknd bef 6th: hdd appr 2 out: rdn to ld again after 2 out: styd on wl: comf* **7/4**[2]

U013 2 2 ¾ **Alizee Javilex (FR)**[31] 2929 6-11-0 0 LeightonAspell 101+
(Lucy Wadham) *trckd ldrs: nt fluent 5th: chsd wnr next: rdn to ld appr 2 out: pckd and hdd after 2 out: mstke last: styd on same pce flat* **10/11**[1]

4606 3 2 ¼ **The Barbury Queen (IRE)**[29] 2952 6-11-0 0 WayneHutchinson 97+
(Alan King) *prom: mstke 2nd: outpcd 7th: styd on flat* **16/1**

6 4 5 **Ballybrowneybridge (IRE)**[35] 2856 6-11-0 0 RichardJohnson 92
(Sam Thomas) *chsd wnr to 6th: remained handy tl rdn after 3 out: styd on same pce* **6/1**[3]

5m 43.3s (32.70) **Going Correction** +0.80s/f (Soft) 4 Ran SP% 108.9
Speed ratings (Par 105): **69,67,67,65**
CSF £3.90 TOTE £2.60; EX 4.90 Trifecta £11.80.
Owner Elite Racing Club **Bred** Elite Racing Club **Trained** Upper Lambourn, Berks

FOCUS
Not many runners, but this was still an interesting mares' novice event. The pace was steady, but the winner scored under a penalty in gritty style.

3486 RACING UK PROFITS RETURNED TO RACING NOVICES' CHASE (19 fncs) 2m 7f 129y

2:10 (2:11) (Class 4) 5-Y-O+ £3,833 (£1,125; £562; £281)

Form RPR

1 **Drumacoo (IRE)**[412] 2627 7-11-0 0[1] NicodeBoinville 155+
(Ben Pauling) *trckd ldr: nt fluent 11th: led 15th: clr appr 2 out: easily* **12/1**[3]

-P23 2 38 **Fletchers Flyer (IRE)**[26] 3013 8-11-0 140 (t) NoelFehily 120
(Harry Fry) *led: j.lft: nt fluent 11th: hdd 15th: wknd appr 2 out* **1/1**[1]

4/12 3 23 **Bonnet's Vino**[17] 3174 8-10-7 0 SamTwiston-Davies 88
(Pam Sly) *hld up: wnt 3rd at 3rd: rdn and wknd after 14th* **66/1**

1-6 4 33 **Ocean Venture (IRE)**[32] 2906 8-11-0 0 KielanWoods 82
(Graeme McPherson) *chsd ldrs: lost pl 3rd: wknd 13th* **100/1**

25-F F **Value At Risk**[41] 2726 7-11-0 0 HarrySkelton
(Dan Skelton) *hld up: slipped into the 2nd and fell* **11/10**[2]

6m 28.6s (18.30) **Going Correction** +1.10s/f (Heav) 5 Ran SP% 107.8
Speed ratings: **113,100,92,81,**
CSF £24.98 TOTE £9.00: £3.10, £1.10; EX 20.50 Trifecta £50.00.
Owner Mrs Robin Birley **Bred** Michael Moakley **Trained** Bourton-On-The-Water, Gloucs

FOCUS
The favourite didn't fire in this useful novice event and the other market leader fell early on, but the winner was impressive on his comeback and this rates as a big step up.

3487 REWARDS4RACING.COM H'CAP HURDLE (QUALIFIER FOR THE CHALLENGER TWO MILE HURDLE SERIES FINAL) (8 hdls) 1m 7f 171y

2:40 (2:41) (Class 3) (0-125,125) 4-Y-O+ £5,393 (£1,583; £791; £395)

Form RPR

0/63 1 **Kings Bayonet**[31] 2926 9-11-4 117 WayneHutchinson 128+
(Alan King) *hld up: hdwy after 5th: led appr and j.rt last: rdn out* **14/1**

211 2 1 ¼ **Tara Flow**[9] 3318 6-11-8 121 7ex AidanColeman 131+
(Venetia Williams) *a.p: led bef 2 out: hdd appr last: carried rt flat: no ex towards fin* **1/1**[1]

F0 3 8 **King Muro**[26] 3015 6-10-12 111 (t) PaddyBrennan 112
(Fergal O'Brien) *hld up: hdwy appr 3 out: rdn after next: wknd flat* **16/1**

13 4 5 **Iftiraaq (IRE)**[34] 2860 5-11-11 124 (p) ConorO'Farrell 121
(Seamus Durack) *trckd ldrs: rdn after 3 out: wknd appr last* **16/1**

52-P 5 1 ½ **Rude And Crude (IRE)**[21] 3117 7-11-1 114 TomCannon 110
(Chris Gordon) *led tl after 3rd: led again 5th: rdn and hdd appr 2 out: wknd bef last* **10/1**[3]

0-12 6 ½ **Qasser (IRE)**[25] 3035 7-11-12 125 GavinSheehan 119
(Harry Whittington) *chsd ldrs: rdn after 3 out: wknd appr last* **7/1**[2]

2640 7 ½ **Fields Of Glory (FR)**[71] 2123 6-9-13 103 AlanJohns(5) 98
(Tim Vaughan) *hld up: hdwy 5th: rdn and wknd appr last* **33/1**

0424 8 ½ **Crookstown (IRE)**[25] 3045 9-11-9 122 KielanWoods 116
(Ben Case) *prom: mstke 2nd: rdn appr 2 out: wkng whn mstke last* **16/1**

P02- 9 ½ **Steel City**[300] 4731 8-11-10 123 (p) RyanMahon 116
(Seamus Mullins) *chsd ldr tl led after 3rd: hdd 5th: rdn after 3 out: wknd bef last* **25/1**

211- 10 nk **Apterix (FR)**[159] 5158 6-11-8 121 DannyCook 113
(Brian Ellison) *hld up: hdwy 3 out: rdn and wknd appr last* **12/1**

115B 11 ¾ **Midnight Shot**[54] 2472 6-11-12 125 RichardJohnson 116
(Charlie Longsdon) *hld up in tch: rdn and swtchd lft after 3 out: mstke next: sn wknd* **12/1**

263F 12 2 **Newton Geronimo**[65] 2246 7-10-13 112 NicodeBoinville 101
(Ben Pauling) *hld up: plld hrd: effrt after 3 out: sn wknd* **20/1**

6-0P 13 ½ **Landscape (FR)**[16] 3196 8-10-6 105 MattieBatchelor 94
(Sheena West) *hld up: bhd fr 4th* **100/1**

24P0 14 11 **Full Blast (FR)**[27] 2989 5-10-11 110 (t) MarcGoldstein 88
(Chris Gordon) *hld up: rdn and wknd after 5th* **66/1**

2100 15 ½ **Watt Broderick (IRE)**[18] 3152 7-11-0 116 (tp) RobMcCarth(3) 93
(Ian Williams) *hld up: rdn after 5th: wknd bef next* **100/1**

3/-4 16 4 ½ **Unex Modigliani (IRE)**[51] 2543 7-10-11 110 (t) JamesDavies 85
(Derek Shaw) *hld up: hit 5th: sn rdn and wknd* **33/1**

116/ P **Herod The Great**[781] 2500 6-11-2 120 DanielHiskett(5)
(Richard Phillips) *prom tl rdn and wknd after 5th: bhd whn p.u bef 2 out* **33/1**

4m 4.9s (10.00) **Going Correction** +0.80s/f (Soft) 17 Ran SP% 132.2
Speed ratings (Par 107): **107,106,102,99,99 98,98,98,98,97 97,96,96,90,90 88,**
CSF £29.66 CT £274.75 TOTE £15.20: £2.70, £1.10, £3.90, £4.70; EX 39.60 Trifecta £746.30.
Owner W H Ponsonby **Bred** Mickley Stud & C J Whiston **Trained** Barbury Castle, Wilts

FOCUS
The hot favourite couldn't quite defy a penalty in this big-field handicap, but the first two finished clear and the form looks solid. The winner is entitled to rate a lot higher on Flat form.

3488 RACINGUK.COM/ANYWHERE H'CAP CHASE (19 fncs) 2m 7f 129y

3:10 (3:11) (Class 5) (0-100,92) 5-Y-O+ £2,469 (£725; £362; £181)

Form RPR

-052 1 **Tanner Hill (IRE)**[17] 3178 8-11-1 81 (b[1]) MarkQuinlan 94+
(James Evans) *hld up: hmpd bnd after 12th: hdwy next: chsd ldr 14th: rdn to ld appr 2 out: clr whn wnt lft last* **85/40**[2]

4P-P 2 13 **Triggers Ginger**[27] 2997 11-11-3 88 CiaranGethings(5) 88
(Paul Cowley) *prom: led 12th: rdn and hdd appr 2 out: wknd bef last* **50/1**

P411 3 35 **Xenophon**[11] 3222 8-11-4 91 ThomasCheesman(7) 59
(Olly Williams) *chsd ldrs: rdn after 12th: pckd next: mstke and wknd 14th* **15/8**[1]

30-P 4 4 ½ **Dixie Bull (IRE)**[24] 3062 11-11-8 88 (p) JamesDavies 49
(Tom Symonds) *chsd ldr tl rdn and nt fluent 14th: wknd after next: bhd whn j.lft 3 out* **9/2**

5P35 5 16 **Silver Dragon**[24] 3067 8-11-12 92 (tp) DenisO'Regan 37
(Tony Coyle) *led: drvn along at various stages: hdd 12th: wknd after next* **4/1**[3]

6m 41.9s (31.60) **Going Correction** +1.10s/f (Heav) 5 Ran SP% 106.9
Speed ratings: **91,86,75,73,68**
CSF £37.41 TOTE £2.40: £1.30, £11.50; EX 54.80 Trifecta £186.40.
Owner PWrightBevans SMatner PSmith & APidgeon **Bred** Patrick John Devereux **Trained** Broadwas, Worcs

FOCUS
They finished well strung out in this minor staying handicap. Probably a step up from the winner.

3489 RACING UK DAY PASS JUST £10 NOVICES' H'CAP HURDLE (12 hdls) 3m 1f 10y
3:40 (3:41) (Class 5) (0-100,100) 4-Y-0+ **£2,274** (£667; £333; £166)

Form RPR
0-62 **1** **Dandy Duke (IRE)**[29] 2964 5-11-12 **100** PaddyBrennan 111+
(Tom George) *chsd ldrs: led 3 out: clr whn j.rt next: styd on wl* **11/4**[1]
00-4 **2** *11* **Glendermot (IRE)**[24] 3067 7-11-6 **94** [1] AdamWedge 93
(Paul Cowley) *prom: chsd wnr after 3 out: sn rdn: styd on same pce fr next* **11/2**
63P2 **3** *½* **Ballochmyle (IRE)**[20] 3128 6-10-11 **85** (t) JackQuinlan 84
(Caroline Fryer) *chsd ldrs: mstke 4th: rdn after 9th: styd on same pce fr 2 out* **3/1**[2]
-P60 **4** *10* **El Indio (IRE)**[11] 3220 9-10-2 **79** (vt) ConorShoemark(3) 67
(Claire Dyson) *w ldr tl rdn appr 3 out: sn wknd* **7/1**
6-P3 **5** *1 ¾* **Kavanaghs Corner (IRE)**[20] 3128 7-10-10 **89** KevinJones(5) 75
(Simon Earle) *hld up: hdwy 9th: rdn after 3 out: wknd after next* **4/1**[3]
-600 **P** **Kingscombe (USA)**[17] 3177 7-10-0 **74** oh5 (t) MarcGoldstein
(Linda Jewell) *hld up: rdn and wknd 8th: bhd whn p.u bef 2 out* **33/1**
53F **P** **Element Quartet (IRE)**[23] 3087 7-10-0 **74** oh5 (t) BrendanPowell
(Brendan Powell) *led: rdn and hdd 3 out: sn wknd: bhd whn p.u bef last* **12/1**

6m 58.4s (35.50) **Going Correction** +0.80s/f (Soft) **7** Ran **SP% 110.2**
Speed ratings (Par 103): **75,71,71,68,67 ,**
CSF £16.84 CT £43.51 TOTE £3.50: £1.50, £2.70; EX 15.10 Trifecta £37.00.
Owner Dermot O'Donohoe & Sharon C Nelson **Bred** Abergwaun Farms **Trained** Slad, Gloucs

FOCUS
Six maidens lined up in this ordinary handicap, but it was won in emphatic style but an unexposed 5yo who is on the upgrade.
T/Plt: £23.70 to a £1 stake. Pool: £52,098.51 - 1,601.69 winning units. T/Qpdt: £17.30 to a £1 stake. Pool: £4,206.07 - 179.20 winning units. **Colin Roberts**

3159 NEWCASTLE (L-H)
Thursday, January 7
3490 Meeting Abandoned - waterlogged

3126 TOWCESTER (R-H)
Thursday, January 7

OFFICIAL GOING: Heavy
Wind: Strong across Weather: Sunshine and showers

3497 HAYGAIN HAY STEAMERS CLEAN HEALTHY FORAGE H'CAP CHASE (11 fncs) 2m 70y
1:05 (1:05) (Class 5) (0-100,98) 5-Y-0+ **£3,249** (£954; £477; £238)

Form RPR
-1FP **1** **Mr Bachster (IRE)**[36] 2855 11-11-3 **89** (p) JamieMoore 103+
(Kerry Lee) *chsd ldr tl led 4th: rdn out* **12/1**
2PP1 **2** *3* **Winged Express (IRE)**[8] 3368 7-10-9 **81** IanPopham 91
(Alexandra Dunn) *hld up: hdwy to chse wnr 8th: ev ch after 3 out: sn rdn: styd on same pce fr next* **11/10**[1]
40-0 **3** *32* **Bertenbar**[56] 2453 12-11-6 **92** AndrewThornton 75
(Lawney Hill) *chsd ldrs tl rdn and wknd appr 2 out: blnd last* **16/1**
-333 **4** *10* **Carhue Princess (IRE)**[21] 3131 10-10-10 **85** BenPoste(3) 56
(Tom Symonds) *led to 4th: chsd wnr to 8th: sn rdn and wknd* **6/1**[3]
1251 **P** **Chankillo**[12] 3237 7-11-12 **98** (p) SamTwiston-Davies
(Sarah-Jayne Davies) *hld up: reminder after 3rd: blnd next: sn rdn and wknd: bhd whn p.u bef 7th* **6/1**[3]
-P06 **U** **It's Oscar (IRE)**[12] 3222 9-10-5 **77** (bt) MarkQuinlan 55
(James Evans) *hld up: hdwy 8th: rdn and wknd after 3 out: poor 4th whn uns rdr last* **7/2**[2]

4m 28.2s (12.10) **Going Correction** +0.75s/f (Soft) **6** Ran **SP% 112.0**
Speed ratings: **99,97,81,76,**
CSF £27.16 TOTE £9.00: £6.20, £1.80; EX 28.80 Trifecta £309.20.
Owner Richard Lee **Bred** Mrs Anne Caplice **Trained** Byton, H'fords

FOCUS
Hurdle course dolled out to middle position, adding approximately 12yds to each circuit. The ground was predictably very testing. The front pair came clear in what was a lowly handicap chase, but this was a step up from the winner.

3498 SHERSTON WINE COMPANY LTD H'CAP HURDLE (8 hdls) 1m 7f 181y
1:35 (1:35) (Class 4) (0-110,110) 4-Y-0+ **£4,548** (£1,335; £667; £333)

Form RPR
-031 **1** **Eminent Poet**[8] 3374 5-11-11 **109** AidanColeman 124+
(Venetia Williams) *a.p: led appr 2 out: sn clr: eased nr fin* **4/5**[1]
P011 **2** *8* **Arquebusier (FR)**[35] 2862 6-11-3 **104** (p) JamesBanks(3) 107
(Emma Baker) *chsd ldrs: led 5th: rdn and hdd appr 2 out: sn btn* **10/1**
0013 **3** *4 ½* **American Life (FR)**[7] 3383 9-11-2 **105** (vt) CharlieDeutsch(5) 105
(Sophie Leech) *prom: rdn after 3 out: sn outpcd: hmpd next: styd on to go 3rd appr last* **6/1**[2]
6031 **4** *6* **Catchin Time (IRE)**[7] 3376 8-11-3 **104** 7ex (t) KieronEdgar(3) 98
(Laura Hurley) *hld up: hdwy after 3 out: wknd next* **8/1**
0603 **5** *1* **Bishop Wulstan (IRE)**[24] 3080 5-11-10 **108** (b) SeanBowen 103
(Peter Bowen) *led to 2nd: chsd ldrs: ev ch 3 out: sn rdn: wknd next: j.lft last* **11/1**
-3P1 **P** **Taroum (IRE)**[210] 695 9-11-5 **103** (bt) RhysFlint
(John Flint) *mid-div: hdwy 5th: wknd after 3 out: bhd whn p.u bef next* **66/1**
031/ **P** **My Miss Lucy**[758] 3005 10-11-12 **110** SamTwiston-Davies
(Richard Phillips) *chsd ldr: led 2nd to 5th: sn rdn and wknd: bhd whn p.u bef next* **33/1**
P003 **P** **Dardanella**[17] 3198 9-10-12 **96** DaveCrosse
(Hugo Froud) *hld up: rdn and wknd appr 3 out: bhd whn p.u bef next* **40/1**
0600 **P** **Mystery Drama**[30] 2956 6-11-1 **99** AdamWedge
(Alexandra Dunn) *hld up: rdn and wknd after 5th: bhd whn p.u bef last* **66/1**
1-20 **P** **Aces Over Eights (IRE)**[39] 2812 7-11-7 **105** JamieMoore
(Kerry Lee) *hld up: hdwy 4th: rdn and wknd after 3 out: bhd whn p.u bef last* **15/2**[3]

4m 19.3s (11.40) **Going Correction** +0.75s/f (Soft) **10** Ran **SP% 118.5**
Speed ratings (Par 105): **101,97,94,91,91 , , , ,**
CSF £10.02 CT £32.58 TOTE £1.70: £1.10, £1.60, £2.00; EX 10.70 Trifecta £33.50.
Owner B C Dice **Bred** George Strawbridge **Trained** Kings Caple, H'fords

FOCUS
A race that revolved around the favourite, who was well in on his recent win, and the form is only modest.

3499 HAYGAIN HAY STEAMERS CLEAN HEALTHY HAY H'CAP CHASE (QUAL FOR CHALLENGER MIDDLE DISTANCE FINAL) (13 fncs) 2m 3f 179y
2:05 (2:06) (Class 4) (0-120,116) 5-Y-0+ **£6,330** (£1,870; £935; £468; £234)

Form RPR
53-3 **1** **Sunny Ledgend**[21] 3123 11-10-11 **108** MrJMartin(7) 120
(Andrew J Martin) *led to 6th: led again next: shkn up appr last: styd on wl* **12/1**
463F **2** *2* **Cloudy Bob (IRE)**[10] 3315 9-11-10 **114** LeightonAspell 124
(Pat Murphy) *a.p: chsd wnr appr 2 out: sn rdn: j.rt last: hung lft flat: styd on same pce* **3/1**[3]
3-45 **3** *15* **Son Of Suzie**[27] 3014 8-11-11 **115** PaddyBrennan 113
(Fergal O'Brien) *chsd ldrs: led 6th: hdd next: rdn and ev ch after 3 out: wknd appr last* **7/4**[1]
-413 **4** *9* **Rosa Fleet (IRE)**[27] 3007 8-11-12 **116** LiamTreadwell 106
(Venetia Williams) *chsd wnr to 5th: outpcd 8th: rallied appr 3 out: rdn and wknd bef next* **9/2**
0012 **5** *20* **Kings Cross (FR)**[26] 3044 6-11-9 **113** LeeEdwards 79
(Tony Carroll) *hld up: hdwy 6th: rdn and wknd after 3 out* **5/2**[2]

5m 32.3s (14.10) **Going Correction** +0.75s/f (Soft) **5** Ran **SP% 115.8**
Speed ratings: **101,100,94,90,82**
CSF £48.51 TOTE £13.50: £4.70, £1.70; EX 52.70 Trifecta £157.10.
Owner Andrew J Martin **Bred** A And Mrs Martin **Trained** Chipping Norton, Oxon

FOCUS
A couple of the fancied runners failed to give their running and the front pair came clear. The winner has run to his mark.

3500 HAYGAIN HAY STEAMERS CLEAN HEALTHY FORAGE MARES' "NATIONAL HUNT" MAIDEN HURDLE (8 hdls) 1m 7f 181y
2:35 (2:35) (Class 5) 4-Y-0+ **£2,599** (£763; £381; £190)

Form RPR
2202 **1** **Pulling Power**[22] 3110 6-11-2 0 (t) DavidBass 111+
(Kim Bailey) *led: hdd appr 3rd: remained handy: pushed along to chse ldr appr 2 out: rdn to ld flat: styd on* **11/10**[1]
0-2F **2** *2* **Happy Diva (IRE)**[44] 2697 5-11-2 0 JamieMoore 110+
(Kerry Lee) *a.p: chsd ldr 3rd: led appr 2 out: nt fluent last: rdn and hdd flat: styd on same pce* **11/10**[1]
4005 **3** *35* **A Touch Of Sass (IRE)**[21] 3126 6-10-11 0 [1] CharlieDeutsch(5) 73
(John Spearing) *hld up: plld hrd: hdwy to ld appr 3rd: sn clr: rdn: hdd & wknd appr 2 out* **20/1**[3]
-005 **4** *21* **Miss Mash**[45] 2689 5-11-2 0 AndrewTinkler 52
(Henry Daly) *hld up: hdwy after 5th: rdn and wknd appr 2 out* **14/1**[2]
66 **5** *31* **Premier Rose (IRE)**[7] 3388 7-10-9 0 MrJNixon(7) 21
(Katy Price) *chsd ldrs: lost pl 3rd: bhd next: rdn and wknd appr 3 out* **28/1**
PPP- **P** **Maetrufel Annie**[280] 5108 7-11-2 0 (p) MarkQuinlan
(Paul Webber) *w ldr to appr 3rd: rdn and wknd after 5th: bhd whn p.u bef 2 out* **100/1**

4m 20.7s (12.80) **Going Correction** +0.75s/f (Soft) **6** Ran **SP% 111.1**
Speed ratings (Par 103): **98,97,79,69,53**
CSF £2.53 TOTE £2.00: £1.10, £1.10; EX 3.20 Trifecta £8.50.
Owner Turf Club 2014 & The Real Partnership **Bred** Mrs S Steer-Fowler & Mrs P Hedden **Trained** Andoversford, Gloucs

FOCUS
The market leaders dominated this mares' hurdle. The first two were closely matched and are rated to their marks.

3501 EBF/TBA MARES' NOVICES' H'CAP CHASE (9 fncs 4 omitted) 2m 3f 179y
3:05 (3:07) (Class 4) (0-110,107) 5-Y-0+ **£5,325** (£1,653; £890)

Form RPR
3-31 **1** **Black Narcissus (IRE)**[24] 3088 7-10-12 **93** RhysFlint 104+
(Alexandra Dunn) *hld up in tch: chsd ldr appr 3rd: led last (normal 3 out): shkn up and c clr fr normal last* **2/1**[2]
1PF4 **2** *12* **Bobble Boru (IRE)**[9] 3337 8-11-12 **107** (b[1]) LiamTreadwell 109+
(Venetia Williams) *led: j.big 2nd: j.lft 7th: hung lft and hdd last (normal 3 out): styd on same pce after normal 2 out* **11/4**[3]
02/2 **3** *50* **September Blaze**[27] 3007 9-11-11 **106** CharliePoste 55
(Paul Webber) *chsd ldrs: rdn and ev ch after last (normal 3 out): wknd bef normal 2 out* **5/1**
0-6P **U** **Maybe Plenty**[35] 2865 7-11-7 **102** TomCannon
(Giles Smyly) *chsd ldrs: mstke 2nd: lost pl after 4th: rdn and detached whn mstke and uns rdr last (normal 3 out)* **15/8**[1]

5m 29.1s (10.90) **Going Correction** +0.75s/f (Soft) **4** Ran **SP% 111.4**
Speed ratings: **108,103,83,**
CSF £7.89 TOTE £2.60; EX 8.10 Trifecta £12.00.
Owner Team Dunn **Bred** Patrick Davern **Trained** West Buckland, Somerset

FOCUS
The two fences in the home straight were omitted due to low sun. Moderate chasing form, arguably a pb from the winner.

3502 HAYGAIN HAY STEAMERS CLEAN HEALTHY FORAGE MAIDEN OPEN NATIONAL HUNT FLAT RACE 1m 7f 181y
3:40 (3:40) (Class 6) 4-6-Y-0 **£1,949** (£572; £286; £143)

Form RPR
1 **Billy Bronco** 5-11-5 0 TrevorWhelan 115
(Debra Hamer) *sn prom: rdn to ld ins fnl f: styd on wl* **20/1**
2 **2** *2 ¼* **Pride Of Lecale**[33] 2909 5-11-5 0 (t) PaddyBrennan 113
(Fergal O'Brien) *hld up in tch: led over 3f out: rdn and hdd ins fnl f: styd on same pce* **4/5**[1]
3 **3** *12* **What A Diva**[24] 3082 5-10-12 0 SeanBowen 94
(Peter Bowen) *led: hdd 7f out: rdn and ev ch over 2f out: wknd over 1f out* **11/2**[3]
2-33 **4** *17* **Briac (FR)**[17] 3200 5-11-5 0 SamTwiston-Davies 84
(Jim Best) *chsd ldrs: led 7f out: rdn and hdd over 3f out: wknd 2f out* **3/1**[2]

2- 5 4 1/2 **King Uther**[346] 3905 6-11-5 0 TomCannon 80
(Chris Gordon) *hld up: pushed along over 7f out: wknd over 4f out* **7/1**
6 11 **Silent Doctor (IRE)**[312] 6-11-2 0 JamesBanks(3) 69
(Roy Brotherton) *prom: pushed along over 6f out: wknd over 4f out* **66/1**
0 7 36 **Balmoral Prince**[28] 2991 5-11-5 0 BrendanPowell 33
(Shaun Lycett) *chsd ldr over 7f: rdn and wknd over 4f out* **100/1**
4m 10.9s (8.60) **Going Correction** +0.75s/f (Soft) **7** Ran SP% **115.7**
Speed ratings: **108,106,100,92,90 84,66**
CSF £37.64 TOTE £26.20: £6.90, £1.20; EX 47.50 Trifecta £259.90.
Owner Mrs D A Hamer **Bred** Mickley Stud **Trained** Nantycaws, Carmarthens

FOCUS
A bit of a turn up in what was an average bumper.
T/Plt: £90.60 to a £1 stake. Pool of £78649.51 - 633.43 winning tickets. T/Qpdt: £48.60 to a £1 stake. Pool of £5686.82 - 86.55 winning tickets. **Colin Roberts**

3333 DONCASTER (L-H)
Friday, January 8

OFFICIAL GOING: Soft (heavy in places; chs 6.3, hdl 6.3)
Wind: moderate 1/2 against Weather: fine but cold, soon becoming sunny

3503 KEYHOLE VISUALS FUTURE OF DIGITAL MEDIA H'CAP HURDLE (11 hdls) 3m 96y
12:15 (12:15) (Class 5) (0-100,100) 4-Y-0+ **£2,599** (£763; £381; £190)

Form RPR
00-5 1 **Redkalani (IRE)**[29] 2980 8-11-8 **96** JamesReveley 106+
(Keith Reveley) *mde all: nt fluent 2 out: forged clr between last 2: eased nr fin* **5/2**[1]
0-24 2 11 **Blue Cove**[55] 2488 11-10-0 **74** oh9 SeanQuinlan 73
(Lynn Siddall) *chsd ldrs: pushed along 7th: 2nd 3 out: 10 l down whn mstke last* **40/1**
1F32 3 7 **Jumpandtravel (IRE)**[11] 3312 7-11-9 **100** JoeColliver(3) 91
(Micky Hammond) *jnd ldr 4th: 2nd bef 8th: upsides appr next: one pce* **9/2**[2]
552 4 10 **Triumph Davis (IRE)**[7] 3402 7-11-0 **88** SamTwiston-Davies 69
(Micky Hammond) *in rr: hdwy to chse ldrs 8th: modest 4th next: wknd appr last* **15/2**
2PP2 5 8 **Harleys Max**[29] 2983 7-9-13 **80** JamesCorbett(7) 53
(Susan Corbett) *t.k.h: j. slowly: trcking ldrs 2nd: lost pl bef 3 out* **10/1**
5404 5 dht **Irish Octave (IRE)**[8] 3382 6-10-0 **77** BenPoste(3) 50
(Rosemary Gasson) *t.k.h: trckd ldrs 2nd: drvn along 6th: lost pl 8th* **14/1**
0035 7 4 **Tickanrun (IRE)**[42] 2751 6-11-0 **93** (p) DiarmuidO'Regan(5) 62
(Chris Grant) *prom: drvn 4th: outpcd 8th: lost pl bef next* **7/1**[3]
P545 8 2 **Lady Vivona**[13] 3234 8-9-9 **74** oh10 CallumBewley(5) 41
(Lisa Harrison) *hld up in rr: lost pl after 8th: sn bhd: wknd between last 2* **50/1**
0344 P **Minden March**[19] 3177 11-9-9 **74** JamieHamilton(5)
(Peter Maddison) *w ldrs: drvn 9th: sn lost pl: t.o whn p.u bef 3 out* **16/1**
-P5R R **Madam Lilibet (IRE)**[40] 2800 7-11-5 **100** (b[1]) FinianO'Toole(7)
(Sharon Watt) *chsd ldrs: drvn and lost pl after 4th: sn bhd: t.o 7th: ref next* **12/1**
5/PP F **Cleve Cottage**[33] 2937 8-10-6 **83** AdamNicol(3)
(Philip Kirby) *hld up in rr: fell 2nd* **11/1**
6m 24.5s (25.50) **Going Correction** +0.525s/f (Soft) **11** Ran SP% **113.1**
Speed ratings (Par 103): **78,74,72,68,66 66,64,64,,**
CSF £85.80 CT £427.51 TOTE £3.50: £1.50, £5.80, £1.80; EX 97.00 Trifecta £452.30.
Owner Cristiana's Crew **Bred** Mrs M C Reveley **Trained** Lingdale, Redcar & Cleveland

FOCUS
Distance changes as follows; R1 add 24yds, R2 & 5 add 6yds, R3, 4, 6 & 7 add 15yds. James Reveley said of the ground "It's horrible, testing, if not quite bottomless." Moderate handicap form, and it proved quite hard work in the conditions, despite a steady early pace. A personal-best from the winner.

3504 CROWNHOTEL-BAWTRY.COM NOVICES' CHASE (15 fncs) 2m 3f 44y
12:45 (12:45) (Class 4) 5-Y-0+ **£3,898** (£1,144; £572; £286)

Form RPR
0-05 1 **Bouvreuil (FR)**[34] 2913 5-10-7 136 (t) SamTwiston-Davies 140+
(Paul Nicholls) *t.k.h in rr: hdwy to trck ldrs 6th: 2nd gng wl 3 out: effrt next: led last: drvn rt out* **7/2**[2]
42-1 2 1 1/2 **Vyta Du Roc (FR)**[28] 3006 7-11-4 0 NicodeBoinville 149+
(Nicky Henderson) *w ldr: led after 11th: sn pushed along: hdd narrowly last: styd on same pce last 100yds* **2/5**[1]
0P-U 3 28 **Monbeg Theatre (IRE)**[35] 2881 7-10-12 130 (t) BrendanPowell 116
(Jamie Snowden) *chsd ldrs: outpcd and lost pl 3 out: distant 3rd and j. bdly rt last* **16/1**
0/ 4 26 **Legal Exit (IRE)**[362] 3644 9-10-12 0 RichardJohnson 93
(Tom Lacey) *j.rt: led: hdd after 11th: wknd bef 2 out* **9/1**[3]
P **Overtheedge (IRE)**[259] 7-10-9 0 JoeColliver(3)
(Simon West) *chsd ldrs: lost pl 9th: t.o 4 out: p.u bef 2 out* **150/1**
4m 49.3s (0.30) **Going Correction** +0.25s/f (Yiel)
WFA 5 from 7yo+ 3lb **5** Ran SP% **110.2**
Speed ratings: **109,108,96,85,**
CSF £5.68 TOTE £5.30: £1.70, £1.10; EX 5.40 Trifecta £17.80.
Owner Chris Giles & Potensis Bloodstock Ltd **Bred** Mme Nicolas Devilder & Fernand Sellier **Trained** Ditcheat, Somerset

FOCUS
Two good novices came clear and it was no great shock to see the favourite turned over, with there being little between the pair at the weights on hurdle ratings. Both are rated similar to their best hurdles figures.

3505 MORAN MARES' H'CAP HURDLE (10 hdls) 2m 3f 120y
1:20 (1:20) (Class 4) (0-120,112) 4-Y-0+ **£3,249** (£954; £477; £238)

Form RPR
3-21 1 **Iron Butterfly**[28] 3025 7-11-12 **112** JackQuinlan 121+
(James Eustace) *trckd ldrs: led 6th: clr sn after 2 out: smoothly* **15/8**[1]
-502 2 6 **Fountains Blossom**[43] 2732 7-11-0 **107** (t) HarryCobden(7) 107
(Anthony Honeyball) *trckd ldrs: chsd wnr fr 7th: sn drvn: no imp* **10/3**[3]
2-32 3 29 **Donna's Pride**[10] 3333 7-11-9 **109** JamesReveley 84
(Keith Reveley) *chsd ldrs: outpcd 7th: lost pl next* **85/40**[2]
4-00 4 10 **Kashstaree**[13] 3233 5-10-3 **94** CallumBewley(5) 55
(Lisa Harrison) *in rr: hdwy and handy 3rd 5th: drvn and outpcd 7th: sn lost pl: distant 4th after 3 out* **20/1**
6346 5 17 **Taylor (IRE)**[40] 2802 7-11-9 **112** JoeColliver(3) 56
(Micky Hammond) *led: hdd 6th: lost pl after 7th: poor 4th whn mstke 3 out: sn wl bhd* **6/1**
4m 59.1s (7.80) **Going Correction** +0.525s/f (Soft) **5** Ran SP% **108.9**
Speed ratings (Par 105): **105,102,91,87,80**
CSF £8.35 TOTE £2.50: £1.10, £2.00; EX 8.60 Trifecta £14.40.
Owner Harold Nass **Bred** Rockville Pike Partnership **Trained** Newmarket, Suffolk

FOCUS
Two in-form types came clear in what was a modest handicap, with the front pair clear. A personal best from the winner.

3506 PREMIER QUALITY FOODS "NATIONAL HUNT" NOVICES' HURDLE (8 hdls) 2m 140y
1:50 (1:50) (Class 4) 4-Y-0+ **£3,249** (£954; £477; £238)

Form RPR
21 1 **Le Prezien (FR)**[23] 3105 5-11-12 130 (t) SamTwiston-Davies 142+
(Paul Nicholls) *hld up: trckd ldrs 3rd: upsides on bit 2 out: led between last 2: wnt clr: v easily* **1/4**[1]
-1F0 2 19 **Desertmore Hill (IRE)**[65] 2265 6-11-5 0 SeanBowen 110
(Peter Bowen) *trckd ldrs: 2nd 3rd: led appr 3 out: hdd between last 2: no ch w wnr* **12/1**[3]
0-11 3 5 **Unbuckled (IRE)**[28] 3022 6-11-5 0 TrevorWhelan 105
(Neil King) *pushed along 3rd: handy 4th 5th: modest 3rd between last 2: hit last* **7/2**[2]
00-5 4 11 **Busy Baro (IRE)**[22] 3130 6-11-5 0 CharliePoste 94
(Paul Cowley) *led: hdd appr 3 out: wknd between last 2* **25/1**
-400 5 23 **Temple Tiger**[11] 3309 6-11-5 0 PeterBuchanan 71
(James Turner) *chsd ldrs: drvn after 4th: reminders and lost pl bef 3 out: bhd whn j.lft 3 out: sn t.o* **100/1**
66F- 6 10 **Caldey**[550] 886 7-10-9 0 RobMcCarth(3) 54
(Ian Williams) *trckd ldrs: drvn 4th: sn lost pl: wl bhd bef 3 out: t.o* **100/1**
0 7 1 1/2 **St Lewis**[205] 761 6-11-5 0 SeanQuinlan 60
(Jennie Candlish) *stdd s: hld up towards rr: bhd fr 5th: t.o bef next* **200/1**
4m 13.3s (8.60) **Going Correction** +0.525s/f (Soft) **7** Ran SP% **116.2**
Speed ratings (Par 105): **100,91,88,83,72 68,67**
CSF £5.08 TOTE £1.30: £1.10, £3.50; EX 3.50 Trifecta £9.60.
Owner Million In Mind Partnership **Bred** Jean-Raymond Breton & Thomas Trapenard **Trained** Ditcheat, Somerset

FOCUS
No depth to this novice hurdle and the favourite bolted up. He looks to be improving.

3507 TRUEMAN FAMILY NOVICES' H'CAP CHASE (18 fncs) 3m 6y
2:25 (2:25) (Class 4) (0-120,120) 5-Y-0+ **£3,898** (£1,144; £572; £286)

Form RPR
-412 1 **Askamore Darsi (IRE)**[20] 3160 7-11-3 **111** (p) HenryBrooke 124
(Donald McCain) *led: drvn 13th: hdd 4 out: rallied appr last: led fnl strides* **11/1**
3P-2 2 hd **Lovely Job (IRE)**[30] 2973 6-11-8 **116** PaddyBrennan 131+
(Fergal O'Brien) *trckd ldrs: cl 2nd whn pckd landing 15th: led next: drvn 3 out: 3 l ahd last: hdd and no ex fnl strides* **5/4**[1]
10/1 3 18 **Mysteree (IRE)**[34] 2918 8-11-12 **120** TomScudamore 118
(Lucinda Russell) *chsd ldrs: cl 3rd whn blnd 4 out: mstke 2 out: wknd between last 2* **9/2**[2]
4444 4 12 **Manballandall (IRE)**[20] 3162 8-11-1 **116** (tp) JamesCorbett(7) 103
(Susan Corbett) *mid-div: chsd ldrs 5th: pushed along 8th: lost pl 15th: hmpd and lft poor 4th 3 out* **25/1**
1650 5 2 1/2 **Mercers Court (IRE)**[21] 3137 8-11-9 **117** (t) TrevorWhelan 98
(Neil King) *mid-div: chsd ldrs 7th: lost pl 14th: lft poor 5th 3 out* **25/1**
6/02 6 3/4 **Joseph Mercer (IRE)**[34] 2922 9-10-4 **98** JonathanEngland 78
(Tina Jackson) *chsd ldrs: pushed along 7th: lost pl 10th: reminders next: rallied 14th: lost pl 15th: lft poor 6th 3 out* **16/1**
FP12 F **Pure Poteen (IRE)**[65] 2272 8-10-12 **113** (t) MrMartinMcIntyre(7)
(Neil Mulholland) *nt fluent in rr: blnd 1st: sn bhd: pushed along 9th: hdwy 14th: rdn next: modest 5th and one pce whn fell 4 out* **7/1**[3]
-113 F **Leanna Ban**[34] 2917 9-11-4 **117** (t) CallumBewley(5)
(Tristan Davidson) *hld up in rr: hdwy 10th: chsng ldrs next: 4th and keeping on same pce whn fell 3 out* **16/1**
/04F P **The Ramblin Kid**[20] 3162 8-11-9 **117** SamTwiston-Davies
(Micky Hammond) *w ldr: drvn 11th: reminders 13th: lost pl next: sn bhd: t.o whn p.u bef 3 out* **7/1**[3]
6m 19.5s (7.50) **Going Correction** +0.25s/f (Yiel) **9** Ran SP% **115.4**
Speed ratings: **97,96,90,86,86 85,,,**
CSF £26.53 CT £72.67 TOTE £8.60: £2.10, £1.10, £1.80; EX 34.90 Trifecta £136.50.
Owner Deva Racing Darsi Partnership **Bred** William McGladdery **Trained** Cholmondeley, Cheshire
■ Stewards' Enquiry : Henry Brooke seven-day ban; used whip above the permitted level (22nd-28th Jan)
Paddy Brennan two-day ban; used whip above the permitted level (22nd, 24th Jan)

FOCUS
A fair chase and, as ever in these novice handicaps, jumping was a key factor. The winner was on a good mark and has been rated close to his best.

3508 1STSECURITYSOLUTIONS.CO.UK MAIDEN HURDLE (DIV I) (10 hdls) 2m 3f 120y
3:00 (3:00) (Class 5) 4-Y-0+ **£2,599** (£763; £381; £190)

Form RPR
4 1 **Baoulet Delaroque (FR)**[65] 2265 5-11-6 0 SamTwiston-Davies 124+
(Paul Nicholls) *trckd ldrs 2nd: 2nd appr 3 out: led between last 2: drvn out* **15/8**[2]
1 2 3 3/4 **Divine Spear (IRE)**[242] 242 5-11-6 0 NicodeBoinville 121+
(Nicky Henderson) *t.k.h: trckd ldr: led 3rd: j.rt 7th: hit next: hdd between last 2: kpt on same pce* **1/1**[1]
3 18 **Dalkadam (FR)**[44] 5-11-6 120 RichardJohnson 103
(J R Jenkins) *set slow pce: hdd 3rd: j.lft: wknd 2 out: tired 3rd whn hit last* **7/2**[3]
-600 4 1/2 **Kara Tara**[28] 3022 6-10-13 0 BrianHughes 93
(Lawrence Mullaney) *hld up towards rr: hdwy 5th: outpcd appr 3 out: kpt on appr last* **25/1**
4 5 4 **Looksnowtlikebrian (IRE)**[78] 2044 5-11-1 0 AlanJohns(5) 96
(Tim Vaughan) *rn wout declared tongue strap: chsd ldrs: outpcd 3 out: sn lost pl* **33/1**
0005 6 2 3/4 **Paris Snow**[11] 3316 6-11-3 0 RobMcCarth(3) 94
(Ian Williams) *in rr: hdwy 7th: reminder appr 3 out: sn outpcd: wknd bef 2 out* **66/1**
6-0 7 1 1/4 **Scooby (IRE)**[42] 2750 5-11-3 0 RyanHatch(3) 93
(Graeme McPherson) *prom: drvn appr 3 out: sn lost pl* **100/1**

16 P **Improved (IRE)**[42] 2750 6-11-3 0 AdamNicol(3)
(Philip Kirby) *chsd ldrs: lost pl after 7th: sn bhd: t.o whn p.u bef 2 out* **25/1**
0- P **Lady Brienne (IRE)**[393] 3030 7-10-10 0 JoeColliver(3)
(Simon West) *chsd ldrs: lost pl 5th: sn bhd: t.o 7th: p.u bef next* **200/1**
5m 3.6s (12.30) **Going Correction** +0.525s/f (Soft) **9** Ran SP% **120.6**
Speed ratings (Par 103): **96,94,87,87,85 84,83,**
CSF £4.41 TOTE £2.80: £1.20, £1.10, £1.30; EX 5.50 Trifecta £10.30.
Owner Potensis Bloodstock Limited **Bred** Mme Genevieve Mongin **Trained** Ditcheat, Somerset

FOCUS
They dawdled through the early stages of this maiden hurdle, which featured two potentially useful sorts who drew clear.

3509 1STSECURITYSOLUTIONS.CO.UK MAIDEN HURDLE (DIV II) (10 hdls) 2m 3f 120y
3:30 (3:30) (Class 5) 4-Y-0+ **£2,599** (£763; £381; £190)

Form RPR
332 1 **Chase End Charlie (IRE)**[42] 2750 5-11-6 0 RichardJohnson 130+
(Tom Lacey) *led to 3rd: j.rt next: drvn 7th: led 3 out: styd on wl run-in: drvn out* **9/2**[3]
5-42 2 3 **Ami Desbois (FR)**[27] 3037 6-11-6 0 KielanWoods 126
(Graeme McPherson) *trckd ldrs: handy 3rd appr 3 out: 2nd 2 out: upsides between last 2: kpt on same pce run-in* **2/1**[1]
-330 3 12 **Moidore**[31] 2961 7-11-6 115 AdamPogson 115
(Charles Pogson) *hld up in rr: hdwy to trck ldrs 6th: handy 4th and swtchd lft 3 out: modest 3rd appr last* **7/1**
2 4 6 **Caged Lightning (IRE)**[11] 3309 6-11-6 0 TomScudamore 109
(Steve Gollings) *w ldr: led 3rd: drvn 7th: hdd next: wknd bef last* **5/2**[2]
22-6 5 13 **Sir Will (IRE)**[65] 2270 5-11-6 0 (p) SeanBowen 96
(Peter Bowen) *chsd ldrs: drvn 7th: lost pl bef next: sn bhd* **5/1**
44U 6 14 **Exactly What**[7] 3397 7-11-6 0 HenryBrooke 81
(Donald McCain) *trckd ldrs 3rd: lost pl appr 3 out: sn bhd* **66/1**
7 10 **Man From Seville**[832] 6-11-6 0 PaddyBrennan 71
(Fergal O'Brien) *trckd ldrs: outpcd and modest 5th whn bot fluent 3 out: sn wknd and bhd: eased clsng stages* **25/1**
1/00 8 32 **Heritage Way**[13] 3239 7-11-6 0 BrianHughes 39
(Henry Hogarth) *t.k.h in rr: hdwy 6th: lost pl next: sn wl bhd: t.o 3 out* **66/1**
5m 2.9s (11.60) **Going Correction** +0.525s/f (Soft) **8** Ran SP% **116.1**
Speed ratings (Par 103): **97,95,91,88,83 77,73,61**
CSF £14.52 TOTE £4.90: £1.60, £1.20, £2.40; EX 12.60 Trifecta £80.50.
Owner Tudor Street Partnership **Bred** Eoin Fenton **Trained** Ledbury, H'fords

FOCUS
The weaker of the two divisions and a big step up from the winner..
T/Plt: £3.80 to a £1 stake. Pool: £67,340.69 - 12,700.11 winning tickets T/Qpdt: £2.50 to a £1 stake. Pool: £6,803.93 - 1,939.23 winning tickets **Walter Glynn**

2917 WETHERBY (L-H)
Friday, January 8
3510 Meeting Abandoned - Waterlogged

2903 CHEPSTOW (L-H)
Saturday, January 9
OFFICIAL GOING: Heavy (chs 4.5; hdl 4.3)
Wind: almost nil Weather: overcast, intermittent heavy rain after race 1

3516 DOWNLOAD THE CORAL MOBILE APP NOVICES' HURDLE (9 hdls 2 omitted) 2m 3f 100y
12:35 (12:35) (Class 4) 4-Y-0+ **£3,898** (£1,144; £572; £286)

Form RPR
0-32 1 **Millanisi Boy**[44] 2725 7-11-6 125 TomO'Brien 125+
(Richard Woollacott) *trckd ldrs: wnt 2nd on extended run between last 2: led last: edgd rt and drvn out flat* **9/4**[1]
421 2 1 **Never Equalled (IRE)**[26] 3077 7-11-5 125 JordanWilliams(7) 130
(Bernard Llewellyn) *led: wnt 7 l clr after 6th: reduced ld 2 out: rdn on extended run between last 2: hdd last: kpt on wl u.p flat* **4/1**[2]
3-4 3 1 3/4 **Ballybane (IRE)**[93] 1829 6-11-6 0 (p) SeanBowen 122
(Rebecca Curtis) *racd in 2nd: 7 l off ldr after 6th: clsd 2 out: lost 2nd on extended run between last 2: flashed tail flat but styd on u.p* **9/1**[3]
1-1 4 3 **Maxanisi (IRE)**[52] 2564 6-11-12 0 AdamWedge 125
(Evan Williams) *mid-div: hdwy to chse ldrs 4th: rdn after 3 out: one pce on extended run between last 2* **9/4**[1]
3 5 11 **Minella Daddy (IRE)**[30] 2998 6-11-6 0 JamieMoore 108
(Peter Bowen) *chsd ldrs: rdn appr 3 out: wknd on extended run between last 2* **10/1**
-2P0 6 21 **Mad About The Boy**[22] 3133 6-11-6 115 AidanColeman 87
(Robert Walford) *nt far away: rdn along 6th: wknd 3 out* **20/1**
2-0P 7 2 3/4 **Oskar's Eva (IRE)**[42] 2776 6-10-8 0 AlanJohns(5) 78
(Tim Vaughan) *chsd ldrs: nt fluent 6th: wkng whn mstke 3 out* **66/1**
44 8 6 **Very Extravagant (IRE)**[14] 3252 7-10-13 0 MarkQuinlan 74
(Neil Mulholland) *mid-div: outpcd by ldrs 5th: wknd after next* **16/1**
5065 9 23 **Court King (IRE)**[26] 3077 5-11-1 0 CiaranGethings(5) 56
(Peter Bowen) *a in rr: lost tch 6th: t.o* **66/1**
0 10 nk **Ayla's Emperor**[26] 3077 7-10-13 0 RobertDunne 48
(John Flint) *hld up in rr: sme hdwy after 6th: wknd appr 3 out: t.o* **100/1**
030 11 49 **The Model County (IRE)**[23] 3132 6-10-6 0 MrAlexEdwards(7)
(Alan Phillips) *tended to jump big: mid-div tl dropped towards rr after 3rd: sn rdn along: lost tch 6th: t.o* **66/1**
54P0 12 7 **Run Bob Run**[26] 3077 5-11-6 0 RhysFlint
(John Flint) *a in rr: lost tch 6th: t.o* **150/1**
-0P3 P **Pursuitofhappiness (IRE)**[14] 3255 8-11-6 0 BrendanPowell
(Neil Mulholland) *mid-div tl dropped towards rr after 3rd: lost tch 6th: t.o whn p.u bef 3 out* **150/1**
5m 2.6s (0.80) **Going Correction** +0.225s/f (Yiel) **13** Ran SP% **118.1**
Speed ratings (Par 105): **107,106,105,104,99 91,89,87,77,77 56,54,**
CSF £11.28 TOTE £3.00: £1.20, £1.60, £3.00; EX 9.60 Trifecta £77.70.
Owner D Stevens & Mrs S Stevens **Bred** Mrs Audrey Goodwin **Trained** South Molton, Devon

FOCUS
Although it was a wet week the sun came out in time and this already rescheduled meeting was given the go ahead, with a proviso it was obviously very taxing underfoot. This opening novice event proved a real test thanks to the runner-up and the form should work out well enough. The second-last flight was omitted in all hurdle races.

3517 CORAL PROUD SUPPORTERS OF BRITISH HORSE RACING H'CAP HURDLE (12 hdls) 2m 7f 131y
1:10 (1:10) (Class 2) (0-145,145) 4-Y-0+ **£12,660** (£3,740; £1,870; £936; £468)

Form RPR
66-0 1 **Awaywiththegreys (IRE)**[35] 2906 9-10-9 128 (b) SeanBowen 130
(Peter Bowen) *led to 4th: styd cl up: led again 3 out: rdn on extended run between last 2: 3 l up last: drvn flat: jst hld on* **10/1**
P-52 2 shd **Moorlands Mist**[35] 2906 9-10-4 128 ConorRing(5) 129
(Evan Williams) *hld up: bmpd 2nd: rdn 3 out: stl only sixth 2 out: hdwy u.p on extended run between last 2: chsd wnr flat: styd on wl: jst failed* **11/2**[3]
-056 3 3 1/4 **Filatore (IRE)**[26] 3078 7-9-7 119 oh9 (p) JordanWilliams(7) 118
(Bernard Llewellyn) *cl up: led 4th: rdn and hdd 3 out: mstke and lost 2nd next: kpt on u.p* **66/1**
2113 4 hd **Sykes (IRE)**[43] 2759 7-10-1 125 CiaranGethings(5) 123
(Philip Hobbs) *mid-div: j.rt 2nd: hdwy after 7th: chsd wnr 2 out: one pce and lost 2 pls flat* **6/4**[1]
2412 5 4 1/2 **Captainofindustry (IRE)**[26] 3078 7-10-0 119 oh1 (p) BrendanPowell 112
(Mark Pitman) *chsd ldrs: mstke and rdn 3 out: no ex appr last* **6/1**
F4-5 6 2 3/4 **Hansupfordetroit (IRE)**[41] 2809 11-10-6 128 (tp) RobertWilliams(3) 118
(Bernard Llewellyn) *s.i.s: hld up: stdy hdwy after 7th: rdn and wknd appr last* **10/1**
-254 7 1 3/4 **Kayf Moss**[19] 3197 8-11-9 142 (bt) RhysFlint 131
(John Flint) *chsd ldrs: nt fluent 5th: rdn and lost pl next: one pce and no imp fr 3 out* **16/1**
05/0 8 1 **Ballyrock (IRE)**[66] 2268 10-10-0 124 (t) AlanJohns(5) 112
(Tim Vaughan) *hld up: rdn appr 3 out: no imp* **66/1**
5001 9 2 **Gevrey Chambertin (FR)**[28] 3045 8-11-7 145 (p) DavidNoonan(5) 131
(David Pipe) *mid-div: rdn after 7th: wknd 3 out* **5/1**[2]
6m 21.7s (19.50) **Going Correction** +0.775s/f (Soft) **9** Ran SP% **113.4**
Speed ratings (Par 109): **98,97,96,96,95 94,93,93,92**
CSF £63.25 CT £3389.61 TOTE £8.20: £2.30, £1.70, £11.00; EX 69.30 Trifecta £2752.40 Part won..
Owner Karen Bowen, Saith O Ni & The Hedonists **Bred** Domenico Fonzo **Trained** Little Newcastle, Pembrokes
■ Stewards' Enquiry : Jordan Williams four-day ban; used whip above the permitted level (24th-27th Jan)

FOCUS
There was a sound enough gallop on on this fair staying handicap. The first three are rated pretty much to their marks.

3518 CORAL WELSH GRAND NATIONAL (A H'CAP CHASE) (GRADE 3) (22 fncs) 3m 5f 110y
1:45 (1:46) (Class 1) 5-Y-0+
£68,340 (£25,644; £12,840; £6,396; £3,216; £1,608)

Form RPR
-536 1 **Mountainous (IRE)**[35] 2916 11-10-6 **132** (p) JamieMoore 147
(Kerry Lee) *mid-div: hdwy to chse ldrs 4th: wnt 2nd 5 out: rdn to ld 3 out: sn c clr: drvn out to hold dwindling advantage flat* **9/1**[2]
0-P3 2 2 3/4 **Firebird Flyer (IRE)**[35] 2907 9-10-7 **133** AdamWedge 144
(Evan Williams) *hld up: hmpd 2nd: stdy hdwy 14th: rdn 5 out: chsd wnr appr 2 out: styd on and clsng flat* **25/1**
UP-5 3 11 **Shotgun Paddy (IRE)**[56] 2482 9-11-5 **145** GavinSheehan 146
(Emma Lavelle) *mid-div: hdwy to chse ldrs 14th: rdn 5 out: no ex fr 2 out* **12/1**
0-15 4 8 **Saroque (IRE)**[42] 2790 9-10-6 **132** LiamTreadwell 125
(Venetia Williams) *prom: blnd 8th: led 11th tl hdd and mstke 3 out: wknd 2 out* **33/1**
0-61 5 nk **Woodford County**[36] 2878 9-9-12 **129** 4ex (p) CiaranGethings(5) 121
(Philip Hobbs) *mid-div: hdwy to chse ldrs 6th: mstke 8th: rdn 5 out: wknd 3 out* **12/1**
-0PF 6 21 **Portrait King (IRE)**[35] 2899 11-10-6 **132** (p) DerekFox 102
(Patrick Griffin, Ire) *towards rr: hmpd 2nd: j. slowly 4th: sme hdwy 14th: wknd 5 out* **16/1**
U-2P P **Masters Hill (IRE)**[42] 2790 10-11-4 **144** (p) BrendanPowell
(Colin Tizzard) *towards rr: lost tch 15th: t.o whn p.u bef 3 out* **33/1**
-P43 U **Allez Vic (IRE)**[35] 2908 10-9-11 **128** ConorRing(5)
(Evan Williams) *mid-div tl blnd and uns rdr 2nd* **33/1**
50-0 U **Black Thunder (FR)**[56] 2482 9-11-5 **152** (t) HarryCobden(7)
(Paul Nicholls) *chsd ldrs: hmpd 8th: mstke 12th: rdn whn blnd and uns rdr next* **12/1**
33-3 P **Fourovakind**[46] 2701 11-10-1 **127** (b) NicodeBoinville
(Harry Whittington) *towards rr: hdwy 7th: wknd 14th: bhd whn p.u bef 17th* **16/1**
41-1 P **Emperor's Choice (IRE)**[49] 2638 9-11-1 **141** AidanColeman
(Venetia Williams) *mid-div: j. slowly 5th: rdn whn mstke 12th: p.u bef next* **10/1**[3]
35/1 P **Tour Des Champs (FR)**[35] 2907 9-9-13 **130** 4ex JamieBargary(5)
(Nigel Twiston-Davies) *prom: mstke 1st: j. slowly 4th: mstke and lost pl 5th: blnd 15th: bhd whn p.u bef 17th* **12/1**
0-64 P **Bertie Boru (IRE)**[35] 2916 9-10-6 **132** TomO'Brien
(Philip Hobbs) *a towards rr: lost tch 15th: t.o whn p.u bef 3 out* **25/1**
P-P5 P **Benvolio (IRE)**[35] 2907 9-11-2 **142** (b) NickScholfield
(Paul Nicholls) *led to 1st: styd prom: led again 5th to next: wknd 15th: t.o whn p.u bef 3 out* **20/1**
P-P1 F **Bob Ford (IRE)**[26] 3079 9-10-11 **137** 4ex SeanBowen
(Rebecca Curtis) *mounted on crse: chsd ldrs: led 6th to 11th: disputing 4th and wkng whn fell 4 out* **10/1**[3]
00-5 P **Return Spring (IRE)**[57] 2473 9-10-6 **132** JamesBest
(Philip Hobbs) *nvr really travelling: in rr and rdn along by 3rd: t.o whn p.u bef 17th* **25/1**
-212 P **Upswing (IRE)**[56] 2482 8-10-13 **139** BarryGeraghty
(Jonjo O'Neill) *a towards rr: struggling whn p.u after 11th* **10/1**[3]
PP-2 P **Chase The Spud**[46] 2701 8-10-0 **126** (t[1]) BrianHughes
(Fergal O'Brien) *a towards rr: hmpd bnd after 1st: struggling 11th: p.u bef next* **25/1**
6F-4 P **Cogry**[56] 2482 7-10-8 **137** RyanHatch(3)
(Nigel Twiston-Davies) *chsd ldrs: mstke 7th: rdn along after: lost tch 16th: t.o whn p.u bef 4 out* **8/1**[1]

11-2 **U** **Red Devil Lads (IRE)**[24] 3109 7-10-10 136.............................. JJBurke
(Rebecca Curtis) *prom: led 1st: mstke and hdd 5th: blnd and uns rdr 8th* **14/1**

8m 26.6s (506.60) **Going Correction** +1.40s/f (Heav) **20** Ran SP% **126.6**
Speed ratings: **113,112,109,107,107 101,,,, ,,,,, ,,,,,**
CSF £223.24 CT £2707.39 TOTE £11.20: £2.60, £5.10, £3.70, £7.60; EX 258.10 Trifecta £4341.90.
Owner Hartley Phillips Roseff Shields **Bred** Lady Melissa Brooke **Trained** Byton, H'fords

FOCUS
Moved forward from an originally intended 3.25pm off time to ensure it was the first chase on the card, this was another fiercely competitive and gruelling Welsh National. It was run in driving rain. Only six managed to get home. Mountainous is back to his previous winning mark in this race, with a pb in defeat from Firebird Flyer.

3519 CORAL.CO.UK FUTURE CHAMPIONS FINALE JUVENILE HURDLE (GRADE 1) (6 hdls 2 omitted) 2m 11y
2:20 (2:21) (Class 1) 4-Y-0
£28,475 (£10,685; £5,350; £2,665; £1,340; £670)

Form RPR
22 **1** **Adrien Du Pont (FR)**[28] 3028 4-11-0 140.......................(t) NickScholfield 136+
(Paul Nicholls) *t.k.h: chsd ldng pair: wnt 2nd after 4th: hit 3 out: rdn and clsd on extended run between last 2: wandered and led last: drvn out* **11/8[1]**

2143 **2** 2 ¾ **Chic Name (FR)**[28] 3028 4-11-0 127..................................(v) AlainCawley 132
(Richard Hobson) *trckd ldr tl led 4th: sn 8 l clr: rdn on extended run between last 2: hdd last: kpt on same pce* **22/1**

60-2 **3** 8 **Coo Star Sivola (FR)**[56] 2480 4-11-0 0.......................... AidanColeman 125
(Nick Williams) *chsd ldrs: rdn bef 3 out: one pce: 3rd and hld whn blnd last* **3/1[2]**

11 **4** 22 **Jaboltiski (SPA)**[48] 2662 4-11-0 135.......................... TomO'Brien 101
(Philip Hobbs) *mid-div: wnt 4th appr 3 out: no further imp: wknd 2 out* **5/1[3]**

22 **5** 36 **Forgiving Glance**[35] 2896 4-10-7 123.......................... DenisO'Regan 58
(Alan King) *hld up: wknd appr 3 out: t.o* **11/1**

31 **6** 18 **Borak (IRE)**[26] 3076 4-11-0 120.............................. RobertWilliams 47
(Bernard Llewellyn) *hld up: nt fluent 4th: wknd appr 3 out: t.o* **12/1**

2 **7** 99 **Nabhan**[26] 3076 4-11-0 0.............................. MichaelByrne
(Bernard Llewellyn) *in rr: hit 1st: struggling whn j. slowly 3rd: lost tch after next: virtually p.u: t.o* **50/1**

3 **P** **Major Mac**[43] 2757 4-11-0 0..............................(t) NicodeBoinville
(Hughie Morrison) *led tl hdd and mstke 4th: wknd qckly: wl bhd whn p.u bef 3 out* **14/1**

4m 15.9s (5.30) **Going Correction** +0.775s/f (Soft) **8** Ran SP% **112.8**
Speed ratings: **117,115,111,100,82 73,24,**
CSF £32.16 TOTE £2.20: £1.20, £3.90, £1.60; EX 28.10 Trifecta £115.60.
Owner Mrs Johnny de la Hey **Bred** Thierry Cypres **Trained** Ditcheat, Somerset

FOCUS
A weak Grade 1 for juveniles and an extreme text. Adrien Du Pont is rated similar to his Cheltenham mark and stepped up on that compared to Chic Name.

3520 CORAL.CO.UK MONEY BACK IF YOUR HORSE FALLS NOVICES' LIMITED H'CAP CHASE (14 fncs 4 omitted) 2m 7f 131y
2:55 (2:56) (Class 3) 5-Y-0+ **£6,498** (£1,908; £954; £477)

Form RPR
6/05 **1** **Racing Pulse (IRE)**[74] 2122 7-11-5 130.............................. JJBurke 142+
(Rebecca Curtis) *hld up wl in tch: clsd 4th: chal 2 out: led last: drvn out* **6/1**

3-31 **2** 3 ¾ **Subtle Grey (IRE)**[27] 3055 7-11-1 126.......................... BarryGeraghty 134+
(Donald McCain) *trckd ldr: led 2 out: sn rdn: hdd last: one pce flat* **9/4[1]**

-332 **3** 2 ½ **Jennys Surprise (IRE)**[19] 3197 8-10-13 127.............. ConorShoemark(3) 132
(Fergal O'Brien) *led tl drvn and hdd 2 out: kpt on same pce* **15/2**

/364 **4** 9 **Berea Boru (IRE)**[35] 2905 8-10-11 122..........................(t) SeanBowen 118
(Peter Bowen) *mainly chsd ldrs: nt fluent 9th: wknd 3 out* **12/1**

6-3P **5** 3 ¼ **Heronshaw (IRE)**[36] 2878 9-10-12 123.......................... TomO'Brien 118
(Henry Daly) *in tch towards rr: mstke 10th: rdn appr 4 out: wknd 3 out* **11/2[3]**

1P11 **P** **Courtown Oscar (IRE)**[35] 2922 7-10-12 123.................. JamesReveley
(Philip Kirby) *hld up: mstke 3rd: hdwy 8th: wknd qckly after 10th: bhd whn p.u bef 4 out* **4/1[2]**

-512 **P** **Wizards Bridge**[42] 2785 7-11-8 133..............................(p) BrendanPowell
(Colin Tizzard) *chsd ldrs: lost pl whn blnd 7th: anther blunder next: sn no ch: wl bhd whn j. slowly 3 out and p.u* **13/2**

6m 48.9s (26.90) **Going Correction** +1.40s/f (Heav) **7** Ran SP% **113.2**
Speed ratings: **111,109,108,105,104**
CSF £20.30 CT £101.71 TOTE £6.50: £3.40, £1.90; EX 21.00 Trifecta £140.40.
Owner Carl Hinchy **Bred** Thomas O'Keeffe **Trained** Newport, Pembrokeshire

FOCUS
A fair staying handicap for novices, run at an average gallop, and they got sorted out with three to jump. The second and third fences in the back straight and the second in the home straight were omitted due to standing water. The winner improved to his hurdles mark.

3521 CORAL.CO.UK BEST PRICE GUARANTEED ON HORSE RACING H'CAP CHASE (12 fncs 4 omitted) 2m 3f 98y
3:25 (3:28) (Class 2) 5-Y-0+ **£19,165** (£5,785; £2,980; £1,579)

Form RPR
2-21 **1** **Otago Trail (IRE)**[36] 2877 8-11-12 141.......................... AidanColeman 157+
(Venetia Williams) *led to 2nd: styd cl up: led again after 4th: drew wl clr on extended run to 2 out: eased towards fin* **6/5[1]**

-425 **2** 36 **Saint Raph (FR)**[28] 3046 8-10-8 123..............................(t) JamieMoore 96
(Robert Walford) *cl up: led 2nd tl after 4th: styd in 2nd: mstke 7th: no ch w wnr fr 2 out: tired whn blnd last: jst hld 2nd* **6/1[2]**

31F2 **3** ½ **Fourth Act (IRE)**[24] 3106 7-10-12 127..........................(t) BrendanPowell 97
(Colin Tizzard) *hld up: rdn and sme hdwy 4 out: plugged on u.p: clsng on 2nd nr fin* **6/1[2]**

-642 **4** 15 **Going Concern (IRE)**[28] 3030 9-11-5 134.......................... AdamWedge 89
(Evan Williams) *chsd ldrs: u.p whn stmbld 4 out: sn wknd* **7/1[3]**

2615 **P** **Rouge Et Blanc (FR)**[36] 2877 11-10-12 130..............(p) ThomasGarner(3)
(Oliver Sherwood) *t.k.h early: chsd ldrs tl wknd after 10th: wl bhd whn p.u bef 3 out* **16/1**

-06P **P** **Quincy Des Pictons (FR)**[216] 660 12-11-5 141.............. HarryCobden(7)
(Alan Jones) *chsd ldrs tl lost pl after 4th: no ch fr 8th: t.o whn p.u bef 3 out* **9/1**

FF4- **P** **Fayette County (IRE)**[357] 3740 9-11-4 133..........................[1] BarryGeraghty
(Tim Vaughan) *hld up: rdn along fr 5th: j. slowly next: losing tch whn slow again 8th: sn p.u* **8/1**

5m 33.7s (22.40) **Going Correction** +1.40s/f (Heav) **7** Ran SP% **113.5**
Speed ratings: **108,92,92,86, ,**
CSF £9.11 TOTE £1.80: £1.30, £2.90; EX 10.30 Trifecta £33.60.
Owner Mrs Marie Shone **Bred** Dan O'Brien **Trained** Kings Caple, H'fords

FOCUS
This wasn't a bad handicap, but it proved one-way traffic as most found the going too much. The winner is a smart novice in this ground, but this easn't form to put a figure on.

3522 CORAL FUNDRAISING FOR "CHILDREN WITH CANCER UK" STANDARD OPEN NATIONAL HUNT FLAT RACE 2m 11y
4:00 (4:00) (Class 4) 5-7-Y-0 **£3,249** (£954; £477; £238)

Form RPR
1 **Ballymalin (IRE)**[91] 6-10-11 0.............................. RyanHatch(3) 118+
(Nigel Twiston-Davies) *prom: rdn along in 3rd 6f out: wnt 2nd 4f out and sn drew clr w ldr: led ins fnl f: styd on* **11/2[3]**

0-6 **2** 2 **Druid's Folly (IRE)**[44] 2729 6-11-0 0.............................. JJBurke 116+
(Rebecca Curtis) *led: drew clr w wnr fr 4f out: gng the bttr 2f out: sn wandered u.p: hdd ins fnl f: no ex* **7/4[1]**

/1 **3** 24 **Matchaway (IRE)**[29] 3012 7-11-2 0.............................. CiaranGethings(5) 99
(Kerry Lee) *prom: rdn 4f out: wknd 3f out and sn lost 3rd: tk modest 3rd again ins fnl f* **11/4[2]**

2 **4** 4 **Canton Prince (IRE)**[96] 1797 5-10-9 0.............................. AlanJohns(5) 88
(Tim Vaughan) *mid-div: rdn 5f out: sn no ch w ldrs: wnt mod 3rd over 2f out tl ins fnl f* **16/1**

5 23 **Dylanseoghan (IRE)**[321] 7-10-7 0.................. WilliamFeatherstone(7) 65
(Zoe Davison) *t.k.h towards rr: modest 5th whn drvn 5f out: grad wknd: t.o* **25/1**

6 hd **Cougar's Gold (IRE)** 5-11-0 0.............................. SeanBowen 65
(Peter Bowen) *hld up: rdn along at times: wknd 5f out: t.o* **8/1**

7 9 **Top And Drop** 5-10-7 0.............................. AidanColeman 49
(Venetia Williams) *a towards rr: lost tch 5f out: t.o* **13/2**

0 **8** 8 **Jack Henri (FR)**[35] 2909 5-11-0 0.............................. LeeEdwards 48
(Ian Williams) *t.k.h in mid-div: wknd 5f out: t.o* **50/1**

4m 21.7s (16.70) **Going Correction** +0.775s/f (Soft)
WFA 5 from 6yo+ 3lb **8** Ran SP% **114.5**
Speed ratings: **89,88,76,74,62 62,57,53**
CSF £15.59 TOTE £7.30: £2.60, £1.02, £1.50; EX 19.70 Trifecta £57.10.
Owner N A Twiston-Davies **Bred** Ms Anne Daly And Ms Laura Devitt **Trained** Naunton, Gloucs

FOCUS
An ordinary bumper, dominated by the first two home, who are probably decent.
T/Plt: £235.20 to a £1 stake. Pool: £156,529.95 - 485.81 winning units. T/Qpdt: £29.90 to a £1 stake. Pool: £16,273.84 - 402.36 winning units. **Richard Lowther**

3279 KEMPTON (R-H)
Saturday, January 9

OFFICIAL GOING: Soft (heavy in places; chs 4.8; hdl 4.3)
Wind: light, behind Weather: overcast

3523 WILLIAM HILL - IN THE APP STORE JUVENILE HURDLE (8 hdls) 2m
12:15 (12:15) (Class 4) 4-Y-0 **£3,249** (£954; £477; £238)

Form RPR
1 **Seven Kingdoms (IRE)**[137] 4-10-12 0.............................. NoelFehily 120+
(David Dennis) *nt a fluent: chsd ldng pair tl after 2nd: j.rt and cannoned into rival 3rd: smooth hdwy to trck ldrs after 3 out: led next: sn clr: v easily* **5/2[3]**

6110 **2** 17 **Golden Gate Bridge (GER)**[8] 3409 4-10-12 0.............. RichardJohnson 99
(Mark Pitman) *chsd ldr: clsd after 4th: pushed into ld bef 2 out: hdd 2 out and immediately brushed aside by wnr: plugged on to hold 2nd* **6/4[1]**

3 2 **Gild Master**[37] 4-10-12 0.............................. WayneHutchinson 101+
(Alan King) *plld hrd: mstkes: hld up in last pair: wnt 3rd after 2nd: mstke 5th: cl 4th after 3 out: 3rd and wl hld 2 out: plugged on* **9/4[2]**

2 **4** 13 **Directional**[212] 690 4-10-12 0.............................. TomCannon 85
(Tim Vaughan) *led: clr tl after 4th: rdn and hdd bef 2 out: sn btn: 4th and wkng next* **16/1**

65 **5** 47 **Satin And Lace (IRE)**[14] 3213 4-10-5 0..........................(t) MarcGoldstein 30
(Michael Madgwick) *a in last pair: j. bdly lft 1st: last whn j.lft and cannoned into rival 3rd: bhd after next: rdn and struggling after 5th: t.o 2 out* **66/1**

4m 13.15s (15.15) **Going Correction** +0.50s/f (Soft) **5** Ran SP% **106.7**
Speed ratings: **82,73,72,66,42**
CSF £6.44 TOTE £3.40: £1.60, £1.20; EX 8.00 Trifecta £10.70.
Owner Professor L P Hardwick & Partner **Bred** Ballygallon Stud Limited **Trained** Hanley Swan, Worcestershire

FOCUS
Allowing for rail movements, this race was run over 49yds further than advertised. The testing ground made it hard work for these 4yos in what was a modest juvenile event for the track, with Seven Kingdoms coming from off the pace to run out an easy winner. He looks a fair recruit.

3524 WILLIAM HILL - DOWNLOAD THE APP H'CAP CHASE (13 fncs) 2m 2f
12:50 (12:50) (Class 3) (0-140,137)
5-Y-0+ **£6,498** (£1,908; £954; £477)

Form RPR
-200 **1** **Un Beau Roman (FR)**[13] 3284 8-11-7 132.............. WayneHutchinson 144+
(Paul Henderson) *hld up in last pair: clsd to trck ldrs 9th: swtchd lft and jnd ldrs 3 out: sn led: pushed along and asserted last: styd on wl: rdn out* **20/1**

24-4 **2** 4 ½ **Galway Jack (IRE)**[246] 184 11-11-9 134.............. AndrewThornton 140
(Caroline Bailey) *in tch: clsd to trck ldrs 9th: ev ch 3 out: clr w wnr next: no ex u.p between last: kpt in same pce flat* **6/1**

6-PF **3** 15 **The Clock Leary (IRE)**[47] 2686 8-10-10 126..........(b[1]) CharlieDeutsch(5) 116
(Venetia Williams) *racd keenly: led after 1st tl rdn and hdd sn after 3 out: 3rd and btn whn j.lft next: wknd* **4/1[3]**

-6P2 **4** 3 ¼ **Comeonginger (IRE)**[29] 3014 9-11-1 126..........(t) TomCannon 114
(Chris Gordon) *racd keenly: led tl after 1st: rdn 10th: 4th and btn whn j.rt 2 out: wknd* **11/4[2]**

341U **5** 34 **Balgarry (FR)**[11] 3351 9-11-12 137.............................. TomScudamore 104
(David Pipe) *chsd ldrs: blnd 2nd: mstke and lost pl 8th: struggling in 5th and u.p next: lost tch 3 out: t.o* **2/1[1]**

/22- P **Starkie**[280] 2147 9-11-0 125............................ RichardJohnson
(Paul Henderson) *a last: mstke 2nd: detached after 6th: lost tch and j.v.slowly 10th: t.o whn p.u next* 7/1
4m 38.8s (278.80) 6 Ran SP% **111.5**
CSF £122.21 TOTE £22.00: £7.80, £4.20; EX 141.40 Trifecta £1212.90.
Owner John H W Finch & The Romans **Bred** Jaques Cypres **Trained** Whitsbury, Hants
■ A new race distance for Kempton.
FOCUS
Allowing for rail movements, this race was run over 39yds further than advertised. A fair handicap, although the market leaders failed to run up to their best, with the early pace a good one and first pair home sitting off it. The winner is on the upgrade.

3525 WILLIAM HILL - BET AND WATCH NOVICES' HURDLE (12 hdls) 3m 121y
1:25 (1:25) (Class 3) 4-Y-O+ **£5,393** (£1,583; £791; £395)

Form RPR
4-14 1 **The Boss's Dream (IRE)**[49] 2630 8-11-12 125............ TrevorWhelan 129
(Neil King) *led: jnd and rdn 3 out: hdd and jst over 1 l down 2 out: battled on u.p to ld again last: hld on towards fin: all out* 8/1
311 2 ½ **Tapaculo**[35] 2904 5-11-12 130.......................... RichardJohnson 130+
(Philip Hobbs) *in tch: hdwy to join wnr and travelling wl 3 out: led and jst over 1 l ahd whn nt fluent next: sn rdn: hdd last: kpt on again towards fin: hld cl home* 5/6[1]
6-31 3 4½ **Weststreet (IRE)**[27] 3064 6-11-8 119..................(p) LeightonAspell 120
(Oliver Sherwood) *chsd ldrs: wnt 2nd 8th tl bef next: 3rd and styd on same pce u.p fr bef 2 out* 5/1[3]
-401 4 54 **Brod Na Heireann (IRE)**[23] 3126 7-11-8 123........ WayneHutchinson 66
(Alan King) *chsd wnr tl after 8th: 4th and wknd next: t.o* 3/1[2]
P0 P **Kent Ragstone (USA)**[3] 3483 7-11-2 0.................. MattieBatchelor
(Sheena West) *nt fluent: in tch in rr tl 9th: sn lost tch: t.o whn p.u 2 out* 200/1
00-4 P **Dun Bay Creek**[26] 3085 5-10-13 0........................ TomBellamy[(3)]
(Alan King) *in tch: 5th and struggling bef 3 out: wknd and t.o whn p.u 2 out* 40/1
6m 31.8s (11.80) **Going Correction** +0.50s/f (Soft) 6 Ran SP% **110.3**
Speed ratings (Par 107): **101,100,99,82,**
CSF £15.33 TOTE £7.80: £2.40, £1.20; EX 15.00 Trifecta £55.70.
Owner SLIS Ltd, M Gibbons & D Nott **Bred** Paul Barden **Trained** Barbury Castle, Wiltshire
FOCUS
Allowing for rail movements, this race was run over 99yds further than advertised. A fair novice hurdle where the best horse finished second. The winner is rated up 4lb.

3526 WILLIAMHILL.COM CHASE (LISTED RACE) (16 fncs) 2m 4f 110y
2:00 (2:00) (Class 1) 5-Y-O+ **£18,690** (£8,016)

Form RPR
/P3- 1 **Triolo D'Alene (FR)**[371] 3508 9-11-0 150.............. JeremiahMcGrath 160+
(Nicky Henderson) *led tl 10th: j. bk into ld 12th: bttr jump than rival and def advantage 3 out: 1 l ld and travelling best whn lft wl clr next* 8/1[3]
0-23 2 49 **Wishfull Thinking**[34] 2927 13-11-10 165..................(t) RichardJohnson 150
(Philip Hobbs) *hld up in tch in 3rd: rdn after 13th: sn lost tch: lft poor 2nd 2 out: t.o* 10/3[2]
-12F U **Ptit Zig (FR)**[34] 2927 7-11-10 162.......................... SamTwiston-Davies 163
(Paul Nicholls) *pressed wnr on inner tl led 10th: out j. and hdd 12th: out j. by wnr next 2 fences: jst over 1 l down and drvn whn mstke and uns rdr 2 out* 2/5[1]
5m 22.15s (10.15) **Going Correction** +0.85s/f (Soft) 3 Ran SP% **105.6**
Speed ratings: **114,95,**
CSF £24.63 TOTE £5.10; EX 14.70 Trifecta £14.40.
Owner Mr & Mrs Sandy Orr **Bred** Louis Couteaudier **Trained** Upper Lambourn, Berks
FOCUS
Allowing for rail movements, this race was run over 39yds further than advertised. A good race despite the three runners, but there was a bit of a turn up with it going to the outsider of three. Triolo D'Alene is rated back to his best.

3527 WILLIAM HILL LANZAROTE HURDLE (H'CAP) (LISTED RACE) (10 hdls) 2m 5f
2:35 (2:35) (Class 1) 4-Y-O+
£22,780 (£8,548; £4,280; £2,132; £1,072; £536)

Form RPR
2-15 1 **Yala Enki (FR)**[49] 2641 6-9-12 130...................... CharlieDeutsch[(5)] 142+
(Venetia Williams) *led and handed clr ld at s: hit 5th: rdn bef last: styd on gamely flat* 11/4[1]
P21 2 2 **Westren Warrior (IRE)**[19] 3194 7-10-0 127................ WillKennedy 138+
(Dr Richard Newland) *mstkes: mostly chsd wnr: effrt and hit 2 out: drvn between last 2: kpt on but a hld flat* 9/2[2]
64-2 3 1¾ **Ibis Du Rheu (FR)**[42] 2781 5-10-8 135..............(t) SamTwiston-Davies 142
(Paul Nicholls) *hld up in last trio: clsd and in tch 5th: hdwy and mstke 3 out: effrt and cl 3rd 2 out: styd on same pce u.p flat* 11/2
1-13 4 9 **Brother Tedd**[49] 2634 7-11-12 153.......................... RichardJohnson 152
(Philip Hobbs) *racd wd: hld up in last pair: clsd and in tch 5th: cl 4th and rdn 2 out: wknd bef last* 7/1
-4F0 5 3¼ **Little Boy Boru (IRE)**[14] 3254 8-9-11 127 oh5............ HarryBannister[(3)] 122
(Suzy Smith) *hld up in rr: clsd and in tch 5th: struggling u.p 7th bef 2 out: plugged on but no ch* 16/1
PF-P 6 2½ **Deep Trouble (IRE)**[35] 2914 9-10-13 140..................(t) KielanWoods 133
(Ben Case) *t.k.h: mostly 3rd tl 5th and outpcd jst bef 2 out: wknd between last 2* 33/1
2-42 7 2¾ **Un Ace (FR)**[35] 2901 8-11-3 144.......................... (t) DavidBass 134
(Kim Bailey) *midfield: clsd and in tch 5th: nt fluent next: 6th and struggling u.p bef 2 out: wknd 2 out* 10/1
3135 8 16 **Dell' Arca (IRE)**[43] 2760 7-11-1 142.................(p) TomScudamore 123
(David Pipe) *hld up in midfield: clsd and in tch 5th: dropped to last and struggling u.p 3 out: wknd bef next: t.o* 11/1
3-01 P **Bivouac (FR)**[60] 2411 5-11-0 141.......................... NoelFehily
(Nicky Henderson) *hld up in midfield: clsd and in tch 5th: mstke 3 out: sn rdn and btn: fading whn hung lft bef 2 out: sn p.u* 5/1[3]
5m 25.1s (4.10) **Going Correction** +0.50s/f (Soft) 9 Ran SP% **115.6**
Speed ratings (Par 111): **112,111,110,107,105 104,103,97,**
CSF £15.99 CT £63.14 TOTE £4.20: £1.50, £1.70, £1.90; EX 13.50 Trifecta £86.30.
Owner Hills Of Ledbury (Aga) **Bred** Esteve Rouchvarger Et Al **Trained** Kings Caple, H'fords

FOCUS
Allowing for rail movements, this race was run over 70yds further than advertised. Bit of an unsatisfactory race, with the winner gifted a several-lengths lead at the start and the eventual second, in turn with another, racing a few lengths ahead of the main bunch. A step up from the winner.

3528 WILLIAM HILL - BET ON THE MOVE H'CAP CHASE (18 fncs) 3m
3:10 (3:10) (Class 2) (0-150,147) 5-Y-O+ **£12,021** (£3,529; £1,764; £882)

Form RPR
/02- 1 **Kruzhlinin (GER)**[342] 4001 9-11-3 138.................. RichardJohnson 153+
(Philip Hobbs) *j.lft: chsd ldrs: blnd 1st: led 5th: mde rest: j.lft and cannoned into rival 14th: clr 2 out: styd on: readily* 5/2[1]
3-P0 2 5 **Le Reve (IRE)**[56] 2482 8-11-12 147.......................(p) LeightonAspell 153
(Lucy Wadham) *hld up in tch: pushed along to chse ldrs 13th: drvn bef 3 out: outpcd 2 out: wnt 2nd last: no imp* 7/2[2]
3-1F 3 1¼ **Harry's Farewell**[13] 3282 9-10-5 133.................. MrJoshuaNewman[(7)] 140
(Polly Gundry) *led tl 4th: mostly chsd wnr after: ev ch and bmpd 14th: rdn and flashed tail u.p fr after next: no ex 2 out: lost 2nd last* 11/2
P0-0 4 36 **Grandads Horse**[35] 2916 10-11-2 137......................(p) NoelFehily 105
(Charlie Longsdon) *hld up in tch: rdn and btn after 15th: wknd next: t.o* 8/1
-2US 5 15 **Shangani (USA)**[13] 3282 10-10-6 132....................(b) CharlieDeutsch[(5)] 85
(Venetia Williams) *chsd ldrs: rdn 14th: wknd after next: t.o* 5/1[3]
P-60 P **Poole Master**[35] 2902 11-11-7 142.......................(bt) TomScudamore
(David Pipe) *led tl 4th: lost pl and blnd 9th: bhd and reminders bef next: t.o 12th tl p.u 14th* 12/1
500/ F **Seefood (IRE)**[162] 1173 9-11-3 138.......................... WillKennedy
(Dr Richard Newland) *chsd ldrs 6th: 5th and rdn whn fell 12th* 15/2
6m 22.2s (13.20) **Going Correction** +0.85s/f (Soft) 7 Ran SP% **113.4**
Speed ratings: **112,110,109,97,92**,
CSF £11.88 CT £42.28 TOTE £2.90: £1.50, £2.50; EX 7.60 Trifecta £30.50.
Owner Paul & Clare Rooney **Bred** Gestut Kussaburg **Trained** Withycombe, Somerset
FOCUS
A good-quality staying handicap that was won in taking fashion by the favourite. He was well in old form.

3529 WILLIAM HILL - HOME OF BETTING H'CAP HURDLE (8 hdls) 2m
3:45 (3:45) (Class 3) (0-140,135) 4-Y-O+ **£5,393** (£1,583; £791; £395)

Form RPR
3-25 1 **Mr Fitzroy (IRE)**[39] 2831 6-9-12 110.......................(t) JamesBanks[(3)] 122+
(Jo Davis) *chsd ldrs: mstke 2nd: led 3 out: clr and in command whn mstke last: r.o: readily* 11/2[2]
-511 2 6 **Hollywood All Star (IRE)**[22] 3140 7-9-10 112........... ArchieBellamy[(7)] 116
(Graeme McPherson) *in tch in midfield: hdwy 3 out: chsd wnr and drvn bef 2 out: styd on same pce between last 2* 5/1[1]
-104 3 3¾ **War Singer (USA)**[34] 2926 9-11-7 130...................(bt) LeightonAspell 130
(Johnny Farrelly) *hld up in tch towards rr: hdwy to trck ldrs bef 2 out: effrt in 3rd 2 out: sn btn: wknd flat* 14/1
0F11 4 4 **Dormouse**[19] 3196 11-10-11 120.......................(p) RichardJohnson 114
(Anabel K Murphy) *sn bhd and struggling: niggled along after 5th: styd on to pass btn horses bef 2 out: snatched 4th on line: nvr trbld ldrs* 9/1
P320 5 nse **Exitas (IRE)**[13] 3284 8-11-1 129.......................(t) CharlieDeutsch[(5)] 124
(Phil Middleton) *in tch in midfield: hdwy to chse ldrs after 3 out: 4th and btn whn j.lft next: lost 4th on line* 16/1
-400 6 19 **Stars Over The Sea (USA)**[77] 2060 5-11-12 135......(t) TomScudamore 112
(David Pipe) *led: hit 5th: mstke and hdd 3 out: wknd bef next* 11/2[2]
46-3 7 2 **Jumps Road**[23] 3120 9-11-6 129.............................(t) NoelFehily 104
(Colin Tizzard) *hld up in tch towards rr: short-lived effrt after 3 out: sn wl btn and bhd 2 out* 9/1
43-2 8 1 **Tara Bridge**[28] 3047 8-10-11 120.......................... TomCannon 92
(Chris Gordon) *t.k.h: hld up in tch in midfield: rdn and btn sn after 3 out: wl bhd next* 11/2[2]
-U54 9 6 **Last Supper**[35] 2901 7-10-12 124.......................... JoeColliver[(3)] 90
(James Bethell) *chsd ldr tl lost pl qckly bef 3 out: wl bhd bef 2 out: t.o* 9/1
-342 10 1½ **Heath Hunter (IRE)**[26] 3080 9-11-8 134..................(bt) KieronEdgar[(3)] 98
(David Pipe) *chsd ldrs: ev ch and blnd 3 out: wknd u.p bef next: fdd: t.o* 6/1[3]
4m 5.0s (7.00) **Going Correction** +0.50s/f (Soft) 10 Ran SP% **119.7**
Speed ratings (Par 107): **102,99,97,95,95 85,84,84,81,80**
CSF £34.61 CT £372.67 TOTE £7.80: £2.30, £1.40, £4.80; EX 35.70 Trifecta £730.10.
Owner Mrs Patricia Brown **Bred** Mrs D M Solomon **Trained** East Garston, Berks
FOCUS
Ordinary handicap form. A big hurdles best from the winner.
T/Jkpt: not won. JACKPOT PLACEPOT £2,322.70. Pool: £3,181.90 - 0.95 winning units. T/Plt: £302.00 to a £1 stake. Pool: £87,141.47 - 210.58 winning units. T/Qpdt: £34.10 to a £1 stake. Pool: £8,313.76 - 180.04 winning units. **Steve Payne**

3252 WINCANTON (R-H)
Saturday, January 9

3530 Meeting Abandoned -

3536 - 3538a (Foreign Racing) - See Raceform Interactive

3389 PUNCHESTOWN (R-H)
Saturday, January 9

OFFICIAL GOING: Heavy

3539a SKY BET MOSCOW FLYER NOVICE HURDLE (GRADE 2) (9 hdls) 2m
2:05 (2:07) 5-Y-O+ **£18,529** (£5,867; £2,779; £926; £617)

RPR
1 **Min (FR)**[30] 3003 5-11-0 0...................................... RWalsh 152+
(W P Mullins, Ire) *chsd ldrs tl wnt 2nd fr 1st: racd freely early and led fr 3rd: extended advantage bef next: reduced ld 3 out and pressed next: stl travelling wl into st and extended advantage bef last where in command: easily* 1/7[1]
2 9½ **Attribution**[34] 2938 6-11-2 132..........................(p) BJCooper 142
(Henry De Bromhead, Ire) *chsd ldr tl dropped to 3rd fr 1st: wnt 2nd bef 3 out: disp cl 2nd next where nt fluent: rdn in 2nd between last 2 and sn no imp on easy wnr: kpt on one pce* 9/2[2]
3 1¼ **Ball D'Arc (FR)**[12] 3326 5-11-0 0.......................... DavyRussell 139
(Gordon Elliott, Ire) *hld up towards rr: impr into 3rd bef 3 out: disp cl 2nd 2 out: rdn in 3rd between last 2 and sn no imp on easy wnr: kpt on one pce* 12/1[3]

4 *37* **Gars Bar Dine (FR)** 21 [3170] 5-11-0 123........................ AndrewRing 104
(Mrs S A Bramall, Ire) *hld up in rr: detached in rr 4th: pushed along into mod 4th after 3 out and no imp: mstke last: t.o* **100/1**

5 *17* **Tongie (IRE)** 14 [3269] 6-11-2 109........................ DannyMullins 87
(P A Fahy, Ire) *led tl hdd fr 3rd and settled bhd ldr: pushed along and lost pl bef 3 out where nt fluent in 4th: wknd: eased and slt mstke last: completely t.o* **100/1**

4m 0.7s (-4.30) **Going Correction** +0.10s/f (Yiel) **5 Ran SP% 115.3**
Speed ratings: **114,109,108,90,81**
CSF £1.66 TOTE £1.10: £1.02, £1.30; DF 1.60 Trifecta £2.10.
Owner Mrs S Ricci **Bred** Madame Marie-Therese Mimouni **Trained** Muine Beag, Co Carlow

FOCUS
A very impressive performance from Min considering the manner in which he raced although it has to be said that he was beating horses that should be well short of his calibre. The time was the pick of the card.

3540 - 3542a (Foreign Racing) - See Raceform Interactive

3076 FFOS LAS (L-H)
Sunday, January 10

3543 Meeting Abandoned - waterlogged

3549 - 3551a (Foreign Racing) - See Raceform Interactive

3429 FAIRYHOUSE (R-H)
Sunday, January 10

OFFICIAL GOING: Heavy

3552a UNDERWRITING EXCHANGE DAN MOORE MEMORIAL H'CAP CHASE (GRADE A) (13 fncs) 2m 1f
2:20 (2:22) 4-Y-0+

£44,117 (£13,970; £6,617; £2,205; £1,470; £735)

RPR

1 **Nearly Nama'd (IRE)** 43 [2794] 8-10-5 **134**........................ BarryGeraghty 145+
(Ms Sandra Hughes, Ire) *settled bhd ldrs: clsr in 2nd 3 out (normal 4 out) and disp appr st: led after 2 out and rdn clr run-in: kpt on wl* **4/1** 2

2 *4 ½* **Mozoltov** 29 [3031] 10-11-5 **148**........................ DavidMullins 154+
(W P Mullins, Ire) *hld up towards rr: cl 6th whn slt mstke 5 out (normal 6 out): impr bhd ldrs into 4th into st: slt mstke in 3rd 2 out: no imp on wnr bef last: kpt on u.p into 2nd cl home* **14/1**

3 *1* **Guitar Pete (IRE)** 57 [2504] 6-10-3 **132** oh2........................(vt) MsNCarberry 137
(Ms Sandra Hughes, Ire) *mid-div early tl tk clsr order bhd ldrs bef 3rd: disp appr st and hdd after 2 out: rdn and no imp on wnr bef last: kpt on same pce and dropped to 3rd cl home* **8/1**

4 *9* **Tennis Cap (FR)** 50 [2655] 9-10-11 **140**........................ RWalsh 135
(W P Mullins, Ire) *mid-div early: j.big 2nd: dropped to rr at 5th: sme hdwy after 7th: rdn briefly after 3 out (normal 4 out): cl 6th bef 2 out: sn rdn and no imp on ldrs: kpt on one pce in mod 4th run-in* **7/1** 3

5 *4* **Days Hotel (IRE)** 27 [3092] 11-11-4 **147**........................ AELynch 139
(Henry De Bromhead, Ire) *disp early and settled bhd ldrs fr 1st: 4th whn mstke 6th: pushed along into st and no ex u.p in 4th after 2 out where j.big: one pce in 5th run-in* **8/1**

6 *5* **Draycott Place (IRE)** 273 [5303] 7-9-12 **132** oh4........................ DonaghMeyler(5) 118
(John Patrick Ryan, Ire) *chsd ldrs tl led narrowly bef 5 out (normal 6 out): hdd bef st: sn rdn in 3rd and wknd 2 out* **16/1**

7 *8 ½* **Bright New Dawn (IRE)** 27 [3092] 9-11-0 **148**........................(t) JackKennedy(5) 126
(Gordon Elliott, Ire) *hld up in rr: mstke and hmpd 2nd: tk clsr order bef 3 out (normal 4 out): squeezed for room and lost pl at bypassed 3 out: pushed along in 7th appr st and sn no imp on ldrs: one pce after* **9/4** 1

8 *8* **Clarcam (FR)** 14 [3293] 6-11-10 **153**........................(tp) BJCooper 123
(Gordon Elliott, Ire) *chsd ldrs: 6th bef 6th: dropped to 9th bef 3 out (normal 4 out) and no imp: mod 8th bef 2 out: one pce after* **11/1**

P **Baily Green (IRE)** 165 [1152] 10-11-5 **148**........................(t) MarkEnright
(M F Morris, Ire) *disp early and led fr 1st: hdd bef 5 out (normal 6 out) mstke in 4th 3 out (normal 4 out): sn wknd and eased: p.u bef 2 out* **16/1**

F **Irish Thistle (IRE)** 15 [3270] 9-9-10 **132** oh4........................(t) JonathanMoore(7)
(H Rogers, Ire) *hld up in tch: mstke 1st and dropped towards rr: clsr in 6th bef next where fell* **14/1**

4m 39.3s (8.30) **Going Correction** +0.825s/f (Soft) **10 Ran SP% 118.9**
Speed ratings: **113,110,110,106,104 101,97,94, ,**
CSF £57.43 CT £434.81 TOTE £5.00: £1.30, £3.50, £2.30; DF 58.10 Trifecta £744.20.
Owner John P McManus **Bred** Prospect Stables Ltd **Trained** Kildare, Co Kildare

FOCUS
There were two fences omitted - the third and seventh on the circuit - due to ground conditions.\n\x\x A competitive renewal of this handicap with five of the field rated 147 or higher. The early gallop was quite strong given the conditions and the winner won decisively.

3553 - 3555a (Foreign Racing) - See Raceform Interactive

3436 AYR (L-H)
Monday, January 11

3556 Meeting Abandoned - waterlogged

3417 FAKENHAM (L-H)
Tuesday, January 12

3562 Meeting Abandoned - waterlogged

3464 LUDLOW (R-H)
Tuesday, January 12

OFFICIAL GOING: Heavy (soft in places; 4.8)
Wind: Fresh half-against Weather: Cloudy

3568 RACINGUK.COM/ANYWHERE "NATIONAL HUNT" NOVICES' HURDLE (8 hdls 1 omitted) 1m 7f 169y
1:30 (1:30) (Class 5) 4-Y-0+ **£2,599** (£763; £381; £190)

Form RPR

-41F 1 **The Gipper (IRE)** 38 [2904] 6-11-11 0........................ AdamWedge 129+
(Evan Williams) *mde all: j.lft 2nd: shkn up flat: styd on wl* **4/11** 1

-P25 2 *1 ¾* **Itshard To No (IRE)** 35 [2961] 7-11-11 115........................(t) RichardJohnson 126+
(Kerry Lee) *sn prom: chsd wnr 4th: hit 3 out: j.lft next: rdn and hung lft flat: styd on* **4/1** 2

0P 3 *28* **Jack Snipe** 13 [3370] 7-11-5 0........................ LiamHeard 90
(Jeremy Scott) *hld up in tch: rdn appr 3 out: sn wknd* **100/1**

0- 4 *shd* **Kapgarde King (FR)** 307 [4715] 5-11-5 0........................ 1 BrendanPowell 90
(Jamie Snowden) *prom: rdn appr 3 out: sn wknd* **66/1**

3-04 5 *8* **Weyburn (IRE)** 66 [2338] 5-11-5 0........................ AndrewTinkler 82
(Martin Keighley) *hld up: hdwy appr 3 out: sn wknd* **12/1**

60 6 *1 ¼* **Adeenne De Sevres (FR)** 42 [2840] 6-11-5 0........................ WayneHutchinson 81
(Tom Lacey) *chsd wnr to 4th: remained handy tl rdn and wknd 3 out* **25/1**

000 7 *1 ¾* **The Minkle (IRE)** 11 [3411] 5-11-5 0........................ TomScudamore 79
(David Pipe) *hld up and bhd: rdn appr 3 out: sn wknd* **50/1**

5500 8 *1* **Definately Vinnie** 27 [3105] 6-11-0 0........................ ConorRing(5) 78
(Jane Mathias) *hld up and bhd: nvr on terms* **100/1**

0 9 *1 ½* **Bandon Roc** 33 [2995] 5-11-5 0........................ DavidBass 76
(Kim Bailey) *prom tl rdn after 5th: wknd bef next* **8/1** 3

FUUF 10 *6* **Seeanythingyoulike (IRE)** 55 [2563] 5-11-2 0........................ MattGriffiths(3) 70
(Jeremy Scott) *hld up and bhd: plld hrd: hdwy on outer appr 3 out: sn wknd* **66/1**

0P0P 11 *5* **Kaddys Girl** 12 [3386] 6-10-7 0........................ ChrisWard(5) 58
(Robin Dickin) *hld up: j. slowly 4th: nt fluent next: hdwy appr 3 out: sn rdn and wknd* **66/1**

00 P **Manton Boy** 62 [2440] 7-11-5 0........................ KielanWoods
(Michael Mullineaux) *prom: mstke 5th: sn rdn and wknd: bhd whn p.u bef next* **80/1**

4m 8.4s (18.90) **Going Correction** +1.475s/f (Heav) **12 Ran SP% 125.6**
Speed ratings (Par 103): **101,100,86,86,82 81,80,80,79,76 73,**
CSF £2.50 TOTE £1.30: £1.10, £1.50, £20.50; EX 2.30 Trifecta £112.40.
Owner POS Partnership **Bred** James Nolan **Trained** Llancarfan, Vale Of Glamorgan

FOCUS
Race distance 24yds further than advertised. Testing ground, described by Adam Wedge as "pretty deep and hard work", and by Tom Scudamore as "very, very holding and hardish work". There was no depth to this novice hurdle, which was dominated by the two penalised runners.

3569 RACING UK 3 DEVICES 1 PRICE H'CAP CHASE (22 fncs) 3m 1f 125y
2:00 (2:00) (Class 4) (0-115,115) 5-Y-0+ **£5,198** (£1,526; £763; £381)

Form RPR

4313 1 **Still Believing (IRE)** 64 [2403] 8-11-11 **114**........................ AdamWedge 120
(Evan Williams) *hld up: racd keenly: hdwy appr 4 out: chsd ldr and j.rt next: led appr last: rdn out* **3/1** 2

5-52 2 *nk* **Take The Mick** 32 [3008] 9-11-12 **115**........................(p) AidanColeman 124+
(Venetia Williams) *led: mstke 12th: hdd after 14th: sn rdn: lost 2nd 16th: rallied to ld 4 out: blnd 2 out: hdd bef last: styd on u.p* **1/1** 1

/P04 3 *32* **Raduis Bleu (FR)** 12 [3385] 11-9-9 **91**........................ MissLBrooke(7) 65
(Lady Susan Brooke) *chsd ldrs: mstke 12th: rdn 17th: wknd 4 out* **20/1**

/111 4 *¾* **Celtic Intrigue (IRE)** 177 [1049] 9-11-8 **111**........................(p) TomScudamore 84
(David Bridgwater) *chsd ldr tl led after 14th: rdn and hdd 4 out: wknd appr 2 out* **9/2** 3

25-P U **Ghost Of A Smile (IRE)** 59 [2491] 8-10-13 **102**........................ WillKennedy
(Ian Williams) *hld up: hdwy 14th: chsd ldr 16th: ev ch appr 4 out: sn rdn and wknd: pulling up whn rn into the last and uns rdr* **7/1**

7m 21.6s (46.30) **Going Correction** +1.55s/f (Heav) **5 Ran SP% 110.4**
Speed ratings: **90,89,80,79,**
CSF £6.82 TOTE £3.90: £1.80, £1.20; EX 7.60 Trifecta £35.30.
Owner R E R Williams **Bred** Declan Moran **Trained** Llancarfan, Vale Of Glamorgan

FOCUS
Race distance 48yds further than advertised. This proved a slog, and was a race of fluctuating fortunes. The winner is rated to her mark.

3570 RACINGUK.COM/WINTERSEASONTICKET MAIDEN HURDLE (10 hdls 1 omitted) 2m 5f 55y
2:30 (2:30) (Class 5) 4-Y-0+ **£2,599** (£763; £381; £190)

Form RPR

1 **Battle Of Shiloh (IRE)** 345 7-11-6 0........................ WayneHutchinson 112+
(Tom George) *hld up in tch: led 3 out: rdn and hung lft appr last: edgd rt flat: styd on u.p* **9/4** 1

06 2 *2* **Another Frontier (IRE)** 44 [2807] 5-11-1 0........................ JamieBargary(5) 109
(Nigel Twiston-Davies) *a.p: chsd ldr 7th: ev ch fr 3 out: rdn appr last: no ex towards fin* **15/2** 3

3 *5* **One Style (FR)** 422 6-11-6 0........................ AidanColeman 104
(Venetia Williams) *chsd ldrs: rdn appr last: no ex flat* **4/1** 2

0-F3 4 *1 ½* **Baraka De Thaix (FR)** 29 [3077] 5-11-6 119........................(t) TomScudamore 103
(David Pipe) *hld up: hdwy 7th: rdn after 3 out: styd on same pce appr last: styd on same pce* **9/4** 1

/4-0 5 *½* **Crowd Control (IRE)** 8 [3467] 7-10-13 0........................ MissLBrooke(7) 102
(Lady Susan Brooke) *led: hdd 3 out: styd on same pce appr last* **200/1**

0- 6 *3* **Driftwood Haze** 263 [5511] 8-11-1 0........................ MrBMoorcroft(5) 100
(Phillip Dando) *hld up: hdwy 7th: rdn and wknd 2 out* **66/1**

7 *13* **Late Shipment** 57 5-11-1 0........................ ChrisWard(5) 89
(Nikki Evans) *hld up: hdwy appr 3 out: rdn and wkng whn mstke next: hung lft flat* **25/1**

05 8 *56* **Midnight Jade (IRE)** 8 [3467] 7-10-13 0........................ LeeEdwards 23
(John Groucott) *hld up: hdwy appr 3 out: sn rdn and wknd* **125/1**

60/5 9 *8* **Viking Mistress** 12 [3386] 8-10-13 0........................ AndrewTinkler 15
(Martin Keighley) *hld up: hdwy after 7th: rdn and wknd bef next* **50/1**

-F4P P **Rock Of Ages** 10 [2838] 7-11-1 100........................(bt) CiaranGethings(5)
(Steve Flook) *chsd ldr to 6th: rdn and wknd after next: bhd whn p.u bef 3 out* **50/1**

60 **P** **Penny Option (IRE)**[224] 594 7-10-13 0............................ TomO'Brien
(Robert Stephens) *mid-div: hit 4th: wknd after 7th: bhd whn p.u bef 3 out* **100/1**

054 **P** **Midnight Target**[12] 3381 6-10-13 0............................ LiamHeard
(John Groucott) *hld up: hit 2nd: mstke 5th: bhd fr 7th: p.u bef 3 out* **25/1**

P **Allstar Vinnie (IRE)**[44] 6-10-13 0.......................... MrTommieMO'Brien[(7)]
(Tom Lacey) *chsd ldrs tl rdn and wknd after 7th: bhd whn p.u bef next* **16/1**

5m 39.5s (24.70) **Going Correction** +1.475s/f (Heavy) **13** Ran SP% **114.6**
Speed ratings (Par 103): **101,100,98,97,97 96,91,70,67, , ,**
CSF £19.01 TOTE £3.00: £1.30, £2.20, £1.70; EX 17.00 Trifecta £66.50.
Owner Paul & Clare Rooney **Bred** Mrs Evelyn Sheridan **Trained** Slad, Gloucs

FOCUS
Race distance 48yds further than advertised. A modest event in which they went what looked a steady pace. The fourth is rated a stone off.

3571 RACING UK WINTER SEASON TICKET NOVICES' CHASE (12 fncs) 1m 7f 212y
3:00 (3:01) (Class 3) 5-Y-0+ **£6,657** (£2,067; £1,113)

Form RPR

1-11 **1** **Garde La Victoire (FR)**[58] 2510 7-11-10 151.............. RichardJohnson 153+
(Philip Hobbs) *trckd ldr: nt fluent 3rd: j.lft 6th: led and wnt rt appr 2 out: rdn and hung rt bef last: pushed out* **1/6**[1]

1/02 **2** *5* **Doctor Harper (IRE)**[9] 3451 8-11-0 0.......................... TomScudamore 133+
(David Pipe) *chsd ldrs: outpcd 7th: reminder after next: styd on to go 2nd towards fin* **6/1**[2]

1- **3** *nk* **Gino Trail (IRE)**[348] 3934 9-11-0 0.............................. TomCannon 134
(David Bridgwater) *led: hdd appr 2 out: mstke and no ex last* **18/1**[3]

P **Beallandendall (IRE)**[226] 8-10-7 0...................... MrStanSheppard[(7)]
(Matt Sheppard) *hld up: plld hrd: mstke 3rd: nt fluent 7th: sn bhd: p.u bef 2 out* **150/1**

4m 21.0s (22.50) **Going Correction** +1.55s/f (Heavy) **4** Ran SP% **105.9**
Speed ratings: **105,102,102,**
CSF £1.67 TOTE £1.10; EX 1.70 Trifecta £1.90.
Owner Mrs Diana L Whateley **Bred** Mlle Laure Godet **Trained** Withycombe, Somerset

FOCUS
Race distance 48yds further than advertised. Much of the interest in this novice chase centred around the long odds-on favourite, already a Grade 2 winner over fences. He's rated below his best.

3572 RACING UK DAY PASS JUST £10 CONDITIONAL JOCKEYS' H'CAP HURDLE (10 hdls 2 omitted) 2m 7f 174y
3:30 (3:30) (Class 4) (0-110,110) 4-Y-0+ **£3,898** (£1,144; £572; £286)

Form RPR

F-55 **1** **Fishing Bridge (IRE)**[29] 3078 11-11-6 **104**............(vt) KieronEdgar 110+
(David Rees) *hld up: blnd 7th: hdwy appr 3 out: led flat: drvn out* **5/1**[3]

U52U **2** *9* **Market Option (IRE)**[26] 3127 10-11-3 **104**............(p) CharlieDeutsch[(3)] 100
(Venetia Williams) *led to 7th: led again appr 3 out: rdn and hdd flat: wknd towards fin* **9/2**[2]

335 **3** *3/4* **Captain Flash (IRE)**[12] 3377 7-11-0 **98**................(t) JeremiahMcGrath 93
(Jo Davis) *chsd ldr tl led 7th: hdd bef next: rdn and wknd flat* **9/2**[2]

5516 **4** *3 3/4* **Rainbow Haze**[33] 2985 10-11-0 **103**.......................... GeorgeBlackwell[(5)] 93
(Phillip Dando) *chsd ldrs: rdn after 7th: outpcd bef next: styd on u.p flat* **3/1**[1]

6 **5** *2* **Romeo Is Bleeding (IRE)**[247] 216 10-11-10 **108**......... CiaranGethings 98
(David Rees) *hld up: hdwy 7th: rdn and wknd bef next* **16/1**

6-6U **6** *11* **Try It Sometime (IRE)**[29] 3081 8-11-1 **102**.................(t) MikeyHamill[(3)] 79
(Sheila Lewis) *hld up: hdwy 5th: rdn appr 7th: wknd bef next* **16/1**

500- **P** **Bhakti (IRE)**[281] 5183 9-11-9 **107**.............................. KillianMoore
(Mark Rimell) *hld up: rdn and wknd after 5th: bhd whn p.u bef next* **11/1**

F6U4 **P** **Shy John**[29] 3086 10-11-6 **109**................................ LewisGordon[(5)]
(Jennifer Mason) *hld up: rdn and wknd appr 3 out: bhd whn p.u next* **11/1**

/3P- **P** **Castletown (IRE)**[390] 3155 8-11-7 **110**.....................(t) JordanWilliams[(5)]
(Sheila Lewis) *chsd ldrs: rdn: hung lft and lost pl after 5th: wknd 7th: bhd whn p.u bef 3 out* **16/1**

0/0- **P** **The Perfect Crime (IRE)**[446] 2027 7-10-0 **92**............... TobyWheeler[(8)]
(Ian Williams) *plld hrd and prom: wknd after 6th: bhd whn p.u bef 3 out* **40/1**

6m 40.0s (47.70) **Going Correction** +1.475s/f (Heavy) **10** Ran SP% **114.8**
Speed ratings (Par 105): **79,76,75,74,73 70, , , ,**
CSF £27.81 CT £108.01 TOTE £6.20: £2.10, £2.10, £1.80; EX 37.30 Trifecta £170.00.
Owner D Rees **Bred** George Ward **Trained** Clarbeston, Pembrokes

FOCUS
Race distance 48yds further than advertised. This modest handicap proved quite a test. The winner is rated back to his best.

3573 RACING UK PROFITS RETURNED TO RACING STANDARD OPEN NATIONAL HUNT FLAT RACE 1m 7f 169y
4:00 (4:00) (Class 5) 4-6-Y-0 **£2,599** (£763; £381; £190)

Form RPR

53 **1** **Alf 'N' Dor (IRE)**[99] 1797 5-11-5 0.............................(t) SeanBowen 119+
(Peter Bowen) *disp ld tl wnt on over 4f out: pushed clr fr over 2f out* **15/8**[2]

2 *21* **Diamond Rock** 5-11-5 0.................................... JamesDavies 98
(Henry Oliver) *prom: rdn over 2f out: sn outpcd* **13/2**

20 **3** *hd* **Handpicked**[79] 2086 5-10-12 0............................ RichardJohnson 91
(Henry Daly) *hld up: hdwy 4f out: rdn over 2f out: sn outpcd* **13/8**[1]

30 **4** *10* **Rebel Beat**[33] 2998 5-11-5 0.................................. BrianHughes 90
(David Dennis) *hld up: racd keenly: hdwy 5f out: rdn and wknd over 2f out* **11/2**[3]

00/0 **5** *30* **Over The Bridge**[38] 2909 6-10-12 0............................[1] MrJNixon[(7)] 58
(Steve Flook) *disp ld tl over 4f out: rdn and wknd 3f out* **100/1**

0 **6** *1/2* **Over To Midnight**[8] 3469 6-10-5 0................................ MissLBrooke[(7)] 51
(Lady Susan Brooke) *chsd ldrs over 11f* **66/1**

7 *80* **Two Many Words (IRE)** 4-10-5 0 ow3........................ JakeHodson[(5)]
(Bill Turner) *sn prom: rdn over 4f out: sn wknd* **20/1**

0 **8** *47* **Piccomore**[83] 2016 6-10-12 0..................................(t) NickScholfield
(Polly Gundry) *hld up: pushed along over 7f out: sn wknd* **25/1**

4m 10.8s (26.90) **Going Correction** +1.475s/f (Heavy)
WFA 4 from 5yo+ 11lb **8** Ran SP% **112.7**
Speed ratings: **91,80,80,75,60 60,20,**
CSF £13.53 TOTE £2.60: £1.10, £2.10, £1.10; EX 13.40 Trifecta £25.50.
Owner John Andrews **Bred** James Browne **Trained** Little Newcastle, Pembrokes

FOCUS
Race distance 24yds further than advertised. A moderate bumper with a big step up from the winner.
T/Plt: £5.40 to a £1 stake. Pool: £65,354.18 - 8,756.06 winning tickets. T/Qpdt: £3.50 to a £1 stake. Pool: £5,304.08 - 1,105.76 winning tickets. **Colin Roberts**

[3159]NEWCASTLE (L-H)
Wednesday, January 13
3574 Meeting Abandoned - Waterlogged

[3368]TAUNTON (R-H)
Wednesday, January 13

OFFICIAL GOING: Heavy (4.2)
Wind: virtually nil Weather: sunny with cloudy periods

3580 SOMERSET CHAMBER OF COMMERCE MAIDEN HURDLE (12 hdls) 2m 7f 198y
1:10 (1:10) (Class 5) 5-Y-0+ **£3,249** (£954; £477; £238)

Form RPR

F **1** **Churchtown Champ (IRE)**[16] 3316 6-10-12 0................ HarrySkelton 132+
(Dan Skelton) *hld up: smooth hdwy 3 out: sn led: clr next: wl in command whn blnd bdly last: pushed out* **5/1**[3]

F-20 **2** *11* **Say My Name (IRE)**[25] 3146 5-10-12 115...............(p) LiamHeard 118+
(Bob Buckler) *trckd ldrs: rdn after 9th: edgd rt whn gng hld 2nd 2 out: styd on but nvr any ch w wnr* **5/1**[3]

P **3** *14* **Miss Gotaway**[259] 16 7-10-5 0.............................. TomScudamore 95
(David Pipe) *trckd ldrs: rdn appr 2 out: wnt 3rd bef the last: styd on same pce* **18/1**

00 **4** *10* **Kanturk Bank (IRE)**[70] 2265 6-10-12 0.......................(p) SeanBowen 94
(Rebecca Curtis) *led: mstke 7th: rdn and hdd after 3 out: grad fdd fr next* **80/1**

52 **5** *12* **A Plein Temps (FR)**[27] 3124 6-10-12 0.......................... NoelFehily 80
(Harry Fry) *hld up in tch on outer: hdwy after 8th: short-lived effrt after 3 out: wknd bef next* **9/4**[1]

452 **6** *6* **Petite Power (IRE)**[35] 2972 7-10-12 0......................... GavinSheehan 74
(Ali Stronge) *hld up in tch on outer: pushed along after 7th: hdwy after 9th: drvn to chse ldrs after 3 out: sn btn* **5/2**[2]

53 **7** *1/2* **Highway Storm (IRE)**[27] 3124 6-10-12 0...................... AidanColeman 74
(Rebecca Curtis) *prom: rdn after 9th: wknd sn after 3 out* **8/1**

0/5 **8** *2 1/4* **Bel Ami Rich**[34] 2986 6-10-9 0.................................. JamesBanks[(3)] 71
(Sally Randell) *chsd ldrs: dropped to last pair and pushed along but stl in tch 6th: rdn after 8th: btn 3 out* **66/1**

00 **P** **De Bene Esse (IRE)**[12] 3411 6-10-12 0.......................... AdamWedge
(Evan Williams) *trckd ldrs tl wknd 3 out: t.o whn p.u bef last* **25/1**

6m 28.9s (24.90) **Going Correction** +1.125s/f (Heavy) **9** Ran SP% **115.6**
Speed ratings: **103,99,94,91,87 85,85,84,**
CSF £30.17 TOTE £6.30: £2.00, £2.00, £4.30; EX 29.20 Trifecta £1600.90.
Owner Priority Racing Partnership **Bred** J Gordon & W Barrett **Trained** Alcester, Warwicks

FOCUS
Chase and hurdle bends were out and the distance of this race was increased by 156yds. Liam Heard described the ground as "tacky and heavy - hard work." Modest maiden hurdle form and they finished well strung out despite a steady gallop. A big step up from the easy winner.

3581 BROADWAY & HORTON CRICKET CLUB "NATIONAL HUNT" NOVICES' HURDLE (DIV I) (10 hdls) 2m 3f 1y
1:40 (1:40) (Class 4) 4-Y-0+ **£3,898** (£1,144; £572; £286)

Form RPR

6 **1** **Fionn Mac Cul (IRE)**[67] 2331 5-11-5 0.......................... AidanColeman 120+
(Venetia Williams) *trckd ldrs: pressed ldr fr 4th: led for str chal fr 2 out: led narrowly and edgd lft run-in: won on nod: all out* **11/2**[3]

1 **2** *nse* **Rolling Dylan (IRE)**[41] 2875 5-11-5 0.......................... RichardJohnson 121+
(Philip Hobbs) *racd wd most of way: led 4th: hrd pressed fr 2 out: rdn whn nt fluent last: sn v narrowly hdd: strly drvn and kpt on gamely: lost on nod* **4/6**[1]

-162 **3** *23* **Morthanalegend**[40] 2879 7-11-5 0..........................(t) BrendanPowell 100
(Brendan Powell) *prom fr 4th: rdn after 3 out: dropped to hld 3rd bef next: grad fdd* **2/1**[2]

3-03 **4** *1* **In The Hold (IRE)**[46] 2769 6-11-5 0............................ AdamWedge 96
(Evan Williams) *trckd ldrs tl lost pl after 7th: rdn after 3 out: wnt wl hld 4th bef 2 out* **25/1**

0 **5** *1 1/4* **Zero Grand (IRE)**[48] 2729 5-11-5 0............................ RichieMcLernon 95
(Johnny Farrelly) *hld up in tch: trckd ldrs after 5th: rdn after 3 out: wknd bef next* **100/1**

00 **6** *7* **Mr Medic**[14] 3370 5-11-5 0.. TomCannon 90
(Robert Walford) *in tch on outer: trcking ldrs whn blnd 3 out: wknd bef next* **66/1**

00 **7** *25* **Brin D'Avoine (FR)**[12] 3411 5-11-5 0........................ MarkQuinlan 63
(Neil Mulholland) *racd keenly: hld up: hdwy 3rd: sn prom: wknd after 3 out: t.o whn mstke last* **100/1**

454 **8** *63* **Oneforthenure (IRE)**[41] 2870 7-10-12 0...................... TomO'Brien
(Richard Woollacott) *struggling in last fr 4th: t.o fr 7th* **16/1**

2300 **9** *8* **Junior Package**[28] 3105 5-11-5 0................................ TomScudamore
(David Pipe) *in tch tl rdn after 6th: t.o* **40/1**

6 **P** **Monet Moor**[41] 2870 7-10-5 0...................................... PaulO'Brien[(7)]
(Jimmy Frost) *led tl 4th: sn struggling in last pair: t.o 7th: p.u bef 2 out* **100/1**

5m 12.0s (26.00) **Going Correction** +1.125s/f (Heavy) **10** Ran SP% **125.3**
Speed ratings (Par 105): **102,101,92,91,91 88,77,51,47,**
CSF £10.82 TOTE £8.80: £1.70, £1.10, £1.10; EX 17.50 Trifecta £35.80.
Owner Trevor Hemmings **Bred** Joseph Smiddy **Trained** Kings Caple, H'fords

FOCUS
Race distance increased by 117yds. The first and faster division of an ordinary novice hurdle, run at a steady gallop, and the front pair, who are both promising types, came clear, enjoying a good tussle up the straight which prompted a stewards' inquiry being called. The winner produced a big step up.

3582 BROADWAY & HORTON CRICKET CLUB "NATIONAL HUNT" NOVICES' HURDLE (DIV II) (10 hdls) 2m 3f 1y
2:10 (2:10) (Class 4) 4-Y-0+ **£3,898** (£1,144; £572; £286)

Form RPR

5 **1** **Stop The Press**[18] 3258 7-11-5 0.................................. DenisO'Regan 101+
(Mark Pitman) *prom tl 2nd: trckd ldrs: lft in ld after 6th: rdn and hdd 2 out: led after last: sn drifted lft u.p: styd on: drvn out* **6/1**[2]

3305 **2** 3/4 **Grand Introduction (IRE)**[43] 2838 6-11-2 0..........(t) ConorShoemark(3) 100+
(Fergal O'Brien) *led tl 2nd: trckd ldr: lft pressing wnr after 6th: rdn to ld 2 out: sn hung rt: hdd after last: no ex* **8/11**[1]

-440 **3** 9 **Justatenner**[39] 2904 5-11-2 0.......................... MauriceLinehan(3) 93
(Colin Tizzard) *mid-div: hdwy after 7th: rdn to chse ldng pair appr 2 out: sn hld: keeping on at same pce whn mstke last* **8/1**

0 **4** 1 3/4 **Present Times (IRE)**[51] 2683 5-11-5 0.......................... AdamWedge 89
(Evan Williams) *mid-div: hdwy after 7th: rdn to chse ldrs appr 2 out: sn one pce* **16/1**

4-30 **5** 4 **Lift The Lid (IRE)**[12] 3411 6-11-5 0.......................... NoelFehily 85
(Neil Mulholland) *trckd ldrs: rdn after 3 out: one pce fr next* **10/1**

0 **6** 25 **Shouting Hill (IRE)**[30] 3077 6-11-5 0.......................... LiamHeard 59
(Johnny Farrelly) *hld up: awkward 7th: sn rdn: wknd after next: t.o* **40/1**

U5PP **7** 8 **Hill Forts Gypse (IRE)**[40] 2881 5-11-5 0..........(t) AndrewThornton 51
(Seamus Mullins) *kpt to outer: trckd ldrs tl 5th: bhd whn sltly hmpd next: t.o* **100/1**

8 1/2 **Tactical Manoeuvre (IRE)**[53] 5-11-5 0.......................... RhysFlint 51
(Alexandra Dunn) *hld up: rdn after 7th: v awkward 3 out: sn wknd: t.o* **15/2**[3]

U **Red Red Rover (IRE)**[45] 6-10-12 0.......................... MrLDrowne(7)
(Nigel Hawke) *hld up: awkward whn rdr lost both irons 1st: nvr rcvrd: led 2nd tl uns rdr after 6th* **25/1**

5m 22.2s (36.20) **Going Correction** +1.125s/f (Heav) **9** Ran SP% **117.3**
Speed ratings (Par 105): **68,67,63,63,61 50,47,47,**
CSF £11.27 TOTE £7.20: £2.00, £1.10, £2.10; EX 15.00 Trifecta £58.40.
Owner Malcolm C Denmark **Bred** M C Denmark **Trained** Upper Lambourn, Berks

FOCUS
Race distance increased by 30yds. As in division one, the race was dominated by two, with the odds-on favourite again suffering defeat. It certainly looked a lesser race than the first leg and the time was over 10sec slower. The form is suspect but could be rated a stone higher through the second.

3583 BATHWICK TYRES H'CAP CHASE (17 fncs) 2m 7f 3y
2:40 (2:40) (Class 3) (0-140,138) 5-Y-0+ **£8,305** (£2,507; £1,291; £684)

Form RPR

P-F3 **1** **Wychwoods Brook**[30] 3079 10-11-3 **129**.......................... AdamWedge 142+
(Evan Williams) *trckd ldrs: led bef 3 out: rdn after 2 out: 1 l up whn mstke last: styd on: drvn out* **11/2**

-P60 **2** 1/2 **Easter Day (FR)**[47] 2759 8-11-12 **138**..........(p) SamTwiston-Davies 152+
(Paul Nicholls) *in tch: hdwy 4 out: rdn to chse wnr bef next: ev ch 2 out: 1 l down last: styd on but a being jst hld* **5/1**[3]

-23F **3** 27 **Murrayana (IRE)**[39] 2908 6-10-12 **124**..........(t) NoelFehily 113
(Colin Tizzard) *j.lft: in tch: rdn after 12th: lft hld 4th 3 out: wnt 3rd bef next: nvr threatened ldrs* **4/1**[2]

24-2 **4** 13 **Top Wood (FR)**[39] 2907 9-11-9 **135**..........(bt) TomScudamore 113
(David Pipe) *pressed ldr: led 10th: rdn and hdd after 4 out: lft hld 3rd next: wknd 2 out* **11/4**[1]

5521 **F** **Paddy The Oscar (IRE)**[13] 3385 13-10-2 **119**.......................... ConorRing(5)
(Grace Harris) *led tl 10th: pressed ldr: led after 4 out: rdn: hdd and looking hld in 3rd whn fell next* **16/1**

-1P2 **P** **Union Jack D'Ycy (FR)**[14] 3373 8-11-2 **128**.......................... AidanColeman
(Venetia Williams) *trckd ldrs tl 4th: struggling in last 7th: t.o whn p.u bef 13th* **10/1**

2215 **P** **St Dominick (IRE)**[40] 2878 9-11-6 **132**.......................... JamesBest
(Jackie Du Plessis) *hld up: hdwy after 7th: rdn after 4 out: nvr threatened: wknd next: p.u bef last* **10/1**

641 **P** **Morney Wing (IRE)**[14] 3365 7-10-10 **122**..........(tp) DenisO'Regan
(Charlie Mann) *in tch: pckd 1st: nt fluent 8th: in last pair 10th: rdn next: wknd 12th: t.o whn p.u bef last* **17/2**

6m 18.6s (2.60) **Going Correction** +0.35s/f (Yiel) **8** Ran SP% **113.3**
Speed ratings: **109,108,99,94,**
CSF £32.78 CT £120.81 TOTE £7.60: £2.20, £1.90, £1.60; EX 37.30 Trifecta £160.40.
Owner Kevin & Anne Glastonbury **Bred** D T And A T Goldsworthy **Trained** Llancarfan, Vale Of Glamorgan

FOCUS
Race distance increased by 117yds. A decent handicap chase, with the front pair both back to form. They were both on good marks.

3584 BATHWICK TYRES H'CAP HURDLE (10 hdls) 2m 3f 1y
3:10 (3:10) (Class 3) (0-140,135) 4-Y-0 **£6,330** (£1,870; £935; £468; £234)

Form RPR

-33F **1** **Winning Spark (USA)**[12] 3414 9-10-6 **115**.......................... JamesBest 119+
(Jackie Du Plessis) *hld up: smooth hdwy after 3 out: led sn after next: shkn up run-in: styd on wl: readily* **9/2**[3]

2P-3 **2** 2 1/4 **Norse Legend**[32] 3045 5-11-1 **124**.......................... TomCannon 125
(Chris Gordon) *prom: hit 6th: led 3 out: rdn whn narrowly hdd next: kpt on fr last but a being readily hld by wnr* **20/1**

51-1 **3** 3 1/4 **Pull The Chord (IRE)**[63] 2445 6-11-12 **135**.......................... RichardJohnson 134
(Philip Hobbs) *in tch: slt advantage whn blnd 2 out: sn rdn and hdd: disputing hld 2nd whn mstke last: styd on same pce* **13/8**[1]

2-30 **4** 1 **Ascendant**[33] 3015 10-11-4 **132**..........(t) JamieBargary(5) 128
(Johnny Farrelly) *led tl after 3 out: rdn bef next: styd on same pce* **20/1**

632F **5** 1 **Here's Herbie**[24] 3176 8-10-8 **120**..........(t) LucyGardner(3) 116
(Sue Gardner) *in tch on outer: effrt appr 2 out: styd on same pce* **8/1**

33- **6** 8 **The Brock Again**[418] 2647 6-11-0 **123**..........(t) SamTwiston-Davies 110
(Paul Nicholls) *in tch: cl up 3 out: rdn bef 2 out: sn one pce* **7/2**[2]

30F5 **7** 3/4 **My Brother Sylvest**[28] 3107 10-10-7 **116**.......................... TomScudamore 102
(David Pipe) *hld up: hdwy 3 out: rdn bef next: sn one pce* **33/1**

P-23 **8** 7 **Tornado In Milan (IRE)**[51] 2691 10-11-6 **129**.......................... AdamWedge 108
(Evan Williams) *prom tl rdn after 3 out: grad fdd* **12/1**

P **9** 1 1/4 **Lord Adare (IRE)**[39] 2906 8-10-1 **115**..........(t) CharlieDeutsch(5) 93
(Nikki Evans) *trckd ldrs tl rdn after 7th: fdd bef 2 out* **100/1**

001/ **P** **Adelar (GER)**[894] 1185 11-10-5 **117**.......................... CallumWhillans(3)
(Venetia Williams) *in tch: nt fluent 4th: struggling after 6th: wknd after next: t.o whn p.u after 3 out* **25/1**

5m 11.9s (25.90) **Going Correction** +1.125s/f (Heav) **10** Ran SP% **114.6**
Speed ratings (Par 107): **90,89,87,87,86 83,83,80,79,**
CSF £85.14 CT £203.91 TOTE £5.30: £1.70, £4.50, £1.20; EX 89.90 Trifecta £413.60.
Owner Miss J Du Plessis **Bred** Haras De Bernesq & Jean Zorbibe **Trained** Trehan, Cornwall

FOCUS
Race distance increased by 30yds. Again no great gallop on for what was just an ordinary handicap. The winner is rated to his best.

3585 GEOFFREY BOSLEY "TALLY HO" OPEN HUNTERS' CHASE (17 fncs) 2m 7f 3y
3:40 (3:40) (Class 6) 5-Y-0+ **£1,975** (£607; £303)

Form RPR

642/ **1** **Dark Lover (GER)**[632] 5446 11-11-5 130.......................... MissPFuller(7) 131+
(Jamie Snowden) *travelled and j.w: trckd ldrs: pressed ldr fr 11th: led appr 3 out: styd on wl* **9/1**

145- **2** 2 3/4 **Richmond (FR)**[291] 5026 11-11-13 125.......................... MissLMTurner(7) 135
(P P C Turner) *j.lft: prom: disputing ld whn hit 6th: rdn and hdd appr 3 out: styd on but a being hld by wnr fr 2 out* **16/1**

060/ **3** 17 **Join Together (IRE)**[31] 11-11-7 139.......................... MissBFrost(5) 111
(Mrs Rose Loxton) *led tl 1st: mid-div after 3rd: hdwy after 11th: pushed along whn lft 4th 4 out: wnt 3rd bef 3 out: nvr threatened front pair and outpcd fr 2 out* **6/4**[1]

P34- **4** 4 **Ballyallia Man (IRE)**[16] 11-11-9 125..........(tp) MrEdBailey(7) 111
(Mrs N Sheppard) *hld up: stdy prog after 10th: lft 3rd 4 out: sn rdn: wknd next* **25/1**

550- **5** 32 **Chance Du Roy (FR)**[277] 5275 12-11-5 139..........(p) MissNatalieParker(7) 82
(K J Parker) *mid-div: hdwy 9th: rdn after 11th: wknd after 12th: t.o* **4/1**[3]

534- **P** **Sangfroid**[16] 12-11-5 88.......................... MissTWorsley(7)
(Andrew Quick) *awkward 1st: a towards rr: losing tch whn p.u bef 12th* **200/1**

41-3 **U** **Pearlysteps**[257] 75 13-12-3 132.......................... MissJCWilliams(3)
(Henry Daly) *mid-div: hdwy fr 11th: pushed along in cl enough 3rd whn awkward and uns rdr 4 out* **11/4**[2]

2PP- **P** **Viking Blond (FR)**[38] 11-11-12 108..........(b) MrWBiddick
(Dafydd Jones) *prom: disp 5th tl after 10th: wknd after next: t.o whn p.u bef 2 out* **25/1**

5503 **P** **Alf Wright (IRE)**[75] 2168 10-11-7 116.......................... MrJoshuaNewman(5)
(Tracey L Bailey) *racd keenly: led 1st tl hmpd after 3rd: mstke next: trckd ldrs tl wknd u.p after 10th: p.u after next* **33/1**

6206 **P** **Mr Moss (IRE)**[147] 1288 11-11-5 120.......................... MrJAndrews(7)
(S Rea) *trckd ldrs tl wknd qckly 12th: p.u next* **40/1**

PP- **P** **Devon Mead**[38] 10-11-5 0.......................... MrPBryan(7)
(Andrew Quick) *trckd ldrs: led 4th tl 10th: lost pl 10th: t.o whn p.u 13th* **250/1**

PP0- **P** **Sustainability (IRE)**[288] 5084 11-11-5 115.......................... MrJSKnox(7)
(Miss B Eckley) *trcking ldrs whn hmpd 1st and rdr lost irons: mstke 2nd and sddle slipped: nvr rcvrd and p.u after 3rd* **100/1**

24-6 **P** **Allerton (IRE)**[16] 9-11-9 103.......................... MissLMPinchin(7)
(Fergal O'Brien) *mid-div: hdwy after 10th: rdn after 12th: wknd 4 out: t.o whn p.u bef 2 out* **40/1**

P- **P** **Fiasco**[255] 7-11-5 0.......................... MrHFNugent(7)
(A Campbell) *reminders after 7th: a in rr: t.o whn p.u bef 11th* **100/1**

6m 30.0s (14.00) **Going Correction** +0.35s/f (Yiel) **14** Ran SP% **120.9**
Speed ratings: **89,88,82,80,69 , , , , , , , ,**
CSF £120.57 TOTE £10.30: £2.80, £4.20, £1.10; EX 157.80 Trifecta £706.40.
Owner The Dark Lovers **Bred** W Lohmann Jr **Trained** Lambourn, Berks

FOCUS
Race distance increased by 117yds. The first hunter chase of the season and it proved quite a test, with only five of the 14 runners completing and the front pair clear of the favourite. The form is rated through the second.

3586 ROA/RACING POST OWNERS JACKPOT H'CAP HURDLE (9 hdls) 2m 104y
4:10 (4:10) (Class 5) (0-100,100) 4-Y-0+ **£3,249** (£954; £477; £238)

Form RPR

22-3 **1** **Olympian Boy (IRE)**[251] 161 12-11-3 **94**..........(t) KillianMoore(3) 106+
(Sophie Leech) *hld up towards rr: stdy prog fr 5th: rdn to ld between the last 2: styd on wl: rdn out* **16/1**

0040 **2** 5 **In The Crowd (IRE)**[48] 2730 7-11-1 **92**..........(p) JamesBanks(3) 98
(Roy Brotherton) *mid-div: hdwy 5th: led next: rdn and hdd between last 2: no ex run-in* **10/1**

-306 **3** 13 **Brise Coeur (FR)**[34] 2997 5-11-7 **100**.......................... LizzieKelly(5) 96
(Nick Williams) *mid-div: hdwy 5th: rdn and ev ch appr 2 out: sn hld: fdd run-in* **5/2**[1]

/000 **4** 4 **Chakisto (FR)**[48] 2736 8-11-3 **91**.......................... NickScholfield 80
(Katie Stephens) *hld up towards rr: hdwy fr 5th: rdn after 3 out: wnt hld 4th bef 2 out: nvr trbld ldrs* **8/1**

-63P **5** 2 3/4 **Allchilledout**[41] 2871 7-11-5 **100**..........(t) PaulO'Brien(7) 86
(Colin Tizzard) *trckd ldrs in chsng gp: chal briefly after 3 out: sn rdn: one pce fr next* **22/1**

5003 **6** 2 1/2 **Triple Chief (IRE)**[14] 3368 5-11-5 **98**..........(tp) CiaranGethings(5) 82
(Chris Down) *mid-div: hdwy 5th to trck ldrs next: rdn after 3 out: one pce fr next* **4/1**[2]

3-3P **7** 12 **The Sneezer (IRE)**[39] 2908 13-10-13 **92**.......................... CharlieDeutsch(5) 67
(Nikki Evans) *led chsng gp: clsd on ldng pair 4th: rdn and wknd after 3 out* **12/1**

2-34 **8** 1 **Entry To Evrywhere (IRE)**[30] 3089 8-10-5 **79**.......................... ConorO'Farrell 50
(Alexandra Dunn) *racd v keenly: led tl after 4th: trckd ldrs tl wknd 3 out: eased whn btn* **14/1**

0652 **9** hd **Vering (FR)**[18] 3256 10-10-3 **77**..........(tp) MichealNolan 48
(Carroll Gray) *mid-div: hdwy 5th: rdn and wknd after 6th* **14/1**

P000 **10** 15 **Lough Derg Island (IRE)**[14] 3368 8-11-2 **90**.......................... RhysFlint 46
(Alexandra Dunn) *a towards rr* **20/1**

444P **11** 3 **Goal (IRE)**[18] 3242 8-11-5 **100**..........(bt) MissBHampson(7) 53
(Sally Randell) *trckd ldrs in chsng gp: hdwy 4th: led sn after: rdn and hdd 6th: wknd after 3 out: t.o* **16/1**

355P **12** 7 **The Bugler (IRE)**[42] 2851 9-11-7 **95**..........(t) AdamWedge 41
(Evan Williams) *hung lft thrght: towards rr of midfield tl wknd bef 3 out: t.o* **15/2**[3]

P005 **13** 6 **Surprise Us**[41] 2040 9-9-7 **74** oh6.......................... ArchieBellamy(7) 14
(Mark Gillard) *pressed ldr tl rdn after 4th: wknd after next: t.o* **100/1**

4 **14** 14 **Sussex Road (IRE)**[26] 3143 6-11-0 **88**..........(p) LeeEdwards 14
(Aytach Sadik) *mid-div: hdwy after 4th: wknd next: t.o* **25/1**

4m 29.6s (21.60) **Going Correction** +1.125s/f (Heav) **14** Ran SP% **122.0**
Speed ratings (Par 103): **91,88,82,80,78 77,71,70,70,63 61,58,55,48**
CSF £159.59 CT £545.34 TOTE £10.70: £3.30, £3.80, £2.10; EX 140.20 Trifecta £1259.70.
Owner J Cocks & C J Leech **Bred** Mrs Mary O'Connor **Trained** Elton, Gloucs
■ Stewards' Enquiry : Rhys Flint ten-day ban: failed to take all reasonable and permissable measures to obtain the best possible placing (Jan 27-Feb 5)

FOCUS
Run at a good gallop, the front pair drew clear from the favourite late on in this moderate hurdle. The winner is rated similar to his old hurdles mark.

T/Plt: £46.60 to a £1 stake. Pool: £94,135.18 - 1473.96 winning units. T/Qpdt: £8.10 to a £1 stake. Pool: £9,563.53 - 864.59 winning units. **Tim Mitchell**

3397 CATTERICK (L-H)

Thursday, January 14

OFFICIAL GOING: Soft (heavy in places; chs 5.5; hdl 6.0)

Wind: fresh 1/2 against Weather: overcast, breezy and cold

3587 RACINGUK.COM FILLIES' JUVENILE HURDLE (8 hdls) 1m 7f 156y

12:50 (12:50) (Class 4) 4-Y-O **£3,898** (£1,144; £572; £286)

Form RPR

21 **1** **Pemba (FR)**[16] 3338 4-11-3 0........................... WayneHutchinson 109+
(Alan King) *trckd ldrs: shkn up appr 2 out: sn upsides: led between last 2: drvn clr run-in: readily* **1/2**[1]

2 **2** *6* **Miss Ranger (IRE)**[30] 3099 4-10-10 0........................... DannyCook 94+
(Brian Ellison) *trckd ldrs: led appr 2 out: hung rt and hdd between last 2: j.lft last: kpt on same pce* **2/1**[2]

234P **3** *3 ¾* **Our Kylie (IRE)**[40] 2896 4-10-10 98........................... DenisO'Regan 90
(Tony Coyle) *w ldrs: led briefly after 3 out: kpt on one pce fr next* **14/1**

434 **4** *1 ½* **Multi Grain**[17] 3309 4-10-5 97........................... JamieBargary[(5)] 88
(Micky Hammond) *hld up towards rr: hdwy 5th: one pce appr 2 out* **12/1**[3]

66 **5** *2 ½* **Lucie Rie (IRE)**[12] 2537 4-10-10 0........................... HenryBrooke 86
(K R Burke) *led: hdd after 3 out: one pce* **33/1**

6 *20* **Wishing Well**[83] 4-10-7 0........................... JoeColliver[(3)] 66
(Micky Hammond) *stdd s: t.k.h in rr: nt fluent: bhd fr 5th: t.o 2 out* **16/1**

005 **7** *1* **Bond Starprincess**[50] 2718 4-10-7 93........................... AdamNicol[(3)] 65
(George Moore) *chsd ldrs: drvn and reminder 3 out: wknd appr next: t.o last* **66/1**

8 *19* **Q Twenty Girl (IRE)**[136] 4-10-5 0........................... StephenMulqueen[(5)] 46
(John Norton) *t.k.h in rr: bhd whn mstke 3 out: sn t.o* **100/1**

4m 8.5s (16.00) **Going Correction** +1.05s/f (Soft) **8** Ran SP% **125.7**
Speed ratings: **102,99,97,96,95 85,84,75**
CSF £2.17 TOTE £1.40: £1.10, £1.10, £3.00; EX 1.70 Trifecta £7.80.
Owner Million In Mind Partnership **Bred** M L Bloodstock Ltd **Trained** Barbury Castle, Wilts

FOCUS
Some starts have been moved at this track following remeasuring, so some races will not have speed figures until there is sufficient data to calculate updated median times. Both bends moved out 6yds and races 1, 3, 4 & 7 increased by 36yds, race 2 by 72yds, race 5 by 90yds and race 6 by 54yds. The runners got through the deep going well enough in the opening juvenile event for fillies, but winning rider Wayne Hutchinson afterwards still described it as "hard work". The cosy winner set a fair standard and is rated to his mark.

3588 BHEST RACING TO SCHOOL NOVICES' HURDLE (12 hdls) 3m 1f 71y

1:20 (1:20) (Class 4) 4-Y-O+ **£3,249** (£954; £477; £238)

Form RPR

635 **1** **Quinto**[46] 2801 6-11-2 0........................... TomO'Brien 113+
(John Quinn) *w ldrs: led 4th: qcknd pce 8th: drvn and styd on fr 2 out: hit last* **9/4**[2]

2-23 **2** *3* **Gully's Edge**[84] 2031 6-11-2 0...........................(t) BrianHughes 111+
(Malcolm Jefferson) *trckd ldrs: drvn 9th: chsd wnr sn after next: kpt on same pce* **5/4**[1]

-334 **3** *14* **Bryden Boy (IRE)**[202] 837 6-11-2 118...........................(p) SeanQuinlan 97
(Jennie Candlish) *led to 2nd: trckd ldrs: drvn bef 2 out: wknd appr last* **4/1**[3]

06 **4** *24* **Kerry's Lord (IRE)**[32] 3063 7-10-9 0........................... RomainClavreul[(7)] 71
(Joanne Thomason-Murphy) *w ldrs: led 2nd: hdd 4th: drvn and lost pl 3 out: sn bhd: t.o next* **250/1**

2033 **P** **Sign Manual**[30] 3101 7-11-3 112........................... JamesCowley[(5)]
(Donald McCain) *hld up in last: pushed along after 7th: lost pl and reminders 9th: sn bhd: t.o 2 out: p.u bef last* **15/2**

7m 9.1s (41.50) **Going Correction** +1.05s/f (Soft) **5** Ran SP% **107.4**
Speed ratings (Par 105): **79,78,73,65,**
CSF £5.37 TOTE £3.00: £1.10, £1.10; EX 5.40 Trifecta £10.30.
Owner S W Knowles **Bred** Beechwood Grange Stud **Trained** Settrington, N Yorks

FOCUS
A modest little staying novice event in which they went very steadily early on. The winner is rated to his mark. Race distance 72 yards further than advertised.

3589 W.L. AND HECTOR CHRISTIE MEMORIAL TROPHY H'CAP CHASE (12 fncs) 1m 7f 145y

1:50 (1:51) (Class 3) (0-130,125) 5-Y-O+ **£7,988** (£2,480; £1,335)

Form RPR

4651 **1** **Cloudy Joker (IRE)**[13] 3401 8-11-7 120........................... HenryBrooke 131+
(Donald McCain) *j. soundly: w ldrs: led after 4th: clr 8th: reminders and 8 l ahd 3 out: rdn next: 5 l ahd last: all out* **6/1**

-P52 **2** *¾* **Uno Valoroso (FR)**[13] 3401 8-10-6 110........................... JamieHamilton[(5)] 117
(Mark Walford) *trckd ldrs: led 3rd: hdd after next: hit 7th: chsd wnr fr next: drvn bef 3 out: kpt on between last 2: jst hld* **11/2**[3]

-126 **3** *3 ¾* **Grey Life**[40] 2920 10-11-12 125........................... BrianHughes 128
(Malcolm Jefferson) *hld up: trckd ldrs 5th: 5th whn blnd 7th: wnt modest 3rd bef 3 out: kpt on same pce run-in* **9/1**

3004 **F** **Gin Cobbler**[35] 2979 10-9-7 99 oh2........................... ThomasDowson[(7)]
(Victor Thompson) *in rr: fell 2nd* **40/1**

-443 **U** **Crafty Roberto**[33] 3042 8-11-2 115........................... RichardJohnson
(Alex Hales) *chsd ldrs: 4th and outpcd whn blnd bdly and uns rdr 8th* **3/1**[1]

4434 **F** **Sleepy Haven (IRE)**[15] 3365 6-11-9 122...........................(tp) SeanQuinlan
(Jennie Candlish) *trckd ldrs: hit 5th: lost pl and reminders 7th: lft modest 3rd 9th: 4th and wl hld whn fell 2 out* **15/2**

5542 **F** **Mr Burbidge**[29] 3115 8-11-11 124........................... MarkQuinlan
(Neil Mulholland) *led: stmbld on landing 1st: hdd 3rd: hit 6th: modest 4th whn fell 9th: fatally injured* **7/2**[2]

3345 **P** **Vodka Wells (FR)**[10] 3475 6-11-6 124........................... JamieBargary[(5)]
(Micky Hammond) *in rr: bhd 3rd: hit 7th: t.o 9th: p.u bef next* **9/1**

4m 10.1s (10.00) **Going Correction** +0.85s/f (Soft) **8** Ran SP% **111.1**
Speed ratings: **109,108,106, , ,**
CSF £36.76 CT £283.33 TOTE £5.60: £1.70, £1.50, £2.30; EX 30.80 Trifecta £170.10.
Owner On Cloud Eight **Bred** Miss Penny Downes **Trained** Cholmondeley, Cheshire
■ Stewards' Enquiry : Jamie Hamilton two-day ban: used whip above permitted level (Jan 28-29)

FOCUS
Race distance 36yds further than advertised. This modest handicap was run at a brisk gallop and most were taken out of their comfort zones as a result. The winner was value for further and rated back to his best.

3590 WATCH ON 3 DEVICES RACINGUK.COM/ANYWHERE NOVICES' HURDLE (8 hdls) 1m 7f 156y

2:20 (2:20) (Class 4) 4-Y-O+ **£3,249** (£954; £477; £238)

Form RPR

4 **1** **William Of Orange**[17] 3306 5-11-5 0........................... WayneHutchinson 108+
(Donald McCain) *chsd ldrs: 2nd sn after 3 out: kpt on same pce fr next: lft in ld last: drvn clr* **9/2**[3]

0 **2** *11* **Un Prophete (FR)**[52] 2689 5-11-5 0........................... AidanColeman 98
(Venetia Williams) *stdd s: sn trcking ldrs: 3rd sn after 3 out: fdd appr last: lft 4 l 2nd and hit last* **20/1**

00 **3** *19* **Thyne For Gold (IRE)**[29] 3105 5-11-5 0........................... WillKennedy 78
(Donald McCain) *in rr-div: sme hdwy 5th: kpt on fr 2 out: lft poor 3rd last* **40/1**

0 **4** *8* **Ping (IRE)**[215] 727 5-11-0 0........................... RyanDay[(5)] 70
(Nicky Richards) *in rr-div: sme hdwy 4th: lost pl 3 out: bhd whn blnd next: tk poor 4th in clsng stages* **200/1**

5 *¾* **Satellite (IRE)**[118] 5-11-5 0........................... RichardJohnson 71
(Tim Vaughan) *trckd ldr: led 4th: hdd sn after next: wknd 3 out: lft poor 4th last* **9/4**[2]

23 **6** *¾* **Who's Micky Brown (IRE)**[24] 3194 6-11-5 0........................... MarkQuinlan 69
(Neil Mulholland) *in rr-div: hmpd appr 2 out: nvr on terms* **14/1**

7 *1 ¼* **Sthenic (FR)**[210] 4-10-4 0........................... JoeColliver[(3)] 56
(Micky Hammond) *in rr: drvn 3rd: hmpd appr next: nvr a factor* **100/1**

5144 **8** *1 ¾* **Boldbob (IRE)**[13] 3423 4-10-7 110........................... FinianO'Toole[(7)] 61
(Micky Hammond) *led: mstke and hdd 4th: distant 4th bef 2 out: sn wknd* **25/1**

60 **9** *13* **Seraffimo**[17] 3306 4-10-2 0........................... JamesCowley[(5)] 41
(Sharon Watt) *in rr: mstke 1st: sme hdwy 4th: wknd 3 out: sn bhd* **250/1**

P0 **10** *29* **Hugh's Secret (IRE)**[17] 3306 4-10-2 0........................... NathanMoscrop[(5)] 12
(Philip Kirby) *in rr: bhd fr 4th: t.o 3 out: mstke next* **250/1**

0 **P** **Tom Hall**[34] 3021 6-11-5 0...........................[1] TrevorWhelan
(Neil King) *rn wout declared tongue strap: in rr: bhd fr 5th: heavily eased and p.u bef 2 out* **250/1**

1 **F** **Always Resolute**[17] 3309 5-11-12 0........................... DannyCook 135+
(Brian Ellison) *trckd ldrs: led after 5th: wnt clr between last 2: 15 l ahd whn fell last* **11/10**[1]

PP **P** **Raknruin (IRE)**[41] 2890 6-11-5 0...........................(t) HenryBrooke
(Joanne Foster) *in rr: drvn 3rd: bhd next: t.o 3 out: p.u bef next* **250/1**

4m 6.1s (13.60) **Going Correction** +1.05s/f (Soft)
WFA 4 from 5yo+ 11lb **13** Ran SP% **117.4**
Speed ratings (Par 105): **108,102,93,89,88 88,87,86,80,65 , ,**
CSF £75.29 TOTE £5.30: £1.50, £4.70, £9.30; EX 93.10 Trifecta £4043.50.
Owner T W Johnson & G Maxwell **Bred** Coln Valley Stud **Trained** Cholmondeley, Cheshire

FOCUS
Race distance 36yds further than advertised. They went a sound gallop in this novice contest and only three mattered before final-flight drama. The faller set a fair standard but was heading for a 20l+ win. The winner is rated to his C&D mark.

3591 WATT FENCES NORTH YORKSHIRE GRAND NATIONAL H'CAP CHASE (24 fncs) 3m 5f 214y

2:50 (2:50) (Class 3) (0-135,133) 5-Y-O+ **£12,558** (£3,742; £1,894; £970; £508)

Form RPR

0224 **1** **Lackamon**[34] 3024 11-11-4 125........................... DannyCook 136+
(Sue Smith) *j. slowly 2nd: in rr: hdwy 9th: blnd 12th: hdwy 16th: chsng ldrs next: 3rd appr 3 out: 2nd 2 out: styd on run-in: led clsng stages* **12/1**

4531 **2** *½* **Alto Des Mottes (FR)**[26] 3160 6-11-4 125........................... BrianHughes 133+
(Henry Hogarth) *mid-div: trcking ldrs 7th: led 4 out: 5 l ahd whn stmbld on landing last: tired bdly and hdd in clsng stages* **10/1**

P-PP **3** *16* **Gorgehous Lliege (FR)**[41] 2878 10-10-2 109...........................(p) AidanColeman 100
(Venetia Williams) *w ldr: led 9th to 13th: led 16th: hdd 4 out: wknd 2 out* **10/1**

F/62 **4** *2 ¼* **Pete The Feat (IRE)**[37] 2955 12-11-1 132...........................(t) TomHumphries[(10)] 120
(Charlie Longsdon) *chsd ldrs: wknd 2 out* **9/1**

-4P3 **5** *26* **Barton Gift**[19] 3236 9-10-4 111...........................(b) NicodeBoinville 73
(John Spearing) *led to 9th: led 13th: hdd 16th: wknd 10th* **7/1**[3]

P0P5 **P** **Pinerolo**[28] 3127 10-10-9 116........................... SeanQuinlan
(Joanne Foster) *prom: lost pl 7th: sn reminders and bhd: t.o 11th: p.u bef 16th* **100/1**

4421 **U** **Valleyofmilan (IRE)**[17] 3312 9-10-8 120........................... JamesCowley[(5)]
(Donald McCain) *mstke 3rd: in rr whn blnd and uns rdr 4th* **12/1**

4031 **P** **West Of The Edge (IRE)**[19] 3236 8-9-7 107 oh1.. ThomasCheesman[(7)]
(Dai Williams) *in rr: bhd and drvn 10th: t.o 16th: p.u bef 18th* **9/1**

U03U **P** **Silver Tassie (IRE)**[12] 3439 8-11-5 133........................... FinianO'Toole[(7)]
(Micky Hammond) *in rr: mstke 5th: bhd 14th: blnd 17th: mstke 20th: sn wknd: t.o 3 out: 6th whn p.u bef last* **20/1**

4/42 **P** **Nail 'M (IRE)**[41] 2878 8-10-5 112...........................(v[1]) TomScudamore
(Nigel Hawke) *chsd ldrs: lost pl 16th: t.o whn p.u bef next* **4/1**[1]

322U **P** **Delgany Demon**[29] 3113 8-11-12 133........................... TrevorWhelan
(Neil King) *mid-div: lost pl after 16th: t.o whn p.u bef 19th* **14/1**

-1R2 **F** **Jac The Legend**[17] 3310 7-10-6 113...........................(p) WillKennedy
(Brian Ellison) *in rr: hit 9th: lost pl 13th: fell next* **5/1**[2]

8m 17.2s (497.20) **12** Ran SP% **115.2**
CSF £122.53 CT £1246.99 TOTE £10.10: £3.00, £2.80, £2.90; EX 88.10 Trifecta £931.40.
Owner Mrs S Smith **Bred** W P Jenks **Trained** High Eldwick, W Yorks
■ The 1,000th winner of Sue Smith's career.

FOCUS
Race distance 90yds further than advertised. There was no hiding place in this marathon handicap and it saw changing fortunes after the last. Only five finished. The winner's best figure since 2013.

3592 YORKSHIRE-OUTDOORS.CO.UK ADVENTURE ACTIVITIES H'CAP HURDLE (10 hdls) 2m 3f 66y

3:25 (3:31) (Class 4) (0-115,115) 4-Y-O+ **£3,898** (£1,144; £572; £286)

Form RPR

6400 **1** **Tanarpino**[29] 3114 5-11-2 105........................... PeterCarberry 121+
(Jennie Candlish) *chsd ldrs: led appr last: forged clr run-in* **9/1**

5322 **2** *11* **Beat The Tide**[41] 2880 6-11-2 105........................... RichardJohnson 106
(Tim Vaughan) *mid-div: chsd ldrs 6th: hit 3 out: kpt on same pce appr last* **4/1**[2]

5-03 **3** *¾* **Sandford Castle (IRE)**[13] 3411 6-11-12 115........................... BrendanPowell 114
(Johnny Farrelly) *chsd ldrs: led 7th: drvn appr 2 out: hdd appr last: kpt on same pce* **5/2**[1]

24-4 **4** *9* **Stilo Blue Native (IRE)**[96] 1852 8-11-11 **114**.................... BrianHughes 104
(John Wade) *in rr: hdwy 6th: sn chsng ldrs: wknd appr 2 out* **10/1**

0/06 **5** *7* **Roman Numeral (IRE)**[19] 3242 8-11-3 **109**.................... JoeColliver(3) 92
(David Thompson) *chsd ldrs: lost pl 8th: kpt on between last 2* **33/1**

3400 **6** *6* **Harvey's Hope**[33] 3035 10-11-2 **108**.........................(b) HarryChalloner(3) 85
(Keith Reveley) *in rr: bhd and drvn 3 out: nvr on terms* **16/1**

1302 **7** *12* **Prince Khurram**[19] 3242 6-11-1 **114**.............................(t) RonanShort(10) 79
(Donald McCain) *trckd ldrs 4th: 5th and wkng whn mstke 2 out: eased appr last* **13/2**[3]

3-53 **8** *3 ¾* **Attention Seaker**[16] 3342 6-10-13 **109**.................... MrWEasterby(7) 70
(Tim Easterby) *chsd ldrs: drvn 7th: lost pl after next* **9/1**

5F **9** *9* **Lord Ballim (FR)**[58] 2560 6-11-1 **104**.............................(t) TomScudamore 56
(Nigel Hawke) *in rr: j. slowly 1st: hdwy after 5th: lost pl after 3 out* **11/1**

-P06 **P** **Hail The Brave (IRE)**[16] 3346 7-10-1 **95**.................... JamieHamilton(5)
(Michael Smith) *led: drvn and hdd 7th: sn lost pl: bhd whn eased 2 out: t.o whn p.u bef last* **16/1**

-F30 **P** **Fair To Middling**[70] 2287 6-10-13 **102**.............................(tp) SeanBowen
(Peter Bowen) *in rr: bhd and drvn after 5th: t.o whn p.u bef 2 out* **14/1**

5m 1.0s (24.90) **Going Correction** +1.05s/f (Soft) **11** Ran SP% **120.7**
Speed ratings (Par 105): **89,84,84,80,77 74,69,68,64,**
CSF £47.01 CT £120.56 TOTE £12.80: £3.60, £1.60, £1.80; EX 72.00 Trifecta £505.70.
Owner P and Mrs G A Clarke **Bred** R W Huggins **Trained** Basford Green, Staffs

FOCUS
Race distance 54yds further than advertised. A moderate handicap, but it was run at a fair gallop and should prove sound form for the class. The winner took a winner massive step up on his previous hurdles form.

3593 RACING AGAIN 27TH JANUARY STANDARD NATIONAL HUNT FLAT RACE (CONDITIONALS/AMATEURS) 1m 7f 156y
3:55 (3:57) (Class 6) 4-6-Y-O **£1,949** (£572; £286; £143)

Form RPR

1 **1** **Tomngerry (IRE)**[19] 3245 6-11-7 0.............................. MeganCarberry(5) 117+
(Brian Ellison) *sn trcking ldrs: 2nd 8f out: effrt 3f out: led 2f out: pushed clr 1f out: heavily eased in clsng stages* **8/13**[1]

6 **2** *1 ¼* **Sungai Long**[35] 2991 4-10-4 0.............................. ThomasGarner(3) 92
(Michael Scudamore) *trckd ldrs: drvn and modestr 3rd over 4f out: 2nd 1f out: kpt on* **25/1**

2 **3** *10* **Loch Linnhe**[40] 2923 4-10-2 0.............................. JamieHamilton(5) 82
(Mark Walford) *in rr: bhd and pushed along after 4f: reminders and sme hdwy 6f out: lost pl over 4f out: poor 4th over 1f out: kpt on to take modest 3rd last 50yds* **8/1**[3]

- **4** *3 ¾* **Move To The Groove (IRE)**[334] 6-10-9 0.................... RonanShort(10) 90
(Donald McCain) *w ldr: led after 7f: hdd 2f out: wknd appr fnl f* **7/2**[2]

6-0 **5** *20* **Beyond The Glen**[41] 2895 6-10-7 0.............................. DiarmuidO'Regan(5) 63
(Chris Grant) *led 7f: reminders 7f out: lost pl over 2f out* **80/1**

6 *8* **Miss Barbossa (IRE)**[244] 5-10-9 0.............................. GrahamWatters(3) 55
(Martin Todhunter) *trckd ldrs: pushed along 7f out: outpcd over 5f out: wknd 3f out* **22/1**

7 *½* **Reverant Cust (IRE)** 5-10-12 0.............................. FinianO'Toole(7) 62
(Peter Atkinson) *chsd ldrs: reminders and outpcd over 4f out: wknd over 2f out* **16/1**

8 *63* **Night In London (IRE)** 6-10-7 0.............................. MrJohnDawson(5)
(Keith Reveley) *in rr: hdwy after 5f: reminders and lost pl 7f out: sn bhd and eased: t.o 5f out: eventually completed* **17/2**

4m 1.9s (15.00) **Going Correction** +1.05s/f (Soft)
WFA 4 from 5yo 11lb 5 from 6yo 3lb **8** Ran SP% **121.1**
Speed ratings: **104,103,98,96,86 82,82,50**
CSF £26.02 TOTE £1.80: £1.10, £3.90, £1.70; EX 18.80 Trifecta £146.60.
Owner Mrs J A Martin **Bred** Mrs E Tector **Trained** Norton, N Yorks
■ Stewards' Enquiry : Ronan Short two-day ban: used whip above permitted level (Jan 28-29)

FOCUS
Race distance 36yds further than advertised. There was a fair gallop on in this modest bumper. The winner is rated in line with his recent easy win.
T/Plt: £184.90 to a £1 stake. Pool of £60246.80 - 237.78 winning tickets. T/Qpdt: £88.50 to a £1 stake. Pool of £5768.34 - 48.20 winning tickets. **Walter Glynn**

3313 LEICESTER (R-H)
Thursday, January 14

3594 Meeting Abandoned - waterlogged

3600 - 3602a (Foreign Racing) - See Raceform Interactive

3180 THURLES (R-H)
Thursday, January 14

OFFICIAL GOING: Soft

3603a LADBROKES IRELAND KINLOCH BRAE CHASE (GRADE 2) (14 fncs) 2m 4f
2:10 (2:10) 6-Y-O+ **£18,750** (£5,937; £2,812; £937)

RPR

1 **Don Cossack (GER)**[19] 3231 9-11-10 175.............................(t) BJCooper 175+
(Gordon Elliott, Ire) *trckd ldrs: disp 2nd briefly fr 4th: disp ld bef 8th: cl 2nd 4 out and niggled along briefly: reminder after next and travelling wl on terms again bef 2 out: sn led and rdn clr bef last: styd on strly* **1/8**[1]

2 *9 ½* **Wounded Warrior (IRE)**[261] 10 7-11-8 153.................... SeanFlanagan 160
(Noel Meade, Ire) *settled bhd ldr in cl 2nd: jnd for 2nd briefly fr 4th: dropped to 3rd bef 8th: mstke 5 out and dropped to rr: rdn after 2 out and no imp on wnr stl in rr: wnt 2nd fr last and kpt on one pce: nt trble wnr* **10/1**[2]

3 *1* **Rubi Light (FR)**[56] 2606 11-11-3 148.............................(t) AELynch 155
(Robert Alan Hennessy, Ire) *sn led narrowly: jnd bef 8th: narrow advantage bef 4 out: jnd bef 2 out where sltly hmpd and slt mstke: sn hdd and no imp on wnr in 2nd bef last where slow and lost pl: one pce run-in* **20/1**[3]

4 *10* **Mount Colah (IRE)**[49] 2742 10-11-3 148.................... MrNMcParlan 148
(J G Cosgrave, Ire) *w.w in rr: impr into 3rd briefly fr 8th: wnt 3rd fr 5 out: rdn on inner bef 2 out where bad mstke: no imp u.p in 3rd after and dropped to rr of quartet bef last* **20/1**[3]

5m 30.9s (2.70) **4** Ran SP% **107.5**
CSF £2.22 TOTE £1.10; DF 1.90 Trifecta £3.30.
Owner Gigginstown House Stud **Bred** Gestut Etzean **Trained** Longwood, Co Meath

FOCUS
A more workmanlike performance than anything from the long odds-on Don Cossack, and it should help restore some jumping confidence after his Kempton tumble. He's rated a few pounds off his best.

3604a OCOVANGO COOLMORE NATIONAL HUNT SIRES EUROPEAN BREEDERS FUND MARES NOVICE CHASE (GRADE 2) (14 fncs) 2m 4f
2:40 (2:40) 5-Y-O+ **£24,264** (£7,683; £3,639; £1,213; £808)

RPR

1 **Aunt Nora (IRE)**[13] 3434 9-11-0 113.............................. DavidMullins 125
(P A Fahy, Ire) *hld up: clsr in 4th at 1/2-way: mod 5th bef 3 out where lft 4th: impr into 2nd bef 2 out: no imp on ldr: u.p in 2nd bef last: styd on wl nr side fr last to ld fnl strides* **33/1**

2 *½* **Queens Wild (IRE)**[31] 3093 6-11-3 125.............................. APHeskin 127
(Edward P Harty, Ire) *chsd ldrs: 3rd 1/2-way: wnt 2nd after 4 out and lft in front fr next: extended ld gng wl bef 2 out: pushed along and stl clr bef last: rdn far side run-in and reduced advantage in clsng stages: hdd fnl strides* **10/1**[3]

3 *12* **Melbourne Lady**[11] 3457 8-11-0 124.............................. MatthewBowes 112
(P Fegan, Ire) *chsd ldrs: slt mstke 6th: wnt 4th 4 out: lft 3rd next and rdn: no imp on ldr into st and one pce in 3rd fr 2 out* **16/1**

4 *16* **Annamatopoeia (IRE)**[17] 3321 8-11-0 0.............................. AELynch 96
(Brian Jordan, Ire) *led and disp: hdd after 3rd: dropped to 3rd after 4 out: lft in 2nd next tl sn no ex and wknd into 4th bef 2 out where pckd sltly* **33/1**

5 *36* **Perfect Woman (IRE)**[25] 3184 8-11-0 124.............................(p) MarkWalsh 60
(Michael Winters, Ire) *chsd ldrs: sltly hmpd by faller at 4th: slt mstke towards rr at 7th and reminder after: pushed along in rr bef 8th and no imp next: t.o* **8/1**[2]

U **Bitofapuzzle**[28] 3122 8-11-0 0.............................(t) NoelFehily 131+
(Harry Fry) *cl up: racd keenly early and disp bef 1st: led after 3rd: nt fluent 7th: stl gng wl and over 2 l clr bef 3 out where blnd and uns rdr* **30/100**[1]

F **Emcon (IRE)**[31] 3093 7-11-0 123.............................. KevinSexton
(W J Austin, Ire) *chsd ldrs: 3rd whn fell 4th* **10/1**[3]

F **I'm All You Need (IRE)**[19] 3270 6-11-0 125.............................(p) RobbiePower
(Paul Nolan, Ire) *w.w in rr: hmpd by faller at 4th: tk clsr order after 9th and disp 4th whn fell 5 out* **10/1**[3]

5m 34.5s (6.30) **8** Ran SP% **127.1**
CSF £331.80 TOTE £38.30: £8.80, £1.90, £3.50; DF 223.10 Trifecta £1856.20.
Owner Mrs J Kealy **Bred** Fintan Kealy **Trained** Leighlinbridge, Co Carlow

FOCUS
A race that was meant to be a straightforward task for the odds-on favourite but turned into a race of some drama. Aunt Nora is progressive and the runner-up has been rated to the better view of her form.

3605 - 3606a (Foreign Racing) - See Raceform Interactive

3483 HUNTINGDON (R-H)
Friday, January 15

OFFICIAL GOING: Hurdle course - soft (heavy in places; 5.3); chase course - heavy (4.9)
Wind: fresh, half behind Weather: sunny and bright

3607 32RED CASINO CONDITIONAL JOCKEYS' H'CAP HURDLE (10 hdls) 2m 3f 137y
1:20 (1:21) (Class 4) (0-115,115) 4-Y-O+ **£3,249** (£954; £477; £238)

Form RPR

1/44 **1** **Daliance (IRE)**[36] 2997 7-10-2 **96**.........................(b) WilliamFeatherstone(5) 109+
(Noel Williams) *hld up in last pair: hdwy 5th: chsd clr ldr next: steadily clsd: rdn bef 3 out: led wl bef 2 out: sn clr: eased flat* **4/1**[2]

2000 **2** *9* **Argot**[20] 3238 5-10-12 **111**.............................. TomHumphries(10) 112
(Charlie Longsdon) *chsd ldrs: rdn after 2nd: lost pl after 4th: rallied into modest 3rd 7th: plugged on steadily to chse clr wnr between last 2: no imp* **12/1**

0PP **3** *16* **Bobble Emerald (IRE)**[36] 2985 8-10-13 **105**..............(bt[1]) ConorSmith(3) 94+
(Martin Keighley) *chsd ldr tl led 2nd: sn clr: rdn after 7th: hdd wl bef 2 out and sn btn: lost 2nd between last 2: wknd* **28/1**

0P51 **4** *25* **Ballinalacken (IRE)**[20] 3223 8-11-3 **109**.............(v) ThomasCheesman(3) 69
(Clare Ellam) *hld up in midfield: lost tch w ldrs after 5th: no ch 7th: wnt modest 4th 2 out: t.o* **7/1**

02-6 **5** *16* **Wake Your Dreams (IRE)**[38] 2962 8-11-7 **115**............(p) ConorWalsh(5) 59
(Jennie Candlish) *led tl 2nd: chsd ldr tl mstke 6th: hit next: 5th and wkng whn mstke 3 out: t.o* **17/2**

/PP3 **6** *19* **Indian Daudaie (FR)**[14] 3420 9-10-5 **104**..............(p) RomainClavreul(10) 29
(Sarah Humphrey) *midfield: hdwy but nt on terms w ldr after 5th: wknd after 7th: t.o* **50/1**

P-13 **P** **Kleitomachos (IRE)**[36] 2985 8-11-3 **109**..............(b) HarryCobden(3)
(Stuart Kittow) *chsd ldrs tl lost pl and no rspnse to riding after 4th: bhd and lost tch after next: t.o whn p.u bef 7th: burst blood vessel* **7/2**[1]

P32 **P** **Vaillant Creek (FR)**[57] 2595 7-11-5 **115**.............................. ArchieBellamy(7)
(Alex Hales) *hld up in tch in midfield: dropped to rr and rdn after 5th: sn lost tch: t.o whn p.u bef 3 out* **11/2**

0-56 **P** **The Hon Mackinlay (IRE)**[35] 3022 7-10-11 **105**.......(t) LiamMcKenna(5)
(Ben Pauling) *hld up towards rr: sme hdwy but nt on terms w ldr after 5th: lost tch 7th: t.o whn p.u last* **9/2**[3]

5m 11.8s (12.80) **Going Correction** +0.775s/f (Soft) **9** Ran SP% **111.9**
Speed ratings (Par 105): **105,101,95,85,78 71, , ,**
CSF £47.43 CT £1157.03 TOTE £4.80: £1.50, £2.90, £5.80; EX 53.10 Trifecta £683.50.
Owner EPDS Racing Partnership 15 **Bred** Societa Agricola Gem Srl **Trained** Blewbury, Oxon

FOCUS
Shared bend for the chase & hurdle courses on the stable bend, requiring the fence after the road crossing to be omitted. This conditional riders' handicap was a funny race in that they went hard early and few got involved on the demanding surface. Suspect form. Race distance 128yds further than advertised. The easy winner is rated in line with his 2013 hurdle best.

3608 32RED EBF "NATIONAL HUNT" MAIDEN HURDLE (QUALIFIER) (8 hdls) 1m 7f 171y
1:50 (1:50) (Class 4) 4-7-Y-O **£3,573** (£1,049; £524; £262)

Form RPR

2/06 **1** **Scooter Boy**[29] 3130 7-11-5 0.............................. KielanWoods 111
(Alex Hales) *t.k.h: hld up in last pair: hdwy after 5th: 4th and rdn bef 2 out: no imp on ldr: lft jst over 1 l 2nd last: led flat: styd on: drvn out* **20/1**

31-0 **2** *nk* **The Unit (IRE)**[61] 2514 5-11-5 0........................ WayneHutchinson 113+
(Alan King) *t.k.h: hld up in midfield: j.big 2nd: hdwy to chse ldr bef 3 out: rdn and no imp bef 2 out: 12 l down whn lft in ld and j.lft last: hdd flat: kpt on but hld fnl 100yds* **5/4**[2]

05 **3** *8* **Britanio Bello (FR)**[66] 2417 5-11-5 0........................ JoshuaMoore 103
(Gary Moore) *t.k.h: hld up in rr: hdwy after 5th: 5th and no imp after 3 out: lft 8 l 3rd and wnt rt last: no imp flat* **16/1**[3]

0 **4** *1 1/4* **Hollow Bay**[72] 2277 6-10-12 0........................ LiamTreadwell 95
(Paul Webber) *hld up in tch in midfield: effrt after 5th: 6th and no imp after 3 out: lft 10 l 4th and wnt rt last: plugged on same pce flat* **66/1**

/65P **5** *21* **Max The Minister**[30] 3117 6-11-5 0........................ TomO'Brien 81
(Hughie Morrison) *hld up in tch in midfield: mstke 5th: sn struggling u.p: wl btn after 3 out: lft poor 5th last* **25/1**

20 **6** *3 1/4* **Cashanova (IRE)**[20] 3227 5-11-5 0........................ TomCannon 78
(Nick Gifford) *t.k.h: hld up towards rr: effrt after 5th: no imp and wl hld whn blnd next: wknd* **16/1**[3]

222 **F** **Tippmanboy (IRE)**[18] 3306 6-11-5 123........................ WillKennedy 127+
(Dr Richard Newland) *taken down early: t.k.h: chsd ldrs tl lft after 2nd: clr fr 3rd: in command 2 out: 12 l up whn fell last: fatally injured* **1/1**[1]

F6 **F** **Bingo D'Olivate (FR)**[14] 3411 5-11-2 0........................ JamesBanks(3) 111
(Noel Williams) *prom in main gp: wnt 3rd 4th: rdn after 3 out: no imp on ldr: wl hld but plugging on whn lft jst over 1 l 2nd and fell last* **33/1**

0- **P** **No Bad News**[300] 4921 6-11-5 0........................ JamesDavies
(Henry Oliver) *hld up in tch towards rr: j.big 3rd: rdn and rapidly lost tch after 5th: t.o whn p.u 2 out* **66/1**

P **Centreofexcellence (IRE)**[75] 5-11-5 0........................ JamieMoore
(Gary Moore) *t.k.h: mostly chsd ldr tl after 5th: sn dropped out and eased: t.o whn p.u 2 out* **20/1**

U40 **P** **Mesut (FR)**[79] 2136 5-11-5 103........................ JackQuinlan
(Sarah Humphrey) *t.k.h: led: j.big 1st: sn hdd: chsd ldrs tl lost pl rapidly u.p and bhd 5th: t.o whn p.u 2 out* **100/1**

4m 7.45s (12.55) **Going Correction** +0.775s/f (Soft) **11** Ran SP% **126.5**
Speed ratings: **99,98,94,94,83 82, , , ,**
CSF £48.83 TOTE £39.30: £3.50, £1.10, £3.50; EX 118.90 Trifecta £1699.30.
Owner The Scooter Boy Partnership **Bred** Mrs S C Welch **Trained** Edgcote, Northamptonshire

FOCUS
There was late drama in this modest maiden and the form should be treated with a pinch of salt. The winner is entitled to be this good on his bumper debut run. Race distance 105yds further than advertised.

3609 32RED CASINO H'CAP CHASE (17 fncs 2 omitted) 2m 7f 129y
2:20 (2:21) (Class 4) (0-105,104) 5-Y-0+ **£3,898** (£1,144; £572; £286)

Form RPR

-4P4 **1** **Arbeo (IRE)**[17] 3349 10-11-12 104........................ MarcGoldstein 115
(Diana Grissell) *chsd ldr: rdn 12th: lft upsides ldr 14th: outpcd after next: rallied between last 2: led flat: sn clr: styd on* **6/5**[1]

5P5P **2** *9* **Basford Ben**[28] 3144 8-11-8 100........................(b) PeterCarberry 107+
(Jennie Candlish) *j.lft: led and sn clr: j.lft: mstke and jnd 14th: wnt clr again after next: j.lft 2 out: sn rdn: lft again last: sn hdd and no ex* **7/1**

-54P **3** *11* **Miss Oscarose (IRE)**[16] 3369 9-11-3 95........................ TomO'Brien 88
(Paul Henderson) *a 3rd: mstke and pckd 10th: clsd 12th: rdn and wknd after 3 out* **12/1**

6433 **4** *12* **Veauce De Sivola (FR)**[32] 3081 7-11-0 95........................(t) TomBellamy(3) 76
(Mark Gillard) *off the pce in last trio: clsd and in tch 12th: j. slowly 3 out: sn wknd* **7/2**[2]

3012 **P** **Bus Named Desire**[28] 3144 8-10-7 92........................(tp) MrStanSheppard(7)
(Matt Sheppard) *off the pce in last trio: clsd and in tch whn mstke 13th: wknd 3 out: t.o whn p.u next: burst blood vessel* **4/1**[3]

00-F **P** **Steel A Tune**[32] 3081 7-10-7 78 oh5........................ ConorO'Farrell
(Nick Mitchell) *a bhd: j. slowly 3rd: j.lft and nt fluent 8th: losing tch whn p.u 10th* **25/1**

6m 38.5s (28.20) **Going Correction** +1.175s/f (Heav) **6** Ran SP% **111.7**
Speed ratings: **100,97,93,89, ,**
CSF £9.94 TOTE £2.30: £1.30, £2.80; EX 13.90 Trifecta £47.20.
Owner Nigel & Barbara Collison **Bred** William J O'Doherty **Trained** Brightling, E Sussex

FOCUS
This moderate staying handicap was 125yds further than the advertised distance and served up a thorough test. The winner is rated 3lb off last year's win.

3610 32RED CHATTERIS FEN JUVENILE HURDLE (8 hdls) 1m 7f 171y
2:50 (2:50) (Class 2) 4-Y-0 **£12,512** (£3,696; £1,848; £924; £462)

Form RPR

1211 **1** **Sceau Royal (FR)**[34] 3028 4-11-6 142........................ DarylJacob 136+
(Alan King) *chsd ldr: jnd ldr and hit 2 out: sn led: cruised clr last: nt extended* **2/11**[1]

21 **2** *7* **Perceus**[28] 3139 4-10-12 124........................ JackQuinlan 115
(James Eustace) *nt a fluent: led: hdd sn after 2 out: easily brushed aside by wnr last: kpt on* **4/1**[2]

1P15 **3** *14* **Darebin (GER)**[19] 3279 4-11-6 125........................ JamieMoore 111
(Gary Moore) *hld up in tch: trckd ldrs 5th: shkn up after next: sn outpcd and wl hld between last 2* **9/1**[3]

04 **4** *19* **Burner (IRE)**[13] 3443 4-10-12 0........................ TomCannon 83
(Olly Williams) *j.lft: t.k.h: hld up in rr: outpcd and rdn after 3 out: 4th and wl hld whn mstke next: j.lft and mstke last* **100/1**

5 *21* **Diamond Reflection (IRE)**[210] 4-10-12 0........................ KillianMoore 60
(Tom Weston) *t.k.h: hld up in tch: outpcd and pushed along after 3 out: last and wl btn next* **40/1**

4m 6.95s (12.05) **Going Correction** +0.775s/f (Soft) **5** Ran SP% **118.0**
Speed ratings: **100,96,89,80,69**
CSF £1.86 TOTE £1.10: £1.10, £1.60; EX 1.50 Trifecta £2.20.
Owner Simon Munir & Isaac Souede **Bred** Guy Vimont **Trained** Barbury Castle, Wilts

FOCUS
Race distance 105yds further than advertised. A weak renewal of this long-established juvenile prize, but the first pair both continue on the up. The easy winner didn't need to improve to lands the odds, with the first three pretty much to their marks.

3611 32RED.COM CHASE (A NOVICES' LIMITED H'CAP) (15 fncs 1 omitted) 2m 3f 189y
3:20 (3:20) (Class 3) 5-Y-0+ **£6,657** (£2,067; £1,113)

Form RPR

312F **1** **Buckhorn Timothy**[20] 3228 7-11-0 132........................ TomScudamore 137
(Colin Tizzard) *mde most: mstke 11th: rdn 2 out: hdd last: sn lft in ld again: styd on to assert fnl 75yds: ridden out* **15/2**

11-3 **2** *2 3/4* **Three Faces West (IRE)**[27] 3156 8-10-12 130........................ RichardJohnson 132
(Philip Hobbs) *mounted on crse: chsd ldrs: effrt after 3 out: drvn and ev ch between last 2: no ex fnl 75yds* **6/4**[1]

-304 **3** *3/4* **Ballybolley (IRE)**[28] 3134 7-10-10 128........................(t) SamTwiston-Davies 131
(Nigel Twiston-Davies) *chsd ldr: mstke 3 out: stl ev ch but unable qck between last 2: lft 3rd and j.rt last: kpt on same pce* **8/1**

12/4 **U** **Ubak (FR)**[49] 2760 8-11-8 140........................ JoshuaMoore 150+
(Gary Moore) *hld up in rr: wnt 4th 10th: hit next: clsd 2 out: rdn to ld: blnd bdly and uns rdr last* **11/4**[2]

0334 **P** **L'Unique (FR)**[20] 3229 7-11-5 137........................ WayneHutchinson
(Alan King) *in tch in 4th: pushed along after 7th: dropped to last 10th: sn lost tch: t.o whn p.u after 3 out* **5/1**[3]

5m 23.55s (18.25) **Going Correction** +1.175s/f (Heav) **5** Ran SP% **106.2**
Speed ratings: **110,108,108, ,**
CSF £18.60 TOTE £9.50: £2.70, £1.10; EX 21.10 Trifecta £87.80.
Owner The Buckhorn Racing Team **Bred** M M Hooker **Trained** Milborne Port, Dorset

FOCUS
A decent little novice handicap. It was run at a sound gallop and four were pretty much upsides at the last. The winner is rated to his mark. Race distance 92yds further than advertised.

3612 £10 FREE AT 32RED.COM MARES' MAIDEN HURDLE (10 hdls) 2m 4f 145y
3:50 (3:52) (Class 4) 4-Y-0+ **£3,249** (£954; £477; £238)

Form RPR

P-03 **1** **Briery Belle**[34] 3034 7-11-4 120........................ TomO'Brien 121+
(Henry Daly) *chsd ldr: j. path after 5th: lft in ld bnd bef next: hdd bef 3 out: drvn bef 2 out: led: j.rt and mstke last: styd on: rdn out* **4/5**[1]

/04- **2** *2 1/2* **Caitys Joy (GER)**[404] 2969 6-11-4 0........................ DarylJacob 118
(Warren Greatrex) *hld up in tch in midfield: trckd ldrs 6th: cl 3rd and swtchd lft 2 out: swtchd between last 2: j.rt last: wnt 2nd flat: kpt on but no imp on wnr* **3/1**[2]

1445 **3** *1 1/2* **Potters Midnight**[26] 3179 6-11-4 108........................ RichardJohnson 116
(Lucy Wadham) *chsd ldrs 5th: lft chsng wnr bnd bef next: led bef 3 out: rdn 2 out: hdd and mstke last: no ex and one pce flat* **7/1**

-334 **4** *26* **Midnight Silver**[20] 3217 6-11-4 112........................(t) BrendanPowell 89
(Jamie Snowden) *led: hung lft and hdd bnd after 5th: cl 4th 7th: rdn and wknd sn after 3 out* **6/1**[3]

2-44 **5** *36* **Miss Tongabezi**[15] 3386 7-11-4 99........................(t) LiamTreadwell 53
(Paul Webber) *t.k.h: chsd ldrs tl after 5th: lost pl and last trio next: t.o 3 out* **25/1**

0- **P** **Arsenale (GER)**[29] 4923 5-11-4 0........................ JonathanEngland
(Michael Appleby) *hld up in tch in rr: struggling 7th: sn lost tch: t.o whn p.u 2 out* **100/1**

060- **P** **Weston Flame**[289] 5093 6-11-4 0........................ KielanWoods
(Ben Case) *in tch in midfield: chsd ldrs 5th: mstke 7th: sn wknd: t.o whn p.u 2 out* **100/1**

0 **P** **En Passe (IRE)**[77] 2164 7-11-4 0........................(t) AidanColeman
(Charlie Longsdon) *mstkes: hld up in last pair: blnd 3rd: lost tch after 6th: t.o whn p.u 3 out* **16/1**

5m 29.5s (18.90) **Going Correction** +0.775s/f (Soft) **8** Ran SP% **119.0**
Speed ratings (Par 105): **95,94,93,83,69 , ,**
CSF £3.78 TOTE £1.40: £1.10, £1.70, £2.00; EX 2.90 Trifecta £6.70.
Owner Mrs H Plumbly J Trafford K Deane S Holme **Bred** Simon And Helen Plumbly **Trained** Stanton Lacy, Shropshire

FOCUS
This wasn't a bad mares' maiden by any means, the winner setting a decent standard. Race distance 128yds further than advertised.
T/Plt: £46.20 to a £1 stake. Pool: £62,861.43 - 993.09 winning tickets T/Qpdt: £3.70 to a £1 stake. Pool: £6,653.29 - 1,301.43 winning tickets **Steve Payne**

3239 SEDGEFIELD (L-H)
Friday, January 15
3613 Meeting Abandoned - snow

3382 WARWICK (L-H)
Saturday, January 16
OFFICIAL GOING: Heavy (chs 4.7, hdl 4.9)
Wind: Almost nil Weather: Fine

3619 BETFRED "GOALS GALORE" NOVICES' H'CAP HURDLE (8 hdls) 2m
12:40 (12:40) (Class 4) (0-110,110) 4-Y-0+ **£3,249** (£954; £477; £238)

Form RPR

-453 **1** **Bold Duke**[17] 3374 8-11-7 108........................ BenPoste(3) 117
(Edward Bevan) *hld up in tch: rdn after 3 out: led next: styd on* **15/2**

0-00 **2** *3/4* **Red Hott Robbie**[17] 3363 7-11-2 100........................ AndrewThornton 107
(Giuseppe Fierro) *hld up: hdwy 5th: j.rt 2 out: sn rdn: styd on u.p* **66/1**

-130 **3** *8* **Back By Midnight**[37] 2987 7-11-6 107........................(t) JamesBanks(3) 108
(Emma Baker) *led 2nd: hdd after next: led again 4th: mstke 5th: hdd and mstke 2 out: nt fluent last: wknd flat* **9/1**

066- **4** *1 3/4* **No Ceiling (IRE)**[314] 4654 6-10-3 97........................ TobyWheeler(10) 96
(Ian Williams) *prom: racd keenly: rdn after 2 out: wknd last* **12/1**

6056 **5** *18* **Tullow Tonic (IRE)**[47] 2823 5-11-4 102........................ RichardJohnson 82
(Charlie Longsdon) *hld up: hdwy after 5th: rdn and wknd after 3 out* **9/1**

5-22 **6** *1 1/4* **Georgieshore (IRE)**[29] 3143 8-10-13 104........................ WilliamFeatherstone(7) 83
(Zoe Davison) *led to 2nd: chsd ldrs: j. slowly 4th: sn drvn along: wknd appr 3 out* **6/1**[2]

/3B4 **7** *4 1/2* **Spa's Dancer (IRE)**[54] 2689 9-11-12 110........................ JackQuinlan 84
(James Eustace) *trckd ldrs: racd keenly: wnt 2nd 5th tl rdn after 3 out: sn wknd* **7/1**[3]

-5P2 **8** *1 1/2* **Get Ready Freddy**[26] 3194 6-11-0 98........................ NickScholfield 72
(Nick Mitchell) *chsd ldr: led after 3rd tl next: mstke 5th: wknd next* **12/1**

050 **9** *1 3/4* **Hallingham**[31] 3114 6-10-13 97........................ TomCannon 68
(Chris Gordon) *hld up: mstke 1st: rdn after 4th: wknd next: in rr whn hmpd 3 out* **33/1**

43-0 **10** *3/4* **Belize**[95] 1893 5-11-2 105........................ AlanJohns(5) 75
(Tim Vaughan) *mid-div: mstke 2nd: hdwy appr 4th: wknd next* **18/1**

365- **11** *8* **Polo (GER)**[331] 4311 6-10-11 100........................ CharlieDeutsch(5) 62
(Venetia Williams) *hld up: hdwy appr 4th: rdn and wknd after 3 out* **11/4**[1]

44P **12** *9* **Nordical (IRE)**[31] 3117 6-11-4 102........................(t) AdamWedge 55
(Evan Williams) *hld up: wknd after 5th* **25/1**

2P2P **13** *34* **Flash Crash**[17] 3362 7-11-1 106........................ MrZBaker(7) 25
(Barry Brennan) *hld up: j. slowly 3rd: sn drvn along: bhd fr next* **20/1**

3300 **14** *1* **Fauve (IRE)**[73] 2271 5-11-4 **109**................................ MrRobertHawker(7) 27
(Richard Hawker) *hld up: sme hdwy appr 5th: sn wknd* **100/1**
4m 5.8s (6.80) **Going Correction** +0.525s/f (Soft) **14** Ran SP% **119.9**
Speed ratings (Par 105): **104,103,99,98,89 89,86,86,85,84 80,76,59,58**
CSF £436.97 CT £4469.61 TOTE £7.40: £2.20, £17.30, £3.20; EX 779.60 Trifecta £1570.10.
Owner E G Bevan **Bred** Pullen Farm Stud **Trained** Ullingswick, H'fords

FOCUS

All starts have been moved at this track following remeasuring, so there will be no speed figures here until there is sufficient data to calculate updated median times. Frost covers had been deployed overnight and with temperatures dipping to just -3 the track passed a morning inspection. Rail realignment increased races 1, 5 & 7 by 11yds, race 2 by 46yds, race 4 by 22yds and races 3 & 6 by 92yds. A competitive opener, in which Polo was fancied to provide Venetia Williams with a third win in the race since 2011. It looked hard work and they came home at long intervals. The winner has been rated back to his best, and the fourth as running a pb.

3620 BETFRED "JANUARY SALE" H'CAP CHASE (FOR THE EDWARD COURAGE CUP) (12 fncs) 2m

1:15 (1:15) (Class 3) (0-135,132) 5-Y-0+ **£6,498** (£1,908; £954; £477)

Form RPR
-P32 **1** **Big Jim**[29] 3141 7-10-5 **111**.. KielanWoods 128+
(Alex Hales) *led to 2nd: led again and mstke 4th: shkn up and j.rt 2 out: drvn out* **5/1**[3]

2U33 **2** *8* **Morning Reggie**[21] 3257 7-10-12 **118**..........................(p) LeightonAspell 128
(Oliver Sherwood) *hld up: hdwy 5th: chsd wnr 9th: nt fluent next: sn rdn: no ex flat* **9/2**[2]

22 **3** *4 1/2* **Walk In The Mill (FR)**[42] 2908 6-11-1 **121**.................. AndrewThornton 124
(Robert Walford) *hld up: hdwy 8th: rdn after 3 out: wknd appr last* **9/1**

P-U3 **4** *4 1/2* **Vivaccio (FR)**[31] 3107 7-11-8 **128**.............................. LiamTreadwell 130
(Venetia Williams) *led 2nd to 4th: chsd wnr: mstke 7th: lost 2nd 9th: rdn and wknd appr 2 out: mstke last* **14/1**

0065 **5** *8* **Owen Na View (IRE)**[35] 3030 8-10-13 **122**..............(t) ConorShoemark(3) 113
(Fergal O'Brien) *hld up: hdwy 8th: rdn and wknd 2 out* **25/1**

2312 **6** *11* **All Together (FR)**[29] 3134 5-11-8 **131**............................... JamesBest 113
(Johnny Farrelly) *chsd ldrs: mstke 7th: wknd after next* **9/2**[2]

14-3 **7** *35* **Lanceur (FR)**[37] 2993 7-11-2 **122**.............................. RichardJohnson 67
(Lucy Wadham) *chsd ldrs: nt fluent and lost pl 6th: sn bhd* **6/1**

6PB0 **8** *22* **Le Bacardy (FR)**[35] 3036 10-11-12 **132**............................ HarrySkelton 55
(Dan Skelton) *hld up: bhd fr 4th* **18/1**

61-3 **P** **Laser Hawk (IRE)**[49] 2779 9-11-12 **132**............................. AdamWedge
(Evan Williams) *prom: nt fluent 3rd: blnd and lost pl next: bhd whn p.u bef 6th* **4/1**[1]

4m 12.5s (2.50) **Going Correction** +0.375s/f (Yiel)
WFA 5 from 6yo+ 3lb **9** Ran SP% **113.1**
Speed ratings: **108,104,101,99,95 90,72,61,**
CSF £27.81 CT £194.54 TOTE £5.30: £2.40, £1.40, £3.10; EX 23.60 Trifecta £231.40.
Owner Gumbrills Racing Partnership **Bred** John S C And Mrs K A Fry **Trained** Edgcote, Northamptonshire

■ Stewards' Enquiry : Kielan Woods six-day ban; used his whip above the permitted level and without giving his horse time to respond (30th Jan - 4th Feb)

FOCUS

Race distance increased by 46yds. This looked every bit as competitive on paper as the market suggested. Venetia Williams, who was represented by Vivaccio, was bidding for a hat-trick in the race. A big chase pb from the winner, with the third rated to his mark.

3621 BETFRED MOBILE HAMPTON NOVICES' CHASE (LISTED RACE) (18 fncs) 3m

1:50 (1:50) (Class 1) 5-Y-0+ **£13,252** (£5,069; £2,615; £1,380)

Form RPR
010- **1** **Black Hercules (IRE)**[33] 3095 7-11-4 147.......................... DannyMullins 159+
(W P Mullins, Ire) *chsd ldrs: led 2nd: shkn up flat: styd on: comf* **5/6**[1]

P-21 **2** *2 3/4* **Definitly Red (IRE)**[15] 3399 7-11-0 0........................ RichardJohnson 150
(Brian Ellison) *hld up: nt fluent 5th: hdwy 9th: nt fluent 12th: chsd wnr after 3 out: sn rdn: styd on same pce flat* **9/2**[2]

-112 **3** *20* **Emily Gray (IRE)**[18] 3337 8-11-0 145.................................... DavidBass 131
(Kim Bailey) *chsd wnr 2nd tl rdn after 3 out: wknd appr last* **6/1**[3]

6112 **4** *10* **Silsol (GER)**[41] 2932 7-11-7 150.........................(tp) SamTwiston-Davies 131
(Paul Nicholls) *prom: pushed along 14th: wknd appr 3 out* **6/1**[3]

-116 **P** **Bally Beaufort (IRE)**[21] 3229 8-11-4 143.............................. RyanHatch
(Nigel Twiston-Davies) *led to 2nd: chsd ldrs tl rdn and wknd appr 12th: bhd whn p.u bef 2 out* **12/1**

6m 32.9s (-1.10) **Going Correction** +0.375s/f (Yiel) **5** Ran SP% **109.0**
Speed ratings: **116,115,108,105,**
CSF £5.01 TOTE £1.60: £1.10, £1.80; EX 5.10 Trifecta £8.00.
Owner Andrea & Graham Wylie **Bred** Spencer Hawkins **Trained** Muine Beag, Co Carlow

FOCUS

Race distance increased by 92yds. An intriguing Listed chase. Black Hercules justified favouritism and took Willie Mullins' impressive record at the track to 5-7. The winner has been rated as a top-class novice and is obvious Festival material, while the second has been rated as running a pb in defeat. There's a case for rating the race a lot higher through the third and fourth, but neither got home.

3622 PERTEMPS NETWORK H'CAP HURDLE (SERIES QUALIFIER) (12 hdls) 3m 2f

2:25 (2:25) (Class 2) 5-Y-0+
£11,573 (£3,418; £1,709; £854; £427; £214)

Form RPR
P-P0 **1** **Flintham**[36] 3018 7-11-12 **138**.......................................(p) NicodeBoinville 143
(Mark Bradstock) *led after 1st: rdn appr 2 out: hdd last: rallied to ld flat: styd on gamely* **7/1**

3-51 **2** *3/4* **Pobbles Bay (IRE)**[33] 3078 6-10-8 **120**............................... AdamWedge 124
(Evan Williams) *hld up: hdwy 6th: chsd wnr 3 out: hit next: led last: rdn and hdd flat: kpt on* **11/2**[3]

11F1 **3** *11* **Isaacstown Lad (IRE)**[28] 3158 9-11-8 **134**....................... BrianHarding 127
(Nicky Richards) *hld up: hdwy 9th: rdn and wknd appr last* **9/2**[2]

-P4P **4** *5* **Rolling Maul (IRE)**[39] 2960 8-11-11 **137**....................(b) SeanBowen 124
(Peter Bowen) *led tl after 1st: chsd ldrs: wnt 2nd after 7th tl mstke 9th: sn rdn: wknd after 3 out* **10/1**

0321 **5** *23* **Howaboutnever (IRE)**[16] 3383 8-9-13 **121**..............(p) TobyWheeler(10) 86
(Ian Williams) *hld up: hdwy appr 8th: wknd bef 3 out* **7/1**

5111 **6** *1/2* **Arctic Gold (IRE)**[12] 3465 5-11-4 **130**................... SamTwiston-Davies 98
(Nigel Twiston-Davies) *hld up in tch: mstke 8th: chsd ldr next tl 3 out: sn rdn and wknd* **4/1**[1]

-P20 **7** *45* **According To Trev (IRE)**[15] 3407 10-11-2 **133**.............. JakeHodson(5) 52
(David Bridgwater) *prom: nt fluent and lost pl 2nd: hdwy and racd wd appr 8th: wknd next* **20/1**

-503 **P** **Floral Spinner**[12] 3465 9-9-9 **112** oh2.................................. RyanWhile(5)
(Bill Turner) *in rr: pushed along and hdwy after 7th: wknd after next: bhd whn p.u bef 3 out* **25/1**

1041 **P** **Volcanic (FR)**[36] 3010 7-11-1 **127**..............................(t) WayneHutchinson
(Donald McCain) *chsd wnr 2nd tl pushed along after 7th: wknd bef next: bhd whn p.u bef 3 out* **11/1**

3-FP **P** **Kingscourt Native (IRE)**[55] 2660 8-11-12 **138**....................(t) NoelFehily
(Colin Tizzard) *hld up: wkng whn mstke 9th: bhd whn p.u bef 2 out* **8/1**

6m 52.8s (15.80) **Going Correction** +0.875s/f (Soft) **10** Ran SP% **115.7**
Speed ratings: **110,109,106,104,97 97,83,,,**
CSF £45.44 CT £193.50 TOTE £9.00: £2.80, £2.40, £1.80; EX 49.60 Trifecta £433.50.
Owner The Rasher Partnership **Bred** Lord Oaksey **Trained** Letcombe Bassett, Oxon

FOCUS

Race distance increased by 22yds. This devilishly competitive handicap hurdle featured five last-time-out winners. The winner, returning to hurdles after an unsuccessful stint over fences, ran them ragged under top weight. The winner has been rated back to the best of last season's form.

3623 NEPTUNE INVESTMENT MANAGEMENT NOVICES' HURDLE (REG' AS THE LEAMINGTON NOVICES' HURDLE) (GRADE 2) (11 hdls) 2m 5f

3:00 (3:00) (Class 1) 5-Y-0+ **£17,165** (£6,491; £3,290; £1,679; £884)

Form RPR
2 **1** **Thomas Hobson**[37] 3002 6-11-7 0...................................... DannyMullins 148+
(W P Mullins, Ire) *mde all: clr fr 7th tl mstke 2 out: rdn and nt fluent last: hung rt flat: all out* **5/1**[2]

2 **2** *2 1/2* **Open Eagle (IRE)**[21] 3227 7-11-7 137.............................. DavidMullins 142
(W P Mullins, Ire) *hld up: hdwy 8th: chsd wnr appr 2 out: rdn bef last: no ex nr fin* **7/1**[3]

1-31 **3** *6* **Definite Outcome (IRE)**[70] 2331 7-11-4 0......................... SeanBowen 133
(Rebecca Curtis) *chsd wnr: nt fluent 6th: rdn and lost 2nd appr 2 out: sn outpcd: styd on flat* **9/1**

1 **4** *5* **Born Survivor (IRE)**[37] 2995 5-11-4 0............................... HarrySkelton 128
(Dan Skelton) *hld up in tch: rdn after 3 out: wknd bef next* **6/4**[1]

2112 **5** *2 3/4* **Final Nudge (IRE)**[35] 3032 7-11-4 137................................... NoelFehily 126
(David Dennis) *hld up: hdwy 7th: wknd next* **7/1**[3]

23-3 **P** **Ballagh (IRE)**[42] 2910 7-11-0 133..................................... MrMJPKendrick
(Ben Case) *chsd ldrs: nt fluent 5th: lost pl after next: wknd 7th: bhd whn p.u bef 2 out* **16/1**

1142 **P** **Viens Chercher (IRE)**[57] 2626 5-11-4 137......................... RichardJohnson
(Brian Ellison) *prom to 7th: bhd whn p.u bef 2 out* **16/1**

4-11 **U** **Wishing And Hoping (IRE)**[57] 2614 6-11-7 130........ WayneHutchinson
(Alan King) *hld up: rdn and wknd 7th: bhd whn mstke and uns rdr 3 out* **20/1**

-311 **P** **Mckenzie's Friend (IRE)**[33] 3085 5-11-4 130................. LeightonAspell
(Oliver Sherwood) *prom tl wknd after 7th: bhd whn p.u bef 2 out* **14/1**

5m 30.7s (9.70) **Going Correction** +0.875s/f (Soft) **9** Ran SP% **114.9**
Speed ratings: **116,115,112,110,109 ,,,**
CSF £39.58 TOTE £6.20: £2.10, £2.50, £3.20; EX 18.40 Trifecta £297.20.
Owner Mrs S Ricci **Bred** Mount Coote Stud And M H Dixon **Trained** Muine Beag, Co Carlow

FOCUS

Race distance increased by 11yds. A strong renewal of this novice contest, the finish of which was dominated by a pair of Willie Mullins-trained runners. The winner is better than the bare result and is a potential 150+ hurdler on his Flat form. He rates as serious Festival material, with the second stepping up for the longer trip and the third running a pb.

3624 BETFRED CLASSIC CHASE (H'CAP) (GRADE 3) (22 fncs) 3m 5f

3:35 (3:35) (Class 1) 5-Y-0+ **£34,330** (£12,982; £6,580; £3,358; £1,768)

Form RPR
-625 **1** **Russe Blanc (FR)**[36] 3008 9-10-7 **127**..........................(p) CharliePoste 138+
(Kerry Lee) *hld up in tch: led appr 16th: pckd 2 out: drvn out* **20/1**

/0-4 **2** *3 3/4* **Midnight Prayer**[49] 2780 11-10-12 **135**........................... TomBellamy(3) 143+
(Alan King) *hld up: hdwy 13th: hmpd 15th: chsd wnr 17th: stmbld next: rdn appr 2 out: ev ch last: styd on same pce flat* **15/2**[2]

-350 **3** *24* **Dromnea (IRE)**[20] 3296 9-11-2 **136**................................. MarkEnright 124
(M F Morris, Ire) *hld up: hmpd 11th: mstke next: hdwy appr 16th: rdn and wknd bef 2 out* **16/1**

-000 **4** *6* **Houblon Des Obeaux (FR)**[28] 3150 9-11-12 **146**.......... LiamTreadwell 122
(Venetia Williams) *prom: mstke 2nd: nt fluent and lost pl 4th: in rr and pushed along 12th: no ch after* **15/2**[2]

2P-1 **5** *41* **Vivaldi Collonges (FR)**[41] 2935 7-11-8 **142**.........(t) SamTwiston-Davies 77
(Paul Nicholls) *mid-div: hmpd 11th: hdwy after 15th: rdn and wknd 3 out* **10/1**

-041 **F** **Rigadin De Beauchene (FR)**[17] 3364 11-10-13 **133**....(b) RobertDunne
(Venetia Williams) *chsd ldrs: led 9th to 13th: cl up whn hmpd by loose horse and fell 15th* **10/1**

5-24 **U** **Foxbridge (IRE)**[20] 3282 10-10-1 **126**............................(t) JamieBargary(5)
(Nigel Twiston-Davies) *hld up: hmpd 11th: hmpd and uns rdr 15th* **9/1**[3]

2U26 **U** **Loose Chips**[20] 3282 10-10-13 **133**.................................(b) NoelFehily
(Charlie Longsdon) *led 2nd to 9th: wkng whn blnd and uns rdr 17th* **28/1**

6-F1 **P** **What A Good Night (IRE)**[66] 2436 8-10-11 **131**..................(t) HarrySkelton
(Dan Skelton) *hld up: rdn after 13th: hmpd and wknd 15th: bhd whn p.u bef next* **16/1**

-501 **F** **Sego Success (IRE)**[35] 3038 8-11-12 **146**.............(p) WayneHutchinson
(Alan King) *hld up: fell 2nd* **7/1**[1]

11-U **F** **De Kerry Man (IRE)**[15] 3404 8-10-0 **125**............................ JakeHodson(5)
(David Bridgwater) *chsd ldrs: led 13th: hdd appr 16th: rdn and wknd 3 out: bhd whn fell next* **15/2**[2]

3-30 **P** **Ballyheigue Bay (IRE)**[20] 3282 9-10-12 **132**.......................(t) TomCannon
(Chris Gordon) *prom tl wknd appr 13th: bhd whn p.u after 15th* **25/1**

0-2U **F** **Algernon Pazham (IRE)**[42] 2899 7-11-5 **142**...................... RyanHatch(3)
(Nigel Twiston-Davies) *hld up: hdwy 8th: fell 11th* **10/1**

1-2U **P** **Red Devil Lads (IRE)**[7] 3518 7-11-4 **138**.............................. SeanBowen
(Rebecca Curtis) *led to 2nd: chsd ldr to 9th: remained handy tl wknd after 17th: bhd whn p.u bef next* **12/1**

8m 3.1s (7.10) **Going Correction** +0.375s/f (Yiel) **14** Ran SP% **116.6**
Speed ratings: **105,103,97,95,84 ,,,,, ,,,**
CSF £157.48 CT £2468.91 TOTE £21.60: £5.10, £2.50, £5.40; EX 191.10 Trifecta £3580.90.
Owner Mark Jackson **Bred** B De La Motte Saint-Pierre & Jean-Francois Lambert **Trained** Byton, H'fords

FOCUS
Race distance increased by 92yds. An incident packed feature, run in gruelling conditions. Due to rail movements it was run over 96 yards further than officially advertised. Only five of the 14 runners completed. A pb from the winner on his first attempt at 3m4f+.

3625 BETFRED TV "NEWCOMERS" STANDARD OPEN NATIONAL HUNT FLAT RACE 2m
4:05 (4:09) (Class 6) 4-6-Y-O **£1,949** (£572; £286; £143)

Form RPR
1 **Thisonetime (IRE)** 5-11-4 0 AndrewTinkler 108+
(John Quinn) *hld up in tch: pushed along over 5f out: chsd ldr 4f out: rdn to ld 2f out: sn hung lft: styd on* **3/1**[2]

2 *6* **Opera Rock (FR)** 5-10-13 0 CharlieDeutsch[(5)] 102+
(Venetia Williams) *hld up: hdwy 5f out: rdn to chse wnr and hung rt over 1f out: no ex fnl f* **9/4**[1]

3 *1* **Cheltenam De Vaige (FR)** 4-10-7 0 DavidEngland 89
(Giles Smyly) *disp ld tl wnt on 7f out: rdn and hdd 2f out: styd on same pce* **14/1**

4 *9* **Sydney De Baune (FR)** 5-11-4 0 AndrewThornton 91
(Robert Walford) *prom 12f* **6/1**

5 *2 ¾* **Miss Maiden Over (IRE)** 4-9-11 0 ConorShoemark[(3)] 70
(Fergal O'Brien) *chsd ldrs tl rdn and wknd over 3f out* **9/2**[3]

6 *25* **Indian Secret (IRE)** 6-10-11 0 JamieMoore 56
(Jim Best) *prom: pushed along and lost pl over 10f out: bhd fr 1/2-way* **6/1**

7 *40* **Canton Massini** 5-11-4 0 CharliePoste 23
(John Holt) *disp ld 9f: wknd 5f out* **33/1**

4m 16.7s (31.30) **Going Correction** +0.875s/f (Soft)
WFA 4 from 5yo+ 11lb **7 Ran SP% 112.1**
Speed ratings: **56,53,52,48,46 34,14**
CSF £9.77 TOTE £3.40: £1.40, £1.80; EX 10.90 Trifecta £85.50.
Owner Steven McKie **Bred** Miss Laura Devitt **Trained** Settrington, N Yorks

FOCUS
Race distance increased by 11yds. An informative bumper, featuring seven newcomers. The first three home broke nicely clear. With nothing to go on the race has only been given a token rating.
T/Plt: £508.20 to a £1 stake. Pool: £148,121.08 - 212.74 winning tickets T/Qpdt: £39.50 to a £1 stake. Pool: £12,765.21 - 238.88 winning tickets **Colin Roberts**

2917 WETHERBY (L-H)
Saturday, January 16

OFFICIAL GOING: Heavy (soft in places; 4.8)
Wind: light 1/2 behind Weather: fine but cold

3626 PREMIER LEAGUE BETTING AT 188BET EBF "NATIONAL HUNT" NOVICES' HURDLE (QUALIFIER) 2m 3f 154y
12:25 (12:25) (Class 4) 4-7-Y-O **£3,898** (£1,144; £572; £286)

Form RPR
1 **Sharpasaknife (IRE)** 6-11-2 0 BrianHughes 128+
(Malcolm Jefferson) *trckd ldrs: led appr 3 out: wnt clr run-in: v readily* **16/1**

41 2 *11* **Road To Gold (IRE)**[41] 2931 7-11-8 116 LucyAlexander 120
(N W Alexander) *led: hdd and hit 3 out: kpt on same pce between last 2* **5/1**[2]

P 3 *2* **Barenice (FR)**[72] 2299 5-10-13 0 (t) KillianMoore[(3)] 112
(Alex Hales) *in rr-div: hdwy 4 out: kpt on to take modest 3rd appr last* **25/1**

-4F4 4 *9* **Return Flight**[32] 3101 5-11-2 0 AidanColeman 103
(Micky Hammond) *hld up in mid-div: hdwy to trck ldrs 5th: 3rd appr 3 out: wknd appr last* **16/1**

325 5 *1 ¾* **Petethepear (IRE)**[29] 3133 6-11-2 0 JoshuaMoore 101
(Stuart Edmunds) *chsd ldrs: drvn 4 out: wknd between last 2* **6/5**[1]

4-26 6 *20* **Tara The Tiger**[34] 3054 5-10-9 0 JamesReveley 79
(Tim Easterby) *in rr: bhd fr 4th: distant 6th 2 out* **40/1**

63-3 7 *21* **Along Came Theo (IRE)**[34] 3056 6-10-13 0 JohnKington[(3)] 60
(Andrew Crook) *sn chsng ldrs: lost pl bef 3 out: t.o* **50/1**

232 8 *13* **Shine Away (IRE)**[45] 2847 6-10-9 105 DannyCook 40
(Sue Smith) *chsd ldrs: drvn 4 out: lost pl bef next: sn bhd: t.o whn j. bdly lft last* **7/1**[3]

54 9 *18* **Lough Salt (IRE)**[15] 3397 5-11-2 0 JakeGreenall 29
(Mark Walford) *prom: lost pl 4 out: sn bhd: t.o next* **12/1**

00-5 P **More Play**[45] 2849 5-10-6 0 AdamNicol[(3)]
(George Moore) *in last: mstke 2nd: drvn next: t.o 4 out: sn p.u* **200/1**

2 P **Rolling Thunder (IRE)**[21] 3245 6-11-2 0 DarylJacob
(Donald McCain) *chsd ldrs: lost pl after 5th: sn bhd: t.o whn p.u after 4 out* **9/1**

62-P P **Mr K (IRE)**[19] 3316 5-11-2 0 TomO'Brien
(Paul Webber) *chsd ldrs: drvn 4 out: sn lost pl and bhd: t.o whn p.u bef 2 out* **80/1**

46 U **What A Game (IRE)**[15] 3397 5-10-9 0 MrWEasterby[(7)]
(Tim Easterby) *in rr: mstke 5th: sn bhd: t.o 3 out: bdly hmpd and uns rdr last* **100/1**

5m 24.0s (17.00) **Going Correction** +1.175s/f (Heav) **13 Ran SP% 115.0**
Speed ratings: **113,108,107,104,103 95,87,81,74, , ,**
CSF £89.85 TOTE £32.00: £9.70, £1.70, £6.10; EX 125.70 Trifecta £2000.60.
Owner The Mount Fawcus Partnership **Bred** Gerry Carroll **Trained** Norton, N Yorks

FOCUS
Testing conditions. The last flight in the back straight was omitted in all hurdle races. After rail movements, the actual distance of the opener was 2m4f 87yds. The pace was just steady in what was an ordinary novice hurdle, with the time 50sec slower than standard. The second and fourth are probably a better guide to the level than the below-par fifth.

3627 LIVE BETTING AT 188BET.CO.UK NOVICES' CHASE (12 fncs 4 omitted) 2m 3f 85y
12:55 (12:58) (Class 4) 5-Y-0+ **£3,898** (£1,144; £572; £286)

Form RPR
14-1 1 **L'Ami Serge (IRE)**[13] 3451 6-11-7 0 DarylJacob 156+
(Nicky Henderson) *mde all: clr fr 3 out: j.lft 2 out: smoothly* **1/6**[1]

-413 2 *6* **Run Ructions Run (IRE)**[18] 3337 7-11-0 135 (p) BrianHughes 137+
(Tim Easterby) *chsd ldng pair: 2nd 4th: pushed along 4 out: kpt on: no ch w wnr* **6/1**[2]

11-P 3 *8* **Central Flame**[32] 3100 8-10-9 133 MissCWalton[(5)] 127
(James Walton) *chsd wnr to 4th: outpcd 6th: one pce appr 4 out: tk modest 3rd run-in* **33/1**[3]

5/U3 4 *1* **Only Orsenfoolsies**[34] 3055 7-10-7 123 FinianO'Toole[(7)] 127
(Micky Hammond) *nt fluent in rr: outpcd 6th: modest 3rd 4 out: one pce* **50/1**

5m 38.8s (31.00) **Going Correction** +1.325s/f (Heav) **4 Ran SP% 104.9**
Speed ratings: **87,84,81,80**
CSF £1.58 TOTE £1.10; EX 1.50 Trifecta £2.60.
Owner Simon Munir & Isaac Souede **Bred** P Ryan **Trained** Upper Lambourn, Berks

FOCUS
Actual race distance 2m4f. The last two fences in the back straight were omitted in all the chases. After the race Daryl Jacob described the ground on the chase track as "hard work and very gluey." This proved easy pickings for the short-priced favourite. The easy winner has been rated in line with his hurdle mark, but is a potential 160+ chaser. It's been rated around the balance of the second and fourth.

3628 188BET.CO.UK H'CAP HURDLE (8 hdls 1 omitted) 2m
1:30 (1:30) (Class 4) (0-110,110) 4-Y-0+ **£3,249** (£954; £477; £238)

Form RPR
1 **Seamus Mor (IRE)**[65] 2462 8-11-0 98 JamesDavies 105+
(Henry Oliver) *trckd ldrs: 3rd 3 out: upsides between last 2: edgd rt and led narrowly last: drvn rt out* **7/4**[1]

064 2 *1 ¾* **Veinard (FR)**[17] 3366 7-10-13 102 CallumBewley[(5)] 106
(Robert Bewley) *mid-div: chsd ldrs 4th: upsides 3 out: led narrowly 2 out: hdd and n.m.r last: styd on same pce* **12/1**

2412 3 *3 ¾* **Nebula Storm (IRE)**[44] 2869 9-11-4 109 (v) HarryCobden[(7)] 108
(Michael Blake) *chsd ldrs: kpt on one pce fr 2 out* **11/2**[2]

666- 4 *2 ½* **Fingers Crossed (IRE)**[268] 5496 6-11-12 110 TomO'Brien 108
(Paul Webber) *jnd ldrs 3rd: sn led: hdd 2 out: 3rd whn hit last: fdd* **14/1**

0040 5 *1 ¼* **Hey Bob (IRE)**[32] 3099 4-10-9 104 JakeGreenall 88
(Chris Grant) *hld up in rr: hdwy to chse ldrs appr 3 out: hung rt between last 2: fdd and j.lft last* **50/1**

-52P 6 *¾* **Mondo Cane (IRE)**[21] 3236 9-11-6 104 (b) AdamPogson 99
(Charles Pogson) *t.k.h in rr: hdwy bef 3 out: one pce fr 2 out* **12/1**

2366 7 *1 ¼* **Presenting Streak (IRE)**[63] 2496 7-11-5 110 (t) MrRWinks[(7)] 103
(Peter Winks) *t.k.h: led: hdd sn after 3rd: drvn 5th: one pce fr 3 out* **17/2**[3]

P/PP 8 *13* **Moscow Presents (IRE)**[29] 3142 8-11-9 107 (p) JamesReveley 87
(Philip Kirby) *mid-div: chsd ldrs 3rd: drvn appr 3 out: lost pl bef 2 out: bhd whn j.lft last* **16/1**

0360 9 *1 ¼* **Bold Henmie (IRE)**[41] 2933 5-10-11 98 AdamNicol[(3)] 77
(Philip Kirby) *chsd ldrs: drvn 5th: chsng ldrs next: sn wknd* **20/1**

4052 10 *1 ½* **Strait Run (IRE)**[19] 3307 5-10-0 87 JoeColliver[(3)] 65
(Micky Hammond) *chsd ldrs to 3rd: in rr and drvn next: sme hdwy appr 3 out: sn lost pl* **18/1**

0006 11 *79* **Zakety Zak**[19] 3306 5-11-2 100 PeterBuchanan
(James Turner) *in rr: hdwy 4th: chsng ldrs next: lost pl bef 3 out: sn wl bhd: tailed rt off: eventually completed* **50/1**

46-P P **Air Chief**[19] 3307 11-10-7 94 (t) JohnKington[(3)]
(Andrew Crook) *chsd ldrs: reminders after 5th: wknd qckly bef 3 out: t.o whn p.u after 3 out* **80/1**

4-30 F **Walser (IRE)**[233] 520 9-11-7 105 (b) BrianHughes
(John Wade) *chsd ldrs: blnd 1st: lost pl and in rr whn fell 4th* **9/1**

4m 22.2s (26.40) **Going Correction** +1.175s/f (Heav)
WFA 4 from 5yo+ 11lb **13 Ran SP% 115.4**
Speed ratings (Par 105): **81,80,78,77,76 76,75,68,68,67 28, ,**
CSF £22.04 CT £98.36 TOTE £2.70: £1.20, £4.50, £2.10; EX 27.00 Trifecta £143.10.
Owner Oscar Singh & Miss Priya Purewal **Bred** Victor Treacy **Trained** Abberley, Worcs
■ Stewards' Enquiry : James Davies caution; careless riding

FOCUS
Modest handicap hurdle form, but it looks sound enough. Actual race distance 2m 99yds. A big step up from the second on his handicap debut, with the third and fifth helping to set the level.

3629 188BET H'CAP CHASE (11 fncs 2 omitted) 1m 7f 36y
2:05 (2:05) (Class 2) (0-150,144) 5-Y-0+ **£11,710** (£3,459; £1,729; £865; £432)

Form RPR
13-P 1 **Gardefort (FR)**[49] 2784 7-11-0 132 AidanColeman 144+
(Venetia Williams) *hld up wl in tch: hdwy 4 out: upsides 2 out: led between last 2: pushed clr run-in: v readily* **7/2**[1]

1115 2 *7* **Sir Valentino (FR)**[20] 3281 7-11-11 143 (t) DarylJacob 148
(Tom George) *trckd ldr 3rd: led 3 out: jnd next: hdd between last 2: styd on same pce* **9/2**[2]

055F 3 *12* **Mwaleshi**[42] 2902 11-10-13 131 DannyCook 125
(Sue Smith) *j.rt: led: drvn bef 4 out: hdd 3 out: one pce* **9/2**[2]

-544 4 *2* **Yorkist (IRE)**[42] 2920 8-11-2 134 BrianHughes 125
(Micky Hammond) *trckd ldrs: effrt 4 out: sn rdn: one pce fr 3 out* **6/1**[3]

3-06 5 *6* **Upsilon Bleu (FR)**[15] 3426 8-11-12 144 JamesReveley 131
(Pauline Robson) *trckd ldrs: effrt appr 4 out: outpcd and nt fluent 4 out: sn lost pl* **7/2**[1]

-02F P **Whispering Harry**[28] 3155 7-10-11 129 JamesDavies
(Henry Oliver) *chsd ldrs: drvn 6th: hit next and reminders: sn lost pl: eased and t.o omitted 5 out: p.u bef 4 out* **6/1**[3]

4m 11.5s (15.70) **Going Correction** +1.325s/f (Heav) **6 Ran SP% 109.4**
Speed ratings: **111,107,100,99,96**
CSF £18.29 TOTE £4.80: £2.40, £1.60; EX 19.40 Trifecta £76.40.
Owner A Brooks **Bred** S A R L Carion Emm **Trained** Kings Caple, H'fords

FOCUS
A good handicap, run at what looked a fair gallop given the conditions. The actual race distance was 1m7f 117yds. A small step up from the winner, with the second probably the best guide to the level.

3630 ASIAN H'CAPS AT 188BET.CO.UK HANDICAP HURDLE 2m 3f 154y
2:40 (2:40) (Class 3) (0-140,138) 4-Y-0+ **£6,498** (£1,908; £954; £477)

Form RPR
2-1P 1 **One For Harry (IRE)**[56] 2641 8-11-4 133 AdamNicol[(3)] 142+
(Nicky Richards) *prom: 2nd appr normal 3 out: hit 3 out: led appr last: hit last: drvn out* **15/2**

-215 2 *3 ¼* **Waterclock (IRE)**[104] 1776 7-10-7 122 JoeColliver[(3)] 126+
(Micky Hammond) *in rr: effrt and 4th appr normal 3 out: 3rd bef last: styd on to tk 2nd last 75yds* **11/1**

0201 3 *4 ½* **Vendor (FR)**[42] 2921 8-11-12 138 DannyCook 138
(Sue Smith) *trckd ldrs: hit 3rd: led appr normal 3 out: hdd appr last: fdd last 100yds* **4/1**[1]

-041 4 *9* **Maxie T**[18] 3346 5-10-11 130 FinianO'Toole[(7)] 121
(Micky Hammond) *hld up in rr: effrt normal 3 out: modest 4th last: nvr a factor* **9/2**[2]

6-11 5 *4 ½* **Divine Port (USA)**[21] 3242 6-10-7 119 JakeGreenall 106
(Alan Swinbank) *chsd ldrs: one pce fr normal 3 out* **11/2**

5460 **6** *2 1/4* **Rival D'Estruval (FR)**[15] 3428 11-10-2 **117**................ GrahamWatters(3) 101
(Pauline Robson) *in rr: pushed along 6th: outpcd appr normal 3 out: kpt on between last 2: nvr a factor* **14/1**

0/60 **7** *18* **Swnymor (IRE)**[21] 3232 7-10-11 **123**........................(t) MarkGrant 89
(Kevin Frost) *t.k.h in rr: stdy hdwy 4th: modest 3rd normal 3 out: fnd nil and sn lost pl: eased clsng stages* **10/1**

24P- **8** *3 1/2* **Spanish Fleet**[287] 5139 8-11-6 **132**........................ BrianHughes 94
(John Wade) *chsd ldrs: drvn 6th: lost pl bef 3 out: sn bhd* **25/1**

-4P0 **9** *22* **Medicine Hat**[36] 3027 5-10-13 **125**........................ RichieMcLernon 65
(George Moore) *chsd ldrs: drvn after 5th: lost pl bef normal 3 out: sn bhd: t.o whn eased run-in* **22/1**

11 **10** *58* **Master Jake (IRE)**[53] 2699 8-10-11 **128**................ BridgetAndrews(5) 10
(Dan Skelton) *led: hdd appr 3 out: sn lost pl and bhd: t.o last: virtually p.u: eventually completed* **5/1**[3]

5m 25.5s (18.50) **Going Correction** +1.175s/f (Heav) **10** Ran SP% **114.3**
Speed ratings (Par 107): **110,108,106,103,101 100,93,92,83,60**
CSF £83.60 CT £376.52 TOTE £8.90: £3.00, £3.50, £2.20; EX 92.70 Trifecta £464.30.
Owner The Fife Boys + 1 **Bred** Berry Farms **Trained** Greystoke, Cumbria

FOCUS
Actual race distance 2m4f 87yds. The second-last flight was bypassed as it had been damaged. It represents decent handicap hurdle form. The third has been rated 4lb off his recent win.

3631 FREE BET AT 188BET H'CAP CHASE (12 fncs 4 omitted) 2m 3f 85y
3:15 (3:15) (Class 4) (0-120,118) 5-Y-0+ **£3,898** (£1,144; £572; £286)

Form RPR

0111 **1** **Caraline (FR)**[18] 3343 5-11-0 **113**........................ JoeColliver(3) 123+
(Micky Hammond) *trckd ldrs 5th: effrt and cl 3rd 4 out: led and blnd next: hdd narrowly 2 out: styd on to ld towards fin* **4/1**[2]

P-P4 **2** *hd* **Azert De Coeur (FR)**[12] 3466 6-11-4 **110**................ AidanColeman 123+
(Venetia Williams) *hld up: trckd ldrs 5th: cl 2nd 4 out: upsides whn hit next: led narrowly 2 out: hdd nr fin* **7/2**[1]

P-P0 **3** *15* **Voyage A New York (FR)**[17] 3364 7-11-6 **112**................ DerekFox 109
(Lucinda Russell) *t.k.h: led: hdd appr 4 out: outpcd and lost pl 3 out: kpt on run-in: tk poor 3rd clsng stages* **6/1**

P332 **4** *6* **Trust Thomas**[18] 3343 8-11-1 **112**................ JamieHamilton(5) 103
(Ann Hamilton) *chsd ldrs: outpcd bef 4 out: modest 3rd after 3 out: edgd lft and wknd last 150yds* **9/2**[3]

P-44 **5** *6* **Little Glenshee (IRE)**[41] 2935 10-11-12 **118**................ LucyAlexander 106
(N W Alexander) *chsd ldrs: stmbld on landing 5th: mstke 6th: sn drvn: lost pl bef 4 out: sn wl bhd: kpt on appr last* **9/1**

-522 **6** *7* **Red Danaher (IRE)**[21] 3243 9-10-12 **104**................ DannyCook 88
(Sue Smith) *w ldr: drvn 8th: led appr 4 out: hdd 3 out: sn lost pl: bhd whn eased clsng stages* **4/1**[2]

-U50 **7** *2 1/4* **Too Much Too Soon (IRE)**[29] 3134 7-11-3 **109**.....(tp) RichieMcLernon 87
(Paul Webber) *in rr: mstke 2nd: hdwy 5th: hit 8th: lost pl bef 4 out: sn bhd* **20/1**

2P65 **8** *1 1/4* **Vayland**[18] 3345 7-11-3 **109**........................ CraigNichol 83
(Micky Hammond) *in rr: pushed along and sme hdwy 8th: lost pl bef 4 out: sn bhd: b.b.v* **40/1**

5m 39.7s (31.90) **Going Correction** +1.325s/f (Heav)
WFA 5 from 6yo+ 3lb **8** Ran SP% **111.9**
Speed ratings: **85,84,78,76,73 70,69,69**
CSF £18.15 CT £80.28 TOTE £3.30: £1.70, £2.10, £2.60; EX 15.00 Trifecta £110.60.
Owner Give Every Man His Due **Bred** Mme Caroline Elizabeth Huni **Trained** Middleham, N Yorks

FOCUS
Actual race distance 2m4f. A fair handicap chase which produced a fine finish, the first two clear. Another step forward from the winner, and a much bigger one from the second. There's a case for rating the race up to 10lb higher through the rest, but the fourth has been rated in line with his recent runs and this is probably high enough.

3632 FREE SPINS AT 188BET CASINO FILLIES' "JUNIOR" STANDARD OPEN NATIONAL HUNT FLAT RACE 1m 4f 77y
3:50 (3:50) (Class 6) 4-Y-0 **£1,949** (£572; £286; £143)

Form RPR

1 **1** **Woolstone One**[31] 3118 4-11-3 0........................ GavinSheehan 120+
(Harry Whittington) *trckd ldr: led after 3f: pushed along over 3f out: drvn clr over 1f out: styd on wl* **1/2**[1]

2 *13* **Poisoned Berry (IRE)** 4-10-3 0................ MissBHampson(7) 95
(Fergal O'Brien) *chsd ldng pair: modest 3rd over 3f out: 2nd over 2f out: no ch w wnr* **50/1**

22 **3** *10* **Passmore**[72] 2304 4-10-10 0........................ AidanColeman 81
(Alan King) *hld up towards rr: modest 3rd over 5f out: chsd wnr over 3f out: wknd over 1f out* **9/4**[2]

4 *1 3/4* **Dance And Romance** 4-10-10 0........................ BrianHughes 79
(Tim Easterby) *mid-div: outpcd and lost pl over 3f out* **10/1**[3]

5 *28* **Cupid's Quest (IRE)** 4-10-3 0................ JamesCorbett(7) 39
(Susan Corbett) *in rr: pushed along 6f out: lost pl over 4f out: sn wl bhd* **100/1**

5 **6** *29* **Another (IRE)**[42] 2923 4-10-10 0........................ AlainCawley
(David C Griffiths) *led 3f: chsd wnr: lost pl over 3f out: sn bhd: eased whn t.o 2f out* **50/1**

3m 18.5s (198.50) **6** Ran SP% **111.4**
CSF £30.77 TOTE £1.60: £1.10, £7.30; EX 26.20 Trifecta £46.60.
Owner Paul G Jacobs **Bred** D R Tucker **Trained** Sparsholt, Oxfordshire

FOCUS
Actual race distance 1m4f 158yds. There wasn't much depth to this fillies' bumper, but it produced an impressive wide-margin winner. The winner set a good standard, but this still looks a step up, and there's a case for rating him a lot higher through the third.
T/Plt: £152.00 to a £1 stake. Pool: £66,987.44 - 321.52 winning tickets T/Qpdt: £22.90 to a £1 stake. Pool: £7,394.13 - 238.01 winning tickets **Walter Glynn**

3633 - (Foreign Racing) - See Raceform Interactive

3457 NAAS (L-H)
Saturday, January 16

OFFICIAL GOING: Soft to heavy

3634a LIMESTONE LAD HURDLE (GRADE 3) (10 hdls) 2m 3f
1:20 (1:20) 5-Y-0+ **£14,338** (£4,191; £1,985; £661)

RPR

1 **Sempre Medici (FR)**[35] 3033 6-11-10 **156**........................ RWalsh 148+
(W P Mullins, Ire) *hld up bhd ldrs in 3rd: nt fluent 3rd and 6th: tk clsr order bhd ldrs bef 2 out where wnt 2nd: travelling wl and led bef last where slt mstke: pushed out to assert run-in and styd on wl: comf* **1/8**[1]

2 *5* **Massini's Trap (IRE)**[16] 3391 7-11-1 127........................ MarkWalsh 134
(J A Nash, Ire) *w.w in rr: tk clsr order bhd ldrs gng wl into st: rdn after 2 out and wnt 3rd between last 2: wnt 2nd bef last and pressed wnr briefly: no imp on wnr run-in: kpt on same pce* **14/1**[3]

3 *15* **He'llberemembered (IRE)**[57] 2049 13-11-8 144................ PaddyKennedy 125
(P G Fahey, Ire) *chsd ldr: clsr in 2nd bef 4 out where disp: led narrowly into st: rdn after 2 out and hdd u.p bef last where dropped to 3rd: no ex and one pce run-in* **7/1**[2]

4 *5 1/2* **Lindenhurst (IRE)**[16] 3391 6-11-1 127................(t) MarkBolger 113
(John C McConnell, Ire) *led: slt mstke 4th: pressed clly bef 4 out where jnd: rdn and hdd into st: no ex whn mstke 2 out and sn dropped to rr: one pce after* **50/1**

4m 46.6s (-5.00) **4** Ran SP% **110.0**
CSF £3.22 TOTE £1.10; DF 2.30 Trifecta £3.60.
Owner Mrs S Ricci **Bred** Mlle M Bollack, N Forgeard Et Al **Trained** Muine Beag, Co Carlow

FOCUS
The favourite managed to get the job done, not impressively, but adequately enough. The runner-up limits the form.

3635a WOODLANDS PARK 100 CLUB NOVICE CHASE (GRADE 2) (16 fncs) 3m
1:55 (1:55) 5-Y-0+ **£18,750** (£5,937; £2,812)

RPR

1 **Roi Des Francs (FR)**[28] 3167 7-11-5 0........................ BJCooper 151+
(W P Mullins, Ire) *hld up bhd ldrs: impr to dispute 2nd into st and disp ld bef 2 out: led narrowly fr last and kpt on wl u.p run-in where edgd sltly rt to assert clsng stages* **13/8**[2]

2 *1 1/2* **Pont Alexandre (GER)**[41] 2942 8-11-5 0........................ RWalsh 149+
(W P Mullins, Ire) *led and disp: nt fluent 1st: j. sltly rt next: 2nd fr bef 9th: in rr of trio briefly into st: disp ld 2 out where pckd sltly: hdd narrowly fr last where nt fluent: kpt on wl wout matching wnr* **4/7**[1]

3 *4 1/2* **Sub Lieutenant (IRE)**[28] 3167 7-11-5 142................(tp) JJBurke 145
(Ms Sandra Hughes, Ire) *led and disp: in front fr bef 9th: rdn and hdd 2 out: no imp on ldrs fr last: kpt on same pce* **12/1**[3]

6m 42.6s (-5.50) **3** Ran SP% **109.4**
CSF £3.12 TOTE £2.20; DF 2.20 Trifecta £2.90.
Owner Gigginstown House Stud **Bred** Ecurie Maulepaire **Trained** Muine Beag, Co Carlow

FOCUS
A surprise reversal for the favourite, but a result that enhances the Cheltenham claims of the winner. It was slowly run and the first two are rated to their latest form.

3340 KELSO (L-H)
Sunday, January 17

3640 Meeting Abandoned - waterlogged & frozen

3647 - 3649a (Foreign Racing) - See Raceform Interactive

3354 LEOPARDSTOWN (L-H)
Sunday, January 17

OFFICIAL GOING: Soft (soft to heavy in places)

3650a CORAL.IE HURDLE (EXTENDED H'CAP HURDLE - RATED 0-150) (GRADE B) (8 hdls) 2m
2:25 (2:25) (0-150,145) 4-Y-0+ **£44,117** (£13,970; £6,617; £2,205; £1,470; £735)

RPR

1 **Henry Higgins (IRE)**[50] 2797 6-10-10 **131**........................ RobbiePower 145+
(Charles O'Brien, Ire) *hld up towards rr: gd hdwy on inner after 3 out to chse ldrs travelling wl after next: impr to ld fr last and rdn out run-in: kpt on wl: comf* **16/1**

2 *2 1/4* **Kalkir (FR)**[310] 4736 5-11-0 **137**........................ JacquesRicou 146
(W P Mullins, Ire) *hld up in tch: tk clsr order bhd ldrs bef 4 out: cl 2nd bef next: prog to ld bef last where hdd and sn no ch w wnr: kpt on wl run-in* **12/1**

3 *2* **Desoto County**[28] 3183 7-10-0 **126**................(t) JackKennedy(5) 135+
(Gordon Elliott, Ire) *hld up towards rr: hdwy after 3 out: n.m.r into st and rdn in 10th: clsd u.p between horses into 6th bef last and kpt on wl into 3rd: nvr trbld ldrs* **11/2**[2]

4 *5 1/2* **Tigris River (IRE)**[20] 3329 5-10-7 **133**................(t) JodyMcGarvey(3) 135
(A P O'Brien, Ire) *in rr of mid-div: prog after 3 out to chse ldrs fr next: rdn into 6th between last 2 and no imp on ldrs u.p in 5th bef last: kpt on one pce into mod 4th run-in* **25/1**

5 *1/2* **Good As Gold**[16] 3431 8-9-12 **119**........................ MsKWalsh 122
(P A Fahy, Ire) *disp early tl sn settled bhd ldrs: 4th after 3 out: rdn disputing 2nd after 2 out and no ex u.p in 3rd between last 2: dropped to 4th bef last and one pce run-in* **25/1**

6 *3/4* **Bentelimar (IRE)**[35] 3071 7-11-3 **141**................ LPDempsey(3) 143
(J R Barry, Ire) *settled bhd ldr in 2nd tl led after 2nd: nt fluent 4 out: slt mstke 2 out: rdn and strly pressed between last 2: hdd u.p bef last where dropped to 3rd and mstke: wknd run-in* **16/1**

7 *hd* **Bishopslough (IRE)**[171] 1161 8-9-11 **118**................(t) AELynch 120+
(Alan Fleming, Ire) *towards rr: n.m.r on inner after 2 out where sltly hmpd and swtchd rt: 17th between last 2: r.o wl fr last: nvr nrr* **25/1**

8 *1 1/4* **Whatsforuwontgobyu (IRE)**[20] 3323 6-10-6 **127**................ MarkWalsh 128
(A J Martin, Ire) *mid-div: hdwy after 2 out to chse ldrs bef last where nt fluent in 7th: one pce run-in* **12/1**

9 *3 3/4* **Cliff House (IRE)**[28] 3183 6-10-13 **134**................ SeanFlanagan 131
(John J Walsh, Ire) *chsd ldrs: rdn after 2 out and sn no ex: wknd bef last* **16/1**

10 *2 3/4* **Colla Pier (IRE)**[50] 2778 7-10-1 **122**................(t) RobertDunne 116
(Patrick Mooney, Ire) *mid-div: rdn and no ex after 2 out: kpt on one pce* **14/1**

11 *shd* **After Rain (FR)**[50] 2797 6-10-4 **125**................ BarryGeraghty 119
(J R Barry, Ire) *chsd ldrs: racd keenly: rdn in 7th between last 2 and no ex bef last: wknd run-in* **9/2**[1]

12 *5 1/2* **The Plan Man (IRE)**[50] 2797 6-10-11 **132**................(t) DavyRussell 121
(A J Martin, Ire) *mid-div: rdn and no ex after 2 out: one pce after* **33/1**

13 *1 1/4* **Archive (FR)**[19] 3359 6-10-10 **131**................ BJCooper 118
(Eoin Griffin, Ire) *towards rr: niggled along after 2nd: tk clsr order after 2 out: no imp in mod 13th bef last: kpt on one pce* **25/1**

14 1 **Ancient Sands (IRE)**21 3295 8-10-1 **122** BrianHayes 108
(John E Kiely, Ire) *in rr of mid-div: rdn and no imp after 2 out* **20/1**
15 ½ **Ivan Grozny (FR)**636 5470 6-11-10 **145** DannyMullins 131
(W P Mullins, Ire) *chsd ldrs: slt mstke 3 out: tk clsr order in 4th gng wl fr 2 out: rdn in 5th and no ex bef last where wknd qckly and slt mstke* **33/1**
16 shd **Waxies Dargle**29 3151 7-10-10 **138** (t) JonathanMoore(7) 124
(Noel Meade, Ire) *hld up in mid-div: slt mstke 1st: rdn and wknd after 3 out* **20/1**
17 19 **Misty Lady (IRE)**35 3071 7-10-6 **127** MarkEnright 94
(John Laurence Cullen, Ire) *led: j.big 1st and hdd after next: slt mstke 3rd: 3rd after 3 out: rdn and wknd bef 2 out where nt fluent: eased and j.rt last* **25/1**
18 7½ **Princely Conn (IRE)**35 3071 7-10-10 **131** JJBurke 90
(Thomas Mullins, Ire) *chsd ldrs: pushed along in mid-div bef 2 out and sn no ex: wknd bef last* **33/1**
19 10 **Vive La France (FR)**170 1172 7-10-10 **131** (t) APHeskin 80
(Alan Fleming, Ire) *mid-div: rdn and wknd after 2 out: eased st: t.o* **9/1**3
20 2½ **Sir Scorpion (IRE)**287 5174 7-9-13 **120** AlanCrowe 67
(Thomas Mullins, Ire) *hld up: mstke towards rr 3 out: rdn and no ex on outer after 2 out: wknd and eased: t.o* **20/1**
21 27 **Gladiator King (IRE)**21 3295 7-10-2 **128** (t) DonaghMeyler(5) 48
(A J Martin, Ire) *in rr of mid-div: rdn and wknd bef 2 out: eased st: completely t.o* **50/1**
22 12 **Buiseness Sivola (FR)**224 665 5-11-0 **137** RWalsh 43
(W P Mullins, Ire) *in tch: clsr in 4th after 3 out: rdn and wknd after 2 out: eased bef last: completely t.o* **10/1**
P **Bamako Moriviere (FR)**20 3329 5-10-10 **133** DavidMullins
(W P Mullins, Ire) *chsd ldrs: racd keenly: 6th bef 2nd: lost pl and slt mstke 4th: wknd bef 3 out: trailing whn p.u bef 2 out* **20/1**

4m 8.9s (1.40) **Going Correction** +0.375s/f (Yiel) 23 Ran SP% **141.4**
Speed ratings: **111,109,108,106,105 105,105,104,102,101 101,98,98,97,97 97,87,84,79,77 64,58,**
CSF £183.74 CT £1235.95 TOTE £26.30: £4.80, £3.00, £2.20, £5.60; DF 387.70 Trifecta £6089.60.
Owner John P McManus **Bred** Glending Bloodstock **Trained** Straffan, Co Kildare

FOCUS
A typically competitive running of this event, the winner scoring well in the end under a really fine ride. The standard is set around the fourth down to the seventh.

3651a CORAL.IE LEOPARDSTOWN H'CAP CHASE (GRADE A) (14 fncs) 2m 5f
3:00 (3:00) 5-Y-O+
£44,117 (£13,970; £6,617; £2,205; £1,470; £735)

RPR
1 **Empire Of Dirt (IRE)**21 3296 9-9-11 **133** JonathanMoore(7) 142
(C A Murphy, Ire) *chsd ldrs: cl 4th 5 out: prog on inner fr 2 out to ld narrowly gng wl into st: rdn and styd on wl fr last* **8/1**
2 2¼ **Killer Crow (IRE)**21 3302 7-10-1 **130** (t) BJCooper 137
(Gordon Elliott, Ire) *hld up towards rr: hdwy in 9th 2 out to chse ldrs gng wl into st: wnt 2nd fr last and rdn: sn no imp on wnr: kpt on same pce* **6/1**3
3 2½ **Seabass (IRE)**17 3391 13-10-6 **135** MsKWalsh 140
(T M Walsh, Ire) *led: rdn and hdd into st: no imp on wnr fr last where dropped to 3rd: kpt on same pce* **8/1**
4 1¼ **Fine Rightly (IRE)**35 3073 8-11-4 **147** AELynch 150
(S R B Crawford, Ire) *chsd ldrs: tk clsr order between horses 2 out: sn rdn and no imp on wnr u.p in 4th fr last: kpt on same pce* **9/2**1
5 3½ **Blood Cotil (FR)**261 69 7-11-10 **153** RWalsh 153
(W P Mullins, Ire) *hld up: cl 8th out wd gng wl bef 2 out: pushed along into st and wnt 5th bef last where pckd sltly: no ex u.p and one pce run-in* **7/1**
6 4½ **Hash Brown (IRE)**22 3270 7-9-12 **127** NiallPMadden 122
(Michael Hourigan, Ire) *chsd ldrs early: slt mstke 1st and dropped towards rr bef next: tk clsr order on outer bef 2 out: rdn in 6th out wd into st and sn no imp on ldrs: one pce after* **10/1**
7 ½ **Los Amigos (IRE)**21 3296 9-10-8 **137** (b) APHeskin 132
(Dermot Anthony McLoughlin, Ire) *settled bhd ldr in cl 2nd: rdn after 2 out and lost pl into st: swtchd lft disputing 4th bef last and sn no ex: wknd run-in* **8/1**
8 8½ **Fever Pitch (IRE)**35 3073 10-9-5 **125** (t) JackKennedy(5) 111
(A L T Moore, Ire) *chsd ldrs: cl up between horses 4 out: nt fluent next and pushed along in 6th after: rdn and no ex after 2 out: dropped to 8th bef last* **8/1**
9 12 **Heathfield (IRE)**21 3296 9-10-4 **133** BarryGeraghty 107
(A J Martin, Ire) *chsd ldrs out wd: almost on terms bef 8th: stl gng wl bef 2 out: rdn and wknd after 2 out* **5/1**2
10 1 **Cause Of Causes (USA)**21 3296 8-10-13 **142** (tp) MarkWalsh 115
(Gordon Elliott, Ire) *hld up in tch: niggled along briefly fr 6th: pushed along in rr 4 out: rdn and no ex after 2 out* **20/1**
U **Rivage D'Or (FR)**37 3017 11-10-5 **134** (t) DavidMullins
(A J Martin, Ire) *hld up: in rr whn blnd and uns rdr 7th* **50/1**

5m 37.3s (1.30) **Going Correction** +0.125s/f (Yiel) 11 Ran SP% **121.9**
Speed ratings: **102,101,100,99,98 96,96,93,88,88**
CSF £58.41 CT £407.24 TOTE £9.10: £3.40, £2.70, £2.70; DF 59.60 Trifecta £606.30.
Owner Gigginstown House Stud **Bred** Sean Harnedy **Trained** Gorey, Co Wexford

FOCUS
The winner always was one with a chance if he could come back to form, and that he did. The standard is set by the fourth and fifth.

3652a "MONEY BACK ON FALLERS" AT CORAL.IE NOVICE CHASE (GRADE 2) (12 fncs) 2m 3f
3:30 (3:30) 5-Y-O+
£18,529 (£5,867; £2,779; £926)

RPR
1 **Killultagh Vic (IRE)**29 3166 7-11-5 0 RWalsh 156+
(W P Mullins, Ire) *led: nt fluent 2nd: 6 l clr at 1/2-way: reduced ld after 3 out: stl gng wl after next and in command bef last where pitched on landing and c to a standstl: rdr lost iron and rallied in 3rd: styd on again to ld cl home* **2/7**1
2 ¾ **Blair Perrone (IRE)**20 3321 7-11-5 0 (t) DenisO'Regan 145
(A J Martin, Ire) *w.w in rr: 4th 1/2-way: tk clsr order bef 7th: wnt 2nd bef 3 out: clsr in 2nd bef next where sit mstke: hld in 2nd bef last where lft in front: sn rdn and strly pressed cl home where hdd* **10/1**3
3 1¾ **Lord Scoundrel (IRE)**35 3069 7-11-8 142 BJCooper 145
(Gordon Elliott, Ire) *chsd ldr in cl 2nd tl dropped to 3rd bef 3 out: rdn in 3rd bef last and no imp on clr ldr whn lft 2nd: kpt on same pce run-in and dropped to 3rd again clsng stages* **8/1**2
4 27 **Walk To Freedom (IRE)**35 3072 6-11-5 139 RobbiePower 115
(Mrs John Harrington, Ire) *hld up bhd ldrs in 3rd: nt fluent 6th: mstkes 5 out and next in rr: pushed along after 3 out and no imp on ldrs fr next: wknd* **8/1**2
F **Captain Hox (IRE)**29 3153 7-11-5 123 (t) JJBurke
(Patrick Griffin, Ire) *hld up towards rr: last at 1/2-way: in rr whn fell 5 out* **66/1**

4m 53.8s (-4.20) **Going Correction** +0.125s/f (Yiel) 5 Ran SP% **110.6**
Speed ratings: **113,112,111,100,**
CSF £4.18 TOTE £1.10: £1.02, £2.20; DF 3.70 Trifecta £10.20.
Owner Mrs R Boyd, Mrs M J Armstrong & J B Anderson **Bred** F Boyd **Trained** Muine Beag, Co Carlow

FOCUS
A truly extraordinary finish to a race that looked absolutely routine coming to the last. The standard is set by the third, who has been rated to his mark.

3653 - (Foreign Racing) - See Raceform Interactive

3076 FFOS LAS (L-H)
Monday, January 18
3654 Meeting Abandoned - Waterlogged

3450 PLUMPTON (L-H)
Monday, January 18

OFFICIAL GOING: Heavy (chs 3.6; hdl 4.4)
Wind: Almost nil Weather: Fine but cloudy, cold

3660 DOWNLOAD THE TIMEFORM APP NOVICES' HURDLE (9 hdls) 1m 7f 195y
1:45 (1:45) (Class 4) 4-Y-O+
£5,198 (£1,526; £763; £381)

Form RPR
-012 1 **Sunshine Corner (IRE)**30 3154 5-11-3 124 LeightonAspell 120+
(Lucy Wadham) *w ldrs: led 6th: drew clr 2 out: shkn up and styd on after last* **30/100**1
35 2 7 **Jajamcool (IRE)**20 3353 6-11-4 0 JamesBest 114+
(Caroline Keevil) *mde most to 6th: w wnr tl bef 2 out and wl clr of rest: kpt on one pce* **8/1**3
606 3 18 **Bolister (FR)**15 3450 5-11-4 0 JamieMoore 98
(Gary Moore) *hld up: prog 6th: chsd clr ldng pair bef 3 out: urged along and no imp after* **33/1**
00 4 4 **Red Orator**23 3227 7-11-4 0 BrendanPowell 91
(Jim Best) *w ldrs to 5th: lost pl suddenly and sn in last pair of main gp: kpt on again bef 2 out: nt disgracd* **25/1**
0-04 5 ¾ **Sir Hubert**15 3450 6-11-4 0 AndrewThornton 90
(Richard Rowe) *settled in midfield: lost tch w ldrs 6th: pushed along after: keeping on whn mstke 2 out: n.d* **66/1**
60-6 6 16 **Mount Shamsan**35 3083 6-11-4 0 JoshuaMoore 75
(Gary Moore) *hld up: last whn impeded 1st: prog into midfield 5th: pushed along and no imp on ldrs after: wknd last* **12/1**
01 7 ½ **Dalaki (IRE)**17 3418 5-11-10 0 PeterCarberry 84
(Des Donovan) *j. slowly 1st: chsd ldrs: lft bhd by ldng pair 6th: wknd after 3 out: mstke next* **4/1**2
P 8 34 **Little Buxted (USA)**15 3450 6-11-4 0 AndrewGlassonbury 40
(Jim Best) *in tch to 6th: sn wknd: virtually p.u nr fin* **50/1**
6060 9 1 **Cougar Kid (IRE)**35 3083 5-11-4 0 RichieMcLernon 39
(Philip Hide) *lost tch 5th: sn t.o* **20/1**

4m 20.6s (19.80) **Going Correction** +1.475s/f (Heav) 9 Ran SP% **130.7**
Speed ratings (Par 105): **109,105,96,94,94 86,85,68,68**
CSF £4.77 TOTE £1.20: £1.10, £1.80, £7.90; EX 5.20 Trifecta £90.70.
Owner P A Philipps & Mrs G J Redman **Bred** John Crean **Trained** Newmarket, Suffolk

FOCUS
Hurdle top bend out 8yds, bottom bend out 10yds. Chase top bend out 4yds. As a result this race was run over 64yds further than normal. The ground was certainly hard work. Little depth to this novice hurdle and the red-hot favourite ran out just a workmanlike winner. The winner set the standard and has been rated close to her mark.

3661 "MY DASHBOARD" ON THE TIMEFORM APP H'CAP CHASE (12 fncs) 2m 214y
2:15 (2:15) (Class 5) (0-100,99) 5-Y-O+
£3,898 (£1,144; £572; £286)

Form RPR
/3PU 1 **Goring Two (IRE)**35 3088 11-10-2 **80** CharlieDeutsch(5) 96+
(Anna Newton-Smith) *cl up: led 3rd: hdd after 8th: gd jump to ld again 3 out: drvn clr fr next: styd on wl* **5/2**2
5-2F 2 12 **Slidecheck (IRE)**17 3419 9-11-5 **92** (tp) RhysFlint 96
(Alexandra Dunn) *led to 3rd: chsd ldng pair after: nt fluent 5th: rdn to cl 3 out: chsd wnr 2 out but no imp: fin tired* **9/1**
P0-5 3 6 **Virtuose Du Chenet (FR)**18 3379 7-11-8 **95** AidanColeman 97+
(Venetia Williams) *w ldrs gng wl: led after 8th: nt fluent 3 out and hdd: sn rdn and no rspnse: lost 2nd 2 out: fin weakly* **13/8**1
-PP5 4 31 **Topthorn**23 3225 10-11-5 **99** (p) MrZBaker(7) 65
(Martin Bosley) *hld up: lost tch 7th: bhd and pushed along next: wknd 4 out: t.o* **14/1**
/42U U **Highbury High (IRE)**23 3214 9-11-9 **96** (p) NoelFehily
(Neil Mulholland) *last whn mstke 3rd: detached whn blnd and uns rdr next* **11/1**
F553 P **Head Spin (IRE)**35 3088 8-11-3 **90** (tp) AndrewThornton
(Seamus Mullins) *chsd ldrs: reminders after 5th: wknd 7th: wl bhd whn p.u bef next* **4/1**3

4m 38.4s (15.40) **Going Correction** +0.975s/f (Soft) 6 Ran SP% **111.7**
Speed ratings: **102,96,93,78,**
CSF £22.47 TOTE £3.40: £1.60, £4.10; EX 17.60 Trifecta £51.00.
Owner George Goring **Bred** James A Slattery **Trained** Jevington, E Sussex

FOCUS
Lowly chase form, with the favourite not getting home. The race was run over 24yds further than advertised. The second and third have been rated as running personal bests.

3662 "MY TIMEFORM" ON THE TIMEFORM APP H'CAP HURDLE (14 hdls) 3m 217y
2:45 (2:45) (Class 4) (0-115,110) 4-Y-0+ **£3,898** (£1,144; £572; £286)

Form RPR
-013 **1** **Extreme Impact**[31] 3142 10-11-10 **108**............................(v) KielanWoods 110
(Graeme McPherson) *in tch in midfield: rdn 8th: struggling to stay in tch fr 11th: stl only 5th and 10 l down 2 out: tk 3rd last: styd on stoutly to ld fnl 75yds* **16/1**
5-4P **2** *2* **Major Milborne**[52] 2758 8-11-5 **110**.................................... MissPFuller[(7)] 112
(Jamie Snowden) *trckd ldrs gng wl: led 11th: rdn after mstke 3 out: kpt on and looked like holding on tl hdd last 75yds* **20/1**
-P23 **3** *1 ¼* **Reblis (FR)**[35] 3086 11-11-8 **106**.........................(b) JoshuaMoore 105
(Gary Moore) *trckd ldr: led 5th: drvn fr 9th: hdd 11th: kpt on to chal fr 2 out: no ex after last* **8/1**
5-06 **4** *4 ½* **Darkestbeforedawn (IRE)**[23] 3220 9-11-4 **107**.......... JackSherwood[(5)] 102
(Caroline Keevil) *in rr and pushed along 4th: prog fr 8th: chsd ldng trio 11th: drvn to go 3rd bef 2 out: no imp after* **10/1**
-402 **5** *4* **Onwiththeparty**[19] 3369 7-11-4 **102**..................(p) TomCannon 93
(Chris Gordon) *prog to chse ldrs 5th: drvn fr 10th: no imp on ldrs fr 3 out: plugged on* **4/1[1]**
U-55 **P** **Aviador (GER)**[23] 3220 10-10-6 **100**.............................. LukeIngram[(10)]
(Lucy Wadham) *lost pl and in rr fr 4th: bhd fr 10th: t.o whn p.u after 3 out* **9/2[2]**
614- **P** **Baldadash (IRE)**[273] 5429 11-11-9 **107**.........................(p) JamesDavies
(Jose Santos) *chsd ldrs: wknd 7th: in rr whn mstke 10th: t.o whn p.u bef next* **25/1**
2451 **P** **Flemi Two Toes (IRE)**[23] 3220 10-10-3 **97**..........(p) RomainClavreul[(10)]
(Sarah Humphrey) *drvn in midfield after 4th: struggling in rr 10th: t.o whn p.u bef next* **12/1**
423 **P** **Sky Watch (IRE)**[56] 2692 9-11-11 **109**..............................(t) GavinSheehan
(Brian Barr) *hld up in last: nvr a factor: rdn 8th: t.o whn p.u bef 11th* **12/1**
6035 **P** **Bishop Wulstan (IRE)**[11] 3498 5-11-9 **107**..........................(tp) SeanBowen
(Peter Bowen) *led to 5th: chsd ldr to 10th: wknd rapidly: t.o whn p.u after 3 out* **14/1**
-402 **P** **Bassarabad (FR)**[61] 2569 5-11-12 **110**........................... RichardJohnson
(Tim Vaughan) *dropped to rr 4th: effrt and jst in tch bef 11th: sn wknd: t.o whn p.u bef 2 out* **8/1**
-446 **P** **Speredek (FR)**[38] 3023 5-11-9 **107**.................................(tp) ConorO'Farrell
(Nigel Hawke) *mstke 1st: in tch: chsd ldng pair and mstke 11th: upsides briefly sn after 3 out: wknd rapidly and p.u bef 2 out* **7/1[3]**

7m 13.3s (48.30) **Going Correction** +1.60s/f (Heavy) 12 Ran SP% **118.5**
Speed ratings (Par 105): **86,85,84,83,82** , , , , , ,
CSF £288.96 TOTE £17.50: £4.80, £6.10, £2.80; EX 313.20 Trifecta £5687.20 Part won..
Owner Extreme Racing Fans **Bred** Juddmonte Farms Ltd **Trained** Upper Oddington, Gloucs

FOCUS
Less than half the field managed to complete in this staying handicap that proved a good old test in the ground. Race run over 138yds further than advertised. The second, third and fourth have been rated close to their marks.

3663 EPDS RACING WELFARE BTO SERIES 2016 H'CAP CHASE (18 fncs) 3m 1f 152y
3:15 (3:16) (Class 5) (0-100,100) 5-Y-0+ **£3,898** (£1,144; £572; £286)

Form RPR
4023 **1** **Bebinn (IRE)**[23] 3222 9-11-3 **91**..............................(p) DarylJacob 101+
(Ben Case) *sn dropped to last but wl in tch: prog to trck ldrs 11th: wnt 2nd 14th: led after 3 out and gng best: drvn out after last* **3/1[1]**
P226 **2** *1 ¼* **Burgess Dream (IRE)**[35] 3087 7-10-13 **87**.................. AndrewThornton 95
(Anna Newton-Smith) *hld up in tch: mstke 4th: prog after 14th: rdn 3 out: tk 2nd next: tried to chal after last: kpt on but no imp nr fin* **9/2[3]**
3124 **3** *1 ¼* **Cheat The Cheater (IRE)**[23] 3236 9-11-2 **90**..............(tp) BrendanPowell 95
(Claire Dyson) *in tch: rdn 14th: kpt on for press fr 4 out and tk 3rd 2 out: styd on but nvr able to chal* **9/2[3]**
34P5 **4** *20* **Kinari (IRE)**[49] 2827 6-11-1 **89**..............................(tp) SeanBowen 75
(Peter Bowen) *led to 2nd: pressed ldr tl led again after 12th: hdd after 3 out: wknd qckly next* **7/2[2]**
-11P **5** *2 ½* **Leith Hill Legasi**[18] 3385 7-11-12 **100**..................(bt) SamTwiston-Davies 84
(Charlie Longsdon) *led 2nd but had to work to get there: hdd after 12th: sn rdn: lost pl after 14th: wknd 4 out* **8/1**
4334 **6** *21* **Veauce De Sivola (FR)**[3] 3609 7-11-4 **95**..................(t) TomBellamy[(3)] 65
(Mark Gillard) *wl in tch: rdn bef 4 out: wknd sn after* **15/2**
PPP4 **P** **Ravens Brook (IRE)**[17] 3419 10-11-7 **95**...................(p) TrevorWhelan
(Neil King) *reminders after 4th: styd in tch but u.p tl wknd qckly 10th: p.u bef next* **16/1**

7m 23.8s (33.10) **Going Correction** +1.10s/f (Heavy) 7 Ran SP% **112.3**
Speed ratings: **93,92,92,86,85 78,**
CSF £16.50 TOTE £3.80: £2.30, £2.60; EX 17.50 Trifecta £69.10.
Owner The Polk Partnership **Bred** James Gill **Trained** Edgcote, Northants

FOCUS
Moderate chasing form. The race was run over 36yds further than advertised. The first three have all been rated within a few pounds of their marks.

3664 DAVID GEORGE MEMORIAL MAIDEN HURDLE (12 hdls) 2m 4f 114y
3:45 (3:45) (Class 5) 4-Y-0+ **£3,898** (£1,144; £572; £286)

Form RPR
33-P **1** **Saucysioux**[28] 3194 6-10-12 0.................................. AndrewThornton 100+
(Michael Roberts) *nt fluent: hld up and last tl after 8th: rapid prog to press ldrs and mstke 3 out: rallied to ld 2 out: drvn clr fr last* **33/1**
0 **2** *8* **Bold Runner**[86] 1234 5-11-5 0.....................................(p) JamesDavies 98
(Jose Santos) *hld up in tch: prog to chse ldr after 8th: led after 3 out: drvn and hdd 2 out and sn in 3rd: btn last but tk 2nd nr fin* **16/1**
41 **3** *¾* **Champagne George (IRE)**[54] 2715 6-11-5 0.......................... NoelFehily 96
(Neil Mulholland) *cl up: mstke 3rd: trckd ldr 6th tl after 8th: sn urged along: rallied to chal 2 out: stl ch last: hung lft and wknd flat: lost 2nd fnl strides* **6/5[1]**
5220 **4** *18* **Linguine (FR)**[21] 2888 6-11-5 116.............................(p) ConorO'Farrell 78
(Seamus Durack) *nt a fluent: racd towards inner: mde most tl after 3 out: wknd qckly bef next* **2/1[2]**
03-2 **P** **Holbrook Park**[18] 3388 6-11-5 0.................................... TrevorWhelan
(Neil King) *racd towards inner: wl in tch tl wknd qckly 3 out: t.o whn p.u bef next* **9/2[3]**

5P5P **P** **Contempt Of Court (IRE)**[39] 2995 7-11-5 0...................(v) DenisO'Regan
(Mark Pitman) *chsd ldr to 6th: wknd 8th: t.o whn p.u bef 3 out* **25/1**

5m 58.4s (41.40) **Going Correction** +1.725s/f (Heav) 6 Ran SP% **109.6**
Speed ratings (Par 103): **90,86,86,79,**
CSF £351.59 TOTE £13.70: £2.70, £4.30; EX 68.70 Trifecta £200.40.
Owner Mike Roberts **Bred** E R Hanbury **Trained** Bodle Street Green, E Sussex

FOCUS
Bit of a turn up here with the market leaders disappointing. The race was run over 108yds further than advertised. The second has the potential to rate a lot higher on his Flat form, while the third has been rated 10lb off his bumper mark.

3665 ANISE CATERING H'CAP HURDLE (9 hdls) 1m 7f 195y
4:10 (4:10) (Class 5) (0-100,100) 4-Y-0+ **£3,898** (£1,144; £572; £286)

Form RPR
6203 **1** **Guaracha**[17] 3417 5-11-5 **100**..................................... MikeyHamill[(7)] 106
(Alexandra Dunn) *hld up: prog 6th: chal after 3 out: led 2 out to last: kpt on wl to ld again nr fin* **11/2[3]**
P-13 **2** *½* **Torero**[23] 3219 7-10-13 **87**.....................................(p) JoshuaMoore 92
(Gary Moore) *in tch: urged along 6th: effrt 3 out: jnd ldrs next: drvn to ld last: hdd nr fin* **2/1[1]**
0P4F **3** *2 ¼* **Tuffstuff**[32] 3125 8-11-7 **95**.......................................(tp) GavinSheehan 99
(Brian Barr) *led to 3rd: styd w ldrs: urged along 6th: led 3 out to 2 out: one pce fr last* **8/1**
4-F3 **4** *18* **Willshebetrying**[48] 2829 5-11-10 **98**.................................. JamieMoore 85
(Jim Best) *hld up in rr: pushed along 6th: rapid prog downhill to press ldr next (3 out): wknd bef 2 out* **9/1**
003P **5** *9* **Dardanella**[11] 3498 9-11-1 **89**...(t) DaveCrosse 65
(Hugo Froud) *trckd ldr: led 3rd to 3 out: wknd bef 2 out* **25/1**
05P **6** *8* **Man Of God (IRE)**[33] 3108 8-10-11 **85**.......................... RichardJohnson 53
(Tim Vaughan) *nt fluent: hld up in last: lost tch 5th: wl t.o 3 out: r.o fr last* **20/1**
22P5 **7** *3 ¾* **Henry Oliver (IRE)**[31] 3140 8-11-2 **90**...........................(tp) SeanBowen 54
(John O'Shea) *wl in tch: trckd ldrs after 6th: shkn up and wknd sn after 3 out: eased flat* **16/1**
-P35 **P** **Asker (IRE)**[23] 3219 8-10-0 **74** oh2.............................(vt) NicodeBoinville
(Zoe Davison) *in tch to 4th: wknd qckly next: t.o whn p.u after 6th* **12/1**
0022 **P** **Warrant Officer**[35] 3089 6-11-3 **91**................................. MarcGoldstein
(Sheena West) *w ldrs: rdn 6th: wknd qckly 3 out: t.o whn p.u bef last* **7/2[2]**

4m 29.5s (28.70) **Going Correction** +1.85s/f (Heav) 9 Ran SP% **114.2**
Speed ratings (Par 103): **102,101,100,91,87 83,81, ,**
CSF £17.21 CT £87.08 TOTE £7.00: £1.80, £1.50, £2.60; EX 26.00 Trifecta £194.50.
Owner West Buckland Bloodstock Ltd **Bred** Michael E Broughton **Trained** West Buckland, Somerset

FOCUS
Modest handicap form, but the first three were clear. The race was run over 64yds further than usual. The first three have been rated to their marks.
T/Plt: £4,382.40 to a £1 stake. Pool: £70,118.70 - 11.68 winning units. T/Qpdt: £1,178.20 to a £1 stake. Pool: £6,846.43 - 4.30 winning units. **Jonathan Neesom**

3436 AYR (L-H)
Tuesday, January 19

OFFICIAL GOING: Heavy (soft in places on chase course; hdl 5.6; chs 5.9)
Wind: Breezy, half behind Weather: Overcast, dry

3666 COTTER'S EDGE MARES' MAIDEN HURDLE (12 hdls) 3m 70y
12:55 (12:56) (Class 5) 4-Y-0+ **£2,469** (£725; £362; £181)

Form RPR
U/63 **1** **Cinder Rua (IRE)**[24] 3260 9-10-9 103.............................. LiamMcKenna[(7)] 109+
(J J Lambe, Ire) *nt fluent: t.k.h in rr: smooth hdwy to ld appr 3 out: nt fluent next: shkn up and kpt on strly fr last* **4/1[2]**
2 **2** *4* **Conquer Gold (IRE)**[37] 3060 6-11-2 0.............................. BrianHarding 103
(Nicky Richards) *trckd ldrs: wnt 2nd 7th: disp ld bef 3 out: rdn next: 1 l down whn pckd last: kpt on same pce* **10/11[1]**
43-4 **3** *4* **Knocklayde Sno Cat (IRE)**[36] 3091 7-10-9 105..............(t) AdamShort[(7)] 100
(S R B Crawford, Ire) *hld up in tch: smooth hdwy 4 out: effrt and disp ld briefly next: drvn and outpcd between last 2* **4/1[2]**
002P **4** *24* **The Toft**[45] 2922 7-10-11 93.................................. GrantCockburn[(5)] 75
(Lucinda Russell) *led to 3rd: pressed ldr to 7th: sn pushed along: rallied: wknd bef 3 out* **12/1[3]**
3/3- **5** *2* **Waltz Legend (IRE)**[24] 3260 10-11-2 103.............................. BrianHughes 73
(Liam Lennon, Ire) *w ldr: led 3rd: rdn and hdd appr 3 out: sn wknd* **12/1[3]**

6m 43.4s (11.60) **Going Correction** +0.575s/f (Soft) 5 Ran SP% **107.8**
Speed ratings (Par 103): **103,101,100,92,91**
CSF £8.08 TOTE £4.10: £2.40, £1.10; EX 10.50 Trifecta £29.30.
Owner Bohilla Racing Partnership **Bred** John Jobson **Trained** Dungannon, Co Tyrone

FOCUS
Some starts have been moved at this track following remeasuring, so some races will not have speed figures until there is sufficient data to calculate updated median times. The bend on the home turn was shared, and the stands' bend divided. This was a very modest maiden hurdle, run at a a reasonable gallop in the testing conditions. The time was nearly a minute slower than standard. The winner has been rated in line with her recent chase form, and the third to her mark.

3667 ANNICK GARDENS "NATIONAL HUNT" MAIDEN HURDLE (DIV I) (12 hdls) 2m 4f 100y
1:25 (1:26) (Class 5) 5-Y-0+ **£2,469** (£725; £362; £181)

Form RPR
1 **Master Ruffit (IRE)**[24] 3267 8-11-0 0.............................. BrianHughes 113+
(Neil McKnight, Ire) *trckd ldrs: chal 8th: led bef 3 out: rdn and kpt on strly fr next* **16/1**
5-2 **2** *3 ¼* **Sevenballs Of Fire (IRE)**[21] 3340 7-11-0 0.......................... HenryBrooke 110+
(Iain Jardine) *in tch on outside: hdwy to press wnr 3 out: sn rdn and edgd lft: kpt on fr next: nt pce to chal* **15/8[1]**
5020 **3** *7* **Herecomesnelson (IRE)**[21] 3346 7-10-9 108............. CallumBewley[(5)] 102
(Katie Scott) *hld up: rdn and outpcd after 4 out: rallied 2 out: kpt on run-in: nt rch first two* **10/1**
60 **4** *1* **Orioninverness (IRE)**[17] 3442 5-11-0 0.......................(t) PeterBuchanan 101
(Lucinda Russell) *hld up in tch: rdn bef 3 out: sn outpcd: rallied after next: no imp fr last* **80/1**
0 **5** *7* **Benarty Hill (IRE)**[24] 3262 6-10-7 0.......................... RachaelBlackmore[(7)] 96
(Liam Lennon, Ire) *t.k.h: led to bef 3 out: rdn and hung rt after next: sn btn* **40/1**
6 *1 ½* **Infrontofthejudge (IRE)**[24] 3262 7-10-7 0.................(p) LiamMcKenna[(7)] 93
(J J Lambe, Ire) *cl up: rdn along 4 out: outpcd bef next: n.d after* **2/1[2]**

54 7 1 1/2 **Bertalus (IRE)**[55] 2716 7-11-0 0 LucyAlexander 91
(N W Alexander) *t.k.h early: w ldrs: nt fluent 2nd: rdn and wknd 3 out*
13/2[3]

8 31 **Wicked Games (IRE)**[297] 5-10-7 0 CraigNichol 53
(Rose Dobbin) *prom: rdn after 4 out: wknd bef next*
14/1

00-5 9 7 **Titian Boy (IRE)**[69] 2428 7-11-0 0 BrianHarding 53
(N W Alexander) *t.k.h: hld up: rdn and outpcd bef 3 out: sn btn: no ch whn mstke last*
250/1

0 10 18 **Farewelltocheyenne (IRE)**[251] 285 8-10-9 0 StephenMulqueen(5) 35
(N W Alexander) *nt fluent in rr: struggling 4 out: wknd bef next*
25/1

5m 39.2s (339.20) 10 Ran SP% 111.0
CSF £45.14 TOTE £13.30: £2.50, £1.20, £2.80; EX 50.70 Trifecta £439.60.
Owner Norman McKnight **Bred** Joseph Smiddy **Trained** Banbridge, Co. Down
■ The first winner in Britain for Neil McKnight.

FOCUS
This weak maiden hurdle was run at a very steady pace. As a consequence most were still in with a shout turning for home, and the form may not be entirely reliable. It was the slower division by 6.5sec. It's been rated around the first two.

3668 ANNICK GARDENS "NATIONAL HUNT" MAIDEN HURDLE (DIV II) (12 hdls) 2m 4f 100y
2:00 (2:00) (Class 5) 5-Y-0+ **£2,469** (£725; £362; £181)

Form RPR

1FF 1 **Lake View Lad (IRE)**[17] 3436 6-10-9 0 StephenMulqueen(5) 121+
(N W Alexander) *t.k.h early: cl up: led gng wl 2 out: qcknd clr on bridle run-in: readily*
2/5[1]

2 5 **Nendrum (IRE)**[18] 3429 7-11-0 0 (t) AELynch 109
(S R B Crawford, Ire) *led: rdn and hdd 2 out: rallied: no ch w ready wnr run-in*
33/1

-54P 3 10 **The Bishop (IRE)**[43] 2950 8-11-0 99 BrianHarding 100
(N W Alexander) *hld up: hdwy and prom after 4 out: rdn and flashed tail after next: keeping on same pce whn mstke last*
14/1

/4-3 4 4 **Superior Command (IRE)**[15] 3471 7-10-9 0 GrantCockburn(5) 95
(Lucinda Russell) *hld up: stdy hdwy after 4 out: effrt 2 out: sn outpcd* 9/2[2]

5 5 14 **Ash Park (IRE)**[24] 3240 8-10-7 0 SamColtherd(7) 80
(Stuart Coltherd) *in tch: effrt bef 3 out: wkng whn hung rt after next* 66/1

P-4P 6 3 **Bolton Blue (IRE)**[21] 3340 7-10-11 96 (t) AdamNicol(3) 77
(Katie Scott) *cl up tl rdn and wknd bef 3 out* 66/1

33 7 4 1/2 **Final Fling (IRE)**[46] 2895 5-11-0 0 CraigNichol 73
(Rose Dobbin) *hld up: stdy hdwy 4 out: rdn and wknd after next* 9/1[3]

0366 8 2 1/4 **Court Baloo (IRE)**[17] 3436 5-11-0 0 HenryBrooke 70
(Alistair Whillans) *prom: hit and lost pl 7th: struggling fr 4 out* 100/1

6-34 9 46 **Heilan Rebel (IRE)**[17] 3442 6-11-0 0 LucyAlexander 24
(N W Alexander) *hld up: rdr lost iron sn after s: rcvrd iron whn mstke 2nd: rdn and outpcd after 4 out: lost tch next: t.o*
9/1[3]

5m 32.7s (332.70) 9 Ran SP% 123.2
CSF £22.75 TOTE £1.40: £1.10, £5.10, £2.80; EX 27.20 Trifecta £177.80.
Owner Alistair Cochrane **Bred** Peter Magnier **Trained** Kinneston, Perth & Kinross

FOCUS
This division was 6.5sec quicker than the first. There was little depth to it. The third and fifth helps set the level.

3669 VILLAFIELD NOVICES' H'CAP CHASE (13 fncs 4 omitted) 2m 4f 110y
2:35 (2:35) (Class 4) (0-120,117) 5-Y-0+ **£4,028** (£1,182; £591; £295)

Form RPR

-341 1 **Un Noble (FR)**[37] 3061 6-11-11 116 CraigNichol 130+
(Nicky Richards) *led or disp ld tl def advantage 3 out: 2 l up whn hit last: drvn and styd on strly*
2/1[1]

36/2 2 3 1/4 **Kilbree Chief (IRE)**[21] 3345 8-11-12 117 PeterBuchanan 125
(Lucinda Russell) *hld up in tch on outside: stdy hdwy 1/2-way: drvn and outpcd after 4 out (usual 5 out): rallied to chse wnr bef 2 out: kpt on same pce run-in*
6/1[2]

36-4 3 2 **Vinny Gambini (IRE)**[21] 3343 9-10-11 105 GrahamWatters(3) 111
(Rose Dobbin) *trckd ldrs: effrt and rdn after 3 out: edgd lft after next: kpt on same pce*
7/1

0-31 4 20 **Gold Opera (IRE)**[31] 3164 7-11-8 113 LucyAlexander 99
(N W Alexander) *hld up on outside: stdy hdwy and prom 9th: drvn and outpcd 4 out (usual 5 out): struggling fr next*
13/2[3]

15P5 5 1 3/4 **Wolf Sword (IRE)**[22] 3311 7-11-6 111 RichieMcLernon 98
(George Moore) *cl up: chal 8th to 3 out: rdn and wknd bef next* 18/1

0-23 U **The Orange Rogue (IRE)**[31] 3160 9-10-11 107 StephenMulqueen(5)
(N W Alexander) *prom: hit 4th: mstke and lost pl 8th: last and drvn along whn blnd and uns rdr 10th*
8/1

4U3U P **Kilmainham (IRE)**[74] 2320 8-10-5 96 (p) HenryBrooke
(Martin Todhunter) *bhd: struggling 10th: no ch whn blnd 2 out: sn p.u*
14/1

P-33 U **Hellorboston (IRE)**[24] 3224 8-11-2 107 (p) AdrianLane
(Donald McCain) *led or disp ld to 8th: sn drvn along 5 l sixth and outpcd whn mstke and uns rdr 4 out (usual 5 out)*
6/1[2]

5m 43.7s (343.70) 8 Ran SP% 110.8
CSF £13.79 CT £64.79 TOTE £2.50: £1.20, £1.60, £2.70; EX 12.00 Trifecta £42.30.
Owner Mrs C A Torkington **Bred** Richard Godefroy **Trained** Greystoke, Cumbria

FOCUS
The middle fence in the back straight and the first fence in the home straight were omitted in all chases. After this first race over fences Craig Nichol said the ground was "less testing than the hurdle track, and more consistent." The form of this novice handicap chase has a sound look to it. The second has been rated to his mark.

3670 BURNGREEN BRAE H'CAP CHASE (10 fncs 2 omitted) 1m 7f 112y
3:05 (3:07) (Class 4) (0-115,115) 5-Y-0+ **£4,028** (£1,182; £591; £295)

Form RPR

P221 1 **Willie Hall**[17] 3441 12-9-9 89 CallumBewley(5) 101+
(Lisa Harrison) *hld up: stdy hdwy to trck ldrs after 4 out: shkn up bef 2 out: led and pricked ears bef last: qcknd clr run-in*
6/1

1362 2 6 **Quick Decisson (IRE)**[17] 3441 8-11-3 111 GrantCockburn(5) 118
(Stuart Coltherd) *led: hdd whn hit 4 out (usual 5 out): rallied: effrt and chsng wnr whn hit last: sn no ex*
9/2[3]

/5-3 3 2 3/4 **Young Palm (IRE)**[19] 3390 9-10-13 102 (t) AELynch 106
(S R B Crawford, Ire) *cl up: led bef 4 out (usual 5 out): rdn and hdd bef last: hit last: sn btn*
7/2[2]

2445 4 44 **Duhallowcountry (IRE)**[24] 3243 10-9-8 90 oh11 ow1 (p) ThomasDowson(7) 48
(Victor Thompson) *prom: hit 3rd: drvn and outpcd 6th: lost tch after next: t.o*
40/1

16/ F **Glen Gyle (IRE)**[24] 3260 9-9-12 94 RachaelBlackmore(7)
(Liam Lennon, Ire) *in tch: fell 1st* 16/1

-P04 P **Scimon Templar (FR)**[17] 3441 8-10-7 96 CraigNichol
(Rose Dobbin) *nt fluent: hld up in tch: stdy hdwy whn sprawled bdly 6th: sn p.u*
5/1

5-P3 B **Supreme Asset (IRE)**[22] 3313 8-11-12 115 BrianHarding
(Donald McCain) *hld up in tch: b.d jst after 1st* 10/3[1]

555P F **Pekanheim (IRE)**[67] 2475 8-11-2 105 HenryBrooke
(Martin Todhunter) *trckd ldrs: fell 6th* 14/1

4m 9.6s (-1.10) **Going Correction** +0.075s/f (Yiel) 8 Ran SP% 109.4
Speed ratings: **105,102,100,78, , ,**
CSF £30.74 CT £98.76 TOTE £6.50: £1.80, £1.40, £1.90; EX 24.50 Trifecta £91.10.
Owner R H Hall **Bred** G E Leech **Trained** Aldoth, Cumbria

FOCUS
An ordinary handicap chase. The fences thinned out the field, with the favourite one of two on the deck at the first. The second and third have been rated to their marks.

3671 ELLISTON PARK H'CAP CHASE (15 fncs 4 omitted) 3m 67y
3:40 (3:40) (Class 4) (0-120,120) 5-Y-0+ **£4,028** (£1,182; £591; £295)

Form RPR

0/3F 1 **Art Lord (IRE)**[15] 3472 10-10-9 106 (t) GrahamWatters(3) 121+
(Karl Thornton, Ire) *t.k.h: hld up in tch: stdy hdwy 1/2-way: led 10th: mde rest: jnd whn lft 7 l clr 3 out: drew further clr: easily*
7/1[2]

63U5 2 15 **More Madness (IRE)**[21] 3341 9-10-2 103 (v[1]) MrKitAlexander(7) 98
(N W Alexander) *cl up: led 2nd to 10th: drvn and outpcd whn lft 7 l 2nd 3 out: sn no imp*
12/1

P0-1 3 7 **Blue Kascade (IRE)**[81] 2173 9-11-3 111 BrianHughes 98
(Sandy Thomson) *nt fluent on occasions: w ldrs to 10th: nt fluent 4 out (usual 5 out): outpcd whn lft 11 l 3rd 3 out: no imp*
11/4[1]

44-5 4 1 1/2 **Oil Burner**[66] 2500 11-9-9 94 oh2 GrantCockburn(5) 81
(Stuart Coltherd) *blnd 1st: hld up: stdy hdwy and pushed along 11th: outpcd next: n.d after*
7/1[2]

5451 5 1 1/4 **My Friend George**[24] 3243 10-10-6 100 (p) HenryBrooke 83
(Kenneth Slack) *nt fluent: hld up: effrt on outside 10th: outpcd 4 out (usual 5 out): btn whn lft modest 4th 3 out*
14/1

F444 6 19 **Chanceofa Lifetime (IRE)**[21] 3341 9-10-10 111 ThomasDowson(7) 75
(Victor Thompson) *bhd: struggling 10th: btn after next* 16/1

-5U3 P **Chavoy (FR)**[21] 3341 11-11-5 120 (tp) FinianO'Toole(7)
(Rebecca Menzies) *hld up in tch: drvn and outpcd whn mstke 4 out (usual 5 out): sn btn: p.u bef next*
7/1[2]

P/26 F **Rocking Blues (FR)**[39] 3014 11-10-6 110 LorcanMurtagh(10)
(Rose Dobbin) *prom: smooth hdwy and ev ch whn fell 3 out* 16/1

2-21 P **Cobajayisland (IRE)**[75] 2295 8-11-8 116 DerekFox
(Lucinda Russell) *led to 2nd: cl up: lost pl after 8th: struggling fr 10th: lost tch and p.u bef 3 out*
8/1[3]

-242 P **Kalastar (IRE)**[74] 2320 7-9-9 94 oh1 (b[1]) CallumBewley(5)
(Katie Scott) *prom: lost pl whn hit 6th: reminders and hung lft next: struggling fnl circ: t.o whn p.u bef 3 out*
7/1[2]

6m 48.2s (-1.70) 10 Ran SP% 113.9
CSF £82.79 CT £285.38 TOTE £9.20: £2.60, £4.90, £1.10; EX 124.20 Trifecta £690.50.
Owner P McNamee & D Harvey **Bred** Paul McNamee **Trained** Skerries, Co Dublin

FOCUS
They went a reasonable gallop in this fair handicap chase. The winner has been rated to his 2013 best.

3672 DAWN HOMES ASSURED MOVE H'CAP HURDLE (9 hdls) 2m
4:15 (4:16) (Class 5) (0-100,100) 4-Y-0+ **£2,469** (£725; £362; £181)

Form RPR

6355 1 **Hatton Springs (IRE)**[70] 2427 5-10-9 90 SamColtherd(7) 95
(Stuart Coltherd) *chsd clr ldr: clsd 1/2-way: led bef 3 out: drvn and drifted rt run-in: hld on wl cl home*
16/1

P463 2 hd **Landmeafortune (IRE)**[56] 2706 7-11-2 90 HenryBrooke 95
(Martin Todhunter) *hld up: hdwy to chse clr ldng pair bef 3 out: wnt 2nd last: carried rt and kpt on wl run-in: jst hld*
10/1

300- 3 9 **Galleons Way**[373] 3635 7-11-9 100 AdamNicol(3) 96
(Katie Scott) *led and clr to 1/2-way: hdd bef 3 out: rallied and ev ch next: drvn and outpcd fr last*
20/1

-004 4 1 1/4 **Kashstaree**[11] 3505 5-10-11 90 CallumBewley(5) 85
(Lisa Harrison) *hld up: drvn and outpcd after 4 out: pluged on fr 2 out: nvr able to chal*
18/1

0522 5 6 **Discoverie**[18] 3398 8-10-7 84 (p) HarryChalloner(3) 73
(Kenneth Slack) *prom: drvn and outpcd bef 4 out: no imp fr next* 1/1[1]

FP30 6 1 1/2 **Redpender (IRE)**[40] 2982 10-11-6 94 BrianHughes 81
(James Moffatt) *hld up in midfield: stdy hdwy and prom 1/2-way: rdn and outpcd 3 out: btn next*
15/2[2]

P/0P 7 shd **Academy (IRE)**[75] 2292 8-10-1 75 LucyAlexander 62
(N W Alexander) *hld up: mstke 1st: pushed along and shortlived effrt bef 3 out: edgd lft and sn btn*
12/1

0-4P 8 1/2 **Higgs Boson**[18] 3427 11-10-7 86 (p) DiarmuidO'Regan(5) 73
(Jim Goldie) *prom: drvn and outpcd after 4 out: struggling fr next* 16/1

500 9 3 **Suzy's Music (IRE)**[59] 8-11-4 92 AELynch 75
(S R B Crawford, Ire) *hld up: mstke 4th: struggling after 4 out: nvr on terms*
17/2[3]

5P00 10 3 3/4 **Question Of Faith**[24] 3239 5-11-2 90 BrianHarding 70
(Martin Todhunter) *hld up: hit 1st: rdn and struggling 4 out: btn next* 50/1

4m 16.9s (256.90) 10 Ran SP% 112.8
CSF £158.73 CT £3180.48 TOTE £26.00: £4.60, £1.90, £3.50; EX 141.60 Trifecta £683.00.
Owner Binnie Dunbar Murray Sheil **Bred** L Queally **Trained** Selkirk, Borders
■ Stewards' Enquiry : Sam Coltherd one-day ban: careless riding (Feb 3); seven-day ban: used whip above permitted level (Feb 4,6,7,9,10,12,15)

FOCUS
A very moderate handicap hurdle. The winner and third have been rated to their marks.
T/Jkpt: Not won. JACKPOT PLACEPOT £2,157.30 - 0.15 winning units. T/Plt: £17.20 to a £1 stake. Pool: £69,949.04 - 2951.96 winning units. T/Qpdt: £9.20 to a £1 stake. Pool: £8,144.15 - 649.00 winning units. **Richard Young**

3410 EXETER (R-H)
Tuesday, January 19
3673 Meeting Abandoned - Waterlogged

3470 MUSSELBURGH (R-H)

Wednesday, January 20

OFFICIAL GOING: Soft

Wind: Almost nil Weather: Overcast, dry

3679 ROA/RACING POST OWNERS JACKPOT CONDITIONAL JOCKEYS' H'CAP CHASE (15 fncs 3 omitted) 2m 7f 170y

1:10 (1:10) (Class 5) (0-100,91) 5-Y-0+ £3,249 (£954; £477; £238)

Form RPR

540U 1 **Solway Bay**[16] 3472 14-11-2 **84**....(t) CallumBewley(3) 96
(Lisa Harrison) *chsd ldrs: rdn and outpcd bef 3 out: rallied next: drifted lft run-in: led last 50yds: styd on strly* **25/1**

-2F1 2 2 1/4 **Runswick Relax**[23] 3308 10-10-6 **76**....(tp) ThomasDowson(5) 88
(Kenneth Slack) *cl up: wnt 2nd 7th: ev ch bef 3 out: blnd next: sn led: hdd last 50yds: kpt on same pce* **11/4**[1]

0/ 3 3 1/4 **Itsnoteasyted (IRE)**[41] 3001 9-11-12 **91**.... GrahamWatters 100
(C A McBratney, Ire) *hld up in tch: hdwy and cl up after 4 out: effrt whn bmpd next: sn rdn: rallied and chsd ldr last: no ex last 75yds* **10/1**

P054 4 3/4 **Under The Red Sky (IRE)**[19] 3399 9-10-8 **73**....(p) HarryBannister 79
(Kenny Johnson) *hld up: stdy hdwy after 4 out: rdn next: kpt on fr 2 out: no imp* **8/1**

-253 5 3 **Trouble In Paris (IRE)**[23] 3308 9-9-13 **69**....(bt) LorcanMurtagh(5) 75
(Barry Murtagh) *hld up in midfield: mstke 9th: rallied and cl up whn n.m.r bnd after 4 out: rdn and cl 3rd whn j.rt next: edgd rt and outpcd next* **12/1**

P652 6 6 **Top Cat Dj (IRE)**[19] 3427 8-10-8 **76**....(v) DiarmuidO'Regan(3) 73
(Chris Grant) *led: j. slowly 2nd: rdn and hdd 2 out: cl 3rd but outpcd whn mstke last: sn wknd* **15/2**[3]

0-0F 7 1 1/4 **Proud Gamble (IRE)**[19] 3427 7-11-5 **84**....(t) CraigNichol 80
(Rose Dobbin) *hld up: hit 2nd: pushed along bef 4 out: nvr able to chal* **25/1**

-5U1 8 8 **Wakhan (IRE)**[19] 3427 8-11-12 **91**.... DerekFox 80
(Sandy Thomson) *chsd ldr: hit 6th: lost 2nd next struggling fr 4 out: btn bef next* **7/2**[2]

P0/P 9 5 **Tears From Heaven (USA)**[16] 3472 10-10-9 **79**....(p) FinianO'Toole(5) 62
(Chris Grant) *hld up in midfield: pushed along after 4 out: wknd bef next* **40/1**

10-1 10 15 **Flaming Thistle (IRE)**[256] 204 12-11-3 **82**.... GrantCockburn 50
(John Hodge) *chsd ldrs: lost pl after 5th: struggling fnl circ: t.o* **18/1**

4253 P **Benefit In Kind (IRE)**[16] 3472 8-11-9 **88**....(tp) JamieHamilton
(Katie Scott) *bhd: pushed along fr 5th: struggling fnl circ: lost tch and p.u bef 3 out* **8/1**

6m 28.6s (25.20) **Going Correction** +0.975s/f (Soft) **11 Ran SP% 115.1**
Speed ratings: **97,96,95,94,93 91,91,88,87,82**
CSF £93.26 CT £759.54 TOTE £26.40: £5.60, £1.50, £3.90; EX 133.30 Trifecta £702.70.
Owner Exors of the Late David Alan Harrison **Bred** D A Harrison **Trained** Aldoth, Cumbria
■ Stewards' Enquiry : Thomas Dowson one-day ban: careless riding (Feb 3)

FOCUS
Chase out 4yds from inner, adding 35yds to the distance of this race. Callum Bewley said of the ground: "It's soft but I'd also say it's a bit dead." Low-grade handicap form with a surprise winner, who was on a good mark.

3680 M-PACT BUILDING SERVICES H'CAP HURDLE (12 hdls) 2m 3f 81y

1:45 (1:45) (Class 4) (0-105,105) 4-Y-0+ £3,249 (£954; £477; £238)

Form RPR

3-14 1 **Almost Gemini (IRE)**[22] 3344 7-11-4 **97**....(p) HenryBrooke 104+
(Kenneth Slack) *prom: rdn and outpcd bef 3 out: rallied to ld between last 2: edgd lft run-in: rdn out* **9/4**[1]

033P 2 1 1/4 **Snowed In (IRE)**[25] 3244 7-10-13 **92**....(p) SeanQuinlan 96
(Barry Murtagh) *hld up in midfield: shkn up and outpcd bef 3 out: rallied next: chsd wnr run-in: kpt on* **20/1**

PP65 3 3 3/4 **Definitely Better (IRE)**[52] 2812 8-10-4 **88**.... JamieBargary(5) 90
(Tom George) *hld up: hdwy and cl up 4 out: led next: sn hung rt: hdd between last 2: no ex and lost 2nd run-in* **5/1**[2]

4015 4 3 1/2 **Nafaath (IRE)**[35] 3108 10-11-5 **105**....(p) MrTGillard(7) 103
(Donald McCain) *cl up: rdn and ev ch whn mstke 3 out: kpt on same pce between last 2* **14/1**

02/0 5 1 1/2 **Roycano**[50] 2840 6-11-9 **105**.... HarryBannister(3) 102
(Michael Easterby) *t.k.h in midfield: smooth hdwy to ld 4 out: rdn and hdd next: one pce fr 2 out: hld whn nt fluent last* **7/1**[3]

5400 6 17 **Solway Prince**[19] 3428 7-11-5 **103**.... CallumBewley(5) 81
(Lisa Harrison) *hld up: drvn and outpcd after 4 out: no imp fr next* **8/1**

P050 7 1/2 **Rioja Day (IRE)**[16] 3473 6-10-11 **90**.... DannyCook 68
(Jim Goldie) *led: rdn along and hdd 4 out: wknd bef next* **14/1**

-650 8 hd **Sky Full Of Stars (IRE)**[16] 3471 6-11-5 **98**.... LucyAlexander 75
(James Ewart) *cl up: rdn and outpcd after 4 out: wknd bef next* **16/1**

160 9 3 1/2 **Roc De Prince**[44] 2948 7-11-0 **98**....(tp) DiarmuidO'Regan(5) 72
(James Ewart) *bhd: drvn and struggling 1/2-way: nvr on terms* **25/1**

34U 10 7 **May's Boy**[144] 1404 8-11-12 **105**....(p) BrianHughes 72
(James Moffatt) *hld up: rdn after 4 out: wknd bef next* **25/1**

4-20 11 4 1/2 **Towerburn (IRE)**[88] 2066 7-11-5 **103**.... JamieHamilton(5) 65
(Alison Hamilton) *midfield: lost pl 1/2-way: struggling bef 4 out: sn btn* **8/1**

5P4- 12 3 **Dr Beaujolais (IRE)**[343] 4165 10-11-2 **98**.... HarryChalloner(3) 57
(Richard Ford) *t.k.h early: cl up tl rdn and wknd bef 3 out* **33/1**

0 13 hd **Shalamzar (FR)**[19] 3398 7-11-4 **104**.... FinianO'Toole(7) 63
(Micky Hammond) *bhd: drvn and struggling fnl circ: nvr on terms* **50/1**

4m 56.7s (5.20) **Going Correction** +0.10s/f (Yiel) **13 Ran SP% 118.7**
Speed ratings (Par 105): **93,92,90,89,88 81,81,81,79,76 75,73,73**
CSF £53.29 CT £212.44 TOTE £3.20: £1.50, £3.80, £2.10; EX 30.00 Trifecta £159.10.
Owner E G Tunstall **Bred** Rockhart Trading Ltd **Trained** Hilton, Cumbria

FOCUS
A moderate but competitive handicap. There may still be more to come from the winner.

3681 M-PACT DEVELOPMENTS COSMIC CASE MARES' ONLY NOVICES' HURDLE (9 hdls) 1m 7f 124y

2:20 (2:20) (Class 4) 4-Y-0+ £3,249 (£954; £477; £238)

Form RPR

2-36 1 **Storming Strumpet**[76] 2302 6-10-9 115.... JamieBargary(5) 96+
(Tom George) *t.k.h early: cl up: nt fluent 4th: effrt and ev ch bef 3 out: hung rt next: led last: rdn out* **11/8**[1]

P 2 1 **Milan Lady (IRE)**[45] 2936 5-11-0 0....(t) BrianHughes 94
(Chris Grant) *cl up: ev ch after 4 out: rdn next: hung lft and chsd wnr last: kpt on: hld nr fin* **33/1**

26-4 3 3 1/4 **Definitely Glad (IRE)**[16] 3471 9-10-7 98....(t[1]) JamesCorbett(7) 92
(Susan Corbett) *cl up: led after 4 out: hrd pressed fr next: rdn and hdd last: kpt on same pce* **10/1**

24 4 2 **Mo Chailin (IRE)**[16] 3469 5-11-0 0.... HenryBrooke 89
(Donald McCain) *nt fluent on occasions: prom: effrt and rdn bef 2 out: kpt on same pce fr last* **17/2**

2110 5 1 1/4 **Stoneham**[39] 3034 5-11-2 114.... RyanDay(5) 95
(Iain Jardine) *in tch: drvn and outpcd bef 3 out: rallied after next: kpt on fr last: no imp* **7/2**[2]

0 6 1 **Sweet Holly**[54] 2756 5-10-9 0.... GrantCockburn(5) 87
(Lucinda Russell) *hld up in tch on outside: rdn and outpcd bef 3 out: plugged on fr last: nvr able to chal* **33/1**

-046 7 9 **Norfolk Sound**[22] 3342 5-10-7 0.... SamColtherd(7) 78
(Stuart Coltherd) *hld up: shkn up and sme hdwy 3 out: no imp fr next* **100/1**

-060 8 3/4 **Miss Mackie (IRE)**[16] 3470 5-10-9 0.... CallumBewley(5) 78
(R Mike Smith) *hld up towards rr: pushed along after 4 out: no imp fr next* **200/1**

30-5 9 5 **Theatre Act**[250] 316 5-10-9 0.... DiarmuidO'Regan(5) 72
(Chris Grant) *hld up towards rr: rdn whn nt fluent 3 out: sn btn* **40/1**

6- 10 6 **Miss Blanche**[271] 5520 5-11-0 0.... DerekFox 66
(Lucinda Russell) *t.k.h: led to after 4 out: outpcd whn nt fluent next: sn btn* **14/1**

11 shd **Regal Ways (IRE)**[95] 4-10-3 0.... DannyCook 61
(Brian Ellison) *t.k.h: prom: smooth hdwy bef 3 out: rdn and wknd next* **5/1**[3]

46- 12 35 **Beau Marsh**[556] 936 7-11-0 0.... SeanQuinlan 31
(Barry Murtagh) *nt fluent in rr: outpcd whn mstke 3 out: struggling fr next: t.o* **100/1**

3m 56.2s (7.80) **Going Correction** +0.10s/f (Yiel)
WFA 4 from 5yo+ 11lb **12 Ran SP% 118.1**
Speed ratings (Par 105): **84,83,81,80,80 79,75,74,72,69 69,51**
CSF £57.01 TOTE £2.20: £1.10, £4.80, £3.20; EX 42.00 Trifecta £275.90.
Owner PJL Racing **Bred** Janet Greenway **Trained** Slad, Gloucs

FOCUS
A modest mares' hurdle that provided the favourite with an excellent opportunity to finally get off the mark. It's been rated through the third, with the winner a stone plus off her best.

3682 LOGANBET BRECHIN BIG LAYERS ON FOOTBALL BETS H'CAP HURDLE (9 hdls) 1m 7f 124y

2:55 (2:55) (Class 3) (0-140,134) 4-Y-0+ £7,797 (£2,289; £1,144; £572)

Form RPR

2611 1 **Holly Bush Henry (IRE)**[39] 3035 5-11-12 **134**....(t) KielanWoods 139
(Graeme McPherson) *prom: drvn along bef 3 out: rallied and chsd ldr next: led run-in: drvn and hld on wl* **5/2**[1]

-502 2 nk **Teo Vivo (FR)**[19] 3424 9-11-0 **122**....(b) BrianHughes 127
(Pauline Robson) *trckd ldrs: smooth hdwy to ld bef 3 out: rdn after next: hdd run-in: kpt on: hld nr fin* **8/1**

50-1 3 1/2 **Shrewd**[16] 3473 6-10-7 **120**.... RyanDay(5) 126+
(Iain Jardine) *hld up on ins: hdwy bef 3 out: effrt whn nt fluent next: rallied and pressed ldrs last: edgd rt and kpt on run-in* **11/4**[2]

-F23 4 7 **Zaidiyn (FR)**[19] 3426 6-11-12 **134**.... DannyCook 133
(Brian Ellison) *hld up: hdwy to chse ldrs 4 out: effrt and ev ch next: drvn and outpcd fr 2 out* **9/2**[3]

0454 5 4 **Silver Duke (IRE)**[19] 3426 5-10-9 **117**.... JamesReveley 111
(Jim Goldie) *hld up: effrt whn n.m.r briefly and stmbld appr 3 out: nt fluent and rdn 3 out: no imp fr next* **16/1**

60-0 6 1 **Frederic**[19] 3426 5-10-7 **115**.... BrianHarding 108
(Micky Hammond) *cl up: effrt and drvn along 3 out: outpcd fr next* **18/1**

2402 7 14 **Domtaline (FR)**[25] 3238 9-10-7 **122**.... MrRWinks(7) 101
(Peter Winks) *trckd ldrs: nt fluent 3rd: effrt and rdn bef 3 out: sn wknd* **14/1**

2426 8 nse **Claude Carter**[19] 3424 12-9-12 **109**....(p) CallumWhillans(3) 90
(Alistair Whillans) *led: mstke 4 out: rdn and hdd bef next: sn wknd* **40/1**

-156 9 5 **Jet Master (IRE)**[60] 2639 10-11-3 **125**.... LucyAlexander 98
(N W Alexander) *pressed ldr tl rdn and wknd bef 3 out* **18/1**

3m 46.3s (-2.10) **Going Correction** +0.10s/f (Yiel) **9 Ran SP% 110.0**
Speed ratings (Par 107): **109,108,108,105,103 102,95,95,93**
CSF £21.17 CT £53.04 TOTE £3.00: £1.40, £2.00, £1.40; EX 20.90 Trifecta £74.90.
Owner Lady Bamford & Alice Bamford **Bred** John Connolly **Trained** Upper Oddington, Gloucs

FOCUS
The front three came clear in what was an ordinary hurdle. The winner is still on the upgrade, but this was a stone plus off what would be required at the Festival. The second has been rated to his best.

3683 MACKIEMOTORS.COM NUMBER ONE RENAULT, DACIA, NISSAN DEALER H'CAP CHASE (14 fncs 2 omitted) 2m 3f 193y

3:30 (3:30) (Class 4) (0-105,97) 5-Y-0+ £3,249 (£954; £477; £238)

Form RPR

PP25 1 **Harleys Max**[12] 3503 7-9-11 **75**.... JamesCorbett(7) 88+
(Susan Corbett) *hld up: hmpd 1st: hdwy to chse ldrs whn lft 2 l 2nd 4 out: effrt next: edgd rt and 1 l down whn mstke last: led run-in: styd on wl* **15/2**

-P64 2 2 1/4 **Asuncion (FR)**[38] 3059 6-10-3 **74**....(p) BrianHughes 86
(Rebecca Menzies) *pressed wnr and clr of rest: lft 2 l in front 4 out: rdn and 1 l up whn mstke last: hdd run-in: kpt on same pce* **6/1**

P434 3 23 **Reverse The Charge (IRE)**[81] 2191 9-10-0 **71** oh2.... PeterBuchanan 58
(Jane Walton) *hld up in tch: shkn up whn lft 5 l 3rd 4 out: struggling fr next* **12/1**

4562 4 1 1/2 **Rosquero (FR)**[23] 3308 11-10-1 **79**....(b) ThomasDowson(7) 64
(Kenny Johnson) *chsd clr ldng pair: drvn and outpcd bef 10th: lft modest 4th next: btn whn mstke 3 out* **9/2**[3]

-P33 U **On The Case**[25] 3241 8-10-12 **88**....(t) JamieBargary(5)
(Tom George) *in tch: nt fluent and uns rdr 1st* **4/1**[2]

64FP F **Parlour Of Dreams (IRE)**[44] 2947 9-11-5 **97**.... SamColtherd(7)
(Andrew Hamilton) *hld up: fell 9th: fatally injured* **66/1**

U536 F **Court Of Law (IRE)**[33] 3140 8-11-11 **96**....(p) HenryBrooke
(Donald McCain) *trckd ldrs: fell 1st* **11/2**

44-P F **Home For Tea**[208] 841 7-10-7 **78**....(p) CraigNichol
(Keith Dalgleish) *j. sltly lft on occasions: led 1 l in front and gng wl whn fell 4 out* **3/1**[1]

5m 19.3s (18.10) **Going Correction** +0.975s/f (Soft) **8 Ran SP% 113.8**
Speed ratings: **102,101,91,91, , ,**
CSF £50.98 CT £533.64 TOTE £8.00: £2.10, £2.10, £3.00; EX 45.40 Trifecta £366.50.
Owner Girsonfield Racing Club **Bred** Girsonfield Stud **Trained** Otterburn, Northumberland

FOCUS
Race run over 35yds further than advertised. Half of the eight runners failed to complete, including three of the first four in the betting, and therefore the form of this lowly handicap chase is worth little. The winner has been rated to his hurdle mark, and the runner-up recording a chase pb.

3684 MACBETSPORTS.CO.UK H'CAP HURDLE (14 hdls) 2m 7f 180y
4:05 (4:06) (Class 4) (0-105,105) 4-Y-O+ **£3,249** (£954; £477; £238)

Form RPR

P566 **1** **Arctic Court (IRE)**[19] 3428 12-11-12 **105**.......................... JamesReveley 108
(Jim Goldie) *hld up: stdy hdwy to chse ldng trio 9th: effrt and wnt 2nd 2 out: swtchd rt appr last: kpt on wl u.p to ld towards fin* **7/1**[3]

0350 **2** *1/2* **Tickanrun (IRE)**[12] 3503 6-10-11 **90**..........................(p) BrianHughes 93
(Chris Grant) *trckd ldng pair and clr of rest: hdwy to ld after 3 out: rdn and wandered fr next: kpt on u.p run-in: hdd and no ex towards fin* **12/1**

-012 **3** *8* **Omid**[97] 1925 8-11-9 **105**..........................(tp) JohnKington(3) 101
(Kenneth Slack) *mde most tl hdd after 3 out: drvn and outpcd by first two fr next* **6/1**[2]

3001 **4** *14* **Simarthur**[16] 3474 9-11-12 **105**..........................(v) PeterBuchanan 89
(Lucinda Russell) *w ldr: drvn and ev ch 3 out: wknd after next* **5/1**[1]

P506 **5** *1 3/4* **Toarmandowithlove (IRE)**[23] 3307 8-10-3 **89**..........(t) JamesCorbett(7) 68
(Susan Corbett) *hld up: rdn and struggling fr 8th: plugged on fr 3 out: nvr on terms* **50/1**

6F44 **6** *2* **Dutch Canyon (IRE)**[56] 2720 6-10-13 **92**..................(v[1]) LucyAlexander 69
(N W Alexander) *chsd clr ldng trio to 9th: drvn and outpcd next: n.d after* **17/2**

F3-2 **7** *3/4* **Ganbei**[38] 3064 10-11-1 **97**.......................... HarryBannister(3) 73
(Michael Easterby) *hld up on outside: stdy hdwy 4 out: hung lft and rn wd bnd bef next: sn wknd* **5/1**[1]

431P **8** *7* **Itstimeforapint (IRE)**[16] 3472 8-11-11 **104**..........................(t) DerekFox 73
(Lucinda Russell) *midfield: drvn and outpcd 1/2-way: shortlived effrt after 4 out: btn next* **8/1**

1-54 **9** *4 1/2* **High Fair**[203] 869 10-10-11 **97**.......................... MrTHamilton(7) 62
(Sandy Forster) *hld up: pushed along 8th: hdwy bef 3 out: rdn and wknd bef next* **25/1**

3233 **10** *1 1/2* **Solway Sam**[16] 3474 13-11-0 **98**.......................... CallumBewley(5) 61
(Lisa Harrison) *hld up: drvn and outpcd bef 8th: nvr on terms* **17/2**

0030 **11** *14* **Mister Don (IRE)**[38] 3067 6-11-4 **100**..........................(t) GrahamWatters(3) 49
(Rose Dobbin) *hld up in midfield: drvn and outpcd after 4 out: wknd bef next* **16/1**

0/5P **P** **Forty Something (IRE)**[22] 3340 11-10-2 **88**.......................... SamColtherd(7)
(Stuart Coltherd) *midfield: hit 5th: struggling fr next: lost tch and p.u 8th* **80/1**

3P3P **P** **Solway Legend**[25] 3235 9-11-3 **96**.......................... BrianHarding
(Lisa Harrison) *hld up: struggling fr 8th: t.o whn p.u bef 3 out* **20/1**

6m 2.2s (20.10) **Going Correction** +0.10s/f (Yiel) **13** Ran SP% **117.7**
Speed ratings (Par 105): **70,69,67,62,61 61,61,58,57,56 52, ,**
CSF £82.77 CT £537.79 TOTE £7.60: £2.80, £4.10, £2.30; EX 86.80 Trifecta £921.80.
Owner Mr & Mrs Raymond Anderson Green **Bred** Paul Doyle **Trained** Uplawmoor, E Renfrews
■ Stewards' Enquiry : Brian Hughes two-day ban: used whip above permitted level (Feb 3-4)

FOCUS
Moderate hurdle form, the front pair clear. The winner has been rated in line with the best of this season's form.
T/Plt: £407.60 to a £1 stake. Pool: £63058.83 - 112.91 winning tickets T/Qpdt: £62.70 to a £1 stake. Pool: £7746.73 - 91.3 winning tickets **Richard Young**

3347 NEWBURY (L-H)
Wednesday, January 20
3685 Meeting Abandoned - Frost

3691 - 3697a (Foreign Racing) - See Raceform Interactive

3568 LUDLOW (R-H)
Thursday, January 21
3698 Meeting Abandoned -

3252 WINCANTON (R-H)
Thursday, January 21
OFFICIAL GOING: Soft (heavy in places; chs: 5.9, hdl: 5.7)
Wind: mild breeze against Weather: overcast with occasional showers

3705 HIGOS INSURANCE SERVICES SOMERTON H'CAP HURDLE (10 hdls 1 omitted) 2m 5f 82y
1:35 (1:37) (Class 3) (0-125,123) 4-Y-O+ **£5,523** (£1,621; £810; £405)

Form RPR

3605 **1** **Pilgrims Bay (IRE)**[20] 3411 6-10-13 **110**.......................... ConorO'Farrell 121+
(David Pipe) *hld up towards rr: smooth hdwy fr after 6th: led between last 2: looked wl in command after last but idling u.str.p towards fin: jst hld on* **16/1**

P-33 **2** *hd* **Zephyros Bleu (IRE)**[35] 3126 6-10-10 **107**.......................... GavinSheehan 116
(Harry Whittington) *towards rr: hdwy fr after 6th: rdn to chse ldrs after 3 out: chsng wnr whn nt fluent last: kpt on wl towards fin: jst failed* **13/2**[2]

30-0 **3** *4* **Albert D'Olivate (FR)**[70] 2456 6-10-8 **105**..........................(p) SeanBowen 109
(Robert Walford) *mid-div: stdy prog after 3 out: nt fluent next: styd on strly fr last: nt quite rch fr pair* **11/1**

/3-P **4** *2 1/4* **Light Well (IRE)**[31] 3196 8-11-2 **113**.......................... JamieMoore 116
(Gary Moore) *mid-div: hdwy after 7th: rdn to chse ldrs between last 2: styd on same pce* **14/1**

0410 **5** *1/2* **Kap Jazz (FR)**[33] 3146 6-11-1 **112**.......................... AidanColeman 114
(Venetia Williams) *mid-div: reminders after 3rd: drvn along fr 6th where chsng ldrs: led after 3 out tl between last 2: no ex fr last* **8/1**[3]

0-22 **6** *3/4* **Present Man (IRE)**[63] 2603 6-11-5 **116**..........(t) SamTwiston-Davies 117+
(Paul Nicholls) *mid-div: hdwy 6th: trckd ldr 3 out: effrt bef next: sn one pce* **2/1**[1]

2PP- **7** *2* **Rendl Beach (IRE)**[301] 4993 9-11-12 **123**..........................(t) TomO'Brien 122
(Robert Stephens) *trckd ldr: rdn after 6th: one pce fr 2 out* **33/1**

P-35 **8** *3/4* **Its A Long Road**[44] 2962 8-10-8 **105**..........................(p) NickScholfield 105
(Tim Dennis) *bhd: struggling after 5th: stdy prog after 3 out: styng on but no threat whn stmbld bdly last* **12/1**

P-P0 **9** *8* **Ambion Wood (IRE)**[26] 3254 10-11-7 **118**..........................(p) IanPopham 108
(Victor Dartnall) *mid-div: struggling after 5th: nvr threatened: wknd between last 2* **20/1**

P-15 **10** *13* **Mountain Of Mourne (IRE)**[47] 2904 7-10-13 **117**.......... ConorSmith(7) 94
(Linda Blackford) *in tch: rdn after 7th: wknd after 3 out* **16/1**

6P05 **11** *5* **Motts Cross (IRE)**[35] 3124 5-10-4 **101**.......................... JamesDavies 73
(Chris Down) *mid-div: rdn after 5th: towards rr next: nvr bk on terms* **33/1**

5-P0 **12** *4 1/2* **Brook (FR)**[42] 2989 5-11-4 **120**..........................(t) DavidNoonan(5) 87
(David Pipe) *mid-div tl rdn after 3 out: sn wknd* **50/1**

0522 **13** *3/4* **Benbecula**[35] 3120 7-11-4 **118**..........................(b) TomBellamy(3) 85
(Richard Mitchell) *led tl after 3 out: sn wknd: eased whn btn* **12/1**

/10U **P** **Ashbrittle**[60] 2669 9-11-10 **121**..........................(tp) TrevorWhelan
(Neil King) *trckd ldr tl rdn after 6th: wknd after 3 out: t.o whn p.u bef next* **20/1**

-P4F **P** **Letemgo (IRE)**[26] 3253 8-11-8 **119**.......................... TomCannon
(Giles Smyly) *trckd ldrs tl wknd after 7th: t.o whn p.u bef 2 out* **16/1**

60-F **P** **Geton Xmoor (IRE)**[22] 3371 9-11-7 **118**.......................... DarylJacob
(Richard Woollacott) *mid-div tl wknd after 3 out: p.u bef next* **66/1**

5m 41.2s (14.70) **Going Correction** +0.90s/f (Soft) **16** Ran SP% **124.7**
Speed ratings (Par 107): **108,107,106,105,105 105,104,104,100,96 94,92,92, ,**
CSF £112.67 CT £1225.77 TOTE £21.20: £3.70, £2.00, £3.10, £3.20; EX 155.60 Trifecta £589.40.
Owner Clifford, Gosden & House **Bred** Michael Kirwan **Trained** Nicholashayne, Devon

FOCUS
The hurdle on the stables bend was omitted, and the race distance for the opener was approximately 30yds further than advertised. Plenty of runners started this competitive handicap, but the betting clearly settled on just one runner. However, he failed to come up to market expectations. Big steps up from the first two, with the third, fourth and fifth helping to set the level.

3706 HIGOS INSURANCE SERVICES PLATINUM H'CAP CHASE (17 fncs) 2m 4f 35y
2:10 (2:10) (Class 3) (0-130,128) 5-Y£7,912 (£2,337; £1,168; £585; £292)

Form RPR

P331 **1** **Quite By Chance**[26] 3257 7-11-0 **123**.......................... PaulO'Brien(7) 138+
(Colin Tizzard) *trckd ldrs: lft in ld 12th: rdn whn strly pressed fr 3 out: edgd lft bef last: kpt on wl to assert run-in* **8/1**

-052 **2** *1 3/4* **Wuff (IRE)**[36] 3113 8-11-11 **127**..........................(tp) SamTwiston-Davies 139+
(Paul Nicholls) *trckd ldrs: rdn to chal 3 out: ev ch last where nt fluent: no ex fnl 120yds* **9/4**[1]

P-40 **3** *19* **Ballinvarrig (IRE)**[25] 3282 9-11-6 **122**..........................(p) PaddyBrennan 116
(Tom George) *chsd ldrs: wnt cl 3rd after 13th: rdn appr 3 out: hld bef 2 out: wknd bef last* **7/1**[3]

P-5P **4** *1 1/2* **Renard (FR)**[19] 3448 11-11-11 **127**.......................... AidanColeman 117
(Venetia Williams) *led tl 10th: prom tl rdn appr 4 out: outpcd bef 3 out: styd on again fr 2 out but no ch* **7/1**[3]

-344 **5** *3/4* **Umberto D'Olivate (FR)**[26] 3253 8-11-6 **122**..........................(p) TomCannon 114
(Robert Walford) *chsd ldrs: rdn after 11th: outpcd bef 3 out: styd on again but no ch fr 2 out* **10/1**

-410 **6** *5* **Toowoomba (IRE)**[19] 3445 8-11-0 **116**..........................(t) TomO'Brien 105
(Philip Hobbs) *hld up in tch: hdwy 13th: rdn after 4 out: hld in 4th whn blnd bdly 2 out: wknd* **8/1**

-2F6 **7** *35* **Wadswick Court (IRE)**[36] 3106 8-11-7 **128**..........(p) CharlieDeutsch(5) 77
(Neil Mulholland) *hld up in tch: j.ft at times: hit 2nd and 10th: wknd after 4 out: t.o* **25/1**

3333 **B** **Gores Island (IRE)**[33] 3148 10-11-8 **124**.......................... JoshuaMoore
(Gary Moore) *hld up bhd: making stdy prog whn b.d 12th* **6/1**[2]

-311 **F** **Alder Mairi (IRE)**[40] 3044 9-11-6 **122**.......................... AndrewThornton
(Seamus Mullins) *trckd ldrs: nt fluent 1st: led 10th tl fell 12th* **10/1**

5m 27.3s (9.80) **Going Correction** +0.70s/f (Soft) **9** Ran SP% **114.3**
Speed ratings: **108,107,99,99,98 96,82, ,**
CSF £27.23 CT £133.80 TOTE £8.20: £3.00, £1.30, £2.10; EX 36.30 Trifecta £205.70.
Owner T Hamlin,J M Dare,J W Snook,J T Warner **Bred** Mrs S M Newell **Trained** Milborne Port, Dorset

FOCUS
This race distance was approximately 25yds further than advertised. Quite a decent handicap chase, with a few of the runners seemingly on fair marks if performing to their best. Personal bests from the winner and runner-up.

3707 HIGOS INSURANCE SERVICES SOMERSET NATIONAL H'CAP CHASE (22 fncs) 3m 2f 162y
2:45 (2:45) (Class 3) (0-130,130) 5-Y£12,558 (£3,742; £1,894; £970; £508)

Form RPR

-124 **1** **Golden Chieftain (IRE)**[19] 3448 11-11-10 **128**..........(bt) BrendanPowell 138+
(Colin Tizzard) *led 2nd: rdn and narrowly hdd briefly 3 out: sn bk in command: styd on wl* **14/1**

2-3U **2** *2 3/4* **Dawson City**[47] 2905 7-11-7 **125**.......................... AndrewThornton 135+
(Polly Gundry) *led tl 2nd: chsd ldrs: pushed along fr 15th: rdn to ld whn mstke 3 out and stmbld bdly: hld after: hit 2 out: nt fluent last: styd on* **7/2**[1]

31-0 **3** *2 3/4* **Krackatoa King**[71] 2442 8-11-0 **121**..........................(b[1]) JamesBanks(3) 125+
(Noel Williams) *pressed wnr: nt fluent 7th: mstke 13th: rdn along fr 16th: lost 3nd after 4 out: styd on but hld fr next* **8/1**[3]

U-F1 **4** *17* **Rocky Bender (IRE)**[20] 3412 11-10-10 **117**.......... CallumWhillans(3) 109
(Venetia Williams) *mid-div: pushed along but no imp whn v awkward 17th: wnt wl hld 4th bef 2 out: nvr threatened ldrs* **20/1**

-25P **5** *24* **Royal Palladium (FR)**[38] 3079 8-11-9 **127**.......................... AidanColeman 87
(Venetia Williams) *trckd ldrs tl rdn after 16th: wknd after 18th: t.o* **9/1**

35-4 **P** **Upham Atom**[49] 2872 13-10-11 **115**.......................... LiamTreadwell
(Kate Buckett) *trckd ldrs early: towards rr 11th: t.o whn p.u bef 15th* **22/1**

-P34 **P** **Monkerty Tunkerty**[51] 2838 13-11-7 **130**.......................... AliceMills(5)
(Jess Westwood) *a bhd: t.o whn p.u after 4 out* **14/1**

1-P0 **P** **Leo Luna**[47] 2916 7-11-12 **130**..........................(vt) JamieMoore
(Gary Moore) *pressed wnr tl 15th: sn rdn along in tch: wknd appr 3 out: p.u next* **12/1**

2241 **P** **Shockingtimes (IRE)**[26] 3253 9-11-9 **127**..........................(bt) TomO'Brien
(Jamie Snowden) *mid-div: blnd 2nd: wnt 5th 17th: 7th whn blnd bdly next: sn p.u* **12/1**

0P00 **P** **Tales Of Milan (IRE)**[47] 2916 9-10-7 **118**..........(bt) HarryCobden(7)
(Phil Middleton) *mstke 2nd: a towards rr: t.o whn p.u 15th* **14/1**

-P13 **P** **Big Society (IRE)**[23] 3349 10-11-8 **126**..........................(p) GavinSheehan
(Harry Whittington) *nvr travelling in detached last: mstke 1st: nt fluent after: losing tch whn p.u bef 10th* **15/2**[2]

5U-P **P** **Letbeso (IRE)**[67] 2517 8-11-3 **121**..........................(v) SeanBowen
(Peter Bowen) *mid-div: hit 13th: wknd 15th: t.o whn p.u 17th* **16/1**

36-0 **P** **Strollawaynow (IRE)**[42] 2996 9-10-12 **116**..........................[1] TomCannon
(David Arbuthnot) *mid-div: reminder after 4th: dropped in rr 14th: bhd whn p.u bef 2 out* **14/1**

6-62 **P** **Onderun (IRE)**[40] 3046 7-10-9 **113**..........................(p) DarylJacob
(Emma Lavelle) *towards rr of mid-div: reminders after 9th: sn in rr: p.u after 13th* **10/1**

7m 32.8s (24.60) **Going Correction** +0.70s/f (Soft) **14** Ran SP% **121.2**
Speed ratings: **91,90,89,84,77** ,,,, ,,,
CSF £64.91 CT £436.52 TOTE £9.80: £3.40, £1.80, £2.90; EX 59.20 Trifecta £619.70.
Owner Brocade Racing **Bred** Robert Donaldson **Trained** Milborne Port, Dorset

FOCUS
This race was approximately 42yds further than advertised. This always looked likely to be a good test with such a competitive line-up, and not many finished. The winner was a 145 chaser at his peak but this is his best figure since Aintree 2014.

3708 HIGOS INSURANCE SERVICES YEOVIL H'CAP HURDLE (QUALIFIER FOR CHALLENGER TWO MILE HURDLE SERIES) (7 hdls 1 omitted) 1m 7f 65y

3:20 (3:20) (Class 3) (0-130,128) 4-Y-O **£6,498** (£1,908; £954; £477; £015)

22-2 **1** **Floresco (GER)**[56] 2734 6-10-13 **115**..........................(t) DarylJacob 120+
(Richard Woollacott) *trckd clr ldrs: led appr 2 out: rdn and edgd lft after last: kpt on wl* **5/1**[2]

130- **2** 1 1/4 **Rafafie**[310] 4821 8-10-0 **105** ow1.......................... LucyGardner(3) 109+
(Sue Gardner) *mid-div: hdwy 3 out: wnt cl 2nd 2 out: sn rdn: hit last: kpt on same pce* **11/1**

0-14 **3** 2 **Baby King (IRE)**[33] 3156 7-11-12 **128**..........................(t) PaddyBrennan 129
(Tom George) *hld up: hdwy 3 out: wnt 3rd 2 out: rdn bef last: kpt on same pce* **9/2**[1]

-002 **4** 1/2 **Eddiemaurice (IRE)**[24] 3318 5-10-8 **110**.......................... TomO'Brien 111
(John Flint) *hld up: hdwy after 3 out: wnt 4th next: rdn to dispute cl 3rd at the last: kpt on but no ex* **14/1**

3205 **5** 11 **Exitas (IRE)**[12] 3529 8-11-9 **128**..........................(t) ConorShoemark(3) 118
(Phil Middleton) *mid-div: in tch 3 out: effrt bef next: sn one pce* **14/1**

-330 **6** 1 1/2 **Leviathan**[19] 3449 9-11-6 **122**.......................... AidanColeman 110
(Venetia Williams) *chsd ldrs: rdn after 3 out: wknd between last 2* **8/1**

6-30 **7** 2 **Jumps Road**[12] 3529 9-11-9 **125**..........................(t) BrendanPowell 111
(Colin Tizzard) *led tl after 2nd: chsd ldr tl after 3 out: wknd between last 2* **12/1**

41-2 **8** 1/2 **Needless Shouting (IRE)**[26] 3216 5-11-3 **119**.......................... GavinSheehan 107
(Mick Channon) *racd wd: led after 2nd: rdn and hdd appr 2 out: sn hld: wkng whn stmbld last* **6/1**[3]

11U0 **9** 8 **Kalifourchon (FR)**[41] 3027 5-11-2 **123**.......................... DavidNoonan(5) 101
(David Pipe) *a towards rr* **12/1**

4-14 **10** nk **All Set To Go (IRE)**[34] 3135 5-11-10 **126**..........................(t) SamTwiston-Davies 104
(Paul Nicholls) *mainly towards rr: drvn after 3 out: wknd next* **5/1**[2]

2-0F **11** shd **Global Thrill**[38] 3080 7-11-3 **122**.......................... RobertWilliams(3) 99
(Bernard Llewellyn) *mid-div: hdwy after 3 out: effrt bef next: wknd between last 2* **40/1**

0-P4 **P** **Thundering Home**[71] 2445 9-11-1 **120**..........................(t) TomBellamy(3)
(Richard Mitchell) *trckd ldrs tl after 4th: wknd qckly after mstke 3 out: sn p.u* **20/1**

3m 59.4s (10.50) **Going Correction** +0.90s/f (Soft) **12** Ran SP% **121.2**
Speed ratings (Par 107): **108,107,106,106,100 99,98,98,93,93 93,**
CSF £60.32 CT £270.77 TOTE £6.10: £2.20, £3.80, £2.40; EX 72.10 Trifecta £701.20.
Owner D G Staddon **Bred** Hauptgestut Graditz **Trained** South Molton, Devon

FOCUS
The hurdle on the stables bend was omitted. This race distance was approximately 20yds further than advertised. With a few in-form horses taking their chance, this should be decent form. The third and fourth set the level in a solid-looking handicap.

3709 HIGOS INSURANCE SERVICES STREET NOVICES' LIMITED H'CAP CHASE (17 fncs) 2m 4f 35y

3:55 (3:56) (Class 4) (0-120,120) 5-Y-O+ **£6,498** (£1,908; £954; £477)

Form RPR

-603 **1** **Daveron (IRE)**[21] 3379 8-11-2 **117**.......................... MattGriffiths(3) 126+
(Jeremy Scott) *in tch: hit 6th: tk clsr order 13th: led 3 out: styd on: pushed out* **10/1**

5233 **2** 2 1/2 **Marden Court (IRE)**[26] 3253 6-10-11 **109**..........................(tp) PaddyBrennan 114
(Colin Tizzard) *prom: led 11th tl 13th: led after 4 out: rdn and hdd next: styd on but a being hld fr 2 out* **9/2**[2]

5-PF **3** 14 **Sidbury Hill**[42] 2988 8-10-12 **115**.......................... KevinJones(5) 104
(Seamus Mullins) *hld up in tch: hdwy after 4 out: wnt cl 3rd next: sn rdn and hld: kpt on same pce* **3/1**[1]

2P-1 **4** 4 1/2 **Merchant Of Milan**[21] 3387 8-10-3 **101**..........................(p) TomO'Brien 89
(John Flint) *in tch tl dropped to last 13th: rdn after 4 out: stdy prog fr next but nt pce to get involved* **5/1**[3]

0-61 **5** 3 **John Louis**[71] 2435 8-11-3 **120**.......................... CharlieDeutsch(5) 104
(Venetia Williams) *led: mstke 8th: hdd 11th tl 13th: rdn and hdd after 4 out: hld whn blnd bdly 2 out: wknd* **9/2**[2]

F52P **6** 1 **Saint Breiz (FR)**[22] 3371 10-10-7 **105**..........................(t) IanPopham 87
(Carroll Gray) *in tch: hdwy 11th: rdn after 13th: wknd after 3 out* **25/1**

4456 **P** **Too Scoops (IRE)**[42] 2990 9-11-2 **114**..........................(t) DarylJacob
(Richard Woollacott) *trckd ldrs: nt fluent 2nd and lost pl: in last pair whn nt fluent 5th: tailing off whn p.u bef 11th* **14/1**

3/2- **P** **Netherby**[563] 885 10-11-3 **115**.......................... JoshuaMoore
(Gary Moore) *hld up: pckd 4th: blnd 11th: sn p.u* **14/1**

0-53 **P** **Abigail Lynch (IRE)**[33] 3155 8-11-5 **117**..........................(t) SamTwiston-Davies
(Nigel Twiston-Davies) *trckd ldrs: rdn after 4 out: wkng whn blnd 3 out: sn p.u* **14/1**

P2-0 **R** **Lewis**[44] 2963 7-11-8 **120**.......................... JamesDavies
(Tom Symonds) *trckd ldrs: rdn after 13th: wknd 3 out: ref next* **16/1**

5m 35.6s (18.10) **Going Correction** +0.70s/f (Soft) **10** Ran SP% **116.8**
Speed ratings: **91,90,84,82,81 81,**,,,
CSF £56.06 CT £170.99 TOTE £7.50: £2.40, £4.60, £1.70; EX 42.30 Trifecta £583.60.
Owner Nigel Holder **Bred** C B Poots **Trained** Brompton Regis, Somerset

FOCUS
This race distance was approximately 25yds further than advertised. Probably just an ordinary race of its type. The second sets the level.

3710 HIGOS INSURANCE SERVICES CREWKERNE "NATIONAL HUNT" NOVICES' HURDLE (7 hdls 1 omitted) 1m 7f 65y

4:25 (4:26) (Class 4) 4-Y-O+ **£3,249** (£954; £477; £238)

Form RPR

F62 **1** **Gala Ball (IRE)**[20] 3411 6-11-4 118.......................... TomO'Brien 132+
(Philip Hobbs) *trckd ldr: led after 3 out: styd on strly: pushed out* **3/1**[2]

222 **2** 12 **Casper King (IRE)**[36] 3105 5-11-4 0.......................... RichardJohnson 121+
(Philip Hobbs) *in tch: stmbld 2nd: tk clsr order after 4th: rdn to chse wnr after 2 out: a being readily hld* **6/4**[1]

42 **3** 6 **Shadow Blue (IRE)**[42] 2987 7-10-11 115.......................... MrGTreacy(7) 112
(Steven Dixon) *led: rdn and hdd after 3 out: kpt on same pce fr next* **7/1**

55 **4** 8 **The Fresh Prince (IRE)**[22] 3370 6-11-4 0.......................... LeightonAspell 107
(Oliver Sherwood) *racd keenly: trckd ldrs: rdn whn outpcd after 3 out: styd on into 4th bef last but nt pce to get on terms w ldrs* **9/1**

5P50 **5** 6 **Trans Express (IRE)**[20] 3411 6-11-1 0.......................... LucyGardner(3) 98
(Sue Gardner) *hld up: styd on fr bef last: fin wl to snatch wl hld 5th fnl stride* **100/1**

5-0 **6** nse **Bound Hill**[257] 213 7-10-11 0.......................... MrMLegg(7) 98
(Fiona Shaw) *mid-div tl outpcd after 3 out: styd on again after 2 out but nt a danger* **33/1**

7 3/4 **Leg Lock Luke (IRE)**[95] 6-11-4 0.......................... PaddyBrennan 99+
(Colin Tizzard) *trckd ldrs: rdn and hld whn nt fluent 2 out: wknd last* **6/1**[3]

6 **8** 8 **Coeur Tantre (IRE)**[22] 3370 5-11-4 0.......................... DaveCrosse 89
(Hugo Froud) *mid-div: rdn after 3 out: wknd next* **100/1**

236 **9** 3 **Who's Micky Brown (IRE)**[7] 3590 6-10-11 0.......................... MrShaneQuinlan(7) 86
(Neil Mulholland) *a towards rr* **50/1**

000 **10** 17 **Brin D'Avoine (FR)**[8] 3581 5-11-4 0.......................... MarkQuinlan 69
(Neil Mulholland) *a towards rr* **250/1**

3000 **11** 10 **Junior Package**[8] 3581 5-10-13 0.......................... DavidNoonan(5) 59
(David Pipe) *mid-div tl after 2nd: drvn along in detached last next: t.o* **100/1**

32- **12** 7 **Beau Phil (FR)**[287] 5248 5-11-4 0..........................(t) SamTwiston-Davies 52
(Paul Nicholls) *mid-div: rdn after 3 out: wknd bef next: t.o* **11/1**

00- **P** **Le Capricieux (FR)**[306] 4921 5-11-4 0.......................... JamieMoore
(Gary Moore) *plld v hrd: a in rr: wknd after 3 out: p.u bef next* **100/1**

4m 1.1s (12.20) **Going Correction** +0.90s/f (Soft) **13** Ran SP% **119.4**
Speed ratings (Par 105): **103,96,93,89,85 85,85,81,79,70 65,61,**
CSF £8.09 TOTE £5.00: £1.60, £1.30, £2.50; EX 11.50 Trifecta £51.40.
Owner Robert & Janet Gibbs **Bred** Thomas James **Trained** Withycombe, Somerset

FOCUS
The hurdle on the stables bend was omitted. This race distance was approximately 20yds further than advertised. Thistlecrack won this last year, Baltimore Rock in 2014 and Shutthefrontdoor in 2013, so this is a race that can go to a horse with a decent future. A step up from the winner, while the second, fifth and ninth help set the level. It could be rated higher through the third and fourth, but not on time compared with the earlier handicap.
T/Plt: £95.40 to a £1 stake. Pool of £72409.04 - 553.69 winning tickets. T/Qpdt: £7.80 to a £1 stake. Pool of £8430.13 - 790.55 winning tickets. **Tim Mitchell**

3711 - 3712a (Foreign Racing) - See Raceform Interactive

2651 GOWRAN PARK (R-H)

Thursday, January 21

OFFICIAL GOING: Heavy

3713a JOHN MULHERN GALMOY HURDLE (GRADE 2) (13 hdls) 3m

2:00 (2:00) 5-Y-O+ **£18,750** (£5,937; £2,812; £937; £625)

RPR

1 **Alpha Des Obeaux (FR)**[24] 3322 6-11-3 152..........................(p) BJCooper 159+
(M F Morris, Ire) *settled bhd ldrs tl wnt 2nd fr 7th: led narrowly 4 out tl sn jnd and disp: mstke 3 out: regained advantage bef 2 out: extended ld between last 2 and styd on wl: comf* **13/8**[1]

2 11 **At Fishers Cross (IRE)**[315] 4719 9-11-3 157..........................(b) BarryGeraghty 147+
(Rebecca Curtis) *trckd ldr tl led briefly after 4th: nt fluent in 2nd at 6th: lost pl after next and dropped to 4th bef 3 out: impr on inner into 3rd bef 2 out: no imp on wnr bef last where slt mstke: kpt on into 2nd run-in* **11/2**

3 1 3/4 **Martello Tower (IRE)**[24] 3322 8-11-10 149.......................... APHeskin 154
(Ms Margaret Mullins, Ire) *jinked lft briefly at s and led narrowly: hdd briefly after 5th: narrow advantage whn bad mstke 4 out and hdd: sn disp tl hdd bef 2 out: no imp on wnr bef last: dropped to 3rd run-in and kpt on one pce* **5/2**[2]

4 16 **Briar Hill (IRE)**[340] 4258 8-11-3 150.......................... RWalsh 131
(W P Mullins, Ire) *hld up bhd ldrs in 4th: dropped to rr fr 5th: niggled along after 7th: wnt 4th after 3 out: sn pushed along and no imp on ldrs bef next: one pce after* **7/2**[3]

5 40 **Noble Emperor (IRE)**[21] 3391 8-11-3 139.......................... MarkWalsh 99
(A J Martin, Ire) *w.w in rr: wnt 4th fr 5th: nt fluent 9th: cl 4th fr 4 out and wnt 3rd bef next: pushed along after 3 out and no ex u.p bef next where dropped to rr: wknd and eased: t.o* **12/1**

6m 43.6s (14.70) **5** Ran SP% **112.0**
CSF £10.90 TOTE £2.50: £1.30, £1.60; DF 10.80 Trifecta £25.30.
Owner Gigginstown House Stud **Bred** Marie Devilder & Stephanie Fasquelle **Trained** Fethard, Co Tipperary

FOCUS
A decisive performance from the winner, showing that he's a high-class stayer and one that doesn't necessarily need testing ground to be seen at his best.

3714a (Foreign Racing) - See Raceform Interactive

3715a GOFFS THYESTES H'CAP CHASE (GRADE A) (17 fncs) 3m 1f

3:10 (3:10) 5-Y-O+ **£44,117** (£13,970; £6,617; £2,205; £1,470; £735)

RPR

1 **My Murphy (IRE)**[25] 3296 10-10-5 **139**.......................... RobbiePower 151+
(W J Burke, Ire) *trckd ldrs: almost on terms fr bef 4th: cl 3rd fr 6th: cl 2nd after 5 out and disp bef 3 out where led narrowly: rdn and strly pressed fr 2 out: kpt on wl w narrow advantage run-in to assert in clsng stages* **16/1**

2 1 1/4 **Mala Beach (IRE)**[33] 3147 8-10-8 **142**.......................... DavyRussell 153+
(Gordon Elliott, Ire) *chsd ldrs: tk clsr order and disp 4th 4 out: nt fluent next and impr to chal 2 out where mstke and pckd: rdn in cl 2nd and ev ch nr side fr last: kpt on wl wout matching wnr in clsng stages* **5/1**[1]

3 5 1/2 **Ucello Conti (FR)**[25] 3296 8-10-9 **143**..........................(t) JacquesRicou 149
(Gordon Elliott, Ire) *mid-div early: racd out wd and impr bhd ldrs after 6th: disp on outer bef 3 out where mstke: pckd sltly disputing 3rd next and sn no imp on ldrs in 3rd: kpt on one pce* **11/1**

4 4 **The Job Is Right**[12] 3542 8-10-6 **140**..........................(b) MarkEnright 143
(Michael Hourigan, Ire) *chsd ldrs: slt mstke 6th: 5th bef 10th: rdn after 4 out and no imp u.p in 7th after 3 out: mstke next: kpt on into mod 4th after last: nvr trbld ldrs* **12/1**

5 4 **Rule The World**[23] 3357 9-10-9 **148**.......................... JackKennedy(5) 146
(M F Morris, Ire) *chsd ldrs: rdn in 6th after 3 out and no imp on ldrs fr next: kpt on one pce* **9/1**

6 1 1/2 **Buckers Bridge (IRE)**[39] 3073 10-10-6 **140**.......................... JJBurke 138
(Henry De Bromhead, Ire) *led narrowly and extended advantage briefly after 2nd: jnd bef 4th: nt fluent 6th where hdd: 3rd bef 10th: rdn disputing 3rd after 3 out and no ex fr next where slt mstke in 4th: wknd run-in* **12/1**

7 2 1/4 **Urano (FR)**[25] 3296 8-10-2 136 PaulTownend 131
(W P Mullins, Ire) *hld up towards rr: mstke 8th: tk clsr order after 5 out: nt fluent 3 out and pushed along in 9th: no imp after 2 out: mstke last: kpt on one pce into mod 7th cl home* 25/1

8 hd **Leavethelighton (IRE)**[25] 3302 9-10-0 134 (p) MPButler 131
(Eoin Doyle, Ire) *chsd ldrs: rdn bef 3 out where slt mstke: no imp in 8th bef next: kpt on one pce* 16/1

9 4 3/4 **Ballycasey (IRE)**[264] 95 9-11-1 149 RWalsh 142
(W P Mullins, Ire) *cl up and disp bef 4th: cl 2nd fr 6th tl led next: mstke 9th: jnd bef 3 out where hdd: rdn and wknd bef 2 out: eased* 11/2[2]

10 45 **Thunder And Roses (IRE)**[47] 2899 8-10-6 145 (p) JonathanMoore(5) 89
(Ms Sandra Hughes, Ire) *chsd ldrs: 4th bef 10th: rdn in 4th bef 4 out and sn no ex: wknd u.p bef next: eased: completely t.o* 20/1

11 3 1/4 **Folsom Blue (IRE)**[25] 3296 9-10-1 135 (p) BJCooper 79
(M F Morris, Ire) *cl up early: nt fluent 2nd: disp 6th bef 10th where slow and lost pl: reminders after next and no imp after 5 out: u.p in 10th after 4 out: wknd and eased bef next: completely t.o* 8/1[3]

12 11 **Letter Of Credit (IRE)**[20] 3432 11-10-3 137 PhillipEnright 69
(James Joseph Mangan, Ire) *hld up towards rr: rdn and no imp bef 3 out: one pce after and eased fr after 2 out: completely t.o* 33/1

P **Vics Canvas (IRE)**[47] 2899 13-10-11 145 (p) RobertDunne
(Dermot Anthony McLoughlin, Ire) *mid-div: pushed along bef 4 out and wknd qckly: eased and t.o whn p.u bef next* 16/1

P **Boston Bob (IRE)**[176] 1152 11-11-8 156 DannyMullins
(W P Mullins, Ire) *in rr of mid-div: mstke 2nd: niggled along after 11th and no imp fr 5 out: lost tch and t.o whn p.u bef 3 out* 28/1

R **Malt Gem (IRE)**[24] 3320 8-9-11 131 AELynch
(Miss Mary Louise Hallahan, Ire) *towards rr: mstke 11th: tk clsr order briefly fr 4 out: wknd bef next where slow: trailing whn ref at last* 16/1

P **Unic De Bersy (FR)**[12] 3538 8-9-11 134 (b) LPDempsey(3)
(Gordon Elliott, Ire) *mid-div early: mstke 6th and dropped to rr: reminders in rr after 8th: mstke next and p.u after 9th* 16/1

P **Suntiep (FR)**[681] 4741 10-10-4 138 DavidMullins
(W P Mullins, Ire) *mid-div best: rdn towards rr after 12th and no ex after 5 out: wknd and p.u bef 3 out* 20/1

P **Nickname Exit (FR)**[20] 3432 6-9-7 132 ow2 (p) ChrisTimmons(5)
(Gordon Elliott, Ire) *mid-div best: mstke 4 out and wknd towards rr: eased and p.u after 3 out* 12/1

7m 11.7s (431.70) **18 Ran SP% 133.7**
CSF £97.60 CT £968.03 TOTE £21.50: £4.40, £2.00, £2.40, £2.50; DF 158.10 Trifecta £5277.50.
Owner Hans Joerg Zindel **Bred** S P Tindall **Trained** Mallow, Co Cork
■ Stewards' Enquiry : Chris Timmons one-day ban: weighed-in 2lb heavy (tbn)

FOCUS
A game and tough performance from a winner that deserved to get his turn in a race like this. The first and third have been rated as running personal bests.

3716a PMF ACCOUNTANTS BEGINNERS CHASE (12 fncs) 2m 2f
3:45 (3:46) 5-Y-0+ £6,849 (£1,588; £694; £397)

RPR

1 **Tell Us More (IRE)**[24] 3321 7-11-12 0 BJCooper 140+
(W P Mullins, Ire) *settled bhd ldrs: j. sltly lft 3rd and at times after: led after 4th and slow next: jnd briefly bef 7th: extended advantage after 4 out: j.lft next and 2 out: in command at last: nt extended* 4/6[1]

2 6 **Mount Gunnery**[590] 668 8-11-12 0 DavidMullins 129
(P A Fahy, Ire) *cl up and led briefly fr 4th tl sn hdd: dropped to 4th bef next: impr out wd to dispute briefly bef 7th: rdn fr 2 out where slt mstke and pckd in 3rd: no imp on wnr bef last: kpt on into 2nd run-in* 20/1

3 4 1/2 **Young Finnegan (IRE)**[980] 346 10-11-12 0 PhillipEnright 127
(Robert Tyner, Ire) *chsd ldrs: pressed wnr in 2nd bef 3 out: rdn after next where nt fluent and no imp on wnr bef last: one pce run-in where dropped to 3rd* 12/1[3]

4 44 **Robin Des People (IRE)**[33] 3166 6-11-12 0 MPFogarty 80
(Barry John Murphy, Ire) *chsd ldrs: 5th whn mstke and pckd sltly at 5th: pushed along in 4th bef 3 out and sn no ex: wknd bef 2 out* 66/1

5 4 3/4 **Kansas City Chief (IRE)**[74] 2384 7-11-12 0 AELynch 75
(Miss Mary Louise Hallahan, Ire) *towards rr: no imp in remote 7th bef 3 out: wnt remote 5th fr last: t.o* 50/1

6 2 **Back Door Johnny (IRE)**[46] 5-11-6 0 RobbiePower 67
(Paul Nolan, Ire) *hld up: slt mstke towards rr 1st: no imp in remote 6th bef 3 out: t.o* 16/1

7 11 **Marinero (IRE)**[54] 2792 7-11-12 0 (t) DavyRussell 62
(A J Martin, Ire) *led narrowly tl hdd fr 4th: dropped to 5th and no imp fr 5 out: wknd and eased bef 3 out: t.o* 2/1[2]

8 25 **Busty Brown (IRE)**[32] 3183 10-11-12 0 (p) SeanFlanagan 37
(M O Cullinane, Ire) *mid-div best: wknd 5 out and no imp in remote 8th bef 3 out: completely t.o* 33/1

9 36 **Wildcatted (GER)**[75] 2355 7-11-12 0 RobbieColgan
(Michael J McDonagh, Ire) *hld up in mid-div: slt mstke 3rd: wknd 5 out: completely t.o* 100/1

P **Run For Firth (IRE)**[24] 3327 9-11-12 0 (t) BrianO'Connell
(Kieran Purcell, Ire) *towards rr: nt fluent 5th: rdn after next and no imp trailing bef 7th: p.u bef 4 out* 25/1

F **Simple Joys**[42] 2999 6-11-5 0 (t) MarkEnright
(Mrs Denise Foster, Ire) *hld up: towards rr whn fell 7th* 100/1

5m 11.7s (27.70)
WFA 5 from 6yo+ 3lb **11 Ran SP% 123.9**
CSF £19.58 TOTE £1.80: £1.02, £3.70, £2.60; DF 18.90 Trifecta £115.40.
Owner Gigginstown House Stud **Bred** Tim Conroy **Trained** Muine Beag, Co Carlow

FOCUS
With the 2-1 second-favourite running a stinker, this did not take much winning.

3717a (Foreign Racing) - See Raceform Interactive

3516 CHEPSTOW (L-H)
Friday, January 22
3718 Meeting Abandoned - Waterlogged

3233 MARKET RASEN (R-H)
Friday, January 22

OFFICIAL GOING: Chase course - soft (good to soft in places); hurdle course - good to soft (soft in places) changing to soft (heavy in places) all round after race 1 (1.15), changing to heavy after race 3 (2.20)
moderate 1/2 behind
rain up to start of 1st race (1.15), then overcast and damp, fine last 2

3724 WALKING THE COURSES NOVICES' HURDLE (10 hdls) 2m 2f 140y
1:15 (1:16) (Class 4) 4-Y-0+ £3,249 (£954; £477; £238)

Form RPR

4F 1 **Paddy's Field (IRE)**[84] 2163 6-11-5 0 NicodeBoinville 124+
(Ben Pauling) *trckd ldrs: upsides 2 out: pckd landing last: styd on wl to ld last 75yds* 3/1[2]

2 3 1/4 **Frightened Rabbit (USA)**[155] 4-10-7 0 CraigNichol 107
(Keith Dalgleish) *hld up in mid-div: hdwy 5th: trcking ldrs 3 out: led appr last: hdd and no ex last 75yds* 66/1

22P- 3 1 **Sakhee's City (FR)**[251] 5255 5-11-2 0 AdamNicol(3) 119
(Philip Kirby) *trckd ldr: led bef 2 out: hdd appr last: styd on same pce* 50/1

-204 4 6 **Vivas (FR)**[63] 2612 5-11-5 0 RichardJohnson 114
(Charlie Longsdon) *chsd ldrs: upsides whn mstke 2 out: wknd last 100yds* 9/1

P 5 1 1/2 **Bonne Question (FR)**[72] 2437 7-11-5 0 LiamTreadwell 111
(Venetia Williams) *hld up in rr: t.k.h: hdwy 3 out: one pce appr 2 out* 40/1

3-6 6 9 **The Last Bar**[55] 2776 6-10-12 0 HarrySkelton 95
(Dan Skelton) *chsd ldrs: drvn 3 out: wknd appr next* 25/1

-213 7 2 3/4 **Abbreviate (GER)**[44] 2972 5-11-12 130 DavidBass 107
(Kim Bailey) *led: hit 4th: hdd bef 2 out: sn wknd* 9/4[1]

54- P **Mr Snoozy**[12] 2950 7-11-5 0 JakeGreenall
(Mark Walford) *chsd ldrs: lost pl after 7th: t.o whn p.u after next* 33/1

2 P **Travertine (IRE)**[16] 3484 6-11-5 0 BarryGeraghty
(Alan King) *trckd ldrs: drvn 3 out: sn wknd: distant 8th whn p.u bef next* 7/2[3]

130/ P **Two Jabs**[65] 5264 6-11-5 0 JamieMoore
(Michael Appleby) *j. poorly in rr: bhd 5th: t.o next: p.u bef 2 out* 6/1

02 P **Duc De Seville (IRE)**[35] 3139 4-10-2 0 (p) GaryDerwin(5)
(Michael Chapman) *in rr: bhd 5th: t.o next: p.u bef 2 out* 200/1

60-0 P **Snow Prince**[25] 3306 5-10-12 0 TrevorRyan(7)
(Steve Gollings) *mid-div: drvn 5th: sn lost pl and bhd: t.o 3 out: p.u bef next: b.b.v* 125/1

03-P P **The Conn (IRE)**[77] 2319 6-11-5 0 BrianHughes
(Chris Grant) *mid-div: lost pl and stmbld on landing 5th: sn bhd: t.o whn p.u bef 7th* 100/1

-005 P **Hey Up Ashey**[64] 2597 6-11-5 0 DannyCook
(Michael Mullineaux) *mstke 1st: hdwy to chse ldrs 4th: sn drvn: lost pl 6th: sn bhd: t.o 3 out: p.u bef next* 200/1

4m 53.5s (14.10) **Going Correction** +0.95s/f (Soft)
WFA 4 from 5yo+ 11lb **14 Ran SP% 117.7**
Speed ratings (Par 105): **108,106,106,103,103 99,98,,, ,,,,**
CSF £182.43 TOTE £3.80: £2.00, £13.10, £5.60; EX 284.90 Trifecta £5914.20.
Owner Paul & Clare Rooney **Bred** Gerard Coleman **Trained** Bourton-On-The-Water, Gloucs

FOCUS
Rail set out 3 yards on the Wood bend adding approximately 27 yards to races 1, 2 and 6 and approximately 36 yards to races 3, 4 and 5. The 2.5mm of morning rain certainly looked to have got into the ground as runners ploughed through the opening novice event. The going was then changed to soft, heavy in places on the hurdle course. The winner built on his latest form but the second and third are concerns.

3725 RACING UK WINTER SEASON TICKET H'CAP HURDLE (8 hdls) 2m 148y
1:50 (1:50) (Class 4) (0-120,119) 4-Y-0+ £3,249 (£954; £477; £238)

Form RPR

5/53 1 **Herons Heir (IRE)**[42] 3009 8-10-13 106 (t) HarrySkelton 112+
(Dan Skelton) *hld up wl in tch: smooth hdwy to trck ldrs 3 out: 2nd bef 2 out: upsides whn nt fluent last: led last 150yds: drvn out* 2/1[1]

-650 2 3 1/4 **Ourmanmassini (IRE)**[43] 2987 8-11-0 107 (t) TomO'Brien 108
(Suzy Smith) *led: hit 2nd: reminders after 3 out: jnd next: hdd and no ex last 150yds* 9/2[2]

66F2 3 2 1/4 **Sailors Warn (IRE)**[49] 2893 9-11-8 115 (t) DenisO'Regan 116+
(Ronald Thompson) *hld up wl in tch: hdwy to chse ldrs 4th: outpcd and modest 3rd whn mstke 2 out: styd on last 150yds* 11/2[3]

4 18 **Mercian King (IRE)**[47] 5-11-10 117 RichardJohnson 99
(Charlie Longsdon) *chsd ldr: upsides 5th: drvn next: lost pl bef 2 out* 11/2[3]

5213 5 3 **Renoyr (FR)**[24] 3346 11-11-5 112 BrianHughes 90
(Malcolm Jefferson) *chsd ldrs: pushed along and nt fluent 4th: lost pl 3 out: j.lft last* 11/2[3]

11 6 1 1/2 **Edward Elgar**[44] 2974 5-11-12 119 AndrewThornton 95
(Caroline Bailey) *nt jump wl: hit 1st: sn chsng ldrs: mstke and lost pl 4th: chsd ldrs 3 out: sn wknd* 11/1

440 7 12 **My Anchor**[42] 3023 5-10-8 108 TommyDowling(7) 72
(Charlie Mann) *trckd ldrs: t.k.h: upsides sn after 3 out: lost pl bef 2 out: bhd whn mstke 2 out: sn eased* 20/1

4m 28.4s (21.70) **Going Correction** +1.225s/f (Heav) **7 Ran SP% 110.8**
Speed ratings (Par 105): **97,95,94,85,84 83,78**
CSF £10.89 CT £38.79 TOTE £2.50: £1.50, £3.10; EX 11.30 Trifecta £47.20.
Owner HighclereThoroughbredRacing-Herons Heir **Bred** Seamus Larkin **Trained** Alcester, Warwicks

FOCUS
Not a bad handicap. It was run at an average gallop and they got sorted out from the home turn. The winner improved to his bumper mark.

3726 WEATHERBYS HAMILTON GRADUATION CHASE (14 fncs) 2m 5f 89y
2:20 (2:20) (Class 2) 5-Y-0+ £12,777 (£3,857; £1,987; £1,053)

Form RPR

-222 1 **Aso (FR)**[34] 3153 6-10-10 137 AidanColeman 153+
(Venetia Williams) *trckd ldng pair: 2nd 3rd: led 11th: drvn and styd on run-in* 2/1[1]

2/U6 2 1 3/4 **Ballyalton (IRE)**[70] 2469 9-10-10 140 RichardJohnson 149+
(Ian Williams) *trckd ldrs: j.lft 2nd: chsd wnr bef 3 out: hit last: styd on same pce last 100yds* 11/4[3]

3F1F **3** *21* **Kalane (IRE)**[24] 3337 7-10-3 0 .... BrianHughes 126
(Charlie Longsdon) *trckd ldr: mstke 7th: drvn 11th: lost pl next: bhd whn j.lft last 2* **85/40**[2]

-2F4 **4** *23* **Straidnahanna (IRE)**[41] 3038 7-11-7 131 .... DannyCook 122
(Sue Smith) *led: pushed along 8th: drvn and hdd whn hit 11th: lost pl bef next: sn wl bhd* **17/2**

P- **P** **Buche De Noel (FR)**[75] 5-10-6 134 .... BrendanPowell
(Jamie Snowden) *trckd ldrs: pushed along after 7th: outpcd next: wkng whn mstke 9th: sn eased: bhd whn p.u bef next* **16/1**

6m 1.3s (15.30) **Going Correction** +1.00s/f (Soft)
WFA 5 from 6yo+ 4lb **5** Ran SP% **108.4**
Speed ratings: **110,109,101,92,**
CSF £7.79 TOTE £3.00: £1.50, £1.70; EX 8.00 Trifecta £15.10.
Owner The Bellamy Partnership **Bred** I Pacault, A Pacault & M Pacault **Trained** Kings Caple, H'fords

FOCUS
A very interesting affair that served up a real test.

3727 WATCH RACING UK ON 3 DEVICES H'CAP CHASE (14 fncs) 2m 5f 89y
2:55 (2:57) (Class 4) (0-115,115) 5-Y-0+ **£3,898** (£1,144; £572; £286)

Form RPR

3-31 **1** **Sunny Ledgend**[15] 3499 11-11-1 **111** .... MrJMartin(7) 120+
(Andrew J Martin) *j. soundly: mde virtually all: jnd 3 out: kpt on gamely run-in* **8/1**

211P **2** *1 ½* **Thinger Licht (FR)**[194] 961 7-10-13 **102** ....(p) HarrySkelton 109
(Dan Skelton) *in rr: hdwy to chse ldrs after 4th: upsides 3 out: kpt on same pce last 100yds* **5/1**[3]

5652 **3** *17* **Gold Ingot**[25] 3313 9-11-12 **115** .... AndrewThornton 104
(Caroline Bailey) *chsd ldrs: outpcd and lost pl 3 out: tk remote 3rd last* **7/1**

0/5 **4** *1 ½* **Sizing Sahara**[33] 3176 8-10-13 **102** .... TomO'Brien 90
(Paul Henderson) *in rr: hdwy to chse ldrs after 4th: one pce fr 3 out* **25/1**

3-21 **5** *1 ¾* **Kassis**[42] 3007 7-11-1 **104** .... BrendanPowell 90
(Jamie Snowden) *chsd ldrs: upsides 8th: outpcd 3 out: fdd last* **9/2**[2]

/U44 **6** *16* **Tiny Dancer (IRE)**[27] 3243 8-10-10 **99** ....(v[1]) BrianHughes 71
(Chris Grant) *kicked s: trckd ldrs: drvn whn mstke 4 out: lost pl bef next: sn bhd* **17/2**

25-6 **7** *18* **Hindon Road (IRE)**[44] 2973 9-11-9 **112** .... WayneHutchinson 64
(Alan King) *in rr: hdwy to chse ldrs after 4th: drvn 9th: modest 3rd 3 out: wknd bef next: sn bhd* **7/1**

33/3 **P** **Father Probus**[52] 2839 10-11-2 **105** .... JonathanEngland
(Michael Appleby) *chsd ldrs: drvn 9th: sn lost pl: t.o whn p.u bef 3 out* **9/1**

50/0 **P** **Silver Eagle (IRE)**[56] 2749 8-11-9 **112** ....(t) DavidBass
(Kim Bailey) *w ldrs: pushed along 5th: sn in rr: drvn 9th: bhd next: p.u bef 2 out* **4/1**[1]

6m 17.2s (31.20) **Going Correction** +1.275s/f (Heav) **9** Ran SP% **115.3**
Speed ratings: **91,90,83,83,82 76,69,,**
CSF £48.38 CT £296.03 TOTE £9.90: £3.20, £1.80, £2.10; EX 44.10 Trifecta £244.90.
Owner Andrew J Martin **Bred** A And Mrs Martin **Trained** Chipping Norton, Oxon

FOCUS
The going was further downgraded to heavy all over prior to this modest handicap. It was run at a routine gallop and only two mattered from the third-last. The winner may still be capable of better than this and there's a case for rating the form higher.

3728 THANK YOU & FAREWELL JANE HEDLEY H'CAP HURDLE (10 hdls) 2m 4f 139y
3:30 (3:31) (Class 3) (0-130,128) 4-Y-0+ **£5,393** (£1,583; £791; £395)

Form RPR

P3-5 **1** **Salmanazar**[44] 2977 8-11-10 **126** .... WayneHutchinson 135+
(Alan King) *chsd ldrs: led appr 2 out: styd on wl run-in* **10/1**

0/11 **2** *6* **Cotillion**[21] 3417 10-10-12 **124** ....(p) TobyWheeler(10) 129+
(Ian Williams) *trckd ldrs: chal on ins whn hmpd bnd bef 2 out: sn chsng wnr: hung rt between last 2: kpt on same pce last 150yds* **9/2**[3]

-124 **3** *6* **Great Link**[25] 3315 7-10-13 **115** ....(b) HarrySkelton 112
(Dan Skelton) *set str pce: hit 2nd: reminders bef 6th: j.lft 7th and next: hdd appr 2 out: one pce* **15/2**

-613 **4** *25* **Palm Grey (IRE)**[27] 3235 8-10-13 **115** .... DannyCook 92
(Sue Smith) *chsd ldrs: nt fluent and lost pl 4th: sn drvn: chsng ldrs 3 out: lost pl bef next: sn bhd* **12/1**

15B0 **5** *47* **Midnight Shot**[16] 3487 6-11-6 **122** .... RichardJohnson 47
(Charlie Longsdon) *hld up detached in last: sme hdwy whn nt fluent 4th: bhd fr 7th: t.o 3 out* **8/1**

-0F3 **P** **Rumble Of Thunder (IRE)**[127] 1448 10-11-8 **127** ....(p) AdamNicol(3)
(Philip Kirby) *prom: reminders and lost pl 6th: bhd whn hit 3 out: sn eased: t.o whn sn p.u* **22/1**

0360 **P** **Phare Isle (IRE)**[48] 2912 11-10-11 **120** ....(tp) MrMJPKendrick(7)
(Ben Case) *chsd ldrs: drvn 5th: sn lost pl: bhd next: t.o 7th: p.u after next* **28/1**

124/ **P** **Captain Kelly (IRE)**[850] 1642 9-10-6 **113** ....(t) BridgetAndrews(5)
(Dan Skelton) *in rr: lost pl and bhd 6th: sn t.o: p.u bef 3 out* **20/1**

5241 **P** **Away For Slates (IRE)**[21] 3424 6-11-0 **121** .... RyanDay(5)
(Keith Dalgleish) *mid-div: chsd ldrs 5th: lost pl next: rallied to chse ldrs 3 out: sn lost pl: wl bhd whn p.u bef next* **7/2**[1]

13 **P** **Crosspark**[52] 2838 6-11-10 **126** .... JamieMoore
(Caroline Bailey) *chsd ldrs: drvn 7th: reminders next: lost pl and wl bhd whn p.u bef 2 out* **4/1**[2]

5m 30.1s (21.30) **Going Correction** +1.225s/f (Heav) **10** Ran SP% **112.6**
Speed ratings (Par 107): **108,105,103,93,76 ,,,,**
CSF £52.02 CT £357.79 TOTE £11.00: £3.30, £2.20, £2.60; EX 56.40 Trifecta £332.70.
Owner Top Brass Partnership **Bred** Wood Farm Stud **Trained** Barbury Castle, Wilts

FOCUS
A competitive handicap on paper, but the majority couldn't cope with the going due to the solid gallop. The winner is rated in line with his old hurdle mark.

3729 NEXT MEETING 9TH FEBRUARY CONDITIONAL JOCKEYS' H'CAP HURDLE (10 hdls) 2m 2f 140y
4:00 (4:01) (Class 4) (0-110,112) 4-Y-0+ **£3,249** (£954; £477; £238)

Form RPR

4001 **1** **Tanarpino**[8] 3592 5-12-0 **112** 7ex .... ConorWalsh(5) 120+
(Jennie Candlish) *chsd ldrs: pushed along 5th: nt fluent and lost pl next: rallied 3 out: chsng ldng pair appr next: edgd rt between last 2: lost styd on to ld last 150yds* **10/11**[1]

0351 **2** *2 ¼* **Milly Baloo**[27] 3234 5-11-7 **100** .... DerekFox 104
(Tim Easterby) *trckd ldrs: t.k.h: led bef 2 out: hdd and no ex last 150yds* **5/1**[2]

6-05 **3** *8* **Yasir (USA)**[22] 3376 8-10-13 **95** .... KillianMoore(3) 92
(Sophie Leech) *in rr but wl in tch: pushed along 5th: chsng ldrs 3 out: 2nd bef 2 out: wknd last* **10/1**

4-01 **4** *13* **Glenarm**[49] 2876 7-11-12 **105** .... JeremiahMcGrath 87
(Seamus Mullins) *w ldrs: lost pl bef 2 out* **11/2**[3]

6453 **5** *nse* **Molko Jack (FR)**[22] 3376 12-9-6 **79** oh1 .... LewisStones(8) 61
(Michael Mullineaux) *t.k.h: trckd ldrs: lost pl after 7th: rallied next: lost pl bef 2 out* **22/1**

4504 **P** **Alys Rock (IRE)**[66] 2559 7-11-3 **99** .... JonathanEngland(3)
(Michael Appleby) *in rr: chsd ldrs 7th: lost pl rapidly bef 2 out: wl bhd whn p.u sn after 2 out* **16/1**

550 **U** **Moon Arc (IRE)**[51] 2845 4-10-4 **98** ....(p) CraigNichol(3)
(Keith Dalgleish) *led: hdd bef 2 out: 5th and wkng whn blnd and uns rdr 2 out* **16/1**

4m 59.8s (20.40) **Going Correction** +1.225s/f (Heav)
WFA 4 from 5yo+ 11lb **7** Ran SP% **109.6**
Speed ratings (Par 105): **106,105,101,96,96 ,**
CSF £5.63 CT £22.85 TOTE £1.60: £1.40, £2.50; EX 6.10 Trifecta £30.50.
Owner P and Mrs G A Clarke **Bred** R W Huggins **Trained** Basford Green, Staffs

FOCUS
This conditional riders' handicap was run at a sound gallop and the principals came clear. The winner was a little below his Catterick level.
T/Plt: £184.70 to a £1 stake. Pool: £65,569.84 - 259.12 winning tickets T/Qpdt: £10.90 to a £1 stake. Pool: £8,376.58 - 566.02 winning tickets **Walter Glynn**

3146 ASCOT (R-H)
Saturday, January 23

OFFICIAL GOING: Soft (heavy in places; chs 5.5, hdl 5.3)
Wind: Moderate, half against Weather: Cloudy

3730 ASCOT SUPPORTING OUR LOCAL COMMUNITY JUVENILE HURDLE (8 hdls) 1m 7f 152y
12:40 (12:42) (Class 3) 4-Y-0 **£6,498** (£1,908; £954; £477)

Form RPR

1 **1** **Gibralfaro (IRE)**[27] 3279 4-11-4 0 .... WayneHutchinson 136+
(Alan King) *t.k.h: mde all: stuttered into 3rd and wandered bef next: shkn up whn pressed last: styd on wl: readily* **4/5**[1]

1- **2** *1 ¾* **Connetable (FR)**[261] 4-11-4 139 .... NickScholfield 134+
(Paul Nicholls) *str: bit bkwd: cl up: chsd wnr bef 2 out: rdn to chal last: styd on but no imp fnl 150yds* **9/4**[2]

0-32 **3** *25* **Swincombe Toby**[62] 2662 4-10-12 122 .... WillKennedy 108
(Nick Williams) *w'like: lengthy: t.k.h: cl up: chsd wnr after 4th tl bef 2 out: wknd* **5/1**[3]

5 **4** *42* **Sea Serpent (FR)**[25] 3347 4-10-12 0 .... JoshuaMoore 61
(Gary Moore) *pressed wnr tl after 4th: shkn up and lost tch next: t.o whn blnd last: rdn out to win battle for 4th* **33/1**

3 **5** *1 ¼* **Jinsha Lake (IRE)**[50] 2883 4-10-12 0 ....(t) AdamWedge 60
(Evan Williams) *str: swtg: a last: lost tch and nudged along 5th: t.o 2 out: rdn to chal for 4th pl after last* **25/1**

4m 1.5s (14.10) **Going Correction** +0.675s/f (Soft) **5** Ran SP% **109.8**
Speed ratings: **91,90,77,56,56**
CSF £2.97 TOTE £1.50: £1.10, £1.40; EX 2.90 Trifecta £3.80.
Owner McNeill Family **Bred** Sarl Darpat France **Trained** Barbury Castle, Wilts

FOCUS
Rail movements resulted in this race being run over 28yds further than advertised. Nick Scholfield described the ground as "soft, heavy in places and hard work." Two very useful juveniles dominated this small-field hurdle, which could be rated higher through the third.

3731 THAMES MATERIALS AMATEUR RIDERS' H'CAP CHASE (16 fncs) 2m 2f 175y
1:15 (1:15) (Class 3) (0-135,134) 5-Y-0+ **£9,358** (£2,902; £1,450; £726)

Form RPR

0156 **1** **Johnny Og**[35] 3148 7-10-1 **116** ....(b) MrHHunt(7) 133+
(Martin Keighley) *lw: trckd ldr: led 12th and sn scampered clr: 12 l up 2 out: tired bef last but nvr in any danger* **14/1**

63F2 **2** *6* **Cloudy Bob (IRE)**[16] 3499 9-10-2 **115** .... MrTGreatrex(5) 124
(Pat Murphy) *hld up: rdn 11th: outpcd after next: prog to take remote 2nd bef 2 out: steadily clsd on wnr but nvr any threat* **5/1**[3]

0125 **3** *¾* **Kings Cross (FR)**[16] 3499 6-9-13 **112** .... MrTommieMO'Brien(5) 120
(Tony Carroll) *hld up in last: prog 11th: outpcd next: tk remote 3rd bef 2 out: kpt on but nvr any ch* **16/1**

/F13 **4** *12* **Elenika (FR)**[24] 3365 8-10-5 **120** .... MissLMTurner(7) 118
(Venetia Williams) *in tch: rdn and outpcd fr 12th: no ch after* **9/1**

P320 **5** *1 ¾* **Fairy Rath (IRE)**[17] 3445 10-11-1 **128** .... MrJoshuaNewman(5) 123
(Nick Gifford) *chsd ldng pair: outpcd fr 12th: wknd bef 2 out* **8/1**

6442 **6** *8* **Mountain King**[35] 3148 7-11-5 **134** .... MrSeanHoulihan(7) 122
(Philip Hobbs) *nt a fluent: hld up in rr: rdn 11th: outpcd fr next: no real prog bef 2 out: wknd* **7/2**[2]

1122 **7** *nse* **Capilla (IRE)**[23] 3380 8-9-12 **113** ....(t) MrConorOrr(7) 100
(Evan Williams) *led: t.k.h fr 7th: hdd 12th and sn outpcd by wnr: lost 2nd bef 2 out: eased and qckly dropped to last* **10/1**

1-14 **F** **Brody Bleu (FR)**[225] 715 9-11-6 **131** .... MrMLegg(3)
(Robert Walford) *hld up in rr: fell 2nd* **7/1**

21 **P** **Bold Bachelor (IRE)**[22] 3419 7-10-1 **109** ....(p) MissGAndrews
(Dr Richard Newland) *trckd ldng pair: pushed along 11th: blnd bdly next: dropped to last and t.o whn j.v.slowly 4 out: p.u bef next* **5/2**[1]

4m 53.3s (6.90) **Going Correction** +0.375s/f (Yiel) **9** Ran SP% **113.7**
Speed ratings: **100,97,97,92,91 88,87,,**
CSF £82.28 CT £1139.08 TOTE £21.50: £4.10, £1.60, £4.20; EX 100.30 Trifecta £1700.60.
Owner T Hanlon M Boothright S Hanlon N Martin **Bred** R T Crellin **Trained** Condicote, Gloucs
■ A first winner over jumps for Hugo Hunt.

FOCUS
Rail movements resulted in this race being run over 41yds further than advertised. They got racing a fair way out in this amateur riders' handicap, with the winner receiving an enterprising ride. He produced a definite step up.

3732 OLBG.COM MARES' HURDLE (REGISTERED AS WARFIELD MARES' HURDLE RACE) (GRADE 2) (11 hdls) 2m 7f 118y
1:50 (1:50) (Class 1) 4-Y-0+
£28,475 (£10,685; £5,350; £2,665; £1,340; £670)

Form RPR

11-1 **1** **Vroum Vroum Mag (FR)**[32] 3209 7-11-3 149 .... RWalsh 151+
(W P Mullins, Ire) *str: racd wd: hld up: prog to trck ldrs 6th: led 2 out gng easily: pushed along to assert after last: v comf* **4/6**[1]

F4-5 **2** 3½ **Jennies Jewel (IRE)**[14] 3542 9-11-0 138 IanMcCarthy 137
(Jarlath P Fahey, Ire) *hld up in rr: prog fr 8th: chsd ldrs bef 2 out: sn hrd rdn: chsd wnr bef last: styd on but n.d* **33/1**

2421 **3** 6 **Cannon Fodder**[27] 3283 9-11-0 131 MarcGoldstein 131
(Sheena West) *chsd ldr: rdn fr 8th: chal and upsides 2 out: chsd wnr briefly after: one pce bef last* **40/1**

-104 **4** 1¾ **Dark Spirit (IRE)**[37] 3122 8-11-0 140 AdamWedge 129
(Evan Williams) *lw: hld up: rdn in 8th pl bef 3 out: kpt on fr 2 out to take 4th after last* **25/1**

-3F2 **5** 2 **The Govaness**[21] 3444 7-11-3 144 WillKennedy 131
(Dr Richard Newland) *taken down early: trckd ldrs: rdn to chal and upsides whn mstke 2 out: fdd after* **7/1[3]**

5125 **6** 6 **Rons Dream**[22] 3407 6-11-3 140 SeanBowen 125
(Peter Bowen) *in tch: rdn whn blnd 3 out: sn btn* **16/1**

-P12 **7** ½ **Desert Queen**[27] 3283 8-11-0 148 (t) NoelFehily 122
(Harry Fry) *led in s: led: nt fluent 6th and hit 8th: hdd & wknd 2 out* **13/2[2]**

2-33 **8** 8 **Fairytale Theatre (IRE)**[21] 3444 9-11-0 133 (t) RyanMahon 113
(Dan Skelton) *chsd ldrs: lost pl 6th: struggling fr 8th: sn bhd* **33/1**

21-4 **9** 15 **Aurore D'Estruval (FR)**[22] 3408 6-11-5 144 BarryGeraghty 103
(Rebecca Curtis) *in tch: prog to go prom after 5th tl wknd qckly 3 out: t.o* **15/2**

-10P **P** **Molly's A Diva**[33] 3197 9-11-0 141 (p) DavidBass
(Kim Bailey) *lw: chsd ldrs tl dropped to rr and nt fluent 6th: sn t.o: p.u bef 8th* **40/1**

6m 2.2s (6.20) **Going Correction** +0.675s/f (Soft) **10** Ran SP% **118.1**
Speed ratings (Par 115): **116,114,112,112,111 109,109,106,101,**
CSF £36.17 TOTE £1.50: £1.10, £5.10, £7.10; EX 27.40 Trifecta £364.10.
Owner Mrs S Ricci **Bred** Comte A Maggiar & Mlle A Maggiar **Trained** Muine Beag, Co Carlow

FOCUS
Rail movements resulted in this race being run over 45yds further than advertised. A good-quality mares' event that was won in pretty impressive fashion by favourite Vroum Vroum Mag. She can rate 155+ over hurdles.

3733 "40 YEARS OF KELTBRAY" HOLLOWAY'S H'CAP HURDLE (GRADE 3) (10 hdls) 2m 3f 58y
2:25 (2:25) (Class 1) 4-Y-0+
£28,475 (£10,685; £5,350; £2,665; £1,340; £670)

Form RPR

P-21 **1** **Rock The Kasbah (IRE)**[63] 2639 6-11-5 **144** RichardJohnson 152+
(Philip Hobbs) *racd on inner: chsd ldrs: mstke 7th: rdn and prog after 3 out: chsd ldr 2 out: clsd to ld last and sn 2 l ahd: drvn out to hold on nr fin* **7/1[1]**

-111 **2** ½ **Baron Alco (FR)**[28] 3232 5-10-9 **134** JamieMoore 142+
(Gary Moore) *racd freely: led: mstke 4th: mod pce tl 1/2-way: stretched on after 6th: sent for home 2 out: hdd last: rallied nr fin: jst hld* **10/1[3]**

3312 **3** 3 **Lil Rockerfeller (USA)**[22] 3408 5-11-12 **151** (p) TrevorWhelan 156
(Neil King) *prom: nt fluent 5th: tk cl 3rd 2 out: sn drvn: styd on same pce after and nvr quite able to chal* **10/1[3]**

-312 **4** 9 **Simply A Legend**[28] 3232 7-10-6 **134** TomBellamy[(3)] 129
(Alan King) *lw: hld up towards rr: prog and hit 6th: chsd ldrs and in tch 3 out: sn rdn: kpt on to win battle for 4th fr last* **14/1**

-311 **5** ¾ **Theo's Charm (IRE)**[20] 3450 6-10-7 **132** TomCannon 126
(Nick Gifford) *prom: rdn after 3 out: one pce u.p fr 2 out* **7/1[1]**

1-F **6** shd **Kilcrea Vale (IRE)**[64] 2614 6-11-8 **147** JeremiahMcGrath 142
(Nicky Henderson) *lw: hld up in rr: gd prog fr 6th: rdn and last of 8 w a ch on long run after 3 out: kpt on to take 4th briefly last: no ex* **10/1[3]**

1-F1 **7** hd **Zulu Oscar**[27] 3284 7-11-1 **140** (t) NoelFehily 134
(Harry Fry) *hld up in rr: lft bhd whn pce lifted fr 6th: prog fr next but v modest 9th after 3 out: kpt on but no ch to be involved* **12/1**

-520 **8** 9 **Unanimite (FR)**[35] 3151 5-10-6 **136** (p) DavidNoonan[(5)] 121
(David Pipe) *hld up in rr: pushed along 6th and lost tch fr next: nvr on terms after* **16/1**

5-FF **9** 1¼ **Value At Risk**[17] 3486 7-11-3 **142** IanPopham 126
(Dan Skelton) *lw: t.k.h: prom: chsd ldr fr 5th tl jst bef 2 out: wknd* **8/1[2]**

-102 **10** 1½ **Dubawi Island (FR)**[28] 3254 7-10-11 **136** LiamTreadwell 118
(Venetia Williams) *nvr bttr than midfield: shkn up and lost tch bef 7th: no ch after* **33/1**

14-6 **11** 8 **Sugar Baron (IRE)**[28] 3232 6-10-6 **131** NicodeBoinville 105
(Nicky Henderson) *chsd ldrs: rdn and lost tch fr 7th: sn no ch* **7/1[1]**

5414 **12** 1½ **Minstrels Gallery (IRE)**[21] 3449 7-10-1 **126** LeightonAspell 99
(Lucy Wadham) *a in rr: rdn and struggling 6th: no ch after next* **33/1**

-006 **13** 1¼ **Ebony Express**[21] 3449 7-9-12 **133** CharlieHammond[(10)] 105
(Dr Richard Newland) *mostly chsd ldr to 5th: styd prom and stl disputing 2nd 3 out: btn whn mstke 2 out: wknd* **20/1**

251 **14** 17 **Mr Fitzroy (IRE)**[14] 3529 6-9-11 **125** oh3 (t) JamesBanks[(3)] 79
(Jo Davis) *mstke 1st: drvn in midfield after 6th: wknd next: t.o* **25/1**

0-P1 **P** **Royal Guardsman (IRE)**[56] 2781 9-10-7 **132** BarryGeraghty
(Ali Stronge) *prom on outer tl wknd qckly bef 6th: wl bhd whn p.u bef next* **25/1**

11-3 **P** **Theinval (FR)**[88] 2122 6-11-7 **151** FreddieMitchell[(5)]
(Nicky Henderson) *hld up towards rr: prog fr 6th: jst in tch bef 3 out: sn wknd rapidly: t.o whn p.u bef 2 out* **25/1**

1-P6 **P** **Monsieur Gibraltar (FR)**[27] 3284 5-10-10 **135** (t) NickScholfield
(Paul Nicholls) *hld up in rr: pushed along after 6th: wl bhd after mstke next: t.o whn p.u bef last* **16/1**

4m 53.9s (9.20) **Going Correction** +0.675s/f (Soft) **17** Ran SP% **124.2**
Speed ratings (Par 113): **107,106,105,101,101 101,101,97,96,96 92,92,91,84,**
CSF £69.27 CT £711.30 TOTE £6.00: £2.10, £3.20, £2.20, £2.90; EX 86.30 Trifecta £1326.10.
Owner Mrs Diana L Whateley **Bred** Joe Rogers **Trained** Withycombe, Somerset

FOCUS
Due to rail movements this race was run over 37yds further than advertised. A really good handicap featuring any number of progressive, promising types, and the form looks solid. They didn't go much of a gallop early, though, and those racing prominently were favoured. The first two are very progressive on soft ground.

3734 SODEXO CLARENCE HOUSE CHASE (GRADE 1) (13 fncs) 2m 192y
3:00 (3:02) (Class 1) 5-Y-0+ **£71,187** (£26,712; £13,375; £6,662; £3,350)

Form RPR

1-1F **1** **Un De Sceaux (FR)**[27] 3293 8-11-7 168 RWalsh 172+
(W P Mullins, Ire) *mde all: stl gng easily bef 2 out: briefly pressed bef last and shkn up: pushed along and readily drew clr flat* **1/2[1]**

-512 **2** 5 **Sire De Grugy (FR)**[27] 3281 10-11-7 169 JamieMoore 166
(Gary Moore) *lw: chsd wnr: shkn up after 3 out: drvn to try to chal after 2 out: sn no imp and btn: jst hld on for 2nd* **11/4[2]**

113- **3** shd **Traffic Fluide (FR)**[287] 5272 6-11-7 154 JoshuaMoore 165
(Gary Moore) *lw: hld up in last: prog after 3 out to take 3rd 2 out: shkn up bef last: r.o flat and nrly snatched 2nd* **33/1**

-133 **4** 5 **Vibrato Valtat (FR)**[27] 3281 7-11-7 161 (t) NoelFehily 162
(Paul Nicholls) *trckd ldrs: slt mstke 7th: rdn after 3 out: no hdwy and btn 2 out: fdd* **12/1[3]**

-142 **5** 1¾ **Simply Ned (IRE)**[27] 3293 9-11-7 160 BrianHarding 158
(Nicky Richards) *chsd ldrs: rdn after 3 out: no hdwy and btn 2 out: fdd* **20/1**

4m 14.7s (0.10) **Going Correction** +0.375s/f (Yiel) **5** Ran SP% **108.7**
Speed ratings: **114,111,111,109,108**
CSF £2.30 TOTE £1.30: £1.10, £2.30; EX 2.50 Trifecta £12.70.
Owner E O'Connell **Bred** Haras De La Rousseliere Et Al **Trained** Muine Beag, Co Carlow

FOCUS
Due to rail movements this race was run over 41yds further than advertised. A fascinating clash that provided the favourite with his biggest task to date over fences and he ran out a ready winner. He's rated up 7lb on his previous best.

3735 BET365 H'CAP CHASE (17 fncs) 2m 5f 8y
3:35 (3:35) (Class 2) 5-Y-0+
£43,792 (£12,936; £6,468; £3,234; £1,617; £812)

Form RPR

FP-P **1** **Dare Me (IRE)**[73] 2436 12-11-1 **139** AlainCawley 150
(Venetia Williams) *chsd clr ldng pair fr 2nd: mstke 10th: grad clsd fr 12th: tk 2nd 3 out: clsd to chal 2 out: narrow ld last: drvn out* **25/1**

-651 **2** 2¼ **Royal Regatta (IRE)**[35] 3147 8-11-11 **149** (bt) RichardJohnson 158
(Philip Hobbs) *pressed ldr and clr of rest: led 12th: rdn after 3 out: pressed next: narrowly hdd last: no ex fnl 100yds* **7/2[1]**

-PP1 **3** 5 **Bennys Mist (IRE)**[49] 2902 10-11-7 **145** LiamTreadwell 148
(Venetia Williams) *led at gd pce and clr w one rival: hdd 12th: lost 2nd 3 out and btn after: kpt on gamely to hold 3rd* **10/1**

1-16 **4** 4½ **Salubrious (IRE)**[35] 3150 9-11-8 **146** NickScholfield 144
(Paul Nicholls) *hld up in rr: no imp on ldrs 12th: rdn and tried to cl bef 2 out: no hdwy after* **5/1[2]**

41-F **5** ½ **Minella Reception (IRE)**[24] 3365 10-10-1 **130** (t) JamieBargary[(5)] 128
(Nigel Twiston-Davies) *lw: hld up: mstke 12th and no imp on ldrs: tried to cl u.p bef 2 out: sn no hdwy* **12/1**

0200 **6** 13 **Aerlite Supreme (IRE)**[28] 3254 9-10-8 **132** (t) AdamWedge 118
(Evan Williams) *prom in chsng gp: disp 3rd pl 11th: no hdwy next: wknd 3 out* **14/1**

53F1 **P** **Regal Encore (IRE)**[40] 3084 8-11-6 **144** (t) BarryGeraghty
(Anthony Honeyball) *hld up: mstke 7th: blnd 10th and wknd: sn t.o: p.u bef 2 out* **6/1[3]**

-521 **R** **Bernardelli (IRE)**[35] 3162 8-10-8 **132** CraigNichol
(Nicky Richards) *lw: nt fluent and dropped to last after 5th: sn struggling: t.o whn rn out 10th* **8/1**

-136 **R** **Cold March (FR)**[42] 3030 6-11-7 **150** CharlieDeutsch[(5)]
(Venetia Williams) *hld up in rr: in tch whn rn out 10th* **7/1**

-0PP **P** **Tara Road**[77] 2335 8-10-0 **124** oh1 (t) SeanBowen
(Rebecca Curtis) *hld up: no prog bef 12th: sn btn: poor 7th whn p.u bef 3 out* **8/1**

5m 27.4s (1.40) **Going Correction** +0.375s/f (Yiel) **10** Ran SP% **115.2**
Speed ratings: **112,111,109,107,107 102,,,,**
CSF £113.11 CT £958.81 TOTE £20.90: £4.50, £1.70, £3.20; EX 130.40 Trifecta £2579.20.
Owner Shire Birds **Bred** Aaron Metcalfe **Trained** Kings Caple, H'fords

FOCUS
Due to rail movements this race was run over 49yds further than advertised. An open handicap run at a good gallop with two soon clear. It went to the complete outsider and proved a thorough test in the conditions. Arguably a small pb from the winner.

3736 EBF STALLIONS "NATIONAL HUNT" NOVICES' HURDLE (QUALIFIER) (10 hdls) 2m 5f 141y
4:10 (4:10) (Class 3) 4-7-Y-0 **£6,498** (£1,908; £954; £477)

Form RPR

-212 **1** **Duke Des Champs (IRE)**[36] 3137 6-11-8 135 RichardJohnson 142+
(Philip Hobbs) *trckd ldrs: cl 3rd fr 6th tl led bef 2 out: sn drew rt away: eased nr fin* **10/11[1]**

141 **2** 14 **Western Cape (IRE)**[36] 3133 5-11-7 130 KevinJones[(5)] 126
(Seamus Mullins) *lw: prom: trckd ldr 6th: shkn up to chal bef 2 out: sn lft bhd by wnr: kpt on* **8/1[3]**

00-P **3** 20 **Pawn Star (IRE)**[81] 2257 6-11-2 0 LeightonAspell 94
(Emma Lavelle) *hld up in last: sme prog 6th but nvr on terms w ldrs: pushed along and kpt on wl fr last to take 3rd nr fin: shaped w promise* **50/1**

4-42 **4** 3 **What A Moment (IRE)**[34] 3179 6-11-2 126 TomScudamore 91
(David Pipe) *lw: hld up in midfield: nt on terms w ldrs fr 6th: pushed along and kpt on steadily fr last to take 4th nr fin: shaped w promise* **8/1[3]**

2131 **5** ¾ **Masterplan (IRE)**[36] 3137 6-11-5 127 GrahamWatters[(3)] 98
(Charlie Longsdon) *led: mstke 6th: clr w 2 rivals after: hdd bef 2 out and wknd rapidly: lost pls nr fin* **10/1**

0-33 **6** 1¼ **Minstrel Royal**[36] 3133 6-11-2 0 DavidBass 89
(Nicky Henderson) *hld up: nt fluent 4th: chsd ldng trio after 6th but no imp: shkn up and fdd fr 2 out* **10/1**

1-22 **P** **King Kayf**[36] 3133 7-10-13 126 (t) JamesBanks[(3)]
(Noel Williams) *prom: chsd ldr 4th to 6th: wknd v rapidly: p.u bef next* **5/1[2]**

FP **P** **Swizzler (IRE)**[67] 2558 7-11-2 0 WillKennedy
(Ian Williams) *hld up in rr: lost tch 6th: wl bhd fr next: t.o whn p.u bef 2 out* **100/1**

P **P** **Yanmare (IRE)**[74] 2417 6-10-11 0 JamieBargary[(5)]
(Nigel Twiston-Davies) *pressed ldr to 4th but often pushed along: lost pl rapidly and mstke 5th: sn t.o: p.u after 6th* **66/1**

0-51 **P** **Expedite (IRE)**[28] 3221 5-11-1 0 TommyDowling[(7)]
(Charlie Mann) *in tch on outer to 5th: wknd after next: t.o whn p.u bef 2 out* **16/1**

5m 39.6s (13.60) **Going Correction** +0.675s/f (Soft) **10** Ran SP% **119.8**
Speed ratings: **102,96,89,88,88 87,,,,**
CSF £9.63 TOTE £1.70: £1.10, £2.20, £5.40; EX 8.50 Trifecta £415.60.
Owner Diana Whateley & Tim Syder **Bred** David & Leonard O'Brennan **Trained** Withycombe, Somerset
■ Richard Johnson's 3,000th winner over jumps in Britain and Ireland.

FOCUS
Due to rail movement this race was run over 45yds further than advertised. A decent novice but the ground had really cut up by this stage and it took a toll on the runners. Another step up from the winner.

T/Jkpt: Not won. JACKPOT PLACEPOT £119.40. Pool: £2783 - 23.30 winning units. T/Plt: £69.10 to a £1 stake. Pool: £143,030.78 - 1,509.46 winning tickets T/Qpdt: £6.70 to a £1 stake. Pool: £12,383.56 - 1,350.32 winning tickets **Jonathan Neesom**

3361 HAYDOCK (L-H)
Saturday, January 23

OFFICIAL GOING: Heavy (2.7)
Wind: light 1/2 behind Weather: fine but overcast and cold last 3

3737 NRC CHELTENHAM PREVIEW NIGHT HERE H'CAP HURDLE (12 hdls) 2m 6f 177y
1:00 (1:00) (Class 3) (0-140,137) 4-Y-0+ **£6,498** (£1,908; £954; £477)

Form RPR
-111 1 **Baywing (IRE)**[36] 3142 7-10-9 **125** .... RyanDay(5) 135+
(Nicky Richards) *in rr-div: blnd 7th: drvn 9th: hdwy to chse ldrs next: led between last 2: forged clr last 150yds* **11/4**[1]
01F4 2 5 **Goodbye Dancer (FR)**[36] 3137 5-11-5 **130** .... SamTwiston-Davies 132
(Nigel Twiston-Davies) *in rr: hdwy to chse ldrs 6th: chal 3 out: outpcd sn after 2 out: 4th last: styd on to take 2nd nr fin* **9/1**
1-03 3 ¾ **Shades Of Midnight**[64] 2624 6-10-10 **124** ....(t) CallumWhillans(3) 124
(Donald Whillans) *in rr: hdwy to chse ldrs 6th: drvn bef 3 out: kpt on same pce to take 2nd last 50yds* **7/2**[2]
-115 4 2 ¼ **Island Heights (IRE)**[41] 3058 7-11-5 **130** .... DerekFox 129
(Lucinda Russell) *trckd ldrs: led appr 3 out: hdd between last 2: wknd last 100yds* **10/1**
1-43 5 6 **Sa Suffit (FR)**[21] 3440 13-11-5 **135** ....(p) DiarmuidO'Regan(5) 127
(James Ewart) *chsd ldrs: led 6th: hdd appr 3 out: wknd between last 2* **25/1**
-265 6 11 **Shotavodka (IRE)**[25] 3352 10-11-4 **132** ....(b[1]) KieronEdgar(3) 116
(David Pipe) *prom: lost pl 2nd: sn pushed along: drvn whn hmpd bnd after 6th: brief effrt to chse ldrs 9th: sn reminders and lost pl* **12/1**
-PP6 7 6 **Barafundle (IRE)**[41] 3058 12-11-10 **135** ....(b) SeanQuinlan 110
(Jennie Candlish) *chsd ldrs: lost pl and pushed along 5th: bhd fr 9th* **14/1**
3PP- 8 3 ¼ **Corrin Wood (IRE)**[287] 5275 9-11-10 **135** .... AidanColeman 107
(Donald McCain) *led to 6th: chsd ldrs: lost pl appr 3 out: sn bhd* **20/1**
-4F4 9 36 **Horizontal Speed (IRE)**[22] 3407 8-11-12 **137** .... BrianHughes 73
(David Dennis) *chsd ldrs: lost pl bef 3 out: sn wl bhd: t.o 2 out* **11/2**[3]
0P-0 F **Bold Sir Brian (IRE)**[63] 2641 10-11-0 **125** ....(t) PeterBuchanan
(Lucinda Russell) *in rr: chsd ldrs 6th: 7th and outpcd whn fell 3 out* **16/1**

6m 10.5s (10.50) **Going Correction** +0.40s/f (Soft) **10 Ran SP% 112.2**
Speed ratings (Par 107): **97,95,95,94,92 88,86,85,72,**
CSF £26.77 CT £86.59 TOTE £3.00: £1.30, £2.40, £1.90; EX 23.70 Trifecta £159.20.
Owner David & Nicky Robinson **Bred** Hugh Suffern Bloodstock **Trained** Greystoke, Cumbria

FOCUS
Running rail moved out on bends after the winning post: Chase out 12yds; Hurdle out 14yds. Out of back straight: Chase out 6yds; Hurdle on innermost. They went a sound enough gallop in this fair handicap and got sorted out from the third-last. The race distance was 84 yards further than advertised and the riders afterwards reported the ground was hard work. Another step up from the progressive winner.

3738 START YOUR RACINGUK FREE TRIAL NOW NOVICES' CHASE (REGISTERED AS ALTCAR NOVICES' CHASE) (GRADE 2) (17 fncs) 2m 3f 203y
1:30 (1:30) (Class 1) 5-Y-0+ **£18,438** (£7,052; £3,638; £1,920)

Form RPR
2121 1 **Bristol De Mai (FR)**[26] 3317 5-11-0 146 .... DarylJacob 161+
(Nigel Twiston-Davies) *led to 1st: led after 2nd: hdd 11th: led next: drew clr fr 3 out: 18 l ahd last: eased fnl 100yds* **7/4**[2]
-42U 2 32 **Amore Alato**[36] 3136 7-11-0 0 .... HarrySkelton 137+
(Johnny Farrelly) *j.rt at times: led 1st: hdd after 2nd: jnd wnr 8th: led 11th: sn drvn: hdd next: wknd 3 out: heavily eased last 100yds* **8/1**[3]
-211 3 10 **Otago Trail (IRE)**[14] 3521 8-11-7 154 .... AidanColeman 120
(Venetia Williams) *chsd ldrs: hit 7th: lost pl and bhd 9th: remote 3rd sn after last* **11/8**[1]
25-3 4 3 **Zamdy Man**[40] 3084 7-11-0 0 .... BrianHughes 111
(Venetia Williams) *t.k.h in rr: hdwy to trck wnr 3rd: outpcd and modest 3rd 9th: j.rt 11th: bhd whn j.rt 2 out: j.rt and blnd last* **10/1**
1P-1 P **Boru's Brook (IRE)**[70] 2495 8-11-0 136 .... SamTwiston-Davies
(Jim Best) *chsd ldrs: hit 6th: sn reminders: lost pl and bhd whn p.u bef 8th* **12/1**

5m 23.6s (323.60)
WFA 5 from 7yo+ 4lb **5 Ran SP% 106.4**
CSF £13.22 TOTE £2.50: £1.40, £3.10; EX 10.50 Trifecta £21.60.
Owner Simon Munir & Isaac Souede **Bred** Jean-Yves Touzaint **Trained** Naunton, Gloucs

FOCUS
Race run over 72 yards further than advertised. This Grade 2 novice saw a very useful line up, but only two mattered off the home turn as the race fell apart with the mud flying. The winner is a top-class novice in heavy ground.

3739 SKY BET SUPREME TRIAL NOVICES' HURDLE (REGISTERED AS ROSSINGTON MAIN NOVICES' HURDLE) (GRADE 2) (9 hdls) 1m 7f 144y
2:05 (2:05) (Class 1) 4-Y-0+ **£17,085** (£6,411; £3,210; £1,599; £804; £402)

Form RPR
11 1 **Its'afreebee (IRE)**[24] 3366 6-11-8 134 .... HarrySkelton 144+
(Dan Skelton) *led: drvn clr 3 out: hit next: jnd last: hld on gamely run-in: all out* **7/2**[2]
211 2 ¾ **Le Prezien (FR)**[15] 3506 5-11-8 140 ....(t) SamTwiston-Davies 142
(Paul Nicholls) *trckd ldrs: chsd wnr appr 3 out: upsides last: sn rdn: no ex nr fin* **15/8**[1]
-111 3 3 ¼ **Vieux Lille (IRE)**[22] 3413 6-11-8 138 .... TomO'Brien 140
(Philip Hobbs) *t.k.h: trckd ldrs: pushed along 6th: kpt on one pce fr next* **4/1**[3]
121 4 12 **Bigmartre (FR)**[24] 3363 5-11-8 134 .... GavinSheehan 127
(Harry Whittington) *chsd ldrs: 2nd after 3rd: lost pl bef 2 out* **9/2**
4-12 5 4 **Baby Bach (IRE)**[35] 3156 6-11-4 129 .... BrianHughes 119
(S R B Crawford, Ire) *in rr but wl in tch: mstke 3rd: pushed along 5th: drvn next: lost pl and mstke 3 out: sn bhd* **8/1**
02 6 13 **Ballypoint (IRE)**[37] 3130 5-11-4 0 .... RyanHatch 109
(Nigel Twiston-Davies) *hld up in rr: hdwy to trck ldrs 3rd: effrt 6th: outpcd and lost pl next* **33/1**

4m 4.5s (0.30) **Going Correction** +0.40s/f (Soft) **6 Ran SP% 109.2**
Speed ratings (Par 115): **115,114,113,107,105 98**
CSF £10.22 TOTE £4.40: £2.10, £1.50; EX 10.40 Trifecta £24.30.
Owner Rebel Jumping **Bred** Edward Sexton **Trained** Alcester, Warwicks

FOCUS
Race run over 42 yards further than advertised. A traditionally strong Grade 2 novice hurdle, won by Peddlers Cross in 2010 before he took the Neptune, and Cinders And Ashes followed up his 2012 success in that season's Supreme Novice. There was a fair gallop on and it proved a real test in the home straight. Solid form but the winner is still 10lb shy of what will be needed at the festival.

3740 STANJAMES.COM CHAMPION HURDLE TRIAL (GRADE 2) (9 hdls) 1m 7f 144y
2:40 (2:40) (Class 1) 4-Y-0+ **£42,712** (£16,027; £8,025; £3,997; £2,010; £1,005)

Form RPR
5-12 1 **The New One (IRE)**[28] 3230 8-11-12 161 .... SamTwiston-Davies 162+
(Nigel Twiston-Davies) *trckd ldng pair: 2nd 5th: led 2 out: sn drvn: edgd rt run-in: kpt rt up to work* **8/13**[1]
3201 2 2 ¼ **Rayvin Black**[21] 3449 7-11-4 146 .... ThomasGarner 153+
(Oliver Sherwood) *led: clr whn hung rt and reminders bnd after 3rd: reluctant and drvn bef next: hdd 2 out: swtchd rt last 150yds: kpt on* **8/1**[3]
2343 3 4 ½ **Melodic Rendezvous**[21] 3449 10-11-4 150 .... MattGriffiths 147
(Jeremy Scott) *chsd ldrs: 3rd and pushed along after 6th: outpcd next: kpt on same pce* **13/2**[2]
13P/ 4 18 **Captain Conan (FR)**[682] 4753 9-11-4 145 .... AndrewTinkler 128
(Nicky Henderson) *mid-div: chsd ldrs 6th: sn drvn: lost pl appr next: remote 4th 2 out* **10/1**
33B5 5 ¾ **Strongpoint (IRE)**[22] 3426 12-11-4 138 .... PeterBuchanan 129
(S R B Crawford, Ire) *chsd ldr to 5th: lost pl next: sn bhd* **40/1**
2-04 6 8 **Fou Et Sage (FR)**[63] 2640 5-11-6 143 ....(t) HarrySkelton 131+
(Dan Skelton) *t.k.h in rr: hdwy to trck ldrs 6th: 4th and outpcd whn blnd and lost pl next: hung rt: bhd whn eased clsng stages* **10/1**

4m 5.1s (0.90) **Going Correction** +0.40s/f (Soft) **6 Ran SP% 107.0**
Speed ratings (Par 115): **113,111,109,100,100 96**
CSF £5.49 TOTE £1.40: £1.10, £2.30; EX 5.10 Trifecta £13.30.
Owner S Such & Cg Paletta **Bred** R Brown & Ballylinch Stud **Trained** Naunton, Gloucs
■ Stewards' Enquiry : Sam Twiston-Davies two-day ban: use of whip (7-8 Feb)

FOCUS
Race run over 42 yards further than advertised. A mixed bag contested this Grade 2 contest. There was no hanging about and the first pair dominated from two out. The New One is rated similar to his Kempton run, with another step up from Rayvin Black.

3741 PETER MARSH CHASE (A LIMITED H'CAP) (GRADE 2) (18 fncs) 3m 24y
3:15 (3:15) (Class 1) 5-Y-0+ **£28,475** (£10,685; £5,350; £2,665; £1,340; £670)

Form RPR
0P03 1 **Cloudy Too (IRE)**[35] 3157 10-10-4 **139** oh2 .... DannyCook 154+
(Sue Smith) *chsd ldrs: 2nd 10th: lft in ld 15th: drew clr fr 3 out: eased clsng stages* **6/1**
-022 2 15 **Virak (FR)**[35] 3150 7-11-3 **159** .... HarryCobden(7) 156
(Paul Nicholls) *chsd ldr 2nd: lft 2nd 15th: kpt on same pce fr 3 out* **9/2**[2]
-243 3 5 **Fingal Bay (IRE)**[35] 3150 10-10-7 **142** .... TomO'Brien 134
(Philip Hobbs) *mid-div: lft modest 4th 15th: 3rd next: j.lft and one pce last 3* **5/1**[3]
4215 4 7 **Seventh Sky (GER)**[22] 3406 9-11-5 **154** ....(tp) GavinSheehan 142
(Charlie Mann) *led to 2nd: chsd ldrs: lost pl 10th: rallied and lft modest 5th 15th: poor 4th and one pce whn hit 3 out* **14/1**
0-62 5 16 **Reve De Sivola (FR)**[35] 3149 11-10-4 **139** .... JamesReveley 123
(Nick Williams) *mid-div: hit 4th: hdwy to chse ldrs 6th: nt fluent 9th: lft 3rd 15th: wknd and hit next: sn bhd and eased* **3/1**[1]
2236 6 24 **Third Intention (IRE)**[49] 2915 9-11-3 **159** ....(t) PaulO'Brien(7) 104
(Colin Tizzard) *in rr: pushed along 9th: bhd fr 13th: t.o 4 out* **20/1**
P-3P P **Universal Soldier (IRE)**[209] 855 11-10-4 **139** oh16 ....(p) HarrySkelton
(Peter Bowen) *in rr: reminders after 1st: sn drvn: bhd 5th: t.o whn p.u bef next* **25/1**
3303 P **Presenting Junior (IRE)**[21] 3439 9-10-1 **139** oh5 .... HarryChalloner(3)
(Martin Todhunter) *in rr: drvn 9th: bhd next: t.o 13th: p.u bef 3 out* **33/1**
P4F- U **Gas Line Boy (IRE)**[287] 5275 10-10-5 **140** ....(v[1]) BrianHughes
(Jim Best) *led 2nd: travelling strly whn mstke and uns rdr 15th* **25/1**
-00U P **Splash Of Ginge**[56] 2783 8-10-8 **146** .... RyanHatch(3)
(Nigel Twiston-Davies) *in rr: blnd 7th: sn drvn: bhd 10th: t.o 13th: p.u bef 3 out* **12/1**
-2UF P **Algernon Pazham (IRE)**[7] 3624 7-10-7 **142** .... SamTwiston-Davies
(Nigel Twiston-Davies) *in rr: reminders 9th: sn bhd: t.o whn p.u bef next* **8/1**
-6P4 U **Man With Van (IRE)**[21] 3439 10-9-11 **139** oh10 ....(tp) AdamShort(7)
(S R B Crawford, Ire) *chsd ldrs: mstke and uns rdr 5th* **25/1**

6m 42.0s (11.50) **Going Correction** +0.85s/f (Soft) **12 Ran SP% 118.8**
Speed ratings: **114,109,107,105,99 91, , , , ,**
CSF £31.57 CT £147.64 TOTE £7.50: £2.50, £1.60, £2.00; EX 41.00 Trifecta £183.00.
Owner Formulated Polymer Products Ltd **Bred** E J O'Sullivan **Trained** High Eldwick, W Yorks
■ Stewards' Enquiry : Sam Twiston-Davies jockey said that the gelding was never travelling

FOCUS
Race run over 108 yards further than advertised. This well-established staying handicap proved another war of attrition, but the form looks fair rated around the placed horses. The winner is rated back to his best, and could be pitched 10lb+ higher.

3742 LYMM H'CAP CHASE (13 fncs) 2m 67y
3:50 (3:50) (Class 3) (0-130,120) 5-Y-0+ **£6,498** (£1,908; £954; £477)

Form RPR
-P63 1 **Ubaltique (FR)**[28] 3237 8-11-6 **114** ....(bt) AidanColeman 129+
(Donald McCain) *hld up in rr but wl in tch: hdwy to trck ldrs 4 out: upsides next: led 2 out: drvn clr run-in* **11/2**
-322 2 6 **Goohar (IRE)**[19] 3466 7-11-9 **117** ....(p) TomO'Brien 125
(Henry Daly) *chsd ldrs: pushed along 9th: kpt on to take 2nd last: no imp* **3/1**[1]
1422 3 2 ½ **Morning Royalty (IRE)**[24] 3362 9-11-12 **120** .... BrianHughes 126
(James Moffatt) *trckd ldrs: led 3 out: hdd next: one pce between last 2* **7/2**[2]
443U 4 ¾ **Crafty Roberto**[9] 3589 8-11-7 **115** .... KielanWoods 121
(Alex Hales) *led: hdd 3 out: 4th and one pce whn hit last* **6/1**
63-2 5 4 **Island Confusion (IRE)**[35] 3164 8-11-11 **119** .... PeterBuchanan 122
(Lucinda Russell) *chsd ldrs: hit 2nd: drvn 4 out: edgd lft and wknd 2 out* **4/1**[3]
1-31 6 18 **Little Jimmy**[23] 3380 9-10-12 **106** ....(tp) FelixDeGiles 97
(Tom Gretton) *hld up in rr but wl in tch: outpcd 8th: stmbld on landing 4 out: lost pl and j.lft 2 out: bhd whn eased run-in* **8/1**

4m 37.6s (18.60) **Going Correction** +0.85s/f (Soft) **6 Ran SP% 108.0**
Speed ratings: **87,84,82,82,80 71**
CSF £20.93 TOTE £6.80: £3.50, £2.10; EX 21.50 Trifecta £75.60.

Owner T G Leslie **Bred** Arnaud Chaille-Chaille **Trained** Cholmondeley, Cheshire

FOCUS

Race run over 54 yards further than advertised. A modest handicap, run at a routine gallop. The first five all had a chance in the home straight. The winner is rated to the best of his chase form.

3743 BROWN SHIPLEY "FIXED BRUSH" NOVICES' HURDLE (10 hdls) 2m 2f 191y

4:20 (4:20) (Class 4) 4-7-Y-O £3,898 (£1,144; £572; £286)

Form RPR

14 1 **Bun Doran (IRE)**[57] 2763 5-11-5 0 PaddyBrennan 140+
(Tom George) *mde all: wnt clr 3 out: eased clsng stages: unchal* 9/4[2]

-212 2 6 **Vintage Clouds (IRE)**[24] 3363 6-11-11 132 DannyCook 137
(Sue Smith) *trckd wnr: t.k.h: drvn 7th: one pce appr next* 13/8[1]

422 3 36 **Baratineur (FR)**[35] 3152 5-11-5 125 HarrySkelton 94
(Dan Skelton) *hld up in rr: hdwy 6th: lft 3rd 3 out: sn remote: mstke next: wknd run-in* 3/1[3]

3-04 4 ½ **High Hopper (IRE)**[42] 3037 6-11-5 0 BrianHughes 93
(Malcolm Jefferson) *chsd ldng pair: outpcd and lost pl whn lft poor 4th 3 out* 14/1

-420 5 5 **Sartorial Elegance**[50] 2879 5-10-12 0 (b) PaulO'Brien(7) 88
(Colin Tizzard) *chsd ldrs: drvn 5th: reminders 7th: sn lost pl and bhd* 40/1

0-04 6 9 **Pink Tara**[56] 2769 5-10-9 0 CallumWhillans(3) 72
(Venetia Williams) *rr-div: nt fluent 6th: sn bhd: blnd 3 out* 40/1

0F 7 9 **Craiganboy (IRE)**[21] 3436 7-10-12 0 AdamShort(7) 70
(S R B Crawford, Ire) *stdd s: hld up in rr: brief effrt 7th: sn lost pl and bhd* 200/1

221F F **Raise A Spark**[28] 3240 6-11-5 114 SamTwiston-Davies 106+
(Donald McCain) *in rr: hdwy 6th: drvn to chse ldrs next: 3rd and keeping on whn fell 3 out* 16/1

02 F **Robinshill (IRE)**[24] 3366 5-11-2 0 RyanHatch(3)
(Nigel Twiston-Davies) *mid-div: chsd ldrs 3rd: lost pl and in rr whn fell heavily next* 25/1

5m 10.0s (17.00) **Going Correction** +0.40s/f (Soft) 9 Ran SP% 115.6
Speed ratings: **80,77,62,62,60 56,52, ,**
CSF £6.42 TOTE £3.30: £1.40, £1.10, £2.00; EX 7.30 Trifecta £16.60.
Owner Crossed Fingers Partnership **Bred** Mrs Mary F Griffin **Trained** Slad, Gloucs

FOCUS

Race run over 42 yards further than advertised. Few got into this novice event as those held up were at a distinct disadvantage. The impressive winner looks a decent prospect and the second sets the level.

T/Plt: £22.40 to a £1 stake. Pool: £91,646.1 - 2,982.85 winning tickets T/Qpdt: £7.10 to a £1 stake. Pool: £6,579.54 - 685.58 winning tickets **Walter Glynn**

3580 TAUNTON (R-H)

Saturday, January 23

OFFICIAL GOING: Heavy (soft in places; 4.7)

Wind: strong half across Weather: cloudy with sunny periods Rails: Chase bends moved out 6 yards from innermost positions. Hurdle bends moved out 18 yards from innermost positions. Races 1, 2 and 5 adds 162 yards. Race 3 adds 72 yards. Races 4 and 6 adds 54 yards.

3744 EBF STALLIONS "NATIONAL HUNT" NOVICES' HURDLE (QUALIFIER) (10 hdls) 2m 3f 1y

1:35 (1:36) (Class 4) 4-7-Y-O £4,548 (£1,335; £667; £333)

Form RPR

33 1 **Mr Mix (FR)**[50] 2879 5-11-2 120 ConorO'Farrell 143+
(Paul Nicholls) *mid-div: smooth hdwy fr 6th: led on bit appr 2 out: drew clr between last 2: rn green and kpt up to work run-in: easily* 5/1[3]

4552 2 17 **Mountain Eagle (IRE)**[41] 3063 7-10-9 118 (t) LiamMcKenna(7) 127+
(Harry Fry) *hld up: hdwy fr 6th: wnt 3rd 3 out: chalng whn nt fluent 2 out: sn hld: mstke last: kpt on same pce* 8/1

31 3 3¾ **Miles To Milan (IRE)**[24] 3370 6-11-8 134 MichealNolan 127
(Philip Hobbs) *trckd ldr: led 7th: rdn and hdd appr 2 out: sn one pce* 7/4[1]

5311 4 ½ **Barney Dwan (IRE)**[28] 3239 6-11-9 130 ConorShoemark(3) 132
(Fergal O'Brien) *trckd ldrs: chalng whn hit 7th: rdn after 3 out: one pce fr next* 15/8[2]

0 5 31 **Behind Time (IRE)**[57] 2763 5-11-2 0 RichieMcLernon 88
(Harry Fry) *hld up: nt fluent 6th: wknd after 3 out: t.o* 16/1

2-60 6 20 **Miss Mobot**[48] 2929 6-10-4 0 CiaranGethings(5) 61
(Philip Hobbs) *trckd ldrs tl wknd after 3 out: t.o* 8/1

-305 7 69 **Lift The Lid (IRE)**[10] 3582 6-11-2 0 MarkQuinlan
(Neil Mulholland) *led tl 7th: wknd next: t.o* 66/1

U F **Red Red Rover (IRE)**[10] 3582 6-10-9 0 MrLDrowne(7)
(Nigel Hawke) *trcking ldr whn fell 5th* 80/1

00 U **Sahara Haze**[52] 2856 7-10-4 0 MrBMoorcroft(5)
(Phillip Dando) *in tch tl dropped to detached last after 5th: bhd whn wnt lft and uns rdr 3 out* 100/1

5m 10.2s (24.20) **Going Correction** +1.70s/f (Heav) 9 Ran SP% 119.6
Speed ratings: **117,109,108,108,95 86,57, ,**
CSF £45.16 TOTE £6.20: £2.00, £1.90, £1.10; EX 50.40 Trifecta £227.00.
Owner Ian Fogg & Potensis Bloodstock Ltd **Bred** Lucas Gombeau **Trained** Ditcheat, Somerset

FOCUS

Race run over 162 yards further than advertised. The going was heavy, soft in places. A fair contest which was won in good style by the unexposed winner.

3745 BATHWICK TYRES BATH NOVICES' HURDLE (9 hdls) 2m 104y

2:10 (2:10) (Class 4) 4-Y-O+ £4,548 (£1,335; £667; £333)

Form RPR

P561 1 **Allee Bleue (IRE)**[17] 3484 6-11-10 135 JamesBest 134+
(Philip Hobbs) *mde all: kpt on wl: pushed out* 5/2[2]

120 2 3¼ **Air Horse One**[61] 2683 5-10-11 0 LiamMcKenna(7) 122+
(Harry Fry) *mid-div: hdwy after 5th: wnt cl 3rd after 3 out: rdn next: edgd lft: styd on but nt pce to get on terms w wnr: snatched 2nd fnl stride* 2/1[1]

164 3 hd **Fountains Windfall**[68] 2549 6-11-4 0 BrendanPowell 121
(Anthony Honeyball) *mid-div: hdwy 3 out: sn trcking wnr: nodded 2 out: sn rdn: kpt on same pce: lost 2nd fnl stride* 7/1[3]

3U40 4 15 **Chief Brody**[40] 3077 5-11-4 0 DenisO'Regan 109
(Grace Harris) *trckd ldrs: rdn in cl enough 4th appr 2 out: fading whn nt fluent last* 14/1

5 1¾ **Clic Work (FR)**[247] 4-10-7 0 (t) ConorO'Farrell 94
(Paul Nicholls) *mid-div: rdn after 3 out: wknd bef next* 5/2[2]

05 6 shd **Zero Grand (IRE)**[10] 3581 5-11-4 0 RichieMcLernon 104
(Johnny Farrelly) *mid-div: rdn after 3 out: wknd bef next* 50/1

6-0 7 10 **Teachmetobougie**[49] 2909 6-11-4 0 RhysFlint 94
(Alexandra Dunn) *trckd ldrs: pressed wnr 6th tl rdn after 3 out: wknd bef next* 40/1

0-6 8 ½ **Driftwood Haze**[11] 3570 8-10-13 0 MrBMoorcroft(5) 94
(Phillip Dando) *rdn after 6th: nvr bttr than mid-div* 20/1

60 9 18 **Mondello (GER)**[24] 3370 5-11-4 0 MichealNolan 81
(Richard Woollacott) *a towards rr* 66/1

0 10 2½ **Beau Knight**[22] 3418 4-10-0 0 MikeyHamill(7) 62
(Alexandra Dunn) *a towards rr* 66/1

00-0 11 ¾ **The Big Mare**[66] 2564 7-10-11 0 RobertDunne 65
(Laura Young) *a towards rr* 100/1

1-40 12 3 **Nutcracker Prince**[17] 3483 5-11-4 0 (t) PeterCarberry 69
(Shaun Lycett) *struggling 6th: a towards rr* 25/1

60UP 13 32 **Acajou Des Bieffes (FR)**[38] 3117 6-11-4 0 AndrewThornton 37
(Anthony Honeyball) *trckd ldrs: rdn after 6th: wknd after 3 out: t.o* 50/1

6P/0 14 1½ **Primo Milano**[38] 3114 7-10-13 0 ConorRing(5) 36
(Evan Williams) *pressed wnr tl 5th: sn bhd: t.o* 66/1

4m 34.0s (26.00) **Going Correction** +1.70s/f (Heav)
WFA 4 from 5yo+ 11lb 14 Ran SP% 130.1
Speed ratings (Par 105): **103,101,101,93,92 92,87,87,78,77 76,75,59,58**
CSF £8.48 TOTE £3.20: £1.40, £1.40, £2.00; EX 10.00 Trifecta £35.50.
Owner Andrew L Cohen **Bred** Wood Hall Stud **Trained** Withycombe, Somerset

FOCUS

Race run over 162 yards further than advertised. An uncompetitive hurdle run at a sensible gallop.

3746 BATHWICK TYRES YEOVIL NOVICES' H'CAP CHASE (17 fncs) 2m 7f 3y

2:45 (2:45) (Class 4) (0-105,105) 5-Y-O+ £5,198 (£1,526; £763; £381)

Form RPR

05-3 1 **Badger Wood**[28] 3256 7-11-5 98 DenisO'Regan 108+
(Giles Smyly) *j.lft thrght: mde virtually all: drifted lft then rt run-in: styd on wl: rdn out* 13/2[2]

/0-0 2 ¾ **Residence And Spa (IRE)**[72] 2454 8-9-9 79 oh4 GaryDerwin(5) 88+
(Helen Rees) *towards rr: pushed along in last fr 9th: gd hdwy after 4 out: chal after 2 out: ev ch last: sltly hmpd whn swtchd rt run-in: styd on but a being hld* 25/1

2362 3 9 **Somerset Lias (IRE)**[22] 3412 8-11-10 103 (p) LiamHeard 102
(Bob Buckler) *in tch: chal after 4 out tl rdn bef next: styd on same pce fr 2 out* 4/1[1]

0-24 4 8 **Eaton Rock (IRE)**[23] 3387 7-11-10 103 (t) JamesDavies 94
(Tom Symonds) *mid-div: hdwy after 12th: cl 3rd after 4 out: rdn next: fdd after 2 out* 14/1

4124 5 14 **Bredon Hill Lad**[22] 3412 9-11-3 99 LucyGardner(3) 78
(Sue Gardner) *in tch: effrt after 4 out: wknd next* 15/2

0-0F 6 4 **Tikkapick (IRE)**[66] 2582 6-11-1 94 (p) BrendanPowell 75
(Colin Tizzard) *pressed wnr most of way tl rdn after 4 out: disp cl 3rd whn stmbld bdly 3 out: no ch after* 12/1

50S2 7 2½ **Johns Luck (IRE)**[22] 3419 7-11-5 98 (b) MarkQuinlan 70
(Neil Mulholland) *hld up: hdwy fr 12th: wnt 5th and rdn after 4 out: wknd bef next* 7/1[3]

5P-3 8 12 **Mount Prospex (IRE)**[22] 3410 7-11-1 94 AndrewThornton 53
(Tim Dennis) *mid-div: nt fluent 8th: hdwy 11th: wknd after 13th* 10/1

-054 P **Garde Fou (FR)**[23] 3383 10-11-12 105 (t) RobertDunne
(Paul Henderson) *struggling 10th: a towards rr: tailing off whn p.u bef 12th* 9/1

335P U **Rebel Benefit (IRE)**[26] 3310 8-10-12 98 (p) GarethMalone(7)
(David Dennis) *trcking ldrs whn blnd and uns rdr 11th* 13/2[2]

006 P **Some Finish (IRE)**[26] 3316 7-10-6 85 CharliePoste
(Robin Dickin) *hit 7th: a towards rr: t.o whn p.u after 4 out* 12/1

P-02 P **What Larks (IRE)**[44] 2988 8-11-9 102 DaveCrosse
(Hugo Froud) *hld up: pushed along after 10th: no imp and u.p whn blnd 4 out: sn p.u* 12/1

000 F **Trehan Cross**[37] 3124 7-10-0 79 oh3 JamesBest
(Jackie Du Plessis) *in tch whn fell 4th* 33/1

6m 34.4s (18.40) **Going Correction** +0.925s/f (Soft) 13 Ran SP% 126.6
Speed ratings: **105,104,101,98,93 92,91,87, , ,**
CSF £154.98 CT £751.33 TOTE £9.60: £4.20, £6.50, £2.30; EX 174.10 Trifecta £1414.70 Part won. Pool of £941.33 carried forward to Saturday.
Owner Anthony Ward-Thomas **Bred** G A Greaves **Trained** Wormington, Worcs

FOCUS

Race run over 72 yards further than advertised. They went a decent gallop for this open handicap.

3747 BATHWICK TYRES TAUNTON NOVICES' LIMITED H'CAP CHASE (12 fncs) 2m 12y

3:20 (3:22) (Class 3) (0-135,135) 5-Y-O+ £8,533 (£2,735; £1,519)

Form RPR

3-03 1 **Pressurize (IRE)**[43] 3006 10-10-3 116 oh1 RobertDunne 130+
(Venetia Williams) *chsd ldr: hit 7th: rdn to ld 2 out: awkward on landing last: styd on wl: rdn out* 14/1

0012 2 3 **Sandy Beach**[25] 3348 6-10-9 122 BrendanPowell 130
(Colin Tizzard) *chsd ldrs: rdn along fr 7th: clsd on front pair 3 out: chsd wnr after 2 out: styd on same pce fr last* 3/1[2]

1-3P 3 13 **Laser Hawk (IRE)**[7] 3620 9-10-12 130 ConorRing(5) 130+
(Evan Williams) *led: clr 8th tl 3 out: hdd next: sn no ex* 9/2

PP-1 P **Richardofdoccombe (IRE)**[261] 160 10-9-12 116 oh3 (t) AliceMills(5)
(Gail Haywood) *trckd ldr tl wknd 8th: tailing off whn p.u after next* 25/1

-51F U **Sea Wall (FR)**[25] 3351 8-10-9 122 [1] DenisO'Regan
(Chris Gordon) *hld up bhd ldrs: stmbld bdly 5th whn unseating rdr* 7/2[3]

60-6 P **Some Buckle (IRE)**[43] 3015 7-11-8 135 (t) ConorO'Farrell
(Paul Nicholls) *nvr travelling bhd ldrs: pushed along fr 5th: wnt 4th u.p 4 out: sn wknd: p.u bef next* 15/8[1]

4m 24.9s (10.90) **Going Correction** +0.925s/f (Soft) 6 Ran SP% 110.7
Speed ratings: **109,107,101, ,**
CSF £54.52 TOTE £10.20: £4.50, £1.50; EX 40.80 Trifecta £400.40.
Owner Mrs Sarah Williams **Bred** Dr J O'Keeffe **Trained** Kings Caple, H'fords

FOCUS

Race run over 54 yards further than advertised. Not a strong contest for the grade.

3748 BATHWICK TYRES SENIORS' H'CAP HURDLE (10 hdls) 2m 3f 1y

3:55 (3:55) (Class 2) 8-Y-O+
£11,573 (£3,418; £1,709; £854; £427; £214)

Form RPR

-230 1 **Tornado In Milan (IRE)**[10] 3584 10-10-4 127 ConorRing(5) 133
(Evan Williams) *mde all: styd on wl: drifted sltly lft run-in: drvn out* 11/1

32F5 **2** *1* **Here's Herbie**[10] 3584 8-9-12 **119** ow1..........................(t) LucyGardner(3) 124
(Sue Gardner) *mid-div on outer: hdwy 6th: trckd wnr after 3 out: rdn after next: swtchd rt run-in: styd on but a being hld by wnr towards fin* **9/2**[3]

-321 **3** *nk* **Spice Fair**[28] 3238 9-10-8 **126**.................................. RichieMcLernon 131
(Mark Usher) *hld up: hdwy after 7th: rdn to chse ldng pair appr 2 out: styd on to press for 2nd run-in: kpt on but hld towards fin* **8/1**

33F1 **4** *6* **Winning Spark (USA)**[10] 3584 9-10-3 **121**........................... JamesBest 121
(Jackie Du Plessis) *hld up: hdwy 6th: rdn to chse ldng pair appr 2 out: nvr threatened: no ex fr last* **3/1**[1]

-1U5 **5** *19* **Blue Buttons (IRE)**[42] 3034 8-10-12 **137**....................(t) LiamMcKenna(7) 120
(Harry Fry) *trckd ldrs: rdn after 3 out: wknd next* **4/1**[2]

0120 **6** *43* **Foxcub (IRE)**[22] 3407 8-11-12 **144**................................. JamesDavies 81
(Tom Symonds) *mid-div tl wknd 3 out: t.o* **10/1**

P2PP **P** **Handy Andy (IRE)**[38] 3109 10-10-2 **120**.......................... BrendanPowell
(Colin Tizzard) *trckd ldr tl after 6th: rdn after next: sn wknd: t.o whn p.u bef 2 out* **14/1**

3P16 **P** **Wilton Milan (IRE)**[35] 3157 8-10-10 **133**..................(tp) BridgetAndrews(5)
(Dan Skelton) *trckd ldrs: rdn after 7th: wknd after 3 out: t.o whn p.u next* **12/1**

0-20 **P** **Lightentertainment (IRE)**[49] 2912 8-10-11 **129**.............. DenisO'Regan
(Chris Gordon) *mid-div: hdwy 7th: wknd after 3 out: t.o whn p.u bef next* **8/1**

5m 12.9s (26.90) **Going Correction** +1.70s/f (Heav) **9** Ran SP% **117.2**
Speed ratings: **111,110,110,107,99 81,,,**
CSF £61.55 CT £426.19 TOTE £14.40: £3.50, £1.70, £2.60; EX 73.20 Trifecta £721.30.
Owner Mrs C Williams **Bred** Garry Hadden **Trained** Llancarfan, Vale Of Glamorgan
■ The first running of this veterans' hurdle race.

FOCUS
Race run over 162 yards further than advertised. A decent handicap run at a fair gallop.

3749 BATHWICK TYRES BRIDGWATER H'CAP CHASE (12 fncs) 2m 12y
4:30 (4:30) (Class 3) (0-140,140) 4-Y-0+ **£8,305** (£2,507; £1,291; £684)

Form RPR

0104 **1** **Wings Of Smoke (IRE)**[149] 1382 11-11-2 **135**..............(t) AlanJohns(5) 138+
(Tim Vaughan) *nvr really travelling in last: stdy prog fr 7th: chsd ldr appr 3 out: 5 l down whn lft in ld and hmpd 2 out: drvn out to assert run-in* **11/1**

2-42 **2** *6* **Ut Majeur Aulmes (FR)**[28] 3257 8-10-13 **127**..............(t) DenisO'Regan 122
(Victor Dartnall) *hld up: hdwy fr 7th: wnt 2nd after next tl rdn bef 3 out: looked hld in 3rd whn lft w ev ch after 2 out: no ex fr last* **13/8**[1]

1134 **3** *16* **Helium (FR)**[35] 3153 11-11-4 **132**..................................... RhysFlint 111
(Alexandra Dunn) *trckd eladers: rdn after 8th: wknd 4 out: lft modest 3rd 2 out* **7/1**

5-00 **4** *21* **Enjoy Responsibly (IRE)**[21] 3446 7-11-4 **139**......(t) HarrisonBeswick(7) 95
(Sam Thomas) *led tl after 5th: wknd after 8th: t.o* **14/1**

-233 **F** **Cash And Go (IRE)**[21] 3446 9-11-12 **140**........................ RobertDunne
(Venetia Williams) *prom: led after 5th: fell 7th* **9/4**[2]

140U **F** **Bullet Street (IRE)**[28] 3257 8-10-10 **129**........................ ConorRing(5) 132
(Evan Williams) *trckd ldrs: lft in ld 7th: pushed along appr 3 out: 5 l clr whn fell 2 out* **9/2**[3]

4m 30.1s (16.10) **Going Correction** +0.925s/f (Soft) **6** Ran SP% **114.5**
Speed ratings (Par 107): **96,93,85,74,**
CSF £31.47 TOTE £10.80: £3.70, £1.20; EX 46.30 Trifecta £136.40.
Owner Pearn's Pharmacies Ltd **Bred** Fred Mackey **Trained** Aberthin, Vale of Glamorgan

FOCUS
Race run over 54 yards further than advertised. The gallop was sound for this dramatic handicap.
T/Plt: £76.20 to a £1 stake. Pool: £60,447.37 - 578.73 winning tickets T/Qpdt: £33.50 to a £1 stake. Pool: £4,169.31 - 92.0 winning tickets **Tim Mitchell**

3750 - 3756a (Foreign Racing) - See Raceform Interactive

3213 FONTWELL (L-H)
Sunday, January 24

3757 Meeting Abandoned - waterlogged

3764 - (Foreign Racing) - See Raceform Interactive

3647 LEOPARDSTOWN (L-H)
Sunday, January 24

OFFICIAL GOING: Soft (soft to heavy in places)

3765a NATHANIEL LACY & PARTNERS SOLICITORS NOVICE HURDLE (GRADE 2) (10 hdls) 2m 4f
1:20 (1:21) 5-Y-0+

£18,529 (£5,867; £2,779; £926; £617; £308)

RPR

1 **A Toi Phil (FR)**[29] 3267 6-11-3 0.................................... BJCooper 152+
(W P Mullins, Ire) *settled bhd ldr in 2nd: clsr in 2nd 4 out and sn led narrowly: gng best between last 2 and extended advantage travelling wl bef last: rdn briefly run-in and styd on strly: easily* **6/4**[1]

2 *7* **Acapella Bourgeois (FR)**[26] 3355 6-11-3 129........................... JJBurke 143
(Ms Sandra Hughes, Ire) *led: over 2 l clr at 1/2-way: reduced advantage 4 out and sn hdd narrowly: dropped to cl 4th 2 out tl wnt 2nd gng wl appr st: sn rdn and no imp on wnr: kpt on same pce* **11/4**[3]

3 *11* **Woodland Opera (IRE)**[28] 3294 6-11-3 0........................... RobbiePower 132
(Mrs John Harrington, Ire) *chsd ldrs: slt mstke in 3rd at 4th: cl 4th after 3 out and impr into 3rd briefly next where nt fluent: sn rdn in 4th and no imp on wnr into st: mod 3rd whn nt fluent last: kpt on one pce* **5/2**[2]

4 *3 ¼* **Chain Gang**[27] 3319 5-11-0 0.. APHeskin 126
(Alan Fleming, Ire) *hld up bhd ldrs in 4th: clsr in 4th bef 4 out and impr into 2nd after next: rdn in cl 2nd after 2 out and sn no ex u.p in 3rd: dropped to 4th bef last* **8/1**

5 *22* **Cardinal Palace (IRE)**[22] 3449 6-11-3 132................................ RWalsh 107
(J A Nash, Ire) *w.w towards rr: dropped to rr bef 5th: slt mstke 4 out: pushed along and no imp after 3 out: one pce after: t.o* **18/1**

6 *38* **Chitu (IRE)**[58] 2754 6-11-3 0.. AELynch 69
(S R B Crawford, Ire) *hld up in rr: wnt 5th bef 5th: tk clsr order stl in 5th bef 2 out where slt mstke: sn rdn and no ex: wknd into st and sn eased: completely t.o* **25/1**

5m 5.9s (-0.50) **Going Correction** -0.25s/f (Good) **6** Ran SP% **115.5**
Speed ratings: **91,88,83,82,73 58**
CSF £6.42 TOTE £2.30: £1.50, £1.80; DF 6.20 Trifecta £11.80.
Owner Gigginstown House Stud **Bred** Docteur Vet Philippe Raphael Legault **Trained** Muine Beag, Co Carlow

FOCUS
Perhaps not the strongest renewal ever but the winner was pretty sensational. Improvement from the first two.

3766a FRANK WARD SOLICITORS ARKLE NOVICE CHASE (GRADE 1) (11 fncs) 2m 1f
1:55 (1:55) 5-Y-0+ **£39,705** (£12,573; £5,955)

RPR

1 **Douvan (FR)**[29] 3271 6-11-12 160.. RWalsh 161+
(W P Mullins, Ire) *mde all: stl travelling wl after 2 out: pushed out briefly fr last and qcknd clr: easily* **1/14**[1]

2 *15* **Velvet Maker (FR)**[29] 3271 7-11-12 143................................ APHeskin 144
(Alan Fleming, Ire) *w.w in rr of trio tl wnt 2nd bef 3rd: pckd on landing at 5th: nt fluent 7th: gng wl into st: slt mstke last and no imp on easy wnr run-in: kpt on one pce* **16/1**[3]

3 *13* **Domesday Book (USA)**[27] 3327 6-11-12 138............................ AELynch 133
(Henry De Bromhead, Ire) *settled bhd ldr in 2nd under dropped to rr of trio bef 3rd: nt fluent 4th: slt mstke 3 out and pushed along: no ex u.p after 2 out: one pce after* **14/1**[2]

4m 17.9s (-4.10) **Going Correction** +0.225s/f (Yiel) **3** Ran SP% **105.9**
Speed ratings: **118,110,104**
CSF £2.02 TOTE £1.10; DF 1.70 Trifecta £1.90.
Owner Mrs S Ricci **Bred** S A R L Haras De La Faisanderie **Trained** Muine Beag, Co Carlow

FOCUS
This might be deemed an uncompetitive renewal, but not so. The winner is potentially the best chaser since Arkle and Velvet Maker is rated 143. He helps with the standard.

3767a (Foreign Racing) - See Raceform Interactive

3768a BHP INSURANCES IRISH CHAMPION HURDLE (GRADE 1) (8 hdls) 2m
3:05 (3:05) 4-Y-0+ **£48,529** (£15,367; £7,279; £2,426; £1,617)

RPR

1 **Faugheen (IRE)**[29] 3230 8-11-10 174.................................... RWalsh 177+
(W P Mullins, Ire) *mde all: under 1 l clr at 1/2-way: narrow ld after 3 out: extended advantage fr 2 out stl travelling wl: wl clr whn mstke last: eased cl home: easily* **30/100**[1]

2 *15* **Arctic Fire (GER)**[27] 3322 7-11-10 166............................ DannyMullins 161
(W P Mullins, Ire) *chsd ldrs: mstke in 3rd 4 out: wnt 2nd after 2 out and sn no imp on easy wnr: kpt on one pce* **8/1**[3]

3 *13* **Nichols Canyon**[26] 3358 6-11-10 160.............................. PaulTownend 152+
(W P Mullins, Ire) *settled bhd ldr: cl 2nd after 3 out: slt mstke next and sn dropped to 3rd u.p: no imp and one pce after* **10/3**[2]

4 *24* **King Of The Picts (IRE)**[28] 3301 7-11-10 134.................... LPDempsey 123
(John Patrick Shanahan, Ire) *w.w: reminders in rr after 4th: no imp u.p and lost tch fr 4 out: kpt on one pce fr last into remote 4th cl home* **150/1**

5 *½* **Plinth (IRE)**[26] 3358 6-11-10 141..........................(bt) BarryGeraghty 123
(A P O'Brien, Ire) *in tch: niggled along briefly after 4th where wnt 4th: pushed along after 3 out and no imp on ldrs: one pce in remote 4th into st: dropped to remote 5th cl home* **100/1**

3m 54.0s (-13.50) **Going Correction** -0.25s/f (Good) **5** Ran SP% **112.8**
Speed ratings: **123,115,109,97,96**
CSF £3.99 TOTE £1.10: £1.02, £2.10; DF 4.00 Trifecta £4.10.
Owner Mrs S Ricci **Bred** Dr John Waldron **Trained** Muine Beag, Co Carlow

FOCUS
The best hurdle race run this season, and any doubts about Faugheen were truly demolished. Arctic Fire is rated in line with the best view of this season's form.

3769 - 3770a (Foreign Racing) - See Raceform Interactive

3523 KEMPTON (R-H)
Monday, January 25

OFFICIAL GOING: Soft (chs 5.2; hdl 4.7)
Wind: Moderate, across Weather: Fine becoming overcast, mild

3771 WATCH RACINGUK WITH FREE TRIAL NOW CONDITIONAL JOCKEYS' H'CAP HURDLE (12 hdls) 3m 121y
1:05 (1:05) (Class 5) (0-100,100) 4-Y-0+ **£2,599** (£763; £381; £190)

Form RPR

05PP **1** **Flugzeug**[42] 3087 8-11-0 **88**.................................. JeremiahMcGrath 95
(Seamus Mullins) *hld up in last trio: gd prog after 8th: tk 3rd after 3 out and rdn to chse ldr 2 out: clsd to chal last: drvn to ld flat* **33/1**

5305 **2** *½* **Shoofly Milly (IRE)**[24] 3410 7-11-2 **93**..................(b[1]) MattGriffiths(3) 101
(Jeremy Scott) *mde most: drew clr 3 out and stl gng strly: rdn whn mstke 2 out: hrd pressed last: hdd flat: kpt on* **9/1**[3]

3523 **3** *8* **Storm Alert**[36] 3174 9-11-0 **93**........................ WilliamFeatherstone(5) 94
(Sue Gardner) *racd wd in midfield: reminders 6th: prog next: chsd ldr bef 3 out but sn drvn: lost 2nd 2 out: fdd* **13/2**[2]

0211 **4** *3 ½* **Snowball (IRE)**[26] 3369 9-11-3 **94**................................ HarryCobden(3) 89
(David Arbuthnot) *hld up in rr: prog after 8th: in chsng gp bef 3 out but u.p: plugged on fr 2 out: n.d* **9/2**[1]

421 **5** *6* **Maccabees**[42] 3087 7-10-2 **79**................................ ThomasCheesman(3) 68
(Linda Jewell) *in tch in midfield: rdn after 6th and struggling next: prog 9th: urged along in chsng gp 3 out: one pce after* **12/1**

0033 **6** *½* **Jackfield**[63] 2693 6-9-13 **76** ow1................................... ConorSmith(3) 65
(Robin Dickin) *racd wd: pressed ldrs: rdn bef 3 out: wknd bef 2 out* **20/1**

-524 **7** *15* **Moon Trip**[42] 3087 7-11-10 **98**...................................(t) ConorShoemark 72
(Geoffrey Deacon) *wl in tch in midfield tl rdn and struggling 9th: wl off the pce in 10th 3 out* **14/1**

-0PP **8** *2 ¼* **Coolking**[27] 3349 9-11-6 **94**.. ThomasGarner 65
(Chris Gordon) *w ldr to 8th: stl jst in tch 3 out: sn wknd* **16/1**

5-5P **9** *½* **Strawberry Hill (IRE)**[64] 2658 10-11-12 **100**...............(tp) JackSherwood 71
(Caroline Keevil) *chsd ldrs: rdn and in tch bef 3 out: wknd bef 2 out* **25/1**

-343 **10** *½* **The Last Bridge**[26] 3369 9-10-7 **81**...........................(b[1]) TomBellamy 53
(Susan Johnson) *chsd ldrs: u.p fr 1/2-way: dropped to rr and wl bhd 9th* **10/1**

-45P **11** *3 ¼* **Burgundy Betty (IRE)**[39] 3128 6-11-1 **89**........................ DanielHiskett 56
(Ben Pauling) *kpt away fr others at s: early reminders and nvr gng wl in rr: bhd fr 8th* **20/1**

P00P **12** *4 ½* **Follow The Tracks (IRE)**[36] 3178 8-11-2 **95**.......... MrShaneQuinlan(5) 58
(Brian Barr) *trckd ldrs: lost pl bef 1/2-way: lost tch w ldrs fr 9th: wl bhd 3 out* **12/1**

5004 **13** *9* **Whispering Speed (IRE)**[39] 3128 6-10-10 **84**............(b[1]) DavidNoonan 38
(Lucy Wadham) *w ldrs: stl cl up bef 3 out but rdn: wknd qckly bef 2 out* **12/1**

P50 **14** *8* **Tisfreetdream (IRE)**[53] 2858 15-10-1 **80**..................(tp) ArchieBellamy(5) 26
(Peter Pritchard) *w ldrs tl wknd qckly u.p after 8th: sn wl in rr* **25/1**

066U **15** *7* **Toast And Jam (IRE)**[60] 2735 7-10-4 **78**.....................(t) CharlieDeutsch 17
(Claire Dyson) *hld up in rr: nt fluent 3rd: n.m.r bnd after 6th: pushed along and no prog after 8th: sn bhd* **33/1**

05/P **P** **Subtle Approach (IRE)**[26] 3369 11-9-9 **74** oh2........ HarrisonBeswick(5)
(Emma Baker) *a in rr: mstke 4th: wknd 7th: wl t.o whn p.u after 3 out* **66/1**

P524 **P** **Ride On Time (IRE)**[67] 2596 6-11-9 **100**............... MauriceLinehan(3)
(Ben Pauling) *prom to 1/2-way: wknd 7th: bhd whn blnd 9th: t.o whn p.u bef 2 out* **10/1**

-000 **P** **Guiting Power**[30] 3221 5-11-3 **94**.................................... RyanHatch(3)
(Nigel Twiston-Davies) *a towards rr: shkn up after 6th: toiling in rr 9th: t.o whn p.u bef 2 out* **20/1**

6m 35.8s (15.80) **Going Correction** +0.70s/f (Soft) **18** Ran SP% **124.7**
Speed ratings (Par 103): **102,101,99,98,96 96,91,90,90,90 89,87,84,82,80 , ,**
CSF £287.48 CT £2207.17 TOTE £33.70: £4.40, £2.30, £2.10, £1.50; EX 480.80 Trifecta £2959.10 Part won..
Owner New Forest Racing Partnership **Bred** Mrs J N Humphreys **Trained** Wilsford-Cum-Lake, Wilts

FOCUS
All starts have been moved at this track following remeasuring, so there will be no speed figures until there is sufficient data to calculate updated median times. Both courses out from their innermost configurations and as a result this race was run over 127yds further than advertised. No hanging around and most of these were on the stretch from a long way out in what was a moderate handicap hurdle. The first three have been rated pretty much to their marks, with the fourth below the level of recent win.

3772 BELLSHILL WINS ALL #THEFINALFURLONG NOVICES' HURDLE (DIV I) (8 hdls) 2m
1:35 (1:35) (Class 4) 4-Y-O+ **£3,249** (£954; £477; £238)

Form RPR

3-21 **1** **Wait For Me (FR)**[40] 3114 6-11-11 139.................. RichardJohnson 135+
(Philip Hobbs) *mstkes: trckd ldrs: clsd to ld after 5th: blnd 2 out and sn rdn: mstke last: drvn out* **1/5**[1]

2 *2* **Querry Horse (FR)**[134] 4-10-9 0.............................. JackSherwood(5) 119
(Oliver Sherwood) *led tl after 5th: dropped to 3rd 3 out but chsd wnr bef 2 out: drvn and lft w a ch last: kpt on but hld fnl 100yds* **8/1**[3]

3 *20* **Hell's Kitchen** 5-11-4 0.. BarryGeraghty 108+
(Harry Fry) *hld up in tch: prog 5th: chsd wnr 3 out whn gng strly but running green: lost 2nd bef 2 out and wknd: shaped w promise* **6/1**[2]

UUF0 **4** *8* **Seeanythingyoulike (IRE)**[13] 3568 5-11-1 0.............. MattGriffiths(3) 95
(Jeremy Scott) *hld up and detached in last tl 5th: sme prog into 7th whn wd bnd bef 2 out: nudged along after: racd shade awkwardly but kpt on steadily to snatch 4th last strides: possible improver* **100/1**

4-U0 **5** *nk* **Mr Kit Cat**[59] 2747 6-11-4 0.. AdamWedge 96
(Evan Williams) *trckd ldrs: outpcd fr 3 out: pushed along and wl hld whn blnd 2 out: lost 4th nr fin* **16/1**

/05- **6** *6* **Shareni (IRE)**[291] 2882 7-10-11 0.............................. WilliamFeatherstone(7) 89
(Zoe Davison) *towards rr: lost tch w ldrs bef 5th: nvr on terms after* **100/1**

5 **7** *3/4* **Bol D'Air (FR)**[79] 2351 5-11-4 0.............................. SamTwiston-Davies 88
(Paul Nicholls) *trckd ldrs: shkn up and outpcd 3 out: steadily fdd* **8/1**[3]

5- **8** *1/2* **Followmybuttons (IRE)**[408] 3086 6-11-4 0...................... TomCannon 88
(David Arbuthnot) *chsd ldrs: shkn up and struggling sn after 5th: no ch fr 3 out* **25/1**

0 **9** *1 1/4* **Guantoshol (IRE)**[19] 3484 5-11-4 0.............................. AidanColeman 87
(Venetia Williams) *taken steadily towards rr: rchd 6th pl after 5th but nt on terms: no prog after: fdd fr 2 out: nt totally disgracd* **25/1**

6 **P** **Bobby Benton (IRE)**[24] 3418 5-11-4 0............................ JamieMoore
(Jim Best) *t.k.h: w ldr to 4th: wknd rapidly and t.o in last pl after next: p.u bef 2 out* **33/1**

4m 7.4s (9.40) **Going Correction** +0.70s/f (Soft)
WFA 4 from 5yo+ 11lb **10** Ran SP% **138.3**
Speed ratings (Par 105): **104,103,93,89,88 85,85,85,84,**
CSF £4.48 TOTE £1.30: £1.02, £1.30, £2.20; EX 4.10 Trifecta £12.20.
Owner Andrew L Cohen **Bred** Haras D'Etreham **Trained** Withycombe, Somerset

FOCUS
Due to rail movements this race was run over 65yds further than advertised. Not a bad little novice hurdle, the front pair coming clear, but it proved mighty hard work for the red-hot favourite. They went a good pace from the off and the time was over 7secs faster than division two. There's a case for rating this a few pound higher through the winner.

3773 BELLSHILL WINS ALL #THEFINALFURLONG NOVICES' HURDLE (DIV II) (8 hdls) 2m
2:10 (2:10) (Class 4) 4-Y-O+ **£3,249** (£954; £477; £238)

Form RPR

16-4 **1** **Legend Lady**[89] 2136 5-10-11 0.................................... LeightonAspell 112+
(Oliver Sherwood) *trckd ldrs: led 4th and injected sme pce: mde rest: shkn up after 2 out: rdn and styd on wl flat: readily* **5/2**[2]

2F2 **2** *1* **Authorized Too**[25] 3375 5-11-4 120.......................... WayneHutchinson 118+
(Noel Williams) *led at modest pce to 4th: chsd wnr after: rdn 2 out: chal and nt fluent last: styd on but a hld* **1/1**[1]

0-6 **3** *9* **Centurius**[86] 2183 6-11-4 0.. AidanColeman 112+
(Venetia Williams) *t.k.h: trckd ldng pair: pushed along fr 2 out: hld whn mstke last: kpt on* **8/1**[3]

6-00 **4** *4* **Scooby (IRE)**[17] 3508 5-11-4 0.................................. KielanWoods 105
(Graeme McPherson) *t.k.h: hld up towards rr: pushed along bef 2 out: sme hdwy into 4th bef last: nt disgracd* **33/1**

4 **5** *2 1/4* **Burning Desire (IRE)**[27] 2723 5-11-4 0........................ BrendanPowell 103
(Richard Hughes) *chsd ldrs: lost pl after 4th: rdn after 3 out: nvr on terms after: plugged on* **12/1**

0 **6** *1 1/4* **Gone Viral (IRE)**[25] 3375 5-11-4 0..............................(t) TrevorWhelan 102
(George Baker) *in tch: shkn up on long run bef 2 out: no imp on ldrs after* **20/1**

160 **7** *3* **Grandmaster George (IRE)**[27] 3353 7-11-4 0............ JeremiahMcGrath 99
(Seamus Mullins) *trckd ldr to 4th: shkn up after 3 out: steadily wknd fr 2 out* **10/1**

0 **8** *30* **Tactical Manoeuvre (IRE)**[12] 3582 5-11-4 0.................. AdamWedge 69
(Alexandra Dunn) *hld up and a in last pair: no prog after 3 out and nvr involved: heavily eased fr 2 out: t.o* **66/1**

9 *13* **Ann Maries Reject (IRE)**[92] 7-10-8 0.......................... ThomasGarner(3) 49
(Brian Barr) *tk fierce hold early: hld up in last: lost tch 3 out: t.o* **100/1**

4m 14.7s (16.70) **Going Correction** +0.70s/f (Soft) **9** Ran SP% **116.7**
Speed ratings (Par 105): **86,85,81,79,77 77,75,60,54**
CSF £5.50 TOTE £3.50: £1.50, £1.10, £2.20; EX 6.70 Trifecta £24.40.
Owner Legend Lady Partnership **Bred** Simon Dutfield **Trained** Upper Lambourn, Berks

FOCUS
Due to rail movements this race was run over 65yds further than advertised. Dominated by the market leaders, this looked the lesser of the two divisions and was run in a time over 7secs slower than the first leg. The winner is rated in line with her bumper mark, rated through the second and fifth, with steps up from the third and fourth, but the form is suspect.

3774 RACINGUK.COM/ANYWHERE NOVICES' CHASE (18 fncs) 3m
2:40 (2:40) (Class 4) 5-Y-O+ **£4,659** (£1,446; £779)

Form RPR

12-1 **1** **Local Show (IRE)**[40] 3113 8-11-6 138.......................... NicodeBoinville 152+
(Ben Pauling) *j.w: mde all: 3 l clr after 4 out: rdn after next: hrd pressed fr last: hld on wl* **11/4**[2]

1-12 **2** *hd* **Onenightinvienna (IRE)**[45] 3013 7-11-6 151.................. TomO'Brien 153+
(Philip Hobbs) *j. quite big early: trckd wnr: shkn up and 3 l bhd after 4 out: rdn and grad clsd fr 2 out: str chal after last: jst hld* **10/11**[1]

1-56 **3** *98* **Closing Ceremony (IRE)**[65] 2641 7-11-0 145................ DarylJacob
(Emma Lavelle) *nt that fluent: a 3rd: rdn and lost tch after 11th: wl t.o whn clambered over 4 out* **9/2**[3]

2-1U **U** **Padge (IRE)**[44] 3029 7-11-6 143.................................... AdamWedge
(Evan Williams) *j. awkwardly and uns rdr 1st* **8/1**

6m 15.0s (6.00) **Going Correction** +0.65s/f (Soft) **4** Ran SP% **108.3**
Speed ratings: **116,115,83,**
CSF £5.94 TOTE £3.90; EX 6.50 Trifecta £10.10.
Owner Nicholas Piper & Claire E Piper **Bred** J J Harty **Trained** Bourton-On-The-Water, Gloucs

FOCUS
Due to rail movements this race was run over 81yds further than advertised. A small field, but an interesting race none the less, with two really useful staying novice chasers putting on a fine show of jumping. There's a case for rating this 4lb higher through the second.

3775 RACINGUK.COM/FREETRIAL NOVICES' HURDLE (10 hdls) 2m 5f
3:10 (3:11) (Class 4) 5-Y-O+ **£3,249** (£954; £477; £238)

Form RPR

4/14 **1** **A Hare Breath (IRE)**[45] 3015 8-11-5 134.................... NicodeBoinville 138+
(Ben Pauling) *trckd ldrs: led sn after 5th: drew clr fr next: in n.d after: pckd 2 out: nrly 15 l clr last: eased: dismntd after fin* **4/9**[1]

6-43 **2** *10* **Midnight Cowboy**[50] 2928 5-10-12 0.......................... WayneHutchinson 115+
(Alan King) *trckd ldrs: chsd clr wnr fr 3 out: no ch whn nt fluent 2 out: kpt on steadily* **9/2**[2]

3 *16* **Oneida Tribe (IRE)**[295] 7-10-12 0................................ AidanColeman 98
(Venetia Williams) *trckd ldrs: outpcd along w rest fr 7th: rdn in chsng gp after 3 out: no ch but kpt on to win battle for 3rd nr fin* **20/1**

4 *hd* **Noble Ned**[302] 7-10-5 0.. LiamMcKenna(7) 99
(Harry Fry) *hld up wl in rr: stdy prog fr 7th: jnd chsng gp 3 out: chsd ldng pair bef 2 out: nt fluent last: lost 3rd nr fin: shaped w sme promise* **14/1**

5 *15* **Meme's Horse (IRE)**[295] 5172 6-10-12 0..........................(t) NoelFehily 86
(Harry Fry) *nt a fluent: trckd ldrs: sltly impeded 5th: chsd clr wnr fr 7th tl 3 out: wknd bef 2 out: nt disgracd* **9/1**[3]

5 **6** *18* **Dylanseoghan (IRE)**[16] 3522 7-10-5 0.............. WilliamFeatherstone(7) 65
(Zoe Davison) *towards rr: lost tch w chsng gp 7th: poor 6th after: t.o* **100/1**

7 *2 1/4* **Restless Rebel**[631] 7-10-12 0.. DavidBass 63
(Polly Gundry) *hld up in rr: lost tch after 6th: t.o in last pair fr next* **66/1**

8 *29* **Day Of Roses (IRE)**[261] 7-10-12 0.............................. NickScholfield 34
(Jeremy Scott) *led to 4th: lft in ld briefly next: wknd rapidly 7th: t.o* **66/1**

3 **P** **That's Gonna Sting (IRE)**[194] 1003 5-10-9 0.............. MattGriffiths(3)
(Jeremy Scott) *nt a fluent: a in last pair: t.o 7th: p.u bef 2 out* **50/1**

-562 **F** **Fin D'Espere (IRE)**[42] 3085 5-10-12 0........................(t) GavinSheehan
(Suzy Smith) *pressed ldr: led 4th tl fell heavily next* **25/1**

5m 29.6s (8.60) **Going Correction** +0.70s/f (Soft) **10** Ran SP% **118.6**
Speed ratings: **111,107,101,101,95 88,87,76, ,**
CSF £2.70 TOTE £1.20: £1.02, £1.80, £3.40; EX 3.30 Trifecta £21.50.
Owner Mrs S N J Embiricos **Bred** Martin Byrne **Trained** Bourton-On-The-Water, Gloucs
■ Atirelarigo was withdrawn. Price at time of withdrawal 14/1. Rule 4 applies to all bets - deduction 5p in the pound.

FOCUS
Due to rail movements this race was run over 92yds further than advertised. No great depth to this and the winner took the race by the scruff of the neck some way out. The easy winner stood out and rates a decent sort although a stone+ off what will be required to win a festival novice. The second helps set the level.

3776 INTERACTIVE H'CAP CHASE (16 fncs) 2m 4f 110y
3:45 (3:45) (Class 2) (0-145,142) 5-Y-O+
£11,573 (£3,418; £1,709; £854; £427; £214)

Form RPR

-01P **1** **Roc D'Apsis (FR)**[59] 2761 7-11-1 131..........................(p) PaddyBrennan 142+
(Tom George) *in tch in midfield: prog to chse ldr 11th: rdn 3 out: led bef last: drvn and styd on wl* **14/1**

4-42 **2** *2* **Galway Jack (IRE)**[16] 3524 11-11-4 134........................ AndrewThornton 140
(Caroline Bailey) *j.w: led: rdn 3 out: hrd pressed next: hdd and one pce bef last* **15/2**

0-24 **3** *2 3/4* **Barrakilla (IRE)**[23] 3446 9-11-6 136............................ AdamWedge 141+
(Evan Williams) *prom: disp 2nd pl after 11th: shkn up in cl 3rd whn mstke 3 out: kpt on same pce after* **9/2**[3]

0P1P **4** *3* **Gallery Exhibition (IRE)**[40] 3109 9-11-8 138....................(t) DavidBass 138
(Kim Bailey) *hld up in rr: prog after 9th: jnd ldrs 4 out: sn rdn: one pce fr 3 out* **14/1**

024U **5** *6* **Ericht (IRE)**[58] 2780 10-10-13 129................................ NicodeBoinville 128
(Nicky Henderson) *blnd 2nd and dropped to last: renewed effrt fr 11th: rdn and in tch after 4 out: wknd 2 out* **6/1**

-565 **6** *10* **For Two (FR)**[40] 3106 7-10-2 118..................................(t) MarcGoldstein 104
(Chris Gordon) *hld up in rr: mstke 6th: nt fluent 8th: stl in tch 4 out: pushed along and wknd sn after* **14/1**

00-P **7** *6* **Stellar Notion (IRE)**[58] 2784 8-11-5 135..............(t) SamTwiston-Davies 115
(Paul Nicholls) *nt a fluent: trckd ldrs on outer: shkn up 4 out: sn wknd: b.b.v* **7/2**[1]

11-5 **P** **Opening Batsman (IRE)**[29] 3282 10-11-12 142................(bt) NoelFehily
(Harry Fry) *racd wd: hld up: nt fluent 8th and 9th and sn bhd: t.o whn p.u bef 11th* **4/1**[2]

22PP **P** **Atlantic Roller (IRE)**[40] 3113 9-10-5 121......................(tp) TomCannon
(Chris Gordon) *chsd ldr to 11th: wknd rapidly and sn t.o: p.u bef 3 out* **20/1**

5m 20.1s (8.10) **Going Correction** +0.65s/f (Soft) **9** Ran SP% **111.2**
Speed ratings: **110,109,108,107,104 100,98, ,**
CSF £107.55 CT £537.42 TOTE £12.10: £2.90, £2.10, £1.80; EX 105.40 Trifecta £629.30.
Owner David Rea & Miss Diane Fudge **Bred** N Colliere, C Verry et al **Trained** Slad, Gloucs

FOCUS
Due to rail movements this race was run over 65yds further than advertised. Fair chasing form. A step up from the winner, with the second to fourth helping to set the level.

3777 RACING UK 3 DEVICES 1 PRICE H'CAP HURDLE (8 hdls) 2m
4:20 (4:20) (Class 4) (0-120,119) 4-Y-0+ **£3,573** (£1,049; £524; £262)

Form RPR
213- **1** **Debdebdeb**[295] [5161] 6-11-8 **115**.. HarrySkelton 130+
(Dan Skelton) *j.w: trckd ldr: led 4th: mde rest: shkn up whn pressed bef last where anther gd jump: styd on wl* **2/1**[1]
041 **2** *1 3/4* **Harley Rebel**[30] [3213] 4-10-13 **117**.. NoelFehily 119+
(Neil Mulholland) *racd wd: hld up in midfield: prog bef 3 out: chsd wnr bef 2 out: rdn to cl and ch bef last: styd on but no imp flat* **12/1**
2340 **3** *12* **While You Wait (IRE)**[72] [2490] 7-11-3 **113**........................ LucyGardner(3) 112+
(Sue Gardner) *hld up in rr: sme prog 3 out but stl only 8th bef next: urged along and styd on wl after: tk 3rd last strides: no ch to threaten* **16/1**
-614 **4** *1* **Canadian Diamond (IRE)**[29] [3284] 9-11-3 **117**............... MikeyHamill(7) 116
(Richard Rowe) *trckd ldrs: wnt 2nd briefly on long run bef 2 out: sn btn: fdd and lost 3rd last strides* **8/1**
5112 **5** *3 3/4* **Hollywood All Star (IRE)**[16] [3529] 7-11-1 **115**........... ArchieBellamy(7) 109
(Graeme McPherson) *cl up: on terms 3 out: rdn and fdd fr 2 out* **13/2**[2]
345- **6** *2 3/4* **Albahar (FR)**[12] [5043] 5-11-3 **110**.. TomCannon 103
(Chris Gordon) *prom: chsd wnr 3 out tl bef next: steadily fdd* **20/1**
3-05 **7** *13* **Bountiful Sin**[44] [3047] 5-11-3 **110**.................................(p) LeightonAspell 90
(Oliver Sherwood) *chsd ldrs: rdn after 3 out: wknd bef 2 out* **50/1**
24- **8** *2 3/4* **Perfect Summer (IRE)**[55] [5090] 6-10-13 **106**...................(p) WillKennedy 82
(Ian Williams) *t.k.h: trckd ldrs tl wknd on long run after 3 out* **8/1**
4P00 **9** *3/4* **Full Blast (FR)**[19] [3487] 5-11-0 **107**..............................(t) MarcGoldstein 82
(Chris Gordon) *hld up wl in rr: shkn up 3 out: modest prog but nvr a factor* **40/1**
U-02 **10** *5* **Right Step**[48] [2956] 9-10-8 **108**.....................................(t) PaddyBradley(7) 78
(Pat Phelan) *led to 4th: chsd wnr to 3 out: drvn and wknd bef 2 out: virtually p.u after last* **8/1**
324- **11** *14* **Gaelic Myth**[395] [3265] 6-11-12 **119**.. DavidBass 75
(Kim Bailey) *hld up towards rr: pushed along after 3 out: no prog bef next: eased* **7/1**[3]
4F0 **12** *6* **Antiphony (IRE)**[19] [3483] 5-10-12 **105**........................ RichardJohnson 55
(Philip Hobbs) *plld hrd: hld up in last trio: nvr a factor: wknd after 3 out: t.o* **16/1**
44P0 **P** **Nordical (IRE)**[9] [3619] 6-10-5 **98**.....................................(t) AdamWedge
(Evan Williams) *hld up: a in last trio: wknd 3 out: last and t.o whn p.u bef 2 out* **66/1**

4m 10.9s (12.90) **Going Correction** +0.70s/f (Soft)
WFA 4 from 5yo+ 11lb **13** Ran SP% **122.6**
Speed ratings (Par 105): **95,94,88,87,85 84,77,76,76,73 66,63,**
CSF £27.12 CT £320.84 TOTE £2.80: £1.40, £3.90, £5.00; EX 30.10 Trifecta £334.30.
Owner The Sea Breeze Partnership **Bred** C C And Mrs D J Buckley **Trained** Alcester, Warwicks
FOCUS
Race distance increased by 65 yards. Modest hurdle form, the front pair dominating. The winner and second improved, with the fourth to his mark.
T/Plt: £20.50 to a £1 stake. Pool: £83421.36 - 2960.18 winning tickets T/Qpdt: £8.40 to a £1 stake. Pool: £6571.76 - 578.0 winning tickets **Jonathan Neesom**

3159 NEWCASTLE (L-H)
Monday, January 25
3778 Meeting Abandoned - waterlogged

3313 LEICESTER (R-H)
Tuesday, January 26
OFFICIAL GOING: Hurdle course - heavy (4.5); chase course - soft (heavy in places; 6.0)
Wind: very blustery Weather: overcast and drizzly; 10 degrees

3784 HUMBERSTONE H'CAP HURDLE (8 hdls) 1m 7f 113y
1:20 (1:20) (Class 4) (0-110,110) 4-Y-0+ **£4,548** (£1,335; £667; £333)

Form RPR
P622 **1** **Norse Light**[27] [3368] 5-10-9 **100**..................................(p) GarethMalone(7) 102+
(David Dennis) *settled towards rr: hdwy after 5th: sustained effrt fr next: hrd rdn to ld last: idling in front and all out* **4/1**[1]
2420 **2** *nk* **Akula (IRE)**[31] [3238] 9-11-3 **106**.. CiaranGethings(5) 106
(Barry Leavy) *led: hrd drvn 2 out: jst hdd last: hld fnl 75yds* **5/1**[2]
44 **3** *2 3/4* **Sean Ban (IRE)**[27] [3363] 6-11-12 **110**........................ WayneHutchinson 107
(Donald McCain) *cl up: pressed ldng fr bef 2 out but racing awkwardly and edging rt: nvr making any imp fr between last two* **4/1**[1]
0314 **4** *3 1/4* **Catchin Time (IRE)**[19] [3498] 8-11-4 **105**........................(t) KieronEdgar(3) 99
(Laura Hurley) *settled towards rr: rdn and sme prog bef 2 out: nvr making any imp fr bef last* **11/2**[3]
0000 **5** *2 1/4* **Powderonthebonnet (IRE)**[31] [3223] 8-10-8 **97**.............. DanielHiskett(5) 90
(Richard Phillips) *midfield: rdn 3 out: plugged on and n.d fr next* **20/1**
65 **6** *3 3/4* **Aza Run (IRE)**[182] [1137] 6-11-2 **100**.. TrevorWhelan 89
(Shaun Harris) *towards rr: sme prog in 4th whn hit 3 out: sn reluctant and racing v awkwardly: no ch fr next* **25/1**
-235 **7** *15* **Malanos (IRE)**[31] [3216] 8-11-4 **107**.. NickSlatter(5) 80
(Tony Carroll) *pressed ldr tl 3 out: rdn and dropped out qckly* **4/1**[1]
U155 **8** *20* **Dainty Diva (IRE)**[49] [2956] 8-11-8 **106**.............................. NickScholfield 59
(Jeremy Scott) *dropped bk last and slow 3rd: nvr travelling: t.o bef 3 out: b.b.v* **8/1**

4m 12.4s (11.40) **Going Correction** +0.65s/f (Soft) **8** Ran SP% **111.8**
Speed ratings (Par 105): **97,96,95,93,92 90,83,73**
CSF £23.37 CT £82.23 TOTE £4.20: £1.70, £2.60, £2.20; EX 22.80 Trifecta £87.70.
Owner The Dobbin Club & Partner **Bred** Littleton Stud **Trained** Hanley Swan, Worcestershire
■ Gareth Malone's first winner in Britain.

FOCUS
Rail movement increased races 1, 2 & 5 by 10yds, race 3 by 6yds, races 4 & 6 by 14yds. Moderate hurdling form. The winner looked to have a bit in hand, rated in line with Taunton run, and the second in line with pre-Christmas C&D run.

3785 BRITISH STALLION STUDS EBF MARES' "NATIONAL HUNT" NOVICES' HURDLE (8 hdls) 1m 7f 113y
1:55 (1:55) (Class 3) 4-Y-0+ **£6,330** (£1,870; £935; £468)

Form RPR
2112 **1** **Tara Flow**[20] [3487] 6-11-12 **130**.. AidanColeman 133+
(Venetia Williams) *tall: wl-mde: 2nd tl led gng best sn after 3 out: rdn after next but comf holding rival after* **5/4**[2]
111 **2** *6* **The Organist (IRE)**[31] [3215] 5-11-12 **0**........................ LeightonAspell 128+
(Oliver Sherwood) *str: workmanlike: led at decent pce: hit 3 out: immediately hdd and rdn: no imp fr next and looked laboured in grnd* **4/6**[1]
5-55 **3** *40* **Appletree Lane**[31] [3252] 6-11-2 **0**.. TommyPhelan 82
(Tom Gretton) *a 3rd: 20 l fr ldng pair at 5th: nvr on terms but kpt gng steadily* **150/1**[3]
0 **4** *48* **Stoical Patient (IRE)**[40] [3132] 7-11-2 **0**........................... KielanWoods 27
(Mark Wall) *stmbld 2nd: a last: t.o after 5th* **200/1**

4m 7.6s (6.60) **Going Correction** +0.65s/f (Soft) **4** Ran SP% **105.6**
Speed ratings (Par 107): **109,106,86,62**
CSF £2.39 TOTE £1.90; EX 2.90 Trifecta £3.20.
Owner Kate & Andrew Brooks **Bred** Miss A Gibson Fleming **Trained** Kings Caple, H'fords
FOCUS
The two market leaders duly dominated this small-field mares' hurdle which lacked depth. The winner is probably still on the upgrade.

3786 DICK CHRISTIAN NOVICES' CHASE (12 fncs) 1m 7f 201y
2:30 (2:30) (Class 3) 5-Y-0+ **£6,498** (£1,908; £954)

Form RPR
/022 **1** **Doctor Harper (IRE)**[14] [3571] 8-11-0 **0**........................... TomScudamore 147+
(David Pipe) *cl up and travelled wl: jnd ldr 3 out tl sauntered clr fr last: v easily* **8/11**[1]
F-P6 **2** *4 1/2* **Deep Trouble (IRE)**[17] [3527] 9-11-0 **133**...........................(t) KielanWoods 133
(Ben Case) *t.k.h: led tl 9th: rdn after: w wnr on sufferance fr 3 out tl last: kpt on same pce after* **15/8**[2]
1F44 **3** *24* **Gentleman Jon**[41] [3113] 8-11-10 **124**..............................(t) PaddyBrennan 128
(Colin Tizzard) *pressed ldr: nt fluent 4th and 5th: led 9th tl hdd by rival pair and rdn next: tired fr 2 out* **13/2**[3]

4m 14.9s (6.70) **Going Correction** +0.65s/f (Soft) **3** Ran SP% **106.0**
Speed ratings: **109,106,94**
CSF £2.41 TOTE £1.60; EX 2.00 Trifecta £1.70.
Owner The Johnson Family **Bred** Stephen O'Flynn **Trained** Nicholashayne, Devon
FOCUS
One key non-runner made this much more winnable, but it was still a reasonable little novice chase. The easy winner improving in line with best of hurdle form, and the eased-down third is rated close to his mark.

3787 CROXTON PARK NOVICES' HURDLE (10 hdls) 2m 4f 110y
3:00 (3:02) (Class 4) 4-Y-0+ **£4,548** (£1,335; £667; £333)

Form RPR
21 **1** **Hit The Highway (IRE)**[29] [3316] 7-11-12 **130**........................ TomCannon 133+
(Giles Smyly) *mde all: pushed along bef 3 out: rdn 2 out: kpt on gamely to assert fr last* **5/4**[1]
2-21 **2** *3* **Knockgraffon (IRE)**[58] [2807] 6-11-12 **127**........................ HarrySkelton 132+
(Dan Skelton) *settled promly: t.k.h: pressed wnr fr 3 out and sn wl clr w him: hit next: ev ch tl edgd lft u.p last: tired and no ex flat* **7/4**[2]
0-F3 **3** *16* **Pine Warbler**[29] [3316] 7-11-0 **0**.. CiaranGethings(5) 107
(Stuart Edmunds) *towards rr: lost tch w ldng trio fr 3 out: kpt on steadily to go poor 3rd at last* **14/1**
0-1F **4** *2* **Briery Queen**[38] [3154] 7-11-5 **0**..................................[1] WayneHutchinson 105
(Noel Williams) *settled handy: effrt 7th: disp 2nd home turn: rdn and fdd bdly after 3 out: lost tired and mod 3rd at last* **4/1**[3]
050 **5** *60* **Midnight Jade (IRE)**[14] [3570] 7-10-12 **0**........................... LeeEdwards 38
(John Groucott) *dropped bk last at 5th: rdn and lost tch after 7th: t.o bef 2 out: fin tired* **100/1**
0300 **P** **The Model County (IRE)**[17] [3516] 6-10-5 **0**.................. MrAlexEdwards(7)
(Alan Phillips) *prom tl rdn and lost pl 6th: t.o and p.u 2 out* **100/1**
0-50 **P** **Sir Bentley**[25] [3418] 6-11-5 **0**.. TomScudamore
(Caroline Bailey) *bhd: rdn and lost tch 7th: bdly t.o whn p.u 3 out* **100/1**

5m 36.5s (11.80) **Going Correction** +0.65s/f (Soft) **7** Ran SP% **110.4**
Speed ratings (Par 105): **103,101,95,95,72 ,**
CSF £3.56 TOTE £2.70: £1.30, £1.40; EX 5.90 Trifecta £15.10.
Owner Anthony Ward-Thomas **Bred** Ballymorris Stables **Trained** Wormington, Worcs
FOCUS
The two at the head of the market dominated, coming nicely clear. The winner is on the upgrade, the second is rated to his mark and there's a case for rating 5lb+ higher through the third.

3788 SIS H'CAP CHASE (18 fncs) 2m 6f 151y
3:35 (3:35) (Class 4) (0-110,110) 5-Y-0+ **£4,548** (£1,335; £667; £333)

Form RPR
-435 **1** **Ballyrath (IRE)**[47] [2996] 6-11-10 **108**.....................(p) SamTwiston-Davies 126+
(Nigel Twiston-Davies) *pressed ldr fr 4th: led bef 15th: pushed along and drew rt away fr next: idling whn wl in command: eased flat* **5/2**[1]
-625 **2** *9* **Buckhorn Tom**[25] [3412] 8-11-9 **107**..............................(b) PaddyBrennan 107
(Colin Tizzard) *cl up tl rdn 8th: nvr on bridle and j. modly after: 3 l 3rd bef 15th: nvr making any imp after: hit last: swtchd lft and drvn into mod 2nd cl home* **9/2**[3]
-F61 **3** *3/4* **Kings Apollo**[27] [3373] 7-11-9 **110**.. BenPoste(3) 106
(Tom Symonds) *led: hdd bef 15th: pushed along and sn outpcd by wnr: lost 2nd nr fin* **4/1**[2]
5-51 **4** *65* **Call The Detective (IRE)**[31] [3218] 7-11-12 **110**.............. TomScudamore 41
(Ali Stronge) *half w.r.s and lost 12 l: in tch by 4th: rdn 10th and nvr looking keen enough after: lost tch after 14th: t.o whn j.lft 3 out and next* **5/2**[1]
404P **P** **Eco Warrior**[27] [3362] 6-11-7 **105**..............................(b) AidanColeman
(Venetia Williams) *in last pair: rdn 9th: nt fluent next: lost tch 11th: t.o and p.u 15th* **6/1**

6m 18.4s (14.40) **Going Correction** +0.65s/f (Soft) **5** Ran SP% **109.6**
Speed ratings: **100,96,96,74,**
CSF £13.38 TOTE £3.50: £1.80, £2.10; EX 12.70 Trifecta £65.00.
Owner The Stirling Partnership **Bred** Ballymorris Stables **Trained** Naunton, Gloucs

FOCUS
This had looked quite an open handicap, despite the small field, but the winner took it well. It was a big step up from the winner, with the second to his mark.

3789 BROOK CONDITIONAL JOCKEYS' MARES' H'CAP HURDLE (10 hdls) 2m 4f 110y
4:10 (4:10) (Class 5) (0-100,98) 4-Y-0+ £3,249 (£954; £477; £238)

Form RPR
-311 1 **Black Narcissus (IRE)**[19] 3501 7-11-3 **95**...................... MikeyHamill(6) 103
(Alexandra Dunn) *cl up and gng wl: led 2 out: 3 l clr last: sn rdn: hld on gamely* **9/4**[1]
-042 2 *nk* **Loves Destination**[31] 3219 5-10-12 **84**.................. ThomasGarner 92
(Chris Gordon) *towards rr but wl in tch: effrt on inner whn hit 3 out and rdn: hit next: wnt 2nd at last: drvn and kpt on steadily: jst hld fnl 50yds* **6/1**
-525 3 *15* **Kayf Charmer**[27] 3368 6-10-0 **75**........................ ConorSmith(3) 69
(Linda Blackford) *prom: led bef 3 out: rdn and hdd next: tired and wl btn in 3rd whn nt fluent last* **5/1**[3]
5303 4 *1 3/4* **Young Lou**[26] 3382 7-10-5 **77**......................(p) ConorShoemark 67
(Robin Dickin) *midfield: effrt 3 out: rdn and struggling bef next: plodded on* **14/1**
-164 5 *42* **Helamis**[46] 3011 6-11-5 **91**............................ CiaranGethings 39
(Barry Leavy) *towards rr of cl bunch: effrt 7th: fdd bdly bef 2 out: t.o whn blnd last* **13/2**
6022 6 *8* **Rebekah Rabbit (IRE)**[26] 3382 6-10-13 **85**..................(t) DavidNoonan 25
(Tom Lacey) *towards rr: rdn 7th: no rspnse: t.o 2 out* **4/1**[2]
00P2 7 *29* **Petite Fantasie**[25] 3410 7-10-5 **77**.........................(t) CharlieDeutsch
(Mark Gillard) *led tl 2nd: led 6th tl rdn bef 3 out: fdd bdly bef next: sn t.o* **12/1**
3334 8 *19* **Carhue Princess (IRE)**[19] 3497 10-10-6 **81**.......... ThomasCheesman(3)
(Tom Symonds) *led 2nd tl 6th: last next: continued bdly t.o* **16/1**

5m 41.3s (16.60) **Going Correction** +0.65s/f (Soft) **8** Ran SP% **115.3**
Speed ratings (Par 103): **94,93,88,87,71 68,57,50**
CSF £16.61 CT £60.96 TOTE £3.00: £1.40, £2.80, £2.00; EX 21.10 Trifecta £117.50.
Owner Team Dunn **Bred** Patrick Davern **Trained** West Buckland, Somerset

FOCUS
Lowly hurdles form, but the front pair did pull a long way clear. A hurdles pb from the winner, with the second improving in line with her bumper mark.
T/Plt: £39.60 to a £1 stake. Pool: £55,878.09 - 1029.24 winning units. T/Qpdt: £18.20 to a £1 stake. Pool: £45,22.57 - 4522.57 winning units. **Iain Mackenzie**

3626 WETHERBY (L-H)
Tuesday, January 26

OFFICIAL GOING: Heavy (soft in places; chs 5.5; hdl 5.6)
Wind: strong 1/2 behind Weather: very windy, light showers

3790 RACINGUK.COM/ANYWHERE JUVENILE MAIDEN HURDLE (8 hdls 1 omitted) 2m
1:10 (1:10) (Class 5) 4-Y-0 £2,599 (£763; £381; £190)

Form RPR
20 1 **Pinkie Brown (FR)**[107] 1881 4-10-12 **124**...................... NoelFehily 113+
(Neil Mulholland) *hld up: hit 2nd: hdwy to trck ldrs bef 3 out: sn chsng ldr: led last: drvn rt out* **5/6**[1]
6 2 *1 3/4* **Baraymi (FR)**[41] 3112 4-10-12 0.........................(p) MichealNolan 109
(Jamie Snowden) *led: drvn 3 out: hdd last: kpt on same pce* **10/1**[3]
36 3 *13* **Kisumu**[42] 3099 4-10-5 0................................ FinianO'Toole(7) 97
(Micky Hammond) *chsd ldng pair: one pce appr 2 out* **14/1**
2 4 *63* **For Goodness Sake (IRE)**[47] 2992 4-10-5 0................ GavinSheehan 26
(Warren Greatrex) *w ldr: j.lft 1st: drvn and wknd appr 3 out: sn bhd: t.o whn eased between last 2: eventually completed* **7/4**[2]
5 P **Diamond Reflection (IRE)**[11] 3610 4-10-9 0.................. KillianMoore(3)
(Tom Weston) *detached in last: drvn 5th: t.o whn p.u bef 3 out* **40/1**
P **Austin Friars**[278] 4-10-12 0..................................(v[1]) JamieMoore
(Jim Best) *chsd ldrs: drvn 5th: wknd qckly and t.o whn p.u bef 3 out* **18/1**

4m 26.5s (30.70) **Going Correction** +1.70s/f (Heavy) **6** Ran SP% **114.4**
Speed ratings: **91,90,83,52,**
CSF £10.67 TOTE £1.60: £1.10, £4.70; EX 13.10 Trifecta £78.70.
Owner B Dunn **Bred** S A Scuderia Del Bargelo **Trained** Limpley Stoke, Wilts

FOCUS
The going was officially heavy, soft in places. Last hurdle and last fence in back straight omitted. Away chase bend out 9yds and away hurdles bend out 18yds from innermost line, Shared 'A1' bend out 21yds from innermost line. Race distances increased as a result with the actual distance of the opener 2m 117yds. The winner set a fair standard and is rated to his mark.

3791 BRAMHAM HALL FOR CONFERENCES & EVENTS H'CAP HURDLE 2m 3f 154y
1:45 (1:45) (Class 5) (0-100,100) 4-Y-0+ £2,599 (£763; £381; £190)

Form RPR
6-14 1 **Transient Bay (IRE)**[39] 3140 6-10-6 **83**..................(p) AdamNicol(3) 92+
(Philip Kirby) *w ldrs: bmpd 1st: 2nd appr 3 out: led 2 out: drvn 6 l clr run-in: heavily eased clsng stages* **3/1**[1]
640F 2 *1 3/4* **Naburn**[92] 2103 8-11-5 **98**.................................. RyanDay(5) 101+
(Andrew Wilson) *in rr-div: sme hdwy whn nt fluent 5th: hdwy next: sn chsng ldrs: 3rd appr 3 out: kpt on to take 2nd clsng stages* **14/1**
20-2 3 *3/4* **Oscar O'Scar (IRE)**[51] 2937 8-11-5 **100**.............. FinianO'Toole(7) 100
(Micky Hammond) *chsd ldrs: led appr 3 out: hdd 2 out: kpt on same pce run-in* **10/3**[2]
5-43 4 *23* **Cadgers Hole**[247] 466 9-10-0 **74** oh1...................... SeanQuinlan 51
(Lynn Siddall) *trckd ldrs: n.m.r and mstke 1st: lost pl appr 3 out: distant 4th appr last* **11/1**
0324 5 *11* **Blake Dean**[25] 3402 8-10-9 **90**............................ MrRHogg(7) 56
(Sue Smith) *trckd ldrs: led 4th: sn clr: drvn and hdd appr 3 out: sn lost pl: wknd between last 2* **5/1**[3]
-006 6 *24* **Wayward Sun (IRE)**[62] 2716 5-10-13 **90**............... JoeColliver(3) 32
(Micky Hammond) *in rr: reminders after 4th: bhd fr 6th: t.o 3 out* **20/1**
160- 7 *15* **Simmply Sam**[287] 5330 9-10-11 **85**.................. JeremiahMcGrath 12
(Marjorie Fife) *in rr: bhd fr 5th: t.o next* **10/1**
6260 8 *14* **Poet Mark (IRE)**[42] 3099 4-10-13 **99**...................(b) JakeGreenall
(Tim Easterby) *prom: reminders 5th: lost pl 3 out: t.o whn heavily eased run-in: virtually p.u* **14/1**
0-P0 P **Mubrook (USA)**[29] 3307 11-10-11 **85**......................(b) AlainCawley
(John David Riches) *led: j.lft 1st: 2: hdd 4th: reluctant and lost pl next: t.o 6th: sn p.u* **25/1**
034/ P **Saddlers' Secret (IRE)**[1082] 4118 11-9-9 **74** oh6.......... JamieHamilton(5)
(Mark Campion) *trckd ldrs: t.k.h: hmpd and lost pl 6th: sn bhd: t.o whn p.u bef 3 out* **66/1**
6/P0 P **Sory**[29] 3309 9-10-11 **85**.................................. JonathanEngland
(Tina Jackson) *in rr: hdwy 5th: j.rt next: sn chsng ldrs: lost pl bef 3 out: sn bhd: t.o whn p.u bef 2 out* **25/1**
040 P **Mr Jalfrazy (IRE)**[40] 3130 7-10-13 **90**...................... KillianMoore(3)
(Tom Weston) *chsd ldrs: reminders and lost pl after 4th: sn bhd: t.o whn p.u bef next* **10/1**
0050 P **Bond Starprincess**[12] 3587 4-10-0 **86** oh1.................. RichieMcLernon
(George Moore) *chsd ldrs: reminders 5th: sn lost pl and bhd: t.o whn p.u after 6th* **33/1**

5m 39.8s (32.80) **Going Correction** +1.70s/f (Heavy)
WFA 4 from 5yo+ 12lb **13** Ran SP% **121.5**
Speed ratings (Par 103): **102,101,101,91,87 77,71,66, , , ,**
CSF £42.04 CT £152.59 TOTE £3.60: £1.50, £5.50, £1.80; EX 48.70 Trifecta £249.90.
Owner The Waking Ned Partnership **Bred** Kenneth Parkhill **Trained** East Appleton, N Yorks

FOCUS
Actual race distance 2m4f 114yds. A modest handicap hurdle which was quite a test in the conditions and they finished well spread out. The winner was well in on recent win but this was probably a step up and he can rate higher still. The second posted a pb, with the third close to his mark.

3792 TOTEPOOL MEDIEVAL DAY - SATURDAY 6TH FEBRUARY H'CAP CHASE (17 fncs 2 omitted) 3m 45y
2:20 (2:20) (Class 4) (0-120,120) 5-Y-0+ £3,898 (£1,144; £572; £286)

Form RPR
3-41 1 **Armedanddangerous (IRE)**[39] 3144 11-10-3 **97**..........(b) JamesDavies 113+
(Tom Gretton) *chsd ldrs: led 13th: styd on wl fr 2 out: drvn clr run-in* **7/1**
113F 2 *10* **Leanna Ban**[18] 3507 9-11-6 **114**........................(t) JonathanEngland 120
(Tristan Davidson) *hld up towards rr: hdwy 10th: sn trcking ldrs: chsd wnr sn after 3 out: kpt on same pce between last 2* **12/1**
-522 3 *5* **Take The Mick**[14] 3569 9-11-8 **116**..........................(b[1]) LiamTreadwell 119
(Venetia Williams) *j.rt: led: hdd 13th: lost pl and modest 4th bef 3 out: wnt 3rd between last 2* **7/2**[2]
3621 4 *12* **Longueville Flier (IRE)**[73] 2500 7-10-3 **100**............. JoeColliver(3) 90
(Micky Hammond) *chsd ldrs: pushed along 8th: lost pl sn after 4 out* **4/1**[3]
F/P- 5 *nse* **Merlin's Wish**[329] 4545 11-11-12 **120**........................ IanPopham 110
(Martin Keighley) *trckd ldrs: reminders 13th: lost pl next: bhd whn blnd last* **10/1**
0-06 6 *10* **Pay The King (IRE)**[25] 3427 9-10-3 **97**...................... BrianHughes 76
(Micky Hammond) *chsd ldrs: 2nd 13th: wknd bef 2 out: bhd whn eased run-in* **8/1**
33-F P **Rowdy Rocher (IRE)**[25] 3425 10-11-12 **120**..................... DerekFox
(Lucinda Russell) *in rr: drvn 9th: chsng ldrs 11th: lost pl after 13th: sn wl bhd: t.o whn p.u bef next* **14/1**
PPP- P **Tutchec (FR)**[317] 4783 9-11-7 **115**.............................. BrianHarding
(Nicky Richards) *chsd ldrs: nt fluent and lost pl 10th: j. slowly and reminders next: sn wl bhd: t.o whn p.u bef 4 out* **3/1**[1]

7m 17.3s (29.30) **8** Ran SP% **114.3**
CSF £79.82 CT £342.74 TOTE £6.90: £2.30, £4.50, £1.10; EX 115.80 Trifecta £343.50.
Owner Not The Peloton Partnership **Bred** Tony McKiernan **Trained** Holberrow Green, Worcs

FOCUS
Actual race distance 3m1f 5yds. A fair handicap chase and a true test in the conditions. The winner was a 113 horse in 2013 and is seemingly back to his best, with the second to his mark.

3793 WETHERBYRACING.CO.UK H'CAP HURDLE (10 hdls 2 omitted) 3m 26y
2:50 (2:53) (Class 5) (0-100,100) 4-Y-0+ £2,599 (£763; £381; £190)

Form RPR
-200 1 **Newyearsresolution (IRE)**[47] 2980 12-9-7 **74** oh3....... MissAWaugh(7) 85
(Simon Waugh) *hld up towards rr: t.k.h: hdwy to ld after 5th: styd on wl fr 3 out: drew clr last 75yds* **25/1**
P-36 2 *5* **Jonny Eager (IRE)**[25] 3402 7-11-7 **95**........................ CraigNichol 103
(Alistair Whillans) *trckd ldrs: chsd wnr sn after 5th: 3 l down whn mstke 2 out: 2 l down last: wknd last 100yds* **14/1**
/PPF 3 *4 1/2* **Cleve Cottage**[18] 3503 8-10-6 **83**........................... AdamNicol(3) 85
(Philip Kirby) *hld up in rr: hdwy 6th: modest 4th bef 3 out: 3rd last: kpt on same pce* **10/1**
0-33 4 *16* **Rocky Stone (IRE)**[25] 3402 8-11-8 **96**.......................... NoelFehily 87
(Donald McCain) *trckd ldrs: wknd bef 2 out* **5/1**[2]
P-33 5 *9* **Mr McGregor (IRE)**[39] 3144 8-10-12 **86**...............(p) RichardJohnson 62
(Heather Dalton) *led: drvn 3rd: hdd next: lost pl after 5th: distant 5th bef 3 out* **11/2**[3]
5431 6 *11* **Optical High**[54] 2868 7-10-6 **90**........................ StephenMcCarthy(10) 55
(Sue Smith) *chsd ldr: led 4th: hdd after next: drvn 6th: sn lost pl: distant 6th bef 3 out* **4/1**[1]
5524 7 *6* **Triumph Davis (IRE)**[18] 3503 7-10-11 **88**.................. JoeColliver(3) 47
(Micky Hammond) *in rr: drvn after 2nd: bhd after 6th* **12/1**
6-P1 8 *49* **Gorey Lane (IRE)**[26] 3378 10-11-4 **95**..............(vt) ColmMcCormack(3)
(John Norton) *mid-div: chsd ldrs 6th: reminders next: sn lost pl and bhd: t.o whn heavily eased run-in: eventually completed* **11/1**
-PU0 P **Notonebuttwo (IRE)**[22] 3474 9-10-9 **83**...................(tp) BrianHughes
(Chris Grant) *trckd ldrs: drvn 7th: sn lost pl: wl bhd whn p.u bef 3 out* **8/1**
-242 P **Blue Cove**[18] 3503 11-10-0 **74** oh2.............................. SeanQuinlan
(Lynn Siddall) *chsd ldrs: lost pl sn after 7th: bhd 3 out: p.u bef next* **12/1**
01-4 P **Prairie Lad**[58] 2806 8-11-5 **100**..............................(p) StevenFox(7)
(Sandy Thomson) *rr-div: hdwy 4th: nt fluent 6th: sn lost pl: t.o whn p.u bef 3 out* **13/2**

7m 6.8s (50.30) **Going Correction** +1.80s/f (Heavy) **11** Ran SP% **119.8**
Speed ratings (Par 103): **88,86,84,79,76 72,70,54, ,**
CSF £333.53 CT £3717.41 TOTE £36.40: £8.00, £4.80, £4.70; EX 457.80 Trifecta £5445.80 Part won..
Owner S Waugh **Bred** Daniel Fogarty **Trained** Mitford, Northumberland

FOCUS
Actual race distance 3m1f 40yds. An ordinary staying handicap hurdle that was hard work to watch, let alone take part in. Again they finished well spread out. The winner is rated to the level of his 2015 chase form, with the second back to 2014 winning mark.

3794 RACING UK DAY PASS JUST £10.00 H'CAP CHASE (QUAL' FOR THE CHALLENGER MIDDLE DISTANCE CHASE FINAL) (14 fncs 2 omitted) 2m 3f 85y
3:25 (3:25) (Class 3) (0-130,127) ~~£6,498~~ (£1,908; £954; £477; £15; £Form)

-202 1 **Cultram Abbey**[24] 3439 9-11-11 **126**........................ BrianHarding 140+
(Nicky Richards) *in rr: chsd ldrs 3rd: reminder 6th: drvn next: reminders 9th: outpcd next: modest 5th 4 out: hdwy bef next: 2nd 2 out: led between last 2: drvn clr last* **7/1**[3]

2210 **2** *8* **Dartford Warbler (IRE)**[38] 3148 9-11-7 **122**.................. DannyCook 128
(Sue Smith) *chsd ldrs: hit 5th: drvn upsides 10th: led bef next: sn rdn: hdd between last 2: no ex* **10/1**

3043 **3** *3/4* **Ballybolley (IRE)**[11] 3611 7-11-12 **127**..................(t) DarylJacob 131
(Nigel Twiston-Davies) *hld up in rr: hdwy to trck ldrs 10th: 3rd 2 out: one pce* **9/2**[2]

1151 **4** *3 1/2* **Throthethatch (IRE)**[27] 3362 7-11-1 **116**.................. PeterBuchanan 120
(Lucinda Russell) *led to 4th: chsd ldrs: nt fluent 8th: chalng whn mstke 3 out: wknd bef next* **9/2**[2]

-324 **5** *12* **Plus Jamais (FR)**[38] 3157 9-11-2 **117**.................. BrianHughes 106
(Jim Goldie) *hld up in rr: hdwy 10th: lost pl next* **11/1**

PF1 **6** *2 1/4* **Ballyadeen (IRE)**[31] 3235 8-11-2 **120**.................. JamesBanks(3) 108
(Dai Williams) *t.k.h: trckd ldrs: led 4th: hdd bef 4 out: wknd bef 2 out* **7/1**[3]

12-4 **P** **Somchine**[85] 2243 8-11-5 **120**.................. AndrewThornton
(Seamus Mullins) *in rr: hmpd 2nd: hdwy 10th: lost pl bef next: hit 4 out: p.u bef next* **11/1**

-P42 **F** **Azert De Coeur (FR)**[10] 3631 6-11-0 **115**.................. LiamTreadwell
(Venetia Williams) *trckd ldrs: fell 2nd* **5/2**[1]

5m 45.8s (38.00) **Going Correction** +2.20s/f (Heavy) **8 Ran SP% 115.7**
Speed ratings: **108,104,104,102,97 96, ,**
CSF £70.86 CT £350.67 TOTE £7.50: £1.90, £3.50, £1.80; EX 81.10 Trifecta £295.90.
Owner The Roper Family **Bred** C G And Mrs Johnson **Trained** Greystoke, Cumbria

FOCUS
Actual race distance 2m4f 18yds. A decent handicap chase in which all seven remaining runners still had some sort of a chance turning in. This is rated around the balance of second to fourth and looks solid despite the favourite falling.

3795 RACINGUK.COM/FREETRIAL "NATIONAL HUNT" NOVICES' HURDLE (8 hdls 1 omitted) 2m
4:00 (4:01) (Class 4) 4-Y-0+ **£3,573** (£1,049; £524; £262)

Form RPR

2 **1** **The Dutchman (IRE)**[24] 3436 6-11-4 0.................. DannyCook 130+
(Sandy Thomson) *trckd ldrs: led bef 3 out: hit 3 out: stmbld bdly on landing and wnt rt 2 out: edgd lft run-in: fnd ex nr fin* **11/4**[2]

2 **2** *1 1/4* **No Comment**[41] 3111 5-11-4 0.................. RichardJohnson 128+
(Philip Hobbs) *hld up in rr: t.k.h: hdwy 4th: sn trcking ldrs: 2nd appr 3 out: hmpd sn after 2 out: swtchd lft: abt 1 l down last: sn drvn and carried lft: no ex clsng stages* **7/4**[1]

61 **3** *18* **Fionn Mac Cul (IRE)**[13] 3581 5-11-11 0.................. LiamTreadwell 117
(Venetia Williams) *trckd ldrs: drvn 5th: modest 3rd appr next* **3/1**[3]

5142 **4** *18* **Lamanver Alchemy**[26] 3386 5-10-11 0.................. NoelFehily 90
(Tom Lacey) *led: j.lft: hdd bef 3 out: wknd between last 2* **7/1**

3234 **5** *29* **Rushvale (IRE)**[31] 3238 7-10-11 116.................. MrMJPKendrick(7) 61
(Ben Case) *chsd ldrs: reminders 4th and next: lost pl bef 3 out: sn distant 5th* **6/1**

004 **6** *4* **Smuggler's Stash (IRE)**[31] 3239 6-11-4 0.................. CraigNichol 57
(Rose Dobbin) *chsd ldrs: lost pl sn after 5th: bhd next* **100/1**

0 **7** *12* **Rhythm Of Sound (IRE)**[25] 3397 6-10-8 0.... HugoThompsonBrown(10) 45
(Micky Hammond) *chsd ldrs: drvn 4th: lost pl next: sn bhd* **100/1**

000/ **8** *22* **Jasani**[650] 5354 8-10-11 0.................. GLavery(7) 23
(Alan Brown) *in rr: reminders 3rd: sn bhd: t.o 5th* **150/1**

P **9** *4 1/2* **Violoniste (FR)**[26] 3375 7-11-4 0.................. JonathanEngland 19
(Richard Drake) *in rr: bhd fr 4th: t.o next* **100/1**

360/ **P** **Charming Grace (IRE)**[1024] 5202 10-10-6 92.......... JamieHamilton(5)
(Mark Campion) *in rr: sn drvn along: bhd 3rd: t.o next: p.u bef 5th* **150/1**

-045 **P** **Weyburn (IRE)**[14] 3568 5-11-4 0.................. AndrewTinkler
(Martin Keighley) *prom: lost pl 4th: bhd next: t.o whn p.u bef 3 out* **50/1**

4m 22.0s (26.20) **Going Correction** +1.80s/f (Heavy) **11 Ran SP% 121.1**
Speed ratings (Par 105): **106,105,96,87,72 70,64,53,51,**
CSF £8.69 TOTE £3.80: £1.30, £1.20, £1.60; EX 12.20 Trifecta £27.70.
Owner Sprayclad UK **Bred** Regina Anne Hennessy **Trained** Lambden, Berwicks
■ Stewards' Enquiry : Danny Cook three-day ban: careless riding (Feb 9-11)

FOCUS
Actual race distance 2m 117yds. The market leaders dominated in this novices' hurdle and the first two look nice sorts. There was some argy bargy between the first two from the second-last flight, but the result was left unchanged. There's a case for rating a few pound higher through the third and fourth.
T/Plt: £1028.00 to a £1 stake. Pool: £61,695.60 - 43.81 winning units. T/Qpdt: £298.70 to a 31 stake. Pool: £6,297.26 - 15.60 winning units. **Walter Glynn**

3006 BANGOR-ON-DEE (L-H)
Wednesday, January 27

3796 Meeting Abandoned - Waterlogged

3587 CATTERICK (L-H)
Wednesday, January 27

OFFICIAL GOING: Soft (heavy in places; chs 5.1, hdl 6.0)
Wind: strong, half behind Weather: very windy, mostly dry

3802 YORKSHIRE-OUTDOORS.CO.UK NOVICES' HURDLE (10 hdls) 2m 3f 66y
1:20 (1:21) (Class 4) 5-Y-0+ **£3,249** (£954; £477; £238)

Form RPR

3161 **1** **Point The Way (IRE)**[32] 3240 5-11-5 0.................. DannyCook 131+
(Brian Ellison) *mde all: drvn clr 6th: hit 2 out: drvn rt out* **7/4**[2]

1 **2** *5* **Vinciaettis (FR)**[72] 2549 5-10-12 0.................. GavinSheehan 118+
(Warren Greatrex) *nt fluent: chsd ldng pair: drvn to chse wnr bef 2 out: kpt on same pce appr last* **8/11**[1]

26 **3** *8* **Golden Investment (IRE)**[60] 2791 7-10-12 0.................. WayneHutchinson 109
(Donald McCain) *chsd wnr: drvn 3 out: one pce bef 2 out* **8/1**[3]

4 *35* **San Pietro (FR)**[66] 8-10-9 0.................. HarryChalloner(3) 74
(Richard Ford) *in rr 4th: distant 4th 3 out* **33/1**

0 **5** *20* **Sybil Grey**[63] 2721 7-10-0 0.................. JonathonBewley(5) 47
(George Bewley) *j.rt 2nd: bhd 4th: t.o 6th* **200/1**

6 *12* **Roxy The Rebel** 6-10-0 0.................. GrantCockburn(5) 35
(Simon Waugh) *bhd 4th: hit 7th: sn t.o* **150/1**

5m 3.1s (27.00) **Going Correction** +0.875s/f (Soft) **6 Ran SP% 109.5**
Speed ratings: **78,75,72,57,49 44**
CSF £3.33 TOTE £3.00: £1.40, £1.10; EX 4.60 Trifecta £6.40.
Owner P J Martin **Bred** Mrs Kay Cottrell **Trained** Norton, N Yorks

FOCUS
Bends were out 6yds and as a result this race was run over 54yds further than advertised. A combination of soft ground and strong winds made it hard work for the runners. Not a bad little novice hurdle for the track and the winner is on the upgrade. The second was below the level of his bumper win, with the third to his bumper mark.

3803 CATTERICKBRIDGE.CO.UK H'CAP CHASE (18 fncs 1 omitted) 3m 1f 54y
1:50 (1:50) (Class 5) (0-100,100) 5-Y-0+ **£3,249** (£954; £477; £238)

Form RPR

-PP0 **1** **Auldthunder (IRE)**[56] 2844 9-10-13 **90**.................. JoeColliver(3) 102+
(Micky Hammond) *hdwy to chse ldrs 7th: led 5 out: j.rt last 2: styd on strly: readily* **10/1**

6-45 **2** *8* **Treliver Manor (IRE)**[26] 3427 8-10-10 **84**..................(t) GavinSheehan 87
(Rose Dobbin) *chsd ldrs 8th: 2nd sn after 4 out: kpt on same pce fr 2 out: no imp* **8/1**[3]

013P **3** *21* **Urban Gale (IRE)**[30] 3310 11-11-8 **96**..................(p) DannyCook 77
(Joanne Foster) *chsd ldrs: led 5th: drvn 12th: hdd 5 out: outpcd after next: tk poor 3rd last* **9/1**

5453 **4** *2* **Veroce (FR)**[45] 3059 7-11-2 **90**.................. JakeGreenall 70
(Mark Walford) *chsd ldrs: outpcd after 4 out: sn lost pl* **7/2**[1]

/P-3 **5** *1/2* **Admiral Blake**[66] 2661 9-10-10 **84**.................. RobertDunne 64
(Laura Young) *nt fluent in rr: hdwy 12th: modest 3rd sn after 4 out: wknd last* **8/1**[3]

4-PU **P** **Samson Collonges (FR)**[45] 3059 10-10-0 **74** oh2.........(p) BrianHughes
(Rebecca Menzies) *chsd ldrs: lost pl and hit 13th: sn bhd: t.o 6th whn p.u bef 3 out* **12/1**

1354 **P** **Over And Above (IRE)**[64] 2708 10-10-12 **89**.........(tp) GrahamWatters(3)
(Henry Hogarth) *led to 5th: hit 11th and reminders: sn lost pl and bhd: t.o 5 out: p.u bef 3 out* **11/2**[2]

5246 **P** **Cara Court (IRE)**[45] 3062 10-10-0 **77** ow1............(v) ColmMcCormack(3)
(Joanne Foster) *chsd ldrs: lost pl after 11th: sn bhd: t.o 5 out: p.u bef 3 out* **16/1**

1-P6 **P** **Debt To Society (IRE)**[220] 798 9-11-9 **100**..............(t) HarryChalloner(3)
(Richard Ford) *pushed along in last: bhd fr 10th: t.o 12th: p.u bef 3 out* **18/1**

3P12 **F** **Thatildee (IRE)**[54] 2892 8-10-12 **91**..................(p) DiarmuidO'Regan(5)
(Chris Grant) *sn pushed along: sn chsng ldrs: fell 6th: fatally injured* **11/2**[2]

7m 3.0s (21.00) **Going Correction** +0.875s/f (Soft) **10 Ran SP% 113.1**
Speed ratings: **101,98,91,91,90 , , , ,**
CSF £84.54 CT £745.58 TOTE £14.10: £4.10, £2.70, £1.10; EX 103.40 Trifecta £876.30.
Owner The Rat Pack Racing Club **Bred** Miss Jill Farrell **Trained** Middleham, N Yorks

FOCUS
Bends were out 6yds and as a result this race was run over 72yds further than advertised. Only half the runners managed to complete with conditions making it a thorough test. The winner was well in on last season's Sedgefield success and is rated to a similar level, with the second to his mark.

3804 HAPPY RETIREMENT GEORGE MOORE H'CAP HURDLE (10 hdls) 2m 3f 66y
2:25 (2:25) (Class 3) (0-140,140) 4-Y-0+ **£6,498** (£1,908; £954; £477)

Form RPR

041 **1** **Tomkevi (FR)**[28] 3367 5-10-2 **116**.................. BrianHughes 121+
(Rebecca Menzies) *chsd ldrs: 2nd sn after 3 out: upsides last: kpt on to ld last 50yds* **9/2**[3]

364 **2** *3/4* **Forest Bihan (FR)**[46] 3041 5-11-12 **140**.................. DannyCook 143
(Brian Ellison) *chsd ldrs: led 3 out: rdr dropped whip between last 2: jnd last: hdd and no ex last 50yds* **9/4**[2]

1-3 **3** *26* **Driftashore (IRE)**[267] 127 9-10-9 **130**.................. MissBHampson(7) 107
(Sally Randell) *chsd ldr: hmpd 5th: drvn 6th: led next: hdd and reminder 8th: sn lost pl: poor 3rd whn hit 2 out* **14/1**

4-04 **4** *nk* **Desert Cry (IRE)**[25] 3440 10-11-7 **135**.................. WayneHutchinson 112
(Donald McCain) *nt fluent 6th: sn drvn: lost pl sn after 3 out* **10/1**

2330 **P** **Egmont**[97] 2029 4-10-0 **126** oh18..................(p) RichieMcLernon
(George Moore) *chsd ldrs: hit 4th: sn drvn: lost pl and reminders next: sn bhd: t.o 3 out: p.u bef last* **66/1**

-011 **F** **Poulanassy (IRE)**[43] 3101 6-10-4 **118**.................. AdamWedge
(Evan Williams) *led: j.rt 5th: hdd 7th: drvn and hit next: sn wknd: t.o 5th whn fell last: fatally injured* **11/8**[1]

4m 55.1s (19.00) **Going Correction** +0.875s/f (Soft)
WFA 4 from 5yo+ 11lb **6 Ran SP% 108.3**
Speed ratings (Par 107): **95,94,83,83,**
CSF £14.30 TOTE £4.80: £2.40, £2.00; EX 15.60 Trifecta £98.90.
Owner P J Howe & R G Oliver **Bred** Y Molliere **Trained** Stearsby, N Yorks

FOCUS
Bends were out 6yds and as a result this race was run over 54yds further than advertised. An ordinary handicap hurdle, but there's a case for rating it a bit higher.

3805 RACINGUK.COM NOVICES' CHASE (16 fncs) 2m 3f 51y
3:00 (3:00) (Class 4) 5-Y-0+ **£4,882** (£1,669)

Form RPR

F-63 **1** **Out Sam**[40] 3136 7-10-11 0.................. GavinSheehan 137+
(Warren Greatrex) *mde all: hit 10th: pushed along 4 out: lft dist clr 2 out* **1/4**[1]

000- **2** *80* **Halcyon Days**[289] 5312 7-10-6 88.................. JamieHamilton(5) 57
(Rebecca Menzies) *a last: pushed along 7th: sme hdwy 9th: hit next: lost pl 12th: t.o whn lft distant 2nd 2 out: eventually completed* **40/1**[3]

3324 **F** **Major Ivan (IRE)**[39] 3158 7-10-11 0.................. BrianHughes 129
(Malcolm Jefferson) *trckd ldrs: effrt 3 out: abt 3 l down and looking hld whn fell next* **10/3**[2]

5m 11.7s (311.70) **3 Ran SP% 105.5**
CSF £4.91 TOTE £1.10; EX 6.60.
Owner Swanee River Partnership **Bred** D & N Leggate, R Kent & I Henderson **Trained** Upper Lambourn, Berks

FOCUS
Bends were out 6yds and as a result this race was run over 54yds further than advertised. Only two of the three mattered and the favourite was seemingly in control when left clear.

3806 SCORTON H'CAP CHASE (12 fncs) 1m 7f 145y
3:35 (3:35) (Class 3) (0-125,124) 5-Y-0+ **£7,797** (£2,289; £1,144; £572)

Form RPR

3031 **1** **Star Presenter (IRE)**[43] 3103 8-10-7 **105**.................. JonathanEngland 114+
(Sam Drake) *trckd ldrs: led sn after 4th: drvn and hld on fnl 75yds* **9/2**[3]

2411 **2** *nk* **Nautical Twilight**[30] 3311 6-11-8 **120**..................(b) BrianHughes 129+
(Malcolm Jefferson) *trckd ldrs: effrt appr 2 out: wnt 2nd between last 2: styd on towards fin: jst hld* **7/2**[2]

-P3P 3 *11* **Money For Nothing**[32] 3237 7-10-3 **104**............(t[1]) ColmMcCormack(3) 103
(Harriet Bethell) *in rr: pckd landing 6th: effrt and modest 4th sn after 9th: kpt on one pce to take modest 3rd nr fin* **14/1**

P522 4 *2* **Uno Valoroso (FR)**[13] 3589 8-10-7 **110**.................... JamieHamilton(5) 110
(Mark Walford) *nt fluent: led: hdd after 4th: hit next: mstke 8th: wknd appr last* **5/2**[1]

-P52 5 *14* **Aye Well**[23] 3475 11-11-12 **124**........................... JamesReveley 106
(Stuart Coltherd) *mid-div: chsd ldrs after 4th: drvn 9th: sn lost pl* **11/2**

224F 6 *shd* **Ever So Much (IRE)**[61] 2746 7-11-0 **112**......................(p) AndrewTinkler 96
(Ben Haslam) *in rr-div: drvn 7th: lost pl 9th: sn bhd* **18/1**

/U34 P **Only Orsenfoolsies**[11] 3627 7-11-4 **123**.................. FinianO'Toole(7)
(Micky Hammond) *sn in rr: nvr travelling: eased after 4th: bhd and p.u bef next* **11/2**

4m 11.3s (11.20) **Going Correction** +0.875s/f (Soft) **7** Ran SP% **111.7**
Speed ratings: **107,106,101,100,93 93,**
CSF £20.05 TOTE £5.60: £2.70, £1.90; EX 18.10 Trifecta £188.50.
Owner Mrs J Drake **Bred** J R Weston **Trained** Guiseley, West Yorkshire
■ Sam Drake's first winner and runner since taking over the licence from her father Richard.

FOCUS
Bends were out 6yds and as a result this race was run over 36yds further than advertised. The front pair, both in form, pulled clear in this moderate handicap. The winner is rated to the level of recent C&D win, with the second still on the upgrade.

3807 DINE AND VIEW AT CATTERICK RACES H'CAP HURDLE (8 hdls) 1m 7f 156y
4:05 (4:08) (Class 5) (0-100,100) 4-Y-O+ **£2,599** (£763; £381; £190)

Form RPR

00P1 1 **Notebook**[30] 3307 5-10-10 **91**......................(p) ThomasCheesman(7) 106+
(Martin Smith) *t.k.h: sn trcking ldrs: led 2nd: styd on wl fr 2 out: clr last: eased clsng stages* **5/1**[2]

2040 2 *7* **Astrum**[32] 3223 6-11-2 **100**..........................(b) RonanShort(10) 105
(Donald McCain) *chsd ldrs: kpt on to take modest 2nd appr last: no ch w wnr* **5/1**[2]

5-03 3 *2 3/4* **Copt Hill**[32] 3244 8-10-7 **81**..............................(p) BrianHughes 83
(Tracy Waggott) *sn trcking ldrs: 2nd 3 out: one pce between last 2* **4/1**[1]

2244 4 *17* **Gunner Lindley (IRE)**[32] 3244 9-10-9 **90**................ SamColtherd(7) 74
(Stuart Coltherd) *chsd ldrs: drvn 3 out: lost pl appr next* **11/1**

0P04 5 *6* **Captain Sharpe**[32] 3241 8-10-0 **81**.................(b) ThomasDowson(7) 59
(Kenny Johnson) *chsd ldrs: drvn 3 out: wknd next* **20/1**

0520 6 *5* **Strait Run (IRE)**[11] 3628 5-10-10 **87**..................... JoeColliver(3) 60
(Micky Hammond) *in rr: drvn after 3rd: bhd fr 3 out* **16/1**

P0/0 7 *14* **Shivsingh**[54] 2880 7-11-3 **91**............................... RobertDunne 50
(Laura Young) *in rr: bhd fr 3 out* **33/1**

226- P **Deny**[297] 5163 8-10-11 **88**..............................(p) GrahamWatters(3)
(Henry Hogarth) *hld up towards rr: sme hdwy 3 out: poor 8th whn bdly hmpd next: sn p.u: lame* **8/1**

-651 U **Fiddler's Flight (IRE)**[32] 3244 10-10-7 **84**.............. ColmMcCormack(3)
(John Norton) *in rr: drvn 3 out: poor 7th whn mstke and uns rdr 2 out: b.b.v* **8/1**

53-P P **Dye Of A Needle (IRE)**[78] 2413 6-11-12 **100**..............(p) GavinSheehan
(Evan Williams) *led to 2nd: drvn next: reminders 5th: sn lost pl: t.o whn p.u bef 2 out* **7/1**[3]

P-0 P **Bolero Collonges (FR)**[23] 3473 5-11-5 **98**............... CallumBewley(5)
(Simon Waugh) *chsd ldrs: nt fluent and lost pl 4th: bhd next: t.o whn p.u bef 2 out* **22/1**

4m 5.4s (12.90) **Going Correction** +0.875s/f (Soft) **11** Ran SP% **114.3**
Speed ratings (Par 103): **102,98,97,88,85 83,76,, ,**
CSF £28.95 CT £108.89 TOTE £5.80: £2.20, £2.00, £2.00; EX 33.00 Trifecta £168.90.
Owner Little Princess Racing **Bred** Mr & Mrs G Middlebrook **Trained** Newmarket, Suffolk

FOCUS
Bends were out 6yds and as a result this race was run over 36yds further than advertised. Lowly handicap form but a progressive winner.
T/Plt: £53.40 to a £1 stake. Pool: £53,347.89. 728.80 winning tickets. T/Qpdt: £9.60 to a £1 stake. Pool: £5,375.42. 411.70 winning tickets. **Walter Glynn**

3808 - 3814a (Foreign Racing) - See Raceform Interactive

PAU (R-H)
Wednesday, January 27

OFFICIAL GOING: Turf: very soft

3815a PRIX DU PONT-LONG (HURDLE) (CLAIMER) (5YO) (TURF) 2m 3f
2:40 (12:00) 5-Y-O **£6,352** (£3,176; £1,852; £1,257; £595)

RPR

1 **Caprice De Nuit (FR)**[208] 5-10-3 0.......................... EdgarLabaisse(9)
(P Chevillard, France) **16/1**

2 *1* **First Moon (FR)**[70] 5-10-1 0............................ ChristopherCouillaud(9)
(Y Fertillet, France) **5/1**[2]

3 *1/2* **Rockozal (FR)**[97] 5-9-13 0.............................(b) TheoChevillard(9)
(P Chevillard, France) **10/1**

4 *1* **Le Sacre Coeur (GER)** 5-10-12 0...................... CorentinSmeulders(9)
(C Cheminaud, France) **31/1**

5 *10* **Belladone (FR)** 5-10-2 0 ow1.........................(p) VincentChatellier(9)
(L Cadot, France) **86/1**

6 *3* **Monsieur Oliver (FR)**[78] 5-10-10 0..........(b) MlleClementineChevallier(9)
(E Leray, France) **78/10**[3]

7 *4* **First Bag (FR)**[282] 5-10-3 0.............................(p) JeremyRey(9)
(Anthony Clement, France) **22/1**

8 *8* **Brise Coeur (FR)**[14] 3586 5-10-10 0.......................... LizzieKelly(9)
(Nick Williams) *midfield in tch: clsd and prom 7th: rdn and lost pl fr 4 out: sn btn: wknd* **15/1**

F **Azastar (FR)**[753] 5-10-6 0.................................. RaphaelMayeur(8)
(F-M Cottin, France) **59/1**

P **Beautiful King's (FR)**[136] 5-10-3 0.......................(p) MaximeCamus(9)
(G Taupin, France) **14/1**

P **Picasso Do Brasil (FR)**[95] 5-10-6 0.................(b) MaximilienFarcinade(8)
(P Chevillard, France) **19/5**[1]

P **Simba De Teillee (FR)**[145] 5-10-10 0...................(b) GregoryDenuault(9)
(E Leenders, France) **83/10**

P **Powerful Blue (FR)**[452] 5-10-6 0............................... KevinNabet
(F-M Cottin, France) **9/1**

P **Aquitania (FR)** 5-10-10 0...................................... DamienDevesse
(C Gourdain, France) **14/1**

P **Luckydom (FR)** 5-10-6 0.................................... ArmelLotout(8)
(E Leray, France) **24/1**

P **Arcanciel Val (FR)** 5-10-6 0................................. RichardLeStang(8)
(X-L Le Stang, France) **140/1**

\n\x\x PARI-MUTUEL (all including 1 euro stake): WIN 6.70 (coupled with Rockozal);
Owner P Chevillard & Andralus **Bred** Y Fremiot & Mme Y Fremiot **Trained** France

3417
FAKENHAM (L-H)
Thursday, January 28

OFFICIAL GOING: Soft (5.4)
Wind: Light breeze Weather: Very bright and sunny

3816 TAVERHAM HALL RACING TO SCHOOL H'CAP HURDLE (9 hdls) 2m 3y
1:25 (1:25) (Class 5) (0-100,107) 4-Y-O+ **£3,898** (£1,144; £572; £286)

Form RPR

P06U 1 **It's Oscar (IRE)**[21] 3497 9-10-13 **87**........................(b) MarkQuinlan 100+
(James Evans) *tended to jump rt: led 3rd: sn sent 10 l clr: pressed 2 out: rdn to forge clr despite idling between last two: 8 l ahd whn j.rt last* **10/1**

02 2 *9* **Lake Chapala (IRE)**[43] 3108 7-10-11 **90**..................... AlanJohns(5) 92
(Tim Vaughan) *3rd or 4th pl tl wnt 2nd bef 3 out: chal u.p next: fnd little and a hld after* **4/1**[2]

5036 3 *1/2* **Brinestine (USA)**[29] 3368 7-11-3 **98**..............(t) HarrisonBeswick(7) 99
(Emma Baker) *detached in 7th pl tl 1/2-way: picked up struggling rivals fr 3 out: drvn and chal for mod 2nd at last: styd on* **5/1**[3]

2036 4 *5* **Irondale Express**[75] 2494 5-11-5 **100**.......................... HarryCobden(7) 96
(Barry Brennan) *prom tl drvn bef 6th: dropped out bef next: disp poor 3rd 2 out* **8/1**

34F2 5 *shd* **Ogaritmo**[39] 3177 7-11-9 **100**..............................(t) JamesBanks(3) 96
(Alex Hales) *last and nvr travelling: sn 15 l adrift: pushed along 4th: no ch fr 3 out: mstke last* **4/1**[2]

2031 6 *22* **Guaracha**[10] 3665 5-11-12 **107** 7ex..........................(p) MikeyHamill(7) 81
(Alexandra Dunn) *towards rr: rdn 3 out: a struggling after: blnd last* **7/2**[1]

4-34 7 *33* **Flichity (IRE)**[58] 2836 11-9-11 **74** oh22..........................(p) BenPoste(3) 15
(John Cornwall) *led tl 3rd: lost pl rapidly u.p 5th: sn t.o* **100/1**

600P P **Culworth Boy (IRE)**[33] 3221 6-10-4 **78**............................(t) JamesBest
(Sophie Leech) *prom: hit 6th: 5 l 3rd bef 3 out: sn rdn and dropped out: t.o and p.u bef 2 out* **15/2**

4m 17.4s (4.40) **Going Correction** +0.325s/f (Yiel) **8** Ran SP% **111.8**
Speed ratings (Par 103): **102,97,97,94,94 83,67,**
CSF £48.17 CT £223.23 TOTE £8.60: £2.70, £1.60, £1.70; EX 38.40 Trifecta £248.20.
Owner Miss S Troughton **Bred** James Silk **Trained** Broadwas, Worcs

FOCUS
There was a fresh two-yard strip of ground the whole way around on the hurdles course. The official race distance had an additional 113 yards added to it. A moderate contest to start the meeting with, but it was run at a good gallop. The winner was a 110 hurdler at his peak but this is his best figure since 2013.

3817 RACING TO SCHOOL INSPIRING YOUNG MINDS NOVICES' HURDLE (13 hdls) 2m 7f 95y
2:00 (2:00) (Class 4) 5-Y-O+ **£5,198** (£1,526; £763; £381)

Form RPR

35 1 **Minella Daddy (IRE)**[19] 3516 6-10-12 0............................. SeanBowen 129+
(Peter Bowen) *prom: hit 7th: led or disp ld fr 10th: drvn 2 l ahd 2 out: edgd clr and 5 l up at last: flashed tail briefly but a in command* **4/1**[3]

-115 2 *6* **Girly Girl (IRE)**[29] 3372 7-10-6 0........................ BridgetAndrews(5) 120
(Dan Skelton) *hdwy to press ldrs 7th: cl up 3 out: rdn to chse wnr and gng clr of rest fr next: wknd bef last but remained clr of rest* **9/4**[2]

24FU 3 *14* **Road To Freedom**[30] 3348 7-11-4 120............................ TomO'Brien 116
(Lucy Wadham) *settled trcking ldrs: effrt bef 3 out:mstke next: sn rdn and outpcd: tk poor 3rd at last* **7/1**

32P 4 *7* **Vaillant Creek (FR)**[13] 3607 7-10-12 115......................... KielanWoods 104
(Alex Hales) *j.rt: led: reminder 6th: jnd 10th: ev ch tl hrd rdn and nt run on fr bef 2 out: lost poor 3rd at last* **16/1**

-313 5 *36* **Weststreet (IRE)**[19] 3525 6-11-4 120........................(p) LeightonAspell 70
(Oliver Sherwood) *prom tl rdn and slowed rapidly bef 3 out: sn t.o* **6/4**[1]

400 P **Mahlers Spirit (IRE)**[33] 3221 6-10-12 0.......................... JackQuinlan
(Sarah Humphrey) *cl up tl 7th: rdn and lost tch bef 9th: reluctant to continue: t.o and p.u 10th* **200/1**

2-PP P **Far From Defeat (IRE)**[49] 2995 6-10-12 0....................... LiamTreadwell
(Michael Scudamore) *bhd: struggling 10th: t.o and p.u after 3 out* **33/1**

664 P **Brave Cupid**[47] 3043 6-10-5 0.................................. JeremiahMcGrath
(Michael Roberts) *j. slowly: sn tailed herself off: p.u 9th* **100/1**

6m 22.0s **Going Correction** +0.325s/f (Yiel) **8** Ran SP% **113.6**
Speed ratings: **113,110,106,103,91 , ,**
CSF £13.64 TOTE £5.30: £1.50, £1.30, £1.80; EX 13.00 Trifecta £77.80.
Owner Roddy Owen & Paul Fullagar **Bred** R McCarthy **Trained** Little Newcastle, Pembrokes

FOCUS
There was a fresh two-yard strip of ground the whole way around on the hurdles course. The official race distance had an additional 170 yards added to it. Probably just a fair race of its type, but there's a case for rating this 5lb higher through the second.

3818 WENDLING H'CAP CHASE (18 fncs) 3m 38y
2:30 (2:30) (Class 3) (0-130,125) 5-Y-O+ **£6,498** (£1,908; £954; £477)

Form RPR

30P- 1 **Beforeall (IRE)**[299] 5138 8-11-11 **124**........................(t) LeightonAspell 132
(Oliver Sherwood) *last pair: rdn 11th: outpcd 14th: effrt and drvn bef 3 out: 8 l 3rd next: clsd grad for str driving to chal last: forced ahd fnl stride* **5/1**[3]

6155 2 *shd* **Regal Flow**[26] 3445 9-11-10 **123**................................... JamesBest 131
(Caroline Keevil) *cl up: wnt 2nd at 11th: led next: rdn fr 2 out: jnd last: battled on gamely w slt advantage tl pipped on post* **12/1**

0P12 3 *8* **Amidon (FR)**[30] 3349 6-11-11 **124**............................... HarrySkelton 126
(Lucy Wadham) *nt a fluent in midfield: mstke 10th: clsd to 2nd at 14th: led briefly 3 out: rdn and ev ch next: lost 2nd bef last and wknd* **7/2**[1]

2/3P 4 *22* **Bucking The Trend**[47] 3046 8-11-4 **122**......................... AlanJohns(5) 101
(Tim Vaughan) *last pair tl effrt 11th: sn pushed along: 3 l 3rd bef 15th: rdn and floundering bef 2 out* **12/1**

2-33 5 *4 1/2* **Listen Boy (IRE)**[29] 3364 10-11-6 **122**........................... RyanHatch(3) 95
(Nigel Twiston-Davies) *lft in ld briefly 3rd: pressed ldr tl 11th: rdn bef 14th: sn dropped out* **4/1**[2]

0P13 P **Fruity O'Rooney**[47] 3046 13-11-11 **124**........................(b) JamieMoore
(Gary Moore) *led: j. slowly 3rd and hdd briefly: hdd again 12th: sn hrd drvn: nt run on: t.o and p.u sn after 3 out* **12/1**

-220 P **Ultimatum Du Roy (FR)**[33] 3236 8-11-5 **118**.....................(tp) NoelFehily
(Alex Hales) *lacked fluency in last pair: rdn 12th: t.o and p.u 15th* **9/1**

6-4B **P** **Aigle De La See (FR)**[30] 3348 6-11-12 125 .... NicodeBoinville
(Nicky Henderson) *tended to lack fluency in midfield: slow 8th and 9th: hit 12th: dropped bk last at 14th: p.u next* **7/2**[1]

6m 45.7s (10.00) **Going Correction** +0.60s/f (Soft) **8** Ran SP% **114.2**
Speed ratings: **107,106,104,96,95 , ,**
CSF £58.08 CT £235.63 TOTE £5.90: £1.80, £3.90, £1.50; EX 70.90 Trifecta £276.60.
Owner Beforeall Partnership **Bred** Ms Barbara Johnston **Trained** Upper Lambourn, Berks

FOCUS
The official race distance had an additional 221 yards (over a furlong) added to it. This looked competitive and it was run at a fair gallop. The winner is rated back to his best.

3819 LIFE IS GOOD IN NORFOLK MAIDEN HURDLE (9 hdls) 2m 3y
3:05 (3:05) (Class 4) 4-Y-O+ **£5,198** (£1,526; £763; £381)

Form RPR
6 **1** **Gwafa (IRE)**[33] 3227 5-11-4 .... RichieMcLernon 137+
(Paul Webber) *ldng pair mostly: led 6th: cl 2nd whn mstke 3 out: sn led: drew 10 l clr bef last: easily* **7/2**[3]
52 **2** 15 **Magic Dancer**[27] 3423 4-10-4 ....(tp) GrahamWatters(3) 110
(Charlie Longsdon) *midfield: drvn to go 4th 3 out: last of four who were clr at next: sn 2nd but no ch wout threatening to go poor 2nd at last* **7/1**
03 **3** 1 ½ **Instant Karma (IRE)**[27] 3418 5-11-4 .... TomO'Brien 120
(Michael Bell) *t.k.h: led bef 5th tl next: w wnr tl bef 2 out: sn outpcd by him: lost poor 2nd at last* **16/1**
-102 **4** 9 **Late Night Lily**[33] 3221 5-10-11 .... HarrySkelton 106
(Dan Skelton) *a abt same pl: rdn after 3 out: fdd between last two* **9/4**[1]
-334 **5** 24 **Briac (FR)**[21] 3502 5-11-4 .... JamieMoore 90
(Jim Best) *midfield: on outside 1/2-way: nudged along and lost tch fr 3 out* **22/1**
5- **6** 4 **Maybell**[291] 5299 5-10-8 .... JamesBanks(3) 75
(Alex Hales) *mstke 2nd: nvr bttr than midfield: t.o 3 out* **66/1**
P0 **7** 12 **Little Buxted (USA)**[10] 3660 6-11-4 .... AndrewGlassonbury 70
(Jim Best) *led tl hdd bef 5th: lost pl qckly: t.o 3 out* **200/1**
0 **8** 19 **Iman (GER)**[31] 3306 6-11-4 .... JakeGreenall 61
(Sophie Leech) *taken down early: unruly s and slowly away: a bhd: t.o 3 out* **200/1**
5-50 **9** 38 **Gabriel Oats**[22] 3483 7-11-4 .... KielanWoods
(Graeme McPherson) *a last and wl off pce: t.o fr 1/2-way* **150/1**
P **Honey Badger**[59] 5-11-4 ....[1] JackQuinlan
(Eugene Stanford) *mstkes in rr: t.o and p.u 3 out* **100/1**
4-63 **P** **Rock Chick Supremo (IRE)**[57] 2847 5-10-6 .... BridgetAndrews(5)
(Dan Skelton) *midfield tl p.u after 5th and dismntd* **40/1**
3 **F** **Haut Bages (FR)**[78] 2439 4-10-7 .... LeightonAspell
(Oliver Sherwood) *fell 1st* **12/1**
P **Barman (FR)**[88] 5-11-4 .... NicodeBoinville
(Nicky Henderson) *cl up: sing to struggle whn mstke 3 out: mod 5th whn p.u next* **5/2**[2]

4m 18.3s (5.30) **Going Correction** +0.325s/f (Yiel)
WFA 4 from 5yo+ 11lb **13** Ran SP% **118.6**
Speed ratings (Par 105): **99,91,90,86,74 72,66,56,37, , ,**
CSF £27.73 TOTE £5.10: £2.20, £1.10, £4.50; EX 38.80 Trifecta £329.00.
Owner Saleh Al Homaizi & Imad Al Sagar **Bred** Kenilworth House Stud **Trained** Mollington, Oxon

FOCUS
There was a fresh two-yard strip of ground the whole way around on the hurdles course. The official race distance had an additional 113 yards added to it. An interesting maiden, with three potentially useful prospects heading the market.

3820 EAST BILNEY H'CAP CHASE (16 fncs) 2m 5f 44y
3:40 (3:40) (Class 5) (0-100,100) 5-Y-O+ **£4,548** (£1,335; £667; £333)

Form RPR
323B **1** **Halo Moon**[27] 3421 8-11-11 99........................(p) NoelFehily 120+
(Neil Mulholland) *taken steadily in rr: j.v.slowly 13th: stl 4th but effrt whn nt fluent 3 out: sn swept into ld and drew wl clr: heavily eased flat* **11/10**[1]
P-PP **2** 17 **Midnight Charmer**[92] 2140 10-11-12 100........................(t) RichieMcLernon 99
(Emma Baker) *cl up: ev ch and nudged along 3 out: sn lost tch w wnr: rdn to go poor 2nd sn after last* **17/2**
/333 **3** 2 ¼ **Salut Honore (FR)**[24] 3468 10-10-6 83........................(t) JamesBanks(3) 83
(Alex Hales) *led: pckd 10th: drvn 3 out: sn hdd and outpcd by wnr: pckd last and lost 2nd* **7/2**[2]
3F **4** 21 **Glenwood For Ever (IRE)**[27] 3421 8-11-8 96........................(tp) TomO'Brien 72
(Paul John Gilligan, Ire) *cl up: lost pl 10th: struggling bef 13th: t.o between last two and fin v slowly* **5/1**[3]
2140 **5** 2 ¾ **Minella Bliss (IRE)**[33] 3220 11-11-2 97........................(b) WilliamFeatherstone(7) 70
(James Evans) *bhd tl 7th: clsd to join ldr briefly 10th: cl 2nd tl rdn 3 out: fnd nil: t.o between last two* **17/2**
34P- **P** **That's The Deal (IRE)**[286] 5374 12-10-4 81........................ BenPoste(3)
(John Cornwall) *last fr 7th: u.p 11th: sn lost tch: t.o whn climbed 13th and p.u* **33/1**

6m 0.4s (18.60) **Going Correction** +0.60s/f (Soft) **6** Ran SP% **110.5**
Speed ratings: **88,81,80,72,71**
CSF £10.34 TOTE £1.90: £1.30, £3.70; EX 12.20 Trifecta £61.80.
Owner Level Par Racing **Bred** David Jenks **Trained** Limpley Stoke, Wilts

FOCUS
The official race distance had an additional 185 yards added to it. Four of these runners failed to finish last time, two the last twice, so this isn't likely to be strong form, but it was a big chase pb from the winner.

3821 LONGHAM CONDITIONAL JOCKEYS' H'CAP HURDLE (11 hdls) 2m 4f 1y
4:10 (4:11) (Class 5) (0-100,100) 4-Y-O+ **£3,898** (£1,144; £572; £286)

Form RPR
2431 **1** **Hassadin**[33] 3219 10-11-5 96........................(p) HarryCobden(3) 102
(Michael Blake) *led: jnd 7th: duelled for ld tl slt advantage and rdn 2 out: gaining command whn gd jump last: styd on steadily* **5/2**[1]
-0P3 **2** 3 ¼ **Vent Nivernais (FR)**[70] 2596 7-10-0 79........................(b) WilliamFeatherstone(5) 83
(James Evans) *sn prom: jnd wnr 7th: upsides tl rdn between last two: kpt on same pce and all out to hold 2nd* **9/2**[3]
-2F2 **3** ½ **Slidecheck (IRE)**[10] 3661 9-10-11 91........................(tp) MikeyHamill(6) 95
(Alexandra Dunn) *settled in 3rd or 4th pl: 8 l 3rd and hrd drvn bef 3 out: effrt after next: disputing 2nd and trying to rch wnr whn hit last: no ch after: game effrt* **8/1**
F323 **4** 8 **Jumpandtravel (IRE)**[20] 3503 7-11-9 100........................ JoeColliver(3) 95
(Micky Hammond) *midfield: pushed along and nt travelling 3rd: nt fluent 4th: u.p after 5th: n.d fr 8th: plodded on* **9/2**[3]
-P12 **5** 20 **Running Wolf (IRE)**[8] 3098 5-11-11 99........................(t) KillianMoore 74
(Alex Hales) *settled in rr trio: short-lived effrt bef 3 out* **10/3**[2]
040P **6** 11 **Betsy Boo Boo**[51] 2952 7-11-0 88........................ JeremiahMcGrath 52
(Michael Roberts) *last tl 3 out where t.o* **16/1**

POUP **7** 21 **Whatsupjack (IRE)**[56] 2868 9-9-9 74 oh2........................(b) GrahamCarson(5) 17
(Shaun Harris) *j. poorly: prom tl lost pl and j. slowly 6th: rdn and wknd 7th: nt run on: t.o last 3 out* **14/1**

5m 34.7s (14.30) **Going Correction** +0.325s/f (Yiel) **7** Ran SP% **111.7**
Speed ratings (Par 103): **84,82,82,79,71 66,58**
CSF £13.66 TOTE £3.40: £1.90, £2.80; EX 17.30 Trifecta £102.50.
Owner Wayne Clifford **Bred** Mrs S Clifford **Trained** Trowbridge, Wilts

FOCUS
There was a fresh two-yard strip of ground the whole way round on the hurdle course. The official race distance had an additional 141yds added to it. A low-grade handicap. Winner similar to recent win, with the second to his mark and the third to the level of his chase form.
T/Plt: £191.60 to a £1 stake. Pool of £62,080.47 - 236.43 winning tickets. T/Qpdt: £46.20 to a £1 stake. Pool of £5,055.03 - 80.82 winning tickets. **Iain Mackenzie**

3619 WARWICK (L-H)
Thursday, January 28

OFFICIAL GOING: Soft (heavy in places, 5.2)
Wind: fresh 1/2 behind Weather: overcast, shower race 6 (4.30)

3822 LIGHTHORNE LAMB JUVENILE HURDLE (8 hdls) 2m
1:50 (1:50) (Class 4) 4-Y-O **£3,898** (£1,144; £572; £286)

Form RPR
1 **1** **Fixe Le Kap (FR)**[30] 3347 4-11-5 133........................ DarylJacob 142+
(Nicky Henderson) *led to 3rd: led 5th: wnt clr bef 2 out: eased in clsng stages: v easily* **30/100**[1]
2 28 **Three Colours Red (IRE)**[123] 4-10-12 0........................ GavinSheehan 101
(Warren Greatrex) *t.k.h: trckd wnr: led 3rd to 5th: drvn bef 2 out: kpt on: no ch w wnr* **8/1**[3]
13 **3** 7 **Mystery Code**[54] 2896 4-10-12 123........................ WayneHutchinson 96
(Alan King) *trckd ldrs: 3rd 4th: drvn 3 out: wl hld whn blnd next* **7/2**[2]
4 7 **Deebaj (IRE)**[182] 4-10-12 0........................ RichardJohnson 89
(Richard Price) *hld up towards rr: hdwy 3rd: wnt modest 4th 5th: wknd next* **25/1**
04 **5** 14 **Mister Dick (FR)**[49] 2992 4-10-5 0........................ PatrickCowley(7) 73
(Jonjo O'Neill) *chsd ldrs: drvn and lost pl 5th: bhd next* **25/1**
35 **P** **Jinsha Lake (IRE)**[5] 3730 4-10-7 0........................(t) ConorRing(5)
(Evan Williams) *in rr: hit 4th: sn bhd: t.o next: p.u after 3 out* **33/1**
P **Live Miracle (USA)**[235] 4-10-5 0........................ AidanColeman
(Venetia Williams) *trckd ldrs: drvn and lost pl after 4th: sn bhd: t.o next: p.u bef 2 out* **10/1**
35 **P** **Renaissance Red**[55] 2882 4-10-12 0........................(t) BrendanPowell
(Brendan Powell) *in rr: pushed along 3rd: sn bhd: t.o 5th: p.u after next* **33/1**

4m 10.0s (11.00) **Going Correction** +0.85s/f (Soft) **8** Ran SP% **132.9**
Speed ratings: **106,92,88,85,78 , ,**
CSF £5.22 TOTE £1.30: £1.02, £2.30, £1.10; EX 4.90 Trifecta £11.20.
Owner Simon Munir & Isaac Souede **Bred** Olivier Tricot & Max Hennau **Trained** Upper Lambourn, Berks

FOCUS
A dry night and the ground remained soft with heavy places. An uncompetitive juvenile hurdle run at a fair gallop but a useful effort from the winner. Rail movements added 11yds to the advertised distance and the winning rider commented: "It's soft and a bit gluey." The winner was very impressive and rates a high-class juvenile on soft ground.

3823 D W CLARK DRAINAGE H'CAP CHASE (20 fncs) 3m 1f 100y
2:20 (2:20) (Class 4) (0-120,120) 5-Y-O+ **£4,223** (£1,240; £620; £310)

Form RPR
-52P **1** **As De Fer (FR)**[55] 2878 10-10-7 106........................(t) DavidNoonan(5) 135+
(Anthony Honeyball) *chsd ldr: led 14th: clr fr 16th: stmbld appr 2 out: hit 2 out: heavily eased run-in* **7/1**
11/F **2** 26 **Willoughby Hedge**[30] 3348 9-11-12 120........................ WayneHutchinson 117
(Alan King) *in rr: hdwy to trck ldrs 8th: chsd wnr 14th: one pce fr next* **3/1**[1]
3-41 **3** nk **Bears Rails**[39] 3178 6-11-0 108........................ TomScudamore 105
(Colin Tizzard) *chsd ldrs: hit 10th: 3rd next: outpcd and lost pl 15th: kpt on fr 2 out* **6/1**[3]
1-06 **4** 8 **Itoldyou (IRE)**[39] 3176 10-11-5 116........................(tp) ThomasGarner(3) 107
(Linda Jewell) *in rr: pushed along 4th: hdwy 8th: drvn 14th: lost pl next: sn bhd* **33/1**
521F **5** 25 **Paddy The Oscar (IRE)**[15] 3583 13-11-6 119........................ ConorRing(5) 87
(Grace Harris) *led: hdd and blnd 14th: lost pl 16th: sn wl bhd* **14/1**
-223 **P** **Smart Exit (IRE)**[42] 3127 9-11-2 115........................ CiaranGethings(5)
(Stuart Edmunds) *chsd ldrs: reminder 6th: lost pl 14th: sn bhd: t.o whn p.u bef 2 out* **8/1**
3/U0 **P** **Tidal Dance (IRE)**[30] 3348 9-11-6 119........................(b[1]) CharlieDeutsch(5)
(Venetia Williams) *in rr: mstke 1st: bhd and reminders 5th: t.o 11th: p.u after 13th: b.b.v* **16/1**
2-F1 **P** **Newton Thistle**[42] 3127 9-11-12 120........................(t) DavidBass
(Ben Pauling) *in rr-div: chsd ldrs 8th: lost pl 15th: wl bhd 4 out: p.u bef last* **10/1**
3P46 **U** **Themanfrom Minella (IRE)**[33] 3236 7-10-11 112(tp) MrMJPKendrick(7)
(Ben Case) *chsd ldrs: 4th whn stumnled landing and uns rdr 13th* **9/1**
11-6 **P** **Castarnie**[71] 2566 8-11-3 111........................ TomCannon
(Robert Walford) *j.rt: mid-div: mstke 1st: drvn 7th: lost pl next: sn bhd: t.o whn p.u bef 14th* **5/1**[2]

7m 6.2s (7.20) **Going Correction** +0.45s/f (Soft) **10** Ran SP% **114.1**
Speed ratings: **106,97,97,95,87 , , , ,**
CSF £28.72 CT £133.88 TOTE £5.70: £2.10, £1.90, £2.00; EX 38.90 Trifecta £182.50.
Owner Midd Shire Racing **Bred** Didier Leviel **Trained** Mosterton, Dorset

FOCUS
Mainly exposed sorts in a fair handicap in which rail movements saw 104yds added to the race distance. The gallop was sound throughout. The impressive winner was a 146 chaser at his best and there's a case for rating this race up to 5lb higher.

3824 BIGCASINOBONUSES.CO.UK H'CAP HURDLE (12 hdls) 3m 2f
2:55 (2:55) (Class 3) (0-130,130) 4-Y-O+ **£6,498** (£1,908; £954; £477)

Form RPR
-141 **1** **The Boss's Dream (IRE)**[19] 3525 8-11-12 130........................ TrevorWhelan 140+
(Neil King) *w ldrs: led 3rd to next: led 8th: styd on wl fr 3 out: hld on gamely run-in* **8/1**
0132 **2** 1 ¾ **Tambura**[33] 3217 6-10-8 119........................ MrZBaker(7) 126
(G C Maundrell) *in rr: bhd and nt fluent 7th: safter 8th: chsd wnr sn after 3 out: swtchd lft sn after last: styd on same pce last 100yds* **9/2**[1]

6P30 **3** *35* **Sybarite (FR)**[27] 3407 10-11-7 **125**........ SamTwiston-Davies 97
(Nigel Twiston-Davies) *in last: bhd and drvn 4th: t.o 6th: styd on fr 3 out: distant 6th last: tk poor 3rd in clsng stages* **20/1**

-210 **4** *2 1/2* **Dan Emmett (USA)**[27] 3407 6-11-7 **125**........ BrendanPowell 96
(Michael Scudamore) *trckd ldrs: outpcd 3 out: distant 3rd whn blnd 2 out* **9/1**

212 **5** *17* **Battle Dust (IRE)**[28] 3383 7-11-7 **125**........(p) DavidBass 78
(Kim Bailey) *chsd ldrs: reminders after 6th: drvn 6th: lost pl appr 3 out* **7/1**[3]

5P1P **6** *6* **Earcomesthedream (IRE)**[33] 3220 13-9-8 **105**........(b) ArchieBellamy[(7)] 52
(Peter Pritchard) *chsd ldrs: reminders 2nd: sn drvn lost pl 4th: sn bhd: t.o 6th: kpt on after 3 out* **50/1**

-5PP **P** **Tara Tavey (IRE)**[67] 2658 11-9-13 **110**........(t) ConorSmith[(7)]
(Kevin Bishop) *in rr: reminders 2nd: t.o 6th: p.u bef 8th* **40/1**

-33F **P** **Vice Et Vertu (FR)**[30] 3348 7-11-5 **123**........(p) AndrewTinkler
(Henry Daly) *led to 3rd: led next: hdd 8th: lost pl next: t.o whn p.u bef 2 out* **16/1**

0142 **P** **Knight ofthe Realm**[40] 3146 7-10-7 **111**........ IanPopham
(Caroline Keevil) *nt fluent: chsd ldrs: 2nd 9th: wknd next: wl bhd whn p.u bef last* **6/1**[2]

2-05 **P** **Princess Tara (IRE)**[59] 2825 6-11-2 **120**........ AidanColeman
(Peter Bowen) *chsd ldrs: lost pl bef 7th: t.o whn p.u bef 8th* **10/1**

-2P2 **P** **An Poc Ar Buile (IRE)**[221] 798 7-10-3 **112**........(p) CiaranGethings[(5)]
(Sophie Leech) *trckd ldrs: lost pl bef 3 out: sn bhd: t.o whn p.u bef 2 out* **20/1**

42U4 **P** **Auvergnat (FR)**[48] 3008 6-11-9 **127**........(t) RichardJohnson
(Jonjo O'Neill) *in rr-div: hdwy to trck ldrs 6th: lost pl 8th: bhd whn p.u bef next* **10/1**

1-U0 **P** **Herbert Park (IRE)**[33] 3254 6-11-12 **130**........(b[1]) TomScudamore
(David Pipe) *in rr: hdwy to trck ldrs 6th: lost pl after 9th: sn bhd: t.o whn p.u bef 2 out* **7/1**[3]

7m 1.4s (24.40) **Going Correction** +1.15s/f (Heav) **13 Ran SP% 116.6**
Speed ratings (Par 107): **108,107,96,95,90 88,,,,,,,**
CSF £41.68 CT £702.05 TOTE £9.00: £2.80, £2.10, £6.50; EX 50.80 Trifecta £1005.20.
Owner SLIS Ltd, M Gibbons & D Nott **Bred** Paul Barden **Trained** Barbury Castle, Wiltshire

FOCUS
A reasonable staying handicap which was increased by 22yds owing to rail movements. The betting suggested this was a competitive event but the first two pulled clear in the last half mile. There's a case for rating this at least 6lb higher.

3825 BRITISH STALLION STUDS EBF MARES' "NATIONAL HUNT" NOVICES' HURDLE (11 hdls) 2m 5f
3:30 (3:31) (Class 4) 4-Y-O+ **£4,548** (£1,335; £667; £333)

Form RPR

12 **1** **Savingforvegas (IRE)**[39] 3175 6-11-0 0........ BrendanPowell 117+
(Stuart Edmunds) *trckd ldrs: mstke 8th: led bef 2 out: j. last last: drvn rt out* **4/1**[3]

-113 **2** *3/4* **Surtee Du Berlais (IRE)**[29] 3372 6-11-9 127........ ThomasGarner[(3)] 125
(Oliver Sherwood) *w ldrs: led bef 7th: hdd bef 2 out: hit last: rallied: styd on to take 2nd nr fin* **3/1**[2]

5- **3** *1* **Buttercup (FR)**[217] 5-11-0 0........ AidanColeman 113+
(Venetia Williams) *trckd ldrs: hit 3rd: chal bef 2 out: carried lft last: kpt on same pce* **5/1**

2 **4** *8* **Mia's Storm (IRE)**[53] 2929 6-11-0 0........ WayneHutchinson 108+
(Alan King) *trckd ldrs: clipped heels: stmbld bdly and lost pl 8th: rallied and modest 4th appr 2 out: kpt on same pce bef 2 out* **11/8**[1]

2-6 **5** *73* **Meyrem Ana**[245] 526 6-10-7 0........ MrWillPettis[(7)] 31
(Natalie Lloyd-Beavis) *led: hdd bef 7th: lost pl 3 out: sn bhd: t.o whn lft 5th 2 out* **100/1**

P **Treaty Girl (IRE)**[270] 5-11-0 0........ DavidBass
(Ben Pauling) *chsd ldrs: drvn 6th: lost pl next: sn bhd: t.o 5th whn p.u bef 2 out* **12/1**

5U **P** **Hawaian Rose**[33] 3258 6-10-7 0........ PaulO'Brien[(7)]
(Colin Tizzard) *chsd ldrs: lost pl 5th: sn drvn: bhd whn j.lft 7th: sn t.o: p.u after 3 out* **80/1**

5m 51.9s (30.90) **Going Correction** +1.45s/f (Heav) **7 Ran SP% 113.7**
Speed ratings (Par 105): **99,98,98,95,67**
CSF £16.57 TOTE £5.70: £2.40, £2.00; EX 16.20 Trifecta £69.20.
Owner Ben Turner **Bred** David Byrne **Trained** Newport Pagnell, Bucks

FOCUS
Not the strongest of novice hurdles and a steady gallop to the end of the back straight means this form isn't entirely reliable. Eleven yards were added onto the official distance due to rail movement. The second sets the level.

3826 SANDRA LLOYD MEMORIAL WILLOUGHBY DE BROKE OPEN HUNTERS' CHASE (FOR WILLOUGHBY DE BROKE TROPHY) (18 fncs) 3m
4:00 (4:04) (Class 6) 5-Y-O+ **£1,247** (£387; £193; £96)

Form RPR

220- **1** **Mendip Express (IRE)**[324] 4690 10-11-11 146........(t) MrDavidMaxwell[(5)] 145+
(Philip Hobbs) *hld up towards rr: hdwy 5th: sn trcking ldrs: led 3 out: clr next: pushed out* **1/2**[1]

45-2 **2** *3 3/4* **Richmond (FR)**[15] 3585 11-11-9 125........ MissLMTurner[(7)] 135
(P P C Turner) *w ldr: led 2nd: mstke and hdd 8th: outpcd 12th: kpt on 4 out to take modest 3rd appr 2 out: 2nd appr last* **7/2**[2]

53/0 **3** *13* **Clonbanan Lad (IRE)**[242] 576 10-11-9 0........ MrJSole[(3)] 120
(Miss Louise Allan) *w ldrs: led 8th: hdd 3 out: one pce* **20/1**

/P6- **4** *10* **Night Alliance (IRE)**[460] 2062 11-11-5 122........(t) MrLeoMahon[(7)] 110
(P R M Philips) *chsd ldrs 6th: outpcd and lost pl 12th: bhd fr 4 out: poor 4th bef 2 out* **25/1**

34P- **P** **Bally Sands (IRE)**[344] 4299 12-11-9 99........ MrZBaker[(3)]
(Robin Mathew) *led to 2nd: drvn 10th: lost pl 12th: sn bhd: p.u 3 out* **33/1**

U- **P** **Kalmonto (FR)**[217] 10-12-1 0........(b) MrMatthewHampton[(5)]
(R J Alford) *prom: lost pl 8th: towards rr and reminders 11th: sn t.o: p.u bef next* **9/1**[3]

310/ **P** **Barel Of Laughs (IRE)**[888] 1362 10-11-12 115........ MrWBiddick
(Philip Rowley) *hld up in rr: hdwy to join ldrs 12th: wknd appr 3 out: sn bhd: t.o whn p.u bef 2 out* **12/1**

P0-P **P** **Sustainability (IRE)**[15] 3585 11-11-5 115........(p) MrJSKnox[(7)]
(Miss B Eckley) *in rr: bhd: mstke and reminders 11th: t.o whn p.u bef next* **66/1**

P **Equity Swap (IRE)**[168] 1248 7-11-5 120........(t) MrLWilliams[(7)]
(Chris Williams) *in rr: mstke 11th: sn bhd: p.u bef next* **20/1**

6m 54.1s (20.10) **Going Correction** +0.75s/f (Soft) **9 Ran SP% 124.4**
Speed ratings: **96,94,90,87,,,,,**
CSF £2.88 TOTE £1.70: £1.10, £1.40, £4.20; EX 2.90 Trifecta £27.50.
Owner David Maxwell Racing Limited **Bred** Miss E Hamilton **Trained** Withycombe, Somerset

FOCUS
A wide display of ability on show but a reasonable gallop and a thorough test of stamina in the conditions in a race where 104yds were added to the official distance. The winner was a 154 chaser at best and will be tough to beat in this grade.

3827 DELI CAFE INTERMEDIATE OPEN NATIONAL HUNT FLAT RACE 2m
4:30 (4:31) (Class 6) 5-6-Y-O **£1,624** (£477; £238; £119)

Form RPR

3 **1** **Shambougg**[44] 3104 5-10-12 0........ RichardJohnson 108+
(Philip Hobbs) *trckd ldr: effrt 3f out: led over 1f out: drvn out* **4/1**[3]

2 *1* **Shrewd Tactics (IRE)**[95] 5-10-7 0........ ConorRing[(5)] 105
(Evan Williams) *hld up in rr: hdwy 6f out: cl 3rd 3f out: outpcd over 1f out: styd on wl to take 2nd towards fin* **7/2**[2]

3 *1 3/4* **Reilly's Minor (IRE)**[116] 5-10-12 0........ GavinSheehan 103
(Warren Greatrex) *led: drvn 3f out: hdd over 1f out: kpt on same pce* **4/1**[3]

5 **4** *6* **Red Infantry (IRE)**[63] 2729 6-10-9 0........ RobMcCarth[(3)] 97
(Ian Williams) *t.k.h in rr: hdwy 6f out: sn pushed along: lost pl over 3f out* **16/1**

5 *30* **Katara Bay** 5-10-12 0........ AidanColeman 72
(Venetia Williams) *mid-div: chsd ldrs 7f out: drvn 4f out: sn lost pl* **3/1**[1]

6 *99* **Eclectica Girl** 5-10-5 0........ LeeEdwards
(Kevin Frost) *in rr: pushed along after 6f: lost pl 7f out: sn bhd: t.o 4f out* **50/1**

P **Ballycash (IRE)**[124] 5-10-12 0........ SamTwiston-Davies
(Nigel Twiston-Davies) *trckd ldrs: drvn and lost pl over 4f out: sn wl bhd: t.o whn p.u 2f out* **4/1**[3]

4m 10.3s (24.90) **Going Correction** +1.75s/f (Heav) **7 Ran SP% 115.1**
Speed ratings: **107,106,105,102,87 38,**
CSF £18.62 TOTE £3.80: £2.30, £2.30; EX 15.50 Trifecta £28.20.
Owner M G St Quinton **Bred** Mrs A F Tullie **Trained** Withycombe, Somerset
■ Mixelle Days was withdrawn. Price at time of withdrawal 50/1. Rule 4 does not apply.

FOCUS
Not much to go on in the way of Rules form and just an ordinary gallop in which the first three pulled clear in the straight. Eleven yards were added to the distance of this race. The winner built on his debut and the fourth helps set the level.
T/Plt: £27.50 to a £1 stake. Pool of £58917.52 - 1562.39 winning tickets. T/Qpdt: £16.70 to a £1 stake. Pool of £3790.35 - 167.82 winning tickets. **Walter Glynn**

3828 - 3829a (Foreign Racing) - See Raceform Interactive

3808 THURLES (R-H)
Thursday, January 28

OFFICIAL GOING: Heavy

3830a THURLES RACECOURSE SUPPORTERS CLUB CHASE (LISTED RACE) (13 fncs) 2m 2f
2:15 (2:15) 5-Y-O+ **£12,426** (£3,632; £1,720)

RPR

1 **Smashing (FR)**[68] 2655 7-11-3 147........ DavyRussell 155+
(Henry De Bromhead, Ire) *mde all: stl gng wl whn stdd 3 out: mstke next and pckd: sn rdn and asserted: wandered sltly bef last: drvn out run-in and styd on wl* **9/10**[1]

2 *5* **Tennis Cap (FR)**[18] 3552 9-11-3 140........ PaulTownend 149+
(W P Mullins, Ire) *settled bhd ldr in 2nd: jnd for 2nd fr 4th: dropped to rr bef 1/2-way: lft 3rd fr 3 out and rdn in 2nd next: sn no imp on wnr u.p: kpt on same pce* **20/1**

3 *9* **Nearly Nama'd (IRE)**[18] 3552 8-11-3 143........ BarryGeraghty 142+
(Ms Sandra Hughes, Ire) *w.w in rr of quartet: j. sltly lft 3rd: slt mstke 6th and impr into 2nd after next: slt mstke 5 out: dropped to 3rd bef 3 out where lft 2nd: rdn and no imp on wnr in 3rd fr 2 out: one pce after* **4/1**[3]

F **Avant Tout (FR)**[32] 3301 6-11-3 144........ RWalsh
(W P Mullins, Ire) *hld up bhd ldrs: disp 2nd fr 4th: 3rd 1/2-way: niggled along in 3rd after 4 out and wnt 2nd bef next where fell* **9/4**[2]

5m 4.4s (21.80) **4 Ran SP% 108.2**
CSF £11.61 TOTE £1.70; DF 14.80 Trifecta £37.60.
Owner Ann & Alan Potts Partnership **Bred** Jacques Seror **Trained** Knockeen, Co Waterford

FOCUS
A small field but not a race short of incident. The winner and second are rated to their marks.

3831 - 3833a (Foreign Racing) - See Raceform Interactive

3503 DONCASTER (L-H)
Friday, January 29

OFFICIAL GOING: Good to soft (good in places; chs 7.5, hdl 7.7)
Wind: strong 1/2 against Weather: fine and sunny but very windy

3834 SKY BET NOVICES' H'CAP CHASE (15 fncs) 2m 3f 44y
12:50 (12:50) (Class 4) (0-105,105) 5-Y-O+ **£4,548** (£1,335; £667; £333)

Form RPR

3300 **1** **Native Robin (IRE)**[50] 2987 6-11-10 **103**........ NickScholfield 117+
(Jeremy Scott) *led tl hdd appr 8th: led appr 2 out: styd on wl* **20/1**

43/F **2** *3 1/2* **The Mumper (IRE)**[52] 2957 9-11-9 **102**........ WayneHutchinson 110
(Alan King) *mid-div: trckd ldrs 7th: led 4 out: hdd appr 2 out: kpt on same pce run-in* **8/1**[3]

P-53 **3** *shd* **Coozan George**[59] 2841 7-11-7 **100**........(t) BrianHughes 109
(Malcolm Jefferson) *hld up in rr: hdwy 10th: chsng ldrs 2 out: hit last: kpt on clsng stages* **7/1**[2]

6432 **4** *2* **Theflyingportrait (IRE)**[34] 3241 7-11-5 **98**........(t) SeanQuinlan 104
(Jennie Candlish) *in rr: hdwy 11th: styd on fr 3 out: nt rch ldrs* **12/1**

F551 **5** *1 3/4* **Pandy Wells**[34] 3224 7-10-3 **89**........ ArchieBellamy[(7)] 93
(Graeme McPherson) *mid-div: hdwy 11th: chsng ldrs 3 out: kpt on same pce* **12/1**

-444 **6** *3/4* **Under The Phone (IRE)**[51] 2973 7-11-7 **105**........ ChrisWard[(5)] 110
(Robin Dickin) *chsd ldrs: one pce fr 3 out* **13/2**[1]

32-1 **7** *1 1/4* **Supreme Bob (IRE)**[46] 3081 10-11-7 **100**........ TrevorWhelan 103
(Debra Hamer) *chsd ldrs: one pce fr 3 out* **7/1**[2]

P251 **8** *7* **Harleys Max**[9] 3683 7-9-10 **82** 7ex........ JamesCorbett[(7)] 80
(Susan Corbett) *hld up in rr: hdwy to trck ldrs 7th: upsides whn hmpd 9th: wknd 3 out* **11/1**

1-PP **9** *2 3/4* **Passing Fiesta**[72] 2565 7-10-5 **87**........ JamesBanks[(3)] 82
(Sarah-Jayne Davies) *mid-div: hdwy 6th: led 8th: j.rt next: hdd 4 out: sn wknd: mstke last* **66/1**

4P43 **10** *3 ¾* **Wish In A Well (IRE)**[29] 3387 7-10-7 **86**..........(t) KielanWoods 77
(Ben Case) *chsd ldrs: wknd 3 out* **12/1**
-040 **11** *25* **Our Phylli Vera (IRE)**[32] 3311 7-10-3 **85**.......... ColmMcCormack(3) 53
(Joanne Foster) *in rr: bhd fr 5th: t.o 11th* **66/1**
544 **12** *nk* **Glacial Rock (IRE)**[31] 3345 10-11-12 **105**..........(v[1]) HenryBrooke 76
(Alistair Whillans) *mstkes: chsd ldrs: blnd 10th: lost pl next: sn bhd: t.o* **12/1**
600 **13** *4* **Inchcolm (IRE)**[91] 2169 6-10-7 **89**.......... JoeColliver(3) 53
(Micky Hammond) *in rr: hdwy 7th: lost pl 9th: bhd fr 11th: t.o* **25/1**
4006 **F** **Harvey's Hope**[15] 3592 10-11-12 **105**.......... JamesReveley
(Keith Reveley) *in rr: fell 8th* **20/1**
/3-U **U** **Generous Helpings (IRE)**[48] 3042 7-11-10 **103**.......... JoshuaMoore
(Gary Moore) *in rr: hdwy 10th: hit next: keeping on whn blnd and uns rdr 3 out* **12/1**
-414 **P** **Albatros De Guye (FR)**[66] 2698 6-10-3 **82**..........(tp) JeremiahMcGrath
(Anna Newton-Smith) *chsd ldrs: nt fluent 1st: mstke 8th: lost pl 8th: bhd whn blnd 10th: sn t.o: p.u bef 3 out* **16/1**

4m 53.5s (4.50) **Going Correction** -0.15s/f (Good) **16** Ran SP% **118.5**
Speed ratings: **84,82,82,81,80 80,80,77,75,74 63,63,62, ,**
CSF £163.01 CT £1246.72 TOTE £31.50: £3.40, £2.10, £2.30, £2.10; EX 153.90 Trifecta £1407.50.
Owner The Punchestown Syndicate **Bred** Barry O'Connor **Trained** Brompton Regis, Somerset

FOCUS
This novice handicap was wide open and it saw a host of chances down the home straight. The winner was up a stone on the best of his hurdles figures.

3835 SKY BET NOVICES' HURDLE (8 hdls) 2m 140y
1:25 (1:25) (Class 4) 4-Y-0+ **£4,548** (£1,335; £667; £333)

Form RPR
P21P **1** **Cyrius Moriviere (FR)**[27] 3447 6-11-7 130..........(t) MauriceLinehan(3) 129+
(Ben Pauling) *trckd ldr: led 4th: c clr on bit after 2 out: rdn out run-in: easily* **10/3**[2]
2 *19* **Moabit (GER)**[176] 4-10-7 0..........(t) SamTwiston-Davies 96+
(Paul Nicholls) *in tch: hit 1st: hdwy to chse ldr appr 3 out: rdn 2 out: one pce and sn no ch w wnr* **7/2**[3]
0 **3** *3 ½* **Brian Boranha (IRE)**[63] 2756 5-11-4 0.......... BrianHughes 101+
(Peter Niven) *hld up: pushed along appr 3 out: styd on fr appr last: wnt 3rd fnl 110yds* **66/1**
46 **4** *2 ¾* **Kauto Riko (FR)**[30] 3363 5-11-4 0.......... JamesDavies 99
(Tom Gretton) *midfield: rdn appr 3 out: plugged on* **100/1**
0-20 **5** *1 ¾* **Give Him A Glance**[43] 3130 5-11-4 0.......... WayneHutchinson 97
(Alan King) *hld up: racd keenly: nt fluent 2nd: pushed along and hdwy after 3 out: plugged on* **14/1**
6 *nk* **Levelling** 4-10-0 0.......... DavidEngland 79
(Dan Skelton) *trckd ldrs: rdn 3 out: sn outpcd: plugged on run-in* **28/1**
7 *6* **Big Thunder**[111] 6-11-4 0.......... CraigNichol 91
(Micky Hammond) *in tch: rdn 3 out: wknd run-in* **14/1**
0 **8** *nk* **Camakasi (IRE)**[44] 3114 5-11-4 0..........(t) DaveCrosse 91
(Ali Stronge) *hld up in midfield: hdwy after 5th: wnt 3rd 3 out: sn rdn: stl 3rd last: wknd* **66/1**
34 **9** *4* **Adman Sam (IRE)**[34] 3226 5-11-4 0.......... DarylJacob 87
(Ian Williams) *in tch: pushed along bef 3 out: sn wknd* **25/1**
003 **10** *1 ¼* **Thyne For Gold (IRE)**[15] 3590 5-11-4 0.......... HenryBrooke 86
(Donald McCain) *hld up: sme hdwy 3 out: nvr threatened* **40/1**
0-02 **11** *11* **Cassie**[34] 3215 6-10-11 0..........(t) NicodeBoinville 69
(Ben Pauling) *in tch: wknd after 5th* **14/1**
00 **12** *7* **St Lewis**[21] 3506 6-11-4 0.......... SeanQuinlan 70
(Jennie Candlish) *hld up: nvr threatened* **150/1**
10 **13** *3* **Royal Sea (IRE)**[91] 2163 7-11-4 0.......... KielanWoods 67
(Michael Mullineaux) *hld up: nvr threatened* **40/1**
3-20 **14** *1 ¾* **Bendomingo (IRE)**[78] 2450 5-10-13 0..........(t) JamieBargary(5) 66
(Nigel Twiston-Davies) *led narrowly: hit 4th and hdd: rdn after 5th: wknd bef 3 out* **25/1**
0 **15** *1 ¼* **Sarazen Bridge**[30] 3363 5-11-4 0.......... BarryGeraghty 65
(Jonjo O'Neill) *midfield: wknd appr 3 out* **25/1**
0-0 **16** *shd* **Vic's Last Stand (IRE)**[25] 3476 6-10-8 0.......... HarryChalloner(3) 58
(Keith Reveley) *a in rr* **66/1**
10-2 **17** *7* **Dashing Oscar (IRE)**[94] 2123 6-11-4 0..........(t) RyanMahon 58
(Harry Fry) *trckd ldr: rdn after 5th: hit 3 out: sn outpcd: btn whn mstke last: wknd and eased* **9/4**[1]
0 **18** *39* **Lynda's Boy**[63] 2750 5-11-4 0.......... RobertDunne 23
(Dan Skelton) *midfield: hit fnal 5th: wknd 3 out* **100/1**

4m 4.0s (-0.70) **Going Correction** -0.15s/f (Good)
WFA 4 from 5yo+ 11lb **18** Ran SP% **123.1**
Speed ratings (Par 105): **95,86,84,83,82 82,79,79,77,76 71,68,66,66,65 65,62,43**
CSF £14.23 TOTE £4.60: £1.80, £1.80, £7.90; EX 18.20 Trifecta £1150.40.
Owner The Pillar P Partnership **Bred** Patrick Harroin **Trained** Bourton-On-The-Water, Gloucs

FOCUS
A modest novice hurdle. The winner set a decent standard and this was probably a step up on his Huntingdon win.

3836 SKY BET H'CAP CHASE (QUALIFIER FOR THE CHALLENGER STAYING CHASE SERIES FINAL) (18 fncs) 3m 6y
2:00 (2:00) (Class 4) (0-120,120) 5-Y-0+ **£5,848** (£1,717; £858; £429)

Form RPR
5/P1 **1** **Gonalston Cloud (IRE)**[32] 3310 9-10-7 **101**.......... AndrewTinkler 117+
(Nick Kent) *chsd ldrs: outpcd and mstke 11th: chsng ldrs next: rdn appr 4 out: led appr 3 out: forged clr last 150yds* **4/1**[1]
PP56 **2** *9* **Hollow Blue Sky (FR)**[28] 3404 9-11-1 **114**..........(tp) JamieBargary(5) 120
(Nigel Twiston-Davies) *hld up in rr: hdwy to trck ldrs 11th: drvn upsides 4 out: chsd wnr next: kpt on same pce run-in* **11/1**
3-S4 **3** *½* **Baku Bay (IRE)**[69] 2631 8-11-10 **118**.......... WayneHutchinson 122
(Ali Stronge) *chsd ldrs: kpt on same pce fr 3 out* **8/1**
5P-0 **4** *1 ¼* **Oliver's Hill (IRE)**[51] 2973 7-11-1 **109**..........(tp) TomCannon 115+
(Lawney Hill) *trckd ldrs: led 14th: hdd appr 3 out: kpt on same pce* **33/1**
421U **5** *8* **Valleyofmilan (IRE)**[15] 3591 9-11-7 **120**.......... JamesCowley(5) 117
(Donald McCain) *in rr: kpt on fr 4 out: nvr a factor* **14/1**
-623 **6** *24* **Gamain (IRE)**[29] 3385 7-11-5 **113**..........(b) DarylJacob 97
(Ben Case) *led to 2nd: chsd ldrs: 5th and wkng whn hit 3 out: t.o whn blnd last* **16/1**
P-11 **7** *29* **Cyrien Star**[58] 2848 9-11-8 **116**.......... RichardJohnson 84
(Henry Daly) *mstke 1st: led 2nd: mstke 13th: hdd next: lost pl 4 out: eased after 2 out: t.o* **6/1**[3]
3-12 **P** **Present Lodger (IRE)**[83] 2341 8-11-9 **117**..........(t) DerekFox
(Lucinda Russell) *in rr: bhd 8th: t.o 12th: p.u bef 3 out* **12/1**
612P **P** **Spending Time**[50] 2988 7-11-6 **114**..........(tp) ConorO'Farrell
(David Pipe) *in rr: bhd fr 10th: t.o whn p.u bef 3 out* **11/1**
-401 **P** **Golanova**[74] 2539 8-11-4 **112**..........(b) JoshuaMoore
(Gary Moore) *in rr: mstke 1st: bdly hmpd 9th: sn t.o: p.u bef 12th* **16/1**
064 **U** **Grove Silver (IRE)**[30] 3362 7-11-9 **117**.......... SeanQuinlan
(Jennie Candlish) *hld up in rr: hdwy to trck ldrs 6th: outpcd whn blnd and uns rdr 13th* **10/1**
3-1P **F** **Globalisation (IRE)**[64] 2727 6-11-12 **120**..........(t) BarryGeraghty
(Rebecca Curtis) *in rr: sn pushed along: bhd whn fell 9th* **5/1**[2]

6m 4.7s (-7.30) **Going Correction** -0.15s/f (Good) **12** Ran SP% **116.9**
Speed ratings: **106,103,102,102,99 91,82, , ,**
CSF £46.92 CT £338.66 TOTE £4.50: £1.70, £4.60, £2.80; EX 51.80 Trifecta £675.70.
Owner R J Jackson **Bred** Conna Stud **Trained** Brigg, Lincs

FOCUS
This modest staying handicap served up a decent test. The winner built on his recent win.

3837 SKY BET H'CAP HURDLE (11 hdls) 3m 96y
2:30 (2:31) (Class 4) (0-120,120) 4-Y-0+ **£4,548** (£1,335; £667; £333)

Form RPR
6003 **1** **Night In Milan (IRE)**[28] 3428 10-11-8 **119**..........(b) HarryChalloner(3) 130+
(Keith Reveley) *trckd ldrs: 2nd 8th: upsides 2 out: sn led and drew clr* **6/1**[3]
-1P0 **2** *8* **Horsted Valley**[67] 2687 6-11-2 **113**..........(p) HarryBannister(3) 117
(Warren Greatrex) *hld up in mid-div: hdwy 4th: modest 3rd appr 2 out: kpt on to take 2nd last* **20/1**
0-40 **3** *7* **Sebastian Beach (IRE)**[42] 3137 5-11-8 **116**..........(t) RichardJohnson 114
(Jonjo O'Neill) *mid-div: hdwy appr 3 out: kpt on to take modest 3rd nr fin* **14/1**
-3P6 **4** *1 ½* **San Telm (IRE)**[42] 3137 11-11-10 **118**..........(p) JoshuaMoore 113
(Stuart Edmunds) *led: hdd sn after 2 out: wknd last* **8/1**
3-25 **5** *2 ¾* **Allbarnone**[219] 833 8-11-4 **112**.......... DenisO'Regan 105
(William Kinsey) *in rr: kpt on fr 3 out: nvr a factor* **25/1**
4366 **6** *6* **Echo Springs**[31] 3344 6-11-2 **110**.......... BrianHughes 97
(Danielle McCormick) *sn chsng ldrs: wknd appr 2 out* **5/1**[2]
P654 **7** *4* **Sinbad The Sailor**[55] 2125 11-11-4 **112**..........(t) AndrewTinkler 96
(George Baker) *in rr: sme hdwy appr 3 out: wknd appr 2 out* **20/1**
-010 **8** *¾* **Giveitachance (IRE)**[67] 2687 9-10-9 **103**..........(t) BrendanPowell 86
(Claire Dyson) *chsd ldrs: lost pl bef 2 out* **25/1**
6-43 **9** *hd* **Achimota (IRE)**[48] 3038 10-11-10 **118**.......... KielanWoods 105
(Graeme McPherson) *chsd ldrs: reminders 7th: lost pl bef 2 out* **8/1**
3-0P **10** *1 ¾* **Howaboutnow (IRE)**[55] 2922 9-11-11 **119**..........(p) WayneHutchinson 100
(Ian Williams) *in rr: kpt on fr 3 out: nvr on terms* **16/1**
2032 **11** *¾* **Chantara Rose**[49] 3025 7-11-2 **110**..........(p) BarryGeraghty 91
(Neil Mulholland) *mid-div: trckd ldrs 5th: 3rd appr 3 out: lost pl 2 out: eased between last 2: b.b.v* **9/2**[1]
-500 **12** *15* **Hada Men (USA)**[28] 3428 11-11-4 **112**..........(b[1]) HenryBrooke 79
(Rebecca Menzies) *in rr: wl bhd and drvn 7th: sn t.o* **25/1**
P514 **13** *1 ¼* **Ballinalacken (IRE)**[14] 3607 8-11-1 **109**..........(v) DavidEngland 75
(Clare Ellam) *in rr: hdwy 6th: drvn next: lost pl after 8th: sn wl bhd* **33/1**
3PP0 **14** *17* **Wolf Shield (IRE)**[76] 2496 9-11-6 **114**..........(t) SeanBowen 65
(George Moore) *chsd ldrs: drvn 8th: sn lost pl and bhd* **11/1**
4444 **P** **Manballandall (IRE)**[21] 3507 8-11-5 **120**..........(tp) JamesCorbett(7)
(Susan Corbett) *chsd ldrs: lost pl after 7th: sn bhd: t.o whn p.u bef last* **33/1**
44 **P** **Dukes Den**[25] 3467 5-11-1 **109**..........(tp) DarylJacob
(Charlie Mann) *in rr: bhd fr 7th: t.o whn p.u bef last* **20/1**

5m 57.7s (-1.30) **Going Correction** -0.15s/f (Good) **16** Ran SP% **123.9**
Speed ratings (Par 105): **96,93,91,90,89 87,86,86,85,85 85,80,79,74,**
CSF £123.80 CT £1625.87 TOTE £7.50: £2.00, £4.80, £3.40, £2.80; EX 179.40 Trifecta £1552.60.
Owner Richard Collins **Bred** Commandant Brendan Healy **Trained** Lingdale, Redcar & Cleveland
■ Wolf Shield was the final runner of George Moore's successful training career.

FOCUS
This looked competitive, but there was uneven gallop on and it paid to race handily. A hurdles best from the winner.

3838 SKY BET NOVICES' CHASE (17 fncs 1 omitted) 3m 6y
3:05 (3:05) (Class 4) 5-Y-0+ **£5,325** (£1,653; £890)

Form RPR
6-12 **1** **Thomas Brown**[42] 3136 7-11-6 138.......... BrianHughes 147+
(Harry Fry) *trckd ldr: hit 1st: mstke 4 out: sn pushed along: led bef 2 out: styd on* **7/4**[1]
-1F4 **2** *10* **Vintage Vinnie (IRE)**[76] 2481 7-11-6 141.......... BarryGeraghty 141
(Rebecca Curtis) *led: mstke 3 out: sn rdn: hdd bef 2 out: sn btn* **9/2**
1-0P **3** *45* **Wicked Spice (IRE)**[54] 2932 7-11-0 127.......... BrianHarding 98
(Nicky Richards) *hld up in tch: pushed along after 10th: lft bhd after 12th* **9/1**
/F-1 **P** **Saint Roque (FR)**[64] 2733 10-11-6 140..........(t) SamTwiston-Davies
(Paul Nicholls) *trckd ldr: blnd 2nd: slithered on landing and p.u* **7/2**[3]
-034 **F** **The Tourard Man (IRE)**[44] 3109 10-11-0 134.......... WayneHutchinson
(Alan King) *trckd ldr: fell 2nd* **3/1**[2]

6m 9.0s (-3.00) **Going Correction** -0.15s/f (Good) **5** Ran SP% **111.8**
Speed ratings: **99,95,80, ,**
CSF £10.00 TOTE £2.40: £1.60, £1.90; EX 8.80 Trifecta £38.10.
Owner The Corse Lawners **Bred** Elms Stud Co Ltd **Trained** Seaborough, Dorset

FOCUS
Only the first pair mattered down the home straight in what had promised to be a decent novice event. Arguably a small pb from the winner.

3839 SKY BET THANKS JEN NOBLE MAIDEN HURDLE (10 hdls) 2m 3f 120y
3:40 (3:40) (Class 5) 4-Y-0+ **£4,106** (£1,197; £598)

Form RPR
-232 **1** **Big Chief Benny (IRE)**[44] 3117 5-11-5 133.......... DenisO'Regan 131+
(Alan King) *hld up in mid-div: hdwy appr 3 out: led last: edgd rt: drvn out* **2/1**[1]
2 *2* **Cottersrock (IRE)**[91] 2181 6-11-5 0.......... AndrewTinkler 128+
(Martin Keighley) *trckd ldrs: 2nd 3 out: led appr next: hdd last: sn swtchd lft: styd on same pce* **25/1**
214- **3** *7* **Rainy City (IRE)**[385] 3592 6-11-5 0..........(t) SamTwiston-Davies 122
(Paul Nicholls) *chsd ldrs: 3rd appr 3 out: upsides 2 out: wknd last* **15/2**
3303 **4** *3* **Moidore**[21] 3509 7-11-5 113.......... AdamPogson 119
(Charles Pogson) *led and sn clr: hdd appr 2 out: wknd appr last* **25/1**
3 **5** *9* **Royal Milan (IRE)**[31] 3334 6-11-5 0..........(t) RichardJohnson 112
(Philip Hobbs) *hld up in mid-div: effrt appr 3 out: one pce* **7/2**[2]
00 **6** *4* **Jack Henri (FR)**[20] 3522 5-11-5 0.......... BrianHughes 107+
(Ian Williams) *in rr: hdwy 6th: kpt on fr 2 out* **200/1**

-640 **7** *1* **Movie Legend**[54] 2928 6-11-5 0........................(t) KielanWoods 106
(Ben Case) *rr-div: hdwy 7th: fdd 3 out* **100/1**

8 *5* **Kk Lexion (IRE)**[160] 1335 5-11-0 0........................ JamieBargary[(5)] 105
(Tom George) *mid-div: hdwy 7th: wknd and blnd 2 out* **33/1**

6 **9** *4 ½* **Behind The Wire (IRE)**[69] 2636 5-11-5 0........................ PaddyBrennan 97
(Tom George) *mid-div: hdwy 7th: chsng ldrs appr next: wknd 2 out* **10/1**

5 **10** *1 ½* **Tipperairy (IRE)**[69] 2636 5-11-5 0........................ RyanMahon 96
(Dan Skelton) *chsd ldrs: wknd appr 3 out* **50/1**

5 **11** *½* **Lord Golan**[32] 3309 8-11-2 0........................ MauriceLinehan[(3)] 97
(Nick Kent) *chsd ldrs: drvn 7th: lost pl bef 2 out* **200/1**

244 **12** *1* **Egret (IRE)**[31] 3340 6-11-5 0........................ DerekFox 95
(Lucinda Russell) *chsd ldrs: lost pl appr 3 out* **100/1**

14-4 **13** *2* **Kingussie**[43] 3130 8-11-5 0........................ NicodeBoinville 93
(Ben Pauling) *chsd ldrs: lost pl 7th* **18/1**

14 *7* **Derksen (IRE)** 6-11-5 0........................ JeremiahMcGrath 87
(Nicky Henderson) *in rr: sme hdwy 7th: sn lost pl and bhd* **22/1**

6-43 **P** **Definitely Glad (IRE)**[9] 3681 9-10-5 98........................(t) JamesCorbett[(7)]
(Susan Corbett) *chsd ldrs: lost pl 7th: sn bhd: t.o whn p.u bef last* **100/1**

01-1 **F** **Emperor Sakhee**[237] 640 6-11-5 0........................ BrianHarding
(Karen McLintock) *in rr: fell 4th* **33/1**

35- **P** **Tropical Sunshine (IRE)**[403] 3231 8-11-0 0........................ NickSlatter[(5)]
(Pippa Bickerton) *mid-div: drvn and lost pl 7th: sn bhd: t.o whn p.u bef last* **200/1**

1-3 **P** **See The World**[64] 2723 6-11-5 0........................ DarylJacob
(Emma Lavelle) *chsd ldrs: wknd 7th: blnd next: t.o whern p.u bef last: b.b.v* **11/2**[3]

P **U** **Tango Unchained (IRE)**[59] 2842 7-11-2 0........................ HarryBannister[(3)]
(Charlie Mann) *in rr: blnd and uns rdr 1st* **125/1**

0 **P** **Night In London (IRE)**[15] 3593 6-10-9 0........................ HarryChalloner[(3)]
(Keith Reveley) *in rr: t.o 7th: p.u bef next* **200/1**

P **Onlyfoolsownhorses (IRE)** 5-11-5 0........................ CraigNichol
(Micky Hammond) *gave problems befhand: sn detached in rr: t.o 3rd: p.u after 7th* **100/1**

4m 43.0s (-8.30) **Going Correction** -0.15s/f (Good) **21 Ran SP% 123.7**
Speed ratings (Par 103): **110,109,106,105,101 100,99,97,95,95 95,94,93,91, , , , ,**
CSF £60.37 TOTE £2.90: £1.40, £8.40, £3.10; EX 58.50 Trifecta £553.80.
Owner Oitavos Partnership **Bred** Brian And Mrs Bronagh Lawler **Trained** Barbury Castle, Wilts

FOCUS
There was no hanging about in this fair maiden. It was run in a good time for the grade and should produce winners.

3840 SKY BET NOVICES' H'CAP HURDLE (8 hdls) 2m 140y
4:10 (4:10) (Class 5) (0-100,100) 4-Y-O+ **£3,249** (£954; £477; £238)

Form RPR

4463 **1** **Quill Art**[25] 3473 4-11-1 97........................ BrianHughes 95+
(Richard Fahey) *trckd ldrs: 3rd and rdn between last 2: led sn after last: forged clr last 75yds* **3/1**[1]

4-56 **2** *4* **Mazovian (USA)**[31] 621 8-11-10 95........................(p) MarkQuinlan 97
(Neil Mulholland) *mid-div: nt fluent and drvn 3rd: chsng ldrs 5th: led appr 2 out: hdd sn after last: kpt on same pce* **9/2**[2]

3 *10* **Bourbon Prince**[148] 1463 5-11-12 97........................ JonathanEngland 89
(Sam Drake) *led: hdd 3 out: 3rd and one pce whn j.lft last* **25/1**

05-0 **4** *3 ¼* **Surging Seas (IRE)**[100] 2015 7-11-9 94........................(tp) SamTwiston-Davies 83
(Ali Stronge) *mid-div: hdwy 3 out: 4th appr last: one pce* **6/1**[3]

044 **5** *7* **Burner (IRE)**[14] 3610 4-11-1 97........................ TomCannon 69
(Olly Williams) *chsd ldrs: wknd between last 2* **20/1**

000 **6** *1 ¾* **Ultimate Dream (FR)**[43] 3130 5-11-2 87........................ JoshuaMoore 68+
(Jonjo O'Neill) *mid-div: kpt on fr 3 out: nvr a factor* **7/1**

6055 **7** *4* **Skyfire**[34] 3233 9-11-1 86........................ DarylJacob 65
(Nick Kent) *in rr: kpt on fr 3 out: nvr on terms* **14/1**

0-P3 **8** *1 ¾* **Agesilas (FR)**[41] 3161 8-9-13 73 oh2 ow2........................(p) JohnKington[(3)] 49
(Andrew Crook) *in rr: wl bhd 7th: sme hdwy fr 2 out: nvr on terms* **33/1**

UP25 **9** *1 ¾* **Mister Hendre**[25] 3473 8-10-7 78........................(t) HenryBrooke 52
(Susan Corbett) *trckd ldrs: led 3 out: wandered and hdd appr next: sn wknd* **15/2**

P00 **10** *5* **Qatea (IRE)**[32] 3309 4-11-4 100........................(t) AdrianLane 59
(Donald McCain) *in rr whn j.lft and mstke 1st: sme hdwy 5th: lost pl bef next* **33/1**

600 **11** *3 ½* **Seraffimo**[15] 3590 4-10-1 88........................ JamesCowley[(5)] 44
(Sharon Watt) *chsd ldrs: lost pl bef 3 out* **40/1**

-200 **12** *¾* **First Of Never (IRE)**[63] 2745 10-10-0 71........................ SeanQuinlan 41
(Lynn Siddall) *hld up in mid-div: chsng ldrs whn hit 5th: wknd 2 out: bhd whn j.lft last* **10/1**

0060 **13** *17* **Zakety Zak**[13] 3628 5-11-7 92........................ PeterBuchanan 43
(James Turner) *in rr: bhd fr 5th: t.o whn j.lft 2 out* **33/1**

5/0- **14** *20* **Lordship (IRE)**[477] 1812 12-10-5 76........................ TommyPhelan 9
(Tom Gretton) *hld up in rr: hdwy appr 5th: sn lost pl and bhd* **40/1**

-6P0 **15** *8* **Dounya's Boy**[23] 3484 7-10-13 84........................ DaveCrosse 10
(Christopher Kellett) *in rr: wl bhd 5th: sn t.o* **100/1**

4m 4.8s (0.10) **Going Correction** -0.15s/f (Good) **15 Ran SP% 120.8**
WFA 4 from 5yo+ 11lb
Speed ratings (Par 103): **93,91,86,84,81 80,78,78,77,74 73,72,64,55,51**
CSF £15.26 CT £291.13 TOTE £3.20: £1.20, £2.10, £7.40; EX 13.70 Trifecta £282.40.
Owner P S Cresswell & Mrs P A Morrison **Bred** Jeremy Gompertz **Trained** Musley Bank, N Yorks

FOCUS
They got sorted out from the penultimate flight in this ordinary handicap. Fair form for the class, with a step up from the winner.
T/Jkpt: Not won. JACKPOT PLACEPOT: £654.00 to a £1 stake. Pool of £2,374.40 - 2.65 winning units. T/Plt: £171.30 to a £1 stake. Pool: £86,737.79 - 369.43 winning tickets. T/Qpdt: £32.60 to a £1 stake. Pool: £8,979.47 - 203.67 winning tickets. **Walter Glynn & Andrew Sheret**

3607 HUNTINGDON (R-H)
Friday, January 29

OFFICIAL GOING: Chase course - soft (good to soft in places); hurdle course - good to soft (soft in places)
Wind: Strong, across Weather: Cloudy and mild

3841 RACINGUK HD COMING SOON "NATIONAL HUNT" NOVICES' H'CAP HURDLE (10 hdls) 2m 3f 137y
1:00 (1:00) (Class 4) (0-105,105) 4-Y-O+ **£3,249** (£954; £477; £238)

Form RPR

5453 **1** **Zanstra (IRE)**[28] 3414 6-11-10 103........................ TomScudamore 110+
(Colin Tizzard) *settled in 2nd or 3rd pl: led bef 2 out: idling in front after and sn rdn: a in command fr last* **15/8**[1]

4P33 **2** *6* **Trespassers Will (IRE)**[23] 3483 5-11-12 105........................(t[1]) PaddyBrennan 108
(Fergal O'Brien) *cl up: rdn to chse wnr bef 2 out: no imp and wl hld fr last* **9/2**[3]

2P-4 **3** *7* **Summer Sounds (IRE)**[49] 3023 7-11-8 104........................ BenPoste[(3)] 102
(Tom Symonds) *led: hit 5th: sn hdd: led again after 7th: hit 3 out: rdn and hdd bef 2 out: wl-hld 3rd whn mstke last* **5/1**

0000 **4** *17* **Blue Prairie**[43] 3130 5-10-9 88........................(p) HarrySkelton 70
(Dan Skelton) *towards rr: nt fluent 3rd and 5th: rdn and outpcd 7th: no ch whn mstke next: plugged on into poor 4th 2 out* **14/1**

-P52 **5** *9* **Arthur Mc Bride (IRE)**[59] 2833 7-11-8 104........................ RyanHatch[(3)] 76
(Nigel Twiston-Davies) *midfield: rdn 7th: last of 4 gng clr bef 3 out: rdn and dropped out rapidly bef next* **4/1**[2]

4PP4 **6** *9* **Glenariff**[30] 3374 7-11-5 103........................ KevinJones[(5)] 67
(Seamus Mullins) *chsd ldrs: rdn and lost tch bef 3 out: t.o* **12/1**

43PP **7** *3* **The Lion Man (IRE)**[58] 2855 6-11-7 100........................ CharliePoste 62
(Robin Dickin) *sn in last pair: rdn 7th: struggling after: t.o bef 2 out* **20/1**

UPP4 **8** *3 ½* **League Of His Own (IRE)**[34] 3234 7-9-11 79 oh15(t) ConorShoemark[(3)] 37
(Claire Dyson) *last early: rushed up to ld after 5th and sn 8 l clr: hdd after 7th: rdn and nt run on: lost pl rapidly: t.o* **66/1**

5m 12.2s (13.20) **Going Correction** +0.85s/f (Soft) **8 Ran SP% 110.2**
Speed ratings (Par 105): **107,104,101,95,91 87,86,85**
CSF £10.21 CT £32.18 TOTE £2.60: £1.10, £2.00, £1.70; EX 12.10 Trifecta £46.70.
Owner Moonrakers **Bred** Mrs Darina Kelly **Trained** Milborne Port, Dorset

FOCUS
Ground conditions weren't too bad, but the wind was strong and blustery, making it tough for the runners. Amended bends resulted in this race being run over 136yds further than advertised. Moderate form, with the runners finishing well strung out. Small steps up from the first two.

3842 RACING UK NOVICES' HURDLE (8 hdls) 1m 7f 171y
1:35 (1:35) (Class 4) 4-Y-O+ **£3,249** (£954; £477; £238)

Form RPR

24-1 **1** **Buveur D'Air (FR)**[63] 2763 5-11-11 0........................ NoelFehily 141+
(Nicky Henderson) *tall: cl up and gng wl: led on bit 2 out: clr last: v easily* **2/11**[1]

040 **2** *7* **Breath Of Blighty (FR)**[34] 3227 5-11-4 0........................ LiamTreadwell 119
(Paul Webber) *prom: disp 4th and rdn home turn: no imp tl styd on after last to take wl-hld 2nd* **33/1**

2-5 **3** *1 ½* **Ten Sixty (IRE)**[63] 2762 6-11-4 0........................ TomO'Brien 119
(Philip Hobbs) *settled in midfield: nudged along after 5th: disp 4th and rdn home turn: effrt between last 2: kpt on steadily flat* **5/1**[2]

-431 **4** *3 ½* **Mystic Sky**[40] 3175 5-11-4 116........................ LeightonAspell 114
(Lucy Wadham) *cl up: effrt bef 3 out: rdn and disp ld home turn: 3rd 2 out: kpt on same pce* **5/1**[2]

5 *¾* **Minella Experience (IRE)**[327] 5-11-4 0........................ HarrySkelton 113
(Dan Skelton) *led or disp ld: rdn and hdd whn hit 2 out: one pce and btn last* **10/1**[3]

0-5 **6** *25* **Dragon De La Tour (FR)**[75] 2519 5-10-13 0........................ BridgetAndrews[(5)] 88
(Dan Skelton) *led or disp ld tl 3 out: dropped out qckly* **50/1**

64 **7** *47* **Coco Flower (FR)**[72] 2583 4-9-11 0........................ KillianMoore[(3)] 23
(Alex Hales) *lost tch bef 4th: t.o after 3 out* **100/1**

0 **8** *51* **Pennine Panther**[57] 2860 5-10-11 0........................(t) HarrisonBeswick[(7)]
(Sam Thomas) *sn bhd: lost tch bef 4th: t.o next* **100/1**

/0-4 **P** **Terra Firma**[262] 271 6-11-1 0........................ ConorShoemark[(3)]
(Claire Dyson) *mstke 1st: chsd ldrs tl drvn after 5th: wkng whn mstke next: t.o and p.u 2 out* **100/1**

4m 4.8s (9.90) **Going Correction** +0.85s/f (Soft)
WFA 4 from 5yo+ 11lb **9 Ran SP% 134.9**
Speed ratings (Par 105): **109,105,104,103,102 90,66,41,**
CSF £18.07 TOTE £1.10: £1.02, £8.10, £1.40; EX 19.60 Trifecta £82.90.
Owner Potensis Bloodstock Ltd & Chris Giles **Bred** Gerard Ferte **Trained** Upper Lambourn, Berks

FOCUS
Amended bends resulted in this race being run over 188yds further than advertised. All about the favourite and he didn't disappoint with an easy success. He is a potential 150+ hurdler but didn't need to run to his Newbury mark.

3843 START YOUR RACINGUK FREE TRIAL NOW H'CAP CHASE (16 fncs) 2m 3f 189y
2:10 (2:11) (Class 3) (0-130,127) 5-Y-O+ **£6,498** (£1,908; £954; £477)

Form RPR

-244 **1** **Cadoudoff (FR)**[48] 3046 6-11-10 125........................ TomO'Brien 137+
(Charlie Longsdon) *pushed along early: bhd: effrt in 3rd at 13th: gng wl after: led 2 out: rdn clr whn plunged through last: pushed out* **9/2**[2]

10-0 **2** *8* **Special Agent**[64] 2727 7-11-8 123........................ DavidBass 128
(Nicky Henderson) *dropped towards rr 7th: hdwy in 2nd at 12th: rdn to ld wl bef 2 out: jst hdd u.p whn sprawled on landing 2 out: no ch w wnr after but remained clr of rest* **7/1**

1-22 **3** *13* **Mr Muddle**[27] 3445 9-11-5 120........................ MarcGoldstein 112
(Sheena West) *lost 8 l at s: stdy prog to go 3rd at 7th: rdn 10th: 4th and losing tch w ldng pair after 3 out: plodded on* **9/1**

4123 **4** *22* **Artifice Sivola (FR)**[56] 2884 6-11-12 127........................ LeightonAspell 95
(Lucy Wadham) *pressed ldr: led 10th: rdn and hdd wl bef 2 out: sn wknd and lost tch w ldng pair* **8/1**

3/23 **5** *1 ¾* **Denali Highway (IRE)**[50] 2996 9-11-5 120........................ AndrewThornton 89
(Caroline Bailey) *cl up tl rdn and struggling 10th: t.o last 3 out* **4/1**[1]

0-3P **6** *3 ¼* **Dusky Lark**[42] 3134 6-11-10 125........................ NoelFehily 89
(Colin Tizzard) *midfield: rdn and struggling 3 out: t.o* **13/2**[3]

0351 **P** **Sonofagun (FR)**[34] 3225 10-11-4 119........................(p) WillKennedy
(Ian Williams) *dropped to rr and rdn 7th: t.o whn j.lft 9th and p.u* **14/1**

-PF3 **P** **The Clock Leary (IRE)**[20] 3524 8-11-8 123........................(b) AidanColeman
(Venetia Williams) *led tl 10th: rdn and lost pl tamely: t.o and p.u after 3 out* **13/2**[3]

1/P6 **P** **Mountain Tunes (IRE)**[31] 3348 7-11-7 122........................ RichieMcLernon
(Jonjo O'Neill) *last after v slow jump 2nd: nvr travelling or jumping after: j. bdly lft 6th and again 9th where t.o and p.u* **9/1**

5m 18.6s (13.30) **Going Correction** +0.85s/f (Soft) **9 Ran SP% 115.1**
Speed ratings: **107,103,98,89,89 87, , ,**
CSF £35.90 CT £271.49 TOTE £5.70: £2.10, £2.40, £2.50; EX 45.00 Trifecta £255.70.
Owner The Four Kings **Bred** Franck Van Haaren & Philippe Lefevre **Trained** Over Norton, Oxon

FOCUS
Amended bends resulted in this race being run over 95yds further than advertised. A fair chase run at a good gallop. There's a case for rating it 10lb+ higher.

3844 PERTEMPS NETWORK H'CAP HURDLE (SERIES QUALIFIER) (12 hdls) — 3m 1f 10y
2:40 (2:41) (Class 2) 5-Y-O+
£11,573 (£3,418; £1,709; £854; £427; £214)

Form — RPR
44-0 **1** **Taj Badalandabad (IRE)**[55] 2912 6-10-10 **126**..........(p) TomScudamore 132+
(David Pipe) *nt fluent 2nd: settled towards rr: stdy prog 8th: led bef 2 out: styd on wl flat: pushed out* **12/1**
P212 **2** 1 **Westren Warrior (IRE)**[20] 3527 7-11-3 **133**.......... WillKennedy 138+
(Dr Richard Newland) *prom: rdn and pressed wnr fr bef 2 out: 2 l down whn clipped last: a hld flat* **6/1**[2]
/016 **3** 4 ½ **So Fine (IRE)**[28] 3407 10-10-13 **129**.......... JamesBest 129
(Philip Hobbs) *chsd ldrs: rdn 9th: 3rd and hrd drvn bef 2 out: kpt on same pce wout threatening* **14/1**
-306 **4** 7 **Invicta Lake (IRE)**[44] 3113 9-10-8 **124**.......... TomO'Brien 124
(Suzy Smith) *led tl rdn and hdd bef 2 out: one pce and btn between last 2* **20/1**
-420 **5** 2 ½ **Un Ace (FR)**[20] 3527 8-11-12 **142**..........(t) DavidBass 140
(Kim Bailey) *midfield: outpcd 3 out: 5th and hrd drvn bef next: no imp after* **11/1**
0311 **6** 11 **Eminent Poet**[22] 3498 5-10-5 **126**.......... CharlieDeutsch(5) 115
(Venetia Williams) *chsd ldr after 2nd tl rdn and hit 3 out: sn wknd* **14/1**
-304 **7** 2 ½ **Ascendant**[16] 3584 10-10-10 **131**..........(t) DavidNoonan(5) 117
(Johnny Farrelly) *midfield: rdn 9th: btn next* **50/1**
P233 **8** 68 **Kerisper (FR)**[31] 3336 7-10-8 **127**.......... RyanHatch(3) 51
(Nigel Twiston-Davies) *midfield: blnd bdly 9th: nvr rcvr: t.o and virtually p.u last* **10/1**[3]
31 **P** **Amiral Collonges (FR)**[41] 3146 6-10-8 **124**.......... LiamTreadwell
(James Evans) *a bhd: lost tch 9th: t.o and p.u 2 out* **11/4**[1]
2211 **P** **Singlefarmpayment**[28] 3407 6-11-3 **133**.......... DavyRussell
(Tom Lacey) *bhd: last whn mstke 5th: nvr gng wl enough in rr after: t.o and p.u 2 out* **11/4**[1]

6m 38.6s (15.70) **Going Correction** +0.85s/f (Soft) **10** Ran SP% **112.8**
Speed ratings: **108,107,106,106,105 101,101,79, ,**
CSF £80.19 CT £1019.68 TOTE £13.90: £3.70, £3.30, £3.70; EX 99.60 Trifecta £589.80.
Owner W Frewen **Bred** Patrick Kelly **Trained** Nicholashayne, Devon

FOCUS
Amended bends resulted in this race being run over 172yds further than advertised. No great gallop on here, with none of the runners wanting to lead, and questionable what the form is worth with the market leaders disappointing. The winner belatedly built on his novice form from 2014. The first six qualify for the final of the series at the festival.

3845 RACINGUK.COM/FREETRIAL NOVICES' H'CAP CHASE (12 fncs) — 2m 104y
3:15 (3:16) (Class 4) (0-105,105) 5-Y-O+ £3,994 (£1,240; £667)

Form — RPR
141P **1** **Sir Note (FR)**[189] 1096 6-11-2 **95**.......... JackQuinlan 110+
(James Eustace) *j. soundly: led at decent pce and nvr less than 6 l clr: only one on bridle wl bef 2 out: unchal* **7/2**[2]
434P **2** 13 **Agentleman (IRE)**[31] 3345 6-11-7 **100**.......... DannyCook 97
(Tim Easterby) *4th and off the pce tl lft 12 l 3rd bef 6th: drvn after 3 out: wnt 2nd at next: nvr nr wnr* **7/2**[2]
304 **3** 33 **Mandy's Boy (IRE)**[45] 3103 6-11-2 **98**..........(tp) JamesBanks(3) 80
(Sally Randell) *chsd wnr but nvr win 6 l of him: nt fluent 8th: rdn after 3 out: lost 2nd and nt fluent next: fin tired and heavily eased flat* **6/1**
0410 **P** **Neworld (FR)**[25] 3473 7-11-9 **102**.......... AlainCawley
(Richard Hobson) *mod last and nvr gng wl: t.o 3 out: p.u next* **11/2**[3]
5-44 **P** **At The Top (FR)**[59] 2840 6-11-12 **105**.......... HarrySkelton
(Dan Skelton) *mstke 2nd: 3rd tl dug her toes in and plld herself up bef 6th* **7/4**[1]

4m 30.8s (20.60) **Going Correction** +0.85s/f (Soft) **5** Ran SP% **110.5**
Speed ratings: **82,75,59, ,**
CSF £15.77 TOTE £4.40: £2.50, £1.70; EX 18.60 Trifecta £69.30.
Owner G F Chesneaux **Bred** Jean-Pierre Coiffier **Trained** Newmarket, Suffolk

FOCUS
Amended bends resulted in this race being run over 93yds further than advertised. Weak form and it was made even more winnable after the favourite pulled herself up racing out on to the final circuit. Seemingly a big step up from the winner.

3846 WATCH THE CHELTENHAM FESTIVAL ON RACINGUK H'CAP HURDLE (10 hdls) — 2m 4f 145y
3:50 (3:52) (Class 4) (0-120,120) 4-Y-O+ £3,249 (£954; £477; £238)

Form — RPR
4F13 **1** **Abricot De L'Oasis (FR)**[69] 2647 6-11-7 **120**.......... BridgetAndrews(5) 127+
(Dan Skelton) *led: blnd 3 out: sn rdn and 3 l clr: jnd next: level whn clipped last: r.o gamely to assert fnl strides* **3/1**[1]
-40U **2** nk **Poker School (IRE)**[78] 2449 6-11-5 **113**.......... WillKennedy 118+
(Ian Williams) *hld up in rr: gd prog 6th: wnt 5th and mstke 3 out: sn chsng wnr: upsides and rdn fr 2 out tl jst outpcd clsng strides* **16/1**
P-50 **3** 7 **Wintered Well (IRE)**[34] 3242 8-10-13 **107**..........(p) PeterCarberry 106
(Jennie Candlish) *chsd ldrs: rdn and styd on after 3 out: lft 3rd next but nvr trbld ldng pair* **9/1**
-655 **4** 6 **Kamool (GER)**[71] 2595 6-11-5 **113**.......... NoelFehily 108
(Jonjo O'Neill) *pressed ldrs: rdn 3 out: 3rd and no imp whn blnd bdly next* **16/1**
/441 **5** 12 **Daliance (IRE)**[14] 3607 7-10-11 **105**..........(b) AndrewThornton 87
(Noel Williams) *prom: disp 2nd and rdn 7th: fdd after next* **6/1**[3]
0PU2 **6** 9 **Drombeg West**[34] 3223 9-10-11 **105**.......... TrevorWhelan 78
(Anna Brooks) *bhd: passed btn horses fr 3 out but nvr nr ldrs* **16/1**
15 **7** 4 ½ **Church Field (IRE)**[25] 3465 8-11-4 **115**.......... ConorShoemark(3) 84
(Phil Middleton) *towards rr: rdn and struggling bef 6th: plodded on* **20/1**
14 **8** 7 **Handsome Sam**[32] 3316 5-11-3 **118**.......... WilliamFeatherstone(7) 81
(Alan King) *midfield: rdn 7th: btn next: t.o* **9/2**[2]
9 1 **Speed Demon (IRE)**[161] 1315 7-11-12 **120**.......... IanPopham 82
(Richard Phillips) *2nd or 3rd pl tl rdn and lost pl qckly after 7th: t.o* **33/1**
-032 **10** 43 **Rustamabad (FR)**[105] 1952 6-10-11 **110**..........(t) AlanJohns(5) 33
(Tim Vaughan) *prom: chsd wnr fr 5th tl rdn and fdd qckly after 3 out: t.o* **25/1**
05P/ **P** **Fuhgeddaboudit**[1037] 4977 9-10-3 **102**.......... KevinJones(5)
(Seamus Mullins) *nvr bttr than midfield: t.o and p.u 3 out* **50/1**
126/ **P** **Pink Gin**[700] 4535 8-11-6 **114**..........(t) MarkGrant
(Nigel Twiston-Davies) *nt jump wl in last pair: t.o 7th: p.u next* **11/1**
15-1 **P** **Vif Argent (FR)**[267] 176 7-11-9 **120**.......... BenPoste(3)
(Andrew Reid) *midfield: wknd bef 6th: t.o next: p.u 3 out* **25/1**
-330 **P** **Sandygate (IRE)**[41] 3152 6-11-6 **114**.......... TomO'Brien
(Philip Hobbs) *dropped to rr and drvn 1/2-way: nvr travelling after: t.o and p.u 3 out: lame* **10/1**

5m 24.5s (13.90) **Going Correction** +0.85s/f (Soft) **14** Ran SP% **119.9**
Speed ratings (Par 105): **107,106,104,101,97 93,92,89,89,72 , , ,**
CSF £46.81 CT £398.95 TOTE £3.70: £1.70, £6.10, £3.50; EX 70.60 Trifecta £637.30.
Owner Frank McAleavy **Bred** S Blanchais, N Blanchais Et Al **Trained** Alcester, Warwicks

FOCUS
Amended bends resulted in this race being run over 136yds further than advertised. Modest handicap form, although the front pair came clear late and the form is solid at its level.

3847 RACING UK ANYWHERE STANDARD OPEN NATIONAL HUNT FLAT RACE — 1m 5f 148y
4:20 (4:21) (Class 6) 4-6-Y-O £1,559 (£457; £228; £114)

Form — RPR
2 **1** **Bags Groove (IRE)**[69] 2636 5-11-4 0.......... NickScholfield 111+
(Harry Fry) *prom: wnt 2nd 6f out: led wl over 1f out: pushed along and kpt on wl: readily* **7/4**[1]
2 2 ¼ **Silverhow (IRE)** 5-11-4 0.......... PeterCarberry 107+
(Nicky Henderson) *chsd ldrs: rdn and outpcd in 5th home turn: rallied and styd on strly to go 2nd ins fnl f: nt rch wnr: promising* **16/1**
3 2 **Zipple Back (IRE)** 4-10-7 0.......... NoelFehily 93
(Alan King) *rrd over in paddock: chsd ldrs: effrt 6f out: 4th home turn: rdn to dispute 2nd 1f out: nt qckn after* **4/1**[2]
4 **4** 1 ¾ **Mr Fenton (IRE)**[55] 2909 5-11-4 0.......... AidanColeman 102
(Emma Lavelle) *tk str hold: prom: 4th and rdn home turn: kpt on steadily at same pce* **10/1**
6 **5** ¾ **Al Reesha (IRE)**[86] 2277 5-10-11 0.......... HarrySkelton 94
(Dan Skelton) *led at stdy pce: rdn and hdd wl over 1f out: one pce after* **33/1**
6 shd **Midnight Jitterbug** 4-10-7 0.......... IanPopham 90
(Noel Williams) *towards rr and pushed along 1/2-way: effrt in 6th home turn: sn rdn: pressing ldrs over 1f out: kpt on gamely after* **33/1**
7 nk **Thomas Campbell** 4-10-7 0.......... DavidBass 89
(Nicky Henderson) *hld up towards rr: effrt in 7th home turn: sn rn green and hanging lft: kpt on steadily wout threatening* **9/2**[3]
2- **8** 13 **Ritual Of Senses (IRE)**[414] 3037 6-11-4 0.......... GavinSheehan 84
(Warren Greatrex) *chsd ldrs tl rdn and wknd over 3f out: t.o* **13/2**
20 **9** ¾ **Shining Romeo**[62] 2777 4-10-7 0.......... WillKennedy 72
(Denis Quinn) *a bhd: struggling 5f out: t.o* **50/1**
3 **10** 1 ¾ **Fella**[48] 3048 4-10-7 0.......... JamieMoore 69
(Gary Moore) *trckd ldrs for 10f: t.o* **20/1**
11 12 **Primo Time** 5-11-1 0.......... KillianMoore(3) 65
(Michael Appleby) *t.k.h in midfield: lost tch 5f out: t.o* **150/1**
12 2 ¾ **Kristal Star** 4-9-11 0.......... JamesBanks(3) 43
(Alex Hales) *chsd ldrs 10f: t.o* **66/1**
13 99 **Kylie's Kenny** 6-11-4 0..........[1] JamesDavies
(Derek Shaw) *bhd and hanging bdly lft: t.o 5f out tl virtually rn off crse on home turn* **150/1**

3m 27.1s (7.10) **13** Ran SP% **118.3**
CSF £33.33 TOTE £3.00: £2.00, £4.60, £1.70; EX 27.20 Trifecta £129.40.
Owner Michael Pescod **Bred** Mrs Valerie Dalgetty **Trained** Seaborough, Dorset

FOCUS
Amended bends resulted in this race being run over 55yds further than advertised. Just a steady pace but this was still a decent bumper that should produce winners. Bags Groove didn't need to improve on his Ascot run.

T/Plt: £200.70 to a £1 stake. Pool: £54,347.43 - 197.65 winning tickets. T/Qpdt: £128.70 to a £1 stake. Pool: £4,871.86 - 28.00 winning tickets. **Iain Mackenzie**

3403 CHELTENHAM (L-H)
Saturday, January 30

OFFICIAL GOING: Heavy (6.4)
Wind: quite strong against Weather: sunny with cloudy periods

3848 JCB TRIUMPH HURDLE TRIAL (JUVENILE HURDLE) (REGISTERED AS THE FINESSE JUVENILE HURDLE) (GRADE 2) (8 hdls) — 2m 179y
12:40 (12:40) (Class 1) 4-Y-O
£17,085 (£6,411; £3,210; £1,599; £804; £402)

Form — RPR
1 **Protek Des Flos (FR)**[136] 1561 4-11-0 0.......... NoelFehily 133+
(Nicky Henderson) *tall: lw: trckd ldrs: outpcd in 6th 2 out: hdwy appr last where wnt 4 l 4th: led fnl 120yds: styd on strly* **25/1**
1 **2** 1 ¼ **Clan Des Obeaux (FR)**[45] 3112 4-11-4 0.......... SamTwiston-Davies 134
(Paul Nicholls) *str: lw: travelled wl most of way: trckd ldrs: led narrowly after 2 out: hrd drvn fnl f: hdd fnl 120yds: kpt on but no ex* **11/8**[1]
3 1 ¾ **Consul De Thaix (FR)**[126] 4-11-0 0.......... BarryGeraghty 129
(Nicky Henderson) *lengthy: trckd ldrs: wnt cl 3rd after 2 out: big jump at the last: sn rdn: kpt on but nt quite pce to chal* **10/1**[3]
11 **4** nk **Who Dares Wins (IRE)**[49] 3039 4-11-7 148.......... RichardJohnson 135
(Alan King) *racd keenly: pressed ldr tl led 3rd: nt fluent 3 out: rdn whn narrowly hdd after 2 out: stl ch last: kpt on but no ex fnl f* **13/8**[2]
212 **5** 8 **Duke Of Medina (IRE)**[34] 3279 4-11-4 138..........(b) GavinSheehan 124
(Harry Whittington) *led tl 3rd: trckd ldr: rdn after 3 out: nt pce to chal: fdd fnl f* **14/1**
11 **6** 60 **Wolf Of Windlesham (IRE)**[77] 2480 4-11-7 137.......... JoshuaMoore 67
(Stuart Edmunds) *trckd ldrs: rdn after 2 out: sn wknd and eased* **12/1**

4m 29.0s (17.70) **Going Correction** +1.425s/f (Heavy) **6** Ran SP% **107.5**
Speed ratings: **115,114,113,113,109 81**
CSF £57.18 TOTE £27.60: £6.30, £1.40; EX 60.00 Trifecta £420.40.
Owner Potensis Bloodstock Limited **Bred** Clovis Bardin & Mme Florence Bardin **Trained** Upper Lambourn, Berks

FOCUS
Despite 15mm of overnight rain the course passed a morning inspection. The hurdle bends were dolled out 14 yards and chase bends 16 yards. Race distance increased 84 yards. This is always an informative affair and has proved a leading trial for the Triumph Hurdle, as was highlighted by year's winner Peace And Co following up in the big one at the festival. There was a muddling finish, with changing fortunes up the run-in. The first four are all decent juveniles but the level of the form is 10lb+ shy of what will be required in the Triumph Hurdle.

3849 TIMEFORM NOVICES' H'CAP CHASE (13 fncs 4 omitted) 2m 4f 166y
1:15 (1:15) (Class 2) 5-Y-0+
£15,640 (£4,620; £2,310; £1,155; £577; £290)

Form RPR
1-31 1 **King's Odyssey (IRE)**[35] 3255 7-10-13 139 LeightonAspell 155+
(Evan Williams) *lw: mid-div: trckd ldrs 4th: led after 2 out (usual 3 out): styd on gamely fr last: drifted rt fnl f: drvn out* **8/1**

4-11 2 1 3/4 **Waldorf Salad**[31] 3371 8-10-1 127 AlainCawley 139
(Venetia Williams) *led: rdn and hdd after 2 out: styd on gamely fr last: clsng again on wnr towards fin but a being hld* **11/1**

-21F 3 7 **Smooth Stepper**[49] 3040 7-10-4 130 DannyCook 135
(Sue Smith) *trckd ldrs: rdn after 3 out (usual 4 out): styd on same pce fr next* **10/1**

-122 4 8 **Un Temps Pour Tout (IRE)**[65] 2726 7-11-12 152 (bt) TomScudamore 149
(David Pipe) *lw: mid-div: rdn along after 10th: nvr threatened ldrs: wnt hld 4th at the last (usual 2 out)* **3/1**[1]

-133 5 24 **One For Arthur (IRE)**[55] 2932 7-10-9 135 PeterBuchanan 108
(Lucinda Russell) *trckd ldr tl 4th: mid-div: lft hld 4th 2 out (usual 3 out): wknd last (usual 2 out)* **14/1**

2-12 6 3 1/2 **Viva Steve (IRE)**[34] 3282 8-10-5 131 GavinSheehan 103
(Mick Channon) *mid-div: wnt cl 4th after 5th: rdn after 10th: sn wknd: t.o* **15/2**[3]

-432 7 9 **Astigos (FR)**[35] 3253 9-10-0 126 oh6 (b[1]) AidanColeman 88
(Venetia Williams) *nt fluent 5th: a towards rr: struggling after 6th: wknd 10th: t.o* **10/1**

3F1P P **Regal Encore (IRE)**[7] 3735 8-11-3 143 (t) BarryGeraghty
(Anthony Honeyball) *mid-div tl 8th: sn struggling towards rr: wknd 3 out (usual 4 out): p.u after next* **16/1**

1561 P **Johnny Og**[7] 3731 7-10-0 126 oh2 (b) AndrewTinkler
(Martin Keighley) *mid-div: struggling in last after 4th: detached whn mstke 7th: p.u next* **20/1**

501F P **Kilronan High (IRE)**[50] 3014 7-10-6 132 (t) SamTwiston-Davies
(Nigel Twiston-Davies) *a towards rr: tailing off whn p.u bef 10th* **28/1**

1-01 P **Imagine The Chat**[32] 3348 7-10-1 127 SeanBowen
(Rebecca Curtis) *lw: a towards rr: struggling 8th: wknd out (usual 4 out): p.u after next* **11/2**[2]

F **Rezorbi (FR)**[87] 5-10-8 138 JoshuaMoore
(Jonjo O'Neill) *lw: hld up towards rr: stdy prog fr 7th: pushed along disputing 4th whn fell 2 out (usual 3 out)* **22/1**

5m 39.1s (23.40) **Going Correction** +1.425s/f (Heav)
WFA 5 from 7yo+ 4lb **12** Ran SP% **114.9**
Speed ratings: **112,111,108,105,96 95,91,,,**
CSF £86.21 CT £888.05 TOTE £10.50: £3.20, £2.50, £3.00; EX 110.90 Trifecta £839.00.

Owner Mr & Mrs William Rucker **Bred** The Hon Mrs V M A Tower **Trained** Llancarfan, Vale Of Glamorgan

FOCUS
Fences two, five and seven (last) were omitted in all chases. On paper this was a very strong novice handicap, run over a distance 96 yards further than advertised, which has often been a leading pointer to the 0-140 novice handicap on the opening day of the festival. However, most struggled to go the gallop on the attritional going and only two mattered from the usual third-last fence. The winner rates a smart soft-ground novice.

3850 BETBRIGHT TRIAL COTSWOLD CHASE (GRADE 2) (18 fncs 3 omitted) 3m 1f 56y
1:50 (1:51) (Class 1) 5-Y-0+ £57,218 (£21,638; £10,968; £5,598; £2,948)

Form RPR
-114 1 **Smad Place (FR)**[35] 3231 9-11-6 168 RichardJohnson 173+
(Alan King) *mde all: j.w: jnd 3 out tl last: styd on strly to draw clr again fr last: rdn out: v game* **9/2**[2]

1-62 2 12 **Many Clouds (IRE)**[56] 2900 9-11-10 166 LeightonAspell 166
(Oliver Sherwood) *lw: trckd ldrs: jnd wnr 3 out tl rdn jst bef last: styd on for clr 2nd but sn hld by wnr* **6/1**[3]

R-32 3 24 **Theatre Guide (IRE)**[63] 2783 9-11-6 139 (tp) AidanColeman 140
(Colin Tizzard) *lw: j. sltly rt at times: hld up: crept clsr 13th: rdn after 3 out (usual 4 out): wnt 4th 2 out: wnt hld 3rd at the last (usual 2 out): nvr trbld front pair* **33/1**

-F00 4 7 **The Giant Bolster**[42] 3150 11-11-0 145 (tp) TomScudamore 124
(David Bridgwater) *chsd ldrs tl 5th: sn pushed along in last pair: no ch fr 3 out (usual 4 out) but kpt on fr last to snatch wl hld 4th towards fin* **25/1**

PP-4 5 3 1/2 **Sam Winner (FR)**[91] 2200 9-11-10 160 (bt) SamTwiston-Davies 132
(Paul Nicholls) *chsd ldrs: rdn along fr 11th and lost pl: regained 3rd 15th tl after next: wknd on long run-in: lost 4th towards fin* **20/1**

5/P1 P **O'Faolains Boy (IRE)**[45] 3116 9-11-6 156 (t) NoelFehily
(Rebecca Curtis) *trckd ldrs: losing pl whn nt fluent 15th: sn wknd: t.o whn p.u bef 2 out (usual 3 out)* **15/2**

-111 P **Wakanda (IRE)**[42] 3150 7-11-6 155 DannyCook
(Sue Smith) *sn trcking wnr: rdn after 13th: mstke next: wknd 15th: t.o whn p.u after 2 out (usual 3 out)* **12/1**

2-21 F **Djakadam (FR)**[55] 2941 7-11-10 170 RWalsh
(W P Mullins, Ire) *lw: in tch on outer: cl up and travelling wl whn fell 10th* **5/6**[1]

6m 58.1s (19.90) **Going Correction** +1.425s/f (Heav) **8** Ran SP% **118.0**
Speed ratings: **125,121,113,111,110 ,,**
CSF £31.23 TOTE £4.60: £1.50, £1.70, £7.80; EX 22.30 Trifecta £1170.90.

Owner Mrs Peter Andrews **Bred** Eric Aubree & Mme Maryse Aubree **Trained** Barbury Castle, Wilts

FOCUS
Race distance increased by 192 yards. Unsurprisingly this Grade 2 proved a war of attrition and the first pair had it to themselves from a long way out, but it's form to be positive about. Smad Place is rated back to his Hennessy form.

3851 FREEBETS.COM TROPHY CHASE (H'CAP) (GRADE 3) (13 fncs 4 omitted) 2m 4f 166y
2:25 (2:25) (Class 1) 5-Y-0+
£34,170 (£12,822; £6,420; £3,198; £1,608; £804)

Form RPR
F-16 1 **Annacotty (IRE)**[49] 3031 8-11-9 151 (p) IanPopham 159
(Alan King) *lw: trckd ldr: rdn after 3 out (usual 4 out): led last: idling whn briefly pressed ent fnl f: styd on again to assert towards fin* **13/2**[3]

-132 2 1 1/4 **Tenor Nivernais (FR)**[29] 3406 9-11-6 148 AidanColeman 156
(Venetia Williams) *j. sltly rt: led: rdn and hdd appr last where mstke: rallied ent fnl f: styd on but hld towards fin* **11/2**[2]

1044 3 31 **Lost Legend (IRE)**[29] 3406 9-11-0 142 (v) RichieMcLernon 118
(Jonjo O'Neill) *mid-div: lft 4th after 8th: rdn and lost pl after 3 out (usual 4 out): plugged on after last to go 3rd on long run-in but no ch w front pair* **28/1**

P006 4 1 **Johns Spirit (IRE)**[29] 3406 9-11-6 148 JoshuaMoore 124
(Jonjo O'Neill) *hld up in last pair: struggling and detached 10th: no ch but plugged on fr last* **10/1**

314U 5 13 **Final Assault (IRE)**[42] 3157 7-10-11 139 DerekFox 101
(Lucinda Russell) *lw: hld up: hdwy after 8th: rdn after 3 out (usual 4 out): chalng for hld 3rd whn hit 2 out (usual 3 out): wknd on long run-in* **10/1**

-164 6 14 **Salubrious (IRE)**[7] 3735 9-11-2 144 (b[1]) SamTwiston-Davies 92
(Paul Nicholls) *lw: mid-div: wnt 3rd after 8th: rdn after 10th: nvr quite on terms w front pair: wknd on long run-in* **9/1**

2001 P **Un Beau Roman (FR)**[21] 3524 8-10-9 137 TomO'Brien
(Paul Henderson) *mid-div: wnt 5th after 9th: rdn after 3 out (usual 4 out): wknd next: p.u bef last (usual 2 out)* **20/1**

2F-2 P **Champagne West (IRE)**[49] 3031 8-11-12 154 RichardJohnson
(Philip Hobbs) *trckd ldrs: travelling wl and abt to mount chal whn short of room and mstke 8th: virtually fell and dropped to rr: nt fluent after and nvr rcvrd: p.u after 10th* **7/4**[1]

2155 P **Irish Cavalier (IRE)**[35] 3231 7-11-12 154 (p) BarryGeraghty
(Rebecca Curtis) *chsd ldrs: pushed along whn hit 5th: dropped to rr qckly: p.u whn losing tch after 7th* **7/1**

5m 42.0s (26.30) **Going Correction** +1.425s/f (Heav) **9** Ran SP% **114.0**
Speed ratings: **106,105,93,93,88 83,,,**
CSF £42.02 CT £930.26 TOTE £7.50: £2.10, £1.80, £5.70; EX 44.80 Trifecta £1560.80.

Owner Mrs Peter Prowting **Bred** Patrick Crotty Jnr **Trained** Barbury Castle, Wilts

FOCUS
This good-quality handicap was another race where the first pair dominated the finish, as the ground again played a big part. The runner-up sets a decent standard. It was run over distance 192 yards further than advertised. A small pb from the winner with the second to his best, and the rest 2st+ off.

3852 NEPTUNE INVESTMENT MANAGEMENT NOVICES' HURDLE (REGISTERED AS CLASSIC NOVICES' HURDLE) (GRADE 2) (10 hdls) 2m 4f 56y
3:00 (3:00) (Class 1) 4-Y-0+
£17,085 (£6,411; £3,210; £1,599; £804; £402)

Form RPR
-111 1 **Yanworth**[43] 3135 6-11-12 148 BarryGeraghty 160+
(Alan King) *lw: travelled strly thrght: hld up: smooth prog fr 6th: little green whn having a look at the 3rd last: jnd ldr gng best appr last: led run-in: drew clr: unextended and most impressive* **2/1**[1]

1-11 2 7 **Shantou Village (IRE)**[78] 2470 6-11-12 146 RWalsh 147
(Neil Mulholland) *in tch: rdn and hdwy to ld after 2 out: hdd after last: styd on but sn hld by impressive wnr* **9/4**[2]

1211 3 10 **Champers On Ice (IRE)**[29] 3403 6-11-12 143 TomScudamore 140
(David Pipe) *trckd ldr: blnd 2 out: sn rdn and ev ch: styd on same pce fr last* **6/1**[3]

31 4 3 3/4 **Chef D'Oeuvre (FR)**[49] 3043 5-11-9 0 GavinSheehan 130
(Warren Greatrex) *prom: led after 2nd: rdn after 2 out: hdd bef last: styd on but no ex* **8/1**

2 5 12 **Baden (FR)**[50] 3019 5-11-5 0 AndrewTinkler 115
(Nicky Henderson) *str: hld up: hdwy 3 out: trckd ldrs 2 out: rdn bef last: nt quite pce to chal: fdd run-in* **16/1**

2-14 6 4 1/2 **Royal Vacation (IRE)**[64] 2762 6-11-9 128 (t) AidanColeman 114
(Colin Tizzard) *hld up: pushed along after 7th: outpcd after 2 out: nvr trbld ldrs* **50/1**

2114 7 2 **Clondaw Cian (IRE)**[57] 2886 6-11-9 135 TomO'Brien 112
(Suzy Smith) *in tch: in last pair 3 out: sn rdn: outpcd after next* **25/1**

0121 P **Charmix (FR)**[45] 3117 6-11-12 145 NoelFehily
(Harry Fry) *lw: trckd ldrs: mstke 7th: rdn appr 2 out: sn wknd: p.u bef last* **9/1**

5m 23.0s (25.60) **Going Correction** +1.425s/f (Heav) **8** Ran SP% **111.2**
Speed ratings (Par 115): **105,102,98,96,91 90,89,**
CSF £6.50 TOTE £2.50: £1.20, £1.30, £1.60; EX 6.70 Trifecta £23.70.

Owner John P McManus **Bred** Wood Farm Stud **Trained** Barbury Castle, Wilts

FOCUS
A strong Grade 2 novice contest, run at a solid gallop and the form is rock-solid. Yanworth showed a level good enough to win all bar one of the last ten Neptunes. The race distance was increased by 84 yards.

3853 GALLIARDHOMES.COM CLEEVE HURDLE (GRADE 2) (12 hdls) 2m 7f 213y
3:35 (3:36) (Class 1) 5-Y-0+
£34,170 (£12,822; £6,420; £3,198; £1,608; £804)

Form RPR
-211 1 **Thistlecrack**[42] 3149 8-11-8 168 TomScudamore 172+
(Colin Tizzard) *racd wd: travelled strly thrght: trckd ldrs: led bef last: drew effrtlessly clr: v impressive* **4/5**[1]

12FU 2 12 **Ptit Zig (FR)**[21] 3526 7-11-0 159 SamTwiston-Davies 149
(Paul Nicholls) *lw: racd wd: in last pair: nt fluent 6th: wnt 4th at the 8th: disp cl 3rd after 2 out: rdn to chse wnr jst bef last: nvr any ch w impressive wnr but kpt on* **7/1**[3]

-00F 3 2 **The Romford Pele (IRE)**[50] 3016 9-11-0 136 (b) NoelFehily 145
(Rebecca Curtis) *racd wd: in last pair: hdwy after 3 out: disp cl 3rd after next: rdn jst bef last: styd on same pce* **50/1**

0P-2 **4** ¾ **Knockara Beau (IRE)**[29] 3407 13-11-0 140........................ JanFaltejsek 144
(George Charlton) *kpt to inner: led tl 7th: pressed ldr fr 9th tl rdn after 2 out: styd on same pce fr last* **20/1**

4-U1 **5** *11* **Camping Ground (FR)**[29] 3408 6-11-8 163...................(t) LeightonAspell 145
(Robert Walford) *racd keenly and kpt wd: prom: led 7th: rdn and hdd bef last: wknd run-in* **5/2**[2]

-2U4 **6** *17* **The Young Master**[42] 3150 7-11-0 144....................(p) MrSWaley-Cohen 116
(Neil Mulholland) *lw: kpt to inner: trckd ldr tl 7th: in tch tl outpcd after 3 out: nt a threat after* **25/1**

66-3 **7** *11* **Guitar Pete (IRE)**[20] 3552 6-11-0 146..........................(vt) BarryGeraghty 105
(Ms Sandra Hughes, Ire) *racd wd: hld up in tch: effrt after 2 out: wknd bef last* **33/1**

6m 26.2s (25.20) **Going Correction** +1.425s/f (Heavy) **7** Ran SP% **110.1**
Speed ratings: **115,111,110,110,106 100,97**
CSF £6.29 TOTE £1.60: £1.30, £2.30; EX 5.20 Trifecta £85.00.
Owner John and Heather Snook **Bred** R F And S D Knipe **Trained** Milborne Port, Dorset

FOCUS
Race distance increased by 148 yards. This wasn't such a competitive edition of the Cleeve hurdle, but it was impossible not to be impressed with the high-class winner who confirmed the merit of his Ascot form. The fourth is a fair benchmark.

3854 STEEL PLATE AND SECTIONS H'CAP HURDLE (8 hdls) 2m 179y
4:10 (4:12) (Class 2) 4-Y-O+ **£16,245** (£4,770; £2,385; £1,192)

Form RPR

1111 **1** **Solstice Star**[50] 3015 6-9-11 **127** oh5..............................(t) KillianMoore(3) 132+
(Martin Keighley) *mde all: hit 3rd: r.o wl fr last: rdn out* **13/2**[3]

1-65 **2** *4* **Cheltenian (FR)**[49] 3033 10-11-12 **153**................................ RichardJohnson 153+
(Philip Hobbs) *hld up: pushed along after 2 out: nt clrest of runs whn rdn after last: r.o into 2nd fnl 140yds: no threat to wnr* **13/2**[3]

1-5 **3** *1 ¼* **Frodon (FR)**[84] 2360 4-10-0 **138** oh1......................... SamTwiston-Davies 126
(Paul Nicholls) *str: lw: hld up: hdwy after 3 out: disp 2nd next: rdn bef last: kpt on but no ex fnl 140yds* **13/2**[3]

1620 **4** *shd* **Prairie Town (IRE)**[33] 3318 5-10-2 **129**................................ LeeEdwards 129
(Tony Carroll) *trckd wnr: rdn after 2 out: kpt on same pce fnl 120yds* **25/1**

-521 **5** *1 ½* **Champagne At Tara**[33] 3306 7-10-2 **129**........................ RichieMcLernon 126
(Jonjo O'Neill) *hld up: hdwy 2 out: disp 2nd at the last: kpt on tl no ex fnl 140yds* **6/1**[2]

0600 **6** *hd* **Olofi (FR)**[50] 3015 10-9-9 **127** oh3..................................(bt[1]) JamieBargary(5) 125
(Tom George) *trckd ldrs: rdn appr last: kpt on tl no ex fnl 140yds* **7/1**

211- **7** *4* **Clean Sheet (IRE)**[351] 4205 7-10-8 **135**................................ BarryGeraghty 129
(Nicky Henderson) *lw: racd keenly: in tch: hdwy 2 out: disputing 2nd whn blnd last: wknd fnl f* **11/4**[1]

-P01 **8** *5* **Prouts Pub (IRE)**[35] 3216 7-10-4 **131**................................ LeightonAspell 119
(Nick Gifford) *in tch: dropped to last 5th: rdn 2 out: wknd bef last* **12/1**

4/1- **P** **Maestro Royal**[386] 3600 7-10-0 **127**.................................... PeterCarberry
(Nicky Henderson) *racd keenly: trckd ldrs: p.u whn sddle slipped appr 3 out* **10/1**

4m 30.0s (18.70) **Going Correction** +1.425s/f (Heavy)
WFA 4 from 5yo+ 11lb **9** Ran SP% **114.1**
Speed ratings (Par 109): **113,111,110,110,109 109,107,105,**
CSF £47.70 CT £285.18 TOTE £6.50: £2.00, £2.10, £2.10; EX 42.10 Trifecta £573.50.
Owner E&G Racing Ltd **Bred** David Allen **Trained** Condicote, Gloucs

FOCUS
Race distance increased by 84 yards. This fair handicap was run at a muddling gallop and the bang in-form winner dictated. The third to sixth were close to their marks.
T/Jkpt: Not Won. JACKPOT PLACEPOT £187.40 to a £1 stake. Pool: £3684.98 - 14.35 winning tickets. T/Plt: £194.50 to a £1 stake. Pool: £199915.28 - 750.01 winning tickets T/Qpdt: £16.50 to a £1 stake. Pool: £15447.35 - 691.65 winning tickets **Tim Mitchell**

3834 DONCASTER (L-H)
Saturday, January 30

OFFICIAL GOING: Good (good to soft in places; chs 7.6, hdl 8.0)
Wind: fresh across Weather: mixture of sunshine and cloud, shower before 6th

3855 PHILIP SHACKLEY 60TH BIRTHDAY CELEBRATION H'CAP HURDLE (10 hdls) 2m 3f 120y
12:30 (12:30) (Class 4) (0-120,120) 4-Y-O+ **£4,548** (£1,335; £667; £333)

Form RPR

5302 **1** **McCabe Creek (IRE)**[51] 2989 6-10-8 **112**............................ JamieInsole(10) 121+
(Alan King) *racd keenly: sn in tch: trckd ldrs after 6th: led appr 3 out: nt fluent 2 out: sn rdn: wandered between last 2: hit last and rdr lost iron: jnd run-in: styd on* **9/1**

-053 **2** *2 ¼* **Charlie Cook (IRE)**[35] 3238 7-11-0 **108**................................ DavidBass 111
(Graeme McPherson) *prom: chal 3 out: rdn bef 2 out: ev ch run-in: one pce and hld towards fin* **5/1**[1]

2/05 **3** *4* **Roycano**[10] 3680 6-10-6 **103**................................ HarryBannister(3) 103
(Michael Easterby) *hld up: pushed along and hdwy bef 3 out: wnt 3rd 2 out: styd on* **12/1**

-505 **4** *½* **City Supreme (IRE)**[66] 2713 6-10-4 **103**..........................[1] DavidNoonan(5) 102
(Anthony Honeyball) *midfield: rdn and hdwy bef 3 out: kpt on* **12/1**

2-22 **5** *4 ½* **Deputy Commander (IRE)**[42] 3159 7-10-12 **109**................ RyanHatch(3) 104
(Nigel Twiston-Davies) *hld up in midfield: drvn bef 3 out: styd on after 2 out* **13/2**[3]

4-F3 **6** *nse* **Degooch (IRE)**[66] 2711 7-11-11 **119**................................ BrendanPowell 113
(Johnny Farrelly) *hld up: hdwy and in tch 6th: rdn 3 out: one pce* **10/1**

F0P5 **7** *7* **Tekthelot (IRE)**[29] 3424 10-11-0 **111**................................ HarryChalloner(3) 100
(Keith Reveley) *midfield: rdn bef 3 out: nt fluent 2 out: wknd last* **14/1**

1F02 **8** *9* **Desertmore Hill (IRE)**[22] 3506 6-11-2 **110**........................ PaddyBrennan 90
(Peter Bowen) *racd keenly: prom: led narrowly after 6th: hdd appr 3 out: wknd after 2 out* **11/2**[2]

23 **9** *nk* **Le Legro (IRE)**[105] 1968 6-11-1 **109**................................ DenisO'Regan 90
(Charlie Mann) *led: hit 4th: hdd after 6th: rdn 3 out: sn wknd* **20/1**

550P **10** *3 ¼* **She's Late**[52] 2973 6-11-2 **117**................................ PatrickCowley(7) 94
(Jonjo O'Neill) *midfield: rdn bef 3 out: sn wknd* **25/1**

3410 **11** *1 ½* **Scoppio Del Carro**[35] 3238 5-10-13 **107**.......................(t) AdamPogson 83
(Charles Pogson) *trckd ldrs: wknd after 3 out* **33/1**

-321 **12** *2* **Bells Of Ailsworth (IRE)**[211] 893 6-11-2 **110**........................ TomCannon 84
(Tim Vaughan) *midfield: rdn after 7th: wknd after 2 out* **20/1**

/PP0 **13** *1 ¼* **Moscow Presents (IRE)**[14] 3628 8-10-5 **102**........................ AdamNicol(3) 75
(Philip Kirby) *hld up: rdn after 6th: sn struggling* **40/1**

P/43 **14** *4 ½* **Kind Of Easy (IRE)**[32] 3344 10-10-10 **104**........................ CraigNichol 73
(Alistair Whillans) *in tch: pushed along after 6th: wknd bef 3 out* **25/1**

00 **15** *10* **Shalamzar (FR)**[10] 3680 7-10-2 **99**................................ JoeColliver(3) 59
(Micky Hammond) *hld up: nvr threatened* **100/1**

6P-2 **16** *6* **Smadynium (FR)**[55] 2933 8-11-12 **120**..............................(t) HenryBrooke 74
(Julia Brooke) *midfield: wknd bef 3 out* **20/1**

-U26 **17** *4 ½* **Swivel**[150] 1455 5-10-13 **110**................................ MattGriffiths(3) 60
(Mark Wall) *hld up: rdn bef 3 out: sn wknd* **33/1**

4122 **18** *nk* **Polarbrook (IRE)**[50] 3023 9-10-11 **105**..............................(vt) JamesDavies 55
(Derek Shaw) *a towards rr* **12/1**

4m 45.9s (-5.40) **Going Correction** -0.025s/f (Good) **18** Ran SP% **125.5**
Speed ratings (Par 105): **109,108,106,106,104 104,101,98,97,96 96,95,94,92,88 86,84,84**
CSF £48.44 CT £563.88 TOTE £9.80: £2.50, £2.20, £4.00, £3.30; EX 67.10 Trifecta £863.90.
Owner Ian Payne & Kim Franklin **Bred** John P A Kenny **Trained** Barbury Castle, Wilts

FOCUS
Chases increased by 12yds and Hurdles by 24yds. After just 0.6mm of overnight rain the official going remained good, good to soft in places. The opener was a fair handicap hurdle and they finished well strung out, despite the gallop being ordinary. The winner is better than the bare result and this rates a step up.

3856 GRAND-NATIONAL2016.CO.UK LIGHTNING NOVICES' CHASE (GRADE 2) (12 fncs) 2m 90y
1:00 (1:00) (Class 1) 5-Y-O+ **£19,932** (£7,479; £3,745; £1,865; £938)

Form RPR

5-12 **1** **Vaniteux (FR)**[34] 3280 7-11-0 152................................ NicodeBoinville 162+
(Nicky Henderson) *trckd ldr: nt fluent 6 out and briefly pushed along: led 3 out: rdn to assert next: drvn out run-in* **6/4**[2]

0113 **2** *3 ¼* **Arzal (FR)**[34] 3280 6-11-4 149................................ DavidBass 160
(Harry Whittington) *led: nt fluent 5 out and sn pushed along: rdn whn hdd 3 out: kpt on* **11/2**[3]

-112 **3** *10* **Fox Norton (FR)**[76] 2510 6-11-4 148................................ DarylJacob 152
(Neil Mulholland) *in tch: mstke 4 out: sn rdn: one-pced in 3rd after 3 out* **16/1**

21-3 **4** *1 ¾* **Shaneshill (IRE)**[27] 3458 7-11-4 152................................ PaulTownend 149
(W P Mullins, Ire) *in tch: pushed along whn mstke 4 out: rdn next: sn btn* **11/8**[1]

-051 **5** *14* **Bouvreuil (FR)**[22] 3504 5-10-11 139..............................(t) NickScholfield 135
(Paul Nicholls) *hld up: nt fluent 4th: hit 3 out: a in rr* **25/1**

3m 57.3s (-7.70) **Going Correction** -0.025s/f (Good)
WFA 5 from 6yo+ 3lb **5** Ran SP% **107.2**
Speed ratings: **118,116,111,110,103**
CSF £9.21 TOTE £2.30: £1.20, £2.60; EX 12.00 Trifecta £41.60.
Owner Mr & Mrs R Kelvin-Hughes **Bred** Jacques Cypres **Trained** Upper Lambourn, Berks

FOCUS
An interesting novice chase with the festival in mind and it was run at a reasonable gallop. The form looks solid even with the market leader running below par. Vaniteux is a high-class novice and is rated similar to his previous two chase runs.

3857 PLAY CHANNEL 4 RACING'S PICK 6 H'CAP CHASE (12 fncs) 2m 90y
1:30 (1:30) (Class 2) 5-Y-O+ **£31,280** (£9,240; £4,620; £2,310; £1,155; £580)

Form RPR

1 **Dandridge**[63] 2794 7-9-11 **125**..................................(t) DonaghMeyler(5) 139+
(A L T Moore, Ire) *midfield: smooth hdwy 5 out: led gng wl 3 out: pushed clr after 2 out: rdn out run-in* **8/1**[3]

1-26 **2** *5* **Just Cameron**[28] 3446 9-11-8 **148**..................................(t) JoeColliver(3) 154
(Micky Hammond) *led: hdd bef 6th: remained prom: rdn 4 out: styd on* **9/1**

3-P1 **3** *4 ½* **Gardefort (FR)**[14] 3629 7-11-4 **141**................................ LiamTreadwell 143
(Venetia Williams) *in tch: hdwy and in tch 5 out: rdn after 4 out: one pce: wnt 3rd last* **9/1**

1-11 **4** *1 ¾* **Red Spinner (IRE)**[51] 2993 6-11-6 **143**................................ DavidBass 146
(Kim Bailey) *trckd ldr: led bef 6th: mstke 6 out: hdd 3 out: sn rdn: grad wknd fr appr last* **4/1**[1]

1152 **5** *½* **Sir Valentino (FR)**[14] 3629 7-11-6 **143**..............................(t) PaddyBrennan 144
(Tom George) *trckd ldrs: nt a fluent: rdn and outpcd after 4 out: plugged on run-in* **8/1**[3]

3511 **6** *6* **Dresden (IRE)**[70] 2635 8-11-12 **149**................................ JamesDavies 144
(Henry Oliver) *midfield: rdn after 5 out: sn no imp* **8/1**[3]

6-50 **7** *¾* **Turn Over Sivola (FR)**[49] 3031 9-10-11 **134**........................ DenisO'Regan 130
(Alan King) *midfield: rdn after 4 out: nvr threatened* **9/2**[2]

6441 **8** *½* **Chestnut Ben (IRE)**[26] 3475 11-9-8 **124** oh7 ow1.............. MrRWinks(7) 118
(Peter Winks) *hld up: rdn after 5 out: nvr threatened* **66/1**

0-11 **9** *16* **On Tour (IRE)**[62] 2803 8-11-1 **138**................................ BrianHarding 117
(Evan Williams) *hld up: pushed along after 4th: reminder after 5th: nt fluent 6 out: a in rr* **9/2**[2]

23-P **10** *26* **Ifandbutwhynot (IRE)**[49] 3041 10-11-1 **138**........................ BrianHughes 94
(Tim Easterby) *hld up: wknd after 5 out* **20/1**

4m 1.6s (-3.40) **Going Correction** -0.025s/f (Good) **10** Ran SP% **116.0**
Speed ratings: **107,104,102,101,101 98,97,97,89,76**
CSF £76.48 CT £663.72 TOTE £9.10: £2.60, £3.50, £2.60; EX 101.70 Trifecta £717.40.
Owner R A Bartlett **Bred** Boyce Bloodstock **Trained** Naas, Co Kildare

FOCUS
A competitive-looking handicap chase, but the winner was travelling by far the best some way from home. This rates a step up from him, with the second back to his best.

3858 OLBG.COM MARES' HURDLE (REGISTERED AS DONCASTER MARES' HURDLE) (GRADE 2) (8 hdls) 2m 140y
2:05 (2:05) (Class 1) 4-Y-O+ **£28,475** (£10,685; £5,350; £2,665; £1,340; £670)

Form RPR

1131 **1** **Smart Talk (IRE)**[42] 3154 6-11-5 134................................ PaddyBrennan 145+
(Brian Ellison) *trckd ldr: jnd ldr 5th: led narrowly whn mstke 3 out and hdd: sn rdn: led again last: styd on wl* **7/1**[3]

6111 **2** *3 ¼* **Lily Waugh (IRE)**[49] 3034 9-11-0 140..............................(t) DavidNoonan 134
(Anthony Honeyball) *hld up in tch: rdn and outpcd in 4th appr 3 out: styd on after 2 out: wnt 2nd towards fin* **7/1**[3]

11-3 **3** *1 ¼* **Morning Run (IRE)**[32] 3356 7-11-5 148................................ PaulTownend 138
(W P Mullins, Ire) *led: jnd 5th: hdd narrowly bef 3 out: led again after 3 out: drvn after 2 out: hdd last: wknd fnl 110yds: lost 2nd towards fin* **5/6**[1]

-02P **4** *½* **Pass The Time**[24] 3034 7-11-0 138..................................(p) MarkQuinlan 134
(Neil Mulholland) *in tch: rdn to chse ldng pair bef 3 out: nt fluent 2 out: edgd lft and sn one pce: j.lft last* **12/1**

0-62 **5** *9* **Rock On The Moor (IRE)**[32] 3356 8-11-3 140................ RobbiePower 127
(Mrs John Harrington, Ire) *in tch: lost pl 5th: rdn and bdly outpcd on run to 3 out: plugged on after 2 out* **6/1**[2]

The Form Book Jumps 2015-16, Raceform Ltd, Newbury, RG14 5SJ

5-25 **6** *7* **Intense Tango**[15] 2789 5-11-5 138 .... BrianHughes 124
(K R Burke) *hld up: pushed along bef 3 out: sn btn* **8/1**
-323 **7** *33* **Donna's Pride**[22] 3505 7-11-0 108 .... HarryChalloner 88
(Keith Reveley) *a bhd* **100/1**
3m 59.2s (-5.50) **Going Correction** -0.025s/f (Good) **7** Ran SP% **113.6**
Speed ratings (Par 115): **111,109,108,108,104 101,85**
CSF £52.08 TOTE £9.10: £3.10, £3.30; EX 50.40 Trifecta £74.30.
Owner Mrs J A Martin **Bred** Roland Rothwell **Trained** Norton, N Yorks

FOCUS
A useful mares' hurdle and a progressive and smart winner.

3859 ALBERT BARTLETT NOVICES' HURDLE (REGISTERED AS RIVER DON NOVICES' HURDLE) (GRADE 2) (11 hdls) 3m 96y
2:40 (2:40) (Class 1) 5-Y-O+ **£17,165** (£6,491; £3,290; £1,679; £884)

Form RPR
1-11 **1** **Barters Hill (IRE)**[32] 3350 6-11-7 150 .... DavidBass 147+
(Ben Pauling) *mde all: nt fluent 4th: hit 4 out: pushed along bef 3 out: pressed bef last: drvn run-in: edgd lft: kpt on gamely* **4/7**[1]
-211 **2** *¾* **Ballydine (IRE)**[63] 2787 6-11-7 132 .... BrianHughes 143
(Charlie Longsdon) *trckd ldng pair: pushed along to chal between last 2: drvn run-in: kpt on but a hld* **28/1**
-422 **3** *9* **Ami Desbois (FR)**[22] 3509 6-11-0 125 .... RyanHatch 129
(Graeme McPherson) *hld up: hdwy and in tch appr 3 out: sn rdn: wnt 3rd whn mstke last: wknd run-in* **100/1**
0-31 **4** *11* **Up For Review (IRE)**[30] 3393 7-11-7 151 .... PaulTownend 130+
(W P Mullins, Ire) *pressed ldr: mstke 4 out: rdn after 3 out: wknd last* **7/4**[2]
021 **5** *77* **Minella Charmer (IRE)**[27] 3452 5-11-7 141 ....(t) TomBellamy 56
(Alan King) *hld up in tch: rdn after 4 out: sn wknd: mstke 3 out* **22/1**[3]
31 **P** **Ephraim**[49] 3037 5-11-4 129 .... PaddyBrennan
(Charlie Mann) *trckd ldng pair: lost pl whn nt fluent 5th: sn pushed along and struggling in rr: t.o whn p.u bef 3 out* **28/1**
5m 54.7s (-4.30) **Going Correction** -0.025s/f (Good) **6** Ran SP% **112.3**
Speed ratings: **106,105,102,99,73**
CSF £16.72 TOTE £1.60: £1.50, £4.90; EX 11.30 Trifecta £127.50.
Owner Circle Of Friends **Bred** Lady J Fowler **Trained** Bourton-On-The-Water, Gloucs

FOCUS
A fascinating novices' staying hurdle, featuring the two market leaders for the Albert Bartlett. Barters Hill is rated below the level of his Newbury win.

3860 SKY BET CHASE (H'CAP) (FORMERLY GREAT YORKSHIRE CHASE) (LISTED RACE) (18 fncs) 3m 6y
3:15 (3:15) (Class 1) 5-Y-O+
£45,560 (£17,096; £8,560; £4,264; £2,144; £1,072)

Form RPR
-P31 **1** **Ziga Boy (FR)**[32] 3339 7-10-0 **133** oh1 .... BrendanPowell 144+
(Alan King) *pressed ldr: led narrowly 11th: asserted gng wl bef 4 out: rdn appr 2 out: drvn and kpt on run-in* **8/1**[2]
-132 **2** *3¼* **Coologue (IRE)**[49] 3040 7-10-6 **139** .... BrianHughes 145
(Charlie Longsdon) *trckd ldng pair: nt fluent 5 out: wnt 2nd 4 out: rdn after 3 out: styd on but a hld* **9/1**[3]
-324 **3** *½* **Buywise (IRE)**[49] 3031 9-11-4 **151** .... BrianHarding 158
(Evan Williams) *hld up: stdy hdwy after 6 out: rdn 3 out: wnt 3rd 2 out: sn drvn: kpt on same pce* **8/1**[2]
4P-P **4** *6* **Pass The Hat**[30] 3394 9-9-13 **137** ....(t) DonaghMeyler(5) 140
(A L T Moore, Ire) *midfield: hdwy and in tch 6 out: rdn to go 3rd jst after 4 out: lost 3rd 2 out: grad wknd* **10/1**
66-1 **5** *13* **Ikorodu Road**[50] 3024 13-10-0 **133** ....(p) HarrySkelton 122
(Graeme McPherson) *midfield: rdn after 6 out: plugged on after 2 out: nvr threatened* **16/1**
-P02 **6** *¾* **Le Reve (IRE)**[21] 3528 8-10-13 **146** ....(p) NicodeBoinville 135
(Lucy Wadham) *hld up in rr: mstke 1st: rdn after 6 out: plugged on after 3 out: nvr threatened* **10/1**
00-3 **7** *6* **Dolatulo (FR)**[56] 2899 9-10-13 **146** ....(tp) DenisO'Regan 131
(Warren Greatrex) *in tch: rdn after 5 out: wknd after 3 out* **12/1**
32/0 **8** *4½* **Gullinbursti (IRE)**[42] 3150 10-10-1 **134** ....(v) ConorO'Farrell 114
(Emma Lavelle) *racd keenly: trckd ldng pair: rdn after 5 out: sn wknd* **14/1**
-245 **9** *3¾* **Double Ross (IRE)**[56] 2902 10-11-3 **153** .... RyanHatch(3) 128
(Nigel Twiston-Davies) *midfield: rdn 5 out: sn wknd* **16/1**
0136 **10** *6* **Distime (IRE)**[29] 3425 10-10-0 **133** oh4 .... JonathanEngland 103
(Sam Drake) *trckd ldrs: lost pl 9th: wknd after 12th* **66/1**
4112 **11** *3¼* **Aachen**[28] 3448 12-10-13 **151** .... CharlieDeutsch(5) 118
(Venetia Williams) *led narrowly: hdd 11th: rdn after 5 out: wknd after 4 out* **22/1**
2P-2 **P** **Court By Surprise (IRE)**[111] 1871 11-10-7 **140** .... DarylJacob
(Emma Lavelle) *midfield: mstkes 8th (water) and 9th: slow 10th: sn struggling: p.u bef 12th* **25/1**
1P3U **P** **No Planning**[56] 2899 9-10-4 **137** .... PaddyBrennan
(Sue Smith) *a towards rr: p.u bef 5 out* **11/1**
3-54 **P** **Holywell (IRE)**[70] 2642 9-11-12 **159** ....(p) WillKennedy
(Jonjo O'Neill) *hld up: pushed along and struggling after 7th: t.o whn p.u bef 5 out* **8/1**[2]
-113 **P** **Le Mercurey (FR)**[29] 3405 6-10-9 **142** ....(t) NickScholfield
(Paul Nicholls) *hld up: rdn 11th: sn btn: p.u bef 3 out* **6/1**[1]
6m 2.9s (-9.10) **Going Correction** -0.025s/f (Good) **15** Ran SP% **119.9**
Speed ratings: **114,112,112,110,106 106,104,102,101,99 98, , , ,**
CSF £76.68 CT £604.00 TOTE £8.50: £2.90, £3.30, £3.40; EX 91.20 Trifecta £1012.10.
Owner Axom Ll **Bred** Guy Cherel **Trained** Barbury Castle, Wilts

FOCUS
A competitive renewal of this valuable Listed handicap chase and solid form, with the first three coming clear. Probably another step up from Ziga Boy.

3861 STEVIE BOW'S 50TH BIRTHDAY CELEBRATION BRITISH STALLIONS EBF MARES' STANDARD OPEN NH FLAT (DIV I) 2m 140y
3:50 (3:50) (Class 6) 4-7-Y-O **£1,949** (£572; £286; £143)

Form RPR
3 **1** **Queen Odessa (IRE)**[81] 2421 5-11-0 0 .... NickScholfield 109
(Harry Fry) *mde most: set stdy pce: rdn over 2f out: sn 3 l clr: reduced advantage fnl 110yds: hld on all out* **8/1**
33- **2** *hd* **Kayf Grace**[289] 5359 6-11-0 .... NicodeBoinville 109+
(Nicky Henderson) *trckd ldng pair: rdn 3f out: styd on wl fnl f: jst failed* **6/5**[1]
5 **3** *4½* **Atlanta Ablaze**[44] 3132 5-11-0 0 .... JakeGreenall 104
(Henry Daly) *trckd ldng pair: 3f out: kpt on same pce* **20/1**
24 **4** *6* **Cajun Fiddle (IRE)**[44] 3132 5-10-11 0 .... TomBellamy(3) 98
(Alan King) *midfield: rdn over 3f out: plugged on* **9/2**[2]
35-3 **5** *¾* **Sainte Ladylime (FR)**[269] 152 5-11-0 0 .... DavidBass 98
(Kim Bailey) *in tch: rdn 3f out: plugged on* **10/1**
1 **6** *7* **Mcgregor's Cottage (IRE)**[57] 2895 5-11-7 0 .... BrianHughes 98
(Malcolm Jefferson) *midfield: pushed along over 4f out: wknd 2f out* **5/1**[3]
7 *shd* **Innovate (FR)** 4-10-3 0 .... MarkQuinlan 79
(Paul Webber) *pressed ldr: pushed along over 5f out: wknd over 2f out* **20/1**
4 **8** *7* **Dance And Romance**[14] 3632 4-10-3 0 .... BrianHarding 72
(Tim Easterby) *midfield: rdn and outpcd over 4f out: no threat after* **40/1**
9 *½* **Lady Longshot** 5-10-11 0 .... MattGriffiths(3) 83
(Jeremy Scott) *hld up: hdwy over 3f out: rdn over 2f out: sn wknd* **25/1**
10 *28* **Must Meet Mrsgrath (IRE)**[69] 5-10-9 0 .... ChrisWard(5) 55
(Robin Dickin) *hld up: nvr threatened* **100/1**
0 **11** *3¼* **Little Miss Flossy**[268] 159 7-10-11 0 .... JohnKington(3) 52
(Andrew Crook) *midfield on outer: rdn over 3f out: sn wknd* **100/1**
4m 17.3s (18.20) **Going Correction** -0.025s/f (Good)
WFA 4 from 5yo+ 11lb **11** Ran SP% **118.3**
Speed ratings: **56,55,53,50,50 47,47,43,43,30 29**
CSF £17.17 TOTE £7.90: £2.20, £1.20, £4.00; EX 24.70 Trifecta £255.40.
Owner J K Whymark **Bred** The Hon Mrs V M A Tower **Trained** Seaborough, Dorset

FOCUS
The first two pulled a little way clear in the first division of an ordinary mares' bumper, run in a very slow time. A big step up from the winner.

3862 STEVIE BOW'S 50TH BIRTHDAY CELEBRATION BRITISH STALLIONS EBF MARES' STANDARD OPEN NH FLAT (DIV II) 2m 140y
4:25 (4:25) (Class 6) 4-7-Y-O **£1,949** (£572; £286; £143)

Form RPR
2 **1** **Miss Spent (IRE)**[26] 3469 6-11-0 0 .... HarrySkelton 109+
(Lucy Wadham) *trckd ldr: led over 2f out: sn rdn: styd on wl* **7/1**
2 *1¾* **Raised On Grazeon** 5-11-0 0 .... DarylJacob 106
(John Quinn) *in tch: smooth hdwy into 2nd 2f out: rdn over 1f out: kpt on but a hld* **16/1**
6 **3** *10* **Viking Queen**[81] 2421 5-11-0 0 .... MarkQuinlan 97
(Paul Webber) *led: rdn whn hdd over 2f out: sn one-pced in 3rd* **20/1**
3 **4** *3¾* **Kir Royal**[65] 2729 5-10-11 0 .... TomBellamy(3) 94
(Alan King) *racd keenly in midfield: pushed along and lost pl over 5f out: hdwy over 3f out: rdn over 2f out: one pce* **2/1**[1]
421 **5** *½* **Kalaniti (IRE)**[64] 2756 5-11-7 0 .... BrianHughes 101
(Chris Grant) *midfield: rdn over 3f out: plugged on: nvr threatened* **5/1**[3]
6 *4½* **Floramoss** 5-11-0 0 .... JonathanEngland 90
(Keith Reveley) *hld up in rr: pushed along over 6f out: bhd tl styd on fnl 2f* **20/1**
4- **7** *17* **Little Acorn**[327] 4687 5-11-0 0 .... NickScholfield 74
(Harry Fry) *midfield: rdn over 2f out: wknd over 1f out* **10/3**[2]
50- **8** *1* **Wishing Wind**[289] 5359 6-11-0 0 .... NicodeBoinville 73
(Nicky Henderson) *in tch: pushed along over 5f out: wknd over 2f out* **17/2**
0-5 **9** *3¼* **Marvellous Monty (IRE)**[77] 2493 6-11-0 0 .... BrendanPowell 70
(Johnny Farrelly) *in tch: rdn over 3f out: sn wknd* **33/1**
10 *¾* **Fact Of Life** 4-9-12 0 ....(t) DavidNoonan(5) 59
(Anthony Honeyball) *a towards rr* **20/1**
0 **11** *54* **Kaddys Dream**[45] 3111 5-10-9 0 .... ChrisWard(5) 21
(Robin Dickin) *a in rr: t.o fnl 3f* **100/1**
4m 6.5s (7.40) **Going Correction** -0.025s/f (Good)
WFA 4 from 5yo+ 11lb **11** Ran SP% **120.2**
Speed ratings: **81,80,75,73,73 71,63,62,61,61 35**
CSF £103.46 TOTE £7.30: £2.70, £5.00, £6.40; EX 127.30 Trifecta £1300.60.
Owner The Wynn Partnership **Bred** Alice Kehoe **Trained** Newmarket, Suffolk

FOCUS
The second division of the mares' bumper was run 10.8sec quicker than the first. The winner built on the promise of her debut run.
T/Plt: £504.10 to a £1 stake. Pool: £115942.85 - 167.88 winning tickets T/Qpdt: £100.60 to a £1 stake. Pool: £10123.03 - 74.4 winning tickets **Andrew Sheret**

3375 UTTOXETER (L-H)
Saturday, January 30

OFFICIAL GOING: Heavy (4.9)
Wind: fresh 1/2 against Weather: fine and sunny but cold

3863 MOORLANDS RACING CONDITIONAL JOCKEYS' MAIDEN HURDLE (6 hdls 3 omitted) 1m 7f 168y
1:45 (1:45) (Class 4) 4-Y-O+ **£3,798** (£1,122; £561; £280; £140)

Form RPR
-635 **1** **Will O'The West (IRE)**[45] 3105 5-11-4 0 .... JackSherwood 122+
(Henry Daly) *in tch: drvn bef 2 out (normal 3 out): lft 2nd: led bef omitted last: drvn rt out* **15/8**[1]
3-2P **2** *13* **Danvinnie**[40] 3194 7-11-1 0 .... ThomasGarner(3) 110
(Oliver Sherwood) *led: drvn 4th: hdd appr 2 out (normal 3 out): lft in ld: hdd bef omitted last: kpt on same pce* **9/4**[2]
52 **3** *13* **Nam Hai (IRE)**[29] 3397 5-11-4 0 .... ConorShoemark 100
(Kim Bailey) *trckd ldrs: rdn: lft handy 3rd and hit 2 out (normal 3 out): one pce* **7/2**[3]
00 **4** *11* **Leaving Las Vegas**[31] 3363 5-11-4 0 .... JeremiahMcGrath 86
(William Kinsey) *prom: lost pl bef 2 out (normal 3 out): sn bhd* **33/1**
33-5 **5** *2½* **Jaunty Thor**[30] 3375 6-10-13 0 .... WilliamFeatherstone(5) 83
(Brian Eckley) *chsd ldrs: drvn and lost pl bef 2 out (normal 3 out)* **7/1**
0 **6** *73* **Pettal**[30] 3381 5-10-6 0 .... CharlieHammond(5)
(Sarah-Jayne Davies) *trckd ldrs: lost pl 3rd: sn bhd: t.o 2 out (normal 3 out): eventually completed* **66/1**
P00 **7** *46* **Hugh's Secret (IRE)**[16] 3590 4-10-7 0 .... CallumBewley
(Philip Kirby) *in rr: drvn 3rd: sn lost pl: bhd fr 4th: sn t.o: eventually completed* **150/1**
22/0 **U** **Georgian Firebird**[30] 3375 6-10-11 0 .... CiaranGethings
(Barry Leavy) *w ldr: led appr 2 out (normal 3 out): stmbld on landing and uns rdr 2 out* **20/1**
605U **P** **Sadiks Boy (IRE)**[59] 2850 7-11-1 0 ....(p) MikeyHamill(3)
(Aytach Sadik) *chsd ldrs: reluctant and lost pl bef 3rd: sn reminders and wl bhd: t.o whn p.u bef 4th* **150/1**
4m 31.2s (33.80) **Going Correction** +2.05s/f (Heav)
WFA 4 from 5yo+ 11lb **9** Ran SP% **110.8**
Speed ratings (Par 105): **97,90,84,78,77 40,17, ,**
CSF £6.02 TOTE £2.90: £1.20, £1.10, £1.50; EX 7.30 Trifecta £14.60.
Owner Strachan,Connell,Salwey,Griffith&Gabb **Bred** Mrs L Suenson-Taylor **Trained** Stanton Lacy, Shropshire

FOCUS
On the hurdles course the chute hurdle was not used in the two-mile races at 1.45 and 2.55 and the final hurdle (number three) is out in all races. With the rails moved out add 22yds to the 1.45 and 2.55 and 32yds to the 4.35. On the chase course the last in the back straight (fence eight) was omitted in all chases. A very ordinary conditional jockeys' maiden hurdle. They went a sensible gallop on desperately heavy ground. The form could be up to 7lb out either way.

3864 ASHLEIGH BUILDERS NOVICES' H'CAP CHASE (16 fncs 2 omitted) 3m 2y
2:20 (2:20) (Class 4) (0-105,105) 5-Y-0+ £7,279

Form RPR
-6U6 1 **Try It Sometime (IRE)**[18] 3572 8-10-13 95........................(t) BenPoste(3) 107+
(Sheila Lewis) *chsd ldrs: hit 4th and reminders: clr 2nd 10th: led appr 4 out: lft alone 2 out: mstke last* 14/1

5252 P **Kapricorne (FR)**[35] 3222 9-10-6 90............................(tp) DannyBurton(5)
(Sophie Leech) *chsd ldrs: lost pl 9th: clr 3rd 12th: wknd 4 out: chsd wnr appr 3 out: distant 2nd whn p.u 2 out* 4/1[1]

2-23 P **Over My Head**[30] 3378 8-10-3 85........................(t) ConorShoemark(3)
(Claire Dyson) *chsd ldrs: wknd 10th: t.o whn p.u bef 12th* 4/1[1]

-265 P **Lawless Island (IRE)**[123] 1693 7-11-7 105........................ AlanJohns(5)
(Tim Vaughan) *in rr: bhd and pushed along 9th: sn t.o: p.u bef 12th* 11/1

35PU P **Rebel Benefit (IRE)**[7] 3746 8-11-5 98............................(p) TrevorWhelan
(David Dennis) *prom: drvn 5th: lost pl 6th: sn bhd: t.o whn p.u bef 8th* 4/1[1]

63P1 P **Gowanauthat (IRE)**[26] 3468 8-10-7 93............(tp) TommyDowling(7)
(Charlie Mann) *j.rt: chsd ldrs: drvn 9th: lost pl next: t.o whn p.u bef 12th* 11/2[2]

006P P **Some Finish (IRE)**[7] 3746 7-10-6 85........................(v[1]) CharliePoste
(Robin Dickin) *j.rt: led: clr 4th: hdd appr 4 out: sn lost pl and bhd: distant 3rd whn p.u 3 out* 16/1

-35U P **Cul Dealga (IRE)**[64] 2749 7-11-9 102........................(t) TomMessenger
(Chris Bealby) *in rr: drvn 5th: bhd 9th: t.o next: p.u bef 11th* 11/1

006- P **Maz Majecc (IRE)**[84] 7-10-10 92................................[1] CallumWhillans(3)
(Noel C Kelly, Ire) *hld up in rr: hdwy 9th: lft modest 4th 12th: wknd and p.u 4 out* 8/1[3]

7m 30.9s (82.80) **Going Correction** +2.475s/f (Heav) **9 Ran SP% 115.7**
Speed ratings: **61, , , , , , , ,**
TOTE £19.80: £13.70; EX 18.20 Trifecta £20.80.
Owner Brian Davies **Bred** Mrs P And Philip Heaney **Trained** Brecon, Powys

FOCUS
A modest novice handicap chase. They went quite a good gallop considering the desperate conditions and it took its toll with only one horse completing the course. The winner is rated to the level of his hurdles form.

3865 MOORLANDS RACING NOVICES' H'CAP HURDLE (6 hdls 3 omitted) 1m 7f 168y
2:55 (2:55) (Class 4) (0-120,114) 4-Y-0+ £3,638 (£1,068; £534; £267)

Form RPR
0002 1 **Argot**[15] 3607 5-11-6 111........................ GrahamWatters(3) 114
(Charlie Longsdon) *led tl after 1st: chsd ldr: hung lft and upsides 2 out (normal 3 out): hung lft and led over 1f out: all out* 7/2[3]

0003 2 hd **Just So Cool (IRE)**[26] 3467 5-11-8 110........................ TrevorWhelan 112
(David Dennis) *trckd ldrs: nt fluent 4th: n.m.r bnd appr 2 out (normal 3 out): 3rd and outpcd appr last (normal 2 out): rallied on inner 1f out: str late chal: jst hld* 11/2

-111 3 1 1/2 **Clan Legend**[28] 3438 6-11-11 113........................ LucyAlexander 115
(N W Alexander) *led after 1st: jnd whn blnd 2 out (normal 3 out): hdd over 1f out: kpt on same pce fnl f* 9/4[1]

-002 4 50 **Red Hott Robbie**[14] 3619 7-11-6 108........................ AndrewThornton 59
(Giuseppe Fierro) *trckd ldrs: n.m.r bnd and hit 2 out (normal 3 out): wknd bef next: sn bhd: t.o whn j.lft last* 13/2

5 1 1/2 **Noble Galileo (GER)**[202] 6-11-7 114........................ AlanJohns(5) 63
(Tim Vaughan) *chsd ldrs: drvn 4th: lost pl bef 2 out (normal 3 out): sn bhd: t.o* 20/1

4122 6 39 **Vicky's Charm (IRE)**[30] 3377 7-11-1 106........................ JamesBanks(3) 16
(Barry Brennan) *swvd bdly lft s and v.s.a: sn t.o: hdwy 3rd: chsng ldrs sn after next: lost pl bef 2 out (normal 3 out): sn wl bhd: t.o whn eased over 1f out: eventually completed* 3/1[2]

4m 27.9s (30.50) **Going Correction** +2.05s/f (Heav) **6 Ran SP% 111.5**
Speed ratings (Par 105): **105,104,104,79,78 58**
CSF £21.88 TOTE £6.60: £2.30, £2.60; EX 32.20 Trifecta £124.60.
Owner Westbourne Racing Club **Bred** Millsec Limited **Trained** Over Norton, Oxon

FOCUS
An ordinary novice handicap hurdle run at an even gallop. The third is the best guide.

3866 EBF/TBA MARES' NOVICES' LIMITED H'CAP CHASE (14 fncs 2 omitted) 2m 6f 108y
3:30 (3:30) (Class 3) (0-125,121) 5-Y-0+ £7,830 (£2,541; £1,432)

Form RPR
2-15 1 **Blameitalonmyroots (IRE)**[45] 3113 6-11-5 121........ ThomasGarner(3) 136+
(Oliver Sherwood) *chsd ldr: drvn to ld appr 4 out: jnd last: fnd ex clsng stages* 13/8[1]

-P4P 2 2 **Streets Of Promise (IRE)**[61] 2825 7-11-4 117................(p) JamieMoore 128+
(Michael Scudamore) *trckd ldrs: hit 8th: drvn 10th: chsd wnr next: upsides last: no ex clsng stages* 8/1

/123 3 27 **Bonnet's Vino**[24] 3486 8-10-13 115........................ MissGAndrews(3) 106
(Pam Sly) *trckd ldrs: nt fluent 1st: mstke 9th: handy 3rd 4 out: j.rt and wknd 2 out: sn wl bhd: t.o whn j.rt last* 6/1[3]

4-53 P **Nosey Box (IRE)**[35] 3259 10-10-9 111....................(bt) CallumWhillans(3)
(Noel C Kelly, Ire) *in rr: lost pl and reminders 5th: sn wl bhd: t.o whn p.u after 7th* 6/1[3]

31P5 P **Teochew (IRE)**[42] 3160 8-10-8 112........................(tp) KevinJones(5)
(Mark Shears) *in rr: drvn 4th: bhd and reminders next: t.o 7th: p.u bef next* 22/1

PF42 P **Bobble Boru (IRE)**[23] 3501 8-10-6 105........................(b) LiamTreadwell
(Venetia Williams) *led: mstke 7th: drvn 10th: hdd appr next: t.o whn p.u after 3 out* 4/1[2]

50-P P **Koolala (IRE)**[55] 2925 8-11-5 118........................(p) JamesBest
(Paul Webber) *chsd ldrs: shkn up 3rd: reminders 6th: lost pl 8th: bhd whn p.u bef next* 10/1

6m 40.8s (58.10) **Going Correction** +2.475s/f (Heav) **7 Ran SP% 111.2**
Speed ratings: **93,92,82, , ,**
CSF £14.07 TOTE £2.20: £1.30, £2.80; EX 15.30 Trifecta £58.70.
Owner Tim Syder **Bred** Thomas Stacey **Trained** Upper Lambourn, Berks
■ Stewards' Enquiry : Thomas Garner two-day ban: use of whip (TBC)

FOCUS
The feature race was a fair mares' novice handicap chase. They went a respectable gallop and the winner is on the upgrade.

3867 BESPOKE CREATIONS H'CAP CHASE (13 fncs 2 omitted) 2m 4f
4:05 (4:05) (Class 4) (0-120,120) 5-Y-0+ £5,432 (£2,043)

Form RPR
1113 1 **Truckers Highway (IRE)**[33] 3311 7-11-5 116............ HarryChalloner(3) 128+
(John Groucott) *trckd ldr: led bef 4 out: forged clr between last 2: kpt on* 9/2

-013 2 21 **Long John**[29] 3412 9-11-2 110........................ JamesBest 104
(Jackie Du Plessis) *in rr: hdwy 8th: chsd wnr 3 out: 8 l down and wl btn whn blnd last* 3/1[2]

4-14 P **Winston Churchill (IRE)**[49] 3044 10-10-11 105........(t) AndrewThornton
(Sophie Leech) *led: pushed along 7th: hdd bef 4 out: sn lost pl and bhd: lft distant 3rd and p.u last* 11/4[1]

413/ P **Ace Fighter Pilot**[773] 3162 10-11-12 120........................ JamieMoore
(Jim Best) *sn chsng ldrs: hit 5th: drvn 9th: 3rd and wl btn whn j.lft and blnd 2 out: distant 3rd whn p.u appr last* 15/2

0-52 P **Jaunty Inflight**[30] 3379 7-10-8 102........................ RobertDunne
(Brian Eckley) *trckd ldrs 3rd: lost pl bef 4 out: sn bhd: t.o 5th whn p.u sn after 2 out* 4/1[3]

32-P P **Alberto's Dream**[30] 3384 7-10-8 102........................ JamesDavies
(Tom Symonds) *hdwy to chse ldrs 6th: reminders next: sn lost pl and bhd: t.o whn p.u bef 4 out* 9/1

5m 55.9s (46.10) **Going Correction** +2.475s/f (Heav) **6 Ran SP% 111.6**
Speed ratings: **106,97, , ,**
CSF £18.45 TOTE £4.30: £2.40, £1.80; EX 21.50 Trifecta £17.00.
Owner C J Tipton **Bred** David Pim **Trained** Bourton, Shropshire

FOCUS
A fair handicap chase. They went a solid gallop considering the heavy underfoot conditions. The winner is back on the upgrade.

3868 BC EVENTS H'CAP HURDLE (8 hdls 2 omitted) 2m 3f 207y
4:35 (4:35) (Class 5) (0-100,100) 4-Y-0+ £2,859 (£839; £419; £209)

Form RPR
U11 1 **Marlee Massie (IRE)**[51] 2980 7-11-7 95........................ LucyAlexander 102+
(N W Alexander) *racd wd: trckd ldrs: 2nd bef 2 out (normal 3 out): led 2f out: drvn rt out* 6/4[1]

P05- 2 1 1/4 **Zayfire Aramis**[344] 4339 7-11-7 95........................ LiamTreadwell 100
(Michael Scudamore) *t.k.h in rr: hdwy appr 2 out (normal 3 out): chsd wnr over 1f out: kpt on same pce last 100yds* 12/1

2-P2 3 9 **Pret A Thou (FR)**[30] 3376 13-11-9 100................(p) HarryChalloner(3) 96
(John Groucott) *trckd ldrs: t.k.h: led 2 out (normal 3 out): hdd 2f out: wknd fnl 2f* 11/4[2]

5-34 4 11 **Old Magic (IRE)**[35] 3219 11-10-2 76........................ JamesBest 61
(Sophie Leech) *led: hdd 2 out (normal 3 out): wknd fnl 2f* 4/1[3]

F4PP 5 7 **Rock Of Ages**[18] 3570 7-11-0 95........................(bt) MrJNixon(7) 72
(Steve Flook) *chsd ldrs: wknd over 2f out* 25/1

40 6 27 **Sussex Road (IRE)**[17] 3586 6-10-2 83................(p) MikeyHamill(7) 33
(Aytach Sadik) *chsd ldrs: hit 6th: sn drvn: lost pl bef next: sn bhd: t.o* 12/1

-P26 7 32 **Izzy Piccolina (IRE)**[115] 1816 8-11-10 98........................ MarkGrant 16
(Geoffrey Deacon) *in rr: pushed along 5th: lost pl bef 2 out (normal 3 out): sn bhd: blnd last (normal 2 out): t.o* 18/1

5m 58.6s (55.40) **Going Correction** +2.05s/f (Heav) **7 Ran SP% 111.2**
Speed ratings (Par 103): **71,70,66,62,59 48,36**
CSF £17.91 TOTE £2.10: £1.30, £4.20; EX 18.50 Trifecta £58.60.
Owner Nicholas Alexander **Bred** Tom Baker **Trained** Kinneston, Perth & Kinross

FOCUS
The concluding contest was another modest handicap hurdle, run at a sensible gallop. The winner is rated close to his recent wins.
T/Plt: £5524.10 to a £1 stake. Pool: £60538.50 - 8 winning tickets T/Qpdt: £51.30 to a £1 stake. Pool: £4996.31 - 71.95 winning tickets **Walter Glynn**

3869 - 3872a (Foreign Racing) - See Raceform Interactive

3691
FAIRYHOUSE (R-H)
Saturday, January 30
OFFICIAL GOING: Heavy (soft to heavy in places)

3873a COOLMORE N.H. SIRES MARES NOVICE HURDLE (GRADE 3) (10 hdls) 2m 2f
3:05 (3:05) 4-Y-0+ £16,727 (£4,889; £2,316; £772)

RPR
1 **Limini (IRE)**[259] 342 5-10-11 0........................ DannyMullins 141+
(W P Mullins, Ire) *chsd ldrs: racd keenly early: nt fluent in 3rd at 5th: disp bef 3 out where slt mstke: travelling wl and led fr next: eased clr bef last: easily* 4/5[1]

2 11 **Cashelard Lady (IRE)**[29] 3430 6-10-13 0........................ RobbieColgan 130
(Shane Crawley, Ire) *led and clr: slt mstke and j.lft 4th: over 5 l clr bef 1/2-way: reduced ld bef 5th: jnd bef 3 out: rdn on terms bef 2 out where hdd and no ch w wnr: slt mstke last: kpt on one pce* 5/1[3]

3 6 **Whistle Dixie (IRE)**[47] 3091 6-10-13 119........................(t) BJCooper 124
(Gordon Elliott, Ire) *settled bhd ldr tl disp bef 3 out: rdn appr st and sn no imp on easy wnr u.p in 3rd: slt mstke last and one pce run-in* 4/1[2]

4 12 **Ten Times Better (IRE)**[69] 2672 6-10-13 0........................ DavidMullins 112
(P A Fahy, Ire) *chsd ldrs: 4th 1/2-way: rdn in 4th bef 3 out and no imp on clr ldrs: one pce* 8/1

5 6 **Jodies Miss (IRE)**[10] 3693 7-10-13 0........................(t) PhillipEnright 106
(P M Lynch, Ire) *hld up: last at 1/2-way: rdn and no imp 3 out: nt fluent next and kpt on one pce into mod 5th run-in* 50/1

6 1 3/4 **The Brock Inn (IRE)**[32] 3356 5-10-11 113........................ MarkEnright 102
(John W Nicholson, Ire) *hld up: 6th 1/2-way: no imp on clr ldrs bef 3 out: kpt on one pce in mod 6th fr next* 66/1

7 nk **Rosie Alice (IRE)**[34] 3305 5-11-1 119........................ DavyRussell 106
(C Byrnes, Ire) *hld up: 5th 1/2-way: pushed along and no imp on clr ldrs in 5th bef 2 out: wknd and eased run-in* 12/1

4m 52.5s (3.10) **Going Correction** +0.675s/f (Soft) **7 Ran SP% 114.5**
Speed ratings: **120,115,112,107,104 103,103**
CSF £5.52 TOTE £1.60: £1.20, £2.40; DF 5.60 Trifecta £14.60.
Owner Mrs S Ricci **Bred** Sir E J Loder **Trained** Muine Beag, Co Carlow

FOCUS
A facile victory for the odds-on favourite and she certainly didn't do her Cheltenham prospects any harm. She improved as per her Flat form.

The Form Book Jumps 2015-16, Raceform Ltd, Newbury, RG14 5SJ

3874 - 3875a (Foreign Racing) - See Raceform Interactive

3815 **PAU** (R-H)

Saturday, January 30

OFFICIAL GOING: Turf: very soft

3876a PRIX DE LARUNS (HURDLE) (CONDITIONS) (5YO) (TURF) 2m 3f

3:25 (12:00) 5-Y-O £11,294 (£5,647; £3,294; £2,235; £1,058)

RPR

1 **Spirit Ness (FR)** 5-10-8 0 ErvanChazelle (J-P Daireaux, France) **80/1**

2 ½ **Saint Lino (FR)**[26] 3467 5-10-10 0 LizzieKelly(4) (Nick Williams) *a.p: led after 4 out: rdn clr turning in: clsd down whn mstke last: strly pressed flat: styd on gamely but hdd nring fin: jst hld* **53/10**[2]

3 6 **Baron Du Seuil (FR)**[62] 5-10-12 0 JacquesRicou (F-M Cottin, France) **58/10**[3]

4 nk **Whip Dancer (FR)**[756] 5-10-10 0 AlejandroRuizGonzalez(4) (D Guillemin, France) **11/1**

5 3 **Ganndar (FR)**[660] 5-10-8 0 FelixDeGiles (P Cottin, France) **83/10**

6 nse **Balisha (FR)** 5-10-8 0 AlexisPoirier (S Foucher, France) **3/1**[1]

7 7 **Sacre Tsar (FR)**[222] 5-10-12 0 ArnaudDuchene (Mlle I Gallorini, France) **13/1**

8 7 **Norma (SPA)**[13] 5-10-6 0 ErwanBureller (T Callejo-Solana, Spain) **11/1**

9 2 **Castor Solaire (FR)**[295] 5-10-3 0 AlexisMercurol (Mlle I Gallorini, France) **26/1**

F **My My My Diliza**[736] 5-10-8 0 JeremyRey(4) (Mlle M Henry, France) **83/10**

P **Vanvidd (FR)**[34] 5-10-4 0 ow1 (p) VincentChatellier(5) (Remy Nerbonne, France) **89/1**

P **Mister Gregorium (IRE)**[89] 5-10-8 0 JoAudon (P Cottin, France) **65/1**

P **Dragonstone (FR)**[725] 5-10-8 0 KevinNabet (D De Watrigant, France) **14/1**

P **Belak Chop (FR)**[267] 5-11-0 0 GaetanOlivier (F Cellier, France) **64/1**

P **Brindor Des Iles (FR)** 5-10-3 0 HernanRodriguezNunez(5) (M Nicolau, France) **204/1**

P **Balinas D'Airy (FR)** 5-10-8 0 DavyLesot (J Ortet, France) **45/1**

P **Flyinga De Liaf (FR)** 5-10-3 0 PaulinBlot (C Pautier, France) **204/1**

PARI-MUTUEL (all including 1 euro stake): WIN 80.80; PLACE 11.90, 2.50, 2.40; DF 228.40; SF 540.90

Owner Mlle Caroline Brunaud **Bred** Scea Montigny & Mlle C Brunaud **Trained** France

3213 **FONTWELL** (L-H)

Sunday, January 31

3877 Meeting Abandoned - waterlogged

3239 **SEDGEFIELD** (L-H)

Sunday, January 31

OFFICIAL GOING: Good to soft (5.7)

Wind: Almost nil Weather: Overcast

3883 BETFRED NOVICES' HURDLE (BETFRED HURDLE SERIES QUALIFIER) 2m 3f 188y

1:45 (1:46) (Class 4) 4-Y-O+ £3,798 (£1,122; £561; £280; £140)

Form RPR

22 1 **Waiting Patiently (IRE)**[64] 2772 5-11-2 120 HarryChalloner(3) 123+ (Keith Reveley) *hld up: stdy hdwy whn nt clr run briefly after 3 out: effrt and led next: drvn and styd on strly fr last* **5/2**[3]

31-1 2 3½ **Libby Mae (IRE)**[68] 2704 6-10-9 0 JoeColliver(5) 109 (Micky Hammond) *chsd ldrs: pushed along appr 3 out: rallied and led briefly bef next: kpt on fr last to take 2nd cl home: nt pce of wnr* **2/1**[2]

0-21 3 hd **Western Rules (IRE)**[49] 3056 6-11-11 122 BrianHarding 122 (Nicky Richards) *in tch: hdwy to ld briefly 2 out: w wnr to after last: one pce and lost 2nd cl home* **7/4**[1]

5 4 4½ **General Mahler (IRE)**[27] 3476 6-11-5 0 DannyCook 111 (Brian Ellison) *hld up: pushed along and hdwy after 3 out: rdn and kpt on fr next: nvr able to chal* **12/1**

55 5 3¼ **Ash Park (IRE)**[12] 3668 8-10-12 0 SamColtherd(7) 108 (Stuart Coltherd) *hld up: hdwy and cl up on outside 3rd: led 3 out to bef next: rdn: edgd rt and wknd after last* **150/1**

6 6 16 **Oak Vintage (IRE)**[58] 2895 6-11-0 0 JamieHamilton(5) 94 (Ann Hamilton) *chsd ldrs: ev ch 3 out to bef next: sn rdn and wknd* **100/1**

-200 7 shd **Ten Trees**[30] 3397 6-10-12 0 JakeGreenall 85 (Alan Swinbank) *hld up on outside: drvn and outpcd bef 3 out: btn bef next* **20/1**

60 8 1¼ **Nortonthorpelegend (IRE)**[36] 3239 6-11-5 0 BrianHughes 91 (John Wade) *cl up: rdn and lost pl bef 3 out: sn wknd* **150/1**

P360 9 30 **Bertielicious**[34] 3307 8-10-12 61 (p) ThomasDowson(7) 61 (Jonathan Haynes) *t.k.h: led to 3 out: sn rdn and wknd* **250/1**

P P **Killone (IRE)**[43] 3153 7-11-5 0 DerekFox (Stuart Coltherd) *midfield: lost pl 4 out: sn struggling: t.o whn p.u bef 2 out* **80/1**

5m 8.4s (14.30) **Going Correction** +0.575s/f (Soft) **10** Ran SP% **114.7**

Speed ratings (Par 105): **94,92,92,90,89 83,82,82,70,**

CSF £8.00 TOTE £3.30: £1.20, £1.20, £1.30; EX 7.30 Trifecta £13.20.

Owner Richard Collins **Bred** Vincent Finn **Trained** Lingdale, Redcar & Cleveland

FOCUS

The ground had dried out and the going was now good to soft all over, though after the first Brian Harding said: "If you were being kind you would say it is good to soft, but it's hard work." Hurdles towards the centre and common bends. All bends bar the one going up the hill towards the cross fence dolled off the inner to provide fresh ground. Rail movement meant that the actual distance of the opener was 2m4f 126yds.\n\x\x Not the deepest of races, but some interesting prospects took part in this novices' hurdle and there wasn't much separating the trio at the head of the market. There wasn't much between them jumping two out either.

3884 HAPPY 80TH DON ROBSON "BONNIE LAD" H'CAP HURDLE 2m 3f 188y

2:15 (2:16) (Class 4) (0-120,117) 4-Y-O+ £3,898 (£1,144; £572; £286)

Form RPR

3336 1 **Captain Redbeard (IRE)**[30] 3398 7-10-8 106 SamColtherd(7) 120+ (Stuart Coltherd) *hld up in midfield: hdwy to ld bef 6th: mde rest: pushed clr fr 2 out* **9/1**[3]

5222 2 8 **Good Vibration (FR)**[36] 3240 5-11-5 110 DannyCook 112 (Sue Smith) *wnt rt s: chsd ldrs: rdn after 5th: rallied to chse wnr 4 out: effrt and drvn after 3 out: plugged on fr next: no ch w wnr* **13/8**[1]

3503 3 nse **Falcarragh (IRE)**[59] 2867 9-11-5 110 RichardJohnson 112 (Tim Vaughan) *hld up: stdy hdwy 4 out: effrt and disp ld fr bef 2 out: edgd lft after last: kpt on same pce* **9/1**[3]

-216 4 12 **Carlo Rocks (IRE)**[43] 3146 6-11-6 111 HarrySkelton 103 (Caroline Bailey) *chsd ldrs: drvn and lost pl 1/2-way: rallied and prom bef 3 out: rdn and wknd bef next* **3/1**[2]

4P3F 5 12 **Lord Usher (IRE)**[36] 3243 9-10-10 101 JanFaltejsek 79 (George Charlton) *hld up: nt fluent and outpcd 6th: n.d after* **16/1**

3250 6 shd **Ben Cee Pee M (IRE)**[36] 3238 11-11-4 114 (b) CraigGallagher(5) 92 (Brian Ellison) *hld up: pushed along after 4 out: struggling bef next* **22/1**

2-65 7 ½ **Wake Your Dreams (IRE)**[16] 3607 8-11-7 112 SeanQuinlan 89 (Jennie Candlish) *chsd ldrs: rdn after 6th: wknd fr 3 out* **16/1**

-P44 P **Up And Go (FR)**[32] 3361 8-11-12 117 (b[1]) WillKennedy (Donald McCain) *led to 3rd: cl up tl lost pl 6th: struggling fr next: t.o whn p.u bef 2 out* **11/1**

/065 P **Roman Numeral (IRE)**[17] 3592 8-10-12 106 AdamNicol(3) (David Thompson) *hld up on outside: hdwy to ld 3rd: hdd bef 6th: wknd bef 3 out: lost tch and p.u bef next* **20/1**

5m 4.4s (10.30) **Going Correction** +0.575s/f (Soft) **9** Ran SP% **112.3**

Speed ratings (Par 105): **102,98,98,93,89 89,88, ,**

CSF £23.95 CT £136.67 TOTE £9.60: £2.80, £1.10, £2.50; EX 30.10 Trifecta £219.70.

Owner S Coltherd **Bred** Derrymore House Syndicate **Trained** Selkirk, Borders

FOCUS

Actual distance 2m4f 126yds. Just a fair handicap hurdle and they finished well spread out. The winning time was four seconds quicker than the opener.

3885 JEAN DAWSON MEMORIAL CHASE (NOVICES' LIMITED H'CAP) (18 fncs 3 omitted) 3m 2f 59y

2:45 (2:45) (Class 3) (0-135,131) 5-Y-O+ £6,498 (£1,908; £954; £477)

Form RPR

4121 1 **Askamore Darsi (IRE)**[23] 3507 7-10-10 116 (p) HenryBrooke 124 (Donald McCain) *led: rdn and hdd 2 out (usual 3 out): rallied u.p and regained ld passing omitted last: kpt on gamely* **5/1**[3]

1112 2 ½ **Not A Bother Boy (IRE)**[36] 3236 8-10-3 116 TrevorRyan(7) 123 (Sue Smith) *nt fluent on occasions: cl up: led 2 out (usual 3 out): sn hrd pressed: hdd passing omitted last: kpt on u.p: hld cl home* **4/1**[2]

-452 3 ½ **Racing Europe (IRE)**[47] 3100 7-11-8 128 DannyCook 135 (Brian Ellison) *prom: stdy hdwy whn hit 2 out (usual 3 out): effrt and chal after next to passing omitted last: no ex u.p cl home* **5/4**[1]

3F14 4 17 **Cyclop (IRE)**[32] 3364 5-11-6 131 (tp) AidanColeman 118 (David Dennis) *cl up: effrt and ev ch briefly bef last (usual 2 out): edgd lft and wknd bef omitted last* **4/1**[2]

0-33 5 7 **Lucematic**[64] 2785 10-10-9 115 BrianHughes 98 (Chris Grant) *hld up in tch: hit 7th: rdn and outpcd 3 out (usual 4 out): struggling fr next* **10/1**

7m 20.6s (9.60) **Going Correction** +0.575s/f (Soft)

WFA 5 from 7yo+ 5lb **5** Ran SP% **110.2**

Speed ratings: **108,107,107,102,100**

CSF £23.88 TOTE £6.10: £2.20, £1.40; EX 16.20 Trifecta £54.60.

Owner Deva Racing Darsi Partnership **Bred** William McGladdery **Trained** Cholmondeley, Cheshire

■ Stewards' Enquiry : Trevor Ryan two-day ban: used whip above permitted level (Feb 14-15)

Danny Cook two-day ban: used whip above permitted level (Feb 14-15)

FOCUS

Actual distance 3m2f 185yds and normal last fence omitted on each circuit. A decent staying novices' handicap chase and a thrilling outcome, with the front three battling in a line across the track all the way up the long run-in from the last fence (normal second-last).

3886 DENYS SMITH CELEBRATING 145 SEDGEFIELD WINNERS H'CAP HURDLE (8 hdls) 2m 178y

3:15 (3:15) (Class 4) (0-120,120) 4-Y-O+ £3,898 (£1,144; £572; £286)

Form RPR

4335 1 **Card Game (IRE)**[36] 3242 7-10-9 103 BrianHughes 115+ (Malcolm Jefferson) *in tch: shkn up and hdwy to ld between last 2: nt fluent last: sn pushed clr* **8/1**

24-1 2 12 **Mixboy (FR)**[58] 2893 6-11-12 120 BrianHarding 122 (Keith Dalgleish) *hld up: stdy hdwy bef 3 out: cl 3rd and gng wl whn nt fluent next: sn rdn: kpt on to take 2nd towards fin: no ch w wnr* **6/4**[1]

1615 3 2¼ **Fair Loch**[34] 3318 8-11-2 115 MeganCarberry(5) 114 (Brian Ellison) *led: qcknd bef 2 out: hdd between last 2: sn no ch w wnr: no ex and lost 2nd towards fin* **16/1**

-534 4 1 **Orchard Road (USA)**[29] 3438 9-10-9 103 (t) JonathanEngland 102 (Tristan Davidson) *hld up in midfield: stdy hdwy 3 out: pushed along and outpcd next: no imp whn nt fluent last* **10/1**

1024 5 9 **Perseid (IRE)**[73] 2595 6-10-8 102 SeanQuinlan 92 (Sue Smith) *chsd ldr to 3 out: sn drvn along: rallied: wknd bef next* **7/1**[3]

-115 6 2 **Divine Port (USA)**[15] 3630 6-11-11 119 TomScudamore 107 (Alan Swinbank) *chsd ldrs: wnt 2nd briefly 3 out: rdn and wknd bef next* **5/1**[2]

0405 7 29 **Hey Bob (IRE)**[15] 3628 4-9-11 105 oh3 AdamNicol(3) 56 (Chris Grant) *s.i.s: hld up: stdy hdwy 4 out: rdn and struggling bef next: nvr on terms* **25/1**

PF 8 30 **Telex Du Berlais (FR)**[78] 2495 7-10-11 110 (t) CallumBewley(5) 45 (Simon Waugh) *hld up: pushed along and outpcd bef 3 out: sn wknd* **80/1**

-30F P **Walser (IRE)**[15] 3628 9-10-11 105 (b) HenryBrooke (John Wade) *bhd on outside: struggling bef 4th: lost tch and p.u bef 3 out* **33/1**

P04P P **Scimon Templar (FR)**[12] 3670 8-10-8 102 CraigNichol (Rose Dobbin) *hld up in midfield: nt fluent and lost pl 4th: sn struggling: t.o whn p.u bef 2 out* **25/1**

323P P **Shout It Aloud**[139] 1549 7-11-1 109 (t) RichardJohnson (Tim Vaughan) *prom on outside: struggling bef 3 out: sn wknd: p.u bef next* **14/1**

4m 13.9s (7.00) **Going Correction** +0.575s/f (Soft)

WFA 4 from 6yo+ 11lb **11** Ran SP% **113.8**

Speed ratings (Par 105): 106,100,99,98,94 93,80,65, ,

CSF £19.69 CT £190.01 TOTE £9.30: £3.00, £1.10, £3.50; EX 25.10 Trifecta £217.70.

Owner Messrs Hales Dodd Wood & Dickinson **Bred** David Connors **Trained** Norton, N Yorks
FOCUS
Actual distance 2m1f 116yds. A fair handicap hurdle and they went a good pace.

3887 JEAN TAYLOR MEMORIAL H'CAP CHASE (14 fncs 2 omitted) 2m 3f 65y
3:50 (3:50) (Class 3) (0-140,137) 5-Y-O+ **£6,498** (£1,908; £954; £477)

Form RPR
2-62 **1** **Firth Of The Clyde**[56] 2935 11-11-12 **137**........................(b1) BrianHughes 149+
(Malcolm Jefferson) *prom: stdy hdwy bef 2 out (usual 3 out): shkn up to ld bef omitted last: sn rdn clr* **4/1**[3]
1R2F **2** *7* **Jac The Legend**[17] 3591 7-10-2 **113**..............................(p) WillKennedy 118
(Brian Ellison) *nt fluent on occasions: hld up in tch: hdwy to chse ldrs 2 out (usual 3 out): rdn whn nt fluent last: wnt 2nd passing omitted last: no ch w wnr* **4/1**[3]
-435 **3** *3/4* **Sa Suffit (FR)**[8] 3737 13-11-6 **136**.........................(p) DiarmuidO'Regan(5) 141
(James Ewart) *chsd ldrs: drvn and outpcd bef 2 out (usual 3 out): rallied and hung lft bef omitted last: kpt on: no imp* **6/1**
55F3 **4** *5* **Mwaleshi**[15] 3629 11-11-0 **125**... DannyCook 129
(Sue Smith) *chsd ldr: hit 8th: effrt 2 out (usual 3 out): led last to bef omitted last: no ex and lost two pls last 50yds* **7/2**[2]
4-24 **5** *13* **Top Wood (FR)**[18] 3583 9-11-10 **135**..........................(t) TomScudamore 123
(David Pipe) *bhd: reminders after 5th: drvn and outpcd fr 8th: sn lost tch: sme late hdwy: nvr on terms* **3/1**[1]
P515 **6** *1/2* **Noble Legend**[34] 3315 9-11-7 **132**....................................(p) HarrySkelton 119
(Caroline Bailey) *led: rdn 2 out (usual 3 out): hdd last: sn wknd* **9/1**
5m 14.4s (11.40) **Going Correction** +0.575s/f (Soft) **6** Ran **SP% 111.5**
Speed ratings: **99,96,95,93,88 87**
CSF £19.92 TOTE £5.20: £2.20, £2.40; EX 22.40 Trifecta £119.90.
Owner Robert H Goldie **Bred** Robert H Goldie **Trained** Norton, N Yorks
FOCUS
Actual distance 2m3f 183yds and normal last fence omitted on each circuit. A decent handicap chase and they went a solid pace throughout.

3888 PHOENIX SECURITY MARES' H'CAP HURDLE (8 hdls) 2m 178y
4:20 (4:21) (Class 5) (0-100,100) 4-Y-O+ **£2,599** (£763; £381; £190)

Form RPR
4044 **1** **Flemerina (IRE)**[168] 1271 7-10-12 **86**................................ SeanQuinlan 90+
(Sue Smith) *chsd ldrs: rdn bef 3 out: rallied and led bef next: edgd lft and hdd appr last: regained ld last 50yds: styd on wl* **9/2**[3]
P000 **2** *1/2* **Question Of Faith**[12] 3672 5-10-8 **82**............................ HenryBrooke 85
(Martin Todhunter) *hld up: stdy hdwy and prom after 3 out: effrt and led appr last: edgd lft and hdd last 50yds: kpt on* **25/1**
6004 **3** *3/4* **Kara Tara**[23] 3508 6-11-12 **100**.......................................(p) BrianHughes 102
(Lawrence Mullaney) *trckd ldrs: effrt and rdn 2 out: edgd lft: kpt on run-in* **11/4**[1]
3U02 **4** *8* **Louloumills**[79] 2476 6-10-1 **82**.............................. ThomasDowson(7) 77
(Maurice Barnes) *hld up bhd ldng gp: rdn bef 3 out: rallied bef next: sn no imp* **7/1**
3551 **5** *12* **Hatton Springs (IRE)**[12] 3672 5-11-1 **96**..................... SamColtherd(7) 82
(Stuart Coltherd) *nt fluent on occasions: chsd ldrs: chal after 3rd to after 3 out: rdn and wknd appr next* **4/1**[2]
2442 **6** *8* **Beyondtemptation**[43] 3163 8-10-7 **86**..................(t) DiarmuidO'Regan(5) 67
(Jonathan Haynes) *led tl rdn and hdd bef 2 out: sn wknd* **9/2**[3]
0-10 **P** **Ellistrin Belle**[27] 3473 8-11-3 **94**..........................(t) CallumWhillans(3)
(Donald Whillans) *hld up on outside: drvn and outpcd bef 4 out: struggling fr next: t.o whn p.u bef 2 out* **17/2**
/5P- **P** **Present Trend (IRE)**[425] 2873 7-10-10 **87**.................... HarryChalloner(3)
(Richard Ford) *hld up: rdn and outpcd bef 3 out: lost tch and p.u bef next* **25/1**
4m 24.2s (17.30) **Going Correction** +0.575s/f (Soft) **8** Ran **SP% 113.7**
Speed ratings (Par 103): **82,81,81,77,72 68, ,**
CSF £90.30 CT £360.44 TOTE £5.60: £2.60, £5.90, £1.10; EX 110.70 Trifecta £459.40.
Owner Mrs S Smith **Bred** Robert McCarthy **Trained** High Eldwick, W Yorks
FOCUS
Actual distance 2m1f 116yds. A moderate mares' handicap hurdle and a dour battle between the front three up the run-in.
T/Jkpt: Not Won. JACKPOT PLACEPOT £37.40 to a £1 stake. Pool: £4,128.92 - 80.51 winning tickets. T/Plt: £40.40 to a £1 stake. Pool: £116,310.28 - 2,101.00 winning tickets. T/Qpdt: £35.70 to a £1 stake. Pool: £8,391.79 - 173.80 winning tickets. **Richard Young**

3889 & 3891a- (Foreign Racing) - See Raceform Interactive

3536 PUNCHESTOWN (R-H)
Sunday, January 31

OFFICIAL GOING: Soft to heavy

3890a I.N.H. STALLION OWNERS EUROPEAN BREEDERS FUND NOVICE HURDLE (LISTED RACE) (9 hdls) 2m
2:00 (2:01) 4-Y-O+ **£14,338** (£4,191; £1,985; £661)

RPR
1 **Ball D'Arc (FR)**[22] 3539 5-11-7 131.. BJCooper 137+
(Gordon Elliott, Ire) *chsd ldrs in 3rd: tk clsr order bef 2 out: travelled wl to ld bef last and sn clr: styd on wl* **9/2**[3]
2 *3* **Royal Caviar (IRE)**[66] 2740 8-11-9 130............................ PaulTownend 133
(W P Mullins, Ire) *chsd ldr in 2nd: clsr appr 3 out: rdn and nt qckn in 2nd afer 2 out: kpt on same pce* **4/1**[2]
3 *6* **Monbeg Rose (IRE)**[17] 3601 6-11-2 0..............................[1] DavidMullins 121
(W P Mullins, Ire) *led: pressed bef 2 out and hdd bef last where dropped to 3rd: kpt on one pce* **25/1**
4 *5* **Staker Wallace (IRE)**[64] 2796 5-11-3 0.......................(t) BarryGeraghty 116
(E Bolger, Ire) *hld up in rr: niggled along bef 4th: no imp bef 2 out: kpt on one pce into 4th run-in* **20/1**
5 *12* **Myska (IRE)**[32] 3372 6-11-5 0.. RWalsh 121+
(W P Mullins, Ire) *hld up in 4th: nt fluent 4th: clsd appr 2 out: sn rdn and nt qckn: wknd bef last: eased run-in: coughing* **8/13**[1]
4m 8.9s (3.90) **Going Correction** +0.525s/f (Soft) **5** Ran **SP% 108.7**
Speed ratings: **111,109,106,104,98**
CSF £21.13 TOTE £4.80: £1.80, £1.40; DF 17.40 Trifecta £43.30.
Owner Gigginstown House Stud **Bred** S C E A Le Fragneau & Nicole Terriere **Trained** Longwood, Co Meath
FOCUS
A good performance from an apparently improving horse, albeit one for whom these underfoot conditions are probably very important.

3892a BOYLESPORTS TIED COTTAGE CHASE (GRADE 2) (11 fncs) 2m
3:00 (3:01) 5-Y-O+

£18,750 (£5,937; £2,812; £937; £625; £312)

RPR
1 **Felix Yonger (IRE)**[48] 3092 10-11-12 160...................................... RWalsh 164+
(W P Mullins, Ire) *hld up towards inner in 5th: tk clsr order to trck ldrs after 2 out: led appr last: kpt on wl* **1/1**[1]
2 *1 3/4* **Flemenstar (IRE)**[35] 3293 11-11-12 160..................................... AELynch 162
(Anthony Curran, Ire) *sn trckd ldr in 2nd: led after 4 out: hdd last: kpt on wl in 2nd: no imp on wnr in clsng stages* **3/1**[2]
3 *2 1/2* **Mozoltov**[21] 3552 10-11-4 152.. BJCooper 152
(W P Mullins, Ire) *hld up in 4th: nt fluent in 5th 2 out: swtchd to inner appr last in 3rd: kpt on same pce wout rching principals* **3/1**[2]
4 *1 1/2* **Days Hotel (IRE)**[21] 3552 11-11-4 146.................................. DavyRussell 150
(Henry De Bromhead, Ire) *trckd ldrs in 3rd: dropped to 4th 2 out: sn rdn and no ex appr last: kpt on same pce* **14/1**[3]
5 *12* **Twinlight (FR)**[48] 3092 9-11-12 156................................ PaulTownend 149
(W P Mullins, Ire) *led 1st: mstke 5th: hdd after 4 out: rdn in 2nd after 2 out: no ex in 5th appr last: wknd* **14/1**[3]
6 *19* **Draycott Place (IRE)**[15] 3637 7-11-4 128............................ DannyMullins 119
(John Patrick Ryan, Ire) *a in rr: detached after 3 out: sn no threat* **100/1**
4m 12.0s (-6.60) **Going Correction** -0.05s/f (Good) **6** Ran **SP% 114.3**
Speed ratings: **114,113,111,111,105 95**
CSF £4.80 TOTE £1.70: £1.10, £1.40; DF 3.40 Trifecta £6.30.
Owner Andrea & Graham Wylie **Bred** J Brophy **Trained** Muine Beag, Co Carlow
FOCUS
A very good performance from the winner, a horse that's proving totally reliable and now seems to handle any ground with equal effectiveness. The second and fourth set the standard.

3894a RACINGUK.COM/FREETRIAL GRAND NATIONAL TRIAL H'CAP CHASE (GRADE C) 3m 4f
4:05 (4:05) 5-Y-O+ **£15,294** (£4,470; £2,117; £705)

RPR
1 **Bonny Kate (IRE)**[64] 2792 6-10-1 **125**.................................. SeanFlanagan 137+
(Noel Meade, Ire) *mde all: j.w: extended advantage after 2 out: ld briefly reduced last: kpt on wl to reassert in clsng stages* **4/1**[3]
2 *6* **Baie Des Iles (FR)**[22] 3538 5-10-4 **136**...................................... RWalsh 134+
(Ross O'Sullivan, Ire) *chsd ldrs in 4th: wnt 2nd w a circ to r: rdn to cl on wnr appr last: no imp in clsng stages: kpt on same pce* **3/1**[1]
3 *18* **Folsom Blue (IRE)**[10] 3715 9-10-11 **135**..............................(p) BJCooper 123
(M F Morris, Ire) *sn chsd clr ldr in 2nd: reminders in 4th w over a circ to r: prog again in 3rd bef 3 out: no imp in 4th after next: kpt on one pce into 3rd at last* **10/1**
4 *4 1/4* **Bothair Clei (IRE)**[34] 3328 11-9-10 **120**.............................. MarkEnright 104
(Daniel G Murphy, Ire) *hld up: tk clsr order bef 3 out: rdn and no imp in 5th bef next: kpt on one pce into mod 4th at last* **8/1**
5 *12* **Captain Von Trappe (IRE)**[35] 3296 7-10-12 **136**.............. DavidMullins 108
(Gordon Elliott, Ire) *sn chsd clr ldr in 3rd: rdn in 4th bef 3 out: briefly wnt 3rd after next: wknd into 5th at last* **16/1**
6 *2 3/4* **Embracing Change (IRE)**[31] 3391 11-10-6 **130**............(p) PhillipEnright 99
(Robert Tyner, Ire) *hld up: rdn and no imp bef 3 out: kpt on one pce in 6th fr next* **12/1**
7 *26* **Down Under (IRE)**[33] 3354 9-9-5 **120** oh4..................(p) DonaghMeyler(5) 63
(F Flood, Ire) *hld up: rdn and no imp after 3 out: mstke next and no ex* **14/1**
8 *6 1/2* **Lyreen Legend (IRE)**[34] 3320 9-11-5 **148**.............(tp) JonathanMoore(5) 85
(Ms Sandra Hughes, Ire) *racd in mid-div tl rdn and nt qckn after 3 out: no ex* **16/1**
P **Riverside City (IRE)**[35] 3296 7-9-10 **123**..................... JackKennedy(3)
(Gordon Elliott, Ire) *hld up in rr: nt fluent 4th: rdn after 5 out: nt fluent next and sn detached: p.u after 2 out* **7/2**[2]
7m 50.5s (470.50)
WFA 5 from 6yo+ 5lb **9** Ran **SP% 113.5**
CSF £16.77 CT £109.38 TOTE £4.60: £2.20, £1.02, £2.50; DF 14.30 Trifecta £164.40.
Owner Mrs Patricia Hunt **Bred** R Guiry **Trained** Castletown, Co Meath
FOCUS
The two mares at the head of the market looked unexposed and one of them proved much better handicapped than the other. They finished clear and the winner set a pb.

3893 & 3895a (Foreign Racing) - See Raceform Interactive

3666 AYR (L-H)
Monday, February 1

3896 Meeting Abandoned - waterlogged

3660 PLUMPTON (L-H)
Monday, February 1

OFFICIAL GOING: Heavy (hdl 3.4; chs 3.7)
Wind: strong, against Weather: overcast, drizzly

3902 BLUERIBANDBET.COM 1/4 ODDS E/W EVERY RACE MAIDEN HURDLE (9 hdls) 1m 7f 195y
1:35 (1:35) (Class 5) 4-Y-O+ **£3,898** (£1,144; £572; £286)

Form RPR
202 **1** **Clayton**[29] 3450 7-11-3 122... JoshuaMoore 123+
(Gary Moore) *led 2nd: mde rest: drew clr fr 3 out: more than 20 l ahd last: eased* **10/11**[1]
22-3 **2** *16* **Generous Jack (IRE)**[46] 3130 7-11-3 0................................ JamieMoore 103
(Jim Best) *chsd ldrs: pushed along fr 4th: chsd wnr 6th: rdn and no imp after 3 out: no ch whn j.lft last* **11/4**[2]
P **3** *3 1/4* **Karens Lad (IRE)**[29] 3452 6-11-3 0.................................. TomCannon 98+
(Nick Gifford) *chsd ldrs but urged along fr 3rd: lost pl after nt fluent 5th: struggling bdly next: picked up bef 2 out: styd on stoutly to take 3rd after last* **33/1**
00 **4** *4* **Talk Of The South (IRE)**[34] 3353 7-11-3 0.................... NickScholfield 93
(Paul Henderson) *hld up: sn detached in last: pushed along fr 3rd: virtually t.o in 11th pl 6th: suddenly sed to run on fr 3 out: fin w sme relish* **14/1**

P00 **5** *4* **Little Buxted (USA)**[4] 3819 6-11-3 0 AndrewGlassonbury 92
(Jim Best) *led to 2nd: chsd wnr to 6th: wl clr of rest in 3rd pl after tl wknd fr 2 out and lost pls flat* **100/1**
-364 **6** *3 1/4* **Shake Devaney (IRE)**[72] 2646 6-11-3 0 PaddyBrennan 86
(Fergal O'Brien) *hld up in midfield: lft bhd by ldrs 5th but gng bttr than many: nt fluent next but sn poor 4th: no imp on ldrs: fdd fr last* **13/2**[3]
0/4- **7** *22* **Swanage Bay (IRE)**[522] 1365 9-11-3 0 RichieMcLernon 64
(Sophie Leech) *nvr beyond midfield: lost tch w ldrs 5th: pushed along and no prog after next* **66/1**
P **Yur Next (IRE)**[619] 8-10-10 0 LeightonAspell
(Alison Batchelor) *hld up in rr: prog into midfield 5th: sn lost tch w ldrs: wknd after next: t.o in 11th whn p.u bef 2 out* **100/1**
- **P** **Aramadyh**[676] 5-10-10 0 TomO'Brien
(Jim Best) *hld up in rr: lft bhd by ldrs 5th: prog fr next to press for poor 4th 3 out: fdd and p.u bef 2 out* **66/1**
P **The Child (IRE)**[743] 7-11-3 0 AndrewThornton
(Anna Newton-Smith) *a wl in rr: t.o in last pl after 5th tl p.u bef last* **100/1**
6P **P** **Bobby Benton (IRE)**[7] 3772 5-11-3 0 LiamTreadwell
(Jim Best) *t.k.h: hld up in midfield: lost tch w ldrs 5th: wl bhd after: poor 8th whn p.u bef last* **100/1**
30 **P** **Arcamante (ITY)**[25] 2754 5-11-3 0 BrendanPowell
(Jamie Snowden) *w ldrs to 4th: wknd rapidly fr next: t.o in 10th 2 out: p.u bef last* **12/1**

4m 22.7s (21.90) **Going Correction** +1.55s/f (Heavy) **12 Ran SP% 116.6**
Speed ratings (Par 103): **107,99,97,95,93 91,80, , ,**
CSF £3.38 TOTE £2.50: £1.20, £1.10, £5.30; EX 4.10 Trifecta £43.20.
Owner Ashley Head **Bred** G Reed **Trained** Lower Beeding, W Sussex

FOCUS
Due to rail movements this race was run over 57yds further than advertised. Josh Moore described the ground as "hard work, and holding enough." Little depth to this maiden hurdle and the field were strung out a long way from the finish. The winner stood out and is rated close to his mark.

3903 BLUERIBANDBET.COM 0800 014 7304 TELEPHONE BETTING NOVICES' H'CAP CHASE (12 fncs) 2m 214y
2:10 (2:11) (Class 4) (0-105,105) 5-Y-0+ **£4,548** (£1,335; £667; £333)

Form RPR
-P31 **1** **Very Live (FR)**[42] 3199 7-11-5 98 (p) RichieMcLernon 108+
(Paul Webber) *disp ld fr 3rd to 8th and fr next: drvn 2 out: narrow ld last: hld on wl* **11/4**[2]
-453 **2** *3/4* **Like Sully (IRE)**[46] 3129 8-11-9 102 LeightonAspell 111+
(Richard Rowe) *disp ld fr 3rd: led 8th to next: w wnr after: narrowly hdd last: kpt on but jst hld* **9/4**[1]
-F66 **3** *3* **Golan Dancer (IRE)**[46] 3129 8-11-7 105 JakeHodson(5) 112
(David Bridgwater) *nt fluent: chsd ldrs: reminder after 6th: drvn to stay cl up fr 8th: responded and stl in w a ch 2 out: no ex* **10/1**
-1F3 **4** *38* **Zero Visibility (IRE)**[42] 3195 9-10-6 85 ConorO'Farrell 52
(Alexandra Dunn) *led: outj. and hdd 3rd: in 4th pl fr 1/2-way: nudged along and lost tch w ldrs after 8th: wknd 2 out* **10/3**[3]
5445 **P** **Ennisnag (IRE)**[77] 2548 11-11-1 94 TomO'Brien
(Paul Henderson) *in tch in rr to 8th: wknd after next: t.o whn p.u bef 2 out* **16/1**
006/ **F** **Gold Carrot**[661] 5258 8-10-10 89 JamieMoore
(Gary Moore) *jumping lacked fluency: sn last: jst in tch whn fell 8th* **13/2**

4m 50.0s (27.00) **Going Correction** +1.675s/f (Heavy) **6 Ran SP% 108.8**
Speed ratings: **103,102,101,83, ,**
CSF £9.11 TOTE £3.60: £1.80, £1.70; EX 9.30 Trifecta £36.90.
Owner R V Shaw **Bred** Patrick Ansault And Claudine Ansault **Trained** Mollington, Oxon

FOCUS
Due to rail movements this race was run over 48yds further than advertised. A competitive little heat, despite there being just the six runners. The form is pretty modest, though, the winner similar to his Lingfield win.

3904 CRYSTAL SERVICES CONDITIONAL JOCKEYS' H'CAP HURDLE (QUAL FOR CHALLENGER STAYING HURDLE FINAL) (14 hdls) 3m 217y
2:45 (2:45) (Class 4) (0-120,119) 4-Y-0+ **£6,498** (£1,908; £954; £477)

Form RPR
031P **1** **West Of The Edge (IRE)**[18] 3591 8-10-5 101 (p) ThomasCheesman(3) 110+
(Dai Williams) *trckd ldr: led 10th: 4 l clr bef 2 out: drvn sn after: kpt on wl fr last* **16/1**
P-01 **2** *2 1/2* **Royale Knight**[95] 2146 10-11-4 119 CharlieHammond(8) 123
(Dr Richard Newland) *prom: rdn after 11th: tk 2nd bef 2 out and kpt on gamely to cl on wnr last: one pce flat* **5/1**
0133 **3** *5* **American Life (FR)**[25] 3498 9-11-2 112 (vt) KillianMoore(3) 110
(Sophie Leech) *hld up: prog to trck ldrs after 10th: rdn 3 out: tk 3rd 2 out but no imp on ldng pair after* **9/2**[3]
2114 **4** *1 1/2* **Snowball (IRE)**[7] 3771 9-9-12 94 HarryCobden(3) 91
(David Arbuthnot) *in tch: rdn bef 3 out: no imp on ldrs after: kpt on* **3/1**[1]
0222 **5** *37* **Twenty Eight Guns**[42] 3198 6-11-1 108 ThomasGarner 68
(Michael Scudamore) *cl up: chsd wnr 11th: rdn after 3 out: lost 2nd and wknd rapidly jst bef 2 out: virtually p.u nr fin* **10/1**
03P5 **P** **Iora Glas (IRE)**[46] 3129 7-11-5 115 ConorShoemark(3)
(Fergal O'Brien) *in tch tl rdn and wknd after 8th: t.o whn p.u after 10th* **14/1**
04-1 **P** **Mogestic (IRE)**[46] 3125 7-10-6 99 JeremiahMcGrath
(Seamus Mullins) *led: hit 9th: hdd next: wknd qckly after 11th: t.o whn p.u bef 2 out* **4/1**[2]
40-5 **P** **Ginny's Tonic (IRE)**[55] 2952 7-10-10 103 (t) FreddieMitchell
(Suzy Smith) *in tch: blnd 6th: nvr gng wl after: t.o whn p.u after 10th* **8/1**

7m 13.7s (48.70) **Going Correction** +1.55s/f (Heavy) **8 Ran SP% 112.6**
Speed ratings (Par 105): **84,83,81,81,69 , ,**
CSF £91.06 CT £424.57 TOTE £17.70: £3.90, £1.90, £1.10; EX 105.70 Trifecta £491.90.
Owner F Michael **Bred** Michael Lee **Trained** Broad Hinton, Wilts

FOCUS
Due to rail movements this race was run over 81yds further than advertised. This was always likely to prove a thorough test given the ground, even if the early pace was steady. A fair handicap for the grade.

3905 ALICE'S NOODLE BAR H'CAP HURDLE (9 hdls) 1m 7f 195y
3:20 (3:20) (Class 5) (0-100,99) 4-Y-0+ **£3,898** (£1,144; £572; £286)

Form RPR
0422 **1** **Loves Destination**[6] 3789 5-10-11 84 TomCannon 93+
(Chris Gordon) *cl up: trckd ldr 6th: rdn to ld after 3 out: styd on wl and drew clr fr next* **2/1**[1]
00FP **2** *10* **Kayflin (FR)**[204] 977 8-10-9 85 (p) ThomasGarner(3) 84
(Linda Jewell) *t.k.h early: hld up in rr: prog fr 6th: rdn to chse wnr bef 2 out: one pce and sn wl hld* **22/1**
-045 **3** *12* **Sir Hubert**[14] 3660 6-11-12 99 LeightonAspell 90
(Richard Rowe) *wl in tch: cl up 3 out: rdn to chse ldng pair jst bef 2 out but sn lft bhd: eased whn wl hld after last* **9/1**
5P20 **4** *9* **Get Ready Freddy**[16] 3619 6-11-9 96 GavinSheehan 73
(Nick Mitchell) *nt a fluent: mde most tl after 3 out: wknd next* **15/2**
-F34 **5** *6* **Willshebetrying**[14] 3665 5-11-9 96 (v[1]) JamieMoore 67
(Jim Best) *chsd ldr to 3rd: in tch but rdn 6th: wknd after 3 out* **12/1**
022P **6** *15* **Warrant Officer**[14] 3665 6-11-3 90 MarcGoldstein 46
(Sheena West) *racd wd thrght: prom: chsd ldr 3rd to 6th: wknd qckly 3 out* **6/1**[3]
0P4P **7** *14* **Rior (IRE)**[43] 3178 9-11-4 98 MrMartinMcIntyre(7) 40
(Paul Henderson) *in tch in rr tl drvn and wknd after 5th: sn t.o: hit last* **12/1**
0P **F** **Honourable Exit (IRE)**[58] 2904 9-11-2 89 SamTwiston-Davies
(Alexandra Dunn) *trckd ldrs: cl 6th whn fell 6th* **7/2**[2]

4m 26.5s (25.70) **Going Correction** +1.55s/f (Heavy) **8 Ran SP% 111.3**
Speed ratings (Par 103): **97,92,86,81,78 71,64,**
CSF £38.27 CT £313.86 TOTE £2.70: £1.10, £5.80, £2.90; EX 45.30 Trifecta £407.80.
Owner Chris Gordon Racing Club **Bred** Hazeley Stud **Trained** Morestead, Hampshire

FOCUS
Due to rail movements this race was run over 57yds further than advertised. The runners finished strung out in what was a moderate handicap. The winner is rated similar to her last couple of runs.

3906 BLUERIBANDBET.COM ALL ANTE POST SINGLES NRNB H'CAP CHASE (18 fncs) 3m 1f 152y
3:50 (3:51) (Class 5) (0-100,98) 5-Y-0+ **£3,994** (£1,240; £667)

Form RPR
0231 **1** **Bebinn (IRE)**[14] 3663 9-11-10 96 (p) DarylJacob 112+
(Ben Case) *cl up: trckd ldr fr 8th: disp ld bef 14th tl drew rt away fr 2 out: comf* **2/1**[2]
2262 **2** *29* **Burgess Dream (IRE)**[14] 3663 7-11-1 87 AndrewThornton 79
(Anna Newton-Smith) *cl up: trckd ldr fr 8th: mstke next: disp ld bef 14th tl wknd qckly 2 out: fin tired* **15/8**[1]
526- **3** *1 1/2* **Wayward Frolic**[295] 5291 10-11-12 98 (v[1]) JamieMoore 83
(Jim Best) *j.lft: led: drvn 13th: hdd bef next: wl btn after 4 out* **11/4**[3]
64PP **P** **Red Anchor (IRE)**[37] 3218 12-10-5 77 (b) LeightonAspell
(Linda Jewell) *chsd ldr to 8th: sn drvn: wknd 11th: t.o whn p.u bef 14th* **13/2**

7m 34.4s (43.70) **Going Correction** +1.675s/f (Heavy) **4 Ran SP% 108.1**
Speed ratings: **99,90,89,**
CSF £6.20 TOTE £2.70; EX 5.10 Trifecta £7.50.
Owner The Polk Partnership **Bred** James Gill **Trained** Edgcote, Northants

FOCUS
Due to rail movements this race was run over 72yds further than advertised. This had looked a trappy heat, despite just the four runners, but the winner scored as she pleased. There's a case for rating her up to 5lb higher, but this isn't form to be confident about.

3907 ANISE CATERING MAIDEN OPEN NATIONAL HUNT FLAT RACE 2m 1f 164y
4:25 (4:25) (Class 6) 4-6-Y-O **£1,624** (£477; £238; £119)

Form RPR
1 **Clondaw Bisto (IRE)**[72] 5-11-3 0 TomO'Brien 116+
(Suzy Smith) *cl up: jnd ldr 1/2-way: led over 6f out and gng bttr than rest: rdn over 2f out: styd on steadily* **5/2**[2]
2-5 **2** *8* **King Uther**[25] 3502 6-11-3 0 TomCannon 108
(Chris Gordon) *pressed ldr to 1/2-way: rdn 7f out: kpt in tch: rallied to go 2nd 3f out: no imp on wnr fnl 2f* **11/1**
3 *22* **Costante Via (IRE)** 5-10-10 0 MarkGrant 79
(Dominic Ffrench Davis) *led to over 6f out: sn rdn: w wnr tl over 3f out: sn lost 2nd and wknd* **25/1**
4 *5* **Cinderfella** 5-11-0 0 JamesBanks(3) 81
(Noel Williams) *cl up: rdn 7f out: kpt in tch tl wknd over 3f out* **9/1**
5 *59* **Doasuwouldbedoneby (IRE)** 5-11-3 0 LeightonAspell 22
(David Arbuthnot) *cl up: rdn 7f out: sn wknd: t.o 4f out* **5/1**[3]
6 *51* **Carqalin (FR)** 4-10-7 0 TomScudamore
(David Pipe) *trckd ldrs: rdn 7f out: sn wknd: t.o over 5f out* **7/4**[1]
P **Beauchamp Eagle** 4-10-7 0 BrendanPowell
(Jamie Snowden) *hld up: rdn and wknd 1/2-way: t.o whn p.u 6f out* **12/1**

4m 49.1s (23.80) **Going Correction** +1.55s/f (Heavy)
WFA 4 from 5yo+ 9lb **7 Ran SP% 111.5**
Speed ratings: **109,105,95,93,67 44,**
CSF £27.62 TOTE £5.80: £1.60, £3.60; EX 29.90 Trifecta £171.50.
Owner J Gordon-Watson **Bred** William J M McGaffin **Trained** Lewes, E Sussex

FOCUS
Due to rail movements this race was run over 48yds further than advertised. Little depth to this bumper and the poor display of the favourite made it easier for the winner, but none the less he created a good impression.
T/Plt: £36.60 to a £1 stake. Pool: £82,297.25 - 1637.01 winning units. T/Qpdt: £20.20 to a £1 stake. Pool: £6,388.58 - 233.80 winning units. **Jonathan Neesom**

3194 LINGFIELD (L-H)
Tuesday, February 2
3908 Meeting Abandoned - Waterlogged

3744 TAUNTON (R-H)
Tuesday, February 2

OFFICIAL GOING: Heavy (4.5)
Wind: strong across Weather: sunny periods with showers

3914 OPENBET CONDITIONAL JOCKEYS' H'CAP HURDLE (12 hdls) 2m 7f 198y
2:15 (2:16) (Class 5) (0-100,100) 4-Y-0+ **£3,249** (£954; £477; £238)

Form RPR
1146 **1** **Oscar Jane (IRE)**[38] 3256 9-11-2 90 (bt) DavidNoonan 99+
(Johnny Farrelly) *mde virtually all: styd on wl: rdn out* **5/1**[3]
0-42 **2** *8* **Glendermot (IRE)**[27] 3489 7-11-6 94 CiaranGethings 96
(Paul Cowley) *trckd ldrs: nt fluent 9th: rdn to chse wnr after 3 out: styd on same pce fr next* **9/4**[1]
0P60 **3** *8* **Lunar Flow**[50] 3077 5-10-12 94 GrahamCarson(8) 88
(Jamie Snowden) *cl up: rdn after 9th: chsd ldng pair bef 2 out but nvr any threat* **16/1**

-P06 **4** *17* **Comical Red**[34] 3369 8-11-2 **90**........................(b) TomBellamy 68
(Mark Gillard) *led 3rd tl 5th: pressed wnr most of way tl rdn after 9th: wknd appr 2 out* **7/1**

-UP0 **5** *11* **Safran De Cotte (FR)**[38] 3220 10-11-12 **100**..............(b[1]) JackSherwood 65
(Henry Daly) *trckd ldrs tl rdn after 9th: wknd after next: t.o* **3/1[2]**

P45/ **P** **Normally**[1323] 747 12-10-3 **80**........................(p) ThomasCheesman[(3)]
(Hywel Evans) *reminders after 3rd: a towards rr: losing tch whn p.u after 7th* **50/1**

4600 **P** **I'llhavealook (IRE)**[47] 3125 11-11-7 **95**........................(p) RobertWilliams
(Katie Stephens) *trckd ldrs tl lost pl between 3rd and 4th: in last trio: wknd after 9th: t.o whn p.u bef last* **14/1**

5005 **P** **Karl Marx (IRE)**[47] 3125 6-10-13 **87**........................(b) JakeHodson
(Mark Gillard) *trckd ldrs tl wknd after 9th: t.o whn p.u bef 2 out* **12/1**

4P00 **P** **Run Bob Run**[24] 3516 5-11-3 **91**........................ KieronEdgar
(John Flint) *reminder after 3rd: a towards rr: wknd after 9th: t.o whn p.u bef 2 out* **16/1**

6m 41.4s (37.40) **Going Correction** +1.475s/f (Heav) **9** Ran SP% **113.0**
Speed ratings (Par 103): **96,93,90,85,81** ,,,
CSF £16.74 CT £163.92 TOTE £6.20: £2.00, £1.10, £4.30; EX 16.10 Trifecta £243.90.
Owner P Tosh **Bred** J R Weston **Trained** Enmore, Somerset

FOCUS
The course passed an inspection the previous day and it was tough going on a windy afternoon. The bend into home straight was shared and the bend out of home straight divided. The opening handicap for conditional riders was a moderate affair run over a distance 138 yards further than advertised. Winning jockey David Noonan afterwards said the ground was "very tacky as it's drying out". The second is the best guide to the form.

3915 OPENBET NOVICES' HURDLE (9 hdls) 2m 104y
2:45 (2:45) (Class 4) 4-Y-0+ **£3,898** (£1,144; £572; £286)

Form RPR

1 **Bloody Mary (FR)**[139] 5-11-2 0........................ BarryGeraghty 125+
(Nicky Henderson) *trckd ldrs: led after 3 out: rdn between last 2: kpt on wl to assert fnl 120yds* **4/6[1]**

1P **2** *2 1/4* **Banyu (FR)**[35] 3353 5-11-9 0........................ RichardJohnson 128+
(Philip Hobbs) *plld hrd: hld up bhd: hdwy fr 5th: trckd wnr after 3 out: rdn w ev ch between last 2: kpt on but hld fnl 120yds* **11/2[3]**

056 **3** *11* **Zero Grand (IRE)**[10] 3745 5-11-3 0........................ RichieMcLernon 111
(Johnny Farrelly) *trckd ldrs: chal briefly 3 out: sn rdn: nt pce of ldrs: styd on into 3rd run-in* **25/1**

4 *2* **Lou Vert (FR)**[325] 4-10-7 0........................(t) SamTwiston-Davies 100+
(Paul Nicholls) *mid-div: hdwy after 3 out: rdn to chse ldng pair next: nvr threatened: no ex run-in* **2/1[2]**

600 **5** *15* **Mondello (GER)**[10] 3745 5-11-3 0........................(t) ConorO'Farrell 94
(Richard Woollacott) *prom: ev ch 3 out: sn rdn: wknd after next* **100/1**

3050 **6** *1 3/4* **Lift The Lid (IRE)**[10] 3744 6-11-3 0........................ NoelFehily 92
(Neil Mulholland) *trckd ldrs: chal 6th tl rdn after 3 out: wknd between last 2* **50/1**

0600 **7** *1 1/2* **Cougar Kid (IRE)**[15] 3660 5-11-3 0........................(p) LeightonAspell 91
(Philip Hide) *hld up towards rr: hdwy 3 out: sn rdn: wknd next* **50/1**

0-00 **8** *2 3/4* **The Big Mare**[10] 3745 7-10-10 0........................ RobertDunne 81
(Laura Young) *mid-div tl 3 out: sn wknd* **100/1**

0UP0 **9** *3/4* **Acajou Des Bieffes (FR)**[10] 3745 6-11-3 0........................ RyanMahon 87
(Anthony Honeyball) *mid-div: rdn after 3 out: wknd bef next* **150/1**

04 **10** *2* **Present Times (IRE)**[20] 3582 5-10-12 0........................ ConorRing[(5)] 85
(Evan Williams) *a towards rr* **20/1**

55 **11** *1/2* **Rocknrobin (IRE)**[30] 3452 5-11-3 0........................ TomCannon 85
(Chris Gordon) *led tl after 5th: wknd 3 out* **50/1**

4m 27.6s (19.60) **Going Correction** +1.475s/f (Heav)
WFA 4 from 5yo+ 9lb **11** Ran SP% **125.8**
Speed ratings (Par 105): **110,108,103,102,94 94,93,91,91,90 90**
CSF £5.77 TOTE £1.40: £1.10, £1.60, £6.00; EX 6.40 Trifecta £87.20.
Owner John P McManus **Bred** Jacques Cypres & Arnaud Poirier **Trained** Upper Lambourn, Berks

FOCUS
Rail movement increased this race distance by 69yds. After an ordinary gallop the field got sorted out from the third-last in this interesting novice event. The first two should go on to rate higher.

3916 SOUTHWEST RACING CLUB NOVICES' LIMITED H'CAP CHASE (14 fncs) 2m 2f 40y
3:15 (3:15) (Class 4) (0-120,120) 5-Y-0+ **£5,198** (£1,526; £763; £381)

Form RPR

/42U **1** **Gallic Warrior (FR)**[32] 3412 9-10-5 **103**........................(t) PaddyBrennan 117+
(Fergal O'Brien) *trckd ldrs: led after 8th: in control whn mstke last: styd on wl* **2/1[2]**

0323 **2** *6* **Vic De Touzaine (FR)**[31] 3445 7-11-8 **120**........................ AidanColeman 127+
(Venetia Williams) *trckd ldrs: rdn to chse wnr after 3 out: sn hld: kpt on same pce* **15/8[1]**

P/25 **3** *7* **Fountains Flypast**[243] 614 12-10-9 **112**........................(t) DavidNoonan[(5)] 111
(Anthony Honeyball) *hld up: rdn after 4 out: stdy prog into hld 3rd at the last: nvr gng pce to threaten ldrs* **16/1**

2P06 **4** *4 1/2* **Mad About The Boy**[24] 3516 6-10-12 **110**........................ JamieMoore 106
(Robert Walford) *trckd ldr: pressed ldr after 7th tl rdn after 4 out: 3rd and hld whn v awkward 3 out: one pce after* **14/1**

-52P **5** *14* **Jaunty Inflight**[5] 3867 7-10-4 **102**........................ RobertDunne 92
(Brian Eckley) *trckd ldrs: pressed ldrs 8th tl rdn after 4 out: hld next: wknd last* **16/1**

331- **F** **Seranwen (IRE)**[530] 1273 9-10-10 **108**........................ SamTwiston-Davies
(Nigel Twiston-Davies) *led tl after 8th: fell next* **8/1**

1 **F** **Seamus Mor (IRE)**[17] 3628 8-11-6 **118**........................ JamesDavies
(Henry Oliver) *trcking ldrs whn fell 9th* **5/1[3]**

5m 8.9s (16.90) **Going Correction** +1.025s/f (Soft) **7** Ran SP% **114.3**
Speed ratings: **103,100,97,95,89** ,
CSF £6.51 TOTE £3.60: £1.80, £1.20; EX 6.50 Trifecta £51.00.
Owner The Gud Times Partnership **Bred** Mme Jean Hodgkiss **Trained** Naunton, Gloucs

FOCUS
Rail movement increased this race distance by 90yds. Not a bad handicap for the class. After drama on the far side the first pair had it to themselves in the home straight. The winner is rated in line with his hurdles best.

3917 BATHWICK TYRES H'CAP HURDLE (9 hdls) 2m 104y
3:45 (3:45) (Class 3) (0-135,132) 4-Y-0 **£6,330** (£1,870; £935; £468; £234)

Form RPR

51FU **1** **Sea Wall (FR)**[10] 3747 8-11-0 **120**........................ TomCannon 132+
(Chris Gordon) *racd keenly: trckd ldrs: led appr 2 out: sn in command: rdn out* **8/1**

3420 **2** *10* **Heath Hunter (IRE)**[24] 3529 9-11-7 **132**........................(bt) DavidNoonan[(5)] 132
(David Pipe) *trckd ldrs: led 3 out: sn rdn: hdd bef next: sn hld by wnr: keeping on at same pce whn awkward last* **15/2[3]**

1U-0 **3** *4 1/2* **Lochnagar (GER)**[31] 3449 7-10-11 **117**........................ LiamTreadwell 112
(Venetia Williams) *hld up bhd ldrs: mstke 3 out: sn rdn: styd on fr next to go 3rd at the last: nvr gng pce to get on terms* **14/1**

3551 **4** *2* **After Hours (IRE)**[45] 3152 7-11-0 **120**........................ JamesDavies 113
(Henry Oliver) *disp tl 3rd: chsd ldrs: rdn along fr 6th: styd on at same pce fr next* **9/4[2]**

6010 **5** *7* **De Faoithesdream (IRE)**[60] 2884 10-11-1 **128**........................ LewisGordon[(7)] 117
(Evan Williams) *led tl 3 out: sn rdn and hld: wknd last* **9/1**

1043 **6** *1/2* **War Singer (USA)**[24] 3529 9-11-10 **130**........................(bt) NoelFehily 116
(Johnny Farrelly) *hld up bhd ldrs: effrt after 3 out: nvr threatened: wknd last* **9/1**

/3F- **P** **Master Red (IRE)**[444] 2508 7-11-4 **124**........................(t) TomScudamore
(David Pipe) *trckd ldrs: rdn after 3 out: wknd qckly and p.u bef next* **2/1[1]**

4m 28.0s (20.00) **Going Correction** +1.475s/f (Heav) **7** Ran SP% **113.6**
Speed ratings (Par 107): **109,104,101,100,97 97,**
CSF £62.26 TOTE £10.70: £4.40, £3.60; EX 64.00 Trifecta £354.90.
Owner Draper Edmonds Draper **Bred** Ian Hanamy **Trained** Morestead, Hampshire

FOCUS
Rail movement increased this race distance by 69yds. A modest handicap in which the majority found the going too much. The second sets the level.

3918 BATHWICK TYRES H'CAP CHASE (17 fncs) 2m 7f 3y
4:15 (4:15) (Class 3) (0-140,134) 5-Y-~~£8,229~~ (£2,431; £1,215; £608; £304)

Form RPR

-242 **1** **Sonny The One**[34] 3371 6-10-6 **114**........................ BrendanPowell 124+
(Colin Tizzard) *trckd ldr: led after 11th: rchd for next: rdn appr 3 out: styd on wl run-in: drvn out* **11/4[2]**

0- **2** *1/2* **Cork Citizen**[301] 5233 8-11-3 **125**........................(tp) TomScudamore 132
(David Pipe) *chsd ldrs: pushed along fr 10th: chsd wnr after 4 out: styd on wl fr last but a being jst hld* **12/1**

60-0 **3** *nk* **Ballyoliver**[93] 2213 12-11-5 **127**........................ LiamTreadwell 134
(Venetia Williams) *trckd ldrs: rdn and ev ch after 4 out: dropped to 5 l 3rd next: nt fluent last: styd on wl towards fin* **16/1**

5/1P **4** *10* **Tour Des Champs (FR)**[24] 3518 9-11-6 **131**........................(v) RyanHatch[(3)] 129
(Nigel Twiston-Davies) *led tl after 11th: chsd ldr: rdn 4 out: styd on same pce fr next* **5/1[3]**

FP-6 **5** *17* **Minellahalfcentury (IRE)**[81] 2473 8-11-9 **131**....(bt) SamTwiston-Davies 115
(Paul Nicholls) *trckd ldrs: rdn after 13th: sn hld in 5th: wknd bef last* **6/1**

-F31 **P** **Wychwoods Brook**[20] 3583 10-11-7 **134**........................ ConorRing[(5)]
(Evan Williams) *trckd ldrs: nt travelling fr 5th: p.u bef 8th* **6/4[1]**

6m 34.3s (18.30) **Going Correction** +1.025s/f (Soft) **6** Ran SP% **111.2**
Speed ratings: **109,108,108,105,99**
CSF £29.29 TOTE £3.70: £2.00, £2.90; EX 19.40 Trifecta £129.90.
Owner R E Nuttall **Bred** Mrs S F Maude **Trained** Milborne Port, Dorset

FOCUS
Rail movement increased this race distance by 120yds. This was a fair little staying handicap. They went a routine gallop and it saw a tight three-way finish. The winner's recent course run behind a well in-rival could be rated to this level.

3919 OPENBET H'CAP HURDLE (10 hdls) 2m 3f 1y
4:45 (4:45) (Class 4) (0-110,109) 4-Y-0+ **£3,898** (£1,144; £572; £286)

Form RPR

3-62 **1** **Join The Navy**[34] 3374 11-11-1 **101**........................ KieronEdgar[(3)] 106
(Kate Buckett) *hld up bhd: pushed along and hdwy after 3 out: styd on wl fr next: led run-in: pushed out* **6/1[3]**

4405 **2** *2 1/4* **Bishops Court**[76] 2564 6-11-9 **106**........................ NoelFehily 109
(Neil Mulholland) *mid-div: hdwy 3 out: led 2 out: sn rdn: hdd run-in: kpt on but no ex* **9/2[2]**

PP12 **3** *2 3/4* **Winged Express (IRE)**[26] 3497 7-11-4 **101**........................ IanPopham 101
(Alexandra Dunn) *in tch: rdn to chse ldrs after 3 out: wnt 3rd bef last: styd on same pce run-in* **9/4[1]**

4-42 **4** *7* **Jully Les Buxy**[61] 2870 6-11-7 **104**........................ AidanColeman 98
(Robert Walford) *prom: disp ld 3 out tl next: sn one pce* **6/1[3]**

-331 **5** *3 1/2* **Precious Ground**[32] 3410 6-10-12 **95**........................ JamesBest 86
(Kevin Bishop) *prom: mstke 2nd: disp ld 3 out tl next: no ex fr last* **7/1**

6145 **6** *1 1/2* **Exemplary**[34] 3374 9-11-4 **106**........................(t) DavidNoonan[(5)] 94
(Johnny Farrelly) *hld up: hdwy after 7th: rdn to chse ldrs after 3 out: no ex appr last* **12/1**

PFU0 **7** *3/4* **Sheer Poetry (IRE)**[38] 3256 5-10-9 **92**........................ ConorO'Farrell 80
(Richard Woollacott) *trckd ldrs: rdn after 3 out: wkng whn hit last* **33/1**

524P **8** *20* **Only Gorgeous (IRE)**[32] 3414 7-11-2 **102**........................ LucyGardner[(3)] 69
(Sue Gardner) *led tl 3 out: sn wknd: t.o* **10/1**

-P00 **9** *24* **Hoist The Colours (IRE)**[238] 669 5-11-5 **102**........................ JamieMoore 45
(Robert Walford) *nt fluent 1st: mid-div tl wknd after 3 out: t.o* **40/1**

3160 **P** **Milestone (IRE)**[54] 2989 6-11-5 **109**........................(t) LewisGordon[(7)]
(Evan Williams) *in tch: effrt after 3 out: wknd bef next: p.u bef last* **20/1**

5m 17.7s (31.70) **Going Correction** +1.475s/f (Heav) **10** Ran SP% **116.9**
Speed ratings (Par 105): **92,91,89,86,85 84,84,76,66,**
CSF £33.11 CT £79.33 TOTE £6.80: £2.10, £2.00, £1.60; EX 35.90 Trifecta £136.70.
Owner Mrs D Buckett **Bred** Mrs F Wilson **Trained** Upham, Hants

FOCUS
Rail movement increased this race distance by 69yds. A moderate handicap which was run at an ordinary gallop yet the winner still came from last to first. The winner is rated to his very best.
T/Plt: £64.30 to £1 stake. Pool: £95,280.16 - 1,080.48 winning tickets. T/Qpdt: £20.70 to a £1 stake. Pool: £7,542.67 - 268.79 winning tickets. **Tim Mitchell**

3784 LEICESTER (R-H)
Wednesday, February 3

OFFICIAL GOING: Hurdle course - heavy (4.3); chase course - soft (heavy in places; 5.7)
Wind: Light behind Weather: Fine

3920 EBF STALLIONS "NATIONAL HUNT" NOVICES' HURDLE (QUALIFIER) (8 hdls 2 omitted) 2m 4f 110y
1:50 (1:52) (Class 3) 4-7-Y-0 **£6,498** (£1,908; £954; £477)

Form RPR

4/22 **1** **Allysson Monterg (FR)**[33] 3403 6-11-2 132........................ AlainCawley 135+
(Richard Hobson) *mde all: set stdy pce tl qcknd after 6th: shkn up appr last: styd on wl* **10/11[1]**

1221 **2** *9* **Potters Legend**[28] 3483 6-11-8 132 ... LeightonAspell 135+
(Lucy Wadham) *racd keenly: w wnr to 3rd: settled into 2nd: hit 2 out: rdn appr last: eased whn btn flat* **13/8**[2]

6P **3** *54* **Three Of A Kind (IRE)**[61] 2879 7-11-2 0 ...(t) PaddyBrennan 72
(Fergal O'Brien) *hld up: hdwy 5th: wknd appr 2 out* **150/1**

4 *83* **Hang Fire (IRE)**[45] 3185 6-10-9 0 ... LeeEdwards
(Tony Carroll) *hld up: a in rr: bhd fr 4th* **250/1**

P **Just Acting (IRE)**[416] 6-11-2 0 ... BarryGeraghty
(Paul Nicholls) *chsd ldrs tl wknd after 6th: bhd whn p.u bef last* **7/1**[3]

3 **P** **Ambion Lane (IRE)**[39] 3258 6-11-2 0 ... IanPopham
(Victor Dartnall) *prom to 5th: bhd whn p.u bef last* **50/1**

5m 32.4s (7.70) **Going Correction** +0.425s/f (Soft) **6** Ran SP% **106.0**
Speed ratings: **102,98,78,46,**
CSF £2.39 TOTE £1.90: £1.10, £1.10; EX 2.90 Trifecta £32.60.
Owner D W Fox **Bred** S C E A La Haute Perriere **Trained** Stow-On-The-Wold, Gloucs

FOCUS
The bends were moved out, so it increased this distance by 28yds. Flight one (the second-last) was bypassed for all hurdle races. Only three of these made any great appeal, and the whole field was slow to start when asked to set off. The market leaders dominated the outcome after pulling well way from the rest. The winner didn't need to improve.

3921 BURTON LAZARS NOVICES' CLAIMING HURDLE (6 hdls 2 omitted) 1m 7f 113y
2:25 (2:25) (Class 5) 4-Y-O+ **£2,599** (£763; £381; £190)

Form RPR

3-P4 **1** **Light Well (IRE)**[13] 3705 8-11-11 113 ... AndrewGlassonbury 113
(Gary Moore) *chsd ldrs: led and hit 2 out: drvn out: jst hld on* **3/1**[2]

2032 **2** *nk* **Bar A Mine (FR)**[37] 3314 7-11-5 105 ...(v) SamTwiston-Davies 106
(Nigel Twiston-Davies) *prom: outpcd after 4th: rallied appr last: hmpd flat: styd on u.p* **4/1**[3]

1213 **3** *4 1/2* **Anda De Grissay (FR)**[39] 3217 6-11-2 122 ...(t) DavidNoonan(5) 105
(Anthony Honeyball) *trckd ldrs: racd keenly: ev ch 2 out: sn rdn: nt fluent last: no ex flat* **10/11**[1]

0P26 **4** *27* **El Massivo (IRE)**[37] 3318 6-11-8 118 ... PaddyBrennan 78
(Harriet Bethell) *hld up: rdn and wknd appr 2 out* **8/1**

P **P** **Water For Life**[45] 3175 5-10-5 0 ... ThomasCheesman(7)
(Martin Smith) *disp ld tl wnt on 3rd: hdd 2 out: sn rdn and wknd: bhd whn p.u bef last* **150/1**

0/0 **P** **Sprogzilla**[34] 3381 7-10-12 0 ... TrevorWhelan
(Hannah James) *disp ld: j.rt 2nd: j.rt and lost pl next: wknd next: bhd whn p.u bef last* **200/1**

00 **P** **Teme Trixie**[119] 831 6-10-12 0 ... LeightonAspell
(Miss Imogen Pickard) *hld up: hdwy after 3rd: rdn and wknd appr 2 out: bhd whn p.u bef last* **200/1**

4m 10.2s (9.20) **Going Correction** +0.425s/f (Soft) **7** Ran SP% **110.2**
Speed ratings (Par 103): **94,93,91,78,**
CSF £14.23 TOTE £6.60: £3.40, £1.60; EX 14.20 Trifecta £34.50.
Owner B Siddle & B D Haynes **Bred** March Thoroughbreds **Trained** Lower Beeding, W Sussex

FOCUS
The bends were moved out, so it increased this distance by 16yds. Flight one (the second-last) was bypassed for all hurdle races. Probably a fair race of its type. The first two are rated pretty much to their marks, with the third a stone+ off.

3922 OTTER NOVICES' LIMITED H'CAP CHASE (18 fncs) 2m 6f 151y
3:00 (3:00) (Class 3) 5-Y-O+ **£7,213** (£2,623)

Form RPR

310/ **1** **Prideofthecastle (IRE)**[690] 4805 9-10-6 124 ... TomScudamore 131
(David Pipe) *hld up: hmpd 1st: nt fluent 12th: hdwy to chse ldr 4 out: sn ev ch: upsides and gng best whn lft wl clr last* **8/1**

311- **2** *81* **Lessons In Milan (IRE)**[334] 4613 8-11-8 140 ... PeterCarberry 66
(Nicky Henderson) *chsd ldrs: j.rt 1st: pushed along after 11th: wkng whn hit 4 out: lft remote 3rd 3 out: lft 2nd and j. slowly last* **2/1**[2]

1-50 **U** **Gunner Fifteen (IRE)**[39] 3232 8-9-10 121 ... MrMLegg(7)
(Harry Fry) *led: racd keenly: clr 5th to 10th: hdd appr 4 out: sn rdn: 3rd and wkng whn mstke and uns rdr next* **3/1**[3]

3-11 **F** **April Dusk (IRE)**[57] 2963 7-10-13 131 ... GavinSheehan 138
(Warren Greatrex) *chsd ldr tl led appr 4 out: jnd bef next: sn rdn: slt ld whn fell last* **13/8**[1]

6m 5.8s (1.80) **Going Correction** +0.40s/f (Soft) **4** Ran SP% **107.5**
Speed ratings: **112,83,,**
CSF £23.42 TOTE £7.90; EX 13.20 Trifecta £13.70.
Owner Bryan Drew **Bred** Patrick Cronin **Trained** Nicholashayne, Devon

FOCUS
The bends were moved out, so it increased this distance by 10yds. This had the look of a strong race despite the lack of chasing experience between the four runners , but two failed to complete and another was disappointing, so caution with regards to form is advised in the short-term. The winner is rated in line with his hurdles mark.

3923 GOLDEN MILLER H'CAP HURDLE (8 hdls 2 omitted) 2m 4f 110y
3:35 (3:35) (Class 3) (0-125,125) 4-Y-O+ **£7,912** (£2,337; £1,168; £585; £292)

Form RPR

0604 **1** **The Artful Cobbler**[28] 3484 5-10-6 105 ... JakeGreenall 120+
(Henry Daly) *racd keenly: a.p: led appr last: styd on wl* **8/1**

6051 **2** *13* **Pilgrims Bay (IRE)**[13] 3705 6-11-8 121 ... TomScudamore 123
(David Pipe) *hld up: hdwy 6th: rdn appr last: wknd flat* **4/1**[1]

030P **3** *14* **Rock On Rocky**[27] 3407 8-11-12 125 ...(p) CharliePoste 112
(Matt Sheppard) *led: hit 5th: rdn: hdd and wkng whn mstke last* **8/1**

/F-3 **4** *25* **Lower Hope Dandy**[36] 3352 9-11-5 123 ... CharlieDeutsch(5) 85
(Venetia Williams) *chsd ldrs tl rdn and wknd after 6th* **4/1**[1]

02-0 **5** *3 3/4* **Steel City**[28] 3487 8-11-7 120 ... RyanMahon 78
(Seamus Mullins) *hld up: hdwy after 6th: hit 2 out: sn rdn and wknd* **10/1**

1003 **6** *3 3/4* **Brave Helios**[37] 3318 6-11-4 122 ... DanielHiskett(5) 77
(Richard Phillips) *hld up: hdwy 5th: rdn bef next: wknd appr 2 out* **13/2**[3]

5125 **7** *37* **Milord (GER)**[36] 3336 7-11-12 125 ...(p) DavidBass 43
(Kim Bailey) *prom: rdn after 6th: wknd bef 2 out* **9/2**[2]

-333 **8** *33* **Fort Smith (IRE)**[33] 3397 7-11-1 121 ...(t) HarrisonBeswick(7) 6
(Sam Thomas) *racd keenly: w ldr: nt fluent 6th: rdn and wknd bef next* **17/2**

5m 29.9s (5.20) **Going Correction** +0.425s/f (Soft) **8** Ran SP% **113.4**
Speed ratings (Par 107): **107,102,96,87,85 84,70,57**
CSF £39.79 CT £264.79 TOTE £9.10: £2.30, £1.60, £3.10; EX 36.60 Trifecta £364.40.
Owner Exors of the Late Mrs A Timpson **Bred** Richard S Keeley **Trained** Stanton Lacy, Shropshire

FOCUS
The bends were moved out, so it increased this distance by 28yds. Flight one (the second-last) was bypassed for all hurdle races. A few of these were easy to make a case for if they ran up to their best, so it's probably wise to rate the form positively until proven otherwise. There should be more to come from the winner.

3924 RUNNING HARE H'CAP CHASE (QUALIFIER FOR THE CHALLENGER MIDDLE DISTANCE CHASE SERIES FINAL) (15 fncs) 2m 4f 45y
4:10 (4:10) (Class 4) (0-120,120) 5-Y-O+ **£4,548** (£1,335; £667; £333)

Form RPR

4-42 **1** **Cernunnos (FR)**[54] 3020 6-11-12 120 ...(tp) BarryGeraghty 138+
(Tom George) *hld up: hdwy 7th: led appr last: rdn clr flat* **7/2**[3]

4351 **2** *7* **Ballyrath (IRE)**[8] 3788 6-11-7 115 7ex ...(p) SamTwiston-Davies 126
(Nigel Twiston-Davies) *chsd ldr: pushed along to ld 4 out: rdn and hdd appr last: styd on same pce flat* **9/4**[1]

6-51 **3** *9* **Troika Steppes**[62] 2861 8-11-2 113 ...(t) ConorShoemark(3) 114
(Fergal O'Brien) *led: clr 3rd to 7th: hdd 4 out: rdn next: wknd last* **6/1**

-54P **4** *9* **Thedrinkymeister (IRE)**[34] 3384 7-11-5 113 ... DavidBass 106
(Kim Bailey) *chsd ldrs: wnt 2nd 6th tl 8th: sn pushed along: wknd bef 4 out* **9/2**

223 **5** *7* **Walk In The Mill (FR)**[18] 3620 6-11-11 119 ... AndrewThornton 113
(Robert Walford) *prom: pushed along appr 4 out: blnd and wknd next* **10/3**[2]

5m 23.7s (4.80) **Going Correction** +0.40s/f (Soft) **5** Ran SP% **108.5**
Speed ratings: **106,103,99,96,93**
CSF £11.67 TOTE £4.50: £2.50, £1.30; EX 10.70 Trifecta £27.90.
Owner John P McManus **Bred** Patrick Montfort & San Gabriel Inv Inc **Trained** Slad, Gloucs

FOCUS
The bends were moved out, so it increased this distance by 10yds. A tight handicap, run at a decent gallop. A big step up from the winner.

3925 ROA/RACING POST OWNERS JACKPOT H'CAP HURDLE (6 hdls 2 omitted) 1m 7f 113y
4:40 (4:41) (Class 5) (0-100,98) 4-Y-O+ **£3,249** (£954; £477; £238)

Form RPR

-243 **1** **Global Dream**[33] 3422 6-11-8 94 ... AdamPogson 98
(Caroline Bailey) *chsd ldr to 3rd: remained handy: rdn to ld appr last: styd on u.p* **10/3**[2]

0402 **2** *1/2* **In The Crowd (IRE)**[21] 3586 7-11-9 98 ...(p) JamesBanks(3) 102
(Roy Brotherton) *hld up in tch: chsd ldr 3rd: ev ch whn nt fluent last: rdn and hung rt flat: nt qckn towards fin* **3/1**[1]

5004 **3** *15* **Aaman (IRE)**[35] 3368 10-10-8 83 ... RobertWilliams(3) 71
(Bernard Llewellyn) *led: clr after 1st tl 4th: rdn: hdd & wknd appr last* **9/1**

-065 **4** *3* **Little James (IRE)**[34] 3382 7-11-5 91 ... SamTwiston-Davies 76
(Nigel Twiston-Davies) *hld up: rdn appr 2 out: sn wknd* **7/2**[3]

P633 **5** *26* **Gud Day (IRE)**[39] 3233 8-11-2 88 ...(p) PaddyBrennan 47
(Conor Dore) *prom tl rdn and wknd after 2 out* **4/1**

500- **P** **Recway Lass**[458] 2226 8-11-2 88 ...(t) TrevorWhelan
(Hannah James) *hld up: rdn and wknd appr 2 out: bhd whn p.u bef last* **33/1**

24 **P** **Directional**[25] 3523 4-11-2 98 ... TomCannon
(Tim Vaughan) *chsd ldrs: nt fluent 1st: rdn after 4th: wknd bef 2 out: bhd whn p.u bef last* **12/1**

4m 9.8s (8.80) **Going Correction** +0.425s/f (Soft)
WFA 4 from 6yo+ 9lb **7** Ran SP% **110.9**
Speed ratings (Par 103): **95,94,87,85,72 ,**
CSF £13.21 TOTE £4.40: £2.10, £1.60; EX 17.30 Trifecta £101.20.
Owner Mrs Susan Carsberg **Bred** Mrs S Carsberg **Trained** Holdenby, Northants

FOCUS
The bends were moved out, so it increased this distance by 16yds. Flight one (the second-last) was bypassed for all hurdle races. This looked pretty competitive for a moderate event and was run at a decent gallop. The first two are rated in line with their previous bests.
T/Plt: £218.40 to a £1 stake. Pool: £53,106.33 - 177.46 winning units. T/Qpdt: £80.60 to a £1 stake. Pool: £4,926.09 - 45.20 winning units. **Colin Roberts**

3568 LUDLOW (R-H)
Wednesday, February 3

OFFICIAL GOING: Soft (good to soft in places; 5.3)
Wind: fresh half against Weather: sunny spells

3926 OPENBET JUVENILE HURDLE (9 hdls) 1m 7f 169y
1:10 (1:10) (Class 4) 4-Y-O **£3,249** (£954; £477; £238)

Form RPR

1 **1** **St Saviour**[30] 3464 4-11-5 0 ... RichardJohnson 125+
(Philip Hobbs) *racd keenly: prom: w ldr 2nd to 3rd: led appr 5th: blnd 3 out: sn drvn: styd on wl flat* **4/6**[1]

13 **2** *2 1/4* **Berland (IRE)**[38] 3279 4-11-5 126 ... AidanColeman 120
(John Ferguson) *hld up: clsd 4th: rdn 2 out: wnt 2nd last: kpt on same pce flat* **7/2**[2]

316 **3** *8* **Borak (IRE)**[25] 3519 4-10-12 120 ...(t) JordanWilliams(7) 113
(Bernard Llewellyn) *chsd clr ldng pair: clsd 4th: wnt 2nd bef next: rdn 3 out: lost 2nd last: wknd flat* **11/1**

4 *9* **Brotherly Company (IRE)**[108] 4-10-12 0 ... NoelFehily 97+
(Harry Fry) *hld up: nudged along and outpcd by ldng trio appr 3 out: no ch after but kpt on steadily* **7/1**[3]

P4 **F** **Blackadder**[7] 3076 4-10-5 0 ... MrTGillard(7)
(Mark Gillard) *plld hrd: led: tended to jump rt: mstke 1st: hdd appr 5th: wknd rapidly: t.o whn fell heavily last: winded* **250/1**

4 **P** **Me Voila (FR)**[36] 3347 4-10-7 0 ... LizzieKelly(5)
(Nick Williams) *wnt bdly lft whn tape rose and lost 15 l: racd keenly and in tch by 3rd: wknd after 5th: bhd whn p.u bef 3 out* **16/1**

4m 8.6s (19.10) **Going Correction** +1.125s/f (Heav) **6** Ran SP% **109.3**
Speed ratings: **97,95,91,87,**
CSF £3.19 TOTE £1.50: £1.10, £1.70; EX 3.20 Trifecta £10.40.
Owner Highclere Thoroughbred Racing-St Saviour **Bred** Floors Farming **Trained** Withycombe, Somerset

■ Stewards' Enquiry : Mr T Gillard 28-day ban: continued to race contrary to gelding's welfare (Feb 17-24,27-Mar 3,5,9,11,13-15,17-18,20-21,24,28,30,Apr 1)

FOCUS
Due to rail movements this race was run over 9yds further than advertised. Richard Johnson described the ground as "very hard work" and a headwind in the straight made it more difficult. A useful juvenile hurdle, with the market leaders dominating. The winner and third set the standard.

3927 OPENBET "NATIONAL HUNT" MAIDEN HURDLE (DIV I) (9 hdls) 1m 7f 169y
1:40 (1:40) (Class 5) 4-Y-0+ £2,599 (£763; £381; £190)

Form RPR
12 1 **Divine Spear (IRE)**[26] 3508 5-11-5 0.................. NicodeBoinville 120+
(Nicky Henderson) *trckd ldrs: led 3 out: pushed along fr next and steadily drew clr: comf* 1/4[1]
2 5 **Bay Sly (IRE)**[464] 2116 9-11-5 0.................. ConorO'Farrell 110
(Seamus Durack) *wnt to post early: led tl rdn, hung lft and hdd 3 out: one pce fr next: hld whn j.rt last* 10/1[3]
3-PP 3 1 3/4 **Deadly Move (IRE)**[84] 2437 7-11-5 0.................. SeanBowen 108
(Peter Bowen) *towards rr: hdwy 5th: chsd ldng pair bef 3 out: rdn between last 2: styd on flat* 25/1
04 4 9 **North Hill (IRE)**[39] 3258 5-11-5 0..................[1] WillKennedy 99
(Ian Williams) *towards rr: pushed along and hdwy after 6th: rdn 3 out: btn in 4th whn mstke last* 22/1
00 5 3/4 **Bonvilston Boy**[49] 3105 5-11-0 0.................. AlanJohns(5) 101
(Tim Vaughan) *chsd ldrs: mstke 4th: mstke and lost grnd next: hit 3 out: kpt on same pce* 50/1
6P 6 14 **Whos De Baby (IRE)**[30] 3467 8-11-2 0.................. JamesBanks(3) 87
(Sarah-Jayne Davies) *chsd ldr to 3rd: styd prom: rdn and wkng whn blnd 3 out* 25/1
6-3P 7 9 **Hoponandsee**[78] 2561 5-10-12 0.................. AndrewTinkler 69
(George Baker) *mid-div: hdwy 5th: rdn 3 out: sn wknd* 40/1
00 8 32 **Apache Pearl (IRE)**[78] 2562 5-11-2 0..................(t) HarryBannister(3) 44
(Warren Greatrex) *racd keenly: prom: trckd ldr 3rd tl wknd qckly appr 3 out: t.o whn mstke last* 50/1
9 5 **Fled Or Pled (IRE)** 4-10-9 0.................. AidanColeman 29
(David Dennis) *t.k.h in rr: rdn and lost tch after 6th: t.o* 14/1
100- P **Rose Revived**[298] 5277 5-10-12 0.................. RichardJohnson
(Jonjo O'Neill) *hld up: j.rt: struggling fr 5th: j. slowly next: t.o whn p.u bef 3 out* 6/1[2]

4m 6.9s (17.40) **Going Correction** +1.125s/f (Heav)
WFA 4 from 5yo+ 9lb 10 Ran SP% **128.4**
Speed ratings (Par 103): **101,98,97,93,92 85,81,65,62,**
CSF £4.47 TOTE £1.20: £1.02, £2.80, £5.10; EX 5.70 Trifecta £63.80.
Owner Middleham Park Racing LXII **Bred** Miss Elizabeth Kennedy **Trained** Upper Lambourn, Berks

FOCUS
Due to rail movements this race was run over 9yds further than advertised. Division one of a maiden hurdle lacking depth. The easy winner was below his Doncaster mark.

3928 OPENBET "NATIONAL HUNT" MAIDEN HURDLE (DIV II) (9 hdls) 1m 7f 169y
2:10 (2:10) (Class 5) 4-Y-0+ £2,599 (£763; £381; £190)

Form RPR
053 1 **Britanio Bello (FR)**[19] 3608 5-11-5 114.................. JoshuaMoore 121+
(Gary Moore) *hld up: gd hdwy appr 3 out: chal 2 out: sn led: rdn and asserted flat* 4/1[3]
5-00 2 2 1/4 **Set In My Ways (IRE)**[36] 3334 5-11-5 0.................. RichardJohnson 118
(Jonjo O'Neill) *hld up: nt fluent 3rd or 4th: hdwy next: rdn 3 out: 4th over last: styd on wl flat: tk 2nd fnl 50yds* 9/1
P 3 2 1/4 **Beallandendall (IRE)**[22] 3571 8-10-12 0.................. MrStanSheppard(7) 116
(Matt Sheppard) *chsd ldrs: nt fluent 3 out: sn rdn: ev ch 2 out tl one pce flat: lost 2nd fnl 50yds* 100/1
4 3 1/2 **Space Oddity (FR)**[506] 5-11-5 0..................[1] NoelFehily 112
(Harry Fry) *t.k.h: led to 4th: styd cl up: led again 3 out: jnd next: hdd appr last where mstke: no ex* 6/4[1]
0/F- 5 22 **Beatu (IRE)**[344] 4414 7-11-5 0.................. WillKennedy 89
(Donald McCain) *t.k.h: hld up: hdwy 5th: rdn bef 3 out: wknd 2 out* 7/1
P-2 6 7 **Boolavard King (IRE)**[64] 2840 7-11-2 0.................. TomBellamy(3) 86
(Kim Bailey) *racd keenly: w ldr: led and mstke 4th: rdn and hdd 3 out: sn wknd* 11/4[2]
60-P 7 2 1/4 **Weston Flame**[19] 3612 6-10-12 0..................(t) DarylJacob 73
(Ben Case) *chsd ldrs tl wknd 3 out* 150/1
0-00 8 11 **Another Cobbler (FR)**[35] 3363 6-10-12 0.................. AndrewTinkler 62
(Henry Daly) *t.k.h: chsd ldrs: j.rt 2nd: rdn along after next: last and struggling by 5th* 50/1

4m 7.2s (17.70) **Going Correction** +1.125s/f (Heav) 8 Ran SP% **112.8**
Speed ratings (Par 103): **100,98,97,96,85 81,80,74**
CSF £36.37 TOTE £3.70: £1.50, £2.20, £7.60; EX 33.80 Trifecta £1166.20.
Owner Ashley Head **Bred** Remi Boucret & Arnaud Charrie **Trained** Lower Beeding, W Sussex

FOCUS
Due to rail movements this race was run over 9yds further than advertised. One key non-runner resulted in division two of this maiden hurdle having an open look to it. A small step up from the winner.

3929 OPENBET NOVICES' LIMITED H'CAP CHASE (19 fncs) 2m 7f 171y
2:45 (2:45) (Class 3) (0-135,135) 5-Y-0+ £6,498 (£1,908; £954; £477)

Form RPR
02/1 1 **Another Hero (IRE)**[74] 2631 7-11-4 131.................. RichardJohnson 140+
(Jonjo O'Neill) *j.lft: hld up: hdwy 11th: chal 4 out: ev ch whn lft in command 2 out: rdn out* 3/1[1]
3131 2 4 1/2 **Still Believing (IRE)**[22] 3569 8-9-10 116.................. MrConorOrr(7) 119
(Evan Williams) *hld up: rdn 13th: last and struggling 15th: hdwy 4 out: chsd wnr appr last: styd on flat* 5/1[3]
-116 3 8 **Royale Django (IRE)**[190] 1138 7-11-3 135.................. AlanJohns(5) 133
(Tim Vaughan) *in tch towards rr: stdy hdwy 14th: rdn 3 out: 3rd whn stmbld bdly next: no ex* 12/1
P1-0 4 2 1/2 **Carningli (IRE)**[116] 1848 7-11-6 133.................. AidanColeman 127
(Rebecca Curtis) *chsd ldrs: rdn after 15th: wkng whn mstke 4 out: plugged on to go 4th post* 11/2
3P14 5 shd **Uhlan Bute (FR)**[76] 2592 8-10-7 120..................(p) LiamTreadwell 113
(Venetia Williams) *led: mstke 14th: rdn: hdd and rdr dropped whip appr 3 out: grad wknd: lost 4th post* 11/1
2P3P U **Belmount (IRE)**[36] 3349 7-10-8 124.................. RyanHatch(3)
(Nigel Twiston-Davies) *chsd ldrs: bmpd 1st: mstke 13th: wknd after 15th: bhd whn blnd and uns rdr 3 out* 9/2[2]
1-U6 U **Ivy Gate (IRE)**[32] 3445 8-10-6 119..................(v[1]) RichieMcLernon 122
(Jonjo O'Neill) *chsd ldr: j.lft 1st: rdn after 15th: led 3 out: narrowly ahd whn blnd and uns rdr next* 16/1
-23F P **Souriyan (FR)**[39] 3255 5-11-1 132..................(p) MichealNolan
(Jamie Snowden) *mid-div: mstke 6th: reminder next: rdn 12th: sn struggling: last whn p.u w tack problems bef 15th* 13/2

6m 32.4s (392.40)
WFA 5 from 7yo+ 3lb 8 Ran SP% **110.5**
CSF £17.44 CT £144.23 TOTE £3.00: £1.50, £1.90, £3.30; EX 10.40 Trifecta £51.20.
Owner John P McManus **Bred** Miss Noreen Hayes **Trained** Cheltenham, Gloucs

FOCUS
Due to rail movements this race was run over 30yds further than advertised. Fair chasing form, with the winner improving. The second is rated similar to her recent level.

3930 OPENBET MARES' H'CAP HURDLE (QUALIFIER FOR THE CHALLENGER MARES' HURDLE SERIES FINAL) (11 hdls) 2m 5f 55y
3:20 (3:20) (Class 4) (0-110,110) 4-Y-0+ £3,249 (£954; £477; £238)

Form RPR
5533 1 **Timon's Tara**[34] 3377 7-11-6 104.................. JackQuinlan 113
(Robin Dickin) *mid-div: hdwy 5th: rdn to chal 3 out: led appr last: styd on to assert fnl 100yds* 7/1[3]
-P45 2 1 1/2 **Dolly Diamond**[73] 2661 7-9-9 86.................. ArchieBellamy(7) 94
(Graeme McPherson) *mid-div: hdwy 4th: chsd ldr 7th: led narrowly appr 3 out where mstke: hdd appr last: no ex fnl 100yds* 10/1
6-60 3 8 **Lilywhite Gesture (IRE)**[39] 3234 7-9-13 90.................. GarethMalone(7) 89+
(Fergal O'Brien) *in rr: rdn after 8th: stl last of those continuing 3 out: styd on wl fr next: wnt 3rd flat* 50/1
F2P4 4 4 **Magic Money**[66] 2812 8-11-5 106.................. TomBellamy(3) 101
(Kim Bailey) *led tl rdn and hdd appr 3 out: sn outpcd by ldng pair: lost modest 3rd flat* 11/2[2]
-046 5 7 **Pink Tara**[11] 3743 5-11-4 105.................. CallumWhillans(3) 94
(Venetia Williams) *chsd ldrs: rdn after 8th: grad wknd fr 3 out* 25/1
-20P 6 shd **Aces Over Eights (IRE)**[27] 3498 7-11-4 102.................. JamieMoore 89
(Kerry Lee) *mid-div: hdwy to chse ldrs after 8th: sn one pce: stl modest 4th over last: wknd flat* 8/1
145/ 7 9 **Crazy (GER)**[21] 1321 7-10-12 96..................(p) AidanColeman 74
(David Dennis) *hld up: hdwy whn nt fluent 8th: rdn appr 3 out: sn wknd* 8/1
P434 8 3/4 **Mini Muck**[44] 3198 10-11-7 108.................. RyanHatch(3) 86
(Nigel Twiston-Davies) *chsd ldrs: rdn appr 3 out: sn wknd* 9/1
052P 9 36 **Midnight Gem**[85] 2413 6-11-7 105.................. DarylJacob 47
(Charlie Longsdon) *racd keenly: prom: hit 5th: wknd qckly appr 3 out: t.o* 7/1[3]
503P P **Floral Spinner**[18] 3622 9-11-7 110.................. RyanWhile(5)
(Bill Turner) *mid-div: rdn 7th and sn in rr: wl bhd whn p.u bef 3 out* 20/1
U03P P **Goodoldhonkytonk (IRE)**[37] 3312 8-11-4 102..................(b) LiamTreadwell
(James Evans) *t.k.h: prom to 4th: in rr fr 6th: t.o whn p.u bef 3 out* 20/1
440 P **Very Extravagant (IRE)**[25] 3516 7-11-12 110.................. NoelFehily
(Neil Mulholland) *mid-div: rdn 7th: struggling whn nt fluent next: sn lost tch: t.o whn p.u bef 3 out* 9/2[1]

5m 40.3s (25.50) **Going Correction** +1.125s/f (Heav) 12 Ran SP% **115.2**
Speed ratings (Par 105): **96,95,92,90,88 88,84,84,70, , ,**
CSF £68.47 CT £3203.51 TOTE £9.70: £2.80, £3.90, £13.30; EX 71.80 Trifecta £3412.30 Part won..
Owner Mark James **Bred** A P James **Trained** Alcester, Warwicks

FOCUS
Due to rail movements this race was run over 9yds further than advertised. A moderate mares' hurdle, the front pair coming clear. A step up from the winner.

3931 OPENBET H'CAP CHASE (12 fncs) 1m 7f 212y
3:55 (3:55) (Class 4) (0-115,113) 5-Y-0+ £4,548 (£1,335; £667; £333)

Form RPR
2-53 1 **Grimley Girl**[83] 2449 10-11-5 106.................. JamesDavies 118+
(Henry Oliver) *led to 2nd: styd prom: rdn after 9th: rallied to chal last: led flat: styd on wl* 6/1
423- 2 2 1/2 **Explained (IRE)**[522] 1394 9-11-12 113.................. RichardJohnson 120
(Tim Vaughan) *t.k.h in rr: hdwy to ld 2nd: j.lft and hdd 4 out: sn rdn: ev ch last: one pce flat* 14/1
5-23 3 1 3/4 **Frizzo (FR)**[64] 2837 9-11-12 113..................(b) NicodeBoinville 118
(Harry Whittington) *chsd ldrs: led 4 out: rdn next: jnd last: sn hdd and no ex* 7/2[1]
/4-4 4 4 1/2 **Agincourt Reef (IRE)**[57] 2957 7-11-9 110.................. JoshuaMoore 114+
(Gary Moore) *hld up: mstke 5th (water): hdwy after 9th: rdn 4 out: wknd appr last* 11/2[3]
0432 5 12 **Guanciale**[39] 3224 9-10-12 99.................. RobertDunne 89
(Dai Burchell) *in tch: hdwy 9th: rdn 3 out: wknd 2 out* 8/1
4531 6 2 1/4 **Zama Zama**[93] 2249 9-10-7 104..................(v) CianMaher(10) 94
(Evan Williams) *hld up: struggling after 9th: sn no ch* 6/1
0304 7 9 **Kerryhead Storm (IRE)**[37] 3313 11-11-3 111........(t) MrStanSheppard(7) 99
(Matt Sheppard) *hld up: reminder 4th: sme hdwy after 9th: wkng whn mstke 3 out: mstke 2 out* 9/2[2]
26- P **Lemon's Gent**[426] 2891 9-11-4 105..................(p) RichieMcLernon
(Paul Webber) *chsd ldrs to 9th: sn lost tch: wl bhd whn p.u bef 4 out* 11/1

4m 21.3s (22.80) **Going Correction** +1.55s/f (Heav) 8 Ran SP% **110.5**
Speed ratings: **105,103,102,100,94 93,89,**
CSF £72.30 CT £319.56 TOTE £9.60: £2.40, £2.80, £1.80; EX 100.00 Trifecta £289.90.
Owner R M Phillips **Bred** R M And Mrs Phillips **Trained** Abberley, Worcs

FOCUS
Due to rail movements this race was run over 15yds further than advertised. Quite a lowly chase but it was competitive. A big step up from the winner on her previous chase run.

3932 OPENBET AMATEUR RIDERS' H'CAP HURDLE (9 hdls) 1m 7f 169y
4:30 (4:30) (Class 4) (0-115,115) 4-Y-0+ £3,119 (£967; £483; £242)

Form RPR
05P4 1 **Hear The Chimes**[33] 3398 7-10-12 108.................. AidenBlakemore(7) 116+
(Shaun Harris) *hld up: hdwy 6th: rdn 2 out: chal last: sn led: r.o* 9/1
0-23 2 2 **Reyno**[111] 1931 8-10-13 102..................(bt) MissGAndrews 107
(Stuart Edmunds) *prom: chsd ldr 3rd: chal 3 out: led narrowly next: hdd jst after last: one pce* 15/2
4000 3 2 1/4 **Anton Dolin (IRE)**[81] 2492 8-9-13 95.................. MrHFNugent(7) 98
(Michael Mullineaux) *mid-div tl dropped to rr 5th: clsd again after next: rdn 3 out: 6th over last: styd on flat* 25/1
3514 4 1 1/2 **Hill Fort**[37] 3318 6-11-7 113..................(t) MrStanSheppard(3) 114
(Matt Sheppard) *chsd ldrs tl lost pl 4th: clsd again after 6th: rdn 3 out: styd on flat* 5/1[2]
02 5 1/2 **Un Prophete (FR)**[20] 3590 5-10-9 105.................. MissLMTurner(7) 107
(Venetia Williams) *mid-div: hdwy 5th: wnt 2nd after next: led appr 3 out to 2 out: no ex appr last: lost 2 pls flat* 5/1[2]

0321 **6** *1* **Danceintothelight**[50] 3098 9-10-9 **105**..............(t) MissAMcCain(7) 105
(Donald McCain) *led tl hdd appr 3 out: one pce* **7/2**[1]
0134 **7** *4 ½* **Worldor (FR)**[119] 1810 10-10-5 **101**..............(t) MrWGordon(7) 97+
(Alexandra Dunn) *hld up in rr: styd on steadily fr 2 out: nvr trbld ldrs* **20/1**
1F26 **8** *1 ½* **Scales (IRE)**[49] 3108 10-10-13 **109**.............. MissTWorsley(7) 103
(Kerry Lee) *hld up: pushed along 5th: hdwy after next: rdn 3 out: sn wknd* **7/1**[3]
4111 **9** *nse* **Grams And Ounces**[45] 1810 9-11-5 **115**..............(t) MissNatalieParker(7) 109
(Grace Harris) *hld up: hdwy after 6th: rdn 3 out: wknd 2 out* **16/1**
3633 **10** *15* **Akinspirit (IRE)**[17] 3108 12-10-7 **103**..............(t) MissRDagge(7) 82
(Nikki Evans) *t.k.h: chsd ldrs: rdn 3 out: wknd* **20/1**
2155 **11** *10* **Pandorica**[51] 3080 8-10-10 **104**..............(p) MrRhysHughes(5) 73
(Bernard Llewellyn) *chsd ldrs tl wknd 6th* **20/1**
0540 **12** *shd* **Sun Quest**[69] 2730 12-9-7 **89** oh22.............. MrBParis-Crofts(7) 58
(Steven Dixon) *mid-div: wknd after 6th* **100/1**
01/P **13** *24* **Adelar (GER)**[21] 3584 11-11-4 **114**.............. MrJSKnox(7) 59
(Venetia Williams) *hld up: sme hdwy after 6th: wknd 3 out: t.o* **22/1**
36-3 **P** **Acapulco Bay**[268] 237 12-9-13 **93**..............(p) MissJodieHughes(5)
(Dai Burchell) *chsd ldrs tl wknd after 6th: t.o whn p.u bef 3 out* **40/1**
5-50 **P** **Finch Flyer (IRE)**[47] 806 9-9-11 **89** oh14..............(p) MrAlexEdwards(3)
(Aytach Sadik) *chsd ldrs tl wknd after 6th: t.o whn p.u bef 3 out* **100/1**
4m 5.3s (15.80) **Going Correction** +1.125s/f (Heav) **15** Ran SP% **122.6**
Speed ratings (Par 105): **105,104,102,102,101 101,99,98,98,90 85,85,73, ,**
CSF £68.63 CT £1652.07 TOTE £14.10: £3.70, £2.40, £8.30; EX 113.00 Trifecta £1837.40.
Owner Miss H Ward **Bred** Mrs P Badger **Trained** Carburton, Notts

FOCUS
Due to rail movements this race was run over 9yds further than advertised. An open handicap. The winner was back to the level of last year's Huntingdon win.
T/Plt: £561.30 to a £1 stake. Pool: £53130.09 - 69.09 winning tickets T/Qpdt: £167.50 to a £1 stake. Pool: £4030.15 - 17.8 winning tickets **Richard Lowther**

3159 NEWCASTLE (L-H)

Wednesday, February 3

OFFICIAL GOING: Soft (heavy in places; 4.9)
Wind: Breezy, half behind Weather: Dry, fine

3933 PHOENIX SECURITY NOVICES' H'CAP CHASE (19 fncs) 2m 7f 91y
1:30 (1:30) (Class 4) (0-120,119) 5-Y-0+ **£3,994** (£1,240; £667)

Form RPR
0/13 **1** **Mysteree (IRE)**[26] 3507 8-11-3 119.............. GrantCockburn(5) 131
(Lucinda Russell) *pressed ldr and clr of rest to 1/2-way: led 10th: nt fluent and hdd 5 out: rallied and regained ld next: kpt on gamely u.p fr last* **2/1**[1]
-23U **2** *1* **The Orange Rogue (IRE)**[15] 3669 9-10-3 105.....[1] StephenMulqueen(5) 115
(N W Alexander) *led: hit 1st: hdd 10th: cl up: regained ld 5 out: hdd next but upsides wnr to last: styd on: hld nr fin* **3/1**[2]
-005 **3** *34* **Golans Choice (IRE)**[36] 3344 7-10-8 105.............. CraigNichol 85
(Rose Dobbin) *nt fluent first circ in rr: hdwy to chse ldrs 1/2-way: drvn and outpcd after 5 out: lost tch w ldrs fr next* **6/1**[3]
0-51 **P** **Redkalani (IRE)**[26] 3503 8-10-8 108.............. HarryChalloner(3)
(Keith Reveley) *nt fluent on occasions: chsd clr ldng pair: hdwy and cl up whn nt fluent 10th: hit and outpcd 12th: rallied: wknd 5 out: p.u 3 out* **2/1**[1]
6m 41.2s (18.70) **Going Correction** +0.80s/f (Soft) **4** Ran SP% **106.0**
Speed ratings: **99,98,86,**
CSF £7.76 TOTE £2.40; EX 5.10 Trifecta £23.20.
Owner Mrs Lynne Maclennan **Bred** Lar & Fiona Cloke **Trained** Arlary, Perth & Kinross

FOCUS
A chaseOnly card as the hurdles track was waterlogged. Approximately 35 yards was added to the race distance. The winning jockey described the ground as 'sticky' after this, which was run in a decidedly slow time - they went no great pace either but conditions were clearly testing. Neither of the newcomers to fences ultimately figured so that this novice handicap was even less competitive than the size of the field might suggest. The form is rated around the winner.

3934 PHOENIX EYE H'CAP CHASE (19 fncs) 2m 7f 91y
2:00 (2:00) (Class 4) (0-120,119) 5-Y-0+ **£6,498** (£1,908; £954; £477)

Form RPR
/26F **1** **Rocking Blues (FR)**[15] 3671 11-10-7 **110**.............. LorcanMurtagh(10) 131+
(Rose Dobbin) *t.k.h: trckd ldrs: wnt 2nd 6 out: led gng wl bef 4 out: clr on bridle next: easily* **11/4**[1]
-445 **2** *9* **Little Glenshee (IRE)**[18] 3631 10-11-8 **115**.............. LucyAlexander 124
(N W Alexander) *in tch on outside: drvn and outpcd 5 out: rallied to chse wnr next: plugged on fr 2 out: nt pce to chal* **9/2**
2321 **3** *36* **Presented (IRE)**[32] 3439 9-11-7 **119**.............. CallumBewley(5) 91
(Lisa Harrison) *w ldr: ev ch 5 out to bef next: outpcd 3 out: btn whn nt fluent 2 out* **4/1**[3]
5456 **4** *28* **Moyode Wood**[116] 1855 11-10-9 **102**..............(p) DannyCook 46
(Brian Ellison) *led: drvn along fnl circ: rallied: hdd bef 4 out: rdn and wknd bef next* **6/1**
4P-P **P** **Frank The Slink**[37] 3310 10-10-9 **109**.............. FinianO'Toole(7)
(Micky Hammond) *hld up in tch: hit 10th: drvn and outpcd fr 13th: lost tch and p.u bef 2 out* **11/1**
U321 **P** **Total Assets**[36] 3341 8-11-4 **111**.............. BrianHughes
(Simon Waugh) *in tch: hdwy to chse ldrs 1/2-way: lost grnd 12th: rallied whn nt fluent 6 out: wknd bef 4 out: t.o whn p.u bef 2 out* **7/2**[2]
6m 38.2s (15.70) **Going Correction** +0.80s/f (Soft) **6** Ran SP% **109.7**
Speed ratings: **104,100,88,78,**
CSF £14.68 TOTE £3.40: £2.30, £2.40; EX 13.10 Trifecta £84.40.
Owner The Friday Lions **Bred** Mme Genevieve Mongin **Trained** South Hazelrigg, Northumbria

FOCUS
Approximately 35 yards was added to the race distance. A potentially fair race for the grade, as two of these had won last time and another might have done had he not fallen. A step up from the winner.

3935 HOMECARE PLUS NOVICES' CHASE (12 fncs 1 omitted) 2m 75y
2:35 (2:35) (Class 4) 5-Y-0+ **£3,898** (£1,144; £572)

Form RPR
-531 **1** **Pain Au Chocolat (FR)**[46] 3153 5-11-2 140.............. HarrySkelton 150+
(Dan Skelton) *mde all: drew clr fr 5 out: nt fluent 3 out and last: v easily* **2/7**[1]
1-3F **2** *20* **Captain Hox (IRE)**[17] 3652 7-10-12 125..............(t) BrianHughes 116
(Patrick Griffin, Ire) *nt fluent on occasions: prom: hdwy to chse wnr 7th: outpcd after 5 out: no imp fr next* **9/2**[2]
3622 **3** *25* **Quick Decisson (IRE)**[15] 3670 8-10-7 111.............. GrantCockburn(5) 99
(Stuart Coltherd) *chsd wnr to 7th: drvn and struggling fr 5 out* **10/1**[3]
4m 27.1s (6.00) **Going Correction** +0.80s/f (Soft)
WFA 5 from 7yo+ 1lb **3** Ran SP% **105.0**
Speed ratings: **117,107,94**
CSF £1.90 TOTE £1.20; EX 1.60 Trifecta £2.20.
Owner Mike And Eileen Newbould **Bred** Mme Karine Du Pont De Romemont **Trained** Alcester, Warwicks

FOCUS
Got The Nac's absence left this an uncompetitive novice chase, which was run over approximately 20 yards further than the usual distance, with the cross fence omitted due to low sun. A smart effort from the winner and the form could rate higher.

3936 NORTHRIDGE NOVICES' H'CAP CHASE (15 fncs 1 omitted) 2m 4f 19y
3:10 (3:10) (Class 3) (0-135,130) 5-Y-0+ **£9,097** (£2,671; £1,335; £667)

Form RPR
0/P2 **1** **Special Catch (IRE)**[55] 2981 9-11-0 **125**.............. HarryChalloner(3) 133+
(Keith Reveley) *in tch: stdy hdwy to chse ldrs 1/2-way: nt fluent 9th: pushed along and outpcd bef 4 out: rallied and led next: sn hrd pressed: pushed out fr last* **11/4**[2]
1-P3 **2** *1 ¼* **Central Flame**[18] 3627 8-11-3 **130**.............. MissCWalton(5) 138+
(James Walton) *led to after 6th: chsd ldr tl mstke 8th: rallied on outside and led bef 4 out: hdd next: upsides w wnr to bef last: kpt on run-in* **4/1**[3]
0013 **3** *26* **Tikkandemickey (IRE)**[59] 2934 10-10-12 **125**.............. DaraghBourke(5) 104
(Raymond Shiels) *cl up: hdwy to chal 5th: led after next: hdd bef 4 out: rdn and wknd after next* **6/1**
21P2 **4** *¾* **Present Flight (IRE)**[36] 3341 7-10-10 **118**..............(t) DerekFox 96
(Lucinda Russell) *hld up in last pl: stdy hdwy 5 out: effrt and pushed along next: edgd lft and sn outpcd: btn fnl 2* **11/2**
4P-0 **5** *1* **Spanish Fleet**[18] 3630 8-11-7 **129**..............(p) BrianHughes 106
(John Wade) *cl up on outside: wnt 2nd 8th to bef 4 out: rdn and sn wknd* **14/1**
15F1 **P** **Lord Wishes (IRE)**[36] 3345 9-11-5 **127**..............(p) BrianHarding
(James Ewart) *chsd ldrs: nt fluent 6th: sn drvn: struggling fr next: lost tch and p.u 6 out* **5/2**[1]
5m 38.9s (11.70) **Going Correction** +0.80s/f (Soft) **6** Ran SP% **111.6**
Speed ratings: **108,107,97,96,96**
CSF £14.04 TOTE £3.60: £1.90, £1.80; EX 18.00 Trifecta £74.10.
Owner Mike Browne & William McKeown **Bred** Thistletown Stud **Trained** Lingdale, Redcar & Cleveland

FOCUS
Several potentially fair chasers in this novice handicap, which had approximately 30 yards added to the race distance, with the cross fence omitted due to low sun. A big chase best from the winner.

3937 BAR B H'CAP CHASE (16 fncs) 2m 4f 19y
3:45 (3:53) (Class 4) (0-110,110) 5-Y-0+ **£3,898** (£1,144; £572; £286)

Form RPR
23B1 **1** **Halo Moon**[6] 3820 8-11-8 106 7ex..............(p) MarkQuinlan 120+
(Neil Mulholland) *hld up: blkd 8th: mstke 11th: smooth hdwy to ld appr 2 out: qcknd clr on bridle bef last: readily* **7/4**[1]
-456 **2** *3* **Bonzo Bing (IRE)**[67] 2788 8-11-12 110.............. HenryBrooke 112
(Martin Todhunter) *cl up: led 9th: rdn bef 4 out: hdd appr 2 out: plugged on fr last: no ch w ready wnr* **9/1**
P6/P **3** *½* **Tipsy Dara (IRE)**[36] 3341 12-10-7 96.............. StephenMulqueen(5) 98
(N W Alexander) *led to 5th: cl up: lft in ld 7th: hdd 9th: styd upsides ldr to bef 2 out: kpt on fr last: no imp* **25/1**
4-54 **4** *½* **Oil Burner**[15] 3671 11-10-3 92.............. GrantCockburn(5) 93
(Stuart Coltherd) *hld up: stdy hdwy to chse ldrs after 5 out: pushed along next: kpt on fr last* **11/2**[3]
/026 **5** *8* **Joseph Mercer (IRE)**[26] 3507 9-10-8 92..............(p) JonathanEngland 87
(Tina Jackson) *bhd: outpcd 5th: rallied 1/2-way: rdn and effrt bef 4 out: 5th and no imp whn blnd 2 out* **16/1**
-113 **6** *26* **What A Dream**[36] 3345 10-10-6 95..............(tp) JamieHamilton(5) 62
(Alison Hamilton) *trckd ldrs to 5 out: rdn and wknd bef next: t.o* **10/1**
U446 **7** *25* **Tiny Dancer (IRE)**[12] 3727 8-10-13 97..............(v) BrianHughes 39
(Chris Grant) *prom: stdy hdwy 1/2-way: rdn and wknd bef 4 out: t.o* **10/1**
24P6 **F** **Amethyst Rose (IRE)**[36] 3343 9-11-3 108.............. SamColtherd(7)
(Stuart Coltherd) *hld up: fell 7th* **22/1**
0544 **R** **Under The Red Sky (IRE)**[14] 3679 9-9-7 84 oh11(p) ThomasDowson(7)
(Kenny Johnson) *racd wd: prom: hdwy to ld 5th: tk wrong crse 7th* **16/1**
564 **U** **Nakadam (FR)**[32] 3437 6-10-6 95..............(t) CallumBewley(5)
(R Mike Smith) *hld up: stdy hdwy on outside 1/2-way: prom whn blnd and uns rdr 5 out* **5/1**[2]
5m 44.8s (17.60) **Going Correction** +0.80s/f (Soft) **10** Ran SP% **116.6**
Speed ratings: **96,94,94,94,91 80,70,**
CSF £18.54 CT £295.96 TOTE £2.60: £1.80, £2.80, £3.80; EX 20.40 Trifecta £351.60.
Owner Level Par Racing **Bred** David Jenks **Trained** Limpley Stoke, Wilts
■ Stewards' Enquiry : Thomas Dowson 12-day ban: took wrong course (Feb 17-28)

FOCUS
Approximately 30 yards were added to the distance. Several of these had something to prove in a handicap less competitive than the size of the field might suggest. Plenty were still in contention five out, but that was a reflection of the fact they had gone no more than a fair gallop to that point. The easy winner was value for further.

3938 YOLO H'CAP CHASE (13 fncs) 2m 75y
4:20 (4:22) (Class 4) (0-110,108) 5-Y-0+ **£3,898** (£1,144; £572; £286)

Form RPR
5624 **1** **Rosquero (FR)**[14] 3683 11-9-7 82 oh3..............(b) MrWHRReed(7) 93+
(Kenny Johnson) *in tch: hdwy 1/2-way: led bef 4 out: sn pushed along: idled run-in: kpt on* **20/1**
2315 **2** *1 ¼* **Retrieve The Stick**[36] 3343 7-11-12 108..............(b) BrianHughes 114
(Malcolm Jefferson) *nt fluent on occasions: hld up: hit 4th: hdwy 5 out: rdn to chse wnr whn nt fluent 3 out: kpt on fr last* **9/2**[3]
55PF **3** *6* **Pekanheim (IRE)**[15] 3670 8-11-9 105.............. HenryBrooke 105
(Martin Todhunter) *hld up: stdy hdwy 5 out: rdn next: kpt on fr 2 out: nt rch first two* **18/1**
3525 **4** *7* **Pamak D'Airy (FR)**[32] 3441 13-11-0 103..............(p) FinianO'Toole(7) 97
(Henry Hogarth) *hld up: stdy hdwy bef 4 out: pushed along and lft 6 l 3rd next: outpcd bef 2 out* **14/1**
2211 **5** *20* **Willie Hall**[15] 3670 12-10-9 96.............. CallumBewley(5) 72
(Lisa Harrison) *hld up: stdy hdwy 5 out: checked and rdn next: sn btn* **5/1**
FPP0 **P** **Suprise Vendor (IRE)**[36] 3346 10-11-0 103.............. SamColtherd(7)
(Stuart Coltherd) *prom: outpcd 5th: struggilng fr next: lost tch and p.u 4 out* **9/1**

004F **U** **Gin Cobbler**[20] 3589 10-10-8 97.................................. ThomasDowson(7)
(Victor Thompson) *cl up: led bef 4th to 6th: chsd ldr to after 5 out: 6 l sixth and outpcd whn fell next* **20/1**

4-PF **F** **Home For Tea**[14] 3683 7-10-0 82 oh4.......................(p) CraigNichol
(Keith Dalgleish) *prom on ins: stdy hdwy and ev ch briefly bef 4 out: nrly 4 l 3rd and outpcd whn fell next* **4/1**[2]

0-U1 **U** **Clan Chief**[46] 3161 7-10-11 93.................................. LucyAlexander
(N W Alexander) *nt fluent on occasions: led to bef 4th: led 6th: mstke next: hdd bef 4 out: 7 l 5th and outpcd whn hmpd and uns rdr next* **11/4**[1]

4m 32.2s (11.10) **Going Correction** +0.80s/f (Soft) **9** Ran **SP% 113.0**
Speed ratings: **104,103,100,96,86 , , ,**
CSF £107.35 CT £1659.14 TOTE £17.80: £4.20, £1.90, £4.20; EX 143.80 Trifecta £2216.60.
Owner Alan Kidd Dave Bamlet Racing R Johnson **Bred** Denis Fontaine **Trained** Newburn, Tyne & Wear

■ The first training success for Kenny Johnson, who took over the licence from his father Bob.

FOCUS
Not a bad race for a 0-110, with several of interest at the weights. Approximately 20 yards was added to the distance of a race in which the early leaders set a strong pace, which helped those coming from behind. The idling winner was value for further.
T/Plt: £232.90 to a £1 stake. Pool: £49,803.04 - 156.10 winning units. T/Qpdt: £33.80 to a £1 stake. Pool: £4,421.59 - 96.60 winning units. **Richard Young**

3939 - 3945a (Foreign Racing) - See Raceform Interactive

3497 TOWCESTER (R-H)
Thursday, February 4

OFFICIAL GOING: Soft (7.2)
Wind: breezy Weather: overcast; 12 degrees

3946 TOTEPOOL RACING'S BIGGEST SUPPORTER H'CAP HURDLE (11 hdls) 2m 4f 217y
1:10 (1:11) (Class 5) (0-100,96) 4-Y-O+ **£3,573** (£1,049; £524; £262)

Form RPR

0-00 **1** **Navanman (IRE)**[55] 3011 7-11-8 **95**.................................. KieronEdgar(3) 109+
(David Pipe) *hld up in midfield: stl 8th 3 out but gng strly: wnt 2nd home turn: led travelling best bef last where sltly awkward: sn pushed clr: readily* **6/1**

0024 **2** *5* **Distant Sound (IRE)**[112] 1927 9-10-10 **80**.......................(b) MichealNolan 87+
(Grace Harris) *trckd ldrs: effrt 3 out and sn led gng wl: rdn and hdd bef last: sn outpcd by wnr but clr of rest* **13/2**

006 **3** *13* **Ceann Sibheal (IRE)**[49] 3126 7-11-11 **95**.......................... GavinSheehan 88
(Warren Greatrex) *towards rr: rdn and effrt bef 8th: tk mod 3rd after 2 out: plugged on* **5/1**[2]

3P23 **4** *2 ½* **Ballochmyle (IRE)**[29] 3489 6-11-1 **85**................................(t) JackQuinlan 76
(Caroline Fryer) *prom: rdn and ev ch 3 out: 12 l 3rd and fading next* **11/2**[3]

4311 **5** *5* **Hassadin**[7] 3821 10-11-5 **96**..(p) HarryCobden(7) 81
(Michael Blake) *led tl jnd 4th: hdd 6th: rdn bef 3 out: wknd tamely* **9/4**[1]

050 **6** *6* **Jopaan (IRE)**[91] 2299 9-9-9 **70** oh1................................(t) GaryDerwin(5) 49
(Brian Barr) *chsd ldrs tl rdn and fdd bef 3 out* **40/1**

-PP0 **7** *2 ¾* **Memory Of Light (IRE)**[36] 3369 7-10-7 **77**.....................(t) BrendanPowell 53
(Claire Dyson) *hld up in midfield: effrt 8th: pressed ldrs briefly 3 out: sn rdn and struggling* **16/1**

5/PP **8** *nse* **Subtle Approach (IRE)**[10] 3771 11-9-13 **72**......................(p) JamesBanks(3) 48
(Emma Baker) *chsd ldrs: effrt 8th: cl up but rdn 3 out: sn dropped out* **100/1**

0165 **9** *10* **Monty's Revenge (IRE)**[49] 3131 11-10-1 **71**.......................(p) IanPopham 37
(Martin Keighley) *cl 2nd: disp ld 4th tl led 6th: rdn and hdd after 3 out: dropped out qckly* **10/1**

500 **P** **Tisfreetdream (IRE)**[10] 3771 15-10-7 **80**.......................(tp) TomBellamy(3)
(Peter Pritchard) *wl bhd: rdn and toiling after 7th: t.o and p.u 2 out* **50/1**

4-4P **P** **Bob Will (IRE)**[257] 438 11-10-0 **70** oh7.........................(bt) WillKennedy
(John Flint) *bhd: struggling bef 3 out: t.o and p.u next* **40/1**

02P **P** **Duc De Seville (IRE)**[13] 3724 4-9-12 **86**.......................(p) GrahamCarson(7)
(Michael Chapman) *dropped to rr 5th: rdn and wknd bef 8th: t.o and p.u 2 out* **66/1**

0305 **P** **Minmore Grey (IRE)**[54] 3043 7-11-0 **87**.......................(p) ThomasGarner(3)
(Nick Lampard) *lost tch u.p bef 6th: t.o and p.u 8th* **50/1**

5m 33.4s (6.20) **Going Correction** -0.05s/f (Good)
WFA 4 from 6yo+ 10lb **13** Ran **SP% 116.7**
Speed ratings (Par 103): **86,84,79,78,76 74,72,72,69, ,**
CSF £42.60 CT £210.85 TOTE £8.90: £5.10, £3.00, £1.70; EX 63.10 Trifecta £367.30.
Owner Mrs Yvonne Fleet **Bred** Aidan Ryan **Trained** Nicholashayne, Devon

FOCUS
Hurdles course on the inside line, on fresher ground. This didn't look an overly strong race despite the number of runners, and two pulled a long way in front of the remainder. The cosy winner improved to the level of his bumper form.

3947 HAYGAIN HAY STEAMERS CLEAN HEALTHY FORAGE MARES' NOVICES' HURDLE (10 hdls) 2m 3f 34y
1:40 (1:43) (Class 4) 4-Y-O+ **£3,898** (£1,144; £572; £286)

Form RPR

04-2 **1** **Caitys Joy (GER)**[20] 3612 6-11-0 0................................ DarylJacob 121+
(Warren Greatrex) *trckd ldrs tl led 5th: mstke 3 out: steadily drew clr: 15 l ahd last: v easily* **4/5**[1]

2 *9* **Bagging Turf (IRE)**[327] 6-11-0 0................................ JamieMoore 105+
(Gary Moore) *tall chser type: cl up: rdn to go 2nd sn after 2 out: wnr already clr: styd on steadily wout threatening* **20/1**

23 **3** *7* **Graceful Legend**[35] 3381 5-10-11 0................................ RyanHatch(3) 100
(Ben Case) *midfield: rdn and effrt 7th: wnt 2nd 3 out: u.p home turn: tired whn hit 2 out: sn lost 2nd: v tired whn mstke last* **14/1**

4 *44* **On The Couch (IRE)**[277] 7-11-0 0................................ JakeGreenall 53
(Sam Thomas) *midfield: struggling whn ldng trio wnt wl clr fr 3 out: sn t.o* **66/1**

6 **5** *½* **Princess Tiana (IRE)**[79] 2561 5-11-0 0........................... RichieMcLernon 53
(Jonjo O'Neill) *chsd ldrs: rdn and wknd bef 3 out: sn t.o* **50/1**

30P **6** *7* **Midnight Folie**[73] 2690 6-11-0 0................................ NicodeBoinville 46
(Ben Pauling) *led 2nd tl 5th: wknd rapidly fr 3 out: 30 l 4th and v tired home turn: continued t.o* **16/1**

120 **7** *12* **Mozo**[50] 3110 5-11-0 0................................ ConorO'Farrell 34
(David Pipe) *sn pushed along: j. slowly 3rd: nvr travelling and wl bhd: mstke 6th: t.o fr 7th* **11/2**[3]

4P **P** **Zarosa (IRE)**[40] 3221 7-11-0 0................................ JackQuinlan
(John Berry) *j.lft 3rd: midfield early: struggling after 6th: t.o and p.u 2 out* **66/1**

63-P **P** **Triumvirate**[34] 3398 6-11-0 105................................(p) LiamTreadwell
(Venetia Williams) *led tl 2nd: cl up tl lost pl and j. slowly 6th: t.o and p.u 2 out* **16/1**

P **Felice (IRE)**[54] 6-10-7 0................................ GLavery(7)
(Scott Dixon) *chsd ldrs early: struggling fr 7th: t.o and p.u 2 out* **100/1**

0-45 **P** **Lady Persephone (FR)**[68] 2778 5-11-0 0................................ DenisO'Regan
(Alan King) *chsd ldrs tl 7th: rdn fdd bef next: t.o and v tired whn p.u 2 out* **4/1**[2]

0 **P** **Ann Maries Reject (IRE)**[10] 3773 7-10-11 0................................ ThomasGarner(3)
(Brian Barr) *dropped to rr and rdn after 5th: t.o and p.u 2 out* **100/1**

26 **P** **Miss Giselle**[35] 3381 7-10-7 0................................ HarrisonBeswick(7)
(Sam Thomas) *nvr travelling: sn lost tch and rdn: t.o fr 5th: p.u 2 out* **66/1**

5m 5.1s (-4.50) **Going Correction** -0.05s/f (Good) **13** Ran **SP% 122.6**
Speed ratings (Par 105): **107,103,100,81,81 78,73, , , ,**
CSF £22.85 TOTE £1.60: £1.10, £5.20, £2.80; EX 18.50 Trifecta £159.80.
Owner Diamond Club **Bred** Gestut Erlenhof **Trained** Upper Lambourn, Berks

FOCUS
Hurdles course on inside line, on fresher ground. Not many of these made any great appeal, so this is weak form behind the winner. She set a decent standard and can win again.

3948 SKYBET CHELTENHAM PREVIEW HERE MARCH 7TH H'CAP CHASE (17 fncs) 3m 102y
2:10 (2:12) (Class 5) (0-100,100) 5-Y-O+ **£3,573** (£1,049; £524; £262)

Form RPR

1243 **1** **Cheat The Cheater (IRE)**[17] 3663 9-11-1 **89**.............(tp) BrendanPowell 106
(Claire Dyson) *rdn to begin: prom: 2nd 9th tl 3 out: sn 4th and looking lazy: rallied to ld bef last: sn plodded clr* **6/1**

P5P2 **2** *8* **Basford Ben**[20] 3609 8-11-12 **100**.......................(b) SeanQuinlan 110
(Jennie Candlish) *led at decent pce: pushed along 8th: pckd bdly 12th: drvn and hdd after 3 out: btn between last two but regained 2nd fnl 75yds* **9/2**[1]

4656 **3** *2 ½* **Jolly Boys Outing (IRE)**[49] 3131 13-9-12 **75**....................... BenPoste(3) 82
(Rosemary Gasson) *trckd ldrs: effrt 11th: rdn to ld after 3 out: hdd and edgd rt and slow last: plodded on and lost 2nd cl home* **12/1**

-23P **4** *shd* **Nalim (IRE)**[65] 2836 10-10-13 **87**.......................(v[1]) JonathanEngland 92
(Harriet Bethell) *bhd: reluctant early: hdwy 9th and sn prom: rdn and ev ch bef 3 out: sn fnd little: btn after next but nrly snatched 3rd* **11/2**[3]

3U34 **5** *24* **Georgian King**[49] 3127 13-11-5 **100**.......................(p) TomHumphries(7) 85
(Martin Keighley) *rn in snatches early: 2nd 6th tl 9th: rdn and wknd and hit 11th: t.o bef 2 out* **5/1**[2]

PP2P **P** **Mansonien L'As (FR)**[40] 3222 10-10-10 **84**.......................(tp) WillKennedy
(Donald McCain) *blnd 2nd: prom: rdn and ev ch nring 3 out: stopped v qckly: t.o and p.u next* **8/1**

6004 **P** **Carhue (IRE)**[52] 3081 9-9-8 **75**.......................... MrMartinMcIntyre(7)
(Sheila Lewis) *bhd and nt travelling: t.o 9th: blnd 11th: p.u 12th* **12/1**

P-35 **F** **Admiral Blake**[8] 3803 9-10-10 **84**................................ RobertDunne
(Laura Young) *fell 1st* **13/2**

-335 **P** **Mr McGregor (IRE)**[9] 3793 8-10-10 **91**.......................(bt) FinianO'Toole(7)
(Heather Dalton) *chsd ldrs: mstke 10th and rdn: nt gng wl after: lost tch 12th: t.o 3 out: p.u next* **8/1**

6m 51.9s (15.00) **Going Correction** +0.375s/f (Yiel) **9** Ran **SP% 115.5**
Speed ratings: **90,87,86,86,78 , , ,**
CSF £33.89 CT £314.87 TOTE £4.60: £1.80, £1.80, £3.50; EX 14.50 Trifecta £533.20.
Owner Pink Fizz Fillies **Bred** Mrs Elizabeth Grant **Trained** Cleeve Prior, Worcs

■ Stewards' Enquiry : Brendan Powell two-day ban: used whip above permitted level (Feb 18-19)

FOCUS
Chase course dolled out wide on all bends, adding approximately 55yds to this race distance. A moderate event for stayers. The winner's Lingfield form could be rated to this sort of level.

3949 HAYGAIN HAY STEAMERS CLEAN HEALTHY FORAGE "NATIONAL HUNT" NOVICES' HURDLE (8 hdls) 1m 7f 181y
2:40 (2:41) (Class 4) 4-Y-O+ **£3,898** (£1,144; £572; £286)

Form RPR

-613 **1** **Flashjack (IRE)**[36] 3363 6-11-10 127.......................... JakeGreenall 130+
(Henry Daly) *tall: confidently rdn in midfield: 4th and gng wl 3 out: effrt to ld between last two: sn pushed clr* **6/4**[2]

2 *3 ¼* **Mahlers Star (IRE)**[309] 6-10-12 0.......................... JakeHodson(5) 115
(David Bridgwater) *prom: led bef 2 out: sn rdn: hdd between last two: comf outpcd by wnr* **16/1**

1-01 **3** *7* **Suit Yourself (IRE)**[53] 3054 7-11-10 0.......................(t) BarryGeraghty 117
(Jonjo O'Neill) *towards rr: rdn 4th: nt fluent next: sme hdwy after 3 out but nvr gng wl enough: drvn into mod 3rd after last* **5/4**[1]

P26P **4** *nk* **Christmas Twenty (IRE)**[34] 3420 6-11-3 111.......................(p) BrendanPowell 109
(Stuart Edmunds) *mounted outside paddock: trckd ldr tl led 3 out: rdn and hdd bef 2 out: wkng whn edgd lft between last two: lost 3rd flat* **10/1**

0-54 **5** *16* **Busy Baro (IRE)**[27] 3506 6-11-3 0.......................... CharliePoste 94
(Paul Cowley) *led tl 3 out: rdn and fdd tamely bef next* **25/1**

6 *12* **King Cool**[95] 5-11-3 0.......................... JamieMoore 80
(Gary Moore) *a in fnl trio: struggling bef 3 out* **13/2**[3]

0P **7** *13* **Paradis Blanc (FR)**[38] 3316 5-10-12 0.......................... JamieBargary(5) 67
(Nigel Twiston-Davies) *towards rr: losing tch whn mstke 3 out: t.o: fin lame* **50/1**

3-5P **P** **Real Gone Kid**[60] 2928 5-11-3 0.......................... AndrewTinkler
(Martin Keighley) *small: j.lft 1st: reminder 2nd: cl up tl lost pl 4th: nt fluent 5th: t.o whn mstke 2 out: p.u last* **40/1**

4m 3.6s (-4.30) **Going Correction** -0.05s/f (Good) **8** Ran **SP% 121.0**
Speed ratings (Par 105): **108,106,102,102,94 88,82,**
CSF £24.97 TOTE £2.40: £1.10, £3.00, £1.10; EX 24.40 Trifecta £62.40.
Owner Charles Whittaker & Belinda Clarke **Bred** Seamus Murphy **Trained** Stanton Lacy, Shropshire

■ Stewards' Enquiry : Jamie Bargary vet said gelding was lame off-fore

FOCUS
Hurdles course on inside line, on fresher ground. The betting suggested only two of these could be seriously fancied, but one of those principals failed to run up to his best. The winner was back to the level of his Leicester win.

3950 TOTEPOOLLIVEINFO.COM H'CAP HURDLE (8 hdls) 1m 7f 181y
3:15 (3:15) (Class 4) (0-110,110) 4-Y-O+ **£6,498** (£1,908; £954; £477)

Form RPR

52P6 **1** **Mondo Cane (IRE)**[19] 3628 9-11-4 **102**.......................(p) AdamPogson 111+
(Charles Pogson) *settled trcking ldrs: wnt 2nd bef 5th: chsd ldr wl bef 2 out: sn rdn: styd on gamely to ld fnl 50yds* **7/1**

1104 **2** *½* **Hope's Wishes**[40] 3223 6-11-0 **105**.......................... HarryCobden(7) 112
(Barry Brennan) *trckd ldrs: effrt 5th: disp ld next: forged 2 l clr: rdn and over 1 l ahd whn hit last: kpt on tl hdd 50yds out* **11/2**[3]

/0-P 3 13 **Seymour Eric**[35] 3377 11-11-12 **110**....................(p) IanPopham 104
(Martin Keighley) *led tl 2nd: prom tl 3rd and rdn 3 out: 10 l 3rd and wkng next* **13/2**

600P 4 6 **Romeo Americo (IRE)**[34] 3414 9-11-6 **104**.................. AndrewThornton 92
(Seamus Mullins) *detached in last pl: btn bef 3 out: plodded into remote 4th 2 out: no ch* **10/1**

-226 5 1 1/4 **Georgieshore (IRE)**[19] 3619 8-10-11 **102**........... WilliamFeatherstone(7) 89
(Zoe Davison) *nt a fluent: mde most fr 2nd tl drvn after 5th: dropped out qckly next* **8/1**

6530 6 17 **Palmaria**[67] 2812 6-11-4 **102**.................................1 JamesBest 72
(Caroline Keevil) *blnd 2nd: prom: rdn 5th: struggling next: b.b.v* **20/1**

0P11 R **Notebook**[8] 3807 5-10-7 **98** 7ex..........................(p) ThomasCheesman(7)
(Martin Smith) *ref to r* **9/4**[1]

63F0 R **Newton Geronimo**[29] 3487 7-11-11 **109**.......................... NicodeBoinville
(Ben Pauling) *taken to post v early: unruly and ref to r* **5/1**[2]

4m 8.3s (0.40) **Going Correction** -0.05s/f (Good) **8 Ran SP% 113.6**
Speed ratings (Par 105): **97,96,90,87,86 78,,**
CSF £44.52 CT £261.66 TOTE £8.90: £2.90, £1.90, £2.60; EX 50.80 Trifecta £385.20.
Owner C T Pogson **Bred** David And Ann Mooney **Trained** Farnsfield, Notts

FOCUS
Hurdles course on inside line, on fresher ground. The start for this modest handicap had a bizarre look to it, as market leader \bNotebook\p went left as the field jumped off and flatly refused to take part, while \bNewton Geronimo\p, who had a handler at the start, never went a yard either. The latter had been stood away from his rivals. A hurdles pb from the winner.

3951 FOLLOW @TOTEPOOL ON TWITTER CONDITIONAL JOCKEYS' H'CAP CHASE (11 fncs) 2m 70y
3:50 (3:50) (Class 5) (0-100,100) 5-Y-0+ **£3,249** (£954; £477; £238)

Form RPR

4-PP 1 **High Aspirations (IRE)**[34] 3421 8-9-12 **75**.....................1 HarryCobden(3) 84
(Michael Blake) *cl up in 3rd or 4th pl: drvn 2 out: led bef last: a jst holding chalr flat: all out* **10/3**[1]

6-5P 2 1 1/4 **Edlomond (IRE)**[38] 3314 10-11-4 **92**....................(t) JakeHodson 101
(Bill Turner) *racd wd: trckd ldrs: mstke 4th: wnt 2nd bef 3 out: urged along and ev ch appr last: n.g.t flat* **10/1**

PP2U 3 5 **Lamb's Cross**[45] 3199 10-10-8 **82**.......................... HarryBannister 85
(Brian Barr) *led: rdn 2 out: hdd bef last: plugged on same pce flat* **11/1**

31-P 4 14 **Princesse Fleur**[35] 3387 8-11-8 **96**.......................... ThomasGarner 87
(Michael Scudamore) *t.k.h towards rr: effrt bef 3 out: sn wknd: tired jump last* **10/1**

3P-P 5 27 **Castletown (IRE)**[23] 3572 8-11-9 **100**......................1 MikeyHamill(3) 62
(Sheila Lewis) *taken down early: last whn j. bdly rt 4th and lost tch: mstke next: nt keen: hmpd 8th: t.o next* **8/1**

1FP1 6 31 **Mr Bachster (IRE)**[28] 3497 11-11-12 **100**....................(p) TomBellamy 61
(Kerry Lee) *pressed ldr tl rdn bef 3 out: nt run on: remote whn rdr nrly c off at last and virtually p.u* **4/1**[2]

0PP0 F **Wicklewood**[70] 2736 10-11-9 **100**...................(bt) ThomasCheesman(3)
(Mark Gillard) *chsd ldrs: 5th and rdn 7th: becoming outpcd whn fell next* **20/1**

2-31 P **Olympian Boy (IRE)**[22] 3586 12-11-8 **99**...................(t) KillianMoore(3)
(Sophie Leech) *towards rr: rdn and struggling after 8th: t.o and p.u 2 out* **9/2**[3]

025U U **Lost In Newyork (IRE)**[34] 3419 9-10-0 **74**..................(p) ConorShoemark
(Nick Kent) *bhd: rdn 7th: struggling whn bdly hmpd and uns rdr next* **10/1**

3P-P P **Up Your Game (IRE)**[64] 2851 8-10-3 **77**.........................(t) RyanHatch
(Roy Brotherton) *midfield: 6th and rdn and outpcd whn almost uns rdr 3 out: t.o and p.u next* **25/1**

0-40 P **Big Night Out**[57] 2976 10-11-2 **90**..............................(t) KieronEdgar
(Laura Hurley) *dropped to rr after 4th: mstke 6th and struggling: t.o and p.u last* **20/1**

4m 22.1s (6.00) **Going Correction** +0.375s/f (Yiel) **11 Ran SP% 121.3**
Speed ratings: **100,99,96,89,76 60,,,,,**
CSF £36.58 CT £339.96 TOTE £5.60: £2.20, £3.40, £3.50; EX 56.60 Trifecta £490.80.
Owner Mrs J M Haines **Bred** David Moran **Trained** Trowbridge, Wilts

FOCUS
Chase course dolled out wide on all bends, adding approximately 30yds to this distance. With the winner officially rated just 75, this is moderate form, and not a race to be confident about.

3952 HAYGAIN HAY STEAMERS CLEAN HEALTHY FORAGE INTERMEDIATE OPEN NATIONAL HUNT FLAT RACE 1m 7f 181y
4:25 (4:25) (Class 6) 4-6-Y-0 **£1,949** (£572; £286; £143)

Form RPR

3 1 **Informationisking (IRE)**[35] 3388 5-11-3 **0**.................... BarryGeraghty 113+
(Alan King) *tall scopey: chsd ldrs: effrt over 3f out: sn rdn: led wl over 1f out: in command fnl f and styd on gamely* **4/1**[3]

1 2 1 3/4 **Ballymalin (IRE)**[26] 3522 6-11-7 **0**.............................. RyanHatch(3) 118
(Nigel Twiston-Davies) *workmanlike chser type: prom: led over 3f out: sn rdn: hdd wl over 1f out: kpt on steadily whn hld ins fnl f* **85/40**[2]

2 3 1 1/2 **Boudry (FR)**[84] 2460 5-11-3 **0**.................................... GavinSheehan 110
(Warren Greatrex) *prom: last of four gng clr over 2f out: 3rd and styd on nicely although hld ins fnl f* **7/4**[1]

063 4 3 1/4 **Druids Lodge**[90] 2330 5-11-3 **0**................................. LeightonAspell 106
(Don Cantillon) *hld up: tk clsr order 1/2-way: shkn up 4f out: 5th rdn and outpcd home turn: kpt on wout threatening ins fnl f* **20/1**

5 1 **Jot'em Down (IRE)**[263] 5-10-12 **0**.............................. JakeHodson(5) 105
(David Bridgwater) *cl up: wnt 2nd over 3f out: sn rdn: lost 2nd wl over 1f out: no ex ins fnl f* **10/1**

6 15 **Arian (IRE)** 4-10-0 **0**... WillKennedy 73
(John Flint) *midfield: wl in tch tl drvn over 3f out: wknd over 2f out: fin tired* **14/1**

602 7 22 **Tara Well (IRE)**[35] 3381 6-10-5 **0**............................... ChrisWard(5) 61
(Robin Dickin) *led or disp ld tl rdn and dropped out qckly over 3f out: t.o* **16/1**

0 8 76 **Gold Thief (IRE)**[204] 1003 6-11-3 **0**............................ RobertDunne
(Laura Young) *in tch tl rdn 5f out: sn struggling: t.o* **100/1**

0- 9 7 **More More More**[392] 3585 6-10-10 **0**.............................. GLavery(7)
(Scott Dixon) *w ldr tl rdn and fdd rapidly 4f out: sn t.o* **80/1**

10 78 **Nomadrush** 6-10-10 **0**... CharliePoste
(John Holt) *tiny: bhd: t.o after 6f* **100/1**

00 11 89 **Annie'sboydave**[94] 2250 6-11-0 **0**............................ TomBellamy(3)
(Peter Pritchard) *v small: bhd: rdn after 5f: sn t.o* **100/1**

3m 59.5s (-2.80) **Going Correction** -0.05s/f (Good) **11 Ran SP% 119.0**
WFA 4 from 5yo 9lb 5 from 6yo 1lb
Speed ratings: **105,104,103,101,101 93,82,44,41,2**
CSF £12.91 TOTE £5.00: £1.40, £1.40, £1.20; EX 15.00 Trifecta £21.30.
Owner John P McManus **Bred** Robert McCarthy **Trained** Barbury Castle, Wilts

FOCUS
Just an ordinary race of its type and the early gallop didn't look strong. A big step up from the winner.
T/Jkpt: Not won. T/Plt: £134.90 to a £1 stake. Pool: £66595.87 - 360.23 winning tickets T/Qpdt: £48.20 to a £1 stake. Pool: £6223.26 - 95.4 winning tickets **Iain Mackenzie**

3705 WINCANTON (R-H)
Thursday, February 4

OFFICIAL GOING: Heavy (soft in places; chs:5.2, hdl:5.5)
Wind: mild behind Weather: overcast

3953 CARLING EUROPEAN BREEDERS' FUND MARES' "NATIONAL HUNT" NOVICES' HURDLE (10 hdls 1 omitted) 2m 5f 82y
1:30 (1:30) (Class 4) 4-Y-0+ **£3,994** (£1,240; £667)

Form RPR

0-1P 1 **Lifeboat Mona**[36] 3372 6-11-6 **0**...........................(t) SamTwiston-Davies 127+
(Paul Nicholls) *trckd ldr: disp 6th tl drew ahd appr 2 out: kpt up to work run-in: styd on* **6/4**[2]

-223 2 3 1/2 **Brise Vendeenne (FR)**[61] 2911 5-11-0 **115**................. RichardJohnson 115
(Philip Hobbs) *led: jnd whn hit 6th: rdn and hdd bef 2 out: styd on but sn hld* **11/10**[1]

-124 3 16 **Kentford Myth**[66] 2825 6-10-9 **103**............................... KevinJones(5) 100
(Seamus Mullins) *trckd ldrs: rdn to chse ldng pair after 3 out: outpcd next* **14/1**

0/ P **Mylittlemouse (IRE)**[673] 5130 8-10-9 **0**........................... ConorRing(5)
(Helen Nelmes) *hld up bhd ldrs: nt fluent 2nd: wknd after 3 out: p.u bef next* **100/1**

-133 P **Drumviredy (IRE)**[40] 3252 7-11-6 **113**........................... AidanColeman
(Venetia Williams) *trckd ldrs: disp cl 3rd after 3 out: wknd qckly whn rdn and p.u bef next* **11/2**[3]

60P P **Penny Option (IRE)**[23] 3570 7-11-0 **0**............................. TomO'Brien
(Robert Stephens) *chsd ldrs tl pushed along in last pair 6th: wknd after 3 out: p.u bef next* **200/1**

5m 48.3s (21.80) **Going Correction** +1.25s/f (Heav) **6 Ran SP% 111.2**
Speed ratings (Par 105): **108,106,100,,,**
CSF £3.56 TOTE £2.50: £1.50, £1.50; EX 3.90 Trifecta £12.30.
Owner Axom LV **Bred** Bryan & Sandra Mayoh, Eskdale Stud **Trained** Ditcheat, Somerset

FOCUS
Due to rail movements this race was run over 36yds further than advertised. The hurdle on the stables bend was omitted. Sam Twiston-Davies described the ground as "heavy and very holding". The two at the head of the market dominated what was a decent mares' hurdle. The winner looks above average.

3954 CW ACCOUNTANCY SERVICES NOVICES' LIMITED H'CAP CHASE (10 fncs 3 omitted) 1m 7f 149y
2:00 (2:03) (Class 3) (0-135,132) 5-Y-0+ **£8,086** (£2,957)

Form RPR

-031 1 **Pressurize (IRE)**[12] 3747 10-10-5 **120**........................ CharlieDeutsch(5) 136+
(Venetia Williams) *trckd ldrs: disp after 7th: rdn bef 3 out: led bef 2 out: in command whn blnd bdly last* **5/4**[1]

33-6 2 5 **The Brock Again**[22] 3584 6-10-11 **121**................(t) SamTwiston-Davies 130
(Paul Nicholls) *trckd ldr: pressed ldr fr 4th (usual 6th): disp after 7th: rdn appr 3 out: hdd bef 2 out: kpt on same pce* **9/2**[2]

1-3 P **Gino Trail (IRE)**[23] 3571 9-11-8 **132**.............................. TomScudamore
(David Bridgwater) *led: tended to go sltly lft whn jnd 4th: rdn and hdd after 7th: sn wknd: p.u bef next* **5/4**[1]

P-1P F **Richardofdoccombe (IRE)**[12] 3747 10-9-12 **113** oh4......(t) AliceMills(5)
(Gail Haywood) *trcking ldrs whn fell 1st (usual 2nd)* **25/1**[3]

4m 16.3s (16.40) **Going Correction** +1.25s/f (Heav) **4 Ran SP% 110.9**
Speed ratings: **109,106,,**
CSF £6.97 TOTE £2.10; EX 5.30 Trifecta £4.70.
Owner Mrs Sarah Williams **Bred** Dr J O'Keeffe **Trained** Kings Caple, H'fords

FOCUS
Due to rail movements this race was run over 84yds further than advertised. Fair chasing form, even if one of the joint-favourites stopped as if shot. A step up from the winner.

3955 WORTHINGTON NOVICES' HURDLE (7 hdls 1 omitted) 1m 7f 65y
2:30 (2:31) (Class 3) 4-Y-0+ **£5,523** (£1,621; £810; £405)

Form RPR

1 **Unison (IRE)**[108] 6-10-13 **0**..................................... MattGriffiths(3) 106+
(Jeremy Scott) *in tch: wnt 2nd at the 3rd: led after 3 out: stmbld 2 out: kpt on wl fr last: pushed out* **6/1**[3]

00 2 6 **Guantoshol (IRE)**[10] 3772 5-11-2 **0**.............................. AidanColeman 98
(Venetia Williams) *hld up: hdwy appr 3 out: chal 2 out: sn edgd lft and hld: kpt on same pce fr last* **14/1**

2360 3 3 1/4 **Who's Micky Brown (IRE)**[14] 3710 6-11-2 **0**.................... NoelFehily 94
(Neil Mulholland) *mid-div: dropped to last pair 3 out and reminder: hdwy bef next where wnt 3rd: styd on wout threatening* **10/1**

4 7 **Crin Au Vent (FR)**[131] 4-11-2 **0**..........................1 SamTwiston-Davies 89
(Paul Nicholls) *racd freely: j.lft most of way: led: hdd after 3 out: rdn bef next: sn hld: wknd last* **2/7**[1]

0 5 12 **Closer To Home (IRE)**[50] 3112 4-10-6 **0**..................(p) TomScudamore 66
(David Pipe) *in tch: rdn to chse ldrs after 3 out: wknd next* **5/1**[2]

-560 6 shd **Royal Salute**[69] 2763 6-11-2 **0**...................................... NickScholfield 75
(Anthony Honeyball) *chsd ldr tl 3rd: rdn after 3 out: wknd next* **20/1**

0000 7 6 **Brin D'Avoine (FR)**[14] 3710 5-10-9 **0**......................... MrShaneQuinlan(7) 71
(Neil Mulholland) *trckd ldrs: rdn after 3 out: wknd next* **50/1**

P/ P **Highest Red**[928] 1059 7-10-9 **0**...................................... MrWillPettis(7)
(Natalie Lloyd-Beavis) *a towards rr: struggling 3rd: lost tch after next: t.o whn p.u bef 2 out* **100/1**

4m 3.5s (14.60) **Going Correction** +1.25s/f (Heav) **8 Ran SP% 132.2**
Speed ratings (Par 107): **111,107,106,102,95 95,92,**
CSF £83.93 TOTE £11.60: £1.70, £3.50, £2.00; EX 200.00 Trifecta £1475.60.
Owner J P Carrington **Bred** Alan Dargan **Trained** Brompton Regis, Somerset

FOCUS

Due to rail movements this race was run over 24yds further than advertised. No depth to this novice hurdle and the heavy odds-on favourite flopped. The winner should go on to rate higher.

3956 LATESTFREEBETOFFERS.COM H'CAP HURDLE (9 hdls 1 omitted) 2m 3f 166y

3:05 (3:05) (Class 3) (0-140,138) 4-Y-0+

£9,384 (£2,772; £1,386; £693; £346; £174)

Form				RPR
41	1		**Baoulet Delaroque (FR)**[27] 3508 5-10-12 **124**....... SamTwiston-Davies (Paul Nicholls) *hld up in tch: tk clsr order 6th: ldng whn wnt rt 2 out: in command whn nt fluent last: easily* **13/8**[1]	139+
-353	2	*8*	**Sir Ivan**[40] 3254 6-11-5 **131**.......... NoelFehily (Harry Fry) *prom: rdn and hdd whn hit 2 out: sn hld by wnr: wnt lft last: styd on but nt pce of wnr* **5/1**[2]	135
-62P	3	*½*	**Dolores Delightful (FR)**[49] 3122 6-10-8 **120**.............(t) RichardJohnson (Nick Williams) *pushed along in last fr 4th but in tch: hdwy after 3 out: rdn and ch bef next: styd on but nt pce of wnr* **6/1**[3]	123
2414	4	*16*	**The Geegeez Geegee (IRE)**[63] 2867 7-9-12 **115**......(t) DavidNoonan(5) (Anthony Honeyball) *hld up in tch: hdwy after 6th: rdn to dispute cl 4th after 3 out: wknd next* **6/1**[3]	102
3-PP	5	*shd*	**Shammick Boy (IRE)**[62] 2877 11-11-7 **138**.............(p) CiaranGethings(5) (Victor Dartnall) *led: j.rt at times: hdd bef 3rd: prom: rdn after 3 out: wknd next* **16/1**	124
4-2P	6	*47*	**Space Walker (IRE)**[57] 2977 5-10-8 **120**..........(p) DavidBass (Ben Pauling) *chsd ldrs: rdn after 3 out: wknd bef next: t.o* **10/1**	59
F/50	P		**Phantom Prince (IRE)**[157] 1432 7-10-9 **128**.......... MissBFrost(7) (Jimmy Frost) *in tch tl wknd 6th: p.u bef next* **33/1**
P-32	P		**Norse Legend**[22] 3584 5-11-0 **126**.......... TomCannon (Chris Gordon) *chsd ldrs tl rdn after 5th: sn lost pl: wknd 3 out: t.o whn p.u bef 2 out* **7/1**

5m 14.3s (314.30) **8 Ran SP% 113.7**

CSF £10.46 CT £38.02 TOTE £2.80: £1.30, £1.80, £1.90; EX 11.00 Trifecta £38.60.

Owner Potensis Bloodstock Limited **Bred** Mme Genevieve Mongin **Trained** Ditcheat, Somerset

FOCUS

Due to rail movements this race was run over 36yds further than advertised. An ordinary handicap that was taken apart by the well handicapped winner. He can rate higher and win again.

3957 DICK HUNT H'CAP CHASE (FOR THE DICK HUNT TROPHY) (14 fncs 3 omitted) 2m 4f 35y

3:40 (3:40) (Class 3) (0-140,140) 5-Y-0+

£13,763 (£4,065; £2,032; £1,016; £508; £255)

Form				RPR
52P1	1		**As De Fer (FR)**[7] 3823 10-9-9 **113** 7ex..........(t) DavidNoonan(5) (Anthony Honeyball) *mde virtually all: rdn and hdd briefly 3 out: styd on: drvn out* **9/4**[1]	124+
3311	2	*¾*	**Quite By Chance**[14] 3706 7-10-8 **129**.......... PaulO'Brien(7) (Colin Tizzard) *trckd ldrs: blnd bdly 2nd: rdn in cl 4th whn lft 2nd 3 out: styd on towards fin but a being hld* **4/1**[2]	138
333B	3	*11*	**Gores Island (IRE)**[14] 3706 10-10-10 **124**.......... JoshuaMoore (Gary Moore) *hld up: hdwy on long run after 11th: rdn whn lft hld 3rd 3 out: kpt on same pce* **6/1**[3]	120
0-6U	4	*1½*	**Unique De Cotte (FR)**[40] 3228 8-11-12 **140**.............(t[1]) TomScudamore (David Pipe) *in tch: trckd ldrs 8th: travelling jst as wl as ldr and tight on his heels in 3rd whn bdly hmpd 3 out: j.lft after and nvr rcvrd but kpt on past 2 horses to regain 4th last* **7/1**	146+
-143	5	*2½*	**The Italian Yob (IRE)**[38] 3315 8-10-5 **124**..............(b) LizzieKelly(5) (Nick Williams) *chsd ldrs: rdn after 11th: hld in one pce 6th whn lft 4th 3 out: one pce fr next* **12/1**	116
-14F	6	*5*	**Brody Bleu (FR)**[12] 3731 9-11-3 **131**.......... TomCannon (Robert Walford) *cl up: nt fluent 7th: rdn after 11th: lft hld 5th 3 out: one pce fr next* **33/1**	120
4252	7	*11*	**Saint Raph (FR)**[26] 3521 8-10-8 **122**..........(tp) PaddyBrennan (Robert Walford) *pressed wnr tl 11th: sn btn* **8/1**	99
P-0P	8	*3¼*	**Majala (FR)**[68] 2780 10-11-10 **138**..........(t) SeanBowen (Tom George) *mstke 1st: pushed along after 6th: a towards rr: wknd on long run bef 3 out* **50/1**	114
22-P	P		**Starkie**[26] 3524 9-10-9 **123**.......... TomO'Brien (Paul Henderson) *in tch tl wknd after 11th: t.o whn p.u bef next* **25/1**
-312	F		**Stilletto (IRE)**[37] 3351 7-11-4 **132**.......... SamTwiston-Davies (Paul Nicholls) *hld up: smooth hdwy to join wnr 11th: travelling strly in narrow ld whn fell 3 out* **6/1**[3]	140+

5m 41.9s (24.40) **Going Correction** +1.25s/f (Heavy) **10 Ran SP% 119.4**

Speed ratings: **101,100,96,95,94 92,88,87, ,**

CSF £12.39 CT £48.52 TOTE £2.90: £1.30, £2.10, £1.80; EX 14.90 Trifecta £77.20.

Owner Midd Shire Racing **Bred** Didier Leviel **Trained** Mosterton, Dorset

FOCUS

Due to rail movements this race was run over 102yds further than advertised. The outcome of this race changed three out when the strongest travelling pair saw their challenge come to an end. Fair form.

3958 STEWART TORY MEMORIAL OPEN HUNTERS' CHASE (FOR THE STEWART TORY MEMORIAL CHALLENGE TROPHY) (17 fncs 4 omitted) 3m 1f 30y

4:15 (4:16) (Class 6) 5-Y-0+

£935 (£290; £145; £72)

Form				RPR
60/3	1		**Join Together (IRE)**[22] 3585 11-11-7 134.......... MissBFrost(5) (Mrs Rose Loxton) *prom: led after 10th tl after next: dropped to cl 4th 14th: led again bef next: strly pressed fr 3 out: styd on: rdn out* **8/15**[1]	114+
3/	2	*1¼*	**Big Georgie (IRE)**[18] 9-11-7 0.......... MrLouisMuspratt(5) (J M Ridley) *hld up: hdwy 10th: tk clsr order after 11th: rdn for str chal fr 3 out: styd on w ev ch tl no ex run-in* **11/2**[3]	111
/P0-	3	*17*	**Tullyraine (IRE)**[38] 12-11-13 116.......... MrLWilliams(7) (Dean Coleman) *j.lft at times: led: hdd after 10th tl after next: rdn and hdd on long run bef 3 out: grad fdd* **33/1**	104
32-1	4	*4*	**Parkam Jack**[249] 10-11-9 113.......... MrJLThomas(7) (Mrs Kayley Woollacott) *trckd ldrs: chal after 14th: sn rdn and hld bef 3 out: grad fdd* **9/2**[2]	98
065/	P		**Battle Bridge (IRE)**[18] 11-11-5 83.......... MissCSwaffield(7) (Mrs H M Tory) *sn pushed along in 5 l last: lost tch after 12th: p.u bef 14th* **50/1**
123/	P		**Otto The Great (FR)**[256] 8-11-5 119.......... MrFHenderson(7) (J H Henderson) *trckd ldrs: upsides 10th tl next: struggling 14th: sn wknd: p.u bef 3 out* **17/2**

7m 29.1s (49.60) **Going Correction** +1.25s/f (Heavy) **6 Ran SP% 114.2**

Speed ratings: **70,69,64,62,**

CSF £4.49 TOTE £1.60: £1.10, £2.70; EX 5.00 Trifecta £36.50.

Owner Ian J Fogg & Mrs Wendy Fogg **Bred** J D Flood **Trained** Bruton, Somerset

FOCUS

Due to rail movements this race was run over 120yds further than advertised. The front pair came clear in this ordinary hunter chase. The winner is rated close to his recent run.

3959 BIGCASINOBONUSES.CO.UK STANDARD OPEN NATIONAL HUNT FLAT RACE 1m 7f 65y

4:50 (4:50) (Class 6) 4-6-Y-0

£1,624 (£477; £238; £119)

Form				RPR
1		**Chalonnial (FR)** 4-10-7 0.......... NoelFehily (Harry Fry) *a.p: led wl over 2f out: styd on wl to assert fr over 1f out: rdn out* **5/2**[2]	105+
2	*5*	**Crank Em Up (IRE)**[74] 5-11-3 0.......... AidanColeman (David Dennis) *mid-div: trckd ldrs 4f out: rdn and ev ch over 2f out tl over 1f out: kpt on same pce fnl f* **9/2**	107
1	3	*3½*	**Steel Express (IRE)**[62] 2882 4-10-7 0.......... ConorSmith(7) (Linda Blackford) *mid-div: trckd ldrs 6f out: ev ch 3f out: sn rdn: kpt on same pce fnl 2f* **16/1**	100
4	4	*5*	**Burton Boru (IRE)**[34] 3416 4-10-7 0.......... PaddyBrennan (Colin Tizzard) *mid-div: outpcd 3f out: styd on again fr over 1f out but nt any danger* **14/1**	88
5	*nk*	**Bradford Bridge (IRE)** 4-10-7 0.......... RichardJohnson (Philip Hobbs) *trckd ldrs: jnd ldrs over 4f out: led v briefly 3f out: sn edgd lft and outpcd* **3/1**[3]	88
6	*3¾*	**Baby Sherlock** 5-11-3 0.......... TomScudamore (David Pipe) *hld up: hdwy fr 4f out: effrt 3f out: nt pce to get involved: wknd over 1f out* **9/4**[1]	94
7	*18*	**Pomicide** 6-11-0 0.......... LucyGardner(3) (Sue Gardner) *led at stdy pce tl qcknd up 1/2-way: hdd over 3f out: sn wknd* **50/1**	76
8	*12*	**That Will Do** 6-10-12 0.......... ConorRing(5) (Helen Nelmes) *a towards rr: t.o fnl 2f* **66/1**	64
9	*44*	**Inthenicoftime** 6-10-12 0.......... AliceMills(5) (Jess Westwood) *pressed ldrs tl 4f out: sn wknd: t.o* **100/1**	20

4m 6.8s (23.50) **Going Correction** +1.25s/f (Heavy) **9 Ran SP% 119.5**

Speed ratings: **87,84,82,79,79 77,68,61,38**

CSF £14.89 TOTE £3.70: £1.30, £1.90, £2.40; EX 22.00 Trifecta £195.00.

Owner Chris Giles & Potensis Bloodstock Ltd **Bred** Francis Maze **Trained** Seaborough, Dorset

FOCUS

Due to rail movements this race was run over 24yds further than advertised. Probably just an average bumper but a good winner. The third sets the level.

T/Plt: £153.20 to a £1 stake. Pool of £48285.98 - 229.97 winning tickets. T/Qpdt: £18.40 to a £1 stake. Pool of £3922.52 - 157.60 winning tickets. **Tim Mitchell**

3960 - 3961a (Foreign Racing) - See Raceform Interactive

3208 CLONMEL (R-H)

Thursday, February 4

OFFICIAL GOING: Heavy

3962a SUREHAUL MERCEDES-BENZ NOVICE HURDLE (GRADE 3) (14 hdls) 2m 6f

2:25 (2:25) 4-Y-0+ **£16,957** (£5,238; £2,481; £1,102; £413)

| | | | RPR
---|---|---|---|---
| 1 | | **Arkwrist (FR)**[21] 3601 6-11-2.......... RWalsh (W P Mullins, Ire) *chsd ldrs: clsr 5 out where nt fluent bef led next: nt fluent 3 out: extended ld to 5 l appr last: rdn out in clsng stages* **12/1** | 138
| 2 | *2½* | **Westend Star (IRE)**[21] 3601 7-11-5 133.......... (t) LPDempsey (Gordon Elliott, Ire) *hld up: nt fluent 4th: rdn to take clsr order in 3rd after 3 out: wnt 2nd appr next: no imp last: kpt on same pce* **10/3**[3] | 138+
| 3 | *8* | **Dont Tell No One (IRE)**[34] 3429 8-11-2.......... DavyRussell (D K Weld, Ire) *trckd ldrs in 3rd tl nt qckn in 4th after 3 out: wnt mod 3rd bef last: nt trble principals* **3/1**[2] | 127
| 4 | *29* | **Stone Hard (IRE)**[32] 3459 6-11-2.......... BJCooper (W P Mullins, Ire) *chsd ldrs in 4th: clsr to chse ldr in 2nd after 3 out: dropped to 3rd appr next: sn no ex and dropped to 4th* **9/4**[1] | 102
| 5 | *58* | **Last Encounter (IRE)**[32] 3459 6-11-2 135.......... DannyMullins (Ms Margaret Mullins, Ire) *led tl hdd 4 out: wknd qckly after next* **4/1** | 40
| P | | **Roman Gold (IRE)**[60] 2938 6-11-5 125.......... JackKennedy (Gordon Elliott, Ire) *a in rr: rdn and detached bef 4 out where p.u* **20/1** |
| P | | **Side Saddle (IRE)**[15] 3693 6-10-9.......... MarkWalsh (Ms Sandra Hughes, Ire) *sn trckd ldr in 2nd: rdn in 3rd 4 out: dropped to rr at next and sn no ex: sn p.u* **33/1** |

6m 11.7s (371.70) **7 Ran SP% 114.2**

CSF £52.17 TOTE £11.60: £4.30, £1.90; DF 25.50 Trifecta £77.40.

Owner Gigginstown House Stud **Bred** E R Hanbury **Trained** Muine Beag, Co Carlow

FOCUS

Undoubtedly an improved performance from the winner, very much helped by a wonderfully clever ride from the champion jockey. Another pb from the progressive winner, with the second and third to their marks.

3963 - 3966a (Foreign Racing) - See Raceform Interactive

3802 CATTERICK (L-H)

Friday, February 5

OFFICIAL GOING: Good to soft (good in places; chs 7.3, hdl 7.6)

Wind: fresh 1/2 behind Weather: fine but breezy. becoming overcast and cold

3967 RACINGUK.COM JUVENILE HURDLE (8 hdls) 1m 7f 156y

1:20 (1:21) (Class 4) 4-Y-0 **£3,249** (£954; £477; £238)

Form				RPR
12	1		**Jaleo (GER)**[51] 3112 4-11-5 123.......... AidanColeman (John Ferguson) *trckd ldrs: 2nd 2 out: shkn up to ld appr last: wnt clr: easily* **8/11**[1]	133+
13	2	*11*	**Our Thomas (IRE)**[98] 2172 4-11-5 133.......... BrianHughes (Tim Easterby) *t.k.h: trckd ldrs: nt fluent 6th: led next: sn drvn: hdd appr last: kpt on same pce* **7/4**[2]	118
3	*11*	**Invictus (GER)**[125] 4-10-9 0.......... JoeColliver(3) (Micky Hammond) *t.k.h: led to 3rd: led briefly appr 2 out: wknd and modest 3rd whn hit last* **12/1**[3]	102
5	4	*7*	**Hubal (POL)**[52] 3099 4-10-12 0.......... JanFaltejsek (George Charlton) *chsd ldrs: outpcd after 6th: lost pl next: poor 4th appr last* **33/1**	94

3 **5** *24* **Pariyan (FR)**[151] [1495] 4-10-12 0.......................... AdrianLane 69
(Donald McCain) *stdd s: t.k.h: sn trcking ldrs: led 3rd: hdd appr 2 out: 4th and wkng whn hit 2 out: sn bhd* **66/1**

6 **P** **Silver Glaze (IRE)**[38] [2216] 4-10-12 0.......................... DannyCook
(Brian Ellison) *chsd ldrs: drvn and lost pl 3rd: brief effrt whn nt fluent next: sn bhd: t.o 6th: p.u bef next* **200/1**

3m 54.0s (1.50) **Going Correction** +0.175s/f (Yiel) **6** Ran SP% **106.9**
Speed ratings: **103,97,92,88,76**
CSF £2.05 TOTE £1.50: £1.10, £1.10; EX 2.30 Trifecta £4.80.
Owner Bloomfields **Bred** Gestut Karlshof **Trained** Cowlinge, Suffolk

FOCUS
The ground was officially good in places at a course that drains quickly and which reported plenty of windy weather recently. It was described as 'deadish' by the jockeys. The winner's time was 14 seconds over standard, but rail movement meant that 24yds was added to the race distance and they went no gallop. There were two potentially progressive winners and an interesting recruit from the Flat in the field for what is usually a good juvenile hurdle for the track, but they went only a steady pace, with several racing keenly early on, and the principals are probably better than their proximity to the remainder might suggest. The second and fourth have been rated pretty much to their marks.

3968 FREE RACEDAYS WITH THE RACEGOERS CLUB NOVICES' H'CAP CHASE (12 fncs) 1m 7f 145y
1:50 (1:50) (Class 4) (0-105,104) 5-Y-0+ **£4,548** (£1,335; £667; £333)

Form RPR

5224 **1** **Bollin Line**[39] [3308] 9-10-3 **86**.......................... DeanPratt(5) 99+
(Lucinda Egerton) *mid-div: hdwy to trck ldrs 5th: led 2 out: drvn clr sn after last: eased last 50yds* **6/1**

5225 **2** *2* **Discoverie**[17] [3672] 8-10-0 **78**..........................(p) HenryBrooke 85
(Kenneth Slack) *chsd ldrs: 2nd 3rd: drvn appr 3 out: upsides 2 out: kpt on same pce appr last* **10/3**[1]

0-23 **3** *2 ¼* **Oscar O'Scar (IRE)**[10] [3791] 8-11-1 **100**.......................... FinianO'Toole(7) 105
(Micky Hammond) *rr-div: hdwy appr 3 out: 4th 2 out: 3rd last: kpt on one pce* **9/2**[2]

222- **4** *4* **Casual Cavalier (IRE)**[381] [3783] 8-11-8 **100**.......................... BrianHughes 103
(John Wade) *chsd ldrs: drvn 9th: one pce and 4th last 100yds* **9/1**

0-65 **5** *4 ½* **Bennylicious (IRE)**[65] [2844] 7-11-3 **95**.......................... CraigNichol 94
(Rose Dobbin) *led: hdd 2 out: wknd fnl 150yds* **11/2**[3]

640U **6** *7* **Miss Conway**[52] [3098] 5-10-3 **83** ow1.......................... JakeGreenall 72
(Mark Walford) *mid-div: chsd ldrs 8th: outpcd appr 3 out* **28/1**

34P2 **7** *nk* **Agentleman (IRE)**[7] [3845] 6-11-8 **100**.......................... DannyCook 94
(Tim Easterby) *nt fluent: chsd ldrs: 3rd whn blnd 5th: lost pl 8th* **13/2**

604 **8** *5* **Devon River (FR)**[92] [2294] 6-11-0 **97**..........................(p) CallumBewley(5) 84
(Simon Waugh) *j.rt: in rr: hit 2nd: sme hdwy after 9th: sn lost pl* **33/1**

P3P3 **9** *¾* **Money For Nothing**[9] [3806] 7-11-9 **104**..........................(t) ColmMcCormack(3) 92
(Harriet Bethell) *in rr: last whn blnd 7th: nvr on terms* **8/1**

3F-4 **10** *12* **New Academy**[48] [3161] 8-11-3 **95**.......................... AndrewThornton 73
(John Wade) *mid-div: pushed along 6th: lost pl 8th: bhd fr 3 out* **33/1**

3m 59.1s (-1.00) **Going Correction** +0.025s/f (Yiel)
WFA 5 from 6yo+ 1lb **10** Ran SP% **114.7**
Speed ratings: **103,102,100,98,96 93,92,90,90,84**
CSF £26.30 CT £96.97 TOTE £10.60: £2.30, £1.40, £1.80; EX 37.80 Trifecta £126.70.
Owner Miss L Egerton **Bred** Mrs J Broad **Trained** Malton, North Yorks

FOCUS
A typically uncompetitive 0-105 novice handicap, with half of the field making their chasing debut and none of the others having shown abundant promise over fences. Few got into things in a contest run at a fair clip, with the distance extended by 24yds. The second has been rated to his mark.

3969 INTERACTIVE H'CAP CHASE (19 fncs) 3m 1f 54y
2:25 (2:25) (Class 4) (0-110,105) 5-Y-0+ **£3,768** (£1,106; £553; £276)

Form RPR

PP01 **1** **Auldthunder (IRE)**[9] [3803] 9-11-1 97 7ex.......................... JoeColliver(3) 117+
(Micky Hammond) *nt fluent in rr: shkn up 4th: sn bhd: hdwy and modest 6th 12th: outpcd next: modest 5th 3 out: styd on and 2nd last: led last 150yds: readily* **4/1**[1]

2F12 **2** *5* **Runswick Relax**[16] [3679] 10-10-2 81..........................(tp) HenryBrooke 92
(Kenneth Slack) *chsd ldr: led 14th: clr bef 2 out: fdd and hdd last 150yds* **4/1**[1]

00P5 **3** *1 ½* **Houndscourt (IRE)**[35] [3401] 9-11-8 101..........................(t) BrianHughes 110
(Joanne Foster) *chsd ldrs: outpcd 15th: hung lft: kpt on one pce and 3rd between last 2* **16/1**

5226 **4** *10* **Red Danaher (IRE)**[20] [3631] 9-11-8 101.......................... DannyCook 105
(Sue Smith) *chsd ldrs: pushed along 11th: 4th and hld whn mstke 2 out: sn wknd* **8/1**

-452 **5** *11* **Treliver Manor (IRE)**[9] [3803] 8-10-5 84..........................(t) CraigNichol 77
(Rose Dobbin) *chsd ldrs: 2nd 15th: wknd between last 2* **9/2**[2]

3-P6 **P** **Whats Up Woody (IRE)**[39] [3310] 11-11-2 100.......(p) JonathonBewley(5)
(George Bewley) *led: hdd 14th: lost pl 3 out: poor 6th whn p.u bef next* **11/2**[3]

354P **P** **Over And Above (IRE)**[9] [3803] 10-10-5 89..........................(tp) RyanDay(5)
(Henry Hogarth) *in rr: bhd and pushed along 4th: reminders 6th and 10th: t.o after 11th: p.u bef 13th* **20/1**

-33U **P** **Hellorboston (IRE)**[17] [3669] 8-11-12 105..........................(b) WillKennedy
(Donald McCain) *chsd ldrs 3rd: pushed along 8th: mstke and lost pl 10th: bhd whn hit 12th: t.o 14th: p.u bef last* **6/1**

6m 42.3s (0.30) **Going Correction** +0.025s/f (Yiel) **8** Ran SP% **109.6**
Speed ratings: **100,98,97,94,91** , ,
CSF £19.13 CT £206.67 TOTE £4.00: £1.50, £1.60, £3.30; EX 16.80 Trifecta £161.70.
Owner The Rat Pack Racing Club **Bred** Miss Jill Farrell **Trained** Middleham, N Yorks

FOCUS
Plenty with questions to answer in a race run over an extra 48yds, a 0-110 open handicap in which all bar three were still eligible for novice chases. They went a good pace for the grade. The second, third and fourth have been rated pretty much to their marks.

3970 DINE AND VIEW AT CATTERICK RACES H'CAP HURDLE (QUALIFIER FOR THE CHALLENGER STAYING HURDLE) (12 hdls) 3m 1f 71y
2:55 (2:56) (Class 3) (0-125,123) 4-Y-0+ **£6,498** (£1,908; £954; £477)

Form RPR

-042 **1** **Hainan (FR)**[37] [3367] 5-11-4 **115**.......................... DannyCook 120+
(Sue Smith) *chsd ldrs: reminders appr 8th: led narrowly 2 out: styd on wl to forge clr run-in: eased towards fin* **7/2**[2]

-211 **2** *4 ½* **Iron Butterfly**[28] [3505] 7-11-12 **123**.......................... JackQuinlan 123
(James Eustace) *chsd ldrs: drvn appr 2 out: 2nd last: styd on same pce* **9/2**[3]

1322 **3** *1 ½* **Tambura**[8] [3824] 6-11-1 **119**.......................... MrZBaker(7) 118+
(G C Maundrell) *in rr: bhd 3rd: nt fluent and pushed along next: hdwy and in tch 8th: hit next: outpcd and lost pl after 3 out: lft modest 6th last: kpt on to take 3rd nr fin* **5/2**[1]

22P3 **4** *hd* **Shantou Tiger (IRE)**[35] [3399] 7-11-4 **120**..........................(p) JamesCowley(5) 116
(Donald McCain) *w ldr: hung lft fr 8th: led appr 3rd: hdd 2 out: one pce run-in* **16/1**

0142 **5** *7* **Maggie Blue (IRE)**[34] [3437] 8-10-3 **105**.......................... CallumBewley(5) 95
(Harriet Graham) *chsd ldrs: upsides 2 out: wknd appr last* **20/1**

0-65 **6** *18* **Bell Weir**[37] [3361] 8-10-9 **109**.......................... HarryChalloner(3) 83
(Dianne Sayer) *in rr: drvn 7th: chsng ldrs next: lost pl sn after 3 out* **16/1**

0123 **7** *7* **Omid**[16] [3684] 8-10-5 **105**..........................(tp) JohnKington(3) 73
(Kenneth Slack) *led: hdd appr 3rd: sn drvn: lost pl 3 out: sn bhd* **13/2**

3465 **8** *6* **Taylor (IRE)**[28] [3505] 7-10-8 **108**.......................... JoeColliver(3) 70
(Micky Hammond) *in rr: lost pl 8th: bhd fr 3 out* **16/1**

-330 **F** **Hartforth**[54] [3058] 8-11-6 **120**.......................... CallumWhillans(3) 109
(Donald Whillans) *chsd ldrs: drvn 7th: outpcd appr 2 out: modest 6th and wl hld whn fell last* **12/1**

6m 27.4s (-0.20) **Going Correction** +0.175s/f (Yiel) **9** Ran SP% **112.4**
Speed ratings (Par 107): **107,105,105,105,102 97,94,92,**
CSF £19.34 CT £44.52 TOTE £3.60: £1.40, £2.10, £1.30; EX 21.30 Trifecta £45.90.
Owner Mrs J Morgan & Mrs Lindsey J Shaw **Bred** Marc Staels **Trained** High Eldwick, W Yorks

FOCUS
Not a bad handicap hurdle, with several of the field coming into the race (which was run over an extra 48yds) in some sort of form and they went a decent pace. A small step up from the winner and another pb in defeat from the second.

3971 EUROPEAN BREEDERS' FUND "NATIONAL HUNT" NOVICES' HURDLE (QUALIFIER) (10 hdls) 2m 3f 66y
3:25 (3:25) (Class 4) 4-7-Y-0 **£3,898** (£1,144; £572; £286)

Form RPR

32F1 **1** **Wade Harper (IRE)**[38] [3334] 6-11-8 132.......................... AidanColeman 123+
(David Dennis) *w ldr: led 4th: drvn clr between last 2: drvn rt out* **7/4**[1]

3232 **2** *¾* **Double W's (IRE)**[69] [2773] 6-11-2 121.......................... BrianHughes 125+
(Malcolm Jefferson) *trckd ldrs: t.k.h: bdly hmpd and lost pl 7th: modest 4th appr 2 out: 6 l 2nd and hit last: styd on wl: nt quite rch wnr* **7/4**[1]

5- **3** *8* **Banny's Lad**[279] 7-10-13 0.......................... HarryBannister(3) 107
(Michael Easterby) *hld up in rr: hdwy 6th: lft modest 4th next: 3rd next: one pce and 3rd last* **40/1**

232 **4** *16* **Just Georgie**[41] [3239] 6-11-2 115.......................... DannyCook 99+
(Sue Smith) *chsd ldrs: lft 2nd 7th: drvn next: wknd appr last: eased clsng stages* **7/2**[2]

23 **5** *7* **Loch Linnhe**[22] [3593] 4-10-5 0.......................... JakeGreenall 74
(Mark Walford) *mid-div: lft poor 5th 7th: fdd appr 2 out* **33/1**

4-32 **6** *nk* **Mr Witmore (IRE)**[60] [2951] 6-11-2 0.......................... CraigNichol 85
(Michael Smith) *chsd ldrs: lft modest 3rd 7th: wknd appr 2 out* **22/1**

44U6 **7** *1 ¼* **Exactly What**[28] [3509] 7-11-2 0.......................... AdrianLane 88
(Donald McCain) *mid-div: sme hdwy 7th: lost pl and poor 7th whn blnd 2 out* **125/1**

0 **8** *34* **Just Like Dylan (IRE)**[39] [3309] 5-11-2 0.......................... BrianHarding 53
(Barry Murtagh) *in rr: lft poor 6th 7th: wknd next: t.o bef 2 out* **200/1**

F **9** *hd* **Pretty Miss Mahler (IRE)**[35] [3397] 5-10-9 0.......................... HenryBrooke 59+
(Martin Todhunter) *in rr: blnd bdly and collided w rail 2nd: t.o after 2nd* **28/1**

05 **10** *11* **Sybil Grey**[9] [3802] 7-10-4 0.......................... JonathonBewley(5) 36
(George Bewley) *in rr: bhd 4th: hung lft and t.o 6th* **200/1**

11 *60* **Anna Grey** 7-10-2 0.......................... MissAWaugh(7)
(Simon Waugh) *in rr: bhd fr 4th: t.o 6th: blnd bdly 2 out* **200/1**

1-0 **F** **Beggars Cross (IRE)**[38] [3334] 6-11-2 0.......................... WillKennedy
(Jonjo O'Neill) *led to 4th: 2nd and upsides whn fell 7th* **12/1**[3]

4m 47.8s (11.70) **Going Correction** +0.175s/f (Yiel)
WFA 4 from 5yo+ 9lb **12** Ran SP% **118.1**
Speed ratings: **82,81,78,71,68 68,67,53,53,48 23,**
CSF £4.74 TOTE £2.60: £1.10, £1.10, £7.20; EX 5.20 Trifecta £106.90.
Owner Favourites Racing (Syndication) Ltd 4 **Bred** Mrs J O'Callaghan **Trained** Hanley Swan, Worcestershire

FOCUS
Three of these had proven themselves fair hurdlers and another had won a bumper so this was potentially a reasonable novice event, run over an extra 24yds. They went a good pace and the field was soon well strung out, but an incident four out put two of the principals out of contention. The winner has been rated to his best.

3972 RACING UK ANYWHERE H'CAP CHASE (QUALIFIER FOR THE CHALLENGER MIDDLE DISTANCE CHASE SERIES) (16 fncs) 2m 3f 51y
4:00 (4:00) (Class 3) (0-125,125) 5-Y-0+ **£7,797** (£2,289; £1,144; £572)

Form RPR

4303 **1** **Raktiman (IRE)**[65] [2846] 9-11-8 **121**..........................(t) JonathanEngland 138+
(Sam Drake) *trckd ldr: led after 5th: clr bef 3 out: drvn out* **9/2**[3]

4224 **2** *10* **Ballydague Lady (IRE)**[56] [3007] 9-10-12 **111**..........................(p) MarkQuinlan 117
(Neil Mulholland) *hdwy to chse ldrs 4th: pushed along 9th: outpcd 12th: distant 4th 3 out: styd on appr last: tk modest 2nd last 50yds* **16/1**

-213 **3** *1 ¾* **Rear Admiral (IRE)**[35] [3401] 10-11-4 **117**..........................(t) JakeGreenall 121
(Michael Easterby) *hld up: hdwy to trck ldrs 9th: lft 3rd 12th: 2nd 2 out: one pce* **13/2**

-U13 **4** *5* **The Cobbler Swayne (IRE)**[56] [3014] 7-11-9 **122**.......... PeterBuchanan 125
(Lucinda Russell) *in rr: hit 5th: j. slowly 7th: pushed along to chse ldrs 9th: lft 2nd 12th: wknd last 150yds* **4/1**[2]

36P3 **5** *13* **Special Wells**[37] [3362] 7-10-13 **112**.......................... DannyCook 103
(Sue Smith) *chsd ldrs: hmpd and lost pl 12th: hit next: sn bhd* **11/4**[1]

6065 **6** *18* **Strongly Suggested**[48] [3155] 9-11-11 **124**.......................... RichieMcLernon 96
(Jonjo O'Neill) *chsd ldrs: drvn 10th: lost pl and hit next: sn bhd* **14/1**

4-PP **7** *63* **Swift Arrow (IRE)**[114] [1902] 10-11-11 **124**..........................(p) WillKennedy 39
(Donald McCain) *chsd ldrs: wknd 13th: sn bhd: t.o next* **33/1**

6511 **F** **Cloudy Joker (IRE)**[22] [3589] 8-11-12 **125**.......................... HenryBrooke
(Donald McCain) *led tl after 5th: cl 2nd whn fell heavily 12th* **9/2**[3]

4m 59.4s (299.40) **8** Ran SP% **111.9**
CSF £62.12 CT £458.33 TOTE £4.20: £1.40, £5.30, £2.40; EX 68.60 Trifecta £403.70.
Owner J C England and Valerie Beattie **Bred** Kilbride Stud Ltd **Trained** Guiseley, West Yorkshire

FOCUS
Several with decent form of late in a fair handicap chase, which was run over an extra 24yds. They went a decent pace too and there is no reason to think the winner won anything other than on merit. The second and third have been rated pretty much to their marks.

3973 YORKSHIRE-OUTDOORS.CO.UK CONDITIONAL JOCKEYS' H'CAP HURDLE (10 hdls) 2m 3f 66y
4:30 (4:30) (Class 5) (0-100,99) 4-Y-0+ £2,599 (£763; £381; £190)

Form RPR
-45P 1 **Perfect Poison (IRE)**[59] 2964 8-11-4 99 .... RonanShort(8) 104
(Donald McCain) *led: hit 7th: hung bdly lft between last 2: jst hld on* 5/1[3]
33-5 2 *shd* **Diego Suarez (FR)**[279] 90 6-10-10 88 .... TrevorRyan(5) 93
(Chris Bealby) *t.k.h: trckd ldrs: chsd wnr appr 2 out: 1 l down last: styd on towards fin: jst failed* 9/2[2]
-562 3 *11* **Mazovian (USA)**[7] 3840 8-11-8 95 ....(p) CiaranGethings 90
(Neil Mulholland) *mid-div: chsd ldrs 6th: drvn and outpcd 3 out: tk modest 3rd whn hit last: one pce* 11/8[1]
U000 4 *3* **Alchimix (FR)**[35] 3398 6-10-12 95 .... HugoThompsonBrown(10) 86
(Micky Hammond) *chsd ldrs: drvn 3 out: one pce* 33/1
/P0P 5 *nk* **Sory**[10] 3791 9-10-12 85 .... JonathanEngland 76
(Tina Jackson) *chsd wnr: upsides 4th: lost pl bef 3 out: kpt on clsng stages: tk modest 5th clsng stages* 25/1
3P0P 6 *2 ½* **The Late Shift**[35] 3402 6-10-7 85 .... LorcanMurtagh(5) 76
(Barry Murtagh) *hdwy to trck ldrs 4th: clr 3rd bef 2 out: 4th whn blnd last: wknd last 75yds* 11/1
05P- 7 *7* **Quite Sparky**[14] 5030 9-9-11 73 oh7 ....(b) DeanPratt(3) 58
(Lucinda Egerton) *hld up in rr: hdwy 6th: outpcd and lost pl 3 out* 22/1
U3UP 8 *15* **Kilmainham (IRE)**[17] 3669 8-11-9 96 .... GrahamWatters 65
(Martin Todhunter) *in rr: bhd fr 6th: t.o 3 out* 10/1
6UPP 9 *12* **Brunello**[57] 2980 8-10-12 85 .... RyanDay 43
(Michael Smith) *chsd ldrs: drvn and lost pl 7th: sn bhd: eased clsng stages* 18/1
520/ P **Mootabar (IRE)**[660] 5359 9-10-6 79 .... JoeColliver
(Chris Fairhurst) *in rr: nt fluent 5th: bhd next: t.o 3 out: p.u bef next* 14/1
4m 54.2s (18.10) **Going Correction** +0.175s/f (Yiel) 10 Ran SP% **117.4**
Speed ratings (Par 103): **68,67,63,62,61 60,57,51,46,**
CSF £27.80 CT £47.29 TOTE £6.20: £2.00, £1.70, £1.10; EX 25.30 Trifecta £89.00.
Owner John Gwynne **Bred** Michael Lee **Trained** Cholmondeley, Cheshire

FOCUS
As uncompetitive as you would expect for a 0-100 conditional jockeys' race (run over an extra 24yds), with most having something to prove on recent efforts and six of the ten runners pulled up last time out. With the favourite seemingly below his recent form, it probably did not take a great deal of winning. A pb from the runner-up, with the third rated 7lb off his recent Doncaster second.
T/Plt: £11.10 to a £1 stake. Pool: £68,045.51 - 4,455.42 winning tickets. T/Qpdt: £7.20 to a £1 stake. Pool: £5,489.95 - 561.3 winning tickets. **Walter Glynn**

3516 CHEPSTOW (L-H)
Friday, February 5

OFFICIAL GOING: Heavy (soft in places; 5.0)
Wind: slight half behind Weather: light rain

3974 EBF/32RED ONLINE CASINO "NATIONAL HUNT" NOVICES' HURDLE (QUALIFIER) (8 hdls) 2m 11y
1:40 (1:40) (Class 4) 4-7-Y-0 £3,898 (£1,144; £572; £286)

Form RPR
3 1 **Pougne Bobbi (FR)**[261] 407 5-11-3 0 .... AndrewTinkler 135+
(Nicky Henderson) *racd in 3rd tl impr a pl 4 out: shkn up whn nt fluent next: rdn to ld appr last: styd on wl* 8/1[3]
421 2 *5* **Robin Of Locksley (IRE)**[54] 3063 6-11-4 123 .... BridgetAndrews(5) 134
(Dan Skelton) *t.k.h: led: hit 2 out: drvn whn hdd appr last: one pce flat* 11/10[1]
4-13 3 *9* **Aurillac (FR)**[82] 2514 6-11-3 0 .... LeightonAspell 119+
(Rebecca Curtis) *trckd ldr: j.rt 2nd: lost 2nd and rdn 4 out: one pce fr 2 out* 6/5[2]
45 4 *35* **Looksnowtlikebrian (IRE)**[28] 3508 5-11-3 0 .... RichardJohnson 82
(Tim Vaughan) *hld up in last: lost tch 4th: t.o* 33/1
4m 17.5s (6.90) **Going Correction** +0.70s/f (Soft) 4 Ran SP% **107.1**
Speed ratings: **110,107,103,85**
CSF £17.55 TOTE £9.50; EX 17.30 Trifecta £30.00.
Owner Juergen Meyer **Bred** John Nye **Trained** Upper Lambourn, Berks

FOCUS
Both bends were railed out approximately four metres from the inside line. Race distance increased by 22yds. It's a shame Nansaroy defected, but this was still an interesting novice event and the runner-up sets the level. Winning rider Andrew Tinkler afterwards said: "I'd say it's more soft than heavy and isn't as deep as I've known it here". The runner-up sets the standard, with the third rated 8lb off his bumper mark.

3975 £10 FREE AT 32RED.COM NOVICES' CHASE (12 fncs) 2m 11y
2:10 (2:10) (Class 4) 5-Y-0+ £4,223 (£1,240; £620; £310)

Form RPR
1-22 1 **Oscar Sunset (IRE)**[35] 3415 9-10-7 138 .... ConorRing(5) 147+
(Evan Williams) *trckd ldr fr 2nd: mstke 6th: led after 3 out: rdn flat: r.o strly to draw clr fnl 100yds* 7/4[2]
04-1 2 *3 ¼* **Baltimore Rock (IRE)**[38] 3335 7-11-4 143 ....(t) NoelFehily 149
(Neil Mulholland) *t.k.h in last: impr into 3rd bef 5 out: nt fluent next: wnt cl 2nd 2 out: sn drvn: outpcd by wnr fnl 100yds* 6/5[1]
3 *15* **Lockstockandbarrel (IRE)**[358] 4197 7-10-12 0 .... RichardJohnson 130+
(Jonjo O'Neill) *hld up: in 3rd fr 7th tl appr 5 out: rdn and rallied 3 out: wnt 3rd again next: no imp and wknd last* 7/2[3]
62-3 4 *13* **Kiama Bay (IRE)**[57] 2981 10-10-12 134 .... JamieMoore 115
(Jim Best) *led: 5 l clr after 7th: reduced ld and rdn 4 out: hdd after next: sn wknd* 20/1
-150 5 *10* **Mountain Of Mourne (IRE)**[15] 3705 7-10-5 115 ....(p) ConorSmith(7) 106
(Linda Blackford) *chsd ldrs tl dropped to rr 7th: sn rdn: no ch fr 5 out* 100/1
4m 19.2s (2.10) **Going Correction** +0.425s/f (Soft) 5 Ran SP% **109.8**
Speed ratings: **111,109,101,95,90**
CSF £4.44 TOTE £2.60: £1.10, £1.30; EX 6.20 Trifecta £9.30.
Owner Geoff & Anne Price **Bred** E J Fagan **Trained** Llancarfan, Vale Of Glamorgan

FOCUS
Race distance increased by 22yds. They went a solid gallop in this fair novice chase.

3976 32RED ON THE APP STORE NOVICES' HURDLE (12 hdls) 2m 7f 131y
2:45 (2:45) (Class 4) 5-Y-0+ £3,898 (£1,144; £572; £286)

Form RPR
2F3 1 **Wild West Wind (IRE)**[35] 3400 7-10-12 0 ....(t) PaddyBrennan 119+
(Tom George) *trckd ldrs: chal 4 out: led appr last: drvn and styd on wl to assert fnl 100yds* 9/4[2]
0315 2 *2* **You Say What (IRE)**[35] 3400 6-11-5 0 .... TrevorWhelan 121
(Neil King) *prom: rdn to ld appr 4 out: sn jnd: hdd appr last: no ex u.p fnl 100yds* 7/1
P 3 *9* **Just Bill (IRE)**[62] 2903 8-10-5 0 .... LewisGordon(7) 106
(Evan Williams) *hld up: hdwy to go 3rd 3 out: hit next: one pce after and no ch w ldng pair* 33/1
35 4 *4 ½* **Mister Kalanisi (IRE)**[56] 3021 7-10-12 0 .... HarrySkelton 102
(Dan Skelton) *hld up: hit 5th: hdwy after 8th: one pce fr 2 out* 5/1[3]
-202 5 *12* **Say My Name (IRE)**[23] 3580 5-10-12 115 ....(p) LiamHeard 91
(Bob Buckler) *towards rr: rdn after 7th: wknd 4 out: sme late hdwy past btn rivals* 2/1[1]
-253 6 *2 ¾* **Bindon Mill**[35] 3413 7-10-12 0 .... IanPopham 87
(Victor Dartnall) *t.k.h early: trckd ldrs tl lost pl 7th: wknd 3 out* 12/1
3P 7 *5* **Master Ally (IRE)**[99] 2152 6-10-12 0 .... LeightonAspell 83
(Rebecca Curtis) *led: tended to jump rt: wandered and hdd appr 4 out: sn rdn and wknd* 25/1
51 8 *12* **Stop The Press**[23] 3582 7-11-5 0 .... DenisO'Regan 76
(Mark Pitman) *trckd ldr: lost 2nd appr 4 out where mstke: wknd 3 out* 16/1
064 9 *15* **Kerry's Lord (IRE)**[22] 3588 7-10-5 0 .... RomainClavreul(7) 54
(Joanne Thomason-Murphy) *hld up: hdwy 3rd: j. slowly 6th: rdn after 7th: wknd 4 out* 200/1
0/50 10 *29* **Bel Ami Rich**[23] 3580 6-10-9 0 .... BenPoste(3) 25
(Sally Randell) *midfield: dropped to rr and struggling 8th: t.o fr 4 out* 125/1
6m 40.4s (38.20) **Going Correction** +0.70s/f (Soft) 10 Ran SP% **114.9**
Speed ratings: **64,63,60,58,54 53,52,48,43,33**
CSF £17.93 TOTE £3.10: £1.20, £2.00, £5.60; EX 17.20 Trifecta £354.30.
Owner Simon W Clarke **Bred** Ms Margaret Treacy **Trained** Slad, Gloucs

FOCUS
Race distance increased by 34yds. Not a bad staying novice event. It was run at an ordinary gallop and two came clear. The winner has been rated back to the level of his course fall, with the fourth in line with his Doncaster form.

3977 32RED CASINO H'CAP CHASE (16 fncs) 2m 3f 98y
3:15 (3:17) (Class 4) (0-110,110) 5-Y-0+ £4,223 (£1,240; £620; £310)

Form RPR
04FF 1 **Tea Caddy**[41] 3214 10-11-6 104 ....(bt) BrendanPowell 109
(Jamie Snowden) *mid-div: tk clsr order 11th: led 4 out: mstke next: drvn and hdd last: rallied u.p to ld 100yds out* 16/1
0F63 2 *2 ½* **Modeligo (IRE)**[49] 3141 7-10-6 90 ....(t) CharliePoste 93
(Matt Sheppard) *hld up: clsd after 11th: mstke, hmpd and rdn 5 out: chsd wnr 2 out: drvn to ld last: hdd 100yds out: no ex* 12/1
1-0P 3 *8* **Forgivienne**[57] 2988 9-11-11 109 .... TomO'Brien 103
(Evan Williams) *mid-div: hdwy after 5th: rdn 4 out: kpt on same pce fr next* 16/1
-F26 4 *¾* **Rouquine Sauvage**[36] 3379 8-11-7 110 ....(t) DavidNoonan(5) 104
(Anthony Honeyball) *hld up: hdwy 11th: led 5 out: nt fluent and hdd next: sn one pce: rallied to go 4th nr fin* 10/1
3146 5 *nk* **Matrow's Lady (IRE)**[46] 3195 9-9-13 90 ....(t) MrMartinMcIntyre(7) 82
(Neil Mulholland) *towards rr: clsd after 11th: wnt 2nd briefly appr 2 out: one pce bef 2 pls flat* 10/1
-064 6 *9* **Darkestbeforedawn (IRE)**[18] 3662 9-11-5 103 .... JamesBest 90
(Caroline Keevil) *chsd ldrs: hit 10th: drvn along fr next: no ch fr 4 out* 9/2[2]
201P 7 *11* **Kings River (FR)**[35] 3412 7-10-7 96 .... CharlieDeutsch(5) 70
(Venetia Williams) *chsd ldrs: mstke 11th: wknd 3 out* 11/4[1]
-3P0 P **The Sneezer (IRE)**[23] 3586 13-10-2 91 .... ChrisWard(5)
(Nikki Evans) *cl up: led 3rd tl hdd & wknd qckly appr 5 out: bhd whn p.u bef 4 out* 50/1
PP45 P **Tom Bach (IRE)**[89] 2366 12-10-0 84 oh9 ....(b) LiamTreadwell
(Hywel Evans) *in rr: last and struggling fr 5th: wl bhd whn p.u bef 8th* 16/1
4431 P **Ballyegan (IRE)**[50] 3131 11-10-8 92 .... LiamHeard
(Bob Buckler) *prom tl blnd bdly 5th: stl in tch whn p.u bef 7th* 13/2[3]
24-4 P **Bravo Riquet (FR)**[86] 2441 10-11-2 105 ....(vt) JakeHodson(5)
(Robin Mathew) *in rr: sltly hmpd 7th: mstke 9th: p.u bef next* 20/1
0P/P P **Kilrush (IRE)**[35] 3415 10-11-3 108 .... HarryTeal(7)
(John Berwick) *towards rr: j. slowly 6th and 8th: wl bhd whn p.u bef 10th* 66/1
0234 U **Third Act (IRE)**[55] 3042 7-11-9 107 ....(tp) TomScudamore
(Colin Tizzard) *prom: trckd ldr fr 7th: led appr 5 out where blnd and uns rdr* 13/2[3]
0-FP U **Steel A Tune**[21] 3609 7-10-0 84 oh15 ....(v[1]) ConorO'Farrell
(Nick Mitchell) *led to 3rd: mstke next: losing pl whn blnd and uns rdr 7th* 50/1
5m 31.1s (19.80) **Going Correction** +1.15s/f (Heav) 14 Ran SP% **125.2**
Speed ratings: **104,102,99,99,99 95,90,, , ,**
CSF £194.94 CT £3139.33 TOTE £19.90: £4.40, £3.90, £4.00; EX 288.60 Trifecta £3693.40.
Owner R Matthews **Bred** Richard Matthews **Trained** Lambourn, Berks
■ Stewards' Enquiry : Brendan Powell 7-day ban; used whip above permitted level (20th-26th Feb)

FOCUS
Race distance increased by 22yds. A moderate handicap which saw two forge clear from the last. The first two have been rated to their best.

3978 32RED.COM H'CAP HURDLE (11 hdls) 2m 3f 100y
3:50 (3:51) (Class 4) (0-120,120) 4-Y-0+ £4,548 (£1,335; £667; £333)

Form RPR
0412 1 **Harley Rebel**[11] 3777 4-10-12 117 .... RichardJohnson 119+
(Neil Mulholland) *chsd ldrs: rdn 4 out: led 2 out: sn drvn: hdd jst after last: rallied to ld again towards fin* 9/4[1]
2 *nk* **Ayalor (FR)**[670] 6-11-6 114 .... NoelFehily 127+
(Harry Fry) *hld up towards rr: stdy hdwy 4 out: hung lft between last 2: led sn after last and hung lft u.p: hdd nr fin* 4/1[2]
1-22 3 *3 ½* **Alberobello (IRE)**[251] 553 8-11-9 120 ....(t) MattGriffiths(3) 128
(Jeremy Scott) *led to 2 out: kpt on u.p tl unable qck flat* 11/2[3]

4 21 **Le Boizelo (FR)**[111] 1981 5-11-10 118 .... JamieMoore 105
(Robert Walford) *t.k.h: chsd ldrs: rdn 3 out: 4th whn mstke next: sn wknd: wl hld whn j.lft last* **11/1**

300P 5 14 **Midnight Belle**[37] 3365 9-11-7 118 ....(p) BenPoste(3) 91
(Tom Symonds) *prom: ev ch 3 out: sn drvn: wknd 2 out* **28/1**

4-36 6 3 1/2 **L Frank Baum (IRE)**[37] 3374 9-9-11 94 oh1 ....(p) RobertWilliams(3) 64
(Bernard Llewellyn) *prom tl wknd 3 out* **33/1**

4P-0 7 4 1/2 **Agreement (IRE)**[62] 2906 6-10-11 110 ....(p) ChrisWard(5) 75
(Nikki Evans) *wnt to post early: chsd ldr tl rdn and wknd 4 out: wl bhd whn mstke last* **80/1**

0563 8 2 3/4 **Filatore (IRE)**[27] 3517 7-11-3 118 ....(p) JordanWilliams(7) 80
(Bernard Llewellyn) *towards rr: mstke 2nd: last and rdn along fr 4th: lost tch 4 out* **7/1**

3-65 9 1 3/4 **Stiff Upper Lip (IRE)**[55] 3045 6-11-6 114 .... LeightonAspell 75
(Oliver Sherwood) *a towards rr: rdn and wknd after 7th: wl bhd whn mstke 2 out* **14/1**

5400 F **Lava Lamp (GER)**[49] 3137 9-10-11 115 .... CianMaher(10)
(Evan Williams) *mid-div: rdn whn fell 4 out* **16/1**

-551 P **Fishing Bridge (IRE)**[24] 3572 11-11-0 111 ....(vt) KieronEdgar(3)
(David Rees) *hld up: nt fluent 2nd: bdly hmpd 4 out: p.u bef next* **12/1**

5m 20.5s (18.70) **Going Correction** +0.70s/f (Soft)
WFA 4 from 5yo+ 9lb 11 Ran SP% 114.9
Speed ratings (Par 105): **88,87,86,77,71 70,68,67,66,**
CSF £11.43 CT £43.14 TOTE £2.30: £1.40, £1.70, £1.90; EX 8.80 Trifecta £36.20.
Owner Mrs Gloria Seymour **Bred** Stephen & Gloria Seymour **Trained** Limpley Stoke, Wilts

FOCUS
Race distance increased by 22yds. The principals had this to themselves from two out and it's form to be positive about for the class. A hurdle pb from the runner-up, but in line with the best of his chase form.

3979 32RED H'CAP CHASE (18 fncs) 2m 7f 131y
4:20 (4:22) (Class 4) (0-120,120) 5-Y-O+ £5,198 (£1,526; £763; £381)

Form RPR

3644 1 **Berea Boru (IRE)**[27] 3520 8-11-11 119 ....(t) SeanBowen 137+
(Peter Bowen) *prom: lost 2nd whn stmbld 4 out: rallied to chse ldr 2 out: chal last: sn led: styd on wl* **6/1[3]**

51-P 2 3 1/2 **Emma Soda**[26] 3385 11-10-9 103 ....(b) PeterCarberry 112
(Paul Davies) *led: jnd 3rd: hdd 11th: styd prom: rdn to ld again bef 4 out: jnd last: hdd and unable qck flat* **25/1**

4-46 3 22 **Drumshambo (USA)**[51] 3109 10-11-4 117 .... CharlieDeutsch(5) 110
(Venetia Williams) *chsd ldrs: lost pl 12th: rallied 5 out: chsd ldr 4 out tl wknd appr 2 out* **6/1[3]**

-522 4 11 **Moorlands Mist**[27] 3517 9-11-4 117 .... ConorRing(5) 94
(Evan Williams) *hld up in rr: mstke 9th and rdn along: lost tch 12th* **2/1[1]**

-14P 5 15 **Thatchers Gold (IRE)**[36] 3384 8-11-1 109 .... DenisO'Regan 70
(Henry Oliver) *prom whn mstke 1st: chsd ldrs: mstke and reminder 6th: mstke 8th: rdn after 13th: wknd 5 out* **14/1**

6252 P **Buckhorn Tom**[10] 3788 8-10-13 107 ....(b) PaddyBrennan
(Colin Tizzard) *chsd ldrs: mstke 4th: rdn and struggling fr 7th: j. slowly 12th: sn wl bhd: p.u bef 4 out* **11/2[2]**

P12F P **Pure Poteen (IRE)**[28] 3507 8-11-3 111 ....(t) NoelFehily
(Neil Mulholland) *hld up in rr: mstke 4th: struggling 13th: bhd whn p.u bef 4 out* **6/1[3]**

0PPP F **Tara Road**[13] 3735 8-11-12 120 ....(tp) LeightonAspell
(Rebecca Curtis) *prom: w ldr 3rd tl led 11th: hdd appr 4 out: 4th and wkng qckly whn fell next: winded* **8/1**

6m 50.2s (28.20) **Going Correction** +1.15s/f (Heavy) 8 Ran SP% 113.2
Speed ratings: **99,97,90,86,81 , ,**
CSF £110.85 CT £931.39 TOTE £7.70: £2.50, £5.90, £2.00; EX 155.20 Trifecta £1435.60.
Owner H Jones **Bred** Mrs E Thompson **Trained** Little Newcastle, Pembrokes

FOCUS
Race distance increased by 34yds. A modest staying handicap, rated around the runner-up.

3980 32REDSPORT.COM STANDARD OPEN NATIONAL HUNT FLAT RACE 2m 11y
4:50 (4:54) (Class 6) 4-6-Y-O £1,949 (£572; £286; £143)

Form RPR

22 1 **Pride Of Lecale**[29] 3502 5-11-3 0 ....(t) PaddyBrennan 130+
(Fergal O'Brien) *racd on ins: a.p: led over 3f out: shkn up and sn drew clr: eased fnl 50yds* **3/1[2]**

531 2 14 **Alf 'N' Dor (IRE)**[24] 3573 5-11-10 0 ....(t) SeanBowen 120
(Peter Bowen) *t.k.h early: prom: rdn to chse wnr over 3f out: one pce and lost 2nd 2f out: rallied to go modest 2nd post* **6/1[3]**

0 3 shd **Instingtive (IRE)**[251] 558 5-11-3 0 ....(t) NoelFehily 113
(Harry Fry) *led tl hdd over 3f out: kpt on same pce: wnt mod 2nd 2f out: no ch w wnr: ct for 2nd post* **20/1**

22 4 3/4 **Desert Retreat (IRE)**[93] 2270 5-11-3 0 .... RichardJohnson 112
(Philip Hobbs) *chsd ldrs tl rdn and lost pl over 4f out: styd on fnl 2f* **10/11[1]**

5 nk **Wylde Magic (IRE)** 5-11-3 0 .... LeightonAspell 112
(Evan Williams) *hld up in rr: clsd 6f out: rdn 4f out: styd on same pce* **10/1**

6 10 **Muffins For Tea** 6-11-3 0 .... DarylJacob 102
(Colin Tizzard) *chsd ldrs: rdn 3f out: wknd 2f out* **28/1**

7 44 **Port Navas (IRE)** 5-11-3 0 .... TomScudamore 58
(David Pipe) *hld up: rdn 6f out: lost tch 4f out: t.o* **16/1**

8 99 **Double Miss** 5-10-10 0 .... TomO'Brien
(Robert Stephens) *towards rr: rdn along 1/2-way: t.o fnl 6f* **50/1**

4m 12.6s (7.60) **Going Correction** +0.70s/f (Soft) 8 Ran SP% 116.8
Speed ratings: **109,102,101,101,101 96,74,24**
CSF £21.27 TOTE £3.80: £1.20, £1.50, £4.20; EX 17.20 Trifecta £153.00.
Owner Paul & Clare Rooney **Bred** Mrs B Hanna **Trained** Naunton, Gloucs

FOCUS
Race distance increased by 22yds. A modest bumper that served up a real test. The second and fourth have been rated close to their marks.
T/Plt: £1,747.30 to a £1 stake. Pool: £78,607.37 - 32.84 winning tickets. T/Qpdt: £216.10 to a £1 stake. Pool: £9,608.58 - 32.9 winning tickets. **Richard Lowther**

3076 FFOS LAS (L-H)
Saturday, February 6
3981 Meeting Abandoned - waterlogged

3443 SANDOWN (R-H)
Saturday, February 6

OFFICIAL GOING: Hurdle course - soft (heavy in places in home straight, good to soft in places in back straight; 4.5) chase course - good to soft (good in places, soft in places downhill section; 5.3)
Wind: strong, mostly against Weather: overcast

3988 BETFRED "HOME OF GOALS GALORE" JUVENILE HURDLE (8 hdls) 1m 7f 216y
12:40 (12:42) (Class 3) 4-Y-O £6,657 (£2,067; £1,113)

Form RPR

61 1 **Akavit (IRE)**[73] 2718 4-11-4 0 .... DavidBass 122+
(Ed de Giles) *mde all and set gd pce: shkn up whn pressed bef 2 out: 4 l ld and in command whn lft clr last: drvn out* **10/1**

1 2 8 **Seven Kingdoms (IRE)**[28] 3523 4-11-4 0 .... AidanColeman 115
(David Dennis) *hld up in 4th: rdn and tried to cl bef 2 out but no great imp: wl hld whn lft in 2nd pl last* **6/4[2]**

2 3 9 **Searching (IRE)**[42] 3213 4-10-12 0 .... JoshuaMoore 105
(Gary Moore) *trckd wnr: shkn up and lost 2nd whn blnd 2 out: sltly hmpd last and wknd* **6/1[3]**

P P **Austin Friars**[11] 3790 4-10-12 0 .... JamieMoore
(Jim Best) *nt fluent: a in last: lost tch 3 out: shkn up and wknd bef 2 out: wl bhd whn p.u bef last* **100/1**

51 F **Fingertips (FR)**[64] 2883 4-11-8 129 ....(t) DarylJacob 122
(David Pipe) *trckd ldng pair: nt fluent 4th: shkn up to take 2nd 2 out: sn drvn: 4 l down and hld whn fell last* **5/4[1]**

4m 13.7s (6.50) **Going Correction** +0.625s/f (Soft) 5 Ran SP% 108.8
Speed ratings: **108,104,99, ,**
CSF £25.61 TOTE £8.90: £3.00, £1.20; EX 21.80 Trifecta £81.70.
Owner Simon Treacher **Bred** Tenuta Genzianella Di Manuela Martinelli **Trained** Ledbury, H'fords

FOCUS
The going on the hurdle course was soft, with heavy patches in the straight and good to soft areas down the back. Daryl Jacob felt it wasn't too bad, although there was a slight headwind in the straight. All distances as advertised. Not a strong juvenile hurdle, although it was run at a good gallop thanks to the winner. The second and the faller help set the level.

3989 BETFRED RACING "FOLLOW US ON TWITTER" CONTENDERS HURDLE (LISTED RACE) (8 hdls) 1m 7f 216y
1:15 (1:15) (Class 1) 4-Y-O+ £14,237 (£5,342; £2,675; £1,332)

Form RPR

1-2 1 **Connetable (FR)**[14] 3730 4-10-4 139 .... SamTwiston-Davies 135
(Paul Nicholls) *lw: trckd clr ldr: clsd 3 out: rdn 2 out: narrow ld last but exagant jump and jnd: drvn ahd again fnl 75yds* **15/2[3]**

2012 2 nk **Rayvin Black**[14] 3740 7-11-0 149 ....(p) ThomasGarner 144
(Oliver Sherwood) *led and clr: stdd pce 3rd: drvn for home bef 2 out: hdd last but sn upsides wnr again: kpt on wl but jst hld fnl 75yds* **11/4[2]**

11-6 3 2 **Peace And Co (FR)**[56] 3033 5-11-4 159 .... DarylJacob 147
(Nicky Henderson) *lw: hld up in 3rd: dropped to last 3 out but stl gng wl: chsd ldng pair again 2 out: sn rdn and nt qckn: kpt on fr last* **4/7[1]**

3130 4 1 1/4 **Kayf Blanco**[35] 3449 7-11-0 138 .... KielanWoods 141
(Graeme McPherson) *hld up in last: nt fluent 5th: chsd ldng pair 3 out to 2 out: sn rdn: stl cl up last: one pce flat* **20/1**

4m 11.4s (4.20) **Going Correction** +0.625s/f (Soft)
WFA 4 from 5yo+ 9lb 4 Ran SP% 106.8
Speed ratings (Par 111): **114,113,112,112**
CSF £25.77 TOTE £5.20; EX 18.10 Trifecta £22.10.
Owner Chris Giles **Bred** Serge Barthelemy **Trained** Ditcheat, Somerset

FOCUS
Run at a stop-start gallop, the 138-rated outsider of the field finished a close-up last of four and the form isn't strong, but none the less it was a good effort by the winning juvenile. A messy race, and a token rating has been given through the fourth.

3990 BETFRED "TREBLE ODDS ON LUCKY 15'S" H'CAP CHASE (13 fncs) 1m 7f 119y
1:50 (1:50) (Class 2) 5-Y-O+ £15,640 (£4,620; £2,310; £1,155)

Form RPR

1-12 1 **Arthur's Oak**[35] 3446 8-10-13 144 .... AidanColeman 151
(Venetia Williams) *led: j.lft 3rd: kicked for home after 3 out: pressed and mstke last: hdd flat: rallied wl to ld again nr fin: jst hld on* **6/4[1]**

1-P0 2 nse **Ulck Du Lin (FR)**[56] 3030 8-10-8 139 ....(bt) NickScholfield 145
(Paul Nicholls) *lw: trckd wnr: clsd 2 out: drvn to chal last: led flat: kpt on but hdd nr fin: jst pipped* **7/1**

F4-U 3 10 **Chris Pea Green**[127] 1735 7-10-11 142 .... JoshuaMoore 141
(Gary Moore) *mstke 2nd: last fr 4th: shkn up after 4 out: no imp fr next: tk 3rd 2 out: n.d* **11/4[3]**

-001 4 35 **Bold Henry**[35] 3446 10-10-13 144 .... RichardJohnson 121
(Philip Hobbs) *hld up: trckd ldng pair fr 4th: gng easily tl mstke 9th: shkn up to dispute 2nd 3 out: sn wknd: virtually p.u after last* **9/4[2]**

4m 3.5s (1.70) **Going Correction** +0.275s/f (Yiel) 4 Ran SP% 109.9
Speed ratings: **106,105,100,83**
CSF £10.26 TOTE £2.30; EX 11.90 Trifecta £38.20.
Owner Mrs J K Burt **Bred** J L Burt **Trained** Kings Caple, H'fords
■ Stewards' Enquiry : Nick Scholfield two-day ban; excessive use of whip (21st-22nd Feb)

FOCUS
The ground on the chase course wasn't as testing as on the hurdles track, given as good to soft with soft patches downhill and good areas in the back straight. The front pair came clear in what was a decent small-field chase, although the winner's main market rival did disappoint. The winner has been rated up 3lb on his previous best, with the second rated back to his best.

3991 BETFRED TV SCILLY ISLES NOVICES' CHASE (GRADE 1) (17 fncs) 2m 4f 10y
2:25 (2:25) (Class 1) 5-Y-O+ £25,627 (£9,616; £4,815; £2,398)

Form RPR

1211 1 **Bristol De Mai (FR)**[14] 3738 5-11-0 151 .... DarylJacob 158+
(Nigel Twiston-Davies) *lw: mde all: pressed 2 out: sn drew clr: shkn up and r.o wl flat: comf* **10/11[1]**

223F 2 6 **As De Mee (FR)**[42] 3229 6-11-3 140 .... SamTwiston-Davies 153
(Paul Nicholls) *chsd wnr to 7th: styd cl up: wnt 2nd again 2 out and tried to chal: sn brushed aside: one pce* **10/1**

6011 3 1 **Tea For Two**[42] 3229 7-11-3 153 .... LizzieKelly 153
(Nick Williams) *trckd wnr 7th: shkn up and lost 2nd 2 out: sn outpcd: kpt on fr last* **7/4[2]**

2/4U **4** *19* **Ubak (FR)**[22] 3611 8-11-3 144.. JoshuaMoore 138
(Gary Moore) *a last: mstke 7th: nt fluent 10th and 4 out: shkn up and no imp sn after: wknd flat* **9/1**[3]

5m 14.65s (-3.75) **Going Correction** +0.275s/f (Yiel)
WFA 5 from 6yo+ 2lb **4** Ran SP% **107.8**
Speed ratings: **118,115,115,107**
CSF £8.32 TOTE £1.50; EX 7.30 Trifecta £12.40.
Owner Simon Munir & Isaac Souede **Bred** Jean-Yves Touzaint **Trained** Naunton, Gloucs

FOCUS
Billed as a match between two high-class novice chasers, the duel never really developed with the favourite winning with plenty in hand. Sound form, although the runner-up does carry a rating of just 140. The winner has been rated in line with his Haydock romp, but there's a case for rating this higher.

3992 BETFRED MOBILE HEROES H'CAP HURDLE (GRADE 3) (11 hdls 1 omitted) 2m 7f 98y
3:00 (3:00) (Class 1) 4-Y-0+ **£28,609** (£10,819; £5,484; £2,799; £1,474)

Form RPR
11/5 **1** **Saddlers Encore (IRE)**[42] 3254 7-10-5 **129**.......................... RichardJohnson 135
(Philip Hobbs) *lw: trckd ldr: pushed along sn after bypassed 3 out: rdn to ld after 2 out: hrd pressed fr: hld on wl: all out* **5/1**[3]

0-53 **2** *3/4* **Join The Clan (IRE)**[40] 3317 7-10-5 **136**.................. PatrickCowley[(7)] 141
(Jonjo O'Neill) *trckd ldrs: nt fluent 3rd: lost pl bypassing 3 out and pushed along: renewed effrt to press ldng pair bef 2 out: chal last: kpt on but jst hld* **9/1**

-151 **3** *hd* **Yala Enki (FR)**[28] 3527 6-11-0 **138**............................ AidanColeman 143
(Venetia Williams) *lw: led and clr early: pressed after bypassed 3 out: hdd after 2 out: 3rd jumping last: kpt on wl but jst hld* **7/2**[1]

4F05 **4** *25* **Little Boy Boru (IRE)**[28] 3527 8-9-11 **124** oh2............ HarryBannister[(3)] 104
(Suzy Smith) *hld up in rr: rdn and lost tch w ldrs on long run after bypassed 3 out: tk poor 4th after 2 out: no ch* **14/1**

4-23 **5** *7* **Ibis Du Rheu (FR)**[28] 3527 5-11-1 **139**...................(t) SamTwiston-Davies 112
(Paul Nicholls) *lw: wl in tch: chsd ldng pair after bypassed 3 out tl bef 2 out where mstke and wknd: fin tired* **4/1**[2]

214- **P** **Medinas (FR)**[413] 3181 9-11-5 **150**........................ WilliamFeatherstone[(7)]
(Alan King) *settled in last: urged along fr 8th and struggling: sme modest prog bef 2 out but nvr on terms: poor 6th whn p.u bef last* **8/1**

3064 **P** **Invicta Lake (IRE)**[8] 3844 9-10-0 **124** oh2........................ GavinSheehan
(Suzy Smith) *towards rr: nt fluent 7th: urged along after 9th: sn wknd: wl bhd whn p.u bef 2 out* **15/2**

-343 **P** **Anteros (IRE)**[36] 3407 8-10-8 **132**....................................(t) PaddyBrennan
(Sophie Leech) *hld up in rr: hit 4th: prog to chse ldrs 9th: rdn and wknd wl bef 2 out: poor 7th whn p.u bef last* **9/1**

-331 **P** **Donna's Diamond (IRE)**[36] 3428 7-10-6 **135**.............. DiarmuidO'Regan[(5)]
(Chris Grant) *reluctant to s: urged along and rcvrd to chse ldng pair fr 2nd tl wknd sn after bypassing 3 out: poor 8th whn p.u bef last* **11/1**

6m 5.45s (365.45) **9** Ran SP% **116.8**
CSF £49.14 CT £178.49 TOTE £5.50: £1.80, £2.80, £1.80; EX 56.80 Trifecta £162.00.
Owner Robert & Janet Gibbs **Bred** Kevin Neville **Trained** Withycombe, Somerset
■ Stewards' Enquiry : Patrick Cowley two-day ban; used whip above permitted level (21st-22nd Feb)

FOCUS
Good handicap form, the right horses coming a long way clear in a race that proved a thorough test. A step up from the winner.

3993 BETFRED MASTERS H'CAP CHASE (22 fncs) 3m 37y
3:30 (3:32) (Class 2) 5-Y-0+
£31,280 (£9,240; £4,620; £2,310; £1,155; £580)

Form RPR
P026 **1** **Le Reve (IRE)**[7] 3860 8-11-4 **144**...............................(b[1]) HarrySkelton 154+
(Lucy Wadham) *wl in tch: trckd ldng pair 16th: gng strly 4 out: chsd ldr next: chal 2 out: led last: drvn out* **4/1**[1]

/624 **2** *2 1/4* **Pete The Feat (IRE)**[23] 3591 12-10-4 **130**..................(t) RichardJohnson 139
(Charlie Longsdon) *lw: led at gd pce: mstke 12th: drvn and jnd 2 out: hdd last: kpt on gamely* **15/2**

0-00 **3** *4* **Unioniste (FR)**[49] 3150 8-11-10 **150**........................... NickScholfield 155
(Paul Nicholls) *hld up in rr: last whn nt fluent 14th and looked to be struggling: prog 17th: chsd ldng pair after 3 out: shkn up and styd on same pce after* **8/1**

-154 **4** *13* **Saroque (IRE)**[28] 3518 9-10-5 **131**.................................. AidanColeman 127
(Venetia Williams) *chsd ldr: rdn 4 out: lost 2nd next: sn wknd* **11/2**

UU-2 **5** *1 1/4* **Summery Justice (IRE)**[63] 2916 12-10-7 **138**.........(p) CharlieDeutsch[(5)] 130
(Venetia Williams) *last whn awkward 1st: mostly in rr: jst in tch but rdn 4 out: btn bef next* **7/1**

0-0U **6** *22* **Black Thunder (FR)**[28] 3518 9-11-9 **149**..............(t) SamTwiston-Davies 120
(Paul Nicholls) *chsd ldng pair tl 16th where mstke and dropped to rr: rdn and jst in tch 4 out: wknd bef next* **5/1**[3]

2154 **7** *5* **Seventh Sky (GER)**[14] 3741 9-11-12 **152**........................(tp) DarylJacob 118
(Charlie Mann) *lw: pressed ldrs: lost pl fr 15th: struggling in last pl out: sn wknd* **12/1**

-214 **F** **Knock House (IRE)**[57] 3016 7-11-4 **144**............................ GavinSheehan
(Mick Channon) *slow jump 4th: in tch in last trio tl fell 12th* **9/2**[2]

6m 26.5s (-1.30) **Going Correction** +0.275s/f (Yiel) **8** Ran SP% **113.3**
Speed ratings: **113,112,110,106,106 98,97,**
CSF £32.76 CT £226.49 TOTE £4.40: £1.80, £2.70, £2.90; EX 42.00 Trifecta £305.00.
Owner P H Betts **Bred** J D Flood **Trained** Newmarket, Suffolk

FOCUS
A useful staying handicap run at a sound gallop throughout courtesy of the runner-up. The winner has been rated to his best.

3994 BETFRED "DOWNLOAD THE APP" NOVICES' H'CAP HURDLE (8 hdls 1 omitted) 2m 3f 173y
4:05 (4:05) (Class 3) (0-125,124) 4-Y-0+ **£6,498** (£1,908; £954; £477)

Form RPR
3541 **1** **Pinnacle Panda (IRE)**[37] 3375 5-11-9 **121**.................. RichardJohnson 130+
(Tom Lacey) *hld up in last: prog bef usual 3 out: chal and mstke usual 2 out (actual last): sn led: hanging lft flat then edgd rt: 2 l up whn swvd sharply lft 50yds out: jst hld on* **9/2**[2]

0-11 **2** *1/2* **Bon Enfant (FR)**[63] 2917 5-11-10 **122**............................ GavinSheehan 128
(Warren Greatrex) *lw: trckd ldrs: wnt 2nd after usual 3 out: rdn to ld bef usual 2 out (actual last): hdd sn after it: kpt on u.p and nrly ct wandering wnr nr fin* **7/2**[1]

P56- **3** *25* **Birch Hill (IRE)**[370] 3999 6-11-12 **124**............................ AndrewTinkler 104
(Nicky Henderson) *lw: nt a fluent: hld up in tch: pushed along and prog after usual 3 out: rdn and hanging bef usual 2 out (actual last): tk 3rd on extended run-in but lost grnd on ldng pair* **7/2**[1]

212 **4** *3 1/4* **Perceus**[22] 3610 4-11-1 **124**.. JackQuinlan 89
(James Eustace) *in tch: prog to chse ldng pair after usual 3 out: wknd qckly bef usual 2 out (actual last)* **7/2**[1]

3-05 **5** *16* **Coup De Grace (IRE)**[20] 3042 7-11-3 **115**..................(v[1]) JoshuaMoore 75
(Pat Phelan) *in tch: drvn and struggling after usual 3 out: wl btn bef usual 2 out (actual last)* **14/1**

0112 **6** *66* **Arquebusier (FR)**[30] 3498 6-10-9 **110**.........................(p) JamesBanks[(3)] 4
(Emma Baker) *led: mstke 2nd: hdd & wknd rapidly usual 3 out: t.o* **12/1**

6203 **7** *5* **Manhattan Mead**[34] 3452 6-11-5 **117**.........................(v[1]) MarcGoldstein 6
(Michael Madgwick) *chsd ldr to 3rd: lost pl and rdn next: wknd bef usual 3 out: sn t.o* **33/1**

3-20 **8** *42* **Tara Bridge**[28] 3529 8-11-8 **120**... TomCannon
(Chris Gordon) *trckd ldr: led usual 3 out gng strly: hdd bef usual 2 out (actual last) and wknd rapidly: remote 6th whn grnd to a halt after it: eventually fin* **16/1**

6063 **9** *48* **Bolister (FR)**[19] 3660 5-9-11 **102**.................................. GeorgeGorman[(7)]
(Gary Moore) *in tch in rr: wknd qckly after usual 6th: sn t.o* **8/1**[3]

5m 15.2s (15.60) **Going Correction** +0.625s/f (Soft)
WFA 4 from 5yo+ 10lb **9** Ran SP% **119.1**
Speed ratings (Par 107): **93,92,82,81,75 48,46,29,10**
CSF £21.86 CT £62.36 TOTE £4.90: £1.80, £1.40, £1.80; EX 21.00 Trifecta £117.80.
Owner Mr Hinds & Galloping on the South Downs **Bred** Daniel Furini **Trained** Ledbury, H'fords

FOCUS
The front pair came well clear in a fair handicap, although there was late drama with the runners being waved around the omitted last hurdle and the winner then darting left nearing the line and nearly throwing it away. Seemingly big steps up from the first two, but the form could be at least 5lb out either way.
T/Plt: £234.90 to a £1 stake. Pool: £110,344.12 - 342.91 wining units. T/Qpdt: £10.80 to a £1 stake. Pool: £10,905.18 - 740.70 winning units. **Jonathan Neesom**

3790 WETHERBY (L-H)
Saturday, February 6

OFFICIAL GOING: Soft (heavy in places back straight) changing to heavy after race 2 (1.35)
Wind: moderate 1/2 against, becoming fresh 1/2 behind Weather: light rain

3995 WILMOT-SMITH MEMORIAL MARES' NOVICES' HURDLE (9 hdls) 2m
1:00 (1:01) (Class 4) 4-Y-0+ **£3,249** (£954; £477; £238)

Form RPR
-221 **1** **Pink Play (IRE)**[55] 3066 5-11-6 117.............................. NicodeBoinville 122+
(Harry Whittington) *chsd ldrs: cl 2nd bef 3 out: sn drvn upsides: led narrowly 2 out: fnd ex clsng stages* **1/2**[1]

32 **2** *1 1/2* **Secret Door (IRE)**[55] 3066 5-11-0 0.. NoelFehily 113
(Harry Fry) *chsd clr ldr: led 5th: jnd 3 out: hdd 2 out: upsides last: no ex clsng stages* **2/1**[2]

43 **3** *59* **Stickee Fingers**[66] 2856 5-11-0 0................................... TomScudamore 54
(Warren Greatrex) *chsd ldrs: drvn bef 3 out: sn wknd and bhd: t.o 2 out* **14/1**[3]

6 **4** *70* **Wishing Well**[23] 3587 4-10-1 0.. JoeColliver[(3)]
(Micky Hammond) *j.rt: t.k.h in rr: remote 4th 5th: t.o whn mstke 3 out: j. bdly rt last 2: eventually completed* **66/1**

0-0P **P** **Turtleplex**[55] 3054 5-10-9 0......................................[1] DaraghBourke[(5)]
(Maurice Barnes) *j. bdly rt: led sn clr tl after 4th: hdd & wknd qckly next: sn t.o: p.u after 6th* **300/1**

6 **P** **Miss Barbossa (IRE)**[23] 3593 5-11-0 0.............................. HenryBrooke
(Martin Todhunter) *in rr: bhd fr 4th: t.o 6th: sn p.u* **100/1**

0P **P** **Night In London (IRE)**[8] 3839 6-10-11 0......................... HarryChalloner[(3)]
(Keith Reveley) *in rr: bhd fr 4th: blnd next: sn t.o: p.u after 6th* **150/1**

4m 38.1s (42.30) **Going Correction** +2.80s/f (Heav)
WFA 4 from 5yo+ 9lb **7** Ran SP% **110.1**
Speed ratings (Par 105): **106,105,75,40, ,**
CSF £1.69 TOTE £1.50: £1.10, £1.40; EX 1.60 Trifecta £2.50.
Owner Paul G Jacobs **Bred** Berry Farms **Trained** Sparsholt, Oxfordshire

FOCUS
The A1 bend had been set 24yds from the innermost line. The 'away' chase bend had been set 12yds from the innermost line and the 'away' hurdle bend has been set 20yds from the innermost line. The effect on the official distance of this contest was an extra 132yds. Only two mattered in the betting and they came clear. The first two have been rated pretty much to their Southwell marks.

3996 TOTESCOOP6 H'CAP CHASE (14 fncs 2 omitted) 2m 3f 85y
1:35 (1:37) (Class 2) (0-150,148) 5-Y-0+ **£11,734** (£3,579; £1,869; £1,015)

Form RPR
3005 **1** **Sew On Target (IRE)**[75] 2686 11-10-10 **132**........................ BrendanPowell 146+
(Colin Tizzard) *mde all: drew clr fr 4 out: 35 l ahd last: heavily eased last 75yds* **15/2**

-5P4 **2** *32* **Renard (FR)**[16] 3706 11-10-2 **124**....................................... LiamTreadwell 98
(Venetia Williams) *chsd wnr: 3rd and drvn 4 out: remote 2nd appr 2 out* **4/1**[3]

3511 **3** *12* **Katkeau (FR)**[52] 3109 9-11-12 **148**...............................(t) TomScudamore 108
(David Pipe) *in rr: modest 4th 8th: lost pl and reminders 10th: sn wl bhd: lft poor 4th appr last: tk 3rd nr fin* **5/2**[1]

5122 **4** *3/4* **Friendly Royal (IRE)**[38] 3365 7-10-1 **123**............................. SeanQuinlan 85
(Sue Smith) *mstkes: chsd ldrs: blnd 6th: lost pl 8th: reminders next: remote 4th whn blnd 3 out: 3rd appr last: fin tired* **3/1**[2]

6000 **P** **Rathlin**[36] 3425 11-10-6 **135**..(tp) FinianO'Toole[(7)]
(Micky Hammond) *trckd ldrs: chsd wnr bef 4 out: wknd and remote tired 4th whn p.u appr last* **17/2**

545- **P** **Mr Syntax (IRE)**[300] 5297 12-10-0 **122** oh3.............................. BrianHughes
(Chris Grant) *prom: lost pl 8th: t.o after 10th: p.u bef 4 out* **33/1**

U112 **P** **Indian Voyage (IRE)**[63] 2920 8-10-7 **134**........................(t) DaraghBourke[(5)]
(Maurice Barnes) *in rr: nt fluent and lost pl 8th: sn bhd: t.o whn p.u bef 4 out* **7/1**

5m 51.4s (43.60) **Going Correction** +2.60s/f (Heav) **7** Ran SP% **111.3**
Speed ratings: **112,98,93,93,** ,
CSF £35.76 TOTE £8.60: £3.90, £2.80; EX 44.90 Trifecta £165.20.
Owner A Selway **Bred** Gerry Canavan **Trained** Milborne Port, Dorset

FOCUS
The A1 bend had been set 24yds from the innermost line. The 'away' chase bend had been set 12yds from the innermost line and the 'away' hurdle bend has been set 20yds from the innermost line. The effect on the official distance of this contest was an extra 180yds. The final fence down the back straight was bypassed throughout the meeting. Quite a competitive handicap and the form can prove to be reliable in similar conditions.

3997 TOTEPOOLLIVEINFO.COM NOVICES' HURDLE (12 hdls) 2m 5f 56y
2:10 (2:10) (Class 4) 5-Y-O+ £3,249 (£954; £477; £238)

Form RPR
11 **1** **Tomngerry (IRE)**[23] 3593 6-10-12 0.................................... DannyCook 121+
(Brian Ellison) *trckd ldrs: nt fluent and dropped bk 9th: drvn to chse ldng pair bef next: led narrowly 2 out: edgd lft between last 2: forged clr last 75yds* **1/1**[1]

1 **2** *6* **Bigirononhiship (IRE)**[35] 3436 5-11-5 0.............................. CraigNichol 122
(Rose Dobbin) *hld up in last: trckd ldrs: cl 2nd after 9th: led and nt fluent 3 out: hdd next: swtchd rt between last 2: kpt on same pce last 100yds* **5/2**[2]

1-20 **3** *28* **Bronco Billy (IRE)**[40] 3316 6-10-12 0.................................... NoelFehily 87
(Jonjo O'Neill) *trckd ldrs: drvn and lost pl bef 3 out: tk distant 3rd appr last* **3/1**[3]

-620 **4** *10* **Infinityandbeyond (IRE)**[39] 3334 5-10-12 0.................. TrevorWhelan 79
(Neil King) *w ldr: led 2nd: drvn and hdd 3 out: wknd and hit next: fin tired* **20/1**

5P **P** **Pikes Peak (IRE)**[97] 2210 7-10-12 0.................................... BrianHughes
(Chris Grant) *led to 2nd: w ldr: drvn 9th: lost pl and wl bhd whn p.u bef next* **100/1**

6m 23.7s (56.90) **Going Correction** +2.80s/f (Heav) 5 Ran SP% 109.3
Speed ratings: **103,100,90,86,**
CSF £3.89 TOTE £1.70: £1.10, £1.50; EX 5.70 Trifecta £5.20.
Owner Mrs J A Martin **Bred** Mrs E Tector **Trained** Norton, N Yorks

FOCUS
The A1 bend had been set 24yds from the innermost line. The 'away' chase bend had been set 12yds from the innermost line and the 'away' hurdle bend has been set 20yds from the innermost line. The effect on the official distance of this contest was an extra 204yds. This was slowly run and the form is far from reliable. A small step up from the second, with the third again well below form.

3998 TOTEPOOL TOWTON NOVICES' CHASE (GRADE 2) (17 fncs 2 omitted) 3m 45y
2:45 (2:45) (Class 1) 5-Y-O+ £19,221 (£7,835; £4,421)

Form RPR
4F12 **1** **Blaklion**[36] 3405 7-11-7 150.. RyanHatch 162+
(Nigel Twiston-Davies) *trckd ldrs: 2nd bef 4 out: sn upsides: led last: drvn clr* **4/1**

-212 **2** *8* **Definitly Red (IRE)**[21] 3621 7-11-0 0.................................... DannyCook 150
(Brian Ellison) *chsd ldrs: hit 7th: mstke next: 2nd 13th: led bef 4 out: sn hrd drvn: hdd and j.lft last: sn wknd* **3/1**[3]

3113 **3** *10* **Native River (IRE)**[42] 3229 6-11-7 153.............................. BrendanPowell 146
(Colin Tizzard) *chsd ldrs: pushed along 6th: drvn and lost pl bef 4 out: poor 3rd 3 out* **11/4**[2]

-116 **P** **Kingswell Theatre**[38] 3364 7-11-4 142.............................. TomScudamore
(Michael Scudamore) *led: hdd after 5th: lost pl after 9th: sn bhd: t.o 11th: p.u after 13th* **28/1**

1-1U **P** **Bitofapuzzle**[23] 3604 8-10-11 148..(t) NoelFehily
(Harry Fry) *t.k.h: trckd ldrs: led after 5th: hdd bef 4 out: sn wknd: distant 4th whn blnd 2 out: immediately p.u* **9/4**[1]

4132 **P** **Run Ructions Run (IRE)**[21] 3627 7-10-7 135.................(p) BrianHughes
(Tim Easterby) *nt fluent: in tch: hit 8th: outpcd 10th: bhd 13th: t.o whn p.u bef 4 out* **16/1**

7m 19.5s (31.50) 6 Ran SP% 111.8
CSF £16.54 TOTE £4.80: £2.50, £2.00; EX 15.60 Trifecta £43.60.
Owner S Such & Cg Paletta **Bred** Mrs M D W Morrison **Trained** Naunton, Gloucs

FOCUS
The A1 bend had been set 24yds from the innermost line. The 'away' chase bend had been set 12yds from the innermost line and the 'away' hurdle bend has been set 20yds from the innermost line. The effect on the official distance of this contest was an extra 216yds. The final fence down the back straight was bypassed throughout the meeting. This looked a really strong contest, and it developed into a gruelling test. Another small step up from the winner.

3999 FOLLOW @TOTEPOOLRACING ON TWITTER H'CAP HURDLE (12 hdls) 3m 26y
3:20 (3:21) (Class 3) (0-140,135) 4-Y-O+ £5,523 (£1,621; £810; £405)

Form RPR
P-30 **1** **Sir Vinski (IRE)**[36] 3428 7-10-11 **120**..............................(b[1]) CraigNichol 132+
(Nicky Richards) *w ldrs: led after 9th: drew clr fr 2 out: styd on wl: hit last: drvn out* **9/4**[1]

0121 **2** *8* **Another Mattie (IRE)**[39] 3344 9-10-12 **121**..................(t) LucyAlexander 124
(N W Alexander) *racd wd: hld up: jnd ldrs 8th: chsd wnr after 9th: sn drvn: hit 2 out: kpt on one pce* **7/1**[2]

2152 **3** *nk* **Waterclock (IRE)**[21] 3630 7-10-13 **125**.................................. JoeColliver[(3)] 129
(Micky Hammond) *hld up towards rr: sme hdwy 7th: chsng ldrs in 4th whn hit 3 out: sn outpcd: styd on appr last: gng on at fin* **9/4**[1]

-262 **4** *9* **Quel Elite (FR)**[55] 3058 12-10-8 **117**..............................(p) BrianHughes 111
(James Moffatt) *chsd ldrs 3rd: 3rd 3 out: hung rt and wknd run-in* **7/1**[2]

PR-P **5** *14* **Alpha Victor (IRE)**[87] 2431 11-11-7 **135**.................(t) CiaranGethings[(5)] 114
(William Kinsey) *chsd ldrs: led 8th: hdd after next: wknd 3 out* **12/1**[3]

P/5F **P** **Victor Hewgo**[39] 3339 11-11-0 **126**.............................. HarryChalloner[(3)]
(Keith Reveley) *nt fluent in rr: j.lft 2nd: sme hdwy 8th: sn lost pl and bhd: t.o whn p.u bef 3 out* **16/1**

2220 **P** **Snapping Turtle (IRE)**[36] 3428 11-10-4 **116**.................. CallumWhillans[(3)]
(Donald Whillans) *led: blnd 4th: hdd 8th: sn lost pl and bhd: t.o whn p.u bef 3 out* **14/1**

0612 **P** **Fresh By Nature (IRE)**[67] 2839 9-10-4 **113**.................. JonathanEngland
(Harriet Bethell) *in rr: drvn and mstke 8th: sn bhd: t.o whn p.u bef 3 out* **25/1**

7m 23.3s (66.80) **Going Correction** +2.80s/f (Heav) 8 Ran SP% 110.6
Speed ratings (Par 107): **100,97,97,94,89** , ,
CSF £17.22 CT £35.79 TOTE £3.00: £1.30, £1.90, £1.20; EX 19.80 Trifecta £38.90.
Owner Anne Marie Melville/The Northern Raiders **Bred** James F Barry **Trained** Greystoke, Cumbria

FOCUS
The A1 bend had been set 24yds from the innermost line. The 'away' chase bend had been set 12yds from the innermost line and the 'away' hurdle bend has been set 20yds from the innermost line. The effect on the official distance of this contest was an extra 264yds. A competitive handicap run at a predictably ordinary gallop considering the conditions. The second and third have been rated close to their marks.

4000 KENNETH FOSTER 60TH BIRTHDAY OPEN HUNTERS' CHASE (17 fncs 2 omitted) 3m 45y
3:55 (3:55) (Class 6) 6-Y-O+ £1,317 (£405; £202)

Form RPR
111- **1** **Palypso De Creek (FR)**[20] 13-12-1 130.............................. MissCVHart[(3)] 132+
(M N Dawson) *chsd ldrs: 2nd 8th: led bef 2 out: forged wl clr run-in* **4/7**[1]

210- **2** *21* **Big Fella Thanks**[27] 14-11-7 135.......................................(t) MrNGeorge[(7)] 112
(Tom George) *trckd ldrs: blnd 12th: 2nd 2 out: 6 l down last: tired bdly* **7/2**[2]

622- **3** *1 ½* **Jaunty Journey**[55] 13-11-10 103.................................... MrJohnDawson 103
(P Foster) *w ldr: led 5th: drvn 3 out: hdd next: sn wknd: poor 3rd last: kpt on clsng stages* **33/1**

P/P- **4** *25* **Robin Will (FR)**[13] 11-11-5 102.. MrRSmith[(5)] 77
(Miss G E J Anderson) *towards rr: hdwy to chse ldrs 10th: hit 3 out and sn lost pl: sn wl bhd* **25/1**

4/2- **5** *dist* **Mister Philson (IRE)**[27] 11-11-11 111...............(p) MrGregoryWalters[(7)] 40
(Mrs L Pomfret) *led: hdd 5th: lost pl 12th: sn bhd: t.o 4 out: virtually p.u run-in* **66/1**

PP6- **P** **Herdsman (IRE)**[289] 5497 11-11-11 126................................(p) MrRHogg[(7)]
(D J Dickenson) *chsd ldrs: drvn 6th: lost pl and reminders next: bhd whn mstke 8th: p.u bef next* **14/1**

11-0 **P** **Wayupinthesky (IRE)**[13] 9-12-1 113.................................. MrTHamilton[(3)]
(J P G Hamilton) *chsd ldrs: blnd 4 out: lost pl and sn bhd: t.o 5th whn p.u bef 2 out* **10/1**[3]

7m 48.8s (60.80) 7 Ran SP% 109.9
CSF £2.74 TOTE £1.40: £1.10, £1.90; EX 4.10 Trifecta £26.20.
Owner M N Dawson **Bred** Suc Yves Chopin & Mme Francoise Roux **Trained** Grainthorpe, Lincolnshire

FOCUS
The A1 bend had been set 24yds from the innermost line. The 'away' chase bend had been set 12yds from the innermost line and the 'away' hurdle bend has been set 20yds from the innermost line. The effect on the official distance of this contest was an extra 216yds. The final fence down the back straight (fence number 9) was bypassed throughout the meeting. Not for the first time on the card, only two made much appeal and they dominated late on. The winner has been rated to his mark.

4001 AUNT BESSIE'S STANDARD OPEN NATIONAL HUNT FLAT RACE 2m
4:30 (4:30) (Class 6) 4-6-Y-O £1,949 (£572; £286; £143)

Form RPR
1 **Sam's Adventure** 4-10-2 0.. CraigGallagher[(5)] 115+
(Brian Ellison) *mid-div: puished along to chse ldrs 7f out: led over 3f out: wandered and drew wl clr over 1f out: eased clsng stages* **10/1**

31 **2** *19* **Spirit Of Kayf**[35] 3442 5-11-10 0.. DannyCook 110
(Sandy Thomson) *led 5f: w ldrs: led 6f out: kpt on same pce fnl 2f* **9/4**[2]

15 **3** *17* **Burlington Bert (FR)**[50] 3138 5-11-3 0.............................. MrTGreatrex[(7)] 95
(Warren Greatrex) *chsd ldrs: 3rd and drvn over 3f out: one pce* **11/10**[1]

43 **4** *4* **Eastview Boy**[42] 3245 5-10-12 0................................ NathanMoscrop[(5)] 82
(Philip Kirby) *chsd ldrs: drvn 7f out: modest 4th over 3f out: one pce* **33/1**

5 *1 ¼* **Bering Upsun** 5-11-0 0...[1] GrahamWatters[(3)] 81
(James Ewart) *t.k.h: w ldr: led after 5f: hdd 6f out: one pce fnl 4f* **66/1**

5 **6** *27* **Spirit Of Hale (IRE)**[57] 3012 5-11-3 0................................ PeterCarberry 54
(Jennie Candlish) *chsd ldrs: drvn and lost pl 7f out: sn wl bhd* **66/1**

7 *24* **Smart Boy (IRE)** 5-11-3 0.. LucyAlexander 30
(Tim Easterby) *in rr: drvn and n.m.r bnd after 5f: sme hdwy 8f out: sn lost pl: wl bhd fnl 6f* **12/1**

8 *35* **Len's Legacy (IRE)** 4-10-7 0.. BrianHughes
(Tim Easterby) *prom: lost pl 7f out: sn wl bhd: t.o whn eased fnl 2f* **8/1**[3]

9 *1* **Hollins Hill** 6-11-3 0.. JonathanEngland
(Sam Drake) *w ldrs: reminders and lost pl 7f out: sn wl bhd: t.o 4f out* **40/1**

4 **F** **Flying Jack**[74] 2709 6-10-12 0.. DaraghBourke[(5)]
(Maurice Barnes) *rr-div: detached last whn fell 7f out* **66/1**

P **Lady Broome** 5-10-10 0.. AlainCawley
(John David Riches) *t.k.h in last: drvn and nt keen after 3f: sn wl bhd: t.o whn p.u after 6f* **66/1**

4m 30.5s (40.30) **Going Correction** +2.80s/f (Heav)
WFA 4 from 5yo+ 9lb 11 Ran SP% 117.6
Speed ratings: **111,101,93,91,90 76,64,47,46,**
CSF £32.37 TOTE £13.80: £3.50, £1.10, £1.10; EX 37.40 Trifecta £160.10.
Owner Mrs J A Martin **Bred** R Johnson **Trained** Norton, N Yorks
■ Stewards' Enquiry : Jonathan England two-day ban; used his whip without giving his mount time to respond (20th-21st Feb)

FOCUS
The A1 bend had been set 24yds from the innermost line. The 'away' chase bend had been set 12yds from the innermost line and the 'away' hurdle bend has been set 20yds from the innermost line. The effect on the official distance of this contest was an extra 132yds. This didn't look a particularly strong race of its type but the gallop was honest. The second has been rated to his recent win, but there's a case for rating the race higher through the third and fourth.
T/Plt: £19.90 to a £1 stake. Pool: £63,143.18 - 2,313.14 winning tickets T/Qpdt: £3.30 to a £1 stake. Pool: £4,964.67 - 1,089.42 winning tickets **Walter Glynn**

3764 LEOPARDSTOWN (L-H)
Saturday, February 6
OFFICIAL GOING: Soft to heavy changing to heavy after race 4 (2.30)

4002a GAIN SPRING JUVENILE HURDLE (GRADE 1) (8 hdls) 2m
12:55 (12:56) 4-Y-O
£36,875 (£11,875; £5,625; £2,500; £1,250; £625)

RPR
1 **Footpad (FR)**[16] 3711 4-11-0 134..[1] DannyMullins 142+
(W P Mullins, Ire) *settled in rr: 7th 1/2-way: hdwy 3 out into cl 5th bef next: impr on outer into st and rdn to ld bef last: kpt on wl run-in* **14/1**

2 2 3/4 **Allblak Des Places (FR)**[49] 3168 4-11-0 0........................ PaulTownend 139
(W P Mullins, Ire) *chsd ldrs: 4th 1/2-way: pushed along in 3rd bef 2 out where slt mstke: impr to chal between horses bef last: no imp on wnr in 2nd run-in: kpt on same pce: jst hld on for 2nd* **10/1**

3 nse **Let's Dance (FR)**[41] 3291 4-10-7 0........................ RWalsh 132+
(W P Mullins, Ire) *led 1st where j.big: jnd 3 out and sn hdd: impr gng wl to regain ld between last 2: rdn and hdd bef last where slt mstke: no imp on wnr whn swtchd in 3rd: r.o again cl home: jst failed for 2nd* **5/1**[2]

4 7 **Ivanovich Gorbatov (IRE)**[41] 3291 4-11-0 0................(t) BarryGeraghty 134
(A P O'Brien, Ire) *hld up in tch: mstke in 5th 4 out: impr into 4th after next and disp 3rd bef 2 out where slt mstke: sn pushed along and n.m.r bhd horses into st: no ex in 4th bef last and one pce run-in* **8/13**[1]

5 hd **Jer's Girl (IRE)**[42] 3268 4-10-7 133........................ RobbiePower 125
(Gavin Cromwell, Ire) *prom tl settled bhd ldr fr 1st where slt mstke: cl 2nd whn nt fluent 4 out: disp next and sn led: rdn and strly pressed after 2 out: hdd between last 2 and wknd bef last* **6/1**[3]

6 24 **Rashaan (IRE)**[42] 3268 4-11-0 133........................ MPFogarty 108
(Colin Kidd, Ire) *hld up in tch: 6th 1/2-way: bad mstke 3 out and lost tch: no imp in mod 7th bef 2 out: eased* **16/1**

P **Lagostovegas (IRE)**[21] 3633 4-10-7 119........................ SeanFlanagan
(David Harry Kelly, Ire) *chsd ldrs: j. sltly rt at times: mstke 4th: slt mstke in 4th 4 out: rdn and wknd fr next: eased 2 out and t.o whn p.u bef last* **25/1**

P **Best Kept Secret (IRE)**[21] 3633 4-11-0 0........................(t) MarkWalsh
(A P O'Brien, Ire) *a bhd: slt mstke in rr at 4th: slt mstke 3 out and wknd: t.o whn p.u bef 2 out* **100/1**

4m 2.0s (-5.50) **Going Correction** 0.0s/f (Good) **8** Ran SP% **119.3**
Speed ratings: **113,111,111,108,108 96, ,**
CSF £143.08 TOTE £8.70: £1.70, £2.00, £1.70; DF 106.10 Trifecta £358.60.
Owner Simon Munir & Isaac Souede **Bred** Mlle Louise Collet & Mlle Camille Collet **Trained** Muine Beag, Co Carlow

FOCUS
Winning jockey Danny Mullins said the ground was hard work but there was some juice in the surface and it wasn't as tacky as it might have been were it a little drier. Our Conor was the last horse to win this and follow up in the JCB Triumph Hurdle back in 2013. Willie Mullins completed a 1-2-3 here but in the opposite order to the way the betting suggested. This muddied the Triumph Hurdle waters as Ivanovich Gorbatov failed to perform to the level expected of him. The time was fast compared with the later handicap.

4004a DELOITTE NOVICE HURDLE (GRADE 1) (9 hdls) 2m 2f
1:55 (1:55) 5-Y-O+ £39,044 (£12,573; £5,955; £2,647; £1,323)

RPR

1 **Bleu Et Rouge (FR)**[41] 3294 5-11-9 145........................ BarryGeraghty 151+
(W P Mullins, Ire) *trckd ldrs tl wnt 2nd 3 out: sn disp and led narrowly gng best between horses bef last: jnd fr last and rdn: sn regained advantage u.p and styd on wl to assert clsng stages* **11/1**

2 3 **Tombstone (IRE)**[41] 3294 6-11-10 147........................[1] BJCooper 150
(Gordon Elliott, Ire) *hld up bhd ldrs: 4th 1/2-way: niggled along briefly after 3 out and sn tk clsr order in 3rd: rdn after 2 out and wnt cl 2nd bef last: sn disp tl hdd u.p run-in: no imp on wnr clsng stages* **3/1**[2]

3 15 **Bellshill (IRE)**[34] 3459 6-11-10 150........................ RWalsh 137+
(W P Mullins, Ire) *led: bad mstke 1st: 1 l clr at 1/2-way: jnd after 3 out: rdn and hdd bef last where dropped to 3rd and slt mstke: wknd qckly and eased run-in* **4/6**[1]

4 5 1/2 **Petit Mouchoir (FR)**[41] 3294 5-11-9 145........................ PaulTownend 129
(W P Mullins, Ire) *w.w: slt mstke in rr at 3rd: mstke in rr at 5th: pushed along bef 2 out and sn no imp: rdn into remote 4th fr last* **6/1**[3]

5 5 1/2 **Coney Island (IRE)**[42] 3266 5-11-9 130........................ MarkWalsh 122
(Edward P Harty, Ire) *trckd ldr tl lost pl 3 out: dropped to 4th bef next: rdn and no imp on ldrs after 2 out: sn wknd* **20/1**

4m 38.7s (-2.10) **Going Correction** +0.20s/f (Yiel) **5** Ran SP% **112.4**
Speed ratings: **112,110,104,101,99**
CSF £43.52 TOTE £10.40: £2.20, £2.30; DF 56.90 Trifecta £32.80.
Owner John P McManus **Bred** Haras De La Rousseliere **Trained** Muine Beag, Co Carlow

FOCUS
An informative race and won by clearly a much-improved horse in Bleue Et Rouge. Tombstone is rated to his mark.

4005a FLOGAS NOVICE CHASE (GRADE 1) (14 fncs) 2m 5f 60y
2:30 (2:31) 5-Y-O+ £36,875 (£11,875; £5,625; £2,500; £1,250; £625)

RPR

1 **Outlander (IRE)**[41] 3301 8-11-10 149........................ BJCooper 156+
(W P Mullins, Ire) *settled bhd ldr in cl 2nd: gng best into st and led bef last: rdn clr run-in and kpt on wl* **13/8**[1]

2 2 3/4 **Monksland (IRE)**[39] 3357 9-11-10 147........................ SeanFlanagan 152
(Noel Meade, Ire) *hld up towards rr: clsr in 4th bef 7th: tk clsr order 4 out: rdn in 3rd after 2 out and no imp on ldrs bef last where mstke: kpt on wl u.p into 2nd run-in: nt trble wnr* **6/1**

3 2 **Pont Alexandre (GER)**[21] 3635 8-11-10 149........................ RWalsh 152
(W P Mullins, Ire) *led: j. sltly rt at times: extended advantage bef 7th: nt fluent next where reduced ld: narrow advantage 3 out: rdn and hdd bef last where bad mstke: no ex run-in and dropped to 3rd* **9/4**[2]

4 19 **Zabana (IRE)**[40] 3321 7-11-10 0........................ DavyRussell 131
(Andrew Lynch, Ire) *chsd ldrs: slt mstke 6th: mstke in 4th at 8th: mstke 5 out where lost pl: rdn in 5th after 2 out and no imp on ldrs: one pce after* **4/1**[3]

5 11 **Blair Perrone (IRE)**[20] 3652 7-11-10 145........................(t) DenisO'Regan 118
(A J Martin, Ire) *hld up in rr: pushed along after 2 out and no imp into st: wnt mod 5th bef last* **20/1**

6 46 **McKinley**[27] 3553 6-11-10 139........................ PaulTownend 72
(W P Mullins, Ire) *chsd ldrs: mstke in 5th at 9th and pushed along: 4th 3 out: rdn in 4th after 2 out and no imp on ldrs: wknd bef last: eased run-in* **12/1**

5m 50.3s (14.30) **6** Ran SP% **115.6**
CSF £12.31 TOTE £2.40: £1.30, £2.80; DF 13.10 Trifecta £20.80.
Owner Gigginstown House Stud **Bred** Ronnie O'Neill **Trained** Muine Beag, Co Carlow

FOCUS
A race of real depth and quality with the winner producing a performance of real merit. The second and third are rated to the best view of their recent chase form.

4007a IRISH GOLD CUP (CHASE) (GRADE 1) (17 fncs) 3m 60y
3:40 (3:41) 5-Y-O+
£62,316 (£20,955; £9,926; £4,411; £2,205; £551)

RPR

1 **Carlingford Lough (IRE)**[40] 3324 10-11-10 160........................ MarkWalsh 170+
(John E Kiely, Ire) *hld up: rdn in rr after 2 out and clsd u.p to chse ldrs in 3rd bef last: lft in 2nd at last and sn led: styd on strly to assert run-in* **20/1**

2 12 **Road To Riches (IRE)**[86] 2464 9-11-10 165........................ BJCooper 161+
(Noel Meade, Ire) *led tl hdd bef 2nd where slt mstke: dropped to 3rd fr 6th: led bef 11th where jnd and hdd: regained ld fr 2 out: rdn and hdd bef last where lft in ld briefly: sn hdd and no imp on wnr in 2nd run-in* **5/4**[1]

3 8 **Fine Rightly (IRE)**[20] 3651 8-11-10 148........................ AELynch 150
(S R B Crawford, Ire) *hld up towards rr: sme hdwy fr bef 12th gng wl in cl 8th bef 2 out: prog into 4th between last 2: dropped to 5th bef last where lft 3rd: no imp on wnr and kpt on one pce run-in* **33/1**

4 2 1/2 **Foxrock (IRE)**[40] 3324 8-11-10 160........................(bt) APHeskin 149
(T M Walsh, Ire) *chsd ldrs: wnt 2nd fr 6th: reminder disputing 2nd after 4 out: rdn in 3rd after 2 out and u.p in 4th whn slt mstke last and lft 3rd briefly: kpt on one pce in 4th run-in* **9/1**

5 3 **Gilgamboa (IRE)**[41] 3296 8-11-10 154........................(p) BarryGeraghty 145
(E Bolger, Ire) *w.w towards rr: tk clsr order on outer fr 10th: pushed along in 6th after 3 out and no imp on ldrs u.p in 7th after next: lft mod 6th at last and kpt on one pce* **6/1**[3]

6 1/2 **Wounded Warrior (IRE)**[23] 3603 7-11-10 155........................ SeanFlanagan 145
(Noel Meade, Ire) *chsd ldrs: slt mstke 3rd: rdn in 4th after 2 out where slt mstke and no ex u.p in 6th bef last where lft mod 5th: one pce run-in* **12/1**

7 6 **Sir Des Champs (FR)**[40] 3324 10-11-10 157........................ PaulTownend 138
(W P Mullins, Ire) *hld up in tch: rdn after 2 out and no imp on ldrs u.p in 8th bef last where lft mod 7th: one pce* **14/1**

8 34 **On His Own (IRE)**[40] 3324 12-11-10 157........................(b) MrPWMullins 109
(W P Mullins, Ire) *cl up tl led bef 2nd and sn extended ld: nt fluent 4th and next: j. sltly rt at times: bad mstke 10th and hdd tl regained ld next: over 1 l clr whn bad mstke 2 out and hdd: no imp after: wknd* **16/1**

P **First Lieutenant (IRE)**[40] 3324 11-11-10 160........................(p) DavyRussell
(M F Morris, Ire) *hld up in tch: tk clsr order into 5th bef 10th: rdn in 5th out wd after 2 out and sn no ex: wknd and eased into st: p.u bef last* **10/1**

U **Valseur Lido (FR)**[42] 3231 7-11-10 156........................ RWalsh 164+
(W P Mullins, Ire) *mid-div: hdwy on outer into 4th bef 10th: cl 2nd after 2 out and led travelling wl nr side bef last where blnd and uns rdr* **5/1**[2]

6m 38.0s (-1.00) **10** Ran SP% **122.4**
CSF £50.23 TOTE £29.60: £5.50, £1.10, £7.60; DF 71.00 Trifecta £1417.60.
Owner John P McManus **Bred** Kenilworth House Stud **Trained** Dungarvan, Co Waterford

FOCUS
A truly extraordinary race. The winning rider was on he verge of pulling up before two out, the probable winner capsized at the last and the tactics employed on the favourite didn't make a lot of sense. Carlingford Lough is gradually progressing with age. Valseur Lido has been rated as finishing second.

4003, 4008 & 4009a (Foreign Racing) - See Raceform Interactive

[3679]MUSSELBURGH (R-H)
Sunday, February 7

OFFICIAL GOING: Good to soft (good in places) changing to soft (good to soft in places) after race 1 (1.00)
Wind: Fairly strong, across Weather: Overcast, showers

4010 SKY BET SUPREME SCOTTISH TRIAL NOVICES' HURDLE (9 hdls) 1m 7f 124y
1:00 (1:00) (Class 2) 4-Y-O+
£14,388 (£4,250; £2,125; £1,062; £531; £266)

Form RPR

4122 1 **Charbel (IRE)**[51] 3135 5-11-11 137........................ DavidBass 150+
(Kim Bailey) *mde all: rdn and hung rt 2 out: drew clr: eased nr fin* **4/1**[2]

10-1 2 11 **Brain Power (IRE)**[76] 2683 5-11-8 0........................ BarryGeraghty 138+
(Nicky Henderson) *nt fluent on occasions: t.k.h: trckd ldrs: wnt 2nd 4 out: effrt and jst over 1 l down whn hit 2 out: sn outpcd* **5/4**[1]

F224 3 6 **Impulsive American**[84] 2516 4-10-7 118........................(p) TomScudamore 115
(David Pipe) *hld up: hdwy bef 3 out: rdn and no imp fr next* **50/1**

1F 4 7 **Always Resolute**[24] 3590 5-11-8 0........................ DannyCook 123
(Brian Ellison) *prom: pushed along after 4 out: shortlived effrt next: sn btn* **4/1**[2]

5 3/4 **Azzuri**[142] 4-10-7 0........................ HarrySkelton 107
(Dan Skelton) *hld up: pushed along and outpcd 5th: n.d after* **20/1**

-134 6 17 **Simon Squirrel (IRE)**[43] 3227 6-11-8 138........................(t) SamTwiston-Davies 112
(Paul Nicholls) *t.k.h early: cl up tl rdn and wknd bef 3 out* **13/2**[3]

114 P **Altruism (IRE)**[79] 2626 6-11-11 133........................ RichardJohnson
(James Moffatt) *plld hrd in rr: struggling after 3rd: lost tch next: p.u 5th* **14/1**

-541 P **Lac Leman (GER)**[34] 3470 5-11-8 125........................(t) BrianHughes
(Pauline Robson) *t.k.h early: trckd ldrs: pushed along and outpcd whn mstke and sprawled bdly 3 out: sn p.u* **28/1**

3m 45.1s (-3.30) **Going Correction** +0.125s/f (Yiel)
WFA 4 from 5yo+ 9lb **8** Ran SP% **114.6**
Speed ratings (Par 109): **113,107,104,101,100 92, ,**
CSF £9.62 TOTE £4.30: £1.40, £1.10, £9.30; EX 11.00 Trifecta £271.60.
Owner Mrs Julie Martin And David R Martin **Bred** Peter & Sandra McCarthy **Trained** Andoversford, Gloucs

FOCUS
After 3mm of rain in the morning the ground had eased to good to soft, good in places, while the runners were also buffeted by a strong wind. All hurdles and fences moved in to fresh ground. Bottom hurdle bend out 5yds, chase 2yds. The opening race was run over 16yds further than advertised. An interesting novices' hurdle and a powerful front-running display from the winner. The winner rates a smart novice, while the second improved on his debut win.

4011 TOTEEXACTA SCOTTISH CHAMPION CHASE (H'CAP) (FOR THE BOWES-LYON TROPHY) (10 fncs 2 omitted) 1m 7f 182y
1:30 (1:30) (Class 3) (0-140,136) 5-Y-O+ £12,996 (£3,816; £1,908; £954)

Form RPR

4410 1 **Chestnut Ben (IRE)**[8] 3857 11-9-12 115........................ MrRWinks(7) 128
(Peter Winks) *hld up: stdy hdwy 1/2-way: effrt and chsng ldrs 3 out: led run-in: edgd lft: styd on strly* **18/1**

5444 **2** 3 ½ **Yorkist (IRE)**[22] 3629 8-11-7 **131**....................(t) BrianHughes 141
(Micky Hammond) *hld up in tch: stdy hdwy gng wl to press ldrs 4 out: ev ch next: shkn up to ld bef last: edgd rt and hdd run-in: kpt on same pce nr fin* **12/1**

4243 **3** 13 **Quito Du Tresor (FR)**[37] 3425 12-10-5 **115**..............(p) PeterBuchanan 112
(Lucinda Russell) *bhd: pushed along and sme hdwy 1/2-way: rdn and plugged on fr 2 out: nvr able to chal* **18/1**

-413 **4** 6 **The Grey Taylor (IRE)**[40] 3335 7-11-12 **136**.................. DannyCook 130
(Brian Ellison) *chsd ldr: led bef 3 out: hdd whn nt fluent last: wknd run-in* **7/2**[3]

P525 **5** 3 **Aye Well**[11] 3806 11-10-13 **123**.................. DerekFox 111
(Stuart Coltherd) *prom to 1st: sn lost pl: struggling fnl circ: nvr on terms* **25/1**

22-1 **6** 3 ¼ **Got The Nac (IRE)**[59] 2981 7-10-13 **123**.................. BrianHarding 107
(Keith Dalgleish) *t.k.h: led: clr 3rd to next: rdn and hdd bef 3 out: wknd bef next* **3/1**[2]

4-0F **7** 10 **Irish Thistle (IRE)**[28] 3552 9-11-1 **128**.................. JamesBanks(3) 102
(Dai Williams) *hld up: drvn and outpcd 1/2-way: nvr on terms* **22/1**

0F50 **P** **My Brother Sylvest**[25] 3584 10-11-2 **126**..............(b) TomScudamore
(David Pipe) *hld up in tch on outside: stdy hdwy bef 4th: struggling bef 4 out: lost tch and p.u next* **17/2**

-001 **P** **Full Shift (FR)**[43] 3228 7-11-11 **135**.................. BarryGeraghty
(Nicky Henderson) *chsd clr ldrs: drvn outpcd after 3rd: struggling next: nt fluent 6th and sn p.u* **5/2**[1]

4m 1.6s (9.20) **Going Correction** +0.80s/f (Soft) **9** Ran SP% **112.7**
Speed ratings: **109,107,100,97,96 94,89,,**
CSF £198.60 CT £3887.01 TOTE £21.20: £4.30, £2.60, £4.00; EX 277.60 Trifecta £2318.70.
Owner P Winks **Bred** Sean Deu Burca **Trained** Little Houghton, S Yorks

FOCUS
This race was run over 7yds further than advertised. After the opener the ground was changed to soft, good to soft in places. A decent handicap chase and there was no hanging about. The winner has been rated back to his best.

4012 TOTETRIFECTA SCOTTISH TRIUMPH HURDLE TRIAL (JUVENILE HURDLE) (LISTED RACE) (9 hdls) 1m 7f 124y
2:00 (2:00) (Class 1) 4-Y-O **£17,085** (£6,411; £3,210; £1,599)

Form RPR

2 **1** **Tommy Silver (FR)**[40] 3347 4-11-0 0.................. SamTwiston-Davies 128+
(Paul Nicholls) *j.lft thrght: mde all at ordinary gallop: shkn up 3 out: drew clr fr next: edgd lft bef last: readily* **4/6**[1]

14 **2** 11 **Ashoka (IRE)**[42] 3279 4-11-5 124.................. HarrySkelton 120
(Dan Skelton) *chsd wnr thrght: effrt and jst over 1 l down 3 out: rdn whn nt fluent next: sn outpcd* **7/1**[3]

131 **3** 2 ¾ **Sir Chauvelin**[37] 3423 4-11-8 130.................. RichardJohnson 120
(Jim Goldie) *nt fluent on occasions: chsd ldrs: rdn bef 4th: struggling after 4 out: rallied bef last: drifted rt run-in: no imp* **2/1**[2]

6133 **4** 8 **Sikandar (IRE)**[37] 3423 4-11-5 114.................. DannyCook 111
(Brian Ellison) *nt fluent on occasions: t.k.h: hld up in last pl: drvn and tk modest 3rd bef 3 out: no imp: hld whn nt fluent last* **28/1**

3m 50.5s (2.10) **Going Correction** +0.125s/f (Yiel) **4** Ran SP% **109.3**
Speed ratings: **99,93,92,88**
CSF £5.70 TOTE £1.70; EX 4.50 Trifecta £10.30.
Owner Potensis Bloodstock Limited & Ged Mason **Bred** Francis Dunn **Trained** Ditcheat, Somerset

FOCUS
This race was run over 16yds further than advertised. The quartet weren't that keen to jump off when the tape went across, but they did go a fair pace once under way. A small step up from the winner, with the third and fourth rated close to their marks.

4013 TOTEPOOLLIVE.COM SCOTTISH FUTURE CHAMPIONS NOVICES' CHASE (14 fncs 2 omitted) 2m 3f 193y
2:30 (2:30) (Class 3) 5-Y-O+ **£7,988** (£2,480; £1,335)

Form RPR

5-10 **1** **Five In A Row (IRE)**[37] 3428 8-10-12 0.................. DannyCook 137
(Brian Ellison) *led at modest gallop to 6th: nt fluent next: outpcd and lost 2nd 4 out: plenty to do next: rallied but stl 8 l down last: styd on strly to ld cl home* **17/2**[3]

/1U2 **2** ½ **Sametegal (FR)**[57] 3029 7-11-3 145.................. SamTwiston-Davies 143
(Paul Nicholls) *pressed ldr: hit 4th: led 6th: qcknd 8th: pushed along after 3 out: kpt on u.p fr last: hdd cl home* **1/2**[1]

3114 **3** 1 ¾ **Ittirad (USA)**[42] 3280 8-11-8 146.................. AidanColeman 148
(John Ferguson) *hld up in tch: nt fluent 1st: lft 3rd and clsd 3rd: wnt 2nd 4 out: clsng whn mstke next: rcvrd and effrt 2 out: rdn and nrly 2 l down whn hit last: kpt on run-in* **5/2**[2]

P **F** **Overtheedge (IRE)**[30] 3504 7-10-12 0.................. RichieMcLernon
(Simon West) *t.k.h: chsd ldrs: fell 3rd* **150/1**

5m 14.3s (13.10) **Going Correction** +0.80s/f (Soft) **4** Ran SP% **106.4**
Speed ratings: **105,104,104,**
CSF £13.95 TOTE £8.00; EX 14.50 Trifecta £16.00.
Owner P J Martin **Bred** Ms M Maher **Trained** Norton, N Yorks

FOCUS
This race was run over 33yds further than advertised. Basically a three-horse race, but as dramatic as they come, especially for those who laid the winner at the maximum 999-1 in-running on the exchanges, albeit to small money. There's a case for rating the race 7lb higher through the second and third, but the winner has already been rated 3lb up on his best hurdle figures, and this is probably high enough.

4014 TOTEPOOL SUPPORTING SCOTTISH RACING SCOTTISH COUNTY HURDLE (H'CAP) (LISTED RACE) (9 hdls) 1m 7f 124y
3:00 (3:00) (Class 1) 4-Y-O+
£14,237 (£5,342; £2,675; £1,332; £670; £335)

Form RPR

0-13 **1** **Shrewd**[18] 3682 6-9-9 **124** oh1.................. ShaneShortall(5) 132+
(Iain Jardine) *hld up on ins: smooth hdwy on ins bef 3 out: rdn to ld last: kpt on strly run-in* **5/1**[2]

2013 **2** 2 **Vendor (FR)**[22] 3630 8-11-0 **138**.................. DannyCook 141
(Sue Smith) *chsd clr ldr: clsd 1/2-way: led appr 3 out to last: kpt on run-in: nt pce of wnr* **15/2**

215- **3** ¾ **Cardinal Walter (IRE)**[303] 5250 7-11-1 **139**.................. AndrewTinkler 141
(Nicky Henderson) *t.k.h in midfield: smooth hdwy bef 3 out: effrt whn nt fluent next: disp ld last: kpt on same pce run-in* **11/2**[3]

F234 **4** nk **Zaidiyn (FR)**[18] 3682 6-10-10 **134**.................. AidanColeman 136
(Brian Ellison) *hld up: hdwy bef 3 out: effrt and rdn bef next: kpt on fr last* **10/1**

320- **5** 10 **Hawk High (IRE)**[331] 4737 6-11-7 **145**..............(p) BrianHughes 139
(Tim Easterby) *t.k.h: in tch: lost pl after 4 out: rallied but no imp whn hit last* **20/1**

F111 **6** 2 **Aristo Du Plessis (FR)**[37] 3426 6-11-7 **150**.............. DiarmuidO'Regan(5) 142
(James Ewart) *led and clr to 1/2-way: hdd bef 3 out: rallied and ev ch next: wknd fr last* **7/2**[1]

10-0 **7** 3 ¾ **Days Of Heaven (FR)**[84] 2512 6-11-5 **143**.................. BarryGeraghty 131
(Nicky Henderson) *prom: effrt and rdn bef 3 out: wknd bef next* **5/1**[2]

142P **8** 1 ½ **Viens Chercher (IRE)**[22] 3623 5-10-13 **137**.................. PaddyBrennan 124
(Brian Ellison) *nt fluent on occasions: hld up: hdwy and cl up 4 out: rdn and wknd fr next: hld whn mstke last* **16/1**

40-2 **9** 1 ¾ **Pearl Castle (IRE)**[15] 3426 6-10-9 **140**.................. FinianO'Toole(7) 125
(K R Burke) *hld up on outside: stdy hdwy bef 3 out: sn rdn: edgd rt and wknd bef next* **12/1**

3 **10** 4 ½ **Mango Cap (FR)**[56] 3054 5-10-2 **126**..............(t) TomScudamore 109
(David Pipe) *chsd ldrs: hit 4 out: rdn and wknd bef next* **16/1**

312 **11** 13 **Serenity Now (IRE)**[52] 2326 8-9-9 **124** oh3.................. CraigGallagher(5) 93
(Brian Ellison) *bhd: struggling 1/2-way: nvr on terms* **33/1**

3m 45.4s (-3.00) **Going Correction** +0.125s/f (Yiel) **11** Ran SP% **119.0**
Speed ratings (Par 111): **112,111,110,110,105 104,102,101,100,98 92**
CSF £43.19 CT £216.75 TOTE £7.90: £2.30, £2.50, £2.00; EX 52.50 Trifecta £329.60.
Owner Tapas Partnership **Bred** Darley **Trained** Carrutherstown, D'fries & G'way

FOCUS
This race was run over 16yds further than advertised. A competitive handicap hurdle run at a serious pace and the first four pulled well clear. The second, third and fourth set the level.

4015 ALBERT BARTLETT SCOTTISH TRIAL (NOVICES' HURDLE) (14 hdls) 2m 7f 180y
3:30 (3:30) (Class 2) 4-Y-O+ **£14,388** (£4,250; £2,125; £1,062)

Form RPR

-112 **1** **O O Seven (IRE)**[36] 3447 6-11-13 145.................. AndrewTinkler 144+
(Nicky Henderson) *trckd ldr: nt fluent 1st: effrt whn nt fluent 3 out: led next: edgd rt u.p after last: styd on gamely* **11/10**[1]

-111 **2** ¾ **Fagan**[62] 2945 6-11-10 0.................. RichardJohnson 138
(Gordon Elliott, Ire) *chsd ldrs: stdy hdwy after 4 out: effrt and pressed wnr last: sn rdn and ev ch: kpt on: hld nr fin* **6/4**[2]

2131 **3** 1 ¼ **Delusionofgrandeur (IRE)**[37] 3400 6-11-13 133.................. DannyCook 140
(Sue Smith) *led: rdn after 4 out: hdd 2 out: kpt on u.p fr last: hld whn rdr lost irons cl home* **5/1**[3]

2110 **4** 55 **Calivigny (IRE)**[71] 2787 7-11-13 125.................. LucyAlexander 91
(N W Alexander) *hld up: pushed along and outpcd after 5th: struggling fnl circ: t.o* **33/1**

5m 59.9s (17.80) **Going Correction** +0.125s/f (Yiel) **4** Ran SP% **107.2**
Speed ratings (Par 109): **75,74,74,56**
CSF £3.13 TOTE £1.80; EX 3.20 Trifecta £4.00.
Owner Triermore Stud **Bred** Robert McCarthy **Trained** Upper Lambourn, Berks

FOCUS
This race was run over 33yds further than advertised. Despite the small field this staying novices' hurdle was run at a fair pace and it produced a thrilling finish between the three principals. The winner has been rated below the level of his Tolworth second, with small steps up from the runner-up and third.

4016 NORTHERN AREA POINT TO POINT SCOTTISH FOXHUNTER CHASE (AN OPEN HUNTERS' CHASE) (12 fncs 3 omitted) 3m 2f 139y
4:00 (4:00) (Class 3) 5-Y-O+ **£6,269** (£2,146; £1,209)

Form RPR

22-U **1** **Railway Dillon (IRE)**[21] 11-11-7 114.................. MissETodd(5) 115
(Mrs C Drury) *hld up in tch: stdy hdwy bef 11th: effrt and pushed along 3 out: led run-in: edgd lft: styd on wl* **4/1**[1]

/112 **2** ¾ **Pena Dorada (IRE)**[170] 1309 9-11-13 115.................. MissRMcDonald(5) 121
(Alan J Brown) *disp ld: wnt on 11th: pushed along whn nt fluent 2 out and last: hdd run-in: rallied: hld nr fin* **6/1**[3]

2U-2 **3** 8 **Nowurhurlin (IRE)**[14] 9-11-11 118..............(v) MrNOrpwood(7) 113
(Mrs S J Stilgoe) *chsd ldrs: wnt 2nd bef 12th: chal 4 out to next: drvn 2 out: outpcd fr last* **4/1**[1]

P-44 **P** **Isla Pearl Fisher**[99] 2192 13-12-1 116..............(t) MrKitAlexander(3)
(N W Alexander) *sn wl bhd: no ch fnl circ: p.u bef 3 out* **14/1**

P3U- **P** **No Loose Change (IRE)**[35] 11-11-10 130..............(t) MrDavidMaxwell(5)
(Mrs Kim Smyly) *hld up: stdy hdwy and prom bef 11th: struggling 4 out: lost tch and p.u bef next* **4/1**[1]

4445 **P** **Nearest The Pin (IRE)**[112] 1989 11-11-13 130.................. MrTGreatrex(5)
(Dai Williams) *nt fluent on occasions: hld up in tch: struggling bef 4 out: lost tch and p.u bef 2 out* **11/2**[2]

F0-6 **U** **Little Fritz (FR)**[281] 80 9-11-5 99.................. MrRyanNichol(7)
(L Kerr) *hld up: blnd and uns rdr 1st* **66/1**

P **Pharawaydante (IRE)**[14] 8-11-5 0.................. MrRWilson(7)
(Norman Sanderson) *in tch: outpcd 7th: struggling whn mstke next: sn p.u* **40/1**

P **Damiens Dilemma (IRE)**[252] 8-11-9 0.................. MrTHamilton(3)
(Mrs L A Coltherd) *mstkes: mde most to 11th: sn lost pl: wknd and p.u bef 4 out* **7/1**

7m 7.7s (18.90) **Going Correction** +0.80s/f (Soft) **9** Ran SP% **112.8**
Speed ratings: **104,103,101, , , , , ,**
CSF £27.84 TOTE £4.50: £2.10, £2.50, £1.70; EX 31.50 Trifecta £147.30.
Owner Paul Drury **Bred** Miss Laura Duggan **Trained** Sheriff Hutton, N Yorks

FOCUS
This race was run over 14yds further than advertised. A decent hunter chase, but a solid pace meant it became a war of attrition in the conditions and only three completed. It's been rated around the balance of the finishers.

4017 PERTEMPS NETWORK H'CAP HURDLE (SERIES QUALIFIER) (15 hdls) 3m 2f 26y
4:30 (4:34) (Class 2) 5-Y-O+ **£12,996** (£3,816; £1,908; £954)

Form RPR

/31- **1** **Cup Final (IRE)**[428] 2945 7-10-4 **132**.................. BarryGeraghty 137+
(Nicky Henderson) *hld up in midfield: stdy hdwy bef 3 out: effrt and pressed ldr bef last: drvn to ld run-in: edgd lft: kpt on wl* **11/8**[1]

2-2P **2** 1 ½ **Warriors Tale**[54] 3100 7-10-9 **137**.................. SamTwiston-Davies 139
(Paul Nicholls) *hld up in tch: smooth hdwy to ld 2 out: rdn and hdd run-in: kpt on* **14/1**

4340 **3** 3 **Taglietelle**[23] 3149 7-11-12 **154**..............(b) RichardJohnson 154+
(Gordon Elliott, Ire) *replated bef s: hld up: hdwy on outside whn hit 3 out: sn rdn: kpt on fr last: nt pce to chal* **12/1**

-223 **4** ½ **Seldom Inn**[54] 3100 8-10-2 **130**..............(p) BrianHughes 128
(Sandy Thomson) *chsd ldrs: chal 11th to 2 out: hung rt: kpt on same pce fr last* **17/2**

5200 **5** *nse* **Unanimite (FR)**[15] 3733 5-10-6 **134** ....(p) TomScudamore 132
(David Pipe) *hld up: rdn whn hit 3 out: kpt on fr last: nt pce to chal* **10/1**
1261 **6** *hd* **Sky Khan**[80] 2594 7-10-7 **135** ....(p) PeterBuchanan 133
(Lucinda Russell) *hld up: pushed along bef 3 out: kpt on run-in: nvr rchd ldrs* **20/1**
-016 **7** *3 3/4* **Tap Night (USA)**[36] 3440 9-10-1 **129** ....(p) RichieMcLernon 123
(Lucinda Russell) *mde most to 2 out: sn rdn and outpcd* **33/1**
112- **8** *1* **Call The Cops (IRE)**[304] 5241 7-11-11 **153** .... AndrewTinkler 146+
(Nicky Henderson) *t.k.h: hld up: pushed along and outpcd bef 3 out: n.d after* **8/1**[3]
1142 **9** *8* **Oscar Blue (IRE)**[50] 3158 6-10-0 **128** .... PaddyBrennan 113
(Brian Ellison) *trckd ldrs: nt fluent 10th: rdn after 4 out: wknd bef next* **13/2**[2]
2-16 **10** *22* **Drum Valley**[58] 3018 8-10-5 **140** .... BenFfrenchDavis(7) 103
(Oliver Sherwood) *w ldr to 4 out: sn drvn and outpcd: wknd bef next* **16/1**

6m 45.4s (30.30) **Going Correction** +0.125s/f (Yiel) **10 Ran SP% 114.1**
Speed ratings: **58,57,56,56,56 56,55,54,52,45**
CSF £21.04 CT £167.25 TOTE £2.30: £1.30, £3.20, £2.70; EX 26.10 Trifecta £217.80.
Owner John P McManus **Bred** Mrs C A Moore **Trained** Upper Lambourn, Berks

FOCUS
This race was run over 33yds further than advertised. The pace was modest and the field were still bunched together rounding the home bend, so it developed into something of a sprint. The first six all qualify for next month's Pertemps Final. The second has been rated as improving towards his chase mark, with a small pb from the third.
T/Jkpt: Not won. T/Plt: £1,939.40 to a £1 stake. Pool of £80188.72 - 30.18 winning tickets. T/Qpdt: £151.80 to a £1 stake. Pool of £5747.19 - 28.0 winning tickets. **Richard Young**

4018 - (Foreign Racing) - See Raceform Interactive

3633 NAAS (L-H)
Sunday, February 7

OFFICIAL GOING: Soft (soft to heavy in places)

4019a BBA IRELAND LIMITED OPERA HAT MARES CHASE (LISTED RACE) (10 fncs) 2m
2:20 (2:20) 5-Y-O+ £14,696 (£4,540; £2,150)

RPR
1 **Gitane Du Berlais (FR)**[36] 3444 6-11-7 149 .... RWalsh 149+
(W P Mullins, Ire) *mde all: j. sltly rt 1st: nt fluent 4th: pressed after 3 out: stl gng best after next: slt mstke last and drvn clr run-in: kpt on wl* **6/5**[1]
2 *7* **I'm All You Need (IRE)**[24] 3604 6-10-7 125 ....(tp) RobbiePower 126
(Paul Nolan, Ire) *w.w in rr of quartet: tk clsr order bhd ldrs stl in rr after 3 out: lft 3rd 2 out where sltly hmpd by faller: rdn into 2nd bef last and no imp on wnr run-in: kpt on same pce* **8/1**
3 *5* **Queens Wild (IRE)**[24] 3604 6-10-13 125 .... APHeskin 127
(Edward P Harty, Ire) *settled bhd ldr: rdn in 2nd after 2 out and no imp on wnr bef last where dropped to 3rd: one pce run-in* **6/1**[3]
F **Carrigmoorna Rock (IRE)**[10] 3829 8-10-7 0 .... PhillipEnright 125
(Robert Tyner, Ire) *hld up bhd ldrs in 3rd: nt fluent 4 out: tk clsr order bhd ldr after 3 out: niggled along between horses disputing cl 2nd bef 2 out where fell: fatally injured* **13/8**[2]

4m 24.8s (1.50) **4 Ran SP% 108.9**
CSF £9.19 TOTE £2.00; DF 8.70 Trifecta £20.40.
Owner Simon Munir & Isaac Souede **Bred** J M Lucas, L Collet & C Collet **Trained** Muine Beag, Co Carlow

FOCUS
A smart mares' race and it was hard to believe that the favourite went off almost the same price as she was in the Ryanair Gold Cup last year. The third limits the form, with the first two just off their best.

4020 - 4024a - (Foreign Racing) - See Raceform Interactive

3816 FAKENHAM (L-H)
Monday, February 8

OFFICIAL GOING: Soft (good to soft in places on chase course; 5.6)
Wind: gusty, strong at times, against Weather: overcast, gusty wind

4025 FAKENHAM RACECOURSE SUPPORTS RACING TO SCHOOL MAIDEN H'CAP HURDLE (9 hdls) 2m 3y
1:45 (1:45) (Class 5) (0-100,100) 4-Y-O+ £3,898 (£1,144; £572; £286)

Form RPR
0P32 **1** **Vent Nivernais (FR)**[11] 3821 7-9-13 **80** ....(b) WilliamFeatherstone(7) 85
(James Evans) *in tch in 4th: stmbld 2nd: rdn after 6th: finding nil and sn outpcd: 6 l 3rd 2 out: plugged on to ld bypassing last: doing little in front and drifting lft cl home: rdn out* **2/1**[1]
0402 **2** *nk* **Astrum**[12] 3807 6-11-2 **100** ....(b) RonanShort(10) 105
(Donald McCain) *mde most: nt fluent 3 out: 4 l clr next: rdn and finding little whn drifted rt bnd ent st: hdd bypassing last: ev ch after but nvr finding enough to regain ld* **2/1**[1]
04-0 **3** *4* **Fifi L'Amour (IRE)**[250] 597 10-10-0 **74** oh5 .... BrendanPowell 75
(Linda Jewell) *pressed ldr: nt fluent 1st: rdn and unable qck after 3 out: 4 l 2nd next: plugged on u.p and stl cl enough in 3rd bypassing last: no ex and wknd fnl 150yds* **11/1**[3]
022 **4** *21* **Lake Chapala (IRE)**[11] 3816 7-10-12 **91** ....(vt[1]) AlanJohns(5) 74
(Tim Vaughan) *chsd ldng pair: rdn and struggling whn nt fluent 3 out: dropped to 4th and wknd bef next* **11/4**[2]
005 **P** **Sawwala**[10] 1694 6-10-6 **80** .... JamesDavies
(J R Jenkins) *a in rr: hit 1st: pushed along after 3rd: nvr travelling after: u.p after 5th: losing tch whn wnt bdly rt 6th: immediately p.u* **18/1**

4m 20.45s (7.45) **Going Correction** +0.45s/f (Soft) **5 Ran SP% 106.9**
Speed ratings (Par 103): **99,98,96,86,**
CSF £6.17 TOTE £2.60: £1.10, £1.50; EX 6.50 Trifecta £35.80.
Owner Elegant Clutter Ltd **Bred** Rene Beaunee **Trained** Broadwas, Worcs

FOCUS
Race distance increased by 90yds. The opening contest was a modest maiden handicap hurdle. They went an honest gallop on ground officially described as soft, good to soft in places on the chase course on a particularly blustery afternoon. The final hurdle got damaged and was bypassed the last twice. The first two are rated pretty much to their marks.

4026 RACING TO SCHOOL ARE HERE TODAY "NATIONAL HUNT" NOVICES' HURDLE (9 hdls) 2m 3y
2:20 (2:20) (Class 4) 4-Y-O+ £4,548 (£1,335; £667; £333)

Form RPR
31 **1** **Prince Of Steal (IRE)**[50] 3179 6-11-10 0 .... LiamTreadwell 136+
(James Evans) *in tch in 4th: hdwy to chse ldr bef 3 out: reminder after 3 out and sn led: mstke 3 out: gng clr and flashing tail ent st: styd on wl* **8/1**[3]
1-12 **2** *8* **Hollies Pearl**[82] 2579 6-11-3 124 ....(bt[1]) SeanBowen 120
(Peter Bowen) *led tl 1st: chsd ldr: nt fluent 3rd: led again after 5th: wnt clr w wnr after next: hdd and rdn bef 2 out: nt fluent 2 out: wl hld between last 2: plugged on* **6/4**[2]
F6F **3** *38* **Bingo D'Olivate (FR)**[24] 3608 5-11-3 0 .... LeightonAspell 82
(Noel Williams) *mstkes: bhd: lost tch 6th: plugged on into poor 3rd between last 2: t.o* **20/1**
3 **4** *11* **Dalkadam (FR)**[31] 3508 5-11-3 115 .... JamesDavies 71
(J R Jenkins) *chsd ldng pair: rdn after 5th: struggling after next: 3rd and losing tch whn mstke 3 out: dropped to last between last 2: t.o* **12/1**
-304 **P** **Dexcite (FR)**[59] 3019 5-11-3 127 .... PaddyBrennan
(Tom George) *v keen: dashed into ld 1st: hdd after 5th: lost pl qckly after next: t.o whn p.u 2 out* **5/4**[1]

4m 15.5s (2.50) **Going Correction** +0.45s/f (Soft) **5 Ran SP% 108.0**
Speed ratings (Par 105): **111,107,88,82,**
CSF £20.29 TOTE £7.40: £2.70, £1.40; EX 16.70 Trifecta £110.80.
Owner The Cheltenham Flyers **Bred** A Ryan **Trained** Broadwas, Worcs

FOCUS
Race distance increased by 90yds. A fair little novice hurdle. They went a decent gallop. The winner rates a fair novice and there's a case for rating this a bit higher through the second.

4027 RACING WELFARE H'CAP CHASE (16 fncs) 2m 5f 44y
2:50 (2:50) (Class 4) (0-115,117) 5-Y-O+ £5,198 (£1,526; £763; £381)

Form RPR
3B11 **1** **Halo Moon**[5] 3937 8-12-0 **117** 7ex ....(p) NoelFehily 125+
(Neil Mulholland) *hld up in tch in last pair: clsd to trck ldrs 13th: led between last 2: sn clr: easily* **4/6**[1]
/563 **2** *4 1/2* **Fine Parchment (IRE)**[40] 3373 13-11-6 **112** ....(tp) HarryBannister(3) 109
(Charlie Mann) *led: rdn after 3 out: hdd between last 2: sn brushed aside by wnr: kpt on for clr 2nd* **15/2**[3]
14-0 **3** *34* **Alanjou (FR)**[51] 3146 6-11-7 **115** ....(p) FreddieMitchell(5) 80
(Henry Tett) *chsd ldrs: wnt 2nd and mstke 12th: 3rd and stl cl enough 2 out: wknd wl bef last: mstke last: eased flat: t.o* **9/1**
1114 **4** *2 3/4* **Celtic Intrigue (IRE)**[27] 3569 9-11-6 **109** ....(b) TomScudamore 71
(David Bridgwater) *chsd ldr: mstke 11th: sn rdn: dropped to last and struggling bef 13th: lost tch after 3 out: t.o* **4/1**[2]
PP4P **P** **Ravens Brook (IRE)**[21] 3663 10-10-3 **92** ....(p) TrevorWhelan
(Neil King) *in tch in rr: rdn 12th: sn lost tch: t.o whn p.u 3 out: burst blood vessel* **16/1**

5m 53.4s (11.60) **Going Correction** +0.725s/f (Soft) **5 Ran SP% 107.6**
Speed ratings: **106,104,91,90,**
CSF £5.81 TOTE £1.60: £1.10, £4.40; EX 6.50 Trifecta £20.50.
Owner Level Par Racing **Bred** David Jenks **Trained** Limpley Stoke, Wilts

FOCUS
Race distance increased by 154yds. The feature contest was an ordinary handicap chase. They went a sensible gallop. The winner stood out on recent form and is rated to a similar level.

4028 EPDS RACING WELFARE BTO SERIES H'CAP HURDLE (11 hdls) 2m 4f 1y
3:20 (3:20) (Class 4) (0-105,105) 4-Y-O+ £4,548 (£1,335; £667; £333)

Form RPR
4415 **1** **Daliance (IRE)**[10] 3846 7-11-4 **104** ....(b) WilliamFeatherstone(7) 111
(Noel Williams) *prom: wnt 2nd 4th tl after 7th: outpcd in 3rd and urged along hands and heels after 8th: 6 l down 2 out: chsd clr wnr between last 2: plugged on and clsd to jump into ld last: jst doing enough under hands and heels riding fla* **5/2**[1]
5514 **2** *hd* **Lee Side Lady (IRE)**[153] 1509 6-10-13 **92** .... NoelFehily 100+
(Neil Mulholland) *w ldr whn lft in ld 1st: clr w rival after 8th: wnt clr 2 out: rdn between last 2: out j. and hdd last: kpt on u.p but a jst hld flat* **4/1**[3]
103P **3** *21* **Tara Mac**[44] 3217 7-11-2 **100** .... AlanJohns(5) 86
(Tim Vaughan) *hld up in rr: struggling after 7th: no ch w ldrs 3 out: plugged on past btn horse fr 2 out: wnt modest 3rd last* **11/1**
4 *8* **Daphiglote (FR)**[225] 7-11-12 **105** ....[1] JackQuinlan 86
(Eugene Stanford) *chsd ldrs: lft 2nd 1st tl 4th: styd prom: wnt 2nd again after 7th: clr w ldr after next: ev ch and hit 3 out: drvn and btn next: lost 2nd between last 2: wknd* **7/2**[2]
603 **5** *4* **Fine Tune (IRE)**[36] 3450 5-11-7 **103** ....(t) ThomasGarner(3) 77
(Linda Jewell) *in tch in midfield: u.p after 7th: sn struggling: wl btn 3 out* **18/1**
6145 **6** *11* **Kayfton Pete**[64] 2924 10-11-10 **103** .... AdamPogson 66
(Charles Pogson) *t.k.h: chsd ldrs tl 4th and wl outpcd after 8th: t.o and v tired flat* **8/1**
035P **7** *11* **Bishop Wulstan (IRE)**[21] 3662 5-11-12 **105** ....(tp) SeanBowen 57
(Peter Bowen) *led: j.v.slowly: hdd and dropped to last trio 1st: rdn and losing tch in last after 7th: t.o 3 out* **6/1**

5m 34.5s (14.10) **Going Correction** +0.80s/f (Soft) **7 Ran SP% 109.8**
Speed ratings (Par 105): **103,102,94,91,89 85,80**
CSF £12.06 TOTE £2.70: £1.80, £2.00; EX 11.40 Trifecta £102.80.
Owner EPDS Racing Partnership 15 **Bred** Societa Agricola Gem Srl **Trained** Blewbury, Oxon

FOCUS
Race distance increased 113yds. A modest handicap hurdle. They went a sensible gallop in deteriorating conditions. The winner is rated to his best.

4029 KING'S LYNN H'CAP CHASE (12 fncs) 2m 59y
3:50 (3:50) (Class 5) (0-100,96) 5-Y-O+ £3,898 (£1,144; £572; £286)

Form RPR
340 **1** **Entry To Evrywhere (IRE)**[26] 3586 8-10-7 **77** ....(t[1]) ConorO'Farrell 95
(Alexandra Dunn) *led to s: chsd ldr: clsd qckly to jump into ld 2 out: readily wnt clr between last 2: rdn out flat* **7/2**[3]
043 **2** *40* **Mandy's Boy (IRE)**[10] 3845 6-11-9 **96** ....(tp) JamesBanks(3) 84
(Sally Randell) *led tl out j. and hdd 2 out: sn brushed aside and wl btn whn mstke last* **12/1**

4555 3 22 **Tenby Jewel (IRE)**[49] 3195 11-9-12 **73**..............(tp) CharlieDeutsch(5) 29
(Mark Gillard) *hld up in tch in rr: hmpd 4th: rdn and struggling 8th: losing tch and mstke next: t.o 3 out: wnt poor 3rd last* **8/1**
PP54 4 17 **Topthorn**[21] 3661 10-11-3 **94**..............(p) MrZBaker(7) 40
(Martin Bosley) *chsd ldrs 3rd: rdn after 9th: racing awkwardly u.p and wknd sn after next: t.o whn lost 3rd last* **20/1**
06U1 F **It's Oscar (IRE)**[11] 3816 9-10-10 **80**..............(b) MarkQuinlan
(James Evans) *in tch in midfield: j.rt and fell 4th* **7/4**[1]
P33U P **On The Case**[19] 3683 8-11-4 **88**..............(t) PaddyBrennan
(Tom George) *mstkes: in tch: pushed rt and hmpd 4th: rdn 8th: sn struggling and losing tch whn mstke next: t.o whn p.u 2 out: burst blood vessel* **11/4**[2]

4m 27.8s (11.20) **Going Correction** +0.725s/f (Soft) **6** Ran SP% **108.8**
Speed ratings: **101,81,70,61,**
CSF £34.94 TOTE £4.10: £2.00, £3.00; EX 24.90 Trifecta £137.90.
Owner G Butler & West Buckland Bloodstock **Bred** Patrick O'Riordan **Trained** West Buckland, Somerset

FOCUS
Race distance increased 123yds. A moderate handicap chase. They went an honest gallop. This was a big step up from the winner; we've split the difference between the first two but could be 10lb+ out either way.

4030 WELLS NEXT THE SEA H'CAP HURDLE (13 hdls) 2m 7f 95y
4:20 (4:20) (Class 5) (0-100,102) 4-Y-0+ **£3,898** (£1,144; £572; £286)

Form RPR
-001 1 **Navanman (IRE)**[4] 3946 7-12-1 **102** 7ex.............. TomScudamore 112+
(David Pipe) *pressed ldr on inner and a gng wl: led after 3 out: wnt clr between last 2: eased flat: v easily* **8/13**[1]
0040 2 3 ½ **Whispering Speed (IRE)**[14] 3771 6-10-7 **80**..............(b) LeightonAspell 79
(Lucy Wadham) *in tch in rr: rdn after 9th: wnt 3rd bef 3 out: chsd wnr last: plugged on but no ch* **8/1**[3]
00P1 3 9 **Izbushka (IRE)**[38] 3422 5-11-5 **92**..............(b) PeterCarberry 82
(David Thompson) *racd wd: mde most but on and off the bridle: hdd and drvn after 3 out: outpcd after 2 out: lost 2nd last: wknd flat* **4/1**[2]
1405 4 18 **Minella Bliss (IRE)**[11] 3820 11-11-5 **99**..............(b) WilliamFeatherstone(7) 71
(James Evans) *hld up in tch: effrt in 4th bef 3 out: outpcd after 3 out: wknd next* **20/1**
0650 P **Court King (IRE)**[30] 3516 5-11-12 **99**..............(t) SeanBowen
(Peter Bowen) *chsd ldrs: wnt cl up 4th: lost pl after 10th: last whn hit 3 out: sn lost tch: t.o whn p.u between last 2* **8/1**[3]

6m 40.75s (18.75) **Going Correction** +0.80s/f (Soft) **5** Ran SP% **108.9**
Speed ratings (Par 103): **99,97,94,88,**
CSF £5.90 TOTE £1.40: £1.10, £4.10; EX 5.20 Trifecta £11.70.
Owner Mrs Yvonne Fleet **Bred** Aidan Ryan **Trained** Nicholashayne, Devon

FOCUS
Race distance increased 136yds. The concluding contest was a modest staying handicap hurdle. They went a respectable gallop. The winner stood out in a weak race and the second posted a small pb.
T/Plt: £40.00 to a £1 stake. Pool: £58,648.89 - 1,068.8 winning tickets T/Qpdt: £19.10 to a £1 stake. Pool: £4,788.05 - 184.60 winning tickets **Steve Payne**

4010 MUSSELBURGH (R-H)
Monday, February 8

OFFICIAL GOING: Soft
Wind: Light, half against Weather: Cloudy, bright

4031 TOTEPLACEPOT BRITISH STALLIONS EBF "NATIONAL HUNT" MAIDEN HURDLE (QUALIFIER) (9 hdls) 1m 7f 124y
1:00 (1:00) (Class 5) 4-Y-0+ **£3,898** (£1,144; £572; £286)

Form RPR
1 **Ascot De Bruyere (FR)**[124] 6-11-6 **0**..............(p) JakeGreenall 115+
(James Ewart) *mde all at ordinary gallop: qcknd clr bef 3 out: shkn up briefly run-in: easily* **11/4**[2]
3 2 4 ½ **Dubai Devils (IRE)**[23] 3639 5-11-1 **0**.............. JonathanMoore(5) 105
(Paul Stafford, Ire) *prom: hdwy to chse (clr) wnr 3 out: kpt on fr last: nt pce to chal* **8/1**
5432 3 3 ¼ **Theatrical Style (IRE)**[59] 3011 7-11-6 **104**..............(p) BrianHarding 101
(Donald McCain) *pressed wnr: drvn after 4 out: lost 2nd and outpcd next: plugged on fr 2 out: no imp* **6/4**[1]
06 4 4 **Sweet Holly**[19] 3681 5-10-13 **0**.............. BrianHughes 90
(Lucinda Russell) *hld up: stdy hdwy gng wl bef 3 out: shkn up next: nvr nr ldrs* **6/1**[3]
6 5 7 **Benjamin Tree (IRE)**[76] 2709 5-11-6 **0**.............. CraigNichol 91
(Rose Dobbin) *midfield: drvn and outpcd bef 3 out: no imp fr next: hld whn mstke last* **20/1**
660- 6 ½ **This Thyne Jude**[402] 3483 8-10-8 **0**.............. GrantCockburn(5) 83
(Lucy Normile) *hld up: drvn and outpcd 1/2-way: plugged on fr 2 out: nvr on terms* **33/1**
330 7 ½ **Final Fling (IRE)**[20] 3668 5-11-3 **0**.............. AdamNicol(3) 89
(Rose Dobbin) *prom to 1/2-way: sn lost pl and struggling: no imp fr 3 out* **14/1**
6 8 2 **Mahler Bay (IRE)**[55] 3104 6-11-6 **0**.............. HenryBrooke 87
(Michael Smith) *t.k.h: in tch: drvn and outpcd bef 3 out: btn next* **50/1**
5 9 8 **Red Piano**[37] 3436 7-10-13 **0**.............. MrWHRReed(7) 79
(Andrew Hamilton) *hld up: drvn and outpcd 1/2-way: nvr on terms* **125/1**
40-0 10 1 **Ange Des Malberaux (FR)**[278] 145 6-11-1 **0**.............. DiarmuidO'Regan(5) 81
(James Ewart) *nt fluent: trckd ldrs: pckd 5th: nt fluent next: outpcd 3 out: wkng whn mstke next* **33/1**
P 11 25 **Secret Act (IRE)**[64] 2931 7-11-6 **0**.............. LucyAlexander 53
(N W Alexander) *hld up: pushed along and outpcd 1/2-way: nvr on terms* **50/1**

3m 59.2s (10.80) **Going Correction** +0.225s/f (Yiel) **11** Ran SP% **114.1**
Speed ratings (Par 103): **82,79,78,76,72 72,72,71,67,66 54**
CSF £22.14 TOTE £3.00: £1.20, £2.40, £1.10; EX 22.70 Trifecta £44.80.
Owner The Steel Bonnets **Bred** E A R L La Bruyere & Alain Ziegler **Trained** Langholm, Dumfries & G'way

FOCUS
All fences and hurdles were moved on to fresh ground. Race distance increased by 16yds. 3mm of rain in the morning eased the ground from the previous day's going description. This was a weak maiden, run at an uneven gallop. The winner is rated similar to his French chase form, with the second to fourth close to their marks.

4032 TOTEEXACTA PICK THE 1ST AND 2ND H'CAP CHASE (15 fncs 3 omitted) 2m 7f 170y
1:30 (1:30) (Class 5) (0-100,98) 5-Y-0+ **£3,249** (£954; £357; £357)

Form RPR
-263 1 **Vision De La Vie (FR)**[38] 3427 6-11-5 **91**..............(b) JamesReveley 101+
(Pauline Robson) *hld up: hdwy to ld bef 3 out: sn rdn: kpt on gamely fr last* **10/3**[2]
-0F0 2 2 ½ **Proud Gamble (IRE)**[19] 3679 7-10-4 **76**..............(t) CraigNichol 80
(Rose Dobbin) *in tch: effrt and pushed along bef 3 out: chsd wnr last: kpt on: nt pce to chal* **15/2**
4664 3 1 **Foot The Bill**[55] 3102 11-11-0 **89**.............. JohnKington(3) 94
(Patrick Holmes) *sn cl up: drvn and outpcd 4 out: rallied 2 out: kpt on fr last: nt rch first two* **14/1**
3U52 3 dht **More Madness (IRE)**[20] 3671 9-11-5 **98**..............(v) MrKitAlexander(7) 104
(N W Alexander) *chsd ldrs: drvn and outpcd whn nt fluent 3 out: rallied next: kpt on towards fin* **5/2**[1]
0465 5 ¾ **Apache Pilot**[42] 3310 8-10-4 **83**..............(tp) ThomasDowson(7) 87+
(Maurice Barnes) *j.lft thrght: mde most to 3 out: drvn and one pce fr last: no ex and lost two pls cl home* **6/1**[3]
4343 6 37 **Reverse The Charge (IRE)**[19] 3683 9-10-0 **72** oh6.............. PeterBuchanan 49
(Jane Walton) *hld up: mstke 10th: stdy hdwy and in tch 4 out: rdn and wknd fr next* **14/1**
-00P 7 14 **West Ship Master (IRE)**[50] 3181 12-10-12 **91**..............(p) MissLBrooke(7) 42
(Paul Stafford, Ire) *t.k.h: cl up tl rdn and wknd fr 4 out* **16/1**
0/P0 P **Tears From Heaven (USA)**[19] 3679 10-9-9 **72** oh1(p) DiarmuidO'Regan(5)
(Chris Grant) *hld up: nt fluent 5th: drvn along 1/2-way: wknd and p.u bef 4 out* **18/1**
0004 P **Resolute Reformer (IRE)**[35] 3472 7-11-11 **97**.............. DerekFox
(Stuart Coltherd) *in tch: lost pl bef 6th: sn rdn: lost tch and p.u 10th* **7/1**

6m 26.0s (22.60) **Going Correction** +0.95s/f (Soft) **9** Ran SP% **114.7**
Speed ratings: **100,99,98,98,98 86,81,,**
PLACE: More Madness £0.70, Foot The Bill £2.10; TC: VDLV-PG-MM 35.84, VDLV-PG-FTB 153.45; TF: VDLV-PG-MM £29.20 VDLV-PG-FTB £212.70 CSF £28.41 TOTE £4.00: £1.30, £2.00; EX 20.30.
Owner I Couldn't Switch Club **Bred** P Journiac, T Journiac Et Al **Trained** Kirkharle, Northumberland

FOCUS
Race distance increased by 14yds. This moderate staying handicap saw a bunched finish behind the winner, who built on his recent C&D run, with the second to his C&D mark.

4033 TOTEQUADPOT FOUR PLACES IN FOUR RACES NOVICES' HURDLE (12 hdls) 2m 3f 81y
2:00 (2:01) (Class 4) 4-Y-0+ **£3,249** (£954; £477; £238)

Form RPR
0-2 1 **Jetstream Jack (IRE)**[39] 3393 6-12-0 **134**.............. RichardJohnson 137+
(Gordon Elliott, Ire) *cl up: led bef 3 out: shkn up after next: rdn and hrd pressed run-in: styd on gamely towards fin* **30/100**[1]
3 2 ½ **Blue Rambler**[42] 3306 6-11-7 **0**.............. AidanColeman 127
(John Ferguson) *prom: stdy hdwy to chse wnr bef 3 out: effrt after next: drvn and ev ch run-in: hld nr fin* **3/1**[2]
54 3 19 **General Mahler (IRE)**[8] 3883 6-11-7 **0**.............. DannyCook 109
(Brian Ellison) *hld up in tch: stdy hdwy 4 out: pushed along and outpcd fr next* **25/1**
4 46 **Lycidas (GER)**[212] 7-11-7 **0**.............. LucyAlexander 62
(James Ewart) *plld hrd: prom: hdwy to ld bef 7th: hdd whn mstke 3 out: sn wknd* **20/1**[3]
4-0 5 14 **Daytripper**[277] 159 5-11-0 **0**.............. BrianHughes 41
(Lucinda Russell) *nt fluent on occasions: in tch: outpcd fr 8th: btn bef 3 out* **80/1**
06 6 4 ½ **Applejack Lad**[35] 3471 5-11-7 **0**.............. HenryBrooke 44
(Michael Smith) *bhd: struggling whn mstke 8th: nvr on terms* **80/1**
4/00 7 24 **Latin Rebel (IRE)**[35] 3471 9-11-7 **0**.............. JamesReveley 20
(Jim Goldie) *bhd and detached: nvr on terms* **200/1**
FP-0 P **Flying Native (IRE)**[35] 3471 7-11-2 **0**..............(b[1]) JonathonBewley(5)
(George Bewley) *led to bef 7th: struggling fr next: t.o whn p.u 3 out* **200/1**

4m 51.4s (-0.10) **Going Correction** +0.225s/f (Yiel) **8** Ran SP% **114.0**
Speed ratings (Par 105): **109,108,100,81,75 73,63,**
CSF £1.52 TOTE £1.20: £1.10, £1.10, £2.50; EX 2.00 Trifecta £4.80.
Owner Mrs Diana L Whateley **Bred** Miss E Hamilton **Trained** Longwood, Co Meath

FOCUS
Race distance increased by 33yds. This novice event served up a decent test and the two clear market leaders had the finish to themselves. The winner set a decent standard and is rated to his best.

4034 TOTETRIFECTA PICK THE 1 2 3 NOVICES' H'CAP CHASE (14 fncs 2 omitted) 2m 3f 193y
2:30 (2:30) (Class 4) (0-105,102) 5-Y-0+ **£4,790** (£1,396; £698)

Form RPR
2510 1 **Harleys Max**[10] 3834 7-9-9 **78**.............. JamesCorbett(7) 88
(Susan Corbett) *hld up: stdy hdwy to chse ldrs 1/2-way: led gng wl 3 out: rdn and edgd rt after next: styd on wl run-in* **7/2**[2]
-223 2 3 ¾ **Mumgos Debut (IRE)**[37] 3441 8-11-3 **93**..............(t) PeterBuchanan 99
(Lucinda Russell) *led to 5th: cl up: effrt and ev ch fr 3 out to run-in: kpt on: hld nr fin* **7/2**[2]
P642 3 19 **Asuncion (FR)**[19] 3683 6-10-0 **76** oh2..............(b[1]) BrianHughes 65
(Rebecca Menzies) *w ldrs: hit 10th: led next to 3 out: rdn and wknd fr 2 out* **11/4**[1]
536F 4 6 **Court Of Law (IRE)**[19] 3683 8-11-6 **96**..............(p) HenryBrooke 81
(Donald McCain) *j.lft: prom: hdwy to ld 5th: hdd 4 out: hung lft and wknd fr next* **6/1**[3]
-660 P **No Such Number**[73] 2751 8-10-6 **89**.............. MrTHamilton(7)
(Sandy Forster) *chsd ldrs: lost pl 1/2-way: sn struggling: t.o whn p.u bef 3 out* **8/1**
5350 P **Attention Please (IRE)**[73] 2745 6-10-9 **85**.............. CraigNichol
(Rose Dobbin) *nt fluent in rr: struggling 5 out: btn after next: t.o whn p.u bef 3 out* **17/2**
2-0P P **Clenagh Castle (IRE)**[64] 2937 6-10-4 **85**.............. DiarmuidO'Regan(5)
(Chris Grant) *prom tl rdn and wknd fr 4 out: lost tch and p.u bef next* **18/1**

5m 19.2s (18.00) **Going Correction** +0.95s/f (Soft) **7** Ran SP% **112.3**
Speed ratings: **102,100,92,90,**
CSF £15.96 CT £36.80 TOTE £5.90: £1.90, £2.10; EX 16.90 Trifecta £32.30.

Owner Girsonfield Racing Club **Bred** Girsonfield Stud **Trained** Otterburn, Northumberland
FOCUS
Race distance increased by 14yds. An ordinary novice handicap. There was a fair gallop on and two came well clear from the penultimate fence. The winner looks on the upgrade with the second to his mark.

4035 TOTEPOOLLIVEINFO.COM H'CAP HURDLE (14 hdls) 2m 7f 180y
3:00 (3:00) (Class 4) (0-115,109) 4-Y-0+ £5,198 (£1,526; £763; £381)

Form RPR
-563 1 **Rocklim (FR)**[35] 3470 6-11-5 102 .... LucyAlexander 109+
(James Ewart) *hld up: pushed along and hdwy bef 3 out: led run-in: styd on wl* 14/1
-141 2 2 **Almost Gemini (IRE)**[19] 3680 7-11-8 105 .... (p) HenryBrooke 111+
(Kenneth Slack) *hld up: smooth hdwy to ld 2 out: sn rdn and hung lft: hdd run-in: kpt on same pce* 7/4[1]
1-0P 3 5 **Bop Along (IRE)**[41] 3346 9-11-9 109 .... (p) AdamNicol(3) 109
(Alistair Whillans) *mde most to 2 out: one pce whn mstke last* 12/1
4353 4 5 **Down Time (USA)**[44] 3243 6-11-4 101 .... (b) DannyCook 96
(Brian Ellison) *hld up: hdwy and prom 5th: effrt and ev ch 3 out to next: rdn and outpcd fr last* 11/2[3]
6500 5 10 **Sky Full Of Stars (IRE)**[19] 3680 6-10-7 95 .... NathanMoscrop(5) 79
(James Ewart) *t.k.h: hld up: nt fluent 2nd: hdwy and rdn bef 3 out: edgd rt bef next: sn wknd* 18/1
4006 6 3/4 **Solway Prince**[19] 3680 7-10-12 100 .... CallumBewley(5) 83
(Lisa Harrison) *prom tl rdn and wknd bef 2 out* 8/1
243 7 2 3/4 **What Happens Now (IRE)**[44] 3239 7-11-10 107 .... BrianHarding 89
(Donald McCain) *t.k.h: w ldr: rdn bef 3 out: 5th and wkng whn nt fluent last* 9/2[2]
6000 8 2 **Ethan (IRE)**[35] 3474 7-10-4 92 .... MissCWalton(5) 71
(Sheena Walton) *in tch: stdy hdwy 1/2-way: rdn and wknd bef 3 out* 18/1
6422 9 29 **Bescot Springs (IRE)**[41] 3344 11-11-5 102 .... (p) DerekFox 52
(Lucinda Russell) *prom: drvn and outpcd 4 out: lost tch fr next: t.o* 10/1
6m 14.0s (31.90) **Going Correction** +0.50s/f (Soft) 9 Ran SP% 115.0
Speed ratings (Par 105): **66,65,63,62,58 58,57,56,47**
CSF £39.96 CT £315.85 TOTE £9.60: £2.50, £1.20, £3.70; EX 37.40 Trifecta £505.10.
Owner The Rocklim Partnership **Bred** S C E A Haras Du Puy **Trained** Langholm, Dumfries & G'way
FOCUS
Race distance increased by 33yds. A modest staying handicap, run to suit the closers. Fair form for the class. This was a big step up from the winner, with the second back to his best.

4036 TOTEPOOL SUPPORTING SCOTTISH RACING H'CAP HURDLE (9 hdls) 1m 7f 124y
3:30 (3:30) (Class 4) (0-110,108) 4-Y-0+ £4,548 (£1,335; £667; £333)

Form RPR
4553 1 **So Satisfied**[38] 3424 5-11-4 107 .... StevenFox(7) 122+
(Sandy Thomson) *cl up: led bef 3 out: rdn clr fr next* 5/2[1]
2/00 2 13 **Jonny Delta**[38] 3424 9-11-12 108 .... JamesReveley 106
(Jim Goldie) *t.k.h: in tch: smooth hdwy to press wnr 3 out: shkn up and outpcd next: 9 l down whn mstke last* 9/2[2]
4260 3 4 **Claude Carter**[19] 3682 12-11-8 107 .... (p) CallumWhillans(3) 100
(Alistair Whillans) *led to 4 out: rdn and outpcd bef next: plugged on fr 2 out: no imp* 10/1
-434 4 4 **Near To Tears (IRE)**[51] 3163 6-10-8 90 .... PeterBuchanan 79
(Lucinda Russell) *hld up: stdy hdwy bef 3 out: pushed along and hung rt after next: no imp* 12/1
0600 5 2 **Miss Mackie (IRE)**[19] 3681 5-10-6 93 .... CallumBewley(5) 81
(R Mike Smith) *in tch: outpcd whn mstke 5th: rallied 2 out: plugged on fr last: nvr able to chal* 50/1
0500 6 1 **Rioja Day (IRE)**[19] 3680 6-10-5 87 .... HenryBrooke 73
(Jim Goldie) *bhd: struggling after 3rd: sme late hdwy: nvr on terms* 11/1
2060 7 1/2 **Celestino (FR)**[64] 2933 5-11-3 99 .... LucyAlexander 85
(N W Alexander) *hld up: pushed along and outpcd after 4 out: rdn and no imp fr next* 17/2
42F 8 17 **Lady Clitico (IRE)**[14] 1684 5-11-9 105 .... BrianHughes 74
(Rebecca Menzies) *cl up: led 4 out to bef next: rdn and wknd bef 2 out* 5/1[3]
-43P 9 4 1/2 **Definitely Glad (IRE)**[10] 3839 9-10-10 99 .... (t) JamesCorbett(7) 63
(Susan Corbett) *hld up: stdy hdwy after 4 out: rdn and wknd bef next* 14/1
23-3 10 24 **Sultana Belle (IRE)**[258] 482 8-11-9 108 .... AdamNicol(3) 48
(R Mike Smith) *hld up: struggling bef 4 out: sn btn* 14/1
3m 54.6s (6.20) **Going Correction** +0.50s/f (Soft) 10 Ran SP% 114.4
Speed ratings (Par 105): **104,97,95,93,92 92,91,83,81,69**
CSF £14.23 CT £93.88 TOTE £3.30: £1.50, £2.20, £2.50; EX 16.80 Trifecta £119.10.
Owner M Wright **Bred** Cavendish Inv Ltd & Mr & Mrs B W Hills **Trained** Lambden, Berwicks
FOCUS
Race distance increased by 16yds. They went a sound gallop in this moderate handicap yet still it paid to race handily, and this was a big step up from the easy winner.

4037 TOTEPOOL BETTING ON ALL UK RACING MAIDEN OPEN NATIONAL HUNT FLAT RACE 1m 7f 124y
4:00 (4:00) (Class 6) 4-6-Y-0 £1,949 (£572; £286; £143)

Form RPR
2 1 **Atomix (GER)**[55] 3104 5-11-7 0 .... BrianHughes 109+
(Peter Niven) *hld up in midfield: smooth hdwy to ld over 2f out: rdn over 1f out: edgd lft ins fnl f: kpt on strly* 6/4[1]
2 1 **Moonman (IRE)**[106] 6-11-7 0 .... (t) RichardJohnson 106+
(Gordon Elliott, Ire) *hld up: stdy hdwy gng wl over 3f out: effrt and ev ch over 1f out: sn drvn: kpt on fnl f: hld nr fin* 4/1[2]
3 nk **Ballycrystal (IRE)**[120] 5-11-0 0 .... GLavery(7) 106+
(Brian Ellison) *hld up: hdwy to press ldrs over 1f out: edgd lft ins fnl f: kpt on: hld nr fin* 5/1[3]
4 4 6 **Grays Choice (IRE)**[73] 2756 5-11-2 0 .... JonathonBewley(5) 100
(George Bewley) *led at stdy pce to over 5f out: regained ld over 3f out to over 2f out: outpcd over 1f out* 20/1
5 5 1 **Multipede**[72] 2777 4-10-11 0 .... LucyAlexander 89
(James Ewart) *hld up: stmbld after 2f: rdn over 3f out: kpt on fr 2f out: nt pce to chal* 28/1
0- 6 1/2 **Monfass (IRE)**[324] 4915 5-11-7 0 .... CraigNichol 99
(Rose Dobbin) *plld hrd: cl up: chal over 3f out to over 2f out: rdn and no ex over 1f out* 50/1
2 7 nk **Fenlon's Hill (IRE)**[35] 3476 5-11-2 0 .... JonathanMoore(5) 98
(Paul Stafford, Ire) *hld up: hdwy and in tch over 5f out: effrt and rdn over 2f out: edgd rt and no ex over 1f out* 12/1
5 8 hd **Cupid's Quest (IRE)**[23] 3632 4-9-11 0 .... JamesCorbett(7) 81
(Susan Corbett) *hld up: hdwy and prom 2f out: rdn and wknd fnl f* 200/1
9 1/2 **Motion To Strike (IRE)**[71] 6-11-7 0 .... AidanColeman 98
(Rebecca Menzies) *t.k.h: cl up: effrt and ev ch over 2f out: rdn and no ex over 1f out* 14/1
10 1 1/4 **Loud And Clear** 5-11-7 0 .... HenryBrooke 96
(Iain Jardine) *hld up: pushed along and hdwy over 3f out: outpcd whn edgd rt over 1f out: sn btn* 6/1
0 11 22 **Knysna Bay**[132] 1688 5-10-9 0 .... DiarmuidO'Regan(5) 67
(Chris Grant) *t.k.h: pressed ldr led over 5f out to over 3f out: sn wknd* 100/1
3m 55.4s (12.60) **Going Correction** +0.50s/f (Soft)
WFA 4 from 5yo+ 9lb 11 Ran SP% 117.0
Speed ratings: **88,87,87,84,83 83,83,83,83,82 71**
CSF £7.02 TOTE £2.30: £1.02, £2.20, £5.80; EX 9.90 Trifecta £25.40.
Owner G C Wragg **Bred** Gestut Auenquelle **Trained** Barton-le-Street, N Yorks
FOCUS
Race distance increased by 16yds. This modest bumper saw a messy finish due to a steady gallop, but the winner, fourth, fifth and seventh all pretty much ran to their marks.
T/Plt: £7.80 to a £1 stake. Pool: £65,056.68 - 6,062.06 winning tickets T/Qpdt: £6.90 to a £1 stake. Pool: £5,359.44 - 571.70 winning tickets **Richard Young**

3724 MARKET RASEN (R-H)
Tuesday, February 9

OFFICIAL GOING: Heavy (soft in places on hurdle course; chs 6.3, hdl 5.5)
Wind: moderate 1/2 against Weather: fine and sunny

4038 RACING UK WINTER SEASON TICKET JUVENILE HURDLE (8 hdls) 2m 148y
2:00 (2:00) (Class 4) 4-Y-0 £3,249 (£954; £477; £238)

Form RPR
13 1 **Kasakh Noir (FR)**[42] 3347 4-11-5 133 .... HarrySkelton 126+
(Dan Skelton) *hld up: trckd ldrs 3rd: nt fluent next: effrt and upsides 2 out: styd on to ld post* 5/4[2]
1 2 shd **Wolfcatcher (IRE)**[68] 2863 4-11-5 0 .... AidanColeman 126+
(John Ferguson) *hld up: trckd ldrs 3rd: led on bit appr 2 out: drvn and mstke last: hdd post* 4/5[1]
0 3 17 **Alhamareer (IRE)**[13] 2992 4-10-12 0 .... JamesBest 102
(Paul Webber) *nt fluent: w ldrs: led after 3rd: hdd appr 2 out: one pce* 100/1
2 4 2 **Three Colours Red (IRE)**[12] 3822 4-10-12 0 .... GavinSheehan 101
(Warren Greatrex) *led: j.lft: hdd after 3rd: drvn 3 out: one pce: fdd nr fin* 11/1[3]
35P 5 65 **Jinsha Lake (IRE)**[12] 3822 4-10-7 0 .... (t) ConorRing(5) 35
(Evan Williams) *t.k.h: trckd ldrs: lost pl 4th: sn bhd: t.o 2 out: eventually completed* 80/1
4m 22.4s (15.70) **Going Correction** +1.15s/f (Heav) 5 Ran SP% 110.6
Speed ratings: **109,108,100,100,69**
CSF £2.70 TOTE £2.20: £1.10, £1.10; EX 2.00 Trifecta £19.60.
Owner T P Radford **Bred** P Jabot, G Harari & H De Watrigant **Trained** Alcester, Warwicks
FOCUS
Following 4mm of overnight rain the going on the hurdles course was eased to heavy, soft in places. The actual race distance was 2m196yds. This looked a match on the book and the market leaders pulled clear after the second last. This was a step up from the winner, with the second building on easy course win, and there's a case for rating a bit higher through the fourth, but this was a big step up from the suprise third.

4039 BRITISH STALLION STUDS EBF MARES' "NATIONAL HUNT" MAIDEN HURDLE (8 hdls) 2m 148y
2:30 (2:30) (Class 4) 4-Y-0+ £3,898 (£1,144; £572; £286)

Form RPR
53-5 1 **Superfection (IRE)**[73] 2770 7-11-3 0 .... WillKennedy 112+
(Donald McCain) *chsd ldrs: hit 3 out: led appr next: hit last: drvn out* 40/1
6 2 4 1/2 **Pennywell (IRE)**[77] 2697 6-11-3 0 .... GavinSheehan 106
(Warren Greatrex) *led: pushed along 4th: hdd appr 2 out: kpt on same pce run-in* 17/2[3]
1-0 3 4 1/2 **Midnight Tour**[65] 2929 6-11-3 0 .... SamTwiston-Davies 102
(David Loder) *trckd ldrs: upsides 3 out: effrt and cl 3rd whn nt fluent next: kpt on one pce* 5/1[2]
5-3 4 13 **Buttercup (FR)**[12] 3825 5-11-3 125 .... AidanColeman 91
(Venetia Williams) *hld up: effrt appr 2 out: sn rdn and wknd* 2/5[1]
-63P 5 7 **Rock Chick Supremo (IRE)**[12] 3819 5-11-3 0 .... HarrySkelton 81
(Dan Skelton) *in rr: drvn and outpcd 3 out* 11/1
5 6 40 **Lovefromabove (IRE)**[218] 928 5-11-3 0 .... RobertDunne 41
(Dan Skelton) *in rr: drivcen 3 out: sn bhd: t.o* 33/1
4m 27.0s (20.30) **Going Correction** +1.15s/f (Heav) 6 Ran SP% 112.3
Speed ratings (Par 105): **98,95,93,87,84 65**
CSF £303.18 TOTE £26.40: £10.30, £3.80; EX 224.20 Trifecta £1136.90.
Owner Chasing Gold Racing Club **Bred** Mrs A Connolly **Trained** Cholmondeley, Cheshire
FOCUS
An uncompetitive maiden hurdle which saw a shock winner, who made a big step up on her bumper form. The actual race distance was 2m196yds.

4040 EBF STALLIONS "NATIONAL HUNT" NOVICES' HURDLE (QUALIFIER) (10 hdls) 2m 4f 139y
3:05 (3:06) (Class 3) 4-7-Y-0 £6,173 (£1,812; £906; £453)

Form RPR
1611 1 **Point The Way (IRE)**[13] 3802 5-11-7 125 .... MeganCarberry(5) 136+
(Brian Ellison) *led: qcknd gallop 5th: drvn 3 out: hung lft run-in: styd on wl towards fin* 4/1[3]
1 2 1 1/2 **Sharpasaknife (IRE)**[24] 3626 6-11-8 0 .... BrianHughes 128
(Malcolm Jefferson) *trckd wnr: upsides 3 out: upsides 2 out and last: kpt on same pce last 50yds* 13/8[2]
0011 3 28 **Tanarpino**[18] 3729 5-11-8 122 .... PeterCarberry 100
(Jennie Candlish) *chsd ldng pair: pushed along 6th: lost pl 3 out: j. bdly lft last: tk distant 3rd last 100yds* 9/1
1-13 4 7 **Onefitzall (IRE)**[72] 2807 6-11-8 130 .... RichardJohnson 97
(Philip Hobbs) *chsd ldng pair: nt fluent 7th: pushed along next: sn wl outpcd and bhd: wknd and lost distant 3rd last 150yds: b.b.v* 11/8[1]
5m 27.9s (19.10) **Going Correction** +1.15s/f (Heav) 4 Ran SP% 110.2
Speed ratings: **109,108,97,95**
CSF £11.12 TOTE £4.10; EX 10.50 Trifecta £38.80.
Owner P J Martin **Bred** Mrs Kay Cottrell **Trained** Norton, N Yorks

FOCUS
An interesting contest despite the small field. The actual race distance was 2m4f199yds. Another step up from the winner, with the second building on his easy debut win. This could be rated a bit higher.

4041 ERIC AND LUCY PAPWORTH H'CAP HURDLE (10 hdls) 2m 4f 139y
3:35 (3:36) (Class 4) (0-120,114) 4-Y-0+ **£3,249** (£954; £477; £238)

Form RPR
516/ **1** **Spencer Lea**[704] 4662 8-11-12 **114** JamesDavies 122+
(Henry Oliver) *hld up in last: t.k.h: trcking ldrs 4th: nt fluent 6th: led appr 2 out: nt fluent last: drvn out* **9/4**[2]
3512 **2** *3 3/4* **Milly Baloo**[18] 3729 5-11-1 **103** BrianHughes 105
(Tim Easterby) *trckd ldrs: t.k.h: chsd wnr appr last: hit last: kpt on same pce* **11/4**[3]
-642 **3** *13* **Petrou (IRE)**[60] 3009 6-11-11 **113** KielanWoods 102
(Ben Case) *led: hung lft most of way: pushed along 6th: hdd appr 2 out: wknd last 200yds* **2/1**[1]
1220 **4** *14* **Polarbrook (IRE)**[10] 3855 9-11-2 **104** (v) RichardJohnson 78
(Derek Shaw) *chsd ldrs: pushed along 7th: lost pl bef 2 out: sn bhd* **8/1**
24/P **F** **Captain Kelly (IRE)**[18] 3728 9-11-11 **113** (t) HarrySkelton
(Dan Skelton) *in rr: pushed along and outpcd 3 out: sn lost pl and bhd: t.o whn fell heavily next* **10/1**

5m 35.8s (27.00) **Going Correction** +1.15s/f (Heavy) **5 Ran SP% 111.0**
Speed ratings (Par 105): **94,92,87,82,**
CSF £9.02 TOTE £2.80: £1.60, £1.90; EX 11.60 Trifecta £18.30.
Owner Mrs Carol Davis **Bred** Mrs C Davis **Trained** Abberley, Worcs

FOCUS
An interesting handicap run at a steady gallop. The actual race distance was 2m4f199yds. The winner was well in on old form but this was arguably a small pb for new yard, with the second similar to recent course run.

4042 ROA/RACING POST OWNERS JACKPOT NOVICES' LIMITED H'CAP CHASE (14 fncs) 2m 3f 34y
4:10 (4:10) (Class 4) (0-120,118) 5-Y-0+ **£3,994** (£1,240; £667)

Form RPR
PF16 **1** **Ballyadeen (IRE)**[14] 3794 8-11-5 **118** JamesBanks(3) 135+
(Dai Williams) *j.lft: t.k.h: trcking ldr whn hit 2nd: led 4th: drvn 3 out: hit last: styd on wl: eased clsng stages* **5/2**[2]
5251 **2** *11* **Pembroke House**[50] 3195 9-10-10 **106** (p) RichardJohnson 109
(Sarah-Jayne Davies) *t.k.h: trckd ldrs 7th: 2nd and hit 11th: drvn next: kpt on same pce appr last* **3/1**[3]
P42F **3** *7* **Azert De Coeur (FR)**[14] 3794 6-11-5 **115** LiamTreadwell 115
(Venetia Williams) *hld up in rr: hdwy to trck ldrs 6th: 2nd 9th: pushed along 11th: rdn next: outpcd appr 2 out: wknd appr last* **11/8**[1]
331P **P** **Ivans Back (IRE)**[43] 3308 11-10-3 **99** oh5 GavinSheehan
(Nick Kent) *led: nt fluent and hdd 4th: outpcd 9th: sn lost pl and bhd: t.o after 11th: p.u bef 2 out: b.b.v* **13/2**

5m 32.1s (26.40) **Going Correction** +1.55s/f (Heavy) **4 Ran SP% 109.0**
Speed ratings: **106,101,98,**
CSF £9.87 TOTE £3.40; EX 8.70 Trifecta £20.90.
Owner F Michael **Bred** Michael Woodlock & Seamus Kennedy **Trained** Broad Hinton, Wilts

FOCUS
Following 4mm of overnight rain the going on the chase track was eased to heavy. A steadily run handicap. The actual race distance was 2m3f82y. The winner's Christmas course win could be rated this high. The second is rated to his mark.

4043 MARKET RASEN 2016 ANNUAL BADGEHOLDERS OPEN HUNTERS' CHASE (17 fncs) 2m 7f 191y
4:40 (4:41) (Class 6) 5-Y-0+ **£1,559** (£483; £241; £121)

Form RPR
42/1 **1** **Dark Lover (GER)**[27] 3585 11-11-11 130 MissPFuller(5) 128+
(Jamie Snowden) *trckd ldrs: led bef 3 out: hit 2 out: drew clr run-in* **4/9**[1]
14/P **2** *5* **Farmer Matt (IRE)**[43] 10-12-3 114 (t) MissAEStirling(3) 124
(Fergal O'Brien) *chsd ldrs: led 5th: 2 l down last: kpt on same pce* **11/1**
1/3- **3** *31* **Doubledisdoubledat (IRE)**[454] 2436 9-12-1 0 MissRMcDonald(5) 94
(Stuart Coltherd) *t.k.h: led to 5th: outpcd appr 3 out: hit 2 out: sn wknd* **20/1**
/10- **4** *12* **Soleil D'Avril (FR)**[306] 5239 10-11-9 106 MrWEasterby(5) 77
(Mrs Sarah Easterby) *in rr: jnd ldrs 12th: drvn next: outpcd and lost pl bef 3 out: sn bhd* **10/1**[3]
/24- **P** **Locked Inthepocket (IRE)**[290] 12-11-5 112 (p) MrHMorshead(7)
(Mrs Anthea Morshead) *in rr: chsd ldrs 7th: mstke next: drvn 12th: lost pl 13th: sn bhd: t.o whn p.u bef 3 out* **40/1**
U **Lord Heathfield (IRE)**[43] 10-11-9 118 (p) MissCVHart(3)
(Miss C L Mews) *chsd ldrs: blnd and uns rdr 3rd* **9/2**[2]

7m 7.1s (35.80) **Going Correction** +1.55s/f (Heavy) **6 Ran SP% 112.1**
Speed ratings: **102,100,90,86,**
CSF £6.45 TOTE £1.20: £1.10, £2.10; EX 5.50 Trifecta £34.80.
Owner The Dark Lovers **Bred** W Lohmann Jr **Trained** Lambourn, Berks

FOCUS
A steadily run hunter chase. The actual race distance was 3m31yds. The winner didn't need to match his recent win, with the second rated to his old mark.
T/Plt: £1,581.60 to a £1 stake. Pool: £50,070.46 - 23.11 winning units. T/Qpdt: £42.50 to a £1 stake. Pool: £5,016.08 - 87.20 winning units. **Walter Glynn**

3883 SEDGEFIELD (L-H)
Tuesday, February 9

OFFICIAL GOING: Soft (heavy in places; 4.7)
Wind: fairly strong behind Weather: Overcast

4044 BETFRED NOVICES' HURDLE (BETFRED HURDLE SERIES QUALIFIER) 2m 3f 188y
1:50 (1:50) (Class 4) 4-Y-0+ **£3,898** (£1,144; £572)

Form RPR
-213 **1** **Yes I Did (IRE)**[52] 3154 6-10-12 125 BridgetAndrews(5) 122+
(Dan Skelton) *mde all: nudged clr after 2 out* **1/3**[1]
41 **2** *9* **William Of Orange**[26] 3590 5-11-10 116 HenryBrooke 114
(Donald McCain) *trckd ldr in 2nd: rdn appr 2 out: drvn between last 2: one pce and sn no ch w wnr* **9/4**[2]
0 **3** *15* **Nine Altars (IRE)**[92] 2401 7-11-1 0 GrahamWatters(3) 96
(Ann Hamilton) *in tch in 3rd: nt fluent 5th: rdn appr 2 out: sn wknd* **100/1**[3]

5m 18.5s (24.40) **Going Correction** +1.475s/f (Heavy) **3 Ran SP% 106.8**
Speed ratings (Par 105): **110,106,100**
CSF £1.48 TOTE £1.20; EX 1.50 Trifecta £1.40.
Owner The Can't Say No Partnership **Bred** Mrs C J Power **Trained** Alcester, Warwicks

FOCUS
All distances as advertised. The opening contest was an ordinary little novice hurdle. They went a respectable gallop on ground officially described as soft, heavy in places. The easy winner stood out - token rating through the second and it makes sense on time compared with following handicap.

4045 WILLS PROPERTY SERVICES H'CAP HURDLE 2m 3f 188y
2:20 (2:20) (Class 5) (0-100,93) 4-Y-0+ **£2,729** (£801; £400; £200)

Form RPR
-015 **1** **Chasma**[39] 3402 6-11-4 **85** (t) JakeGreenall 93+
(Michael Easterby) *midfield: rdn after 3 out: chsd ldr appr 2 out: nt fluent 2 out: led between last 2: drvn out run-in* **3/1**[1]
654/ **2** *2 1/2* **Charlie Wingnut (IRE)**[304] 9-11-5 **93** MrRHogg(7) 98+
(Sue Smith) *trckd ldr: led 3 out: rdn 2 out: hdd appr last: one pce* **7/2**[3]
4405 **3** *10* **Seventeen Black (IRE)**[38] 3438 8-10-10 **77** JamesReveley 73
(Stuart Coltherd) *hld up: rdn after 3 out: plugged on: hit last: wnt modest 3rd run-in* **10/3**[2]
U024 **4** *6* **Louloumills**[9] 3888 6-10-8 **82** ThomasDowson(7) 75
(Maurice Barnes) *trckd ldr: rdn after 3 out: mstke 2 out: sn wknd: nt fluent last: lost 3rd run-in* **15/2**
2P1- **5** *83* **See The Legend**[293] 5473 11-11-5 **93** MrTHamilton(7)
(Sandy Forster) *led: hdd 3 out: sn rdn and wknd* **12/1**
6P5P **P** **He's A Hawker (IRE)**[79] 2666 11-11-3 **87** (v) BrianToomey(3)
(Michael Mullineaux) *trckd ldr: lost pl 3rd: reminders after next: sn struggling: p.u bef 6th* **33/1**
3600 **P** **Bertielicious**[9] 3883 8-9-11 **67** oh6 (p) HarryChalloner(3)
(Jonathan Haynes) *trckd ldr: hit 3rd: hit 7th: sn rdn along and wknd: p.u bef 2 out* **50/1**
-434 **R** **Cadgers Hole**[14] 3791 9-10-5 **72** (t) SeanQuinlan
(Lynn Siddall) *ref to r* **7/1**
6000 **P** **Seraffimo**[11] 3840 4-10-6 **84** HenryBrooke
(Sharon Watt) *hld up: rdn after 6th: sn struggling: t.o whn p.u bef 2 out* **22/1**

5m 22.9s (28.80) **Going Correction** +1.475s/f (Heavy)
WFA 4 from 6yo+ 10lb **9 Ran SP% 111.5**
Speed ratings (Par 103): **101,100,96,93,60 , , ,**
CSF £13.44 CT £34.42 TOTE £3.60: £1.60, £1.70, £2.20; EX 14.60 Trifecta £49.10.
Owner B Padgett & Lord Daresbury **Bred** Sandicroft Stud **Trained** Sheriff Hutton, N Yorks

FOCUS
A moderate handicap hurdle. They went an even gallop. A step up from the winner.

4046 PAXTONS SPRING SHOW 16 & 17 FEBRUARY H'CAP CHASE (17 fncs) 2m 5f 28y
2:55 (2:55) (Class 4) (0-120,117) 5-Y-0+ **£4,418** (£1,297; £648; £324)

Form RPR
4515 **1** **My Friend George**[21] 3671 10-10-7 **98** (p) HenryBrooke 112+
(Kenneth Slack) *hld up in tch: hdwy bef 3 out: sn chsd ldr: rdn to ld jst after 2 out: idled appr last: kpt on run-in* **4/1**[2]
1114 **2** *6* **Verko (FR)**[43] 3310 7-10-6 **104** FinianO'Toole(7) 112
(Micky Hammond) *hld up in rr: hdwy 5 out: rdn bef 3 out: wnt 2nd between last 2: one pce* **11/4**[1]
2034 **3** *11* **Bennys Well (IRE)**[79] 2668 10-10-13 **104** SeanQuinlan 103
(Sue Smith) *led: hdd 5 out: led again bef 3 out: sn rdn: hdd jst after 2 out: wknd* **11/2**
4252 **4** *4 1/2* **Court Dismissed (IRE)**[45] 3235 6-11-4 **114** JamesCowley(5) 107
(Donald McCain) *prom: hit 1st: reminders after 9th: led 5 out: hdd bef 3 out: wknd bef 2 out* **4/1**[2]
-34P **5** *4* **No Through Road**[57] 3086 9-11-6 **111** TomScudamore 100
(Michael Scudamore) *trckd ldng pair: rdn and lost pl after 4 out: wknd bef 2 out* **9/2**[3]
455- **P** **Edmund (IRE)**[362] 4183 9-11-7 **117** (t) JamieHamilton(5) 104
(Ann Hamilton) *trckd ldng pair: rdn after 3 out: wknd after 2 out: eased and p.u bef last* **9/1**

5m 47.0s (14.00) **Going Correction** +0.825s/f (Soft) **6 Ran SP% 110.2**
Speed ratings: **106,103,99,97,96**
CSF £15.19 TOTE £4.80: £2.20, £2.30; EX 13.90 Trifecta £47.10.
Owner A Slack **Bred** G A Slack And H D Sayer **Trained** Hilton, Cumbria

FOCUS
The feature contest was an ordinary handicap chase. They went a decent gallop. A pb from the winner, with the second probably the best guide to the level.

4047 HARDWICK ARMS H'CAP HURDLE (13 hdls) 3m 3f 9y
3:25 (3:25) (Class 5) (0-100,99) 4-Y-0+ **£2,729** (£801; £400; £200)

Form RPR
P-65 **1** **Snuker**[53] 3144 9-11-0 **87** (bt[1]) LucyAlexander 91
(James Ewart) *trckd ldr: nt fluent 4 out and reminder: rdn after 3 out: led last: sn drvn: all out* **9/1**[3]
4316 **2** *nk* **Optical High**[14] 3793 7-10-7 **90** StephenMcCarthy(10) 93
(Sue Smith) *midfield: rdn bef 3 out: styd on wl fr 2 out: wnt 2nd run-in: jst hld* **11/1**
445- **3** *3 3/4* **Leney Cottage (IRE)**[324] 4938 9-11-7 **99** DaraghBourke(5) 98
(Maurice Barnes) *in tch: hdwy to go prom after 8th: led 4 out: rdn bef 2 out: hdd last: no ex* **9/1**[3]
242P **4** *5* **Blue Cove**[14] 3793 11-10-0 **73** oh1 (t) SeanQuinlan 66
(Lynn Siddall) *in tch: rdn and outpcd bef 3 out: plugged on after 2 out* **16/1**
-334 **5** *nk* **Rocky Stone (IRE)**[14] 3793 8-10-12 **95** (t) RonanShort(10) 88
(Donald McCain) *hld up: stdy hdwy fr 8th: rdn after 3 out: no ex in 4th after 2 out* **10/3**[1]
-0P0 **6** *23* **Tomahawk Wood**[36] 3474 7-10-7 **83** (t) CallumWhillans(3) 65
(Donald Whillans) *hld up: reminders after 6th: hdwy after 8th: chsd ldr 3 out: mstke 2 out: wknd* **10/1**
-540 **7** *37* **High Fair**[20] 3684 10-11-1 **95** MrTHamilton(7) 28
(Sandy Forster) *midfield: rdn along fr 7th: bhd after 4 out* **25/1**
-024 **P** **Wellforth (IRE)**[40] 3378 12-11-6 **93** (p) DavidEngland
(Clare Ellam) *in tch on outer: wknd after 4 out: p.u after next* **14/1**
13P3 **P** **Urban Gale (IRE)**[13] 3803 11-11-4 **91** (tp) JonathanEngland
(Joanne Foster) *trckd ldr: wknd after 3 out: p.u bef 2 out* **12/1**
13P6 **P** **Heart O Annandale (IRE)**[223] 869 9-11-8 **95** (t) HenryBrooke
(Iain Jardine) *led: hdd 4 out: wknd qckly: p.u bef next* **11/2**[2]
5-56 **P** **Deportation**[54] 3128 9-10-0 **76** ow3 (b[1]) ColmMcCormack(3)
(John Norton) *a in rr: p.u after 3 out* **22/1**
165P **P** **Darsi Dancer (IRE)**[39] 3402 8-11-8 **95** (p) DerekFox
(Stuart Coltherd) *midfield: mstke 2nd: sn pushed along: bhd fr 9th: p.u bef 2 out* **14/1**

0-05 P **Messina Straights**[106] 2103 8-9-12 76.................(tp) JonathonBewley(5)
(George Bewley) *a in rr: p.u bef 9th* 40/1
7m 30.0s (38.00) **Going Correction** +1.475s/f (Heav) 13 Ran SP% 113.4
Speed ratings (Par 103): **102,101,100,99,99 92,81, , , , ,**
CSF £96.26 CT £913.78 TOTE £10.70: £2.40, £3.30, £3.50; EX 122.50 Trifecta £474.20.
Owner J Percy,D Down,R Boyd,CraigFarmSyndicate **Bred** Mr And Mrs N M L Ewart **Trained** Langholm, Dumfries & G'way

FOCUS
A moderate staying handicap hurdle. They went an even gallop. The winner is rated in line with his hurdle best and there's a case for rating this a bit higher.

4048 WINDPOWER ENERGY H'CAP CHASE (13 fncs) 2m 77y
4:00 (4:00) (Class 5) (0-100,97) 5-Y-O+ £2,989 (£877; £438; £219)

Form RPR
P045 1 **Captain Sharpe**[13] 3807 8-9-12 76.............................(b) MrWHRReed(7) 86
(Kenny Johnson) *chsd ldr: rdn after 3 out: 4th between last 2: styd on wl fr appr last: led towards fin* 14/1
4314 2 ½ **Roxyfet (FR)**[39] 3401 6-11-2 94.............................. FinianO'Toole(7) 104
(Micky Hammond) *midfield: mstke 8th: rdn and hdwy after 3 out: led between last 2: drvn and one pce run-in: hdd towards fin* 5/2[1]
04FU 3 4 ½ **Gin Cobbler**[6] 3938 10-11-5 97.............................. ThomasDowson(7) 103
(Victor Thompson) *led: hit 7th: rdn whn hdd between last 2: no ex run-in* 11/1
P030 4 3 **Odds On Dan (IRE)**[43] 3308 10-9-12 74.........................(tp) DeanPratt(5) 76
(Lucinda Egerton) *hld up: hdwy to trck ldr 4 out: rdn bef 2 out: wknd last* 9/2[3]
2RP0 5 3 **Dundee Blue (IRE)**[56] 3103 8-10-2 80.........................(tp) MissETodd(7) 78
(Henry Hogarth) *midfield: rdn bef 4 out: outpcd bef next and no threat after* 7/1
4535 6 6 **Molko Jack (FR)**[18] 3729 12-10-2 73.............................. SeanQuinlan 67
(Michael Mullineaux) *chsd ldr: rdn after 4 out: wknd bef 2 out* 8/1
P333 7 12 **Rupert Bear**[42] 3343 10-10-11 87.........................(tp) MissCWalton(5) 67
(James Walton) *hld up in rr: reminders after 5th: a bhd* 3/1[2]
4m 25.8s (11.80) **Going Correction** +0.825s/f (Soft) 7 Ran SP% 110.4
Speed ratings: **103,102,100,99,97 94,88**
CSF £47.25 TOTE £16.70: £6.00, £1.50; EX 53.00 Trifecta £932.90.
Owner Alan Kidd **Bred** Bumble Bloodstock & Mrs S Nicholls **Trained** Newburn, Tyne & Wear

FOCUS
A moderate handicap chase. They went an honest gallop. The winner was a 100+ hurdler at his best but this his best chase figure by a long way.

4049 SEDGEFIELD BOOKMAKERS H'CAP HURDLE (8 hdls) 2m 178y
4:30 (4:31) (Class 5) (0-100,94) 4-Y-O+ £2,729 (£801; £400; £200)

Form RPR
651U 1 **Fiddler's Flight (IRE)**[13] 3807 10-10-13 84............ ColmMcCormack(3) 90+
(John Norton) *hld up in rr: hit 1st: nt fluent 4th: pushed along and hdwy after 3 out: 3rd whn mstke 2 out: anther mstke last and rdr lost irons: stl 3 l down 110yds out: r.o to ld nr fin* 8/1
2045 2 ½ **King's Chorister**[45] 3244 10-10-1 76.........................(t) LorcanMurtagh(7) 78
(Barry Murtagh) *trckd ldrs: jnd ldr after 3 out: hit 2 out but led narrowly: rdn and edgd rt run-in: one pce fnl 110yds: hdd nr fin* 8/1
-033 3 nse **Copt Hill**[13] 3807 8-10-11 79.............................(p) BrianHarding 80
(Tracy Waggott) *pressed ldr: led bef 3 out: rdn whn hdd narrowly 2 out: drvn and one pce run-in* 5/2[2]
5206 4 39 **Strait Run (IRE)**[13] 3807 5-11-1 86.........................(tp) JoeColliver(3) 48
(Micky Hammond) *hld up: hdwy to chse ldrs 3 out: rdn bef 2 out: sn wknd* 13/2[3]
3540 P **Hi Dancer**[76] 2720 13-11-0 87.........................(b[1]) FreddieMitchell(5)
(Ben Haslam) *led narrowly: hdd bef 3 out: rdn after 3 out: sn wknd: p.u bef 2 out* 9/1
3-5P P **Azure Glamour (IRE)**[45] 3242 7-11-3 88.....................(p) HarryChalloner(3)
(Kenneth Slack) *pressed ldr: rdn after 3 out: wknd qckly appr 2 out and p.u* 9/4[1]
0460 P **Norfolk Sound**[20] 3681 5-11-12 94.............................. DerekFox
(Stuart Coltherd) *trckd ldrs: nt fluent 5th: sn pushed along and wknd bef next: p.u bef 2 out* 16/1
4m 31.8s (24.90) **Going Correction** +1.475s/f (Heav) 7 Ran SP% 110.8
Speed ratings (Par 103): **100,99,99,81,**
CSF £62.16 TOTE £7.40: £3.70, £3.80; EX 34.10 Trifecta £81.40.
Owner Fellowship Of The Rose Partnership **Bred** Joe Magee **Trained** High Hoyland, S Yorks

FOCUS
The concluding race was another moderate handicap hurdle. The second and third were on decent marks and set the level.
T/Plt: £86.90 to a £1 stake. Pool: £60,969.57 - 511.93 winning units. T/Qpdt: £53.50 to a £1 stake. Pool: £5,413.25 - 74.80 winning units. **Andrew Sheret**

3054 CARLISLE (R-H)
Wednesday, February 10

OFFICIAL GOING: Heavy (chs 5.3; hdl 5.1)
Wind: Breezy, half behind Weather: Fine, dry

4050 RACING TO SCHOOL NOVICES' HURDLE (10 hdls) 2m 1f
1:50 (1:57) (Class 4) 4-Y-O+ £3,249 (£954; £477; £238)

Form RPR
0-23 1 **Dakota Grey**[43] 3340 5-11-0 111.............................. JoeColliver(3) 123+
(Micky Hammond) *t.k.h: cl up: led bef 3 out: pushed clr fr next* 15/8[2]
2422 2 8 **Berkshire Downs**[43] 3342 6-10-7 112.............................. AdamNicol(3) 108
(Lucy Normile) *led to 3rd: cl up: ev ch 3 out: rdn and outpcd bef next: rallied to chse (clr) wnr bef last: kpt on: no imp* 11/8[1]
3 18 **Dubai Celebrity**[188] 4-10-7 0.............................. BrianHughes 90+
(John Wade) *cl up: chal bef 2 out: rdn and outpcd bef last: wknd run-in* 20/1
04 4 12 **Red Story**[66] 2931 5-11-3 0.............................. CraigNichol 85
(Alistair Whillans) *hld up: outpcd 1/2-way: plugged on fr 2 out: nvr able to chal* 25/1
00 5 1 **Rhythm Of Sound (IRE)**[15] 3795 6-10-10 0.............................. FinianO'Toole(7) 84
(Micky Hammond) *cl up: led 3rd to bef 3 out: rdn and wknd bef next* 100/1
6 21 **Breezemount (IRE)**[80] 6-11-3 0.............................. HenryBrooke 63
(Donald McCain) *in tch: pushed along and outpcd bef 4 out: n.d after* 5/1[3]
7 16 **Here Comes Love (IRE)**[18] 3750 6-11-3 0.............................. DerekFox 47
(Patrick Griffin, Ire) *in tch: outpcd after 4th: drvn and btn fr 3 out* 50/1
40 8 13 **Been Decided (IRE)**[62] 2984 6-11-3 0.............................. LucyAlexander 34
(N W Alexander) *midfield on outside: struggling 4 out: sn btn* 33/1
26/ B **Thackeray**[55] 1268 9-11-0 0.............................. JohnKington(3)
(Chris Fairhurst) *mstke 1st: bhd: b.d 4 out* 50/1
46-0 P **Beau Marsh**[21] 3681 7-10-10 0.............................. SeanQuinlan
(Barry Murtagh) *midfield: struggling after 4th: lost tch and p.u bef 2 out* 250/1
F **Wazowski** 7-10-12 0.............................. JamesCowley(5)
(Donald McCain) *hld up in midfield on outside: stdy hdwy whn fell 4 out* 28/1
4m 33.9s (4.70) **Going Correction** +0.45s/f (Soft)
WFA 4 from 5yo+ 9lb 11 Ran SP% 113.9
Speed ratings (Par 105): **106,102,93,88,87 77,70,64, ,**
CSF £4.42 TOTE £2.50: £1.10, £1.10, £3.50; EX 5.80 Trifecta £43.80.
Owner Still Game Associates **Bred** C F C Jackson **Trained** Middleham, N Yorks

FOCUS
Testing conditions for a meeting that passed a morning inspection. The new inner hurdles course was used, with the inside rail moved out and hurdles in the middle of the course. The first three had this modest event to themselves a long way out. The race was run over 52yds further than advertised. The easy winner is rated to the level of his upgraded Wetherby run, with the second to her mark.

4051 LLOYD LAND ROVER NOVICES' H'CAP CHASE (18 fncs) 3m 110y
2:20 (2:26) (Class 4) (0-105,105) 5-Y-O+ £3,898 (£1,144; £572; £286)

Form RPR
-362 1 **Jonny Eager (IRE)**[15] 3793 7-11-2 95.............................. CraigNichol 119+
(Alistair Whillans) *mde virtually all: rdn and drew clr fr 3 out: nt fluent next: kpt on strly* 7/2[1]
54P3 2 20 **The Bishop (IRE)**[22] 3668 8-10-10 89.............................. LucyAlexander 93
(N W Alexander) *cl up: chal 6th to 3 out: rdn and one pce bef next* 11/2[3]
6-43 3 4 **Vinny Gambini (IRE)**[22] 3669 9-11-12 105.............. SamTwiston-Davies 105
(Rose Dobbin) *hld up in midfield: pushed along and outpcd 11th: rallied to chse clr ldng pair whn pckd 4 out: rdn and no imp fr next* 7/2[1]
2330 4 2 ¾ **Solway Sam**[21] 3684 13-10-1 85.............................. CallumBewley(5) 82
(Lisa Harrison) *chsd ldrs: rdn and outpcd 10th: n.d after* 14/1
04-4 5 hd **Spring Over (IRE)**[40] 3427 10-10-7 86.........................(t) BrianHughes 83
(Ian Duncan) *t.k.h early: prom tl rdn and outpcd bef 4 out: sn btn* 6/1
0300 6 31 **Mister Don (IRE)**[21] 3684 6-11-5 98.........................(t) BrianHarding 64
(Rose Dobbin) *hld up: reminders after 6th: shortlived effrt 11th: struggling fr 5 out: t.o* 25/1
5440 P **Under The Red Sky (IRE)**[7] 3937 9-9-7 79 oh6...(p) ThomasDowson(7)
(Kenny Johnson) *prom: outpcd whn nt fluent 4 out: sn lost tch and p.u bef next* 5/1[2]
P4-0 F **Simply Lucky (IRE)**[37] 3474 7-9-7 79 oh10.............................. MrWHRReed(7)
(W T Reed) *hld up: outpcd 10th: no ch whn fell 4 out* 66/1
6214 P **Longueville Flier (IRE)**[15] 3792 7-11-2 98.............................. JoeColliver(3)
(Micky Hammond) *hld up: struggling bef 10th: wknd and p.u bef 13th* 7/1
6m 55.1s (12.50) **Going Correction** +0.45s/f (Soft) 9 Ran SP% 115.3
Speed ratings: **98,91,90,89,89 79, , ,**
CSF £23.53 CT £71.58 TOTE £5.00: £1.80, £1.90, £1.60; EX 25.60 Trifecta £126.40.
Owner Paul & Clare Rooney **Bred** Mrs R H Lalor **Trained** Newmill-On-Slitrig, Borders

FOCUS
Race over 66yds further than advertised. The winner proved much too strong in this fairly modest event. The second sets the level, but this could be a bit higher through the third and fourth.

4052 BRITISH STALLION STUDS EBF MARES' "NATIONAL HUNT" NOVICES' HURDLE (11 hdls) 2m 3f 61y
2:55 (3:00) (Class 4) 4-Y-O+ £3,898 (£1,144; £572; £286)

Form RPR
-266 1 **Tara The Tiger**[25] 3626 5-11-0 103.........................(b[1]) BrianHughes 112+
(Tim Easterby) *hld up in tch: stdy hdwy 1/2-way: squeezed through to ld after 2 out: rdn clr* 6/1[3]
2 19 **Cherry Bomb (IRE)**[7] 3939 5-11-0 0.........................(p) JamesReveley 93
(S R B Crawford, Ire) *led to 3rd: w ldr: led after 5th to after 2 out: no ch w wnr* 9/1
0 3 23 **Wicked Games (IRE)**[22] 3667 5-11-0 0.............................. CraigNichol 70
(Rose Dobbin) *hld up in tch: stdy hdwy 1/2-way: pressed wnr after 3 out: rdn and wknd fr next* 18/1
00 4 29 **Fairlee Grace**[37] 3476 5-11-0 0.............................. JanFaltejsek 41
(George Charlton) *pressed ldr: led 3rd to after 5th: cl up tl rdn and wknd qckly bef 2 out* 150/1
3-43 F **Knocklayde Sno Cat (IRE)**[22] 3666 7-11-0 105.....................(t) AELynch
(S R B Crawford, Ire) *hld up in tch on outside: stdy hdwy 6th: cl 3rd and gng wl whn fell 3 out* 3/1[2]
6-2 P **Miss Tiggy (IRE)**[66] 2936 6-11-0 0.............................. PeterBuchanan
(Lucinda Russell) *hld up: struggling fr 6th: lost tch and p.u bef 2 out* 2/1[1]
244 U **Mo Chailin (IRE)**[21] 3681 5-11-0 0.............................. SamTwiston-Davies
(Donald McCain) *hld up bhd ldng gp: shkn up whn bdly hmpd and uns rdr 3 out* 3/1[2]
P **Tikkskinned (IRE)**[21] 3697 5-11-0 0.............................. DerekFox
(Benjamin Arthey, Ire) *chsd ldrs tl lost pl bef 4th: lost tch next: sn p.u* 150/1
5m 15.6s (6.80) **Going Correction** +0.45s/f (Soft) 8 Ran SP% 114.2
Speed ratings (Par 105): **103,95,85,73, , ,**
CSF £56.50 TOTE £5.70: £1.40, £2.00, £5.30; EX 45.00 Trifecta £380.60.
Owner Reality Partnerships **Bred** Jocelyn Targett & Overbury Stallions Ltd **Trained** Great Habton, N Yorks

FOCUS
Race run over 58yds further than advertised. A big step up from the winner with the second in line with her bumper form.

4053 LLOYDS BMW NOVICES' LIMITED H'CAP CHASE (12 fncs) 1m 7f 207y
3:30 (3:35) (Class 4) (0-120,120) 5-Y-O+ £4,548 (£1,335; £667; £333)

Form RPR
4223 1 **Morning Royalty (IRE)**[18] 3742 9-11-8 120.............................. BrianHughes 130+
(James Moffatt) *t.k.h: trckd ldrs: effrt and wnt 2nd after 3 out: rdn to ld run-in: sn clr* 7/4[1]
263 2 8 **Dr Moloney (IRE)**[7] 3944 9-10-10 108.............................. AELynch 112
(S R B Crawford, Ire) *led to 5th: pressed ldr: regained ld 4 out: nt fluent and rdn 2 out: hdd run-in: nt pce of wnr* 5/2[2]
0121 3 14 **Moscow Me (IRE)**[44] 3313 9-11-1 113.............................. JeremiahMcGrath 105
(Henry Oliver) *pressed ldr: led 5th to 4 out: rdn next: outpcd whn j.rt 2 out: sn btn* 5/2[2]

4-44 **4** *41* **Stilo Blue Native (IRE)**[27] 3592 8-11-0 112................. AndrewThornton 59
(John Wade) *nt fluent: prom to 5 out: lost tch fr next* **6/1**[3]
4m 21.1s (5.00) **Going Correction** +0.45s/f (Soft) **4** Ran SP% **107.8**
Speed ratings: **105,101,94,73**
CSF £6.41 TOTE £2.30; EX 6.70 Trifecta £11.50.
Owner Mrs Eileen M Milligan **Bred** Miss Marie Murphy **Trained** Cartmel, Cumbria
FOCUS
Race run over 34yds further than advertised. Just a fair novice handicap. A small chase pb from the cosy winner but he was a 132 hurdler at his peak, and the second sets the level.

4054 LLOYDS LAWN AND LEISURE NOVICES' LIMITED H'CAP CHASE (18 fncs) 3m 110y
4:05 (4:10) (Class 3) (0-135,129) 5-Y-0+ **£6,498** (£1,908; £954)

Form RPR
-312 **1** **Subtle Grey (IRE)**[32] 3520 7-11-8 129................................. WillKennedy 144+
(Donald McCain) *trckd ldrs: rn in snatches fnl circ: effrt and drvn 4 out: led 2 out: idled run-in: hld on* **4/5**[1]
6/22 **2** *½* **Kilbree Chief (IRE)**[22] 3669 8-10-12 119......................... PeterBuchanan 128
(Lucinda Russell) *nt fluent on occasions: led to 4th: pressed ldr: led 4 out: rdn and hdd 2 out: rallied run-in: hld towards fin* **11/4**[2]
P11P **3** *2* **Courtown Oscar (IRE)**[32] 3520 7-11-0 121......................... JamesReveley 130
(Philip Kirby) *cl up: led 4th: hit and hdd 4 out: hit next: drvn and outpcd 2 out: plugged on fr last* **3/1**[3]
6m 48.5s (5.90) **Going Correction** +0.45s/f (Soft) **3** Ran SP% **107.2**
Speed ratings: **108,107,107**
CSF £3.19 TOTE £1.40; EX 2.90 Trifecta £3.40.
Owner Deva Racing Subtle Grey Partnership **Bred** James A Slattery **Trained** Cholmondeley, Cheshire
FOCUS
Race run over 66yds further than advertised. A poor turnout numerically for this, but it was still a decent little race and the time was 6.6sec quicker than the earlier 0-105. The winner is on the upgrade, with the second and third to their marks.

4055 LLOYD MOTOR GROUP H'CAP HURDLE (QUALIFIER FOR THE CHALLENGER TWO MILE HURDLE SERIES FINAL) (10 hdls) 2m 1f
4:35 (4:41) (Class 4) (0-120,115) 4-Y-0+ **£3,249** (£954; £477; £238)

Form RPR
6U25 **1** **Pistol (IRE)**[43] 3346 7-10-10 106................................. MrJDixon(7) 121
(John Dixon) *w ldr: led 4 out: drvn clr after next: kpt on wl fr 2 out: unchal* **14/1**
0642 **2** *26* **Veinard (FR)**[25] 3628 7-11-4 107................................. HenryBrooke 96
(Robert Bewley) *nt fluent on occasions: hld up: pushed along 4 out: rallied bef 2 out: chsd (clr) wnr run-in: no imp* **4/1**[2]
6420 **3** *2¼* **Hartside (GER)**[60] 3035 7-11-1 111................................. MrRWinks(7) 98
(Peter Winks) *hld up: pushed along and outpcd bef 3 out: rallied to chse (clr) wnr briefly run-in: one pce* **11/2**[3]
3361 **4** *4* **Captain Redbeard (IRE)**[10] 3884 7-11-10 113 7ex......... JamesReveley 98
(Stuart Coltherd) *chsd clr ldng pair: stdy hdwy to chse (clr) wnr whn nt fluent 2 out: sn no imp: no ex and lost two pls run-in* **3/1**[1]
1-45 **5** *11* **Age Of Glory**[236] 780 7-11-12 115................................. SeanQuinlan 87
(Barry Murtagh) *hld up: pushed along bef 3 out: no imp bef next* **25/1**
4F44 **6** *1* **Return Flight**[25] 3626 5-11-2 105.................................[1] AidanColeman 76
(Micky Hammond) *t.k.h: hld up in tch: lost pl 1/2-way: rallied bef 2 out: sn wknd* **3/1**[1]
3-23 **7** *¾* **Diamond D'Amour (IRE)**[39] 3438 10-10-10 104........ JonathonBewley(5) 74
(George Bewley) *led at decent gallop to 4 out: rdn and wknd bef 2 out* **7/1**
0203 **8** *3¾* **Herecomesnelson (IRE)**[22] 3667 7-11-0 108............. CallumBewley(5) 74
(Katie Scott) *hld up: drvn along after 4 out: sn wknd* **11/1**
4m 35.9s (6.70) **Going Correction** +0.45s/f (Soft) **8** Ran SP% **116.7**
Speed ratings (Par 105): **102,89,88,86,81 81,80,79**
CSF £71.37 CT £354.18 TOTE £16.80: £3.80, £1.40, £2.20; EX 84.60 Trifecta £1166.40.
Owner Mrs S F Dixon **Bred** Mrs Eleanor Commins **Trained** Thursby, Cumbria
FOCUS
Race run over 52yds further than advertised. Only the winner and the seventh ever figured in this ordinary handicap, in which the field was quickly spread out, and the form is questionable, but it could be rated higher. All eight qualify for the series final at Haydock on Easter Saturday.
T/Plt: £670.40 to a £1 stake. Pool: £71,317.82 - 77.65 winning units. T/Qpdt: £238.40 to a £1 stake. Pool: £4,366.07 - 13.55 winning units. **Richard Young**

3926 LUDLOW (R-H)
Wednesday, February 10
4056 Meeting Abandoned - Waterlogged

3855 DONCASTER (L-H)
Thursday, February 11
OFFICIAL GOING: Good to soft (soft in places on chase course) changing to good to soft after race 2 (1.45).
Wind: light 1/2 against Weather: fine and sunny but very cool

4062 CHALLENGER TRACKED TRACTOR H'CAP CHASE (18 fncs) 3m 6y
1:15 (1:15) (Class 4) (0-120,120) 5-Y-0+ **£6,498** (£1,908; £954; £477)

Form RPR
1/F2 **1** **Willoughby Hedge**[14] 3823 9-11-9 120................................. TomBellamy(3) 131+
(Alan King) *chsd ldrs: 2nd 4 out: hit next: led 2 out: nt fluent last: drvn out* **4/1**[1]
4446 **2** *3* **Under The Phone (IRE)**[13] 3834 7-10-4 103......................... ChrisWard(5) 109
(Robin Dickin) *in rr: hdwy to chse ldrs 11th: led 13th: clr 4 out: mstke next: hdd 2 out: kpt on same pce* **13/2**[3]
064U **3** *6* **Grove Silver (IRE)**[13] 3836 7-11-9 117......................... AidanColeman 118
(Jennie Candlish) *in rr: hdwy 13th: poor 4th 3 out: 3rd last: kpt on one pce* **7/1**
F613 **4** *6* **Kings Apollo**[16] 3788 7-11-1 109................................. JamesDavies 103
(Tom Symonds) *led: hit 1st: hdd 13th: outpcd 3 out: wknd last* **16/1**
-322 **5** *4½* **St Johns Point (IRE)**[56] 3129 8-11-12 120.................(bt[1]) BrianHughes 109
(Charlie Longsdon) *hdwy 3rd: sn chsng ldrs: outpcd and lost pl 14th* **5/1**[2]
26- **6** *4* **Solstice Son**[464] 2266 7-11-4 117.................................(t) DavidNoonan(5) 103
(Anthony Honeyball) *chsd ldrs: drvn 11th: lost pl 13th: sn bhd* **15/2**
-P03 **U** **Firm Order (IRE)**[69] 2887 11-11-5 113.................................(tp) RichieMcLernon
(Paul Webber) *chsd ldrs: blnd and uns rdr 4th* **7/1**
4113 **P** **Xenophon**[36] 3488 8-9-9 94 oh5................................. ThomasCheesman(5)
(Olly Williams) *chsd ldrs: stmbld on landing 8th: reminders and lost pl 10th: sn bhd: t.o whn j. bdly rt 12th: p.u bef 4 out* **22/1**
6-UP **P** **Imperial Leader (IRE)**[54] 3160 8-11-4 115.................................(vt) RyanHatch(3)
(Nigel Twiston-Davies) *in rr: hit 2nd: bhd fr 11th: t.o whn p.u bef 3 out* **18/1**
6-0P **P** **Strollawaynow (IRE)**[21] 3707 9-11-4 112.................................(tp[1]) JamieMoore
(David Arbuthnot) *chsd ldrs: lost pl 8th: sn drvn: chsd ldrs 11th: lost pl next: sn bhd: t.o whn p.u bef 4 out* **14/1**
P **P** **Didntitellya (IRE)**[64] 2975 7-11-9 117................................. DavidBass
(Kim Bailey) *chsd ldrs: drvn 11th: reminders and lost pl bef next: sn bhd: t.o whn p.u bef 4 out* **25/1**
6m 4.1s (-7.90) **Going Correction** -0.15s/f (Good) **11** Ran SP% **112.8**
Speed ratings: **107,106,104,102,100 99, , , ,**
CSF £29.46 CT £173.74 TOTE £4.70: £2.30, £8.80, £3.30; EX 36.20 Trifecta £195.50.
Owner Trevor Hemmings **Bred** East Burrow Farm **Trained** Barbury Castle, Wilts
FOCUS
Race distance increased by 12yds. The going was good to soft, soft in places on the chase track. An open handicap run at a decent gallop. The winner improved to the level of his hurdles form, with the second and third to their marks.

4063 EBF STALLIONS "NATIONAL HUNT" NOVICES' HURDLE (QUALIFIER) (10 hdls) 2m 3f 120y
1:45 (1:45) (Class 4) 4-7-Y-O **£3,898** (£1,144; £572; £286)

Form RPR
6-22 **1** **Rock On Oscar (IRE)**[63] 2986 6-11-2 124.................................(t) NickScholfield 136+
(Paul Nicholls) *racd on ins: mde all: t.k.h: wnt clr between last 2: v comf* **3/1**[3]
1-54 **2** *10* **Newsworthy (IRE)**[111] 2056 6-11-2 0................................. BarryGeraghty 128+
(Nicky Henderson) *chsd ldrs: 2nd appr 3 out: rdn bef 2 out: kpt on same pce between last 2* **5/2**[1]
3321 **3** *13* **Chase End Charlie (IRE)**[34] 3509 5-11-8 0......................... RichardJohnson 119
(Tom Lacey) *trckd ldrs: drvn 3 out: sn outpcd: kpt on between last 2: tk modest 3rd post* **11/4**[2]
062 **4** *hd* **Another Frontier (IRE)**[30] 3570 5-10-11 0......................... JamieBargary(5) 114
(Nigel Twiston-Davies) *chsd ldrs: clr 3rd whn hit 3 out: blnd next: wknd in clsng stages* **16/1**
3 **5** *15* **Sonneofpresenting (IRE)**[47] 3221 6-11-2 0......................... DavidBass 101
(Kim Bailey) *sn chsng ldrs: drvn appr 3 out: sn wknd* **20/1**
5 **6** *44* **Easy Street (IRE)**[41] 3413 6-11-2 0................................. RichieMcLernon 59
(Jonjo O'Neill) *hld up in rr-div: hdwy 6th: lost pl appr 3 out: sn bhd: t.o* **66/1**
-3PP **P** **Anti Cool (IRE)**[36] 3483 7-11-2 0................................. CharliePoste
(Robin Dickin) *in rr: bhd 6th: j. bdly rt next: sn t.o: p.u bef 3 out* **200/1**
24 **P** **Galveston (IRE)**[117] 1966 7-10-13 0................................. ConorShoemark(3)
(Fergal O'Brien) *mid-div: drvn 6th: sn lost pl and bhd: t.o whn p.u bef 3 out* **66/1**
0/40 **U** **Henrybrowneyes (IRE)**[85] 2581 7-11-2 0.................................[1] WillKennedy
(Ian Williams) *gave problems befhand: in rr: blnd bdly and uns rdr 6th* **150/1**
3/1- **P** **Score Card (IRE)**[348] 4485 6-10-13 0................................. KieronEdgar(3)
(Alastair Ralph) *nt fluent in rr: bhd fr 6th: t.o whn p.u sn after 3 out* **14/1**
2-44 **U** **Kerrow (IRE)**[55] 3133 6-10-13 123................................. TomBellamy(3)
(Alan King) *hld up towards rr: sme hdwy whn blnd and uns rdr 6th* **11/2**
4m 44.5s (-6.80) **Going Correction** -0.15s/f (Good) **11** Ran SP% **117.1**
Speed ratings: **107,103,97,97,91 74, , , ,**
CSF £11.04 TOTE £4.20: £1.50, £1.60, £1.40; EX 11.70 Trifecta £47.00.
Owner I Fogg,C Barber,D Bennett & D Macdonald **Bred** T J Whitley **Trained** Ditcheat, Somerset
FOCUS
Race distance increased by 30yds. A fair novice hurdle run at an honest gallop. A big step up from the winner, with the second building on the promise of his bumper debut win, the third rated below form, with small steps up from the fourth and fifth.

4064 EVENTMASTERS.CO.UK NOVICES' HURDLE (DIV I) (8 hdls) 2m 140y
2:20 (2:20) (Class 4) 5-Y-0+ **£3,898** (£1,144; £572; £286)

Form RPR
1 **1** **Winter Escape (IRE)**[62] 3021 5-11-5 0................................. BarryGeraghty 137+
(Alan King) *trckd ldr: led between last 2: v easily* **1/5**[1]
122F **2** *6* **Bantam (IRE)**[103] 2199 6-11-5 130................................. RichardJohnson 126+
(Henry Daly) *led: hdd between last 2: kpt on: no ch w wnr* **7/2**[2]
-55P **3** *23* **Lime Street (IRE)**[41] 3411 5-10-12 0................................. JamesDavies 95
(Tom Symonds) *trckd ldng pair: outpcd appr 3 out: poor 3rd between last 2* **14/1**
4 *4* **Celtic Tune (FR)**[112] 5-10-12 0................................. RichieMcLernon 91
(Jonjo O'Neill) *chsd ldrs: hit 4th: 3rd 5th: outpcd next: wknd appr last* **12/1**
P **5** *1½* **Texas Forever (IRE)**[38] 3467 7-10-12 0................................. DavidBass 91
(Kim Bailey) *mid-div: outpcd whn mstke 5th: one pce appr next* **15/2**[3]
34 **6** *3¾* **Captain Mowbray**[66] 2951 5-10-12 0................................. HenryBrooke 87
(Rebecca Menzies) *in rr: sme hdwy 6th: outpcd appr next: bhd whn j.lft last* **50/1**
-500 **7** *½* **Gabriel Oats**[14] 3819 7-10-12 0................................. KielanWoods 88
(Graeme McPherson) *mid-div: outpcd 5th: poor 5th whn hit 3 out and next* **66/1**
00 **8** *82* **Iman (GER)**[14] 3819 6-10-12 0................................. JakeGreenall 12
(Sophie Leech) *led into s: most reluctant to jump off: continued t.o: in tch 4th: lost pl next: sn t.o: eventually completed* **125/1**
4m 8.6s (3.90) **Going Correction** -0.15s/f (Good) **8** Ran SP% **135.9**
Speed ratings: **84,81,70,68,67 66,65,27**
CSF £2.34 TOTE £1.10: £1.02, £1.40, £4.20; EX 2.20 Trifecta £10.70.
Owner John P McManus **Bred** Oliver And Salome Brennan **Trained** Barbury Castle, Wilts
FOCUS
Race distance increased by 30yds. The going changed to good to soft prior to the this race. The gallop was steady for an uncompetitive novice hurdle, in which the market leaders were in control of a long way out. The easy winner is on the upgrade and looks a smart prospect, and the second and third are rated pretty much to their marks.

4065 EVENTMASTERS.CO.UK NOVICES' HURDLE (DIV II) (8 hdls) 2m 140y
2:55 (2:55) (Class 4) 5-Y-0+ **£3,898** (£1,144; £572; £286)

Form RPR
4042 **1** **Muthabir (IRE)**[36] 3483 6-10-12 120................................. IanPopham 118+
(Richard Phillips) *trckd ldrs: 3rd appr 3 out: led appr last: styd on wl last 75yds* **13/8**[2]
3-66 **2** *1¾* **The Last Bar**[20] 3724 6-10-0 0................................. BridgetAndrews(5) 107+
(Dan Skelton) *mid-div: outpcd and pushed along 4th: drvn next: hdwy and modest 5th 3 out: styd on and upsides last: no ex last 50yds* **16/1**

50 **3** *6* **Lord Golan**[13] 3839 8-10-9 0...... MauriceLinehan(3) 109
(Nick Kent) *trckd ldrs: swtchd lft appr 2 out: kpt on one pce to take modest 3rd in clsng stages* **80/1**

2 **4** *¾* **Deadly Approach**[76] 2747 5-10-12 0...... RichardJohnson 108
(Sarah-Jayne Davies) *led: hdd appr last: fdd in clsng stages* **7/1**[3]

-004 **5** *6* **Scooby (IRE)**[17] 3773 5-10-12 0...... KielanWoods 103
(Graeme McPherson) *mid-div: outpcd and lost pl 5th: kpt on between last 2* **12/1**

1-1F **6** *½* **Younevercall (IRE)**[93] 2409 5-11-5 0...... DavidBass 111
(Kim Bailey) *chsd ldrs: hung rt thrght: j.rt 5th: sn drvn: cl 2nd appr 3 out: rdn and ducked lft 2 out: wknd between last 2* **10/11**[1]

000 **7** *45* **St Lewis**[13] 3835 6-10-12 0...... SeanQuinlan 62
(Jennie Candlish) *in rr: hit 3rd: pushed along next: sn bhd: t.o 3 out: eventually completed* **125/1**

P **First Sargeant**[26] 6-10-12 0...... BrianHughes
(Lawrence Mullaney) *in rr: bhd fr 5th: t.o whn p.u bef last* **25/1**

4m 6.0s (1.30) **Going Correction** -0.15s/f (Good) **8** Ran SP% **122.4**
Speed ratings: **90,89,86,86,83 82,61,**
CSF £27.25 TOTE £2.50: £1.10, £3.60, £11.30; EX 24.90 Trifecta £921.30.
Owner The Adlestrop Experience **Bred** Darley **Trained** Adlestrop, Gloucs

FOCUS
Race distance increased by 30yds. This second division of this novice hurdle was run at a sound gallop. The winner is rated similar to his Huntingdon run, with step ups from the second and third, and the fourth and fifth helping set the level.

4066 EVENTMASTERS CATERING SERVICES H'CAP HURDLE (QUALIFIER FOR THE CHALLENGER STAYING HURDLE FINAL)
(11 hdls) **3m 96y**
3:30 (3:30) (Class 3) (0-130,130) 4-Y-0+ **£9,747** (£2,862; £1,431; £715)

Form RPR

13 **1** **Emerging Force (IRE)**[57] 3117 6-11-10 **128**...... RichardJohnson 139
(Harry Whittington) *mid-div: hdwy 7th: chsd ldr after 3 out: styd on run-in: led post* **9/2**[2]

31 **2** *nse* **Whataknight**[63] 2986 7-11-11 **129**......(t) NickScholfield 142+
(Harry Fry) *chsd ldrs: led sn after 3 out: 3 l ahd whn hit last: hdd post* **7/1**[3]

4FU3 **3** *16* **Road To Freedom**[14] 3817 7-10-11 **115**...... JoshuaMoore 113
(Lucy Wadham) *in rr: hdwy appr 3 out: modest 3rd between last 2: one pce* **14/1**

P1-3 **4** *8* **Royal Native (IRE)**[280] 174 8-10-10 **119**......(t) DavidNoonan(5) 108
(Anthony Honeyball) *w ldrs: led briefly bef 3 out: wknd between last 2* **25/1**

6351 **5** *¾* **Quinto**[28] 3588 6-10-13 **117**...... WillKennedy 107
(John Quinn) *mid-div: chsd ldrs 7th: drvn next: one pce fr 3 out* **10/1**

3063 **6** *¾* **I Just Know (IRE)**[43] 3366 6-10-6 **110**...... SeanQuinlan 98
(Sue Smith) *chsd ldrs: led 8th: hdd bef 3 out: wknd between last 2* **25/1**

0-P0 **7** *1 ½* **Al Co (FR)**[41] 3404 11-11-6 **124**...... SeanBowen 111
(Peter Bowen) *led: hdd 8th: outpcd and lost pl next: kpt on between last 2* **20/1**

PP-0 **8** *¾* **Rendl Beach (IRE)**[21] 3705 9-10-13 **122**......(t) CiaranGethings(5) 108
(Robert Stephens) *mid-div: hdwy to chse ldrs 7th: one pce 3 out* **40/1**

006F **9** *1* **Harvey's Hope**[13] 3834 10-9-12 **105**......(b) HarryChalloner(3) 90
(Keith Reveley) *towards rr: sme hdwy appr 3 out: outpcd 2 out: kpt on run-in* **40/1**

-225 **10** *hd* **Shadarpour (IRE)**[55] 3137 7-11-0 **125**......(p) WilliamFeatherstone(7) 110
(Alan King) *chsd ldrs: drvn appr 3 out: edgd lft between last 2: one pce* **14/1**

4124 **11** *1 ½* **Aviator (GER)**[123] 1325 8-11-7 **125**...... JackQuinlan 109
(James Eustace) *chsd ldrs: drvn 8th: one pce bef next* **16/1**

-260 **12** *3 ¾* **Mantou (IRE)**[111] 2058 5-11-11 **129**......(t) AidanColeman 109
(John Ferguson) *mid-div: hdwy 8th: chsng ldrs whn hit 3 out: wknd between last 2* **25/1**

3512 **13** *6* **Harry Hunt**[41] 3428 9-11-5 **123**...... KielanWoods 98
(Graeme McPherson) *mid-div: bhd and drvn 7th: nvr on terms* **14/1**

PP60 **14** *3 ½* **Barafundle (IRE)**[19] 3737 12-11-12 **130**...... BrianHughes 102
(Jennie Candlish) *in rr: drvn and detached 6th: nvr on terms* **25/1**

-046 **15** *5* **Balmusette**[44] 3336 7-11-11 **129**...... JamesReveley 96
(Keith Reveley) *in rr: sme hdwy whn j.lft 3 out: sn bhd* **20/1**

2/2- **16** *12* **Zalgarry (FR)**[432] 2940 9-10-7 **118**...... JoshWall(7) 74
(Arthur Whitehead) *chsd ldrs: lost pl 8th: bhd next: collapsed after line* **16/1**

20-0 **P** **Western Jo (IRE)**[120] 1903 8-11-1 **126**......(p) GLavery(7)
(Alan Brown) *in rr: bhd fr 8th: sn t.o: p.u bef 2 out: sddle slipped* **33/1**

3-00 **P** **Walk On Al (IRE)**[80] 2687 8-11-0 **118**......(p) IanPopham
(Dan Skelton) *chsd ldrs: blnd 1st: drvn and lost pl 7th: sn bhd: t.o bef 3 out: p.u bef 2 out* **16/1**

6041 **P** **The Artful Cobbler**[8] 3923 5-10-8 **112** 7ex...... JakeGreenall
(Henry Daly) *in rr: mstke 7th: drvn and mstke next: sn bhd: t.o bef 3 out: p.u bef 2 out* **4/1**[1]

6m 4.3s (5.30) **Going Correction** -0.15s/f (Good) **19** Ran SP% **130.1**
Speed ratings (Par 107): **85,84,79,76,76 76,75,75,75,75 74,73,71,70,68 64,,,**
CSF £33.12 CT £429.21 TOTE £5.50: £1.80, £2.00, £3.40, £6.50; EX 45.20 Trifecta £417.50.
Owner Webb Holt Carpenter Tucker **Bred** Castletown & Partners **Trained** Sparsholt, Oxfordshire

FOCUS
Race distance increased by 30yds. The gallop was sound for this competitive handicap. The winner's Fontwell win upgraded but this still rates a step up.

4067 LARKSHILL ENGINEERING NOVICES' CHASE (6 fncs 9 omitted) 2m 3f 44y
4:05 (4:06) (Class 4) 5-Y-0+ **£5,198** (£1,526; £763; £381)

Form RPR

10-4 **1** **Nexius (IRE)**[107] 2122 7-11-0 0...... NickScholfield 140+
(Paul Nicholls) *led 1f: trckd ldrs: outpcd 6f out: hdwy and handy 3rd 3f out: 2nd 2f out: sn led: drvn clr* **10/3**[2]

01 **2** *8* **Hollywoodien (FR)**[55] 3134 5-11-3 131...... JamesDavies 135
(Tom Symonds) *w ldrs: led after 4f: clr 10f out: drvn over 3f out: hdd over 1f out: one pce* **6/1**[3]

-622 **3** *1 ½* **Pine Creek**[62] 3026 8-11-0 0...... AidanColeman 132
(John Ferguson) *trckd ldrs: hit 2nd (normal 7th): 2nd over 3f out: sn drvn: one pce fnl 2f* **11/8**[1]

561- **4** *15* **Midnight Monty**[334] 4756 6-11-0 112...... JamesReveley 115
(Keith Reveley) *in rr-div: outpcd and lost pl and bhd 8f out: tk remote 4th 2f out* **28/1**

4000 **5** *2 ½* **Gambol (FR)**[54] 3146 6-11-0 104...... WillKennedy 112
(Ian Williams) *hld up in rr: lost pl and bhd 8f out: tk remote 5th 2f out* **100/1**

0P-P **6** *49* **Blue Fashion (IRE)**[54] 3147 7-11-0 139......(t) DavidBass 63
(Nicky Henderson) *led after 1f: hdd after 4f: chsd clr ldr: wknd over 3f out: wl bhd whn heavily eased 2f out: virtually p.u: b.b.v* **10/3**[2]

4m 40.0s (-9.00) **Going Correction** -0.15s/f (Good) **6** Ran SP% **107.0**
Speed ratings: **112,108,108,101,100 80**
CSF £20.35 TOTE £4.20: £2.00, £2.70; EX 17.80 Trifecta £35.70.
Owner Owners Group 012 **Bred** Juergen Imm **Trained** Ditcheat, Somerset

FOCUS
Race distance increased by 12yds. The four fences in the home straight and the water jump on the first circuit were omitted leaving just six to jump. An interesting chase run at a sound gallop. The winner is rated in line with the best of his hurdles form.

4068 EVENTMASTERS HOSPITALITY CONDITIONAL JOCKEYS' H'CAP HURDLE (4 hdls 4 omitted) 2m 140y
4:40 (4:40) (Class 5) (0-100,100) 4-Y-0+ **£3,422** (£997; £499)

Form RPR

66-4 **1** **No Ceiling (IRE)**[26] 3619 6-11-0 **96**......[1] TobyWheeler(8) 110+
(Ian Williams) *trckd ldrs: 2nd over 4f out: led 3f out: pushed clr over 1f out: eased clsng stages* **3/1**[1]

50-0 **2** *6* **Bertie Lugg**[277] 219 8-10-11 **85**...... JeremiahMcGrath 88
(Henry Oliver) *chsd ldrs: 3rd and reminder 4f out: 2nd over 1f out: no ch w wnr* **9/2**[3]

P11R **3** *11* **Notebook**[7] 3950 5-11-9 **100**......(p) ThomasCheesman(3) 94
(Martin Smith) *led: hdd after 4f: led 8f out: drvn over 3f out: sn hdd: wknd over 1f out* **7/2**[2]

34P3 **4** *12* **Our Kylie (IRE)**[28] 3587 4-11-0 **98**...... CraigNichol 69
(Tony Coyle) *chsd ldrs: outpcd 5f out: sn lost pl and bhd: kpt on over 2f out: remote 4th over 1f out* **8/1**

P000 **5** *6* **Qatea (IRE)**[13] 3840 4-10-9 **96**......(t) JamesCowley(3) 62
(Donald McCain) *chsd ldrs: outpcd over 4f out: sn lost pl* **40/1**

-4P6 **6** *34* **Diamond Gesture (IRE)**[224] 882 8-10-2 **79**...... GarethMalone(3) 24
(Fergal O'Brien) *in rr: bhd fnl 8f: t.o* **12/1**

-PP3 **7** *7* **Prince Of Thieves (IRE)**[77] 2730 6-10-10 **84**......(bt) DavidNoonan 23
(Anthony Honeyball) *chsd ldrs: lost pl over 4f out: sn bhd: t.o* **7/2**[2]

0P6 **8** *dist* **Midnight Thomas**[198] 1133 7-10-5 **79**......(t) KillianMoore
(Martin Keighley) *t.k.h: trckd ldrs: led after 4f: hdd 8f out: wknd qckly over 5f out: sn eased and t.o: virtually p.u: eventually completed* **12/1**

4m 10.1s (5.40) **Going Correction** -0.15s/f (Good)
WFA 4 from 5yo+ 9lb **8** Ran SP% **116.6**
Speed ratings (Par 103): **81,78,73,67,64 48,45,**
CSF £17.64 CT £48.95 TOTE £4.00: £1.40, £1.80, £1.60; EX 17.00 Trifecta £73.80.
Owner The Ferandlin Peaches **Bred** James Hennelly **Trained** Portway, Worcs

FOCUS
Race distance increased by 30yds. The hurdles in the home straight were omitted due to the low sun, leaving just four to jump. The gallop was steady for this modest handicap. Big step ups from the first two, but not one to be confident about.
T/Jkpt: Not won. T/Plt: £47.80 to a £1 stake. Pool of £94970.62 - 1447.92 winning tickets.
T/Qpdt: £14.40 to a £1 stake. Pool of £8332.85- 428.0 winning tickets. **Walter Glynn**

3841 HUNTINGDON (R-H)
Thursday, February 11

OFFICIAL GOING: Hurdle course - good to soft (soft in places; 6.8); chase course - soft (6.3)
Wind: Breeze Weather: Bright and sunny

4069 32RED CASINO H'CAP HURDLE (12 hdls) 3m 1f 10y
1:25 (1:25) (Class 4) (0-110,109) 4-Y-0+ **£3,249** (£954; £477; £238)

Form RPR

3-20 **1** **Ganbei**[22] 3684 10-10-11 **97**...... HarryBannister(3) 105
(Michael Easterby) *settled in rr: 8th and pushed along to make stdy prog 9th: rdn to ld 2 out where clr w one other: asserted last: kpt on gamely* **11/2**[2]

0100 **2** *1* **Giveitachance (IRE)**[13] 3837 9-11-5 **102**......(t) BrendanPowell 109
(Claire Dyson) *cl up: effrt 8th: led after 3 out: drvn and hdd next: jst outpcd by wnr but clr of rest last: plugged on* **15/2**

0-66 **3** *19* **Beauboreen (IRE)**[68] 2919 9-11-11 **108**......(v[1]) PeterCarberry 99
(Jennie Candlish) *midfield: rdn and effrt 9th: kpt on after 2 out: nvr rchd ldrs: wnt poor 3rd and hit last* **11/1**

0006 **4** *4 ½* **Still Together (IRE)**[36] 3483 6-11-6 **103**...... TomScudamore 90
(David Pipe) *settled towards rr: effrt 8th: chal and nt fluent 3 out: sn rdn and outpcd: lost 8 l 3rd after 2 out: lost 3rd at last and fin tired* **9/2**[1]

4025 **5** *4 ½* **Onwiththeparty**[24] 3662 7-11-5 **102**......(p) TomCannon 84
(Chris Gordon) *j. modly: led or disp ld tl nt run on u.p fr 8th* **6/1**[3]

451P **6** *3 ¼* **Flemi Two Toes (IRE)**[24] 3662 10-10-3 **96**......(p) RomainClavreul(10) 75
(Sarah Humphrey) *nvr travelling in rr: hit 2nd and rdn: nvr nr front nk* **12/1**

52U2 **7** *½* **Market Option (IRE)**[30] 3572 10-11-7 **104**......(p) LiamTreadwell 84
(Venetia Williams) *led or disp ld tl hdd and nt fluent 8th: losing pl whn mstke next* **7/1**

15-0 **8** *2* **Knockalongi**[63] 2985 10-11-3 **107**...... BenFfrenchDavis(7) 84
(Dominic Ffrench Davis) *midfield: effrt 8th: led on outer next: rdn and hdd sn after 3 out: lost pl qckly: fin v tired* **16/1**

6165 **9** *20* **Flemensbay**[62] 3025 8-11-4 **106**......(p) DanielHiskett(5) 65
(Richard Phillips) *cl up tl 5th: lost tch and j. slowly 8th: sn t.o* **11/1**

/51- **P** **Squeeze Me**[620] 552 9-10-12 **100**...... NickSlatter(5)
(Gary Hanmer) *pckd bdly 3rd: midfield and gng wl 7th: effrt and cl up briefly 9th: slowed v rapidly after next: sn t.o and p.u 2 out* **33/1**

634P **P** **Maypole Lass**[47] 3220 6-10-12 **100**...... MikeyEnnis(5)
(Clare Hobson) *cl up tl lost pl and j. slowly 8th: t.o and p.u 9th* **25/1**

44P **P** **Dukes Den**[13] 3837 5-11-12 **109**......(tp) DenisO'Regan
(Charlie Mann) *mstke 2nd: nvr travelling in rr: t.o and p.u 3 out* **28/1**

6m 37.2s (14.30) **Going Correction** +0.25s/f (Yiel) **12** Ran SP% **112.6**
Speed ratings (Par 105): **87,86,80,79,77 76,76,75,69,**
CSF £43.27 CT £433.66 TOTE £8.70: £2.20, £2.60, £3.50; EX 43.20 Trifecta £395.60.
Owner N W A Bannister **Bred** Wood Farm Stud **Trained** Sheriff Hutton, N Yorks

FOCUS
Due to bends being moved out, this race distance had approximately 123yds added to it. A moderate staying handicap run at a good gallop. The winner did much bigger figures over fences and may be more to come, the second is rated to best of C&D form, and the third was 125+ hurdler at best.

4070 32RED.COM H'CAP HURDLE (10 hdls) 2m 3f 137y
1:55 (1:56) (Class 2) 4-Y-O+ £12,996 (£3,816; £1,908; £954)

Form RPR
411 1 **Baoulet Delaroque (FR)**[7] 3956 5-10-12 **131** 7ex.. SamTwiston-Davies 143+
(Paul Nicholls) settled cl up: chal ldr 2 out: sn led and rdn: kpt on stoutly and a holding rival flat **15/8**[1]

-FF0 2 2 **Value At Risk**[19] 3733 7-11-6 **139**............ HarrySkelton 149
(Dan Skelton) led: drvn and hrd pressed whn hit 2 out: sn hdd: chsd wnr vainly flat **9/2**[2]

3152 3 8 **San Benedeto (FR)**[44] 3352 5-11-5 **145**...........(t) HarryCobden(7) 147
(Paul Nicholls) trckd ldrs: wnt 3rd after 3 out: sn rdn w little rspnse: abt 8 l down and wl hld fr next **9/1**

20/5 4 6 **Totalize**[88] 2512 7-11-2 **135**............ NoelFehily 133
(Brian Ellison) midfield: rdn and looked outpcd 7th: kpt on into modest 4th and mstke 2 out **11/1**

-125 5 10 **After Eight Sivola (FR)**[46] 3284 6-10-4 **128** ow2............ LizzieKelly(5) 118
(Nick Williams) a bhd: no ch fr 3 out **20/1**

14 6 7 **Theatre Flame (IRE)**[203] 1082 6-10-4 **123**............ TomScudamore 104
(David Bridgwater) pressed ldr tl 8th: struggling after 3 out: mstke next **40/1**

/1-P 7 hd **Maestro Royal**[12] 3854 7-10-8 **127**............ PeterCarberry 108
(Nicky Henderson) t.k.h: bhd and nt a fluent: struggling fr 3 out **16/1**

1-53 8 47 **Blue Bear (IRE)**[79] 2700 7-10-3 **122**............ MarcGoldstein 61
(Diana Grissell) bhd fr 1/2-way: t.o 3 out **50/1**

-20P P **Lightentertainment (IRE)**[19] 3748 8-10-8 **127**............ TomCannon
(Chris Gordon) bhd: rdn and no rspnse 7th: t.o and p.u 2 out **50/1**

0130 P **Cusheen Bridge (IRE)**[67] 2926 8-10-11 **130** ow2............(t) AdamPogson
(Charles Pogson) cl up tl 5th: sn lost pl: t.o and p.u 2 out **33/1**

110- U **One For The Guv'Nr (IRE)**[306] 5276 7-11-2 **135**............ AndrewTinkler 128
(Nicky Henderson) chsd ldrs: rdn and outpcd after 3 out: 20 l 5th whn hit last: stmbld and uns rdr **11/1**

13-4 P **Champagne Express**[89] 2485 6-11-0 **133**............ NicodeBoinville
(Nicky Henderson) chsd ldrs tl rdn and lost pl 7th: nvr really travelling: t.o and p.u 2 out **5/1**[3]

5166 P **Gallic Destiny (IRE)**[98] 2301 5-10-2 **124**............(tp) JamesBanks(3)
(Jo Davis) prom: mstke 7th and drvn: fdd rapidly: t.o and p.u 2 out **125/1**

4m 58.2s (-0.80) **Going Correction** +0.25s/f (Yiel) **13 Ran SP% 117.0**
Speed ratings (Par 109): **111,110,107,104,100 97,97,78,,,**
CSF £9.91 CT £60.83 TOTE £2.10: £1.40, £1.90, £2.80; EX 11.70 Trifecta £56.60.
Owner Potensis Bloodstock Limited **Bred** Mme Genevieve Mongin **Trained** Ditcheat, Somerset

FOCUS
Due to bends being moved out, this race distance had approximately 99yds added to it. With quite a few of these seemingly in good heart, this should be decent form. Two pulled nicely away from their rivals and the winning time was 5.7 seconds faster than the small-field Listed event later on the card. The winner was well in but this still rates a step up, while the second posted a pb, with the third to his best and the fourth close to his mark.

4071 32RED ON THE APP STORE CHASE (A NOVICES' LIMITED H'CAP) (19 fncs) 2m 7f 129y
2:30 (2:30) (Class 4) (0-120,118) 5-Y-O+ £4,873 (£1,431; £715; £357)

Form RPR
53-0 1 **Fight Commander (IRE)**[102] 2222 7-11-0 **110**............ LeightonAspell 122+
(Oliver Sherwood) settled towards rr: stdy prog 11th: chal 16th: lft clr next: rdn bef last: alwys gng to hold dwindling advantage flat **10/1**

4105 2 6 **Kap Jazz (FR)**[21] 3705 6-11-2 **112**............ LiamTreadwell 116+
(Venetia Williams) wl bhd: rdn 13th: mstke 15th: stl remote 7th and drvn after 3 out: 20 l bhd wnr next: fin v strly to go 2nd fnl 50yds but wnr flown **15/2**

431- 3 1 **Vazaro Delafayette (FR)**[441] 2748 7-10-12 **108**........(b) TomScudamore 116+
(David Pipe) tended to jump lft: tk str hold and led 3rd: wnt bdly lft 16th: sn hdd and wnt bdly lft next: sn regained 2nd but wnr clr: fnd nil flat and lost 2nd cl home **5/2**[1]

-13P 4 6 **Millicent Silver**[44] 3348 7-11-3 **113**............(p) SamTwiston-Davies 112
(Nigel Twiston-Davies) nt a fluent and nt travelling: sn lost gd pl: bhd fr 8th: mstke 10th: hit 12th: n.d after: 15 l 6th after 3 out: plodded on **14/1**

55-5 5 ½ **Heroes Or Ghosts (IRE)**[269] 380 7-10-8 **107**............ JamesBanks(3) 105
(Jo Davis) t.k.h and cl up: lost pl and mstke 13th: 6 l 4th after 3 out: plugged on **20/1**

5455 6 64 **Lord Grantham (IRE)**[75] 2774 9-11-8 **118**............ TomO'Brien 50
(Henry Daly) pressed ldrs tl 16th: rdn and dropped out v tamely next: t.o 2 out **6/1**[3]

-35P 7 17 **Ballycoe**[47] 3253 7-10-7 **103**............(t) TomCannon 18
(Chris Gordon) cl up: lft 2nd 3 out: sn rdn: fdd bef next: eased and t.o **14/1**

0/15 P **Squire Trelawney**[83] 2615 10-11-3 **113**............(tp) HarrySkelton
(Dan Skelton) j. sluggishly in last: nvr travelling: rdn after 12th: t.o and p.u 15th: lame **8/1**

PP-2 P **Castle Cheetah (IRE)**[112] 2039 8-11-5 **115**............ NicodeBoinville
(Ben Pauling) hit 1st: mde most tl 3rd: mstke 7th: pressed ldr tl 14th: blnd next: t.o and p.u after 3 out **4/1**[2]

6m 24.3s (14.00) **Going Correction** +0.75s/f (Soft) **9 Ran SP% 112.9**
Speed ratings: **106,104,103,101,101 80,74,,**
CSF £79.92 CT £245.14 TOTE £9.30: £2.40, £2.40, £1.10; EX 73.90 Trifecta £593.20.
Owner J Rathbone **Bred** Mrs B Collins **Trained** Upper Lambourn, Berks

FOCUS
Due to bends being moved out, this race distance had approximately 80yds added to it. Just an ordinary race for the level, but it did contain an interesting runner from the David Pipe stable. The winner made a big step up on his best hurdles form, with the second similar to his hurdles mark.

4072 32RED SIDNEY BANKS MEMORIAL NOVICES' HURDLE (LISTED RACE) (10 hdls) 2m 3f 137y
3:05 (3:07) (Class 1) 4-Y-O+ £14,860 (£5,565; £2,780; £1,387)

Form RPR
2-11 1 **Ma Du Fou (FR)**[62] 3009 6-11-4 137............ GavinSheehan 140+
(Warren Greatrex) 2nd tl led briefly after 5th: slow pce: led again after 7th: rdn and jnd 2 out tl last: fnd plenty to edge clr flat **3/1**[3]

21 2 1 ¼ **North Hill Harvey**[62] 3019 5-11-8 140............ HarrySkelton 142
(Dan Skelton) mstke 2nd: settled trcking ldrs: effrt after 3 out: drvn and sustained chal 2 out tl last: jst outpcd flat **11/4**[2]

1125 3 11 **Final Nudge (IRE)**[26] 3623 7-11-4 137............ DarylJacob 128
(David Dennis) settled in 3rd pl: slow 6th: mstke next: wnt 2nd 3 out tl rdn bef next: sn btn **11/2**

0-1P 4 1 ½ **Justanother Muddle**[61] 3032 7-11-4 0............ MarcGoldstein 126
(Sheena West) mde nrly all tl nt fluent 7th: set slow pce: rdn and outpcd fr 3 out: n.d after **28/1**

2 5 5 **Minella Awards (IRE)**[76] 2762 5-11-4 0............ NoelFehily 120
(Nicky Henderson) a in rr trio: rdn 7th: struggling fr next **13/8**[1]

505/ 6 32 **Vinniewhitefoot**[648] 9-11-4 0............ NickSlatter 88
(Gary Hanmer) reluctant to line up and led in: a last: lost tch 3 out: t.o whn mstke last **250/1**

5m 3.9s (4.90) **Going Correction** +0.25s/f (Yiel) **6 Ran SP% 109.0**
Speed ratings (Par 111): **100,99,95,94,92 79**
CSF £11.18 TOTE £4.00: £1.70, £1.60; EX 9.40 Trifecta £26.50.
Owner Walters Plant Hire & James & Jean Potter **Bred** Scea Ecurie Jc Laisis **Trained** Upper Lambourn, Berks

FOCUS
Due to bends being moved out, this race distance had approximately 99yds added to it. Plenty of decent performers have won this race down the years, like Refinement and Time For Rupert, so the winner is sure to be well above average despite the time being over five seconds slower than the classy handicap earlier on the card. The winner is still on the upgrade and should go on to rate higher, but is still a stone off required festival level, and the second posted a small pb.

4073 32RED £10 FREE H'CAP CHASE (16 fncs) 2m 3f 189y
3:40 (3:41) (Class 4) (0-110,110) 5-Y-O+ £3,898 (£1,144; £572; £286)

Form RPR
414P 1 **Albatros De Guye (FR)**[13] 3834 6-10-0 **84** oh4............(tp) TrevorWhelan 90+
(Anna Newton-Smith) led tl 2nd: remained prom: 3rd and hrd drvn bef 2 out: styd on to ld last: idling whn holding rival flat **22/1**

2-PP 2 3 ¼ **Alberto's Dream**[12] 3867 7-10-8 **99**............ MrJNixon(7) 104+
(Tom Symonds) hld up trcking ldrs: wnt 3rd at 11th: led 14th: rdn and wavering fr 2 out: hdd last: plugged on but fin tired **8/1**

552/ 3 11 **Genstone Trail**[672] 5246 10-10-12 **96**............ BrendanPowell 87
(Alan King) settled towards rr: effrt 14th: rdn and nt qckn after 3 out: wnt mod 3rd after last **10/3**[1]

35P2 4 2 **Trapper Peak (IRE)**[41] 3417 7-11-11 **109**............ RhysFlint 98
(Alexandra Dunn) t.k.h: cl up: pressed ldr 14th tl rdn 2 out: fnd little bef last: lost 3rd flat **9/2**[3]

1-35 5 2 **Classinaglass**[96] 2342 9-11-9 **110**............ HarryBannister(3) 97
(Michael Easterby) bhd: mstke 13th: struggling after **7/2**[2]

2-P0 P **George Nympton (IRE)**[70] 2859 10-10-3 **87**......(tp) SamTwiston-Davies
(Zoe Davison) last whn j. slowly 2nd: a in rr: t.o after 3 out: p.u last **25/1**

3/3P P **Father Probus**[20] 3727 10-11-4 **102**............(p) JonathanEngland
(Michael Appleby) led 2nd tl 7th: v slow next and sn dropped himself out: rdn in last after next: t.o and p.u after 3 out **7/1**

44-P U **Jamrham (IRE)**[45] 3316 9-9-7 **84** oh1............(t) HarrisonBeswick(7)
(Sam Thomas) hit 4th: rdr unbalanced and c off **12/1**

-02P P **Stars Royale (IRE)**[98] 2300 7-11-4 **102**............ LeightonAspell
(Nick Gifford) wnt 3rd at 3rd: led 7th: blnd 9th: mstke next: hdd 14th and dropped out v rapidly: t.o and p.u 2 out **9/1**

5m 28.6s (23.30) **Going Correction** +0.75s/f (Soft) **9 Ran SP% 113.0**
Speed ratings: **83,81,77,76,75 ,,,,**
CSF £179.83 CT £742.41 TOTE £12.20: £4.30, £2.50, £1.20; EX 142.40 Trifecta £884.70.
Owner George Goring **Bred** G A E C Delorme Gerard & Vincent **Trained** Jevington, E Sussex

FOCUS
Due to bends being moved out, this race distance had approximately 62yds added to it. This looked nothing more than a moderate contest. A step up from the winner, with the second similar to his hurdles mark.

4074 32RED BRITISH STALLION STUDS EBF MARES' STANDARD OPEN NATIONAL HUNT FLAT RACE (DIV I) 1m 7f 171y
4:15 (4:15) (Class 6) 4-6-Y-O £1,949 (£572; £286; £143)

Form RPR
2 1 **My Khaleesi**[99] 2277 5-10-12 0............ DenisO'Regan 112+
(Alan King) small: racd enthusiastically and gng wl in midfield: tk 2nd home turn: sn rdn: responded wl and got up 50yds out: gamely **2/1**[1]

2 2 **Storm Patrol** 5-10-12 0............(t) TomO'Brien 110
(Suzy Smith) tall str: prom: led 3f out: rdn 2f out: kpt on steadily tl hdd and no ex fnl 100yds: promising **7/2**[3]

3 3 9 **Chilli Romance (IRE)**[56] 3132 5-10-7 0............ NickSlatter(5) 101
(Fergal O'Brien) settled towards rr: effrt 5f out: 3rd and drvn home turn: no imp on ldng pair after **14/1**

1 4 2 ¼ **Royal Debutante (IRE)**[38] 3469 5-11-5 0............ LiamTreadwell 106
(Paul Webber) cl up: rdn 4f out: plugged on wout threatening fnl 2f **3/1**[2]

5 nse **Phoeniciana** 5-10-12 0............ LeightonAspell 99
(Lucy Wadham) v tall: sweating: bhd: pushed along fr 1/2-way: running v green after: styd on ins fnl f: should do bttr in time **22/1**

35- 6 1 ¼ **Fit The Brief**[297] 5439 6-10-12 0............(t) PaddyBrennan 97
(Tom George) t.k.h: hld up: sme prog to rr of main bunch whn jinked rt towards rail over 3f out: rdn and nvr trbld ldrs after **12/1**

00 7 5 **Lady Markby (IRE)**[56] 3132 5-10-12 0............ DarylJacob 92
(Emma Lavelle) midfield: rdn 4f out: sn btn **40/1**

63 8 17 **Deauville Dame**[38] 3469 4-10-2 0............ MichealNolan 65
(Sir Mark Prescott Bt) led: rdn 4f out: hdd 3f out: sn lost pl: t.o and eased **16/1**

9 4 ½ **Kokomo** 5-10-9 0............ JamesBanks(3) 71
(Noel Williams) small: midfield: midfield: lost tch 4f out: t.o **50/1**

10 26 **Peal Of Bells** 5-10-12 0............ AndrewTinkler 45
(Henry Daly) small: rdn and struggling 6f out: t.o fnl 4f **33/1**

11 42 **Be Here Now** 5-10-12 0............(t) MarcGoldstein 3
(Jo Davis) tall: prom tl rdn 7f out: t.o fnl 4f **66/1**

3m 57.1s (8.00) **Going Correction** +0.25s/f (Yiel)
WFA 4 from 5yo+ 9lb **11 Ran SP% 114.0**
Speed ratings: **90,89,84,83,83 82,80,71,69,56 35**
CSF £8.21 TOTE £3.20: £1.40, £1.60, £3.70; EX 9.40 Trifecta £80.80.
Owner Mrs M C Sweeney **Bred** Mrs M C Sweeney **Trained** Barbury Castle, Wilts

FOCUS
Due to bends being moved out, this race distance had approximately 97yds added to it. The first of the concluding bumpers was run in a slightly quicker time. Big step up from winner, rated round balance of 3rd/4th/6th/7th.

4075 32RED BRITISH STALLION STUDS EBF MARES' STANDARD OPEN NATIONAL HUNT FLAT RACE (DIV II) 1m 7f 171y

4:50 (4:50) (Class 6) 4-6-Y-O **£1,949** (£572; £286; £143)

Form RPR
00 **1** **Beyond Measure (IRE)**[67] 2929 5-10-12 0 DenisO'Regan 111+
(Don Cantillon) *ly: taken down early: mde all and travelled wl: pushed clr fnl f: readily* **5/1[3]**
52- **2** *5* **Song Saa**[344] 4562 6-10-12 0 PaddyBrennan 104
(Tom George) *midfield: effrt 4f out: wnt 2nd wl over 2f out: sn rdn: clr of rest over 1f out but wl hld by wnr* **13/2**
6 **3** *22* **Parisian Star**[57] 3118 4-9-9 0 PaddyBradley(7) 72
(J R Jenkins) *small: hld up in last tl 1/2-way: sme prog fnl 4f: plugged into poor 3rd ins fnl f* **50/1**
3 **4** *4 1/2* **Miss Yeats (IRE)**[78] 2721 5-10-12 0 TomCannon 78
(Laura Mongan) *small: prom tl rdn and wknd wl over 2f out: lost remote 3rd ins fnl f* **12/1**
0 **5** *3 3/4* **Choochoobugaloo**[57] 3118 4-10-2 0 JamesBest 64
(Tom Symonds) *tall light-framed: t.k.h: chsd ldrs: 4th and rdn and outpcd by ldng pair on home turn: plugged on: t.o* **100/1**
6 *4 1/2* **Bright Eyes** 5-10-12 0 AndrewTinkler 69
(Nicky Henderson) *small: prom: 2nd and rdn 3f out: fdd tamely over 2f out: t.o* **6/4[1]**
7 *14* **Flights** 5-10-12 0 JamieMoore 55
(Robert Walford) *small: rdn 1/2-way: struggling after: t.o fnl 2f* **16/1**
8 *shd* **Willaldoo** 5-10-12 0 TomO'Brien 55
(Henry Daly) *small: rdn 1/2-way: struggling after: t.o* **20/1**
9 *15* **Rumour Has It** 5-10-12 0 SamTwiston-Davies 40
(Mark Rimell) *tall: mounted outside paddock: chsd ldrs: rdn 5f out: sn struggling: t.o fnl 2f* **16/1**
60- **10** *17* **Hold Hands**[332] 4812 5-10-12 0 BrendanPowell 23
(Brendan Powell) *tall rngy: prom: rdn over 3f out: sn dropped rt out: t.o* **50/1**
0- **11** *79* **Milanese Queen**[311] 5193 5-10-12 0 GavinSheehan
(Warren Greatrex) *small: lost gd pl after 5f: t.o 1/2-way: virtually p.u over 3f out* **9/2[2]**

3m 57.6s (8.50) **Going Correction** +0.25s/f (Yiel)
WFA 4 from 5yo+ 9lb **11 Ran SP% 117.3**
Speed ratings: **88,85,74,72,70 68,61,61,53,45 5**
CSF £36.48 TOTE £6.20: £1.90, £1.90, £4.90; EX 19.70 Trifecta £1457.60.
Owner Don Cantillon **Bred** Don Cantillon **Trained** Newmarket, Suffolk

FOCUS
Due to bends being moved out, this race distance had approximately 97yds added to it. The winner dominated and did it nicely, and the second is rated to her mark.
T/Plt: £118.80 to a £1 stake. Pool of £57,955.27 - 355.95 winning units T/Qpdt: £15.10 to a £1 stake. Pool of £5,848.18 - 284.84 winning units **Iain Mackenzie**

3914 TAUNTON (R-H)
Thursday, February 11
4076 Meeting Abandoned - waterlogged

4082 - 4088a (Foreign Racing) - See Raceform Interactive

3006 BANGOR-ON-DEE (L-H)
Friday, February 12
4089 Meeting Abandoned - waterlogged

3771 KEMPTON (R-H)
Friday, February 12

OFFICIAL GOING: Soft (good to soft in places on chase course, heavy lakeside bend on hurdle course; chs 4.9, hdl 4.2)
Wind: moderate, across Weather: overcast, cold

4096 RACINGUK.COM/ANYWHERE CONDITIONAL JOCKEYS' H'CAP HURDLE (8 hdls) 2m

1:05 (1:05) (Class 4) (0-115,115) 4-Y-O+ **£3,249** (£954; £477; £238)

Form RPR
13 **1** **Taweyla (IRE)**[262] 491 5-11-7 **110** JamieBargary 120+
(Pam Sly) *trckd ldrs: cl up after 3 out: led sn after 2 out and rdn clr: styd on wl* **10/1**
206 **2** *3 1/2* **Disputed (IRE)**[48] 3216 6-11-12 **115** ThomasGarner 118
(Chris Gordon) *hld up and in last pair to 4th: tried to make prog 3 out but sn drvn and only 10th on long run after it: gd hdwy u.p after 2 out: tk 2nd flat: nt rch wnr* **10/1**
5P6P **3** *5* **Very Noble (FR)**[48] 3257 7-10-8 **102** (t) WilliamFeatherstone(5) 100
(Chris Gordon) *hld up and in last pair to 4th: rdn 3 out and only 11th on long run after it: styd on u.p fr 2 out: snatched 3rd last stride* **16/1**
4P1 **4** *shd* **Darwins Theory (IRE)**[70] 2880 8-11-10 **113** (t) JackSherwood 111
(Fiona Shaw) *trckd ldrs: prog after 3 out to ld 2 out: sn hdd and btn: wknd flat* **12/1**
-003 **5** *4 1/2* **Abyaat (IRE)**[64] 2987 5-10-8 **103** (t) DavidPrichard(6) 96
(Victor Dartnall) *settled in midfield: rdn 3 out: tried to cl bef 2 out: sn no imp on ldrs* **8/1**
324 **6** *nk* **Sky Lino (FR)**[62] 3028 4-10-11 **113** LizzieKelly(3) 97
(Nick Williams) *free to post: t.k.h: led: hdd 2 out: wknd bef last* **9/2[1]**
-P4P **7** *1* **Thundering Home**[22] 3708 9-11-4 **112** (t) ArchieBellamy(5) 106
(Richard Mitchell) *hld up in midfield: rdn 3 out: struggling in 9th bef 2 out: modest late prog* **16/1**
50P0 **8** *1* **She's Late**[13] 3855 6-11-3 **114** PatrickCowley(8) 105
(Jonjo O'Neill) *hld up in rr: dropped to last pair after 4th and rdn next: sn lost tch* **25/1**
5000 **9** *7* **Brown Bear (IRE)**[37] 3483 5-10-13 **102** DavidNoonan 86
(Nick Gifford) *hld up in midfield: rdn bef 3 out: tried to cl bef 2 out: sn wknd* **13/2[3]**
-334 **10** *1 3/4* **Cotswold Road**[42] 3413 6-11-6 **115** (t) PaulO'Brien(6) 97
(Colin Tizzard) *pressed ldr tl rdn and wknd sn after 3 out* **11/2[2]**
00/0 **11** *2 3/4* **Deepsand (IRE)**[68] 2926 7-11-12 **115** (p) ConorShoemark 95
(Ali Stronge) *chsd ldrs: hit 2nd: blnd 4th: drvn and wknd wl bef 2 out* **33/1**
24-0 **12** *13* **Gaelic Myth**[18] 3777 6-11-11 **114** TomBellamy 86
(Kim Bailey) *pckd 1st: chsd ldrs: rdn in 3rd pl bef 3 out: wknd qckly bef 2 out* **9/1**
P-55 **P** **Chill (IRE)**[203] 1099 8-11-8 **111** (p) HarryBannister
(Zoe Davison) *a in rr: wknd after 4th: t.o after next: p.u after 3 out* **100/1**

4m 6.3s (8.30) **Going Correction** +0.65s/f (Soft)
WFA 4 from 5yo+ 9lb **13 Ran SP% 113.4**
Speed ratings (Par 105): **105,103,100,100,98 98,97,97,93,92 91,85,**
CSF £99.37 CT £1577.64 TOTE £7.90: £2.40, £4.20, £3.40; EX 95.20 Trifecta £2976.00 Part won..
Owner Pam's People **Bred** Darley **Trained** Thorney, Cambs

FOCUS
All starts have been moved at this track following remeasuring, so there will be no speed figures here until there is sufficient data to calculate updated median times. Hurdle races run on Winter Course. Add 79yds to advertised race distance. This was a truly run handicap hurdle and the form appears sound. A fresh breeze helped dry up the ground a little but didn't necessarily help the horses get home, with jockeys reporting the surface to be "soft, but tacky" and "gluey". A big step up from the winner on her handicap debut, with the second rated to his mark.

4097 RACINGUK.COM/WINTERSEASONTICKET NOVICES' HURDLE (10 hdls) 2m 5f

1:35 (1:35) (Class 4) 4-Y-O+ **£3,249** (£954; £477; £238)

Form RPR
11-6 **1** **Ballyhenry (IRE)**[77] 2762 6-11-4 0 NicodeBoinville 120+
(Ben Pauling) *pressed ldr: led 4th: rdn and narrowly hdd whn lft in ld 2 out: drvn out after last and kpt on wl* **11/4[2]**
213 **2** *2 1/4* **Label Des Obeaux (FR)**[45] 3350 5-11-11 139 DenisO'Regan 126+
(Alan King) *trckd ldrs on inner: shkn up after 3 out: drvn to chse ldng pair bef 2 out: kpt on but nvr quite able to chal: tk 2nd nr fin* **10/11[1]**
3 *nk* **Atirelarigo (FR)**[467] 6-11-4 0 RichardJohnson 121+
(Philip Hobbs) *t.k.h: hld up but in tch on outer: prog to go prom 3 out: led and blnd 2 out: hdd but stl upsides wnr whn pckd last: nt rcvr and lost 2nd nr fin* **20/1**
56 **4** *6* **Dylanseoghan (IRE)**[18] 3775 7-10-11 0 WilliamFeatherstone(7) 112
(Zoe Davison) *trckd ldrs: lost pl 6th: effrt again and shkn up after 3 out: nt pce to threaten but kpt on to take 4th after last* **100/1**
3 **5** *2 3/4* **What's The Scoop (IRE)**[84] 2612 6-11-4 0 BarryGeraghty 111
(Nicky Henderson) *mstke 1st: t.k.h and sn prom: trckd ldr 5th tl after 3 out: wknd bef last* **9/2[3]**
4526 **6** *4 1/2* **Petite Power (IRE)**[30] 3580 7-11-4 0 GavinSheehan 105
(Ali Stronge) *hld up in rr: lost tch in last pair sn after 3 out: pushed along and kpt on steadily after 2 out: nt disgracd* **50/1**
02 **7** *1/2* **Bold Runner**[25] 3664 5-11-4 0 (p) JamesDavies 104
(Jose Santos) *trckd ldrs: wl there after 3 out: wknd qckly bef 2 out* **33/1**
40 **8** *1/2* **Crockery**[83] 2644 6-10-6 0 BridgetAndrews(5) 97
(Dan Skelton) *trckd ldrs: lost pl sn after 3 out: pushed along and steadily lft bhd* **100/1**
1-P **9** *3* **Duke Arcadio (IRE)**[69] 2898 7-11-4 0 LeightonAspell 101
(Oliver Sherwood) *hld up in tch: trckd ldrs 3 out: wknd bef 2 out* **16/1**
3P **10** *1 1/4* **Celldomfed (IRE)**[57] 3126 6-11-4 0 NoelFehily 99
(Jonjo O'Neill) *racd wd: hld up: in tch in rr and gng bttr than many 3 out: pushed along bef 2 out: steadily dropped away* **50/1**
3345 **11** *1 1/4* **Briac (FR)**[15] 3819 5-11-4 0 JamieMoore 100
(Jim Best) *hld up: stl in tch in rr 3 out: no prog and wl btn bef next: nt fluent 2 out and mstke last* **100/1**
0 **12** *13* **Hinxworth (IRE)**[111] 2062 7-11-4 0 SamTwiston-Davies 85
(Nick Mitchell) *hld up: a in rr: lost tch 3 out: t.o* **100/1**
0 **P** **Onurbike**[46] 3316 8-11-4 0 MarkGrant
(John O'Neill) *led to 4th: wknd rapidly 6th: t.o next: p.u bef 2 out* **100/1**

5m 31.9s (10.90) **Going Correction** +0.65s/f (Soft) **13 Ran SP% 119.7**
Speed ratings (Par 105): **105,104,104,101,100 98,98,98,97,96 96,91,**
CSF £5.62 TOTE £3.50: £1.80, £1.10, £4.10; EX 9.10 Trifecta £53.40.
Owner The Vestey Family Partnership **Bred** Paddy Kennedy **Trained** Bourton-On-The-Water, Gloucs

FOCUS
Add 113yds to advertised race distance. A decent novice hurdle, although the pace only looked steady. The fifth, sixth and seventh have been rated close to their marks.

4098 RACING UK IN HD NEXT MONTH NOVICES' LIMITED H'CAP CHASE (12 fncs) 2m

2:05 (2:05) (Class 4) (0-120,120) 5-Y-O+ **£3,898** (£1,144; £572; £286)

Form RPR
1224 **1** **Always On The Run (IRE)**[43] 3384 6-11-8 **120** PaddyBrennan 134+
(Tom George) *mde all at decent pce: nt fluent 8th: rdn and pressed 2 out: 2 l ahd and looked in command whn lft clr last* **7/2[1]**
0523 **2** *12* **Trojan Star (IRE)**[71] 2859 6-10-13 **111** (t) DavidBass 113
(Kim Bailey) *trckd wnr: mstke 9th and sn rdn: lost 2nd 3 out: wl hld after: lft 2nd again last* **7/1[3]**
25-5 **3** *3/4* **Saffron Prince**[92] 2449 8-11-4 **116** TomScudamore 116
(David Bridgwater) *hld up in rr: prog fr 7th: chsd ldrs after 4 out: rdn and no imp 3 out: lft 4th next and 3rd last* **12/1**
22-3 **4** *15* **Dollar Bill**[40] 3451 7-10-12 **110** TomCannon 95
(Nick Gifford) *hld up in rr: lost tch 6th and bhd after: lft 4th by defections in st: kpt on* **16/1**
P-40 **5** *6* **Money Talks**[70] 2885 6-11-7 **119** (t) MarcGoldstein 99
(Michael Madgwick) *chsd ldrs: struggling to hold pl fr 6th: wl btn after blunder 4 out: wknd bef next: fin tired* **33/1**
3-01 **6** *8* **Cappielow Park**[43] 3379 7-11-8 **120** (tp) GavinSheehan 93
(Ali Stronge) *chsd ldrs: slow jump 5th: struggling to keep in tch after next: wknd fr 4 out* **10/1**
3-12 **7** *13* **Buy Back Bob (IRE)**[262] 491 9-11-5 **117** (t) RichardJohnson 75
(Tim Vaughan) *nt fluent 1st and 2nd whn in last pl: effrt fr 7th: no prog 4 out: wknd and t.o* **10/1**
/P-F **F** **Devil To Pay**[71] 2857 10-10-10 **111** TomBellamy(3) 124
(Alan King) *wl in tch: trckd ldng pair 7th: wnt 2nd 3 out: rdn to chal 2 out: 2 l down and looked hld whn fell last* **7/1[3]**
06-P **F** **Dellbuoy**[16] 2712 7-10-3 **101** oh2 (t) JoshuaMoore
(Pat Phelan) *j. bdly: last and bhd whn fell heavily 6th* **66/1**
4-30 **F** **Lanceur (FR)**[27] 3620 7-11-8 **120** LeightonAspell 120
(Lucy Wadham) *hld up: prog fr 7th: chsd ldng trio after 4 out: shkn up next: 6 l bhd wnr in 4th whn fell 2 out* **9/1**

-311 **U** **Exmoor Mist**[58] 3115 8-11-7 **119**...(t) IanPopham
(Victor Dartnall) *trckd ldng pair to 7th: 4th and wl in tch whn propped on landing and uns rdr next* **4/1**[2]

4m 5.2s (10.20) **Going Correction** +0.475s/f (Soft) **11** Ran SP% **113.4**
Speed ratings: **93,87,86,79,76 72,65,,,**
CSF £27.70 CT £260.85 TOTE £4.00: £1.80, £2.20, £4.30; EX 26.80 Trifecta £232.80.
Owner Paul & Clare Rooney **Bred** Island Bridge Racing Club **Trained** Slad, Gloucs

FOCUS
Add 57yds to advertised race distance. An incident-strewn novice handicap chase. A big step up from the winner.

4099 TODAY'S RACING JUST £10 WITH RACINGUK NOVICES' H'CAP HURDLE (10 hdls) 2m 5f

2:40 (2:40) (Class 4) (0-110,110) 4-Y-O+ **£3,249** (£954; £477; £238)

Form RPR

405- **1** **Malibu Rock**[413] 3241 8-11-2 **100**...TomCannon 109+
(Chris Gordon) *hld up: prog 7th: cl up gng easily whn nt fluent 3 out: sn trckd ldr: led after 2 out: rdn whn nt fluent last: kpt on wl* **16/1**

0-03 **2** 1 ¼ **Albert D'Olivate (FR)**[22] 3705 6-11-9 **107**...(p) SeanBowen 114
(Robert Walford) *trckd ldrs: nt fluent 7th: disp 2nd after 3 out but sn hrd rdn: looked wl hld in 3rd fr 2 out tl styd on wl fr last to take 2nd nr fin* **5/1**[3]

4531 **3** ¾ **Zanstra (IRE)**[14] 3841 6-11-11 **109**...TomScudamore 114
(Colin Tizzard) *cl up: trckd ldr 6th: led 3 out: hrd rdn and hdd after 2 out: kpt on but lost 2nd nr fin* **7/4**[1]

4-4P **4** 89 **Kahdian (IRE)**[44] 3369 6-10-8 **97**...GaryDerwin(5) 13
(Helen Rees) *in tch: mstke 5th and pushed along: lost tch u.p bef 3 out: t.o bef 2 out* **25/1**

05-6 **P** **Shareni (IRE)**[18] 3772 7-10-4 **95**...WilliamFeatherstone(7)
(Zoe Davison) *prom on outer: pressed ldr 5th tl blnd 6th: wknd rapidly next: wl t.o in 8th whn p.u after 3 out* **40/1**

0P2- **P** **Twin Barrels**[364] 4203 9-11-12 **110**...(p) RichardJohnson
(Sarah-Jayne Davies) *led to 4th: wknd qckly next: t.o in last pl 6th: p.u after 3 out* **20/1**

0000 **P** **Montecito (FR)**[60] 3083 6-10-11 **95**...MarcGoldstein
(Chris Gordon) *hld up: lost tch fr 7th: t.o in 6th pl whn p.u bef 2 out* **100/1**

450- **F** **Oh So Fruity**[329] 4883 6-11-6 **104**...JamieMoore
(Gary Moore) *trckd ldrs tl fell heavily 3rd* **6/1**

P300 **P** **Daulys Anthem (IRE)**[44] 3374 8-11-3 **101**...AidanColeman
(David Dennis) *hld up in tch: mstke 5th: wknd after 7th: t.o in 7th whn p.u bef 2 out* **50/1**

4052 **P** **Bishops Court**[10] 3919 6-11-8 **106**...NoelFehily
(Neil Mulholland) *pressed ldr: led 4th: hdd 3 out and wknd rapidly: t.o in 5th whn p.u bef 2 out* **3/1**[2]

5m 28.1s (7.10) **Going Correction** +0.65s/f (Soft) **10** Ran SP% **112.2**
Speed ratings (Par 105): **112,111,111,77, , , , ,**
CSF £86.13 CT £212.25 TOTE £11.80: £2.90, £1.70, £1.10; EX 78.80 Trifecta £274.40.
Owner Chris Gordon Racing Club **Bred** Brook Stud Bloodstock & Leydens Farm Stud **Trained** Morestead, Hampshire

FOCUS
Add 113yds to advertised race distance. This became something of a slog, but the form among the first three ought to prove sound. The winner was well in on his old form and has been rated similar to that level following a long absence.

4100 RACING UK 3 DEVICES 1 PRICE GRADUATION CHASE (16 fncs) 2m 4f 110y

3:15 (3:15) (Class 2) 5-Y-O+ **£12,996** (£3,816; £1,908; £954)

Form RPR

34-F **1** **Josses Hill (IRE)**[69] 2915 8-11-0 158...NicodeBoinville 160+
(Nicky Henderson) *mde virtually all: j. deliberately early but bttr whn asked to stretch on fr 10th: jnd and rdn 2 out: sn drew clr: styd on wl* **10/11**[1]

2F-3 **2** 8 **God's Own (IRE)**[101] 2259 8-11-7 159...(t) PaddyBrennan 162+
(Tom George) *nt fluent 1st: 2nd and 4th: hld up bhd ldng pair: wnt 2nd 11th: rdn to chal and upsides 2 out: sn btn off: nt fluent last* **2/1**[2]

2221 **3** 2 ¼ **Aso (FR)**[21] 3726 6-11-3 145...AidanColeman 153
(Venetia Williams) *t.k.h: hld up in tch: wnt 3rd after 11th but outpcd fr next and nudged along: nvr on terms after but kpt on steadily fr 2 out* **4/1**[3]

3204 **4** 29 **Kings Lad (IRE)**[55] 3147 9-11-7 143...(t) TomScudamore 126
(Colin Tizzard) *pressed wnr to 10th: wknd after next: t.o* **20/1**

5m 14.1s (2.10) **Going Correction** +0.475s/f (Soft) **4** Ran SP% **110.5**
Speed ratings: **115,111,111,100**
CSF £3.31 TOTE £1.90; EX 3.40 Trifecta £4.60.
Owner A D Spence **Bred** I W Moore **Trained** Upper Lambourn, Berks

FOCUS
Add 79yds to actual race distance. A good graduation chase. It's been rated around the balance of the second and third.

4101 RASHER FRITH MEMORIAL H'CAP CHASE (18 fncs) 3m

3:50 (3:50) (Class 3) (0-140,137) 5-Y-O+ **£6,498** (£1,908; £954; £477)

Form RPR

2-U1 **1** **Silvergrove**[45] 3349 8-11-5 **130**...(t) NicodeBoinville 141+
(Ben Pauling) *j. solidly: mde all: clr w runner-up bef 3 out: rdn 2 out: kpt on stoutly* **3/1**[1]

-530 **2** 2 ¼ **A Good Skin (IRE)**[42] 3406 7-11-10 **135**...PaddyBrennan 143
(Tom George) *mstke 1st: hld up in last trio: prog and nt fluent 12th: chsd wnr 14th: drvn and tried to cl fr 3 out: kpt on but nvr really able to chal* **9/2**[3]

512P **3** 11 **Wizards Bridge**[34] 3520 7-11-7 **132**...(b[1]) AidanColeman 131
(Colin Tizzard) *hld up in tch and gng wl: prog to chse ldng pair sn after 4 out: rdn and no imp bef 3 out: wl hld after: mstke last* **15/2**

3-4P **4** 4 ½ **Sun Wild Life (FR)**[66] 2955 6-10-11 **122**...(p) JamieMoore 114
(Robert Walford) *trckd ldrs: rdn and outpcd fr 4 out: n.d after* **20/1**

-60P **5** 19 **Ned Stark (IRE)**[47] 3282 8-11-12 **137**...(p) DenisO'Regan 114
(Alan King) *occasionally j.lft: pressed wnr tl lost pl and blnd 14th: wl hld fr next (4 out): wknd 3 out* **4/1**[2]

4145 **6** 1 ¾ **Shuil Royale (IRE)**[63] 3016 11-11-5 **137**...(t) LiamMcKenna(7) 111
(Harry Fry) *chsd ldrs: mstke 11th: lost tch whn j. bdly rt 14th: bhd after: t.o* **11/1**

0-P1 **7** 1 ½ **Tinker Time (IRE)**[72] 2853 8-11-7 **132**...LiamHeard 101
(Bob Buckler) *j. slowly 2nd: 3rd and 4th and reminder: styd in tch in rr to 13th: sn wknd: t.o* **7/1**

450P **8** 10 **Kilbree Kid (IRE)**[63] 3017 9-11-2 **132**...(tp) JamieBargary(5) 91
(Tom George) *j. stickily and nvr really gng wl: a in rr: lost tch fr 13th: t.o* **33/1**

-063 **P** **Financial Climate (IRE)**[42] 3404 9-11-4 **132**...(p) ThomasGarner(3)
(Oliver Sherwood) *trckd ldrs: rdn and outpcd in 6th whn terrible blunder 4 out: nt rcvr and p.u bef next* **16/1**

/1-P **U** **Seebright**[48] 3232 9-11-9 **134**...IanPopham
(Victor Dartnall) *in tch: hmpd and mstke 7th: rdn and outpcd fr 13th: 6th and wl hld whn blnd and uns rdr 3 out* **16/1**

6m 21.9s (12.90) **Going Correction** +0.625s/f (Soft) **10** Ran SP% **115.2**
Speed ratings: **103,102,98,97,90 90,89,86,,**
CSF £17.32 CT £91.54 TOTE £2.60: £1.30, £1.90, £2.60; EX 20.10 Trifecta £91.60.
Owner Nicholas Piper & Claire E Piper **Bred** Elms Stud Co Ltd & Miss J Winter **Trained** Bourton-On-The-Water, Gloucs

FOCUS
Add 100yds to advertised race distance. A decent handicap chase, won in good style from the front. The second was well in on last year's Cheltenham win and has been rated back to that level.

4102 RACINGUK.COM/ANYWHERE MAIDEN OPEN NATIONAL HUNT FLAT RACE (DIV I) 2m

4:25 (4:25) (Class 5) 4-6-Y-O **£2,274** (£667; £333; £166)

Form RPR

1 **Sir Antony Browne** 4-10-5 0...TomBellamy(3) 103+
(Alan King) *t.k.h: hld up wl in rr: prog 4f out: rdn to chse ldng trio over 2f out: looked hld tl str burst fnl f to ld 100yds out: sn clr* **9/1**

2 2 ¼ **Ridgeway Flyer** 5-11-4 0...NickScholfield 110
(Harry Fry) *w ldrs: led over 3f out: drvn and hrd pressed fr 2f out: hdd 1f out: dropped to 3rd ins fnl f: kpt on to take 2nd last stride* **16/1**

3 hd **Whoshotwho (IRE)** 5-11-4 0...AndrewTinkler 110
(Nicky Henderson) *t.k.h: hld up wl in rr: smooth prog on outer fr 4f out: rdn to chal jst over 2f out: led 1f out: hdd and outpcd 100yds out: lost 2nd last stride* **20/1**

2 **4** 2 ¼ **Peppay Le Pugh (IRE)**[280] 188 5-11-4 0...NoelFehily 108
(Nicky Henderson) *hld up in rr: smooth prog 4f out: jnd ldrs and rdn to chal 2f out: one pce fnl f* **7/2**[1]

5 4 **Thomas Shelby (IRE)** 5-11-4 0...DenisO'Regan 104
(Alan King) *t.k.h: hld up in rr: prog 4f out: shkn up wl over 2f out: no hdwy after but kpt on* **9/2**[2]

6 3 ¾ **Phobiaphiliac (IRE)** 5-11-4 0...JeremiahMcGrath 101
(Nicky Henderson) *hld up in midfield: trckd ldrs gng strly over 3f out: rdn and wknd jst over 2f out* **11/1**

7 1 ¾ **Faheem** 5-11-4 0...MarcGoldstein 99
(Lydia Richards) *hld up wl in rr: urged along over 3f out: rn green but kpt on fnl 2f* **100/1**

8 nk **Daytime Ahead (IRE)** 5-10-11 0...LeightonAspell 91
(Oliver Sherwood) *in tch: shkn up over 3f out: sn outpcd and btn: plugged on* **28/1**

9 7 **Bigpipenotobacee (IRE)**[68] 5-11-4 0...PaddyBrennan 93
(Tom George) *t.k.h: hld up in tch: prog to press ldrs 4f out: rdn and wknd over 2f out* **7/1**

10 4 ½ **Belmont Park (FR)** 5-11-4 0...TomScudamore 87
(David Bridgwater) *pressed ldrs tl rdn and wknd 3f out* **33/1**

11 5 **Herdswick Holloa (IRE)** 5-11-4 0...TrevorWhelan 82
(Neil King) *wl in tch: rdn and wknd jst over 3f out* **16/1**

3 **12** 6 **Cheltenam De Vaige (FR)**[27] 3625 4-10-8 0...DavidEngland 66
(Giles Smyly) *w ldr: led briefly 4f out: wknd qckly 3f out* **20/1**

13 28 **King Charlie (IRE)**[96] 6-11-4 0...TomO'Brien 48
(Suzy Smith) *led to 4f out: wknd rapidly: t.o* **20/1**

0 **14** 11 **Tonythetarmacker (IRE)**[88] 2549 5-11-4 0...GavinSheehan 37
(Ali Stronge) *a in rr: lost tch 1/2-way: sn t.o* **150/1**

P **15** 25 **Fell Runner**[280] 187 5-11-4 0...NicodeBoinville 12
(Nicky Henderson) *t.k.h: in tch: reminder 5f out: sn wknd rapidly: t.o and eased 3f out* **11/2**[3]

4m 4.6s (12.20) **Going Correction** +0.80s/f (Soft)
WFA 4 from 5yo+ 9lb **15** Ran SP% **120.7**
Speed ratings: **101,99,99,98,96 94,93,93,90,88 85,82,68,63,50**
CSF £132.90 TOTE £12.40: £4.60, £4.30, £5.00; EX 169.80 Trifecta £1762.60.
Owner Incipe Partnership **Bred** R W Russell **Trained** Barbury Castle, Wilts

FOCUS
Add 79yds to advertised race distance. This bumper should produce winners. Cheltenian won it en route to taking the Champion Bumper at Cheltenham in 2011.

4103 RACINGUK.COM/ANYWHERE MAIDEN OPEN NATIONAL HUNT FLAT RACE (DIV II) 2m

4:55 (4:55) (Class 5) 4-6-Y-O **£2,274** (£667; £333; £166)

Form RPR

1 **Stowaway Magic (IRE)**[327] 5-11-4 0...NicodeBoinville 121+
(Nicky Henderson) *t.k.h: hld up in midfield: prog 6f out on outer to chse ldng pair over 4f out: clsd and drvn over 2f out: led wl over 1f out: sn pressed: kpt on wl fnl f* **5/1**[3]

4 **2** 1 ½ **Onthewesternfront (IRE)**[78] 2729 6-11-4 0...RichardJohnson 119+
(Jonjo O'Neill) *t.k.h: trckd ldrs on outer: lost pl after 7f and in rr 6f out: prog over 4f out to rch 6th over 3f out but nt on terms w ldrs: clsd over 2f out: chsd wnr over 1f out: kpt on wl but a jst hld* **3/1**[2]

3 12 **Golden Birthday (FR)**[120] 1940 5-11-4 0...NickScholfield 107
(Harry Fry) *t.k.h: w ldrs: wnt 2nd 1/2-way: clr of rest over 4f out: rdn to ld over 2f out: hdd wl over 1f out: wknd but clung on for 3rd* **9/4**[1]

4 nse **Le Dauphin (IRE)** 5-11-4 0...DavidBass 107
(Nicky Henderson) *hld up towards rr: prog 7f out: jnd ldrs 4f out: rdn to chal 2f out: wknd over 1f out* **8/1**

62 **5** 3 **Sungai Long**[29] 3593 4-10-8 0...TomScudamore 94
(Michael Scudamore) *led 3f: led again 9f out: clr w one rival over 4f out: rdn and hdd over 2f out: wknd over 1f out* **20/1**

2 **6** ¾ **Walt (IRE)**[73] 2835 5-11-4 0...NoelFehily 103
(Nicky Henderson) *t.k.h: racd wd: led after 3f tl 9f out: lost pl fr 7f out: no ch 4f out: kpt on steadily fnl 2f: nt disgracd* **10/1**

7 1 **Grand Coureur (FR)** 4-10-3 0...LizzieKelly(5) 92
(Nick Williams) *wl in tch: prog to join ldrs 5f out: lft bhd by ldng quartet and pushed along 3f out: steadily fdd: nt disgracd* **16/1**

8 nse **Midnight Merlot** 4-10-8 0...IanPopham 92
(Noel Williams) *hld up wl in rr: sme prog 4f out but sn pushed along and nt on terms w ldrs: no hdwy over 2f out: kpt on* **25/1**

6- **9** 5 **Hoo Bally Diva (IRE)**[298] 5439 5-10-11 0...LiamHeard 90
(Bob Buckler) *prom tl wknd over 3f out* **100/1**

10 21 **Ermyn's Edith** 5-10-4 0...PaddyBradley(7) 69
(Pat Phelan) *t.k.h: hld up wl in rr: pushed along over 4f out: wknd 3f out: t.o* **100/1**

11 1 ¼ **Too Far Gone (IRE)** 5-10-11 0...WilliamFeatherstone(7) 75
(Alan King) *hld up in midfield: rdn and wknd wl over 3f out: t.o* **18/1**

0 **12** ½ **Baron Du Plessis (FR)**[78] 2729 5-11-4 0...WillKennedy 74
(Ian Williams) *t.k.h: hld up in rr: prog into midfield 6f out: wknd 4f out: t.o* **100/1**

13 *5* **Catena Alta (IRE)** 5-11-4 0 AndrewTinkler 69
(Martin Keighley) *hld up wl in rr: sltly hmpd bnd over 12f out: struggling 5f out: wknd and t.o* **50/1**

0 14 *40* **Galice Du Ciel**[97] 2351 5-10-11 0 MrDavidTurner(7) 29
(Giles Smyly) *plld hrd: lost pl after 5f: struggling bef 1/2-way: wl t.o 5f out* **200/1**

4 15 *19* **The Racing Duke (IRE)**[62] 3048 4-10-8 0 KielanWoods
(Graeme McPherson) *chsd ldrs tl wknd rapidly over 4f out: t.o and eased* **50/1**

4m 4.7s (12.30) **Going Correction** +0.80s/f (Soft)
WFA 4 from 5yo+ 9lb **15 Ran SP% 119.8**
Speed ratings: **101,100,94,94,92 92,91,91,89,78 78,77,75,55,45**
CSF £19.24 TOTE £5.80: £2.30, £1.90, £1.30; EX 29.00 Trifecta £125.20.
Owner Grech & Parkin **Bred** B O'Driscoll & A O'Brien **Trained** Upper Lambourn, Berks

FOCUS
Add 79yds to advertised race distance. The first two finished clear in this useful bumper, which was run in an almost identical time to the first division. The first two look well above average, while the third, fifth, sixth and ninth help set the level.
T/Plt: £133.60 to a £1 stake. Pool: £87,976.01 - 480.51 winning tickets. T/Qpdt: £14.80 to a £1 stake. Pool: £9,373.10 - 468.47 winning tickets. **Jonathan Neesom**

3995 WETHERBY (L-H)
Friday, February 12

OFFICIAL GOING: Heavy (soft in places home bend and home straight; 5.3)
Wind: almost nil Weather: fine but cold

4104 RACING UK IN HD NEXT MONTH JUVENILE MAIDEN HURDLE (9 hdls) 2m
1:20 (1:21) (Class 5) 4-Y-O £2,599 (£763; £381; £190)

Form RPR

53 1 **Cobra De Mai (FR)**[58] 3112 4-10-12 0 HarrySkelton 109+
(Dan Skelton) *trckd ldr: effrt appr 2 out: upsides last: led last 150yds: drvn out* **8/13**[1]

U 2 *1 1/2* **Ikrapol (FR)**[82] 2662 4-10-12 119 (t) DarylJacob 107+
(David Pipe) *set stdy pce: increased gallop 3 out: drvn 2 out: jnd last: hdd and no ex last 100yds* **13/8**[2]

P 3 *9* **Fibre Optic**[98] 2324 4-10-12 0 CraigNichol 98
(Rose Dobbin) *hld up in last: wnt handy 3rd 3rd: drvn appr 2 out: wknd appr last* **22/1**

40 4 *16* **Dance And Romance**[13] 3861 4-10-5 0 BrianHughes 75
(Tim Easterby) *in rr: mstke 5th: hdwy to chse ldng trio next: lost pl 3 out: sn bhd* **20/1**[3]

00 5 *49* **Lipstickandpowder (IRE)**[46] 3306 4-10-2 0 HarryChalloner(3) 26
(Dianne Sayer) *t.k.h in rr: sme hdwy 6th: drvn and lost pl bef next: sn bhd: t.o 2 out* **200/1**

4m 22.2s (26.40) **Going Correction** +0.825s/f (Soft) **5 Ran SP% 109.6**
Speed ratings: **67,66,61,53,29**
CSF £1.92 TOTE £1.30: £1.02, £1.40; EX 1.80 Trifecta £4.20.
Owner Norman Lake & Susan Carsberg **Bred** Jean-Yves Touzaint **Trained** Alcester, Warwicks

FOCUS
The going was officially heavy, soft in places on home bend and straight. Shared 'A1' bend back on innermost line. Shared 'away' bend 20yds out from innermost chase line and 3yds out from innermost hurdle line. As a result this race was run over 9yds shorter than the advertised distance. This looked a two-horse race on paper and they duly battled out the finish in a race where they went a steady pace until after turning for home. Daryl Jacob said of the ground that it was "hard work". Small steps up from the first two.

4105 RACINGUK.COM/ANYWHERE (S) HURDLE 2m 3f 154y
1:50 (1:52) (Class 5) 5-Y-O+ £2,599 (£763; £381; £190)

Form RPR

/112 1 **Cotillion**[8] 3728 10-11-3 126 (p) RobMcCarth(3) 128+
(Ian Williams) *trckd ldrs: led between last 2: wnt clr sn after last: eased clsng stages* **4/7**[1]

4302 2 *4* **Maybe I Wont**[64] 2980 11-10-10 104 (p) BrianHughes 107
(James Moffatt) *trckd ldr: led 3 out: hdd between last 2: kpt on same pce* **13/2**[3]

-P13 3 *hd* **Ministerofinterior**[66] 2962 11-10-11 114 (b) CiaranGethings(5) 112
(Barry Leavy) *mid-div: drvn to chse ldrs 8th: upsides 2 out: kpt on clsng stages* **8/1**

2-03 4 *2 1/2* **Calculated Risk**[75] 2808 7-10-5 116 NathanMoscrop(5) 104
(Iain Jardine) *hld up in rr: t.k.h: hdwy to trck ldrs 3 out: upsides next: sn pushed along: hung lft and fnd little: fdd last 150yds* **4/1**[2]

PP 5 *40* **Local Celebrity (IRE)**[180] 1269 12-10-3 115 (t[1]) MissBHampson(7) 63
(Sally Randell) *led: pushed along 6th: j.rt and hdd 3 out: lost pl bef next: sn wl bhd: t.o* **66/1**

-P6P 6 *4* **Debt To Society (IRE)**[16] 3803 9-10-7 109 (vt) HarryChalloner(3) 59
(Richard Ford) *mid-div: pushed along 7th: lost pl next: wl bhd 3 out: sn t.o* **28/1**

5m 31.7s (24.70) **Going Correction** +0.825s/f (Soft) **6 Ran SP% 113.0**
Speed ratings: **83,81,81,80,64 62**
CSF £5.26 TOTE £1.50: £1.10, £3.40; EX 4.50 Trifecta £14.30.There was no bid for the winner.
Owner Jamie Robert Roberts **Bred** Mr & Mrs G Middlebrook **Trained** Portway, Worcs

FOCUS
This race was run over 9yds shorter than the advertised distance. A modest selling hurdle, but the outsider made sure it was run at a fair pace and the favourite dotted up. The second and third set the level.

4106 RACING UK DAY PASS JUST £10 H'CAP CHASE (13 fncs) 1m 7f 36y
2:25 (2:25) (Class 4) (0-120,120) 5-Y-O+ £3,898 (£1,144; £572; £286)

Form RPR

4320 1 **Astigos (FR)**[13] 3849 9-11-7 120 CharlieDeutsch(5) 137+
(Venetia Williams) *mde all: drew clr appr 4 out: 12 l ahd whn blnd 2 out: pushed rt out: unchal* **15/8**[2]

01-2 2 *25* **Bawden Rocks**[53] 3195 7-10-4 103 JakeHodson(5) 100
(David Bridgwater) *chsd wnr: blnd 5th: nt fluent next: reminders 8th: btn appr 4 out: fin tired* **6/4**[1]

2PPP 3 *7* **Cody Wyoming**[77] 2758 10-11-12 120 (tp) DarylJacob 105
(Charlie Mann) *chsd ldng pair: drvn 9th: wknd 3 out* **7/2**[3]

00P4 4 *31* **Formidableopponent (IRE)**[39] 3475 9-10-11 105 DerekFox 89
(William Young Jnr) *reluctant and virtually ref to r: eventually set off t.o: eased 3 out* **8/1**

4m 20.9s (25.10) **Going Correction** +0.775s/f (Soft) **4 Ran SP% 108.1**
Speed ratings: **64,50,46,30**
CSF £5.22 TOTE £2.70; EX 4.20 Trifecta £7.80.
Owner A Brooks **Bred** Marcello Randelli **Trained** Kings Caple, H'fords

■ Stewards' Enquiry : Derek Fox two-day ban: use of whip (26-27 Feb)

Jake Hodson jockey said that the gelding stopped quickly

FOCUS
This race was run over 60yds further than the advertised distance. A small field for this fair handicap chase and a race that completely fell apart. A new pb from the winner.

4107 RACING UK PROFITS RETURNED TO RACING H'CAP HURDLE 2m 3f 154y
3:00 (3:00) (Class 3) (0-140,132) 4-Y-O+ £5,523 (£1,621; £810; £405)

Form RPR

4140 1 **Minstrels Gallery (IRE)**[20] 3733 7-11-5 125 HarrySkelton 130
(Lucy Wadham) *trckd ldr: led 7th: styd on wl fr 2 out: drvn rt out* **6/4**[1]

0414 2 *2 1/4* **Maxie T**[27] 3630 5-11-3 130 FinianO'Toole(7) 133
(Micky Hammond) *hld up wl in tch: trckd ldrs 6th: effrt between last 2: styd on run-in: unable to chal* **13/8**[2]

1152 3 *4* **Bowdler's Magic**[42] 3420 9-10-11 120 AdamNicol(3) 119
(David Thompson) *led to 7th: drvn 3 out: kpt on one pce* **4/1**[3]

230- 4 *12* **The Wallace Line (IRE)**[105] 4707 5-11-7 132 AlanJohns(5) 119
(Tim Vaughan) *hld up wl in tch: trcking ldrs 6th: effrt appr 3 out: wknd bef 2 out: eased clsng stages* **9/1**

5m 27.5s (20.50) **Going Correction** +0.825s/f (Soft) **4 Ran SP% 108.1**
Speed ratings (Par 107): **92,91,89,84**
CSF £4.41 TOTE £2.40; EX 3.80 Trifecta £6.90.
Owner G Pascoe & S Brewer **Bred** Morecool Stud **Trained** Newmarket, Suffolk

FOCUS
This race was run over 9yds shorter than the advertised distance. A disappointing turnout for this decent handicap hurdle and they only went a steady pace, with the contest developing into a sprint over the last three flights. The winner has been rated back to his best.

4108 HIGH DEFINITION RACING UK NEXT MONTH NOVICES' HURDLE 2m 3f 154y
3:35 (3:36) (Class 4) 4-Y-O+ £3,249 (£954; £477; £238)

Form RPR

1FF1 1 **Lake View Lad (IRE)**[24] 3668 6-11-6 121 StephenMulqueen(5) 138+
(N W Alexander) *trckd ldrs: 2nd 3rd: chal 3 out: led next: drvn and styd on wl run-in* **5/2**[2]

1-5 2 *4* **Walking In The Air (IRE)**[101] 2257 6-11-4 0 HarrySkelton 126+
(Dan Skelton) *led: drvn 3 out: hdd next: kpt on same pce run-in* **8/13**[1]

2233 3 *37* **Bollin Ace**[48] 3240 5-11-4 115 (b[1]) BrianHughes 96
(Tim Easterby) *chsd ldr to 3rd: modest 3rd whn blnd 8th: sn no ch w first 2: hit 2 out* **4/1**[3]

4 4 *23* **San Pietro (FR)**[16] 3802 8-11-1 0 HarryChalloner(3) 66
(Richard Ford) *in rr: distant 5th appr 3 out: remote 4th between last 2* **33/1**

14-P 5 *14* **Dalaman (IRE)**[94] 2417 5-10-13 0 (t) AlanJohns(5) 52
(Tim Vaughan) *mid-div: distant 4th 8th: wknd 2 out* **20/1**

00/0 6 *16* **Jasani**[17] 3795 8-10-11 0 (p) GLavery(7) 36
(Alan Brown) *mid-div: wknd 8th: sn wl bhd* **200/1**

-PR5 7 *55* **Ashes Corner (IRE)**[45] 3340 6-11-1 0 JohnKington(3)
(Julia Brooke) *in rr: bhd and reminders 6th: t.o 8th* **100/1**

P0 8 *2 3/4* **Violoniste (FR)**[17] 3795 7-11-4 0 JonathanEngland
(Sam Drake) *chsd ldrs: wknd qckly and lost pl after 5th: sn wl bhd: t.o 8th* **100/1**

00-P P **Bold Prince Rupert (IRE)**[85] 2591 6-10-13 0 NathanMoscrop(5)
(Sara Ender) *in rr: bhd whn 4th: sn given reminders: t.o 8th: p.u bef next* **150/1**

0- P **Wee Holio (IRE)**[322] 5020 5-11-4 0 JakeGreenall
(Marjorie Fife) *in rr: bhd 6th: t.o 8th: p.u bef next* **50/1**

5m 19.4s (12.40) **Going Correction** +0.825s/f (Soft) **10 Ran SP% 123.3**
Speed ratings (Par 105): **108,106,91,82,76 70,48,47,,**
CSF £4.84 TOTE £3.40: £1.10, £1.10, £1.10; EX 5.60 Trifecta £10.20.
Owner Alistair Cochrane **Bred** Peter Magnier **Trained** Kinneston, Perth & Kinross

FOCUS
This race was run over 9yds shorter than the advertised distance. Not a particularly competitive novice hurdle with them betting 20-1 bar three. The trio dominated from the start, but the race became a match from the home bend and the front pair pulled miles clear. A big step up from the winner, with the second rated to the level he had promised when an impressive bumper winner.

4109 RACINGUK.COM H'CAP CHASE (QUALIFIER FOR THE CHALLENGER STAYING CHASE SERIES FINAL) (19 fncs) 3m 45y
4:10 (4:10) (Class 3) (0-130,130) 5-Y-O+ £6,498 (£1,908; £954; £477)

Form RPR

0-2P 1 **Goodtoknow**[58] 3109 8-11-4 122 (p) JakeGreenall 145+
(Kerry Lee) *trckd ldrs: led bef 4 out: j.rt 4 out: clr fr next: 17 l clr whn j.rt last: heavily eased* **5/1**[3]

-234 2 *15* **King Of The Wolds (IRE)**[83] 2638 9-11-12 130 BrianHughes 133
(Malcolm Jefferson) *trckd ldrs: led 3rd to 5th: outpcd appr 4 out: modest 2nd between last 2: no ch w wnr* **9/4**[1]

-P03 3 *3/4* **Voyage A New York (FR)**[27] 3631 7-10-6 110 DerekFox 111
(Lucinda Russell) *chsd ldrs: 3rd and outpcd appr 4 out: kpt on one pce to take modest 3rd appr last* **9/2**[2]

0-03 4 *8* **Ballyoliver**[10] 3918 12-11-9 127 LiamTreadwell 123
(Venetia Williams) *led to 3rd: hit 10th: sn drvn: hit 12th: outpcd 15th: poor 4th last* **5/1**[3]

5433 5 *19* **Epic Warrior (IRE)**[45] 3348 7-11-1 122 (b) KieronEdgar(3) 103
(David Pipe) *w ldrs: led 5th: hdd bef 4 out: wknd between last 2: disputing 4th but wkng whn blnd last: fin tired* **5/1**[3]

2100 6 *7* **Jack Steel (IRE)**[39] 3475 6-11-6 124 RichieMcLernon 91
(Lucinda Russell) *chsd ldrs: lost pl 11th: wl bhd fr 15th* **16/1**

/1P4 P **Glen Countess (IRE)**[44] 3367 9-11-2 120 SeanQuinlan
(Sue Smith) *prom: mstke 4th: reminders 8th: lost pl 10th: sn bhd: t.o whn p.u bef 12th* **14/1**

7m 14.3s (26.30) **Going Correction** +0.775s/f (Soft) **7 Ran SP% 111.5**
Speed ratings: **108,103,102,100,93 91,**
CSF £16.48 TOTE £5.60: £2.00, £2.40; EX 18.60 Trifecta £75.40.
Owner Burling Daresbury MacEchern Nolan Potter **Bred** P J Hughes Berkswell **Trained** Byton, H'fords

The Form Book Jumps 2015-16, Raceform Ltd, Newbury, RG14 5SJ

FOCUS
This race was run over 120yds further than the advertised distance. A decent handicap chase and although they remained in a bunch for the first circuit, they got sorted out on the second and the winner hosed up. Seemingly a big step up from the easy winner, with the second again below his best but in line with his Haydock run.

4110 YORKSHIRE POST LADIES NIGHT - 24TH MAY H'CAP HURDLE (12 hdls) 3m 26y
4:40 (4:42) (Class 5) (0-100,109) 4-Y-0+ **£2,599** (£763; £381; £190)

Form RPR
0011 **1** **Navanman (IRE)**[4] 4030 7-12-0 **109** 14ex .... MichaelHeard(7) 117+
(David Pipe) *trckd ldrs: 2nd 8th: led 3 out: 3 l ahd whn hit last: drvn out* **4/7**[1]
P011 **2** 1½ **Auldthunder (IRE)**[7] 3969 9-11-8 **99** .... JoeColliver(3) 105+
(Micky Hammond) *chsd ldrs: n.m.r and dropped bk briefly 8th: chsd wnr appr 2 out: swtchd lft between last 2: kpt on same pce run-in* **7/2**[2]
3513 **3** 23 **Turtle Cask (IRE)**[46] 3312 7-11-12 **100** .... (p) BrianHughes 85
(Dianne Sayer) *led: hdd bef 3 out: hit 2 out: sn wknd* **13/2**[3]
60-0 **4** 26 **Simmply Sam**[17] 3791 9-10-9 **83** .... JakeGreenall 39
(Marjorie Fife) *chsd ldrs: outpcd 8th: lost pl bef 3 out: lft distant 4th last* **22/1**
-5PP **5** 5 **Master Murphy (IRE)**[120] 1925 11-10-10 **84** .... (p) PeterBuchanan 35
(Jane Walton) *chsd ldrs: lost pl bef 3 out: sn bhd: t.o whn lft 5th last* **33/1**
3-PP **P** **Castley Lane**[236] 798 10-10-7 **86** .... NathanMoscrop(5)
(Sara Ender) *chsd ldrs: lost pl and reminders 6th: sn bhd: t.o whn p.u bef next* **40/1**
5065 **U** **Toarmandowithlove (IRE)**[23] 3684 8-10-6 **87** .... (t) JamesCorbett(7) 72
(Susan Corbett) *in rr: hdwy 5th: sn chsng ldrs: modest 4th and outpcd appr 3 out: distant 4th whn blnd and uns rdr last* **20/1**

6m 50.1s (33.60) **Going Correction** +0.825s/f (Soft) **7 Ran SP% 113.7**
Speed ratings (Par 103): **77,76,68,60,58**
CSF £2.95 CT £5.71 TOTE £1.40: £1.10, £1.80; EX 3.60 Trifecta £6.00.
Owner Mrs Yvonne Fleet **Bred** Aidan Ryan **Trained** Nicholashayne, Devon

FOCUS
This race was run over 18yds shorter than the advertised distance. An ordinary staying handicap hurdle and the betting had a rather lopsided look to it, but in a race run at a moderate pace the two in-form horses came clear. Another pb from the well-in winner, with the second running a hurdle pb but below his chase mark.
T/Plt: £24.60 to a £1 stake. Pool: £58,125.51 - 1,718.78 winning tickets. T/Qpdt: £18.70 to a £1 stake. Pool: £4,973.83 - 196.3 winning tickets. **Walter Glynn**

3347 NEWBURY (L-H)
Saturday, February 13

OFFICIAL GOING: Hurdle course - heavy (soft in places; 4.1) chase course - soft (heavy in places; 4.8)
Wind: Fresh, behind Weather: Damp

4111 READ PAUL NICHOLLS EXCLUSIVELY AT BETFAIR NOVICES' HURDLE (8 hdls) 2m 69y
1:20 (1:20) (Class 3) 4-Y-0+ **£6,498** (£1,908; £954; £477)

Form RPR
125 **1** **Meet The Legend**[49] 3227 5-11-2 0 .... HarrySkelton 136+
(Dan Skelton) *hld up in rr: hdwy 5th: led appr last: sn clr: rdn out* **7/2**[2]
2-41 **2** 3½ **Emerging Talent (IRE)**[43] 3411 7-11-8 135 .... (t) NickScholfield 138
(Paul Nicholls) *t.k.h: pressed ldr: led 3rd tl 2 out: kpt on run-in* **8/15**[1]
3 8 **Argante (FR)**[147] 7-11-2 0 .... NicodeBoinville 124
(Nicky Henderson) *led tl 3rd: w ldr after: slt ld 2 out: hdd and outpcd appr last* **16/1**
4 3 **Herewego Herewego (IRE)** 5-11-2 0 .... BarryGeraghty 122
(Alan King) *in tch tl outpcd 2 out* **6/1**[3]
45 **5** 37 **Burning Desire (IRE)**[7] 3773 5-11-2 0 .... (t) BrendanPowell 84
(Richard Hughes) *chsd ldrs: j.lft 1st: wknd after 5th* **66/1**
6PP **P** **Bobby Benton (IRE)**[12] 3902 5-11-2 0 .... JoshuaMoore
(Jim Best) *t.k.h: chsd ldrs: blnd and lost pl 4th: lost tch next: t.o whn p.u bef last* **250/1**
-214 **P** **Shanandoa**[55] 3175 5-10-2 0 .... MichaelHeard(7)
(Brian Barr) *towards rr: hmpd 1st: wknd appr 3 out: wl bhd whn p.u bef last* **50/1**

4m 12.6s (2.60) **Going Correction** +0.30s/f (Yiel) **7 Ran SP% 111.5**
Speed ratings (Par 107): **105,103,99,97,79**
CSF £5.69 TOTE £4.10: £1.50, £1.20; EX 7.60 Trifecta £20.50.
Owner Highclere Thoroughbred Racing - Legend **Bred** B G Hellyer & H D J Daly **Trained** Alcester, Warwicks

FOCUS
Add 43yds to the advertised distance. A damp start to the day saw the going downgraded to heavy, soft in places on the hurdle course. This was a good-quality novice event, run at a sound gallop. A step up from the winner, while the third and fourth look sure to win over hurdles.

4112 BETFAIR ACCA EDGE H'CAP HURDLE (12 hdls) 3m 52y
1:50 (1:51) (Class 2) (0-145,144) 4-Y-0+
£12,512 (£3,696; £1,848; £924; £462; £232)

Form RPR
U-2P **1** **Count Guido Deiro (IRE)**[70] 2916 9-10-4 **129** .... MrJJSlevin(7) 135+
(Nigel Twiston-Davies) *mde all: kicked on 3 out: hrd rdn appr last: hld on gamely* **11/1**
1134 **2** 2¾ **Sykes (IRE)**[35] 3517 7-10-7 **125** .... RichardJohnson 128
(Philip Hobbs) *towards rr: mstke 4th: hdwy 2 out: drvn to press wnr last: hld fnl 50yds* **7/2**[1]
5-63 **3** 3¾ **Keltus (FR)**[49] 3232 6-11-2 **134** .... (t) SamTwiston-Davies 132
(Paul Nicholls) *hld up in 6th: hdwy 3 out: briefly wnt 2nd at next: one pce* **7/1**
-201 **4** ½ **Zeroeshadesofgrey (IRE)**[46] 3336 7-11-11 **143** .... TrevorWhelan 141
(Neil King) *prom: rdn 2 out: one pce appr last* **9/2**[2]
-03P **5** 5 **Batavir (FR)**[43] 3407 7-10-9 **127** .... (t) TomScudamore 120
(David Pipe) *chsd wnr tl after 3 out: sn wknd* **13/2**
-321 **6** 1¼ **Millanisi Boy**[35] 3516 7-10-7 **125** .... TomO'Brien 118
(Richard Woollacott) *chsd ldrs tl wknd appr 2 out* **9/2**[2]
0010 **7** 13 **Gevrey Chambertin (FR)**[35] 3517 8-11-7 **144** .... (b) DavidNoonan(5) 124
(David Pipe) *hld up in rr: pushed along after 9th: lost tch appr 2 out* **14/1**
025- **8** 2¾ **Argocat (IRE)**[255] 604 8-11-2 **134** .... DavidBass 111
(Nicky Henderson) *in tch tl wknd 3 out* **6/1**[3]

6m 29.9s (389.90) **8 Ran SP% 113.7**
CSF £49.63 CT £292.45 TOTE £13.50: £2.60, £1.50, £2.80; EX 52.50 Trifecta £168.30.
Owner R N Bevis **Bred** Raymond McDonnell **Trained** Naunton, Gloucs

FOCUS
This fair staying handicap was run at an uneven gallop and the winner bossed it. The race distance was 86yds further than advertised. The second, third and fourth have been rated pretty much to their marks.

4113 BETFAIR DENMAN CHASE (GRADE 2) (18 fncs) 2m 7f 86y
2:25 (2:26) (Class 1) 5-Y-0+ **£28,977** (£11,187; £5,852; £3,167)

Form RPR
0004 **1** **Houblon Des Obeaux (FR)**[28] 3624 9-11-0 146 .... (p) AidanColeman 164+
(Venetia Williams) *sn prom: led 12th: rdn wl clr 4 out: eased run-in* **3/1**[2]
F004 **2** 28 **The Giant Bolster**[14] 3850 11-11-0 139 .... JakeHodson 131
(David Bridgwater) *chsd ldrs: rdn 10th: outpcd 14th: styd on to take remote 2nd appr 2 out* **9/1**[3]
00UP **3** 21 **Splash Of Ginge**[21] 3741 8-11-6 141 .... (v[1]) RyanHatch 120
(Nigel Twiston-Davies) *led tl 2nd: led 4th tl 12th: easily outpcd by wnr and blnd 4 out: wknd and lost 2nd appr 2 out* **16/1**
P-2P **4** ½ **Rocky Creek (IRE)**[70] 2902 10-11-6 158 .... SamTwiston-Davies 115
(Paul Nicholls) *chsd ldrs tl wknd 14th* **2/1**[1]
0450 **P** **Midnight Appeal**[175] 1322 11-11-0 127 .... (t) RichieMcLernon
(Sophie Leech) *bhd: struggling 10th: t.o whn p.u bef 2 out* **100/1**
535P **P** **Ballynagour (IRE)**[49] 3231 10-11-0 159 .... (t) TomScudamore
(David Pipe) *hld up: hdwy 12th: wknd appr 3 out: 5th and no ch whn p.u next* **3/1**[2]
-P1F **P** **Bob Ford (IRE)**[35] 3518 9-11-4 142 .... NicodeBoinville
(Rebecca Curtis) *led 2nd tl 4th: lost pl 8th: wl bhd whn p.u bef 14th* **10/1**

6m 17.4s (11.40) **Going Correction** +0.80s/f (Soft) **7 Ran SP% 109.3**
Speed ratings: **112,102,94,94,**
CSF £25.80 TOTE £4.40: £3.10, £3.80; EX 26.60 Trifecta £137.90.
Owner Mrs Julian Blackwell **Bred** Mme Marie Devilder & Benjamin Devilder **Trained** Kings Caple, H'fords

FOCUS
Add 44yds to the distance. A disappointing edition of this well-established Grade 2 chase which served up a severe test. The winner has been rated back to his best.

4114 BETFAIR EXCHANGE CHASE (REGISTERED AS THE GAME SPIRIT CHASE) (GRADE 2) (13 fncs) 2m 92y
3:00 (3:00) (Class 1) 5-Y-0+ **£28,475** (£10,685; £5,350; £2,665)

Form RPR
-P33 **1** **Top Gamble (IRE)**[43] 3406 8-11-5 155 .... RichardJohnson 165+
(Kerry Lee) *chsd ldr: led 8th: clr fr 3 out* **11/10**[1]
111- **2** 10 **Dodging Bullets**[339] 4705 8-11-10 171 .... (t) SamTwiston-Davies 158
(Paul Nicholls) *trckd ldrs: wnt 2nd at 9th: outpcd and btn 3 out* **6/5**[2]
3P/4 **3** 27 **Captain Conan (FR)**[21] 3740 9-11-0 150 .... AndrewTinkler 128
(Nicky Henderson) *led tl 8th: stmbld on landing and lost 2nd at next: sn rdn and wknd* **15/2**[3]
001P **4** 75 **Un Beau Roman (FR)**[14] 3851 8-11-0 137 .... TomO'Brien 46
(Paul Henderson) *a last: no ch fr 9th* **50/1**

4m 20.1s (12.10) **Going Correction** +0.80s/f (Soft) **4 Ran SP% 106.8**
Speed ratings: **101,96,82,45**
CSF £2.83 TOTE £2.00; EX 2.70 Trifecta £4.20.
Owner Walters Plant Hire & James & Jean Potter **Bred** J D Cantillon **Trained** Byton, H'fords

FOCUS
Add 22yds to the distance. This was all about the reigning Champion Chaser Dodging Bullets but he was below par on the testing ground and the form is best rated around the 155-rated winner. A small pb from the winner, with the third in line with his recent hurdle run.

4115 BETFAIR HURDLE (H'CAP) (GRADE 3) (8 hdls) 2m 69y
3:35 (3:38) (Class 1) 4-Y-0+
£88,272 (£33,123; £16,585; £8,261; £4,154; £2,077)

Form RPR
5213 **1** **Agrapart (FR)**[42] 3447 5-10-5 **137** .... LizzieKelly(5) 151+
(Nick Williams) *prom: led appr last: lft clr: styd on wl* **16/1**
24F- **2** 11 **Starchitect (IRE)**[310] 5236 5-10-8 **135** .... (bt) TomScudamore 143+
(David Pipe) *prom: jnd ldr 2nd: led 5th tl hdd and blnd bdly last: nt rcvr* **16/1**
1235 **3** 1¼ **Flying Angel (IRE)**[49] 3232 5-10-1 **131** ow3 .... RyanHatch(3) 133
(Nigel Twiston-Davies) *in tch: wnt prom at 5th: one pce fr 2 out* **25/1**
2 **4** ¾ **Affaire D'Honneur (FR)**[48] 3284 5-10-5 **132** .... GavinSheehan 133+
(Harry Whittington) *s.s: bhd: styd on fr 3 out* **8/1**[2]
13P0 **5** hd **Waxies Dargle**[27] 3650 7-10-10 **142** .... JonathanMoore(5) 144
(Noel Meade, Ire) *towards rr: hdwy after 5th: wnt 3rd 2 out: one pce* **33/1**
2P-2 **6** 3 **Kalkir (FR)**[27] 3650 5-11-3 **147** .... DavidMullins(3) 145
(W P Mullins, Ire) *towards rr: drvn along fr 5th: styd on fr 2 out* **16/1**
-652 **7** ½ **Cheltenian (FR)**[14] 3854 10-11-12 **153** .... TomO'Brien 151
(Philip Hobbs) *mid-div: styd on same pce fr 2 out: nvr able to chal* **20/1**
5215 **8** 1¼ **Champagne At Tara**[14] 3854 7-10-2 **129** .... AidanColeman 125
(Jonjo O'Neill) *towards rr: sme hdwy 3 out: no imp fr next* **33/1**
9 4 **Blazer (FR)**[7] 4006 5-10-4 **131** 5ex .... BarryGeraghty 124
(W P Mullins, Ire) *in tch: short of room on 1st bnd: chsd ldrs 5th: wknd 2 out* **3/1**[1]
/44- **10** 12 **Montbazon (FR)**[574] 1010 9-10-13 **140** .... DenisO'Regan 122+
(Alan King) *bhd: sme hdwy 2 out: no further prog* **50/1**
5-36 **11** 3¾ **Zarib (IRE)**[56] 3151 5-10-2 **134** .... (p) BridgetAndrews(5) 113
(Dan Skelton) *in tch: tk clsr order 5th: wknd appr 2 out* **16/1**
10-1 **12** 19 **War Sound**[280] 197 7-11-2 **148** .... CiaranGethings(5) 106
(Philip Hobbs) *towards rr: drvn along appr 3 out: nvr nr ldrs* **12/1**[3]
3113 **13** ¾ **Modus**[45] 3370 6-10-12 **139** .... NickScholfield 96
(Paul Nicholls) *towards rr: hmpd 4th: no ch fr 3 out* **8/1**[2]
-143 **14** 4 **Baby King (IRE)**[23] 3708 7-10-1 **128** .... (t) PaddyBrennan 81
(Tom George) *s.s: bhd: sme hdwy 3 out: sn wknd* **25/1**
0124 **15** 8 **Matorico (IRE)**[49] 3232 5-10-9 **136** .... (b[1]) RichieMcLernon 81
(Jonjo O'Neill) *mid-div: sme hdwy appr 3 out: sn wknd* **25/1**
01/0 **16** 22 **Ivan Grozny (FR)**[27] 3650 6-11-4 **145** .... MPFogarty 68
(W P Mullins, Ire) *in tch tl wknd after 5th* **40/1**
-202 **17** 9 **Mad Jack Mytton (IRE)**[64] 3015 6-10-13 **140** .... JoshuaMoore 54
(Jonjo O'Neill) *mid-div: short of room on 1st bnd: hmpd 4th: n.d fr next* **20/1**
-111 **P** **Sternrubin (GER)**[56] 3151 5-11-1 **142** .... RichardJohnson
(Philip Hobbs) *led 1st tl 5th: wknd and p.u appr 3 out* **8/1**[2]
-P36 **P** **Chieftain's Choice (IRE)**[46] 3352 7-10-2 **129** .... BrianHughes
(Kevin Frost) *prom tl wknd 5th: wl bhd whn p.u bef 3 out* **16/1**
-250 **F** **Buiseness Sivola (FR)**[27] 3650 5-11-1 **142** .... SamTwiston-Davies
(W P Mullins, Ire) *hld up in midfield: sme hdwy after 5th: wkng whn fell 3 out* **50/1**

04- **F** **Dicosimo (FR)**[47] 3329 5-11-9 **150**.................... DannyMullins
(W P Mullins, Ire) *plld hrd: led tl blnd 1st: stdd next: in tch whn fell 4th* **16/1**

3642 **P** **Forest Bihan (FR)**[17] 3804 5-10-13 **140**.................... DannyCook
(Brian Ellison) *mid-div: nt fluent 2nd: btn whn hmpd 3 out: wl bhd whn p.u bef last* **18/1**

4m 8.7s (-1.30) **Going Correction** +0.30s/f (Yiel) **22** Ran SP% **135.5**
Speed ratings (Par 113): **115,109,108,108,108 106,106,106,104,98 96,86,86,84,80 69,64,,,**
CSF £237.94 CT £6315.24 TOTE £23.30: £5.00, £4.70, £7.50, £2.60; EX 450.90 Trifecta £16048.30.
Owner The Gascoigne Brookes Partnership Iii **Bred** Jean-Marc Lucas **Trained** George Nympton, Devon

FOCUS
Add 43yds to the advertised distance. The richest handicap hurdle run in Europe. Predictably there was no hanging about, although for the third year running it proved very hard to make any headway from off the leaders. The third helps to set the level. A pb from the winner, with the race rated around the balance of the third, fourth and fifth.

4116 BETTER ODDS WITH BETFAIR NOVICES' CHASE (18 fncs) 2m 7f 86y
4:10 (4:11) (Class 3) 5-Y-0+ **£7,797** (£2,289; £1,144)

Form RPR

-631 **1** **Out Sam**[17] 3805 7-11-4 0.................... GavinSheehan 153+
(Warren Greatrex) *trckd ldr: led after 14th and travelled on bit: shkn up run-in: readily* **3/1**[2]

1-34 **2** *3 ½* **Milansbar (IRE)**[67] 2960 9-11-0 142.................... TrevorWhelan 143
(Neil King) *led tl pckd 14th: sn outpcd in 3rd: styd on to chse wnr run-in* **4/1**[3]

-021 **3** *13* **Activial (FR)**[43] 3415 6-11-4 149....................(t) NoelFehily 137
(Harry Fry) *hld up in 3rd: wnt 2nd after 14th: chal 4 out: rdn and hld 2 out: wknd last* **8/13**[1]

6m 30.7s (24.70) **Going Correction** +0.80s/f (Soft) **3** Ran SP% **106.9**
Speed ratings: **89,87,83**
CSF £10.97 TOTE £3.00; EX 6.50 Trifecta £15.00.
Owner Swanee River Partnership **Bred** D & N Leggate, R Kent & I Henderson **Trained** Upper Lambourn, Berks

FOCUS
Add 44yds to the distance. An interesting little staying novice chase. A big step up on his previous best from the winner, with the second rated to his mark.

4117 TAP TAP BOOM BUMPER (A STANDARD OPEN NATIONAL HUNT FLAT RACE) (LISTED RACE) 2m 69y
4:45 (4:45) (Class 1) 4-6-Y-0
£11,390 (£4,274; £2,140; £1,066; £536; £268)

Form RPR

112 **1** **Ballyandy**[57] 3138 5-11-7 0.................... SamTwiston-Davies 137+
(Nigel Twiston-Davies) *trckd ldr: led 4f out: clr over 1f out: rdn out* **11/8**[1]

1 **2** *9* **Positively Dylan**[70] 2909 5-10-10 0.................... LewisGordon(7) 124
(Evan Williams) *hld up in rr: hdwy 3f out: chsd wnr fnl 2f: no ex ins fnl f* **22/1**

11 **3** *6* **Gayebury**[43] 3416 6-11-3 0.................... BarryGeraghty 118
(Tom Symonds) *led tl 4f out: wknd 2f out* **9/1**

4 **4** *7* **One Of Us**[43] 3409 4-10-7 0.................... RichardJohnson 101
(Nick Williams) *towards rr: hdwy 6f out: wknd 3f out* **6/1**[3]

1 **5** *11* **Lithic (IRE)**[74] 2842 5-11-3 0.................... JoshuaMoore 100
(Jonjo O'Neill) *t.k.h: in tch: outpcd 5f out: sn bhd* **8/1**

13 **6** *2 ¾* **Full Irish (IRE)**[57] 3138 5-11-3 0.................... AidanColeman 97
(Emma Lavelle) *prom tl wknd 3f out* **10/1**

7 *2 ¾* **Bleu Berry (FR)**[476] 5-11-3 0.................... PaulTownend 95
(W P Mullins, Ire) *chsd ldrs tl wknd 3f out* **3/1**[2]

4m 13.0s (8.70) **Going Correction** +0.30s/f (Yiel) **7** Ran SP% **115.9**
WFA 4 from 5yo+ 9lb
Speed ratings: **90,85,82,79,73 72,70**
CSF £35.59 TOTE £2.10: £1.10, £6.70; EX 38.20 Trifecta £160.90.
Owner Options O Syndicate **Bred** Pleasure Palace Racing **Trained** Naunton, Gloucs

FOCUS
Add 43yds to the advertised distance. Traditionally a very strong bumper. Another step up from the winner, with the third and fourth helping to set the level.
T/Plt: £601.30 to a £1 stake. Pool: £146,130.02 - 177.38 winning units. T/Qpdt: £258.30 to a £1 stake. Pool: £8,712.59 - 24.96 winning units. **Lee McKenzie**

3863 UTTOXETER (L-H)
Saturday, February 13
4118 Meeting Abandoned - waterlogged

3822 WARWICK (L-H)
Saturday, February 13

OFFICIAL GOING: Soft (heavy in places; chs 5.4, hdl 5.7)
Wind: light breeze Weather: grey and overcast; 4 degrees

4123 CAROLINE BERMINGHAM & CLAIRE GIBBS BIRTHDAY NOVICES' HURDLE (11 hdls) 2m 5f
1:00 (1:00) (Class 3) 4-Y-0+ **£6,498** (£1,908; £954; £477)

Form RPR

22 **1** **Open Eagle (IRE)**[28] 3623 7-11-10 138.................... PaulTownend 140+
(W P Mullins, Ire) *wore ear plugs: pressed ldr gng strly in slowly run r: led on bit nring 2 out: 3 l clr whn hit last: v easily* **4/7**[1]

1 **2** *3 ¾* **Mystical Knight**[44] 3388 7-11-4 0.................... MarkWalsh 123+
(Rebecca Curtis) *settled handy in 3rd: effrt bef 2 out: sn chsng wnr: wl hld fr last* **6/4**[2]

2-4 **3** *10* **Kilcullen Flem (IRE)**[141] 1648 6-11-4 0.................... LeightonAspell 116
(Rebecca Curtis) *nt a fluent: led at slow pce: mstke out: rdn and hdd nring 2 out: wknd last* **25/1**[3]

/4-6 **4** *99* **Just Like Beth**[45] 3366 8-10-11 0.................... AndrewThornton 7
(Giuseppe Fierro) *sn detached: toiling 5th: stl appr 2 out as wnr fin* **200/1**

5m 33.7s (12.70) **Going Correction** +0.60s/f (Soft) **4** Ran SP% **108.0**
Speed ratings (Par 107): **99,97,93,56**
CSF £1.80 TOTE £1.40; EX 1.50 Trifecta £1.70.
Owner Supreme Horse Racing Club/Colin Gray **Bred** F Bayrou **Trained** Muine Beag, Co Carlow

FOCUS
All starts have been moved at this track following remeasuring, so there will be no speed figures here until there is sufficient data to calculate updated median times. Hurdle races run on the inner hurdles course. Rail movements added 6yds to the advertised race distance. This was steadily run before becoming a dash from the home turn. Winning rider Paul Townend reported the ground to be riding "a little dead, while Leighton Aspell called it "soft." The second has been rated to his bumper mark, with the third similar to his Worcester run.

4124 7BETS4FREE.COM NOVICES' CHASE (20 fncs) 3m 1f 100y
1:30 (1:30) (Class 3) 5-Y-0+ **£10,077** (£3,465)

Form RPR

P-15 **1** **Vivaldi Collonges (FR)**[28] 3624 7-11-10 139....................(t) SeanBowen 157+
(Paul Nicholls) *travelled wl: led tl 7th: disp fr 9th tl led 16th: great jump to go clr 3 out: 20 l ahd next: eased last* **3/1**[3]

-3U2 **2** *62* **Dawson City**[23] 3707 7-11-0 129.................... AndrewThornton 117
(Polly Gundry) *j. slowly 4th: cl 2nd tl led 7th tl 9th: sn pushed along: w wnr tl rdn and outpcd 16th: wl bhd after next: eased last* **13/8**[2]

/051 **P** **Racing Pulse (IRE)**[35] 3520 7-11-6 139.................... LeightonAspell
(Rebecca Curtis) *lft 2nd 4th tl 6th: pushed along and nt gng wl in last after 10th: mstke 13th and sn rdn and struggling: lost tch and mstke 15th: t.o whn climbed next and p.u* **5/4**[1]

7m 0.7s (1.70) **Going Correction** +0.325s/f (Yiel) **3** Ran SP% **107.5**
Speed ratings: **110,90,**
CSF £7.63 TOTE £3.00; EX 5.70 Trifecta £6.80.
Owner The Gi Gi Syndicate **Bred** G A E C Delorme Freres **Trained** Ditcheat, Somerset

FOCUS
Rail movements added 82yds to the advertised race distance. Godsmejudge won this event on the way to his Scottish National victory in 2013, and the following year's winner Midnight Prayer added the National Hunt Chase. With the favourite not running his race, this was somewhat uncompetitive. The easy winner has been rated back to the level he promised by his Kelso reappearance win.

4125 OLBG.COM MARES' HURDLE (LISTED RACE) (11 hdls) 2m 5f
2:05 (2:05) (Class 1) 4-Y-0+
£13,098 (£4,915; £2,461; £1,225; £616; £308)

Form RPR

1416 **1** **Flute Bowl**[42] 3444 6-11-0 132....................(p) JamieMoore 139
(Gary Moore) *pressed ldr: nt fluent 3 out: hrd drvn bef next: chal and lft in ld last: styd on gamely* **8/1**[3]

4112 **2** *1 ¼* **Jessber's Dream (IRE)**[45] 3372 6-11-0 135....................(t) NoelFehily 140+
(Harry Fry) *led: rdn bef 2 out where 2 l ahd: wavering sltly and almost jnd whn hit last and stmbld: sn hdd and a hld after* **13/8**[1]

4-52 **3** *1 ¾* **Jennies Jewel (IRE)**[21] 3732 9-11-0 138.................... IanMcCarthy 137+
(Jarlath P Fahey, Ire) *settled trcking ldrs: 5 l 3rd at 8th: mstke next: sn rdn: no imp fr 2 out tl styd on stoutly fnl 100yds* **11/4**[2]

1020 **4** *7* **Petite Parisienne (FR)**[42] 3444 5-11-5 144....................[1] PaulTownend 133
(W P Mullins, Ire) *trckd ldrs: rdn 8th: fnd little after next and continued in wl-hld 4th* **11/4**[2]

-1PP **5** *12* **Grape Tree Flame**[46] 3336 8-11-0 131.................... SeanBowen 117
(Peter Bowen) *nt a fluent: in last pair fr 5th: lost tch 7th: almost t.o 3 out but mod late prog to go 5th cl home: finshed lame bhd* **16/1**

-P6F **6** *½* **Bobs Lady Tamure**[42] 3440 9-11-0 124....................(t) DaraghBourke 115
(Maurice Barnes) *hld up in last pair tl effrt 8th: wnt 3rd briefly after 3 out: rdn and sn wknd* **33/1**

5m 28.4s (7.40) **Going Correction** +0.60s/f (Soft) **6** Ran SP% **111.4**
Speed ratings (Par 111): **109,108,107,105,100 100**
CSF £21.82 TOTE £11.20: £2.70, £1.40; EX 25.30 Trifecta £48.40.
Owner C E Stedman **Bred** C E Stedman **Trained** Lower Beeding, W Sussex

FOCUS
Rail movements added 6yds to the advertised race distance. This Listed event was run in a time 5.3secs quicker than the opening novice hurdle. A small pb from the winner, and a bigger one from the unlucky runner-up.

4126 7BETS4FREE.COM KINGMAKER NOVICES' CHASE (GRADE 2) (12 fncs) 2m
2:40 (2:40) (Class 1) 5-Y-0+ **£22,780** (£8,548; £4,280)

Form RPR

1211 **1** **Violet Dancer**[46] 3351 6-11-4 143....................(p) JamieMoore 157+
(Gary Moore) *mde all: racd enthusiastically and j. w great gusto: 4 l clr 3 out: sn rdn: in command after next and r.o strly* **8/1**[3]

4-11 **2** *11* **L'Ami Serge (IRE)**[28] 3627 6-11-4 0.................... DarylJacob 149+
(Nicky Henderson) *nt fluent 6th: wnt 2nd at next: slow 8th: rdn after 3 out: sn fnd v little: btn between last 2: 7 l 2nd whn landed v awkwardly last* **1/5**[1]

1123 **3** *9* **Fox Norton (FR)**[14] 3856 6-11-4 148.................... NoelFehily 138
(Neil Mulholland) *2nd tl last fr 7th: 15 l adrift and struggling 3 out* **13/2**[2]

4m 10.3s (0.30) **Going Correction** +0.325s/f (Yiel) **3** Ran SP% **107.8**
Speed ratings: **112,106,102**
CSF £10.99 TOTE £6.90; EX 9.70 Trifecta £5.20.
Owner D Bessell & Galloping On The South Downs **Bred** Jeremy Hinds **Trained** Lower Beeding, W Sussex

FOCUS
Rail movements added 41yds to the advertised race distance. A disappointing turnout, and with the favourite below-par the form might not prove all that robust. Douvan's grip on the Racing Post Arkle looks even tighter now. The winner is on the upgrade and will be worth his place in the Arkle, although this is still 7lb+ off what would be required in an average year.

4127 GUY SALMON LAND ROVER H'CAP HURDLE (12 hdls) 3m 2f
3:15 (3:16) (Class 4) (0-120,120) 4-Y-0+ **£4,548** (£1,335; £667; £333)

Form RPR

0131 **1** **Extreme Impact**[26] 3662 10-11-4 **112**....................(v) KielanWoods 117
(Graeme McPherson) *cajoled along early: 2nd or 3rd tl led briefly after 7th: sn drvn: outpcd u.str driving after 3 out: 6 l 5th 2 out: stl 5 l 5th at last: fnlly responded w a late spurt to get up 50yds out* **5/1**[3]

-F03 **2** *nk* **Saint John Henry (FR)**[61] 3078 6-11-9 **120**....................(b[1]) KieronEdgar(3) 126
(David Pipe) *nt a fluent: 2nd or 3rd tl led 8th: only one on bridle bef 2 out and nt fluent: 2 l ahd and stl hld together last: sn rdn: outbattled and ct cl home* **3/1**[1]

U-PP **3** *1 ¼* **Letbeso (IRE)**[23] 3707 8-11-5 **113**....................(tp) SeanBowen 118
(Peter Bowen) *settled trcking ldrs: effrt after 3 out: rdn to go 2nd after next: kpt on same pce fr last* **7/1**

31P1 **4** *1* **West Of The Edge (IRE)**[12] 3904 8-10-10 **107**..........(p) JamesBanks(3) 110
(Dai Williams) *trckd ldrs: wnt cl 2nd at 9th: drvn next: remained w ev ch tl 3rd and nt qckn bef last* **4/1**[2]

1333 **5** 1 1/4 **American Life (FR)**[12] 3904 9-10-13 **112**..................(vt) CharlieDeutsch(5) 114
(Sophie Leech) *hld up in rr: effrt after 3 out: tried to chal on inner bef next: no imp bef last* **8/1**

P1P6 **6** 45 **Earcomesthedream (IRE)**[16] 3824 13-10-7 **104**.........(b) TomBellamy(3) 60
(Peter Pritchard) *hrd drvn 2nd: last fr next: sn lost tch: t.o after 6th: plugged rnd u.str riding* **28/1**

0322 **P** **Bar A Mine (FR)**[10] 3921 7-10-9 **108**..................(v) JamieBargary(5)
(Nigel Twiston-Davies) *led: nt fluent 4th: mstke next: hdd briefly after 7th and again next where mstke: dropped out rapidly: t.o and eased 3 out: p.u next* **13/2**

1P-2 **P** **Golden Milan (IRE)**[64] 3010 8-11-12 **120**........................ LeightonAspell
(Rebecca Curtis) *handy tl rdn 7th: rdn and dropped out v tamely and sn t.o: p.u next* **8/1**

6m 55.6s (18.60) **Going Correction** +0.60s/f (Soft) **8** Ran SP% **113.2**
Speed ratings (Par 105): **95,94,94,94,93 79, ,**
CSF £20.43 CT £103.41 TOTE £4.80: £1.40, £1.90, £2.80; EX 17.00 Trifecta £608.00.
Owner Extreme Racing Fans **Bred** Juddmonte Farms Ltd **Trained** Upper Oddington, Gloucs

FOCUS
Rail movements added 13yds to the advertised race distance. Something of a bunch finish, but the form seems sound enough. The fourth and fifth are probably the best guide to the level.

4128 7BETS4FREE.COM WARWICK CASTLE H'CAP CHASE (17 fncs) 2m 4f
3:50 (3:51) (Class 2) 5-Y-O+
£18,768 (£5,544; £2,772; £1,386; £693; £348)

Form RPR

P40- **1** **Taquin Du Seuil (FR)**[338] 4718 9-11-12 **152**........................ LeightonAspell 160+
(Jonjo O'Neill) *settled towards rr: effrt in cl 5th 3 out: surged into ld bef next and sn 5 l clr: in command after: j.rt last: pushed out* **5/1**[3]

10-P **2** 3 3/4 **Niceonefrankie**[78] 2761 10-11-0 **145**........................ CharlieDeutsch(5) 145
(Venetia Williams) *2nd or 3rd tl jnd ldr 12th: led 14th: rdn and hdd and j.rt 2 out: sn outpcd by wnr: kpt trying flat* **8/1**

F-4P **3** 5 **Cogry**[35] 3518 7-10-6 **137**..................................(v[1]) JamieBargary(5) 136
(Nigel Twiston-Davies) *blnd 2nd: cl up: 3rd and u.p after 3 out: btn whn sltly impeded next: plugged on same pce* **7/2**[1]

-422 **4** 17 **Galway Jack (IRE)**[19] 3776 11-10-10 **136**.................... AndrewThornton 114
(Caroline Bailey) *led: jnd 12th: rdn and hdd 14th: lost pl qckly after next* **11/2**

454- **5** nk **Band Of Blood (IRE)**[239] 789 8-10-9 **135**........................(t) WillKennedy 114
(Dr Richard Newland) *towards rr: nt fluent 10th: sn rdn and nt gng wl enough after: struggling whn mstke 13th* **4/1**[2]

12/0 **6** 8 **Marcilhac (FR)**[56] 3148 7-10-6 **132**........................ LiamTreadwell 104
(Venetia Williams) *cl up tl rdn and lost pl 3 out: sn wl bhd* **4/1**[2]

1P0- **P** **Headly's Bridge (IRE)**[350] 4496 10-9-13 **130**................ DavidNoonan(5)
(Simon Earle) *j. deliberately early: a last: t.o 14th: p.u 3 out* **12/1**

5m 18.4s (0.40) **Going Correction** +0.325s/f (Yiel) **7** Ran SP% **113.1**
Speed ratings: **112,110,108,101,101 98,**
CSF £40.87 TOTE £3.80: £2.50, £5.60; EX 38.00 Trifecta £88.10.
Owner Martin Broughton & Friends 1 **Bred** Marc Boudot **Trained** Cheltenham, Gloucs

FOCUS
Rail movements added 56yds to the advertised race distance. A good handicap chase, and the form should work out.

4129 WHITSON BLOODSTOCK LTD H'CAP HURDLE (8 hdls) 2m
4:25 (4:25) (Class 4) (0-120,119) 4-Y-O+ **£3,898** (£1,144; £572; £286)

Form RPR

5-31 **1** **Clyne**[61] 3080 6-11-12 **119**........................ LeightonAspell 134+
(Evan Williams) *settled cl up: pushed along briefly 5th: effrt 3 out: led on outside and wnt lft bef 2 out: clr bef last: eased flat* **4/1**[2]

3144 **2** 11 **Catchin Time (IRE)**[18] 3784 8-10-8 **104**..................(t) KieronEdgar(3) 107
(Laura Hurley) *hld up in rr: effrt after 5th: wnt 2nd bef 2 out: sn rdn: one pce and no imp fr bef last* **25/1**

1125 **3** 2 1/2 **Hollywood All Star (IRE)**[19] 3777 7-10-13 **113**.......... ArchieBellamy(7) 113
(Graeme McPherson) *cl up: led 5th: rdn and hdd bef 2 out: 6 l 3rd and btn whn blnd last* **12/1**

6221 **4** 3/4 **Norse Light**[18] 3784 5-10-4 **104**..................(p) GarethMalone(7) 102
(David Dennis) *midfield: effrt 5th: 4th and rdn and racing v awkwardly bef 2 out: rdr lost whip: nt run on and sn btn: hit last and hung bdly rt flat* **8/1**

4202 **5** 10 **Akula (IRE)**[18] 3784 9-11-2 **109**........................ DarylJacob 96
(Barry Leavy) *a abt same pl: rdn and struggling after 3 out* **18/1**

06 **6** 11 **Wells De Lune (FR)**[56] 3152 5-11-7 **117**.................... GrahamWatters(3) 93
(Charlie Longsdon) *t.k.h in rr: brief effrt bef 3 out: nt hrd pushed whn btn bef next* **11/1**

F114 **7** 7 **Dormouse**[35] 3529 11-11-12 **119**..................(p) IanPopham 88
(Anabel K Murphy) *last and pushed along 3rd: nvr travelling in grnd: t.o 3 out* **20/1**

1303 **8** 2 1/2 **Back By Midnight**[28] 3619 7-10-11 **107**..................(t) JamesBanks(3) 73
(Emma Baker) *tended to errors: led tl 5th: rdn and dropped out qckly next: t.o* **10/1**

-064 **9** 25 **Beau Lake (IRE)**[49] 3216 12-11-1 **111**..................(p) HarryBannister(3) 52
(Suzy Smith) *midfield: struggling bef 3 out: t.o* **14/1**

/F-5 **P** **Fatcatinthehat**[56] 3152 7-11-12 **119**........................ NicodeBoinville
(Harry Whittington) *pressed ldr tl bef 4th: fdd qckly: t.o and p.u 2 out* **11/4**[1]

2-P5 **P** **Rude And Crude (IRE)**[38] 3487 7-11-6 **113**.................... TomCannon
(Chris Gordon) *hit 1st: prom tl mstke 4th: sn lost pl: t.o and p.u 2 out* **11/2**[3]

4m 5.9s (6.90) **Going Correction** +0.60s/f (Soft) **11** Ran SP% **118.8**
Speed ratings (Par 105): **106,100,99,98,93 88,84,83,71,**
CSF £93.78 CT £1117.96 TOTE £3.60: £1.20, £8.20, £3.80; EX 125.30 Trifecta £782.10.
Owner David M Williams **Bred** The Kathryn Stud **Trained** Llancarfan, Vale Of Glamorgan

FOCUS
Rail movements added 6yds to the advertised race distance. A fair handicap hurdle run in gloomy conditions as the rain came down. A big step up from the easy winner, with the second, third and fourth helping to set the level.

T/Jkpt: Not won. T/Plt: £909.90 to a £1 stake. Pool: £62,935.32 - 50.49 winning units. T/Qpdt: £146.60 to a £1 stake. Pool: £3,942.58 - 19.90 winning units. **Iain Mackenzie**

4130 - (Foreign Racing) - See Raceform Interactive

3711 GOWRAN PARK (R-H)
Saturday, February 13

OFFICIAL GOING: Heavy

4131a RED MILLS CHASE (GRADE 2) (14 fncs) 2m 4f
2:15 (2:15) 5-Y-O+ **£19,522** (£6,286; £2,977; £1,323)

RPR

1 **Smashing (FR)**[16] 3830 7-11-6 **147**........................ DavyRussell 164+
(Henry De Bromhead, Ire) *mde all: jnd briefly 4 out: stl travelling wl bef 3 out where j. sltly rt: in command fr after next and styd on wl: nt extended: easily* **9/10**[1]

2 11 **Morning Assembly (IRE)**[14] 3871 9-11-3 **149**........................ BJCooper 147+
(P A Fahy, Ire) *settled bhd ldr: slt mstke in 3rd at 3rd: niggled along and tk clsr order in 2nd appr st: rdn in 2nd after 3 out and no imp on wnr fr 2 out where nt fluent: kpt on one pce* **4/1**[3]

3 4 **Ballycasey (IRE)**[23] 3715 9-11-3 **149**........................ RWalsh 143
(W P Mullins, Ire) *settled bhd ldr: tk clsr order after 7th and disp briefly 4 out where j.big: niggled along bef st where dropped to 3rd: sn rdn and no imp on wnr u.p bef 2 out: kpt on one pce* **15/8**[2]

4 70 **Glenwood For Ever (IRE)**[16] 3820 8-11-3 **91**..................(t) BMCash 73
(Paul John Gilligan, Ire) *in rr thrght: trailing fr 2nd and t.o bef 1/2-way: j. sltly rt at times: nvr a factor* **250/1**

5m 35.5s (24.20) **4** Ran SP% **107.8**
CSF £4.80 TOTE £1.60; DF 3.80 Trifecta £5.00.
Owner Ann & Alan Potts Partnership **Bred** Jacques Seror **Trained** Knockeen, Co Waterford

FOCUS
A really impressive performance from the winner, showing what a serious operator he is on testing ground. The second, third and fourth have been rated close to their recent form.

4132 - (Foreign Racing) - See Raceform Interactive

4133a RED MILLS TRIAL HURDLE (GRADE 2) (9 hdls) 2m
3:25 (3:25) 4-Y-O+ **£19,522** (£6,286; £2,977; £1,323)

RPR

1 **Sempre Medici (FR)**[28] 3634 6-11-10 **156**........................ RWalsh 158+
(W P Mullins, Ire) *chsd ldrs: 3rd 1/2-way: tk clsr order almost on terms between horses gng wl into st: sn rdn in 2nd after 2 out and impr to dispute bef last: led u.p run-in and sn in command: kpt on wl* **2/7**[1]

2 7 **Bentelimar (IRE)**[27] 3650 7-11-4 **141**........................ BrianO'Connell 148
(J R Barry, Ire) *w.w: last at 1/2-way: wnt 4th after 4 out: tk clsr order gng wl next where nt fluent: wnt 2nd into st and disp bef 2 out where lft in front: jnd u.p bef last and hdd run-in: sn no ex and eased* **5/1**[2]

3 34 **Rory O'Moore (IRE)**[30] 3602 11-11-4 **127**........................ MrJWO'Neill 111
(Ronald O'Neill, Ire) *trckd ldr tl sn led: narrow advantage at 1/2-way: hdd bef 4 out: wknd into 4th after 3 out: lft mod 3rd next where nt fluent* **50/1**

4 12 **King Of The Picts (IRE)**[20] 3768 7-11-4 **134**........................ LPDempsey 99
(John Patrick Shanahan, Ire) *chsd ldrs: nt fluent 1st: 4th 1/2-way: pushed along after 4 out and no ex u.p in rr bef next: wknd and lft remote 4th 2 out* **50/1**

F **Sizing Tennessee (IRE)**[21] 3751 8-11-4 **140**........................ DavyRussell 133
(Henry De Bromhead, Ire) *led narrowly tl sn hdd: cl 2nd at 1/2-way: led bef 4 out: niggled along and jnd 2 out where fell* **6/1**[3]

4m 25.7s (24.80) **5** Ran SP% **112.6**
CSF £2.52 TOTE £1.30: £1.02, £1.60; DF 1.90 Trifecta £14.80.
Owner Mrs S Ricci **Bred** Mlle M Bollack, N Forgeard Et Al **Trained** Muine Beag, Co Carlow

FOCUS
An interesting enough race, the winner doing it well enough in the end after making hard work of it initially. The first two have been rated to their best.

4134 - 4136a (Foreign Racing) - See Raceform Interactive

3410 EXETER (R-H)
Sunday, February 14

OFFICIAL GOING: Heavy
Wind: mild breeze across Weather: cloudy

4137 BATHWICK TYRES BARNSTAPLE "NATIONAL HUNT" NOVICES' HURDLE (8 hdls 2 omitted) 2m 2f 111y
2:10 (2:10) (Class 4) 4-Y-O+ **£3,249** (£954; £477; £238)

Form RPR

F **1** **Overtown Express (IRE)**[88] 2581 8-11-4 0........................ NoelFehily 131+
(Harry Fry) *patiently rdn: mid-div: nt fluent 5th: hdwy after 6th: chalng whn hit last: w.w bhd front pair: swtchd lft and pushed into ld fnl 175yds: drew clr: easily* **6/1**[3]

12 **2** 10 **Rolling Dylan (IRE)**[32] 3581 5-11-4 0........................ RichardJohnson 121+
(Philip Hobbs) *led 2nd: j. bdly lft fr next: rdn between last 2: hdd fnl 175yds: no ex* **8/11**[1]

4205 **3** 11 **Sartorial Elegance**[22] 3743 5-11-4 0..................(b) TomScudamore 109
(Colin Tizzard) *trckd ldrs: chal appr 2 out: rdn and ev ch last (usual 2 out): no ex* **20/1**

3P **4** 10 **Ambion Lane (IRE)**[11] 3920 6-11-4 0..................(p) IanPopham 97
(Victor Dartnall) *trckd ldrs: rdn after 6th: sn hld: plugged on to regain 4th run-in* **66/1**

5-06 **5** 7 **Bound Hill**[24] 3710 7-10-11 0........................ MrMLegg(7) 90
(Fiona Shaw) *mid-div: rdn after 6th: nvr threatened ldrs* **33/1**

3433 **6** 4 **Western Sunrise (IRE)**[78] 2770 7-10-11 0........................ AlainCawley 81
(Johnny Farrelly) *led tl 2nd: chsd ldr: rdn appr 2 out: hld in 4th between last 2: wknd run-in* **20/1**

0 **7** 44 **Day Of Roses (IRE)**[20] 3775 7-11-4 0........................ NickScholfield 42
(Jeremy Scott) *chsd ldrs: drifted lft 3rd: wknd after next: sn bhd: t.o* **33/1**

U6- **P** **Doris De Silver**[311] 5248 7-10-11 0........................[1] JamesBest
(Jackie Du Plessis) *a in rr: t.o whn p.u bef 2 out (usual 3 out)* **100/1**

00 **P** **Tactical Manoeuvre (IRE)**[20] 3773 5-11-4 0........................ RhysFlint
(Alexandra Dunn) *towards rr: pushed along in midfield 4th: wknd 2 out (usual 3 out): p.u bef last* **200/1**

P **Brelan D'As (FR)**[114] 5-11-11 0........................[1] BarryGeraghty
(Paul Nicholls) *racd keenly: mid-div: hmpd 3rd: sme hdwy next: wknd after 6th: p.u bef next* **15/8**[2]

006 **P** **Mr Medic**[32] 3581 5-11-4 0........................ TomCannon
(Robert Walford) *mid-div tl 4th: sn wknd: t.o whn p.u bef 2 out (usual 3 out)* **50/1**

P **Dunnicks Boris** 7-11-1 0........................ LucyGardner(3)
(Sue Gardner) *a in rr: t.o whn p.u after 6th* **200/1**

P **Inspiring (IRE)** 5-10-11 0............................ LiamHeard
(Johnny Farrelly) *bhd fr 3rd: tailing off whn p.u bef 6th* 66/1
5m 29.0s (46.30) **Going Correction** +2.80s/f (Heav) 13 Ran SP% 129.3
Speed ratings (Par 105): **114,109,105,100,98 96,77,, , , ,**
CSF £11.73 TOTE £9.10: £1.80, £1.10, £3.30; EX 21.20 Trifecta £174.10.
Owner Mrs Lorna Squire & Richard Metherell **Bred** Jimter Stud **Trained** Seaborough, Dorset

FOCUS
All races were run on the chase bends. The last two fences in the back back straight and last fence in the home straight and the last hurdle were omitted. This wasn't a bad novice hurdle. It was run over a distance 90yds further than advertised.

4138 BATHWICK TYRES NOVICES' HURDLE (LISTED RACE) (6 hdls 2 omitted) 2m 175y
2:40 (2:40) (Class 1) 4-Y-0+ **£11,524** (£4,408; £2,274; £1,200)

Form RPR
U2 1 **Politologue (FR)**[47] 3350 5-11-11 142.................... SamTwiston-Davies 141+
(Paul Nicholls) *prom: led 3rd: in command whn lft wl clr 2 out (usual 3 out): v easily* 2/9[1]
505 2 59 **Trans Express (IRE)**[24] 3710 6-11-3 0............................ LucyGardner 68
(Sue Gardner) *led: wnt lft 1st: hdd 3rd: sn lost tch w front pair: lft remote 2nd 2 out (usual 3 out)* 10/1[3]
0P20 3 16 **Petite Fantasie**[19] 3789 7-10-10 75....................(t) CharlieDeutsch 41
(Mark Gillard) *struggling in detached last at the 1st: nvr on terms: lft remote 4th 2 out (usual 3 out): t.o* 50/1
00 4 13 **Beau Knight**[22] 3745 4-10-7 0............................ ConorO'Farrell 30
(Alexandra Dunn) *chsd ldrs: mstke 1st: sn struggling in detached 4th: lft poor 3rd 2 out (usual 3 out): t.o* 33/1
110- F **Ghost River**[340] 4708 6-11-3 0............................ SeanBowen 123
(Peter Bowen) *trckd ldrs: upsides wnr fr 3rd: tiring in hld 2nd whn knuckled on landing and fell 2 out* 7/2[2]
4m 58.2s (42.70) **Going Correction** +2.80s/f (Heav)
WFA 4 from 5yo+ 9lb 5 Ran SP% 118.0
Speed ratings (Par 111): **111,83,75,69,**
CSF £4.48 TOTE £1.20: £1.02, £4.10; EX 4.40 Trifecta £22.50.
Owner J Hales **Bred** Mme Henri Devin **Trained** Ditcheat, Somerset

FOCUS
Race distance increased by 90yds. This Listed event has been won by some top notchers in the past. It was uncompetitive this season, but the winner is a smart prospect.

4139 PERTEMPS NETWORK H'CAP HURDLE (SERIES QUALIFIER) (10 hdls 2 omitted) 2m 7f 25y
3:10 (3:11) (Class 2) 5-Y-0+ **£11,616** (£3,461; £1,752; £897; £470)

Form RPR
111 1 **Unowhatimeanharry**[64] 3032 8-11-10 138........................(t) NoelFehily 145+
(Harry Fry) *hld up: stdy prog after 8th to chal 2 out: sn led: styd on wl fr last: rdn out* 7/2[2]
-035 2 4 1/2 **West Approach**[44] 3403 6-10-11 125............................ RichardJohnson 125
(Colin Tizzard) *in tch: hdwy to ld 5th: wnt lft and nt fluent 2 out (usual 3 out): sn rdn and hdd: styd on but a being hld by wnr fr last* 6/1
-1UU 3 12 **Padge (IRE)**[20] 3774 7-11-10 138............................ LeightonAspell 128
(Evan Williams) *mid-div: hdwy 8th: chalng whn awkward 2 out: sn rdn: styd on same pce* 20/1
3-51 4 7 **Salmanazar**[23] 3728 8-11-5 133............................ DenisO'Regan 115
(Alan King) *trckd ldrs: rdn after 8th: styd on same pce fr next* 8/1
1F42 5 13 **Goodbye Dancer (FR)**[22] 3737 5-10-11 130............... JamieBargary[(5)] 101
(Nigel Twiston-Davies) *mid-div: rdn after 8th: nvr threatened ldrs: wknd bef last* 12/1
034F P **The Tourard Man (IRE)**[16] 3838 10-11-7 138............... TomBellamy[(3)]
(Alan King) *hld up: drvn in 6th after 8th: sn wknd: p.u bef next* 28/1
1350 P **Dell' Arca (IRE)**[36] 3527 7-11-11 139........................(p) TomScudamore
(David Pipe) *a in r: j. sltly lft: t.o whn p.u bef 2 out (usual 3 out)* 20/1
-124 P **The Eaglehaslanded (IRE)**[65] 3018 6-10-11 125(tp)
SamTwiston-Davies
(Paul Nicholls) *chsd ldrs: mstke 7th: nt fluent next: sn drvn: wknd after next: p.u bef last* 11/2[3]
P216 P **Lady Of Longstone (IRE)**[71] 2911 6-10-4 125............... MichaelHeard[(7)]
(David Pipe) *led tl 5th: sn pushed along to press ldr: rdn after 8th: wknd appr 2 out (usual 3 out): p.u bef last* 33/1
14-3 P **Scoop The Pot (IRE)**[91] 2513 6-10-10 124..................(t) BarryGeraghty
(Philip Hobbs) *in tch: hit 2nd: rdn and wknd after 8th: tailing off whn p.u bef next* 13/8[1]
7m 0.4s (61.40) **Going Correction** +2.80s/f (Heav) 10 Ran SP% 124.7
Speed ratings: **105,103,99,96,92 , , , ,**
CSF £25.51 CT £383.86 TOTE £4.60: £1.60, £2.20, £5.50; EX 31.90 Trifecta £413.40.
Owner Harry Fry Racing Club **Bred** R J Smith **Trained** Seaborough, Dorset

FOCUS
Race distance increased by 135yds. A good-quality staying handicap, run at a fair enough gallop, and it proved a war of attrition in the home straight. The first five qualify for a run in the final of this series next month.

4140 BATHWICK TYRES VETERANS' H'CAP CHASE (QUALIFIER) (LEG 1 OF THE 2016 VETERANS' CHASE SERIES) (12 fncs 6 omitted) 3m 54y
3:40 (3:40) (Class 2) (0-150,139) 10-Y-0+ **£29,511**

Form RPR
0-42 1 **Midnight Prayer**[29] 3624 11-11-12 139............................ RichardJohnson 143
(Alan King) *trckd ldrs: wnt 2nd at the 5th: rdn on long run after 9th: looked hld in 2nd whn lft wl clr 3 out (usual 4 out): fin alone and v tired* 1/1[1]
2US5 P **Shangani (USA)**[36] 3528 10-11-2 129........................(p) AidanColeman
(Venetia Williams) *trckd ldr tl lost pl rapidly 5th: t.o whn p.u bef 8th* 7/1
1241 F **Golden Chieftain (IRE)**[24] 3707 11-11-8 135..............(bt) BrendanPowell 149
(Colin Tizzard) *led: looked in command whn fell 3 out (usual 4 out)* 5/1[2]
P0-0 P **Victors Serenade (IRE)**[71] 2907 11-10-13 131..............(t) DavidNoonan[(5)]
(Anthony Honeyball) *hld up in tch: blnd 3rd: mstke 7th: sn lost tch u.p: p.u next* 10/1
26-0 P **Howard's Legacy (IRE)**[74] 2853 10-10-13 126..............(p) LiamTreadwell
(Venetia Williams) *trckd ldrs: struggling after 7th: wknd 9th: sn p.u* 8/1
2656 U **Shotavodka (IRE)**[22] 3737 10-11-3 130...................(b) TomScudamore
(David Pipe) *hld up in tch: wnt 3rd after 7th: wknd on long run after 9th: lft remote 2nd whn blnd bdly and uns rdr 3 out (usual 4 out)* 11/2[3]
7m 25.5s (76.20) **Going Correction** +2.675s/f (Heav) 6 Ran SP% 114.8
Speed ratings: **80, , , ,**
TOTE £1.90: £2.00; EX 1.50 Trifecta £1.80.
Owner The Legends Partnership **Bred** J P L Reynolds **Trained** Barbury Castle, Wilts

FOCUS
Race distance increased by 10yds. This veterans' chase proved highly eventful as only the winner completed.

4141 BATHWICK TYRES BRIDGWATER GRADUATION CHASE (10 fncs 8 omitted) 3m 54y
4:10 (4:10) (Class 2) 5-Y-0+ **£12,820** (£4,004; £2,156)

Form RPR
P-2P 1 **Chase The Spud**[36] 3518 8-11-5 130............................ PaddyBrennan 141
(Fergal O'Brien) *prom: led 5th: mde rest: rdn between last 2: styd on gamely fr last (usual 2 out): rdn out* 11/1[3]
2433 2 7 **Fingal Bay (IRE)**[22] 3741 10-11-5 141............................ RichardJohnson 134
(Philip Hobbs) *j.lft at times: led tl 5th: trckd wnr: rdn and flattered briefly sn after last (usual 2 out): sn no ex* 11/10[1]
-2PP 3 4 1/2 **Masters Hill (IRE)**[36] 3518 10-11-8 141........................(p) AidanColeman 133
(Colin Tizzard) *trckd ldrs: rdn bef omitted 4 out: nvr quite threatened: styd on same pce fr last (usual 2 out)* 11/4[2]
P602 P **Easter Day (FR)**[32] 3583 8-11-8 142........................(p) SamTwiston-Davies
(Paul Nicholls) *trckd ldrs: rdn appr omitted 4 out: wknd qckly and p.u bef 2 out (usual 3 out)* 11/4[2]
7m 18.6s (69.30) **Going Correction** +2.675s/f (Heav) 4 Ran SP% 109.3
Speed ratings: **91,88,87,**
CSF £24.49 TOTE £9.10; EX 26.50 Trifecta £34.70.
Owner Mrs C Banks **Bred** Mrs C J Banks **Trained** Naunton, Gloucs

FOCUS
Race distance increased by 10yds. A decent graduation chase despite the non-runners, but the form should be treated with some caution.

4142 BATHWICK TYRES BIDEFORD NOVICES' CHASE (9 fncs 6 omitted) 2m 3f 48y
4:40 (4:40) (Class 3) 5-Y-0+ **£6,498** (£1,908)

Form RPR
00P 1 **De Bene Esse (IRE)**[32] 3580 6-10-13 0............................ TomO'Brien 135
(Evan Williams) *mde all: kpt on wl: rdn out* 5/1[2]
3-22 2 5 **Southfield Vic (IRE)**[50] 3255 7-10-13 145...........(p) SamTwiston-Davies 133
(Paul Nicholls) *nvr fluent or travelling: chsd wnr: reminder after 5th: drvn between last 2: hit last: a being hld* 1/8[1]
5m 42.5s (45.20) **Going Correction** +2.675s/f (Heav) 2 Ran SP% 105.6
Speed ratings: **111,108**
TOTE £3.30.
Owner Mr & Mrs William Rucker **Bred** Ms Margaret Treacy **Trained** Llancarfan, Vale Of Glamorgan

FOCUS
Race distance increased by 10yds. A disappointing turn out and a right turn up.

4143 BATHWICK TYRES TAUNTON INTERMEDIATE OPEN NATIONAL HUNT FLAT RACE 2m 175y
5:10 (5:10) (Class 6) 4-6-Y-0 **£1,624** (£477; £238; £119)

Form RPR
1 1 **Westend Story (IRE)**[50] 3226 5-11-11 0............................ RichardJohnson 127+
(Philip Hobbs) *mde all: in command fr 2f out: comf* 8/15[1]
2 18 **Man From Mars** 4-10-3 0............................ LizzieKelly[(5)] 92
(Nick Williams) *trckd ldrs: pushed along 5f out: rdn to chse wnr over 2f out: styd on same pce fnl 2f* 7/1
1 3 hd **My Liege (IRE)**[50] 3258 5-11-11 0............................ LeightonAspell 109
(Evan Williams) *trckd ldrs: rdn to chse wnr over 2f out: styd on same pce fnl 2f* 5/1[3]
4 51 **Molineaux (IRE)** 5-11-4 0............................ TomScudamore 51
(Colin Tizzard) *trckd wnr: rdn over 2f out: sn wknd: t.o* 7/2[2]
5 21 **The Last Melon** 4-10-8 0............................ GavinSheehan 20
(James Bennett) *hld up bhd ldrs: lost tch over 4f out: t.o* 25/1
5m 2.4s (53.60) **Going Correction** +2.80s/f (Heav)
WFA 4 from 5yo+ 9lb 5 Ran SP% 120.5
Speed ratings: **85,76,76,52,42**
CSF £6.09 TOTE £1.60: £1.10, £2.30; EX 5.50 Trifecta £15.40.
Owner Mick Fitzgerald Racing Club **Bred** James F Barry **Trained** Withycombe, Somerset

FOCUS
Race distance increased by 90yds. The testing ground played its part in this modest bumper and there was an impressive winner.
T/Plt: £1,080.70 to a £1 stake. Pool: £66,697.26 - 45.05 winning tickets. T/Qpdt: £412.10 to a £1 stake. Pool: £4,845.57 - 8.70 winning tickets. **Tim Mitchell**

4144 - (Foreign Racing) - See Raceform Interactive

3750

NAVAN (L-H)
Sunday, February 14

OFFICIAL GOING: Heavy

4145a FLYINGBOLT NOVICE CHASE (GRADE 2) (12 fncs) 2m 1f
2:30 (2:30) 5-Y-0+ **£18,437** (£5,937)

RPR
1 **Sambremont (FR)**[44] 3433 6-11-4 137............................ RWalsh 132+
(W P Mullins, Ire) *settled bhd ldrs in 3rd: detached fr bef 5th: niggled along fr 5 out and tk clsr order bhd ldrs 3 out where mstke: lft 2nd 2 out and clsd u.p fr bef last to ld in clsng stages: kpt on wl* 4/1[3]
2 1 **Ttebbob (IRE)**[50] 3271 7-11-7 151............................ RobbiePower 136+
(Mrs John Harrington, Ire) *led narrowly tl jnd bef 3rd: regained advantage after 3 out: pressed fr 4 out: bmpd sltly 3 out: rdn and hdd bef next where lft in front: wknd fr bef last and rdn: no ex u.p clsng stages where hdd* 8/11[1]
F **Tell Us More (IRE)**[24] 3716 7-11-4 139............................ BJCooper 145+
(W P Mullins, Ire) *cl up in 2nd: j.lft thrght: disp bef 3rd tl settled in 2nd after 3rd: slt mstke 7th: tk clsr order 4 out: j.lft 3 out and bmpd rival: led travelling wl bef 2 out where j.lft and fell* 9/4[2]
4m 55.4s (22.10) 3 Ran SP% 108.7
CSF £7.52 TOTE £5.60; DF 7.90.
Owner Shanakiel Racing Syndicate **Bred** Richard Corveller **Trained** Muine Beag, Co Carlow

The Form Book Jumps 2015-16, Raceform Ltd, Newbury, RG14 5SJ

FOCUS
A disappointing renewal. Tell Us More would have scored emphatically had he not departed at the second-last. He traded at 1.08 on the exchanges. The winner traded at a high of 49-1 having looked booked for third for much of the journey. It's been rated around the faller to the best of his hurdling form.

4146a LADBROKES IRELAND BOYNE HURDLE (GRADE 2) (12 hdls) 2m 5f
3:00 (3:00) 5-Y-0+ **£19,522** (£6,286; £2,977)

RPR

1 **Snow Falcon (IRE)**[48] 3322 6-11-3 145 SeanFlanagan 150+
(Noel Meade, Ire) *w.w in rr of trio: disp 2nd for most fr 1/2-way: pressed ldr 3 out where slt mstke: n.m.r on inner bef 2 out where swtchd in 3rd: rdn into 2nd between last 2 gng best and led narrowly fr last: kpt on wl* **11/4**[3]

2 *2 ¾* **Lieutenant Colonel**[290] 49 7-11-10 150 (t) DavidMullins 152+
(Ms Sandra Hughes, Ire) *attempted to make all: j.big 4th: 3 l clr at 1/2-way: pressed clly 3 out: rdn after next and hdd narrowly fr last: kpt on wl run-in wout matching wnr in clsng stages* **5/2**[2]

3 *11* **Dedigout (IRE)**[314] 5221 10-11-8 157 (t) BJCooper 139+
(A J Martin, Ire) *settled bhd ldr in 2nd: disp 2nd for most fr 1/2-way: tk clsr order fr 3 out and wnt cl 2nd bef next: rdn and dropped to 3rd between last 2: sn no imp on ldrs and one pce run-in: eased in clsng stages* **10/11**[1]

5m 49.7s (33.70) **3 Ran SP% 107.6**
CSF £8.44 TOTE £4.10; DF 8.30 Trifecta £6.90.
Owner Mrs Patricia Hunt **Bred** Sean Gorman **Trained** Castletown, Co Meath
■ Stewards' Enquiry : David Mullins one-day ban: careless riding (tbn)
Sean Flanagan caution: careless riding

FOCUS
The absence of Val De Ferbet and in particular Prince Of Scars erased plenty of the intrigue from this. The odds-on favourite was having his first start since last April and got tired. The winner was value for more than the winning margin. The winner has been rated in line with his best, with the runner-up below his best on his return from a break.

4147a - (Foreign Racing) - See Raceform Interactive

4148a TEN UP NOVICE CHASE (GRADE 2) (17 fncs) 3m
4:00 (4:00) 5-Y-0+ **£18,437** (£5,937; £2,812; £1,250)

RPR

1 **Measureofmydreams (IRE)**[36] 3536 8-11-3 0 PaulTownend 151
(W P Mullins, Ire) *hld up in tch: impr on outer to dispute 3rd after 4 out: slt mstke next: wnt cl 2nd gng wl bef 2 out: rdn in 2nd and hld by ldr bef last where lft in front and clr: rdn out run-in* **12/1**

2 *5* **Noble Endeavor (IRE)**[50] 3259 7-11-3 140 (p) DavyRussell 146
(Gordon Elliott, Ire) *chsd ldrs: cl 5th after 4 out: cl 4th bef 2 out: sn rdn and no imp on ldrs u.p in 3rd bef last where lft 2nd: kpt on same pce: nt trble wnr* **6/1**[2]

3 *18* **Pleasant Company (IRE)**[45] 3389 8-11-3 0 DavidMullins 129
(W P Mullins, Ire) *led: jnd briefly fr 6th: hdd narrowly after 3 out: pushed along in 4th after 2 out and no imp: wknd and lft mod 3rd at last* **12/1**

4 *11* **Sub Lieutenant (IRE)**[29] 3635 7-11-3 142 (tp) BJCooper 122
(Ms Sandra Hughes, Ire) *settled bhd ldr in 2nd: slt mstke 10th: niggled along briefly fr 4 out and wknd fr next: lft remote 4th at last where slow* **9/1**[3]

F **Black Hercules (IRE)**[29] 3621 7-11-3 152 RWalsh 156+
(W P Mullins, Ire) *chsd ldrs: disp briefly fr 6th: led narrowly travelling wl after 3 out: in command and 1 l clr at last where fell* **4/11**[1]

P **Shantou Flyer (IRE)**[77] 2817 6-11-8 143 (t) MrBO'Neill
(Colin Bowe, Ire) *hld up in tch: slt mstke in rr at 6th: last at 1/2-way: detached fr 9th: j.big 3 out and wknd: j.lft next and t.o whn p.u bef last* **25/1**

6m 51.6s (22.30) **6 Ran SP% 116.8**
CSF £78.53 TOTE £15.60: £4.20, £2.50; DF 80.30 Trifecta £291.30.
Owner Gigginstown House Stud **Bred** Richard Keane **Trained** Muine Beag, Co Carlow

FOCUS
It was a pity that both Monksland and Wrath Of Titans were withdrawn as this looked a top-notch renewal with their presence. There was late drama as Black Hercules crashed out at the last having looked sure to score. The fourth-last fence was omitted due to ground conditions. A fair pb from the winner.

4149 - 4150a (Foreign Racing) - See Raceform Interactive

3967
CATTERICK (L-H)
Monday, February 15

OFFICIAL GOING: Soft (good to soft in places; chs 6.7, hdl 7.3)
Wind: fresh 1/2 against Weather: fine and sunny but very cool

4151 RACINGUK.COM MARES' NOVICES' HURDLE (12 hdls) 3m 1f 71y
2:10 (2:11) (Class 4) 5-Y-0+ **£3,249** (£954; £477; £238)

Form RPR

2131 1 **Yes I Did (IRE)**[6] 4044 6-11-7 125 BridgetAndrews(5) 129+
(Dan Skelton) *mde all: t.k.h: wnt clr between last 2: 8 l ahd last: sn eased: cruised home* **8/11**[1]

P22- 2 *9* **Kilas Girl (IRE)**[342] 4696 6-10-12 0 RichardJohnson 102
(John Quinn) *nt fluent: trckd ldrs: 3rd 3 out: mstke next: chsd wnr between last 2: no ch w wnr* **4/1**[2]

046 3 *5* **Nancy's Trix (IRE)**[61] 3110 7-10-7 0 JackSherwood(5) 95
(David Loder) *trckd ldng pair: drvn and outpcd appr 2 out: one pce and modest 3rd nr fin* **12/1**

P3 4 *¾* **Miss Gotaway**[33] 3580 7-10-12 0 (t) TomScudamore 96
(David Pipe) *chsd wnr: mstke 6th: drvn sn after 3 out: wknd appr last* **9/2**[3]

04FU 5 *88* **Latest Fashion (IRE)**[239] 803 10-10-9 64 (t) ColmMcCormack(3) 6
(Christopher Wilson) *chsd ldrs: drvn 7th: reminders and lost pl bef next: sn bhd: t.o 3 out: eased between last 2: virtually p.u: eventually completed* **250/1**

64 P **Ballybrowneybridge (IRE)**[40] 3485 6-10-12 0 AlainCawley
(Sam Thomas) *in rr: bhd fr 8th: blnd 3 out: sn t.o: p.u bef next* **22/1**

0PP P **Night In London (IRE)**[9] 3995 6-10-9 HarryChalloner(3)
(Keith Reveley) *racd in last: drvn after 7th: t.o 9th: p.u bef 2 out* **200/1**

6m 31.1s (3.50) **Going Correction** +0.30s/f (Yiel) **7 Ran SP% 109.0**
Speed ratings: **106,103,101,101,73 ,**
CSF £3.63 TOTE £1.50: £1.10, £4.40; EX 3.80 Trifecta £14.60.
Owner The Can't Say No Partnership **Bred** Mrs C J Power **Trained** Alcester, Warwicks

FOCUS
All distances as advertised. An ordinary mares' novice hurdle. The second, third and fourth have been rated pretty much to their marks

4152 DINE AND VIEW AT CATTERICK RACES H'CAP HURDLE (10 hdls) 2m 3f 66y
2:40 (2:40) (Class 4) (0-115,115) 4-Y-0+ **£3,249** (£954; £477; £238)

Form RPR

033P 1 **Sign Manual**[32] 3588 7-11-7 110 (b[1]) RichardJohnson 119+
(Donald McCain) *chsd ldng pair: 2nd 5th: led between last 2: drvn out* **8/1**

4536 2 *9* **Kuda Huraa (IRE)**[51] 3238 8-11-8 114 HarryBannister(3) 116
(Harriet Bethell) *in rr: pushed along 3rd: drvn 5th: chsng ldrs 7th: 2nd appr last: kpt on same pce* **12/1**

0-06 3 *11* **Jokers And Rogues (IRE)**[83] 2705 8-10-5 94 (t) HenryBrooke 85+
(Kenneth Slack) *led: clr 3rd: drvn appr 2 out: hdd between last 2: sn wknd* **9/4**[1]

54-P 4 *2* **Mr Snoozy**[24] 3724 7-11-4 107 (p) JakeGreenall 94
(Mark Walford) *chsd ldrs: lost pl 7th: kpt on fr 2 out: tk modest 4th last 75yds* **25/1**

0P50 5 *3* **Tekthelot (IRE)**[16] 3855 10-11-0 108 MrJohnDawson(5) 93
(Keith Reveley) *in rr-div: hdwy 6th: 3rd next: wknd appr 2 out* **13/2**

46U 6 *2 ½* **What A Game (IRE)**[30] 3626 5-10-9 98 BrianHughes 80
(Tim Easterby) *mid-div: lost pl 6th: sn bhd* **16/1**

6F23 7 *6* **Sailors Warn (IRE)**[24] 3725 9-11-7 115 (t) ThomasCheesman(5) 91
(Ronald Thompson) *chsd ldrs: lost pl 6th: sn bhd* **6/1**[3]

100 U **Royal Sea (IRE)**[17] 3835 7-10-8 107 LewisStones(10)
(Michael Mullineaux) *in rr: detached last whn bdly hmpd and uns rdr 6th* **66/1**

23 F **Air Glider (IRE)**[211] 1044 6-11-8 111 HarrySkelton
(Dan Skelton) *in rr: bhd fr 7th: t.o 2 out: fell last* **11/2**[2]

544F F **Benny's Secret (IRE)**[48] 3346 6-11-2 105 LucyAlexander
(N W Alexander) *in rr: hdwy 5th: handy 4th whn fell next* **17/2**

4m 51.6s (15.50) **Going Correction** +0.30s/f (Yiel) **10 Ran SP% 114.3**
Speed ratings (Par 105): **79,75,70,69,68 67,64, , ,**
CSF £95.40 CT £286.56 TOTE £6.90: £2.50, £3.60, £1.40; EX 111.00 Trifecta £699.30.
Owner Graham & Carole Worsley **Bred** The Queen **Trained** Cholmondeley, Cheshire

FOCUS
A moderate handicap, run at a brisk gallop. A pb from the winner, with the second rated in line with the best of his form for this yard.

4153 WEATHERBYS BANK CHASE (A NOVICES' LIMITED H'CAP) (19 fncs) 3m 1f 54y
3:10 (3:11) (Class 4) (0-120,120) 5-Y-0+ **£6,498** (£1,908; £954; £477)

Form RPR

/P11 1 **Gonalston Cloud (IRE)**[17] 3836 9-11-3 115 AndrewTinkler 129+
(Nick Kent) *chsd ldrs 6th: 2nd sn after 12th: blnd 15th: sn drvn: 3 l down whn hit 3 out: rallied and upsides last: eased clsng stages* **15/8**[1]

13F2 2 *3 ¼* **Leanna Ban**[20] 3792 9-11-2 114 (t) JonathanEngland 121
(Tristan Davidson) *led: drvn appr 3 out: jnd last: sn hdd: kpt on same pce* **9/2**[3]

1211 3 *57* **Askamore Darsi (IRE)**[15] 3885 7-11-6 118 (p) HenryBrooke 67
(Donald McCain) *chsd ldrs: shkn up 3rd: nt fluent and reminders 5th: chsng ldrs 11th: lost pl next: sn bhd: t.o 4 out* **9/4**[2]

3F26 4 *15* **Ueueteotl (FR)**[66] 3024 8-11-8 120 (b[1]) LucyAlexander 54
(James Ewart) *chsd ldr: mstke 2nd: drvn 12th: reminders next: sn lost pl and bhd: t.o 4 out: wknd between last 2: fin tired* **6/1**

-P00 F **Brook (FR)**[25] 3705 5-11-0 115 (bt) TomScudamore
(David Pipe) *in rr: last whn fell 7th* **9/1**

6m 44.1s (2.10) **Going Correction** +0.075s/f (Yiel)
WFA 5 from 7yo+ 3lb **5 Ran SP% 108.0**
Speed ratings: **99,97,79,74,**
CSF £10.00 TOTE £2.60: £1.60, £2.20; EX 8.20 Trifecta £18.30.
Owner R J Jackson **Bred** Conna Stud **Trained** Brigg, Lincs

FOCUS
A modest staying novice handicap, run at a decent gallop. Another step forward from the winner, and there's a case for rating the race 3lb higher through the second, but not on time compared with the later handicap.

4154 GORGEOUS JOSIE BINNIE IS 50 TODAY H'CAP HURDLE (8 hdls) 1m 7f 156y
3:40 (3:40) (Class 4) (0-115,115) 4-Y-0+ **£3,898** (£1,144; £572; £286)

Form RPR

4203 1 **Hartside (GER)**[5] 4055 7-11-1 111 (v) MrRWinks(7) 119
(Peter Winks) *chsd ldrs: drvn and outpcd 3 out: handy 3rd next: upsides last: kpt on to ld clsng stages: all out* **9/2**[2]

5531 2 *nk* **So Satisfied**[7] 4036 5-11-4 114 7ex StevenFox(7) 122
(Sandy Thomson) *led to 3rd: w ldr: led appr 2 out: rdn between last 2: hdd and no ex clsng stages* **8/11**[1]

1/0- 3 *9* **Rhymers Stone**[485] 1955 8-10-8 102 (p) CallumBewley(5) 101+
(Harriet Graham) *chsd ldrs: drvn and outpcd 3 out: handy 4th next: kpt on one pce: tk modest 3rd nr fin* **50/1**

3020 4 *½* **Prince Khurram**[32] 3592 6-11-10 113 (t) HenryBrooke 111+
(Donald McCain) *w ldr: led 3rd: hdd appr 2 out: one pce* **12/1**

1440 5 *1* **Boldbob (IRE)**[32] 3590 4-10-3 108 FinianO'Toole(7) 97
(Micky Hammond) *chsd ldrs to 3rd: hdwy 3 out: one pce appr next* **25/1**

-620 6 *3 ½* **It's A Mans World**[93] 2499 10-11-7 115 MeganCarberry(5) 111
(Brian Ellison) *nt fluent: chsd ldrs: mstke 5th: outpcd next: chsng ldrs 2 out: wknd appr last* **14/1**

000 7 *20* **Shalamzar (FR)**[16] 3855 7-10-3 95 JoeColliver(3) 69
(Micky Hammond) *in rr: bhd fr 3 out* **28/1**

-U4P 8 *6* **Frankie's Promise (IRE)**[48] 3345 8-11-6 109 (p) LucyAlexander 77
(N W Alexander) *t.k.h in rr: drvn 4th: sn bhd* **17/2**[3]

4050 9 *18* **Hey Bob (IRE)**[15] 3886 4-10-2 100 BrianHughes 41
(Chris Grant) *sn chsng ldrs: nt fluent 4th: lost pl sn after 3 out: sn wl bhd* **20/1**

3m 55.1s (2.60) **Going Correction** +0.30s/f (Yiel)
WFA 4 from 5yo+ 9lb **9 Ran SP% 115.0**
Speed ratings (Par 105): **105,104,100,100,99 97,87,84,75**
CSF £8.10 CT £137.97 TOTE £7.40: £1.90, £1.10, £6.60; EX 10.70 Trifecta £222.20.
Owner P Winks **Bred** Gestut Ammerland **Trained** Little Houghton, S Yorks
■ Stewards' Enquiry : Steven Fox two-day ban: used whip above permitted level (Feb 29-Mar 1)

FOCUS
This modest handicap was run at a solid gallop and it saw two pull well clear from the last. The winner has been rated back to his C&D mark from last year. Solid form for the level.

4155 WEATHERBYS HAMILTON H'CAP CHASE (19 fncs) 3m 1f 54y
4:10 (4:10) (Class 3) (0-140,138) 5-Y-O+ **£7,797** (£2,289; £1,144; £572)

Form | | | | RPR
2F44 **1** **Straidnahanna (IRE)**[24] 3726 7-11-2 **128**........ DannyCook 139+
(Sue Smith) *chsd ldrs: led after 9th: hit 12th: hdd 15th: led again next: drvn bef 3 out: hit last: fnd ex clsng stages* **9/2**[2]
R2F2 **2** *2* **Jac The Legend**[15] 3887 7-10-1 **113**........(p) TomScudamore 121
(Brian Ellison) *in rr: hdwy 9th: sn chsng ldrs: clr 2nd between last 2: chal 1f out: no ex clsng stages* **9/2**[2]
1360 **3** *6* **Distime (IRE)**[16] 3860 10-11-3 **129**........ JonathanEngland 130
(Sam Drake) *chsd ldrs: drvn 4 out: one pce fr 2 out* **25/1**
-362 **4** *7* **Beeves (IRE)**[66] 3024 9-11-3 **129**........(v) HenryBrooke 125
(Jennie Candlish) *trckd ldrs: led 3rd tl after 9th: wknd appr 2 out* **9/1**
-164 **5** *29* **Shimla Dawn (IRE)**[65] 3036 8-11-6 **132**........ JakeGreenall 97
(Mark Walford) *chsd ldrs: drvn and outpcd 13th: lost pl next: sn bhd: t.o* **12/1**
1P-0 **P** **Scotswell**[44] 3440 10-10-12 **124**........ LucyAlexander
(Harriet Graham) *chsd ldrs: blnd and lost pl 6th: bhd and drvn 10th: t.o whn p.u after 11th* **33/1**
P16P **P** **Wilton Milan (IRE)**[23] 3748 8-11-7 **133**........(tp) HarrySkelton
(Dan Skelton) *in rr: hdwy 6th: sn chsng ldrs: drvn 12th: wknd 15th: wl bhd whn p.u bef 3 out* **25/1**
0-41 **U** **Warrantor (IRE)**[56] 3197 7-11-5 **138**........(t) MrTGreatrex[(7)]
(Warren Greatrex) *in rr: blnd and uns rdr 1st* **6/1**[3]
-042 **F** **Looking Well (IRE)**[45] 3399 7-10-11 **123**........ BrianHarding
(Nicky Richards) *hld up: hdwy 11th: trcking ldrs whn fell 14th* **9/4**[1]

6m 37.2s (-4.80) **Going Correction** +0.075s/f (Yiel) **9 Ran SP% 109.7**
Speed ratings: **110,109,107,105,95 , , ,**
CSF £23.33 CT £412.18 TOTE £5.30: £1.40, £2.00, £5.40; EX 23.30 Trifecta £413.20.
Owner M B Scholey & R H Scholey **Bred** Mrs Eleanor Hadden **Trained** High Eldwick, W Yorks

FOCUS
The feature handicap proved a decent test and the first pair fought it out from the last. A pb from the winner, with the second and third rated to their marks.

4156 RACING AGAIN 1ST MARCH MAIDEN NATIONAL HUNT FLAT RACE (CONDITIONAL JOCKEYS'/AMATEUR RIDERS') 1m 7f 156y
4:40 (4:40) (Class 6) 4-6-Y-O **£1,949** (£572; £286; £143)

Form | | | | RPR
1 **Sam Spinner** 4-10-5........ JoeColliver[(3)] 108+
(Jedd O'Keeffe) *trckd ldrs: led 4f out: drvn rt out* **5/1**[3]
2 **2** *1 ¼* **Raised On Grazeon**[16] 3862 5-10-5........ DeanPratt[(5)] 108
(John Quinn) *hld up in rr: hdwy 7f out: sn trcking ldrs: 3rd over 2f out: chal over 1f out: no ex last 75yds* **7/2**[2]
3 *1 ¼* **Captain Moirette (FR)** 4-10-1........ TrevorRyan[(7)] 105+
(Sue Smith) *t.k.h towards rr: hdwy 7f out: 5th over 2f out: 3rd over 1f out: edgd lft and kpt on same pce last 150yds* **12/1**
062 **4** *2* **Very First Time**[58] 3165 4-10-1........ MrWEasterby[(7)] 103
(Tim Easterby) *hld up towards rr: hdwy 7f out: chsng ldrs over 4f out: 4th over 2f out: kpt on one pce* **5/1**[3]
5 **5** *3 ¾* **Patience Tony (IRE)**[67] 2984 5-10-12........ CallumBewley[(5)] 108
(Alan Swinbank) *mid-div: chsng ldrs 7f out: 2nd over 3f out: wknd fnl f* **14/1**
0 **6** *21* **Reverant Cust (IRE)**[32] 3593 5-10-10........ FinianO'Toole[(7)] 87
(Peter Atkinson) *led: hung rt bnd after 5f: hdd 4f out: wknd over 2f out* **80/1**
7 *5* **Persian Steel (IRE)** 4-10-3........ CraigGallagher[(5)] 73
(Brian Ellison) *in rr: pushed along after 6f: sme hdwy 5f out: sn lost pl and bhd* **9/4**[1]
35 **8** *1 ¼* **Grow Nasa Grow (IRE)**[80] 2750 5-10-10........ MrRWinks[(7)] 81
(Peter Winks) *chsd ldrs: lost pl over 3f out: sn bhd* **8/1**
0 **9** *½* **Primo Time**[17] 3847 5-11-3........ JonathanEngland 80
(Michael Appleby) *chsd ldrs: lost pl over 4f out: sn bhd* **80/1**
0 **10** *77* **Mini Frank**[58] 3165 4-10-3........ DiarmuidO'Regan[(5)]
(Chris Grant) *chsd ldrs: drvn after 7f: lost pl 6f out: sn wl bhd: t.o 3f out: eased over 1f out: eventually completed* **200/1**
11 *5* **Dave The Rave (IRE)** 6-10-12........ ThomasCheesman[(5)]
(Ronald Thompson) *mid-div: drvn 8f out: reminders and lost pl 6f out: sn bhd: t.o 3f out: eased over 1f out: eventually completed* **33/1**

3m 51.1s (4.20) **Going Correction** +0.30s/f (Yiel) **11 Ran SP% 117.7**
WFA 4 from 5yo+ 9lb
Speed ratings: **101,100,99,98,96 86,83,83,83,44 42**
CSF £22.81 TOTE £8.90: £2.50, £1.50, £4.00; EX 27.40 Trifecta £209.80.
Owner Caron & Paul Chapman **Bred** Wriggle Valley TBs & R Eccleshall **Trained** Middleham Moor, N Yorks

FOCUS
This bumper was run at a fair gallop and the form looks sound. An above average bumper for the track, rated around the second and fourth.
T/Plt: £55.70 to a £1 stake. Pool: £67,748.90 - 887.85 winning units. T/Qpdt: £19.90 to a £1 stake. Pool: £5,639.49 - 209.20 winning units. **Walter Glynn**

3902 PLUMPTON (L-H)
Monday, February 15

OFFICIAL GOING: Heavy (chs 4.1, hdl 3.9)
Wind: Moderate, behind Weather: Fine, cold

4157 AT THE RACES VIRGIN 535 MARES' NOVICES' HURDLE (7 hdls 2 omitted) 1m 7f 195y
2:00 (2:00) (Class 4) 4-Y-O+ **£3,898** (£1,144; £572; £286)

Form | | | | RPR
15P1 **1** **Bella (FR)**[75] 2852 5-11-7 119........(t) DavidNoonan[(5)] 118+
(David Pipe) *trckd ldr: upsides fr 3rd tl led 3 out: sn jnd: shkn up to assert bef 2 out: pushed out flat: comf* **11/10**[1]
00 **2** *9* **Ayla's Emperor**[37] 3516 7-10-12 0........ RobertDunne 94
(John Flint) *prom in chsng gp: chsd ldng pair 4th: wnt 2nd after 3 out and sn w wnr: shkn up and one pce bef 2 out* **16/1**
-P **3** *3 ½* **Aramadyh**[14] 3902 5-10-12 0........ JamieMoore 92
(Jim Best) *hld up in last trio: stdy prog fr 3rd: tk 4th bef 3 out and in tch: chsd ldng pair after 3 out: sn outpcd: pushed along and one pce after* **20/1**
0 **4** *7* **Top And Drop**[37] 3522 5-10-12 0........ AidanColeman 84
(Venetia Williams) *hld up in rr: prog after 4th: tk 4th after 3 out but sn shkn up and outpcd: no imp after* **8/1**[3]
60P/ **5** *29* **Mrs Winchester (IRE)**[667] 5389 7-10-12 0........ IanPopham 59
(Caroline Keevil) *hld up in last: t.o after 4th: kpt on steadily after: no inroads on ldrs but hint of promise* **100/1**
P **Patronne (FR)**[129] 4-10-3 0........ GavinSheehan
(Harry Whittington) *led: jnd 3rd: hdd and hit 3 out: wknd qckly: wl bhd in 6th whn p.u bef 2 out* **6/4**[2]
P **Spanish Danser (IRE)**[135] 4-10-0 0........(t) JamesBanks[(3)]
(Jo Davis) *a in rr: t.o after 4th: last whn p.u bef 2 out* **66/1**
-00P **P** **Sunley Spirit**[51] 3252 6-10-12 0........ TomCannon
(Chris Gordon) *chsd ldng pair to 4th: wknd qckly on long run bef 3 out: wl bhd in 7th whn p.u bef 2 out* **14/1**
46 **P** **Sweet'N'Chic (IRE)**[77] 2828 6-10-12 0........ LeightonAspell
(Richard Rowe) *nt jump wl: a in rr: t.o after 4th: 8th whn p.u bef 2 out* **28/1**
04 **P** **Stoical Patient (IRE)**[20] 3785 7-10-12 0........ KielanWoods
(Mark Wall) *rdn after 3rd and sn wknd: t.o after next: 9th whn p.u bef 2 out* **50/1**

4m 11.2s (10.40) **Going Correction** +0.85s/f (Soft)
WFA 4 from 5yo+ 9lb **10 Ran SP% 123.9**
Speed ratings (Par 105): **108,103,101,98,83 , , , ,**
CSF £20.67 TOTE £1.90: £1.10, £3.80, £3.30; EX 18.10 Trifecta £147.20.
Owner Prof Caroline Tisdall **Bred** Dr Vet R Y Simon & N Simon **Trained** Nicholashayne, Devon

FOCUS
Bend rails from innermost line: Chase top & bottom out 5yds. Hurdle top & bottom out 7yds. David Noonan described the ground as "very soft with the best ground at the end of the back straight". As a result this race was run over 63yds further than advertised. Little depth to this mares' hurdle and the favourite won well. The easy winner set the standard, with a big step up from the second.

4158 DOWNLOAD THE AT THE RACES APP NOVICES' LIMITED H'CAP CHASE (14 fncs) 2m 3f 164y
2:30 (2:31) (Class 3) 5-Y-O+ **£6,498** (£1,908; £954)

Form | | | | RPR
6111 **1** **Ar Mad (FR)**[50] 3280 6-11-8 **155**........ JoshuaMoore 160+
(Gary Moore) *smetimes j. sltly rt: mde all and sn clr: 15 l up 1/2-way: drew further ahd fr 4 out: easily* **2/7**[1]
311F **2** *25* **Alder Mairi (IRE)**[25] 3706 9-10-3 **136** oh14........ JeremiahMcGrath 116
(Seamus Mullins) *chsd clr wnr fr 5th: nvr any ch: hit last* **9/1**[3]
P0-1 **3** *6* **Chill Factor (IRE)**[291] 29 7-10-3 **136** oh2........(t) AidanColeman 110
(Anthony Honeyball) *chsd wnr to 5th: rdn 3 out: no imp on runner-up after* **5/1**[2]

5m 11.4s (4.10) **Going Correction** +0.70s/f (Soft) **3 Ran SP% 104.4**
Speed ratings: **119,109,106**
CSF £2.79 TOTE £1.20; EX 3.50 Trifecta £3.80.
Owner Ashley Head **Bred** Michel Le Meur **Trained** Lower Beeding, W Sussex

FOCUS
This was run over 60yds further than advertised. All about the favourite, who was trialling for the Arkle, and he never had a moment's concern.

4159 EXCLUSIVE BARRY GERAGHTY BLOG ON ATTHERACES.COM H'CAP HURDLE (9 hdls 3 omitted) 2m 4f 114y
3:00 (3:00) (Class 3) (0-130,130) 4-Y-O+ **£5,588** (£1,640; £820; £410)

Form | | | | RPR
/120 **1** **Billy No Name (IRE)**[51] 3232 8-11-4 **122**........ PaddyBrennan 132+
(Colin Tizzard) *trckd ldng pair: mstke 4th: wnt 2nd after 7th: led bypassing omitted 3 out and gng best: drew clr 2 out: 8 l ahd last: urged along nr fin* **9/4**[1]
31- **2** *2 ½* **Rock Gone (IRE)**[423] 3172 8-11-8 **126**........ WillKennedy 128
(Dr Richard Newland) *trckd ldrs: cl up after 7th: chsd wnr after 3 out: shkn up 2 out: hanging and nt qckn bef last: styd on flat and clsng at fin* **4/1**[2]
4213 **3** *3 ¼* **Cannon Fodder**[23] 3732 9-11-12 **130**........ MarcGoldstein 130
(Sheena West) *chsd ldr: mstke 4th: led after 7th: sn urged along: hdd bypassing 3 out: dropped to 3rd bef next: kpt on wl fr last* **5/1**[3]
-300 **4** *10* **Jumps Road**[25] 3708 9-11-3 **121**........(b[1]) BrendanPowell 111
(Colin Tizzard) *mstke 1st: hld up: trckd ldng trio on long run after 7th and wl in tch: rdn and fdd wl bef 2 out* **9/1**
-002 **5** *48* **First Avenue**[65] 3045 11-11-4 **122**........ TomCannon 63
(Laura Mongan) *in tch: rdn sn after 7th: wknd on v long run after: t.o* **16/1**
22P6 **P** **Warrant Officer**[14] 3905 6-10-0 **104** oh18........ MattieBatchelor
(Sheena West) *j.rt: led: hdd & wknd after 7th: t.o whn p.u bef 2 out* **66/1**
P010 **P** **Prouts Pub (IRE)**[16] 3854 7-11-12 **130**........ LeightonAspell
(Nick Gifford) *sn in last: shkn up and no rspnse after 4th: t.o whn p.u bef 6th* **13/2**
5022 **P** **Fountains Blossom**[38] 3505 7-10-0 **109**........(t) DavidNoonan[(5)]
(Anthony Honeyball) *in tch: nt fluent 5th and 6th and wknd u.p: sn t.o: p.u bypassing omitted 3 out* **6/1**

5m 30.2s (13.20) **Going Correction** +0.85s/f (Soft) **8 Ran SP% 112.4**
Speed ratings (Par 107): **108,107,105,102,83 , , ,**
CSF £11.59 CT £38.84 TOTE £3.20: £1.20, £1.90, £1.60; EX 12.60 Trifecta £51.10.
Owner Mrs Jean R Bishop **Bred** Seamus O'Farrell **Trained** Milborne Port, Dorset

FOCUS
This was run over 84yds further than advertised. The third-last had to be omitted. The right horses came to the fore in this fair handicap hurdle, with the winner value for further than it looked. A pb from the winner, with the second rated to his mark.

4160 AT THE RACES SKY 415 NOVICES' H'CAP CHASE (17 fncs 1 omitted) 3m 1f 152y
3:30 (3:31) (Class 4) (0-105,102) 5-Y-O+ **£4,328** (£1,574)

Form | | | | RPR
-623 **1** **The Cider Maker**[105] 2254 6-11-9 **99**........(t) BrendanPowell 125+
(Colin Tizzard) *trckd ldrs: mstke 3rd: in tch 9th: wnt 2nd 3 out and led bef next: sn drew rt away fr exhausted rivals* **5/1**
2114 **2** *26* **Arthamint**[51] 3224 8-11-12 **102**........(t) DavidEngland 98
(Dan Skelton) *plld hrd: hld up: sltly impeded 9th: in tch tl urged along and no rspnse bef 4 out: wl btn after: blnd 2 out: tk remote 2nd last* **9/2**[3]
/5PP **P** **Molly Oscar (IRE)**[51] 3218 10-10-4 **80**........(b) TomCannon
(Johnny Farrelly) *led: hdd and rdn 13th: led again and hit 4 out: hdd bef 2 out: immediately wknd qckly: lost remote 2nd and p.u bef last* **9/1**
0646 **U** **Darkestbeforedawn (IRE)**[10] 3977 9-11-10 **100**........(b[1]) JamesBest 89
(Caroline Keevil) *trckd ldr: led 13th: rdn and hdd 4 out: wknd qckly after next: remote 3rd whn clambered over last and uns rdr* **11/4**[2]
3-UU **F** **Generous Helpings (IRE)**[17] 3834 7-11-11 **101**........ JoshuaMoore
(Gary Moore) *nt a fluent: in tch: 5th whn fell 8th* **5/2**[1]

 The Form Book Jumps 2015-16, Raceform Ltd, Newbury, RG14 5SJ

6660 P **Bridal Suite (IRE)**[51] 3220 7-10-10 **93**..........................(tp) TommyDowling[(7)]
(Charlie Mann) *lost tch 6th: sn t.o: p.u bef 10th* **13/2**
7m 9.9s (19.20) **Going Correction** +0.70s/f (Soft) **6** Ran SP% **113.4**
Speed ratings: **98, , ,**
CSF £27.45 TOTE £5.10: £2.40, £2.20; EX 17.70 Trifecta £18.50.
Owner Mrs C Djivanovic, Joanna Tizzard, KSB **Bred** Barrow Hill **Trained** Milborne Port, Dorset
FOCUS
This was run over 90yds further than advertised. Moderate chase form, with only two runners completing. A seemingly massive step up from the winner, with the second and unseater rated in line with their latest runs.

4161 AT THE RACES APP ON IPHONE CONDITIONAL JOCKEYS' H'CAP HURDLE (7 hdls 2 omitted) 1m 7f 195y
4:00 (4:01) (Class 5) (0-100,95) 4-Y-O+ **£3,249** (£954; £477; £238)

Form RPR
0036 1 **Triple Chief (IRE)**[33] 3586 5-11-12 **95**..........................(tp) CiaranGethings 98
(Chris Down) *patiently rdn: hld up in last pair: prog to go 4th 3 out: clsd on ldrs and tk 2nd 2 out: sn rdn: narrow ld last: drvn rt out* **10/3**[2]
15/P 2 2 **Clonusker (IRE)**[77] 2826 8-11-2 **85**..........................(t) CharlieDeutsch 87
(Linda Jewell) *led to 3rd: shkn up briefly after next: led on long run bef 3 out: drvn bef 2 out: hdd last: kpt on* **7/1**[3]
-132 3 3¼ **Torero**[28] 3665 7-11-0 **91**..........................(p) GeorgeGorman[(8)] 90
(Gary Moore) *hld up in tch: prog to trck ldr 3 out to next: sn rdn and nt qckn: kpt on fr last but unable to chal* **6/4**[1]
0043 4 10 **Aaman (IRE)**[12] 3925 10-10-9 **81**.......................... RobertWilliams[(3)] 70
(Bernard Llewellyn) *mstke 1st: led 3rd: hit next: hdd on long run bef 3 out: stl on terms in cl 4th 2 out: wknd* **17/2**
5036 5 17 **Up Four It (IRE)**[51] 3219 8-10-0 **76**.......................... FrankiePenford[(7)] 47
(Jamie Poulton) *trckd ldrs: wkng whn mstke 3 out: sn bhd* **9/1**
0500 6 9 **Hallingham**[30] 3619 6-11-9 **92**.......................... ThomasGarner 54
(Chris Gordon) *hld up in last pair: lost tch on long run to 3 out: bhd after* **8/1**
-00P P **Moving Waves (IRE)**[51] 3219 5-10-11 **80**.......................... DavidNoonan
(Johnny Farrelly) *cl up: pushed along fr 4th: sn struggling: bhd after 3 out: p.u bef last* **16/1**
4m 19.8s (19.00) **Going Correction** +0.85s/f (Soft) **7** Ran SP% **113.1**
Speed ratings (Par 103): **86,85,83,78,69 65,**
CSF £25.54 TOTE £4.50: £2.30, £2.50; EX 24.60 Trifecta £74.00.
Owner G Thompson **Bred** Breda Wall & Timothy Cleary **Trained** Mutterton, Devon
FOCUS
This was run over 63yds further than advertised. Lowly hurdles form. The winner has been rated to the best of this season's form.

4162 AT THE RACES APP ON ANDROID STANDARD OPEN NATIONAL HUNT FLAT RACE 2m 1f 164y
4:30 (4:31) (Class 6) 4-6-Y-O **£1,559** (£457; £228; £114)

Form RPR
1 **Mickieblueeyes (IRE)** 4-10-8 [0].......................... MarcGoldstein 83+
(Diana Grissell) *cl up: jnd ldrs 4f out: rn green and hanging over 2f out: shkn up to ld wl over 1f out: urged along and kpt on* **20/1**
4 2 1½ **Lord Bryan (IRE)**[271] 407 5-11-3 [0].......................... SeanBowen 90
(Peter Bowen) *cl up: jnd ldrs 4f out: urged along and dropped to 3rd over 2f out: hrd rdn to chse wnr jst over 1f out: kpt on but a hld* **13/8**[2]
3 5 **Samdibien (FR)** 4-10-8 [0].......................... AidanColeman 77
(Sam Thomas) *mde most: pressed 4f out: rdn and hdd wl over 1f out: one pce* **5/1**[3]
4 32 **Passing Du Moulin (FR)** 5-11-3 [0].......................... GavinSheehan 53
(Harry Whittington) *rn green and struggling in last bef 1/2-way: lost tch 5f out: t.o* **6/4**[1]
5 1¾ **Remember Forever (IRE)**[282] 6-11-3 [0].......................... LeightonAspell 51
(Richard Rowe) *w ldr to 4f out: wknd qckly: t.o* **11/1**
4m 53.1s (27.80) **Going Correction** +0.85s/f (Soft)
WFA 4 from 5yo+ 9lb **5** Ran SP% **107.9**
Speed ratings: **72,71,69,54,54**
CSF £51.02 TOTE £19.40: £6.90, £1.40; EX 63.70 Trifecta £244.30.
Owner Keith Dilworth **Bred** H & P Byrne **Trained** Brightling, E Sussex
FOCUS
This was run over 84yds further than advertised. Quite a weak bumper and it went to the outsider of the field. The runner-up is the best guide to the level.
T/Plt: £28.70 to a £1 stake. Pool: £61,657.78 - 1563.94 winning units. T/Qpdt: £16.90 to a £1 stake. Pool: £5,247.14 - 229.35 winning units. **Jonathan Neesom**

3666 AYR (L-H)
Tuesday, February 16
OFFICIAL GOING: Soft (good to soft in places on chase course) changing to heavy after race 1 (2.20)
Wind: Strong, half-against Weather: Overcast, raining

4163 DAWN HOMES ASSURED MOVE CONDITIONAL JOCKEYS' H'CAP HURDLE (12 hdls) 2m 4f 100y
2:20 (2:21) (Class 5) (0-100,100) 4-Y-O+ **£2,599** (£763; £381; £190)

Form RPR
3-P6 1 **W Six Times**[83] 2720 10-10-9 **83**..........................(p) KieronEdgar 91+
(Alistair Whillans) *chsd ldrs: chal 7th: led bef 3 out: rdn clr fr last* **8/1**[2]
0-50 2 9 **Titian Boy (IRE)**[28] 3667 7-10-1 **75**.......................... JoeColliver 76+
(N W Alexander) *led to 4th: cl up: regained ld 7th: hdd bef 3 out: rallied: 2 l down and one pce whn mstke last: sn no ex* **25/1**
0046 3 2¾ **Smuggler's Stash (IRE)**[21] 3795 6-11-12 **100**.......................... CraigNichol 97+
(Rose Dobbin) *hld up in tch: blkd by faller 7th: effrt after 4 out: rdn next: kpt on fr last: no imp* **12/1**[3]
0-30 4 1¾ **Cruachan (IRE)**[68] 2980 7-11-8 **96**.......................... JonathanEngland 90
(Lucy Normile) *hld up: stdy hdwy and in tch bef 3 out: sn rdn: kpt on same pce fr next* **11/2**[1]
-54P 5 18 **Massini's Lady**[72] 2936 5-11-0 **91**.......................... StephenMulqueen[(3)] 67
(N W Alexander) *midfield: drvn and lost pl 4th: struggling fr 6th: plugged on fr 3 out: no ch w ldrs* **66/1**
5000 6 nk **Suzy's Music (IRE)**[28] 3672 8-10-7 **86**.......................... AdamShort[(5)] 61
(S R B Crawford, Ire) *nt fluent in rr: sme hdwy after 4 out: rdn and wknd fr next* **22/1**
6400 7 5 **Beer Goggles (IRE)**[43] 3474 5-11-4 **100**.......................... FinianO'Toole[(8)] 70
(Micky Hammond) *hld up towards rr: drvn along 7th: outpcd next: btn bef 3 out* **8/1**[2]
FP6- 8 1 **De Bee Keeper (IRE)**[275] 8-10-11 **90**.......................... RossChapman[(5)] 59
(Russell Ross) *cl up: led 4th to 7th: cl up tl rdn and wknd fr 3 out* **11/2**[1]
600 9 8 **Whatsthestoryman (IRE)**[107] 2210 8-11-3 **94**..........................(t) StevenFox[(3)] 55
(Katie Scott) *hld up: drvn along bef 7th: nvr on terms* **50/1**
PP-5 10 2¾ **Blueside Boy (IRE)**[108] 2191 8-10-5 **84**.......................... ThomasDowson[(5)] 42
(Harriet Graham) *prom: pushed along 7th: rdn and wknd bef 3 out* **25/1**
-4P0 11 40 **Higgs Boson**[28] 3672 11-10-2 **81**..........................(p) RonanShort[(5)]
(Jim Goldie) *midfield: drvn and struggling 7th: btn after next: t.o* **14/1**
3UP0 12 29 **Kilmainham (IRE)**[11] 3973 8-11-5 **93**.......................... GrahamWatters
(Martin Todhunter) *bhd: struggling fnl circ: t.o* **33/1**
40F2 F **Naburn**[21] 3791 8-11-12 **100**.......................... RyanDay
(Andrew Wilson) *t.k.h: hld up on ins: stdy hdwy and in tch whn fell 7th* **8/1**[2]
30-2 P **Molly Milan**[45] 3438 8-11-1 **89**.......................... DiarmuidO'Regan
(Jim Goldie) *prom tl rdn and wknd bef 3 out: p.u bef last* **11/2**[1]
0044 P **Kashstaree**[28] 3672 5-10-12 **89**.......................... CallumBewley[(3)]
(Lisa Harrison) *hld up in midfield: struggling 1/2-way: lost tch and p.u bef 3 out* **25/1**
5-3P P **The Squinty Bridge**[72] 2937 8-10-13 **90**..........................(tp) GrantCockburn[(3)]
(Lucinda Russell) *in tch: drvn along 6th: struggling fr next: lost tch and p.u bef 3 out* **18/1**
5m 45.1s (345.10) **16** Ran SP% **121.4**
CSF £194.82 CT £2394.40 TOTE £10.80: £2.00, £7.30, £3.80, £1.80; EX 261.30 Trifecta £3644.70 Part won..
Owner Mrs L M Whillans **Bred** East Burrow Farm **Trained** Newmill-On-Slitrig, Borders
FOCUS
Some starts have been moved at this track following remeasuring, so some races will not have speed figures until there is sufficient data to calculate updated median times. Hurdle distances increased by 48yds per circuit. Horrible blustery conditions made it hard work for the runners, with the ground being changed to heavy after this opening handicap. Lowly form. The winner has been rated back to her C&D winning mark, with big steps up from the second and third.

4164 DAWN HOMES ASSISTED MOVE MARES' MAIDEN HURDLE (9 hdls) 2m
2:55 (2:59) (Class 5) 4-Y-O+ **£2,599** (£763; £381; £190)

Form RPR
2- 1 **Danielle's Journey**[30] 3647 6-11-2 [0]..........................(t) AELynch 113+
(S R B Crawford, Ire) *chsd ldr: led 3 out: shkn up and drew clr fr next: easily* **11/8**[1]
5-1P 2 17 **My Little Cracker (IRE)**[72] 2936 6-11-2 [0].......................... BrianHarding 96
(Iain Jardine) *nt fluent on occasions: led: hit 4th: hdd 3 out: plugged on same pce fr next* **4/1**[2]
3 5 **Milan Dancer (IRE)**[24] 3750 5-10-9 [0].......................... MrSPKelly[(7)] 91
(Noel C Kelly, Ire) *hld up in tch: effrt bef 3 out: rdn and no imp fr next* **14/1**
4 3¾ **Liannastarr (IRE)**[31] 3639 6-10-9 [0].......................... AlisonClarke[(7)] 87
(J J Lambe, Ire) *chsd ldrs: rdn bef 3 out: wknd fr next* **100/1**
F0 5 2¾ **Pretty Miss Mahler (IRE)**[11] 3971 5-11-2 [0].......................... HenryBrooke 85
(Martin Todhunter) *nt fluent on occasions: hld up on outside: pushed along after 4 out: wknd bef next* **33/1**
10-4 6 1½ **Verona Opera (IRE)**[30] 3647 5-10-9 [0].......................... AdamShort[(7)] 83
(S R B Crawford, Ire) *chsd ldrs tl rdn and wknd fr 3 out* **6/1**
56 7 9 **Lovefromabove (IRE)**[7] 4039 5-11-2 [0].......................... HarrySkelton 74
(Dan Skelton) *hld up: rdn after 4 out: nvr on terms* **25/1**
464 8 ½ **Rivabodiva (IRE)**[49] 3342 6-11-2 **109**.......................... DerekFox 74
(Lucinda Russell) *hld up: struggling after 4 out: btn next* **9/2**[3]
6-0 9 33 **Miss Blanche**[27] 3681 5-11-2 [0]..........................[1] PeterBuchanan 41
(Lucinda Russell) *hld up: drvn and struggling after 4 out: btn next* **40/1**
4m 30.1s (270.10) **9** Ran SP% **111.5**
CSF £6.58 TOTE £2.30: £1.10, £1.60, £3.60; EX 7.50 Trifecta £60.50.
Owner Realta Horseracing Club **Bred** Mrs R I Vaughan **Trained** Larne, Co Antrim
FOCUS
Hurdle distances increased by 48yds per circuit. No depth to this moderate mares' hurdle. The winner has been rated to her mark.

4165 DAWN HOMES PART EXCHANGE H'CAP HURDLE (12 hdls) 3m 70y
3:30 (3:30) (Class 4) (0-120,120) 4-Y-O+ **£3,573** (£1,049; £524; £262)

Form RPR
540 1 **Bertalus (IRE)**[28] 3667 7-10-8 **102**.......................... LucyAlexander 110+
(N W Alexander) *in tch: hdwy bef 4 out: sn chsng ldr: effrt and ev ch 2 out: led last: pushed clr: readily* **9/2**
1 2 6 **Master Ruffit (IRE)**[28] 3667 8-11-10 **118**.......................... BrianHughes 120
(Neil McKnight, Ire) *nt fluent on occasions: cl up: led 7th: rdn and edgd lft 3 out: hdd last: kpt on same pce* **4/1**[3]
-031 3 15 **Lochnell (IRE)**[45] 3437 7-10-0 **94** oh1.......................... BrianHarding 79
(Ian Duncan) *hld up: stdy hdwy and cl up 4 out: rdn next: wknd between last 2* **3/1**[2]
220P 4 10 **Snapping Turtle (IRE)**[10] 3999 11-11-3 **114**.......................... CallumWhillans[(3)] 89
(Donald Whillans) *led to 7th: sn drvn along: wknd bef 3 out* **15/2**
P-0F 5 10 **Bold Sir Brian (IRE)**[24] 3737 10-11-12 **120**..........................(t) PeterBuchanan 90
(Lucinda Russell) *trckd ldrs: rdn and outpcd bef 3 out: sn wknd* **5/2**[1]
6-05 P **Trucking Along (IRE)**[13] 3940 10-11-7 **115**.......................... AELynch
(S R B Crawford, Ire) *hld up: rdn and outpcd 4 out: sn lost tch: p.u next* **11/1**
7m 12.8s (41.00) **Going Correction** +1.875s/f (Heav) **6** Ran SP% **111.9**
Speed ratings (Par 105): **106,104,99,95,92**
CSF £22.37 TOTE £6.20: £2.60, £2.80; EX 22.10 Trifecta £79.10.
Owner Lord Cochrane And Partners **Bred** David Lalor **Trained** Kinneston, Perth & Kinross
FOCUS
Hurdle distances increased by 48yds per circuit. The front pair came clear late in a race that proved to be a thorough test, even if the early pace was a slow one. The first two are probably on the upgrade, while the third has been rated a stone off his recent C&D win, but it could be at least 5lb out either way.

4166 DAWN HOMES FUTURE DEVELOPMENTS H'CAP CHASE (10 fncs 2 omitted) 1m 7f 112y
4:05 (4:07) (Class 4) (0-115,112) 5-Y-O+ **£4,223** (£1,240; £620; £310)

Form RPR
3324 1 **Trust Thomas**[31] 3631 8-11-7 **112**.......................... JamieHamilton[(5)] 122+
(Ann Hamilton) *hld up in tch: hit 6th: effrt bef 2 out: shkn up to ld last: rdn and r.o wl* **15/2**
6223 2 1¾ **Quick Decisson (IRE)**[13] 3935 8-11-11 **111**.......................... DannyCook 117
(Stuart Coltherd) *pressed ldr and sn clr of rest: led 6th: hit next and 4 out: rdn 3 out: hdd last: kpt on run-in* **6/1**
2115 3 2¾ **Willie Hall**[13] 3938 12-10-5 **96**.......................... CallumBewley[(5)] 100
(Lisa Harrison) *hld up: stdy hdwy 1/2-way: effrt and chsd ldrs bef 2 out: kpt on same pce fr last* **11/1**

05 **4** ½ **Finea (IRE)**[13] 3944 9-11-7 107....................(tp) BrianHughes 113+
(R K Watson, Ire) *chsd clr ldng pair: stdy hdwy to take 2nd 3 out: effrt and ev ch whn blnd next: sn one pce* **4/1**[1]

-U1U **5** ½ **Clan Chief**[13] 3938 7-10-5 91....................[1] LucyAlexander 92
(N W Alexander) *nt fluent: hld up in rr: stdy hdwy 1/2-way: effrt and kpt on fr 2 out: nt pce to chal* **8/1**

4562 **6** 10 **Bonzo Bing (IRE)**[13] 3937 8-11-10 110....................(p) HenryBrooke 101
(Martin Todhunter) *in tch: rdn 4 out: wknd bef next* **9/2**[2]

0P44 **7** 2 **Formidableopponent (IRE)**[4] 4106 9-11-5 105....................(b[1]) DerekFox 94
(William Young Jnr) *towards rr: struggling 1/2-way: nvr on terms* **33/1**

4/ **8** 15 **The Shepherd King (IRE)**[109] 2180 12-11-2 105....(t) CallumWhillans(3) 79
(R K Watson, Ire) *led at decent gallop to 6th: pressed ldr to 3 out: wknd fr next* **20/1**

F-0F **9** 35 **Why But Why (USA)**[45] 3438 8-11-5 108....................(b) GrahamWatters(3) 47
(Ian Duncan) *bhd: struggling fr 1/2-way: nvr on terms* **50/1**

-406 **P** **Too Cool To Fool (IRE)**[45] 3441 13-11-0 100....................(p) JamesReveley
(Jim Goldie) *midfield: struggling 1/2-way: t.o whn p.u bef 3 out* **16/1**

5-33 **F** **Young Palm (IRE)**[28] 3670 9-11-1 101....................(tp) AELynch
(S R B Crawford, Ire) *hld up: fell 1st* **11/2**[3]

4m 22.6s (11.90) **Going Correction** +0.875s/f (Soft) **11** Ran SP% **114.6**
Speed ratings: **105,104,102,102,102 97,96,88,71,**
CSF £50.44 CT £494.09 TOTE £7.00: £2.50, £2.10, £3.20; EX 48.80 Trifecta £346.90.
Owner Ian Hamilton **Bred** Wood Farm Stud **Trained** Great Bavington, Northumberland

FOCUS
Chase distances increased by 30yds per circuit. A few had their chance in this modest chase, with the leaders racing clear early. The second and third have been rated pretty much to their marks.

4167 DAWN HOMES PERCETON H'CAP CHASE (13 fncs 4 omitted) 2m 4f 110y
4:40 (4:41) (Class 3) (0-140,138) 5-Y-0+ **£7,797** (£2,289; £1,144; £572)

Form RPR

5210 **1** **Bernardelli (IRE)**[24] 3735 8-11-6 132....................(b[1]) CraigNichol 143+
(Nicky Richards) *trckd ldrs: pushed along after 4 out: led next: clr after 2 out: rdn out run-in* **7/2**[3]

3245 **2** 3 **Plus Jamais (FR)**[21] 3794 9-10-3 115.................... BrianHughes 121
(Jim Goldie) *led to bef 3 out: rallied and chsd wnr after next: kpt on fr last: nt pce to chal* **5/2**[2]

P631 **3** 8 **Ubaltique (FR)**[24] 3742 8-10-9 121....................(bt) AidanColeman 120
(Donald McCain) *hld up in tch: effrt and rdn bef 3 out: no imp fr next* **7/2**[3]

-PP1 **4** 1¼ **Yes Tom (IRE)**[45] 3440 11-11-12 138....................(p) AELynch 140+
(S R B Crawford, Ire) *nt fluent: chsd ldr: chal 5 out: led briefly bef 3 out: wknd bef last* **15/8**[1]

1560 **5** 18 **Jet Master (IRE)**[27] 3682 10-11-11 137.................... LucyAlexander 116
(N W Alexander) *t.k.h: hld up: struggling bef 4 out: btn next* **22/1**

6m 3.9s (363.90) **5** Ran SP% **112.1**
CSF £13.04 TOTE £4.30: £1.70, £2.00; EX 12.80 Trifecta £37.90.
Owner Henriques & LLoyd-Bakers **Bred** Minch Bloodstock **Trained** Greystoke, Cumbria

FOCUS
Chase distances increased by 30yds per circuit. Fair chase form. The second has been rated to his mark.

4168 DAWN HOMES KILSYTH MARES' INTERMEDIATE OPEN NATIONAL HUNT FLAT RACE 2m
5:10 (5:15) (Class 6) 4-6-Y-0 **£1,624** (£477; £238; £119)

Form RPR

65 **1** **Al Reesha (IRE)**[18] 3847 5-11-2 0.................... HarrySkelton 113+
(Dan Skelton) *pressed ldr and clr of rest after 4f: led 1/2-way: clr over 5f out: shkn up and kpt on wl fr over 2f out: unchal* **11/4**[2]

0 **2** 23 **Undisputed (IRE)**[86] 2677 5-11-2 0.................... MrSCrawford 90
(S R B Crawford, Ire) *t.k.h early: chsd clr ldng pair: hdwy to chse (clr) wnr over 4f out: rdn and no imp fnl 2f* **4/6**[1]

3 3¼ **Little Missserious (IRE)**[31] 3639 5-10-9 0.................... LiamMcKenna(7) 85
(J J Lambe, Ire) *hld up: pushed along 1/2-way: hdwy over 4f out: sn drvn and no imp fr 3f out* **8/1**[3]

02- **4** 87 **Missesgeejay**[375] 4065 6-10-13 0.................... HarryChalloner(3)
(Richard Ford) *led to 1/2-way: chsd wnr tl wknd over 4f out: t.o* **16/1**

5 99 **Supreme Gael** 5-11-2 0.................... HenryBrooke
(Iain Jardine) *sn towards rr: lost tch fnl circ: virtually p.u fnl 4f* **25/1**

4m 28.0s (268.00) **5** Ran SP% **107.5**
CSF £4.73 TOTE £2.80: £1.50, £1.10; EX 4.60 Trifecta £10.70.
Owner Nick Allsop **Bred** George Clohessy **Trained** Alcester, Warwicks

FOCUS
No depth to this bumper and the winner proved much too good for the favourite. A big step up from the winner, with the second and third rated close to their marks.
T/Jkpt: Not won. T/Plt: £91.00 to a £1 stake. Pool: £87,305.93 - 700.16 winning tickets. T/Qpdt: £18.20 to a £1 stake. Pool: £7,656.34 - 310.78 winning tickets. **Richard Young**

3194 LINGFIELD (L-H)
Tuesday, February 16
4169 Meeting Abandoned - waterlogged

4031 MUSSELBURGH (R-H)
Wednesday, February 17

OFFICIAL GOING: Soft (good to soft in places)
Wind: Breezy, half against Weather: Overcast

4175 WILLIAM HILL - BET AND WATCH H'CAP CHASE (13 fncs 5 omitted) 2m 7f 97y
1:40 (1:41) (Class 5) (0-100,98) 5-Y-0+ **£3,249** (£954; £477; £238)

Form RPR

0F02 **1** **Proud Gamble (IRE)**[9] 4032 7-10-4 76....................(t) CraigNichol 86+
(Rose Dobbin) *hld up: hdwy to trck ldrs 4 out: effrt and hung rt 2 out: rallied to ld run-in: styd on strly* **4/1**[2]

13-4 **2** ¾ **Whiskey Chaser (IRE)**[75] 2894 8-11-12 98.................... WillKennedy 106
(Donald McCain) *w ldr: nt fluent 1st: led 9th: rdn 2 out: hdd run-in: r.o: hld cl home* **8/1**

5U10 **3** 1¾ **Wakhan (IRE)**[28] 3679 8-11-3 89.................... DerekFox 96
(Sandy Thomson) *led to 9th: w ldr: drvn along 2 out: kpt on run-in* **11/2**

4655 **4** 7 **Apache Pilot**[9] 4032 8-10-6 83....................(tp) DaraghBourke(5) 82
(Maurice Barnes) *hld up: outpcd 8th: rallied after 4 out: drvn and no imp fr next* **5/1**[3]

40U1 **5** ½ **Solway Bay**[28] 3679 14-11-1 92....................(t) CallumBewley(5) 91
(Lisa Harrison) *chsd ldrs: drvn and outpcd after 4 out: no imp fr next* **10/1**

-544 **6** 19 **Oil Burner**[14] 3937 11-10-13 92.................... SamColtherd(7) 79
(Stuart Coltherd) *chsd ldrs: mstkes 3rd and 9th: rdn and wknd bef 3 out* **11/2**

/P0P **7** 25 **Tears From Heaven (USA)**[9] 4032 10-10-0 72 oh1.......(p) BrianHughes 27
(Chris Grant) *chsd ldrs: drvn and outpcd 8th: strugglign after next* **25/1**

2631 **P** **Vision De La Vie (FR)**[9] 4032 6-11-12 98 7ex....................(b) JamesReveley
(Pauline Robson) *hld up in tch: lost pl 6th: outpcd fr next: lost tch and p.u bef 3 out* **7/2**[1]

6m 6.8s (366.80) **8** Ran SP% **113.7**
CSF £34.63 CT £174.99 TOTE £5.60: £2.00, £2.30, £1.90; EX 35.50 Trifecta £220.00.
Owner Major General C A Ramsay **Bred** Ned Whitty **Trained** South Hazelrigg, Northumbria

FOCUS
Last fence and the last fence in back straight were omitted. Chase distances as advertised. Craig Nichol described the ground as "soft". Moderate chasing form. The first three have been rated pretty much to their marks.

4176 RACINGUK.COM/ANYWHERE MAIDEN HURDLE (12 hdls) 2m 3f 81y
2:15 (2:15) (Class 5) 4-Y-0+ **£3,249** (£954; £477; £238)

Form RPR

2243 **1** **Impulsive American**[10] 4010 4-10-11 118....................(p) TomScudamore 109+
(David Pipe) *hld up: smooth hdwy to trck ldrs bef 3 out: led gng wl last: shkn up and kpt on strly* **1/1**[1]

56 **2** 8 **Some Are Lucky (IRE)**[97] 2450 5-11-7 0.................... PaddyBrennan 107
(Tom George) *cl up: led and rdn 2 out: hdd whn nt fluent last: no ch w wnr* **2/1**[2]

2P **3** 7 **Rolling Thunder (IRE)**[32] 3626 6-11-7 0.................... HenryBrooke 100
(Donald McCain) *nt fluent on occasions: led: rdn bef 3 out: hdd next: sn outpcd* **9/1**

0 **4** 3½ **Shanroe Street (IRE)**[46] 3442 6-11-7 0.................... PeterBuchanan 96
(Lucinda Russell) *cl up: drvn and outpcd after 4 out: edgd rt and plugged on fr 2 out: no imp* **11/2**[3]

4-43 **5** 11 **Officer Hoolihan**[63] 3111 6-11-2 0....................(t) AlanJohns(5) 85
(Tim Vaughan) *t.k.h: trckd ldrs on outside tl rdn and wknd fr 3 out* **14/1**

50 **6** 22 **Red Piano**[9] 4031 7-11-0 0.................... MrWHRReed(7) 63
(Andrew Hamilton) *hld up: outpcd 7th: n.d after: btn bef 3 out* **66/1**

-340 **7** 29 **Heilan Rebel (IRE)**[29] 3668 6-11-7 0.................... LucyAlexander 34
(N W Alexander) *nt fluent in rr: struggling fnl circ: nvr on terms* **20/1**

P **Hop 'n Pop (IRE)**[59] 3185 9-11-0 0.................... CraigNichol
(Hugh Burns) *prom: lost pl bef 7th: struggling fr next: t.o whn p.u 3 out* **80/1**

4m 54.9s (3.40) **Going Correction** +0.425s/f (Soft)
WFA 4 from 5yo+ 9lb **8** Ran SP% **122.9**
Speed ratings (Par 103): **109,105,102,101,96 87,75,**
CSF £3.67 TOTE £1.80: £1.10, £1.10, £2.50; EX 3.40 Trifecta £14.20.
Owner Mrs Jo Tracey **Bred** D Brocklehurst **Trained** Nicholashayne, Devon

FOCUS
This race was run over 7yds further than advertised. Ordinary maiden hurdle form, with the ex-Flat race winner having too much pace for a trio of ex-pointers. The second and third have been rated in line with their bumper marks.

4177 BOOGIE IN THE MORNING H'CAP CHASE (12 fncs 4 omitted) 2m 3f 120y
2:50 (2:50) (Class 4) (0-110,110) 5-Y-0+ **£5,325** (£1,653; £890)

Form RPR

054 **1** **Finea (IRE)**[1] 4166 9-11-9 107....................(tp) BrianHughes 118+
(R K Watson, Ire) *cl up: led 3 out: shkn up and clr bef last: kpt on wl run-in* **7/2**[3]

4-21 **2** 4 **Oscar Lateen (IRE)**[69] 2983 8-10-12 96....................(p) DannyCook 101
(Sandy Thomson) *led: rdn 4 out: hdd whn mstke next: rallied: kpt on same pce fr last* **2/1**[1]

4446 **3** 12 **Chanceofa Lifetime (IRE)**[29] 3671 9-11-3 108.................... MrRSmith(7) 104
(Victor Thompson) *t.k.h: prom: rdn whn lft cl 3rd 3 out: mstke and outpcd fr next* **15/2**

2241 **F** **Bollin Line**[12] 3968 9-10-4 93.................... DeanPratt(5) +
(Lucinda Egerton) *hld up in tch: smooth hdwy on outside to chal whn fell 3 out* **10/3**[2]

31P0 **P** **Itstimeforapint (IRE)**[28] 3684 8-11-12 110....................(t) DerekFox
(Lucinda Russell) *nt fluent on occasions: hld up: outpcd 1/2-way: lost tch fnl circ: t.o whn p.u bef 3 out* **9/1**

265P **B** **Lawless Island (IRE)**[18] 3864 7-10-12 101.................... AlanJohns(5)
(Tim Vaughan) *trckd ldrs: stl gng wl whn b.d 3 out* **14/1**

P650 **U** **Vayland**[32] 3631 7-11-6 104.................... CraigNichol
(Micky Hammond) *hld up: sixth and in tch whn mstke: sprawled bdly and uns rdr 7th* **12/1**

5m 10.3s (310.30) **7** Ran SP% **114.8**
CSF £11.55 TOTE £3.40: £2.30, £1.60; EX 11.40 Trifecta £47.50.
Owner R K Watson **Bred** W J Vance **Trained** Killylea, Co Armagh

FOCUS
The complexion of this chase changed at the third-last when the strong-travelling Bollin Line fell, bringing down Lawless Island, who very much looked to be going well also. The form, as a result, isn't worth much. A step up from the winner, with the runner-up rated 3lb off following a break.

4178 RACING UK PROFITS RETURNED TO RACING H'CAP HURDLE (12 hdls) 2m 3f 81y
3:25 (3:25) (Class 4) (0-105,104) 4-Y-0+ **£3,249** (£954; £477; £238)

Form RPR

3216 **1** **Danceintothelight**[14] 3932 9-11-12 104....................(t) AdrianLane 110+
(Donald McCain) *led: nt fluent 4 out: hdd appr next: rallied and swtchd rt bef last: led run-in: styd on strly* **14/1**

0234 **2** 2½ **Hunters Belt (IRE)**[50] 3346 12-11-3 100....................(vt) JonathonBewley(5) 103
(George Bewley) *hld up: pushed along after 4 out: rallied 2 out: chsd wnr last 50yds: r.o* **20/1**

4-00 **3** ¾ **Imperial Prince (IRE)**[81] 2791 7-11-1 100.................... StevenFox(7) 103+
(Sandy Thomson) *hld up: rdn after 4 out: hdwy after next: kpt on fr last* **18/1**

P653 **4** 2¼ **Definitely Better (IRE)**[28] 3680 8-10-10 88.................... PaddyBrennan 89
(Tom George) *hld up: hdwy to chse ldrs 4 out: led after next: rdn 2 out: hung lft and hdd run-in: sn no ex* **13/2**[2]

400 **5** ¾ **Morning Time (IRE)**[44] 3473 10-10-5 88....................(tp) GrantCockburn(5) 88
(Lucinda Russell) *hld up in midfield: effrt and rdn bef 3 out: kpt on same pce fr last* **66/1**

-PFF **6** 1¾ **Home For Tea**[14] 3938 7-10-0 78....................(p) BrianHarding 75
(Keith Dalgleish) *cl up: jst led whn hit 3 out: sn hdd: cl up tl rdn and wknd after last* **12/1**

33P2 **7** *3* **Snowed In (IRE)**[28] 3680 7-11-4 **96**....................(p) SeanQuinlan 91
(Barry Murtagh) *prom: effrt and drvn along bef 3 out: wknd after last* **11/1**

6-41 **8** *1 1/4* **No Ceiling (IRE)**[6] 4068 6-10-8 **96**.................... TobyWheeler(10) 90
(Ian Williams) *hld up: stdy hdwy bef 3 out: sn pushed along: nt fluent next: sn wknd* **11/10**[1]

3023 **9** *4 1/2* **Roll Of Thunder**[118] 2029 7-10-12 **95**.................... MissCWalton(5) 84
(James Walton) *prom tl rdn and wknd bef 3 out* **33/1**

3455 **10** *1 1/2* **Stay In My Heart (IRE)**[127] 1897 7-10-7 **92**.................... JamesCorbett(7) 79
(Susan Corbett) *midfield: outpcd after 4 out: struggling fr next* **33/1**

4050 **11** *8* **Crinkle Crags (IRE)**[44] 3474 6-11-4 **96**.................... CraigNichol 75
(Nicky Richards) *bhd: outpcd 7th: nvr on terms* **9/1**[3]

4534 **12** *1 1/4* **Sendiym (FR)**[51] 3307 9-10-8 **86**....................(p) BrianHughes 64
(Dianne Sayer) *midfield: rdn after 4 out: wknd bef next* **16/1**

4m 55.6s (4.10) **Going Correction** +0.425s/f (Soft) **12** Ran SP% **116.9**
Speed ratings (Par 105): **108,106,106,105,105 104,103,102,100,100 96,96**
CSF £251.08 CT £4965.41 TOTE £12.80: £3.10, £6.80, £5.50; EX 196.10 Trifecta £2727.40.
Owner Mrs Sian McCain **Bred** Mrs David Low **Trained** Cholmondeley, Cheshire

FOCUS
This was run over 7yds further than advertised. Those at the head of the weights came to the fore in this modest handicap, with the picture changing late as the leaders stopped. The winner and fifth have been rated to their marks.

4179 WILLIAM HILL DOWNLOAD THE APP H'CAP HURDLE (QUALIFIER FOR CHALLENGER TWO MILE HURDLE FINAL) (9 hdls) 1m 7f 124y

4:00 (4:00) (Class 3) (0-130,130) 4-Y-O+ **£6,498** (£1,908; £954; £477)

Form RPR

5022 **1** **Teo Vivo (FR)**[28] 3682 9-11-7 **125**....................(b) BrianHughes 127+
(Pauline Robson) *chsd ldr: effrt and rdn 2 out: led last: drvn out run-in* **7/4**[1]

/002 **2** *1 1/4* **Jonny Delta**[9] 4036 9-10-4 **108**.................... HenryBrooke 108
(Jim Goldie) *led and sn clr: rdn 3 out: edgd lft and hdd last: rallied: hld nr fin* **15/2**

120 **3** *3 1/4* **Serenity Now (IRE)**[10] 4014 8-11-3 **121**.................... AidanColeman 117
(Brian Ellison) *hld up: hdwy to chse ldrs 2 out: sn rdn: kpt on same pce fr last* **14/1**

222- **4** *3 1/4* **El Beau (IRE)**[106] 4674 5-11-12 **130**.................... DannyCook 124
(John Quinn) *prom: blnd 3rd: effrt and rdn 3 out: nt fluent last: kpt on same pce* **11/2**[3]

-315 **5** *1 1/4* **Quick Brew**[118] 2027 8-10-9 **118**....................(t) DaraghBourke(5) 110
(Maurice Barnes) *in tch: rdn bef 3 out: outpcd fr next* **25/1**

5-44 **6** *2* **Marcus Antonius**[44] 3473 9-10-0 **104**.................... DerekFox 93
(Lucinda Russell) *hld up: rdn and effrt after 3 out: no imp fr next* **10/1**

-140 **7** *1 1/4* **Venue**[249] 727 6-11-9 **127**.................... WillKennedy 115
(Donald McCain) *hld up: effrt bef 3 out: outpcd fr next: hld whn hit last* **16/1**

4545 **8** *3/4* **Silver Duke (IRE)**[28] 3682 5-10-13 **117**.................... JamesReveley 104
(Jim Goldie) *hld up: hdwy 3 out: wknd fr next* **5/1**[2]

0 **9** *19* **First Post (IRE)**[14] 3941 9-11-0 **118**.................... PaddyBrennan 93
(Adrian McGuinness, Ire) *hld up in tch: drvn along bef 3 out: sn outpcd: hld whn nt fluent next* **12/1**

3m 51.8s (3.40) **Going Correction** +0.425s/f (Soft) **9** Ran SP% **113.4**
Speed ratings (Par 107): **108,107,105,104,103 102,101,101,92**
CSF £15.39 CT £136.98 TOTE £2.60: £1.40, £2.10, £2.30; EX 15.90 Trifecta £117.10.
Owner It's A Bargain Syndicate **Bred** E Chevalier Du Fau Et Al **Trained** Kirkharle, Northumberland

FOCUS
This was run over 3yds further than advertised. No hanging around here courtesy of the runner-up and the form is sound for the level. The second, third and fourth have been rated pretty much to their marks.

4180 EILDON HILL STABLES HUNTERS' CHASE (12 fncs 4 omitted) 2m 3f 120y

4:35 (4:40) (Class 6) 5-Y-O+ **£1,247** (£387; £193; £96)

Form RPR

0-00 **1** **Klepht (IRE)**[199] 1186 11-11-4 0....................(t) MrDHolmes(7) 120+
(D Holmes) *mde all: clr bef 4th: keeping on whn hung lft after last: unchal* **10/3**[2]

312- **2** *2 1/4* **Fredo (IRE)**[346] 4655 12-12-0 121....................(p) MrRyanBird(5) 123
(Ian Williams) *chsd wnr: rdn bef 3 out: kpt on wl fr last: nt rch wnr* **4/1**[3]

533- **3** *5* **Coeur De Fou (FR)**[24] 11-11-4 99....................(p) MrNGeorge(7) 110
(Tom George) *hld up: pushed along after 4 out: kpt on fr 2 out: nvr able to chal* **2/1**[1]

P **4** *7* **Damiens Dilemma (IRE)**[10] 4016 8-11-4 0.................... SamColtherd(7) 104
(Mrs L A Coltherd) *bhd: pushed along bef 4 out: hmpd next: kpt on fr 2 out: no imp* **11/2**

0-6U **5** *2 3/4* **Little Fritz (FR)**[10] 4016 9-11-4 99.................... MrRyanNichol(7) 100
(L Kerr) *nt fluent on occasions: hld up: hdwy 1/2-way: effrt bef 3 out: no ex bef last* **16/1**

40F5 **6** *25* **Emkae (IRE)**[130] 1853 8-11-8 87....................(t) MrTHamilton(3) 75
(J P G Hamilton) *hld up in tch: outpcd fr 8th: btn bef 3 out* **33/1**

16P/ **7** *19* **Molten Brown**[326] 11-11-6 0.................... MissJWalton(5) 56
(Tony Hogarth) *hld up in tch: nt fluent and outpcd 8th: sn struggling* **50/1**

PP-4 **F** **Brokethegate**[287] 140 11-11-6 84.................... MrRSmith(5)
(Chris Grant) *uns rdr and loose bef s: t.k.h: hld up: fell 2nd* **50/1**

P04- **U** **Lachlan Mor**[66] 7-11-4 68.................... MissPoppi-JayneShepherd(7)
(Stuart Coltherd) *prom to 1/2-way: sn struggling: no ch whn mstke and uns rdr last* **150/1**

302 **U** **Wind Of Hope (IRE)**[145] 1646 7-11-6 115.................... MissRMcDonald(5)
(Alan J Brown) *prom: pushed along after 4 out: 13 l 4th and outpcd whn blnd and uns rdr next* **11/4**[1]

5m 6.5s (306.50) **10** Ran SP% **115.2**
CSF £17.16 TOTE £3.70: £1.30, £1.80, £2.00; EX 17.70 Trifecta £67.70.
Owner D Holmes **Bred** Hugh O'Connor **Trained** Morpeth, Northumberland

FOCUS
The two with back class came to the fore in this hunters' chase. The third and fifth help set the level.

4181 WILLIAMHILL.COM OPEN NATIONAL HUNT FLAT RACE 1m 7f 124y

5:05 (5:05) (Class 6) 4-6-Y-O **£1,949** (£572; £286; £143)

Form RPR

1 **Boyhood (IRE)**[283] 5-11-2 0.................... PaddyBrennan 105+
(Tom George) *hld up in tch: shkn up and hdwy to ld over 1f out: pushed out fnl f* **9/4**[2]

05 **2** *3* **Desert Sensation (IRE)**[60] 3165 4-10-7 0....................(t) BrianHughes 92
(Tracy Waggott) *t.k.h: led at modest gallop: qcknd over 2f out: rdn and hdd over 1f out: kpt on same pce ins fnl f* **16/1**

U0 **3** *2 3/4* **Dubai Shen (IRE)**[82] 2756 5-11-2 0.................... CraigNichol 98
(Alistair Whillans) *cl up: drvn and outpcd over 2f out: rallied over 1f out: no imp fnl f* **15/2**

4 *9* **Up North (IRE)** 4-10-4 0.................... JoeColliver(3) 80
(Micky Hammond) *hld up in tch on outside: hdwy 3f out: rdn and edgd rt wl over 1f out: sn wknd* **2/1**[1]

23 **5** *5* **Selkirk's Island**[66] 3060 5-10-9 0.................... PeterBuchanan 77
(Lucinda Russell) *cl up: drvn and outpcd over 2f out: btn over 1f out* **5/2**[3]

3m 50.8s (8.00) **Going Correction** +0.425s/f (Soft)
WFA 4 from 5yo 9lb **5** Ran SP% **110.3**
Speed ratings: **97,95,94,89,87**
CSF £30.19 TOTE £3.80: £2.70, £3.90; EX 29.70 Trifecta £75.50.
Owner H Stephen Smith & The Gabbertas Family **Bred** Mrs A Murphy **Trained** Slad, Gloucs

FOCUS
This was run over 3yds further than advertised. Little depth to this weak bumper. The third sets the level.
T/Plt: £187.00 to a £1 stake. Pool: £59260.8 - 231.22 winning tickets T/Qpdt: £46.10 to a £1 stake. Pool: £4181.38 - 67.1 winning tickets **Richard Young**

3946 TOWCESTER (R-H)

Wednesday, February 17

OFFICIAL GOING: Soft (heavy in places)
Wind: Fresh across Weather: Raining

4182 HAYGAIN HAY STEAMERS CLEAN HEALTHY FORAGE NOVICES' HURDLE (DIV I) (8 hdls) 1m 7f 181y

1:20 (1:20) (Class 4) 4-Y-O+ **£3,898** (£1,144; £572; £286)

Form RPR

-212 **1** **William H Bonney**[50] 3353 5-11-8 136.................... RichardJohnson 129+
(Alan King) *hld up: hdwy 4th: led appr 2 out: rdn out* **1/4**[1]

1-04 **2** *1 3/4* **Chic Theatre (IRE)**[70] 2972 6-10-11 0.................... DavidNoonan(5) 119
(David Pipe) *chsd ldr tl led 4th: rdn and hdd appr 2 out: styd on same pce flat* **4/1**[2]

50 **3** *20* **Tipperairy (IRE)**[19] 3839 5-11-2 0.................... HarrySkelton 99
(Dan Skelton) *hld up: hdwy 4th: rdn after next: wknd appr 2 out* **12/1**[3]

-U20 **4** *3* **Viva Rafa (IRE)**[49] 3370 6-11-2 0.................... IanPopham 96
(Richard Phillips) *led to 4th: ev ch 3 out: rdn and wknd bef next* **20/1**

0-4P **5** *11* **Terra Firma**[19] 3842 6-11-2 0.................... BrendanPowell 85
(Claire Dyson) *chsd ldrs tl rdn and wknd appr 2 out* **100/1**

5 **6** *nse* **Good Man Hughie (IRE)**[74] 2909 7-10-13 0.................... BenPoste(3) 85
(Sally Randell) *hld up and bhd: rdn after 3 out: nvr on terms* **25/1**

00- **7** *2 3/4* **Gray Wolf River**[31] 5-10-2 0.................... MrRHogg(7) 75
(Richard Harper) *chsd ldrs: j. slowly 3rd: rdn and wknd after 3 out* **66/1**

4m 18.4s (10.50) **Going Correction** +0.70s/f (Soft) **7** Ran SP% **118.8**
Speed ratings (Par 105): **101,100,90,88,83 83,81**
CSF £1.92 TOTE £1.10: £1.10, £1.80; EX 2.20 Trifecta £5.00.
Owner Mr & Mrs R Scott **Bred** Pitchall Stud **Trained** Barbury Castle, Wilts

FOCUS
Hurdles on inside line and distances as advertised. Very testing conditions and it looked really hard work for most of these novice hurdlers in the opener. This looked a shallow affair and the pair that dominated the betting did so in the race itself, drawing a long way clear. The winner set a high standard and has been rated below his best, with the second rated similar to his bumper mark and the third and fourth helping to set the level.

4183 HAYGAIN HAY STEAMERS CLEAN HEALTHY FORAGE NOVICES' HURDLE (DIV II) (8 hdls) 1m 7f 181y

1:50 (1:51) (Class 4) 4-Y-O+ **£3,898** (£1,144; £572; £286)

Form RPR

2/0U **1** **Georgian Firebird**[18] 3863 6-10-4 0.................... CiaranGethings(5) 111+
(Barry Leavy) *led: hdd after 2nd: chsd ldr: nt fluent next: shkn up to ld again appr last: edgd lft flat: styd on wl* **11/1**

3F-U **2** *2 3/4* **Go West Young Man (IRE)**[99] 2412 8-11-2 125.................... JakeGreenall 115+
(Henry Daly) *trckd ldrs: wnt 2nd and shkn up flat: styd on same pce* **13/8**[2]

1 **3** *4* **Que Sera (IRE)**[62] 3130 6-11-8 0.................... TomO'Brien 117
(Philip Hobbs) *chsd ldrs: led appr 2 out: rdn and hdd bef last: wknd flat* **11/8**[1]

4P **4** *10* **Me Voila (FR)**[14] 3926 4-10-2 0.................... LizzieKelly(5) 93
(Nick Williams) *hld up: plld hrd: hdwy to ld after 2nd: rdn and hdd appr 2 out: wknd bef last* **9/1**[3]

0030 **5** *4 1/2* **Thyne For Gold (IRE)**[19] 3835 5-11-2 0.................... SamTwiston-Davies 97
(Donald McCain) *hld up: rdn and wknd after 3 out* **25/1**

6 *1/2* **Lord Of The Island (IRE)**[73] 8-11-2 0.................... DavidBass 96
(Sally Randell) *hld up: rdn after 3 out: nvr on terms* **33/1**

30P6 **7** *1 3/4* **Midnight Folie**[13] 3947 6-10-9 0.................... NicodeBoinville 87
(Ben Pauling) *hld up: rdn and wknd after 3 out* **33/1**

05 **8** *1 3/4* **Closer To Home (IRE)**[13] 3955 4-10-2 0....................(p) DavidNoonan(5) 84
(David Pipe) *hld up: nt fluent 4th: rdn after next: wknd appr 2 out* **20/1**

0-56 **9** *10* **Dragon De La Tour (FR)**[19] 3842 5-11-2 0.................... HarrySkelton 83
(Dan Skelton) *hld up: hdwy after 5th: rdn and wknd bef 2 out* **25/1**

4m 23.7s (15.80) **Going Correction** +0.70s/f (Soft)
WFA 4 from 5yo+ 9lb **9** Ran SP% **116.9**
Speed ratings (Par 105): **88,86,84,79,77 77,76,75,70**
CSF £28.99 TOTE £11.90: £2.80, £1.10, £1.10; EX 39.20 Trifecta £64.60.
Owner Mrs Lizzy Wilson **Bred** Brown Moss Stud **Trained** Forsbrook, Staffs

FOCUS
This looked a bit of a match on paper given the top two in the betting set quite a good standard on form. The slower of the two divisions. The winner has been rated in line with her Flat form, with the second 10lb off.

4184 SKYBET CHELTENHAM PREVIEW HERE MARCH 7TH H'CAP HURDLE (10 hdls) 2m 3f 34y

2:25 (2:28) (Class 5) (0-100,100) 4-Y-O+ **£3,249** (£954; £477; £238)

Form RPR

0P45 **1** **Kelsey (IRE)**[48] 3378 6-11-1 **89**....................(t) RichardJohnson 102+
(Tom Lacey) *hld up: hdwy 3 out: led bef next: clr last: styd on wl* **6/1**[3]

3034 **2** *12* **Young Lou**[22] 3789 7-10-0 **77**....................(p) ConorShoemark(3) 78
(Robin Dickin) *hld up: hdwy after 6th: rdn and ev ch appr 2 out: nt fluent 2 out: styd on same pce* **20/1**

-55P **3** *14* **Aviador (GER)**[30] 3662 10-11-7 **100**.................... DavidNoonan(5) 87
(Lucy Wadham) *chsd ldr: rdn and ev ch appr 2 out: wknd bef last* **10/1**

-141 **4** *9* **Transient Bay (IRE)**[22] 3791 6-11-2 **93**....................(p) AdamNicol(3) 70
(Philip Kirby) *prom: lost pl 6th: hdwy after 3 out: rdn and wknd next* **4/1**[2]

-F0P **5** *10* **Mother Meldrum (IRE)**[47] 3414 7-11-5 **100**................ DavidPrichard(7) 67
(Victor Dartnall) *mid-div: hdwy 5th: rdn and wknd after 3 out* **20/1**

506 **6** *1 ½* **Jopaan (IRE)**[13] 3946 9-9-9 **74** oh5.......................(t) GaryDerwin(5) 40
(Brian Barr) *led: rdn and hdd appr 2 out: sn wknd* **33/1**

22P3 **7** *17* **Camillas Wish (IRE)**[46] 3437 7-10-9 **88**................(p) JonathanMoore(5) 37
(J T R Draper, Ire) *hld up: bhd fr 7th* **12/1**

0242 **8** *1* **Distant Sound (IRE)**[13] 3946 9-10-11 **85**......................(b) MichealNolan 33
(Grace Harris) *hld up: hdwy 7th: rdn and wknd after 3 out* **7/2**[1]

6335 **9** *16* **Gud Day (IRE)**[14] 3925 8-10-10 **84**...................................(p) TomO'Brien 16
(Conor Dore) *hld up: a in rr: bhd fr 7th* **25/1**

-053 **P** **Yasir (USA)**[26] 3729 8-11-5 **93**.................................(t) RichieMcLernon
(Sophie Leech) *hld up: rdn and wknd appr 3 out: bhd whn p.u bef next* **12/1**

6531 **P** **Solidago (IRE)**[48] 3382 9-11-3 **96**.......................... CiaranGethings(5)
(Barry Leavy) *hld up: bhd fr 7th: p.u bef 2 out* **10/1**

534P **P** **Sylvan Legend**[44] 3468 8-10-4 **78**...........................(tp) TrevorWhelan
(Matt Sheppard) *hld up: rdn and wknd appr 3 out: bhd whn p.u bef next* **33/1**

0005 **P** **Powderonthebonnet (IRE)**[22] 3784 8-11-1 **94**............ DanielHiskett(5)
(Richard Phillips) *prom: lost pl 5th: bhd fr 7th: p.u bef 2 out* **20/1**

434R **P** **Cadgers Hole**[8] 4045 9-10-0 **74** oh2......................... TomMessenger
(Lynn Siddall) *hld up: rdn and appr 3 out: bhd whn p.u bef next* **50/1**

PP00 **P** **Memory Of Light (IRE)**[13] 3946 7-10-0 **74**...............(t) BrendanPowell
(Claire Dyson) *mid-div: hdwy 6th: rdn and wknd after 3 out: bhd whn p.u bef next* **16/1**

-020 **P** **Cassie**[19] 3835 6-11-9 **97**...(t) DavidBass
(Ben Pauling) *chsd ldrs tl rdn and wknd after 3 out: bhd whn p.u bef next* **12/1**

000- **P** **Mon Petit Ange (FR)**[345] 4674 5-10-6 **85**.....................(p) JakeHodson(5)
(David Bridgwater) *mid-div: lost pl appr 6th: bhd fr next: p.u bef 2 out* **66/1**

5m 17.2s (7.60) **Going Correction** +0.70s/f (Soft) **17 Ran SP% 131.1**
Speed ratings (Par 103): **112,106,101,97,93 92,85,84,78, , , , ,**
CSF £128.51 CT £1223.75 TOTE £10.40: £2.90, £4.80, £2.50, £1.40; EX 192.90 Trifecta £3260.00 Part won..
Owner Tom Lacey & Heather Haddock **Bred** Gerry O'Dowd **Trained** Ledbury, H'fords

FOCUS
A wide-open handicap which was run at what appeared quite an even gallop. Very little had landed a blow on the leading pair until the home turn but, by the time they reached the second-last flight, the picture was changing quickly and the leaders began to fold. A big step up from the winner, with the second the best guide to the level.

4185 JIM DIMMOCK 50 YEARS IN RACING MEMORIAL H'CAP CHASE (15 fncs 2 omitted) 3m 102y

3:00 (3:04) (Class 4) (0-110,110) 5-Y-0+ **£6,330** (£1,870; £935; £468; £234)

Form RPR

1-P2 **1** **Emma Soda**[12] 3979 11-11-6 **104**.................................(b) PeterCarberry 112
(Paul Davies) *chsd ldr to 4th: remained handy: rdn to go 2nd again appr 2 out: led bef last: styd on wl* **11/2**[3]

11P5 **2** *7* **Leith Hill Legasi**[30] 3663 7-10-6 **97**..........................(bt) MissCVHart(7) 100+
(Charlie Longsdon) *led: rdn appr 2 out: hdd whn mstke last: no ex flat* **10/1**

-514 **3** *6* **Call The Detective (IRE)**[22] 3788 7-11-12 **110**.............. GavinSheehan 104
(Ali Stronge) *hld up: hdwy 12th: rdn after 3 out: wknd next* **11/2**[3]

2311 **4** *19* **Bebinn (IRE)**[16] 3906 9-11-7 **105**...................................(p) DarylJacob 80
(Ben Case) *prom tl rdn and wknd after 3 out* **13/2**

5-44 **5** *7* **Gibbstown (IRE)**[20] 3833 10-10-9 **98**.....................(p) JonathanMoore(5) 66
(Paul Stafford, Ire) *hld up: mstke 2nd: hdwy 9th: mstke next: rdn and wknd appr 3 out* **9/1**

4/P- **6** *9* **Our Island (IRE)**[45] 11-11-12 **110**..................................(p) DaveCrosse 69
(Hugo Froud) *hld up: drvn along 8th: wknd after 11th* **40/1**

3623 **P** **Somerset Lias (IRE)**[25] 3746 8-11-4 **102**.......................... LiamHeard
(Bob Buckler) *hld up: hdwy 4th: lost pl 8th: sme hdwy 11th: wknd appr 3 out: bhd whn p.u bef last* **7/2**[2]

5-31 **P** **Badger Wood**[25] 3746 7-11-8 **106**.................................. TomCannon
(Giles Smyly) *prom: chsd ldr 4th tl rdn appr 2 out: stmbld on landing 2 out: sn wknd and p.u* **3/1**[1]

7m 5.1s (28.20) **Going Correction** +1.275s/f (Heav) **8 Ran SP% 112.9**
Speed ratings: **104,101,99,93,91 88, ,**
CSF £54.39 CT £313.98 TOTE £6.70: £2.20, £2.80, £1.80; EX 69.70 Trifecta £294.90.
Owner P S Davies **Bred** Richard Mathias **Trained** Bromyard, H'fords

FOCUS
They bypassed what would have been the first fence as the ground continued to deteriorate. Race distance increased by 65yds. This turned into a real war of attrition and most of these were cooked a long way out. A small pb from the winner, with the second rated back to form.

4186 HAYGAIN HAY STEAMERS CLEAN HEALTHY FORAGE MARES' H'CAP HURDLE (12 hdls) 2m 7f 211y

3:35 (3:35) (Class 3) (0-125,120) 4-Y-0+ **£6,498** (£1,908; £954; £477)

Form RPR

P4P2 **1** **Streets Of Promise (IRE)**[18] 3866 7-11-12 **120**.........(p) LiamTreadwell 131
(Michael Scudamore) *led to 4th: led again 7th: hdd 9th: led appr 2 out: styd on wl* **8/1**

5331 **2** *7* **Timon's Tara**[14] 3930 7-11-2 **110**.................................. JackQuinlan 113
(Robin Dickin) *hld up: hdwy appr 8th: rdn after 3 out: styd on same pce appr last: wnt 2nd flat* **7/1**[3]

62P3 **3** *1* **Dolores Delightful (FR)**[13] 3956 6-11-11 **119**........(t) RichardJohnson 123
(Nick Williams) *hld up in tch: jnd wnr 8th: led next: rdn and hdd appr 2 out: no ex last* **15/8**[1]

3-42 **4** *15* **Altesse De Guye (FR)**[88] 2632 6-11-1 **109**.................. AndrewTinkler 101
(Martin Keighley) *hld up: hdwy appr 3 out: wknd bef next* **7/2**[2]

-236 **5** *26* **Jean Fleming (IRE)**[68] 3025 9-11-7 **115**.....................(v[1]) BrendanPowell 76
(Jamie Snowden) *chsd ldrs: rdn after 9th: wknd 3 out* **8/1**

31/P **U** **My Miss Lucy**[41] 3498 10-10-6 **105**............................. DanielHiskett(5)
(Richard Phillips) *chsd wnr tl led 4th: hdd 7th: rdn and lost pl bef next: wkng whn tried to refuse and uns rdr 9th* **25/1**

612P **P** **Fresh By Nature (IRE)**[11] 3999 9-10-13 **110**.............. HarryBannister(3)
(Harriet Bethell) *hld up: a in rr: rdn and lost tch after 7th: bhd whn p.u bef 3 out* **14/1**

542 **P** **Lakeshore Lady (IRE)**[62] 3126 6-10-11 **110**................... JakeHodson(5)
(David Bridgwater) *chsd ldrs tl rdn and wknd after 3 out: bhd whn p.u bef next* **8/1**

6m 49.2s (34.20) **Going Correction** +0.70s/f (Soft) **8 Ran SP% 113.4**
Speed ratings (Par 107): **71,68,68,63,54 , ,**
CSF £60.56 CT £147.76 TOTE £8.30: £1.90, £1.90, £1.50; EX 49.80 Trifecta £172.40.
Owner Gempro **Bred** Gareth Adair **Trained** Bromsash, H'fords

FOCUS
A competitive mares' hurdle, but conditions were worsening and only four of the eight runners had any sort of chance by the home turn. The winner has been rated to her best, with the second and third rated to their marks.

4187 HAYGAIN HAY STEAMERS CLEAN HEALTHY FORAGE H'CAP CHASE (12 fncs 1 omitted) 2m 3f 179y

4:10 (4:12) (Class 5) (0-100,100) 5-Y-0+ **£3,249** (£954; £477; £238)

Form RPR

1245 **1** **Bredon Hill Lad**[25] 3746 9-11-6 **97**............................ LucyGardner(3) 111+
(Sue Gardner) *prom: lost pl 3rd: hdwy 9th: rdn after 3 out: led bef next: pckd 2 out: styd on* **5/2**[1]

431P **2** *1 ½* **Ballyegan (IRE)**[12] 3977 11-11-4 **92**.................................. LiamHeard 100
(Bob Buckler) *a.p: rdn after 3 out: chsd wnr appr last: styd on u.p* **11/2**

3212 **3** *15* **Riddlestown (IRE)**[62] 3131 9-11-9 **97**..........................(b) HarrySkelton 90
(Caroline Fryer) *sn prom: j.rt 5th: chsd ldr next: led 7th: rdn and hdd appr 2 out: wknd last* **3/1**[2]

P2U3 **4** *nk* **Lamb's Cross**[13] 3951 10-10-6 **83**........................... HarryBannister(3) 75
(Brian Barr) *led to 7th: led again after 3 out: rdn and hdd bef next: wknd last* **4/1**[3]

PP0F **P** **Wicklewood**[13] 3951 10-11-11 **99**.................................(t) TomCannon
(Mark Gillard) *hld up: a in rr: bhd fr 5th: p.u bef 3 out* **20/1**

3P0P **P** **The Sneezer (IRE)**[12] 3977 13-10-7 **86**..........................(p) ChrisWard(5)
(Nikki Evans) *chsd ldr: nt fluent 4th: lost 2nd 6th: wknd next: bhd whn p.u bef 3 out* **40/1**

3P-4 **P** **Parting Way (IRE)**[48] 3379 8-11-12 **100**....................... RichardJohnson
(Tim Vaughan) *hld up: a in rr: hit 5th: bhd fr 7th: mstke 2 out: sn p.u* **9/2**

5m 45.8s (27.60) **Going Correction** +1.275s/f (Heav) **7 Ran SP% 114.3**
Speed ratings: **95,94,88,88,**
CSF £16.73 TOTE £3.30: £1.80, £2.60; EX 18.50 Trifecta £38.60.
Owner R W & Mrs J M Mitchell **Bred** R W And Mrs Mitchell **Trained** Longdown, Devon

FOCUS
Race distance increased by 35yds. A modest handicap chase that represented a drop in class for the winner. It's been rated around the first two.

4188 HAYGAIN HAY STEAMERS CLEAN HEALTHY FORAGE STANDARD OPEN NATIONAL HUNT FLAT RACE 1m 7f 181y

4:45 (4:46) (Class 6) 4-6-Y-0 **£1,949** (£572; £286; £143)

Form RPR

1 **Laser Light (IRE)**[87] 5-11-2 0.. DarylJacob 118+
(Alan King) *w ldrs: led over 2f out: c readily clr fnl f* **4/6**[1]

2 *7* **Western Wave (FR)** 4-10-7 0.. NoelFehily 95+
(David Loder) *hld up: hdwy over 4f out: chsd wnr 2f out: sn rdn: outpcd fnl f* **11/4**[2]

3 *18* **Big Time Frank (IRE)** 5-11-2 0....................................... KielanWoods 86
(Alex Hales) *disp ld tl wnt on over 3f out: rdn and hdd over 2f out: wknd over 1f out* **16/1**

0 **4** *23* **Pomicide**[13] 3959 6-10-13 0... LucyGardner(3) 63
(Sue Gardner) *disp ld tl rdn over 3f out: wknd over 2f out* **20/1**

5 *14* **Booted Eagle (IRE)** 6-11-2 0.. IanPopham 49
(Anabel K Murphy) *prom: rdn over 4f out: sn wknd* **6/1**[3]

6 **6** *78* **Eclectica Girl**[20] 3827 5-10-9 0..................................(b[1]) LeeEdwards
(Kevin Frost) *hld up: reminder after 3f: rdn over 5f out: wknd over 4f out* **66/1**

4m 12.6s (10.30) **Going Correction** +0.70s/f (Soft)
WFA 4 from 5yo 9lb 5 from 6yo 1lb **6 Ran SP% 113.1**
Speed ratings: **102,98,89,78,71 32**
CSF £2.79 TOTE £1.60: £1.10, £1.40; EX 2.70 Trifecta £12.00.
Owner Simon Munir & Isaac Souede **Bred** Clongiffin Stud **Trained** Barbury Castle, Wilts

FOCUS
This looked no more than an ordinary bumper, but the winner looked decent and should win more races.
T/Plt: £54.40 to a £1 stake. Pool: £65777.02 - 882.54 winning tickets T/Qpdt: £42.00 to a £1 stake. Pool: £5292.0 - 93.2 winning tickets **Colin Roberts**

4189 - 4195a (Foreign Racing) - See Raceform Interactive

3213 FONTWELL (L-H)

Thursday, February 18

OFFICIAL GOING: Heavy (3.6)
Wind: almost nil Weather: sunny Rails: Fences and Hurdles outer. Top bend common (adds 78yds). Bottom bends divided adds 54yds. Additional distances (approx) Races 1, 2 & 5 - add 264 yards. Races 3 & 4 - add 318 yards. Race 6 - add 186 yards.

4196 EBF STALLIONS "NATIONAL HUNT" NOVICES' HURDLE (QUALIFIER) (9 hdls) 2m 1f 145y

2:20 (2:20) (Class 4) 4-7-Y-0 **£3,898** (£1,144; £572; £286)

Form RPR

1446 **1** **Alcala (FR)**[54] 3254 6-11-8 125...................................(t[1]) SeanBowen 126+
(Paul Nicholls) *trckd ldrs: led between last 2: jnd briefly last: drifted lft fnl 120yds but r.o wl to assert: rdn out* **1/2**[1]

554 **2** *2 ¼* **The Fresh Prince (IRE)**[28] 3710 6-11-2 0................... LeightonAspell 118+
(Oliver Sherwood) *trckd ldrs: cl 3rd 3 out: shkn up to chal last: styd on but nt quite pce of wnr fnl 120yds* **7/2**[2]

0-35 **3** *24* **Wabanaki (IRE)**[50] 3363 6-11-2 0....................................... AdamWedge 98
(Evan Williams) *led: rdn and hdd after 2 out: wknd run-in* **11/2**[3]

2-65 **4** *27* **Meyrem Ana**[21] 3825 6-10-2 0..................................... MrWillPettis(7) 60
(Natalie Lloyd-Beavis) *trckd ldr tl rdn after 3 out: wknd next: t.o* **200/1**

0-60 **P** **Rob Robin (IRE)**[65] 3101 6-11-2 0.................................... TomCannon
(Chris Gordon) *hld up bhd ldrs: lost tch after 6th: t.o whn p.u after next (b.b.vs)* **33/1**

5m 6.8s (32.50) **Going Correction** +1.775s/f (Heav) **5 Ran SP% 107.7**
Speed ratings: **98,97,86,74,**
CSF £2.56 TOTE £1.30: £1.10, £1.50; EX 2.10 Trifecta £2.80.
Owner Andrea & Graham Wylie **Bred** Francois Rimaud **Trained** Ditcheat, Somerset

FOCUS
Fences and hurdles outer. Top bend common (adds 78yds), bottom bend common (adds 54yds). As a result this race was run over 264yds further than advertised. Leighton Aspell described the ground as "heavy but not holding" adding that rain the previous night probably helped. No great depth to this novice hurdle and the front pair ended up well clear. The cosy winner didn't need to be at his best to land the odds, while the second has been rated as running a small pb.

4197 ROA/RACING POST OWNERS JACKPOT H'CAP CHASE (13 fncs) 2m 1f 96y
2:55 (2:55) (Class 4) (0-115,109) 5-Y-O+ **£4,548** (£1,335; £667; £333)

Form RPR
10-6 **1** **Cloudy Beach (IRE)**[76] 2885 9-11-7 **109**.................. CharlieDeutsch[(5)] 122+
(Venetia Williams) *j.w: a.p: led 7th: jnd 2 out: styd on wl to assert fnl 75yds: rdn out* **3/1**[2]

4-44 **2** *6* **Agincourt Reef (IRE)**[15] 3931 7-11-11 **108**.................. JoshuaMoore 114
(Gary Moore) *trckd ldrs: nt fluent 1st: rdn along fr 7th: chal 2 out: ev ch fr last tl no ex fnl 75yds* **11/4**[1]

1465 **3** *1* **Matrow's Lady (IRE)**[13] 3977 9-10-6 **89**..................(tp) NoelFehily 95
(Neil Mulholland) *hld up bhd ldrs: j.lft at times: hit 3rd: wnt 4th after 4 out: rdn after next: styd on same pce fr 2 out* **7/2**[3]

0314 **4** *1* **Thepartysover**[63] 3125 11-11-8 **105**..................(t) TomO'Brien 110
(Paul Henderson) *j.lft at times: hld up last but in tch: hit 9th: rdn appr 3 out: no imp tl styd on fr last: wnt 4th towards fin* **8/1**

-31P **5** *2* **Olympian Boy (IRE)**[14] 3951 12-11-2 **99**..................(t) RichieMcLernon 101
(Sophie Leech) *hld up bhd ldrs: wnt 2nd travelling wl after 9th: rdn bef 3 out: styd on same pce* **12/1**

3PU1 **P** **Goring Two (IRE)**[31] 3661 11-10-7 **90**.................. TrevorWhelan
(Anna Newton-Smith) *led tl 7th: sn drvn along: dropped to last after 4 out but stl in tch: p.u next* **9/2**

5m 13.8s (39.10) **Going Correction** +2.35s/f (Heav) **6** Ran SP% **110.9**
Speed ratings: **102,99,98,98,97**
CSF £11.71 TOTE £3.00: £1.30, £4.70; EX 11.80 Trifecta £37.40.
Owner The Beachcombers **Bred** Jim Dempsey **Trained** Kings Caple, H'fords

FOCUS
Race run over 264yds further than advertised. Modest chase form, but a winner on the up. The winner has been rated up a stone plus on the best of his hurdle figures, with the second, third and fourth all pretty close to their marks.

4198 GEORGE SMITH HORSEBOXES NOVICES' HURDLE (11 hdls) 2m 5f 139y
3:30 (3:30) (Class 4) 5-Y-O+ **£3,898** (£1,144; £572; £286)

Form RPR
314 **1** **Chef D'Oeuvre (FR)**[19] 3852 5-11-5 135.................. GavinSheehan 136+
(Warren Greatrex) *mde all: tended to jump v sltly rt at times: jnd 3 out tl shkn up to draw clr fr next: comf* **2/11**[1]

0-03 **2** *21* **Norman The Red**[68] 3043 6-10-12 0.................. MattieBatchelor 100
(Jamie Poulton) *trckd ldrs: nt fluent 6th: chal 3 out tl rdn bef next: kpt on for clr 2nd but sn no ch w wnr* **100/1**

-034 **3** *22* **In The Hold (IRE)**[36] 3581 6-10-12 0.................. AdamWedge 76
(Evan Williams) *j.lft at times: hld up: v awkward and nrly uns rdr 2nd: rdn in wl hld 4th after 3 out: wnt modest 3rd towards fin* **16/1**

0-P3 **4** *2 1/4* **Pawn Star (IRE)**[26] 3736 6-10-12 0.................. LeightonAspell 74
(Emma Lavelle) *hld up: hmpd 3rd: hdwy after 7th: rdn after 3 out: wknd next: lost modest 3rd towards fin* **15/2**[2]

64-1 **P** **Blackdown Hills**[266] 526 6-10-5 0.................. NicodeBoinville
(Mark Bradstock) *racd keenly: trckd wnr tl wknd rapidly after 7th: sn p.u* **12/1**[3]

3-2P **P** **Holbrook Park**[31] 3664 6-10-12 0..................(t) TrevorWhelan
(Neil King) *trckd ldrs: nt fluent 4th: wknd 3 out: t.o whn p.u bef next* **33/1**

P **Crack On Tom (IRE)** 7-10-12 0.................. NoelFehily
(Emma Lavelle) *hld up in tch: tk clsr order 5th: struggling 8th: wknd bef next: t.o whn p.u bef 2 out* **20/1**

6m 16.6s (34.10) **Going Correction** +1.775s/f (Heav) **7** Ran SP% **118.6**
Speed ratings: **109,101,93,92,** ,
CSF £48.47 TOTE £1.10: £1.10, £17.70; EX 47.50 Trifecta £371.30.
Owner McNeill Family **Bred** Ecurie Winning **Trained** Upper Lambourn, Berks

FOCUS
Race run over 318yds further than advertised. No depth at all to this novice hurdle, with the red-hot favourite gradually pulling clear. The runner-up has been rated as taking a step up.

4199 BUY A GEORGE SMITH HORSEBOX H'CAP CHASE (16 fncs) 2m 5f 31y
4:05 (4:05) (Class 4) (0-110,110) 5-Y-O+ **£4,882** (£1,669)

Form RPR
401P **1** **Golanova**[20] 3836 8-11-12 **110**..................(b) JoshuaMoore 118
(Gary Moore) *disp ld most of way: rdn appr 3 out: edgd ahd run-in: drvn out* **4/1**[3]

-P11 **2** *12* **Showboater (IRE)**[54] 3214 7-11-11 **109**..................(p) NicodeBoinville 107
(Ben Pauling) *disp ld most of way: j.rt 3rd: 4th: 9th and 10th: rdn after 3 out: pckd next: hdd run-in: wknd fnl 50yds: dismntd (tired)* **4/5**[1]

3111 **F** **Black Narcissus (IRE)**[23] 3789 7-11-9 **107**.................. RhysFlint
(Alexandra Dunn) *trcking ldng pair whn fell 12th* **9/4**[2]

6m 30.0s (47.00) **Going Correction** +2.35s/f (Heav) **3** Ran SP% **106.3**
Speed ratings: **104,99,**
CSF £7.60 TOTE £3.90; EX 7.70 Trifecta £4.80.
Owner Mrs Elizabeth Kiernan **Bred** R D And Mrs J S Chugg **Trained** Lower Beeding, W Sussex

FOCUS
Race run over 318yds further than advertised. This form isn't worth much at all, with one falling and the odds-on favourite clearly performing below his best. This might be a step up from the winner, but the form is suspect.

4200 CONGRATULATIONS GEORGE DIGWEED WINNING 26 WORLD CHAMPIONSHIPS H'CAP HURDLE (10 hdls) 2m 3f 33y
4:40 (4:40) (Class 4) (0-110,107) 4-Y-O+ **£3,898** (£1,144; £572; £286)

Form RPR
5142 **1** **Lee Side Lady (IRE)**[10] 4028 6-10-11 **92**.................. NoelFehily 100
(Neil Mulholland) *trckd ldrs: jnd ldrs 3 out tl rdn bef next: led last: styd on strly: rdn out* **15/8**[1]

4400 **2** *5* **Ashkoun (FR)**[49] 3376 5-10-9 **95**..................(t) AlanJohns[(5)] 98
(Tim Vaughan) *led: clr tl 3rd: jnd 3 out: rdn and hdd bef next: ev ch briefly between last 2: hld last: styd on same pce* **16/1**

-530 **3** *4 1/2* **Itsaboutime (IRE)**[62] 3133 6-11-2 **102**.................. ConorRing[(5)] 101
(Helen Nelmes) *hld up in tch: nt fluent 3rd: hdwy after 7th: rdn after 3 out: no further imp tl styd on fr last: wnt 3rd nring fin* **25/1**

04PP **4** *1 1/2* **Eco Warrior**[23] 3788 6-11-5 **105**.................. CharlieDeutsch[(5)] 104
(Venetia Williams) *trckd ldr: rdn to ld appr 2 out where blnd bdly: sn hdd and hld: no ex fr last: lost 3rd nring fin* **7/2**[3]

5 *51* **Claire Pet (IRE)**[61] 3171 9-11-2 **107**.................. CharlieHammond[(10)] 52
(Dr Richard Newland) *hld up last but in tch: hdwy 6th: effrt in cl 4th after 3 out: wknd bef last: fin v tired* **2/1**[2]

4PP **P** **Zarosa (IRE)**[14] 3947 7-10-12 **93**.................. JackQuinlan
(John Berry) *hld up in tch: struggling 7th: wknd after next: t.o whn p.u bef last* **33/1**

550 **P** **Rocknrobin (IRE)**[16] 3915 5-11-2 **97**.................. TomCannon
(Chris Gordon) *hld up in tch: struggling after 6th: wknd after 3 out: t.o whn p.u bef last* **12/1**

5m 38.1s (38.70) **Going Correction** +1.775s/f (Heav) **7** Ran SP% **110.7**
Speed ratings (Par 105): **89,86,85,84,62** ,
CSF £26.75 TOTE £2.60: £1.50, £4.40; EX 21.70 Trifecta £218.60.
Owner The Affordable (2) Partnership **Bred** Michael Lane **Trained** Limpley Stoke, Wilts
■ Stewards' Enquiry : Charlie Deutsch two-day ban: used whip above permitted level (Mar 3-4)

FOCUS
Race run over 264yds further than advertised. Lowly hurdles form and the runners finished tired. The winner has been rated to a similar level as her recent reappearance.

4201 LEASE A HORSEBOX FROM GEORGE SMITH INTERMEDIATE NATIONAL HUNT FLAT RACE (COND. JOCKEYS & AMATEURS) 1m 5f 143y
5:10 (5:10) (Class 6) 4-6-Y-O **£1,559** (£457; £228; £114)

Form RPR
1 **Admiral Kid (IRE)**[144] 5-10-11 0.................. MrShaneQuinlan[(7)] 110+
(Neil Mulholland) *mde all: kpt on wl and in command fnl 2f* **4/5**[1]

2 *1 1/4* **River Of Intrigue (IRE)** 6-10-8 0.................. AlanDoyle[(10)] 106+
(Nicky Henderson) *hld up last but wl in tch: hdwy 5f out to trck wnr: rdn over 2f out: kpt on but a being hld* **7/4**[2]

3 *11* **Alice Pink (IRE)** 6-10-4 0.................. MrBParis-Crofts[(7)] 85
(Paul Henderson) *trckd ldrs: rdn over 2f out: kpt on same pce fnl f* **20/1**

4 *18* **Chasing Fairies** 5-10-4 0.................. MrWGordon[(7)] 62
(Alexandra Dunn) *chsd ldrs tl outpcd 5f out: no ch and hanging rt but regained 4th ent fnl f* **20/1**

5 *9* **Tengri** 4-10-4 0.................. FreddieMitchell[(5)] 48
(John Ryan) *trckd ldrs: rdn 3f out: wknd ent fnl f* **12/1**[3]

3m 50.8s (19.70) **5** Ran SP% **109.1**
CSF £2.35 TOTE £1.70: £1.10, £1.20; EX 2.30 Trifecta £7.80.
Owner Equi ex Incertis Partners **Bred** Michael Conlon **Trained** Limpley Stoke, Wilts

FOCUS
Race run over 186yds further than advertised. The big two in the market dominated this pretty modest bumper.
T/Plt: £33.30 to a £1 stake. Pool: £47,634.64 - 1,042.22 winning tickets. T/Qpdt: £19.00 to a £1 stake. Pool: £3,028.05 - 117.4 winning tickets. **Tim Mitchell**

[3340]KELSO (L-H)
Thursday, February 18

OFFICIAL GOING: Heavy (soft in places)
Wind: Fresh, half against Weather: Sunny

4202 KELSO ANNUAL MEMBERS NOVICES' HURDLE (6 hdls 2 omitted) 2m 51y
1:20 (1:20) (Class 4) 4-Y-O+ **£3,249** (£954; £477; £238)

Form RPR
412 **1** **Road To Gold (IRE)**[33] 3626 7-11-9 116.................. LucyAlexander 129+
(N W Alexander) *pressed ldr: drvn 3 out (usual 4 out): outpcd next: rallied after omitted 2 out: edgd rt and led run-in: styd on strly* **3/1**[3]

-213 **2** *5* **Western Rules (IRE)**[18] 3883 6-11-9 122.................. BrianHarding 123
(Nicky Richards) *led: nt fluent 2nd: rdn and hrd pressed bef last: edgd rt and hdd run-in: sn no ex* **5/4**[1]

3 *1 3/4* **Water Sprite (IRE)**[14] 3961 5-11-2 0..................(t) RichardJohnson 114
(Gordon Elliott, Ire) *in tch: stdy hdwy 2 out (usual 3 out): effrt and ev ch last: edgd lft and no ex run-in* **15/8**[2]

3300 **4** *28* **Final Fling (IRE)**[10] 4031 5-11-2 0.................. CraigNichol 86
(Rose Dobbin) *hld up: outpcd 3rd: shkn up and hdwy bef 2 out (usual 3 out): sn no imp: btn passing omitted 2 out* **80/1**

46-5 **5** *26* **Red Mystique (IRE)**[67] 3054 7-10-11 79..................(t) DaraghBourke[(5)] 60
(Maurice Barnes) *prom: drvn and outpcd 2 out (usual 3 out): wknd passing omitted 2 out* **200/1**

P **Scrutiny**[125] 5-11-2 0.................. BrianHughes
(Barry Murtagh) *bhd: struggling 3rd: lost tch next: t.o whn p.u bef last* **33/1**

0 **P** **Anna Grey**[13] 3971 7-10-2 0.................. MissAWaugh[(7)]
(Simon Waugh) *bhd on outside: struggling fr 3rd: lost tch and p.u bef last* **250/1**

4m 23.1s (21.30) **Going Correction** +1.525s/f (Heav)
WFA 4 from 5yo+ 9lb **7** Ran SP% **109.3**
Speed ratings (Par 105): **107,104,103,89,76** ,
CSF £6.78 TOTE £6.10: £1.90, £1.10; EX 6.00 Trifecta £9.50.
Owner Mrs J Douglas Miller **Bred** Kevin Whelan **Trained** Kinneston, Perth & Kinross

FOCUS
Testing ground, with even the clerk of the course suggesting that the drying sun would make conditions 'hard work' - the winner's time underlined how heavy the ground was. Three previous winners who had shown fair form made this a potentially decent novice hurdle for the track, one run over an extra 36yds due to rail movement. The usual second-last hurdle was omitted. The second, third and fourth have been rated close to their marks.

4203 BORDER HOTEL KIRK YETHOLM H'CAP CHASE (15 fncs 2 omitted) 2m 7f 96y
1:55 (1:55) (Class 3) (0-125,125) 5-Y-O+ **£6,498** (£1,908; £954; £477)

Form RPR
26F1 **1** **Rocking Blues (FR)**[15] 3934 11-10-11 120.................. LorcanMurtagh[(10)] 143+
(Rose Dobbin) *pressed ldr: led 2 out (usual 3 out): qckd clr bef last: readily* **7/4**[1]

P602 **2** *20* **Carrigdhoun (IRE)**[61] 3162 11-11-7 125..................(t) DaraghBourke[(5)] 128
(Maurice Barnes) *led at ordinary gallop: rdn and hdd 2 out (usual 3 out): rallied: no ex bef last* **9/4**[2]

-314 **3** *14* **Gold Opera (IRE)**[30] 3669 7-10-12 111.................. LucyAlexander 102
(N W Alexander) *nt fluent: in tch: stdy hdwy 1/2-way: effrt on outside bef omitted 2 out: hung lft and sn wknd* **5/1**[3]

-335 **4** *13* **Lucematic**[18] 3885 10-11-1 114.................. BrianHughes 90
(Chris Grant) *hld up in tch: effrt after 2 out (usual 3 out): wknd passing omitted 2 out* **8/1**

-51P **P** **Redkalani (IRE)**[15] 3933 8-10-9 108..................(b[1]) JamesReveley
(Keith Reveley) *chsd ldrs: hit 7th: lost pl whn hit next: struggling fr 10th: lost tch and p.u bef 3 out (usual 4 out)* **8/1**

6m 54.7s (46.70) **Going Correction** +2.225s/f (Heav) **5** Ran SP% **106.0**
Speed ratings: **107,100,95,90,**
CSF £5.79 TOTE £2.30: £1.90, £1.20; EX 6.80 Trifecta £22.30.

Owner The Friday Lions **Bred** Mme Genevieve Mongin **Trained** South Hazelrigg, Northumbria

FOCUS

Only a couple of proven, in-form chasers in this small-field handicap, which was run over an extra 48yds with the usual second-last fence omitted. The impressive winner is on the upgrade and there's a case for rating him 7lb+ higher given the fast finishing split in the ground.

4204 TIMEFORM MOREBATTLE HURDLE (8 hdls 2 omitted) 2m 2f 25y

2:30 (2:30) (Class 2) 4-Y-0+ **£16,245** (£4,770; £2,385; £1,192)

Form RPR

-225 **1** **Top Notch (FR)**[48] 3408 5-11-4 158................................ DarylJacob 159+
(Nicky Henderson) *trckd ldrs: smooth hdwy to ld bef last: shkn up briefly and qckd clr run-in: readily* **4/11**[1]

-1P1 **2** *12* **One For Harry (IRE)**[33] 3630 8-11-2 140.................... BrianHarding 142
(Nicky Richards) *prom: niggled along after 4th: nt fluent 2 out (usual 3 out): hdwy to ld passing omitted 2 out: drvn and hdd bef last: no ch w ready wnr* **4/1**[2]

1432 **3** *22* **Chic Name (FR)**[40] 3519 4-10-7 139.....................(v) AlainCawley 110
(Richard Hobson) *pressed ldr: led briefly bef omitted 2 out: sn rdn and wknd* **10/1**[3]

P-36 **4** *59* **Croco Bay (IRE)**[95] 2511 9-11-2 140........................ KielanWoods 60
(Ben Case) *nt fluent early: led at ordinary gallop: rdn and hdd bef omitted 2 out: sn wknd* **18/1**

4m 56.2s (29.20) **Going Correction** +1.70s/f (Heav)
WFA 4 from 5yo+ 9lb **4** Ran SP% **107.7**
Speed ratings (Par 109): **103,97,87,61**
CSF £2.24 TOTE £1.10; EX 2.40 Trifecta £3.50.

Owner Simon Munir & Isaac Souede **Bred** Haras Des Sablonnets & Dr Vet B Gabeur **Trained** Upper Lambourn, Berks

FOCUS

A range of abilities over hurdles among the four runners assembled for a contest that had fallen to the high-class Peddlers Cross and Simonsig in previous years. The usual second-last hurdle was omitted and the race was run over an extra 36yds. The easy winner has been rated back to something like his best, while the second sets the level.

4205 IVAN STRAKER MEMORIAL CHASE (16 fncs 3 omitted) 3m 2f 39y

3:05 (3:05) (Class 2) 5-Y-0+ **£14,102** (£4,404; £2,371)

Form RPR

-003 **1** **Unioniste (FR)**[12] 3993 8-11-2 149.......................... NickScholfield 154+
(Paul Nicholls) *prom: hdwy to ld 4th: hdd 2 out (usual 3 out): shkn up to ld bef last: sn clr and styd on strly* **10/11**[1]

0-21 **2** *9* **Neptune Equester**[74] 2934 13-10-12 130........................(p) DerekFox 138
(Sandy Thomson) *chsd ldrs: pushed along and hdwy to chse wnr bef 11th: led 2 out (usual 3 out) to bef last: kpt on same pce: collapsed fatally after r* **14/1**

-041 **3** *66* **Soll**[47] 3448 11-11-2 152...(bt) TomScudamore 92
(David Pipe) *chsd ldr tl hit 2nd: cl up: drvn and outpcd after 10th: rallied 4 out (usual 5 out): wknd fr next: eased whn no ch passing omitted 2 out* **6/4**[2]

PP-0 **P** **Corrin Wood (IRE)**[26] 3737 9-10-12 141.......................... BrianHarding
(Donald McCain) *led to 4th: cl up: drvn and outpcd 10th: lost tch and p.u bef 4 out (usual 5 out)* **8/1**[3]

7m 47.1s (59.90) **Going Correction** +2.40s/f (Heav) **4** Ran SP% **110.2**
Speed ratings: **103,100,79,**
CSF £10.10 TOTE £2.40; EX 9.20 Trifecta £17.10.

Owner J Hales **Bred** Haras De Saint-Voir Et Al **Trained** Ditcheat, Somerset

FOCUS

This quartet had all shown very useful form over fences, albeit the BHA ratings suggested a couple were significantly disadvantaged at the weights, but only two horses gave their running in a contest run over an extra 48yds. The usual second-last fence was omitted. The cosy winner has been rated similar to the level of his recent Sandown run, and the second to his best.

4206 KELSO ANNUAL MEMBERS H'CAP HURDLE (5 hdls 6 omitted) 2m 6f 151y

3:40 (3:41) (Class 3) (0-125,124) 4-Y-0+ **£6,498** (£1,908; £954; £477)

Form RPR

033 **1** **Shades Of Midnight**[26] 3737 6-11-9 **124**..................(t) CallumWhillans(3) 140+
(Donald Whillans) *hld up on ins: hdwy to ld after last (usual 3 out): rdn clr after omitted 2 out: kpt on strly* **4/1**[1]

/430 **2** *26* **Kind Of Easy (IRE)**[19] 3855 10-10-6 **104**........................ CraigNichol 94
(Alistair Whillans) *mde most to after last (usual 3 out): sn drvn along: plugged on passing omitted last: tk 2nd cl home: no ch w wnr* **16/1**

0512 **3** *shd* **Pilgrims Bay (IRE)**[15] 3923 6-11-9 **121**........................ TomScudamore 111
(David Pipe) *hld up: hdwy to chse ldrs 1/2-way: effrt and wnt 2nd bef omitted 2 out: sn one pce: lost 2nd cl home* **4/1**[1]

F2-2 **4** *28* **Teddy Tee (IRE)**[82] 2764 7-11-6 **123**............................ RyanDay(5) 85
(Nicky Richards) *hld up in tch: effrt bef last (usual 3 out): wknd passing omitted 2 out* **5/1**[3]

-604 **5** *11* **Landecker (IRE)**[48] 3428 8-11-7 **119**..........................(v) LucyAlexander 70
(N W Alexander) *cl up: drvn and outpcd after last (usual 3 out): wknd passing omitted 2 out* **9/2**[2]

444P **6** *6* **Manballandall (IRE)**[20] 3837 8-10-12 **117**..................(t) JamesCorbett(7) 62
(Susan Corbett) *hld up: rdr lost iron briefly after 3rd: rdn 2 out (usual 4 out): wknd fr last (usual 3 out)* **20/1**

5032 **7** *24* **Rock Relief (IRE)**[50] 3361 10-10-1 **104**..................(v) DiarmuidO'Regan(5) 25
(Chris Grant) *rn in snatches: prom tl rdn and wknd fr 2 out* **12/1**

-2P0 **8** *8* **Always Tipsy**[48] 3428 7-11-3 **120**............................ StephenMulqueen(5) 33
(N W Alexander) *hld up: stdy hdwy and prom 1/2-way: rdn and wknd after last (usual 3 out)* **12/1**

PU/5 **9** *dist* **Kris Cross (IRE)**[48] 3428 9-11-5 **122**........................(tp) GrantCockburn(5)
(Lucinda Russell) *chsd ldrs: struggling 2 out (usual 4 out): sn btn: virtually p.u passing omitted 2 out* **10/1**

/56- **P** **Mr Blue Nose**[395] 3775 6-10-9 **112**.................................. CallumBewley(5)
(Simon Waugh) *chsd ldrs: struggling bef 3 out (usual 5 out): lost tch and p.u bef last (usual 3 out)* **16/1**

6m 19.6s (38.60) **Going Correction** +1.875s/f (Heav) **10** Ran SP% **115.9**
Speed ratings (Par 107): **107,97,97,88,84 82,73,71,,**
CSF £63.30 CT £272.81 TOTE £4.80: £1.90, £4.70, £1.60; EX 74.80 Trifecta £348.40.

Owner The Potassium Partnership **Bred** Potassium Partnership II **Trained** Hawick, Borders

FOCUS

Plenty of these had form credentials to make them of interest in a competitive handicap hurdle. It was run over an extra 32yds but the usual last and second-last hurdles were both omitted, so the run-in was nearly 5f and this was a true test of stamina - they finished well strung out. The winner was quite impressive and recorded a fast finishing split, but this seems a big step up and nothing else got home, with the second and third rated 10lb off.

4207 P & G ALLAN CATERING OPEN HUNTERS' CHASE (12 fncs 5 omitted) 2m 7f 96y

4:15 (4:15) (Class 5) 5-Y-0+ **£2,495** (£774; £386; £193)

Form RPR

4-4 **1** **Durban Gold**[263] 9-10-12 0.. MrNOrpwood(7) 113
(Mrs D Walton) *in tch: hdwy to chse ldr bef 8th: led bef omitted 2 out: drvn and styd on wl* **25/1**

03U- **2** *6* **Wicklow Lad**[25] 12-12-3 122.................................(v) MrKitAlexander(3) 122
(N W Alexander) *cl up: led bef 7th: hdd bef omitted 2 out: one pce passing omitted last* **5/1**[3]

5F-P **3** *5* **Mister Marker (IRE)**[287] 156 12-12-6 121........................ MissCWalton 118
(Nicky Richards) *cl up: pushed along 2 out (usual 4 out): one pce passing omitted 2 out* **4/1**[2]

120- **4** *12* **Barachois Silver**[25] 12-11-4 94.................................. MissRMcDonald(5) 94
(Mrs J M Hollands) *led to bef 7th: sn drvn along: rallied: outpcd fr last (usual 3 out)* **25/1**

1-0P **5** *½* **Wayupinthesky (IRE)**[12] 4000 9-12-3 113........................ MrTHamilton(3) 105
(J P G Hamilton) *prom: drvn along and outpcd bef 2 out (usual 4 out): btn bef omitted 2 out* **13/2**

0 **6** *59* **Havana Jack (IRE)**[67] 6-11-5 0.................................. MrRyanNichol(7) 38
(L Kerr) *hld up: pushed along 3 out (usual 5 out): struggling fr next: t.o* **66/1**

50-4 **7** *99* **Bobcatbilly (IRE)**[290] 100 10-12-1 137.......................... MrRyanBird(5)
(Ian Williams) *plld hrd early in rr: nt fluent on occasions: stdy hdwy and prom whn mstke 7th: rdn last (usual 3 out): wknd bef omitted 2 out: virtually p.u* **11/10**[1]

-1PP **P** **Kings Grey (IRE)**[200] 1186 12-12-6 130......................(tp) MrJohnDawson
(Philip Kirby) *hld up: hit 6th: struggling bef 3 out (usual 5 out): wknd and p.u bef next* **10/1**

7m 1.3s (53.30) **Going Correction** +2.575s/f (Heav) **8** Ran SP% **115.9**
Speed ratings: **110,107,106,102,101 81,46,**
CSF £144.98 TOTE £19.50: £4.90, £1.90, £1.60; EX 171.30 Trifecta £1151.30.

Owner Mrs D Walton **Bred** R J And Mrs E M D Chugg **Trained** Chathill, Northumberland

FOCUS

Not a race to go overboard about as although there were plenty with form under rules, they all had questions to answer. This hunter chase was run over an extra 48yds and the usual second-last fence plus last were omitted, making for a lengthy run-in. A big step up from the winner, with the second rated to the best of last season's form.

4208 RACING UK IN HD NEXT MONTH STANDARD OPEN NATIONAL HUNT FLAT RACE 2m 51y

4:50 (4:50) (Class 6) 4-6-Y-O **£1,624** (£477; £238; £119)

Form RPR

1 **Lady Beaufort** 5-10-9 0.. RichardJohnson 101+
(John Quinn) *prom: hdwy to ld 2f out: rdn and kpt on strly fnl f* **9/4**[2]

2 *3* **Randy Pike (IRE)** 6-11-2 0.. BrianHarding 105+
(Nicky Richards) *t.k.h: trckd ldrs: checked bnd after 6f: smooth hdwy to chal over 2f out: rdn over 1f out: kpt on same pce ins fnl f* **6/5**[1]

3 *15* **Brackenmoss Rory** 4-10-7 0.. CraigNichol 81
(Alistair Whillans) *hld up: stdy hdwy over 4f out: effrt over 2f out: plugged on fnl f: nt rch first two* **8/1**

-4 **4** *7* **Move To The Groove (IRE)**[35] 3593 6-11-2 0.................... AdrianLane 83
(Donald McCain) *t.k.h: led at modest gallop: rdn and hdd 2f out: sn wknd* **7/1**[3]

0 **5** *6* **Coachie Bear**[288] 145 5-10-13 0.................................. AdamNicol(3) 77
(Katie Scott) *chsd ldr: faltered bnd after 6f: rdn along over 3f out: sn wknd* **50/1**

6 *¾* **Cully Mac (IRE)** 5-10-11 0.. RyanDay(5) 76
(Andrew Wilson) *t.k.h: hld up: drvn and outpcd over 3f out: btn fnl 2f* **16/1**

7 *2¼* **Speranza** 4-9-7 0.. JamesCorbett(7) 58
(Susan Corbett) *hld up: drvn and outpcd over 3f out: sn btn* **25/1**

8 *46* **Winter Link** 6-10-2 0.. MrTHamilton(7) 21
(Sandy Forster) *hld up: struggling 4f out: sn lost tch: t.o* **28/1**

4m 30.2s (34.00) **Going Correction** +2.05s/f (Heav)
WFA 4 from 5yo 9lb 5 from 6yo 1lb **8** Ran SP% **115.0**
Speed ratings: **97,95,88,84,81 81,80,57**
CSF £5.23 TOTE £3.10: £1.10, £1.10, £2.00; EX 6.00 Trifecta £25.70.

Owner The Desperados **Bred** R W Russell **Trained** Settrington, N Yorks

FOCUS

Nothing out of the ordinary among the two with experience and this bumper, run over an extra 36yds, was ripe for taking by a newcomer, as the market leaders proved by fighting out the finish. The fourth helps set the level.

T/Plt: £34.10 to a £1 stake. Pool: £46,489.54 - 994.53 winning tickets. T/Qpdt: £21.20 to a £1 stake. Pool: £3,370.50 - 117.62 winning tickets. **Richard Young**

3920 LEICESTER (R-H)

Thursday, February 18

OFFICIAL GOING: Heavy

Wind: Light across Weather: Fine

4209 WREN H'CAP CHASE (12 fncs) 1m 7f 201y

2:10 (2:10) (Class 4) (0-115,115) 5-Y-0+ **£4,548** (£1,335; £667; £333)

Form RPR

-P23 **1** **Pret A Thou (FR)**[19] 3868 13-11-4 **110**.................... HarryChalloner(3) 119
(John Groucott) *chsd ldr tl after 2nd: remained handy: wnt 2nd again 8th tl 4 out: chsd ldr 3 out: led appr last: rdn out* **6/1**[3]

6523 **2** *4½* **Gold Ingot**[27] 3727 9-11-12 **115**.................................. AndrewThornton 120
(Caroline Bailey) *racd wd: led to 4th: chsd ldr to 8th: rdn to go 2nd again 4 out tl next: styd on same pce appr last: wnt 2nd flat* **9/2**[2]

42U1 **3** *2¾* **Gallic Warrior (FR)**[16] 3916 9-11-7 **110**....................(t) PaddyBrennan 113
(Fergal O'Brien) *prom: chsd ldr after 2nd: led and nt fluent 4th: rdn and hdd appr last: wknd flat* **8/11**[1]

-1PF **4** *21* **Richardofdoccombe (IRE)**[14] 3954 10-11-6 **109**.........(t) DenisO'Regan 89
(Gail Haywood) *sn bhd: j. slowly 4 out* **16/1**

31-F **P** **Seranwen (IRE)**16 3916 9-11-5 **108** .... SamTwiston-Davies
(Nigel Twiston-Davies) *hld up: j.rt 7th: wknd 4 out: bhd whn p.u bef last* **13/2**

4m 20.2s (12.00) **Going Correction** +0.80s/f (Soft) **5** Ran SP% **109.6**
Speed ratings: **102,99,98,87,**
CSF £30.20 TOTE £5.80: £2.50, £1.60; EX 23.40 Trifecta £47.30.
Owner C J Tipton **Bred** Mme Robert Jeannin **Trained** Bourton, Shropshire

FOCUS
This all-chase card went ahead in spite of 13mm of overnight rain, which saw the ground change from soft, heavy in places to heavy all over before the opener. Sam Twiston-Davies reported after the first 'it's heavy,' while Andrew Thornton stated 'it's soft and heavy on the crossings - it's not too bad.' The bends were moved out, so 39yds needs adding to the official race distance. Quite a competitive race to start off with even though it was a small field. It's been rated around the balance of the first three.

4210 FERNIE NOVICES' LIMITED H'CAP CHASE (12 fncs) 1m 7f 201y
2:45 (2:45) (Class 3) (0-140,137) 5-Y-O+ **£7,596** (£2,244; £1,122)

Form RPR
3126 **1** **All Together (FR)**33 3620 5-11-1 **131** .... JamesBest 135+
(Johnny Farrelly) *chsd ldr tl led 3 out: rdn appr last: styd on wl* **5/2**3

61U2 **2** *3* **Jayo Time (IRE)**64 3107 7-11-3 **137** ....(p) CiaranGethings(5) 140
(Kerry Lee) *hld up: hdwy to dispute 2nd 6th tl appr 4 out: rallied to chse wnr last: sn rdn: styd on same pce flat* **2/1**2

1131 **3** *12* **Truckers Highway (IRE)**19 3867 7-10-7 **125** .... HarryChalloner(3) 117
(John Groucott) *led at stdy pce: nt fluent 2nd: j.lft 4th: qckned appr 4 out: hdd next: sn rdn: wknd flat* **5/4**1

4m 25.1s (16.90) **Going Correction** +0.80s/f (Soft)
WFA 5 from 7yo 1lb **3** Ran SP% **106.3**
Speed ratings: **89,87,81**
CSF £7.00 TOTE £3.30; EX 10.60 Trifecta £9.30.
Owner Mrs Z Wentworth **Bred** Maurice Hassan **Trained** Enmore, Somerset

FOCUS
The bends were moved out, so 39yds needs adding to the official race distance. Not form to go over the top about but none of the three could be safely discounted before the start. It's been rated around the first two.

4211 WEATHERBYS NOVICES' H'CAP CHASE (12 fncs) 1m 7f 201y
3:20 (3:20) (Class 4) (0-105,103) 5-Y-O+ **£5,198** (£1,526; £763; £381)

Form RPR
2431 **1** **Global Dream**15 3925 6-11-8 **99** .... AdamPogson 109
(Caroline Bailey) *chsd ldr: led and hit 2nd: sn hdd: lost 2nd 6th: dropped to rr next: rallied to ld after 8th: nt fluent 4 out: hdd next: rdn appr 2 out: styd on to ld fnl 110yds* **13/8**2

5/00 **2** *½* **Diamond Life**72 2958 10-11-4 **95** .... DenisO'Regan 104
(Mark Pitman) *a.p: nt fluent 1st: chsd ldr 6th tl led 8th: sn hdd: led again 3 out: j.lft next: rdn and hdd fnl 110yds: styd on same pce* **7/1**

3401 **3** *15* **Entry To Evrywhere (IRE)**10 4029 8-10-7 **84** 7ex........(t) ConorO'Farrell 81
(Alexandra Dunn) *plld hrd: led to 2nd: sn led again: hdd 8th: wknd after 2 out: hit last* **11/8**1

2350 **4** *2¾* **Malanos (IRE)**23 3784 8-11-12 **103** .... LeeEdwards 94
(Tony Carroll) *hld up: racd keenly: hdwy 7th: nt fluent next: rdn appr 4 out: wknd next* **6/1**3

4m 24.8s (16.60) **Going Correction** +0.80s/f (Soft) **4** Ran SP% **107.0**
Speed ratings: **90,89,82,80**
CSF £10.66 TOTE £2.50; EX 11.30 Trifecta £21.30.
Owner Mrs Susan Carsberg **Bred** Mrs S Carsberg **Trained** Holdenby, Northants

FOCUS
The bends were moved out, so 39yds needs adding to the official race distance. Probably a weak contest. The second has been rated to his hurdle mark.

4212 SIS CAVALRY H'CAP CHASE (15 fncs) 2m 4f 45y
3:55 (3:55) (Class 3) (0-140,138) 5-Y-0+ **£7,596** (£2,244; £1,122; £561; £280)

Form RPR
312F **1** **Stilletto (IRE)**14 3957 7-11-6 **132** .... SamTwiston-Davies 150+
(Paul Nicholls) *hld up: mstke 3rd: hdwy 6th: chsd ldr 4 out: led after 2 out: clr last: pushed out* **7/4**1

P1FP **2** *10* **Simply Wings (IRE)**51 3339 12-11-6 **132** ....(p) JamieMoore 132
(Kerry Lee) *prom: chsd ldr 6th: led 8th: rdn appr 3 out: nt fluent 2 out: sn hdd: wknd last* **8/1**

14F6 **3** *17* **Brody Bleu (FR)**14 3957 9-11-4 **130** .... LiamTreadwell 111
(Robert Walford) *chsd ldr to 6th: wknd 10th* **33/1**

10/1 **4** *1½* **Prideofthecastle (IRE)**15 3922 9-10-10 **127** .... DavidNoonan(5) 108
(David Pipe) *hld up: hdwy 5th: chsd ldr after 11th: rdn and lost 2nd bef next: wknd 3 out* **2/1**2

5156 **5** *13* **Noble Legend**18 3887 9-11-3 **129** ....(p) HarrySkelton 96
(Caroline Bailey) *led to 8th: rdn after 11th: wknd 4 out* **14/1**

-P1U **P** **Valid Point (IRE)**51 3339 10-10-13 **125** ....(vt1) MarkGrant
(Nigel Twiston-Davies) *chsd ldrs: lost pl 5th: bhd fr next: p.u bef 8th* **7/1**3

-00U **P** **Silver Roque (FR)**75 2902 10-11-5 **138** .... MissAEStirling(7)
(Fergal O'Brien) *prom: lost pl 6th: wknd 9th: bhd whn p.u bef 2 out* **10/1**

5m 29.9s (11.00) **Going Correction** +0.80s/f (Soft) **7** Ran SP% **112.0**
Speed ratings: **110,106,99,98,93**
CSF £15.27 CT £327.09 TOTE £2.20: £2.30, £1.90; EX 14.10 Trifecta £112.80.
Owner R S Brookhouse **Bred** W Powell-Harris **Trained** Ditcheat, Somerset

FOCUS
The bends were moved out, so 51yds needs adding to the official race distance. This was the best race on the card, with plenty of these having a chance for one reason or another. Another step up from the winner, with the second rated close to his mark. The time was very fast compared with the later handicap.

4213 DICK SAUNDERS NOVICES' HUNTERS' CHASE (18 fncs) 2m 6f 151y
4:30 (4:30) (Class 6) 6-Y-O+ **£1,559** (£483; £241; £121)

Form RPR
1 **Carlton Ryan (IRE)**32 8-11-9 0 .... MrWEasterby(5) 106+
(Mrs Stephanie Easterby) *hld up: pckd 12th: hdwy next: chal 4 out: rdn appr last: hmpd flat: styd on u.p to ld nr fin* **8/11**1

P40- **2** *nk* **Gentle Duke**310 5337 9-11-11 0 .... MrStanSheppard(3) 105
(Miss L Wallace) *chsd ldr: led 13th: hdd after next: led again bef 3 out: rdn and j.lft 2 out: edgd lft flat: hdd nr fin* **20/1**

5/2- **3** *7* **Mister Teddy**39 11-11-7 103 ....(p) MrHFNugent(7) 98
(F A Hutsby) *led to 13th: led again after next: hdd 4 out: sn rdn: styd on same pce appr last* **8/1**3

3/2 **4** *7* **Big Georgie (IRE)**14 3958 9-11-9 0 .... MrJMRidley(5) 93
(J M Ridley) *chsd ldrs: rdn appr 3 out: wknd after next* **9/4**2

P **Cab On Times (IRE)**25 7-11-7 0 .... MrJNailor(7)
(S Rea) *chsd ldrs: led 4 out: hdd bef next: sn rdn: wknd 2 out: p.u bef last* **33/1**

6m 26.7s (22.70) **Going Correction** +0.80s/f (Soft) **5** Ran SP% **107.5**
Speed ratings: **92,91,89,87,**
CSF £12.06 TOTE £1.50: £1.10, £6.80; EX 13.20 Trifecta £52.10.
Owner S A Hollings **Bred** Frank Sinnott **Trained** Sherriff Hutton, N Yorks
■ Stewards' Enquiry : Mr Stan Sheppard two-day ban: careless riding (Mar 3,9)

FOCUS
The bends were moved out, so 51yds needs adding to the official race distance. The early pace wasn't quick and it developed into a bit of a sprint down the home straight. Seemingly a step up from the runner-up.

4214 CHARNWOOD H'CAP CHASE (15 fncs) 2m 4f 45y
5:00 (5:00) (Class 5) (0-100,98) 5-Y-0+ **£3,898** (£1,144; £572; £286)

Form RPR
06PP **1** **Some Finish (IRE)**19 3864 7-10-5 **77** ....(v) CharliePoste 89+
(Robin Dickin) *chsd ldr 2nd tl j.rt 4 out: rallied appr last: led 110yds out: styd on wl* **7/2**2

4324 **2** *6* **Theflyingportrait (IRE)**20 3834 7-11-12 **98** ....(t) SeanQuinlan 104
(Jennie Candlish) *hld up: racd keenly: hdwy 8th: chsd ldr and hmpd 4 out: led appr last: rdn and hdd 110yds out: no ex* **11/4**1

26-3 **3** *4* **Wayward Frolic**17 3906 10-11-10 **96** .... JamieMoore 99
(Jim Best) *led: j.lft at times: clr fr 4th tl 4 out: blnd next: rdn and hdd appr last: wknd flat* **6/1**3

-3FP **4** *99* **Expanding Universe (IRE)**54 3218 9-11-6 **92** .... LeeEdwards
(Tony Carroll) *chsd ldr and blnd 1st: lost 2nd next: lost pl and pushed along after 5th: wknd 10th: j. bdly lft fnl 4 fences* **15/2**

-PP2 **P** **Midnight Charmer**21 3820 10-11-8 **97** ....(t) JamesBanks(3)
(Emma Baker) *hld up: hdwy 9th: rdn and wknd after 11th: bhd whn p.u bef 3 out* **6/1**3

0-53 **P** **Virtuose Du Chenet (FR)**31 3661 7-11-5 **91** .... AidanColeman
(Venetia Williams) *hld up: hdwy after 5th: lost pl whn blnd 9th: wknd 11th: bhd whn p.u bef next* **7/2**2

5m 40.7s (21.80) **Going Correction** +0.80s/f (Soft) **6** Ran SP% **111.4**
Speed ratings: **88,85,84,44,,**
CSF £13.69 CT £52.30 TOTE £4.00: £2.90, £1.60; EX 13.00 Trifecta £54.90.
Owner Mrs C Dickin & The Some Finish Partners **Bred** Liam Cullinan **Trained** Alcester, Warwicks

FOCUS
The bends were moved out, so 51yds needs adding to the official race distance. This was a really moderate event. A big step up from the winner on his previous Rules form, with the second setting the level.
T/Plt: £356.70 to a £1 stake. Pool: £49,529.92 - 101.34 winning tickets. T/Qpdt: £15.40 to a £1 stake. Pool: £4,379.96 - 210.36 winning tickets. **Colin Roberts**

4215 - 4221a (Foreign Racing) - See Raceform Interactive

4025 FAKENHAM (L-H)
Friday, February 19

OFFICIAL GOING: Good to soft (soft in places; 5.5)
Wind: fresh breeze Weather: very bright and sunny; 6 degrees

4222 ANDY DON MEMORIAL NOVICES' CHASE (16 fncs) 2m 5f 44y
1:30 (1:30) (Class 4) 5-Y-0+ **£5,198** (£1,526)

Form RPR
1/14 **1** **Willow's Saviour**76 2913 9-11-7 138 .... HarrySkelton 129+
(Dan Skelton) *mde all at slow pce: nt fluent 6th and 12th but gd otherwise: nvr in the remotest danger* **1/20**1

0554 **2** *12* **Larteta (FR)**49 3422 7-10-4 96 .... RomainClavreul(10) 102
(Sarah Humphrey) *j. deliberately in 2nd: struggling 13th: drvn 2 out: v flattered by proximity to wnr* **12/1**2

5m 56.6s (14.80) **Going Correction** +0.175s/f (Yiel)
WFA 5 from 7yo+ 2lb **2** Ran SP% **102.9**
Speed ratings: **78,73**
TOTE £1.10.
Owner Triple F Partnership **Bred** Mrs M Cuff **Trained** Alcester, Warwicks

FOCUS
The ground had dried out on a dry and quite breezy day, the meeting having survived two morning inspections. The race distance was increased by 154yds. A total miss-match for this novices' chase. The easy winner is a potential 150+ chaser.

4223 RICHARD FARQUHAR (A GOOD MAN) WALKING COURSES (S) H'CAP HURDLE (8 hdls 1 omitted) 2m 3y
2:00 (2:00) (Class 5) (0-100,100) 4-Y-0+ **£4,106** (£1,197; £598)

Form RPR
/040 **1** **Razzle Dazzle 'Em**51 2492 7-10-2 **76** .... BrendanPowell 87
(Shaun Harris) *lft in ld 3rd: only one stl travelling whn hit 2 out: sn drew clr: hrd rdn bef last: all out* **11/2**3

410P **2** *10* **Neworld (FR)**21 3845 7-11-9 **100** ....(p1) ConorShoemark(3) 102
(Richard Hobson) *lft 2nd at 4th: rdn bef 3 out: sn fnd nil and chsd wnr vainly fr next: jst hld on in duel for poor 2nd* **2/1**1

40-P **3** *shd* **Bernisdale**35 2565 8-10-10 **84** .... RobertDunne 86
(John Flint) *lft 3rd at 3rd: rdn bef 3 out: sn fnd nil: disp wl hld 2nd after next tl fnl stride* **11/2**3

2P50 **4** *42* **Henry Oliver (IRE)**32 3665 8-10-13 **90** ....(tp) KillianMoore(3) 54
(John O'Shea) *j. modly and nvr travelling in last: reluctant fr 1/2-way: t.o after 3 out: heavily eased flat* **5/1**2

0-01 **B** **Vertueux (FR)**28 3233 11-10-8 **82** ....(p) LeeEdwards
(Tony Carroll) *cl up tl b.d 3rd* **5/1**2

PP36 **U** **Indian Daudaie (FR)**35 3607 9-11-1 **99** ....(b) RomainClavreul(10)
(Sarah Humphrey) *trckd ldrs tl bdly hmpd and uns rdr 3rd* **14/1**

F-F0 **F** **Run Hurricane (IRE)**152 1604 8-11-0 **88** ....(t) DaveCrosse
(John O'Shea) *led tl j.rt and fell 3rd* **12/1**

4m 11.6s (-1.40) **Going Correction** -0.125s/f (Good) **7** Ran SP% **111.8**
Speed ratings (Par 103): **98,93,92,71, ,**
CSF £16.65 TOTE £6.40: £2.90, £1.40; EX 26.10 Trifecta £126.90.There was no bid for the winner.
Owner Shaun Harris Racing Club **Bred** Winterbeck Manor Stud **Trained** Carburton, Notts

FOCUS
A run-of-the-mill selling handicap hurdle run over an extra 68yds. The field was depleted when three exited at the third hurdle. The third-last hurdle had to be omitted. The winner is rated in line with his best form.

4224 EBF STALLIONS "NATIONAL HUNT" NOVICES' HURDLE (QUALIFIER) (10 hdls 1 omitted) 2m 4f 1y
2:30 (2:31) (Class 3) 4-7-Y-0 £6,498 (£1,908; £954; £477)

Form RPR
-126 1 **Work In Progress (IRE)**[92] [2594] 6-11-8 135 HarrySkelton 143+
(Dan Skelton) *mde all: set stdy pce tl drew rt away bef 2 out: clipped last: sn heavily eased* **10/11**[1]
311P 2 31 **Mckenzie's Friend (IRE)**[34] [3623] 5-11-2 130 HarrisonBeswick(10) 117
(Oliver Sherwood) *a 2nd or 3rd: drvn and chsd wnr bef omitted 3 out: completely outpcd fr next: hit last* **85/40**[2]
21FF 3 2½ **Raise A Spark**[27] [3743] 6-11-2 114 HenryBrooke 105
(Donald McCain) *t.k.h in last tl 8th: j.rt at times: drvn to go 3rd after omitted 3 out: j.rt next and struggling: j.rt last* **10/1**
0 4 9 **Leg Lock Luke (IRE)**[29] [3710] 6-11-2 0 PaddyBrennan 99
(Colin Tizzard) *last pair tl wnt 3rd and drvn bef 8th: fdd after omitted next* **8/1**[3]
-51P P **Expedite (IRE)**[27] [3736] 5-11-1 120 TommyDowling(7)
(Charlie Mann) *2nd or 3rd tl rdn 7th: sn carrying hd awkwardly: nt run on: t.o and p.u passing omitted 3 out* **20/1**
5m 12.8s (-7.60) **Going Correction** -0.125s/f (Good) **5 Ran SP% 109.3**
Speed ratings: **110,97,96,93,**
CSF £3.15 TOTE £2.00: £2.00, £1.10; EX 3.00 Trifecta £7.70.
Owner Donlon & Doyle **Bred** Mrs M O'Driscoll **Trained** Alcester, Warwicks

FOCUS
On paper quite an interesting novices' hurdle but it turned out to be a one-horse contest. It was run over an extra 85yds. Arguably a step up from the winner.

4225 TIM BARCLAY MEMORIAL H'CAP CHASE (QUALIFIER FOR CHALLENGER MIDDLE DISTANCE CHASE SERIES FINAL) (16 fncs) 2m 5f 44y
3:05 (3:05) (Class 3) (0-125,125) 5-Y-0+ £7,797 (£2,289; £1,144; £572)

Form RPR
6236 1 **Gamain (IRE)**[21] [3836] 7-10-10 **109** (b) KielanWoods 114
(Ben Case) *2nd tl lft in front whn clr ldr fell 10th: hdd bef 13th: sn hrd drvn: 3 l 2nd and looked hld 2 out tl last: plodded past stopping ldr nr fin* **6/1**
1435 2 ½ **The Italian Yob (IRE)**[15] [3957] 8-11-5 **123** (b) LizzieKelly(5) 130
(Nick Williams) *rn in snatches first circ: j. slowly 7th: clsd and lft 2nd at 10th: led bef 13th: rdn clr after 2 out: wnt lft and tried to pull himself up flat: jst ct and threw it away* **5/1**[3]
1253 3 26 **Kings Cross (FR)**[27] [3731] 6-10-13 **112** LeeEdwards 93
(Tony Carroll) *towards rr and nvr looked to be gng wl enough: urged along and struggling fr 13th* **7/2**[2]
0/54 4 39 **Sizing Sahara**[28] [3727] 8-10-0 **99** GavinSheehan 45
(Paul Henderson) *j. slowly in last: immediately lost tch: t.o fr 7th: plugged rnd in own time* **10/1**
/4-6 F **Kazlian (FR)**[95] [2545] 8-11-10 **123** (p) BrendanPowell
(Johnny Farrelly) *led: drew clr 9th: travelling wl and 9 l ahd whn fell next* **14/1**
1564 U **Rock N Rhythm (IRE)**[55] [3228] 6-11-12 **125** (t) RichieMcLernon
(Jonjo O'Neill) *trckd ldrs: lft 3rd at 10th: nrly fell and uns rdr next* **10/1**
2332 F **Marden Court (IRE)**[29] [3709] 6-10-11 **110** (bt[1]) PaddyBrennan
(Colin Tizzard) *mstkes: effrt to press ldrs whn fell 6th: fatally injured* **9/4**[1]
5m 41.3s (-0.50) **Going Correction** +0.175s/f (Yiel) **7 Ran SP% 108.8**
Speed ratings: **107,106,96,82,**
CSF £32.24 TOTE £5.40: £3.10, £3.10; EX 39.30 Trifecta £166.80.
Owner Mrs A Allen **Bred** P J Fortune **Trained** Edgcote, Northants
■ Stewards' Enquiry : Kielan Woods two-day ban; used his whip above the permitted level (4th-5th Feb)

FOCUS
A weak handicap chase run over an extra 154yds. An eventful event with just three in serious contention on the final circuit. The winner improved to his hurdles mark.

4226 SNELLING GROUP NOVICES' H'CAP HURDLE (13 hdls) 2m 7f 95y
3:40 (3:40) (Class 4) (0-115,115) 4-Y-0+ £4,548 (£1,335; £667; £333)

Form RPR
/053 1 **Roycano**[20] [3855] 6-10-11 **103** HarryBannister(3) 117+
(Michael Easterby) *taken steadily towards rr: effrt and hmpd 3 out: led next: sn pushed clr: plenty in reserve* **15/8**[1]
0032 2 14 **Just So Cool (IRE)**[20] [3865] 5-11-9 **112** TrevorWhelan 112
(David Dennis) *trckd ldrs: chal and lft in ld 3 out: rdn and jnd and hit next: immediately outpcd by wnr* **4/1**[3]
P-43 3 23 **Summer Sounds (IRE)**[21] [3841] 7-10-13 **102** JamesDavies 81
(Tom Symonds) *t.k.h: pressed ldr tl led bef 3 out where rdn and j.rt and hdd: struggling in 3rd fr next: fin weakly* **7/2**[2]
-4P2 4 3 **Major Milborne**[32] [3662] 8-11-2 **112** MissPFuller(7) 87
(Jamie Snowden) *cl up tl rdn bef 3 out: wknd tamely wl bef next* **9/2**
4FP- 5 27 **Hard To Swallow (IRE)**[389] [3896] 10-11-9 **115** KillianMoore(3) 65
(Tom Weston) *set leisurely pce: hit 5th and 9th: drvn and hdd bef 3 out: t.o next: eased last* **16/1**
230 P **Le Legro (IRE)**[20] [3855] 6-11-3 **106** GavinSheehan
(Charlie Mann) *detached last and nt travelling: drvn 9th: no rspnse: mstke next: t.o and p.u 3 out* **8/1**
6m 16.0s (-6.00) **Going Correction** -0.125s/f (Good) **6 Ran SP% 112.2**
Speed ratings (Par 105): **105,100,92,91,81**
CSF £9.94 TOTE £3.30: £1.80, £1.40; EX 10.90 Trifecta £31.60.
Owner M J R Bannister **Bred** G H Sparkes And M W Easterby **Trained** Sheriff Hutton, N Yorks

FOCUS
A very modest novices' handicap hurdle run at a steady pace until the final circuit. It was run over an extra 102yds. The race soon fell apart and in the end produced a facile winner. Seemingly a big step up from him.

4227 BETFAIR SWITCHING SADDLES "GRASSROOTS" FOX HUNTERS' CHASE (FOR WILLIAM BULWER-LONG MEMORIAL TROPHY) (18 fncs) 3m 38y
4:10 (4:10) (Class 6) 5-Y-0+ £1,871 (£580; £290; £145)

Form RPR
PP-0 1 **Vasco Du Mee (FR)**[26] 7-11-11 130 (bt) MissJosephineBanks(7) 119+
(Martin Weston) *settled towards rr: blnd 8th and rdr did wl to rcvr: blnd 14th: stl in last 3 out: urged into 4 l 2nd next: led gng strly bef last: sn clr* **8/1**
6/0- 2 6 **Good Egg (IRE)**[26] 13-11-11 106 MissSRippon(7) 110
(Miss Sarah Rippon) *j. safely in ld: awkward 2nd: 4 l clr 2 out: bmpd along between last two: hdd bef last and immediately outpcd* **11/2**[2]
2-1P 3 22 **Can Mestret (IRE)**[19] 9-11-11 116 MrJAndrews(7) 97
(S R Andrews) *t.k.h: hld up pressing ldrs: effrt 15th: wnt 2nd next tl rdn 2 out: tired bef last: fin weakly* **6/1**[3]
U0F- 4 14 **Wiffy Chatsby (IRE)**[307] 9-11-9 117 (t) MissJodieHughes(5) 74
(Dafydd Jones) *cl up: wnt 2nd at 13th: hit 14th: rdn bef 15th: hrd drvn and lost 2nd next: fdd v qckly* **22/1**
12-3 U **Pacha Du Polder (FR)**[19] 9-11-11 141 MsVLPendleton(7)
(Paul Nicholls) *j.w in last: cl up whn rdr c off at 7th* **8/13**[1]
F/45 U **Baltic Blue**[12] 9-11-5 0 (p) MissCareyWilliamson(5)
(B Dowling) *slow 1st: cl up tl hit 7th hrd and uns rdr* **40/1**
6m 50.2s (14.50) **Going Correction** +0.175s/f (Yiel) **6 Ran SP% 109.5**
Speed ratings: **82,80,72,68,**
CSF £46.10 TOTE £7.80: £3.00, £2.00; EX 50.80 Trifecta £84.80.
Owner Mrs C Banks **Bred** Jacques Hersent & Mrs Jacqueline Hersent **Trained** Hindlip, Worcs

FOCUS
This was run over an extra 185yds. A weak hunters' chase after the unfortunate early departure of Pacha Du Polder and double Olympic gold medallist Victoria Pendleton. The winning rider deserves full marks. The winner was a 135 chaser at his peak and is probably still capable of rating higher than this.

4228 BRITISH STALLION STUDS EBF MARES' MAIDEN OPEN NATIONAL HUNT FLAT RACE 2m 3y
4:45 (4:45) (Class 5) 4-7-Y-0 £2,737 (£798; £399)

Form RPR
4 1 **Potters Lady Jane**[65] [3118] 4-10-12 0 HarrySkelton 94
(Lucy Wadham) *stocky: midfield and gng wl: effrt 6f out: led 3f out: rdn fnl f: hld on gamely* **7/2**[2]
2 2 1 **Postbridge (IRE)**[114] [2141] 5-11-7 0 GavinSheehan 102
(Warren Greatrex) *small: led: rdn over 4f out: hdd 3f out: dropped bk 4th on home turn: rallied wl 1f out: wnt 2nd ins fnl f: drvn and no imp fnl 75yds* **4/5**[1]
6 3 2¾ **Llantara**[64] [3132] 5-11-7 0 JamesDavies 100
(Tom Symonds) *pressed ldrs: effrt 5f out: rdn 3f out: no ex over 1f out* **9/2**[3]
0 4 ½ **Focusing**[79] [2856] 6-11-7 0 (t) PaddyBrennan 100
(Stuart Edmunds) *str scopey: settled towards rr: effrt 5f out: last of four gng wl clr 4f out: drvn and nt qckn fr wl over 1f out* **20/1**
5 47 **Winola**[362] 6-11-7 0 DavidBass 57
(Charlie Wallis) *tall: prom 10f: t.o in 5th 3f out* **33/1**
6 9 **Tilsworth Phyllis** 4-10-12 0 BrendanPowell 40
(J R Jenkins) *small: bhd: rdn and struggling 6f out: t.o fnl 4f* **25/1**
0- 7 15 **Busy Lilly**[534] [1436] 7-11-7 0 AdamPogson 36
(Charles Pogson) *prom tl rdn and fdd rapidly 4f out: sn t.o* **66/1**
8 94 **Our Savannah (IRE)** 4-10-5 0 PaddyBradley(7)
(J R Jenkins) *last pair and nt travelling: pushed along 1/2-way: t.o fnl 6f* **12/1**
9 nk **Hooley Time (IRE)** 4-10-12 0 JackQuinlan
(Olly Williams) *cl up: drvn 7f out: sn t.o* **33/1**
4m 13.5s (6.10) **Going Correction** -0.125s/f (Good)
WFA 4 from 5yo+ 9lb **9 Ran SP% 119.6**
Speed ratings: **79,78,77,76,53 48,41,,**
CSF £6.62 TOTE £4.20: £1.40, £1.02, £1.70; EX 8.90 Trifecta £28.20.
Owner Mrs J May **Bred** Mrs J May **Trained** Newmarket, Suffolk

FOCUS
Probably a very ordinary mares' bumper, run over an extra 68yds, and only the first four were in serious contention in the final half-mile. The form looks believable.
T/Plt: £64.20 to a £1 stake. Pool: £48,120.65 - 546.83 winning tickets T/Qpdt: £18.40 to a £1 stake. Pool: £4,679.28 - 188.00 winning tickets **Iain Mackenzie**

3988 SANDOWN (R-H)
Friday, February 19

OFFICIAL GOING: Chase course - soft (good to soft in places); hurdle course - heavy (soft in places in back straight)
Wind: Moderate, half against Weather: Fine becoming overcast; light rain race 4 onwards

4229 COBHAM CONDITIONAL JOCKEYS' H'CAP HURDLE (8 hdls) 1m 7f 216y
1:40 (1:40) (Class 4) (0-120,120) 4-Y-0+ £3,898 (£1,144; £572; £286)

Form RPR
6144 1 **Canadian Diamond (IRE)**[25] [3777] 9-11-5 **116** MikeyHamill(3) 118
(Richard Rowe) *hld up in last pair: prog after 3 out: clsd on ldrs after 2 out: led sn after last: rdn out and kpt on wl* **11/2**[3]
2-40 2 1¼ **Smart Catch (IRE)**[82] [2810] 10-10-7 **104** NickSlatter(3) 105
(Tony Carroll) *trckd ldrs: led sn after 2 out gng strly: j.lft last and sn hdd: nt qckn flat* **16/1**
032- 3 ¾ **Aston Cantlow**[348] [4654] 8-11-9 **120** (t) CiaranGethings(3) 120
(Philip Hobbs) *t.k.h: hld up in rr: prog 2 out: chsd ldng pair and mstke last: kpt on but unable to chal* **11/2**[3]
2-05 4 3½ **Steel City**[16] [3923] 8-11-10 **118** (v[1]) JeremiahMcGrath 116
(Seamus Mullins) *led: rdn whn j.rt 2 out: sn hdd and nt qckn: kpt on same pce fr last* **5/1**[2]
P4P0 5 9 **Thundering Home**[7] [4096] 9-10-13 **112** (t) ArchieBellamy(5) 101
(Richard Mitchell) *trckd ldrs: rdn to chal 2 out: sn btn off: wkng whn mstke last* **7/1**

U-03 **6** 4 ½ **Lochnagar (GER)**[17] 3917 7-11-4 **115**.................. CharlieDeutsch(3) 100
(Venetia Williams) *hld up towards rr: j. slowly 4th: rdn and no prog bef 2 out* **3/1**[1]

66-4 **7** 1 ¾ **Fingers Crossed (IRE)**[34] 3628 6-11-2 **110**.................. TomBellamy 90
(Paul Webber) *trckd ldr: rdn to chal whn nt fluent 2 out: wknd qckly* **6/1**

P065 **8** 18 **Franciscan**[135] 1814 8-11-7 **118**..................(p) JamesCowley(3) 80
(Donald McCain) *hld up in last pair: rdn after 3 out: wknd and bhd bef 2 out: t.o* **16/1**

4m 21.9s (14.70) **Going Correction** +1.075s/f (Soft) **8** Ran SP% **111.0**
Speed ratings (Par 105): **106,105,105,103,98 96,95,86**
CSF £75.89 CT £485.79 TOTE £6.70: £2.00, £3.50, £2.00; EX 74.80 Trifecta £373.60.
Owner Nicholls Family **Bred** J S Bolger **Trained** Sullington, W Sussex

FOCUS
This open-looking handicap was run at an average gallop and they got sorted out from the second-last. The first three were close to their marks.

4230 "UBIQUE" H'CAP CHASE (13 fncs) 1m 7f 119y
2:10 (2:10) (Class 3) (0-130,130) 5-Y-0+ **£6,498** (£1,908; £954; £477)

Form RPR

3205 **1** **Fairy Rath (IRE)**[27] 3731 10-11-8 **126**.................. TomCannon 133+
(Nick Gifford) *cl up: trckd ldr 6th to next and fr 4 out: led 3 out: shkn up and in command bef last: styd on wl* **15/2**[3]

-201 **2** 2 ¼ **Blandfords Gunner**[78] 2857 7-11-9 **127**.................. AdamWedge 131
(Evan Williams) *hld up towards rr: prog after 4 out: chsd wnr bef 2 out: rdn and styd on but nvr able to chal* **7/2**[1]

1343 **3** ¾ **Helium (FR)**[27] 3749 11-11-12 **130**.................. RhysFlint 133
(Alexandra Dunn) *prom: chsd ldr 7th to 4 out: shkn up after 3 out: chsd ldng pair after: rdn and kpt on flat: nvr chal* **25/1**

-P44 **4** 2 ¼ **Minella Definitely (IRE)**[55] 3257 9-11-7 **125**..................(p) MarkQuinlan 127
(Neil Mulholland) *led to 2nd: reminders after next: styd in tch: cl enough 3 out: one pce after* **8/1**

PF3P **5** 1 ¾ **The Clock Leary (IRE)**[21] 3843 8-11-2 **120**..................(p) AidanColeman 121
(Venetia Williams) *wl in tch: mstke 4 out whn cl up: rdn after 3 out: one pce and no imp* **8/1**

0/4 **6** 20 **Legal Exit (IRE)**[42] 3504 9-11-7 **125**..................(t) RichardJohnson 104
(Tom Lacey) *hld up: rapid prog to ld after 2nd: hdd & wknd qckly 3 out* **7/2**[1]

-311 **7** 1 **Sunny Ledgend**[28] 3727 11-10-8 **119** ow1.................. MrJMartin(7) 97
(Andrew J Martin) *smetimes j.lft: a in rr: mstke 2nd: struggling fr 7th: no ch bef 3 out* **9/1**

F233 **F** **Bodega**[50] 3384 8-10-9 **113**..................(p) WillKennedy
(Ian Williams) *mstke 2nd: in tch in last tl fell 6th* **9/2**[2]

1133 **P** **Lord Lir (IRE)**[110] 2220 10-10-0 **104**..................(b) TomScudamore
(Tim Vaughan) *led briefly 2nd: chsd ldr to 6th: lost pl qckly: t.o whn p.u bef last* **33/1**

4m 11.0s (9.20) **Going Correction** +0.80s/f (Soft) **9** Ran SP% **113.4**
Speed ratings: **109,107,107,106,105 95,95, ,**
CSF £34.36 CT £622.72 TOTE £7.70: £2.30, £1.80, £2.90; EX 37.00 Trifecta £344.40.
Owner Mrs C L Kyle **Bred** Miss Mary G Cotter **Trained** Findon, W Sussex

FOCUS
A fair handicap, run at a sound gallop.It was run over 10 yards further than advertised. Solid form, the winner rated 3lb off the best of his form over longer.

4231 WEATHERBYS GSB JANE SEYMOUR MARES' NOVICES' HURDLE (GRADE 2) (9 hdls) 2m 3f 173y
2:45 (2:45) (Class 1) 4-Y-0+
£17,085 (£6,411; £3,210; £1,599; £804; £402)

Form RPR

1122 **1** **Jessber's Dream (IRE)**[6] 4125 6-11-2 135..................(t) NoelFehily 143+
(Harry Fry) *mde all: drew clr bef 2 out and stl gng easily: hit last 2: rdn out* **9/2**[3]

0-11 **2** 8 **Katie Too (IRE)**[50] 3386 5-11-2 132.................. RichardJohnson 132
(Alan King) *hld up in last trio: prog 3 out: rdn wl bef 2 out: hit 2 out: kpt on to take 2nd last: no ch w wnr* **13/8**[1]

2111 **3** ¾ **Actinpieces**[49] 3420 5-11-2 130.................. MissGAndrews 132
(Pam Sly) *trckd ldng trio: urged along sn after 3 out: kpt on to take 2nd briefly bef last: one pce flat* **6/1**

0121 **4** 11 **Sunshine Corner (IRE)**[32] 3660 5-11-2 126.................. LeightonAspell 121
(Lucy Wadham) *pressed wnr: rdn and lft bhd bef 2 out: wknd and lost 2nd bef last* **7/1**

3-42 **5** 15 **Coco Des Champs (IRE)**[76] 2911 6-11-2 114........ SamTwiston-Davies 106
(Oliver Sherwood) *in tch in last trio tl rdn and mstke 3 out: sn wknd and bhd* **66/1**

1121 **6** 1 ¼ **Tara Flow**[24] 3785 6-11-2 135.................. AidanColeman 104
(Venetia Williams) *nt a fluent: chsd ldng pair tl after 3 out: sn rdn and wknd: bhd fr 2 out* **7/2**[2]

24 **P** **Mia's Storm (IRE)**[22] 3825 6-11-2 0.................. DenisO'Regan
(Alan King) *in tch in rr: mstke 4th: rdn and lost tch on long run after 3 out: wknd 2 out: last whn p.u bef last* **20/1**

5m 15.1s (15.50) **Going Correction** +1.075s/f (Soft) **7** Ran SP% **111.5**
Speed ratings (Par 115): **112,108,108,104,98 97,**
CSF £12.03 TOTE £5.10: £2.30, £1.60; EX 14.20 Trifecta £76.10.
Owner Chris Giles & Potensis Bloodstock Ltd **Bred** Denis Noonan **Trained** Seaborough, Dorset

FOCUS
This Grade 2 mares' event fell apart in the home straight, but the winner impressed and rates a small pb. The third helps sets the level.

4232 ROYAL ARTILLERY GOLD CUP (A CHASE FOR MILITARY AMATEUR RIDERS) (22 fncs) 3m 37y
3:20 (3:20) (Class 3) 6-Y-0+ **£6,239** (£1,935; £967; £484)

Form RPR

3323 **1** **Jennys Surprise (IRE)**[41] 3520 8-11-4 127.............. MissBHampson(3) 121+
(Fergal O'Brien) *j.lft: pressed ldr tl j. bdly lft 12th: pushed along fr 15th: only 4th after 4 out and looked btn: tk 3rd bef 3 out: stl 15 l bhd ldr 2 out: styd on to ld last 75yds* **5/4**[1]

-F1P **2** 1 ½ **Newton Thistle**[22] 3823 9-11-7 118..................(tp) CaptHarryWallace(7) 124
(Ben Pauling) *prom: pressed ldr 12th: led next and mde most after: drew clr 2 out: hung lft and wknd after last: hdd fnl 75yds* **10/1**

641P **3** 4 **Morney Wing (IRE)**[37] 3583 7-11-12 122..............(tp) CaptMaxChenery(7) 124
(Charlie Mann) *bhd and nt a jumping in tune w rdr: lost tch 12th: urged along and kpt on fr 4 out: tk 3rd nr fin* **16/1**

-4PP **4** 1 ½ **Cowards Close (IRE)**[76] 2899 9-11-12 127...(t) OCdtOswaldWedmore(7) 126
(Chris Gordon) *mde most to 13th: pressed ldr after: stl upsides 3 out and clr of rest: mstke 2 out and btn: mstke last and wknd* **13/2**[3]

-0F0 **5** 15 **Irish Thistle (IRE)**[12] 4011 9-11-7 128.................. SACSamWilliams(7) 103
(Dai Williams) *early errors and bhd: rapid prog 12th to press ldrs next: more errors and lost tch again 16th* **14/1**

P014 **P** **High Kite (IRE)**[75] 10-11-7 108..................(b) LtColEricaBridge(7)
(T D B Underwood) *sn detached: t.o whn p.u bef 12th* **66/1**

3/03 **P** **Clonbanan Lad (IRE)**[22] 3826 10-11-11 117.................. MrJSole(3)
(Miss Louise Allan) *cl up: jnd ldng pair 17th: stl upsides 4 out and clr of rest: wknd rapidly sn after: p.u bef 3 out: dismntd* **8/1**

-316 **P** **Bob Tucker (IRE)**[91] 2616 9-11-7 128.................. MrGDisney(7)
(Charlie Longsdon) *pressed ldrs: mstke 11th and lost pl: mstkes and lost tch fr 13th: wl adrift whn p.u after 3 out* **5/1**[2]

P311 **P** **Very Live (FR)**[18] 3903 7-11-7 102..................(p) CaptJackStamp(7)
(Paul Webber) *in tch to 1/2-way: bhd fr 13th: t.o whn p.u bef 3 out* **20/1**

6m 49.1s (21.30) **Going Correction** +0.80s/f (Soft) **9** Ran SP% **113.4**
Speed ratings: **96,95,94,93,88 , , ,**
CSF £14.63 TOTE £1.90: £1.10, £3.80, £4.60; EX 16.50 Trifecta £147.30.
Owner Mark Hampson **Bred** Denis J Reddan **Trained** Naunton, Gloucs

FOCUS
A fair edition of this long-established Military chase, which proved a thorough test. It was run over 20 yards further than advertised. The second is probably the best guide.

4233 DAVID LINDON & CO NOVICES' HURDLE (8 hdls) 1m 7f 216y
3:50 (3:51) (Class 4) 4-Y-0+ **£3,898** (£1,144; £572; £286)

Form RPR

1 **1** **Protek Des Flos (FR)**[20] 3848 4-11-0 0.................. NoelFehily 126+
(Nicky Henderson) *hld up: prog 4th: chsd clr ldr and nt fluent 3 out: pushed along to cl 2 out: shkn up to ld last: styd on wl* **2/7**[1]

4/03 **2** 4 ½ **Starving Marvin**[44] 3484 8-11-2 0.................. LeightonAspell 122+
(Rod Millman) *led: nt fluent 4th but clr: stl 6 l up bef 2 out: sn c bk to wnr: hdd last: kpt on same pce and no ch w wnr after* **8/1**[3]

0-63 **3** 21 **Centurius**[25] 3773 6-11-2 0.................. AidanColeman 101+
(Venetia Williams) *t.k.h: hld up in last: prog 3 out: chsd clr ldng pair on long run bef 2 out: sn rdn and no imp: wknd last but hld on for 3rd* **6/1**[2]

4 **4** 3 ½ **Byron Flyer**[30] 188 5-11-2 0.................. WillKennedy 96
(Ian Williams) *in tch towards rr: outpcd in last and pushed along 3 out: kpt on steadily fr 2 out to take modest 4th last* **11/1**

4-40 **5** 4 **Kingussie**[21] 3839 8-11-2 0.................. NicodeBoinville 92
(Ben Pauling) *prom: chsd ldr 4th to 3 out: sn shkn up and outpcd: wknd and mstke last* **12/1**

6 5 **The Venerable Bede (IRE)** 5-11-2 0.................. JakeGreenall 87
(Paul Webber) *early mstkes in rr: in tch tl outpcd fr 3 out: no ch after: kpt on* **33/1**

30P **7** 1 **Arcamante (ITY)**[18] 3902 5-10-6 0.................. GrahamCarson(10) 86
(Jamie Snowden) *chsd ldr to 4th: lost pl 3 out and rdn: no ch sn after* **25/1**

-060 **8** 2 ¼ **Better Days (IRE)**[75] 2928 5-11-2 0.................. SamTwiston-Davies 84
(Nigel Twiston-Davies) *prom: disp 2nd pl fr 4th to 3 out: sn outpcd and rdn: no ch after: mstke last and wknd* **50/1**

3450 **9** 1 **Briac (FR)**[7] 4097 5-11-2 0.................. JamieMoore 83
(Jim Best) *in tch: sme prog 3 out: sn rdn and outpcd: wknd 2 out* **33/1**

4m 19.1s (11.90) **Going Correction** +1.075s/f (Soft)
WFA 4 from 5yo+ 9lb **9** Ran SP% **130.9**
Speed ratings (Par 105): **113,110,100,98,96 94,93,92,91**
CSF £4.75 TOTE £1.20: £1.10, £2.80, £1.80; EX 5.70 Trifecta £17.40.
Owner Potensis Bloodstock Limited **Bred** Clovis Bardin & Mme Florence Bardin **Trained** Upper Lambourn, Berks

FOCUS
An uncompetitive novice event by course standards. There's a case for rating the form the best partof 10lb higher.

4234 ASCOT UNDERWRITING H'CAP CHASE (QUALIFIER FOR THE CHALLENGER STAYING CHASE SERIES FINAL) (22 fncs) 3m 37y
4:20 (4:20) (Class 3) (0-135,134) 5-Y-0+ **£7,797** (£2,289; £1,144; £572)

Form RPR

-332 **1** **Beg To Differ (IRE)**[49] 3404 6-11-11 **133**..................(v[1]) RichardJohnson 147+
(Jonjo O'Neill) *nvr that fluent but trckd ldng pair gng strly: wnt 2nd bef 3 out: led last: qckly drew clr: v comf* **5/2**[1]

U26U **2** 4 ½ **Loose Chips**[34] 3624 10-11-10 **132**..................(b) NoelFehily 139
(Charlie Longsdon) *won battle for ld and set decent pce: clr w wnr after 3 out: hdd last: styd on but qckly outpcd* **7/1**

4P41 **3** 12 **Arbeo (IRE)**[35] 3609 10-10-5 **113**.................. MarcGoldstein 107
(Diana Grissell) *chsd ldr: tried to chal 13th: btn off sn after: lost 2nd bef 3 out: steadily outpcd but kpt on* **10/1**

2-42 **4** 1 ¼ **Dancing Shadow (IRE)**[77] 2885 7-11-0 **122**.................. IanPopham 118
(Victor Dartnall) *chsd ldrs: drvn to chal for 3rd after 3 out: one pce and mstke 2 out* **6/1**[3]

-64P **5** ¾ **Bertie Boru (IRE)**[41] 3518 9-11-8 **130**.................. TomO'Brien 126+
(Philip Hobbs) *mstkes in rr: struggling in 8th pl fr 12th: blnd 4 out in same position: styd on fr 2 out: nvr nrr* **9/2**[2]

4133 **6** 12 **Sands Cove (IRE)**[54] 3282 9-11-5 **127**.................. LiamTreadwell 111
(James Evans) *towards rr: tried to make prog fr 14th: no imp on ldrs in 5th bef 3 out: wknd and blnd last* **8/1**

125P **7** 9 **Buachaill Alainn (IRE)**[76] 2899 9-11-12 **134**..................(bt) SeanBowen 105
(Peter Bowen) *mstkes and a in rr: last and struggling bdly after 12th: t.o* **16/1**

F134 **8** 2 ¾ **Elenika (FR)**[27] 3731 8-10-10 **118**.................. AidanColeman 89
(Venetia Williams) *chsd ldng trio to 14th: slow and mstke next and lost pl: struggling in rr after: tried to rally 3 out: wknd qckly bef 2 out* **12/1**

3413 **P** **Fond Memory (IRE)**[78] 2872 8-10-13 **121**..............(t) SamTwiston-Davies
(Nigel Twiston-Davies) *in tch: chsd ldrs 17th: wknd sn after 4 out: clambered over 2 out: last whn p.u bef last* **12/1**

6m 41.4s (13.60) **Going Correction** +0.80s/f (Soft) **9** Ran SP% **115.0**
Speed ratings: **109,107,103,103,102 98,95,94,**
CSF £20.66 CT £148.74 TOTE £2.60: £1.50, £1.80, £3.70; EX 20.00 Trifecta £182.30.
Owner Mrs John Magnier, D Smith & M Tabor **Bred** Robert McCarthy **Trained** Cheltenham, Gloucs

FOCUS
It paid to race handily in this fair staying handicap. It was run over 20 yards further than advertised. The cosy winner is on the upgrade.

4235 OXSHOTT NOVICES' H'CAP HURDLE (9 hdls) 2m 3f 173y
4:50 (4:52) (Class 4) (0-120,120) 4-Y-0+ **£3,898** (£1,144; £572; £286)

Form RPR

4 **1** **Le Boizelo (FR)**[14] 3978 5-11-7 **115**.................. JamieMoore 125+
(Robert Walford) *trckd ldrs: wnt 2nd on long run after 3 out: chalng whn lft in clr ld 2 out: drvn further ahd bef last* **3/1**[1]

056- **2** *19* **Ruperra Tom**[482] 2053 8-10-3 **97**.................. TomScudamore 90
(Sophie Leech) *hld up in last pair: nt fluent 4th: j.lft 3 out: prog to chse ldng pair bef 2 out: no imp whn lft 2nd and sltly hmpd 2 out: no ch w wnr after* **20/1**

350- **3** *7* **Buckontupence (IRE)**[475] 2186 8-10-9 **103**.................. LiamTreadwell 88
(James Evans) *t.k.h: hld up in last pair: nt fluent 4th and mstke next: urged along 3 out: plugged on and lft in 3rd 2 out: no real hdwy after* **5/1**

3 **4** *38* **One Style (FR)**[38] 3570 6-11-7 **120**.................. CharlieDeutsch(5) 64
(Venetia Williams) *t.k.h: cl up tl wknd on long run bef 2 out: t.o and fin tired* **10/3[2]**

U404 **5** *21* **Chief Brody**[27] 3745 5-11-5 **118**.................. DavidNoonan(5) 41
(Grace Harris) *in tch: rdn 3 out: brief effrt sn after: wknd wl bef 2 out: t.o* **10/1**

2345 **P** **Rushvale (IRE)**[24] 3795 7-10-13 **114**.................. MrMJPKendrick(7)
(Ben Case) *t.k.h: led at mod pce to 6th: lost 2nd after 3 out and wknd qckly: t.o whn p.u bef last* **8/1**

352 **F** **Jajamcool (IRE)**[32] 3660 6-11-11 **119**.................. JamesBest 123
(Caroline Keevil) *trckd ldr: led and mstke 6th: hrd pressed but clr of rest whn fell heavily 2 out: fatally injured* **7/2[3]**

5m 29.1s (29.50) **Going Correction** +1.075s/f (Soft) **7 Ran SP% 111.9**
Speed ratings (Par 105): **84,76,73,58,50**
CSF £48.45 TOTE £3.20: £1.80, £9.30; EX 49.30 Trifecta £393.00.
Owner Dr & Mrs John Millar **Bred** Jocelyn Chasserio & Jean-Louis Chasserio **Trained** Child Okeford, Dorset

FOCUS
A modest novice handicap, run at a routine gallop. There's probably more to come from the winner.
T/Plt: £24.10 to a £1 stake. Pool: £91,630.86 - 2,772.58 winning tickets T/Qpdt: £3.10 to a £1 stake. Pool: £8,583.95 - 2,045.87 winning tickets **Jonathan Neesom**

3730
ASCOT (R-H)
Saturday, February 20

OFFICIAL GOING: Soft (chs 6.5, hdl 6.3)
Wind: moderate, half against Weather: steady rain most of the afternoon

4236 NEPTUNE INVESTMENT MANAGEMENT NOVICES' HURDLE (AN ASCOT APPEARANCE MONEY SCHEME RACE) (10 hdls) 2m 3f 58y
1:15 (1:15) (Class 2) 5-Y-O+ **£15,640** (£4,620; £2,310; £1,155; £577)

Form RPR

1513 **1** **Yala Enki (FR)**[14] 3992 6-11-8 142.................. AidanColeman 147
(Venetia Williams) *mde all: sent for home bef 2 out: sn drvn: jnd last: battled on really wl to gain upper hand flat* **7/4[1]**

331 **2** *3/4* **Mr Mix (FR)**[28] 3744 5-11-5 135.................. SamTwiston-Davies 143
(Paul Nicholls) *t.k.h: trckd ldng pair: chsd wnr 3 out: chal fr 2 out gng strly: rdn and upsides last: kpt on but nt qckn flat* **7/2[3]**

-111 **3** *2 1/2* **Aloomomo (FR)**[84] 2780 6-11-0 129.................. HarryBannister 136
(Warren Greatrex) *in tch: effrt to dispute 2nd 3 out: drvn bef 2 out: kpt on same pce after* **15/2**

1-21 **4** *4* **Premier Bond**[53] 3353 6-11-5 137.................. NicodeBoinville 138
(Nicky Henderson) *chsd wnr: nt fluent 7th: lost pl next and sn rdn: dropped to last and wl btn bef 2 out: kpt on again nr fin* **9/4[2]**

2321 **5** *hd* **Big Chief Benny (IRE)**[22] 3839 5-11-5 133.................. DenisO'Regan 138
(Alan King) *mostly in last: sltly outpcd 3 out and rdn: rallied and in tch 2 out: hld whn nt fluent last: fdd nr fin* **12/1**

4m 48.5s (3.80) **Going Correction** +0.475s/f (Soft) **5 Ran SP% 108.8**
Speed ratings: **111,110,109,107,107**
CSF £8.06 TOTE £2.60: £1.30, £2.10; EX 7.40 Trifecta £24.90.
Owner Hills Of Ledbury (Aga) **Bred** Esteve Rouchvarger Et Al **Trained** Kings Caple, H'fords

FOCUS
Conditions were unpleasant with Nico de Boinville confirming it to be "hard work". A good-quality novice, even after the defection of the top-rated runner, and it was run at a true gallop courtesy of the winner, who is worth his place at the festival.

4237 SODEXO REYNOLDSTOWN NOVICES' CHASE (AN ASCOT APPEARANCE MONEY SCHEME RACE) (GRADE 2) (20 fncs) 2m 7f 180y
1:50 (1:50) (Class 1) 5-Y-O+ **£22,887** (£8,655; £4,387; £2,239; £1,179)

Form RPR

2-12 **1** **Vyta Du Roc (FR)**[43] 3504 7-11-0 145.................. DarylJacob 151
(Nicky Henderson) *trckd ldrs: clsd after 3 out: sltly impeded 2 out but sn in 2nd: quick jump last and sn led: drvn out and hld on* **9/2[3]**

-3P6 **2** *1/2* **Minella Rocco (IRE)**[50] 3405 6-11-0 143.................. (t) NoelFehily 151
(Jonjo O'Neill) *settled in last: stl there after 3 out: r.o fr 2 out: tk 3rd last and 2nd fnl 150yds: clsd on wnr nr fin* **12/1**

113P **3** *3 1/2* **Le Mercurey (FR)**[21] 3860 6-11-7 140.................. (tp) SamTwiston-Davies 155
(Paul Nicholls) *trckd ldrs: clsd after 3 out: j. sltly rt 2 out but sn led: 2 l clr bef last: hdd sn after last and one pce flat* **12/1**

1 **4** *7* **Drumacoo (IRE)**[45] 3486 7-11-0 143.................. NicodeBoinville 142
(Ben Pauling) *j. sltly erratically early: led to 3rd: chsd ldr: chal fr 14th tl led after 3 out: drvn and hdd after 2 out: wknd last* **7/4[1]**

-122 **5** *7* **Onenightinvienna (IRE)**[26] 3774 7-11-4 149.................. (p) TomO'Brien 138
(Philip Hobbs) *j.w: led 3rd: hdd after 3 out: sn rdn: wknd 2 out* **9/4[2]**

/U62 **F** **Ballyalton (IRE)**[29] 3726 9-11-0 140.................. AidanColeman
(Ian Williams) *in tch in rr tl fell heavily 7th* **12/1**

6m 14.1s (10.60) **Going Correction** +0.725s/f (Soft) **6 Ran SP% 108.4**
Speed ratings: **111,110,109,107,105**
CSF £43.66 TOTE £5.10: £1.80, £5.00; EX 58.20 Trifecta £235.50.
Owner Simon Munir & Isaac Souede **Bred** Andre Le Gall **Trained** Upper Lambourn, Berks

FOCUS
Following chase course rail movements this race was run over 6yds further than advertised. A competitive edition of the race, even if not the strongest in terms of quality, with most of these, if not all, set for a career in handicaps. It proved a right old test and set up for those who sat off the leaders. Small pbs from the winner and third and a much bigger one from the second.

4238 APPLETISER 50 YEAR CELEBRATION CHASE (A LIMITED H'CAP) (LISTED RACE) (20 fncs) 2m 7f 180y
2:25 (2:25) (Class 1) 5-Y-O+ **£25,627** (£9,616; £4,815; £2,398; £1,206)

Form RPR

-P12 **1** **Sausalito Sunrise (IRE)**[66] 3116 8-11-10 **150**.................. TomO'Brien 163+
(Philip Hobbs) *settled in last: prog to trck ldng pair after 14th: clsd to ld bef 2 out: styd on strly and drew rt away after* **3/1[2]**

111U **2** *12* **Vieux Lion Rouge (FR)**[71] 3016 7-11-6 **146**.................. TomScudamore 148
(David Pipe) *wl in tch: mstke 13th and dropped to last: cl up again 15th: chal gng strly bef 2 out: sn brushed aside by wnr* **3/1[2]**

-112 **3** *6* **Waldorf Salad**[21] 3849 8-10-6 **132**.................. AidanColeman 130
(Venetia Williams) *led: pressed and urged along fr 15th: kpt on tl hdd and btn bef 2 out: fin tired* **11/4[1]**

-412 **4** *3* **Spookydooky (IRE)**[63] 3157 8-11-2 **142**.................. (t) JoshuaMoore 135
(Jonjo O'Neill) *in tch: nudged along fr 11th: last after 14th: lost tch 4 out: no ch after: kpt on to snatch 4th fnl strides* **4/1[3]**

116P **5** *nk* **Bally Beaufort (IRE)**[35] 3621 8-10-13 **142**.................. (p) RyanHatch(3) 134
(Nigel Twiston-Davies) *pressed ldr: chal fr 15th tl btn off after 3 out: wknd 2 out* **7/1**

6m 15.6s (12.10) **Going Correction** +0.725s/f (Soft) **5 Ran SP% 109.2**
Speed ratings: **108,104,102,101,100**
CSF £12.16 TOTE £3.80: £1.80, £1.80; EX 10.60 Trifecta £19.50.
Owner Mrs Diana L Whateley **Bred** Thomas Corish **Trained** Withycombe, Somerset

FOCUS
Following chase course rail movements this race was run over 6yds further than advertised. A good staying handicap, even if there were only the five runners. The leaders got tired late in a race where stamina was at a premium and the winner powered away from some tired rivals late. The form is rated around the first two.

4239 LES AMBASSADEURS CASINO H'CAP HURDLE (10 hdls) 2m 3f 58y
3:00 (3:01) (Class 2) 4-Y-O+
£28,152 (£8,316; £4,158; £2,079; £1,039; £522)

Form RPR

411- **1** **Different Gravey (IRE)**[309] 5360 6-11-12 **149**.................. NicodeBoinville 164+
(Nicky Henderson) *hld up in chsng gp: prog 7th: wnt 2nd after 3 out: led 2 out: drew wl clr bef last: pushed out: impressive* **5/1[3]**

51F **2** *16* **Fingertips (FR)**[14] 3988 4-10-2 **135**.................. (t) TomScudamore 124
(David Pipe) *in tch in chsng gp: dropped to last and reminder 6th: struggling next: rallied fr 3 out: kpt on wl to take 2nd last strides* **16/1**

0-11 **3** *nk* **Montdragon (FR)**[63] 3156 6-10-12 **135**.................. (t) JoshuaMoore 135
(Jonjo O'Neill) *prom in chsng gp: clsd 3 out: shkn up bef 2 out: chsd wnr between last 2 but no ch: lost 2nd last strides* **4/1[1]**

1122 **4** *15* **Sirop De Menthe (FR)**[49] 3449 6-10-6 **132**.................. LucyGardner(3) 116
(Sue Gardner) *t.k.h: trckd ldr and sn clr of rest: led 6th: hdd & wknd 2 out* **8/1**

1-13 **5** *shd* **Pull The Chord (IRE)**[38] 3584 6-10-12 **135**.................. JamesBest 119
(Philip Hobbs) *hld up in last: mstke 4th: rdn bef 3 out: sme prog after but nvr on terms w ldrs* **8/1**

1116 **6** *4 1/2* **Arctic Gold (IRE)**[35] 3622 5-10-4 **130**.................. RyanHatch(3) 109
(Nigel Twiston-Davies) *prom in chsng gp: rdn bef 3 out: wknd bef 2 out* **12/1**

-P23 **7** *5* **Sirabad (FR)**[56] 3228 6-10-11 **134**.................. (t) SamTwiston-Davies 108
(Paul Nicholls) *hld up in chsng gp: prog 7th but lost pl 3 out and sn bhd* **13/2**

1115 **8** *13* **Roadie Joe (IRE)**[78] 2886 7-10-9 **139**.................. LewisGordon(7) 100
(Evan Williams) *hld up in chsng gp: effrt 6th: lost pl next: bhd fr 3 out* **11/1**

13-1 **F** **Debdebdeb**[26] 3777 6-9-12 **126**.................. BridgetAndrews(5)
(Dan Skelton) *racd v freely: led and clr w one rival: hdd 6th: lost 2nd after 3 out: 4th and wkng qckly whn fell 2 out: winded* **9/2[2]**

4m 49.6s (4.90) **Going Correction** +0.675s/f (Soft)
WFA 4 from 5yo+ 9lb **9 Ran SP% 112.3**
Speed ratings (Par 109): **116,109,109,102,102 100,98,93,**
CSF £73.90 CT £346.70 TOTE £4.70: £1.90, £3.30, £2.00; EX 72.30 Trifecta £600.60.
Owner Mr & Mrs R Kelvin-Hughes **Bred** Seamus Murphy **Trained** Upper Lambourn, Berks

FOCUS
No hanging around here, with two soon racing clear, and the race produced a most impressive winner, although again ground conditions may have accentuated his superiority. He's rated up a stone+ on the best of his novice form. The form is believable.

4240 BETFAIR ASCOT CHASE (GRADE 1) (17 fncs) 2m 5f 8y
3:35 (3:36) (Class 1) 5-Y-O+
£85,425 (£32,055; £16,050; £7,995; £4,020; £2,010)

Form RPR

-22P **1** **Silviniaco Conti (FR)**[56] 3231 10-11-7 164.................. (b[1]) NoelFehily 175
(Paul Nicholls) *trckd ldr: clr of rest 4 out: led bef 2 out: shkn up and drew wl clr: fine jump last: impressive* **2/1[1]**

0230 **2** *20* **Dynaste (FR)**[63] 3149 10-11-7 162.................. (bt[1]) TomScudamore 156
(David Pipe) *tended to jump lft: trckd ldrs: wnt 3rd 3 out but nt on terms w ldng pair: kpt on to take modest 2nd after last: no ch w wnr* **9/2[2]**

6512 **3** *2 1/4* **Royal Regatta (IRE)**[28] 3735 8-11-7 152.................. (bt) TomO'Brien 156
(Philip Hobbs) *led: mstke 12th: clr w wnr 4 out: hdd bef 2 out and immediately btn: tired after and lost 2nd after last* **9/1**

42U2 **4** *14* **Amore Alato**[28] 3738 7-11-7 139.................. AidanColeman 141
(Johnny Farrelly) *in tch on outer: pushed along and lft bhd fr 12th: no ch 3 out* **33/1**

P3-1 **5** *18* **Triolo D'Alene (FR)**[42] 3526 9-11-7 155.................. JeremiahMcGrath 121
(Nicky Henderson) *hld up in last pair: nudged along and lft bhd fr 12th: wl adrift after 3 out* **5/1[3]**

3412 **6** *50* **Flemenstar (IRE)**[20] 3892 11-11-7 160.................. AELynch 71
(Anthony Curran, Ire) *trckd ldrs: mstke 8th: lost pl qckly fr 10th: last after next: sn t.o: eventually completed* **5/1[3]**

0434 **P** **Savello (IRE)**[77] 2914 10-11-7 154.................. BridgetAndrews
(Dan Skelton) *t.k.h: hld up in last: pushed along and no prog after 11th: wl bhd in 7th whn p.u bef 3 out* **20/1**

6301 **P** **Ma Filleule (FR)**[53] 3337 8-11-0 150.................. DarylJacob
(Nicky Henderson) *wl in tch: chsd ldng pair 11th: no imp 13th: lost 3rd and wknd 3 out: poor 5th jumping 2 out: p.u bef last* **8/1**

5m 29.1s (3.10) **Going Correction** +0.725s/f (Soft) **8 Ran SP% 113.7**
Speed ratings: **123,115,114,109,102 83, ,**
CSF £11.45 CT £63.75 TOTE £2.70: £1.20, £1.90, £2.20; EX 9.60 Trifecta £70.60.
Owner Potensis Bloodstock Ltd & Chris Giles **Bred** Patrick Joubert **Trained** Ditcheat, Somerset

FOCUS
Following chase course rail movements this race was run over 6yds further than advertised. Plenty of these had questions to answer and a couple of the major contenders failed to give their running, so it remains to be seen what the form is worth, but none the less it was good to see Silviniaco Conti back in top form. He now looks one of the better handicapped horses in the Grand National.

4241 TWO WEEKS UNTIL RACING UK HD H'CAP HURDLE (QUALIFIER FOR CHALLENGER STAYING HURDLE SERIES FINAL) (11 hdls) 2m 7f 118y
4:10 (4:10) (Class 3) (0-125,125) 4-Y-O+ **£9,747** (£2,862; £1,431; £715)

Form RPR

42-2 **1** **Bangkok Pete (IRE)**[64] 3142 11-10-10 **109**.................. MattieBatchelor 114
(Jamie Poulton) *hld up in rr: stdy prog fr 7th: rdn to chse ldng pair on long run after 3 out: clsd 2 out: led bef last: drvn and hld on wl* **12/1**

/330 **2** 1 1/2 **Billy Dutton**[50] 3407 10-11-7 **125**........ CiaranGethings(5) 128
(Chris Down) *hld up towards rr: prog fr 7th: rdn to chse ldng trio after 3 out: nt fluent 2 out: rallying whn nt fluent last: kpt on to take 2nd fnl 150yds: no imp on wnr nr fin* **11/2**[1]

3255 **3** 1 **Petethepear (IRE)**[35] 3626 6-11-8 **121**........ JoshuaMoore 122
(Stuart Edmunds) *prom: chsd ldr after 7th: led briefly 3 out and drvn to ld again 2 out: hdd bef last: no ex* **6/1**[2]

P303 **4** nk **Sybarite (FR)**[23] 3824 10-11-10 **123**........ SamTwiston-Davies 124
(Nigel Twiston-Davies) *hld up in last: rousted along after 5th: lost tch 7th: wl bhd next: passed toiling rivals to take modest 6th 2 out: styd on wl fr last: all too late* **25/1**

-012 **5** 1/2 **Royale Knight**[19] 3904 10-10-13 **122**........ CharlieHammond(10) 123
(Dr Richard Newland) *led: mstke 3 out and briefly hdd: hdd 2 out: one pce u.p* **8/1**

-32P **6** 12 **Norse Legend**[16] 3956 5-11-12 **125**........ MarcGoldstein 113
(Chris Gordon) *trckd ldrs: last of 5 in tch after 3 out: wknd bef 2 out* **33/1**

4125 **7** 6 **Captainofindustry (IRE)**[42] 3517 7-11-5 **118**........(p) DenisO'Regan 100
(Mark Pitman) *prom: losing pl whn mstke 8th: n.d after 3 out: plugged on* **12/1**

-424 **8** 25 **What A Moment (IRE)**[28] 3736 6-11-12 **125**........(t[1]) TomScudamore 82
(David Pipe) *hld up in rr: tried to make prog bef 8th: sn rdn and no hdwy: wknd 3 out: t.o* **6/1**[2]

-1P2 **9** 1 **Decimus (IRE)**[87] 2711 9-11-12 **125**........(p) LiamHeard 81
(Jeremy Scott) *in tch on outer: struggling after 7th: wknd bef 3 out: t.o* **40/1**

3052 **10** 1 1/4 **Grand Introduction (IRE)**[38] 3582 6-10-13 **115**....(t) ConorShoemark(3) 70
(Fergal O'Brien) *pressed ldr tl after 7th: wkng whn blnd next: t.o* **20/1**

2F52 **11** 5 **Here's Herbie**[28] 3748 8-11-6 **122**........(t) LucyGardner(3) 72
(Sue Gardner) *hld up in rr: effrt after 7th: sn btn: t.o* **10/1**

-4BP **12** 44 **Aigle De La See (FR)**[23] 3818 6-11-12 **125**........ DarylJacob 31
(Nicky Henderson) *hld up in rr: brief effrt after 7th: sn wknd rapidly: t.o* **15/2**[3]

05/2 **P** **Muhtaris (IRE)**[41] 2202 6-11-6 **119**........(p) LiamTreadwell
(James Evans) *t.k.h: trckd ldrs: stmbld 2nd: wknd qckly bef 7th: t.o whn p.u bef next* **9/1**

4014 **S** **Brod Na Heireann (IRE)**[42] 3525 7-11-7 **123**........ TomBellamy(3)
(Alan King) *in tch in midfield whn slipped up bnd bef 6th* **16/1**

6m 11.4s (15.40) **Going Correction** +0.675s/f (Soft) **14** Ran SP% **121.2**
Speed ratings (Par 107): **101,100,100,100,99 95,93,85,85,84 83,68, ,**
CSF £75.23 CT £447.62 TOTE £16.60: £4.60, £2.00, £2.30; EX 116.20 Trifecta £905.00.
Owner Miss Stephanie Young **Bred** Christopher Maye **Trained** Telscombe, E Sussex

FOCUS
A modest staying handicap that was always likely to prove a gruelling test with conditions worsening. The form looks solid enough at its level.

4242 NEPTUNE INVESTMENT MANAGEMENT MARES' STANDARD OPEN NATIONAL HUNT FLAT RACE 1m 7f 152y
4:45 (4:46) (Class 4) 4-6-Y-O **£4,548** (£1,335; £667; £333)

Form RPR

1 **1** **Tearsofclewbay**[51] 3381 5-10-13 0........ ConorSmith(7) 120+
(Philip Hobbs) *t.k.h: hld up in midfield: prog to trck ldr 6f out: led 3f out gng strly: drvn and pressed over 1f out: styd on wl fnl f* **5/1**[3]

3 **2** 3 1/4 **Theatre Territory (IRE)**[98] 2486 6-10-13 0........ MrSWaley-Cohen(3) 113
(Nicky Henderson) *t.k.h: hld up in rr: prog 6f out: chsd ldng pair 3f out: wnt 2nd 2f out and sn chalng: drvn and one pce fnl f* **15/8**[1]

3 15 **Calling Des Blins (FR)**[328] 4-10-11 0........ NoelFehily 93
(Harry Fry) *led at mod pce: stretched on fr 7f out: hdd and shkn up 3f out: lost 2nd and wknd 2f out* **15/8**[1]

4 2 **River Arrow** 5-10-11 0........ CiaranGethings(5) 96
(Susan Johnson) *chsd ldr to 1/2-way: rdn 4f out: sn outpcd by ldrs: no ch after but kpt on to snatch 4th last strides* **66/1**

5 hd **Isle Of Ewe** 5-11-2 0........ NicodeBoinville 96
(Tom Lacey) *prom: chsd ldr 1/2-way to 6f out: rdn and lost 3rd 3f out: btn after: fdd fnl f* **16/1**

1- **6** 34 **Grand Turina**[368] 4289 5-11-6 0........ AidanColeman 66
(Venetia Williams) *t.k.h: hld up in last: tk 6th 6f out and in tch: nudged along and wknd over 4f out: t.o* **4/1**[2]

5 **7** 13 **Dewberry**[262] 602 5-11-2 0........ MarkGrant 49
(Geoffrey Deacon) *hld up in last: lost tch sn after 1/2-way: t.o* **66/1**

8 19 **Lady Ash (IRE)** 6-11-2 0........ DarylJacob 30
(Robert Walford) *t.k.h: trckd ldrs: wknd 1/2-way: t.o* **33/1**

4m 1.5s (20.70) **Going Correction** +0.675s/f (Soft)
WFA 4 from 5yo+ 9lb **8** Ran SP% **118.0**
Speed ratings: **75,73,65,64,64 47,41,31**
CSF £15.32 TOTE £5.30: £1.60, £1.10, £1.20; EX 11.70 Trifecta £36.60.
Owner Mrs Caren Walsh & Mrs Kathleen Quinn **Bred** W P Jenks **Trained** Withycombe, Somerset

FOCUS
The front pair came clear in what was quite a decent mares' bumper, although once again conditions made it very tough going. The first two built on good debut runs.
T/Plt: £171.70 to a £1 stake. Pool: £141,360.64 - 600.97 winning units. T/Qpdt: £25.50 to a £1 stake. Pool: £13,004.30 - 377.17 winning units. **Jonathan Neesom**

3737 HAYDOCK (L-H)
Saturday, February 20

OFFICIAL GOING: Heavy (chs 2.7; hdl 2.9)
Wind: fresh 1/2 against Weather: raining

4243 RAY GILPIN VICTOR LUDORUM JUVENILE HURDLE (SPONSORED BY BETFRED) (9 hdls) 1m 7f 144y
1:30 (1:30) (Class 2) 4-Y-O **£9,747** (£2,862; £1,431; £715)

Form RPR

1-53 **1** **Frodon (FR)**[21] 3854 4-11-6 138........ SeanBowen 136+
(Paul Nicholls) *trckd ldr: upsides 2 out: led last: sn wnt lft: drvn rt out* **4/1**[2]

11 **2** 3/4 **Fixe Le Kap (FR)**[23] 3822 4-11-6 145........ DavidBass 136+
(Nicky Henderson) *led: qcknd pce gng to 3 out: hdd last: sn nt clr run and swtchd rt: tk 2nd last 75yds: styd on same pce* **1/4**[1]

3 1 1/2 **Messire Des Obeaux (FR)**[90] 4-10-12 0........ RichardJohnson 126+
(Alan King) *t.k.h: trckd ldng pair: hit 2nd: lft 2nd sn after last: kpt on same pce last 100yds* **16/1**[3]

4 **4** 30 **Deebaj (IRE)**[23] 3822 4-10-12 0........ RobertDunne 101
(Richard Price) *t.k.h in rr: hdwy to trck ldrs 6th: pushed along next: lost pl 2 out: sn bhd: t.o* **100/1**

4m 19.8s (15.60) **Going Correction** +1.225s/f (Heav) **4** Ran SP% **106.9**
Speed ratings: **110,109,108,93**
CSF £5.70 TOTE £4.50; EX 5.30 Trifecta £8.10.
Owner Ian Fogg & Potensis Bloodstock Ltd **Bred** Philippe Gasdoue **Trained** Ditcheat, Somerset

FOCUS
Due to rail movements this was run over 57 yards further than advertised. This was always likely to be tactical and so it proved, resulting in a messy finish. Suspect juvenile form, with a very fast finishing split. The winner built on his Cheltenham run.

4244 BETFRED "HOME OF GOALS GALORE" HURDLE (REGISTERED AS RENDLESHAM HURDLE) (GRADE 2) (12 hdls) 2m 6f 177y
2:05 (2:05) (Class 1) 4-Y-O+
£22,780 (£8,548; £4,280; £2,132; £1,072; £536)

Form RPR

-625 **1** **Reve De Sivola (FR)**[28] 3741 11-11-10 160........ RichardJohnson 163
(Nick Williams) *mde all: pushed along 8th: drvn 3 out: hld on gamely* **7/2**[2]

1-51 **2** 3/4 **One Track Mind (IRE)**[53] 3352 6-11-2 147........ GavinSheehan 154
(Warren Greatrex) *chsd ldrs: 2nd 2 out: 3 l down sn after last: styd on clsng stages* **5/2**[1]

1124 **3** 13 **Silsol (GER)**[35] 3621 7-11-2 154........(tp) JackSherwood 142
(Paul Nicholls) *in rr: nt fluent 6th: outpcd next: sn drvn: hdwy 3 out: 3rd between last 2: one pce* **9/2**[3]

54-2 **4** 10 **At Fishers Cross (IRE)**[30] 3713 9-11-2 157........(b) BarryGeraghty 135
(Rebecca Curtis) *chsd ldrs: drvn and outpcd 3 out: wknd between last 2* **7/2**[2]

-F23 **5** 25 **Deputy Dan (IRE)**[63] 3149 8-11-2 151........(b) LeightonAspell 115
(Oliver Sherwood) *hld up in rr: hdwy 6th: 2nd 9th: 4th and wkng whn nt fluent 2 out: sn wknd: heavily eased run-in: collapsed fatally sn after line* **9/2**[3]

1206 **6** 41 **Foxcub (IRE)**[28] 3748 8-11-2 142........(p) DavidBass 64
(Tom Symonds) *chsd ldrs: lost pl 7th: bhd and reminders 9th: t.o whn j. bdly rt 3 out and last: virtually p.u* **40/1**

6m 20.1s (20.10) **Going Correction** +1.225s/f (Heav) **6** Ran SP% **111.8**
Speed ratings (Par 115): **114,113,109,105,97 82**
CSF £12.85 TOTE £4.40: £2.30, £1.80; EX 14.20 Trifecta £51.70.
Owner Paul Duffy Diamond Partnership **Bred** Gilles Trapenard & Thomas Trapenard **Trained** George Nympton, Devon

FOCUS
Due to rail movements this was run over 114 yards further than advertised.This looked a tight edition of the Grade 2 Rendlesham, often a big pointer for the World Hurdle next month. However, the first pair are not entered and it was a race for mud-lovers. The winner was close to his best in much the the fastest of the races over the trip.

4245 BETFRED GRAND NATIONAL TRIAL (A H'CAP CHASE) (GRADE 3) 3m 4f 97y
2:40 (2:40) (Class 1) 5-Y-O+ **£45,050** (£18,365; £10,362)

Form RPR

-001 **1** **Bishops Road (IRE)**[49] 3445 8-11-7 **144**........ RichardJohnson 157
(Kerry Lee) *in rr: hit 2nd: chsng ldrs 5th: drvn 13th: mstke 16th: led 4 out: forged clr run-in* **13/2**

26-5 **2** 9 **Broadway Buffalo (IRE)**[105] 2361 8-11-4 **141**........(bt) MsKWalsh 148
(David Pipe) *hld up in rr: hdwy 11th: hit next 2nd 3 out: j.ft next: 2 l down last: sn fdd* **4/1**[1]

P031 **3** 22 **Cloudy Too (IRE)**[28] 3741 10-11-12 **149**........ DannyCook 136
(Sue Smith) *chsd ldrs: hit 13th: wknd appr 2 out: lft distant 3rd last* **11/2**[3]

041F **P** **Rigadin De Beauchene (FR)**[35] 3624 11-10-10 **133**....(b) RobertDunne
(Venetia Williams) *led: hdd and mstke 15th: lost pl and mstke 17th: sn bhd: t.o 5th whn p.u bef 3 out* **5/1**[2]

5361 **P** **Mountainous (IRE)**[42] 3518 11-11-5 **142**........(p) JamieMoore
(Kerry Lee) *chsd ldrs: pushed along 11th: lost pl after 13th: reminders next: sn bhd: p.u bef 16th* **5/1**[2]

F332 **P** **Harry The Viking**[52] 3364 11-10-5 **128**........(p) DerekFox
(Sandy Thomson) *in rr: drvn along 3rd: reminders 12th: sn bhd: t.o 14th: t.o 6th whn p.u bef 3 out* **7/1**

4F-U **P** **Gas Line Boy (IRE)**[28] 3741 10-11-3 **140**........(v) LeightonAspell
(Jim Best) *w ldr: drvn 15th: sn lost pl and bhd: t.o whn p.u bef 18th* **6/1**

-233 **P** **Minella On Line (IRE)**[66] 3113 7-10-2 **125**........(b[1]) BrianHughes
(Rebecca Curtis) *chsd ldrs: led 15th: hdd 4 out: wknd 2 out: distant 3rd whn p.u appr last* **22/1**

8m 33.1s (61.50) **Going Correction** +2.25s/f (Heav) **8** Ran SP% **113.2**
Speed ratings: **102,99,93, , , , ,**
CSF £32.66 CT £151.63 TOTE £6.20: £1.60, £1.90, £2.00; EX 34.10 Trifecta £222.20.
Owner Alan Halsall **Bred** P J Morrissey **Trained** Byton, H'fords

FOCUS
Due to rail movements this was run over 132 yards further than advertised. Once again this Grand National trial proved a severe stamina examination. The runner-up sets the standard, with another big step forward from the winner.

4246 PERTEMPS NETWORK H'CAP HURDLE (SERIES QUALIFIER) (12 hdls) 2m 6f 177y
3:15 (3:16) (Class 2) 5-Y-O+ **£12,021** (£3,529; £1,764; £882)

Form RPR

PPP- **1** **Mr Moonshine (IRE)**[392] 3860 12-11-6 **133**........ DannyCook 139+
(Sue Smith) *w ldr: led after 9th: clr 2 out: drvn out* **33/1**

2624 **2** 12 **Quel Elite (FR)**[14] 3999 12-10-3 **116**........ HenryBrooke 110
(James Moffatt) *chsd ldrs: lost pl 8th: hdwy to chse ldrs bef 3 out: 2nd 2 out: kpt on same pce* **25/1**

1F13 **3** 1 **Isaacstown Lad (IRE)**[35] 3622 9-11-7 **134**........ BrianHarding 127
(Nicky Richards) *hld up towards rr: hdwy appr 3 out: styd on to take modest 3rd clsng stages* **9/1**

4-01 **4** 1 1/4 **Taj Badalandabad (IRE)**[22] 3844 6-11-6 **133**........(p) ConorO'Farrell 125
(David Pipe) *hld up in rr: hdwy appr 3 out: 3rd last: kpt on same pce* **11/2**[3]

/0P- **5** 3 3/4 **Champagne James (IRE)**[28] 3755 8-11-0 **127**........(t) APHeskin 115
(T M Walsh, Ire) *in rr-div: hdwy 7th: outpcd appr 3 out: kpt on between last 2* **6/1**

1-12 **6** 5 **Top Billing**[53] 3336 7-11-7 **139**........ RyanDay(5) 122
(Nicky Richards) *led: hdd after 9th: wknd last 150yds* **12/1**

5-13 **7** 11 **Tradewinds (FR)**[119] 2062 8-10-10 **128**........ GrantCockburn(5) 100
(Lucinda Russell) *chsd ldrs: lost pl bef 3 out* **25/1**

4F40 **8** 10 **Horizontal Speed (IRE)**[28] 3737 8-11-8 **135**........ BrianHughes 99
(David Dennis) *trckd ldrs: wkng whn hit 3 out: bhd next* **20/1**

/P6P **9** 4 **Mountain Tunes (IRE)**[22] 3843 7-10-11 **124**........(v[1]) RichieMcLernon 84
(Jonjo O'Neill) *chsd ldrs: lost pl and nt fluent 3 out: sn bhd* **25/1**

-634 **P** **Box Office (FR)**[77] 2912 5-11-8 **135**........(t) BarryGeraghty
(Jonjo O'Neill) *in rr: lost pl bef 3 out: sn bhd: p.u bef 2 out* **4/1**[2]

3 **P** **Woodford Island (IRE)**[28] 3753 5-10-13 **126**..............(t) RichardJohnson
(Gordon Elliott, Ire) *in rr: blnd 7th: mstke 9th: sn bhd: t.o whn p.u bef 2 out* **5/2**[1]

6m 30.7s (30.70) **Going Correction** +1.60s/f (Heav) **11** Ran SP% **115.2**
Speed ratings: **110,105,105,105,103 102,98,94,93,**
CSF £616.44 CT £7795.73 TOTE £26.20: £5.90, £6.70, £3.00; EX 841.50 Trifecta £15709.40.
Owner DG Pryde,J Beaumont,DP Van Der Hoeven 1 **Bred** T McIlhagga **Trained** High Eldwick, W Yorks

FOCUS
Due to rail movements this was run over 114 yards further than advertised. This looked very competitive, but the bad ground played a big part and it's suspect form. The winner was well treated on his best hurdle form and is rated back to that level.

4247 BETFRED "DOUBLE DELIGHT" NOVICES' LIMITED H'CAP CHASE (17 fncs) 2m 3f 203y

3:50 (3:50) (Class 3) 5-Y-0+ **£8,122** (£2,385; £1,192; £596)

Form RPR

-311 **1** **Kylemore Lough**[65] 3121 7-11-8 **147**.................................. JamieMoore 155+
(Kerry Lee) *lft in ld 1st: j. soundly: clr 9th: 6 l ahd whn blnd 2 out: edgd lft and forged clr run-in* **4/5**[1]

-352 **2** *5* **Kayfleur**[65] 3122 7-10-3 **128** oh2.. JakeGreenall 127
(Henry Daly) *hld up in tch: hdwy and handy 3rd 11th: bmpd 4 out: chsd wnr appr 2 out: 3 l down last: kpt on same pce* **5/1**[3]

1-15 **3** *15* **Capard King (IRE)**[49] 3439 7-11-0 **139**......................... RichardJohnson 128
(Jonjo O'Neill) *chsd ldng pair: mstke 6th: 2nd 9th: drvn and j.lft 4 out: hit next: wknd appr 2 out* **3/1**[2]

1514 **4** *8* **Throthethatch (IRE)**[25] 3794 7-10-3 **128** oh12.................. PeterBuchanan 109
(Lucinda Russell) *j. slowly: led: mstke and hdd 1st: chsd wnr: lost pl 9th: bhd 11th* **8/1**

5m 50.2s (350.20) **4** Ran SP% **108.3**
CSF £5.02 TOTE £1.50; EX 5.30 Trifecta £11.40.
Owner M J McMahon & Denis Gallagher **Bred** M J McMahon **Trained** Byton, H'fords

FOCUS
Due to rail movements this was run over 75 yards further than advertised. A fair novice handicap, run at a decent gallop. The mud-loving winner rates value for plenty further and is a smart novice.

4248 ALBERT BARTLETT NOVICES' HURDLE (REGISTERED AS PRESTIGE NOVICES' HURDLE) (GRADE 2) (12 hdls) 2m 6f 177y

4:25 (4:25) (Class 1) 5-Y-0+ **£17,138** (£6,587; £3,392; £1,793)

Form RPR

1212 **1** **Jonniesofa (IRE)**[50] 3400 6-11-4 135.................................. CraigNichol 140
(Rose Dobbin) *w ldr: t.k.h: led narrowly 2 out: forged clr last 100yds* **8/1**

2122 **2** *3* **Vintage Clouds (IRE)**[28] 3743 6-11-7 132.......................... DannyCook 140
(Sue Smith) *led: hit 3 out: hdd narrowly next: styd on same pce fnl 150yds* **5/1**[3]

2121 **3** *4* **Duke Des Champs (IRE)**[28] 3736 6-11-7 146.................. RichardJohnson 137
(Philip Hobbs) *racd wd: trckd ldrs: handy 3rd whn hit 7th: upsides 2 out: 2 l down whn stmbld on landing last: kpt on one pce* **10/11**[1]

F1 **4** *76* **Churchtown Champ (IRE)**[38] 3580 6-11-0 130.................... IanPopham 78
(Dan Skelton) *chsd ldrs: pushed along 9th: sn outpcd: bhd bef next: t.o whn virtually p.u run-in: eventually completed* **10/1**

1111 **P** **Baywing (IRE)**[28] 3737 7-11-7 135.. BrianHarding
(Nicky Richards) *nt fluent: chsd ldrs: pushed along 8th: lost pl next: sn bhd: t.o whn p.u bef last* **7/2**[2]

6m 35.5s (35.50) **Going Correction** +1.60s/f (Heav) **5** Ran SP% **111.5**
Speed ratings: **102,100,99,73,**
CSF £43.55 TOTE £8.60: £2.90, £2.20; EX 37.70 Trifecta £151.40.
Owner R & Mrs A Houghton & A Houghton **Bred** T Finn **Trained** South Hazelrigg, Northumbria

FOCUS
Due to rail movements this was run over 114 yards further than advertised. This Grade 2 novice proved extremely hard work. The first three were all a stone+ off what is likely to be required to win at the festival.

4249 BETFRED "HAT TRICK HEAVEN" WALRUS OPEN HUNTERS' CHASE (18 fncs) 3m 24y

5:00 (5:00) (Class 3) 5-Y-0+ **£6,964** (£2,660)

Form RPR

1-3U **1** **Pearlysteps**[38] 3585 13-12-1 132.................................. MissJCWilliams(3) 135+
(Henry Daly) *j.rt: led 2nd: wl clr bef 2 out: pushed out* **7/4**[1]

P/F3 **2** *85* **Ace High**[27] 12-11-12 115.. MrDEdwards
(Mrs Janet Ackner) *chsd ldrs: hit 8th: chsd wnr 4 out: wknd 2 out: 20 l 2nd whn clambered over last: stopped to walk: eventually completed* **9/2**[3]

22-3 **P** **Jaunty Journey**[14] 4000 13-11-12 103..............................(p) MrJohnDawson
(P Foster) *led to 3rd: lost pl 10th: bhd whn blnd and reminders next: t.o whn blnd 11th: sn p.u* **25/1**

P5-P **P** **Chartreux (FR)**[294] 95 11-11-11 129..............(t) MrSDavies-Thomas(7)
(Mrs Julie Marles) *chsd ldrs: blnd 1st: lost pl bef 4 out: sn bhd: remote 3rd whn p.u bef last* **20/1**

5-22 **P** **Richmond (FR)**[23] 3826 11-11-11 125.............................. MissLMTurner(7)
(P P C Turner) *chsd ldrs: lost pl bef 4 out: bhd whn j.rt 3 out: 5th whn p.u bef 2 out* **11/4**[2]

31P- **P** **Grove Pride**[302] 5518 11-11-11 125.................................. MrLeoMahon(7)
(Mrs D J Ralph) *in rr: hit 4th: chsd ldrs 6th: 2nd 13th: drvn and lost pl 4 out: remote 4th whn hit 2 out: sn p.u* **16/1**

32 **P** **Connies Cross (IRE)**[27] 9-11-7 125.................................. MrJNixon(5)
(Mrs Sheila Crow) *chsd ldrs: lost pl 10th: bhd 15th: t.o whn p.u bef 3 out* **5/1**

7m 18.7s (48.20) **Going Correction** +2.25s/f (Heav) **7** Ran SP% **112.4**
Speed ratings: **109,80,,,**
CSF £9.98 TOTE £2.70: £1.60, £2.70; EX 10.60 Trifecta £13.00.
Owner The Glazeley Partnership **Bred** W P Jenks **Trained** Stanton Lacy, Shropshire

FOCUS
Due to rail movements this was run over 132 yards further than advertised. This hunter chase proved another war of attrition as only two got home. The winner is rated in line with the best of last season's runs.

T/Plt: £3919.70 to a £1 stake. Pool: £85,965.36 - 16.01 winning units. T/Qpdt: £345.60 to a £1 stake. Pool: £7,427.12 - 15.90 winning units. **Walter Glynn**

3953 WINCANTON (R-H)

Saturday, February 20

OFFICIAL GOING: Soft (heavy in places; chs 5.2, hdl 6.1)
Wind: strong breeze half across Weather: showers

4250 BATHWICK TYRES SALISBURY H'CAP HURDLE (10 hdls 1 omitted) 2m 5f 82y

1:40 (1:40) (Class 4) (0-105,105) 4-Y-0+ **£3,249** (£954; £477; £238)

Form RPR

-P0P **1** **Somerset Jem**[50] 3413 7-10-1 **87**.................................. ConorSmith(7) 102+
(Kevin Bishop) *hld up towards rr: stdy prog fr 6th: wnt 3rd after 3 out: led next: styd on wl to draw clr: pushed out* **10/1**

4552 **2** *13* **Craiganee (IRE)**[50] 3414 9-11-7 **103**..............................(t) KieronEdgar(3) 106
(Chris Down) *chsd ldrs: rdn to chal whn hung in bhd ldr appr 2 out: regained 2nd at the last: styd on same pce* **8/1**

600P **3** *11* **I'llhavealook (IRE)**[18] 3914 11-10-4 **90**..............................(p) MissPFuller(7) 78
(Katie Stephens) *mid-div: rdn after 3 out: stdy prog into 4th 2 out: styd on into 3rd run-in: nvr threatened ldrs* **66/1**

14-P **4** *3* **Baldadash (IRE)**[33] 3662 11-11-12 **105**..............................(p) JamesDavies 96+
(Jose Santos) *chsd ldrs: led 7th: rdn and hdd whn nt fluent 2 out: 3rd and hld whn blnd bdly last: no ex* **28/1**

3603 **5** *14* **Who's Micky Brown (IRE)**[16] 3955 6-11-4 **104**........ MrShaneQuinlan(7) 75
(Neil Mulholland) *mid-div: rdn after 3 out: nvr any imp on ldrs: chal for wl hld 4th 2 out: no ex fr last* **9/2**[2]

005P **6** *24* **Karl Marx (IRE)**[18] 3914 6-10-0 **84**..............................(b) CharlieDeutsch(5) 31
(Mark Gillard) *prom tl 7th: sn rdn: wknd bef 2 out where hmpd* **18/1**

5222 **7** *15* **Very Intense (IRE)**[50] 3422 5-11-2 **102**..............(p) MrTommieMO'Brien(7) 34
(Tom Lacey) *hld up towards rr: hdwy into midfield 3 out: sn rdn: wknd bef next: t.o* **4/1**[1]

6-P4 **8** *67* **Kudu Shine**[50] 3410 10-11-0 **100**..........................(tp) MrMatthewHampton(7)
(Richard Woollacott) *led tl 7th: rdn after 3 out: wkng whn hmpd 2 out: eased: t.o* **9/1**

5P/P **F** **Fuhgeddaboudit**[22] 3846 9-11-4 **102**.................................. KevinJones(5)
(Seamus Mullins) *mid-div on outer: hdwy after 3 out: rdn and wkng in 6th whn fell next* **50/1**

-350 **P** **Its A Long Road**[30] 3705 8-11-11 **104**..............................(p) NickSchofield
(Tim Dennis) *struggling fr 5th: a bhd: t.o whn p.u bef 2 out* **5/1**[3]

-633 **P** **Mrsrobin (IRE)**[51] 3386 6-11-0 **103**.................................. RichieO'Dea(10)
(Emma Lavelle) *mid-div tl wknd 3 out: t.o whn p.u bef next* **14/1**

6005 **P** **Mondello (GER)**[18] 3915 5-11-10 **103**.................................. PaddyBrennan
(Richard Woollacott) *a towards rr: t.o whn p.u after 3 out* **16/1**

4646 **P** **Morestead Screamer**[124] 2002 7-11-11 **104**.................................. TomCannon
(Chris Gordon) *mid-div tl wknd 6th: t.o whn p.u after 3 out* **25/1**

-5FP **P** **Whiskey John**[74] 2964 6-10-7 **91**.................................. ThomasCheesman(5)
(Laura Young) *mid-div tl wknd bef 3 out: t.o whn p.u bef next* **66/1**

0P3 **P** **Jack Snipe**[39] 3568 7-11-3 **99**.................................. MattGriffiths(3)
(Jeremy Scott) *mid-div: struggling whn hit 7th: wknd next: t.o whn p.u bef 2 out* **16/1**

5m 58.0s (31.50) **Going Correction** +1.20s/f (Heav) **15** Ran SP% **121.0**
Speed ratings (Par 105): **88,83,78,77,72 63,57,32,, ,,,,**
CSF £85.15 CT £4968.56 TOTE £12.40: £3.60, £2.90, £17.80; EX 108.60 Trifecta £2323.10.
Owner Slabs And Lucan **Bred** Chris Macey **Trained** Spaxton, Somerset

FOCUS
The hurdle course was out wide on 80% fresh ground, plus the hurdle on the stables bend was omitted. Add 54 yards to the official race distance. The early gallop for this weak handicap didn't seem strong. The second sets the level.

4251 BATHWICK TYRES TAUNTON H'CAP CHASE (14 fncs 3 omitted) 2m 4f 35y

2:15 (2:15) (Class 3) (0-135,126) 5-Y-0+ **£6,963** (£2,057; £1,028; £514; £257)

Form RPR

1F23 **1** **Fourth Act (IRE)**[42] 3521 7-11-12 **126**..............................(t) PaddyBrennan 141+
(Colin Tizzard) *trckd ldrs: led 4 out: drew clr fr next: comf* **2/1**[1]

-213 **2** *11* **Cresswell Breeze**[65] 3122 6-11-7 **126**..............................(t) DavidNoonan(5) 126+
(Anthony Honeyball) *j.lft thrght: prom: stmbld 5th: rdn after 4 out: chsd wnr fr next but a being readily hld: styd on same pce* **2/1**[1]

2PPP **3** *2* **Atlantic Roller (IRE)**[26] 3776 9-11-3 **117**..............................(p) TomCannon 112
(Chris Gordon) *hld up in last pair but wl in tch: stmbld 3rd: hdwy 4 out: sn rdn: styd on same pce fr next* **10/1**

2520 **4** *3/4* **Saint Raph (FR)**[16] 3957 8-11-6 **120**..............................(t) AdamWedge 115
(Robert Walford) *led tl mstke 4 out: sn rdn: styd on same pce fr next* **7/1**[3]

2-4P **5** *45* **Somchine**[25] 3794 8-11-5 **119**.................................. AndrewThornton 68
(Seamus Mullins) *hld up in last pair but wl in tch: hit 6th: effrt after 10th: wknd after 4 out: t.o* **12/1**

4106 **6** *11* **Toowoomba (IRE)**[30] 3706 8-11-1 **115**..............................(t) MichealNolan 53
(Philip Hobbs) *chsd ldrs: rdn after 10th: wknd after 4 out: t.o* **5/1**[2]

5m 52.7s (35.20) **Going Correction** +1.575s/f (Heav) **6** Ran SP% **112.6**
Speed ratings: **92,87,86,86,68 64**
CSF £6.79 TOTE £2.80: £1.80, £1.50; EX 6.40 Trifecta £45.30.
Owner Wendy & Malcolm Hezel **Bred** Kenilworth House Stud **Trained** Milborne Port, Dorset

FOCUS
The water jump and last open ditch were omitted, and the chases were run on the hurdle bend leaving the back straight. Add 78 yards to the official race distance. Probably not a strong race for the grade. The easy winner's Carlisle win could be rated to this sort of level.

4252 BATHWICK TYRES YEOVIL H'CAP HURDLE 2m 5f 82y

2:50 (2:50) (Class 3) (0-135,128) 4-Y-0+ **£6,498** (£1,908; £954; £477)

Form RPR

06-6 **1** **Tagrita (IRE)**[55] 3283 8-10-13 **122**..............................(t) HarryCobden(7) 128+
(Paul Nicholls) *trckd ldr: led sn after 2 out: styd on wl: rdn out* **5/2**[2]

2-40 **2** *2* **Oscarteea (IRE)**[71] 3018 7-11-12 **128**..............................(t) HarrySkelton 132
(Neil Mulholland) *j. sltly lft thrght: led tl after 5th: led after 3 out: nt fluent and hdd 2 out: sn rdn: styd on but a being hld fr last* **9/4**[1]

2441 **3** *4 1/2* **Cadoudoff (FR)**[22] 3843 6-11-8 **127**..............................(p) GrahamWatters(3) 128
(Charlie Longsdon) *chsd ldrs: pushed along fr 7th: rdn after 3 out: chal for hld 3rd fr 2 out: styd on same pce* **7/2**[3]

30-5 **4** *1 1/4* **Queen Of The Stage (IRE)**[49] 3444 6-11-5 **126**.............. LizzieKelly(5) 125
(Nick Williams) *trckd ldrs: nudged along after mstke 7th: rdn and ch appr 2 out: sn hld: disputing 3rd whn mstke last: no ex* **7/2**[3]

1110 **5** *49* **Grams And Ounces**[17] 3932 9-10-12 **114**..............................(t) MichealNolan 62
(Grace Harris) *trckd ldrs: led after 5th: rdn and hdd after 3 out: wknd bef next: t.o* **25/1**

/50P 6 21 **Phantom Prince (IRE)**[16] 3956 7-11-2 **125**........................ PaulO'Brien(7) 52
(Jimmy Frost) *trckd ldrs tl wknd after 3 out: t.o next* **50/1**
5m 58.3s (31.80) **Going Correction** +1.20s/f (Heavy) **6** Ran SP% **109.6**
Speed ratings (Par 107): **87,86,84,84,65 57**
CSF £8.36 TOTE £3.20: £1.80, £1.40; EX 7.50 Trifecta £24.90.

Owner Axom XLVIII **Bred** John Kidd **Trained** Ditcheat, Somerset

FOCUS
The hurdle course was out wide on 80% fresh ground, plus the hurdle on the stables bend was omitted. Add 54 yards to the official race distance. This looked one of the stronger handicaps on the card, despite the topweight being 7lb below the ceiling rating for the race, but they went slow early. The winner was a 135 hurdler at her peak and may still be capable of better than this.

4253 BATHWICK TYRES KINGWELL HURDLE (GRADE 2) (7 hdls 1 omitted) 1m 7f 65y
3:20 (3:21) (Class 1) 4-Y-0+ **£34,170** (£12,822; £6,420; £3,198)

Form RPR
0122 1 **Rayvin Black**[14] 3989 7-11-2 149............................(p) ThomasGarner 151+
(Oliver Sherwood) *mde all: rdn after 3 out: kpt on v gamely fr last: drvn out* **10/3**[2]
3433 2 5 **Melodic Rendezvous**[28] 3740 10-11-2 146....................(p) MattGriffiths 147
(Jeremy Scott) *trckd ldrs: pushed along fr 4th: drvn after 3 out: styd on to chse wnr bef last: a being hld run-in* **6/1**
5311 3 2 ½ **Pain Au Chocolat (FR)**[17] 3935 5-11-2 145........................ HarrySkelton 145
(Dan Skelton) *trckd wnr: looked to be gng best after 3 out: rdn bef next: nt pce to chal: no ex appr last* **11/2**[3]
-116 4 48 **Irving**[84] 2789 8-11-10 162.. NickScholfield 132
(Paul Nicholls) *trckd ldrs: nudged along after 3 out: drvn bef 2 out: sn btn: eased run-in* **8/11**[1]
4m 1.6s (12.70) **Going Correction** +1.20s/f (Heavy) **4** Ran SP% **110.7**
Speed ratings (Par 115): **114,111,110,84**
CSF £19.00 TOTE £4.80; EX 14.20 Trifecta £26.30.

Owner R White & V J Walsh **Bred** Mystic Meg Limited **Trained** Upper Lambourn, Berks

FOCUS
The hurdle course was out wide on 80% fresh ground, plus the hurdle on the stables bend was omitted. Add 36 yards to the official race distance. Only a small field lined up for a this classy race, but it was a fascinating contest. Rayvin Black is rated similar to his previous best.

4254 BATHWICK TYRES SALISBURY H'CAP CHASE (11 fncs 2 omitted) 1m 7f 149y
3:55 (3:56) (Class 2) (0-150,143) 5-Y-0+ **£12,627** (£3,811; £1,963; £1,039)

Form RPR
-F40 1 **Ultragold (FR)**[49] 3445 8-10-3 **120**..............................(t) PaddyBrennan 135+
(Colin Tizzard) *trckd ldrs: led 4 out: drew clr after next: nt fluent last: comf* **2/1**[1]
-P13 2 17 **Gardefort (FR)**[21] 3857 7-11-5 **141**........................ CharlieDeutsch(5) 140
(Venetia Williams) *racd keenly: hld up last in chsng gp: tk clsr order after 4th: rdn after 4 out: chsd wnr next: hld 2 out: fdd* **5/2**[2]
F443 3 23 **Gentleman Jon**[25] 3786 8-10-0 **124**..............................(t) PaulO'Brien(7) 97
(Colin Tizzard) *chsd ldr: nt fluent 1st: rdn bef 4 out: wknd bef 3 out: t.o* **5/1**
5140 4 11 **Keel Haul (IRE)**[49] 3446 8-10-13 **130**..............................(p) JamesDavies 92
(Henry Oliver) *chsd ldrs: drvn along fr 5th: wknd bef 4 out: t.o whn lft 4th bef 3 out* **7/2**[3]
31P- P **Sail By The Sea (IRE)**[347] 4689 8-11-10 **141**........................ MarkQuinlan
(Neil Mulholland) *racd keenly: led: clr tl 6th: hdd 4 out: wknd qckly: p.u next* **6/1**
4m 20.8s (20.90) **Going Correction** +1.575s/f (Heavy) **5** Ran SP% **115.1**
Speed ratings: **110,101,90,84,**
CSF £8.03 TOTE £3.10: £1.60, £1.90; EX 9.20 Trifecta £25.10.

Owner Brocade Racing J P Romans Terry Warner **Bred** Gilles Chaignon **Trained** Milborne Port, Dorset

FOCUS
The water jump and last open ditch were omitted, and the chases were run on the hurdle bend leaving the back straight. Add 51 yards to the official race distance. The pace was sound for this probably just fair contest. A pb from the winner.

4255 BATHWICK TYRES BRIDGWATER H'CAP CHASE (17 fncs 4 omitted) 3m 1f 30y
4:30 (4:32) (Class 4) (0-115,112) 5-Y-0+ **£5,770** (£2,098)

Form RPR
4P35 1 **Barton Gift**[37] 3591 9-11-9 **109**..............................(b) AndrewThornton 115+
(John Spearing) *pressed ldrs tl dropped to 3rd u.p after 4 out: lft 5 l 2nd and hmpd next: rallied after 2 out: 3 l down last: str run fnl 140yds: led nring fin* **3/1**[1]
14P 2 ½ **Winston Churchill (IRE)**[21] 3867 10-11-1 **104**............(t) KillianMoore(3) 107
(Sophie Leech) *in tch: hdwy 10th: chalng whn lft in ld and mstke 3 out: 6 l clr 2 out: 3 l clr last: no ex whn hdd nring fin* **11/1**
5632 P **Fine Parchment (IRE)**[12] 4027 13-11-9 **112**..........(tp) HarryBannister(3)
(Charlie Mann) *led tl 12th: wknd after next: t.o whn p.u after 4 out* **8/1**
6134 P **Kings Apollo**[9] 4062 7-11-9 **109**.. JamesDavies
(Tom Symonds) *chsd ldrs: struggling after 10th: wknd next: tailing off whn p.u bef 12th* **5/1**
4P-F F **The Chuckmeister (IRE)**[284] 266 7-11-8 **108**........................ TomCannon
(Chris Gordon) *trcking ldrs whn fell 8th* **11/1**
-0F6 F **Tikkapick (IRE)**[28] 3746 6-10-6 **92**........................ PaddyBrennan 95+
(Colin Tizzard) *hld up: hdwy 11th: led next: jnd but looked to be travelling wl enough whn fell 3 out* **4/1**[3]
P064 P **Mad About The Boy**[18] 3916 6-11-5 **105**........................ AdamWedge
(Robert Walford) *bhd: struggling 7th: losing tch whn p.u next* **10/3**[2]
7m 36.2s (56.70) **Going Correction** +1.575s/f (Heavy) **7** Ran SP% **112.5**
Speed ratings: **72,71, , , ,**
CSF £31.56 TOTE £4.00: £2.00, £5.70; EX 37.80 Trifecta £32.40.

Owner Mercy Rimell & Kate Ive **Bred** Mrs Mercy Rimell **Trained** Kinnersley, Worcs

■ Stewards' Enquiry : Andrew Thornton seven-day ban: used whip above permitted level (Sat 5th - Fri 11th March)

Adam Wedge vet said gelding had bled from the nose

FOCUS
The water jump and last open ditch were omitted, and the chases were run on the hurdle bend leaving the back straight. Add 90 yards to the official race distance. A modest staying chase. The winner is rated close to his best.

4256 BEN WAKELEY "NATIONAL HUNT" NOVICES' HURDLE (7 hdls 1 omitted) 1m 7f 65y
5:05 (5:08) (Class 4) 4-Y-0+ **£3,898** (£1,144; £572; £286)

Form RPR
F621 1 **Gala Ball (IRE)**[30] 3710 6-11-8 133........................ MichealNolan 135
(Philip Hobbs) *led tl after 3rd: pressed ldr: led after 3 out: rdn after last: styd on wl* **5/6**[1]
1643 2 ¾ **Fountains Windfall**[28] 3745 6-10-11 0........................ DavidNoonan(5) 127
(Anthony Honeyball) *mid-div: hdwy after 3 out: rdn to chse wnr bef last: styd on wl but a being hld nring fin* **9/2**[3]
3 13 **Black Corton (FR)**[157] 5-11-2 0........................ NickScholfield 115
(Paul Nicholls) *racd keenly: trckd ldrs: rdn to chse wnr appr 2 out tl appr last: styd on same pce* **4/1**[2]
0 4 16 **Valhalla (IRE)**[64] 3133 6-11-2 0..............................(t) PaddyBrennan 100
(Colin Tizzard) *racd wd: trckd ldrs: rdn to chse wnr briefly appr 2 out: wknd between last 2* **7/1**
423 5 4 ½ **Shadow Blue (IRE)**[30] 3710 7-10-9 114........................ MrGTreacy(7) 94
(Steven Dixon) *w wnr: led after 3rd tl after 3 out: wknd between last 2* **16/1**
6 7 **Bennys King (IRE)** 5-10-11 0........................ CharlieDeutsch(5) 87
(Venetia Williams) *a towards rr* **20/1**
65-3 7 23 **Monkey Rum**[284] 271 6-11-2 0........................ PeterCarberry 64
(Brendan Powell) *a towards rr: t.o* **50/1**
P **Final Flow** 7-10-9 0........................ PaulO'Brien(7)
(Colin Tizzard) *mid-div tl wknd 4th: t.o whn p.u bef 2 out* **40/1**
4m 7.7s (18.80) **Going Correction** +1.20s/f (Heavy) **8** Ran SP% **120.3**
Speed ratings (Par 105): **97,96,89,81,78 75,62,**
CSF £5.49 TOTE £1.90: £1.10, £1.50, £1.60; EX 7.70 Trifecta £16.10.
Owner Robert & Janet Gibbs **Bred** Thomas James **Trained** Withycombe, Somerset
■ Stewards' Enquiry : Paul O'Brien vet said the gelding had bled from the nose.

FOCUS
The hurdle course was out wide on 80% fresh ground, plus the hurdle on the stables bend was omitted. Add 36 yards to the official race distance. Quite an interesting race of its type, run at a fair pace. Straightforward form.
T/Plt: £400.00 to a £1 stake. Pool: £62,232.64 - 113.57 winning units. T/Qpdt: £40.20 to a £1 stake. Pool: £4,440.55 - 81.60 winning units. **Tim Mitchell**

4257 - 4259a (Foreign Racing) - See Raceform Interactive

3869 FAIRYHOUSE (R-H)
Saturday, February 20

OFFICIAL GOING: Heavy

4260a AT THE RACES BOBBYJO CHASE (GRADE 2) (20 fncs) 3m 1f
3:25 (3:26) 5-Y-0+
£19,522 (£6,286; £2,977; £1,323; £661; £330)

RPR
1 **Boston Bob (IRE)**[30] 3715 11-11-3 155........................ RWalsh 155
(W P Mullins, Ire) *hld up bhd ldrs: 5th 1/2-way: clsr in 4th bef 3 out and wnt 3rd gng wl bef next where lft 2nd: led narrowly bef last: sn rdn and strly pressed fr last where jnd: all out clsng stages where led narrowly* **4/1**[3]
2 hd **On His Own (IRE)**[14] 4007 12-11-6 155..............................(p) MrPWMullins 158
(W P Mullins, Ire) *led tl hdd fr 1st: disp for most after next: slt mstkes 10th and 13th and hdd: disp bef next tl hdd 4 out: hmpd 2 out: sn rdn in 3rd and clsd u.p to dispute: kpt on wl: hdd cl home* **8/1**
3 8 ½ **Turban (FR)**[297] 24 9-11-3 150........................ PaulTownend 147
(W P Mullins, Ire) *w.w: 6th 1/2-way: tk clsr order bhd ldrs fr 4 out: almost on terms 2 out where lft in front: sn jnd and hdd bef last: kpt on one pce run-in* **16/1**
4 ½ **Baie Des Iles (FR)**[20] 3894 5-10-3 142........................ RobbiePower 132
(Ross O'Sullivan, Ire) *chsd ldrs: 4th 1/2-way: clsr in 4th fr 13th: mstke 4 out: rdn bef 2 out where lft 4th and no imp on ldrs bef last: kpt on one pce* **3/1**[2]
5 8 **Thunder And Roses (IRE)**[30] 3715 8-11-3 145..............................(p) BJCooper 138
(Ms Sandra Hughes, Ire) *cl up and led briefly fr 1st: jnd after next and disp for most: cl 2nd bef 11th tl led fr 13th: jnd bef 5 out: reminder on outer after 5 out where slt mstke and hdd next where slt mstke: wknd 2 out* **16/1**
6 8 **Vics Canvas (IRE)**[30] 3715 13-11-3 143..............................(p) MarkWalsh 130
(Dermot Anthony McLoughlin, Ire) *hld up: last at 1/2-way: rdn and no imp on ldrs after 3 out: sltly hmpd next and one pce after* **25/1**
F **Mala Beach (IRE)**[30] 3715 8-11-3 148........................ DavyRussell 157+
(Gordon Elliott, Ire) *trckd ldrs: 3rd 1/2-way: almost on terms between horses after 5 out and led fr next: stl gng wl whn fell 2 out* **5/4**[1]
7m 21.3s (19.30) **Going Correction** +1.175s/f (Heavy)
WFA 5 from 8yo+ 3lb **7** Ran SP% **116.2**
Speed ratings: **116,115,113,113,110 107,**
CSF £34.87 TOTE £5.00: £2.20, £3.10; DF 18.80 Trifecta £125.20.
Owner Andrea & Graham Wylie **Bred** Burgage Stud **Trained** Muine Beag, Co Carlow
■ Stewards' Enquiry : Mr P W Mullins three-day ban: used whip with excessive force and failed to give gelding time to respond (tbn)
R Walsh caution: used whip without giving gelding time to respond

FOCUS
A fortunate one-two-three in the race for Willie Mullins, but all three look Aintree bound and enhanced their claims to varying degrees. The front-running runner-up helps set the standard, with most of these out of form. The winner has been rated close to his old best.

4261 - 4263a (Foreign Racing) - See Raceform Interactive

3076

FFOS LAS (L-H)

Sunday, February 21

OFFICIAL GOING: Heavy (3.3)

Wind: medium against Weather: drizzle and mist, heavier rain from race 5

4264 EBF STALLIONS "NATIONAL HUNT" NOVICES' HURDLE (QUALIFIER) (8 hdls 2 omitted) 2m 4f

2:00 (2:00) (Class 4) 4-7-Y-0 **£4,548** (£1,335; £667; £333)

Form RPR

1 **Ballyoptic (IRE)**[57] 3265 6-11-3 0 SamTwiston-Davies 133+
(Nigel Twiston-Davies) *t.k.h: hdwy to trck ldr 2nd: disp ld fr 4th tl led appr 2 out: mstke last: drvn out to assert fnl 100yds* **16/1**

3-13 **2** 3 1/4 **Potters Corner (IRE)**[130] 1901 6-11-9 127 DenisO'Regan 134
(Paul Morgan) *hld up: hdwy 6th: rdn after 2 out: stl 4th over last: styd on flat to go 2nd towards fin* **7/2**[3]

-323 **3** 3 3/4 **Preseli Rock (IRE)**[51] 3403 6-11-3 128 LeightonAspell 126
(Rebecca Curtis) *mid-div: hdwy after 3rd: rdn to chal 2 out: no ex fnl 100yds: lost 2nd towards fin* **15/8**[1]

4212 **4** 2 3/4 **Never Equalled (IRE)**[43] 3516 7-11-2 129 JordanWilliams(7) 127
(Bernard Llewellyn) *trckd ldrs: rdn 2 out: sn hld by ldng pair: lost 3rd flat* **3/1**[2]

2 **5** 27 **Apache Outlaw (IRE)**[72] 3012 7-11-3 0 TomScudamore 96
(Rebecca Curtis) *led: jnd 4th: hdd appr 2 out: wknd qckly: t.o* **7/1**

454 **6** 7 **Looksnowtlikebrian (IRE)**[16] 3974 5-10-12 0 AlanJohns(5) 87
(Tim Vaughan) *mid-div tl wknd after 6th: t.o* **100/1**

3-55 **7** hd **Jaunty Thor**[22] 3863 6-11-3 0 RobertDunne 87
(Brian Eckley) *hld up: lost tch 6th: t.o* **50/1**

P **Days Like These**[694] 7-10-7 0 BenPoste(3)
(Adrian Wintle) *a in rr: tended to jump rt: lost tch 4th: p.u bef next* **125/1**

4-05 **P** **Crowd Control (IRE)**[40] 3570 7-10-10 105 MissLBrooke(7)
(Lady Susan Brooke) *j.rt at times: trckd ldr to 2nd: styd prom to 4th: lost tch 6th: p.u bef 2 out* **66/1**

P **Redmond (IRE)**[91] 6-11-3 0 AidanColeman
(Venetia Williams) *hld up towards rr: lost tch 6th: wl bhd whn p.u bef 2 out* **7/1**

5m 19.4s (319.40) **10 Ran SP% 118.1**
CSF £73.68 TOTE £19.50: £4.20, £1.60, £1.10; EX 103.60 Trifecta £332.40.

Owner N A Twiston-Davies **Bred** Roger Ryan **Trained** Naunton, Gloucs

FOCUS

Hurdle bends at innermost position, and the last hurdle in the home straight was omitted in hurdle races, meaning there was a long run from what was the last to the winning line. With three runners having official marks in the 120s, this was a decent race, although the ground was incredibly testing and they are not likely to face similar conditions too often.

4265 DRIBUILD LTD NOVICES' H'CAP CHASE (11 fncs 4 omitted) 2m 3f 83y

2:35 (2:35) (Class 4) (0-105,99) 5-Y-0+ **£3,898** (£1,144; £572; £286)

Form RPR

2-10 **1** **Supreme Bob (IRE)**[23] 3834 10-11-12 99 TrevorWhelan 112+
(Debra Hamer) *hld up wl in tch in last pair: clsd on extended run to 2 out: led last: rdn out* **11/4**[2]

0S20 **2** nk **Johns Luck (IRE)**[29] 3746 7-11-4 96 (b) DavidNoonan(5) 108
(Neil Mulholland) *hld up wl in tch in last pair: clsd 2 out: ev ch last: r.o u.p flat* **4/1**[3]

-PP1 **3** 2 **High Aspirations (IRE)**[17] 3951 8-10-3 83 HarryCobden(7) 92
(Michael Blake) *trckd ldrs: slipped bypassing normal 3rd-last: chal 2 out: stl ev ch last: unable qck flat* **2/1**[1]

2F23 **4** 5 **Slidecheck (IRE)**[24] 3821 9-11-4 91 (tp) RhysFlint 96
(Alexandra Dunn) *trckd ldrs: nt fluent 8th: led narrowly appr 2 out where mstke: hdd last: no ex* **8/1**

3346 **5** 14 **Veauce De Sivola (FR)**[34] 3663 7-11-5 92 (tp) TomCannon 86
(Mark Gillard) *several slow jumps: led to 6th: led again 8th: rdn home turn: hdd appr 2 out: sn wknd* **12/1**

6U61 **U** **Try It Sometime (IRE)**[22] 3864 8-11-6 96 (t) BenPoste(3) 99
(Sheila Lewis) *cl up: led 6th: nt fluent next: hdd 8th: styd cl up: rdn home turn: disputing 3rd whn blnd and uns rdr 2 out* **6/1**

5m 31.8s (30.70) **Going Correction** +1.125s/f (Heav) **6 Ran SP% 113.1**
Speed ratings: **80,79,79,76,71**
CSF £14.44 TOTE £3.50: £1.70, £2.40; EX 15.10 Trifecta £39.30.

Owner Mrs J M Edmonds **Bred** Tom Murray **Trained** Nantycaws, Carmarthens

FOCUS

Chase bends at innermost position, and the first and second fences in the home straight were omitted, as they were in all the chases. A moderate contest in which four jumped the last almost in unison.

4266 FFOS LAS RACECOURSE (S) HURDLE (6 hdls 2 omitted) 1m 7f 202y

3:10 (3:10) (Class 5) 4-7-Y-0 **£2,599** (£763; £381; £190)

Form RPR

-034 **1** **Calculated Risk**[9] 4105 7-10-11 111 NathanMoscrop(5) 117+
(Iain Jardine) *hld up in last: clsd into 3rd 2 out: led on bit last: shkn up as runner-up clsd nr fin: v comf* **7/4**[2]

5P54 **2** 1/2 **Lac Sacre (FR)**[69] 3080 7-11-2 114 (bt) RhysFlint 112
(John Flint) *chsd ldrs: wnt 2nd and rdn bef 2 out: ev ch last: kpt on u.p flat: clsng nr fin but a hld by easy wnr* **11/8**[1]

35P0 **3** 10 **Bishop Wulstan (IRE)**[13] 4028 5-11-5 101 (vt) SeanBowen 105
(Peter Bowen) *cl up: w ldr 2nd tl led bef 2 out: sn rdn: hdd last: wknd flat* **10/3**[3]

4 56 **Drip Tray (IRE)**[266] 6-11-2 0 (t) RobertDunne 46
(John Flint) *racd on inner: hld up wl in tch: wknd qckly bef 2 out: t.o* **16/1**

06 **5** 16 **Over To Midnight**[40] 3573 6-10-2 0 MissLBrooke(7) 23
(Lady Susan Brooke) *led: jnd 2nd: j.rt 4th: hdd bef 2 out: wknd qckly: t.o* **50/1**

4m 9.5s (21.00) **Going Correction** +1.45s/f (Heav) **5 Ran SP% 109.4**
Speed ratings: **105,104,99,71,63**
CSF £4.65 TOTE £2.50: £1.10, £2.30; EX 4.60 Trifecta £5.70.The winner sold to Paul Hamer for 3,000gns.

Owner S Middleton **Bred** Newsells Park Stud **Trained** Carrutherstown, D'fries & G'way

FOCUS

Hurdle bends at innermost position, and the last hurdle in the home straight was omitted in hurdle races, meaning there was a long way from what was the last to the winning line. This was a poor seller.

4267 DRIBUILD CONSTRUCTION H'CAP CHASE (14 fncs 4 omitted) 2m 7f 177y

3:45 (3:45) (Class 3) (0-130,129) 5-Y-0+ **£6,498** (£1,908; £954; £477)

Form RPR

6441 **1** **Berea Boru (IRE)**[16] 3979 8-11-7 124 (t) SeanBowen 140+
(Peter Bowen) *chsd ldrs tl lost pl 5th: pushed along 8th: hdwy 10th: wnt 2nd bypassing normal 3rd-last: led last: drvn out* **3/1**[1]

2540 **2** 3/4 **Kayf Moss**[43] 3517 8-11-8 125 (bt) RhysFlint 139
(John Flint) *trckd ldr: led 10th: 5 l clr bypassing normal 4th-last: rdn bef 2 out: hdd last: no ex nr fin* **8/1**

P13P **3** 9 **Big Society (IRE)**[31] 3707 10-11-9 126 (p) DavidBass 132
(Harry Whittington) *mid-div tl dropped to rr 3rd: rdn along fr 5th: hdwy after 12th: one pce and no further imp fr 2 out* **12/1**

/1P4 **4** 3 **Tour Des Champs (FR)**[19] 3918 9-11-12 129 SamTwiston-Davies 132
(Nigel Twiston-Davies) *led: mstke 9th: hdd next: rdn whn mstke 11th: sn lost 2nd: tried to rally bypassing normal 3rd-last: one pce fr 2 out* **6/1**

04-2 **5** 31 **Horatio Hornblower (IRE)**[143] 1722 8-11-3 125 LizzieKelly(5) 109
(Nick Williams) *hld up: nt fluent 5th: slow 8th: hdwy 10th: chsd ldr 12th tl wknd bypassing normal 3rd-last: t.o* **9/2**[2]

5530 **P** **Copper Birch (IRE)**[92] 2638 8-10-8 111 AdamWedge
(Evan Williams) *hld up: mstke 6th: sme hdwy 10th: wknd home turn: wl bhd whn p.u bef 2 out* **7/1**

-3P5 **P** **Heronshaw (IRE)**[43] 3520 9-11-3 120 (b[1]) PaddyBrennan
(Henry Daly) *in rr: hdwy to chse ldrs 5th: blnd 10th: losing pl whn mstke next: wl bhd whn p.u bef 2 out* **11/2**[3]

51-5 **P** **Ashford Wood (IRE)**[54] 3348 8-11-3 125 (v) AlanJohns(5)
(Tim Vaughan) *mid-div: nt fluent 1st: rdn along fr 7th: lost tch 10th: wl bhd whn p.u bef 12th* **25/1**

153P **P** **How About It (IRE)**[57] 3228 7-11-9 126 (p) LeightonAspell
(Rebecca Curtis) *chsd ldrs: nt fluent 7th: rdn and wknd after 12th: wl bhd whn p.u bef 2 out* **11/1**

6m 39.4s (22.00) **Going Correction** +1.125s/f (Heav) **9 Ran SP% 116.3**
Speed ratings: **108,107,104,103,93 , , ,**
CSF £27.52 CT £253.14 TOTE £3.10: £1.50, £2.30, £4.40; EX 24.40 Trifecta £320.50.

Owner H Jones **Bred** Mrs E Thompson **Trained** Little Newcastle, Pembrokes

■ Stewards' Enquiry : Rhys Flint two-day ban: used whip without giving gelding time to respond (Mar 6-7)

FOCUS

Chase bends at innermost position, and the first and second fences in the home straight were omitted. A decent contest run at a respectable gallop considering the conditions.

4268 FFOS LAS RACECOURSE MARES' H'CAP HURDLE (9 hdls 2 omitted) 2m 5f 192y

4:15 (4:15) (Class 4) (0-115,113) 4-Y-0+ **£4,548** (£1,335; £667; £333)

Form RPR

3344 **1** **Midnight Silver**[37] 3612 6-11-9 110 (t) MichealNolan 115+
(Jamie Snowden) *t.k.h: w ldr: led 7th: rdn between last 2: styd on wl* **9/4**[2]

2225 **2** 1 1/4 **Twenty Eight Guns**[20] 3904 6-11-4 105 (p) TomScudamore 107
(Michael Scudamore) *hld up in cl 4th: impr a pl after 4th: chsd wnr appr 2 out: sn rdn: nt qckn flat* **3/1**[3]

133P **3** 41 **Drumviredy (IRE)**[17] 3953 7-11-12 113 AidanColeman 74
(Venetia Williams) *led narrowly: hit 3rd and stmbld: hdd 7th: sn rdn and btn: regained poor 3rd flat* **7/2**

4245 **4** 1 1/2 **Barton Rose**[57] 3217 7-11-4 112 HarryCobden(7) 72
(Michael Blake) *trckd ldrs: relegated to cl last after 4th: rdn and wknd after 7th: in poor 3rd between last 2 tl flat* **15/8**[1]

6m 1.2s (41.20) **Going Correction** +1.45s/f (Heav) **4 Ran SP% 112.8**
Speed ratings (Par 105): **83,82,67,67**
CSF £9.31 TOTE £3.10; EX 10.30 Trifecta £26.50.

Owner Foxtrot Nh Racing Partnership Ix **Bred** G Staniek **Trained** Lambourn, Berks

FOCUS

Hurdle bends at innermost position, and the last hurdle in the home straight was omitted in hurdle races, meaning there was a long way from what was the last to the winning line. This was weak for the race type.

4269 DUNRAVEN WELSH FOXHUNTERS OPEN HUNTERS' CHASE (14 fncs 4 omitted) 2m 7f 177y

4:50 (4:53) (Class 4) 5-Y-0+ **£4,991** (£1,548; £773; £387)

Form RPR

P6-4 **1** **Night Alliance (IRE)**[24] 3826 11-11-3 113 (bt) MrLFerguson(7) 124+
(P R M Philips) *hld up: mstke 7th: hdwy 10th: rdn bypassing normal 3rd-last: wnt 2nd 2 out: led appr last: styd on wl* **8/1**

520- **2** 5 **Dineur (FR)**[416] 3444 10-11-3 124 [1] MrJamesKing(7) 118
(Mickey Bowen) *hld up: stdy hdwy 10th: shkn up to go 3rd 2 out: sn rdn: chsd wnr flat: one pce* **9/2**[2]

3P-1 **3** 3 1/2 **Monkey Kingdom**[288] 209 8-11-9 132 (tp) MrHHunt(5) 119
(Rebecca Curtis) *t.k.h: prom in chsng gp: chsd clr ldr 5th: led 9th: hit 11th whn gng 6 l clr: reduced ld 2 out: hdd bef last: no ex* **11/10**[1]

/3P- **4** 6 **Churchtown Love (IRE)**[7] 8-11-3 95 MrTomDavid 102
(Miss A Griffiths) *hld up: hdwy 10th: wknd between last 2* **16/1**

P0-3 **5** 14 **Tullyraine (IRE)**[17] 3958 12-11-11 116 MrLWilliams(7) 104
(Dean Coleman) *mid-div: mstkes 6th and 8th: struggling fr 10th* **12/1**

0U0/ **6** shd **Oscar Delta (IRE)**[7] 13-11-5 115 MrJNixon(5) 96
(C Price) *prom in chsng gp: chsd ldr 11th: mstke 12th: rdn bypassing normal 3rd-last: wknd 2 out* **13/2**[3]

5/ **7** 38 **Mangans Turn**[28] 9-11-5 0 MrRhysHughes(5) 56
(Miss Karen A Williams) *chsd clr ldr: j.rt 3rd: lost 2nd at 5th: struggling fr 11th: t.o* **100/1**

154- **P** **Arctic Ben (IRE)**[303] 5509 12-11-11 123 MissJCWilliams(3)
(Henry Daly) *led: racd keenly and sn a long way clr: much reduced ld fr 7th tl hdd 9th: mstke next: wknd after 12th: t.o whn p.u bef 2 out* **10/1**

-1PP **P** **The Happy Warrior**[7] 8-11-13 98 MrJMartin(5)
(C Price) *urged along to s: prom in chsng gp: mstkes 2nd and 10th: sn wknd: wl bhd whn p.u bef 2 out* **33/1**

6m 57.1s (39.70) **Going Correction** +1.125s/f (Heav) **9 Ran SP% 116.8**
Speed ratings: **78,76,75,73,68 68,55, ,**
CSF £45.31 TOTE £7.80: £2.00, £1.70, £1.20; EX 44.10 Trifecta £148.30.

Owner P R M Philips **Bred** Mrs Mary Doyle And Peter Sherry **Trained** Claines, Worcestershire

FOCUS
Chase bends at innermost position, and the first and second fences in the home straight were omitted. This is probably decent enough form, but one runner went off too quickly.

4270 FFOS LAS RACECOURSE MAIDEN OPEN NATIONAL HUNT FLAT RACE 1m 7f 202y
5:20 (5:22) (Class 6) 4-6-Y-O £1,949 (£572; £286; £143)

Form RPR

0-62 **1** **Druid's Folly (IRE)**[43] 3522 6-11-2 0........................ LeightonAspell 110+
(Rebecca Curtis) *mde all: rdn 2f out: styd on wl to draw clr fnl f* 8/13[1]

54 **2** *10* **Beggar's Wishes (IRE)**[75] 2965 5-11-2 0........................(t) SeanBowen 100
(Peter Bowen) *trckd wnr tl lost 2nd 6f out: rallied u.p fnl 2f: styd on to go 2nd again 100yds out: no imp* 8/1

3 *1 ¾* **Winning Ticket (IRE)** 5-11-2 0........................ DenisO'Regan 98
(Paul Morgan) *hld up in 4th: gd hdwy to trck wnr 3f out: rdn 2f out: no ex appr fnl f: lost 2nd 100yds out* 4/1[2]

0- **4** *12* **Tudors Treasure**[309] 5402 5-11-2 0........................ MichealNolan 86
(Robert Stephens) *racd in 3rd: wnt 2nd 6f out tl wknd 3f out* 33/1

5 *23* **Fille Des Champs (IRE)** 5-10-2 0........................ LewisGordon(7) 56
(Evan Williams) *a in last: lost tch 6f out* 9/2[3]

4m 11.2s (28.30) **Going Correction** +1.45s/f (Heav) **5 Ran SP% 114.2**
Speed ratings: **87,82,81,75,63**
CSF £6.85 TOTE £1.50: £1.10, £2.20; EX 6.00 Trifecta £16.10.
Owner C R Trembath **Bred** Thomas Kent **Trained** Newport, Pembrokeshire

FOCUS
Poor visibility. The pace for this bumper wasn't that bad considering the ground conditions, but the form isn't worth a great deal.
T/Plt: £49.10 to a £1 stake. Pool: £89,671.15 - 1,331.37 winning tickets T/Qpdt: £11.60 to a £1 stake. Pool: £6,610.65 - 418.95 winning tickets **Richard Lowther**

4038 MARKET RASEN (R-H)
Sunday, February 21

OFFICIAL GOING: Soft (hdl 5.8, chs 6.2)
Wind: fresh 1/2 against Weather: overcast and breezy

4271 32RED CASINO MARES' NOVICES' HURDLE (8 hdls) 2m 148y
2:10 (2:11) (Class 4) 4-Y-O+ £3,249 (£954; £477; £238)

Form RPR

12- **1** **Chocca Wocca**[316] 5277 6-11-2 0........................ NicodeBoinville 113+
(Nicky Henderson) *t.k.h: trckd ldr sn after 1st: effrt 2 out: drvn to ld narrowly last: fnd ex clsng stages* 8/15[1]

2131 **2** *nk* **Awesome Rosie**[57] 3252 5-11-6 117........................ TomBellamy(3) 119
(Alan King) *trckd ldrs: effrt and handy 3rd bef 2 out: styd on to go cl 2nd last 150yds: no ex towards fin* 3/1[2]

24 **3** *3* **For Goodness Sake (IRE)**[26] 3790 4-10-7 0........................ GavinSheehan 101
(Warren Greatrex) *led: drvn appr 2 out: hdd and nt fluent last: rdr sn dropped whip: wknd fnl 75yds* 6/1

22 **4** *17* **Miss Ranger (IRE)**[38] 3587 4-10-7 109........................ DannyCook 85
(Brian Ellison) *nt jump wl: mid-div: hdwy 3 out: sn chsng ldrs: outpcd and modest 4th whn blnd 2 out* 5/1[3]

0-50 **5** *1 ¾* **Theatre Act**[32] 3681 5-10-11 0........................ DiarmuidO'Regan(5) 90
(Chris Grant) *chsd ldrs: drvn 3 out: lost pl bef next* 50/1

0-P0 **6** *1 ¾* **Weston Flame**[18] 3928 6-11-2 0........................(t) DarylJacob 89
(Ben Case) *in rr: sme hdwy 4th: outpcd and lost pl sn after 3 out* 150/1

0-00 **7** *nse* **Vic's Last Stand (IRE)**[23] 3835 6-10-13 0........................ HarryChalloner(3) 88
(Keith Reveley) *in rr: sme hdwy 3 out: sn outpcd and lost pl* 66/1

640 **8** *37* **Coco Flower (FR)**[23] 3842 4-10-4 0........................ KillianMoore(3) 42
(Alex Hales) *in rr: detached and drvn 4th: t.o 2 out* 100/1

0 **9** *16* **Q Twenty Girl (IRE)**[38] 3587 4-10-4 0........................ ColmMcCormack(3) 26
(John Norton) *in rr: bhd fr 3 out: t.o next* 150/1

4m 24.6s (17.90) **Going Correction** +0.90s/f (Soft) **9 Ran SP% 127.0**
WFA 4 from 5yo+ 9lb
Speed ratings (Par 105): **93,92,91,83,82 81,81,64,56**
CSF £3.19 TOTE £1.40: £1.10, £1.20, £1.70; EX 4.00 Trifecta £11.00.
Owner Mr & Mrs R Kelvin-Hughes **Bred** Mr & Mrs R Kelvin-Hughes **Trained** Upper Lambourn, Berks

FOCUS
All bends were moved. Wood bend out 9yds and stands bend out 7yds, adding approximately 75yds to this race. This was a solid test and it's sound mares' form. Afterwards rider Killian Moore said "the ground is tacky".

4272 32RED ON THE APP STORE MARES' H'CAP HURDLE (QUALIFIER FOR CHALLENGER MARES' HURDLE FINAL) (10 hdls) 2m 2f 140y
2:45 (2:46) (Class 4) (0-115,115) 4-Y-O+ £3,249 (£954; £477; £238)

Form RPR

3351 **1** **Card Game (IRE)**[21] 3886 7-11-7 115........................ JamieHamilton(5) 127+
(Malcolm Jefferson) *chsd ldrs: lost pl 3rd: sn pushed along: drvn 6th: hdwy 3 out: upsides next: led appr last: rdr dropped whip sn after last: kpt on* 6/1[3]

322 **2** *4 ½* **Secret Door (IRE)**[15] 3995 5-11-6 109........................ DarylJacob 113
(Harry Fry) *trckd ldrs: led 2 out: hdd appr last: kpt on same pce* 9/4[1]

23P- **3** *4* **Miss Estela (IRE)**[353] 4576 6-11-6 109........................ GavinSheehan 110
(Warren Greatrex) *trckd ldrs: led 7th: hdd 2 out: fdd run-in* 11/4[2]

1212 **4** *17* **Alizee De Janeiro (FR)**[54] 3346 6-11-10 113........................ PeterBuchanan 98
(Lucinda Russell) *chsd ldrs: hit 2nd: drvn and outpcd 6th: bhd fr 3 out: tk poor 4th last* 11/1

0543 **5** *1 ¼* **Stepover**[63] 3175 5-11-2 105........................ KielanWoods 87
(Alex Hales) *t.k.h in rr: hdwy 7th: trcking ldrs next: lost pl bef 2 out* 20/1

24U **6** *7* **Roja Dove (IRE)**[113] 2199 7-11-8 114........................ AdamNicol(3) 89
(David Thompson) *stdd s: in rr: sme hdwy 3 out: lost pl bef next* 50/1

3230 **7** *10* **Donna's Pride**[22] 3858 7-11-2 108........................ HarryChalloner(3) 77
(Keith Reveley) *mid-div: lost pl and hit 3 out: sn wl bhd* 20/1

31 **P** **Miss Tiger Lily**[143] 1716 6-11-5 115........................ MissPFuller(7)
(Jamie Snowden) *led: hdd 6th: lost pl and hit next: sn bhd: t.o whn p.u after 3 out* 16/1

F11 **P** **Clemency**[46] 3485 5-11-12 115........................ AndrewTinkler
(Nicky Henderson) *w ldr: led 6th: hdd next: lost pl and hit 3 out: sn wl bhd: t.o whn p.u bef next* 6/1[3]

4m 53.8s (14.40) **Going Correction** +0.90s/f (Soft) **9 Ran SP% 111.7**
Speed ratings (Par 105): **105,103,101,94,93 93,89, ,**
CSF £19.29 CT £44.04 TOTE £8.20: £2.50, £1.10, £1.30; EX 22.90 Trifecta £78.50.
Owner Messrs Hales Dodd Wood & Dickinson **Bred** David Connors **Trained** Norton, N Yorks

FOCUS
Add 75 yards to the advertised race distance. Not a bad mares' handicap. The principals came clear.

4273 32RED.COM H'CAP HURDLE (8 hdls) 2m 148y
3:20 (3:21) (Class 3) (0-135,132) 4-Y-O+ £5,848 (£1,717; £858; £429)

Form RPR

1121 **1** **Cotillion**[9] 4105 10-10-10 126........................(p) TobyWheeler(10) 131+
(Ian Williams) *hld up in mid-div: trckd ldrs 4th: 2nd sn after 3 out: led last: hung rt: drvn clr* 3/1[2]

11-0 **2** *5* **Apterix (FR)**[46] 3487 6-11-0 120........................ DannyCook 120
(Brian Ellison) *trckd ldr: t.k.h: led appr 4th: nt fluent next: hdd last: kpt on same pce* 4/1[3]

6UFP **3** *3 ½* **Minellaforleisure (IRE)**[57] 3232 8-11-2 122........................ DarylJacob 118
(Alex Hales) *hld up in rr: hdwy 5th: trcking ldrs next: clr 3rd and drvn 2 out: one pce* 16/1

434F **4** *½* **Sleepy Haven (IRE)**[38] 3589 6-11-8 128........................(tp) SeanQuinlan 124
(Jennie Candlish) *mid-div: chsng ldrs 3 out: outpcd next: kpt on run-in* 14/1

1314 **5** *32* **Template (IRE)**[62] 3196 5-10-12 125........................ LiamMcKenna(7) 88
(Harry Fry) *led tl appr 4th: hit 3 out: lost pl bef next: blnd 2 out: t.o whn eased clsng stages* 11/2

04 **6** *20* **Monyjean (FR)**[54] 3335 5-11-10 130........................ TomO'Brien 73
(Evan Williams) *chsd ldrs: lost pl 3 out: sn bhd: t.o whn eased run-in* 33/1

F-10 **P** **Winner Massagot (FR)**[64] 3151 5-11-12 132........................ NoelFehily
(Alan King) *hld up towards rr: p.u sn after 1st: lame* 7/4[1]

4m 24.7s (18.00) **Going Correction** +0.90s/f (Soft) **7 Ran SP% 112.2**
Speed ratings (Par 107): **93,90,89,88,73 64,**
CSF £15.03 TOTE £3.50: £1.80, £2.20; EX 17.50 Trifecta £121.30.
Owner Jamie Robert Roberts **Bred** Mr & Mrs G Middlebrook **Trained** Portway, Worcs

FOCUS
Add 75 yards to the advertised race distance. This fair handicap changed complexion when the favourite sadly went wrong early on.

4274 32RED NOVICES' CHASE (14 fncs) 2m 5f 89y
3:55 (3:56) (Class 3) 5-Y-O+ £7,988 (£2,480; £1,335)

Form RPR

3 **1** **Lockstockandbarrel (IRE)**[16] 3975 7-11-0 0........................ RichardJohnson 145+
(Jonjo O'Neill) *hld up: wnt 2nd 9th: hmpd and lft in ld 10th: clr bef 2 out: coasted home* 11/8[1]

1413 **2** *33* **Wings Attract (IRE)**[63] 3176 7-11-7 127........................(p) TomMessenger 112
(Chris Bealby) *trckd ldr: nt fluent 3rd: sddle slipped after 7th: shkn up next: sn drvn: lft 3rd 10th: 2nd sn after next: wknd qckly appr 2 out: sn wl bhd* 9/2[3]

0- **3** *51* **Frontline (IRE)**[141] 1765 8-10-9 123........................ CiaranGethings(5) 65
(Paul Cowley) *hld up: chsng ldrs 9th: hmpd and lft 2nd next: lost pl next: sn wl bhd: t.o 3 out: eventually completed* 8/1

-P62 **U** **Deep Trouble (IRE)**[26] 3786 9-11-0 133........................(t) DarylJacob
(Ben Case) *led: qcknd pce 7th: blnd bdly and uns rdr 10th* 13/8[2]

6m 17.0s (31.00) **Going Correction** +1.675s/f (Heav) **4 Ran SP% 109.5**
Speed ratings: **107,94,75,**
CSF £7.44 TOTE £2.40; EX 6.40 Trifecta £18.70.
Owner John P McManus **Bred** Gerry Carroll **Trained** Cheltenham, Gloucs

FOCUS
Add 96 yards to the advertised race distance. This novice chase fell apart from the tenth fence, but the winner is a bright prospect.

4275 MARK HAWKS 39TH BIRTHDAY H'CAP CHASE (14 fncs) 2m 3f 34y
4:25 (4:25) (Class 4) (0-110,110) 5-Y-O+ £3,994 (£1,240; £667)

Form RPR

3/F2 **1** **The Mumper (IRE)**[23] 3834 9-11-3 104........................ TomBellamy(3) 114+
(Alan King) *trckd ldrs: led appr 3 out: drvn clr last 75yds* 6/4[1]

5515 **2** *7* **Pandy Wells**[23] 3834 7-10-4 88........................ KielanWoods 90
(Graeme McPherson) *led: j.lft 4th: sn hdd: chsd ldrs: upsides 3 out: kpt on same pce fr next* 9/4[2]

-PP0 **3** *35* **Passing Fiesta**[23] 3834 7-9-13 86 ow1........................ JamesBanks(3) 58
(Sarah-Jayne Davies) *chsd ldrs: drvn 9th: led sn after 11th: hdd appr next: sn wknd and bhd* 8/1

3302 **P** **Safari Journey (USA)**[57] 3225 12-11-3 106........................(p) DeanPratt(5)
(Lucinda Egerton) *chsd ldrs: hit 2nd and sn lost pl: drvn 8th: sn bhd: t.o 11th: sn p.u* 9/1

5224 **P** **Uno Valoroso (FR)**[25] 3806 8-11-12 110........................ JakeGreenall
(Mark Walford) *t.k.h in rr: hit 3rd: hdwy to ld after 4th: hit 7th and 11th: hdd sn after 11th: wknd qckly: t.o next: p.u bef 2 out* 4/1[3]

5m 35.4s (29.70) **Going Correction** +1.675s/f (Heav) **5 Ran SP% 111.9**
Speed ratings: **104,101,86, ,**
CSF £5.62 TOTE £2.50: £1.50, £1.60; EX 4.60 Trifecta £21.00.
Owner The Weighed In Partnership **Bred** Patrick Day **Trained** Barbury Castle, Wilts

FOCUS
Add 75 yards to the advertised race distance. The form of this modest handicap is straightforward.

4276 32RED £10 FREE H'CAP CHASE (17 fncs) 2m 7f 191y
5:00 (5:01) (Class 5) (0-100,100) 5-Y-O+ £2,599 (£763; £381; £190)

Form RPR

4534 **1** **Veroce (FR)**[25] 3803 7-10-10 89........................ JamieHamilton(5) 106+
(Mark Walford) *trckd ldrs: mstke 7th: cl 2nd sn after 4 out: led 2 out: drvn clr run-in* 9/2[2]

5P22 **2** *7* **Basford Ben**[17] 3948 8-11-12 100........................(b) SeanQuinlan 109
(Jennie Candlish) *led: clr 7th: drvn 12th: jnd next: hdd sn after 4 out: one pce next: modest 3rd appr 2 out: kpt on to take 2nd last 50yds* 9/2[2]

3333 **3** *6* **Salut Honore (FR)**[24] 3820 10-10-3 80........................(t) JamesBanks(3) 84
(Alex Hales) *hld up: hdwy to trck ldrs 9th: led sn after 4 out: hdd 2 out: wknd last: fin tired* 6/1[3]

P430 **4** *18* **Wish In A Well (IRE)**[23] 3834 7-10-8 82........................(t) KielanWoods 69
(Ben Case) *prom: lost pl 6th: hdwy 4 out: modest 3rd next: wknd appr 2 out: sn bhd* 8/1

4564 **P** **Moyode Wood**[18] 3934 11-11-10 98........................(p) DannyCook
(Brian Ellison) *trckd ldrs: 2nd 11th: wknd 12th: poor 5th whn p.u bef 3 out* 10/1

0521 **P** **Tanner Hill (IRE)**[46] 3488 8-11-6 94........................(b) MarkQuinlan
(James Evans) *nt fluent in rr: drvn 8th: sme hdwy 11th: sn lost pl: bhd whn p.u bef 3 out* 7/2[1]

P-6P **P** **Brave Buck**[65] 3144 8-11-8 96........................ JakeGreenall
(Henry Daly) *chsd ldr to 11th: wknd next: bhd 3 out: t.o whn p.u bef next* 13/2

P-P2 **U** **Triggers Ginger**[46] 3488 11-10-6 **85**........................ CiaranGethings(5)
(Paul Cowley) *mid-div: lost pl and blnd 11th: reminders 13th: bhd whn blnd and uns rdr next* **14/1**

7m 9.5s (38.20) **Going Correction** +1.675s/f (Heav) **8** Ran SP% **113.1**
Speed ratings: **103,100,98,92,** , ,
CSF £24.92 CT £120.51 TOTE £5.30: £1.80, £1.60, £1.80; EX 25.50 Trifecta £132.00.
Owner The 4 Amigos & Partner **Bred** E A R L Trinquet, M & O Trinquet **Trained** Sherriff Hutton, N Yorks

FOCUS
Add 96 yards to the advertised race distance. A moderate handicap, run at a decent gallop.
T/Jkpt: Not won. T/Plt: £20.80 to a £1 stake. Pool: £84,590.74 - 2,959.91 winning tickets T/Qpdt: £8.10 to a £1 stake. Pool: £4,818.20 - 438.60 winning tickets **Walter Glynn**

4277 - 4278a (Foreign Racing) - See Raceform Interactive

4018 NAAS (L-H)
Sunday, February 21

OFFICIAL GOING: Soft to heavy changing to heavy on the chase course after race 3 (2.55)

4279a WOODLANDS 100 CLUB NAS NA RIOGH NOVICE H'CAP CHASE (GRADE B) (13 fncs) 2m 4f
2:55 (2:55) 5-Y-0+
£21,691 (£6,985; £3,308; £1,470; £735; £367)

RPR

1 **Marlbrook (IRE)**[42] 3554 8-11-3 **132**........................ BarryGeraghty 146+
(C A Murphy, Ire) *mde all: stl gng wl after 3 out: pressed next where slt mstke: asserted bef last and pushed out run-in: eased clsng stages: comf* **2/1**[1]

2 *6* **Vicangelome (FR)**[17] 3965 7-10-3 **118**........................ PhillipEnright 124
(Robert Tyner, Ire) *hld up towards rr: slt mstke 3rd: tk clsr order at 1/2-way: impr into 4th bef 5 out: wnt 2nd after 3 out: rdn in 2nd bef 2 out where pressed wnr: no imp on wnr bef last: kpt on same pce* **6/1**[2]

3 *4* **Captain Von Trappe (IRE)**[21] 3894 7-11-2 **134**.......(b[1]) JackKennedy(3) 135+
(Gordon Elliott, Ire) *hld up bhd ldrs: 4th 1/2-way: clsr in 3rd fr 7th: rdn in 4th after 3 out and no imp on wnr struggling in 3rd fr next: kpt on one pce* **8/1**

4 *15* **Wrath Of Titans (IRE)**[54] 3357 7-10-13 **128**........................ BJCooper 114
(Ms Sandra Hughes, Ire) *chsd ldrs tl wnt 2nd after 2nd: mstke and j.rt 7th where dropped to 4th: rdn in 3rd after 3 out and no imp on wnr whn mstke next and lost pl: one pce in 4th after* **9/1**

5 *27* **Marvellous Moment (IRE)**[14] 4021 7-10-3 **118** oh2........ AELynch 77
(J H Culloty, Ire) *towards rr: tk clsr order after 1/2-way: rdn in 5th after 3 out and no imp on ldrs u.p in mod 5th bef next: wknd: t.o* **14/1**

6 *2 1/4* **Queens Wild (IRE)**[14] 4019 6-10-10 **125**........................ APHeskin 82
(Edward P Harty, Ire) *w.w in rr: tk clsr order after 1/2-way: slt mstke in 5th 4 out and lost pl: wknd bef next where slt mstke: t.o* **11/1**

P **Salsa Sensation (IRE)**[77] 2942 7-10-4 **119**........................ MarkWalsh
(T M Walsh, Ire) *bhd: slt mstke in rr at 6th and pushed along: slt mstke next: no imp fr 8th where nt fluent: trailing whn p.u bef 4 out* **16/1**

P **Mr Diablo (IRE)**[43] 3536 7-10-13 **131**........................ LPDempsey(3)
(J P Dempsey, Ire) *chsd ldrs: mstke 1st: 3rd 1/2-way: pushed along in 4th bef 4 out and sn lost pl: wknd: trailing whn slt mstke 2 out: p.u bef last* **13/2**[3]

P **Un Noble (FR)**[33] 3669 6-10-7 **122**........................ CraigNichol
(Nicky Richards) *chsd ldrs: pushed along briefly after 5th: 5th 1/2-way: pushed along after 7th and lost tch bef next: t.o 4 out: p.u after next* **6/1**[2]

5m 49.2s (20.20) **9** Ran SP% **117.2**
CSF £15.28 CT £80.30 TOTE £2.50: £1.10, £1.70, £2.60; DF 15.00 Trifecta £111.30.
Owner John P McManus **Bred** Kenneth Parkhill **Trained** Gorey, Co Wexford

FOCUS
The non-runners thieved this race of some of its depth. It was not an especially hot race for the grade, but it was a proper test. The first two are rated to their hurdle bests. The chase track's going was changed to heavy after this.

4280a PADDY POWER SHOPS BETTER VALUE NOVICE HURDLE (GRADE 2) (8 hdls) 2m
3:30 (3:30) 4-Y-0+
£20,172 (£6,496; £3,077; £1,367; £683; £341)

RPR

1 **Ball D'Arc (FR)**[21] 3890 5-11-3 135........................ BJCooper 143+
(Gordon Elliott, Ire) *hld up: nt fluent 1st: 6th 1/2-way: impr bhd ldrs gng wl bef 2 out: led narrowly after 2 out tl hdd bef last and pushed along: regained advantage run-in and rdn clr: kpt on wl* **5/1**[3]

2 *2* **Moon Over Germany (IRE)**[69] 3090 5-11-3 0........................ DavyRussell 141+
(Edward P Harty, Ire) *w.w towards rr: mstke in 7th at 3rd: impr bhd ldrs gng wl bef 2 out: prog between horses to ld narrowly bef last: hdd after last and sn no imp on wnr: kpt on same pce* **7/1**

3 *13* **Don't Touch It (IRE)**[28] 3764 6-11-4 0........................ BarryGeraghty 132+
(Mrs John Harrington, Ire) *hld up bhd ldrs: slt mstke in 5th at 2nd: slt mstke 3rd: 5th 1/2-way: n.m.r in 4th between horses appr st and ckecked sltly: almost on terms whn hit 2 out: rdn bef last and wknd in 3rd fr last* **13/8**[1]

4 *2 1/4* **Au Quart De Tour (FR)**[31] 3712 6-11-4 139........................ RWalsh 127+
(W P Mullins, Ire) *chsd ldrs: 4th 1/2-way: impr on outer into 3rd appr st: rdn and no ex after 2 out: sn wknd and eased in 4th bef last* **4/1**[2]

5 *9* **All The Answers**[183] 1341 5-11-3 0........................(t[1]) MarkWalsh 117+
(A P O'Brien, Ire) *hld up in rr: last at 1/2-way: pushed along in 7th after 2 out and wnt mod 6th between last 2: one pce after* **50/1**

6 *1/2* **Marakoush (IRE)**[49] 3459 5-11-3 0........................ APHeskin 116
(Alan Fleming, Ire) *sn disp: slt mstke 1st and led: j.big 2nd: extended advantage bef 3rd: reduced ld and 2 l clr at 1/2-way: rdn and hdd bef 2 out: sn wknd* **5/1**[3]

7 *13* **Yes Sir Brian (IRE)**[22] 3870 7-11-4 125........................ MarkEnright 104
(Garrett James Power, Ire) *keen bef s: chsd ldrs: slt mstke in 3rd at 2nd: impr between horses to ld bef 2 out where nt fluent and hdd: no ex and wknd qckly bef last* **16/1**

8 *3/4* **Hurry Henry (IRE)**[49] 3460 7-11-4 0........................(p) AELynch 104
(Henry De Bromhead, Ire) *led and disp tl settled in 2nd after 1st: niggled along in 2nd bef 4 out: slt mstke next: rdn bef 2 out where n.m.r and sltly hmpd: sn wknd to rr* **14/1**

4m 14.1s (10.60) **8** Ran SP% **118.4**
CSF £40.70 TOTE £5.80: £1.50, £2.30, £1.02; DF 36.10 Trifecta £93.80.
Owner Gigginstown House Stud **Bred** S C E A Le Fragneau & Nicole Terriere **Trained** Longwood, Co Meath

FOCUS
An intriguing race in which many had a chance turning in but, the gallop having been generous, most of them stopped quickly.

4281a PADDY POWER OVER 260 SHOPS NATIONWIDE CHASE (GRADE 2) (10 fncs) 2m
4:05 (4:05) 5-Y-0+
£20,606 (£6,636; £3,143; £1,397; £698; £349)

RPR

1 **Days Hotel (IRE)**[21] 3892 11-11-4 146........................ AELynch 157
(Henry De Bromhead, Ire) *mde all: slt mstke 3rd: nt fluent 3 out: stl gng wl bef 2 out: over 3 l clr gng best bef last: drvn further clr and styd on wl run-in: comf* **7/2**[2]

2 *7 1/2* **Twinlight (FR)**[21] 3892 9-11-12 153........................ RWalsh 160+
(W P Mullins, Ire) *edgd sltly rt s: settled in 2nd: j.rt thrght: kpt out wd for most: pushed along bef 2 out where dropped to 3rd: dropped to mod 4th bef last tl kpt on again into mod 2nd run-in: nt trble wnr* **9/2**[3]

3 *2 1/2* **Simply Ned (IRE)**[29] 3734 9-11-4 159........................ BrianHarding 148
(Nicky Richards) *chsd ldrs: racd keenly early: 4th 1/2-way: impr into 2nd bef 2 out: rdn between last 2 and no imp on wnr bef last: one pce run-in and dropped to mod 3rd cl home* **11/10**[1]

4 *1 3/4* **Mount Colah (IRE)**[38] 3603 10-11-4 148........................ MrNMcParlan 146
(J G Cosgrave, Ire) *chsd ldrs: 3rd 1/2-way: pushed along in 4th after 3 out and no imp on wnr u.p in 3rd bef last: dropped to mod 4th and one pce run-in* **13/2**

5 *13* **Cause Of Causes (USA)**[35] 3651 8-11-4 140............(tp) BarryGeraghty 136
(Gordon Elliott, Ire) *hld up towards rr: 5th 1/2-way: niggled along in 5th after 5th: no imp on ldrs bef 5 out: one pce after* **14/1**

6 *56* **Glenwood For Ever (IRE)**[8] 4131 8-11-4 91........(bt) RobbieColgan 76
(Paul John Gilligan, Ire) *in rr thrght: slt mstke 3rd: trailing fr bef 5th and t.o bef 5 out* **200/1**

4m 27.8s (4.50) **6** Ran SP% **108.5**
CSF £18.00 TOTE £4.70: £1.90, £1.70; DF 13.70 Trifecta £36.50.
Owner James Treacy **Bred** James Treacy **Trained** Knockeen, Co Waterford

FOCUS
A proper slog. It seemed to break the favourite's heart and was probably exactly what the winner wanted. He's rated back to form.

4282 - 4283a (Foreign Racing) - See Raceform Interactive

4050 CARLISLE (R-H)
Monday, February 22

OFFICIAL GOING: Heavy (chs 4.9, hdl 5.2)
Wind: Breezy, half against Weather: Overcast, showers

4284 RACING UK NOVICES' HURDLE (11 hdls) 2m 3f 61y
2:00 (2:00) (Class 4) 4-Y-0+ £3,249 (£715; £715; £238)

Form RPR

613 1 **Fionn Mac Cul (IRE)**[27] 3795 5-11-10 125........................ AidanColeman 117+
(Venetia Williams) *trckd ldrs: wnt 2nd 3rd: smooth hdwy to ld after 2 out: pushed out fr last: comf* **8/15**[1]

3215 2 *3 1/4* **Howaboutnever (IRE)**[37] 3622 8-11-0 120................(p) TobyWheeler(10) 111+
(Ian Williams) *led: rdn and hdd after 2 out: kpt on u.p fr last* **2/1**[2]

03 2 *dht* **Wicked Games (IRE)**[12] 4052 5-10-10 0........................ CraigNichol 97
(Rose Dobbin) *hld up: stdy hdwy after 3 out: effrt next: chsd wnr last: kpt on: nt gng pce to chal* **20/1**[3]

4 *5* **Too Many Chiefs (IRE)**[71] 5-10-10 0........................ FinianO'Toole(7) 99
(Sharon Watt) *prom: rdn after 3 out: rallied: outpcd fr next* **100/1**

66 5 *hd* **Oak Vintage (IRE)**[22] 3883 6-10-12 0........................ JamieHamilton(5) 99
(Ann Hamilton) *trckd ldrs: rdn 2 out: outpcd fr last* **40/1**

F05 6 *4* **Pretty Miss Mahler (IRE)**[6] 4164 5-10-10 0........................ HenryBrooke 88
(Martin Todhunter) *hld up: stdy hdwy 3 out: rdn next: sn outpcd: hld whn nt fluent last* **28/1**

4 7 *18* **Baby Ticker**[71] 3060 7-10-7 0........................ CallumWhillans(3) 70
(Donald Whillans) *nt fluent: hld up: stdy hdwy 6th: rdn and outpcd next: rallied after 3 out: wknd bef next* **40/1**

5m 17.8s (9.00) **Going Correction** +0.60s/f (Soft) **7** Ran SP% **112.6**
Speed ratings (Par 105): **105,103,103,101,101 99,92**
WIN: 1.40 Fionn Mac Cul; PL: 1.10 Fionn Mac Cul, .60 Howaboutnever, 2.10 Wicked Games; EX: 1.20, 6.00; CSF: .90, 6.09; TC: ; TF: 3.00, 10.10;.
Owner Trevor Hemmings **Bred** Joseph Smiddy **Trained** Kings Caple, H'fords

FOCUS
The going was heavy after the track passed a morning inspection. Due to rail movements the actual race distance was 2m3f 133yds. An uncompetitive hurdle, run at a steady gallop, and the winner probably didn't need to improve to land the odds.

4285 RACING UK DAY PASS JUST £10 H'CAP HURDLE (10 hdls) 2m 1f
2:35 (2:35) (Class 4) (0-120,120) 4-Y-0+ **£3,898** (£1,144; £572; £286)

Form RPR

443 1 **Sean Ban (IRE)**[27] 3784 6-11-2 **110**........................ WillKennedy 114
(Donald McCain) *pressed ldr: led 3rd: rdn and hrd pressed fr 2 out: styd on gamely fr last* **3/1**[2]

4-12 2 *1 3/4* **Mixboy (FR)**[22] 3886 6-11-12 **120**........................ BrianHarding 122
(Keith Dalgleish) *trckd ldrs: wnt 2nd 4 out: clsd after next: effrt and ev ch bef last: drvn and kpt on same pce run-in* **6/4**[1]

6422 3 *31* **Veinard (FR)**[12] 4055 7-10-8 **107**........................ CallumBewley(5) 78
(Robert Bewley) *hld up in tch: outpcd whn nt fluent 4th: no imp fr 3 out* **3/1**[2]

6030 4 *3 3/4* **Circus Star (USA)**[65] 3152 8-11-2 **117**........................ MrJDixon(7) 85
(John Dixon) *t.k.h: led to 3rd: chsd wnr to 4 out: rdn and struggling fr next* **9/2**[3]

4m 35.2s (6.00) **Going Correction** +0.60s/f (Soft) **4** Ran SP% **108.2**
Speed ratings (Par 105): **109,108,93,91**
CSF £8.01 TOTE £4.10; EX 6.60 Trifecta £11.70.
Owner Matthew Taylor **Bred** J P White **Trained** Cholmondeley, Cheshire

FOCUS
A steadily run contest with the front two in control a long way from home and the winner is on the upgrade. Due to rail movements the actual race distance was 2m1f 60yds.

4286 WEATHERBYS HAMILTON H'CAP CHASE (14 fncs 4 omitted) 3m 110y
3:05 (3:05) (Class 3) (0-140,138) 5-Y-0+ **£9,747** (£2,862; £1,431; £715)

Form RPR

11P3 1 **Courtown Oscar (IRE)**[12] 4054 7-10-5 **120**........................ AdamNicol(3) 134+
(Philip Kirby) *pressed ldr: rdn after 3 out (usual 4 out): rallied and led last: drew clr run-in* **9/2**[3]

1335 **2** *12* **One For Arthur (IRE)**[23] 3849 7-11-7 **133**........................ PeterBuchanan 134
(Lucinda Russell) *hld up: hit 4th: pushed along after 7th: rallied and prom 10th: led 3 out (usual 4 out) sn rdn clr: hdd whn nt fluent last: sn no ex*
4/1[2]

P600 **3** *5* **Barafundle (IRE)**[11] 4066 12-11-9 **135**..............................(b) SeanQuinlan 131
(Jennie Candlish) *led to 3 out (usual 4 out): sn rdn and outpcd* **20/1**

0133 **4** *24* **Tikkandemickey (IRE)**[19] 3936 10-10-6 **123**............ DaraghBourke(5) 98
(Raymond Shiels) *t.k.h early: hld up: outpcd whn nt fluent 9th: lft modest 4th 4 out (usual 5 out): nvr on terms* **14/1**

5312 **P** **Alto Des Mottes (FR)**[39] 3591 6-11-6 **132**.............................. BrianHughes
(Henry Hogarth) *nt fluent on occasions: prom: outpcd 9th: struggling fr next: lost tch and p.u bef last* **3/1**[1]

-41U **F** **Warrantor (IRE)**[7] 4155 7-11-5 **138**..............................(t) MrTGreatrex(7)
(Warren Greatrex) *hld up in tch on outside: stdy hdwy 1/2-way: nrly 5 l down and outpcd whn fell 4 out (usual 5 out)* **9/2**[3]

1224 **R** **Friendly Royal (IRE)**[16] 3996 7-10-10 **122**.............................. DannyCook
(Sue Smith) *chsd ldrs: drvn along 9th: struggling fr next: last and no ch whn ref last* **9/2**[3]

6m 45.2s (2.60) **Going Correction** +0.375s/f (Yiel) **7** Ran SP% **111.0**
Speed ratings: **110,106,104,96, ,**
CSF £21.72 TOTE £5.50: £2.00, £3.00; EX 28.60 Trifecta £401.30.
Owner Nobaj Ltd **Bred** Lorcan Allen **Trained** East Appleton, N Yorks

FOCUS
A competitive handicap run at a decent gallop in the conditions and there is probably still more to come from the winner. Due to rail movements the actual race distance was 3m2f 206yds.

4287 WATCH RACING UK ON 3 DEVICES H'CAP HURDLE (11 hdls) 2m 3f 61y
3:40 (3:40) (Class 3) (0-140,140) 4-Y-O+ **£6,498** (£1,908; £954; £477)

Form RPR

U251 **1** **Pistol (IRE)**[12] 4055 7-9-13 **120**.. MrJDixon(7) 124
(John Dixon) *mde all: pushed along 4 out: drvn after next: hrd pressed fr 2 out: hld on gamely run-in* **11/4**[2]

4142 **2** *1 1/4* **Maxie T**[10] 4107 5-10-9 **130**.. FinianO'Toole(7) 133
(Micky Hammond) *trckd ldrs: smooth hdwy to take 2nd bef 2 out: effrt and ev ch last: kpt on run-in: hld nr fin* **5/6**[1]

4353 **3** *9* **Sa Suffit (FR)**[22] 3887 13-11-4 **132**...........................(p) LucyAlexander 126
(James Ewart) *pressed wnr tl rdn and outpcd bef 2 out: no imp fr last* **6/1**[3]

500- **4** *35* **Clondaw Kaempfer (IRE)**[319] 5241 8-11-12 **140**.................... WillKennedy 99
(Donald McCain) *t.k.h: hld up in tch: outpcd bef 4 out: lost tch next: t.o* **13/2**

5m 15.1s (6.30) **Going Correction** +0.60s/f (Soft) **4** Ran SP% **108.8**
Speed ratings (Par 107): **110,109,105,90**
CSF £5.72 TOTE £3.60; EX 5.60 Trifecta £7.70.
Owner Mrs S F Dixon **Bred** Mrs Eleanor Commins **Trained** Thursby, Cumbria
■ Stewards' Enquiry : Finian O'Toole two-day ban: used whip above permitted level (Mar 7-8)

FOCUS
This was competitive enough, despite the small field, and the winner has been rated in line with the best of his old form. Due to rail movements the actual race distance was 2m3f 133yds.

4288 CHELTENHAM FREE BETS @BOOKIES.COM H'CAP CHASE (12 fncs 4 omitted) 2m 4f
4:10 (4:10) (Class 4) (0-120,120) 5-Y-O+ **£4,548** (£1,335; £667; £333)

Form RPR

33U3 **1** **Swing Hard (IRE)**[56] 3310 8-11-0 **108**.................................... DannyCook 118+
(Sue Smith) *j.lft on occasions: mde virtually all: rdn and hrd pressed bef last: hld on gamely run-in* **5/4**[1]

6/P3 **2** *2 1/4* **Tipsy Dara (IRE)**[19] 3937 12-9-11 **96**.................... StephenMulqueen(5) 105
(N W Alexander) *pressed wnr to bef 3 out (usual 4 out): rallied and regained 2nd next: effrt and ev ch bef last: kpt on run-in: hld towards fin* **9/2**[3]

-615 **3** *19* **John Louis**[32] 3709 8-11-7 **120**.. CharlieDeutsch(5) 111
(Venetia Williams) *trckd ldrs: wnt 2nd bef 3 out (usual 4 out) to next: wknd bef last* **3/1**[2]

/31- **4** *1/2* **Abbey Storm (IRE)**[508] 1697 10-11-7 **115**................................ BrianHarding 103
(Micky Hammond) *hld up in tch: outpcd 4 out (usual 5 out): no imp fr next* **10/1**

5PF3 **5** *1 1/2* **Pekanheim (IRE)**[19] 3938 8-10-8 **102**...................................... HenryBrooke 89
(Martin Todhunter) *prom: rdn and outpcd 4 out (usual 5 out): btn fr next* **6/1**

5m 35.1s (7.70) **Going Correction** +0.375s/f (Yiel) **5** Ran SP% **111.0**
Speed ratings: **99,98,90,90,89**
CSF £7.39 TOTE £2.20: £1.30, £2.30; EX 7.20 Trifecta £18.10.
Owner DP van der Hoeven, DG Pryde & J Beaumont **Bred** Paddy Kinsella **Trained** High Eldwick, W Yorks

FOCUS
Not a strong contest for the grade, but the winner has been rated back to his best. Due to rail movements the actual race distance was 2m4f 60yds.

4289 EXPERT CHELTENHAM TIPS @BOOKIES.COM H'CAP HURDLE (14 hdls) 3m 1f
4:45 (4:45) (Class 4) (0-105,103) 4-Y-O+ **£3,249** (£954; £477; £238)

Form RPR

-P61 **1** **W Six Times**[6] 4163 10-10-3 **83**..............................(p) KieronEdgar(3) 96+
(Alistair Whillans) *t.k.h: pressed ldr: led bef 6th: rdn 2 out: j.lft last: drvn and hld on wl* **15/8**[1]

PPF3 **2** *3/4* **Cleve Cottage**[27] 3793 8-10-3 **83**.. AdamNicol(3) 95+
(Philip Kirby) *chsd ldrs: rdn and outpcd after 3 out: rallied after next: cl 2nd whn nt fluent and hmpd last: r.o u.p* **9/4**[2]

065U **3** *16* **Toarmandowithlove (IRE)**[10] 4110 8-10-0 **84**...........(t) JamesCorbett(7) 78
(Susan Corbett) *hld up: pushed along and outpcd 4 out: rallied to chse wnr bef 2 out: rdr dropped whip after 2 out: sn lost 2nd: wknd fr last* **14/1**

5PP5 **4** *nk* **Master Murphy (IRE)**[10] 4110 11-10-2 **79**....................(p) PeterBuchanan 73
(Jane Walton) *in tch: rdn after 3 out: wknd bef next* **25/1**

2001 **5** *16* **Newyearsresolution (IRE)**[27] 3793 12-9-9 **79**.................. MissAWaugh(7) 57
(Simon Waugh) *hld up: hdwy to chse wnr bef 8th: rdn and outpcd bef 2 out: sn wknd* **13/2**

5-45 **P** **Raid Stane (IRE)**[241] 838 10-11-3 **94**..............................(p) HenryBrooke
(Julia Brooke) *prom: lost pl 3rd: struggling bef 4 out: lost tch and p.u after 2 out* **11/1**

0053 **P** **Golans Choice (IRE)**[19] 3933 7-11-12 **103**.............................. CraigNichol
(Rose Dobbin) *led to bef 6th: hit next: outpcd bef 4 out: sn struggling: lost tch and p.u after 2 out* **6/1**[3]

7m 4.1s (25.10) **Going Correction** +0.60s/f (Soft) **7** Ran SP% **112.0**
Speed ratings (Par 105): **83,82,77,77,72 , ,**
CSF £6.46 CT £40.08 TOTE £3.00: £1.80, £2.20; EX 6.50 Trifecta £58.40.
Owner Mrs L M Whillans **Bred** East Burrow Farm **Trained** Newmill-On-Slitrig, Borders

FOCUS
A modest handicap run at a steady gallop with the first two running pretty much to their marks. Due to rail movements the actual race distance was 3m1f 96yds.
T/Plt: £149.30 to a £1 stake. Pool: £61,269.02 - 299.40 winning tickets T/Qpdt: £35.50 to a £1 stake. Pool: £4,626.54 - 96.22 winning tickets **Richard Young**

3914 TAUNTON (R-H)
Tuesday, February 23

OFFICIAL GOING: Heavy (soft in places; 4.0)
Wind: almost nil Weather: sunny Rails: Both bends divided effecting distances as follows; Race 1 add 168 yards. Races 2, 4, 5 & 7 add 93 yards. Races 3 & 6 add 30 yards.

4290 ASPEN WAITE COMPLETE BUSINESS GROWTH SERVICE MARES' H'CAP HURDLE (12 hdls) 2m 7f 198y
2:00 (2:00) (Class 5) (0-100,98) 4-Y-O+ **£3,249** (£954; £477; £238)

Form RPR

3052 **1** **Shoofly Milly (IRE)**[29] 3771 7-11-8 **97**...........................(b) MattGriffiths(3) 107+
(Jeremy Scott) *disp ld most of way: nt fluent 3rd: rdn along whn idling after 7th: outrt ldr next: dropped to 3rd u.str.p after 3 out: led next: styd on: drvn out* **13/8**[1]

1461 **2** *3 1/2* **Oscar Jane (IRE)**[21] 3914 9-11-6 **97**..........................(bt) DavidNoonan(5) 101
(Johnny Farrelly) *disp ld most of way tl rdn after 8th: dropped to 3rd next: styd on same pce fr 2 out: regained 2nd run-in* **7/4**[2]

03P3 **3** *1* **Tara Mac**[15] 4028 7-11-7 **98**.. AlanJohns(5) 102
(Tim Vaughan) *trckd ldrs: led 9th: rdn and hdd bef 2 out: no ex run-in* **8/1**[3]

-000 **4** *44* **The Big Mare**[21] 3915 7-11-8 **94**.. RobertDunne 62
(Laura Young) *trckd ldrs: rdn after 7th: wknd after 3 out: t.o* **40/1**

04-0 **P** **Lady A**[143] 1756 6-11-2 **88**.. TomCannon
(Chris Gordon) *hld up in tch: reminders after 3rd: nt fluent 6th: t.o whn p.u after 8th* **8/1**[3]

0046 **P** **Omgnotanother (IRE)**[74] 3011 5-11-1 **92**.........................(p) ConorRing(5)
(Evan Williams) *chsd ldrs: rdn after 8th: wknd bef 3 out: t.o whn p.u bef 2 out* **8/1**[3]

6m 38.7s (34.70) **Going Correction** +1.125s/f (Heav) **6** Ran SP% **110.2**
Speed ratings (Par 103): **87,85,85,70, ,**
CSF £4.85 TOTE £2.20: £1.30, £1.70; EX 4.80 Trifecta £10.40.
Owner Gale Force One **Bred** Michael Whitty **Trained** Brompton Regis, Somerset

FOCUS
Rail movements resulted in this being run over 168yds further than advertised. Lowly mares' form, but the winner is on the upgrade.

4291 MERCEDES-BENZ OF TAUNTON H'CAP HURDLE (10 hdls) 2m 3f 1y
2:30 (2:30) (Class 5) (0-100,99) 4-Y-O+ **£3,249** (£954; £477; £238)

Form RPR

63P5 **1** **Allchilledout**[41] 3586 7-11-3 **97**..............................(t) PaulO'Brien(7) 106+
(Colin Tizzard) *mid-div: hdwy after 6th: rdn to ld 2 out: idling but fnd plenty whn briefly threatened fnl 75yds: rdn out* **9/2**[2]

5P6 **2** *1* **Man Of God (IRE)**[36] 3665 8-10-7 **85**.................................. AlanJohns(5) 92
(Tim Vaughan) *hld up bhd: plenty to do after 3 out: hdwy between last 2: 6 l 4th last: rdn and styd on strly run-in: wnt 2nd nring fin* **33/1**

24P0 **3** *1 1/2* **Only Gorgeous (IRE)**[21] 3919 9-11-9 **99**.......................... LucyGardner(3) 105
(Sue Gardner) *a.p: rdn and hanging rt but ev ch appr 2 out: swtchd rt run-in: hld last: styd on but no ex towards fin where lost 2nd* **11/1**

434- **4** *7* **Edeiff's Lad**[383] 4056 9-9-9 **75**...................................... MrJoshuaNewman(7) 75
(Polly Gundry) *mid-div on outer: hdwy after 3 out: sn rdn: styd on same pce: wnt 4th run-in* **15/2**

P4P0 **5** *2 1/4* **Rior (IRE)**[22] 3905 9-11-1 **95**.. MrGTreacy(7) 91
(Paul Henderson) *mid-div: hdwy into 4th after 3 out: rdn bef next: nvr threatened: no ex run-in* **22/1**

5400 **6** *8* **Sun Quest**[20] 3932 12-9-7 **73** oh6.. MrJPearce(7) 62
(Steven Dixon) *chsd ldrs: rdn after 3 out: grad fdd* **22/1**

0326 **7** *5* **Drummond**[111] 2264 7-9-9 **75**.. MissPFuller(7) 58
(Katie Stephens) *hld up towards rr: sme prog u.p after 3 out: no further imp fr next* **8/1**

-P64 **8** *1/2* **Aristocracy**[70] 3098 5-11-4 **94**.. JamesBanks(3) 79
(Sally Randell) *led 3rd tl rdn and hdd appr 2 out: sn wknd* **10/1**

9 *17* **Drive On Locky (IRE)**[73] 3050 9-11-3 **90**..........................(tp) AlainCawley 56
(Johnny Farrelly) *a towards rr* **5/1**[3]

060- **10** *3 1/4* **Knight's Reward**[383] 4055 6-11-12 **99**.................................... JamesBest 62
(Tim Vaughan) *a towards rr* **20/1**

0PF **P** **Honourable Exit (IRE)**[22] 3905 9-11-2 **89**................................ RhysFlint
(Alexandra Dunn) *trckd ldrs tl wknd 3 out: t.o whn p.u bef next* **3/1**[1]

5PP0 **P** **Hill Forts Gypse (IRE)**[41] 3582 5-10-1 **79**.........................(t) KevinJones(5)
(Seamus Mullins) *mid-div: struggling after 5th: sn wknd: t.o whn p.u bef 7th* **22/1**

5m 12.0s (26.00) **Going Correction** +1.125s/f (Heav) **12** Ran SP% **120.9**
Speed ratings (Par 103): **90,89,88,86,85 81,79,79,72,70**
CSF £150.78 CT £1562.17 TOTE £5.10: £2.10, £7.00, £3.40; EX 137.70 Trifecta £716.70.
Owner Gale Force Six **Bred** J B Property Developments (midlands) Ltd **Trained** Milborne Port, Dorset

FOCUS
Rail movements resulted in this being run over 93yds further than advertised. Moderate handicap form and a step up from the winner.

4292 ROYAL BATH & WEST NOVICES' H'CAP CHASE (12 fncs) 2m 12y
3:05 (3:05) (Class 4) (0-120,120) 5-Y-O+ **£5,198** (£1,526; £763; £381)

Form RPR

3-62 **1** **The Brock Again**[19] 3954 6-11-12 **120**..................(t) SamTwiston-Davies 130+
(Paul Nicholls) *j.w: trckd ldr: chal 4 out: led next: kpt on wl to assert towards fin: rdn out* **15/8**[2]

2421 **2** *1 3/4* **Sonny The One**[21] 3918 6-11-8 **116**..............................(p) TomScudamore 125+
(Colin Tizzard) *led: stirrup leather broke after 8th: jnd next where jockey kicked out irons: hdd 3 out: stl ev ch at the last: no ex cl home: gd effrt but nvr rcvrd* **11/10**[1]

0/35 **3** *17* **Valseur Du Granval (FR)**[104] 2437 7-11-0 **108**.................(t) SeanBowen 100
(Tom George) *trckd ldrs: wnt cl 3rd 3 out: sn rdn: wknd after next* **10/1**

1PF4 **4** *20* **Richardofdoccombe (IRE)**[5] 4209 10-11-1 **109**..........(t) DenisO'Regan 80
(Gail Haywood) *in last pair: wkng whn lft 4th 3 out: t.o* **25/1**

1456 **F** **Exemplary**[21] 3919 9-10-10 **104**...(t) AlainCawley
(Johnny Farrelly) *in last pair: wknd bef 3 out: fell 2 out* **22/1**

-361 **F** **Storming Strumpet**[34] 3681 6-11-7 **115**..........................(t) PaddyBrennan
(Tom George) *trckd ldrs: pushed along in cl 4th whn fell 3 out* **8/1**[3]

4m 22.1s (8.10) **Going Correction** +0.675s/f (Soft) **6** Ran SP% **110.8**
Speed ratings: **106,105,96,86,**
CSF £4.43 TOTE £2.50: £1.70, £1.10; EX 4.80 Trifecta £17.70.
Owner Axom Liv **Bred** Mette Campbell-Andenaes **Trained** Ditcheat, Somerset

FOCUS
Rail movements resulted in this being run over 30yds further than advertised. The market leaders dominated this modest chase, but the winner looked fortunate.

4293 BRITISH STALLION STUDS EBF MARES' "NATIONAL HUNT" NOVICES' HURDLE (10 hdls) 2m 3f 1y
3:40 (3:40) (Class 4) 4-Y-O+ **£4,548** (£1,335; £667; £333)

Form RPR
6-2U **1** **Antartica De Thaix (FR)**[59] 3252 6-10-12 0.........(t) SamTwiston-Davies 110+
(Paul Nicholls) *travelled wl: hld up in tch: hdwy to ld and qcknd pce after 5th: kpt on wl fr last: rdn out* **3/1**[2]

102 **2** *1 ¼* **Robinesse (IRE)**[68] 3119 5-10-12 0.............................. LeightonAspell 109+
(Oliver Sherwood) *trckd ldr: led 4th tl after next: chsd wnr: pushed along fr 7th: rdn after 3 out: styd on fr last but nt pce to mount chal* **1/3**[1]

4 **3** *33* **On The Couch (IRE)**[19] 3947 7-10-12 0.............................. AidanColeman 76
(Sam Thomas) *trckd ldrs: outpcd after 3 out: wnt modest 3rd at the last* **33/1**

-040 **4** *5* **Mari Me Oscar (IRE)**[69] 3110 6-10-7 0.............................. CharlieDeutsch(5) 71
(Nikki Evans) *trckd ldrs: rdn after 3 out: wknd bef next* **100/1**

4540 **5** *18* **Oneforthenure (IRE)**[41] 3581 7-10-12 0.............................. TomO'Brien 53
(Richard Woollacott) *led tl 4th: pressed ldr tl 6th: wknd after 3 out: t.o* **20/1**[3]

P **Wallawallabingbang** 7-10-12 0.............................. AdamWedge
(Alexandra Dunn) *hld up in tch: wknd after 7th: t.o whn p.u after 3 out* **33/1**

5m 14.1s (28.10) **Going Correction** +1.125s/f (Heav) **6** Ran SP% **111.7**
Speed ratings (Par 105): **85,84,70,68,60**
CSF £4.55 TOTE £4.00: £1.50, £1.10; EX 5.90 Trifecta £19.70.
Owner D Macdonald, C Barber, I Fogg & R Webb **Bred** Michel Bourgneuf **Trained** Ditcheat, Somerset

FOCUS
Rail movements resulted in this being run over 93yds further than advertised. As expected the big two in the market dominated this mares' novice, but they didn't finish in the order the market suggested they would, with the riding of Sam Twiston-Davies making the difference.

4294 BATHWICK TYRES H'CAP HURDLE (8 hdls 1 omitted) 2m 104y
4:10 (4:10) (Class 2) 4-Y-O+
£11,573 (£3,418; £1,709; £854; £427; £214)

Form RPR
-146 **1** **Royal Vacation (IRE)**[24] 3852 6-11-1 **125**..........................(p) PaddyBrennan 131+
(Colin Tizzard) *trckd ldr: nudged along after 6th: rdn sn after 2 out (usual 3 out): led sn after last: drvn rt out* **7/4**[1]

-060 **2** *½* **Qualando (FR)**[80] 2901 5-11-5 **136**.............................. HarryCobden(7) 142+
(Paul Nicholls) *trckd ldr: rdn after 3 out (usual 2 out): led bef last: hdd run-in: kpt on* **3/1**[2]

2301 **3** *3 ¼* **Tornado In Milan (IRE)**[31] 3748 10-11-1 **130**.............................. ConorRing(5) 132
(Evan Williams) *led: rdn bypassing omitted 2 out: hdd bef last: no ex run-in* **13/2**[3]

531 **4** *12* **Cobra De Mai (FR)**[11] 4104 4-9-12 **122**.............................. BridgetAndrews(5) 103
(Dan Skelton) *trckd ldrs: rdn after 6th: nt quite pce to chal: wknd last* **13/2**[3]

1FU1 **5** *2 ½* **Sea Wall (FR)**[21] 3917 8-11-8 **132**.............................. TomCannon 121
(Chris Gordon) *hld up last but in tch: hdwy appr omitted 2 out: sn rdn: wknd last* **13/2**[3]

-036 **6** *16* **Lochnagar (GER)**[4] 4229 7-10-0 **115**.............................. CharlieDeutsch(5) 87
(Venetia Williams) *hld up in tch: hit 3rd: wknd 2 out (usual 3 out)* **10/1**

4m 22.1s (14.10) **Going Correction** +1.125s/f (Heav)
WFA 4 from 5yo+ 9lb **6** Ran SP% **110.5**
Speed ratings (Par 109): **109,108,107,101,99 91**
CSF £7.37 TOTE £2.40: £1.20, £2.20; EX 7.50 Trifecta £27.70.
Owner Mrs Jean R Bishop **Bred** Tim Hegarty **Trained** Milborne Port, Dorset

FOCUS
Rail movements resulted in this being run over 93yds further than advertised. A fair handicap, the right horses coming to the fore. The winner is on a decent mark and is back to his best.

4295 RICHARD WILLIAMS MEMORIAL "GRASSROOTS" HUNTERS' CHASE (FOR THE RICHARD WILLIAMS MEMORIAL TROPHY) (12 fncs) 2m 12y
4:45 (4:45) (Class 6) 6-Y-O+ **£1,975** (£607; £303)

Form RPR
5-20 **1** **Delta Borget (FR)**[23] 11-11-2 109..............................(p) MissJBuck(5) 110
(L Jefford) *in tch whn hmpd 2nd: towards rr: hdwy fr 7th: rdn to ld jst bef last: drifted lft briefly run-in: r.o: rdn out* **17/2**

-466 **2** *1 ¼* **Swallows Delight (IRE)**[57] 11-11-11 103.............................. MrDMansell 113
(Mrs Julie Mansell) *chsd ldrs: wnt 2nd 4 out: rdn next: ev ch last: jinked lft run-in: hld cl home* **18/1**

0/P- **3** *10* **Decade Player (IRE)**[30] 8-11-7 0.............................. MissGAndrews 98
(Miss Kelly Morgan) *j.lft: led: clr tl rdn after 3 out: hdd bef last: no ex* **3/1**[2]

60- **4** *19* **Ambitious Pursuit (IRE)**[30] 8-11-0 0.............................. MissPGlanville(7) 79
(Mrs L Glanville) *hld up towards rr: struggling and no ch 4 out: wnt modest 4th sn after last* **20/1**

P **5** *3 ¾* **Triggywinkle (FR)**[9] 7-10-9 0..............................(tp) MrMartinMcIntyre(5) 68
(Roderick Chelton) *chsd ldr tl 4 out: sn rdn: wknd next: lft modest 4th briefly at the last* **66/1**

466- **6** *9* **Rio De Sivola (FR)**[16] 7-11-0 107..............................(t) MrJLThomas(7) 66
(Miss V J Nicholls) *mid-div tl wknd after 8th: t.o* **10/1**

34-P **F** **Sangfroid**[41] 3585 12-11-4 88.............................. MrZBaker(3)
(Andrew Quick) *mid-div tl wknd after 8th: bhd whn fell 3 out* **50/1**

20/ **U** **Firmount Beech (IRE)**[268] 12-11-0 0..............................[1] MrSEllicott(7)
(Mrs E Scott) *chsd ldrs tl 6th: fading whn mstke and uns rdr 8th* **100/1**

2354 **P** **Dr Anubis (IRE)**[30] 11-11-0 80.............................. MissKatyLyons(7)
(Miss Hannah Taylor) *mid-div tl wknd after 7th: t.o whn p.u bef 4 out* **33/1**

PP-P **R** **Devon Mead**[41] 3585 10-11-2 0..............................(p) MissPFuller(5)
(Andrew Quick) *ref to r: tk no part* **150/1**

U **Griesenau (IRE)**[51] 10-11-0 0.............................. MrBParis-Crofts(7)
(Paul Henderson) *dwlt: a in rr: mstke and uns rdr 4 out* **66/1**

/6-1 **F** **The Wealerdealer (IRE)**[86] 9-11-8 110.............................. MrIChanin(3)
(I Chanin) *trcking ldrs whn fell 2nd* **6/4**[1]

00/3 **F** **Anglingforcharlie**[285] 293 7-11-0 0.............................. MrNLawton(7) 94
(Miss Beth Childs) *chsd ldrs: bdly hmpd 2nd and lost pl: eventually rcvrd: wnt 3rd 3 out: sn rdn: hld in one pce 4th whn fell last* **11/2**[3]

4m 26.4s (12.40) **Going Correction** +0.675s/f (Soft) **13** Ran SP% **119.6**
Speed ratings: **96,95,90,80,79 74, , , , ,**
CSF £130.57 TOTE £9.20: £2.60, £3.80, £1.50; EX 180.20 Trifecta £886.00.
Owner Here Come The Girls **Bred** Xavier Goupil & Laurent Boron **Trained** Kentisbeare, Devon
■ Stewards' Enquiry : Mr D Mansell two-day ban: used whip above permitted level (tbn)

FOCUS
Rail movements resulted in this being run over 30yds further than advertised. Less than half the field managed to complete in what was a moderate hunter chase, with the favourite departing early. The front pair were put off by a loose horse on the run-in, but it had no impact on the result.

4296 SOMERSET COUNTY GAZETTE STANDARD NATIONAL HUNT FLAT RACE (CONDITIONAL JOCKEYS AND AMATEUR RIDERS) 2m 104y
5:20 (5:20) (Class 5) 4-6-Y-O **£2,395** (£698; £349)

Form RPR
1 **Captain Buck's (FR)**[294] 4-10-2 0..............................(t) MrStanSheppard(7) 105+
(Paul Nicholls) *trckd ldrs: chal wl over 2f out: led over 1f out: kpt on wl fnl f: readily* **11/4**[2]

4 **2** *3 ½* **Misterton**[103] 2460 5-10-11 0.............................. LiamMcKenna(7) 108+
(Harry Fry) *led: rdn whn jnd wl over 2f out: hdd over 1f out: styd on but no ex fnl f* **7/4**[1]

0 **3** *6* **Cucklington**[135] 1872 5-10-11 0..............................(t) PaulO'Brien(7) 102
(Colin Tizzard) *trckd ldr: rdn to chal briefly 3f out: sn outpcd: styd on to go 3rd fnl f* **7/1**

4 *4* **Admiral's Secret** 5-10-11 0..............................(t) DavidPrichard(7) 98
(Victor Dartnall) *hld up: hdwy on outer fnl bnd: effrt 3f out: styd on same pce fnl 2f* **7/1**

1 **5** *1 ¼* **Mac Gregory**[113] 2250 5-11-4 0.............................. LewisGordon(7) 104
(Evan Williams) *trckd ldrs: effrt 3f out: styd on same pce fnl 2f* **5/1**[3]

6 *4* **Next Lot**[275] 6-10-13 0.............................. DanielHiskett(5) 93
(Richard Phillips) *trckd ldrs: rdn 3f out: styd on same pce fnl 2f* **25/1**

0 **7** *26* **Yenston (IRE)**[99] 2549 5-10-11 0..............................(t) MrEDoggrell(7) 67
(Colin Tizzard) *trckd ldrs: struggling in last 1/2-way: wknd 4f out* **40/1**

4 **8** *nk* **Cove Lodge**[82] 2875 6-10-11 0.............................. MrMatthewHampton(7) 66
(Richard Woollacott) *trckd ldrs: effrt 3f out: sn wknd* **33/1**

4m 23.2s (20.80) **Going Correction** +1.125s/f (Heav)
WFA 4 from 5yo+ 9lb **8** Ran SP% **113.9**
Speed ratings: **93,91,88,86,85 83,70,70**
CSF £7.79 TOTE £3.60: £1.50, £1.10, £2.60; EX 9.80 Trifecta £38.30.
Owner Donlon & Doyle **Bred** Mme Marie Pallot **Trained** Ditcheat, Somerset

FOCUS
Rail movements resulted in this being run over 93yds further than advertised. The two at the head of the market dominated and both could be useful.
T/Plt: £32.90 to a £1 stake. Pool: £63,966.51 - 1418.28 winning units. T/Qpdt: £7.70 to a £1 stake. Pool: £5,720.60 - 545.90 winning units. **Tim Mitchell**

4104 WETHERBY (L-H)
Tuesday, February 23

OFFICIAL GOING: Soft (heavy in places in back straight; 5.2)
Wind: moderate 1/2 behind Weather: fine but cold

4297 RACING UK CLUB DAY HERE TODAY CONDITIONAL JOCKEYS' H'CAP HURDLE (9 hdls) 2m
2:10 (2:10) (Class 5) (0-100,100) 4-Y-O+ **£2,599** (£763; £381; £190)

Form RPR
4426 **1** **Beyondtemptation**[23] 3888 8-10-9 **83**..............................(t) DiarmuidO'Regan 91+
(Jonathan Haynes) *mde all: wl clr fr 4th: eased clsng stages: unchal* **16/1**

P250 **2** *17* **Mister Hendre**[25] 3840 8-9-10 **78**..............................(t) JamesCorbett(8) 69
(Susan Corbett) *chsd ldrs: modest 2nd 6th: kpt on: no threat* **13/2**[3]

/53- **3** *1 ½* **Flobury**[641] 430 8-11-4 **92**.............................. CiaranGethings 83
(Barry Leavy) *in rr: hdwy whn hit 2 out: styd on to take modest 3rd towards fin* **20/1**

0333 **4** *¾* **Copt Hill**[14] 4049 8-10-6 **80**..............................(p) CraigNichol 71
(Tracy Waggott) *chsd wnr: blnd 4th: one pce fr 3 out* **11/4**[1]

4565 **5** *1 ½* **Dalby Spook (IRE)**[93] 2670 6-10-3 **80**.............................. EmmaSayer(3) 67
(Dianne Sayer) *chsd ldrs: modest 4th 3 out: 3rd last: wknd clsng stages* **11/1**

00P/ **6** *3 ¼* **Hydrant**[10] 5302 10-10-10 **84**.............................. KieronEdgar 68
(Richard Guest) *t.k.h in rr: effrt 3 out: kpt on: nvr a factor* **11/1**

004 **7** *3 ¾* **Leaving Las Vegas**[24] 3863 5-11-12 **100**..............................(t) JeremiahMcGrath 81
(William Kinsey) *chsd ldrs: wknd 2 out* **12/1**

-P30 **8** *3* **Agesilas (FR)**[25] 3840 8-10-0 **74** oh5..............................(p) JonathanEngland 53
(Andrew Crook) *chsd ldng pair: outpcd 6th* **50/1**

005 **9** *2* **Rhythm Of Sound (IRE)**[13] 4050 6-10-13 **97**.............................. BillyGarritty(10) 72
(Micky Hammond) *in rr: bhd and drvn 6th: sme late hdwy* **18/1**

540P **10** *¾* **Hi Dancer**[14] 4049 13-10-8 **82**.............................. FreddieMitchell 57
(Ben Haslam) *in rr: nvr on terms* **18/1**

05-2 **11** *9* **Zayfire Aramis**[24] 3868 7-11-10 **98**.............................. ThomasGarner 69
(Michael Scudamore) *trckd ldrs: modest 3rd 3 out: 4th whn blnd last: heavily eased last 100yds* **7/2**[2]

0000 **12** *6* **Shalamzar (FR)**[8] 4154 7-10-11 **95**.............................. HugoThompsonBrown(10) 55
(Micky Hammond) *in rr: pushed along 4th: nvr on terms* **33/1**

4m 15.8s (20.00) **Going Correction** +1.30s/f (Heav) **12** Ran SP% **112.7**
Speed ratings (Par 103): **102,93,92,92,91 90,88,86,85,85 80,77**
CSF £109.79 CT £2085.37 TOTE £12.50: £3.40, £2.80, £5.40; EX 77.10 Trifecta £1421.10.
Owner J C Haynes **Bred** J C Haynes **Trained** Low Row, Cumbria

FOCUS
A drying day although the going was still deep underfoot. After winning the first Diarmuid O'Regan said it was "tacky, holding ground." This race distance was increased by 15yds. This moderate handicap for conditional riders was a messy race with the winner coming home unchallenged.

4298 EBF/TBA MARES' NOVICES' H'CAP CHASE (18 fncs) 2m 5f 75y
2:45 (2:45) (Class 4) (0-105,104) 5-Y-O+ **£4,659** (£1,446; £779)

Form RPR
0006 **1** **Suzy's Music (IRE)**[7] 4163 8-10-8 **86**.............................. AELynch 96+
(S R B Crawford, Ire) *trckd ldng pair: cl 2nd sn after 14th: j.lft next: effrt 2 out: stchd rt between last 2: styd on wl to ld last 75yds* **5/2**[2]

F20P **2** *2* **Lily Little Legs (IRE)**[74] 3025 7-11-2 **94**.............................. BrianHughes 101
(Mike Sowersby) *led: pushed along 4 out: jst over 1 l ahd last: hdd and no ex last 75yds* **5/2**[2]

0400 3 58 **Our Phylli Vera (IRE)**[25] 3834 7-10-0 **81** ow1........ ColmMcCormack(3) 43
(Joanne Foster) *racd in last wl in tch: pushed along 11th: reminders 13th: sn lost pl and bhd: t.o 4 out: lft distant 3rd bef 2 out* **12/1**[3]

4-02 P **Goldray**[207] 1165 10-11-12 **104**.................................... JamieMoore
(Kerry Lee) *w ldr: hung lft thrght: drvn 14th: lost pl bef next: distant 3rd whn p.u bef 2 out* **11/8**[1]

6m 18.5s (41.50) **Going Correction** +1.55s/f (Heav) **4** Ran SP% **106.9**
Speed ratings: **82,81,59,**
CSF £8.75 TOTE £3.50; EX 8.80 Trifecta £38.20.
Owner R McGaw **Bred** R J A McGaw **Trained** Larne, Co Antrim

FOCUS
An ordinary little mares' novice handicap, run at a routine gallop. Due to rail movement it was run over 90yds further than advertised.

4299 WATCH THE CHELTENHAM FESTIVAL ON RACING UK NOVICES' HURDLE 2m 3f 154y
3:20 (3:20) (Class 4) 4-Y-0+ **£3,249** (£954; £477; £238)

Form RPR

14 1 **Born Survivor (IRE)**[38] 3623 5-11-9 142.................. HarrySkelton 133+
(Dan Skelton) *mde all: nt fluent 2 out: pushed along and styd on strly run-in: unchal* **1/8**[1]

2324 2 6 **Just Georgie**[18] 3971 6-11-3 113............................ DannyCook 113
(Sue Smith) *trckd ldrs: 3rd 7th: chsd wnr 3 out: kpt on: no imp* **4/1**[2]

540 3 12 **Lough Salt (IRE)**[38] 3626 5-11-3 0........................ JakeGreenall 101
(Mark Walford) *trckd ldrs: 2nd 7th: drvn bef 3 out: one pce* **16/1**[3]

P00 4 28 **Violoniste (FR)**[11] 4108 7-11-3 0........................ JonathanEngland 71
(Sam Drake) *chsd wnr: pushed along 8th: sn lost pl and bhd: t.o* **150/1**

6 P **Roxy The Rebel**[27] 3802 6-10-5 0.......................... GrantCockburn(5)
(Simon Waugh) *trckd ldrs: nt fluent 2nd and 7th: drvn and lost pl 8th: t.o whn blnd next: p.u between last 2* **200/1**

5m 27.8s (20.80) **Going Correction** +1.30s/f (Heav) **5** Ran SP% **115.9**
Speed ratings (Par 105): **110,107,102,91,**
CSF £1.46 TOTE £1.10: £1.10, £1.40; EX 1.50 Trifecta £2.00.
Owner Mrs G Widdowson & Mrs R Kelvin-Hughes **Bred** Liam Brady **Trained** Alcester, Warwicks

FOCUS
Straightforward novice form, with the winner not needing to be at his best to land the odds and rated around the runner-up. This race distance was increased by 24yds.

4300 RACING UK IN HD NEXT MONTH H'CAP CHASE (13 fncs) 1m 7f 36y
3:50 (3:50) (Class 4) (0-120,120) 5-Y-0+ **£5,198** (£1,526; £763; £381)

Form RPR

3152 1 **Retrieve The Stick**[20] 3938 7-11-0 **108**...............(b) BrianHughes 120+
(Malcolm Jefferson) *hdwy to trck ldrs 9th: effrt next: chsd ldr 3 out: j.lft next: kpt on run-in: led last 50yds: drvn out* **7/2**[2]

P321 2 1 ½ **Big Jim**[38] 3620 7-11-12 **120**.................................. KielanWoods 131+
(Alex Hales) *w ldr: hit 7th: led next: hdd and no ex last 50yds* **5/4**[1]

330 3 4 ½ **Rupert Bear**[14] 4048 10-9-9 **94** oh7...........................(p) MissCWalton(5) 99
(James Walton) *chsd ldng pair 3rd: reminders after 9th: sn lost pl: kpt on fr 2 out: tk modest 3rd last: styd on* **33/1**

2232 4 12 **Quick Decisson (IRE)**[7] 4166 8-11-3 **111**................... DannyCook 108
(Stuart Coltherd) *led: hdd 8th: pushed along next: lost pl 2 out: wknd last* **7/2**[2]

5254 5 11 **Pamak D'Airy (FR)**[20] 3938 13-10-7 **101**...............(p) BrianHarding 83
(Henry Hogarth) *hld up in rr: outpcd and lost pl 8th: sn bhd* **22/1**

-33F 6 1 ¼ **Young Palm (IRE)**[7] 4166 9-10-7 **101**.........................(tp) AELynch 81
(S R B Crawford, Ire) *hld up in rr: hdwy to trck ldrs 6th: drvn 3 out: fnd little and lost pl bef next: bhd whn j.rt last* **6/1**[3]

4m 16.5s (20.70) **Going Correction** +1.55s/f (Heav) **6** Ran SP% **110.5**
Speed ratings: **106,105,102,96,90 89**
CSF £8.47 TOTE £3.90: £1.60, £1.30; EX 9.80 Trifecta £118.60.
Owner Newstead Racing Partnership **Bred** Mrs M Barker **Trained** Norton, N Yorks

FOCUS
A modest handicap in which the leaders went off hard and set it up for a closer. Due to rail movement it was run over 81yds further than advertised.

4301 STAR SPORTS CHELTENHAM PREVIEW NIGHT - 8TH MARCH H'CAP HURDLE (12 hdls) 2m 5f 56y
4:25 (4:25) (Class 4) (0-115,114) 4-Y-0+ **£3,898** (£1,144; £572; £286)

Form RPR

6134 1 **Palm Grey (IRE)**[32] 3728 8-11-12 **114**........................ DannyCook 117+
(Sue Smith) *w ldr: led 5th: styd on fr 3 out: edgd lft run-in: drvn rt out* **3/1**[2]

-332 2 1 ¼ **Zephyros Bleu (IRE)**[33] 3705 6-11-11 **113**.................. GavinSheehan 116+
(Harry Whittington) *chsd ldrs: shkn up 7th: 2nd after 8th: drvn 3 out: swtchd rt 75yds out: kpt on* **10/11**[1]

PP00 3 19 **Moscow Presents (IRE)**[24] 3855 8-10-7 **98**..............(p) AdamNicol(3) 83
(Philip Kirby) *chsd ldrs: drvn 8th: 3rd appr 3 out: wknd appr last* **15/2**[3]

20/P 4 14 **Mootabar (IRE)**[18] 3973 9-10-0 **88** oh13.................. JonathanEngland 57
(Chris Fairhurst) *hld up in rr: hdwy 9th: wknd bef 2 out: j.lft last: lame* **125/1**

5140 5 1 **Ballinalacken (IRE)**[25] 3837 8-11-4 **106**..................(v) DavidEngland 74
(Clare Ellam) *chsd ldrs: drvn 9th: lost pl next: sn bhd* **25/1**

2465 6 9 **Shaiyzar (IRE)**[50] 3474 7-10-11 **99**.........................(p) PeterCarberry 58
(David Thompson) *chsd ldrs: reminders after 9th: lost pl bef next* **11/1**

26/P 7 2 **Pink Gin**[25] 3846 8-11-8 **110**.................................(t) MarkGrant 67
(Nigel Twiston-Davies) *led: hdd 5th: lost pl appr 3 out: sn bhd* **16/1**

5m 51.2s (24.40) **Going Correction** +1.30s/f (Heav) **7** Ran SP% **108.0**
Speed ratings (Par 105): **105,104,97,91,91 88,87**
CSF £5.58 TOTE £3.40: £1.70, £1.10; EX 7.80 Trifecta £22.00.
Owner Mrs S Smith **Bred** Patrick Doyle **Trained** High Eldwick, W Yorks
■ Stewards' Enquiry : Danny Cook caution: careless riding

FOCUS
This moderate handicap was run at an average gallop and the first pair dominated the finish. This race distance was increased by 24yds.

4302 RACING UK DAY PASS JUST £10 MARES' STANDARD OPEN NATIONAL HUNT FLAT RACE 2m
5:00 (5:00) (Class 6) 4-6-Y-0 **£2,053** (£598; £299)

Form RPR

1 **Listen To The Man (IRE)**[79] 6-11-0 0......................... HarrySkelton 100+
(Dan Skelton) *set stdy pce: increased gallop 6f out: shkn up over 2f out: clr over 1f out: pushed out* **2/7**[1]

5 2 7 **Wildehearted Woman (IRE)**[90] 2715 5-11-0 0...........(t) MichealNolan 90
(Jamie Snowden) *trckd ldng pair: 2nd over 3f out: sn drvn: one pce* **25/1**

3 ½ **State Sovereignty** 4-10-5 0.................................. LiamTreadwell 81
(Michael Scudamore) *hld up in last but wl in tch: effrt over 3f out: sn 3rd: drvn over 2f out: one pce* **7/1**[3]

4 9 **Oscar's Prospect (IRE)** 4-10-5 0............................. BrianHarding 72
(Jedd O'Keeffe) *trckd wnr: pushed along over 5f out: drvn over 3f out: lost pl over 2f out* **13/2**[2]

4m 14.0s (23.80) **Going Correction** +1.30s/f (Heav)
WFA 4 from 5yo 9lb 5 from 6yo 1lb **4** Ran SP% **107.4**
Speed ratings: **92,88,88,83**
CSF £8.43 TOTE £1.20; EX 6.40 Trifecta £14.00.
Owner M Boothright **Bred** P J Kelly **Trained** Alcester, Warwicks

FOCUS
An ordinary little mares' bumper, run at an uneven tempo. This race distance was increased by 15yds.
T/Plt: £67.50 to a £1 stake. Pool: £47,126.68 - 509.02 winning units. T/Qpdt: £2.00 to a £1 stake. Pool: £4,219.44 - 1543.39 winning units. **Walter Glynn**

4062 DONCASTER (L-H)
Wednesday, February 24

OFFICIAL GOING: Good (good to soft in places on chase course; chs 7.6, hdl 7.8)
Wind: light, half against Weather: fine and sunny

4303 EBF STALLIONS BETBRIGHT #REALFANSONLY "NATIONAL HUNT" NOVICES' HURDLE (QUALIFIER) (8 hdls) 2m 140y
2:00 (2:06) (Class 4) 4-7-Y-O **£3,898** (£1,144; £572; £286)

Form RPR

-042 1 **Chic Theatre (IRE)**[7] 4182 6-11-2 0........................ TomScudamore 120+
(David Pipe) *chsd ldrs: led 5th: blnd last: kpt on: all out* **15/2**

1-02 2 shd **The Unit (IRE)**[40] 3608 5-10-13 0........................... TomBellamy(3) 120+
(Alan King) *stdd s: hld up in rr: hdwy after 4th: chal 2 out: upsides whn nt fluent last: kpt on: jst hld* **9/2**[2]

121 3 2 ½ **Divine Spear (IRE)**[21] 3927 5-11-8 127...................... NicodeBoinville 123+
(Nicky Henderson) *trckd ldrs: t.k.h: upsides 3 out: kpt on same pce appr last* **8/11**[1]

4 1 ½ **Peter The Mayo Man (IRE)**[308] 5488 6-11-2 0................. NoelFehily 115+
(Neil Mulholland) *hld up in mid-div: t.k.h: hdwy to trck ldrs 3 out: edgd lft appr last: kpt on same pce* **11/2**[3]

0-30 5 7 **The Missus**[57] 3334 5-10-6 0............................... MrSWaley-Cohen(3) 101
(Warren Greatrex) *chsd ldrs: one pce fr 2 out* **66/1**

0 6 1 **Kk Lexion (IRE)**[26] 3839 5-11-2 0............................ PaddyBrennan 108
(Tom George) *mid-div: hdwy to chse ldrs 5th: one pce fr 2 out* **25/1**

434 7 nk **Eastview Boy**[18] 4001 5-10-13 0.............................. AdamNicol(3) 107
(Philip Kirby) *chsd ldrs: one pce fr 3 out* **100/1**

0F0 8 5 **Definitly Grey (IRE)**[75] 3021 5-10-13 0.................. GrahamWatters(3) 102
(Charlie Longsdon) *led to 5th: wknd 2 out* **200/1**

03 9 1 ½ **Brian Boranha (IRE)**[26] 3835 5-11-2 0....................... BrianHughes 101
(Peter Niven) *mid-div: outpcd 5th: hdwy next: fdd 2 out* **33/1**

35 10 7 **Sonneofpresenting (IRE)**[13] 4063 6-11-2 0................... HenryBrooke 97
(Kim Bailey) *t.k.h: trckd ldrs: cl up whn stmbld on landing 3 out: wknd next* **50/1**

400 11 18 **Crockery**[12] 4097 6-10-9 0..................................... HarrySkelton 69
(Dan Skelton) *chsd ldrs: hit 5th: sn drvn: lost pl next* **40/1**

12 19 **Bored Or Bad (IRE)** 4-10-7 0................................... AidanColeman 48
(David Dennis) *in rr: j.lft 2nd: bhd fr 4th* **100/1**

13 4 ½ **Change Or Go (IRE)** 4-10-7 0.................................. MichealNolan 43
(David Dennis) *nt fluent in rr: bhd fr 4th* **150/1**

-00P 14 1 ½ **Up The Junction**[56] 3370 5-11-2 0............................ TomCannon 51
(Tim Vaughan) *in rr: bhd fr 4th: hmpd 2 out* **250/1**

/40U F **Henrybrowneyes (IRE)**[13] 4063 7-11-2 0...................... WillKennedy
(Ian Williams) *mid-div: sme hdwy 3 out: modest 11th whn stmbld on landing and fell next* **200/1**

4m 0.9s (-3.80) **Going Correction** -0.075s/f (Good)
WFA 4 from 5yo+ 9lb **15** Ran SP% **120.0**
Speed ratings: **105,104,103,103,99 99,99,96,96,92 84,75,73,72,**
CSF £40.40 TOTE £8.90: £2.10, £1.40, £1.10; EX 48.10 Trifecta £92.00.
Owner Bryan Drew **Bred** Kevin Conaty **Trained** Nicholashayne, Devon

FOCUS
The track passed an inspection for overnight frost and the ground was officially good, something that has been in very short supply in recent months. After winning the first race Tom Scudamore said the going was good, good to soft in places on the hurdles track. They went what looked a fairly steady gallop in this ordinary novice hurdle, which was run over about 18yds further than advertised. The first three were pretty close to their marks.

4304 WATCH LIVE RACING ON BETBRIGHT.COM JUVENILE HURDLE (8 hdls) 2m 140y
2:30 (2:35) (Class 4) 4-Y-O **£3,898** (£1,144; £572; £286)

Form RPR

5P 1 **Ardamir (FR)**[70] 3112 4-11-5 120.............................. DenisO'Regan 120+
(Alan King) *hld up towards rr: hdwy 5th: trcking ldrs next: led appr 2 out: drvn last: styd on wl last 150yds* **4/1**

132 2 1 ½ **Our Thomas (IRE)**[19] 3967 4-11-5 128.......................... BrianHughes 118
(Tim Easterby) *trckd ldrs: nt fluent 4th: upsides bef 2 out: drvn between last 2: kpt on same pce last 100yds* **15/8**[1]

03 3 26 **Alhamareer (IRE)**[15] 4038 4-10-12 0............................ JamesBest 85
(Paul Webber) *chsd ldrs: led 3 out: hdd appr next: wknd between last 2* **25/1**

62 4 7 **Baraymi (FR)**[29] 3790 4-10-12 0............................(p) MichealNolan 78
(Jamie Snowden) *led: hdd 3 out: wknd between last 2* **7/2**[3]

4 5 12 **Lou Vert (FR)**[22] 3915 4-10-12 0..........................(t) SamTwiston-Davies 66
(Paul Nicholls) *hld up towards rr: hdwy to chse ldrs 3 out: sn drvn and lost pl* **5/2**[2]

0 6 47 **Fled Or Pled (IRE)**[21] 3927 4-10-12 0......................... NoelFehily 19
(David Dennis) *t.k.h in rr: j.rt 4th: bhd next: t.o 3 out* **125/1**

P **Fraser Canyon**[295] 4-10-12 0.................................. TomCannon
(Tim Vaughan) *chsd ldrs: lost pl sn after 5th: sn bhd: t.o 3 out: p.u bef next* **100/1**

4m 0.8s (-3.90) **Going Correction** -0.075s/f (Good) **7** Ran SP% **111.2**
Speed ratings: **106,105,93,89,84 62,**
CSF £11.61 TOTE £6.20: £4.70, £1.10; EX 10.60 Trifecta £98.10.
Owner The Dunkley & Reilly Partnership **Bred** Christophe Jouandou **Trained** Barbury Castle, Wilts

FOCUS
This was run over about 18yds further than advertised. Not a bad juvenile hurdle, and it was run in a time very similar to that recorded by the older novices. The first two finished well clear and winner's performance was believable on his French form.

4305 BETBRIGHTBOOST H'CAP HURDLE (11 hdls) 3m 96y
3:00 (3:05) (Class 3) (0-130,129) 4-Y-0 £6,330 (£1,870; £935; £468; £234)

Form — RPR

2140 **1** **Fingeronttheswitch (IRE)**[75] 3018 6-11-6 123 NoelFehily 132+
(Neil Mulholland) *hld up in mid-div: t.k.h: hdwy 8th: sn trcking ldrs: 2nd bef 2 out: led between last 2: styd on wl: drvn out* **9/4**[1]

5411 **2** 3 **Pinnacle Panda (IRE)**[18] 3994 5-11-12 129 RichardJohnson 133
(Tom Lacey) *towards rr: hit 4th: hdwy appr 3 out: chsng ldrs 2 out: 3rd appr last: styd on same pce last 150yds* **9/2**[2]

3331 **3** nse **Theatre Goer**[76] 2985 7-10-6 112 JamesBanks(3) 116
(Noel Williams) *chsd ldrs: drvn 3 out: 2nd appr last: styd on same pce last 150yds* **20/1**

6P-2 **4** 6 **Nightline**[120] 2125 6-11-3 120 (t) AidanColeman 121+
(Charlie Longsdon) *led: hdd between last 2: wknd last 75yds* **8/1**

3152 **5** 6 **You Say What (IRE)**[19] 3976 6-11-8 125 TrevorWhelan 118
(Neil King) *chsd ldrs: 2nd 3 out: wknd between last 2* **20/1**

13P **6** 16 **Crosspark**[33] 3728 6-11-9 126 HarrySkelton 105
(Caroline Bailey) *in rr-div: hdwy 7th: wknd bef 2 out* **12/1**

360P **7** 1¼ **Phare Isle (IRE)**[33] 3728 11-10-7 117 (tp) MrMJPKendrick(7) 95
(Ben Case) *prom: drvn appr 3 out: wknd appr 2 out* **66/1**

041P **8** 2 **Volcanic (FR)**[39] 3622 7-11-8 125 (t) WillKennedy 101
(Donald McCain) *chsd ldr: wknd bef 2 out* **40/1**

30-1 **9** ¾ **Mount Haven (IRE)**[51] 3467 6-11-5 122 TomScudamore 97
(David Pipe) *mid-div: chsd ldrs 3rd: mstke 3 out: lost pl appr next* **17/2**

212P **10** 2½ **Henllan Harri (IRE)**[57] 3349 8-11-11 128 (v[1]) SeanBowen 101
(Peter Bowen) *prom: effrt 3 out: lost pl bef next* **16/1**

/5FP **11** 12 **Victor Hewgo**[18] 3999 11-11-5 122 JamesReveley 84
(Keith Reveley) *chsd ldrs: lost pl 5th: sn in rr and reminders* **22/1**

4F20 **P** **Fort Worth (IRE)**[81] 2901 7-11-12 129 PaddyBrennan
(Jonjo O'Neill) *in rr: blnd 2nd: rdn and lost tch after 8th: t.o whn p.u bef next: b.b.v* **6/1**[3]

5m 52.2s (-6.80) **Going Correction** -0.075s/f (Good) **12 Ran SP% 116.3**
Speed ratings (Par 107): **108,107,106,104,102 97,97,96,96,95 91,**
CSF £11.64 CT £159.72 TOTE £3.90: £2.10, £1.60, £4.10; EX 17.20 Trifecta £455.00.
Owner Cahill, Atwell & Crofts **Bred** Denis Cleary **Trained** Limpley Stoke, Wilts

FOCUS
A competitive handicap hurdle contested by some improving types and the right horses came to the fore. It was run over about 18yds further than advertised.

4306 BETBRIGHT BEST FOR FESTIVAL BETTING VETERANS' H'CAP CHASE (QUALIFIER) (LEG 2 OF VETERANS' SERIES) (18 fncs) 3m 6y
3:30 (3:35) (Class 2) (0-150,147)
10-Y-0+ £18,768 (£5,544; £2,772; £1,386; £693; £3415)

2-60 **1** **Saint Are (FR)**[81] 2899 10-11-11 146 (tp) PaddyBrennan 155
(Tom George) *led to 5th: led 10th: drvn 4 out: styd on: hld on gamely run-in* **10/1**

0-04 **2** ¾ **Grandads Horse**[46] 3528 10-10-13 134 (p) AidanColeman 141
(Charlie Longsdon) *chsd ldrs: chsd wnr fr 14th: kpt on same pce run-in: keeping on at fin* **13/2**[3]

054P **3** 2¾ **Baileys Concerto (IRE)**[74] 3038 10-10-7 128 (t) BrianHughes 134
(Dianne Sayer) *hld up in rr-div: hdwy 14th: 4th 4 out: 3rd 2 out: kpt on same pce run-in* **16/1**

656U **4** 1½ **Shotavodka (IRE)**[10] 4140 10-10-9 130 (p) TomScudamore 135
(David Pipe) *mid-div: hdwy 10th: sn chsng ldrs: 3rd 4 out: kpt on same pce fr 2 out* **12/1**

-002 **5** 11 **Godsmejudge (IRE)**[57] 3339 10-10-8 129 (t) NoelFehily 124
(David Dennis) *chsd ldrs: lft 2nd at 2nd: led 5th to 10th: wknd 4 out* **3/1**[1]

2-23 **6** 1¼ **Reaping The Reward (IRE)**[53] 3448 12-10-13 134 (t) PeterBuchanan 126
(Lucinda Russell) *in rr: hdwy 12th: chsng ldrs 4 out: wknd 2 out: j.lft last* **8/1**

351P **7** 3¼ **Sonofagun (FR)**[26] 3843 10-10-0 121 oh2 WillKennedy 111
(Ian Williams) *in rr: nvr on terms* **66/1**

0105 **8** 2¼ **Benbens (IRE)**[53] 3448 11-11-4 142 RyanHatch(3) 131
(Nigel Twiston-Davies) *chsd ldrs: drvn and lost pl 10th: rallied 12th: lost pl bef 4 out* **7/1**

-62P **9** 3¾ **French Opera**[53] 3448 13-11-12 147 AndrewTinkler 132
(Nicky Henderson) *prom: outpcd 14th: lost pl bef next* **14/1**

0031 **F** **Night In Milan (IRE)**[26] 3837 10-11-4 139 (b) JamesReveley
(Keith Reveley) *chsd wnr: 2nd whn fell 2nd* **7/2**[2]

5m 55.7s (-16.30) **Going Correction** -0.375s/f (Good) **10 Ran SP% 115.0**
Speed ratings: **112,111,110,110,106 106,105,104,103,**
CSF £73.08 CT £1035.08 TOTE £9.70: £3.10, £2.70, £5.70; EX 86.40 Trifecta £1243.10.
Owner D W Fox **Bred** Jacques Cypres **Trained** Slad, Gloucs

FOCUS
A decent veterans' chase, run over about 6yds further than advertised. A personal best from the winner, and the form should work out.

4307 BETBRIGHT APP OPEN HUNTERS' CHASE (9 fncs 10 omitted) 3m 2f 14y
4:05 (4:10) (Class 6) 5-Y-0+ £1,871 (£580; £290; £145)

Form — RPR

34-2 **1** **Paint The Clouds**[271] 535 11-12-4 138 MrSWaley-Cohen 132+
(Warren Greatrex) *trckd ldrs: 2nd after 4f: led 9f out: clr whn shkn up over 1f out: eased clsng stages* **1/3**[1]

UF0- **2** 3¼ **One More Tune (IRE)**[31] 8-11-7 0 (p) MrAlexEdwards(3) 116+
(Philip Rowley) *chsd ldrs: chsd wnr over 2f out: no imp* **100/1**

F-11 **3** 8 **Cave Hunter (IRE)**[276] 457 9-12-1 118 (tp) MrTHamilton(3) 117
(Mrs Wendy Hamilton) *led: stmbld bdly 1st: hdd 9f out: sn drvn: one pce fnl 4f* **6/1**[2]

10/P **4** 1½ **Barel Of Laughs (IRE)**[10] 10-11-7 109 (p) MrPGerety(3) 106
(Philip Rowley) *chsd ldrs: 2nd 6f out: one pce fnl 2f* **17/2**

4-1P **5** 17 **Major Malarkey (IRE)**[271] 535 13-11-11 127 (v) MrJJSlevin(7) 102
(Nigel Twiston-Davies) *chsd ldrs early: lost pl and blnd 2nd: bhd and reminders 12f out* **8/1**[3]

2-U1 **6** 20 **Railway Dillon (IRE)**[17] 4016 11-11-13 114 MissETodd(5) 87
(Mrs C Drury) *mid-div: outpcd and lost pl 12f out* **12/1**

206P **7** 7 **Mr Moss (IRE)**[42] 3585 11-11-7 118 MissCVHart(3) 62
(S Rea) *trckd ldrs: lost pl 5f out: sn bhd* **28/1**

445P **8** 15 **Nearest The Pin (IRE)**[17] 4016 11-12-4 120 MrTomDavid 55
(Dai Williams) *in rr-div: sme hdwy 12f out: lost pl 6f out: sn bhd: hung bdly rt and heavily eased fnl 2f: eventually completed* **28/1**

6m 28.2s (-14.80) **Going Correction** -0.375s/f (Good) **8 Ran SP% 126.5**
Speed ratings: **107,106,103,103,97 91,89,84**
CSF £66.03 TOTE £1.30: £1.02, £12.90, £1.40; EX 72.90 Trifecta £274.90.
Owner Peter Deal & Jill & Robin Eynon **Bred** Guy Reed And Mrs A H Daniels **Trained** Upper Lambourn, Berks

FOCUS
This hunter chase was run over about 6yds further than advertised. All the fences in the home straight were omitted due to the low sun, as well as one of the ditches which had been damaged. It made for a very long run-in, and the form obviously isn't as solid as it might have been. Paint The Clouds is rated a stone off.

4308 BETBRIGHT CASINO STANDARD OPEN NATIONAL HUNT FLAT RACE (DIV I) 2m 140y
4:40 (4:45) (Class 6) 4-6-Y-0 £1,949 (£572; £286; £143)

Form — RPR

3 **1** **Ballycrystal (IRE)**[16] 4037 5-11-2 0 DannyCook 91+
(Brian Ellison) *trckd ldrs: led 3f out: drvn and styd on wl over 1f out* **4/5**[1]

2 3 **Man O'Words (IRE)** 5-11-2 0 RichardJohnson 87
(Tom Lacey) *chsd ldrs: drvn over 3f out: sn outpcd: hdwy over 1f out: styd on to take 2nd fnl strides* **5/1**[2]

3 hd **Focaccia (IRE)** 5-11-2 0 HarrySkelton 87
(Dan Skelton) *trckd ldrs: effrt over 3f out: kpt on to take 2nd last 150yds: kpt on same pce* **11/1**[3]

3 **4** 2¼ **Jack Lamb**[81] 2923 4-10-4 0 AdamNicol(3) 76
(Sally Hall) *trckd ldrs: upsides 4f out: kpt on one pce fnl 2f* **28/1**

6 **5** ½ **Cougar's Gold (IRE)**[46] 3522 5-11-2 0 SeanBowen 85
(Peter Bowen) *led 2f: w ldrs: led 8f out: hdd 3f out: sn outpcd: rallied and kpt on fnl f* **33/1**

6 2½ **Toosey** 5-11-2 0 JamesDavies 82
(Tom Symonds) *w ldr: led after 2f: hdd 8f out: one pce fnl 3f* **66/1**

6 **7** 1 **William Hunter**[106] 2414 4-10-4 0 TomBellamy(3) 72
(Alan King) *hld up towards rr: t.k.h: hdwy over 3f out: chsd wnr over 1f out: sn fdd* **12/1**

10 **8** 2½ **Vive Le Roi (IRE)**[101] 2514 5-11-9 0 BrianHughes 86
(Charlie Longsdon) *trckd ldrs: t.k.h: effrt over 2f out: sn outpcd: wknd over 1f out* **5/1**[2]

9 3½ **He Likes Tobougie** 5-11-2 0 TrevorWhelan 75
(Neil King) *hld up in rr: hdwy 4f out: wknd fnl 2f* **50/1**

10 ½ **Popelys Gull (IRE)** 4-10-7 0 KielanWoods 66
(Pam Sly) *in rr: drvn 4f out: sn lost pl* **50/1**

4m 11.3s (12.20) **Going Correction** -0.075s/f (Good)
WFA 4 from 5yo 9lb **10 Ran SP% 116.7**
Speed ratings: **68,66,66,65,65 64,63,62,60,60**
CSF £4.83 TOTE £1.80: £1.10, £1.60, £2.40; EX 6.30 Trifecta £34.90.
Owner P J Martin **Bred** Lucy Norton & Norris Mount Stud **Trained** Norton, N Yorks

FOCUS
They went a very sedate early pace in this bumper, which was run over about 18yds further than advertised. It was run no less than 16.3sec slower than the other division and they finished in a heap.

4309 BETBRIGHT CASINO STANDARD OPEN NATIONAL HUNT FLAT RACE (DIV II) 2m 140y
5:10 (5:15) (Class 6) 4-6-Y-0 £1,949 (£572; £286; £143)

Form — RPR

1 **Snow Leopardess** 4-10-0 0 AidanColeman 105+
(Charlie Longsdon) *chsd ldr: drvn over 3f out: 2nd over 2f out: styd on fnl 150yds: led nr fin* **9/1**[3]

U1 **2** ½ **Rather Be (IRE)**[70] 3111 5-11-9 0 AndrewTinkler 128+
(Nicky Henderson) *trckd ldr: led over 3f out: drvn over 1f out: rdn last 75yds: hdd and no ex nr fin* **11/8**[2]

3 15 **Frankly Speaking** 6-11-2 0 JamesDavies 106
(Tom Symonds) *chsd ldrs: effrt over 3f out: modest 3rd over 1f out: one pce* **22/1**

6 **4** ¾ **Midnight Jitterbug**[26] 3847 4-10-7 0 IanPopham 96
(Noel Williams) *trckd ldrs: effrt over 3f out: modest 4th over 1f out: one pce* **12/1**

2 **5** 3¾ **Groundunderrepair (IRE)**[132] 1926 5-11-2 0 GavinSheehan 101
(Warren Greatrex) *led: drvn along 7f out: hdd over 3f out: wknd fnl f* **6/5**[1]

4 **6** nk **Moon Jet (IRE)**[88] 2777 4-10-7 0 AlainCawley 92
(John Mackie) *in rr: hdwy 7f out: chsng ldrs 4f out: wknd fnl 2f* **14/1**

7 9 **Mustang On** 6-11-2 0 [1] SeanBowen 92
(Nick Kent) *hld up in rr: hdwy 6f out: chsng ldrs over 3f out: wknd over 2f out* **50/1**

0 **8** 42 **Canton Massini**[39] 3625 5-11-2 0 AndrewThornton 50
(John Holt) *hld up: drvn and sme hdwy 6f out: sn lost pl: bhd fnl 4f: t.o whn eased over 1f out* **150/1**

9 4½ **Ogwen Valley Girl** 5-9-13 0 LewisStones(10) 39
(Michael Mullineaux) *in rr: sn drvn along: lost pl 7f out: sn bhd: t.o fnl 3f* **150/1**

3m 54.8s (-4.30) **Going Correction** -0.075s/f (Good)
WFA 4 from 5yo+ 9lb **9 Ran SP% 119.6**
Speed ratings: **107,106,99,99,97 97,93,73,71**
CSF £22.62 TOTE £8.70: £2.00, £1.10, £4.40; EX 28.70 Trifecta £311.20.
Owner Mrs O Fox-Pitt **Bred** O And Mrs Fox-Pitt **Trained** Over Norton, Oxon

FOCUS
This was run over about 18yds further than advertised. In contrast to the other division, this was solidly run from the off. The time was no less than 16.3sec quicker, the first two pulling well clear.
T/Plt: £33.10 to a £1 stake. Pool: £89,597.28. 1,970.98 winning tickets. T/Qpdt: £15.70 to a £1 stake. Pool: £6,653.06. 311.90 winning tickets. **Walter Glynn**

3926 LUDLOW (R-H)
Wednesday, February 24
4310 Meeting Abandoned - frozen track

4069 HUNTINGDON (R-H)

Thursday, February 25

OFFICIAL GOING: Chase course - soft (good to soft in places; 6.0); hurdle course - good to soft (soft in places; 6.3)

Wind: fresh breeze Weather: bright and sunny; 6 degrees

4317 HIGH DEFINITION RACING UK NEXT MONTH NOVICES' HURDLE (8 hdls) 1m 7f 171y

1:45 (1:46) (Class 4) 4-Y-0+ £3,249 (£954; £477; £238)

Form RPR

61 1 **Gwafa (IRE)**[28] 3819 5-11-9 0 RichieMcLernon 140+
(Paul Webber) *mounted outside paddock: prom: effrt 3 out: led gng best next: rdn clr last: styd on wl* 2/1[2]

32 2 6 **Blue Rambler**[17] 4033 6-11-2 124 AidanColeman 126
(John Ferguson) *mde most: rdn and drawing clr w wnr whn hdd 2 out: jst getting outpcd by him whn hit last: hld after* 8/11[1]

P5 3 5 **Bonne Question (FR)**[34] 3724 7-11-2 0 LiamTreadwell 120+
(Venetia Williams) *pressed ldrs: effrt 3 out: 3rd and rdn home turn: one-pced and n.d to ldng pair after* 16/1

4 9 **Persian Breeze**[104] 4-10-0 0 HarrySkelton 95
(Lucy Wadham) *chsd ldrs: rdn after 3 out: wl hld by ldrs fr next* 14/1

044 5 6 **North Hill (IRE)**[22] 3927 5-11-2 0 TomO'Brien 107
(Ian Williams) *hld up: mstke 5th: effrt 3 out: 6th and rdn home turn: sn btn: mstke last* 50/1

06 6 3 ¼ **Gone Viral (IRE)**[31] 3773 5-11-2 0 (t) AndrewTinkler 102
(George Baker) *last after 3rd: nvr on terms* 66/1

40 7 9 **Ebadani (IRE)**[55] 3411 6-11-2 0 DarylJacob 93
(Jamie Snowden) *w ldr tl 3 out: rdn and dropped out tamely bef next* 10/1[3]

5-6 8 ¾ **Maybell**[28] 3819 5-10-6 0 JamesBanks(3) 85
(Alex Hales) *nvr trbld ldrs: btn 3 out* 200/1

203 9 hd **Handpicked**[44] 3573 5-10-9 0 RichardJohnson 85
(Henry Daly) *sweating: nvr bttr than midfield: outpcd 3 out: sn hung lft: mstke last* 25/1

54 10 4 **Mixchievous**[50] 3483 5-10-11 0 CharlieDeutsch(5) 89
(Venetia Williams) *tall: nvr on terms: mstke 5th: hanging rt* 66/1

00 11 7 **Bandon Roc**[44] 3568 5-11-2 0 DavidBass 81
(Kim Bailey) *tall str: midfield: rdn and btn bef 3 out* 100/1

0-4 12 13 **Kapgarde King (FR)**[44] 3568 5-11-2 0 MichealNolan 68
(Jamie Snowden) *nvr trbld ldrs: wl btn 3 out* 100/1

00 13 1 ¼ **Sarazen Bridge**[27] 3835 5-11-2 0 JoshuaMoore 67
(Jonjo O'Neill) *str chser type: a bhd: t.o 3 out* 100/1

0 14 1 ¾ **Cocker**[55] 3418 4-10-7 0 JackQuinlan 56
(Alan Blackmore) *t.k.h: prom tl nt fluent 5th and lost pl rapidly: t.o* 200/1

0 P **Arroyeau (FR)**[109] 2375 6-11-2 0 (p) LeightonAspell
(Nick Gifford) *unruly s: last away: plld v hrd and led briefly 3rd: hung bdly lft bef next and almost unrideable: lost tch and p.u 4th* 200/1

3m 54.4s (-0.50) **Going Correction** +0.225s/f (Yiel)
WFA 4 from 5yo+ 9lb 15 Ran SP% 126.1
Speed ratings (Par 105): **110,107,104,100,97 95,90,90,90,88 84,78,77,76,**
CSF £4.04 TOTE £3.60: £2.00, £1.10, £3.30; EX 5.30 Trifecta £26.60.
Owner Saleh Al Homaizi & Imad Al Sagar **Bred** Kenilworth House Stud **Trained** Mollington, Oxon
■ Stewards' Enquiry : Charlie Deutsch £140 fine: failed to report that the gelding hung right handed

FOCUS
There was no need for the planned inspection. Due to rail movements this race was run over 68yds further than advertised. Probably a decent novice, with the winner (a potential 145+ novice on Flat form) putting up a useful effort under his penalty.

4318 RACING UK CLUB DAY HERE TODAY H'CAP HURDLE (10 hdls) 2m 3f 137y

2:15 (2:16) (Class 5) (0-100,90) 4-Y-0+ £2,599 (£763; £381; £190)

Form RPR

330/ 1 **Shaddaii (FR)**[693] 5143 10-10-9 73 (t) JamieMoore 80
(Robert Walford) *settled trcking ldrs: wnt 3rd at 7th: led bef 2 out: 3 l clr last: drvn and idling after: kpt rt up to work but a holding rival* 13/2[3]

-366 2 1 ½ **L Frank Baum (IRE)**[20] 3978 9-11-9 90 (p) RobertWilliams(3) 96
(Bernard Llewellyn) *ldng trio and slt advantage at times: pressing wnr and rdn whn flattened last: sn jst outpcd: plugging on as rival idled flat but a hld* 8/1

P-PP 3 18 **Up Your Game (IRE)**[21] 3951 8-10-9 76 (t) RyanHatch(3) 66
(Roy Brotherton) *settled trcking ldrs: effrt 3 out: sn drvn: wl hld fr next* 25/1

0006 4 1 **Ultimate Dream (FR)**[27] 3840 5-11-7 85 JoshuaMoore 76
(Jonjo O'Neill) *nt jump wl: trckd ldrs: effrt whn mstkes 7th and next: plodded on and wl btn after* 2/1[1]

4640 5 13 **Rolling Dough (IRE)**[73] 3089 8-11-7 85 MarcGoldstein 67
(Diana Grissell) *prom: mde most fr 4th tl hrd rdn and hdd bef 2 out: btn whn mstke 2 out: disputing poor 4th at last: sn eased* 13/2[3]

P-5P P **Noir Girl**[129] 2004 7-10-5 76 (p) WilliamFeatherstone(7)
(Zoe Davison) *nt fluent 1st: led or vied for ld tl 5th: last and struggling whn slow next: sn t.o: p.u after 7th* 20/1

66U0 U **Toast And Jam (IRE)**[31] 3771 7-10-4 73 (t) DanielHiskett(5)
(Claire Dyson) *unwilling to set off: wl in tch whn uns rdr 2nd* 8/1

50P P **Tommy The Rascal**[61] 3239 6-11-7 85 (p) PeterCarberry
(Jennie Candlish) *in tch: last and shkn up after 5th: fnd nil whn drvn bef next: t.o bef 3 out: p.u last* 7/2[2]

5m 12.9s (13.90) **Going Correction** +0.575s/f (Soft) 8 Ran SP% 113.1
Speed ratings (Par 103): **95,94,87,86,81 , ,**
CSF £54.63 CT £1207.09 TOTE £5.20: £2.10, £1.90, £5.80; EX 26.80 Trifecta £330.10.
Owner Mrs Christine E Davies **Bred** Mme & Nicolas Devilder **Trained** Child Okeford, Dorset
■ Stewards' Enquiry : Robert Williams two-day ban: use of whip (10-11 March)

FOCUS
Due to rail movements this race was run over 78yds further than advertised. Low-grade hurdling form with the winner rated in line with his old mark.

4319 RACING UK LADY PROTECTRESS MARES' CHASE (LISTED RACE) (16 fncs) 2m 3f 189y

2:45 (2:46) (Class 1) 5-Y-0+ £17,085 (£6,411; £3,210; £1,599; £804)

Form RPR

1123 1 **Emily Gray (IRE)**[40] 3621 8-11-10 145 DavidBass 141+
(Kim Bailey) *led at stdy pce: rdn after 3 out: jnd next but kpt battling on: edgd lft u.str driving flat: hdd briefly: regained advantage cl home* 5/2[2]

0241 2 nk **Gitane Du Berlais (FR)**[18] 4019 6-11-10 150 DarylJacob 139
(W P Mullins, Ire) *cl up and gng wl in 2nd much of way: rdn and effrt to draw upsides wnr 2 out tl last: in front briefly 100yds out: jst outbattled nr fin* 1/2[1]

01FP 3 16 **Kilronan High (IRE)**[26] 3849 7-11-0 130 (t) SamTwiston-Davies 116
(Nigel Twiston-Davies) *tended to lack fluency: last pair tl wnt 3rd after 3 out: sn rdn and effrt short-lived: 7 l 3rd and btn next* 10/1[3]

-215 4 1 ¼ **Kassis**[34] 3727 7-11-0 103 MichealNolan 113
(Jamie Snowden) *j. slowly 3rd: prom tl rdden after 3 out: 4th and outpcd by ldng pair whn hit next: hit last* 100/1

4134 5 15 **Rosa Fleet (IRE)**[49] 3499 8-11-0 115 LiamTreadwell 100
(Venetia Williams) *mstkes in last: struggling 12th: t.o whn mstke next* 40/1

5m 12.9s (7.60) **Going Correction** +0.70s/f (Soft) 5 Ran SP% 107.8
Speed ratings: **112,111,105,104,98**
CSF £4.18 TOTE £3.30: £1.60, £1.10; EX 5.00 Trifecta £8.20.
Owner J Perriss **Bred** Robert McCarthy **Trained** Andoversford, Gloucs
■ Stewards' Enquiry : David Bass two-day ban: use of whip (10-11 March)

FOCUS
Due to rail movements this race was run over 50yds further than advertised. The first running of this, it saw the rematch between the big two in the market, having contested a similar race at Carlisle in November, and the outcome was the same.

4320 WATCH RACING UK TODAY JUST £10 BRAMPTON MARES' H'CAP HURDLE (8 hdls) 1m 7f 171y

3:20 (3:21) (Class 4) (0-115,113) 4-Y-0+ £3,249 (£954; £477; £238)

Form RPR

1042 1 **Hope's Wishes**[21] 3950 6-11-1 109 HarryCobden(7) 112+
(Barry Brennan) *dug toes in briefly and lost 10 l at s: sn rcvrd and wnt 3rd at 3rd: tk 2nd and hit 3 out: rdn bef last: led fnl 100yds and styd on stoutly* 7/2[2]

32 2 2 **Deja Bougg**[61] 3252 5-11-8 109 MarkQuinlan 110
(Neil Mulholland) *settled towards rr: mstke 5th and pushed along: drvn into 3rd home turn: no real imp fr last but wnt 2nd cl home: wnr in command* 12/1

4-51 3 nk **May Hay**[68] 3163 6-11-12 113 JackQuinlan 113
(Anthony Carson) *led 2nd: j.w: 3 l clr 2 out: rdn bef last: hdd fnl 100yds: wkng whn lost 2nd nr fin* 4/1[3]

2005 4 3 ¾ **Midtech Valentine**[55] 3418 5-10-13 100 RichardJohnson 97
(Ian Williams) *midfield: 5th and rdn home turn: one-pced and nvr threatened to get on terms after* 13/2

1105 5 4 **Stoneham**[17] 3681 5-11-7 111 KieronEdgar(3) 104
(Iain Jardine) *a abt same pl: rdn after 3 out and disp 3rd briefly home turn: plugged on and n.d after* 10/1

PU26 6 4 ½ **Drombeg West**[27] 3846 9-11-1 102 AndrewTinkler 91
(Anna Brooks) *last pair: drvn 3 out: nvr looked like getting in a blow* 10/1

1 7 63 **Comragh (IRE)**[106] 2428 6-11-7 108 NickScholfield 40
(Jeremy Scott) *plld hrd: led tl 2nd: chsd wnr tl bef 3 out where wkng whn j. slowly: sn eased and t.o* 9/4[1]

4m 2.1s (7.20) **Going Correction** +0.575s/f (Soft) 7 Ran SP% 112.2
Speed ratings (Par 105): **105,104,103,101,99 97,66**
CSF £39.19 TOTE £3.90: £1.70, £4.70; EX 48.60 Trifecta £134.20.
Owner M J Hills **Bred** Edward Spurrier **Trained** Upper Lambourn, Berks
■ Stewards' Enquiry : Nick Scholfield trainer said that the mare had a breathing problem

FOCUS
Due to rail movements this race was run over 68yds further than advertised. Modest mares' form, with the first four running pretty much to their marks, and they went steady early.

4321 RACING UK JOHN BIGG OXO H'CAP CHASE (16 fncs) 2m 3f 189y

3:55 (3:55) (Class 4) (0-115,115) 5-Y-0+ £3,898 (£1,144; £572; £286)

Form RPR

31-3 1 **Vazaro Delafayette (FR)**[14] 4071 7-11-6 109 (b) TomScudamore 131+
(David Pipe) *jumping lacked conviction early: last tl impr grad fr 7th: wnt 2nd wl bef 2 out where j. ahd: 3 l clr next: cruising along after and nvr knew he'd had a r* 13/8[1]

4331 2 11 **Here I Am (IRE)**[144] 1767 9-11-5 108 MarcGoldstein 115
(Diana Grissell) *led: 12 l clr at 5th: pressed fr 10th: passed briefly 3 out: rdn and hdd and nt fluent 2 out: plugged on gamely but nt in league of wnr after: j.lft last* 9/1

P562 3 8 **Hollow Blue Sky (FR)**[27] 3836 9-11-7 115 (tp) JamieBargary(5) 115
(Nigel Twiston-Davies) *v slow 1st: tended to jump indifferently: chsd ldrs: effrt after 3 out: little rspnse and sn lost tch w ldrs: poor 5th whn hit 2 out: plodded into poor 3rd after last* 11/4[2]

4325 4 7 **Guanciale**[22] 3931 9-10-9 98 RobertDunne 88
(Dai Burchell) *chsd ldrs: effrt 13th: rdn and wknd bef 2 out* 16/1

2-PP 5 27 **Its A Sting (IRE)**[78] 2973 7-11-12 115 LeightonAspell 76
(Oliver Sherwood) *chsd clr ldr: clsd 10th: led briefly 3 out: rdn and fdd tamely bef next* 9/2[3]

3-46 P **Morgan's Bay**[83] 2884 11-11-12 115 TomCannon
(Laura Mongan) *towards rr: struggling after mstke 10th: mstke 13th: t.o and p.u after 3 out* 20/1

34 P **Dalkadam (FR)**[17] 4026 5-11-5 110 AidanColeman
(J R Jenkins) *tall mgy: bhd: struggling 10th: t.o 13th: p.u 2 out* 12/1

5m 15.4s (10.10) **Going Correction** +0.70s/f (Soft)
WFA 5 from 7yo+ 2lb 7 Ran SP% 111.3
Speed ratings: **107,102,99,96,85**
CSF £15.38 TOTE £1.90: £1.20, £3.30; EX 13.40 Trifecta £34.10.
Owner Bryan Drew **Bred** Mrs Jean-Jacques Augier **Trained** Nicholashayne, Devon

FOCUS
Due to rail movements this race was run over 50yds further than advertised. No hanging around early courtesy of the runner-up and the race rather fell apart. The form therefore isn't worth much, though still a big step up from the winner.

4322 WATCH THE CHELTENHAM FESTIVAL ON RACINGUK "NATIONAL HUNT" MAIDEN HURDLE (DIV I) (10 hdls) 2m 4f 145y

4:30 (4:33) (Class 5) 4-Y-0+ £2,599 (£763; £381; £190)

Form RPR

-234 1 **Board Of Trade**[57] 3370 5-11-1 132 TomBellamy(3) 119+
(Alan King) *cl up in 4th pl: effrt bef 3 out: sn pressing ldr: rdn to ld last: a jst doing enough after* 6/5[1]

2-2 2 1 **Boy In A Bentley (IRE)**[290] 242 6-11-4 0 DavidBass 118+
(Kim Bailey) *2nd mostly tl led 3 out: sn drvn: nt fluent next: hdd last: kpt on steadily after but a jst hld* 12/1

2-53 3 1 ½ **Ten Sixty (IRE)**[27] 3842 6-11-4 0 RichardJohnson 115
(Philip Hobbs) *pressed ldrs: effrt 3 out: abt 4 l 3rd fr bef next: drvn and kpt styng on after last* 2/1[2]

PU **4** *8* **Tango Unchained (IRE)**[27] 3839 7-11-1 0.................. HarryBannister(3) 107
(Charlie Mann) *bhd: shkn up in last but one after 5th: passed btn horses fr after 3 out: mstke next: nvr rchd ldrs* **150/1**

6- **5** *3½* **Micks Lad (IRE)**[372] 4296 6-11-4 0.................. HarrySkelton 105
(Dan Skelton) *nt fluent: settled towards rr: hdwy 7th: 4th and rdn after 3 out: btn bef next* **9/1**

0 **6** *6* **Derksen (IRE)**[27] 3839 6-11-4 0.................. JeremiahMcGrath 98
(Nicky Henderson) *tall str: pressed ldrs tl rdn and wknd after 3 out: mstke next* **40/1**

6 **7** *¾* **Neumond (GER)**[96] 2630 5-11-4 0.................. NicodeBoinville 98
(Nicky Henderson) *midfield: rdn 3 out: sn btn but rallied and styng on nicely after last* **9/2**[3]

4/ **8** *1* **Truckers First**[974] 842 8-10-11 0.................. TomO'Brien 89
(Ian Williams) *hld up towards rr: lost tch bef 3 out* **100/1**

16P **9** *3½* **Improved (IRE)**[48] 3508 6-11-1 0.................. AdamNicol(3) 92
(Philip Kirby) *hld up last tl 6th: nvr nr ldrs* **66/1**

5 **10** *25* **Doasuwouldbedoneby (IRE)**[24] 3907 5-11-4 0.................. TomCannon 67
(David Arbuthnot) *t.k.h: mstke 3rd: 3rd tl wnt 2nd briefly at 6th: rdn and lost pl qckly bef 3 out: t.o* **100/1**

00 **11** *33* **Heighnow**[113] 2277 5-10-11 0.................. PaulMoloney 27
(Conrad Allen) *led: hdd 3 out: lost pl rapidly: t.o and eased bef last* **200/1**

P **King Of Milan (IRE)**[284] 6-11-4 0.................. PeterCarberry
(Des Donovan) *tall chser type: midfield tl wknd and blnd 7th: t.o and p.u 2 out* **100/1**

5m 34.2s (23.60) **Going Correction** +0.575s/f (Soft) **12 Ran SP% 122.7**
Speed ratings (Par 103): **78,77,77,74,72 70,70,69,68,58 46,**
CSF £19.08 TOTE £1.70: £1.10, £2.50, £1.10; EX 15.20 Trifecta £35.90.
Owner Ian Payne & Kim Franklin **Bred** Mrs S C Welch **Trained** Barbury Castle, Wilts
■ Stewards' Enquiry : Harry Skelton jockey said that the gelding lugged left under pressure
Nico de Boinville jockey said that the gelding ran too freely

FOCUS
Due to rail movements this race was run over 78yds further than advertised. No gallop on here in division one of a fair maiden hurdle and hard to be confident about the form. It still looked the stronger of the two legs, though.

4323 WATCH THE CHELTENHAM FESTIVAL ON RACINGUK "NATIONAL HUNT" MAIDEN HURDLE (DIV II) (10 hdls) 2m 4f 145y
5:05 (5:06) (Class 5) 4-Y-0+ £2,599 (£763; £381; £190)

Form RPR

P **1** **Treaty Girl (IRE)**[28] 3825 5-10-11 0.................. NicodeBoinville 124+
(Ben Pauling) *settled in 3rd or 4th pl: rdn after 3 out: chal and lft in ld and bmpd next: 3 l clr last: kpt up to work but in command after* **33/1**

2 **2** *10* **Cottersrock (IRE)**[27] 3839 6-11-4 0.................. AndrewTinkler 125
(Martin Keighley) *3rd or 4th tl wnt 2nd 3 out: dropped bk 3rd and rdn whn lft 2nd and sltly impeded next: hld whn ungainly jump last* **11/4**[2]

3 *1¾* **Clondaw Fonz (IRE)**[88] 5-11-1 0.................. TomBellamy(3) 119
(Alan King) *midfield: 5th and drvn and outpcd home turn: 12 l 3rd at last: wnt 3rd flat and kpt on steadily* **12/1**

1-P0 **4** *2¼* **Duke Arcadio (IRE)**[13] 4097 7-11-4 0.................. LeightonAspell 120+
(Oliver Sherwood) *hit 2nd: disp ld tl bef 6th: pressed ldr tl 3 out: rdn and no ex next: hung lft and lost 3rd flat* **16/1**

-336 **5** *28* **Minstrel Royal**[33] 3736 6-11-4 0.................. DavidBass 97
(Nicky Henderson) *hld up in midfield: mstke 6th: lost tch after next: nt fluent last: sn eased: t.o* **4/1**[3]

63P5 **6** *4½* **Rock Chick Supremo (IRE)**[16] 4039 5-10-11 0.................. HarrySkelton 81
(Dan Skelton) *hld up towards rr: struggling bef 3 out: t.o* **66/1**

4-10 **7** *22* **Top Priority (FR)**[76] 3022 5-11-4 0.................. RichardJohnson 68
(Jonjo O'Neill) *chsd ldrs: rdn whn hit 3 out: no ch after: t.o* **9/1**

8 *4* **Funny Irish (FR)**[74] 5-11-4 0.................. TomMessenger 65
(Fiona Kehoe) *towards rr: lost tch bef 3 out: t.o* **100/1**

0-P **9** *nse* **Midnight Owle**[300] 56 6-11-4 0..................(t) JoshuaMoore 65
(Claire Dyson) *midfield tl 6th: struggling bef 3 out: t.o* **200/1**

3-13 **F** **Penn Lane (IRE)**[74] 3063 5-11-4 0.................. GavinSheehan 126+
(Warren Greatrex) *disp ld tl led 6th: rdn bef 2 out where fell whn hrd pressed* **6/4**[1]

6-0P **P** **Silver Ticket (IRE)**[69] 3133 5-11-4 0.................. TomCannon
(Laura Mongan) *a last: hit 5th: hung lft bef next and rdn: t.o 7th: p.u next* **200/1**

5m 24.8s (14.20) **Going Correction** +0.575s/f (Soft) **11 Ran SP% 116.7**
Speed ratings (Par 103): **95,91,90,89,79 77,68,67,67,**
CSF £125.63 TOTE £25.20: £4.80, £1.10, £2.30; EX 138.40 Trifecta £885.20.
Owner The Bourtoneers **Bred** Anthony P Butler **Trained** Bourton-On-The-Water, Gloucs
■ Stewards' Enquiry : Richard Johnson jockey said that the gelding made a significant jumping error at the third last

FOCUS
Due to rail movements this race was run over 78yds further than advertised. Much more pace on here than in division one and those who raced up on the speed were left vulnerable in the straight, resulting in a surprise winner.
T/Plt: £21.90 to a £1 stake. Pool: £53331.11 - 1777.5 winning tickets T/Qpdt: £4.30 to a £1 stake. Pool: £3488.26 - 597.86 winning tickets **Iain Mackenzie**

4044 SEDGEFIELD (L-H)
Thursday, February 25

OFFICIAL GOING: Good to soft (soft in places; 5.9)
Wind: light 1/2 behind Weather: fine but cold

4324 BETFRED CONDITIONAL JOCKEYS' NOVICES' HURDLE (BETFRED HURDLE SERIES QUALIFIER) (8 hdls) 2m 178y
2:25 (2:25) (Class 4) 4-Y-0+ £3,508 (£1,030; £515; £257)

Form RPR

F **1** **Flemensfirthleader**[58] 3340 7-10-6 0.................. PaulO'Brien(3) 121+
(Keith Dalgleish) *mde all: t.k.h: pushed clr sn after 3 out: shkn up between last 2: readily* **8/11**[1]

12 **2** *9* **Samtu (IRE)**[141] 1806 5-11-5 116..................(t) ThomasCheesman(3) 123+
(Dan Skelton) *trckd ldrs: sddle slipped after 2nd: outpcd sn after 6th: kpt on to take modest 2nd appr last: no ch w wnr* **7/1**

24 **3** *5* **Caged Lightning (IRE)**[48] 3509 6-10-13 115..........(p) MichaelHeard(3) 111
(Steve Gollings) *chsd ldrs: drvn 6th: sn outpcd: kpt on to take poor 3rd last 75yds* **3/1**[2]

3 **4** *6* **Invictus (GER)**[20] 3967 4-9-13 0.................. FinianO'Toole(8) 100
(Micky Hammond) *trckd ldrs: chsd wnr sn after 3 out: reminders bef next: 8 l down whn blnd 2 out: wknd appr last* **13/2**[3]

P3 **5** *9* **Fibre Optic**[13] 4104 4-9-13 0.................. LorcanMurtagh(8) 88
(Rose Dobbin) *trckd ldrs 4th: drvn along next: wknd between last 2* **12/1**

346 **6** *13* **Captain Mowbray**[14] 4064 5-10-13 0.................. ConorSmith(3) 83
(Rebecca Menzies) *in rr: bhd and drvn 4th* **100/1**

005P **P** **Hey Up Ashey**[34] 3724 6-10-13 0.................. JoshWall(3)
(Michael Mullineaux) *in rr: pushed along after 2nd: lost pl and p.u bef 4th: fatally injured* **100/1**

4m 16.6s (9.70) **Going Correction** +0.80s/f (Soft)
WFA 4 from 5yo+ 9lb **7 Ran SP% 118.4**
Speed ratings (Par 105): **109,104,102,99,95 89,**
CSF £7.56 TOTE £1.40: £1.10, £2.40; EX 6.90 Trifecta £10.80.
Owner Tom Young **Bred** David Williams **Trained** Carluke, S Lanarks

FOCUS
All race distances as advertised. The first three were all taking a drop in trip, some by quite a lot, so it remains to be seen how strong this form is.

4325 WILLS PROPERTY SERVICES H'CAP CHASE (16 fncs) 2m 3f 65y
2:55 (2:55) (Class 5) (0-100,100) 5-Y-0+ £3,119 (£915; £457; £228)

Form RPR

-233 **1** **Oscar O'Scar (IRE)**[20] 3968 8-11-5 100.................. FinianO'Toole(7) 121+
(Micky Hammond) *mid-div: hdwy 10th: 2nd 13th: led 2 out: wnt clr bef last: eased clsng stages* **10/3**[2]

2252 **2** *16* **Discoverie**[20] 3968 8-10-6 80..................(b) HenryBrooke 85
(Kenneth Slack) *chsd ldr: led 12th: hdd 2 out: kpt on same pce: no ch w wnr* **9/4**[1]

00-2 **3** *2* **Halcyon Days**[29] 3805 7-10-9 88.................. JamieHamilton(5) 91+
(Rebecca Menzies) *sn chsng ldrs: mstke 4th: blnd bdly and rdr lost irons 12th: regained them bef 3 out: modest 3rd between last 2* **16/1**

RP05 **4** *3* **Dundee Blue (IRE)**[16] 4048 8-9-9 76..................(tp) MissETodd(7) 74
(Henry Hogarth) *in rr: hit 6th: sme hdwy 11th: tk poor 4th appr last* **10/1**

36F4 **5** *1¾* **Court Of Law (IRE)**[17] 4034 8-11-0 93..................(p) JamesCowley(5) 88
(Donald McCain) *led: reminders 11th: hdd next: wknd between last 2* **6/1**[3]

350P **6** *7* **Attention Please (IRE)**[17] 4034 6-10-9 83..................(b[1]) CraigNichol 72
(Rose Dobbin) *chsd ldrs: nt fluent 2nd: lost pl 12th: sn bhd* **11/1**

6040 **7** *4* **Devon River (FR)**[20] 3968 6-10-13 92..................(p) CallumBewley(5) 77
(Simon Waugh) *chsd ldrs: hit 7th: lost pl 11th: sn bhd* **28/1**

6241 **8** *3* **Rosquero (FR)**[22] 3938 11-10-5 86..................(b) MrWHRReed(7) 67
(Kenny Johnson) *chsd ldrs: drvn 8th: lost pl 10th: sn bhd* **15/2**

-R0P **P** **Zazamix (FR)**[59] 3308 11-9-11 74 oh6..................(b) JohnKington(3)
(Andrew Crook) *in rr: bhd 7th: t.o 10th: p.u bef 3 out* **50/1**

-UPR **P** **Hi Bob**[55] 3419 8-11-2 90..................(p) DannyCook
(Lucinda Egerton) *sn bhd: nt fluent 2nd: reminders 7th: t.o whn p.u bef 9th* **20/1**

5m 7.8s (4.80) **Going Correction** +0.25s/f (Yiel) **10 Ran SP% 113.4**
Speed ratings: **99,92,91,90,89 86,84,83,,**
CSF £11.15 CT £100.09 TOTE £3.70: £1.70, £2.60, £4.10; EX 12.50 Trifecta £117.50.
Owner Newroc 1 **Bred** Miss Christine Keymer **Trained** Middleham, N Yorks

FOCUS
A really weak contest, with the top weight and winner coming into it a 16-raced maiden. The gallop set by the leaders appeared to be strong.

4326 JOHN WADE GROUP H'CAP HURDLE (8 hdls) 2m 178y
3:30 (3:30) (Class 4) (0-105,105) 4-Y-0+ £3,508 (£1,030; £515; £257)

Form RPR

-063 **1** **Jokers And Rogues (IRE)**[10] 4152 8-11-1 94..................(t) HenryBrooke 114+
(Kenneth Slack) *mde all: clr 5th: 10 l ahd whn blnd bdly 2 out: eased clsng stages* **5/2**[1]

0154 **2** *10* **Nafaath (IRE)**[36] 3680 10-11-1 104..................(p) RonanShort(10) 112
(Donald McCain) *chsd ldrs: 2nd 5th: kpt on fr 2 out: no ch w wnr* **5/1**[2]

2444 **3** *13* **Gunner Lindley (IRE)**[29] 3807 9-10-1 87..................(p) SamColtherd(5) 82
(Stuart Coltherd) *chsd wnr to 5th: one pce fr 6th* **12/1**

3534 **4** *½* **Down Time (USA)**[17] 4035 6-11-1 99..................(b) MeganCarberry(5) 94
(Brian Ellison) *chsd ;ldrs: drvn 5th: one pce fr next* **6/1**[3]

0452 **5** *1¾* **King's Chorister**[16] 4049 10-9-7 79 oh2..................(t) LorcanMurtagh(5) 71
(Barry Murtagh) *mid-div: hdwy to chse ldrs 3 out: poor 4th whn mstke last* **10/1**

5530 **6** *3¼* **Karisma King**[61] 3242 7-11-2 105.................. StephenMcCarthy(10) 95
(Sue Smith) *chsd ldrs: mstke 1st: lost pl after 5th: kpt on fr 2 out* **5/1**[2]

1600 **7** *5* **Bertie Moon**[43] 1677 6-11-5 98.................. BrianHarding 82
(Keith Dalgleish) *hld up in rr: hdwy 5th: chsng ldrs next: wknd 2 out* **13/2**

346P **8** *nk* **Endeavor**[58] 3343 11-11-6 102.................. EmmaSayer(3) 85
(Dianne Sayer) *in rr: drvn 5th: sme hdwy next: sn lost pl* **25/1**

2064 **9** *¾* **Strait Run (IRE)**[16] 4049 5-10-1 83..................(p) JoeColliver(3) 67
(Micky Hammond) *in rr: pushed along and hit 4th: nvr on terms* **28/1**

205/ **P** **Magic Haze**[1056] 5164 10-11-1 94.................. BrianHughes
(Sally Hall) *chsd ldrs: drvn 5th: sn lost pl: bhd bef 2 out: t.o whn p.u bef last* **33/1**

4m 16.8s (9.90) **Going Correction** +0.80s/f (Soft) **10 Ran SP% 116.5**
Speed ratings (Par 105): **108,103,97,96,96 94,92,92,91,**
CSF £15.43 CT £126.03 TOTE £3.60: £2.40, £1.50, £2.10; EX 18.40 Trifecta £89.20.
Owner A Slack **Bred** J P Russell **Trained** Hilton, Cumbria

FOCUS
A moderate contest, in which the highest-rated runner was a seven-raced maiden. A big step up from the winner.

4327 WEATHERBYS BANK CHASE (A NOVICES' LIMITED H'CAP) (17 fncs) 2m 5f 28y
4:05 (4:05) (Class 4) (0-120,120) 5-Y-0+ £4,158 (£1,221; £610; £305)

Form RPR

1142 **1** **Verko (FR)**[16] 4046 7-9-13 104.................. FinianO'Toole(7) 114+
(Micky Hammond) *detached in last: blnd 9th: hdwy 12th: 3rd 13th: chsng ldrs 2 out: sn swtchd rt: styd on to ld appr last: drvn out* **7/4**[1]

0541 **2** *1* **Finea (IRE)**[8] 4177 9-11-2 114 7ex..................(tp) BrianHughes 121
(R K Watson, Ire) *trckd ldrs: 2nd after 12th: upsides and rdn between last 2: kpt on same pce clsng stages* **2/1**[2]

4463 **3** *2* **Chanceofa Lifetime (IRE)**[8] 4177 9-10-3 108.................. MissPFuller(7) 114
(Victor Thompson) *led to 2nd: led 3rd: hdd and hit last: kpt on same pce* **9/2**[3]

10UP **4** *55* **Ashbrittle**[35] 3705 9-11-8 120..................(bt) TrevorWhelan 69
(Neil King) *w ldr: led 2nd to next: reminders 4th: drvn next: hit 12th: lost pl next: t.o 4th 3 out* **5/1**

P-0P **P** **Bolero Collonges (FR)**[29] 3807 5-9-12 103..................(b[1]) CallumBewley(5)
(Simon Waugh) *chsd ldrs: drvn 11th: lost pl next: t.o whn j.rt 3 out: p.u bef last* **25/1**

5m 34.7s (1.70) **Going Correction** +0.25s/f (Yiel)
WFA 5 from 7yo+ 2lb **5 Ran SP% 108.4**
Speed ratings: **106,105,104,83,**
CSF £5.69 TOTE £2.40: £1.40, £1.30; EX 5.70 Trifecta £10.90.
Owner David Green **Bred** E A R L Trinquet, M & O Trinquet **Trained** Middleham, N Yorks

The Form Book Jumps 2015-16, Raceform Ltd, Newbury, RG14 5SJ

FOCUS
A well-run if modest chase. The winner overcame a few errors and ran to his best.

4328 WEATHERBYS HAMILTON H'CAP HURDLE 2m 3f 188y
4:40 (4:40) (Class 4) (0-120,117) 4-Y-0+ **£3,508** (£1,030; £515; £257)

Form RPR
1412 1 **Almost Gemini (IRE)**[17] 4035 7-11-6 **110**..........(p) HenryBrooke 119+
(Kenneth Slack) *trckd ldrs: 2nd bef 2 out: led between last 2: hit last: drvn out* **11/4**[1]
54/2 2 *6* **Charlie Wingnut (IRE)**[16] 4045 9-10-6 **96**.......... DannyCook 98
(Sue Smith) *led: drvn bef 2 out: hdd between last 2: kpt on same pce* **3/1**[2]
1263 3 *6* **Grey Life**[42] 3589 10-11-10 **114**.......... BrianHughes 109
(Malcolm Jefferson) *hld up towards rr: stdy hdwy appr 8th: 3rd appr 2 out: kpt on one pce* **6/1**
3456 4 *11* **Morning With Ivan (IRE)**[59] 3308 6-10-2 **95**..........(p) JoeColliver(3) 79
(Martin Todhunter) *hld up towards rr: hdwy 5th: outpcd sn after 3 out: poor 4th appr last* **12/1**
2506 5 *10* **Ben Cee Pee M (IRE)**[25] 3884 11-11-2 **111**..........(b) CraigGallagher(5) 88
(Brian Ellison) *chsd ldrs: upsides whn hit 8th: sn drvn: wknd 2 out* **28/1**
5325 6 *5* **Touch Back (IRE)**[61] 3238 10-11-5 **116**.......... MrTommieMO'Brien(7) 87
(Chris Bealby) *chsd ldrs: drvn whn hit 7th: lost pl next* **6/1**
3-30 7 *32* **Sultana Belle (IRE)**[17] 4036 8-11-2 **106**.......... PeterBuchanan 43
(R Mike Smith) *hld up in rr: effrt whn hit 7th: sn wknd: t.o 2 out* **66/1**
33P1 8 *16* **Sign Manual**[10] 4152 7-11-13 **117** 7ex..........(b) WillKennedy 38
(Donald McCain) *chsd ldrs: lost pl 3 out: sn bhd: t.o next* **9/2**[3]
1-26 9 *13* **Stow**[257] 726 11-11-6 **115**..........(p) DeanPratt(5) 23
(Lucinda Egerton) *chsd ldrs: lost pl bef 5th: sn bhd: t.o 8th* **40/1**

5m 7.1s (13.00) **Going Correction** +0.80s/f (Soft) 9 Ran SP% **113.5**
Speed ratings (Par 105): **106,103,101,96,92 90,78,71,66**
CSF £11.40 CT £43.75 TOTE £4.00: £1.50, £1.40, £2.10; EX 17.40 Trifecta £48.50.
Owner E G Tunstall **Bred** Rockhart Trading Ltd **Trained** Hilton, Cumbria

FOCUS
Quite a competitive race for the level. The winner is closing in on the level you would expect on the best of his Flat form.

4329 NO WIN NO FEE RACING SYNDICATE H'CAP CHASE (13 fncs) 2m 77y
5:15 (5:15) (Class 5) (0-100,99) 5-Y-0+ **£2,989** (£877; £438; £219)

Form RPR
3142 1 **Roxyfet (FR)**[16] 4048 6-11-4 **98**.......... FinianO'Toole(7) 115+
(Micky Hammond) *hld up towards rr: hdwy 7th: trcking ldrs 10th: cl 2nd appr 2 out: led appr last: styd on strly to go clr: eased towards fin* **9/1**
4454 2 *9* **Duhallowcountry (IRE)**[37] 3670 10-9-12 **78**..........(p) MissAWaugh(7) 85
(Victor Thompson) *chsd ldrs: 2nd 6th: led bef 3 out: hdd appr last: kpt on: no ch w wnr* **20/1**
0304 3 *6* **Odds On Dan (IRE)**[16] 4048 10-9-9 **73**..........(tp) DeanPratt(5) 74
(Lucinda Egerton) *nt fluent: sn detached in last: hit 6th: reminders 8th: t.o 10th: hdwy appr next: lft poor 4th last: tk 3rd nr fin* **9/1**
4053 4 *¾* **Seventeen Black (IRE)**[16] 4045 8-9-10 **76**.......... SamColtherd(7) 77
(Stuart Coltherd) *in rr: blnd 1st: sn bhd: kpt on fr 3 out: lft poor 3rd last* **5/1**[3]
0451 5 *6* **Captain Sharpe**[16] 4048 8-10-1 **81**..........(b) MrWHRReed(7) 73
(Kenny Johnson) *chsd ldrs 5th: one pce fr 3 out* **12/1**
4FU3 6 *11* **Gin Cobbler**[16] 4048 10-11-2 **96**.......... MissPFuller(7) 80
(Victor Thompson) *led: hdd bef 3 out: wknd between last 2* **14/1**
6423 7 *2 ¾* **Asuncion (FR)**[17] 4034 6-10-1 **74**..........(b) BrianHughes 54
(Rebecca Menzies) *chsd ldrs: lost pl after 10th: sn bhd* **9/2**[2]
40U6 8 *16* **Miss Conway**[20] 3968 5-10-6 **80**.......... JakeGreenall 42
(Mark Walford) *chsd ldrs: lost pl bef 3 out: sn bhd* **14/1**
306P U **Calton Entry (IRE)**[90] 2755 7-11-7 **99**.......... CallumBewley(5) 102
(Katie Scott) *mid-div: hdwy to chse ldrs 10th: 3rd appr 2 out: modest 3rd and one pce whn blnd last: sn uns rdr* **33/1**
6000 P **Inchcolm (IRE)**[27] 3834 6-10-8 **84**.......... JoeColliver(3)
(Micky Hammond) *in rr: prom whn hit 5th: lost pl 7th: sn bhd: t.o whn p.u bef 2 out* **20/1**
-655 P **Bennylicious (IRE)**[20] 3968 7-11-4 **91**.......... CraigNichol
(Rose Dobbin) *chsd ldrs: drvn and lost pl 9th: bhd after next: t.o whn p.u bef 2 out* **5/2**[1]

4m 16.3s (2.30) **Going Correction** +0.25s/f (Yiel)
WFA 5 from 6yo+ 1lb 11 Ran SP% **116.9**
Speed ratings: **104,99,96,96,93 87,86,78, ,**
CSF £163.16 CT £1665.02 TOTE £6.10: £1.90, £4.60, £2.60; EX 132.10 Trifecta £1400.80.
Owner R J Ball **Bred** Jacky Thomas **Trained** Middleham, N Yorks

FOCUS
A moderate contest that the winner took with plenty in hand. He is in line with his French rating.
T/Plt: £8.60 to a £1 stake. Pool: £65,605.08 - 5530.96 winning units. T/Qpdt: £5.00 to as £1 stake. Pool: £4,539.95 - 666.77 winning units. **Walter Glynn**

4330 - 4331a (Foreign Racing) - See Raceform Interactive

4082 THURLES (R-H)
Thursday, February 25

OFFICIAL GOING: Soft (soft to heavy in places on chase course)

4332a AT THE RACES MICHAEL PURCELL MEMORIAL NOVICE HURDLE (GRADE 2) (12 hdls) 2m 4f
3:15 (3:15) 5-Y-0+ **£19,522** (£6,286; £2,977)

RPR
1 **Acapella Bourgeois (FR)**[32] 3765 6-11-3 **132**.......... RWalsh 139+
(Ms Sandra Hughes, Ire) *led 1st where slt mstke: jnd briefly next: pushed along and 1 l up into st: slt mstke 2 out and jnd: rdn to regain ld between last 2: over 1 l clr whn bad mstke last: pressed briefly tl kpt on wl to assert* **5/2**[2]
2 *5* **Nambour (GER)**[56] 3393 6-11-3 **0**..........(t) BJCooper 134+
(W P Mullins, Ire) *settled bhd ldr: disp briefly 2nd: settled in 3rd after next: impr bhd ldr and disp cl 2nd whn lft 2nd 3 out: rdn to dispute ld fr 2 out: hdd u.p between last 2: no ex in 2nd run-in* **7/2**[3]
3 *74* **Road To Respect (IRE)**[14] 4086 5-11-1 **130**.......... DavyRussell 63
(Eoin Griffin, Ire) *w.w in rr of quintet: j.big 1st: wnt 4th at 4th: disp 3rd briefly bef 6th: pushed along in 4th bef 4 out and sn lost tch: lft remote 3rd 3 out: t.o* **14/1**
F **Edwulf**[40] 3636 7-11-3 **130**..........(t) BarryGeraghty 128+
(A P O'Brien, Ire) *chsd ldrs in 4th tl impr into 2nd after 3rd: niggled along in 2nd after 4 out: disp cl 2nd whn fell next* **10/1**
P **Our Duke (IRE)**[39] 3648 6-11-3 **0**.......... RobbiePower
(Mrs John Harrington, Ire) *settled bhd ldrs: almost on terms bef 3rd: dropped to 4th after 3rd and niggled along: dropped to rr next and pushed along: lost tch bef 7th where eased and slt mstke: p.u after 7th* **6/5**[1]

5m 9.9s (309.90) 5 Ran SP% **112.0**
CSF £11.71 TOTE £2.40: £1.02, £2.00; DF 10.10 Trifecta £27.60.
Owner Slaneyville Syndicate **Bred** Jean-Paul Bannier & Mme Michele Bannier **Trained** Kildare, Co Kildare

FOCUS
A gutsy performance in the end from the winner despite a mistake at the final flight, and he's certainly improving.

4333 - 4336a (Foreign Racing) - See Raceform Interactive

4137 EXETER (R-H)
Friday, February 26

OFFICIAL GOING: Soft (6.3)
Wind: strong behind Weather: overcast Rails: Races 1, 2, 3 & 7 add 65yds; Race 4 add 60yds; Race 5 add 45yds; Race 6 add 115yds. All races to be run on chase bends.

4337 CALL STAR SPORTS ON 08000 521 321 MARES NOVICES' HURDLE (8 hdls) 2m 175y
2:20 (2:21) (Class 4) 4-Y-0+ **£3,328** (£1,033; £556)

Form RPR
1152 1 **Girly Girl (IRE)**[29] 3817 7-11-5 **120**.......... HarrySkelton 120+
(Dan Skelton) *j.lft at times: mde virtually all: wnt lft 3 out: sn drvn: jnd next: bmpd sn after: narrowly hdd whn lft wl clr last* **2/5**[1]
62 2 *41* **Pennywell (IRE)**[17] 4039 6-10-12 **0**.......... GavinSheehan 91
(Warren Greatrex) *trckd wnr most of way tl rdn appr 3 out: wknd 2 out: lft 2nd at the last* **7/2**[2]
00U 3 *8* **Sahara Haze**[34] 3744 7-10-7 **0**.......... MrBMoorcroft(5) 66
(Phillip Dando) *j.lft: trckd ldrs: j. v bdly lft last 3: rdn appr 3 out: sn wknd: lft modest 3rd at the last* **100/1**
530 P **Purple Genie (GR)**[72] 3118 4-10-3 **0**.......... JamesDavies
(Patrick Chamings) *chsd ldrs: struggling 4th: wknd next: t.o whn p.u bef 3 out* **28/1**
4-0 F **Lapalala (IRE)**[301] 67 5-10-12 **0**.......... TomO'Brien 111
(Philip Hobbs) *trckd ldrs: tk clsr order after 5th: chal 2 out: sn drifted lft and bmpd wnr: pushed into narrow advantage whn knuckled on landing and fell last* **8/1**[3]
0 P **Shady Grey**[85] 2875 6-10-12 **0**.......... JamesBest
(Kevin Bishop) *last but in tch: struggling 3rd: wknd bef 3 out: t.o whn p.u bef last* **100/1**

4m 49.3s (33.80) **Going Correction** +1.95s/f (Heav)
WFA 4 from 5yo+ 9lb 6 Ran SP% **110.2**
Speed ratings (Par 105): **98,78,74, ,**
CSF £2.13 TOTE £1.40: £1.10, £1.40; EX 2.30 Trifecta £33.70.
Owner T Crowe **Bred** Sean McNamara **Trained** Alcester, Warwicks

FOCUS
A windy day, with it behind runners down the home straight. All races were run on the chase bends. This probably wasn't a bad little mares' novice hurdle and the winner has been rated in line with her previous best. Due to rail movements the race was run over 65yds further than advertised.

4338 LATESTFREEBETOFFERS.COM MARES' H'CAP HURDLE (QUALIFIER FOR CHALLENGER MARES' HURDLE SERIES FINAL) (10 hdls) 2m 2f 111y
2:50 (2:50) (Class 3) (0-130,129) 4-Y-0+ **£5,848** (£1,717; £858; £429)

Form RPR
2-64 1 **Hannah's Princess (IRE)**[90] 2775 7-11-8 **125**.......... GavinSheehan 133+
(Warren Greatrex) *hld up last: hdwy appr 3 out: rdn to chal between last 2: led last: styd on wl to assert fnl 100yds* **5/2**[2]
3-34 2 *6* **Midnight Jazz**[76] 3034 6-11-12 **129**.......... DarylJacob 133
(Ben Case) *a.p: led appr 3 out: rdn whn jnd between last 2: narrowly hdd last: no ex fnl 100yds* **7/2**[3]
0465 3 *22* **Pink Tara**[23] 3930 5-9-11 **103**.......... CallumWhillans(3) 85
(Venetia Williams) *led: rdn and hdd appr 3 out: sn outpcd: plugged on to regain 3rd run-in* **18/1**
2133 4 *¾* **Anda De Grissay (FR)**[23] 3921 6-11-5 **122**..........(t) NickScholfield 102
(Anthony Honeyball) *trckd ldrs: rdn appr 3 out: sn outpcd: plugged on to regain 4th run-in* **16/1**
211 5 *1 ½* **Pemba (FR)**[43] 3587 4-10-7 **120**.......... WayneHutchinson 88
(Alan King) *trckd ldrs: rdn appr 3 out: sn hld: fdd fr 2 out: lost modest 3rd run-in* **7/4**[1]
4-56 6 *23* **Loyaute (FR)**[116] 2247 9-11-4 **121**..........(t) JamesDavies 76
(Chris Down) *chsd ldrs tl rdn 7th: sn bhd: t.o* **8/1**

5m 15.6s (32.90) **Going Correction** +1.95s/f (Heav)
WFA 4 from 5yo+ 9lb 6 Ran SP% **109.4**
Speed ratings (Par 107): **108,105,96,95,95 85**
CSF £11.17 TOTE £6.80: £2.90, £1.30; EX 12.50 Trifecta £79.20.
Owner Swanee River Partnership **Bred** Gary Adams **Trained** Upper Lambourn, Berks

FOCUS
Due to rail movements the race was run over 65yds further than advertised. A fair mares' handicap and they went an ordinary gallop. Two came well clear from the penultimate hurdle and the winner is up 5lb on her previous best.

4339 STARSPORTSBET.CO.UK "NATIONAL HUNT" NOVICES' HURDLE (10 hdls) 2m 2f 111y
3:20 (3:20) (Class 4) 4-Y-0+ **£3,249** (£954; £477; £238)

Form RPR
-120 1 **Captain Chaos (IRE)**[56] 3403 5-11-10 **141**.......... HarrySkelton 115+
(Dan Skelton) *hld up: hdwy but nt best of runs bef 3 out: hrd drvn after 2 out: chal last: jockey dropped whip run-in: kpt on: won on nod* **4/6**[1]
2536 2 *nse* **Bindon Mill**[21] 3976 7-11-3 **0**.......... IanPopham 108+
(Victor Dartnall) *trckd ldr: narrow advantage whn hit 2 out: sn rdn: kpt on whn strly and chal fr last: lost on nod* **7/1**[3]
05 3 *shd* **Behind Time (IRE)**[34] 3744 5-11-3 **0**.......... BarryGeraghty 108+
(Harry Fry) *trckd ldrs: nudged along after 7th: rdn to chal bef 2 out: kpt on w ev ch fr last: jst hld* **9/1**
UF 4 *10* **Red Red Rover (IRE)**[34] 3744 6-11-3 **0**.......... DaveCrosse 98
(Nigel Hawke) *led at stdy pce: rdn after 3 out: narrowly hdd next: cl 4th but hld whn awkward last* **50/1**
5 *4 ½* **Firsty (IRE)**[478] 5-11-3 **0**.......... SamTwiston-Davies 92
(Paul Nicholls) *in tch: hdwy 3 out: sn drvn: ch next: no ex appr last* **15/8**[2]

0-60 6 23 **Driftwood Haze**34 3745 8-10-12 0 MrBMoorcroft(5) 69
(Phillip Dando) *trckd ldrs: rdn appr 3 out: wknd bef 2 out* 28/1
00 7 19 **Day Of Roses (IRE)**12 4137 7-11-3 0 NickScholfield 50
(Jeremy Scott) *hld up: struggling 7th: sn lost tch: t.o* 50/1
0 8 3/4 **Tell Tony (IRE)**151 1673 6-11-3 0 MichealNolan 50
(Tim Dennis) *in tch: trckd ldr after 3rd tl rdn bef 3 out: sn wknd: t.o* 100/1
5m 21.6s (38.90) **Going Correction** +1.95s/f (Heav) 8 Ran SP% 125.6
Speed ratings (Par 105): **96,95,95,91,89 80,72,71**
CSF £7.60 TOTE £1.70: £1.02, £2.80, £2.10; EX 11.10 Trifecta £28.60.
Owner Mike And Eileen Newbould **Bred** Conor Hickey **Trained** Alcester, Warwicks

FOCUS
Due to rail movements the race was run over 65yds further than advertised. A novice hurdle that was run at a sedate gallop, resulting in a very tight three-way finish and slow winning time. The race has been rated around the balance of the first three.

4340 HIGOS INSURANCE SERVICES DEVON NATIONAL H'CAP CHASE (21 fncs) 3m 6f 153y
3:55 (3:55) (Class 3) (0-135,131) 5-Y-0+ £14,245 (£5,429)

Form RPR
3-3P 1 **Fourovakind**48 3518 11-11-5 124 (b) GavinSheehan 140+
(Harry Whittington) *mid-div: hdwy 15th: led appr 4 out: in command fr 3 out: comf* 9/2[1]
1544 2 17 **Saroque (IRE)**20 3993 9-11-10 129 LiamTreadwell 133
(Venetia Williams) *led: hit 4th: hdd 14th: rdn in 4th after 17th: regained 3rd next: wnt 2nd 2 out: styd on but nvr any threat to wnr* 8/1[3]
-310 P **Thomas Wild**243 855 11-11-7 126 MichealNolan
(Philip Hobbs) *hld up: struggling 14th: lost tch 17th: p.u bef next* 16/1
-411 F **Armedanddangerous (IRE)**31 3792 11-10-3 108 (b) JamesDavies
(Tom Gretton) *fell heavily 1st* 14/1
R-P5 R **Alpha Victor (IRE)**20 3999 11-11-3 122 (t) PeterBuchanan
(William Kinsey) *in tch: drvn along fr 16th: nvr threatened ldrs: chal for btn 4th 2 out: tired 4th whn ref last* 12/1
/P-5 B **Merlin's Wish**31 3792 11-10-12 117 (p) IanPopham
(Martin Keighley) *b.d 1st* 12/1
332P P **Finish The Story (IRE)**82 2934 10-10-10 115 (bt) AlainCawley
(Johnny Farrelly) *trckd ldrs: led 14th: rdn and hdd bef 4 out: grad fdd: tired 5th whn bdly hmpd and p.u last* 10/1
1P5P P **Teochew (IRE)**27 3866 8-10-5 110 (t) AndrewGlassonbury
(Mark Shears) *trckd ldr tl drvn along after 9th: sn bhd: t.o whn p.u bef 14th* 100/1
0-5P P **Return Spring (IRE)**48 3518 9-11-8 127 (p) JamesBest
(Philip Hobbs) *nvr travelling and sn scrubbed along towards rr: t.o whn p.u after 17th* 9/1
-223 P **Alberobello (IRE)**21 3978 8-11-3 125 (t) MattGriffiths(3)
(Jeremy Scott) *hld up bhd: hdwy 10th: lost pl 14th: rdn into 5th appr 4 out: nvr threatened: p.u bef 2 out* 8/1[3]
/42P F **Nail 'M (IRE)**43 3591 8-10-7 112 (p) SamTwiston-Davies
(Nigel Hawke) *trckd ldrs: bdly hmpd 1st: hit 6th and 9th: rdn after 15th: chsd ldr after 17th tl 3 out: 3rd and hld whn hit 2 out: fell heavily last* 6/1[2]
12P3 P **Wizards Bridge**14 4101 7-11-12 131 (b) DarylJacob
(Colin Tizzard) *trckd ldrs: hit 10th: struggling 14th: wknd after 17th: p.u bef next* 9/2[1]
8m 50.4s (61.80) **Going Correction** +1.95s/f (Heav) 12 Ran SP% 120.9
Speed ratings: **98,93, , , , , , , , , ,**
CSF £41.86 TOTE £7.20: £3.60, £5.50; EX 43.10.
Owner Andrew F Sawyer,G W Hazell & C Bosley **Bred** M G Hazell **Trained** Sparsholt, Oxfordshire

FOCUS
A severe test of stamina, run over 60 yards further than advertised, and only two of the 12-strong field completed.

4341 ANDREW WEST MEMORIAL NOVICES' LIMITED H'CAP CHASE (16 fncs 2 omitted) 3m 54y
4:25 (4:25) (Class 3) 5-Y-0+ £6,564 (£2,104; £1,169)

Form RPR
342 1 **Milansbar (IRE)**13 4116 9-11-3 137 TrevorWhelan 151+
(Neil King) *j.w: trckd ldr: led 4th: rdn after 13th: styd on strly and in command on long run fr last (usual 2 out)* 9/4[2]
1-32 2 8 **Three Faces West (IRE)**42 3611 8-10-10 130 TomO'Brien 136
(Philip Hobbs) *trckd ldrs: rdn appr 3 out (usual 4 out): sn chsng wnr: styd on but a being readily hld on long run fr last (usual 2 out)* 2/1[1]
116P 3 52 **Kingswell Theatre**20 3998 7-11-8 142 (p) TomScudamore 118
(Michael Scudamore) *led tl 4th: trckd wnr: chal after 13th tl rdn bef next where lost 3rd: wknd last (usual 2 out): eased* 7/1
-01P P **Imagine The Chat**27 3849 7-10-7 127 BarryGeraghty
(Rebecca Curtis) *awkward 1st: last but wl in tch: wnt 4th after 9th: nudged after 12th: wknd qckly 3 out (usual 4 out): p.u bef next* 10/3[3]
F144 P **Cyclop (IRE)**26 3885 5-10-7 130 (tp) SamTwiston-Davies
(David Dennis) *trckd ldrs: struggling in last after 9th: losing tch whn p.u next* 12/1
6m 49.5s (40.20) **Going Correction** +1.95s/f (Heav)
WFA 5 from 7yo+ 3lb 5 Ran SP% 107.4
Speed ratings: **111,108,91, ,**
CSF £7.03 TOTE £2.90: £1.20, £2.10; EX 7.00 Trifecta £33.60.
Owner Robert Bothway **Bred** T J Wyatt **Trained** Barbury Castle, Wiltshire

FOCUS
A good-quality staying novice handicap, run at a sound gallop, and the winner is on the upgrade. The race was run over 45 yards further than advertised and the last fence was bypassed.

4342 ROA/RACING POST OWNERS JACKPOT H'CAP HURDLE (12 hdls) 2m 7f 25y
5:00 (5:00) (Class 4) (0-120,120) 4-Y-0+ £3,249 (£954; £477; £238)

Form RPR
2025 1 **Say My Name (IRE)**21 3976 5-11-7 115 (p) LiamHeard 127+
(Bob Buckler) *led 2nd: mde rest: styd on strly fr 3 out: unchal* 12/1
-032 2 15 **Albert D'Olivate (FR)**14 4099 6-11-2 110 (p) SeanBowen 106
(Robert Walford) *led tl 2nd: trckd ldrs: rdn to chse wnr appr 3 out: nvr threatened to get on terms but styd on for clr 2nd* 11/4[1]
3315 3 28 **Precious Ground**24 3919 6-10-1 95 JamesBest 60
(Kevin Bishop) *mid-div: hdwy 6th: sn rdn: nvr threatened to get on terms but plugged on fr 3 out: wnt modest 3rd towards fin: t.o* 13/2[3]
-F34 4 2 1/2 **Baraka De Thaix (FR)**45 3570 5-11-9 117 (t) DarylJacob 80
(David Pipe) *hld up bhd: stdy prog fr 6th: wnt cl enough 3rd after 9th: rdn bef 3 out: fnd nil: lost modest 3rd towards fin: t.o* 17/2
-204 5 64 **Captain McGinley (IRE)**54 3452 6-11-4 112 (p) LeightonAspell 11
(Rebecca Curtis) *trckd ldrs: cl 2nd after 9th: rdn bef next: wknd qckly: t.o* 16/1
/04- P **Royal Charm (FR)**357 4607 11-11-10 118 (b) ConorO'Farrell
(Alexandra Dunn) *mid-div: struggling 8th: sn wknd: t.o whn p.u bef 3 out* 50/1
-P00 P **Ambion Wood (IRE)**36 3705 10-11-7 115 (p) IanPopham
(Victor Dartnall) *chsd ldrs tl dropped to rr on long run after 5th: bhd fr next: t.o whn p.u after 9th* 8/1
5164 P **Rainbow Haze**45 3572 10-10-4 103 ow1 MrBMoorcroft(5)
(Phillip Dando) *a towards rr: struggling and detached 6th: t.o whn p.u bef 9th* 18/1
5PPP P **Tara Tavey (IRE)**29 3824 11-10-9 110 (t) ConorSmith(7)
(Kevin Bishop) *chsd ldrs tl after 6th: wknd after 9th: t.o whn p.u bef 3 out* 33/1
/U0P P **Tidal Dance (IRE)**29 3823 9-11-12 120 (p) LiamTreadwell
(Venetia Williams) *chsd ldrs tl lost pl u.p on long run after 5th: t.o whn p.u bef 9th* 33/1
350P P **Its A Long Road**6 4250 8-10-10 104 (b1) NickScholfield
(Tim Dennis) *a bhd: t.o whn p.u bef 3 out* 16/1
-225 P **Deputy Commander (IRE)**27 3855 7-11-0 108 SamTwiston-Davies
(Nigel Twiston-Davies) *mid-div: sme hdwy 7th: drvn after next: wknd after 9th: p.u bef 3 out* 3/1[2]
6m 43.6s (44.60) **Going Correction** +1.95s/f (Heav) 12 Ran SP% 119.2
Speed ratings (Par 105): **100,94,85,84,61 , , , , , ,**
CSF £45.86 CT £243.23 TOTE £10.40: £3.50, £1.60, £2.30; EX 55.50 Trifecta £263.10.
Owner T S MacDonald **Bred** R H Buckler **Trained** Henley, Somerset

FOCUS
A modest handicap, run at a routine gallop, and the runner-up sets the level. Due to rail movements it was run over 115yds further than advertised.

4343 RACING UK DAY PASS JUST £10 H'CAP HURDLE (8 hdls) 2m 175y
5:30 (5:30) (Class 5) (0-100,100) 4-Y-0+ £2,274 (£667; £333; £166)

Form RPR
-000 1 **On The Road (IRE)**62 3256 6-10-0 74 oh1 PaulMoloney 86+
(Evan Williams) *mid-div: hdwy after 4th: wnt 2nd 3 out: chal 2 out: led last: kpt on wl: readily* 5/1[2]
2420 2 6 **Distant Sound (IRE)**9 4184 9-10-11 85 (b) MichealNolan 87
(Grace Harris) *mid-div: hdwy 3rd: rdn to ld after 3 out: hdd last: kpt on but no ex* 15/2
-344 3 15 **Old Magic (IRE)**27 3868 11-10-0 74 (t) JamesBest 60
(Sophie Leech) *trckd ldr tl rdn after 5th: one pce fr 3 out* 12/1
0P0- 4 2 1/2 **Bring Back Charlie**310 5481 6-10-5 79 SamTwiston-Davies 63
(Nigel Twiston-Davies) *trckd ldrs: led 4th tl after 3 out: grad fdd* 6/1[3]
0361 5 11 **Triple Chief (IRE)**11 4161 5-11-2 95 (tp) CiaranGethings(5) 68
(Chris Down) *hld up towards rr: hdwy and in tch 5th: rdn bef 3 out: wknd qckly* 13/8[1]
406 P **On Demand**62 3252 5-11-5 93 1 DarylJacob
(Simon Hodgson) *hld up: sme hdwy 5th: sn rdn: wknd bef next: p.u bef 2 out* 20/1
6-33 P **Wayward Frolic**8 4214 10-11-12 100 JoshuaMoore
(Jim Best) *prom: led 2nd where mstke: hdd 4th: sn rdn: wknd bef 3 out: t.o whn p.u bef last* 14/1
P-30 P **Mount Prospex (IRE)**34 3746 7-11-3 91 NickScholfield
(Tim Dennis) *t.o 2nd: p.u bef 4th* 8/1
-400 P **Culm Counsellor**115 2258 7-10-9 86 (p1) GilesHawkins(3)
(Chris Down) *led tl hit 2nd: wknd after 4th: t.o whn p.u bef 3 out* 33/1
000- P **Water Rail**338 4984 7-11-10 98 TomScudamore
(Simon Earle) *a towards rr: t.o whn p.u bef 3 out* 33/1
4m 54.4s (38.90) **Going Correction** +1.95s/f (Heav) 10 Ran SP% 116.9
Speed ratings (Par 103): **86,83,76,74,69 , , , , ,**
CSF £41.31 CT £424.16 TOTE £5.90: £2.10, £2.90, £3.70; EX 47.50 Trifecta £453.40.
Owner Mrs C Williams **Bred** G T Greene **Trained** Llancarfan, Vale Of Glamorgan

FOCUS
A moderate handicap, in which the going again played a big part, and a big personal best from the winner. It was run over 65 yards further than advertised.
T/Jkpt: Not won. T/Plt: £48.00 to a £1 stake. Pool: £59,635.78 - 905.16 winning tickets T/Qpdt: £21.30 to a £1 stake. Pool: £4,977.23 - 172.30 winning tickets **Tim Mitchell**

4123 WARWICK (L-H)
Friday, February 26

OFFICIAL GOING: Soft (good to soft in places; chs 5.9, hdl 5.6)
Wind: light breeze Weather: weak sun; 8 degrees

4344 EBF STALLIONS "NATIONAL HUNT" NOVICES' HURDLE (QUALIFIER) (9 hdls) 2m 3f
2:10 (2:11) (Class 4) 4-7-Y-0 £3,898 (£1,144; £572; £286)

Form RPR
6351 1 **Will O'The West (IRE)**27 3863 5-11-2 123 JakeGreenall 129+
(Henry Daly) *trckd ldrs gng wl: wnt 3rd 3 out: sn clr of rest: led after next: slt advantage last: rdn and styd on gamely flat* 4/1[2]
026 2 3/4 **Ballypoint (IRE)**34 3739 5-10-11 0 JamieBargary(5) 127+
(Nigel Twiston-Davies) *tall: rangy: chasing type: led or cl 2nd: def advantage 6th: drvn on home turn: hdd after 2 out: stl cl 2nd whn hit last: kpt on wl although jst hld after* 8/1
4F1 3 10 **Paddy's Field (IRE)**35 3724 6-11-8 0 NicodeBoinville 124+
(Ben Pauling) *cl 3rd or 4th: effrt 3 out: 2nd and ev ch bef next: drvn appr last: sn wknd* 7/4[1]
54 4 16 **Red Infantry (IRE)**29 3827 6-11-2 0 WillKennedy 100
(Ian Williams) *hld up in midfield: effrt but no ch w ldrs fr 3 out: wnt poor 4th at last* 66/1
/061 5 hd **Scooter Boy**42 3608 7-11-8 0 KielanWoods 106
(Alex Hales) *settled towards rr: effrt 8th: rdn and lost tch w ldrs bef 2 out: lost 4th at last* 20/1
-205 6 5 **Give Him A Glance**28 3835 5-11-2 0 1 DenisO'Regan 97
(Alan King) *small: nvr bttr than midfield: btn 3 out: hit next* 20/1
3 7 nk **Oneida Tribe (IRE)**32 3775 7-11-2 0 AidanColeman 95
(Venetia Williams) *big: str: alternated in ld tl bef 6th: rdn and wknd 3 out: over 15 l 4th and nt hrd pushed whn btn next* 16/1
006 8 3 **Jack Henri (FR)**28 3839 5-11-2 0 BrianHughes 92
(Ian Williams) *hld up and bhd: 9th and styng on nicely whn mstke 3 out: no ch after: looks sure to do bttr* 50/1
9 1 1/2 **Distant Rain (IRE)**201 1220 6-10-11 0 JackSherwood(5) 90
(Henry Oliver) *hld up in last tl 6th: sme prog into midfield at 8th: btn next: nt disgracd* 100/1
5 10 13 **Minella Experience (IRE)**28 3842 5-11-2 0 PaddyBrennan 78
(Dan Skelton) *prom: 3rd and rdn bef 6th: fdd bef 3 out: t.o* 6/1[3]

11 12 **Perfect Swing (IRE)** 5-11-2 0........................ RichieMcLernon 65
(Jonjo O'Neill) *str: novicey and nvr bttr than midfield: wknd after 8th: t.o: slt signs of ability* **50/1**

203 12 4 1/2 **Walkami (FR)**[87] 2840 5-11-2 0........................ RichardJohnson 61
(Jonjo O'Neill) *nvr bttr than midfield: wknd after 8th: t.o* **15/2**

560 13 16 **Lovefromabove (IRE)**[10] 4164 5-10-9 0........................ RobertDunne 38
(Dan Skelton) *chsd ldrs tl 1/2-way: t.o* **150/1**

06 P **Pettal**[27] 3863 5-10-2 0........................ CharlieHammond(7)
(Sarah-Jayne Davies) *tall: rangy: t.k.h early: dropped to rr 6th: tailing off whn jinked lft bef 7th: p.u 3 out: b.b.v* **250/1**

46 P **Hooghly River (IRE)**[70] 3145 6-11-2 0........................ DavidBass
(Jennifer Mason) *on toes: t.k.h early: hit 2nd: cl up tl 6th: slowed v rapidly next and sn t.o: p.u 3 out* **200/1**

4m 54.3s (8.30) **Going Correction** +0.625s/f (Soft) **15** Ran SP% **116.9**
Speed ratings: **107,106,102,95,95 93,93,92,91,86 81,79,72, ,**
CSF £32.77 TOTE £3.70: £1.40, £2.40, £3.90; EX 33.00 Trifecta £88.40.
Owner Strachan,Corbett,Salwey,Griffith&Gabb **Bred** Mrs L Suenson-Taylor **Trained** Stanton Lacy, Shropshire
■ Stewards' Enquiry : Robert Dunne four-day ban: weighed in heavy (11-14 Mar)

FOCUS
All starts have been moved at this track following remeasuring, so there will be no speed figures here until there is sufficient data to calculate updated median times. All hurdle races and the bumper were run on the outer hurdles track, over standard distances. After the first, the jockeys had differing opinions on the ground, with Jamie Bargary calling it "good" and Nico De Boinville "soft." A fairly ordinary novice hurdle, run 28.3sec slower than standard, but the first two are on the upgrade.

4345 SIMON BUTLER CELEBRATING 25 YEARS JUVENILE HURDLE (8 hdls) 2m
2:40 (2:40) (Class 4) 4-Y-O **£3,249** (£954; £477; £238)

Form RPR

225 1 **Forgiving Glance**[48] 3519 4-10-5 120........................ DenisO'Regan 112+
(Alan King) *small: neat: settled towards rr: effrt in 3rd at 5th: 2nd gng wl after 3 out: led and clipped next: readily drew clr: in command whn clipped last: v easily* **5/2[1]**

2 2 6 **Pillard (FR)**[55] 3443 4-11-5 129........................ RichardJohnson 116
(Jonjo O'Neill) *chsd ldrs: wnt 2nd at 5th: led after next: rdn and hdd and hit 2 out: sn outpcd by wnr* **5/2[1]**

24 3 18 **Three Colours Red (IRE)**[17] 4038 4-10-9 106.........(t) HarryBannister(3) 95
(Warren Greatrex) *chsd ldrs: last of five gng clr at 5th: drvn into 3rd after next: 7 l 3rd and btn whn j.rt 2 out* **11/4[2]**

P 4 25 **Solstalla**[137] 975 4-9-12 0........................ MrChrisMeehan(7) 64
(David Weston) *in rr early but t.k.h and racd up to join ldr 3rd: led bef 4th tl rdn and hdd sn after 3 out: tired qckly: t.o* **25/1**

P 5 10 **Live Miracle (USA)**[29] 3822 4-10-5 0........................ AidanColeman 49
(Venetia Williams) *prom bhd tearaway: clsd 3rd: rdn and fdd tamely 5th: t.o after next* **16/1**

F P **Darkening Night**[74] 3076 4-10-9 0........................ JamesBanks(3)
(Sarah-Jayne Davies) *v free to post: tk ferocious hold: led: 12 l clr at 2nd but jnd next: slowed rapidly bef 4th: t.o and p.u 5th* **100/1**

6 P **Levelling**[28] 3835 4-10-0 0........................ BridgetAndrews(5)
(Dan Skelton) *midfield: wknd after 4th: t.o and p.u 3 out* **10/1[3]**

P **Rebel Yell**[192] 4-10-9 0........................ BenPoste(3)
(Richard Price) *j. poorly: last after 2nd: t.o and p.u 5th* **100/1**

P **Sanok (POL)**[153] 4-10-12 0........................ DannyCook
(Paul Cowley) *hit 2nd: chsd tearaway ldr tl jnd him 3rd: slowed rapidly after next: t.o and p.u 2 out* **12/1**

4m 10.7s (19.70) **Going Correction** +1.00s/f (Soft) **9** Ran SP% **112.3**
Speed ratings: **90,87,78,65,60 , , ,**
CSF £8.87 TOTE £2.80: £1.30, £1.10, £1.30; EX 6.60 Trifecta £11.10.
Owner Mrs K Holmes **Bred** Pitchall Stud **Trained** Barbury Castle, Wilts

FOCUS
They went a strong gallop in this fair juvenile hurdle and only a couple saw it out. The winner set a fair standard.

4346 LISTERS AUDI NOVICES' H'CAP CHASE (18 fncs) 3m
3:10 (3:10) (Class 4) (0-105,98) 5-Y-0+ **£3,898** (£1,144; £572; £286)

Form RPR

2431 1 **Cheat The Cheater (IRE)**[22] 3948 9-11-10 96.........(tp) RichardJohnson 106
(Claire Dyson) *racd freely: led tl 2nd: w ldr tl rdn bef 12th: idling and lost pl next: 8 l 4th 3 out: rallied u.p after next: styd on stoutly to ld sn after last: forged clr* **4/1[1]**

-422 2 3 1/2 **Glendermot (IRE)**[24] 3914 7-11-8 94........................ DannyCook 104+
(Paul Cowley) *settled in 3rd or 4th: effrt 14th: led next: gd jump 3 out and 6 l clr briefly: sn idling and hrd drvn: half a l ld at last but sn hdd and outbattled: eased cl home* **4/1[1]**

F632 3 14 **Modeligo (IRE)**[21] 3977 7-11-8 94........................(t) CharliePoste 91
(Matt Sheppard) *hld up towards rr: effrt in 3rd and bad mstke 13th: on heels of ldrs and bmpd along whn squeezed for room bef 2 out: wknd last: jst hld on to 3rd pl* **5/1[2]**

252P 4 nk **Kapricorne (FR)**[27] 3864 9-11-4 90........................(bt1) RichieMcLernon 88
(Sophie Leech) *racd keenly: slt ld 2nd tl 15th: 2nd and outpcd by wnr after mstke next: 4th whn blnd 2 out: nrly regained poor 3rd* **5/1[2]**

00P0 5 35 **Follow The Tracks (IRE)**[32] 3771 8-10-8 85........................ MichaelHeard(5) 57
(Brian Barr) *j. deliberately 5th: cl up tl rdn and lost pl 12th: t.o 3 out* **9/1**

2622 P **Burgess Dream (IRE)**[25] 3906 7-11-1 87........................ AndrewThornton
(Anna Newton-Smith) *j.v.slowly 5th and lost tch: rallied 8th: rdn bef 12th: no rspnse and p.u next* **15/2**

353 F **Captain Flash (IRE)**[45] 3572 7-11-12 98........................(t) MarcGoldstein
(Jo Davis) *3rd whn fell heavily 3rd* **11/2[3]**

6m 30.4s (-3.60) **Going Correction** -0.15s/f (Good) **7** Ran SP% **110.5**
Speed ratings: **100,98,94,94,82 ,**
CSF £19.23 CT £75.21 TOTE £4.90: £2.40, £2.20; EX 10.30 Trifecta £20.30.
Owner Pink Fizz Fillies **Bred** Mrs Elizabeth Grant **Trained** Cleeve Prior, Worcs

FOCUS
Rail movements meant this was run over 94 yards further than advertised. An ordinary event run at a generous gallop and a chase personal best from the winner.

4347 BIGCASINOBONUSES.CO.UK BUDBROOKE CHASE (A H'CAP) (17 fncs) 2m 4f
3:45 (3:45) (Class 2) (0-150,140) 5£18,887 (£5,613; £2,841; £1,455; £762)

Form RPR

1-F5 1 **Minella Reception (IRE)**[34] 3735 10-10-13 127........................(t) NoelFehily 145+
(Nigel Twiston-Davies) *settled cl up: wnt 2nd gng wl at 10th: delayed effrt tl pushed into ld w ears pricked between last two: immediately asserted: hit last: v readily* **7/2[1]**

5P42 2 8 **Renard (FR)**[20] 3996 11-10-7 121........................(p) AidanColeman 127
(Venetia Williams) *led and set str gallop: 8 l clr at 3rd: pressed fr 1/2-way: hrd drvn bef 2 out: hdd between last two: kpt on steadily but no match for wnr* **7/2[1]**

-530 3 3/4 **Araldur (FR)**[55] 3448 12-10-9 126........................ TomBellamy(3) 134
(Alan King) *hld up: blnd 7th: mstke 14th: rdn and effrt in 3 l 3rd 3 out: hld whn hit next: tried hrd to get 2nd flat* **7/2[1]**

51FP 4 18 **Howlongisafoot (IRE)**[61] 3282 7-11-5 140........................(b) HarryCobden(7) 129
(Paul Nicholls) *tended to lack fluency and rn in snatches: nt fluent and rdn 11th: struggling bef 3 out* **7/2[1]**

-60P 5 1 3/4 **Poole Master**[48] 3528 11-11-5 138........................(p) DavidNoonan(5) 125
(David Pipe) *blnd 2nd: pressed ldr tl 10th but nt a fluent: rdn next: hit 13th: struggling bef 3 out* **12/1[3]**

P62U P **Deep Trouble (IRE)**[5] 4274 9-11-5 133........................(t) KielanWoods
(Ben Case) *pressed ldrs tl 4 l 4th and rdn 3 out: fdd bef next: p.u last: lame* **11/2[2]**

5m 13.8s (-4.20) **Going Correction** -0.15s/f (Good) **6** Ran SP% **112.0**
Speed ratings: **102,98,98,91,90**
CSF £16.19 CT £44.00 TOTE £3.50: £2.00, £2.00; EX 15.70 Trifecta £53.70.
Owner Options O Syndicate **Bred** Elms Stud Co Ltd **Trained** Naunton, Gloucs

FOCUS
Due to rail movements, this was run over 73 yards further than advertised. A valuable handicap chase, if not the most competitive for the grade, with an impressive winner.

4348 MIDSHIRE H'CAP CHASE (QUALIFIER FOR CHALLENGER STAYING CHASE SERIES FINAL) (18 fncs) 3m
4:15 (4:15) (Class 3) (0-130,129) 5-Y-0+ **£6,498** (£1,908; £954; £477)

Form RPR

-P0P 1 **Leo Luna**[36] 3707 7-11-7 124........................(tp) JamieMoore 142
(Gary Moore) *mde all at fast gallop: at least 4 l clr fr 12th: hrd drvn bef 2 out and hit fence hrd: styd on gamely u.str.p after* **7/1[3]**

3-0P 2 6 **No Duffer**[84] 2887 9-11-8 125........................(t) PaddyBrennan 137
(Tom George) *j. deliberately 6th: a 2nd or 3rd: chsd wnr fr 13th: j.rt 15th: 6 l 2nd and rdn whn slipped on bnd bef 2 out: drvn and kpt on steadily but nvr looked like catching wnr* **7/1[3]**

-430 3 11 **Achimota (IRE)**[28] 3837 10-11-5 122........................ KielanWoods 121
(Graeme McPherson) *blnd 3rd: shkn up 8th: midfield: rdn and outpcd 13th: 20 l 6th 2 out: plugged past tiring rivals wout threatening after* **9/1**

-1PP 4 5 **Winged Crusader (IRE)**[96] 2663 8-10-10 116........................(v) RyanHatch(3) 109
(Nigel Twiston-Davies) *pressed ldrs: rdn 12th: 10 l 3rd and outpcd 15th: lost 3rd flat* **20/1**

2P11 5 3 1/4 **As De Fer (FR)**[22] 3957 10-11-3 125........................(t) DavidNoonan(5) 116
(Anthony Honeyball) *chsd wnr: rdn 12th: wknd next: 15 l 4th at 15th* **9/2[1]**

5223 6 nk **Take The Mick**[31] 3792 9-10-13 116........................(p) AidanColeman 106
(Venetia Williams) *chsd ldrs: slow 10th: dropped to rr next: no ch fr 12th: styd on after last and nrly snatched remote 5th* **9/1**

/235 7 3 **Denali Highway (IRE)**[28] 3843 9-11-2 119........................(p) AndrewThornton 107
(Caroline Bailey) *midfield: rdn bef 12th: no rspnse: plugged on same pce and n.d after* **16/1**

3445 8 1 1/4 **Umberto D'Olivate (FR)**[36] 3706 8-11-2 119........................(p) TomCannon 104
(Robert Walford) *a bhd: rdn 9th: struggling bef 12th* **8/1**

P-PP 9 1 **Farbreaga (IRE)**[58] 3373 10-11-10 127........................(p) JeremiahMcGrath 111
(Harry Whittington) *nt jump wl and nvr travelling in rr: last at 11th: t.o 13th* **6/1[2]**

-F1P P **What A Good Night (IRE)**[41] 3624 8-11-12 129.........(tp) DavidEngland
(Dan Skelton) *midfield: rdn bef 12th: struggling after: t.o and p.u 2 out* **16/1**

2-13 P **Hi Vic (IRE)**[77] 3008 11-11-5 122........................ NoelFehily
(David Loder) *lacked fluency in last trio: rdn and lost tch bef 12th: t.o next: p.u 2 out* **8/1**

6m 25.6s (-8.40) **Going Correction** -0.15s/f (Good) **11** Ran SP% **116.2**
Speed ratings: **108,106,102,100,99 99,98,98,97,**
CSF £55.29 CT £447.48 TOTE £6.20: £2.60, £2.60, £3.20; EX 59.90 Trifecta £563.50.
Owner P B Moorhead **Bred** Juddmonte Farms Ltd **Trained** Lower Beeding, W Sussex

FOCUS
Rail movements added 94 yards to the advertised race distance. This looked competitive, but they finished well strung out and the winner has slipped to a very good mark..

4349 WALKING THE COURSES "HANDS AND HEELS" H'CAP HURDLE (CONDITIONALS/AMATEURS) (12 hdls) 3m 2f
4:50 (4:50) (Class 5) (0-100,100) 4-Y-0+ **£2,274** (£667; £333; £166)

Form RPR

0PP0 1 **Coolking**[32] 3771 9-11-1 89........................(b1) DavidNoonan 102
(Chris Gordon) *led 4th tl mstke 7th: w ldr after tl lft 8 l in ld and rdn 3 out: pushed along to maintain 3 l advantage fr next* **10/1**

0342 2 6 **Young Lou**[9] 4184 7-9-12 77........................(v1) CathalCourtney(5) 87
(Robin Dickin) *mstke 3rd: a ldng quartet: 3 l 3rd at 8th: rdn after next: lft 8 l 2nd after being hmpd 3 out: urged and tried to rally bef next but no imp whn awkward fnl two* **7/1[3]**

0063 3 10 **Ceann Sibheal (IRE)**[22] 3946 7-11-2 95........................ MrBHicks(5) 92
(Warren Greatrex) *towards rr tl 8th: pushed along and sn outpcd: nrly 20 l 3rd 2 out: plugged on* **11/2[2]**

233 4 21 **Storm Alert**[32] 3771 9-11-5 93........................ MrMatthewHampton 69
(Sue Gardner) *wl bhd tl 8th: plugged on into remote 4th cl home: nvr nr ldrs* **8/1**

P234 5 nk **Ballochmyle (IRE)**[22] 3946 6-10-6 85........................ MrJAndrews(5) 61
(Caroline Fryer) *chsd ldrs: rdn bef 8th: outpcd next: 30 l 4th 2 out* **10/1**

P451 6 13 **Kelsey (IRE)**[9] 4184 6-11-8 96 7ex........................ MrTommieMO'Brien 59
(Tom Lacey) *midfield at 6th: rdn and lost pl after next: nt travelling after: t.o 3 out* **7/4[1]**

P604 7 hd **El Indio (IRE)**[51] 3489 9-9-12 75........................(vt) CharlieHammond(3) 38
(Claire Dyson) *led briefly after 1st: last and rdr bumping up and down fr 6th: continued t.o* **16/1**

P064 8 1 1/4 **Comical Red**[24] 3914 8-10-11 88........................(bt) MrTGillard(3) 49
(Mark Gillard) *cl up tl rdn after 7th: 15 l 4th and losing tch bef 3 out* **25/1**

51P6 9 12 **Flemi Two Toes (IRE)**[15] 4069 10-11-4 95........................(v) RomainClavreul(3) 44
(Sarah Humphrey) *bhd: rdn 3rd: nvr gng sweetly: t.o after 7th* **25/1**

0052 F **Warsaw Pact (IRE)**[71] 3125 13-10-0 79........................ MrBParis-Crofts(5)
(Steven Dixon) *led or disp ld fr 2nd tl fell 3 out whn stl upsides wnr and gng equally wl and 4 l clr of rest* **25/1**

6F-6 P **Caldey**[49] 3506 7-10-9 88........................ MrAMcGlinchey(5)
(Ian Williams) *bhd: prog to midfield 5th: rdn and wknd after 7th: sn t.o: p.u 2 out* **25/1**

7m 2.3s (25.30) **Going Correction** +1.00s/f (Soft) **11** Ran SP% **114.8**
Speed ratings (Par 103): **101,99,96,89,89 85,85,85,81,**
CSF £72.49 CT £423.58 TOTE £11.10: £2.90, £2.20, £3.10; EX 77.00 Trifecta £460.00.
Owner Sir Peter & Lady Forwood **Bred** Goldford Stud **Trained** Morestead, Hampshire

FOCUS
They appeared to go a solid gallop up front, but very few got into this modest event. The winner has been a 111-rated hurdler at his best and ran to 117 over fences here last season.

4350 BRITISH STALLION STUDS EBF MARES' STANDARD OPEN NATIONAL HUNT FLAT RACE 2m

5:20 (5:20) (Class 6) 4-7-Y-0 **£1,949** (£572; £286; £143)

Form | | | | RPR
2 **1** **Little Miss Poet**[72] 3118 4-10-5 0 RichardJohnson 97+
(Philip Hobbs) *wl mde: hld up in rr in slow r: effrt on inner 4f out: chal 2f out: edgd lft and kpt on to ld fnl 75yds: readily* **2/5**[1]
2 *1 1/4* **Nightfly** 5-11-0 0 AidanColeman 105+
(Charlie Longsdon) *cl up and gng wl: effrt to ld 300yds out: sn rdn: hdd and outpcd fnl 75yds* **9/2**[2]
3 *6* **Lamanver Odyssey** 4-10-5 0 NicodeBoinville 90
(Tom Lacey) *hld up: effrt 3f out: sn drvn: kpt on same pce fr over 1f out* **6/1**[3]
4 *2 3/4* **Dalton Glance** 6-10-11 0 KillianMoore(3) 96
(Martin Keighley) *small: trckd ldrs: effrt 4f out: rdn and ev ch 2f out: wknd ins fnl f* **16/1**
3 **5** *nk* **Primrose Court (IRE)**[173] 1491 6-11-0 0 KielanWoods 96
(Shaun Lycett) *bhd: hdwy over 2f out: kpt on wout threatening ins fnl f* **10/1**
6 *3/4* **Up Till Midnight** 7-11-0 0 MarcGoldstein 95
(Lydia Richards) *prom: led narrowly over 2f out: rdn and hdd over 1f out: no ex* **66/1**
7 *5* **Time Wise** 6-10-9 0 DanielHiskett(5) 90
(Richard Phillips) *towards rr: rdn and btn over 2f out* **16/1**
60-0 **8** *1 3/4* **Romann Angel**[57] 3381 7-11-0 0 SeanQuinlan 89
(Michael Mullineaux) *bhd: lost tch wl over 2f out* **40/1**
9 *8* **Venture Lagertha (IRE)** 7-10-9 0 GaryDerwin(5) 81
(Brian Barr) *in tch tl fdd wl over 2f out: t.o* **10/1**
0 **10** *21* **Annie Hughes (IRE)**[57] 3381 7-10-11 0 BenPoste(3) 60
(Adrian Wintle) *on toes: swtg: mde most at v stdy pce tl rdn and hdd over 2f out: sn t.o* **100/1**

4m 19.6s (34.20) **Going Correction** +1.00s/f (Soft)
WFA 4 from 5yo 9lb 5 from 6yo+ 1lb **10 Ran SP% 131.2**
Speed ratings: **54,53,50,49,48 48,45,45,41,30**
CSF £3.43 TOTE £1.30: £1.02, £1.20, £2.70; EX 3.50 Trifecta £10.40.
Owner M J Tuckey **Bred** M J Tuckey **Trained** Withycombe, Somerset

FOCUS
This mares' bumper was run at a steady pace and they were still well bunched on the home turn.
T/Plt: £120.60 to a £1 stake. Pool: £70,766.24 - 428.07 winning tickets T/Qpdt: £58.40 to a £1 stake. Pool: £4,678.92 - 59.26 winning tickets **Iain Mackenzie**

3974
CHEPSTOW (L-H)
Saturday, February 27

OFFICIAL GOING: Soft (good to soft in places; chs 5.1, hdl 5.4)
Wind: fresh half against Weather: sunny spells

4351 MPS NETWORK MAIDEN HURDLE (9 hdls 2 omitted) 2m 3f 100y

2:05 (2:05) (Class 4) 4-Y-0+ **£4,873** (£1,431; £715; £357)

Form | | | | RPR
-133 **1** **Aurillac (FR)**[22] 3974 6-11-0 0 DavidMullins(3) 132+
(Rebecca Curtis) *trckd ldrs: nt fluent 4th: pushed along 3 out: chsd ldr next: led on extended run between last 2: c clr flat: comf* **5/2**[2]
10-F **2** *7* **Ghost River**[13] 4138 6-11-3 0 JamieMoore 125
(Peter Bowen) *t.k.h: trckd ldr: chal 5th to next: rdn 3 out: mstke next and briefly lost 2nd: hld whn nt fluent last* **11/4**[3]
F0 **3** *8* **Red Hanrahan (IRE)**[98] 2630 5-11-3 0 (t) SeanBowen 116
(Paul Nicholls) *led: jnd 5th to next: rdn and hdd on extended run between last 2: wkng in 3rd by last* **7/4**[1]
-PPP **4** *10* **Far From Defeat (IRE)**[30] 3817 6-11-3 0 TomScudamore 105
(Michael Scudamore) *hld up in last trio: sme hdwy after 6th: no imp on ldrs: styd on to go 4th nr fin* **40/1**
P3 **5** *1/2* **Barenice (FR)**[42] 3626 5-11-0 0 (t) KillianMoore(3) 105
(Alex Hales) *mid-div: rdn and outpcd by ldng trio bef 3 out: lost 4th nr fin* **6/1**
005 **6** *14* **Bonvilston Boy**[24] 3927 5-10-12 0 AlanJohns(5) 91
(Tim Vaughan) *chsd ldrs tl rdn and wknd bef 3 out* **33/1**
4 **7** *7* **Sydney De Baune (FR)**[42] 3625 5-11-3 0 AndrewThornton 84
(Robert Walford) *a in last trio: mstke 4th: wknd after 6th* **33/1**
56-3 **P** **Jaslamour (FR)**[263] 682 5-11-3 0 ConorO'Farrell
(Alexandra Dunn) *a in last trio: struggling 5th: lost tch after mstke next: t.o whn p.u bef 3 out* **66/1**

5m 4.7s (2.90) **Going Correction** +0.15s/f (Yiel) **8 Ran SP% 115.7**
Speed ratings (Par 105): **99,96,92,88,88 82,79,**
CSF £9.98 TOTE £3.40: £1.40, £1.20, £1.10; EX 9.00 Trifecta £18.20.
Owner D Mossop, P John & R White **Bred** Mme J Besnouin & J Besnouin **Trained** Newport, Pembrokeshire
■ The first winner in Britain for David Mullins.

FOCUS
The secon-last flight was omitted in all hurdles. Far bend dolled out by 8yds and the stable bend by 7yds, adding approximately 41yds to an opening contest which can number Hey Big Spender, Holywell and Annacotty among its seven most recent previous winners. They appeared to go a reasonable early gallop on ground subsequently described variously as "good to softish" and "a bit dead". There's probably more to come from the winner, with the second and fourth the best guides.

4352 PERTEMPS NETWORK LTD NOVICES' LIMITED H'CAP CHASE (18 fncs) 2m 7f 131y

2:40 (2:41) (Class 3) (0-125,123) 5-Y-0+ **£6,498** (£1,908; £954; £477)

Form | | | | RPR
464U **1** **Henri Parry Morgan**[60] 3348 8-11-7 122 (tp) SeanBowen 145+
(Peter Bowen) *towards rr: gd hdwy after 13th: wnt 2nd 4 out: sn led: drew clr fr 2 out: easily* **10/1**
-413 **2** *10* **Bears Rails**[30] 3823 6-10-7 108 BrendanPowell 118
(Colin Tizzard) *prom: rdn 5 out and briefly outpcd by ldrs: rallied to chse wnr bef 2 out: sn one pce and no imp* **5/1**[2]
64U3 **3** *8* **Grove Silver (IRE)**[16] 4062 7-11-1 116 SeanQuinlan 116
(Jennie Candlish) *a.p: rdn and one pce fr 3 out* **11/2**[3]
-F13 **4** *1* **Wild Bill (IRE)**[60] 3339 7-11-8 123 PaulMoloney 122
(Evan Williams) *chsd ldrs: rdn to chse wnr briefly 3 out: wknd next* **3/1**[1]
F630 **5** *12* **Doitforthevillage (IRE)**[70] 3146 7-10-6 107 JamieMoore 98
(Paul Henderson) *t.k.h in rr: hdwy 4th: led appr 5 out: mstke next and sn hdd: wknd 3 out* **12/1**
P00F **6** *20* **Brook (FR)**[12] 4153 5-10-11 115 (bt) TomScudamore 79
(David Pipe) *in rr: hdwy 11th: wknd 3 out: t.o* **20/1**
-U6U **7** *3/4* **Ivy Gate (IRE)**[24] 3929 8-11-7 122 (b[1]) RichieMcLernon 88
(Jonjo O'Neill) *chsd along to get gng s: mid-div: reminder 5th: mstke next: rdn along 9th: struggling fr 13th: t.o* **11/1**
1254 **8** *3 1/2* **Ready Token (IRE)**[59] 3371 8-11-1 116 (tp) KielanWoods 79
(Charlie Longsdon) *led tl mstke and hdd 8th: mstke 10th: sn drvn: wknd after 13th: t.o* **11/1**
FP-5 **P** **Hard To Swallow (IRE)**[8] 4226 10-10-9 110 (b[1]) AndrewThornton
(Tom Weston) *a towards rr: wknd after 13th: t.o whn p.u bef 5 out* **50/1**
34P/ **U** **Potters Cross**[738] 4347 9-11-7 122 TrevorWhelan
(Rebecca Curtis) *chsd ldrs: led 8th tl mstke and hdd 13th: 8th and wkng whn blnd and uns rdr 4 out* **12/1**
-025 **F** **Relentless Dreamer (IRE)**[98] 2631 7-11-5 123 (p) DavidMullins(3)
(Rebecca Curtis) *cl up: led 13th tl hdd appr 5 out: wkng whn mstke 4 out: mod 6th whn fell heavily last* **9/1**
2P2P **P** **An Poc Ar Buile (IRE)**[30] 3824 7-10-13 114 (p) DenisO'Regan
(Sophie Leech) *kicked at s: a in rr: lost tch 13th: t.o whn p.u bef 5 out* **20/1**

6m 24.3s (2.30) **Going Correction** +0.15s/f (Yiel)
WFA 5 from 6yo+ 3lb **12 Ran SP% 119.7**
Speed ratings: **102,98,96,95,91 85,84,83, , ,**
CSF £60.00 CT £372.72 TOTE £11.70: £3.70, £1.90, £2.00; EX 67.90 Trifecta £1241.30.
Owner Ednyfed & Elizabeth Morgan **Bred** J R Bryan **Trained** Little Newcastle, Pembrokes

FOCUS
A well-stocked novice handicap, run over about 65yds further than the advertised distance due to bend readjustments.

4353 PERTEMPS NETWORK INDUSTRIAL H'CAP HURDLE (QUALIFIER FOR THE CHALLENGER TWO MILE HURDLE SERIES) (6 hdls 2 omitted) 2m 11y

3:10 (3:13) (Class 3) (0-135,135) 4-Y-0+ **£6,498** (£1,908; £954; £477)

146 **1** **Theatre Flame (IRE)**[16] 4070 6-10-11 120 TomScudamore 126+
(David Bridgwater) *trckd ldr tl led 4th: drvn after last (usual 3 out): styd on wl u.p on extended run-in* **6/1**[3]
4531 **2** *2* **Bold Duke**[42] 3619 8-10-5 117 BenPoste(3) 120
(Edward Bevan) *chsd ldrs: rdn after 2 out (usual 4 out): wnt 2nd early on extended run-in: styd on wl but hld fnl f* **7/1**
02FP **3** *8* **Whispering Harry**[42] 3629 7-10-8 117 JeremiahMcGrath 113
(Henry Oliver) *chsd ldrs: wnt 2nd at 4th: mstke 2 out (usual 4 out): sn rdn: lost 2nd early on extended run-in: one pce* **8/1**
-0F0 **4** *1 3/4* **Global Thrill**[37] 3708 7-10-4 116 RobertWilliams(3) 109
(Bernard Llewellyn) *hld up in last pair: rdn 2 out (usual 4 out): no imp tl styd on wl fnl f* **8/1**
2-21 **5** *3/4* **Floresco (GER)**[37] 3708 6-10-12 121 (t) IanPopham 118
(Richard Woollacott) *chsd ldrs: mstke 3rd and briefly rdn along: 4th whn mstke last (usual 3 out): one pce and btn extended run-in* **11/4**[1]
4240 **6** *3/4* **Crookstown (IRE)**[52] 3487 9-10-12 121 KielanWoods 113
(Ben Case) *hld up in last pair: rdn 2 out (usual 4 out): one pce and btn extended run-in* **8/1**
2-34 **7** *33* **Kiama Bay (IRE)**[22] 3975 10-11-12 135 (v[1]) JamieMoore 94
(Jim Best) *led tl hdd 3rd and dropped to 3rd: wknd bef 2 out (usual 4 out): t.o* **20/1**
2036 **F** **Ballyglasheen (IRE)**[29] 1868 6-11-10 133 PaulMoloney
(Evan Williams) *fell 1st: fatally injured* **4/1**[2]

4m 8.7s (-1.90) **Going Correction** +0.15s/f (Yiel) **8 Ran SP% 111.5**
Speed ratings (Par 107): **110,109,105,104,103 103,86,**
CSF £44.46 CT £329.50 TOTE £6.50: £2.00, £2.20, £2.20; EX 55.10 Trifecta £310.60.
Owner CWB LLP **Bred** Liam Brady **Trained** Icomb, Gloucs

FOCUS
Far bend dolled out by 8yds and the stable bend by 7yds, adding approximately 41yds to this contest. An already modest contest for the grade lost much of its interest when Ballyglasheen, one of only two competitors rated less than a stone below the ceiling, took a terrible fall at the first. The omission of the same flight on the final circuit gave rise to a run-in of over 2f. A step up from the winner.

4354 PERTEMPS NETWORK GROUP H'CAP HURDLE (SERIES QUALIFIER) (10 hdls 2 omitted) 2m 7f 131y

3:45 (3:48) (Class 2) 5-Y-0+
£12,512 (£3,696; £1,848; £924; £462; £232)

Form | | | | RPR
1-2P **1** **Arpege D'Alene (FR)**[73] 3116 6-11-1 140 (t) SeanBowen 149+
(Paul Nicholls) *nvr far away: led narrowly 3 out: drvn on extended run between last 2: mstke last: sn hdd and a l down: rallied to ld last strides* **13/2**[2]
2104 **2** *1/2* **Dan Emmett (USA)**[30] 3824 6-10-0 125 oh1 LiamTreadwell 131
(Michael Scudamore) *prom tl lost pl 4th: hdwy 6th: 4th and rdn whn mstke 2 out: wnt 2nd bef last: led early on run-in and wnt a l up: hdd last strides* **25/1**
03P5 **3** *7* **Batavir (FR)**[14] 4112 7-10-0 125 (bt[1]) ConorO'Farrell 126
(David Pipe) *hld up: gd hdwy 7th: mstke and rdn 3 out: no ex appr last* **8/1**[3]
4-56 **4** *8* **Hansupfordetroit (IRE)**[49] 3517 11-9-7 125 (t) JordanWilliams(7) 118
(Bernard Llewellyn) *s.i.s: hld up in rr: hdwy after 7th: ev ch 2 out: wknd on extended run to last* **20/1**
F131 **5** *2 3/4* **Abricot De L'Oasis (FR)**[29] 3846 6-9-11 127 BridgetAndrews(5) 116
(Dan Skelton) *cl up: led 1st to 3 out: rdn and wkng whn j.lft next* **9/1**
-222 **6** *shd* **Southfield Vic (IRE)**[13] 4142 7-11-4 148 (b[1]) JackSherwood(5) 136
(Paul Nicholls) *drvn along s to r in mid-div: rdn 6th: lost tch w ldrs 3 out: styd on u.p fr next* **16/1**
552P **7** *6* **A Vos Gardes (FR)**[57] 3407 6-10-7 132 (t) RichieMcLernon 114
(Charlie Longsdon) *s.s: in rr: hdwy after 7th: rdn 2 out: sn wknd* **20/1**
/P1P **8** *9* **O'Faolains Boy (IRE)**[28] 3850 9-11-9 151 DavidMullins(3) 124
(Rebecca Curtis) *led to 1st: styd prom to 5th: rdn and struggling after 7th* **10/1**
0100 **9** *3* **Gevrey Chambertin (FR)**[14] 4112 8-10-12 142 (b) MichaelHeard(5) 112
(David Pipe) *s.i.s: sn w ldrs: rdn and wknd appr 3 out* **25/1**
343P **10** *1/2* **Anteros (IRE)**[21] 3992 8-10-5 130 (t) DenisO'Regan 99
(Sophie Leech) *in rr: trying to cl into midfield whn hmpd bnd after 4th: struggling fr 7th* **16/1**
6-01 **11** *10* **Awaywiththegreys (IRE)**[49] 3517 9-10-6 131 (b) JamieMoore 95
(Peter Bowen) *mid-div: hdwy to chse ldrs 2nd: rdn and wknd 3 out* **16/1**

The Form Book Jumps 2015-16, Raceform Ltd, Newbury, RG14 5SJ

0-66 **12** *4 1/2* **Rebeccas Choice (IRE)**[84] 2907 13-9-7 **125** oh11(p) MissJodieHughes(7) 80
(Dai Burchell) *chsd ldrs tl lost pl and rdn after 4th: bhd fr 6th* **100/1**

264P **13** *15* **Audacious Plan (IRE)**[105] 2482 7-10-1 **126**......................(p) IanPopham 66
(Rebecca Curtis) *chsd ldrs to 2nd: mid-div after: hmpd bnd after 4th: wknd after 7th* **20/1**

P43U **14** *36* **Allez Vic (IRE)**[49] 3518 10-10-2 **127**...................................... PaulMoloney 31
(Evan Williams) *hld up: hdwy and j.big 4th: wknd after 7th: t.o* **33/1**

02F1 **P** **Pineau De Re (FR)**[76] 3058 13-11-2 **141**........................ BrendanPowell
(Dr Richard Newland) *s.i.s: a towards rr: struggling fr 7th: t.o whn p.u bef last* **20/1**

16-0 **P** **Kings Palace (IRE)**[105] 2483 8-11-8 **147**..................(t) TomScudamore
(David Pipe) *wnt to post early: mid-div: hdwy 4th: wkng whn mstke 3 out: p.u bef next* **3/1**[1]

1411 **P** **The Boss's Dream (IRE)**[30] 3824 8-11-0 **139**.................. TrevorWhelan
(Neil King) *cl up tl lost pl 6th: bhd fr next: t.o whn p.u bef 3 out* **8/1**[3]

6m 11.6s (9.40) **Going Correction** +0.15s/f (Yiel) **17 Ran SP% 128.0**
Speed ratings: **90,89,87,84,83 83,81,78,77,77 74,72,67,55, ,**
CSF £167.03 CT £1351.90 TOTE £7.50: £2.30, £4.70, £3.00, £2.50; EX 176.60 Trifecta £2642.30 Part won. .
Owner Mr & Mrs P K Barber & Potensis Bloodstock Ltd **Bred** Louis Couteaudier **Trained** Ditcheat, Somerset

FOCUS
Far bend dolled out by 8yds and the stable bend by 7yds, adding approximately 65yds to this series qualifier. A step up from the lightly raced winner.

4355 OFFICE VISIONS H'CAP CHASE (12 fncs) 2m 11y
4:20 (4:20) (Class 2) 5-Y-O+ **£25,554** (£7,714; £3,974; £2,106)

Form RPR

-121 **1** **Arthur's Oak**[21] 3990 8-11-7 **148**................................ LiamTreadwell 154+
(Venetia Williams) *mde all: shkn up after 3 out: clr 2 out: drvn out and styd on wl flat* **11/4**[2]

-P1P **2** *5* **Grey Gold (IRE)**[56] 3446 11-11-12 **153**........................ JamieMoore 155
(Kerry Lee) *hld up bhd ldrs: rdn to go 2nd 4 out: no imp 2 out: kpt on flat and clsng on wnr but a hld* **9/2**[3]

-221 **3** *10* **Oscar Sunset (IRE)**[22] 3975 9-11-1 **142**........................ PaulMoloney 134
(Evan Williams) *hld up bhd ldrs: mstke 3rd: in 2nd appr 5 out tl mstke 4 out: no ch w first two fr next* **11/8**[1]

5116 **4** *6* **Dresden (IRE)**[28] 3857 8-11-8 **149**.............................. JamesDavies 136
(Henry Oliver) *hld up wl in tch in last: squeezed along at times: rdn 4 out: no ch w first two fr next: mstkes 2 out and last* **7/1**

113- **P** **Dance Floor King (IRE)**[420] 3505 9-10-3 **130**.............. TomScudamore
(Nick Mitchell) *racd keenly: chsd wnr: nt fluent 4th: lost 2nd appr 5 out: wknd qckly: wl bhd whn p.u bef 3 out* **10/1**

4m 14.0s (-3.10) **Going Correction** +0.15s/f (Yiel) **5 Ran SP% 108.5**
Speed ratings: **113,110,105,102,**
CSF £14.30 TOTE £3.80: £1.80, £1.40; EX 15.40 Trifecta £32.70.
Owner Mrs J K Burt **Bred** J L Burt **Trained** Kings Caple, H'fords

FOCUS
Far bend dolled out by 8yds and the stable bend by 7yds, adding approximately 41yds to this contest. No Sire De Grugy this year, but still a decent quintet of runners and a well-run event enlivened by the sublime jumping display of the winner. He's till on the upgrade, the solid second setting the level.

4356 PERTEMPS NETWORK H'CAP CHASE (12 fncs) 2m 11y
4:55 (4:55) (Class 5) (0-100,100) 5-Y-O+ **£3,249** (£954; £477; £238)

Form RPR

P123 **1** **Winged Express (IRE)**[25] 3919 7-10-13 **87**........................ IanPopham 105+
(Alexandra Dunn) *mid-div: rdn and hdwy after 7th: chsd ldr 3 out: 2 l down last: styd on wl u.p to ld fnl 100yds* **5/2**[2]

0-F **2** *1 1/2* **Not For You (IRE)**[150] 1703 8-11-2 **90**..........................[1] PaulMoloney 105
(C Byrnes, Ire) *t.k.h: chsd ldrs: led 4 out: 2 l up last: sn rdn: hdd and unable qck fnl 100yds* **9/4**[1]

4-PU **3** *16* **Jamrham (IRE)**[16] 4073 9-10-9 **83**........................(t) LiamTreadwell 82
(Sam Thomas) *chsd ldrs: led 2nd to 5th: styd prom tl wknd 3 out: hld on for mod 3rd* **33/1**

52P5 **4** *3/4* **Jaunty Inflight**[25] 3916 7-11-5 **100**................ WilliamFeatherstone(7) 101
(Brian Eckley) *towards rr: mstke 3rd: hdwy 7th: rdn and wknd 3 out* **14/1**

06/F **5** *1 1/4* **Gold Carrot**[26] 3903 8-10-13 **87**................................ JamieMoore 86
(Gary Moore) *t.k.h: prom: mstke 4th: led next: mstke 6th: rdn whn mstke and hdd 4 out: sn wknd* **7/1**[3]

1-P4 **6** *2 1/2* **Princesse Fleur**[23] 3951 8-11-5 **93**............................ TomScudamore 88
(Michael Scudamore) *hld up: hdwy after 5th: mstke 5 out: shkn up next: one pce and sn no ch w ldrs* **9/1**

6233 **7** *10* **The Omen**[109] 2416 10-10-7 **86**.................................... AlanJohns(5) 71
(Tim Vaughan) *led to 2nd: styd prom tl wknd 5 out* **20/1**

-P24 **8** *18* **Bonds Conquest**[68] 3195 7-10-0 **74**...................... JeremiahMcGrath 41
(Seamus Mullins) *chsd ldrs: reminders 4th: sn lost pl: struggling fr 7th: t.o whn blnd last* **12/1**

P-P5 **9** *2* **Castletown (IRE)**[23] 3951 8-11-6 **94**.......................... MarkQuinlan 59
(Sheila Lewis) *wnt to post early: chsd ldrs: drvn along and grad lost pl fr 5th: bhd fr 7th: t.o* **33/1**

300 **10** *11* **Sabroclair (FR)**[59] 3368 7-11-9 **97**........................(t[1]) MichealNolan 51
(Richard Woollacott) *mid-div tl rdn and wknd after 7th: t.o* **25/1**

5553 **P** **Tenby Jewel (IRE)**[19] 4029 11-9-9 **74** oh5..................(p) MichaelHeard(5)
(Mark Gillard) *a towards rr: mstke 5th: lost tch after 7th: t.o whn p.u bef 2 out* **40/1**

34PP **P** **Sylvan Legend**[10] 4184 8-10-4 **78**............................(tp) TrevorWhelan
(Matt Sheppard) *a in rr: lost tch 7th: t.o whn p.u bef 5 out* **20/1**

4m 19.9s (2.80) **Going Correction** +0.15s/f (Yiel) **12 Ran SP% 117.9**
Speed ratings: **99,98,90,89,89 88,83,74,73,67 ,**
CSF £7.96 CT £145.47 TOTE £3.50: £1.90, £1.80, £8.60; EX 10.20 Trifecta £147.00.
Owner J Burley & The Bucklanders **Bred** Sean And Orla Gannon **Trained** West Buckland, Somerset

FOCUS
Far bend dolled out by 8yds and the stable bend by 7yds, adding approximately 41yds. A weak event, and a winning time 5.9 seconds slower than that clocked by the 61lb superior-rated scorer in the preceding C&D race. The winner improved in line with his hurdles mark.

4357 COUNTY MARQUEES MAIDEN NATIONAL HUNT FLAT RACE (CONDITIONAL JOCKEYS' AND AMATEUR RIDERS') 2m 11y
5:30 (5:30) (Class 6) 4-6-Y-O **£1,949** (£572; £286; £143)

Form RPR

1 **Big Meadow (IRE)**[112] 5-11-2 0.................................. KillianMoore(3) 126+
(Neil King) *mid-div: hdwy to chse ldrs 6f out: led over 3f out: sn drew clr: eased nr fin* **7/2**[3]

2 *14* **Geordie Des Champs (IRE)** 5-11-2 0.......................... DavidMullins(3) 111
(Rebecca Curtis) *prom: rdn in 4th 4f out: wnt 2nd over 2f out: styd on but no real imp on easy wnr* **15/2**

3-32 **3** *5* **Bacchanel (FR)**[57] 3416 5-11-0 0.............................. ThomasCheesman(5) 107
(Philip Hobbs) *chsd ldrs: wnt 2nd 1/2-way: drvn 5f out: lost 2nd over 2f out: one pce* **5/2**[2]

6 **4** *7* **Muffins For Tea**[22] 3980 6-10-12 0.................................. PaulO'Brien(7) 99
(Colin Tizzard) *towards rr whn hmpd and stmbld bnd after 2f: sme hdwy 7f out: drvn in mod 5th 5f out: plugged on* **20/1**

5 *17* **Starlight Court (IRE)**[76] 5-11-0 0.............................. BridgetAndrews(5) 84
(Dan Skelton) *racd keenly: led and set gd gallop: hdd over 3f out: sn rdn and wknd* **7/4**[1]

6 *25* **Let's Tango (IRE)** 5-10-12 0.. MrMLegg(7) 57
(Caroline Keevil) *towards rr whn forced wd and hmpd bnd after 2f: struggling fr 1/2-way: t.o* **33/1**

7 *25* **Courting Harry** 5-10-12 0.. CharlieHammond(7) 32
(Sarah-Jayne Davies) *t.k.h in mid-div: rdn and struggling 1/2-way: t.o* **50/1**

8 *9* **Francophile (FR)** 4-10-5 0...................................... JackSherwood(5) 14
(David Loder) *mid-div: n.m.r bnd after 2f: wknd 6f out: t.o* **12/1**

0 **9** *28* **Armement (FR)**[98] 2650 5-11-2 0.................................. ConorShoemark(3)
(James Grassick) *prom: rdn along 1/2-way: wknd over 5f out: t.o* **150/1**

0 **10** *nk* **Surfing The Stars (IRE)**[105] 2493 5-11-2 0.................. KieronEdgar(3)
(Laura Young) *a in rr: t.o* **125/1**

P **Lure Des Pres (IRE)** 4-10-3 0.................................... ConorSmith(7)
(Linda Blackford) *chsd ldrs tl wknd qckly 1/2-way: t.o whn p.u 5f out* **66/1**

4m 7.5s (2.50) **Going Correction** +0.15s/f (Yiel)
WFA 4 from 5yo+ 9lb **11 Ran SP% 119.2**
Speed ratings: **99,92,89,86,77 65,52,48,34,33**
CSF £28.84 TOTE £4.50: £1.20, £2.60, £1.50; EX 29.40 Trifecta £99.00.
Owner Peter Beadles **Bred** Padraic Ryan **Trained** Barbury Castle, Wiltshire

FOCUS
Far bend dolled out by 8yds and the stable bend by 7yds, adding approximately 41yds to this contest. Not many to consider in this bumper, and only four still in contention turning for home. The winner impressed and looks a decent recruit.
T/Jkpt: Not won. T/Plt: £79.50 to a £1 stake. Pool: £84,319.16 - 773.49 winning tickets T/Qpdt: £44.40 to a £1 stake. Pool: £5,554.83 - 92.46 winning tickets **Richard Lowther**

4096 KEMPTON (R-H)
Saturday, February 27

OFFICIAL GOING: Good to soft (good in places)
Wind: Fresh, across Weather: Cloudy, cold

4358 BETBRIGHT #REALFANSONLY ADONIS JUVENILE HURDLE (GRADE 2) (8 hdls) 2m
2:00 (2:00) (Class 1) 4-Y-O
£17,085 (£6,411; £3,210; £1,599; £804; £402)

Form

1 **Zubayr (IRE)**[264] 4-10-12 0...................................... NickScholfield 139+
(Paul Nicholls) *hld up in last: stl only 6th 3 out and wl off the pce: gd prog to take 2nd 2 out: shkn up and sn clsd on ldr: led last and pushed clr: readily* **9/1**

5 **2** *3 3/4* **Azzuri**[20] 4010 4-10-12 0.. HarrySkelton 134
(Dan Skelton) *led and clr: stl nrly 20 l up whn mstke 3 out: c bk to rivals 2 out: hdd last: no ch w wnr but hld on wl for 2nd* **25/1**

3 *3/4* **Khezerabad (FR)**[195] 4-10-12 0...................................... DarylJacob 133+
(Nicky Henderson) *hld up in chsng gp: nt fluent 4th: prog 3 out: chsd clr ldr bef 2 out tl 2 out: kpt on same pce after* **8/1**[3]

11 **4** *5* **Gibralfaro (IRE)**[35] 3730 4-11-5 **151**........................ WayneHutchinson 134
(Alan King) *hld up in chsng gp: prog 3 out: sn rdn: dropped to 5th and btn bef 2 out: plugged on* **1/1**[1]

12 **5** *2* **Wolfcatcher (IRE)**[18] 4038 4-11-2 **132**........................ AidanColeman 130
(John Ferguson) *prom in chsng gp to 3 out: wknd steadily bef 2 out* **13/2**[2]

11 **6** *7* **St Saviour**[24] 3926 4-11-2 **134**................................ RichardJohnson 125
(Philip Hobbs) *chsd clr ldr: mstke 3 out: lost 2nd on long run bef 2 out: wknd* **8/1**[3]

7 *3/4* **Pilansberg**[125] 4-10-12 0.................................... SamTwiston-Davies 118
(Paul Nicholls) *in tch in chsng gp: nt fluent 2nd: sing to struggle whn bad mstke 3 out: sn no ch: plugged on* **13/2**[2]

3m 49.9s (-8.10) **Going Correction** -0.45s/f (Good) **7 Ran SP% 112.7**
Speed ratings: **102,100,99,97,96 92,92**
CSF £153.41 TOTE £11.70: £3.70, £8.90; EX 208.40 Trifecta £970.30.
Owner P J Vogt **Bred** His Highness The Aga Khan's Studs S C **Trained** Ditcheat, Somerset

FOCUS
All starts have been moved at this track following remeasuring, so there will be no speed figures here until there is sufficient data to calculate updated median times. The chase course and the winter hurdle course were on their innermost configurations, with all distances as advertised. No hiding place for these juveniles in what looked a good edition of the race, with the runner-up having them on the stretch from a long way out. The favourite disappointed, but still worth rating the race quite highly. Zubayr is a smart recruit but will need to improve best part of a stone to win an average Triumph.

4359 BETBRIGHT BEST FOR FESTIVAL BETTING PENDIL NOVICES' CHASE (GRADE 2) (16 fncs) 2m 4f 110y
2:35 (2:35) (Class 1) 5-Y-O+ **£19,078** (£7,692; £4,278)

Form RPR

-144 **1** **Killala Quay**[71] 3136 9-11-4 **136**............................(p) RichardJohnson 151+
(Charlie Longsdon) *j.lft: mde all: jnd and drvn 2 out: bttr jump and asserted last: kpt on wl* **5/1**[3]

/1PP **2** *3 3/4* **Twelve Roses**[93] 2726 8-11-0 **140**.................................(p) DavidBass 142
(Kim Bailey) *cl up in 3rd: pushed along whn lft 2nd 4 out: drvn to chal and w wnr 2 out: outj. last: kpt on same pce* **11/2**

5021 **3** *21* **Cloonacool (IRE)**[54] 3466 7-11-4 **139**.......................... JoshuaMoore 135
(Stuart Edmunds) *settled in last: blnd 9th: rdn 4 out: tried to mount a chal 3 out: no imp next: wknd last* **7/2**[2]

-025 **F** **The Saint James (FR)**[62] 3280 5-10-12 **142**..................(t) BarryGeraghty
(Jonjo O'Neill) *trckd ldng trio: lft 3rd 4 out: stl to be asked a serious question and cl up whn fell 3 out* **5/2**[1]

2210 **F** **Mon Successeur (FR)**[57] 3406 5-11-2 **145**.............. SamTwiston-Davies
(Paul Nicholls) *trckd wnr: cl up whn fell 4 out* **5/2**[1]

5m 8.3s (-3.70) **Going Correction** -0.05s/f (Good)
WFA 5 from 7yo+ 2lb **5 Ran SP% 111.4**
Speed ratings: **105,103,95, ,**
CSF £29.29 TOTE £6.00: £2.20, £2.60; EX 24.80 Trifecta £82.00.
Owner Richard & Mrs Susan Perkins **Bred** N Franklin **Trained** Over Norton, Oxon

FOCUS
Not a strong edition of the race, and with the two market leaders falling, it ultimately didn't take much winning, the winner making all at a decent gallop. He was entitled to rate this high on the best of his hurdle form.

4360 SKY BET DOVECOTE NOVICES' HURDLE (GRADE 2) (8 hdls) 2m
3:05 (3:05) (Class 1) 4-Y-0+ **£17,085** (£6,411; £3,210; £1,599; £804)

Form RPR
11 **1** **Winter Escape (IRE)**[16] 4064 5-11-6 142........................ BarryGeraghty 140+
(Alan King) *trckd ldr: shkn up to cl 2 out: chal and outj. last: rdn to ld fnl 150yds: styd on and in command nr fin* **4/6**[1]
-113 **2** 1 1/4 **Marracudja (FR)**[63] 3227 5-11-9 136....................(t) SamTwiston-Davies 140
(Paul Nicholls) *led: rdn 2 out: pressed last: kpt on but hdd and hld fnl 150yds* **9/2**[2]
-214 **3** 1 1/4 **Welsh Shadow (IRE)**[56] 3447 6-11-9 134.................. HarrySkelton 139
(Dan Skelton) *chsd ldng pair: rdn sn after 3 out: cl up fr 2 out: kpt on wl but nvr quite able to chal* **5/1**[3]
114 **4** 15 **Oceane (FR)**[105] 2480 4-11-0 132.......................... WayneHutchinson 118
(Alan King) *chsd ldrs: rdn after 3 out: wknd 2 out* **12/1**
1360 **5** 12 **Cold March (FR)**[35] 3735 6-11-2 0.................................. AidanColeman 112
(Venetia Williams) *in last whn mstke 4th: lost tch and mstke next: no ch fr 3 out* **14/1**

3m 49.6s (-8.40) **Going Correction** -0.45s/f (Good)
WFA 4 from 5yo+ 9lb **5** Ran SP% **109.2**
Speed ratings (Par 115): **103,102,101,94,88**
CSF £4.06 TOTE £1.50: £1.10, £1.90; EX 4.50 Trifecta £6.40.
Owner John P McManus **Bred** Oliver And Salome Brennan **Trained** Barbury Castle, Wilts
FOCUS
As with the previous contest, this didn't look a terribly strong edition and a pair of mid-130s rated novices bustled up the favourite, to whom they were conceding 3lb. It was run at a good gallop. A small step up from the winner who looks sure to rate higher.

4361 BETBRIGHT CHASE (H'CAP) (GRADE 3) (18 fncs) 3m
3:35 (3:37) (Class 1) 5-Y-0+
£56,950 (£21,370; £10,700; £5,330; £2,680; £1,340)

Form RPR
-323 **1** **Theatre Guide (IRE)**[28] 3850 9-10-6 **139**....................(tp) PaddyBrennan 154+
(Colin Tizzard) *cl up in midfield: nt fluent 6th: prog to join ldrs 13th: trckd ldr after 4 out: led after 3 out and sn clr: drvn bef last: styd on strly* **6/1**[2]
1-5P **2** 10 **Opening Batsman (IRE)**[33] 3776 10-10-1 **141** ow1(bt) LiamMcKenna(7) 147
(Harry Fry) *hld up in last quartet: gd prog after 4 out: styd on wl to take 2nd last: no imp on clr wnr* **20/1**
01P1 **3** 3/4 **Roc D'Apsis (FR)**[33] 3776 7-10-3 **136**.................(p) RichardJohnson 142
(Tom George) *nt fluent in last quartet: blnd 9th: stl wl in rr bef 3 out: prog after: styd on wl to take 3rd nr fin* **16/1**
114P **4** 1 3/4 **Ballykan**[91] 2790 6-10-0 **136**.............................(t) RyanHatch(3) 140
(Nigel Twiston-Davies) *pressed ldrs: upsides 14th: rdn after 4 out and outpcd by ldng pair: one pce after* **20/1**
0261 **5** 3/4 **Le Reve (IRE)**[21] 3993 8-11-2 **149**.............................(b) HarrySkelton 151
(Lucy Wadham) *trckd ldrs: prog to ld 4 out: clr w wnr bef 3 out: hdd after 3 out and sn btn: lost 2nd and wknd last* **9/1**
-126 **6** nk **Viva Steve (IRE)**[28] 3849 8-9-11 **133** oh2........... HarryBannister(3) 135
(Mick Channon) *trckd ldrs: cl up 4 out: rdn and outpcd bef next: one pce after* **14/1**
/6P- **7** 1 3/4 **Hadrian's Approach (IRE)**[392] 3978 9-11-0 **147**............ NicodeBoinville 147
(Nicky Henderson) *settled in midfield: rdn after 4 out and tried to cl on ldrs: no imp 3 out: one pce after* **20/1**
P311 **8** 3 1/2 **Ziga Boy (FR)**[28] 3860 7-10-5 **141**......................... TomBellamy(3) 139
(Alan King) *led or disp ld to 4 out: sn rdn: fdd fr 3 out* **8/1**
-330 **9** 1/2 **Fox Appeal (IRE)**[70] 3150 9-11-3 **150**........................... DarylJacob 147
(Emma Lavelle) *in tch in midfield: mstke 11th: sme prog fr 14th: no imp on ldrs 3 out: wl btn whn blnd last* **25/1**
-2P4 **10** 2 1/2 **Rocky Creek (IRE)**[14] 4113 10-11-11 **158**.........(bt[1]) SamTwiston-Davies 152
(Paul Nicholls) *racd on outer: pressed ldrs: rt on terms 14th: lost pl and rdn next (4 out): wknd 3 out* **16/1**
0222 **11** 3/4 **Virak (FR)**[35] 3741 7-11-5 **159**........................... HarryCobden(7) 153
(Paul Nicholls) *pressed ldrs: rdn 4 out: sn btn: wknd 3 out* **12/1**
/15- **12** 7 **Ruben Cotter (IRE)**[323] 5253 10-10-7 **140**.................. NickScholfield 127
(Paul Nicholls) *a in last quartet: no prog 4 out: wl btn after* **16/1**
1322 **P** **Tenor Nivernais (FR)**[28] 3851 9-11-5 **152**.................. AidanColeman
(Venetia Williams) *disp ld to 12th: wknd qckly 14th: t.o whn p.u bef 3 out* **16/1**
F-2P **F** **Champagne West (IRE)**[28] 3851 8-11-7 **154**.................. TomO'Brien 149
(Philip Hobbs) *t.k.h: hld up in midfield: in tch whn mstke 14th: no prog after next: wl btn in 10th whn fell 2 out* **7/1**[3]
-121 **U** **Thomas Brown**[29] 3838 7-10-7 **140**..............................(p) NoelFehily
(Harry Fry) *nt a fluent: settled in last quartet: stl there but wl in tch whn blnd and uns rdr 11th* **4/1**[1]

5m 59.0s (-10.00) **Going Correction** -0.05s/f (Good) **15** Ran SP% **123.9**
Speed ratings: **114,110,110,109,109 109,108,107,107,106 106,104, , ,**
CSF £125.19 CT £1853.89 TOTE £7.80: £2.50, £7.60, £6.30; EX 161.90 Trifecta £2960.40.
Owner Mrs Jean R Bishop **Bred** Kenilworth House Stud **Trained** Milborne Port, Dorset
FOCUS
Traditionally a strong handicap chase, this year's edition had looked really competitive, but it was won in runaway fashion. There was early competition for the lead and it was certainly truly run, suiting the closers. The winner is rated back to his very best, with the next three pretty much to their marks.

4362 WATCH RACING UK ON 3 DEVICES H'CAP HURDLE (10 hdls) 2m 5f
4:10 (4:12) (Class 3) (0-135,135) 4-Y-0+ **£5,393** (£1,583; £791; £395)

Form RPR
40U2 **1** **Poker School (IRE)**[29] 3846 6-10-0 **119**.................. TobyWheeler(10) 125
(Ian Williams) *hld up in last: smooth prog fr 3 out to trck ldrs 2 out: clsd to ld last: drvn out and hld on* **11/1**
3532 **2** nk **Sir Ivan**[23] 3956 6-11-8 **131**....................................(t) NoelFehily 138
(Harry Fry) *mde most: hdd and rdn 2 out: sn led again: hdd last: battled on wl flat: jst hld* **8/1**
3021 **3** 7 **McCabe Creek (IRE)**[28] 3855 6-10-1 **120**................ JamieInsole(10) 121
(Alan King) *hld up towards rr: prog 7th: drvn after 3 out: hdwy to ld 2 out: sn hdd: hld whn mstke last: one pce* **10/1**
/530 **4** 1 **Vicenzo Mio (FR)**[70] 3151 6-10-13 **129**....................(t) HarryCobden(7) 129
(Paul Nicholls) *wl in tch: prog to trck ldrs 3 out: cl up and rdn 2 out: one pce after* **6/1**[2]
-22P **5** 3 1/4 **King Kayf**[35] 3736 7-11-0 **126**..............................(t) JamesBanks(3) 122
(Noel Williams) *w ldr: stl upsides after 3 out: sn drvn: lost pl and fdd 2 out* **25/1**
11-0 **6** 4 **Clean Sheet (IRE)**[28] 3854 7-11-10 **133**.................. BarryGeraghty 126
(Nicky Henderson) *trckd ldrs: hit 7th: shkn up after 3 out: rdn and cl up 2 out: wknd bef last* **15/8**[1]
0-16 **7** 2 1/4 **Thunder Sheik (IRE)**[88] 2831 8-10-8 **120**......................(t) RyanHatch(3) 111
(Nigel Twiston-Davies) *trckd ldrs: rdn sn after 3 out: steadily wknd jst bef 2 out* **33/1**
4-4P **8** 6 **Blue Atlantic (USA)**[282] 418 5-10-13 **125**.................. HarryBannister(3) 110
(Warren Greatrex) *in tch: pressed ldrs on outer bef 3 out: sn drvn: styd in tch tl wknd jst bef 2 out* **50/1**
5-1P **9** 24 **Vif Argent (FR)**[29] 3846 7-10-7 **116**.................................. TomCannon 79
(Andrew Reid) *in tch: prog after 6th: jnd ldrs after next: disp ld briefly 3 out: wknd qckly bef next* **100/1**
-PP5 **10** 3/4 **Shammick Boy (IRE)**[23] 3956 11-11-4 **134**..............(p) DavidPrichard(7) 97
(Victor Dartnall) *w ldrs on outer: wd bnd bef 5th: wknd qckly and slow jump 7th: sn t.o* **25/1**
1-01 **11** 18 **Kublai (FR)**[96] 2694 6-10-13 **122**.............................. RichardJohnson 69
(Philip Hobbs) *mstkes: in rr: stmbld bdly 6th: lost tch next: t.o* **10/1**
1F1/ **P** **Hannibal The Great (IRE)**[816] 2875 8-10-13 **122**.........(t) AidanColeman
(Charlie Longsdon) *trckd ldrs: pushed along 5th: lost pl rapidly next: t.o whn p.u bef 7th* **7/1**[3]
-FPP **P** **Kingscourt Native (IRE)**[42] 3622 8-11-12 **135**.............(t) PaddyBrennan
(Colin Tizzard) *hld up in rr: lost tch fr 7th: sn t.o: p.u bef 2 out* **20/1**

5m 6.5s (-14.50) **Going Correction** -0.45s/f (Good) **13** Ran SP% **117.5**
Speed ratings (Par 107): **109,108,106,105,104 103,102,99,90,90 83, ,**
CSF £87.40 CT £917.42 TOTE £12.30: £3.00, £2.80, £3.60; EX 110.70 Trifecta £621.00.
Owner Aniol Chandler Medcroft Turner Westwood **Bred** Mrs Mary Doyle **Trained** Portway, Worcs
FOCUS
No great gallop on here, but two were still able to draw away late on. Fair handicap form, the third to fifth setting a solid level.

4363 WATCH LIVE RACING ON BETBRIGHT.COM H'CAP CHASE (16 fncs) 2m 4f 110y
4:45 (4:45) (Class 3) (0-130,129) 5-Y-0+ **£6,498** (£1,908; £954; £477)

Form RPR
24U5 **1** **Ericht (IRE)**[33] 3776 10-11-9 **126**..............................(p) NicodeBoinville 142+
(Nicky Henderson) *j.lft: often quite markedly: mde virtually all: shkn up and kpt on wl fr 3 out: in command after last* **5/1**[2]
-421 **2** 5 **Cernunnos (FR)**[24] 3924 6-11-12 **129**.............................(tp) BarryGeraghty 138
(Tom George) *w.w: prog 10th: urged along after 4 out: lft in 2nd pl next: rdn and no real imp on wnr after* **4/1**[1]
3F22 **3** 3 1/4 **Cloudy Bob (IRE)**[35] 3731 9-10-12 **115**........................ HarrySkelton 120
(Pat Murphy) *hld up towards rr: prog fr 11th: rdn whn lft in 3rd 3 out: kpt on same pce after* **4/1**[1]
-3P6 **4** 1/2 **Dusky Lark**[29] 3843 6-11-5 **122**...................................(t) PaddyBrennan 132+
(Colin Tizzard) *hld up in rr: prog 8th: chsd wnr next: abt 3 l down but stl gng wl enough whn terrible blunder 3 out: no ch after: kpt on fr 2 out* **14/1**
P-1F **5** 13 **West Wizard (FR)**[63] 3228 7-11-7 **124**............ SamTwiston-Davies 118
(Nigel Twiston-Davies) *trckd ldrs: nt fluent 10th and lost pl: rdn and tried to renew effrt after 4 out: no prog 3 out: wl btn after: mstke last* **10/1**
2-F0 **6** nk **Tom Neary (IRE)**[79] 2990 9-11-3 **120**............................(t) JakeGreenall 113
(Robert Walford) *chsd ldrs: outpcd fr 4 out: n.d fr next* **40/1**
U-40 **7** 7 **Roberto Pegasus (USA)**[78] 3014 10-11-2 **122**............(p) TomBellamy(3) 110
(Alan King) *in tch: rdn and no prog after 4 out: wl btn bef next: wknd and mstke last* **25/1**
1-UF **8** 10 **De Kerry Man (IRE)**[42] 3624 8-11-0 **122**...................... JakeHodson(5) 103
(David Bridgwater) *nt fluent 1st: trckd ldrs: mstke 10th: rdn whn mstke 4 out: wknd and bhd after* **5/1**[2]
-223 **U** **Mr Muddle**[29] 3843 9-11-2 **119**.................................. MarcGoldstein
(Sheena West) *towards rr: no prog whn blnd bdly and uns rdr 11th* **16/1**
6P24 **P** **Comeonginger (IRE)**[49] 3524 9-11-8 **125**......................(t) TomCannon
(Chris Gordon) *pressed wnr: stmbld bdly on landing 8th: lost pl qckly and p.u after next* **8/1**[3]
315P **U** **Dursey Sound (IRE)**[87] 2853 8-11-10 **127**.................. RichardJohnson
(Jonjo O'Neill) *settled in last: detached fr 9th: sltly hmpd and uns rdr 11th* **20/1**

5m 11.3s (-0.70) **Going Correction** -0.05s/f (Good) **11** Ran SP% **117.1**
Speed ratings: **99,97,95,95,90 90,87,84, ,**
CSF £25.42 CT £88.36 TOTE £5.70: £2.20, £2.00, £1.50; EX 31.20 Trifecta £151.70.
Owner Mrs Christopher Hanbury **Bred** Mrs M McDonagh **Trained** Upper Lambourn, Berks
FOCUS
Solid handicap form. The winner was back to something like his best.

4364 RACINGUK.COM/ANYWHERE STANDARD OPEN NATIONAL HUNT FLAT RACE 2m
5:20 (5:21) (Class 5) 4-6-Y-0 **£2,599** (£763; £381; £190)

Form RPR
1 **Bolving (IRE)** 5-11-2 0.. NickScholfield 119+
(Victor Dartnall) *prom: trckd ldr over 3f out: led 2f out: sltly green and shkn up over 1f out: styd on wl* **20/1**
221 **2** 3 **Templeross (IRE)**[71] 3145 5-11-9 0.................. SamTwiston-Davies 123
(Nigel Twiston-Davies) *led 2f: pressed ldr: led again 4f out: drvn and hdd 2f out: kpt on same pce* **10/1**
1 **3** nk **Drumcliff (IRE)**[79] 2991 5-11-9 0.................................. BarryGeraghty 124+
(Harry Fry) *t.k.h: trckd ldrs: rdn over 2f out: hanging and nt qckn in 3rd pl over 1f out: kpt on nr fin* **7/4**[1]
4 3 **Azzerti (FR)** 4-10-4 0... TomBellamy(3) 104
(Alan King) *hld up in rr: stdy prog fr 4f out gng wl: rchd 4th over 2f out: pushed along and rn green after: one pce* **9/1**
6-11 **5** 2 **Criq Rock (FR)**[98] 2636 5-11-12 0........................ WayneHutchinson 121
(Alan King) *t.k.h: hld up towards rr: pushed along and tried to make prog over 3f out: kpt on but nvr gng pce to be involved* **7/2**[2]
3-2 **6** nk **Vaillant Nonantais (FR)**[286] 366 5-11-2 0.................... AndrewTinkler 111
(Nicky Henderson) *wl in tch in midfield: pushed along 4f out: outpcd over 2f out* **16/1**
13 **7** 3 1/2 **The Blue Bomber**[57] 3409 4-10-7 0.................................. AidanColeman 99
(Mick Channon) *led after 2f to 4f out: lost 2nd over 3f out: fdd fnl 2f* **8/1**
8 1 1/2 **Sulamani The Late (FR)** 4-10-7 0.................................. HarrySkelton 97
(Dan Skelton) *t.k.h early: hld up in rr: threatened to make prog over 3f out: no hdwy over 2f out* **16/1**
9 5 **Sidbury Fair** 5-10-2 0.. DavidPrichard(7) 95
(Victor Dartnall) *trckd ldrs on outer tl dropped to rr 4f out: no ch over 2f out* **50/1**
05 **10** nk **Twycross Warrior**[99] 2629 4-10-2 0.................................. ChrisWard(5) 92
(Robin Dickin) *hld up in last: lost tch 4f out: no ch over 2f out* **100/1**

11 *11* **Berce (FR)** 5-11-2 0 NicodeBoinville 92
(Nicky Henderson) *wl in tch: first one to be urged along over 4f out: wknd over 3f out* **7/1**[3]
3m 51.3s (-1.10) **Going Correction** -0.45s/f (Good)
WFA 4 from 5yo 9lb **11** Ran SP% **120.8**
Speed ratings: **84,82,82,80,79 79,77,77,74,74 69**
CSF £210.07 TOTE £18.70: £3.80, £3.00, £1.60; EX 183.70 Trifecta £1386.90.
Owner Mrs C Barber **Bred** J R Weston **Trained** Brayford, Devon
FOCUS
A decent bumper that should produce plenty of winners. The first three are well above average.
T/Plt: £3,166.30 to a £1 stake. Pool: £119,888.99 - 27.64 winning tickets T/Qpdt: £24.40 to a £1 stake. Pool: £13,046.19 - 395.42 winning tickets **Jonathan Neesom**

3933 **NEWCASTLE** (L-H)
Saturday, February 27
OFFICIAL GOING: Good to soft (soft in places; 5.9)
Wind: Almost nil Weather: Overcast

4365 BETFRED "GREAT VALUE EVERY DAY" NOVICES' CHASE (19 fncs) 2m 7f 91y
1:50 (1:50) (Class 2) 5-Y-O+ **£12,660** (£3,740; £1,870)

Form RPR
-311 **1** **Seeyouatmidnight**[57] 3405 8-11-7 151 BrianHughes 139+
(Sandy Thomson) *mde all: hit and shkn up 4 out: nt fluent last: drvn out* **1/8**[1]
21F3 **2** *6* **Smooth Stepper**[28] 3849 7-11-4 130 DannyCook 130
(Sue Smith) *chsd wnr: shkn up whn mstke 4 out: effrt next: no ex fr last: eased towards fin* **6/1**[2]
30-5 **3** *28* **Westend Theatre (IRE)**[112] 2339 7-10-13 88 PeterBuchanan 94
(Jane Walton) *chsd ldrs: outpcd 1/2-way: struggling fr 5 out* **100/1**[3]
6m 18.1s (-4.40) **Going Correction** -0.075s/f (Good) **3** Ran SP% **104.2**
Speed ratings: **104,101,92**
CSF £1.29 TOTE £1.10; EX 1.10 Trifecta £1.10.
Owner Mrs A M Thomson **Bred** Fiona Avice Evans **Trained** Lambden, Berwicks
FOCUS
A disappointing numerical turnout given the money on offer, but it did attract one of the best northern-trained jumpers around. After rail movements the actual race distance was 2m7f126yds. The winner didn't need to be near his best.

4366 BETFRED "STILL TREBLE ODDS ON LUCKY 15'S" H'CAP HURDLE (8 hdls 1 omitted) 2m 98y
2:20 (2:20) (Class 2) (0-150,140) 4-Y-O+ **£12,660** (£3,740; £1,870; £936; £468)

Form RPR
2344 **1** **Zaidiyn (FR)**[20] 4014 6-11-7 135 GavinSheehan 144+
(Brian Ellison) *confidently rdn in rr: smooth hdwy bef 2 out: led on bit run-in: shkn up and qcknd clr: readily* **11/2**
P6F6 **2** *4 1/2* **Bobs Lady Tamure**[14] 4125 9-10-5 124 (t) DaraghBourke[(5)] 126
(Maurice Barnes) *hld up: smooth hdwy to ld bef 2 out: nt fluent and rdn last: sn hdd: kpt on: no ch w wnr* **25/1**
0132 **3** *2 1/2* **Vendor (FR)**[20] 4014 8-11-12 140 DannyCook 141
(Sue Smith) *pressed ldr: chal 3rd: drvn and outpcd after 3 out (usual 4 out): rallied next: plugged on fr last* **7/2**[1]
4202 **4** *nse* **Heath Hunter (IRE)**[25] 3917 9-10-13 132 (bt) DavidNoonan[(5)] 132
(David Pipe) *led after 5th: rdn along after next: rallied bef 2 out: cl 3rd whn nt fluent last: sn no ex* **7/1**
3-35 **5** *1* **Cape Caster (IRE)**[78] 3015 5-10-7 121 AdamWedge 119
(Evan Williams) *t.k.h: trckd ldrs: effrt bef 2 out: outpcd fr last* **9/2**[2]
1401 **6** *8* **Minstrels Gallery (IRE)**[15] 4107 7-11-1 129 LeightonAspell 123
(Lucy Wadham) *prom: hdwy to ld after 5th: rdn and hdd bef 2 out: outpcd whn nt fluent last: sn btn* **8/1**
5312 **7** *5* **So Satisfied**[12] 4154 5-10-9 123 BrianHughes 109
(Sandy Thomson) *trckd ldrs: rdn and outpcd bef omitted 3 out: sn btn* **7/1**
-310 **8** *40* **Draytonian (IRE)**[62] 3284 6-10-12 126 JamesBest 76
(Philip Hobbs) *hld up in tch: stdy hdwy and cl up 3rd: effrt and ev ch bef omitted 3 out: sn struggling: last and no ch whn blnd bdly and nrly uns rdr 2 out: eased* **5/1**[3]
4m 4.6s (-5.40) **Going Correction** -0.075s/f (Good) **8** Ran SP% **112.4**
Speed ratings (Par 109): **110,107,106,106,105 101,99,79**
CSF £106.22 CT £543.08 TOTE £6.90: £1.90, £6.50, £1.10; EX 129.10 Trifecta £725.50.
Owner P J Martin **Bred** S C H H The Aga Khan's Studs **Trained** Norton, N Yorks
FOCUS
A pretty useful contest which was soundly run, the easy winner impressive. Solid form. After rail movements the actual race distance was 2m113yds.

4367 BETFRED EIDER (A H'CAP CHASE) (25 fncs) 4m 122y
2:50 (2:51) (Class 2) 5-Y-O+
£53,176 (£15,708; £7,854; £3,927; £1,963; £986)

Form RPR
6F11 **1** **Rocking Blues (FR)**[9] 4203 11-9-12 126 6ex LorcanMurtagh[(10)] 147+
(Rose Dobbin) *hld up in tch: smooth hdwy to ld 4 out: sn clr: jst over 12 l up whn blnd last: easily* **8/1**[3]
P-53 **2** *9* **Shotgun Paddy (IRE)**[49] 3518 9-11-12 144 DavyRussell 154
(Emma Lavelle) *hld up towards rr: hit 11th: nt fluent 16th: hdwy on outside to chse (clr) wnr appr 3 out: kpt on: nt pce to chal* **7/1**[2]
0PF6 **3** *3/4* **Portrait King (IRE)**[49] 3518 11-10-13 131 (p) BrianHughes 140
(Patrick Griffin, Ire) *hld up in midfield: stdy hdwy 19th: effrt and pushed along 4 out: kpt on fr 2 out: no imp* **12/1**
/131 **4** *shd* **Mysteree (IRE)**[24] 3933 8-9-12 121 GrantCockburn[(5)] 130
(Lucinda Russell) *nt fluent on occasions: cl up: rdn along bef 4 out: kpt on fr last: no imp* **20/1**
0-00 **5** *12* **Glenquest (IRE)**[23] 3964 13-10-7 125 (t) PeterBuchanan 123
(S R B Crawford, Ire) *hld up in midfield: effrt and pushed along bef 4 out: outpcd fr next* **33/1**
-615 **6** *15* **Woodford County**[49] 3518 9-10-8 131 (p) CiaranGethings[(5)] 114
(Philip Hobbs) *led to 1st: cl up: regained ld 5 out: hdd next: rdn and wknd fr 3 out* **10/1**
-000 **7** *7* **Milborough (IRE)**[91] 2790 10-11-5 140 GrahamWatters[(3)] 118
(Ian Duncan) *nt fluent on occasions: hld up in midfield: rdn 6 out: wknd bef 4 out* **14/1**
2FP- **8** *3 1/4* **Wyck Hill (IRE)**[322] 5275 12-11-1 133 (bt[1]) WillKennedy 109
(David Bridgwater) *led 1st: hdd 5 out: rallied and ev ch to next: rdn and wknd fr 3 out* **14/1**
2241 **9** *5* **Lackamon**[44] 3591 11-11-1 133 DannyCook 108
(Sue Smith) *nt fluent in rr: struggling fnl circ: nvr on terms* **16/1**
U-25 **10** *5* **Summery Justice (IRE)**[21] 3993 12-10-13 136 (p) CharlieDeutsch[(5)] 103
(Venetia Williams) *nt fluent towards rr: rdn 17th: sn struggling: nvr on terms* **12/1**
3213 **11** *8* **Presented (IRE)**[24] 3934 9-9-10 119 CallumBewley[(5)] 77
(Lisa Harrison) *cl up: rdn 5 out: wknd bef next* **33/1**
6251 **U** **Russe Blanc (FR)**[42] 3624 9-11-7 139 (p) CharliePoste
(Kerry Lee) *in tch: mstke 17th: hit 19th: sn uns rdr* **11/1**
6FP0 **P** **William Money (IRE)**[59] 3364 9-9-13 122 DiarmuidO'Regan[(5)]
(Chris Grant) *bhd: drvn and struggling fr 17th: t.o whn p.u bef last* **16/1**
0-51 **F** **Ballyculla (IRE)**[78] 3008 9-11-4 136 (p) GavinSheehan
(Warren Greatrex) *nt fluent on occasions: mstke 1st: sn towards rr: fell 17th* **13/2**[1]
0P-1 **P** **Beforeall (IRE)**[30] 3818 8-10-13 131 (t) LeightonAspell
(Oliver Sherwood) *nt fluent on occasions: bhd: struggling fr 15th: lost tch and p.u bef 17th* **25/1**
2021 **F** **Cultram Abbey**[32] 3794 9-11-2 134 BrianHarding
(Nicky Richards) *hld up on ins: fell 1st* **16/1**
0-2 **U** **Cork Citizen**[25] 3918 8-10-2 125 (tp) DavidNoonan[(5)]
(David Pipe) *hld up on ins: rdn along fr 11th: outpcd whn hmpd and uns rdr 17th* **9/1**
8m 54.7s (-13.10) **Going Correction** -0.075s/f (Good) **17** Ran SP% **125.2**
Speed ratings: **112,109,109,109,106 103,101,100,99,98 96, , , ,**
CSF £62.69 CT £684.51 TOTE £6.90: £2.20, £2.60, £2.90, £4.30; EX 64.10 Trifecta £1913.00.
Owner The Friday Lions **Bred** Mme Genevieve Mongin **Trained** South Hazelrigg, Northumbria
FOCUS
This looked to be a really competitive renewal of this valuable staying prize but turned out to be anything but, the thriving winner absolutely bolting up. The easy winner should still be competitive when reassessed. After rail movements the actual race distance was 4m162yds.

4368 BETFRED LOTTO NOVICES' HURDLE (11 hdls 2 omitted) 2m 6f
3:25 (3:25) (Class 3) 5-Y-O+ **£6,498** (£1,908; £954; £477)

Form RPR
111 **1** **Tomngerry (IRE)**[21] 3997 6-11-4 0 WillKennedy 134+
(Brian Ellison) *nt fluent on occasions: hld up in tch: hdwy bef 2 out: led appr last: drvn and styd on strly* **6/1**[3]
-11F **2** *2 1/2* **April Dusk (IRE)**[24] 3922 7-11-4 0 GavinSheehan 132+
(Warren Greatrex) *trckd ldrs: nt fluent 8th: led bef 2 out: rdn and jst hdd whn nt fluent last: rallied: kpt on same pce run-in* **8/1**
12 **3** *26* **Bigironhiship (IRE)**[21] 3997 5-11-4 124 CraigNichol 111
(Rose Dobbin) *nt fluent on occasions: in tch: drvn and outpcd bef omitted 3 out: ch w first two fr 2 out* **18/1**
1313 **4** *18* **Delusionofgrandeur (IRE)**[20] 4015 6-11-8 140 DannyCook 98
(Sue Smith) *led: jnd and rdn 3 out (usual 4 out): hdd bef next: sn wknd* **9/4**[2]
141 **5** *57* **Bun Doran (IRE)**[35] 3743 5-11-4 138 DavyRussell 40
(Tom George) *pressed ldr: ev ch 3 out (usual 4 out): wknd bef 2 out: eased bef last* **11/10**[1]
5m 46.5s (10.50) **Going Correction** -0.075s/f (Good) **5** Ran SP% **109.0**
Speed ratings: **77,76,66,60,39**
CSF £43.03 TOTE £5.10: £2.70, £3.00; EX 28.30 Trifecta £100.70.
Owner Mrs J A Martin **Bred** Mrs E Tector **Trained** Norton, N Yorks
FOCUS
Not as competitive a novice hurdle as looked the case beforehand, the two market leaders both well below form, but still plenty to be positive about regards the unbeaten winner. He's clearly on the upgrade. After rail movements the actual race distance was 2m6f30yds.

4369 BETFRED SUPPORTS JACK BERRY HOUSE MARES' NOVICES' HURDLE (8 hdls 1 omitted) 2m 98y
4:00 (4:00) (Class 4) 4-Y-O+ **£4,548** (£1,335; £667; £333)

Form RPR
3P31 **1** **Presenting Rose (IRE)**[60] 3342 6-11-0 113 StephenMulqueen[(5)] 111+
(N W Alexander) *t.k.h: nt fluent on occasions: mde all: rdn 2 out: edgd rt last: styd on wl* **5/2**[2]
-43F **2** *1 3/4* **Knocklayde Sno Cat (IRE)**[17] 4052 7-10-5 105 (t) AdamShort[(7)] 100
(S R B Crawford, Ire) *hld up: nt fluent 3rd and next: hdwy and chsd wnr 2 out: 2 l down last: kpt on run-in: hld nr fin* **7/2**[3]
3-51 **3** *8* **Superfection (IRE)**[18] 4039 7-11-5 0 WillKennedy 102
(Donald McCain) *cl up: wnt 2nd bef 3 out (usual 4 out): rdn and outpcd 2 out: no imp whn nt fluent last* **7/2**[3]
-000 **4** *19* **Vic's Last Stand (IRE)**[6] 4271 6-10-9 0 HarryChalloner[(3)] 77
(Keith Reveley) *in tch: outpcd after 3 out (usual 4 out): plugged on fr last: no ch w ldrs* **25/1**
5 *9* **Amys Choice (IRE)**[666] 6-10-12 0 DavyRussell 67
(Rose Dobbin) *t.k.h: nt fluent on occasions: prom: outpcd after 3 out (usual 4 out): wknd bef 2 out* **9/4**[1]
004 **6** *1* **Fairlee Grace**[17] 4052 5-10-12 0 JanFaltejsek 66
(George Charlton) *cl up: ev ch 4th: rdn and outpcd 3 out (usual 4 out): btn next* **50/1**
0-0 **7** *11* **Spirit Dame (IRE)**[140] 1854 5-10-12 0 CraigNichol 56
(Rose Dobbin) *hld up: stdy hdwy 3 out (usual 4 out): wknd bef next* **100/1**
4m 10.6s (0.60) **Going Correction** -0.075s/f (Good) **7** Ran SP% **110.6**
Speed ratings (Par 105): **95,94,90,80,76 75,70**
CSF £10.97 TOTE £3.10: £1.90, £1.70; EX 15.60 Trifecta £46.30.
Owner Alistair Cochrane **Bred** Patrick Cullinan And Sandra Bromley **Trained** Kinneston, Perth & Kinross
FOCUS
Just an ordinary mares' event. The first two are rated pretty much to their marks. After rail movements the actual race distance was 2m113yds.

4370 BETFRED "THE HOME OF GOALS GALORE" H'CAP CHASE (QUALIFIER FOR THE CHALLENGER CHASE SERIES FINAL) (16 fncs) 2m 4f 19y
4:35 (4:35) (Class 3) (0-135,135) 5-Y-O+ **£9,747** (£2,862; £1,431; £715)

Form RPR
-101 **1** **Five In A Row (IRE)**[20] 4013 8-11-7 130 GavinSheehan 140+
(Brian Ellison) *prom: nt fluent 7th: rdn 5 out: rallied next: chsd ldr 3 out: led last 75yds: styd on gamely* **11/2**[2]
-P32 **2** *nk* **Central Flame**[24] 3936 8-11-4 132 MissCWalton[(5)] 138
(James Walton) *hld up: outpcd 1/2-way: last and plenty to do bef 4 out: gd hdwy 2 out: disp ld last 75yds: jst hld* **7/1**
221 **3** *1 1/2* **Indian Temple (IRE)**[57] 3425 7-10-11 127 MrWHRReed[(7)] 132
(W T Reed) *cl up: led 4 out: rdn and hdd last 75yds: no ex* **9/1**
14U5 **4** *6* **Final Assault (IRE)**[28] 3851 7-11-12 135 DerekFox 135
(Lucinda Russell) *hld up: stdy hdwy and prom 4 out: effrt and rdn next: kpt on same pce after 2 out* **15/2**

2-33 **5** *10* **Blakemount (IRE)**[110] 2399 8-11-9 132 .... DannyCook 123
(Sue Smith) *prom: drvn and outpcd 4 out: rallied 2 out: sn no imp* **5/2**[1]

-0P0 **6** *12* **Majala (FR)**[23] 3957 10-11-2 130 .... (tp) CharlieDeutsch(5) 112
(Tom George) *led: hit 2nd: rdn and hdd 4 out: wknd fr next* **20/1**

/P21 **7** *5* **Special Catch (IRE)**[24] 3936 9-11-4 130 .... HarryChalloner(3) 107
(Keith Reveley) *nt fluent on occasions: in tch: rdn 6 out: wknd fr 4 out* **6/1**[3]

52/4 **8** *19* **Humbie (IRE)**[57] 3425 12-10-11 120 .... BrianHarding 85
(Pauline Robson) *hld up: stdy hdwy on outside 9th: bdly hmpd by faller 5 out: nt rcvr* **12/1**

4112 **F** **Nautical Twilight**[31] 3806 6-11-4 127 .... (b) BrianHughes
(Malcolm Jefferson) *hld up in tch: stdy hdwy to chse ldrs whn hit 6 out: 5th and outpcd whn fell next* **12/1**

5m 25.4s (-1.80) **Going Correction** -0.075s/f (Good) 9 Ran SP% **112.7**
Speed ratings: **100,99,99,96,92 88,86,78,**
CSF £42.40 CT £337.42 TOTE £6.30: £1.90, £2.20, £2.80; EX 46.30 Trifecta £317.60.
Owner P J Martin **Bred** Ms M Maher **Trained** Norton, N Yorks

FOCUS
A fairly useful handicap, the winner confirming the merit of his Musselburgh win. After rail movements the actual race distance was 2m4f44yds.

4371 BETFRED TV BUMPER STANDARD OPEN NATIONAL HUNT FLAT RACE 2m 98y

5:05 (5:07) (Class 6) 4-6-Y-O **£1,949** (£572; £286; £143)

Form RPR

23 **1** **Boudry (FR)**[23] 3952 5-11-2 0 .... GavinSheehan 116+
(Warren Greatrex) *hld up: shkn up briefly over 4f out: smooth hdwy to ld over 1f out: pushed along and drew clr fnl f: easily* **10/11**[1]

16 **2** *9* **Mcgregor's Cottage (IRE)**[28] 3861 5-11-2 0 .... BrianHughes 105
(Malcolm Jefferson) *prom: effrt and pushed along over 2f out: chsd wnr over 1f out: plugged on fnl f: no imp* **9/1**[3]

313 **3** *7* **Applaus (GER)**[70] 3165 4-10-11 0 .... (t) JoeColliver(3) 98
(Micky Hammond) *in tch: stdy hdwy over 5f out: rdn and outpcd over 2f out: rallied and swtchd rt over 1f out: sn no imp* **9/1**[3]

554- **4** *2 1/2* **K O Kenny**[313] 5426 5-10-13 0 .... JohnKington(3) 97
(Andrew Crook) *w ldr: led over 2f out to over 1f out: edgd lft and sn btn* **33/1**

31 **5** *13* **Shambougg**[30] 3827 5-11-4 0 .... CiaranGethings(5) 92
(Philip Hobbs) *led at ordinary gallop: rdn and hdd over 2f out: wknd over 1f out* **2/1**[2]

50 **6** *20* **Cupid's Quest (IRE)**[19] 4037 4-9-7 0 .... JamesCorbett(7) 51
(Susan Corbett) *t.k.h: chsd ldrs: struggling over 3f out: sn btn* **66/1**

0 **7** *17* **Motion To Strike (IRE)**[19] 4037 6-11-2 0 .... HenryBrooke 52
(Rebecca Menzies) *hld up on outside: drvn and outpcd wl over 2f out: sn btn: eased whn no ch fnl f* **28/1**

4m 4.4s **Going Correction** -0.075s/f (Good)
WFA 4 from 5yo+ 9lb 7 Ran SP% **113.6**
Speed ratings: **97,92,89,87,81 71,62**
CSF £10.19 TOTE £1.90: £1.50, £2.60; EX 8.10 Trifecta £27.00.
Owner Power Geneva Ltd **Bred** Jean Sandoz **Trained** Upper Lambourn, Berks
■ Stewards' Enquiry : Ciaran Gethings three-day ban; careless riding (12th-14th March)

FOCUS
Not a strong bumper, particularly with the second favourite clearly well below par, and the winner was a class apart. The third and fourth set the level. After rail movements the actual race distance was 2m113yds.
T/Plt: £235.80 to a £1 stake. Pool: £79,099.88 - 244.86 winning tickets T/Qpdt: £59.70 to a £1 stake. Pool: £6,714.89 - 83.22 winning tickets **Richard Young**

4372 - 4378a (Foreign Racing) - See Raceform Interactive

4196 FONTWELL (L-H)

Sunday, February 28

OFFICIAL GOING: Good to soft (soft in places; 6.3)
Wind: quite strong across Weather: overcast Rails: Rail movement adding 12yds to all races except the 4.20 add 18yds.

4379 TOTEPLACEPOT JOSH GIFFORD MEMORIAL NOVICES' CHASE (FOR THE JOSH GIFFORD CUP) (13 fncs) 2m 1f 96y

2:20 (2:20) (Class 2) 5-Y-O+ **£18,270**

Form RPR

P- **1** **Orbasa (FR)**[116] 5-11-2 132 .... (t) NoelFehily 137+
(Paul Nicholls) *j.w: mde all: drawing clr whn lft wl clr 3 out: fin alone* **1/5**[1]

4-55 **U** **Ma'ire Rua (IRE)**[101] 2604 9-10-12 100 .... JamesBest
(Alan Jones) *detached in 3rd thrght: lost tch 8th: t.o whn mstke and uns rdr 3 out* **20/1**[3]

-530 **F** **Blue Bear (IRE)**[17] 4070 7-10-12 118 .... MarcGoldstein
(Diana Grissell) *trckd wnr: chalng whn stmbld 4 out: rdn and hld whn fell 3 out* **9/2**[2]

4m 46.1s (11.40) **Going Correction** +0.80s/f (Soft) 3 Ran SP% **106.3**
Speed ratings: **105, ,**
TOTE £1.10 Trifecta £1.10.
Owner Potensis Bloodstock Limited **Bred** Marc Bouyssou & Xavier Cheyrou **Trained** Ditcheat, Somerset

FOCUS
Hurdles and fences on inner line, and fresh ground on bends. Race run over 12 yards further than advertised. The official going was changed from soft, good to soft in places before racing. A poor turnout for this valuable novice chase, which used to be run over 2m5f.

4380 TOTEQUADPOT H'CAP CHASE (FOR THE CERTAIN JUSTICE CHALLENGE TROPHY) (16 fncs) 2m 5f 31y

2:50 (2:50) (Class 4) (0-115,115) 5-Y-O+ **£5,198** (£1,526; £763; £381)

Form RPR

11P2 **1** **Thinger Licht (FR)**[37] 3727 7-11-4 107 .... (p) HarrySkelton 129+
(Dan Skelton) *trckd ldrs: led after 4 out: drew clr fr next: v easily* **5/2**[1]

0354 **2** *15* **Venetian Lad**[74] 3115 11-11-3 106 .... MarcGoldstein 104
(Lydia Richards) *chsd ldrs: dropped to hld 5th u.p after 4 out: styd on fr last: snatched 2nd fnl strides: no ch w wnr* **12/1**

01P1 **3** *shd* **Golanova**[10] 4199 8-11-10 113 .... (b) JamieMoore 115
(Gary Moore) *in tch: nudged along fr 4th: drvn in 4th after 4 out: styd on into 2nd at the last but no threat to wnr: no ex whn lost 2nd fnl strides* **7/2**[2]

54P3 **4** *1 1/2* **Miss Oscarose (IRE)**[44] 3609 9-10-2 91 .... (t) TomO'Brien 91
(Paul Henderson) *chsd ldrs: nt fluent 2nd: struggling whn mstke 12th: one pce and hld fr next: wnt 4th run-in* **10/1**

5-00 **5** *3* **Knockalongi**[17] 4069 10-11-2 112 .... (p) BenFfrenchDavis(7) 109
(Dominic Ffrench Davis) *trckd ldrs: rdn after 4 out: 3rd and hld whn mstke 3 out: wknd run-in* **14/1**

5656 **6** *11* **For Two (FR)**[34] 3776 7-11-12 115 .... (t) TomCannon 102
(Chris Gordon) *led: j. sltly lft at times: hdd after 4 out: hld fr next: wknd last* **11/2**

-064 **7** *6* **Itoldyou (IRE)**[31] 3823 10-11-8 114 .... (tp) ThomasGarner(3) 99
(Linda Jewell) *hit 6th: a in last pair: struggling after 10th: nvr threatened to get involved* **4/1**[3]

4-4P **8** *13* **Bravo Riquet (FR)**[23] 3977 10-10-13 102 .... (vt) TomScudamore 75
(Robin Mathew) *prom: nt fluent and lost pl 8th: struggling in last pair after 10th: nvr bk on terms* **22/1**

5m 55.0s (12.00) **Going Correction** +0.80s/f (Soft) 8 Ran SP% **114.0**
Speed ratings: **109,103,103,102,101 97,95,90**
CSF £30.56 CT £104.58 TOTE £2.60: £1.40, £2.70, £1.90; EX 21.50 Trifecta £107.30.
Owner Carl Hodgson **Bred** M Jacques Chapet & Mme Anne Dupont **Trained** Alcester, Warwicks

FOCUS
Race run over 12 yards further than advertised. A wide-margin winner of an ordinary handicap chase, with a big chase pb from the winner.

4381 TOTEPOOL NATIONAL SPIRIT HURDLE (GRADE 2) (10 hdls) 2m 3f 33y

3:20 (3:21) (Class 1) 4-Y-O+
£45,560 (£17,096; £8,560; £4,264; £2,144; £1,072)

Form RPR

3123 **1** **Lil Rockerfeller (USA)**[36] 3733 5-11-7 154 .... (p) TrevorWhelan 156+
(Neil King) *trckd ldr: led 2 out: sn clr: comf* **7/4**[1]

/4U4 **2** *9* **Ubak (FR)**[22] 3991 8-11-3 144 .... JoshuaMoore 143
(Gary Moore) *led: rdn and hdd 2 out: lost 2nd at the last: rallied to regain 2nd fnl 120yds but no ch w wnr* **17/2**

1523 **3** *2 1/4* **San Benedeto (FR)**[17] 4070 5-11-3 145 .... (t) SamTwiston-Davies 140
(Paul Nicholls) *trckd ldrs: rdn and ev ch 2 out: wnt hld 2nd at the last: no ex whn lost 2nd fnl 120yds* **8/1**

6520 **4** *1 1/2* **Cheltenian (FR)**[15] 4115 10-11-7 153 .... RichardJohnson 145
(Philip Hobbs) *hld up in last trio: tk clsr order 6th: mstke 3 out: sn rdn: mstke last: nvr threatened: kpt on same pce* **7/2**[2]

4332 **5** *12* **Melodic Rendezvous**[8] 4253 10-11-3 146 .... (p) MattGriffiths 132
(Jeremy Scott) *trckd ldrs: rdn after 3 out: nt pce to get on terms: fdd run-in* **9/1**

2062 **6** *21* **Disputed (IRE)**[16] 4096 6-11-3 119 .... TomCannon 109
(Chris Gordon) *hld up in last trio: rdn after 3 out: nvr gng pce to get on terms: wknd between last 2* **150/1**

P-45 **7** *21* **Grumeti**[99] 2634 8-11-3 148 .... WayneHutchinson 90
(Alan King) *trckd ldrs: rdn after 7th: wknd 2 out: t.o* **11/2**[3]

14-P **8** *23* **Medinas (FR)**[22] 3992 9-11-11 150 .... DenisO'Regan 77
(Alan King) *hld up in last trio: pushed along after 6th: rdn after next: wknd after 3 out: t.o* **22/1**

4m 59.2s (-0.20) **Going Correction** +0.325s/f (Yiel)
WFA 4 from 5yo+ 9lb 8 Ran SP% **110.6**
Speed ratings (Par 115): **113,109,108,107,102 93,84,75**
CSF £16.41 TOTE £2.40: £1.20, £2.50, £2.30; EX 18.40 Trifecta £159.50.
Owner Davies Smith Govier & Brown **Bred** Brushwood Stable **Trained** Barbury Castle, Wiltshire

FOCUS
Race run over 12 yards further than advertised. A good field for Fontwell's richest-ever race. The winner is rated to his mark in a well run renewal.

4382 TOTEEXACTA SUPPORTS THE RACEHORSE SANCTUARY NOVICES' HURDLE (10 hdls) 2m 3f 33y

3:50 (3:50) (Class 4) 5-Y-O+ **£3,898** (£1,144; £572; £286)

Form RPR

6 **1** **King Cool**[24] 3949 5-10-12 0 .... JamieMoore 113+
(Gary Moore) *sn trcking ldrs: led 3 out: drew clr between last 2: v easily* **11/4**[2]

004 **2** *23* **Talk Of The South (IRE)**[27] 3902 7-10-12 0 .... NickScholfield 86
(Paul Henderson) *hld up: hdwy appr 7th: rdn to chal for 2nd whn mstke 2 out and last: styd on but no ch w wnr* **9/2**[3]

5-30 **3** *1 3/4* **Monkey Rum**[8] 4256 6-10-12 0 .... PeterCarberry 82
(Brendan Powell) *mid-div: hdwy after 6th: travelling wl disputing 2nd 2 out: sn rdn: sn hld: no ex run-in* **33/1**

P **4** *1 1/2* **Yur Next (IRE)**[27] 3902 8-10-5 0 .... TomCannon 76
(Alison Batchelor) *trckd ldr: pushed along whn nt fluent 7th: rdn after 3 out: one pce fr next* **100/1**

4 **5** *12* **Zadok**[76] 3082 6-10-12 0 .... MichealNolan 70
(Jamie Snowden) *trckd ldrs: rdn after 7th: wknd after 2 out* **9/1**

0-03 **6** *18* **Georgies Pip**[64] 3215 5-10-5 0 .... JoshuaMoore 47
(Brendan Powell) *racd wout declared tongue-tie: hld up: hdwy after 7th: rdn after 3 out: wknd between last 2: wnt lft last* **40/1**

3-P1 **7** *46* **Saucysioux**[41] 3664 6-10-12 0 .... AndrewThornton 13
(Michael Roberts) *mid-div: wnt rt 2nd: mstke and reminder after 4th: sn bhd: t.o 7th* **5/1**

503 **8** *4* **Tipperairy (IRE)**[11] 4182 5-10-12 0 .... HarrySkelton 9
(Dan Skelton) *hld up: struggling after 6th: wknd next: t.o* **9/4**[1]

0 **P** **King Charlie (IRE)**[16] 4102 6-10-12 0 .... TomO'Brien
(Suzy Smith) *trckd ldrs: rdn after 7th: wknd after next: t.o whn p.u bef last* **25/1**

-654 **P** **Meyrem Ana**[10] 4196 6-9-12 0 .... MrWillPettis(7)
(Natalie Lloyd-Beavis) *led tl 3 out: sn rdn and wknd: t.o whn p.u bef last* **200/1**

5m 13.7s (14.30) **Going Correction** +0.325s/f (Yiel) 10 Ran SP% **113.0**
Speed ratings: **82,72,71,70,65 58,38,37, ,**
CSF £14.73 TOTE £3.30: £1.20, £1.40, £7.40; EX 18.00 Trifecta £272.60.
Owner P Mott **Bred** Paul Brewer **Trained** Lower Beeding, W Sussex
■ Stewards' Enquiry : Tom Cannon caution; careless riding.

FOCUS
Race run over 12 yards further than advertised. The time was 14.5sec slower than the Grade 2 National Spirit Hurdle. With two of the market leaders below par, there are doubts over this form. The second sets the level.

4383 TOTETRIFECTA FOXHUNTER TRIAL (AN OPEN HUNTERS' CHASE) (FOR THE WHITELAW CHALLENGE CUP) (19 fncs) 3m 1f 106y

4:20 (4:21) (Class 6) 5-Y-O+ **£2,089** (£798)

Form RPR

20-1 **1** **Mendip Express (IRE)**[31] 3826 10-12-1 146 .... (t) MrDavidMaxwell(5) 127+
(Philip Hobbs) *trckd ldrs: disp 4th tl led 7th: jnd again next: 2 l up whn mstke 3 out: narrowly hdd next: styd on to regain ld fnl 50yds* **4/9**[1]

01 **2** *nk* **Impact Area (IRE)**[21] 10-11-9 0.......................(p) MrLouisMuspratt(5) 116
(Mrs Harriet Waight) *led 4th tl 7th: pressed wnr most of way fr next: rdn to take narrow advantage 2 out where wnt sltly rt: wnt sltly rt last: hdd fnl 50yds* **5/1**[2]

/0-2 **U** **Good Egg (IRE)**[9] 4227 13-11-5 106.................... MissSRippon(7)
(Miss Sarah Rippon) *trcking ldrs whn mstke and uns rdr 5th* **14/1**

0/31 **U** **Join Together (IRE)**[24] 3958 11-11-11 134.................... MissBFrost(5)
(Mrs Rose Loxton) *led tl uns rdr 4th* **11/2**[3]

340/ **U** **Featherintheattic (IRE)**[680] 11-11-7 103.................... MrTGreatrex(5)
(A J S Phillips-Hill) *trckd ldrs: struggling after 7th: uns rdr next* **100/1**

7m 14.2s (13.10) **Going Correction** +0.80s/f (Soft) 5 Ran SP% **109.0**
Speed ratings: **111,110, , ,**
CSF £3.24 TOTE £1.40: £1.10, £2.20; EX 4.50 Trifecta £4.50.
Owner David Maxwell Racing Limited **Bred** Miss E Hamilton **Trained** Withycombe, Somerset

FOCUS
Race run over 18 yards further than advertised. This hunter chase was left as a match from as early as the eighth fence, but it produced a fine finish. Not an easy race to put a figure on.

4384 TOTEPOOL LIKE US ON FACEBOOK H'CAP HURDLE (9 hdls) 2m 1f 145y
4:50 (4:50) (Class 4) (0-115,113) 4-Y-0+ **£3,898** (£1,144; £572; £286)

Form RPR

066 **1** **Wells De Lune (FR)**[15] 4129 5-11-11 112.......................(t[1]) RichardJohnson 129+
(Charlie Longsdon) *mde all: blnd 3 out: drew wl clr fr next: unchal* **7/2**[2]

3144 **2** *21* **Thepartysover**[10] 4197 11-11-4 105.......................(t) JamieMoore 98
(Paul Henderson) *towards rr: rdn after 6th: stdy prog after 3 out: styd on fr last: snatched 2nd fnl stride: nvr any ch w wnr* **25/1**

P14 **3** *nse* **Darwins Theory (IRE)**[16] 4096 8-11-5 113.......................(t) MrMLegg(7) 106
(Fiona Shaw) *mid-div: rdn after 7th: stdy prog after 3 out: styd on into hld 2nd run-in: lost 2nd fnl stride* **14/1**

6502 **4** *3 1/4* **Ourmanmassini (IRE)**[37] 3725 8-11-9 110.......................(t) TomO'Brien 102
(Suzy Smith) *trckd ldrs: rdn to chse wnr after 3 out: hld fr next: no ex fr last* **17/2**

4-04 **5** *3 1/4* **Bladoun (FR)**[89] 2831 8-11-6 107.......................(p) TomScudamore 94
(David Pipe) *trckd ldr tl rdn after 3 out: hld fr next: no ex run-in* **8/1**

3-1P **6** *8* **Brave Deed (IRE)**[95] 2712 10-11-1 102.................... NickScholfield 82
(Jeremy Scott) *bhd: struggling after 4th: sme minor late prog: nvr on terms* **10/1**

P6P3 **7** *8* **Very Noble (FR)**[16] 4096 7-11-1 102.......................(t) TomCannon 75
(Chris Gordon) *mid-div tl struggling in last after 5th: nvr bk on terms* **7/1**[3]

/531 **8** *12* **Herons Heir (IRE)**[37] 3725 8-11-12 113.......................(t) HarrySkelton 75
(Dan Skelton) *mid-div: hdwy 5th: rdn after 3 out: qckly btn* **11/4**[1]

/64- **9** *48* **Bushel (USA)**[38] 785 6-11-7 108.................... AndrewThornton 27
(Tony Newcombe) *mid-div: drvn along fr after 5th: bhd fr next: t.o* **50/1**

3403 **10** *18* **While You Wait (IRE)**[34] 3777 7-11-9 113.................... LucyGardner(3) 15
(Sue Gardner) *mid-div tl wknd bef 3 out: t.o: b.b.v* **15/2**

4m 41.6s (7.30) **Going Correction** +0.325s/f (Yiel) 10 Ran SP% **116.4**
Speed ratings (Par 105): **96,86,86,85,83 80,76,71,49,41**
CSF £79.74 CT £1096.67 TOTE £4.40: £1.90, £4.50, £3.80; EX 74.80 Trifecta £1428.70.
Owner Swanee River Partnership **Bred** Francis Picoulet **Trained** Over Norton, Oxon

FOCUS
Race run over 12 yards further than advertised. Not many got into this modest handicap hurdle, the winner making all. This was a massive step up on his British form and he can win again.

4385 MYTOTEPOOL.COM MAIDEN OPEN NATIONAL HUNT FLAT RACE 2m 1f 145y
5:20 (5:22) (Class 6) 4-6-Y-0 **£1,559** (£457; £228; £114)

Form RPR

2-52 **1** **King Uther**[27] 3907 6-11-3 0.................... TomCannon 120+
(Chris Gordon) *mde all: pushed along over 6f out: rdn clr over 2f out: styd on strly* **6/1**[3]

2 **2** *23* **Crank Em Up (IRE)**[24] 3959 5-11-3 0.................... AidanColeman 99
(David Dennis) *chsd ldrs: wnt 2nd over 6f out: rdn 3f out: sn hld* **1/1**[1]

0 **3** *20* **Belmont Park (FR)**[16] 4102 5-11-3 0.................... TomScudamore 81
(David Bridgwater) *chsd wnr tl over 6f out: lost tch 4f out: regained modest 3rd fnl f* **16/1**

4 *13* **Free Stone Hill (IRE)**[145] 1804 6-11-3 0.................... HarrySkelton 70
(Dan Skelton) *hld up: hdwy 1/2-way: wnt cl 3rd over 6f out: rdn 3f out: wknd over 2f out: t.o* **9/4**[2]

5 *103* **Nelson's Victory** 6-11-3 0.................... MarcGoldstein
(Diana Grissell) *chsd ldrs tl dropped to rr u.p 1/2-way: sn t.o* **10/1**

0 **P** **That Will Do**[24] 3959 6-10-12 0.................... ConorRing(5)
(Helen Nelmes) *a last: struggling 1/2-way: sn t.o: p.u over 1f out* **100/1**

4m 40.0s (11.30) **Going Correction** +0.325s/f (Yiel) 6 Ran SP% **111.0**
Speed ratings: **87,76,67,62,**
CSF £12.26 TOTE £6.20: £2.50, £1.40; EX 11.80 Trifecta £66.70.
Owner Anthony Ward-Thomas **Bred** Maggi Searles **Trained** Morestead, Hampshire

FOCUS
Race run over 12 yards further than advertised. The winner set a searching gallop. The form could be at least 7lb out either way.
T/Jkpt: Not won. T/Plt: £59.80 to a £1 stake. Pool: £82,457.01 - 1,006.43 winning tickets. T/Qpdt: £21.20 to a £1 stake. Pool: £7,610.18 - 265.43 winning tickets. **Tim Mitchell**

3061 SOUTHWELL (L-H)
Sunday, February 28

OFFICIAL GOING: Good to soft (soft in places; 7.3)
Wind: moderate 1/2 against Weather: fine and sunny but cold

4386 RACEGOERSCLUB.CO.UK H'CAP CHASE (13 fncs) 1m 7f 153y
2:10 (2:10) (Class 4) (0-120,119) 5-Y-0+ **£4,548** (£1,335; £667; £333)

Form RPR

6-0P **1** **Santa's Secret (IRE)**[89] 2837 8-11-2 109.......................(p) LeightonAspell 124+
(Oliver Sherwood) *chsd ldrs: lft in ld 9th: drvn next: clr whn hit last: drvn out* **11/2**

F42U **2** *11* **Buck Mulligan**[93] 2746 11-11-12 119.................... PaulMoloney 123
(Evan Williams) *hld up in rr: hdwy 8th: 2nd 2 out: kpt on same pce* **7/2**[2]

5P24 **3** *2 1/2* **Trapper Peak (IRE)**[17] 4073 7-10-13 106.................... AdamWedge 108
(Alexandra Dunn) *hld up in rr: trckd ldrs 6th: 2nd appr 3 out: one pce fr 2 out* **11/4**[1]

P231 **4** *6* **Pret A Thou (FR)**[10] 4209 13-11-5 115.................... HarryChalloner(3) 112
(John Groucott) *trckd ldrs: t.k.h: hmpd 9th: sn outpcd: lost pl and hit 3 out* **4/1**[3]

2106 **5** *5* **Blades Lad**[24] 3475 7-11-5 112.......................(p) BrianHughes 108
(Peter Niven) *chsd ldrs: 2nd whn hit 10th: lost pl 2 out: bhd whn j.rt last* **11/2**

02P1 **R** **Marky Bob (IRE)**[103] 2552 11-10-9 102.................... DaveCrosse
(Hugo Froud) *ref to r: tk no part* **12/1**

/2-P **F** **Netherby**[38] 3709 10-11-8 115.................... AndrewGlassonbury
(Gary Moore) *led: hit 7th: fell 9th: fatally injured* **12/1**

4m 11.3s (9.30) **Going Correction** +0.75s/f (Soft) 7 Ran SP% **115.0**
Speed ratings: **106,100,99,96,93**
CSF £25.82 TOTE £8.20: £3.90, £3.20; EX 28.50 Trifecta £87.70.
Owner Barratt, Gumienny, Johnsons & Signys **Bred** John Mulvaney **Trained** Upper Lambourn, Berks

FOCUS
The first jumps meeting of the year at the track and after a dry night the official going was changed to good to soft, soft in places. After riding in the opener both Paul Moloney and Brian Hughes described the ground as 'dead', with Hughes adding 'it is tiring enough out there'. \n\x\x A fair handicap chase and the winner proved too good.

4387 DAVE DEAN 30TH BIRTHDAY BASH NOVICES' H'CAP CHASE (21 fncs) 3m 1f 129y
2:40 (2:40) (Class 4) (0-105,102) 5-Y-0 **£5,651** (£1,684; £852; £436; £228)

Form RPR

0505 **1** **Midnight Jade (IRE)**[33] 3787 7-10-3 79.................... LeeEdwards 87+
(John Groucott) *mde all: drvn bef 3 out: 1 l ahd whn edgd rt: styd on wl* **7/1**

1142 **2** *2* **Arthamint**[13] 4160 8-11-12 102.......................(t) DavidEngland 108
(Dan Skelton) *j.rt: trckd ldrs: 2nd 2 out: kpt on same pce run-in* **7/2**[2]

3345 **3** *2 1/4* **Rocky Stone (IRE)**[19] 4047 8-11-3 93.......................(t) WillKennedy 96
(Donald McCain) *chsd wnr: reminders appr 3 out: drvn and hung lft: one pce appr last* **11/4**[1]

0265 **4** *20* **Joseph Mercer (IRE)**[25] 3937 9-11-0 90.......................(p) JonathanEngland 75
(Tina Jackson) *chsd ldrs: rdn 4 out: sn lost pl and bhd* **7/2**[2]

202/ **5** *9* **Tickatack (IRE)**[35] 11-11-4 94.................... KielanWoods 74
(Graeme McPherson) *in last: drvn and nt fluent 16th: hit next 2: lost pl sn after 4 out: sn bhd: eased clsng stages* **4/1**[3]

-00P **U** **Benability (IRE)**[88] 2851 6-11-0 95.................... AlanJohns(5)
(Tim Vaughan) *in rr: blnd and uns rdr 1st* **10/1**

7m 9.7s (23.70) **Going Correction** +0.75s/f (Soft) 6 Ran SP% **112.7**
Speed ratings: **93,92,91,85,82**
CSF £31.77 TOTE £6.70: £3.50, £1.70; EX 33.10 Trifecta £190.40.
Owner Mrs Robin Birley **Bred** M C McDaniel-Stone **Trained** Bourton, Shropshire

FOCUS
A moderate handicap chase in which the winner was never headed.

4388 RACEGOERSCLUB.CO.UK NOVICES' HURDLE (9 hdls) 1m 7f 153y
3:10 (3:10) (Class 4) 4-Y-0+ **£4,548** (£1,335; £667; £333)

Form RPR

0 **1** **Man From Seville**[51] 3509 6-11-2 0.................... PaddyBrennan 116+
(Fergal O'Brien) *chsd ldrs: 2nd bef 3 out: drvn appr next: hit last and lft abt 8 l ld: drvn out* **20/1**

36 **2** *3 3/4* **Nobel Leader (IRE)**[64] 3226 6-11-2 0.......................(p[1]) LiamTreadwell 110
(James Evans) *chsd ldrs: one pce bef 2 out: lft 4th last: kpt on to take 2nd clsng stages* **12/1**

-006 **3** *shd* **Windy Writer (IRE)**[70] 3179 6-10-13 0.................... RyanHatch(3) 110
(Shaun Lycett) *mid-div: hdwy and modest 5th 3 out: lft 3rd last: kpt on clsng stages* **100/1**

3034 **4** *1/2* **Moidore**[30] 3839 7-11-2 115.................... AdamPogson 110
(Charles Pogson) *led: nt fluent 3rd: mstke 5th and rdr briefly lost iron: hdd next: outpcd 3 out lft modest 2nd last: one pce* **3/1**[2]

00-P **5** *21* **Rose Revived**[25] 3927 5-10-2 0.................... PatrickCowley(7) 83
(Jonjo O'Neill) *mid-div: outpcd bef 7th* **10/1**[3]

0000 **6** *2 3/4* **St Lewis**[17] 4065 6-11-2 0.................... SeanQuinlan 89
(Jennie Candlish) *in rr: sme hdwy after 6th: reminders and outpcd next* **100/1**

00- **7** *5* **Amber Gambler (GER)**[21] 6-11-2 0.................... WillKennedy 83
(Ian Williams) *in rr: nvr on terms* **10/1**[3]

660P **8** *2* **Down The Line (IRE)**[58] 3397 6-11-2 0.................... LeightonAspell 82
(Alan Swinbank) *mid-div: bhd fr 3 out* **66/1**

65 **9** *4* **Princess Tiana (IRE)**[24] 3947 5-10-9 0.................... RichieMcLernon 71
(Jonjo O'Neill) *chsd ldrs: drvn 3 out: sn lost pl* **33/1**

6 **10** *8* **Lord Of The Island (IRE)**[11] 4183 8-11-2 0.................... DavidBass 71
(Sally Randell) *in rr: hdwy 5th: lost pl after next* **33/1**

6 **11** *41* **Breezemount (IRE)**[18] 4050 6-11-2 0.................... BrianHarding 34
(Donald McCain) *bhd and drvn 4th: t.o 3 out: eventually completed* **33/1**

0-13 **U** **Aqua Dude (IRE)**[72] 3135 6-11-8 130.................... PaulMoloney 120+
(Evan Williams) *trckd ldrs: led 6th: drvn appr 2 out: 3 l ahd whn j. bdly rt and stmbld on landing last: uns rdr* **4/6**[1]

00 **P** **Babylone Colombe (FR)**[74] 3105 5-10-6 0.................... BenPoste(3)
(Tom Symonds) *in rr: bhd fr 6th: t.o whn p.u bef 2 out* **125/1**

4m 4.0s (7.00) **Going Correction** +0.60s/f (Soft) 13 Ran SP% **128.7**
Speed ratings (Par 105): **106,104,104,103,93 91,89,88,86,82 61, ,**
CSF £237.05 TOTE £14.70: £2.30, £3.50, £13.10; EX 329.30 Trifecta £5927.00 Part won. Pool: £7,902.78 - 0.16 winning units..
Owner Mr & Mrs William Rucker **Bred** Lady Bamford **Trained** Naunton, Gloucs

FOCUS
A fair novices' hurdle with little strength in depth but there was a dramatic incident late on when the hot favourite unseated his rider at the last when seemingly in command.

4389 SOPER OF LINCOLN BMW & MINI H'CAP HURDLE (13 hdls) 2m 7f 209y
3:40 (3:40) (Class 3) (0-140,137) 4-Y-0 **£7,596** (£2,244; £1,122; £561; £280)

Form RPR

22UP **1** **Delgany Demon**[45] 3591 8-11-1 126.................... SeanBowen 131+
(Neil King) *trckd ldrs: led appr last: drvn out* **8/1**

-P44 **2** *3 3/4* **Pyrshan (IRE)**[71] 3146 7-10-0 111.......................(t) KielanWoods 113
(Graeme McPherson) *hld up towards rr: hdwy to trck ldrs 3 out: 3rd last: kpt on to take 2nd fnl strides* **9/2**[2]

4-10 **3** *hd* **Optimistic Bias (IRE)**[100] 2624 7-10-7 125.................... PatrickCowley(7) 128
(Jonjo O'Neill) *trckd ldrs: led appr 2 out: hdd appr last: hit last: kpt on same pce* **3/1**[1]

31P **4** *8* **Amiral Collonges (FR)**[30] 3844 6-10-13 124.................... LiamTreadwell 120
(James Evans) *sn chsng ldrs: led briefly sn after 3 out: wknd appr last* **5/1**[3]

241P **5** *nk* **Away For Slates (IRE)**[37] 3728 6-10-10 121....................[1] BrianHarding 116
(Keith Dalgleish) *uns rdr and rn loose bef s: hld up in rr: hdwy 10th: drvn to chse ldrs next: j.lft and wknd last* **9/1**

P-4P **6** *29* **Kaysersberg (FR)**[74] 3116 9-11-9 137.................... HarryBannister(3) 105
(Warren Greatrex) *led: j.rt 5th: hdd sn after 3 out: sn lost pl and bhd: t.o* **11/2**

1-33 **7** *3 3/4* **Driftashore (IRE)**[32] 3804 9-10-9 127.................... MissBHampson(7) 92
(Sally Randell) *prom: lost pl 10th: sn bhd: t.o 2 out* **25/1**

P200 **8** *12* **According To Trev (IRE)**[43] 3622 10-11-1 **131**.................. JakeHodson(5) 85
(David Bridgwater) *chsd ldrs: drvn 9th: lost pl after next: sn bhd: t.o* **16/1**
FU33 **9** *6* **Road To Freedom**[17] 4066 7-10-4 **115**..........................(p) LeightonAspell 64
(Lucy Wadham) *chsd ldrs: drvn 3 out: sn lost pl and bhd: t.o next* **11/2**
6m 23.1s (8.10) **Going Correction** +0.60s/f (Soft) **9 Ran SP% 121.5**
Speed ratings (Par 107): **110,108,108,106,105 96,95,91,89**
CSF £46.80 CT £136.44 TOTE £8.00: £2.40, £1.70, £1.60; EX 41.20 Trifecta £306.30.
Owner C M Wilson **Bred** C M Wilson **Trained** Barbury Castle, Wiltshire
FOCUS
A useful handicap hurdle, although it wasn't the strongest for the grade.

4390 DEAN LAUNDRY SYSTEMS (S) H'CAP HURDLE (9 hdls) 1m 7f 153y
4:10 (4:10) (Class 5) (0-100,100) 4-Y-0+ **£3,249** (£954; £477; £238)

Form RPR
44P0 **1** **Goal (IRE)**[46] 3586 8-11-3 **98**..............................(vt) MissBHampson(7) 103+
(Sally Randell) *chsd ldrs: led 7th: 3 l ahd last: drvn rt out* **17/2**
0434 **2** *1 ¼* **Aaman (IRE)**[13] 4161 10-10-0 **77**....................................... RobertWilliams(3) 80
(Bernard Llewellyn) *mid-div: clr 4th and drvn appr 2 out: 2nd last: kpt on* **6/1[3]**
5344 **3** *8* **Orchard Road (USA)**[28] 3886 9-11-7 **100**..............(t) DiarmuidO'Regan(5) 98
(Tristan Davidson) *chsd ldrs: 2nd 2 out: wknd last* **11/4[1]**
1550 **4** *3 ¾* **Pandorica**[25] 3932 8-11-5 **100**...........................(p) JordanWilliams(7) 92
(Bernard Llewellyn) *rr-div: hdwy appr 2 out: kpt on to take modest 4th last 75yds* **12/1**
00-P **5** *3 ¼* **Nicki's Nipper**[303] 65 8-10-0 **74** oh5.................................. DavidEngland 63
(Sam Drake) *chsd ldrs: 3rd 3 out: wknd between last 2* **40/1**
P36U **6** *7* **Indian Daudaie (FR)**[9] 4223 9-11-1 **99**..................(b) RomainClavreul(10) 82
(Sarah Humphrey) *w ldr: led 5th: hdd 3 out: sn wknd* **20/1**
0-66 **7** *8* **Mount Shamsan**[41] 3660 6-11-11 **99**.............................. AndrewGlassonbury 75
(Gary Moore) *chsd ldrs: drvn 4th: 2nd 3 out: lost pl bef next: sn eased* **5/1[2]**
0401 **8** *6* **Razzle Dazzle 'Em**[9] 4223 7-10-10 **84**...................................... BrendanPowell 54
(Shaun Harris) *led to 5th: drvn 3 out: sn lost pl* **5/1[2]**
/0-0 **9** *7* **Lordship (IRE)**[30] 3840 12-10-0 **74**... TommyPhelan 38
(Tom Gretton) *in rr: brief effrt 3 out: sn lost pl* **33/1**
1340 **10** *11* **Worldor (FR)**[25] 3932 10-11-12 **100**....................................(t) AdamWedge 54
(Alexandra Dunn) *in rr: bhd fr 3 out* **12/1**
6-3P **11** *43* **Acapulco Bay**[25] 3932 12-11-2 **90**......................................(p) RobertDunne 6
(Dai Burchell) *prom: lost pl 6th: sn bhd: t.o 2 out* **20/1**
3350 **P** **Gud Day (IRE)**[11] 4184 8-10-7 **81**.......................................(p) PaddyBrennan
(Conor Dore) *in rr: bhd fr 3 out: t.o whn p.u bef next* **10/1**
0050 **P** **Sweet Midnight**[72] 3143 4-10-8 **91**... CharliePoste
(John Holt) *in rr: drvn 4th: bhd fr 6th: t.o whn p.u bef 2 out* **50/1**
4m 8.1s (11.10) **Going Correction** +0.60s/f (Soft)
WFA 4 from 6yo+ 9lb **13 Ran SP% 126.2**
Speed ratings (Par 103): **96,95,91,89,87 84,80,77,73,68 46, ,**
CSF £59.31 CT £183.49 TOTE £14.70: £5.90, £2.80, £1.30; EX 76.50 Trifecta £319.80.
Owner Mark Hampson **Bred** A M F Persse **Trained** Broad Hinton, Wilts
■ The first winner as a trainer for Sally Randell.
FOCUS
A typically moderate selling handicap hurdle and they finished well strung out.

4391 ATTHERACES.COM H'CAP HURDLE (13 hdls) 2m 7f 209y
4:40 (4:40) (Class 5) (0-100,99) 4-Y-0+ **£3,249** (£954; £477; £238)

Form RPR
P-PP **1** **Shinooki (IRE)**[62] 3310 9-11-12 **99**..................................(p) KielanWoods 115+
(Alex Hales) *in rr: hdwy to chse ldrs 6th: led sn after 3 out: wnt wl clr bef next: over 20 l ahd last: heavily eased clsng stages* **10/1**
UF44 **2** *13* **Mission Complete (IRE)**[62] 3312 10-10-12 **95**...............(t) JackSavage(10) 89
(Jonjo O'Neill) *mid-div: hdwy and modest 5th sn after 3 out: kpt on to take poor 2nd after last* **10/1**
01PP **3** *2 ¾* **Vodka Island (IRE)**[60] 3369 7-10-11 **89**................................ AlanJohns(5) 81
(Tim Vaughan) *chsd ldrs: poor 2nd bef 2 out: one pce* **14/1**
2123 **4** *9* **Riddlestown (IRE)**[11] 4187 9-11-7 **99**.....................(b) BridgetAndrews(5) 84
(Caroline Fryer) *mde most to 8th: led briefly 3 out: fdd sn after 2 out* **8/1**
5032 **5** *3* **Black Lily (IRE)**[87] 2868 8-10-0 **73**...............................(p) TomMessenger 54
(Chris Bealby) *in rr: hdwy 10th: one pce fr next* **7/1[3]**
-34P **6** *16* **Uncle Monty (IRE)**[59] 3378 7-11-10 **97**..............................(p) WillKennedy 63
(Donald McCain) *w ldr: led 8th: wknd bef 2 out: sn bhd* **12/1**
0640 **7** *15* **Kerry's Lord (IRE)**[23] 3976 7-11-2 **96**.............................. RomainClavreul(7) 49
(Joanne Thomason-Murphy) *hld up in rr: bhd fr 10th: t.o 2 out* **33/1**
42P4 **8** *15* **Blue Cove**[19] 4047 11-10-0 **73** oh1...(t) SeanQuinlan 12
(Lynn Siddall) *chsd ldrs: drvn 9th: lost pl bef 3 out: sn bhd: t.o* **12/1**
/PP0 **P** **Subtle Approach (IRE)**[24] 3946 11-10-0 **73** oh4......(p) RichieMcLernon
(Emma Baker) *chsd ldrs: lost pl 10th: sn bhd: t.o whn p.u bef 2 out* **50/1**
PF4P **P** **Exit To Freedom**[123] 2139 10-9-11 **73**..................................[1] JoeCollver(3)
(John Wainwright) *sn chsng ldrs: lost pl 9th: sn bhd: t.o whn p.u bef 2 out* **33/1**
-53P **P** **Blurred Lines (IRE)**[193] 1293 7-11-3 **97**..................................... MrJJohnson(7)
(Trevor Wall) *in rr: hdwy to chse ldrs 6th: lost pl 9th: sn bhd: t.o whn p.u bef 3 out* **20/1**
0336 **P** **Jackfield**[34] 3771 6-9-6 **75** oh1 ow2... CathalCourtney(10)
(Robin Dickin) *in rr: drvn 8th: sn bhd: t.o whn p.u after 3 out* **9/2[1]**
0402 **P** **Whispering Speed (IRE)**[20] 4030 6-10-11 **84**.............(b) LeightonAspell
(Lucy Wadham) *in rr: reminders 7th: sn bhd: t.o whn p.u after 3 out* **9/2[1]**
606 **P** **Adeenne De Sevres (FR)**[47] 3568 6-11-11 **98**..................[1] NicodeBoinville
(Tom Lacey) *hld up in rr: hdwy 7th: reminders and lost pl next: t.o whn p.u bef 9th* **6/1[2]**
6m 37.8s (22.80) **Going Correction** +0.60s/f (Soft) **14 Ran SP% 127.1**
Speed ratings (Par 103): **86,81,80,77,76 71,66,61, , , ,**
CSF £108.28 CT £1433.53 TOTE £15.10: £3.90, £2.90, £5.50; EX 162.10 Trifecta £2960.50.
Owner Mrs A Allen **Bred** John Quane **Trained** Edgcote, Northamptonshire
FOCUS
A moderate handicap hurdle and weak form.

4392 FOLLOW @SOUTHWELL_RACES ON TWITTER "NEWCOMERS" STANDARD OPEN NATIONAL HUNT FLAT RACE 1m 7f 153y
5:10 (5:11) (Class 5) 4-5-Y-0 **£1,949** (£572; £286; £143)

Form RPR
1 **Happy Hollow** 4-10-12 0... PaulMoloney 105+
(Alan Swinbank) *t.k.h in rr: hdwy 6f out: 2nd over 2f out: led over 1f out: drvn out* **8/1**
2 *3* **Black Country Boy** 4-10-12 0.. CharliePoste 98
(Robin Dickin) *in rr: pushed along 8f out: hdwy 5f out: 3rd over 1f out: kpt on to take 2nd last 50yds* **20/1**
3 *2 ¾* **Stamp Your Feet (IRE)** 4-10-12 0.. PaddyBrennan 95
(Tom George) *mid-div: hdwy to trck ldrs 5f out: led 3f out: hdd over 1f out: kpt on one pce* **9/2[2]**
4 *3 ¾* **First Du Charmil (FR)** 4-10-12 0...................................... NicodeBoinville 91
(Tom Lacey) *trckd ldrs: drvn over 4f out: one pce fnl 2f* **3/1[1]**
5 *2* **Elgin** 4-10-9 0.. TomBellamy(3) 89
(Alan King) *mid-div: drvn 4f out: one pce fnl 3f* **9/2[2]**
6 *14* **May Mist** 4-9-12 0.. JoshWall(7) 68
(Trevor Wall) *mid-div: chsng ldrs over 3f out: wknd over 2f out* **50/1**
7 *4* **Lickpenny Larry** 5-11-7 0... TommyPhelan 80
(Tom Gretton) *trckd ldrs: led 4f out: hdd 3f out: wknd fnl 2f* **66/1**
8 *7* **Snatchitback** 5-11-4 0... BenPoste(3) 73
(Tom Symonds) *t.k.h in rr: drvn over 4f out: nvr factor* **16/1**
9 *17* **Ask Paddy (IRE)** 4-10-12 0.. JonathanEngland 47
(Sam Drake) *racd wd: w ldrs: wandered and lost pl over 4f out: sn bhd: eased over 1f out* **25/1**
10 *14* **Bella Girino** 4-10-0 0.. BridgetAndrews(5) 26
(Dan Skelton) *t.k.h: led: hdd 4f out: wknd over 2f out: sn bhd* **6/1[3]**
11 *12* **Last To Leave** 5-11-7 0.. BrendanPowell 30
(Stuart Edmunds) *chsd ldrs: drvn 6f out: lost pl over 4f out: sn bhd* **10/1**
12 *5* **Ellerslie Joe** 4-10-12 0.. DougieCostello 16
(Tom Tate) *chsd ldrs: drvn 5f out: lost pl over 3f out: sn bhd* **8/1**
4m 5.1s (13.70) **Going Correction** +0.60s/f (Soft)
WFA 4 from 5yo 9lb **12 Ran SP% 124.9**
Speed ratings: **89,87,86,84,83 76,74,70,62,55 49,46**
CSF £165.40 TOTE £9.10: £2.30, £6.90, £1.90; EX 164.50 Trifecta £1180.70.
Owner Elsa Crankshaw & G Allan **Bred** Stuart McPhee Bloodstock Ltd **Trained** Melsonby, N Yorks
FOCUS
A newcomers' bumper and a wide-open betting heat, in which the winner created a very good impression.
T/Plt: £51,326.60 to a £1 stake. Pool: £91,403.54 - 1.30 winning tickets. T/Qpdt: £6,391.20 to a £1 stake. Pool: £9,414.17 - 1.09 winning tickets. **Walter Glynn**

4393 - 4396a (Foreign Racing) - See Raceform Interactive

4002
LEOPARDSTOWN (L-H)
Sunday, February 28
OFFICIAL GOING: Soft (yielding in places)

4397a TRI EQUESTRIAN H'CAP CHASE (GRADE B) (14 fncs) 2m 5f 60y
4:00 (4:04) 5-Y-0+
£21,691 (£6,985; £3,308; £1,470; £735; £367)

RPR
1 **Colms Dream (IRE)**[58] 3425 7-10-4 **125**.........................(t[1]) DonaghMeyler(5) 143+
(Karl Thornton, Ire) *hld up: clsr in 7th at 1/2-way: impr bhd ldrs into 3rd bef 8th and wnt 2nd after next: almost on terms bef 2 out: rdn to ld bef last and styd on wl to assert run-in* **12/1**
2 *6 ½* **The Mooch (IRE)**[35] 3767 8-9-9 **114**..............................(b) JackKennedy(3) 127
(Paul Nolan, Ire) *trckd ldrs tl led fr 1st: pressed clly bef 2 out: rdn and hdd bef last: no imp on wnr run-in: kpt on same pce* **8/1[3]**
3 *3 ½* **Kylecrue (IRE)**[42] 3649 9-10-3 **119**...................................(b) PhillipEnright 127
(John Patrick Ryan, Ire) *chsd ldrs: nt fluent 3rd and at times after: 3rd 1/2-way: rdn after 2 out and no imp on wnr u.p in 3rd bef last: kpt on one pce run-in: jst hld 3rd* **16/1**
4 *nk* **Rogue Angel (IRE)**[119] 2228 8-11-2 **137**.................(bt) JonathanMoore(5) 145+
(M F Morris, Ire) *chsd ldrs: 5th 1/2-way: rdn in 7th after 2 out and no imp on wnr u.p disputing 6th at last: kpt on again fr last into 4th cl home: jst hld for 3rd* **16/1**
5 *1 ½* **Aurora Bell (IRE)**[10] 4215 8-10-0 **123**.................................... MartinBurke(7) 129
(John M Burke, Ire) *mid-div: 6th 1/2-way: impr bhd ldrs bef 2 out: wnt 4th between last 2 and sn rdn: no imp on wnr bef last and one pce run-in* **6/1[2]**
6 *1 ¼* **Federici**[22] 4006 7-10-10 **126**... RobbieColgan 131
(E Bolger, Ire) *chsd ldrs in 6th early: 9th 1/2-way: rdn in 9th after 2 out and no imp bef last: kpt on u.p run-in* **14/1**
7 *1* **Ballyadam Approach (IRE)**[91] 2816 11-10-10 **129**........ DavidSplaine(3) 133
(Terence O'Brien, Ire) *chsd ldrs: 4th 1/2-way: rdn in 4th into st and sn no ex u.p in 5th: wknd run-in* **8/1[3]**
8 *3 ¾* **Your Busy (IRE)**[57] 3448 13-11-2 **132**.................................(t) MarkEnright 132
(J A Nash, Ire) *led tl hdd fr 1st: 2nd 1/2-way: dropped to 3rd after 9th: rdn and wknd after 2 out* **33/1**
9 *¾* **Bearly Legal (IRE)**[35] 3769 10-10-8 **127**...(t) GerFox(3) 127
(Karl Thornton, Ire) *hld up: 11th 1/2-way: pushed along after 8th: no imp trailing in 11th into st: kpt on again fr last* **8/1[3]**
10 *2 ¾* **Riverside City (IRE)**[28] 3894 7-10-6 **122**................................. MarkWalsh 119
(Gordon Elliott, Ire) *hld up: last at 1/2-way: niggled along after 5 out: tk clsr order after 3 out: rdn in 8th after 2 out and no ex bef last: one pce run-in* **8/1[3]**
11 *13* **Draycott Place (IRE)**[28] 3892 7-10-12 **128**.................................... AELynch 112
(John Patrick Ryan, Ire) *towards rr: 10th 1/2-way: rdn and no imp after 2 out* **20/1**
12 *22* **Malt Gem (IRE)**[21] 4021 8-10-13 **129**...................................(tp) MPFogarty 91
(Miss Mary Louise Hallahan, Ire) *mid-div: 8th 1/2-way: rdn after 4 out and no imp fr next: wknd and eased* **25/1**
P **Dressedtothenines (IRE)**[77] 3073 9-10-9 **125**........................ BarryGeraghty
(Edward P Harty, Ire) *hld up: nt fluent towards rr at 6th: 12th 1/2-way: pushed along in 10th after 3 out and wknd bef next: eased after 2 out and t.o whn p.u bef last* **7/2[1]**
5m 28.0s (-8.00) **Going Correction** -0.125s/f (Good) **13 Ran SP% 118.6**
Speed ratings: **110,107,106,106,105 105,104,103,102,101 96,88,**
CSF £97.59 CT £1349.95 TOTE £13.80: £3.80, £2.50, £5.60; DF 153.10 Trifecta £2451.70.
Owner Colm's Dream Syndicate **Bred** Colm Farrell **Trained** Skerries, Co Dublin
■ Unic De Bersy was withdrawn. Price at time of withdrawal 10/1. Rule 4 applies to all bets - deduction 5p in the pound.
FOCUS
Falls on his two previous starts took nothing out of the winner and didn't affect his confidence at all as he won with considerable authority.

4398 - 4399a (Foreign Racing) - See Raceform Interactive

ANGERS (R-H)

Sunday, February 28

OFFICIAL GOING: Turf: soft

4400a PRIX GEORGES THIBAULT (CHASE) (CLAIMER) (5YO+) (TURF) 2m 3f
3:00 (12:00) 5-Y-0+ £6,352 (£3,176; £1,852; £1,257; £595)

RPR

1 **Holstmaker (FR)**[680] 6-11-3 0 JordanDuchene 116
(P Peltier, France) 7/1[3]

2 4 **Grand Moss (FR)**[91] 2820 5-9-13 0 (b) RomainLoree(9) 103
(S Foucher, France) 14/5[2]

3 20 **Eclair Gris (FR)**[733] 7-10-10 0 (p) ChristopherCouillaud(9) 94
(Y Fertillet, France) 11/10[1]

4 4 **Sagafor (FR)**[297] 5-10-10 0 (b) ThomasBlainville(9) 90
(P Leblanc, France) 36/1

5 ¾ **Siam De La Roque (FR)**[1203] 10-10-8 0 ReesMorganMurphy(9) 87
(Jerome Zuliani, France) 36/5

P **Brise Coeur (FR)**[32] 3815 5-10-8 0 LizzieKelly(9)
(Nick Williams) *w.w towards rr: j. slowly and relegated to last 2nd: pckd 3rd: last and reminders after 5th: lost tch bef next: wl bhd fr 10th: p.u bef next* 162/10

P **Fornebello (FR)** 6-11-3 0 (p) RomainJulliot
(X-L Le Stang, France) 29/1

P **Chou Du Mathan (FR)** 8-10-6 0 YoannMichaux(8)
(Christian Le Galliard, France) 84/10

4m 54.95s (294.95)
WFA 5 from 6yo+ 1lb **8 Ran SP% 121.1**
PARI-MUTUEL (incl. 1 euro stake): WIN: 8.00. PLACES: 1.70, 1.40, 1.30. DF: 24.00. SF: 51.10..
Owner Pierre Coveliers **Bred** Regis Claude **Trained** France

4401a PRIX D'AUTEUIL (CHASE) (CONDITIONS) (5YO) (TURF) 2m 2f 110y
4:15 (12:00) 5-Y-0 £9,176 (£4,588; £2,676; £1,816; £860)

RPR

1 **Hurricancrys (FR)**[334] 5-11-5 0 BaptisteMeme(4)
(J Boisnard, France) 22/5[2]

2 1 **Kilda Six (FR)**[97] 5-10-12 0 MorganRegairaz
(D Bressou, France) 43/5

3 6 **Eagle De L'Aube (FR)** 5-10-10 0 (p) MickaelDanglades
(E Lecoiffier, France) 79/1

4 2½ **Cro Easy (USA)**[263] 5-11-7 0 RomainJulliot
(P Dubois, France) 145/10

5 6 **Quick Eleven (FR)**[97] 5-10-6 0 ow3 Marc-AntoineBillard
(Mlle S Delaroche, France) 71/1

6 1½ **Baby Cat Delaroque (FR)** 5-10-8 0 YoannLecourt
(J Merienne, France) 81/10

U **Saint Lino (FR)**[29] 3876 5-10-3 0 LizzieKelly(5)
(Nick Williams) *after two false ss: w.w towards rr: awkward on landing 2nd: sn settled in midfield on outer: mstke and uns rdr 5th* 2/1[1]

F **Breddy Du Desert (FR)**[459] 5-11-3 0 YoannMichaux(4)
(J Planque, France) 66/10

P **Call Hector (FR)**[113] 2362 5-10-3 0 ArthurBrunetti(5)
(G Chaignon, France) 51/1

U **Lockydor (FR)**[165] 5-11-0 0 AngeloGasnier
(S Foucher, France) 6/1[3]

P **A Tout Propos (FR)**[309] 5-10-4 0 ow1 BenoitClaudic(5)
(M De Montfort, France) 155/10

R **Bargain (FR)** 5-10-8 0 Jean-ChristopherGagnon
(M Postic, France) 50/1

4m 53.18s (293.18) **12 Ran SP% 119.7**
PARI-MUTUEL (incl. 1 euro stake): WIN: 5.40. PLACES: 2.40, 3.00, 11.60. DF: 21.30. SF: 31.60..
Owner Mme Anne Boisnard **Bred** Mme E Masson **Trained** France

4163 AYR (L-H)

Monday, February 29

OFFICIAL GOING: Soft (heavy in places; chs 6.5, hdl: 6.3)
Wind: Fresh, across Weather: Overcast

4402 DAWN HOMES FUTURE DEVELOPMENTS NOVICES' CHASE (11 fncs 1 omitted) 1m 7f 112y
1:40 (1:41) (Class 4) 5-Y-0+ £5,211

Form RPR

-3F2 1 **Captain Hox (IRE)**[26] 3935 7-10-12 125 (t) BrianHughes 127
(Patrick Griffin, Ire) *pressed ldr: lft alone 1st* 2/1[2]

-330 F **Fairytale Theatre (IRE)**[37] 3732 9-10-5 0 (t) IanPopham
(Dan Skelton) *led tl fell 1st* 2/5[1]

4m 25.7s (15.00) **2 Ran SP% 104.8**
TOTE £1.70.
Owner Mrs Siobhan Ryan **Bred** Swordlestown Stud **Trained** Oldtown, Co Dublin

FOCUS
Some starts have been moved at this track following remeasuring, so some races will not have speed figures until there is sufficient data to calculate updated median times. Hurdle bend out eight yards, while the chase equivalent was out seven yards. This race was run over 42yds further than advertised. An already highly uncompetitive novice chase fell apart after the first fence.

4403 DAWN HOMES ASSURED MOVE MAIDEN HURDLE (9 hdls) 2m
2:10 (2:11) (Class 5) 4-Y-0+ £2,599 (£763; £381; £190)

Form RPR

24 1 **Oldgrangewood**[62] 3353 5-11-2 120 HarrySkelton 123+
(Dan Skelton) *pressed ldr: nt fluent 5th: led after next: hrd pressed and rdn bef 2 out: edgd rt run-in: styd on wl* 1/6[1]

0F0 2 1½ **Craiganboy (IRE)**[37] 3743 7-11-2 120 AELynch 120+
(S R B Crawford, Ire) *in tch: hdwy to chse clr ldng pair 4th: effrt and disp ld bef 2 out to last: kpt on run-in* 22/1[3]

604 3 49 **Orioninverness (IRE)**[41] 3667 5-11-2 0 (t) PeterBuchanan 71
(Lucinda Russell) *in tch: pushed along and outpcd 4 out: rallied to chse clr ldng pair next: plugged on: no imp* 9/1[2]

4-05 4 2 **Daytripper**[21] 4033 5-10-9 0 BrianHughes 62
(Lucinda Russell) *hld up: nt fluent 1st: outpcd 4th: rallied 3 out: plugged on: nvr on terms* 50/1

00 5 14 **Farewelltocheyenne (IRE)**[41] 3667 8-10-11 0 StephenMulqueen(5) 55
(N W Alexander) *midfield: outpcd 4th: hdwy bef 3 out: nvr able to chal* 40/1

0-00 6 16 **Ange Des Malberaux (FR)**[21] 4031 6-10-11 0 DiarmuidO'Regan(5) 39
(James Ewart) *hld up: nt fluent 2nd: struggling 4th: nvr on terms* 66/1

7 8 **Bill D'Aron (FR)** 5-11-2 0 JakeGreenall 31
(James Ewart) *in tch: hdwy to chse clr ldng pair briefly bef 3 out: wkng whn blnd bdly 3 out* 25/1

600 8 12 **Fire Rock (IRE)**[97] 2704 5-10-11 0 RyanDay(5) 19
(Nicky Richards) *hld up: struggling 1/2-way: nvr on terms* 66/1

00 9 9 **Just Like Dylan (IRE)**[24] 3971 5-11-2 0 BrianHarding 10
(Barry Murtagh) *bhd: struggling fr 4th: nvr on terms* 125/1

00 P **Mcginty's Dream (IRE)**[81] 2984 5-11-2 0 LucyAlexander
(N W Alexander) *plld hrd in midfield: hdwy to chse ldrs whn hit 3rd: nt fluent and wknd next: lost tch whn p.u bef 3 out* 100/1

50P P **September Son (IRE)**[58] 3436 6-10-13 0 GrahamWatters(3)
(Ian Duncan) *led to after 4 out: wknd bef next: t.o whn p.u bef last* 250/1

4m 14.0s (254.00) **11 Ran SP% 113.5**
CSF £7.70 TOTE £1.20: £1.02, £2.40, £1.80; EX 5.80 Trifecta £15.40.
Owner Chris Giles & Sandra Giles **Bred** Mickley Stud **Trained** Alcester, Warwicks

FOCUS
This race was run over 48yds further than advertised. The first pair had this to themselves from a long way out. The winner has been rated to his mark for the time being.

4404 DAWN HOMES ASSISTED MOVE H'CAP HURDLE (9 hdls) 2m
2:40 (2:41) (Class 5) (0-100,100) 4-Y-0+ £2,599 (£763; £381; £190)

Form RPR

0002 1 **Question Of Faith**[29] 3888 5-10-12 86 HenryBrooke 93+
(Martin Todhunter) *nt fluent: hld up: stdy hdwy whn hit 4th: effrt and chsng ldrs bef 3 out: rdn to ld bef last: nt fluent last: kpt on strly* 17/2

5006 2 3 **Rioja Day (IRE)**[21] 4036 6-10-4 83 DiarmuidO'Regan(5) 84
(Jim Goldie) *chsd ldrs: rdn along 4 out: rallied to ld bef next: hdd bef last: kpt on same pce* 15/2

5515 3 5 **Hatton Springs (IRE)**[29] 3888 5-11-1 96 SamColtherd(7) 93
(Stuart Coltherd) *in tch: effrt and rdn 3 out: one pce whn hit last* 9/1

-230 4 17 **Diamond D'Amour (IRE)**[19] 4055 10-11-7 100 JonathonBewley(5) 81
(George Bewley) *prom: stdy hdwy to press ldr 4 out: ev ch briefly bef next: rdn and wknd fr 2 out* 5/1[1]

0600 5 7 **Celestino (FR)**[21] 4036 5-11-0 95 (p) MrKitAlexander(7) 67
(N W Alexander) *led: nt fluent 4th: hdd bef 3 out: rdn and wknd fr next* 6/1[3]

460P 6 4 **Norfolk Sound**[20] 4049 5-10-7 86 GrantCockburn(5) 54
(Stuart Coltherd) *hld up: smooth hdwy after 4 out: rdn next: wknd 2 out* 50/1

-200 7 3¾ **Towerburn (IRE)**[40] 3680 7-11-7 100 (t) JamieHamilton(5) 64
(Alison Hamilton) *in tch: pushed along 4th: rallied: rdn and wknd bef 3 out* 10/1

4525 8 3 **King's Chorister**[4] 4326 10-9-10 77 (t) LorcanMurtagh(7) 38
(Barry Murtagh) *hld up: stdy hdwy after 4 out: rdn and wknd bef next* 11/2[2]

5340 9 5 **Sendiym (FR)**[12] 4178 9-10-9 83 (t) BrianHughes 39
(Dianne Sayer) *hld up: rdn and outpcd whn nt fluent 4 out: sn btn* 12/1

P04- P **Spinning Away**[366] 4486 8-11-7 95 LucyAlexander
(N W Alexander) *bhd: outpcd whn hit 5th: sn struggling: lost tch and p.u bef 3 out* 25/1

00-3 F **Galleons Way**[41] 3672 7-11-7 100 CallumBewley(5)
(Katie Scott) *pressed ldr to 4 out: rdn and wkng whn mstke next: no ch whn fell heavily last* 7/1

4m 20.4s (260.40) **11 Ran SP% 113.7**
CSF £68.78 CT £587.71 TOTE £5.00: £2.00, £2.80, £3.60; EX 85.40 Trifecta £784.60.
Owner K Fitzsimons & G Fell **Bred** Sir Robert Ogden **Trained** Orton, Cumbria
■ Stewards' Enquiry : Callum Bewley eight-day ban: continued to race contrary to gelding's welfare (Mar 14-21)

FOCUS
This race was run over 48yds further than advertised. There was a fair gallop on in this weak handicap and the form makes sense. The time was slow compared to the previous novice, though.

4405 DAWN HOMES PART EXCHANGE H'CAP HURDLE (QUALIFIER FOR CHALLENGER STAYING HURDLE SERIES FINAL) (12 hdls) 2m 5f 91y
3:15 (3:16) (Class 3) (0-135,128) 4-Y-0+ £5,848 (£1,717; £858; £429)

Form RPR

/2F2 1 **Caledonia**[58] 3440 9-11-1 117 HenryBrooke 121+
(Jim Goldie) *hld up in tch on outside: smooth hdwy to ld after 3 out: rdn after next: kpt on gamely fr last* 9/2[3]

43B3 2 ¾ **Octagon**[61] 3367 6-11-2 118 BrianHughes 122+
(Dianne Sayer) *hld up: smooth hdwy to trck ldrs bef 3 out: wnt 2nd gng wl next: rdn bef last: kpt on run-in: hld nr fin* 8/1

1420 3 10 **Oscar Blue (IRE)**[22] 4017 6-11-12 128 PaddyBrennan 123
(Brian Ellison) *hld up: hdwy to chse ldrs 4 out: drvn and outpcd after next: plugged on fr last: no ch w first two* 7/2[2]

421 4 2 **Takingrisks (IRE)**[62] 3340 7-11-6 122 BrianHarding 116
(Nicky Richards) *nt fluent on occasions: prom: hdwy to ld briefly bef 3 out: rdn next: wknd bef last* 2/1[1]

0160 5 25 **Tap Night (USA)**[22] 4017 9-11-12 128 (p) RichieMcLernon 94
(Lucinda Russell) *led to 3rd: cl up: led 4 out to bef next: sn rdn and wknd* 16/1

316- 6 6 **Golden Sparkle (IRE)**[416] 3595 10-10-12 117 GrahamWatters(3) 77
(Ian Duncan) *hld up: pushed along after 4 out: wknd bef next* 40/1

4606 P **Rival D'Estruval (FR)**[44] 3630 11-10-12 114 (b[1]) CraigNichol
(Pauline Robson) *sn pushed along towards rr: hdwy to ld 3rd: hdd 4 out: rdn and wknd bef next: p.u bef 2 out* 12/1

330F P **Hartforth**[24] 3970 8-10-13 118 CallumWhillans(3)
(Donald Whillans) *chsd ldrs: drvn along bef 6th: dropped in rr and struggling next: lost tch and p.u bef 3 out* 16/1

1104 P **Calivigny (IRE)**[22] 4015 7-11-9 125 LucyAlexander
(N W Alexander) *in tch: drvn and outpcd bef 3 out: sn btn: p.u bef next* 12/1

5m 48.6s (348.60) **9 Ran SP% 114.4**
CSF £39.64 CT £139.34 TOTE £5.40: £1.70, £2.20, £1.40; EX 31.20 Trifecta £146.40.
Owner F J Connor & J S Goldie **Bred** E W Hyslop **Trained** Uplawmoor, E Renfrews

FOCUS
This race was run over 48yds further than advertised. They went just an ordinary gallop in this fair handicap and the first pair came clear from the last. The third has been rated to his mark.

4406 DAWN HOMES PERCETON H'CAP CHASE (15 fncs 2 omitted) 2m 4f 110y
3:50 (3:50) (Class 4) (0-120,119) 5-Y-O+ **£4,028** (£1,182; £591; £295)

Form RPR

4452 **1** **Little Glenshee (IRE)**[26] [3934] 10-11-7 **114**.................... LucyAlexander 124
(N W Alexander) *nt fluent on occasions: chsd ldr: rdn bef 4 out: rallied 2 out: led run-in: styd on wl* **2/1**[1]

406P **2** *1 1/4* **Too Cool To Fool (IRE)**[13] [4166] 13-10-2 **95**.................(v[1]) HenryBrooke 103
(Jim Goldie) *led: 5 l clr and pushed along 3 out: hdd run-in: kpt on same pce towards fin* **11/1**

-21P **3** *4* **Cobajayisland (IRE)**[41] [3671] 8-11-9 **116**.............................. DerekFox 121
(Lucinda Russell) *hld up in tch: outpcd 1/2-way: nt fluent 5 out: rallied after next: styng on whn nt fluent last: nt rch first two* **5/1**[3]

1136 **4** *2 1/2* **What A Dream**[26] [3937] 10-9-10 **94**..........................(tp) JamieHamilton(5) 97
(Alison Hamilton) *chsd ldng pair: pushed along after 4 out: no imp fr 2 out* **15/2**

-05P **5** *27* **Trucking Along (IRE)**[13] [4165] 10-11-3 **110**........................... AELynch 89
(S R B Crawford, Ire) *hld up in tch: mstke 7th: hit 6 out: outpcd whn mstke 4 out: sn btn* **11/1**

4P6F **6** *16* **Amethyst Rose (IRE)**[26] [3937] 9-10-8 **108**..................... SamColtherd(7) 66
(Stuart Coltherd) *bhd: outpcd 1/2-way: nvr on terms* **18/1**

/3F1 **P** **Art Lord (IRE)**[36] [3769] 10-11-9 **119**.........................(t) GrahamWatters(3)
(Karl Thornton, Ire) *s.i.s: sn bucking and kicking and rel to r: p.u bef 1st* **11/4**[2]

5m 45.6s (345.60) **7** Ran SP% **110.4**
CSF £21.05 CT £89.76 TOTE £2.40: £1.60, £4.90; EX 24.10 Trifecta £122.90.
Owner Turcan Barber Douglas Miller Dunning 1 **Bred** Alexander Family **Trained** Kinneston, Perth & Kinross

FOCUS
This race was run over 63yds further than advertised. This modest handicap was run at a decent gallop and the first two home were always up there. The third and fourth have been rated to their marks.

4407 DAWN HOMES KILSYTH H'CAP CHASE (19 fncs 2 omitted) 3m 2f 197y
4:20 (4:21) (Class 4) (0-120,119) 5-Y-O+ **£4,223** (£1,240; £620; £310)

Form RPR

/222 **1** **Kilbree Chief (IRE)**[19] [4054] 8-11-12 **119**......................... PeterBuchanan 131+
(Lucinda Russell) *prom: stdy hdwy 12th: effrt whn hit 4 out: swtchd rt bef next: led last: rdn and edgd lft: hld on wl cl home* **4/1**[2]

564U **2** *nk* **Nakadam (FR)**[26] [3937] 6-10-2 **95**..............................(tp) RichieMcLernon 107+
(R Mike Smith) *prom: hdwy to chse ldr whn mstke 5 out: led and hit 3 out: hdd whn blnd last: swtchd rt run-in: kpt on: hld cl home* **16/1**

3621 **3** *19* **Jonny Eager (IRE)**[19] [4051] 7-11-5 **112**.............................. CraigNichol 108
(Alistair Whillans) *disp ld: wnt on 12th: stmbld bnd bef 4 out: hit and rdn 4 out: hdd whn mstke next: nt fluent 2 out: sn btn* **3/1**[1]

U523 **4** *1 1/4* **More Madness (IRE)**[21] [4032] 9-10-4 **97**...................(v) LucyAlexander 87
(N W Alexander) *prom: drvn and outpcd after 5 out: struggling fr 3 out* **11/2**[3]

5U3P **5** *27* **Chavoy (FR)**[41] [3671] 11-11-11 **118**...............................(tp) HenryBrooke 87
(Rebecca Menzies) *hld up: reminders 1/2-way: rallied: lost tch 6 out: t.o* **9/1**

22-2 **P** **Viking Rebel (IRE)**[299] [141] 14-9-8 **94**.........................(p) MrWHRReed(7)
(W T Reed) *w ldrs to 9th: outpcd after next: lost tch whn j. slowly 12th: sn p.u* **25/1**

PP-P **P** **Tutchec (FR)**[34] [3792] 9-11-4 **111**.. BrianHarding
(Nicky Richards) *mstkes: mde most to 12th: struggling 6 out: lost tch and p.u bef 4 out* **6/1**

111- **U** **Milan Flyer (IRE)**[37] [3756] 10-10-7 **107**..............................(t) MrSPKelly(7)
(Noel C Kelly, Ire) *hld up: stdy hdwy and in tch whn mstke and uns rdr 6 out* **11/2**[3]

7m 35.5s (41.20) **Going Correction** +1.70s/f (Heav) **8** Ran SP% **109.8**
Speed ratings: **106,105,100,99,91 , ,**
CSF £53.77 CT £200.02 TOTE £4.60: £1.70, £3.70, £1.40; EX 59.70 Trifecta £251.30.
Owner John R Adam **Bred** James Griffin **Trained** Arlary, Perth & Kinross
■ Stewards' Enquiry : Peter Buchanan one-day ban: careless riding (Mar 14)

FOCUS
This race was run over 84yds further than advertised. A moderate staying handicap which served up a tight two-way finish. A big British pb from the runner-up, with the third and fourth below the level of their latest runs.

4408 LEAP FOR RYAN AND CHRIS MAIDEN OPEN NATIONAL HUNT FLAT RACE 2m
4:50 (4:54) (Class 6) 4-6-Y-O **£1,642** (£478; £239)

Form RPR

3 **1** **Progress Drive (IRE)**[58] [3442] 5-10-11 0............... StephenMulqueen(5) 93+
(Nicky Richards) *in tch: stdy hdwy 5f out: rdn and outpcd over 2f out: rallied to ld over 1f out: pushed clr fnl f* **8/13**[1]

5 **2** *5* **Bering Upsun**[23] [4001] 5-10-13 0.............................. GrahamWatters(3) 84
(James Ewart) *led at ordinary gallop: rdn and hdd over 2f out: outpcd over 1f out: rallied and chsd (clr) wnr towards fin: no imp* **18/1**

3 *1 1/4* **Jimmy Breekie (IRE)**[301] [118] 6-11-2 0.................................... AELynch 83
(S R B Crawford, Ire) *hld up: smooth hdwy to ld over 2f out: rdn and hdd over 1f out: hung rt and no ex ins fnl f* **14/1**

4 *26* **Knocklayde (IRE)** 4-10-2 0.................................... CallumBewley(5) 48
(Katie Scott) *chsd ldr: drvn and outpcd over 3f out: btn fnl 2f* **33/1**

55 **5** *18* **Multipede**[21] [4037] 4-10-7 0... LucyAlexander 30
(James Ewart) *hld up in touich: stdy hdwy over 5f out: rdn and wknd over 3f out* **9/1**[3]

6 *32* **Bonnie Lizzie** 5-10-6 0.. HarryChalloner(3)
(Dianne Sayer) *t.k.h early: chsd ldrs: drvn and struggling over 6f out: sn lost tch: t.o* **25/1**

44 **U** **Grays Choice (IRE)**[21] [4037] 5-10-11 0................... JonathonBewley(5)
(George Bewley) *hld up on ins: fly-jmpd and uns rdr bnd after 5f* **9/2**[2]

4m 12.7s (252.70)
WFA 4 from 5yo 9lb 5 from 6yo 1lb **7** Ran SP% **108.8**
CSF £12.45 TOTE £1.60: £1.20, £4.40; EX 12.10 Trifecta £81.90.
Owner Alistair Cochrane **Bred** Jay Brennan **Trained** Greystoke, Cumbria

FOCUS
This race was run over 48yds further than advertised. An ordinary bumper. The second is probably the best guide to the level.
T/Plt: £42.90 to a £1 stake. Pool of £46457.67 - 790.36 winning tickets. T/Qpdt: £17.60 to a £1 stake. Pool of £6872.26 - 288.31 winning tickets. **Richard Young**

4157 PLUMPTON (L-H)
Monday, February 29

OFFICIAL GOING: Chase course - good to soft (good in places); hurdle course - soft (good to soft in places)
Wind: Light, behind Weather: Fine but cloudy

4409 188BET MAIDEN HURDLE (9 hdls) 1m 7f 195y
2:00 (2:00) (Class 4) 4-Y-O+ **£3,898** (£1,144; £572; £286)

Form RPR

4223 **1** **Baratineur (FR)**[37] [3743] 5-11-2 125.................................. RobertDunne 130+
(Dan Skelton) *in tch at hd of chsng gp: hit 6th but sn chsd ldng pair: clsd 3 out: led 2 out: rdn clr fr last* **13/8**[1]

2 *5* **Graasten (GER)**[154] 4-10-7 0... JamieMoore 114+
(Gary Moore) *led at gd pce and had field wl str out: clr w wnr after 3 out: hdd 2 out: one pce but stl wl ahd of rest* **11/4**[2]

-200 **3** *13* **Tara Bridge**[23] [3994] 8-11-2 117.. TomCannon 112
(Chris Gordon) *w ldr at gd pce: nt fluent 4th: lost 2nd and rdn sn after 3 out: fdd but stl wl ahd of rest* **7/1**

40PP **4** *14* **Cor Wot An Apple**[57] [3450] 5-11-2 0...................................(t) TomO'Brien 97
(Colin Tizzard) *hld up in midfield and off the pce: wnt remote 5th after 5th and remote 4th 3 out: nvr on terms but shaped w promise* **25/1**

2 **5** *6* **Mahlers Star (IRE)**[25] [3949] 6-11-2 0.............................. TomScudamore 90
(David Bridgwater) *chsd ldng pair tl drvn 6th: sn wl btn and dropped to remote 5th 3 out* **5/1**[3]

P **6** *hd* **Centreofexcellence (IRE)**[45] [3608] 5-10-9 0............. GeorgeGorman(7) 90
(Gary Moore) *hld up wl in rr: bdly hmpd 1st: a wl bhd but mde sme decent hdwy bef 3 out: battled for remote 5th fr 2 out* **66/1**

-06F **7** *22* **Staff Sergeant**[109] [1941] 9-10-9 93.................................. MrDGBurchell(7) 68
(Mark Hoad) *hld up: t.o in last after 3rd: sme prog bef 3 out: pushed along and fin w sme zest after last* **100/1**

-P3 **8** *10* **Aramadyh**[14] [4157] 5-10-9 0.. JoshuaMoore 51
(Jim Best) *hld up in rr and wl bhd: mstke 2nd: nvr a factor and t.o after 5th* **25/1**

6PPP **9** *2 1/4* **Bobby Benton (IRE)**[16] [4111] 5-11-2 0.............................. BrendanPowell 56
(Jim Best) *hld up in last pair and immediately wl bhd: t.o after 5th: sme prog after next but nvr a factor* **100/1**

P **10** *10* **The Child (IRE)**[28] [3902] 7-11-2 0.................................. AndrewThornton 46
(Anna Newton-Smith) *chsd clr ldng trio to 3rd: wknd 5th: sn t.o* **150/1**

PP **11** *35* **Austin Friars**[23] [3988] 4-10-7 0.................................. AndrewGlassonbury
(Jim Best) *a wl bhd: rdn after 2nd: t.o after 5th* **100/1**

U **Glimmer Of Hope**[40] 5-11-2 0... MarcGoldstein
(Mark Hoad) *j. bdly lft 1st and eventually uns rdr* **200/1**

5-5 **P** **Evening Stanley (IRE)**[297] [187] 6-11-2 0............................ LeightonAspell
(Oliver Sherwood) *prom in chsng gp but nt on terms: 6th whn blnd 5th: nt rcvr and t.o after next: p.u bef 2 out* **14/1**

0P **P** **Arroyeau (FR)**[4] [4317] 6-11-2 0...[1] LiamTreadwell
(Nick Gifford) *t.k.h: hld up in midfield and wl off the pce: wknd after 6th: t.o whn p.u bef 2 out* **100/1**

4m 5.5s (4.70) **Going Correction** +0.475s/f (Soft)
WFA 4 from 5yo+ 9lb **14** Ran SP% **114.9**
Speed ratings (Par 105): **107,104,98,91,88 87,76,71,70,65 48, , ,**
CSF £5.62 TOTE £2.80: £1.10, £1.60, £2.00; EX 6.70 Trifecta £28.40.
Owner Grech & Parkin **Bred** Philippe Achard **Trained** Alcester, Warwicks
■ Stewards' Enquiry : Mr D G Burchell Fine: £140, failed to report gelding had hung left and been unsuited by the ground

FOCUS
This race was run over 78yds further than advertised. Quite a modest maiden hurdle that saw the two at the head of the market come clear, and the race set up nicely for the winner, with the runner-up having set a good gallop. A small pb from the winner, and there's a case for rating him a lot higher through the third and fifth.

4410 188BET.CO.UK H'CAP CHASE (12 fncs) 2m 214y
2:30 (2:31) (Class 4) (0-115,113) 5-Y-O+ **£4,548** (£1,335; £667; £333)

Form RPR

-233 **1** **The Green Ogre**[88] [2857] 6-11-11 **112**...........................(b) JoshuaMoore 122
(Gary Moore) *mde all and mostly j.w: drvn clr after 3 out: mstke last: styd on wl* **7/4**[2]

5-53 **2** *8* **Saffron Prince**[17] [4098] 8-11-12 **113**............................... TomScudamore 116
(David Bridgwater) *hld up in 4th: prog to chse wnr after 4 out: rdn and nt qckn bef 2 out: no imp after* **5/4**[1]

11-P **3** *9* **Bobbits Way**[99] [2659] 11-10-11 **98**.................................(p) TomCannon 94
(Alan Jones) *chsd wnr: rdn 4 out: sn lost 2nd: wl hld in 3rd bef 2 out* **14/1**

-P0P **4** *9* **George Nympton (IRE)**[18] [4073] 10-9-7 **87** oh4........(bt) HarryCobden(7) 74
(Zoe Davison) *mostly chsd ldng pair: nt fluent 3rd: lost 3rd pl and pckd 8th: wl btn fr 4 out* **16/1**

02PP **5** *20* **Stars Royale (IRE)**[18] [4073] 7-10-13 **100**........................ LeightonAspell 68
(Nick Gifford) *a in last: rdn and lost tch after 7th: t.o whn j. slowly 3 out* **6/1**[3]

4m 26.1s (3.10) **Going Correction** +0.325s/f (Yiel) **5** Ran SP% **107.6**
Speed ratings: **105,101,97,92,83**
CSF £4.33 TOTE £2.40: £1.20, £1.30; EX 4.10 Trifecta £17.60.
Owner Past The Post Racing & Gary Moore **Bred** Leydens Farm Stud **Trained** Lower Beeding, W Sussex

FOCUS
This race was run over 60yds further than advertised. The runners finished strung out in this ordinary chase, the winner making all. The winner has been rated as improving in line with the best of his hurdle form, with the second rated to his mark.

4411 JOAN COLLISON MEMORIAL H'CAP HURDLE (9 hdls) 1m 7f 195y
3:05 (3:05) (Class 4) (0-115,114) 4-Y-O+ **£5,523** (£1,621; £810; £405)

Form RPR

/26- **1** **Planetoid (IRE)**[307] [2283] 8-11-11 **113**...........................(b) JamieMoore 120+
(Jim Best) *trckd ldrs: hit 6th: cl up 3 out: n.m.r on bnd after: rdn to ld and mstke 2 out: hrd pressed fr last: drvn out and hld on wl* **16/1**

45-6 **2** *3/4* **Albahar (FR)**[11] [3777] 5-11-3 **105**.. TomCannon 109
(Chris Gordon) *hld up in slowly run event: last tl prog after 6th: waiting for a gap on bnd bef 2 out: prog to chse wnr bef last: drvn to chal flat: styd on but a hld and jst too much to do* **3/1**[2]

5P41 **3** *3* **Hear The Chimes**[26] [3932] 7-11-5 **114**.................. WilliamFeatherstone(7) 117
(Shaun Harris) *hld up in last trio in slowly run event: waiting for room on bnd bef 2 out and swtchd out wd: prog to chse ldng pair bef last: styd on but too much to do* **2/1**[1]

1105 **4** 4 ½ **Grams And Ounces**[9] 4252 9-11-10 **112**..........(t) MichealNolan 109
(Grace Harris) *trckd ldrs: cl up 3 out: rdn and nt qckn bef 2 out: one pce after* **20/1**

00P4 **5** 6 **Romeo Americo (IRE)**[25] 3950 9-10-12 **100**.......... AndrewThornton 91
(Seamus Mullins) *mde most: set modest pce to 6th: stl in front of packed field after 3 out: hdd 2 out: fdd* **9/1**

0453 **6** ¾ **Sir Hubert**[28] 3905 6-10-9 **97**.......... LeightonAspell 88
(Richard Rowe) *w ldr at mod pce: rdn and stl rt there on bnd after 3 out: fdd after 2 out* **8/1**

4123 **7** 3 ¼ **Nebula Storm (IRE)**[44] 3628 9-11-1 **110**..........(v) HarryCobden(7) 97
(Michael Blake) *trckd ldrs: cl up on bnd after 3 out: rdn and wknd bef 2 out* **9/2**[3]

533- **8** 21 **Jazzy Lady (IRE)**[357] 4682 5-11-5 **107**.......... JoshuaMoore 73
(Jim Best) *nt fluent: a in rr: pushed along and lost tch after 6th: t.o* **20/1**

-250 **P** **Sebs Sensei (IRE)**[70] 2415 5-11-1 **110**.......... MrDGBurchell(7)
(Mark Hoad) *t.k.h early: trckd ldrs: lost pl fr 6th: 8th whn awkward 3 out and rdr lost irons: p.u bef 2 out* **33/1**

4m 13.0s (12.20) **Going Correction** +0.475s/f (Soft) **9** Ran SP% **116.0**
Speed ratings (Par 105): **88,87,86,83,80 80,78,68,**
CSF £63.88 CT £142.03 TOTE £15.70: £3.10, £1.50, £1.10; EX 93.20 Trifecta £155.90.
Owner Planetoid Partnership **Bred** Bjorn Nielsen **Trained** Lewes, E Sussex

FOCUS
This race was run over 78yds further than advertised. Run at a steady gallop, this is only modest form. The second has been raetd in line with his hurdle best.

4412 HOWDEN INSURANCE BROKERS AMATEUR RIDERS' H'CAP CHASE (FOR THE GAY KINDERSLEY MEMORIAL SALVER) (18 fncs) 3m 1f 152y
3:40 (3:41) (Class 4) (0-115,114) 5-Y-0+ **£4,367** (£1,354; £676; £338)

Form RPR

6231 **1** **The Cider Maker**[14] 4160 6-11-5 **110**..........(t) MrMLegg(3) 127+
(Colin Tizzard) *wl in tch: trckd ldr 13th: led 4 out: pressed 2 out: shkn up and sn drew clr: readily* **5/6**[1]

P233 **2** 9 **Reblis (FR)**[42] 3662 11-10-11 **106**..........(p) MrWRClarke(7) 112
(Gary Moore) *led but needed plenty of urging to stay there: hdd 4 out: rallied and tried to chal 2 out: sn lft bhd* **11/4**[2]

445P **3** 24 **Ennisnag (IRE)**[28] 3903 11-9-12 **93** ow1..........(t¹) MrBParis-Crofts(7) 80
(Paul Henderson) *nt a fluent: hld up: hit 10th: trckd ldng pair after 13th: cl up 4 out: wknd after 3 out* **25/1**

1P14 **4** 13 **West Of The Edge (IRE)**[16] 4127 8-11-0 **107**..........(p) MrJNixon(5) 79
(Dai Williams) *cl up: rdn after 13th and sn outpcd: nvr on terms fr next* **9/2**[3]

65PP **P** **Barra Rotha (IRE)**[74] 3131 9-9-11 **92**..........(p) MrHFNugent(7)
(Laura Hurley) *trckd ldr tl mstke 13th: wknd rapidly and sn t.o: mstke 4 out and p.u bef next* **20/1**

6m 56.3s (5.60) **Going Correction** +0.325s/f (Yiel) **5** Ran SP% **108.0**
Speed ratings: **104,101,93,89,**
CSF £3.53 TOTE £1.70: £1.10, £1.60; EX 2.90 Trifecta £14.10.
Owner Mrs C Djivanovic, Joanna Tizzard, KSB **Bred** Barrow Hill **Trained** Milborne Port, Dorset

FOCUS
This race was run over 90yds further than advertised. Little depth to this handicap and the front pair came well clear. The winner was well in on his recent C&D win and both races could be rated higher, while the second has been rated 10lb off last season's best.

4413 PETER EARL MEMORIAL MARES' H'CAP HURDLE (12 hdls) 2m 4f 114y
4:10 (4:10) (Class 4) (0-105,102) 4-Y-0+ **£4,223** (£1,240; £620; £310)

Form RPR

500- **1** **Mariet**[330] 5157 7-10-12 **93**.......... JackSherwood(5) 95+
(Suzy Smith) *prom: trckd ldr 6th: led 8th: rdn 5 l clr after 3 out: v awkward jumps last 2: drvn out and hld on* **9/1**

-603 **2** nk **Lilywhite Gesture (IRE)**[26] 3930 7-10-7 **90**.......... GarethMalone(7) 91
(Fergal O'Brien) *in tch: urged along fr 8th: prog next to chse wnr 3 out: clsd last: kpt on flat: jst hld* **9/2**[2]

4221 **3** 4 **Loves Destination**[28] 3905 5-11-4 **94**.......... TomCannon 91
(Chris Gordon) *in tch: effrt after 8th: rdn and no imp on ldrs bef 3 out: kpt on to take 3rd bef 2 out: nvr able to chal* **2/1**[1]

-445 **4** 3 **Miss Tongabezi**[45] 3612 7-11-9 **99**..........(t¹) JamesBest 94
(Paul Webber) *hld up in last pair: hit 8th: prog fr next: tried to cl on ldrs but nt on terms whn mstke 3 out: kpt on same pce after* **10/1**

000- **5** 20 **Katarrhini**[325] 5260 7-10-8 **84**.......... SeanBowen 62
(Mark Bradstock) *led to 8th: nudged along fr next and steadily dropped away: bhd whn mstke 2 out* **5/1**[3]

0FP2 **P** **Kayflin (FR)**[28] 3905 8-10-9 **85**..........(p) LeightonAspell
(Linda Jewell) *prom: j.lft 6th: chsd ldr next to 3 out: wknd rapidly: p.u bef 2 out* **7/1**

000- **P** **Frank N Fair**[325] 5260 8-10-0 **83** ow3.......... WilliamFeatherstone(7)
(Zoe Davison) *a in rr: rdn and wknd 8th: t.o in last whn p.u bef 3 out* **25/1**

0-5P **P** **Ginny's Tonic (IRE)**[28] 3904 7-11-12 **102**..........(tp) TomO'Brien
(Suzy Smith) *chsd ldr to 6th: sn wknd u.p: t.o after 9th: p.u bef 2 out* **11/1**

5m 35.3s (18.30) **Going Correction** +0.475s/f (Soft) **8** Ran SP% **112.0**
Speed ratings (Par 105): **84,83,82,81,73**
CSF £47.48 CT £112.26 TOTE £11.10: £3.10, £1.60, £1.20; EX 53.80 Trifecta £217.80.
Owner Miss Suzy Smith **Bred** Pollards Stables **Trained** Lewes, E Sussex
■ Stewards' Enquiry : Gareth Malone four-day ban: used whip above permitted level (Mar 14,19,20,21)

FOCUS
This race was run over 90yds further than advertised. Moderate form. The winner has been rated to her C&D mark under the same jockey, while the third helps set the level.

4414 ANISE CATERING INTERMEDIATE OPEN NATIONAL HUNT FLAT RACE 2m 1f 164y
4:40 (4:40) (Class 6) 4-6-Y-0 **£1,624** (£477; £238; £119)

Form RPR

5 **1** **Jot'em Down (IRE)**[25] 3952 5-11-4 0.......... TomScudamore 111+
(David Bridgwater) *mde virtually all: modest pce tl kicked on 1/2-way: drvn over 2f out: kpt on wl fr over 1f out* **5/2**[2]

1 **2** 3 **Clondaw Bisto (IRE)**[28] 3907 5-11-11 0.......... TomO'Brien 116+
(Suzy Smith) *cl up: trckd wnr 7f out: rdn to chal 2f out: racd awkwardly and nt qckn over 1f out: hld after* **8/11**[1]

1 **3** 5 **Lillian (IRE)**[271] 601 5-10-13 0.......... KevinJones(5) 103
(Seamus Mullins) *hld up in last: in tch whn prog to chse ldng pair 3f out: shkn up and kpt on same pce fnl 2f* **14/1**

4 12 **Ermyn's Emerald** 4-10-2 0.......... PaddyBradley(7) 82
(Pat Phelan) *in tch: effrt to dispute 2nd 6f out: fdd 3f out* **12/1**[3]

2-33 **5** 44 **Relight The Fire**[91] 2828 5-11-4 0.......... WillKennedy 47
(Denis Quinn) *trckd wnr to 7f out: sn shkn up: dropped to last 6f out: t.o* **14/1**

4m 47.0s (21.70) **Going Correction** +0.475s/f (Soft)
WFA 4 from 5yo+ 9lb **5** Ran SP% **107.5**
Speed ratings: **70,68,66,61,41**
CSF £4.46 TOTE £2.90: £1.20, £1.50; EX 4.00 Trifecta £12.30.
Owner Simon Hunt **Bred** Kenilworth House Stud **Trained** Icomb, Gloucs

FOCUS
This race was run over 90yds further than advertised. No depth to this small-field bumper and the two at the head of the market dominated. Straightforward form, rated around the first three.
T/Plt: £5.00 to a £1 stake. Pool of £64235.96 - 9276.74 winning tickets. T/Qpdt: £3.00 to a £1 stake. Pool of £5469.31 - 1344.78 winning tickets. **Jonathan Neesom**

4151 CATTERICK (L-H)
Tuesday, March 1

OFFICIAL GOING: Good to soft (good in places; chs 7.1, hdl 7.3)
Wind: fresh 1/2 against Weather: fine but breezy

4415 RACINGUK.COM H'CAP HURDLE (FOR LADY AMATEUR RIDERS) (10 hdls) 2m 3f 66y
2:00 (2:00) (Class 5) (0-100,100) 4-Y-0+ **£2,495** (£774; £386; £193)

Form RPR

4261 **1** **Beyondtemptation**[7] 4297 8-10-6 **83**..........(t) MissAEStirling(3) 95+
(Jonathan Haynes) *led: hit 2nd: clr next: jnd between last 2: hdd narrowly last: lft 7 l clr: styd on* **9/2**[2]

5344 **2** 13 **Down Time (USA)**[5] 4326 6-11-6 **99**..........(b) MissKBryson(5) 100
(Brian Ellison) *chsd ldrs: drvn 3 out: lft modest 2nd last* **11/2**[3]

5-40 **3** ½ **Lowcarr Motion**[95] 2745 6-11-9 **97**.......... MissCWalton 97
(Micky Hammond) *in rr: hdwy and poor 7th 2 out: lft modest 3rd last: kpt on* **7/1**

36P1 **4** 2 ¾ **Cumbrian Farmer**[60] 3402 9-9-13 **78**..........(bt) MissJWalton(5) 75
(Kenneth Slack) *chsd ldrs: drvn 3 out: outpcd appr next: lft modest 4th last* **9/4**[1]

PP03 **5** 2 ½ **Jimmie Brown (USA)**[77] 3098 8-9-9 **74**.......... MissETodd(5) 69
(Andrew Crook) *in rr-div: hdwy 5th: drvn next: one pce fr 3 out* **80/1**

U3 **6** 1 ½ **When In Roam (IRE)**[84] 2964 7-10-6 **83**..........(p) MissBHampson(3) 77
(John O'Shea) *in rr: kpt on fr 3 out: nvr a factor* **9/1**

UP00 **7** 11 **Kilmainham (IRE)**[14] 4163 8-10-11 **90**.......... MissRMcDonald(5) 74
(Martin Todhunter) *chsd ldrs: drvn 6th: lost pl bef 2 out: sn bhd* **22/1**

3100 **8** 27 **Ardesia (IRE)**[82] 2982 12-9-7 **74**..........(p) MissAWaugh(7) 34
(Tina Jackson) *chsd ldrs: drvn 6th: sn lost pl: wl bhd bef 2 out: t.o* **40/1**

430 **9** 40 **Champagne Ransom (FR)**[138] 1928 4-10-8 **96**.......... MissBeckySmith(5) 11
(Micky Hammond) *in rr: bhd and drvn 6th: t.o 3 out: eventually completed* **33/1**

4022 **F** **Astrum**[22] 4025 6-11-5 **100**..........(b) MissAMcCain(7) 112+
(Donald McCain) *chsd wnr fr 2nd: upsides between last 2: slt advantage whn fell last* **13/2**

4m 51.3s (15.20) **Going Correction** +0.475s/f (Soft)
WFA 4 from 6yo+ 7lb **10** Ran SP% **111.1**
Speed ratings (Par 103): **87,81,81,80,79 78,73,62,45,**
CSF £27.20 CT £163.02 TOTE £4.30: £1.80, £1.40, £2.60; EX 33.70 Trifecta £170.00.
Owner J C Haynes **Bred** J C Haynes **Trained** Low Row, Cumbria

FOCUS
Despite 5mm of overnight rain the ground was still expected to ride on the quick side of good to soft. The far bend was moved out 3yds, while the bend after the winning post was moved out 6yds. This race was run over 20yds further than advertised. Unsurprisingly, this moderate handicap for lady amateur riders was run at a brisk gallop and it saw late drama. The winner has been rated in line with her recent Wetherby win, with the second and third close to their marks.

4416 YORKSHIRE-OUTDOORS.CO.UK ADVENTURE ACTIVITIES MAIDEN HURDLE (DIV I) (8 hdls) 1m 7f 156y
2:30 (2:30) (Class 5) 4-Y-0+ **£2,599** (£763; £381; £190)

Form RPR

2P-3 **1** **Sakhee's City (FR)**[39] 3724 5-10-13 0.......... AdamNicol(3) 117+
(Philip Kirby) *trckd ldrs: 2nd 3rd: led 2 out: drvn and styd on* **2/1**[1]

543 **2** 1 ¾ **General Mahler (IRE)**[22] 4033 6-11-2 113.......... DannyCook 116
(Brian Ellison) *chsd ldrs: drvn appr 2 out: disp 2nd last: styd on same pce* **5/2**[2]

/F-5 **3** 2 ½ **Beatu (IRE)**[27] 3928 7-11-2 0.......... WillKennedy 113
(Donald McCain) *trckd ldrs: effrt and handy 3rd 2 out: disp 2nd last: hung lft: kpt on one pce* **16/1**

363 **4** 6 **Kisumu**[35] 3790 4-10-1 112.......... FinianO'Toole(7) 100
(Micky Hammond) *chsd ldrs: mstke 1st: one pce fr 2 out* **9/1**

-335 **5** 3 ¾ **Leading Score (IRE)**[57] 3471 6-11-2 112.......... LucyAlexander 105
(James Ewart) *led: hdd 2 out: wknd appr last* **9/2**[3]

-P2 **6** 7 **Archipeligo**[17] 3470 5-11-2 0.......... BrianHughes 100
(Iain Jardine) *trckd ldrs: effrt appr 2 out: wknd appr last* **13/2**

26/B **7** 26 **Thackeray**[20] 4050 9-10-13 0.......... JohnKington(3) 75
(Chris Fairhurst) *in rr: sme hdwy 3 out: lost pl and bhd bef next: t.o* **150/1**

6P **8** 17 **Miss Barbossa (IRE)**[24] 3995 5-10-9 0.......... HenryBrooke 53
(Martin Todhunter) *in rr: bhd whn j.rt 5th: t.o 2 out* **250/1**

P **9** 12 **Scrutiny**[12] 4202 5-11-2 0.......... SeanQuinlan 49
(Barry Murtagh) *in rr: bhd fr 4th: t.o 3 out* **150/1**

3m 57.6s (5.10) **Going Correction** +0.475s/f (Soft)
WFA 4 from 5yo+ 7lb **9** Ran SP% **111.0**
Speed ratings (Par 103): **106,105,103,100,99 95,82,74,68**
CSF £6.91 TOTE £2.50: £1.20, £1.30, £3.10; EX 7.20 Trifecta £58.30.
Owner Mrs Jayne Sivills **Bred** Kassala Ltd **Trained** East Appleton, N Yorks

FOCUS
This race was run over 11yds further than advertised. They went steadily in this ordinary maiden and only got sorted out from the second-last. The winner set a fair standard and didn't need to match his Market Rasen figure.

4417 YORKSHIRE-OUTDOORS.CO.UK ADVENTURE ACTIVITIES MAIDEN HURDLE (DIV II) (8 hdls) 1m 7f 156y
3:00 (3:00) (Class 5) 4-Y-0+ **£2,599** (£763; £381; £190)

Form RPR

03 **1** **Nine Altars (IRE)**[21] 4044 7-11-2 0.......... BrianHughes 113+
(Ann Hamilton) *chsd ldrs: 2nd 3rd: led 3 out: drvn and styd on fr 2 out: forged clr run-in* **10/1**

2 6 **Sinakar (IRE)**[65] 5-11-2 0 JakeGreenall 107
(David O'Meara) *in tch: hdwy and handy 4th 2 out: 2nd last: kpt on same pce* 9/2[3]

6562 3 1 ¼ **Myrtle Drive (IRE)**[95] 2752 5-10-9 0 WillKennedy 99
(Donald McCain) *chsd ldrs: cl 3rd 2 out: j.lft last: kpt on same pce* 4/1[2]

52 4 shd **Carthage (IRE)**[57] 3471 5-11-2 0 DannyCook 105
(Brian Ellison) *chsd ldrs: drvn and cl 2nd whn hit 2 out: kpt on same pce run-in* 8/11[1]

3466 5 16 **Captain Mowbray**[5] 4324 5-11-2 0 HenryBrooke 90
(Rebecca Menzies) *stdd s: in rr: poor 5th bef 2 out: nvr on terms* 28/1

6 30 **Coniston Cold** 4-10-5 0 HarryBannister(3) 55
(Michael Easterby) *stdd s: in rr: bhd fr 4th: t.o bef 2 out* 20/1

P 7 47 **Onlyfoolsownhorses (IRE)**[32] 3839 5-10-13 0 JoeColliver(3) 20
(Micky Hammond) *in rr: bhd and drvn after 3rd: t.o 5th: eventually completed* 50/1

P- U **Wannabe King**[453] 2896 10-10-11 0 RyanDay(5)
(Ian Brown) *led: hdd 3 out: wknd qckly: distant 7th whn blnd and uns rdr 2 out* 66/1

P **Tawan**[565] 5-10-11 0 JamieHamilton(5)
(Brian Rothwell) *chsd ldrs to 3rd: sn struggling: wl bhd 3 out: t.o whn p.u bef next* 200/1

P **Belle Peinture (FR)**[119] 5-10-9 0 CraigNichol
(Alan Lockwood) *nt fluent in rr: bhd fr 3rd: t.o whn p.u after 5th* 66/1

3m 58.9s (6.40) **Going Correction** +0.475s/f (Soft)
WFA 4 from 5yo+ 7lb **10** Ran SP% **118.8**
Speed ratings (Par 103): **103,100,99,99,91 76,52, , ,**
CSF £52.42 TOTE £8.30: £2.40, £1.50, £1.60; EX 60.50 Trifecta £180.10.
Owner Ian Hamilton **Bred** Noel James **Trained** Great Bavington, Northumberland

FOCUS
This race was run over 11yds further than advertised. The second division of the ordinary maiden can be rated around the third. A big step up from the winner, with the third and fifth setting the level.

4418 EASBY ABBEY H'CAP CHASE (12 fncs) 1m 7f 145y
3:30 (3:30) (Class 4) (0-120,120) 5-Y-O+ £6,498 (£1,908; £954; £477)

Form RPR

6313 1 **Ubaltique (FR)**[14] 4167 8-11-12 **120** (bt) WillKennedy 133+
(Donald McCain) *in rr: reminders bef 5th: sn chsng ldrs: led appr 3 out: 5 l ahd last: drvn and styd on: eased nr fin* 7/1

5151 2 3 ½ **My Friend George**[21] 4046 10-10-11 **105** (p) HenryBrooke 112
(Kenneth Slack) *chsd ldrs: drvn to chse wnr 2 out: kpt on same pce* 4/1[3]

241F 3 ½ **Bollin Line**[13] 4177 9-9-9 **94** oh1 DeanPratt(5) 101
(Lucinda Egerton) *chsd ldrs: drvn and outpcd after 9th: kpt on and 3rd 2 out: kpt on same pce* 7/4[1]

33-P 4 15 **The Wexfordian (IRE)**[73] 3146 7-11-3 **111** AndrewTinkler 106
(Martin Keighley) *led 2nd: hdd appr 3 out: wknd between last 2* 11/4[2]

302P 5 3 ¾ **Safari Journey (USA)**[9] 4275 12-10-12 **106** (p) BrianHarding 98
(Lucinda Egerton) *led to 2nd: lost pl 8th: hit next: sn bhd* 33/1

55-P 6 13 **Edmund (IRE)**[21] 4046 9-11-2 **115** (t) JamieHamilton(5) 96
(Ann Hamilton) *sn chsng ldrs: drvn 6th: lost pl 8th: sn bhd* 9/1

4m 0.6s (0.50) **Going Correction** +0.20s/f (Yiel) **6** Ran SP% **108.5**
Speed ratings: **106,104,104,96,94 88**
CSF £32.21 TOTE £3.80: £2.20, £1.90; EX 14.90 Trifecta £25.80.
Owner T G Leslie **Bred** Arnaud Chaille-Chaille **Trained** Cholmondeley, Cheshire

FOCUS
This race was run over 11yds further than advertised. A modest handicap run at a sound gallop. A chase pb from the winner, with the second and third rated pretty much to their marks.

4419 RACING UK CLUB DAY HERE TODAY NOVICES' HURDLE (12 hdls) 3m 1f 71y
4:00 (4:00) (Class 4) 4-Y-O+ £3,898 (£1,144; £572; £286)

Form RPR

35 1 **Royal Milan (IRE)**[32] 3839 6-11-3 0 (t) RichardJohnson 121+
(Philip Hobbs) *trckd ldng pair: led 8th: drvn appr 2 out: j.lft last 2: forged clr run-in* 4/6[1]

5-3 2 14 **Banny's Lad**[25] 3971 7-11-0 0 HarryBannister(3) 110
(Michael Easterby) *hld up: hdwy to trck ldrs 8th: cl 2nd 2 out: sn drvn: kpt on same pce appr last* 10/3[2]

-044 3 5 **High Hopper (IRE)**[38] 3743 6-11-3 115 BrianHughes 104
(Malcolm Jefferson) *nt fluent: chsd ldr: pushed along 8th: upsides 3 out: wknd between last 2: j.lft last* 7/2[3]

0-33 4 26 **Cross To Boston (IRE)**[113] 2402 10-10-10 88 MrRHogg(7) 79
(Sue Smith) *led: hdd 8th: drvn and lost pl 3 out: sn bhd: j.lft last 2: t.o* 28/1

0-P P **Wee Holio (IRE)**[18] 4108 5-11-3 0 JakeGreenall
(Marjorie Fife) *hld up detached in last: lost pl 8th: t.o next: p.u bef 2 out* 200/1

6m 47.0s (19.40) **Going Correction** +0.475s/f (Soft) **5** Ran SP% **109.2**
Speed ratings (Par 105): **87,82,80,72,**
CSF £3.33 TOTE £2.00: £1.40, £1.10; EX 3.50 Trifecta £5.50.
Owner The Mount Fawcus Partnership **Bred** Fenlon Brothers **Trained** Withycombe, Somerset

FOCUS
This race was run over 22yds further than advertised. Not a bad little staying novice hurdle. It was very steadily run and this is not form to be confident about.

4420 CATTERICKBRIDGE.CO.UK CHASE (A NOVICES' LIMITED H'CAP) (19 fncs) 3m 1f 54y
4:30 (4:30) (Class 4) (0-120,114) 5-Y-O+ £5,198 (£1,526; £763; £381)

Form RPR

2524 1 **Court Dismissed (IRE)**[21] 4046 6-11-1 **112** JamesCowley(5) 122+
(Donald McCain) *chsd ldr: drvn 14th: styd on run-in: led last 75yds* 10/1

233F 2 1 ¼ **Bodega**[11] 4230 8-11-7 **113** WillKennedy 121
(Ian Williams) *hld up: hdwy to trck ldrs 15th: 3rd whn pckd on landing 3 out: outpcd next: styd on fnl 150yds: tk 2nd clsng stages* 17/2

3F22 3 1 **Leanna Ban**[15] 4153 9-11-8 **114** (t) JonathanEngland 121
(Tristan Davidson) *led: j. soundly: drvn 3 l clr last: fdd and hdd fnl 75yds* 7/4[1]

6P35 4 25 **Special Wells**[25] 3972 7-11-5 **111** DannyCook 95
(Sue Smith) *chsd ldng pair: pushed along 12th: wknd 3 out: sn bhd* 9/2[2]

-433 5 35 **Vinny Gambini (IRE)**[20] 4051 9-10-10 **105** GrahamWatters(3) 57
(Rose Dobbin) *hit 3rd: mstke 6th: hdwy to chse ldrs 9th: pushed along 12th: outpcd and lost pl 4 out: sn bhd: t.o 2 out* 6/1[3]

5626 P **Bonzo Bing (IRE)**[14] 4166 8-11-2 **108** HenryBrooke
(Martin Todhunter) *in rr: lost pl 14th: sn bhd: t.o 4 out: p.u bef next* 6/1[3]

/33- P **Bespoke Lady (IRE)**[556] 1304 7-11-1 **107** BrianHarding
(Micky Hammond) *nt fluent: chsd ldrs: lost pl 4th: sn drvn: bhd and reminders 10th: t.o whn blnd 13th: sn p.u* 20/1

6m 44.9s (2.90) **Going Correction** +0.20s/f (Yiel) **7** Ran SP% **107.5**
Speed ratings: **103,102,102,94,83 ,**
CSF £75.13 TOTE £13.10: £5.10, £3.30; EX 115.10 Trifecta £228.30.
Owner Special Piping Materials Ltd **Bred** Peter Tonery **Trained** Cholmondeley, Cheshire

FOCUS
This race was run over 22yds further than advertised. A modest staying novice handicap run at a fair gallop, and the turf was kicking up. The second and third have been rated pretty much to their marks.

4421 RACING AGAIN 9TH MARCH H'CAP HURDLE (12 hdls) 3m 1f 71y
5:00 (5:00) (Class 4) (0-110,109) 4-Y-O+ £3,249 (£954; £477; £238)

Form RPR

-503 1 **Wintered Well (IRE)**[32] 3846 8-11-10 **107** RichardJohnson 120+
(Jennie Candlish) *hld up in rr-div: hdwy to trck ldrs 8th: led bef 2 out: forged clr appr last: styd on wl* 9/4[1]

2342 2 12 **Hunters Belt (IRE)**[13] 4178 12-11-0 **102** (vt) JonathonBewley(5) 103
(George Bewley) *stdd s: hld up and bhd: stdy hdwy after 7th: trcking ldrs 3 out: 2nd bef next: kpt on same pce between last 2* 16/1

0-P3 3 7 **Seymour Eric**[26] 3950 11-11-10 **107** (p) IanPopham 100
(Martin Keighley) *w ldrs: drvn 3 out: 3rd and outpcd appr 2 out: one pce* 9/1

0441 4 1 ½ **Flemerina (IRE)**[30] 3888 7-10-8 **91** SeanQuinlan 84
(Sue Smith) *chsd ldrs: one pce bef 2 out: modest 4th between last 2* 10/1

5133 5 16 **Turtle Cask (IRE)**[18] 4110 7-11-1 **98** (p) BrianHughes 78
(Dianne Sayer) *chsd ldrs: led sn after 3 out: hdd bef next: wknd between last 2* 17/2[3]

3502 6 20 **Tickanrun (IRE)**[41] 3684 6-10-12 **95** (p) DenisO'Regan 54
(Chris Grant) *chsd ldrs: pushed along 4th: reminders after 7th: lost pl 3 out: sn bhd* 9/1

45-3 7 7 **Leney Cottage (IRE)**[21] 4047 9-10-11 **99** DaraghBourke(5) 52
(Maurice Barnes) *t.k.h: mde most tl hdd sn after 3 out: sn lost pl: wl bhd whn eased run-in* 9/2[2]

3P6P P **Heart O Annandale (IRE)**[21] 4047 9-10-12 **95** (t) HenryBrooke
(Iain Jardine) *sn bhd: reminders 2nd and 7th: t.o next: sn p.u* 33/1

30-0 P **Super Lunar (IRE)**[123] 2174 7-11-3 **105** (t) JamieHamilton(5)
(Henry Hogarth) *mid-div: drvn 7th: lost pl 9th: sn bhd: t.o whn p.u bef last* 80/1

0P13 P **Izbushka (IRE)**[22] 4030 5-10-8 **91** (b) PeterCarberry
(David Thompson) *rel to r: hdwy to chse ldrs 2nd: drvn and lost pl 8th: sn bhd: t.o whn p.u bef 2 out* 25/1

-316 P **Whitsundays (IRE)**[61] 3377 7-11-12 **109** WillKennedy
(Donald McCain) *prom: dropped bk briefly 6th: chsng ldrs next: lost pl sn after 8th: sn bhd: t.o whn p.u bef 2 out* 16/1

5240 P **Triumph Davis (IRE)**[35] 3793 7-9-7 **86** (p) BillyGarritty(10)
(Micky Hammond) *in rr: bhd fr 8th: t.o 3 out: p.u bef last* 14/1

6m 39.0s (11.40) **Going Correction** +0.475s/f (Soft) **12** Ran SP% **115.0**
Speed ratings (Par 105): **100,96,93,93,88 81,79, , ,**
CSF £36.59 CT £275.48 TOTE £2.70: £1.20, £4.90, £3.20; EX 41.80 Trifecta £322.90.
Owner A White **Bred** Mrs Kathleen Leahy **Trained** Basford Green, Staffs

FOCUS
This race was run over 22yds further than advertised. This looked competitive for the class, but the well-backed winner hosed up. The second has been rated in line with his recent runs, although the race could be rated up to 6lb higher through the third and fourth.
T/Jkpt: Not won. T/Plt: £101.30 to a £1 stake.Pool: £58,458.00 - 420.88 winning units. T/Qpdt: £30.00 to a £1 stake. Pool: £4,625.60 - 114.00 winning units. **Walter Glynn**

4209 LEICESTER (R-H)
Tuesday, March 1

OFFICIAL GOING: Heavy (soft in places; 5.6)
Wind: Light behind Weather: Cloudy with sunny spells

4422 SQUIRE OSBALDESTON H'CAP CHASE (18 fncs) 2m 6f 151y
2:20 (2:20) (Class 4) (0-110,110) 5-Y-O+ £4,659 (£1,446; £779)

Form RPR

-322 1 **I Am Colin**[61] 3387 7-11-12 **110** SamTwiston-Davies 126+
(Nigel Twiston-Davies) *chsd ldrs: pushed along 14th: led bef next: drvn out* 2/1[1]

P541 2 9 **Lord Landen (IRE)**[81] 3014 11-11-7 **105** (t) PaddyBrennan 111
(Fergal O'Brien) *hld up: hdwy to chse wnr appr 4 out: nt fluent next: rdn bef last: edgd lft and no ex flat* 9/4[2]

P-14 3 21 **Merchant Of Milan**[40] 3709 8-11-3 **101** (p) RhysFlint 87
(John Flint) *chsd ldr tl rdn appr 4 out: wknd bef last* 4/1[3]

-12P P **Ball Hopper (IRE)**[78] 3088 12-10-3 **87** (p) RichieMcLernon
(Richenda Ford) *hld up: pushed along 5th: reminders after next: wknd 9th: bhd whn p.u bef 11th* 9/1

6-PP P **Our Cat (IRE)**[75] 3123 8-11-7 **108**[1] ConorShoemark(3)
(Fergal O'Brien) *led: rdn: hdd & wknd appr 4 out: bhd whn p.u bef next* 7/1

6m 22.3s (18.30) **Going Correction** +0.90s/f (Soft) **5** Ran SP% **106.6**
Speed ratings: **104,100,93, ,**
CSF £6.64 TOTE £2.30: £1.40, £1.50; EX 5.80 Trifecta £12.10.
Owner Mrs Caroline Beresford-Wylie **Bred** Mrs Caroline Beresford-Wylie **Trained** Naunton, Gloucs

FOCUS
Bends were out, increasing all race distances by 44yds. Paddy Brennan described the ground as "very hard work." Moderate chasing form and something of a slow motion finish. The runner-up has been rated 3lb off.

4423 SILEBY NOVICES' H'CAP CHASE (15 fncs) 2m 4f 45y
2:50 (2:50) (Class 4) (0-105,105) 5-Y-O+ £4,548 (£1,335; £667; £333)

Form RPR

6PP1 1 **Some Finish (IRE)**[12] 4214 7-10-5 **84** (v) CharliePoste 101+
(Robin Dickin) *mde all: j.rt 3 out: clr fr next: pushed out* 6/4[1]

4311 2 11 **Global Dream**[12] 4211 6-11-12 **105** AdamPogson 112
(Caroline Bailey) *chsd wnr to 4th: wnt 2nd again next: rdn after 4 out: mstke next: styd on same pce: nt fluent last* 7/2[3]

2451 3 30 **Bredon Hill Lad**[13] 4187 9-11-5 **101** LucyGardner(3) 81
(Sue Gardner) *hld up in tch: hit 7th: wknd next* 11/4[2]

350P 4 99 **The Society Man (IRE)**[66] 3236 9-10-2 **88** GrahamCarson(7)
(Michael Chapman) *prom: chsd wnr 4th to next: remained handy tl wknd appr 8th* 25/1

The Form Book Jumps 2015-16, Raceform Ltd, Newbury, RG14 5SJ

302/ **U** **Lost Arca (FR)**[852] 2181 10-10-4 **83**........................ TomScudamore
(David Bridgwater) *chsd ldrs: mstke 5th: nt fluent 7th: wknd 4 out: mstke and uns rdr next* **11/2**

5m 40.6s (21.70) **Going Correction** +0.90s/f (Soft) **5** Ran SP% **108.1**
Speed ratings: **92,87,75,36,**
CSF £6.96 TOTE £2.00: £1.10, £1.70; EX 5.40 Trifecta £9.70.
Owner Mrs C Dickin & The Some Finish Partners **Bred** Liam Cullinan **Trained** Alcester, Warwicks

FOCUS
Bends were out, increasing all race distances by 44yds. As in the first race, they finished tired and well strung out. Another big step forward from the winner, with the second rated to his recent course mark.

4424 LEICESTERSHIRE OPEN HUNTERS' CHASE (18 fncs) 2m 6f 151y
3:20 (3:21) (Class 3) 6-Y-O+ **£9,105** (£2,844; £1,422; £711; £355)

Form RPR
31-3 **1** **Penmore Mill (IRE)**[44] 11-11-3 127........................ MrHFNugent(7) 131
(F A Hutsby) *a.p: chsd ldr 5th tl appr 9th: remained handy: led 4 out: clr bef last: rdn out* **10/1**
/03P **2** *8* **Clonbanan Lad (IRE)**[11] 4232 10-11-7 108........................ MrJSole(3) 123
(Miss Louise Allan) *a.p: chsd ldr bef 9th tl led appr 4 out: sn hdd: styd on same pce fr 2 out* **20/1**
630- **3** *10* **Robbie**[16] 12-12-2 144........................ MrJohnDawson 122
(Keith Reveley) *hld up: hmpd 5th: hdwy 8th: rdn and wknd after 2 out* **9/2**[1]
00/ **4** *5* **You Too Pet (IRE)**[16] 8-11-3 0........................ MrPMason(7) 108
(P W Mason) *hld up: hdwy 8th: rdn after 4 out: mstke: hmpd and wknd 3 out* **10/1**
1UF- **5** *16* **Tony Star (FR)**[347] 4884 9-11-9 135........................ MrJamesKing(7) 104
(Mickey Bowen) *hld up: effrt appr 4 out: sn wknd* **7/1**[3]
4-35 **P** **Ray Diamond**[23] 11-11-9 107........................ MissOliviaHutchings(7)
(Jackie Du Plessis) *prom: mstke 4th: sn lost pl: bhd fr 8th: p.u bef last* **50/1**
/1F- **P** **Ockey De Neulliac (FR)**[289] 14-11-3 120........................ SamColtherd(7)
(N Mechie) *led: hdd appr 4 out: wknd next: bhd whn p.u bef last* **17/2**
/F-4 **P** **Warne (IRE)**[23] 12-11-10 127........................ MrSWaley-Cohen
(Robert Waley-Cohen) *hld up: hdwy 8th: wknd after 4 out* **11/2**[2]
6-41 **F** **Night Alliance (IRE)**[9] 4269 11-11-3 113........................(bt) MrLeoMahon(7)
(P R M Philips) *prom tl fell 5th* **7/1**[3]
450P **P** **Midnight Appeal**[17] 4113 11-11-5 127........................(tp) MrRobertHawker(5)
(Sophie Leech) *hld up: hmpd 5th: hdwy 10th: mstke 4 out: sn wknd: bhd whn p.u bef last* **17/2**
PP5 **P** **Local Celebrity (IRE)**[18] 4105 12-11-3 107........................(t) MissLWheeler(7)
(Sally Randell) *hld up: bhd fr 9th: p.u bef 12th* **150/1**
1041 **U** **Wings Of Smoke (IRE)**[38] 3749 11-11-9 135........................(t) MrEDavid(7)
(Tim Vaughan) *hld up: hdwy 14th: disputing cl 2nd whn blnd and uns rdr 3 out* **10/1**
U2-1 **P** **Neverownup (IRE)**[44] 11-11-9 126........................ MrSeanHoulihan(7)
(M J Vanstone) *chsd ldr to 5th: remained handy tl wknd 10th: bhd whn p.u bef 13th* **25/1**
UP-3 **P** **Catch Tammy (IRE)**[277] 536 10-11-7 110........................ MissCVHart(3)
(Mrs I Barnett) *bhd fr 4th: hmpd next: p.u bef 12th* **100/1**

6m 19.1s (15.10) **Going Correction** +0.90s/f (Soft) **14** Ran SP% **119.1**
Speed ratings: **109,106,102,101,95** , , , , , , , , ,
CSF £186.04 TOTE £10.10: £2.80, £3.90, £2.80; EX 202.30 Trifecta £1786.50.
Owner K Hutsby **Bred** P Power **Trained** Stratford-Upon-Avon, Warwicks

FOCUS
Bends were out, increasing all race distances by 44yds. Only five of the 14 runners managed to complete in what had looked a wide-open and decent hunter chase. The winner has been rated to his best, with the second to his Warwick reappearance.

4425 RUTLAND WATER NOVICES' CHASE (18 fncs) 2m 6f 151y
3:50 (3:50) (Class 3) 5-Y-O+ **£7,031** (£2,571)

Form RPR
2203 **1** **Abracadabra Sivola (FR)**[84] 2963 6-11-0 125........................ TomScudamore 138
(David Pipe) *mde all: j.lft at times: nt fluent 11th: rdn after 2 out: styd on u.p* **15/8**[2]
31 **2** *1¾* **Lockstockandbarrel (IRE)**[9] 4274 7-11-6 0........................ AidanColeman 142
(Jonjo O'Neill) *hld up: lft 2nd 6th: chal on bit after 2 out: sn rdn: styd on same pce flat* **8/11**[1]
/12- **F** **Tsar Alexandre (FR)**[427] 3410 9-11-0 117........................(t) GavinSheehan
(Warren Greatrex) *chsd wnr tl fell 6th* **7/1**[3]
PP **U** **Yanmare (IRE)**[38] 3736 6-10-11 0........................(t) RyanHatch(3)
(Nigel Twiston-Davies) *prom tl mstke and uns rdr 6th* **50/1**

6m 17.9s (13.90) **Going Correction** +0.90s/f (Soft) **4** Ran SP% **107.1**
Speed ratings: **111,110, ,**
CSF £3.76 TOTE £3.60; EX 4.50 Trifecta £5.00.
Owner The Arthur White Partnership **Bred** G Trapenard **Trained** Nicholashayne, Devon

FOCUS
Bends were out, increasing all race distances by 44yds. This looked a bit of a match anyway and only the big two were left after the outsiders departed at the sixth.

4426 COTTESMORE "GRASSROOTS" MAIDEN HUNTERS' CHASE (15 fncs) 2m 4f 45y
4:20 (4:20) (Class 6) 6-Y-O+ **£1,871** (£580; £290; £145)

Form RPR
325- **1** **Man Of Steel (IRE)**[38] 7-12-2 96........................ MissGAndrews 112+
(Alan Hill) *hld up in tch: racd wd: chsd ldr appr 4 out: rdn to ld last: rdr dropped whip flat: pushed out* **11/4**[2]
2 *2¼* **Thetalkinghorse (IRE)**[16] 8-11-9 0........................ MrSDavies-Thomas(7) 110+
(G T H Bailey) *chsd ldrs: blnd 7th: led appr 4 out: j.rt next: sn rdn: hdd and mstke last: styd on same pce flat* **15/8**[1]
3 *¾* **Melt The Silver**[703] 10-11-9 0........................ MrLeoMahon(7) 106
(Mrs D J Ralph) *chsd ldr 2nd tl blnd next: sn lost pl: rallied to go 2nd again 6th tl rdn appr 4 out: outpcd after 2 out: styd on wl towards fin* **10/1**
/2-3 **4** *17* **Mister Teddy**[12] 4213 11-11-9 103........................(p) MrHFNugent(7) 89
(F A Hutsby) *chsd ldrs: pushed along at various stages: reminders after 8th: hmpd bnd after 11th: wknd appr 4 out* **7/2**[3]
P **5** *9* **Cooladerry King (IRE)**[9] 8-11-11 0........................ MrJNixon(5) 80
(Mrs Sheila Crow) *led: rdn and hdd appr 4 out: wknd next* **6/1**
P **P** **Cab On Times (IRE)**[12] 4213 7-11-9 0........................ MrJNailor(7)
(S Rea) *hld up: a in rr: bhd fr 6th: p.u bef last* **40/1**
P5 **P** **Triggywinkle (FR)**[7] 4295 7-11-4 0........................(tp) MrMartinMcIntyre(5)
(Roderick Chelton) *hld up: sme hdwy after 11th: sn wknd: bhd whn p.u bef next* **80/1**

5m 44.9s (26.00) **Going Correction** +0.90s/f (Soft) **7** Ran SP% **110.7**
Speed ratings: **84,83,82,76,72** , ,
CSF £8.16 TOTE £2.60: £1.60, £2.20; EX 10.60 Trifecta £51.70.
Owner Alan Hill **Bred** Katie McCarthy **Trained** Aston Rowant, Oxfordshire

FOCUS
Bends were out, increasing all race distances by 44yds. Not a bad little maiden hunters' chase, although again runners finished tired. The winner has been rated in line with his old hurdle mark.

4427 DANIEL LAMBERT H'CAP CHASE (15 fncs) 2m 4f 45y
4:50 (4:50) (Class 4) (0-115,113) 5-Y-O+ **£4,659** (£1,446; £779)

Form RPR
-513 **1** **Troika Steppes**[27] 3924 8-11-9 113........................(t) ConorShoemark(3) 130+
(Fergal O'Brien) *mde virtually all: clr fr 11th: easily* **13/8**[1]
22-P **2** *32* **One For The Boss (IRE)**[104] 2569 9-11-9 110........................(p) RobertDunne 87
(Dai Burchell) *chsd ldrs: wnt 2nd 9th: wknd 3 out* **8/1**
1505 **3** *10* **Mountain Of Mourne (IRE)**[25] 3975 7-11-5 113........................(p) ConorSmith(7) 83
(Linda Blackford) *drvn along thrght: chsd wnr to 9th: wknd 4 out: stmbld last* **9/2**[3]
52/3 **P** **Genstone Trail**[19] 4073 10-10-9 96........................ BrendanPowell
(Alan King) *chsd ldrs: j.lft 7th: mstke 11th: sn rdn and wknd: bhd whn p.u bef 3 out* **9/2**[3]
12PP **P** **Spending Time**[32] 3836 7-11-12 113........................(bt) TomScudamore
(David Pipe) *hld up: nt fluent 7th: wknd 10th: bhd whn p.u bef 3 out* **10/3**[2]

5m 43.6s (24.70) **Going Correction** +0.90s/f (Soft) **5** Ran SP% **108.6**
Speed ratings: **86,73,69, ,**
CSF £12.96 TOTE £3.10: £1.40, £3.50; EX 12.40 Trifecta £43.00.
Owner William Williamson **Bred** William And Mrs Susan Williamson **Trained** Naunton, Gloucs

FOCUS
Bends were out, increasing all race distances by 44yds. This didn't take much winning, with a couple of the key contenders failing to give their running. The winner was seemingly taking a big step up on his recent course run, but the second was back from a long absence and this is not one to be confident about.
T/Plt: £64.20 to a £1 stake. Pool: £58,581.87 - 665.60 winning units. T/Qpdt: £47.80 to a £1 stake. Pool: £4,835.38 - 74.80 winning units. **Colin Roberts**

4428 - (Foreign Racing) - See Raceform Interactive

3006 BANGOR-ON-DEE (L-H)
Wednesday, March 2

OFFICIAL GOING: Heavy (5.2)
Wind: Fairly strong, half behind Weather: Cloudy and very cold, rain late on

4429 STELLA CIDRE NOVICES' H'CAP HURDLE (9 hdls) 2m 145y
2:00 (2:00) (Class 4) (0-120,118) 4-Y-O+ **£3,249** (£954; £477; £238)

Form RPR
4323 **1** **Theatrical Style (IRE)**[23] 4031 7-10-12 104........................(p) WillKennedy 112+
(Donald McCain) *w ldr: rdn bef 5th: led appr 3 out: clr bef 2 out: styd on wl* **3/1**[2]
P2-P **2** *6* **Twin Barrels**[19] 4099 9-10-11 106........................(p) JamesBanks(3) 105
(Sarah-Jayne Davies) *led: rdn appr 4 out: hdd bef 3 out: one pce fr 2 out* **12/1**
3222 **3** *13* **Beat The Tide**[48] 3592 6-10-8 105........................ AlanJohns(5) 92
(Tim Vaughan) *trckd ldrs: nt fluent 5th: rdn after 3 out: no imp fr 2 out* **2/1**[1]
16F6 **4** *1* **Political Quiz**[67] 3221 6-11-12 118........................ NicodeBoinville 105
(Tom Symonds) *hld up: effrt appr 3 out: rdn and btn 2 out* **7/2**[3]
2-33 **P** **What A Scorcher**[80] 3066 5-10-11 103........................ LeightonAspell
(Oliver Sherwood) *chsd ldrs: dropped to last 5th: rdn appr 4 out: t.o 3 out: p.u bef next* **7/2**[3]

4m 33.0s (22.10) **Going Correction** +1.45s/f (Heav) **5** Ran SP% **110.5**
Speed ratings (Par 105): **106,103,97,96,**
CSF £29.59 TOTE £2.70: £1.40, £5.10; EX 34.00 Trifecta £72.10.
Owner Deva Racing Palladium Partnership **Bred** Spratstown Bloodstock Ltd **Trained** Cholmondeley, Cheshire

FOCUS
All race distances were as advertised. Morning rain and sleet turned the ground from soft to heavy, and it looked hard work. Will Kennedy described the ground as "very testing". This very ordinary novice handicap was run at a steady pace. A step up from the winner, and there's a case for rating him up to 6lb higher.

4430 EQUINE LENS MAIDEN HURDLE (11 hdls) 2m 3f 123y
2:30 (2:30) (Class 5) 4-Y-O+ **£2,599** (£763; £381; £190)

Form RPR
3343 **1** **Bryden Boy (IRE)**[48] 3588 6-11-2 115........................ SeanQuinlan 117+
(Jennie Candlish) *mde virtually all: rdn and edgd lft appr last where mstke: pressed fnl 100yds: kpt on wl nr fin* **7/2**[2]
32 **2** *1¼* **Dubai Devils (IRE)**[23] 4031 5-11-2 0........................ BrianHughes 114
(Paul Stafford, Ire) *trckd ldrs: wnt 2nd appr 2 out: rdn and swtchd rt bef last: pressed wnr fnl 100yds: no ex fnl strides* **8/1**
053- **3** *12* **Seymour Star**[340] 5033 8-11-2 108........................ AndrewTinkler 104
(Alastair Ralph) *w ldrs early: prom: rdn and lost pl bef 7th: outpcd 4 out: rallied u.p 2 out: kpt on to take 3rd appr last: no imp on front two* **25/1**
263 **4** *5* **Golden Investment (IRE)**[35] 3802 7-11-2 0........................ WayneHutchinson 98
(Donald McCain) *w wnr: hit 7th: nt fluent 3 out: sn rdn: lost 2nd and wknd appr 2 out* **4/1**[3]
054P **5** *33* **Midnight Target**[50] 3570 6-10-9 0........................ LeeEdwards 60
(John Groucott) *hld up: in midfield after 5th: outpcd bef 4 out: fin wl bhd* **66/1**
F-U2 **6** *34* **Go West Young Man (IRE)**[14] 4183 8-11-2 123........................ JakeGreenall 65
(Henry Daly) *trckd ldrs: wknd after 3 out: bhd whn hung rt and wnt off crse after last: c to standstl: continued: t.o* **9/4**[1]
0/05 **P** **Over The Bridge**[50] 3573 6-10-9 0........................ MrJNixon(7)
(Steve Flook) *midfield: lost pl and mstke 6th: struggling bef 7th: t.o whn p.u bef 2 out* **200/1**
35-P **P** **Tropical Sunshine (IRE)**[33] 3839 8-10-11 0........................ NickSlatter(5)
(Pippa Bickerton) *a bhd: struggling bef 4 out: t.o whn p.u bef 2 out* **200/1**
0-50 **P** **Marvellous Monty (IRE)**[32] 3862 6-10-9 0........................ AlainCawley
(Johnny Farrelly) *a bhd: struggling bef 4 out: t.o whn p.u bef 2 out* **50/1**
-0PP **P** **Adadream**[80] 3064 7-10-13 0........................(t) ConorShoemark(3)
(Claire Dyson) *midfield: lost pl bef 4th: bhd after 5th and struggling: t.o whn p.u bef 6th* **200/1**
3P0 **P** **Master Ally (IRE)**[26] 3976 6-11-2 0........................ SeanBowen
(Rebecca Curtis) *racd keenly: trckd ldrs: j.rt 4th: sn in midfield: lost pl 6th: struggling bef 4 out: t.o whn p.u bef 2 out* **20/1**
P **Bellator (FR)** 5-11-2 0........................ NicodeBoinville
(Nicky Henderson) *hld up in midfield: pushed along appr 7th: sn wknd: t.o whn p.u bef 2 out* **4/1**[3]

5m 20.1s (28.10) **Going Correction** +1.60s/f (Heav) **12** Ran SP% **117.7**
Speed ratings (Par 103): **107,106,101,99,86 72** , , , , , ,
CSF £30.00 TOTE £4.30: £1.60, £2.40, £6.10; EX 35.50 Trifecta £498.70.

Owner Alan Baxter & Brian Hall **Bred** Mrs Mary O'Donoghue **Trained** Basford Green, Staffs
FOCUS
A modest race of its type. The winner and third set the level.

4431 BROXTON GATES H'CAP CHASE (12 fncs) 2m 1f 77y
3:05 (3:07) (Class 4) (0-115,115) 5-Y-O+ £6,498 (£1,908; £954; £477)

Form RPR
-316 **1** **Little Jimmy**[39] 3742 9-11-2 105..........................(tp) BrianHughes 123+
(Tom Gretton) *hld up: impr gng wl bef 3 out: wnt 2nd 2 out: shkn up to ld run-in: readily drew clr* **25/1**
-P3B **2** *4* **Supreme Asset (IRE)**[43] 3670 8-11-12 115.............. WayneHutchinson 125
(Donald McCain) *prom: led appr 2 out: rdn bef last: hdd run-in: kpt on same pce clsng stages* **6/1**[3]
0-F2 **3** *2 ½* **Not For You (IRE)**[4] 4356 8-10-1 90......................... PaulMoloney 101
(C Byrnes, Ire) *hld up: nt fluent 8th: impr bef 3 out: effrt and cl up 2 out: rdn bef last: one pce run-in* **1/1**[1]
0-61 **4** *30* **Cloudy Beach (IRE)**[13] 4197 9-11-7 115................. CharlieDeutsch(5) 98
(Venetia Williams) *led: hdd 3rd: remained prom: regained ld 8th: rdn and hdd appr 2 out: wknd after fence* **2/1**[2]
5-P0 **P** **Satu (IRE)**[77] 3108 12-9-7 89 oh2..............................(t) MissLBrooke(7)
(Lady Susan Brooke) *chsd ldrs: led jst after 3rd: hdd 8th: wknd 3 out: t.o whn p.u bef 2 out* **66/1**
2512 **P** **Pembroke House**[22] 4042 9-10-13 105......................(p) JamesBanks(3)
(Sarah-Jayne Davies) *prom: lost pl 4 out: wknd 3 out: t.o whn p.u bef 2 out* **10/1**

5m 2.3s (40.20) **Going Correction** +2.50s/f (Heav) **6 Ran SP% 112.0**
Speed ratings: **105,103,101,87,**
CSF £152.74 TOTE £11.20: £4.90, £3.40; EX 45.40 Trifecta £206.40.
Owner Tom Gretton Racing & Ownaracehorse Ltd **Bred** Mrs Marigold West **Trained** Holberrow Green, Worcs
FOCUS
Quite a competitive handicap despite the small field. A big step up from the surprise winner, but the second and third are on good marks and he's been given the benefit of the doubt.

4432 BROXTON GATES H'CAP HURDLE (11 hdls) 2m 3f 123y
3:40 (3:40) (Class 4) (0-120,120) 4-Y-O+ £6,498 (£1,908; £954; £477)

Form RPR
-404 **1** **Tanit River (IRE)**[62] 3377 6-10-9 108.......................... AlanJohns(5) 120+
(Tim Vaughan) *trckd ldrs: chsd ldr appr 3 out: led jst bef 2 out: drawing clr whn mstke last: styd on wl* **11/4**[2]
06PP **2** *12* **Quincy Des Pictons (FR)**[53] 3521 12-11-6 114.................. RhysFlint 111
(Alan Jones) *led: wnt abt 5 l clr bef 3 out: reduced advantage after 3 out: rdn and hdd jst bef 2 out: one pce and no ch bef last* **6/1**
5 **3** *27* **Noble Galileo (GER)**[32] 3865 6-11-2 110..................... TomO'Brien 82
(Tim Vaughan) *hld up: outpcd 3 out: wnt mod 3rd bef 2 out: no imp* **28/1**
0024 **4** *21* **Red Hott Robbie**[32] 3865 7-10-11 105..................... AndrewThornton 54
(Giuseppe Fierro) *hld up: struggling whn mstke 3 out: wl btn: t.o* **8/1**
6423 **5** *5* **Petrou (IRE)**[22] 4041 6-11-5 113..............................(p) KielanWoods 57
(Ben Case) *chsd ldrs: wnt 2nd bef 4 out: lost 2nd bef 3 out: sn wknd: t.o* **2/1**[1]
F42P **P** **Bobble Boru (IRE)**[32] 3866 8-10-9 103......................(b) LiamTreadwell
(Venetia Williams) *tk str hold: chsd ldr: lost 2nd appr 4 out where mstke: sn wknd: t.o whn p.u bef 2 out* **7/2**[3]

5m 21.3s (29.30) **Going Correction** +1.60s/f (Heav) **6 Ran SP% 111.1**
Speed ratings (Par 105): **105,100,89,81,79**
CSF £18.45 CT £355.71 TOTE £3.90: £3.50, £2.30; EX 17.30 Trifecta £229.60.
Owner Brian Ead & Martin Moore **Bred** T P Quinlan **Trained** Aberthin, Vale of Glamorgan
FOCUS
They finished well strung out in this modest handicap hurdle. The winner looks back on the upgrade, while the second has been rated to his mark.

4433 ROA/RACING POST OWNERS JACKPOT H'CAP CHASE (21 fncs) 3m 5f 142y
4:15 (4:17) (Class 4) (0-110,110) 5-Y-O+ £5,198 (£1,526; £763; £381)

Form RPR
13P4 **1** **Millicent Silver**[20] 4071 7-11-8 109..........................(p) RyanHatch(3) 128+
(Nigel Twiston-Davies) *in tch: rdn along most of way fr after 6th: bhd 8th: chsd ldrs 11th: wnt 2nd 15th: rdn and upsides 2 out: led last: styd on to draw clr fnl 100yds* **4/1**[2]
53 **2** *7* **Son Of Suzie**[55] 3499 8-11-9 110............................(p) ConorShoemark(3) 124
(Fergal O'Brien) *w ldr: led 2nd: rdn whn jnd 2 out: mstke and hdd last: no ex fnl 100yds* **5/2**[1]
-445 **3** *46* **Gibbstown (IRE)**[14] 4185 10-10-8 92..........................(p) BrianHughes 58
(Paul Stafford, Ire) *hld up: hdwy 9th: rdn and unable to go w front two bef 3 out: plugged on after* **15/2**
23P4 **4** *8* **Nalim (IRE)**[27] 3948 10-10-1 85............................(b) JonathanEngland 43
(Harriet Bethell) *in tch: dropped to rr 5th: mstke 9th: nt travel wl after and bhd: plugged on fr 2 out* **5/1**[3]
2U20 **5** *2 ½* **Market Option (IRE)**[20] 4069 10-11-6 104..................(p) LiamTreadwell 60
(Venetia Williams) *hld up: impr to trck ldrs 6th: mstke 12th: sn rdn and towards rr: hdwy 14th and sn prom: wknd 17th* **6/1**
/P-6 **6** *8* **Our Island (IRE)**[14] 4185 11-11-4 102..........................(p) DaveCrosse 50
(Hugo Froud) *led to 2nd: prom tl pushed along after 6th and lost pl: rn in snatches after: wknd 15th: t.o* **18/1**
-04P **P** **Quilnton (FR)**[108] 2517 12-11-10 108.......................... RichieMcLernon
(Johnny Farrelly) *in tch: chsd ldr fr 9th tl 15th: wknd 4 out: t.o whn p.u bef 2 out* **10/1**
P2PP **P** **Mansonien L'As (FR)**[27] 3948 10-9-9 84 oh3...........(tp) JamesCowley(5)
(Donald McCain) *prom: mstke 5th and 9th: wknd after 14th: lost tch and p.u after 15th* **10/1**

9m 2.7s (67.70) **Going Correction** +2.50s/f (Heav) **8 Ran SP% 114.7**
Speed ratings: **109,107,94,92,92 89, ,**
CSF £15.13 CT £70.81 TOTE £5.40: £3.20, £1.30, £1.40; EX 18.00 Trifecta £101.30.
Owner John Goodman **Bred** Owen Brennan / John Goodman **Trained** Naunton, Gloucs
FOCUS
A real slog, this ordinary marathon handicap being run in a slower time than last season's Grand National. The first two pulled clear. A big step up from the winner, with the second rated back to his best.

4434 STELLA ARTOIS STANDARD NATIONAL HUNT FLAT RACE (CONDITIONAL JOCKEYS' AND AMATEUR RIDERS' RACE) 2m 145y
4:50 (4:52) (Class 6) 4-6-Y-O £1,949 (£572; £286; £143)

Form RPR
4 **1** **Orchard Park (IRE)**[83] 2991 5-10-8 0......................... GrahamCarson(10) 101
(Jamie Snowden) *chsd ldr: rdn 3f out: outpcd by wnr 2f out: abt 4 l down 1f out: styd on ins fnl f: led fnl 50yds: won gng away: uns rdr after line* **2/1**[2]
2 **2** **The Pierre Lark (IRE)**[108] 6-10-13 0.......................... JamesCowley(5) 99
(Donald McCain) *led: wnt clr 2f out: rdn abt 4 l clr 1f out: hdd and no ex fnl 50yds* **10/11**[1]
3 **3** *9* **Rio Bravo (IRE)**[130] 5-11-1 0...................................(t) RyanHatch(3) 90
(Graeme McPherson) *in rr: wnt 3rd 5f out: rdn over 2f out: one pce after* **7/2**[3]
0 **4** *11* **Buachaill Beag**[121] 2250 5-10-11 0...........................(t) PhilipDonovan(7) 79
(Fergal O'Brien) *t.k.h: chsd ldrs: dropped to rr 5f out: pushed along 4f out: lft bhd 2f out* **16/1**

4m 35.2s (29.90) **Going Correction** +1.60s/f (Heav) **4 Ran SP% 113.8**
Speed ratings: **93,92,87,82**
CSF £4.51 TOTE £3.10; EX 4.40 Trifecta £4.50.
Owner D I Ryder **Bred** Daniel O'Sullivan **Trained** Lambourn, Berks
■ Graham Carson's first 'jumps' winner, to go with three as an amateur on the Flat.
FOCUS
A moderate little bumper. It's been rated around the winner and fourth.
T/Plt: £1,020.60 to a £1 stake. Pool: £51,956.33 - 37.16 winning tickets. T/Qpdt: £116.80 to a £1 stake. Pool: £5,909.21 - 37.42 winning tickets. **Darren Owen**

4250 WINCANTON (R-H)
Wednesday, March 2

OFFICIAL GOING: Soft (chs 6.5, hdl 6.9)
Wind: very strong half behind Weather: light showers Rails: Race distances: Races 1 & 6 add 40yds. Races 2 & 3 add 45yds. Races 4 & 5 add 60yds.

4435 BETFAIR ACCA EDGE MARES' NOVICES' HURDLE (7 hdls 1 omitted) 1m 7f 65y
2:10 (2:10) (Class 4) 5-Y-O+ £3,898 (£1,144; £572; £286)

Form RPR
5-35 **1** **Sainte Ladylime (FR)**[32] 3861 5-10-10 0.......................... DavidBass 131+
(Kim Bailey) *trckd ldrs: shkn up to chal bef 2 out: led between last 2: pushed clr: readily* **6/1**[3]
-2U1 **2** *13* **Antartica De Thaix (FR)**[8] 4293 6-11-3 0..........(t) SamTwiston-Davies 124
(Paul Nicholls) *led: jnd 2 out: sn rdn and hdd: no ex* **4/9**[1]
214P **3** *26* **Shanandoa**[18] 4111 5-10-5 0................................ MichaelHeard(5) 90
(Brian Barr) *trckd ldrs: rdn 3 out: wknd next* **16/1**
002 **4** *12* **Ayla's Emperor**[16] 4157 7-10-10 0.................................. RobertDunne 78
(John Flint) *mid-div: wnt 4th 3 out: nvr trbld ldrs: wknd bef next: t.o* **10/1**
0-0 **5** *14* **Apple Pops**[120] 2258 6-10-10 0...................................... MarkQuinlan 64
(Neil Mulholland) *pressed wnr tl after 3rd: wknd after 3 out: t.o* **100/1**
54 **6** *10* **Keep Up Keira (IRE)**[91] 2856 5-10-10 0.................... TomScudamore 54
(Neil Mulholland) *mid-div tl wknd 3 out: t.o* **16/1**
0P/5 **7** *24* **Mrs Winchester (IRE)**[16] 4157 7-10-10 0....................... IanPopham 30
(Caroline Keevil) *a in rr: t.o* **100/1**
036/ **U** **Ella's Promise**[681] 5440 7-10-10 0................................. LiamHeard
(Martin Hill) *last whn running green and uns rdr 1st* **66/1**
0-40 **P** **Biretta**[118] 2302 5-10-10 0..(t) NoelFehily
(Harry Fry) *mid-div: in last trio whn nt fluent 3rd: struggling next: sn wknd: t.o whn p.u 2 out* **4/1**[2]
5UP **P** **Hawaian Rose**[34] 3825 6-10-3 0..................................... PaulO'Brien(7)
(Colin Tizzard) *a towards rr: lost tch 4th: t.o whn p.u bef 2 out* **100/1**

3m 57.5s (8.60) **Going Correction** +0.85s/f (Soft) **10 Ran SP% 128.9**
Speed ratings: **111,104,90,83,76 71,58, , ,**
CSF £10.56 TOTE £8.70: £2.00, £1.10, £4.20; EX 12.30 Trifecta £118.20.
Owner Paul & Clare Rooney **Bred** Har Du Puy **Trained** Andoversford, Gloucs
FOCUS
The hurdle on the stable bend was omitted. Due to rail movements this race was run over 40yds further than advertised. There was quite a headwind in the back straight and the ground looked quite hard work, Sam Twiston-Davies describing it as "tacky and holding." Little depth to this mares' hurdle, in which they finished strung out, and there was a bit of a turn up. The winner was impressive and has been rated positively.

4436 BETFAIR AUTHORISED BETTING PARTNER OF BRITISH RACING H'CAP CHASE (15 fncs 2 omitted) 2m 4f 35y
2:45 (2:45) (Class 3) (0-135,134) 5-Y-O+ £7,666 (£2,314; £1,192; £631)

Form RPR
-635 **1** **La Vaticane (FR)**[74] 3148 7-11-11 133....................(bt[1]) TomScudamore 143
(David Pipe) *trckd ldrs: pressed ldr 11th: led 3 out (usual 4 out): strly pressed whn lft wl clr next: unchal after* **15/8**[1]
0-45 **2** *23* **Ratify**[67] 3223 12-10-4 112.. RobertDunne 99
(Dai Burchell) *led: hdd 9th: chsd ldrs: rdn after 3 out (usual 4 out): wkng whn lft 2nd 2 out* **22/1**
3112 **3** *6* **Quite By Chance**[27] 3957 7-11-12 134........................ PaddyBrennan 114
(Colin Tizzard) *racd wd: in tch: hdwy after 7th: ldng whn mstke 9th: hdd 3 out (usual 4 out): wkng whn lft 3rd 2 out* **11/4**[2]
PPP3 **4** *23* **Atlantic Roller (IRE)**[11] 4251 9-10-6 114.....................(p) TomCannon 70
(Chris Gordon) *hld up: rdn after 12th: wknd next: t.o 2 out* **7/1**
04/P **P** **Si C'Etait Vrai (FR)**[95] 2780 10-11-10 132........................ NoelFehily
(Neil Mulholland) *prom tl 10th: sn rdn: wknd after 12th: p.u after 3 out (usual 4 out)* **12/1**
4F63 **P** **Brody Bleu (FR)**[13] 4212 9-11-7 129................................ JamieMoore
(Robert Walford) *trckd ldrs tl wknd after 10th: t.o whn p.u after 3 out (usual 4 out)* **25/1**
-004 **P** **Enjoy Responsibly (IRE)**[39] 3749 7-11-5 134...(bt[1]) HarrisonBeswick(7)
(Sam Thomas) *prom tl hmpd on bnd after 4th: rdn after 7th: detached in last after next: tailing off whn p.u 12th* **66/1**
3232 **U** **Vic De Touzaine (FR)**[29] 3916 7-10-12 120..................... AidanColeman 130
(Venetia Williams) *hld up: hdwy fr 9th: pushed along to chse wnr after 3 out (usual 4 out): mounting str chal whn mstke: stmbld and uns rdr next* **4/1**[3]

5m 35.9s (18.40) **Going Correction** +1.15s/f (Heav) **8 Ran SP% 111.3**
Speed ratings: **109,99,97,88, , ,**
CSF £35.90 CT £108.56 TOTE £2.50: £1.10, £4.60, £1.40; EX 36.70 Trifecta £173.10.
Owner Ms Maria Bukhtoyarova **Bred** E B De La Motte & Scuderia Del Bargelo **Trained** Nicholashayne, Devon

FOCUS
The first fence in the home straight was omitted in all chases. Due to rail movements this race was run over 45yds further than advertised. Late drama with the favourite looking to have a proper fight on her hands when being left clear. The winner has been rated to her mark, and the unseater was heading for a similar level to his recent form.

4437 BETFAIR SWITCHING SADDLES HUNTERS' CHASE (FOR THE DICK WOODHOUSE TROPHY) (13 fncs 4 omitted) 2m 4f 35y
3:20 (3:20) (Class 6) 5-Y-0+ £1,247 (£387; £193; £96)

Form RPR
2-3U **1** **Pacha Du Polder (FR)**[12] 4227 9-11-11 141 MsVLPendleton(7) 147+
(Paul Nicholls) *mde all: drew wl clr fr 3 out (usual 4 out): v easily* **5/4**[1]
10-2 **2** *29* **Big Fella Thanks**[25] 4000 14-11-11 130 (t) MrNGeorge(7) 117
(Tom George) *trckd ldrs: rdn to chse wnr after 3 out (usual 4 out): wknd next* **15/8**[2]
01-3 **3** *7* **Blinding Lights (IRE)**[10] 11-11-11 104 (tp) MrMatthewHampton(5) 108
(Mary Sanderson) *trckd wnr: rdn after 11th: lost 2nd after 3 out (usual 4 out): wknd bef 2 out* **20/1**
434- **4** *3* **Flaming Gorge (IRE)**[24] 11-12-1 120 (t) MrSDavies-Thomas(7) 112
(Alan Hill) *trckd wnr tl rdn appr 3 out (usual 4 out): sn wknd* **12/1**
40/P **U** **Gauvain (GER)**[276] 14-11-11 129 (t) MissAEStirling(3)
(Miss V Collins) *hld up bhd ldrs: blnd bdly and uns rdr 7th* **14/1**
60-4 **P** **Ambitious Pursuit (IRE)**[8] 4295 8-11-7 0 MissPGlanville(7)
(Mrs L Glanville) *hld up: struggling 9th: wknd after next: t.o whn p.u 3 out (usual 4 out)* **66/1**
P **Never Complain (IRE)**[18] 8-12-1 128 MrCharlieMarshall(7)
(Mrs F Marshall) *hld up bhd ldrs: trckd ldrs 10th: rdn after next: wknd 3 out (usual 4 out): p.u bef next* **11/2**[3]
0F3/ **P** **Ziggie (IRE)**[10] 9-11-7 0 MrRexDingle(7)
(P Ponting) *hld up bhd ldrs: struggling 11th: wknd on long run bef 3 out (usual 4 out): t.o whn p.u bef 2 out* **66/1**

5m 35.3s (17.80) **Going Correction** +1.15s/f (Heav) 8 Ran SP% **116.7**
Speed ratings: **110,98,95,94, , ,**
CSF £4.16 TOTE £2.10: £1.10, £1.10, £5.80; EX 5.40 Trifecta £34.90.
Owner The Stewart Family **Bred** Hubert Honore, & Pierrick Rouxel **Trained** Ditcheat, Somerset
■ The first winner for Olympic gold medal-winning cyclist Victoria Pendleton.

FOCUS
The first fence in the home straight was omitted in all chases and the last in the back straight was bypassed here also. Due to rail movements this race was run over 45yds further than advertised. All eyes on Victoria Pendleton, bidding for a first rules success, and unlike on her first hunter chase ride aboard the same horse 12 days earlier, everything went smoothly this time. The winner has been rated back to something like his best.

4438 CASH OUT WITH BETFAIR H'CAP HURDLE (10 hdls 1 omitted) 2m 5f 82y
3:55 (3:55) (Class 3) (0-130,128) 4-Y-0+ £6,498 (£1,908; £954; £477)

Form RPR
6-61 **1** **Tagrita (IRE)**[11] 4252 8-11-5 128 (t) HarryCobden(7) 136+
(Paul Nicholls) *mde all: r.o wl to assert fr last: pushed out* **5/2**[1]
P0P1 **2** *3½* **Somerset Jem**[11] 4250 7-10-1 103 JamesBest 105
(Kevin Bishop) *trckd wnr: rdn appr 2 out: 1 l down last: kpt on but nt pce of wnr* **9/2**[3]
23F3 **3** *5* **Murrayana (IRE)**[49] 3583 6-11-7 123 (t) RichardJohnson 121
(Colin Tizzard) *trckd wnr: rdn appr 2 out: hld in 3rd whn wnt lft last: kpt on same pce* **3/1**[2]
014S **4** *11* **Brod Na Heireann (IRE)**[11] 4241 7-11-4 123 TomBellamy(3) 109
(Alan King) *in tch: rdn appr 2 out: kpt on same pce* **14/1**
4144 **5** *6* **The Geegeez Geegee (IRE)**[27] 3956 7-10-7 114 (bt1) DavidNoonan(5) 94
(Anthony Honeyball) *hld up: effrt appr 2 out: sn one pce* **10/1**
-352 **6** *6* **Bim Bam Boum (FR)**[63] 3370 5-11-12 128 NoelFehily 105
(Harry Fry) *hld up: rdn and sme hdwy appr 2 out: hung lft and wknd between last 2* **7/1**
3116 **7** *1¾* **Eminent Poet**[33] 3844 5-11-9 125 AidanColeman 97
(Venetia Williams) *in tch: rdn bef 2 out: wknd between last 2* **10/1**
660 **8** *2¾* **Titch Strider (IRE)**[66] 3283 11-10-1 103 ConorO'Farrell 73
(John Panvert) *a towards rr: wknd appr 2 out* **66/1**

5m 56.0s (29.50) **Going Correction** +1.425s/f (Heav) 8 Ran SP% **110.6**
Speed ratings (Par 107): **100,98,96,92,90 88,87,86**
CSF £13.48 CT £31.74 TOTE £4.00: £1.60, £1.10, £1.70; EX 12.80 Trifecta £44.60.
Owner Axom XLVIII **Bred** John Kidd **Trained** Ditcheat, Somerset

FOCUS
The hurdle on the stable bend was omitted. Due to rail movements this was run over 90yds further than advertised. A fair handicap taken by an in-form mare. The winner has been rated back to something like his best.

4439 BETFAIR EXCHANGE NOVICES' HURDLE (10 hdls 1 omitted) 2m 5f 82y
4:30 (4:30) (Class 4) 4-Y-0+ £3,898 (£1,144; £572; £286)

Form RPR
2-15 **1** **Dueling Banjos**[95] 2787 6-11-8 0 DavidBass 134+
(Kim Bailey) *mde virtually all: rdn clr after 3 out: drifted lft between last 2: unchal* **6/5**[1]
1-0 **2** *23* **Fivefortyfive**[83] 2986 8-11-2 0 (t) NickScholfield 95
(Polly Gundry) *chsd ldrs tl lost pl u.p after 5th: stdy hdwy after 3 out: chsd wnr but nvr any ch fr next* **10/1**
0-P0 **3** *8* **Colmers Hill**[83] 2986 6-11-2 0 MattGriffiths 89
(Jeremy Scott) *hld up towards rr: struggling after 6th: disputing last whn blnd 3 out: stdy prog bef next: wnt 3rd between last 2: nvr threatened to get involved* **66/1**
3 **4** *16* **Bugsie Malone (IRE)**[81] 3037 6-11-2 0 SamTwiston-Davies 71
(Paul Nicholls) *trckd ldrs: rdn after 7th: chsd wnr but hld after 3 out: wknd bef next: t.o* **2/1**[2]
5000 **5** *23* **Definately Vinnie**[50] 3568 6-10-11 0 ConorRing(5) 56
(Jane Mathias) *mid-div: struggling 6th: wknd after 3 out: t.o* **100/1**
004 **P** **Beau Knight**[17] 4138 4-10-7 0 AdamWedge
(Alexandra Dunn) *a in rr: struggling 5th: tailing off whn p.u next* **100/1**
P **Time For Champers (IRE)**[354] 4775 6-10-4 0 ChrisWard(5)
(Nikki Evans) *mid-div: sme hdwy into wl hld 3rd after 3 out: hung lft and wknd bef next where p.u* **100/1**
P **P** **Monsieur Murphy (IRE)**[120] 2257 6-11-2 0 MarkQuinlan
(Neil Mulholland) *trckd wnr most of way tl rdn after 3 out: sn wknd: t.o whn p.u bef next* **100/1**
P **Butney Island (IRE)**[87] 6-11-2 0 GavinSheehan
(Nick Mitchell) *chsd ldrs tl mstke 7th: sn wknd: t.o whn p.u bef 2 out* **25/1**
-0 **P** **Morris The Miner**[116] 2351 6-11-2 0 TomScudamore
(Neil Mulholland) *chsd ldrs tl after 6th: sn wknd: p.u bef 3 out* **100/1**
4 **P** **Noble Ned**[37] 3775 7-11-2 0 NoelFehily
(Harry Fry) *mid-div: nt fluent 4th: lost action whn p.u bef 6th* **4/1**[3]
06 **P** **Wun Destination**[90] 2875 7-10-9 0 ConorO'Farrell
(John Panvert) *bhd: struggling 5th: tailing off whn p.u next* **100/1**

6m 2.8s (36.30) **Going Correction** +1.425s/f (Heav)
WFA 4 from 6yo+ 8lb 12 Ran SP% **119.2**
Speed ratings (Par 105): **87,78,75,69,60 , , , ,**
CSF £15.02 TOTE £2.40: £1.40, £2.40, £9.90; EX 16.90 Trifecta £460.10.
Owner J Perriss **Bred** Richard Davies **Trained** Andoversford, Gloucs

FOCUS
The hurdle on the stable bend was omitted. Due to rail movements this was run over 90yds further than advertised. No hanging around here and these novices finished out on their feet. The third has been rated to his mark.

4440 READ PAUL NICHOLLS EXCLUSIVELY ON BETFAIR H'CAP HURDLE (7 hdls 1 omitted) 1m 7f 65y
5:05 (5:05) (Class 5) (0-100,100) 4-Y-0+ £2,924 (£858; £429; £214)

Form RPR
F234 **1** **Slidecheck (IRE)**[10] 4265 9-11-3 91 (tp) AdamWedge 96
(Alexandra Dunn) *trckd ldrs: chal 3 out: disp ld bef next: rdn to ld between last 2 where drifted lft: wnt rt last: kpt on: drvn out* **7/1**[3]
6520 **2** *2¼* **Vering (FR)**[49] 3586 10-9-8 75 (tp) MrSeanHoulihan(7) 77
(Carroll Gray) *trckd ldr: pressed ldr fr 3rd: disp ld bef next: rdn and hdd between last 2: kpt on but a being hld run-in* **7/1**[3]
5606 **3** *10* **Royal Salute**[27] 3955 6-11-7 100 DavidNoonan(5) 92
(Anthony Honeyball) *trckd ldrs: rdn to chal for 3rd 2 out: styd on but nt pce of front* **3/1**[2]
062/ **4** *3½* **Cropley (IRE)**[421] 4779 7-11-2 90 RobertDunne 79
(Dai Burchell) *chsd ldrs: chal for 3rd 2 out: styd on same pce fr last* **20/1**
0035 **5** *8* **Abyaat (IRE)**[19] 4096 5-11-5 100 (t) DavidPrichard(7) 82
(Victor Dartnall) *chsd ldrs: rdn after 3 out: wknd between last 2* **9/4**[1]
0P3F **6** *7* **John Biscuit (IRE)**[91] 2851 8-11-2 90 GavinSheehan 64
(Jo Davis) *led: clr tl after 3rd: rdn and hdd after 3 out: wknd between last 2* **7/1**[3]
5006 **7** *¾* **Hallingham**[16] 4161 6-10-11 85 TomCannon 58
(Chris Gordon) *chsd ldrs: hit 3 out: sn rdn: wknd bef next* **10/1**
-PPP **P** **Dont Call Me Oscar (IRE)**[83] 2987 9-11-5 96 (t) TomBellamy(3)
(Mark Gillard) *w.r.s: detached in last: tagged on to main gp 4th: effrt after 3 out: wknd bef next: p.u bef last* **16/1**

4m 9.2s (20.30) **Going Correction** +1.425s/f (Heav) 8 Ran SP% **113.0**
Speed ratings (Par 103): **102,100,95,93,89 85,85,**
CSF £52.92 CT £177.21 TOTE £6.40: £2.10, £2.00, £1.30; EX 50.20 Trifecta £150.90.
Owner West Buckland Bloodstock Ltd **Bred** Richard Tanner Jnr **Trained** West Buckland, Somerset

FOCUS
The hurdle on the stable bend was omitted. Due to rail movements this race was run over 40yds further than advertised. Moderate handicap form, with only one of the eight runners previous successful over jumps. The first two have been rated pretty much to their marks.
T/Plt: £12.00 to a £1 stake. Pool: £65,473.74 - 3,956.12 winning tickets. T/Qpdt: £6.90 to a £1 stake. Pool: £4,654.24 - 496.46 winning tickets. **Tim Mitchell**

3926 LUDLOW (R-H)
Thursday, March 3

OFFICIAL GOING: Soft
Wind: Light, half behind Weather: Fine

4441 THREE COUNTIES EQUINE HOSPITAL NOVICES' HURDLE (9 hdls) 1m 7f 169y
1:55 (1:55) (Class 4) 4-Y-0+ £3,898 (£1,144; £572; £286)

Form RPR
P3 **1** **Beallandendall (IRE)**[29] 3928 8-10-10 0 MrStanSheppard(7) 125+
(Matt Sheppard) *in tch: trckd ldrs fr 4th: gng wl and moved upsides 3 out: led and hit 2 out: pushed clr ins fnl 150yds* **12/1**
2 **2** *8* **Querry Horse (FR)**[38] 3772 4-10-10 0 JackSherwood(5) 113
(Oliver Sherwood) *wnt lft s: sn handy: wnt 2nd after 4th: led long bef 3 out: rdn and jnd 3 out: hdd 2 out: no ch w wnr* **4/9**[1]
2 **3** *5* **Bay Sly (IRE)**[29] 3927 9-11-3 0 ConorO'Farrell 110
(Seamus Durack) *prom: led 4th: hdd long bef 3 out and pushed along: kpt on same pce fr 2 out* **5/1**[2]
2 **4** *16* **Diamond Rock**[51] 3573 5-11-3 0 RichardJohnson 93
(Henry Oliver) *midfield: mstke 5th: styd on fr last but no ch* **6/1**[3]
44 **5** *nk* **Byron Flyer**[13] 4233 5-11-3 0 WillKennedy 93
(Ian Williams) *racd keenly: hld up: styd on steadily fr 2 out: nvr nr to chal* **8/1**
000P **6** *1* **Opechee (IRE)**[60] 3450 5-10-12 0 JakeHodson(5) 94
(David Bridgwater) *in tch: clsd appr 5th: rdn and btn whn mstke 3 out* **200/1**
4 **7** *11* **Glimpse Of Gold**[189] 1378 5-11-3 0 TomCannon 81
(Tim Vaughan) *hld up in midfield: plugged on bef 3 out: no imp* **50/1**
605- **8** *9* **Ta Ha (IRE)**[468] 2638 8-11-3 0 MarkQuinlan 72
(Malcolm Jones) *chsd ldrs tl rdn and wknd appr 4 out* **200/1**
5P **9** *¾* **Diamond Reflection (IRE)**[37] 3790 4-10-9 0 (t) AdamWedge 63
(Tom Weston) *in rr: plugged on fr 3 out: nvr a danger* **200/1**
6-60 **10** *10* **Isla Di Milano (IRE)**[105] 2591 5-11-3 0 TomO'Brien 61
(Tim Vaughan) *hld up in midfield: rdn after 4 out: no imp* **200/1**
56 **11** *2¾* **Good Man Hughie (IRE)**[15] 4182 7-11-0 0 BenPoste(3) 59
(Sally Randell) *hld up: struggling bef 3 out: nvr on terms* **66/1**
600 **12** *11* **Artiste Du Gouet (FR)**[88] 2928 6-11-0 0 HarryChalloner(3) 48
(Heather Dalton) *hmpd s: a bhd: struggling bef 3 out: nvr on terms* **100/1**
0 **13** *1¾* **Al Fatih (IRE)**[83] 3021 5-10-12 0 JamieHamilton(5) 46
(Steve Flook) *hmpd s: sn in tch: j.lft 4th: pushed along and wknd bef 4 out* **100/1**
00 **14** *19* **Camakasi (IRE)**[34] 3835 5-11-3 0 (t) GavinSheehan 27
(Ali Stronge) *hld up: blnd 3rd: a bhd: t.o* **33/1**
0 **15** *½* **Actiondancer (IRE)**[103] 2636 5-11-3 0 JeremiahMcGrath 26
(Henry Oliver) *midfield: mstke 2nd: pushed along whn mstke 5th: sn wknd: t.o* **100/1**
065 **16** *12* **Over To Midnight**[11] 4266 6-10-3 0 MissLBrooke(7) 7
(Lady Susan Brooke) *led: sddle sn slipped: hdd 4th: lost pl bef 5th: t.o* **200/1**

4m 3.2s (13.70) **Going Correction** +0.875s/f (Soft)
WFA 4 from 5yo+ 7lb 16 Ran SP% **130.9**
Speed ratings (Par 105): **100,96,93,85,85 84,79,74,74,69 68,62,61,52,51 45**
CSF £20.21 TOTE £18.20: £3.40, £1.02, £1.80; EX 41.00 Trifecta £122.50.
Owner D R Bevan **Bred** S J Harrington **Trained** Eastnor, H'fords

FOCUS
The Ludlow bend was out 5 yards, and the stables bend 18 yards. The distance of the opener was 44.5 yards further than advertised. Richard Johnson described the ground as "soft" and Gavin Sheehan as "tacky", with both agreeing that it was "hard work." Few got involved in this modest novice hurdle. A step up from the winner.

4442 HENMAN MARQUEES "NATIONAL HUNT" NOVICES' H'CAP HURDLE (11 hdls) 2m 5f 55y
2:30 (2:30) (Class 3) (0-130,126) 4-Y-0+ **£5,848** (£1,717; £858; £429)

Form RPR
22F0 **1** **Mighty Leader (IRE)**[130] 2085 8-10-4 **104**.................. JeremiahMcGrath 112
(Henry Oliver) *hld up: niggled along appr 7th: rdn and hdwy appr 3 out: 3rd at flight: wnt 2nd run-in: styd on to ld fnl 130yds: sn edgd lft: in command towards fin* **12/1**
32P4 **2** *2 ½* **Vaillant Creek (FR)**[35] 3817 7-10-11 **111**.....................(b[1]) KielanWoods 118+
(Alex Hales) *led: j.rt fnl 3: blnd last: hdd fnl 130yds: no ex towards fin* **16/1**
4113 **3** *10* **Minellacelebration (IRE)**[75] 3146 6-10-6 **113**.................. MrJNixon(7) 109
(Katy Price) *wnt 2nd after 2nd: w ldr bef 7th: rdn and ev ch 3 out: mstke last: sn lost 2nd: no ex* **7/2[3]**
130 **4** *1 ¾* **Max Forte (IRE)**[68] 3232 6-11-9 **126**........................... KieronEdgar(3) 119
(Chris Down) *hld up: hdwy 4 out: rdn appr 3 out: kpt on same pce fr 2 out* **10/3[2]**
5313 **5** *7* **Zanstra (IRE)**[20] 4099 6-10-11 **111**............................... RichardJohnson 99
(Colin Tizzard) *in tch: nt fluent 5th: rdn and wkng whn mstke 3 out* **15/8[1]**
5-55 **6** *59* **Going For Broke (IRE)**[130] 2080 6-11-8 **122**...................(p) SeanBowen 49
(Rebecca Curtis) *in tch: rdn appr 3 out: sn wknd: t.o* **8/1**
-05P **7** *7* **Crowd Control (IRE)**[11] 4264 7-9-12 **105**..................... MissLBrooke(7) 25
(Lady Susan Brooke) *chsd ldr tl after 2nd: wknd after 4 out: t.o* **50/1**
2430 **P** **What Happens Now (IRE)**[24] 4035 7-10-7 **107**.............. WayneHutchinson
(Donald McCain) *hld up: rdn after 5th: t.o whn p.u bef 3 out* **12/1**
5m 29.0s (14.20) **Going Correction** +0.875s/f (Soft) **8** Ran SP% **114.4**
Speed ratings (Par 107): **107,106,102,101,98 76,73,**
CSF £167.21 CT £814.97 TOTE £14.20: £3.20, £4.50, £1.40; EX 230.30 Trifecta £1151.60.
Owner Oscar Singh & Miss Priya Purewal **Bred** John Hore **Trained** Abberley, Worcs

FOCUS
Race run over 62 yards further than advertised. A fair event of its type. A small pb from the winner.

4443 WYE VALLEY BREWERY NOVICES' LIMITED H'CAP CHASE (16 fncs) 2m 4f 11y
3:05 (3:05) (Class 3) (0-135,131) 5-Y-0+ **£6,963** (£2,057; £1,028; £514; £257)

Form RPR
6031 **1** **Daveron (IRE)**[42] 3709 8-11-1 **123**............................... MattGriffiths 133+
(Jeremy Scott) *hld up: racd wd: hdwy 7th: wnt 2nd and chalng whn blnd 2 out: upsides last: sn led: styd on and a jst doing enough* **6/1[2]**
P145 **2** *nk* **Uhlan Bute (FR)**[29] 3929 8-10-10 **118**.................(p) LiamTreadwell 127
(Venetia Williams) *prom: pckd 1st: led and hit 12th: pressed 4 put: jnd whn nt fluent last: sn hdd: styd on and continued chal run-in: a jst hld* **12/1**
-1PF **3** *2 ¾* **Globalisation (IRE)**[34] 3836 6-10-11 **119**......................(tp) SeanBowen 125
(Rebecca Curtis) *in rr: hdwy 10th: mstke 11th: rdn whn chsng ldrs appr 4 out: no imp: styd on u.p to take 3rd fnl 110yds: nt pce to chal front two* **10/1**
012 **4** *½* **Hollywoodien (FR)**[21] 4067 5-11-8 **131**........................ AidanColeman 137+
(Tom Symonds) *chsd ldrs: mstke 7th: mstke 9th (water): wnt 2nd appr 13th: chalng whn dived 3 out: lost 2nd 2 out: no ex run-in* **5/2[1]**
-54P **5** *6* **Brownville**[106] 2566 7-10-9 **117**...........................(t) SamTwiston-Davies 117
(Nigel Twiston-Davies) *hld up: hdwy 12th: effrt to chse ldrs appr 4 out: kpt on same pce fr 2 out* **6/1[2]**
531 **6** *27* **Grimley Girl**[29] 3931 10-10-4 **112**.............................. RichardJohnson 88
(Henry Oliver) *midfield: wknd after 13th* **6/1[2]**
236P **P** **Top Cat Henry (IRE)**[68] 3235 8-11-1 **123**.......................(tp) WillKennedy
(Dr Richard Newland) *midfield: rdn and wknd after 13th: t.o whn p.u bef 2 out* **8/1[3]**
13F6 **P** **By The Boardwalk (IRE)**[98] 2733 8-11-6 **128**......................(t) DavidBass
(Kim Bailey) *hld up: struggling 12th: t.o whn p.u bef 4 out* **14/1**
1313 **R** **Truckers Highway (IRE)**[14] 4210 7-10-12 **123**.............. HarryChalloner(3)
(John Groucott) *led: hdd and j.lft 12th: wkng whn j.lft 4 out: ref 3 out* **11/1**
0-0F **P** **Glenwood Star (IRE)**[77] 3129 8-10-6 **114**.......................(b) TrevorWhelan
(Rebecca Curtis) *sn w ldr: blnd 6th: lost pl 10th: wl bhd whn p.u bef 13th* **66/1**
5m 23.8s (19.40) **Going Correction** +1.175s/f (Heav) **10** Ran SP% **115.8**
Speed ratings: **108,107,106,106,104 93,,,,**
CSF £72.64 CT £708.87 TOTE £7.40: £2.40, £3.80, £3.50; EX 94.80 Trifecta £1210.00.
Owner Nigel Holder **Bred** C B Poots **Trained** Brompton Regis, Somerset

FOCUS
Race run over 75 yards further than advertised. A competitive race of its type, and the form should prove sound. The winner is on the upgrade, the second has been rated back to form, with the third rated in line with his hurdle mark.

4444 FORBRA GOLD CUP H'CAP CHASE (19 fncs) 2m 7f 171y
3:40 (3:40) (Class 3) (0-140,140) 5-Y-0+ **£12,685** (£3,869; £2,021; £1,097)

Form RPR
-245 **1** **Top Wood (FR)**[32] 3887 9-11-5 **133**........................(bt) ConorO'Farrell 145+
(David Pipe) *led bef 2nd (water): hdd 6th: remained prom: led again 11th (water): wnt steadily clr fr 3 out: eased down run-in* **9/1**
4-32 **2** *16* **Foundry Square (IRE)**[294] 294 10-10-13 **127**.................. PeterCarberry 124
(David Evans) *hld up: hdwy 5th: sn trckd ldrs: lft 2nd u.p 3 out: no imp on wnr after* **25/1**
-463 **3** *10* **Drumshambo (USA)**[27] 3979 10-9-11 **114**............(p) CallumWhillans(3) 99
(Venetia Williams) *led: hdd bef 2nd: remained in tch: rdn appr 4 out: lft 3rd 3 out: plugged on but n.d after* **6/1[3]**
342P **4** *6* **Sun Cloud (IRE)**[75] 3157 9-11-12 **140**..........................(t) BrianHughes 121
(Malcolm Jefferson) *hld up in rr: hdwy after 15th: sn rdn and no imp: plugged on after* **7/1**
4224 **F** **Galway Jack (IRE)**[19] 4128 11-11-8 **136**..................... AndrewThornton
(Caroline Bailey) *cl up: led 10th: hdd 11th (water): abt 3 l downs in 2nd whn fell 3 out* **12/1**
50P0 **P** **Kilbree Kid (IRE)**[20] 4101 9-10-10 **129**.....................(tp) JamieBargary(5)
(Tom George) *towards rr: rdn after 11th: t.o whn p.u bef 4 out* **20/1**
0-41 **P** **Nexius (IRE)**[21] 4067 7-11-8 **136**......................... SamTwiston-Davies
(Paul Nicholls) *hld up: rdn appr 15th: wknd bef 4 out and sn p.u* **9/4[1]**
1060 **P** **Big Casino**[75] 3148 10-10-13 **127**........................(v) WayneHutchinson
(Nigel Twiston-Davies) *chsd ldrs: lost pl 5th: struggling 13th: t.o whn p.u bef 4 out* **11/2[2]**
25P5 **P** **Royal Palladium (FR)**[42] 3707 8-10-10 **124**.................... AidanColeman
(Venetia Williams) *prom: led 6th: stmbld and hdd 10th: lost pl 13th: t.o whn p.u bef 4 out* **11/2[2]**
6m 34.9s (394.90) **9** Ran SP% **114.6**
CSF £173.86 CT £1451.38 TOTE £10.40: £2.60, £4.60, £1.90; EX 198.60 Trifecta £771.40.
Owner Mrs Jo Tracey **Bred** Francois Couvreur **Trained** Nicholashayne, Devon

FOCUS
Race run over 120 yards further than advertised. Only four got round in this decent handicap chase, which became a stamina test. A pb from the winner, with the second rated in line with the best of last season's figures.

4445 BARRELS MARES' H'CAP HURDLE (12 hdls) 2m 7f 174y
4:15 (4:15) (Class 3) (0-125,123) 4-Y-0+ **£5,991** (£1,860; £1,001)

Form RPR
2P33 **1** **Dolores Delightful (FR)**[15] 4186 6-11-3 **119**.....................(t) LizzieKelly(5) 131+
(Nick Williams) *hld up: blnd 6th: wnt 3rd after 4 out: chsd ldr appr 3 out: rdn to ld bef 2 out: styd on to draw clr run-in* **2/1[2]**
216P **2** *8* **Lady Of Longstone (IRE)**[18] 4139 6-11-7 **123**............... MichaelHeard(5) 121
(David Pipe) *led: rdn and hdd appr 2 out: no ex fnl 110yds* **9/1**
2232 **3** *5* **Brise Vendeenne (FR)**[28] 3953 5-11-4 **115**................ RichardJohnson 110
(Philip Hobbs) *chsd ldr: pushed along and lost 2nd bef 3 out: one pce and hld whn mstke 2 out* **11/8[1]**
2021 **P** **Pulling Power**[56] 3500 6-11-5 **116**...................................(t) DavidBass
(Kim Bailey) *prom: blnd 8th: nt fluent 4 out: sn wknd: t.o whn p.u bef 3 out* **10/3[3]**
6m 24.0s (31.70) **Going Correction** +0.875s/f (Soft) **4** Ran SP% **108.5**
Speed ratings (Par 107): **82,79,77,**
CSF £14.85 TOTE £3.20; EX 14.50 Trifecta £32.60.
Owner Miss Eliisa Morgan **Bred** I, J P, G & C Garcon **Trained** George Nympton, Devon

FOCUS
Race run over 62 yards further than advertised. The runner-up didn't set a bad pace in this small-field mares' handicap. The idling winner was value for further and this rates a pb under her claiming rider. The runner-up has been rated 5lb off.

4446 GEORGE JONES MEMORIAL HUNTERS' CHASE (16 fncs) 2m 4f 11y
4:50 (4:50) (Class 5) 5-Y-0+ **£2,495** (£774; £386; £193)

Form RPR
0-40 **1** **Daymar Bay (IRE)**[259] 772 10-11-13 117......................... MrAWright(7) 130+
(Gareth Thomas) *hld up: stmbld 1st: j.lft 2nd: hdwy into midfield 5th: hdwy to ld 4 out: asserted last: styd on wl* **50/1**
2P-U **2** *3 ½* **Invisible Man (FR)**[279] 534 11-11-5 122.......(t) MissJosephineBanks(7) 116
(Mrs D J Ralph) *in tch: wnt 2nd appr 4 out: sn chalng tl nt qckn appr last: kpt on u.p run-in but no imp on wnr* **12/1**
0/6- **3** *2 ¾* **Grandioso (IRE)**[673] 27 9-11-9 139.....................(t) MrStanSheppard(3) 114
(Steve Flook) *midfield: hdwy appr 4 out: wnt 3rd and bmpd 2 out: styd on to cl on runner-up appr last: one pce fnl 100yds* **4/1[3]**
160- **4** *nk* **Shoreacres (IRE)**[329] 5239 13-11-9 119........................ MrJDrinkwater(7) 118
(Mrs Gillian Jones) *hld up: rdn appr 3 out: styd on u.p run-in: nvr able to mount serious chal* **11/4[2]**
0-PP **5** *2* **Sustainability (IRE)**[35] 3826 11-11-5 107.......................(p) MrJSKnox(7) 113
(Miss B Eckley) *trckd ldrs: prom 5th: led after 13th: hdd 4 out: stl chsng ldrs whn bmpd 2 out: no ex last* **100/1**
15-3 **6** *17* **Bound For Glory (IRE)**[60] 10-11-9 122.......................... MissHLewis(5) 99
(D M G Fitch-Peyton) *led: dived 4th: hdd after 13th: wknd appr 4 out* **4/1[3]**
/4P- **7** *3 ¼* **De Forgotten Man (IRE)**[95] 11-11-5 108............................(b[1]) MrPBryan(7) 95
(Philip Rowley) *trckd ldrs: nt fluent 9th (water): rdn and wknd appr 4 out* **33/1**
/PP- **P** **Qrackers (FR)**[60] 12-11-13 116..............................(t) MissAEStirling(3)
(Miss V Collins) *prom: lost pl 6th: bhd whn p.u bef last* **33/1**
P4-2 **P** **Fromthetop (IRE)**[39] 10-11-7 76..(t) MrJNixon(5)
(G Slade-Jones) *a bhd: struggling 9th (water): t.o whn p.u bef 13th* **100/1**
PP/0 **P** **Getaway Driver (IRE)**[66] 9-11-5 94..................................(bt) MrNLawton(7)
(Mrs Janet Ackner) *bhd: u.p bef 10th: p.u bef 3 out* **200/1**
3P-5 **P** **Trafalgar (FR)**[295] 282 9-11-7 105.. MrJMahot(5)
(Sarah-Jayne Davies) *midfield: lost pl bef 5th: bhd whn p.u bef last* **50/1**
P-13 **P** **Monkey Kingdom**[11] 4269 8-11-13 132................................(tp) MrMLegg(3)
(Rebecca Curtis) *prom: rdn and wknd after 13th: bhd whn p.u bef 3 out* **9/4[1]**
5m 33.9s (29.50) **Going Correction** +1.175s/f (Heav) **12** Ran SP% **117.4**
Speed ratings: **88,86,85,85,84 77,76,,,,**
CSF £523.61 TOTE £50.50: £9.80, £3.10, £1.70; EX 678.40 Trifecta £5285.90 Part won..
Owner Lee & Rowles **Bred** Barry Noonan **Trained** Bishop's Castle, Shropshire
■ The first training success for Gareth Thomas, with his first runner.

FOCUS
They went off quite hard in this modest hunter chase, which was run over 75 yards further than the advertised distance. There's a case for rating the race 7lb+ higher through a few of these, but the winner has been rated similar to his best already and the fifth in line with the best of last season's runs.

4447 PERROTT PROPERTIES LTD CONDITIONAL JOCKEYS' H'CAP HURDLE (9 hdls) 1m 7f 169y
5:25 (5:25) (Class 4) (0-120,120) 4-Y-0+ **£3,898** (£1,144; £572; £286)

Form RPR
1-02 **1** **Apterix (FR)**[11] 4273 6-11-9 **120**........................... MeganCarberry(3) 128
(Brian Ellison) *hld up: hdwy appr 3 out: wnt 2nd last: styd on to ld fnl 50yds* **3/1[1]**
4333 **2** *¾* **Celestial Magic**[59] 3464 4-10-5 **110**............................ DanielHiskett(3) 110
(Richard Phillips) *chsd ldr: led appr 3 out: nt fluent last: hdd and hld fnl 50yds* **16/1**
0024 **3** *6* **Eddiemaurice (IRE)**[42] 3708 5-11-2 **110**........................ KillianMoore 111
(John Flint) *hld up: rdn and hdwy appr 3 out to go 2nd: lost 2nd last: no ex fnl 75yds* **6/1[2]**
1442 **4** *2 ¼* **Catchin Time (IRE)**[19] 4129 8-10-13 **107**.......................(t) KieronEdgar 106
(Laura Hurley) *jinked lft s: hld up in rr: rdn and hdwy 3 out: kpt on u.p run-in: unable to trble ldrs* **14/1**
-000 **5** *7* **Beatabout The Bush (IRE)**[88] 2926 5-11-12 **120**... JeremiahMcGrath 114
(Henry Oliver) *chsd ldrs: hit 4 out: one pce fr 2 out* **11/1**
002 **6** *6* **Guantoshol (IRE)**[28] 3955 5-10-10 **107**...................... CharlieDeutsch(3) 93
(Venetia Williams) *midfield: lost pl after 4 out: outpcd bef 3 out: plugged on u.p run-in* **7/1[3]**
5144 **7** *¾* **Hill Fort**[29] 3932 6-11-5 **113**.......................................(t) CiaranGethings 98
(Matt Sheppard) *chsd ldrs tl rdn and wknd after 4 out* **8/1**
0464 **8** *½* **Discay**[66] 3311 7-11-4 **120**..[1] CharlieHammond(8) 106
(Dr Richard Newland) *led: hit 4 out: hdd appr 3 out: sn wknd* **12/1**
-323 **9** *½* **Destiny's Gold (IRE)**[262] 745 6-11-12 **120**...................... ThomasGarner 104
(George Baker) *rdn appr 3 out: a bhd* **25/1**

422 **10** *76* **The Coffee Hunter (FR)**[59] 3464 4-10-10 **115**..................(t) LizzieKelly(3) 15
(Nick Williams) *midfield: hdwy to chse ldrs 5th: rdn and wknd bef 4 out*
9/1

-250 **R** **Blue April (FR)**[78] 3114 5-10-8 **105**.................................... MattGriffiths(3)
(Jeremy Scott) *w.r.s: ref to r* **6/1**[2]

4m 4.9s (15.40) **Going Correction** +0.875s/f (Soft)
WFA 4 from 5yo+ 7lb **11** Ran **SP%** **119.6**
Speed ratings (Par 105): **96,95,92,91,88 85,84,84,84,46**
CSF £50.99 CT £279.00 TOTE £3.60: £1.60, £3.90, £2.50; EX 45.00 Trifecta £706.20.
Owner P J Martin **Bred** Joel Chaignon **Trained** Norton, N Yorks

FOCUS
Race run over 44.5 yards further than advertised. The runner-up and the eighth went out clear in this ordinary handicap. The winner has been rated similar to last time out. There's a case for rating him 5lb higher through the third and fourth, but not on time compared with the earlier novice.
T/Jkpt: Not won. T/Plt: £894.90 to a £1 stake. Pool of £63184.45 - 51.54 winning tickets. T/Qpdt: £233.80 to a £1 stake. Pool of £4929.76 - 15.60 winning tickets. **Darren Owen**

4290 TAUNTON (R-H)
Thursday, March 3

OFFICIAL GOING: Soft (5.3)
Wind: mild breeze across Weather: cloudy Rails: Split bends effecting race distances as follows: Races 1, 2, 5 & 7 add 162yds. Race 3 add 216yds. Races 4 & 6 add 12yds.

4448 UK GAME FAIR (S) HURDLE (10 hdls) 2m 3f 1y
2:05 (2:07) (Class 5) 4-Y-0+ **£3,249** (£954; £477; £238)

Form RPR
25 **1** **Apache Outlaw (IRE)**[11] 4264 7-11-2 0.......................... LeightonAspell 111+
(Rebecca Curtis) *led tl 3rd: led 6th: 12 l clr 2 out: sn rdn: enough in hand and a holding on run-in: drvn out* **3/1**[1]

P133 **2** *1 ½* **Ministerofinterior**[20] 4105 11-11-2 112....................(b) CiaranGethings(5) 112
(Barry Leavy) *in tch: rdn after 3 out: hdwy fr next: chsd wnr appr last: styd on run-in but a being hld* **7/2**[2]

65 **3** *5* **Romeo Is Bleeding (IRE)**[51] 3572 10-11-2 105.............. PaulMoloney 106+
(David Rees) *hld up: sme prog 7th: lost pl u.p and hanging rt appr 2 out: styng on into 3rd whn blnd bdly last: no further imp run-in* **8/1**

P542 **4** *2 ¼* **Lac Sacre (FR)**[11] 4266 7-11-2 114.............................(bt) RhysFlint 100
(John Flint) *chsd ldrs: rdn into 3rd after 6th: nvr threatened: kpt on same pce fr 2 out* **7/2**[2]

2025 **5** *2* **Akula (IRE)**[19] 4129 9-11-2 108.............................. AlanJohns(5) 103
(Barry Leavy) *trckd ldr: led 3rd tl 6th: rdn after next: wknd between last 2* **5/1**[3]

3S30 **6** *20* **Tijori (IRE)**[80] 3078 8-10-13 101.......................... RobertWilliams(3) 86
(Bernard Llewellyn) *trckd ldrs: rdn after 3 out: wknd bef next* **14/1**

3324 **7** *63* **Vinnie The Fish (IRE)**[130] 2090 8-11-2 0.........................(p) RobertDunne 15
(Dai Burchell) *in tch: rdn after 3 out: sn wknd: t.o* **11/1**

5m 8.7s (22.70) **Going Correction** +1.05s/f (Soft) **7** Ran **SP%** **112.2**
Speed ratings (Par 103): **94,93,91,90,89 81,54**
CSF £13.43 TOTE £3.10: £2.10, £2.00; EX 16.90 Trifecta £100.50.The winner was bought in for £7,500.
Owner G Costelloe **Bred** Mrs Kathleen Lee **Trained** Newport, Pembrokeshire

FOCUS
Bends were split. Rail movements resulted in this race being run over 162yds further than advertised. The least-exposed runner in the field took this seller. A step up from the winner, with the second setting the level.

4449 CHETWOOD WEALTH MANAGEMENT SUPPORTING GWCT NOVICES' HURDLE (10 hdls) 2m 3f 1y
2:40 (2:40) (Class 4) 4-Y-0+ **£4,548** (£1,335; £667; £333)

Form RPR
4 **1** **Space Oddity (FR)**[29] 3928 5-11-2 0.......................... NoelFehily 103+
(Harry Fry) *trckd ldr: led last: kpt on wl: rdn out* **5/4**[1]

32-0 **2** *nk* **Beau Phil (FR)**[42] 3710 5-10-9 0..............................(t) HarryCobden(7) 103+
(Paul Nicholls) *in tch: hdwy 2 out: rdn in 3rd after last: r.o wl to press wnr fnl 90yds: hld nring fin* **9/1**

510 **3** *1* **Stop The Press**[27] 3976 7-11-9 0.......................... DenisO'Regan 110
(Mark Pitman) *led: mstke 3 out: sn rdn: hdd last: styd on but no ex* **10/1**

4403 **4** *4 ½* **Justatenner**[50] 3582 5-11-2 0.............................. PaddyBrennan 98
(Colin Tizzard) *trckd ldrs: short of room 3 out: rdn whn swtchd lft after 2 out: hit last: kpt on same pce* **9/2**[2]

5 *1* **Nice Thoughts (IRE)**[128] 4-10-7 0.......................... TomScudamore 87
(David Pipe) *hld up towards rr: t.k.h in midfield after 5th: rdn between last 2: kpt on same pce* **8/1**[3]

6 *6* **Dragoon Guard (IRE)**[43] 5-10-11 0.......................... DavidNoonan(5) 90
(Anthony Honeyball) *mid-div: tk clsr order after 3 out: rdn next: sn one pce* **16/1**

0 **7** *1 ¼* **Late Shipment**[51] 3570 5-10-11 0.......................... ChrisWard(5) 89
(Nikki Evans) *trckd ldrs: rdn appr 2 out: hung lft and wknd between last 2* **16/1**

6- **8** *1 ¼* **El Bandit (IRE)**[337] 5104 5-11-2 0.......................... NickScholfield 88
(Paul Nicholls) *hld up towards rr: midfield 3 out: sn rdn: wknd next: blnd last* **8/1**[3]

00 **9** *8* **Tell Tony (IRE)**[6] 4339 6-11-2 0.......................... MichealNolan 80
(Tim Dennis) *mid-div: rdn after 3 out: wknd next* **150/1**

300P **10** *3 ¾* **The Model County (IRE)**[37] 3787 6-10-2 0.......................... MrAlexEdwards(7) 69
(Alan Phillips) *mid-div: pushed along after 5th: lost pl after next: wknd bef 2 out* **150/1**

0 **P** **Inthenicoftime**[28] 3959 6-11-2 0.......................... JamesBest
(Jess Westwood) *a towards rr: struggling after 6th: t.o whn p.u after 3 out* **200/1**

5m 11.4s (25.40) **Going Correction** +1.05s/f (Soft)
WFA 4 from 5yo+ 7lb **11** Ran **SP%** **117.5**
Speed ratings (Par 105): **88,87,87,85,85 82,82,81,78,76**
CSF £13.98 TOTE £2.00: £1.30, £2.10, £1.60; EX 13.30 Trifecta £91.20.
Owner The Rate Chasers **Bred** Antoine Lamotte D'Argy Et Al **Trained** Seaborough, Dorset

FOCUS
Rail movements resulted in this race being run over 162yds further than advertised. Ordinary novice form. It's been rated around the third and fourth, but this is not form to take seriously.

4450 JACKSON-STOPS & STAFF NOVICES' H'CAP HURDLE (12 hdls) 2m 7f 198y
3:15 (3:15) (Class 4) (0-110,108) 4-Y-0+ **£4,548** (£1,335; £667; £333)

Form RPR
525 **1** **A Plein Temps (FR)**[50] 3580 6-11-12 **108**..............................(t) NoelFehily 113+
(Harry Fry) *disp ld tl clr ldr 8th: styd on wl fr last: rdn out* **2/1**[1]

3210 **2** *1* **Bells Of Ailsworth (IRE)**[33] 3855 6-11-6 **107**.................. AlanJohns(5) 110
(Tim Vaughan) *trckd ldrs: rdn to chse wnr appr 2 out: blnd last: styd on but a being hld fnl 100yds* **6/1**

5054 **3** *¾* **City Supreme (IRE)**[33] 3855 6-11-2 **103**...................... DavidNoonan(5) 104
(Anthony Honeyball) *hld up: hdwy 9th: disputing cl 3rd but nt clr run on bnd shortly after: rdn bef next: styd on fnl 100yds but a being hld* **5/2**[2]

1144 **4** *19* **Snowball (IRE)**[31] 3904 9-10-11 **93**................................ LeightonAspell 79
(David Arbuthnot) *trckd ldrs: chal 9th: rdn after 3 out: wknd next* **4/1**[3]

P603 **5** *7* **Lunar Flow**[30] 3914 5-10-11 **93**................................ BrendanPowell 68
(Jamie Snowden) *trckd ldrs tl 3 out: sn rdn: wknd bef next* **8/1**

4-03 **P** **Alanjou (FR)**[24] 4027 6-11-2 **103**..............................(v[1]) FreddieMitchell(5)
(Henry Tett) *disp ld tl 8th: sn rdn: wknd bef 3 out: t.o whn p.u bef 2 out* **25/1**

6m 30.0s (26.00) **Going Correction** +1.05s/f (Soft) **6** Ran **SP%** **111.1**
Speed ratings (Par 105): **98,97,97,91,88**
CSF £13.81 TOTE £2.50: £1.30, £2.70; EX 12.60 Trifecta £30.70.
Owner R P B Michaelson & E M Thornton **Bred** Haras De Saint Voir & Patrick Joubert **Trained** Seaborough, Dorset

FOCUS
Rail movements resulted in this race being run over 216yds further than advertised. Quite a moderate handicap and the pace was a steady one. A small pb from the second, with the third helping to set the level.

4451 CLARKE WILLMOTT NOVICES' LIMITED H'CAP CHASE (17 fncs) 2m 7f 3y
3:50 (3:50) (Class 3) (0-135,133) 5-Y-0+ **£9,140** (£3,342)

Form RPR
1-31 **1** **Vazaro Delafayette (FR)**[7] 4321 7-10-5 **116** 7ex.......(b) TomScudamore 122+
(David Pipe) *trckd ldrs: lft 3rd at the 11th: rdn and looking hld whn lft in ld 3 out: idling next: only doing jst enough but a holding on fr last* **10/11**[1]

3-01 **2** *1* **Fight Commander (IRE)**[21] 4071 7-10-8 **119**.................. LeightonAspell 125+
(Oliver Sherwood) *led: rdn and hdd whn bdly hmpd 3 out: kpt on fr last but a being hld* **9/2**[3]

0122 **U** **Sandy Beach**[40] 3747 6-10-11 **122**...................................... PaddyBrennan
(Colin Tizzard) *trcking ldrs whn blnd bdly and uns rdr 11th* **5/2**[2]

1163 **F** **Royale Django (IRE)**[29] 3929 7-11-3 **133**...................... AlanJohns(5) 138
(Tim Vaughan) *prom tl 8th: reminders: chsd ldr: chal 4 out: shkn up in 1 l ld whn knuckled on landing and fell 3 out* **9/1**

6m 20.2s (4.20) **Going Correction** +0.15s/f (Yiel) **4** Ran **SP%** **109.1**
Speed ratings: **98,97, ,**
CSF £5.27 TOTE £1.80; EX 5.00 Trifecta £4.50.
Owner Bryan Drew **Bred** Mrs Jean-Jacques Augier **Trained** Nicholashayne, Devon

FOCUS
Rail movements resulted in this race being run over 12yds further than advertised. Weakened by the defection of Nitrogen, as had been the case last time the race rather fell into the lap of the favourite. The winner has been rated below his recent win.

4452 EXMOOR TRIM H'CAP HURDLE (10 hdls) 2m 3f 1y
4:25 (4:25) (Class 3) (0-140,130) 4-Y-0 **£6,330** (£1,870; £935; £468; £234)

Form RPR
3013 **1** **Tornado In Milan (IRE)**[9] 4294 10-11-7 **130**...................... ConorRing(5) 137+
(Evan Williams) *racd wd: mde all: hit 5th: blnd bdly next: jnd 2 out tl last: kpt on: rdn out* **4/1**

2431 **2** *2 ¼* **Impulsive American**[15] 4176 4-10-8 **121**..................(p) TomScudamore 115
(David Pipe) *cl up: wnt 2nd 3 out: ev ch next: sn rdn: no ex fr last* **5/2**[1]

1255 **3** *2 ½* **After Eight Sivola (FR)**[21] 4070 6-11-6 **124**...................... NoelFehily 126
(Nick Williams) *cl up: wnt 3rd after 3 out: rdn bef next: nt pce to mount chal* **3/1**[3]

3-63 **4** *15* **Kingfisher Creek**[108] 2545 6-11-11 **129**.........................(p) PaddyBrennan 117
(Colin Tizzard) *trckd ldrs: wnt 2nd 7th tl 3 out: sn hld: wknd between last 2* **11/4**[2]

3040 **5** *7* **Ascendant**[34] 3844 10-11-7 **130**.............................(b) ThomasCheesman(5) 109
(Johnny Farrelly) *trckd ldrs tl rdn after 3 out: sn btn* **12/1**

564U **6** *22* **Rock N Rhythm (IRE)**[13] 4225 6-11-12 **130**..............(t) RichieMcLernon 87
(Jonjo O'Neill) *trckd wnr tl rdn after 6th: wknd bef 3 out: t.o* **16/1**

5m 2.1s (16.10) **Going Correction** +1.05s/f (Soft)
WFA 4 from 6yo+ 7lb **6** Ran **SP%** **113.8**
Speed ratings (Par 107): **108,107,106,99,96 87**
CSF £15.04 TOTE £4.30: £2.00, £3.90; EX 16.60 Trifecta £45.90.
Owner Mrs C Williams **Bred** Garry Hadden **Trained** Llancarfan, Vale Of Glamorgan

FOCUS
Rail movements resulted in this race being run over 162yds further than advertised. The front three came clear in what was a fair little hurdle. The winner has been rated back to his very best, with a hurdle pb from the runner-up and the third close to his mark.

4453 GIBBS H'CAP CHASE (14 fncs) 2m 2f 40y
5:00 (5:00) (Class 4) (0-110,110) 5-Y-0+ **£5,198** (£1,526; £763; £381)

Form RPR
-442 **1** **Agincourt Reef (IRE)**[14] 4197 7-11-10 **108**..................(v[1]) JoshuaMoore 118+
(Gary Moore) *trckd ldrs: chal 2 out: sn led and edgd lft: hanging lft but asserted run-in: rdn out* **15/8**[1]

52P6 **2** *1 ½* **Saint Breiz (FR)**[42] 3709 10-11-5 **103**..........................(tp) IanPopham 110
(Carroll Gray) *disp ld most of way: rdn to ld 3 out: edgd rt: hdd after next: ev ch briefly after last: swtchd rt: kpt on same pce* **8/1**

456P **3** *10* **Too Scoops (IRE)**[42] 3709 9-11-12 **110**.............................(p) DarylJacob 108
(Richard Woollacott) *j.lft thrght: disp ld most of way: rdn and hdd 3 out: styd on same pce fr next* **6/1**

5-44 **4** *21* **Grand March**[85] 2976 7-11-2 **103**.............................(p) TomBellamy(3) 80
(Kim Bailey) *trckd ldrs: nt fluent 6th: sn struggling: wknd bef 3 out: t.o* **3/1**[2]

31P2 **5** *1 ¾* **Ballyegan (IRE)**[15] 4187 11-10-9 **93**.............................. LiamHeard 66
(Bob Buckler) *disp ld tl 4th: chsd ldrs tl outpcd after 6th: wknd appr 3 out* **7/2**[3]

20/P **F** **Sir Pitt**[23] 2435 9-11-9 **107**.................................... RobertDunne 110+
(Mark Brisbourne) *trckd ldrs: rdn and mounting str chal whn fell 3 out* **28/1**

4m 52.9s (0.90) **Going Correction** +0.15s/f (Yiel) **6** Ran **SP%** **110.8**
Speed ratings: **104,103,98,89,88**
CSF £15.82 TOTE £2.70: £1.90, £3.90; EX 15.80 Trifecta £64.50.

Owner A Head, R Lockwood & M Burne **Bred** Lar & Fiona Cloke **Trained** Lower Beeding, W Sussex
■ Stewards' Enquiry : Joshua Moore caution: careless riding

FOCUS
Rail movements resulted in this race being run over 12yds further than advertised. The front pair came clear in what was a modest chase. The winner has been rated as improving to his hurdle mark, with the second similar to his chase best.

4454 A.W. RULE & SON GUN MAKERS LTD H'CAP HURDLE (10 hdls) 2m 3f 1y
5:35 (5:35) (Class 5) (0-100,100) 4-Y-0+ **£3,249** (£954; £477; £238)

Form RPR
0001 1 **On The Road (IRE)**[6] 4343 6-10-6 **80** 7ex. PaulMoloney 94+
(Evan Williams) *trckd ldrs: led briefly after 3 out: jst taken narrow advantage whn lft wl clr next: wnt rt last* **4/6**[1]
0F6F 2 *19* **Tikkapick (IRE)**[12] 4255 6-10-11 **92** PaulO'Brien(7) 86+
(Colin Tizzard) *trckd ldrs: jst taken narrow advantage whn stmbld bdly and hdd 3 out: no ch after: sn rdn: lft wl hld 2nd next* **4/1**[2]
0P/P 3 *4 ½* **Micquus (IRE)**[235] 977 7-10-10 **84** MarkGrant 71
(Jonathan Geake) *mid-div: rdn to dispute hld 3rd after 3 out: lft 3rd next: kpt on same pce* **40/1**
4006 4 *½* **Sun Quest**[9] 4291 12-9-7 **74** oh7 MrJPearce(7) 59
(Steven Dixon) *led tl 6th: outpcd after 7th: styd on again fr 2 out but no ch: wnt 4th towards fin* **16/1**
3P00 5 *1 ¼* **My Diamond (IRE)**[84] 2986 5-11-1 **89** RobertDunne 76
(Laura Young) *mid-div: trcking ldrs whn bdly hmpd 3 out: hld after: rdn to dispute 3rd appr 2 out where 4th: no ex fr last* **33/1**
/060 6 *19* **Up To Al (IRE)**[64] 3370 8-11-12 **100** LiamHeard 65
(Bob Buckler) *hld up: hdwy 5th to trck ldrs: wknd after 7th: t.o* **15/2**[3]
0000 7 *shd* **Junior Package**[42] 3710 5-11-1 **89** (b) TomScudamore 54
(David Pipe) *mid-div on outer: wknd 7th: t.o* **9/1**
030 8 *14* **Fidelity**[84] 2992 4-10-6 **92** ConorShoemark(3) 34
(Jonathan Geake) *prom: led 6th tl after 7th: hmpd 3 out: sn wknd: t.o* **66/1**
5P F **Rosygo (IRE)**[84] 2985 8-11-2 **95** DavidNoonan(5) 104+
(Adrian Wintle) *racd keenly: hld up: hdwy after 6th: led sn after 3 out: narrowly hdd whn fell heavily 2 out* **20/1**

5m 12.5s (26.50) **Going Correction** +1.05s/f (Soft)
WFA 4 from 5yo+ 7lb **9 Ran SP% 119.3**
Speed ratings (Par 103): **86,78,76,75,75 67,67,61,**
CSF £4.12 CT £55.91 TOTE £1.60: £1.02, £1.80, £12.20; EX 4.50 Trifecta £88.80.
Owner Mrs C Williams **Bred** G T Greene **Trained** Llancarfan, Vale Of Glamorgan

FOCUS
Rail movements resulted in this race being run over 162yds further than advertised. Lowly handicap form and the favourite won, as expected. Another step up from the winner, with the second in line with his hurdle mark.
T/Plt: £16.70 to a £1 stake. Pool of £59589.99 - 2592.61 winning tickets. T/Qpdt: £7.80 to a £1 stake. Pool of £4697.65 - 441.41 winning tickets. **Tim Mitchell**

4303 DONCASTER (L-H)
Friday, March 4

OFFICIAL GOING: Soft (good to soft in places) changing to soft after race 1 (2.10)
Wind: light 1/2 against Weather: overcast

4455 WATCH LIVE RACING ON BETBRIGHT.COM H'CAP HURDLE (10 hdls) 2m 3f 120y
2:10 (2:10) (Class 4) (0-110,110) 4-Y-0+ **£4,548** (£1,335; £667; £333)

Form RPR
0500 1 **Drumlee Lad (IRE)**[83] 3035 6-11-5 **103** BrendanPowell 119+
(Johnny Farrelly) *trckd ldrs travelling strly: 2nd on bit 2 out: led bef last: drvn clr* **12/1**
4-P4 2 *10* **Mr Snoozy**[18] 4152 7-11-1 **104** (p) JamieHamilton(5) 109
(Mark Walford) *chsd ldr: led appr 3 out: hdd and 3 l down whn mstke last: kpt on same pce* **8/1**[3]
0545 3 *3 ½* **Kilronan Castle**[63] 3398 5-11-9 **107** WillKennedy 106
(Donald McCain) *chsd ldrs: j.lft last 3: one pce fr 2 out* **6/1**[2]
1025 4 *17* **Pied Du Roi (IRE)**[107] 2577 6-11-12 **110** (p) BrianHughes 94
(Charlie Longsdon) *chsd ldrs: drvn bef 3 out: wknd and remote 4th whn hit 2 out* **11/2**[1]
0045 5 *11* **Scooby (IRE)**[22] 4065 5-11-10 **108** KielanWoods 79
(Graeme McPherson) *in rr: sme hdwy 3 out: nvr on terms* **11/2**[1]
4-P4 6 *nk* **Baldadash (IRE)**[13] 4250 11-11-6 **104** (p) LeightonAspell 75
(Jose Santos) *chsd ldrs: outpcd 7th: sn lost pl and bhd* **9/1**
P505 7 *2 ½* **Tekthelot (IRE)**[18] 4152 10-11-6 **104** JamesReveley 72
(Keith Reveley) *led: hdd appr 3 out: sn lost pl and bhd* **6/1**[2]
2204 8 *9* **Polarbrook (IRE)**[24] 4041 9-11-4 **102** (v) SeanQuinlan 61
(Derek Shaw) *mid-div: lost pl 7th: bhd next* **16/1**
1-50 9 *37* **Tidestream**[65] 3374 6-11-10 **108** (t) RichardJohnson 30
(Tim Vaughan) *in rr: mstke 3rd: bhd and reminders after 7th: t.o next: eventually completed* **6/1**[2]
-26P P **Hillview Lad (IRE)**[111] 2490 8-11-3 **101** AdamWedge
(Nick Kent) *t.k.h in rr: racd wd: hdwy 4th: lost pl and blnd 7th: sn bhd: t.o whn p.u bef next* **40/1**
P0 P **Mille Nautique (FR)**[99] 2725 5-11-5 **106** TomBellamy(3)
(Alan King) *hld up in rr: t.k.h: hdwy bef 7th: lost pl and bhd whn p.u bef 3 out* **9/1**

4m 58.5s (7.20) **Going Correction** +0.475s/f (Soft) **11 Ran SP% 120.8**
Speed ratings (Par 105): **104,100,98,91,87 87,86,82,67,**
CSF £107.35 CT £645.58 TOTE £12.70: £4.40, £3.00, £2.30; EX 155.80 Trifecta £1425.70.
Owner R S Brookhouse **Bred** I McGrath & K McGrath **Trained** Enmore, Somerset

FOCUS
All race distances as advertised. Rain and light snow meant that the ground was considerably softer than had been anticipated, leading to a glut of non-runners. Brendan Powell, rider of the first winner, called conditions "tacky, with big clumps of kickback", while Leighton Aspell said: "There's not a lot of grass on it and they are wheel spinning a bit. They are not going in very far but it's soft." There was a very easy winner of this ordinary handicap hurdle, in which not many got involved. A step up from the winner and a hurdles best from the second.

4456 BETBRIGHT H'CAP CHASE (15 fncs) 2m 3f 44y
2:40 (2:40) (Class 4) (0-120,117) 5-Y-0+ **£6,256** (£1,848; £924; £462)

Form RPR
61-4 1 **Midnight Monty**[22] 4067 6-11-7 **112** JamesReveley 123+
(Keith Reveley) *w ldr: led 6th: mstke 9th: jnd 2 out: hit last: sn forged clr: eased clsng stages* **5/2**[2]
2331 2 *11* **Oscar O'Scar (IRE)**[8] 4325 8-10-9 **107** 7ex. FinianO'Toole(7) 114+
(Micky Hammond) *trckd ldng pair 5th: 3rd whn hit 4 out: upsides 2 out: jst over 1 l down whn blnd last: kpt on same pce* **11/8**[1]
-233 3 *11* **Frizzo (FR)**[30] 3931 9-11-9 **114** (b) NicodeBoinville 102
(Harry Whittington) *trckd ldrs: led 3rd: swtchd outside bef 8th: hit 10th: upsides next: sn drvn: wknd bef 3 out* **3/1**[3]
42F3 4 *22* **Azert De Coeur (FR)**[24] 4042 6-11-8 **113** LiamTreadwell 85
(Venetia Williams) *nt jump wl: led: hdd and mstke 3rd: drvn 8th: reminders and hit next: lost pl and bhd 11th: t.o 3 out* **5/1**

5m 2.8s (13.80) **Going Correction** +0.875s/f (Soft) **4 Ran SP% 112.3**
Speed ratings: **105,100,95,86**
CSF £6.79 TOTE £3.60; EX 7.10 Trifecta £14.40.
Owner Mr & Mrs W J Williams **Bred** W J And Mrs M Williams **Trained** Lingdale, Redcar & Cleveland

FOCUS
A fair handicap chase where the outcome was decided at the final fence. The winner is on the upgrade and the second was below the level of his recent win.

4457 EBF STALLIONS BETBRIGHT APP MARES' "NATIONAL HUNT" NOVICES' HURDLE (10 hdls) 2m 3f 120y
3:15 (3:15) (Class 4) 4-Y-0+ **£3,898** (£1,144; £572; £286)

Form RPR
-1F4 1 **Briery Queen**[38] 3787 7-11-5 123 LeightonAspell 120+
(Noel Williams) *trckd ldrs: n.m.r and hit 3 out: drvn next: led narrowly 2 out: forged clr run-in* **4/7**[1]
6 2 *3 ¾* **Maid Of Milan (IRE)**[101] 2702 5-10-12 0 DenisO'Regan 108
(Charlie Mann) *w ldr: led 4th to 6th: led next: hdd 2 out: kpt on same pce* **16/1**
-535 3 *7* **Miss Crick**[79] 3110 5-10-9 0 TomBellamy(3) 104
(Alan King) *trckd ldrs: drvn upsides 2 out: wkng whn hit last: sddle moved and rdr briefly lost iron* **2/1**[2]
4336 4 *1 ½* **Western Sunrise (IRE)**[19] 4137 7-10-12 0 AlainCawley 101
(Johnny Farrelly) *led to 4th: led 6th to next: wkng whn hit 2 out* **14/1**[3]
04P 5 *81* **Stoical Patient (IRE)**[18] 4157 7-10-12 0 KielanWoods 18
(Mark Wall) *hld up in last: bhd 6th: t.o 3 out: eventually completed* **100/1**

5m 5.2s (13.90) **Going Correction** +0.775s/f (Soft) **5 Ran SP% 110.5**
Speed ratings (Par 105): **103,101,98,98,65**
CSF £10.38 TOTE £1.40: £1.10, £5.20; EX 7.70 Trifecta £19.90.
Owner Helen Plumbly & Kathryn Leadbeater **Bred** Simon And Helen Plumbly **Trained** Blewbury, Oxon

FOCUS
The market had this down as a two-mare race but it didn't pan out like that, with four of them fighting it out at the second-last. The time was relatively slow and the winner is rated 5lb off her best.

4458 BETBRIGHT BEST FOR FESTIVAL BETTING NOVICES' CHASE (15 fncs) 2m 3f 44y
3:50 (3:50) (Class 4) 5-Y-0+ **£5,630** (£1,663; £831)

Form RPR
-110 1 **Presenting Arms (IRE)**[76] 3151 9-11-0 0 (t) RichardJohnson 139+
(Harry Fry) *trckd ldr: j.rt 7th: drvn between last 2: led narrowly last: hld on gamely clsng stages* **5/2**[2]
1322 2 *½* **Coologue (IRE)**[34] 3860 7-11-6 141 (t) BrianHughes 145+
(Charlie Longsdon) *led: j. soundly: qcknd pce 9th: drvn 3 out: rdn between last 2: hdd narrowly last: kpt on: no ex clsng stages* **1/3**[1]
FPP 3 *43* **Swizzler (IRE)**[41] 3736 7-11-0 0 WillKennedy 96
(Ian Williams) *j. bdly rt throught: detached in last: j. slowly 8th: sn bhd: t.o 4 out: eventually completed* **40/1**[3]

4m 59.6s (10.60) **Going Correction** +0.875s/f (Soft) **3 Ran SP% 106.0**
Speed ratings: **112,111,93**
CSF £3.90 TOTE £2.90; EX 3.40 Trifecta £2.60.
Owner J M Dare **Bred** Ms Iona Maguire **Trained** Seaborough, Dorset

FOCUS
A surprise outcome to this decent little novice chase. The winner is rated to his hurdles mark and there's a case for rating the race up to 6lb higher through the runner-up.

4459 BETBRIGHT CASINO MARES' H'CAP HURDLE (QUALIFIER FOR CHALLENGER MARES' HURDLE SERIES FINAL) (8 hdls) 2m 140y
4:20 (4:20) (Class 3) (0-125,123) 4-Y-0+ **£6,498** (£1,908; £954; £477)

Form RPR
131 1 **Taweyla (IRE)**[21] 4096 5-11-2 **118** JamieBargary(5) 124+
(Pam Sly) *trckd ldrs: t.k.h: hit 3 out: 2nd next: led 200yds out: drvn out* **1/1**[1]
-0U5 2 *2* **Favorite Girl (GER)**[32] 3335 8-11-11 **122** JonathanEngland 124
(Michael Appleby) *led: drvn appr 3 out: j.lft last: sn hdd: kpt on same pce* **10/1**
1P-P 3 *3 ¾* **Faerie Reel (FR)**[119] 2314 6-11-12 **123** RichardJohnson 121
(Kim Bailey) *chsd ldrs: pushed along 5th: sn lost pl: rallied appr 2 out: 3rd appr last: kpt on one pce* **17/2**
4314 4 *13* **Mystic Sky**[35] 3842 5-11-5 **116** LeightonAspell 104
(Lucy Wadham) *racd wd: chsd ldrs: nt fluent 3rd: 3rd whn mstke 2 out: wknd bef last* **10/3**[2]
133 5 *23* **Mystery Code**[36] 3822 4-10-12 **120** TomBellamy(3) 83
(Alan King) *t.k.h: sn trcking ldrs: effrt 3 out: wknd next: bhd whn eased last 150yds* **9/2**[3]

4m 14.8s (10.10) **Going Correction** +0.775s/f (Soft)
WFA 4 from 5yo+ 7lb **5 Ran SP% 110.9**
Speed ratings (Par 107): **107,106,104,98,87**
CSF £10.53 TOTE £1.90: £1.40, £3.60; EX 11.20 Trifecta £44.30.
Owner Pam's People **Bred** Darley **Trained** Thorney, Cambs

FOCUS
Just a fair handicap, confined to mares. It was the quickest of the three contests over the trip. The winner is on the upgrade.

4460 BETBRIGHTBOOST NOVICES' H'CAP HURDLE (8 hdls) 2m 140y
4:55 (4:55) (Class 4) (0-105,105) 4-Y-0+ **£3,898** (£1,144; £572; £286)

Form RPR
0-00 1 **Northandsouth (IRE)**[107] 2581 6-10-10 **92** RyanHatch(3) 97+
(Nigel Twiston-Davies) *t.k.h: sn trcking ldrs: led after 4th: pushed along appr 3 out: kpt on wl run-in: drvn rt out* **5/1**[2]
4631 2 *1 ¾* **Quill Art**[35] 3840 4-11-4 **105** BrianHughes 98
(Richard Fahey) *trckd ldrs: 2nd appr 3 out: upsides appr last: edgd lft and kpt on same pce last 150yds* **13/8**[1]

3-05 **3** 3 1/4 **Bibi D'Eole (FR)**[58] 3484 5-11-9 **102**........................ KielanWoods 101
(Graeme McPherson) *mid-div: chsd ldrs 5th: hung lft between last 2: kpt on to take 3rd clsng stages* **5/1**[2]

5-30 **4** 1 **Elkstone**[85] 2987 5-11-12 **105**........................[1] DenisO'Regan 103
(Alan King) *hld up in rr: hdwy 5th: sn trcking ldrs: 3rd appr next: swtchd rt appr 2 out: fdd last 100yds* **7/1**

5623 **5** 22 **Mazovian (USA)**[19] 3973 8-11-6 **99**........................(p) MarkQuinlan 74
(Neil Mulholland) *t.k.h: trckd ldrs: nt fluent 1st: pushed along 4th: outpcd and lost pl next: sn bhd* **11/2**[3]

656 **6** 4 **Aza Run (IRE)**[38] 3784 6-11-1 **94**........................ BrendanPowell 65
(Shaun Harris) *mid-div: chsd ldrs 5th: lost pl bef next: sn bhd* **16/1**

0P/6 **7** 8 **Hydrant**[10] 4297 10-10-2 **84**........................ KieronEdgar[(3)] 47
(Richard Guest) *t.k.h: trckd ldr sn after 2nd: led after 3rd: hdd after next: lost pl bef 2 out: sn bhd* **12/1**

-000 **8** 16 **Another Cobbler (FR)**[30] 3928 6-11-4 **97**........................ JakeGreenall 44
(Henry Daly) *set stdy pce: hdd after 3rd: drvn 5th: sn lost pl and bhd: eased run-in* **20/1**

4m 17.3s (12.60) **Going Correction** +0.775s/f (Soft)
WFA 4 from 5yo+ 7lb **8** Ran SP% **117.6**
Speed ratings (Par 105): **101,100,98,98,87 85,82,74**
CSF £14.47 CT £43.35 TOTE £5.90: £1.90, £1.10, £2.70; EX 19.00 Trifecta £95.10.
Owner Mills & Mason Partnership **Bred** Cyril O'Hara **Trained** Naunton, Gloucs

FOCUS
Modest novice handicap form, but it seems pretty solid.

4461 BETBRIGHT #REALFANSONLY CONDITIONAL JOCKEYS' NOVICES' HURDLE (8 hdls) 2m 140y
5:25 (5:26) (Class 4) 4-Y-0+ **£3,898** (£1,144; £572)

Form RPR

-131 **1** **Shrewd**[26] 4014 6-12-0 130........................ ShaneShortall 129+
(Iain Jardine) *hld up: wnt 2nd 5th: upsides 3 out: led 2 out: rdn between last 2: wnt clr fnl 150yds: v readily* **10/11**[1]

32 **2** 8 **Swansea Mile (IRE)**[138] 1986 6-11-11 137........................ BridgetAndrews[(3)] 124+
(Dan Skelton) *set v stdy pce: increased gallop gng to 3 out: nt fluent 3 out: sn pushed along: hdd 2 out: outpcd sn after last: eased clsng stages* **10/11**[1]

06 **3** 1/2 **Swinton Diamond (IRE)**[111] 2493 5-10-8 0........................ TobyWheeler[(8)] 105
(Ian Williams) *gave problems at s: t.k.h: trckd ldr: outpcd and lost pl 3 out: 8 l down on 2nd last: kpt on clsng stages* **33/1**[2]

4m 46.6s (41.90) **Going Correction** +0.775s/f (Soft) **3** Ran SP% **107.7**
Speed ratings (Par 105): **32,28,28**
CSF £2.14 TOTE £1.90; EX 1.70 Trifecta £1.60.
Owner Tapas Partnership **Bred** Darley **Trained** Carrutherstown, D'fries & G'way

FOCUS
A race that has been won in recent seasons by the likes of Red Merlin, Cockney Sparrow and Sign Of A Victory. There were a couple of useful novices this time despite the small field, but it turned into a sprint from the home turn and isn't form to take seriously. The first two are rated below their marks.
T/Plt: £466.90 to a £1 stake. Pool: £72,078.17 - 112.68 winning tickets T/Qpdt: £14.20 to a £1 stake. Pool: £6,211.16 - 321.77 winning tickets **Walter Glynn**

4111 NEWBURY (L-H)
Friday, March 4

OFFICIAL GOING: Chase course - good to soft (soft in places); hurdle course - soft (good to soft in places)
Wind: Fresh, against Weather: Sunny intervals

4462 FOCUS JUVENILE HURDLE (8 hdls) 2m 69y
2:20 (2:20) (Class 4) 4-Y-0 **£4,548** (£1,335; £667; £333)

Form RPR

20 **1** **Nabhan**[55] 3519 4-10-9 0........................ RobertWilliams[(3)] 126+
(Bernard Llewellyn) *lw: led 1st: jinked on path and wnt wd on 1st bnd: nt fluent 3rd and 4th: rdn appr last: styd on* **25/1**

2 5 **Lutece**[145] 4-10-5 0........................ AidanColeman 114+
(Venetia Williams) *tall: hld up in 6th: hdwy on inner 5th: trckd wnr 3 out: mstke last: unable qck* **6/1**[3]

P **3** 19 **Favorito Buck's (FR)**[68] 3279 4-11-5 0........................(t) SamTwiston-Davies 108
(Paul Nicholls) *str: lengthy: lw: prom: hmpd on 1st bnd: pressed wnr 2nd tl 3 out: wknd next* **10/11**[1]

0 **4** 5 **Vocaliser (IRE)**[121] 2273 4-10-12 0........................ CharliePoste 98
(Robin Dickin) *t.k.h towards rr: hdwy appr 3 out: 4th and wkng whn j.lft 2 out* **16/1**

54 **5** 15 **Sea Serpent (FR)**[41] 3730 4-10-12 0........................ JoshuaMoore 81
(Gary Moore) *bhd: rdn 3 out: n.d* **50/1**

6 3/4 **Zante (FR)**[55] 4-10-12 0........................ JamieMoore 82
(Gary Moore) *chsd ldrs: j. slowly 2nd: wknd appr 3 out* **8/1**

12 **7** 9 **Seven Kingdoms (IRE)**[27] 3988 4-11-5 127........................(t) NoelFehily 78
(David Dennis) *lw: led tl mstke 1st: hmpd on 1st bnd: prom tl wknd after 5th* **7/2**[2]

8 13 **Chief Spirit**[86] 4-10-12 0........................ JackQuinlan 58
(James Eustace) *in tch: outpcd in 5th whn mstke 3 out: sn bhd* **16/1**

4m 18.7s (8.70) **Going Correction** +0.175s/f (Yiel) **8** Ran SP% **117.6**
Speed ratings: **85,82,73,70,63 62,58,51**
CSF £169.63 TOTE £31.80: £5.10, £2.30, £1.02; EX 194.30 Trifecta £513.40.
Owner Gethyn Mills & Alex James **Bred** Rabbah Bloodstock Limited **Trained** Fochriw, Caerphilly

FOCUS
Rail movements added 43yds to the race distance. The going was soft, good to soft in places on the hurdles course and the jockeys said the ground was "a bit tacky". A fair juvenile hurdle that produced a surprise winner, and with a couple disappointing, the form looks worth treating with caution. The winner could be rated 5lb higher through the best of the runner-up's French figures.

4463 RR ELITE "NATIONAL HUNT" NOVICES' HURDLE (IN AID OF WEST BERKSHIRE MENCAP) (10 hdls) 2m 4f 118y
2:50 (2:51) (Class 4) 5-Y-0+ **£4,548** (£1,335; £667; £333)

Form RPR

3 **1** **Hell's Kitchen**[39] 3772 5-10-12 0........................ BarryGeraghty 137+
(Harry Fry) *lengthy: well-made: lw: t.k.h: sn prom: pressed ldr 4th: slt ld on bit last: briefly shkn up and wl on top: easily* **4/1**[2]

1-52 **2** 2 **Walking In The Air (IRE)**[21] 4108 6-10-12 0........................ HarrySkelton 130+
(Dan Skelton) *led tl last: kpt on same pce: easily hld by wnr and flattered by margin* **5/6**[1]

4 **3** 14 **Some Kinda Lama (IRE)**[97] 2772 5-10-12 0........................ DarylJacob 116+
(Charlie Mann) *prom: mstke and sltly lost pl 5th: hit 3 out: 4th and btn whn mstke next* **33/1**

-432 **4** nk **Midnight Cowboy**[39] 3775 5-10-12 119........................ WayneHutchinson 115
(Alan King) *chsd ldrs tl wknd 2 out* **9/2**[3]

1-0F **5** 45 **Beggars Cross (IRE)**[28] 3971 6-10-12 0........................ AidanColeman 75
(Jonjo O'Neill) *str: a towards rr: struggling fr 6th* **25/1**

1-00 **6** 1/2 **Coole Charmer (IRE)**[63] 3403 7-10-12 0........................ NoelFehily 69
(Nicky Henderson) *in tch: trckd ldrs 7th: wknd appr 3 out* **10/1**

P **P** **Redmond (IRE)**[12] 4264 6-10-9 0........................ CallumWhillans[(3)]
(Venetia Williams) *prom: lost pl after 3rd: sn bhd: t.o whn p.u bef 3 out* **50/1**

-065 **P** **Bound Hill**[19] 4137 7-10-5 0........................ MrMLegg[(7)]
(Fiona Shaw) *sn bhd: pushed along after 3rd: no ch 6th: p.u bef last* **100/1**

P **Tuffatthetop (IRE)** 5-10-12 0........................ RichieMcLernon
(Jonjo O'Neill) *bit bkwd: bhd: blnd 5th: t.o 7th: p.u bef last* **66/1**

F **Nice N Easy (IRE)** 6-10-12 0........................ SamTwiston-Davies
(Paul Nicholls) *tall: hld up towards rr: fell 1st* **16/1**

5m 15.5s (-3.50) **Going Correction** +0.175s/f (Yiel) **10** Ran SP% **118.9**
Speed ratings: **113,112,106,106,89 89,,,,**
CSF £8.02 TOTE £4.70: £1.30, £1.20, £6.90; EX 13.50 Trifecta £203.00.
Owner John P McManus **Bred** Netherfield House Stud **Trained** Seaborough, Dorset

FOCUS
Rail movements added 86yds to the race distance. An interesting novices' hurdle whose best recent winner was the subsequent Group 1 scorer Pettifour. The first two pulled well clear and the winner looks to have a decent future. The time was good compared with the later handicap. A step up from the third, with the fourth helping to set the level.

4464 BERRY BROS & RUDD H'CAP CHASE (FOR THE GEOFFREY GILBEY TROPHY) (QUALIFIER) (13 fncs) 2m 92y
3:25 (3:27) (Class 3) (0-130,127) 5-Y-0+ **£6,498** (£1,908; £954; £477)

Form RPR

-422 **1** **Ut Majeur Aulmes (FR)**[41] 3749 8-11-7 **127**........................(t) CiaranGethings[(5)] 136+
(Victor Dartnall) *hld up in midfield: hdwy 4 out: led last: drvn out: jst hld on* **6/1**[3]

2235 **2** nk **Walk In The Mill (FR)**[30] 3924 6-11-2 **117**........................ AndrewThornton 125+
(Robert Walford) *hld up towards rr: hdwy to chse ldrs 8th: cl 3rd whn hit last: clsng at fin: jst failed* **13/2**

2-PP **3** 4 **Starkie**[29] 3957 9-11-5 **120**........................ TomCannon 124
(Chris Gordon) *led tl 7th: led 4 out: hit 2 out: hdd last: ev ch tl no ex fnl 100yds* **10/1**

F-P4 **4** nk **Festive Affair (IRE)**[91] 2884 8-11-7 **122**........................(t) NoelFehily 126
(Jonjo O'Neill) *chsd ldrs: chal 3 out: one pce appr last* **7/2**[1]

1234 **5** 2 **Artifice Sivola (FR)**[35] 3843 6-11-12 **127**........................ HarrySkelton 129
(Lucy Wadham) *lw: trckd ldr: led 7th: blnd and hdd 4 out: one pce fr next* **7/1**

02P0 **6** 2 **Noche De Reyes (FR)**[91] 2884 7-11-5 **120**........................ PaddyBrennan 120
(Tom George) *lw: chsd ldrs tl outpcd fr 3 out* **10/1**

33B3 **7** 11 **Gores Island (IRE)**[29] 3957 10-11-8 **123**........................ JoshuaMoore 118
(Gary Moore) *lw: hld up towards rr: mstke 1st: effrt 3 out: wknd appr last* **9/2**[2]

511F **8** 19 **Cloudy Joker (IRE)**[28] 3972 8-11-10 **125**........................ HenryBrooke 97
(Donald McCain) *prom: lost pl 8th: mstke and wknd 4 out* **10/1**

0656 **9** 28 **Strongly Suggested**[28] 3972 9-11-6 **121**........................ BarryGeraghty 68
(Jonjo O'Neill) *mid-div: hrd rdn and wknd 7th: sn bhd* **20/1**

4P0U **P** **Paddy The Stout (IRE)**[69] 3257 11-10-4 **105**........................(t) TomO'Brien
(Paul Henderson) *j. stickily in rr: struggling 1/2-way: t.o whn p.u bef 3 out* **20/1**

4m 17.8s (9.80) **Going Correction** +0.675s/f (Soft) **10** Ran SP% **117.3**
Speed ratings: **102,101,99,99,98 97,92,82,68,**
CSF £45.50 CT £379.94 TOTE £6.20: £2.10, £2.70, £3.50; EX 42.70 Trifecta £578.20.
Owner Mrs S De Wilde **Bred** Emmanuel Bodard **Trained** Brayford, Devon

FOCUS
The going on the chase course was good to soft, soft in places, and rail movements added 44yds to the race distance. A competitive handicap chase and there were many with chances in the straight. A small pb from the winner, with the second, third and fourth rated pretty much to their marks.

4465 AGETUR UK NOVICES' LIMITED H'CAP CHASE (17 fncs) 2m 6f 93y
4:00 (4:00) (Class 4) (0-125,125) 5-Y-0+ **£6,498** (£1,908; £954; £477)

Form RPR

-151 **1** **Mystifiable**[67] 3315 8-11-3 **120**........................(t) PaddyBrennan 138+
(Fergal O'Brien) *hld up in midfield: hdwy and gng wl 12th: led 3 out: sn clr: easily* **4/1**[2]

-S43 **2** 7 **Baku Bay (IRE)**[35] 3836 8-11-1 **118**........................ GavinSheehan 125
(Ali Stronge) *lw: chsd ldrs: outpcd 3 out: styd on to chse easy wnr run-in* **11/2**[3]

1F22 **3** 3 3/4 **Muckle Roe (IRE)**[64] 3384 7-10-11 **114**........................ SamTwiston-Davies 119
(Nigel Twiston-Davies) *chsd ldrs: led and blnd 4 out: hdd next: sn outpcd by wnr* **10/1**

24-3 **4** 1 1/2 **Nitrogen (IRE)**[99] 2727 9-11-4 **121**........................ NoelFehily 122
(Harry Fry) *lw: bhd: rdn and styd on fr 4 out: nvr nrr* **7/2**[1]

-406 **5** 1 3/4 **Lucky Jim**[27] 2266 5-11-3 **121**........................ WayneHutchinson 120
(David Dennis) *hld up in midfield: smooth hdwy 13th: chsd wnr 3 out tl wknd last* **40/1**

0-PP **6** 20 **Boardwalk Empire (IRE)**[74] 3197 9-10-7 **117**..(t) WilliamFeatherstone[(7)] 99
(Kate Buckett) *prom: outpcd 12th: n.d fr 4 out* **66/1**

0-02 **7** 3/4 **Special Agent**[35] 3843 7-11-6 **123**........................(p) DavidBass 107
(Nicky Henderson) *mid-div: rdn 11th: struggling whn mstke 13th* **15/2**

-44F **8** 1 1/2 **Long Lunch**[66] 3335 7-11-5 **122**........................(t) AidanColeman 102
(Charlie Longsdon) *lw: a bhd* **12/1**

316P **9** 6 **Bob Tucker (IRE)**[14] 4232 9-11-4 **124**........................(p) GrahamWatters[(3)] 101
(Charlie Longsdon) *led tl 6th: blnd 10th: led and rdn 13th: hdd and hit next: sn wknd* **20/1**

F161 **10** 25 **Ballyadeen (IRE)**[24] 4042 8-11-5 **125**........................ JamesBanks[(3)] 87
(Dai Williams) *chsd ldr: led 6th tl 13th: wknd 4 out: 8th and wl btn whn blnd next* **12/1**

1-4P **P** **Elmore Back (IRE)**[69] 3235 7-11-2 **119**........................ DarylJacob
(Charlie Mann) *towards rr: mstke 2nd: wl bhd fr 8th: p.u bef 12th* **16/1**

-143 **F** **Wild Rover (IRE)**[65] 3371 7-11-1 **118**........................ SeanBowen
(Rebecca Curtis) *in tch: lost pl 4th: in rr whn fell 12th* **11/1**

5m 57.8s (10.80) **Going Correction** +0.675s/f (Soft) **12** Ran SP% **116.8**
Speed ratings: **107,104,103,102,101 94,94,94,91,82 ,**
CSF £26.11 CT £206.32 TOTE £5.20: £1.70, £2.30, £2.40; EX 31.20 Trifecta £257.80.
Owner Graham And Alison Jelley **Bred** Overbury Stallions Ltd **Trained** Naunton, Gloucs

FOCUS
Rail movements added 22yds to the race distance. An interesting and competitive novices' handicap chase which produced an impressive winner. Another big step up from the winner, with the second to the fifth pretty much to their marks.

4466 PHYSICOOL H'CAP HURDLE (IN AID OF WEST BERKSHIRE MENCAP) (10 hdls) 2m 4f 118y
4:30 (4:31) (Class 4) (0-120,120) 4-Y-0+ **£4,548** (£1,335; £667; £333)

Form RPR
5/2P **1** **Muhtaris (IRE)**[13] 4241 6-11-4 **119**........................ WilliamFeatherstone(7) 127+
(James Evans) *confidently rdn in rr: gd hdwy 3 out: led appr last: rdn clr* **8/1**

562F **2** *2 1/4* **Fin D'Espere (IRE)**[39] 3775 5-11-1 **109**..........................(t) GavinSheehan 113
(Suzy Smith) *prom: led 2 out tl appr last: kpt on u.p* **12/1**

5522 **3** *1 3/4* **Mountain Eagle (IRE)**[41] 3744 7-11-10 **118**..........................(t) NoelFehily 120+
(Harry Fry) *t.k.h: trckd ldrs: briefly wnt 2nd 2 out: kpt on same pce* **13/8**[1]

1-10 **4** *1/2* **Dazinski**[99] 2734 10-11-3 **116**........................ CiaranGethings(5) 118
(Henry Oliver) *hld up in midfield: effrt and gng wl whn swtchd lft after 2 out: styd on same pce* **7/1**[3]

241/ **5** *13* **Badgers Cove (IRE)**[720] 4809 12-11-2 **110**........................ CharliePoste 99
(Robin Dickin) *lw: led tl after 3rd: prom tl qckly lost pl 3 out* **20/1**

1300 **6** *4* **Dubh Eile (IRE)**[69] 3232 8-11-7 **115**........................ AidanColeman 100
(Tim Vaughan) *in tch: clsd on ldrs after 7th: wknd 2 out* **14/1**

3330 **7** *1* **Fort Smith (IRE)**[30] 3923 7-11-3 **118**..........................(t) HarrisonBeswick(7) 104
(Sam Thomas) *lw: led after 3rd: hit 3 out: hdd & wknd 2 out* **20/1**

-032 **8** *3 1/2* **Guards Chapel**[53] 2924 8-11-4 **112**..........................(v) JamieMoore 92
(Gary Moore) *towards rr: rdn appr 3 out: sme hdwy 2 out: sn wknd* **9/1**

524 **9** *18* **Super Scorpion (IRE)**[79] 3105 6-11-12 **120**........................ TomO'Brien 82
(Debra Hamer) *lw: bhd: effrt on inner appr 3 out: sn wknd* **6/1**[2]

10 *6* **Cleni Wells (FR)**[87] 5-11-6 **114**........................ LiamHeard 70
(Martin Hill) *athletic: lw: in tch tl wknd 3 out* **20/1**

5m 27.1s (8.10) **Going Correction** +0.175s/f (Yiel) **10** Ran SP% **114.6**
Speed ratings (Par 105): **91,90,89,89,84 82,82,81,74,71**
CSF £91.18 CT £230.06 TOTE £9.80: £3.20, £3.50, £1.30; EX 109.90 Trifecta £616.70.
Owner The Cheltenham Boys Racing Club 1 **Bred** Rabbah Bloodstock Limited **Trained** Broadwas, Worcs

FOCUS
Rail movements added 43yds to the race distance. A modest handicap hurdle run at a very steady gallop and the time was much slower than the earlier novices' hurdle. A step up from the winner and a bigger one from the second, with the third rated close to his mark.

4467 TKP SURFACING H'CAP HURDLE (IN AID OF WEST BERKSHIRE MENCAP) (12 hdls) 3m 52y
5:05 (5:06) (Class 4) (0-120,117) 5-Y-0+ **£4,548** (£1,335; £667; £333)

Form RPR
P45P **1** **Get Involved (IRE)**[76] 3146 7-10-11 **102**........................ CharliePoste 112+
(Robin Dickin) *hld up in 5th: hdwy 3 out: led 2 out: edgd lft and hdd last: rallied and led again run-in: drvn out* **9/2**[2]

3313 **2** *1 1/2* **Theatre Goer**[9] 4305 7-11-4 **112**........................ JamesBanks(3) 117
(Noel Williams) *led tl after 2nd: led after 3 out tl 2 out: rallied gamely and led last: hdd run-in: kpt on* **5/4**[1]

3335 **3** *5* **American Life (FR)**[20] 4127 9-11-6 **111**..........................(vt) PaulMoloney 111
(Sophie Leech) *hld up in rr: rdn 3 out: styd on to take 3rd run-in: nvr able to chal* **8/1**

2-43 **4** *3 1/2* **Kilcullen Flem (IRE)**[20] 4123 6-11-12 **117**........................ TomScudamore 114
(Rebecca Curtis) *chsd ldr: led after 2nd tl after 3 out: sn wknd* **5/1**[3]

054P **5** *1 3/4* **Garde Fou (FR)**[41] 3746 10-11-0 **105**..........................(t) TomO'Brien 100
(Paul Henderson) *t.k.h: chsd ldrs tl outpcd fr 3 out* **16/1**

5-63 **6** *4* **Monetary Fund (USA)**[102] 2687 10-11-8 **113**........................ AidanColeman 104
(Venetia Williams) *cl 3rd most of way tl wknd 2 out* **7/1**

4054 **F** **Minella Bliss (IRE)**[25] 4030 11-9-10 **97**..........................(b) JosephWilliamson(10)
(James Evans) *plld hrd: stdd in rr: disputing last but in tch whn fell 8th* **25/1**

6m 33.7s (393.70) **7** Ran SP% **112.6**
CSF £10.61 CT £41.46 TOTE £5.90: £3.10, £1.10; EX 10.90 Trifecta £71.00.
Owner The Point Of Attack Partnership **Bred** L O'Shaughnessy **Trained** Alcester, Warwicks

FOCUS
Rail movements added 86yds to the race distance. An ordinary staying handicap hurdle and just modest form. The winner has been rated back to the level of last year's Southwell run, with the second to her mark.

4468 RICKETY BRIDGE MARES' STANDARD OPEN NATIONAL HUNT FLAT RACE (IN AID OF WEST BERKSHIRE MENCAP) 2m 69y
5:35 (5:38) (Class 6) 4-6-Y-0 **£1,624** (£477; £238; £119)

Form RPR
1 **Canoodle** 4-10-7 0..........................(b[1]) TomO'Brien 98+
(Hughie Morrison) *athletic: plld hrd towards rr: hdwy 4f out: slt ld and swvd rt 2f out: drvn to get on top ins fnl f* **11/1**

2 **2** *2* **Poisoned Berry (IRE)**[48] 3632 4-10-4 0........................ ConorShoemark(3) 94
(Fergal O'Brien) *w'like: led: kicked 4 l clr 4f out: hdd 2f out: kpt on wl tl outpcd by wnr ins fnl f* **15/2**

3 *3 3/4* **Only For Love** 5-10-10 0........................ FreddieMitchell(5) 98
(Nicky Henderson) *lengthy: lw: in tch: rdn 5f out: wnt 4th 3f out: styd on fnl f* **3/1**[2]

16 **4** *10* **Westerbee (IRE)**[77] 3138 5-11-3 0........................ KevinJones(5) 95
(Seamus Mullins) *t.k.h and stdd in last pl: gd hdwy over 3f out: wknd wl over 1f out* **9/1**

5 *1* **Pampanini** 5-11-1 0........................ NoelFehily 87
(Harry Fry) *attractive: prom tl wknd over 2f out* **15/8**[1]

0 **6** *11* **Owners Day**[115] 2421 6-11-1 0........................ TomScudamore 76
(Neil Mulholland) *plld hrd in 6th: wknd 3f out* **25/1**

0 **7** *3 1/2* **Peal Of Bells**[22] 4074 5-11-1 0........................ PaddyBrennan 73
(Henry Daly) *sn towards rr: n.d fnl 4f* **66/1**

4 **8** *4* **My Cousin Rachel (IRE)**[85] 2998 5-11-1 0........................ DavidBass 69
(Kim Bailey) *tall: prom: chsd ldr after 4f tl wknd over 3f out* **5/1**[3]

9 *1* **Staunton** 5-10-10 0........................ CiaranGethings(5) 68
(Susan Johnson) *chsd ldrs tl wknd over 3f out* **25/1**

4m 13.1s (8.80) **Going Correction** +0.175s/f (Yiel)
WFA 4 from 5yo+ 7lb **9** Ran SP% **115.7**
Speed ratings: **85,84,82,77,76 71,69,67,66**
CSF £88.45 TOTE £11.50: £3.00, £2.10, £1.40; EX 54.50 Trifecta £332.30.
Owner Mrs M D W Morrison **Bred** Mrs M D W Morrison **Trained** East Ilsley, Berks

FOCUS
Rail movements added 43yds to the race distance. Nicky Henderson has dominated the previous runnings of this mares' bumper, but another local trainer came out best this time. It's been rated around the second and fourth.

T/Jkpt: Not won. T/Plt: £45.60 to a £1 stake. Pool: £74,406.03 - 1,190.04 winning tickets T/Qpdt: £15.70 to a £1 stake. Pool: £6,531.35 - 306.80 winning tickets **Lee McKenzie**

4455 DONCASTER (L-H)
Saturday, March 5

OFFICIAL GOING: Soft (chs 6.8, hdl 6.8)
Wind: moderate 1/2 behind Weather: mostly fine

4469 WATCH LIVE RACING ON BETBRIGHT.COM H'CAP CHASE (12 fncs) 2m 90y
2:00 (2:00) (Class 2) 5-Y-0+ **£18,768** (£5,544; £2,772; £1,386; £693)

Form RPR
-065 **1** **Upsilon Bleu (FR)**[49] 3629 8-11-12 **140**........................ JamesReveley 151+
(Pauline Robson) *hld up in rr: hdwy after 5th: trcking ldrs 8th: led appr 2 out: wnt clr run-in: smoothly* **10/3**[2]

3315 **2** *4* **Pearls Legend**[63] 3446 9-11-10 **138**........................ JamieMoore 142
(John Spearing) *w ldr: led after 6th: pushed along 8th: hdd 3 out: kpt on to chse wnr between last 2: no imp* **11/4**[1]

4442 **3** *1 1/2* **Yorkist (IRE)**[27] 4011 8-11-6 **134**..........................(t) BrianHughes 137
(Micky Hammond) *hld up towards rr: hdwy to chse ldrs 5th: drvn and outpcd 3 out: kpt on to take 3rd sn after last* **7/2**[3]

12F5 **4** *3 1/4* **Ulis De Vassy (FR)**[195] 1344 8-10-13 **127**........................ RobertDunne 127
(Dan Skelton) *trckd ldng pair: 2nd 8th: drvn to ld 3 out: hdd and hit next: fdd between last 2* **9/2**

3201 **5** *nk* **Astigos (FR)**[22] 4106 9-10-11 **125**..........................(p) AlainCawley 126
(Venetia Williams) *led: drvn 6th: sn hdd: outpcd and reminders 8th: sn lost pl: blnd last: kpt on clsng stages* **9/2**

4m 9.2s (4.20) **Going Correction** +0.325s/f (Yiel) **5** Ran SP% **108.3**
Speed ratings: **102,100,99,97,97**
CSF £12.52 TOTE £5.20: £2.40, £1.80; EX 12.40 Trifecta £25.10.
Owner Mr & Mrs Raymond Anderson Green **Bred** A Peltier, D Juste & J Houdin **Trained** Kirkharle, Northumberland

FOCUS
The ground was officially soft but no worse than that - the first winner's time suggested that conditions were far from gruelling and nothing like as desperate as the plethora of withdrawals on the card might suggest. \n\x\x This was not as strong a race as might have been hoped for, given it was an open handicap, and the topweight was rated just 140. They went a good pace up front which suited the waited-with contenders. Solid form, the winner rated back to his best.

4470 BETBRIGHT CASINO H'CAP HURDLE (11 hdls) 3m 96y
2:35 (2:35) (Class 2) (0-145,142) 4-Y£12,512 (£3,696; £1,848; £924; £462)

Form RPR
4-60 **1** **Sugar Baron (IRE)**[42] 3733 6-10-13 **129**........................ DavidBass 133+
(Nicky Henderson) *t.k.h: sn trcking ldng pair: upsides 8th: drvn to ld 3 out: hung lft: rdn between last 2: edgd lft run-in: fnd ex clsng stages* **5/2**[2]

014 **2** *2 1/4* **Zeroeshadesofgrey (IRE)**[21] 4112 7-11-12 **142**........................ TrevorWhelan 142
(Neil King) *t.k.h: trckd ldr tl 7th: drvn almost upsides last: sn chsng wnr: styd on same pce last 75yds* **9/4**[1]

51F2 **3** *1 3/4* **Fingertips (FR)**[14] 4239 4-10-9 **135**..........................(t) DarylJacob 123
(David Pipe) *led: hdd 3 out: almost upsides and n.m.r last: kpt on same pce* **4/1**

1523 **4** *26* **Waterclock (IRE)**[28] 3999 7-10-6 **125**..........................(p) JoeColliver(3) 96
(Micky Hammond) *chsd ldrs to 2nd: in rr: nt fluent and reminders 5th: sn pushed along: outpcd 8th: poor 4th appr 3 out: sn bhd* **7/2**[3]

/26- **5** *55* **Clerk's Choice (IRE)**[553] 1398 10-11-9 **139**........................ JackQuinlan 55
(Michael Banks) *hld up in rr: trckd ldrs 4th: outpcd and hit 8th: lost pl bef next: sn wl bhd: t.o whn eased sn after last: eventually completed* **14/1**

6m 16.8s (17.80) **Going Correction** +0.575s/f (Soft)
WFA 4 from 6yo+ 9lb **5** Ran SP% **108.2**
Speed ratings (Par 109): **93,92,91,83,64**
CSF £8.39 TOTE £3.20: £1.50, £1.30; EX 10.80 Trifecta £24.60.
Owner Anthony Speelman **Bred** Nelius O'Keeffe **Trained** Upper Lambourn, Berks

FOCUS
The absence of the promising Whataknight plus three others weakened this handicap hurdle, but two or three of the remainder were still open to improvement and a couple of those came clear with a decent yardstick in a contest run at just a fair pace. A small pb from the winner. Rail movement meant they raced over about 12 yards short of the advertised distance.

4471 BETBRIGHT MARES' NOVICES' HURDLE (LISTED RACE) (11 hdls) 3m 96y
3:10 (3:10) (Class 1) 4-Y-0+ **£17,165** (£6,491; £3,290; £1,679; £884)

Form RPR
1112 **1** **The Organist (IRE)**[39] 3785 5-11-2 129........................ LeightonAspell 137+
(Oliver Sherwood) *trckd ldrs: led 3 out: drvn and styd on wl* **5/2**[1]

-031 **2** *3* **Briery Belle**[50] 3612 7-11-2 120........................ JakeGreenall 131
(Henry Daly) *hld up: hdwy to chse ldrs 8th: 2nd last: styd on same pce: no imp* **5/2**[1]

-122 **3** *11* **Hollies Pearl**[26] 4026 6-11-2 128..........................(bt) SeanBowen 128+
(Peter Bowen) *hdwy to chse ldrs whn hit 8th: chsd wnr 3 out: 3rd and wkng whn blnd and wnt lft last* **5/1**[2]

1311 **4** *1/2* **Yes I Did (IRE)**[19] 4151 6-11-2 130........................ RobertDunne 121
(Dan Skelton) *t.k.h: trckd ldr: led briefly appr 3 out: wknd between last 2* **5/2**[1]

233 **5** *59* **Graceful Legend**[30] 3947 5-11-2 0........................ DarylJacob 61
(Ben Case) *racd wd: hdwy 5th: chsng ldrs 8th: wknd 3 out: sn bhd: t.o: eventually completed* **50/1**

5215 **P** **Samedi Soir**[146] 1870 6-11-2 118........................ JamesReveley
(Keith Reveley) *on toes befhand: led: clr to 6th: hdd appr 3 out: sn lost pl and eased: wl bhd whn p.u bef 3 out* **20/1**[3]

5-34 **P** **Buttercup (FR)**[25] 4039 5-11-2 125........................ AlainCawley
(Venetia Williams) *chsd ldrs: lost pl and drvn 7th: sn bhd: t.o whn p.u bef 3 out* **20/1**[3]

6m 12.3s (13.30) **Going Correction** +0.575s/f (Soft) **7** Ran SP% **113.9**
Speed ratings (Par 111): **100,99,95,95,75** ,
CSF £8.99 TOTE £3.00: £1.50, £2.30; EX 9.20 Trifecta £33.10.
Owner Million In Mind Partnership **Bred** John Browne **Trained** Upper Lambourn, Berks

FOCUS
Potentially a decent Listed race, with all bar two of these already winners over hurdles and most of the field seemingly on the up. They went a good pace in a contest run over a distance about 12 yards short of that advertised.

4472 BETBRIGHT GRIMTHORPE CHASE H'CAP CHASE (19 fncs) 3m 2f 14y
3:45 (3:45) (Class 2) 5-Y-O+ **£34,535** (£10,291; £5,209; £2,668; £1,398)

Form RPR
2-31 **1** **The Last Samuri (IRE)**[69] 3282 8-11-6 **149**........................ DavidBass 160+
(Kim Bailey) *trckd ldrs: j. soundly: 2nd 15th: led 3 out: forged clr run-in: eased clsng stages* **2/1**[1]
F-66 **2** *10* **The Druids Nephew (IRE)**[85] 3016 9-11-12 **155**..........(p) DenisO'Regan 153
(Neil Mulholland) *trckd ldrs 6th: hit 11th: 3rd 4 out: chsd wnr appr 2 out: kpt on same pce* **7/1**[3]
54-5 **3** *¾* **Band Of Blood (IRE)**[21] 4128 8-10-3 **132**........................(t) WillKennedy 129
(Dr Richard Newland) *in rr: pushed along 8th: sn outpcd: lost pl and reminders 13th: modest 4th 3 out: tk 3rd sn after last: kpt on* **4/1**[2]
501F **4** *6* **Sego Success (IRE)**[49] 3624 8-11-3 **146**........................(p) TomCannon 137
(Alan King) *w ldr: led 14th: hdd 3 out: wknd last* **4/1**[2]
-411 **5** *51* **Drop Out Joe**[119] 2348 8-11-8 **151**..............................(p) RichardJohnson 89
(Charlie Longsdon) *led: hdd 14th: drvn and wknd appr 4 out: sn bhd: t.o whn eased run-in: eventually completed* **4/1**[2]
1540 **P** **Seventh Sky (GER)**[28] 3993 9-11-7 **150**............................(tp) DarylJacob
(Charlie Mann) *chsd ldrs: pushed along 11th: lost pl and bhd whn j.lft 13th: t.o whn p.u bef 15th* **14/1**

6m 39.9s (-3.10) **Going Correction** +0.325s/f (Yiel) **6** Ran SP% **112.5**
Speed ratings: **117,113,113,111,96**
CSF £15.75 CT £50.04 TOTE £2.80: £1.40, £4.00; EX 18.40 Trifecta £82.10.
Owner Paul & Clare Rooney **Bred** Edmond Coleman **Trained** Andoversford, Gloucs

FOCUS
This is traditionally one of the first big handicap chases run after the ground has begun to dry and has been a fair pointer to the major spring prizes, with one recent winner going on to take the Bet365 Gold Cup and two in the last 12 years landing the Scottish Grand National - with another two placed at Ayr.\n\x\x Soft ground cut the size of the field this year and reduced the race's usual competitiveness but it still featured some serious contenders for big races in the coming months and they went a strong pace, which made for a good test of stamina. The easy winner is on the upgrade.

4473 BETBRIGHT BEST FOR FESTIVAL BETTING NOVICES' HURDLE (10 hdls) 2m 3f 120y
4:20 (4:20) (Class 4) 4-Y-O+ **£4,548** (£1,335; £667; £333)

Form RPR
3 **1** **Cracked Rear View (IRE)**[86] 2978 6-11-4 0........................(t) DavidBass 112+
(Kim Bailey) *trckd ldng pair: 2nd 6th: upsides and drvn 3 out: rdn to ld between last 2: j.lft last: hung rt and forged clr last 75yds* **4/7**[1]
16P0 **2** *5* **Improved (IRE)**[9] 4322 6-11-4 0............................ JamesReveley 106
(Philip Kirby) *led: hdd between last 2: kpt on same pce last 100yds* **7/1**[3]
-PP3 **3** *19* **Deadly Move (IRE)**[31] 3927 7-11-4 0............................(t) SeanBowen 90
(Peter Bowen) *hld up: hit 2nd: chsd ldrs 4th: clr 3rd bef 3 out: lost pl bef 2 out* **9/4**[2]
P **4** *93* **Felice (IRE)**[12] 3947 6-10-4 0............................ GLavery[(7)]
(Scott Dixon) *w ldr: drvn 6th: reminders and lost pl bef 3 out: sn wl bhd: t.o: eventually completed* **33/1**

4m 55.9s (4.60) **Going Correction** +0.575s/f (Soft) **4** Ran SP% **109.9**
Speed ratings (Par 105): **113,111,103,66**
CSF £5.13 TOTE £1.50; EX 3.70 Trifecta £6.40.
Owner Paul & Clare Rooney **Bred** Joe Fogarty **Trained** Andoversford, Gloucs

FOCUS
An uncompetitive novice event, run over about six yards shorter than the advertised distance, with only a couple of these having shown anything other than poor form over hurdles. The winner should go on to rate higher.

4474 GRAND-NATIONAL2016.CO.UK H'CAP HURDLE (11 hdls) 3m 96y
4:55 (4:55) (Class 4) (0-120,117) 4-Y-O+ **£4,185** (£1,431)

Form RPR
5031 **1** **Wintered Well (IRE)**[4] 4421 8-11-9 **114** 7ex................ RichardJohnson 115+
(Jennie Candlish) *mde all: jnd bef 3 out: sn drvn: j.lft last 2: c rt away run-in* **4/9**[1]
6505 **2** *18* **Mercers Court (IRE)**[57] 3507 8-11-12 **117**........................ TrevorWhelan 108
(Neil King) *t.k.h in last: lft 2nd 4th: jnd wnr bef 3 out: one pce bef 2 out: 7 l down whn heavily eased sn after last* **13/2**[3]
5631 **U** **Rocklim (FR)**[26] 4035 6-11-5 **110**........................ LucyAlexander
(James Ewart) *trckd wnr: t.k.h: blnd bdly and uns rdr 4th* **11/4**[2]

6m 35.3s (36.30) **Going Correction** +0.575s/f (Soft) **3** Ran SP% **109.3**
Speed ratings (Par 105): **62,56,**
CSF £3.36 TOTE £1.40; EX 3.10 Trifecta £5.90.
Owner A White **Bred** Mrs Kathleen Leahy **Trained** Basford Green, Staffs

FOCUS
This handicap hurdle, run over a distance about 12 yards shorter than advertised, had looked uncompetitive after declarations were made and two further withdrawals plus the early departure of one of the remaining trio left it a decidedly uninformative affair. Not form to take seriously.

4475 BETBRIGHT #REALFANSONLY STANDARD NATIONAL HUNT FLAT RACE (CONDITIONAL JOCKEYS AND AMATEUR RIDERS) 2m 140y
5:30 (5:30) (Class 6) 4-6-Y-O **£1,949** (£572; £286; £143)

Form RPR
1 **Midnight Maestro** 4-10-3 0........................ WilliamFeatherstone[(7)] 109+
(Alan King) *hld up wl in tch: chal over 4f out: led over 2f out: drvn and edgd lft fnl f: forged clr* **6/4**[1]
2 *4½* **Wenyerreadyfreddie (IRE)** 5-10-11 0................ MrAlexFerguson[(7)] 110
(John Ferguson) *hld up wl in tch: chal over 4f out: 2nd over 1f out: kpt on one pce* **7/4**[2]
P **3** *9* **Ballycash (IRE)**[37] 3827 5-10-11 0........................ MrJJSlevin[(7)] 103
(Nigel Twiston-Davies) *trckd ldng pair: led over 5f out: hdd over 2f out: wknd appr fnl f* **9/2**[3]
4 *43* **Spring Hill (IRE)** 4-10-3 0........................ MrTommieMO'Brien[(7)] 50
(Chris Bealby) *chsd ldr: pushed along over 5f out: sn outpcd: lost pl 3f out: sn bhd: t.o* **8/1**
0-0 **5** *23* **More More More**[30] 3952 6-10-11 0........................ MrKLocking[(7)] 35
(Scott Dixon) *led: pushed along 7f out: hdd over 5f out: lost pl over 4f out: sn wl bhd: t.o whn eased over 1f out: eventually completed* **33/1**

4m 7.7s (8.60) **Going Correction** +0.575s/f (Soft)
WFA 4 from 5yo+ 7lb **5** Ran SP% **108.6**
Speed ratings: **102,99,95,75,64**
CSF £4.28 TOTE £2.60: £1.20, £1.60; EX 5.20 Trifecta £10.70.
Owner Mrs K Holmes **Bred** Pitchall Stud **Trained** Barbury Castle, Wilts

FOCUS
Nothing better than modest form from those to have raced in bumpers and this looked ripe for the taking by one of the newcomers - and so it proved with the two debutants who dominated the betting also dominating the finish. The first two are probably above average.
T/Plt: £24.70 to a £1 stake. Pool: £96,203.26 - 2,841.35 winning tickets T/Qpdt: £8.50 to a £1 stake. Pool: £6,023.16 - 518.87 winning tickets **Walter Glynn**

4202 KELSO (L-H)
Saturday, March 5

4476 Meeting Abandoned - waterlogged

4462 NEWBURY (L-H)
Saturday, March 5

OFFICIAL GOING: Hurdle course - soft (good to soft in places; hdl 5.5) changing to soft after race 4 (3.25); chase course - good to soft (soft in places; chs 5.7) changing to soft (good to soft in places) after race 3 (2. Fresh, across away from standsUnsettled

4482 BETFAIR SUPPORTING GREATWOOD VETERANS' H'CAP HURDLE (10 hdls) 2m 4f 118y
1:45 (1:46) (Class 3) (0-130,128) 8-Y-O+ **£12,996** (£3,816; £1,908; £954)

Form RPR
2152 **1** **Howaboutnever (IRE)**[12] 4284 8-10-10 **119**........................(p) HarryTeal[(7)] 119
(Roger Teal) *chsd ldr: 1 l down and rdn whn mstke and lft in narrow ld 2 out: drvn out* **12/1**
3213 **2** *1½* **Spice Fair**[42] 3748 9-11-11 **127**........................ WayneHutchinson 127+
(Mark Usher) *hld up in rr: mstke 3 out: effrt whn sltly hmpd 2 out: rdn to chal last: r.o* **11/2**[3]
54-0 **3** *9* **Bonobo (IRE)**[108] 2577 9-10-7 **109**........................ PaulMoloney 101
(Evan Williams) *prom: mstke 6th: lft cl 2nd and hmpd 2 out: hrd rdn and wknd appr last* **8/1**
6006 **4** *¾* **Olofi (FR)**[35] 3854 10-11-8 **124**........................(bt) PaddyBrennan 114
(Tom George) *t.k.h towards rr: hdwy 2 out and trckd wnr on bit: rdn and fnd nthing appr last* **9/2**[2]
1/4- **5** *19* **Total Submission**[342] 5049 11-10-12 **114**........................ LiamHeard 85
(John Groucott) *led tl after 3 out: disputing 6th and btn whn sltly hmpd next* **14/1**
0-P0 **6** *2½* **Lexi's Boy (IRE)**[125] 2214 8-11-5 **121**..................(tp) SamTwiston-Davies 95+
(Donald McCain) *in tch: effrt whn bdly hmpd 2 out: nt rcvr* **9/1**
1103 **7** *9* **Cousin Khee**[103] 2684 9-11-12 **128**........................ TomO'Brien 86
(Hughie Morrison) *t.k.h in rr: rdn 3 out: no ch whn hmpd by loose horse next* **15/2**
01-0 **P** **Tiger O'Toole (IRE)**[293] 356 11-11-3 **119**........................ JeremiahMcGrath
(Henry Oliver) *t.k.h in rr: pushed along after 7th: sn bhd: p.u bef 2 out* **7/1**
31-2 **F** **Rock Gone (IRE)**[19] 4159 8-11-12 **128**........................ AidanColeman 128+
(Dr Richard Newland) *trckd ldrs: led after 3 out: 1 l up and gng wl whn fell next* **4/1**[1]

5m 20.4s (1.40) **Going Correction** +0.275s/f (Yiel) **9** Ran SP% **113.3**
Speed ratings: **108,107,104,103,96 95,92,,**
CSF £75.51 CT £563.23 TOTE £13.90: £2.90, £2.10, £3.10; EX 97.70 Trifecta £725.50.
Owner Barry Kitcherside & Roger Teal **Bred** Mrs A Connolly **Trained** Great Shefford, Berks
■ The first jumps winner, to go with one on the Flat, for trainer's son Harry Teal.

FOCUS
Due to rail movements this race was run over 109yds further than advertised. Wayne Hutchinson described the ground as "a bit dead". An ordinary veterans' hurdle, run at a pretty steady gallop, and the favourite appeared in control when falling two out. The winner is rated to his mark.

4483 BETWAY SUPPORTING GREATWOOD VETERANS' H'CAP CHASE (QUALIFIER) (LEG 3 OF THE VETERANS' SERIES) (21 fncs) 3m 1f 214y
2:15 (2:16) (Class 2) (0-150,150) 10-Y-O+
£18,768 (£5,544; £2,772; £1,386; £693; £348)

Form RPR
56U4 **1** **Shotavodka (IRE)**[10] 4306 10-10-3 **127**........................(p) TomScudamore 146+
(David Pipe) *hld up towards rr: stdy hdwy 14th: led 2 out: sn clr: easily* **7/1**[2]
6242 **2** *11* **Pete The Feat (IRE)**[28] 3993 12-10-9 **133**.............(t) SamTwiston-Davies 138
(Charlie Longsdon) *j.rt: led tl 2 out: sn outpcd* **5/1**[1]
2PP3 **3** *1¾* **Masters Hill (IRE)**[20] 4141 10-11-2 **140**........................(tp) TomO'Brien 142
(Colin Tizzard) *mid-div: outpcd and lost pl 13th: styd on fr 3 out* **9/1**
0163 **4** *11* **So Fine (IRE)**[36] 3844 10-10-5 **129**........................(p) JamesBest 123
(Philip Hobbs) *in tch: lost pl 11th: rdr dropped whip 16th: rallied 4 out: wknd next* **12/1**
305 **5** *2½* **Restless Harry**[66] 3364 12-10-9 **133**........................ PaddyBrennan 122
(Henry Oliver) *prom: rdn and lost pl 15th: n.d after* **5/1**[1]
1456 **6** *shd* **Shuil Royale (IRE)**[22] 4101 11-10-11 **135**........................(t) NoelFehily 135+
(Harry Fry) *j.rt: hld up in rr: promising hdwy in 6th whn bdly hmpd and dropped to rr again 17th: styd on fr 3 out* **10/1**
2F1P **7** *15* **Pineau De Re (FR)**[7] 4354 13-11-3 **141**........................(p) NicodeBoinville 119
(Dr Richard Newland) *hld up towards rr on outer: stdy hdwy whn j. slowly 13th: lft 4 l 2nd and gng wl at 17th: wknd 3 out* **12/1**
/54- **8** *25* **Alvarado (IRE)**[329] 5275 11-10-13 **137**........................ PaulMoloney 105
(Fergal O'Brien) *towards rr: pushed along 11th: no ch fr 17th* **14/1**
1120 **9** *7* **Aachen**[35] 3860 12-11-7 **150**........................ CharlieDeutsch[(5)] 97
(Venetia Williams) *in tch tl wknd 16th* **14/1**
415P **10** *5* **Houston Dynimo (IRE)**[63] 3448 11-9-9 **124**.............(bt) DavidNoonan[(5)] 66
(David Pipe) *chsd ldrs tl wknd 4 out* **40/1**
P-0P **U** **Relax (FR)**[63] 3448 11-10-8 **132**........................ LiamTreadwell
(Venetia Williams) *chsd ldr: cl up and ev ch whn blnd and uns rdr 17th* **11/1**
5P/P **P** **Same Difference (IRE)**[66] 3373 10-10-6 **130**........................(p) GavinSheehan
(Warren Greatrex) *towards rr whn mstke 9th: bhd and rdn fr 11th: t.o whn p.u bef 4 out* **15/2**[3]

7m 0.1s (14.10) **Going Correction** +0.625s/f (Soft) **12** Ran SP% **116.2**
Speed ratings: **103,99,99,95,94 94,90,82,80,78 ,**
CSF £42.11 CT £320.42 TOTE £5.80: £2.10, £2.20, £3.30; EX 28.70 Trifecta £456.00.
Owner Mrs Jane Gerard-Pearse **Bred** Alastair Pim **Trained** Nicholashayne, Devon

FOCUS
Due to rail movements this was run over 46yds further than advertised. Run at a fair gallop, what had looked an open handicap was won in clear-cut fashion. The easy winner is rated close to his best.

4484 LADBROKES SUPPORTING GREATWOOD H'CAP HURDLE (8 hdls) 2m 69y
2:50 (2:50) (Class 3) (0-140,140) 4-Y-0+

£12,512 (£3,696; £1,848; £924; £462; £232)

Form / RPR

6211 **1** **Gala Ball (IRE)**[14] [4256] 6-11-5 **133**........................ TomO'Brien 144+
(Philip Hobbs) *in tch: mstke 4th: effrt and led 2 out: rdn clr* **7/1**[3]

212- **2** *7* **Boite (IRE)**[220] [5360] 6-11-5 **133**........................ GavinSheehan 135
(Warren Greatrex) *chsd ldrs: led 4th tl 3 out: outpcd by wnr fr next* **8/1**

642P **3** *4 ½* **Forest Bihan (FR)**[21] [4115] 5-11-12 **140**........................ DannyCook 138
(Brian Ellison) *towards rr: hdwy 5th: led 3 out tl 2 out: wknd appr last* **11/1**

1430 **4** *12* **Baby King (IRE)**[21] [4115] 7-11-1 **129**..................(t) PaddyBrennan 117
(Tom George) *hld up in rr: hdwy appr 3 out: mstke and wknd next* **12/1**

412- **5** *5* **Saint Charles (FR)**[385] [4220] 6-11-3 **131**..................[1] BarryGeraghty 113
(Nicky Henderson) *in tch: effrt 3 out: wknd next* **7/2**[2]

5514 **6** *9* **After Hours (IRE)**[32] [3917] 7-10-6 **120**........................ JeremiahMcGrath 91
(Henry Oliver) *prom tl wknd 3 out* **14/1**

-3F5 **7** *3 ¾* **Red Devil Star (IRE)**[90] [2926] 6-10-10 **124**............(t) SamTwiston-Davies 91
(Suzy Smith) *sn towards rr: rdn and n.d fr 3 out* **33/1**

/631 **8** *2 ¼* **Kings Bayonet**[21] [3487] 9-11-0 **128**........................ WayneHutchinson 94
(Alan King) *t.k.h towards rr: rdn and n.d fr 3 out* **16/1**

31-P **9** *37* **Rathealy (IRE)**[282] [197] 5-10-13 **132**........................ DavidNoonan[(5)] 60
(David Pipe) *prom tl 3rd: wknd rapidly 5th: sn t.o* **25/1**

5F-4 **P** **Gabrial The Great (IRE)**[93] [2873] 7-10-12 **126**..........(t[1]) TomScudamore
(David Pipe) *plld hrd in rr: gd hdwy 4th: jnd ldr next: wknd qckly and p.u bef 3 out* **9/1**

0661 **P** **Wells De Lune (FR)**[6] [4384] 5-10-5 **119** 7ex..............(b[1]) NicodeBoinville
(Charlie Longsdon) *wore blinkers instead of declared eye-shields: led and racd freely: stdd pce 3rd: hdd next: sn p.u* **10/3**[1]

4m 11.5s (1.50) **Going Correction** +0.35s/f (Yiel) **11** Ran SP% **114.3**
Speed ratings (Par 107): **110,106,104,98,95 91,89,88,69,**
CSF £60.35 CT £608.97 TOTE £7.40: £2.40, £3.40, £2.80; EX 72.30 Trifecta £365.20.
Owner Robert & Janet Gibbs **Bred** Thomas James **Trained** Withycombe, Somerset

FOCUS
Due to rail movements this race was run over 82yds further than advertised. Run at a good gallop throughout, the runners finished fairly tired and it went to an improver. The winner is on the upgrade.

4485 STANJAMES.COM SUPPORTING GREATWOOD GOLD CUP H'CAP CHASE (GRADE 3) (16 fncs) 2m 3f 187y
3:25 (3:25) (Class 1) 5-Y-0+

£28,475 (£10,685; £5,350; £2,665; £1,340; £670)

Form / RPR

1U22 **1** **Sametegal (FR)**[27] [4013] 7-11-3 **143**..................(t) SamTwiston-Davies 154+
(Paul Nicholls) *hld up towards rr: hdwy 11th: chal gng wl 2 out: led last: rdn clr* **7/1**[2]

PP13 **2** *4* **Bennys Mist (IRE)**[42] [3735] 10-11-5 **145**........................ LiamTreadwell 151
(Venetia Williams) *prom: lft in ld 12th: hdd 3 out: hrd rdn next: one pce run-in* **10/1**

2006 **3** *¾* **Aerlite Supreme (IRE)**[42] [3735] 9-10-2 **128**..................(t) AdamWedge 133
(Evan Williams) *in tch: effrt appr 2 out: pressed ldrs last: one pce* **20/1**

/U-1 **4** *3 ¼* **Pythagore**[27] 11-11-8 **148**..................(t) FelixDeGiles 151
(Emmanuel Clayeux, France) *hld up towards rr: hdwy 12th: led 2 out tl last: no ex* **10/1**

F401 **5** *6* **Ultragold (FR)**[14] [4254] 8-10-5 **131**..................(t) PaddyBrennan 129
(Colin Tizzard) *chsd ldrs: led 3 out tl 2 out: sn wknd* **8/1**

-005 **6** *12* **Generous Ransom (IRE)**[84] [3038] 8-10-10 **136**..........(p) NicodeBoinville 121
(Nick Gifford) *towards rr: rdn and hdwy 12th: in tch and drvn along 4 out: wknd 2 out* **8/1**

3160 **7** *5* **Art Mauresque (FR)**[84] [3031] 6-11-4 **144**........................ NickScholfield 125
(Paul Nicholls) *mid-div: outpcd 12th: n.d after* **5/1**[1]

F52F **P** **Off The Ground (IRE)**[84] [3036] 10-10-11 **137**........................ TomScudamore
(Charlie Longsdon) *prom: mstke 4th: wknd 10th: losing pl whn mstke next: t.o whn p.u bef 4 out* **20/1**

15-3 **P** **Shutthefrontdoor (IRE)**[119] [2333] 9-11-12 **152**..........(t) BarryGeraghty
(Jonjo O'Neill) *racd wd: dropped to rr 6th: sn rdn along and t.o: p.u bef 12th* **12/1**

-3P3 **P** **Laser Hawk (IRE)**[42] [3747] 9-10-1 **127**........................ PaulMoloney
(Evan Williams) *led: mstke 6th (water): blnd and hdd 12th: 6th and btn whn blnd and p.u 4 out* **10/1**

01P4 **P** **Un Beau Roman (FR)**[21] [4114] 8-10-11 **137**........................ TomO'Brien
(Paul Henderson) *in tch: lost pl 6th: sn bhd: t.o whn p.u bef 3 out* **33/1**

F **Vicomte Du Seuil (FR)**[32] 7-10-8 **134**..................(t) JacquesRicou
(Emmanuel Clayeux, France) *bhd: last whn blnd bdly 1st and 3rd: fell 12th* **14/1**

4100 **P** **Little Jon**[64] [3406] 8-11-3 **143**........................ NoelFehily
(Nigel Twiston-Davies) *mid-div: mstkes 6th (water) and 7th: blnd and p.u 12th* **15/2**[3]

5m 8.9s (5.90) **Going Correction** +0.625s/f (Soft) **13** Ran SP% **117.3**
Speed ratings: **113,111,111,109,107 102,100,, , ,**
CSF £71.70 CT £1338.77 TOTE £9.00: £2.70, £2.90, £7.90; EX 65.10 Trifecta £2300.20.
Owner Mr And Mrs J D Cotton **Bred** Pierre De Maleissye Melun Et Al **Trained** Ditcheat, Somerset

FOCUS
Due to rail movements this race was run over 32yds further than advertised. Often a competitive handicap, several had their chance in the straight and Paul Nicholls was training the winner for the eighth time in 11 years. A step up from the winner, with the second and third setting the level.

4486 MOORE OF DEVIZES LTD SUPPORTING GREATWOOD NOVICES' H'CAP HURDLE (8 hdls) 2m 69y
4:00 (4:01) (Class 4) (0-120,120) 4-Y-0+ **£4,548** (£1,335; £667; £333)

Form / RPR

F6F3 **1** **Bingo D'Olivate (FR)**[26] [4026] 5-11-6 **114**........................ WayneHutchinson 123+
(Noel Williams) *chsd ldrs: led appr 2 out: rdn clr appr last: comf* **14/1**

F03 **2** *8* **King Muro**[59] [3487] 6-11-4 **112**..................(t) PaddyBrennan 112+
(Fergal O'Brien) *mstke 1st: travelled strly towards rr: smooth hdwy 3 out: trckd wnr on bit next: rdn and fnd little appr last* **3/1**[1]

0421 **3** *12* **Muthabir (IRE)**[23] [4065] 6-11-12 **120**........................ IanPopham 110
(Richard Phillips) *hld up in 5th: mstke 1st: outpcd fr 3 out: wnt modest 3rd appr last* **7/2**[2]

U2 **4** *3* **Ikrapol (FR)**[22] [4104] 4-11-3 **119**..................(t) TomScudamore 96
(David Pipe) *led: racd freely and restrained in front: hit 3rd: hdd 3 out: sn wknd* **15/2**

14CP **5** *¾* **Itsnowcato**[70] [3238] 5-11-7 **115**........................ NicodeBoinville 99
(Ben Pauling) *trckd ldrs: led 3 out: sn hdd & wknd* **7/2**[2]

0 **6** *18* **Blackfire (FR)**[68] [3318] 4-11-4 **120**........................ JoshuaMoore 78
(Jonjo O'Neill) *prom tl wknd appr 3 out* **25/1**

1334 **7** *10* **Sikandar (IRE)**[27] [4012] 4-10-12 **114**........................ DannyCook 62
(Brian Ellison) *in rr: nt fluent 2nd and 3rd: n.d fr 5th* **4/1**[3]

4m 20.6s (10.60) **Going Correction** +0.35s/f (Yiel)
WFA 4 from 5yo+ 7lb **7** Ran SP% **111.7**
Speed ratings (Par 105): **87,83,77,75,75 66,61**
CSF £54.07 CT £180.48 TOTE £25.70: £6.90, £1.80; EX 52.50 Trifecta £252.60.
Owner Didntt Partnership **Bred** Jean-Philippe Rivoire **Trained** Blewbury, Oxon

FOCUS
Due to rail movements this race was run over 82yds further than advertised. No great gallop on early and yet the finished tired, with only the winner seeing it out with much purpose. Seemingly a big step up from him.

4487 BETVICTOR SUPPORTING GREATWOOD NOVICES' LIMITED H'CAP CHASE (FOR THE JACKY UPTON TROPHY) (15 fncs) 2m 2f 64y
4:35 (4:36) (Class 3) (0-125,124) 5-Y-0+ **£7,147** (£2,098; £1,049; £524)

Form / RPR

561P **1** **Johnny Og**[35] [3849] 7-11-8 **124**..................(b) AndrewTinkler 134+
(Martin Keighley) *mde all: sn clr: 10 l clr ent st: tiring appr last: hld on gamely* **8/1**

311U **2** *1 ¾* **Exmoor Mist**[22] [4098] 8-11-3 **119**..................(t) IanPopham 126
(Victor Dartnall) *chsd ldrs: wnt 2nd at 10th: 10 l bhd wnr ent st: grad clsd fr 2 out: a hld* **4/1**[2]

5232 **3** *9* **Trojan Star (IRE)**[22] [4098] 6-10-5 **110**..................(tp) TomBellamy[(3)] 107
(Kim Bailey) *t.k.h in 5th: wnt fair 3rd at 11th: no imp fr 3 out* **8/1**

-P1P **4** *57* **Royal Guardsman (IRE)**[42] [3733] 9-11-8 **124**........................ GavinSheehan 64
(Ali Stronge) *prom tl blnd bdly 2nd: dropped to rr 5th: no ch fr 10th* **4/1**[2]

60-P **P** **So Oscar (IRE)**[143] [1911] 8-10-6 **108**..................(t) ConorShoemark[(3)]
(Fergal O'Brien) *chsd ldrs: outpcd 9th: 5th and btn whn blnd 11th: bhd whn p.u bef 4 out* **20/1**

-354 **P** **Florida Calling (IRE)**[86] [2986] 7-10-12 **114**........................ PaddyBrennan
(Tom George) *chsd wnr 2nd: blnd 3rd: lost 2nd at 10th: wknd next: 4th and no ch whn p.u bef 3 out* **7/2**[1]

25-1 **P** **Hughesie (IRE)**[116] [2424] 7-11-7 **123**........................ PaulMoloney
(Evan Williams) *sn towards rr: struggling 1/2-way: wl bhd whn p.u bef 4 out* **5/1**[3]

1456 **P** **Take A Break (FR)**[103] [2688] 5-11-6 **122**..................(tp) TomScudamore
(Nigel Hawke) *hld up: j. slowly 6th: modest 6th whn blnd 10th: wl bhd whn p.u bef next* **20/1**

4m 54.0s (24.00) **Going Correction** +0.625s/f (Soft) **8** Ran SP% **110.6**
Speed ratings: **71,70,66,40,**
CSF £38.17 CT £252.20 TOTE £9.70: £2.70, £1.40, £2.10; EX 38.00 Trifecta £225.90.
Owner T Hanlon M Boothright S Hanlon N Martin **Bred** R T Crellin **Trained** Condicote, Gloucs
■ Stewards' Enquiry : Ian Popham two-day ban; used whip above the permitted level (19th-20th Mar)

FOCUS
Due to rail movements this was run over 23yds further than advertised. Only half of the eight runners managed to complete in a chase that was run at a good gallop with slow finishing fractions. The winner is rated back to his best.

4488 DBS SPRING SALES BUMPER (A STANDARD OPEN NATIONAL HUNT FLAT RACE) 2m 69y
5:10 (5:10) (Class 2) 4-5-Y-0

£29,505 (£9,840; £4,920; £2,455; £1,480; £985)

Form / RPR

1 **1** **Sam's Adventure**[28] [4001] 4-10-13 0........................ DannyCook 116
(Brian Ellison) *trckd ldr: led after 6f: hrd rdn and disp ld fnl 3f: gamely* **4/1**[2]

21 **2** *nse* **Bags Groove (IRE)**[36] [3847] 5-11-7 0..................(t) NoelFehily 124
(Harry Fry) *prom: disp ld fnl 3f: kpt on wl: jst denied* **7/1**

1 **3** *1 ¼* **Sir Antony Browne**[22] [4102] 4-10-13 0........................ WayneHutchinson 115
(Alan King) *in tch: drvn to press ldrs wl over 1f out: kpt on fnl f* **9/4**[1]

22 **4** *6* **Pure Vision (IRE)**[100] [2729] 5-11-3 0..................(t) BarryGeraghty 114
(Anthony Honeyball) *led: green on 1st bnd and early in bk st: hdd after 6f: prom tl wknd over 1f out* **10/1**

5 *¾* **Silver Kayf** 4-10-9 0........................ TomScudamore 104
(Kim Bailey) *mid-div: lost pl 7f out: styd on wl fnl 2f* **16/1**

231 **6** *½* **Boudry (FR)**[7] [4371] 5-11-7 0........................ GavinSheehan 116
(Warren Greatrex) *t.k.h in rr: gd hdwy 3f out: wknd over 1f out* **7/1**

7 *½* **Twist On Ginge (IRE)** 4-10-6 0........................ RyanHatch[(3)] 103
(Nigel Twiston-Davies) *chsd ldrs: rdn 4f out: btn over 2f out* **28/1**

2 **8** *2 ¼* **Prime Venture (IRE)**[82] [3082] 5-11-2 0........................ ConorRing[(5)] 113
(Evan Williams) *bhd: rdn 4f out: styd on fnl 2f* **20/1**

9 *4 ½* **Oxwich Bay (IRE)** 4-10-9 0........................ AdamWedge 97
(Evan Williams) *bhd: rdn 4f out: n.d* **66/1**

3-1 **10** *¾* **Cultivator**[126] [2188] 5-11-7 0..................[1] NicodeBoinville 108
(Nicky Henderson) *hld up in midfield: promising hdwy on bit over 3f out: hrd rdn and wknd 2f out* **6/1**[3]

11 *10* **Tara View** 5-10-7 0........................ TomBellamy[(3)] 87
(Alan King) *a towards rr: rdn and n.d fnl 3f* **25/1**

12 *¾* **Louis' Vac Pouch (IRE)** 4-10-9 0........................ TomO'Brien 85
(Philip Hobbs) *t.k.h: in tch tl wknd 4f out* **33/1**

13 *¾* **Cosmic King (FR)** 4-10-4 0........................ DanielHiskett[(5)] 84
(Richard Phillips) *mid-div: effrt 4f out: wknd 2f out* **50/1**

14 *62* **Legendara** 4-10-2 0........................ JamesBest 15
(Charlie Longsdon) *in tch: clsd on ldrs 7f out: wknd 4f out: sn wl bhd* **66/1**

4m 13.0s (8.70) **Going Correction** +0.35s/f (Yiel)
WFA 4 from 5yo 7lb **14** Ran SP% **125.0**
Speed ratings: **92,91,91,88,87 87,87,86,84,83 78,78,77,46**
CSF £31.51 TOTE £5.60: £2.00, £2.90, £1.40; EX 34.30 Trifecta £138.40.
Owner Mrs J A Martin **Bred** R Johnson **Trained** Norton, N Yorks
■ Stewards' Enquiry : Gavin Sheehan gelding wore earplugs to start which were taken out
Tom O'Brien vet said gelding lost right-hind shoe

FOCUS
Due to rail movement this was run over 82yds further than advertised. Traditionally one of the better bumpers run throughout the season. They went just a steady gallop but the race should again work out well.
T/Jkpt: Not won. T/Plt: £421.70 to a £1 stake. Pool of £156773.26 - 271.36 winning tickets.
T/Qpdt: £66.30 to a £1 stake. Pool of £9798.88 - 109.30 winning tickets. **Lee McKenzie**

2149 **STRATFORD** (L-H)

Saturday, March 5

OFFICIAL GOING: Soft (heavy in places on chase course; chs 5.3, hdl 5.7)

Wind: Fresh across Weather: Cloudy with sunny spells

4489 BET WITH TATTERSALLS BOOKMAKERS JUVENILE MAIDEN HURDLE (8 hdls) 2m 70y

2:20 (2:23) (Class 4) 4-Y-O **£3,898** (£1,144; £572; £286)

Form				RPR
	1		**Sleep Easy**[162] 4-11-0 0 MarkQuinlan (Neil Mulholland) *chsd ldrs: led wl bef last: sn clr: easily* **5/1**[3]	114+
44	2	7	**Deebaj (IRE)**[14] 4243 4-11-0 0 ConorO'Farrell (Richard Price) *a.p: rdn to chse wnr wl bef last: styd on same pce* **16/1**	108+
	3	9	**Red Tornado (FR)**[151] 4-11-0 0 HarrySkelton (Dan Skelton) *chsd ldrs: rdn after 2 out: wkng whn lft 3rd last* **5/2**[2]	97
243	4	17	**For Goodness Sake (IRE)**[13] 4271 4-10-0 112 ConorWalsh(7) (Warren Greatrex) *chsd ldr tl led 3 out: rdn: hdd & wknd wl bef last* **7/4**[1]	76
P-P2	5	8	**Grisedenuit (FR)**[67] 3338 4-10-0 0 JoshWall(7) (Trevor Wall) *hld up: hdwy appr 3 out: rdn and wknd wl bef last* **100/1**	65
6400	6	26	**Coco Flower (FR)**[13] 4271 4-10-4 0 KillianMoore(3) (Alex Hales) *hld up: bhd fr 4th* **250/1**	39
3	7	15	**Samdibien (FR)**[19] 4162 4-11-0 0 RichieMcLernon (Sam Thomas) *led: hdd 3 out: sn rdn and wknd* **25/1**	31
	P		**Recently Acquired**[203] 4-10-9 0 JackSherwood(5) (David Loder) *hld up: rdn after 4th: wknd bef 3 out: whn p.u bef 2 out* **14/1**	
P	U		**Cabernet D'Alene (FR)**[69] 3279 4-10-9 0 LizzieKelly(5) (Nick Williams) *hld up: hdwy 3 out: rdn after next: 12th l 3rd and btn whn blnd and uns rdr last* **7/1**	99+

4m 7.5s (11.50) **Going Correction** +1.275s/f (Heavy) **9 Ran SP% 111.9**

Speed ratings: 122,118,114,105,101 88,81, ,

CSF £70.63 TOTE £6.30: £2.20, £3.10, £1.10; EX 82.80 Trifecta £348.30.

Owner Tony Bloom **Bred** Meon Valley Stud **Trained** Limpley Stoke, Wilts

FOCUS

The hurdle track was railed on the inner most line. Quite an interesting opener, won in good style by a hurdling newcomer. who should win again. The time was fast compared to the next.

4490 SUPPORT YOUR ON COURSE BOOKMAKER CONDITIONAL JOCKEYS' (S) H'CAP HURDLE (8 hdls) 2m 70y

2:55 (2:56) (Class 5) (0-100,100) 4-7-Y-O **£3,249** (£954; £477; £238)

Form				RPR
2450	1		**Symphony Of Pearls**[94] 2850 5-10-2 81 JamieInsole(5) (Dai Burchell) *chsd ldrs: led after 3 out: clr after next: shkn up whn j. slowly last: rdn out* **9/2**[2]	87+
24-0	2	3 1/4	**Perfect Summer (IRE)**[40] 3777 6-11-4 100 (v) TobyWheeler(8) (Ian Williams) *chsd ldr tl led after 5th: blnd next: sn hdd: nt fluent 2 out: sn rdn and looked reluctant: kpt on to go 2nd wl bef last: nt get to wnr* **9/4**[1]	101
00-0	3	16	**Petergate**[66] 3368 5-10-5 82 (p) ConorSmith(3) (Nigel Hawke) *chsd ldrs: ev ch appr 2 out: sn rdn: wknd wl bef last* **15/2**[3]	67
PP40	4	1 3/4	**League Of His Own (IRE)**[36] 3841 7-10-0 74 oh10 (t) MauriceLinehan (Claire Dyson) *hld up: hdwy 5th: rdn and wknd wl bef last* **50/1**	56
0P2P	5	14	**Poetic Presence (IRE)**[92] 2876 6-10-0 74 oh5 (v) JamieBargary (Adrian Wintle) *sn pushed along in rr: bhd fr 3rd: j. slowly 5th* **14/1**	42
P640	6	48	**Aristocracy**[11] 4291 5-11-2 90 (b) ThomasGarner (Sally Randell) *sn pushed along to ld: rdn whn blnd 5th: sn hdd & wknd* **9/2**[2]	10
05	7	26	**Social Climber (IRE)**[42] 1866 4-10-10 100 (b) PhilipDonovan(8) (Fergal O'Brien) *prom: rdn after 4th: wknd next: bhd whn blnd last* **8/1**	
5-6P	P		**Shareni (IRE)**[22] 4099 7-11-0 91 (t) HarryCobden(3) (Zoe Davison) *in rr and rdn 3rd: lost tch after next: bhd whn p.u bef 2 out* **12/1**	

4m 17.0s (21.00) **Going Correction** +1.275s/f (Heavy)

WFA 4 from 5yo+ 7lb **8 Ran SP% 112.7**

Speed ratings: 98,96,88,87,80 56,43,

CSF £15.04 CT £72.07 TOTE £5.50: £3.60, £1.10, £2.10; EX 18.10 Trifecta £86.70.

Owner Brian Williams **Bred** Thomas R Pearson **Trained** Briery Hill, Blaenau Gwent

FOCUS

The hurdle track was railed on the inner most line. Most of these appeared to be out of form, so this was a weak contest even for selling grade. Every runner was wearing headgear of some description. Arguably a pb from the winner, but the time was very slow.

4491 BILL BOOTH 90TH BIRTHDAY CELEBRATION NOVICES' H'CAP CHASE (11 fncs 4 omitted) 2m 4f 205y

3:30 (3:31) (Class 4) (0-105,105) 5-Y-O+ **£7,655** (£2,377; £1,279)

Form				RPR
560	1		**Ballyvaughn (IRE)**[97] 2807 6-11-5 97 HarrySkelton (Caroline Bailey) *a.p: chsd ldr 4th tl led 3 out: mstke next: hdd and rdn sn after: 2 l down and styng on same pce whn lft wl clr last* **5/1**[3]	102+
5-PU	2	34	**Ghost Of A Smile (IRE)**[53] 3569 8-11-5 97 RichieMcLernon (Ian Williams) *hld up: wknd appr 8th: lft remote 2nd last* **9/2**[2]	65
0316	3	76	**Guaracha**[37] 3816 5-11-12 105 RhysFlint (Alexandra Dunn) *hld up: hdwy 7th: wknd next: lft remote 3rd last* **14/1**	
513	P		**Derryogue (IRE)**[86] 2994 11-10-9 94 (t) HarryCobden(7) (Zoe Davison) *mid-div: hdwy appr 8th: wkng whn stmbld 2 out: poor 3rd whn p.u bef last* **10/1**	
P565	P		**Walkabout Creek (IRE)**[68] 3314 9-10-7 88 (v) BenPoste(3) (Derek Frankland) *prom: rdn after 6th: wknd next: bhd whn p.u bef 8th* **20/1**	
1/PU	P		**My Miss Lucy**[17] 4186 10-11-5 100 MauriceLinehan(3) (Richard Phillips) *hld up: bhd fr 7th: p.u bef next* **14/1**	
0P3P	P		**Pursuitofhappiness (IRE)**[56] 3516 8-11-1 93 (p) MarkQuinlan (Neil Mulholland) *chsd ldr after 1st tl 4th: remained handy tl rdn: wknd and p.u bef 8th* **6/1**	
5152	P		**Pandy Wells**[13] 4275 7-10-2 87 ArchieBellamy(7) (Graeme McPherson) *hld up: mstkes 6th and next: rdn and wknd sn after: bhd whn p.u bef 2 out* **5/2**[1]	
5F0	F		**Lord Ballim (FR)**[51] 3592 6-11-9 101 (t) ConorO'Farrell (Nigel Hawke) *led to 3 out: led again after next: 2 l ld and rdn whn fell last* **12/1**	110+

5m 51.8s (36.80) **Going Correction** +1.70s/f (Heavy) **9 Ran SP% 112.6**

Speed ratings: 97,84,55, , ,

CSF £27.58 CT £290.88 TOTE £5.90: £2.10, £1.60, £2.80; EX 36.00 Trifecta £187.60.

Owner C W Booth **Bred** David Pim **Trained** Holdenby, Northants

FOCUS

54 yards was added to the actual race distance, and fence 2 was bypassed due to work done on the take off and landing. Fence 3 was also bypassed due to standing water. The gallop set by Lord Ballim seemed strong, and saw the field strung out early. Not form to be confident about.

4492 GET VALUE ON COURSE AT STRATFORD H'CAP HURDLE (QUALIFIER FOR THE CHALLENGER STAYING HURDLE) (11 hdls) 2m 6f 7y

4:05 (4:06) (Class 4) (0-120,120) 4-Y-O+ **£6,388** (£1,928; £993; £526)

Form				RPR
P-45	1		**Moss On The Mill**[65] 3383 8-10-9 108 (p) CiaranGethings(5) (Tom George) *w ldr tl settled into 2nd after 5th: led 3 out: rdn appr last: c clr flat* **7/2**[2]	113+
P140	2	14	**Uncle Tone (IRE)**[111] 2513 7-11-12 120 MichealNolan (Tim Vaughan) *prom: chsd wnr and mstke last: eased whn btn flat* **10/1**	120+
2114	3	23	**Butlergrove King (IRE)**[86] 2988 7-10-6 107 MissJodieHughes(7) (Dai Burchell) *led: blnd and hdd 3 out: rdn and wknd wl bef last* **4/1**[3]	79
62-P	4	53	**Seas Of Green**[97] 2812 9-10-9 108 BridgetAndrews(5) (Paul Cowley) *hld up and bhd: effrt appr 3 out: hmpd and wknd next* **12/1**	23
1233	B		**Bonnet's Vino**[35] 3866 8-11-2 115 JamieBargary(5) (Pam Sly) *chsd ldrs: pushed along after 8th: cl 5th but rdn whn b.d 2 out* **11/2**	108+
00	F		**Kentucky Star (FR)**[112] 2499 7-11-7 115 HarrySkelton (Dan Skelton) *hld up in tch: racd keenly: cl 3rd and gng wl whn fell 2 out* **7/4**[1]	118+

6m 0.6s (32.50) **Going Correction** +1.275s/f (Heavy) **6 Ran SP% 110.8**

Speed ratings (Par 105): **91,85,77,58,**

CSF £32.77 CT £137.16 TOTE £5.10: £2.70, £3.60; EX 23.70 Trifecta £180.50.

Owner Mr & Mrs R Cornock **Bred** S D Hemstock **Trained** Slad, Gloucs

FOCUS

The hurdle track was railed on the inner most line. Probably just an ordinary race for the level. The pace was modest early. The form is rated through the eased-down runner-up.

4493 STRATFORD BOOKMAKERS DAY H'CAP CHASE (QUALIFIER FOR THE CHALLENGER STAYING CHASE SERIES FINAL) (13 fncs 4 omitted) 2m 6f 125y

4:40 (4:41) (Class 4) (0-120,118) 5-Y-O **£7,346** (£2,217; £1,142; £605; £15)

Form				RPR
33F2	1		**Bodega**[4] 4420 8-11-0 113 TobyWheeler(7) (Ian Williams) *hld up: hdwy 4th: led after 2 out: rdn out* **11/4**[2]	128+
1P21	2	7	**Thinger Licht (FR)**[6] 4380 7-11-3 114 7ex (p) BridgetAndrews(5) (Dan Skelton) *hld up in tch: chsd ldr 10th: led after 3 out: rdn and hdd after next: ev ch last: no ex flat* **2/1**[1]	122
33FP	3	24	**Vice Et Vertu (FR)**[37] 3824 7-11-9 115 (b[1]) RichieMcLernon (Henry Daly) *led: mstke 3 out: sn hdd: rdn and wknd after next* **5/1**	101
3110	4	12	**Sunny Ledgend**[15] 4230 11-11-5 118 MrJMartin(7) (Andrew J Martin) *chsd ldr to appr 10th: wknd 2 out* **14/1**	89
145	F		**Cruchain (IRE)**[162] 1641 13-11-4 115 (p) FreddieMitchell(5) (Dai Burchell) *hld up: wknd 10th: bhd whn fell 2 out* **33/1**	
5-23	P		**Colin's Brother**[99] 2758 6-11-6 117 JamieBargary(5) (Nigel Twiston-Davies) *chsd ldrs: nt fluent 4th: hit next: sn lost pl: j.big 6th: reminders after 9th: wknd appr 3 out: bhd whn p.u bef last* **3/1**[3]	

6m 14.5s (35.30) **Going Correction** +1.70s/f (Heavy) **6 Ran SP% 111.3**

Speed ratings: 106,103,95,91,

CSF £8.90 CT £23.19 TOTE £3.80: £2.00, £1.40; EX 8.50 Trifecta £39.00.

Owner Paul Williams **Bred** Mrs Claire Massey **Trained** Portway, Worcs

FOCUS

54 yards was added to the advertised race distance and fence 2 was bypassed due to work done on the take off and landing. Fence 3 was also bypassed due to standing water. The tempo only increased significantly on the final circuit. There's a case for rating the form a few pounds higher through the second.

4494 BET WITH COURSE BOOKMAKERS MAIDEN HURDLE (9 hdls) 2m 2f 148y

5:15 (5:16) (Class 4) 5-Y-O+ **£3,898** (£1,144; £572; £286)

Form				RPR
13	1		**Three Ways**[78] 3145 5-11-0 0 (t) MichealNolan (Jamie Snowden) *a.p: rdn to ld and edgd lft appr last: styd on* **5/2**[1]	109+
34	2	1 1/4	**One Style (FR)**[15] 4235 6-10-9 117 CharlieDeutsch(5) (Venetia Williams) *a.p: chsd ldr 6th: led 3 out: rdn: hdd and nt clr run appr last: swtchd rt: rallied and ev ch flat: nt qckn towards fin* **7/2**[3]	108
-435	3	1 3/4	**Officer Hoolihan**[17] 4176 6-10-9 0 AlanJohns(5) (Tim Vaughan) *hld up: hdwy appr 2 out: rdn to go 3rd bef last: styd on: nt rch ldrs* **16/1**	106
354	4	nk	**Mister Kalanisi (IRE)**[29] 3976 7-11-0 0 HarrySkelton (Dan Skelton) *chsd ldr tl led 6th: hdd 3 out: rdn after next: outpcd wl bef last: styd on u.p flat* **3/1**[2]	105
5-60	5	28	**Maybell**[9] 4317 5-10-4 0 JamesBanks(3) (Alex Hales) *hld up: blnd 2 out: nvr on terms* **28/1**	75
00P	6	14	**Hardtorock (IRE)**[92] 2879 7-10-11 0 (t) KieronEdgar(3) (Liam Corcoran) *hld up: nvr nrr* **100/1**	66
4	7	2 1/2	**Hang Fire (IRE)**[31] 3920 6-10-7 0 LeeEdwards (Tony Carroll) *mid-div: dropped to rr 6th: sn bhd* **100/1**	53
43	8	1/2	**Mr Banks (IRE)**[70] 3226 5-11-0 0 CharliePoste (Paul Webber) *prom: blnd 1st: lost pl after 5th: wknd next* **8/1**	60
00	9	6	**Badger Run (IRE)**[107] 2597 5-11-0 0 MattieBatchelor (Pat Murphy) *hld up: hdwy 6th: wknd 2 out* **200/1**	54
	10	54	**Urban Moon (IRE)**[144] 5-11-0 0 RichieMcLernon (Jonjo O'Neill) *led: racd keenly: hdd 6th: sn wknd* **10/1**	
3/40	P		**Subordinate (GER)**[114] 2460 7-11-0 0 (t) JamieMoore (Emma Lavelle) *hld up: hdwy after 6th: wknd appr 2 out: bhd whn p.u and dismntd bef last* **20/1**	
36-	P		**Welcome Bach (IRE)**[355] 4809 7-11-0 0 ConorO'Farrell (Liam Corcoran) *sn prom: stl gng okay in 4th whn nt fluent 2 out: sn p.u and dismntd* **17/2**	

4m 52.2s (20.70) **Going Correction** +1.275s/f (Heavy) **12 Ran SP% 123.1**

Speed ratings: 107,106,105,105,93 87,86,86,84,61 ,

CSF £11.89 TOTE £3.80: £1.90, £1.70, £4.70; EX 14.90 Trifecta £171.70.

Owner David Brownlow **Bred** S D Hemstock **Trained** Lambourn, Berks

FOCUS

The hurdle track is railed on the inner most line. Just an ordinary maiden event. There'a a case for rating the race up to 6lb higher through the second.

T/Plt: £170.10 to a £1 stake. Pool: £58,485.76 - 250.91 winning tickets T/Qpdt: £43.80 to a £1 stake. Pool: £4,067.36 - 68.70 winning tickets **Colin Roberts**

4495 - 4501a (Foreign Racing) - See Raceform Interactive

4317
HUNTINGDON (R-H)
Sunday, March 6

OFFICIAL GOING: Soft (heavy in places)
Wind: Light behind Weather: Overcast

4502 BRAD MCKELLAR 50TH BIRTHDAY MAIDEN HURDLE (8 hdls) 1m 7f 171y
2:00 (2:01) (Class 4) 4-Y-0+ **£3,249** (£954; £477; £238)

Form RPR
-633 **1** **Centurius**[16] 4233 6-11-4 112 AidanColeman 109+
(Venetia Williams) *hld up: hdwy after 5th: hit 3 out: chsd ldr bef next: rdn to ld flat: styd on wl* **5/4**[1]
3 **2** 2 3/4 **Red Hammer**[136] 2032 4-10-10 0 DarylJacob 96+
(Nicky Henderson) *hld up: plld hrd: hdwy to ld appr 4th: rdn and hdd flat: no ex* **5/4**[1]
3 14 **My Mistress (IRE)**[115] 4-10-3 0 JackQuinlan 77
(Phil McEntee) *chsd ldr to appr 4th: remained handy: rdn and ev ch appr 2 out: wknd bef last* **33/1**
-4P5 **4** 1 **Terra Firma**[18] 4182 6-11-4 0 BrendanPowell 91
(Claire Dyson) *prom tl rdn and wknd appr 2 out: hit last* **22/1**[3]
6P **5** shd **Levelling**[9] 4345 4-10-3 0 HarrySkelton 75
(Dan Skelton) *hld up: rdn and wknd appr 2 out* **9/1**[2]
5 **6** 10 **Winola**[16] 4228 6-10-11 0 JoshuaMoore 72
(Charlie Wallis) *led: hdd appr 4th: rdn and wknd appr 2 out* **40/1**
00P- **7** 23 **Flamingo Beat**[517] 1783 6-11-4 80 TrevorWhelan 56
(Christine Dunnett) *prom tl rdn and wknd after 3 out* **100/1**

4m 17.6s (22.70) **Going Correction** +1.20s/f (Heavy)
WFA 4 from 5yo+ 7lb **7 Ran SP% 109.6**
Speed ratings (Par 105): **91,89,82,82,82 77,65**
CSF £2.76 TOTE £2.70: £1.60, £1.10; EX 3.90 Trifecta £33.30.
Owner Andrew Brooks & Julian Taylor **Bred** D J Bloodstock, G Roddick & Wrottesley Ltd **Trained** Kings Caple, H'fords

FOCUS
There were 22 non-runners on the card, mostly due to a change in the going. All bends were moved, and the hurdle rail was out 14yds, except the bend into home straight which was out 20yds, adding approximately 145yds to this race. This didn't look a strong race of its type.

4503 RACING UK HD ON SKY432 TOMORROW H'CAP CHASE (16 fncs) 2m 3f 189y
2:30 (2:32) (Class 4) (0-105,102) 5-Y-0+ **£3,898** (£1,144; £572)

Form RPR
-PP2 **1** **Alberto's Dream**[24] 4073 7-11-5 102 MrJNixon(7) 110+
(Tom Symonds) *chsd ldrs: led after 2 out: rdn out* **7/4**[2]
14P1 **2** 8 **Albatros De Guye (FR)**[24] 4073 6-11-0 90 (tp) JeremiahMcGrath 90
(Anna Newton-Smith) *led to 12th: led again appr 2 out: rdn and hdd after 2 out: no ex last* **6/4**[1]
-53P **3** 25 **Virtuose Du Chenet (FR)**[17] 4214 7-10-10 91 (p) CharlieDeutsch(5) 69
(Venetia Williams) *w ldr tl led 12th: rdn and hdd appr 2 out: wknd bef last* **5/2**[3]

5m 32.7s (27.40) **Going Correction** +1.00s/f (Soft) **3 Ran SP% 104.9**
Speed ratings: **85,81,71**
CSF £4.16 TOTE £2.60; EX 3.40 Trifecta £3.60.
Owner Wallys Dream Syndicate **Bred** P J Andrews **Trained** Harewood End, H'fords

FOCUS
Chase rail on inner most position. A moderate event, with the topweight 3lb below the ceiling rating.

4504 ALL 28 CHELTENHAM RACES ON RACINGUK H'CAP HURDLE (10 hdls) 2m 4f 145y
3:00 (3:03) (Class 5) (0-100,100) 4-Y-0+ **£2,599** (£763; £381; £190)

Form RPR
-006 **1** **Champagne Chaser**[133] 2093 6-11-11 99 RichardJohnson 117+
(Tim Vaughan) *a.p: chsd ldr 6th: led after next: clr appr last: easily* **2/1**[1]
-453 **2** 10 **Vinegar Hill**[94] 2868 7-10-12 86 AndrewTinkler 83
(Anna Brooks) *chsd ldrs: mstke 5th: rdn and lost pl 7th: rallied appr 2 out: r.o flat* **11/2**[2]
U05P **3** 4 1/2 **Double Court (IRE)**[80] 3128 5-9-9 74 oh5 (v) JamieBargary(5) 68
(Nigel Twiston-Davies) *chsd ldrs: wnt 2nd after 7th: ev ch and mstke 3 out: sn rdn: nt fluent next: wknd last* **14/1**
65P5 **4** 13 **Max The Minister**[51] 3608 6-11-12 100 TomO'Brien 80
(Hughie Morrison) *hld up: hdwy appr 3 out: rdn and wknd bef next* **6/1**[3]
00P/ **5** 2 **Lombardy Boy (IRE)**[854] 2253 11-10-2 76 TrevorWhelan 54
(Michael Banks) *hld up: hdwy 7th: wknd 3 out* **33/1**
6U0U **6** 3 1/4 **Toast And Jam (IRE)**[10] 4318 7-9-9 74 oh1 (t) DanielHiskett(5) 47
(Claire Dyson) *hld up: sme hdwy appr 3 out: sn wknd* **28/1**
5/P2 **7** 1/2 **Clonusker (IRE)**[20] 4161 8-11-0 88 (t) LeightonAspell 61
(Linda Jewell) *hld up: hdwy 6th: rdn and wknd appr 3 out* **13/2**
P6U0 **8** 31 **Friendly Society (IRE)**[124] 2262 11-11-7 98 (b) JamesBanks(3) 40
(Noel Williams) *w ldr: racd keenly: led 4th: mstke next: hdd after 7th: sn rdn and wknd* **9/1**
335- **U** **Stonemadforspeed (IRE)**[322] 8-11-2 97 HarryTeal(7)
(Roger Teal) *hld up: plld hrd and wnt prom whn stmbld on landing and uns rdr 2nd* **10/1**
/0-P **P** **The Perfect Crime (IRE)**[54] 3572 7-10-9 90 TobyWheeler(7)
(Ian Williams) *led to 4th: remained handy tl rdn and wknd appr 3 out: bhd whn p.u bef next* **20/1**

5m 39.0s (28.40) **Going Correction** +1.20s/f (Heavy) **10 Ran SP% 113.2**
Speed ratings (Par 103): **93,89,87,82,81 80,80,68, ,**
CSF £12.92 CT £117.57 TOTE £3.00: £1.40, £1.70, £3.80; EX 15.30 Trifecta £126.10.
Owner Mrs Monica O'Sullivan **Bred** A M Armitage **Trained** Aberthin, Vale of Glamorgan

FOCUS
All bends were moved, and the hurdle rail was out 14yds, except the bend into home straight which was out 20yds, adding approximately 169yds to this race. This appeared a weak race, and the favourite won with tons to spare.

4505 RACINGUK.COM/HD CAMBRIDGESHIRE NATIONAL H'CAP CHASE (25 fncs) 3m 6f 162y
3:30 (3:31) (Class 3) (0-125,120) 5-Y-0+ **£9,985** (£3,100; £1,669)

Form RPR
-F14 **1** **Rocky Bender (IRE)**[45] 3707 11-11-3 116 CharlieDeutsch(5) 121+
(Venetia Williams) *hld up in tch: nt fluent 18th: rdn after 3 out: chsd ldr bef next: edgd rt and styd on to ld towards fin* **7/2**[3]
2-P1 **2** 2 **Leg Iron (IRE)**[83] 3086 11-11-12 120 (p) LeightonAspell 121
(Sheena West) *hld up: hdwy to 13th: jnd ldr again after next: led 19th: rdn after 3 out: edgd rt flat: hdd towards fin* **9/1**
P413 **3** 7 **Arbeo (IRE)**[16] 4234 10-11-4 112 TomCannon 108
(Diana Grissell) *disp ld tl wnt on 13th: pushed along after 18th: hdd and nt fluent next: rdn and ev ch 3 out: styd on same pce fr next* **9/4**[2]
3512 **U** **Ballyrath (IRE)**[32] 3924 6-11-12 120 (p) SamTwiston-Davies
(Nigel Twiston-Davies) *chsd ldrs tl blnd and uns rdr 5th* **6/5**[1]

8m 38.4s (25.60) **Going Correction** +1.00s/f (Soft) **4 Ran SP% 108.4**
Speed ratings: **106,105,103,**
CSF £23.50 TOTE £5.00; EX 22.80 Trifecta £51.40.
Owner Miss V M Williams **Bred** B Deane **Trained** Kings Caple, H'fords
■ A new slot for this event, previously run in November.

FOCUS
Chase rail on inner most position. The tempo only increased on the final circuit for this small-field staying contest.

4506 BEN BULL 18TH BIRTHDAY H'CAP HURDLE (8 hdls) 1m 7f 171y
4:00 (4:02) (Class 4) (0-115,114) 4-Y-0+ **£3,249** (£954; £477; £238)

Form RPR
6400 **1** **Fields Of Glory (FR)**[60] 3487 6-11-0 102 RichardJohnson 111+
(Tim Vaughan) *chsd ldrs: led appr 2 out: mstke last: drvn out* **5/2**[1]
345- **2** nk **Ivanhoe**[135] 4298 6-11-7 109 NickScholfield 116
(Michael Blanshard) *hld up: hdwy 5th: chsd wnr 2 out: rdn and ev ch flat: r.o* **11/2**
26P4 **3** 5 **Christmas Twenty (IRE)**[31] 3949 6-11-9 111 (p) JoshuaMoore 115
(Stuart Edmunds) *trckd ldr: racd keenly: mstke 3rd: rdn appr 3 out: lost 2nd bef next: styd on same pce last* **7/2**[2]
11R3 **4** 7 **Notebook**[24] 4068 5-10-7 100 (p) ThomasCheesman(5) 97
(Martin Smith) *reluctant to post: led: j. slowly 1st: rdn and hdd appr 2 out: wknd last* **5/1**[3]
/-40 **5** 1/2 **Unex Modigliani (IRE)**[11] 3487 7-11-3 108 (t) JamesBanks(3) 103
(Derek Shaw) *hld up: racd keenly: shkn up after 3 out: nvr trbld ldrs* **12/1**
00/2 **6** 2 **Aldeburgh**[18] 3022 7-11-12 114 MarkGrant 108
(Nigel Twiston-Davies) *hld up: hdwy appr 3 out: rdn and wknd last* **7/1**
-1F0 **7** 38 **Honkytonktennessee (IRE)**[180] 1508 7-11-7 109 DaveCrosse 64
(Hugo Froud) *prom: hit 5th: sn rdn: wknd bef next* **14/1**

4m 11.8s (16.90) **Going Correction** +1.20s/f (Heavy) **7 Ran SP% 109.7**
Speed ratings (Par 105): **105,104,102,98,98 97,78**
CSF £15.25 CT £42.64 TOTE £3.60: £2.20, £4.10; EX 16.80 Trifecta £58.20.
Owner Pearn's Pharmacies Ltd **Bred** Woodcote Stud Limited **Trained** Aberthin, Vale of Glamorgan

FOCUS
All bends were moved, and the hurdle rail was out 14yds, except the bend into home straight which was out 20yds, adding approximately 145yds to this race. Probably an okay race for the level, but it developed into a bit of a dash to the line heading to three out.

4507 WALKING THE COURSES MARES' MAIDEN HURDLE (10 hdls) 2m 3f 137y
4:30 (4:33) (Class 4) 4-Y-0+ **£3,249** (£954; £477; £238)

Form RPR
52-2 **1** **Song Saa**[24] 4075 6-10-9 0 PaddyBrennan 107+
(Tom George) *hld up: hdwy after 6th: chsd ldr whn nt fluent 3 out: sn rdn: hit next: led and nt fluent last: drvn out* **Evs**[1]
1024 **2** 1 1/2 **Late Night Lily**[38] 3819 5-10-9 0 HarrySkelton 106+
(Dan Skelton) *racd keenly: trckd ldr tl led and mstke 4th: nt fluent next: hit 7th: j.rt 2 out: rdn and hdd appr last: unable qck towards fin* **Evs**[1]
P4 **3** 24 **Yur Next (IRE)**[7] 4382 8-10-9 0 TomCannon 80
(Alison Batchelor) *led: nt a fluent: hdd 4th: chsd ldr tl lost pl after 6th: wknd 3 out* **22/1**[2]
00-0 **4** 5 **Gray Wolf River**[18] 4182 5-10-6 0 JamesBanks(3) 75
(Richard Harper) *prom: racd keenly: chsd ldr after 6th tl appr next: rdn and wknd after 3 out* **40/1**[3]

5m 27.7s (28.70) **Going Correction** +1.20s/f (Heavy) **4 Ran SP% 106.8**
Speed ratings (Par 105): **90,89,79,77**
CSF £2.31 TOTE £2.00; EX 2.50 Trifecta £4.20.
Owner Sharon C Nelson & Georgie McGrath **Bred** Copernicus Bloodstock Agency Ltd **Trained** Slad, Gloucs

FOCUS
All bends were moved, and the hurdle rail was out 14yds, except bend into home straight which was out 20yds, adding approximately 169yds to this race. The betting suggested this was a match, and so it proved, the pair pulling miles clear.

4508 RACING UK HD LAUNCHES TOMORROW STANDARD OPEN NATIONAL HUNT FLAT RACE 1m 7f 171y
5:00 (5:04) (Class 6) 4-6-Y-0 **£1,624** (£477; £238; £119)

Form RPR
1 **Tolethorpe** 5-11-2 0 GavinSheehan 114+
(Harry Whittington) *chsd ldrs: shkn up over 4f out: led 3f out: c readily clr fnl 2f* **5/2**[2]
6-3 **2** 11 **Piton Pete (IRE)**[115] 2460 5-11-2 0 LeightonAspell 102
(Oliver Sherwood) *hld up: rdn to chse wnr over 2f: styd on same pce* **5/1**[3]
3 **3** 11 **Kafella**[99] 2777 4-10-8 0 HarrySkelton 83
(Dan Skelton) *led: chsd ldr tl wnt upsides after 3f: led over 3f out: sn hdd: rdn and wknd over 1f out* **8/11**[1]
3-03 **4** 5 **Classic Tune**[86] 3012 6-11-2 0 JoshuaMoore 86
(Claire Dyson) *led: hung lft and hdd over 3f out: sn wknd* **16/1**

4m 7.3s (18.20) **Going Correction** +1.20s/f (Heavy)
WFA 4 from 5yo+ 7lb **4 Ran SP% 109.0**
Speed ratings: **102,96,91,88**
CSF £13.56 TOTE £3.30; EX 12.80 Trifecta £18.20.
Owner Mr & Mrs W J Williams **Bred** W J & Mrs M Williams **Trained** Sparsholt, Oxfordshire

FOCUS
This race was run over approximately 145yds further than advertised. While it's hard to get overly excited about a four-runner race the winner, who was the only one making his debut, did look a decent prospect.

T/Plt: £289.60 to a £1 stake. Pool: £74,213.63 - 187.06 winning tickets. T/Qpdt: £80.50 to a £1 stake. Pool: £5,445.77 - 50.06 winning tickets. **Colin Roberts**

[4324] SEDGEFIELD (L-H)

Sunday, March 6

OFFICIAL GOING: Soft (heavy in places; 5.1)

Wind: moderate 1/2 against Weather: overcast and cold, snow shower race 5 (4.20)

4509 BETFRED NOVICES' HURDLE (BETFRED HURDLE SERIES QUALIFIER) 2m 3f 188y

2:20 (2:20) (Class 4) 4-Y-O+ **£4,158** (£1,221; £610; £305)

Form RPR

665 **1** **Oak Vintage (IRE)**[13] 4284 6-10-11 0........................ JamieHamilton(5) 109+
(Ann Hamilton) *trckd ldrs: 2nd 7th: drvn next: 5 l down and looking hld whn lft clr 2 out: hit last: drvn out* **22/1**

2P3 **2** *6* **Rolling Thunder (IRE)**[18] 4176 6-11-2 0........................ HenryBrooke 100
(Donald McCain) *led tl after 1st: trckd ldr: drvn and outpcd sn after 3 out: lft 12 l 2nd 2 out: kpt on* **5/1**[2]

2653 **3** *18* **Silver Shuffle (IRE)**[71] 3242 9-10-13 100........................ EmmaSayer(3) 89
(Dianne Sayer) *chsd ldrs: pushed along 5th: sn outpcd: lft poor 3rd 2 out* **14/1**

40 **4** *10* **Baby Ticker**[13] 4284 7-10-6 0........................ CallumWhillans(3) 66
(Donald Whillans) *nt jump wl: j.rt in rr: hung rt bnd after 5th: brief effrt 7th: sn lost pl and bhd: lft distant 4th 2 out* **150/1**

404 **5** *12* **Dance And Romance**[23] 4104 4-10-0 0........................ BrianHarding 43
(Tim Easterby) *in rr: bhd and reminders 7th* **125/1**

5/4- **6** *5* **Rock On Bollinski**[131] 1058 6-11-2 0........................(p) DannyCook 59
(Brian Ellison) *j. slowly and lost pl 2nd: nt fluent in rr: hmpd bnd after 5th: bhd and j.rt 6th* **8/1**[3]

-123 **U** **Ryedale Racer**[103] 2704 5-11-2 0........................ BrianHughes 117+
(Malcolm Jefferson) *led after 1st: shkn up after 3 out: 5 l clr and looking in command whn blnd bdly and uns rdr 2 out* **4/9**[1]

5m 11.7s (17.60) **Going Correction** +0.775s/f (Soft)
WFA 4 from 5yo+ 8lb 7 Ran SP% **109.5**
Speed ratings (Par 105): **95,92,85,81,76 74,**
CSF £115.55 TOTE £19.30: £8.00, £2.80; EX 104.80 Trifecta £449.50.
Owner Ian Hamilton **Bred** William Barron **Trained** Great Bavington, Northumbland

FOCUS
The exact distance for this race was 35 yards shorter than advertised on ground described as 'tacky' or 'holding.'\n\x\x Winners in point-to-points, bumpers and on the Flat took part in this novice event, but none had scored over hurdles, and with the odds-on favourite departing this is certainly not form to get carried away with.

4510 BARDI H'CAP HURDLE (13 hdls) 3m 3f 9y

2:50 (2:50) (Class 4) (0-110,110) 4-Y-O+ **£4,158** (£1,221; £610; £305)

Form RPR

4000 **1** **Beer Goggles (IRE)**[19] 4163 5-10-10 97........................ JoeColliver(3) 104+
(Micky Hammond) *in rr: reminder after 3rd: outpcd 7th: hdwy to chse ldrs 3 out: led appr next: fnd ex clsng stages* **4/1**[2]

P003 **2** *1 1/2* **Moscow Presents (IRE)**[12] 4301 8-10-9 96........................(p) AdamNicol(3) 103
(Philip Kirby) *hld up: hdwy to trck ldrs 9th: upsides 2 out: no ex last 50yds* **2/1**[1]

410P **3** *15* **Dusky Bob (IRE)**[69] 3312 11-11-0 98........................ DannyCook 92
(Brian Ellison) *chsd ldrs: pushed along 8th: led 10th: hdd next: wknd after 2 out: hit last* **6/1**[3]

1425 **4** *26* **Maggie Blue (IRE)**[30] 3970 8-11-1 104........................ CallumBewley(5) 69
(Harriet Graham) *w ldrs: led 3 out: hdd appr next: sn wknd* **8/1**

3162 **5** *57* **Optical High**[26] 4047 7-10-10 94........................ SeanQuinlan
(Sue Smith) *led 1st: reminders bef 9th: hdd and blnd 10th: lost pl bef 3 out: sn bhd: t.o 2 out* **4/1**[2]

20P4 **P** **Snapping Turtle (IRE)**[19] 4165 11-11-9 110........................ CallumWhillans(3)
(Donald Whillans) *led to 1st: chsd ldrs: pushed along 7th: lost pl 10th: sn bhd: t.o 5th whn p.u bef 2 out* **6/1**[3]

7m 13.2s (21.20) **Going Correction** +0.90s/f (Soft) 6 Ran SP% **113.0**
Speed ratings (Par 105): **104,103,99,91,74**
CSF £12.98 TOTE £6.60: £4.00, £2.10; EX 14.10 Trifecta £76.90.
Owner Richard & Katherine Gilbert **Bred** Cathal Ennis **Trained** Middleham, N Yorks

FOCUS
Most of these were in some sort of form, ahead of a handicap hurdle run over a distance 44 yards shorter than advertised. They went just a fair pace until the tempo increased going to four out.

4511 BARCA H'CAP CHASE (QUALIFIER FOR THE CHALLENGER STAYING CHASE SERIES FINAL) (18 fncs 3 omitted) 3m 2f 59y

3:20 (3:20) (Class 3) (0-130,122) 5-Y-O+ **£6,388** (£1,928; £993; £526)

Form RPR

0112 **1** **Auldthunder (IRE)**[23] 4110 9-10-6 105........................ JoeColliver(3) 121+
(Micky Hammond) *j.rt: chsd ldng pair: 2nd 13th: led 4 out (normal 5 out): forged 5 l clr bef last: drvn out* **3/1**[2]

2F22 **2** *4* **Jac The Legend**[20] 4155 7-11-7 117........................(p) WillKennedy 126
(Brian Ellison) *nt fluent 1st: in rr: hdwy to chse ldrs whn nt fluent 12th: reminders sn after 3 out: 3 l 2nd next: kpt on same pce between last 2* **13/8**[1]

P-0P **3** *10* **Scotswell**[20] 4155 10-11-4 121........................ ThomasDowson(7) 121
(Harriet Graham) *led to 2nd: w ldr: led 5th: hdd 4 out (normal 5 out): wknd between last 2* **20/1**

2113 **4** *23* **Askamore Darsi (IRE)**[20] 4153 7-11-8 118........................(p) HenryBrooke 93
(Donald McCain) *led 2nd to 5th: sn drvn along: hit 13th: lost pl 3 out (normal 4 out): t.o 2 out* **7/2**[3]

5F34 **U** **Mwaleshi**[35] 3887 11-11-12 122........................ DannyCook
(Sue Smith) *rr-div whn blnd and uns rdr 2nd* **9/2**

7m 21.0s (10.00) **Going Correction** +0.575s/f (Soft) 5 Ran SP% **108.3**
Speed ratings: **107,105,102,95,**
CSF £8.34 TOTE £3.70: £1.90, £1.10; EX 7.70 Trifecta £46.60.
Owner The Rat Pack Racing Club **Bred** Miss Jill Farrell **Trained** Middleham, N Yorks

FOCUS
This was run over 65 yards further than advertised with the cross fence omitted.\n\x\x A couple of in-form, unexposed staying chasers at the foot of this handicap chase, and they fought out the finish.

4512 SANTA PRINCESA MARES' H'CAP HURDLE (QUALIFIER FOR THE CHALLENGER MARES' HURDLE SERIES FINAL) 2m 3f 188y

3:50 (3:50) (Class 4) (0-120,119) 4-Y-O+ **£4,158** (£1,221; £610; £305)

Form RPR

-530 **1** **Attention Seaker**[52] 3592 6-11-1 108........................ BrianHughes 120+
(Tim Easterby) *trckd ldrs: led appr 3 out: drew wl clr between last 2: drvn out* **13/2**

1P4P **2** *23* **Glen Countess (IRE)**[23] 4109 9-11-1 108........................ SeanQuinlan 96
(Sue Smith) *racd wd: chsd ldrs: w wnr 3 out: kpt on one pce to take remote 2nd nr fin* **6/1**[3]

5P11 **3** *hd* **Bella (FR)**[20] 4157 5-11-12 119........................(t) TomScudamore 108
(David Pipe) *chsd ldrs: nt fluent 2nd: nt fluent and drvn 6th: tk 2nd appr 2 out: kpt on one pce: fdd and lost remote 2nd nr fin* **10/11**[1]

-66P **4** *7* **Whatdoesthefoxsay (IRE)**[68] 3333 7-11-0 117........................ RonanShort(10) 98
(Donald McCain) *led: hdd appr 3 out: lost pl bef 2 out: sn bhd* **7/2**[2]

4U6 **5** *19* **Roja Dove (IRE)**[14] 4272 7-11-0 110........................(v) AdamNicol(3) 72
(David Thompson) *chsd ldrs: pushed along 5th: lost pl bef 3 out: sn bhd: j.lft last* **18/1**

5m 15.0s (20.90) **Going Correction** +1.025s/f (Soft) 5 Ran SP% **107.5**
Speed ratings (Par 105): **99,89,89,86,79**
CSF £37.91 TOTE £6.20: £2.30, £2.50; EX 23.20 Trifecta £55.90.
Owner Ryedale Partners No 6 **Bred** Ryedale Partners No 6 **Trained** Great Habton, N Yorks

FOCUS
The withdrawal of Libby Mae left the progressive topweight standing out on recent form in this otherwise uncompetitive affair, which was run over 35 yards shorter than the advertised distance, and the fact she did not seem to be at her best left this a tricky race to assess.

4513 POLONUS H'CAP HURDLE (8 hdls) 2m 178y

4:20 (4:20) (Class 5) (0-100,100) 4-Y-O+ **£2,859** (£839; £419; £209)

Form RPR

1421 **1** **Roxyfet (FR)**[10] 4329 6-11-5 100........................ FinianO'Toole(7) 111+
(Micky Hammond) *mid-div: trckd ldrs 4th: led narrowly 2 out: drvn out* **3/1**[1]

3334 **2** *5* **Copt Hill**[12] 4297 8-10-6 80........................(p) BrianHughes 85
(Tracy Waggott) *led to 1st: trckd ldr: led 3 out: hdd 2 out: kpt on same pce: hung rt run-in* **3/1**[1]

51U1 **3** *11* **Fiddler's Flight (IRE)**[26] 4049 10-10-11 88........................ ColmMcCormack(3) 82
(John Norton) *hld up towards rr: hdwy to trck ldrs 4th: one pce appr 2 out: tk modest 3rd last 75yds* **13/2**[3]

2502 **4** *3/4* **Mister Hendre**[12] 4297 8-10-4 78........................(t) HenryBrooke 70
(Susan Corbett) *trckd ldrs: outpcd 3 out: modest 3rd between last 2: one pce* **8/1**

P555 **5** *13* **Mrs Grass**[103] 2703 9-9-9 74 oh6........................(vt) DiarmuidO'Regan(5) 53
(Jonathan Haynes) *led 1st: hdd 3 out: wknd sn after 2 out: sn bhd* **20/1**

5655 **6** *shd* **Dalby Spook (IRE)**[12] 4297 6-10-3 80........................ EmmaSayer(3) 59
(Dianne Sayer) *in tch: j. slowly and lost pl 4th: bhd fr 3 out* **8/1**

33-1 **7** *nk* **Van Mildert (IRE)**[284] 507 7-10-3 80........................(p) HarryChalloner(3) 59
(Kenneth Slack) *chsd ldrs: nt fluent and lost pl 5th: bhd next* **7/2**[2]

4m 25.3s (18.40) **Going Correction** +1.15s/f (Heav) 7 Ran SP% **112.5**
Speed ratings (Par 103): **102,99,94,94,88 87,87**
CSF £12.33 TOTE £3.80: £1.70, £1.30; EX 10.60 Trifecta £26.70.
Owner R J Ball **Bred** Jacky Thomas **Trained** Middleham, N Yorks

FOCUS
Just a handful with good recent form to their name and they came to the fore in this handicap hurdle, which was run at a fair pace over a distance 24 yards shorter than advertised. The field had to brave a snowstorm.

4514 KIRKELLA H'CAP CHASE (18 fncs 3 omitted) 3m 2f 59y

4:50 (4:50) (Class 4) (0-105,99) 5-Y-O+ **£3,768** (£1,106; £553; £276)

Form RPR

PU0P **1** **Notonebuttwo (IRE)**[40] 3793 9-10-7 80........................(tp) BrianHughes 89
(Chris Grant) *t.k.h: led tl after 2nd: led 4th: kpt on wl fr 2 out: drvn rt out* **8/1**[3]

100P **2** *4 1/2* **Feast Of Fire (IRE)**[69] 3310 9-11-12 99........................ BrianHarding 103
(Joanne Foster) *t.k.h: trckd ldng pair: j.lft and reminder 4th: 2nd 13th: reminders 3 out (normal 4 out): rallied and chsd wnr between last 2: kpt on same pce* **10/1**

4525 **3** *2 3/4* **Treliver Manor (IRE)**[30] 3969 8-10-4 84........................(t) LorcanMurtagh(7) 85
(Rose Dobbin) *hld up: hdwy 10th: sn chsng ldrs: hit 12th: drvn 3 out (normal 4 out): 3rd appr last: one pce* **2/1**[1]

/6P6 **4** *1* **Mia Matriarch**[99] 2771 10-10-0 66........................(t) JonathanEngland 73
(Stuart Coltherd) *in rr: modest 5th whn hit 2 out: kpt on: one pce appr last* **25/1**

066 **5** *1 1/2* **Pay The King (IRE)**[40] 3792 9-10-13 93........................ FinianO'Toole(7) 91
(Micky Hammond) *hld up: hit 2nd: hdwy 10th: sn chsng ldrs: chal appr 2 out: fdd appr last* **5/1**[2]

33UP **6** *17* **Hellorboston (IRE)**[30] 3969 8-11-12 99........................(p) WillKennedy 80
(Donald McCain) *w ldr: led after 2nd: hdd 4th: mstke and reminders 12th: drvn next: lost pl after 4 out (normal 5 out): t.o 2 out* **2/1**[1]

7m 36.3s (25.30) **Going Correction** +0.70s/f (Soft) 6 Ran SP% **107.4**
Speed ratings: **89,87,86,86,86 80**
CSF £65.69 TOTE £8.50: £3.70, £3.50; EX 57.50 Trifecta £231.80.
Owner D&D Armstrong Ltd **Bred** Joe Dolan **Trained** Newton Bewley, Co Durham

FOCUS
Question marks about the entire field in an uncompetitive chase run over a distance 65 yards further than advertised, with the cross fence omitted, so this is unlikely to prove decent form.

4515 SNAEFELL STANDARD OPEN NATIONAL HUNT FLAT RACE 2m 178y

5:20 (5:20) (Class 6) 4-6-Y-O **£1,559** (£457; £228; £114)

Form RPR

1 **Lastbutnotleast (IRE)**[148] 6-10-11 0........................ AdrianLane 105+
(Donald McCain) *mde all: pushed along over 3f out: drvn clr over 1f out: styd on wl* **2/1**[2]

2 *19* **Strike West (IRE)** 4-10-7 0........................ JoeColliver(3) 87
(Micky Hammond) *trckd ldrs: v green: wandered bdly and j. two crossings: rallied 5f out: chsd wnr over 2f out: hung rt: and lost tch w wnr over 1f out* **11/2**[3]

3 *3 1/2* **Shantou Theatre (IRE)** 6-11-4 0........................ JanFaltejsek 90
(George Charlton) *trckd wnr: pushed along over 4f out: wknd 2f out* **9/1**

4 *27* **Moscow Calling (IRE)** 5-11-4 0........................ CraigNichol 63
(Nicky Richards) *trckd ldrs: pushed along 7f out: outpcd and lost pl over 5f out: sn bhd: t.o 3f out* **1/1**[1]

4m 24.4s (23.10) **Going Correction** +1.275s/f (Heav)
WFA 4 from 5yo+ 7lb 4 Ran SP% **108.7**
Speed ratings: 96,87,85,72
CSF £11.79 TOTE £2.80; EX 8.90 Trifecta £36.90.

Owner Mrs B McCain **Bred** Minch Bloodstock **Trained** Cholmondeley, Cheshire
FOCUS
No previous bumper form to go on in this NH Flat race, which was run over a distance 24 yards shorter than advertised.
T/Plt: £2,165.60 to a £1 stake. Pool: £74,312.76 - 25.05 winning tickets. T/Qpdt: £84.10 to a £1 stake. Pool: £7,403.47 - 65.10 winning tickets. **Walter Glynn**

4277 NAAS (L-H)
Sunday, March 6
OFFICIAL GOING: Hurdle course - soft to heavy; chase course - heavy

4516a IRISH RACING WRITERS KINGSFURZE NOVICE HURDLE (LISTED RACE) (8 hdls) 2m
2:10 (2:10) 4-Y-O+ **£12,435** (£3,841; £1,819; £808; £303)

RPR
1 **Sutton Place (IRE)**56 3555 5-11-2 0 BarryGeraghty 137+
(Gordon Elliott, Ire) *chsd ldrs in 4th: t.k.h: nt fluent 4th: tk clsr order on outer 2 out: led last: rdn clr clsng stages* **12/1**
2 6 ½ **Royal Caviar (IRE)**35 3890 8-11-6 131 RWalsh 133
(W P Mullins, Ire) *chsd ldrs on inner in 3rd: prog into 2nd at 4th: rdn to dispute appr last where hdd: no match for wnr clsng stages* **5/1**
3 1 ¾ **Burgas (FR)**24 4085 5-11-6 0 BJCooper 132
(W P Mullins, Ire) *led tl strly pressed appr last and hdd: dropped to 3rd: kpt on one pce* **3/1**3
4 4 ¼ **Gurteen (IRE)**43 3750 6-11-6 0 PhillipEnright 127
(Robert Tyner, Ire) *hld up in rr: sme prog on inner 2 out: nt qckn in 4th appr last: sn one pce: injured rt hind leg* **2/1**1
5 4 ¼ **Attribution**57 3539 6-11-6 135 (p) DavyRussell 125
(Henry De Bromhead, Ire) *trckd ldr in 2nd: dropped to 3rd at 4th: nt qckn and dropped to rr after 2 out: sn no ex* **11/4**2
3m 57.7s (-5.80) **5 Ran SP% 109.4**
CSF £62.86 TOTE £10.20: £3.70, £1.80; DF 24.60 Trifecta £293.20.
Owner John P McManus **Bred** James D Leahy **Trained** Longwood, Co Meath
FOCUS
An intriguing novice hurdle with a surprisingly moribund market. The winner was friendless but made a mockery of that with a bloodless win. The form takes a knock because the last two, neither unfancied, clearly underperformed.

4517a NAAS DIRECTORS PLATE NOVICE CHASE (GRADE 3) (13 fncs) 2m 4f
2:40 (2:40) 5-Y-O+ **£14,696** (£4,540; £2,150; £955; £358)

RPR
1 **Sub Lieutenant (IRE)**21 4148 7-11-2 141 (vt1) DavidMullins 147
(Ms Sandra Hughes, Ire) *led tl briefly jnd 8th: sn bk in front and lft clr 3 out: pressed appr last: kpt on wl clsng stages* **9/1**
2 2 **Tell Us More (IRE)**21 4145 7-11-2 143 RWalsh 145
(W P Mullins, Ire) *racd towards rr: nt fluent 8th on inner: gd hdwy appr 2 out: pressed ldr at last and sn ev ch: no ex w wnr clsng stages* **13/8**1
3 13 **Arctic Skipper (IRE)**43 3755 7-11-2 130 AELynch 133
(Vincent Laurence Halley, Ire) *t.k.h early in mid-div: 4th at 1/2-way: lft 3rd 3 out: rdn and no imp appr last in 4th: kpt on one pce into 3rd run-in* **16/1**
4 5 ½ **Rule The World**45 3715 9-11-2 142 BJCooper 129
(M F Morris, Ire) *racd in mid-div: clsr 5 out in 4th: hmpd 3 out where briefly lft 2nd: nt qckn in 3rd appr last: one pce and sn dropped to 4th* **2/1**2
5 59 **Finea (IRE)**10 4327 9-11-8 112 (tp) LPDempsey 74
(R K Watson, Ire) *chsd ldr in 2nd: clsr and on terms at 8th: rdn and nt qckn after 4 out: sn detached: t.o* **100/1**
F **Montys Meadow (IRE)**38 3831 8-11-2 136 DavyRussell
(James Joseph Mangan, Ire) *chsd ldrs in 3rd: j.w and on terms at 8th: cl 2nd whn fell 3 out* **5/1**3
P **Golantilla (IRE)**197 1338 8-11-2 0 (t) APHeskin
(Alan Fleming, Ire) *hld up towards rr: in rr at 1/2-way: nvr a threat: p.u bef 3 out* **10/1**
5m 37.1s (8.10) **7 Ran SP% 114.1**
CSF £25.14 TOTE £11.10: £3.10, £1.80; DF 32.20 Trifecta £355.50.
Owner Gigginstown House Stud **Bred** Edmond Coleman **Trained** Kildare, Co Kildare
FOCUS
Well up to the status of a Grade 3, this was nevertheless a bit unsatisfactory, with the second-favourite disappointing and a faller in contention three out. A small pb from the winner.

4518 - 4520a (Foreign Racing) - See Raceform Interactive

4521a WOODLANDS 100 CLUB LEINSTER NATIONAL H'CAP CHASE (GRADE B) (16 fncs) 3m
4:40 (4:41) 5-Y-O+
£21,691 (£6,985; £3,308; £1,470; £735; £367)

RPR
1 **Venitien De Mai (FR)**32 3943 7-9-12 127 JonathanMoore(5) 138+
(J T R Dreaper, Ire) *pressed ldr in 2nd: disp fr 4th and sn led: rdn and styd on wl fr bef last: forged clr run-in* **10/3**1
2 6 **Goonyella (IRE)**39 3812 9-11-9 147 (t) JJBurke 152
(J T R Dreaper, Ire) *led: jnd 4th: dropped towards mid-div w a circ to r: rdn in 6th bef 2 out: styd on wl into 2nd run-in: nt rch wnr* **14/1**
3 7 ½ **Futuramic (IRE)**32 3943 9-9-13 123 RobbieColgan 121
(Andrew Lynch, Ire) *racd in mid-div: gd prog to chse ldr in 2nd w a circ to r: almost on terms after 4 out: no imp and dropped to 3rd after last: kpt on same pce* **7/1**
4 1 ¼ **Forever Gold (IRE)**69 3320 9-9-10 120 oh4 (p) PhillipEnright 116
(Edward Cawley, Ire) *hld up: prog to chse ldrs w a circ to r: cl 4th 2 out: no imp after last: kpt on one pce* **5/1**2
5 shd **Gallant Oscar (IRE)**49 3649 10-11-10 148 BarryGeraghty 146
(A J Martin, Ire) *hld up towards rr: last w a circ to r: slt mstke 4 out: prog fr next to chse ldrs 2 out in 5th: kpt on same pce run-in* **10/1**
6 3 ¾ **Ibetellingyoualie (IRE)**22 4132 10-9-5 120 oh5 (tp) AndrewRing(5) 112
(Terence O'Brien, Ire) *chsd ldrs in 3rd tl after 4 out: nt qckn bef next: kpt on one pce fr bef last* **16/1**
7 29 **Ad Idem**8 4377 12-9-3 120 oh4 (p) RachaelBlackmore(7) 83
(Mrs Pauline Gavin, Ire) *hld up tl tk clsr order 5 out: rdn in 4th after 3 out: no imp appr last: wknd run-in and eased* **16/1**
8 5 ½ **Bothair Clei (IRE)**10 4334 11-9-10 120 oh1 MarkEnright 78
(Daniel G Murphy, Ire) *racd in mid-div to 1/2-way: mstke and dropped towards rr 6 out: no imp after 3 out* **14/1**
9 13 **Captain Von Trappe (IRE)**14 4279 7-10-7 134 (b) LPDempsey(3) 79
(Gordon Elliott, Ire) *chsd ldrs tl pckd 4 out: rdn and nt qckn after next: no ex* **9/1**
10 15 **Nickname Exit (FR)**21 4147 6-10-6 130 (b) BJCooper 60
(Gordon Elliott, Ire) *chsd ldrs towards outer: clsr in 3rd w a circ to r: rdn in mid-div 6 out: wknd fr next: t.o* **11/2**3
P **Art Lord (IRE)**6 4406 10-9-5 120 oh7 (t) DonaghMeyler(5)
(Karl Thornton, Ire) *slowly away and detached tl jnd field after 3rd: mid-div at next: bk towards rr w a circ to r: p.u 6 out* **20/1**
P **Golden Wonder (IRE)**65 3432 10-10-13 137 RogerLoughran
(Ms Sandra Hughes, Ire) *hld up: prog to chse ldrs on outer w a circ to r: wknd qckly 3 out and sn p.u* **20/1**
6m 52.4s (4.30) **12 Ran SP% 121.3**
CSF £50.25 CT £310.30 TOTE £3.90: £1.50, £3.20, £2.50; DF 49.10 Trifecta £362.60.
Owner Ann & Alan Potts Partnership **Bred** M Jean-Yves Touzaint **Trained** Greenogue, Co Meath
■ Stewards' Enquiry : Robbie Colgan four-day ban: used whip with excessive frequency (Mar 20, 24, 27-28)
FOCUS
A pretty classy renewal of the race and a superb training effort from Jim Dreaper.

4522 - 4525a (Foreign Racing) - See Raceform Interactive

3194 LINGFIELD (L-H)
Monday, March 7
OFFICIAL GOING: Turf course - heavy (4.1); all-weather - polytrack: standard
Wind: Moderate, against Weather: Fine but cloudy, cold

4526 RACING WELFARE INTRODUCING RACING'S SUPPORT LINE NOVICES' HURDLE (8 hdls) 2m
2:10 (2:10) (Class 4) 4-Y-O+ **£4,659** (£1,446; £779)

Form RPR
F1 1 **Overtown Express (IRE)**22 4137 8-11-7 0 NoelFehily 131+
(Harry Fry) *hld up: trckd ldng pair 4th: led after 2 out: sn clr: easily* **4/6**1
6 2 8 **Grandasowt (IRE)**84 3077 7-11-1 0 PaulMoloney 107
(Evan Williams) *hld up: pushed along in 4th after 3 out: lost tch w ldrs bef next: kpt on steadily after: lft 3rd last and sn tk 2nd: shaped wl* **15/8**2
110 3 7 **Master Jake (IRE)**51 3630 8-11-8 128 BridgetAndrews(5) 112
(Dan Skelton) *mde most: jnd 3 out: hdd after 2 out: tired and lost 2nd after last* **7/2**2
61 F **King Cool**8 4382 5-11-7 0 JamieMoore 113
(Gary Moore) *trckd ldr fr 3rd: upsides fr 3 out: no ch w wnr after 2 out: disputing 6 l 2nd whn fell last* **9/2**3
46P P **Sweet'N'Chic (IRE)**21 4157 6-10-8 0 LeightonAspell
(Richard Rowe) *chsd ldr tl mstke 3rd: sn in last: mstke 5th and wknd: t.o whn p.u bef last* **100/1**
4m 42.6s (14.60) **Going Correction** +1.15s/f (Heavy) **5 Ran SP% 107.3**
Speed ratings (Par 105): **109,105,101, ,**
CSF £10.64 TOTE £1.40: £1.10, £4.50; EX 7.40 Trifecta £20.30.
Owner Mrs Lorna Squire & Richard Metherell **Bred** Jimter Stud **Trained** Seaborough, Dorset
FOCUS
All starts have been moved at this track following remeasuring, so there will be no speed figures here until there is sufficient data to calculate updated median times. Not a bad little novice event, but it was a cakewalk for the winner. Winning rider Noel Fehily said afterwards the going was "very testing and tacky". Due to rail realignments the race distance was 12yds further than advertised. The easy winner confirmed the merit of his Exeter win.

4527 MICK HUGHES 69TH BIRTHDAY NOVICES' H'CAP CHASE (12 fncs) 2m
2:40 (2:40) (Class 4) (0-105,102) 5-Y-O+ **£5,198** (£1,526; £763; £381)

Form RPR
6/F5 1 **Gold Carrot**9 4356 8-10-9 85 JamieMoore 102+
(Gary Moore) *in tch: mstke 6th: trckd ldr 8th: led 3 out: in command next: drvn out fr last* **3/1**1
1-22 2 4 ½ **Bawden Rocks**24 4106 7-11-7 102 (p) JakeHodson(5) 111
(David Bridgwater) *sn trckd ldr: led 6th: hdd 3 out: kpt on fr last but no imp on wnr* **3/1**1
5-20 3 28 **Zayfire Aramis**13 4297 7-11-8 98 LiamTreadwell 87
(Michael Scudamore) *sloppy rnd of jumping: t.k.h in last: effrt after 4 out: tk 3rd next but no imp on ldng pair: wknd after anther mstke last* **5/1**3
4013 4 17 **Entry To Evrywhere (IRE)**18 4211 8-10-12 88 (t) RhysFlint 59
(Alexandra Dunn) *walked to post early: plld hrd early: led to 6th: wknd on long run bef 3 out: t.o* **4/1**2
/002 P **Diamond Life**18 4211 10-11-10 100 DenisO'Regan
(Mark Pitman) *cl up: wl in tch in 3rd on long run after 4 out: wknd bef 3 out: poor 4th 2 out: p.u bef last* **3/1**1
4m 49.2s (9.20) **Going Correction** +0.75s/f (Soft) **5 Ran SP% 111.7**
Speed ratings: **107,104,90,82,**
CSF £12.56 TOTE £2.80: £1.30, £1.60; EX 11.50 Trifecta £32.10.
Owner Tony Head **Bred** R And Mrs Blackman **Trained** Lower Beeding, W Sussex
FOCUS
This moderate handicap was run at a sound gallop and the runner-up gives it a straightforward look. Due to rail realignments the race distance was 12yds further than advertised. A big step up from the winner and a small pb from the second.

4528 SHAKATHEBOOKIESMACKER.COM H'CAP HURDLE (12 hdls) 2m 7f
3:10 (3:10) (Class 5) (0-100,99) 4-Y-O+ **£3,249** (£954; £477; £238)

Form RPR
0633 1 **Ceann Sibheal (IRE)**10 4349 7-11-6 93 GavinSheehan 118+
(Warren Greatrex) *w ldr but chivvied along at various stages: led bef 8th: urged along and drew away bef 2 out: 25 l up last: eased* **5/4**1
0/ 2 15 **Sacre Malta (FR)**47 3695 10-11-5 99 ConorWalsh(7) 89
(Dominic Ffrench Davis) *in tch: chsd wnr 8th to 3 out: sn rdn: no ch fr 2 out: kpt on to win battle for remote 2nd nr fin* **9/2**2
4-03 3 hd **Fifi L'Amour (IRE)**28 4025 10-9-13 75 oh2 ow2 ThomasGarner(3) 68
(Linda Jewell) *often j.rt: in tch: effrt to go 2nd 3 out: lft bhd and wl btn whn mstke 2 out: lost remote 2nd nr fin* **5/1**3
6040 4 7 **El Indio (IRE)**10 4349 9-9-9 73 oh2 (vt) DanielHiskett(5) 57
(Claire Dyson) *led to bef 8th: sn rdn: dropped to last bef 3 out and sn lost tch: kpt on again to press for remote 2nd whn hmpd last: wknd* **5/1**3
0000 P **Lough Derg Island (IRE)**54 3586 8-11-3 90 RhysFlint
(Alexandra Dunn) *hld up in tch: cl up and looked to be gng wl 3 out: sn rdn and wknd rapidly: p.u bef 2 out: dismntd* **6/1**
6400 P **Kerry's Lord (IRE)**8 4391 7-11-2 96 RomainClavreul(7)
(Joanne Thomason-Murphy) *in tch in rr to 7th: sn t.o: p.u bef 9th* **25/1**
7m 2.0s (422.00) **6 Ran SP% 114.1**
CSF £7.77 TOTE £1.90: £1.10, £2.70; EX 8.20 Trifecta £11.80.
Owner The High Kites **Bred** E Wallace **Trained** Upper Lambourn, Berks

■ Stewards' Enquiry : Conor Walsh four-day ban: used whip above permitted level (Mar 21-24)

FOCUS

A very weak staying handicap but the form could be rated up to 10lb higher. Due to rail realignments the race distance was 121yds further than advertised.

4529 INJURED JOCKEYS FUND CONDITIONAL JOCKEYS' TRAINING SERIES H'CAP CHASE (RACING EXC' INITIATIVE) (12 fncs) 2m

3:40 (3:40) (Class 4) (0-120,120) 5-Y-0+ **£5,325** (£1,653; £890)

Form RPR

-UF0 **1** **De Kerry Man (IRE)**[9] 4363 8-11-7 **120** WilliamFeatherstone(5) 132+
(David Bridgwater) *mde all: pressed but stl gng wl 3 out: shkn up bef last: rdn and asserted flat* **11/8**[1]

U2-3 **2** *2 1/4* **De Blacksmith (IRE)**[311] 62 8-11-0 **113** (tp) GeorgeGorman(5) 120
(Gary Moore) *chsd wnr 2nd to 6th and again after 3 out: rdn to chal 2 out: one pce after last* **2/1**[2]

-016 **3** *37* **Cappielow Park**[24] 4098 7-11-12 **120** (tp) CiaranGethings 102
(Ali Stronge) *cl up: chsd wnr 6th: rdn to chal bef 3 out: btn off: lost 2nd and wknd sn after 3 out* **7/2**[3]

PU1P **P** **Goring Two (IRE)**[18] 4197 11-10-0 **94** oh4 FreddieMitchell
(Anna Newton-Smith) *chsd wnr to 2nd: rel to r and j. awkwardly 5th and 6th: lost tch and p.u bef next* **10/1**

4m 49.3s (9.30) **Going Correction** +0.75s/f (Soft) **4 Ran SP% 106.8**

Speed ratings: **106,104,86,**

CSF £4.50 TOTE £1.90; EX 4.50 Trifecta £7.00.

Owner In It For The Crack **Bred** R Goodwin **Trained** Icomb, Gloucs

■ Stewards' Enquiry : Freddie Mitchell seven-day ban: used whip contrary to race conditions (Mar 27-29,Apr 1-3,8)

FOCUS

A modest little handicap, confined to conditional riders. Due to rail realignments the race distance was 12yds further than advertised. A pb from the winner with the second to his mark.

4530 LET US MAKE YOUR GOOD FRIDAY GREAT! MAIDEN HURDLE (10 hdls) 2m 3f 110y

4:10 (4:10) (Class 4) 4-Y-0+ **£4,548** (£1,335; £667; £333)

Form RPR

2265 **1** **Georgieshore (IRE)**[32] 3950 8-10-11 **100** WilliamFeatherstone(7) 113+
(Zoe Davison) *mde most to 8th: styd pressing ldr: led bef 2 out but sn pressed and rdn: styd on wl to draw clr bef last* **5/1**[3]

402P **2** *8* **Bassarabad (FR)**[49] 3662 5-10-13 **108** AlanJohns(5) 104
(Tim Vaughan) *trckd ldrs: pushed along after 3 out: no hdwy bef 2 out: kpt on to take 2nd bef last: drvn and no imp on wnr after* **5/2**[2]

P3 **3** *12* **Just Bill (IRE)**[31] 3976 8-11-4 0 PaulMoloney 93
(Evan Williams) *hld up in tch: trckd ldng pair 5th: led after 3 out and looked to be gng best: hdd bef 2 out: shkn up and no rspnse sn after: wknd bef last* **2/1**[1]

6020 **4** *29* **Tara Well (IRE)**[32] 3952 6-10-11 0 CharliePoste 62
(Robin Dickin) *pressed ldr: led 8th: sn hdd and rdn: wknd qckly bef 2 out* **10/1**

2030 **5** *27* **Manhattan Mead**[30] 3994 6-11-4 **114** MattieBatchelor 35
(Michael Madgwick) *immediately shoved along: chsd ldng pair to 5th: wknd 7th: sn t.o* **11/2**

P6 **6** *8* **Centreofexcellence (IRE)**[7] 4409 5-11-4 0 JoshuaMoore 27
(Gary Moore) *hld up in last: nudged along and lost tch 6th: sn t.o* **10/1**

5m 49.2s (23.20) **Going Correction** +1.15s/f (Heavy) **6 Ran SP% 112.1**

Speed ratings (Par 105): **99,95,91,79,68 65**

CSF £18.19 TOTE £5.90: £3.10, £1.40; EX 20.40 Trifecta £58.30.

Owner The Lump O'Clock Syndicate **Bred** David Valentine **Trained** Hammerwood, E Sussex

FOCUS

A moderate maiden, run at a routine sort of gallop. THe second sets the level. Due to rail realignments the race distance was 121yds further than advertised.

4531 JILL MAYO FOUR SCORE H'CAP CHASE (18 fncs) 2m 7f 110y

4:40 (4:40) (Class 5) (0-100,93) 5-Y-0+ **£3,898** (£1,144; £572; £286)

Form RPR

4-46 **1** **Somerby (IRE)**[66] 3412 13-10-5 **72** (t) RichieMcLernon 84
(Richenda Ford) *mde all and j. soundly: gng best bef 3 out: hrd pressed after last: drvn and hld on gamely nr fin* **5/2**[1]

3465 **2** *1/2* **Veauce De Sivola (FR)**[15] 4265 7-11-7 **88** (t) TomCannon 99
(Mark Gillard) *in tch: pushed along fr 13th: rdn to chse wnr bef 3 out: clsd u.p after last: str chal fnl 150yds: jst hld* **6/1**

4PPP **3** *34* **Red Anchor (IRE)**[35] 3906 12-10-4 **74** ThomasGarner(3) 55
(Linda Jewell) *in tch in rr: mstke 11th: urged along fr 13th: lft bhd on long run after 4 out: tk remote 3rd last* **9/1**

3P1P **4** *32* **Gowanauthat (IRE)**[37] 3864 8-11-5 **93** (tp) TommyDowling(7) 38
(Charlie Mann) *pressed wnr: hit 11th: mstke 4 out and rdn: lost 2nd and wknd bef 3 out: fin v tired* **5/1**[3]

-2PP **P** **Strange Bird (IRE)**[77] 3198 11-11-4 **85** LeightonAspell
(Richard Rowe) *racd wd: prom to 6th: wknd 9th: t.o whn p.u bef next* **6/1**

-33P **P** **Wayward Frolic**[10] 4343 10-11-11 **92** JamieMoore
(Jim Best) *trckd ldrs: awkward jump 12th: urged along fr 14th: wknd on long run after 4 out: bhd whn p.u bef 2 out* **3/1**[2]

7m 27.5s (27.70) **Going Correction** +0.75s/f (Soft) **6 Ran SP% 108.8**

Speed ratings: **83,82,71,60,**

CSF £16.13 TOTE £3.00: £1.40, £3.00; EX 16.30 Trifecta £84.20.

Owner Mr & Mrs K B Snook **Bred** King Bloodstock **Trained** Brockhampton Green, Dorset

■ Stewards' Enquiry : Tom Cannon four-day ban: used whip above permitted level (Mar 21-24)

FOCUS

A weak staying handicap. It was steadily run and only two mattered from the penultimate fence. The first two are rated to their marks. Due to rail realignments the race distance was 66yds further than advertised.

4532 BESTBINGOSITES.CO.UK THE BEST ONLINE BINGO SITE STANDARD OPEN NATIONAL HUNT FLAT RACE (ALL-WEATHER) 2m

5:10 (5:12) (Class 6) 4-6-Y-0 **£1,559** (£457; £228; £114)

Form RPR

1 **Peggies Venture** 5-10-9 0 NickScholfield 94+
(Nick Gifford) *cl up on inner: gng strly 3f out: clsd fr 2f out to ld 1f out: sn rdn clr* **16/1**

1 **2** *4* **Manhattan Spring**[77] 3200 5-11-4 0 KevinJones(5) 104
(Seamus Mullins) *plld hrd: trckd ldr after 5f: rdn to ld over 2f out: hdd and outpcd 1f out* **8/1**

00- **3** *2* **Kalaskadesemilley**[354] 4873 5-10-11 0 ThomasCheesman(5) 95
(Kevin Morgan) *towards rr: pushed along 3f out in 7th: stydon fr 2f out to take 3rd ins fnl f: nt pce to threaten* **20/1**

43-1 **4** *2* **Jennifer Eccles**[156] 1758 6-11-2 0 TomO'Brien 93
(Suzy Smith) *fractious bef lining up: led: rdn and hdd over 2f out: fdd over 1f out* **3/1**[2]

0- **5** *nk* **Good Idea (IRE)**[324] 5402 5-11-2 0 JeremiahMcGrath 93
(Nicky Henderson) *in tch: prog to trck ldrs 6f: disp 3rd and cl up 2f out: rdn and nt qckn over 1f out: sn btn* **9/2**[3]

6 **6** *3/4* **Hard Toffee (IRE)**[184] 1484 5-11-2 0 PaulMoloney 92
(Conrad Allen) *settled in rr: effrt on wd outside 3f out: no prog 2f out: outpcd after* **14/1**

7 *4* **Scarper (IRE)** 4-10-8 0 GavinSheehan 80
(Harry Whittington) *trckd ldr 5f: styd cl up: pushed along over 3f out: steadily wknd over 2f out* **11/4**[1]

4-2 **8** *hd* **Mr Mountain (IRE)**[77] 3200 6-10-6 0 RichieO'Dea(10) 88
(Emma Lavelle) *t.k.h: trckd ldrs: lost pl sn after 1/2-way: pushed along in rr 3f out: sn btn* **5/1**

9 *17* **Wyatt (IRE)** 4-10-3 0 FreddieMitchell(5) 63
(Philip Mitchell) *a in rr: wknd 3f out: t.o* **33/1**

3m 28.8s (208.80)

WFA 4 from 5yo+ 7lb **9 Ran SP% 117.9**

CSF £139.71 TOTE £14.80: £3.60, £1.80, £4.20; EX 110.90 Trifecta £5515.00.

Owner Sir Christopher Wates **Bred** Sir Christopher Stephen Wates **Trained** Findon, W Sussex

■ Stewards' Enquiry : Richie O'Dea five-day ban: used whip when out of contention (Mar 21-24,26)

FOCUS

As ever with bumpers around here this proved a tactical affair. The form is rated around the second to the fourth.

T/Plt: £100.80 to a £1 stake. Pool: £59538.89 - 430.78 winning tickets T/Qpdt: £26.10 to a £1 stake. Pool: £4245.37 - 120.15 winning tickets **Jonathan Neesom**

4386 SOUTHWELL (L-H)

Monday, March 7

OFFICIAL GOING: Heavy (soft in places; 5.6)

Wind: moderate 1/2 behind Weather: fine and sunny, cold

4533 FOLLOW AT THE RACES ON TWITTER NOVICES' LIMITED H'CAP CHASE (10 fncs 3 omitted) 1m 7f 153y

2:00 (2:00) (Class 4) (0-120,120) 5-Y-0+ **£5,325** (£1,653; £890)

Form RPR

S202 **1** **Johns Luck (IRE)**[15] 4265 7-10-3 **101** oh3 (b) MarkQuinlan 108+
(Neil Mulholland) *mde all: drvn appr 2 out (normal 3 out): drew clr appr last* **5/2**[3]

4111 **2** *6* **Ashcott Boy**[112] 2546 8-11-3 **120** DavidNoonan(5) 120
(Neil Mulholland) *j.lft: chsd ldrs: pushed along and clr 2nd 7th: reminders next: one pce fr 2 out (normal 3 out)* **2/1**[2]

4P06 **3** *50* **The Jugopolist (IRE)**[67] 3376 9-10-0 **101** oh33 (b) BenPoste(3) 51
(John Cornwall) *chsd ldrs: reminders bef 6th: sn lost pl and bhd: t.o 8th: lft distant 3rd bef 2 out (normal 3 out)* **100/1**

1213 **P** **Moscow Me (IRE)**[26] 4053 9-11-1 **113** PaddyBrennan
(Henry Oliver) *racd wd: j.rt: chsd ldrs: lost pl 7th: sn bhd: distant 3rd whn p.u bef 2 out (normal 3 out)* **5/4**[1]

4m 17.6s (15.60) **Going Correction** +1.125s/f (Heavy) **4 Ran SP% 107.3**

Speed ratings: **106,103,78,**

CSF £7.80 TOTE £3.30; EX 8.10 Trifecta £35.80.

Owner John Hobbs **Bred** Mrs P Kennedy **Trained** Limpley Stoke, Wilts

FOCUS

Not a strong contest for the grade.

4534 VISIT ATTHERACES.COM H'CAP CHASE (14 fncs 5 omitted) 2m 7f 209y

2:30 (2:30) (Class 4) (0-105,102) 5-Y-0+ **£5,848** (£1,717; £858; £429)

Form RPR

6643 **1** **Foot The Bill**[28] 4032 11-10-9 **88** JohnKington(3) 97
(Patrick Holmes) *chsd ldrs: 3rd whn hit 2 out (normal 3 out): led appr last: drvn out* **4/1**[3]

1422 **2** *2 1/4* **Arthamint**[8] 4387 8-11-12 **102** (tp[1]) DavidEngland 110+
(Dan Skelton) *j.rt: in rr: pushed along fr 5th: wnt cl 2nd 3 out (normal 4 out): led appr next: wandered and carried hd awkwardly: hdd appr last: edgd lft: nt resolute* **3/1**[1]

231P **3** *1 1/4* **Kilcascan**[72] 3222 12-10-11 **90** (p) BenPoste(3) 95
(Rosemary Gasson) *led: hdd appr 2 out (normal 3 out): keepuing on same pce whn crowded sn after last* **7/2**[2]

P3P **4** *4 1/2* **Urban Gale (IRE)**[27] 4047 11-11-5 **95** (p) SeanQuinlan 96
(Joanne Foster) *chsd ldrs: hit 3rd and 8th: drvn 9th: lost pl 2 out: rallied and wnt lft last: wknd and eased towards fin* **6/1**

P355 **5** *9* **Silver Dragon**[61] 3488 8-11-0 **90** (p) BrianHughes 81
(Mike Sowersby) *j.rt: chsd ldrs: drvn 10th: lost pl and hit 3 out (normal 4 out): bhd next* **3/1**[1]

R0PP **P** **Zazamix (FR)**[11] 4325 11-10-0 **76** oh11 (v) JonathanEngland
(Andrew Crook) *detached in last: pushed along 4th: t.o 10th: p.u bef next* **33/1**

6m 55.8s (32.80) **Going Correction** +1.125s/f (Heavy) **6 Ran SP% 109.4**

Speed ratings: **90,89,88,87,84**

CSF £15.84 TOTE £6.10: £2.50, £1.90; EX 15.50 Trifecta £36.70.

Owner Colin Stirling **Bred** Milton Park Stud Partnership **Trained** Middleham, N Yorks

FOCUS

The gallop was steady for this modest handicap. The winner's best figure since December 2014.

4535 SOUTHWELL GOLF CLUB PAY AND PLAY "NATIONAL HUNT" NOVICES' HURDLE (9 hdls 2 omitted) 2m 4f 62y

3:00 (3:00) (Class 4) 4-Y-0+ **£3,898** (£1,144; £572; £286)

Form RPR

1253 **1** **Final Nudge (IRE)**[25] 4072 7-11-9 **135** GarethMalone(7) 137+
(David Dennis) *w ldr: led 2nd: mde rest: qcknd pce after 5th: rdn between last 2: edgd rt run-in: hld on wl* **1/1**[1]

351 **2** *1 1/4* **Minella Daddy (IRE)**[39] 3817 6-11-9 0 (p) SeanBowen 129
(Peter Bowen) *trckd ldng pair: 2nd 5th: drvn bef 2 out : 1 l down last: styd on same pce* **11/8**[2]

0 **3** *42* **Kalanisi Glen (IRE)**[107] 2630 6-11-2 0 DavidBass 92
(Kim Bailey) *t.k.h: trckd ldrs: j.rt: shkn up 5th: clr 3rd next: drvn and lost pl bef 2 out: sn wknd: t.o whn j. violently rt last* **6/1**[3]

0P **4** *61* **Onurbike**[24] 4097 8-11-2 0 MarkGrant 19
(John O'Neill) *led to 2nd: chsd ldrs: pushed along 5th: lost pl bef next: sn t.o: eventually completed* **300/1**

P P **King Of Milan (IRE)**[11] 4322 6-11-2 0 TrevorWhelan
(Des Donovan) *t.k.h in last: pushed along after 4th: lost pl bef 6th: sn bhd: t.o whn blnd 3 out : p.u bef next* 125/1

5m 38.6s (25.60) **Going Correction** +1.375s/f (Heavy) 5 Ran SP% 107.5
Speed ratings (Par 105): **103,102,85,61,**
CSF £2.62 TOTE £1.70: £1.10, £1.10; EX 2.10 Trifecta £2.90.
Owner Corbett Stud **Bred** M W And Mrs M Doran **Trained** Hanley Swan, Worcestershire

FOCUS
A fair novices' hurdle run at a steady gallop. A small pb from the winner.

4536 SOUTHWELL GOLF CLUB WINTER PACKAGES NOVICES' H'CAP HURDLE (9 hdls 2 omitted) 2m 4f 62y
3:30 (3:30) (Class 4) (0-100,106) 4-Y-0+ **£3,249** (£954; £477)

Form RPR

0-02 1 **Bertie Lugg**[25] 4068 8-11-0 **87** RichardJohnson 96+
(Henry Oliver) *set stdy pce: j.rt 3rd: hit 3 out : reminders and clr between last 2: 20 l ahd last: heavily eased* 2/9[1]

P300 2 *23* **Agesilas (FR)**[13] 4297 8-9-12 **74** oh4 ow1 (p) JohnKington(3) 58
(Andrew Crook) *j.rt: wnt 2nd 6th: drvn and ducked bdly lft sn after 3 out : wknd and j. bdly rt last: nt keen* 4/1[2]

6P-6 3 *3 3/4* **Johnnys Legacy (IRE)**[14] 2037 9-10-5 **85** (tp) MrSeanHoulihan(7) 62
(Ken Wingrove) *drvn 6th: lost pl 3 out : sn bhd* 25/1[3]

5m 52.2s (39.20) **Going Correction** +1.375s/f (Heavy) 3 Ran SP% 105.7
Speed ratings (Par 105): **76,66,65**
CSF £1.52 TOTE £1.20; EX 1.40 Trifecta £1.50.
Owner M G Racing **Bred** A Price **Trained** Abberley, Worcs

FOCUS
Two withdrawals took much of the interest out of this weak handicap. The winner is rated in line with the best of his bumper figures.

4537 AT THE RACES SKY 415 H'CAP HURDLE (11 hdls 2 omitted) 2m 7f 209y
4:00 (4:00) (Class 4) (0-120,120) 4-Y-0+ **£3,898** (£1,144; £572; £286)

Form RPR

3256 1 **Touch Back (IRE)**[11] 4328 10-10-12 **113** MrTommieMO'Brien(7) 130+
(Chris Bealby) *trckd ldrs: j.rt 1st: cl 2nd appr 2 out: led between last 2: drvn wl clr run-in* 4/1[3]

2164 2 *16* **Carlo Rocks (IRE)**[36] 3884 6-11-2 **110** RichardJohnson 109
(Caroline Bailey) *led: qcknd pce 7th: hdd between last 2: wl hld whn mstke last* 15/8[1]

12PP 3 *4 1/2* **Fresh By Nature (IRE)**[19] 4186 9-10-9 **106** HarryBannister(3) 99
(Harriet Bethell) *in rr but wl in tch: pushed along 7th: handy 4th 3 out : sn drvn and outpcd: poor 3rd appr last* 9/1

0-10 4 *17* **Mount Haven (IRE)**[12] 4305 6-11-12 **120** TomScudamore 96
(David Pipe) *trckd ldrs: drvn and lost pl appr 2 out : bhd whn eased clsng stages* 2/1[2]

5630 5 *49* **Filatore (IRE)**[31] 3978 7-11-5 **116** (p) RobertWilliams(3) 43
(Bernard Llewellyn) *w ldr: reminders 8th: sn lost pl and bhd: t.o bef 2 out : eventually completed* 8/1

6m 44.2s (29.20) **Going Correction** +1.375s/f (Heavy) 5 Ran SP% 109.2
Speed ratings (Par 105): **106,100,99,93,77**
CSF £11.99 TOTE £6.70: £4.00, £1.40; EX 11.60 Trifecta £45.50.
Owner Miss Laura Morgan **Bred** John O'Connor **Trained** Barrowby, Lincs

FOCUS
A steadily run handicap. The winner was thrown in on his Uttoxeter second and is rated back to that sort of level.

4538 SOUTHWELL GOLF CLUB MEMBERSHIP MARES' H'CAP HURDLE (8 hdls 1 omitted) 1m 7f 153y
4:30 (4:30) (Class 5) (0-100,100) 4-Y-0+ **£3,249** (£954; £477; £238)

Form RPR

6534 1 **Definitely Better (IRE)**[19] 4178 8-11-0 **88** PaddyBrennan 100+
(Tom George) *trckd ldrs: 2nd sn after 3 out: led next: wnt clr between last 2: v easily* 15/8[1]

5PP- 2 *7* **Clara Peggotty**[359] 4763 9-10-8 **82** (p) MarkQuinlan 79
(Tom Gretton) *chsd ldrs: led after 2nd: drvn bef 2 out : hdd between last 2: no ch w wnr* 25/1

45/0 3 *19* **Crazy (GER)**[33] 3930 7-11-7 **95** (v) AidanColeman 73
(David Dennis) *hld up: trckd ldrs 5th: reminders sn after 3 out : sn wknd* 15/2

523- 4 *80* **Solstice Dawn**[359] 4763 8-9-11 **78** MrRWinks(7)
(Peter Winks) *in last: drvn 4th: sn bhd: t.o next: eventually completed* 4/1[3]

5504 F **Pandorica**[8] 4390 8-11-5 **100** (p) JordanWilliams(7)
(Bernard Llewellyn) *chsd ldrs: drvn whn fell 5th: fatally injured* 6/1

0226 P **Rebekah Rabbit (IRE)**[41] 3789 6-10-11 **85** (t) RichardJohnson
(Tom Lacey) *led tl after 2nd: drvn and lost pl: reminders after 4th: sn bhd: t.o whn p.u bef next* 10/3[2]

4m 16.2s (19.20) **Going Correction** +1.375s/f (Heavy) 6 Ran SP% 107.8
Speed ratings (Par 103): **107,103,94,54,**
CSF £32.18 TOTE £2.30: £1.30, £8.50; EX 41.50 Trifecta £181.30.
Owner Mrs Elizabeth Fletcher **Bred** John And Iris Lunny **Trained** Slad, Gloucs

FOCUS
They went an honest gallop for this very modest handicap. The winner had slipped to a very good mark.

T/Plt: £27.90 to a £1 stake. Pool: £53663.44 - 1402.21 winning tickets T/Qpdt: £3.80 to a £1 stake. Pool: £3789.16 - 724.03 winning tickets **Walter Glynn**

4428 ENGHIEN (L-H)
Monday, March 7

OFFICIAL GOING: Turf: very soft

4539a PRIX D'ESSAI DES POULAINS (DIV 1) (HURDLE) (CONDITIONS) (3YO C & G, UNRACED OVER HURDLES/FENCES) 1m 7f 110y
12:15 (12:00) 3-Y-0 **£18,352** (£9,176; £5,352; £3,632; £1,720)

RPR

1 **Mont Lachaux (FR)** 3-10-3 0 HarrySkelton 132
(Dan Skelton) *t.k.h early: hld up in tch: untidy 4th: awkward 7th: trckd ldr fr 4 out: shkn up to ld wl bef 2 out: drvn clr nring last: styd on run-in: comf* 187/10

2 *12* **Flapjack (FR)** 3-10-3 0 ErvanChazelle 120
(C Scandella, France) 57/10[3]

3 *snk* **Jazz In Montreux (FR)** 3-10-3 0 StephanePaillard 120
(Francois Nicolle, France) 89/10

4 *8* **Okay Senam (FR)** 3-10-3 0 KevinNabet 112
(G Macaire, France) 57/10[3]

5 *3* **Gorvino (FR)** 3-10-3 0 JamesReveley 109
(G Macaire, France) 12/5[1]

6 *nk* **Desinvolte (FR)**[71] 3-10-3 0 ThomasBlainville 109
(P Leblanc, France) 58/1

7 *dist* **Saint Pierrot (FR)** 3-10-3 0 RegisSchmidlin
(Francois Nicolle, France) 122/10

P **Starkhov (FR)**[157] 3-10-3 0 BertrandLestrade
(G Macaire, France) 5/1[2]

P **Longuivy De La Mer (FR)** 3-10-3 0 MathieuDelage
(Patrice Quinton, France) 39/1

P **Boum Boum (FR)** 3-10-3 0 DylanUbeda
(M Seror, France) 38/1

F **Winner Saulaie (FR)** 3-10-3 0 GeoffreyRe
(G Cherel, France) 17/2

P **Pecuchet (FR)** 3-10-3 0 AlexisAcker
(T Civel, France) 29/1

\n\x\x PARI-MUTUEL (all including 1 euro stake): WIN 19.70. PLACE: 4.30, 2.20,
Owner Patrick Atkinson **Bred** Earl Haras De La Croix Sonnet, Mlle S Hosselet & H **Trained** Alcester, Warwicks

4540a PRIX DU MONT CENIS (HURDLE) (CONDITIONS) (5YO+) (TURF) 2m 3f
1:50 (12:00) 5-Y-0+ **£21,176** (£10,588; £6,176; £4,191; £1,985)

RPR

1 **Shelford (IRE)**[360] 4741 7-10-12 0 HarrySkelton 140
(Dan Skelton) *chsd two clr ldrs: wnt 20 l 2nd 5 out: making grnd on ldr whn mstke 3 out: continued prog to join ldr 2 out: sn led and 5 l clr at last: drew clr run-in: v comf* 146/10

2 *20* **Onsaijamais (FR)**[83] 5-11-3 0 KevinNabet 125
(G Macaire, France) 41/10[2]

3 *hd* **Djagble (FR)**[99] 2820 5-10-6 0 StevenColas 114
(J Bertran De Balanda, France) 17/2

4 *1 1/4* **Viky Du Reponet (FR)**[120] 2394 7-11-0 0 AngeloGasnier 121
(S Foucher, France) 224/10

5 *1 1/2* **Comas Sola (FR)**[99] 2821 5-10-1 0 ThomasMessina(5) 111
(J-P Gallorini, France) 191/10

6 *15* **Nouma Jelois (FR)**[135] 5-10-8 0 BaptisteMeme(4) 102
(Yannick Fouin, France) 243/10

7 *4* **Lamego (FR)**[106] 2681 9-11-0 0 Jean-LucBeaunez 100
(Mme P Butel, France) 43/1

8 *10* **Korfou De Maspie (FR)**[290] 437 7-10-12 0 BertrandLestrade 88
(S Foucher, France) 59/10

9 *1 3/4* **Singapore Sling (FR)**[178] 7-11-0 0 (p) MorganRegairaz 88
(A Bonin, France) 209/10

10 *5* **Valtor (FR)**[99] 7-10-10 0 Marc-AntoineDragon 79
(E Leray, France) 47/1

P **Plumeur (FR)**[106] 2681 9-11-3 0 DavidCottin
(G Chaignon, France) 13/5[1]

P **Cascavel (GER)**[491] 7-10-12 0 JamesReveley
(Yannick Fouin, France) 31/1

P **Piccolino (FR)**[494] 6-11-0 0 JacquesRicou
(P Peltier, France) 57/10[3]

4m 52.5s (292.50) 13 Ran SP% 119.0
PARI-MUTUEL (all including 1 euro stake): WIN: 15.60. PLACE: 4.40, 2.10, 2.80. DF: 100.90. SF: 184.20..
Owner Carl Hodgson **Bred** Brittas & Minch Bloodstock **Trained** Alcester, Warwicks

4337 EXETER (R-H)
Tuesday, March 8

OFFICIAL GOING: Good to soft (soft in places; chs 6.6, hdl 6.5)
Wind: quite strong behind Weather: cloudy with light showers

4541 RACING UK HD LAUNCHES TODAY CONDITIONAL JOCKEYS' TRAINING SERIES H'CAP HURDLE (8 hdls) 2m 175y
2:00 (2:01) (Class 4) (0-110,109) 4-Y-0+ **£3,249** (£954; £477; £238)

Form RPR

-045 1 **Bladoun (FR)**[9] 4384 8-11-10 **107** (p) MichaelHeard 115+
(David Pipe) *j.lft bdly at times: led after 1st: rdn whn nt fluent 2 out or last: strly pressed run-in: hld on all out* 6/1[3]

2 *nk* **Fort Carson (IRE)**[19] 4220 10-10-10 **100** LeroyLynch(7) 106+
(Neil King) *plld hrd: hld up: hdwy into midfield bef 2nd: pushed along in last trio after 5th: hdwy 3 out: str chal fr last: jst hld* 9/1

F0P5 3 *1 3/4* **Mother Meldrum (IRE)**[20] 4184 7-11-0 **97** (tp) DavidPrichard 99
(Victor Dartnall) *hld up: hmpd 2nd: pushed along after 4th: hdwy after 5th: chsd wnr 2 out tl last: drifted sltly lft: kpt on same pce* 9/1

2214 4 *24* **Norse Light**[24] 4129 5-11-7 **104** (p) GarethMalone 85
(David Dennis) *racd keenly: trckd ldrs: hmpd 5th: sn rdn: wknd 3 out* 6/1[3]

4P05 5 *1* **Thundering Home**[18] 4229 9-11-4 **106** (t) ArchieBellamy(5) 89
(Richard Mitchell) *j.lft bdly at times: trckd ldrs: wnt bdly lft and bmpd 2nd: blnd next: rdn after 5th: wknd bef next* 6/1[3]

0PP- 6 *17* **Comte D'Anjou**[366] 4651 7-11-11 **108** LiamMcKenna 73
(Johnny Farrelly) *a in rr: wknd 3 out: t.o* 20/1

0064 7 *4* **Still Together (IRE)**[26] 4069 6-11-4 **101** (p) DavidNoonan 62
(David Pipe) *mid-div: hdwy 4th: rdn to chse wnr briefly after 5th: wknd 3 out: t.o* 11/2[2]

6/FU P **Twyford**[110] 2601 9-10-8 **91** ThomasCheesman
(Laura Young) *mid-div: rdn after 5th: sn wknd: p.u bef next* 50/1

1550 P **Dainty Diva (IRE)**[42] 3784 8-11-2 **106** TomHumphries(7)
(Jeremy Scott) *led tl 2nd: struggling whn hmpd 5th: sn wknd: p.u bef next* 20/1

5601 P **Milan Of Crystal (IRE)**[143] 1975 7-10-9 **92** CiaranGethings
(Robert Stephens) *mid-div: hdwy 5th: wknd after next: p.u bef 3 out* 16/1

2053 B **Sartorial Elegance**[23] 4137 5-11-12 **109** (b) PaulO'Brien
(Colin Tizzard) *trcking ldrs whn bdly hmpd and b.d 2nd* 5/1[1]

4m 33.5s (18.00) **Going Correction** +1.175s/f (Heavy) 11 Ran SP% 112.3
Speed ratings (Par 105): **104,103,103,91,91 83,81,, ,**
CSF £54.47 CT £477.89 TOTE £9.20: £2.70, £2.40, £3.10; EX 56.40 Trifecta £510.00.
Owner Wayne Clifford **Bred** S Boucheron **Trained** Nicholashayne, Devon

FOCUS
Due to rail movements this was run over 30yds further than advertised. Michael Heard described the ground as "very soft and hard work in places". Modest hurdles form, with a case for rating it a bit higher through the third.

4542 WEATHERBYS HAMILTON NOVICES' LIMITED H'CAP CHASE (18 fncs) 3m 54y
2:35 (2:35) (Class 4) (0-120,120) 5-Y-0+ **£3,898** (£1,144; £572; £286)

Form RPR
P46U **1** **Themanfrom Minella (IRE)**[40] 3823 7-10-6 **112**..(tp) MrMJPKendrick[(7)] 128+
(Ben Case) trckd ldrs: untidy 1st: rdn to chse ldng pair appr 4 out: led between last 2: styd on strly to draw clr: rdn out **9/1**
4212 **2** *8* **Sonny The One**[14] 4292 6-11-5 **118** BrendanPowell 127
(Colin Tizzard) pressed ldr: rdn appr 4 out: 1 l 3rd 2 out: styd on to regain 2nd run-in but no threat to wnr **3/1**[1]
233P **3** *1 ¼* **Minella On Line (IRE)**[17] 4245 7-11-7 **120**..................(b) LeightonAspell 129+
(Rebecca Curtis) led: j.lft thrght: rdn whn nt fluent 4 out: hdd between last 2: mstke last: no ex and lost 2nd run-in **11/2**[3]
-PF3 **4** *50* **Sidbury Hill**[47] 3709 8-10-9 **113**.. KevinJones[(5)] 90
(Seamus Mullins) trckd ldrs: rdn to chse ldng pair appr 4 out tl 3 out: wknd next: t.o **11/2**[3]
P-00 **P** **Rendl Beach (IRE)**[26] 4066 9-11-4 **117**...............................(t) TomO'Brien
(Robert Stephens) trckd ldrs tl dropped to last pair 11th: mstke next: sn wknd: t.o whn p.u bef 4 out **11/1**
-424 **P** **Dancing Shadow (IRE)**[18] 4234 7-11-7 **120**.......................(p) IanPopham
(Victor Dartnall) trckd ldrs: nt fluent 8th and 9th: stmbld next and reminders: rdn after 11th: lost pl 13th: wknd 4 out: t.o whn p.u bef 2 out (b.b.v) **7/2**[2]
4335 **P** **Epic Warrior (IRE)**[25] 4109 7-11-4 **117**.........................(tp) TomScudamore
(David Pipe) struggling 11th: a in last pair: t.o whn p.u after 14th **7/1**
3314 **P** **Calin Du Brizais (FR)**[89] 2989 5-10-7 **108** oh1..............(t) ConorO'Farrell
(Nigel Hawke) hld up in last pair: wnt cl enough 5th after 14th: rdn and wknd bef next where p.u **16/1**

6m 31.3s (22.00) **Going Correction** +0.85s/f (Soft)
WFA 5 from 6yo+ 1lb **8** Ran SP% **114.7**
Speed ratings: **97,94,93,77, , ,**
CSF £37.51 CT £164.83 TOTE £9.70: £2.50, £1.30, £2.10; EX 37.60 Trifecta £207.80.
Owner Mrs Carolyn Kendrick **Bred** G Durrheim And Maria Mulcahy Durrheim **Trained** Edgcote, Northants
■ Stewards' Enquiry : Leighton Aspell six-day ban: used whip above permitted level down the shoulder in the forehand (Mar 22-24,26-28)

FOCUS
Due to rail movements this was run over 76yds further than advertised. This took some getting with conditions such hard work and only four finished. A big chase pb from the winner.

4543 WEATHERBYS CHELTENHAM FESTIVAL BETTING GUIDE H'CAP HURDLE (12 hdls) 2m 7f 25y
3:05 (3:05) (Class 4) (0-115,114) 4-Y-0+ **£3,249** (£954; £477; £238)

Form RPR
446P **1** **Speredek (FR)**[50] 3662 5-11-5 **107**...............................(tp) TomScudamore 112+
(Nigel Hawke) mde most: nvr that fluent: hit 6th: mstke 3 out: sn rdn: hdd bef last: styd on gamely to regain the ld towards fin: drvn rt out **4/1**[2]
3153 **2** *nk* **Precious Ground**[11] 4342 6-10-5 **93** JamesBest 98+
(Kevin Bishop) trckd wnr tl rdn appr 3 out: regained 2nd 2 out: led bef last: no ex whn hdd towards fin **15/2**
60P0 **3** *18* **Phare Isle (IRE)**[13] 4305 11-11-5 **114**..........................(tp) MrMJPKendrick[(7)] 101
(Ben Case) trckd ldrs: rdn after 9th: sn hld: wnt wl btn 3rd run-in **16/1**
-000 **4** *1 ¾* **Aka Doun (FR)**[89] 2995 5-11-2 **104**.......................................(v[1]) DarylJacob 90
(Emma Lavelle) trckd ldrs: rdn to chse wnr after 9th tl 3 out: hld fr next: wknd last **20/1**
551P **5** *7* **Fishing Bridge (IRE)**[32] 3978 11-11-8 **110**......................(bt[1]) PaulMoloney 89
(David Rees) hld up: rdn appr 3 out: nvr threatened to get involved **16/1**
142P **6** *1 ½* **Knight ofthe Realm**[40] 3824 7-11-9 **111**...........................(p) IanPopham 88
(Caroline Keevil) mid-div: hdwy 8th: effrt bef 3 out: sn hld: wknd last **9/2**[3]
1143 **7** *nk* **Tokyo Javilex (FR)**[103] 2732 9-11-2 **111**...........................(t) MrLDrowne[(7)] 88
(Nigel Hawke) hld up towards rr: sme prog 9th: rdn bef next: no further imp fr next: wknd last **14/1**
P/PP **P** **Kilrush (IRE)**[32] 3977 10-11-1 **108**.................................. DannyBurton[(5)]
(John Berwick) trckd ldrs tl 7th: sn bhd: t.o whn p.u bef 3 out **80/1**
6-0P **P** **Tea Time Fred**[107] 2667 7-11-5 **110**..................................... LucyGardner[(3)]
(Sue Gardner) towards rr: rdn after 8th: wknd after next: t.o whn p.u after 3 out **5/1**
1052 **P** **Kap Jazz (FR)**[26] 4071 6-11-10 **112** AidanColeman
(Venetia Williams) nvr travelling in mid-div and reminders fr an early stage: lost tch after 8th: t.o whn p.u bef 3 out **3/1**[1]

6m 30.0s (31.00) **Going Correction** +1.475s/f (Heav) **10** Ran SP% **116.0**
Speed ratings (Par 105): **105,104,98,98,95 95,94, , ,**
CSF £34.13 CT £433.55 TOTE £6.90: £2.70, £2.40, £4.40; EX 34.10 Trifecta £445.40.
Owner Kapinhand **Bred** S C E A Haras Des Monts D'Arree **Trained** Stoodleigh, Devon

FOCUS
Due to rail movements this was run over 45yds further than advertised. The front pair came clear in what was a fairly modest handicap. The winner finally built on the promise of his Carlisle bumper win.

4544 WATCH RACING UK HD FROM TODAY NOVICES' HURDLE (12 hdls) 2m 7f 25y
3:40 (3:40) (Class 4) 4-Y-0+ **£3,249** (£954; £477; £238)

Form RPR
1525 **1** **You Say What (IRE)**[13] 4305 6-11-9 125.................... TrevorWhelan 131+
(Neil King) trckd ldrs: led 3 out: sn rdn: drifted lft fr next: styd on wl fr last: rdn out **6/1**[3]
0 **2** *3 ½* **Bigbadjohn (IRE)**[102] 2762 7-11-3 0.............................. LeightonAspell 120
(Rebecca Curtis) trckd ldrs: disp cl 2nd appr 3 out: sn rdn: ev ch between last 2: no ex fr last **16/1**
312 **3** *14* **Whataknight**[26] 4066 7-11-9 140...(t) NoelFehily 116
(Harry Fry) j. sltly lft at times: led: hdd 3 out: sn rdn: fnd little and hld fr next **4/11**[1]
2125 **4** *23* **Battle Dust (IRE)**[40] 3824 7-11-3 124.......................................(p) DavidBass 87
(Kim Bailey) chsd ldrs: pushed along fr after 5th: drvn along after next: wknd 3 out **5/1**[2]
00 **P** **Hinxworth (IRE)**[25] 4097 7-11-3 0.. DarylJacob
(Nick Mitchell) pressed ldr tl rdn after 9th: wkng whn p.u bef next **100/1**

6m 28.7s (29.70) **Going Correction** +1.475s/f (Heav) **5** Ran SP% **111.1**
Speed ratings (Par 105): **107,105,100,92,**
CSF £64.40 TOTE £8.90: £3.00, £6.20; EX 53.40 Trifecta £157.10.
Owner Turner Webb **Bred** W Dillon **Trained** Barbury Castle, Wiltshire

FOCUS
Due to rail movements this was run over 45yds further than advertised. A bit of a turn up here with the long odds-on favourite well beaten back in third. The winner is rated to his best.

4545 RACING UK HD FROM MARCH 8TH H'CAP CHASE (15 fncs) 2m 3f 48y
4:10 (4:10) (Class 4) (0-120,119) 5-Y-0+ **£6,498** (£1,908; £954; £477)

Form RPR
4132 **1** **Bears Rails**[10] 4352 6-11-1 **108**.................................... TomScudamore 118+
(Colin Tizzard) trckd ldr: led appr 4 out: mstke last: styd on: drvn out **9/4**[1]
P422 **2** *1 ¼* **Renard (FR)**[11] 4347 11-11-12 **119**....................................(p) AidanColeman 124
(Venetia Williams) led: hdd u.p and looked wl hld in 4th appr 4 out: rallied between last 2: styd on into 2nd after last but a being hld by wnr **11/4**[2]
/F21 **3** *1 ¼* **The Mumper (IRE)**[16] 4275 9-11-2 **109**..................... WayneHutchinson 114
(Alan King) trckd ldrs: shkn up briefly after 8th and again after 11th: rdn appr 4 out: styd on but no ex fr last **4/1**[3]
2242 **4** *19* **Ballydague Lady (IRE)**[32] 3972 9-11-4 **111**........................(p) NoelFehily 102
(Neil Mulholland) trckd ldrs: rdn into 3rd appr 4 out: wknd 2 out **12/1**
2533 **5** *13* **Kings Cross (FR)**[18] 4225 6-11-5 **112**.................................. LeeEdwards 92
(Tony Carroll) hld up in last pair: rdn in 5th appr 4 out: nvr threatened ldrs: wknd after 3 out **9/1**
433P **6** *14* **Isthereadifference (IRE)**[122] 2346 9-10-6 **106**...(p) MrMartinMcIntyre[(7)] 69
(Neil Mulholland) racd in cheekpieces nt declared eyeshields: hld up in last pair: last and struggling after 7th: wknd 3 out **20/1**
3-2P **P** **Tolkeins Tango (IRE)**[82] 3123 8-11-11 **118**............................(t) IanPopham
(Victor Dartnall) chsd ldrs: rdn after 9th: wknd bef 4 out: p.u 3 out **15/2**

5m 10.6s (13.30) **Going Correction** +0.85s/f (Soft) **7** Ran SP% **111.7**
Speed ratings: **106,105,104,96,91 85,**
CSF £8.81 TOTE £3.50: £2.90, £1.50; EX 10.30 Trifecta £21.80.
Owner P M Warren **Bred** Brian And Gwen Griffiths **Trained** Milborne Port, Dorset

FOCUS
Due to rail movement this was run over 38yds less than advertised. Solid form for the level and a winner certainly going the right way. He's rated better than the bare result.

4546 BRITISH STALLIONS STUDS / EBF MARES' "NATIONAL HUNT" NOVICES' HURDLE (8 hdls) 2m 175y
4:40 (4:40) (Class 4) 4-Y-0+ **£3,573** (£1,049; £524; £262)

Form RPR
-245 **1** **Eardisland**[82] 3119 6-11-0 113.....................................(t) RichardJohnson 113+
(Philip Hobbs) trckd ldrs: wnt 2nd appr 3 out: chalng whn nt fluent las: sn led: edgd lft: r.o wl: rdn out **2/1**[2]
-311 **2** *1 ¾* **Rene's Girl (IRE)**[83] 3110 6-11-12 123.................................. HarrySkelton 122
(Dan Skelton) hld up: trckd ldrs: 5th: led appr 3 out: sn rdn: hdd run-in: no ex **4/7**[1]
0-34 **3** *25* **Fizzy Dancer**[138] 2033 6-11-0 0.. DavidBass 87
(Kim Bailey) trckd ldrs: pressed ldr 3rd tl rdn appr 3 out: sn outpcd: mstke 2 out **8/1**[3]
0/P **4** *9* **Mylittlemouse (IRE)**[33] 3953 8-11-0 0................................. PaulMoloney 75
(Helen Nelmes) chsd ldr tl 2nd: in tch in last pair but sn nudged along: outpcd 3 out: wnt btn 4th after 2 out **100/1**
43 **5** *3 ¼* **On The Couch (IRE)**[14] 4293 7-11-0 0................................. JakeGreenall 72
(Sam Thomas) led: rdn and hdd appr 3 out: sn outpcd: wknd 2 out **50/1**
U6-P **6** *7* **Doris De Silver**[23] 4137 7-11-0 0... JamesBest 65
(Jackie Du Plessis) hld up: rdn after 5th: outpcd bef next **66/1**

5m 1.5s (46.00) **Going Correction** +1.475s/f (Heav) **6** Ran SP% **112.5**
Speed ratings (Par 105): **50,49,37,33,31 28**
CSF £3.68 TOTE £3.00: £1.20, £1.10; EX 3.60 Trifecta £6.50.
Owner Unity Farm Holiday Centre Ltd **Bred** R Johnson **Trained** Withycombe, Somerset

FOCUS
Due to rail movements this was run over 30yds further than advertised. The big two in the market predictably dominated a mares' hurdle lacking depth, but the odds-on favourite was turned over. It was steadily run with a sprint finish but the form makes sense.
T/Plt: £463.80 to a £1 stake. Pool: £62,296.23 - 98.05 winning units. T/Qpdt: £72.00 to a £1 stake. Pool: £5,926.31 - 60.90 winning units. **Tim Mitchell**

4365 NEWCASTLE (L-H)
Tuesday, March 8

OFFICIAL GOING: Heavy (soft in places; 3.9)
Wind: Breezy, half against Weather: Overcast, dry

4547 HOLLINSHEAD HOP CONDITIONAL JOCKEYS' H'CAP HURDLE (9 hdls 2 omitted) 2m 4f 133y
2:10 (2:10) (Class 5) (0-100,97) 4-Y-0+ **£3,249** (£954; £477; £238)

Form RPR
0404 **1** **Generous Pet (IRE)**[111] 2582 7-10-9 **80**............................ JoeColliver 93+
(Kenneth Slack) pressed ldr: bmpd 2nd: led 4th: mde rest: pushed along whn nt fluent 2 out: kpt on strly fr last **6/1**[3]
65U3 **2** *4 ½* **Toarmandowithlove (IRE)**[15] 4289 8-10-3 **82**...........(t) JamesCorbett[(8)] 87
(Susan Corbett) hld up in midfield: outpcd 6th: rallied to chse wnr 2 out: effrt bef last: kpt on same pce run-in **6/1**[3]
PP02 **3** *10* **Vodka Red (IRE)**[89] 2982 8-11-0 **90**..................(b) ThomasDowson[(5)] 85
(Kenny Johnson) hld up: stdy hdwy to chse ldrs 4 out: effrt and wnt 2nd briefly bef 2 out: shkn up whn nt fluent 2 out: outpcd fr last **11/2**[2]
0066 **4** *nk* **Solway Prince**[29] 4035 7-11-9 **97**............................(p) CallumBewley[(3)] 92
(Lisa Harrison) prom: drvn and outpcd bef omitted 3 out: n.d after **6/1**[3]
0534 **5** *10* **Seventeen Black (IRE)**[12] 4329 8-10-3 **74**..................(p) GrantCockburn 59
(Stuart Coltherd) chsd ldrs: outpcd 3 out (usual 4 out): struggling fr next **7/1**
-502 **6** *8* **Titian Boy (IRE)**[21] 4163 7-10-9 **83**.......................... StephenMulqueen[(3)] 64
(N W Alexander) j.lft on occasions: led: bmpd rival 2nd: hdd 4th: upsides wnr to be omitted 3 out: wknd bef 2 out **3/1**[1]
600P **P** **Bertielicious**[28] 4045 8-10-0 **71** oh7..(p) DerekFox
(Jonathan Haynes) nt fluent in rr: struggling 1/2-way: t.o whn p.u bef 2 out **125/1**
044P **P** **Kashstaree**[21] 4163 5-10-11 **85**...................................... FinianO'Toole[(3)]
(Lisa Harrison) hld up: outpcd 4 out: struggling next: t.o whn p.u bef 2 out **20/1**
04F4 **P** **Warksburn Boy**[89] 2978 6-11-7 **92**....................................... JamieHamilton
(Sheena Walton) midfield: struggling 3 out (usual 4 out): lost tch and p.u bef next **11/1**

5m 37.0s (15.90) **Going Correction** +0.725s/f (Soft) **9** Ran SP% **109.6**
Speed ratings (Par 103): **98,96,92,92,88 85, , ,**
CSF £38.61 CT £191.96 TOTE £6.60: £2.90, £3.40, £2.70; EX 43.60 Trifecta £310.30.
Owner Miss H P Tate **Bred** R J A McGaw **Trained** Hilton, Cumbria

FOCUS
Race run over 31 yards further than advertised. An ordinary handicap, confined to conditional jockeys. The riders reported afterwards that the going was very testing. A big step up from the winner.

4548 JUDAH'S JUMPS "NATIONAL HUNT" NOVICES' HURDLE (8 hdls 1 omitted) 2m 98y
2:45 (2:45) (Class 4) 4-Y-0+ £4,223 (£1,240; £620; £310)

Form RPR
0624 1 **Very First Time**[22] 4156 4-10-7 0 BrianHughes 109+
(Tim Easterby) *trckd ldrs: led gng wl bef 2 out: sn shkn up: clr last: rdn and r.o strly* 7/1[3]
4340 2 3 ½ **Eastview Boy**[13] 4303 5-10-12 0 AdamNicol(3) 112+
(Philip Kirby) *chsd ldr: effrt and pressed wnr whn j.rt 2 out: kpt on fr last: nt pce to chal* 11/1
15 3 2 ¼ **Caius Marcius (IRE)**[114] 2514 5-11-1 0 CraigNichol 108
(Nicky Richards) *trckd ldrs: hit 5th: nt fluent next: effrt bef 2 out: kpt on same pce fr last* 10/11[1]
3 4 15 **Misfits (IRE)**[64] 3476 5-11-1 0 DerekFox 93
(Lucinda Russell) *hld up: stdy hdwy 3 out (usual 4 out): rdn and outpcd bef next: no imp after* 11/1
5 14 **Glenbank King (IRE)**[23] 4144 8-11-1 0 (t) LiamTreadwell 79
(R K Watson, Ire) *prom: lost pl 5th: rallied bef omitted 3 out: sn no imp: btn after 2 out* 100/1
2 6 10 **Nendrum (IRE)**[49] 3668 7-11-1 108 (t) PeterBuchanan 74
(S R B Crawford, Ire) *j.rt on occasions: led at ordinary gallop to bef 2 out: sn rdn and wknd* 11/4[2]
3400 7 11 **Heilan Rebel (IRE)**[20] 4176 6-11-1 0 BrianHarding 58
(N W Alexander) *nt fluent in rr: struggling 4 out: nvr on terms* 100/1
04 8 24 **Ping (IRE)**[54] 3590 5-10-10 0 RyanDay(5) 34
(Nicky Richards) *hld up: pushed along 1/2-way: struggling 3 out (usual 4 out): t.o* 66/1
400 9 13 **Been Decided (IRE)**[27] 4050 6-10-10 0 StephenMulqueen(5) 21
(N W Alexander) *bhd: pushed along and struggling 4 out: t.o* 100/1
064 F **Sweet Holly**[29] 4031 5-10-3 0 GrantCockburn(5) 76
(Lucinda Russell) *hld up in midfield: stdy hdwy 4 out: 11 l 6th and outpcd whn fell 2 out* 16/1

4m 19.1s (9.10) **Going Correction** +0.725s/f (Soft)
WFA 4 from 5yo+ 7lb 10 Ran SP% 118.6
Speed ratings (Par 105): **106,104,103,95,88 83,78,66,59,**
CSF £77.98 TOTE £7.00: £1.70, £2.60, £1.10; EX 80.80 Trifecta £646.10.
Owner Habton Farms **Bred** Conor J Colgan **Trained** Great Habton, N Yorks

FOCUS
Race run over 18 yards further than advertised. A modest novice hurdle, run at an ordinary gallop. The winner is rated similar to his bumper mark.

4549 ISAAC'S CHARGE H'CAP CHASE (19 fncs) 2m 7f 91y
3:15 (3:15) (Class 4) (0-120,120) 5-Y-0+ £6,657 (£2,067; £1,113)

Form RPR
4P21 1 **Streets Of Promise (IRE)**[20] 4186 7-11-9 117 (p) LiamTreadwell 135+
(Michael Scudamore) *cl up: led 2nd: mstke 10th: drew clr fr 3 out: easily* 11/8[1]
1334 2 22 **Tikkandemickey (IRE)**[15] 4286 10-11-7 120 DaraghBourke(5) 108
(Raymond Shiels) *prom: rdn and outpcd after 5 out: rallied to chse (clr) wnr bef last: no imp* 9/1
23U2 3 30 **The Orange Rogue (IRE)**[34] 3933 9-10-6 105 (p[1]) StephenMulqueen(5) 73
(N W Alexander) *led to 2nd: pressed wnr: nt fluent 5 out: sn pushed along: effrt and hung lft 3 out: sn outpcd: wknd and lost 2nd bef last* 7/2[2]
P-PP P **Frank The Slink**[34] 3934 10-10-4 105 FinianO'Toole(7)
(Micky Hammond) *hld up: outpcd 11th: rallied 6 out: struggling after next: lost tch and p.u bef 3 out* 14/1
321P P **Total Assets**[34] 3934 8-10-12 111 CallumBewley(5)
(Simon Waugh) *mstkes in tch: struggling 11th: lost tch and p.u 6 out* 12/1
P **Celtic Thunder (IRE)**[10] 7-10-8 102 (tp) BrianHughes
(R K Watson, Ire) *chsd ldrs: nt fluent 12th: mstke next: sn rdn: wknd bef 4 out: no ch whn p.u appr 2 out* 4/1[3]

6m 44.6s (22.10) **Going Correction** +1.10s/f (Heav) 6 Ran SP% 108.7
Speed ratings: **105,97,86, ,**
CSF £12.54 TOTE £2.20: £2.20, £3.30; EX 13.70 Trifecta £30.00.
Owner Gempro **Bred** Gareth Adair **Trained** Bromsash, H'fords

FOCUS
Race run over 40 yards further than advertised. The going was more testing on the chase course and only three got home on this modest handicap. The form could be rated a lot higher through beaten horses but it's hard to be confident.

4550 NATHANIEL'S HEDGE HOPPING H'CAP HURDLE (8 hdls 1 omitted) 2m 98y
3:50 (3:50) (Class 4) (0-110,110) 4-Y-0+ £4,548 (£1,335; £667; £333)

Form RPR
6000 1 **Bertie Moon**[12] 4326 6-10-12 96 BrianHarding 103+
(Keith Dalgleish) *hld up: pushed along after 3 out (usual 4 out): rallied bef next: led appr last: rdn and r.o strly* 10/1
4223 2 3 ¾ **Veinard (FR)**[15] 4285 7-11-2 105 CallumBewley(5) 107
(Robert Bewley) *t.k.h: hld up in tch: stdy hdwy and cl up bef 4th: led bef 2 out: rdn and hdd appr last: kpt on same pce run-in* 5/1[2]
50P- 3 3 ½ **Mcvicar**[21] 2587 7-11-5 110 (p) FinianO'Toole(7) 109
(John Davies) *hld up: stdy hdwy bef 3 out (usual 4 out): effrt and drvn bef next: kpt on fr last: nt pce to chal* 33/1
-466 4 1 **Cadore (IRE)**[93] 2933 8-10-13 100 (p) AdamNicol(3) 99
(Lucy Normile) *bhd: pushed along 1/2-way: rallied bef 2 out: kpt on wl fr last: nvr able to chal* 12/1
064- 5 ½ **Nicholascopernicus (IRE)**[420] 3659 7-11-6 104 (t) JamieMoore 103
(Kerry Lee) *nt fluent: cl up: led briefly bef 2 out: rdn and wknd run-in* 9/2[1]
4564 6 18 **Morning With Ivan (IRE)**[12] 4328 6-10-8 92 (vt) HenryBrooke 71
(Martin Todhunter) *hld up in tch: stdy hdwy bef 3 out (usual 4 out): rdn and wknd bef 2 out* 15/2
6F35 7 24 **Seven Devils (IRE)**[69] 3367 6-11-8 106 DerekFox 61
(Lucinda Russell) *prom: drvn and outpcd after 3 out (usual 4 out): btn next* 8/1
4/0 8 ¾ **The Shepherd King (IRE)**[21] 4166 12-11-4 102 (t) BrianHughes 56
(R K Watson, Ire) *led tl rdn and hdd bef 2 out: sn wknd* 20/1
4443 9 44 **Gunner Lindley (IRE)**[12] 4326 9-9-8 85 (p) SamColtherd(7)
(Stuart Coltherd) *chsd ldrs: lost pl whn hit 4th: sn struggling: no ch after* 7/1[3]
-005 P **Killiecrankie**[73] 3239 8-10-13 100 ColmMcCormack(3)
(Kenneth Slack) *chsd ldrs: lost pl whn hit 4th: sn struggling: t.o whn p.u bef 2 out* 14/1

4m 20.0s (10.00) **Going Correction** +0.725s/f (Soft) 10 Ran SP% 116.5
Speed ratings (Par 105): **104,102,100,99,99 90,78,78,56,**
CSF £60.12 CT £1600.29 TOTE £14.50: £3.30, £1.50, £6.80; EX 85.60 Trifecta £1448.70.
Owner Equus I **Bred** M E Wates **Trained** Carluke, S Lanarks

FOCUS
Race run over 18 yards further than advertised. An ordinary handicap, run at a sound gallop. The winner is rated in line with his previous hurdle best but is entitled to rate higher on Flat form.

4551 CLARA'S GALLOP H'CAP CHASE (14 fncs 2 omitted) 2m 4f 19y
4:20 (4:22) (Class 3) (0-130,130) 5-Y-0+ £9,985 (£3,100; £1,669)

Form RPR
2-21 1 **De Vous A Moi (FR)**[115] 2497 8-11-12 130 DannyCook 143+
(Sue Smith) *chsd wnr: rdn and outpcd 9th: 6 l down 4 out (usual 5 out): rallied to ld bef 2 out: styd on strly* 11/8[1]
P210 2 5 **Special Catch (IRE)**[10] 4370 9-11-12 130 JamesReveley 136+
(Keith Reveley) *led: clr 9th: 6 l up 4 out (usual 5 out): j.w tl hit 3 out: rdn and hdd bef next: sn no ex* 11/4[3]
5-P6 3 3 ½ **Edmund (IRE)**[7] 4418 9-10-6 115 (t) JamieHamilton(5) 115
(Ann Hamilton) *chsd ldrs: outpcd 7th: rallied 4 out (usual 5 out): drvn and outpcd fr 3 out* 9/1
1111 P **Caraline (FR)**[52] 3631 5-10-13 121 JoeColliver(3)
(Micky Hammond) *nt fluent: in tch: mstke 6th: struggling fr next: lost tch and p.u 10th* 9/4[2]

5m 45.2s (18.00) **Going Correction** +1.10s/f (Heav) 4 Ran SP% 109.5
Speed ratings: **108,106,104,**
CSF £5.59 TOTE £2.40; EX 5.70 Trifecta £16.40.
Owner Mrs J Morgan **Bred** Rene Wattinne **Trained** High Eldwick, W Yorks

FOCUS
Race run over 31 yards further than advertised. A fair little handicap, run at a decent gallop. There should be more to come from the winner.

4552 FORDS FENCES "NEWCOMERS" STANDARD OPEN NATIONAL HUNT FLAT RACE 2m 98y
4:50 (4:51) (Class 6) 4-5-Y-O £1,949 (£572; £286; £143)

Form RPR
1 **Bestiarius (IRE)** 4-10-10 0 JamesReveley 105+
(Keith Reveley) *hld up: stdy hdwy 5f out: rdn and outpcd over 2f out: rallied to ld over 1f out: edgd rt: pushed out fnl f* 6/1
2 4 **Blakerigg (IRE)** 5-11-4 0 BrianHarding 109
(Nicky Richards) *hld up: stdy hdwy on outside 1/2-way: rdn to ld over 2f out: hung lft and hdd over 1f out: kpt on same pce fnl f* 3/1[1]
3 3 ¾ **Black Ivory** 4-10-10 0 BrianHughes 97
(Malcolm Jefferson) *cl up: led briefly after 2f: effrt and rdn over 2f out: 3rd and one pce whn lft 3rd over 1f out: no imp* 7/2[2]
4 4 **Eaton Hill (IRE)** 4-10-10 0 JamieMoore 93
(Kerry Lee) *t.k.h: cl up: led after 2f: rdn and hdd over 2f out: no ex fr over 1f out* 11/2[3]
5 nk **Dear Sire (FR)** 4-10-3 0 AdamShort(7) 93
(S R B Crawford, Ire) *t.k.h: cl up: chal after 5f: rdn and hung lft over 2f out: sn btn* 11/1
6 23 **What Kept You (IRE)** 4-10-10 0 CraigNichol 70
(David Dennis) *hld up bhd ldng gp: drvn and outpcd over 4f out: btn fnl 2f* 6/1
7 7 **Mutawaasel** 4-10-3 0 TrevorRyan(7) 63
(Sue Smith) *led at stdy gallop 2f: cl up tl rdn and wknd fr 3f out* 17/2
8 99 **Colrockin** 5-11-4 0 HenryBrooke
(Russell Ross) *t.k.h: hld up: struggling 5f out: wknd and eased fnl 3f* 66/1
U **Dr West (IRE)** 5-10-13 0 JonathonBewley(5) 103
(George Bewley) *prom on outside: pushed along and effrt over 2f out: cl 3rd and rdn along whn edgd lft and uns rdr over 1f out* 33/1

4m 19.1s (14.70) **Going Correction** +0.725s/f (Soft)
WFA 4 from 5yo 7lb 9 Ran SP% 114.5
Speed ratings: **92,90,88,86,85 74,70,21,**
CSF £24.12 TOTE £6.50: £1.60, £3.10, £1.50; EX 30.00 Trifecta £82.50.
Owner Richard Collins **Bred** Commandant Brendan Healy **Trained** Lingdale, Redcar & Cleveland

FOCUS
Race run over 18 yards further than advertised. No previous form to go on here but it didn't look a bad bumper on paper. The first two could be above average.
T/Plt: £108.30 to a £1 stake. Pool: £70,251.25 - 473.14 winning units. T/Qpdt: £20.80 to a £1 stake. Pool: £5,413.75 - 192.32 winning units. **Richard Young**

4415 CATTERICK (L-H)
Wednesday, March 9

OFFICIAL GOING: Soft (heavy in places; chs 6.4 hdl 6.8)
Wind: fresh 1/2 against Weather: raining

4553 CALL STAR SPORTS ON 08000 521 321 (S) H'CAP HURDLE (8 hdls) 1m 7f 156y
2:00 (2:00) (Class 5) 4-Y-0+ £2,599 (£763; £381; £190)

Form RPR
6153 1 **Fair Loch**[38] 3886 8-11-5 113 MeganCarberry(5) 120+
(Brian Ellison) *mde all: wnt clr bef 2 out: easily* 4/6[1]
350P 2 14 **Gud Day (IRE)**[10] 4390 8-9-7 89 oh8 (p) HarryCobden(7) 76
(Conor Dore) *chsd wnr: kpt on same pce fr 3 out: tk 15 l 2nd appr last* 11/1
-026 3 7 **Tinseltown**[16] 1272 10-10-11 100 HenryBrooke 80
(Harriet Bethell) *chsd ldrs: drvn and outpcd 3 out: sn bhd: kpt on between last 2: 5th last: tk 3rd last 50yds* 10/1[3]
0500 4 2 ½ **Hey Bob (IRE)**[23] 4154 4-9-11 97 oh4 AdamNicol(3) 69
(Chris Grant) *t.k.h in rr: hdwy 5th: chsng ldrs next: effrt whn stmbld on landing 2 out: one pce* 11/1
5 2 ½ **Poetic Lord**[201] 1315 7-11-9 115 (t) TonyKelly(3) 90
(Rebecca Menzies) *t.k.h in rr: hdwy 3 out: sn outpcd: one pce between last 2* 14/1
26-P 6 nk **Deny**[42] 3807 8-10-0 89 oh1 (p) BrianHughes 64
(Henry Hogarth) *chsd ldrs: wknd last* 5/1[2]

4m 8.4s (15.90) **Going Correction** +1.125s/f (Heav)
WFA 4 from 7yo+ 7lb 6 Ran SP% 109.1
Speed ratings (Par 103): **105,98,94,93,92 91**
CSF £8.05 TOTE £1.50: £1.10, £5.20; EX 7.40 Trifecta £35.70.There was no bid for the winner.
Owner Mrs J A Martin **Bred** Steve Hadley **Trained** Norton, N Yorks

FOCUS
The far bend was moved out 8yds, bend past the stands 6yds. As a result of the rail movements this race was run over 42yds further than advertised. Rain overnight and in the run up to racing saw the ground soften further, and it looked to be riding heavy. An uncompetitive handicap and the favourite dominated. Not form to be overly confident about.

4554 FOLLOW US ON TWITTER @STARSPORTS_BET H'CAP CHASE (16 fncs) 2m 3f 51y
2:30 (2:30) (Class 4) (0-110,107) 5-Y-0+ **£5,325** (£1,653; £890)

Form RPR
4211 1 **Roxyfet (FR)**[3] 4513 6-11-5 107 .... FinianO'Toole(7) 117+
(Micky Hammond) *chsd ldrs: drvn appr 3 out: swtchd rt between last 2: upsides last: led last 200yds: styd on* **6/4**[2]
1512 2 2½ **My Friend George**[8] 4418 10-11-10 105 ....(p) HenryBrooke 112
(Kenneth Slack) *chsd ldrs: led narrowly appr 3 out: hdd and no ex last 200yds* **11/10**[1]
4/00 3 6 **The Shepherd King (IRE)**[1] 4550 12-11-4 102 ....(t) CallumWhillans(3) 102
(R K Watson, Ire) *trckd ldrs: led after 5th: hdd appr 3 out: upsides last: wknd last 150yds: eased towards fin* **33/1**
20P2 U **Lily Little Legs (IRE)**[15] 4298 7-10-13 94 .... BrianHughes
(Mike Sowersby) *led tl after 5th: chsd ldrs: handy 4th whn blnd bdly and uns rdr 13th* **5/1**[3]
5m 17.1s (317.10) **4 Ran SP% 107.2**
CSF £3.64 TOTE £2.10; EX 3.20 Trifecta £12.60.
Owner R J Ball **Bred** Jacky Thomas **Trained** Middleham, N Yorks

FOCUS
Due to rail movements this was run over 66yds further than advertised. Just the four runners, but solid form for the level.

4555 ALL 28 CHELTENHAM RACES ON RACINGUK MARES' NOVICES' HURDLE (8 hdls) 1m 7f 156y
3:00 (3:00) (Class 4) 4-Y-0+ **£3,249** (£954; £477; £238)

Form RPR
244U 1 **Mo Chailin (IRE)**[28] 4052 5-10-12 0 .... SamTwiston-Davies 108+
(Donald McCain) *trckd ldr: upsides 3 out: led between last 2: drvn out* **6/1**[2]
0 2 6 **Regal Ways (IRE)**[49] 3681 4-9-13 0 .... CraigGallagher(5) 95
(Brian Ellison) *hld up: nt fluent 4th: trckd ldng pair 3 out: 2nd last: kpt on same pce* **14/1**[3]
F1 3 5 **Flemensfirthleader**[13] 4324 7-10-5 0 .... PaulO'Brien(7) 98
(Keith Dalgleish) *led: t.k.h: nt fluent 3 out and next: hdd between last 2: wknd last* **2/11**[1]
P 4 37 **Hop 'n Pop (IRE)**[21] 4176 9-10-12 0 .... BrianHughes 60
(Hugh Burns) *hld up: lost pl 4th: sn bhd: t.o 2 out* **200/1**
4m 6.2s (13.70) **Going Correction** +1.125s/f (Heavy)
WFA 4 from 5yo+ 7lb **4 Ran SP% 106.1**
Speed ratings (Par 105): **110,107,104,86**
CSF £45.78 TOTE £6.30; EX 23.70 Trifecta £35.30.
Owner Mrs Sarah Leslie **Bred** Cal Flavin **Trained** Cholmondeley, Cheshire

FOCUS
As a result of the rail movements this race was run over 42yds further than advertised. The heavy odds-on favourite disappointed in what looked an uncompetitive mares' hurdle, so the form is worth little. A big step up from the winner.

4556 RACING UK IN GLORIOUS HD NOVICES' H'CAP CHASE (12 fncs) 1m 7f 145y
3:30 (3:30) (Class 4) (0-105,105) 5-Y-0+ **£5,198** (£1,526; £763; £381)

Form RPR
2522 1 **Discoverie**[13] 4325 8-10-1 80 ....(b) HenryBrooke 100+
(Kenneth Slack) *w ldrs: led after 4th: drvn 9th: forged clr bef next: eased clsng stages* **11/8**[1]
4542 2 13 **Duhallowcountry (IRE)**[13] 4329 10-9-7 79 oh1 ....(p) MissAWaugh(7) 83
(Victor Thompson) *led to 2nd: led briefly 4th: chsd wnr: one pce and j.rt last 3* **15/2**
53-0 3 12 **Nefyn Bay**[297] 354 7-11-12 105 ....(t) WillKennedy 96
(Donald McCain) *in rr: bhd and reminders 4th: poor 4th 8th: kpt on and modest 3rd last* **11/2**[3]
22-4 4 4 **Casual Cavalier (IRE)**[33] 3968 8-11-6 99 ....(b) BrianHughes 88
(John Wade) *chsd ldrs: modest 3rd whn blnd 6th: reminders next: poor 4th appr last* **3/1**[2]
5 38 **Nimdani (IRE)**[11] 4376 7-11-12 105 ....(b[1]) BrendanPowell 74
(Mrs Y Dunleavy, Ire) *trckd ldrs 3rd: modest 3rd bef 7th: effrt appr 3 out: sn wknd: hit 2 out: distant 5th whn eased last 100yds: t.o* **14/1**
6000 P **Fire (IRE)**[74] 3234 6-11-2 95 ....(t) TomMessenger
(Chris Bealby) *trckd ldrs: led 2nd to 4th: drvn and lost pl bef next: t.o 8th: p.u bef 3 out: b.b.v* **10/1**
4m 12.3s (12.20) **Going Correction** +0.85s/f (Soft) **6 Ran SP% 110.0**
Speed ratings: **103,96,90,88,69**
CSF £11.33 TOTE £2.20; £1.40, £3.20; EX 9.10 Trifecta £42.00.
Owner A Slack **Bred** Ally And Les Mitchell **Trained** Hilton, Cumbria

FOCUS
As a result of the rail movements this race was run over 42yds further than advertised. Moderate form but a clear-cut winner who was seemingly improved.

4557 GO RACING IN YORKSHIRE H'CAP HURDLE (12 hdls) 3m 1f 71y
4:00 (4:00) (Class 5) (0-100,106) 4-Y-0+ **£2,599** (£763; £381; £190)

Form RPR
-PP1 1 **Shinooki (IRE)**[10] 4391 9-11-12 106 7ex ....(p) HarryCobden(7) 117+
(Alex Hales) *chsd ldrs: drvn 9th: styd on to ld 2 out: forged clr appr last* **10/11**[1]
11P/ 2 6 **Brae On (IRE)**[738] 4577 8-11-3 95 .... JonathonBewley(5) 95
(George Bewley) *t.k.h in rr: hdwy to trck ldrs 3rd: led narrowly 7th: hdd 2 out: kpt on same pce* **12/1**
6P14 3 2 **Cumbrian Farmer**[8] 4415 9-10-2 78 ....(bt) HarryChalloner(3) 76
(Kenneth Slack) *led: hit 6th: hdd 7th: one pce fr 2 out* **11/4**[2]
2P40 4 ½ **Blue Cove**[10] 4391 11-10-0 73 oh1 .... SeanQuinlan 71
(Lynn Siddall) *chsd ldrs 5th: drvn 9th: outpcd appr 2 out: kpt on run-in* **25/1**
002 5 6 **Agent Louise**[69] 3378 8-10-4 80 ....(p) AdamNicol(3) 74
(Mike Sowersby) *chsd ldrs: t.k.h early: one pce bef 2 out* **14/1**
6 40 **Top Man Tim (IRE)**[42] 3813 9-11-8 95 ....(b[1]) AlainCawley 47
(M O Cullinane, Ire) *in rr: drvn 7th: sn bhd: t.o whn eased between last 2: eventually completed* **33/1**
0066 P **Wayward Sun (IRE)**[43] 3791 5-10-9 85 .... JoeColliver(3)
(Micky Hammond) *tiook t.k.h: hdwy 5th: lost pl 7th: sn bhd and p.u* **10/1**[3]
7m 1.7s (34.10) **Going Correction** +1.125s/f (Heavy) **7 Ran SP% 109.3**
Speed ratings (Par 103): **90,88,87,87,85 72,**
CSF £11.15 CT £20.27 TOTE £1.80; £1.10, £3.30; EX 11.20 Trifecta £21.90.
Owner Mrs A Allen **Bred** John Quane **Trained** Edgcote, Northamptonshire

FOCUS
As a result of the rail movements this race was run over 84yds further than advertised. Little depth to this moderate hurdle. The winner should still be competitive when reassessed.

4558 JOHN WADE SKIP HIRE NOVICES' HUNTERS' CHASE (19 fncs) 3m 1f 54y
4:30 (4:30) (Class 6) 5-Y-0+ **£1,871** (£580; £290; £145)

Form RPR
1 1 **Carlton Ryan (IRE)**[20] 4213 8-11-13 0 .... MrWEasterby(3) 118+
(Mrs Stephanie Easterby) *hld up: hdwy to trck ldrs 7th: 2nd 13th: drvn to ld last: hdd last 50yds: rallied to ld again fnl strides* **10/11**[1]
223/ 2 hd **Comedinewithme**[31] 8-11-0 97 .... MrRSmith(5) 109+
(I M Mason) *trckd ldrs: 3rd 15th: hit 4 out and 2 out: 2nd last: led narrowly last 50yds: hdd fnl strides* **4/1**[2]
24-2 3 13 **Forge Valley**[10] 12-11-5 107 ....(p) MrTGreenwood(7) 102
(Miss G Walton) *led: clr briefly whn hit 12th: mstke next: drvn 4 out: hdd last: fdd* **7/1**[3]
-6U5 4 23 **Little Fritz (FR)**[21] 4180 9-11-5 95 .... MrRyanNichol(7) 80
(L Kerr) *in rr: hdwy to chse ldrs 10th: 4th and outpcd 4 out: rallied and 3rd bef next: wknd 2 out* **16/1**
532- 5 5 **Scots Gaelic (IRE)**[24] 9-11-5 119 .... MissFMcSharry(7) 75
(Chris McSharry) *chsd ldrs: mstke 7th: blnd 10th: sn lost pl: wl bhd fr 11th: blnd 2 out* **12/1**
6 ½ **Fureys Bar (IRE)**[10] 8-11-5 0 .... MrJTeal(7) 74
(J Teal) *t.k.h: hdwy to trck ldrs 2nd: 2nd 8th: lost pl and mstke 14th: sn wl bhd* **9/1**
7m 10.8s (28.80) **Going Correction** +0.85s/f (Soft) **6 Ran SP% 108.5**
Speed ratings: **87,86,82,75,73 73**
CSF £4.71 TOTE £1.80; £1.10, £2.50; EX 4.20 Trifecta £12.30.
Owner S A Hollings **Bred** Frank Sinnott **Trained** Sherriff Hutton, N Yorks

FOCUS
As a result of the rail movements this race was run over 84yds further than advertised. The front pair came clear late in what was a modest hunter chase. The winner built on his recent win.

4559 FLAT SEASON NEXT MARES' STANDARD NATIONAL HUNT FLAT RACE (CONDITIONAL JOCKEYS' AND AMATEUR RIDERS') 1m 7f 156y
5:00 (5:00) (Class 6) 4-6-Y-O **£1,949** (£572; £286; £143)

Form RPR
1 **Kelka** 4-9-9 0 .... JamieHamilton(5) 96+
(Malcolm Jefferson) *trckd ldrs: 2nd and effrt over 2f out: led over 1f out: drvn clr* **6/1**
02 2 5 **Undisputed (IRE)**[22] 4168 5-10-8 0 .... MrSCrawford 99+
(S R B Crawford, Ire) *led: drvn over 2f out: hdd over 1f out: styd on same pce* **15/8**[1]
5 3 6 **Supreme Gael**[22] 4168 5-10-3 0 .... RyanDay(5) 92
(Iain Jardine) *trckd ldrs: t.k.h: drvn 4f out: kpt on one pce over 2f out* **66/1**
6 4 2½ **Floramoss**[39] 3862 5-10-8 0 .... JonathanEngland 90
(Keith Reveley) *hld up in rr: hdwy over 6f out: chsng ldrs over 3f out: one pce over 2f out* **9/2**[3]
5 1¾ **Outrageous Romana (IRE)**[25] 5-10-1 0 .... ArchieBellamy(7) 88
(Graeme McPherson) *chsd ldrs: drvn after 6f: outpcd over 2f out: one pce* **14/1**
506 6 3¼ **Cupid's Quest (IRE)**[11] 4371 4-9-7 0 .... JamesCorbett(7) 77
(Susan Corbett) *stdd s: hld up in rr: effrt 4f out: sn prom: wknd appr fnl f* **33/1**
02 7 24 **Lady Of Llanarmon**[98] 2856 5-10-1 0 ....(p) MrJMorris(7) 66
(Kim Bailey) *chsd ldrs: pushed along after 7f: reminders 7f out: lost pl over 2f out: bhd whn eased clsng stages: t.o* **2/1**[2]
8 7 **Beyondtheflame** 6-10-1 0 .... ThomasDowson(7) 54
(Jonathan Haynes) *hld up in mid-div: hdwy to chse ldrs 6f out: drvn over 3f out: lost pl 3f out: sn bhd: t.o* **125/1**
4m 9.2s (22.30) **Going Correction** +1.125s/f (Heavy)
WFA 4 from 5yo+ 7lb **8 Ran SP% 112.5**
Speed ratings: **89,86,83,82,81 79,67,64**
CSF £17.11 TOTE £6.70; £2.00, £1.10, £6.40; EX 24.60 Trifecta £414.50.
Owner The Sisters Partnership **Bred** A W Buller **Trained** Norton, N Yorks

FOCUS
As a result of the rail movements this race was run over 42yds further than advertised. Little got into this ordinary mares' bumper, which is rated around the fourth and sixth.
T/Plt: £78.70 to a £1 stake. Pool: £56,622.49 - 524.73 winning tickets T/Qpdt: £22.00 to a £1 stake. Pool: £4,603.98 - 154.59 winning tickets **Walter Glynn**

4379 FONTWELL (L-H)
Wednesday, March 9
4560 Meeting Abandoned - Waterlogged

4284 CARLISLE (R-H)
Thursday, March 10
OFFICIAL GOING: Soft (heavy in places; chs 5.7, hdl 6.1) changing to soft after race 3 (3.05)
Wind: Almost nil Weather: Overcast

4566 APOLLOBET CHELTENHAM OFFERS "HANDS AND HEELS" H'CAP HURDLE (CONDITIONAL JOCKEYS & AMATEUR RIDERS) (11 hdls) 2m 3f 61y
2:00 (2:00) (Class 4) (0-120,117) 4-Y-0+ **£3,249** (£954; £477; £238)

Form RPR
3614 1 **Captain Redbeard (IRE)**[29] 4055 7-11-6 114 .... SamColtherd(3) 126+
(Stuart Coltherd) *cl up: led 4th to bef 6th: regained ld after 3 out: pushed clr fr next: eased nr fin* **5/1**[3]
F344 2 8 **Baraka De Thaix (FR)**[13] 4342 5-11-9 114 ....(t) DavidNoonan 114
(David Pipe) *j.lft on occasions: led to 4th: regained ld bef 6th: hdd after 3 out: rdn bef next: one pce fr 2 out: hld whn nt fluent last* **11/4**[2]
0050 3 30 **Rhythm Of Sound (IRE)**[16] 4297 6-10-0 94 .... MrJoeWright(3) 62
(Micky Hammond) *chsd ldrs: rdn 1/2-way: rallied: wknd bef 2 out* **20/1**
44P6 4 3½ **Manballandall (IRE)**[21] 4206 8-11-8 113 ....(bt[1]) JamesCorbett 78
(Susan Corbett) *rn in snatches: cl up: lost pl after 5th: struggling next: no imp fr 2 out* **8/1**
1156 5 1 **Divine Port (USA)**[39] 3886 6-11-12 117 ....(t) HarryCobden 81
(Alan Swinbank) *prom: drvn along after 6th: rallied: wknd bef 2 out* **11/8**[1]

1542 6 11 **Nafaath (IRE)**[14] 4326 10-10-10 **104**....(p) MissAMcCain(3) 61
(Donald McCain) *racd wd: hld up: outpcd 4 out: sme hdwy bef 2 out: sn wknd* **8/1**
5m 10.4s (1.60) **Going Correction** +0.35s/f (Yiel) **6 Ran SP% 112.4**
Speed ratings (Par 105): **110,106,94,92,92 87**
CSF £19.44 TOTE £6.30: £3.30, £1.30; EX 20.10 Trifecta £167.20.
Owner S Coltherd **Bred** Derrymore House Syndicate **Trained** Selkirk, Borders

FOCUS
Hurdle races were on the inner course. The hurdle rail was out 9yds and as a result this contest was run over 81yds further than advertised. Modest hurdle form, the front pair well clear. The winner confirmed the merit of his easy Sedgefield win and is the type to win more races.

4567 APOLLOBET "NATIONAL HUNT" NOVICES' HURDLE (11 hdls) 2m 3f 61y
2:35 (2:35) (Class 4) 4-Y-O+ **£3,249** (£954; £477; £238)

Form RPR
-125 1 **Baby Bach (IRE)**[47] 3739 6-11-8 **129**.... BrianHughes 131+
(S R B Crawford, Ire) *trckd ldr: smooth hdwy to ld 2 out: sn clr on bridle: v easily* **4/5**[1]
-231 2 10 **Dakota Grey**[29] 4050 5-11-5 **127**.... JoeColliver(3) 116
(Micky Hammond) *t.k.h: led: rdn and hdd 2 out: no ch w easy wnr* **11/8**[2]
F 3 4 **Wazowski**[29] 4050 7-10-11 0.... JamesCowley(5) 104
(Donald McCain) *nt fluent on occasions: hld up on outside: outpcd 1/2-way: rallied after 3 out: plugged on fr last: nt rch first two* **33/1**
2000 4 ½ **Ten Trees**[39] 3883 6-10-9 99.... PaulMoloney 96
(Alan Swinbank) *nt fluent on occasions: chsd ldrs: outpcd 3 out: rallied bef next: no ex between last 2* **33/1**
4 5 7 **Too Many Chiefs (IRE)**[17] 4284 5-10-9 0.... FinianO'Toole(7) 96
(Sharon Watt) *hld up in tch: outpcd 6th: sn struggling: nvr on terms* **25/1**[3]
6 ½ **Little Bruce (IRE)** 4-10-4 0.... AdamNicol(3) 87
(Philip Kirby) *bhd: struggling 6th: nvr on terms* **50/1**
5m 12.7s (3.90) **Going Correction** +0.35s/f (Yiel)
WFA 4 from 5yo+ 7lb **6 Ran SP% 109.4**
Speed ratings (Par 105): **105,100,99,98,95 95**
CSF £2.09 TOTE £1.70: £1.10, £1.20; EX 2.40 Trifecta £10.60.
Owner Pircan Partnership **Bred** Miss Ann Twomey **Trained** Larne, Co Antrim

FOCUS
The hurdle rail was out 9yds and as a result this contest was run over 81yds further than advertised. Ordinary novice form, with the winner proving much too good. It was a slow time compared with the earlier handicap.

4568 APOLLOBET ENHANCED ODDS H'CAP HURDLE (14 hdls) 3m 1f
3:05 (3:05) (Class 3) (0-140,140) 4-Y-O+ **£6,498** (£1,908; £954; £477)

Form RPR
1000 1 **Gevrey Chambertin (FR)**[12] 4354 8-11-12 **140**....(b) TomScudamore 149+
(David Pipe) *mde all: shkn up and drew clr appr 2 out: pushed out run-in: eased nr fin* **9/2**
F133 2 13 **Isaacstown Lad (IRE)**[19] 4246 9-11-6 **134**.... BrianHarding 126
(Nicky Richards) *prom: wnt 2nd 7th: pushed along after 3 out: outpcd fr next* **5/2**[1]
3025 3 11 **Cloudy Copper (IRE)**[72] 3349 9-11-4 **132**....(tp) RichardJohnson 113
(Jonjo O'Neill) *hld up: stdy hdwy to chse ldrs 4 out: rdn and outpcd fr next: no imp fnl 2* **4/1**[3]
PP4P 4 27 **Knock A Hand (IRE)**[68] 3448 11-11-2 **130**....(v[1]) JamieMoore 84
(Kerry Lee) *w wnr to bef 6th: rdn next: rallied bef 8th: outpcd 4 out: btn bef 2 out* **3/1**[2]
P-05 5 46 **Spanish Fleet**[36] 3936 8-10-12 **126**....(b[1]) BrianHughes 34
(John Wade) *hld up: struggling fnl circ: t.o* **14/1**
2511 U **Pistol (IRE)**[17] 4287 7-10-3 **124**.... MrJDixon(7)
(John Dixon) *chsd ldrs: wnt 2nd bef 6th to next: drvn and outpcd 8th: 7 l 5th whn mstke and uns rdr 4 out* **7/1**
6m 45.0s (6.00) **Going Correction** +0.35s/f (Yiel) **6 Ran SP% 110.9**
Speed ratings (Par 107): **104,99,96,87,72**
CSF £16.07 TOTE £5.80: £2.50, £1.60; EX 15.80 Trifecta £38.70.
Owner Roger Stanley & Yvonne Reynolds III **Bred** M Jean-Marie Prost Alamartine **Trained** Nicholashayne, Devon

FOCUS
The hurdle rail was out 9yds and as a result this contest was run over 108yds further than advertised. A decent handicap in which the runners finished strung out. The easy winner is rated back to his best.

4569 RACING UK DAY PASS JUST £10 NOVICES' H'CAP CHASE (18 fncs) 2m 4f 198y
3:40 (3:40) (Class 4) (0-105,102) 5-Y-O+ **£4,223** (£1,240; £620; £310)

Form RPR
5-30 1 **Leney Cottage (IRE)**[9] 4421 9-11-1 **96**....(t) DaraghBourke(5) 114+
(Maurice Barnes) *t.k.h in rr: hdwy and in tch 1/2-way: led gng wl 5 out: qcknd clr on bridle after 3 out: 7 l up whn nt fluent last: easily* **13/2**[3]
440P 2 8 **Under The Red Sky (IRE)**[29] 4051 9-9-7 **76** oh3.... MrWHRReed(7) 80
(Kenny Johnson) *cl up: led 10th: blkd 13th: hdd 5 out: rallied: edgd rt bef 2 out: kpt on same pce* **16/1**
0- 3 2¼ **One Cool Clarkson**[26] 9-11-3 **93**.... BrianHughes 95
(Neil McKnight, Ire) *cl up: chal 9th to next: rdn after 5 out: kpt on same pce fr 3 out* **8/1**
2232 4 6 **Mumgos Debut (IRE)**[31] 4034 8-11-3 **93**....(t) PeterBuchanan 89
(Lucinda Russell) *cl up: lost grnd 1/2-way: rallied bef 5 out: effrt next: no imp fr 3 out* **10/1**
34-P 5 ½ **Major Ridge (IRE)**[91] 2983 7-11-0 **95**....(t) CallumBewley(5) 91
(Robert Bewley) *prom: drvn and outpcd after 5 out: n.d after* **100/1**
F122 6 12 **Runswick Relax**[34] 3969 10-10-6 **82**....(tp) HenryBrooke 71
(Kenneth Slack) *hld up in tch: hdwy on outside and cl up 10th: blkd 13th: blnd and outpcd next: struggling fr 4 out* **3/1**[1]
5101 7 24 **Harleys Max**[31] 4034 7-10-0 **83**.... JamesCorbett(7) 43
(Susan Corbett) *nt fluent: hld up: hit 11th: rdn after next: struggling bef 4 out: sn btn: t.o* **3/1**[1]
5440 8 23 **Glacial Rock (IRE)**[41] 3834 10-11-10 **100**....(p) CraigNichol 37
(Alistair Whillans) *nt fluent on occasions in rr: struggling fr 10th: t.o* **11/1**
P34- P **Attimo (GER)**[360] 4808 7-11-12 **102**....(t) JonathanEngland
(Sam Drake) *mde most to 10th: cl up tl outpcd after 5 out: sn struggling: t.o whn p.u bef last* **25/1**
5-31 P **Fly Home Harry**[112] 2596 7-11-2 **92**.... PaulMoloney
(Alan Swinbank) *hld up: mstke 3rd: struggling 10th: lost tch and p.u after 12th* **6/1**[2]
4-0F F **Simply Lucky (IRE)**[29] 4051 7-10-0 **76** oh7.... SeanQuinlan
(W T Reed) *nt fluent in rr: struggling 10th: rallied bef 4 out: 15 l sixth and no imp whn fell 2 out* **100/1**
5m 41.1s (4.10) **Going Correction** +0.35s/f (Yiel) **11 Ran SP% 117.9**
Speed ratings: **106,102,102,99,99 95,85,77, ,**
CSF £97.97 CT £846.34 TOTE £8.30: £2.60, £4.00, £3.00; EX 112.80 Trifecta £1034.70.
Owner P Hegarty & P Gaffney **Bred** James Hannon **Trained** Farlam, Cumbria

FOCUS
Moderate chase form. A big chase best from the winner.

4570 ROA/RACING POST OWNERS JACKPOT NOVICES' H'CAP HURDLE (10 hdls) 2m 1f
4:15 (4:15) (Class 4) (0-120,114) 4-Y-O+ **£3,249** (£954; £477; £238)

Form RPR
555 1 **Ash Park (IRE)**[39] 3883 8-10-12 **107**.... SamColtherd(7) 108+
(Stuart Coltherd) *disp ld: led 4 out: rdn after 2 out: hld on wl run-in* **9/1**
4431 2 ¾ **Sean Ban (IRE)**[17] 4285 6-11-12 **114**.... WillKennedy 114+
(Donald McCain) *t.k.h: led to 4 out: drvn after next: rallied: j.rt 2 out: kpt on wl fr last: hld nr fin* **1/1**[1]
0664 3 ¾ **Solway Prince**[2] 4547 7-10-4 **97**.... CallumBewley(5) 96
(Lisa Harrison) *prom: rdn and outpcd bef 2 out: rallied and cl 3rd last: kpt on: hld nr fin* **7/2**[2]
PF35 4 12 **Pekanheim (IRE)**[17] 4288 8-10-8 **96**.... HenryBrooke 83
(Martin Todhunter) *hld up: pushed along after 3rd: drvn and outpcd 4 out: rallied after 2 out: plugged on run-in: nvr able to chal* **11/1**
0004 5 16 **Alchimix (FR)**[34] 3973 6-10-2 **93**.... JoeColliver(3) 64
(Micky Hammond) *trckd ldrs: rdn after 3 out: wknd fr next* **4/1**[3]
4m 32.9s (3.70) **Going Correction** +0.35s/f (Yiel) **5 Ran SP% 110.6**
Speed ratings (Par 105): **105,104,104,98,91**
CSF £19.48 TOTE £12.10: £3.70, £1.10; EX 23.10 Trifecta £59.20.
Owner Coltherd McDougal **Bred** Patrick Moakley **Trained** Selkirk, Borders
■ Stewards' Enquiry : Will Kennedy two-day ban: used whip above permitted level (Mar 24,26)

FOCUS
The hurdle rail was out 9yds and as a result this contest was run over 66yds further than advertised. The front three pulled clear in what was a modest handicap. The first two are rated in line with their recent runs.

4571 WATCH RACING UK IN HD H'CAP CHASE (16 fncs) 2m 4f
4:50 (4:50) (Class 4) (0-120,111) 5-Y-O+ **£4,548** (£1,335; £667; £333)

Form RPR
3U31 1 **Swing Hard (IRE)**[17] 4288 8-11-12 **111**.... DannyCook 118+
(Sue Smith) *j.lft: mde all: pushed along fr 3 out: hld on gamely u.p fr last* **7/4**[1]
0665 2 nk **Pay The King (IRE)**[4] 4514 9-10-5 **93**.... JoeColliver(3) 100+
(Micky Hammond) *hld up in tch: stdy hdwy to chse ldrs 10th: nt fluent and outpcd 4 out: rallied bef last: kpt on wl u.p run-in: jst hld* **9/4**[2]
1421 3 1¾ **Verko (FR)**[14] 4327 7-11-2 **108**.... FinianO'Toole(7) 114+
(Micky Hammond) *chsd ldrs: mstke and lost grnd 8th: rallied and cl up 4 out: effrt and rdn whn blnd 2 out: chsd wnr last: no ex last 50yds* **3/1**[3]
/P32 4 3 **Tipsy Dara (IRE)**[17] 4288 12-10-7 **97**.... StephenMulqueen(5) 98
(N W Alexander) *j.lft on occasions: pressed wnr: rdn along 4 out: lost 2nd last: sn outpcd* **6/1**
5m 31.0s (3.60) **Going Correction** +0.35s/f (Yiel) **4 Ran SP% 106.4**
Speed ratings: **106,105,105,103**
CSF £5.91 TOTE £2.20; EX 5.50 Trifecta £9.90.
Owner DP van der Hoeven, DG Pryde & J Beaumont **Bred** Paddy Kinsella **Trained** High Eldwick, W Yorks

FOCUS
Just the four runners, but each of the quartet was in with a chance at the last. The winner is rated to his recent C&D mark.

4572 APOLLOBET INTERMEDIATE OPEN NATIONAL HUNT FLAT RACE 2m 1f
5:25 (5:25) (Class 6) 4-6-Y-O **£1,559** (£457; £228; £114)

Form RPR
2 1 **Reivers Lad**[68] 3442 5-11-4 0.... BrianHarding 105+
(Nicky Richards) *t.k.h early: trckd ldrs: wnt 2nd over 2f out: drvn to ld ins fnl f: kpt on strly* **6/4**[2]
2 3½ **Powerful Symbol (IRE)**[95] 6-11-4 0.... RichardJohnson 101+
(Jonjo O'Neill) *led at ordinary gallop: rdn over 2f out: hdd ins fnl f: kpt on same pce* **11/10**[1]
5 3 9 **Our Morris (IRE)**[68] 3442 5-10-13 0.... JonathonBewley(5) 92
(George Bewley) *trckd ldrs: wnt 2nd bef 1/2-way to over 2f out: edgd rt and outpcd fr over 1f out* **6/1**[3]
0 4 19 **Speranza**[21] 4208 4-9-10 0.... JamesCorbett(7) 58
(Susan Corbett) *hld up: pushed along and struggling 3f out: btn fnl 2f* **100/1**
5 5 14 **Paddling (FR)**[86] 3104 5-11-1 0.... JoeColliver(3) 59
(Micky Hammond) *t.k.h: prom tl rdn and wknd fr 3f out* **20/1**
05 6 95 **Flowalong (IRE)**[88] 3060 6-10-11 0....(t) BrianHughes
(Bruce Mactaggart) *pressed ldr to bef 1/2-way: sn lost pl and struggling: t.o fr 5f out* **250/1**
4m 33.2s (9.60) **Going Correction** +0.35s/f (Yiel)
WFA 4 from 5yo+ 7lb **6 Ran SP% 108.1**
Speed ratings: **91,89,85,76,69 24**
CSF £3.17 TOTE £2.30: £1.30, £1.10; EX 3.90 Trifecta £6.00.
Owner J M Stenhouse **Bred** W Amos **Trained** Greystoke, Cumbria

FOCUS
The hurdle rail was out 9yds and as a result this contest was run over 66yds further than advertised. The two at the head of the market dominated this modest bumper. The winner is rated similar to his good Ayr run.
T/Plt: £103.60 to a £1 stake. Pool of £69178.12 - 487.35 winning tickets. T/Qpdt: £38.70 to a £1 stake. Pool of £4845.65 - 92.60 winning tickets. **Richard Young**

4435 WINCANTON (R-H)
Thursday, March 10
4573 Meeting Abandoned - waterlogged

[4402]AYR (L-H)

Friday, March 11

OFFICIAL GOING: Soft changing to soft (heavy in places) after race 2 (2.30)

Wind: Fresh, across Weather: Overcast, showers

4580 RACING UK IN HD NOW! MAIDEN HURDLE (12 hdls) 2m 5f 91y

2:00 (2:00) (Class 5) 4-Y-0+ **£2,599** (£763; £381; £190)

Form RPR

04 1 **Shanroe Street (IRE)**[23] 4176 6-11-5 0.............................. PeterBuchanan 121+
(Lucinda Russell) *pressed ldr: led 7th: mde rest: rdn 3 out: hrd pressed bef last: edgd rt run-in: styd on gamely* **20/1**[3]

0F02 2 1 ¼ **Craiganboy (IRE)**[11] 4403 7-11-5 103.............................. BrianHughes 120
(S R B Crawford, Ire) *hld up in tch: stdy hdwy to press wnr 2 out: shkn up and ev ch last: sn rdn: kpt on: hld nr fin* **10/3**[2]

3 9 **Minella Aris (IRE)**[74] 3319 5-11-5 0.............................. PaddyBrennan 115+
(Tom George) *nt fluent: t.k.h: trckd ldrs: wnt 2nd gng wl 4 out: 1 l down whn stmbld bdly 3 out: sn rdn: rallied whn j.lft next: j.lft and wknd last* **30/100**[1]

0 4 35 **Here Comes Love (IRE)**[30] 4050 6-11-5 0.............................. DerekFox 75
(Patrick Griffin, Ire) *led at stdy pce: hdd 7th: chsd wnr to 4 out: rdn and wknd bef 3 out: t.o* **200/1**

6m 11.2s (371.20) 4 Ran SP% **105.3**

CSF £71.75 TOTE £13.30; EX 25.70 Trifecta £53.20.

Owner Netherfield House Stud **Bred** J P Farrell **Trained** Arlary, Perth & Kinross

FOCUS

Some starts have been moved at this track following remeasuring, so some races will not have speed figures until there is sufficient data to calculate updated median times. The going was officially soft and due to rail movement the opening race was run over 99yds further than advertised. Just the four remaining runners for this uncompetitive maiden hurdle, but a more dramatic race than might have been expected. They went no pace until approaching the turn for home on the final circuit and the winning rider said of the ground: "It's soft and though we have had the best of it the rain will help as it means they will get through it better." A big step up on his rules form from the winner.

4581 ROSS CLARK ROOFING CONTRACTOR H'CAP HURDLE (12 hdls) 2m 4f 100y

2:30 (2:30) (Class 4) (0-105,104) 4-Y-0+ **£3,573** (£1,049; £524; £262)

Form RPR

1414 1 **Transient Bay (IRE)**[23] 4184 6-10-10 91..........................(p) AdamNicol[(3)] 107+
(Philip Kirby) *hld up in midfield: stdy hdwy and cl up 7th: led gng wl bef 3 out: sn clr and pushed along: kpt on strly fr 2 out* **4/1**[1]

4220 2 11 **Bescot Springs (IRE)**[32] 4035 11-11-5 102..............(v) GrantCockburn[(5)] 104
(Lucinda Russell) *pressed ldr: lft in ld appr 6th: rdn and hdd bef 3 out: plugged on: no ch w wnr* **25/1**

0-06 3 4 ½ **Rinnagree Rosie**[92] 2980 10-10-7 85..............................(p) AdrianLane 83
(Lucy Normile) *in tch: pushed along 5th: outpcd and lost pl after next: rallied 2 out: drifted rt: styd on wl fr last: no ch w first two* **10/1**

4632 4 3 **Landmeafortune (IRE)**[52] 3672 7-11-3 95.............................. HenryBrooke 90
(Martin Todhunter) *hld up: stdy hdwy and in tch after 7th: rdn and outpcd after next: rallied bef 2 out: no imp bef last* **13/2**[3]

4P00 5 1 ½ **Higgs Boson**[24] 4163 11-9-9 78 oh4.....................(v[1]) DiarmuidO'Regan[(5)] 71
(Jim Goldie) *led tl hmpd by loose horse and hdd appr 6th: sn drvn along: rallied: outpcd after 4 out: no imp fr next* **18/1**

506 6 hd **Red Piano**[23] 4176 7-10-2 87.............................. MrWHRReed[(7)] 80
(Andrew Hamilton) *t.k.h: cl up: effrt and rdn bef 3 out: wknd between last 2* **22/1**

5153 7 12 **Hatton Springs (IRE)**[11] 4404 5-10-11 96.............................. SamColtherd[(7)] 77
(Stuart Coltherd) *prom: drvn and outpcd bef 4 out: btn bef next* **8/1**

044 8 2 ¼ **Red Story**[30] 4050 5-11-6 98.............................. CraigNichol 77
(Alistair Whillans) *hld up in midfield: stdy hdwy and prom 4 out: pushed along and outpcd next: 5th and hld whn nt fluent 2 out* **12/1**

-300 9 18 **Sultana Belle (IRE)**[15] 4328 8-11-10 102.............................. PeterBuchanan 63
(R Mike Smith) *hld up: rdn and struggling after 4 out: sn btn: t.o* **40/1**

1/ P **Jumbo John (IRE)**[23] 4192 10-11-9 101.............................. BrianHarding
(Mrs Lorna Fowler, Ire) *hld up on outside: stdy hdwy and in tch 7th: wknd bef next: lost tch and p.u bef 3 out* **9/2**[2]

0F2F P **Naburn**[24] 4163 8-11-3 100.............................. RyanDay[(5)]
(Andrew Wilson) *hld up: blnd 3rd: stdy hdwy at bk of main gp whn mstke 4 out: sn struggling: p.u bef 2 out* **17/2**

44FF U **Benny's Secret (IRE)**[25] 4152 6-11-12 104.............................. LucyAlexander
(N W Alexander) *t.k.h: hld up: checked: stmbld and uns rdr jst after 3rd* **15/2**

5m 42.5s (342.50) 12 Ran SP% **117.6**

CSF £99.83 CT £942.36 TOTE £5.00: £1.90, £6.00, £2.20; EX 85.20 Trifecta £1319.90.

Owner The Waking Ned Partnership **Bred** Kenneth Parkhill **Trained** East Appleton, N Yorks

FOCUS

Due to rail movement this race was run over 99yds further than advertised. Quite a competitive handicap hurdle and they went a fair pace in the conditions with the field finishing well spread out. A big step up from the winner with the second and third setting the level.

4582 RACING UK LIVE IN HD NOW! NOVICES' LIMITED H'CAP CHASE (15 fncs 2 omitted) 2m 4f 110y

3:05 (3:06) (Class 4) (0-120,116) 5-Y-0+ **£4,223** (£1,240; £620; £310)

Form RPR

3143 1 **Gold Opera (IRE)**[22] 4203 7-11-2 110..............................(p) BrianHarding 122+
(N W Alexander) *hld up in tch: hit and reminder 5th: hdwy to chal briefly after 5 out: rdn and outpcd 3 out: rallied to ld bef last: drvn clr* **3/1**[3]

5144 2 7 **Throthethatch (IRE)**[20] 4247 7-11-8 116.............................. PeterBuchanan 120
(Lucinda Russell) *led: rdn and hdd bef 3 out: rallied: chsd (clr) wnr run-in: no imp* **9/4**[1]

632 3 ¾ **Dr Moloney (IRE)**[30] 4053 9-11-4 112.............................. BrianHughes 115
(S R B Crawford, Ire) *trckd ldrs: wnt 2nd 7th: led gng wl 3 out: shkn up and hdd whn j. awkwardly last: no ex and lost 2nd run-in* **11/4**[2]

1364 4 17 **What A Dream**[11] 4406 10-9-12 97 oh3..............(tp) JamieHamilton[(5)] 81
(Alison Hamilton) *chsd ldr tl hit and lost 2nd 7th: prom: rdn and outpcd after 5 out: btn next* **13/2**

05P5 5 38 **Trucking Along (IRE)**[11] 4406 10-10-9 110..............(t) AdamShort[(7)] 56
(S R B Crawford, Ire) *t.k.h: trckd ldrs: outpcd bef 5 out: sn struggling: no ch whn mstke 3 out* **8/1**

5m 56.2s (356.20) 5 Ran SP% **106.9**

CSF £9.77 TOTE £3.60: £2.30, £1.20; EX 12.80 Trifecta £19.70.

Owner Macdonalds, Cardwell, Castle & Davies **Bred** J W George **Trained** Kinneston, Perth & Kinross

FOCUS

Due to rail movement this race was run over 90yds further than advertised and the open ditch in the back straight was omitted in all chases. A fair novices' handicap chase and plenty of credit must go to the winning jockey on a spare ride. A big step up from the winner.

4583 ALL 28 CHELTENHAM RACES ON RACINGUK H'CAP HURDLE (FOR THE JAMES BARCLAY CHALLENGE TROPHY) (9 hdls) 2m

3:40 (3:40) (Class 4) (0-120,116) 4-Y-0+ **£3,898** (£1,144; £572; £286)

Form RPR

1113 1 **Clan Legend**[41] 3865 6-11-2 113.............................. MrKitAlexander[(7)] 122+
(N W Alexander) *mde all: mstke 4 out: pushed along next: edgd lft last: kpt on strly* **5/4**[1]

-446 2 5 **Marcus Antonius**[23] 4179 9-10-12 102.............................. DerekFox 104
(Lucinda Russell) *t.k.h: trckd ldrs: effrt and rdn bef 2 out: chsd wnr between last 2: kpt on same pce run-in* **13/2**

/U1- 3 2 **See Double You (IRE)**[51] 3696 13-10-13 110........(p) MrRMPMcNally[(7)] 111
(Ronan M P McNally, Ire) *prom: hdwy to chse wnr bef 3 out: effrt and hung lft bef next: kpt on same pce fr last* **7/2**[2]

2324 4 49 **Quick Decisson (IRE)**[17] 4300 8-11-7 116.............................. GrantCockburn[(5)] 78
(Stuart Coltherd) *chsd wnr to bef 3 out: sn rdn and wknd: t.o* **13/2**

2465 P **One For Hocky (IRE)**[95] 2948 8-11-6 110.............................. BrianHarding
(Nicky Richards) *bhd: outpcd 4th: rdn and lost tch 4 out: p.u bef next* **5/1**[3]

4m 20.2s (260.20) 5 Ran SP% **110.0**

CSF £9.36 TOTE £1.80: £1.30, £4.20; EX 7.40 Trifecta £30.60.

Owner Clan Gathering **Bred** Alexander Family **Trained** Kinneston, Perth & Kinross

FOCUS

Due to rail movement this race was run over 66yds further than advertised. A fair handicap hurdle in which the favourite kept it simple and unfortunately another winner missed by Lucy Alexander after her fall in the second race. Her brother proved an able deputy, though. This rates another step up from the winner.

4584 EIGHT EXCLUSIVE CHELTENHAM RACES ON RACINGUK H'CAP CHASE (15 fncs 2 omitted) 2m 4f 110y

4:15 (4:15) (Class 3) (0-130,121) 5-Y-0+ **£7,147** (£2,098; £1,049; £524)

Form RPR

U134 1 **The Cobbler Swayne (IRE)**[35] 3972 7-11-12 120.............................. PeterBuchanan 129+
(Lucinda Russell) *trckd ldrs: gng wl whn hit 4 out: wnt 3 l 2nd and rdn next: hdwy bef last: led run-in: drvn and styd on wl* **3/1**[2]

-403 2 ¾ **Ballinvarrig (IRE)**[50] 3706 9-11-12 120..............................(p) PaddyBrennan 127
(Tom George) *j. sltly rt: pressed ldrs: hdwy to chse ldr whn hit 10th: led 6 out: jst over 3 l clr 3 out: edgd lft bef last: hdd run-in: kpt on: hld nr fin* **6/5**[1]

4521 3 14 **Little Glenshee (IRE)**[11] 4406 10-11-13 121 7ex.............................. BrianHarding 113
(N W Alexander) *cl up: led 3rd to 6 out: rallied and ev ch after next: rdn whn hit 4 out: wknd fr next* **9/2**

06P2 4 33 **Too Cool To Fool (IRE)**[11] 4406 13-10-1 95..............(v) HenryBrooke 67
(Jim Goldie) *led to 3rd: chsd ldr tl rdn and outpcd bef 9th: struggling bef 6 out: lost tch after next: t.o* **4/1**[3]

5m 54.4s (354.40) 4 Ran SP% **108.6**

CSF £7.28 TOTE £4.00; EX 8.80 Trifecta £17.00.

Owner Mrs R Stobart **Bred** Jerry Russell **Trained** Arlary, Perth & Kinross

FOCUS

Due to rail movement this race was run over 90yds further than advertised and the open ditch in the back straight was omitted in all chases. A small field and an ordinary race for the grade with the penalised top weight 9lb below the race ceiling. A rematch between a couple of horses who finished 1-2 here 11 days earlier, but they were well beaten by the other pair this time. The winner is probably the best guide to the level.

4585 WATCH RACINGUK HD TODAY JUST £10 H'CAP HURDLE (9 hdls) 2m

4:50 (4:52) (Class 5) (0-100,99) 4-Y-0+ **£2,599** (£763; £381; £190)

Form RPR

PP0P 1 **Suprise Vendor (IRE)**[37] 3938 10-11-5 99.............................. SamColtherd[(7)] 111+
(Stuart Coltherd) *cl up: led bef 4th: shkn up briefly and qcknd clr bef 3 out: kpt on strly fr next: easily* **11/1**

0-46 2 11 **Verona Opera (IRE)**[24] 4164 5-11-5 99..............................[1] AdamShort[(7)] 96
(S R B Crawford, Ire) *hld up: smooth hdwy to chse ldrs 4 out: effrt and wnt 2nd next: rdn and no imp fr 2 out* **3/1**[3]

0021 3 1 ¾ **Question Of Faith**[11] 4404 5-11-6 93 7ex.............................. HenryBrooke 89
(Martin Todhunter) *hld up in tch: nt fluent 5th: effrt and rdn bef 3 out: kpt on same pce fr last* **7/4**[1]

0062 4 28 **Rioja Day (IRE)**[11] 4404 6-10-5 83.............................. DiarmuidO'Regan[(5)] 50
(Jim Goldie) *nt fluent on occasions: led to bef 4th: rallied: ev ch and rdn after 4 out: outpcd whn hit next: sn wknd* **5/2**[2]

55/- 5 2 **Anitopia**[1188] 2942 11-11-7 94.............................. BrianHughes 59
(Linda Perratt) *cl up tl lost pl bef 3 out: sn struggling* **25/1**

005 6 22 **Morning Time (IRE)**[23] 4178 10-10-9 87..............(tp) GrantCockburn[(5)] 30
(Lucinda Russell) *nt fluent on occasions: hld up in tch: pushed along after 4 out: wknd bef next: t.o* **12/1**

4m 26.3s (266.30) 6 Ran SP% **109.8**

CSF £42.22 TOTE £12.30: £5.40, £1.70; EX 43.60 Trifecta £133.20.

Owner Aidan Gunning **Bred** P Travers **Trained** Selkirk, Borders

FOCUS

Due to rail movement this race was run over 66yds further than advertised. A modest handicap hurdle run at an even pace, featuring another rematch between two horses who finished 1-2 here the previous week. However, as in the previous race the pair didn't figure in the finish on this occasion. The easy winner was thrown in on the best of last season's form.

4586 RACINGUK.COM/WINTERSEASONTICKET AMATEUR RIDERS' H'CAP HURDLE (15 hdls) 3m 2f 110y

5:25 (5:25) (Class 4) (0-120,120) 4-Y-0+ **£3,431** (£1,064; £531; £266)

Form RPR

5-22 1 **Sevenballs Of Fire (IRE)**[52] 3667 7-10-11 112.............................. MrRyanNichol[(7)] 121+
(Iain Jardine) *cl up: effrt bef 3 out: rdn and outpcd next: rallied bef last: led run-in: styd on strly* **5/2**[2]

2F31 2 3 ½ **Wild West Wind (IRE)**[35] 3976 7-11-5 120..............(t) MrNGeorge[(7)] 127
(Tom George) *hld up: hdwy to ld 2 out: sn rdn: hit last: sn hdd: kpt on same pce* **11/10**[1]

4302 3 7 **Kind Of Easy (IRE)**[22] 4206 10-10-3 104.............................. MrGaryBeaumont[(7)] 103
(Alistair Whillans) *led at modest gallop: rdn and hdd 2 out: outpcd fr last* **9/1**

2-24 4 20 **Teddy Tee (IRE)**[22] 4206 7-11-12 120.............................. MrDerekO'Connor 98
(Nicky Richards) *hld up in tch: mstke 5th: rdn and outpcd bef 3 out: sn struggling: no ch whn hit last* **3/1**[3]

7m 58.1s (478.10) 4 Ran SP% **111.2**

CSF £6.02 TOTE £3.10; EX 6.60 Trifecta £23.00.

Owner A Murray Russell **Bred** Mrs Ann Cunningham **Trained** Carrutherstown, D'fries & G'way

FOCUS

Due to rail movement this race was run over 132yds further than advertised. Just the four remaining runners for this fair amateur riders' staying handicap hurdle, but an interesting field including a couple of handicap debutants. Nothing much happened for two circuits, though, and it developed into a bit of a sprint from the home bend. It's rated around the balance of the first three.

T/Plt: £9,887.70 to a £1 stake. Pool: £51,606.17 - 3.81 winning tickets T/Qpdt: £47.50 to a £1 stake. Pool: £5,984.32 - 93.10 winning tickets **Richard Young**

4422 LEICESTER (R-H)

Friday, March 11

OFFICIAL GOING: Heavy (4.3)

Wind: Light across Weather: Fine

4587 SHERWOOD RANGERS YEOMANRY H'CAP CHASE (10 fncs 2 omitted) 1m 7f 201y

2:20 (2:20) (Class 4) (0-110,109) 5-Y-O+ **£5,198** (£1,526; £763; £381)

Form | | | | RPR
3040 **1** **Kerryhead Storm (IRE)**[37] 3931 11-11-5 **109**......(tp) MrStanSheppard(7) 119+
(Matt Sheppard) *hld up in tch: jnd ldrs last: led flat: rdn out* **7/4**[1]
4224 **2** *6* **Take The Crown**[76] 3225 7-11-6 **103**..........................(t) JeremiahMcGrath 107
(Henry Oliver) *chsd ldr: rdn appr 2 out: ev ch last: no ex flat* **9/4**[2]
P16 **3** *1* **Mr Bachster (IRE)**[36] 3951 11-11-3 **100**......................(p) JakeGreenall 104
(Kerry Lee) *led: rdn appr 2 out: hdd: edgd lft and no ex flat* **11/2**
1442 **4** *8* **Thepartysover**[12] 4384 11-11-6 **103**.................................(t) TomO'Brien 98
(Paul Henderson) *prom tl rdn and wknd 2 out* **3/1**[3]

4m 17.5s (9.30) **Going Correction** +0.50s/f (Soft) **4** Ran SP% **107.5**

Speed ratings: **96,93,92,88**

CSF £6.03 TOTE £2.50; EX 5.40 Trifecta £14.20.

Owner Simon Gegg **Bred** James R Browne **Trained** Eastnor, H'fords

FOCUS

Testing conditions for this all-chase card. After riding in the first, Jeremiah McGrath said: "It's terrible ground." The first two fences in the home straight were missed out all day, and all race distances were as advertised. The opener was run at a reasonable pace and the form looks sound enough. The winner is rated to his best.

4588 ROYAL LANCERS BEGINNERS' CHASE (10 fncs 2 omitted) 1m 7f 201y

2:50 (2:50) (Class 4) 5-Y-O+ **£5,198** (£1,526; £763; £381)

Form | | | | RPR
FPP3 **1** **Swizzler (IRE)**[7] 4458 7-11-2 0.. WillKennedy 98+
(Ian Williams) *mde all: shkn up appr last: rdn out* **10/11**[1]
204/ **2** *4* **Hit The Headlines (IRE)**[391] 10-11-2 119........................(t) TomCannon 93
(Luke Dace) *w wnr tl nt fluent 5th: remained in 2nd pl tl appr 2 out: rallied to chse wnr bef last: no ex flat* **5/2**[2]
4PP5 **3** *5* **Rock Of Ages**[41] 3868 7-10-9 0...............................(tp) MrJNixon(7) 87
(Steve Flook) *prom: rdn to chse wnr appr 2 out tl bef last: wknd flat* **14/1**
-024 **4** *1 3/4* **Boston Blue**[21] 3314 9-10-11 110.. NickSlatter(5) 87
(Tony Carroll) *prom: mstke 4th: pushed along after 3 out: rdn and wknd appr last* **4/1**[3]

4m 22.9s (14.70) **Going Correction** +0.50s/f (Soft) **4** Ran SP% **107.6**

Speed ratings: **83,81,78,77**

CSF £3.60 TOTE £2.00; EX 4.30 Trifecta £13.90.

Owner Peter P Elliott **Bred** Mrs Kathleen Hoey **Trained** Portway, Worcs

FOCUS

This very weak event was run 5.4sec slower than the opening handicap. Not form to treat too seriously.

4589 PETE ESCOBAR H'CAP CHASE (11 fncs 4 omitted) 2m 4f 45y

3:25 (3:27) (Class 3) (0-130,127) 5-Y-O+ **£6,498** (£1,908; £954; £477)

Form | | | | RPR
232U **1** **Vic De Touzaine (FR)**[9] 4436 7-11-5 **120**........................ LiamTreadwell 135+
(Venetia Williams) *hld up: hdwy 5th: chsd ldr 9th: led wl bef 2 out: rdn clr appr last: styd on wl* **15/8**[1]
-1P4 **2** *8* **Toby Lerone (IRE)**[85] 3126 9-11-10 **125**......................(b) HarrySkelton 130
(Dan Skelton) *led: rdn and hdd wl bef 2 out: styd on same pce appr last* **7/1**
0/14 **3** *14* **Prideofthecastle (IRE)**[22] 4212 9-11-12 **127**.............. TomScudamore 118
(David Pipe) *hld up: hdwy to chse ldr appr 7th tl 9th: rdn and wknd bef last* **2/1**[2]
5204 **4** *3 1/4* **Saint Raph (FR)**[20] 4251 8-11-2 **117**................................(t) AdamWedge 108
(Robert Walford) *chsd ldr tl appr 7th: wknd after next* **11/2**[3]
41P3 **5** *11* **Morney Wing (IRE)**[21] 4232 7-11-7 **122**....................(tp) DenisO'Regan 102
(Charlie Mann) *chsd ldrs: pushed along appr 4th: lost pl after next: bhd fr 7th* **15/2**

5m 24.9s (6.00) **Going Correction** +0.50s/f (Soft) **5** Ran SP% **107.8**

Speed ratings: **108,104,99,97,93**

CSF £13.25 TOTE £2.40: £1.40, £2.80; EX 11.70 Trifecta £29.10.

Owner A Brooks & G Moore **Bred** Daniel Jandard & Mme Andree Jandard **Trained** Kings Caple, H'fords

FOCUS

A fair handicap chase. Another step forward from the winner.

4590 LEICESTERSHIRE AND DERBYSHIRE YEOMANRY H'CAP CHASE (11 fncs 4 omitted) 2m 4f 45y

4:00 (4:00) (Class 5) (0-100,97) 5-Y-O+ **£3,898** (£1,144; £572)

Form | | | | RPR
5-36 **1** **Beaujolais Bob**[40] 8-9-11 **71** oh5..........................(bt) ConorShoemark(3) 92+
(Richard Hawker) *mde all: rdn clr appr 2 out* **7/2**[3]
1234 **2** *32* **Riddlestown (IRE)**[12] 4391 9-11-12 **97**..........................(b) HarrySkelton 82
(Caroline Fryer) *prom: pushed along after 3 out: sn wknd: wnt 2nd towards fin* **4/5**[1]
1233 **3** *6* **Tachbury**[225] 1158 12-11-1 **86**...(p) TomO'Brien 68
(Tim Vaughan) *chsd wnr: hit 7th: rdn and wkng whn mstke 2 out* **11/4**[2]

5m 33.0s (14.10) **Going Correction** +0.50s/f (Soft) **3** Ran SP% **104.4**

Speed ratings: **91,78,75**

CSF £6.60 TOTE £4.40; EX 6.30 Trifecta £8.00.

Owner Richard Hawker **Bred** Mrs Sarah Hawker **Trained** Rode, Somerset

FOCUS

A weak event run in a time around eight seconds slower than the earlier Class 3 handicap. The winner is rated in line wih his old bumper mark.

4591 SOUTH NOTTS HUSSARS H'CAP CHASE (14 fncs 4 omitted) 2m 6f 151y

4:35 (4:35) (Class 5) (0-100,100) 5-Y-O+ **£3,898** (£1,144; £572)

Form | | | | RPR
3-42 **1** **Whiskey Chaser (IRE)**[23] 4175 8-11-12 **100**........................ WillKennedy 118+
(Donald McCain) *chsd ldr tl led after 7th: wnt clr appr 2 out: easily* **7/2**[3]
P222 **2** *31* **Basford Ben**[19] 4276 8-11-12 **100**..(b) SeanQuinlan 80
(Jennie Candlish) *led: hdd and reminders after 7th: wknd 11th: wnt remote 2nd last* **3/1**[2]
PP11 **3** *39* **Some Finish (IRE)**[10] 4423 7-11-3 **91** 7ex..................(v) CharliePoste 44
(Robin Dickin) *prom: jnd wnr 8th tl mstke 10th: rdn bef 12th: wknd appr 2 out* **8/11**[1]

6m 21.2s (17.20) **Going Correction** +0.50s/f (Soft) **3** Ran SP% **105.1**

Speed ratings: **90,79,65**

CSF £11.06 TOTE £3.60; EX 5.40 Trifecta £5.40.

Owner Deva Racing Flemensfirth Partnership **Bred** P Coghlan **Trained** Cholmondeley, Cheshire

FOCUS

Modest chasing form. They didn't go a bad tempo and finished at wide intervals. A seemingly massive step up from the winner.

4592 H.A.C. PIPELINE OPEN HUNTERS' CHASE (10 fncs 2 omitted) 1m 7f 201y

5:10 (5:10) (Class 6) 5-Y-O+ **£1,871** (£580; £290; £145)

Form | | | | RPR
-201 **1** **Delta Borget (FR)**[17] 4295 11-11-9 108..............................(p) MissVWade(7) 130+
(L Jefford) *disp ld tl wnt on 6th: shkn up appr last: styd on wl* **11/1**
20-2 **2** *4 1/2* **Dineur (FR)**[19] 4269 10-11-5 116.. MrJamesKing(7) 121
(Mickey Bowen) *disp ld to 3rd: remained handy: ev ch 2 out: sn rdn: styd on same pce last* **3/1**[2]
0-40 **3** *23* **Bobcatbilly (IRE)**[22] 4207 10-12-1 137.............................. MrRyanBird(5) 106
(Ian Williams) *chsd ldrs tl rdn and wknd appr 2 out* **4/1**[3]
42B- **4** *5* **Siro Demur (FR)**[68] 10-12-3 120...................................... MrAlexEdwards(3) 101
(Philip Rowley) *hld up: hdwy 7th: rdn and wknd appr 2 out* **5/2**[1]
6050 **5** *19* **Oyster Shell**[236] 1046 9-11-9 0.................................(t) MrEGlassonbury(3) 74
(Oliver Greenall) *hld up: rdn and wknd after 3 out* **9/1**
50PP **6** *10* **Midnight Appeal**[10] 4424 11-11-7 127.......................(vt) MrRobertHawker(5) 64
(Sophie Leech) *disp ld to 6th: mstke next: rdn and wknd appr 2 out* **16/1**
4662 **U** **Swallows Delight (IRE)**[17] 4295 11-11-11 108..................... MissHLewis(5)
(Mrs Julie Mansell) *prom tl blnd and uns rdr 7th* **10/1**
-1P3 **P** **Can Mestret (IRE)**[21] 4227 9-11-13 108................................ MrJAndrews(7)
(S R Andrews) *hld up: wknd 3 out: bhd whn p.u bef 2 out* **11/1**

4m 16.1s (7.90) **Going Correction** +0.50s/f (Soft) **8** Ran SP% **115.2**

Speed ratings: **100,97,86,83,74 69, ,**

CSF £45.84 TOTE £13.70: £2.50, £2.00, £1.20; EX 47.70 Trifecta £287.60.

Owner Here Come The Girls **Bred** Xavier Goupil & Laurent Boron **Trained** Kentisbeare, Devon

FOCUS

The biggest field of the day and a disputed gallop in this hunter chase, which was the quickest of the three races over the trip. The first two came well clear and the form could be rated higher.

T/Plt: £795.90 to a £1 stake. Pool: £50,927.42 - 46.71 winning tickets T/Qpdt: £78.10 to a £1 stake. Pool: £3,759.14 - 35.60 winning tickets **Colin Roberts**

4229 SANDOWN (R-H)

Friday, March 11

OFFICIAL GOING: Chase course - soft (heavy in places, good to soft in places back straight); hurdle course - heavy (soft in places back straight, good to soft in places back straight)

Wind: Almost nil Weather: Fine, emergence of spring

4593 QUEEN ELIZABETH THE QUEEN MOTHER MEMORIAL AMATEUR RIDERS' H'CAP HURDLE (MILITARY AMATEUR RIDERS) (8 hdls) 1m 7f 216y

2:10 (2:12) (Class 4) (0-115,113) 4-Y-O+ **£3,743** (£1,161; £580; £290)

Form | | | | RPR
2213 **1** **Loves Destination**[11] 4413 5-10-6 **94**.......................... OCdtOswaldWedmore(7) 98+
(Chris Gordon) *led to after 2nd: lost pl and in rr bef next: 10 l bhd ldr in 5th on long run after 3 out: urged along and clsd to go 2nd 2 out: led bef last: kpt on wl* **9/2**[2]
-006 **2** *2* **Kastani Beach (IRE)**[94] 2956 10-10-13 **101**..........(v) LtColEricaBridge(7) 104
(Seamus Mullins) *led after 2nd to 3 out: urged along and dropped to 4th 2 out: kpt on fr last to take 2nd flat* **11/2**[3]
025 **3** *4* **Un Prophete (FR)**[37] 3932 5-11-7 **105**.............................. MrJSole(3) 103+
(Venetia Williams) *lw: jnd ldrs 4th: led 3 out: 4 l clr and gng strly on long run after: c bk to rivals and rdn 2 out: hdd bef last: fdd* **7/2**[1]
00/3 **4** *4* **Just When**[101] 2831 7-11-4 **106**.......................................(v) MrGDisney(7) 100
(Patrick Chamings) *w ldrs: chsd ldr 3 out to 2 out: fdd* **8/1**
-402 **5** *3 3/4* **Smart Catch (IRE)**[21] 4229 10-11-3 **105**.................. CaptMaxChenery(7) 96
(Tony Carroll) *chsd ldng trio fr 4th: pushed along to cl and wl on terms 2 out: urged along and wknd bdly fr last* **9/2**[2]
P144 **6** *1 1/4* **West Of The Edge (IRE)**[11] 4412 8-11-5 **107**.......(v[1]) SACSamWilliams(7) 95
(Dai Williams) *w ldrs: lost pl 3rd: struggling in rr 3 out: n.d after: plugged on* **14/1**
-5P6 **7** *67* **Tresor De Bontee (FR)**[72] 3367 9-11-11 **113**.............. LtWillKellard(7) 34
(Kerry Lee) *a in rr: lost tch whn nt fluent 5th: t.o* **12/1**
3F0R **R** **Newton Geronimo**[36] 3950 7-11-7 **109**.......................... CaptHarryWallace(7)
(Ben Pauling) *ref to r* **7/1**

4m 20.7s (13.50) **Going Correction** +0.975s/f (Soft) **8** Ran SP% **111.9**

Speed ratings (Par 105): **105,104,102,100,98 97,64,**

CSF £28.22 CT £94.17 TOTE £4.00: £1.70, £1.10, £3.20; EX 25.90 Trifecta £140.30.

Owner Chris Gordon Racing Club **Bred** Hazeley Stud **Trained** Morestead, Hampshire

■ Ossie Wedmore's first winner under rules.

FOCUS
The home bend was shared by chasers and hurdlers. Hurdle distances remained as advertised, but 2m chases were plus 20 yards, while 3m chases were plus 40 yards. They went a sound gallop in this modest handicap for military amateur riders and the form makes sense. The second sets the level.

4594 OLLIE MCPHAIL'S 1000TH RACING TO SCHOOL "NATIONAL HUNT" NOVICES' HURDLE (8 hdls) 1m 7f 216y
2:40 (2:42) (Class 4) 4-Y-0+ £4,328 (£1,574)

Form RPR
/032 1 **Starving Marvin**[21] 4233 8-11-1 0 LeightonAspell 115
(Rod Millman) *led: styd far side in st: rdn and hdd 2 out: 6 l down and no ch whn lft in ld 100yds out* **2/1**[2]
35 2 6 **What's The Scoop (IRE)**[28] 4097 6-11-1 0 BarryGeraghty 130+
(Nicky Henderson) *lw: hld up bhd other pair: nt fluent 3rd and 5th: c nr side in st and clsd to ld 2 out: sn clr: 6 l ld and cantering whn turned 90°½ lft: careered towards rail 100yds out and stopped: got gng again but no ch to rcvr* **7/2**[3]
1202 U **Air Horse One**[48] 3745 5-11-1 0 NoelFehily
(Harry Fry) *slowed into 1st: j. it bdly lft and uns rdr* **6/4**[1]
P **Bad Boy Du Pouldu (FR)**[54] 5-11-8 0 JoshuaMoore
(Gary Moore) *quite str: lw: trckd ldr: hit 3 out: rdn to chal after it: wknd rapidly on long run to 2 out where mstke: p.u bef last* **8/1**
4m 21.4s (14.20) **Going Correction** +0.975s/f (Soft) **4** Ran SP% **106.7**
Speed ratings (Par 105): **103,100,**
CSF £8.60 TOTE £2.50; EX 8.40 Trifecta £11.70.
Owner Seasons Holidays **Bred** Seasons Holidays Plc **Trained** Kentisbeare, Devon
FOCUS
Only four runners here but it proved highly eventful. There's a case for rating the race up to 7lb higher through the lucky winner.

4595 GRAND MILITARY GOLD CUP (CHASE FOR MILITARY AMATEUR RIDERS) (SPONSORED BY THE MILITARY MUTUAL) (22 fncs) 3m 37y
3:15 (3:23) (Class 3) 6-Y-0+ £6,239 (£1,935; £967; £484)

Form RPR
3231 1 **Jennys Surprise (IRE)**[21] 4232 8-11-5 127 LtColEricaBridge(7) 126+
(Fergal O'Brien) *early errors but cl up: prog to ld bef 12th: mde most after: gng best fr 2 out: pushed out flat* **15/8**[1]
-0P0 2 1½ **Ardkilly Witness (IRE)**[75] 3282 10-12-3 130 (t) CaptHarryWallace(7) 134
(Jamie Snowden) *led 3rd tl j. slowly next: led 9th tl big jump 11th and sn hdd: pressed wnr fr 12th to 3 out: rdn and kpt on to go 2nd again after last* **5/1**
P-65 3 1 **Minellahalfcentury (IRE)**[38] 3918 8-12-2 127 (tp) MrJSole(3) 129
(Paul Nicholls) *lw: hld up in last: prog to trck ldng pair 14th: wnt cl 2nd 3 out: rdn and nt qckn after 2 out: lost 2nd after last* **7/2**[2]
16PP 4 1¾ **Wilton Milan (IRE)**[25] 4155 8-11-12 130 (t) MrGDisney(7) 127
(Dan Skelton) *wl in tch: blnd 15th: outpcd 3 out: kpt on again fr last* **9/1**
1F 5 4½ **Seamus Mor (IRE)**[38] 3916 8-11-7 118 CaptMaxChenery(7) 117
(Henry Oliver) *t.k.h: led after 4th to 9th: lost pl and in rr 12th: effrt again 3 out: on terms and urged along out wd bef 2 out: fdd* **10/1**
4PP4 6 1¾ **Cowards Close (IRE)**[21] 4232 9-11-12 123 (t) OCdtOswaldWedmore(7) 119
(Chris Gordon) *led to 3rd: dropped to rr 13th: lost tch w rest after 4 out: kpt on again fr last* **9/2**[3]
/PP- 7 17 **Dead Or Alive (IRE)**[19] 13-11-7 95 CaptJamesRawdon-Mogg(7) 100
(Miss Rose Grissell) *w ldrs: led briefly 4th and again after 11th: slow jump 14th and dropped to rr: rallied 4 out: wknd bef 3 out* **100/1**
311P U **Very Live (FR)**[21] 4232 7-11-7 102 (b[1]) LtWillKellard(7)
(Paul Webber) *uns rdr 1st* **33/1**
6m 52.3s (24.50) **Going Correction** +1.05s/f (Soft) **8** Ran SP% **114.9**
Speed ratings: **101,100,100,99,98 97,91,**
CSF £12.14 TOTE £2.40: £1.10, £1.80, £2.00; EX 12.10 Trifecta £33.80.
Owner Yes No Wait Sorries and G & P Barker Ltd **Bred** Denis J Reddan **Trained** Naunton, Gloucs
FOCUS
Add 40 yards to race distance. An up-to-scratch running of this long-standing Military Chase. It was a complicated going report on the chase track, with soft, heavy and good to soft in places on the back straight given. The winner is rated similar to her Royal Artillery win.

4596 TEAM ARMY H'CAP HURDLE (11 hdls) 2m 5f 110y
3:50 (3:53) (Class 3) (0-135,133) 4-Y-0+
£8,758 (£2,587; £1,293; £646; £323; £162)

Form RPR
6352 1 **Ballycross**[74] 3316 5-11-0 121 SamTwiston-Davies 129+
(Nigel Twiston-Davies) *lw: trckd ldr: only one to come wd in home st first time: led 5th: mde rest: clr and gng strly bef 2 out: rdn out: unchal* **7/1**[3]
16/1 2 4 **Spencer Lea**[31] 4041 8-10-13 120 RichardJohnson 125+
(Henry Oliver) *hld up in last: mstke 6th: prog fr next: rdn to chse wnr bef 2 out: kpt on wl but no imp fr last* **5/1**[2]
-112 3 8 **Bon Enfant (FR)**[34] 3994 5-11-7 128 GavinSheehan 123
(Warren Greatrex) *lw: prom: lost pl and nt fluent 7th: effrt and drvn bef 2 out: tk 3rd last: one pce after* **9/2**[1]
2-10 4 nk **Bells 'N' Banjos (IRE)**[76] 3232 6-11-9 133 HarryBannister(3) 128
(Warren Greatrex) *led to 5th: chsd wnr to 7th: wnt 2nd again briefly on long run bef 2 out: one pce u.p after* **20/1**
-013 5 1¾ **Suit Yourself (IRE)**[36] 3949 7-11-2 123 (t) BarryGeraghty 117
(Jonjo O'Neill) *hld up in midfield: dropped to rr 6th: shuffled along and prog bef 2 out where 5th: looked to be hanging and no hdwy after* **12/1**
3353 6 2 **American Life (FR)**[7] 4467 9-10-4 111 (vt) PaulMoloney 102
(Sophie Leech) *hld up in last trio: tried to make prog on inner bef 2 out: no real hdwy after 2 out: kpt on* **33/1**
F054 7 ½ **Little Boy Boru (IRE)**[34] 3992 8-10-8 120 JackSherwood(5) 110
(Suzy Smith) *in tch: prog 8th: rdn on long run bef 2 out: sn btn* **12/1**
4413 8 1¾ **Cadoudoff (FR)**[20] 4252 6-11-6 127 (p) AidanColeman 116
(Charlie Longsdon) *settled in midfield: effrt and cl up fr 8th tl rdn and wknd bef 2 out* **14/1**
421 9 5 **Doctor Look Here (IRE)**[92] 2989 6-10-8 118 LucyGardner(3) 103
(Sue Gardner) *hld up: a in last trio: urged along and no prog on long run bef 2 out* **10/1**
2 10 17 **Ayalor (FR)**[35] 3978 6-11-0 121 (t) NoelFehily 93
(Harry Fry) *hld up in midfield: blnd 3rd: rdn on long run bef 2 out and no prog: sn wknd: t.o* **9/2**[1]
41 U **Le Boizelo (FR)**[21] 4235 5-11-4 125 JamieMoore 97
(Robert Walford) *prom: chsd wnr 7th tl wknd rapidly bef 2 out: disputing last whn blnd and uns rdr last* **17/2**
5m 54.1s (31.60) **11** Ran SP% **114.9**
CSF £41.55 CT £175.45 TOTE £9.10: £2.50, £1.90, £1.60; EX 52.80 Trifecta £224.20.
Owner The Autism Rockers **Bred** Mill House Stud (shropshire) Ltd **Trained** Naunton, Gloucs

FOCUS
This looked competitive but it rather fell apart up the home straight as being held up proved a disadvantage in a steadily run race. The first two are on the upgrade.

4597 ALBERT HALL DANCE FLOORS H'CAP CHASE (13 fncs) 1m 7f 119y
4:25 (4:27) (Class 3) (0-125,123) 5-Y-0+ £7,147 (£2,098; £1,049; £524)

Form RPR
0F05 1 **Irish Thistle (IRE)**[21] 4232 9-11-4 118 JamesBanks(3) 126+
(Dai Williams) *stmbld 1st: racd in 4th: mstke 4 out: shkn up to cl on ldng trio bef 3 out: drvn 2 out: styd on wl fr last to ld fnl strides* **4/1**[2]
3504 2 nk **Malanos (IRE)**[22] 4211 8-10-4 101 LeeEdwards 107
(Tony Carroll) *led: jnd 3 out: hdd after 2 out: rallied to ld fnl 100yds: hdd last strides* **10/1**
4101 3 1 **Chestnut Ben (IRE)**[33] 4011 11-11-4 122 MrWinks(7) 128
(Peter Winks) *trckd ldr to 9th: styd cl up: rdn on inner 3 out: clsd to ld after 2 out: hdd u.p fnl 100yds* **6/1**[3]
31P5 4 2½ **Olympian Boy (IRE)**[22] 4197 12-10-0 97 (t) PaulMoloney 102
(Sophie Leech) *hld up in last: stuttered into 6th: detached after: rdn bef 3 out: stl wl off the pce 2 out: fin wl fr last* **6/1**[3]
-621 5 3¾ **The Brock Again**[17] 4292 6-11-12 123 (t) SamTwiston-Davies 122
(Paul Nicholls) *trckd ldng pair: nt fluent 7th (water): wnt 2nd 9th: chal and upsides 3 out and next: sn rdn and fnd nil: wknd qckly fr last* **10/11**[1]
4m 15.7s (13.90) **Going Correction** +1.05s/f (Soft) **5** Ran SP% **110.0**
Speed ratings: **107,106,106,105,103**
CSF £33.50 TOTE £4.50: £1.60, £4.90; EX 36.80 Trifecta £130.80.
Owner F Michael **Bred** Ms C Corrigan & Tom Conway **Trained** Broad Hinton, Wilts
FOCUS
Add 20 yards to race distance. A modest handicap chase, run at a brisk gallop. The winner was very well in on Irish form.

4598 ANNE BOLEYN MARES' NOVICES' HURDLE (9 hdls) 2m 3f 173y
5:00 (5:02) (Class 4) 4-Y-0+ £3,898 (£1,144; £572; £286)

Form RPR
2 1 **Bagging Turf (IRE)**[36] 3947 6-10-12 0 JamieMoore 100+
(Gary Moore) *q str: edgy: nt a fluent: trckd ldrs: led 4th: rdn bef 2 out: hdd after and awkward last: rallied to ld fnl 100yds* **8/13**[1]
04 2 ½ **Hollow Bay**[56] 3608 6-10-12 0 RichieMcLernon 98
(Paul Webber) *lw: hld up in last: produced to chal 2 out: rdn to ld last: hdd and no ex fnl 100yds* **9/2**[2]
0204 3 3½ **Tara Well (IRE)**[4] 4530 6-10-2 0 CathalCourtney(10) 95
(Robin Dickin) *led at mod pce to 4th: cl up after: drvn to chal bef 2 out: one pce bef last* **13/2**
04 4 13 **Top And Drop**[25] 4157 5-10-12 0 AidanColeman 84
(Venetia Williams) *on toes: swtg: cl up: rdn wl bef 2 out: btn whn mstke 2 out: wknd* **6/1**[3]
5m 39.2s (39.60) **Going Correction** +0.975s/f (Soft) **4** Ran SP% **107.7**
Speed ratings (Par 105): **59,58,57,52**
CSF £3.72 TOTE £1.30; EX 4.70 Trifecta £8.10.
Owner Mrs M Devine **Bred** Mrs M Devine **Trained** Lower Beeding, W Sussex
■ Stewards' Enquiry : Jamie Moore two-day ban; used whip above the permitted level (26th-27th Mar)
FOCUS
This was a tactical affair, resulting in a messy finish, and it's probably unreliable form. The winner is rated below her best.
T/Plt: £185.70 to a £1 stake. Pool: £72,517.16 - 285.05 winning tickets T/Qpdt: £34.00 to a £1 stake. Pool: £6,375.81 - 138.50 winning tickets **Jonathan Neesom**

4599 - 4604a (Foreign Racing) - See Raceform Interactive

4580 AYR (L-H)
Saturday, March 12

OFFICIAL GOING: Heavy (soft in places; chs 6.5, hdl 6.8)
Wind: Breezy, half against Weather: Overcast, dry

4605 LELYCENTER IN KILMARNOCK NOVICES' HURDLE (12 hdls) 3m 70y
1:45 (1:46) (Class 4) 4-Y-0+ £3,573 (£1,049; £524)

Form RPR
1 1 **Billy Billy (IRE)**[38] 3939 6-10-10 0 PeterBuchanan 121+
(S R B Crawford, Ire) *led to 2nd: w ldr: led after 4 out: drew clr after next: pushed along whn mstke last: styd on* **3/1**[2]
F441 2 27 **Straidnahanna (IRE)**[26] 4155 7-11-3 0 DannyCook 109
(Sue Smith) *cl up: led 2nd: nt fluent 4 out: sn hdd and rdn: ev ch whn nt fluent and outpcd next: one pce fr 2 out: eased whn hld last 100yds* **8/11**[1]
12 3 39 **Master Ruffit (IRE)**[25] 4165 8-11-10 125 BrianHughes 65
(Neil McKnight, Ire) *trckd ldrs: drvn and outpcd bef 4 out: losing tch whn hit next* **3/1**[2]
7m 16.5s (44.70) **Going Correction** +0.725s/f (Soft) **3** Ran SP% **107.9**
Speed ratings (Par 105): **54,45,32**
CSF £5.73 TOTE £3.80; EX 6.00 Trifecta £4.30.
Owner W Cromie **Bred** William McGladdery **Trained** Larne, Co Antrim
FOCUS
Some starts have been moved at this track following remeasuring, so some races will not have speed figures until there is sufficient data to calculate updated median times. Due to rail movement the actual race distance was 3m1f 6yds. A fair contest despite the small field. Not ratings to have too much confidence in.

4606 ORTUS HOMES H'CAP CHASE (11 fncs 1 omitted) 1m 7f 112y
2:20 (2:21) (Class 3) (0-135,133) 5-Y-0+ £7,797 (£2,289; £1,144; £572)

Form RPR
000P 1 **Rathlin**[35] 3996 11-11-5 133 (tp) FinianO'Toole(7) 143+
(Micky Hammond) *t.k.h: trckd ldrs: wnt 2nd 4th: chal 3 out: shkn up to ld bef last: rdn out run-in* **11/2**
-112 2 4 **Monbeg River (IRE)**[133] 2193 7-11-6 127 HenryBrooke 134
(Martin Todhunter) *led: rdn and hdd bef last: kpt on same pce run-in* **2/1**[1]
112F 3 4½ **Nautical Twilight**[14] 4370 6-11-6 127 (b) BrianHughes 129
(Malcolm Jefferson) *hld up in tch: stdy hdwy to chse ldrs 4 out: pushed along and outpcd after next: sn no imp* **5/1**
112P 4 4½ **Indian Voyage (IRE)**[35] 3996 8-11-7 133 (t) DaraghBourke(5) 131
(Maurice Barnes) *pressed ldr to 4th: prom tl drvn and outpcd after 4 out: btn fnl 2* **9/2**[3]
F13- 5 2¾ **Lord Of Drums (IRE)**[534] 1623 10-10-0 107 oh2 DerekFox 103
(Lucinda Russell) *t.k.h early: hld up in tch: rdn and outpcd bef 4 out: n.d after* **14/1**

3131 **U** **Ubaltique (FR)**[11] 4418 8-11-2 **128**............................(bt) JamesCowley(5)
(Donald McCain) *hld up in tch: cl 5th and gng wl whn mstke and uns rdr 5 out* **4/1**[2]

4m 18.5s (7.80) **Going Correction** +0.725s/f (Soft) **6** Ran SP% **110.2**
Speed ratings: **109,107,104,102,101**
CSF £16.94 TOTE £8.70: £3.60, £1.10; EX 21.90 Trifecta £86.10.
Owner Masters Of The Hall 2 **Bred** Mrs C J Zetter-Wells **Trained** Middleham, N Yorks

FOCUS
Due to rail movement the actual race distance was 1m7f 172y. A decent handicap run at a fair gallop in the conditions. Solid form, the winner well in on the best of last season's efforts.

4607 AJ GALLAGHER PRIVATE CLIENTS H'CAP HURDLE (12 hdls) 2m 5f 91y
2:55 (2:55) (Class 4) (0-120,115) 4-Y-0+ **£3,573** (£1,049; £524; £262)

Form RPR
-0F5 **1** **Bold Sir Brian (IRE)**[25] 4165 10-11-12 **115**..................(t) PeterBuchanan 121
(Lucinda Russell) *hld up in tch: stdy hdwy bef 4 out: wnt 2nd bef next: rdn to ld bef last: edgd rt run-in: styd on strly* **3/1**[3]

U1-3 **2** *¾* **See Double You (IRE)**[1] 4583 13-11-0 **110**............(p) MrRMPMcNally(7) 116
(Ronan M P McNally, Ire) *nt fluent on occasions: cl up: hit 6th: wnt 2nd 8th: led 3 out: sn pushed along: hdd bef last: rallied: kpt on run-in* **9/4**[2]

5401 **3** *22* **Bertalus (IRE)**[25] 4165 7-11-12 **115**.............................. BrianHarding 100
(N W Alexander) *led: blnd 8th: rdn and hdd 3 out: wknd bef next* **2/1**[1]

3022 **4** *18* **Maybe I Wont**[29] 4105 11-11-1 **104**..............................(p) BrianHughes 69
(James Moffatt) *chsd ldr to 8th: nt fluent and outpcd next: lost tch bef 3 out* **9/2**

6m 16.6s (376.60) **4** Ran SP% **107.3**
CSF £9.80 TOTE £4.20; EX 11.30 Trifecta £22.60.
Owner A R Trotter & Peter J S Russell **Bred** Heinz Pollmeier **Trained** Arlary, Perth & Kinross

FOCUS
Due to rail movement the actual race distance was 2m5f 208yds. Not a strong contest for the grade. The winner's best figure since 2013.

4608 ORTUS HOMES MARES' H'CAP HURDLE (FOR THE AYRSHIRE YEOMANRY CUP) (QUAL. FOR MARES' HURDLE FINAL) (12 hdls) 2m 5f 91y
3:30 (3:30) (Class 3) (0-130,128) 4-Y-0+ **£6,498** (£1,908; £954; £477)

Form RPR
P611 **1** **W Six Times**[19] 4289 10-9-11 **102** oh7.......................(p) CallumWhillans(3) 111+
(Alistair Whillans) *mde all: rdn and clr after 3 out: 10 l up whn mstke last: kpt on wl: unchal* **11/2**

P311 **2** *12* **Presenting Rose (IRE)**[14] 4369 6-10-7 **114**.............. StephenMulqueen(5) 111
(N W Alexander) *t.k.h: chsd wnr: effrt and rdn 3 out: kpt on same pce fr next* **11/4**[1]

0313 **3** *¾* **Lochnell (IRE)**[25] 4165 7-9-9 **102** oh10.................... DiarmuidO'Regan(5) 96
(Ian Duncan) *hld up bhd ldng gp: stdy hdwy to chse ldrs 4 out: rdn along next: sn no imp* **14/1**

0514 **4** *11* **Innis Shannon (IRE)**[97] 2936 6-9-12 **105**................ JonathonBewley(5) 92
(George Bewley) *hld up: stdy hdwy after 4 out: rdn and no imp fr next* **15/2**

16-6 **P** **Golden Sparkle (IRE)**[12] 4405 10-10-12 **117**............. GrahamWatters(3)
(Ian Duncan) *prom on outside: struggling bef 4 out: sn wknd qckly and p.u bef next* **17/2**

6F62 **U** **Bobs Lady Tamure**[14] 4366 9-11-3 **124**......................(t) DaraghBourke(5) 97
(Maurice Barnes) *hld up: rdn bef 3 out: sn btn: last and no ch whn mstke and uns rdr last* **3/1**[2]

43F2 **F** **Knocklayde Sno Cat (IRE)**[14] 4369 7-9-10 **105**...........(t) AdamShort(7)
(S R B Crawford, Ire) *hld up in tch: 4 l 3rd and shkn up whn fell 3 out* **9/2**[3]

6m 4.7s (364.70) **7** Ran SP% **114.2**
CSF £21.40 CT £199.73 TOTE £4.50: £1.80, £1.70; EX 21.60 Trifecta £96.70.
Owner Mrs L M Whillans **Bred** East Burrow Farm **Trained** Newmill-On-Slitrig, Borders

FOCUS
Due to rail movement the actual race distance was 2m6f 5yds. Not a strong contest for the grade with the top weight 6lb below the ceiling. Seemingly a big step up from the in-form winner.

4609 MCCARTHY & STONE H'CAP CHASE (FOR THE HUGH BARCLAY CHALLENGE TROPHY) (17 fncs 2 omitted) 3m 67y
4:05 (4:05) (Class 3) (0-140,137) 5-Y-0+ **£7,797** (£2,289; £1,144; £572)

Form RPR
P3UP **1** **No Planning**[42] 3860 9-11-7 **132**.............................. DannyCook 143+
(Sue Smith) *j.w: mde all: rdn bef 3 out: styd on gamely fr last* **9/4**[1]

03UP **2** *2 ¼* **Silver Tassie (IRE)**[58] 3591 8-10-13 **131**.................... FinianO'Toole(7) 140
(Micky Hammond) *hld up: stdy hdwy after 5 out: effrt and pushed along bef 2 out: wnt 2nd last: kpt on same pce* **10/1**

2342 **3** *5* **King Of The Wolds (IRE)**[29] 4109 9-11-4 **129**.................. BrianHughes 133
(Malcolm Jefferson) *prom: wnt 2nd 1/2-way: effrt and rdn 2 out: lost 2nd last: sn outpcd* **7/2**[2]

3352 **4** *10* **One For Arthur (IRE)**[19] 4286 7-11-7 **132**.................. PeterBuchanan 130
(Lucinda Russell) *in tch: pushed along and cl 4th whn blnd 3 out: sn btn* **9/4**[1]

2130 **5** *9* **Presented (IRE)**[14] 4367 9-10-1 **117**...................... CallumBewley(5) 101
(Lisa Harrison) *chsd wnr to 1/2-way: rdn and struggling 5 out: sn btn* **16/1**

2101 **P** **Bernardelli (IRE)**[25] 4167 8-11-12 **137**..............................(b) CraigNichol
(Nicky Richards) *mstkes in rr: hit and outpcd 10th: lost tch bef 5 out: t.o whn p.u after next* **8/1**[3]

7m 3.4s (13.50) **Going Correction** +0.725s/f (Soft) **6** Ran SP% **109.8**
Speed ratings: **106,105,103,100,97**
CSF £21.24 TOTE £3.30: £1.70, £3.70; EX 15.70 Trifecta £52.10.
Owner Mrs Jacqueline Conroy **Bred** Mrs S Johnson **Trained** High Eldwick, W Yorks

FOCUS
Due to rail movement the actual race distance was 3m 187yds. A fair contest run at an honest gallop. The winner is rated in line with the best of last season's runs.

4610 ORTUS HOMES H'CAP HURDLE (FOR THE CRAIGIE CUP) (12 hdls) 2m 4f 100y
4:40 (4:41) (Class 3) (0-140,137) 4-Y-0+ **£9,747** (£2,862; £1,431; £715)

Form RPR
331 **1** **Shades Of Midnight**[23] 4206 6-11-9 **137**..............(t) CallumWhillans(3) 146+
(Donald Whillans) *chsd clr ldr: hdwy to ld 3 out: rdn next: hit last: styd on strly* **7/4**[2]

3533 **2** *2 ¼* **Sa Suffit (FR)**[19] 4287 13-10-13 **129**...............(p) DiarmuidO'Regan(5) 134
(James Ewart) *led and 5 l clr to bef 4 out: rdn and hdd next: rallied: kpt on same pce after last* **8/1**[3]

PP14 **3** *14* **Yes Tom (IRE)**[25] 4167 11-11-3 **135**..............................(p) AdamShort(7) 129
(S R B Crawford, Ire) *hld up in tch: smooth hdwy to chal after 4 out to next: sn rdn: wknd bef last* **10/1**

2132 **4** *16* **Western Rules (IRE)**[23] 4202 6-10-11 **122**..........................(t) BrianHarding 97
(Nicky Richards) *nt fluent on occasions: prom: drvn and outpcd after 4 out: wknd fr next* **11/8**[1]

-535 **5** *21* **De Boitron (FR)**[84] 3156 12-10-11 **122**.............................. DannyCook 76
(Sue Smith) *hld up: struggling after 7th: lost tch bef 3 out: t.o* **9/1**

5m 44.2s (344.20) **5** Ran SP% **108.7**
CSF £13.98 TOTE £2.70: £1.50, £2.60; EX 14.00 Trifecta £34.60.
Owner The Potassium Partnership **Bred** Potassium Partnership II **Trained** Hawick, Borders

FOCUS
Due to rail movement the actual race distance was 2m4f 217yds. Four withdrawals took some interest out of this fair handicap. The winner should still be competitive when reassessed.

4611 KEN BINNIE FINANCIAL LTD STANDARD OPEN NATIONAL HUNT FLAT RACE 2m
5:15 (5:15) (Class 6) 4-6-Y-0 **£1,624** (£477; £238; £119)

Form RPR
44U **1** **Grays Choice (IRE)**[12] 4408 5-10-11 0....................... JonathonBewley(5) 117+
(George Bewley) *chsd clr ldr: hdwy to ld over 2f out: sn clr: kpt on wl* **5/1**[3]

51 **2** *24* **Sammy B**[68] 3476 6-11-9 0.............................. PeterBuchanan 99
(Lucinda Russell) *hld up in tch: hdwy over 5f out: rdn and outpcd over 2f out: lft 2nd over 1f out: no ch w wnr* **5/2**[2]

2 **3** *2 ½* **Randy Pike (IRE)**[23] 4208 6-11-2 0.............................. BrianHarding 88
(Nicky Richards) *t.k.h: prom: drvn and outpcd over 5f out: sme late hdwy: nvr on terms* **10/11**[1]

5 **4** *2* **Breakdown Cover (IRE)**[127] 2330 5-11-2 0.............................. BrianHughes 96+
(S R B Crawford, Ire) *poached 10 l clr s: led: rdn whn hung lft and hdd over 2f out: outpcd whn hung violently lft and lost 2nd over 1f out* **16/1**

5 *38* **Just Brooke** 6-10-4 0.............................. StephenMulqueen(5) 41
(N W Alexander) *prom: drvn and outpcd 1/2-way: nvr on terms after* **28/1**

3 **P** **Brackenmoss Rory**[23] 4208 4-10-8 0.............................. CraigNichol
(Alistair Whillans) *hld up: struggling over 5f out: t.o whn p.u over 1f out* **22/1**

4m 27.6s (267.60)
WFA 4 from 5yo+ 7lb **6** Ran SP% **111.3**
CSF £17.56 TOTE £4.80: £2.20, £1.30; EX 21.40 Trifecta £42.10.
Owner martingrayracing **Bred** Terence P White **Trained** Bonchester Bridge, Borders

FOCUS
Due to rail movement the actual race distance was 2m 78yds. Not a strong contest run at a fair gallop in the conditions. The form could be 5lb out either way.
T/Plt: £938.70 to a £1 stake. Pool: £52,658.31 - T/Qpdt: £59.00 to a £1 stake. Pool: £4,193.83 - **Richard Young**

4351 CHEPSTOW (L-H)
Saturday, March 12

OFFICIAL GOING: Heavy (soft in places; chs 4.8, hdl 5.2)
Wind: slight half behind Weather: fine

4612 SIMPLY EXECUTIVE CHARITY CONDITIONAL JOCKEYS' H'CAP CHASE (18 fncs) 2m 7f 131y
1:50 (1:54) (Class 4) (0-115,115) 5-Y-0+ **£4,548** (£1,335; £667; £333)

Form RPR
/P1- **1** **Wood Yer (IRE)**[510] 1964 10-11-8 **114**.....................(tp) JamieBargary(3) 126+
(Nigel Twiston-Davies) *cl up: led 2nd: jnd after 13th: shkn up whn lft wl clr 5 out: tired 3 out: much reduced ld last where j. slowly: sn hdd: rallied to ld fnl 50yds* **13/2**[2]

2236 **2** *hd* **Take The Mick**[15] 4348 9-11-8 **114**..............................(p) CharlieDeutsch(3) 121
(Venetia Williams) *cl up: nt fluent 6th: lost pl 13th: styd on again fr 4 out: wnt 2nd appr last: led flat: hdd fnl 50yds: jst hld* **10/1**

530P **3** *9* **Copper Birch (IRE)**[20] 4267 8-10-11 **108**.............................. LewisGordon(8) 105
(Evan Williams) *hld up: nt fluent 2nd: hdwy into mid-div 10th: chsd clr ldr 4 out: lost 2nd appr last: no ex flat* **9/1**

4450 **4** *2 ¼* **Umberto D'Olivate (FR)**[15] 4348 8-11-6 **112**..............(b[1]) PaulO'Brien(3) 107
(Robert Walford) *hld up: reminder after 4th: rdn 9th: lost tch w ldrs after 13th: styd on flat* **9/2**[1]

42PF **5** *8* **Nail 'M (IRE)**[15] 4340 8-11-6 **109**..............................(v) TomBellamy 98
(Nigel Hawke) *chsd ldrs: mstke 8th: sn drvn along: lost tch w ldng pair after 13th: plugged on to dispute mod 2nd 4 out: wknd 2 out* **9/2**[1]

-0P3 **6** *17* **Forgivienne**[36] 3977 9-11-2 **108**.............................. ConorRing(3) 80
(Evan Williams) *led to 2nd: styd cl up: mstkes 10th and 13th: sn outpcd by ldng pair: lft mod 2nd 5 out: wknd next* **12/1**

P351 **7** *3 ¼* **Barton Gift**[21] 4255 9-11-8 **111**..............................(b) JeremiahMcGrath 77
(John Spearing) *nt fluent 1st: sn chsng ldrs: lost pl 5th: rdn along fr 8th: no ch fr 13th* **7/1**[3]

223P **P** **Smart Exit (IRE)**[44] 3823 9-11-10 **113**.............................. LizzieKelly
(Stuart Edmunds) *hld up towards rr: rdn along 9th: lost tch 12th: t.o whn p.u bef 3 out* **13/2**[2]

4P/U **F** **Potters Cross**[14] 4352 9-11-12 **115**..............................(t) DavidNoonan
(Rebecca Curtis) *trckd ldrs: wnt 2nd at 12th: disp ld after next tl fell 5 out* **8/1**

6m 26.7s (4.70) **Going Correction** +0.25s/f (Yiel) **9** Ran SP% **113.4**
Speed ratings: **102,101,98,98,95 89,88, ,**
CSF £66.05 CT £582.71 TOTE £7.20: £2.30, £2.30, £3.90; EX 49.30 Trifecta £513.10.
Owner Miss Katharine J Holland **Bred** J Harold-Barry **Trained** Naunton, Gloucs

FOCUS
The far bend and the stable bend are dolled out adding 11yds to races 1,3 and 7 and 8yds to races 2,4,5 and 6.\n\x\x An ordinary conditional jockeys' staying handicap chase. They went a sensible gallop on ground officially described as heavy, soft in places. The idling winner was value for further.

4613 PERTEMPS NETWORK NOVICES' HURDLE (6 hdls 2 omitted) 2m 11y
2:25 (2:26) (Class 4) 4-Y-0+ **£3,898** (£1,144; £572; £286)

Form RPR
41F1 **1** **The Gipper (IRE)**[60] 3568 6-11-13 130.............................. AdamWedge 125+
(Evan Williams) *led: tended to jump lft: clr 2nd: reduced ld 3 out: drew away again on extended run to last: unchal* **1/5**[1]

6 **2** *6* **Bennys King (IRE)**[21] 4256 5-11-1 0.............................. LiamTreadwell 101
(Venetia Williams) *t.k.h early: chsd wnr tl dropped to 3rd bef 3 out: sn shkn up: disp 2nd last: r.o flat but no ch w wnr* **10/1**[2]

60 **3** *1 ¼* **Lord Of The Island (IRE)**[13] 4388 8-10-12 0.............................. JamesBanks(3) 100
(Sally Randell) *t.k.h: hld up in mid-div: chsd wnr sn after 2 out: nudged along and no imp: kpt on same pce flat* **40/1**

0 **4** *1 ¼* **Distant Rain (IRE)**[15] 4344 6-11-1 0.............................. JeremiahMcGrath 100
(Henry Oliver) *t.k.h: towards rr: clsd 4th: shkn up on extended run to last where disp 2nd: one pce* **11/1**[3]

40 5 20 **Sydney De Baune (FR)**[14] 4351 5-11-1 0........................ PaulMoloney 84
(Robert Walford) *mid-div: clsd to chse wnr bef 3 out: lost 2nd and wknd on extended run to last* **20/1**

45 6 13 **Zadok**[13] 4382 6-11-1 0...(p) MichealNolan 66
(Jamie Snowden) *chsd ldrs: j. slowly 2nd and 3rd: rdn along after next: mstke 3 out: sn wknd* **16/1**

-600 7 3 1/4 **Isla Di Milano (IRE)**[9] 4441 5-10-10 0................................ AlanJohns(5) 63
(Tim Vaughan) *a in last: lost tch after 4th* **50/1**

4m 13.3s (2.70) **Going Correction** +0.30s/f (Yiel) **7 Ran SP% 115.8**
Speed ratings (Par 105): **105,102,101,100,90 84,82**
CSF £3.42 TOTE £1.10: £1.10, £3.10; EX 2.70 Trifecta £54.60.
Owner POS Partnership **Bred** James Nolan **Trained** Llancarfan, Vale Of Glamorgan

FOCUS
The far bend and the stable bend are dolled out adding 8yds. The second-last flight was omitted.\n\x\x A fair novices' hurdle run at an honest gallop. The easy winner stood out and didn't need to be at his best.

4614 TESM "NATIONAL HUNT" MAIDEN HURDLE (10 hdls 2 omitted) 2m 7f 131y
3:00 (3:02) (Class 4) 4-Y-O+ **£3,898** (£1,144; £572; £286)

Form RPR
6 1 **Kit Casey (IRE)**[68] 3467 6-11-3 0.................................(p) TrevorWhelan 117+
(Rebecca Curtis) *prom: jnd ldr 7th: led appr 3 out: rdn next: 7 l clr whn sprawled on landing last: drvn out* **20/1**

-606 2 3 1/4 **Driftwood Haze**[15] 4339 8-10-10 102................................ MrTGreatrex(7) 110+
(Phillip Dando) *mid-div: rdn in 4th appr 3 out: sn chsd wnr: 7 l down and hld whn stmbld on landing last: kpt on flat* **33/1**

530 3 2 1/4 **Highway Storm (IRE)**[59] 3580 6-11-3 0...........................(p) SeanBowen 105
(Rebecca Curtis) *hld up towards rr: rdn 7th: sn lost tch w ldrs: styd on fr 2 out* **7/1[3]**

3P4 4 3 **Ambion Lane (IRE)**[27] 4137 6-10-10 0..........................(p) DavidPrichard(7) 104
(Victor Dartnall) *mid-div: rdn along fr 6th: lost tch w ldrs next: plugged on fr 3 out: no ch whn hit 2 out* **16/1**

UF4 5 24 **Red Red Rover (IRE)**[15] 4339 6-11-3 0............................ DaveCrosse 82
(Nigel Hawke) *led: tended to jump rt: jnd 7th: hdd appr 3 out: wknd after 2 out* **18/1**

03 6 5 **Cucklington**[18] 4296 5-10-10 0.......................................(t) PaulO'Brien(7) 73
(Colin Tizzard) *in rr: hdwy whn nt fluent 5th: wknd after 7th* **7/1[3]**

30 7 7 **Oneida Tribe (IRE)**[15] 4344 7-11-3 0.................................... LiamTreadwell 66
(Venetia Williams) *prom tl wknd appr 3 out* **10/3[2]**

P P **Days Like These**[20] 4264 7-10-7 0... BenPoste(3)
(Adrian Wintle) *chsd ldrs to 5th: lost tch 7th: t.o whn p.u bef last* **200/1**

46 P **Semper Invicta (IRE)**[85] 3133 5-11-3 0................................... NickScholfield
(Paul Nicholls) *hld up: hdwy to trck ldrs 5th: rdn 3 out: wknd qckly: bhd whn p.u bef last* **11/10[1]**

00 P **Yenston (IRE)**[18] 4296 5-11-0 0.......................................(t) MauriceLinehan(3)
(Colin Tizzard) *hld up: rdn after 4th: lost tch 6th: t.o whn p.u bef last* **100/1**

6m 14.2s (12.00) **Going Correction** +0.30s/f (Yiel) **10 Ran SP% 116.0**
Speed ratings (Par 105): **92,90,90,89,81 79,77,,,**
CSF £402.98 TOTE £19.40: £4.30, £5.10, £2.00; EX 189.10 Trifecta £3113.30.
Owner Conyers, O'Reilly, Roddis, Zeffman **Bred** John Place **Trained** Newport, Pembrokeshire

FOCUS
The far bend and the stable bend are dolled out adding 11yds. The second-last flight was omitted.\n\x\x An ordinary staying maiden hurdle. They went another honest gallop. A big step up from the winner, who looks the sort to rate higher.

4615 TORI - ALTERNATIVE TO "BIG 4" CONSULTANCY NOVICES' LIMITED H'CAP CHASE (16 fncs) 2m 3f 98y
3:35 (3:37) (Class 4) (0-120,117) 5-Y-O+ **£5,325** (£1,653; £890)

Form RPR
-614 1 **Cloudy Beach (IRE)**[10] 4431 9-11-1 115............................ CharlieDeutsch(5) 125+
(Venetia Williams) *w ldr: led after 11th: shkn up and jnd again whn lft 6 l up 5 out: styd on wl to draw clr fr 2 out: easily* **11/4[2]**

-101 2 22 **Supreme Bob (IRE)**[20] 4265 10-10-11 106............................ TrevorWhelan 101+
(Debra Hamer) *hld up in 3rd: blnd 10th: lft 6 l 2nd 5 out: nt fluent next or 3 out: sn wknd: b.b.v* **6/4[1]**

0343 3 99 **In The Hold (IRE)**[23] 4198 6-10-11 106.............................. PaulMoloney
(Evan Williams) *hld up in last: nt fluent and shkn up 9th: mstke next: lost tch after 11th: lft poor 3rd 5 out: completed in own time: sddle slipped* **3/1[3]**

P-2P U **Golden Milan (IRE)**[28] 4127 8-11-3 117...................(bt[1]) DavidNoonan(5)
(Rebecca Curtis) *led narrowly: mstke 7th: hdd after 11th: clsd again and upsides wnr whn stmbld and uns rdr 5 out* **9/2**

5m 23.2s (11.90) **Going Correction** +0.25s/f (Yiel) **4 Ran SP% 109.8**
Speed ratings: **84,74,33,**
CSF £7.55 TOTE £2.90; EX 4.00 Trifecta £11.50.
Owner The Beachcombers **Bred** Jim Dempsey **Trained** Kings Caple, H'fords

FOCUS
The far bend and the stable bend are dolled out adding 8yds. A modest little novices' handicap chase run at a sensible gallop. It's difficult to know what the winner achieved with nothing else performing.

4616 CQRS CHARITY MARES' H'CAP HURDLE (9 hdls 2 omitted) 2m 3f 100y
4:10 (4:12) (Class 4) (0-120,120) 4-Y-O+ **£4,548** (£1,335; £667; £333)

Form RPR
1226 1 **Vicky's Charm (IRE)**[42] 3865 7-10-9 106........................... JamesBanks(3) 110
(Barry Brennan) *trckd ldrs: hit 3 out: sn rdn: led after 2 out: j.lft last: drvn out to assert and edgd rt flat* **10/1**

1243 2 2 1/4 **Kentford Myth**[37] 3953 6-10-4 103.................................... KevinJones(5) 105
(Seamus Mullins) *prom: w ldr fr 4th: hit 3 out and rdn: ev ch last: unable qck u.p flat* **8/1**

3441 3 12 **Midnight Silver**[20] 4268 6-11-4 112...................................(t) MichealNolan 103
(Jamie Snowden) *led: rdn 3 out: hdd after next: wkng in 3rd whn j.lft last* **7/4[1]**

602 4 4 1/2 **Jester Jet**[95] 2959 6-9-13 98... NickSlatter(5) 84
(Tony Carroll) *t.k.h early: in rr: mstke 3rd: hdwy 3 out: outpcd by ldrs fr next: styd on flat* **9/2[2]**

1334 5 3 3/4 **Anda De Grissay (FR)**[15] 4338 6-11-7 120..........................(t) DavidNoonan(5) 101
(Anthony Honeyball) *mid-div: rdn after 7th: one pce and no ch w ldrs fr 3 out* **7/1[3]**

4653 6 6 **Pink Tara**[15] 4338 5-10-1 100.. CharlieDeutsch(5) 75
(Venetia Williams) *hld up in tch: rdn and clsd after 7th: wknd 3 out* **9/2[2]**

131- 7 20 **Lights Of Broadway (IRE)**[395] 4159 10-10-11 108.(t) RobertWilliams(3) 63
(Bernard Llewellyn) *t.k.h in rr: mstke 5th and shkn up: last and struggling after 7th: lost tch fr 2 out* **12/1**

5m 4.6s (2.80) **Going Correction** +0.30s/f (Yiel) **7 Ran SP% 113.1**
Speed ratings (Par 105): **106,105,100,98,96 94,85**
CSF £80.11 TOTE £12.10: £4.60, £4.20; EX 89.90 Trifecta £335.40.
Owner Dr Ian Cragg **Bred** Anthony Kelleher **Trained** Upper Lambourn, Berks

FOCUS
The far bend and the stable bend are dolled out adding 8yds. The second-last flight omitted. \n\x\x A fair mares' handicap hurdle. They went a respectable gallop. All except the first two were upwaerds of 10lb off.

4617 TORI GLOBAL AND THE SAMARITANS H'CAP CHASE (12 fncs) 2m 11y
4:45 (4:51) (Class 3) (0-140,137) 5-Y-O+ **£12,996** (£3,816; £1,908; £954)

Form RPR
122U 1 **Sandy Beach**[9] 4451 6-10-11 122.. TomScudamore 131+
(Colin Tizzard) *hld up bhd ldrs: clsd to ld 7th: rdn after 2 out: styd on wl flat* **7/2[2]**

0131 2 4 1/2 **Tornado In Milan (IRE)**[9] 4452 10-11-2 127......................... PaulMoloney 131
(Evan Williams) *led to 2nd: led 4th to 7th: chsd wnr after: rdn whn nt fluent last: one pce flat* **9/2[3]**

1400 3 2 **Zarzal (IRE)**[163] 1719 8-11-12 137....................................... AdamWedge 139+
(Evan Williams) *s.i.s fr standing s: in rr: detached in last pair 6th: styd on fr 3 out to go modest 3rd last: r.o flat* **20/1**

1261 4 10 **All Together (FR)**[23] 4210 5-11-9 134................................... JamesBest 127
(Johnny Farrelly) *chsd ldrs: rdn 5 out: sn one pce: lost modest 3rd last* **6/1**

0311 5 4 **Pressurize (IRE)**[37] 3954 10-10-12 128............................ CharlieDeutsch(5) 114
(Venetia Williams) *wnt 150yds after false s: cl up tl dropped to rr 2nd: nvr gng after: stmbld 5th: no ch fr next: styd on flat* **7/2[2]**

2FP3 6 6 **Whispering Harry**[14] 4353 7-11-3 128............................... JeremiahMcGrath 110
(Henry Oliver) *chsd ldrs: rdn after 7th: cl 3rd whn mstke 5 out: wkng whn mstke 3 out* **9/1**

3212 P **Big Jim**[18] 4300 7-10-12 123.. KielanWoods
(Alex Hales) *trckd ldr: led 2nd to 4th: styd prom: 3rd whn lost action: eased and p.u after 7th: dsmntd* **3/1[1]**

4m 17.0s (-0.10) **Going Correction** +0.25s/f (Yiel) **7 Ran SP% 116.7**
Speed ratings: **110,107,106,101,99 96,**
CSF £20.50 TOTE £3.60: £1.60, £2.70; EX 19.30 Trifecta £197.40.
Owner Brocade Racing **Bred** Alan Gibson **Trained** Milborne Port, Dorset

FOCUS
The far bend and the stable bend are dolled out adding 8yds.\n\x\x The feature contest was a decent handicap chase in which they went a proper gallop. The winner is rated to his previous best.

4618 BEN CRUTCHLEY MEMORIAL H'CAP HURDLE (10 hdls 2 omitted) 2m 7f 131y
5:20 (5:21) (Class 4) (0-120,120) 4-Y-O+ **£4,548** (£1,335; £667; £333)

Form RPR
0322 1 **Albert D'Olivate (FR)**[15] 4342 6-11-1 109............................(p) SeanBowen 115+
(Robert Walford) *in share of 2nd tl rdn and outpcd after 7th: styd on fr 2 out to cl gap on ldng pair: chal last: r.o u.p to ld nr fin* **7/4[1]**

5/00 2 nk **Ballyrock (IRE)**[63] 3517 10-11-7 120.................................(t) AlanJohns(5) 126+
(Tim Vaughan) *hld up: pushed along and hdwy after 7th: 3rd whn blnd 3 out: styd on fr 2 out to cl gap on ldng pair: chal last: sn led: hdd nr fin* **6/1**

164P 3 4 **Rainbow Haze**[15] 4342 10-9-13 100...................................... MrTGreatrex(7) 102
(Phillip Dando) *led: j.rt at times: clr to 2nd: nt fluent 3 out: sn rdn: hdd appr last where stl ev ch: one pce flat* **16/1**

0624 4 nk **Another Frontier (IRE)**[30] 4063 5-11-2 115........................ JamieBargary(5) 114
(Nigel Twiston-Davies) *hld up: hdwy 6th: wnt 2nd after 7th: chal 2 out: shkn up to ld narrowly appr last: hdd jst after flight and no ex* **3/1[2]**

51U- 5 27 **Obistar (FR)**[379] 4477 6-11-6 114..(b) TomScudamore 95
(David Pipe) *in share of 2nd tl rdn and wknd appr 3 out* **9/2[3]**

12-6 6 36 **Candide (IRE)**[274] 707 9-11-4 115....................................(p) JamesBanks(3) 51
(Sally Randell) *hld up bhd ldrs: rdn and wknd appr 3 out: t.o* **16/1**

1311 7 1/2 **Extreme Impact**[28] 4127 10-11-0 115.................................(v) MrMEnnis(7) 51
(Graeme McPherson) *rousted along fr s and nvr gng: in rr tl wnt prom 4th: last again next: t.o fr 6th but rdr nvr stopped pushing* **9/1**

6m 14.6s (12.40) **Going Correction** +0.30s/f (Yiel) **7 Ran SP% 115.6**
Speed ratings (Par 105): **91,90,89,89,80 68,68**
CSF £13.21 TOTE £2.70: £1.60, £3.90; EX 14.40 Trifecta £86.00.
Owner Chris Pugsley & Nigel Skinner **Bred** Jean-Philippe Rivoire **Trained** Child Okeford, Dorset

FOCUS
The far bend and the stable bend are dolled out adding 11yds. The second-last flight was omitted.\n\x\x Another fair staying handicap hurdle run at a respectable gallop. The winner is rated similarly to his Kempton run.
T/Plt: £1827.40 to a £1 stake. Pool: £62,960.45 - 25.15 winning units. T/Qpdt: £175.50 to a £1 stake. Pool: £4,032.24 - 17.00 winning units. **Richard Lowther**

[4593] SANDOWN (R-H)
Saturday, March 12

OFFICIAL GOING: Soft (good to soft in back straight on chase course, heavy in places on hurdle course)
Wind: Almost nil Weather: Fine, hazy

4619 ASPALL CYDER JUVENILE H'CAP HURDLE (8 hdls) 1m 7f 216y
1:25 (1:25) (Class 3) (0-125,125) 4-Y-O **£6,498** (£1,908; £954; £477)

Form RPR
4121 1 **Harley Rebel**[36] 3978 4-11-12 125.. NoelFehily 128+
(Neil Mulholland) *lw: mostly chsd ldr: nt fluent 5th: dropped to 3rd next and first one to be pushed along: responded and c through to ld bef 2 out: sn clr: rdn out* **1/1[1]**

033 2 14 **Alhamareer (IRE)**[17] 4304 4-10-9 108.................................. JamesBest 96
(Paul Webber) *racd in 3rd tl chsd ldr 3 out: drvn and dropped to 3rd bef 2 out: kpt on to take 2nd again last: no ch w wnr* **7/1[3]**

55 3 8 **Shintori (FR)**[68] 3464 4-10-4 103....................................... PaddyBrennan 83
(Richard Woollacott) *tended to jump lft: led: looked to be gng best on long run after 3 out: rdn and hdd bef 2 out: sn btn: lost 2nd last: wknd* **11/1**

23 4 11 **Searching (IRE)**[35] 3988 4-11-2 115.................................. JoshuaMoore 87
(Gary Moore) *nt fluent: hld up in last: drvn and no prog wl bef 2 out: sn wknd* **15/8[2]**

4m 11.2s (4.00) **Going Correction** +0.25s/f (Yiel) **4 Ran SP% 105.6**
Speed ratings: **100,93,89,83**
CSF £7.03 TOTE £1.60; EX 5.50 Trifecta £16.10.
Owner Mrs Gloria Seymour **Bred** Stephen & Gloria Seymour **Trained** Limpley Stoke, Wilts

FOCUS
All race distances as advertised. A drying day, which was evident with the going in the opening juvenile handicap and the winning time also backed that up. A step up from the winner and the form could be rating 6lb higher through the second.

4620 30TH EUROPEAN BREEDERS' FUND GREENALL'S GIN "NATIONAL HUNT" NOVICES' H'CAP HURDLE FINAL (GRADE 3) (9 hdls) 2m 3f 173y
2:00 (2:00) (Class 1) 4-7-Y-O
£34,170 (£12,822; £6,420; £3,198; £1,608; £804)

Form RPR

3114 **1** **Barney Dwan (IRE)**[49] 3744 6-11-6 **129**........................ PaddyBrennan 142+
(Fergal O'Brien) *prog fr midfield to trck ldrs 5th: hdwy to ld bef 2 out: rdn clr bef last: readily* **14/1**

2212 **2** *4* **Potters Legend**[38] 3920 6-11-12 **135**........................ LeightonAspell 141
(Lucy Wadham) *lw: hld up in midfield: prog on outer on long run after 3 out: chsd wnr sn after 2 out: no imp but hld on for 2nd* **14/1**

4461 **3** *½* **Alcala (FR)**[23] 4196 6-10-9 **125**........................(t) HarryCobden(7) 130
(Paul Nicholls) *hld up wl in rr: drvn wl bef 2 out: swtchd towards inner but stl only 9th 2 out: styd on wl after: nrst fin* **8/1**[2]

-323 **4** *hd* **Two Taffs (IRE)**[76] 3284 6-11-3 **126**........................ HarrySkelton 133+
(Dan Skelton) *lw: hld up wl in rr: prog and swtchd to inner bef 2 out gng strly: trapped bhd wkng rival after 2 out and lost grnd: drvn and styd on again fr last* **7/1**[1]

0113 **5** *6* **Tanarpino**[32] 4040 5-10-11 **120**........................ PeterCarberry 119
(Jennie Candlish) *lw: pushed along in midfield bef 4th: effrt u.p bef 2 out: plugged on but nvr gng pce to threaten* **25/1**

-132 **6** *1 ¼* **Potters Corner (IRE)**[20] 4264 6-11-7 **130**........................ DenisO'Regan 128
(Paul Morgan) *t.k.h: prom: chsd ldr briefly bef 2 out and looked to be gng strly: sn rdn and wknd bef last* **12/1**

362 **7** *7* **Dark Flame (IRE)**[69] 3452 7-11-5 **128**........................ NoelFehily 119
(Richard Rowe) *wl in tch: drvn bef 2 out and no imp on ldrs: fdd* **33/1**

4F13 **8** *2 ½* **Paddy's Field (IRE)**[15] 4344 6-10-12 **121**........................ DavidBass 109
(Ben Pauling) *w ldrs tl drvn and wknd jst bef 2 out* **14/1**

0421 **9** *3 ¼* **Chic Theatre (IRE)**[17] 4303 6-11-1 **124**........................ TomScudamore 111
(David Pipe) *mde most tl hdd & wknd bef 2 out* **20/1**

1213 **10** *2 ½* **Divine Spear (IRE)**[17] 4303 5-11-4 **127**........................ NicodeBoinville 110
(Nicky Henderson) *in tch in midfield: rdn wl bef 2 out: sn wknd* **11/1**

0262 **11** *7* **Ballypoint (IRE)**[15] 4344 5-11-1 **124**........................ SamTwiston-Davies 101
(Nigel Twiston-Davies) *trckd ldr: mstke 3 out: lost 2nd and wknd qckly bef 2 out* **16/1**

4212 **12** *31* **Robin Of Locksley (IRE)**[36] 3974 6-11-0 **123**........................ IanPopham 100+
(Dan Skelton) *n.m.r 1st: hld up in rr: trying to make prog whn hmpd bef 2 out: no ch after: virtually p.u after last* **9/1**[3]

1412 **13** *5* **Western Cape (IRE)**[49] 3736 5-11-2 **130**........................ KevinJones(5) 100
(Seamus Mullins) *hld up in last pair: sme prog on inner bef 2 out: sn wknd qckly: virtually p.u after last* **16/1**

2F11 **P** **Wade Harper (IRE)**[36] 3971 6-11-9 **132**........................ AidanColeman
(David Dennis) *chsd ldrs tl wknd qckly after 3 out: wl bhd whn p.u bef 2 out* **20/1**

3511 **P** **Will O'The West (IRE)**[15] 4344 5-11-4 **127**........................ JakeGreenall
(Henry Daly) *hld up in rr: rdn and no prog after 3 out: sn wknd: wl bhd whn p.u bef 2 out* **14/1**

6131 **F** **Flashjack (IRE)**[37] 3949 6-11-7 **130**........................ RichardJohnson 117
(Henry Daly) *settled in midfield: blnd 3rd: mstke 4th and dropped to rr: rdn and no real prog bef 2 out: 10th whn fell last* **8/1**[2]

1623 **P** **Morthanalegend**[59] 3581 7-10-13 **122**........................(t) BrendanPowell
(Brendan Powell) *a towards rr: wknd 3 out: t.o in last whn p.u bef 2 out* **50/1**

6111 **P** **Point The Way (IRE)**[32] 4040 5-11-9 **132**........................ GavinSheehan
(Brian Ellison) *lw: trckd ldrs: rdn bef 3 out: wknd qckly sn after it: wl bhd whn p.u bef 2 out* **10/1**

5m 10.8s (11.20) **Going Correction** +0.25s/f (Yiel) **18** Ran SP% **126.5**
Speed ratings: **87,85,85,85,82 82,79,78,77,76 73,60,58, , , ,**
CSF £188.69 CT £1701.28 TOTE £15.70: £4.10, £3.60, £2.40, £2.00; EX 253.30 Trifecta £4387.60 Part won..
Owner Paul & Clare Rooney **Bred** Grange Stud **Trained** Naunton, Gloucs

FOCUS
An ultra-competitive edition of this novice handicap, littered with future chasers. They went a fair gallop and it should prove sound form. The first two are on the upgrade, with the third and fifth the best guides.

4621 KINGS MISTRAL H'CAP CHASE (22 fncs) 3m 37y
2:35 (2:35) (Class 3) (0-135,132) 5-Y-0+
£9,384 (£2,772; £1,386; £693; £346; £174)

Form RPR

62-5 **1** **Mosspark (IRE)**[105] 2780 8-11-9 **129**........................ DarylJacob 141+
(Emma Lavelle) *lw: trckd ldng pair: wnt 2nd after 11th: chal fr 3 out: led after 2 out: sn rdn clr* **5/1**[2]

3U22 **2** *6* **Dawson City**[28] 4124 7-11-9 **129**........................ AndrewThornton 137+
(Polly Gundry) *trckd ldrs: rdn bef 3 out: kpt on to take 2nd last: no imp on wnr* **15/2**

-0PU **3** *2 ¾* **Relax (FR)**[7] 4483 11-11-12 **132**........................ AidanColeman 136
(Venetia Williams) *mostly j.w: led: nt fluent 16th (water): drvn 3 out: hdd after 2 out: fdd* **11/2**[3]

063P **4** *8* **Financial Climate (IRE)**[29] 4101 9-11-5 **128**........................(p) ThomasGarner(3) 123
(Oliver Sherwood) *chsd ldr tl after 11th: lost pl fr next and nvr bttr than midfield after: struggling 4 out: n.d after* **7/1**

-P40 **5** *10* **Desert Joe (IRE)**[92] 3024 10-11-5 **125**........................(p) WayneHutchinson 112
(Alan King) *lw: chsd ldrs: lost pl 13th: sn pushed along: last and wl btn after 4 out* **17/2**

215P **6** *35* **St Dominick (IRE)**[59] 3583 9-11-10 **130**........................ JamesBest 79
(Jackie Du Plessis) *hld up in last: prog whn stmbld on landing 17th: chsd ldng pair 4 out and looked a threat: hrd rdn and no rspnse bef 3 out: wknd rapidly 2 out: fin v tired* **20/1**

64P5 **U** **Bertie Boru (IRE)**[22] 4234 9-11-8 **128**........................(p) RichardJohnson
(Philip Hobbs) *hld up: terrible blunder 4th: tended to jump lft after: disputing 5th whn blnd and uns rdr 15th* **4/1**[1]

-P31 **P** **Benenden (IRE)**[68] 3472 8-11-5 **125**........................ TomScudamore
(Michael Scudamore) *hld up: mstkes 2nd and 5th: blnd 12th: struggling after: bhd whn p.u bef 17th* **4/1**[1]

6m 30.9s (3.10) **Going Correction** +0.375s/f (Yiel) **8** Ran SP% **111.6**
Speed ratings: **109,107,106,103,100 88, ,**
CSF £39.26 CT £207.79 TOTE £5.70: £1.80, £2.70, £2.10; EX 35.30 Trifecta £251.00.
Owner N Mustoe & Tim Syder **Bred** Mrs Anthea Smyth **Trained** Hatherden, Hants

FOCUS
An open-looking staying handicap and it served up a real test. The winner improved to his hurdles mark.

4622 CLOSE BROTHERS IMPERIAL CUP H'CAP HURDLE (GRADE 3) (8 hdls) 1m 7f 216y
3:10 (3:10) (Class 1) 4-Y-0+
£39,865 (£14,959; £7,490; £3,731; £1,876; £938)

Form RPR

2353 **1** **Flying Angel (IRE)**[28] 4115 5-10-7 **133**........................ RyanHatch(3) 145+
(Nigel Twiston-Davies) *lw: hld up early: prog 4th: jnd ldrs 3 out gng strly: rdn to ld bef 2 out: kpt on wl u.p after* **9/1**

1111 **2** *5* **Solstice Star**[42] 3854 6-10-8 **134**........................(t) KillianMoore(3) 142+
(Martin Keighley) *pressed ldr: chal fr 3rd: pressed new ldr fr next: led after 3 out: drvn and hdd bef 2 out: kpt on gamely but no imp fr last* **11/1**

2132 **3** *4 ½* **Spice Fair**[7] 4482 9-10-7 **130**........................ WayneHutchinson 130
(Mark Usher) *hld up in last pair and wl bhd: stl only 10th after 3 out and long way off pce: rdn and gd prog bef 2 out: tk 3rd after 2 out: kpt on but nvr rchd ldng pair* **20/1**

24 **4** *16* **Affaire D'Honneur (FR)**[28] 4115 5-10-10 **133**........................ GavinSheehan 117
(Harry Whittington) *hld up in last pair and wl bhd: shoved along and no prog after 3 out: stl only 10th 2 out: plugged on to take remote 4th nr fin* **9/2**[1]

5611 **5** *1 ¾* **Allee Bleue (IRE)**[49] 3745 6-10-12 **135**........................ RichardJohnson 117
(Philip Hobbs) *trckd ldrs: clr in ldng quartet sn after 3 out: rdn and fdd wl bef 2 out* **12/1**

1221 **6** *2* **Rayvin Black**[21] 4253 7-11-9 **149**........................(p) ThomasGarner(3) 129
(Oliver Sherwood) *led at str pce but pressed: hdd 4th: lost pl 3 out and struggling after* **11/1**

-212 **7** *1* **Knockgraffon (IRE)**[46] 3787 6-10-9 **132**........................ HarrySkelton 111
(Dan Skelton) *hld up in midfield: prog to take 5th after 3 out but nt on terms w ldrs: no hdwy bef 2 out: sn wknd* **11/1**

1224 **8** *½* **Sirop De Menthe (FR)**[21] 4239 6-10-4 **130**........................ LucyGardner(3) 109
(Sue Gardner) *lw: dropped to rr after mstke 3rd and pushed along: nvr on terms after: wl bhd after 3 out: plugged on* **14/1**

6204 **9** *2* **Prairie Town (IRE)**[42] 3854 5-10-6 **129**........................ LeeEdwards 106
(Tony Carroll) *lw: chsd ldrs: hrd rdn and nt on terms in chsng gp after 3 out: wknd bef 2 out* **25/1**

FU15 **10** *1 ½* **Sea Wall (FR)**[18] 4294 8-10-7 **130**........................ TomCannon 106
(Chris Gordon) *hld up wl in rr and off the pce: rdn and sme prog to join chsng gp after 3 out but nt on terms: wknd 2 out* **40/1**

2021 **11** *4 ½* **Clayton**[40] 3902 7-10-0 **123** oh1........................(t) JoshuaMoore 94
(Gary Moore) *lw: pressed ldng pair: led 4th: hdd after 3 out: stl 3rd 2 out: wknd* **7/1**[3]

6011 **12** *15* **For Good Measure (IRE)**[86] 3120 5-10-7 **130**........................ BarryGeraghty 91
(Philip Hobbs) *hld up off the pce and wl in rr: shoved along and no prog 3 out: wl bhd after: eased fr 2 out* **6/1**[2]

0060 **P** **Ebony Express**[49] 3733 7-10-7 **130**........................(tp) WillKennedy
(Dr Richard Newland) *unable to ld: chsd ldrs: mstke 5th: sn rdn: struggling after 3 out: wl bhd whn p.u bef 2 out* **12/1**

5225 **P** **Ozzy Thomas (IRE)**[85] 3134 6-10-0 **123**........................ PaddyBrennan
(Henry Oliver) *pushed along to stay in midfield bef 3rd: bhd 3 out: p.u bef 2 out* **25/1**

4m 5.8s (-1.40) **Going Correction** +0.25s/f (Yiel) **14** Ran SP% **116.9**
Speed ratings (Par 113): **113,110,108,100,99 98,97,97,96,95 93,86, ,**
CSF £96.09 CT £1925.53 TOTE £9.90: £3.10, £3.30, £6.60; EX 111.00 Trifecta £2416.10.
Owner R J Rexton **Bred** Arctic Tack Stud **Trained** Naunton, Gloucs

FOCUS
The feature handicap was another highly competitive affair and predictably there was no hanging about.

4623 EBF BRITISH STALLION STUDS & TBA MARES' STANDARD OPEN NATIONAL HUNT FLAT RACE (LISTED RACE) 1m 7f 216y
3:45 (3:45) (Class 1) 4-7-Y-0
£11,390 (£4,274; £2,140; £1,066; £536; £268)

Form RPR

11 **1** **The Nipper (IRE)**[105] 2770 5-11-0 0........................ GavinSheehan 124+
(Warren Greatrex) *lw: will make a jumper: mde virtually all: edgd lft and brought to nr side rail in st: def advantage 2f out: hung bdly lft whn rail ended jst ins fnl f: nrly jnd but kpt on wl nr fin* **9/2**[2]

4455 **2** *½* **Colin's Sister**[97] 2929 5-10-11 0........................ ConorShoemark(3) 120+
(Fergal O'Brien) *lw: will make a jumper: pressed ldrs 5f: steadily lost pl: rdn in last quartet 5f out: rallied over 3f out: clsd on ldrs over 1f out: hung lft ins fnl f: styd on to take 2nd last strides* **33/1**

1 **3** *1 ¼* **Listen To The Man (IRE)**[18] 4302 6-11-0 0........................ HarrySkelton 118
(Dan Skelton) *bit on the leg: trckd ldr: 2nd in main gp far side fr 3f out: led gp again fnl f: on terms 75yds out: no ex* **25/1**

11 **4** *hd* **Tearsofclewbay**[21] 4242 5-10-7 0........................ ConorSmith(7) 118
(Philip Hobbs) *prog to join ldrs 1/2-way: rdn and hanging rt 3f out: clsd u.p to chal fnl f: no ex nr fin* **9/2**[2]

5 *¾* **Avellino (IRE)**[42] 3875 5-10-9 0........................ MrNMcParlan(5) 117
(Dermot Anthony McLoughlin, Ire) *lw: will make a jumper: trckd ldng pair: led main gp on far side 3f out: lost ld fnl f: fdd nr fin* **7/1**

4-11 **6** *3* **Copper Kay**[119] 2486 6-11-4 0........................ RichardJohnson 118
(Philip Hobbs) *trckd ldng trio: shkn up 3f out: one pce and nvr able to chal fr 2f out: kpt on* **15/8**[1]

244 **7** *16* **Cajun Fiddle (IRE)**[42] 3861 5-11-0 0........................ WayneHutchinson 100
(Alan King) *will make a jumper: hld up in rr: prog 6f out to chse ldng quartet over 4f out: rdn 3f out: sn floundering and btn* **40/1**

14 **8** *11* **Royal Debutante (IRE)**[30] 4074 5-11-0 0........................ RichieMcLernon 87
(Paul Webber) *will make a jumper: hld up in last trio: sme prog over 4f out and gng bttr than a few: rdn and wknd 3f out* **66/1**

1 **9** *½* **Sister Sibyl (IRE)**[86] 3132 5-11-0 0........................ TomO'Brien 87
(Hughie Morrison) *hld up in last trio: rdn 5f out: sn struggling and bhd* **25/1**

4215 **10** *10* **Kalaniti (IRE)**[42] 3862 5-11-0 0........................ NoelFehily 77
(Chris Grant) *nvr bttr than midfield: rdn and struggling 4f out: sn bhd* **66/1**

21 **11** *13* **Midnight Tune**[103] 2828 5-11-0 0........................(t) AidanColeman 64
(Anthony Honeyball) *t.k.h: hld up in last trio: rdn and no prog 4f out: wknd 3f out* **50/1**

53 **12** *44* **Atlanta Ablaze**[42] 3861 5-11-0 0........................ JakeGreenall 20
(Henry Daly) *nvr bttr than midfield: wknd over 4f out: sn t.o* **100/1**

11 13 3 ½ **Woolstone One**[56] 3632 4-10-6 0.. NicodeBoinville 8
(Harry Whittington) *leggy: angular: racd wd: in tch: chsd ldrs 1/2-way: wknd 4f out: t.o* **6/1**[3]
4m 7.2s (5.60) **Going Correction** +0.25s/f (Yiel)
WFA 4 from 5yo+ 7lb **13** Ran SP% **116.9**
Speed ratings: **96,95,95,95,94 93,85,79,79,74 67,45,44**
CSF £147.75 TOTE £5.70: £2.10, £9.20, £4.60; EX 164.70 Trifecta £3656.20.
Owner Smith, Ratcliffe & Bowring **Bred** W L Smith & Partners **Trained** Upper Lambourn, Berks
■ Stewards' Enquiry : Mr N McParlan seven-day ban; used his whip above the permitted level (tba)
Conor Smith seven-day ban; used whip above the permitted level (26th Mar-1st Apr)

FOCUS
Eight last-time-out winners, five of them unbeaten, lined up for this classy mares' bumper. There was a sound gallop on and it saw a muddling finish, but the form is strong. The winner is better than the bare result.

4624 ESHER NOVICES' LIMITED H'CAP CHASE (FOR THE BURNT OAK AND SPECIAL CARGO CHALLENGE TROPHY) (13 fncs) 1m 7f 119y
4:20 (4:20) (Class 3) 5-Y-O+ **£6,498** (£1,908; £954)

Form RPR
3111 1 **Kylemore Lough**[21] 4247 7-11-8 **151**.. JamieMoore 162+
(Kerry Lee) *j.w: mde all: pushed along and readily drew clr bef 2 out: easily* **8/15**[1]
1224 2 8 **Dormello Mo (FR)**[118] 2510 6-11-3 **146**....................(t) SamTwiston-Davies 150
(Paul Nicholls) *chsd wnr 4th to 7th: rdn to go 2nd again 2 out: kpt on but no ch* **11/4**[2]
3433 3 10 **Helium (FR)**[22] 4230 11-10-3 **132** oh1.. LeightonAspell 128
(Alexandra Dunn) *chsd wnr to 4th and fr 7th to 2 out: wknd* **6/1**[3]
4m 5.7s (3.90) **Going Correction** +0.375s/f (Yiel) **3** Ran SP% **106.2**
Speed ratings: **105,101,96**
CSF £2.31 TOTE £1.40; EX 1.90 Trifecta £2.00.
Owner M J McMahon & Denis Gallagher **Bred** M J McMahon **Trained** Byton, H'fords

FOCUS
A good-quality little novice handicap and solid form. Kylemore Lough rates a top-class novice.

4625 KILBRITTAIN CASTLE H'CAP CHASE (17 fncs) 2m 4f 10y
4:55 (4:56) (Class 3) (0-140,140) 5-Y-O+ **£9,384** (£2,772; £1,386; £693)

Form RPR
U332 1 **Morning Reggie**[56] 3620 7-10-6 **120**..(p) LeightonAspell 130
(Oliver Sherwood) *trckd ldng pair: gd jump to ld 8th: mde rest: awkward 10th: hrd pressed fr 2 out: kpt on wl flat: jst hld on* **11/4**[2]
-F51 2 *shd* **Minella Reception (IRE)**[15] 4347 10-11-7 **135**....(t) SamTwiston-Davies 147+
(Nigel Twiston-Davies) *lw: nt a fluent: cl up bhd ldrs: tk 2nd 3 out: chal gng wl whn nt fluent 2 out: sn rdn: upsides last: drvn flat: jst failed* **11/8**[1]
US5P 3 21 **Shangani (USA)**[27] 4140 10-10-10 **124**..(p) AidanColeman 114
(Venetia Williams) *led to 3rd: j. slowly 8th and hdd: sn dropped to last and lost tch: tk remote 3rd last* **3/1**[3]
P24P 4 18 **Comeonginger (IRE)**[14] 4363 9-10-10 **124**..(t) TomCannon 104
(Chris Gordon) *led to 3rd: chsd ldr: pressed new ldr fr 8th tl 3 out: sn wknd qckly* **5/1**
5m 20.8s (2.40) **Going Correction** +0.375s/f (Yiel) **4** Ran SP% **110.4**
Speed ratings: **110,109,101,94**
CSF £7.28 TOTE £3.00; EX 6.90 Trifecta £7.80.
Owner Tim Syder **Bred** R D & Mrs J S Chugg **Trained** Upper Lambourn, Berks

FOCUS
This fair handicap was run at a decent gallop and it saw a cracking finish. The winner is rated to his best.
T/Plt: £937.00 to a £1 stake. Pool: £152,204.97 - 118.58 winning tickets T/Qpdt: £122.20 to a £1 stake. Pool: £12,116.90 - 73.35 winning tickets **Jonathan Neesom**

4626 - 4632a (Foreign Racing) - See Raceform Interactive

4202
KELSO (L-H)
Sunday, March 13

OFFICIAL GOING: Soft (5.9)
Wind: Light, half against Weather: Overcast

4633 TERRY FRAME JOINERS NOVICES' HURDLE (8 hdls) 2m 51y
1:50 (1:50) (Class 4) 4-Y-O+ **£3,249** (£954; £477; £238)

Form RPR
5542 1 **The Fresh Prince (IRE)**[24] 4196 6-11-1 116.. LeightonAspell 121+
(Oliver Sherwood) *t.k.h: cl up: led 3 out: clr next: pushed along bef last: kpt on strly* **10/11**[1]
2 7 **Grexit (IRE)**[112] 5-10-8 0.. MrWHRReed(7) 112
(Lucinda Russell) *hld up in tch: stdy hdwy after 4 out: effrt and chsd (clr) wnr appr 2 out: sn rdn: kpt on: no imp* **66/1**
4222 3 10 **Berkshire Downs**[32] 4050 6-10-5 112.. AdamNicol(3) 99
(Lucy Normile) *nt fluent on occasions: led to 3 out: rdn and outpcd bef next: n.d after* **13/8**[2]
-006 4 14 **Ange Des Malberaux (FR)**[13] 4403 6-10-10 0........ DiarmuidO'Regan(5) 89
(James Ewart) *hld up in tch: drvn and outpcd bef 4 out: n.d after* **50/1**
3 5 7 **Dubai Celebrity**[32] 4050 4-10-7 0.. BrianHughes 75
(John Wade) *chsd ldr: rdn and lost 2nd appr 2 out: sn wknd* **15/2**[3]
05 6 3 ¾ **Coachie Bear**[24] 4208 5-11-1 0.. DannyCook 77
(Katie Scott) *nt fluent in rr: struggling after 4 out: hit next: no ch whn mstke last* **100/1**
P F **Byronegetonefree**[92] 2474 5-10-8 0.. SamColtherd(7)
(Stuart Coltherd) *in tch on outside: fell 1st* **50/1**
4m 19.9s (18.10) **Going Correction** +1.125s/f (Heav) **7** Ran SP% **108.6**
WFA 4 from 5yo+ 7lb
Speed ratings (Par 105): **99,95,90,83,80 78,**
CSF £43.61 TOTE £1.70: £1.10, £12.40; EX 49.80 Trifecta £125.20.
Owner Trevor Hemmings **Bred** Mrs C Sutton **Trained** Upper Lambourn, Berks

FOCUS
Following heavy rain this notable meeting was abandoned eight days earlier, but it was quickly rescheduled by the track, Levy Board and BHA race-planning department. After a dry night the going was changed to soft all over. All race distances were as advertised. The opener was a modest novice hurdle and they finished well strung out. The winner confirmed the mreit of his improved Fontwell run.

4634 CYRIL ALEXANDER MEMORIAL NOVICES' LIMITED H'CAP CHASE (12 fncs) 2m 1f 14y
2:20 (2:20) (Class 3) (0-125,125) 5-Y-O+ **£9,097** (£2,671; £1,335; £667)

Form RPR
4-34 1 **Superior Command (IRE)**[54] 3668 7-10-4 107..........[1] PeterBuchanan 114+
(Lucinda Russell) *nt fluent on occasions: in tch: hdwy to ld 2 out: j.rt last: drvn and styd on wl run-in* **4/1**[3]
23P 2 1 ¼ **Lowanbehold (IRE)**[237] 1067 9-9-12 106 oh1.............. JamieHamilton(5) 110
(Sandy Forster) *trckd ldrs: pushed along and outpcd after 5 out: rallied after 3 out: edgd lft after last: kpt on to take 2nd towards fin: nt rch wnr* **18/1**
1431 3 *nk* **Gold Opera (IRE)**[2] 4582 7-11-0 117 7ex.. BrianHarding 122
(N W Alexander) *nt fluent on occasions: led to 4 out: drvn and outpcd after next: rallied last: kpt on wl towards fin* **6/4**[1]
2231 4 ¾ **Morning Royalty (IRE)**[32] 4053 9-11-8 125.. BrianHughes 127
(James Moffatt) *pressed ldr: led 4 out: rdn and hdd 2 out: rdn whn swtchd rt appr last: no ex and lost two pls towards fin* **2/1**[2]
3155 U **Quick Brew**[25] 4179 8-10-4 112..(t) DaraghBourke(5) 112
(Maurice Barnes) *hld up in tch: stdy hdwy bef 4 out: rdn along 2 out: 4 l 4th and one pce whn blnd and uns rdr last* **7/1**
4m 40.2s (22.20) **Going Correction** +1.125s/f (Heav) **5** Ran SP% **111.1**
Speed ratings: **92,91,91,90,**
CSF £45.40 TOTE £4.80: £1.80, £6.40; EX 44.00 Trifecta £195.70.
Owner Willie Scott & Peter J S Russell **Bred** Ms C Bryson **Trained** Arlary, Perth & Kinross

FOCUS
A fair handicap chase, albeit not the strongest for the grade, and they finished in a bit of a heap. A step up from the winner and he can probably rate higher.

4635 TOTEPOOLLIVEINFO.COM PREMIER CHASE (LISTED RACE) (17 fncs) 2m 7f 96y
2:55 (2:55) (Class 1) 5-Y-O+
£18,508 (£6,945; £3,477; £1,732; £871; £435)

Form RPR
-622 1 **Many Clouds (IRE)**[43] 3850 9-11-8 166.. LeightonAspell 168+
(Oliver Sherwood) *j.w: t.k.h: cl up: led 4th: mde rest: shkn up and clr bef 2 out: eased nr fin: readily* **11/10**[1]
0031 2 10 **Unioniste (FR)**[24] 4205 8-11-4 149.. NickScholfield 150
(Paul Nicholls) *led to 4th: trckd ldrs: outpcd 12th: rallied 2 out: edgd lft and chsd (clr) wnr run-in: styd on wl: no imp* **5/1**[3]
6022 3 ¾ **Carrigdhoun (IRE)**[24] 4203 11-10-12 125..(tp) DaraghBourke 142
(Maurice Barnes) *sn pressing wnr: effrt and drvn along and outpcd 3 out: rallied bef last: kpt on u.p run-in* **200/1**
P121 4 *hd* **Sausalito Sunrise (IRE)**[22] 4238 8-11-4 163.. RichardJohnson 150
(Philip Hobbs) *nt fluent on occasions: hld up on outside: hit 9th: hdwy next: chsd wnr 5 out: rdn bef 2 out: no ex and lost two pls run-in* **2/1**[2]
0313 5 6 **Cloudy Too (IRE)**[22] 4245 10-11-4 148.. DannyCook 144
(Sue Smith) *chsd ldrs: blnd and nrly uns rdr 4th: rdn bef 4 out: wknd bef 2 out* **14/1**
-135 6 7 **Maggio (FR)**[115] 2606 11-10-12 143..(t) BrianHughes 132
(Patrick Griffin, Ire) *prom: nt fluent 5 out: pushed along fr next: outpcd whn nt fluent 2 out: sn btn* **33/1**
1341 7 15 **Gold Futures (IRE)**[141] 2068 7-10-12 144.. BrianHarding 122
(Nicky Richards) *hld up: pushed along and effrt after 3 out: rdn and wknd bef next* **16/1**
6m 24.7s (16.70) **Going Correction** +1.125s/f (Heav) **7** Ran SP% **113.6**
Speed ratings: **115,111,111,111,109 106,101**
CSF £7.41 TOTE £2.20: £1.40, £2.10; EX 7.30 Trifecta £193.50.
Owner Trevor Hemmings **Bred** Aidan Aherne **Trained** Upper Lambourn, Berks

FOCUS
A interesting Listed chase with the future in mind, in which last year's Grand National Many Clouds winner was totally dominant. He was value for further and is rated close to his best. Unioniste is on a decent mark for the Grand National.

4636 TOTESCOOP6 PREMIER KELSO HURDLE (A NOVICES' HURDLE) (GRADE 2) (10 hdls) 2m 2f 25y
3:30 (3:31) (Class 1) 4-Y-O+
£21,356 (£8,013; £4,012; £1,998; £1,005; £502)

Form RPR
2112 1 **Le Prezien (FR)**[50] 3739 5-11-5 140..(t) SamTwiston-Davies 142+
(Paul Nicholls) *prom: smooth hdwy to ld 2 out: drvn out fr last* **13/8**[1]
21 2 3 **The Dutchman (IRE)**[47] 3795 6-11-5 132.. DannyCook 137
(Sandy Thomson) *w ldr and clr of rest: led 6th: hit next: rdn and hdd 2 out: kpt on u.p run-in* **11/1**
1251 3 1 ½ **Meet The Legend**[29] 4111 5-11-8 0.. HarrySkelton 139
(Dan Skelton) *t.k.h: hld up in rr: smooth hdwy and cl up bef 2 out: rdn between last 2: no ex run-in* **9/2**[3]
FF11 4 17 **Lake View Lad (IRE)**[30] 4108 6-11-5 136.. StephenMulqueen 120
(N W Alexander) *t.k.h: led and clr w one other: hit 3rd: hdd 6th: styd w ldr: rdn and outpcd whn mstke 2 out: sn btn* **6/1**
F11 5 8 **Overtown Express (IRE)**[6] 4526 8-11-5 0.. NoelFehily 113
(Harry Fry) *hld up in tch: mstke 1st: rdn along bef 2 out: sn wknd* **7/1**
1113 6 9 **Vieux Lille (IRE)**[50] 3739 6-11-5 138.. RichardJohnson 105
(Philip Hobbs) *chsd clr ldng pair: nt fluent 5th: hit and dropped in rr next: sn struggling: no ch fr 3 out* **4/1**[2]
4m 40.8s (13.80) **Going Correction** +1.125s/f (Heav) **6** Ran SP% **111.4**
Speed ratings: **114,112,112,104,100 96**
CSF £18.99 TOTE £2.50: £1.50, £4.70; EX 16.50 Trifecta £74.90.
Owner Million In Mind Partnership **Bred** Jean-Raymond Breton & Thomas Trapenard **Trained** Ditcheat, Somerset

FOCUS
A good renewal of this Grade 2, with all of them arriving with a progressive profile. The gallop was sound and the first three pulled clear. The winner set a decent standard and is rated to his best.

4637 PREMIER TRAFFIC MANAGEMENT H'CAP CHASE (FOR THE HAMILTON MEMORIAL TROPHY) (16 fncs) 2m 5f 133y

4:05 (4:05) (Class 4) (0-110,109) 5-Y-O+ **£3,898** (£1,144; £572; £286)

Form RPR

P033 **1** **Voyage A New York (FR)**[30] 4109 7-11-12 109..................(t) DerekFox -123+
(Lucinda Russell) *pressed ldr: chal 5 out: led bef 2 out: drvn clr* **9/4**[1]

0061 **2** *12* **Suzy's Music (IRE)**[19] 4298 8-10-7 90.............................. BrianHughes 92
(S R B Crawford, Ire) *nt fluent on occasions: hld up in tch: stdy hdwy 5 out: effrt and rdn after 2 out: chsd (clr) wnr bef last: kpt on: no imp* **7/2**[3]

-212 **3** *10* **Oscar Lateen (IRE)**[25] 4177 8-10-10 100.......................(b[1]) StevenFox[(7)] 92
(Sandy Thomson) *t.k.h: led and clr to 9th: jnd 5 out: hdd bef 2 out: wknd bef last* **3/1**[2]

5446 **4** *30* **Oil Burner**[25] 4175 11-10-7 90.. BrianHarding 62
(Stuart Coltherd) *nt fluent on occasions: hld up in tch: hit and reminders 8th: struggling 11th: btn fr 3 out* **8/1**

F021 **P** **Proud Gamble (IRE)**[25] 4175 7-10-0 83 oh3.....................(t) CraigNichol
(Rose Dobbin) *hld up: pushed along 9th: outpcd after next: wknd and p.u bef 4 out* **7/2**[3]

6m 2.2s (33.00) **Going Correction** +1.125s/f (Heav) **5** Ran SP% **111.3**
Speed ratings: **85,80,77,66,**
CSF £10.59 TOTE £2.60: £1.80, £2.20; EX 10.10 Trifecta £29.50.
Owner Fyffees **Bred** Mme A Ouvry & Dr V Benoit Grosfils **Trained** Arlary, Perth & Kinross

FOCUS
Only a modest handicap chase. The winner is rated back to the level of last season's novice win, but this probably isn't strong form.

4638 ROCKY LION'S PRIDE OF HAZELRIGG H'CAP HURDLE (11 hdls) 2m 6f 151y

4:40 (4:43) (Class 4) (0-110,110) 4-Y-O+ **£3,249** (£954; £477; £238)

Form RPR

U111 **1** **Marlee Massie (IRE)**[43] 3868 7-10-11 102.................. MrKitAlexander[(7)] 109+
(N W Alexander) *trckd ldrs: led bef 2 out: sn rdn: styd on wl fr last* **6/1**

1-32 **2** *1 3/4* **See Double You (IRE)**[1] 4607 13-11-5 110..............(p) MrRMPMcNally[(7)] 116
(Ronan M P McNally, Ire) *t.k.h early: trckd ldrs: stdy hdwy gng wl bef 2 out: effrt and 1 l down whn mstke last: kpt on same pce* **8/1**

3422 **3** *3* **Hunters Belt (IRE)**[12] 4421 12-10-13 102..........(vt) JonathonBewley[(5)] 103
(George Bewley) *hld up in rr: pushed along bef 3rd: hdwy after 4 out: effrt and chal bef 2 out: hit last: edgd rt and no ex run-in* **5/1**[3]

-304 **4** *10* **Cruachan (IRE)**[26] 4163 7-10-8 95..................................... AdamNicol[(3)] 87
(Lucy Normile) *hld up: stdy hdwy bef 3 out: effrt and rdn bef next: sn no imp* **7/2**[1]

P3F5 **5** *7* **Lord Usher (IRE)**[42] 3884 9-10-7 98......................... LorcanMurtagh[(7)] 82
(George Charlton) *hld up bhd ldng gp: hdwy and cl up whn pushed along 4 out: rdn and wknd bef 2 out* **14/1**

-463 **6** *2 3/4* **Kilquiggan (IRE)**[98] 2937 8-10-1 92.......................... MissRMcDonald[(7)] 75
(Sandy Thomson) *in tch: effrt and rdn after 3 out: wknd bef next* **7/1**

0463 **7** *3 1/4* **Smuggler's Stash (IRE)**[26] 4163 6-11-2 100.......................... CraigNichol 78
(Rose Dobbin) *hld up bhd ldng gp: drvn along fr 8th: struggling after next: n.d after* **9/2**[2]

-0P3 **8** *1/2* **Bop Along (IRE)**[34] 4035 9-11-11 109.................................(p) BrianHughes 90
(Alistair Whillans) *mstkes: mde most to 7th: cl up tl rdn and wknd bef 2 out* **7/1**

P1-5 **P** **See The Legend**[33] 4045 11-9-13 90... MissJWalton[(7)]
(Sandy Forster) *cl up: led 8th: rdn and hdd bef 2 out: sn wknd: p.u bef last* **33/1**

6m 9.4s (28.40) **Going Correction** +1.125s/f (Heav) **9** Ran SP% **117.1**
Speed ratings (Par 105): **95,94,93,89,87 86,85,85,**
CSF £53.40 CT £259.63 TOTE £5.00: £1.60, £3.10, £2.60; EX 40.20 Trifecta £178.90.
Owner Nicholas Alexander **Bred** Tom Baker **Trained** Kinneston, Perth & Kinross

FOCUS
A modest but competitive handicap for the grade. Another step up from the winner.
T/Jkpt: Not won. T/Plt: £114.30 to a £1 stake. Pool of £60822.74 - 388.34 winning tickets.
T/Qpdt: £10.30 to a £1 stake. Pool of £5490.90 - 394.48 winning tickets. **Richard Young**

4271 MARKET RASEN (R-H)

Sunday, March 13

OFFICIAL GOING: Soft (good to soft in places on hurdle course; chs 5.8, hdl 6.1)
Wind: light 1/2 behind Weather: fine but cold

4639 32RED CASINO "NATIONAL HUNT" NOVICES' HURDLE (8 hdls) 2m 148y

2:10 (2:12) (Class 4) 4-Y-O+ **£3,249** (£954; £477; £238)

Form RPR

203 **1** **Star Foot (IRE)**[108] 2731 5-11-1 122..................................(p) TomO'Brien 120+
(Jo Davis) *trckd ldr: drvn to ld narrowly 2 out: forged clr appr last: styd on wl* **15/8**[2]

030 **2** *12* **Brian Boranha (IRE)**[18] 4303 5-11-1 0.......................... HenryBrooke 108
(Peter Niven) *trckd ldng pair: clr 3rd sn after 3 out: hit last 2: kpt on to take modest 2nd in clsng stages* **12/1**

3 *1 3/4* **Eyes Of A Tiger (IRE)**[164] 1724 5-11-3 0.................... NathanMoscrop[(5)] 112
(Brian Ellison) *t.k.h: led: j.rt: drvn and hdd 2 out: wknd fnl 150yds* **5/2**[3]

362 **4** *15* **Nobel Leader (IRE)**[14] 4388 6-10-8 0..............(p) WilliamFeatherstone[(7)] 89
(James Evans) *trckd ldng pair: drvn 5th: reminders and lost pl after next: bhd fr 2 out* **7/4**[1]

4m 17.0s (10.30) **Going Correction** +0.80s/f (Soft) **4** Ran SP% **107.4**
Speed ratings (Par 105): **107,101,100,93**
CSF £16.07 TOTE £2.20; EX 18.20 Trifecta £25.80.
Owner John L Marriott & Albert L Marriott **Bred** Keatly Overseas Ltd **Trained** East Garston, Berks

FOCUS
A modest novice hurdle.

4640 32RED.COM NOVICES' HURDLE (10 hdls) 2m 2f 140y

2:45 (2:46) (Class 4) 4-Y-O+ **£3,249** (£954; £477; £238)

Form RPR

6P3 **1** **Three Of A Kind (IRE)**[39] 3920 7-11-2 0.....................(t) PaddyBrennan 111+
(Fergal O'Brien) *best away: sn wl clr: nt fluent 4th: 5th and 3 out: 25 l ahd 2 out: heavily eased in clsng stages: unchal* **6/1**[2]

1422 **2** *14* **Maxie T**[20] 4287 5-11-2 132.. FinianO'Toole[(7)] 98
(Micky Hammond) *trckd ldng pair: hit 5th: effrt and distant 2nd bef 2 out: kpt on: nvr anywhere nr wnr* **2/7**[1]

P **3** *33* **Tawan**[12] 4417 5-11-2 0... HenryBrooke 57
(Brian Rothwell) *in last: drvn 3 out: tk distant 3rd last* **200/1**[3]

121 **4** *10* **Mountainside**[189] 1486 4-11-2 129..................................(p) DeanPratt[(5)] 52
(Lucinda Egerton) *chsd clr ldr: drvn 3 out: lost pl bef next: wknd last* **6/1**[2]

4m 57.6s (18.20) **Going Correction** +0.80s/f (Soft)
WFA 4 from 5yo+ 7lb **4** Ran SP% **106.8**
Speed ratings (Par 105): **93,87,73,69**
CSF £8.66 TOTE £9.90; EX 10.10 Trifecta £49.70.
Owner The Yes No Wait Sorries **Bred** Vincent Doran **Trained** Naunton, Gloucs
■ Stewards' Enquiry : Finian O'Toole ten-day ban; failing to take all reasonable and permissible measures to obtain the best possible placing (27th Mar-5th Apr)

FOCUS
An uncompetitive novice hurdle.

4641 32REDSPORT.COM H'CAP CHASE (17 fncs) 2m 7f 191y

3:20 (3:22) (Class 4) (0-115,115) 5-Y-O+ **£3,898** (£1,144; £572; £286)

Form RPR

/3P4 **1** **Bucking The Trend**[45] 3818 8-11-7 115..........................(p) AlanJohns[(5)] 130+
(Tim Vaughan) *led to 5th: led 7th: mde rest: styd on to forge clr appr last: eased last 75yds* **13/8**[1]

220P **2** *20* **Ultimatum Du Roy (FR)**[45] 3818 8-11-9 115.............(tp) KillianMoore[(3)] 115
(Alex Hales) *chsd ldng pair: 2nd after 10th: drvn 14th: kpt on same pce fr 2 out* **11/4**[2]

0435 **3** *47* **Master Rajeem (USA)**[75] 3339 7-11-8 111......................(p) TrevorWhelan 81
(Neil King) *w ldr: led 5th: hdd 7th: blnd 9th: drvn 11th: reminders and nt fluent next: sn wknd: t.o bef 3 out* **13/8**[1]

50P4 **4** *dist* **The Society Man (IRE)**[12] 4423 9-9-7 89 oh8............ GrahamCarson[(7)]
(Michael Chapman) *racd in last: drvn and lost tch 10th: t.o next: eventually completed* **18/1**[3]

6m 44.8s (13.50) **Going Correction** +0.70s/f (Soft) **4** Ran SP% **108.1**
Speed ratings: **105,98,82,**
CSF £6.36 TOTE £2.50; EX 5.80 Trifecta £6.60.
Owner The Marinades **Bred** Richard R Evans **Trained** Aberthin, Vale of Glamorgan

FOCUS
A modest handicap.

4642 32RED.COM H'CAP CHASE (14 fncs) 2m 3f 34y

3:55 (3:55) (Class 4) (0-120,115) 5-Y-O+ **£3,994** (£1,240; £667)

Form RPR

251P **1** **Chankillo**[66] 3497 7-10-9 98......................................(p) TomScudamore 107+
(Sarah-Jayne Davies) *chsd ldrs: 2nd 3rd: led 9th: drvn 3 out: edgd rt last 75yds: styd on* **8/1**

2U13 **2** *3* **Gallic Warrior (FR)**[24] 4209 9-11-7 110...........................(t) PaddyBrennan 117+
(Fergal O'Brien) *chsd ldrs 3rd: 2nd 10th: drvn 3 out: swtchd rt and almost upsides last: keeping on same pce whn swtchd lft last 75yds* **13/8**[1]

43U4 **3** *32* **Crafty Roberto**[50] 3742 8-11-7 113..............................(t) KillianMoore[(3)] 94
(Alex Hales) *led: hdd and drvn 9th: reminders next: wknd bef 3 out: sn bhd: t.o whn eased last 100yds* **9/2**[3]

23-2 **P** **Explained (IRE)**[39] 3931 9-11-7 115.. AlanJohns[(5)]
(Tim Vaughan) *in tch: nt fluent: outpcd 7th: drvn next: reminders 10th: sn lost pl and bhd: t.o whn p.u bef 3 out* **9/2**[3]

P112 **P** **Showboater (IRE)**[24] 4199 7-11-6 109.............................(p) NicodeBoinville
(Ben Pauling) *chsd ldrs: lost pl and pushed along 4th: hit 6th: reminders and lost pl next: t.o 8th: p.u bef next* **7/2**[2]

5m 21.0s (15.30) **Going Correction** +0.70s/f (Soft) **5** Ran SP% **107.8**
Speed ratings: **95,93,80,,**
CSF £21.27 TOTE £7.50: £2.90, £1.20; EX 20.60 Trifecta £87.40.
Owner Andrew Gough **Bred** Dullingham Park **Trained** Leominster, H'fords

FOCUS
An ordinary handicap, run at a fair gallop.

4643 32RED H'CAP HURDLE (12 hdls) 2m 7f 16y

4:30 (4:30) (Class 3) (0-130,130) 4-Y-O+ **£5,848** (£1,717; £858; £429)

Form RPR

3P64 **1** **San Telm (IRE)**[44] 3837 11-10-12 116.........................(p) JoshuaMoore 119
(Stuart Edmunds) *led: drvn bef 2 out: sn jnd: fnd ex last 75yds* **5/2**[2]

5123 **2** *2 1/4* **Pilgrims Bay (IRE)**[24] 4206 6-11-3 121.......................... TomScudamore 123
(David Pipe) *hld up in last: hdwy to trck ldrs 9th: upsides 2 out: n.m.r bef last: upsides last: drvn: hung lft and fnd v little last 100yds* **9/4**[1]

243 **3** *10* **Caged Lightning (IRE)**[17] 4324 6-10-1 110..............(p) MichaelHeard[(5)] 103
(Steve Gollings) *t.k.h: w wnr: drvn 3 out: upsides last: wknd last 200yds* **9/2**

U6U0 **4** *3 1/2* **Ivy Gate (IRE)**[15] 4352 8-10-8 119..........................(p) PatrickCowley[(7)] 109
(Jonjo O'Neill) *swvd lft s: chsd ldrs: hit 5th and 7th: drvn 9th: hit next: sn outpcd: distant 4th last: kpt on* **13/2**

2125 **5** *31* **Oh Land Abloom (IRE)**[107] 2759 6-11-12 130..................(t) TrevorWhelan 106
(Neil King) *chsd ldrs: hit 7th: hit 3 out: lost pl bef next: sn bhd: eased run-in: t.o* **7/2**[3]

6m 14.0s (23.50) **Going Correction** +0.80s/f (Soft) **5** Ran SP% **113.1**
Speed ratings (Par 107): **91,90,86,85,74**
CSF £8.98 TOTE £3.90: £2.30, £1.60; EX 9.80 Trifecta £35.60.
Owner The Tyringham Partnership **Bred** Miss Kathleen Clinton **Trained** Newport Pagnell, Bucks

FOCUS
Not a bad little handicap, rated around the runner-up.

4644 32RED £10 FREE MARES' H'CAP HURDLE (12 hdls) 2m 7f 16y

5:05 (5:06) (Class 4) (0-110,106) 4-Y-O+ **£3,249** (£954; £477; £238)

Form RPR

3422 **1** **Young Lou**[16] 4349 7-9-6 82 ow2...............................(p) CathalCourtney[(10)] 89+
(Robin Dickin) *hld up in rr: j.lft 1st: hdwy to chse ldrs 9th: drvn bef 2 out: 2nd appr last: led last 200yds: styd on* **9/4**[1]

5122 **2** *2 1/2* **Milly Baloo**[33] 4041 5-11-6 105.. RyanDay[(5)] 110
(Tim Easterby) *t.k.h in rr: hdwy to trck ldrs 6th: mstke 8th: 2nd sn after 3 out: led next: hdd and no ex last 200yds* **9/4**[1]

6063 **3** *7* **The Barbury Queen (IRE)**[67] 3485 6-11-9 103........ WayneHutchinson 100
(Alan King) *chsd ldrs: outpcd and reminders 7th: lost pl sn after 3 out: poor 4th 2 out: hung lft and kpt on to take modest 3rd last 150yds* **8/1**

2252 **4** *3 1/2* **Twenty Eight Guns**[21] 4268 6-11-11 105.......................(p) TomScudamore 103
(Michael Scudamore) *led: qcknd pce 7th: hdd 2 out: handy 3rd whn hit last: hung lft and wknd last 200yds* **4/1**[2]

22-2 **5** *17* **Kilas Girl (IRE)**[27] 4151 6-11-12 106.. TomO'Brien 87
(John Quinn) *trckd ldr: hit 7th: pushed along next: reminders 3 out: sn lost pl: bhd whn eased in clsng stages* **9/2**[3]

6m 18.0s (27.50) **Going Correction** +0.80s/f (Soft) **5** Ran SP% **110.8**
Speed ratings (Par 105): **84,83,80,79,73**
CSF £7.96 TOTE £3.50: £1.30, £2.60; EX 8.60 Trifecta £35.60.

Owner E R C Beech & B Wilkinson **Bred** E R C Beech **Trained** Alcester, Warwicks
■ Cathal Courtney's first winner.
FOCUS
A moderate mares' handicap, run at a steady gallop and is rated around the consistent runner-up.

4645 32RED ON THE APP STORE CONDITIONAL JOCKEYS' H'CAP HURDLE (10 hdls) 2m 2f 140y
5:40 (5:40) (Class 4) (0-105,106) 4-Y-O+ **£3,249** (£954; £477; £238)

Form				RPR
2	1		**Fort Carson (IRE)**[5] 4541 10-10-11 **100**.......................... LeroyLynch[(10)] *(Neil King) trckd ldrs: t.k.h: led 4th: hdd after 3 out: led next: drew clr last 150yds: eased towards fin* **5/2**[2]	117+
50-3	2	7	**Buckontupence (IRE)**[23] 4235 8-11-5 **101**............ WilliamFeatherstone[(3)] *(James Evans) chsd ldrs: reminders 3 out: lost pl and mod 4th next: kpt on and tk modest 2nd in clsng stages* **9/2**[3]	107
0061	3	2	**Champagne Chaser**[7] 4504 6-11-13 **106** 7ex.................. DavidNoonan *(Tim Vaughan) trckd ldrs: nt fluent 6th: led narrowly after 3 out: hdd and hit next: wknd last 150yds* **6/5**[1]	111
-232	4	7	**Reyno**[39] 3932 8-11-12 **105**..................................(bt) LizzieKelly *(Stuart Edmunds) chsd ldrs: drvn 3 out: wknd last* **6/1**	101
P035	5	42	**Jimmie Brown (USA)**[12] 4415 8-9-9 **79** oh7............. ThomasDowson[(5)] *(Andrew Crook) in rr: mstke 2nd: hdwy 5th: outpcd next: lost pl bef 2 out: sn bhd: t.o* **25/1**	32
F4PP	6	5	**Exit To Freedom**[14] 4391 10-10-0 **79** oh10..........................(p[1]) JoeColliver *(John Wainwright) chsd ldrs: lost pl 6th: sn bhd: t.o 2 out* **66/1**	27
02PP	7	22	**Duc De Seville (IRE)**[38] 3946 4-9-9 **88** oh8.............(p) GrahamCarson[(5)] *(Michael Chapman) a in last: j. slowly 1st: sn bhd: t.o 6th* **66/1**	5
0UP0	P		**Whatsupjack (IRE)**[45] 3821 9-10-0 **79** oh7...............(b) JonathanEngland *(Shaun Harris) led to 4th: sn pushed along: lost pl 6th: bhd whn p.u bef next* **16/1**	

4m 59.8s (20.40) **Going Correction** +0.80s/f (Soft)
WFA 4 from 6yo+ 7lb **8 Ran SP% 119.2**
Speed ratings (Par 105): **89,86,85,82,64 62,53,**
CSF £15.00 CT £19.33 TOTE £3.40: £1.30, £1.90, £1.10; EX 15.10 Trifecta £37.90.
Owner The Ridgeway Racing For Fun Partnership **Bred** Ronald O'Neill **Trained** Barbury Castle, Wiltshire
FOCUS
Only the first pair mattered from the home turn in this moderate handicap.
T/Plt: £763.20 to a £1 stake. Pool of £47364.34 - 45.30 winning tickets. T/Qpdt: £12.10 to a £1 stake. Pool of £3997.80 - 244.10 winning tickets. **Walter Glynn**

4344 WARWICK (L-H)
Sunday, March 13

OFFICIAL GOING: Soft (heavy in places on hurdle course; chs 5.2, hdl 4.9)
Wind: nil Weather: sunny

4646 WARWICKSHIRE & NORTHAMPTONSHIRE AIR AMBULANCE NOVICES' HURDLE (8 hdls) 2m
2:00 (2:01) (Class 4) 4-Y-O+ **£3,249** (£954; £477; £238)

Form				RPR
	1		**Belami Des Pictons (FR)**[149] 5-11-7 0.......................... AidanColeman *(Venetia Williams) hld up in tch: wnt 3rd after 3rd: chsd ldr and rdn bef 2 out: drvn last: styd on u.p to ld fnl 50yds* **11/10**[1]	124+
U204	2	1	**Viva Rafa (IRE)**[25] 4182 6-11-1 0.............................. IanPopham *(Richard Phillips) led: rdn after 2 out: wandered appr last: drvn flat: hdd and no ex fnl 50yds* **10/1**[3]	116
0-1U	3	9	**Nansaroy**[74] 3366 6-11-7 0.. PaulMoloney *(Evan Williams) chsd ldr: j.rt and blnd 2nd: j.rt next: rdn after 3 out: 3rd and struggling next: btn whn mstke last* **5/4**[2]	115
-303	4	58	**Monkey Rum**[14] 4382 6-11-1 0.................................. PeterCarberry *(Brendan Powell) in tch in rr: wnt 4th but losing tch bef 4th: t.o 3 out* **14/1**	49
26P	F		**Kendari King (IRE)**[227] 1153 5-11-1 0............................ TomCannon *(Tim Vaughan) chsd ldng pair tl after 3rd: sn dropped to last and struggling next: losing tch whn fell 5th* **66/1**	

4m 12.05s (21.05) **Going Correction** +1.125s/f (Heav) **5 Ran SP% 109.3**
Speed ratings (Par 105): **92,91,87,58,**
CSF £11.38 TOTE £2.00: £1.10, £4.60; EX 10.60 Trifecta £14.40.
Owner Hills Of Ledbury (Aga) **Bred** S C E A Du Marais Des Pictons **Trained** Kings Caple, H'fords
FOCUS
All starts have been moved at this track following remeasuring, so there will be no speed figures here until there is sufficient data to calculate updated median times. The ground had dried out a little and was now soft on the chase course and soft, heavy in places on the hurdles track. All hurdle races run on outer hurdle track. The rail on hurdle course was out approximately 2yds on the exit to the home straight and 2yds on the home bend. Rail on chase track out approximately 4yds on the exit to the home straight, 14yds on the entrance to the back straight and 10yds on the home bend. Rail movement meant that the opening race was run over 8yds further than advertised. \n This novices' hurdle looked a two-horse race, but with one of them running moderately it remains to be seen what the form is worth. Aidan Coleman described conditions as "very gluey out there as the ground dries out" while Ian Popham said the ground was "soft and quite hard work".

4647 EBF/TBA MARES' NOVICES' LIMITED H'CAP CHASE (17 fncs) 2m 4f
2:30 (2:30) (Class 3) (0-125,125) 5-Y-O+ **£7,147** (£2,098; £1,049; £524)

Form				RPR
05-3	1		**Centasia**[298] 394 9-11-6 **123**..................................(t) DenisO'Regan *(Neil Mulholland) chsd ldrs: wnt 2nd 13th tl led on inner after 3 out: rdn between last 2: 2 l in front last: edgd lft u.p sn after last: kpt on: hrd pressed but a jst holding on towards fin* **7/2**[2]	130
2132	2	nk	**Cresswell Breeze**[22] 4251 6-11-8 **125**..........................(t) AidanColeman *(Anthony Honeyball) in tch in midfield: rdn 12th: chsd wnr bef 2 out: 2 l down last: rallied gamely u.p flat and in clsng fnl 150yds: nvr quite getting to wnr* **2/1**[1]	132
3522	3	6	**Kayfleur**[22] 4247 7-11-8 **125**...................................... JakeGreenall *(Henry Daly) hld up in tch in last pair: hdwy to chse ldrs 14th: cl 3rd and u.p 2 out: no ex last and outpcd flat* **4/1**[3]	127
-53P	4	9	**Abigail Lynch (IRE)**[52] 3709 8-10-7 **113**.......................(t) RyanHatch[(3)] *(Nigel Twiston-Davies) in tch in midfield: mstke 3rd: rdn and struggling 13th: lft 5th and hmpd next: n.d after but plugged on to go modest 4th last* **12/1**	109
F264	5	28	**Rouquine Sauvage**[37] 3977 8-10-1 **109**.......................(t) DavidNoonan[(5)] *(Anthony Honeyball) t.k.h: chsd ldr tl j. into ld 1st: hdd after 3 out: sn rdn and btn: wknd qckly 2 out: fin tired: t.o* **11/1**	78
11F2	F		**Alder Mairi (IRE)**[27] 4158 9-11-5 **122**.......................... AndrewThornton *(Seamus Mullins) led tl out j. and hdd 1st: chsd ldr tl 13th: stl handy whn fell next* **9/1**	
20P6	P		**Aces Over Eights (IRE)**[39] 3930 7-10-3 **106** oh6.................. JamieMoore *(Kerry Lee) in tch in rr tl lost tch qckly after 10th: t.o whn p.u next: burst blood vessel* **8/1**	

5m 21.8s (3.80) **Going Correction** +0.25s/f (Yiel) **7 Ran SP% 112.7**
Speed ratings: **102,101,99,95,84 ,**
CSF £11.11 TOTE £5.40: £2.40, £1.50; EX 13.40 Trifecta £36.50.
Owner R S Brookhouse **Bred** Fawley House Stud **Trained** Limpley Stoke, Wilts
FOCUS
Rail movement meant that this race was run over 79yds further than advertised. A decent mares' novices' handicap chase run at a decent pace in the conditions.

4648 WHITES BEST BUYERS FOR COPPER AND BRASS STANDARDS H'CAP HURDLE (11 hdls) 2m 5f
3:05 (3:05) (Class 4) (0-115,113) 4-Y-O+ **£3,249** (£954; £477; £238)

Form				RPR
50	1		**Church Field (IRE)**[44] 3846 8-11-5 **113**.......................(v[1]) HarryCobden[(7)] *(Phil Middleton) chsd ldrs: wnt 2nd 8th: led 2 out: wandered u.p bef last: styd on and drew clr flat* **8/1**	122+
-621	2	6	**Join The Navy**[40] 3919 11-11-3 **107**........................... KieronEdgar[(3)] *(Kate Buckett) hld up in rr: stdy prog after 6th: trckd ldrs and stl hld onto after 3 out: wnt 2nd next and sn rdn: minimal rspnse and wknd flat* **9/1**	109
0322	3	1	**Just So Cool (IRE)**[23] 4226 5-11-11 **112**......................... AidanColeman *(David Dennis) chsd ldrs: effrt after 3 out: drvn and outpcd bef next: keeping on but no ch w wnr whn wnt 3rd and bmpd last: kpt on same pce* **11/2**[2]	114
-663	4	6	**Beauboreen (IRE)**[31] 4069 9-11-5 **106**.............................(v) SeanQuinlan *(Jennie Candlish) chsd ldr tl led 5th: hdd 7th: styd prom tl outpcd u.p after 3 out: plugged on u.p to go 4th flat: no ch w wnr* **12/1**	101
020	5	3 1/2	**Bold Runner**[30] 4097 5-11-7 **108**..................................(p) BrendanPowell *(Jose Santos) led tl mstke and hdd 5th: pressed ldr tl led again 7th: rdn and hdd bef 2 out: 3rd and btn whn j.rt and cannoned into rival last: wknd flat* **7/1**[3]	103
-P10	6	3 1/4	**Gorey Lane (IRE)**[47] 3793 10-10-5 **95**...............(vt) ColmMcCormack[(3)] *(John Norton) midfield: struggling u.p after 6th: plugged on but no threat to ldrs after* **25/1**	83
6-50	7	6	**Bourne**[152] 1897 10-11-4 **105**.......................................(p) AdrianLane *(Donald McCain) midfield tl lost pl u.p after 6th: n.d after* **14/1**	87
F260	8	1/2	**Scales (IRE)**[39] 3932 10-11-7 **108**.................................. JamieMoore *(Kerry Lee) hld up towards rr: hdwy into midfield 6th: chsd ldrs 8th: drvn and btn after 3 out: wknd next* **9/1**	90
P2PP	9	64	**An Poc Ar Buile (IRE)**[15] 4352 7-11-8 **109**......................... PaulMoloney *(Sophie Leech) a in rr: lost tch and t.o 7th* **25/1**	27
2-P4	P		**Seas Of Green**[8] 4492 9-11-5 **106**................................. AdamWedge *(Paul Cowley) chsd ldrs: losing pl whn j.lft 7th: sn dropped out: t.o whn p.u 3 out* **16/1**	
3463	P		**Dun Scaith (IRE)**[199] 1366 8-11-8 **109**............................ JamesBest *(Sophie Leech) taken down early: hld up in rr: lost tch after 6th: sn t.o tl p.u 3 out* **28/1**	
0532	P		**Charlie Cook (IRE)**[43] 3855 7-11-11 **112**.......................... KielanWoods *(Graeme McPherson) hld up in midfield: clsd and in tch 5th: hit 8th and immediately eased and p.u* **3/1**[1]	

5m 41.5s (20.50) **Going Correction** +1.125s/f (Heav) **12 Ran SP% 115.4**
Speed ratings (Par 105): **105,102,102,100,98 97,95,95,70, , ,**
CSF £74.06 CT £431.20 TOTE £8.30: £2.30, £2.40, £2.60; EX 71.00 Trifecta £480.60.
Owner P W Middleton **Bred** Mrs Eleanor Hadden **Trained** Dorton, Bucks
FOCUS
All hurdle races run on outer hurdle track. Rail movement meant that this race was run over 14yds further than advertised. A fair handicap hurdle run at a solid pace and they finished well strung out.

4649 WHITES FREE SKIPS FOR METAL H'CAP CHASE (22 fncs) 3m 5f
3:40 (3:40) (Class 3) (0-125,125) 5-Y-O+ **£7,797** (£2,289; £1,144; £572)

Form				RPR
-U62	1		**Incentivise (IRE)**[73] 3385 13-10-13 **112**.......................... JamieMoore *(Kerry Lee) midfield: rdn after 15th: 7th and drvn after 15th: rallied in 5th next: lft 3rd 3 out: led bef 2 out: kpt on flat: drvn out* **12/1**	119+
4U33	2	3/4	**Grove Silver (IRE)**[15] 4352 7-11-1 **114**........................... SeanQuinlan *(Jennie Candlish) in tch in midfield: hdwy to chse ldrs 15th: lft 2nd 3 out: sn drvn: kpt on u.p flat* **6/1**[3]	118
1-03	3	nk	**Krackatoa King**[52] 3707 8-11-5 **121**...............................(b) JamesBanks[(3)] *(Noel Williams) chsd ldr tl led 16th: rdn and hdd bef 2 out: kpt on u.p flat* **9/2**[2]	125
-P21	4	56	**Emma Soda**[25] 4185 11-10-13 **112**...............................(b) PeterCarberry *(Paul Davies) in tch in midfield: hdwy to chse ldrs 13th: rdn 16th: sn drvn and struggling: wknd 18th: lft poor 4th 3 out: t.o* **12/1**	60
P-5B	P		**Merlin's Wish**[16] 4340 11-11-4 **117**..............................(p) IanPopham *(Martin Keighley) chsd ldr: mstke 2nd: mstke and lost pl 4th: lost tch 7th: t.o whn p.u after 12th* **16/1**	
F141	P		**Rocky Bender (IRE)**[7] 4505 11-11-5 **123** 7ex.................. CharlieDeutsch[(5)] *(Venetia Williams) in tch: dropped to rr 5th: rdn and sme hdwy after 15th: btn whn j. bdly rt and blnd 17th: p.u next* **16/1**	
-3F4	P		**Red Admirable (IRE)**[75] 3339 10-11-8 **121**.......................(p) KielanWoods *(Graeme McPherson) hld up in tch in rr: mstke 9th: hdwy 12th: rdn and btn 16th: wkng whn p.u next* **25/1**	
-110	P		**Cyrien Star**[44] 3836 9-11-3 **116**...................................... JakeGreenall *(Henry Daly) wnt rt and reminder to jump off: bhd: hdwy to chse ldrs after 5th: lost pl 16th: losing tch whn blnd 18th: p.u next* **33/1**	
124P	P		**Loughalder (IRE)**[73] 3385 10-10-9 **108**.........................(bt) CharliePoste *(Matt Sheppard) chsd ldrs tl mstke 6th: bhd but stl in tch whn mstke 12th and: rdn after 15th: wkng whn p.u 17th* **6/1**[3]	
512U	P		**Ballyrath (IRE)**[7] 4505 6-11-6 **122**.................................(p) RyanHatch[(3)] *(Nigel Twiston-Davies) dropped to rr and rdn after 2nd: nvr travelling wl after: lost tch and t.o 7th tl p.u after 12th* **9/1**	
P211	F		**Streets Of Promise (IRE)**[5] 4549 7-11-11 **124** 7ex.....(p) LiamTreadwell *(Michael Scudamore) j.rt: led tl 16th: chsd ldr after: 2 l down whn j.rt and fell 3 out* **3/1**[1]	

7m 57.8s (1.80) **Going Correction** +0.25s/f (Yiel) **11 Ran SP% 115.7**
Speed ratings: **107,106,106,91, , , , , ,**
CSF £82.28 CT £377.92 TOTE £11.80: £3.10, £2.60, £2.10; EX 88.00 Trifecta £763.30.
Owner R Bartlett J Hulston & Mrs B M Ayres **Bred** Thomas Maher **Trained** Byton, H'fords
■ Stewards' Enquiry : Sean Quinlan four-day; used whip above the permitted level (27th-30th Mar)
James Banks five-day ban: used whip above the permitted level (28th-31st Mar)

FOCUS
Rail movement meant that this race was run over 105yds further than advertised. A competitive staying handicap chase and a real test in the conditions, with a slow-motion finish and only four managing to compete.

4650 COLIN E MANDER BRICKLAYERS 75TH BIRTHDAY CONDITIONAL JOCKEYS' H'CAP HURDLE (8 hdls) 2m
4:15 (4:15) (Class 4) (0-105,105) 4-Y-0+ £3,249 (£954; £477; £238)

Form RPR
0054 1 **Midtech Valentine**[17] 4320 5-10-11 **98**.............................. TobyWheeler(8) 107+
(Ian Williams) *midfield: clsd to chse ldrs 3rd: wnt 2nd next: led sn after 3 out: cruising in front after: mstke last: eased towards fin: easily* **11/4**[1]
2144 2 4 ½ **Norse Light**[5] 4541 5-11-5 **104**..............................(p) GarethMalone(6) 101
(David Dennis) *off the pce in last pair: clsd after 3rd: rdn and chsd clr wnr bef 2 out: no imp and wandered between last 2: plugged on* **10/3**[2]
56-2 3 23 **Ruperra Tom**[23] 4235 8-11-3 **96**.............................. MauriceLinehan 71
(Sophie Leech) *j.lft: led: mstke 3 out and sn hdd: 3rd and wl btn next: wknd: wnt lft and mstke last* **4/1**[3]
000 4 10 **Bandon Roc**[17] 4317 5-11-12 **105**.............................. TomBellamy 69
(Kim Bailey) *chsd ldrs: wnt 2nd after 2nd tl rdn and dropped to 3rd 4th: 4th and wknd 3 out: t.o* **10/1**
-01B 5 2 ¼ **Vertueux (FR)**[23] 4223 11-10-0 **82**..............................(p) NickSlatter(3) 44
(Tony Carroll) *chsd ldr tl after 2nd: dropped to 5th and struggling 4th: no ch 3 out: t.o* **16/1**
6-54 6 16 **Cry Fury**[199] 1379 8-11-11 **104**.............................. KieronEdgar 50
(Sophie Leech) *hld up off the pce in rr: nvr on terms: t.o 5th* **9/1**
0B00 U **Same Ole Trix (IRE)**[67] 3484 6-10-4 **89**..............................(t) MikeyHamill(6)
(Kim Bailey) *midfield tl mstke and uns rdr 3rd* **5/1**

4m 20.7s (29.70) **Going Correction** +1.125s/f (Heav) **7 Ran SP% 111.4**
Speed ratings (Par 105): **70,67,56,51,50 42,**
CSF £11.95 TOTE £3.30: £2.20, £1.60; EX 12.10 Trifecta £40.90.
Owner Midtech **Bred** I P Williams **Trained** Portway, Worcs

FOCUS
All hurdle races run on outer hurdle track. Rail movement meant that this race was run over 8yds further than advertised. A modest event and they were soon well spread out.

4651 CHILDREN'S AIR AMBULAN AIR WEDDING OPEN HUNTERS' CHASE (FOR THE AIR WEDDING CHALLENGE TROPHY) (17 fncs) 2m 4f
4:50 (4:52) (Class 6) 5-Y-0+ £1,247 (£387; £193; £96)

Form RPR
U-23 1 **Nowurhurlin (IRE)**[35] 4016 9-12-1 113.............................. MrNOrpwood(5) 125+
(Mrs S J Stilgoe) *a.p: led 14th: drew clr and in command 3 out: r.o strly: easily* **11/2**[2]
U 2 12 **Lord Heathfield (IRE)**[33] 4043 10-11-7 118.....(p) MrTommieMO'Brien(5) 105+
(Miss C L Mews) *chsd ldr early: lost pl and rdn 5th: no ch w wnr and u.p in 4th bef 2 out: styd on to go 2nd flat* **16/1**
13F- 3 1 ¾ **Out Now (IRE)**[76] 12-11-11 130.............................. MrDavidMaxwell(5) 104
(Mrs Kim Smyly) *midfield: hdwy to chse ldrs 8th: outpcd 3 out: chsd clr wnr next: no imp: lost 2nd flat* **6/1**[3]
06P0 4 1 ¼ **Mr Moss (IRE)**[18] 4307 11-11-5 112.............................. MrJNailor(7) 99
(S Rea) *mostly chsd ldr tl 7th: chsd ldrs after: rdn 14th: sn u.p and outpcd by wnr: 3rd and wl hld 2 out: plugged on* **40/1**
12-2 5 10 **Fredo (IRE)**[25] 4180 12-12-1 120..............................(p) MrRyanBird(5) 101
(Ian Williams) *dropped in rr after mstke 2nd: hdwy after 10th: rdn 13th: 6th and no ch w wnr whn mstke 2 out* **9/2**[1]
54-P 6 5 **Arctic Ben (IRE)**[21] 4269 12-11-13 119.............................. MissJCWilliams(3) 89
(Henry Daly) *hld up in midfield: mstke 11th: sn rdn: wknd 14th* **16/1**
110/ 7 1 ¼ **Shales Rock**[49] 10-11-9 122..............................(p) MissImmyRobinson(7) 87
(Mrs C J Robinson) *chsd ldrs: wnt 2nd 7th and sn pressing ldr: led after 12th tl 14th: lost 2nd and wknd bef 2 out: fdd flat* **6/1**[3]
34-4 8 4 ½ **Ballyallia Man (IRE)**[60] 3585 11-11-9 122..............................(tp) MrEdBailey(7) 82
(Mrs N Sheppard) *in tch towards rr: shortlived effrt 2th: bhd 3 out: t.o* **9/1**
P-5P 9 3 **Trafalgar (FR)**[10] 4446 9-11-7 99.............................. MrJMahot(5) 78
(Sarah-Jayne Davies) *midfield: rdn and mstke 14th: sn btn: wknd 3 out: t.o* **100/1**
5-PP P **Chartreux (FR)**[22] 4249 11-11-13 120..............................(t) MrSDavies-Thomas(7)
(Mrs Julie Marles) *bhd 5th: rdn 8th: struggling whn j. awkwardly 11th: losing tch whn p.u 13th* **20/1**
1PPP P **Kings Grey (IRE)**[24] 4207 12-12-1 128..............................(tp) MrMatthewHampton(5)
(Philip Kirby) *led tl after 12th: dropped out rapidly: bhd whn p.u 14th* **25/1**
-PP5 P **Sustainability (IRE)**[10] 4446 11-11-5 105..............................(p) MrJSKnox(7)
(Miss B Eckley) *in tch: mstke 12th: sn btn and p.u next* **25/1**
F-5P U **Pentiffic (NZ)**[49] 12-11-13 119.............................. MissLMTurner(7)
(P P C Turner) *midfield whn stmbld and uns rdr 3rd* **12/1**
4/P2 P **Farmer Matt (IRE)**[33] 4043 10-12-3 114..............................(t) MissAEStirling(3)
(Fergal O'Brien) *bhd and rdn after mstke 9th: lost tch 12th: p.u 14th* **7/1**

5m 29.6s (11.60) **Going Correction** +0.25s/f (Yiel) **14 Ran SP% 120.0**
Speed ratings: **86,81,80,80,76 74,73,71,70, , , ,**
CSF £81.35 TOTE £6.60: £3.00, £5.90, £2.10; EX 112.60 Trifecta £978.90.
Owner Mrs S J Stilgoe **Bred** Thomas Meagher **Trained** Hutton-Le-Hole, North Yorks

FOCUS
Rail movement meant that this race was run over 79yds further than advertised. A competitive hunters' chase, but the winner took it apart.
T/Plt: £186.30 to £1 stake. Pool of £65839.13 - 257.88 winning tickets. T/Qpdt: £44.70 to a £1 stake. Pool of £6107.58 - 100.90 winning tickets. **Steve Payne**

4652 - (Foreign Racing) - See Raceform Interactive

4626 LIMERICK (R-H)
Sunday, March 13

OFFICIAL GOING: Heavy

4653a KERRY GROUP EUROPEAN BREEDERS FUND SHANNON SPRAY MARES NOVICE HURDLE (GRADE 3) (13 hdls) 2m 6f
2:35 (2:36) 4-Y-0+ £16,053 (£4,959; £2,349; £1,044; £391)

1 **Barnahash Rose (IRE)**[36] 4003 8-10-12 110..............................(t) AmbroseMcCurtin 128+
(Jonathan Sweeney, Ire) *chsd ldrs: mid-div at 1/2-way: prog into 3rd after 4 out: rapid hdwy to trck ldrs after next: led bef 2 out where clr: styd on wl run-in* **6/1**[2]
2 11 **Myztique (IRE)**[63] 3550 6-10-12 116..............................(t) KevinSexton 117
(Gordon Elliott, Ire) *chsd ldr in 2nd: clsr w a circ to r: clr 2nd 3 out: briefly on terms bef 2 out but sn hdd and nt qckn w wnr: kpt on same pce whn nt fluent last* **5/2**[1]
3 11 **Court Challenge (IRE)**[21] 4278 7-10-12 110.............................. MartinMooney 106
(Shane Crawley, Ire) *hld up tl prog 4 out to chse ldrs in mod 4th: no imp bef 2 out: kpt on one pce into remote 3rd after 2 out* **14/1**
4 15 **Monbeg Rose (IRE)**[42] 3890 6-10-12 121.............................. PaulTownend 94
(W P Mullins, Ire) *led: advantage reduced after 3 out and hdd bef next: sn no ex and wknd bef last* **5/2**[1]
5 6 **Marygale Bridge (IRE)**[77] 3300 7-10-12 116..............................(t) BrianO'Connell 87
(John J Walsh, Ire) *chsd ldrs: mid-div at 1/2-way: nt qckn in 5th bef 3 out: sn no ex* **13/2**[3]
6 4 **Cheiliuradh (IRE)**[85] 3169 5-10-11 110..............................(t) SeanFlanagan 82
(David Harry Kelly, Ire) *hld up towards rr: sme prog 4 out: wnt mod 6th after next: nvr on terms* **50/1**
7 11 **Kala Brandy (IRE)**[45] 3829 8-10-12 108.............................. JJBurke 70
(Timothy Townend, Ire) *hld up: sme prog bef 4 out: sn no imp* **12/1**
P **Pride Of The Braid (IRE)**[36] 4003 6-10-12 114.............................. MarkWalsh
(John E Kiely, Ire) *hld up towards rr: sme hdwy 1/2-way: rdn and no imp 4 out: sn p.u* **9/1**
P **Ashes Of Love (IRE)**[25] 4193 6-10-12 0.............................. RobbiePower
(Mrs John Harrington, Ire) *chsd ldrs: clsr in 4th at 4th: mstke 5 out and sn wknd: p.u bef 2 out* **16/1**
P **Siberian Vixen (IRE)**[22] 4258 6-10-12 102..............................(b) AELynch
(Edmond Kent, Ire) *sn chsd ldrs in 3rd on inner: rdn and wknd bef 6 out: p.u bef 2 out* **33/1**
P **Scorpy (IRE)** 4-10-1 0 ow2.............................. IanMcCarthy
(David Harry Kelly, Ire) *racd in rr: mstke 5th: mstke again 6 out and p.u 4 out* **100/1**

6m 9.1s (369.10)
WFA 4 from 5yo+ 8lb **11 Ran SP% 120.9**
CSF £22.46 TOTE £7.40: £2.10, £1.40, £4.20; DF 25.30 Trifecta £315.20.
Owner Miss Michelle O'Connor **Bred** C Kenneally **Trained** Kildinan, Co Cork

FOCUS
Stamina proved to be the key here as the leaders went off too quickly and the winner relished her task

4656a 8/1 WILLIE MULLINS TO TRAIN A CHELTENHAM WINNER AT CORAL.IE EBF MARES NOVICE CHASE (GRADE 2) (14 fncs) 2m 6f
4:20 (4:20) 5-Y-0+ £21,691 (£6,985; £3,308; £1,470; £735)

RPR
1 **Bonny Kate (IRE)**[42] 3894 6-11-0 137.............................. SeanFlanagan 138+
(Noel Meade, Ire) *mde all: j.w: pushed clr bef last: styd on wl run-in* **1/2**[1]
2 2 ¼ **Uranna (FR)**[17] 4330 8-11-0 133.............................. PaulTownend 135
(W P Mullins, Ire) *sn chsd clr ldr in 2nd: dropped briefly to 3rd bef 7 out: rdn and nt qckn w wnr bef last: kpt on same pce* **5/2**[2]
3 12 **Emcon (IRE)**[31] 4083 7-11-0 123.............................. KevinSexton 128
(W J Austin, Ire) *sn chsd ldrs in 3rd: slow at 2nd: clsr briefly in 2nd bef 7 out where again slow: nt qckn in 3rd bef 2 out: sn no ex* **9/1**[3]
4 30 **Give Her Bach (IRE)**[147] 1993 7-11-0 116..............................(t) PierceGallagher 92
(Patrick Cronin, Ire) *racd in rr: detached after 4 out: wnt remote 4th at last: nvr a threat* **33/1**
5 13 **Annamatopoeia (IRE)**[17] 4330 8-11-0 113.............................. AELynch 79
(Brian Jordan, Ire) *hld up in 4th: mstke 1st: no imp bef 3 out: sn no ex: dropped to rr at last* **33/1**

6m 37.0s (397.00) **5 Ran SP% 111.1**
CSF £2.30 TOTE £1.50: £1.02, £1.40; DF 1.70 Trifecta £3.30.
Owner Mrs Patricia Hunt **Bred** R Guiry **Trained** Castletown, Co Meath

FOCUS
A very fluent display from the winner, winning as she was entitled to and all roads now surely will lead to Fairyhouse. The first two are rated to their marks.

4655, 4657 - 4661a (Foreign Racing) - See Raceform Interactive

4372 NAVAN (L-H)
Sunday, March 13

OFFICIAL GOING: Soft to heavy

4662a IRISH STALLION FARMS EUROPEAN BREEDERS FUND NOVICE HURDLE (13 hdls) 2m 7f
4:00 (4:00) 5-Y-0+ £7,687 (£2,375; £1,125; £500)

RPR
1 **Mystical Knight**[29] 4123 7-11-0 0.............................. BarryGeraghty 123+
(Rebecca Curtis) *w.w in rr of quartet at mod pce: tk clsr order fr 3 out: rdn into 2nd after next and clsd u.p to ld far side after last: kpt on wl u.p w narrow advantage clsng stages: all out* **2/1**[2]
2 ½ **General Principle (IRE)**[15] 4373 7-11-4 0.............................. BJCooper 126+
(Gordon Elliott, Ire) *hld up bhd ldrs in 3rd at mod pce: tk clsr order on outer bef 3 out where wnt 2nd: sn led: rdn and hdd narrowly u.p after last: kpt on wl clsng stages wout matching wnr* **4/6**[1]
3 12 **Oscar Lantern (IRE)**[46] 3811 7-11-4 0.............................. DavyRussell 114
(C Byrnes, Ire) *trckd ldr tl led fr 2nd at mod pce: jnd briefly next: narrow ld at 1/2-way: jnd bef 8th: nt fluent and bmpd sltly 4 out: sn hdd tl regained ld 3 out: sn hdd and no ex in 3rd after 2 out* **4/1**[3]
4 8 **Give Us A Hand (IRE)**[483] 14-10-7 0.............................. MrJPBerry(7) 102
(J A Berry, Ire) *led at mod pce: slow 1st and next where hdd: disp briefly 3rd: cl 2nd at 1/2-way: disp bef 8th: j.rt 4 out and sn regained ld: hdd 3 out and dropped to rr whn mstke next where rdr lost irons: wknd* **100/1**

6m 43.2s (403.20) **4 Ran SP% 114.3**
CSF £4.16 TOTE £2.60; DF 4.20 Trifecta £6.30.
Owner John P McManus **Bred** The Jacobean Group **Trained** Newport, Pembrokeshire
■ The first winner in Ireland for Rebecca Curtis.

FOCUS
A fascinating novice hurdle that turned into a sprint, and it is difficult to discern which of the first two - if either - were disadvantaged by same.

4663a IRISH STALLION FARMS EUROPEAN BREEDERS FUND NOVICE H'CAP CHASE FINAL (GRADE C) (17 fncs) 3m
4:35 (4:36) 5-Y-0+ £21,691 (£6,985; £3,308)

RPR
1 **Kilford (IRE)**[15] 4377 10-11-4 **123**.............................. LPDempsey(3) 133+
(Leonard Whitmore, Ire) *led and sn clr: wl clr after 6th: slow 4 out and reduced ld bef next: rdn after 2 out and kpt on wl fr last: comf* **4/1**[3]
2 9 ½ **Oscar Knight (IRE)**[14] 4398 7-10-7 **109**.............................. BarryGeraghty 109+
(Thomas Mullins, Ire) *hld up: lft mod 3rd briefly at 7th tl dropped to mod 4th after next: mstke in mod 4th 4 out: rdn in mod 3rd after next and no imp on wnr at last where nt fluent: wnt 2nd run-in* **15/8**[1]

3 *hd* **Imagine The Chat**[16] 4341 7-11-1 **122**....................(p) JonathanMoore(5) 122
(Rebecca Curtis) *chsd ldr: slt mstke 3rd: rdn in mod 2nd bef 3 out and sme hdwy: slt mstke 2 out and no imp on wnr u.p in mod 2nd: one pce run-in where dropped to 3rd* **9/1**

R **Ballyroe Rambler (IRE)**[35] 4023 9-11-0 **116**.................... MPFogarty
(J A Berry, Ire) *hld up: lft 4th at 7th and wnt 3rd after next: dropped to mod 4th briefly after 5 out: wnt mod 3rd bef next: no ex after 3 out: remote 4th whn slt mstke 2 out: ref at last* **20/1**

P **Sunsetstorise (IRE)**[21] 4282 8-10-8 **110**.................... MarkEnright
(F Flood, Ire) *towards rr: nt fluent 2nd: no imp in remote 5th 3 out: wknd and t.o whn p.u bef next* **12/1**

U **Altiepix (FR)**[24] 4219 6-11-0 **119**....................(b) JackKennedy(3)
(Gordon Elliott, Ire) *chsd ldrs: slow in 3rd at 5th: blnd and uns rdr 7th* **7/2**[2]

P **White Arm (FR)**[21] 4282 7-10-6 **108**....................(tp) NiallPMadden
(A J Martin, Ire) *hld up bhd ldrs in 4th early: dropped to 5th bef 5th: niggled along briefly in 6th after 8th: no imp in remote 5th after 3 out: t.o whn p.u bef next* **15/2**

P **Definite Soldier (IRE)**[24] 4218 7-10-2 **109**....................(t) AndrewRing(5)
(P J Rothwell, Ire) *in rr: no imp and t.o whn nt fluent 3 out: eased and p.u bef next* **14/1**

6m 49.5s (20.20) **8** Ran SP% **117.9**
CSF £12.97 CT £63.89 TOTE £4.60: £1.20, £1.30, £2.50; DF 15.00 Trifecta £144.80.
Owner Fort Road Syndicate **Bred** Brittas House Stud **Trained** Enniscorthy, Co Wexford

FOCUS
Only three finishers in this moderate event for the grade, which shows what can happen when a tearaway goes off hard and keeps going. A big pb from the winner.

4664 - 4667a (Foreign Racing) - See Raceform Interactive

4409
PLUMPTON (L-H)
Monday, March 14

OFFICIAL GOING: Soft (hdl 4.4, chs 4.9)
Wind: light to medium, half behind Weather: dry and bright, chilly breeze

4668 YOUR ULTIMATE CHELTENHAM GUIDE AT ATTHERACES.COM/CHELTENHAM "NATIONAL HUNT" NOVICES' HURDLE (12 hdls) 2m 4f 114y
2:10 (2:11) (Class 4) 5-Y-0+ £3,994 (£1,240; £667)

Form RPR
2124 1 **Never Equalled (IRE)**[22] 4264 7-11-2 129.................... RobertWilliams(3) 130+
(Bernard Llewellyn) *mde all: blnd 4th: pushed along bef 2 out: rdn between last 2: mstke last: styd on wl flat: rdn out* **11/4**[2]

1140 2 1 ¼ **Clondaw Cian (IRE)**[44] 3852 6-11-5 133.................... TomO'Brien 128
(Suzy Smith) *wnt rt s: chsd ldr tl lft upsides 4th: ev ch and rdn after 3 out: styd on same pce u.p flat* **8/15**[1]

P0 3 108 **The Child (IRE)**[14] 4409 7-10-12 0.................... AndrewThornton
(Anna Newton-Smith) *in tch in rr: reminders after 8th: sn rdn and lost tch: t.o after next* **150/1**

44 F **Solomn Grundy (IRE)**[74] 3375 6-10-12 0.................... NoelFehily 121
(Neil Mulholland) *t.k.h: trckd ldng pair: mstke 9th: pushed along and mstke next: rdn and styd on to chal whn fell 2 out* **13/2**[3]

5m 29.2s (12.20) **Going Correction** +0.825s/f (Soft) **4** Ran SP% **105.9**
Speed ratings: **109,108,,**
CSF £4.68 TOTE £3.70; EX 6.80 Trifecta £33.50.
Owner Miss I G Tompsett **Bred** Mrs Mary Dicker **Trained** Fochriw, Caerphilly
■ Stewards' Enquiry : Tom O'Brien two-day ban: lined up before being told (28-29 March)
Robert Williams one-day ban: lined up before being told (28 Mar)

FOCUS
Not a bad little novice hurdle with the winner running to his mark. Due to rail movement the actual distance was 54yds further than advertised. The jockeys generally agreed the going was "holding" and it certainly looked to have dried out.

4669 BERNARD O'BRIEN MEMORIAL NOVICES' H'CAP CHASE (14 fncs) 2m 3f 164y
2:40 (2:40) (Class 4) (0-105,105) 5-Y-0+ £3,898 (£1,144; £572; £286)

Form RPR
550P 1 **Rocknrobin (IRE)**[25] 4200 5-10-13 **93**.................... TomCannon 104+
(Chris Gordon) *chsd ldr tl led 8th: hdd next but styd upsides ldr: rdn after 3 out: led and j.lft between last 2: kpt on flat: drvn out* **25/1**

-361 2 1 ¾ **Beaujolais Bob**[3] 4590 8-9-11 **79** 7ex....................(bt) ConorShoemark(3) 92+
(Richard Hawker) *led tl 8th: styd cl up: mstke 10th and 11th: rallied u.p and ev ch 2 out: drifted rt and styd on same pce flat* **85/40**[1]

2021 3 8 **Johns Luck (IRE)**[7] 4533 7-11-7 **105** 7ex....................(b) DavidNoonan(5) 107
(Neil Mulholland) *trckd ldrs: clsd and jnd ldrs 11th: rdn after 3 out: no ex and outpcd between last 2: wknd flat* **5/1**

30-2 4 1 ¾ **Spartilla**[73] 3421 7-10-5 **84**.................... MattieBatchelor 84
(Daniel O'Brien) *chsd ldrs tl pushed along and clsd to join ldrs 8th: led next: drvn after 3 out: hdd and no ex between last 2: j.rt last: wknd flat* **9/1**

4532 5 1 ½ **Like Sully (IRE)**[42] 3903 8-11-12 **105**.................... LeightonAspell 107
(Richard Rowe) *blnd 1st: nt fluent and dropped to rr next: nvr really on terms w ldrs after: rdn 10th: sn outpcd and plugged on same pce fr next* **4/1**[3]

-222 6 20 **Bawden Rocks**[7] 4527 7-11-4 **102**....................(p) JakeHodson(5) 80
(David Bridgwater) *in tch: blnd 6th: dropped to rr and reminders after 8th: nvr travelling after: lost tch after 10th: eased flat* **11/4**[2]

5m 18.6s (11.30) **Going Correction** +0.70s/f (Soft) **6** Ran SP% **109.2**
Speed ratings: **105,104,101,100,99 91**
CSF £76.01 TOTE £23.00: £7.80, £1.20; EX 97.10 Trifecta £599.50.
Owner Mrs Kate Digweed **Bred** William Allen **Trained** Morestead, Hampshire

FOCUS
A moderate novice handicap, but it's not bad form for the grade with the winner stepping up on his hurdles exploits. Due to rail movement the actual distance was 102yds further than advertised.

4670 CHELTENHAM PRICE BOOSTS AT ATTHERACES.COM/TOPOFFERS H'CAP CHASE (12 fncs) 2m 214y
3:15 (3:17) (Class 4) (0-115,113) 5-Y-0+ £3,898 (£1,144; £572; £286)

Form RPR
-256 1 **Sportsreport (IRE)**[102] 2859 8-11-4 **105**....................(p) AndrewThornton 115+
(Seamus Mullins) *hld up in tch in rr: clsd to press ldr and travelling strly 3 out: led next: sn clr: comf* **11/2**[3]

4421 2 5 **Agincourt Reef (IRE)**[11] 4453 7-11-12 **113**....................(v) JoshuaMoore 116+
(Gary Moore) *chsd ldrs: mstke 7th: rdn after 3 out: chsd clr wnr between last 2: no imp* **8/13**[1]

U1PP 3 5 **Goring Two (IRE)**[7] 4529 11-10-3 **90**.................... JeremiahMcGrath 85
(Anna Newton-Smith) *chsd ldr: clsd and jnd ldr after 7th: led 9th: drvn and hdd 2 out: sn btn and lost 2nd between last 2* **9/1**

2P1R 4 41 **Marky Bob (IRE)**[15] 4386 11-10-10 **102**.................... ConorRing(5) 57
(Hugo Froud) *led to s: led tl hdd and mstke 9th: dropped to last next: sn wknd: t.o* **7/2**[2]

4m 32.4s (9.40) **Going Correction** +0.70s/f (Soft) **4** Ran SP% **109.5**
Speed ratings: **105,102,100,81**
CSF £10.08 TOTE £5.10; EX 10.50 Trifecta £17.30.
Owner Chris Baldwin **Bred** Ms S Phelan **Trained** Wilsford-Cum-Lake, Wilts

FOCUS
An ordinary little handicap with the winner rated to his previous best. Due to rail movement the actual distance was 102yds further than advertised.

4671 ASPEN INSURANCE H'CAP HURDLE (14 hdls) 3m 217y
3:45 (3:46) (Class 4) (0-110,110) 4-Y-0+ £3,898 (£1,144; £572; £286)

Form RPR
0042 1 **Talk Of The South (IRE)**[15] 4382 7-11-4 **102**.................... NickScholfield 112+
(Paul Henderson) *hld up in tch: clsd and trckd ldrs gng wl after 10th: led after 2 out: pushed along and drew clr flat: easily* **9/2**[3]

2332 2 7 **Reblis (FR)**[14] 4412 11-11-9 **107**....................(p) JoshuaMoore 107
(Gary Moore) *led: reminders and rdn after 10th: hdd after 2 out: easily brushed aside by wnr last: kpt on same pce* **5/1**

0255 3 8 **Onwiththeparty**[32] 4069 7-11-2 **100**....................(b[1]) TomCannon 93
(Chris Gordon) *chsd ldr but niggled along at times: reminders after 9th: drvn after 10th: 3rd and wknd bef 2 out* **9/4**[1]

55P3 4 33 **Aviador (GER)**[26] 4184 10-11-0 **98**.................... LeightonAspell 56
(Lucy Wadham) *chsd ldrs: cl 4th whn mstke 11th: rdn after next: sn wknd: t.o* **7/2**[2]

5PP1 5 23 **Flugzeug**[49] 3771 8-10-11 **95**.................... JeremiahMcGrath 30
(Seamus Mullins) *hld up in tch in last pair: rdn after 7th: struggling 10th: lost tch after next: t.o 3 out* **9/2**[3]

-P10 6 13 **Saucysioux**[15] 4382 6-11-11 **109**.................... AndrewThornton 31
(Michael Roberts) *nt jump wl: bhd: rdn 6th: blnd next and sn lost tch: t.o fr 9th* **20/1**

6m 52.2s (27.20) **Going Correction** +0.825s/f (Soft) **6** Ran SP% **110.8**
Speed ratings (Par 105): **89,86,84,73,66 62**
CSF £25.62 CT £59.46 TOTE £5.30: £2.70, £2.40; EX 24.60 Trifecta £75.50.
Owner The Rockbourne Partnership **Bred** B Mason **Trained** Whitsbury, Hants

FOCUS
A moderate staying handicap, run at a fair gallop, with the winner taking a big step up for the longer trip. Due to rail movement the actual distance was 87yds further than advertised.

4672 ASPEN INSURANCE MARES' H'CAP HURDLE (10 hdls) 2m 1f 164y
4:15 (4:17) (Class 4) (0-115,114) 4-Y-0+ £5,198 (£1,526; £763; £381)

Form RPR
0421 1 **Hope's Wishes**[18] 4320 6-11-4 **113**.................... HarryCobden(7) 125+
(Barry Brennan) *led into s: chsd ldrs tl wnt 2nd after 6th: led and travelling strly 3 out: rdn clr after next: in command and mstke last: comf* **11/4**[1]

-513 2 10 **May Hay**[18] 4320 6-11-5 **114**.................... GrahamCarson(7) 115
(Anthony Carson) *chsd ldr tl after 6th: rdn to chse clr ldr after 3 out: no imp and wl hld between last 2* **4/1**

1424 3 20 **Lamanver Alchemy**[48] 3795 5-11-5 **107**.................... NicodeBoinville 87
(Tom Lacey) *t.k.h: hld up in last pair: 5th and stl in tch whn mstke 7th: sn rdn and btn: wnt poor 3rd and j.rt 2 out* **7/2**[3]

542P 4 21 **Lakeshore Lady (IRE)**[26] 4186 6-11-1 **108**....................(p) JakeHodson(5) 67
(David Bridgwater) *led: hdd and rdn 3 out: sn dropped to 3rd and wknd: lost poor 3rd and sltly hmpd 2 out: t.o* **8/1**

-P30 P **Aramadyh**[14] 4409 5-10-4 **92**....................(v[1]) JoshuaMoore
(Jim Best) *a in last pair: pushed along after 5th: rdn after next: losing tch whn mstke next: t.o whn p.u after 3 out* **14/1**

322 P **Deja Bougg**[18] 4320 5-11-8 **110**.................... NoelFehily
(Neil Mulholland) *t.k.h: hld up in tch in midfield: mstke 5th: rdn and btn sn after 7th: eased and p.u next* **3/1**[2]

4m 45.0s (14.10) **Going Correction** +0.825s/f (Soft) **6** Ran SP% **111.7**
Speed ratings (Par 105): **101,96,87,78,**
CSF £14.01 TOTE £3.20: £1.70, £2.20; EX 12.20 Trifecta £40.10.
Owner M J Hills **Bred** Edward Spurrier **Trained** Upper Lambourn, Berks

FOCUS
Races distance increased by 54yds. A run-of-the-mill mares' handicap, run at an average gallop.

4673 ASPEN FINPRO H'CAP CHASE (18 fncs) 3m 1f 152y
4:45 (4:46) (Class 5) (0-100,89) 5-Y-0+ £3,328 (£1,033; £556)

Form RPR
5PPP 1 **Molly Oscar (IRE)**[28] 4160 10-10-11 **74**....................(v) TomCannon 88
(Johnny Farrelly) *led tl 5th: pressed ldr after mstke 8th: led next and mde rest: 7 l clr 3 out: rdn bef next: jst over 2 l clr whn lft wl clr last* **3/1**[2]

553P 2 34 **Head Spin (IRE)**[56] 3661 8-11-11 **88**....................(tp) AndrewThornton 75
(Seamus Mullins) *chsd ldrs: wnt 2nd 9th: blnd 15th: lost 2nd and btn next: sn wknd: lft poor 2nd last* **4/1**[3]

622P 3 2 ¼ **Burgess Dream (IRE)**[17] 4346 7-11-8 **85**.................... JeremiahMcGrath 64
(Anna Newton-Smith) *in tch in last pair: rdn and outpcd in 3rd whn mstke 14th: sn lost tch: lft poor 3rd last* **11/4**[1]

52P4 P **Kapricorne (FR)**[17] 4346 9-11-9 **89**....................(t) KillianMoore(3)
(Sophie Leech) *w ldr tl led 5th: hdd and dropped to 3rd 9th: reminder after 11th: drvn and lost pl after 13th: t.o whn p.u after 3 out* **3/1**[2]

4-44 F **Roparta Avenue**[104] 2830 9-10-13 **76**.................... LeightonAspell 86
(Diana Grissell) *in tch in rr: rdn and outpcd after 13th: rallied u.p and wnt 7 l 2nd 3 out: steadily clsd and jst over 2 l down whn fell last* **6/1**

7m 7.4s (16.70) **Going Correction** +0.70s/f (Soft) **5** Ran SP% **111.0**
Speed ratings: **102,91,90,,**
CSF £14.92 TOTE £2.90: £1.40, £2.20; EX 14.80 Trifecta £39.90.
Owner The Lansdowners **Bred** Edward Crow **Trained** Enmore, Somerset

FOCUS
Race distance increased by 153yds. A very weak staying handicap, run at an ordinary gallop, but a big chase personal best from the winner..

4674 CHELTENHAM FORM STUDY AT ATTHERACES.COM/CHELTENHAM H'CAP HURDLE (9 hdls) 1m 7f 195y
5:15 (5:15) (Class 5) (0-100,100) 4-Y-0+ £3,249 (£954; £477; £238)

Form RPR
4P05 1 **Rior (IRE)**[20] 4291 9-11-4 **92**.................... TomO'Brien 101+
(Paul Henderson) *chsd ldr: clsd and upsides gng best after 6th: led next: rdn clr bef 2 out: styd on: readily* **5/1**[3]

0365 2 14 **Up Four It (IRE)**[28] 4161 8-10-0 **74**.................... MattieBatchelor 70
(Jamie Poulton) *hld up: jnd and rdn after 6th: hdd next: btn whn wnt rt and mstke next: plugged on* **6/1**

24P **3** *3 ½* **Directional**[40] 3925 4-10-5 **92**.. AlanJohns(5) 78
(Tim Vaughan) *a chsng ldng pair: mstke 2nd: rdn and no imp 3 out: wl btn bef next* **4/1**[2]

6405 **4** *19* **Rolling Dough (IRE)**[18] 4318 8-10-8 **82**........................ AndrewThornton 54
(Diana Grissell) *j.rt 1st: chsd ldng trio fr next but nvr on terms: lost tch after 6th: t.o bef 2 out* **12/1**

60-0 **5** *2 ¼* **Knight's Reward**[20] 4291 6-11-6 **94**.. TomCannon 63
(Tim Vaughan) *hld up in last pair: rdn after 5th: sn lost tch: t.o after next* **11/2**

0630 **P** **Bolister (FR)**[37] 3994 5-11-12 **100**.. JoshuaMoore
(Gary Moore) *hld up in last pair: rdn after 5th: sn btn and lost tch: t.o after 6th tl p.u 2 out* **7/4**[1]

4m 17.8s (17.00) **Going Correction** +0.825s/f (Soft)
WFA 4 from 5yo+ 7lb **6** Ran SP% **110.4**
Speed ratings (Par 103): **90,83,81,71,70**
CSF £31.93 TOTE £6.30: £2.70, £3.40; EX 33.40 Trifecta £106.30.
Owner The Ray Of Hope Partnership **Bred** Glebe House Stud Ltd **Trained** Whitsbury, Hants

FOCUS
Race distance increased by 60yds. A weak handicap.
T/Jkpt: £33,826.50 to a £1 stake. Pool: £71,465.00 - 1.5 winning tickets T/Plt: £1,354.10 to a £1 stake. Pool: £10,1285.00 - 54.60 winning tickets T/Qpdt: £84.50 to a £1 stake. Pool: £82,78.89 - 72.50 winning tickets **Steve Payne**

4489 STRATFORD (L-H)
Monday, March 14
4675 Meeting Abandoned - waterlogged

4448 TAUNTON (R-H)
Monday, March 14

OFFICIAL GOING: Soft (good to soft in places) changing to good to soft after race 2 (2.50)
Wind: mild breeze across Weather: sunny Rails: Effect of rail positions on distances as follows; Races 1, 3, 5 & 7 add 117yds. Race 2 add 156yds. Race 4 add 18yds. Race 6 add 12yds.

4681 BATHWICK TYRES BATH MAIDEN HURDLE (9 hdls) 2m 104y
2:20 (2:20) (Class 4) 5-Y-0+ £3,249 (£954; £477; £238)

Form RPR

3 **1** **Ozzie The Oscar (IRE)**[95] 2991 5-11-0 0........................ RichardJohnson 129+
(Philip Hobbs) *trckd ldrs: led between last 2: shkn up to qckn clr run-in: readily* **5/2**[2]

P53 **2** *5* **Bonne Question (FR)**[18] 4317 7-11-0 119........................ LiamTreadwell 122+
(Venetia Williams) *trckd ldrs: led appr 2 out: rdn and hdd between last 2: styd on but nt pce of wnr* **11/8**[1]

64 **3** *4 ½* **Muffins For Tea**[16] 4357 6-11-0 0.. DarylJacob 116
(Colin Tizzard) *trckd ldrs: chal for 3rd 2 out: sn rdn: styd on but nt pce of front pair* **20/1**

4235 **4** *3 ¼* **Shadow Blue (IRE)**[23] 4256 7-10-7 114........................ MrGTreacy(7) 113
(Steven Dixon) *led: rdn and hdd appr 2 out: styd on same pce fr last* **9/2**[3]

5 *nse* **Laugharne**[96] 5-11-0 0.. JamieMoore 113
(Luke Dace) *hld up towards rr: hdwy into midfield 3 out: sn rdn: styd on fr last: nrly snatched 4th fnl stride* **50/1**

53/ **6** *2 ¾* **Benzel (IRE)**[743] 4574 8-11-0 0........................ RichieMcLernon 110
(Jonjo O'Neill) *trckd ldr: rdn after 3 out: disputing cl 3rd whn nt fluent 2 out: wknd last* **16/1**

6 **7** *16* **Dragoon Guard (IRE)**[11] 4449 5-11-0 0........................ AidanColeman 94
(Anthony Honeyball) *mid-div: rdn after 3 out: wknd next* **16/1**

0 **8** *15* **Venture Lagertha (IRE)**[17] 4350 7-10-7 0........................ LiamHeard 72
(Brian Barr) *mid-div: rdn after 3 out: sn wknd* **250/1**

3 **9** *11* **Moontripper**[208] 1289 7-10-0 0........................ MrTGreatrex(7) 61
(Phillip Dando) *a towards rr: t.o* **40/1**

5-06 **10** *14* **Quarryman**[89] 3111 5-11-0 0........................ MattGriffiths 54
(Ron Hodges) *mid-div tl 6th: sn wknd: t.o* **100/1**

6-3P **11** *30* **Jaslamour (FR)**[16] 4351 5-11-0 0........................[1] RhysFlint 24
(Alexandra Dunn) *mid-div tl wknd 3 out: t.o* **100/1**

00 **12** *4 ½* **Piccomore**[62] 3573 6-10-7 0........................ JamesBest 13
(Polly Gundry) *struggling 5th: a towards rr: t.o* **250/1**

U **Catch A Thief (IRE)** 5-11-0 0........................ AdamWedge
(Evan Williams) *racd green: towards rr whn awkward and uns rdr 3rd* **40/1**

R **Sutter's Mill (IRE)** 5-11-0 0........................ PaulMoloney
(Evan Williams) *racd green: a in rr: t.o 5th: ref 2 out* **16/1**

4m 15.2s (7.20) **Going Correction** +0.60s/f (Soft) **14** Ran SP% **120.9**
Speed ratings: **106,103,101,99,99 98,90,82,77,70 55,52,,**
CSF £6.32 TOTE £3.30: £1.30, £1.10, £5.70; EX 7.30 Trifecta £76.80.
Owner Bradley Partnership **Bred** William O'Keeffe **Trained** Withycombe, Somerset

FOCUS
Due to rails movement this was run over 117yds further than advertised. Richard Johnson said the ground was "good to soft but dead". Little depth to this maiden hurdle and the front pair in the market dominated, but the winner looks a decent prospect.

4682 BATHWICK TYRES MIDSOMER NORTON H'CAP HURDLE (12 hdls) 2m 7f 198y
2:50 (2:50) (Class 5) (0-100,98) 4-Y-0+ £3,249 (£954; £477; £238)

Form RPR

4612 **1** **Oscar Jane (IRE)**[20] 4290 9-11-12 **98**........................(bt) BrendanPowell 105+
(Johnny Farrelly) *disp ld tl outrt ldr after 3rd: 4 l clr after 3 out: mstke last: styd on: rdn out* **3/1**[2]

00P3 **2** *1 ¾* **I'llhavealook (IRE)**[23] 4250 11-10-10 **89**........................(p) MissBHampson(7) 94
(Katie Stephens) *chsd ldrs: rdn to chse wnr after 8th: nt quite pce to chal: styd on fr last but a being hld* **7/1**

334 **3** *¾* **Storm Alert**[17] 4349 9-11-2 **91**........................ LucyGardner(3) 94
(Sue Gardner) *disp ld tl 3rd: chsd wnr tl rdn after 8th: styd on fr last but a being hld* **11/4**[1]

0640 **4** *14* **Comical Red**[17] 4349 8-10-12 **87**........................(b) TomBellamy(3) 79
(Mark Gillard) *chsd ldrs: rdn along fr 8th: one pce fr 3 out* **10/1**

P/P3 **P** **Micquus (IRE)**[11] 4454 7-10-9 **81**........................ MarkGrant
(Jonathan Geake) *hit 7th: a towards rr: wknd bef 3 out: t.o whn p.u bef next* **16/1**

10-5 **P** **Phar Away Island (IRE)**[75] 3369 8-10-2 **79**........................ DannyBurton(5)
(John Berwick) *mid-div tl rdn after 8th: wknd bef 3 out: t.o whn p.u bef 2 out* **9/1**

P2P5 **P** **Poetic Presence (IRE)**[9] 4490 6-9-11 **72** oh5 ow2........ JamieBargary(5)
(Adrian Wintle) *last: drvn along fr 5th: losing tch whn p.u bef 8th* **20/1**

00PU **P** **Benability (IRE)**[15] 4387 6-11-9 **95**........................ RichardJohnson
(Tim Vaughan) *hld up: drvn along fr 7th: awkward next: nvr any imp: wknd bef 3 out: t.o whn p.u bef 2 out* **4/1**[3]

6m 20.2s (16.20) **Going Correction** +0.60s/f (Soft) **8** Ran SP% **113.9**
Speed ratings (Par 103): **97,96,96,91, , ,**
CSF £24.02 CT £62.82 TOTE £3.40: £1.40, £1.90, £1.30; EX 27.00 Trifecta £84.40.
Owner P Tosh **Bred** J R Weston **Trained** Enmore, Somerset

FOCUS
Due to rails movement this was run over 156yds further than advertised. Moderate form but a game effort from the winner and another small step up from her.

4683 BATHWICK TYRES YEOVIL FILLIES' JUVENILE HURDLE (9 hdls) 2m 104y
3:25 (3:25) (Class 4) 4-Y-O £4,548 (£1,335; £667; £333)

Form RPR

4214 **1** **Culture De Sivola (FR)**[100] 2896 4-10-11 120........................ LizzieKelly(5) 112+
(Nick Williams) *trckd ldrs: pressed ldr fr after 5th: nt fluent 3 out: led next: sn rdn: hdd last: kpt on to regain ld towards fin* **7/2**[3]

2251 **2** *nk* **Forgiving Glance**[17] 4345 4-11-2 123........................ DenisO'Regan 112+
(Alan King) *trckd ldrs: nt fluent 5th: led last: sn rdn: kpt on but no ex whn hdd towards fin* **8/11**[1]

3 *11* **La Paimpolaise (FR)**[61] 4-11-8 134........................ JamieMoore 110
(Gary Moore) *led 3rd: rdn and hdd appr 2 out: styd on same pce fr last* **3/1**[2]

P4 **4** *9* **Solstalla**[17] 4345 4-10-3 0........................ MrChrisMeehan(7) 87
(David Weston) *trckd ldrs: rdn appr 2 out: sn one pce* **33/1**

0UF **5** *3 ½* **Rest Easy**[79] 3213 4-10-5 0........................ KevinJones(5) 84
(Seamus Mullins) *hld up but in tch: rdn after 6th: wknd after 3 out* **100/1**

P5 **6** *7* **Live Miracle (USA)**[17] 4345 4-10-10 0........................ AidanColeman 78
(Venetia Williams) *led tl 3rd: chsd ldr: rdn after 6th: wknd after 3 out* **20/1**

7 *4* **Starlit Night**[135] 4-10-7 0........................ GilesHawkins(3) 75
(Chris Down) *trckd ldrs: mstke 3 out: sn wknd* **66/1**

U **Vanishing**[165] 4-10-10 0........................ AdamWedge
(Alexandra Dunn) *hld up: uns rdr 1st* **11/1**

4m 19.5s (11.50) **Going Correction** +0.60s/f (Soft) **8** Ran SP% **123.6**
Speed ratings: **95,94,89,84,83 79,77,**
CSF £7.25 TOTE £4.70: £1.50, £1.10, £1.20; EX 10.40 Trifecta £21.10.
Owner Larkhills Racing Partnership II **Bred** Gilles Trapenard **Trained** George Nympton, Devon

FOCUS
Due to rails movement this was run over 117yds further than advertised. Run at a steady pace, two old rivals dominated this fillies' hurdle and the winner is back on an upward curve.

4684 BATHWICK TYRES H'CAP CHASE (21 fncs) 3m 4f 85y
3:55 (3:55) (Class 3) (0-140,138) 5-Y-£8,229 (£2,431; £1,215; £608; £304)

Form RPR

-2P1 **1** **Goodtoknow**[31] 4109 8-11-10 **136**........................(p) JakeGreenall 145
(Kerry Lee) *trckd ldrs: rdn whn swtchd rt after 3 out: led last: hld on: all out* **6/1**[3]

PP33 **2** *hd* **Masters Hill (IRE)**[9] 4483 10-11-5 **138**........................(tp) PaulO'Brien(7) 150+
(Colin Tizzard) *tended to jump sltly lft most of way: trckd ldrs: led after 17th: nt fluent and pckd 2 out: hdd narrowly last: styd on* **2/1**[1]

-P5P **3** *1 ¾* **Benvolio (IRE)**[65] 3518 9-11-10 **136**........................(b) SamTwiston-Davies 143
(Paul Nicholls) *trckd ldrs: chal 4 out tl next: sn drvn: styd on fr last but a being hld* **10/3**[2]

0-2U **4** *13* **Cork Citizen**[16] 4367 8-10-13 **125**........................(bt[1]) TomScudamore 122
(David Pipe) *prom: led 6th tl after 17th: sn rdn: one pce fr 3 out* **10/3**[2]

-034 **5** *51* **Ballyoliver**[31] 4109 12-10-9 **126**........................(p) CharlieDeutsch(5) 88
(Venetia Williams) *led tl 6th: chsd ldrs: rdn after 17th: wknd after next: t.o* **7/1**

1-P5 **P** **Lovcen (GER)**[101] 2887 11-10-13 **125**........................(t) PaulMoloney
(Sophie Leech) *chsd ldrs tl dropped to last and nudged along fr 8th: detached 13th: lost tch 15th: p.u after next* **18/1**

7m 30.9s (6.50) **Going Correction** -0.225s/f (Good) **6** Ran SP% **111.5**
Speed ratings: **81,80,80,76,62**
CSF £18.87 TOTE £6.30: £3.80, £1.50; EX 12.00 Trifecta £56.00.
Owner Burling Daresbury MacEchern Nolan Potter **Bred** P J Hughes Berkswell **Trained** Byton, H'fords

FOCUS
Due to rails movement this was run over 18yds further than advertised. A useful marathon handicap that saw three still in with a chance coming to the last. The winner has been rated in line with his Wetherby win.

4685 BATHWICK TYRES TAUNTON H'CAP HURDLE (10 hdls) 2m 3f 1y
4:25 (4:26) (Class 3) (0-125,123) 4-Y-0 £6,330 (£1,870; £935; £468; £234)

Form RPR

F520 **1** **Here's Herbie**[23] 4241 8-11-8 **122**........................(t) LucyGardner(3) 127
(Sue Gardner) *trckd ldrs: rdn after 7th: sltly outpcd after 3 out: styd on between last 2: led sn after last: kpt on wl* **5/1**[3]

641- **2** *1 ½* **May Be Some Time**[184] 4683 8-10-13 **110**........................(t) PaddyBrennan 115+
(Stuart Kittow) *trckd ldrs: led sn after 2 out gng best: hdd sn after last and rdn: kpt on same pce* **6/1**

4-6F **3** *12* **Kazlian (FR)**[24] 4225 8-11-12 **123**........................(p) BrendanPowell 116
(Johnny Farrelly) *disp ld tl clr ldr appr 7th: rdn and hdd after 2 out: sn no ex* **7/2**[2]

1253 **4** *6* **Hollywood All Star (IRE)**[19] 4129 7-10-9 **113**........................ ArchieBellamy(7) 100
(Graeme McPherson) *trckd ldrs: rdn after 3 out: sn one pce* **7/1**

4546 **5** *¾* **Looksnowtlikebrian (IRE)**[22] 4264 5-10-6 **103**........................ JamesBest 90
(Tim Vaughan) *detached in last: rdn after 7th: styd on fr 2 out but nvr gng pce to get involved* **16/1**

0- **F** **Konig Dax (GER)**[431] 3582 6-11-7 **118**........................ TomScudamore
(David Pipe) *disp ld tl 7th: rdn and looking hld in 3rd whn fell 3 out* **13/8**[1]

046 **P** **Monyjean (FR)**[22] 4273 5-11-11 **122**........................(t) PaulMoloney
(Evan Williams) *trckd ldrs: rdn after 7th: wknd after 3 out: p.u bef next* **28/1**

4m 53.8s (7.80) **Going Correction** +0.60s/f (Soft) **7** Ran SP% **113.1**
Speed ratings (Par 107): **107,106,101,98,98**
CSF £33.41 TOTE £6.20: £3.10, £3.20; EX 35.30 Trifecta £122.10.
Owner D V Gardner **Bred** D V Gardner Woodhayes Stud **Trained** Longdown, Devon

FOCUS
Due to rails movement this was run over 117yds further than advertised. Modest form with the winner rated back to his C&D best.

4686 BATHWICK TYRES BRIDGWATER H'CAP CHASE (12 fncs) 2m 12y
4:55 (4:55) (Class 5) (0-100,93) 5-Y-O+ **£3,898** (£1,144; £572; £286)

Form RPR
34-4 1 **Edeiff's Lad**[20] 4291 9-10-1 **75** MrJoshuaNewman(7) 86+
(Polly Gundry) *mid-div: hdwy after 7th: chal 3 out: led last: r.o wl* **4/1**[1]
PP03 2 1 1/2 **Passing Fiesta**[22] 4275 7-10-11 **81** JamesBanks(3) 90
(Sarah-Jayne Davies) *trckd ldrs: led 8th: rdn whn strly pressed appr 3 out: hdd last: no ex* **8/1**
2U34 3 9 **Lamb's Cross**[26] 4187 10-10-12 **82** HarryBannister(3) 85
(Brian Barr) *trckd ldrs: blnd 7th: rdn after 4 out: ev ch next tl after 2 out: no ex* **9/2**[2]
-PU3 4 5 **Jamrham (IRE)**[16] 4356 9-11-0 **81** (t) LiamTreadwell 77
(Sam Thomas) *hld up towards rr: rdn and stdy prog after 4 out: styd on fr next but nt pce to get involved* **5/1**[3]
1P25 5 6 **Ballyegan (IRE)**[11] 4453 11-11-12 **93** LiamHeard 83
(Bob Buckler) *led tl 8th: sn rdn: one pce fr 4 out* **15/2**
0134 6 2 1/2 **Entry To Evrywhere (IRE)**[7] 4527 8-11-7 **88** (t) RhysFlint 79
(Alexandra Dunn) *trckd ldrs: rdn in 4th after 4 out: wknd after next* **7/1**
-160 7 13 **Beauchamp Viking**[277] 699 12-10-4 **71** (t) DaveCrosse 47
(Hugo Froud) *pressed ldr tl 7th: sn rdn: wknd 4 out* **16/1**
P0P4 8 6 **George Nympton (IRE)**[14] 4410 10-10-6 **80** (bt) WilliamFeatherstone(7) 51
(Zoe Davison) *mid-div: rdn after 8th: wknd next* **14/1**
P0FP P **Wicklewood**[26] 4187 10-11-7 **93** (bt) LizzieKelly(5)
(Mark Gillard) *mid-div: struggling 6th: wknd 8th: tailing off whn p.u bef 3 out* **20/1**
0050 P **Surprise Us**[61] 3586 9-9-9 **67** oh3 MichaelHeard(5)
(Mark Gillard) *hld up towards rr: blnd 8th: no imp whn p.u bef 3 out* **28/1**
P60 P **Midnight Thomas**[32] 4068 7-10-10 **77** (t) AndrewTinkler
(Martin Keighley) *a towards rr: wknd 4 out: p.u bef next* **12/1**

4m 9.8s (-4.20) **Going Correction** -0.225s/f (Good) **11 Ran SP% 118.7**
Speed ratings: **101,100,95,93,90 89,82,79, ,**
CSF £36.83 CT £151.76 TOTE £5.70: £2.10, £2.50, £2.10; EX 35.60 Trifecta £208.00.
Owner Hawks And Doves Racing Syndicate **Bred** Hawks And Doves Racing Syndicate **Trained** Ottery St Mary, Devon

FOCUS
Due to rails movement this was run over 12yds further than advertised. Low-grade chasing form, but a personal best from the winner.

4687 BATHWICK TYRES BRISTOL MARES' STANDARD OPEN NATIONAL HUNT FLAT RACE 2m 104y
5:25 (5:25) (Class 6) 4-6-Y-O **£2,053** (£598; £299)

Form RPR
3 1 **Lamanver Odyssey**[17] 4350 4-9-13 0 MrTommieMO'Brien(7) 92+
(Tom Lacey) *mid-div: hdwy over 6f out: rdn to chse ldrs over 2f out: styd on for str chal fnl f: led fnl stride* **13/2**[3]
35-6 2 shd **Fit The Brief**[32] 4074 6-11-0 0 [1] PaddyBrennan 100+
(Tom George) *hld up: smooth hdwy fr over 7f out: short of room on bnd over 4f out: led over 2f out: rdn over 1f out: hdd fnl stride* **6/1**[2]
3 3 2 3/4 **Costante Via (IRE)**[42] 3907 5-11-0 0 MarkGrant 98
(Dominic Ffrench Davis) *trckd ldrs: rdn and ev ch over 2f out tl ent fnl f: kpt on same pce* **25/1**
6-0 4 5 **Hoo Bally Diva (IRE)**[31] 4103 5-11-0 0 LiamHeard 93
(Bob Buckler) *prom tl rdn 5f out: kpt chsng ldrs: styd on same pce fnl 2f* **20/1**
-00 5 1 1/4 **Amber Alert**[99] 2929 6-11-0 0 (t[1]) AidanColeman 92
(Anthony Honeyball) *led: rdn and hdd over 2f out: styd on same pce* **11/1**
6 5 **Theatre Rouge (IRE)** 4-10-6 0 [1] RichardJohnson 80
(Philip Hobbs) *hld up: sme prog fr 4f out: rdn over 2f out: sn one pce* **6/4**[1]
7 4 1/2 **Whatsthatallabout (IRE)** 5-10-7 0 MrShaneQuinlan(7) 83
(Neil Mulholland) *trckd ldrs: rdn whn stmbld on bnd over 4f out: one pce fnl 2f* **20/1**
8 20 **Neetside (IRE)** 4-10-6 0 MichealNolan 57
(Tim Dennis) *mid-div tl over 3f out* **66/1**
9 2 3/4 **Chicksgrove Sprite (IRE)** 5-11-0 0 DarylJacob 65
(Neil Mulholland) *chsd ldrs tl 4f out* **10/1**
10 2 1/4 **Impulse** 6-11-0 0 (t) JamesBest 61
(Philip Hobbs) *hld up: hdwy at 1/2-way: wknd 3f out* **10/1**
11 22 **Actlikeacountess** 5-11-0 0 MarkQuinlan 41
(Neil Mulholland) *mid-div: rdn 1/2-way: wknd 4f out* **14/1**
12 5 **Goingforamooch** 5-10-7 0 MissBHampson(7) 37
(Katie Stephens) *mid-div tl wknd 6f out* **100/1**
13 83 **Final Say** 6-11-0 0 SamTwiston-Davies
(Simon Hodgson) *sn pushed along towards rr: lost tch after 6f: t.o* **20/1**
14 2 3/4 **Lucy Lane**[343] 6-10-7 0 MrTGreatrex(7)
(Phillip Dando) *lost tch 1/2-way: t.o* **66/1**

4m 10.3s (7.90) **Going Correction** +0.60s/f (Soft)
WFA 4 from 5yo+ 7lb **14 Ran SP% 122.9**
Speed ratings: **104,103,102,100,99 96,94,84,83,82 71,68,27,25**
CSF £42.98 TOTE £7.10: £2.40, £2.30, £9.20; EX 37.50 Trifecta £449.30.
Owner Dr Donna Christensen **Bred** Dr Donna Christensen **Trained** Ledbury, H'fords

FOCUS
Due to rails movement this was run over 117yds further than advertised. A modest mares' bumper.
T/Plt: £19.40 to a £1 stake. Pool: £131,387.02 - 4,920.59 winning tickets T/Qpdt: £11.30 to a £1 stake. Pool: £7,422.70 - 484.80 winning tickets **Tim Mitchell**

4688 - 4694a (Foreign Racing) - See Raceform Interactive

3848 CHELTENHAM (L-H)
Tuesday, March 15

OFFICIAL GOING: Good to soft (soft in places; 7.0)
Wind: Moderate, behind Weather: Overcast

4695 SKY BET SUPREME NOVICES' HURDLE (GRADE 1) (8 hdls) 2m 87y
1:30 (1:31) (Class 1) 4-Y-O+ **£68,340** (£25,644; £12,840; £6,396; £3,216; £1,608)

Form RPR
1111 1 **Altior (IRE)**[80] 3227 6-11-7 155 NicodeBoinville 163+
(Nicky Henderson) *lw: travelled and j.w: mid-div: hdwy after 5th: chal after 2 out: rdn to ld bef last: qcknd clr: impressive* **4/1**[2]
1 2 7 **Min (FR)**[66] 3539 5-11-7 153 RWalsh 157+
(W P Mullins, Ire) *lengthy: trckd ldr: mstke 3rd: chal after 2 out: sn rdn: kpt on but readily outpcd by wnr* **15/8**[1]
4-11 3 1 1/2 **Buveur D'Air (FR)**[46] 3842 5-11-7 154 NoelFehily 154+
(Nicky Henderson) *hld up in rr: hdwy fr 3 out: nt fluent 2 out: sn rdn: wnt 3rd at the last: kpt on but nt pce to get on terms* **10/1**[3]
22 4 4 **Tombstone (IRE)**[38] 4004 6-11-7 147 BJCooper 150
(Gordon Elliott, Ire) *q str: lw: mid-div: rdn and hdwy after 3 out: styd on fr last: snatched 4th fnl strides* **12/1**
1221 5 hd **Charbel (IRE)**[37] 4010 5-11-7 147 (t) DavidBass 150
(Kim Bailey) *lw: led: rdn and hdd after 2 out: 4th and hld whn hit last: lost 4th fnl strides* **16/1**
1-11 6 1 1/4 **Mister Miyagi (IRE)**[110] 2731 7-11-7 135 IanPopham 150+
(Dan Skelton) *blnd 1st: hld up towards rr: rdn after 3 out: styd on fr after 2 out but nt pce to get involved* **33/1**
16-0 7 shd **Supasundae**[79] 3292 6-11-7 140 JJBurke 150
(Henry De Bromhead, Ire) *trckd ldrs: hit 5th: rdn after 2 out: sn outpcd: 5th and hld whn hit last: no ex* **12/1**
1-34 8 1 **Petit Mouchoir (FR)**[38] 4004 5-11-7 144 DavidMullins 147
(W P Mullins, Ire) *trckd ldrs: hit 2 out: sn rdn: fdd bef last* **20/1**
212 9 9 **North Hill Harvey**[33] 4072 5-11-7 140 HarrySkelton 141+
(Dan Skelton) *mid-div: hdwy 3 out: chsng ldrs whn mstke 2 out: sn wknd* **25/1**
2121 10 3 **William H Bonney**[27] 4182 5-11-7 136 WayneHutchinson 136
(Alan King) *mid-div: rdn after 3 out: wknd after next* **50/1**
6111 11 1 1/2 **Holly Bush Henry (IRE)**[55] 3682 5-11-7 142 (t) KielanWoods 133
(Graeme McPherson) *on toes: hld up towards rr: midfield after 4th: rdn after 3 out: wknd after next* **40/1**
1113 12 3/4 **Penglai Pavilion (USA)**[123] 2470 6-11-7 146 AidanColeman 133
(John Ferguson) *a towards rr* **33/1**
1113 13 2 1/4 **Bellshill (IRE)**[38] 4004 6-11-7 148 PaulTownend 132
(W P Mullins, Ire) *trckd ldrs: nt fluent 4th: pushed along after next: rdn after 3 out: sn outpcd: wknd after next* **11/1**
/24- 14 hd **Silver Concorde**[79] 3292 8-11-7 135 DavyRussell 131
(D K Weld, Ire) *towards rr of midfield early: struggling in last fr 4th: wknd after 2 out* **16/1**

3m 46.0s (-16.00) **Going Correction** -0.675s/f (Firm) **14 Ran SP% 118.2**
Speed ratings (Par 117): **113,109,108,106,106 106,105,105,100,99 98,98,97,97**
CSF £10.99 CT £70.50 TOTE £4.10: £1.80, £1.40, £3.40; EX 9.30 Trifecta £58.10.
Owner Mrs Patricia Pugh **Bred** Paddy Behan **Trained** Upper Lambourn, Berks

FOCUS
Races on Old course and all distances as advertised. The course had missed any rain in the days leading up to this season's Festival and the fresh ground looked in excellent nick in the opener, although the winning time suggested it was quicker than the official description. Rider Nico de Boinville was complimentary about it afterwards although claimed it was "dead in places". This looked a strong Supreme Novice and it was run at a decent gallop. The principals were nicely clear at the finish and rate high-class prospects. Only the 2013 winner Champagne Fever has been given a higher RPR than Altior in recent years. Min is well up to the standard of an average Supreme winner.

4696 RACING POST ARKLE CHALLENGE TROPHY CHASE (GRADE 1) (13 fncs) 1m 7f 199y
2:10 (2:10) (Class 1) 5-Y-O+ **£85,827** (£32,457; £16,452; £8,397; £4,422)

Form RPR
1-11 1 **Douvan (FR)**[51] 3766 6-11-4 161 RWalsh 165+
(W P Mullins, Ire) *lw: w ldr: led 3rd: mde rest: a travelling strly: powered clr between last 2: mstke last: r.o wl: comf* **1/4**[1]
2-12 2 7 **Sizing John**[80] 3271 6-11-4 150 JJBurke 156
(Henry De Bromhead, Ire) *led: hdd 3rd: remained in cl 2nd pl tl bef 3 out: outpcd on bnd bef hmpd and lft 2nd 2 out: styd on run-in but no ch w wnr* **9/1**[3]
1233 3 3 3/4 **Fox Norton (FR)**[31] 4126 6-11-4 145 RichardJohnson 152
(Neil Mulholland) *trckd ldrs: pushed along and lost pl after 3 out: outpcd after: sltly hmpd 2 out: kpt on to take 3rd fnl 75yds: no ch* **33/1**
2111 4 2 1/4 **The Game Changer (IRE)**[152] 1937 7-11-4 155 (t) BJCooper 153+
(Gordon Elliott, Ire) *hld up: pckd 2nd: hdwy 3 out: chsng ldrs abt 4 l off the pce whn bmpd and lft 3rd 2 out: no imp whn mstke last: wknd fnl 100yds: sn lost 3rd* **14/1**
2213 5 1 **Aso (FR)**[32] 4100 6-11-4 145 (p) AidanColeman 151
(Venetia Williams) *mstke 1st: nt fluent 3rd and dropped to rr: mstke 3 out: u.p and outpcd after: plugged on but n.d run-in* **66/1**
4-12 F **Baltimore Rock (IRE)**[39] 3975 7-11-4 143 (tp) NoelFehily 149
(Neil Mulholland) *lw: racd keenly: hld up: pckd 6th: hdwy appr 3 out: outpcd whn fell 2 out* **40/1**
-121 U **Vaniteux (FR)**[45] 3856 7-11-4 152 NicodeBoinville 158+
(Nicky Henderson) *lw: trckd ldrs: j. slowly 6th: wnt 2nd bef 3 out: rdn and upsides after 3 out: 1 1/2 l down and u.p whn blnd and uns rdr 2 out* **8/1**[2]

3m 48.6s (-9.40) **Going Correction** 0.0s/f (Good) **7 Ran SP% 114.7**
Speed ratings: **123,119,117,116,116**
CSF £3.67 TOTE £1.10: £1.10, £3.00; EX 3.00 Trifecta £28.50.
Owner Mrs S Ricci **Bred** S A R L Haras De La Faisanderie **Trained** Muine Beag, Co Carlow

FOCUS
Just the seven runners and little depth with a lot of possible contenders running scared of Douvan, who in the absence of his stablemate Faugheen from the Champion Hurdle, was by far the shortest price favourite at the meeting. The market leader did what was expected and became the first horse since Flyingbolt way back in 1965 to win this race having taken the Supreme a year earlier. He set a high standard has been rated below the level of his Leopardstown win at Christmas. He's a potential 175+ chaser.

4697 ULTIMA H'CAP CHASE (GRADE 3) (20 fncs) 3m 1f
2:50 (2:51) (Class 1) 5-Y-O+
£56,950 (£21,370; £10,700; £5,330; £2,680; £1,340)

Form RPR
1224 1 **Un Temps Pour Tout (IRE)**[45] 3849 7-11-7 **148** (bt) TomScudamore 164+
(David Pipe) *trckd ldrs: chal after 4 out: led briefly tl hmpd by loose horse after 3 out: sn bk upsides: rdn to ld bef last: drew clr run-in: readily* **11/1**
-54P 2 7 **Holywell (IRE)**[45] 3860 9-11-12 **153** (b) RichieMcLernon 164+
(Jonjo O'Neill) *trckd ldrs: chal 4 out: led after 3 out: sn rdn: hdd bef last: styd on but nt pce of wnr* **8/1**[2]
2U46 3 9 **The Young Master**[45] 3853 7-11-5 **149** (p) MrSWaley-Cohen(3) 152
(Neil Mulholland) *in tch: nt fluent 1st: trckd ldrs 4 out: rdn into 4th after next: styd on to go 3rd run-in but no threat to front pair* **14/1**
3/-2 4 1 **Morning Assembly (IRE)**[31] 4131 9-11-9 **150** DavyRussell 152
(P A Fahy, Ire) *lw: trckd ldrs: travelling wl enough whn mstke 3 out: sn rdn and outpcd by front pair: j.rt last 2: no ex whn lost 3rd run-in* **10/1**

02-1 **5** *6* **Kruzhlinin (GER)**[66] 3528 9-11-7 **148**............................ RichardJohnson 147+
(Philip Hobbs) *trckd ldrs: hit 4 out: sn rdn: outpcd after 3 out: 5th and hld whn hit next* **9/1**[3]

2UFP **6** *nk* **Algernon Pazham (IRE)**[52] 3741 7-10-9 **139**.................(p) RyanHatch(3) 133
(Nigel Twiston-Davies) *lw: mid-div: in tch whn rdn after 4 out: styd on fr 2 out but nvr gng pce to get on terms* **33/1**

6311 **7** *12* **Out Sam**[31] 4116 7-10-12 **139**............................ GavinSheehan 126+
(Warren Greatrex) *lw: detached in last pair fr 3rd: reminders after 12th: nvr any real imp on ldrs but styd on past btn horses fr after 3 out* **13/2**[1]

4-53 **8** *11* **Band Of Blood (IRE)**[10] 4472 8-10-5 **132**...................(bt[1]) WillKennedy 106
(Dr Richard Newland) *in tch: rdn after 16th: wknd sn after 3 out* **20/1**

2450 **9** *1 ½* **Double Ross (IRE)**[45] 3860 10-11-9 **150**........................(p) JamieMoore 122
(Nigel Twiston-Davies) *led tl 3 out: sn rdn: wknd next* **33/1**

14P4 **10** *hd* **Ballykan**[17] 4361 6-10-8 **135**...(t) DarylJacob 107
(Nigel Twiston-Davies) *lw: mid-div: rdn after 4 out: nvr threatened: wknd after 3 out* **16/1**

3300 **11** *2 ½* **Fox Appeal (IRE)**[17] 4361 9-11-6 **147**............................ BrianHughes 122
(Emma Lavelle) *mid-div: rdn after 4 out: nvr threatened: wkng whn mstke 2 out* **40/1**

P-2P **12** *1 ¼* **O Maonlai (IRE)**[87] 3157 8-10-10 **137**..............................(t) TomO'Brien 106
(Tom George) *blnd 1st: towards rr: sme prog after 4 out: wknd after next* **40/1**

/P-P **13** *7* **Katenko (FR)**[87] 3150 10-11-6 **147**.............................. LiamTreadwell 109
(Venetia Williams) *towards rr: midfield 10th: bhd and struggling after 14th: wknd 3 out* **40/1**

F104 **14** *12* **Shanahan's Turn (IRE)**[136] 2206 8-11-12 **153**..................... JJBurke 104
(Henry De Bromhead, Ire) *lw: racd keenly: pressed ldr tl 13th: grad fdd: bhd fr 16th* **50/1**

3231 **F** **Theatre Guide (IRE)**[17] 4361 9-11-9 **150**.....................(tp) PaddyBrennan
(Colin Tizzard) *lw: mid-div whn fell heavily 13th* **14/1**

-000 **U** **Spring Heeled (IRE)**[79] 3296 9-11-5 **146**......................(p) BrianO'Connell
(J H Culloty, Ire) *slowly away and sn pushed along: last tl bdly hmpd and uns rdr 6th* **33/1**

2000 **P** **According To Trev (IRE)**[16] 4389 10-10-4 **131**.............(b[1]) TomCannon
(David Bridgwater) *mid-div: blnd 2nd: nvr travelling after: bhd fr 7th: t.o whn p.u 14th* **66/1**

F1PP **P** **Regal Encore (IRE)**[45] 3849 8-11-1 **142**.....................(t) BarryGeraghty
(Anthony Honeyball) *hld up towards rr: bdly hmpd 6th: nvr travelling after: p.u bef 4 out* **25/1**

5-51 **P** **Carole's Destrier**[101] 2916 8-11-10 **151**............................ NoelFehily
(Neil Mulholland) *mid-div: struggling in last pair whn blnd bdly 15th: sn p.u* **14/1**

2-34 **B** **Southfield Theatre (IRE)**[101] 2900 8-11-9 **150**....... SamTwiston-Davies
(Paul Nicholls) *blnd 1st: towards rr: making hdwy in midfield whn b.d 13th* **16/1**

03P **F** **Doing Fine (IRE)**[129] 2348 8-10-4 **134**.................(bt) DavidMullins(3)
(Rebecca Curtis) *hld up towards rr: struggling whn fell heavily 15th* **20/1**

64P0 **F** **Audacious Plan (IRE)**[17] 4354 7-10-1 **131**................(b[1]) JackKennedy(3)
(Rebecca Curtis) *mid-div whn fell 6th* **40/1**

3321 **U** **Beg To Differ (IRE)**[25] 4234 6-11-2 **143**.............................(v) AidanColeman
(Jonjo O'Neill) *hld up towards rr: making hdwy in midfield whn clipped heels: stmbld and uns rdr on bnd bef 12th* **11/1**

6m 17.8s (-8.20) **Going Correction** 0.0s/f (Good) course record **23** Ran **SP% 127.4**
Speed ratings: **113,110,107,107,105 105,101,98,97,97 96,96,94,90, , , , , , ,**
CSF £85.39 CT £1274.60 TOTE £13.80: £3.50, £2.60, £4.10, £3.00; EX 131.90 Trifecta £2025.10.
Owner Professor Caroline Tisdall & Bryan Drew **Bred** Felix Talbot **Trained** Nicholashayne, Devon

FOCUS
Traditionally an ultra competitive handicap and that again looked the case, but despite them going a really good gallop up front, very little got into the race. Several were inconvenienced by a messy start, but the classier horses came to the fore and the form looks rock-solid with the winner taking a big step up on previous chase form. He's rated to the level expected of an RSA Chase winner.

4698 STAN JAMES CHAMPION HURDLE CHALLENGE TROPHY (GRADE 1) (8 hdls) 2m 87y

3:30 (3:33) (Class 1) 4-Y-O+

£248,302 (£93,173; £46,652; £23,238; £11,684; £5,842)

Form RPR

1F-1 **1** **Annie Power (IRE)**[27] 4189 8-11-3 **162**.............................. RWalsh 164+
(W P Mullins, Ire) *led 1st: mde rest: drew clr last: r.o strly* **5/2**[1]

123/ **2** *4 ½* **My Tent Or Yours (IRE)**[703] 5274 9-11-10 **161**.............. BarryGeraghty 167
(Nicky Henderson) *trckd ldrs travelling strly: wnt 2nd 3rd: ev ch 2 out: rdn and outpcd by wnr bef last: styd on u.p run-in but no ch: jst hld on for 2nd* **10/1**

1113 **3** *hd* **Nichols Canyon**[51] 3768 6-11-10 **161**......................... PaulTownend 168+
(W P Mullins, Ire) *a.p: nt fluent 3rd: rdn and nt qckn between last 2: blnd last: styd on u.p run-in and chalng for 2nd nr fin: no ch w wnr* **15/2**[3]

-121 **4** *4* **The New One (IRE)**[52] 3740 8-11-10 **161**............... SamTwiston-Davies 163
(Nigel Twiston-Davies) *lw: led to 1st: remained prom: shkn up whn ev ch 2 out: rdn and outpcd bef last: edgd lft u.p run-in: kpt on but nt pce of ldrs* **7/2**[2]

2251 **5** *1* **Top Notch (FR)**[26] 4204 5-11-10 **158**.............................. DarylJacob 162
(Nicky Henderson) *midfield: hdwy appr 3 out: 5th whn mstke 2 out: rdn and outpcd bef last: styd on same pce run-in* **14/1**

-112 **6** *9* **Identity Thief (IRE)**[77] 3358 6-11-10 **159**......................... BJCooper 156
(Henry De Bromhead, Ire) *trckd ldrs: hit 4th: rdn bef 2 out: wknd bef last* **8/1**

1231 **7** *1 ¼* **Lil Rockerfeller (USA)**[16] 4381 5-11-10 **157**...............(p) TrevorWhelan 154
(Neil King) *midfield: rdn along fr after 2nd: wknd bef 2 out* **20/1**

2-45 **8** *2 ¾* **Sign Of A Victory (IRE)**[80] 3230 7-11-10 **153**............... AndrewTinkler 151
(Nicky Henderson) *racd keenly in rr: hdwy to trck ldng bunch appr 3 out: rdn after 2 out: wknd bef last* **66/1**

-U15 **9** *nk* **Camping Ground (FR)**[45] 3853 6-11-10 **163**...........(t) LeightonAspell 151
(Robert Walford) *hld up: nt fluent 4 out: sn rdn: nvr a threat* **16/1**

-433 **10** *28* **Hargam (FR)**[80] 3230 5-11-10 **157**.............................. MarkWalsh 133
(Nicky Henderson) *midfield: lost pl after 2nd: struggling after 4 out: wl btn* **16/1**

4211 **P** **Sempre Medici (FR)**[31] 4133 6-11-10 **157**.....................(t) DavidMullins
(W P Mullins, Ire) *hld up: wl bhd whn blnd 2 out: t.o whn p.u bef last* **16/1**

1-63 **P** **Peace And Co (FR)**[38] 3989 5-11-10 **157**..................... NicodeBoinville
(Nicky Henderson) *lw: hld up: pushed along and outpcd after 4 out: t.o whn p.u bef last* **16/1**

3m 45.1s (-16.90) **Going Correction** -0.675s/f (Firm) course record **12** Ran **SP% 119.2**
Speed ratings (Par 117): **115,112,112,110,110 105,105,103,103,89**
CSF £28.87 CT £170.11 TOTE £3.10: £1.70, £2.30, £2.70; EX 23.40 Trifecta £164.10.
Owner Mrs S Ricci **Bred** Eamon Cleary **Trained** Muine Beag, Co Carlow

FOCUS
Due to the shock injury in mid-February of last year's winner Faugheen, and then later also his stablemate Artic Fire, who finished runner-up to him, it was a substandard Champion Hurdle this season. Nonetheless it was still an utterly fascinating contest. There was no hanging about, resulting in a new course record and, while it still paid to race prominently, the form is still very strong. Annie Power has been rated in line with her 2014 World Hurdle second and taking into account her mares' allowance, well up to race-winning standard.

4699 OLBG MARES' HURDLE (REGISTERED AS THE DAVID NICHOLSON MARES' HURDLE RACE) (GRADE 1) (10 hdls) 2m 3f 200y

4:10 (4:10) (Class 1) 4-Y-O+

£58,802 (£22,154; £11,087; £5,538; £2,779; £1,389)

Form RPR

1-11 **1** **Vroum Vroum Mag (FR)**[52] 3732 7-11-5 **154**.............................. RWalsh 146+
(W P Mullins, Ire) *towards rr of midfield: smooth hdwy fr 4 out: trckd ldrs 2 out: led bef last: r.o wl: rdn out* **4/6**[1]

-625 **2** *2 ¾* **Rock On The Moor (IRE)**[45] 3858 8-11-5 **138**.................. RobbiePower 140
(Mrs John Harrington, Ire) *q lengthy: hld up towards rr: hdwy after 4 out: rdn to ld sn after 2 out: hdd bef last: kpt on* **66/1**

114/ **3** *½* **Legacy Gold (IRE)**[27] 4189 8-11-5 **132**............................ AELynch 140
(S R B Crawford, Ire) *str: hld up towards rr: hdwy after 3 out: rdn after next: lft 3rd at the last: styd on* **40/1**

02P4 **4** *1* **Pass The Time**[29] 3858 7-11-5 **138**..............................(p) TomScudamore 141
(Neil Mulholland) *lw: trckd ldrs: hit 5th and 3 out where lost pl: rdn after next: styd on bk into 4th run-in* **80/1**

2412 **5** *1 ½* **Gitane Du Berlais (FR)**[19] 4319 6-11-5 **143**......................... DarylJacob 138
(W P Mullins, Ire) *in tch: tk clsr order 3 out: led briefly after next: lft hld 4th at the last: no ex fnl 120yds* **25/1**

6-01 **6** *1 ¼* **Keppols Queen (IRE)**[77] 3356 8-11-5 **141**......................... DavyRussell 140
(Mrs John Harrington, Ire) *w'like: hld up towards rr: midfield whn hit 5th: rdn after 2 out: styng on wl in 7th whn bdly hmpd last: kpt on but no ch after* **25/1**

P120 **7** *1 ¾* **Desert Queen**[52] 3732 8-11-5 **147**.............................(t) NickScholfield 138+
(Harry Fry) *racd freely: led: hit 2nd: 3rd and next: rdn and hdd after 2 out: sn no ex* **33/1**

2FF **8** *1 ¾* **Stephanie Frances (IRE)**[113] 2684 8-11-5 **138**................. HarrySkelton 134
(Dan Skelton) *hld up towards rr: hdwy after 4 out: ch 2 out: sn rdn and one pce* **40/1**

1256 **9** *1* **Rons Dream**[52] 3732 6-11-5 **139**...................................... SeanBowen 135
(Peter Bowen) *hit 3 out: nvr bttr than mid-div* **50/1**

1-21 **10** *8* **Polly Peachum (IRE)**[73] 3444 8-11-5 **149**......................... DavidBass 125
(Nicky Henderson) *in tch tl pushed along after 4 out: drvn in midfield after 2 out: wknd bef last* **6/1**[2]

4161 **11** *hd* **Flute Bowl**[31] 4125 6-11-5 **139**..(p) JoshuaMoore 125
(Gary Moore) *mid-div: nudged along after 4th: nvr threatened* **80/1**

131- **12** *nk* **Tara Point**[441] 3411 7-11-5 **130**.......................(t) SamTwiston-Davies 131+
(Paul Nicholls) *in tch: nt fluent 3rd: ev ch 2 out: sn rdn: wkng in 10th whn v bdly hmpd last: eased* **25/1**

F410 **13** *1* **Morello Royale (IRE)**[73] 3444 6-11-5 **140**.................(t) AidanColeman 124
(Colin Tizzard) *a towards rr* **100/1**

1112 **14** *1 ¾* **Lily Waugh (IRE)**[45] 3858 9-11-5 **140**..........................(t) DavidNoonan 122
(Anthony Honeyball) *mid-div: rdn after 3 out: wknd after next* **33/1**

1-40 **15** *3 ¾* **Aurore D'Estruval (FR)**[52] 3732 6-11-5 **142**..................... DavidMullins 124
(Rebecca Curtis) *trckd ldr tl after 3 out: sn wknd: eased bef last* **20/1**

330F **16** *1 ¼* **Fairytale Theatre (IRE)**[15] 4402 9-11-5 **130**..................(t) RyanMahon 118
(Dan Skelton) *a towards rr* **200/1**

-1UP **17** *13* **Bitofapuzzle**[38] 3998 8-11-5 **148**..............................(t) NoelFehily 106
(Harry Fry) *mid-div tl wknd appr 3 out* **12/1**[3]

-553 **18** *9* **Melbourne Lady**[27] 4189 8-11-5 **129**.......................... MatthewBowes 98
(P Fegan, Ire) *w'like: trckd ldrs tl wknd 3 out* **150/1**

3F25 **F** **The Govaness**[52] 3732 7-11-5 **142**............................ RichardJohnson 140
(Dr Richard Newland) *towards rr of mid-div: nt fluent 5th: str chal 2 out: sn rdn: disputing 2nd whn fell last: fatally injured* **12/1**[3]

4m 45.0s (-5.00) **Going Correction** +0.075s/f (Yiel) **19** Ran **SP% 124.8**
Speed ratings (Par 117): **113,111,111,111,110 110,109,108,108,105 105,105,104,103,102 101,96,93,**
CSF £85.47 CT £1201.54 TOTE £1.60: £1.20, £15.60, £9.90; EX 90.70 Trifecta £2088.20.
Owner Mrs S Ricci **Bred** Comte A Maggiar & Mlle A Maggiar **Trained** Muine Beag, Co Carlow

FOCUS
No Annie Power this year, who was busy winning the Champion Hurdle earlier in the afternoon, but the same connections had what looked a more than able deputy and the proved a class apart, continuing the Mullins dominance in the race. Unusually for this event, they went a really good gallop and the field was soon strung out. The winner didn't need to improve to win and has been rated below her Ascot success. The form looks solid enough.

4700 146TH YEAR OF THE NATIONAL HUNT CHASE CHALLENGE CUP (AMATEUR RIDERS' NOVICES' CHASE) (LISTED RACE) (25 fncs) 3m 7f 170y

4:50 (4:53) (Class 1) 5-Y-O+ **£69,960** (£18,730; £9,360; £4,680; £2,340; £1,180)

3P62 **1** **Minella Rocco (IRE)**[24] 4237 6-11-6 **143**..................(t) MrDerekO'Connor 160+
(Jonjo O'Neill) *hld up: reminder after 8th: hdwy 4 out: upsides 2 out: led jst bef last: styd on wl and edgd rt run-in: kpt up to work towards fin* **8/1**

1133 **2** *1 ¼* **Native River (IRE)**[38] 3998 6-11-6 **149**..............................(p) MrMLegg 160+
(Colin Tizzard) *in tch: blnd 13th: chsd wnr 19th (water): lost 2nd and rdn after 4 out: outpcd after 3 out: rallied run-in and hung lft: wnt 2nd fnl 120yds: styd on to cl on wnr nr fin* **7/1**[2]

0-01 **3** *6* **Measureofmydreams (IRE)**[30] 4148 8-11-6 **147**................. MsKWalsh 153
(W P Mullins, Ire) *in rr: blnd 4th: hdwy 19th: wnt 2nd after 4 out: led jst bef 3 out: jnd 2 out: rdn and hdd jst bef last: lost 2nd 120yds: one pce* **9/1**

2112 **4** *5* **Southfield Royale**[80] 3229 6-11-6 **147**..............................(p) MsNCarberry 148
(Neil Mulholland) *midfield: hdwy 19th: ev ch 3 out: rdn sn after: cl 3rd whn blnd 2 out: no ex fnl 150yds* **5/1**[1]

1314 **5** *2 ¾* **Vicente (FR)**[95] 3013 7-11-6 **153**.................................. MrWBiddick 150+
(Paul Nicholls) *hld up: stdy hdwy fr 4 out: chsng ldrs whn hmpd by loose horse 3 out: plugged on run-in but n.d* **14/1**

11U2 **6** *5* **Vieux Lion Rouge (FR)**[24] 4238 7-11-6 **146**...............(p) MrRPQuinlan 141
(David Pipe) *midfield: blnd 11th: hdwy appr 3 out: effrt and handy bef 2 out: wknd bef last* **25/1**

2-11 **7** *7* **Local Show (IRE)**[50] 3774 8-11-6 **147**.............................. MrTomDavid 137
(Ben Pauling) *chsd ldrs: hmpd 20th and lost pl: rallied appr 3 out to chse ldng bunch: wknd bef 2 out* **14/1**

1266 **8** *41* **Viva Steve (IRE)**[17] 4361 8-11-6 **130**.............................. MrOHarding 97
(Mick Channon) *chsd ldrs tl wknd after 4 out* **66/1**

16P5 **P** **Bally Beaufort (IRE)**[24] 4238 8-11-6 139..............................(p) MrJJSlevin
(Nigel Twiston-Davies) *chsd ldrs: lost pl bef 14th: hit 21st and rdn: t.o whn p.u bef 2 out* **66/1**

1123 **P** **Waldorf Salad**[24] 4238 8-11-6 131..[1] MrJSKnox
(Venetia Williams) *sn in midfield: lost pl bef 15th: bhd 19th: t.o whn p.u bef 21st* **66/1**

3/23 **P** **Pont Alexandre (GER)**[38] 4005 8-11-6 149...................... MrPWMullins
(W P Mullins, Ire) *hld up: wnt wrong and p.u bef 20th: dismntd: fatally injured* **15/2**[3]

61P1 **F** **Johnny Og**[10] 4487 7-11-6 132..(b) MissCVHart
(Martin Keighley) *racd keenly: chsd ldr after 3rd: led bef 14th: sn clr: reduced advantage 18th: hdd appr 3 out: sn wknd: bhd whn fell 2 out* **100/1**

2122 **F** **Definitly Red (IRE)**[38] 3998 7-11-6 140...................... MrSWaley-Cohen
(Brian Ellison) *midfield: nt fluent 9th: lost pl whn hit 17th: in rr whn blnd 3 out: fell 2 out* **12/1**

-343 **P** **Pleasant Company (IRE)**[30] 4148 8-11-6 141.................... MrDGLavery
(W P Mullins, Ire) *chsd ldrs: mstke 18th: wknd after 4 out: bhd whn p.u bef 2 out* **25/1**

41UF **P** **Warrantor (IRE)**[22] 4286 7-11-6 138........................(t) MrJoshuaNewman
(Warren Greatrex) *midfield: hdwy 15th: in tch 17th: blnd 4 out: rdr lost irons and sddle slipped: wl bhd whn p.u bef 3 out* **66/1**

25-2 **F** **Noble Endeavor (IRE)**[30] 4148 7-11-6 141.......................(p) MrJJCodd 141
(Gordon Elliott, Ire) *hld up: nt fluent 14th: hdwy appr 3 out: rdn in 6th abt 6 l off the pce whn fell 2 out* **15/2**[3]

FF **U** **Ballychorus (IRE)**[33] 4083 7-10-13 143.......................(t) MrSClements
(Ms Margaret Mullins, Ire) *chsd ldrs tl hit and uns rdr 13th* **9/1**

115P **F** **Shantou Flyer (IRE)**[30] 4148 6-11-6 143.......................(t) MrBO'Neill
(Colin Bowe, Ire) *midfield: fell 18th* **25/1**

1F42 **P** **Vintage Vinnie (IRE)**[46] 3838 7-11-6 136............................ MrHDDunne
(Rebecca Curtis) *led: blnd 12th: hdd bef 14th: continued to chse ldr tl 19th (water): blnd 20th and lost pl qckly: t.o whn p.u bef 4 out* **66/1**

53PP **P** **How About It (IRE)**[23] 4267 7-11-6 124.......................(b[1]) MrSGCarey
(Rebecca Curtis) *hld up: in last pl 12th: struggling 16th: t.o whn p.u bef 4 out* **100/1**

8m 14.0s (-7.80) **Going Correction** 0.0s/f (Good) **20 Ran SP% 125.8**
Speed ratings: **109,108,107,105,105 104,102,92, , , , , , , , , , ,**
CSF £61.28 CT £530.55 TOTE £8.40: £3.00, £3.50, £3.40; EX 94.10 Trifecta £564.20.
Owner John P McManus **Bred** Eclipse Bloodstock & C & G Hadden **Trained** Cheltenham, Gloucs

FOCUS
A deep edition of this marathon race for amateur riders. It again proved a thorough test and the form is well worth being positive about with the winner stepping forward for the longer trip.

4701 CLOSE BROTHERS NOVICES' H'CAP CHASE (LISTED RACE) (16 fncs) 2m 4f 78y
5:30 (5:31) (Class 1) (0-140,140) 5-Y-0+
£37,017 (£13,890; £6,955; £3,464; £1,742; £871)

Form RPR

U62F **1** **Ballyalton (IRE)**[24] 4237 9-11-10 **140**..............................(p) BrianHughes 153+
(Ian Williams) *travelled strly most of way: in tch: tk clsr order 4 out: chal gng wl 3 out: led next: rdn and narrowly hdd last: rallied wl u.p to regain ld fnl 120yds: drvn rt out* **12/1**

0515 **2** ½ **Bouvreuil (FR)**[45] 3856 5-11-8 **139**.......................(t) SamTwiston-Davies 151
(Paul Nicholls) *mid-div: hit 5th: gd hdwy after 3 out: chal sn after 2 out: rdn to take narrow advantage last: kpt on but no ex whn hdd fnl 120yds* **14/1**

-241 **3** 4½ **Double Shuffle (IRE)**[90] 3106 6-11-8 **138**........................ PaddyBrennan 145
(Tom George) *lw: trckd ldrs: led 3 out: sn rdn: hdd next: sn hld: no ex fr last* **8/1**[2]

PF/P **4** 2½ **Bridgets Pet (IRE)**[45] 3871 9-11-5 **140**........................ ShaneShortall[(5)] 146
(Alan Fleming, Ire) *mid-div: hdwy 3 out: sn rdn: styd on fr next but nt pce to get on terms: wnt 4th fnl 100yds* **33/1**

1PP2 **5** 1 **Twelve Roses**[17] 4359 8-11-8 **138**..............................(p) DavidBass 142
(Kim Bailey) *hld up towards rr: hdwy after 4 out: rdn after next: styd on fr 2 out but nt pce to threaten: wnt 5th towards fin* **25/1**

1113 **6** 1 **Aloomomo (FR)**[24] 4236 6-11-10 **140**........................ GavinSheehan 144
(Warren Greatrex) *lw: trckd ldrs: led 10th tl 3 out: sn rdn to chse ldrs: lft 4th next: no ex whn lost 2 pls fnl 120yds* **3/1**[1]

121U **7** 9 **Thomas Brown**[17] 4361 7-11-10 **140**..............................(b[1]) NoelFehily 137
(Harry Fry) *prom: disp 10th tl 12th: rdn to chse ldrs after 3 out: one pce fr next* **8/1**[2]

-110 **8** 1½ **On Tour (IRE)**[45] 3857 8-11-8 **138**........................ PaulMoloney 134
(Evan Williams) *mid-div: rdn after 3 out: nt pce to get on terms* **22/1**

2U24 **9** 2½ **Amore Alato**[24] 4240 7-11-9 **139**........................ AidanColeman 131
(Johnny Farrelly) *in tch: chsd ldrs after 3 out: sn rdn: one pce fr next* **12/1**

051P **10** hd **Racing Pulse (IRE)**[31] 4124 7-11-9 **139**..............................(t) JJBurke 130
(Rebecca Curtis) *mid-div tl after 4 out: n.d after* **22/1**

6-3 **11** ¾ **Domesday Book (USA)**[51] 3766 6-11-9 **139**........................ AELynch 130
(Henry De Bromhead, Ire) *trckd ldrs: rdn after 4 out: wknd after next* **28/1**

1U22 **12** 5 **Jayo Time (IRE)**[26] 4210 7-11-2 **137**..............................(p) CiaranGethings[(5)] 129+
(Kerry Lee) *towards rr of midfield: hmpd 9th: styng on but hld whn bdly hmpd and nrly uns rdr 2 out* **33/1**

1011 **13** 2¼ **Five In A Row (IRE)**[17] 4370 8-11-6 **136**........................ DannyCook 120
(Brian Ellison) *mid-div tl 9th: in rr and nvr bk on terms after* **25/1**

1441 **14** 17 **Killala Quay**[17] 4359 9-11-9 **139**..............................(p) RichardJohnson 108
(Charlie Longsdon) *led tl 10th: rdn after 4 out: wknd next* **12/1**

/141 **F** **Willow's Saviour**[25] 4222 9-11-8 **138**........................ HarrySkelton 144
(Dan Skelton) *racd keenly: trckd ldrs: hit 5th: rdn after 3 out: disputing cl 3rd whn fell 2 out* **10/1**[3]

F231 **P** **Fourth Act (IRE)**[24] 4251 7-11-7 **137**..............................(tp) TomScudamore
(Colin Tizzard) *nvr travelling in rr: t.o whn p.u bef 2 out* **33/1**

0-56 **U** **McKinley**[38] 4005 6-11-9 **139**..............................(p) BJCooper
(W P Mullins, Ire) *towards rr of midfield: being pushed along whn v awkward and uns rdr 10th (water)* **14/1**

0-13 **P** **Katgary (FR)**[95] 3026 6-11-7 **137**..............................(p) NickScholfield
(Paul Nicholls) *nvr travelling: a in rr: t.o whn p.u bef 2 out* **20/1**

-1U1 **U** **Javert (IRE)**[94] 3036 7-11-9 **139**........................ SeanBowen
(Emma Lavelle) *a towards rr: lost tch 4 out: blnd and uns rdr next* **16/1**

F **F** **Rezorbi (FR)**[45] 3849 5-11-7 **138**........................ JoshuaMoore 143
(Jonjo O'Neill) *hmpd s: mid-div after 4th: rdn and hdwy after 3 out: styng on and disputing cl enough 5th whn fell 2 out: fatally injured* **20/1**

5m 8.7s (-2.30) **Going Correction** +0.175s/f (Yiel) **20 Ran SP% 136.8**
Speed ratings: **111,110,109,108,107 107,103,103,102,101 101,99,98,91, , , ,**
CSF £161.08 CT £1459.37 TOTE £18.10: £4.40, £3.00, £2.20, £9.20; EX 293.20 Trifecta £2153.70.
Owner John Westwood **Bred** P Doyle **Trained** Portway, Worcs

FOCUS
An extremely compacted handicap, with just 4lb separating the entire field, and two runners with smart festival-placed hurdles form came to the fore. The pace was a decent one. The form looks rock solid and it's a race that should produce winners.
T/Jkpt: £3,227.20 to a £1 stake. Pool: £41,084.56 - 11 winning tickets. T/Plt: £38.90 to a £1 stake. Pool: £1,308,467.20 - 24,516.05 winning tickets. T/Qpdt: £28.60 to a £1 stake. Pool: £43,158.10 - 1,113.02 winning tickets. **Tim Mitchell & Darren Owen**

4509 SEDGEFIELD (L-H)
Tuesday, March 15

OFFICIAL GOING: Soft (5.3)
Wind: Breezy, half against Weather: Overcast

4702 BETFRED MARES' NOVICES' HURDLE (BETFRED HURDLE SERIES QUALIFIER) 2m 3f 188y
1:15 (1:15) (Class 4) 4-Y-0+ £3,768 (£1,106; £553; £276)

Form RPR

3U2- **1** **Monbeg Dolly (IRE)**[349] 5093 6-10-12 0.............................. CraigNichol 103+
(Alistair Whillans) *t.k.h: hld up in tch: hdwy to ld briefly bef 2 out: rdn and hung lft fr 2 out: kpt on wl fr last to ld cl home* **1/1**[1]

-505 **2** hd **Theatre Act**[23] 4271 5-10-7 99........................ DiarmuidO'Regan[(5)] 102
(Chris Grant) *trckd ldrs: effrt whn n.m.r against ins rail after 3 out: effrt bef next: led bef last: edgd lft run-in: kpt on: hld nr fin* **7/1**[3]

-513 **3** 11 **Superfection (IRE)**[17] 4369 7-11-5 110........................ HenryBrooke 102
(Donald McCain) *pressed ldr: led briefly after 3 out: led bef next: hung rt and hdd bef last: nt fluent last: drvn and outpcd run-in* **5/4**[2]

0046 **4** 23 **Fairlee Grace**[17] 4369 5-10-9 0........................ ColmMcCormack[(3)] 67
(George Charlton) *led at modest gallop: rdn and hdd after 3 out: wknd bef next* **50/1**

5m 15.8s (21.70) **Going Correction** +0.975s/f (Soft) **4 Ran SP% 108.9**
Speed ratings (Par 105): **95,94,90,81**
CSF £7.60 TOTE £2.20; EX 7.10 Trifecta £9.00.
Owner Paul & Clare Rooney **Bred** Cathal Ennis **Trained** Newmill-On-Slitrig, Borders

FOCUS
This was run over 166yds further than advertised. It was just an ordinary mares' novice run at a moderate gallop and a bit of a sprint from the third-last. The race has been rated around the balance of the first three.

4703 CHAMPION HURDLE TIPS @ BOOKIES.COM "NATIONAL HUNT" NOVICES' H'CAP HURDLE (7 hdls 1 omitted) 2m 178y
1:45 (1:45) (Class 4) (0-105,105) 4-Y-0 £3,500 (£1,049; £534; £276; £148)

Form RPR

-5PP **1** **Azure Glamour (IRE)**[35] 4049 7-10-7 **86**..............................(b[1]) HenryBrooke 92+
(Kenneth Slack) *mde all at reasonable gallop: rdn bef 2 out: hrd pressed and edgd lft run-in: all out* **9/2**[3]

PFF6 **2** nse **Home For Tea**[27] 4178 7-10-0 **79** oh3..............................(p) CraigNichol 84
(Keith Dalgleish) *trckd ldrs: effrt and wnt 2nd after 3 out: rdn next: str chal run-in: kpt on: jst failed* **13/2**

0-P5 **3** 4 **Nicki's Nipper**[16] 4390 8-10-0 **79** oh10........................ JonathanEngland 80
(Sam Drake) *hld up: stdy hdwy 3 out: lft 6 l 3rd next: rallied and cl up last: outpcd run-in* **25/1**

1U13 **4** 13 **Fiddler's Flight (IRE)**[9] 4513 10-10-6 **88**........................ ColmMcCormack[(3)] 77
(John Norton) *bhd: outpcd fnl circ: sme late hdwy: nvr on terms* **6/1**

000 **5** 60 **Just Like Dylan (IRE)**[15] 4403 5-10-13 **92**........................ BrianHarding 20
(Barry Murtagh) *nt fluent on occasions: hld up: drvn and outpcd bef 4 out: sn lost tch: eased whn no ch bef 2 out* **33/1**

45P1 **B** **Perfect Poison (IRE)**[39] 3973 8-11-2 **105**........................ RonanShort[(10)] 104
(Donald McCain) *chsd wnr to after 3 out: drvn and 7 l 5th whn b.d next* **3/1**[2]

000 **F** **Normandy King (IRE)**[76] 3368 5-10-4 **88**........................ AlanJohns[(5)] 89
(Tim Vaughan) *prom: effrt and rdn after 3 out: 5 l 3rd and one pce whn fell next* **7/4**[1]

4m 22.2s (15.30) **Going Correction** +0.975s/f (Soft) **7 Ran SP% 114.0**
Speed ratings (Par 105): **103,102,101,94,66 ,**
CSF £32.56 TOTE £6.10: £3.00, £2.90; EX 34.70 Trifecta £459.80.
Owner E G Tunstall **Bred** Kenneth Parkhill **Trained** Hilton, Cumbria

FOCUS
The top weight was rated 105 in this ordinary novice handicap hurdle which was run over 167yds further than advertised. The winner has been rated back to the level of his Kelso hurdle debut.

4704 FREE CHELTENHAM BETS @ BOOKIES.COM NOVICES' H'CAP CHASE (14 fncs 2 omitted) 2m 3f 65y
2:25 (2:25) (Class 4) (0-105,102) 5-Y-0+ £4,548 (£1,335; £667; £333)

Form RPR

1226 **1** **Runswick Relax**[5] 4569 10-10-6 **82**..............................(tp) HenryBrooke 103+
(Kenneth Slack) *j.w: mde all: shkn up bef 2 out: kpt on strly to draw clr between last 2* **15/8**[1]

3242 **2** 19 **Theflyingportrait (IRE)**[26] 4214 7-11-8 **98**..............................(t) SeanQuinlan 104+
(Jennie Candlish) *t.k.h early: hld up in tch: nt fluent 6th: hdwy to chse wnr 9th: effrt and rdn bef 2 out: edgd lft and wknd bef last* **85/40**[2]

65PB **3** 23 **Lawless Island (IRE)**[27] 4177 7-11-11 **101**........................ CraigNichol 78
(Tim Vaughan) *chsd ldrs: wnt 2nd bef 8th to next: cl up tl rdn and wknd fr 3 out* **7/2**[3]

34P6 **4** 10 **Uncle Monty (IRE)**[16] 4391 7-11-2 **92**..............................(p) BrianHarding 59
(Donald McCain) *in tch on outside: mstke 8th: struggling whn nt fluent 4 out: lost tch fr next* **8/1**

P054 **5** 27 **Dundee Blue (IRE)**[19] 4325 8-9-11 **76** oh4..............(tp) HarryChalloner[(3)] 16
(Henry Hogarth) *pressed wnr to after 7th: lost pl next: struggling fr 9th: t.o* **8/1**

5m 14.8s (11.80) **Going Correction** +0.85s/f (Soft) **5 Ran SP% 111.2**
Speed ratings: **109,101,91,87,75**
CSF £6.59 TOTE £2.80: £1.50, £1.50; EX 7.00 Trifecta £10.30.
Owner A Slack **Bred** Mrs S Barraclough **Trained** Hilton, Cumbria

FOCUS
Due to rail movements 121yds were added to the distance of this race. Although the pace was only fair there were only two in contention from the third-last. The winner has been rated in line with the best of his old chase form.

4705 CHELTENHAM PRICE BOOSTS @ BOOKIES.COM H'CAP HURDLE (7 hdls 1 omitted) 2m 178y
3:05 (3:05) (Class 4) (0-120,120) 4-Y-O+ £3,638 (£1,068; £534)

Form RPR
41P5 1 **Away For Slates (IRE)**[16] 4389 6-11-12 120 BrianHarding 126+
(Keith Dalgleish) *pressed ldr: led 3 out: shkn up and qckd clr next: pushed out: readily* 6/4[2]
2111 2 7 **Roxyfet (FR)**[6] 4554 6-10-6 107 7ex FinianO'Toole(7) 107
(Micky Hammond) *t.k.h early: trckd ldrs: wnt 2nd 3 out: ev ch briefly bef next: rdn and one pce fr 2 out* 5/4[1]
-P06 3 23 **Lexi's Boy (IRE)**[10] 4482 8-11-12 120 (tp) HenryBrooke 100
(Donald McCain) *led: nt fluent 4 out: hdd and outpcd next: wknd bef 2 out* 3/1[3]
4m 20.6s (13.70) **Going Correction** +0.975s/f (Soft) 3 Ran SP% 109.4
Speed ratings (Par 105): **106,102,91**
CSF £3.81 TOTE £2.70; EX 3.70 Trifecta £3.30.
Owner Equus I **Bred** Mrs Kay Curtis **Trained** Carluke, S Lanarks

FOCUS
The extra distance for this handicap hurdle was 167yds and though there were only three runners, the pace was fair.

4706 COMPARE CHELTENHAM ODDS @ BOOKIES.COM H'CAP HURDLE 2m 3f 188y
3:45 (3:45) (Class 4) (0-105,104) 4-Y-O+ £3,249 (£954; £477; £238)

Form RPR
4041 1 **Generous Pet (IRE)**[7] 4547 7-9-13 80 JoeColliver(3) 102+
(Kenneth Slack) *pressed ldr: led 4 out: shkn up and drew clr after next: j.rt fnl 2: unchal* 8/13[1]
4460 2 9 **Tiny Dancer (IRE)**[41] 3937 8-10-4 87 (v) DiarmuidO'Regan(5) 97
(Chris Grant) *trckd ldrs: pushed along bef 3 out: rallied to chse (clr) wnr bef next: sn no imp* 14/1[3]
1405 3 13 **Ballinalacken (IRE)**[21] 4301 8-11-12 104 (v) DavidEngland 99
(Clare Ellam) *t.k.h: prom: drvn and outpcd 3 out: no imp fr next* 22/1
0451 4 8 **Bladoun (FR)**[7] 4541 8-11-7 104 (p) MichaelHeard(5) 91
(David Pipe) *led to 4 out: sn pushed along: drvn along next: lost 2nd bef 2 out: sn wknd* 9/4[2]
53-3 P **Flobury**[21] 4297 8-10-11 92 HarryChalloner(3)
(Barry Leavy) *t.k.h: prom on outside tl wknd qckly and p.u bef 2 out* 18/1
5m 15.1s (21.00) **Going Correction** +0.975s/f (Soft) 5 Ran SP% 109.0
Speed ratings (Par 105): **97,93,88,85,**
CSF £8.75 TOTE £1.40: £1.10, £3.40; EX 8.60 Trifecta £33.80.
Owner Miss H P Tate **Bred** R J A McGaw **Trained** Hilton, Cumbria

FOCUS
This was run over 166yds further than advertised. It featured two horses running unpenalised for wins in conditional riders' events last week and they bet 14-1 bar the pair. The pace was fair.

4707 EXPERT RACING TIPS @ BOOKIES.COM H'CAP CHASE (11 fncs 2 omitted) 2m 77y
4:25 (4:25) (Class 5) (0-100,97) 5-Y-O+ £2,729 (£801; £400; £200)

Form RPR
5422 1 **Duhallowcountry (IRE)**[6] 4556 10-10-0 78 (p) MissAWaugh(7) 89+
(Victor Thompson) *pressed ldr: led 5th: mde rest: pushed along and clr bef 2 out: kpt on strly* 4/1[2]
4515 2 7 **Captain Sharpe**[19] 4329 8-10-3 81 (b) MrWHRReed(7) 86
(Kenny Johnson) *nt fluent on occasions: prom: hit 1st: pushed along bef 3 out: rallied to chse (clr) wnr bef next: edgd lft and no imp bef last* 7/1[3]
5221 3 13 **Discoverie**[6] 4556 8-11-2 87 7ex (b) HenryBrooke 80
(Kenneth Slack) *cl up: nt fluent and lost pl 2nd: nt fluent next: sn pushed along: hdwy on outside to chse wnr 4 out: rdn and hung lft after next: outpcd bef 2 out: sn btn* 4/5[1]
FU36 4 1 1/2 **Gin Cobbler**[19] 4329 10-11-2 94 ThomasDowson(7) 83
(Victor Thompson) *led to 5th: chsd wnr to 4 out: rdn and wknd fr next* 14/1
2545 5 6 **Pamak D'Airy (FR)**[21] 4300 13-11-7 95 (p) TonyKelly(3) 79
(Henry Hogarth) *prom: drvn and outpcd 6th: n.d after* 10/1
06PU 6 31 **Calton Entry (IRE)**[19] 4329 7-11-7 97 StephenMulqueen(5) 49
(Katie Scott) *hld up: stdy hdwy to chse ldrs 1/2-way: rdn along 4 out: wknd after next: t.o* 10/1
4m 28.3s (14.30) **Going Correction** +0.85s/f (Soft) 6 Ran SP% 112.9
Speed ratings: **98,94,88,87,84 68**
CSF £29.79 TOTE £7.50: £2.90, £4.80; EX 36.80 Trifecta £59.10.
Owner V Thompson **Bred** J Dulohery **Trained** Alnwick, Northumbria

FOCUS
A strongly run handicap chase which was over 132yds further than advertised. A small step up on his previous chase best from the winner.

4708 WEDNESDAY CHELTENHAM TIPS @ BOOKIES.COM MARES' STANDARD OPEN NATIONAL HUNT FLAT RACE 2m 178y
5:00 (5:02) (Class 6) 4-6-Y-0 £1,559 (£457; £228; £114)

Form RPR
1 **Only Orvieto (IRE)** 5-10-9 0 JamieHamilton(5) 108+
(Malcolm Jefferson) *hld up in tch: shkn up and sltly outpcd over 4f out: rallied 3f out: rdn to ld over 1f out: styd on strly* 4/1[2]
3 2 4 **Paper Roses (IRE)**[109] 2756 5-10-11 0 CallumWhillans(3) 104+
(Donald Whillans) *t.k.h early: trckd ldrs: led over 2f out to over 1f out: kpt on same pce ins fnl f* 10/1
2 3 39 **Mount Mizooka**[168] 1688 5-10-9 0 NathanMoscrop(5) 65
(Brian Ellison) *hld up: pushed along over 4f out: rallied 3f out: no imp on first two fr 2f out* 4/1[2]
4 2 1/2 **Shy (CZE)** 4-10-3 0 ColmMcCormack(3) 55
(George Charlton) *prom: pushed along and outpcd over 4f out: n.d after* 20/1
2 5 2 1/4 **Tara Time**[206] 1334 5-10-11 0 AdamNicol(3) 60
(Philip Kirby) *led to over 2f out: rdn and wknd qckly over 1f out* 11/8[1]
6 29 **It's All About Me (IRE)** 4-10-3 0 JoeColliver(3) 23
(Micky Hammond) *hld up in tch: hdwy and cl up 1/2-way: outpcd over 4f out: sn struggling* 11/2[3]
P 7 99 **Lady Broome**[38] 4001 5-11-0 0 (p) AlainCawley
(John David Riches) *pressed ldr: struggling over 6f out: sn lost tch: t.o* 125/1
4m 13.1s (11.80) **Going Correction** +0.975s/f (Soft)
WFA 4 from 5yo 7lb 7 Ran SP% 112.1
Speed ratings: **111,109,90,89,88 74,28**
CSF £40.21 TOTE £5.40: £1.90, £3.50; EX 40.30 Trifecta £142.90.
Owner D M Gibbons **Bred** Cleaboy Stud **Trained** Norton, N Yorks

FOCUS
A reasonable mares' bumper run over 167yds further than advertised and the first two finished clear. The pace was fair.
T/Plt: £153.00 to a £1 stake. Pool: £59,761.68 - 285.06 winning tickets. T/Qpdt: £26.30 to a £1 stake. Pool: £4,915.67 - 137.80 winning tickets. **Richard Young**

4429 BANGOR-ON-DEE (L-H)
Wednesday, March 16

OFFICIAL GOING: Soft (good to soft in places on hurdle course; hdl 6.4, chs 5.7)
Wind: light breeze Weather: sunny; 11 degrees

4709 HORSERADISH-HOSPITALITY.COM MARES' H'CAP HURDLE (11 hdls) 2m 3f 123y
2:25 (2:25) (Class 4) (0-105,105) 4-Y-O+ £3,898 (£1,144; £572; £286)

Form RPR
2P44 1 **Magic Money**[42] 3930 8-11-9 105 TomBellamy(3) 113
(Kim Bailey) *settled in 2nd or 3rd: nt fluent 2nd: drvn bef 2 out where jnd ldr: led narrowly fr last and jst prevailed in sustained duel* 5/2[2]
5341 2 shd **Definitely Better (IRE)**[9] 4538 8-10-11 95 7ex JamieBargary(5) 102
(Tom George) *settled trcking ldrs: effrt after 3 out: chal next: sn rdn: pressed wnr hrd fr last but jst hld on nod* 2/1[1]
PP46 3 3 3/4 **Glenariff**[47] 3841 7-11-1 99 (p) KevinJones(5) 103
(Seamus Mullins) *nt fluent 1st: 2nd or 3rd tl led 5th: rdn and jnd 2 out: jst hdd whn ungainly last: nt qckn after* 10/1
4 3 1/4 **Lilly Of The Moor**[677] 188 8-11-9 102 KielanWoods 102
(Ben Case) *cl up: 3rd and rdn whn mstke 3 out: chsd ldng trio and kpt on same pce after* 16/1
60 5 3 3/4 **Supreme Hope (IRE)**[133] 2267 7-11-1 94 MarkQuinlan 89
(Neil Mulholland) *chsd ldrs: rdn bef 3 out: nvr making any imp after* 9/1
5435 6 24 **Stepover**[24] 4272 5-11-6 102 KillianMoore(3) 75
(Alex Hales) *last pair: blnd 6th: no ch after and sn rdn: t.o after 3 out: plugged on flat* 6/1[3]
51-P 7 1 3/4 **Squeeze Me**[34] 4069 9-10-13 97 (t) NickSlatter(5) 66
(Gary Hanmer) *hld up in midfield: 6th and rdn bef 7th: no rspnse: t.o after 3 out* 20/1
00-P 8 6 **Frank N Fair**[16] 4413 8-9-8 80 (p) MissBFrost(7) 43
(Zoe Davison) *last pair: rdn and struggling bef 6th: t.o after 3 out* 33/1
/11- P **Detour Ahead**[646] 645 8-11-9 102 (p) DavidEngland
(Clare Ellam) *led tl 5th: lost pl rapidly bef 7th: sn t.o: p.u after 3 out* 20/1
5m 5.5s (13.50) **Going Correction** +0.40s/f (Soft) 9 Ran SP% 113.6
Speed ratings (Par 105): **89,88,87,86,84 75,74,71,**
CSF £7.77 CT £39.35 TOTE £3.00: £1.30, £1.50, £2.80; EX 9.50 Trifecta £54.40.
Owner GSTTKPA Charity Partnership & D Jenks **Bred** Hartshill Stud **Trained** Andoversford, Gloucs

FOCUS
An additional meeting that replaced the cancelled Huntingdon card. All distances as advertised. A moderate contest, although it did contain a couple of horses that won when last seen and the race has been rated around the balance of the first five. The early pace wasn't overly strong.

4710 BANGORBET H'CAP CHASE (18 fncs) 3m 30y
3:05 (3:05) (Class 5) (0-100,107) 5-Y-O+ £4,328 (£1,574)

Form RPR
-421 1 **Whiskey Chaser (IRE)**[5] 4591 8-12-0 107 7ex JamesCowley(5) 126+
(Donald McCain) *j. soundly: cl 2nd tl led 10th: drew rt away after 3 out and only one nt out on his feet after* 7/4[1]
4304 2 61 **Wish In A Well (IRE)**[24] 4276 7-10-3 77 (t) KielanWoods 51
(Ben Case) *last pair: pushed along 11th: wnt 3rd bef 13th and 2nd next: 6 l 2nd and nt fluent 3 out: rapidly lost tch w wnr and drvn and barely able to continue fr wl bef next* 6/1[3]
2/14 P **Don't Hang About**[89] 3144 11-11-3 96 NickSlatter(5)
(Gary Hanmer) *unruly paddock and uns rdr: cl up: hit 7th: wnt 2nd at 12th: rdn whn mstke 14th: continued 3rd but t.o and grnd to a halt after 3 out: p.u wl bef next* 6/1[3]
4P34 P **Miss Oscarose (IRE)**[17] 4380 9-11-1 89 (t) LiamTreadwell
(Paul Henderson) *cl up tl rapidly dropped bk last and mstke 6th: t.o and p.u 9th: dismntd* 5/1[2]
-23P P **Over My Head**[46] 3864 8-10-11 85 (t) BrendanPowell
(Claire Dyson) *narrow ldr tl 10th: rdn 12th: dropped out rapidly: v remote 4th whn p.u 3 out* 6/1[3]
-324 P **Jimmy Shan (IRE)**[163] 1795 8-11-7 100 AlanJohns(5)
(Tim Vaughan) *taken down early and led rnd at s: racd in last pair: rdn after 12th: sn t.o: wnt lft whn crawled over next and p.u* 13/2
6m 54.2s (34.40) **Going Correction** +1.55s/f (Heav) 6 Ran SP% 109.2
Speed ratings: **104,83, , ,**
CSF £11.76 TOTE £2.20: £1.20, £2.40; EX 11.40.
Owner Deva Racing Flemensfirth Partnership **Bred** P Coghlan **Trained** Cholmondeley, Cheshire

FOCUS
Nothing more than a moderate staying chase, and only one performed anywhere near his best. The winner was well in on his Leicester win.

4711 RESTAURANT 1539 MAIDEN HURDLE (12 hdls) 2m 7f 32y
3:45 (3:45) (Class 4) 4-Y-O+ £3,898 (£1,144; £572; £286)

Form RPR
-434 1 **Kilcullen Flem (IRE)**[12] 4467 6-11-4 116 (p) TrevorWhelan 120
(Rebecca Curtis) *set stdy pce: hdd 8th: rdn bef 3 out: looked hld home turn: rallied for str driving to ld last: drew clr flat* 11/8[2]
2-22 2 3 **Boy In A Bentley (IRE)**[20] 4322 6-11-1 0 TomBellamy(3) 118
(Kim Bailey) *sn 2nd: led 8th: 2 l in front and gng best home turn: rdn between last two: hdd last: outstyd flat* 6/5[1]
3-P 3 5 **Mahler Lad (IRE)**[78] 3340 6-11-4 0 CraigNichol 113
(Donald McCain) *cl up in 3rd: rdn 8th: plugged on steadily after but nvr making any imp or gng wl enough* 9/2[3]
0-P0 4 52 **Midnight Owle**[20] 4323 6-11-4 0 (t) BrendanPowell 60
(Claire Dyson) *last pair: rdn and lost tch rapidly after 9th: t.o next: hit 2 out* 125/1

P **Armarissis (IRE)**[703] 9-11-4 0 KielanWoods
(Alex Hales) *last pair: rdn and lost tch rapidly after 9th: t.o 3 out: p.u next* **33/1**

6m 8.9s (17.90) **Going Correction** +0.40s/f (Soft) **5 Ran SP% 109.5**
Speed ratings (Par 105): **84,82,81,63,**
CSF £3.48 TOTE £2.30: £1.20, £1.10; EX 3.40 Trifecta £4.50.
Owner Tangledupinblue **Bred** Robert McCarthy **Trained** Newport, Pembrokeshire

FOCUS
The betting suggested only two of these could be seriously fancied, and they pulled away. A small step up from the winner.

4712 SOUTHPORT FLOWER SHOW LADY RIDERS' H'CAP HURDLE (9 hdls) 2m 145y
4:25 (4:28) (Class 4) (0-105,105) 4-Y-0+ **£4,548** (£1,335; £667; £333)

Form RPR
3443 **1** **Old Magic (IRE)**[19] 4343 11-9-7 79 oh7 (t) MissCVHart(7) 89+
(Sophie Leech) *trckd ldrs: effrt 3 out: rdn to ld bef next: sn drew clr: 8 l ahd last* **25/1**
4PP4 **2** *9* **Eco Warrior**[27] 4200 6-11-4 104 (p) MissLMTurner(7) 106
(Venetia Williams) *pressed ldr: rdn and sltly outpcd after 3 out: rallied to go 2nd and mstke next: plugged on and no ch w wnr* **4/1**[2]
-656 **3** *6* **Bell Weir**[40] 3970 8-11-9 105 (p) EmmaSayer(3) 101
(Dianne Sayer) *led at decent pce: hrd pressed 6th: rdn and hdd bef 2 out: sn outpcd: ev ch of wl hld 2nd tl fdd fr last* **7/2**[1]
3163 **4** *8* **Guaracha**[11] 4491 5-11-7 105 BridgetAndrews(5) 91+
(Alexandra Dunn) *midfield: rdn 3 out: sn btn: heavily eased next: hacked on* **11/1**
0004 **5** *1 1/4* **Chakisto (FR)**[63] 3586 8-10-7 89 MissGAndrews(3) 74
(Tim Vaughan) *hld up in midfield: effrt gng wl enough 3 out: rdn and btn bef next* **4/1**[2]
2P54 **6** *45* **Jaunty Inflight**[18] 4356 7-10-12 98 MissTWorsley(7) 38
(Brian Eckley) *last pair: rdn bef 5th: struggling whn mstke next: continued t.o* **13/2**
F-20 **P** **Lindsay's Dream**[133] 2264 10-10-1 87 (p) MissBFrost(7)
(Zoe Davison) *last pair and nt travelling: rdn after 3rd: t.o bef 5th: p.u 3 out* **25/1**
0 **P** **Zarliman (IRE)**[56] 2123 6-10-4 90 (p) MissBHampson(7)
(Neil Mulholland) *towards rr: rdn and struggling 3 out: poor 6th whn lost action and p.u next* **9/1**
4501 **F** **Symphony Of Pearls**[11] 4490 5-10-0 86 MissJodieHughes(7)
(Dai Burchell) *tk off bef s: prom tl lost pl and mstke 5th: mstke next: poor 7th whn crashing fall 3 out* **6/1**[3]

4m 15.7s (4.80) **Going Correction** +0.40s/f (Soft) **9 Ran SP% 115.9**
Speed ratings (Par 105): **104,99,96,93,92 71,,,**
CSF £124.69 CT £444.01 TOTE £25.10: £5.00, £1.90, £1.60; EX 151.70 Trifecta £2452.90.
Owner Cheltenham Racing Club **Bred** Martin J Dibbs **Trained** Elton, Gloucs

FOCUS
A moderate contest for lady riders, but it was run at a decent pace. The winner recorded his best RPR since 2013.

4713 CHOLMONDELEY PAGEANT OF POWER H'CAP CHASE (13 fncs 2 omitted) 2m 4f 72y
5:05 (5:08) (Class 5) (0-100,100) 5-Y-0+ **£3,994** (£1,240; £667)

Form RPR
2341 **1** **Slidecheck (IRE)**[14] 4440 9-11-3 91 (tp) AdamWedge 104+
(Alexandra Dunn) *trckd ldng pair tl wnt 2nd at 9th: led gng best 3 out: pushed along and plugged on gamely to go clr fr next* **5/2**[2]
0525 **2** *8* **Mist The Boat**[119] 2567 8-11-3 96 (v[1]) AlanJohns(5) 103
(Tim Vaughan) *led tl 6th: mstke 7th: led again 9th tl hdd and mstke 3 out: sn drvn and struggling: plodded on in vain pursuit after* **4/1**[3]
213- **3** *26* **Cruising Bye**[328] 5497 10-11-7 100 (t) NickSlatter(5) 83
(Gary Hanmer) *hld up trcking ldrs tl lost tch and blnd 10th: 20 l 3rd whn v unconvincing jump 2 out: t.o and v tired after* **6/1**
3254 **U** **Guanciale**[20] 4321 9-11-8 96 RobertDunne
(Dai Burchell) *uns rdr 2nd* **9/2**
3453 **P** **Rocky Stone (IRE)**[17] 4387 8-11-5 93 (t) CraigNichol
(Donald McCain) *cl 2nd tl led 6th tl 10th: drvn and immediately fnd nil: poor last whn mstke 3 out: continued t.o and gng v slowly tl climbed over next and p.u* **9/4**[1]

5m 42.6s (33.50) **Going Correction** +1.55s/f (Heavy) **5 Ran SP% 111.8**
Speed ratings: **95,91,81,,**
CSF £12.74 TOTE £3.60: £2.20, £2.00; EX 10.70 Trifecta £36.20.
Owner West Buckland Bloodstock Ltd **Bred** Richard Tanner Jnr **Trained** West Buckland, Somerset

FOCUS
One of the fences in the back straight was missed out due to the low sun, so they jumped two less than they should have.

4714 BANGORBET MAIDEN HURDLE (8 hdls 1 omitted) 2m 145y
5:40 (5:40) (Class 5) 4-Y-0+ **£3,249** (£954; £477; £238)

Form RPR
1-03 **1** **Midnight Tour**[36] 4039 6-10-2 0 JackSherwood(5) 110+
(David Loder) *settled trcking ldrs: mstke 5th: wnt 3rd and effrt 3 out: led gng best bef next: sn clr: readily* **9/2**[2]
52-5 **2** *5* **Road To Rome (IRE)**[99] 2965 6-10-11 0 ThomasGarner(3) 110
(William Kinsey) *tall and rngy: midfield: effrt 3 out: rdn to chse wnr fr next: one pce and making no imp after* **33/1**
54P5 **3** *7* **Midnight Target**[14] 4430 6-10-7 0 LeeEdwards 97
(John Groucott) *tall: bhd: rdn and styd on steadily fr bef 2 out where mstke: drvn into wl hld 3rd after last* **100/1**
4 **4** *4* **Peter The Mayo Man (IRE)**[21] 4303 6-11-0 0 MarkQuinlan 104+
(Neil Mulholland) *tall: chsng type: led after 1st tl 3rd: led again bef 5th: rdn and hdd bef 2 out where nt fluent: sn wl btn: blnd last and lost 3rd flat* **4/7**[1]
-550 **5** *1 1/2* **Jaunty Thor**[24] 4264 6-11-0 98 RobertDunne 99
(Brian Eckley) *cl up: 2nd briefly 3 out: sn rdn: fdd bef next* **16/1**
6P6 **6** *13* **Whos De Baby (IRE)**[42] 3927 8-10-7 0 CharlieHammond(7) 85
(Sarah-Jayne Davies) *led tl after 1st: cl up tl rdn 5th: struggling after next* **40/1**
24 **7** *1 3/4* **Diamond Rock**[13] 4441 5-11-0 0 JamesDavies 83
(Henry Oliver) *midfield: mstke 5th: no ch after* **7/1**[3]
6 **8** *19* **The Venerable Bede (IRE)**[26] 4233 5-11-0 0 JakeGreenall 64
(Paul Webber) *big rngy: towards rr: rdn 4th: t.o bef 2 out* **14/1**
5P0 **9** *1 1/2* **Diamond Reflection (IRE)**[13] 4441 4-10-7 0 (t) AdamWedge 55
(Tom Weston) *a wl bhd: t.o fr 5th* **100/1**
-44 **10** *7* **Move To The Groove (IRE)**[27] 4208 6-11-0 0 AdrianLane 55
(Donald McCain) *chsd ldrs tl rdn and lost pl qckly 3 out: t.o bef next* **25/1**
6 **11** *25* **Double Treasure**[81] 3258 5-11-0 0 [1] BrendanPowell 30
(Jamie Snowden) *t.k.h: wnt 2nd after 1st: led 3rd tl bef 5th: slowed v rapidly and sn t.o* **20/1**
4006 **12** *9* **Coco Flower (FR)**[11] 4489 4-9-12 0 ow1 KillianMoore(3)
(Alex Hales) *sn last: t.o fr 4th* **100/1**

4m 12.0s (1.10) **Going Correction** +0.40s/f (Soft)
WFA 4 from 5yo+ 7lb **12 Ran SP% 123.8**
Speed ratings (Par 103): **113,110,107,105,104 98,97,88,88,84 73,68**
CSF £136.19 TOTE £6.80: £2.00, £5.10, £14.80; EX 147.40 Trifecta £3982.90.
Owner James and Jean Potter **Bred** James & Jean Potter **Trained** Bishop's Castle, Shropshire

FOCUS
Despite the big field, the market was dominated by one runner, with plenty of the remainder going off at long prices. One of the hurdles, what would have been flight five, was omitted due to the low sun. The winner has been rated in line with her bumper win.
T/Plt: £75.80 to a £1 stake. Pool £50,726.29. 488.18 winning tickets. T/Qpdt: £35.30 to a £1 stake. Pool: £3,102.21. 64.86 winning tickets. **Iain Mackenzie**

4695 CHELTENHAM (L-H)
Wednesday, March 16

OFFICIAL GOING: Good (good to soft in places; old course 7.3, cross-country 6.9)
Wind: moderate, behind Weather: cloudy

4715 NEPTUNE INVESTMENT MANAGEMENT NOVICES' HURDLE (REGISTERED AS BARING BINGHAM NOV' HURDLE) (GRADE 1) (10 hdls) 2m 5f 26y
1:30 (1:31) (Class 1) 4-Y-0+ **£68,340** (£25,644; £12,840; £6,396; £3,216; £1,608)

11 **1** **Yorkhill (IRE)**[74] 3447 6-11-7 156 RWalsh 158+
(W P Mullins, Ire) *lw: t.k.h: hld up in rr: nt fluent 4th and 7th: n.m.r bnd bef 3 out: proged to trck ldrs 2 out: squeezed through on inner to ld on bnd bef last: 3 l up and fine jump last: edgd rt and rdn out* **3/1**[2]
1111 **2** *1 3/4* **Yanworth**[46] 3852 6-11-7 158 BarryGeraghty 155+
(Alan King) *hld up in rr: prog on wd outside after 7th: cl up whn mstke 3 out: chal after 2 out: chsd wnr bef last: styd on but nt pce to chal* **11/10**[1]
111 **3** *7* **Its'afreebee (IRE)**[53] 3739 6-11-7 141 IanPopham 146
(Dan Skelton) *pressed ldr: n.m.r on inner and nrly forced out after 5th: led 3 out: hdd bnd bef last and readily outpcd by ldng pair* **33/1**
4 **4** *4* **Bello Conti (FR)**[85] 3208 5-11-7 139 DavidMullins 141
(W P Mullins, Ire) *q tall: lw: hld up in rr: prog 3 out: cl up after 2 out: sn rdn and comf outpcd bef last* **20/1**
2143 **5** *shd* **Welsh Shadow (IRE)**[18] 4360 6-11-7 134 HarrySkelton 142
(Dan Skelton) *hld up in rr: bad mstke 4th: prog 3 out: nt pce to cl on ldrs after 2 out: kpt on* **28/1**
5/5- **6** *1/2* **Vigil (IRE)**[24] 4277 7-11-7 139 DavyRussell 141
(D K Weld, Ire) *hld up in detached last: nt fluent 3rd: stl last after 3 out: prog next: nvr on terms w ldrs but kpt on* **16/1**
1 **7** *7* **A Toi Phil (FR)**[52] 3765 6-11-7 146 BJCooper 135
(W P Mullins, Ire) *pressed ldrs: rt there 3 out: lost pl qckly and in rr after 2 out: nt fluent last* **8/1**[3]
1121 **8** *3* **O O Seven (IRE)**[38] 4015 6-11-7 150 AndrewTinkler 132
(Nicky Henderson) *lw: t.k.h: pressed ldrs: jostling match w rival after 6th: stl chalng 2 out: wknd qckly wl bef last* **20/1**
0-F2 **9** *30* **Ghost River**[18] 4351 6-11-7 0 SeanBowen 100
(Peter Bowen) *trckd ldrs: rt on terms 3 out: lost pl and wknd rapidly sn after: t.o* **100/1**
21 **P** **Thomas Hobson**[60] 3623 6-11-7 145 PaulTownend
(W P Mullins, Ire) *led to 3 out: wkng qckly whn mstke 2 out: t.o whn p.u bef last* **14/1**
5131 **P** **Yala Enki (FR)**[25] 4236 6-11-7 142 AidanColeman
(Venetia Williams) *lost pl 3rd: in rr whn bad mstke 4th and qckly p.u* **25/1**

5m 0.89s (-12.51) **Going Correction** -0.175s/f (Good) **11 Ran SP% 117.0**
Speed ratings (Par 117): **116,115,112,111,111 110,108,107,95,**
CSF £6.25 CT £84.27 TOTE £4.10: £1.30, £5.80; EX 5.50 Trifecta £217.60.
Owner Andrea & Graham Wylie **Bred** Patrick Keating **Trained** Muine Beag, Co Carlow

FOCUS
Races on Old Course and distances as advertised. A blustery and drying day ensured the ground was upgraded to good, good to soft in places for this second day of the Festival. A real highlight of the week, this season's Neptune looked a classy edition and it didn't disappoint. The strong early pace steadied passing the stands and it got tight from the fourth-last to the penultimate flight. They got sorted out from there, though, and the form is outstanding with the winner rated well above average for the race.

4716 RSA CHASE (GRADE 1) (20 fncs) 3m 80y
2:10 (2:10) (Class 1) 5-Y-0+
£85,425 (£32,055; £16,050; £7,995; £4,020; £2,010)

Form RPR
F121 **1** **Blaklion**[39] 3998 7-11-4 150 RyanHatch 162+
(Nigel Twiston-Davies) *a cl up: short of room after 3 out: rdn between last 2: led sn after last: styd on v gamely: all out* **8/1**[3]
1-34 **2** *1/2* **Shaneshill (IRE)**[46] 3856 7-11-4 152 PaulTownend 162+
(W P Mullins, Ire) *lw: hld up: hit 2nd and 11th: hdwy after 3 out: chal next: rdn between last 2: j. sltly lft last: led v briefly sn after: styd on wl w ev ch: hld towards fin* **16/1**
3-11 **3** *8* **More Of That (IRE)**[95] 3029 8-11-4 154 BarryGeraghty 155
(Jonjo O'Neill) *lw: hld up in last pair: little slow 5th: nudged along after 15th: short of room whn taking clsr order bef 3 out: rdn and ev ch 2 out: cl 3rd and stl decent ch whn squeezed up last: no ex (b.b.v)* **6/4**[1]
-511 **4** *3/4* **No More Heroes (IRE)**[78] 3357 7-11-4 159 BJCooper 152
(Gordon Elliott, Ire) *trckd ldrs: disp ld 3 out: rdn into narrow advantage between last 2: nodded on landing last and hdd: no ex* **5/2**[2]
-121 **5** *1 1/4* **Vyta Du Roc (FR)**[25] 4237 7-11-4 145 DarylJacob 151
(Nicky Henderson) *trckd ldrs: rchd for 3rd: rdn after 3 out: one pce and hld in 6th whn hit next* **12/1**
P-61 **6** *10* **Roi Des Francs (FR)**[60] 3635 7-11-4 151 RWalsh 142
(W P Mullins, Ire) *trckd ldr: pressed ldr fr 9th: disp ld 3 out: rdn and hdd between last 2: hld in 5th whn blnd last: wknd* **10/1**
3111 **7** *12* **Seeyouatmidnight**[18] 4365 8-11-4 151 BrianHughes 132
(Sandy Thomson) *led: hit 1st and 14th: hdd 3 out: sn wknd* **9/1**
13P3 **8** *2* **Le Mercurey (FR)**[25] 4237 6-11-4 147 (tp) SamTwiston-Davies 126
(Paul Nicholls) *trckd ldrs: rdn whn outpcd after 4 out: wknd after next* **33/1**

6m 6.2s (-12.10) **Going Correction** -0.075s/f (Good) **8 Ran SP% 115.3**
Speed ratings: **117,116,114,113,113 110,106,105**
CSF £111.32 CT £294.44 TOTE £9.40: £2.50, £3.70, £1.30; EX 136.20 Trifecta £370.70.

Owner S Such & Cg Paletta **Bred** Mrs M D W Morrison **Trained** Naunton, Gloucs

FOCUS

A decent edition of this Grade 1 novices' chase, but the two market leaders had excuses and were below par. The pace was solid, certainly on the second circuit, and several were in with a shout heading to the final fence before the first two came clear. Blaklion is rated to his mark with a big step up from Shaneshill. The fifth helps with the level.

4717 CORAL CUP (A H'CAP HURDLE) (GRADE 3) (10 hdls) 2m 5f 26y

2:50 (2:50) (Class 1) 4-Y-O+

£51,255 (£19,233; £9,630; £4,797; £2,412; £1,206)

Form RPR

/0P- **1** **Diamond King (IRE)**[67] 3542 8-11-3 **149**..........................(t) DavyRussell 154+
(Gordon Elliott, Ire) *hld up in midfield: stdy prog on inner bef 2 out gng wl: rdn to ld last: drvn out* **12/1**

1-1U **2** *1 1/4* **Long House Hall (IRE)**[144] 2063 8-10-8 **140**..................(t) HarrySkelton 144+
(Dan Skelton) *lw: hld up in midfield: prog to trck ldrs 5th: cl up fr 3 out: rdn bef last: styd on to take 2nd nr fin* **16/1**

4U42 **3** *nk* **Ubak (FR)**[17] 4381 8-10-12 **144**.................................... JoshuaMoore 148
(Gary Moore) *lw: pressed ldr: nt fluent 4th: rdn to ld bef last: hdd last: styd on same pce* **28/1**

0 **4** *1/2* **Blazer (FR)**[32] 4115 5-10-9 **141**................................ BarryGeraghty 144
(W P Mullins, Ire) *a cl up: nt fluent 3 out: cl to chal and upsides last: drvn and kpt on same pce flat* **8/1**[2]

4111 **5** *nk* **Baoulet Delaroque (FR)**[34] 4070 5-10-8 **140**.................... NoelFehily 142
(Paul Nicholls) *lw: wl plcd: cl up fr 3 out: drvn bef last: styd on but nvr quite able to chal* **11/1**

3P05 **6** *shd* **Waxies Dargle**[32] 4115 7-10-10 **142**............................... MarkWalsh 144
(Noel Meade, Ire) *lw: hld up wl in rr: prog after 7th: chsd ldrs 2 out: sn rdn: tried to mount a chal on outer bef last: styd on same pce* **33/1**

-134 **7** *1 1/4* **Brother Tedd**[67] 3527 7-11-4 **150**................................ TomO'Brien 151
(Philip Hobbs) *hld up in midfield: prog fr 3 out: drvn after 2 out: styd on fr last but nvr gng pce to chal* **25/1**

00F3 **8** *1/2* **The Romford Pele (IRE)**[46] 3853 9-10-8 **140**...............(b) LeightonAspell 141
(Rebecca Curtis) *settled in rr: effrt bef 3 out: rdn 2 out: no imp bef last: styd on wl fnl 150yds* **16/1**

-12F **9** *1/2* **Avant Tout (FR)**[48] 3830 6-10-12 **144**.............................. PaulTownend 144+
(W P Mullins, Ire) *hld up wl in rr: last of main gp bef 3 out: sn rdn: prog fr 2 out: styd on wl under hrd driving fr last: nrst fin* **22/1**

14-2 **10** *nk* **Arbre De Vie (FR)**[48] 3831 6-11-1 **150**.......................... DavidMullins(3) 149+
(W P Mullins, Ire) *hld up wl in rr: sme prog fr 3 out: rdn after 2 out: kpt on but nvr a real threat* **8/1**[2]

-322 **11** *1/2* **Qewy (IRE)**[95] 3041 6-10-10 **142**....................................(p) AidanColeman 141
(John Ferguson) *prom: nt fluent 3 out: rt on terms w ldrs after 2 out tl wknd jst bef last* **33/1**

1112 **12** *3/4* **Baron Alco (FR)**[53] 3733 5-10-8 **140**.............................. JamieMoore 138
(Gary Moore) *led: set mod pce: rdn 2 out: hdd & wknd bef last* **16/1**

02P3 **13** *nse* **Commissioned (IRE)**[130] 2334 6-11-1 **152**......................(b) MikeyEnnis(5) 150
(John Ferguson) *nvr bttr than midfield: in tch but rdn after 2 out: no real prog* **66/1**

1-3P **14** *3* **Theinval (FR)**[53] 3733 6-11-3 **149**.............................. JeremiahMcGrath 145
(Nicky Henderson) *prom: cl up bhd ldrs 2 out: rdn and wknd bef last* **33/1**

3-14 **15** *1 1/2* **Volnay De Thaix (FR)**[75] 3405 7-11-7 **158**...................... FreddieMitchell(5) 152
(Nicky Henderson) *lw: hld up in rr: rdn after 3 out: one pce and no great prog fr 2 out* **40/1**

1-10 **16** *3 1/4* **Hunters Hoof (IRE)**[116] 2639 7-10-7 **139**.......................... NicodeBoinville 131
(Nicky Henderson) *pressed ldrs: stl rt there after 3 out: wknd qckly bef last* **14/1**

12-0 **17** *3* **Call The Cops (IRE)**[38] 4017 7-11-7 **153**.......................... AndrewTinkler 140
(Nicky Henderson) *j.rt 1st: a wl in rr: shkn up and no prog after 3 out* **25/1**

5-40 **18** *nk* **Three Kingdoms (IRE)**[88] 3151 7-10-2 **141**..............(p) MrAlexFerguson(7) 131
(John Ferguson) *racd on outer in midfield: in tch whn nt fluent 3 out: wknd after 2 out* **50/1**

1-00 **19** *shd* **Sgt Reckless**[88] 3151 9-10-8 **140**.................................... BrianHughes 127
(Mick Channon) *hld up wl in rr: stl in rr 3 out but looked to be gng wl enough: shkn up and no prog after 2 out: nvr involved* **33/1**

U21 **20** *2 3/4* **Politologue (FR)**[31] 4138 5-10-10 **142**.......................... SamTwiston-Davies 126
(Paul Nicholls) *trckd ldrs: chal fr 3 out tl wknd qckly sn after 2 out* **9/1**[3]

-415 **21** *17* **Mister Fizz**[11] 2241 8-10-12 **144**...................................... SeanBowen 111
(Miss Imogen Pickard) *swtg: racd on outer: a towards rr: in tch after 7th: wknd 3 out: t.o* **100/1**

-211 **22** *17* **Rock The Kasbah (IRE)**[53] 3733 6-11-6 **152**...................... RichardJohnson 102
(Philip Hobbs) *trckd ldrs: dropped to midfield and pushed along 6th: struggling whn trapped bhd wkng rival after next: sn t.o* **15/2**[1]

0-00 **23** *7* **Days Of Heaven (FR)**[38] 4014 6-10-9 **141**.......................... DavidBass 84
(Nicky Henderson) *taken down early: t.k.h: trckd ldrs on outer: stl in tch whn nt fluent 3 out: wknd qckly: t.o* **33/1**

P-15 **P** **Blood Cotil (FR)**[59] 3651 7-10-13 **145**................................... RWalsh
(W P Mullins, Ire) *hld up wl in rr: pushed along and lost tch after 7th: t.o whn p.u bef 2 out* **14/1**

1P12 **P** **One For Harry (IRE)**[27] 4204 8-10-8 **140**.......................... BrianHarding
(Nicky Richards) *dropped to last and wknd 4th: t.o fr next tl p.u bef 7th* **50/1**

0-UF **P** **Beast Of Burden (IRE)**[111] 2726 7-10-11 **143**.......................... JJBurke
(Rebecca Curtis) *lw: t.k.h: prom tl wknd rapidly and mstke 7th: sn wl t.o: p.u bef 2 out* **33/1**

5m 2.9s (-10.50) **Going Correction** -0.175s/f (Good) **26** Ran SP% **133.0**

Speed ratings (Par 113): **113,112,112,112,112 112,111,111,111,111 110,110,110,109,108 107,106,106,106,105 98,92,89, ,**

CSF £168.76 CT £5256.59 TOTE £11.50: £2.80, £4.60, £9.50, £3.10; EX 208.30 Trifecta £9234.30.

Owner Mrs Diana L Whateley **Bred** Cleaboy Stud **Trained** Longwood, Co Meath

■ Stewards' Enquiry : Davy Russell two-day ban: use of whip (30-31 Mar)

FOCUS

This was a red-hot Coral Cup. However, they didn't go a breakneck gallop and there was a muddling finish with a lot still in with every chance coming to the last. This was another step up from the winner, with the form looking solid.

4718 BETWAY QUEEN MOTHER CHAMPION CHASE (GRADE 1) (13 fncs) 1m 7f 199y

3:30 (3:30) (Class 1) 5-Y-O+

£199,325 (£74,795; £37,450; £18,655; £9,380; £4,690)

Form RPR

2-11 **1** **Sprinter Sacre (FR)**[80] 3281 10-11-10 **170**...................... NicodeBoinville 176+
(Nicky Henderson) *lw: trckd ldrs: nodded 3 out: led bef next: sn in command: nt fluent last: rdn out* **5/1**[2]

-1F1 **2** *3 1/2* **Un De Sceaux (FR)**[53] 3734 8-11-10 **172**................................ RWalsh 170
(W P Mullins, Ire) *trckd ldr: hit 4th: led after 4 out: rdn whn hdd bef 2 out: sn hld by wnr: kpt on same pce* **4/6**[1]

1-42 **3** *nse* **Special Tiara**[102] 2915 9-11-10 **168**.................................... NoelFehily 170
(Henry De Bromhead, Ire) *led: mstke 3rd: hdd after 4 out: rdn and ev ch after 3 out: hld by wnr bef next but kpt pressing for 2nd: styd on same pce* **16/1**

F-32 **4** *5* **God's Own (IRE)**[33] 4100 8-11-10 **159**............................ PaddyBrennan 166
(Tom George) *lw: in tch: wnt 5th after 4 out: rdn and outpcd after 3 out: 4th and hld whn blnd next: kpt on fr last* **20/1**

-244 **5** *5* **Somersby (IRE)**[80] 3281 12-11-10 **156**..........................(p) BrianHughes 162
(Mick Channon) *in tch: wnt 4th 4 out: rdn after 3 out: keeping on a same pce in hld 5th whn bad mstke next* **50/1**

-262 **6** *9* **Just Cameron**[46] 3857 9-11-10 **150**.................................(t) JoeColliver 154
(Micky Hammond) *chsd ldrs tl 9th: sn struggling to go pce: styd on again fr 2 out but nvr any threat* **66/1**

11-2 **7** *4* **Dodging Bullets**[32] 4114 8-11-10 **168**...................(t) SamTwiston-Davies 151
(Paul Nicholls) *in tch: nt fluent 1st: hit 7th (water): chsng ldrs whn hit 9th: outpcd after 3 out: no threat after* **10/1**[3]

5122 **8** *40* **Sire De Grugy (FR)**[53] 3734 10-11-10 **169**.......................... JamieMoore 140
(Gary Moore) *in last trio but in tch: nvr threatened to get involved: wknd after 3 out* **16/1**

-311 **P** **Felix Yonger (IRE)**[45] 3892 10-11-10 **161**.......................... PaulTownend
(W P Mullins, Ire) *in last pair: mstke 2nd: nvr travelling after: lost tch fr 6th: p.u 4 out* **11/1**

1-25 **P** **Sizing Granite (IRE)**[80] 3293 8-11-10 **155**................................ JJBurke
(C A Murphy, Ire) *lw: blnd v bdly 1st and lucky to stand up: nvr rcvrd in detached last: p.u bef 7th* **33/1**

3m 48.9s (-9.10) **Going Correction** -0.075s/f (Good) **10** Ran SP% **117.0**

Speed ratings: **119,117,117,114,112 107,105,85, ,**

CSF £9.00 CT £50.26 TOTE £5.60: £2.00, £1.10, £3.40; EX 9.80 Trifecta £84.70.

Owner Mrs Caroline Mould **Bred** Christophe Masle **Trained** Upper Lambourn, Berks

FOCUS

An intriguing Champion Chase, featuring last year's brilliant Arkle hero up against the last three winners of this event, all of whom had a certain amount to prove. The pace was sound and the first three home dominated from the off. Despite this amazing success Sprinter Sacre has been rated a stone off his absolute best, but still well up to the race standard.

4719 GLENFARCLAS CHASE (A CROSS COUNTRY CHASE) (32 fncs) 3m 6f 37y

4:10 (4:10) (Class 2) 5-Y-O+

£37,140 (£11,028; £5,514; £2,748; £1,380; £696)

Form RPR

3420 **1** **Any Currency (IRE)**[96] 3017 13-11-4 **157**.....................(p) AidanColeman 149
(Martin Keighley) *a in ldng quartet: trckd ldr 24th: led 26th: rdn after 3 out: hrd pressed fr next: edgd rt but asserted after last: kpt on wl* **11/1**

-U11 **2** *1* **Josies Orders (IRE)**[31] 4147 8-11-4 **148**.............................. MsNCarberry 150+
(E Bolger, Ire) *lw: hld up: clsd on ldrs whn hmpd 16th (2nd cheese wedge): in chsng gp after: shkn up after 3 out: tk 6 l 3rd last: r.o wl to go 2nd 75yds out: nt rch wnr* **15/8**[1]

3434 **3** *1 1/4* **Bless The Wings (IRE)**[96] 3017 11-11-4 **141**........................(p) MrJJCodd 147
(Gordon Elliott, Ire) *hld up: wl in tch fr 14th: prog to trck wnr 3 out: str chal fr next: stl upsides last: no ex flat and lost 2nd fnl 75yds* **33/1**

2C-2 **4** *5* **Quantitativeeasing (IRE)**[31] 4147 11-11-4 **140**..................(p) MarkWalsh 146+
(E Bolger, Ire) *nt a fluent: hld up: wl in tch fr 14th: effrt 3 out: rdn and n.m.r between rivals after 2 out: one pce* **9/1**[3]

2366 **5** *7* **Third Intention (IRE)**[53] 3741 9-11-4 **157**............................(t) TomO'Brien 138
(Colin Tizzard) *lw: hld up: wl in tch fr 14th: disp 2nd briefly 3 out: rdn and fdd after 2 out* **16/1**

F3 **6** *5* **Ballyboker Bridge (IRE)**[45] 3893 9-11-4 **139**.....................(p) AELynch 132
(Peter Maher, Ire) *lw: chsd ldrs: on terms in ldng gp fr 23rd tl wknd after 2 out* **16/1**

6452 **7** *20* **Valadom (FR)**[79] 3315 7-11-4 **130**.................................(t) AlainCawley 114
(Richard Hobson) *led at gd pce: hdd 26th: lost 2nd 3 out: wknd rapidly after 2 out: t.o* **50/1**

-PS2 **8** *11* **Sire Collonges (FR)**[96] 3017 10-11-4 **145**................(b) SamTwiston-Davies 104
(Paul Nicholls) *pressed ldrs: rdn 25th: sn struggling: lost tch 4 out: wl bhd whn j. bdly lft last: t.o* **12/1**

0-30 **9** *1 3/4* **Dolatulo (FR)**[46] 3860 9-11-4 **145**................................(tp) GavinSheehan 103
(Warren Greatrex) *hld up: mstke 4th: nvr a factor and wl off the pce fr 19th: t.o* **25/1**

-1SP **10** *3 3/4* **Uncle Junior (IRE)**[45] 3893 15-11-4 **149**...........................(p) MrPWMullins 99
(W P Mullins, Ire) *sweating: sn detached in last: nvr a factor: t.o* **33/1**

0F5R **11** *nse* **Cantlow (IRE)**[45] 3893 11-11-4 **137**.................................... NiallPMadden 99
(E Bolger, Ire) *hld up: wl in tch fr 14th: rdn 26th: wknd 4 out: t.o* **11/1**

P00U **12** *22* **Rivage D'Or (FR)**[59] 3651 11-11-4 **144**...........................(t) DavyRussell 79
(A J Martin, Ire) *a wl in rr: bhd fr 19th: t.o* **25/1**

11F- **F** **Balthazar King (IRE)**[340] 5275 12-11-4 **153**...................... RichardJohnson
(Philip Hobbs) *trckd ldrs: 6th and wl in tch whn fell 16th (2nd cheese wedge)* **9/2**[2]

0/10 **P** **Rossvoss**[45] 3891 8-11-4 **136**......................................(t) MsKWalsh
(T M Walsh, Ire) *a wl in rr: bhd fr 19th: t.o whn p.u bef 24th* **40/1**

0/0U **P** **Love Rory (IRE)**[45] 3893 8-11-4 **141**.............................. RichieMcLernon
(E Bolger, Ire) *pressed ldr to 24th: wknd rapidly: t.o whn p.u bef 26th* **33/1**

P **Utah De La Coquais (FR)**[10] 8-11-4 **137**...........(p) Marc-AntoineDragon
(E Leray, France) *a wl in rr: bhd fr 19th: t.o whn p.u bef 23rd* **66/1**

8m 11.0s (-27.00) **Going Correction** -0.575s/f (Firm) **16** Ran SP% **121.5**

Speed ratings: **113,112,112,111,109 107,102,99,99,98 98,92, ,**

CSF £30.78 CT £702.96 TOTE £13.60: £3.40, £1.60, £6.80; EX 43.00 Trifecta £1338.80.

Owner Cash Is King **Bred** Gerald Mitchell **Trained** Condicote, Gloucs

FOCUS

The inaugural running of this has a non-handicap. There was a strong gallop on and it was a deep race for the discipline. The form makes sense with the first two rated close to the best of their course form.

4720 FRED WINTER JUVENILE H'CAP HURDLE (GRADE 3) (8 hdls) 2m 87y

4:50 (4:52) (Class 1) 4-Y-O

£42,712 (£16,027; £8,025; £3,997; £2,010; £1,005)

Form RPR

1 **Diego Du Charmil (FR)**[133] 4-11-1 **133**................(t) SamTwiston-Davies 135+
(Paul Nicholls) *tall: will make a chaser: mid-div: hdwy appr 3 out: rdn to ld bef last where being strly pressed tl lft 2 l clr last: jst hld on* **13/2**[2]

1325 **2** *hd* **Romain De Senam (FR)**[74] 3449 4-11-4 **136**..................(t) NickScholfield 137+
(Paul Nicholls) *mid-div: rdn after 2 out and plenty to do: hdwy appr last where lft 4th: str run fnl 100yds: jst failed* **20/1**

0-23 **3** 1/2 **Coo Star Sivola (FR)**[67] 3519 4-10-9 **132** .... LizzieKelly(5) 133
(Nick Williams) *a.p: led 3 out: rdn and hdd bef last where lft clr 2nd briefly: kpt on but no ex fnl 75yds* **16/1**

2 **4** 3 1/4 **Missy Tata (FR)**[108] 2813 4-11-0 **132** .... BJCooper 131+
(Gordon Elliott, Ire) *str: mid-div: mstke 5th: hdwy bef next: rdn after 2 out: swtchd rt bef last where hmpd and lft 3rd briefly: no ex* **10/1**

111 **5** 1 **Doubly Clever (IRE)**[207] 1321 4-10-10 **135** ....[1] HarryCobden(7) 131
(Michael Blake) *lw: mid-div: hdwy 2 out but stl plenty to do: rdn bef last: styd on same pce flat* **50/1**

131 **6** 1 1/2 **Kasakh Noir (FR)**[36] 4038 4-11-5 **137** .... HarrySkelton 134+
(Dan Skelton) *lw: mid-div: hdwy after 4th: rdn to chse ldrs after 2 out: styng on at same pce whn hmpd last* **14/1**

3 **7** 3 1/4 **Messire Des Obeaux (FR)**[25] 4243 4-11-0 **132** .... NoelFehily 126+
(Alan King) *lw: mid-div: hdwy after 5th: rdn to chse ldrs after 2 out: kpt on same pce appr last* **16/1**

112 **8** 3/4 **Fixe Le Kap (FR)**[25] 4243 4-11-10 **142** .... DarylJacob 135+
(Nicky Henderson) *mid-div: hdwy 4th: rdn after 2 out: kpt on but nvr gng pce to get on terms* **8/1**[3]

3132 **9** 13 **Duke Street (IRE)**[27] 2371 4-10-10 **128** ....(p) WillKennedy 114+
(Dr Richard Newland) *chsd ldr: led 3rd tl 3 out: rdn and ev ch after next tl appr last: fdd* **25/1**

121 **10** 1 **Jaleo (GER)**[40] 3967 4-11-2 **134** .... AidanColeman 114
(John Ferguson) *in tch tl mstke 4 out: struggling after and nvr bk on terms* **6/1**[1]

125 **11** 1 1/2 **Wolfcatcher (IRE)**[18] 4358 4-11-5 **137** ....(tp) JackQuinlan 118
(John Ferguson) *chsd ldrs: cl up whn bad mstke 2 out: no time to rcvr and sn btn* **33/1**

1211 **12** 10 **Harley Rebel**[4] 4619 4-10-12 **130** 5ex..........(p) TomScudamore 98
(Neil Mulholland) *struggling after 4th: nvr bttr than mid-div* **20/1**

22 **13** 14 **Pillard (FR)**[19] 4345 4-10-11 **129** .... RichardJohnson 85
(Jonjo O'Neill) *a towards rr* **25/1**

2125 **14** 6 **Duke Of Medina (IRE)**[46] 3848 4-11-6 **138** ....(b) GavinSheehan 88
(Harry Whittington) *a towards rr* **40/1**

4323 **15** 12 **Chic Name (FR)**[27] 4204 4-11-6 **138** ....(v) AlainCawley 78
(Richard Hobson) *chsd ldrs: rdn after 4th: wknd after next* **100/1**

16 6 **Le Curieux (FR)**[130] 4-11-4 **136** ....(t) MarkWalsh 70
(Francois Nicolle, France) *unf: mid-div tl after 5th: sn towards rr* **33/1**

1322 **17** 1 1/4 **Our Thomas (IRE)**[21] 4304 4-10-10 **128** .... BrianHughes 61
(Tim Easterby) *mid-div: mstke 2nd: struggling 4th: sn bhd* **16/1**

611 **P** **Akavit (IRE)**[39] 3988 4-11-3 **135** .... DavidBass
(Ed de Giles) *led tl 3rd: wknd after next: t.o whn p.u after 2 out* **33/1**

2112 **P** **Paddys Runner**[32] 2688 4-11-1 **133** .... WayneHutchinson
(Alan King) *struggling in rr fr 4th: t.o whn p.u 3 out* **33/1**

5P1 **P** **Ardamir (FR)**[21] 4304 4-10-12 **130** .... DenisO'Regan
(Alan King) *sltly on toes: a towards rr: t.o whn p.u 3 out* **12/1**

4 **F** **Campeador (FR)**[81] 3268 4-11-9 **141** ....[1] BarryGeraghty 143+
(Gordon Elliott, Ire) *q str: lw: hld up towards rr: hdwy 3 out: nt clr run briefly 2 out: pushed along and mounting str chal whn fell heavily last* **8/1**[3]

F **Voix Du Reve (FR)**[25] 4257 4-11-7 **139** ....[1] RWalsh 141+
(W P Mullins, Ire) *medium sized: hld up towards rr: hdwy fr 3 out: gd run on inner fnl bnd: travelling wl and mounting str chal whn fell last* **7/1**

3m 49.4s (-12.60) **Going Correction** -0.45s/f (Good) **22** Ran SP% **132.0**
Speed ratings: **113,112,112,111,110 109,108,107,101,100 100,95,88,85,79 76,75, , ,**
CSF £138.44 CT £2053.94 TOTE £6.40: £2.40, £5.30, £5.50, £2.50; EX 141.20 Trifecta £2501.20.
Owner Mrs Johnny de la Hey **Bred** Mme Guilhaine Le Borgne **Trained** Ditcheat, Somerset

FOCUS
Any number of unexposed candidates in this competitive event, with around two-thirds of these having begun their careers in France and just three that had already run in a handicap. The pace was sound and there was drama at the final flight. Like last year, Paul Nicholls saddled a 1-2.

4721 WEATHERBYS CHAMPION BUMPER (A STANDARD OPEN NATIONAL HUNT FLAT RACE) (GRADE 1) 2m 87y

5:30 (5:30) (Class 1) 4-6-Y-O

£39,865 (£14,959; £7,490; £3,731; £1,876; £938)

Form RPR

1121 **1** **Ballyandy**[32] 4117 5-11-5 134 .... SamTwiston-Davies 136+
(Nigel Twiston-Davies) *q str: cl up bhd ldrs: trapped bhd wkng rival 4f out and dropped to midfield 3f out: rdn and rallied 2f out: chsd ldr 1f out: led nr fin: jst hld on* **5/1**[2]

2 nse **Battleford**[45] 3895 5-11-5 121 .... MPFogarty 133
(W P Mullins, Ire) *lengthy: will make a jumper: lw: trckd ldng pair: led 4f out: rdn for home over 2f out: hdd nr fin: kpt on wl fnl strides: jst failed* **25/1**

3 2 **Bacardys (FR)**[81] 3272 5-11-5 125 .... RWalsh 131
(W P Mullins, Ire) *w'like: hld up in midfield: prog over 4f out to trck ldrs 3f out: rdn and no imp 2f out: styd on fnl f to take 3rd last 100yds* **16/1**

1- **4** 1 **Castello Sforza (IRE)**[346] 5179 5-11-5 128 .... BarryGeraghty 130+
(W P Mullins, Ire) *wl plcd bhd ldrs: cl up over 2f out: rdn wl over 1f out: wandered u.p and nt qckn: styd on again ins fnl f* **11/1**

11 **5** nk **Westend Story (IRE)**[31] 4143 5-11-5 128 .... RichardJohnson 130
(Philip Hobbs) *will make a jumper: hld up in midfield: ct up in bkwash over 3f out and dropped to rr: rdn and rallied 2f out: kpt on wl fnl f: nrst fin* **20/1**

-311 **6** 1 1/4 **High Bridge**[92] 3104 5-11-5 127 .... AidanColeman 129
(John Ferguson) *lw: prom: trckd ldr over 3f out: rdn to chal wl over 1f out: fdd fnl f* **12/1**

1 **7** 1/2 **Augusta Kate**[115] 2677 5-10-12 129 .... PaulTownend 121
(W P Mullins, Ire) *medium sized: wl in tch bhd ldrs: cl up over 2f out: rdn wl over 1f out: no ex* **7/2**[1]

1/ **8** nse **Very Much So (IRE)**[687] 12 6-11-5 119 .... DavidMullins 128
(W P Mullins, Ire) *medium sized: towards rr: prog 5f out: chsd ldrs over 2f out: sn rdn: kpt on same pce and nvr able to chal* **33/1**

2 **9** 1/2 **First Figaro (GER)**[78] 3360 6-11-5 124 .... DavyRussell 128
(D K Weld, Ire) *w'like: leggy: hld up in last: stl wl in rr 3f out: sme prog over 2f out: rdn and styd on fr over 1f out despite rdr losing an iron* **16/1**

U12 **9** dht **Rather Be (IRE)**[21] 4309 5-11-5 127 .... AndrewTinkler 128
(Nicky Henderson) *athletic: lw: hld up in rr: tried to make prog on inner over 2f out: rdn and kpt on fr over 1f out: nvr gng pce to threaten* **50/1**

2-1 **11** nk **Coeur Blimey (IRE)**[89] 3138 5-11-5 129 .... LucyGardner 127
(Sue Gardner) *wl plcd bhd ldrs: urged along fr 2f out: steadily lost pl fnl f* **16/1**

12 1 **Avenir D'Une Vie (FR)**[24] 4283 6-11-5 127 .... MrPWMullins 126
(W P Mullins, Ire) *prom: poised to chal gng easily over 2f out: rdn and fnd nil over 1f out: wknd qckly fnl f* **10/1**

221 **13** 1/2 **Pride Of Lecale**[40] 3980 5-11-5 120 ....(t) PaddyBrennan 126
(Fergal O'Brien) *str: t.k.h: hld up wl in rr: prog on outer fr 6f out: cl up over 2f out: wknd over 1f out* **50/1**

-115 **14** 5 **Criq Rock (FR)**[18] 4364 5-11-5 128 .... WayneHutchinson 121
(Alan King) *hld up wl in rr: effrt over 3f out: shkn up and no prog over 2f out* **33/1**

3/ **15** 2 1/2 **Turcagua (FR)**[466] 2963 6-11-5 121 .... MsKWalsh 119
(W P Mullins, Ire) *will make a jumper: t.k.h: hld up in midfield: wl in tch bhd ldng gp over 2f out: sn wknd* **33/1**

42 **16** 1 1/2 **Onthewesternfront (IRE)**[33] 4103 6-11-5 123 .... MsNCarberry 117
(Jonjo O'Neill) *q str: will make a jumper: racd wdst of all in rr: sme prog 5f out and in midfield over 3f out: wknd over 2f out* **40/1**

1 **17** 1/2 **Compadre (IRE)**[126] 2440 5-11-5 122 .... NoelFehily 116
(Jonjo O'Neill) *hld up in midfield: no prog 3f out: wknd over 1f out* **25/1**

2 **18** 4 1/2 **Geordie Des Champs (IRE)**[18] 4357 5-11-5 110 .... LeightonAspell 112
(Rebecca Curtis) *hld up wl in rr: lost tch w ldrs 3f out: bhd fnl 2f* **100/1**

51 **19** 1/2 **Jot'em Down (IRE)**[16] 4414 5-11-5 111 .... TomScudamore 111
(David Bridgwater) *str: will make a jumper:: lw: nvr beyond midfield: lost pl and btn 3f out* **100/1**

12 **20** 1 1/4 **Ballymalin (IRE)**[41] 3952 6-11-5 124 .... RyanHatch 110
(Nigel Twiston-Davies) *hld up in rr: no prog 3f out: bhd 2f out* **100/1**

21 2 3/4 **New To This Town (IRE)**[55] 3717 5-11-5 123 .... JJBurke 107
(Mrs John Harrington, Ire) *will make a jumper: nvr bttr than midfield: dropped to rr and btn 4f out* **6/1**[3]

312 **22** 4 **Spirit Of Kayf**[39] 4001 5-11-5 112 .... DannyCook 105
(Sandy Thomson) *lw: led after 4f to 4f out: wknd rapidly over 3f out* **100/1**

23 1/2 **Winsome Bucks (IRE)**[80] 3297 6-11-5 108 ....(t) MrDLQueally 105
(T Hogan, Ire) *will make a jumper: lw: led 4f: chsd ldr tl wknd rapidly over 4f out* **66/1**

3m 47.7s (-8.70) **Going Correction** -0.45s/f (Good) **23** Ran SP% **129.0**
Speed ratings: **103,102,101,101,101 100,100,100,100,100 100,99,99,96,95 94,94,92,92,91 90,88,87**
CSF £136.17 CT £1908.56 TOTE £5.90: £2.20, £9.00, £4.20; EX 169.70 Trifecta £4371.70.
Owner Options O Syndicate **Bred** Pleasure Palace Racing **Trained** Naunton, Gloucs
■ Stewards' Enquiry : M P Fogarty thirteen-day ban: use of whip (30, 31, 1-5, 7-12) and 300euro fine

FOCUS
Always a cracking affair and once again it was a serious test. There were plenty in with a serious chance up the home straight and it ought to prove a rich source of future winners. Ballyandy may be even better than the bare result, with the next three all big improvers.
T/Jkpt: Not won. T/Plt: £36.40 to a £1 stake. Pool: £1,121,521.20. 22,440.28 winning tickets.
T/Qpdt: £20.50 to a £1 stake. Pool: 52,003.26. 1,874.12 winning tickets.
Jonathan Neesom & Tim Mitchell

4502 HUNTINGDON (R-H)

Wednesday, March 16

4722 Meeting Abandoned - Waterlogged

4715 CHELTENHAM (L-H)

Thursday, March 17

OFFICIAL GOING: Good (good to soft in places; 7.0)
Wind: Moderate; behind Weather: Fine Rails: Distances as advertised with the exception of: Races 3 & 5 add 42yds. Race 7 add 84yds.

4729 JLT NOVICES' CHASE (REGISTERED AS THE GOLDEN MILLER NOVICES' CHASE) (GRADE 1) (16 fncs) 2m 3f 198y

1:30 (1:31) (Class 1) 5-Y-O+

£74,035 (£27,781; £13,910; £6,929; £3,484; £1,742)

Form RPR

0-1F **1** **Black Hercules (IRE)**[32] 4148 7-11-4 152 .... RWalsh 164+
(W P Mullins, Ire) *lw: led tl after 2nd: trckd ldr: upsides fr 9th: hit 3 out: rdn in 1 l 2nd whn hmpd next: led narrowly last: styd on wl to draw clr* **4/1**[1]

2111 **2** 3 **Bristol De Mai (FR)**[40] 3991 5-11-4 153 .... DarylJacob 161+
(Nigel Twiston-Davies) *lw: sltly on toes: led after 2nd: awkward 3rd: hit 3 out: rdn and hdd bef next: disputing 3 l 4th jumping last: styd on into 2nd towards fin but no threat to wnr* **4/1**[1]

-112 **3** 1 **L'Ami Serge (IRE)**[33] 4126 6-11-4 148 .... NicodeBoinville 159
(Nicky Henderson) *lw: trckd ldrs: j. into wing uprt 1st: led after 3 out: wnt bdly lft next: sn rdn: hdd last: kpt on tl no ex fnl 75yds* **8/1**[3]

-315 **4** 1 1/4 **Three Musketeers (IRE)**[76] 3405 6-11-4 152 .... HarrySkelton 158
(Dan Skelton) *hld up bhd ldrs: hdwy 3 out: rdn bef next: wnt 2 1/2 l 3rd jumping last: kpt on same pce run-in* **8/1**[3]

23F2 **5** 12 **As De Mee (FR)**[40] 3991 6-11-4 145 .... SamTwiston-Davies 148
(Paul Nicholls) *hld up bhd ldrs: sltly hmpd 4 out: tk clsr order next: outpcd bef 2 out* **20/1**

30/2 **6** 23 **Mount Gunnery**[28] 4218 8-11-4 131 .... DavidMullins 129
(P A Fahy, Ire) *cmpt: prom tl 9th: dropped to last pair after 11th: wknd after 3 out* **50/1**

-311 **F** **Outlander (IRE)**[40] 4005 8-11-4 151 .... BJCooper
(W P Mullins, Ire) *hmpd s: trcking ldrs by 3rd: wnt rt 11th: gng wl enough in cl 4th whn fell 4 out* **6/1**[2]

2-34 **U** **Zabana (IRE)**[40] 4005 7-11-4 150 .... DavyRussell
(Andrew Lynch, Ire) *sideways on whn shied at tapes and uns rdr s* **8/1**[3]

-111 **F** **Garde La Victoire (FR)**[65] 3571 7-11-4 151 .... RichardJohnson
(Philip Hobbs) *hld up bhd ldrs: gng wl enough in cl 6th whn fell 4 out* **4/1**[1]

4m 55.2s (-9.00) **Going Correction** -0.025s/f (Good) **9** Ran SP% **114.3**
Speed ratings: **117,115,115,114,110 100, , ,**
CSF £20.27 CT £120.65 TOTE £4.90: £1.70, £1.80, £3.20; EX 21.40 Trifecta £181.80.
Owner Andrea & Graham Wylie **Bred** Spencer Hawkins **Trained** Muine Beag, Co Carlow

FOCUS
There was 4mm of selective watering overnight, across much of the course from the turn away from the stands to the turn into the home straight. The first race of the week on the New Course and jockeys were unanimous in calling the ground 'good' after the opener. A competitive edition of the race, up to the recent par, with only one of the runners comfortably ruled out and it was run at a fair gallop. There was an incident as the tapes went up, though, the starter letting them go as Zabana was turned sideways, and Davy Russell was unseated, with Outlander being notably impeded by the incident. The winner remains on the upgrade.

4730 PERTEMPS NETWORK FINAL (A H'CAP HURDLE) (LISTED RACE) (12 hdls) 2m 7f 213y
2:10 (2:11) (Class 1) 5-Y-0+

£51,255 (£19,233; £9,630; £4,797; £2,412; £1,206)

Form RPR

1 **Mall Dini (IRE)**[26] 4259 6-10-11 139 (t) DavyRussell 144+
(Patrick G Kelly, Ire) *midfield: hdwy appr 2 out: rdn whn chsng ldrs bef last where j.lft: sn hung lft: styd on to ld fnl 150yds: kpt on wl nr fin* **14/1**

-2P1 2 ¾ **Arpege D'Alene (FR)**[19] 4354 6-11-4 146 (t) SeanBowen 151+
(Paul Nicholls) *in tch: effrt whn chsd ldrs 2 out: edgd rt u.p between last 2: upsides whn j.lft last: sn hung lft and carried that way: styd on u.p: hld fnl strides* **14/1**

P-P1 3 hd **If In Doubt (IRE)**[82] 3254 8-11-4 146 RichardJohnson 155+
(Philip Hobbs) *hld up: hdwy 3 out: effrt and trying to chal whn n.m.r: hmpd and stmbld on long run between last 2: swtchd lft whn nt clr run appr last: styng on whn carried lft run-in: gng on at fin* **10/1**

3403 4 1 ½ **Taglietelle**[39] 4017 7-11-9 154 (b) JackKennedy(3) 157
(Gordon Elliott, Ire) *midfield: effrt and hdwy 2 out: trying to chal last: carried lft run-in: no ex towards fin* **14/1**

-42B 5 ½ **Our Kaempfer (IRE)**[117] 2641 7-10-11 139 NoelFehily 140
(Charlie Longsdon) *lw: hld up: stdy hdwy 3 out: effrt whn chsng ldrs appr last: hung lft run-in: sn edgd rt: styd on but nt pce of ldrs* **9/1**[3]

5-P 6 ½ **Rathpatrick (IRE)**[21] 4334 8-10-7 135 NiallPMadden 136
(Eoin Griffin, Ire) *in tch: chsd ldrs appr 5th: led between last 2: pressed last: hdd fnl 150yds: sn edgd rt: kpt on but hld after* **40/1**

-163 7 3 ½ **Broxbourne (IRE)**[81] 3283 7-10-10 138 (p) NicodeBoinville 136
(Nicky Henderson) *lw: midfield: rdn to go pce after 2 out: styd on fr last: nt pce to chal ldrs* **25/1**

4205 8 4 ½ **Un Ace (FR)**[48] 3844 8-10-12 140 (t) DavidBass 134
(Kim Bailey) *chsd ldrs: rdn on inner 2 out: nt qckn u.p bef last: edgd rt run-in: kpt on same pce* **16/1**

1 9 2 **Leave At Dawn (IRE)**[80] 3320 6-10-9 137 [1] BarryGeraghty 130
(C Byrnes, Ire) *midfield: mstke 3 out: effrt 2 out: kpt on u.p and stdy prog run-in: nvr able to chal* **11/2**[1]

-532 10 ½ **Join The Clan (IRE)**[40] 3992 7-10-5 140 (b) PatrickCowley(7) 132
(Jonjo O'Neill) *midfield: mstke 3rd: hdwy appr 7th: wnt 2nd 3 out: led appr 2 out: rdn and hdd between last 2: sn carried rt: wknd bef last* **25/1**

-2P2 11 3 ¼ **Warriors Tale**[39] 4017 7-10-12 140 SamTwiston-Davies 129
(Paul Nicholls) *lw: hld up: hdwy 2 out: rdn appr and nvr able to get to ldrs: one pce and no imp* **22/1**

634P 12 shd **Box Office (FR)**[26] 4246 5-10-7 135 RichieMcLernon 124
(Jonjo O'Neill) *sltly on toes: hld up in rr: rdn appr 2 out: stdy hdwy u.p bef last: styd on run-in: nt pce to trble ldrs* **28/1**

P4P4 13 ½ **Rolling Maul (IRE)**[61] 3622 8-10-2 135 (b) DavidNoonan(5) 123
(Peter Bowen) *led to 1st: chsd ldr: rdn appr 3 out: sn lost 2nd: wknd bef 2 out* **25/1**

-234 14 ¾ **Ruacana**[82] 3254 7-10-11 146 MrAlexFerguson(7) 133
(John Ferguson) *chsd ldrs: rdn after 2 out: wknd bef last* **66/1**

1UU3 15 1 ½ **Padge (IRE)**[32] 4139 7-10-10 138 PaulMoloney 124
(Evan Williams) *racd keenly: in tch: lost pl 2 out: one pce and edgd lft bef last where nt fluent: wl hld run-in* **33/1**

230- 16 5 **All Hell Let Loose (IRE)**[46] 3891 7-10-7 135 (vt) BJCooper 117
(Ms Sandra Hughes, Ire) *prom: rdn and outpcd appr 2 out: wknd on long run to last* **25/1**

17 hd **Oscar Sam (IRE)**[46] 3891 7-10-10 138 RobbiePower 119
(Mrs John Harrington, Ire) *hld up: outpcd bef 2 out: wl btn bef last* **25/1**

-P01 18 6 **Flintham**[61] 3622 7-11-0 147 (b[1]) CharlieDeutsch(5) 124
(Mark Bradstock) *led 1st: mstke 9th: rdn and hdd appr 2 out: wknd after flight* **50/1**

2122 19 3 ½ **Westren Warrior (IRE)**[48] 3844 7-10-9 137 WillKennedy 113
(Dr Richard Newland) *in rr: blnd 4th: sme hdwy after 3 out: wknd after 2 out* **20/1**

1020 P **Dubawi Island (FR)**[54] 3733 7-10-8 136 AidanColeman
(Venetia Williams) *hld up in midfield: rdn and lost pl appr 9th: wl bhd whn p.u bef 2 out* **50/1**

31-1 P **Cup Final (IRE)**[39] 4017 7-10-11 139 MarkWalsh
(Nicky Henderson) *in tch: lost pl 8th: bhd and toiling bef 2 out: wl bhd whn p.u bef last* **9/1**[3]

1115 P **Kilfinichen Bay (IRE)**[146] 2054 8-10-12 140 BrianHughes
(Charlie Longsdon) *midfield: lost pl appr 3 out: wl bhd whn p.u bef last* **66/1**

1/51 P **Saddlers Encore (IRE)**[40] 3992 7-10-7 135 TomO'Brien
(Philip Hobbs) *chsd ldrs: mstke 6th: wknd bef 2 out: wl bhd whn p.u bef last* **16/1**

13-1 P **Missed Approach (IRE)**[111] 2759 6-11-1 143 GavinSheehan
(Warren Greatrex) *lw: chsd ldrs: lost pl bef 7th: mstke 9th: wl bhd whn p.u bef last* **8/1**[2]

5m 49.2s (-11.80) **Going Correction** -0.325s/f (Good) **24** Ran SP% **131.4**
Speed ratings: **106,105,105,105,105 104,103,102,101,101 100,100,100,99,99 97,97,95,94, , ,**
CSF £171.98 CT £2083.47 TOTE £17.90: £4.10, £4.60, £2.90, £3.20; EX 258.10 Trifecta £2945.60.
Owner Philip J Reynolds **Bred** Mrs Patricia Furlong **Trained** Athenry, Co Galway

FOCUS
A new rule introduced this season meant that you needed to finish in the first six in one of the many qualifiers to gain entry for the Final. As one would expect, it had a wide-open look to it and the gallop was generous from the outset thanks to Flintham in first-time blinkers. Things got very tight in the home straight and the winner had to survive a stewards inquiry. The first two are are on the upgrade.

4731 RYANAIR CHASE (REGISTERED AS THE FESTIVAL TROPHY CHASE) (GRADE 1) (17 fncs) 2m 4f 166y
2:50 (2:51) (Class 1) 5-Y-0+

£178,538 (£66,994; £33,544; £16,709; £8,401; £4,200)

Form RPR

1-12 1 **Vautour (FR)**[82] 3231 7-11-10 176 RWalsh 178+
(W P Mullins, Ire) *warm: travelled wl: a cl up: led after 13th: qcknd clr appr 2 out: pushed along whn looking abt sn after but wl in control: v comf* **1/1**[1]

-2FU 2 6 **Valseur Lido (FR)**[40] 4007 7-11-10 161 DavidMullins 168
(W P Mullins, Ire) *mid-div: hdwy after 13th: sltly outpcd after 3 out: 4th jumping last: styd on wl to snatch 2nd cl home but no ch w wnr* **11/1**

-312 3 ½ **Road To Riches (IRE)**[40] 4007 9-11-10 165 BJCooper 168
(Noel Meade, Ire) *lw: tended to jump lft at times: led tl 3rd: prom: nt fluent 8th (water): rdn and ev ch after 3 out tl outpcd by wnr bef next: no ex whn lost 2nd cl home* **7/1**[2]

2-13 4 1 ¼ **Al Ferof (FR)**[82] 3231 11-11-10 165 HarrySkelton 167
(Dan Skelton) *mid-div: hdwy after 13th: wnt 3rd after 3 out: sn rdn: nt fluent last: kpt on but no ex whn lost 3rd run-in* **9/1**[3]

-345 5 2 ¼ **Gilgamboa (IRE)**[40] 4007 8-11-10 156 BarryGeraghty 165
(E Bolger, Ire) *mid-div: hdwy 9th: pushed along after 12th: outpcd after 3 out: styd on fr next but nt pce to get involved* **28/1**

40-1 6 3 ¼ **Taquin Du Seuil (FR)**[33] 4128 9-11-10 157 NoelFehily 164
(Jonjo O'Neill) *lw: hld up: mstke 4 out: sme hdwy next: sn rdn: hit last: styd on run-in: nvt threatened ldrs* **16/1**

2302 7 7 **Dynaste (FR)**[26] 4240 10-11-10 159 (bt) TomScudamore 155
(David Pipe) *swtg: hld up towards rr: rdn after 4 out: no imp tl r.o fr last: nvr any threat* **20/1**

4-F1 8 2 **Josses Hill (IRE)**[34] 4100 8-11-10 158 (p) NicodeBoinville 155
(Nicky Henderson) *chsd ldrs: nt fluent 12th: sn pushed along: outpcd after 3 out: wknd last* **20/1**

1111 9 3 **Village Vic (IRE)**[76] 3406 9-11-10 157 RichardJohnson 152
(Philip Hobbs) *led 3rd: rchd for 11th: hdd after 13th: cl 3rd whn mstke 3 out: wknd bef next* **20/1**

F-10 10 15 **Oscar Rock (IRE)**[124] 2483 8-11-10 153 (b) BrianHughes 140
(Malcolm Jefferson) *hit 2nd: a towards rr* **66/1**

-161 11 3 ¼ **Annacotty (IRE)**[47] 3851 8-11-10 157 (p) IanPopham 138
(Alan King) *sn pushed along to hold pl in mid-div: lost pl 9th: in rr fr 12th* **40/1**

P/43 12 6 **Captain Conan (FR)**[33] 4114 9-11-10 147 (p) AndrewTinkler 130
(Nicky Henderson) *mid-div: struggling 11th: wknd 4 out* **100/1**

3-11 P **Smashing (FR)**[33] 4131 7-11-10 159 JJBurke
(Henry De Bromhead, Ire) *on toes: trckd ldrs: hit 11th: wknd after 3 out: p.u bef next* **20/1**

-2PF P **Champagne West (IRE)**[19] 4361 8-11-10 154 TomO'Brien
(Philip Hobbs) *a outpcd in rr: t.o whn p.u bef 11th* **50/1**

1334 F **Vibrato Valtat (FR)**[54] 3734 7-11-10 161 (t) SamTwiston-Davies
(Paul Nicholls) *mid-div: travelling comf in 9th whn fell 4 out* **33/1**

5m 5.5s (-10.20) **Going Correction** -0.025s/f (Good) **15** Ran **SP% 119.0**
Speed ratings: **118,115,115,115,114 112,110,109,108,102 101,99, , ,**
CSF £10.23 CT £56.78 TOTE £1.80: £1.50, £3.10, £2.00; EX 13.40 Trifecta £48.60.
Owner Mrs S Ricci **Bred** Haras De Saint Voir & Patrick Joubert **Trained** Muine Beag, Co Carlow
■ Stewards' Enquiry : David Mullins two-day ban: use of whip (31 Mar and 1 Apr)

FOCUS
Due to rail movements this was run over 42yds further than advertised. A very different looking race to the one expected a week or so earlier, but it made for what was undoubtedly the strongest edition of the race to date. Run at a proper good gallop, it produced the most stunning performance of the week until this point, the favourite confirming himself to be the best chaser in training and also becoming the first Irish-trained winner of the race. The winner has been rated similar to his King George run.

4732 RYANAIR WORLD HURDLE (GRADE 1) (12 hdls) 2m 7f 213y
3:30 (3:30) (Class 1) 4-Y-0+

£170,850 (£64,110; £32,100; £15,990; £8,040; £4,020)

Form RPR

2111 1 **Thistlecrack**[47] 3853 8-11-10 168 TomScudamore 178+
(Colin Tizzard) *lw: midfield: hdwy appr 7th: wnt 2nd bef 3 out: led on bit jst bef 2 out: a travelling strly: effrtlessly wnt clr run-in: impressive* **1/1**[1]

2221 2 7 **Alpha Des Obeaux (FR)**[56] 3713 6-11-10 156 BJCooper 170
(M F Morris, Ire) *lw: hld up in tch: trckd ldrs 3 out: wnt 2nd 2 out: rdn and briefly tried to chal on bnd between last 2: outpcd by impressive wnr last: kpt on and clr of others but no ch* **8/1**[3]

-166 3 22 **Bobs Worth (IRE)**[76] 3408 11-11-10 150 DavidBass 150
(Nicky Henderson) *in tch: lost pl 9th: outpcd bef 2 out: edgd lft and styd on appr last: tk 3rd run-in but no ch w front two* **33/1**

2-33 4 1 ¾ **Cole Harden (IRE)**[76] 3408 7-11-10 164 (t) GavinSheehan 148
(Warren Greatrex) *lw: led: rdn and hdd jst bef 2 out: outpcd by front pair between last 2: wl hld and lost 3rd run-in* **15/2**[2]

1- 5 9 **Aux Ptits Soins (FR)**[372] 4704 6-11-10 152 NickScholfield 141
(Paul Nicholls) *hld up: hdwy 3 out: trckd ldrs bef 2 out: rdn and outpcd between last 2: wl hld last: wknd* **16/1**

-155 6 4 ½ **Saphir Du Rheu (FR)**[89] 3149 7-11-10 161 SamTwiston-Davies 138
(Paul Nicholls) *in tch: lost pl 3 out: outpcd whn hit 2 out: wl btn after* **11/1**

1-33 7 ¾ **Martello Tower (IRE)**[56] 3713 8-11-10 150 APHeskin 135
(Ms Margaret Mullins, Ire) *prom: pushed along appr 2 out: wknd after flight* **14/1**

1-5P 8 ¾ **Whisper (FR)**[76] 3408 8-11-10 164 NicodeBoinville 137
(Nicky Henderson) *bit edgy: hld up: mstke 8th: sn pushed along: wknd after 2 out: eased whn wl btn bef last* **9/1**

P-24 P **Knockara Beau (IRE)**[47] 3853 13-11-10 140 LiamTreadwell
(George Charlton) *prom to 4th: bhd and detached after 6th: t.o 9th: p.u bef last* **100/1**

4-24 P **At Fishers Cross (IRE)**[26] 4244 9-11-10 152 (b) BarryGeraghty
(Rebecca Curtis) *nt fluent: midfield: pushed along after 5th: lost pl 7th: bhd 9th: t.o whn p.u bef 3 out* **33/1**

10-1 P **Kilcooley (IRE)**[138] 2198 7-11-10 164 (t) RichardJohnson
(Charlie Longsdon) *trckd ldrs: wnt 2nd 4th: losing pl whn blnd 3 out: t.o whn p.u bef 2 out* **20/1**

0-42 **P** **Lieutenant Colonel**[32] 4146 7-11-10 155........................(t) DavyRussell
(Ms Sandra Hughes, Ire) *hld up: mstke 7th: rdn whn blnd and nrly uns rdr 3 out: nt rcvr and sn p.u* **33/1**

5m 42.6s (-18.40) **Going Correction** -0.325s/f (Good) **12** Ran SP% **118.3**
Speed ratings (Par 117): **117,114,107,106,103 102,102,101, ,**
CSF £8.82 CT £170.82 TOTE £1.70: £1.10, £2.70, £6.90; EX 9.80 Trifecta £500.40.

Owner John and Heather Snook **Bred** R F And S D Knipe **Trained** Milborne Port, Dorset

FOCUS
This race has arguably produced some of the most fondly remembered hurdlers in recent times, mainly because the likes of Baracouda, Inglis Drever and Big Buck's came back and successfully defended their crown at least once. The 2014 renewal saw this year's Champion Hurdle winner Annie Power go close to taking the prize on her first visit to the Cheltenham festival. The pace was good throughout and the winning time was over six seconds faster than the Pertemps Final. This has been rated the best performance by a hurdler on RPRs at the festival in 30 years.

4733 BROWN ADVISORY & MERRIEBELLE STABLE PLATE (A H'CAP CHASE) (GRADE 3) (17 fncs) 2m 4f 166y
4:10 (4:12) (Class 1) 5-Y-O+

£56,950 (£21,370; £10,700; £5,330; £2,680; £1,340)

Form RPR

-FP1 **1** **Empire Of Dirt (IRE)**[60] 3651 9-10-11 **142**............................. BJCooper 154+
(C A Murphy, Ire) *lw: hld up bhd: bdly hmpd 3rd: stdy prog fr 11th: led appr 2 out: sn rdn: wandered run-in but wl in command: readily* **16/1**

161- **2** *4* **Tango De Juilley (FR)**[348] 5130 8-11-1 **149**................. JackKennedy(3) 153
(Venetia Williams) *sltly on toes: mid-div: hdwy after 7th: lft 4th 4 out: rdn to dispute 3rd after 3 out: styd on to go 2nd towards fin but no ch w wnr* **33/1**

6-0P **3** *1 ¼* **Kings Palace (IRE)**[19] 4354 8-11-5 **150**...................(tp) TomScudamore 154
(David Pipe) *lw: racd wd most of way: mid-div: hdwy 8th: pressed ldr fr 12th: slt ld whn hit 3 out: rdn and hdd bef next: ev ch last: sn no ex: lost 2nd towards fin* **11/1**

001P **4** *2 ½* **Full Shift (FR)**[39] 4011 7-10-4 **135**............................ MarkWalsh 137
(Nicky Henderson) *in tch: hit 5th: rdn after 4 out: wnt 6th after 3 out: cl 4th at the next: drifted lft and styd on same pce fr last* **7/1**[2]

-403 **5** *2 ¾* **Ballycasey (IRE)**[33] 4131 9-11-2 **147**..............................(p) RWalsh 146
(W P Mullins, Ire) *hld up towards rr: stdy hdwy fr 13th: hmpd 4 out: disp 5th appr 2 out: rdn between last 2: styd on same pce* **10/1**

1450 **6** *2 ¼* **Astracad (FR)**[96] 3030 10-9-13 **135**.........................(t) JamieBargary(5) 133
(Nigel Twiston-Davies) *in tch: hit 7th: rdn to chse ldrs after 3 out: styng on at same pce disputing 5th whn blnd last* **33/1**

35PP **7** *1* **Ballynagour (IRE)**[33] 4113 10-11-7 **157**..............(t) DavidNoonan(5) 156+
(David Pipe) *hld up bhd: hmpd 8th: hdwy 4 out: rdn to chse ldrs whn nt fluent 2 out: styd on same pce fr last* **20/1**

0051 **8** *15* **Sew On Target (IRE)**[40] 3996 11-10-9 **140**..............(t) BrendanPowell 124
(Colin Tizzard) *led tl 3 out: sn drvn disputing 3rd bef next: wknd between last 2* **25/1**

P-P1 **9** *1 ¾* **Dare Me (IRE)**[54] 3735 12-11-0 **145**.......................... AlainCawley 127
(Venetia Williams) *mid-div: nt fluent 4th: towards rr 8th: no threat after* **50/1**

2-0P **10** *4* **Baily Green (IRE)**[67] 3552 10-11-5 **150**.........................(t) MarkEnright 127
(M F Morris, Ire) *mid-div: hdwy 10th: rdn to dispute 2nd after 3 out tl jst bef next: wknd between last 2* **33/1**

1646 **11** *shd* **Salubrious (IRE)**[47] 3851 9-10-9 **140**......................... SeanBowen 120
(Paul Nicholls) *swtg: mstke 7th: hmpd 3 out: a in rr* **16/1**

0/56 **12** *4* **Buckers Bridge (IRE)**[56] 3715 10-10-10 **141**.................. JJBurke 114
(Henry De Bromhead, Ire) *trckd ldrs: losing pl whn nt fluent 12th: hmpd 4 out: sn wknd* **20/1**

6PP2 **F** **Quincy Des Pictons (FR)**[15] 4432 12-10-6 **137**.............. WillKennedy
(Alan Jones) *a towards rr: fell 4 out* **100/1**

0-P2 **F** **Niceonefrankie**[33] 4128 10-10-9 **145**...................... CharlieDeutsch(5)
(Venetia Williams) *prom: pushed along in cl 3rd whn fell 4 out: fatally injured* **20/1**

1B-P **F** **Darna**[124] 2483 10-10-13 **144**.......................................(t) DavidBass
(Kim Bailey) *trcking ldrs whn fell heavily 8th* **25/1**

2044 **P** **Kings Lad (IRE)**[34] 4100 9-10-9 **140**...........................(t) DarylJacob
(Colin Tizzard) *towards rr of midfield: bdly hmpd 8th: nvr travelling after: blnd v bdly 11th: sn p.u* **33/1**

1040 **B** **Bear's Affair (IRE)**[97] 3018 10-11-3 **148**.................... PeterCarberry
(Nicky Henderson) *mid-div whn b.d 8th* **40/1**

4332 **P** **Fingal Bay (IRE)**[32] 4141 10-10-10 **141**...................(bt[1]) RichardJohnson
(Philip Hobbs) *towards rr of midfield: hit 6th: nt fluent next: v bdly hmpd 8th: p.u bef next* **8/1**[3]

0064 **P** **Johns Spirit (IRE)**[47] 3851 9-11-0 **145**..................... RichieMcLernon
(Jonjo O'Neill) *mid-div: trckd ldrs 7th: nt fluent 9th: mstke next and 11th: losing pl qckly whn p.u after 12th* **11/2**[1]

100P **F** **Little Jon**[12] 4485 8-10-9 **143**.....................................(p) RyanHatch(3)
(Nigel Twiston-Davies) *mid-div: lost pl 3rd: blnd 5th: virtually b.d 4 out: t.o whn fell next* **33/1**

1600 **P** **Art Mauresque (FR)**[12] 4485 6-10-13 **144**................... NickScholfield
(Paul Nicholls) *lw: in tch: lost pl after 7th: towards rr whn mstke next: t.o whn p.u bef 3 out* **11/1**

12F1 **F** **Stilletto (IRE)**[28] 4212 7-10-11 **142**..................... SamTwiston-Davies
(Paul Nicholls) *lw: hld up towards rr: fell 3rd* **11/2**[1]

5m 13.1s (-2.60) **Going Correction** -0.025s/f (Good) **22** Ran SP% **134.0**
Speed ratings: **103,101,101,100,99 98,97,92,91,89 89,88, , , , , , ,**
CSF £471.74 CT £5978.41 TOTE £19.00: £4.30, £7.40, £3.40, £2.90; EX 796.80 Trifecta £11936.70.

Owner Gigginstown House Stud **Bred** Sean Harnedy **Trained** Gorey, Co Wexford

■ Stewards' Enquiry : Charlie Deutsch one-day ban: allowed their horses to break into canter (31 Mar)

David Bass one-day ban: allowed their horses to break into canter (31 Mar)

Jamie Bargary one-day ban: allowed their horses to break into canter (31 Mar)

Mark Enright one-day ban: allowed their horses to break into canter (31 Mar)

J J Burke two-day ban: allowed their horses to break into canter (31 Mar and 1 Apr)

Nick Scholfield one-day ban: allowed their horses to break into canter (31 Mar)

FOCUS
Due to rail movements this was run over 42yds further than advertised. Traditionally an ultra-competitive handicap chase, this year's edition looked no different, with it being run at a good gallop and full of incident, with lots of fallers and mistakes a feature. Plenty had their chance in the straight. This was a step up from the winner who could go on to rate higher.

4734 TRULL HOUSE STUD MARES' NOVICES' HURDLE (REGISTERED AS DAWN RUN MARES' NOVICES' HURDLE) (GRADE 2) (8 hdls) 2m 179y
4:50 (4:51) (Class 1) 4-Y-O+

£42,712 (£16,027; £8,025; £3,997; £2,010; £1,005)

Form RPR

1 **1** **Limini (IRE)**[47] 3873 5-11-7 145... RWalsh 148+
(W P Mullins, Ire) *athletic: trckd ldrs: gng wl whn swtchd lft appr last and led jst bef flight: qcknd clr run-in: r.o impressively* **8/11**[1]

22-2 **2** *4 ½* **Dusky Legend**[106] 2852 6-11-2 123.......................... WayneHutchinson 134
(Alan King) *midfield: hdwy appr 2 out: led on long run to last: hdd jst bef flight: kpt on but unable to go w wnr run-in* **50/1**

1 **3** *2 ½* **Bloody Mary (FR)**[44] 3915 5-11-7 0......................... BarryGeraghty 139+
(Nicky Henderson) *neat: prom: nt fluent 3rd: shkn up appr 2 out: led on bnd between last 2: sn hdd: rdn and stl in cl contention last: styd on same pce fnl 100yds* **7/1**[3]

1-12 **4** *½* **Robins Reef (IRE)**[110] 2776 6-11-2 125........................ AndrewTinkler 133
(Nicky Henderson) *will make a chaser: midfield: j. slowly 4th: outpcd after 5th: rallied bef 2 out: chsng ldrs whn swtchd lft appr last: nt qckn run-in: styd on u.p towards fin* **25/1**

22F2 **5** *1 ¾* **Bantam (IRE)**[35] 4064 6-11-2 130........................... RichardJohnson 130
(Henry Daly) *hld up: hdwy after 2 out: chsd ldrs on inner bef last: styd on same pce fnl 100yds* **50/1**

3 **6** *3* **Water Sprite (IRE)**[28] 4202 5-11-2 114..............................(t) JackKennedy 127
(Gordon Elliott, Ire) *hld up: pushed along after 5th: hdwy 2 out: chsd ldrs appr last: no imp and one pce run-in* **100/1**

1151 **7** *7* **Tea In Transvaal (IRE)**[110] 2778 5-11-7 138.................. PaulMoloney 126
(Evan Williams) *w ldr: led bef 2 out: rdn and hdd on bnd between last 2: wknd appr last* **16/1**

1113 **8** *¾* **Actinpieces**[27] 4231 5-11-2 131........................... MissGAndrews 120
(Pam Sly) *trckd ldrs: lost pl 2 out: sn outpcd: n.d after* **33/1**

1521 **9** *2 ¼* **Girly Girl (IRE)**[20] 4337 7-11-2 127......................... HarrySkelton 120
(Dan Skelton) *hld up: hit 2nd: no bttr than midfield bef last where j.lft: nvr able to trble ldrs* **50/1**

12-1 **10** *1 ¼* **Chocca Wocca**[25] 4271 6-11-2 0...............................(t) NicodeBoinville 117
(Nicky Henderson) *hld up in midfield: effrt after 2 out to chse ldng bunch: unable to chal: wknd bef last* **10/1**

U4-3 **11** *2 ½* **Whistle Dixie (IRE)**[47] 3873 6-11-2 124..............................(t) BJCooper 115
(Gordon Elliott, Ire) *q tall: will make a chaser: midfield: pushed along briefly after 4th: rdn and outpcd after 3 out: hdwy 2 out: nvr able to get to ldrs: wknd bef last* **16/1**

2-1 **12** *9* **Danielle's Journey**[30] 4164 6-11-2 124..........................(t) BrianHughes 108
(S R B Crawford, Ire) *hld up: struggling whn nt fluent 2 out: nvr a threat* **66/1**

1311 **13** *5* **Smart Talk (IRE)**[47] 3858 6-11-7 149.......................... PaddyBrennan 111
(Brian Ellison) *led: hdd bef 2 out: sn wknd* **6/1**[2]

14 *1* **Jaune Et Bleue (FR)**[64] 4-10-9 0................................ NoelFehily 94
(David Dennis) *midfield: lost pl 2 out: n.d after* **66/1**

1312 **15** *1 ¾* **Awesome Rosie**[25] 4271 5-11-2 122............................ TomBellamy 100
(Alan King) *hld up: struggling after 2 out: nvr a threat* **50/1**

P **Why Wait (FR)**[48] 4-10-12 0................................ JamesReveley
(J-Y Artu, France) *w'like: swtg: in tch: chsd ldrs 3rd: wknd qckly appr 2 out: t.o whn p.u bef last* **100/1**

3m 58.0s (-13.30) **Going Correction** -0.325s/f (Good)
WFA 4 from 5yo+ 7lb **16** Ran SP% **125.1**
Speed ratings (Par 115): **118,115,114,114,113 112,108,108,107,106 105,101,99,98,97**
CSF £65.66 CT £194.65 TOTE £1.70: £1.20, £11.90, £1.80; EX 47.90 Trifecta £353.50.

Owner Mrs S Ricci **Bred** Sir E J Loder **Trained** Muine Beag, Co Carlow

FOCUS
The first running of a race designed to bring together the best novice fillies and mares was rewarded with a large field and contained plenty of promising types, not least the market leader. It remains to be seen whether it becomes a trend, but two of the first three were carrying penalties, albeit they were first and third in the betting. The winner is on the upgrade and looks a potential 155 hurdler.

4735 FULKE WALWYN KIM MUIR CHALLENGE CUP H'CAP CHASE (AMATEUR RIDERS) (21 fncs) 3m 2f
5:30 (5:31) (Class 2) (0-145,145) 5-Y-O+

£38,974 (£12,174; £6,084; £3,042; £1,521; £767)

Form RPR

-005 **1** **Cause Of Causes (USA)**[25] 4281 8-11-9 **142**..............(tp) MrJJCodd 156+
(Gordon Elliott, Ire) *hld up towards rr: dropped to last and nudged along 13th: pushed along and sme prog after 4 out: str run u.p after next to ld 2 out: forged clr: easily* **9/2**[2]

5302 **2** *12* **A Good Skin (IRE)**[34] 4101 7-11-2 **138**....................... MrMLegg(3) 142
(Tom George) *mid-div: hit 13th: rdn after 18th: hdwy after 3 out: styd on fr next: snatched 2nd nring fin: no ch w wnr* **14/1**

-U11 **3** *½* **Silvergrove**[34] 4101 8-11-5 **138**................................(t) MrTomDavid 141
(Ben Pauling) *disp ld tl 11th: trckd ldr: disp ld again after 16th tl next: prom: rdn to chse ldr after next: chsd wnr but hld between last 2: no ex whn lost 2nd nring fin* **16/1**

214F **4** *5* **Knock House (IRE)**[40] 3993 7-11-11 **144**........................(p) MsNCarberry 147+
(Mick Channon) *hld up towards rr: in last pair whn bdly hmpd 13th: hdwy after 3 out: nt fluent next: styd on fr last: wnt 4th nring fin* **16/1**

24-4 **5** *1* **Amigo (FR)**[293] 532 9-11-2 **135**..............................(bt) MissGAndrews 133
(David Pipe) *prom: hit 10th: led 17th: rdn clr after 3 out tl hdd next: no ex fr last* **33/1**

-4P5 **6** *2 ¾* **Indian Castle (IRE)**[76] 3404 8-11-1 **134**...........................(p) MrJJKing 129
(Ian Williams) *mid-div: hdwy after 4 out: rdn into 3rd after 3 out tl next: one pce after* **16/1**

-421 **7** *2* **Midnight Prayer**[32] 4140 11-11-4 **142**.................. MrJoshuaNewman(5) 134
(Alan King) *mid-div: hdwy to trck ldrs 14th: blnd 4 out: sn rdn: one pce fr 2 out* **33/1**

4-F1 **8** *3* **Sambremont (FR)**[32] 4145 6-11-6 **139**......................... MrPWMullins 132
(W P Mullins, Ire) *mid-div: hit 13th and 16th: rdn and sme prog after 3 out: nvr threatened ldrs: fdd bef last* **14/1**

212P **9** *4 ½* **Upswing (IRE)**[68] 3518 8-11-6 **139**........................ MrDerekO'Connor 128
(Jonjo O'Neill) *lw: hld up towards rr: hdwy after 4 out: rdn after 3 out: nvr threatened ldrs: wknd next* **8/1**

-251 **10** ¾ **Perfect Candidate (IRE)**[76] 3404 9-11-7 **143**............(t) MissAEStirling[(3)] 132
(Fergal O'Brien) *hmpd 1st: towards rr most of way: sltly hmpd 4 out: styd on past btn horses fr 2 out: nvr any danger* **33/1**

P-0P **11** 12 **Corrin Wood (IRE)**[28] 4205 9-11-2 **135**.................(tp) MrSGCarey 109
(Donald McCain) *trckd ldrs: rdn to dispute 3rd appr 3 out: wknd 2 out* **50/1**

0UP3 **12** 7 **Splash Of Ginge**[33] 4113 8-11-3 **141**..............(v) MrJJSlevin[(5)] 109
(Nigel Twiston-Davies) *disp tl 11th: lost pl 13th: mstke 16th: sn wknd* **25/1**

0042 **13** 4½ **The Giant Bolster**[33] 4113 11-11-6 **139**.................. MrFMaguire 113
(David Bridgwater) *trckd ldrs: hmpd 4 out: outpcd next: no ch whn hmpd 2 out* **7/1**[3]

-042 **14** 7 **Grandads Horse**[22] 4306 10-11-3 **136**...............(p) MrSWaley-Cohen 93
(Charlie Longsdon) *mid-div: rdn appr 3 out: sn wknd* **20/1**

50-3 **15** 9 **Mon Parrain (FR)**[97] 3016 10-11-7 **145**.............(bt) MrDavidMaxwell[(5)] 94
(Paul Nicholls) *trckd ldrs: led 11th tl 16th: wknd after next* **40/1**

4U51 **P** **Ericht (IRE)**[19] 4363 10-11-2 **135**....................(p) MrDGLavery
(Nicky Henderson) *towards rr of mid-div: wknd 13th: p.u bef 17th* **33/1**

2451 **F** **Top Wood (FR)**[14] 4444 9-11-5 **138** 5ex.....................(bt) MsKWalsh
(David Pipe) *lw: mid-div: trckd ldrs 8th: disputing cl 2nd whn fell 4 out* **25/1**

0443 **F** **Lost Legend (IRE)**[47] 3851 9-11-7 **140**.....................(v) MrSClements
(Jonjo O'Neill) *mid-div: disputing 7th and creeping clsr whn fell 4 out* **33/1**

P554 **U** **The Job Is Right**[56] 3715 8-11-2 **142**..............(b) MrRobertJames[(7)]
(Michael Hourigan, Ire) *towards rr of mid-div: virtually fell whn unseating rdr 13th* **25/1**

0221 **U** **Doctor Harper (IRE)**[51] 3786 8-11-8 **141**.................. MrWBiddick 115
(David Pipe) *hld up towards rr: blnd 1st: hit 16th: mid-div: 18th: rdn after 4 out: nvr threatened: wknd after next: awkward whn uns rdr 2 out* **4/1**[1]

-153 **P** **Capard King (IRE)**[26] 4247 7-11-5 **138**.................... MrROHarding
(Jonjo O'Neill) *mid-div: towards rr fr 10th: t.o whn p.u bef 2 out* **50/1**

2314 **P** **Alternatif (FR)**[76] 3404 6-11-4 **137**........................(b) MrRPQuinlan
(David Pipe) *towards rr of midfield: nt fluent 3rd: wknd 4 out: t.o whn p.u bef 2 out* **25/1**

6m 43.8s (-2.20) **Going Correction** -0.025s/f (Good) **22 Ran SP% 134.0**
Speed ratings: **102,98,98,96,96 95,94,93,92,92 88,86,85,82,80 , , , ,**
CSF £60.03 CT £976.89 TOTE £5.40: £1.80, £4.20, £4.30, £4.10; EX 89.90 Trifecta £1583.00.
Owner John P McManus **Bred** Flaxman Holdings Limited **Trained** Longwood, Co Meath

FOCUS
Due to rail movements this was run over 84yds further than advertised. This looked a strong edition of the race, with at least a handful appealing as being really well handicapped, and with plenty wanting to lead it was always going to be run at a true gallop. This was a step up from the winner.
T/Jkpt: £14,200.00 to a £1 stake. Pool: £100,000.00 - 5.00 winning tickets. T/Plt: £62.50 to a £1 stake. Pool: £1,081,279.50 - 12,621.89 winning tickets. T/Qpdt: £8.80 to a £1 stake. Pool: £58,048.35 - 4,872.27 winning tickets. **Tim Mitchell & Darren Owen**

2474 HEXHAM (L-H)
Thursday, March 17

OFFICIAL GOING: Heavy (soft in places; 5.7)
Wind: Light, half against Weather: Fine, dry

4736 BOOK YOUR TICKETS FOR LADIES DAY CONDITIONAL JOCKEYS' MARES' H'CAP HURDLE (8 hdls) 2m 48y
1:55 (1:56) (Class 4) (0-110,110) 4-Y-O+ £3,422 (£997; £499)

Form RPR

2611 **1** **Beyondtemptation**[16] 4415 8-10-9 **93**..............(t) DiarmuidO'Regan 99+
(Jonathan Haynes) *led: hit 3 out: hdd next: drvn and outpcd between last 2: rallied to regain ld run-in: edgd lft: drvn out* **10/11**[1]

4U65 **2** 4½ **Roja Dove (IRE)**[11] 4512 7-11-12 **110**...................(b[1]) JoeColliver 112+
(David Thompson) *chsd clr ldng pair: hdwy 3rd: wnt 2nd after 3 out: led next: rdn and 3 l clr whn hit last: hdd run-in: no ex* **11/1**

60-6 **3** 7 **This Thyne Jude**[38] 4031 8-10-5 **89**.................... GrantCockburn 82
(Lucy Normile) *hld up in last pl: nt fluent 1st: rdn and outpcd 3 out: rallied bef last: sn no imp* **6/1**[3]

5646 **4** 22 **Morning With Ivan (IRE)**[9] 4550 6-10-8 **92**............(b[1]) CraigNichol 63
(Martin Todhunter) *t.k.h: pressed wnr: mstke 1st: rdn and outpcd bef 2 out: wknd bef last* **2/1**[2]

4m 38.2s (20.80) **Going Correction** +1.40s/f (Heav) **4 Ran SP% 108.3**
Speed ratings (Par 105): **104,101,98,87**
CSF £8.86 TOTE £1.90; EX 7.10 Trifecta £17.50.
Owner J C Haynes **Bred** J C Haynes **Trained** Low Row, Cumbria

FOCUS
Race distance increased by 39yds. Officially heavy ground, soft in places and described by the winning rider as tacky, dead in places. This was a ordinary mares-only handicap hurdle but it was run at a fair pace. The winner is in the form of her life.

4737 BECOME AN ANNUAL MEMBER "NATIONAL HUNT" MARES' NOVICES' HURDLE (8 hdls) 2m 48y
2:35 (2:36) (Class 4) 4-Y-O+ £3,422 (£997; £499)

Form RPR

-1P2 **1** **My Little Cracker (IRE)**[30] 4164 6-11-0 0.................... BrianHarding 121+
(Iain Jardine) *chsd ldr: chal 3 out: led next: shkn up and sn drew clr: easily* **2/1**[2]

F13 **2** 33 **Flemensfirthleader**[8] 4555 7-11-0 0.......................... CraigNichol 86
(Keith Dalgleish) *t.k.h: led: jnd 3 out: hdd next: sn rdn and outpcd: hit last: drvn and hld on for 2nd towards fin* **1/2**[1]

4045 **3** 1¼ **Dance And Romance**[11] 4509 4-10-7 0.......................... DerekFox 77
(Tim Easterby) *in tch: drvn and outpcd bef 4 out: plugged on u.p fr 2 out: nvr on terms* **18/1**[3]

6-0P **P** **Beau Marsh**[36] 4050 7-11-0 0.............................. SeanQuinlan
(Barry Murtagh) *nt fluent in rr: hit and struggling fr 3rd: sn lost tch: t.o whn p.u bef last* **100/1**

4m 38.4s (21.00) **Going Correction** +1.40s/f (Heav)
WFA 4 from 6yo+ 7lb **4 Ran SP% 106.3**
Speed ratings (Par 105): **103,86,85,**
CSF £3.42 TOTE £2.50; EX 4.50 Trifecta £4.50.
Owner Paul & Clare Rooney **Bred** Martin Sheridan **Trained** Carruthertown, D'fries & G'way

FOCUS
Race distance increased by 39yds. A mares' novice race run at a fair pace, but an inconclusive result.

4738 RACE SPONSORSHIP TO CELEBRATE ANY OCCASION NOVICES' H'CAP CHASE (17 fncs 2 omitted) 3m 41y
3:15 (3:15) (Class 4) (0-105,101) 5-Y-O+ £3,768 (£1,106; £553; £276)

Form RPR

4P32 **1** **The Bishop (IRE)**[36] 4051 8-10-7 **89**.................... MrKitAlexander[(7)] 99+
(N W Alexander) *w ldrs thrght: led 2 out: sn hrd pressed: styd on gamely u.p fr last* **9/4**[1]

4-45 **2** 2¼ **Spring Over (IRE)**[36] 4051 10-10-9 **84**.........................(t) DerekFox 91
(Ian Duncan) *w ldrs: led 8th to next: pushed along and outpcd 3 out: rallied to chal after next: nt fluent last: kpt on to take 2nd cl home* **14/1**

2535 **3** nk **Trouble In Paris (IRE)**[57] 3679 9-9-7 **75** oh9.........(bt) LorcanMurtagh[(7)] 83
(Barry Murtagh) *hld up: hit 12th: smooth hdwy to trck ldrs after 2 out: chal bef last: rdn and edgd lft run-in: no ex and lost 2nd cl home* **12/1**

4311 **4** 3¾ **Cheat The Cheater (IRE)**[20] 4346 9-11-9 **101**.......(tp) ConorShoemark[(3)] 104
(Claire Dyson) *chsd ldrs: sn pushed along: hdwy to ld 9th: rdn and hdd bef 3 out: outpcd after next: plugged on fr last: no imp* **5/1**[3]

2654 **5** 17 **Joseph Mercer (IRE)**[18] 4387 9-10-8 **83**...........(p) JonathanEngland 71
(Tina Jackson) *led to 8th: cl up: rdn and hdwy to ld bef 3 out to next: sn drvn and outpcd: btn last* **7/1**

0032 **P** **Moscow Presents (IRE)**[11] 4510 8-11-4 **96**..............(p) AdamNicol[(3)]
(Philip Kirby) *prom: stmbld 2nd: shkn up whn j.lft and outpcd 4 out: struggling fr next: lost tch and p.u bef last* **11/4**[2]

5066 **U** **Red Piano**[6] 4581 7-10-5 **87**.............................. MrWHRReed[(7)]
(Andrew Hamilton) *hld up: mstke and uns rdr 2nd* **16/1**

06-P **P** **Maz Majecc (IRE)**[47] 3864 7-10-4 **86**.................... MrSPKelly[(7)]
(Noel C Kelly, Ire) *hld up: hit 6th: outpcd and hung lft 10th: losing tch whn j. slowly 13th: sn p.u* **9/1**

7m 18.2s (46.00) **Going Correction** +1.95s/f (Heav) **8 Ran SP% 116.8**
Speed ratings: **101,100,100,98,93 , ,**
CSF £32.13 CT £316.92 TOTE £3.20: £1.30, £3.10, £3.00; EX 41.50 Trifecta £322.30.
Owner Turcan Barber Fletcher Dunning **Bred** Raymond McGlinchey **Trained** Kinneston, Perth & Kinross

FOCUS
Race distance increased by 78yds. A low-grade but quite competitive staying handicap chase run at just an ordinary gallop.

4739 HAVE YOUR WEDDING AT HEXHAM RACECOURSE H'CAP HURDLE (12 hdls) 2m 7f 63y
3:55 (3:55) (Class 5) (0-100,104) 4-Y-O+ £2,600 (£758; £379)

Form RPR

0001 **1** **Beer Goggles (IRE)**[11] 4510 5-12-2 **104** 7ex.............. JoeColliver[(3)] 118+
(Micky Hammond) *hld up bhd ldng gp: nt fluent 3 out: pushed along and outpcd next: rallied to ld last: edgd rt and pushed clr* **9/4**[1]

0015 **2** 8 **Newyearsresolution (IRE)**[24] 4289 12-10-1 **79**........... MissAWaugh[(7)] 81
(Simon Waugh) *led: pushed along after 2 out: hdd last: plugged on: nt pce of wnr* **8/1**[3]

5234 **3** ¾ **More Madness (IRE)**[17] 4407 9-10-11 **89**..............(v) MrKitAlexander[(7)] 89
(N W Alexander) *chsd ldr to 3 out: rdn and regained 2nd after next: effrt and ev ch briefly bef last: outpcd run-in* **9/4**[1]

54P5 **4** 28 **Massini's Lady**[30] 4163 5-10-13 **89**...................... StephenMulqueen[(5)] 61
(N W Alexander) *rn in snatches: prom: wnt 2nd 3 out to next: drvn and wknd bef last* **9/1**

P000 **5** 25 **Kilmainham (IRE)**[16] 4415 8-11-1 **86**.......................... HenryBrooke 33
(Martin Todhunter) *hld up in tch: outpcd after 3 out: shortlived effrt bef last: sn no imp* **12/1**

PP54 **P** **Master Murphy (IRE)**[24] 4289 11-10-6 **77**..................(p) PeterBuchanan
(Jane Walton) *chsd ldrs: lost pl 7th: struggling after next: t.o whn p.u bef 2 out* **6/1**[2]

-4P6 **P** **Bolton Blue (IRE)**[58] 3668 7-11-4 **92**..........................(t) AdamNicol[(3)]
(Katie Scott) *hld up: outpcd bef 3 out: lost tch next: t.o whn p.u bef last* **16/1**

6m 45.3s (36.30) **Going Correction** +1.675s/f (Heav) **7 Ran SP% 110.5**
Speed ratings (Par 103): **103,100,99,90,81**
CSF £18.68 TOTE £3.00: £1.80, £2.20; EX 16.80 Trifecta £48.30.
Owner Richard & Katherine Gilbert **Bred** Cathal Ennis **Trained** Middleham, N Yorks

FOCUS
Race distance increased by 78yds. A modest staying handicap hurdle run at a fair gallop with a progressive winner.

4740 PERFECT LOCATION FOR YOUR BUSINESS MEETING H'CAP CHASE (21 fncs 4 omitted) 3m 7f 199y
4:35 (4:43) (Class 4) (0-120,110) 5-Y-O+ £3,969 (£1,157; £578)

Form RPR

1P0P **1** **Itstimeforapint (IRE)**[29] 4177 8-11-10 **108**......................(t) DerekFox 118
(Lucinda Russell) *chsd ldrs: wnt 2nd 4 out: chal after 2 out: led run-in: styd on wl u.p towards fin* **8/1**[3]

6213 **2** ¾ **Jonny Eager (IRE)**[17] 4407 7-11-11 **109**.......................... CraigNichol 118
(Alistair Whillans) *trckd ldrs: hdwy to ld 11th: rdn whn hrd pressed after 2 out: hdd run-in: rallied: hld nr fin* **7/2**[2]

214P **3** 21 **Longueville Flier (IRE)**[36] 4051 7-10-11 **98**.............. JoeColliver[(3)] 86
(Micky Hammond) *in tch: drvn and outpcd fr 3 out: no imp fr next* **9/1**

-53P **4** 1½ **Nosey Box (IRE)**[47] 3866 10-11-3 **108**.................(bt) MrSPKelly[(7)] 95
(Noel C Kelly, Ire) *hld up: stdy hdwy bef 3 out: rdn and chsd clr ldng pair after next: wknd fr last* **14/1**

-651 **P** **Snuker**[37] 4047 9-10-8 **92**...................................(bt) BrianHarding
(James Ewart) *rn in snatches and nt fluent on occasions: mostly prom tl lost pl and struggling 16th: p.u bef next* **7/2**[2]

532 **P** **Son Of Suzie**[15] 4433 8-11-9 **110**......................(p) ConorShoemark[(3)]
(Fergal O'Brien) *led: blnd 7th: hdd 11th: cl up tl drvn and outpcd 3 out: struggling after next: t.o whn p.u bef last* **13/8**[1]

9m 54.1s (58.70) **Going Correction** +1.95s/f (Heav) **6 Ran SP% 110.3**
Speed ratings: **104,103,98,98, ,**
CSF £34.68 TOTE £8.10: £3.50, £2.30; EX 35.40 Trifecta £222.00.
Owner IMEJ Racing **Bred** Ms T Doran **Trained** Arlary, Perth & Kinross

FOCUS
Race distance increased by 78yds. Two fences per circuit were omitted in this 4m chase which was run at at ordinary gallop. A personal best from the winner.

4741 HEXHAM INTERACTIVE H'CAP CHASE (11 fncs 4 omitted) 2m 4f 15y
5:10 (5:15) (Class 5) (0-100,103) 5-Y-O+ £2,600 (£758; £379)

Form RPR
0-10 1 **Flaming Thistle (IRE)**[57] 3679 12-10-4 82 GrantCockburn(5) 98+
(John Hodge) *mde all: clr to 1/2-way: rdn after 2 out: over 4 l up whn nt fluent last: kpt on strly* 10/1
P0P1 2 11 **Suprise Vendor (IRE)**[6] 4585 10-11-5 99 SamColtherd(7) 106
(Stuart Coltherd) *chsd clr ldr: hit 2nd: clsd 1/2-way: effrt and rdn after 2 out: jst over 4 l down whn hit last: sn no ex* 5/2[2]
5253 3 21 **Treliver Manor (IRE)**[11] 4514 8-10-4 84 (tp) LorcanMurtagh(7) 67
(Rose Dobbin) *prom: rdn and outpcd 2 out: no ch w first two bef last* 5/1[3]
5356 4 14 **Molko Jack (FR)**[37] 4048 12-10-0 73 oh4 SeanQuinlan 56
(Michael Mullineaux) *prom: drvn and outpcd 3 out: btn after next* 16/1
5165 P **Bayfirth (IRE)**[165] 1775 13-9-12 78 MrWHRReed(7)
(Andrew Hamilton) *hld up: drvn and outpcd sn after 1/2-way: lost tch and p.u bef 7th* 33/1
-301 R **Leney Cottage (IRE)**[7] 4569 9-11-11 103 7ex (t) DaraghBourke(5)
(Maurice Barnes) *t.k.h: hld up on outside: stdy hdwy to chse ldrs 3 out: rdn after next: sn wknd: 5th and no ch whn ref last* 11/10[1]
5m 51.7s (38.20) **Going Correction** +1.95s/f (Heav) 6 Ran SP% 110.8
Speed ratings: **101,96,88,88,**
CSF £35.05 TOTE £7.00: £3.00, £1.40; EX 40.90 Trifecta £114.10.
Owner John Mc C Hodge **Bred** John Noonan **Trained** Cumnock, Ayrshire

FOCUS
Race distance increased by 39yds. Quite a competitive handicap chase featuring two recent winners. Four fences per circuit were omitted. The winner is back on the upgrade.

4742 ADVERTISE YOUR COMPANY AT HEXHAM RACECOURSE "NATIONAL HUNT" MAIDEN HURDLE (10 hdls) 2m 4f 28y
5:40 (5:41) (Class 5) 4-Y-O+ £2,395 (£698; £349)

Form RPR
45 1 **Too Many Chiefs (IRE)**[7] 4567 5-10-8 0 FinianO'Toole(7) 104+
(Sharon Watt) *prom: wnt 2nd 3 out: led next: shkn up to go clr bef last: styd on strly* 8/1
3 2 7 **Milan Dancer (IRE)**[30] 4164 5-10-1 0 MrSPKelly(7) 91
(Noel C Kelly, Ire) *hld up in tch: stdy hdwy to press wnr after 2 out: sn rdn along: kpt on same pce bef last* 13/2
0 3 11 **Smart Boy (IRE)**[40] 4001 5-11-1 0 DerekFox 86
(Tim Easterby) *nt fluent on occasions: hld up: hit and outpcd 4 out: rallied between last 2: plugged on: nvr nrr* 16/1
1-2P 4 5 **Huehuecoytle**[75] 3436 6-11-1 0 (v[1]) CraigNichol 82
(Keith Dalgleish) *nt fluent on occasions and carried hd high: led: hit and hdd 2 out: rallied: wknd between last 2: hld whn j. slowly last* 6/4[1]
2 5 7 **The Pierre Lark (IRE)**[15] 4434 6-11-1 0 HenryBrooke 73
(Donald McCain) *cl up: drvn and outpcd after 2 out: wknd bef last* 6/1[3]
3355 P **Leading Score (IRE)**[16] 4416 6-11-1 108 BrianHarding
(James Ewart) *hld up in tch: drvn and outpcd 3 out: struggling bef next: sn btn: p.u bef last* 3/1[2]
5m 49.9s (37.40) **Going Correction** +1.675s/f (Heav) 6 Ran SP% 109.6
Speed ratings (Par 103): **92,89,84,82,80**
CSF £52.16 TOTE £8.40: £2.40, £2.60; EX 77.60 Trifecta £370.50.
Owner Major E J Watt **Bred** John Gallagher **Trained** Brompton-on-Swale, N Yorks

FOCUS
Race distance increased by 39yds. A modest maiden hurdle.
T/Plt: £312.70 to a £1 stake. Pool: £3,5571.76 - 83.04 winning tickets. T/Qpdt: £37.00 to a £1 stake. Pool: £3,358.62 - 67.00 winning tickets. **Richard Young**

4182 TOWCESTER (R-H)
Thursday, March 17

OFFICIAL GOING: Soft (6.7)
Wind: Light behind Weather: Fine

4743 BRACKLEY MARES' NOVICES' HURDLE (11 hdls) 2m 4f 217y
1:15 (1:16) (Class 4) 5-Y-O+ £3,898 (£1,144; £572; £286)

Form RPR
-351 1 **Sainte Ladylime (FR)**[15] 4435 5-11-0 0 TomBellamy(3) 114+
(Kim Bailey) *led: nt fluent 3rd: sddle slipped bef 6th: hdd after 3 out: rdn and mstke last: led flat: hung lft: styd on wl* 1/4[1]
35 2 2 **Lemtara Bay**[122] 2549 5-10-10 0 LeightonAspell 101
(Oliver Sherwood) *chsd ldrs: wnt 2nd after 7th: led after 3 out: rdn appr last: hdd flat: nt clr run sn after: styd on same pce* 3/1[2]
00 3 15 **Peal Of Bells**[13] 4468 5-10-10 0 JakeGreenall 85
(Henry Daly) *chsd wnr tl after 7th: mstke 3 out: wknd bef next* 20/1[3]
0-04 4 17 **Gray Wolf River**[11] 4507 5-10-10 0 JamesBanks 68
(Richard Harper) *hld up: racd keenly: rdn and wknd after 3 out: j.lft next* 50/1
0P 5 5 **Ann Maries Reject (IRE)**[42] 3947 7-10-10 0 LiamHeard 63
(Brian Barr) *hld up: effrt after 8th: wknd after next: j.lft 2 out* 150/1
5m 42.3s (15.10) **Going Correction** -0.35s/f (Good) 5 Ran SP% 112.4
Speed ratings: **57,56,50,44,42**
CSF £1.51 TOTE £1.20: £1.10, £1.20; EX 1.30 Trifecta £2.30.
Owner Paul & Clare Rooney **Bred** Har Du Puy **Trained** Andoversford, Gloucs

FOCUS
Drying ground that appeared tacky and rather holding. This uncompetitive and slowly run event went to the odds-on favourite, but not without a scare. She has been rated below her best.

4744 GRAFTON BEGINNERS' CHASE (17 fncs) 3m 102y
1:45 (1:45) (Class 4) 5-Y-O+ £4,882 (£1,669)

Form RPR
525P 1 **Spirit Of Shankly**[89] 3157 8-10-9 129 GrahamWatters(3) 138+
(Charlie Longsdon) *led to 4th: remained w ldr: led again 10th: clr appr 2 out: eased flat* 11/10[2]
-122 2 25 **Royalraise (IRE)**[112] 2733 7-10-12 124 LeightonAspell 118
(Oliver Sherwood) *racd in last pl but prom: chsd wnr 10th: wnt upsides next tl nt fluent 14th: sn pushed along: mstke 3 out: wknd bef next: eased flat* 1/1[1]
PPU P **Yanmare (IRE)**[16] 4425 6-10-9 0 (vt[1]) RyanHatch(3)
(Nigel Twiston-Davies) *j.lft at times: chsd ldr tl wnt upsides and nt fluent 2nd: led 4th tl hdd and wnt lft 10th: rdn and wknd 12th: bhd whn lft 14th: p.u bef next* 10/1[3]
6m 33.5s (-3.40) **Going Correction** +0.15s/f (Yiel) 3 Ran SP% 106.7
Speed ratings: **111,102,**
CSF £2.60 TOTE £1.90; EX 1.80.
Owner Alan Halsall **Bred** Mrs S M Newell **Trained** Over Norton, Oxon

FOCUS
Rail movements added approximately 45 yards to this race. A slowly run beginners' chase.

4745 XPRESS RELOCATIONS 20TH ANNIVERSARY YEAR H'CAP HURDLE (8 hdls) 1m 7f 181y
2:25 (2:28) (Class 4) (0-120,118) 4-Y-O+ £3,898 (£1,144; £572; £286)

Form RPR
1054 1 **Grams And Ounces**[17] 4411 9-11-6 112 (t) MichealNolan 114
(Grace Harris) *mde virtually all: rdn appr 2 out: styd on u.p* 20/1
-054 2 3/4 **Steel City**[27] 4229 8-11-9 115 (v) JeremiahMcGrath 117
(Seamus Mullins) *chsd wnr to 4th: remained handy: lft 2nd 3 out: rdn and ev ch whn nt fluent next: styd on* 3/1[2]
6-24 3 1 1/4 **Lettheriverrundry (IRE)**[115] 2683 6-11-12 118 LeightonAspell 120+
(Brendan Powell) *hld up: j.rt 1st: hdwy after 4th: hmpd 3 out: rdn appr last: edgd lft flat: styd on* 9/4[1]
0615 4 2 3/4 **Scooter Boy**[20] 4344 7-11-11 117 KielanWoods 114
(Alex Hales) *hld up: hmpd and stmbld 1st: hdwy after 4th: rdn after 3 out: styd on same pce fr next* 8/1
U24 5 1 **Ikrapol (FR)**[12] 4486 4-11-1 117 KieronEdgar(3) 107
(David Pipe) *hld up: j.big 2nd: pushed along after 5th: nt fluent 3 out: r.o flat: nvr nrr* 8/1
U266 6 2 **Drombeg West**[21] 4320 9-10-8 100 TrevorWhelan 94
(Anna Brooks) *hld up: hdwy appr 2 out: sn rdn: wknd last* 8/1
0F04 7 12 **Global Thrill**[19] 4353 7-11-6 115 RobertWilliams(3) 99
(Bernard Llewellyn) *prom: lost pl after 4th: rdn and wknd after 3 out* 7/1[3]
-020 F **Right Step**[52] 3777 9-10-8 107 (t) PaddyBradley(7)
(Pat Phelan) *prom: chsd wnr 4th: ev ch whn fell 3 out* 12/1
4m 3.6s (-4.30) **Going Correction** -0.35s/f (Good)
WFA 4 from 6yo+ 7lb 8 Ran SP% 114.1
Speed ratings (Par 105): **96,95,95,93,93 92,86,**
CSF £80.65 CT £193.24 TOTE £25.80: £5.00, £1.20, £1.30; EX 115.10 Trifecta £631.40.
Owner Ron C Williams **Bred** Brook Stud Bloodstock Ltd **Trained** Shirenewton, Monmouthshire

FOCUS
An ordinary handicap hurdle with the winner rated similar to his Ludlow win.

4746 HAYGAIN HAY STEAMERS CLEAN HEALTHY FORAGE H'CAP CHASE (17 fncs) 3m 102y
3:05 (3:06) (Class 5) (0-100,95) 5-Y-O+ £3,249 (£954; £477; £238)

Form RPR
-165 1 **Upbeat Cobbler (FR)**[82] 3222 8-11-10 93 JakeGreenall 110+
(Henry Daly) *mde all: c clr appr 2 out: comf* 7/1
U61U 2 19 **Try It Sometime (IRE)**[25] 4265 8-11-5 95 (t) MikeyHamill(7) 94
(Sheila Lewis) *hld up: nt a fluent: hdwy 14th: hit 3 out: rdn and wknd bef next: wnt 2nd flat* 15/2
PPP1 3 2 1/2 **Molly Oscar (IRE)**[3] 4673 10-10-12 81 7ex (v) TomCannon 76
(Johnny Farrelly) *chsd wnr: ev ch 3 out: rdn and wknd after next: lost 2nd flat* 7/4[1]
6563 4 7 **Jolly Boys Outing (IRE)**[42] 3948 13-10-1 73 BenPoste(3) 63
(Rosemary Gasson) *wnt prom 3rd: lost pl bef 9th: hdwy after 13th: rdn 2 out next: sn rdn and wknd* 4/1[2]
521P F **Tanner Hill (IRE)**[25] 4276 8-11-11 94 (p) MarkQuinlan
(James Evans) *chsd ldrs: hit 2nd: cl 3rd but rdn whn fell 14th* 11/2[3]
0P05 P **Follow The Tracks (IRE)**[20] 4346 8-10-6 80 MichaelHeard(5)
(Brian Barr) *chsd ldrs: mstke 1st: pushed along after 8th: wknd 13th: bhd whn p.u bef 2 out* 13/2
6m 39.4s (2.50) **Going Correction** +0.15s/f (Yiel) 6 Ran SP% 109.3
Speed ratings: **101,94,93,91,**
CSF £49.70 TOTE £6.00: £2.70, £3.20; EX 25.40 Trifecta £92.80.
Owner Exors of the Late Mrs A Timpson **Bred** Daniel & Mme Jeannine Laupretre **Trained** Stanton Lacy, Shropshire

FOCUS
Rail movements added approximately 45 yards to this race. Moderate handicap chase form but there's a case for rating it 10lb+ higher.

4747 ABTHORPE CONDITIONAL JOCKEYS' H'CAP HURDLE (10 hdls) 2m 3f 34y
3:45 (3:45) (Class 5) (0-100,100) 4-Y-O+ £2,599 (£763; £381; £190)

Form RPR
B/ 1 **Visible Light (IRE)**[42] 3963 8-11-9 97 CiaranGethings 105+
(Stuart Edmunds) *hld up: blnd 1st: hdwy 7th: led appr and mstke 2 out: shkn up flat: styd on* 5/2[1]
2314 2 2 1/4 **Pret A Thou (FR)**[18] 4386 13-11-12 100 NickSlatter 102
(John Groucott) *led: rdn and hdd appr 2 out: styd on same pce flat* 9/1[3]
50P2 3 1 1/2 **Gud Day (IRE)**[8] 4553 8-10-4 81 (p) HarryCobden(3) 81
(Conor Dore) *hld up in tch: rdn appr 2 out: edgd rt and no ex flat* 12/1
202 4 11 **Distant Sound (IRE)**[20] 4343 9-11-1 89 (p) ConorRing 78
(Grace Harris) *hld up: rdn appr 2 out: styd on to go 4th post: nvr nrr* 7/1[2]
0/2 5 hd **Sacre Malta (FR)**[10] 4528 10-11-6 99 ConorWalsh(5) 90
(Dominic Ffrench Davis) *hld up: mstke 7th: hdwy 3 out: rdn and wknd next* 16/1
3662 6 3 3/4 **L Frank Baum (IRE)**[21] 4318 9-11-4 92 (p) RobertWilliams 77
(Bernard Llewellyn) *hld up: sme hdwy appr 2 out: sn wknd* 10/1
U0U6 7 1/2 **Toast And Jam (IRE)**[11] 4504 7-10-0 74 oh1 (t) DanielHiskett 60
(Claire Dyson) *prom: hit 3 out: rdn and wknd appr 2 out* 25/1
-360 8 3/4 **Proud Times (USA)**[77] 3376 10-11-8 96 ThomasGarner 80
(Ali Stronge) *chsd ldr to 5th: rdn after next: wknd appr 2 out* 20/1
-4P0 9 9 **Bravo Riquet (FR)**[18] 4380 10-11-6 94 (vt) JakeHodson 69
(Robin Mathew) *chsd ldrs: lost pl 7th: wknd 3 out* 33/1
00PP P **Moving Waves (IRE)**[31] 4161 5-10-0 74 (b) KieronEdgar
(Johnny Farrelly) *prom: chsd ldr 5th: hit 7th: ev ch 3 out: sn rdn and wknd: p.u bef next* 16/1
4516 P **Kelsey (IRE)**[20] 4349 6-11-12 100 (t) KillianMoore
(Tom Lacey) *prom: nt fluent 2nd: lost pl after next: pushed along 4th: sn bhd: p.u bef 6th* 5/2[1]
5m 1.5s (-8.10) **Going Correction** -0.35s/f (Good) 11 Ran SP% 119.7
Speed ratings (Par 103): **103,102,101,96,96 95,94,94,90,**
CSF £25.60 CT £234.63 TOTE £3.70: £1.50, £2.50, £2.70; EX 29.50 Trifecta £231.00.
Owner The Sherington Partnership **Bred** Mrs A Kehoe **Trained** Newport Pagnell, Bucks

FOCUS
Modest handicap form with the winner stepping up on the best of his Irish figures.

4748 TOWCESTER OPEN HUNTERS' CHASE (17 fncs) 3m 102y
4:25 (4:26) (Class 6) 5-Y-0+ **£1,247** (£387; £193; £96)

Form RPR
-3U1 **1** **Pearlysteps**[26] 4249 13-12-3 132 .... MissJCWilliams(3) 138+
(Henry Daly) *j.rt: chsd ldrs: lft 2nd 6th: led 8th: c readily clr fr 3 out* **11/10**[1]
P-01 **2** 22 **Vasco Du Mee (FR)**[27] 4227 7-11-13 130 ......(bt) MissJosephineBanks(7) 116
(Martin Weston) *in rr: pushed along 7th: hdwy appr 9th: chsd wnr 10th to next: outpcd fr 14th: wnt 2nd after 3 out* **4/1**[3]
5 **3** 20 **Goodnight Vienna (IRE)**[19] 10-11-7 0 .... MrMJPKendrick(5) 83
(Mrs L Redman) *disp ld tl wnt on 4th: hdd 8th: remained handy: chsd wnr 11th tl rdn and wknd after 3 out* **9/1**
/1-4 **4** 1 1/4 **Legal Legend**[32] 9-11-9 111 .... MrJonathanBailey(5) 84
(Christopher Henn) *hld up: hdwy appr 7th: mstke 9th: wknd appr 11th* **3/1**[2]
/0-P **U** **Grouse Lodge (IRE)**[18] 10-11-5 112 .... MrSDavies-Thomas(7)
(Mrs Emma Clark) *disp ld to 4th: chsd ldr tl blnd and uns rdr 6th* **25/1**
2-U3 **P** **Charles Bruce (IRE)**[25] 13-11-7 96 .... MrJMartin(5)
(A Campbell) *prom: lost pl 5th: sme hdwy appr 9th: sn wknd: bhd whn p.u bef 12th* **50/1**
60-0 **F** **Rev It Up (IRE)**[19] 10-11-9 119 ....(b[1]) MissCVHart(3)
(Mrs K Lawther) *chsd ldrs: wnt 2nd 9th tl next: rdn and wkng whn fell 12th* **33/1**
40-2 **P** **Gentle Duke**[28] 4213 9-11-9 107 .... MrStanSheppard(3)
(Miss L Wallace) *hld up: a in rr: drvn along 12th: bhd whn hit 3 out: p.u bef next* **14/1**
6m 32.2s (-4.70) **Going Correction** +0.15s/f (Yiel) **8** Ran **SP% 118.0**
Speed ratings: **113,105,99,98, , ,**
CSF £6.37 TOTE £2.10: £1.02, £2.10, £2.90; EX 6.00 Trifecta £37.50.
Owner The Glazeley Partnership **Bred** W P Jenks **Trained** Stanton Lacy, Shropshire

FOCUS
Rail movements added approximately 45 yards to this race. They came home at wide margins behind the favourite.

4749 GREENS NORTON H'CAP HURDLE (12 hdls) 2m 7f 211y
5:00 (5:01) (Class 4) (0-110,110) 4-Y-0+ **£4,548** (£1,335; £667; £333)

Form RPR
PPPP **1** **Tara Tavey (IRE)**[20] 4342 11-11-0 **105** ....(t) ConorSmith(7) 114+
(Kevin Bishop) *hld up in tch: drvn along 9th: led appr 2 out: clr last: styd on wl* **14/1**
3343 **2** 6 **Storm Alert**[3] 4682 9-10-4 **91** .... LucyGardner(3) 94
(Sue Gardner) *chsd ldrs: rdn appr 3 out: styd on to go 2nd nr fin* **3/1**[2]
1532 **3** 2 1/4 **Precious Ground**[9] 4543 6-10-9 **93** .... JamesBest 94
(Kevin Bishop) *chsd ldr: rdn after 9th: led 3 out: hdd bef next: no ex last* **2/1**[1]
2P4P **4** 5 **Kapricorne (FR)**[3] 4673 9-10-10 **99** ....(t) CiaranGethings(5) 96
(Sophie Leech) *hld up: hdwy 3 out: rdn and wknd appr last* **20/1**
4053 **5** 17 **Ballinalacken (IRE)**[2] 4706 8-11-6 **104** ....(v) DavidEngland 82
(Clare Ellam) *hld up: hdwy 9th: rdn and wknd after 3 out* **14/1**
6/P0 **6** 6 **Pink Gin**[23] 4301 8-11-7 **105** ....(t) MarkGrant 79
(Nigel Twiston-Davies) *prom tl rdn and wknd after 3 out: bhd whn mstke next* **11/1**
1P66 **7** 5 **Earcomesthedream (IRE)**[33] 4127 13-10-11 **102**...(b) ArchieBellamy(7) 69
(Peter Pritchard) *in rr: drvn along 4th: lost tch after 6th* **25/1**
3FP4 **8** 26 **Expanding Universe (IRE)**[28] 4214 9-10-2 **86** ....(b[1]) LeeEdwards 27
(Tony Carroll) *prom: pushed along 6th: rdn and wknd after 9th* **14/1**
F1P2 **P** **Newton Thistle**[27] 4232 9-11-9 **110** ....(tp) MauriceLinehan(3)
(Ben Pauling) *led to 3 out: sn rdn and wknd: bhd whn p.u bef next* **7/2**[3]
2PP5 **P** **Stars Royale (IRE)**[17] 4410 7-11-3 **101** .... LeightonAspell
(Nick Gifford) *hld up: rdn and wknd after 7th: bhd whn p.u bef 3 out* **25/1**
6m 11.5s (-3.50) **Going Correction** -0.35s/f (Good) **10** Ran **SP% 121.3**
Speed ratings (Par 105): **91,89,88,86,80 78,77,68, ,**
CSF £58.17 CT £123.99 TOTE £16.50: £3.10, £1.50, £1.80; EX 88.90 Trifecta £461.00.
Owner K Bishop **Bred** Christopher Maye **Trained** Spaxton, Somerset

FOCUS
A modest handicap, but the form looks sound enough with the winner well in on the best of her good ground form last year.
T/Plt: £39.20 to a £1 stake. Pool: £43,881.31 - 39.20 winning tickets. T/Qpdt: £17.30 to a £1 stake. Pool: £3,020.83 - 129.10 winning tickets. **Colin Roberts**

4750 - 4763a (Foreign Racing) - See Raceform Interactive

4729 CHELTENHAM (L-H)
Friday, March 18

OFFICIAL GOING: Good (7.6)
Wind: Moderate; behind Weather: Overcast

4764 JCB TRIUMPH HURDLE (GRADE 1) (8 hdls) 2m 179y
1:30 (1:31) (Class 1) 4-Y-O
£68,340 (£25,644; £12,840; £6,396; £3,216; £1,608)

Form RPR
4 **1** **Ivanovich Gorbatov (IRE)**[41] 4002 4-11-0 142 ....(t) BarryGeraghty 152+
(A P O'Brien, Ire) *cmpt: midfield: hdwy 2 out: wnt 2nd appr last: sn upsides and chalng: wnt sltly lft last: led fnl 110yds: sn qcknd up and in command* **9/2**[1]
1 **2** 1 1/4 **Apple's Jade (FR)**[83] 3268 4-10-7 0 .... BJCooper 143
(W P Mullins, Ire) *lw: cl up: wnt 2nd 5th: led bef 2 out: rdn whn pressed and wnt sltly lft last: hdd fnl 110yds: sn outpcd by wnr* **12/1**
31 **3** 6 **Footpad (FR)**[41] 4002 4-11-0 150 .... RWalsh 145+
(W P Mullins, Ire) *bhd: rdn after 2 out to go pce: hdwy sn after: swtchd lft sltly between last 2: wnt 3rd appr last: styd on: nt pce to trble front pair* **5/1**[2]
3 **4** 7 **Let's Dance (FR)**[41] 4002 4-10-7 139 .... PaulTownend 132
(W P Mullins, Ire) *lw: chsd ldr to 5th: remained prom: ev ch 2 out: rdn and nt qckn bef last: styd on same pce run-in and no ch w ldrs* **11/1**
111U **5** nk **Leoncavallo (IRE)**[97] 3028 4-11-0 140 .... AidanColeman 138
(John Ferguson) *hld up: hdwy after 2 out: rdn appr last: kpt on u.p run-in but nvr a danger* **18/1**
12 **6** 1/2 **Clan Des Obeaux (FR)**[48] 3848 4-11-0 144 .... NoelFehily 139
(Paul Nicholls) *lw: trckd ldrs: rdn and outpcd between last 2: j.lft and nt fluent last: kpt on u.p but n.d* **12/1**
21 **7** 1/2 **Tommy Silver (FR)**[40] 4012 4-11-0 138 .... JJBurke 138
(Paul Nicholls) *q tall: chasing type: hld up: rdn and sme hdwy appr last: styd on but nt pce to get competitive* **25/1**
-531 **8** 1 1/4 **Frodon (FR)**[27] 4243 4-11-0 143 .... SeanBowen 136
(Paul Nicholls) *q lengthy: in tch: rdn and outpcd on bnd between last 2: kpt on u.p run-in but n.d* **20/1**
114 **9** 2 3/4 **Gibralfaro (IRE)**[20] 4358 4-11-0 146 ....(p) WayneHutchinson 135
(Alan King) *hld up in midfield: hdwy 3rd: trckd ldrs appr 3 out: effrt on outer and ch whn mstke 2 out: sn rdn: wknd bef last* **25/1**
3 **10** 4 **Consul De Thaix (FR)**[48] 3848 4-11-0 0 .... MarkWalsh 131
(Nicky Henderson) *lw: hld up: niggled along after 5th: effrt into midfield bef last: sn no imp and wl btn* **33/1**
1-21 **11** 1/2 **Connetable (FR)**[41] 3989 4-11-0 150 ....(p) SamTwiston-Davies 130
(Paul Nicholls) *hld up: pushed along after 3 out: rdn and no imp bef last* **14/1**
2111 **12** 1 **Sceau Royal (FR)**[63] 3610 4-11-0 144 .... DarylJacob 130
(Alan King) *sltly on toes: in tch: effrt to chse ldng bunch after 2 out: no imp: wknd bef last* **8/1**
1 **13** 7 **Zubayr (IRE)**[20] 4358 4-11-0 0 .... NickScholfield 126+
(Paul Nicholls) *swtg: racd keenly in midfield: rdn and outpcd between last: wknd after* **11/2**[3]
114 **14** 10 **Who Dares Wins (IRE)**[48] 3848 4-11-0 146 .... RichardJohnson 124
(Alan King) *prom: rdn after 2 out: sn lost pl: wknd bef last: eased whn wl btn run-in* **10/1**
6122 **15** 77 **Big McIntosh (IRE)**[133] 2324 4-11-0 120 .... MattieBatchelor 44
(John Ryan) *led: pushed along and hdd bef 2 out: sn wknd: t.o* **150/1**
3m 55.1s (-16.20) **Going Correction** -0.60s/f (Firm) **15** Ran **SP% 122.1**
Speed ratings: **114,113,110,107,107 106,106,106,104,102 102,102,98,94,57**
CSF £55.50 CT £287.46 TOTE £5.30: £2.00, £3.90, £1.90; EX 59.20 Trifecta £371.40.
Owner John P McManus **Bred** Lynch Bages & Camas Park Stud **Trained** Cashel, Co Tipperary
■ The winner is credited to Aidan O'Brien, but was in effect trained his son Joseph from a satellite yard.
■ Stewards' Enquiry : B J Cooper two-day ban: use of whip (1-2 Apr)

FOCUS
All races on the New Course and distances as advertised. Following a dry week the official going was changed to good all over after the previous day's racing had finished. The temperature dropped below freezing overnight but none of the frost had got into the ground and jockeys riding in the opener described conditions as "good", although Noel Fehily reckoned it was "a bit slower than yesterday". A wide-open running of the juvenile championship, in which no standout performer had emerged during the season. The field was dominated by Paul Nicholls, Willie Mullins and Alan King who were responsible for 11 of the 15 runners, but it was Aidan O'Brien who came out on top. The seemed to go a good gallop, notwithstanding the field choosing to ignore the front-running outsider, and the two principals fought out a terrific finish. Ivanovich Gorbatov stepped up and the race is up to standard.

4765 VINCENT O'BRIEN COUNTY H'CAP HURDLE (GRADE 3) (7 hdls 1 omitted) 2m 179y
2:10 (2:11) (Class 1) 5-Y-0+
£51,255 (£19,233; £9,630; £4,797; £2,412; £1,206)

Form RPR
4-12 **1** **Superb Story (IRE)**[124] 2512 5-10-12 **138** .... HarrySkelton 148+
(Dan Skelton) *lw: mid-div: hdwy after 2 out (usual 3 out): gng wl in 3rd after next: led bef omitted last: r.o strly* **8/1**[2]
20-2 **2** 2 1/2 **Fethard Player (IRE)**[139] 2205 9-11-2 **145** ....(t) DavidMullins(3) 151
(W F Treacy, Ire) *chsd ldr: rdn and ev ch after last (usual 2 out): nt pce of wnr by-passing omitted last but kpt on wl for 2nd* **33/1**
111P **3** 3 1/2 **Sternrubin (GER)**[34] 4115 5-11-2 **142** .... TomO'Brien 144
(Philip Hobbs) *chsd ldr: led after 2 out (usual 3 out): wnt rt last: rdn and hdd turning in: kpt on but nt pce of front pair* **33/1**
-211 **4** hd **Wait For Me (FR)**[53] 3772 6-10-13 **139** ....[1] RichardJohnson 142
(Philip Hobbs) *hld up towards rr: hdwy on outer after 5th: rdn after last (usual 2 out): styd on wl home st but a hld: chal for 3rd towards fin* **7/1**[1]
4F-2 **5** nk **Starchitect (IRE)**[34] 4115 5-11-1 **141** ....(bt) TomScudamore 146+
(David Pipe) *in tch tl nt clr run and lost pl after last (usual 2 out): rdn and styd on in home st but no threat to ldrs* **10/1**[3]
1143 **6** 3 1/4 **Francis Of Assisi (IRE)**[105] 2886 6-10-7 **140** .... MrAlexFerguson(7) 139
(John Ferguson) *mid-div: stdy prog fr 3rd: rdn to chse ldrs after last (usual 2 out): kpt on same pce home st* **40/1**
1304 **7** 3/4 **Kayf Blanco**[41] 3989 7-10-12 **138** .... KielanWoods 136
(Graeme McPherson) *mid-div: outpcd after last (usual 2 out): styd on again fr over 1f out but no ch* **50/1**
1/00 **8** 1 **Ivan Grozny (FR)**[34] 4115 6-11-3 **143** .... PaulTownend 142
(W P Mullins, Ire) *hld up towards rr: hdwy on outer last (usual 2 out): sn rdn: kpt on but nt pce to get on terms* **40/1**
20-5 **9** shd **Hawk High (IRE)**[40] 4014 6-11-3 **143** ....(b[1]) BrianHughes 140
(Tim Easterby) *mid-div tl lost pl appr 3rd: towards rr: styd on in home st but nvr any threat* **25/1**
15-3 **10** shd **Cardinal Walter (IRE)**[40] 4014 7-11-0 **140** .... AndrewTinkler 137
(Nicky Henderson) *hld up towards rr: hdwy last: effrt sn after: nvr threatened: one pce fr over 1f out* **22/1**
0F-6 **11** nk **Draco**[19] 4395 7-11-0 **140** ....(t) MarkWalsh 137
(A P O'Brien, Ire) *mid-div: tk clsr order appr last: (usual 2 out): gd run on inner turning in: sn rdn: wknd over 1f out* **33/1**
51-5 **12** 3/4 **All Yours (FR)**[132] 2350 5-11-7 **147** ....(t) SamTwiston-Davies 145+
(Paul Nicholls) *mid-div: hmpd 2nd: effrt in tch after last (usual 2 out): wknd over 1f out* **16/1**
1620 **13** 3/4 **Devilment**[90] 3151 5-11-9 **149** .... AidanColeman 145
(John Ferguson) *mid-div: hit 1st: effrt after last (usual 2 out): wknd bef omitted last* **33/1**
2020 **14** 1 1/2 **Mad Jack Mytton (IRE)**[34] 4115 6-11-0 **140** .... RichieMcLernon 135
(Jonjo O'Neill) *hld up towards rr: hmpd 2nd: hdwy appr last (usual 2 out): effrt turning in: wknd bef omitted last* **28/1**
5204 **15** 2 **Cheltenian (FR)**[19] 4381 10-11-5 **152** .... ConorSmith(7) 145
(Philip Hobbs) *mid-div on outer: hdwy after 3rd to trck ldrs: rdn after last (usual 2 out): wknd bef omitted last* **40/1**
0-54 **16** 2 1/2 **Some Plan (IRE)**[90] 3151 8-11-0 **145** ....(t) HarryCobden(5) 136
(Paul Nicholls) *mid-div: rdn after last (usual 2 out): nvr threatened: wknd bef omitted last* **12/1**
11-2 **17** 4 **John Constable (IRE)**[113] 2728 5-10-13 **139** .... PaulMoloney 126
(Evan Williams) *towards rr of midfield: rdn after last (usual 2 out): sn wknd* **14/1**
5-34 **18** 1 1/2 **Zamdy Man**[55] 3738 7-11-5 **150** .... CharlieDeutsch(5) 136
(Venetia Williams) *trckd ldrs: hit 3rd: wknd after last (usual 2 out)* **66/1**
-262 **19** 1 3/4 **Bentelimar (IRE)**[34] 4133 7-11-5 **145** .... BrianO'Connell 130
(J R Barry, Ire) *chsd ldrs tl wknd last (usual 2 out)*

05/F **20** *6* **Sizing Tennessee (IRE)**[34] 4133 8-11-3 **143**.................... JJBurke 121
(Henry De Bromhead, Ire) *mid-div tl wknd last (usual 2 out)* **66/1**

0-F1 **21** *6* **Henry Higgins (IRE)**[61] 3650 6-11-7 **147**.................... RobbiePower 124
(Charles O'Brien, Ire) *a bhd* **20/1**

4/ **22** *7* **Blue Hell (FR)**[111] 2797 6-11-6 **146**.................................(t) APHeskin 113
(Alan Fleming, Ire) *lw: a towards rr* **8/1**[2]

1130 **23** *19* **Modus**[34] 4115 6-10-13 **139**.................... NickScholfield 89
(Paul Nicholls) *sn struggling: detached by 3rd: t.o* **14/1**

44-0 **U** **Montbazon (FR)**[34] 4115 9-10-12 **138**.................... WayneHutchinson
(Alan King) *in tch whn blnd and uns rdr 2nd* **25/1**

04-F **F** **Dicosimo (FR)**[34] 4115 5-11-10 **150**....................[1] RWalsh
(W P Mullins, Ire) *towards rr of mid-div whn fell 4th* **16/1**

P **Great Field (FR)**[19] 4395 5-11-7 **147**.................... BarryGeraghty
(W P Mullins, Ire) *q tall: lw: racd freely: sn led: hdd after 2 out (usual 3 out): sn wknd: p.u after next* **7/1**[1]

3m 55.5s (-15.80) **Going Correction** -0.60s/f (Firm) **26** Ran SP% **135.8**
Speed ratings: **113,111,110,110,109 108,108,107,107,107 107,107,106,105,105 103,101,101,100,97 94,91,82, ,**
CSF £260.20 CT £8137.14 TOTE £7.50: £2.50, £8.60, £9.90, £2.50; EX 474.60 Trifecta £15357.70 Part won..

Owner A Holt, J Robinson, A Taylor & S Miller **Bred** Mrs Gilles Forien **Trained** Alcester, Warwicks

■ Stewards' Enquiry : Harry Skelton four-day ban: use of whip (1-4 Apr)

FOCUS

Traditionally a red-hot handicap and it was again thoroughly competitive, although they didn't go a breakneck gallop, with those racing prominently favoured, and the winning time was 0.40secs slower than the Triumph. The last hurdle had to be bypassed resulting in a lengthy run-in with no hurdles to jump in the straight. A typically solid renewal formwise, with Superb Story on the upgrade.

4766 ALBERT BARTLETT NOVICES' HURDLE (REGISTERED AS THE SPA NOVICES' HURDLE) (GRADE 1) (12 hdls) 2m 7f 213y

2:50 (2:51) (Class 1) 4-Y-O+

£68,340 (£25,644; £12,840; £6,396; £3,216; £1,608)

Form RPR

111 **1** **Unowhatimeanharry**[33] 4139 8-11-5 152.................... (t) NoelFehily 149
(Harry Fry) *hld up: hmpd 8th: hdwy after 3 out: pushed along after 2 out: swtchd lft bef last where carried lft: mstke and led: sn hung rt: kpt on wl towards fin* **11/1**

1112 **2** *1 1/4* **Fagan**[40] 4015 6-11-5 138.................... DavyRussell 147
(Gordon Elliott, Ire) *hld up: hdwy for press after 2 out: wnt 4th appr last: styd on to take 2nd fnl 75yds: hld fnl strides* **33/1**

2113 **3** *1 1/2* **Champers On Ice (IRE)**[48] 3852 6-11-5 143.............(p) TomScudamore 147+
(David Pipe) *trckd ldrs: hit 7th: hit and wnt 2nd 9th: w ldr 3 out: stl upsides and chalng fr 2 out tl run-in: styd on same pce fnl 75yds* **20/1**

-111 **4** *1 3/4* **Barters Hill (IRE)**[48] 3859 6-11-5 150.................... DavidBass 146+
(Ben Pauling) *lw: prom: led 4th: hrd pressed 2 out: edgd rt u.p between last 2: edgd lft and hdd last: hmpd and stmbld sn after: no ex fnl 75yds* **4/1**[2]

5 *11* **Balko Des Flos (FR)**[47] 3889 5-11-5 0.................... DavidMullins 135
(W P Mullins, Ire) *hld up: hdwy bef 6th: trckd ldrs appr 2 out: rdn bef last and nt qckn: one pce after* **40/1**

/221 **6** *7* **Allysson Monterg (FR)**[44] 3920 6-11-5 135.................... AlainCawley 128
(Richard Hobson) *prom: mstke 3 out: rdn and wknd bef last* **40/1**

1 **7** *6* **Gangster (FR)**[90] 3169 6-11-5 147.................... BJCooper 124
(W P Mullins, Ire) *w'like: midfield: hdwy after 3 out: chsd ldrs 2 out: rdn and wknd bef last* **15/2**

221 **8** *8* **Open Eagle (IRE)**[34] 4123 7-11-5 142.................... MPFogarty 115
(W P Mullins, Ire) *on toes: hld up: hit 7th: hdwy after 3 out: rdn and no imp on ldrs after 2 out: wknd bef last* **20/1**

2121 **9** *3 1/4* **Jonniesofa (IRE)**[27] 4248 6-11-5 137.................... CraigNichol 112
(Rose Dobbin) *in tch: pushed along appr 2 out: wknd after flight* **40/1**

1331 **10** *hd* **Aurillac (FR)**[20] 4351 6-11-5 133.................... NicodeBoinville 112
(Rebecca Curtis) *lw: in tch: rdn and wknd after 3 out* **33/1**

0352 **11** *10* **West Approach**[33] 4139 6-11-5 130.................... AidanColeman 103
(Colin Tizzard) *midfield tl wknd 3 out* **66/1**

-314 **P** **Up For Review (IRE)**[48] 3859 7-11-5 148.................... PaulTownend
(W P Mullins, Ire) *racd keenly: led: hit 3rd: hdd 4th: remained w ldr tl 9th: wknd after 3 out: t.o whn p.u bef last* **12/1**

111 **U** **Long Dog**[82] 3294 6-11-5 154.................... RWalsh
(W P Mullins, Ire) *midfield tl wnt wrong and uns rdr bef 5th: fatally injured* **5/1**[3]

1105 **P** **Atlantic Gold (IRE)**[97] 3037 6-11-5 130.................... BrianHughes
(Charlie Longsdon) *prom tl wknd 3 out: t.o whn p.u bef last* **100/1**

-313 **P** **Definite Outcome (IRE)**[62] 3623 7-11-5 132.................... JJBurke
(Rebecca Curtis) *str: trckd ldrs: mstke 3rd: lost pl 8th: struggling after 9th: t.o whn p.u after 3 out* **66/1**

2-41 **F** **Bleu Et Rouge (FR)**[41] 4004 5-11-5 149.................... BarryGeraghty
(W P Mullins, Ire) *q lengthy: will make a chaser: lw: midfield: stl hld up whn fell 8th* **10/1**

-112 **P** **Shantou Village (IRE)**[48] 3852 6-11-5 146.................... RichardJohnson
(Neil Mulholland) *lw: midfield: pushed along and sme hdwy after 3 out: nvr rchd ldrs: wknd after 2 out: wl bhd whn p.u bef last* **7/2**[1]

120 **U** **Bachasson (FR)**[82] 3294 5-11-5 151.................... MrPWMullins 124
(W P Mullins, Ire) *hld up in rr: hmpd 8th: hdwy appr 2 out: rdn to go pce after flight: disputing 5th abt 6 l off the pce and keeping on for press whn blnd and uns rdr last* **28/1**

211 **P** **Hit The Highway (IRE)**[52] 3787 7-11-5 135.................... TomCannon
(Giles Smyly) *midfield: losing pl whn nt fluent 6th: t.o whn p.u after 3 out* **100/1**

5m 48.1s (-12.90) **Going Correction** -0.60s/f (Firm) **19** Ran SP% **126.9**
Speed ratings (Par 117): **97,96,96,95,91 89,87,84,83,83 80, , , , , , , ,**
CSF £334.44 CT £7004.24 TOTE £11.20: £2.80, £6.80, £4.60; EX 357.00 Trifecta £5226.00.

Owner Harry Fry Racing Club **Bred** R J Smith **Trained** Seaborough, Dorset

■ Stewards' Enquiry : Paul Townend jockey said that the gelding ran too freely
B J Cooper jockey said the gelding lost its right fore shoe
J J Burke jockey said the gelding had bled from the nose
David Bass two-day ban: use of whip (1-2 Apr)
Richard Johnson vet said the gelding had been been struck into on its left hind
Tom Cannon jockey said the gelding had bled from the nose

FOCUS

This looked a strong renewal on paper, featuring several multiple winners, and Willie Mullins had seven in the field, but some of the big guns failed to fire and the form is rated as below average for the race. The gallop was not overly strong and the front four pulled clear of the rest. Plenty of these will go chasing next season and it's a race to note with the future in mind.

4767 TIMICO CHELTENHAM GOLD CUP CHASE (GRADE 1) (22 fncs) 3m 2f 70y

3:30 (3:30) (Class 1) 5-Y-O+

£327,462 (£122,877; £61,525; £30,647; £15,410; £7,705)

Form RPR

11F1 **1** **Don Cossack (GER)**[64] 3603 9-11-10 175.................... (t) BJCooper 182+
(Gordon Elliott, Ire) *trckd ldrs: upsides after 17th: led after 3 out: shkn up after 2 out: styd on wl and in command fr last: pushed out* **9/4**[1]

-21F **2** *4 1/2* **Djakadam (FR)**[48] 3850 7-11-10 170.................... RWalsh 177
(W P Mullins, Ire) *lw: in tch: trckd ldrs 10th: upsides after 16th: narrow ld after next: rdn and hdd after 3 out: nt fluent next: styd on fr last but no imp on wnr* **9/2**[3]

5-11 **3** *10* **Don Poli (IRE)**[81] 3324 7-11-10 166.................... DavyRussell 168
(W P Mullins, Ire) *lw: hld up in last pair wl off pce: hdwy 3 out: wnt 3rd 2 out: styd on but nvr any threat to front pair* **9/2**[3]

-461 **4** *7* **Carlingford Lough (IRE)**[41] 4007 10-11-10 164.................... BarryGeraghty 164
(John E Kiely, Ire) *lw: hld up in last trio: struggling whn mstke 16th: plenty to do 3 out: styd on fr next but no ch: snatched 4th fnl stride* **25/1**

155P **5** *nse* **Irish Cavalier (IRE)**[48] 3851 7-11-10 153.................... (p) PaulTownend 161
(Rebecca Curtis) *hld up last wl off pce: hdwy 3 out: styd on into hld 4th sn after 2 out but nvr any threat: lost 4th fnl stride* **66/1**

1141 **6** *16* **Smad Place (FR)**[48] 3850 9-11-10 169.................... WayneHutchinson 151
(Alan King) *hit 1st: sn disputing ld: j. sltly rt most of way: hdd after 16th: sn rdn: outpcd after 4 out: lft 4th 3 out: wknd next* **10/1**

P1P0 **7** *15* **O'Faolains Boy (IRE)**[20] 4354 9-11-10 156.................... (p) NoelFehily 133+
(Rebecca Curtis) *led: jnd 3rd: hdd after 17th but stl upsides tl appr 3 out where lft 3rd: sn rdn: wknd next* **40/1**

U402 **8** *1 1/2* **On His Own (IRE)**[27] 4260 12-11-10 157.................... (p) MrPWMullins 133
(W P Mullins, Ire) *chsd ldrs tl 10th: sn pushed along in last trio: outpcd fr 4 out* **50/1**

4111 **F** **Cue Card**[83] 3231 10-11-10 176.................... (t) PaddyBrennan 180+
(Colin Tizzard) *lw: hit 9th: trckd ldrs 14th: disputing ld and travelling wl whn fell 3 out* **5/2**[2]

6m 35.0s (-18.80) **Going Correction** -0.125s/f (Good) **9** Ran SP% **114.5**
Speed ratings: **123,121,118,116,116 111,106,106,**
CSF £12.68 CT £41.17 TOTE £3.00: £1.50, £1.50, £1.80; EX 12.40 Trifecta £34.90.

Owner Gigginstown House Stud **Bred** Gestut Etzean **Trained** Longwood, Co Meath

FOCUS

Rightly viewed as a good edition of the race, even in the absence of the previous year's hero Coneygree and Thursday's Ryanair one-two-three, most notably the brilliant Vautour, they went a proper gallop from the outset and the scene was set perfectly for three of the big four to fight it out when Cue Card crashed out in dramatic fashion at the third from home. Every reason to think the winner is right up there with, if not better, than the most recent winners of the race. Don Cossack is the highest rated Gold Cup winner since Imperial Commander in 2010, similar to level of last year's Aintree/Punchestown wins. The time was very fast.

4768 ST. JAMES'S PLACE FOXHUNTER CHASE CHALLENGE CUP (22 fncs) 3m 2f 70y

4:10 (4:11) (Class 2) 5-Y-O+

£23,984 (£7,492; £3,744; £1,872; £936; £472)

Form RPR

11-1 **1** **On The Fringe (IRE)**[41] 4008 11-12-0 147.................... MsNCarberry 135+
(E Bolger, Ire) *hld up: hdwy appr 4 out: rdn and styng on bef 2 out: led last: kpt on wl run-in: a doing enough towards fin* **13/8**[1]

20-0 **2** *nk* **Marito (GER)**[40] 10-12-0 143.................... MrNMcParlan 134+
(C A McBratney, Ire) *hld up: hdwy appr 3 out: rdn bef 2 out: edgd lft after for press after last: wnt 2nd fnl 150yds: styd on: jst hld towards fin* **14/1**

4-21 **3** *1* **Paint The Clouds**[23] 4307 11-12-0 138.................... MrSWaley-Cohen 132
(Warren Greatrex) *chsd ldrs: rdn and nt qckn after 3 out: swtchd rt after last: r.o and gaining towards fin* **9/2**[2]

-112 **4** *1* **Current Event (FR)**[19] 9-12-0 142.................... MrWBiddick 132
(Mrs Rose Loxton) *hdwy 11th: wnt 2nd appr 4 out: rdn and ev ch last: styd on same pce towards fin* **14/1**

-3U1 **5** *1/2* **Pacha Du Polder (FR)**[16] 4437 9-12-0 141.................... MsVLPendleton 131+
(Paul Nicholls) *lw: hld up in rr: stdy hdwy fr 4 out: gd prog run-in: fin wl* **28/1**

30-P **6** *1 1/2* **Aupcharlie (IRE)**[40] 10-12-0 136.................... MrJJCodd 130
(Henry De Bromhead, Ire) *hld up in midfield: hdwy appr 3 out: slipped sltly on bnd bef 2 out: rdn whn chsng ldrs bef last: swtchd rt run-in: kpt on u.p towards fin but hld* **9/1**[3]

-1P5 **7** *2* **Major Malarkey (IRE)**[23] 4307 13-12-0 118.................... (v) MrSClements 129
(Nigel Twiston-Davies) *hld up early: impr to chse ldrs after 3rd: bmpd 10th: led 11th: clr appr 4 out to 3 out: rdn and hdd last: no ex fnl 75yds* **66/1**

0-11 **8** *3 1/2* **Mendip Express (IRE)**[19] 4383 10-12-0 139.................... (t) MrDavidMaxwell 125
(Philip Hobbs) *midfield: hdwy 14th (water): chsd ldrs 3 out: rdn bef 2 out: kpt on same pce fr bef last* **12/1**

/26- **9** *4 1/2* **Current Exchange (IRE)**[20] 11-12-0 118.................... (tp) MrTimDonworth 119
(Gordon Elliott, Ire) *trckd ldrs: rdn and outpcd after 3 out: no real imp after* **66/1**

20-2 **10** *1 1/2* **Alskamatic**[55] 10-12-0 124.................... (p) MissCVHart 120
(Richard J Bandey) *racd keenly: prom: led 3rd: hdd bef 5th: led again 8th: mstke 9th: hdd 11th: stl handy: 8th and u.p whn mstke 2 out: wl btn after* **66/1**

012 **11** *3/4* **Impact Area (IRE)**[19] 4383 10-12-0 125.................... (p) MrSDavies-Thomas 119
(Mrs Harriet Waight) *prom: led bef 5th tl bef 7th: remained handy: bmpd and mstke 10th: rdn and wknd after 3 out* **66/1**

1-14 **12** *10* **Mr Mercurial (IRE)**[20] 8-12-0 118.................... (t) MrPGerety 109
(Mrs Sheila Crow) *midfield: rdn and outpcd after 3 out: veered lft after 2 out: no imp after* **25/1**

2-15 **13** *5* **Indiana Bay (IRE)**[26] 9-12-0 120.................... MrRobertHawker 103
(Mrs Jill Dennis) *hld up: mstke 16th: struggling and bhd 18th* **125/1**

00-4 **14** *7* **Brackloon High (IRE)**[19] 11-12-0 117.................... MrABarlow 95
(M Kehoe) *chsd ldrs: lost pl 14th (water): rdn bef 4 out: wknd after 3 out* **150/1**

1122 **15** *3/4* **Pena Dorada (IRE)**[40] 4016 9-12-0 115.................... MissRMcDonald 94
(Alan J Brown) *hld up in midfield: struggling after 4 out: nvr a threat* **100/1**

-22P **16** *5* **Richmond (FR)**[27] 4249 11-12-0 125.................... MissLMTurner 89
(P P C Turner) *prom: led bef 7th: hdd 8th: lost pl 15th: bhd after* **150/1**

-465 **17** *13* **Twirling Magnet (IRE)**[141] 2146 10-12-0 133..................(bt) MrMWalton 78
(Jonjo O'Neill) *midfield: swtchd rt appr 3 out: wknd bef 2 out* **33/1**

2/11 **18** *8* **Dark Lover (GER)**[38] 4043 11-12-0 130 MissGAndrews 68
(Jamie Snowden) *midfield: j. slowly 7th: mstke and lost pl 13th: struggling and bhd fr 16th* **25/1**

0-3P **19** *¾* **Temple Grandin (IRE)**[81] 9-12-0 120 MrAlexEdwards 69
(Philip Rowley) *midfield: rdn 16th: mstke and lost pl 17th: bhd after* **100/1**

P-P **20** *½* **Need To Know (IRE)**[26] 8-12-0 121..........................(t) MrDerekO'Connor 67
(John Paul Brennan, Ire) *in rr: hdwy into midfield 4 out: rdn appr 3 out: sn wknd* **40/1**

P12/ **F** **Chapoturgeon (FR)**[47] 12-12-0 138 MrMartinMcIntyre 131
(Jack R Barber) *mstkes: hld up: hdwy 3 out: over 7 l off the pce but no real imp whn fell 2 out* **33/1**

321/ **P** **Camden (IRE)**[19] 10-12-0 128..........................(bt) MrWEasterby
(Mrs Sarah Easterby) *sn in rr: mstkes: t.o whn p.u bef 15th* **66/1**

-113 **U** **Cave Hunter (IRE)**[23] 4307 9-12-0 113..........................(tp) MrTHamilton
(Mrs Wendy Hamilton) *led to 3rd: remained prom: rdn bef 17th: mstke whn u.p 4 out: wl btn whn mstke and uns rdr 2 out* **66/1**

F **It Came To Pass (IRE)**[41] 4008 6-12-0 126 MrBMLinehan
(J H Culloty, Ire) *lw: midfield: stl gng okay whn fell 3 out* **9/1**[3]

6m 53.7s (-0.10) **Going Correction** -0.125s/f (Good) **24** Ran **SP% 129.8**
Speed ratings: **95,94,94,94,94 93,93,91,90,90 89,86,85,83,82 81,77,74,74,74 , , ,**
CSF £24.73 CT £99.74 TOTE £2.30: £1.70, £4.60, £1.90; EX 29.70 Trifecta £141.00.
Owner John P McManus **Bred** Pat Tobin **Trained** Bruree, Co Limerick
■ Stewards' Enquiry : Ms N Carberry seven-day ban: use of whip (TBA) £400 fine
Miss L M Turner five-day ban: use of whip (TBA)

FOCUS
The big hunter chase of the season wasn't as competitive as the numbers would suggest, but it had a very interesting sub-plot, was run at a strong gallop and provided a thrilling finish. The time was slow compared with the Gold Cup even allowing for relative ability.

4769 MARTIN PIPE CONDITIONAL JOCKEYS' H'CAP HURDLE (9 hdls 1 omitted) 2m 4f 56y

4:50 (4:52) (Class 2) (0-145,142) 4-Y-0+

£37,536 (£11,088; £5,544; £2,772; £1,386; £696)

Form RPR

-235 **1** **Ibis Du Rheu (FR)**[41] 3992 5-11-7 139..........................(t) JackSherwood 146
(Paul Nicholls) *mid-div: hdwy turning in: sn rdn: led ent fnl f: r.o wl* **14/1**

3531 **2** *1 ¼* **Flying Angel (IRE)**[6] 4622 5-11-6 138 5ex RyanHatch 144
(Nigel Twiston-Davies) *mid-div: hdwy 5th: trckd ldrs last (usual 2 out): rdn and ev ch over 1f out tl ins fnl f: kpt on* **8/1**[2]

2616 **3** *1 ¼* **Sky Khan**[40] 4017 7-11-3 135..........................(p) DerekFox 140
(Lucinda Russell) *mid-div: hdwy appr last (usual 2 out): rdn to chse ldrs turning in: styd on to go 3rd fnl f* **50/1**

66 **4** *6* **Tully East (IRE)**[82] 3294 6-11-8 140 ShaneShortall 140+
(Alan Fleming, Ire) *hld up towards rr: hdwy after 7th: led turning in: sn drvn: hdd ent fnl f: no ex* **50/1**

1224 **5** *nk* **Whiteout (GER)**[80] 3356 5-11-7 139 JonathanMoore 139
(W P Mullins, Ire) *towards rr of mid-div: hdwy after 2 out (usual 3 out): rdn after next: styd on fnl f: nrly snatched 4th fnl strides* **33/1**

2000 **6** *2 ¾* **Urano (FR)**[29] 4215 8-11-3 135 DonaghMeyler 133
(W P Mullins, Ire) *hld up towards rr: hmpd 4th: hdwy whn hmpd last (usual 2 out): styng on whn nt clr run and hmpd again over 1f out: styd on but nvr any ch* **33/1**

7 *2* **Squouateur (FR)**[27] 4259 5-11-9 141..........................(t) JackKennedy 137
(Gordon Elliott, Ire) *lengthy: will make a chaser: lw: hld up towards rr: midfield 2 out (usual 3 out): rdn after next: styd on same pce fr over 1f out* **9/4**[1]

1261 **8** *3 ¾* **Work In Progress (IRE)**[28] 4224 6-11-7 139 BridgetAndrews 131+
(Dan Skelton) *led: clr 4th tl last (usual 2 out): rdn and hdd turning in: fdd fnl f* **25/1**

0-21 **9** *½* **Jetstream Jack (IRE)**[39] 4033 6-11-3 135..........................[1] KevinSexton 128
(Gordon Elliott, Ire) *lengthy: q tall: hld up towards rr: hmpd last (usual 2 out): styd on in the home st but nvr any danger* **9/1**[3]

-F10 **10** *1 ½* **Zulu Oscar**[55] 3733 7-11-5 140..........................(t) LiamMcKenna[(3)] 130
(Harry Fry) *in tch: rdn after last (usual 2 out): nvr threatened: fdd fnl f* **22/1**

1240 **11** *4* **Matorico (IRE)**[34] 4115 5-10-13 136..........................(p) PatrickCowley[(5)] 126
(Jonjo O'Neill) *swtg: hld up towards rr: pushed along after 7th: sme late prog: nvr any danger* **33/1**

2132 **12** *nk* **Label Des Obeaux (FR)**[35] 4097 5-11-7 139 TomBellamy 126
(Alan King) *mid-div: hit 7th: wknd after last (usual 2 out)* **25/1**

-036 **13** *½* **Handiwork**[81] 2901 6-11-10 142..........................(p) KillianMoore 127
(Steve Gollings) *mid-div: hdwy 5th: chsd ldrs last (usual 2 out): wknd over 1f out* **100/1**

1110 **14** *1 ½* **Nabucco**[124] 2512 7-11-4 136 CraigNichol 120
(John Ferguson) *trckd ldrs: rdn after last (usual 2 out): wknd over 1f out* **28/1**

63-2 **15** *2 ¼* **Westend Star (IRE)**[43] 3962 7-11-6 138..........................(t) LPDempsey 122
(Gordon Elliott, Ire) *a towards rr* **16/1**

0602 **16** *8* **Qualando (FR)**[24] 4294 5-11-7 139..........................(p) HarryCobden 116
(Paul Nicholls) *lw: in tch tl pushd along after 3 out (usual 2 out): wknd turning in* **10/1**

4 **17** *22* **Childrens List (IRE)**[61] 3649 6-11-7 139 DavidMullins 106
(W P Mullins, Ire) *mid-div tl wknd bef last (usual 2 out)* **10/1**

250F **18** *6* **Buiseness Sivola (FR)**[34] 4115 5-11-7 139 LizzieKelly 88
(W P Mullins, Ire) *a towards rr* **50/1**

0-00 **19** *6* **Goodwood Mirage (IRE)**[80] 3336 6-11-3 135 ConorShoemark 79
(Jonjo O'Neill) *hld up towards rr: sme prog whn bdly hmpd last (usual 2 out): no ch after* **33/1**

212U **U** **Laurium**[111] 2781 6-11-6 138 JeremiahMcGrath
(Nicky Henderson) *in tch whn blnd and uns rdr 4th* **20/1**

1150 **F** **Roadie Joe (IRE)**[27] 4239 7-11-5 137 ConorRing 114
(Evan Williams) *chsd ldrs: wkng whn fell last (usual 2 out)* **66/1**

-01P **P** **Bivouac (FR)**[69] 3527 5-11-9 141..........................(p) FreddieMitchell
(Nicky Henderson) *chsd ldrs tl wknd 2 out (usual 3 out): p.u bef next* **50/1**

-113 **P** **Montdragon (FR)**[27] 4239 6-11-3 135..........................(t) JodyMcGarvey
(Jonjo O'Neill) *mid-div tl wknd after 2 out (usual 3 out): p.u after next: collapsed fatally* **20/1**

3312 **F** **Mr Mix (FR)**[27] 4236 5-11-6 138 CharlieDeutsch 127
(Paul Nicholls) *hld up towards rr: blnd 5th: hdwy but u.p in midfield whn fell last (usual 2 out)* **16/1**

4m 51.7s (-5.70) **Going Correction** 0.0s/f (Good) **24** Ran **SP% 135.6**
Speed ratings (Par 109): **111,110,110,107,107 106,105,104,103,103 101,101,101,100,99 96,87,85,83, , ,EM**
CSF £111.34 CT £5506.74 TOTE £14.90: £3.00, £2.10, £13.10, £11.50; EX 202.80 Trifecta £19699.10 Part won..

Owner J Hales **Bred** Claude Duval **Trained** Ditcheat, Somerset
■ Jack Sherwood's first festival winner.

FOCUS
The market got it wrong this time, the well-backed favourite failing to justify the support, and it proved wide open. Tearaway leader Work In Progress was largely ignored but it was truly run and a good test at the trip. As in the County Hurdle the last hurdle had to be bypassed, again resulting in a lengthy run-in with no hurdles jumped in the straight. A dolid renewal.

4770 JOHNNY HENDERSON GRAND ANNUAL CHASE CHALLENGE CUP (H'CAP) (GRADE 3) (14 fncs) 2m 62y

5:30 (5:31) (Class 1) 5-Y-0+

£56,950 (£21,370; £10,700; £5,330; £2,010; £2,010)

Form RPR

3-3P **1** **Solar Impulse (FR)**[92] 3121 6-11-0 140..........(bt[1]) SamTwiston-Davies 152+
(Paul Nicholls) *midfield: hdwy appr 5th: hit 8th: led gng wl appr last: edgd rt run-in: r.o wl and won gng away* **28/1**

1 **2** *3 ¾* **Dandridge**[48] 3857 7-10-11 137..........................(t) DavyRussell 147+
(A L T Moore, Ire) *midfield: blnd 1st: mstke 4 out: rdn and hdwy appr 2 out: edgd lft run-in and tk 2nd: styd on tl no imp on wnr towards fin* **8/1**[2]

-511 **3** *½* **Rock The World (IRE)**[147] 2053 8-11-6 146..........................(t) RobbiePower 154
(Mrs John Harrington, Ire) *in tch: hmpd 6th (water): effrt after 3 out: chsd ldrs appr 2 out: kpt on u.p run-in but hld* **9/2**[1]

434P **4** *1 ¾* **Savello (IRE)**[27] 4240 10-11-5 150..........................(t[1]) BridgetAndrews[(5)] 157
(Dan Skelton) *lw: hld up: mstke 1st: hdwy 9th: chsd ldrs 3 out: ev ch appr 2 out: stl cl up last: styd on same pce fnl 100yds* **25/1**

3152 **5** *2 ¼* **Pearls Legend**[13] 4469 9-10-12 138 JamieMoore 143
(John Spearing) *chsd ldrs: hit 9th: rdn and ch appr 2 out: nt qckn bef last: kpt on same pce* **33/1**

-114 **5** *dht* **Red Spinner (IRE)**[48] 3857 6-11-3 143 DavidBass 147
(Kim Bailey) *chsd ldrs: led after 3 out: rdn and hdd appr last: no ex fnl 100yds* **33/1**

1164 **7** *1* **Dresden (IRE)**[20] 4355 8-11-7 147 JamesDavies 151
(Henry Oliver) *midfield: hmpd 6th (water): mstke 10th and lost pl: rdn and struggling to go pce after 3 out: styd on after last: nt rch ldrs* **33/1**

1263 **8** *1* **Workbench (FR)**[97] 3030 8-11-0 140..........................(t) HarrySkelton 141
(Dan Skelton) *midfield: hdwy appr 5th: rdn whn chsng ldrs bef 2 out: hung lft bef last and no imp on ldrs: one pce after* **33/1**

-P5P **9** *1* **Eastlake (IRE)**[97] 3030 10-11-3 143 BarryGeraghty 147
(Jonjo O'Neill) *midfield: hmpd and lost pl 6th (water): hdwy appr 2 out: no imp bef last* **12/1**[3]

130P **10** *1 ¼* **Lough Kent**[111] 2784 7-10-12 138 NicodeBoinville 137
(Nicky Henderson) *midfield: outpcd after 3 out: rdn bef last: nvr able to chal* **12/1**[3]

-241 **11** *3* **Raven's Tower (USA)**[129] 2412 6-10-11 137 BrendanPowell 135
(Ben Pauling) *midfield: blnd 4 out: hdwy after 3 out: effrt and chsng ldng bunch whn blnd 2 out: no imp: wknd run-in* **25/1**

0-32 **12** *3* **Velvet Maker (FR)**[54] 3766 7-11-6 146 APHeskin 142
(Alan Fleming, Ire) *led: hdd after 3 out: rdn bef next: wkng whn mstke last* **8/1**[2]

3422 **13** *½* **Dunraven Storm (IRE)**[92] 3121 11-11-8 148 TomO'Brien 141
(Philip Hobbs) *hld up: hdwy 8th: chsd ldng bunch 3 out: no imp bef 2 out: wl btn run-in* **50/1**

0000 **14** *½* **Next Sensation (IRE)**[97] 3030 9-11-4 144..........................(t) TomScudamore 136
(Michael Scudamore) *w ldr: rdn and wknd appr 2 out* **8/1**[2]

00P **15** *8* **Surf And Turf (IRE)**[139] 2185 10-11-1 141 BrianHughes 128
(Kevin Frost) *midfield: hmpd and lost pl 6th (water): sn bhd: n.d after* **100/1**

1211 **16** *1* **Arthur's Oak**[20] 4355 8-11-12 152 LiamTreadwell 138
(Venetia Williams) *chsd ldrs: nt fluent 9th: blnd 4 out: sn lost pl: wknd 3 out* **20/1**

1214 **17** *11* **Germany Calling (IRE)**[132] 2336 7-11-0 140 AidanColeman 114
(Charlie Longsdon) *hld up: struggling to keep up whn pckd 4 out: nvr a threat* **33/1**

U220 **18** *23* **Bright New Dawn (IRE)**[43] 3964 9-11-8 148 BJCooper 102
(Gordon Elliott, Ire) *racd keenly: hld up: hdwy into midfield 5th: lost pl 10th: hmpd 3 out: wl bhd after: t.o* **16/1**

-364 **F** **Croco Bay (IRE)**[29] 4204 9-11-7 147 KielanWoods
(Ben Case) *lw: chsd ldrs tl fell 6th (water)* **20/1**

0014 **F** **Bold Henry**[41] 3990 10-11-4 144 RichardJohnson
(Philip Hobbs) *in rr: pckd 4 out: no bttr than midfield whn fell 3 out* **40/1**

P132 **F** **Gardefort (FR)**[27] 4254 7-10-13 139 AlainCawley
(Venetia Williams) *hld up: hdwy appr 10th: stl gng okay in tch whn blnd 4 out: sn lost pl and nt rcvr: bhd whn fell 2 out* **40/1**

4-U3 **P** **Chris Pea Green**[41] 3990 7-10-13 139 JoshuaMoore
(Gary Moore) *in rr: blnd 9th: nvr gng: t.o whn p.u bef 4 out* **16/1**

35-U **U** **Sizing Codelco (IRE)**[75] 3458 7-11-5 145 JJBurke
(Henry De Bromhead, Ire) *lw: racd keenly: hld up: blnd and uns rdr 1st* **16/1**

025F **P** **The Saint James (FR)**[20] 4359 5-11-2 142..........................(t) MarkWalsh
(Jonjo O'Neill) *in rr: nt a fluent: mstke 5th: struggling after: t.o whn p.u after 3 out* **14/1**

3m 59.2s (-7.50) **Going Correction** -0.125s/f (Good) **24** Ran **SP% 134.4**
Speed ratings: **113,111,110,110,108 108,108,107,107,106 105,103,103,103,99 98,93,81, , , ,**
CSF £225.59 CT £1239.31 TOTE £44.40: £9.00, £2.80, £1.80, £7.80; EX 446.70 Trifecta £4325.80.

Owner Andrea & Graham Wylie **Bred** Paul Nataf **Trained** Ditcheat, Somerset

FOCUS
A highly competitive and strong renewal of one of the season's leading 2m handicaps and the oldest race on the National Hunt calendar. They went a good gallop and plenty were in with a chance as they charged down the hill. Solar Impulse was well in on the best of his form and is rated back to that level.

T/Jkpt: Not won. T/Plt: £1,680.90 to a £1 stake. Pool: £1,245,317.00 - 540.82 winning units
T/Qpdt: £129.60 to £1 stake. Pool: £64,126.0 - 366.15 winning units
Darren Owen & Tim Mitchell

[4222] FAKENHAM (L-H)

Friday, March 18

OFFICIAL GOING: Good (6.6) changing to good (good to soft in places) after race 1 (1.55)

Wind: Breezy Weather: Very changeable but feeling chilly; 7 degrees

4771 TOTEPLACEPOT HUGE CHELTENHAM POOL TODAY (S) HURDLE (9 hdls) 2m 3y

1:55 (1:55) (Class 5) 4-Y-0+ **£2,737** (£798; £399)

Form RPR

234 **1** **Changing The Guard**[154] 1945 10-11-0 113................(tp) JamesBanks 107
(Barry Brennan) *set stdy pce: mstke 5th: rdn and hdd and nt fluent 3 out: drvn to ld again bef last: rdn clr* **7/4**[1]

4P01 **2** *5* **Goal (IRE)**[19] 4390 8-10-12 106................(vt) MissBHampson(7) 109
(Sally Randell) *pressed ldr tl led 3 out: 2 l ahd and rdn whn blnd 2 out: hdd bef last: readily outpcd* **7/2**[3]

6206 **3** *11* **It's A Mans World**[32] 4154 10-11-9 112.......................... GavinSheehan 103
(Brian Ellison) *bhd: last whn nt fluent 5th and rdn: nvr travelling and no ch after: struggled into poor 3rd after 2 out* **15/8**[2]

00 **4** *1* **Cocker**[22] 4317 4-10-0 0.......................... MissTWorsley(7) 83
(Alan Blackmore) *t.k.h: prom tl lost pl qckly 6th: rdn in last and toiling next* **100/1**

33 **5** *22* **The Scourge (IRE)**[23] 1636 5-11-5 109.......................... JackQuinlan 75
(Sarah Humphrey) *chsd ldrs: nt a fluent: rdn and lost tch bef 3 out: t.o* **16/1**

6 *5* **Je T'Aime Encore**[9] 4-10-7 0.......................... PeterCarberry 59
(Gay Kelleway) *v small light-framed: chsd ldrs: hit 6th: struggling after: rdn 3 out: 10 l 3rd 2 out: fdd qckly: faltered flat and lost 5th: t.o* **12/1**

4m 10.2s (-2.80) **Going Correction** -0.325s/f (Good)
WFA 4 from 5yo+ 7lb 6 Ran SP% **107.9**
Speed ratings (Par 103): **94,91,86,85,74 72**
CSF £7.76 TOTE £2.50: £1.30, £1.90; EX 9.20 Trifecta £14.10.There was no bid for the winner
Owner M J Hills **Bred** R A Bonnycastle And Marston Stud **Trained** Upper Lambourn, Berks

FOCUS
This was run over 45 yards further than advertised. Afterwards winning jockey James Banks said: "It's tacky as it's old ground," while Brodie Hampson's take on it was: "It's good ground." The first two had this seller between them a long way from home. The winner was 10lb off his best 2015 figure.

4772 EASTER MONDAY RACING AT FAKENHAM BEGINNERS' CHASE (18 fncs) 3m 38y

2:35 (2:35) (Class 3) 5-Y-0+ **£6,989** (£2,170; £1,168)

Form RPR

-222 **1** **Bon Chic (IRE)**[81] 3317 7-10-7 125.......................... RobertDunne 123+
(Dan Skelton) *j. economically: led tl 2nd and fr 5th: lobbed clr fr 15th: nvr out of a canter* **1/5**[1]

4652 **2** *37* **Veauce De Sivola (FR)**[11] 4531 7-11-0 88................(tp) GavinSheehan 102
(Mark Gillard) *j. modly: led 2nd tl 5th: pushed along and chsd wnr but nt travelling wl after: mstke 8th: completely outpcd 15th: lost 2nd between last two but lft remote 2nd at last* **10/1**[3]

0P44 **3** *74* **The Society Man (IRE)**[5] 4641 9-10-7 81.......................... GrahamCarson(7) 30
(Michael Chapman) *last fr 6th: mstke 8th and rdn: hit 13th: continued t.o and crawling along: lft 3rd at last* **40/1**

P063 **P** **The Jugopolist (IRE)**[11] 4533 9-11-0 68................(b) AdamWedge
(John Cornwall) *last whn hmpd 2nd and immediately p.u* **80/1**

/6P- **F** **Steepleofcopper (IRE)**[593] 1158 10-11-0 67................(t) JackQuinlan
(Alan Jessop) *crashing fall 2nd* **100/1**

0-03 **F** **Rhythm Star**[58] 2925 6-10-7 109................(b) MichealNolan 98
(Jamie Snowden) *3rd fr 6th: numerous shoddy jumps: v slow 11th and rdn: nt travelling after: mstke 3 out: drvn into 2nd between last two: 25 l bhd cantering wnr whn fell last* **7/2**[2]

6m 40.1s (4.40) **Going Correction** +0.325s/f (Yiel) 6 Ran SP% **119.3**
Speed ratings: **105,92,68, ,**
CSF £4.14 TOTE £1.20: £1.10, £3.50; EX 3.70 Trifecta £7.10.
Owner Coral Champions Club **Bred** Barry O'Connor **Trained** Alcester, Warwicks

FOCUS
This was run over 111 yards further than advertised. An uncompetitive beginners' chase. The easy winner didn't need to be at her best.

4773 ROBERT CASE MEMORIAL CONDITIONAL JOCKEYS' MAIDEN HURDLE (8 hdls 1 omitted) 2m 3y

3:15 (3:15) (Class 4) 4-Y-0+ **£4,548** (£1,335; £667; £333)

Form RPR

323 **1** **Baltic Storm (IRE)**[112] 2747 5-10-6 114.......................... TommyDowling(8) 121+
(Charlie Mann) *trckd ldrs: hit 5th: wnt 3rd and nt fluent 3 out: led gng much the best passing 2 out: sn pushed clr: unchal* **3/1**[2]

24 **2** *17* **Deadly Approach**[36] 4065 5-10-9 109.......................... CharlieHammond(5) 104
(Sarah-Jayne Davies) *racd keenly in ld: hrd drvn and hdd passing 2 out: immediately outpcd by wnr but jst clung on to 2nd* **5/1**[3]

264P **3** *nk* **Jethro (IRE)**[83] 3242 5-10-11 106.......................... MeganCarberry(3) 105
(Brian Ellison) *plld hrd in 2nd or 3rd: mstke 6th: hrd drvn bef 2 out: little rspnse and wnr sn clr: ev ch of poor 2nd at last: plugged on* **5/1**[3]

4 **4** *½* **Persian Breeze**[22] 4317 4-10-0 0.......................... DavidNoonan 90
(Lucy Wadham) *hld up and bhd: effrt after 6th: 4th and hrd drvn bef 2 out: fnd nil: plugged on same pce after* **2/1**[1]

0 **5** *22* **Chief Spirit**[14] 4462 4-10-7 0.......................... HarryBannister 80
(James Eustace) *bhd: rdn 5th: blnd 6th: no ch after: t.o* **12/1**

6 *7* **Hannington**[7] 5-10-9 0.......................... JamieInsole(5) 77
(Barry Brennan) *blnd 1st: chsd ldrs: rdn 5th: 4th and drvn bef 3 out: sn struggling: t.o* **33/1**

P40 **7** *shd* **Marshgate Lane (USA)**[116] 2689 7-10-6 0.......................... MrShaneQuinlan(8) 78
(Neil Mulholland) *cl up: mstke 4th: rdn and lost pl bef 3 out: t.o* **15/2**

56 **8** *5* **Winola**[12] 4502 6-10-4 0.......................... FinianO'Toole(3) 66
(Charlie Wallis) *bhd after mstke 2nd: t.o fr 6th* **100/1**

6PP0 **9** *15* **Monzino (USA)**[8] 3233 8-10-9 62.......................... GrahamCarson(5) 59
(Michael Chapman) *rdn and reluctant in last: t.o fr 1/2-way* **100/1**

0PP **P** **Arroyeau (FR)**[18] 4409 6-11-0 0................(t) JamieBargary
(Nick Gifford) *wore earplugs: blnd 1st: chsd ldrs tl 1/2-way: sn reluctant u.p: t.o and p.u 3 out* **66/1**

4m 6.5s (-6.50) **Going Correction** -0.325s/f (Good)
WFA 4 from 5yo+ 7lb 10 Ran SP% **117.5**
Speed ratings (Par 105): **103,94,94,94,83 79,79,77,69,**
CSF £18.75 TOTE £3.30: £1.90, £2.00, £2.60; EX 15.80 Trifecta £41.70.
Owner John Heron **Bred** Gestut Ammerland **Trained** Upper Lambourn, Berks

FOCUS
Race run over 45 yards further than advertised. The second-last flight was bypassed. A modest maiden hurdle. The winner is entitled to rate higher on Flat form.

4774 TOTEPOOL FAKENHAM SILVER CUP (A H'CAP HURDLE) (9 hdls) 2m 3y

3:55 (3:56) (Class 3) (0-125,125) 4-Y-0+ **£9,097** (£2,671; £1,335; £667)

Form RPR

033 **1** **Instant Karma (IRE)**[50] 3819 5-10-11 110.......................... LeightonAspell 123+
(Michael Bell) *chsd ldrs: 5th bef 3 out: rdn and qcknd to ld bef next and dashed clr: pushed along and nvr in danger after* **4/1**[1]

4020 **2** *8* **Domtaline (FR)**[58] 3682 9-11-0 120.......................... MrRWinks(7) 125
(Peter Winks) *midfield: 4th bef 3 out where blnd: sn pushed along: 6th at next but fin stoutly to go 2nd at last: no ch w wnr* **14/1**

-126 **3** *2* **Qasser (IRE)**[22] 3487 7-11-11 124.......................... GavinSheehan 128
(Harry Whittington) *hld up towards rr: last of eight gng clr bef 3 out where blnd: effrt and rdn and chsd wnr vainly after hitting 2 out: btn 2nd and tiring whn hit last* **13/2**[3]

0-43 **4** *7* **Boss Des Mottes (FR)**[124] 2516 5-11-12 125................(t[1]) RyanMahon 122
(Dan Skelton) *a abt same pl: rdn bef 2 out: kpt on same pce and n.d after* **4/1**[1]

0123 **5** *nk* **Gin And Tonic**[89] 3177 6-9-10 102.......................... MissBHampson(7) 101+
(Michael Wigham) *lost 20 l at s: a bhd: rdn and struggling bef 3 out* **7/1**

4644 **6** *6* **Occasionally Yours (IRE)**[77] 3417 12-10-2 108.......................... MissTWorsley(7) 99
(Alan Blackmore) *bhd: j. slowly 3rd: rdn and bdly outpcd bef 3 out but running on v strly after last* **50/1**

0-43 **7** *nse* **Officer Drivel (IRE)**[74] 3466 5-11-11 124.......................... AndrewGlassonbury 116
(Jim Best) *racd freely: pressed ldr tl hrd rdn bef 3 out: btn bef next* **25/1**

3B40 **8** *4 ½* **Spa's Dancer (IRE)**[62] 3619 9-10-8 107.......................... JackQuinlan 95
(James Eustace) *hit 4th: chsd ldrs tl 3 out: sn rdn and btn* **12/1**

1531 **9** *nk* **Fair Loch**[9] 4553 8-11-2 120 7ex.......................... MeganCarberry(5) 108
(Brian Ellison) *led at gd pce: rdn and hdd bef 2 out: lost 3rd and tiring between last two* **8/1**

1/26 **10** *15* **Shalambar (IRE)**[56] 354 10-10-9 108................(b) LeeEdwards 83
(Tony Carroll) *lost 15 l at s: rdn and nvr travelling in rr: struggling bef 3 out where blnd: t.o* **33/1**

3-0 **11** *nse* **Vedani (IRE)**[28] 2961 7-9-10 100.......................... NickSlatter(5) 72
(Tony Carroll) *midfield: rdn and outpcd bef 3 out: t.o but running on after last* **25/1**

0005 **12** *½* **Beatabout The Bush (IRE)**[15] 4447 5-10-13 117.(b[1]) CiaranGethings(5) 89
(Henry Oliver) *prom tl rdn and wknd bef 3 out: t.o* **6/1**[2]

-0P4 **13** *15* **Knight's Parade (IRE)**[22] 2150 6-11-2 125................(t) RomainClavreul(10) 83
(Sarah Humphrey) *bhd: drvn 5th: t.o 3 out* **33/1**

116 **P** **Edward Elgar**[56] 3725 5-11-2 115.......................... AdamPogson
(Caroline Bailey) *qckly lost gd pl: j. slowly 3rd and reminder: sn tailed himself off: p.u 6th* **25/1**

4m 4.9s (-8.10) **Going Correction** -0.325s/f (Good) 14 Ran SP% **125.0**
Speed ratings (Par 107): **107,103,102,98,98 95,95,93,92,85 85,85,77,**
CSF £56.40 CT £371.07 TOTE £5.40: £2.60, £2.40, £2.80; EX 66.00 Trifecta £464.10.
Owner L Caine & J Barnett **Bred** Glashare House Stud **Trained** Newmarket, Suffolk
■ Stewards' Enquiry : Megan Carberry one-day ban: allowed horse to break into a canter at the start (1 Apr)

FOCUS
Race run over 45 yards further than advertised. A competitive handicap for a decent prize. The pace was sound and it was the quickest of the C&D races. The winner is on the upgrade.

4775 PRINCE CARLTON H'CAP CHASE (FOR THE PRINCE CARLTON CHALLENGE CUP) (18 fncs) 3m 38y

4:35 (4:35) (Class 3) (0-130,127) 5-Y-0+ **£6,989** (£2,170; £1,168)

Form RPR

4132 **1** **Wings Attract (IRE)**[26] 4274 7-11-12 127................(b[1]) TomMessenger 136+
(Chris Bealby) *trckd ldrs: lft 2nd at 13th: led gng bttr than rival next: wnt 6 l clr 2 out but rdn: stl 6 l ahd at last but already idling bdly: pulling himself up flat but had enough in hand* **3/1**[2]

1565 **2** *3* **Noble Legend**[29] 4212 9-11-11 126................(p) AdamPogson 128
(Caroline Bailey) *led at fast pce: hdd 10th: lft in ld 13th but sn getting reminders: hdd next: outpcd 3 out: clsng on sufferance after last but nvr looked like catching wnr* **5/1**[3]

-112 **3** *18* **Emerald Rose**[89] 3176 9-11-4 119................(p) MarkGrant 110
(Julian Smith) *countless mstkes and smetimes j.rt: blnd bdly 2nd: nvr travelling in rr: t.o fr 14th* **5/1**[3]

1610 **U** **Ballyadeen (IRE)**[14] 4465 8-11-8 123.......................... JamesBanks
(Dai Williams) *2nd tl led 10th: terrible mstke and uns rdr 13th: fatally injured* **5/1**[3]

2361 **F** **Gamain (IRE)**[28] 4225 7-10-5 111................(b) JamieBargary(5)
(Ben Case) *cl 4th whn fell 8th* **11/4**[1]

63U6 **P** **Harristown**[113] 2727 6-11-4 122................(p) GrahamWatters(3)
(Charlie Longsdon) *nvr jumping or travelling in rr: sn getting reminders: t.o and p.u 12th* **10/1**

6m 38.3s (2.60) **Going Correction** +0.325s/f (Yiel) 6 Ran SP% **110.8**
Speed ratings: **108,107,101, ,**
CSF £17.46 TOTE £3.70: £1.50, £2.00; EX 18.80 Trifecta £80.60.
Owner The Rann Family **Bred** John McAleese **Trained** Barrowby, Lincs

FOCUS
Race run over 111 yards further than advertised. A fair handicap chase. The winner is back on the upgrade.

4776 MARHAM H'CAP CHASE (FOR THE WALTER WALES MEMORIAL CUP) (16 fncs) 2m 5f 44y

5:10 (5:10) (Class 5) (0-100,96) 5-Y-0+ **£3,249** (£954; £477; £238)

Form RPR

-P45 **1** **Miss Dimples (IRE)**[98] 3007 7-10-6 76................(b) TomMessenger 81+
(Sarah-Jayne Davies) *2nd tl led 6th: mstke 3 out and rdn: jst hdd whn outj. last: battled on to regain advantage on nod* **10/1**

4P-P **2** *hd* **That's The Deal (IRE)**[50] 3820 12-10-8 78.......................... AdamWedge 81
(John Cornwall) *settled in tch: effrt 13th: wnt cl 2nd 2 out: rdn after: led last: kpt on but repassed fnl stride* **14/1**

2435 **3** *3 ¾* **Petit Ecuyer (FR)**[74] 3468 10-10-3 73.......................... DaveCrosse 74
(Dai Williams) *cl up: 2nd fr 11th tl drvn and blnd 13th: wknd after next* **7/1**

PP2P **4** *24* **Midnight Charmer**[29] 4214 10-11-11 95................(t) MarkGrant 83
(Emma Baker) *led tl 6th: remained cl up tl hrd rdn 13th: no rspnse and wl btn 2 out: eased flat* **9/2**[2]

42UU **U** **Highbury High (IRE)**[60] 3661 9-11-12 96................(tp) MarkQuinlan
(Neil Mulholland) *trckd ldrs: blnd and uns rdr 11th* **5/1**[3]

P321 **U** **Vent Nivernais (FR)**[39] 4025 7-10-6 **83**...........(p) WilliamFeatherstone(7)
(James Evans) *last whn blnd and v nrly uns at 4th: rdr lost irons and nvr regained them: mstke 10th: wnt 3rd but blnd and uns rdr 12th* **11/10**[1]

5m 52.7s (10.90) **Going Correction** +0.325s/f (Yiel) **6** Ran SP% **110.7**
Speed ratings: **92,91,90,81,**
CSF £104.39 TOTE £9.90: £4.00, £4.20; EX 77.90 Trifecta £365.10.
Owner Pippin Bank Partnership **Bred** Alfred B Hanna **Trained** Leominster, H'fords

FOCUS
Race run over 95 yards further than advertised. A weak handicap chase, the first three pretty much to their marks.
T/Plt: £457.30 to a £1 stake. Pool: £66,819.12 - 106.65 winning units T/Qpdt: £282.90 to a £1 stake. Pool: £3,937.97 - 10.30 winning units **Iain Mackenzie**

4379 FONTWELL (L-H)
Saturday, March 19

OFFICIAL GOING: Good (good to soft in places; 7.2)
Wind: almost nil Weather: sunny periods

4777 BRITISH STALLION STUDS EBF MARES' "NATIONAL HUNT" NOVICES' HURDLE (11 hdls) 2m 5f 139y
2:00 (2:00) (Class 4) 4-Y-0+ **£3,898** (£1,144; £572; £286)

Form RPR

P1 **1** **Treaty Girl (IRE)**[23] 4323 5-11-3 0.............. MauriceLinehan(3) 123+
(Ben Pauling) *trckd ldr: prom 6th: led after 3 out: in command last: styd on wl* **1/1**[1]

3144 **2** *7* **Mystic Sky**[15] 4459 5-11-6 115..............(b[1]) LeightonAspell 116
(Lucy Wadham) *hld up: hdwy after 7th: disputing 3rd whn hit next: rdn to chse wnr 2 out: hld whn hit last: jst hld on for 2nd* **5/2**[2]

62 **3** *nse* **Maid Of Milan (IRE)**[15] 4457 5-11-0.............. AidanColeman 108
(Charlie Mann) *j. sltly rt at times: trckd ldrs: led 7th: rdn and hdd after 3 out: chsd ldng pair next: styd on fr last to nrly regain 2nd fnl stride* **3/1**[3]

4 *7* **Gowell (IRE)** 5-10-9 0.............. KevinJones(5) 103
(Seamus Mullins) *cl up: rdn to dispute cl 3rd after 3 out: styd on same pce fr next: drifted rt run-in* **20/1**

46PP **5** *26* **Sweet'N'Chic (IRE)**[12] 4526 6-11-0 0.............. AndrewGlassonbury 78
(Richard Rowe) *j.rt and nt a fluent: led tl 7th: wknd 3 out* **100/1**

06P **6** *4* **Wun Destination**[17] 4439 7-10-7 0.............. PaulO'Brien(7) 75
(John Panvert) *cl up tl nt fluent and dropped to last 4th: struggling 8th: wknd next* **250/1**

5m 45.6s (3.10) **Going Correction** +0.075s/f (Yiel) **6** Ran SP% **109.7**
Speed ratings (Par 105): **97,94,94,91,82 80**
CSF £3.74 TOTE £1.70: £1.10, £2.00; EX 3.10 Trifecta £5.40.
Owner The Bourtoneers **Bred** Anthony P Butler **Trained** Bourton-On-The-Water, Gloucs

FOCUS
The rails were on the middle inner line, adding 42yds to the race distance. Following a dry night the going was Good, good to soft in places, and the winning jockey described it as Good. A modest mares' hurdle in which only three mattered according to the betting, but the winner scored unextended.

4778 SMARTCOMPUTERSBRISTOL.COM H'CAP CHASE (13 fncs) 2m 1f 96y
2:35 (2:35) (Class 5) (0-100,98) 5-Y-0+ **£3,249** (£954; £477; £238)

Form RPR

0-03 **1** **Bertenbar**[72] 3497 12-11-3 **89**.............. AidanColeman 99+
(Lawney Hill) *trckd ldrs: led 3 out: mstke last: rdn out* **15/2**

P30- **2** *3/4* **Withy Mills**[396] 4281 11-10-0 **79** ow2..............(tp) ConorSmith(7) 87
(Kevin Bishop) *disp ld tl after 4 out: bk upsides next tl 2 out: styd on wl fr last: hld nring fin* **15/2**

02/U **3** *11* **Lost Arca (FR)**[18] 4423 10-10-6 **78**.............. TomCannon 75
(David Bridgwater) *disp ld tl after 7th: rdn after 9th: styd on fr 2 out but no threat: wnt 3rd after last* **10/1**

-5P2 **4** *9* **Edlomond (IRE)**[44] 3951 10-11-7 **98**..............(t) JakeHodson(5) 89
(Bill Turner) *trckd ldrs: pushed along after 7th: led after 4 out gng wl: hdd next: fnd little and sn btn* **9/2**[2]

1F34 **5** *17* **Zero Visibility (IRE)**[47] 3903 9-10-10 **82**.............. LeightonAspell 57
(Alexandra Dunn) *disp ld tl after 9th: rdn after 4 out: wknd next* **13/2**[3]

/F51 **6** *1 1/4* **Gold Carrot**[12] 4527 8-11-4 **90**.............. AndrewGlassonbury 69
(Gary Moore) *hld up: trckd ldrs 7th: sn pushed along: hld in 5th whn mstke 3 out: wknd next* **6/4**[1]

/PUP **P** **My Miss Lucy**[14] 4491 10-11-3 **92**.............. MauriceLinehan(3)
(Richard Phillips) *sn detached in last: tailing off whn wnt bdly rt 8th: p.u after next* **16/1**

4m 38.1s (3.40) **Going Correction** +0.075s/f (Yiel) **7** Ran SP% **110.0**
Speed ratings: **95,94,89,85,77 76,**
CSF £54.50 TOTE £9.40: £3.70, £4.00; EX 79.00 Trifecta £1196.70.
Owner Mrs C A Wyatt **Bred** T J Wyatt **Trained** Aston Rowant, Oxon

FOCUS
Rail movements added 36yds to the race distance. A low-grade handicap chase in which the finish was dominated by veterans. Winner rated to level of Huntingdon win.

4779 "@SMARTBRISTOL ON TWITTER" MARES' H'CAP HURDLE (11 hdls) 2m 5f 139y
3:10 (3:10) (Class 3) (0-135,135) 4-Y-0 **£6,330** (£1,870; £935; £468; £234)

Form RPR

1214 **1** **Sunshine Corner (IRE)**[29] 4231 5-11-3 **126**.............. LeightonAspell 135
(Lucy Wadham) *trckd ldrs: mstke 8th: chal 2 out: rdn after last: tk narrow advantage fnl 120yds: hld on: all out* **4/1**[2]

3-25 **2** *shd* **Lady Of Lamanver**[128] 2455 6-9-10 **112**..............(t) MrMLegg(7) 122+
(Harry Fry) *racd keenly bhd ldrs: tk clsr order 8th: chal 2 out: sn rdn: ev ch whn nt fluent last: kpt on wl: jst hld* **15/2**

-424 **3** *1/2* **Altesse De Guye (FR)**[31] 4186 6-9-11 **109**.............. ConorShoemark(3) 117
(Martin Keighley) *hld up: hmpd 1st: trckd ldrs after 7th: led 3 out: rchd for next: sn rdn: hdd fnl 120yds: kpt on but no ex* **10/1**

P331 **4** *3* **Dolores Delightful (FR)**[16] 4445 6-10-11 **125**..............(t) LizzieKelly(5) 131
(Nick Williams) *trckd ldrs: pressed ldr 7th tl 3 out: sn rdn: styd on same pce fr next* **4/1**[2]

5346 **5** *17* **Miss Serious (IRE)**[119] 2632 6-11-3 **126**.............. NickScholfield 117
(Jeremy Scott) *trckd ldrs: nt fluent 2nd: prom 3rd tl 6th: nt fluent 8th: sn rdn: hld after next: wknd between last 2* **16/1**

2133 **6** *3* **Cannon Fodder**[33] 4159 9-11-7 **130**.............. AidanColeman 119
(Sheena West) *pressed ldr tl 8th: sn outpcd: wknd between last 2* **6/1**[3]

-611 **7** *1 3/4* **Tagrita (IRE)**[17] 4438 8-11-7 **135**..............(t) HarryCobden(5) 121
(Paul Nicholls) *led: mstke 8th: hdd next: sn rdn: wknd between last 2* **11/4**[1]

3223 **8** *37* **Tambura**[43] 3970 6-11-2 **125**.............. TomCannon 77
(G C Maundrell) *in last pair: struggling and detached 7th: t.o 3 out* **14/1**

5m 39.1s (-3.40) **Going Correction** +0.075s/f (Yiel) **8** Ran SP% **114.4**
Speed ratings (Par 107): **109,108,108,107,101 100,99,86**
CSF £33.50 CT £278.31 TOTE £5.80: £2.90, £2.00, £2.90; EX 34.00 Trifecta £403.40.
Owner P A Philipps & Mrs G J Redman **Bred** John Crean **Trained** Newmarket, Suffolk

FOCUS
The rails were on the middle inner line, adding 42yds to the race distance. This decent mares' handicap hurdle was run 6.5sec faster than the earlier novices' hurdle and was an exciting contest, with three in line at the last and not much between them at the finish. Winner back to level of good Haydock run.

4780 PETER AND BERYL SCOTT MEMORIAL H'CAP CHASE (19 fncs) 3m 1f 106y
3:45 (3:46) (Class 4) (0-120,120) 5-Y-0+ **£4,548** (£1,335; £667; £333)

Form RPR

6-6 **1** **Solstice Son**[37] 4062 7-11-1 **114**..............(bt[1]) HarryCobden(5) 131+
(Anthony Honeyball) *mde all: 5 l clr 4 out: styd on wl and in command fr 2 out: rdn out* **9/2**[3]

-4P4 **2** *3 1/2* **Sun Wild Life (FR)**[36] 4101 6-11-4 **119**..............(p) PaulO'Brien(7) 130
(Robert Walford) *pressed ldrs tl 3rd: trckd wnr tl rdn after 14th: regained 2nd 3 out: styd on same pce fr next* **6/1**

2311 **3** *1* **The Cider Maker**[19] 4412 6-11-5 **120**..............(t) MrMLegg(7) 133+
(Colin Tizzard) *sn pushed along chsng ldrs: rdn after 13th: chal for hld 2nd 2 out: no ex nring fin* **9/2**[3]

-012 **4** *6* **Fight Commander (IRE)**[16] 4451 7-11-11 **119**.............. LeightonAspell 125
(Oliver Sherwood) *trckd ldrs: rdn to chse wnr after 4 out: hung rt between last 2: fdd run-in* **3/1**[1]

5624 **5** *14* **Bold Conquest (IRE)**[81] 3336 8-11-5 **118**.............. CiaranGethings(5) 110
(Stuart Edmunds) *trckd ldrs: pushed along fr 15th: rdn after 4 out: wknd after next* **7/2**[2]

3225 **6** *82* **St Johns Point (IRE)**[37] 4062 8-11-12 **120**..............(tp) AidanColeman 38
(Charlie Longsdon) *led tl 4th: trckd ldrs: rdn after 14th: wknd after 3 out: stmbld last: eased* **11/1**

-31P **P** **Badger Wood**[31] 4185 7-10-12 **106**.............. TomCannon
(Giles Smyly) *trckd ldrs: hit 3rd: nt fluent next: nvr travelling after: lost tch 7th: p.u next* **11/1**

6m 59.0s (-2.10) **Going Correction** +0.075s/f (Yiel) **7** Ran SP% **114.5**
Speed ratings: **106,104,104,102,98 71,**
CSF £30.91 TOTE £5.30: £2.50, £3.80; EX 42.80 Trifecta £333.60.
Owner The Summer Solstice **Bred** R W Russell **Trained** Mosterton, Dorset

FOCUS
Rail movements added 54yds to the race distance. A competitive staying handicap chase, but the winner ran and jumped his rivals ragged. Winner sets person best, runner-up and fourth close to marks.

4781 SMART COMPUTERS UK LTD ON FACEBOOK H'CAP HURDLE (9 hdls) 2m 1f 145y
4:20 (4:21) (Class 3) (0-135,134) 4-Y-0 **£6,330** (£1,870; £935; £468; £234)

Form RPR

3P-0 **1** **Karinga Dancer**[105] 2901 10-11-5 **134**..............(t) MrMLegg(7) 141+
(Harry Fry) *trckd ldrs: hit 5th: led after 3 out: kpt on wl and in command fr next* **8/1**

1-P0 **2** *6* **Maestro Royal**[37] 4070 7-11-2 **124**.............. PeterCarberry 124
(Nicky Henderson) *hld up: hdwy 6th: wnt 2nd after 3 out: rdn bef next: kpt on but no imp on wnr* **7/1**[3]

1214 **3** *4* **Bigmartre (FR)**[56] 3739 5-11-7 **134**.............. CiaranGethings(5) 132+
(Harry Whittington) *dictated str pce w 2 others: outrt ldr 6th tl rdn after 3 out: sn hld: styd on same pce fr next* **5/2**[1]

0-0 **4** *14* **Nathans Pride (IRE)**[140] 2184 8-11-2 **129**.............. AlanJohns(5) 113
(Tim Vaughan) *in tch: rdn after 3 out: styd on same pce fr next* **20/1**

20PP **5** *8* **Lightentertainment (IRE)**[37] 4070 8-11-2 **124**.............. TomCannon 101
(Chris Gordon) *hld up: struggling 6th: nvr threatened* **12/1**

1-20 **6** *9* **Needless Shouting (IRE)**[58] 3708 5-10-10 **118**.............. LeightonAspell 87
(Mick Channon) *helped dictate str pce: rdn after 5th: hdd next: wknd after 3 out* **10/1**

-P41 **7** *16* **Flashman**[56] 2253 7-9-9 **110**..............(b) GeorgeGorman(7) 64
(Gary Moore) *helped dictate str pce tl rdn after 5th: lost pl next: wknd 3 out* **7/1**[3]

2055 **P** **Exitas (IRE)**[58] 3708 8-11-1 **126**..............(t) ConorShoemark(3)
(Phil Middleton) *in tch tl 6th: sn wknd: t.o whn p.u 2 out* **12/1**

0-64 **P** **Wilberdragon**[114] 2728 6-11-7 **129**..............(t) AidanColeman
(Charlie Longsdon) *chsd ldrs tl after 5th: wknd next: t.o whn p.u 2 out* **7/2**[2]

4m 33.0s (-1.30) **Going Correction** +0.075s/f (Yiel) **9** Ran SP% **116.1**
Speed ratings (Par 107): **105,102,100,94,90 86,79, ,**
CSF £62.89 CT £181.46 TOTE £8.80: £2.30, £1.60, £1.40; EX 57.20 Trifecta £215.40.
Owner H B Geddes **Bred** Mr & Mrs J K S Cresswell **Trained** Seaborough, Dorset

FOCUS
The rails were on the middle inner line, adding 36yds to the race distance. Quite a fair handicap hurdle and they went a pretty strong gallop. Winner well-in on old form and back to somethink like his best.

4782 SMART COMPUTERS I.T. SUPPORT H'CAP HURDLE (10 hdls) 2m 3f 33y
4:55 (4:55) (Class 4) (0-120,120) 4-Y-0+ **£3,898** (£1,144; £572; £286)

Form RPR

0056 **1** **Paris Snow**[71] 3508 6-10-4 **103**.............. JakeHodson(5) 113+
(Ian Williams) *hld up towards rr: hdwy after 3 out: chal 2 out: led bef last: pushed clr: comf* **3/1**[1]

-455 **2** *7* **Paddy The Deejay (IRE)**[101] 2973 7-11-3 **116**.............. CiaranGethings(5) 118
(Stuart Edmunds) *mid-div: hdwy 6th: rdn to chal 2 out: styd on but nt pce of wnr fr last* **8/1**

4041 **3** *3/4* **Tanit River (IRE)**[17] 4432 6-11-4 **117**.............. AlanJohns(5) 117+
(Tim Vaughan) *mid-div: hdwy 7th: chal 3 out: rdn and ev ch next: kpt on but no ex fr last* **7/1**[3]

0320 **4** *6* **Guards Chapel**[15] 4466 8-11-4 **112**..............(v) JamieMoore 107
(Gary Moore) *towards rr: rdn and plenty to do after 3 out: hdwy appr last: styd on flat: wnt 4th fnl 100yds: nvr trbld ldrs* **20/1**

201- **5** *2* **Libeccio (FR)**[342] 5295 5-11-0 **115**..............(t) TommyDowling(7) 109
(Charlie Mann) *hld up towards rr: midfield whn mstke 3 out: sn rdn: no further imp fr next* **33/1**

3F50 **6** *2 1/2* **Red Devil Star (IRE)**[14] 4484 6-11-7 **120**..............(t) JackSherwood(5) 113
(Suzy Smith) *led: rdn after 3 out: hdd bef last: fdd run-in* **12/1**

5350 **7** *1 3/4* **Golden Bird (IRE)**[84] 3220 5-10-13 **107**.............. PeterCarberry 98
(Brendan Powell) *trckd ldrs: hit 5th: rdn appr 7th: wkng whn mstke last* **25/1**

5B05 **8** *12* **Midnight Shot**[57] 3728 6-11-12 **120**........................... AidanColeman 99
(Charlie Longsdon) *mid-div: rdn after 3 out: wknd next* **8/1**

-055 **9** *7* **Coup De Grace (IRE)**[42] 3994 7-11-0 **111**................ MauriceLinehan(3) 83
(Pat Phelan) *prom tl rdn 3 out: wknd bef next* **25/1**

/26- **10** *6* **Salto Chisco (IRE)**[449] 3275 8-11-5 **113**.................. LeightonAspell 86
(Oliver Sherwood) *hld up: hdwy 4th: trckd ldrs 6th: effrt after 3 out: wknd between last 2: eased run-in* **4/1**[2]

4045 **11** *4* **Chief Brody**[29] 4235 5-11-1 **114**..............................(p) DavidNoonan(5) 77
(Grace Harris) *chsd ldrs tl wknd after 7th* **40/1**

0626 **U** **Disputed (IRE)**[20] 4381 6-11-11 **119**................................ TomCannon
(Chris Gordon) *mid-div whn blnd and uns rdr 6th* **9/1**

5m 10.1s (10.70) **Going Correction** +0.075s/f (Yiel) **12 Ran SP% 115.2**
Speed ratings (Par 105): **80,77,76,74,73 72,71,66,63,61 59,**
CSF £24.44 CT £154.78 TOTE £4.60: £2.90, £3.00, £1.80; EX 32.30 Trifecta £185.00.
Owner Paul Mannion **Bred** George Strawbridge **Trained** Portway, Worcs

FOCUS
The rails were on the middle inner line, adding 36yds to the race distance. They went a very slow early pace in this handicap hurdle.

4783 SMART COMPUTERS SUPPORTING RACING CONDITIONAL JOCKEYS' H'CAP HURDLE (13 hdls) — 3m 1f 142y
5:30 (5:30) (Class 5) (0-100,103) 4-Y-0+ **£3,249** (£954; £477; £238)

Form RPR

PP01 **1** **Coolking**[22] 4349 9-12-1 **103**...................................(b) DavidNoonan 115+
(Chris Gordon) *disp fr 2nd: clr ldr after 6th: hit 10th: drew clr fr 2 out: easily* **4/1**[3]

4221 **2** *12* **Young Lou**[6] 4644 7-10-10 **92** 7ex...............................(p) CathalCourtney(8) 90
(Robin Dickin) *trckd ldrs: dropped to last but in tch 3rd: hdwy after 3 out: styd on same pce fr next and no threat to wnr: wnt 2nd cl home* **7/2**[2]

P0OP **3** *½* **Tales Of Milan (IRE)**[58] 3707 9-11-12 **100**.....................(b) HarryCobden 98
(Phil Middleton) *disp ld tl nt fluent 6th: chsd wnr: rdn and ev ch briefly after 3 out: styd on same pce fr next: lost 2nd cl home* **3/1**[1]

F6F2 **4** *21* **Tikkapick (IRE)**[16] 4454 6-10-12 **92**............................. PaulO'Brien(6) 70
(Colin Tizzard) *chsd ldrs disputing 3rd and rdn appr 10th: one pce fr 2 out* **5/1**

40P6 **5** *4* **Betsy Boo Boo**[51] 3821 7-10-9 **83**...............................(p) JeremiahMcGrath 58
(Michael Roberts) *in tch: hdwy 10th: rdn after next to dispute 3rd: one pce fr 2 out* **25/1**

45P0 **6** *33* **Burgundy Betty (IRE)**[54] 3771 6-10-9 **86**................ MauriceLinehan(3) 31
(Ben Pauling) *sn pushed along: ldng whn nt fluent 1st: hdd whn nt fluent 2nd: in last pair 4th: lost tch 9th: t.o* **10/1**

-U3P **7** *43* **Exmoor Challenge**[97] 3062 7-10-8 **82**...........................(p) KillianMoore
(Neil King) *chsd ldrs: hit 9th: reminders: wknd next: t.o* **18/1**

4-0P **P** **Lady A**[25] 4290 6-10-11 **85**..(p) LizzieKelly
(Chris Gordon) *in tch: trckd ldrs 3rd: pushed along after 5th: wknd after 10th: p.u after next* **17/2**

6m 59.1s (6.30) **Going Correction** +0.075s/f (Yiel) **8 Ran SP% 112.6**
Speed ratings (Par 103): **93,89,89,82,81 71,58,**
CSF £18.20 CT £46.26 TOTE £4.40: £1.50, £1.60, £1.50; EX 14.40 Trifecta £46.60.
Owner Sir Peter & Lady Forwood **Bred** Goldford Stud **Trained** Morestead, Hampshire
■ Stewards' Enquiry : Paul O'Brien two-day ban; deliberately faced his horse backwards when instructed to line up at the start (2nd-3rd Apr)

FOCUS
The rails were on the middle inner line, adding 54yds to the race distance. A moderate staying handicap hurdle which the winner dominated.
T/Plt: £209.40 to a £1 stake. Pool of £71994.24 - 250.88 winning tickets. T/Qpdt: £41.30 to a £1 stake. Pool of £5390.78 - 96.56 winning tickets. **Tim Mitchell**

4358

KEMPTON (R-H)
Saturday, March 19

OFFICIAL GOING: Good (chs 7.6, hdl 6.9)
Wind: light, half against Weather: dry, overcast

4784 RACINGUK.COM/ANYWHERE NOVICES' HURDLE (8 hdls) — 2m
2:05 (2:07) (Class 4) 4-Y-0+ **£3,249** (£954; £477; £238)

Form RPR

0-12 **1** **Brain Power (IRE)**[41] 4010 5-11-6 134............................ BarryGeraghty 133+
(Nicky Henderson) *mstkes: t.k.h: chsd ldrs: pushed along to chal and mstke 2 out: rdn to ld bef last: nt fluent last wandered flat but styd on: rdn out* **2/5**[1]

1 **2** *1½* **Imperial Presence (IRE)**[138] 2238 5-11-6 0.................. MichealNolan 128
(Philip Hobbs) *t.k.h: hdwy to chse ldr 1st: led next: jnd and blnd 2 out: hdd bef last: styd on same pce after* **5/1**[2]

04 **3** *1½* **Valhalla (IRE)**[28] 4256 6-11-0 0...................................(t) PaddyBrennan 122
(Colin Tizzard) *chsd ldrs: wnt 2nd 3rd tl bef 2 out: 4th and sltly outpcd between last 2: kpt on to go 3rd again flat* **14/1**

24 **4** *2* **Fouburg (FR)**[98] 3039 4-10-7 0.. HarrySkelton 112
(Dan Skelton) *t.k.h: hld up in tch in midfield: clsd to chse ldrs 3 out: cl enough in 3rd next: no ex last: styd on same pce and lost 3rd flat* **11/2**[3]

066 **5** *26* **Gone Viral (IRE)**[23] 4317 5-11-0 107..............................(t) AndrewTinkler 96
(George Baker) *hld up in midfield: effrt after 3 out: 5th and no imp bef next: btn whn j.rt next: wknd* **33/1**

0-P5 **6** *13* **Rose Revived**[20] 4388 5-10-0 0..................................... PatrickCowley(7) 77
(Jonjo O'Neill) *bhd: lost tch 3 out: no ch but styd on to pass btn horses fr 2 out: t.o* **50/1**

06 **7** *4* **Denny Kerrell**[78] 3416 5-11-0 0...................................... IanPopham 80
(Caroline Keevil) *a towards rr: lost tch 3 out: t.o next* **100/1**

-044 **8** *6* **Burma (FR)**[97] 3066 5-10-7 0.. JamesBest 68
(Paul Webber) *t.k.h: hld up in midfield: mstke 4th: chsd ldrs next: 6th and wknd bef 2 out: fdd between last 2: t.o* **66/1**

100 **9** *1½* **Bentworth Boy**[92] 3138 5-11-0 0..................................[1] NicodeBoinville 74
(Patrick Chamings) *midfield: struggling bef 3 out: sn lost tch: t.o* **50/1**

560 **10** *5* **Good Man Hughie (IRE)**[16] 4441 7-10-7 0.................. MissBHampson(7) 69
(Sally Randell) *t.k.h: hld up in rr: pushed along after 5th: sn lost tch: t.o* **66/1**

1-34 **11** *23* **Preseli Star (IRE)**[156] 1929 6-11-0 0.............................. PaulMoloney 48
(George Baker) *t.k.h: chsd ldrs tl 5th: struggling next: sn wknd: t.o and eased flat* **66/1**

545 **12** *1¼* **Sea Serpent (FR)**[15] 4462 4-10-7 0.................................. JamieMoore 40
(Gary Moore) *led tl 2nd: chsd ldrs tl lost pl after 5th: wl bhd whn mstke 2 out: t.o whn eased flat* **66/1**

P-26 **P** **Boolavard King (IRE)**[45] 3928 7-11-0 0.......................... DavidBass
(Kim Bailey) *hld up towards rr: hdwy 5th: 8th but nt on terms w ldrs whn mstke 3 out: immediately p.u and dismntd* **25/1**

P **Duke Of North (IRE)**[26] 4-10-7 0...................................... LiamTreadwell
(Jim Boyle) *plld hrd: hld up in rr: blnd 2nd: nt fluent and sddle slipped next: eased and p.u after 4th* **100/1**

3m 54.5s (-3.50) **Going Correction** -0.70s/f (Firm)
WFA 4 from 5yo+ 7lb **14 Ran SP% 128.8**
Speed ratings (Par 105): **80,79,78,77,64 58,56,53,52,49 38,37, ,**
CSF £3.21 TOTE £1.40: £1.10, £1.50, £2.70; EX 3.50 Trifecta £18.70.
Owner Michael Buckley **Bred** David Harvey **Trained** Upper Lambourn, Berks

FOCUS
All starts have been moved at this track following remeasuring, so there will be no speed figures here until there is sufficient data to calculate updated median times. The ground had dried out slightly and was now good all over. Chase and hurdle courses at their innermost configurations and all distances as advertised. After the first Barry Geraghty felt the ground was dead and riding a bit slow.\n\x\x An interesting novice hurdle in which they bet 14-1 bar three. The pace was ordinary and it paid to be handy, with the first four pulling a country mile clear of the rest. Winner close to mark he set in defeat in good novice event previously.

4785 RACING UK NOW IN HD NOVICES' LIMITED H'CAP CHASE (12 fncs) — 2m
2:40 (2:40) (Class 3) (0-135,135) 5-Y-0+
£8,132 (£2,402; £1,201; £600; £300; £150)

Form RPR

2241 **1** **Always On The Run (IRE)**[36] 4098 6-11-2 **129**.............. PaddyBrennan 141+
(Tom George) *mde all: jnd but gng best bef 3 out: rdn and wnt 3 l clr bef 2 out: blnd and wnt lft last: styd on and a holding runner-up flat: rdn out* **11/4**[1]

4222 **2** *1½* **Notnowsam**[100] 2993 5-10-11 **124**..................................(p) HarrySkelton 131
(Dan Skelton) *chsd wnr after 3rd: rdn and chalng but wnr gng bttr bef 3 out: outpcd and 3 l down bef 2 out: lft w a ch last and sn swtchd rt: styd on same pce after* **8/1**

1065 **3** *2¾* **Ink Master (IRE)**[75] 3466 6-10-4 **117**................................ JamesBest 123
(Philip Hobbs) *chsd ldr: blnd: lost 2nd bef next but styd chsng ldrs: drvn and unable qck bef 3 out: plugged on same pce after: wnt 3rd between last 2* **11/2**[2]

P230 **4** *3* **Sirabad (FR)**[28] 4239 6-11-1 **128**..............................(t) SamTwiston-Davies 130
(Paul Nicholls) *hld up in tch: effrt in 5th but no imp bef 3 out: plugged on same pce after* **11/4**[1]

301P **5** *4½* **Antony (FR)**[84] 3228 6-11-1 **128**..................................... JamieMoore 129
(Gary Moore) *j.lft at times: chsd ldrs: 3rd and unable qck bef 3 out: lost 3rd between last 2: wknd last* **8/1**

1205 **6** *4½* **Purple 'n Gold (IRE)**[18] 2185 7-11-3 **135**................(p) DavidNoonan(5) 130
(David Pipe) *hld up in tch in last pair: effrt sn after 9th: no imp and btn next: wknd 2 out* **10/1**

51- **7** *¾* **Casino Markets (IRE)**[492] 2466 8-10-3 **116** oh1............ NicodeBoinville 114+
(Emma Lavelle) *hld up in rr: blnd bdly 5th and detached last after: rdn and no hdwy after 9th: wl btn next* **15/2**[3]

3m 52.9s (-2.10) **Going Correction** -0.20s/f (Good) **7 Ran SP% 111.8**
Speed ratings: **97,96,94,93,91 88,88**
CSF £22.90 TOTE £2.50: £1.60, £3.20; EX 21.40 Trifecta £93.10.
Owner Paul & Clare Rooney **Bred** Island Bridge Racing Club **Trained** Slad, Gloucs

FOCUS
A decent novices' handicap chase run at a good clip thanks to the winner, who improved on recent CD win.

4786 RACINGUK.COM/HD KEMPTON PARK SILVER PLATE (A H'CAP HURDLE) (10 hdls) — 2m 5f
3:15 (3:15) (Class 2) 4-Y-0+
£20,644 (£6,098; £3,049; £1,524; £762; £382)

Form RPR

11-5 **1** **Might Bite (IRE)**[127] 2469 7-11-12 **138**.......................... NicodeBoinville 150+
(Nicky Henderson) *hld up wl in tch and a gng wl: trckd ldrs after 7th: led bef 2 out and sn clr: in command and mstke last: styd on: comf* **8/1**[3]

3124 **2** *8* **Simply A Legend**[56] 3733 7-11-5 **134**............................ TomBellamy(3) 137
(Alan King) *hld up in midfield: hdwy after 7th: rdn and styd on to chse ldrs after 3 out: chsd clr wnr and mstke 2 out: kpt on but no threat to wnr* **14/1**

1315 **3** *2* **Abricot De L'Oasis (FR)**[21] 4354 6-11-1 **127**.................. HarrySkelton 128
(Dan Skelton) *led tl rdn and hdd after 3 out: unable qck w wnr and btn 3rd 2 out: kpt on same pce after* **14/1**

F425 **4** *nk* **Goodbye Dancer (FR)**[34] 4139 5-11-4 **130**.................... PaddyBrennan 131
(Nigel Twiston-Davies) *bhd: stl plenty to do whn swtchd rt and effrt after 7th: styd on to pass btn horses after 3 out: wnt 4th after 2 out: kpt on flat: no ch w wnr* **25/1**

-135 **5** *12* **Pull The Chord (IRE)**[28] 4239 6-11-8 **134**........................ JamesBest 123
(Philip Hobbs) *midfield: rdn after 7th: plugged on and pressing for 3rd but no ch w wnr 2 out: wknd bef last* **25/1**

11-P **6** *13* **Gold Present (IRE)**[129] 2438 6-11-10 **136**.................. JeremiahMcGrath 115
(Nicky Henderson) *wl in tch in midfield: hdwy to chse ldrs 5th: wnt 2nd after next tl lost pl after 3 out: wknd next* **18/1**

63-0 **7** *1½* **Vercingetorix (IRE)**[42] 4006 5-11-8 **134**...........................(bt) DarylJacob 111
(Gordon Elliott, Ire) *hld up in rr: effrt and sme prog after 7th: no imp and wl btn bef 2 out: wknd: t.o* **16/1**

010P **8** *12* **Prouts Pub (IRE)**[33] 4159 7-11-3 **129**............................ LiamTreadwell 94
(Nick Gifford) *a bhd: rdn after 6th: lost tch bef 3 out: t.o* **50/1**

F400 **9** *4½* **Horizontal Speed (IRE)**[28] 4246 8-11-6 **132**.................. IanPopham 93
(David Dennis) *chsd ldrs tl lost pl after 7th: wknd bef 2 out: t.o* **40/1**

0110 **10** *11* **For Good Measure (IRE)**[7] 4622 5-11-4 **130**................ BarryGeraghty 81
(Philip Hobbs) *a in rr: pushed along and no hdwy after 6th: t.o after 3 out* **8/1**[3]

313 **11** *shd* **Miles To Milan (IRE)**[56] 3744 6-11-5 **131**........................ MichealNolan 82
(Philip Hobbs) *midfield tl lost pl after 7th: wl bhd after 3 out: t.o* **12/1**

12 *38* **Townshend (GER)**[28] 4259 5-11-9 **135**.................................[1] RWalsh 52
(W P Mullins, Ire) *hld up in rr: short-lived effrt 7th: sn wl btn: t.o and eased 2 out* **2/1**[1]

-514 **P** **Salmanazar**[34] 4139 8-11-6 **132**.................................... WayneHutchinson
(Alan King) *chsd ldr tl 5th: lost pl bef next: t.o whn p.u 2 out* **25/1**

/141 **P** **A Hare Breath (IRE)**[54] 3775 8-11-11 **137**.......................... DavidBass
(Ben Pauling) *chsd ldrs: wnt 2nd 5th tl bef 3 out: lost pl rapidly and t.o 2 out: p.u last* **9/2**[2]

2-40 **P** **No No Mac (IRE)**[114] 2733 7-11-6 **132**..........................(p) NoelFehily
(Charlie Longsdon) *chsd ldrs tl 5th: rdn and lost pl after next: t.o whn p.u 2 out* **40/1**

-633 **U** **Keltus (FR)**[35] 4112 6-11-8 **134**..............................(t) SamTwiston-Davies 120
(Paul Nicholls) *hld up in midfield: effrt after 7th: 5th and no imp u.p bef 2 out: wl btn whn mstke and uns rdr 2 out* **14/1**

3-4P **P** **Champagne Express**[37] 4070 6-11-7 **133**........................ AndrewTinkler
(Nicky Henderson) *midfield: rdn and no rspnse after 6th: no ch after next: t.o whn p.u 2 out* **22/1**

4m 59.0s (-22.00) **Going Correction** -0.70s/f (Firm) **17** Ran SP% **135.3**
Speed ratings (Par 109): **113,109,109,109,104 99,98,94,92,88 88,73, , ,**
CSF £117.31 CT £1600.16 TOTE £9.70: £2.00, £2.40, £3.00, £4.90; EX 137.30 Trifecta £1130.80.
Owner The Knot Again Partnership **Bred** John O'Brien **Trained** Upper Lambourn, Berks

FOCUS
This race was open to all horses that were eliminated at the declaration stage from any handicap hurdle at the Cheltenham Festival. A competitive race in its own right and they went a solid pace, but it was taken apart by the top weight. Winner very progressive; third and fourth help set the level

4787 RACING UK IN HD KEMPTON PARK SILVER BOWL (A H'CAP CHASE) (16 fncs) 2m 4f 110y
3:50 (3:50) (Class 2) 5-Y-0+
£25,024 (£7,392; £3,696; £1,848; £924; £464)

Form RPR

3-0P **1** **Portway Flyer (IRE)**[75] 3466 8-10-4 **115**........................(t) NicodeBoinville 131+
(Ian Williams) *hld up in tch in midfield: hdwy to press ldrs after 9th: jnd ldr 11th: j. into ld next: gng best whn lft clr 3 out: styd on wl: rdn out* **11/2**[2]

4212 **2** *7* **Cernunnos (FR)**[21] 4363 6-11-7 **132**........................(tp) BarryGeraghty 142+
(Tom George) *hld up in last quartet: hdwy 11th: effrt but stl plenty to do bef 3 out: 3rd and u.p between last 2: wnt 2nd flat: kpt on but no ch w wnr* **11/2**[2]

0433 **3** *hd* **Ballybolley (IRE)**[53] 3794 7-11-1 **126**........................(t) DarylJacob 139+
(Nigel Twiston-Davies) *chsd ldr tl lft in ld 1st: clr 6th: mstke 10th and jnd next: hdd 12th but styd upsides ldr: nt travelling as wl whn blnd 3 out: styd on same pce u.p after: lost 2nd flat* **9/2**[1]

P-1 **4** *8* **Orbasa (FR)**[20] 4379 5-11-7 **132**........................(t) SamTwiston-Davies 133
(Paul Nicholls) *hld up in tch in midfield: hdwy 12th: chsd clr ldng pair and rdn bef 3 out: 4th and no imp between last 2: wknd last* **6/1**[3]

-40P **5** *16* **Pumped Up Kicks (IRE)**[128] 2459 9-11-4 **129**........................ HarrySkelton 117
(Dan Skelton) *midfield tl dropped towards rr 6th: rdn and struggling 13th: wl btn next* **14/1**

-P44 **6** *4* **Festive Affair (IRE)**[15] 4464 8-10-11 **122**........................(t) NoelFehily 105
(Jonjo O'Neill) *hld up in last quartet: stdy hdwy after 9th: cl enough in midfield 12th: short-lived effrt after next: sn btn and wknd 3 out* **10/1**

6P12 **7** *4 ½* **Royal Macnab (IRE)**[78] 3425 8-10-8 **122**........................(t) TonyKelly(3) 104
(Rebecca Menzies) *chsd ldrs: blnd 11th: struggling 13th: wknd bef next: t.o* **20/1**

2015 **8** *5* **Astigos (FR)**[14] 4469 9-11-0 **125**........................(p) LiamTreadwell 102
(Venetia Williams) *a bhd: lost tch 13th: t.o bef 3 out* **16/1**

0105 **9** *55* **De Faoithesdream (IRE)**[46] 3917 10-11-5 **130**........................ PaulMoloney 55
(Evan Williams) *led tl mstke and hdd 1st: chsd ldr tl after 9th: midfield and dropping out next: bhd and t.o bef 3 out* **33/1**

3 **10** *24* **Atirelarigo (FR)**[36] 4097 6-10-12 **123**........................ MichealNolan 27
(Philip Hobbs) *midfield: chsd ldrs after 9th: mstke next and sn losing pl: t.o bef 3 out* **6/1**[3]

2051 **P** **Fairy Rath (IRE)**[29] 4230 10-11-6 **131**........................ PaddyBrennan
(Nick Gifford) *chsd ldrs: wnt 2nd after 9th: ev ch 11th tl 13th: wknd rapidly bef next: t.o whn p.u 2 out* **10/1**

13-P **F** **Dance Floor King (IRE)**[21] 4355 9-11-2 **127**........................ IanPopham
(Nick Mitchell) *midfield whn fell 1st* **25/1**

1P4P **P** **Un Beau Roman (FR)**[14] 4485 8-11-12 **137**........................ WayneHutchinson
(Paul Henderson) *hld up in rr: nvr on terms: lost tch 12th: t.o whn p.u 3 out* **33/1**

5m 1.0s (-11.00) **Going Correction** -0.20s/f (Good) **13** Ran SP% **122.7**
Speed ratings: **112,109,109,106,100 98,96,94,74,64 , , ,**
CSF £36.09 CT £150.44 TOTE £6.00: £2.20, £2.30, £1.70; EX 45.80 Trifecta £488.70.
Owner Patrick Kelly **Bred** DDE Syndicate **Trained** Portway, Worcs

FOCUS
This race was open to all horses that were eliminated at the declaration stage from any handicap chase at the Cheltenham Festival. Again they went a decent pace and it resulted in a big-race double for jockey Nico de Boinville. Winner looked well-weighted and returned to best; runner-up and third ran to marks.

4788 EUSTACE SHERRARD MEMORIAL NOVICES' HURDLE (10 hdls) 2m 5f
4:25 (4:25) (Class 4) 4-Y-0+ **£3,249** (£954; £477; £238)

Form RPR

50 **1** **Chartbreaker (FR)**[113] 2762 5-11-1 0........................ SamTwiston-Davies 125+
(Paul Nicholls) *hld up in tch in midfield: effrt in 4th after 3 out: ev ch and gng bttr than rivals whn nt fluent 2 out: pushed ahd between last 2: mstke last: styd on to assert flat: rdn out* **9/1**

-533 **2** *1* **Ten Sixty (IRE)**[23] 4322 6-11-1 125........................ JamesBest 123
(Philip Hobbs) *chsd ldrs: rdn to chse ldr after 3 out: ev ch and mstke next: stl ev ch last: kpt on but nt quite pce of wnr flat* **7/2**[2]

1-61 **3** *10* **Ballyhenry (IRE)**[36] 4097 6-11-7 0........................ NicodeBoinville 120
(Ben Pauling) *mde most tl 5th: styd w ldr: ev ch and rdn 3 out: 4th and btn next: wknd bef last* **6/4**[1]

341 **4** *3 ½* **Crimson Ark (IRE)**[154] 1968 6-11-7 0........................ DarylJacob 116
(Emma Lavelle) *t.k.h: hld up in tch: hdwy to chse ldrs 4th: led 6th: drvn and hrd pressed 2 out: hdd between last 2: 3rd and btn whn wnt rt last: fdd flat* **12/1**

564 **5** *31* **Dylanseoghan (IRE)**[36] 4097 7-11-1 0........................ LiamTreadwell 85
(Zoe Davison) *in tch in rr: hmpd 3rd: rdn after 6th: wl bhd 3 out* **50/1**

30-0 **P** **Mirkat**[138] 2239 6-11-1 0........................ WayneHutchinson
(Alan King) *hld up in tch in rr: rdn and struggling 7th: lost tch next: t.o whn p.u 3 out* **66/1**

22P5 **P** **King Kayf**[21] 4362 7-11-1 125........................(t) IanPopham
(Noel Williams) *w ldr tl 5th: j. slowly and btn 3 out: sn fdd and t.o whn p.u next* **4/1**[3]

22P **F** **He's A Charmer (IRE)**[92] 3133 6-11-1 0........................(t) NoelFehily
(Harry Fry) *hld up in tch in midfield tl fell 3rd* **8/1**

0 **P** **Perfect Swing (IRE)**[22] 4344 5-11-1 0........................ BarryGeraghty
(Jonjo O'Neill) *in tch in rr: hmpd 3rd: struggling and pushed along whn j.lft 5th: j.lft next: tailing off whn p.u bef 7th* **50/1**

5m 9.5s (-11.50) **Going Correction** -0.70s/f (Firm) **9** Ran SP% **116.4**
Speed ratings (Par 105): **93,92,88,87,75 , , ,**
CSF £41.47 TOTE £10.20: £2.50, £1.60, £1.10; EX 46.00 Trifecta £126.60.
Owner Mrs Johnny de la Hey **Bred** Hans Wirth **Trained** Ditcheat, Somerset

FOCUS
An interesting novices' hurdle if not the most competitive, but not the result many would have expected. Big improvement from winner; small personal bests for placed horses.

4789 WATCH RACING UK TODAY JUST £10 H'CAP CHASE (18 fncs) 3m
5:00 (5:01) (Class 4) (0-115,115) 5-Y-0+ **£6,498** (£1,908; £954; £477)

Form RPR

F223 **1** **Cloudy Bob (IRE)**[21] 4363 9-11-12 **115**........................ HarrySkelton 127+
(Pat Murphy) *hld up in tch in midfield: clsd to trck ldrs 14th: rdn and effrt bef 2 out: led bef last: styd on strly: rdn out* **11/2**[1]

P-2P **2** *2 ¾* **Castle Cheetah (IRE)**[37] 4071 8-11-12 **115**........................ NicodeBoinville 127+
(Ben Pauling) *led tl 9th: styd chsng ldr: mstke 11th: rdn to ld again bef 3 out: hdd between last 2: styd on same pce flat* **7/1**[3]

1U-F **3** *7* **Double Whammy**[81] 3339 10-11-5 **113**........................(b) ShaneShortall(5) 118
(Iain Jardine) *chsd ldr after 2nd tl led 9th: mstke 13th: rdn and hdd bef 3 out: 3rd and no ex 2 out: wknd last* **8/1**

-PP6 **4** *4* **Boardwalk Empire (IRE)**[15] 4465 9-11-1 **109**........................(tp) MichaelHeard(5) 110
(Kate Buckett) *midfield tl hdwy to chse ldrs 6th: 4th and outpcd u.p after 15th: wl hld and plugged on same pce after* **40/1**

F223 **5** *5* **Muckle Roe (IRE)**[15] 4465 7-11-10 **113**........................ SamTwiston-Davies 111
(Nigel Twiston-Davies) *chsd ldr tl after 2nd: sn dropped to midfield but wl in tch: effrt and mstke 15th: btn next* **11/2**[1]

24P3 **6** *7* **Orby's Man (IRE)**[262] 873 7-11-12 **115**........................(p) AndrewTinkler 105
(Charlie Longsdon) *chsd ldrs: rdn after 14th: 5th and no imp after next: wknd 3 out* **11/1**

-3PP **7** *22* **Keltic Rhythm (IRE)**[81] 3339 9-11-8 **111**........................ WayneHutchinson 80
(Neil King) *hld up in last quartet: hmpd 4th: lost tch 15th: t.o* **12/1**

-005 **8** *21* **Knockalongi**[20] 4380 10-10-13 **109**........................(p[1]) BenFfrenchDavis(7) 59
(Dominic Ffrench Davis) *hld up in tch: hmpd 4th: rdn along after 11th: wknd 14th: t.o* **28/1**

34P **9** *10* **Dalkadam (FR)**[23] 4321 5-11-3 **107**........................ PaulMoloney 47
(J R Jenkins) *a in rr: bdly hmpd 4th: lost tch 14th: t.o* **50/1**

P03U **P** **Firm Order (IRE)**[37] 4062 11-11-3 **113**........................(tp) MrMJPKendrick(7)
(Paul Webber) *midfield: rdn and lost pl 10th: bhd and mstke 12th: p.u after next* **8/1**

2-34 **P** **Dollar Bill**[36] 4098 7-11-3 **106**........................(p) LiamTreadwell
(Nick Gifford) *bhd: j. bdly lft: wl bhd whn p.u after 6th* **16/1**

-130 **B** **Georgie Lad (IRE)**[100] 2996 8-11-5 **115**........................ MrSeanHoulihan(7)
(Philip Hobbs) *in tch in midfield tl blnd and rdr looked like being uns whn b.d 4th* **6/1**[2]

2U21 **F** **Vendredi Trois (FR)**[128] 2456 7-11-10 **113**........................ DarylJacob
(Emma Lavelle) *chsd ldrs tl fell 4th* **8/1**

0 **U** **Speed Demon (IRE)**[50] 3846 7-11-9 **112**........................ IanPopham
(Richard Phillips) *t.k.h: hld up in tch in midfield tl hmpd and uns rdr 4th* **33/1**

6m 6.4s (-2.60) **Going Correction** -0.20s/f (Good)
WFA 5 from 7yo+ 1lb **14** Ran SP% **123.6**
Speed ratings: **96,95,92,91,89 87,80,73,69, , , ,**
CSF £44.59 CT £316.87 TOTE £6.60: £2.10, £2.90, £4.00; EX 55.10 Trifecta £482.10.
Owner Men Of Stone **Bred** P Shanahan & R Fitzgearld **Trained** East Garston, Berks

FOCUS
A fair handicap chase, but a nasty incident at the fourth fence which saw \bVendredi Trois\p, \bGeorgie Lad\p and \bSpeed Demon\p all exit the contest. Winner made most of lenient mark.

4790 RACING UK 3 DEVICES 1 PRICE MAIDEN OPEN NATIONAL HUNT FLAT RACE 2m
5:35 (5:38) (Class 5) 4-6-Y-0 **£2,599** (£763; £381; £190)

Form RPR

1 **Mere Ironmonger** 4-10-10 0........................ HarrySkelton 113+
(Brendan Powell) *led tl 10f out: styd pressing ldrs tl led again 3f out: rdn 5 l clr over 2f out: pressed ins fnl f: hld on u.p towards fin* **25/1**

32 **2** *½* **Chelsea Flyer (IRE)**[84] 3258 5-11-3 0........................[1] LiamTreadwell 119+
(Emma Lavelle) *t.k.h: hld up in tch: effrt and plenty to do over 3f out: chsd clr wnr and racing awkwardly u.p over 1f out: clsd to press wnr wl ins fnl f: nvr looked like gng by wnr and hld towards fin* **9/1**

3 **3** *14* **Golden Birthday (FR)**[36] 4103 5-11-3 0........................ NickScholfield 110+
(Harry Fry) *hld up in tch in rr: nt clr run over 4f out and plenty to do whn hdwy 3f out: wnt modest 3rd over 1f out: no ch w ldrs* **9/4**[1]

4 *3 ¾* **Whispering Storm (GER)**[322] 97 6-11-3 0........(t[1]) SamTwiston-Davies 103
(Paul Nicholls) *hld up in midfield: effrt and outpcd by ldrs over 3f out: plugged on to go modest 4th 1f out: n.d* **12/1**

2 **5** *3 ¾* **Show On The Road**[300] 459 5-11-3 0........................ MichealNolan 100
(Philip Hobbs) *chsd ldrs tl jnd ldrs 1/2-way: led over 4f out tl hdd and unable qck w wnr over 2f out: lost 2nd over 1f out: wknd* **8/1**[3]

6 *2* **A Bold Move (IRE)**[147] 6-10-10 0........................ MrBGibbs(7) 98
(Paul Morgan) *chsd ldrs: rdn and outpcd over 3f out: wknd over 2f out* **14/1**

5 **7** *5* **Thomas Shelby (IRE)**[36] 4102 5-11-3 0........................ WayneHutchinson 94
(Alan King) *t.k.h: hld up in tch in midfield: rdn and struggling over 3f out: wknd over 2f out* **5/1**[2]

4 **8** *¾* **Kings Walk (IRE)**[323] 67 5-11-3 0........................ PaddyBrennan 93
(Colin Tizzard) *w ldr tl led 10f out tl over 4f out: wknd qckly 3f out* **8/1**[3]

9 *2* **Master Majic (IRE)** 5-11-3 0........................ PaulMoloney 91
(Colin Tizzard) *t.k.h: hld up towards rr: outpcd 4f out: no ch fnl 3f* **25/1**

60 **10** *2 ¼* **Rhianna**[108] 2856 5-10-10 0........................(t) DavidBass 82
(Kim Bailey) *in tch in midfield: rdn and btn 4f out: wknd 3f out* **100/1**

11 *1* **Stealing Mix**[139] 6-11-3 0........................ MarkQuinlan 88
(Neil Mulholland) *chsd ldrs: 4th and rdn over 3f out: sn btn and wknd* **25/1**

0 **12** *9* **Midnight Merlot**[36] 4103 4-10-10 0........................ IanPopham 73
(Noel Williams) *hld up in midfield: rdn 4f out: sn btn: t.o* **50/1**

4 **13** *shd* **Ermyn's Emerald**[19] 4414 4-10-3 0........................ MrSeanHoulihan(7) 73
(Pat Phelan) *hld up in tch in rr: rdn over 4f out: sn bhd: t.o* **100/1**

26 **14** *1* **Walt (IRE)**[36] 4103 5-11-3 0........................ NoelFehily 79
(Nicky Henderson) *t.k.h: wl in tch in midfield: rdn and btn 4f out: bhd 2f out: t.o* **12/1**

0 **15** *1 ¾* **Too Far Gone (IRE)**[36] 4103 5-11-0 0........................ TomBellamy(3) 78
(Alan King) *hld up in tch in rr: rdn 5f out: sn btn: t.o* **100/1**

16 *69* **Bodekin Point (IRE)** 5-11-3 0........................ AndrewTinkler 16
(Charlie Longsdon) *chsd ldrs: rdn 6f out: sn lost pl: t.o fnl 2f* **33/1**

0 **P** **Tower Of Allen (IRE)**[114] 2729 5-11-3 0........................ NicodeBoinville
(Nicky Henderson) *t.k.h: hld up in tch in midfield: lost pl qckly 4f out: p.u and dismntd 3f out* **20/1**

3m 47.4s (-5.00) **Going Correction** -0.70s/f (Firm)
WFA 4 from 5yo+ 7lb **17** Ran SP% **125.9**
Speed ratings: **84,83,76,74,73 72,69,69,68,67 66,62,61,61,60 26,**
CSF £228.78 TOTE £23.60: £5.80, £3.30, £1.80; EX 269.60 Trifecta £838.40.

The Form Book Jumps 2015-16, Raceform Ltd, Newbury, RG14 5SJ

Owner The Arkle Bar Partnership **Bred** Floors Farming **Trained** Upper Lambourn, Berks
FOCUS
An informative bumper that should produce winners. It had gone to Nicky Henderson in three of the past four years, but neither of his representatives could make much impression this time. Winner looks decent prospect and runner-up building on debut promise.
T/Plt: £80.50 to a £1 stake. Pool: £147,903.11 - 1341.07 winning units. T/Qpdt: £31.60 to a £1 stake. Pool: £8,237.56 - 192.90 winning units. **Steve Payne**

4547 NEWCASTLE (L-H)
Saturday, March 19

OFFICIAL GOING: Heavy (soft in places; 4.8)
Wind: Almost nil Weather: Overcast, dry

4791 MTREC RECRUITMENT - PERMANENT TECHNICAL RECRUITMENT SPECIALISTS NOVICES' HURDLE (8 hdls 1 omitted) 2m 98y
2:15 (2:18) (Class 4) 4-Y-0+ **£5,198** (£1,526; £763; £381)

Form RPR
3402 1 **Eastview Boy**[11] 4548 5-11-0 0 .... BrianHughes 119+
(Philip Kirby) *prom: smooth hdwy to chal 2 out: led and lft clr last: pushed out* **3/1**[2]
1F4 2 5 **Always Resolute**[41] 4010 5-11-1 0 .... CraigGallagher(5) 125+
(Brian Ellison) *t.k.h early: chsd ldrs: rdn: hung lft and hdwy to ld bef 2 out: hdd whn blnd and rdr lost irons last: nt rcvr* **4/6**[1]
6 3 7 **Little Bruce (IRE)**[9] 4567 4-10-2 0 .... NathanMoscrop(5) 100
(Philip Kirby) *chsd ldr: led 4th to bef 2 out: sn drvn and outpcd* **80/1**
2 4 11 **Frightened Rabbit (USA)**[11] 3724 4-10-7 0 .... CraigNichol 92+
(Keith Dalgleish) *t.k.h early: in tch: stdy hdwy after 3 out (usual 4 out): rdn and wknd fr next* **3/1**[2]
0 5 16 **Hollins Hill**[42] 4001 6-11-0 0 .... JonathanEngland 80
(Sam Drake) *nt fluent on occasions: hld up: pushed along 4th: struggling after 3 out (usual 4 out)* **100/1**
60 6 1 ½ **Breezemount (IRE)**[20] 4388 6-11-0 0 .... AdrianLane 79
(Donald McCain) *hld up: pushed along and struggling after 3 out (usual 4 out): btn bef next* **33/1**[3]
F **Russian Breeze (IRE)**[143] 4-10-4 0 .... JohnKington(3)
(Julia Brooke) *led at slow pl: qcknd after 2nd: hdd 4th: outpcd and 7 l last whn fell 3 out (usual 4 out)* **66/1**
4m 18.0s (8.00) **Going Correction** +0.425s/f (Soft) **7 Ran SP% 116.6**
WFA 4 from 5yo+ 7lb
Speed ratings (Par 105): **97,94,91,85,77 76,**
CSF £5.88 TOTE £4.20: £1.60, £1.10; EX 6.10 Trifecta £112.90.
Owner Eastview Thoroughbreds **Bred** Eastview Thoroughbreds **Trained** East Appleton, N Yorks
■ Stewards' Enquiry : Nathan Moscrop three-day ban; weighed in 2lb over (2nd-4th Apr)
FOCUS
The ground was officially heavy, soft in places. This wasn't a particularly competitive novice hurdle and they were big prices bar three. The early pace was pedestrian and several pulled hard as a result. Big step up from winner and third and both could be rated higher.

4792 MTREC RECRUITMENT - SPECIALISTS IN TEMPORARY WORKER RECRUITMENT H'CAP CHASE (19 fncs) 2m 7f 91y
2:50 (2:51) (Class 4) (0-110,104) 5-Y-0+ **£6,498** (£1,908; £954; £477)

Form RPR
5341 1 **Veroce (FR)**[27] 4276 7-11-2 **99** .... JamieHamilton(5) 107+
(Mark Walford) *nt fluent on occasions early on: hld up in tch: hdwy to chse ldng pair 4th: wnt 2nd bef 6 out: clsd next: led 3 out: hld on wl fr last* **9/4**[1]
U0P1 2 1 ¼ **Notonebuttwo (IRE)**[13] 4514 9-10-6 **84** .... (tp) BrianHughes 90
(Chris Grant) *led: clr w one other fr 6th: clr 11th to 4 out: hdd next: rallied and ch whn hit last: kpt on towards fin* **7/2**[2]
2123 3 31 **Oscar Lateen (IRE)**[6] 4637 8-11-1 **100** .... (b) StevenFox(7) 78
(Sandy Thomson) *hld up in tch: outpcd whn blnd 13th: rallied after 5 out: rdn and wknd fr 3 out* **9/2**[3]
3503 4 3 ¾ **Big Sound**[135] 2288 9-11-12 **104** .... (p) PeterBuchanan 73
(Mark Walford) *hld up: outpcd 10th: struggling fr next: n.d after* **5/1**
0343 P **Bennys Well (IRE)**[39] 4046 10-11-8 **100** .... SeanQuinlan
(Sue Smith) *disp ld and clr of rest fr 6th: hit 8th: outpcd 11th: lost 2nd bef 6 out: wknd next: t.o whn p.u bef 4 out* **5/1**
P005 P **Higgs Boson**[8] 4581 11-9-9 **78** oh4 .... (b[1]) DiarmuidO'Regan(5)
(Jim Goldie) *chsd ldrs: lost pl whn hit 5th: struggling fr next: lost tch and p.u bef 10th* **14/1**
6m 35.5s (13.00) **Going Correction** +0.65s/f (Soft) **6 Ran SP% 111.2**
Speed ratings: **103,102,91,90,**
CSF £10.56 TOTE £2.70: £1.50, £1.80; EX 9.90 Trifecta £34.80.
Owner The 4 Amigos & Partner **Bred** E A R L Trinquet, M & O Trinquet **Trained** Sherriff Hutton, N Yorks
FOCUS
Race distance increased by 5yds. An ordinary staying handicap with the top weight having a rating of 104. The pace was fair and the first two, who were both last-time out winners, finished well clear of the remainder. Runner-up sets the standard.

4793 MTREC RECRUITMENT - SPECIALISTS IN CARE RECRUITMENT H'CAP HURDLE (8 hdls 1 omitted) 2m 98y
3:25 (3:27) (Class 3) (0-130,130) 4-Y-0+ **£9,747** (£2,862; £1,431; £715)

Form RPR
2124 1 **Nuts Well**[84] 3240 5-11-4 **122** .... BrianHughes 130+
(Ann Hamilton) *hld up in tch: smooth hdwy to ld bef omitted 3 out: nt fluent and pushed along next: j.lft and mstke last: drvn and styd on wl run-in* **5/2**[2]
2024 2 5 **Heath Hunter (IRE)**[21] 4366 9-11-9 **130** .... (bt) KieronEdgar(3) 130
(David Pipe) *trckd ldrs: led briefly bef omitted 3 out: effrt and rdn next: hit last: kpt on same pce run-in* **2/1**[1]
1523 3 1 ½ **Bowdler's Magic**[36] 4107 9-10-10 **117** .... JoeColliver(3) 115
(David Thompson) *in tch: stdy hdwy bef 3 out (usual 4 out): rdn and outpcd next: kpt on fr last: no imp* **8/1**
P413 4 9 **Hear The Chimes**[19] 4411 7-10-11 **115** .... PeterBuchanan 103
(Shaun Harris) *hld up: hdwy and ev ch after 3 out (usual 4 out): rdn and wknd fr next* **11/2**[3]
531- 5 nk **Rock A Doodle Doo (IRE)**[356] 4830 9-10-11 **122** .... FinianO'Toole(7) 112
(Sally Hall) *hld up: blnd 4th: rallied 3 out (usual 4 out): wknd bef next: last and no ch whn hit last* **20/1**
F34U 6 21 **Mwaleshi**[13] 4511 11-10-11 **115** .... SeanQuinlan 87
(Sue Smith) *led: j.rt and big: hdd 3 out (usual 4 out): wknd bef next* **7/1**
1440 P **Brave Spartacus (IRE)**[121] 2594 10-11-4 **125** .... HarryChalloner(3)
(Keith Reveley) *chsd ldr: led after 3 out (usual 4 out) to bef omitted 3 out: sn wknd: p.u 2 out* **11/1**
4m 14.8s (4.80) **Going Correction** +0.425s/f (Soft) **7 Ran SP% 114.0**
Speed ratings (Par 107): **105,102,101,97,97 86,**
CSF £8.16 TOTE £3.00: £1.40, £2.20; EX 8.30 Trifecta £47.30.
Owner Ian Hamilton **Bred** Chesters Stud Ltd **Trained** Great Bavington, Northumbland
FOCUS
Quite a competitive handicap for the grade, the pace was fair but all seven were still in with a chance on the turn for home. Easy winner back to form, second and third give figures a solid look.

4794 MTREC RECRUITMENT - SPECIALISTS IN INDUSTRIAL RECRUITMENT H'CAP HURDLE (11 hdls 2 omitted) 3m 10y
4:00 (4:00) (Class 3) (0-135,135) 4-Y-0+ **£9,747** (£2,862; £1,431; £715)

Form RPR
2561 1 **Touch Back (IRE)**[12] 4537 10-10-9 **123** .... RyanDay(5) 128+
(Chris Bealby) *hld up: stdy hdwy and prom 3 out (usual 4 out): rdn and outpcd next: rallied fr last and led last 50yds: styd on wl* **15/2**
1212 2 1 **Another Mattie (IRE)**[42] 3999 9-10-13 **122** .... (t) PeterBuchanan 126+
(N W Alexander) *w ldrs: led bef 2 out: edgd lft: rdn and 3 l clr whn hung lft run-in: hdd and no ex last 50yds* **12/1**
-130 3 3 ¼ **Tradewinds (FR)**[28] 4246 8-10-13 **127** .... GrantCockburn(5) 127
(Lucinda Russell) *in tch: hdwy to chal 1/2-way: led 8th to bef 2 out: rdn and kpt on same pce fr last* **16/1**
331P 4 nk **Donna's Diamond (IRE)**[42] 3992 7-11-7 **135** .... DiarmuidO'Regan(5) 133
(Chris Grant) *disp ld: led 6th to 8th: upsides ldr to bef 2 out: sn pressing wnr: lost 2nd and kpt on same pce last 100yds* **8/1**
1042 5 3 ½ **Dan Emmett (USA)**[21] 4354 6-11-7 **130** .... DerekFox 125
(Michael Scudamore) *w ldrs: pushed along 3 out (usual 4 out): rallied bef next: outpcd fr last* **5/1**[3]
5FP0 6 8 **Victor Hewgo**[24] 4305 11-10-6 **118** .... HarryChalloner(3) 108
(Keith Reveley) *nt fluent: hld up in tch on ins: drvn and outpcd 3 out (usual 4 out): wknd bef next* **25/1**
2410 7 4 **Lackamon**[21] 4367 11-10-2 **118** .... TrevorRyan(7) 105
(Sue Smith) *led or disp ld to 6th: rdn next: rallied: wknd bef omitted 3 out* **8/1**
2234 8 9 **Seldom Inn**[41] 4017 8-11-7 **130** .... (p) BrianHughes 105
(Sandy Thomson) *hld up: stdy hdwy 3 out (usual 4 out): rdn and wknd bef next* **4/1**[2]
4112 9 48 **Pinnacle Panda (IRE)**[24] 4305 5-11-8 **134** .... HarryBannister(3) 60
(Tom Lacey) *hld up: stdy hdwy bef 3 out (usual 4 out): rdn and wknd bef omitted 3 out: t.o* **11/4**[1]
6m 18.8s (4.80) **Going Correction** +0.425s/f (Soft) **9 Ran SP% 114.7**
Speed ratings (Par 107): **109,108,107,107,106 103,102,99,83**
CSF £89.09 CT £1391.30 TOTE £8.60: £2.60, £2.60, £3.70; EX 94.80 Trifecta £690.20.
Owner Miss Laura Morgan **Bred** John O'Connor **Trained** Barrowby, Lincs
FOCUS
Quite a competitive staying handicap hurdle but no more than a fair gallop and there were still four with a chance at the second last. Winner was well in on recent win and ran to similar level.

4795 MTREC RECRUITMENT - SPECIALISTS IN AUTOMOTIVE RECRUITMENT H'CAP CHASE (13 fncs) 2m 75y
4:35 (4:38) (Class 4) (0-110,109) 5-Y-0+ **£6,498** (£1,908; £954; £477)

Form RPR
4230 1 **Asuncion (FR)**[23] 4329 6-9-9 **83** oh11 .... (b) JamieHamilton(5) 92+
(Rebecca Menzies) *mde all: jnd and rdn 4 out: kpt on strly fr 2 out* **20/1**
-444 2 3 ¼ **Stilo Blue Native (IRE)**[38] 4053 8-11-11 **108** .... BrianHughes 115+
(John Wade) *nt fluent: in tch: hdwy to chse wnr 4th: hit 6 out: effrt and ev ch bef 4 out: 2 l down and one pce whn nt fluent last* **13/2**
3303 3 9 **Rupert Bear**[25] 4300 10-10-4 **92** .... (p) MissCWalton(5) 90
(James Walton) *t.k.h: prom: wnt 2nd briefly bef 4th: rdn and outpcd after 5 out: rallied bef 2 out: sn no imp* **9/2**[3]
24F6 4 11 **Ever So Much (IRE)**[52] 3806 7-11-9 **109** .... (p) KieronEdgar(3) 93
(Ben Haslam) *bhd and detached: struggling 1/2-way: sme late hdwy: nvr on terms* **9/1**
-33P 5 7 **Castlelawn (IRE)**[81] 3343 9-11-11 **108** .... PeterBuchanan 87
(Lucinda Russell) *j.rt: chsd wnr: lost 2nd whn mstke 4th: struggling fr 6 out: btn 4 out* **4/1**[2]
U1U5 P **Clan Chief**[32] 4166 7-10-8 **91** .... AndrewThornton
(N W Alexander) *hld up: nt fluent 3rd: blnd and p.u next* **15/8**[1]
4m 32.0s (10.90) **Going Correction** +0.65s/f (Soft) **6 Ran SP% 101.1**
Speed ratings: **98,96,91,86,82**
CSF £105.28 TOTE £19.50: £6.10, £2.00; EX 95.80 Trifecta £380.20.
Owner Epds Racing Partnership 6 **Bred** Francois-Marie Cottin **Trained** Stearsby, N Yorks
FOCUS
Race distance increased by 2yds. A weak handicap run at an ordinary pace and the winner raced from 11lb out of the handicap. Winner rated back to best.

4796 MTREC RECRUITMENT - NURSING & CARE SPECIALISTS H'CAP HURDLE (9 hdls 2 omitted) 2m 4f 133y
5:10 (5:12) (Class 4) (0-110,108) 4-Y-0+ **£4,548** (£1,335; £667; £333)

Form RPR
-003 1 **Imperial Prince (IRE)**[31] 4178 7-10-12 **101** .... StevenFox(7) 110+
(Sandy Thomson) *hld up in tch: hdwy on outside to ld bef 2 out: pushed clr fr last* **7/4**[1]
0-2P 2 5 **Molly Milan**[32] 4163 8-10-7 **89** .... BrianHughes 91
(Jim Goldie) *prom: hdwy to join ldr after 3rd: led bef 3 out to bef next: kpt on fr last: nt pce of wnr* **9/2**[2]
5U32 3 ½ **Toarmandowithlove (IRE)**[11] 4547 8-9-12 **87** .... (t) JamesCorbett(7) 87
(Susan Corbett) *hld up: outpcd 5th: rallied bef 2 out: kpt on fr last: nvr able to chal* **11/2**[3]
5306 4 2 ½ **Karisma King**[23] 4326 7-11-6 **102** .... SeanQuinlan 100
(Sue Smith) *nt fluent: prom: hit 4th: effrt and rdn after 3 out (usual 4 out): outpcd whn hit last* **8/1**
51PP 5 1 **Redkalani (IRE)**[30] 4203 8-11-9 **108** .... HarryChalloner(3) 106
(Keith Reveley) *led: rdn and hdd bef 3 out (usual 4 out): rallied: outpcd whn hit last* **8/1**
6043 6 49 **Orioninverness (IRE)**[19] 4403 5-11-10 **106** .... (t) PeterBuchanan 53
(Lucinda Russell) *prom: drvn and outpcd bef omitted 3 out: sn lost tch: t.o* **9/1**
4P0 7 25 **Frankie's Promise (IRE)**[33] 4154 8-11-8 **104** .... (p) AndrewThornton 26
(N W Alexander) *nt fluent: in tch on outside: hdwy after 3rd: mstke 6th: ev ch 3 out (usual 4 out): wknd bef omitted 3 out: sn lost tch and eased* **8/1**
5m 33.1s (12.00) **Going Correction** +0.425s/f (Soft) **7 Ran SP% 113.3**
Speed ratings (Par 105): **94,92,91,90,90 71,62**
CSF £10.14 TOTE £2.20: £1.30, £2.40; EX 10.30 Trifecta £22.80.
Owner M Wright **Bred** John Ryan **Trained** Lambden, Berwicks

FOCUS
A leisurely gallop to this 0-110 handicap hurdle with the whole field having a chance going to the second last. Form rated around runner-up and fourth.

4797 MTREC RECRUITMENT - FINANCE RECRUITMENT SPECIALISTS "HANDS AND HEELS" H'CAP HURDLE (8 hdls 1 omitted) 2m 98y

5:45 (5:46) (Class 5) (0-100,100) 4-Y-0+ **£2,729** (£801; £400; £200)

Form RPR

5024 **1** **Mister Hendre**[13] 4513 8-10-2 **76** (t) JamesCorbett 81+
(Susan Corbett) *prom: hdwy to ld bef omitted 3 out: clr after 2 out: pushed along and kpt on wl* **11/1**

5250 **2** 2 ¾ **King's Chorister**[19] 4404 10-9-13 **76** (t) LorcanMurtagh(3) 74
(Barry Murtagh) *hld up in tch: stdy hdwy bef 3 out: chsd wnr bef next: no imp fr last* **10/1**

3443 **3** 1 ½ **Orchard Road (USA)**[20] 4390 9-11-12 **100** (t) SamColtherd 97
(Tristan Davidson) *led to bef 3rd: cl up: led again 3 out (usual 4 out) to bef omitted 3 out: kpt on same pce fr 2 out* **7/2**[2]

6566 **4** ¾ **Aza Run (IRE)**[15] 4460 6-11-0 **91** AidenBlakemore(3) 87
(Shaun Harris) *hld up: stdy hdwy bef 2 out: kpt on fr last: nvr able to chal* **12/1**

25PF **5** nk **Columbanus (IRE)**[80] 3368 5-10-0 **77** (t) MissNatalieParker(3) 73
(Kenneth Slack) *prom: pushed along and outpcd bef 2 out: no imp fr last* **7/4**[1]

40P0 **6** 11 **Hi Dancer**[25] 4297 13-10-2 **79** ArchieBellamy(3) 64
(Ben Haslam) *in tch: drvn and outpcd after 3 out (usual 4 out): n.d after* **16/1**

3002 **7** 4 ½ **Agesilas (FR)**[12] 4536 8-10-0 **74** oh5 (p) ThomasDowson 54
(Andrew Crook) *hld up: pushed along and struggling after 3 out (usual 4 out): sn btn* **28/1**

0320 **8** 2 **Rock Relief (IRE)**[30] 4206 10-11-7 **100** (b) MrLHall(5) 78
(Chris Grant) *t.k.h: cl up: led bef 3rd to 3 out (usual 4 out): rdn and wknd bef next* **13/2**[3]

P06P **9** 12 **Hail The Brave (IRE)**[65] 3592 7-11-3 **91** (b[1]) FinianO'Toole 57
(Michael Smith) *t.k.h early: chsd ldrs tl rdn and wknd bef omitted 3 out* **8/1**

4m 22.9s (12.90) **Going Correction** +0.425s/f (Soft) **9** Ran **SP% 117.5**
Speed ratings (Par 103): **84,82,81,81,81 75,73,72,66**
CSF £114.00 CT £469.15 TOTE £12.80: £2.50, £1.60, £1.70; EX 67.60 Trifecta £342.30.
Owner Gavin Foley **Bred** Shade Oak Stud **Trained** Otterburn, Northumberland

FOCUS
Mainly exposed sorts in this 0-100 handicap hurdle in which the early gallop was steady and the form likely to be weak. Winner was well-in on old form; runner-up to level of December CD run.
T/Plt: £426.80 to a £1 stake. Pool: £62,220.68 - 106.40 winning units. T/Qpdt: £186.50 to a £1 stake. Pool: £4,059.12 - 16.10 winning units. **Richard Young**

3863 UTTOXETER (L-H)

Saturday, March 19

OFFICIAL GOING: Soft (good to soft in places; 5.6)
Wind: moderate, half behind Weather: overcast

4798 BETFRED "RACING'S BIGGEST SUPPORTER" "NATIONAL HUNT" NOVICES' HURDLE (10 hdls) 2m 3f 207y

1:50 (1:50) (Class 4) 4-Y-0+ **£5,064** (£1,496; £748; £374; £187)

Form RPR

1 **1** **Ballyoptic (IRE)**[27] 4264 6-11-5 0 RyanHatch(3) 149+
(Nigel Twiston-Davies) *trckd ldrs: wnt 2nd 4th: led 6th: clr whn hit last: easily* **6/4**[1]

31 **2** 10 **Pougne Bobbi (FR)**[43] 3974 5-11-3 0 FreddieMitchell(5) 139
(Nicky Henderson) *chsd ldrs: 2nd after 7th: kpt on same pce fr 2 out: no ch w wnr* **2/1**[2]

202U **3** 13 **Air Horse One**[8] 4594 5-10-9 0 LiamMcKenna(7) 120
(Harry Fry) *j.rt: midfield: hdwy to chse ldrs 6th: 3rd appr 3 out: one pce* **10/3**[3]

U6 **4** 7 **Fact Of The Matter (IRE)**[121] 2591 6-11-2 0 (t) BrendanPowell 110
(Jamie Snowden) *chsd ldrs: drven after 7th: one pce* **12/1**

0 **5** 15 **Hopefordebest (IRE)**[84] 3221 6-10-9 0 TobyWheeler(7) 95
(Ian Williams) *led to 6th: lost pl bef 3 out* **66/1**

0445 **6** 1 ½ **North Hill (IRE)**[23] 4317 5-11-2 0 TomO'Brien 95
(Ian Williams) *hld up in rr: hdwy 6th: sn drvn: lost pl bef 3 out* **20/1**

6204 **7** 20 **Infinityandbeyond (IRE)**[42] 3997 5-11-2 0 TrevorWhelan 74
(Neil King) *in rr: bhd fr 5th: t.o 7th* **50/1**

04 **8** 29 **Magic Mustard (IRE)**[135] 2299 5-11-2 0 KielanWoods 45
(Charlie Longsdon) *midfield: reminders 4th: sn lost pl: t.o 7th* **40/1**

00P0 **P** **The Model County (IRE)**[16] 4449 6-10-9 0 AdamWedge
(Alan Phillips) *chsd ldr: drvn and lost pl 7th: sn bhd: p.u bef 2 out* **100/1**

5-5P **P** **Evening Stanley (IRE)**[19] 4409 6-10-13 0 ThomasGarner(3)
(Oliver Sherwood) *nt fluent in rr: drvn and t.o 7th: p.u bef last* **33/1**

5m 6.8s (3.60) **Going Correction** +0.50s/f (Soft) **10** Ran **SP% 118.7**
Speed ratings (Par 105): **112,108,102,100,94 93,85,73, ,**
CSF £4.78 TOTE £2.40: £1.30, £1.50, £1.10; EX 6.40 Trifecta £10.90.
Owner Mills & Mason Partnership **Bred** Roger Ryan **Trained** Naunton, Gloucs

FOCUS
All race distances as advertised. There had been no rain at the course in the last nine days and the going was soft, good to soft in places. Little depth to the opening novice hurdle and the two market leaders dominated, with one proving far superior. Runner-up and fourth close to marks and set standard.

4799 BETFRED "HOME OF GOALS GALORE" NOVICES' H'CAP HURDLE (9 hdls) 1m 7f 168y

2:25 (2:27) (Class 3) (0-125,123) 4-Y-0+
£9,384 (£2,772; £1,386; £693; £346; £174)

Form RPR

4034 **1** **Justatenner**[16] 4449 5-10-9 **106** TomScudamore 113+
(Colin Tizzard) *chsd ldrs: hit 2nd: clr 2nd 2 out: styd on to ld last 50yds: all out* **9/1**

P-31 **2** hd **Sakhee's City (FR)**[18] 4416 5-11-2 **116** AdamNicol(3) 123+
(Philip Kirby) *hld up in rr: j.rt 2nd: stdy hdwy 6th: led 2 out: hdd and no ex last 50yds* **8/1**

0541 **3** 5 **Midtech Valentine**[6] 4650 5-10-1 **98** TomO'Brien 98
(Ian Williams) *hld up in rr: hdwy 6th: chsng ldrs 2 out: 3rd and one pce appr last* **7/2**[1]

21 **4** 1 **Fort Carson (IRE)**[6] 4645 10-10-5 **102** TrevorWhelan 103
(Neil King) *in rr: pushed along 4th: hdwy to chse ldrs after 6th: one pce fr 2 out* **6/1**[3]

-001 **5** 1 ¼ **Northandsouth (IRE)**[15] 4460 6-9-10 **98** JamieBargary(5) 97
(Nigel Twiston-Davies) *trckd ldrs: drvn after 6th: one pce fr 2 out* **11/2**[2]

2124 **6** 12 **Perceus**[42] 3994 4-11-4 **122** JackQuinlan 101
(James Eustace) *prom: drvn 6th: lost pl bef next* **9/1**

0631 **7** 2 ¾ **Jokers And Rogues (IRE)**[23] 4326 8-10-9 **106** (t) HenryBrooke 91
(Kenneth Slack) *led: hit 6th: hdd 2 out: sn wknd* **6/1**[3]

1 **8** ¾ **Ascot De Bruyere (FR)**[40] 4031 6-11-8 **119** (p) JakeGreenall 101
(James Ewart) *prom: drvn 6th: sn lost pl and bhd* **8/1**

3432 **9** 47 **Fast Scat (USA)**[124] 2032 4-9-9 **104** oh2 [1] NickSlatter(5) 32
(Steve Flook) *j.rt: chsd ldrs: blnd 4th: drvn next: lost pl 6th: sn bhd: t.o 3 out: eventually completed* **33/1**

-114 **P** **Isaac Bell (IRE)**[81] 3352 8-11-12 **123** (t) KielanWoods
(Alex Hales) *in rr-div: lost pl and bhd 6th: t.o whn p.u bef next* **12/1**

4m 4.6s (7.20) **Going Correction** +0.50s/f (Soft)
WFA 4 from 5yo+ 7lb **10** Ran **SP% 119.0**
Speed ratings (Par 107): **102,101,99,98,98 92,90,90,67,**
CSF £80.28 CT £304.83 TOTE £10.30: £3.20, £2.70, £1.50; EX 95.90 Trifecta £381.40.
Owner Mrs S Tainton **Bred** Mrs Jane Haywood **Trained** Milborne Port, Dorset

FOCUS
Not the strongest handicap for the grade but it was competitive and featured six last-time-out winners. Big improvement by winner but those behind in line with recent runs.

4800 BETFRED TV NOVICES' LIMITED H'CAP CHASE (17 fncs 1 omitted) 3m 2y

3:00 (3:00) (Class 2) 5-Y-0+ **£18,837** (£5,613; £2,841; £1,455; £762)

Form RPR

64U1 **1** **Henri Parry Morgan**[21] 4352 8-11-4 **135** (tp) SeanBowen 157+
(Peter Bowen) *hld up towards rr: hdwy 7th: 2nd appr omitted 4 out: led 3 out: clr next: eased in clsng stages* **7/1**

2UP1 **2** 15 **Delgany Demon**[20] 4389 8-11-0 **131** TrevorWhelan 136+
(Neil King) *led 2nd: hdd 3 out: kpt on one pce* **11/1**

1F32 **3** 22 **Smooth Stepper**[21] 4365 7-10-13 **130** DannyCook 109
(Sue Smith) *chsd ldrs: pushed along 3rd: hmpd 7th: drvn and outrpced 13th: tk distant 3rd nr fin* **6/1**

1143 **4** hd **Butlergrove King (IRE)**[14] 4492 7-9-12 **120** oh8 FreddieMitchell(5) 99
(Dai Burchell) *chsd ldrs: 2nd 6th: wknd omitted 4 out* **66/1**

12F1 **5** 22 **Buckhorn Timothy**[64] 3611 7-11-4 **135** TomO'Brien 92
(Colin Tizzard) *in rr: hdwy to chse ldrs 7th: outpcd 11th: bhd fr 14th: t.o* **11/1**

3F21 **B** **Bodega**[14] 4493 8-9-12 **122** ow2 (p) TobyWheeler(7)
(Ian Williams) *in rr: b.d 7th* **10/1**

16P3 **P** **Kingswell Theatre**[22] 4341 7-11-8 **139** (p) AdamWedge
(Michael Scudamore) *in rr: sme hdwy 8th: lost pl 11th: sn bhd: t.o whn p.u bef omitted 4 out* **25/1**

132P **P** **Run Ructions Run (IRE)**[42] 3998 7-11-2 **133** (p) BrianHarding
(Tim Easterby) *sn detached in rr: t.o 11th: p.u bef 14th* **9/1**

2031 **F** **Abracadabra Sivola (FR)**[18] 4425 6-10-8 **125** (p) TomScudamore
(David Pipe) *led to 2nd: chsd ldr: fell 7th* **9/2**[1]

-151 **U** **Blameitalonmyroots (IRE)**[49] 3866 6-10-4 **124** ThomasGarner(3)
(Oliver Sherwood) *chsd ldrs: hmpd and uns rdr 7th* **11/2**[3]

11F2 **P** **April Dusk (IRE)**[21] 4368 7-11-2 **133** GavinSheehan
(Warren Greatrex) *in rr: j.lft 4th: bhd 9th: t.o 14th: p.u bef omitted 4 out* **5/1**[2]

6m 13.9s (5.80) **Going Correction** +0.50s/f (Soft) **11** Ran **SP% 118.1**
Speed ratings: **110,105,97,97,90 , , , ,**
CSF £80.56 CT £493.88 TOTE £9.70: £3.30, £4.60, £2.60; EX 111.50 Trifecta £881.60.
Owner Ednyfed & Elizabeth Morgan **Bred** J R Bryan **Trained** Little Newcastle, Pembrokes

FOCUS
This looked a useful contest on paper but it was turned into a procession and winner rates a very smart novice.

4801 BETFRED "TREBLE ODDS ON LUCKY15'S" H'CAP HURDLE (10 hdls) 2m 3f 207y

3:35 (3:35) (Class 3) (0-135,135) 4-Y-0+
£12,512 (£3,696; £1,848; £924; £462; £232)

Form RPR

3F33 **1** **Murrayana (IRE)**[17] 4438 6-11-0 **123** (t) BrendanPowell 131
(Colin Tizzard) *in tch: pushed along and hdwy to chal 3 out: rdn to ld appr 2 out: hdd narrowly appr last: styd on wl: led again towards fin* **11/1**

2150 **2** hd **Champagne At Tara**[35] 4115 7-11-4 **127** RichieMcLernon 135
(Jonjo O'Neill) *hld up in midfield: smooth hdwy appr 3 out: trckd ldr gng wl 2 out: pushed along to ld narrowly appr last: drvn and one pce run-in: hdd towards fin* **9/1**[3]

122 **3** 8 **Rolling Dylan (IRE)**[34] 4137 5-11-1 **124** TomO'Brien 124
(Philip Hobbs) *in tch: rdn and outpcd 3 out: styd on wl after 2 out: wnt 3rd run-in* **8/1**[2]

0U21 **4** 4 **Poker School (IRE)**[21] 4362 6-10-9 **125** TobyWheeler(7) 123
(Ian Williams) *hld up: gd hdwy on outer after 7th: led appr 3 out: nt fluent 3 out: rdn whn hdd appr 2 out: wknd appr last* **8/1**[2]

4121 **5** 1 ½ **Almost Gemini (IRE)**[23] 4328 7-10-8 **117** (p) HenryBrooke 111
(Kenneth Slack) *midfield: sme hdwy 3 out: sn rdn: plugged on* **8/1**[2]

1321 **6** 6 **Braavos**[78] 3414 5-10-6 **120** ThomasCheesman(5) 109
(Philip Hobbs) *midfield on outer: rdn to chse ldrs bef 3 out: wknd after 2 out* **8/1**[2]

1U55 **7** 2 ¼ **Blue Buttons (IRE)**[56] 3748 8-11-1 **134** (t) RichieO'Dea(10) 120
(Emma Lavelle) *hld up: rdn bef 3 out: nvr threatened* **25/1**

30P3 **8** 20 **Rock On Rocky**[45] 3923 8-10-7 **123** (p) MrStanSheppard(7) 89
(Matt Sheppard) *trckd ldrs: rdn bef 3 out: sn wknd* **10/1**

1341 **9** 5 **Palm Grey (IRE)**[25] 4301 8-11-0 **123** DannyCook 85
(Sue Smith) *prom: pressed ldr after 6th: rdn after 7th: wknd after 3 out* **16/1**

3141 **10** 2 ½ **Chef D'Oeuvre (FR)**[30] 4198 5-11-12 **135** GavinSheehan 97
(Warren Greatrex) *prom: nt fluent 4th: rdn and lost pl bef 6th: sn struggling* **3/1**[1]

313- **11** 3 **Make Me A Fortune (IRE)**[350] 5139 8-11-6 **132** (p) RyanHatch(3) 88
(Steve Gollings) *midfield: rdn 3 out: sn wknd* **25/1**

PP50 **12** 2 **Shammick Boy (IRE)**[21] 4362 11-11-7 **130** (p) DenisO'Regan 84
(Victor Dartnall) *trckd ldrs: rdn bef 3 out: sn wknd* **50/1**

1315 **13** 50 **Masterplan (IRE)**[56] 3736 6-11-1 **127** GrahamWatters(3) 31
(Charlie Longsdon) *led: jnd after 6th: rdn whn hdd appr 3 out: wknd* **25/1**

/2P1 **B** **Muhtaris (IRE)**[15] 4466 6-10-9 **125** WilliamFeatherstone(7)
(James Evans) *hld up: b.d 5th* **14/1**

06P- **P** **Party Rock (IRE)**[329] 5539 9-11-11 **134** JJBurke
(Jennie Candlish) *hld up: bdly hmpd 5th and wl bhd: p.u bef 2 out* **28/1**

The Form Book Jumps 2015-16, Raceform Ltd, Newbury, RG14 5SJ

0-00 **F** **Seaviper (IRE)**[99] 3027 7-10-8 **122**.......................... DanielHiskett(5)
(Richard Phillips) *midfield: fell 5th* **50/1**
5m 8.3s (5.10) **Going Correction** +0.50s/f (Soft) **16** Ran SP% **128.3**
Speed ratings (Par 107): **109,108,105,104,103 101,100,92,90,89 88,87,67,,**
CSF £104.94 CT £858.83 TOTE £13.50: £3.00, £2.50, £2.20, £2.60; EX 151.70 Trifecta £2391.10.
Owner Mrs S Tainton **Bred** Cleaboy Stud **Trained** Milborne Port, Dorset
■ Stewards' Enquiry : Brendan Powell four-day ban; used whip above the permitted level (2nd-5th Apr)
FOCUS
A decent handicap, in which the favourite disappointed and the front two pulled clear. Winner improved for switch back to left-handed track. Third and fourth set level.

4802 BETFRED MIDLANDS GRAND NATIONAL (A H'CAP CHASE) (LISTED RACE) (24 fncs) 4m 1f 92y
4:10 (4:10) (Class 1) 5-Y-0+ **£73,756** (£28,165; £14,398; £7,495; £4,063)

Form RPR
-P32 **1** **Firebird Flyer (IRE)**[70] 3518 9-11-5 **138**.......................... AdamWedge 144
(Evan Williams) *midfield: hdwy 17th: 2nd 2 out: lft in ld last: drvn out* **16/1**
421 **2** *2* **Milansbar (IRE)**[22] 4341 9-11-12 **145**.......................... TrevorWhelan 151
(Neil King) *chsd clr ldr fr 3rd: led 4 out to next: 3rd whn mstke 2 out: kpt on same pce: lft 2nd last* **10/1[3]**
-4P3 **3** *3* **Cogry**[35] 4128 7-11-0 **136**..........................(p) RyanHatch(3) 139
(Nigel Twiston-Davies) *prom: chsd ldrs 4 out: lft 3rd and hmpd last: one pce* **6/1[2]**
4124 **4** *2* **Spookydooky (IRE)**[28] 4238 8-11-8 **141**..........................(t) JoshuaMoore 143
(Jonjo O'Neill) *in rr: mstke 1st: hit 17th: chsd ldrs appr 4 out: one pce fr next: lft 4th last* **11/1**
3UP1 **5** *7* **No Planning**[7] 4609 9-11-5 **138** 6ex.......................... DannyCook 134
(Sue Smith) *midfield: hdwy 17th: chsd ldrs appr 4 out: wknd after next* **20/1**
241F **F** **Golden Chieftain (IRE)**[34] 4140 11-11-2 **135**..........(bt) BrendanPowell 149+
(Colin Tizzard) *hit 1st: midfield: hdwy 8th: led 3 out: 7 l clr whn fell last* **14/1**
-3P1 **P** **Fourovakind**[22] 4340 11-11-2 **135**..........................(b) GavinSheehan
(Harry Whittington) *chsd ldrs: blnd 3rd: lost pl 14th: sn bhd: p.u bef 19th* **11/1**
-532 **P** **Shotgun Paddy (IRE)**[21] 4367 9-11-11 **144**.......................... DenisO'Regan
(Emma Lavelle) *in rr-div: bhd and drvn 16th: t.o whn p.u bef next* **10/1[3]**
426/ **P** **Mad Brian (IRE)**[34] 4147 10-11-5 **138**..........................(t) RobertDunne
(Mrs Gillian Callaghan, Ire) *hld up: hdwy to chse ldrs 14th: led after 19th: hdd 4 out: wknd qckly: p.u bef 2 out* **16/1**
1303 **P** **Standing Ovation (IRE)**[146] 2089 9-11-1 **134**..........(bt) RichieMcLernon
(David Pipe) *in rr: bhd fr 17th: t.o whn p.u bef 20th* **20/1**
5113 **P** **Katkeau (FR)**[42] 3996 9-11-12 **145**..........................(t) ConorO'Farrell
(David Pipe) *in rr: hdwy 17th: chsng ldrs appr 4 out: lost pl and p.u bef 3 out* **14/1**
-2P1 **P** **Count Guido Deiro (IRE)**[35] 4112 9-10-5 **129**.......................... JamieBargary(5)
(Nigel Twiston-Davies) *chsd ldrs: lost pl 18th: sn bhd: p.u bef 20th* **14/1**
P1FP **P** **Bob Ford (IRE)**[35] 4113 9-11-6 **139**.......................... SeanBowen
(Rebecca Curtis) *mstke 1st: led to 3rd: lost pl after 17th: sn bhd: t.o whn p.u bef 2 out* **50/1**
021F **P** **Cultram Abbey**[21] 4367 9-11-1 **134**.......................... BrianHarding
(Nicky Richards) *in rr and sn drvn along: t.o whn p.u bef 16th* **25/1**
3-P **P** **Sizing Coal (IRE)**[21] 4374 8-11-8 **134**.......................... JJBurke
(J T R Dreaper, Ire) *in rr: sme hdwy 17th: wknd appr 4 out: bhd whn p.u bef 3 out* **5/1[1]**
-2UP **P** **Red Devil Lads (IRE)**[63] 3624 7-11-2 **135**.......................... TomO'Brien
(Rebecca Curtis) *t.k.h: led 3rd: wl clr fr 8th: drvn 18th: hdd after 19th: sn wknd: eased and p.u bef next* **25/1**
1P31 **P** **Courtown Oscar (IRE)**[26] 4286 7-10-8 **130**.......................... AdamNicol(3)
(Philip Kirby) *in rr: bhd whn mstke 10th: t.o 17th: p.u bef 20th* **16/1**
3121 **P** **Subtle Grey (IRE)**[38] 4054 7-11-2 **135**.......................... WillKennedy
(Donald McCain) *midfield: hdwy 10th: sn chsng ldrs: wknd 4 out: bhd whn p.u bef next* **16/1**
9m 11.8s (28.20) **Going Correction** +0.50s/f (Soft) **18** Ran SP% **128.5**
Speed ratings: **85,84,83,83,81 ,,,,, ,,,,, ,,,**
CSF £164.20 CT £1097.53 TOTE £17.30: £3.50, £2.80, £2.20, £2.40; EX 227.50 Trifecta £1992.60.
Owner R E R Williams **Bred** Paul McWilliams **Trained** Llancarfan, Vale Of Glamorgan
FOCUS
As usual plenty of runners for the Midlands National and they went a sensible gallop, with the field choosing to ignore the runaway leader. There was a late incident that changed the complexion of the race and only five finished. Lucky winner rated to mark with runner-up and fourth close to form.

4803 BETFRED "BE PART OF THE ACTION" H'CAP CHASE (15 fncs) 2m 4f
4:45 (4:45) (Class 4) (0-115,115) 5-Y-0+ **£6,330** (£1,870; £935; £468; £234)

Form RPR
P354 **1** **Special Wells**[18] 4420 7-11-4 **107**.......................... DannyCook 119+
(Sue Smith) *led to 3rd: w ldr: led 2 out: drvn out* **11/2[3]**
34P5 **2** *2 3/4* **No Through Road**[39] 4046 9-11-5 **108**.......................... RichieMcLernon 118
(Michael Scudamore) *w ldr: t.k.h: led 3rd: mstke 9th: hdd 2 out: kpt on same pce* **33/1**
/353 **3** *5* **Valseur Du Granval (FR)**[25] 4292 7-11-3 **106**..........(t) SeanBowen 112
(Tom George) *hld up towards rr: stdy hdwy 10th: upsides 4 out: one pce appr 2 out* **9/1**
00F6 **4** *9* **Brook (FR)**[21] 4352 5-11-4 **107**..........................(bt) ConorO'Farrell 103
(David Pipe) *in rr: drvn 6th: hdwy to chse ldrs 11th: wknd 3 out* **12/1**
4151 **5** *7* **Daliance (IRE)**[40] 4028 7-11-2 **112**..........(b) WilliamFeatherstone(7) 101
(Noel Williams) *in rr: hdwy 9th: lost pl 11th: kpt on between last 2* **7/1**
-352 **6** *1 1/4* **Iona Days (IRE)**[97] 3061 11-11-8 **111**..........................(p) MarkGrant 98
(Julian Smith) *mid-div: hdwy 10th: wkng whn mstke 2 out* **12/1**
2-P2 **7** *7* **One For The Boss (IRE)**[18] 4427 9-11-5 **108**..........(p) RobertDunne 90
(Dai Burchell) *mid-div: hdwy to chse ldrs 6th: wknd between last 2* **14/1**
4/25 **8** *4* **Oscar Magic (IRE)**[98] 3044 9-11-9 **115**..........................(t) RyanHatch(3) 91
(Nigel Twiston-Davies) *t.k.h in rr-div: hdwy to trck ldrs whn hit 7th: wknd 4 out* **7/2[1]**
14P5 **9** *1 1/2* **Thatchers Gold (IRE)**[43] 3979 8-11-3 **106**.......................... DenisO'Regan 82
(Henry Oliver) *chsd ldrs: lost pl 9th: sn bhd* **12/1**
0005 **P** **Gambol (FR)**[37] 4067 6-11-1 **104**.......................... TomO'Brien
(Ian Williams) *in rr: bhd whn mstke 8th: t.o 11th: p.u bef 3 out* **5/1[2]**
-244 **P** **Eaton Rock (IRE)**[56] 3746 7-10-13 **102**..........................(t) JamesDavies
(Tom Symonds) *in rr: drvn 5th: t.o whn p.u bef 11th* **9/1**
5m 23.4s (13.60) **Going Correction** +0.50s/f (Soft) **11** Ran SP% **119.5**
Speed ratings: **92,90,88,85,82 82,79,77,77,**
CSF £148.76 CT £1618.00 TOTE £6.70: £2.30, £10.40, £3.70; EX 189.60 Trifecta £2568.90 Part won..
Owner D Sutherland **Bred** Mrs C J Zetter-Wells **Trained** High Eldwick, W Yorks
FOCUS
A fair handicap chase and the front two disputed the lead throughout. Winner on decent mark and rated back to best.

4804 BETFRED MOBILE MARES' H'CAP HURDLE (12 hdls) 2m 7f 70y
5:20 (5:20) (Class 5) (0-100,99) 4-Y-0+ **£3,898** (£1,144; £572; £286)

Form RPR
36 **1** **When In Roam (IRE)**[18] 4415 7-10-7 **80**..........................(p) DaveCrosse 91+
(John O'Shea) *trckd ldr: pressed ldr fr 8th: led 3 out: rdn and styd on wl* **8/1**
2P30 **2** *5* **Camillas Wish (IRE)**[31] 4184 7-10-12 **85**.......................... JJBurke 91
(J T R Dreaper, Ire) *led: pressed fr 8th: nt fluent 3 out and hdd: rdn and one pce* **6/1**
6032 **3** *7* **Lilywhite Gesture (IRE)**[19] 4413 7-11-1 **95**.......................... PhilipDonovan(7) 93
(Fergal O'Brien) *hld up: rdn after 8th: styd on after 3 out: wnt 3rd jst after last: no threat to ldng pair* **3/1[1]**
0025 **4** *nk* **Agent Louise**[10] 4557 8-10-4 **80**..........................(p) AdamNicol(3) 77
(Mike Sowersby) *hld up: rdn after 4 out: styd on after 2 out: nrst fin* **10/1**
4514 **5** *6* **Amber Flush**[152] 1897 7-11-7 **99**.......................... ThomasCheesman(5) 91
(Martin Smith) *midfield: hdwy to trck ldrs after 7th: rdn and outpcd in 3rd bef 3 out: lost 3rd jst after last: wknd* **9/2[2]**
1PP3 **6** *15* **Vodka Island (IRE)**[20] 4391 7-11-1 **88**.......................... TomO'Brien 69
(Tim Vaughan) *t.k.h in midfield: rdn after 4 out: wknd after 2 out* **5/1[3]**
4-PP **7** *9* **Vintage Vixon (IRE)**[79] 3378 9-10-0 **76**.......................... BenPoste(3) 45
(Adrian Wintle) *trckd ldrs: lost pl 6th: reminders after 7th: struggling after 8th* **33/1**
0-04 **8** *2 1/4* **Simmply Sam**[36] 4110 9-10-6 **79**.......................... JakeGreenall 43
(Marjorie Fife) *trckd ldr: rdn and outpcd after 4 out: wknd after 3 out* **16/1**
4466 **9** *21* **Harriet's Ark**[84] 3234 9-10-0 **73** oh1.......................... MarkGrant 16
(Julian Smith) *hld up: nt fluent 6th and 7th: minor hdwy into midfield 4 out: wknd bef 3 out* **16/1**
P406 **10** *15* **Tara's Rainbow**[113] 2745 6-10-8 **88**..........................(t) MikeyHamill(7) 16
(Kim Bailey) *in tch: rdn bef 4 out: sn wknd* **13/2**
6m 21.9s (23.10) **Going Correction** +0.50s/f (Soft) **10** Ran SP% **122.4**
Speed ratings (Par 103): **79,77,74,74,72 67,64,63,56,50**
CSF £58.62 CT £181.45 TOTE £8.70: £2.70, £2.80, £1.60; EX 72.20 Trifecta £366.90.
Owner J R Salter **Bred** Robert McCarthy **Trained** Elton, Gloucs
FOCUS
Only a moderate handicap for mares. First two home were on decent marks, third and fourth similar to best of recent runs.

4805 BETFRED "FOLLOW US ON TWITTER" STANDARD OPEN NATIONAL HUNT FLAT RACE 1m 7f 168y
5:55 (5:55) (Class 4) 4-6-Y-O **£3,898** (£1,144; £572; £286)

Form RPR
1 **Mr Big Shot (IRE)** 5-11-2 0.......................... ConorO'Farrell 127+
(David Pipe) *s.i.s: in rr and sn drvn along: hdwy 6f out: chsng ldrs over 3f out: 3rd over 2f out: led appr fnl f: forged clr* **8/1**
1 **2** *8* **Big Meadow (IRE)**[21] 4357 5-11-9 0.......................... TrevorWhelan 126
(Neil King) *trckd ldrs: drvn 6f out: led over 3f out: hdd appr fnl f: kpt on same pce* **5/4[1]**
3 *1/2* **Black Mischief** 4-10-2 0.......................... LiamMcKenna(7) 112
(Harry Fry) *in rr: hdwy 6f out: chal 3f out: kpt on same pce appr fnl f* **6/1[3]**
1 **4** *9* **Stowaway Magic (IRE)**[36] 4103 5-11-4 0.......................... NedCurtis(5) 117
(Nicky Henderson) *in rr: hdwy 6f out: chsng ldrs over 3f out: wknd over 1f out* **5/2[2]**
5 *30* **Skipthecuddles (IRE)** 5-11-2 0.......................... KielanWoods 80
(Graeme McPherson) *mid-div: pushed along after 6f: hdwy to chse ldrs over 3f out: wknd over 1f out* **25/1**
56 **6** *30* **Spirit Of Hale (IRE)**[42] 4001 5-10-9 0.......................... ConorWalsh(7) 50
(Jennie Candlish) *chsd ldrs: lost pl 7f out: sn bhd: t.o* **66/1**
0 **7** *36* **Falcons Fall (IRE)**[126] 2493 5-11-2 0.......................... JamesDavies 14
(Tom Symonds) *chsd ldrs: lost pl 7f out: sn bhd: t.o* **50/1**
8 *16* **Bueno Rica (FR)** 5-11-2 0.......................... AlainCawley
(Richard Hobson) *w ldr: lost pl over 3f out: sn bhd: t.o* **25/1**
3 **9** *3* **Big Time Frank (IRE)**[31] 4188 5-11-2 0.......................... TomO'Brien
(Alex Hales) *mid-div: lost pl 6f out: sn bhd: t.o* **20/1**
52 **10** *4* **Bering Upsun**[19] 4408 5-11-2 0.......................... JakeGreenall
(James Ewart) *led: hdd over 3f out: sn lost pl: bhd whn eased 2f out: t.o* **33/1**
11 *77* **Gasoline (IRE)** 4-10-9 0.......................... RichieMcLernon
(Ian Williams) *in rr: t.o 8f out: eventually completed* **25/1**
3m 57.1s (5.30) **Going Correction** +0.50s/f (Soft)
WFA 4 from 5yo 7lb **11** Ran SP% **121.1**
Speed ratings: **106,102,101,97,82 67,49,41,39,37**
CSF £17.85 TOTE £8.90: £2.70, £1.10, £2.60; EX 30.10 Trifecta £118.80.
Owner Prof Caroline Tisdall **Bred** James McGrath **Trained** Nicholashayne, Devon
FOCUS
Something of a shock in the bumper considering the betting, but the winner looks a nice type.Runner-up and fourth close to marks.
T/Jkpt: Not won. T/Plt: £113.70 to a £1 stake. Pool of £219298.32 - 1407.69 winning tickets.
T/Qpdt: £42.70 to a £1 stake. Pool of £11748.15 - 203.30 winning tickets.
Walter Glynn & Andrew Sheret

4806 - 4814a (Foreign Racing) - See Raceform Interactive

4566 CARLISLE (R-H)
Sunday, March 20

OFFICIAL GOING: Good to soft (good in places on chase course; hdl 6.7, chs 7.4)
Wind: Light; half behind Weather: Dry, fine

4815 APOLLOBET HOME OF CASHBACK OFFERS NOVICES' H'CAP HURDLE (11 hdls) 2m 3f 61y
2:15 (2:16) (Class 4) (0-120,115) 4-Y-0+ **£3,898** (£1,144; £572; £286)

Form RPR
1126 **1** **Bruce Almighty (IRE)**[81] 3361 5-11-12 **115**.......................... WayneHutchinson 121+
(Donald McCain) *trckd ldrs: effrt 2 out: led bef last: pushed clr run-in* **9/1**
3431 **2** *5* **Bryden Boy (IRE)**[18] 4430 6-11-12 **115**.......................... SeanQuinlan 117
(Jennie Candlish) *j.lft on occasions: chsd ldr: led 2 out: hdd bef last: kpt on same pce run-in* **13/8[1]**
F354 **3** *3 1/4* **Pekanheim (IRE)**[10] 4570 8-10-3 **92**.......................... HenryBrooke 89
(Martin Todhunter) *hld up: shkn up and stdy hdwy after 4 out: rdn after next: kpt on fr last: nt rch first two* **16/1**

0230 **4** *10* **Roll Of Thunder**[32] 4178 7-9-13 **93**.............................. MissCWalton(5) 82
(James Walton) *led: rdn and hdd 2 out: wknd fr last* **12/1**

4F4P **5** *20* **Warksburn Boy**[12] 4547 6-9-10 **90**.............................. JamieHamilton(5) 60
(Sheena Walton) *hld up in tch: outpcd bef 4 out: lost tch bef 2 out* **28/1**

3442 **6** *28* **Baraka De Thaix (FR)**[10] 4566 5-11-10 **113**....................(tp) DarylJacob 58
(David Pipe) *prom: outpcd whn nt fluent 3 out: sn struggling: t.o* **7/4**[2]

0536 **P** **Buckled**[78] 3438 6-11-1 **104**.............................. BrianHughes
(Sandy Thomson) *hld up on ins: drvn and outpcd 6th: struggling fr next: t.o whn p.u bef last* **15/2**[3]

0000 **P** **Ethan (IRE)**[41] 4035 7-10-0 **89** oh1.............................. BrianHarding
(Sheena Walton) *hld up: broke down bdly bef 6th: fatally injured* **50/1**

4m 49.2s (-19.60) **Going Correction** -0.90s/f (Hard) **8** Ran SP% **115.2**
Speed ratings (Par 105): **105,102,101,97,88 77,,**
CSF £25.10 CT £237.22 TOTE £7.90: £2.60, £1.80, £2.80; EX 27.10 Trifecta £301.20.
Owner G Hunt **Bred** Cathal Ennis **Trained** Cholmondeley, Cheshire

FOCUS
An ordinary novices' handicap hurdle. They went a sound gallop on ground officially described as good to soft, good in places.

4816 APOLLOBET DAILY RACING REFUNDS NOVICES' CHASE (12 fncs) 1m 7f 207y
2:45 (2:46) (Class 3) 5-Y-0+ **£6,498** (£1,908; £954; £477)

Form RPR

4226 **1** **Tomorrow's Legend**[96] 3103 6-10-9 102.............................. JohnKington(3) 122
(Patrick Holmes) *prom: nt fluent 4th and 6th: stdy hdwy 4 out: led gng wl appr last edgd lft and pushed out run-in: comf* **25/1**

3F21 **2** *2* **Captain Hox (IRE)**[20] 4402 7-11-5 125..............................(t) BrianHughes 127
(Patrick Griffin, Ire) *t.k.h: trckd ldrs: wnt 2nd 6th: effrt and pushed along whn nt fluent 2 out: pressed wnr last: edgd rt and kpt on u.p: hld nr fin* **9/2**[3]

2122 **3** *½* **Katachenko (IRE)**[82] 3335 7-11-5 134.............................. WayneHutchinson 129
(Donald McCain) *j.lft: cl up: led 2nd: rdn and hdd bef last: kpt on u.p run-in* **8/13**[1]

53-P **4** *17* **Tambour Major (FR)**[105] 2937 9-10-12 95..............................(tp) HenryBrooke 104
(Alison Hamilton) *hld up: outpcd 5th: rallied 5 out: rdn and wknd fr 3 out* **66/1**

00P1 **5** *99* **De Bene Esse (IRE)**[35] 4142 6-11-5 0.............................. PaulMoloney 22
(Evan Williams) *nt fluent: led to 2nd: chsd ldr to 6th: sn lost pl: lost tch bef 4 out: t.o* **3/1**[2]

4m 1.6s (-14.50) **Going Correction** -0.95s/f (Hard) **5** Ran SP% **110.4**
Speed ratings: **98,97,96,88,38**
CSF £120.64 TOTE £14.60: £7.20, £2.80; EX 61.70 Trifecta £129.30.
Owner Mrs Mary Hatfield & Mrs Susan Kramer **Bred** Michael And Sara Paul **Trained** Middleham, N Yorks

FOCUS
A fairly decent novice chase. They went a respectable gallop on ground riding genuinely good on the chase track.

4817 APOLLOBET BET THROUGH YOUR MOBILE NOVICES' HURDLE (10 hdls) 2m 1f
3:20 (3:21) (Class 4) 4-Y-0+ **£3,898** (£1,144; £572; £286)

Form RPR

1 **Mister Kit**[336] 8-10-9 0.............................. DiarmuidO'Regan(5) 117+
(Chris Grant) *chsd ldr: led after 1st: mde rest: clr 4 out: shkn up and kpt on strly fr 2 out: unchal* **14/1**

2312 **2** *9* **Dakota Grey**[10] 4567 5-11-3 127.............................. JoeColliver(3) 114
(Micky Hammond) *nt fluent on occasions: led to after 1st: chsd wnr: rdn along and effrt bef 2 out: plugged on fr last: nt pce to chal* **13/8**[2]

3-14 **3** *1 ¾* **Imada (IRE)**[85] 3221 6-11-6 126.............................. BrianHarding 111
(Nicky Richards) *nt fluent: chsd ldrs: mstke 2nd: effrt and drvn appr 2 out: kpt on same pce fr last* **8/13**[1]

P **4** *25* **Feather Lane (IRE)**[113] 2769 6-11-0 0.............................. WayneHutchinson 80
(Donald McCain) *hld up in tch: rdn and outpcd 3 out: hdwy bef next: sn rdn and wknd after 2 out* **10/1**[3]

6P0 **5** *1 ¼* **Miss Barbossa (IRE)**[19] 4416 5-10-7 0.............................. HenryBrooke 72
(Martin Todhunter) *nt fluent on occasions in rr: struggling 4 out: nvr on terms* **66/1**

6/B0 **6** *¾* **Thackeray**[19] 4416 9-10-11 0.............................. JohnKington(3) 78
(Chris Fairhurst) *hld up: outpcd 4 out: shortlived effrt after next: wknd bef 2 out* **40/1**

P0 **7** *22* **Scrutiny**[19] 4416 5-11-0 0.............................. SeanQuinlan 56
(Barry Murtagh) *nt fluent on occasions in rr: struggling bef 4 out: nvr on terms* **33/1**

0 **P** **Green Zone (IRE)**[146] 1568 5-10-7 0.............................. FinianO'Toole(7)
(Lisa Harrison) *hld up: outpcd whn blnd 3 out: sn struggling: mstke and p.u next* **33/1**

4m 18.2s (-11.00) **Going Correction** -0.90s/f (Hard) **8** Ran SP% **125.6**
Speed ratings (Par 105): **89,84,83,72,71 71,60,**
CSF £41.66 TOTE £16.80: £3.10, £1.10, £1.10; EX 59.40 Trifecta £100.00.
Owner Mrs H N Eubank **Bred** A Eubank **Trained** Newton Bewley, Co Durham

FOCUS
A fair novice hurdle. They went a respectable gallop once the winner got to the lead after the first.

4818 APOLLOBET WEEKLY GOLF REFUNDS VETERANS' H'CAP CHASE (QUALIFIER) (LEG 4 OF VETERANS' CHASE SERIES) (18 fncs) 3m 110y
3:55 (3:56) (Class 2) (0-150,142) 10-Y-0+ **£18,768** (£5,544; £2,772; £1,386; £693; £348)

-621 **1** **Firth Of The Clyde**[49] 3887 11-11-12 **142**..............................(b) BrianHughes 151+
(Malcolm Jefferson) *hld up: stdy hdwy into midfield 1/2-way: chsng ldrs gng wl whn nt fluent 4 out: led bef last: rdn and edgd rt run-in: styd on wl* **9/1**[3]

0000 **2** *2 ¼* **Milborough (IRE)**[22] 4367 10-11-2 **135**.............................. GrahamWatters(3) 142
(Ian Duncan) *hld up in midfield: hdwy to chse ldr 12th: rdn 4 out: chsd wnr last: styd on* **11/2**[2]

PP-1 **3** *3 ¼* **Mr Moonshine (IRE)**[29] 4246 12-11-8 **138**.............................. DannyCook 143
(Sue Smith) *cl up: led 6th: asserted 10th: rdn bef 3 out: hdd bef last: kpt on same pce run-in* **11/4**[1]

6003 **4** *23* **Barafundle (IRE)**[27] 4286 12-11-1 **131**..............................(bt) SeanQuinlan 116
(Jennie Candlish) *nt fluent on occasions: led to 6th: w ldr to 10th: cl up tl drvn and outpcd 5 out: plugged on fr 3 out: no ch w first three* **16/1**

U105 **5** *5* **Settledoutofcourt (IRE)**[85] 3236 10-10-3 **119**.............................. DerekFox 97
(Lucinda Russell) *hld up in midfield: outpcd and lost pl 1/2-way: sme late hdwy: nvr on terms* **16/1**

055 **6** *1 ½* **Restless Harry**[15] 4483 12-10-11 **127**.............................. JamesDavies 104
(Henry Oliver) *chsd ldrs: drvn and outpcd after 13th: struggling after next* **11/2**[2]

1616 **7** *shd* **Tullamore Dew (IRE)**[78] 3448 14-10-13 **132**.............................. JoeColliver(3) 108
(Micky Hammond) *hld up: drvn and outpcd fr 6th: no ch fnl circ* **10/1**

11-1 **8** *1* **Anay Turge (FR)**[317] 184 11-11-3 **140**..............................(t) ConorSmith(7) 116
(Nigel Hawke) *hld up: stdy hdwy 1/2-way: rdn and edgd rt after 3 out: wknd bef next* **14/1**

-0P3 **9** *½* **Scotswell**[14] 4511 10-9-9 **118**.............................. ThomasDowson(7) 96
(Harriet Graham) *chsd ldrs: drvn and outpcd bef 5 out: struggling fr next* **14/1**

6-0P **10** *43* **Howard's Legacy (IRE)**[35] 4140 10-10-5 **121**..............................(p) LiamTreadwell 57
(Venetia Williams) *prom: lost pl after 2nd: rallied bef 6 out: wknd after next: t.o* **9/1**[3]

332P **P** **Harry The Viking**[29] 4245 11-10-12 **128**..............................(p) CraigNichol
(Sandy Thomson) *bhd and sn struggling: lost tch and p.u after 9th* **12/1**

6m 11.8s (-30.80) **Going Correction** -0.95s/f (Hard) **11** Ran SP% **119.3**
Speed ratings: **111,110,109,101,100 99,99,99,99,85**
CSF £59.89 CT £175.71 TOTE £5.00: £1.30, £3.10, £1.70; EX 61.30 Trifecta £323.50.
Owner Robert H Goldie **Bred** Robert H Goldie **Trained** Norton, N Yorks

FOCUS
The feature race was a decent contest and they went an honest gallop.

4819 APOLLOBET ONLINE CASINO & GAMES H'CAP HURDLE (10 hdls) 2m 1f
4:30 (4:30) (Class 4) (0-115,115) 4-Y-0+ **£3,898** (£1,144; £572; £286)

Form RPR

5000 **1** **Iniciar (GER)**[74] 3484 6-11-8 **111**.............................. DarylJacob 119+
(David Pipe) *hld up in tch: pushed along and outpcd 4 out: rallied after next: rdn and hdwy to ld bef last: pushed out on strly run-in* **11/4**[1]

3P20 **2** *5* **Snowed In (IRE)**[32] 4178 7-10-5 **94**..............................(p) SeanQuinlan 96
(Barry Murtagh) *cl up: led 3rd: clr 4 out: rdn and hdd bef last: kpt on same pce run-in* **6/1**

25-0 **3** *13* **Never Never (IRE)**[36] 3424 6-11-7 **115**.............................. ShaneShortall(5) 104
(Iain Jardine) *chsd ldrs: wnt 2nd after 4 out: rdn and outpcd 2 out: btn bef last* **3/1**[2]

2161 **4** *24* **Danceintothelight**[32] 4178 9-11-6 **109**..............................(t) AdrianLane 77
(Donald McCain) *j.lft on occasions: led to 3rd: chsd ldr tl lost pl after 4 out: struggling after next: plugged on fr last: no ch w first three* **9/2**[3]

0-3F **5** *4* **Galleons Way**[20] 4404 7-10-3 **95**.............................. AdamNicol(3) 59
(Katie Scott) *hld up: nt fluent 3rd: rdn and outpcd whn hit 4 out: sn struggling: nvr on terms* **10/1**

4405 **6** *6* **Boldbob (IRE)**[34] 4154 4-10-5 **108**.............................. FinianO'Toole(7) 60
(Micky Hammond) *in tch: nt fluent 2nd: effrt after 3 out: rdn and wknd bef next* **10/1**

3340 **7** *6* **Baraboy (IRE)**[79] 3398 6-10-9 **105**.............................. LorcanMurtagh(7) 58
(Barry Murtagh) *hld up: hdwy and prom 4 out: rdn and wknd bef 2 out* **9/1**

4m 16.5s (-12.70) **Going Correction** -0.90s/f (Hard)
WFA 4 from 6yo+ 7lb **7** Ran SP% **112.3**
Speed ratings (Par 105): **93,90,84,73,71 68,65**
CSF £18.74 TOTE £4.10: £3.20, £2.30; EX 20.30 Trifecta £62.90.
Owner Simon Munir & Isaac Souede **Bred** Gestut Schlenderhan **Trained** Nicholashayne, Devon

FOCUS
An ordinary handicap hurdle. They went an, at best, respectable gallop.

4820 APOLLOBET BET ON LOTTERIES OPEN HUNTERS' CHASE (18 fncs) 3m 110y
5:00 (5:01) (Class 6) 5-Y-0+ **£1,646** (£506; £253)

Form RPR

30-3 **1** **Robbie**[19] 4424 12-12-6 138.............................. MrJohnDawson 130+
(Keith Reveley) *hld up in tch: stdy hdwy to chse ldrs 1/2-way: smooth hdwy 2nd gng wl 4 out: hit next: sn rcvrd: effrt and rdn bef last: kpt on to ld cl home* **7/2**[2]

1F-P **2** *hd* **Ockey De Neulliac (FR)**[19] 4424 14-12-1 117.............................. SamColtherd(5) 129
(N Mechie) *j.lft on occasions: led to 1st: chsd ldr: regained ld 5 out: rdn after 2 out: kpt on fr last: hdd cl home* **8/1**[3]

20-4 **3** *25* **Barachois Silver**[21] 12-11-4 94.............................. MissRMcDonald(5) 94
(Mrs J M Hollands) *in tch: outpcd 6th: rallied 12th: outpcd 5 out: kpt on fr last to take modest 3rd cl home* **33/1**

4-41 **4** *shd* **Durban Gold**[21] 9-11-4 113.............................. MissJWalton(5) 94
(Mrs D Walton) *hld up on outside: struggling fr 1/2-way: sme late hdwy: nvr on terms* **16/1**

/30- **5** *1 ½* **Long Run (FR)**[672] 379 11-12-6 149..............................(p) MrSWaley-Cohen 111+
(Robert Waley-Cohen) *cl up: led 1st: mstke 10th: nt fluent next two: hdd 5 out: rallied: outpcd bef 2 out: 3rd and clr of rest whn eased last 100yds: shkn up but lost two pls cl home* **1/2**[1]

0-13 **6** *55* **Call Me Mulligan (IRE)**[21] 12-11-11 92..............................(p) MrNOrpwood(5) 50
(Ms Jackie Williamson) *in tch: nt fluent 7th: outpcd fr 12th: btn bef 4 out* **40/1**

/P-4 **P** **Robin Will (FR)**[43] 4000 11-11-7 100.............................. MrRSmith(5)
(Miss G E J Anderson) *hld up: struggling fr 10th: t.o whn p.u 4 out* **40/1**

6m 22.7s (-19.90) **Going Correction** -0.95s/f (Hard) **7** Ran SP% **113.7**
Speed ratings: **93,92,84,84,84 66,**
CSF £28.17 TOTE £3.70: £2.10, £3.50; EX 18.90 Trifecta £111.10.
Owner Mrs Susan McDonald **Bred** Mrs Susan McDonald **Trained** Lingdale, Redcar & Cleveland
■ Stewards' Enquiry : Mr S Waley-Cohen seven-day ban: failed to obtain the best possible placing in that he failed to ride out on a horse that could have finished third (TBC)
Mr John Dawson four-day ban: use of whip (TBC)

FOCUS
A decent hunters' chase. They went a respectable gallop.
T/Plt: £164.10 to a £1 stake. Pool: £84,057.20 - 373.90 winning units T/Qpdt: £16.80 to a £1 stake. Pool: £7,320.66 - 320.91 winning units **Richard Young**

4264 FFOS LAS (L-H)
Sunday, March 20

OFFICIAL GOING: Good to soft (soft in places; chs 7.2, hdl 7.4)
Wind: Slight; half behind Weather: Sunny

4821 HEINEKEN "NATIONAL HUNT" MAIDEN HURDLE (9 hdls 1 omitted) 2m 4f
2:00 (2:00) (Class 4) 4-Y-0+ **£3,249** (£954; £477; £238)

Form RPR

2330 **1** **Kerisper (FR)**[51] 3844 7-10-12 126.............................. RyanHatch(3) 128+
(Nigel Twiston-Davies) *mde virtually all: tended to jump rt: hrd pressed fr 3 out: asserted appr last: styd on wl u.p flat* **4/1**[3]

3233 **2** *6* **Preseli Rock (IRE)**[28] 4264 6-11-1 126..............................(p) AidanColeman 123
(Rebecca Curtis) *w ldr: ev ch fr 3 out tl no ex u.p appr last: kpt on same pce* **9/4**[2]

00U3 3 7 **Sahara Haze**[23] 4337 7-10-1 0 MrTGreatrex(7) 108
(Phillip Dando) *hld up in last pair: clsd 5th: pushed along and outpcd bef 3 out: wnt modest 3rd last: styd on wl* 100/1

-2P2 4 8 **Danvinnie**[50] 3863 7-11-1 116 LeightonAspell 111
(Oliver Sherwood) *trckd ldrs: rdn bef 3 out: one pce* 8/1

12 5 40 **Catcher On The Go (IRE)**[221] 1234 6-11-1 0 AdamWedge 72
(Evan Williams) *hld up in last pair: rdn and wknd bef 3 out: t.o* 11/1

4-P5 6 8 **Dalaman (IRE)**[37] 4108 5-10-10 0 (t) AlanJohns(5) 65
(Tim Vaughan) *hld up bhd ldrs: pushed along 5th: wknd bef 3 out: t.o* 33/1

2U6 F **Hawkhurst (IRE)**[79] 3403 6-11-1 0 SamTwiston-Davies 110
(Paul Nicholls) *racd keenly: trckd ldrs: 3rd whn rdn after 3 out: wknd between last 2: disputing 4th whn fell heavily last* 5/4[1]

04 F **Pomicide**[32] 4188 6-10-12 0 LucyGardner(3)
(Sue Gardner) *towards rr whn fell 1st* 100/1

5m 11.2s (311.20) 8 Ran SP% 119.6
CSF £14.55 TOTE £4.10: £1.40, £1.60, £15.20; EX 17.40 Trifecta £1488.30.
Owner The Autism Rockers **Bred** Bernard Forges **Trained** Naunton, Gloucs

FOCUS
Some starts have been moved at this track following remeasuring, so some races will not have speed figures until there is sufficient data to calculate updated median times. Both bends on the hurdle and chase courses were railed out 3yds from the inside line. This added approximately 30yds to this advertised races distance. Just an ordinary race of its type, with two coming nicely clear. The fourth-last was omitted due to an injured jockey.

4822 HEINEKEN H'CAP HURDLE (11 hdls) 2m 5f 192y
2:30 (2:30) (Class 4) (0-110,109) 4-Y-0+ £3,249 (£954; £477; £238)

Form RPR

6062 1 **Driftwood Haze**[8] 4614 8-11-5 109 MrTGreatrex(7) 128+
(Phillip Dando) *trckd ldrs: led 7th: rdn 2 out: sn c clr: easily* 9/2[2]

5P03 2 12 **Bishop Wulstan (IRE)**[28] 4266 5-11-4 101 (bt) SeanBowen 105
(Peter Bowen) *hld up towards rr: clsd 4th: wnt 2nd after 8th: 2 l down whn rdn 3 out: outpcd by wnr fr next: hld modest 2nd flat* 6/1[3]

653 3 1 1/4 **Romeo Is Bleeding (IRE)**[17] 4448 10-11-3 105 CiaranGethings(5) 107
(David Rees) *hld up in last: hdwy after 8th: shkn up appr 2 out where wnt 3rd: kpt on same pce to press for 2nd flat but nvr threatened wnr* 15/2

4-03 4 12 **Bonobo (IRE)**[15] 4482 9-11-12 109 AdamWedge 100
(Evan Williams) *mid-div: clsd 6th: 3rd whn rdn 3 out: grad wknd fr next* 4/1[1]

54P5 5 1 **Garde Fou (FR)**[16] 4467 10-11-6 103 (t) TomO'Brien 94
(Paul Henderson) *chsd ldrs: led 3rd to next: styd prom: mstke 7th: wknd fr 3 out* 7/1

51P5 6 8 **Fishing Bridge (IRE)**[12] 4543 11-11-9 109 (bt) KieronEdgar(3) 92
(David Rees) *hld up: hdwy whn awkward jump 7th: shkn up and wknd bef 3 out* 12/1

2045 7 45 **Captain McGinley (IRE)**[23] 4342 6-11-10 107 (p) LeightonAspell 50
(Rebecca Curtis) *chsd ldrs: led 4th to 7th: rdn and wknd after next: t.o* 4/1[1]

45/P P **Normally**[47] 3914 12-10-0 83 oh8 (b) JamesBest
(Hywel Evans) *led to 3rd: sn rdn along: bhd by 5th: lost tch next: t.o whn p.u after 8th* 50/1

S306 P **Tijori (IRE)**[17] 4448 8-10-9 99 (t) JordanWilliams(7)
(Bernard Llewellyn) *cl up tl lost pl after 2nd: in rr and hrd rdn 4th: wl bhd whn p.u after next* 18/1

111F P **Black Narcissus (IRE)**[31] 4199 7-11-11 108 RhysFlint
(Alexandra Dunn) *mid-div: niggled along 3rd: mstke 7th: sn struggling: wl bhd whn p.u bef 3 out* 9/1

5m 37.1s (17.10) **Going Correction** +0.90s/f (Soft) 10 Ran SP% 121.6
Speed ratings (Par 105): **104,99,99,94,94 91,75, , ,**
CSF £33.58 CT £203.89 TOTE £8.50: £2.30, £2.30, £2.20; EX 43.00 Trifecta £280.10.
Owner P Dando **Bred** Phillip C And Mrs Kathryn M Dando **Trained** Peterston-Super-Ely, S Glamorg

FOCUS
Both bends on the hurdle and chase courses were railed out 3yds from the inside line. This added approximately 30yds to this advertised races distance. Moderate form, but the winner was really impressive.

4823 HEINEKEN H'CAP CHASE (17 fncs) 2m 4f 199y
3:05 (3:05) (Class 4) (0-105,104) 5-Y-0+ £3,898 (£1,144; £572; £286)

Form RPR

5422 1 **Magical Man**[76] 3468 9-10-6 84 (v) TrevorWhelan 95+
(Debra Hamer) *cl up: led 2nd to 9th: lft in ld 10th: hdd 12th: rdn to ld 4 out: slow jump 2 out: styd on wl* 7/2[1]

5316 2 8 **Zama Zama**[46] 3931 9-11-2 104 (b) CianMaher(10) 107
(Evan Williams) *hld up bhd ldrs: hmpd 10th: wnt 3rd bef 4 out: rdn to chse wnr 3 out: nt fluent next: sn no ex* 12/1

-P50 3 12 **Castletown (IRE)**[22] 4356 8-10-9 87 (b[1]) MarkQuinlan 77
(Sheila Lewis) *led to 2nd: losing pl whn j.rt next: mstke and reminder 7th: rdn along fr 10th: plugged on u.p to go modest 3rd 2 out* 16/1

35P6 4 3 1/2 **Humbel Ben (IRE)**[83] 3314 13-10-4 82 (p) RobertDunne 72
(John Flint) *trckd ldrs: led 12th to 4 out: grad wknd* 10/1

4653 5 55 **Matrow's Lady (IRE)**[31] 4197 9-10-6 89 (tp) DavidNoonan(5) 26
(Neil Mulholland) *towards rr: mstke 2nd: wl bhd 11th: sme hdwy u.p after 13th: wknd 3 out: t.o whn clambered over last* 6/1[3]

P45P P **Tom Bach (IRE)**[44] 3977 12-10-0 78 oh8 (b) JamesBest
(Hywel Evans) *mid-div: rdn 9th: lost tch 13th: t.o whn p.u bef 4 out* 16/1

2330 P **The Omen**[22] 4356 10-10-1 84 AlanJohns(5)
(Tim Vaughan) *hld up: lost tch 11th: t.o whn p.u bef 4 out* 9/1

1-FP P **Seranwen (IRE)**[31] 4209 9-11-12 104 SamTwiston-Davies
(Nigel Twiston-Davies) *hld up: mstke 6th: blnd bdly next: nt fluent and rdn 9th: bhd whn p.u bef 11th* 8/1

-143 F **Merchant Of Milan**[19] 4422 8-11-7 99 (b[1]) RhysFlint
(John Flint) *cl up: led 9th tl fell next: fatally injured* 8/1

3612 F **Beaujolais Bob**[6] 4669 8-10-3 84 (bt) ConorShoemark(3)
(Richard Hawker) *trckd ldrs: 3rd whn rdn after 13th: 6th and wkng whn fell 3 out* 4/1[2]

5m 42.2s (13.60) **Going Correction** +0.55s/f (Soft) 10 Ran SP% 117.3
Speed ratings: **96,92,88,87,66 , , , ,**
CSF £44.34 CT £598.99 TOTE £4.60: £1.70, £3.00, £6.20; EX 44.70 Trifecta £848.50.
Owner C A Hanbury **Bred** A W Buller **Trained** Nantycaws, Carmarthens

FOCUS
Both bends on the hurdle and chase courses were railed out 3yds from the inside line. This added approximately 30yds to this advertised races distance. Nothing more than a moderate contest.

4824 HEINEKEN H'CAP HURDLE (10 hdls) 2m 4f
3:40 (3:40) (Class 3) (0-125,125) 4-Y-0+ £5,848 (£1,717; £858; £429)

Form RPR

330 1 **Driftashore (IRE)**[21] 4389 9-11-3 123 MissBHampson(7) 130+
(Sally Randell) *mde all: clr after 1st: 20 l up at 5th: shkn up 3 out where 14 l clr: j.lft last 2: unchal* 25/1

3P53 2 11 **Batavir (FR)**[22] 4354 7-11-12 125 (bt) ConorO'Farrell 121
(David Pipe) *hld up in mid-div: rdn 3 out: sn wnt mod 2nd: styd on u.p but nvr threatened wnr* 5/2[1]

-650 3 5 **Stiff Upper Lip (IRE)**[44] 3978 6-10-11 110 (p) LeightonAspell 101
(Oliver Sherwood) *hld up in mid-div: nt fluent and rdn 6th: one pce fr 3 out: tk modest 3rd flat but nvr nr wnr* 14/1

30-2 4 3/4 **Rafafie**[59] 3708 8-10-7 109 LucyGardner(3) 100
(Sue Gardner) *hld up in rr: rdn and sme prog whn hit 3 out: wnt modest 3rd appr last tl flat* 6/1

P11F 5 3 1/2 **Never Says Never**[107] 2880 8-10-10 114 (t) HarryCobden(5) 102
(Anthony Honeyball) *hld up in rr: hdwy into 3rd bef 2 out but nvr nr wnr: lost 3rd appr last* 7/2[2]

035- 6 18 **Church Hall (IRE)**[456] 3178 8-11-1 114 BrendanPowell 88
(Emma Baker) *mid-div: hdwy 6th: wnt 2nd after 7th tl appr 2 out where mstke: wknd* 8/1

400F 7 19 **Lava Lamp (GER)**[44] 3978 9-11-2 115 AdamWedge 68
(Evan Williams) *hld up towards rr: wknd bef 3 out* 20/1

00P 8 29 **Auenwirbel (GER)**[90] 3196 5-11-7 120 (t) RobertDunne 47
(Laura Young) *disp 2nd bhd wnr who was sn clr: wknd 3 out: t.o* 50/1

122 9 8 **Number One London (IRE)**[184] 1570 6-11-2 120 AlanJohns(5) 40
(Tim Vaughan) *hld up in rr: wknd bef 3 out: t.o* 16/1

3002 P **Crazy Jack (IRE)**[76] 3465 8-11-9 122 (p) DavidBass
(Kim Bailey) *disp 2nd bhd wnr who was sn clr: rdn and wknd after 7th: wl bhd whn p.u bef 3 out* 4/1[3]

5m 13.1s (313.10) 10 Ran SP% 119.3
CSF £89.97 CT £958.37 TOTE £25.60: £5.20, £1.50, £4.20; EX 119.00 Trifecta £1372.60.
Owner Power Geneva Ltd **Bred** James Paul O'Malley **Trained** Broad Hinton, Wilts

FOCUS
Both bends on the hurdle and chase courses were railed out 3yds from the inside line. This added approximately 30yds to this advertised races distance. The winner was left alone in front while holding a good advantage, and never looked likely to be caught. The time was 70.2 seconds slower than standard, which was much slower than the seller over the same trip.

4825 HEINEKEN CONDITIONAL JOCKEYS' (S) HURDLE (10 hdls) 2m 4f
4:15 (4:16) (Class 5) 4-7-Y-0 £2,599 (£763; £381; £190)

Form RPR

0341 1 **Calculated Risk**[28] 4266 7-11-4 112 TomBellamy 115+
(Debra Hamer) *hld up in last: stdy hdwy 7th: led gng wl 2 out: shkn up and sn clr: rdn out flat* 9/2[3]

6305 2 11 **Filatore (IRE)**[13] 4537 7-11-1 110 (t) RobertWilliams(3) 106
(Bernard Llewellyn) *trckd ldrs: led 7th to 3 out: no ch w wnr but kpt on u.p to regain 2nd bef last* 8/1

630P 3 7 **Brise Coeur (FR)**[21] 4400 5-10-12 98 (b[1]) LizzieKelly(3) 98
(Nick Williams) *reluctant to line up: t.k.h towards rr: hdwy 6th: rdn to ld 3 out: hdd next: no ex and lost 2nd bef last* 12/1

5424 4 14 **Lac Sacre (FR)**[17] 4448 7-11-1 109 (tp) KieronEdgar 86
(John Flint) *chsd ldrs: mstke 6th: rdn 3 out: wknd appr 2 out* 5/1

160P 5 10 **Milestone (IRE)**[47] 3919 6-11-1 106 (tp) ConorRing(3) 79
(Evan Williams) *trckd ldrs: rdn and wkng whn mstke 3 out* 16/1

322P 6 6 **Bar A Mine (FR)**[36] 4127 7-10-12 108 (v) RyanHatch(3) 69
(Nigel Twiston-Davies) *w ldr tl wknd qckly after 7th* 7/2[2]

251 7 43 **Apache Outlaw (IRE)**[17] 4448 7-11-1 0 PaulO'Brien(3) 33
(Rebecca Curtis) *narrow ld tl wknd qckly after 7th: t.o* 2/1[1]

P **So It Begins (IRE)**[43] 6-10-8 0 (p) KillianMoore
(John Flint) *hld up in rr: lost tch after 7th: t.o whn p.u bef 3 out* 40/1

5m 14.5s (314.50) 8 Ran SP% 117.5
CSF £40.50 TOTE £6.50: £1.60, £1.70, £4.80; EX 44.90 Trifecta £401.20.There was no bid for the winner
Owner W A Thomas **Bred** Newsells Park Stud **Trained** Nantycaws, Carmarthens

FOCUS
Both bends on the hurdle and chase courses were railed out 3yds from the inside line. This added approximately 30yds to this advertised races distance. The winner was in a different league to the remainder.

4826 HEINEKEN H'CAP CHASE (18 fncs) 2m 7f 177y
4:45 (4:45) (Class 3) (0-135,129) 5-Y-0+ £6,498 (£1,908; £954; £477)

Form RPR

4-25 1 **Horatio Hornblower (IRE)**[28] 4267 8-11-1 123 LizzieKelly(5) 135
(Nick Williams) *chsd ldrs: wnt 2nd at 10th: rdn to chal 3 out: led narrowly last: hld on wl u.p* 4/1[2]

P3PU 2 hd **Belmount (IRE)**[46] 3929 7-11-3 120 SamTwiston-Davies 132
(Nigel Twiston-Davies) *led: rdn 4 out: jnd next: narrowly hdd last: battled on u.p: jst hld* 7/2[1]

0-0P 3 25 **Victors Serenade (IRE)**[35] 4140 11-11-8 125 AidanColeman 114
(Anthony Honeyball) *prom: outpcd by ldng pair 4 out: plugged on to hold mod 3rd* 14/1

-660 4 3/4 **Rebeccas Choice (IRE)**[22] 4354 13-11-9 126 (p) RobertDunne 115
(Dai Burchell) *hld up towards rr: struggling after 14th: styd on fr 3 out: tk mod 4th flat* 33/1

1PF3 5 3 **Globalisation (IRE)**[17] 4443 6-11-3 120 (p) SeanBowen 106
(Rebecca Curtis) *mid-div: rdn along after 9th: clsd 12th: wknd after 14th: disputing mod 3rd whn blnd 3 out* 9/2[3]

P-1P 6 39 **Beforeall (IRE)**[22] 4367 8-11-12 129 (tp) LeightonAspell 80
(Oliver Sherwood) *chsd ldrs tl rdn and wknd after 14th: t.o* 11/1

-010 F **Awaywiththegreys (IRE)**[22] 4354 9-11-5 122 (b) TomO'Brien
(Peter Bowen) *chsd ldrs: mstke 9th: j. slowly next: rdn and wknd 4 out: 5th and no ch whn fell 2 out* 9/1

13P3 P **Big Society (IRE)**[28] 4267 10-11-7 124 (p) GavinSheehan
(Harry Whittington) *prom to 5th: rdn along after 9th: struggling 12th: lost tch 14th: t.o whn p.u bef 4 out* 7/1

1312 P **Still Believing (IRE)**[46] 3929 8-10-13 116 AdamWedge
(Evan Williams) *hld up in rr: sme hdwy 11th: wknd after 14th: wl bhd whn p.u bef 4 out* 8/1

-13P F **Hi Vic (IRE)**[23] 4348 11-10-12 **120**........ JackSherwood(5)
(David Loder) *hld up: fell 8th* 14/1

6m 25.6s (8.20) **Going Correction** +0.55s/f (Soft) **10** Ran SP% **118.6**
Speed ratings: **108,107,99,99,98 85, , , ,**
CSF £19.48 CT £180.61 TOTE £5.10: £2.10, £1.70, £4.50; EX 23.70 Trifecta £251.50.
Owner Huw & Richard Davies **Bred** H Davies & R Davies **Trained** George Nympton, Devon
■ Stewards' Enquiry : Lizzie Kelly two-day ban: use of whip (3 & 4 Apr)

FOCUS
Both bends on the hurdle and chase courses were railed out 3yds from the inside line. This added approximately 35yds to this advertised races distance. The first two came well clear of the remainder down the home straight.

4827 HEINEKEN STANDARD OPEN NATIONAL HUNT FLAT RACE 1m 7f 202y
5:15 (5:16) (Class 6) 4-6-Y-O **£1,949** (£572; £286; £143)

Form RPR

4 **1** **Savoy Court (IRE)**[320] 124 5-11-2 0........ GavinSheehan 120+
(Warren Greatrex) *mde all: rdn over 2f out: styd on wl u.p* 11/4[2]

2 **2** 2 **Tommy Rapper (IRE)**[110] 2842 5-11-2 0........ HarrySkelton 117+
(Dan Skelton) *hld up towards rr: gd hdwy 5f out: wnt 2nd over 3f out: wandered u.p fnl 2f: kpt on but a hld* 9/4[1]

3 17 **Eamon An Cnoic (IRE)**[336] 5-11-2 0........ ConorO'Farrell 102
(David Pipe) *t.k.h towards rr: hdwy over 4f out: outpcd by ldrs 3f out: styd on to go modest 3rd 1f out* 5/1[3]

2 **4** 6 **Western Wave (FR)**[32] 4188 4-10-4 0........ JackSherwood(5) 89
(David Loder) *prom: rdn over 3f out: sn outpcd by ldrs: lost modest 3rd 1f out* 11/1

10- **5** 6 **Red Six (IRE)**[333] 5468 5-11-9 0........ SeanBowen 98
(Peter Bowen) *chsd wnr tl over 3f out: grad wknd* 11/1

5 **6** 4 1/2 **Le Coeur Net (FR)**[79] 3409 4-10-9 0........[1] AidanColeman 80
(Anthony Honeyball) *mid-div: hdwy to trck ldrs 1/2-way: wknd over 2f out* 6/1

3-0 **7** 2 1/4 **Wicked Willy (IRE)**[178] 1640 5-11-2 0........ SamTwiston-Davies 85
(Nigel Twiston-Davies) *hld up in mid-div: shkn up over 4f out: wknd over 3f out* 14/1

8 55 **Paul (FR)**[42] 5-11-2 0........ LeightonAspell 35
(Rebecca Curtis) *mid-div: rdn and wknd over 4f out: t.o* 12/1

9 1 1/4 **Middle Barn (IRE)** 6-11-2 0........(t) BrendanPowell 34
(Sirrell Griffiths) *towards rr: wknd over 5f out: t.o* 50/1

10 30 **River Haze** 6-10-9 0........ MrTGreatrex(7) 7
(Phillip Dando) *a in rr: rn green and pushed along after 4f: lost tch over 5f out: t.o* 25/1

5 **11** 22 **Anythingmayhappen (IRE)**[101] 2991 5-11-2 0........ NickScholfield
(Jeremy Scott) *prom tl wknd qckly over 5f out: t.o* 20/1

3m 53.3s (10.40) **Going Correction** +0.90s/f (Soft)
WFA 4 from 5yo+ 7lb **11** Ran SP% **130.0**
Speed ratings: **110,109,100,97,94 92,91,63,63,48 37**
CSF £10.36 TOTE £3.50: £1.40, £1.60, £2.00; EX 10.80 Trifecta £70.00.
Owner Mrs T Brown **Bred** Alistair Corrigan **Trained** Upper Lambourn, Berks

FOCUS
Both bends on the hurdle and chase courses were railed out 3yds from the inside line. This added approximately 20yds to this advertised races distance. The winner made all in the concluding bumper.
T/Plt: £318.20 to a £1 stake. Pool: £123,832.52 - 284.05 winning units T/Qpdt: £70.80 to a £1 stake. Pool: £9,000.22 - 94.04 winning units **Richard Lowther**

4828 - 4834a (Foreign Racing) - See Raceform Interactive

4633 KELSO (L-H)
Monday, March 21

OFFICIAL GOING: Good to soft (good in places; 6.3)
Wind: Fresh, half against Weather: Overcast Rails: shared bends, effect of rail positions: Races 1, 2 & 4 adds 15 yards, Races 3& 5 adds 99 yards, Race 6 adds 42 yards.

4835 BRAEHEAD COMMERCIAL FINANCE "NATIONAL HUNT" MAIDEN HURDLE (10 hdls) 2m 2f 25y
2:00 (2:01) (Class 5) 4-Y-O+ **£2,599** (£763; £381; £190)

Form RPR

4FFU **1** **Benny's Secret (IRE)**[10] 4581 6-11-0 104........ BrianHarding 110+
(N W Alexander) *hld up in midfield: smooth hdwy after 4 out: led gng wl bef 2 out: rdn bef last: kpt on wl run-in* 9/4[1]

2 3 3/4 **Ryalex (IRE)**[155] 5-11-0 0........ DerekFox 110+
(Lucinda Russell) *chsd clr ldr: rdn and ev ch bef 2 out: j. bdly rt last: kpt on same pce run-in* 5/2[2]

404 **3** 11 **Baby Ticker**[15] 4509 7-10-4 0........ CallumWhillans(3) 90+
(Donald Whillans) *hld up: outpcd 4 out: plenty to do after next: kpt on fr 2 out: no ch w first two* 50/1

00 **4** 9 **Motion To Strike (IRE)**[23] 4371 6-10-11 0........(t[1]) TonyKelly(3) 93
(Rebecca Menzies) *t.k.h: led and sn 5 l clr: rdn and hdd bef 2 out: wknd between last 2* 10/1

0 **5** 6 **Broad Spectrum (IRE)**[79] 3442 5-11-0 0........(t) AdrianLane 87
(Donald McCain) *midfield: drvn and outpcd 6th: no imp u.p fr 3 out* 18/1

6P **6** 3 1/4 **Roxy The Rebel**[27] 4299 6-10-2 0........ GrantCockburn(5) 75
(Simon Waugh) *prom: pushed along after 4 out: wknd after next* 200/1

60 **7** 45 **Mahler Bay (IRE)**[42] 4031 6-11-0 0........ HenryBrooke 40
(Michael Smith) *chsd ldrs: drvn and struggling 4 out: lost tch fr next: t.o* 22/1

325- **F** **Ca Le Ferra (FR)**[363] 4975 6-11-0 0........ CraigNichol
(James Ewart) *cl up: fell heavily 1st* 9/1

2000 **P** **Towerburn (IRE)**[21] 4404 7-10-7 96........(t) MrTHamilton(7)
(Alison Hamilton) *prom: struggling fr 6th: lost tch and p.u after 2 out* 9/2[3]

056 **P** **Coachie Bear**[8] 4633 5-10-11 0........ AdamNicol(3)
(Katie Scott) *nt fluent in rr: struggling fnl circ: t.o whn p.u bef 4 out* 100/1

0 **P** **Bill D'Aron (FR)**[21] 4403 5-10-9 0........ DiarmuidO'Regan(5)
(James Ewart) *bhd: p.u after 5th* 40/1

P0 **P** **Secret Act (IRE)**[42] 4031 7-10-9 0........(t) StephenMulqueen(5)
(N W Alexander) *hld up: struggling fnl circ: t.o whn p.u bef 3 out* 100/1

4m 41.9s (14.90) **Going Correction** +0.675s/f (Soft) **12** Ran SP% **113.1**
Speed ratings (Par 103): **93,91,86,82,79 78,58, , ,**
CSF £7.52 TOTE £3.20: £1.20, £1.30, £4.60; EX 8.40 Trifecta £228.70.
Owner Brian Castle **Bred** James Mulhall **Trained** Kinneston, Perth & Kinross

FOCUS
Bends out 2yds - add 9yds to race distance. A modest maiden hurdle. They went a decent gallop on ground officially described as good to soft, good in places. A step up from the winner, with the third rated to her bumper mark.

4836 BELHAVEN BREWERY NOVICES' H'CAP CHASE (17 fncs) 2m 7f 96y
2:30 (2:31) (Class 4) (0-120,118) 4-Y-O+ **£3,898** (£1,144; £572; £286)

Form RPR

3312 **1** **Oscar O'Scar (IRE)**[17] 4456 8-10-13 **112**........ FinianO'Toole(7) 121+
(Micky Hammond) *in tch: smooth hdwy 5 out: led bef last: drvn and hld on wl run-in* 2/1[1]

1P24 **2** 3/4 **Present Flight (IRE)**[47] 3936 7-11-11 **117**........(t) DerekFox 124
(Lucinda Russell) *hld up in tch: smooth hdwy and cl up 5 out: led bef 2 out: hung lft and hdd bef last: rallied and swtchd rt run-in: kpt on* 5/2[2]

3342 **3** 25 **Tikkandemickey (IRE)**[13] 4549 10-11-7 **118**........ DaraghBourke(5) 103
(Raymond Shiels) *nt fluent: trckd ldrs tl rdn and outpcd 3 out: no imp bef next* 5/1

0-23 **4** 55 **Halcyon Days**[25] 4325 7-9-12 **92** oh7 ow1........(p) TonyKelly(3) 63
(Rebecca Menzies) *pressed ldr: led 5 out to bef 2 out: sn rdn and wknd: eased whn no ch run-in* 15/2

F264 **P** **Ueueteotl (FR)**[35] 4153 8-11-12 **118**........(b) CraigNichol
(James Ewart) *nt fluent on occasions: led: reminders after 10th: hdd whn hit and stmbld 5 out: sn struggling: lost tch and p.u bef 2 out* 4/1[3]

6m 18.1s (10.10) **Going Correction** +0.60s/f (Soft) **5** Ran SP% **110.3**
Speed ratings (Par 105): **106,105,97,77,**
CSF £7.63 TOTE £3.10: £1.50, £1.50; EX 7.00 Trifecta £13.20.
Owner Newroc 1 **Bred** Miss Christine Keymer **Trained** Middleham, N Yorks

FOCUS
Bends out 2yds - add 14yds to race distance. An ordinary novices' handicap chase. They went a respectable gallop at best. The first two have been rated to their marks.

4837 BERWICK SPEEDWAY EVERY SATURDAY KIDS FREE MARES' NOVICES' HURDLE (11 hdls) 2m 6f 151y
3:00 (3:02) (Class 4) 4-Y-O+ **£3,249** (£954; £477; £238)

Form RPR

3511 **1** **Sainte Ladylime (FR)**[4] 4743 5-11-12 0........ DavidBass 132+
(Kim Bailey) *trckd ldrs: wnt 2nd 2nd: led and hit 4 out: hit next: drew clr on bridle bef 2 out: nt fluent last: easily* 2/5[1]

4550 **2** 19 **Stay In My Heart (IRE)**[33] 4178 7-10-7 90........(t) JamesCorbett(7) 95
(Susan Corbett) *hld up: stdy hdwy 1/2-way: effrt and chsd (clr) wnr 2 out: j.rt last: no imp* 14/1

6-2P **3** 7 **Miss Tiggy (IRE)**[40] 4052 6-11-0 0........ PeterBuchanan 92+
(Lucinda Russell) *early mstkes: chsd ldr to 2nd: cl up: effrt and regained 2nd briefly bef 2 out: drvn and outpcd between last 2* 7/2[2]

5 **4** 21 **Amys Choice (IRE)**[23] 4369 6-11-0 0........ CraigNichol 67
(Rose Dobbin) *led to 4 out: rallied: outpcd after next: btn 2 out* 9/1[3]

0-00 **P** **Spirit Dame (IRE)**[23] 4369 5-10-7 0........[1] LorcanMurtagh(7)
(Rose Dobbin) *hld up: outpcd whn mstke 3 out: sn lost tch: p.u bef next* 100/1

5m 59.3s (18.30) **Going Correction** +0.675s/f (Soft) **5** Ran SP% **111.3**
Speed ratings (Par 105): **95,88,85,78,**
CSF £7.27 TOTE £1.40: £1.10, £6.30; EX 6.90 Trifecta £12.40.
Owner Paul & Clare Rooney **Bred** Har Du Puy **Trained** Andoversford, Gloucs

FOCUS
Bends out 2yds - add 14yds to race distance. An ordinary mares' novices' hurdle. They went a steady gallop. A small pb from the winner, with the second, third and fourth all rated close to their marks.

4838 CHAMPAGNE JOSEPH PERRIER H'CAP CHASE (12 fncs) 2m 1f 14y
3:30 (3:30) (Class 3) (0-140,136) 5-Y-O+ **£9,097** (£2,671; £1,335; £667)

Form RPR

5255 **1** **Aye Well**[43] 4011 11-10-11 **121**........ DerekFox 133+
(Stuart Coltherd) *cl up: wnt 2nd after 5 out: ev ch and rdn whn nt fluent 2 out: led last: styd on wl u.p* 11/1

12P4 **2** 12 **Indian Voyage (IRE)**[9] 4606 8-11-3 **132**........(t) DaraghBourke(5) 134
(Maurice Barnes) *j.w: led: rdn and hdd last: kpt on same pce: wknd and eased towards fin* 8/1

5605 **3** 3/4 **Jet Master (IRE)**[34] 4167 10-11-11 **135**........(t) BrianHarding 137
(N W Alexander) *nt fluent in rr: outpcd 5th: rallied 3 out: kpt on fr last: nrst fin* 11/1

6443 **4** 3/4 **Lightening Rod**[77] 3475 11-10-12 **125**........ HarryBannister(3) 124
(Michael Easterby) *hld up: pushed along after 4 out: rdn and tk modest 3rd bef last to run-in: no imp* 7/2[2]

4423 **5** 1 **Yorkist (IRE)**[16] 4469 8-11-7 **134**........(tp) JoeColliver(3) 133
(Micky Hammond) *in tch: drvn and outpcd bef 3 out: no imp fr next* 9/1

1013 **6** 7 **Chestnut Ben (IRE)**[10] 4597 11-10-5 **122**........ MrRWinks(7) 117
(Peter Winks) *hld up in tch: hdwy to chse ldrs whn hit 4 out: rdn and wknd after next* 8/1

4134 **7** 41 **The Grey Taylor (IRE)**[43] 4011 7-11-12 **136**........(t) DannyCook 126
(Brian Ellison) *pressed ldr to after 5 out: rdn and outpcd bef 2 out: lost 3rd bef last: eased whn btn run-in* 2/1[1]

4m 27.3s (9.30) **Going Correction** +0.60s/f (Soft) **7** Ran SP% **114.4**
Speed ratings: **102,96,96,95,95 91,72**
CSF £88.52 TOTE £13.80: £4.90, £3.60; EX 108.10 Trifecta £442.50.
Owner Mrs Catherine Hogg **Bred** John Hogg **Trained** Selkirk, Borders

FOCUS
Bends out 2yds - add 9yds to race distance. The feature contest was a decent handicap chase. They went an even gallop. A small pb from the winner, with the second rated close to his mark.

4839 QUEENS HEAD HOTEL KELSO BEST BAR NONE H'CAP HURDLE (11 hdls) 2m 4f 189y
4:00 (4:00) (Class 3) (0-130,130) 4-Y-O+ **£5,848** (£1,717; £858; £429)

Form RPR

6141 **1** **Captain Redbeard (IRE)**[11] 4566 7-10-13 **124**........ SamColtherd(7) 138+
(Stuart Coltherd) *hld up: stdy hdwy 4 out: led 2 out: sn pushed clr: eased run-in* 4/1[3]

32P **2** 7 **Boruma (IRE)**[83] 3344 6-10-6 **113**........ HarryChalloner(3) 115
(Dianne Sayer) *chsd ldrs: hit and outpcd 4 out: plenty to do after next: rallied 2 out: kpt on run-in: tk 2nd cl home: nt rch easy wnr* 9/1

6045 **3** shd **Landecker (IRE)**[32] 4206 8-10-9 **118**........(p) StephenMulqueen(5) 121
(N W Alexander) *hld up in tch on outside: stdy hdwy 1/2-way: rdn to ld briefly bef 2 out: hung lft between last 2: kpt on same pce fr last: lost 2nd cl home* 13/2

-044 **4** 12 **Desert Cry (IRE)**[54] 3804 10-11-12 **130**........(b[1]) HenryBrooke 123
(Donald McCain) *hld up: rdn bef 4 out: rallied and edgd rt bef 2 out: sn no imp* 16/1

The Form Book Jumps 2015-16, Raceform Ltd, Newbury, RG14 5SJ

15-0 **5** *16* **Jacks Last Hope**[101] 3027 7-10-10 **119**........................ DiarmuidO'Regan(5) 96
(Chris Grant) *hld up: pushed along bef 7th: rallied: rdn after 3 out: wknd bef next* **14/1**

5F1P **6** *4* **Lord Wishes (IRE)**[47] 3936 9-11-11 **129**........................(b[1]) BrianHarding 103
(James Ewart) *nt fluent on occasions: led to after 4 out: rdn and wknd after next* **12/1**

-204 **7** *1 1/4* **L'Aigle Royal (GER)**[77] 3465 5-11-10 **128**........................(p) DannyCook 100
(John Quinn) *cl up: led after 4 out to bef 2 out: sn rdn and wknd: eased whn no ch run-in* **3/1**[1]

-53B **P** **Uriah Heep (FR)**[142] 2194 7-11-4 **122**........................ CraigNichol
(R Mike Smith) *hld up: drvn and outpcd bef 7th: sn struggling: lost tch and p.u bef 3 out* **20/1**

31 **P** **Cracked Rear View (IRE)**[16] 4473 6-11-2 **120**....................(tp) DavidBass
(Kim Bailey) *nt fluent: prom: hit and drvn 4 out: wknd after next: lost tch and p.u bef 2 out* **7/2**[2]

5m 23.5s (15.50) **Going Correction** +0.675s/f (Soft) **9 Ran SP% 115.6**
Speed ratings (Par 107): **97,94,94,89,83 82,81, ,**
CSF £39.35 CT £229.40 TOTE £7.50: £2.10, £3.10, £2.30; EX 39.40 Trifecta £238.40.
Owner S Coltherd **Bred** Derrymore House Syndicate **Trained** Selkirk, Borders

FOCUS
Bends out 2yds - add 14yds to race distance. A fairly decent handicap hurdle. They went a respectable gallop. Another step up from the winner, with the second helping to set the level.

4840 NEWCASTLE ARMS COLDSTREAM H'CAP HURDLE (13 hdls) 3m 1f 170y
4:30 (4:30) (Class 4) (0-115,114) 4-Y-O+ **£3,249** (£954; £477; £238)

Form RPR

-201 **1** **Ganbei**[39] 4069 10-11-0 **105**........................ HarryBannister(3) 116+
(Michael Easterby) *hld up: hdwy to press ldr 4 out: led 2 out: rdn bef last: drew clr run-in* **5/1**[3]

4254 **2** *6* **Maggie Blue (IRE)**[15] 4510 8-10-7 **102**........................ ThomasDowson(7) 107
(Harriet Graham) *chsd ldrs: led 9th: rdn and hdd 2 out: kpt on same pce fr last* **20/1**

0P4P **3** *15* **Snapping Turtle (IRE)**[15] 4510 11-11-0 **105**.............. CallumWhillans(3) 99
(Donald Whillans) *hld up: drvn and outpcd 1/2-way: rallied 3 out: tk modest 3rd bef last: plugged on: no imp* **22/1**

631U **4** *5* **Rocklim (FR)**[16] 4474 6-11-3 **110**........................ DiarmuidO'Regan(5) 98
(James Ewart) *trckd ldrs: drvn after 3 out: outpcd bef next: wknd and lost 3rd bef last* **4/1**[1]

4223 **5** *3* **Hunters Belt (IRE)**[8] 4638 12-10-9 **102**....................(vt) JonathonBewley(5) 86
(George Bewley) *hld up: pushed along 1/2-way: sme hdwy u.p after 3 out: edgd rt and no further imp bef next* **7/1**

4636 **6** *6* **Kilquiggan (IRE)**[8] 4638 8-9-11 **92**........................ MissRMcDonald(7) 71
(Sandy Thomson) *bhd: plenty to do sing fnl circ: sme hdwy after 3 out: nvr nrr* **18/1**

2202 **7** *9* **Bescot Springs (IRE)**[10] 4581 11-10-7 **102**....................(v) MrWHRReed(7) 72
(Lucinda Russell) *disp ld tl hit and rdn 9th: rallied: wknd after 3 out* **16/1**

U3P5 **8** *21* **Chavoy (FR)**[21] 4407 11-11-9 **114**....................(tp) TonyKelly(3) 66
(Rebecca Menzies) *sn wl bhd: struggling 1/2-way: nvr on terms* **28/1**

3023 **P** **Kind Of Easy (IRE)**[10] 4586 10-10-10 **103**........................ DaraghBourke(5)
(Alistair Whillans) *led or disp ld to 9th: drvn and wknd after next: no ch whn p.u after 2 out* **8/1**

1230 **P** **Omid**[45] 3970 8-10-13 **104**........................(bt) JohnKington(3)
(Kenneth Slack) *in tch: drvn and outpcd 1/2-way: lost tch and p.u bef 3 out* **15/2**

23/P **P** **Moscow Menace (IRE)**[136] 2321 9-10-6 **94**........................ SeanQuinlan
(Katie Scott) *chsd ldrs: drvn and struggling bef 9th: lost tch and p.u bef 3 out* **33/1**

350 **P** **Sonneofpresenting (IRE)**[26] 4303 6-11-2 **104**........................ DavidBass
(Kim Bailey) *hld up bhd ldng gp: effrt and rdn after 4 out: wknd after next: lost tch and p.u bef 2 out* **9/2**[2]

6m 54.2s (14.20) **Going Correction** +0.675s/f (Soft) **12 Ran SP% 116.9**
Speed ratings (Par 105): **105,103,98,97,96 94,91,85, , ,**
CSF £100.92 CT £2010.55 TOTE £6.20: £3.10, £6.40, £7.00; EX 114.00 Trifecta £2820.50 Part won..
Owner N W A Bannister **Bred** Wood Farm Stud **Trained** Sheriff Hutton, N Yorks

FOCUS
Bends out 2yds - add 16yds to race distance. An ordinary staying handicap hurdle. They went a decent, contested gallop. Another hurdle pb from the winner, but in line with last year's hunter chase mark. The second has been rated to her mark.
T/Plt: £221.70 to a £1 stake. Pool: £68,751.38 - 226.36 winning tickets T/Qpdt: £134.10 to a £1 stake. Pool: £4,949.46 - 27.30 winning tickets **Richard Young**

4533

SOUTHWELL (L-H)
Monday, March 21

OFFICIAL GOING: Good (good to soft in places; 7.5)
Wind: light 1/2 behind Weather: overcast

4841 SOUTHWELL GOLF CLUB MEMBERSHIP H'CAP CHASE (13 fncs) 1m 7f 153y
2:20 (2:20) (Class 4) (0-120,118) 5-Y-O+ **£5,198** (£1,526; £763; £381)

Form RPR

5634 **1** **Midnight Chorister**[109] 2859 8-10-13 **105**....................(t) KielanWoods 118+
(Alex Hales) *trckd ldrs: 2nd appr 3 out: led appr last: styd on wl: readily* **13/2**

0655 **2** *3* **Owen Na View (IRE)**[65] 3620 8-11-12 **118**....................(t) PaddyBrennan 124
(Fergal O'Brien) *led: hdd briefly appr 4th: drvn 10th: hdd appr last: kpt on same pce* **5/4**[1]

0-15 **3** *1/2* **Allow Dallow (IRE)**[96] 3115 9-11-11 **117**........................ JoshuaMoore 123
(Jonjo O'Neill) *hld up in rr: hdwy and handy 4th bef 9th: effrt 3 out: kpt on same pce* **4/1**[2]

-532 **4** *2 1/2* **Saffron Prince**[21] 4410 8-11-1 **112**........................ JakeHodson(5) 116
(David Bridgwater) *chsd ldrs: pushed along 7th: one pce bef 3 out* **9/2**[3]

PPP3 **5** *14* **Cody Wyoming**[38] 4106 10-11-11 **117**....................(tp) DenisO'Regan 109
(Charlie Mann) *chsd ldrs: lost pl bef 9th: bhd bef 3 out* **8/1**

06UP **P** **Another Journey**[77] 3466 7-11-2 **108**........................ TomMessenger
(Sarah-Jayne Davies) *chsd ldrs: led briefly appr 4th: nt fluent and reminders 8th: sn lost pl and bhd: t.o whn p.u bef 3 out* **28/1**

4m 9.4s (7.40) **Going Correction** +0.60s/f (Soft) **6 Ran SP% 110.5**
Speed ratings: **105,103,103,102,95**
CSF £15.44 TOTE £8.30: £2.50, £1.80; EX 17.50 Trifecta £59.70.
Owner The Choristers **Bred** Mrs J Way **Trained** Edgcote, Northamptonshire

FOCUS
Fences and hurdles were outside the line raced at the previous meeting on the March 7 with both bends moved to fresh ground. They went a sound gallop in this modest handicap and it's fair form for the class. Afterwards winning rider Kielan Woods reported the going was on the soft side of good. A pb from the winner and a small pb from the fourth.

4842 ROBERT BURLEY 83RD BIRTHDAY CELEBRATION H'CAP CHASE (16 fncs) 2m 4f 62y
2:50 (2:50) (Class 4) (0-120,120) 5-Y-O+
£6,256 (£1,848; £924; £462; £231; £116)

Form RPR

2 **1** **Thoonavolla (IRE)**[103] 2976 8-10-0 **94** oh1........................ AdamWedge 103+
(Tom Weston) *trckd ldrs 3rd: j.rt 4th: 2nd appr 3 out: styd on to ld last 50yds* **5/2**[1]

-4P5 **2** *2 1/4* **Somchine**[30] 4251 8-11-9 **117**........................ AndrewThornton 125
(Seamus Mullins) *hld up in rr: hdwy to trck ldrs 10th: led after 13th: over 2 l ahd whn hit last: hdd and no ex last 50yds* **16/1**

4556 **3** *7* **Lord Grantham (IRE)**[39] 4071 9-11-4 **112**........................ JakeGreenall 112
(Henry Daly) *trckd ldrs: t.k.h: one pce appr 3 out* **5/1**

2350 **4** *1/2* **Denali Highway (IRE)**[24] 4348 9-11-5 **113**....................(p) HarrySkelton 112
(Caroline Bailey) *led: reminders 12th: hdd after 13th: one pce appr next* **3/1**[2]

1066 **5** *27* **Toowoomba (IRE)**[30] 4251 8-11-4 **112**........................ TomO'Brien 94
(Philip Hobbs) *j.rt: chsd ldrs: outpcd and lost pl 13th: sn bhd* **15/2**

-0P1 **6** *62* **Santa's Secret (IRE)**[22] 4386 8-11-10 **118**....................(p) LeightonAspell 37
(Oliver Sherwood) *nt fluent: chsd ldr: drvn 10th: hit next: sn lost pl and bhd: t.o bef 3 out: eventually completed* **4/1**[3]

5m 27.2s (10.20) **Going Correction** +0.625s/f (Soft) **6 Ran SP% 107.9**
Speed ratings: **104,103,100,100,89 64**
CSF £30.42 CT £159.59 TOTE £3.40: £3.00, £5.70; EX 23.50 Trifecta £132.10.
Owner The Troubled Pink Partnership **Bred** Mark Jackson **Trained** Hindlip, Worcs

FOCUS
This modest handicap saw the first pair come clear late in the day. The second sets the level.

4843 SOUTHWELL GOLF CLUB PAY & PLAY "NATIONAL HUNT" MAIDEN HURDLE (DIV I) (11 hdls) 2m 4f 62y
3:20 (3:20) (Class 4) 4-Y-O+ **£3,898** (£1,144; £572; £286)

Form RPR

562 **1** **Some Are Lucky (IRE)**[33] 4176 5-11-1 0........................ PaddyBrennan 120+
(Tom George) *t.k.h: led: hdd bef 5th: led 6th: drvn clr bef 2 out: styd on wl* **2/1**[1]

21-3 **2** *12* **Monkhouse (IRE)**[96] 3105 6-10-12 0........................ TomBellamy(3) 109+
(Kim Bailey) *j.rt: chsd wnr: led bef 5th: hdd 6th: reminders next: outpcd and modest 3rd after 3 out: 2nd appr last: no ch w wnr* **5/2**[2]

02F **3** *1* **Robinshill (IRE)**[58] 3743 5-10-12 0........................ RyanHatch(3) 107
(Nigel Twiston-Davies) *chsd ldrs: 3rd 6th: hmpd 8th and lost pl: modest 2nd after 3 out: one pce* **15/2**

330P **4** *9* **Sandygate (IRE)**[52] 3846 6-11-1 114........................ TomO'Brien 101
(Philip Hobbs) *nt fluent: chsd ldrs: reminders 2nd and 4th: outpcd 6th: poor 5th whn blnd 2 out* **10/1**

5-5 **5** *1 1/4* **Ted's Lad**[151] 2044 6-11-1 0....................(t) WayneHutchinson 96
(Alan King) *hld up in rr: hdwy 6th: outpcd and lost pl 8th* **16/1**

0 **6** *9* **Bored Or Bad (IRE)**[26] 4303 4-10-7 0........................ AidanColeman 80
(David Dennis) *in rr: bhd fr 6th* **100/1**

5-6 **7** *20* **Beneficial Joe (IRE)**[83] 3334 6-11-1 0........................ KielanWoods 70
(Graeme McPherson) *in rr: outpcd 6th: bhd fr 8th: t.o 3 out: lame* **25/1**

2-0R **F** **Lewis**[60] 3709 7-10-12 0........................ BenPoste(3)
(Tom Symonds) *hld up in rr: fell 6th: fatally injured* **13/2**[3]

0-05 **U** **Sugar Mix**[81] 3388 5-11-1 0....................(p) AndrewTinkler
(Martin Keighley) *chsd ldrs: hit 2nd: j.lft: hmpd and uns rdr 6th* **100/1**

6 **U** **Early Retirement (IRE)**[102] 2992 4-10-7 0........................ SeanBowen 80
(Caroline Bailey) *in rr: pushed along 4th: outpcd 6th: bhd fr next: blnd and uns rdr last* **25/1**

5m 20.1s (7.10) **Going Correction** +0.60s/f (Soft)
WFA 4 from 5yo+ 8lb **10 Ran SP% 111.6**
Speed ratings (Par 105): **109,104,103,100,99 96,88, ,**
CSF £6.69 TOTE £2.80: £1.30, £1.60, £2.30; EX 10.10 Trifecta £33.30.
Owner Power Panels Electrical Systems Ltd **Bred** Timothy Nolan **Trained** Slad, Gloucs

FOCUS
There was no hanging about in this ordinary maiden. The third helps set the level.

4844 SOUTHWELL GOLF CLUB PAY & PLAY "NATIONAL HUNT" MAIDEN HURDLE (DIV II) (11 hdls) 2m 4f 62y
3:50 (3:50) (Class 4) 4-Y-O+ **£3,898** (£1,144; £572; £286)

Form RPR

045P **1** **Weyburn (IRE)**[55] 3795 5-11-1 0........................ AndrewTinkler 113+
(Martin Keighley) *wore ear plugs: chsd ldrs: drvn and 3rd sn after 3 out: led next: 4 l clr last: drvn rt out* **14/1**

50 **2** *2* **Minella Experience (IRE)**[24] 4344 5-11-1 0........................ HarrySkelton 110
(Dan Skelton) *led: hit 3 out: hdd narrowly next: styd on same pce* **4/1**[3]

13 **3** *6* **Dante's Way (IRE)**[133] 2401 7-11-1 0........................ BrianHughes 106
(Malcolm Jefferson) *chsd ldrs: drvn and outpcd 3 out: kpt on fr next: modest 3rd last* **6/5**[1]

60 **4** *1 3/4* **Behind The Wire (IRE)**[52] 3839 5-11-1 0........................ PaddyBrennan 103
(Tom George) *t.k.h in rr: trckd ldrs 6th: nt fluent next: drvn and outpcd 3 out: kpt on fr next: tk modest 4th clsng stages* **11/4**[2]

24P **5** *1* **Galveston (IRE)**[39] 4063 7-10-12 0........................ ConorShoemark(3) 101
(Fergal O'Brien) *chsd ldr: drvn 3 out: fdd between last 2* **11/1**

PP **6** *22* **Cab On Times (IRE)**[20] 4426 7-11-1 0........................ JakeGreenall 80
(Mark Walford) *chsd ldrs: lost pl bef 3 out: sn bhd: t.o whn blnd last* **66/1**

0 **P** **Change Or Go (IRE)**[26] 4303 4-10-7 0........................ AidanColeman
(David Dennis) *t.k.h in rr: j.rt 3rd: hdwy to chse ldrs 9th: sn drvn: bhd whn j.rt next: t.o whn j.rt 3 out: p.u after next* **100/1**

5m 21.2s (8.20) **Going Correction** +0.60s/f (Soft)
WFA 4 from 5yo+ 8lb **7 Ran SP% 109.6**
Speed ratings (Par 105): **107,106,103,103,102 93,**
CSF £63.56 TOTE £11.20: £5.30, £2.20; EX 69.70 Trifecta £199.10.
Owner M Boothright **Bred** Padraig Watters **Trained** Condicote, Gloucs

FOCUS
The second division of the maiden was more competitive than the first. The winner has been rated as improving to his bumper mark, while the fourth helps set the level.

4845 AT THE RACES SKY 415 H'CAP HURDLE (11 hdls) 2m 4f 62y
4:20 (4:20) (Class 5) (0-100,100) 4-Y-0+ **£3,249** (£954; £477; £238)

Form RPR
2342 **1** **Riddlestown (IRE)**[10] 4590 9-11-7 **95**..........(b) HarrySkelton 107
(Caroline Fryer) *chsd ldrs: 2nd 6th: led 3 out: jnd next: hdd narrowly last 150yds: crowded: fnd ex and led fnl strides* **10/1**

B/1 **2** *nse* **Visible Light (IRE)**[4] 4747 8-11-4 **97**.......... CiaranGethings(5) 110
(Stuart Edmunds) *chsd ldrs: 3rd 8th: jnd wnr gng wl appr 2 out: j.rt last: sn led narrowly: edgd lft: hdd fnl strides* **1/1**[1]

52P0 **3** *25* **Midnight Gem**[47] 3930 6-11-12 **100**.......... WayneHutchinson 90
(Charlie Longsdon) *w ldrs: led 6th: hdd 3 out: wknd 2 out* **14/1**

P125 **4** *16* **Running Wolf (IRE)**[53] 3821 5-11-6 **97**..........(t) KillianMoore(3) 72
(Alex Hales) *chsd ldrs: outpcd 3 out: clr 4th after 3 out: wknd appr next* **14/1**

5600 **5** *13* **Lovefromabove (IRE)**[24] 4344 5-10-12 **91**.......... BridgetAndrews(5) 54
(Dan Skelton) *hld up in rr: hdwy 7th: drvn and wknd 3 out* **22/1**

3-52 **6** *1 3/4* **Diego Suarez (FR)**[45] 3973 6-11-5 **93**..........(p) TomMessenger 55
(Chris Bealby) *t.k.h: trckd ldrs: lost pl 3 out* **7/1**[3]

533 **7** *2 1/4* **Cahill (IRE)**[36] 2092 4-11-4 **100**..........(p) PaddyBrennan 52
(Fergal O'Brien) *in rr: nt fluent 2nd: hdwy 8th: lost pl next* **6/1**[2]

0 **8** *4 1/2* **Drive On Locky (IRE)**[27] 4291 9-10-12 **86**..........(tp) AlainCawley 42
(Johnny Farrelly) *in rr: drvn after 6th: bhd fr 3 out* **18/1**

41/0 **9** *14* **Ohms Law**[156] 1961 11-9-9 **76** oh1 ow2.......... CathalCourtney(7) 19
(Anthony Day) *chsd ldrs: drvn 6th: lost pl 3 out: sn bhd* **33/1**

0004 **10** *shd* **The Big Mare**[27] 4290 7-11-0 **88**.......... RobertDunne 31
(Laura Young) *chsd ldrs: reminders 5th: lost pl after 8th: sn bhd* **50/1**

P404 **11** *2 1/2* **League Of His Own (IRE)**[16] 4490 7-9-11 **74** oh10(t) MauriceLinehan(3) 15
(Claire Dyson) *stdd s: t.k.h in rr: bhd fr 8th* **66/1**

U **12** *1 3/4* **Griesenau (IRE)**[27] 4295 10-10-7 **88**.......... MrGTreacy(7) 27
(Paul Henderson) *j.rt: led to 6th: lost pl sn after 3 out: wl bhd whn eased clsng stages* **33/1**

5m 19.2s (6.20) **Going Correction** +0.60s/f (Soft)
WFA 4 from 5yo+ 8lb **12** Ran SP% **118.2**
Speed ratings (Par 103): **111,110,100,94,89 88,87,85,80,80 79,78**
CSF £20.25 CT £152.21 TOTE £9.90: £3.00, £1.10, £3.10; EX 30.40 Trifecta £194.80.
Owner J Ward **Bred** Jeremiah O'Brien **Trained** Wymondham, Norfolk
■ Stewards' Enquiry : Ciaran Gethings caution: careless riding
FOCUS
Few got seriously into this moderate handicap and the first pair came well clear in a bobbing finish. Solid form, with a hurdle pb from the winner.

4846 DOWNLOAD THE AT THE RACES APP H'CAP HURDLE (9 hdls) 1m 7f 153y
4:50 (4:50) (Class 4) (0-110,110) 4-Y-0+ **£3,898** (£1,144; £572; £286)

Form RPR
3063 **1** **Being Global (FR)**[86] 3223 5-11-8 **105**.......... HarrySkelton 111
(Caroline Bailey) *chsd ldrs: hmpd 6th: led 3 out: sn drvn: kpt on wl run-in: hld on towards fin* **4/1**[1]

4F00 **2** *1* **Antiphony (IRE)**[56] 3777 5-10-10 **100**.......... ConorSmith(7) 105
(Philip Hobbs) *nt fluent in rr: mstke 1st: hdwy 3 out: 5th next: styd on and 3rd last: tk end clsng stages* **11/1**

0U00 **3** *nk* **Sarpech (IRE)**[75] 3484 5-11-1 **98**.......... AidanColeman 103
(Charlie Longsdon) *trckd ldrs: 3rd between last 2: kpt on wl run-in: no ex clsng stages* **16/1**

2P61 **4** *3 1/2* **Mondo Cane (IRE)**[46] 3950 9-11-10 **107**..........(p) AdamPogson 111+
(Charles Pogson) *trckd ldrs: drvn to chse wnr appr 2 out: 4th whn hit last: fdd* **5/1**[2]

-304 **5** *6* **Elkstone**[17] 4460 5-11-8 **105**.......... DenisO'Regan 101
(Alan King) *hld up in rr: stdy hdwy 6th: trcking ldrs next: cl 3rd whn blnd 2 out: fnd little between last 2* **6/1**[3]

4P4 **6** *12* **Me Voila (FR)**[33] 4183 4-11-0 **109**.......... LizzieKelly(5) 88
(Nick Williams) *in rr: hdwy 6th: sn prom: lost pl appr next* **15/2**

045 **7** *8* **Mister Dick (FR)**[53] 3822 4-11-6 **110**.......... JoshuaMoore 80
(Jonjo O'Neill) *chsd ldrs: pushed along 4th: lost pl appr 2 out* **14/1**

1606 **8** *8* **Miss Fortywinks**[108] 2888 7-11-5 **102**.......... RyanMahon 72
(Seamus Mullins) *chsd ldrs: drvn 3 out: lost pl appr next* **12/1**

-P25 **9** *2 1/2* **Grisedenuit (FR)**[16] 4489 4-10-7 **104**.......... JoshWall(7) 67
(Trevor Wall) *sn trcking ldrs: lost pl appr 2 out* **50/1**

1215 **10** *2 1/2* **Empty The Tank (IRE)**[166] 1810 6-11-9 **106**.......... LeightonAspell 71
(Jim Boyle) *mid-div: drvn 3 out: sn lost pl* **8/1**

6U1F **11** *8* **It's Oscar (IRE)**[42] 4029 9-11-1 **98**..........(p) MarkQuinlan 56
(James Evans) *led: j.rt 6th: hdd next: sn lost pl* **16/1**

36-0 **P** **Shimba Hills**[33] 1893 5-11-7 **109**..........(p) DavidNoonan(5)
(Lawney Hill) *in rr: lost pl bef 3 out: t.o whn p.u bef 2 out* **12/1**

4m 4.7s (7.70) **Going Correction** +0.60s/f (Soft)
WFA 4 from 5yo+ 7lb **12** Ran SP% **117.9**
Speed ratings (Par 105): **104,103,103,101,98 92,88,84,83,82 78,**
CSF £47.58 CT £641.81 TOTE £4.10: £2.10, £4.20, £4.80; EX 55.40 Trifecta £946.70.
Owner Mrs Susan Carsberg **Bred** Pierre Julienne **Trained** Holdenby, Northants
FOCUS
A competitive handicap, run at a fair gallop. The first three are on the upgrade, while the fourth helps set the level.

4847 SOUTHWELL MARES' STANDARD NATIONAL HUNT FLAT RACE (CONDITIONAL JOCKEYS AND AMATEUR RIDERS) 1m 7f 153y
5:20 (5:20) (Class 6) 4-6-Y-0 **£2,053** (£598; £299)

Form RPR
320 **1** **Scorpion Princess (IRE)**[106] 2929 5-10-11 0.......... GrahamWatters(3) 107+
(Charlie Longsdon) *hld up in rr-div: hdwy to trck ldrs 7f out: qcknd to ld over 2f out: styd on wl fnl f: readily* **5/1**[2]

2 *3 1/2* **Book At Bedtime** 5-10-9 0.......... MrJohnDawson(5) 104+
(Keith Reveley) *in rr: reminders after 7f: hdwy to chse ldrs over 3f out: 2nd over 1f out: kpt on same pce* **12/1**

3 **3** *3 3/4* **Alice Pink (IRE)**[32] 4201 6-10-7 0.......... MrBParis-Crofts(7) 100
(Paul Henderson) *t.k.h: led 3f: trckd ldrs: led briefly 3f out: kpt on same pce over 1f out* **50/1**

22 **4** *1/2* **Raised On Grazeon**[35] 4156 5-11-0 0.......... JeremiahMcGrath 100
(John Quinn) *trckd ldrs: t.k.h: drvn over 3f out: one pce and edgd rt over 1f out* **2/1**[1]

0 **5** *1/2* **Daytime Ahead (IRE)**[38] 4102 5-10-10 0 ow3.......... BenFfrenchDavis(7) 102
(Oliver Sherwood) *mid-div: drvn to chse ldrs over 3f out: one pce fnl 2f* **9/1**

6 *1/2* **Mythical Legend** 5-10-9 0.......... DavidNoonan(5) 99
(Emma Lavelle) *mid-div: drvn along after 7f: chsng ldrs over 3f out: one pce fnl 2f* **8/1**

10 **7** *1/2* **Miss Fleming**[80] 3409 4-10-9 0..........(v[1]) JackSherwood(5) 98
(David Loder) *mid-div: hdwy to chse ldrs over 3f out: one pce fnl 2f* **18/1**

162 **8** *1 1/4* **Mcgregor's Cottage (IRE)**[23] 4371 5-11-2 0.......... JamieHamilton(5) 104
(Malcolm Jefferson) *w ldrs: led over 4f out: hdd 3f out: wknd fnl 150yds* **6/1**[3]

0- **9** *1 1/4* **Ruby Wilde (IRE)**[366] 4901 5-10-9 0.......... ConorRing(5) 96
(Graeme McPherson) *mid-div: drvn to chse ldrs over 3f out: edgd rt and one pce fnl 2f* **50/1**

10 *4 1/2* **Moorstone** 4-10-0 0.......... MrMJPKendrick(7) 84
(Giles Bravery) *chsd ldrs: drvn 6f out: lost pl over 2f out* **18/1**

5 **11** *2* **Miss Maiden Over (IRE)**[65] 3625 4-10-4 0.......... ConorShoemark(3) 82
(Fergal O'Brien) *mid-div: drvn 6f out: lost pl over 2f out* **10/1**

35 **12** *27* **Primrose Court (IRE)**[24] 4350 6-10-11 0.......... RyanHatch(3) 62
(Shaun Lycett) *w ldr: led after 3f: drvn and hdd over 4f out: lost pl over 2f out: eased whn bhd: t.o* **25/1**

13 *dist* **Striking Nigella** 6-10-7 0.......... GrahamCarson(7)
(Michael Chapman) *in rr: lost pl 7f out: sn bhd: t.o whn virtually p.u over 3f out: eventually completed* **150/1**

4m 3.5s (12.10) **Going Correction** +0.60s/f (Soft)
WFA 4 from 5yo+ 7lb **13** Ran SP% **121.1**
Speed ratings: **93,91,89,89,88 88,88,87,87,84 83,70,**
CSF £63.59 TOTE £5.40: £2.20, £5.20, £11.80; EX 65.30 Trifecta £3292.70.
Owner J N Greenley **Bred** Mrs Patricia Furlong **Trained** Over Norton, Oxon
■ Water Willow was withdrawn. Price at time of withdrawal 11-2. Rule 4 applies to bets placed prior to withdrawal, but not to SP bets. Deduction 15p in the pound. New market formed.
FOCUS
A modest mares' bumper, confined to conditional and amateur riders. The winner has been rated similar to her pre-race mark.
T/Jkpt: Not won. T/Plt: £144.40 to a £1 stake. Pool: £97,956.04 - 495.06 winning tickets T/Qpdt: £27.10 to a £1 stake. Pool: £7,940.65 - 216.55 winning tickets **Walter Glynn**

4681 TAUNTON (R-H)
Monday, March 21

OFFICIAL GOING: Good (7.2)
Wind: almost nil Weather: sunny Rails: Shared bends, effect of rail positions: Races 1, 2 & 4 adds 15 yards, Races 3 & 5 adds 99 yards, Race 6 adds 42 yards.

4848 C & S ELECTRICAL WHOLESALE ANSELL LIGHTING "NATIONAL HUNT" NOVICES' HURDLE (10 hdls) 2m 3f 1y
2:10 (2:10) (Class 4) 4-Y-0+ **£3,898** (£1,144; £572; £286)

Form RPR
-221 **1** **Rock On Oscar (IRE)**[39] 4063 6-11-8 135..........(t) SamTwiston-Davies 131+
(Paul Nicholls) *mde all: wl in command after 3 out: easily* **2/9**[1]

03-4 **2** *11* **Fortunate George (IRE)**[140] 2239 6-11-1 0.......... DarylJacob 108
(Emma Lavelle) *in tch: hdwy 6th: rdn to chal for 2nd appr 2 out: styd on fr last but no ch w wnr* **11/4**[2]

60 **3** *3 1/2* **Coeur Tantre (IRE)**[60] 3710 5-11-1 0.......... DaveCrosse 105
(Hugo Froud) *hld up in last pair: hdwy 6th: rdn to chse wnr appr 2 out but hld: no ex run-in* **12/1**

00 **4** *2 3/4* **Baron Du Plessis (FR)**[38] 4103 5-11-1 0.......... LiamTreadwell 102
(Ian Williams) *chsd wnr tl 3 out: sn rdn: styd on same pce fr next* **25/1**

6-00 **5** *27* **Teachmetobouggie**[58] 3745 6-11-1 0.......... RhysFlint 74
(Alexandra Dunn) *chsd ldrs: pushed along fr 6th: wknd after 3 out: t.o* **10/1**[3]

0 **6** *6* **Seayoujimmy**[183] 1590 6-10-8 0..........[1] MrJPearce(7) 68
(Daniel O'Brien) *in tch: pushed along fr 6th: wknd after 3 out: t.o* **80/1**

06 **F** **Fled Or Pled (IRE)**[26] 4304 4-10-7 0..........[1] MichealNolan
(David Dennis) *hld up: fell 4th* **33/1**

P **P** **Final Flow**[30] 4256 7-11-1 0..........(t) BrendanPowell
(Colin Tizzard) *in tch tl 6th: sn struggling: wknd after next: t.o whn p.u after 3 out* **18/1**

4m 31.8s (-14.20) **Going Correction** -0.75s/f (Firm)
WFA 4 from 5yo+ 7lb **8** Ran SP% **138.6**
Speed ratings (Par 105): **99,94,92,91,80 77, ,**
CSF £2.07 TOTE £1.20: £1.02, £1.10, £3.30; EX 2.40 Trifecta £5.60.
Owner I Fogg,C Barber,D Bennett & D Macdonald **Bred** T J Whitley **Trained** Ditcheat, Somerset
FOCUS
Shared bends and as a result this was run over 15yds further than advertised. Daryl Jacob described the ground as being "on the quick side of good". No depth to this novice hurdle the heavy odds-on favourite dominated. The second and third help set the level.

4849 C & S ELECTRICAL WHOLESALE TERMINATION TECHNOLOGY NOVICES' HURDLE (9 hdls) 2m 104y
2:40 (2:43) (Class 4) 4-Y-0+ **£3,898** (£1,144; £572; £286)

Form RPR
-140 **1** **All Set To Go (IRE)**[60] 3708 5-11-6 125..........(t) SamTwiston-Davies 123+
(Paul Nicholls) *trckd ldrs: chal after 2 out: led last: r.o wl: rdn out* **2/1**[2]

1P2 **2** *3/4* **Banyu (FR)**[48] 3915 5-11-6 130..........[1] RichardJohnson 122+
(Philip Hobbs) *led: rdn between last 2: hdd last: kpt on* **6/5**[1]

4 **3** *3* **Brotherly Company (IRE)**[47] 3926 4-10-7 0.......... NoelFehily 106
(Harry Fry) *mid-div: hdwy fr 6th: rdn in cl 3rd appr 2 out: kpt on but nt quite pce of front pair* **7/2**[3]

4343 **4** *9* **Jarlath**[169] 1766 5-11-1 110.......... KevinJones(5) 111
(Seamus Mullins) *mid-div: hdwy fr 5th: disp cl 3rd after 3 out: rdn bef next: sn one pce* **12/1**

/40P **5** *24* **Subordinate (GER)**[16] 4494 7-11-0 0..........(t) DarylJacob 80
(Emma Lavelle) *trckd ldrs tl wknd after 3 out* **33/1**

000 **6** *1 1/2* **Camakasi (IRE)**[18] 4441 5-11-0 0..........(t) GavinSheehan 79
(Ali Stronge) *nvr bttr than mid-div* **50/1**

0PP **7** *13* **Dinky Challenger**[80] 3411 8-11-0 0.......... LiamTreadwell 66
(Mark Gillard) *trckd ldrs tl 3 out: sn wknd* **150/1**

P56 **8** *1* **Kingston Mimosa**[83] 3347 4-10-7 95.......... TrevorWhelan 58
(Mark Gillard) *in tch tl 3 out: sn wknd* **50/1**

00 **9** *3 1/4* **Late Shipment**[18] 4449 5-10-9 0.......... ChrisWard(5) 61
(Nikki Evans) *mid-div tl 3 out* **33/1**

PPP0 **10** *1 1/2* **Bobby Benton (IRE)**[21] 4409 5-11-0 0.......... BrendanPowell 60
(Jim Best) *a in last trio: nvr any danger* **100/1**

0P/ **11** *96* **Aster's Approval**[557] 5174 6-11-0 0.......... NickScholfield
(Grant Cann) *racd keenly: a towards rr: t.o* **150/1**

P **Mister Uno (IRE)**[221] 5-11-0 0 (t) MichealNolan
(Carroll Gray) *a bhd: t.o whn p.u bef 3 out* **100/1**

3m 52.0s (-16.00) **Going Correction** -0.75s/f (Firm)
WFA 4 from 5yo+ 7lb 12 Ran SP% **121.8**
Speed ratings (Par 105): **110,109,108,103,91 90,84,83,82,81 33,**
CSF £5.03 TOTE £3.50: £1.50, £1.10, £1.30; EX 5.40 Trifecta £11.50.
Owner C G Roach **Bred** Mrs S M Rogers & Sir Thomas Pilkington **Trained** Ditcheat, Somerset

FOCUS
Shared bends and as a result this was run over 15yds further than advertised. Little got into this, the market leaders dominating. The second and fourth have been rated close to their marks.

4850 C & S ELECTRICAL WHOLESALE HAGER DESIGN H'CAP CHASE (12 fncs) 2m 12y

3:10 (3:10) (Class 5) (0-100,100) 5-Y-0+ £3,898 (£1,144; £572; £286)

Form				RPR
1634	1		**Guaracha**[5] 4712 5-11-12 100 (v[1]) RhysFlint (Alexandra Dunn) *trckd ldrs: rdn to chal whn lft 3 l clr 2 out: kpt on: rdn out* **14/1**	112+
1600	2	5	**Beauchamp Viking**[7] 4686 12-10-2 74 oh3 ow2 (t) DaveCrosse (Hugo Froud) *chsd ldrs: rdn after 4 out: lft 3 l 2nd 2 out: styd on same pce* **33/1**	83
4-41	3	7	**Edeiff's Lad**[7] 4686 9-10-1 82 7ex MrJoshuaNewman(7) (Polly Gundry) *in tch: nt fluent 3rd: rdn after 4 out: nvr threatened: styd on same pce fr next: lft 3rd 2 out* **2/1**[2]	81
23-P	4	15	**Green Du Ciel (FR)**[31] 3369 11-10-12 86 (tp) MichealNolan (Carroll Gray) *trckd ldrs: rdn after 4 out: wknd after next: lft 4th 2 out* **16/1**	74
P032	5	4	**Passing Fiesta**[7] 4686 7-10-7 81 SamTwiston-Davies (Sarah-Jayne Davies) *nvr travelling: a in rr* **13/8**[1]	63
P544	6	2 3/4	**Topthorn**[42] 4029 10-10-7 88 (p) MrZBaker(7) (Martin Bosley) *a in rr: nvr gng pce to get involved* **25/1**	65
0432	7	43	**Mandy's Boy (IRE)**[42] 4029 6-11-6 94 (tp) NickScholfield (Sally Randell) *chsd ldrs tl 7th: sn bhd: t.o* **10/1**	28
4PPP	U		**Sylvan Legend**[23] 4356 8-10-1 75 (bt[1]) TrevorWhelan (Matt Sheppard) *led: jnd after 3 out: stmbld bdly and uns rdr next* **7/1**[3]	81

4m 2.2s (-11.80) **Going Correction** -0.75s/f (Firm) 8 Ran SP% **112.4**
Speed ratings: **99,96,93,85,83 82,60,**
CSF £278.15 CT £1310.16 TOTE £10.80: £2.80, £6.90, £1.20; EX 205.60 Trifecta £1286.50.
Owner West Buckland Bloodstock Ltd **Bred** Michael E Broughton **Trained** West Buckland, Somerset

FOCUS
Shared bends and as a result this was run over 99yds further than advertised. No hanging around here but it still paid to race handily. A step up on the best of his hurdle figures from the winner, while the second and unseater set the level.

4851 C & S ELECTRICAL WHOLESALE LEWDEN PALAZZOLI H'CAP HURDLE (9 hdls) 2m 104y

3:40 (3:40) (Class 3) (0-140,131) 4-Y-0 £6,330 (£1,870; £935; £468; £234)

Form				RPR
22U6	1		**Nesterenko (GER)**[107] 2914 7-11-10 129 NicodeBoinville (Nicky Henderson) *trckd ldrs: rdn between last 2: chal last: kpt on wl to ld towards fin: rdn out* **7/4**[2]	128+
5304	2	3/4	**Vicenzo Mio (FR)**[23] 4362 6-11-9 128 (t) SamTwiston-Davies (Paul Nicholls) *trckd ldr: led 2 out: sn drvn: kpt on but no ex whn hdd towards fin* **6/4**[1]	127
1152	3	1/2	**General Ginger**[130] 2457 6-11-12 131 (t) NoelFehily (Harry Fry) *racd keenly: led tl nt fluent 2 out: sn rdn: ev ch fr last: no ex towards fin* **4/1**[3]	130
1132	4	7	**Retro Valley (IRE)**[200] 1456 4-10-3 120 (p) JamieBargary(5) (David Dennis) *trckd ldrs: rdn and ev ch appr 2 out: hld between last 2: kpt on same pce run-in* **16/1**	104
-500	5	22	**Tamarillo Grove (IRE)**[100] 3035 9-10-7 112 (t) PaulMoloney (Sophie Leech) *trckd ldrs: rdn after 3 out: nt pce to get on terms: wkng whn wnt rt last* **16/1**	87

3m 56.0s (-12.00) **Going Correction** -0.75s/f (Firm)
WFA 4 from 6yo+ 7lb 5 Ran SP% **108.1**
Speed ratings (Par 107): **100,99,99,95,84**
CSF £4.75 TOTE £2.60: £1.50, £1.30; EX 4.20 Trifecta £9.90.
Owner Juergen Meyer **Bred** A Pereira **Trained** Upper Lambourn, Berks

FOCUS
Shared bends and as a result this was run over 15yds further than advertised. Fair handicap form, although they didn't go overly fast and any of the first three had a chance late on. The winner has been rated 5lb off his best.

4852 C & S ELECTRICAL WHOLESALE BG ELECTRICAL H'CAP CHASE (14 fncs) 2m 2f 40y

4:10 (4:10) (Class 3) (0-125,124) 5-Y-£8,229 (£2,431; £1,215; £608; £304)

Form				RPR
F50P	1		**My Brother Sylvest**[43] 4011 10-11-6 123 (b) MichaelHeard(5) (David Pipe) *led: sn clr: blnd 4 out: rdn after 2 out: hdd sn after last: rallied to regain ld fnl 50yds: drvn out* **7/1**	131+
-3FP	2	1/2	**Bilbrook Blaze**[95] 3123 6-11-0 112 RichardJohnson (Philip Hobbs) *trckd ldrs: blnd bdly and hmpd 4 out: rdn after next: chal bef last: led narrowly run-in: no ex whn hdd fnl 50yds* **9/4**[1]	120+
-321	3	10	**Rothman (FR)**[209] 1351 6-11-12 124 (t) SamTwiston-Davies (Paul Nicholls) *trckd wnr: rdn appr 3 out: ch 2 out: no ex bef last* **7/2**[2]	118
45P0	4	1/2	**Nearest The Pin (IRE)**[26] 4307 11-10-10 108 GavinSheehan (Dai Williams) *hld up in last pair: rdn after 8th: nvr any imp: lft 4th 4 out* **4/1**[3]	101
0401	5	20	**Kerryhead Storm (IRE)**[10] 4587 11-10-9 114 (tp) MrStanSheppard(7) (Matt Sheppard) *a detached in last: reminder after 8th: nvr any imp* **6/1**	92
642U	F		**Honey Pound (IRE)**[83] 3351 8-11-10 122 JamieMoore (Tim Vaughan) *trckd ldrs: travelling wl enough disputing cl 2nd whn fell heavily 4 out* **8/1**	

4m 37.9s (-14.10) **Going Correction** -0.75s/f (Firm) 6 Ran SP% **110.9**
Speed ratings: **101,100,96,96,87**
CSF £23.25 TOTE £8.40: £3.10, £1.90; EX 27.50 Trifecta £100.90.
Owner Teddington Racing Club **Bred** David Brace **Trained** Nicholashayne, Devon

FOCUS
Shared bends and as a result this was run over 99yds further than advertised. An ordinary chase with the key moment of the race coming four out, where Honey Pound fell heavily and hampered the runner-up, who did well to stand up himself having hit that fence also.

4853 C & S ELECTRICAL WHOLESALE NATIONAL VENTILATION H'CAP HURDLE (12 hdls) 2m 7f 198y

4:40 (4:40) (Class 4) (0-120,118) 4-Y-0+ £3,898 (£1,144; £572; £286)

Form				RPR
1133	1		**Minellacelebration (IRE)**[18] 4442 6-10-13 112 MrJNixon(7) (Katy Price) *mde all: styd on gamely fr 2 out: drvn out* **7/2**[2]	118
-226	2	3/4	**Present Man (IRE)**[60] 3705 6-11-10 116 (tp) SamTwiston-Davies (Paul Nicholls) *trckd ldrs: chal after 2 out: sn rdn: ev ch last: drifted lft run-in: styd on but hld towards fin* **5/4**[1]	121
-424	3	7	**Jully Les Buxy**[48] 3919 6-10-12 104 GavinSheehan (Robert Walford) *chsd ldrs: pushed along in last but in tch after 8th: stdy prog after 3 out: wnt 3rd at the last: styd on but no threat to ldrs* **10/1**	102
440P	4	2 1/2	**Very Extravagant (IRE)**[47] 3930 7-11-4 110 NoelFehily (Neil Mulholland) *hld up: tk clsr order 7th: rdn to chse ldrs after 3 out: styd on same pce fr next* **10/1**	106
-3F4	5	9	**According To Harry (IRE)**[95] 3124 7-11-12 118 RichardJohnson (Philip Hobbs) *prom: rdn and ev ch appr 2 out where nt fluent: wknd last* **7/1**[3]	105
P32	6	6	**Leath Acra Mor (IRE)**[86] 3220 10-10-8 107 (p) TobyWheeler(7) (Ian Williams) *trckd ldrs: rdn after 8th: wknd bef 2 out* **7/1**[3]	88

5m 47.6s (-16.40) **Going Correction** -0.75s/f (Firm) 6 Ran SP% **109.8**
Speed ratings (Par 105): **97,96,94,93,90 88**
CSF £8.24 TOTE £3.50: £1.60, £1.50; EX 9.10 Trifecta £47.00.
Owner Nick Elliott **Bred** M Doran **Trained** Hay-On-Wye, Powys

FOCUS
Shared bends and as a result this was run over 42yds further than advertised. A race in which it paid to race handy, the winner again making all. A step up from the winner.
T/Plt: £16.00 to a £1 stake. Pool: £80,779.37 - 3,679.96 winning tickets T/Qpdt: £14.10 to a £1 stake. Pool: £5,195.72 - 272.50 winning tickets **Tim Mitchell**

4541 EXETER (R-H)

Tuesday, March 22

OFFICIAL GOING: Good (7.6)
Wind: mild breeze across Weather: overcast Rails: All races will be run on the chase bend turning into home straight. Race distances: Races 1 & 2 +55yds. 3, 4 & 5 -18yds. 6 +95yds.

4854 HIGOS FOR YOUR COMMERCIAL INSURANCE NOVICES' (S) HURDLE (8 hdls) 2m 175y

2:00 (2:00) (Class 5) 4-Y-0+ £2,274 (£667; £333; £166)

Form				RPR
0P53	1		**Mother Meldrum (IRE)**[14] 4541 7-10-0 97 (tp) DavidPrichard(7) (Victor Dartnall) *sn mid-div in chsng gp: hdwy after 4th: led 3 out: kpt on wl to assert fr last: rdn out* **6/4**[1]	106+
4	2	6	**Mr Caffrey**[25] 3213 4-10-7 0 TomO'Brien (Robert Stephens) *trckd ldrs in chsng gp: clsd on ldrs 4th: rdn and ev ch 2 out: kpt on same pce fr last* **5/1**[3]	101
4-02	3	8	**Perfect Summer (IRE)**[17] 4490 6-10-7 100 (v) RichardJohnson (Ian Williams) *led chsng gp in 3rd: hdwy after 3rd: led after 5th tl next: sn one pce* **7/4**[2]	95
6	4	10	**West Hill Legend**[115] 2770 5-10-7 0 ConorO'Farrell (Richard Woollacott) *racd keenly: trckd ldrs in chsng gp: rdn appr 3 out: sn wknd: mstke 2 out* **66/1**	84
-660	5	35	**Mount Shamsan**[23] 4390 6-11-0 99 JoshuaMoore (Gary Moore) *mstke 1st: a towards rr: t.o* **9/1**	70
5202	6	6	**Vering (FR)**[20] 4440 10-10-7 77 (tp) MrSeanHoulihan(7) (Carroll Gray) *mid-div: rdn after 4th: hdwy after next: wknd 3 out: t.o* **18/1**	55
00-0	7	23	**Sangram (IRE)**[327] 30 9-10-7 95 PaulO'Brien(7) (Jimmy Frost) *mid-div tl 4th: sn bhd: t.o* **40/1**	34
0-00	P		**Lordship (IRE)**[23] 4390 12-11-0 69 (t) JamesDavies (Tom Gretton) *mid-div: rdn after 4th: wknd after next: t.o whn p.u bef 2 out* **150/1**	
P/P	P		**Highest Red**[47] 3955 7-10-7 0 (p) MrWillPettis(7) (Natalie Lloyd-Beavis) *mid-div: rdn after 2nd: wknd after 4th: t.o whn p.u bef 3 out* **300/1**	
-F0F	P		**Run Hurricane (IRE)**[32] 4223 8-10-7 88 (t) GrahamCarson(7) (John O'Shea) *chsd clr ldr in clr 2nd tl after 3rd: wknd after next: t.o whn p.u bef 3 out* **50/1**	
P4F	U		**Blackadder**[48] 3926 4-10-7 0 BrendanPowell (Mark Gillard) *racd freely: led: sn 20 l clr: hdd bef 3 out: wknd qckly: bhd whn blnd and uns rdr 2 out* **125/1**	
	P		**Mildmay Arms**[13] 4-10-7 0 MarkQuinlan (Simon Hodgson) *a bhd: t.o whn p.u bef 3 out* **125/1**	
000	P		**Piccomore**[8] 4681 6-10-7 0 JamesBest (Polly Gundry) *bhd fr 2nd: t.o whn p.u bef 3 out* **250/1**	

4m 10.1s (-5.40) **Going Correction** -0.10s/f (Good)
WFA 4 from 5yo+ 7lb 13 Ran SP% **117.2**
Speed ratings (Par 103): **108,105,101,96,80 77,66, , ,**
CSF £9.72 TOTE £2.50: £1.02, £2.40, £1.20; EX 13.40 Trifecta £30.50.No bid for the winner.
Owner G D Hake **Bred** John Bourke **Trained** Brayford, Devon

FOCUS
All races were run on the chase turning into the home straight. This was run over 55yds further than advertised. Lowly selling form. The winner and third set the level.

4855 HIGOS INSURANCE SERVICES PLYMSTOCK H'CAP HURDLE (DIV I) (10 hdls) 2m 2f 111y

2:30 (2:30) (Class 4) (0-110,109) 4-Y-0+ £3,249 (£954; £477; £238)

Form				RPR
050	1		**Closer To Home (IRE)**[20] 4183 4-10-7 103 (b) MichaelHeard(5) (David Pipe) *towards rr: pushed along at times: hdwy on inner whn rdn appr 3 out: led sn after 2 out: kpt on: rdn out* **8/1**	100
-21P	2	2 3/4	**Upton Wood**[117] 2732 10-11-10 107 (p) JamesDavies (Chris Down) *led: rdn and hdd after 2 out: kpt on but no ex fr last* **20/1**	110
5PF	3	8	**Rosygo (IRE)**[19] 4454 8-10-12 100 DavidNoonan(5) (Adrian Wintle) *hld up: hit 3rd: hdwy after 7th: ch 3 out: sn rdn: keeping on at same pce in hld 3rd whn wnt rt last* **14/1**	97

4305 **4** *2* **Lookslikerainted (IRE)**[208] 1382 9-11-9 **106**..............(t) RichieMcLernon 101
(Sophie Leech) *mid-div: hdwy whn short of room chsng ldrs 3 out: sn rdn: kpt on same pce fr next* **12/1**

06-0 **5** *3¾* **Wolftrap (IRE)**[320] 180 7-10-9 **92**.......................... LiamHeard 85
(Philip Hobbs) *mid-div: hdwy after 7th: rdn and ch whn hit next: kpt on tl no ex fr last* **3/1**[1]

-04P **6** *6* **Auckland De Re (FR)**[81] 3414 6-11-12 **109**.......................... NoelFehily 94
(Neil Mulholland) *prom: rdn and ev ch briefly appr 3 out: one pce fr 2 out* **4/1**[2]

0600 **7** *1¾* **Better Days (IRE)**[32] 4233 5-11-5 **102**..................(t) SamTwiston-Davies 86
(Nigel Twiston-Davies) *trckd ldrs: nt fluent 4th: effrt 3 out: wknd after 2 out* **9/2**[3]

4022 **8** *32* **In The Crowd (IRE)**[48] 3925 7-11-2 **102**..................(p) RyanHatch(3) 57
(Roy Brotherton) *mid-div: rdn after 5th: sn bhd: t.o* **8/1**

3P1P **9** *18* **Taroum (IRE)**[75] 3498 9-11-6 **103**.......................................(bt) RhysFlint 42
(John Flint) *mid-div: rdn after 7th: wknd bef next: t.o* **33/1**

-000 **P** **Hurricane Ridge (IRE)**[103] 2990 7-11-8 **105**..................(p) TomO'Brien
(Jimmy Frost) *trckd ldrs: struggling 4th: sn bhd: t.o whn p.u 3 out* **25/1**

U260 **P** **Swivel**[52] 3855 5-11-10 **107**.. MattGriffiths
(Mark Wall) *trckd ldrs tl after 5th: sn wknd: t.o whn p.u 3 out* **25/1**

4m 39.9s (-2.80) **Going Correction** -0.10s/f (Good)
WFA 4 from 5yo+ 7lb **11** Ran SP% **115.2**
Speed ratings (Par 105): **101,99,96,95,94 91,90,77,69,**
CSF £149.72 CT £2186.04 TOTE £10.50: £1.90, £5.20, £3.20; EX 188.50 Trifecta £1962.60.

Owner Andrew Cohen & Alan Kaplan **Bred** Haras Du Logis Saint Germain **Trained** Nicholashayne, Devon

FOCUS
This was run over 55yds further than advertised. The complexion of this moderate hurdle changed late on. A big hurdle pb from the winner, while the second sets the level.

4856 HIGOS INSURANCE SERVICES PLYMSTOCK H'CAP HURDLE (DIV II) (10 hdls) 2m 2f 111y

3:05 (3:05) (Class 4) (0-110,108) 4-Y-0+ **£3,249** (£954; £477; £238)

Form RPR

6055 **1** **Quieto Sol (FR)**[79] 3450 5-11-12 **108**.......................... RichardJohnson 112+
(Charlie Longsdon) *trckd ldrs: led 3 out: wnt rt last: kpt on wl: rdn out* **11/2**[3]

66P/ **2** *2* **Superman De La Rue (FR)**[812] 3431 10-11-7 **103**.......... SeanBowen 102
(Mary Evans) *led: rdn and hdd 3 out: kpt on but hld fr last* **20/1**

55P3 **3** *nk* **Lime Street (IRE)**[40] 4064 5-11-7 **103**.......................... JamesDavies 101
(Tom Symonds) *trckd ldr: rdn after 7th: kpt on fr 2 out but nt quite pce to mount chal* **6/1**

1600 **4** *3½* **Grandmaster George (IRE)**[57] 3773 7-11-11 **107**.......... TomO'Brien 103
(Seamus Mullins) *trckd ldrs: chal after 7th tl rdn bef next: kpt on same pce fr 2 out* **13/2**

P055 **5** *1¾* **Thundering Home**[14] 4541 9-11-3 **102**..................(b1) TomBellamy(3) 99+
(Richard Mitchell) *j.lft thrght bdly at times: hld up: hdwy after 4th: rdn to chse ldrs bef 3 out: styd on same pce fr 2 out* **9/1**

-4P4 **6** *19* **Kahdian (IRE)**[39] 4099 6-10-6 **93**.......................... GaryDerwin(5) 72
(Helen Rees) *mid-div: rdn after 7th: nvr threatened: wknd 2 out* **14/1**

P/14 **7** *nk* **Sir Dylan**[28] 364 7-11-4 **100**.......................... NickScholfield 76
(Polly Gundry) *mid-div: hdwy after 7th: rdn to chse ldrs next: wknd 2 out* **12/1**

004P **P** **Beau Knight**[20] 4439 4-10-6 **96**.......................... AdamWedge
(Alexandra Dunn) *mid-div: rdn in last trio after 6th: wknd after next: bhd whn p.u bef last* **25/1**

-405 **P** **Kingussie**[32] 4233 8-11-10 **106**..................(p) NicodeBoinville
(Ben Pauling) *mid-div tl after 6th: struggling next: wknd after 7th: t.o whn p.u 3 out* **9/2**[2]

0000 **P** **Brown Bear (IRE)**[39] 4096 5-10-12 **99**.......................... DavidNoonan(5)
(Nick Gifford) *lost tch 4th: t.o 6th: p.u after next* **4/1**[1]

4m 44.6s (1.90) **Going Correction** -0.10s/f (Good)
WFA 4 from 5yo+ 7lb **10** Ran SP% **114.2**
Speed ratings (Par 105): **92,91,91,89,88 80,80, , ,**
CSF £100.07 CT £678.98 TOTE £5.80: £2.10, £4.30, £2.10; EX 112.50 Trifecta £1149.70.

Owner Mrs S Longsdon **Bred** Martin Rhyn **Trained** Over Norton, Oxon

FOCUS
This was run over 55yds further than advertised. A couple of the leading fancies disappointing in division two of this moderate handicap. It was again won by an unexposed handicap debutant. A step up from the winner, with the third and fourth helping to set the level.

4857 HIGOS INSURANCE SERVICES BRAUNTON NOVICES' CHASE (15 fncs) 2m 3f 48y

3:40 (3:40) (Class 3) 5-Y-0+ **£6,498** (£1,908; £954; £477)

Form RPR

5-12 **1** **Henryville**[165] 1840 8-11-3 0.. NoelFehily 150+
(Harry Fry) *hld up bhd ldrs: trcking ldrs whn nt fluent 11th: led 3 out: kpt on wl: pushed out* **5/4**[1]

-224 **2** *3* **Golden Doyen (GER)**[109] 2881 5-10-12 136.............. RichardJohnson 139
(Philip Hobbs) *j. sltly lft: disp ld most of way: hit 4th and 8th: rdn and ev ch 3 out: kpt on same pce fr next* **4/1**[2]

0300 **3** *1¼* **Thomas Crapper**[81] 3406 9-10-12 135.......................... CharliePoste 138
(Robin Dickin) *hld up bhd ldrs: trckd ldrs 9th: rdn after 4 out: short of room next: kpt on same pce fr 2 out* **9/2**[3]

2-24 **4** *4½* **Union Saint (FR)**[81] 3415 8-10-5 128.......................... MissBFrost(7) 131
(Jimmy Frost) *hld up: hdwy 4 out: styd on fr 3 out but nt pce to chal: wnt 4th between last 2* **50/1**

2P3P **5** *9* **Wizards Bridge**[25] 4340 7-11-3 129..................(b) TomO'Brien 132
(Colin Tizzard) *disp ld most of way: hit 3rd: blnd bdly 7th: rdn after 4 out: hdd next: grad fdd* **11/1**

3-13 **6** *3½* **Port Melon (IRE)**[117] 2726 8-11-3 140..................(b1) SamTwiston-Davies 125
(Paul Nicholls) *trckd ldrs: rdn appr 4 out: sn hld: wknd bef 2 out* **4/1**[2]

4m 47.8s (-9.50) **Going Correction** -0.225s/f (Good) **6** Ran SP% **112.9**
Speed ratings: **111,109,109,107,103 102**
CSF £7.01 TOTE £2.10: £1.10, £2.10; EX 7.20 Trifecta £20.20.

Owner R P B Michaelson & E M Thornton **Bred** Karen George **Trained** Seaborough, Dorset

FOCUS
This was run over 18yds shorter than advertised. A good-quality novice chase, run at a sound gallop, and the winner did it nicely. A pb from the second, with the third and fourth pretty much to their marks.

4858 HIGOS INSURANCE SERVICES H'CAP CHASE (18 fncs) 3m 54y

4:10 (4:10) (Class 2) (0-150,148) 5-Y-0+

£11,573 (£3,418; £1,709; £854; £427; £214)

Form RPR

-322 **1** **Three Faces West (IRE)**[25] 4341 8-10-7 **129**.............. RichardJohnson 139+
(Philip Hobbs) *a.p: rchd for 5th: led 11th: drawing clr whn dived at 3 out: styd on strly* **6/4**[1]

1-00 **2** *4½* **Just A Par (IRE)**[108] 2916 9-11-11 **147**.......................... SeanBowen 150
(Paul Nicholls) *in tch: nudged along after 10th: hdwy next: rdn to chse wnr fr 4 out: styd on but nvr gng pce to get on terms* **17/2**

4P5U **3** *1¾* **Bertie Boru (IRE)**[10] 4621 9-10-6 **128**..................(p) TomO'Brien 132+
(Philip Hobbs) *hld up: hit 9th: rdn but in tch fr 13th: hdwy after 4 out: lft 3rd whn hmpd 2 out: styd on* **9/1**

1FP4 **4** *11* **Howlongisafoot (IRE)**[25] 4347 7-11-2 **138**..........(b) SamTwiston-Davies 129
(Paul Nicholls) *hld up: hdwy 14th: rdn appr 4 out: lft 4th 2 out: fdd* **10/1**

100P **5** *2¾* **Azure Fly (IRE)**[97] 3109 8-10-8 **133**..................(tp) GrahamWatters(3) 121
(Charlie Longsdon) *trckd ldrs: effrt 4 out: wknd 2 out* **14/1**

0025 **6** *5* **Godsmejudge (IRE)**[27] 4306 10-10-5 **127**..................(p) WayneHutchinson 112
(David Dennis) *prom tl 9th: rdn along in last pair fr 13th: btn 4 out* **6/1**[2]

4115 **7** *12* **Drop Out Joe**[17] 4472 8-11-12 **148**..................(p) NoelFehily 121
(Charlie Longsdon) *j. sltly lft: led tl 11th: chsd wnr tl rdn appr 4 out: wknd 3 out* **8/1**[3]

6PP4 **F** **Wilton Milan (IRE)**[11] 4595 8-10-5 **127**..................(t) HarrySkelton 128
(Dan Skelton) *hld up: hdwy appr 4 out: wnt 3rd 3 out: shkn up and hld in 3rd whn fell 2 out* **8/1**[3]

6m 3.7s (-5.60) **Going Correction** -0.225s/f (Good) **8** Ran SP% **112.8**
Speed ratings: **100,98,97,94,93 91,87,**
CSF £14.52 CT £84.59 TOTE £2.50: £1.30, £2.10, £2.50; EX 15.30 Trifecta £107.40.
Owner Paul & Clare Rooney **Bred** Patrick Hayes **Trained** Withycombe, Somerset

FOCUS
This was run over 18yds shorter than advertised. A really decent staying handicap that went to the least exposed runner. The second has been rated to his mark.

4859 HIGOS INSURANCE SERVICES EXETER NOVICES' H'CAP CHASE (18 fncs) 3m 54y

4:40 (4:40) (Class 4) (0-105,105) 5-Y-0+ **£3,898** (£1,144; £572; £286)

Form RPR

333P **1** **Railway Storm (IRE)**[81] 3412 11-10-11 **97**.......................... MissBFrost(7) 106+
(Jimmy Frost) *in tch: hdwy 4 out: chal 3 out: led next: clr last: styd on wl: pushed out* **11/1**

623P **2** *3¼* **Somerset Lias (IRE)**[34] 4185 8-11-7 **100**.......................... LiamHeard 104
(Bob Buckler) *j. sltly lft at times: led: rdn whn strly chal fr 4 out: hdd 2 out: styd on but no ex* **9/2**[2]

5-04 **3** *¾* **Surging Seas (IRE)**[53] 3840 7-11-0 **93**..................(tp) SamTwiston-Davies 96
(Ali Stronge) *mid-div: hdwy after 14th: rdn to dispute 4th fr 4 out: styd on but nt pce to mount chal: wnt 3rd towards fin* **12/1**

-30P **4** *½* **Mount Prospex (IRE)**[25] 4343 7-10-11 **90**.......................... NickScholfield 93
(Tim Dennis) *hld up towards rr: hdwy 14th: rdn bef 4 out: nt pce to get on terms but styd on fr 3 out: snatched 4th fnl strides* **14/1**

-F66 **5** *nk* **Free Of Charge (IRE)**[116] 2749 7-11-7 **100**.......................... RichardJohnson 108+
(Philip Hobbs) *trckd ldr: hmpd 10th and lost pl: bdly hmpd 12th and dropped to rr: hdwy after 14th: rdn to dispute cl 4th fr 3 out: no ex fr last* **5/2**[1]

1PPP **6** *6* **Mor Brook**[103] 2994 8-11-11 **104**..................(tp) DavidBass 100
(Kim Bailey) *trckd ldrs: chal 13th: rdn whn it 4 out: kpt pressing ldrs w ev ch tl last: wknd run-in* **7/1**

P0P- **7** *72* **Sisterbrooke (IRE)**[356] 5098 7-9-11 **81**.......................... ThomasCheesman(5) 13
(John Panvert) *mid-div: lost pl after 10th: hmpd 12th: hdwy after 14th: rdn bef 4 out: sn wknd: t.o* **50/1**

633P **8** *1¾* **Mrsrobin (IRE)**[31] 4250 6-11-9 **102**.......................... DarylJacob 32
(Emma Lavelle) *struggling 11th: a towards rr: t.o after 14th* **12/1**

P5-P **P** **Lupita (IRE)**[315] 269 12-10-0 **79** oh30..................(t) BrendanPowell
(Derrick Scott) *mid-div tl 11th: sn bhd: t.o whn p.u bef 4 out* **200/1**

PP5P **P** **Local Celebrity (IRE)**[21] 4424 12-11-7 **103**..................(tp) BenPoste(3)
(Sally Randell) *prom: pushed along fr 11th: wknd u.p after 14th: p.u bef next* **66/1**

0-PP **P** **So Oscar (IRE)**[17] 4487 8-11-7 **103**..................(tp) ConorShoemark(3)
(Fergal O'Brien) *in tch: rdn after 14th: sn wknd: bhd whn p.u bef next* **16/1**

42U4 **F** **Titans Approach (IRE)**[107] 2930 7-11-2 **95**..................(p) KielanWoods
(Graeme McPherson) *mid-div: hdwy 11th: trcking ldrs whn fell 12th* **6/1**[3]

1650 **P** **Flemensbay**[40] 4069 8-11-12 **105**..................(p) IanPopham
(Richard Phillips) *a bhd: detached and struggling fr 7th: t.o whn p.u after 14th* **16/1**

6m 15.8s (6.50) **Going Correction** -0.225s/f (Good) **13** Ran SP% **119.6**
Speed ratings: **80,78,78,78,78 76,52,51, , , ,**
CSF £61.66 CT £619.68 TOTE £12.00: £3.00, £2.30, £3.30; EX 65.70 Trifecta £801.70.
Owner Chris Coward **Bred** John Byrne **Trained** Buckfast, Devon
■ Stewards' Enquiry : Liam Heard four-day ban: used whip above permitted level (Apr 5,10-12)

FOCUS
This was run over 18yds shorter than advertised. A fairly eventful race and any number held a chance in the straight. It's been rated around the first two.

4860 HIGOS INSURANCE SERVICES BIDEFORD NOVICES' H'CAP HURDLE (12 hdls) 2m 7f 25y

5:15 (5:15) (Class 4) (0-115,115) 4-Y-0+ **£3,249** (£954; £477; £238)

Form RPR

32 **1** **Cailleach Annie (IRE)**[81] 3413 7-10-11 **105**..................(t) DavidNoonan(5) 108+
(Jackie Du Plessis) *sn mid-div: rdn and hdwy after 9th: chal for 10 l 2nd 3 out: 4 l down last: str run to ld towards fin* **8/1**

46P1 **2** *1½* **Speredek (FR)**[14] 4543 5-11-5 **115**..................(tp) ConorSmith(7) 119+
(Nigel Hawke) *led: sn clr: nt fluent 6th: 10 l clr 3 out: stl travelling wl in 4 l ld whn blnd bdly last: nt rcvr and hdd towards fin* **4/1**[1]

45P1 **3** *1* **Get Involved (IRE)**[18] 4467 7-11-8 **111**.......................... CharliePoste 114+
(Robin Dickin) *hld up towards rr: sme prog 8th: rdn and hdwy after 9th: chal for 10 l 2nd 3 out: styd on fr last but a being hld* **7/1**

P050 **4** *24* **Motts Cross (IRE)**[61] 3705 5-10-10 **99**..................(p) JamesDavies 79
(Chris Down) *chsd ldrs: rdn in 4th after 9th: wknd 2 out* **12/1**

264F **5** *1½* **Thegreendalerocket (IRE)**[83] 3371 7-11-7 **110**.......................... TomO'Brien 88
(Jimmy Frost) *j. sltly rt: chsd ldrs: hit 3rd: clr 2nd after 5th: rdn 9th: sn hld: wknd 2 out* **20/1**

4-20 **6** *15* **Zephyr**[16] 5-10-10 **106** MrCWilliams(7) 71
(Nick Williams) *mid-div: hdwy 6th: lost pl 9th: no ch after* **25/1**

0P12 **7** *18* **Somerset Jem**[20] 4438 7-11-4 **107** JamesBest 55
(Kevin Bishop) *mid-div: hdwy 6th: rdn in hld 3rd after 9th: wknd next: t.o* **11/2**[2]

3340 **8** *13* **Cotswold Road**[39] 4096 6-11-11 **114** (t) NoelFehily 51
(Colin Tizzard) *a towards rr: t.o* **12/1**

1430 **P** **Tokyo Javilex (FR)**[14] 4543 9-11-0 **110** (t) MrLDrowne(7)
(Nigel Hawke) *a towards rr: struggling 6th: t.o whn p.u bef 3 out* **33/1**

P442 **F** **Pyrshan (IRE)**[23] 4389 7-11-9 **112** (t) KielanWoods
(Graeme McPherson) *hld up towards rr: fell 8th* **6/1**[3]

-UUF **P** **Generous Helpings (IRE)**[36] 4160 7-11-1 **104** JoshuaMoore
(Gary Moore) *chsd ldrs tl 7th: sn bhd: t.o whn p.u bef 3 out* **15/2**

30P0 **P** **Arcamante (ITY)**[32] 4233 5-10-13 **109** (p) CharlieHammond(7)
(Mike Hammond) *mid-div: hdwy 6th: wnt 3rd 7th tl rdn after 9th: sn wknd: p.u bef last* **66/1**

306 **P** **Viaduct Jack (IRE)**[101] 3037 7-11-11 **114** (p) DavidBass
(Kim Bailey) *trckd ldrs: losing pl whn mstke 9th: sn wknd: t.o whn p.u bef 3 out* **25/1**

3446 **P** **Airpur Desbois (FR)**[93] 3174 6-10-13 **102** (p) PaddyBrennan
(Charlie Mann) *mid-div: rdn after 9th: wknd bef next: t.o whn p.u bef last* **16/1**

5m 58.2s (-0.80) **Going Correction** -0.10s/f (Good) **14** Ran SP% **123.2**
Speed ratings (Par 105): **97,96,96,87,87 82,75,71,, ,,,**
CSF £39.40 CT £244.58 TOTE £8.40: £2.60, £1.90, £2.70; EX 41.50 Trifecta £157.80.
Owner Miss J Du Plessis **Bred** Jay Leahy **Trained** Trehan, Cornwall

FOCUS
This was run over 95yds further than advertised. The favourite opened up a clear lead without appearing to have to go too hard to do so and little got into it. The winner has been rated similar to her recent course run over shorter.
T/Jkpt: Not won. T/Plt: £138.50 to a £1 stake. Pool: £96,544.14 - 508.67 winning units. T/Qpdt: £17.20 to a £1 stake. Pool: £7,080.27 - 303.00 winning units. **Tim Mitchell**

4297 WETHERBY (L-H)
Tuesday, March 22

OFFICIAL GOING: Good to soft (6.7)
Wind: almost nil Weather: overcast

4861 WATCH RACING UK IN HD (S) HURDLE (12 hdls) 2m 5f 56y
2:10 (2:10) (Class 5) 4-8-Y-O **£3,249** (£954; £477; £238)

Form RPR

6U04 **1** **Ivy Gate (IRE)**[9] 4643 8-11-7 119 (v) AidanColeman 115+
(Jonjo O'Neill) *trckd ldrs: effrt 9th: reminders appr next: 2nd 2 out: edgd lft between last 2: styd on to ld last 50yds* **11/10**[1]

5362 **2** *½* **Kuda Huraa (IRE)**[36] 4152 8-11-1 113 DannyCook 108+
(Harriet Bethell) *trckd ldrs: upsides 3 out: sn led: over 1 l ahd last: hdd and no ex last 50yds* **11/10**[1]

4003 **3** *19* **Our Phylli Vera (IRE)**[28] 4298 7-10-8 76 (p1) SeanQuinlan 82
(Joanne Foster) *trckd ldrs: t.k.h: led briefly appr 3 out: wknd 2 out* **33/1**

U/ **4** *2½* **Kyllachykov (IRE)**[54] 3288 8-11-1 0 BrianHughes 89
(Rebecca Bastiman) *nt jump wl in rr: hdwy to chse ldrs 9th: outpcd and modest 4th next: one pce* **66/1**

P034 **5** *15* **The Ice Factor**[119] 2703 8-10-10 87 (p) JamieHamilton(5) 71
(Alison Hamilton) *rn wout declared tongue strap: w ldr: drvn 9th sn lost pl and bhd* **22/1**[2]

PP **6** *8* **Le Saumon (IRE)**[99] 3085 6-11-1 0 (t) JackQuinlan 63
(Sarah Humphrey) *led: pushed along 8th: hdd appr 3 out: sn lost pl and bhd* **28/1**[3]

5m 36.7s (9.90) **Going Correction** +0.30s/f (Yiel) **6** Ran SP% **107.5**
Speed ratings: **93,92,85,84,78 75**
CSF £2.35 TOTE £1.90: £1.10, £1.10; EX 2.50 Trifecta £11.80.Ivy Gate was bought by Phil Middleton for £7,000
Owner Jeremy & Germaine Hitchins **Bred** W Powell-Harris **Trained** Cheltenham, Gloucs
■ Stewards' Enquiry : Aidan Coleman two-day ban: used whip above permitted level (Apr 5,10)

FOCUS
The A1 bend was out 6yds from the innermost line. The 'away' bend reverted back to separate chase and hurdles bends, set at their innermost lines. This was run over 36yds further than advertised. This typically ordinary seller was run at an ordinary gallop and the market leaders fought it out. Afterwards rider Danny Cook said: "It's horrible ground, it's nearly heavy down the far side and good to firm in the straight." The winner has been rated close to his mark.

4862 RACING UK DAY PASS JUST £10.00 NOVICES' H'CAP HURDLE (DIV I) 2m 3f 154y
2:45 (2:45) (Class 5) (0-100,100) 4-Y-O+ **£3,249** (£954; £477; £238)

Form RPR

4005 **1** **Temple Tiger**[74] 3506 6-11-1 **89** PeterBuchanan 92+
(James Turner) *chsd ldrs: hmpd and 3rd appr 3 out: led appr last: drvn out* **8/1**

0151 **2** *2¾* **Chasma**[42] 4045 6-11-5 **93** (t) JakeGreenall 93
(Michael Easterby) *hld up towards rr: hdwy 7th: chsng ldrs 3 out: 4th last: styd on to take 2nd nr fin* **7/2**[2]

-56P **3** *¾* **Jellied Eel Jack (IRE)**[85] 3316 7-11-12 **100** AdrianLane 99
(Donald McCain) *led to 2nd: w ldr: led briefly appr 3 out: kpt on same pce appr last* **11/1**

-P53 **4** *9* **Nicki's Nipper**[7] 4703 8-10-0 **74** oh5 JonathanEngland 68
(Sam Drake) *hld up in rr: drvn 8th: hdwy to ld next: hdd appr last: wknd fnl 75yds* **6/1**[3]

2040 **5** *5* **Polarbrook (IRE)**[18] 4455 9-11-10 **98** (v) DannyCook 85
(Derek Shaw) *chsd ldrs: outpcd appr 3 out: wknd between last 2* **6/1**[3]

50PP **6** *14* **Tommy The Rascal**[26] 4318 6-10-9 **83** (p) SeanQuinlan 61
(Jennie Candlish) *w ldrs: led 2nd: hdd appr 3 out: blnd and lost pl 3 out* **16/1**

-P06 **7** *14* **Weston Flame**[30] 4271 6-11-10 **98** (t) GavinSheehan 72
(Ben Case) *hld up in rr: hdwy 8th: modest 6th whn blnd 2 out: bhd whn eased run-in* **28/1**

-021 **8** *19* **Bertie Lugg**[15] 4536 8-11-8 **96** JeremiahMcGrath 55
(Henry Oliver) *nt fluent: chsd ldrs: hung lft and lost pl appr 3 out: sn bhd: eased run-in: b.b.v* **10/3**[1]

3P3- **P** **Needwood Park**[422] 3886 8-10-0 **74** (p) BrianHughes
(Ray Craggs) *chsd ldrs: lost pl bef 8th: wl bhd whn p.u bef 3 out* **12/1**

5m 3.3s (-3.70) **Going Correction** -0.125s/f (Good) **9** Ran SP% **110.3**
Speed ratings (Par 103): **102,100,100,97,95 89,83,76,**
CSF £34.37 CT £291.35 TOTE £9.40: £2.80, £1.80, £3.00; EX 37.30 Trifecta £379.00.
Owner J R Turner **Bred** J R Turner **Trained** Norton-le-Clay, N Yorks

FOCUS
This was run over 36yds further than advertised. A moderate novice handicap, run at a routine gallop. A big hurdle pb from the winner, but in line with his bumper mark. The second and third set the level.

4863 RACING UK DAY PASS JUST £10.00 NOVICES' H'CAP HURDLE (DIV II) 2m 3f 154y
3:20 (3:20) (Class 5) (0-100,100) 4-Y-O+ **£3,249** (£954; £477; £238)

Form RPR

0/06 **1** **Jasani**[39] 4108 8-10-7 **88** (p) GLavery(7) 93+
(Alan Brown) *chsd ldrs: led narrowly 2 out: drvn out* **40/1**

34RP **2** *½* **Cadgers Hole**[34] 4184 9-10-0 **74** oh4 SeanQuinlan 76
(Lynn Siddall) *hld up in rr: hdwy 8th: 5th last: styd on to take 2nd nr fin* **28/1**

P0P6 **3** *½* **The Late Shift**[46] 3973 6-10-2 **83** (p) LorcanMurtagh(7) 86
(Barry Murtagh) *chsd ldrs: 3rd 3 out: kpt on run-in: no ex clsng stages* **11/2**[2]

F446 **4** *½* **Return Flight**[41] 4055 5-11-5 **100** FinianO'Toole(7) 101
(Micky Hammond) *hld up towards rr: hdwy 7th: drvn to chse ldrs next: 4th 3 out: kpt on run-in* **7/4**[1]

26PP **5** *2¾* **Hillview Lad (IRE)**[18] 4455 8-11-5 **96** MauriceLinehan(3) 95
(Nick Kent) *t.k.h: led tl after 2nd: w ldrs: lft in ld 7th: hdd 2 out: 2nd last: sn fdd* **9/1**

531P **6** *11* **Solidago (IRE)**[34] 4184 9-11-2 **95** CiaranGethings(5) 84
(Barry Leavy) *chsd ldrs: lost pl 3 out* **12/1**

5R0P **7** *shd* **Downtown Boy (IRE)**[81] 3398 8-11-12 **100** (b) AndrewThornton 92
(Ray Craggs) *in rr: sme hdwy 8th: outpcd whn hit next: wknd and wnt lft 2 out* **20/1**

/050 **8** *12* **Trooper Royal**[144] 2169 6-9-13 **80** ow1 TrevorRyan(7) 60
(Sue Smith) *prom: lost pl 7th: bhd fr 3 out* **15/2**[3]

3600 **F** **Bold Henmie (IRE)**[66] 3628 5-11-2 **93** AdamNicol(3)
(Philip Kirby) *w ldrs: led after 2nd: fell 7th* **15/2**[3]

5m 3.2s (-3.80) **Going Correction** -0.125s/f (Good) **9** Ran SP% **111.3**
Speed ratings (Par 103): **102,101,101,101,100 95,95,91,**
CSF £751.49 CT £6811.28 TOTE £30.90: £5.90, £4.60, £2.20; EX 672.10 Trifecta £5139.20 Part won..
Owner A D Brown **Bred** Mrs Patricia Ann Dobson **Trained** Yedingham, N Yorks
■ Stewards' Enquiry : G Lavery four-day ban: used whip above permitted level (Apr 5,10-12)

FOCUS
This was run over 36yds further than advertised. The second division of the moderate novice handicap was run at a fair gallop. A big pb from the surprise winner, while the second and third help set the level.

4864 WATCH RACING UK IN GLORIOUS HD NOVICES' CHASE (19 fncs) 3m 45y
3:50 (3:50) (Class 3) 5-Y-O+ **£6,498** (£1,908; £954)

Form RPR

-51F **1** **Ballyculla (IRE)**[24] 4367 9-11-5 136 (p) GavinSheehan 143+
(Warren Greatrex) *chsd ldr: shkn up 12th: reminders 14th: styd on appr 3 out: led appr 2 out: drvn clr run-in* **8/13**[1]

2225 **2** *10* **Chase The Wind (IRE)**[111] 2846 7-10-12 121 SeanQuinlan 127
(Joanne Foster) *t.k.h: led: rdn after 3 out: hdd appr next: fdd run-in* **14/1**[3]

11-2 **3** *6* **Lessons In Milan (IRE)**[48] 3922 8-10-12 138 PeterCarberry 119
(Nicky Henderson) *racd in last: nudged along 2nd: drvn after 10th: hdwy to dispute 2nd 14th: reminders next: lost pl bef 4 out: sn bhd* **13/8**[2]

6m 18.0s (-30.00) **3** Ran SP% **106.7**
CSF £5.49 TOTE £1.50; EX 5.90 Trifecta £5.80.
Owner No Dramas & Robert Aplin **Bred** J Mangan **Trained** Upper Lambourn, Berks

FOCUS
This was run over 18yds further than advertised. A fair little staying novice chase. The first two have been rated pretty much to their marks.

4865 RACINGUK.COM H'CAP HURDLE (9 hdls) 2m
4:20 (4:22) (Class 4) (0-120,119) 4-Y-O+ **£4,548** (£1,335; £667; £333)

Form RPR

2031 **1** **Hartside (GER)**[36] 4154 7-11-3 **117** (v) MrRWinks(7) 118
(Peter Winks) *mid-div: outpcd and pushed along 4th: reminders 6th: hdwy appr next: upsides 2 out: styd on to ld last 100yds* **10/3**[1]

33P- **2** *1¼* **Thankyou Very Much**[19] 5470 6-10-3 **99** (p) JoeColliver(3) 99
(James Bethell) *chsd ldrs: led appr 3 out: hdd and no ex last 100yds* **8/1**

503 **3** *1* **Lord Golan**[40] 4065 8-11-0 **110** MauriceLinehan(3) 109
(Nick Kent) *trckd ldrs: led narrowly after 6th: hdd appr next: upsides 2 out: kpt on run-in to take 3rd nr fin* **15/2**

10-4 **4** *hd* **Arthurs Secret**[49] 2499 6-11-7 **119** NathanMoscrop(5) 120+
(John Quinn) *chsd ldrs: upsides 2 out: kpt on same pce run-in* **4/1**[2]

432- **5** *3¾* **Weapon Of Choice (IRE)**[14] 4830 8-11-4 **111** HenryBrooke 108
(Dianne Sayer) *t.k.h: led to 4th: upsides 2 out: wknd clsng stages* **11/1**

302 **6** *9* **Absolute (IRE)**[130] 2474 5-10-12 **105** DannyCook 103+
(Sue Smith) *trckd ldrs: upsides 2 out: upsides whn blnd last: nt rcvr: sn wknd and eased* **4/1**[2]

5 **7** *1* **Poetic Lord**[13] 4553 7-10-13 **109** (t) TonyKelly(3) 96
(Rebecca Menzies) *in rr: hdwy to chse ldrs appr 3 out: sn outpcd: wknd and hung lft bef 2 out* **28/1**

0P00 **8** *16* **She's Late**[39] 4096 6-11-5 **112** AidanColeman 84
(Jonjo O'Neill) *in rr: wl bhd fr 5th* **6/1**[3]

P **9** *49* **Chambord Du Loir (FR)**[101] 3047 6-11-3 **110** JackQuinlan 38
(Sarah Humphrey) *t.k.h: sn trcking ldr: hdd after 6th: lost pl bef next: sn bhd: eventually completed: t.o* **40/1**

3m 58.0s (2.20) **Going Correction** +0.30s/f (Yiel) **9** Ran SP% **114.5**
Speed ratings (Par 105): **106,105,104,104,102 98,97,89,65**
CSF £29.84 CT £185.49 TOTE £3.90: £1.60, £2.50, £2.40; EX 30.60 Trifecta £209.80.
Owner P Winks **Bred** Gestut Ammerland **Trained** Little Houghton, S Yorks

FOCUS
This was run over 36yds further than advertised. Modest handicap form, with any one six in with a chance in between the last two hurdles. They finished in a bit of a heap but the form is solid enough with the first three and fifth rated close to their marks.

4866 RACING UK PROFITS RETURNED TO RACING H'CAP CHASE (18 fncs) 2m 5f 75y
4:55 (4:55) (Class 4) (0-120,120) 5-Y-O+ **£6,498** (£1,908; £954; £477)

Form RPR

36PP **1** **Top Cat Henry (IRE)**[19] 4443 8-11-12 **120** (vt1) WillKennedy 133+
(Dr Richard Newland) *hld up in rr: hdwy 13th: 2nd sn after 4 out: swtchd lft between last 2: upsides whn lft clr last* **17/2**

5232 **2** *8* **Gold Ingot**[33] 4209 9-11-6 **114** AndrewThornton 120
(Caroline Bailey) *chsd ldrs: 2nd 4 out: swtchd rt next: kpt on one pce: lft 7 l 2nd last* **8/1**

/3-3 **3** *1 1/2* **Doubledisdoubleat (IRE)**[42] 4043 9-10-1 **102**........... SamColtherd(7) 107+
(Stuart Coltherd) *chsd ldrs: drvn 9th: outpcd 4 out: modest 4th between last 2: lft 3rd last* **11/2**[3]

0P5P **4** *1* **Pinerolo**[68] 3591 10-11-6 **114**..............................(tp) SeanQuinlan 117
(Joanne Foster) *led: pushed along 9th: hdd next: lost pl 13th: kpt on fr 3 out: lft modest 4th last* **66/1**

1340 **5** *8* **Elenika (FR)**[32] 4234 8-11-10 **118**..............................(p) LiamTreadwell 114
(Venetia Williams) *chsd ldrs: pushed along 13th: outpcd 4 out: wknd between last 2* **12/1**

6560 **6** *13* **Strongly Suggested**[18] 4464 9-11-11 **119**.................... AidanColeman 101
(Jonjo O'Neill) *in rr: pushed along 11th: bhd fr 14th* **25/1**

6652 **U** **Pay The King (IRE)**[12] 4571 9-9-11 **94**.......................... JoeColliver(3)
(Micky Hammond) *in rr: blnd and uns rdr 5th* **5/1**[2]

5P55 **F** **Wolf Sword (IRE)**[63] 3669 7-11-0 **108**........................ DannyCook 121+
(Sue Smith) *trckd ldrs: nt fluent 2nd: 2nd 6th: led 10th: j.lft 14th: edgd rt between last 2: jnd whn fell last* **5/4**[1]

5m 35.8s (-1.20) **Going Correction** +0.10s/f (Yiel) **8** Ran **SP% 111.2**
Speed ratings: **106,102,102,102,98 94, ,**
CSF £67.96 CT £395.61 TOTE £8.50: £2.60, £2.20, £2.90; EX 63.00 Trifecta £251.20.
Owner Off The Clock Partners & Dr RDP Newland **Bred** Mrs Mary Margaret Roche **Trained** Claines, Worcs

FOCUS
This was run over 18yds further than advertised. Late drama with the short-priced favourite blundering and falling at the last when in with every chance. The winner has been rated back to form, with the second to his mark.

4867 WETHERBY FAMILY FUNDAY - SUNDAY 17TH APRIL STANDARD OPEN NATIONAL HUNT FLAT RACE 2m
5:25 (5:25) (Class 6) 4-6-Y-0 **£1,949** (£572; £286; £143)

Form RPR

1 **1** **Happy Hollow**[23] 4392 4-11-2 0................................ PaulMoloney 111+
(Alan Swinbank) *hld up in rr: hdwy 7f out: trcking ldrs on outside over 3f out: 2nd over 1f out: hung lft: led last 150yds: wnt clr: v readily* **7/2**[1]

2 *4 1/2* **Competition** 4-10-9 0...................................... AndrewTinkler 97
(Brian Rothwell) *trckd ldrs: led gng wl over 2f out: hdd and no ex last 150yds* **16/1**[3]

3 **3** *1/2* **Captain Moirette (FR)**[36] 4156 4-10-9 0.................... DannyCook 96
(Sue Smith) *in rr: hdwy 6f out: chsng ldrs over 3f out: kpt on same pce over 1f out* **4/1**[2]

4 *1 1/2* **Yewlands (IRE)** 5-11-2 0.................................. AidanColeman 102
(Jonjo O'Neill) *trckd ldrs: t.k.h: led over 3f out: hdd over 2f out: hung lft and kpt on same pce* **16/1**[3]

5 *nk* **Disturb** 4-10-6 0.. JohnKington(3) 95
(Andrew Crook) *mid-div: hdwy to chse ldrs 4f out: kpt on one pce fnl 2f* **18/1**

6 *1 3/4* **Mayo Star (IRE)** 4-10-9 0................................. BrianHughes 92
(Kevin Ryan) *trckd ldrs: one pce fnl 2f* **4/1**[2]

34 **7** *3/4* **Jack Lamb**[27] 4308 4-10-6 0................................ JoeColliver(3) 92
(Sally Hall) *chsd ldrs: drvn 6f out: wknd fnl f* **20/1**

8 *3* **Monthyne** 5-11-2 0.. GavinSheehan 96
(Warren Greatrex) *trckd ldrs: drvn over 3f out: wknd over 1f out* **7/2**[1]

0-6 **9** *1/2* **Monfass (IRE)**[43] 4037 5-11-2 0...............................[1] CraigNichol 95
(Rose Dobbin) *hld up in rr: hdwy 6f out: chsng ldrs 4f out: wknd over 1f out* **22/1**

0 **10** *3/4* **Popelys Gull (IRE)**[27] 4308 4-10-4 0.................... JamieBargary(5) 87
(Pam Sly) *led: drvn 4f out: sn hdd: wknd fnl 2f* **125/1**

11 *nk* **Montydarkdestroyer** 5-10-9 0.......................... FinianO'Toole(7) 94
(John Davies) *hld up in rr: t.k.h: hdwy 6f out: chsng ldrs over 3f out: wknd over 1f out* **50/1**

0-2 **12** *1* **Majestic Touch (IRE)**[304] 444 5-11-2 0.................... DenisO'Regan 93
(Tracey L Bailey) *trckd ldrs: lost pl over 1f out* **16/1**[3]

13 *9* **Rocku**[367] 6-10-9 0.. MrRyanNichol(7) 84
(Russell Ross) *in rr: hdwy over 4f out: sn drvn: lost pl over 2f out* **125/1**

220 **14** *dist* **Black Ink**[78] 3476 5-11-2 0.................................. HenryBrooke
(Michael Smith) *chsd ldrs: pushed along after 6f: lost pl 6f out: sn bhd and reminders: t.o 4f out: virtually p.u over 2f out: eventually completed* **25/1**

4m 0.4s (10.20) **Going Correction** +0.30s/f (Yiel) **14** Ran **SP% 123.9**
WFA 4 from 5yo+ 7lb
Speed ratings: **86,83,83,82,82 81,81,79,79,79 79,78,74,**
CSF £60.18 TOTE £3.90: £1.80, £5.10, £2.00; EX 84.60 Trifecta £428.60.
Owner Elsa Crankshaw & G Allan **Bred** Stuart McPhee Bloodstock Ltd **Trained** Melsonby, N Yorks

FOCUS
Probably a fair little bumper and the only previous winner in the field defied the penalty. Not form to be confident about, but the winner, third, ninth and 12th help set the level.
T/Plt: £380.40 to a £1 stake. Pool: £64,278.31 - 123.34 winning units. T/Qpdt: £79.90 to a 31 stake. Pool: £5,488.52 - 50.80 winning units. **Walter Glynn**

4243 HAYDOCK (L-H)
Wednesday, March 23

OFFICIAL GOING: Good (chs 6.0, hdl 5.9)
Wind: Light, against Weather: Overcast

4868 LEIGH CENTURIONS MARES' "NATIONAL HUNT" NOVICES' HURDLE (10 hdls) 2m 2f 191y
2:20 (2:20) (Class 4) 4-Y-0+ **£3,898** (£1,144; £572; £286)

Form RPR

1223 **1** **Hollies Pearl**[18] 4471 6-11-6 128..........................(p) SeanBowen 116+
(Peter Bowen) *led: nt fluent 3 out: jnd fr 2 out: rdn after last: narrowly hdd briefly run-in: rallied gamely fnl 110yds: kpt on wl* **8/15**[1]

313P **2** *3/4* **Mardale (IRE)**[95] 3154 6-11-6 125.......................(t) BrianHarding 111
(Nicky Richards) *trckd ldrs: wnt 2nd appr 3 out: upsides and chalng fr 2 out: rdn after last: nosed ahd briefly run-in: no ex fnl strides* **5/2**[2]

34F0 **3** *3 1/2* **Ethelwyn**[116] 2776 6-11-0 0................................ BrianHughes 102
(Malcolm Jefferson) *hld up in rr: impr to go 3rd 2 out: no imp on front pair last: kpt on u.p run-in* **11/1**[3]

-343 **4** *nk* **Fizzy Dancer**[15] 4546 6-11-0 0............................... DavidBass 102
(Kim Bailey) *hld up: dropped to last 4 out: niggled along bef 2 out: 4th and no imp on ldrs last: kpt on run-in but n.d* **25/1**

433 **5** *16* **Stickee Fingers**[46] 3995 5-10-11 0..................... HarryBannister(3) 88
(Warren Greatrex) *racd in 2nd pl: pushed along and lost pl appr 3 out: bhd fr last* **25/1**

4m 54.6s (1.60) **Going Correction** -0.55s/f (Firm) **5** Ran **SP% 109.8**
Speed ratings (Par 105): **74,73,72,72,65**
CSF £2.22 TOTE £1.40: £1.10, £1.90; EX 2.90 Trifecta £4.90.
Owner Roy Swinburne **Bred** Shade Oak Stud And D Jenks **Trained** Little Newcastle, Pembrokes

FOCUS
Shared bends on both tracks, with the bend after the winning post out 23yds and the bend out of the back straight out two yards. This was run over 81yds further than advertised. The ground had been watered the previous week and Brian Harding after the first described it as: "A bit of everything - it is quick in some places, good to soft in others". An uncompetitive mares' event which took place over 81yds further than advertised. The winner and second have been rated below their best, with the third, fourth and fifth a better guide to the level.

4869 MOLSON COORS (WHIZZ KIDS) NOVICES' HURDLE (9 hdls) 1m 7f 144y
2:55 (2:55) (Class 4) 4-Y-0+ **£3,898** (£1,144; £572; £286)

Form RPR

2322 **1** **Double W's (IRE)**[47] 3971 6-11-0 126........................ BrianHughes 123+
(Malcolm Jefferson) *chsd ldr: hit 4th: nt fluent 6th: rdn after 3 out: hit 2 out: rdn to ld 1f out on run-in: drvn out* **1/2**[1]

114P **2** *2 1/4* **Altruism (IRE)**[45] 4010 6-11-12 130........................... HenryBrooke 130
(James Moffatt) *racd keenly: led: rdn appr last: hdd 1f out on run-in: no ex fnl 110yds* **7/1**[2]

1- **3** *8* **Mere Anarchy (IRE)**[144] 5454 5-11-0 0........................ RobertDunne 112
(Robert Stephens) *chsd ldrs: mstke 5th: rdn appr 3 out: sn no imp* **12/1**

56 **4** *1/2* **Boston De La Roche (FR)**[103] 3019 5-11-0 0................ SeanBowen 110
(David Loder) *hld up: pushed along bef 3 out: no imp: rdn bef 2 out: nvr a threat* **9/1**[3]

P5 **5** *23* **Texas Forever (IRE)**[41] 4064 7-11-0 0........................ DavidBass 91
(Kim Bailey) *hld up: struggling bef 3 out: mstke 2 out: n.d whn j.rt last: wl btn* **33/1**

01 **6** *4* **Man From Seville**[24] 4388 6-11-6 0........................ PaulMoloney 94
(Fergal O'Brien) *hld up: nt fluent 6th: struggling bef 3 out: nvr a threat* **9/1**[3]

3m 51.1s (-13.10) **Going Correction** -0.55s/f (Firm) **6** Ran **SP% 109.8**
Speed ratings (Par 105): **110,108,104,104,93 91**
CSF £4.43 TOTE £1.40: £1.10, £2.40; EX 3.60 Trifecta £16.30.
Owner Wharton & Wilson **Bred** Michael Bolger **Trained** Norton, N Yorks

FOCUS
Bar the well-backed odds-on favourite, most of these had questions to answer, but it still looked a decent race of its type. The distance was extended by 75yds due to rail movement. The winner has been rated close to his mark, along with the second, fourth and fifth.

4870 APOLLOBET HOME OF CASHBACK OFFERS NOVICES' LIMITED H'CAP CHASE (17 fncs) 2m 4f 135y
3:30 (3:35) (Class 3) (0-140,133) 5-Y-0+ **£6,498** (£1,908; £954; £477)

Form RPR

0-6P **1** **Some Buckle (IRE)**[60] 3747 7-11-8 **133**....................(t) NickScholfield 146+
(Paul Nicholls) *chsd ldrs: wnt 2nd appr 11th: led bef last: r.o wl to draw clr fnl 110yds* **5/2**[1]

1645 **2** *3 1/4* **Shimla Dawn (IRE)**[37] 4155 8-11-4 **129**.................... JakeGreenall 137
(Mark Walford) *chsd ldr: led 3rd: hdd appr last: kpt on same pce fnl 110yds* **9/2**

0311 **3** *8* **Daveron (IRE)**[20] 4443 8-11-4 **129**........................ MattGriffiths 132
(Jeremy Scott) *in tch: nt fluent 8th: mstke 9th: rdn whn chsng ldrs bef 2 out: one pce run-in* **5/1**

16-1 **4** *15* **Deadly Sting (IRE)**[306] 430 7-11-4 **129**..................(p) DenisO'Regan 118
(Neil Mulholland) *in rr: nt travel wl after 8th: in tch but unable to chal 4 out: lft bhd bef last* **3/1**[2]

F223 **P** **Leanna Ban**[22] 4420 9-10-7 **118**........................(t) JonathanEngland
(Tristan Davidson) *led: hdd 3rd: chsd ldr tl appr 11th where j. slowly: bhd 12th: lost tch qckly after 13th: sn p.u whn t.o* **7/2**[3]

5m 24.4s (324.40) **5** Ran **SP% 110.6**
CSF £13.57 TOTE £3.30: £1.40, £2.70; EX 14.00 Trifecta £43.00.
Owner R S Brookhouse **Bred** James A Slattery **Trained** Ditcheat, Somerset

FOCUS
Despite the small field this looked quite competitive and, with a good pace set, it could work out to be okay form. They went 81yds further than advertised due to rail movements. The second has been rated back to form, with the third a bit below the level of his latest win.

4871 ROA/RACING POST OWNERS JACKPOT H'CAP HURDLE (9 hdls) 1m 7f 144y
4:00 (4:02) (Class 4) (0-110,110) 4-Y-0+ **£3,898** (£1,144; £572; £286)

Form RPR

F-53 **1** **Beatu (IRE)**[22] 4416 7-11-12 **110**........................ WillKennedy 113
(Donald McCain) *chsd ldr: led 3 out but a pressed: rdn run-in: all out towards fin* **7/2**[2]

3030 **2** *1/2* **Back By Midnight**[39] 4129 7-11-9 **107**..................(t) NickScholfield 109
(Emma Baker) *racd keenly: led: clr fr 2nd: mstke 4th: reduced advantage 6th: hdd 3 out: continued to chse ldrs and cl up: rallied to take 2nd fnl 150yds: styd on towards fin* **8/1**

243 **3** *nk* **Three Colours Red (IRE)**[26] 4345 4-10-12 **106**.......(t) HarryBannister(3) 101
(Warren Greatrex) *racd keenly: in tch: rdn bef 3 out: effrt and ev ch 2 out: hung lft bef last: nt qckn early run-in: styd on u.p fnl 110yds: hld towards fin* **11/4**[1]

42F0 **4** *6* **Lady Clitico (IRE)**[44] 4036 5-11-4 **105**.................... TonyKelly(3) 102
(Rebecca Menzies) *hld up: mstke 5th: hdwy to chse ldrs appr 3 out: ev ch 2 out: stl there last: styd on same pce run-in* **14/1**

250R **5** *4 1/2* **Blue April (FR)**[20] 4447 5-11-7 **105**....................(p) MattGriffiths 96
(Jeremy Scott) *chsd ldrs: effrt and ev ch whn blnd 3 out: stl ev ch 2 out: u.p bef last: fdd run-in* **13/2**

-P26 **6** *2 1/2* **Archipeligo**[22] 4416 5-11-7 **105**............................. HenryBrooke 94
(Iain Jardine) *hld up: rdn bef 2 out: no imp* **6/1**[3]

100U **7** *24* **Royal Sea (IRE)**[37] 4152 7-11-6 **104**........................ SeanQuinlan 71
(Michael Mullineaux) *hld up in midfield: lost pl 5th: struggling and lost tch 6th* **25/1**

60P0 **P** **Down The Line (IRE)**[24] 4388 6-10-11 **95**.................. PaulMoloney
(Alan Swinbank) *hld up: mstke 2nd: nt fluent and j. slowly 3rd: struggling 6th: t.o whn p.u bef 2 out* **6/1**[3]

3m 57.7s (-6.50) **Going Correction** -0.55s/f (Firm) **8** Ran **SP% 112.4**
WFA 4 from 5yo+ 7lb
Speed ratings (Par 105): **94,93,93,90,88 87,75,**
CSF £29.97 CT £85.70 TOTE £3.70: £1.70, £2.10, £1.50; EX 25.80 Trifecta £57.20.
Owner T G Leslie **Bred** J Travers **Trained** Cholmondeley, Cheshire

FOCUS
A low-grade handicap with a tight finish, but mainly unexposed performers and a few of these could progress. The event took place over 75yds further than advertised. Small personal bests from the first two, with the third and fourth helping to set the level.

4872 HOWDENS JOINERY VETERANS' H'CAP CHASE (18 fncs) 2m 6f 204y
4:30 (4:30) (Class 4) (0-120,117) 10-Y-O+ £4,548 (£1,335; £667; £333)

Form RPR
/25- **1** **Fiddlers Reel**[654] 633 13-11-10 **115** BrianHughes 128
(Jane Clark) *chsd ldrs: mstke 4th: wnt 2nd 2 out: led run-in: kpt on u.p towards fin* 12/1
632P **2** 1 **Fine Parchment (IRE)**[32] 4255 13-11-4 **112** (tp) HarryBannister(3) 123
(Charlie Mann) *led: shkn up 12th: rdn appr 3 out: hdd run-in: continued to chal for press: hld nr fin* 12/1
5412 **3** 15 **Lord Landen (IRE)**[22] 4422 11-10-13 **104** (t) PaddyBrennan 105
(Fergal O'Brien) *hld up: hdwy to trck ldrs 11th: wnt 2nd after 14th: making effrt whn lost 2nd 2 out: no ex after last* 5/2[2]
45-P **4** 13 **Mr Syntax (IRE)**[46] 3996 12-11-5 **115** DiarmuidO'Regan(5) 102
(Chris Grant) *in tch: trcking ldrs 14th: no imp fr 2 out: wknd bef last* 14/1
-335 **5** 9 **Listen Boy (IRE)**[55] 3818 10-11-9 **117** RyanHatch(3) 95
(Nigel Twiston-Davies) *chsd ldr tl after 14th: rdn appr 4 out: wknd 3 out* 7/4[1]
2433 **6** 37 **Quito Du Tresor (FR)**[45] 4011 12-11-9 **114** (p) PeterBuchanan 76
(Lucinda Russell) *hld up: cl up bhd ldrs 14th: wknd sn after 4 out* 9/1[3]
0U15 **P** **Solway Bay**[35] 4175 14-9-10 **92** (t) CallumBewley(5)
(Lisa Harrison) *hld up: detached after 9th: lost tch 14th: t.o whn p.u bef 3 out* 16/1
P54- **P** **Whiskey Ridge (IRE)**[453] 3261 10-10-8 **99** DannyCook
(Sue Smith) *chsd ldrs: blnd 8th: rdn after 10th and lost pl: lost tch 14th: wl bhd whn p.u bef 4 out* 9/1[3]

6m 7.6s (-6.40) **Going Correction** -0.125s/f (Good) **8** Ran SP% **112.9**
Speed ratings: **106,105,100,95,92 79, ,**
CSF £130.14 CT £475.28 TOTE £10.80: £2.70, £3.30, £1.40; EX 74.10 Trifecta £379.50.
Owner Mrs Jane Clark **Bred** Mrs Jane Clark **Trained** Kelso, Borders

FOCUS
A typical veterans' chase with a number of these looking potentially well handicapped in this company. The trip was extended by 150yds due to rail movements. The winner has been rated to his mark, with the third 6lb off his latest mark.

4873 APOLLOBET DAILY RACING REFUNDS "FIXED BRUSH" NOVICES' H'CAP HURDLE (10 hdls) 2m 2f 191y
5:00 (5:00) (Class 3) (0-135,125) 4-8-Y-0 £8,122 (£2,385; £1,192; £596)

Form RPR
12 **1** **Sharpasaknife (IRE)**[43] 4040 6-11-12 **125** BrianHughes 131+
(Malcolm Jefferson) *prom: wnt 2nd 4 out: chalng 2 out: rdn appr last: styd on for press to ld towards fin* 5/4[1]
56-3 **2** 3/4 **Birch Hill (IRE)**[46] 3994 6-11-9 **122** AndrewTinkler 125
(Nicky Henderson) *led: hdd after 1st: regained ld 2nd: rdn appr 3 out: hdd and hld towards fin* 9/2[3]
24 **3** 3 1/2 **Beware The Bear (IRE)**[104] 2995 6-11-2 **120** FreddieMitchell(5) 122
(Nicky Henderson) *in tch: nt fluent 4 out: rdn and outpcd bef 3 out: styd on to take 3rd fnl 75yds: nt pce to trble front two* 9/2[3]
4312 **4** 1 1/4 **Impulsive American**[20] 4452 4-10-11 **123** (p) DavidNoonan(5) 115
(David Pipe) *hld up: hdwy 4 out: rdn whn cl up bhd ldrs appr last: swtchd rt run-in: nt qckn sn after: no ex fnl 75yds* 7/2[2]
1FF3 **5** 31 **Raise A Spark**[33] 4224 6-11-1 **114** HenryBrooke 91
(Donald McCain) *led after 1st: hdd 2nd: chsd ldr to 4 out: rdn appr 3 out: lft bhd bef next* 14/1

4m 47.4s (-5.60) **Going Correction** -0.55s/f (Firm)
WFA 4 from 6yo 7lb **5** Ran SP% **109.7**
Speed ratings: **89,88,87,86,73**
CSF £7.23 TOTE £2.30: £1.10, £3.00; EX 7.00 Trifecta £16.60.
Owner The Mount Fawcus Partnership **Bred** Gerry Carroll **Trained** Norton, N Yorks
■ Stewards' Enquiry : Andrew Tinkler four-day ban: used whip above permitted level (Apr 10-13)

FOCUS
Top weight was 10lb under ceiling, but it was still a fair race of its type. They were well grouped until late on and due to rail movements they went 81yds further than the official distance. The second, third and fourth have been rated to their marks.
T/Plt: £20.00 to a £1 stake. Pool: £63,866.81 - 2,321.38 winning tickets T/Qpdt: £22.60 to a £1 stake. Pool: £3,524.79 - 115.40 winning tickets **Darren Owen**

4646 WARWICK (L-H)
Wednesday, March 23

OFFICIAL GOING: Good (good to soft in places on hurdle course; chs 7.3, hdl 7.0)
Wind: virtually nil Weather: overcast

4874 MHM MAIDEN HURDLE (11 hdls) 2m 5f
2:10 (2:10) (Class 4) 4-Y-0+ £3,249 (£954; £477; £238)

Form RPR
-522 **1** **Walking In The Air (IRE)**[19] 4463 6-11-1 **127** HarrySkelton 132+
(Dan Skelton) *mde all and sn clr: in command whn blnd last: v easily* 2/5[1]
544 **2** 11 **Red Infantry (IRE)**[26] 4344 6-11-1 0 TomO'Brien 116+
(Ian Williams) *chsd ldrs: chsd clr wnr after 8th: no imp whn j.lft 2 out: wl hld and wnt bdly lft last: no ch w wnr but hld on for 2nd flat* 50/1
6-0 **3** 1 1/2 **El Bandit (IRE)**[20] 4449 5-11-1 0 SamTwiston-Davies 112
(Paul Nicholls) *hld up towards rr: stdy hdwy after 6th: wnt modest 4th after 3 out: styd on steadily: no ch w wnr* 25/1
32-0 **4** 11 **Robert's Star (IRE)**[140] 2265 6-11-1 0 [1] AidanColeman 103
(Mark Bradstock) *hld up in midfield: hdwy after 6th and prom in chsng gp next: 3rd and no imp after 3 out: wknd between last 2* 12/1
430 **5** 27 **Mr Banks (IRE)**[18] 4494 5-11-1 0 (p) CharliePoste 79
(Paul Webber) *chsd wnr tl after 8th: 4th and wkng whn blnd next: fdd 2 out: t.o* 66/1
3 **6** hd **Clondaw Fonz (IRE)**[27] 4323 5-11-1 0 WayneHutchinson 78
(Alan King) *prom in chsng gp tl struggling whn mstke 8th: wl btn next: wknd: t.o* 8/1[2]
0-4 **7** 9 **Tudors Treasure**[31] 4270 5-11-1 0 MichealNolan 69
(Robert Stephens) *hld up in midfield: nvr on terms w wnr: wknd 8th: t.o* 150/1
8 1 1/2 **Glengra (IRE)**[472] 7-10-12 0 MauriceLinehan(3) 67
(Ian Williams) *hld up in rr: hdwy after 5th: midfield after next: struggling whn mstke 7th: wknd next: t.o* 50/1
1-02 **9** 1 1/4 **Fivefortyfive**[21] 4439 8-11-1 0 (t) NoelFehily 66
(Polly Gundry) *prom in chsng gp tl wknd 8th: t.o* 16/1
60 **10** 1 1/4 **Neumond (GER)**[27] 4322 5-11-1 0 NicodeBoinville 65
(Nicky Henderson) *hld up towards rr: nvr on terms w wnr: lost tch 8th: t.o* 16/1
06 **11** 23 **Derksen (IRE)**[27] 4322 6-11-1 0 JeremiahMcGrath 44
(Nicky Henderson) *midfield but nvr on terms w wnr: struggling 7th: bhd next: t.o* 33/1
06F **12** 3 1/2 **Fled Or Pled (IRE)**[2] 4848 4-10-2 0 JamieBargary(5) 33
(David Dennis) *taken down early: hld up in rr: j.rt 4th: mstke and lost tch 7th: t.o* 200/1
0P/0 **P** **Aster's Approval**[2] 4849 6-11-1 0 AndrewThornton
(Grant Cann) *mstkes: a in rr: t.o whn blnd 3 out: p.u next* 200/1
/05P **U** **Over The Bridge**[21] 4430 6-10-8 0 MrJNixon(7)
(Steve Flook) *towards rr whn mstke and uns rdr 3rd* 200/1
P **Scoresheet (IRE)**[157] 5-11-1 0 RichardJohnson
(Philip Hobbs) *midfield but nvr on terms w wnr: mstke 2nd: lost pl 8th: t.o whn p.u 2 out (fatally injured)* 10/1[3]
50 **P** **Doasuwouldbedoneby (IRE)**[27] 4322 5-11-1 0 DarylJacob
(David Arbuthnot) *hld up in rr: lost tch after 7th: t.o whn p.u 2 out* 200/1
P **P** **Bellator (FR)**[21] 4430 5-11-1 0 PeterCarberry
(Nicky Henderson) *hld up in midfield: rdn after 5th: bhd 8th: t.o whn p.u 2 out* 50/1

5m 10.72s (-10.28) **Going Correction** -0.275s/f (Good)
WFA 4 from 5yo+ 8lb **17** Ran SP% **127.9**
Speed ratings (Par 105): **108,103,103,99,88 88,85,84,84,83 74,73, , ,**
CSF £47.60 TOTE £1.30: £1.02, £9.60, £5.70; EX 30.40 Trifecta £456.70.
Owner Mrs Barbara Hester **Bred** Vincent Finn **Trained** Alcester, Warwicks

FOCUS
All starts have been moved at this track following remeasuring, so there will be no speed figures here until there is sufficient data to calculate updated median times. The hurdles and the bumper were run on the outer hurdles track. Not many got into this maiden hurdle, which was run over 2m5f 14yds. Harry Skelton, who rode the winner, said: "It's good ground in the main but there are some dead patches." Big steps up from the second and third, with the fourth helping to set the level.

4875 JCB NOVICES' HURDLE (8 hdls) 2m
2:40 (2:40) (Class 4) 4-Y-0+ £3,249 (£954; £477; £238)

Form RPR
2U34 **1** **Drumlee Sunset (IRE)**[82] 3403 6-11-0 133 RichardJohnson 134+
(Philip Hobbs) *chsd wnr tl led 2nd: jnd and mstke 4th: hit next: pushed along and readily wnt clr after 3 out: in command next: styd on: comf* 8/13[1]
341F **2** 17 **Crickel Wood (FR)**[124] 2617 6-11-6 122 (t) AidanColeman 121
(Charlie Longsdon) *hld up in tch in midfield: effrt 3 out: battling for 2nd but outpcd by wnr bef 2 out: wnt clar 2nd last but no ch w wnr* 9/2[2]
-200 **3** 4 **Bendomingo (IRE)**[54] 3835 5-10-9 0 (t) JamieBargary(5) 111
(Nigel Twiston-Davies) *chsd ldr after 3rd: ev ch 4th tl rdn and outpcd after 3 out: btn next: lost 2nd last: plugged on* 50/1
6-5 **4** 2 1/2 **Micks Lad (IRE)**[27] 4322 6-11-0 0 (t) HarrySkelton 108
(Dan Skelton) *hld up wl in tch in midfield: effrt to go 3rd after 3 out: 4th and btn whn j.rt 2 out: plugged on* 8/1
4 **5** 12 **Celtic Tune (FR)**[41] 4064 5-11-0 0 RichieMcLernon 97
(Jonjo O'Neill) *led tl 2nd: chsd wnr tl after next: styd handy and jnd wnr 4th tl after next: struggling u.p 3 out: wknd bef next* 33/1
0402 **6** 1 **Breath Of Blighty (FR)**[54] 3842 5-11-0 121 LiamTreadwell 97
(Paul Webber) *in tch in midfield: struggling 3 out: 6th and wknd bef next* 6/1[3]
7 1 1/4 **Bertie Barnes (IRE)** 5-11-0 0 IanPopham 96
(Richard Phillips) *hld up in last trio: rdn and outpcd 5th: no ch next: mstke last* 100/1
8 7 **Pao De Acuca (IRE)**[19] 4-10-7 0 (t[1]) MarkGrant 85
(Jose Santos) *in tch in midfield: mstke 4th: sn rdn and wknd bef 3 out: no ch whn mstke last: t.o* 40/1
50 **9** 5 **Bol D'Air (FR)**[58] 3772 5-11-0 0 SamTwiston-Davies 87
(Paul Nicholls) *in tch in midfield: effrt after 5th: sn btn: wknd wl bef 2 out: t.o* 16/1
5600 **10** 20 **Good Man Hughie (IRE)**[4] 4784 7-10-11 0 BenPoste(3) 67
(Sally Randell) *hld up in rr: lost tch 4th: t.o 3 out* 100/1
06-6 **11** 15 **Royal Roo**[315] 279 7-10-7 0 (t) DarylJacob 46
(Mark Rimell) *hld up in last pair: lost tch after 4th: t.o 3 out* 100/1
0-P **P** **No Bad News**[68] 3608 6-11-0 0 JamesDavies
(Henry Oliver) *t.k.h: hld up in midfield: lost pl 7th: bhd and mstke next: t.o whn p.u after 3 out* 200/1

3m 54.3s (3.30) **Going Correction** -0.175s/f (Good)
WFA 4 from 5yo+ 7lb **12** Ran SP% **122.2**
Speed ratings (Par 105): **104,95,93,92,86 85,85,81,79,69 61,**
CSF £3.97 TOTE £1.50: £1.10, £2.30, £7.70; EX 4.80 Trifecta £61.20.
Owner R S Brookhouse **Bred** I McGrath & K McGrath **Trained** Withycombe, Somerset

FOCUS
Actual race distance 2m 8yds. A second easy odds-on winner on the card. The winner set a decent standard and has been rated back to his best, with the second and fourth pretty much to their marks.

4876 BRANDON HIRE GROUP NOVICES' H'CAP CHASE (FOR THE STEPHEN ALLDAY PERPETUAL PLATE) (18 fncs) 3m
3:15 (3:15) (Class 4) (0-120,113) 5-Y-0+ £3,898 (£1,144; £572; £286)

Form RPR
335P **1** **Epic Warrior (IRE)**[15] 4542 7-11-8 **113** (b) ConorO'Farrell 125+
(David Pipe) *mostly trckd ldrs: wnt 2nd and travelling strly after 3 out: pushed into ld between last 2: hit last: drvn and a holding runner-up flat* 10/1
5-55 **2** 1 3/4 **Heroes Or Ghosts (IRE)**[41] 4071 7-10-11 **102** JeremiahMcGrath 109
(Jo Davis) *in tch: chsd ldrs 5th tl led 10th: rdn bef 2 out: hdd between last 2: kpt on but a hld flat* 6/1[2]
12FP **3** 12 **Pure Poteen (IRE)**[47] 3979 8-11-4 **109** (t) NoelFehily 107
(Neil Mulholland) *hld up in tch: stdy hdwy 13th: wnt 3rd 2 out: sn rdn and no ex: btn whn mstke last: wknd flat* 8/1
2540 **4** 3 3/4 **Ready Token (IRE)**[25] 4352 8-11-7 **112** AidanColeman 107
(Charlie Longsdon) *led after 1st tl hdd 10th: pressed ldr again 12th: drvn and no ex bef 2 out: 4th and btn whn j. slowly last* 9/1

4462 **5** *2* **Under The Phone (IRE)**[41] 4062 7-11-2 **107** .... CharliePoste 98
(Robin Dickin) *in tch in last trio: drvn 15th: no imp: wl hld but plugged on u.p flat* **7/2**[1]

54P5 **6** *shd* **Brownville**[20] 4443 7-11-8 **113** ....(tp) SamTwiston-Davies 106
(Nigel Twiston-Davies) *led tl after 1st: chsd ldrs after: j. slowly 3rd: outpcd u.p after 3 out: wknd after next* **7/2**[1]

51P6 **7** *10* **Bayley's Dream**[121] 2687 7-11-4 **109** .... LiamTreadwell 95
(Paul Webber) *in tch in midfield: dropped to rr and j.rt 13th: j.rt and mstke next: wknd after 3 out* **25/1**

PP31 **8** *43* **Swizzler (IRE)**[12] 4588 7-10-10 **101** .... TomO'Brien 64
(Ian Williams) *nt fluent: hld up towards rr: j.rt 1st: mstke 2nd: hdwy into midfield 6th: chsd ldrs after 11th: mstke next: lost pl 14th: bhd 2 out: t.o* **12/1**

-4PP **P** **Elmore Back (IRE)**[19] 4465 7-11-8 **113** ....(p) GavinSheehan
(Charlie Mann) *dropped to rr 4th: in tch: rdn and struggling 13th: lost tch 15th: t.o whn p.u 2 out* **7/1**[3]

6m 13.4s (-20.60) **Going Correction** -0.725s/f (Firm) **9** Ran SP% **113.0**
Speed ratings: **105,104,100,99,98 98,95,80,**
CSF £67.55 CT £504.37 TOTE £12.20: £3.00, £2.00, £2.90; EX 80.50 Trifecta £928.70.
Owner Stuart & Simon Mercer & Peter Green **Bred** Thomas Hannon **Trained** Nicholashayne, Devon

FOCUS
Actual race distance 3m 62yds. A fair novice handicap chase run at a reasonable gallop. A small pb from the winner, with the second rated in line with his best hurdle form.

4877 RICOH ARENA H'CAP HURDLE (11 hdls 1 omitted) 3m 2f
3:50 (3:50) (Class 4) (0-110,110) 4-Y-0+ **£3,249** (£954; £477; £238)

Form RPR

6331 **1** **Ceann Sibheal (IRE)**[16] 4528 7-11-4 **102** ....(p) GavinSheehan 118+
(Warren Greatrex) *mde all: j. slowly 7th: reminder bef next: forged clr after 3 out: in command next: styd on* **7/2**[2]

0421 **2** *13* **Talk Of The South (IRE)**[9] 4671 7-11-11 **109** 7ex..... WayneHutchinson 112+
(Paul Henderson) *trckd ldrs: wnt 3rd bypassing 8th: chsd wnr next: pressing wnr and rdn sn after 3 out: fnd little and sn btn: wl hld whn j. slowly last* **9/4**[1]

5P-3 **3** *8* **Springhill Lad**[104] 2997 9-11-9 **107** .... MarkGrant 100
(Geoffrey Deacon) *hld up in tch: hdwy bypassing 8th: wnt 3rd bef 3 out: no imp and wl btn 2 out* **10/1**

4-54 **4** *7* **Carn Rock**[150] 2081 8-11-0 **105** .... MikeyHamill[(7)] 92
(Michael Gates) *in tch in midfield: hmpd 2nd: rdn and outpcd bypassing 8th: no ch after: modest 4th bef 2 out* **4/1**[3]

P6P6 **5** *10* **Debt To Society (IRE)**[40] 4105 9-11-3 **104** ....(tp) HarryChalloner[(3)] 82
(Richard Ford) *in tch in midfield: hmpd 2nd: hdwy to chse ldrs after 7th: outpcd u.p bypassing next: mstke 9th: no ch 3 out: t.o* **33/1**

0PP- **P** **Stickers**[380] 4668 9-10-1 **85** oh2 ow1 .... JackQuinlan
(Alan Jessop) *hld up in rr: hmpd 2nd: rdn after 6th: mstke next: lost tch bypassing 8th: t.o whn p.u 3 out* **100/1**

4P6- **P** **Oscars Way (IRE)**[441] 3571 8-10-10 **97** ....(tp) BenPoste[(3)]
(Tom Symonds) *chsd ldrs: rdn after 7th: lost pl qckly and wl bhd whn p.u 9th* **22/1**

5PPP **P** **Barra Rotha (IRE)**[23] 4412 9-10-9 **96** ....(p) KieronEdgar[(3)]
(Laura Hurley) *hld up in rr: short-lived effrt bypassing 8th: sn wl btn: t.o 3 out: p.u last* **100/1**

23F **P** **Air Glider (IRE)**[37] 4152 6-11-12 **110** ....(b[1]) HarrySkelton
(Dan Skelton) *chsd ldrs tl lft chsng wnr 2nd: lost 2nd 9th and sn dropped out u.p: t.o whn p.u 2 out* **8/1**

0463 **F** **Nancy's Trix (IRE)**[37] 4151 7-11-2 **105** .... JackSherwood[(5)]
(David Loder) *chsd ldr tl fell 2nd* **10/1**

6m 31.7s (-5.30) **Going Correction** -0.075s/f (Good) **10** Ran SP% **111.6**
Speed ratings (Par 105): **105,101,98,96,93 , , , ,**
CSF £11.30 CT £66.81 TOTE £3.90: £1.50, £1.50, £2.70; EX 9.30 Trifecta £76.30.
Owner The High Kites **Bred** E Wallace **Trained** Upper Lambourn, Berks

FOCUS
Actual race distance 3m2f 17yds. The form horses came to this fore in this modest staying handicap. The first two have been rated in line with their recent wins.

4878 EXECUTIVE HIRE SHOW THANKS FOR ATTENDING MARES' H'CAP HURDLE (11 hdls) 2m 5f
4:20 (4:21) (Class 4) (0-115,115) 4-Y-0+ **£3,249** (£954; £477; £238)

Form RPR

0320 **1** **Chantara Rose**[54] 3837 7-11-7 **110** ....(p) NoelFehily 114
(Neil Mulholland) *hld up in tch in last quartet: hdwy to chse ldng pair after 3 out: swtchd lft between last 2: pressing ldr last: styd on u.p to ld towards fin* **7/1**

2365 **2** *1* **Jean Fleming (IRE)**[35] 4186 9-11-9 **112** ....(b[1]) BrendanPowell 114
(Jamie Snowden) *led: rdn and clr w rival after 3 out: hdd next: rallied u.p and upsides whn lft in ld last: hdd and no ex towards fin* **13/2**[3]

3006 **3** *3 3/4* **Dubh Eile (IRE)**[19] 4466 8-11-10 **113** .... RichardJohnson 113
(Tim Vaughan) *hld up in tch in last quartet: hdwy on inner bef 2 out: rdn to go 4th 2 out: lft 3rd last: kpt on same pce flat* **5/1**[2]

4454 **4** *3 1/2* **Miss Tongabezi**[23] 4413 7-10-9 **98** ....(t) JamesBest 94
(Paul Webber) *chsd ldrs: drvn and mstke 8th: outpcd 2 out: btn and keeping on same pce and hld whn lft 4th last* **16/1**

4340 **5** *23* **Mini Muck**[49] 3930 10-11-2 **105** ....(t) SamTwiston-Davies 85
(Nigel Twiston-Davies) *chsd ldrs: 4th and no ex u.p after 3 out: wknd bef next* **7/1**

011P **6** *5* **Kentford Heiress**[93] 3198 6-10-7 **101** .... KevinJones[(5)] 74
(Seamus Mullins) *in tch in midfield: rdn bef 3 out: wknd bef 2 out: no ch whn hmpd last* **20/1**

233B **7** *3 1/2* **Bonnet's Vino**[18] 4492 8-11-7 **115** .... JamieBargary[(5)] 85
(Pam Sly) *chsd ldr tl after 6th: styd handy and wnt 2nd again 8th: rdn and wknd after 3 out: no ch whn hmpd last* **10/1**

655 **8** *9* **Quantum Of Solace**[116] 2772 6-10-10 **99** .... WayneHutchinson 58
(Noel Williams) *in tch in midfield: effrt after 3 out: sn btn and wknd bef next: t.o* **9/1**

2043 **9** *6* **Tara Well (IRE)**[12] 4598 6-10-1 **100** .... CathalCourtney[(10)] 56
(Robin Dickin) *mstkes: t.k.h: chsd ldrs 2nd tl lost pl after 6th: dropped to rr 8th: lost tch after 3 out: t.o* **16/1**

-006 **10** *1 3/4* **Cosmic Diamond**[101] 3066 6-9-12 **90** oh3 ow1 .... BenPoste[(3)] 42
(Paul Webber) *hld up in tch towards rr: effrt bef 3 out: sn btn: wknd wl bef 2 out: t.o* **33/1**

40P **P** **Big Night Out**[48] 3951 10-9-8 **90** ....(t) MikeyHamill[(7)]
(Laura Hurley) *hld up in tch: hdwy to chse ldr after 6th tl lost pl qckly 8th: t.o whn p.u 2 out* **50/1**

-662 **F** **The Last Bar**[41] 4065 6-11-5 **108** .... HarrySkelton 110
(Dan Skelton) *hld up in tch: hdwy 8th: jnd ldr and travelling bttr after 3 out: led and mstke next: sn rdn and stl jst ahd whn fell last* **4/1**[1]

5m 18.7s (-2.30) **Going Correction** +0.025s/f (Yiel) **12** Ran SP% **115.5**
Speed ratings (Par 105): **105,104,103,101,93 91,89,86,84,83 ,**
CSF £50.15 CT £249.02 TOTE £8.90: £2.40, £2.70, £1.90; EX 72.10 Trifecta £389.30.
Owner Steve & Jackie Fleetham **Bred** David Jenks **Trained** Limpley Stoke, Wilts

FOCUS
Actual race distance 2m5f 14yds. This mares' handicap hurdle was run at a strong gallop, and the form has a sound look to it. The winner and faller have been rated as running personal bests, with the third and fourth helping to set the level.

4879 EXECUTIVE HIRE NEWS PASSIONATE INDUSTRY VOICE H'CAP CHASE (22 fncs) 3m 5f
4:50 (4:50) (Class 4) (0-105,105) 5-Y-0+ **£3,898** (£1,144; £572; £286)

Form RPR

F442 **1** **Mission Complete (IRE)**[24] 4391 10-10-2 **91** ....(tp) JackSavage[(10)] 105+
(Jonjo O'Neill) *chsd ldr 5th tl jnd ldr 14th: led 16th: rdn bef 2 out: styd on: rdn out* **9/2**[2]

3114 **2** *4* **Bebinn (IRE)**[35] 4185 9-11-11 **104** ....(p) DarylJacob 112
(Ben Case) *chsd ldrs: lft 3rd after 10th: chsd wnr 17th: drvn after 3 out: styd on same pce fr next* **20/1**

2PF5 **3** *nk* **Nail 'M (IRE)**[11] 4612 8-11-8 **104** ....(vt) TomBellamy[(3)] 114
(Nigel Hawke) *hld up in tch towards rr: mstke 12th: hdwy after 15th: mstke 18th: effrt to go 3rd sn after 3 out: drvn and styd on same pce flat* **4/1**[1]

14PP **4** *8* **Crack Of Thunder (IRE)**[88] 3220 7-11-12 **105** ....(p) AidanColeman 107
(Charlie Longsdon) *in tch in midfield: reminder after 16th: 4th and drvn after 3 out: no imp next* **4/1**[1]

3430 **5** *6* **The Last Bridge**[58] 3771 9-10-12 **91** ....(p) RichardJohnson 87
(Susan Johnson) *in tch in midfield: rdn after 12th and lost pl next: dropped to rr u.p and lost nr side cheek piece after 15th: rallied briefly 18th: no imp 3 out: wl btn next* **8/1**

P043 **6** *54* **Raduis Bleu (FR)**[71] 3569 11-9-11 **83** .... MissLBrooke[(7)] 30
(Lady Susan Brooke) *hld up in tch: hdwy to chse ldrs 11th: lost pl 16th: struggling u.p next: wl bhd after 3 out: t.o* **25/1**

65P4 **7** *1* **Tinelyra (IRE)**[79] 3468 10-10-3 **85** ....(t) ConorShoemark[(3)] 31
(Fergal O'Brien) *hld up in tch in last pair: effrt 17th: sn struggling: wl bhd after 3 out: t.o* **16/1**

41/5 **P** **Badgers Cove (IRE)**[19] 4466 12-11-11 **104** .... CharliePoste
(Robin Dickin) *chsd ldr tl 5th: clsd 3rd whn lost action after 10th: p.u and dismntd (fatally injured)* **13/2**[3]

263P **P** **Handsome Buddy (IRE)**[104] 2996 9-10-8 **94** ....(v) MikeyHamill[(7)]
(Michael Gates) *s.i.s: nvr gng wl in rr: lost tch and p.u 16th* **10/1**

1P52 **P** **Leith Hill Legasi**[35] 4185 7-10-12 **98** ....(bt) MissCVHart[(7)]
(Charlie Longsdon) *led tl 16th: rdn 18th: 5th and wknd qckly after 3 out: t.o whn p.u last* **11/1**

7m 40.5s (-15.50) **Going Correction** -0.625s/f (Firm) **10** Ran SP% **114.5**
Speed ratings: **96,94,94,92,90 76,75, , ,**
CSF £81.08 CT £387.97 TOTE £4.40: £1.80, £3.90, £2.10; EX 54.60 Trifecta £406.10.
Owner John P McManus **Bred** Hubert Carter **Trained** Cheltenham, Gloucs

FOCUS
Actual race distance 3m5f 62yds. This long-distance handicap chase was run at a sound gallop. It's been rated around the balance of the second, third and fourth.

4880 EXECUTIVE HIRE STILL CELEBRATING SHOW 10 STANDARD OPEN NATIONAL HUNT FLAT RACE 2m
5:20 (5:21) (Class 6) 4-6-Y-0 **£1,624** (£477; £238; £119)

Form RPR

1 **Robin Roe (IRE)**[122] 5-11-4 0 .... HarrySkelton 113+
(Dan Skelton) *hld up wl in tch in midfield: hdwy to ld 4f out: rn green and edgd rt over 1f out: r.o wl: rdn out* **11/4**[1]

2 *1 1/2* **Royal Supremo (IRE)**[136] 5-11-4 0 .... DavidBass 109
(Kim Bailey) *hld up in tch in midfield: hdwy 5f out: effrt to chse wnr wl over 1f out: kpt on but a hld ins fnl f* **25/1**

3 *2* **Post War**[122] 5-11-4 0 .... NicodeBoinville 107
(Nicky Henderson) *chsd ldrs: effrt ent fnl 2f: wnt 3rd 1f out: styd on same pce ins fnl f* **25/1**

4 *1 3/4* **Bastien (FR)** 5-11-4 0 .... WayneHutchinson 106
(Alan King) *chsd ldrs: effrt u.p 3f out: 4th and styd on same pce fnl f* **16/1**

6 **5** *4* **Phobiaphiliac (IRE)**[40] 4102 5-11-4 0 .... JeremiahMcGrath 104+
(Nicky Henderson) *in tch in midfield: stmbld path after 4f: effrt to chse ldrs 3f out: no ex over 1f out: wknd ins fnl f* **9/1**

6 *shd* **Hoke Colburn (IRE)** 4-10-11 0 .... GavinSheehan 95
(Harry Whittington) *in tch in midfield: pushed along 1/2-way: rdn and lost pl 5f out: rallied over 2f out: no ch w wnr but styd on steadily ins fnl f* **9/1**

7 *1/2* **Beau Du Brizais (FR)** 4-10-11 0 .... RichardJohnson 94
(Philip Hobbs) *hld up in tch: hdwy 10f out: chsd wnr over 2f out: lost 2nd wl over 1f out: sn rn green and edgd lft: wknd ins fnl f* **5/1**[2]

8 *8* **Alpine Secret (IRE)** 4-10-11 0 .... BrendanPowell 87
(Ben Pauling) *t.k.h: pressed ldrs for 3f: chsd ldrs tl no ex u.p 3f out: wknd 2f out* **20/1**

9 *4* **Summerhill Boy (IRE)** 5-11-4 0 .... SamTwiston-Davies 91
(Nigel Twiston-Davies) *chsd ldrs tl no ex u.p 3f out: wknd 2f out* **20/1**

2 **10** *1 1/4* **Man From Mars**[38] 4143 4-10-6 0 .... LizzieKelly[(5)] 83
(Nick Williams) *t.k.h: w ldr tl led 5f out tl 4f out: lost pl over 2f and sn wknd* **14/1**

11 *4 1/2* **Dance In The Dust (IRE)**[122] 5-11-4 0 .... AidanColeman 85
(Jonjo O'Neill) *in tch in midfield: rdn 5f out: outpcd and btn 3f out: sn wknd* **6/1**[3]

12 *6* **Silent Warrior** 4-10-8 0 .... GrahamWatters[(3)] 73
(Charlie Longsdon) *in tch towards rr: rdn and btn over 3f out: bhd over 2f out* **14/1**

0 **13** *9* **Jump And Jump (IRE)**[286] 696 6-10-11 0 .... CharliePoste 65
(Robin Dickin) *hld up in rr: lost tch 8f out: sn wl bhd: t.o* **200/1**

14 *3/4* **Sound The Bugle** 6-10-13 0 .... JakeHodson[(5)] 71
(Anthony Day) *mde most tl 5f out: sn dropped out: t.o* **200/1**

15 *10* **Hippiart** 4-10-11 0 .... TomO'Brien 55
(David Bridgwater) *in tch in midfield tl lost pl and rdn 6f out: t.o* **66/1**

16 *7* **Homers Odyssey** 6-11-4 0 .... DarylJacob 56
(Simon Hodgson) *led to s: hld up in rr: lost tch 6f out: t.o* **100/1**

0 **17** *3/4* **Lickpenny Larry**[24] 4392 5-11-4 0 .... JamesDavies 55
(Tom Gretton) *hld up towards rr: lost tch 6f out: t.o* **100/1**

18 *75* **Crosshare** 5-11-4 0...(tp) JoshuaMoore
(Lawney Hill) *a towards rr: bhd and lost tch 7f out: t.o* **100/1**

3m 49.0s (3.60) **Going Correction** +0.125s/f (Yiel)
WFA 4 from 5yo+ 7lb **18** Ran SP% **119.5**
Speed ratings: **96,95,94,93,91 91,91,87,85,84 82,79,74,74,69 65,65,27**
CSF £83.20 TOTE £3.80: £1.50, £7.90, £5.80; EX 74.10 Trifecta £1881.00.
Owner Mrs Barbara Hester **Bred** John O'Leary **Trained** Alcester, Warwicks

FOCUS
Actual race distance 2m 8yds. Winners should emerge from this big-field bumper, which wasn't run at a bad pace.
T/Plt: £43.80 to a £1 stake. Pool: £78,268.56 - 1,301.70 winning tickets T/Qpdt: £27.60 to a £1 stake. Pool: £5,351.19 - 143.46 winning tickets **Steve Payne**

4612 CHEPSTOW (L-H)
Thursday, March 24

OFFICIAL GOING: Good changing to good (good to soft in places) after race 5 (4.25)
Wind: almost nil Weather: light rain, misty

4881 ECIC MARES' NOVICES' HURDLE (7 hdls 1 omitted) 2m 11y
2:05 (2:06) (Class 4) 4-Y-0+ **£3,249** (£954; £477; £238)

Form RPR
-305 **1** **The Missus**[29] 4303 5-10-12 0.. RichardJohnson 110+
(Warren Greatrex) *mde all: 12 l clr 4th: reduced advantage on extended run between last 2 but stl gng wl: rdn out flat* **15/8**[2]
-02P **2** *1 ¼* **Goldray**[30] 4298 10-10-12 104.. JakeGreenall 106
(Kerry Lee) *prom: chsd wnr fr 3rd: rdn bef 3 out: clsd gap on extended run between last 2: hung lft bef last: r.o flat* **4/1**[3]
30 **3** *19* **Moontripper**[10] 4681 7-10-5 0.. MrConorOrr(7) 90
(Phillip Dando) *trckd ldr to 3rd: styd in ldng gp: rdn in mod 4th 3 out: hld after but styd on to go 3rd flat* **20/1**
/30- **4** *¾* **Ivor's Queen (IRE)**[376] 4755 7-10-12 0.......................................(t) NoelFehily 88
(Harry Fry) *hld up in rr: hdwy after 4th: wnt modest 3rd bef last but nvr threatened ldrs: no ex flat* **7/4**[1]
00 **5** *6* **Kaddys Dream**[54] 3862 5-10-12 0.. CharliePoste 83
(Robin Dickin) *mid-div: clsd 2nd: chsd ldng pair 4th: rdn 3 out: wknd and lost 2 pls appr last* **100/1**
0 **6** *14* **Cottonwool Baby (IRE)**[274] 831 5-10-12 0.. RobertDunne 70
(Michael Scudamore) *hld up: a towards rr* **40/1**
000/ **7** *nk* **Crazy Train**[600] 5528 7-10-5 0.. MrJoshuaNewman(7) 70
(Robert Walford) *t.k.h in rr: hdwy into mid-div after 1st: no ch fr 3 out* **100/1**
05-0 **8** *2 ¾* **Miss Minx**[140] 2302 5-10-5 0.. WilliamFeatherstone(7) 67
(Alan King) *mid-div: rdn after 4th: no ch fr 3 out* **12/1**
0-50 **9** *2 ¾* **Beautiful People (FR)**[84] 3381 5-10-12 0.. IanPopham 65
(Richard Phillips) *hld up: a in rr* **66/1**
10 *8* **Bowberry**[268] 5-10-12 0.. DaveCrosse 58
(Ali Stronge) *hld up: a in rr* **20/1**
6-P6 **11** *60* **Doris De Silver**[16] 4546 7-10-12 0.......................................(t) JamesBest 4
(Jackie Du Plessis) *chsd ldrs: pushed along 3rd: wknd after next: t.o* **100/1**

3m 57.8s (-12.80) **Going Correction** -0.725s/f (Firm) **11** Ran SP% **115.3**
Speed ratings (Par 105): **103,102,92,92,89 82,82,80,79,75 45**
CSF £9.32 TOTE £3.70: £2.30, £1.80, £4.00; EX 9.30 Trifecta £75.00.
Owner Robert Waley-Cohen **Bred** Upton Viva Stud **Trained** Upper Lambourn, Berks

FOCUS
The far bend was railed out by 6 metres from the inside and the stables bend by 5 metres. The rail movements added approximately 30yds to this advertised race distance. This looked a weak contest for the race type and the field was strung out soon after the start. Winning rider Richard Johnson felt the ground was on soft side of good. The winner is on the upgrade, while the second and third set the level.

4882 TRIFLEX NOVICES' H'CAP HURDLE (9 hdls 2 omitted) 2m 3f 100y
2:40 (2:45) (Class 4) (0-110,110) 4-Y-0+ **£3,573** (£1,049; £524; £262)

Form RPR
6443 **1** **Florrie Boy (IRE)**[128] 2560 5-11-2 105.. JamieBargary(5) 121+
(Nigel Twiston-Davies) *mid-div: clsd 4th: chal 3 out: led next: sn drew clr: in command whn blnd last: easily* **2/1**[1]
052P **2** *15* **Bishops Court**[41] 4099 6-11-11 109.......................................(t[1]) MarkQuinlan 109
(Neil Mulholland) *t.k.h towards rr: hdwy after 6th: rdn 3 out: wnt 2nd on extended run between last 2: no real imp on easy wnr* **14/1**
0254 **3** *6* **Pied Du Roi (IRE)**[20] 4455 6-11-7 108.......................................(p) GrahamWatters(3) 104
(Charlie Longsdon) *chsd ldrs: wnt cl 2nd after 6th: led 3 out to 2 out: wknd and lost 2nd on extended run between last 2* **15/2**[3]
UF45 **4** *2* **Red Red Rover (IRE)**[12] 4614 6-11-7 105.......................................(p) DaveCrosse 100
(Nigel Hawke) *led: rdn and hdd 3 out: 4th and wkng whn mstke next: wnt 4th again nr fin* **25/1**
5-0P **5** *½* **Acadian (FR)**[89] 3256 6-9-8 85.......................................(p) ConorSmith(7) 77
(Nigel Hawke) *hld up: hdwy after 6th: rdn 3 out: wnt mod 4th between last 2 tl nr fin* **15/2**[3]
006P **6** *1 ¾* **Mr Medic**[39] 4137 5-10-13 97.. DarylJacob 88
(Robert Walford) *chsd ldrs: rdn 3 out: grad wknd* **33/1**
-13P **7** *1 ½* **Kleitomachos (IRE)**[69] 3607 8-11-11 109.......................................(b) SeanBowen 98
(Stuart Kittow) *chsd ldr tl lost pl after 5th: sn rdn: no ch fr 3 out: r.o again flat* **14/1**
-413 **8** *16* **Fuse Wire**[275] 828 9-10-8 92.. RobertDunne 67
(Dai Burchell) *hld up: wknd after 3 out* **20/1**
0501 **9** *1 ¼* **Closer To Home (IRE)**[2] 4855 4-10-13 110 7ex.......(b) MichaelHeard(5) 79
(David Pipe) *mid-div but lost grnd w slow jumps: rdn after 6th: no ch fr 3 out* **3/1**[2]
040 **F** **Present Times (IRE)**[51] 3915 5-11-7 105.. PaulMoloney
(Evan Williams) *hld up toward rr: j.rt and fell 4th* **33/1**

4m 47.5s (-14.30) **Going Correction** -0.725s/f (Firm)
WFA 4 from 5yo+ 7lb **10** Ran SP% **109.7**
Speed ratings (Par 105): **103,96,94,93,93 92,91,85,84,**
CSF £23.46 CT £128.41 TOTE £2.90: £1.20, £3.90, £2.00; EX 39.90 Trifecta £160.10.
Owner Options O Syndicate **Bred** Laurence G Kennedy **Trained** Naunton, Gloucs
■ One Cool Scorpion was withdrawn. Price at time of withdrawal 6/1. Rule 4 applies to board prices before the withdrawal but not to SP bets - deduction 10p in the pound.

FOCUS
The far bend was railed out by 6 metres from the inside and the stables bend by 5 metres. The rail movements added approximately 30yds to this advertised race distance. A moderate race. A big step up from the winner, with the second and fourth rated pretty close to their marks.

4883 RECTICEL H'CAP HURDLE (10 hdls 2 omitted) 2m 7f 131y
3:15 (3:17) (Class 4) (0-120,120) 4-Y-0+ **£4,548** (£1,335; £667; £333)

Form RPR
PPP1 **1** **Tara Tavey (IRE)**[7] 4749 11-10-11 112 7ex.......................................(t) ConorSmith(7) 118+
(Kevin Bishop) *chsd ldng pair: rdn along fr 5th: led narrowly bef 3 out: nt fluent last: styd on gamely u.p flat: asserted nr fin* **12/1**
64P3 **2** *1 ½* **Rainbow Haze**[12] 4618 10-9-13 100.. MrTGreatrex(7) 104
(Phillip Dando) *led: j.rt 5th: rdn and hdd bef 3 out: rallied next: ev ch last: kpt on tl no ex nr fin* **12/1**
14S4 **3** *7* **Brod Na Heireann (IRE)**[22] 4438 7-11-9 120.. TomBellamy(3) 118
(Alan King) *hld up in mid-div: clsd 6th: wnt 3rd and rdn 2 out: styd on same pce on extended run between last 2: hld whn nt fluent last* **10/1**
-002 **4** *17* **Set In My Ways (IRE)**[50] 3928 5-11-9 117.. RichardJohnson 100
(Jonjo O'Neill) *hld up in mid-div: mstke 5th: clsd next: outpcd 3 out: no ch after: styd on flat* **11/8**[1]
P-24 **5** *3 ½* **Nightline**[29] 4305 6-11-9 120.......................................(t) GrahamWatters(3) 102
(Charlie Longsdon) *chsd ldr: ev ch 3 out where nt fluent: wknd next* **9/2**[2]
5266 **6** *1 ¼* **Petite Power (IRE)**[41] 4097 7-11-1 116.......................................(p) MrJoshuaNewman(7) 94
(Ali Stronge) *hld up in last trio: rdn and wknd bef 3 out* **33/1**
3562 **7** *32* **Royal Chief (IRE)**[105] 2985 7-10-11 105.......................................(p) RhysFlint 54
(Alexandra Dunn) *hld up in last trio: rdn and wknd bef 3 out: t.o* **20/1**
1P02 **8** *15* **Horsted Valley**[55] 3837 6-11-5 113.......................................(p) GavinSheehan 49
(Warren Greatrex) *racd in 4th sme way off ldng trio: clsd 6th: rdn and wknd bef 3 out: t.o* **5/1**[3]
PPP4 **P** **Far From Defeat (IRE)**[26] 4351 6-11-1 109.. RobertDunne
(Michael Scudamore) *hld up in last trio: rdn and wknd bef 3 out: t.o whn p.u after 2 out* **33/1**

5m 56.2s (-6.00) **Going Correction** -0.725s/f (Firm) **9** Ran SP% **112.1**
Speed ratings (Par 105): **89,88,86,80,79 78,68,63,**
CSF £130.54 CT £1483.80 TOTE £10.90: £3.30, £2.90, £2.80; EX 112.70 Trifecta £1086.70.
Owner K Bishop **Bred** Christopher Maye **Trained** Spaxton, Somerset

FOCUS
The far bend was railed out by 6 metres from the inside and the stables bend by 5 metres. The rail movements added approximately 48yds to this advertised race distance. This modest contest was run at a respectable gallop. The second has been rated to his mark.

4884 ROCKWOOL H'CAP CHASE (18 fncs) 2m 7f 131y
3:50 (3:52) (Class 4) (0-115,113) 5-Y-0+ **£5,198** (£1,526; £763; £381)

Form RPR
353F **1** **Captain Flash (IRE)**[27] 4346 7-10-11 98.......................................(p) JeremiahMcGrath 106+
(Jo Davis) *mde all: mstke 11th: stmbld 5 out: sn rdn: 4 l up last: drvn out to hold on flat* **4/1**[3]
5053 **2** *½* **Mountain Of Mourne (IRE)**[23] 4427 7-11-3 111.. ConorSmith(7) 115
(Linda Blackford) *mainly chsd ldr: rdn fr 5 out: 4 l down last: styd on wl u.p flat* **6/1**
0/0P **3** *8* **Silver Eagle (IRE)**[62] 3727 8-11-4 108.......................................(tp) TomBellamy(3) 106
(Kim Bailey) *disp 2nd tl lost pl 8th: rdn fr 11th: last and outpcd 5 out: rallied and styd on fr 2 out* **9/4**[1]
0132 **4** *3* **Long John**[54] 3867 9-11-7 108.. JamesBest 104
(Jackie Du Plessis) *hld up in last pair: hdwy 5 out: wnt 3rd 3 out: one pce fr next* **3/1**[2]
2P62 **5** *3 ¼* **Saint Breiz (FR)**[21] 4453 10-11-4 105.......................................(t) IanPopham 98
(Carroll Gray) *racd in 4th tl hdwy 8th: rdn bef 5 out: mstke 4 out: grad wknd* **6/1**
45F **6** *67* **Cruchain (IRE)**[19] 4493 13-11-12 113.......................................(p) RobertDunne 79
(Dai Burchell) *hld up in last pair: hdwy 8th: wnt 3rd 5 out: wknd after 3 out: eased bef last: t.o* **16/1**

6m 12.8s (-9.20) **Going Correction** -0.40s/f (Good) **6** Ran SP% **110.2**
Speed ratings: **99,98,96,95,94 71**
CSF £25.62 TOTE £5.20: £2.20, £3.00; EX 22.80 Trifecta £75.00.
Owner John L & Albert L Marriott & Jo Davis **Bred** Allan A Brown **Trained** East Garston, Berks
■ Stewards' Enquiry : Tom Bellamy nine-day ban: used whip above permitted level (Apr 7-15)

FOCUS
The far bend was railed out by 6 metres from the inside and the stables bend by 5 metres. The rail movements added approximately 48yds to this advertised race distance. An ordinary contest. A step up on his hurdle form from the winner, with the second closing in on his best hurdle form.

4885 ICB H'CAP HURDLE (DIV I) (7 hdls 1 omitted) 2m 11y
4:25 (4:25) (Class 5) (0-100,98) 4-Y-0+ **£2,599** (£763; £381; £190)

Form RPR
4P46 **1** **Alottarain (IRE)**[101] 3089 6-11-3 94.. KevinJones(5) 102+
(Seamus Mullins) *hld up in rr: gd hdwy 3 out: wnt 2nd next: led appr last: shkn up and r.o wl flat* **12/1**
P0-4 **2** *3* **Bring Back Charlie**[27] 4343 6-10-2 79.. JamieBargary(5) 81
(Nigel Twiston-Davies) *towards rr: hdwy 3 out: rdn next: wnt 2nd jst after last but hld by wnr* **11/4**[1]
0363 **3** *2* **Brinestine (USA)**[56] 3816 7-11-5 98.......................................(tp) HarrisonBeswick(7) 99
(Emma Baker) *mid-div: hdwy 3 out: sn rdn: styd on same pce: wnt 3rd flat* **8/1**[3]
050 **4** *2* **Social Climber (IRE)**[19] 4490 4-10-9 91.. ConorShoemark(3) 84
(Fergal O'Brien) *prom: led after 1st: rdn 3 out: hdd appr last where hit flight: wknd flat* **14/1**
4431 **5** *1 ½* **Old Magic (IRE)**[8] 4712 11-10-0 79 7ex.......................................(t) MissCVHart(7) 76
(Sophie Leech) *prom: chsd ldr 6th to 2 out: one pce* **11/4**[1]
P3F6 **6** *11* **John Biscuit (IRE)**[22] 4440 8-11-0 86.. GavinSheehan 73
(Jo Davis) *led tl after 1st: styd prom: pushed along 3 out: wknd on extended run between last 2* **13/2**[2]
-3P0 **7** *1 ¾* **Acapulco Bay**[25] 4390 12-10-10 85.......................................(p) RobertWilliams(3) 72
(Dai Burchell) *chsd ldrs tl wknd 2 out* **25/1**
0600 **8** *20* **Padova**[89] 3256 10-11-6 92.. TommyPhelan 60
(Dr Jeremy Naylor) *mid-div: sme hdwy whn nt fluent 3 out: wknd next* **66/1**
F000 **9** *6* **Top Set (IRE)**[89] 3221 6-11-0 91.. DanielHiskett(5) 53
(Richard Phillips) *in tch towards rr: wknd 3 out* **33/1**
P05P **10** *47* **Myroundorus (IRE)**[84] 3382 6-11-8 94.. CharliePoste 14
(Robin Dickin) *t.k.h in rr: mstke 3rd: lost tch bef 3 out: t.o* **14/1**

FUP- **P** **Jawahal Du Mathan (FR)**[533] 1802 8-9-8 **73** ow1..(t) TommyDowling[7]
(Arthur Whitehead) *t.k.h: prom tl rdn and wknd 3 out: wl bhd whn p.u bef last* **10/1**

4m 3.5s (-7.10) **Going Correction** -0.725s/f (Firm)
WFA 4 from 6yo+ 7lb **11** Ran **SP% 116.2**
Speed ratings (Par 103): **88,86,85,84,83 78,77,67,64,40**
CSF £45.07 CT £288.23 TOTE £14.60: £3.70, £1.60, £2.40; EX 54.70 Trifecta £656.20.
Owner S Mullins Racing Club **Bred** J Day **Trained** Wilsford-Cum-Lake, Wilts

FOCUS
The far bend was railed out by 6 metres from the inside and the stables bend by 5 metres. The rail movements added approximately 30yds to this advertised race distance. A competitive race at a moderate level. The winner has been rated back to her best, with the third rated to her latest mark.

4886 ICB H'CAP HURDLE (DIV II) (7 hdls 1 omitted) 2m 11y
5:00 (5:00) (Class 5) (0-100,98) 4-Y-0+ **£2,599** (£763; £381; £190)

Form RPR
5253 **1** **Kayf Charmer**[58] 3789 6-9-13 **78** ow3................................ ConorSmith[7] 89
(Linda Blackford) *chsd ldrs: led after 4th: rdn 2 out: kpt on wl flat* **3/1**[1]
30/1 **2** *7* **Shaddaii (FR)**[28] 4318 10-10-7 **79**..............................(t) SeanBowen 86+
(Robert Walford) *hld up: clsd 4th: rdn 3 out: wnt 3rd next: chsd wnr between last 2: 4 l down whn stmbld on landing last: no ex* **3/1**[1]
0024 **3** *3/4* **Ayla's Emperor**[22] 4435 7-11-5 **94**..............................(p) KillianMoore[3] 97
(John Flint) *mid-div: hdwy 3 out: wnt 3rd bef last: styd on flat* **8/1**[3]
4342 **4** *13* **Aaman (IRE)**[25] 4390 10-10-9 **84**.............................. RobertWilliams[3] 78
(Bernard Llewellyn) *chsd ldrs: outpcd by ldng pair bef 3 out: wknd on extended run between last 2* **7/1**[2]
C-62 **5** *1* **Blue Top**[141] 2264 7-10-10 **82**.............................. RobertDunne 74+
(Dai Burchell) *mainly chsd ldr: rdn 2 out: no ex and lost 2nd bef last: wknd flat* **8/1**[3]
0000 **6** *6* **Brin D'Avoine (FR)**[49] 3955 5-11-8 **94**.............................. MarkQuinlan 79
(Neil Mulholland) *in rr: shkn up and sme hdwy bef 3 out: sn no imp* **14/1**
3400 **7** *6* **Worldor (FR)**[25] 4390 10-11-12 **98**..............................(t) RhysFlint 78
(Alexandra Dunn) *hld up towards rr: no imp fr 3 out* **14/1**
U060 **8** *10* **Saint Elm (FR)**[160] 1957 6-11-6 **92**.............................. DarylJacob 63
(Richard Woollacott) *in tch in mid-div tl wknd bef 3 out* **16/1**
4-0P **9** *49* **Star Benefit (IRE)**[114] 2840 6-10-10 **85**.............................. BenPoste[3] 12
(Adrian Wintle) *prom: outpcd by ldrs fr 4th: wknd 3 out: t.o* **20/1**
400P **10** *3 1/2* **Culm Counsellor**[27] 4343 7-10-4 **79**..............................(p) KieronEdgar[3]
(Chris Down) *led: wandered and reminder after 2nd: rdn and hdd after 4th: wknd qckly bef 3 out: t.o* **20/1**
3P06 **P** **Spurned Girl**[146] 2162 6-9-7 **75** oh3 ow3..............(t) CathalCourtney[10]
(Robin Dickin) *wnt sideways as tapes rose and s.s: hit 1st: a bhd: t.o whn p.u bef 3 out* **33/1**

4m 3.4s (-7.20) **Going Correction** -0.725s/f (Firm) **11** Ran **SP% 116.4**
Speed ratings (Par 103): **89,85,85,78,78 75,72,67,42,40**
CSF £12.02 CT £64.49 TOTE £4.00: £1.50, £1.10, £2.50; EX 8.80 Trifecta £63.10.
Owner Mrs V W Jones **Bred** Brian & Gwen Griffiths **Trained** Rackenford, Devon

FOCUS
The far bend was railed out by 6 metres from the inside and the stables bend by 5 metres. The rail movements added approximately 30yds to this advertised race distance. The going was changed to good, good to soft in places prior to this race. Not many got into this weak race. A small step up from the winner, with the second setting the level.

4887 IKO OPEN HUNTERS' CHASE (18 fncs) 2m 7f 131y
5:30 (5:30) (Class 6) 5-Y-0+ **£1,317** (£405; £202)

Form RPR
-5PU **1** **Pentiffic (NZ)**[11] 4651 12-11-10 119.............................. MissLMTurner[7] 126+
(P P C Turner) *hld up towards rr: hdwy 8th: led 4 out: c clr between last 2: styd on strly* **22/1**
F31- **2** *14* **Vincitore (FR)**[39] 10-12-0 118..............................(p) MissCVHart[3] 113
(Miss C V Hart) *cl up: led 6th to 8th: outpcd in 4th bef 5 out: rallied 2 out: wnt 2nd appr last: no ch w wnr* **7/1**[3]
163F **3** *4* **Royale Django (IRE)**[21] 4451 7-11-10 133.............................. MrEDavid[7] 114+
(Tim Vaughan) *hld up bhd ldrs: clsd 12th: wnt 3rd and rdn 5 out: chsd wnr 3 out where mstke: sn one pce: lost 2nd bef last* **11/8**[1]
/31U **4** *7* **Join Together (IRE)**[18] 11-11-8 134.............................. MissBFrost[5] 101
(Mrs Rose Loxton) *led: mstke 2nd: hdd 6th: lost pl and rdn along 8th: no ch fr 5 out: styd on to go mod 4th nr fin* **7/2**[2]
/33- **5** *2* **Barlow (IRE)**[32] 9-11-8 123.............................. MrJoshuaNewman[5] 100
(Miss Chloe Roddick) *cl up: led 8th: hit 11th: rdn and hdd 4 out: wknd bef 2 out: lost mod 4th nr fin* **14/1**
54 **6** *22* **Cecile De Volanges**[60] 8-10-11 0.............................. MrRobertHawker[5] 67
(Michael Hawker) *in last: wl bhd by 6th: styd on past btn rivals fr 5 out but nvr any ch* **28/1**
50-5 **7** *4 1/2* **Chance Du Roy (FR)**[71] 3585 12-11-2 134.........(p) MissNatalieParker[7] 70
(K J Parker) *a towards rr: wknd bef 5 out* **8/1**
221- **P** **Double Bank (IRE)**[25] 13-11-12 124.............................. MrMWoodward[5]
(Mrs Emma Oliver) *chsd ldrs: rdn 11th: wknd bef 5 out: bhd whn p.u bef 2 out* **9/1**
0F-4 **P** **Wiffy Chatsby (IRE)**[34] 4227 9-11-2 105..............................(t) MrConorOrr[7]
(Dafydd Jones) *a towards rr: rdn and wknd bef 5 out: bhd whn p.u bef 3 out* **50/1**

6m 19.1s (-2.90) **Going Correction** -0.40s/f (Good) **9** Ran **SP% 114.4**
Speed ratings: **88,83,82,79,79 71,70, ,**
CSF £162.39 TOTE £25.50: £5.80, £2.40, £1.02; EX 200.70 Trifecta £1034.40.
Owner Miss L M Turner **Bred** C Devine,L & S Hampton & L Stevenson **Trained** Hoarwithy, H'fords

FOCUS
The far bend was railed out by 6 metres from the inside and the stables bend by 5 metres. The rail movements added approximately 48yds to this advertised race distance. This was run at a decent pace. The winner has been rated back to his best, with the second 8lb off last year's level.
T/Plt: £435.80 to a £1 stake. Pool: £96199.32 - 161.11 winning tickets T/Qpdt: £116.50 to a £1 stake. Pool: £7289.9 - 46.3 winning tickets **Richard Lowther**

4441 LUDLOW (R-H)
Thursday, March 24

OFFICIAL GOING: Good
Wind: light breeze Weather: overcast; 11 degrees

4888 G C RICKARDS NOVICES' HURDLE (9 hdls) 1m 7f 169y
2:30 (2:30) (Class 4) 4-Y-0+ **£4,548** (£1,335; £667; £333)

Form RPR
6 **1** **Rejaah**[148] 2137 4-9-11 0..............................(t) DavidNoonan[5] 102+
(Nigel Hawke) *v small: trckd ldrs in muddling r: nt fluent 2nd: disp 4th home turn: chal and hanging bef last: swtchd lft after last: drvn ahd fnl 120yds: kpt on gamely* **25/1**
P31 **2** *1 1/4* **Beallandendall (IRE)**[21] 4441 8-11-2 133.............................. MrStanSheppard[7] 122+
(Matt Sheppard) *settled cl up: mstke 3rd: disp 4th home turn: swtchd lft after 3 out: drvn to chal and mstke 2 out: led last: hdd and nt qckn fnl 120yds* **6/5**[1]
110 **3** *nse* **Ascotdeux Nellerie (FR)**[117] 2772 6-11-9 0.............................. DavidBass 118
(Kim Bailey) *settled cl up tl rdn and outpcd in 6th home turn: rallied bef last: drvn and styd on wl flat: nrly snatched 2nd* **15/8**[2]
52 **4** *3/4* **Magic Music Man**[41] 2689 5-11-2 0.............................. WayneHutchinson 110
(Alan King) *t.k.h and prom: led bef 3 out: sn wavered rt and drvn: stl gng rt 2 out: ev ch last: nt qckn flat* **6/1**[3]
/1-P **5** *nk* **Score Card (IRE)**[42] 4063 6-11-2 0.............................. RyanMahon 112
(Alastair Ralph) *2nd or 3rd: rdn 3 out: ev ch whn mstke next: kpt on wl flat* **12/1**
65 **6** *15* **Lovely Bubbly**[159] 1968 5-10-11 0..............................(t) AlanJohns[5] 98
(Tim Vaughan) *midfield: outpcd bef 3 out* **66/1**
5216 **7** *7* **Tour De Ville (IRE)**[137] 2375 6-11-2 0..............................(t[1]) ConorO'Farrell 92
(Seamus Durack) *sn detached in last pl: mstke 6th: nvr a factor: blnd 2 out* **12/1**
0650 **8** *4* **Over To Midnight**[21] 4441 6-10-2 0.............................. MissLBrooke[7] 82
(Lady Susan Brooke) *small: t.k.h in rr: mstke 5th: btn bef 3 out but kpt plugging on gamely tl mstke next* **100/1**
9 *25* **Scot Daddy (USA)**[8] 4-10-9 0.............................. SamTwiston-Davies 57
(David Dennis) *tall: taken down early and v free to post: plld hrd: a towards rr: nt a fluent: lost tch bef 3 out: t.o* **33/1**
5 **10** *7* **My Son Max**[43] 2035 8-10-13 0.............................. RobertWilliams[3] 58
(Nikki Evans) *led and sn 7 l clr but setting modest pce: being ct whn blnd 6th: rdn and hdd bef next: sn lost pl: blnd 2 out* **80/1**
P **11** *47* **Inspiring (IRE)**[39] 4137 5-10-9 0.............................. RichieMcLernon 8
(Johnny Farrelly) *midfield: mstke 6th and fdd rapidly: t.o 3 out: sn eased* **100/1**
00 **12** *1 1/2* **Actiondancer (IRE)**[21] 4441 5-11-2 0.............................. JamesDavies 14
(Henry Oliver) *in rr and rdn bef 5th: t.o bef 3 out where mstke: sn eased* **100/1**
5P **F** **Put The Boot In (IRE)**[29] 2439 4-10-2 0.............................. JamieInsole[7] 79
(Barry Brennan) *midfield: pushed along bef 3 out: 15 l 7th whn crashing fall next* **66/1**

3m 45.9s (-3.60) **Going Correction** 0.0s/f (Good)
WFA 4 from 5yo+ 7lb **13** Ran **SP% 123.9**
Speed ratings (Par 105): **105,104,104,103,103 96,92,90,78,74 51,50,**
CSF £154.30 TOTE £48.20: £8.90, £1.10, £1.10; EX 154.30 Trifecta £399.20.
Owner Mrs K Hawke & W Simms **Bred** Rabbah Bloodstock Limited **Trained** Stoodleigh, Devon

FOCUS
Some starts have been moved at this track following remeasuring, so some races will not have speed figures until there is sufficient data to calculate updated median times. The distance of this race was increased by 28yds. David Noonan said of the ground: "it's good but on the quicker side in a few places." A pretty ordinary novice and there was a surprise winner, with the finish quite a messy one. There's a case for rating the race a bit higher through the second and third, but the fourth and fifth are probably better guides.

4889 ALFA AGGREGATES PRODUCTS NOVICES' LIMITED H'CAP CHASE (12 fncs) 1m 7f 212y
3:05 (3:05) (Class 4) (0-120,120) 5-Y-0+ **£7,988** (£2,480; £1,335)

Form RPR
1112 **1** **Ashcott Boy**[17] 4533 8-11-3 **120**.............................. DavidNoonan[5] 128
(Neil Mulholland) *tended to jump lft: pckd 1st: chsd ldrs: pushed along 6th: outpcd in 4th bef 10th: drvn and rallied 3 out: 2 l 2nd whn lft in ld next: sn clr: wnt sltly lft last: idling flat and pushed out* **7/1**[3]
4640 **2** *9* **Discay**[21] 4447 7-11-3 **115**..............................(p) JoshuaMoore 115
(Dr Richard Newland) *mounted on crse: t.k.h: 2nd whn mstke 5th (water): mstke next: rdn 10th: outpcd 3 out: drvn into modest 2nd cl home* **9/2**[2]
361F **3** *1/2* **Storming Strumpet**[30] 4292 6-11-0 **112**.............................. PaddyBrennan 111
(Tom George) *hld up trcking ldrs: hit 7th: 3rd and pushed along bef 10th: no imp whn lft 2nd 2 out: wl hld after and looking tired: lost 2nd cl home* **9/2**[2]
-42P **P** **Old Pride (IRE)**[83] 3420 8-10-12 **110**.............................. SamTwiston-Davies
(David Loder) *led tl wnt wrong after 1st: p.u* **5/2**[1]
42PP **U** **Bobble Boru (IRE)**[22] 4432 8-10-3 **101**..............................(p) LiamTreadwell
(Venetia Williams) *bhd: struggling 1/2-way: 10 l last whn hit 3 out and uns rdr* **8/1**
0-P2 **F** **Oficial Ben (IRE)**[87] 3311 7-10-1 **106**..............................(t) PatrickCowley[7] 117
(Jonjo O'Neill) *lft in ld after 1st: stl 2 l in front and probably gng best whn fell 2 out* **9/2**[2]
456P **P** **Take A Break (FR)**[19] 4487 5-11-6 **118**..............................(vt[1]) ConorO'Farrell
(Nigel Hawke) *chsd ldrs: dropped to rr and mstke 6th: t.o and p.u 9th* **14/1**

4m 1.4s (2.90) **Going Correction** +0.05s/f (Yiel) **7** Ran **SP% 113.4**
Speed ratings: **94,89,89, ,**
CSF £37.68 CT £156.98 TOTE £6.30: £3.20, £5.50; EX 38.00 Trifecta £159.90.
Owner John Hobbs **Bred** Mrs J A Gawthorpe **Trained** Limpley Stoke, Wilts

FOCUS
The distance of this race was increased by 56yds. Half of the eight runners failed to complete in what was a modest but eventful chase.

4890 LUDLOW FOOD CENTRE MARES' H'CAP HURDLE (9 hdls) 1m 7f 169y
3:40 (3:40) (Class 3) (0-135,120) 4-Y-0+ **£6,498** (£1,908; £954; £477)

Form RPR
5413 **1** **Midtech Valentine**[5] 4799 5-10-5 **98**.............................. TomO'Brien 100
(Ian Williams) *cl 2nd in slow r: jnd ldr 5th: nt fluent next: led narrowly bef 3 out: rdn and clipped next: hld on wl flat* **11/8**[1]

-113 **2** ½ **Unbuckled (IRE)**[76] 3506 6-11-3 **110**........................ TrevorWhelan 112+
(Neil King) *cl bhd ldng pair tl rdn and sltly outpcd 2 out: disp 2 l 3rd and hit last: hrd drvn and styd on best flat but jst hld* **11/4**[2]

2-2P **3** ½ **Avispa**[139] 2314 7-11-12 **119**........................ WayneHutchinson 120
(Alan King) *cl bhd ldng pair tl effrt to chal 3 out: clipped next: stl ev ch last: kpt on same pl and lost 2nd fnl 100yds* **7/2**[3]

316 **4** 2¾ **Grimley Girl**[21] 4443 10-10-8 **106**........................ JackSherwood[(5)] 105
(Henry Oliver) *led at slow pce: jnd 5th: rdn and hdd bef 3 out: remained cl up tl no ex fr last* **8/1**

14P3 **5** 16 **Shanandoa**[22] 4435 5-10-5 **103**........................ DavidNoonan[(5)] 90
(Brian Barr) *nt fluent but on heels of ldrs tl rdn bef 3 out: sn btn* **8/1**

3m 49.1s (-0.40) **Going Correction** 0.0s/f (Good) **5** Ran SP% **113.2**
Speed ratings (Par 107): **97,96,96,95,87**
CSF £5.94 TOTE £2.10: £1.40, £1.60; EX 5.10 Trifecta £9.80.

Owner Midtech **Bred** I P Williams **Trained** Portway, Worcs

FOCUS
The distance of this was increased by 28yds. Modest form, with them going no gallop, and it developed into a bit of a dash. The winner has been rated similar to her Warwick win allowing for the jockey's claim. The third has been rated to her mark.

4891 BROMFIELD SAND & GRAVEL H'CAP CHASE (11 fncs 1 omitted) 1m 7f 212y
4:15 (4:15) (Class 3) (0-140,139) 5-Y-0+ **£12,996** (£3,816; £1,908; £954)

Form RPR

2P06 **1** **Noche De Reyes (FR)**[20] 4464 7-10-4 **117**........................ PaddyBrennan 126
(Tom George) *2nd or 3rd: pushed along bef 3 out (normal 10th): led 3 out: jnd next: tk slt ld sn after last: drvn and battled on gamely: all out* **9/2**[3]

F4-P **2** ½ **Fayette County (IRE)**[75] 3521 9-11-2 **129**........................ TomO'Brien 139+
(Tim Vaughan) *settled towards rr: rdn and outpcd in 8 l 5th after 8th: rallied bef 2 out: 2 l 3rd at last: drvn and styd on stoutly but jst hld* **7/1**

0213 **3** ½ **Cloonacool (IRE)**[26] 4359 7-11-12 **139**........................ JoshuaMoore 147
(Stuart Edmunds) *trckd ldrs: effrt 3 out (normal 10th): rdn and w wnr 2 out tl last: outbattled flat* **5/2**[1]

2345 **4** 14 **Artifice Sivola (FR)**[20] 4464 6-10-13 **126**........................ HarrySkelton 123
(Lucy Wadham) *racd freely and led at brisk pce: pushed along bef 3 out (normal 10th) where hdd: fdd tamely next* **9/2**[3]

1101 **5** 17 **Presenting Arms (IRE)**[20] 4458 9-11-9 **136**........................(t) NoelFehily 132+
(Harry Fry) *2nd or 3rd and ev ch tl nrly uns rdr 3 out (normal 10th) and lost all ch* **11/4**[2]

4003 **6** 25 **Zarzal (IRE)**[12] 4617 8-11-9 **136**........................ AdamWedge 94
(Evan Williams) *last after demolishing 2nd fence: nt fluent 5th (water): nt travelling after: lost tch 7th: t.o next* **8/1**

10FP **R** **Arkaim**[87] 3318 8-11-3 **135**........................[1] ThomasCheesman[(5)]
(Olly Williams) *mulish s and ref to r* **25/1**

3m 57.0s (-1.50) **Going Correction** +0.05s/f (Yiel) **7** Ran SP% **119.1**
Speed ratings: **105,104,104,97,89 76,**
CSF £36.24 CT £96.83 TOTE £6.40: £2.40, £4.00; EX 35.40 Trifecta £124.70.

Owner David Rea & Express Contract Drying Ltd **Bred** Dr Vet R Y Simon & N Simon **Trained** Slad, Gloucs

FOCUS
The distance of this was increased by 56yds. Run at a decent clip, three came clear in what was a fair chase. The open ditch in the home straight (usual three out) had to be bypassed on the final circuit. The first three have been rated pretty much to their marks in a straightforward handicap.

4892 ABBERLEY HALL OLD PUPILS ASSOCIATION OPEN HUNTERS' CHASE (FOR THE LUDLOW GOLD CUP) (17 fncs 2 omitted) 2m 7f 171y
4:50 (4:50) (Class 5) 5-Y-0+ **£3,119** (£967; £483; £242)

Form RPR

0530 **1** **On The Bridge (IRE)**[153] 2054 11-11-4 132........................(tp) MissVWade[(7)] 140+
(Jeremy Scott) *blnd 1st: wl in rr tl gd prog after 6th: tk cl 2nd gng wl 14th: led bef 2 out and mstke: 5 l ahd whn j.rt last: rdn and easily drew clr* **4/1**[2]

3U11 **2** 13 **Pearlysteps**[7] 4748 13-12-2 132........................ MissJCWilliams[(3)] 136+
(Henry Daly) *nt fluent 8th: led or contested ld tl led 12th: mstke 14th and pushed along: rdn and hdd bef 2 out: rdn and readily outpcd fr last* **6/4**[1]

P4-0 **3** nk **Hazy Tom (IRE)**[116] 10-11-4 124........................ MrAWright[(7)] 127
(Gareth Thomas) *chsd ldrs: wnt 2nd at 10th: rdn and outpcd in 6 l 3rd after 14th: n.d after but drvn and jst failed to snatch mod 2nd* **16/1**

/6-3 **4** 54 **Grandioso (IRE)**[21] 4446 9-11-8 135........................(t) MrStanSheppard[(3)] 88
(Steve Flook) *bhd: already detached in rr gp after 6th: 20 l 4th after 14th: plugged on but t.o next* **7/1**

60-4 **5** 17 **Shoreacres (IRE)**[21] 4446 13-11-10 114........................ MissHLewis[(5)] 65
(Mrs Gillian Jones) *impeded 1st: a in detached rr gp: blnd 7th: t.o fr 10th* **5/1**[3]

0-2U **6** 3½ **Good Egg (IRE)**[25] 4383 13-11-4 106........................ MrSDavies-Thomas[(7)] 58
(Miss Sarah Rippon) *j. poorly: sn labouring in rr: t.o last at 10th but plodded on* **25/1**

-41F **P** **Night Alliance (IRE)**[23] 4424 11-11-8 119........................(bt) MrJoeHill[(7)]
(P R M Philips) *midfield: rdn and outpcd 10th: t.o 12th: p.u 2 out* **25/1**

3U-P **P** **No Loose Change (IRE)**[46] 4016 11-11-10 119....(t) MrDavidMaxwell[(5)]
(Mrs Kim Smyly) *w ldr tl 12th: downed tools and lost pl rapidly: t.o and p.u after 14th* **14/1**

4-40 **P** **Ballyallia Man (IRE)**[11] 4651 11-11-8 122........................(tp) MrEdBailey[(7)]
(Mrs N Sheppard) *cl up tl lost pl rapidly 4th: nt keen: blnd 6th: t.o 11th: p.u 3 out: lame* **50/1**

2-1 **P** **Sam Cavallaro (IRE)**[330] 12 10-11-12 115........................ MrJarrett[(3)]
(Miss H Brookshaw) *nt fluent 3rd: detached in rr gp: struggling 10th: t.o 12th: p.u 3 out* **16/1**

0-2P **P** **Gentle Duke**[7] 4748 9-11-4 107........................ MrJSmith-Maxwell[(7)]
(Miss L Wallace) *chsd ldrs tl rdn 10th: sn struggling: mstke 12th: continued t.o: p.u bef last* **50/1**

5m 58.4s (358.40) **11** Ran SP% **119.2**
CSF £10.74 TOTE £4.40: £1.80, £1.30, £4.50; EX 13.60 Trifecta £61.30.

Owner Kit James **Bred** J & D Melody **Trained** Brompton Regis, Somerset

■ Stewards' Enquiry : Mr Ed Bailey seven-day ban: failed to dismount when gelding went lame (tbn)

FOCUS
The distance of this race was increased by 48yds. Not a bad hunter chase, run at a sound gallop. The open ditch in the straight (usual three out) was omitted. The second and third have been rated to their marks.

4893 EFG HARRIS ALLDAY STOCKBROKERS MARES' NOVICES' HURDLE (11 hdls) 2m 5f 55y
5:20 (5:23) (Class 4) 4-Y-0+ **£4,548** (£1,335; £667; £333)

Form RPR

0-04 **1** **Morning Herald**[99] 3110 5-10-12 0........................ AndrewTinkler 113+
(Martin Keighley) *t.k.h in 2nd: led bef 3 out: clattered 3 out and next: 13 l ahd whn flattened last: unchal* **15/8**[1]

-2PP **2** 15 **Just A Feeling**[84] 3386 6-11-0 0 ow2........................ TomO'Brien 97
(Paul Webber) *chsd ldrs: rdn and outpcd after 8th: rallied in 5th bef last: styd on to go 2nd flat but nvr nr wnr* **25/1**

2030 **3** 1¾ **Handpicked**[28] 4317 5-10-12 0........................ JakeGreenall 94
(Henry Daly) *prom: shkn up after 8th: lost tch wnr after mstke next: plugged on same pce* **14/1**

44U1 **4** 3¼ **Mo Chailin (IRE)**[15] 4555 5-11-5 0........................ SamTwiston-Davies 99
(Donald McCain) *led at stdy pce: rdn and hdd bef 3 out: grad wknd: lost 3rd after last* **5/2**[2]

-0P0 **5** 1 **Oskar's Eva (IRE)**[75] 3516 6-10-7 0........................ AlanJohns[(5)] 90
(Tim Vaughan) *bhd: rdn and effrt 3 out: mstke next: nvr rchd ldrs* **40/1**

-45P **6** ½ **Lady Persephone (FR)**[49] 3947 5-10-12 0........................ DenisO'Regan 89
(Alan King) *chsd ldrs: effrt 8th: 3rd and drvn home turn: sn btn* **5/1**[3]

546 **7** 4 **Keep Up Keira (IRE)**[22] 4435 5-10-12 0........................ NoelFehily 86
(Neil Mulholland) *bhd: struggling wl bef 3 out* **16/1**

4P **8** 39 **Baby Bee Jay**[98] 3119 5-10-9 0........................ RyanHatch[(3)] 50
(Nigel Twiston-Davies) *towards rr: rdn and struggling after mstke 8th: t.o and eased next* **5/1**[3]

0-P0 **P** **Velvet Edge**[133] 2452 7-10-7 0........................ JakeHodson[(5)]
(Anthony Day) *mstke 2nd: t.k.h: cl up tl slowed v rapidly after 8th: t.o and p.u next* **100/1**

4 **P** **Chasing Fairies**[35] 4201 5-10-12 0........................ AdamWedge
(Alexandra Dunn) *small light-framed: blnd 1st: t.k.h and j. modly in rr: lost tch 6th: t.o 8th: p.u next* **66/1**

5m 16.1s (1.30) **Going Correction** 0.0s/f (Good) **10** Ran SP% **118.0**
Speed ratings (Par 105): **97,91,90,89,89 88,87,72, ,**
CSF £49.33 TOTE £3.10: £1.30, £4.80, £3.30; EX 59.20 Trifecta £660.80.

Owner Mrs Charles Lloyd-Baker **Bred** C G M Lloyd-Baker **Trained** Condicote, Gloucs

■ Stewards' Enquiry : Tom O'Brien three-day ban: weighed-in 2lb heavy (Apr 7-9)

FOCUS
The distance of this was increased by 56yds. An ordinary mares' hurdle that produced a clear-cut winner. They went very steady early. A big step up from the winner, with the second improving to her bumper mark.

4894 SOUTH SHROPSHIRE HUNT STANDARD OPEN NATIONAL HUNT FLAT RACE 1m 7f 169y
5:50 (5:50) (Class 4) 4-6-Y-O **£3,898** (£1,144; £572; £286)

Form RPR

2 **1** **Ridgeway Flyer**[41] 4102 5-11-0 0........................ NoelFehily 111+
(Harry Fry) *small: wore earplugs: mde all: rdn over 2f out: kpt on gamely and a looked like holding on after* **15/8**[1]

2 1¾ **Bandsman** 5-11-0 0........................ HarrySkelton 110+
(Dan Skelton) *gd-bodied: effrt 3f out: rn green and swvd rt wl over 1f out: rdn and styd on strly to chse wnr fnl f: a jst hld: promising* **20/1**

3 8 **New Member (IRE)** 5-11-0 0........................ NicodeBoinville 102
(Nicky Henderson) *workmanlike: cl up: rdn over 2f out: one pce and hld over 1f out* **5/1**[3]

41 **4** ½ **Blu Cavalier**[133] 2460 6-11-7 0........................ ConorO'Farrell 110+
(Alexandra Dunn) *bhd: outpcd 6f out: hdwy 3f out and chsd ldrs briefly: nt given hrd time after being sltly impeded wl over 1f out* **4/1**[2]

5 6 **Lieutenant Gruber (IRE)** 5-11-0 0........................ JakeGreenall 96
(Henry Daly) *tall: plld hrd: pressed ldrs tl rdn and btn over 2f out* **25/1**

6 ½ **Tinted Rose** 4-10-0 0........................ RichieMcLernon 85+
(Charlie Longsdon) *chsd ldrs: effrt over 3f out: hmpd and stmbld bdly wl over 1f out: sn rdn and btn* **14/1**

24 **7** 2¾ **Ballyhill (FR)**[128] 2562 5-11-0 0........................ SamTwiston-Davies 93
(Nigel Twiston-Davies) *midfield: rdn 3f out: n.d after* **13/2**

24 **8** ¾ **Canton Prince (IRE)**[75] 3522 5-10-9 0........................ AlanJohns[(5)] 93
(Tim Vaughan) *a bhd: no ch fnl 4f* **28/1**

9 ½ **Braqueur D'Or (FR)** 5-11-0 0........................ PaddyBrennan 92
(Rebecca Curtis) *midfield: rdn fr 1/2-way: btn 3f out* **14/1**

10 1½ **Eloped** 5-10-7 0........................ DavidBass 84
(Ben Pauling) *str: prom: rdn 6f out: wknd 4f out* **20/1**

11 25 **Pray For A Rainbow**[312] 5-11-0 0........................ AdamWedge 68
(Evan Williams) *prom tl rdn and fdd over 3f out: t.o* **20/1**

12 5 **Glenlyon** 4-10-7 0........................ TomO'Brien 57
(Paul Webber) *chsd ldrs: rdn 6f out: sn btn: t.o* **22/1**

0 **13** 2½ **He Likes Tobougie**[29] 4308 5-11-0 0........................ TrevorWhelan 62
(Neil King) *nvr bttr than midfield: t.o* **100/1**

14 3¼ **Sidsteel (IRE)** 5-11-0 0........................ LiamHeard 59
(John Groucott) *small: bhd: struggling 6f out: t.o fnl 3f* **80/1**

3m 38.3s (-5.60) **Going Correction** 0.0s/f (Good)
WFA 4 from 5yo+ 7lb **14** Ran SP% **126.3**
Speed ratings: **110,109,105,104,101 101,100,99,99,98 86,83,82,81**
CSF £50.97 TOTE £2.70: £1.20, £7.70, £2.60; EX 40.90 Trifecta £177.50.

Owner A J Norman **Bred** Mrs Audrey Goodwin **Trained** Seaborough, Dorset

FOCUS
The distance of this was increased by 28yds. Not a bad little bumper, it should produce winners. The winner, fourth and eighth set the level.

T/Plt: £103.60 to a £1 stake. Pool of £78021.79 - 549.62 winning tickets. T/Qpdt: £27.90 to a £1 stake. Pool of £6825.60 - 180.50 winning tickets. **Iain Mackenzie**

4895 - 4901a (Foreign Racing) - See Raceform Interactive

4815

CARLISLE (R-H)

Saturday, March 26

OFFICIAL GOING: Good (good to firm in places in last 1m on chase course (chs 8.2, hdl 7.5)

Wind: Light, half against Weather: Overcast

4902 TOTESCOOP6 THE MILLIONAIRE MAKER "NATIONAL HUNT" NOVICES' HURDLE (11 hdls) 2m 3f 61y

1:45 (1:45) (Class 4) 4-Y-0+ **£3,249** (£954; £477; £238)

Form RPR

1251 **1** **Baby Bach (IRE)**[16] 4567 6-11-13 132 AELynch 127+
(S R B Crawford, Ire) *trckd ldrs: mstke 5th: hdwy to chse ldr whn nt fluent 2 out: rallied and led appr last: edgd rt run-in: drvn out* **1/4**[1]

2 ½ **Jovial Joey (IRE)**[174] 5-10-10 0 DaraghBourke(5) 112+
(Maurice Barnes) *cl up: led bef 3rd: hit 4 out: rdn along 2 out: hdd last: rallied: hld nr fin* **25/1**

0043 **3** 11 **Kara Tara**[55] 3888 6-10-3 103 (p) JamieHamilton(5) 94
(Lawrence Mullaney) *hld up: rdn and effrt after 3 out: outpcd next: plugged on fr last: no ch w first two* **5/1**[2]

36 **4** ½ **Ballinvegga (IRE)**[156] 2031 6-10-12 0 TonyKelly(3) 101
(Jackie Stephen) *led to bef 3rd: chsd ldr to bef 2 out: sn rdn: outpcd between last 2* **33/1**

F3 **5** 3¼ **Wazowski**[16] 4567 7-11-1 0 AdrianLane 98
(Donald McCain) *hld up in tch: stdy hdwy bef 6th: effrt and ev ch briefly bef 2 out: wknd bef last* **16/1**

U03 **6** nse **Dubai Shen (IRE)**[38] 4181 5-10-12 0 KieronEdgar(3) 101+
(Alistair Whillans) *nt fluent in rr: struggling bef 4 out: nvr on terms* **14/1**[3]

3-PP **7** 18 **The Conn (IRE)**[64] 3724 6-11-1 0 (b[1]) BrianHarding 82
(Chris Grant) *hld up in tch: stdy hdwy 1/2-way: rdn and wknd bef 2 out* **66/1**

4m 50.1s (-18.70) **Going Correction** -0.75s/f (Firm) 7 Ran SP% **117.5**
Speed ratings (Par 105): **109,108,104,103,102 102,94**
CSF £11.52 TOTE £1.20: £1.10, £8.50; EX 13.40 Trifecta £31.20.
Owner Pircan Partnership **Bred** Miss Ann Twomey **Trained** Larne, Co Antrim

FOCUS

The ground had dried out especially in the home straight on the chase course but it started raining about half an hour before racing. Race distance increased by 19yds. A weak novices' hurdle but the long odds-on favourite had to work hard. There's a case for rating the race a few pounds higher through the winner, third and fifth, but the fourth and sixth might be a better guide.

4903 TOTEPOOLLIVEINFO.COM H'CAP CHASE (19 fncs) 3m 2f 34y

2:20 (2:20) (Class 4) (0-105,101) 5-Y-0+ **£3,898** (£1,144; £572; £286)

Form RPR

2222 **1** **Basford Ben**[15] 4591 8-11-11 100 (b) SeanQuinlan 111
(Jennie Candlish) *mde virtually all: rdn fr 3 out: hrd pressed after last: styd on gamely cl home* **7/2**[1]

0043 **2** nk **Mo Rouge (IRE)**[141] 2327 8-11-4 96 (p) TonyKelly(3) 107
(Jackie Stephen) *hld up in tch: drvn and outpcd after 5 out: rallied bef 2 out: wnt 2nd last: drvn and disp ld last 100yds: kpt on: jst hld* **9/2**[2]

3304 **3** 11 **Solway Sam**[45] 4051 13-9-13 79 CallumBewley(5) 82
(Lisa Harrison) *hld up: hdwy to press ldr after 5 out: ev ch bef next: rdn whn mstke 2 out: edgd rt and outpcd after last* **13/2**

066U **4** 4½ **Red Piano**[9] 4738 7-10-1 83 MissRMcDonald(7) 79
(Andrew Hamilton) *hld up: stdy hdwy and prom 1/2-way: rdn and outpcd 4 out: rallied 2 out: kpt on fr last: no imp* **14/1**

6431 **5** 2 **Foot The Bill**[19] 4534 11-11-0 92 JohnKington(3) 90
(Patrick Holmes) *hld up in tch: hit and outpcd 12th: mstke and struggling 14th: rallied 2 out: sn no imp* **13/2**

242P **6** 1¼ **Kalastar (IRE)**[67] 3671 7-10-5 87 (b) MrTHamilton(7) 80
(Katie Scott) *chsd ldrs: rdn along 5 out: rallied: wknd fr last* **5/1**[3]

P-50 **7** 6 **Blueside Boy (IRE)**[39] 4163 8-9-11 79 ThomasDowson(7) 68
(Harriet Graham) *hld up in tch: rdn along bef 5 out: rallied: wknd bef 2 out* **10/1**

2-2P **8** 7 **Viking Rebel (IRE)**[26] 4407 14-10-7 89 (p) MrWHRReed(7) 72
(W T Reed) *mostly chsd wnr to 5 out: drvn and outpcd bef 3 out: wknd next* **14/1**

6P64 **9** 27 **Mia Matriarch**[20] 4514 10-9-8 76 oh9 ow1 (t) SamColtherd(7) 48
(Stuart Coltherd) *hld up: smooth hdwy to trck ldrs befroe 4 out: rdn and wknd 2 out: btn whn blnd last* **12/1**

P0P0 **P** **Tears From Heaven (USA)**[38] 4175 10-9-9 75 oh17(v[1]) JamieHamilton(5)
(Chris Grant) *chsd ldrs: lost pl 6th: struggling fnl circ: t.o whn p.u 4 out* **33/1**

6m 43.7s (-23.50) **Going Correction** -1.00s/f (Hard) 10 Ran SP% **116.8**
Speed ratings: **96,95,92,91,90 90,88,86,77,**
CSF £20.36 CT £98.28 TOTE £3.80: £1.80, £2.10, £2.10; EX 22.00 Trifecta £92.00.
Owner Alan Baxter **Bred** Carmel Stud **Trained** Basford Green, Staffs

FOCUS

Race distance increased by 30yds. A modest stayers' handicap chase run at a sound pace thanks to the winner. Runner-up on his four most recent starts, the course specialist battled back bravely. The winner has been rated close to last season's C&D best, with the third close to his mark and the fourth in line with his hurdle rating.

4904 TOTEQUADPOT MARES' H'CAP HURDLE (10 hdls) 2m 1f

2:55 (2:55) (Class 4) (0-105,105) 4-Y-0+ **£3,249** (£954; £477; £238)

Form RPR

4P34 **1** **Our Kylie (IRE)**[44] 4068 4-10-5 96 MeganCarberry(5) 95+
(Brian Ellison) *hld up: pushed along and hdwy after 3 out: led between last 2: sn rdn and edgd rt: kpt on wl run-in* **5/1**[3]

3035 **2** 4½ **My Escapade (IRE)**[123] 2706 5-10-10 96 MissAWaugh(7) 98+
(Simon Waugh) *led at decent gallop: rdn and hdd between last 2: rallied: edgd lft and outpcd run-in* **12/1**

-553 **3** 11 **Appletree Lane**[60] 3785 6-10-13 99 MrShaneQuinlan(7) 91
(Tom Gretton) *chsd clr ldng pair: effrt and rdn bef 2 out: sn outpcd: plugged on fr last: no ch w first two* **16/1**

6005 **4** 1½ **Miss Mackie (IRE)**[47] 4036 5-10-6 90 StephenMulqueen(5) 83
(R Mike Smith) *nt fluent on occasions: in tch: smooth hdwy and cl up bef 2 out: sn rdn: 3rd and outpcd whn nt fluent last: sn btn* **16/1**

6556 **5** 2¾ **Dalby Spook (IRE)**[20] 4513 6-9-11 79 oh2 EmmaSayer(3) 67
(Dianne Sayer) *hld up: pushed along and outpcd after 4 out: kpt on fr 2 out: nvr able to chal* **9/1**

-462 **6** 2¼ **Verona Opera (IRE)**[15] 4585 5-10-13 99 AdamShort(7) 86
(S R B Crawford, Ire) *hld up: rdn and outpcd bef 3 out: sme hdwy next: nvr on terms* **3/1**[1]

3000 **7** 2½ **Sultana Belle (IRE)**[15] 4581 8-11-1 97 AdamNicol(3) 81
(R Mike Smith) *hld up in midfield: drvn and outpcd bef 4 out: n.d after* **22/1**

60P6 **8** 1¼ **Norfolk Sound**[26] 4404 5-9-10 82 (t) SamColtherd(7) 66
(Stuart Coltherd) *hld up: pushed along and shortlived effrt after 3 out: btn next* **12/1**

6464 **9** 6 **Morning With Ivan (IRE)**[9] 4736 6-10-6 85 (v) BrianHarding 62
(Martin Todhunter) *pressed ldr and clr of rest: rdn after 3 out: wknd fr next* **12/1**

032 **10** 60 **Wicked Games (IRE)**[33] 4284 5-11-5 105 LorcanMurtagh(7) 28
(Rose Dobbin) *chsd clr ldng trio: rdn after 3 out: wknd bef next* **9/2**[2]

43P0 **11** 1½ **Definitely Glad (IRE)**[47] 4036 9-10-9 95 (t) JamesCorbett(7) 17
(Susan Corbett) *hld up in midfield: drvn along and effrt after 3 out: wknd fr next* **25/1**

44PP **P** **Kashstaree**[18] 4547 5-9-10 80 CallumBewley(5)
(Lisa Harrison) *hld up: struggling bef 4 out: nvr on terms: no ch whn p.u after 2 out* **16/1**

4m 12.1s (-17.10) **Going Correction** -0.75s/f (Firm)
WFA 4 from 5yo+ 7lb 12 Ran SP% **118.8**
Speed ratings (Par 105): **110,107,102,102,100 99,98,97,95,66 66,**
CSF £63.55 CT £902.50 TOTE £5.00: £1.60, £2.90, £4.30; EX 80.20 Trifecta £537.90 Part won..
Owner Morecool & Cool Racing **Bred** Lynn Lodge Stud **Trained** Norton, N Yorks

FOCUS

Race distance increased by 17yds. A strongly run mares' handicap hurdle. The two clear-cut leaders took each other on and the runner-up deserves credit. A step up from the winner, while the second, third and fourth help set the level.

4905 TOTESCOOP6 NOVICES' CHASE (16 fncs) 2m 4f

3:30 (3:30) (Class 3) 5-Y-0+ **£6,498** (£1,908; £954; £477)

Form RPR

-335 **1** **Blakemount (IRE)**[28] 4370 8-10-12 128 SeanQuinlan 140+
(Sue Smith) *mde all: pushed along bef 3 out: styd on strly fr next* **13/8**[1]

32PP **2** 2½ **Run Ructions Run (IRE)**[7] 4800 7-10-11 130 (b[1]) BrianHarding 133
(Tim Easterby) *nt fluent on occasions: chsd ldrs: hit and outpcd 8th: rallied 3 out: chsd (clr) wnr run-in: no imp* **9/4**[2]

-126 **3** 3¾ **Top Billing**[35] 4246 7-10-7 130 RyanDay(5) 130
(Nicky Richards) *chsd wnr: rdn along after 3 out: one pce fr next: hld whn lost 2nd run-in* **10/3**[3]

F212 **4** 21 **Captain Hox (IRE)**[6] 4816 7-11-4 125 (t) AELynch 122
(Patrick Griffin, Ire) *hld up in tch: stdy hdwy bef 4 out: disp 2nd pl next: rdn and hung rt whn hit 2 out: sn btn* **9/2**

-0FF **5** 76 **Simply Lucky (IRE)**[16] 4569 7-10-12 61 AndrewThornton 42
(W T Reed) *bhd and sn detached: struggling on fnl circ: t.o* **200/1**

5m 4.8s (-22.60) **Going Correction** -1.00s/f (Hard) 5 Ran SP% **110.6**
Speed ratings: **105,104,102,94,63**
CSF £5.93 TOTE £2.20: £1.30, £1.70; EX 6.90 Trifecta £14.40.
Owner Mrs Jacqueline Conroy **Bred** T Horgan **Trained** High Eldwick, W Yorks

FOCUS

Race distance increased by 20yds. A fair novices' chase run at a sound pace thanks to the winner. The winner is better than the bare result and has been rated in line with the best of his hurdle figures. The second has been rated 6lb off, with the third in line with his hurdle form.

4906 TOTEEXACTA H'CAP HURDLE (14 hdls) 3m 1f

4:05 (4:05) (Class 3) (0-125,122) 4-Y-0+ **£5,848** (£1,717; £858; £429)

Form RPR

4214 **1** **Takingrisks (IRE)**[26] 4405 7-11-12 122 BrianHarding 125+
(Nicky Richards) *hld up: smooth hdwy and ev ch bef 2 out: sn pressing ldr: jst over 1 l down and styng on whn lft 2 l clr last: edgd rt: styd on strly* **5/1**

0311 **2** 5 **Wintered Well (IRE)**[21] 4474 8-11-7 117 SeanQuinlan 119+
(Jennie Candlish) *hld up: stdy hdwy bef 8th: hit and rdn next: rallied bef 2 out: 3rd and one pce whn lft 2 l 2nd last: sn outpcd* **9/2**[3]

3515 **3** 7 **Quinto**[44] 4066 6-11-6 116 TrevorWhelan 111
(John Quinn) *in tch: effrt and rdn bef 4 out: one pce whn lft 3 l 3rd last: sn wknd* **7/2**[1]

4/22 **4** 21 **Charlie Wingnut (IRE)**[30] 4328 9-9-6 98 StephenMcCarthy(10) 73
(Sue Smith) *cl up: rdn and ev ch bef 2 out: outpcd after 2 out: btn whn lft modest 4th and hit last* **9/2**[3]

0P30 **5** 4 **Bop Along (IRE)**[13] 4638 9-10-10 109 (p) AdamNicol(3) 79
(Alistair Whillans) *led to 4th: nt fluent next: cl up tl outpcd 8th: n.d after* **14/1**

1446 **6** 1 **West Of The Edge (IRE)**[15] 4593 8-10-6 107 (v) ThomasCheesman(5) 78
(Dai Williams) *t.k.h: prom: hdwy to ld 8th: hdd 3 out: rallied: wknd fr next* **25/1**

PP00 **P** **Wolf Shield (IRE)**[57] 3837 9-10-11 110 (t) JohnKington(3)
(Patrick Holmes) *cl up: led 4th to 8th: struggling next: lost tch and p.u bef 2 out* **7/1**

-221 **F** **Sevenballs Of Fire (IRE)**[15] 4586 7-11-3 120 MrRyanNichol(7) 123+
(Iain Jardine) *hld up bhd ldng gp: hdwy to dispute ld after 8th: led 3 out: shkn up and jst over 1 l in front whn fell last* **4/1**[2]

6m 17.9s (-21.10) **Going Correction** -0.75s/f (Firm) 8 Ran SP% **118.3**
Speed ratings (Par 107): **103,101,99,92,91 90, ,**
CSF £29.07 CT £89.96 TOTE £5.90: £2.00, £1.70, £1.60; EX 30.40 Trifecta £133.40.
Owner Frank Bird **Bred** James Murray **Trained** Greystoke, Cumbria

FOCUS

Race distance increased by 25yds. A stayers' handicap hurdle run at a sound pace and the issue was still in the balance when the leader crashed out at the last. The first three have been rated pretty much to their marks.

4907 TOTETRIFECTA H'CAP CHASE (16 fncs) 2m 4f

4:40 (4:40) (Class 3) (0-125,125) 5-Y-0+ **£6,498** (£1,908; £954; £477)

Form RPR

32-5 **1** **Full Jack (FR)**[307] 458 9-11-2 115 JamesReveley 140+
(Pauline Robson) *j.w: hld up in tch: smooth hdwy to ld 4 out: qcknd clr on bridle bef next: v easily* **5/1**[2]

0223 **2** 12 **Carrigdhoun (IRE)**[13] 4635 11-11-7 125 (tp) DaraghBourke(5) 130
(Maurice Barnes) *led or disp ld to 9th: cl up: drvn and outpcd 5 out: rallied bef 3 out: chsd (clr) wnr run-uin: no imp* **7/4**[1]

U311 **3** nse **Swing Hard (IRE)**[16] 4571 8-11-2 115 SeanQuinlan 119
(Sue Smith) *led or disp ld tl wnt on 9th: hld and rdn 4 out: sn no imp w wnr but hung on to 2nd pl to run-in: kpt on* **13/2**

F051 **4** *18* **Irish Thistle (IRE)**[15] 4597 9-11-7 **120**.......................... AndrewThornton 110
(Dai Williams) *in tch: stdy hdwy 1/2-way: drvn and outpcd bef 3 out: sn btn* **9/1**

21P3 **5** *hd* **Cobajayisland (IRE)**[26] 4406 8-11-2 **115**.......................... BrianHarding 103
(Lucinda Russell) *nt fluent on occasions: hld up: stdy hdwy after 7th: rdn and outpcd 11th: n.d after* **7/1**

P1UP **6** *7* **Valid Point (IRE)**[37] 4212 10-11-10 **123**..........................(t) MarkGrant 106
(Nigel Twiston-Davies) *nt fluent: hld up: drvn and outpcd 1/2-way: rallied bef 4 out: wknd bef next* **11/2**[3]

-P63 **7** *38* **Edmund (IRE)**[18] 4551 9-10-7 **111**..........................(t) JamieHamilton(5) 58
(Ann Hamilton) *chsd ldrs: drvn and lost pl bef 8th: struggling fr 10th: t.o* **8/1**

5m 3.5s (-23.90) **Going Correction** -1.00s/f (Hard) **7** Ran SP% **115.4**
Speed ratings: **107,102,102,94,94 92,76**
CSF £15.17 TOTE £6.20: £2.60, £1.70; EX 19.50 Trifecta £160.50.
Owner Mr & Mrs Raymond Anderson Green **Bred** Andre Duboe **Trained** Kirkharle, Northumberland

FOCUS
Race distance increased by 20yds. What looked quite a competitive handicap chase turned out to be a one-horse race. A big step up from the winner on his previous British runs, but he threatened this sort of figure in France. The third has been rated to his mark.

4908 TOTEPOOL HAPPY EASTER MARES' STANDARD OPEN NATIONAL HUNT FLAT RACE 2m 1f
5:15 (5:17) (Class 6) 4-6-Y-O **£1,559** (£457; £228; £114)

Form				RPR

52 **1** **Wildehearted Woman (IRE)**[32] 4302 5-11-0 **0**..........(t) BrendanPowell 93+
(Jamie Snowden) *trckd ldrs: rdn over 2f out: led over 1f out: styd on wl* **12/1**

2 *2* **Bannow Storm (IRE)** 5-10-9 **0**.......................... JonathonBewley(5) 91
(George Bewley) *hld up: hdwy and cl up 1/2-way: led over 2f out to over 1f out: rallied: one pce last 100yds* **16/1**

64 **3** *2 1/4* **Floramoss**[17] 4559 5-11-0 **0**.......................... JamesReveley 90
(Keith Reveley) *hld up in tch: effrt and rdn over 2f out: kpt on same pce fnl f* **6/1**[3]

5 **4** *6* **Toquickly**[147] 2195 4-10-2 **0**.......................... CallumBewley(5) 77
(Harriet Graham) *led at modest gallop: rdn and hdd over 2f out: outpcd wl over 1f out* **66/1**

53 **5** *37* **Supreme Gael**[17] 4559 5-10-9 **0**.......................... RyanDay(5) 50
(Iain Jardine) *t.k.h early: cl up: rdn and outpcd wl over 2f out: btn over 1f out* **16/1**

6 *5* **Missy Myrtle** 5-10-9 **0**.......................... JamieHamilton(5) 46
(Peter Niven) *hld up in tch: outpcd bef 1/2-way: n.d after* **14/1**

3 **7** *nk* **Largy Girl (IRE)**[147] 2195 5-11-0 **0**.......................... AELynch 46
(S R B Crawford, Ire) *hld up in tch: smooth hdwy and cl up over 2f out: rdn and wknd qckly over 1f out: eased whn btn ins fnl f* **3/1**[2]

P **Lethegoodtimesroll (IRE)**[350] 5-10-9 **0**.......................... MeganCarberry(5)
(Brian Ellison) *plld hrd and hung lft fr outset: cl up: lost pl after 6f: sn struggling: p.u 1/2-way* **10/11**[1]

4m 16.9s (-6.70) **Going Correction** -0.75s/f (Firm)
WFA 4 from 5yo 7lb **8** Ran SP% **119.3**
Speed ratings: **85,84,83,80,62 60,60,**
CSF £185.78 TOTE £12.80: £2.90, £5.20, £2.50; EX 226.20 Trifecta £571.00.
Owner EPDS Racing Partnership 13 **Bred** T J Whitley **Trained** Lambourn, Berks

FOCUS
Race distance increased by 17yds. A weak mares' bumper, the first three clear at the line. It's been rated through the third.
T/Plt: £48.90 to a £1 stake. Pool of £59674.57 - 890.35 winning tickets. T/Qpdt: £19.60 to a £1 stake. Pool of £3106.90 - 116.99 winning tickets. **Richard Young**

4868 HAYDOCK (L-H)
Saturday, March 26

OFFICIAL GOING: Good (chs 6.3, hdl 6.3)
Wind: Strong, across Weather: Overcast, wet late on

4909 APOLLOBET WEEKLY GOLF REFUNDS CHALLENGER MARES' HURDLE SERIES FINAL (A MARES' H'CAP HURDLE) (10 hdls) 2m 2f 191y
1:25 (1:25) (Class 2) 4-Y-O+
£30,950 (£9,190; £4,595; £2,290; £1,150; £580)

Form				RPR

16P2 **1** **Lady Of Longstone (IRE)**[23] 4445 6-11-0 **123**..........(p) MichaelHeard(5) 135+
(David Pipe) *j.w: mde all at str pce: clr last: r.o strly: comf* **20/1**

-342 **2** *8* **Midnight Jazz**[29] 4338 6-11-11 **129**.......................... KielanWoods 134
(Ben Case) *hld up in midfield: hdwy 4 out: wnt 2nd 3 out: hit 2 out: rdn appr last: no imp on wnr* **8/1**[3]

3222 **3** *2* **Secret Door (IRE)**[34] 4272 5-10-7 **111**.......................... DarylJacob 112
(Harry Fry) *hld up: mstke 6th: pushed along to go pce after 4 out: hdwy 2 out: styd on run-in: unable to chal* **4/1**[1]

0525 **4** *1/2* **Woodland Walk**[112] 2911 8-11-2 **120**.......................... AidanColeman 122
(Emma Lavelle) *chsd wnr: nt fluent 4th: rdn appr 4 out: nt fluent and lost 2nd 3 out: kpt on same pce u.p fr bef last* **14/1**

-641 **5** *2 1/4* **Hannah's Princess (IRE)**[29] 4338 7-11-13 **131**.......................... GavinSheehan 133+
(Warren Greatrex) *hld up: blnd 2nd: hdwy u.p appr 2 out: no real imp on ldrs: kpt on same pce run-in* **4/1**[1]

66P4 **6** *1 1/4* **Whatdoesthefoxsay (IRE)**[20] 4512 7-10-9 **113**.......... WayneHutchinson 111
(Donald McCain) *chsd ldrs: rdn appr 4 out: sn outpcd: plugged on fr 2 out but no imp* **40/1**

P113 **7** *13* **Bella (FR)**[20] 4512 5-10-10 **119**..........................(t) DavidNoonan(5) 105
(David Pipe) *chsd ldrs: u.p after 4 out: wknd bef 2 out: sltly hmpd whn no ch last* **16/1**

5301 **8** *nk* **Attention Seaker**[20] 4512 6-11-0 **118**.......................... JamesReveley 104
(Tim Easterby) *hld up: rdn appr 2 out: nvr on terms w ldrs* **16/1**

2124 **9** *12* **Alizee De Janeiro (FR)**[34] 4272 6-10-7 **111**.......................... PeterBuchanan 87
(Lucinda Russell) *midfield: mstke 5th: sn niggled along: rdn and wknd after 4 out* **25/1**

2124 **10** *10* **Carinena (IRE)**[104] 3065 7-10-12 **116**.......................... CraigNichol 83
(Nicky Richards) *in tch: nt fluent 4 out: wknd 3 out: no ch whn mstke last* **28/1**

3511 **11** *3/4* **Card Game (IRE)**[34] 4272 7-11-4 **122**.......................... BrianHughes 88
(Malcolm Jefferson) *nt fluent: midfield: lost pl bef 4 out: struggling after* **5/1**[2]

2300 **12** *25* **Donna's Pride**[34] 4272 7-10-0 **104**.......................... HarrySkelton 47
(Keith Reveley) *a in rr: pushed along after 4 out: nvr on terms: t.o* **33/1**

P-P3 **P** **Faerie Reel (FR)**[22] 4459 6-11-4 **122**..........................(t) DavidBass
(Kim Bailey) *midfield: rdn after 5th: lost pl next: t.o 3 out: p.u bef 2 out* **33/1**

1311 **F** **Taweyla (IRE)**[22] 4459 5-11-1 **124**.......................... JamieBargary(5) 122
(Pam Sly) *midfield: pushed along after 4 out: 5th abt 12 l off the pce and no imp whn fell last* **8/1**[3]

4m 34.4s (-18.60) **Going Correction** -0.80s/f (Firm) **14** Ran SP% **117.7**
Speed ratings (Par 109): **107,103,102,102,101 101,95,95,90,86 85,75,,**
CSF £159.31 CT £781.97 TOTE £23.30: £5.90, £3.20, £2.10; EX 195.10 Trifecta £2489.60.
Owner Miss S E Hartnell **Bred** David Crimmins **Trained** Nicholashayne, Devon

FOCUS
Some starts have been moved at this track following remeasuring, so some races will not have speed figures until there is sufficient data to calculate updated median times. Bend movements resulted in this being run over 42yds further than advertised. Jockeys generally agreed the ground was good with a few dead patches. A reasonable mares' hurdle, run at a good gallop, that was won in good style by one of the outsiders. A step up from the winner, with the second and fifth rated in line with their recent Exeter form, and the third and fourth close to their marks.

4910 CHALLENGER MIDDLE DISTANCE CHASE SERIES FINAL (A H'CAP CHASE) (17 fncs) 2m 3f 203y
2:00 (2:00) (Class 2) 5-Y-O+
£30,970 (£9,210; £4,615; £2,310; £1,170; £600)

Form				RPR

4333 **1** **Ballybolley (IRE)**[7] 4787 7-11-5 **129**..........................(t) DarylJacob 148+
(Nigel Twiston-Davies) *prom: led 6th: mde rest: c clr on bit after 3 out: easily* **4/1**[1]

0110 **2** *8* **Five In A Row (IRE)**[11] 4701 8-11-12 **136**.......................... GavinSheehan 143
(Brian Ellison) *led narrowly: hdd 6th: remained cl up: rdn 4 out: styd on but no ch w wnr after 3 out* **10/1**

2102 **3** *3 3/4* **Dartford Warbler (IRE)**[60] 3794 9-10-12 **122**.......................... DannyCook 125
(Sue Smith) *trckd ldrs: rdn bef 4 out: plugged on* **8/1**[3]

1341 **4** *8* **The Cobbler Swayne (IRE)**[15] 4584 7-10-13 **123**.......... PeterBuchanan 119
(Lucinda Russell) *midfield: nt fluent 5th: rdn 4 out: one pce and nvr threatened* **8/1**[3]

5335 **5** *3 1/4* **Kings Cross (FR)**[18] 4545 6-10-0 **110**..........................(p) LeeEdwards 106
(Tony Carroll) *midfield: hmpd by faller 5 out: rdn 4 out: no imp* **20/1**

2231 **6** *11* **Cloudy Bob (IRE)**[7] 4789 9-11-0 **124**.......................... HarrySkelton 109
(Pat Murphy) *trckd ldrs: rdn to dispute 2nd 4 out: j.rt 2 out: wknd* **13/2**[2]

3031 **7** *15* **Raktiman (IRE)**[50] 3972 9-11-6 **130**..........................(t) JonathanEngland 99
(Sam Drake) *midfield: rdn 4 out: wknd after 2 out* **8/1**[3]

2452 **P** **Plus Jamais (FR)**[39] 4167 9-10-7 **117**.......................... BrianHughes
(Jim Goldie) *trckd ldrs towards outer: lost pl 8th: bhd after 5 out: p.u bef 3 out* **16/1**

2102 **P** **Special Catch (IRE)**[18] 4551 9-11-6 **130**.......................... JamesReveley
(Keith Reveley) *hld up: hmpd by faller 5 out: p.u bef 3 out* **9/1**

1452 **F** **Uhlan Bute (FR)**[23] 4443 8-10-11 **121**..........................(p) LiamTreadwell
(Venetia Williams) *pressed ldr: fell 5 out* **11/1**

4352 **F** **The Italian Yob (IRE)**[36] 4225 8-10-10 **125**..........................(b) LizzieKelly(5)
(Nick Williams) *j. slowly towards rr: fell 9th* **8/1**[3]

5m 3.8s (303.80) **11** Ran SP% **115.8**
CSF £43.01 CT £306.34 TOTE £3.90: £2.00, £3.20, £2.30; EX 45.50 Trifecta £341.30.
Owner Simon Munir & Isaac Souede **Bred** The Red Marble Syndicate **Trained** Naunton, Gloucs

FOCUS
Bend movements resulted in this being run over 24yds further than advertised. A decent chase in which it paid to race prominently, the winner making a lot of the running. The winner rates a decent novice and is on the upgrade, and the race has been rated around the balance of the second and third.

4911 APOLLOBET CASH BACK IF 2ND CHALLENGER STAYERS HURDLE SERIES FINAL (A H'CAP HURDLE) (12 hdls) 2m 6f 177y
2:35 (2:35) (Class 2) 4-Y-O+
£30,950 (£9,190; £4,595; £2,290; £1,150; £580)

Form				RPR

2553 **1** **Petethepear (IRE)**[35] 4241 6-10-8 **122**..........................(p) JoshuaMoore 129+
(Stuart Edmunds) *trckd ldrs: wnt 2nd 3rd: nt fluent 7th: led appr 4 out: tried to go clr bef 3 out: hdd sn after 3 out: 3 l down u.p whn lft 5 l clr last: styd on and in command after* **8/1**

1401 **2** *4* **Fingerontheswitch (IRE)**[31] 4305 6-11-9 **137**.......................... NoelFehily 138
(Neil Mulholland) *hld up: nt fluent 2nd: hdwy into midfield 5th: clsd bef 3 out: rdn and lft 5 l 2nd last: kpt on but no imp on wnr after* **13/2**[3]

3302 **3** *4 1/2* **Billy Dutton**[35] 4241 10-11-0 **128**.......................... AidanColeman 124
(Chris Down) *in tch: rdn bef 3 out: lft 3rd last: styd on u.p run-in: no imp on front two* **12/1**

2F21 **4** *3/4* **Caledonia**[26] 4405 9-10-9 **123**.......................... HenryBrooke 118
(Jim Goldie) *midfield: u.p appr 3 out: stdy hdwy whn mstke 2 out: styd on towards fin: nt pce to trble ldrs* **14/1**

0421 **5** *1 3/4* **Hainan (FR)**[50] 3970 5-10-11 **125**.......................... DannyCook 119
(Sue Smith) *midfield: impr to chse ldrs 4th: outpcd after 4 out: kpt on u.p fr last* **14/1**

41P0 **6** *3/4* **Volcanic (FR)**[31] 4305 7-10-9 **123**..........................(t) WayneHutchinson 115
(Donald McCain) *led: hdd appr 4 out: outpcd bef 3 out: kpt on u.p run-in* **25/1**

1342 **7** *hd* **Sykes (IRE)**[42] 4112 7-10-9 **128**.......................... CiaranGethings(5) 123+
(Philip Hobbs) *hld up: hdwy into midfield 3rd: effrt whn nt fluent and ev ch 3 out: mstke 2 out: outpcd bef last: kpt on run-in* **5/1**[1]

F-03 **8** *2 1/2* **Alzammaar (USA)**[106] 3027 5-10-10 **124**..........................(tp) GavinSheehan 116
(Warren Greatrex) *chsd ldrs: nt fluent 5th: outpcd after 4 out: plugged on but n.d after* **7/1**

1605 **9** *53* **Tap Night (USA)**[26] 4405 9-10-13 **127**..........................(p) RichieMcLernon 69
(Lucinda Russell) *midfield early: towards rr whn pushed along and nt fluent 8th: t.o* **33/1**

5120 **10** *17* **Harry Hunt**[14] 4066 9-10-9 **123**.......................... KielanWoods 50
(Graeme McPherson) *hld up: blnd and nrly uns rdr 1st: rdr lost iron briefly: mstke 6th: struggling 8th: t.o* **33/1**

U/50 **P** **Kris Cross (IRE)**[37] 4206 9-10-3 **122**..........................(tp) GrantCockburn(5)
(Lucinda Russell) *in tch: nt fluent 4th: dropped to midfield 5th: struggling 8th: t.o whn p.u bef 3 out* **33/1**

5224 **P** **Moorlands Mist**[50] 3979 9-10-11 **130**.......................... ConorRing(5)
(Evan Williams) *nvr gng wl in rr: t.o whn p.u bef 3 out* **33/1**

-301 **P** **Sir Vinski (IRE)**[49] 3999 7-11-4 **132**..........................(b) CraigNichol
(Nicky Richards) *w ldr to 3rd: lost pl qckly after: t.o whn p.u bef next* **14/1**

3B32 **P** **Octagon**[26] 4405 6-10-9 **123**.......................... BrianHughes
(Dianne Sayer) *hld up: no imp whn p.u bef 3 out* **14/1**

4203 **P** **Oscar Blue (IRE)**[26] 4405 6-11-0 **128**..........................(b[1]) WillKennedy
(Brian Ellison) *in tch: rdn and lost pl after 3rd: t.o whn p.u bef 2 out* **12/1**

131 U Emerging Force (IRE)[44] 4066 6-11-12 140 .... NicodeBoinville 148
(Harry Whittington) trckd ldrs fr 2nd: pushed along after 4 out: led after 3 out: rdn abt 3 l up whn blnd and uns rdr last 11/2[2]

5m 35.3s (-24.70) **Going Correction** -0.80s/f (Firm) course record 16 Ran SP% 126.7
Speed ratings (Par 109): **110,108,107,106,106 105,105,104,86,80 ,,,,,**
CSF £59.19 CT £628.19 TOTE £9.20: £2.70, £2.00, £2.70, £3.60; EX 72.70 Trifecta £1138.10.
Owner KTDA Consultancy Limited **Bred** Dick White **Trained** Newport Pagnell, Bucks

FOCUS

Bend movements resulted in this being run over 42yds further than advertised. Fair handicap form, although a changing picture late on, with the winner fortunate. A step up from the winner, with the third, fourth and fifth helping to set the level.

4912 CHALLENGER STAYING CHASE SERIES FINAL (A H'CAP CHASE) (18 fncs) 3m 24y

3:10 (3:10) (Class 2) 5-Y-0+
£30,950 (£6,892; £6,892; £2,290; £1,150; £580)

Form RPR

-0P2 1 No Duffer[29] 4348 9-11-3 125 ....(t) PaddyBrennan 140+
(Tom George) prom: led narrowly 11th: rdn to assert after 4 out: styd on: eased towards fin 11/2[2]

P111 2 3 ¾ Gonalston Cloud (IRE)[40] 4153 9-11-2 124 .... AndrewTinkler 132
(Nick Kent) midfield on outer: lost pl and dropped to rr bef 10th: rallied appr 4 out: styd on wl 15/2[3]

F222 2 dht Jac The Legend[20] 4511 7-10-9 117 ....(b[1]) WillKennedy 126+
(Brian Ellison) sn led: hdd 11th: remained cl up: bit slow 4 out and sn outpcd in 2nd: plugged on after 3 out: jnd for 2nd post 11/1

S432 4 ½ Baku Bay (IRE)[22] 4465 8-10-10 118 ....(p) GavinSheehan 125
(Ali Stronge) trckd ldrs: rdn and outpcd after 5 out: plugged on after 3 out 5/1[1]

3414 5 13 King Massini (IRE)[115] 2853 10-11-1 123 .... AdamWedge 120
(Evan Williams) trckd ldrs: rdn after 5 out: wknd after 2 out 16/1

F21B 6 24 Bodega[7] 4800 8-10-12 120 ....(p) BrianHughes 94
(Ian Williams) midfield: mstke 9th: rdn after 5 out: wknd after 3 out 8/1

1PP4 7 2 ¾ Winged Crusader (IRE)[29] 4348 8-10-1 112 ....(v) RyanHatch(3) 83
(Nigel Twiston-Davies) trckd ldrs: rdn after 5 out: wknd after 4 out 18/1

5623 8 1 Hollow Blue Sky (FR)[30] 4321 9-10-2 115 ....(tp) JamieBargary(5) 85
(Nigel Twiston-Davies) hld up: rdn after 5 out: wknd after 4 out 9/1

P0P1 P Leo Luna[29] 4348 7-11-10 132 ....(tp) JoshuaMoore
(Gary Moore) midfield: slow 3rd and sn dropped to rr: bhd 6th: p.u after 9th 8/1

1336 P Sands Cove (IRE)[36] 4234 9-11-3 125 .... LiamTreadwell
(James Evans) midfield: mstke 13th: rdn bef 4 out: sn wknd: p.u bef last 25/1

P212 P Thinger Licht (FR)[21] 4493 7-10-11 119 ....(p) HarrySkelton
(Dan Skelton) midfield: hit 10th: rdn after 5 out: wknd after 4 out and p.u bef next 11/1

4U54 P Final Assault (IRE)[28] 4370 7-11-12 134 .... DerekFox
(Lucinda Russell) hld up: sme hdwy 5 out: mstke 3 out: wknd: p.u bef last 12/1

1006 P Jack Steel (IRE)[43] 4109 6-11-0 122 .... RichieMcLernon
(Lucinda Russell) hld up: mstke 2nd: rdn and struggling after 9th: p.u bef next 25/1

6m 16.9s (-13.60) **Going Correction** -0.325s/f (Good) 13 Ran SP% 119.2
Speed ratings: **109,107,107,107,103 95,94,94,,**
WIN: £6.60. Gonalston Cloud: £2.20, Jac The Legend £3.10; EX: ND/GC £21.50, JTL £30.90; CSF: ND/GC £23.57, ND/JTL £32.34; TRICAST: ND/GC/JTL £219.32, ND/JLT/GC £227.83; TRIFECTA: ND/GC/JTL £262.50, ND/JTL/GC £284.90..
Owner David Robey **Bred** Mrs R Crank **Trained** Slad, Gloucs

FOCUS

Bend movements resulted in this being run over 48yds further than advertised. Another race where those racing prominently fared best. A small pb from the winner, with the second, third and fourth rated pretty much to their marks.

4913 CHALLENGER TWO MILE HURDLE SERIES FINAL (A H'CAP HURDLE) (8 hdls 1 omitted) 1m 7f 144y

3:45 (3:45) (Class 2) 4-Y-0+
£30,950 (£9,190; £4,595; £2,290; £1,150; £580)

Form RPR

-160 1 Thunder Sheik (IRE)[28] 4362 8-10-4 119 ....(tp) RyanHatch(3) 128+
(Nigel Twiston-Davies) in tch: hit 4th: effrt and upsides 2 out: rdn appr last: led run-in: styd on strly to go clr fnl 100yds 15/2[3]

6310 2 3 ½ Kings Bayonet[21] 4484 9-11-0 126 .... WayneHutchinson 131
(Alan King) hld up: hdwy appr 2 out: styd on to take 2nd fnl 110yds: no imp on wnr 25/1

-021 3 nk Apterix (FR)[23] 4447 6-11-0 126 .... GavinSheehan 131
(Brian Ellison) hld up in midfield: hmpd 2nd: hdwy appr 2 out: rdn bef last: styd on u.p run-in: no imp on wnr 6/1[1]

-215 4 2 ½ Floresco (GER)[28] 4353 6-10-8 120 ....(t) DarylJacob 124+
(Richard Woollacott) trckd ldrs: hmpd 1st: led bef 2 out but a pressed: hdd run-in: no ex fnl 75yds 14/1

0242 5 4 Heath Hunter (IRE)[7] 4793 9-10-13 130 ....(p) DavidNoonan(5) 128
(David Pipe) midfield: hdwy to trck ldrs after 6th: effrt bef 2 out: styd on same pce run-in 7/1[2]

0221 6 1 Teo Vivo (FR)[38] 4179 9-11-4 130 ....(b) BrianHughes 127
(Pauline Robson) cl up: effrt whn chsng ldrs 2 out: one pce fr bef last 10/1

2406 7 1 ¼ Crookstown (IRE)[28] 4353 9-10-7 119 ....(p) NicodeBoinville 116
(Ben Case) hld up: rdn appr last: no imp 8/1

22-4 8 shd El Beau (IRE)[38] 4179 5-11-4 130 .... SeanBowen 126
(John Quinn) trckd ldrs: lost pl and outpcd after 6th: n.d after 8/1

5312 9 nk Bold Duke[28] 4353 8-10-5 120 .... BenPoste(3) 115
(Edward Bevan) lft in ld 1st: hdd 4th: remained prom: ev ch appr 2 out: rdn bef last: one pce after 33/1

1323 10 7 Vendor (FR)[28] 4366 8-11-12 138 .... DannyCook 132
(Sue Smith) in tch: effrt 2 out: outpcd bef last: btn after 8/1

1400 11 19 Venue[38] 4179 6-10-12 124 ....(t) WillKennedy 96
(Donald McCain) prom: led 4th: hdd appr 2 out: wknd u.p bef last 25/1

5450 12 8 Silver Duke (IRE)[38] 4179 5-10-3 115 .... HenryBrooke 80
(Jim Goldie) hld up: hmpd 2nd: nvr a threat 16/1

0022 F Jonny Delta[38] 4179 9-9-9 112 .... DiarmuidO'Regan(5)
(Jim Goldie) led tl fell 1st 14/1

203 F Serenity Now (IRE)[38] 4179 8-10-9 121 .... AidanColeman
(Brian Ellison) hld up: fell 2nd 10/1

3m 46.2s (-18.00) **Going Correction** -0.80s/f (Firm) 14 Ran SP% 119.9
Speed ratings (Par 109): **113,111,111,109,107 107,106,106,106,103 93,89,,**
CSF £180.32 CT £1207.00 TOTE £9.80: £3.80, £6.20, £2.30; EX 251.70 Trifecta £3358.80.
Owner R J Rexton **Bred** Janus Bloodstock Inc **Trained** Naunton, Gloucs

FOCUS

Bend movements resulted in this being run over 21yds further than advertised. Ordinary handicap form. The winner has been rated to the level of his Kempton win, with the second, third and fourth pretty much to their marks.

4914 TIM MOLONY H'CAP CHASE 3m 4f 97y

4:20 (4:25) (Class 3) (0-130,129) 5-Y-0+ £8,122 (£2,385; £1,192; £596)

Form RPR

-3PP 1 Universal Soldier (IRE)[63] 3741 11-11-6 123 .... SeanBowen 143+
(Peter Bowen) mde most: nt fluent 16th: rdn to go clr appr last: styd on wl and in command after 4/1[1]

144P 2 20 Cyclop (IRE)[29] 4341 5-11-3 126 ....(tp) JamieBargary(5) 133
(David Dennis) prom: nt fluent 9th: lost pl 12th: wnt 2nd appr 4 out and sn chalng: ev ch whn mstke 3 out: rdn and unable to go w wnr whn mstke last: one pce and no ch run-in 20/1

312P 3 18 Alto Des Mottes (FR)[33] 4286 6-11-12 129 ....(p) BrianHughes 119
(Henry Hogarth) in tch: bhd and outpcd after 18th: kpt on to take 3rd run-in: no ch w front two 12/1

P1PP 4 1 ¾ Whats Left (IRE)[101] 3113 8-11-8 125 ....(p) NoelFehily 113
(Neil Mulholland) hld up: rdn and outpcd after 18th: no imp 4 out: kpt on but no ch fr last 6/1[2]

0P0P 5 7 Kilbree Kid (IRE)[23] 4444 9-11-4 121 ....(tp) PaddyBrennan 104
(Tom George) hld up: hdwy bef 10th: prom: wnt 2nd 15th: lost 2nd appr 4 out: sn outpcd: wl hld after 7/1[3]

FP0P 6 6 William Money (IRE)[28] 4367 9-11-0 117 .... HenryBrooke 95
(Chris Grant) midfield: rdn and wknd after 18th 7/1[3]

4303 F Achimota (IRE)[29] 4348 10-11-2 119 .... KielanWoods
(Graeme McPherson) in tch: rdn whn fell 18th 4/1[1]

6156 P Woodford County[28] 4367 9-11-7 129 ....(p) CiaranGethings(5)
(Philip Hobbs) sweating: chsd ldr: blnd 3rd: mstke 11th: lost pl 17th: rdn whn hmpd 18th: nt rcvr and sn p.u 4/1[1]

8m 0.3s (28.70) **Going Correction** -0.325s/f (Good)
WFA 5 from 6yo+ 1lb 8 Ran SP% 111.7
Speed ratings: **46,40,35,34,32 30,,**
CSF £64.83 CT £863.30 TOTE £4.10: £1.90, £4.90, £2.40; EX 84.80 Trifecta £373.70.
Owner Mrs Lindie King **Bred** John McAleese **Trained** Little Newcastle, Pembrokes

FOCUS

Bend movements resulted in this being run over 48yds further than advertised. They came home at intervals in this marathon chase, The second has been rated back to the level of his Warwick win.

4915 APOLLOBET BET THROUGH YOUR MOBILE STANDARD OPEN NATIONAL HUNT FLAT RACE 1m 7f 144y

4:50 (4:56) (Class 5) 4-6-Y-0 £2,274 (£667; £333; £166)

Form RPR

5 1 Elgin[27] 4392 4-10-9 0 .... WayneHutchinson 107+
(Alan King) midfield: hdwy 6f out: wnt 2nd gng wl over 3f out: led over 2f out whn pressed: rdn over 1f out: styd on gamely fnl 100yds 12/1

224 2 1 ½ Desert Retreat (IRE)[50] 3980 5-11-2 0 .... TomO'Brien 113
(Philip Hobbs) led: hdd over 5f out: rdn over 4f out: u.p 4f out: rdn and outpcd over 2f out: hung lft u.p and styd on to take 2nd ins fnl 75yds: nt get to wnr 4/1[2]

3 2 ¼ River Wylde (IRE)[146] 5-11-2 0 .... NicodeBoinville 111+
(Nicky Henderson) racd keenly: in tch: gng wl over 4f out: wnt chalng 2nd over 2f out: rdn and hung lft whn nt qckn over 1f out: no ex and lost 2nd fnl 75yds 1/1[1]

4 1 ½ Arctic Destination (IRE)[55] 5-11-2 0 .... WillKennedy 110
(Donald McCain) chsd ldr: led over 5f out: rdn and hdd over 2f out: styd on same pce fnl 110yds 8/1[3]

5 8 Nicholas T 4-10-9 0 .... HenryBrooke 95
(Jim Goldie) hld up: green after 4f: hdwy over 4f out: chsd ldrs after: one pce under fr over 2f out 80/1

6 6 Derrick D'Anjou (IRE) 5-11-2 0 .... KielanWoods 97
(Graeme McPherson) hld up: u.p 4f out: effrt over 2f out: no imp on ldrs 100/1

7 ½ Newtown Lad (IRE)[125] 6-10-11 0 .... GrantCockburn(5) 97
(Lucinda Russell) trckd ldrs: outpcd and lost pl over 4f out: plugged on ins fnl f: n.d after 16/1

46 8 2 ¼ Moon Jet (IRE)[31] 4309 4-10-9 0 .... BrianHughes 88
(John Mackie) prom: pushed along over 4f out: wknd over 3f out 33/1

9 16 Quietly (IRE) 5-11-2 0 .... DannyCook 80
(Sue Smith) midfield: rdn and wknd 4f out 14/1

10 ¾ Egypt Mill Rebel 6-11-2 0 .... PaddyBrennan 79
(Tom George) hld up: rdn 5f out: sme hdwy over 2f out: nt trble ldrs: wknd over 1f out: eased whn wl btn ins fnl f 12/1

0 11 24 Last To Leave[27] 4392 5-11-2 0 .... JoshuaMoore 58
(Stuart Edmunds) midfield: lost pl after 3f: struggling 4f out: t.o 80/1

12 8 Fieldsofsilk (IRE) 4-10-9 0 .... PeterCarberry 44
(Jennie Candlish) hld up: pushed along 6f out: t.o 25/1

3m 52.7s (-5.90) **Going Correction** -0.80s/f (Firm)
WFA 4 from 5yo+ 7lb 12 Ran SP% 119.3
Speed ratings: **82,81,80,79,75 72,72,71,63,62 50,46**
CSF £58.84 TOTE £13.80: £3.40, £2.00, £1.10; EX 60.00 Trifecta £151.00.
Owner Elite Racing Club **Bred** Elite Racing Club **Trained** Barbury Castle, Wilts

FOCUS

Bend movements resulted in this being run over 21yds further than advertised. A fair bumper dominated by the southern stables. A big step up from the winner, with the second rated to his mark.

T/Jkpt: Not won. T/Plt: £414.90 to a £1 stake. Pool of £187586.17 - 330.03 winning tickets.
T/Qpdt: £77.40 to a £1 stake. Pool of £16252.25 - 155.30 winning tickets. **D Owen & A Sheret**

1837 **NEWTON ABBOT** (L-H)

Saturday, March 26

OFFICIAL GOING: Good to soft (good in places; 6.0) changing to soft (good to soft in places) after race 3 (3.15)

Wind: strong against Weather: rain Rails: Hurdle course set wide, Chase course down the innermost position. Effect on distances: Race 1 adds 108yds, Race 2 adds 138yds, Races 4 & 6 adds 162yds.

4916 SIS MARES' MAIDEN HURDLE (8 hdls) 2m 167y

2:05 (2:06) (Class 5) 4-Y-0+ £3,898 (£1,144; £572; £286)

Form				RPR
3364	1		**Western Sunrise (IRE)**[22] 4457 7-11-0 0 AlainCawley (Johnny Farrelly) *disp ld: clr ldr after 5th: drvn whn strly pressed after 3 out: hung rt but edgd ahd after 2 out: kpt on gamely: drvn out* **10/3**[2]	111+
4-0F	2	2 3/4	**Lapalala (IRE)**[29] 4337 5-11-0 0 RichardJohnson (Philip Hobbs) *in tch: hdwy 3 out: chal after 3 out: rdn and ev ch next: 1 l 2nd whn hmpd between last 2: kpt on same pce* **1/1**[1]	111+
00	3	32	**Venture Lagertha (IRE)**[12] 4681 7-11-0 0 LiamHeard (Brian Barr) *trckd ldrs: wnt rt and hit 3 out: outpcd by front pair sn after: wknd between last 2* **66/1**	80
0P	4	9	**Berwin (IRE)**[100] 3119 7-11-0 0 DaveCrosse (Sarah Robinson) *mid-div: rdn after 5th: wnt btn 4th after 4 out: nvr any danger* **200/1**	72
0-05	5	8	**Apple Pops**[24] 4435 6-11-0 0 MarkQuinlan (Neil Mulholland) *disp ld tl rdn after 5th: wknd after next* **25/1**	65
0U33	6	4 1/2	**Sahara Haze**[6] 4821 7-10-7 0 MrTGreatrex(7) (Phillip Dando) *in tch: rdn along fr 4th: wknd 3 out* **4/1**[3]	64
0	7	1	**Starlit Night**[12] 4683 4-10-4 0 GilesHawkins(3) (Chris Down) *trckd ldrs: rdn after 5th: wknd after next* **50/1**	53
	8	39	**Kipuka**[343] 4-10-7 0 (t) JamesBest (Nigel Hawke) *a towards rr: t.o* **25/1**	18
U	9	21	**Vanishing**[12] 4683 4-10-7 0 IanPopham (Alexandra Dunn) *slow 1st: a in rr: t.o* **6/1**	
36/U	P		**Ella's Promise**[24] 4435 7-10-9 0 AliceMills(5) (Martin Hill) *chsd ldrs tl 4th: sn bhd: t.o whn p.u bef next* **40/1**	

4m 18.0s (12.30) **Going Correction** +0.875s/f (Soft)
WFA 4 from 5yo+ 7lb **10 Ran SP% 121.4**
Speed ratings (Par 103): **106,104,89,85,81 79,79,60,50,**
CSF £7.46 TOTE £4.90: £1.50, £1.02, £22.30; EX 8.40 Trifecta £389.40.
Owner David J Adams **Bred** Paddy Behan Jnr **Trained** Enmore, Somerset

FOCUS

The rain was getting into the ground according to Alain Cawley, who rode the opening winner. The first two finished well clear in a weak maiden hurdle. The hurdles course was set wide, and this was run over 108yds further than advertised. A step up from the winner, with the second rated to her best.

4917 CYSTIC FIBROSIS TRUST "NATIONAL HUNT" NOVICES' HURDLE (9 hdls) 2m 2f 110y

2:40 (2:42) (Class 4) 4-Y-0+ £4,548 (£1,335; £667; £333)

Form				RPR
2120	1		**Knockgraffon (IRE)**[14] 4622 6-11-2 132 BridgetAndrews(5) (Dan Skelton) *trckd ldrs: led after 3 out: kpt on wl: pushed out* **10/11**[1]	137+
643	2	14	**Muffins For Tea**[12] 4681 6-10-8 0 PaulO'Brien(7) (Colin Tizzard) *disp ld tl clr ldr 6th: rdn and hdd after 3 out: styd on but nt pce of wnr* **7/1**	117
2-02	3	5	**Beau Phil (FR)**[23] 4449 5-11-1 0 (t) SamTwiston-Davies (Paul Nicholls) *mid-div: hdwy 6th: cl 3rd 3 out: sn rdn: kpt on same pce fr next* **5/1**[3]	111
36-P	4	26	**Welcome Bach (IRE)**[21] 4494 7-11-1 0 NickScholfield (Liam Corcoran) *hld up towards rr: wnt modest 4th after 3 out: nvr any danger: t.o* **16/1**	88
PF44	5	9	**Richardofdoccombe (IRE)**[32] 4292 10-11-2 0 (t) AliceMills(5) (Gail Haywood) *chsd ldrs tl after 5th: wknd 3 out: t.o* **50/1**	85
0PP4	6	59	**Cor Wot An Apple**[26] 4409 5-11-1 0 (t) IanPopham (Colin Tizzard) *chsd ldrs: rdn after 6th: wknd next: t.o* **20/1**	26
P	P		**Shift It Franklin**[128] 2603 7-10-8 0 MrNLawton(7) (Philip Hobbs) *a in rr: pushed along fr 3rd: t.o whn p.u after 6th* **66/1**	
/3-0	P		**Spring Wolf**[122] 2710 8-11-1 0 DaveCrosse (John Ryall) *in tch: trckd ldr after 5th tl rdn bef 3 out: sn wknd: p.u bef 2 out* **66/1**	
13	P		**Que Sera (IRE)**[38] 4183 6-11-7 126 RichardJohnson (Philip Hobbs) *hld up towards rr: hdwy after 5th: nvr threatened: wknd after 3 out: p.u bef next* **7/2**[2]	
06PP	P		**Bogoss Du Perret (FR)**[85] 3414 5-11-1 100 AndrewGlassonbury (Jimmy Frost) *mid-div: hmpd on bnd and pushed wd after 3rd: rdn after 6th: wknd after next: t.o whn p.u bef 2 out* **100/1**	
0	P		**Port Navas (IRE)**[50] 3980 5-11-1 0 ConorO'Farrell (David Pipe) *a towards rr: t.o 6th: p.u next* **40/1**	
00	P		**Surfing The Stars (IRE)**[28] 4357 5-11-1 0 [1] RobertDunne (Laura Young) *mid-div tl wknd rapidly 4th: p.u after next* **200/1**	
00	P		**Primary Suspect (IRE)**[85] 3416 6-11-1 0 MichealNolan (Linda Blackford) *sn bhd: t.o whn p.u after 4th* **200/1**	
0	P		**Cleni Wells (FR)**[22] 4466 5-11-1 110 LiamHeard (Martin Hill) *disp ld tl after 5th: wknd next: t.o whn p.u after 3 out* **40/1**	

4m 50.1s (20.10) **Going Correction** +1.075s/f (Soft) **14 Ran SP% 126.2**
Speed ratings (Par 105): **100,94,92,81,77 52,,,, ,,,**
CSF £8.72 TOTE £1.70: £1.02, £2.60, £2.60; EX 12.50 Trifecta £39.20.
Owner Mrs Barbara Hester **Bred** R McCarthy **Trained** Alcester, Warwicks

FOCUS

Race run over 138yds further than advertised. An ordinary novice hurdle which went the way of the favourite. The first two have been rated pretty much to their marks.

4918 FRANK LOOSEMORE MEMORIAL H'CAP CHASE (13 fncs) 2m 75y

3:15 (3:18) (Class 2) (0-150,143) 5-Y-0+ £13,293 (£3,927; £1,963; £982; £491)

Form				RPR
4221	1		**Ut Majeur Aulmes (FR)**[22] 4464 8-10-8 132 (t) DavidPrichard(7) (Victor Dartnall) *hld up: hdwy 9th: led after 4 out: kpt on wl fr 2 out: rdn out* **9/2**[3]	139+
-P02	2	2	**Ulck Du Lin (FR)**[49] 3990 8-11-12 143 (bt) SamTwiston-Davies (Paul Nicholls) *trckd ldrs: rdn to chse wnr appr 2 out: kpt on but nt quite pce to get on terms* **11/2**	146
1404	3	22	**Keel Haul (IRE)**[35] 4254 8-10-11 128 (v[1]) JamesDavies (Henry Oliver) *trckd ldrs: chal 4 out tl rdn next: wknd 2 out: lft 3rd bef last* **11/2**	110
221	4	8	**Miss Tenacious**[206] 1451 9-10-7 129 HarryCobden(5) (Ron Hodges) *trckd ldrs: rdn after 4 out: wknd bef 2 out: lft 4th bef last* **16/1**	106
3-PF	5	6	**Dance Floor King (IRE)**[7] 4787 9-10-10 127 NickScholfield (Nick Mitchell) *trckd ldr tl after 6th: lost pl 8th: sn bhd* **8/1**	97
1123	P		**Easily Pleased (IRE)**[176] 1735 10-10-5 122 RichardJohnson (Martin Hill) *racd keenly: hld up: rein broke after 5th: hdwy into 2nd next: nvr rcvrd and p.u bef 9th* **4/1**[2]	
-PP3	P		**Starkie**[22] 4464 9-10-4 121 TomCannon (Chris Gordon) *led: j.rt thrght: rdn and hdd after 4 out: stl ev ch next tl appr 2 out: wkng in 3rd whn p.u bef last* **9/4**[1]	

4m 13.0s (6.50) **Going Correction** +0.70s/f (Soft) **7 Ran SP% 116.7**
Speed ratings: **111,110,99,95,92**
CSF £29.94 TOTE £5.90: £2.70, £2.70; EX 33.90 Trifecta £209.20.
Owner Mrs S De Wilde **Bred** Emmanuel Bodard **Trained** Brayford, Devon

FOCUS

The chase track was down the innermost position, and the race distance was as advertised. A decent handicap chase, if not the strongest form for the grade. The second sets the level.

4919 ATTHERACES NOVICES' H'CAP HURDLE (DIV I) (10 hdls) 2m 5f 122y

3:50 (3:51) (Class 5) (0-100,100) 4-Y-0+ £3,898 (£1,144; £572; £286)

Form				RPR
3-00	1		**Belize**[70] 3619 5-11-12 100 RichardJohnson (Tim Vaughan) *hld up in tch: hdwy 7th: led bef 2 out: pushed clr: v easily* **11/4**[1]	110+
P4-P	2	24	**Tresor De La Vie (FR)**[190] 1576 9-10-0 74 oh6 (tp) IanPopham (Victor Dartnall) *led tl 3rd: prom: led 3 out: rdn and hdd bef 2 out: sn wknd* **10/1**	59
5000	3	3 3/4	**Song Of The Night (IRE)**[91] 3221 5-11-4 92 (p) SamTwiston-Davies (Charlie Longsdon) *cl up: effrt in cl 3rd after 3 out: wknd bef next* **3/1**[2]	73
000	4	1	**Tell Tony (IRE)**[23] 4449 6-11-3 91 (t) MichealNolan (Tim Dennis) *trckd ldrs: nt fluent 6th: rdn after next: nvr threatened: wknd bef 2 out* **11/1**	73
3260	5	3 1/2	**Drummond**[32] 4291 7-9-7 74 JordanWilliams(7) (Katie Stephens) *dwlt: sn chsng ldrs: rdn appr 7th: nvr threatened: wknd bef 2 out* **7/1**	51
0P3P	6	31	**Jack Snipe**[35] 4250 7-11-8 96 MattGriffiths (Jeremy Scott) *prom: led 3rd tl 3 out: sn wknd: t.o* **9/2**[3]	42
6P-P	7	8	**Unify**[107] 2997 6-10-2 79 HarryBannister(3) (Grant Cann) *racd keenly on outer: prom tl rdn 7th: wknd after next: t.o* **16/1**	17
0606	P		**Up To Al (IRE)**[23] 4454 8-11-7 95 LiamHeard (Bob Buckler) *hld up: hdwy 7th: wknd after 3 out: p.u bef last* **8/1**	

5m 59.3s (39.10) **Going Correction** +1.275s/f (Heav) **8 Ran SP% 116.8**
Speed ratings (Par 103): **79,70,68,68,67 56,53,**
CSF £30.24 CT £88.31 TOTE £2.80: £1.60, £3.00, £1.20; EX 34.50 Trifecta £149.10.
Owner D R Passant **Bred** Juddmonte Farms Ltd **Trained** Aberthin, Vale of Glamorgan

FOCUS

Race run over 162yds further than advertised. All of these were maidens and the paper favourite didn't run, so this was a pretty weak contest. The winner has been rated up a stone for the step up in trip.

4920 ATTHERACES NOVICES' H'CAP HURDLE (DIV II) (10 hdls) 2m 5f 122y

4:25 (4:25) (Class 5) (0-100,99) 4-Y-0+ £3,898 (£1,144; £572; £286)

Form				RPR
0P32	1		**I'llhavealook (IRE)**[12] 4682 11-10-11 91 (p) MissPFuller(7) (Katie Stephens) *disp ld most of way tl clr ldr 7th: styd on wl fr 2 out: pushed out* **7/2**[2]	99+
5066	2	9	**Jopaan (IRE)**[38] 4184 9-9-11 73 oh4 (t) HarryBannister(3) (Brian Barr) *trckd ldrs: rdn to chse wnr appr 2 out: kpt on but a being hld* **8/1**	72
4-1P	3	4 1/2	**Mogestic (IRE)**[54] 3904 7-11-7 99 KevinJones(5) (Seamus Mullins) *hld up: hdwy after 6th: rdn to chse wnr after 3 out tl next: kpt on same pce* **4/1**[3]	94
30P6	4	58	**Watchmetail (IRE)**[121] 2736 10-10-0 73 oh9 (b) ConorO'Farrell (John Panvert) *disp ld tl 7th: sn wknd: lft poor 4th after 2 out: t.o* **25/1**	10
6P52	S		**Mexican Border (GER)**[121] 2730 7-11-8 95 RichardJohnson (Martin Hill) *racd keenly: hld up: wnt 5th 3 out: sn rdn and wknd: stmbld on bnd and fell bef 2 out* **7/4**[1]	
00P6	P		**Hardtorock (IRE)**[21] 4494 7-11-7 94 (t) SamTwiston-Davies (Liam Corcoran) *chsd ldrs: rdn appr 7th: wknd after 3 out: p.u bef next* **12/1**	
P005	P		**My Diamond (IRE)**[23] 4454 5-10-12 85 (p) RobertDunne (Laura Young) *in tch: rdn after 7th: wknd next: t.o whn p.u after 2 out* **10/1**	
46P	P		**Whimsical Notion**[143] 2265 6-11-0 87 (tp) JamesBest (Nigel Hawke) *trckd ldrs: rdn to chse ldng trio after 3 out: sn wknd: tired whn blnd next: p.u bef last* **8/1**	

5m 57.1s (36.90) **Going Correction** +1.475s/f (Heav) **8 Ran SP% 121.4**
Speed ratings (Par 103): **91,87,86,65,**
CSF £33.13 CT £119.98 TOTE £4.10: £1.40, £2.40, £2.00; EX 35.20 Trifecta £115.00.
Owner Mrs K J Stephens **Bred** Seamus O'Farrell **Trained** Allensmore, H'fords

FOCUS

Race run over 162 yards further than advertised. A poor event run in increasingly testing conditions. The winner has been rated to his best.

4921 ST AUSTELL BREWERY H'CAP CHASE (16 fncs) 2m 4f 216y

4:55 (4:56) (Class 5) (0-100,95) 5-Y-0+ £4,223 (£1,240; £620; £310)

Form				RPR
PP13	1		**High Aspirations (IRE)**[34] 4265 8-10-10 84 HarryCobden(5) (Michael Blake) *trckd ldrs: wnt 2nd 3 out: led after next: sn clr: v easily* **5/2**[1]	106+
U343	2	16	**Lamb's Cross**[12] 4686 10-10-9 81 HarryBannister(3) (Brian Barr) *prom: led 10th: rdn after 3 out: stmbld and hdd next: sn hld* **4/1**[2]	88
P054	3	10	**Haughtons Bridge (IRE)**[194] 1546 8-11-7 95 (t) AliceMills(5) (Martin Hill) *hld up: struggling bef 4 out: hdwy after 3 out: styd on fr next: nvr trbld ldrs* **14/1**	88
2333	4	8	**Tachbury**[15] 4590 12-10-13 82 (p) RichardJohnson (Tim Vaughan) *trckd ldrs: rdn in 4th after 4 out: one pce fr next* **8/1**	67
PP13	5	5	**Molly Oscar (IRE)**[9] 4746 10-10-11 80 (v) TomCannon (Johnny Farrelly) *prom tl 6th: sn lost pl: nvr bk on terms* **9/2**[3]	60
2P0-	6	6	**Miller's Maverick**[370] 4944 8-11-1 84 (t) NickScholfield (Grant Cann) *a towards rr* **14/1**	58

3000 **7** *6* **Sabroclair (FR)**[28] 4356 7-11-10 **93**........................(t) MichealNolan 61
(Richard Woollacott) *stmbld 1st: in tch: short of room 5th: rdn after 4 out: wknd next* **14/1**

PU34 **8** *2 ½* **Jamrham (IRE)**[12] 4686 9-10-9 **78**........................(t) JakeGreenall 44
(Sam Thomas) *led tl 10th: chsd ldrs: rdn after 4 out: wkng whn wnt bdly rt and stmbld 2 out* **9/2**[3]

0FPP **P** **Wicklewood**[12] 4686 10-10-13 **89**........................(bt) MrTGillard[(7)]
(Mark Gillard) *in tch tl 5th: reminders and sn in rr: lost tch 8th: p.u after next* **33/1**

5m 37.0s (15.60) **Going Correction** +0.775s/f (Soft) **9** Ran SP% **119.0**
Speed ratings: **101,94,91,88,86 83,81,80,**
CSF £14.00 CT £118.00 TOTE £3.20: £1.20, £2.00, £4.00; EX 11.70 Trifecta £119.90.
Owner Mrs J M Haines **Bred** David Moran **Trained** Trowbridge, Wilts

FOCUS
Race distance as advertised. A modest handicap. It didn't look quite so hard work on the chase track as the hurdles course. Another step up from the winner, and there's a case for rating him 5lb higher through the second and third.

4922 SOUTH WEST RACING CLUB H'CAP HURDLE (10 hdls) 2m 5f 122y
5:25 (5:27) (Class 4) (0-115,116) 4-Y-0+ **£4,548** (£1,335; £667; £333)

Form RPR

3135 **1** **Zanstra (IRE)**[23] 4442 6-11-0 **110**........................ PaulO'Brien[(7)] 116+
(Colin Tizzard) *trckd ldrs: led after 3 out: sn rdn: strly pressed whn mstke last: kpt on: all out* **9/2**[3]

2150 **2** *nk* **Western Miller (IRE)**[85] 3403 5-11-11 **114**........................ RichardJohnson 119
(Charlie Longsdon) *hld up: gd hdwy after 3 out: rdn to mount chal whn blnd last: kpt on* **9/4**[2]

4-5 **3** *2 ¾* **Carre Noir (FR)**[121] 2732 7-11-2 **105**........................ LiamHeard 106
(Martin Hill) *hld up: hdwy 7th: rdn and ev ch 2 out: kpt on same pce fr last* **33/1**

/126 **4** *5* **Our Folly**[121] 2732 8-11-0 **103**........................(t) NickScholfield 100
(Stuart Kittow) *trckd ldrs: wnt 2nd after 3 out: rdn whn pckd next: kpt on same pce* **16/1**

2454 **5** *17* **Barton Rose**[34] 4268 7-11-2 **110**........................(p) HarryCobden[(5)] 90
(Michael Blake) *mid-div: rdn after 3 out: nvr any imp: wknd between last 2* **20/1**

1P54 **6** *3 ¾* **Olympian Boy (IRE)**[15] 4597 12-10-13 **105**........................(t) KillianMoore[(3)] 80
(Sophie Leech) *mid-div tl dropped to rr 3 out: nvr bk on terms* **33/1**

0621 **7** *nk* **Driftwood Haze**[6] 4822 8-11-6 **116** 7ex........................ MrTGreatrex[(7)] 91
(Phillip Dando) *led: sn clr: hung rt on bnds at times: rdn and hdd after 3 out: sn wknd* **7/4**[1]

0555 **8** *1 ¾* **Thundering Home**[4] 4856 9-10-10 **102**........................(b) TomBellamy[(3)] 77
(Richard Mitchell) *hld up towards rr: hit 7th: hdwy next: sn rdn to chse ldrs: wkng whn blnd next* **10/1**

5303 **9** *6* **Itsaboutime (IRE)**[37] 4200 6-10-12 **101**........................ ConorO'Farrell 68
(Helen Nelmes) *a towards rr* **20/1**

456F **10** *10* **Exemplary**[32] 4292 9-11-0 **103**........................(t) AlainCawley 60
(Johnny Farrelly) *mid-div: rdn 3 out: sn wknd* **33/1**

5610 **P** **Ice Konig (FR)**[144] 2263 7-10-10 **99**........................ SamTwiston-Davies
(Jimmy Frost) *trckd ldr: rdn 7th: sn wknd: t.o whn p.u bef 2 out* **22/1**

5m 54.2s (34.00) **Going Correction** +1.675s/f (Heav) **11** Ran SP% **123.0**
Speed ratings (Par 105): **105,104,103,102,95 94,94,93,91,87**
CSF £14.81 CT £298.49 TOTE £5.30: £2.00, £1.20, £11.40; EX 17.00 Trifecta £576.70.
Owner Moonrakers **Bred** Mrs Darina Kelly **Trained** Milborne Port, Dorset

FOCUS
Race run over 162yds further than advertised. They went a reasonable gallop in this fair handicap and it was the quickest of the three races over the trip. The winner has been rated to form, with a small pb from the second.
T/Plt: £12.20 to a £1 stake. Pool of £89242.65 - 5308.31 winning tickets. T/Qpdt: £7.00 to a £1 stake. Pool of £5756.9 - 602.90 winning tickets. **Tim Mitchell**

4489 STRATFORD (L-H)
Saturday, March 26

4923 Meeting Abandoned - Patches of unsafe ground from earlier flooding

4668 PLUMPTON (L-H)
Sunday, March 27

OFFICIAL GOING: Soft changing to soft (heavy in places) after race 3 (3.25)
Wind: Strong, against Weather: changeable with showers; heavy downpours races 1 & 3

4930 TOTEPLACEPOT NOVICES' HURDLE (12 hdls) 2m 4f 114y
2:15 (2:15) (Class 4) 4-Y-0+ **£3,898** (£1,144; £572; £286)

Form RPR

1461 **1** **Royal Vacation (IRE)**[33] 4294 6-11-13 130........................(tp) PaddyBrennan 127+
(Colin Tizzard) *mde virtually all and set stdy pce: pressed after 3 out: rdn and jnd 2 out: sing to assert whn flattened last: drvn out* **1/2**[1]

61F **2** *2 ¼* **King Cool**[20] 4526 5-11-7 123........................ JoshuaMoore 117
(Gary Moore) *trckd wnr: chal after 3 out: upsides and rdn 2 out: kpt on but hld fr last* **9/4**[2]

P **3** *6* **Butney Island (IRE)**[25] 4439 6-11-1 0........................ ConorO'Farrell 105+
(Nick Mitchell) *hld up in 4th: lost tch w ldng pair fr 9th: tk 3rd after 3 out gng strly: 15 l bhd 2 out: rdn and styd on in encouraging style* **20/1**[3]

5 **4** *25* **Remember Forever (IRE)**[41] 4162 6-11-1 0........................ AndrewGlassonbury 80
(Richard Rowe) *hld up in last: lost tch w ldng pair 9th: rdn bef next: sn wknd* **40/1**

0P **5** *30* **King Charlie (IRE)**[28] 4382 6-11-1 0........................(t) TomO'Brien 50
(Suzy Smith) *racd in 3rd: lost tch w ldng pair 9th: wknd rapidly 3 out: t.o* **20/1**[3]

5m 42.3s (25.30) **Going Correction** +0.475s/f (Soft) **5** Ran SP% **109.4**
Speed ratings (Par 105): **70,69,66,57,45**
CSF £1.88 TOTE £1.40: £1.10, £1.20; EX 1.50 Trifecta £3.60.
Owner Mrs Jean R Bishop **Bred** Tim Hegarty **Trained** Milborne Port, Dorset

FOCUS
The Sussex track's premier meeting of the season, the most valuable in its history, was decimated by non-runners after a deluge of overnight rain forced a significant change in the going. The track passed a morning inspection, despite the concerns of some standing water. Race distance increased by 54yds. There were four absentees in this weakened opener, which was run in driving rain. The top two in the market dominated throughout.

4931 TOTEEXACTA H'CAP CHASE (14 fncs) 2m 3f 164y
2:50 (2:51) (Class 5) (0-100,101) 5-Y-0+ **£3,328** (£1,033; £556)

Form RPR

3411 **1** **Slidecheck (IRE)**[11] 4713 9-11-10 **98**........................(tp) AdamWedge 105+
(Alexandra Dunn) *hld up in tch: cl 3rd after 9th tl wnt 2nd after 3 out: rdn to ld 2 out: 3 l ahd last: idled fnl 100yds: jst hld on* **11/8**[1]

P240 **2** *½* **Bonds Conquest**[29] 4356 7-10-0 **74** oh4........................ JeremiahMcGrath 78
(Seamus Mullins) *led 3rd tl after next: led again 9th: drvn and hdd 2 out: 3 l down last: kpt on wl flat: jst hld* **5/1**[3]

1PP3 **3** *72* **Goring Two (IRE)**[13] 4670 11-10-12 **86**........................ AndrewThornton 18
(Anna Newton-Smith) *nvr gng wl but rousted along to ld after 4th: hdd and j. slowly 9th: sn dropped to last and t.o: lft remote 3rd after 2 out* **15/2**

50P1 **P** **Rocknrobin (IRE)**[13] 4669 5-11-8 **101**........................ DavidNoonan[(5)]
(Chris Gordon) *led to 3rd: rdn to press ldr bef 10th: lost 2nd and btn after 3 out: wkg qckly in 3rd whn p.u after 2 out* **7/4**[2]

5m 37.9s (30.60) **Going Correction** +1.275s/f (Heav) **4** Ran SP% **106.9**
Speed ratings: **89,88,60,**
CSF £7.66 TOTE £1.80; EX 9.00 Trifecta £47.80.
Owner West Buckland Bloodstock Ltd **Bred** Richard Tanner Jnr **Trained** West Buckland, Somerset

FOCUS
Race distance increased by 24yds. Another race badly hit by non-runners. The favourite scrambled home in front in an attritional test.

4932 TOTEQUADPOT NOVICES' H'CAP CHASE (12 fncs) 2m 214y
3:25 (3:26) (Class 4) (0-105,105) 5-Y-0+ **£3,994** (£1,240; £667)

Form RPR

5325 **1** **Like Sully (IRE)**[13] 4669 8-11-11 **104**........................ AndrewGlassonbury 110
(Richard Rowe) *cl up: chsd ldr 6th: rdn after next: lft in narrow ld 3 out: sn jnd: dour battle w runner-up after: jst asserted fr last* **9/4**[1]

3615 **2** *3* **Triple Chief (IRE)**[30] 4343 5-11-2 **100**........................(tp) CiaranGethings[(5)] 103
(Chris Down) *hld up early: trckd ldrs fr 6th: lft in cl 2nd 3 out: str chal fr next: no ex fnl 100yds* **7/2**[3]

-55U **3** *37* **Ma'ire Rua (IRE)**[28] 4379 9-11-7 **100**........................ NickScholfield 66
(Alan Jones) *set off bhd rest: a detached and jumping lacked fluency: nvr involved: lft remote 3rd 2 out* **7/1**

P243 **P** **Trapper Peak (IRE)**[28] 4386 7-11-11 **104**........................ RhysFlint
(Alexandra Dunn) *led to 5th: wknd after 8th: lft 3rd 3 out: wknd and p.u bef 2 out: dismntd* **5/2**[2]

3-PP **U** **Loukhaar (IRE)**[129] 2604 8-10-11 **90**........................ MarkGrant
(Jonathan Geake) *trckd ldr: led 5th: blnd 8th: mstke next: narrow ld whn mstke and uns rdr 3 out* **10/1**

PP0P **P** **Hill Forts Gypse (IRE)**[33] 4291 5-10-0 **79** oh1........................ JeremiahMcGrath
(Seamus Mullins) *unruly to post: hld up early: mstke 2nd: lost tch 7th: t.o after next: p.u bef 2 out* **12/1**

4m 42.5s (19.50) **Going Correction** +1.275s/f (Heav) **6** Ran SP% **110.8**
Speed ratings: **105,103,86,,**
CSF £10.50 CT £42.76 TOTE £3.30: £1.80, £1.20; EX 9.70 Trifecta £50.50.
Owner Winterfields Farm Ltd **Bred** Donie Hennessy **Trained** Sullington, W Sussex

FOCUS
Race distance increased by 24yds. This was run on ever-worsening ground and proved a grueling test. It served up an exciting finish as a pair of runners slugged it out. Like Sully provided local trainer Richard Rowe with a welcome winner.

4933 TOTEPOOL SUSSEX CHAMPION HURDLE (A H'CAP HURDLE) (9 hdls) 1m 7f 195y
4:00 (4:03) (Class 2) 4-Y-0+ **£18,837** (£5,613; £2,841; £1,455; £762)

Form RPR

626U **1** **Disputed (IRE)**[8] 4782 6-10-7 **119**........................ TomCannon 129+
(Chris Gordon) *hld up in tch: prog to trck ldng pair 3 out: swept into the ld 2 out: clr whn fine jump last: bounded home* **16/1**

P153 **2** *14* **Darebin (GER)**[39] 3610 4-10-6 **125**........................ JoshuaMoore 115
(Gary Moore) *cl up: trckd ldr after 6th: upsides fr 3 out tl wnr swept past 2 out: wl hld whn blnd last* **20/1**

3042 **3** *6* **Vicenzo Mio (FR)**[6] 4851 6-11-2 **128**........................(t) SamTwiston-Davies 119
(Paul Nicholls) *prom: trckd ldr 5th: led after next: jnd 3 out: hdd & wknd 2 out: mstke last* **3/1**[2]

U150 **4** *4 ½* **Sea Wall (FR)**[15] 4622 8-10-11 **128**........................ DavidNoonan[(5)] 113
(Chris Gordon) *set off bhd rest in last: in tch fr 4th tl pushed along and outpcd after 3 out: no ch fr 2 out* **8/1**

1201 **5** *36* **Billy No Name (IRE)**[41] 4159 8-11-7 **133**........................ PaddyBrennan 82
(Colin Tizzard) *nt fluent: led: rdn and hdd after 6th: wknd and t.o after 3 out* **9/2**[3]

1-P0 **P** **Rathealy (IRE)**[22] 4484 5-10-13 **130**........................(p) MichaelHeard[(5)]
(David Pipe) *chsd ldr to 5th: sn wknd: t.o whn p.u bef 2 out* **14/1**

2231 **P** **Baratineur (FR)**[27] 4409 5-11-0 **126**........................ HarrySkelton
(Dan Skelton) *hld up: clsd and wl in tch 6th: rdn and wknd 3 out: wl bhd whn p.u bef 2 out* **11/8**[1]

4m 4.5s (3.70) **Going Correction** +0.475s/f (Soft)
WFA 4 from 5yo+ 7lb **7** Ran SP% **113.7**
Speed ratings (Par 109): **109,102,99,96,78 ,**
CSF £232.53 CT £1221.52 TOTE £21.30: £6.40, £3.40; EX 108.60 Trifecta £762.40.
Owner Gilbert & Gamble **Bred** John O'Dwyer **Trained** Morestead, Hampshire

FOCUS
Race distance increased by 42yds. Last year's winner Dormello Mo was one of four notable absentees and it's dubious that this feature was up the standard of recent renewals. They came home at long intervals behind the surprise winner.

4934 TOTEPOOL SUPPORTING PLUMPTON'S RICHEST EVER DAY MAIDEN HURDLE (9 hdls) 1m 7f 195y
4:35 (4:38) (Class 5) 4-Y-0+ **£3,328** (£1,033; £556)

Form RPR

2F22 **1** **Authorized Too**[62] 3773 5-11-3 120........................(p) WayneHutchinson 123+
(Noel Williams) *mde all: gng best after 3 out: shkn up 2 out: clr last: rdn out* **4/7**[1]

2003 **2** *6* **Tara Bridge**[27] 4409 8-11-3 115........................ TomCannon 115
(Chris Gordon) *trckd ldng pair: wnt 2nd after 6th: mstke 3 out: sn rdn and no imp on wnr: kpt on same pce* **2/1**[2]

6 3 21 **Carqalin (FR)**[55] 3907 4-10-10 0.......................... ConorO'Farrell 86
(David Pipe) *trckd wnr tl after 6th: pushed along and steadily fdd* **8/1[3]**

U P **Glimmer Of Hope**[27] 4409 5-11-0 0.......................... KieronEdgar[(3)]
(Mark Hoad) *nt fluent: t.k.h early: hld up in 4th: lost tch 1/2-way: mstke 6th: wl bhd whn p.u bef 2 out* **50/1**

25/ P **Sutton Sid**[422] 2038 6-10-10 0..........................(p) MissBHampson[(7)]
(Michelle Bryant) *hld up in 5th: lost tch 1/2-way and sn rdn: wl bhd whn p.u bef 2 out* **40/1**

000/ P **Foreverbest (IRE)**[711] 5367 7-10-10 0.......................... MattieBatchelor
(Roger Ingram) *nt fluent: hld up in last: lost tch 1/2-way: mstke 6th: t.o after: p.u bef 2 out* **66/1**

4m 10.9s (10.10) **Going Correction** +0.475s/f (Soft)
WFA 4 from 5yo+ 7lb **6 Ran SP% 114.0**
Speed ratings (Par 103): **93,90,79, ,**
CSF £2.16 TOTE £1.50: £1.10, £1.70; EX 2.20 Trifecta £3.90.
Owner Stonepoint Racing Club **Bred** Almagro De Actividades Commerciales **Trained** Blewbury, Oxon

FOCUS
Race distance increased by 42yds. This lacked depth and proved relatively plain sailing for the odds-on market leader.

4935 AT THE RACES SUSSEX NATIONAL (A H'CAP CHASE) (20 fncs) 3m 4f 102y
5:10 (5:14) (Class 3) (0-130,128) 5-Y-0+ **£12,685** (£3,869; £2,021; £1,097)

Form RPR

1P44 1 **Tour Des Champs (FR)**[35] 4267 9-11-11 **127**.....(p) SamTwiston-Davies 146+
(Nigel Twiston-Davies) *a in ldng trio: led 11th to 14th: led again 16th: drew clr fr 4 out: in n.d after: eased after last* **11/2**

-033 2 16 **Krackatoa King**[14] 4649 8-11-5 **121**..........................(b) WayneHutchinson 123
(Noel Williams) *stmbld 3rd and reminders: pressed ldrs: drvn fr 15th: chsd wnr fr next: mstke 4 out: no ch after next: hld on for 2nd* **3/1[1]**

32PP 3 3/4 **Finish The Story (IRE)**[30] 4340 10-10-11 **113**..........................(bt) AlainCawley 113
(Johnny Farrelly) *hld up in last: rdn and struggling 15th: rallied fr 4 out: pressing for 2nd whn mstke and bmpd last: kpt on* **14/1**

151U 4 19 **Blameitalonmyroots (IRE)**[8] 4800 6-11-8 **124**.......................... AidanColeman 102
(Oliver Sherwood) *in tch: effrt 16th: pressed for a pl fr next but no ch w wnr: wknd after 2 out* **4/1[2]**

P011 P **Coolking**[8] 4783 9-10-1 **108**..........................(b) DavidNoonan[(5)]
(Chris Gordon) *led to 11th: led 14th to 16th: wknd rapidly: p.u bef 3 out* **9/2[3]**

5442 P **Saroque (IRE)**[30] 4340 9-11-12 **128**.......................... LiamTreadwell
(Venetia Williams) *pressed ldrs: lost pl and struggling 7th: lost tch 10th: bhd whn mstke 11th and p.u* **6/1**

640 P **Itoldyou (IRE)**[28] 4380 10-10-8 **110**..........................(vt[1]) TomCannon
(Linda Jewell) *nt a fluent: in tch to 9th: sn t.o: p.u after 12th* **12/1**

1P13 P **Golanova**[28] 4380 8-10-10 **112**..........................(b) JoshuaMoore
(Gary Moore) *in tch: mstke 7th: effrt fr 16th: cl up in chsng gp 4 out but no ch w wnr: no prog after: wl btn 5th whn p.u after 2 out* **16/1**

8m 7.9s (29.90) **Going Correction** +1.275s/f (Heav)
WFA 5 from 6yo+ 1lb **8 Ran SP% 113.1**
Speed ratings: **108,103,103,97, , ,**
CSF £22.64 CT £216.47 TOTE £7.00: £2.00, £1.70, £3.20; EX 29.00 Trifecta £299.30.
Owner Mrs Caroline Mould **Bred** Bruno Vagne **Trained** Naunton, Gloucs

FOCUS
Race distance increased by 36yds. A well contested staying handicap chase, in which stamina was at a premium. Only four of the eight starters completed.

4936 TOTEPOOL HAPPY EASTER CONDITIONAL JOCKEYS' H'CAP HURDLE (12 hdls) 2m 4f 114y
5:45 (5:47) (Class 5) (0-100,99) 4-Y-0+ **£3,249** (£954; £477; £238)

Form RPR

2131 1 **Loves Destination**[16] 4593 5-11-12 **99**.......................... DavidNoonan 107+
(Chris Gordon) *w ldr: led 3 out and sn pushed clr: in n.d after: eased nr fin: comf* **13/8[1]**

FP2P 2 8 **Kayflin (FR)**[27] 4413 8-10-12 **85**..........................(p) JackSherwood 81
(Linda Jewell) *hld up in last but wl in tch: prog to trck ldng pair 9th: cl up whn mstke 3 out: sn outpcd: drvn to take 2nd 2 out: no ch w wnr* **8/1**

05P3 3 3/4 **Double Court (IRE)**[21] 4504 5-9-11 **73** oh4..........................(v) JamieBargary[(3)] 68
(Nigel Twiston-Davies) *j.rt 1st: wl in tch: cl up whn mstke 3 out: sn outpcd: drvn to press for 2nd fr 2 out but no ch w wnr* **7/4[2]**

P-66 4 4 **Snippetydoodah**[265] 930 8-11-1 **88**.......................... CiaranGethings 78
(Michael Roberts) *racd wd: bmpd 1st: pressed ldrs: lost pl 9th: stl in tch 3 out: pushed along and outpcd after: kpt on fr last to take 4th nr fin* **16/1**

-033 5 1 3/4 **Fifi L'Amour (IRE)**[20] 4528 10-9-11 **75**.......................... TommyDowling[(5)] 64
(Linda Jewell) *mde most at stdy pce: hdd and drvn 3 out: lost 2nd and wknd 2 out* **5/1[3]**

-30P P **Bondi Mist (IRE)**[102] 3108 7-11-11 **98**.......................... ConorShoemark
(Jonathan Geake) *in tch: dropped to last and pushed along 8th: stl in tch 3 out: wknd qckly and p.u bef 2 out* **25/1**

5m 47.1s (30.10) **Going Correction** +0.475s/f (Soft) **6 Ran SP% 112.0**
Speed ratings (Par 103): **61,57,57,56,55**
CSF £14.36 CT £24.00 TOTE £2.20: £1.30, £3.00; EX 13.20 Trifecta £38.50.
Owner Chris Gordon Racing Club **Bred** Hazeley Stud **Trained** Morestead, Hampshire

FOCUS
Race distance increased by 54yds. They went very steadily in this concluding handicap hurdle and it paid to be handy.
T/Jkpt: Not won. T/Plt: £298.90 to a £1 stake. Pool: £85,317.03 - 208.32 winning tickets T/Qpdt: £78.00 to a £1 stake. Pool: £7,011.83 - 66.50 winning tickets **Jonathan Neesom**

4702 SEDGEFIELD (L-H)
Sunday, March 27

OFFICIAL GOING: Soft (6.5)
Wind: strong 1/2 behind, wintry showers race 3 (3.00) and 4 Weather: changeable, very windy

4937 BETFRED TV CONDITIONAL JOCKEYS' NOVICES' HURDLE (8 hdls) 2m 178y
1:50 (1:51) (Class 4) 4-Y-0+ **£3,508** (£1,030; £515; £257)

Form RPR

1103 1 **Master Jake (IRE)**[20] 4526 8-11-11 128.......................... BridgetAndrews[(3)] 130+
(Dan Skelton) *mde all: qcknd gallop 3rd: clr next: pushed along bef 2 out: rdn clr bef last: drvn out* **10/3[3]**

3 2 6 **Eyes Of A Tiger (IRE)**[14] 4639 5-11-4 119..........................[1] CraigGallagher[(3)] 118
(Brian Ellison) *chsd wnr: effrt and 2 l down 2 out: kpt on same pce* **5/2[2]**

4222 3 18 **Maxie T**[14] 4640 5-10-11 132.......................... HugoThompsonBrown[(10)] 101
(Micky Hammond) *hld up: hit 2nd: wnt 3rd at next: outpcd and pushed along after 5th: nvr a threat* **10/11[1]**

4 51 **Harmonic Lady**[14] 6-10-7 0.......................... RyanDay 34
(Mike Sowersby) *in rr: t.o 4th sn after 5th: eventually completed* **250/1**

00/ P **Jimsneverright**[385] 8-11-0 0.......................... JamieHamilton
(Ian Brown) *t.k.h: trckd ldrs: lost pl 3rd: sn bhd: t.o whn p.u bef 3 out* **200/1**

35 P **Dubai Celebrity**[14] 4633 4-10-7 0.......................... CraigNichol
(John Wade) *chsd ldrs: outpcd and lost pl 4th: sn bhd: t.o whn p.u bef 2 out* **20/1**

4m 9.6s (2.70) **Going Correction** +0.10s/f (Yiel)
WFA 4 from 5yo+ 7lb **6 Ran SP% 109.7**
Speed ratings (Par 105): **97,94,85,61,**
CSF £11.59 TOTE £4.10: £1.80, £1.30; EX 10.60 Trifecta £12.00.
Owner Craig Buckingham **Bred** Tyrone Molloy **Trained** Alcester, Warwicks

FOCUS
All distances as advertised. After 6mm of overnight rain the official going was changed to soft. Only three mattered in the opening conditional jockeys' novices' hurdle and they finished well strung out, with the favourite disappointing.

4938 BETFRED "SUPPORTS JACK BERRY HOUSE" H'CAP CHASE (16 fncs) 2m 3f 65y
2:25 (2:26) (Class 5) (0-100,98) 5-Y-0+ **£2,989** (£877; £438; £219)

Form RPR

2261 1 **Runswick Relax**[12] 4704 10-11-6 **92**..........................(tp) HenryBrooke 104
(Kenneth Slack) *mde all: drvn clr bef 2 out: 5 l ahd last: wknd clsng stages: jst hld on* **3/1[1]**

34-P 2 nk **Attimo (GER)**[17] 4569 7-11-11 **97**..........................(t) JonathanEngland 109
(Sam Drake) *chsd ldrs: 2nd 4th: styd on wl last 50yds: jst hld* **8/1**

5152 3 5 **Captain Sharpe**[12] 4707 8-10-1 **80**..........................(b) MrStanSheppard[(7)] 86
(Kenny Johnson) *wnt prom 5th: 3rd bef 3 out: kpt on same pce bef next* **15/2**

F363 4 5 **King Of The Dark (IRE)**[99] 3159 9-11-5 **98**.......................... ThomasDowson[(7)] 100
(Victor Thompson) *gave problems s: chsd ldrs: hit 2nd: outpcd 13th: rallied 2 out: modest 4th appr last* **22/1**

136- 5 3 1/4 **Runswick Days (IRE)**[431] 3797 9-11-3 **89**..........................(p) BrianHughes 87
(John Wade) *chsd ldrs: reminders after 12th: sn drvn: one pce fr next* **14/1**

41F3 6 4 1/2 **Bollin Line**[26] 4418 9-11-5 **96**.......................... DeanPratt[(5)] 90
(Lucinda Egerton) *in rr: hdwy sn after 13th: modest 6th 3 out: one pce* **7/1[3]**

143- 7 2 **Hurricane Ivan (IRE)**[28] 4398 8-11-1 **92**.......................... LizzieKelly[(5)] 85
(S Wilson, Ire) *in rr: last whn blnd 9th: sn reminders: sme hdwy next: reminders 11th: nvr on terms* **5/1[2]**

P4-0 8 6 **Dr Beaujolais (IRE)**[67] 3680 10-11-6 **95**.......................... HarryChalloner[(3)] 80
(Richard Ford) *chsd ldrs: lost pl 13th* **33/1**

3400 9 3 **Sendiym (FR)**[27] 4404 9-10-9 **84**..........................(p) ColmMcCormack[(3)] 66
(Dianne Sayer) *in rr: drvn 10th: nvr on terms* **20/1**

332- 10 5 **Crown And Glory (IRE)**[429] 3839 9-10-10 **85**.......................... AdamNicol[(3)] 62
(Chris Fairhurst) *in rr: bhd fr 13th* **5/1[2]**

POPP 11 2 **Stitched In Time (IRE)**[180] 1691 9-10-13 **90**..........................(t) NathanMoscrop[(5)] 65
(Sara Ender) *in rr: blnd 1st: hdwy to chse ldrs 5th: lost pl 11th: sn bhd* **28/1**

5m 4.9s (1.90) **Going Correction** +0.15s/f (Yiel) **11 Ran SP% 115.9**
Speed ratings: **102,101,99,97,96 94,93,91,89,87 86**
CSF £25.41 CT £165.10 TOTE £3.40: £1.60, £2.80, £3.00; EX 33.70 Trifecta £222.90.
Owner A Slack **Bred** Mrs S Barraclough **Trained** Hilton, Cumbria

FOCUS
A moderate handicap chase and the winner just lasted home.

4939 BETFRED MOBILE MARES' H'CAP HURDLE (8 hdls) 2m 178y
3:00 (3:01) (Class 3) (0-125,118) 4-Y-0+ **£6,498** (£1,908; £954; £477)

Form RPR

6111 1 **Beyondtemptation**[10] 4736 8-9-10 **95**..........................(t) ThomasDowson[(7)] 103+
(Jonathan Haynes) *mde all: pushed along 5th: styd on wl fr 2 out* **6/1[3]**

215P 2 3 1/4 **Samedi Soir**[22] 4471 6-11-7 **118**.......................... MrJohnDawson[(5)] 123
(Keith Reveley) *hld up in rr: hdwy to chse ldrs 4th: lft handy 3rd 3 out: 2nd last: kpt on same pce* **17/2**

3010 3 3 1/2 **Attention Seaker**[1] 4909 6-11-12 **118**.......................... BrianHughes 120
(Tim Easterby) *chsd ldrs: lft handy 2nd 3 out: hit next: kpt on same pce* **5/2[1]**

0004 4 4 **Ten Trees**[17] 4567 6-10-8 **100**.......................... PaulMoloney 100
(Alan Swinbank) *chsd ldrs: drvn and outpcd whn hmpd and lft modest 4th 3 out: kpt on between last 2* **7/2[2]**

4650 5 5 **Taylor (IRE)**[51] 3970 7-11-0 **106**.......................... HenryBrooke 99
(Micky Hammond) *hld up in rr: sme hdwy and lft poor 5th 3 out: kpt on between last 2* **18/1**

0 6 19 **Feel The Air (IRE)**[169] 1854 6-11-4 **110**.......................... DerekFox 84
(Mark Michael McNiff, Ire) *chsd ldrs: drvn 4th: lost pl next: bhd 3 out* **10/1**

465R 7 7 **Gold Chain (IRE)**[86] 3424 6-10-3 **98**.......................... EmmaSayer[(3)] 65
(Dianne Sayer) *prom: lost pl bef 3rd: sn bhd: t.o and reminders 5th* **12/1**

2320 F **Shine Away (IRE)**[71] 3626 6-10-13 **105**.......................... DannyCook
(Sue Smith) *chsd wnr: upsides 5th: fell next* **6/1[3]**

4m 12.8s (5.90) **Going Correction** +0.50s/f (Soft) **8 Ran SP% 111.9**
Speed ratings (Par 107): **106,104,102,100,98 89,86,**
CSF £51.98 CT £157.70 TOTE £5.00: £2.10, £2.90, £1.50; EX 58.30 Trifecta £124.70.
Owner J C Haynes **Bred** J C Haynes **Trained** Low Row, Cumbria

FOCUS
A wide-open handicap for mares but not a great race for the grade with the topweight 7lb below the race ceiling.

4940 BETFRED LOTTO H'CAP CHASE (17 fncs) 2m 5f 28y
3:35 (3:36) (Class 4) (0-110,107) 5-Y-0+ **£4,938** (£1,450; £725; £362)

Form RPR

0P2U 1 **Lily Little Legs (IRE)**[18] 4554 7-10-13 **94**.......................... BrianHughes 103+
(Mike Sowersby) *chsd ldrs: nt fluent 7th: drvn 14th: outpcd and reminders bef 2 out: styd on to ld appr last: drvn out* **14/1**

5122 2 3 **My Friend George**[18] 4554 10-11-11 **106**..........................(p) HenryBrooke 112
(Kenneth Slack) *w ldr: nt fluent 3rd: led 9th to 14th: led narrowly bef next: hdd appr last: kpt on same pce* **9/4[1]**

4633 3 1 1/2 **Chanceofa Lifetime (IRE)**[31] 4327 9-11-5 **107**.......................... MissAWaugh[(7)] 112
(Victor Thompson) *completed full circ bef s: chsd ldrs: led briefly 8th: led 14th: hdd bef next: upsides between last 2: kpt on one pce* **5/1**

0P53 **4** *9* **Houndscourt (IRE)**[51] 3969 9-11-6 **101**..............................(t) DannyCook 99
(Joanne Foster) *chsd ldrs: pushed along 8th: lost pl 12th: kpt on fr 2 out* **7/2**[2]

6554 **5** *29* **Apache Pilot**[39] 4175 8-9-9 **83** ow2........................(tp) ThomasDowson(7) 49
(Maurice Barnes) *led to 8th: drvn and lost pl 11th: bhd whn reminders next: t.o 3 out* **9/2**[3]

652U **P** **Pay The King (IRE)**[5] 4866 9-10-13 **94**.................................... WillKennedy
(Micky Hammond) *in rr whn j. violently lft 1st: stirrup leather pin broke and rdr lost iron: eased and p.u bef next* **5/1**

4442 **U** **Stilo Blue Native (IRE)**[8] 4795 8-11-12 **107**.................................... CraigNichol
(John Wade) *hld up in last: wl in tch whn mstke and uns rdr 10th* **10/1**

5m 44.0s (11.00) **Going Correction** +0.55s/f (Soft) **7** Ran SP% **120.3**
Speed ratings: **101,99,99,95,84** ,
CSF £50.36 CT £190.16 TOTE £11.90: £6.60, £2.40; EX 36.00 Trifecta £159.20.
Owner Mrs Janet Cooper **Bred** James Wickham **Trained** Goodmanham, E Yorks

FOCUS
A modest handicap chase and it paid to race prominently.

4941 BETFRED HURDLE SERIES FINAL (HANDICAP HURDLE) 2m 3f 188y
4:10 (4:11) (Class 2) 4-Y-0+

£15,640 (£4,620; £2,310; £1,155; £577; £290)

Form RPR

5432 **1** **General Mahler (IRE)**[26] 4416 6-11-3 **113**.................... RichieMcLernon 121+
(Brian Ellison) *racd wd: chsd ldrs 3rd: cl 2nd appr 2 out: led last: sddle slipped clsng stages: hld on wl* **9/2**[1]

2333 **2** *1* **Bollin Ace**[44] 4108 5-11-0 **110**..............................(b) BrianHarding 117
(Tim Easterby) *trckd ldrs: led bef 2 out: hdd last: no ex clsng stages* **8/1**[3]

123U **3** *13* **Ryedale Racer**[21] 4509 5-11-12 **122**.................................... BrianHughes 117
(Malcolm Jefferson) *trckd ldrs: stmbld sn after 3 out: one pce appr 2 out* **9/2**[1]

3242 **4** *6* **Just Georgie**[33] 4299 6-11-5 **115**.................................... DannyCook 105
(Sue Smith) *in rr: hdwy 3 out: one pce* **9/2**[1]

122 **5** *11* **Samtu (IRE)**[31] 4324 5-11-9 **119**..............................(t) IanPopham 96
(Dan Skelton) *t.k.h: sn trcking ldrs: drvn 3 out: wknd bef next* **10/1**

412 **6** *nk* **William Of Orange**[47] 4044 5-11-8 **118**..............................(t) HenryBrooke 96
(Donald McCain) *led: hit 7th: hdd bef 2 out: sn wknd* **6/1**[2]

6533 **7** *16* **Silver Shuffle (IRE)**[21] 4509 9-9-13 **98**.................................... EmmaSayer(3) 59
(Dianne Sayer) *in rr: drvn 7th: nvr on terms* **18/1**

3-1P **8** *1 ½* **Ardmay (IRE)**[114] 2893 7-10-12 **113**.................................... RyanDay(5) 72
(Kevin Ryan) *hld up in rr: hdwy 7th: lost pl bef 2 out* **28/1**

3026 **P** **Absolute (IRE)**[5] 4865 5-10-2 **105**.................................... TrevorRyan(7)
(Sue Smith) *prom: lost pl after 4th: drvn 3 out: sn bhd: t.o whn p.u bef next* **8/1**[3]

6651 **P** **Oak Vintage (IRE)**[21] 4509 6-10-11 **112**.................................... JamieHamilton(5)
(Ann Hamilton) *w ldr: hit 5th: drvn 7th: lost pl sn after 3 out: t.o whn p.u bef next: lame* **14/1**

5m 11.6s (17.50) **Going Correction** +0.90s/f (Soft)
WFA 4 from 5yo+ 8lb **10** Ran SP% **115.5**
Speed ratings (Par 109): **101,100,95,93,88 88,82,81,** ,
CSF £40.05 CT £171.13 TOTE £6.80: £2.30, £3.70, £1.70; EX 69.80 Trifecta £467.50.
Owner P J Martin **Bred** Noel O'Brien **Trained** Norton, N Yorks

FOCUS
A competitive renewal but the two principals pulled a long way clear of the rest.

4942 BETFRED "HAPPY EASTER" H'CAP HURDLE (13 hdls) 3m 3f 9y
4:45 (4:45) (Class 5) (0-100,100) 4-Y-0+ **£2,729** (£801; £400; £200)

Form RPR

0254 **1** **Agent Louise**[8] 4804 8-10-1 **78**..............................(p) AdamNicol(3) 91+
(Mike Sowersby) *hld up towards rr: reminder after 4th: hdwy 8th: sn trcking ldrs: led appr 2 out: drvn clr between last 2* **9/1**[3]

/ **2** *14* **Spiker The Biker (IRE)**[122] 2743 12-11-2 **90**..............................(tp) RichieMcLernon 91
(Nigel Thomas Slevin, Ire) *trckd ldrs: chsd wnr appr 2 out: kpt on same pce* **14/1**

46U6 **3** *7* **What A Game (IRE)**[41] 4152 5-11-5 **93**.................................... BrianHughes 86
(Tim Easterby) *trckd ldrs: 3rd and drvn appr 2 out: one pce* **7/2**[2]

240P **4** *7* **Triumph Davis (IRE)**[26] 4421 7-10-10 **84**.................................... HenryBrooke 69
(Micky Hammond) *hld up in rr: hdwy to chse ldrs 6th: one pce appr 2 out* **14/1**

P143 **5** *34* **Cumbrian Farmer**[18] 4557 9-10-0 **77**..............................(bt) HarryChalloner(3) 28
(Kenneth Slack) *chsd ldrs: lost pl bef 3 out: lft distant 4th appr 2 out: t.o* **9/4**[1]

P6PP **P** **Heart O Annandale (IRE)**[26] 4421 9-10-12 **91**....(bt[1]) NathanMoscrop(5)
(Iain Jardine) *led: hdd 9th: sn lost pl and bhd: t.o whn p.u bef 3 out* **14/1**

P404 **P** **Blue Cove**[18] 4557 11-10-0 **74** oh5.................................... WillKennedy
(Lynn Siddall) *in rr: hdwy 6th: lost pl 8th: sn bhd: t.o whn p.u bef 2 out* **9/1**[3]

3555 **P** **Silver Dragon**[20] 4534 8-11-4 **97**..............................(p) RyanDay(5)
(Mike Sowersby) *nt fluent in rr: reminders 7th: sme hdwy next: lost pl after 10th: sn bhd: t.o whn p.u bef 2 out* **12/1**

1625 **P** **Optical High**[21] 4510 7-10-10 **94**.................................... StephenMcCarthy(10)
(Sue Smith) *chsd ldrs: drvn 5th: lost pl next: sn detached in last: p.u bef 9th* **9/1**[3]

P13P **P** **Izbushka (IRE)**[26] 4421 5-11-1 **89**..............................(b) PeterCarberry
(David Thompson) *chsd ldrs: led 9th: hdd appr 2 out: sn lost pl and distant 6th whn eased and p.u 2 out* **16/1**

7m 26.5s (34.50) **Going Correction** +1.30s/f (Heav) **10** Ran SP% **116.6**
Speed ratings (Par 103): **100,95,93,91,81**
CSF £122.84 CT £527.78 TOTE £6.90: £2.40, £4.30, £2.40; EX 128.70 Trifecta £682.70.
Owner M E Sowersby **Bred** Mrs C J Zetter-Wells **Trained** Goodmanham, E Yorks

FOCUS
A moderate staying handicap hurdle but a clear-cut winner.

4943 BETFRED RACING "FOLLOW US ON TWITTER" H'CAP HURDLE (8 hdls) 2m 178y
5:20 (5:24) (Class 5) (0-100,99) 4-Y-0+ **£2,729** (£801; £400; £200)

Form RPR

5PP1 **1** **Azure Glamour (IRE)**[12] 4703 7-11-2 **89**..............................(b) HenryBrooke 98+
(Kenneth Slack) *mde all: drvn 4th: reminders next: clr appr 2 out: 8 l ahd whn hit last: tired bdly: all out* **3/1**[2]

0640 **2** *1 ¼* **Strait Run (IRE)**[31] 4326 5-9-11 **80**.................................... BillyGarritty(10) 85
(Micky Hammond) *chsd ldrs: 2nd 5th: styd on fr last: no ex clsng stages* **12/1**

5004 **3** *¾* **Hey Bob (IRE)**[18] 4553 4-10-7 **90**.................................... TonyKelly(3) 87
(Chris Grant) *hld up in rr: hdwy and hung lft fr 3 out: modest 5th 2 out: 3rd last: styd on wl clsng stages* **20/1**

3342 **4** *3 ¼* **Copt Hill**[21] 4513 8-10-9 **82**..............................(p) BrianHughes 83
(Tracy Waggott) *chsd ldrs: drvn 3 out: one pce* **11/4**[1]

0600 **5** *16* **Zakety Zak**[58] 3840 5-10-12 **85**..............................(p) PeterBuchanan 74
(James Turner) *mid-div: hdwy 4th: modest 4th 2 out: sn wknd* **16/1**

6/0- **P** **Court Jester (IRE)**[67] 3695 10-11-7 **99**.................................... LizzieKelly(5)
(S Wilson, Ire) *in rr: bhd fr 5th: t.o whn p.u bef next* **11/2**

0/05 **P** **Grammar**[138] 2422 7-11-0 **90**.................................... AdamNicol(3)
(David Thompson) *prom: drvn and lost pl 3rd: sn bhd: t.o whn p.u bef 5th* **28/1**

FF62 **P** **Home For Tea**[12] 4703 7-10-9 **82**..............................(p) CraigNichol
(Keith Dalgleish) *chsd ldrs: lost pl 3 out: sn bhd: t.o whn p.u bef 2 out* **9/2**[3]

2600 **P** **Poet Mark (IRE)**[61] 3791 4-11-0 **94**..............................(b) BrianHarding
(Tim Easterby) *sn in rr: distant 6th bef 2 out: t.o whn p.u bef last* **22/1**

0005 **P** **Qatea (IRE)**[45] 4068 4-10-2 **92**..............................(t) CaiWilliams(10)
(Donald McCain) *rr-div: bhd fr 5th: t.o whn p.u bef 2 out* **25/1**

4300 **P** **Champagne Ransom (FR)**[26] 4415 4-10-6 **93**........ MissBeckySmith(7)
(Micky Hammond) *in rr: mstke 1st: sme hdwy 3rd: lost pl 5th: sn bhd: t.o whn p.u bef 2 out* **66/1**

4m 34.2s (27.30) **Going Correction** +1.70s/f (Heav)
WFA 4 from 5yo+ 7lb **11** Ran SP% **116.7**
Speed ratings (Par 103): **103,102,102,100,93** , , , ,
CSF £34.13 CT £616.20 TOTE £4.00: £1.40, £5.40, £4.20; EX 43.80 Trifecta £811.00.
Owner E G Tunstall **Bred** Kenneth Parkhill **Trained** Hilton, Cumbria

FOCUS
Only a moderate handicap hurdle.
T/Plt: £280.90 to a £1 stake. Pool: £84,419.36 - 219.38 winning tickets. T/Qpdt: £63.90 to a £1 stake. Pool: £7,488.88 - 86.70 winning tickets. **Walter Glynn**

4944 - 4948a (Foreign Racing) - See Raceform Interactive

4688
CORK (R-H)
Sunday, March 27

OFFICIAL GOING: Heavy

4949a IMPERIAL CALL CHASE (GRADE 3) (16 fncs) 3m
5:05 (5:06) 5-Y-0+ **£14,696** (£4,540; £2,150; £955)

RPR

1 **Fine Rightly (IRE)**[10] 4754 8-11-6 149.................................... AELynch 150+
(S R B Crawford, Ire) *hld up in 4th: clsr 5 out in 3rd: travelled best to dispute 3 out and sn led: clr appr last: kpt on strly: easily* **4/5**[1]

2 *10* **Toon River (IRE)**[22] 4498 11-11-6 144..............................(t) PhillipEnright 140
(Miss Mary Louise Hallahan, Ire) *led tl jnd 3 out and sn hdd: nt fluent next and sn no match for wnr: kpt on same pce run-in* **4/1**[3]

3 *6* **Arctic Skipper (IRE)**[21] 4517 7-10-10 130.................................... PatrickMangan 124
(Vincent Laurence Halley, Ire) *chsd ldrs in 3rd: shaded 2nd fr 3rd: rdn and almost on terms 3 out: nt qckn in 3rd bef next: sn one pce* **4/1**[2]

4 *16* **Boxing Along (IRE)**[45] 4087 12-11-0 104..............................(t) RogerLoughran 112
(Vincent Laurence Halley, Ire) *chsd ldr in 2nd: dropped to 3rd after 3rd: rdn in 4th after 4 out and dropped to rr at next: no ex whn lft remote 4th 2 out* **50/1**

U **Malt Gem (IRE)**[28] 4397 8-11-3 127.................................... DonaghMeyler
(Miss Mary Louise Hallahan, Ire) *hld up in rr: sme prog into mod 4th 3 out: no ex whn j. v big and uns rdr 2 out* **16/1**

F **Toubaloo (IRE)**[22] 4498 8-11-0 127.................................... DavidSplaine
(Andrew Lee, Ire) *hld up in 5th tl fell 8th* **8/1**[3]

7m 21.6s (85.20) **6** Ran SP% **114.5**
CSF £4.89 TOTE £1.70: £1.50, £1.30; DF 4.60 Trifecta £10.10.
Owner Miss Patricia Duffin **Bred** Miss Patricia Duffin **Trained** Larne, Co Antrim

FOCUS
A fine performance here from an improving chaser and, while he was entitled to win on ratings, he did it very smoothly. The winner sets the standard.

4950 - 4953a (Foreign Racing) - See Raceform Interactive

4257
FAIRYHOUSE (R-H)
Sunday, March 27

OFFICIAL GOING: Yielding (soft in places)

4954a IRISH STALLION FARMS EUROPEAN BREEDERS FUND MARES NOVICE HURDLE CHAMPIONSHIP FINAL (GRADE 1) (12 hdls) 2m 4f
3:05 (3:08) 4-Y-0+

£43,382 (£13,970; £6,617; £2,941; £1,470; £735)

RPR

1 **Jer's Girl (IRE)**[50] 4002 4-10-8 133.................................... BarryGeraghty 132+
(Gavin Cromwell, Ire) *settled in mid-div: gng wl in 5th 4 out: tk clsr order after next and disp bef 2 out: led fr 2 out and drvn clr: styd on strly run-in* **3/1**[1]

2 *13* **Jessber's Dream (IRE)**[37] 4231 6-11-7 137..............................(t) NoelFehily 130
(Harry Fry) *chsd ldrs: 4th 1/2-way: rdn in 4th bef 2 out and no imp on wnr u.p in 2nd bef last: kpt on one pce run-in and all out to jst hold mod 2nd* **7/2**[2]

3 *shd* **Asthuria (FR)**[397] 5-11-6.................................... RWalsh 129
(W P Mullins, Ire) *w.w in rr: hdwy bef 3 out to chse ldrs in 5th gng wl into st: swtchd rt bef 2 out where slt mstke: rdn into 3rd bef last and no imp on wnr: kpt on one pce run-in: jst failed for mod 2nd* **4/1**[3]

4 *3 ¼* **Cashelard Lady (IRE)**[57] 3873 6-11-7 130.................................... DenisO'Regan 127
(Shane Crawley, Ire) *sn settled bhd ldr in 2nd: rdn appr st and lost pl bef 2 out where nt fluent in 4th: sn swtchd rt in 5th and no imp on wnr: kpt on one pce in 4th run-in* **7/1**

5 *6* **Monbeg Rose (IRE)**[14] 4653 6-11-7 120.................................... JJBurke 121
(W P Mullins, Ire) *sn led: rdn and jnd bef 2 out: hdd fr 2 out and sn no imp on easy wnr: wknd into 5th bef last* **50/1**

6 *6 ½* **Billy's Hope (IRE)**[52] 3961 5-11-6 118.................................... RobbiePower 113
(Mrs John Harrington, Ire) *hld up towards rr: rdn in 8th after 3 out and no imp in mod 6th fr next: kpt on one pce* **33/1**

7 *26* **Ten Times Better (IRE)**[57] 3873 6-11-7 123.................................... MsKWalsh 88
(P A Fahy, Ire) *prom: sn settled bhd ldrs: nt fluent in 3rd at 3rd and next: mstke in mod 3rd 4 out: nt fluent next and wknd bef 2 out where mstke in mod 7th: t.o* **25/1**

P **Whistle Dixie (IRE)**[10] 4734 6-11-7 119..............................(t) BJCooper
(Gordon Elliott, Ire) *hld up: towards rr whn p.u qckly bef 5th* **20/1**

P **Myztique (IRE)**[14] 4653 6-11-7 116 ... (t) JackKennedy
(Gordon Elliott, Ire) *hld up: pushed along in 7th after 4 out and sn no ex: rdn in mod 9th after 3 out and wknd: eased and p.u bef 2 out* **16/1**

P **Myska (IRE)**[56] 3890 6-11-7 140 ... PaulTownend
(W P Mullins, Ire) *hld up: nt fluent 1st: slt mstke towards rr at 5th: tk clsr order in 6th fr 4 out: wknd after next and trailing whn p.u bef 2 out* **5/1**

P **Miss Me Now (IRE)**[15] 4626 6-11-7 ... DavidMullins
(W P Mullins, Ire) *settled in mid-div: 5th 1/2-way: mstke in 6th 4 out and lost pl: wknd to rr bef 3 out: p.u after 3 out* **20/1**

5m 10.7s (-12.30) **Going Correction** -0.275s/f (Good)
WFA 4 from 5yo+ 8lb **11** Ran SP% **120.5**
Speed ratings: **113,107,107,106,104 101,91,,,**
CSF £13.28 TOTE £3.50: £1.50, £1.60, £1.60; DF 15.00 Trifecta £47.40.
Owner John P McManus **Bred** E A Bourke M R C V S **Trained** Navan, Co. Meath

FOCUS
The average mark of those with a rating here was just higher than 126, showing that such races are often Grade 1s in name only, but it was still an interesting contest. The winner had proper juvenile form, while the second was progressing coming here.

4955a AGNELLI MOTOR PARK NOVICE HURDLE (GRADE 2) (12 hdls) 2m 4f
3:40 (3:42) 4-Y-O+
£19,522 (£6,286; £2,977; £1,323; £661; £330)

RPR

1 **Acapella Bourgeois (FR)**[31] 4332 6-11-10 137 ... JJBurke 143
(Ms Sandra Hughes, Ire) *disp early tl narrow advantage fr 1st: over 2 l clr at 1/2-way: slt mstke 3 out: rdn and strly pressed fr 2 out: jnd u.p run-in: kpt on best clsng stages to ld fnl stride* **5/1**[2]

2 *hd* **Nambour (GER)**[31] 4332 6-11-5 131 ... (t) BJCooper 138
(W P Mullins, Ire) *chsd ldrs: 3rd 1/2-way: cl 2nd bef 3 out: gng wl bhd ldr bef next: rdn bef last where almost on terms: disp u.p run-in and ev ch: hdd fnl stride* **8/1**

3 *2* **Our Duke (IRE)**[31] 4332 6-11-5 0 ... RobbiePower 136
(Mrs John Harrington, Ire) *towards rr early: slt mstke in mid-div at 2nd: 6th 1/2-way: slt mstke 6th: impr bhd ldrs after 4 out: rdn in 4th fr 2 out and no imp on ldrs in 3rd fr bef last: kpt on same pce* **7/1**

4 *4* **Haymount (IRE)**[22] 4496 7-11-5 128 ... PaulTownend 132
(W P Mullins, Ire) *hld up: niggled along in rr after 2nd and reminder: last at 1/2-way: hdwy 4 out to chse ldrs on outer: mstke next: rdn in 5th fr 2 out and no imp on ldrs: kpt on one pce in 4th run-in* **33/1**

5 *4¼* **Lift The Latch (IRE)**[8] 4809 6-11-5 140 ... BarryGeraghty 128+
(A J Martin, Ire) *chsd ldrs early: 7th 1/2-way: impr bhd ldrs fr 4 out: slt mstke next: gng wl in 4th bef st: sn rdn in 3rd and no ex between last 2: wknd into 5th fr last* **2/1**[1]

6 *9½* **American (FR)**[127] 2630 6-11-5 141 ... NoelFehily 118
(Harry Fry) *hld up: 8th 1/2-way: tk clsr order bef 3 out: pushed along in 6th after 3 out and no ex u.p fr next: one pce after* **13/2**[3]

7 *5½* **Alto Esqua (FR)**[38] 4217 6-11-5 0 ... DenisO'Regan 113
(C Byrnes, Ire) *hld up towards rr: 9th 1/2-way: tk clsr order bef 3 out: pushed along in 5th after 3 out and no imp on ldrs bef next where mstke: wknd* **16/1**

8 *13* **Crafty Power (IRE)**[28] 4395 5-11-4 130 ... SeanFlanagan 99
(Sabrina J Harty, Ire) *chsd ldrs: nt fluent 1st: 5th 1/2-way: rdn and wknd bef 2 out where mstke in mod 8th* **40/1**

9 *23* **Fire In Soul (IRE)**[52] 3960 5-11-4 0 ... RWalsh 76
(W P Mullins, Ire) *hld up: 10th 1/2-way: rdn and no imp after 3 out: wknd bef next: eased: t.o* **8/1**

10 *15* **Crest**[14] 4661 5-11-4 0 ... JackKennedy 61
(Gordon Elliott, Ire) *towards rr: 11th 1/2-way: pushed along briefly after 6th: stmbld sltly after 4 out and pushed along in rr: slt mstke towards rr 3 out and no imp after: eased after next: t.o* **16/1**

P **Moylisha Tim (IRE)**[87] 3393 6-11-8 125 ... APHeskin
(R P Rath, Ire) *disp early tl settled in 2nd fr 1st: slt mstke and j. sltly rt 4th: pushed along after 6th: rdn and wknd after 4 out: t.o whn p.u after 3 out* **66/1**

P **Last Encounter (IRE)**[52] 3962 6-11-5 133 ... DavidMullins
(Ms Margaret Mullins, Ire) *chsd ldrs: 4th 1/2-way: wknd to rr after 4 out and trailing whn p.u bef next* **25/1**

5m 9.9s (-13.10) **Going Correction** -0.275s/f (Good) **12** Ran SP% **120.5**
Speed ratings: **115,114,114,112,110 107,104,99,90,84**
CSF £44.32 TOTE £4.40: £1.80, £2.50, £2.50; DF 43.10 Trifecta £244.40.
Owner Slaneyville Syndicate **Bred** Jean-Paul Bannier & Mme Michele Bannier **Trained** Kildare, Co Kildare

FOCUS
Despite its proximity to Cheltenham, this was well up to scratch. There was a nice blend of unexposed winners of maiden hurdles combined with more battle-hardened sorts. The winner made all but set a generous gallop. The winner and third help set the standard.

4956a RYANAIR GOLD CUP NOVICE CHASE (GRADE 1) (16 fncs) 2m 4f
4:15 (4:16) 5-Y-O+ £43,382 (£13,970; £6,617; £2,941; £1,470)

RPR

1 **Kylemore Lough**[15] 4624 7-11-10 155 ... BarryGeraghty 158+
(Kerry Lee) *settled bhd ldrs in 3rd: nt fluent 9th: lft 2nd at 11th: cl 2nd fr 5 out: disp 2 out where nt fluent: rdn to ld fr last and kpt on wl to assert run-in* **7/4**[2]

2 *1* **Outlander (IRE)**[10] 4729 8-11-10 150 ... BJCooper 156
(W P Mullins, Ire) *disp early tl settled in cl 2nd fr 1st: slt mstke 4th: led narrowly 10th: jnd 2 out and rdn: hdd u.p fr last and sn no imp on wnr: kpt on same pce* **1/1**[1]

3 *6* **Blair Perrone (IRE)**[50] 4005 7-11-10 144 ... (t) DenisO'Regan 150
(A J Martin, Ire) *w.w in rr: clsr in 5th fr 5th: sltly hmpd 11th where lft 3rd: lost pl and slt mstke in rr 4 out: gng wl in 3rd bef 2 out where slt mstke: sn rdn and no ex bef last: one pce run-in* **16/1**

4 *24* **McKinley**[12] 4701 6-11-10 139 ... (b[1]) RWalsh 126
(W P Mullins, Ire) *hld up in tch: nt fluent and reminders after 10th: lft 4th fr next: rdn in rr after 4 out and no imp on ldrs bef next where wknd* **14/1**

5 *13* **Vedettariat (FR)**[36] 4261 7-11-10 137 ... PaulTownend 117
(W P Mullins, Ire) *chsd ldrs early: j. sltly in rr at 5th and next: rdn briefly on outer fr 5 out: bad mstke and j.rt u.p in 4th 3 out: no imp after and wknd whn slt mstke next: eased* **12/1**[3]

U **Sizing Platinum (IRE)**[31] 4331 8-11-10 145 ... JJBurke
(Henry De Bromhead, Ire) *disp early tl narrow advantage fr 1st: hdd 10th: cl 2nd whn blnd and uns rdr next* **14/1**

5m 22.9s (-1.10) **Going Correction** +0.05s/f (Yiel) **6** Ran SP% **113.3**
Speed ratings: **104,103,101,91,86**
CSF £4.17 TOTE £2.40: £1.40, £1.02; DF 3.50 Trifecta £21.70.
Owner M J McMahon & Denis Gallagher **Bred** M J McMahon **Trained** Byton, H'fords

FOCUS
This was not the highest-quality renewal of this Grade 1 but the right horses fought out the finish and they pulled 6l clear of the third. The went a decent clip throughout so the form looks reasonably solid. The second and third set the standard.

4957 - 4958a (Foreign Racing) - See Raceform Interactive

4813 AUTEUIL (L-H)
Sunday, March 27

OFFICIAL GOING: Turf: very soft

4959a PRIX VIRELAN (HURDLE) (CONDITIONS) (4YO) (TURF) 2m 2f
1:00 (12:00) 4-Y-O £24,705 (£12,352; £7,205; £4,889; £2,316)

RPR

1 **Saint Goustan Blue (FR)**[125] 4-10-8 0 ... KevinNabet 134
(G Macaire, France) **23/10**[2]

2 *½* **Protek Des Flos (FR)**[37] 4233 4-10-10 0 ... JamesReveley 135
(Nicky Henderson) *cl up: led 6th: kicked 5 l clr fnl bnd wl bef 2 out and sn niggled along: rdn whn chal last: hdd 150yds out: rallied u.p but a hld* **4/5**[1]

3 *18* **Dottore (FR)**[126] 4-10-6 0 ... WilfridDenuault 113
(E Leenders, France) **27/1**

4 *1¼* **Ponte Fortune (FR)**[26] 4-10-6 0 ... GaetanMasure 112
(Francois Nicolle, France) **47/10**[3]

5 *15* **Kelforest (FR)**[125] 2695 4-10-6 0 ... AlainDeChitray 97
(Gabriel Leenders, France) **226/10**

P **Goudevivre (FR)**[119] 4-10-3 0 ... (p) HakimTabet
(Frau S Weis, Germany) **40/1**

P **Speed Rock (FR)**[20] 4-10-10 0 ... ErvanChazelle
(P Cottin, France) **12/1**

4m 39.04s (279.04) **7** Ran SP% **121.3**
PARI-MUTUEL (all including 1 euro stake): WIN 2.10 (coupled with Ponte Fortune); PLACE 1.90, 1.50; SF 9.90.
Owner Simon Munir & Isaac Souede **Bred** A Bassi **Trained** Les Mathes, France

4960a PRIX HUBERT D'AILLIERES (HURDLE) (LISTED RACE) (5YO+) (TURF) 2m 5f 110y
4:10 (12:00) 5-Y-O+ £30,000 (£15,000; £8,750; £5,937; £2,812)

RPR

1 **Park Light (FR)**[21] 4523 6-11-0 0 ... Marc-OlivierBelley 146
(B Lefevre, France) **71/10**[3]

2 *snk* **Maximiser (IRE)**[121] 2760 8-10-8 0 ... JoeColliver 140
(Simon West) *trckd ldr: awkward 1st and led: clr ent bk st: pressed after 3 out: hdd next and rallied: rdn and styd on run-in to go virtually upsides wnr: jst hld* **114/10**

3 *2* **Plumeur (FR)**[20] 4540 9-10-12 0 ... ThomasBeaurain 142
(G Chaignon, France) **44/5**

4 *1½* **Rhialco (FR)**[21] 11-10-10 0 ... FelixDeGiles 139
(Emmanuel Clayeux, France) **49/10**[2]

5 *1¾* **Corscia (FR)**[126] 2679 5-10-3 0 ... BertrandLestrade 130
(G Macaire, France) **7/10**[1]

6 *15* **Monsamou (IRE)**[21] 4525 7-11-3 0 ... (b) DylanUbeda 129
(P Chevillard, France) **124/10**

P **Roches Cross (IRE)**[917] 8-10-12 0 ... JVanaJr
(Josef Vana, Czech Republic) **156/10**

5m 31.39s (331.39) **7** Ran SP% **119.9**
PARI-MUTUEL (all including 1 euro stake): WIN 8.10; PLACE 3.60, 4.20; SF 75.40.
Owner Ecurie Patrick Boiteau & Carlos Pappi **Bred** P Boiteau **Trained** France

4881 CHEPSTOW (L-H)
Monday, March 28

OFFICIAL GOING: Heavy (4.6)
Wind: Moderate; half against Weather: Sunny spells

4961 DEAN CLOSE SCHOOL MARES' NOVICES' HURDLE (9 hdls 2 omitted) 2m 3f 100y
1:45 (1:47) (Class 4) 4-Y-O+ £3,898 (£1,144; £572; £286)

Form RPR

2-21 1 **Song Saa**[22] 4507 6-11-4 0 ... PaddyBrennan 111+
(Tom George) *t.k.h: trckd ldr: hit 1st: led bef 3 out: shkn up appr last: rdn out flat* **1/4**[1]

2 *3½* **Two Smokin Barrels**[359] 7-10-12 0 ... LiamTreadwell 100
(Michael Scudamore) *trckd ldng pair: wnt 2nd bef 3 out: rdn on extended run between last 2: kpt on same pce* **9/2**[2]

3 *27* **Blue Court (IRE)** 5-10-5 0 ... MrConorOrr(7) 73
(Evan Williams) *hld up in last: hit 6th: sn impr a pl: wnt 3rd 3 out: one pce and qckly lft bhd by ldng pair* **10/1**[3]

5 4 *25* **Fille Des Champs (IRE)**[36] 4270 5-10-5 0 ... LewisGordon(7) 48
(Evan Williams) *racd in 4th: j. slowly 4th: rdn next: dropped to last after 6th: lost tch 3 out: t.o* **20/1**

0404 5 *54* **Mari Me Oscar (IRE)**[34] 4293 6-10-7 0 ... ChrisWard(5)
(Nikki Evans) *led tl hdd bef 3 out: wknd qckly: t.o whn mstke last* **25/1**

5m 12.3s (10.50) **Going Correction** +0.30s/f (Yiel) **5** Ran SP% **115.9**
Speed ratings (Par 105): **89,87,76,65,42**
CSF £2.26 TOTE £1.10: £1.10, £1.90; EX 2.40 Trifecta £5.20.
Owner Sharon C Nelson & Georgie McGrath **Bred** Copernicus Bloodstock Agency Ltd **Trained** Slad, Gloucs

FOCUS
The far bend (home turn) was railed out by 6 metres from the inside rail and the stables bend (past the stands) was out by 2 metres. The usual second-last was omitted on each circuit. This race was run over 23yds further than advertised. No depth to this mares' hurdle and the front pair came a long way clear. The winner set a fair standard.

4962 HEDGEHOGS NURSERY NOVICES' H'CAP CHASE (16 fncs 2 omitted) 2m 7f 131y

2:20 (2:21) (Class 4) (0-120,117) 5-Y-0+ **£5,198** (£1,526; £763; £381)

Form RPR

-02P **1** **What Larks (IRE)**[65] 3746 8-10-4 **100**................................ ConorRing(5) 114+
(Hugo Froud) *hld up in last: hdwy 6th: outpcd in 4th whn j.lft 4 out: rallied to go 2nd on extended run to next: led bef last: styd on strly to draw clr flat* **12/1**

1434 **2** *7* **Butlergrove King (IRE)**[9] 4800 7-11-7 **112**...................... RobertDunne 120
(Dai Burchell) *led: jnd 4th to 7th: rdn after 3 out: hdd bef last: one pce flat* **9/2**[2]

1345 **3** *7* **Rosa Fleet (IRE)**[32] 4319 8-11-7 **112**............................ LiamTreadwell 113
(Venetia Williams) *trckd ldrs tl lost pl and rdn along after 6th: mstke 10th: slow jump 12th: styd on fr 3 out: wnt 3rd next: no imp* **8/1**[3]

1321 **4** *½* **Bears Rails**[20] 4545 6-11-9 **114**................................ BrendanPowell 118+
(Colin Tizzard) *chsd ldrs: mstke 3rd: dropped to last 6th: rdn along to cl 8th: mstke 12th: last and drvn 4 out: styd on fr 2 out* **5/4**[1]

-2PU **5** *11* **Golden Milan (IRE)**[16] 4615 8-11-12 **117**.........................(bt) SeanBowen 108
(Rebecca Curtis) *chsd ldrs: blnd 2nd: rdn and wknd 3 out* **9/2**[2]

0P36 **6** *10* **Forgivienne**[16] 4612 9-11-0 **105**................................ AdamWedge 85
(Evan Williams) *trckd ldr: disp ld 4th to 7th: styd in 2nd tl extended run to 3 out: wkng in 4th whn pckd 2 out* **8/1**[3]

6m 34.4s (12.40) **Going Correction** +0.45s/f (Soft) **6** Ran SP% **110.7**
Speed ratings: **97,94,92,92,88 85**
CSF £61.01 TOTE £15.80: £4.80, £3.40; EX 76.40 Trifecta £759.30.
Owner Mrs Heather Heal **Bred** Peter Doyle **Trained** Bruton, Somerset

FOCUS
This was run over 41yds further than advertised. The open ditch in the home straight was omitted on each circuit. Modest form with the favourite disappointing.

4963 ST JOHN'S ON-THE-HILL SCHOOL "NATIONAL HUNT" NOVICES' HURDLE (7 hdls 1 omitted) 2m 11y

2:55 (2:55) (Class 4) 4-Y-0+ **£3,898** (£1,144; £572; £286)

Form RPR

12 **1** **Vinciaettis (FR)**[61] 3802 5-11-0 0................................ GavinSheehan 134+
(Warren Greatrex) *nt a fluent: led tl after 1st: trckd ldr tl led again after 4th: drew clr on extended run between last 2: shkn up flat: easily* **4/5**[1]

1-14 **2** *5* **Maxanisi (IRE)**[79] 3516 6-11-6 127................................ AdamWedge 127
(Evan Williams) *trckd ldng pair: j.rt 4th: sn wnt 2nd: rdn after 3 out: kpt on same pce: hld whn awkward jump last* **7/4**[2]

04 **3** *27* **Leg Lock Luke (IRE)**[38] 4224 6-11-0................................ PaddyBrennan 96
(Colin Tizzard) *t.k.h: hdwy to ld after 1st: shied crossing path sn after: hdd and dropped to 3rd after 4th: wknd 2 out* **17/2**[3]

540 **4** *21* **Mixchievous**[32] 4317 5-11-0 0................................ LiamTreadwell 73
(Venetia Williams) *hld up in last pair: j.rt: lost tch 4th: t.o* **20/1**

40 **5** *84* **Glimpse Of Gold**[25] 4441 5-11-0 0................................ PaulMoloney
(Tim Vaughan) *hld up in last pair: hdwy 3rd: hit next: nudged along and qckly lost tch w 1st 3: t.o* **40/1**

60 **6** *68* **Goonjim (IRE)**[274] 853 5-11-0 0................................(t) RhysFlint
(Alexandra Dunn) *hld up in 4th: slow jump and dropped to last 3rd: t.o fr next* **66/1**

4m 10.9s (0.30) **Going Correction** +0.30s/f (Yiel) **6** Ran SP% **111.1**
Speed ratings (Par 105): **111,108,95,84,42 8**
CSF £2.48 TOTE £1.80: £1.30, £1.10; EX 3.10 Trifecta £5.70.
Owner Mrs J & Miss C Shipp **Bred** Michel Leger & F Verger **Trained** Upper Lambourn, Berks

FOCUS
The usual second-last was omitted on each circuit. This race was run over 23yds further than advertised. Two decent types drew clear. and the winner fulfilled the promise of his bumper form.

4964 BATHWICK TYRES H'CAP CHASE (14 fncs 2 omitted) 2m 3f 98y

3:30 (3:30) (Class 2) 5-Y-0+
£15,640 (£4,620; £2,310; £1,155; £577; £290)

Form RPR

3115 **1** **Pressurize (IRE)**[16] 4617 10-10-2 **128**................................ RobertDunne 138+
(Venetia Williams) *led tl after 4th: trckd ldr: mstke 7th: rdn 4 out: led appr last: drvn out* **12/1**

1123 **2** *3¾* **Quite By Chance**[26] 4436 7-9-13 **132**................................ PaulO'Brien(7) 138
(Colin Tizzard) *wl in tch towards rr: hdwy 8th: led bef 4 out: nt fluent 2 out: hdd appr last: one pce* **9/2**[2]

P1P2 **3** *9* **Grey Gold (IRE)**[30] 4355 11-11-7 **152**.............................. CiaranGethings(5) 148
(Kerry Lee) *hld up: rdn after 10th: hdwy on extended run to 3 out: sn in 3rd but one pce and no imp on ldng pair* **9/2**[2]

U34 **4** *½* **Vivaccio (FR)**[72] 3620 7-10-0 **126** oh1................................ LiamTreadwell 123
(Venetia Williams) *cl up: mstke 4th: rdn and wknd next: styd on again flat* **8/1**

2012 **5** *1½* **Blandfords Gunner**[38] 4230 7-10-3 **129**................................ AdamWedge 124
(Evan Williams) *chsd ldrs: outpcd in 5th bef 4 out: rallied into 3rd whn mstke 3 out: wknd 2 out: lost 4th flat* **5/1**[3]

041U **6** *55* **Wings Of Smoke (IRE)**[27] 4424 11-10-9 **135**.........................(t) PaulMoloney 73
(Tim Vaughan) *hld up: lost tch after 10th: j.rt 4 out: t.o* **16/1**

131U **P** **Ubaltique (FR)**[16] 4606 8-10-2 **128**................................(bt) WillKennedy
(Donald McCain) *racd keenly: chsd ldrs tl led after 4th: hdd bef 4 out: wknd on extended run to 3 out: bhd whn p.u bef 2 out* **16/1**

22U1 **U** **Sandy Beach**[16] 4617 6-10-1 **127**................................ BrendanPowell
(Colin Tizzard) *chsd ldrs tl blnd bdly and uns rdr 6th* **9/4**[1]

5m 13.5s (2.20) **Going Correction** +0.45s/f (Soft) **8** Ran SP% **114.4**
Speed ratings: **113,111,107,107,106 83, ,**
CSF £65.84 CT £283.53 TOTE £16.20: £3.60, £1.60, £1.60; EX 98.90 Trifecta £497.00.
Owner Mrs Sarah Williams **Bred** Dr J O'Keeffe **Trained** Kings Caple, H'fords
■ Stewards' Enquiry : Robert Dunne two-day ban: used whip above permitted level (Apr 11-12)

FOCUS
This race was run over 23yds further than advertised. The open ditch in the home straight was omitted on each circuit. Fair chasing form with the winner back on the upgrade.

4965 RACEHORSE OWNERSHIP WITH DIAMONDRACING.CO.UK H'CAP HURDLE (9 hdls 2 omitted) 2m 3f 100y

4:05 (4:06) (Class 4) (0-120,120) 4-Y-0+ **£4,548** (£1,335; £667; £333)

Form RPR

-23P **1** **Colin's Brother**[23] 4493 6-11-9 **117**................................ SamTwiston-Davies 124+
(Nigel Twiston-Davies) *trckd ldng pair: led after 6th: rdn and jnd whn hit 2 out: upsides whn outj. last and wnt a l down: rallied u.p to ld post* **3/1**[2]

0P30 **2** *nse* **Rock On Rocky**[9] 4801 8-11-4 **119**............................(tp) MrStanSheppard(7) 124
(Matt Sheppard) *t.k.h: cl up: led 4th tl after 6th: upsides 2 out: bttr jump last and wnt a l up: kpt on: hdd post* **5/2**[1]

5UU3 **3** *14* **Owen Glendower (IRE)**[130] 2593 11-11-4 **117**........(t) CiaranGethings(5) 108
(Sophie Leech) *hld up: hdwy after 6th: rdn after 3 out: styd on to go mod 3rd on extended run between last 2* **11/1**

2151 **4** *10* **Panis Angelicus (FR)**[155] 2087 7-11-9 **117**................................ SeanBowen 98
(Tim Vaughan) *led: hit 1st: hdd 4th: rdn in 3rd 3 out: wknd on extended run between last 2* **5/1**[3]

0-0P **5** *7* **Asockastar (IRE)**[163] 1977 8-10-9 **103**................................ RobertDunne 77
(Tim Vaughan) *mid-div: clsd to go 3rd bef 3 out: sn no imp on ldng pair: wknd on extended run between last 2* **25/1**

0450 **6** *1* **Chief Brody**[9] 4782 5-10-10 **109**................................ ConorRing(5) 82
(Grace Harris) *chsd ldrs: rdn and outpcd 3 out: wkng whn nt fluent next* **14/1**

463P **7** *nk* **Dun Scaith (IRE)**[15] 4648 8-10-13 **107**................................ AdamWedge 80
(Sophie Leech) *wnt to post early: hld up: rdn 3 out: sn lost tch* **20/1**

-546 **8** *26* **Cry Fury**[15] 4650 8-10-2 **99**................................ KillianMoore(3) 46
(Sophie Leech) *hld up: rdn whn hit 3 out: sn wknd: t.o* **16/1**

1143 **9** *37* **In On The Act**[173] 1806 6-11-12 **120**................................ PaulMoloney 30
(Evan Williams) *chsd ldrs: rdn 3 out: sn wknd: t.o* **7/1**

5m 8.8s (7.00) **Going Correction** +0.30s/f (Yiel) **9** Ran SP% **112.2**
Speed ratings (Par 105): **97,96,91,86,83 83,83,72,56**
CSF £10.81 CT £68.24 TOTE £3.70: £1.80, £1.40, £2.80; EX 11.50 Trifecta £102.20.
Owner Mrs Caroline Beresford-Wylie **Bred** Mrs Caroline Beresford-Wylie **Trained** Naunton, Gloucs

FOCUS
This race was run over 23yds further than advertised. The usual second-last was omitted on each circuit. The front pair came clear, enjoying a good tussle, and a big hurdle personal best from the winner.

4966 GREAT VALUE BETTING ON COURSE - CHEPSTOW BOOKMAKERS H'CAP CHASE (16 fncs 2 omitted) 2m 7f 131y

4:40 (4:41) (Class 3) (0-140,134) 5-Y-0+ **£9,495** (£2,805; £1,402; £702; £351)

Form RPR

4411 **1** **Berea Boru (IRE)**[36] 4267 8-11-9 **131**................................(t) SeanBowen 145+
(Peter Bowen) *hld up in 5th: hdwy 7th: wnt cl 2nd after 12th: led and hit 4 out: rdn and jnd next: lft in command 2 out: tired jump last: drvn out* **5/2**[1]

5402 **2** *5* **Kayf Moss**[36] 4267 8-11-8 **130**................................(bt) RhysFlint 139+
(John Flint) *chsd ldrs: led after 12th: narrowly hdd next: upsides and ev ch whn blnd 2 out: kpt on same pce* **4/1**[3]

2P1 **3** *10* **Chase The Spud**[43] 4141 8-11-12 **134**................................ PaddyBrennan 131
(Fergal O'Brien) *led tl after 2nd: led 4th: j.rt 8th: hdd after 12th: wknd on extended run to 3 out: styd on flat* **3/1**[2]

33P3 **4** *7* **Minella On Line (IRE)**[20] 4542 7-10-11 **119**..................(b) AdamWedge 110
(Rebecca Curtis) *chsd ldrs: mstke 3rd: outpcd whn rdn 4 out: no ch whn blnd next* **4/1**[3]

FP-0 **5** *10* **Wyck Hill (IRE)**[30] 4367 12-11-5 **127**..............................(bt) WillKennedy 106
(David Bridgwater) *cl up: led 2nd tl after 4th: styd prom tl lost pl 9th: rdn and outpcd next: no ch fr 4 out* **13/2**

F63P **P** **Brody Bleu (FR)**[26] 4436 9-11-5 **127**................................ LiamTreadwell
(Robert Walford) *in rr: rdn along 7th: blnd next: lost tch 12th: t.o whn p.u bef 4 out* **25/1**

6m 30.5s (8.50) **Going Correction** +0.45s/f (Soft) **6** Ran SP% **110.8**
Speed ratings: **103,101,98,95,92**
CSF £12.65 CT £28.20 TOTE £2.70: £1.80, £2.10; EX 13.00 Trifecta £29.20.
Owner H Jones **Bred** Mrs E Thompson **Trained** Little Newcastle, Pembrokes

FOCUS
This was run over 41yds further than advertised. The open ditch in the straight was omitted on each circuit. A decent staying handicap chase which resulted in a battle between two old rivals.

4967 BATHWICK TYRES MARES' STANDARD OPEN NATIONAL HUNT FLAT RACE 2m 11y

5:15 (5:15) (Class 6) 4-6-Y-0 **£1,949** (£572; £286; £143)

Form RPR

1 **Bells On Sunday**[36] 5-11-0 0................................ SamTwiston-Davies 111+
(Tom Lacey) *hld up towards rr: hdwy to go 2nd over 3f out: led gng wl 2f out: rdn out fnl f* **9/4**[2]

22 **2** *3¾* **Postbridge (IRE)**[38] 4228 5-11-0 0................................ GavinSheehan 105
(Warren Greatrex) *mainly in 2nd tl drvn and sltly outpcd over 3f out: rallied to chse wnr over 1f out: styd on* **13/8**[1]

0 **3** *5* **Sweetlittlekitty (IRE)**[102] 3132 6-11-0 0................................ SeanBowen 99
(Rebecca Curtis) *chsd ldrs tl dropped to detached last 6f out: rallied u.p 4f out: outpcd by ldrs 3f out: styd on to go 3rd fnl 75yds* **10/1**

1-6 **4** *2¼* **Grand Turina**[37] 4242 5-11-7 0................................ LiamTreadwell 105
(Venetia Williams) *t.k.h: led tl rdn and hdd 2f out: one pce after: lost 3rd fnl 75yds* **9/2**[3]

63 **5** *20* **Llantara**[38] 4228 5-10-11 0................................ BenPoste(3) 77
(Tom Symonds) *hld up: hdwy after 4f: wknd 3f out* **7/1**

0 **6** *26* **Time Wise**[31] 4350 6-10-9 0................................ DanielHiskett(5) 51
(Richard Phillips) *t.k.h in rr: hdwy after 4f: wknd over 4f out: t.o* **28/1**

4m 9.7s (4.70) **Going Correction** +0.30s/f (Yiel) **6** Ran SP% **112.1**
Speed ratings: **100,98,95,94,84 71**
CSF £6.29 TOTE £3.70: £1.60, £1.30; EX 6.60 Trifecta £29.20.
Owner Mrs S M Newell **Bred** Mrs S M Newell **Trained** Ledbury, H'fords

FOCUS
This race was run over 23yds further than advertised. The two at the head of the market dominated this mares' bumper and the winner looks a nice prospect.

T/Plt: £48.30 to a £1 stake. Pool: £83,924.59 - 1,268.38 winning units T/Qpdt: £6.40 to a £1 stake. Pool: £6,495.25 - 740.10 winning units **Richard Lowther**

4771 **FAKENHAM** (L-H)
Monday, March 28

OFFICIAL GOING: Soft
Wind: very strong winds beginning to abate slightly Weather: becoming quite sunny; 6 degrees

4968 LADIES DAY FAKENHAM 22ND MAY (S) HURDLE (11 hdls) 2m 4f 1y
2:15 (2:15) (Class 4) 4-Y-0+ **£3,764** (£1,097; £548)

Form RPR
25P **1** **Athou Du Nord (FR)**[88] 3375 6-11-1 110..........(t) AlainCawley 115+
(Richard Hobson) *hld up last in slow r tl wnt 2nd bef 3 out: sat jst bhd ldr gng best tl led bef last: sn pushed clr but nt doing much in front* **7/4**[2]
1332 **2** *6* **Ministerofinterior**[25] 4448 11-11-0 112..........(b) AlanJohns(5) 112
(Barry Leavy) *nt fluent 3rd: cl 2nd tl led bef 8th: drvn to hold advantage on suffernce tl bef last: immediately outpcd* **5/6**[1]
3600 **3** *42* **Proud Times (USA)**[11] 4747 10-10-12 92..........(b) RyanHatch(3) 65
(Ali Stronge) *set slow pce tl drvn and hdd bef 8th: sn last and reluctant: t.o after 3 out tl drvn into remote 3rd flat* **8/1**[3]
36U6 **4** *2 3/4* **Indian Daudaie (FR)**[29] 4390 9-10-5 94.......... RomainClavreul(10) 62
(Sarah Humphrey) *nt fluent 4th: cl up in 3rd tl rdn and fnd nil 3 out: t.o after next: pulling himself up whn lost 3rd after last* **16/1**

5m 25.1s (4.70) **Going Correction** +0.375s/f (Yiel) **4** Ran SP% **107.9**
Speed ratings (Par 105): **105,102,85,84**
CSF £3.72 TOTE £2.50; EX 2.70 Trifecta £4.30.The winner sold to Mr S Stronge for £6,000.
Owner Richard Hobson **Bred** Daniel Auroux **Trained** Stow-On-The-Wold, Gloucs

FOCUS
All rails on inner running line for hurdle course. Fresh ground the whole way round on both courses. Distances increased as follows; Race 2 - 31yds, Races 4 & 6 - 37yds. A modest selling hurdle. They went a sensible gallop on soft ground and this was a step up from the winner.

4969 ROBERT HOARE NOVICES' HUNTERS' CHASE (FOR THE ROBERT HOARE MEMORIAL TROPHY) (16 fncs) 2m 5f 44y
2:50 (2:50) (Class 5) 5-Y-0+ **£2,495** (£774; £386; £193)

Form RPR
03P2 **1** **Clonbanan Lad (IRE)**[27] 4424 10-11-7 114.......... MrJSole(3) 121+
(Miss Louise Allan) *cl 2nd tl jnd ldr 6th: led 10th: wnt 3 l clr bef 13th: outj. chalr 2 out and a gng best after: comf* **8/13**[1]
25-1 **2** *2 3/4* **Man Of Steel (IRE)**[27] 4426 7-11-7 105.......... MrJoeHill(7) 119
(Alan Hill) *hld up in last pair: mstke 12th: wnt 2nd next: rdn and tried to chal and outj. 2 out: wl hld after* **15/8**[2]
U-04 **3** *dist* **Talkin Thomas (IRE)**[16] 10-11-3 100..........(p) MrSCroft(7) 80
(S Croft) *led: jnd 6th: hdd 10th: dropped bk last after next and sn struggling: t.o after 3 out: lft remote 3rd at last* **14/1**[3]
040- **4** *3 1/2* **Mackeys Forge (IRE)**[65] 12-11-7 100..........(t) MissBHampson(3) 77
(P E Froud) *last pair: nt fluent 9th or whn pushed along bef 13th: sn struggling: t.o after 2 out: blnd bdly last and lost remote 3rd* **33/1**

5m 58.8s (17.00) **Going Correction** +0.525s/f (Soft) **4** Ran SP% **106.3**
Speed ratings: **88,86,73,72**
CSF £2.12 TOTE £1.60; EX 2.10 Trifecta £3.80.
Owner Robert Clifton-Brown **Bred** Eamonn Heagney **Trained** Exning, Suffolk

FOCUS
Race distance increased by 31yds. An ordinary little novice hunter chase. They went a sensible gallop on soft ground and the winner set a decent standard.

4970 CECIL AND SHEILA BUTTIFANT MEMORIAL NOVICES' H'CAP HURDLE (9 hdls) 2m 3y
3:25 (3:25) (Class 4) (0-105,105) 4-Y-0+ **£6,498** (£1,908; £954; £477)

Form RPR
1235 **1** **Gin And Tonic**[10] 4774 6-11-5 101.......... RyanHatch(3) 109+
(Michael Wigham) *gng wl in last pair: effrt 3 out: led on bit after next: 5 l clr last: v easily* **11/8**[1]
4440 **2** *9* **Dylan's Storm (IRE)**[161] 2000 4-9-13 90..........(t) MikeyEnnis(5) 84
(David Dennis) *2nd or 3rd tl rdn to ld briefly 2 out: sn outpcd by wnr: no ch whn hit last* **9/1**
0056 **3** *4* **Bonvilston Boy**[30] 4351 5-11-7 105.......... AlanJohns(5) 101
(Tim Vaughan) *nt often fluent: 2nd or 3rd tl led briefly bef 2 out: rdn and btn between last two: plodded on* **6/1**
3F12 **4** *13* **Maid Of Tuscany (IRE)**[158] 2043 5-11-12 105..........(b) NickScholfield 87
(Neil Mulholland) *last pair: clsd briefly after 3 out: sn rdn: little rspnse: wl btn after next* **5/1**[3]
33-0 **P** **Jazzy Lady (IRE)**[28] 4411 5-11-9 102.......... AndrewGlassonbury
(Jim Best) *chsd ldrs tl rdn 1/2-way: nt travelling after: lost tch 3 out: t.o and p.u last* **25/1**
10P2 **P** **Neworld (FR)**[38] 4223 7-11-7 100..........(t) AlainCawley
(Richard Hobson) *led: rdn and hdd bef 2 out: dropped out tamely: t.o and p.u last* **11/4**[2]

4m 24.1s (11.10) **Going Correction** +0.375s/f (Yiel)
WFA 4 from 5yo+ 7lb **6** Ran SP% **113.6**
Speed ratings (Par 105): **87,82,80,74,** ,
CSF £13.92 CT £56.61 TOTE £2.20: £1.30, £4.00; EX 19.10 Trifecta £110.60.
Owner The Gin & Tonic Partnership **Bred** Winterbeck Manor Stud **Trained** Newmarket, Suffolk

FOCUS
A modest novice handicap hurdle. They went a respectable gallop and the winner was on a good mark.

4971 DAVID KEITH MEMORIAL H'CAP CHASE (18 fncs) 3m 38y
4:00 (4:00) (Class 3) (0-125,124) 5-Y-0+ **£9,747** (£2,862; £1,431; £715)

Form RPR
1P35 **1** **Morney Wing (IRE)**[17] 4589 7-11-4 119..........(tp) HarryBannister(3) 128
(Charlie Mann) *trckd ldrs: rdn 12th: jnd ldr 2 out and drvn after: tk slt advantage gng sltly bttr nring last: styd on steadily but all out* **7/1**
361F **2** *1 3/4* **Gamain (IRE)**[10] 4775 7-10-10 111..........(b) RyanHatch(3) 118
(Ben Case) *trckd ldrs: nt fluent 7th: slow 9th and rdn briefly: wnt 2nd at 14th: led 3 out: jnd next and hrd drvn after: hdd whn nt fluent last: outbattled and edgd lft flat* **6/1**
PP34 **3** *1 1/4* **Atlantic Roller (IRE)**[26] 4436 9-10-12 110..........(p) TomCannon 116
(Chris Gordon) *trckd ldrs tl rdn and outpcd 3 out: 7 l 3rd and btn next: kpt on u.p fr bef last: nt get in a blow* **8/1**
3P41 **4** *6* **Bucking The Trend**[15] 4641 8-11-7 124..........(p) AlanJohns(5) 123
(Tim Vaughan) *pressed ldr 2nd tl 11th: 5 l 5th and rdn bef 15th: sn outpcd: plugged on wout threatening fr 2 out* **3/1**[2]
5652 **5** *25* **Noble Legend**[10] 4775 9-11-5 124..........(p) MrSDavies-Thomas(7) 98
(Caroline Bailey) *led: rdn and hdd and nt fluent 3 out: dropped out rapidly and sn last* **9/2**[3]
P123 **P** **Amidon (FR)**[60] 3818 6-11-12 124.......... NickScholfield
(Lucy Wadham) *mstke 3rd: last pair: lost tch and rdn 10th: nvr wnt a yard after: t.o 14th: p.u 3 out* **9/4**[1]
34P0 **P** **Dalkadam (FR)**[9] 4789 5-9-10 100.......... MikeyEnnis(5)
(J R Jenkins) *last pair: losing tch qckly whn blnd 15th and p.u* **20/1**

6m 43.6s (7.90) **Going Correction** +0.525s/f (Soft)
WFA 5 from 6yo+ 1lb **7** Ran SP% **116.6**
Speed ratings: **107,106,106,104,95** ,
CSF £48.39 TOTE £8.30: £3.80, £3.00; EX 50.60 Trifecta £147.10.
Owner The Steeple Chasers **Bred** G Bell **Trained** Upper Lambourn, Berks

FOCUS
Race distance increased by 37yds. The feature race was a fair staying handicap chase. They went an even gallop and the first two ran pretty much to their marks.

4972 HEYHO AWAY WEGO ANDY BETHELL MEMORIAL H'CAP HURDLE (13 hdls) 2m 7f 95y
4:35 (4:35) (Class 4) (0-110,110) 4-Y-0+ **£6,498** (£1,908; £954; £477)

Form RPR
6035 **1** **Who's Micky Brown (IRE)**[37] 4250 6-11-5 103..........(p) NickScholfield 120+
(Neil Mulholland) *trckd ldrs: effrt 10th: led bef next and only one travelling after: drew rt away after 2 out w rest out on their feet* **11/2**[3]
-560 **2** *45* **Heresmynumber (IRE)**[109] 2995 6-10-10 97..........(tp) RyanHatch(3) 64
(Ali Stronge) *awkward jump 4th: trckd ldrs: ev ch bef 3 out: sn chsng wnr and drvn: 7 l 2nd and btn next: hopped over last and fin really tired* **7/1**
1P60 **3** *7* **Flemi Two Toes (IRE)**[31] 4349 10-9-12 92.......... RomainClavreul(10) 52
(Sarah Humphrey) *cl up tl dropped himself bk into last pair at 7th: rdn and lost tch next: t.o 3 out: tk v remote 3rd flat* **20/1**
05-1 **4** *8* **Malibu Rock**[45] 4099 8-11-8 106.......... TomCannon 73
(Chris Gordon) *chsd ldr: clsd on him to ld 10th: rdn and sn hdd and hanging bdly rt: 20 l 3rd 2 out: desperately tired and almost walking whn lost 3rd flat* **11/8**[1]
2333 **P** **Skint**[113] 2924 10-11-7 110..........(p) MikeyEnnis(5)
(Ali Stronge) *last pair and awkward hd carriage: pushed along 7th: lost tch next: t.o whn mstke 10th and p.u next* **11/1**
102 **P** **Bells Of Ailsworth (IRE)**[25] 4450 6-11-7 110.......... AlanJohns(5)
(Tim Vaughan) *led at decent pce and up to 8 l clr tl rdn bef 10th where hdd: dropped out rapidly: 4th and t.o whn p.u 2 out* **9/4**[2]

6m 29.9s (7.90) **Going Correction** +0.375s/f (Yiel) **6** Ran SP% **113.9**
Speed ratings (Par 105): **101,85,82,80,** ,
CSF £40.96 TOTE £6.40: £2.60, £2.80; EX 36.40 Trifecta £280.10.
Owner Qdos Racing **Bred** Patrick Murphy **Trained** Limpley Stoke, Wilts

FOCUS
A modest staying handicap hurdle. They went an honest gallop and this looked a big step up from the winner.

4973 QUEEN'S CUP, AN EASTERN COUNTIES HUNTERS' CHASE (18 fncs) 3m 38y
5:10 (5:11) (Class 5) 5-Y-0+ **£2,634** (£810; £405)

Form RPR
0/ **1** **Mr Madeit (IRE)**[29] 10-11-5 0.......... MrGGreenock(7) 121+
(G T H Bailey) *pressed ldr: mstke 6th: led narrowly 11th: a being urged fr 15th: fiddled next but great jump 2 out to go 3 l clr: kpt on v gamely after* **11/10**[1]
31-U **2** *1 1/4* **Master Workman (IRE)**[36] 10-11-7 113..........(p) MrSDavies-Thomas(7) 119
(David Kemp) *led at decent pce tl 11th: w wnr tl chsd him fr 14th: rdn fr next: outpcd fr 2 out but kpt on steadily and clsd fr last although a jst hld* **13/2**[3]
/2-P **3** *80* **Good Order**[8] 11-11-5 0..........(tp) MrRStearn(7) 37
(E Turner) *hit 1st hrd: blnd 2nd and 8th: cl up tl rdn and fdd rapidly 13th: sn t.o: coming to last as ldrs fin* **28/1**
11/ **U** **It Was Me**[30] 11-11-5 0.......... MrAWright(7)
(N R W Wright) *cl up in last pair tl v awkward and uns rdr 11th* **5/4**[2]

6m 53.5s (17.80) **Going Correction** +0.525s/f (Soft) **4** Ran SP% **108.8**
Speed ratings: **91,90,63,**
CSF £7.62 TOTE £2.20; EX 9.30 Trifecta £35.90.
Owner Countess Cathcart **Bred** Robert McCarthy **Trained** Holdenby, Northants

FOCUS
Race distance increased by 37yds. A fair little hunters' chase. They went a respectable gallop and the winner could be decent.

4974 HAPPY EASTER MARES' MAIDEN OPEN NATIONAL HUNT FLAT RACE 2m 3y
5:45 (5:47) (Class 4) 4-6-Y-0 **£3,422** (£997; £499)

Form RPR
33-2 **1** **Kayf Grace**[58] 3861 6-11-4 0.......... NicodeBoinville 118+
(Nicky Henderson) *led and set true pce: 10 l clr 1/2-way: virtually solo wout coming off bit fnl 3f* **1/5**[1]
2 *53* **Indulgence** 4-10-6 0.......... JamieBargary(5) 58
(Pam Sly) *small: chsd wnr after 6f: drvn and brief effrt 5f out: wl btn 3f out: rdn rest of way: fin v tired but game debut* **5/1**[2]
0 **3** *12* **Kokomo**[46] 4074 5-11-4 0.......... NickScholfield 53
(Noel Williams) *chsd ldrs: wknd 1/2-way: t.o fnl 6f* **25/1**
63 **4** *8* **Parisian Star**[46] 4075 4-10-6 0.......... MikeyEnnis(5) 38
(J R Jenkins) *chsd ldrs: rdn 7f out: t.o fnl 5f* **14/1**
P **Arcadiana (IRE)** 6-11-4 0.......... PeterCarberry
(John Gallagher) *chsd clr ldr tl rdn 1/2-way: stopped qckly and t.o 6f out: p.u 4f out* **12/1**[3]

4m 8.3s (0.90) **Going Correction** +0.375s/f (Yiel)
WFA 4 from 5yo+ 7lb **5** Ran SP% **118.2**
Speed ratings: **112,85,79,75,**
CSF £2.15 TOTE £1.20: £1.10, £1.70; EX 1.90 Trifecta £11.60.
Owner James and Jean Potter **Bred** James & Jean Potter **Trained** Upper Lambourn, Berks

FOCUS
An ordinary mares' bumper. They went an even gallop and the front-runner was in a different league.

T/Plt: £439.60 to a £1 stake. Pool: £45,925.31 - 76.25 winning tickets. T/Qpdt: £260.10 to a £1 stake. Pool: £3,269.82 - 9.30 winning tickets. **Iain Mackenzie**

4502 HUNTINGDON (R-H)

Monday, March 28

OFFICIAL GOING: Soft (chs 6.3, hdl 6.5)

Wind: strong, across, easing from race 4 Weather: bright spells, windy until race 4 after a very wet morning

4975 LANCASTER LOOP CONDITIONAL JOCKEYS' TRAINING SERIES H'CAP HURDLE (10 hdls) 2m 4f 145y

2:10 (2:12) (Class 4) (0-110,112) 4-Y-0+ £3,249 (£954; £477; £238)

Form RPR

0P/5 1 **Lombardy Boy (IRE)**[22] 4504 11-9-11 84 oh8.......... MrShaneQuinlan(3) 85+
(Michael Banks) *mde all: set stdy gallop but clr tl jnd after 7th: pushed along and asserted between last 2: in command and pushed out flat* 9/2[3]

42P4 2 7 **Lakeshore Lady (IRE)**[14] 4672 6-11-7 105..........(p) WilliamFeatherstone 99
(David Bridgwater) *t.k.h: hld up in rr: clsd 7th: chsd wnr 2 out: rdn and unable qck between last 2: wl hld and kpt on same pce flat* 9/4[2]

/06- 3 7 **Garde Ville (FR)**[540] 1772 6-9-11 86.......................... GrahamCarson(5) 73
(Lisa Williamson) *racd in 3rd pl: wnt 2nd and clsd on wnr 7th: ev ch next: 3rd and unable qck 2 out: sn outpcd and wl hld last* 14/1

145/ 4 1¾ **Upthemsteps (IRE)**[1200] 3044 11-11-1 105.................(p) TobyWheeler(6) 90
(Ian Williams) *t.k.h: chsd clr wnr tl 7th: clsd 4th next: dropped to last and rdn 2 out: sn outpcd and wl btn last* 6/4[1]

1/P- 5 shd **Max Milano (IRE)**[377] 4821 11-10-10 99.................... CharlieHammond(5) 84
(Alan Jessop) *t.k.h: hld up in last pair: clsd and wl in tch 3 out: rdn next: sn outpcd and wl btn last* 6/1

5m 46.0s (35.40) **Going Correction** +0.75s/f (Soft) 5 Ran SP% **109.9**
Speed ratings (Par 105): **62,59,56,56,55**
CSF £15.11 TOTE £4.70: £1.50, £2.40; EX 14.40 Trifecta £62.00.

Owner M C Banks **Bred** P M Prior-Wandesforde **Trained** Waresley, Cambs

FOCUS
After 6mm of overnight rain the going was changed to soft (from good to soft, soft in places) before racing, with the GoingStick 6.3 on the chase track and 6.5 on the hurdle course. Consequently, there were a plethora of non-runners, resulting in seven small-field races and those that did race faced very blustery conditions. This opening modest conditional jockeys' event, which cut up considerably, was run at a very sedate gallop and very little changed throughout the contest. Race distance increased by 60yds.

4976 LEXUS HYBRID NOVICES' HURDLE (8 hdls) 1m 7f 171y

2:45 (2:46) (Class 4) 4-Y-0+ £3,249 (£954; £477; £238)

Form RPR

6115 1 **Allee Bleue (IRE)**[16] 4622 6-11-12 135.......................... RichardJohnson 134+
(Philip Hobbs) *mde all: hit 3 out: drew clr bef next: wnt rt and mstke last: v easily* 1/4[1]

2 27 **Monsart (IRE)**[370] 4-10-2 0.. JamieBargary(5) 81
(Shaun Lycett) *hld up off the pce in last pair: rdn to go 3rd bef 3 out: no ch w wnr but plugged on steadily after: j.rt last: snatched 2nd on post* 66/1

56 3 nse **Easy Street (IRE)**[46] 4063 6-11-0 0................................ RichieMcLernon 87
(Jonjo O'Neill) *chsd wnr: rdn and btn after 3 out: wnt rt and j. slowly last: pushed along flat: lost 2nd on post* 8/1[3]

25 4 16 **Mahlers Star (IRE)**[28] 4409 6-10-9 0............................. JakeHodson(5) 71
(David Bridgwater) *chsd ldrs: rdn and wknd qckly after 5th: t.o bef 2 out* 4/1[2]

P **Chorlton House**[35] 4-10-7 0... KielanWoods
(Ian Williams) *hld up off the pce in last pair: nvr on terms: lost tch and t.o after 5th: p.u 2 out* 25/1

4m 3.15s (8.25) **Going Correction** +0.75s/f (Soft)
WFA 4 from 6yo 7lb 5 Ran SP% **116.4**
Speed ratings (Par 105): **109,95,95,87,**
CSF £15.63 TOTE £1.40: £1.10, £14.70; EX 19.40 Trifecta £41.20.

Owner Andrew L Cohen **Bred** Wood Hall Stud **Trained** Withycombe, Somerset

FOCUS
A non event in terms of a race as Allee Bleue was in a different league to these rivals and his rider kept things simple by taking it up from an early stage. He was value for further.

4977 BEEHIVE HALF CENTURY NOVICES' CHASE (19 fncs) 2m 7f 129y

3:20 (3:20) (Class 4) 5-Y-0+ £3,898 (£1,144; £572)

Form RPR

5052 1 **Mercers Court (IRE)**[23] 4474 8-10-12 112.......................... TrevorWhelan 130+
(Neil King) *hld up in 3rd: clsd to press ldr 8th: led next tl out j. and hdd 11th: led again after next: mstke 14th: gd jump and clr 3 out: in n.d next: easily* 6/4[2]

5131 2 37 **Troika Steppes**[27] 4427 8-11-7 123..............(t) ConorShoemark(3) 112
(Fergal O'Brien) *led tl 9th: w ldr tl led again 11th: hdd after next: rdn 16th: out j. next: wl btn bef next* 1/2[1]

063P 3 95 **The Jugopolist (IRE)**[10] 4772 9-10-12 68......................(b) DaveCrosse
(John Cornwall) *j.lft: chsd ldr: j.lft and reminder 2nd: dropped to 3rd 8th: rdn and struggling after 10th: t.o fr 12th* 50/1[3]

6m 25.7s (15.40) **Going Correction** +0.85s/f (Soft) 3 Ran SP% **108.6**
Speed ratings: **108,95,64**
CSF £2.78 TOTE £2.10; EX 2.80 Trifecta £3.10.

Owner David Nott, Ken Lawrence, Tim Messom **Bred** Alistair Thompson **Trained** Barbury Castle, Wiltshire

FOCUS
This turned into a procession for the winner who outjumped his main market rival throughout and it was over as a contest leaving the far side. Race distance increased by 51yds.

4978 ST IVES TOYOTA H'CAP CHASE (16 fncs) 2m 3f 189y

3:55 (3:58) (Class 3) (0-125,125) 5-Y-0+ £6,657 (£2,067; £1,113)

Form RPR

3P64 1 **Dusky Lark**[30] 4363 6-11-12 122..................................(t) DarylJacob 140+
(Colin Tizzard) *mde all and j. bttr than rivals: drew wl clr after 3 out: mstke next: v easily* 7/4[2]

1-41 2 24 **Midnight Monty**[24] 4456 6-11-11 121.............................. JamesReveley 109
(Keith Reveley) *nt a fluent: chsd wnr: mstke 6th and 7th: rdn and hit 3 out: wl btn and j.lft last 2* 6/5[1]

PP21 3 21 **Alberto's Dream**[22] 4503 7-10-3 106................................ MrJNixon(7) 79
(Tom Symonds) *hld up in tch: 3rd whn stmbld on landing 10th: sn struggling: lost tch 12th: t.o* 9/2[3]

5P04 P **Nearest The Pin (IRE)**[7] 4852 11-10-12 108..............(tp) AndrewTinkler
(Dai Williams) *chsd ldrs tl j. slowly and dropped to last 8th: struggling whn mstke 11th: immediately p.u* 10/1

5m 18.65s (13.35) **Going Correction** +0.85s/f (Soft) 4 Ran SP% **109.1**
Speed ratings: **107,97,89,**
CSF £4.45 TOTE £2.40; EX 4.60 Trifecta £4.70.

Owner Mrs Sara Biggins & Mrs Celia Djivanovic **Bred** Sir Thomas Pilkington **Trained** Milborne Port, Dorset

■ Indian Stream (6-1) was withdrawn. Rule 4 applies to bets struck priot to withdrawal but not to SP bets. Deduction - 10p in the pound. New market formed.

FOCUS
Jumping won the day here as Dusky Lark jumped with much more fluency than any of his rivals and he had this in safe keeping from some way out.

4979 TOYOTA HILUX JUVENILE H'CAP HURDLE (8 hdls) 1m 7f 171y

4:30 (4:30) (Class 4) (0-120,120) 4-Y-0 £3,249 (£954; £477)

Form RPR

32 1 **Red Hammer**[22] 4502 4-11-3 111.. DarylJacob 108+
(Nicky Henderson) *led: travelling best bef 2 out: flattened 2 out and hdd: battled on wl u.p flat to ld again cl home* 11/8[2]

522 2 hd **Magic Dancer**[60] 3819 4-11-2 113.................(tp) GrahamWatters(3) 109
(Charlie Longsdon) *chsd ldr: jnd ldr bef 3 out: rdn bef 2 out: lft in ld 2 out: mstke last: kpt on u.p flat tl hdd and no ex cl home* 1/1[1]

06 3 17 **Blackfire (FR)**[23] 4486 4-11-7 115.............................. RichardJohnson 98
(Jonjo O'Neill) *hld up in tch in 3rd: mstke 3 out: sn rdn: wknd between last 2* 11/2[3]

4m 8.3s (13.40) **Going Correction** +0.75s/f (Soft) 3 Ran SP% **107.5**
Speed ratings: **96,95,87**
CSF £3.18 TOTE £2.00; EX 3.10 Trifecta £3.20.

Owner Simon Munir & Isaac Souede **Bred** Pontchartrain Stud **Trained** Upper Lambourn, Berks

FOCUS
This was run at a fairly steady gallop and it developed into a head-to-head up the straight, with this being a step up from the winner. Race distance increased by 51yds.

4980 CAMBRIDGE LEXUS H'CAP CHASE (19 fncs) 2m 7f 129y

5:05 (5:08) (Class 5) (0-100,98) 5-Y-0+ £2,662 (£826; £445)

Form RPR

152P 1 **Pandy Wells**[23] 4491 7-11-1 87.. KielanWoods 92+
(Graeme McPherson) *w ldr: mstke 1st: j. slowly next and lost pl: in tch in rr after: lft 3rd after 13th: wnt 2nd after next: ev ch whn lft clr 2 out: carried lft and hmpd by loose horse bef last: styd on: rdn out* 2/1[1]

4353 2 11 **Petit Ecuyer (FR)**[10] 4776 10-9-8 73................................ MissPFuller(7) 68
(Dai Williams) *led: j. slowly and hdd 2nd: dropped to last pair but wl in tch after: lft 2nd after 13th tl after 14th: drvn and rallied after 3 out: lft 2nd 2 out: 3 l down last: carried rt and hmpd by loose horse flat: no ch after* 7/2[3]

P443 3 57 **The Society Man (IRE)**[10] 4772 9-9-7 72 oh10.......... GrahamCarson(7) 3
(Michael Chapman) *chsd ldrs: hmpd 2nd: jnd ldr after 3rd tl 11th: dropped to last and rdn after mstke 14th: lost tch 16th: t.o whn lft 3rd 2 out* 11/1

0U60 U **Toast And Jam (IRE)**[11] 4747 7-10-0 72 oh8................(t) LeeEdwards 77
(Claire Dyson) *j.rt at times: t.k.h: lft in ld 2nd: jnd whn jinked rt and uns rdr 2 out* 6/1

0-23 U **Smartmax (FR)**[106] 3061 7-11-12 98................................ TomMessenger
(Caroline Bailey) *t.k.h: hmpd 1st: chsd ldrs 3rd tl wnt 2nd 11th: stmbld and uns rdr after 13th* 9/4[2]

6m 39.6s (29.30) **Going Correction** +0.85s/f (Soft) 5 Ran SP% **108.9**
Speed ratings: **85,81,62, ,**
CSF £9.18 TOTE £2.70: £1.10, £2.30; EX 8.40 Trifecta £27.10.

Owner Mike & Linda Paul **Bred** M R Paul **Trained** Upper Oddington, Gloucs

FOCUS
An eventful handicap chase, but this wouldn't be the most reliable piece of form on offer.

4981 DATA TECHNIQUES REDEMPTION INTERMEDIATE OPEN NATIONAL HUNT FLAT RACE 1m 7f 171y

5:40 (5:42) (Class 6) 4-6-Y-0 £1,624 (£477; £238; £119)

Form RPR

1 **Laval Noir (FR)** 5-11-2 0... DavidBass 108+
(Kim Bailey) *hld up in 3rd: lft 2nd after 5f: rdn over 2f out: led 1f out: sn asserted but hung lft: styd on* 7/2[3]

2 6 **Bardd (IRE)** 4-10-9 0.. AndrewTinkler 95
(Nicky Henderson) *chsd ldr tl lft in ld after 5f: gng best over 2f out: shkn up 2f out: rn green whn rdn over 1f out: hdd 1f out: sn btn: wknd ins fnl f* 5/6[1]

3 19 **Max Dynamo** 6-11-2 0... RyanMahon 83
(Jim Wilson) *hld up in last pair: lft cl 3rd 5f out: dropped to last and outpcd 4f out: no ch w ldng pair but styd on 1f out to go modest 3rd ins fnl f* 50/1

00 4 8 **He Likes Tobouggie**[4] 4894 5-11-2 0..........................(t) TrevorWhelan 75
(Neil King) *hld up in rr: lft cl 4th after 5f: rdn 3f out: 3rd and wl btn 2f out: wknd and lost 3rd ins fnl f* 33/1

3 5 2½ **Frankly Speaking**[33] 4309 6-11-2 0................................ JamesDavies 84+
(Tom Symonds) *led: hung lft after 3f: racing on stands' rail whn hdd dropped to last after 5f: rallied and bk in tch 1/2-way: wnt 3rd over 4f out: rdn and btn 3f out: 4th and wl btn whn hung lft again 1f out: wknd* 9/4[2]

4m 0.75s (11.65) **Going Correction** +0.75s/f (Soft)
WFA 4 from 5yo+ 7lb 5 Ran SP% **112.4**
Speed ratings: **100,97,87,83,82**
CSF £7.08 TOTE £4.30: £2.10, £1.40; EX 8.70 Trifecta £74.90.

Owner The Mindy Partnership **Bred** Pierre Jabot **Trained** Andoversford, Gloucs

FOCUS
This turned into a straight scrap in the straight, with the front two drawing a mile clear. Race distance increased by 51yds.

T/Plt: £90.30 to a £1 stake. Pool: £38,136.60 - 308.20 winning tickets. T/Qpdt: £46.80 to a £1 stake. Pool: £2,057.00 - 32.50 winning tickets. **Steve Payne**

4639 MARKET RASEN (R-H)
Monday, March 28

OFFICIAL GOING: Soft
Wind: strong 1/2 against Weather: changeable, breezy and very cool

4982 WATCH RACING UK IN HD "NATIONAL HUNT" NOVICES' HURDLE (10 hdls) 2m 2f 140y
1:20 (1:20) (Class 4) 4-Y-0+ **£3,898** (£1,144; £572)

Form RPR
44F **1** **Solomn Grundy (IRE)**[14] [4668] 6-11-1 123 NoelFehily 112+
(Neil Mulholland) *mde all: inclined to jump lft: increased gallop 6th: pushed along 3 out: drew clr run-in* **1/4**[1]
2030 **2** *8* **Walkami (FR)**[31] [4344] 5-11-1 0 AidanColeman 104
(Jonjo O'Neill) *chsd wnr thrght: pushed along 8th: hung rt and kpt on one pce fr 2 out* **10/3**[2]
0-P6 **3** *8* **Sirius Star**[121] [2772] 7-10-10 0 JamieHamilton(5) 96
(Brian Rothwell) *wore ear plugs: a in last: pushed along 7th: chsng ldng pair appr 2 out: wknd last* **33/1**[3]
5m 4.0s (24.60) **Going Correction** +1.375s/f (Heav) **3 Ran SP% 106.0**
Speed ratings (Par 105): **103,99,96**
CSF £1.47 TOTE £1.30; EX 1.50 Trifecta £1.40.
Owner R S Brookhouse **Bred** Mrs Kay Cottrell **Trained** Limpley Stoke, Wilts

FOCUS
After 14mm of rain overnight the going was soft and there was a headwind up the home straight. The stable bend was moved out 15 yards, and the wood bend was out 16 yards, adding approximately 141yds to the race distance. The hot favourite had only two rivals to beat in this opening event, but he was never in any danger under a positive ride and is a potentially useful type.

4983 SUE IS 60 H'CAP HURDLE (12 hdls) 2m 7f 16y
1:50 (1:50) (Class 4) (0-120,120) 4-Y-0+ **£3,898** (£1,144; £572; £286)

Form RPR
0344 **1** **Moidore**[29] [4388] 7-11-7 115 AdamPogson 117+
(Charles Pogson) *t.k.h: trckd ldrs: led 3 out: hdd narrowly next: upsides last: led last 200yds: drvn out* **11/2**
0P03 **2** *2 3/4* **Phare Isle (IRE)**[20] [4543] 11-10-11 112 (tp) MrMJPKendrick(7) 110
(Ben Case) *trckd ldr: led narrowly 2 out: hung lft and hdd last 200yds: no ex* **5/1**
1222 **3** *3/4* **Milly Baloo**[15] [4644] 5-11-1 109 BrianHughes 106
(Tim Easterby) *hld up in last: hdwy to trck ldrs bef 2 out: effrt appr last: styd on same pce* **2/1**[1]
U330 **4** *2 1/2* **Road To Freedom**[29] [4389] 7-11-5 113 DannyCook 108
(Lucy Wadham) *trckd ldrs: one pce appr 2 out* **10/3**[2]
PP11 **5** *3 1/4* **Shinooki (IRE)**[19] [4557] 9-11-3 116 (p) DavidNoonan(5) 108
(Alex Hales) *set v stdy pce: qcknd gallop 8th: drvn and hdd 3 out: wknd between last 2* **7/2**[3]
7m 1.0s (70.50) **Going Correction** +1.375s/f (Heav) **5 Ran SP% 110.7**
Speed ratings (Par 105): **32,31,30,29,28**
CSF £30.32 TOTE £5.30: £1.70, £2.90; EX 41.40 Trifecta £82.30.
Owner C T Pogson **Bred** The Queen **Trained** Farnsfield, Notts

FOCUS
Race distance was increased by 186yds. They went a very steady pace and there was only about 10l separating all the runners at the finish. The winner has run to his mark.

4984 RACING UK PROFITS RETURNED TO RACING CHASE (A NOVICES' LIMITED H'CAP) (12 fncs) 2m 1f 43y
2:25 (2:29) (Class 4) (0-120,118) 5-Y-0+ **£5,325** (£1,653; £890)

Form RPR
41P1 **1** **Sir Note (FR)**[59] [3845] 6-10-11 107 JackQuinlan 110
(James Eustace) *j. boldly: led: hrd drvn and hdd narrowly appr 3 out: 3 l clr sn after last: hrd rdn: tired and hld on all out nr fin* **7/2**[3]
4065 **2** *1/2* **Lucky Jim**[24] [4465] 5-11-6 116 AidanColeman 121+
(David Dennis) *drvn to chse ldng pair 9th: hmpd and lft 2nd next: kpt on run-in: jst hld* **5/2**[2]
-533 **3** *1* **Coozan George**[59] [3834] 7-10-7 103 BrianHughes 106
(Malcolm Jefferson) *racd in last: dropped bk and reminders 5th: nt fluent next: reminders and outpcd 8th: kpt on fr 2 out: one pce last 75yds* **15/8**[1]
546- **P** **Neck Or Nothing (GER)**[329] [112] 7-11-1 111 NoelFehily
(Neil Mulholland) *t.k.h: trckd wnr sn after 2nd: 3rd and outpcd whn blnd 8th: sn wknd: t.o whn p.u bef 3 out* **9/2**
56PP **F** **Take A Break (FR)**[4] [4889] 5-11-8 118 (vt) JamesBest 121
(Nigel Hawke) *trckd ldrs: 2nd 6th: upsides 9th: led narrowly appr next only to fall: fell heavily last whn running loose* **14/1**
4m 57.5s (22.50) **Going Correction** +1.475s/f (Heav) **5 Ran SP% 110.4**
Speed ratings: **106,105,105,,**
CSF £12.84 TOTE £3.30: £1.60, £1.60; EX 11.60 Trifecta £23.50.
Owner G F Chesneaux **Bred** Jean-Pierre Coiffier **Trained** Newmarket, Suffolk

FOCUS
Race distance increased by 141yds. There was some drama and a tight finish in this fair handicap. The winner has run to his mark.

4985 RACING UK DAY PASS JUST £10 H'CAP CHASE (14 fncs) 2m 5f 89y
3:00 (3:02) (Class 4) (0-110,110) 5-Y-0+ **£4,393** (£1,364; £734)

Form RPR
343P **1** **Bennys Well (IRE)**[9] [4792] 10-10-12 96 DannyCook 103
(Sue Smith) *nt fluent: led tl after 4th: w ldr: reminders 8th: sn pushed along: outpcd 11th: chsd clr ldr next: styd on run-in: led last 50yds* **13/8**[1]
2424 **2** *3* **Ballydague Lady (IRE)**[20] [4545] 9-11-12 110 (p) NoelFehily 117+
(Neil Mulholland) *hit 1st: trckd ldng pair: led 9th: wnt clr sn after 11th: reminders appr next: j.lft last 2: 12 l ahd last: tired bdly: wknd and hdd last 50yds* **5/2**[2]
456 **3** *70* **Kayfton Pete**[49] [4028] 10-11-10 108 AdamPogson 72
(Charles Pogson) *t.k.h: trckd ldr: led after 4th: hdd 9th: sn lost pl and bhd: t.o 11th: lft distant 3rd sn after 2 out: eased run-in: eventually completed* **11/2**
4P20 **P** **Agentleman (IRE)**[52] [3968] 6-10-13 97 BrianHughes
(Tim Easterby) *hld up in last: chsd ldr 10th: wknd 3 out: poor 3rd whn blnd next: immediately p.u* **11/4**[3]
6m 20.9s (34.90) **Going Correction** +1.475s/f (Heav) **4 Ran SP% 108.7**
Speed ratings: **92,90,64,**
CSF £6.06 TOTE £2.30; EX 6.70 Trifecta £20.80.
Owner Mrs A Ellis **Bred** J Costello **Trained** High Eldwick, W Yorks

FOCUS
The race distance was increased by 186yds. A weak event but the winner produced a remarkable performance to register an unlikely victory even though he was nowhere near his best.

4986 RACING UK NOW IN HD! H'CAP HURDLE (10 hdls) 2m 2f 140y
3:35 (3:37) (Class 3) (0-135,129) 4-Y-0+
£9,384 (£2,772; £1,386; £693; £346; £174)

Form RPR
-131 **1** **Cloudy Dream (IRE)**[121] [2772] 6-11-5 122 BrianHughes 132+
(Malcolm Jefferson) *trckd ldrs: t.k.h: smooth hdwy to ld last: hung rt: qcknd clr: v readily* **5/2**[2]
00F **2** *6* **Kentucky Star (FR)**[23] [4492] 7-10-12 115 IanPopham 115+
(Dan Skelton) *hld up in last but wl in tch: hdwy to trck ldrs 3 out: 4th last: styd on to take modest 2nd last 50yds* **3/1**[3]
4016 **3** *1* **Minstrels Gallery (IRE)**[30] [4366] 7-11-12 129 DannyCook 129
(Lucy Wadham) *chsd ldrs: hit 7th: 2nd next: kpt on same pce run-in* **11/1**
13-0 **4** *3/4* **Make Me A Fortune (IRE)**[9] [4801] 8-11-5 129 (p) TrevorRyan(7) 127
(Steve Gollings) *hld up in rr but wl in tch: hdwy to chse ldrs 3 out: 6th last: styd on fnl 100yds* **14/1**
322 **5** *nk* **Blue Rambler**[32] [4317] 6-11-7 124 AidanColeman 122
(John Ferguson) *trckd ldrs: 5th last: styd on last 100yds* **2/1**[1]
0541 **6** *4 1/2* **Grams And Ounces**[11] [4745] 9-10-8 116 (t) DavidNoonan(5) 110
(Grace Harris) *chsd ldr: led bef 3 out: hdd last: wknd last 200yds* **20/1**
0U52 **7** *68* **Favorite Girl (GER)**[24] [4459] 8-11-7 124 JonathanEngland 49
(Michael Appleby) *led: hdd bef 3 out: sn lost pl and bhd: t.o last: heavily eased: eventually completed* **20/1**
5m 1.6s (22.20) **Going Correction** +1.375s/f (Heav) **7 Ran SP% 111.4**
Speed ratings (Par 107): **108,105,105,104,104 102,74**
CSF £10.15 CT £63.87 TOTE £2.70: £1.50, £2.10; EX 12.10 Trifecta £84.70.
Owner Trevor Hemmings **Bred** Eimear Purcell **Trained** Norton, N Yorks

FOCUS
Race distance increased by 141yds. They went a stop-start gallop but the winner was impressive under a hold-up ride in this decent handicap.

4987 HIGH DEFINITION RACING UK CONDITIONAL JOCKEYS' H'CAP HURDLE (10 hdls) 2m 2f 140y
4:10 (4:13) (Class 5) (0-100,99) 4-Y-0+ **£2,599** (£763; £381; £190)

Form RPR
5P62 **1** **Man Of God (IRE)**[34] [4291] 8-11-3 90 DavidNoonan 94+
(Tim Vaughan) *t.k.h: led tl after 1st: chsd ldr: drvn and briefly outpcd after 3 out: rallied and 2nd next: led appr last: drvn rt out* **11/8**[1]
25UU **2** *3* **Lost In Newyork (IRE)**[53] [3951] 9-10-0 73 oh1 (p) MauriceLinehan 75
(Nick Kent) *in rr but wl in tch: nt fluent 5th: drvn 7th: hdwy and cl 3rd 2 out: rpt on to take 2nd clsng stages* **5/2**[2]
050P **3** *1/2* **Sweet Midnight**[29] [4390] 4-10-1 89 (p) CathalCourtney(7) 82
(John Holt) *t.k.h: nt fluent: led after 1st: hdd sn after 3 out: led appr next: hdd whn stmbld on landing last: edgd lft: kpt on same pce* **16/1**[3]
0P23 **4** *26* **Gud Day (IRE)**[11] [4747] 8-10-8 81 (p) KieronEdgar 55
(Conor Dore) *chsd ldrs: led sn after 3 out: drvn and hdd appr next: sn lost pl and bhd: t.o* **5/2**[2]
0P-0 **5** *88* **Flamingo Beat**[22] [4502] 6-9-11 77 GeorgeGorman(7)
(Christine Dunnett) *trckd ldrs: outpcd 6th: hdwy to chse ldrs sn after 3 out: lost pl bef next: sn bhd: t.o whn virtually p.u run-in: walked home last 75yds: eventually completed* **16/1**[3]
5m 9.0s (29.60) **Going Correction** +1.375s/f (Heav)
WFA 4 from 5yo+ 7lb **5 Ran SP% 111.0**
Speed ratings (Par 103): **92,90,90,79,42**
CSF £5.44 TOTE £2.20: £1.50, £2.00; EX 7.90 Trifecta £37.90.
Owner optimumracing.co.uk **Bred** Premier Bloodstock **Trained** Aberthin, Vale of Glamorgan
■ Stewards' Enquiry : Cathal Courtney seven-day ban: used whip above permitted level (Apr 11-17)

FOCUS
Race distance increased by 141yds. This was weakened by numerous withdrawals, but the well-backed favourite showed plenty of tenacity to record his breakthrough hurdles win.

4988 RACING UK DAY PASS JUST £10 MAIDEN OPEN NATIONAL HUNT FLAT RACE 2m 148y
4:45 (4:49) (Class 6) 4-6-Y-0 **£1,559** (£457; £228; £114)

Form RPR
44 **1** **Debece**[169] [1873] 5-11-3 0 NoelFehily 116+
(Tim Vaughan) *trckd ldr: upsides after 7f: led over 5f out: wnt wl clr over 1f out: easily* **11/4**[3]
2 *19* **Johanos (FR)** 5-10-12 0 DavidNoonan(5) 97
(Nigel Hawke) *hld up in rr: drvn over 7f out: reminders and outpcd 6f out: hdwy 3f out: tk remote 2nd over 1f out* **5/2**[2]
0 **3** *4 1/2* **Mustang On**[33] [4309] 6-11-0 0 MauriceLinehan(3) 92
(Nick Kent) *hld up in mid-div: trckd ldrs after 6f: drvn over 5f out: chsd wnr over 2f out: wknd over 1f out* **20/1**
3 **4** *3 3/4* **Black Ivory**[20] [4552] 4-10-10 0 BrianHughes 81
(Malcolm Jefferson) *trckd ldrs: 2nd over 4f out: drvn 3f out: sn btn* **5/4**[1]
0 **5** *28* **Mutawaasel**[20] [4552] 4-10-10 0 DannyCook 53
(Sue Smith) *led: hdd over 5f out: lost pl 3f out: wl bhd over 1f out: t.o* **17/2**
0 **6** *8* **Ask Paddy (IRE)**[29] [4392] 4-10-10 0 (t) JonathanEngland 45
(Sam Drake) *hld up in mid-div: drvn over 5f out: sn bhd: t.o over 2f out* **22/1**
4m 23.6s (22.50) **Going Correction** +1.375s/f (Heav)
WFA 4 from 5yo+ 7lb **6 Ran SP% 119.3**
Speed ratings: **102,93,90,89,76 72**
CSF £10.92 TOTE £3.90: £2.10, £2.30; EX 14.60 Trifecta £111.90.
Owner Robert Kirkland **Bred** Brian J Griffiths And John Nicholson **Trained** Aberthin, Vale of Glamorgan

FOCUS
Race distance increased by 141yds. There were several non-runners in this bumper, but the promising winner hammered his rivals.
T/Plt: £87.40 to a £1 stake. Pool: £34,382.29 - 286.90 winning units T/Qpdt: £16.80 to a £1 stake. Pool: £2,161.89 - 94.92 winning units **Walter Glynn**

4930 PLUMPTON (L-H)
Monday, March 28
4989 Meeting Abandoned - Waterlogged

4996 - 5000a (Foreign Racing) - See Raceform Interactive

4952 FAIRYHOUSE (R-H)

Monday, March 28

OFFICIAL GOING: Yielding to soft (soft in places)

5001a REA GRIMES PROPERTY CONSULTANTS JUVENILE HURDLE (GRADE 2) (10 hdls) 2m

2:40 (2:40) 4-Y-O

£19,522 (£6,286; £2,977; £1,323; £661; £330)

RPR

1 **Slowmotion (FR)**[15] 4652 4-10-7 0 BarryGeraghty 138+
(A P O'Brien, Ire) *chsd ldrs at mod early pce: mod 3rd at 1/2-way: tk clsr order bhd ldr 3 out and disp travelling wl bef next: led fr 2 out and sn extended advantage: pushed out run-in: easily* **2/1**[1]

2 *7* **Rashaan (IRE)**[51] 4002 4-11-3 133 MPFogarty 133
(Colin Kidd, Ire) *chsd ldrs at mod early pce: mod 4th at 1/2-way: tk clsr order bhd ldr gng wl 3 out: disp bef 2 out where nt fluent and hdd: sn no imp on easy wnr: kpt on same pce* **9/4**[2]

3 *8* **Newberry New (IRE)**[37] 4257 4-11-3 127 RobbiePower 125
(Mrs John Harrington, Ire) *led at mod early pce tl hdd fr 1st: nt fluent next and at times after: mod 2nd at 1/2-way: clsr in 2nd 3 out: sn pushed along and dropped to 4th bef st: no imp on easy wnr fr 2 out: wnt mod 3rd at last* **9/2**

4 *6½* **Tocororo (IRE)**[37] 4257 4-10-7 119 BJCooper 111
(Gordon Elliott, Ire) *cl up at mod early pce and led fr 1st: extended ld fr next: rn arnd bef 3rd: slt mstke next: reduced ld bef 3 out where nt fluent: rdn and hdd bef next and sn no imp in 3rd: dropped to mod 4th at las* **4/1**[3]

5 *12* **Alterno (IRE)**[11] 4757 4-11-0 0 DavyRussell 104
(Desmond McDonogh, Ire) *hld up at mod early pce: mod 5th at 1/2-way: tk clsr order bhd ldrs 3 out: sn pushed along and no imp on ldrs bef st: one pce* **25/1**

6 *4½* **Sound Money**[170] 4-11-0 0 AELynch 99
(E J O'Grady, Ire) *chsd ldrs early at mod early pce: nt fluent 1st: nt fluent in rr at 5th: rdn in 6th after 3 out and no imp on ldrs bef next: one pce after* **33/1**

7 *19* **Calin Des Ongrais (FR)**[30] 4372 4-11-0 0 JackKennedy 80
(Gordon Elliott, Ire) *w.w in rr at mod early pce: mod 6th at 1/2-way: pushed along towards rr bef 3 out and no imp bef st: wknd: t.o* **33/1**

8 *11* **Lake Champlain (IRE)**[38] 2203 4-11-0 120 MarkBolger 69
(Mrs John Harrington, Ire) *hld up at mod early pce: nt fluent 3rd: mod 7th at 1/2-way: pushed along towards rr bef 3 out and no imp u.p in 7th bef st: wknd bef 2 out: t.o* **20/1**

4m 5.7s (-6.30) **Going Correction** -0.225s/f (Good) **8 Ran SP% 116.8**
Speed ratings: **106,102,98,95,89 87,77,72**
CSF £6.87 TOTE £2.90: £1.02, £1.30, £1.40; DF 8.80 Trifecta £22.20.

Owner John P McManus **Bred** Adrian Von Gunten **Trained** Cashel, Co Tipperary

FOCUS
Both Barry Geraghty and Robbie Power agreed that the ground was livelier than on Sunday. This Grade 2 suffered from its proximity to Cheltenham, but it produced a promising winner who was much the best. Tocororo set a scorching clip and it did not relent at any stage. The winner is improving.

5002a RATHBARRY & GLENVIEW STUDS NOVICE HURDLE (GRADE 2) (10 hdls) 2m

3:15 (3:15) 4-Y-O+

£19,522 (£6,286; £2,977; £1,323; £661; £330)

RPR

1 **Sutton Place (IRE)**[22] 4516 5-11-4 135 BarryGeraghty 144+
(Gordon Elliott, Ire) *hld up: slt mstke 4th: 5th 1/2-way: impr to chal bef 2 out: led narrowly between last 2 tl jnd bef last where mstke and sn hdd: rallied far side run-in to regain advantage clsng stages: kpt on wl* **13/8**[1]

2 *½* **Royal Caviar (IRE)**[22] 4516 8-11-4 134 (t[1]) RWalsh 142+
(W P Mullins, Ire) *hld up towards rr: 6th 1/2-way: hdwy in 6th bef 2 out where swtchd lft: rdn to chal on outer between last 2 and disp bef last where mstke: sn led tl hdd u.p clsng stages: no ex* **7/1**[3]

3 *10* **Moon Over Germany (IRE)**[36] 4280 5-11-4 140 DavyRussell 132
(Edward P Harty, Ire) *chsd ldrs: racd keenly: 4th 1/2-way: tk clsr order bhd ldrs gng wl into st: n.m.r bhd horses bef 2 out: rdn in 4th after 2 out and no imp on ldrs bef last: kpt on one pce in 3rd run-in* **10/3**[2]

4 *2* **Jett (IRE)**[29] 4393 5-11-4 0 RobbiePower 130
(Mrs John Harrington, Ire) *trckd ldr: slt mstke 1st: racd keenly: disp fr 3rd and led after next: pushed along w narrow advantage after 3 out: strly pressed next and hdd after 2 out: wknd bef last where mstke* **8/1**

5 *1¾* **Babbling Stream**[50] 4018 5-11-4 0 PaulTownend 128
(W P Mullins, Ire) *hld up towards rr: 7th 1/2-way: slt mstke in rr 4 out: rdn and no imp in mod 8th after next: kpt on one pce fr after 2 out* **14/1**

6 *2½* **General Principle (IRE)**[15] 4662 7-11-4 132 BJCooper 126
(Gordon Elliott, Ire) *chsd ldrs: slt mstke 3rd: 3rd 1/2-way: tk clsr order in cl 2nd fr 3 out: rdn between horses bef next and wknd after 2 out* **7/1**[3]

7 *½* **Attribution**[22] 4516 6-11-4 133 AELynch 125
(Henry De Bromhead, Ire) *led tl jnd fr 3rd and hdd after next: rdn in cl 3rd appr st and sn no ex: dropped to 6th 2 out and wknd* **14/1**

8 *3¾* **Drumcliff (IRE)**[30] 4364 5-11-4 0 MarkWalsh 122
(Harry Fry) *hld up in rr: slt mstkes 1st and next: last at 1/2-way: pushed along in 7th appr st and no imp on ldrs bef next* **33/1**

4m 3.2s (-8.80) **Going Correction** -0.225s/f (Good) **8 Ran SP% 113.6**
Speed ratings: **113,112,107,106,105 104,104,102**
CSF £13.61 TOTE £2.50: £1.20, £1.60, £1.40; DF 13.60 Trifecta £23.00.

Owner John P McManus **Bred** James D Leahy **Trained** Longwood, Co Meath

FOCUS
None of these showed up at Cheltenham. The winner attracted good support and justified favouritism despite making a complete mess of the last. He is progressive and recorded a fair personal best.

5004a KEELINGS IRISH STRAWBERRY HURDLE (GRADE 2) (12 hdls) 2m 4f

4:20 (4:22) 5-Y-O+

£26,029 (£8,382; £3,970; £1,764; £882; £441)

RPR

1 **Value At Risk**[46] 4070 7-11-3 144 HarrySkelton 151
(Dan Skelton) *trckd ldr: racd keenly early: disp fr 5th and led fr next: gng wl 3 out where slt mstke: pushed along and pressed bef next: sn rdn and kpt on wl u.p fr last* **11/4**[2]

2 *1½* **Marchese Marconi (IRE)**[29] 4396 7-11-3 138 (t) BarryGeraghty 150+
(A P O'Brien, Ire) *chsd ldrs: j.big 1st: nt fluent in cl 3rd 4 out: wnt 2nd after next and pressed wnr fr bef 2 out: mstke last and kpt on wl wout matching wnr run-in* **12/1**

3 *1* **Dedigout (IRE)**[43] 4146 10-11-8 157 (t) BJCooper 154+
(A J Martin, Ire) *chsd ldrs: 4th 1/2-way: rdn in 3rd into st and no imp on wnr u.p bef last: kpt on same pce run-in* **5/2**[1]

4 *3½* **Sort It Out (IRE)**[100] 3151 7-11-6 143 MarkWalsh 148
(Edward P Harty, Ire) *hld up in tch: 6th 1/2-way: rdn in 5th after 3 out and impr into 4th appr st: no imp on ldrs after 2 out: kpt on one pce fr last* **12/1**

5 *25* **Plinth (IRE)**[64] 3768 6-11-8 140 (bt) JodyMcGarvey 125
(A P O'Brien, Ire) *settled in rr early: 7th 1/2-way: rdn in 6th after 3 out and no imp on ldrs: one pce after* **33/1**

6 *8½* **Gwencily Berbas (FR)**[120] 2815 5-11-7 151 (t) APHeskin 116
(Alan Fleming, Ire) *trckd ldrs: racd keenly early and led 2nd: jnd fr 5th and hdd fr next: dropped to 3rd after 3 out and wknd into 5th bef st: bad mstke in mod 6th 2 out: distressed post r* **4/1**[3]

7 *3¾* **Taglietelle**[11] 4730 7-11-6 152 (b) DavyRussell 111
(Gordon Elliott, Ire) *a bhd: last at 1/2-way: pushed along in rr after 4 out and no imp after next* **9/2**

8 *64* **Sheamus (IRE)**[29] 4395 7-11-3 132 RWalsh 44
(Ms Sandra Hughes, Ire) *led tl hdd 2nd: dropped to 5th bef 5th where nt fluent: mstke in 5th 4 out and lost pl: wknd to rr bef 3 out and eased: t.o* **12/1**

5m 13.0s (-10.00) **Going Correction** -0.225s/f (Good) **8 Ran SP% 119.4**
Speed ratings: **111,110,110,108,98 95,93,68**
CSF £35.68 TOTE £3.20: £1.40, £2.90, £1.30; DF 37.90 Trifecta £152.20.
Owner D M Huglin **Bred** D M Huglin **Trained** Alcester, Warwicks
■ Stewards' Enquiry : Harry Skelton caution: failed to give gelding time to respond to the whip

FOCUS
This was a proper Grade 2, but the three horses rated in the 150s ran below best and two of them flopped. A small personal best from the winner from the front.

5005a BOYLESPORTS IRISH GRAND NATIONAL CHASE (EXTENDED H'CAP CHASE) (GRADE A) (24 fncs) 3m 5f

5:00 (5:00) 5-Y-O+

£111,764 (£38,970; £18,750; £8,639; £4,595; £2,573)

RPR

1 **Rogue Angel (IRE)**[29] 4397 8-10-6 137 (bt) GerFox(3) 150
(M F Morris, Ire) *disp early and led bef 3rd: strly pressed 2 out: hdd narrowly u.p fr last where bmpd sltly: rallied far side run-in to regain narrow advantage clsng stages: all out: jst* **16/1**

2 *shd* **Bless The Wings (IRE)**[12] 4719 11-10-7 135 (p) RWalsh 148+
(Gordon Elliott, Ire) *hld up in mid-div: prog 4 out to chse ldrs next: impr steadily to ld narrowly fr last where j. sltly rt and sltly bmpd rival: strly pressed run-in and hdd narrowly clsng stages: kpt on wl: jst hld* **12/1**

3 *3¾* **Ballyadam Approach (IRE)**[29] 4397 11-9-12 129 DavidSplaine(3) 138
(Terence O'Brien, Ire) *chsd ldrs: slt mstke 5 out: effrt in 2nd bef 2 out: dropped to 3rd fr last and sn no imp on ldrs: kpt on same pce run-in* **33/1**

4 *2½* **Folsom Blue (IRE)**[57] 3894 9-10-1 134 AndrewRing(5) 141
(M F Morris, Ire) *chsd ldrs: slt mstke 6 out: rdn in 5th after 3 out and dropped to 6th bef next: kpt on again u.p into mod 4th bef last: no imp on ldrs run-in: kpt on same pce* **20/1**

5 *6* **Bearly Legal (IRE)**[29] 4397 10-9-8 127 (t) DonaghMeyler(5) 130
(Karl Thornton, Ire) *mid-div early: rdn in 3rd after 4 out and no imp on wnr bef 2 out where bad mstke and lost pl: no ex u.p in 5th bef last and one pce run-in* **40/1**

6 *2¼* **Baie Des Iles (FR)**[37] 4260 5-10-7 141 MsKWalsh 134
(Ross O'Sullivan, Ire) *hld up in mid-div: nt fluent 4 out and rdn: kpt on u.p in 10th fr after next: nvr trbld ldrs* **20/1**

7 *3¾* **Killer Crow (IRE)**[71] 3651 7-10-3 134 (t) JackKennedy(3) 129
(Gordon Elliott, Ire) *hld up towards rr: hdwy gng wl bef 4 out where n.m.r on inner: tk clsr order bef next: rdn in 6th after 3 out and no imp on ldrs fr next: one pce after* **10/1**[3]

8 *½* **Tulsa Jack (IRE)**[8] 4831 7-9-5 124 JonathanMoore(5) 118
(Noel Meade, Ire) *hld up: hdwy in 12th on outer after 4 out: rdn in 8th after next and no imp on ldrs: kpt on one pce* **25/1**

9 *2½* **Venitien De Mai (FR)**[22] 4521 7-10-9 137 JJBurke 129
(J T R Dreaper, Ire) *disp early tl sn settled bhd ldrs: niggled along after 5 out and no ex fr u.p in 6th after next: wknd 3 out* **7/1**[2]

10 *2¾* **Wrath Of Titans (IRE)**[36] 4279 7-9-13 127 (p) AlanCrowe 116
(Ms Sandra Hughes, Ire) *in tch: pckd sltly out wd 4 out: rdn in 8th into st and no ex fr 3 out: one pce after* **20/1**

11 *1¾* **Cantlow (IRE)**[12] 4719 11-10-6 134 MarkWalsh 121
(E Bolger, Ire) *hld up in tch: pushed along bef 4 out: sn rdn and no imp bef 3 out where bad mstke in 10th: one pce after* **33/1**

12 *4½* **Portrait King (IRE)**[30] 4367 11-10-2 130 (p) APHeskin 113
(Patrick Griffin, Ire) *chsd ldrs: niggled along bef 5 out: rdn and no imp bef next: kpt on one pce in 12th fr after 3 out* **25/1**

13 *27* **Raz De Maree (FR)**[14] 4691 11-10-5 133 (b) AELynch 89
(Gavin Cromwell, Ire) *mid-div: bmpd sltly 10th: rdn after 4 out and no imp in mod 16th into st: t.o* **33/1**

P **Russe Blanc (FR)**[30] 4367 9-10-9 137 (p) CharliePoste
(Kerry Lee) *towards rr: bad mstke 5th and struggling in rr after: trailing bef 1/2-way: p.u after 14th* **25/1**

P **My Murphy (IRE)**[67] 3715 10-11-6 148 RobbiePower
(W J Burke, Ire) *mid-div: pushed along after 15th and dropped towards rr after next: t.o whn p.u bef 5 out* **25/1**

P **Jarob**[29] 4394 9-10-2 130 LPDempsey
(Andrew Lynch, Ire) *in rr of mid-div: slt mstke towards rr 5 out: wknd and p.u bef next* **33/1**

P **Living Next Door (IRE)**[88] 3394 10-11-3 **145**..................(t) DenisO'Regan
(A J Martin, Ire) *w.w towards rr: tk clsr order after 1/2-way: mstke 16th: struggling towards rr 6 out: t.o whn p.u bef next* **20/1**

P **Futuramic (IRE)**[8] 4831 9-9-7 **124** oh1.................. ConorMaxwell[(3)]
(Andrew Lynch, Ire) *in rr of mid-div: hmpd by faller at 11th: niggled along fr 14th and no imp after 5 out: t.o whn p.u bef 2 out* **25/1**

P **Thunder And Roses (IRE)**[37] 4260 8-11-3 **145**............(b[1]) DavidMullins
(Ms Sandra Hughes, Ire) *sn chsd ldrs: niggled along briefly after 17th (normal 18th): rdn after 5 out and wknd next: eased next and p.u bef 2 out* **33/1**

P **Kilford (IRE)**[15] 4663 10-10-5 **133** 10ex.................. PaulTownend
(Leonard Whitmore, Ire) *chsd ldrs early: no imp towards rr 6 out: slow next and t.o whn p.u bef 4 out* **20/1**

P **Mala Beach (IRE)**[37] 4260 8-11-8 **150**.................. DavyRussell
(Gordon Elliott, Ire) *chsd ldrs: 9th 1/2-way: rdn and no ex after 5 out: wknd and p.u after next* **12/1**

U **Unic De Bersy (FR)**[17] 4604 8-10-0 **133**..................(p) ChrisTimmons[(5)]
(Gordon Elliott, Ire) *hld up: 19th bef 13th: tk clsr order in mid-div at bypassed 17th: wknd fr 6 out and p.u bef next* **50/1**

P **Sub Lieutenant (IRE)**[22] 4517 7-11-3 **145**..................(vt) BJCooper
(Ms Sandra Hughes, Ire) *disp early and led bef 2nd tl hdd bef next: slt mstke 15th: mstke and pckd sltly 4 out: wknd bef next where mstke in mod 12th: eased and p.u bef 2 out* **14/1**

F **Another Hero (IRE)**[54] 3929 7-10-8 **136**.................. BarryGeraghty
(Jonjo O'Neill) *hld up: in rr of mid-div whn fell 11th* **12/1**

P **Riverside City (IRE)**[8] 4831 7-9-10 **124** oh2.................. MsNCarberry
(Gordon Elliott, Ire) *lost grnd s and detached in rr: struggling towards rr 6 out: p.u bef next* **20/1**

P **Captain Von Trappe (IRE)**[22] 4521 7-10-5 **133**..............(b) KevinSexton
(Gordon Elliott, Ire) *towards rr: bad mstke 1st and almost uns rdr: rdn in mid-div bef 5 out where bad mstke: eased and p.u bef next* **33/1**

P **Bonny Kate (IRE)**[15] 4656 6-10-9 **137**.................. SeanFlanagan
(Noel Meade, Ire) *cl ldrs: impr bhd ldrs gng wl fr 5 out: pushed along bef next and sn no ex: wknd after 4 out and eased: p.u bef 3 out* **13/2**[1]

7m 55.7s (-10.30) **Going Correction** -0.05s/f (Good)
WFA 5 from 6yo+ 1lb **27** Ran SP% **140.4**
Speed ratings: **112,111,110,110,108 107,106,106,106,105 104,103,96, , , , , ,EM**
CSF £162.04 CT £6251.31 TOTE £20.20: £4.30, £2.50, £7.40, £6.00; DF 276.70.
Owner Gigginstown House Stud **Bred** Mrs R H Lalor **Trained** Fethard, Co Tipperary
■ Stewards' Enquiry : R Walsh one-day ban: failed to give gelding time to respond to the whip (tbn)
Ger Fox one-day ban: failed to give gelding time to respond to the whip (tbn)

FOCUS
This looked a pretty standard, open Irish National. Again, if you can get into a rhythm up front, you can be hard to catch in this race. Above all, it proved the genius of Mouse Morris, who saddled the first and fourth. The winner recorded a personal best from the front.

5006a JOHN & CHICH FOWLER MEMORIAL EUROPEAN BREEDERS FUND MARES CHASE (GRADE 3) (16 fncs) 2m 4f
5:35 (5:36) 5-Y-0+ **£16,957** (£5,238; £2,481; £1,102; £413)

RPR

1 **Emily Gray (IRE)**[32] 4319 8-11-3 148.................. JJBurke 145+
(Kim Bailey) *led and disp early: dropped to 4th bef 6 out: rdn in 4th bef st and impr on outer to ld fr after 3 out: pressed clly u.p bef last: kpt on wl run-in* **1/1**[1]

2 1 1/4 **Uranna (FR)**[15] 4656 8-10-11 133.................. RWalsh 138+
(W P Mullins, Ire) *w.w towards rr: gng wl in cl 5th bef 6 out: slt mstke 3 out: rdn into 2nd after next and pressed wnr clly bef last: kpt on wl run-in wout matching wnr* **9/4**[2]

3 9 1/2 **Perfect Promise (IRE)**[92] 3296 8-11-0 129.................. DavyRussell 130
(James Joseph Mangan, Ire) *cl up and disp after 1st tl settled in 2nd bef 3rd: disp bef 5th and led narrowly bef 7th tl sn jnd: disp for most tl hdd after 4 out: no imp on wnr in 3rd after 2 out: one pce after* **8/1**[3]

4 6 **Dressedtothenines (IRE)**[29] 4397 9-10-11 125.................. BarryGeraghty 121
(Edward P Harty, Ire) *prom tl settled bhd ldrs fr 1st: almost on terms bef 9th: disp fr 6 out tl hdd 3 out where slt mstke: no imp on wnr in 5th 2 out: one pce after* **8/1**[3]

5 2 1/4 **Emcon (IRE)**[15] 4656 7-10-11 123.................. KevinSexton 119
(W J Austin, Ire) *chsd ldrs: cl up bhd ldrs bef 7th: disp fr bef 6 out tl hdd after 3 out: sn rdn and struggling in 3rd whn mstke next: no imp after and wknd bef last* **14/1**

6 61 **Give Her Bach (IRE)**[15] 4656 7-10-11 116..............(t) PierceGallagher 58
(Patrick Cronin, Ire) *in rr thrght: j. sltly lft at times: lost tch fr 8th where slt mstke: j.w lft 5 out and t.o bef next: nvr a factor* **66/1**

5m 23.1s (-0.90) **Going Correction** -0.05s/f (Good) **6** Ran SP% **111.2**
Speed ratings: **99,98,94,92,91 67**
CSF £3.69 TOTE £2.00: £1.20, £1.30; DF 3.60 Trifecta £12.20.
Owner J Perriss **Bred** Robert McCarthy **Trained** Andoversford, Gloucs

FOCUS
This was a worthy Grade 3 and an exciting spectacle. The winner, second and fourth have been rated around their recent efforts.

5003, 5007 - 5008a (Foreign Racing) - See Raceform Interactive

4736 HEXHAM (L-H)
Tuesday, March 29

OFFICIAL GOING: Soft (good to soft in places; 5.1)
Wind: Breezy, half against Weather: Overcast

5009 SIS NOVICES' HURDLE (8 hdls) 2m 48y
2:00 (2:00) (Class 4) 4-Y-0+ **£3,422** (£997; £499)

Form RPR

4 1 **Kid Valentine (IRE)**[167] 1901 6-11-0 0.................. DannyCook 114+
(Michael Smith) *mde all: rdn between last 2: styd on strly run-in* **11/8**[1]

414 2 1 3/4 **Storm Forecast (IRE)**[94] 3245 5-11-0 0.................. BrianHughes 111
(Malcolm Jefferson) *t.k.h early: trckd ldrs: effrt and chsd wnr between last 2: sn rdn: kpt on fr last: nt pce to chal* **7/2**[3]

-054 3 2 **Daytripper**[29] 4403 5-10-2 0.................. GrantCockburn[(5)] 102
(Lucinda Russell) *pressed wnr tl rdn and outpcd between last 2: kpt on fr last: nt rch first two* **33/1**

2232 4 7 **Veinard (FR)**[21] 4550 7-10-9 107.................. CallumBewley[(5)] 107+
(Robert Bewley) *wore hood in paddock and taken early to post: hld up: stdy hdwy and in tch after 3 out: effrt on outside between last 2: 4 l 3rd and hld whn mstke last* **11/4**[2]

24 5 12 **Frightened Rabbit (USA)**[10] 4791 4-10-7 0.................. CraigNichol 84
(Keith Dalgleish) *prom: hit and rdn 2 out: wknd between last 2* **7/1**

005 6 nse **Farewelltocheyenne (IRE)**[29] 4403 8-11-0 0.................. PeterBuchanan 91
(N W Alexander) *nt fluent: hld up: rdn and outpcd after 3 out: nvr on terms* **25/1**

4F 7 5 **Flying Jack**[52] 4001 6-10-7 0.................. ThomasDowson[(7)] 85
(Maurice Barnes) *hld up: rdn and struggling 3 out: btn next* **125/1**

4000 8 13 **Been Decided (IRE)**[21] 4548 6-10-9 0.................. StephenMulqueen[(5)] 75
(N W Alexander) *in tch: hit 4 out: rdn and struggling next: sn btn* **200/1**

P **Tonto's Spirit**[251] 4-10-7 0.................. HenryBrooke
(Kenneth Slack) *t.k.h early: nt jump wl in rr: struggling fr 3rd: t.o whn p.u 2 out* **28/1**

4m 21.9s (4.50) **Going Correction** +0.55s/f (Soft)
WFA 4 from 5yo+ 7lb **9** Ran SP% **115.0**
Speed ratings (Par 105): **110,109,108,104,98 98,96,89,**
CSF £6.43 TOTE £2.10: £1.20, £1.20, £6.70; EX 7.50 Trifecta £81.40.
Owner D Gilbert, M Lawrence, A Bruce **Bred** Mrs Christopher Dunn **Trained** Kirkheaton, Northumberland

FOCUS
This wasn't a bad novice event by track standards. The winning time suggested the going was no quicker than advertised. Race distance increased by 30yds.

5010 HEXHAM BOOKMAKERS H'CAP CHASE (15 fncs) 2m 4f 15y
2:30 (2:31) (Class 5) (0-100,100) 5-Y-0+ **£3,285** (£957; £479)

Form RPR

-P6P 1 **Whats Up Woody (IRE)**[53] 3969 11-11-2 **95**.................. JonathonBewley[(5)] 112+
(George Bewley) *mde all: nt fluent 3 out: sn jnd and rdn: asserted again after next: drvn out fr last* **4/1**[2]

0-53 2 5 **Westend Theatre (IRE)**[31] 4365 7-11-0 **88**.................. PeterBuchanan 97
(Jane Walton) *in tch: hit and outpcd 4 out: rdn and rallied after 2 out: hit last: wnt 2nd last 100yds: nt rch wnr* **15/2**

40P2 3 1 3/4 **Under The Red Sky (IRE)**[19] 4569 9-9-9 **76**..............(p) MrWHRReed[(7)] 83
(Kenny Johnson) *t.k.h early: trckd ldrs: wnt 2nd 5th: chal after 3 out to after next: 2 l down whn hit last: hung rt and lost 2nd last 100yds* **11/4**[1]

1010 4 3 1/4 **Harleys Max**[19] 4569 7-10-2 **83**.................. JamesCorbett[(7)] 88
(Susan Corbett) *hld up: stdy hdwy and prom 7th: effrt 3 out: drvn and outpcd after next: no imp fr last* **6/1**[3]

00PP P **Bertielicious**[21] 4547 8-9-9 **76** oh18 ow2..................[1] ThomasDowson[(7)]
(Jonathan Haynes) *bhd: blnd and rdr lost iron briefly 2nd: hit 7th: struggling fr 9th: t.o whn p.u bef last* **125/1**

5353 P **Trouble In Paris (IRE)**[12] 4738 9-9-8 **75**..............(bt) LorcanMurtagh[(7)]
(Barry Murtagh) *hld up: struggling 9th: lost tch 4 out: t.o whn p.u after next* **7/1**

1335 P **Turtle Cask (IRE)**[28] 4421 7-11-5 **93**..............(p) BrianHughes
(Dianne Sayer) *chsd wnr tl j. v awkwardly 5th: j. slowly and lost pl next: sn struggling: lost tch and p.u bef 9th* **10/1**

6005 P **Celestino (FR)**[29] 4404 5-11-5 **100**..............(p) MrKitAlexander[(7)]
(N W Alexander) *t.k.h: prom: drvn and outpcd 4 out: wknd bef next: lost tch and p.u bef last* **16/1**

021P P **Proud Gamble (IRE)**[16] 4637 7-10-6 **80**..............(t) CraigNichol
(Rose Dobbin) *hld up: pushed along 7th: struggling 9th: p.u next* **9/1**

5m 30.8s (17.30) **Going Correction** +0.925s/f (Soft) **9** Ran SP% **111.0**
Speed ratings: **102,100,99,98, , , ,**
CSF £32.00 CT £90.72 TOTE £5.40: £1.80, £2.90, £1.70; EX 34.00 Trifecta £154.40.
Owner G T Bewley **Bred** Michael Hayes **Trained** Bonchester Bridge, Borders

FOCUS
A weak handicap in which only four completed and the winner had slipped to a good mark. Race distance increased by 45yds.

5011 LWC NOVICES' HURDLE (12 hdls) 2m 7f 63y
3:05 (3:05) (Class 4) 5-Y-0+ **£3,422** (£997; £499)

Form RPR

-232 1 **Gully's Edge**[75] 3588 6-10-12 0.................. BrianHughes 127+
(Malcolm Jefferson) *trckd ldr: shkn up to ld bef last: sn clr: nudged out run-in: readily* **2/1**[1]

011P 2 17 **Net Work Rouge (FR)**[108] 3032 7-11-12 135..............(t) DavidBass 125
(Kim Bailey) *led: pushed along whn nt fluent 2 out: hdd bef last: no ch w ready wnr* **9/4**[2]

104P 3 1/2 **Calivigny (IRE)**[29] 4405 7-11-7 122.................. StephenMulqueen[(5)] 122
(N W Alexander) *hld up in tch: stdy hdwy 4 out: rdn and outpcd 2 out: kpt on fr last: no imp* **12/1**[3]

3P5P 4 1 1/4 **Iora Glas (IRE)**[57] 3904 7-11-2 113..............(t) ConorShoemark[(3)] 114
(Fergal O'Brien) *t.k.h: sn prom: stdy hdwy after 3 out: rdn and outpcd between last 2: no imp fr last* **33/1**

6-1P 5 71 **Mahler And Me (IRE)**[88] 3400 6-11-5 0.................. HenryBrooke 43
(Alistair Whillans) *nt fluent on occasions: hld up: stdy hdwy 4 out: rdn and wknd 2 out: sn lost tch: t.o* **28/1**

11 P **Billy Billy (IRE)**[17] 4605 6-10-12 124.................. PeterBuchanan
(S R B Crawford, Ire) *trckd ldrs: lost pl qckly 7th: struggling and p.u next* **9/4**[2]

6m 27.2s (18.20) **Going Correction** +0.825s/f (Soft) **6** Ran SP% **109.0**
Speed ratings: **101,95,94,94,69**
CSF £6.60 TOTE £2.40: £1.50, £1.70; EX 6.10 Trifecta £26.00.
Owner Mrs K S Gaffney & Mrs Alix Stevenson **Bred** Mrs K S Gaffney & Mrs Alix Stevenson **Trained** Norton, N Yorks

FOCUS
A modest staying novice hurdle and a big step up from the winner. Race distance increased by 60yds.

5012 FOLLOW HEXHAM ON FACEBOOK H'CAP HURDLE (10 hdls) 2m 4f 28y
3:40 (3:40) (Class 4) (0-120,120) 4-Y-0+ **£6,498** (£1,908; £954; £477)

Form RPR

-322 1 **See Double You (IRE)**[16] 4638 13-11-0 **115**.................. MrRMPMcNally[(7)] 121+
(Ronan M P McNally, Ire) *in tch: stdy hdwy bef 2 out: shkn up to ld bef last: kpt on strly* **15/2**

4P64 2 3 1/2 **Manballandall (IRE)**[19] 4566 8-10-8 **109**..............(bt) JamesCorbett[(7)] 110
(Susan Corbett) *led tl rdn and hdd 3 out: rallied and led briefly between last 2: kpt on same pce run-in* **9/2**[2]

5144 3 8 **Innis Shannon (IRE)**[17] 4608 6-10-3 **102**.................. JonathonBewley[(5)] 98
(George Bewley) *mstkes: in tch: pushed along after 6th: rallied and cl up whn hit 2 out: rdn and outpcd bef last* **13/2**

322 4 3 **Dubai Devils (IRE)**[10] 4806 5-11-5 **113**.................. BrianHughes 103
(Paul Stafford, Ire) *cl up: rdn and outpcd after 2 out: no imp bef last* **7/2**[1]

-063 5 3 **Rinnagree Rosie**[18] 4581 10-10-0 **94** oh10..............(p) AdrianLane 81
(Lucy Normile) *in tch: drvn and outpcd after 3 out: plugged on fr last: nvr rchd ldrs* **18/1**

3133 **6** *nk* **Lochnell (IRE)**[17] 4608 7-10-3 **100**............................ GrahamWatters(3) 87
(Ian Duncan) *prom: hdwy 6th: led 3 out to between last 2: sn rdn and wknd* **11/1**

P-20 **7** *9* **Smadynium (FR)**[59] 3855 8-11-0 **118**........................(p) RossTurner(10) 97
(Julia Brooke) *hld up: pushed along bef 3 out: shortlived effrt bef next: sn wknd* **14/1**

-416 **8** *¾* **Grey Monk (IRE)**[152] 2145 8-11-7 **120**......................(t) NathanMoscrop(5) 97
(Sara Ender) *hld up: outpcd whn hit 4 out: struggling fr next* **10/1**

5000 **9** *9* **Hada Men (USA)**[60] 3837 11-10-8 **105**..............................(p) TonyKelly(3) 73
(Rebecca Menzies) *cl up: outpcd and lost pl 5th: struggling after next: sn n.d* **16/1**

6563 **10** *10* **Bell Weir**[13] 4712 8-10-5 **102**.. EmmaSayer(3) 60
(Dianne Sayer) *nt fluent on occasions: hld up: outpcd whn hit 3 out: nvr on terms* **6/1**[3]

5m 25.9s (13.40) **Going Correction** +0.825s/f (Soft) **10 Ran SP% 115.0**
Speed ratings (Par 105): **106,104,101,100,99 98,95,94,91,87**
CSF £41.31 CT £232.62 TOTE £5.30: £1.50, £1.70, £2.40; EX 41.30 Trifecta £258.60.
Owner Bricky Lobe Syndicate **Bred** Michael And Mrs B C Lenihan **Trained** Armagh, Northern Ireland

FOCUS
This moderate handicap took some getting and the winner ran his best figiure since recording a 125 here in 2014. Race distance increased by 45yds.

5013 PRIMARY WEBSITES H'CAP CHASE (19 fncs) 3m 41y
4:15 (4:15) (Class 5) (0-100,97) 5-Y-0+ **£3,119** (£915; £457; £228)

Form RPR

4453 **1** **Gibbstown (IRE)**[27] 4433 10-11-3 **88**..............................(p) BrianHughes 102+
(Paul Stafford, Ire) *t.k.h: in tch: stdy hdwy 1/2-way: led gng wl bef last: pushed along and qcknd clr run-in: readily* **7/2**[2]

-101 **2** *5* **Flaming Thistle (IRE)**[12] 4741 12-11-1 **91**................ GrantCockburn(5) 98
(John Hodge) *led to 3rd: cl up: hit 7th and lost grnd: nt fluent and outpcd 4 out: rallied 2 out: chsd wnr bef last: kpt on run-in: nt pce to chal* **11/2**[3]

3P44 **3** *14* **Nalim (IRE)**[27] 4433 10-10-11 **82**....................................(b) DannyCook 77
(Harriet Bethell) *bhd: nt fluent and reminders 2nd: outpcd 1/2-way: rallied 2 out: no imp fr last* **17/2**

P321 **4** *2* **The Bishop (IRE)**[12] 4738 8-11-1 **93**........................ MrKitAlexander(7) 83
(N W Alexander) *cl up: led bef 3 out to bef last: sn rdn and wknd* **2/1**[1]

P3P4 **5** *15* **Urban Gale (IRE)**[22] 4534 11-11-9 **94**.........................(p) HenryBrooke 72
(Joanne Foster) *cl up: led 3rd to bef 3 out: rallied: rdn and wknd between last 2* **20/1**

00P2 **6** *1¾* **Feast Of Fire (IRE)**[23] 4514 9-11-7 **97**................................ RyanDay(5) 75
(Joanne Foster) *hld up in tch: stdy hdwy and cl up 4 out: drvn and outpcd whn hit 3 out: nt fluent and wknd next* **6/1**

-452 **F** **Spring Over (IRE)**[12] 4738 10-10-11 **85**....................(t) GrahamWatters(3)
(Ian Duncan) *trckd ldrs: fell 3rd* **7/1**

7m 5.1s (32.90) **Going Correction** +1.20s/f (Heav) **7 Ran SP% 113.0**
Speed ratings: **93,91,86,86,81 80,**
CSF £22.31 CT £148.88 TOTE £3.90: £2.40, £2.20; EX 22.40 Trifecta £130.10.
Owner Mrs L Skelly **Bred** John And Ann Goold **Trained** Oldtown, Co. Dublin

FOCUS
A competitive handicap for the class which saw a pair of former winners fill the first two places. Race distance increased by 60yds.

5014 FOLLOW HEXHAM ON TWITTER MAIDEN OPEN NATIONAL HUNT FLAT RACE 2m 48y
4:50 (4:50) (Class 6) 4-6-Y-O **£2,053** (£598; £299)

Form RPR

1 **Imperial Eloquence (IRE)** 4-10-8 0............................ ConorShoemark(3) 104+
(Fergal O'Brien) *hld up: stdy hdwy over 4f out: led and shkn up over 1f out: rdn and kpt on ins fnl f* **6/1**

5 **2** *1¾* **Isle Of Ewe**[38] 4242 5-10-11 0.. DavidBass 99+
(Tom Lacey) *prom: hdwy 3f out: chsd wnr over 1f out: drifted lft but clsd ins fnl f: kpt on: no ex nr fin* **9/2**[2]

54 **3** *6* **Breakdown Cover (IRE)**[17] 4611 5-11-4 0.................. PeterBuchanan 99
(S R B Crawford, Ire) *in tch: stdy hdwy 1/2-way: rdn and effrt over 2f out: hung lft and outpcd over 1f out* **18/1**

U **4** *4* **Dr West (IRE)**[21] 4552 5-10-13 0............................ JonathonBewley(5) 96
(George Bewley) *t.k.h: promd: led over 2f out: hung lft and hdd over 1f out: btn ins fnl f* **5/1**[3]

5 *3¾* **Tiger Mountain (IRE)** 5-11-4 0.. BrianHughes 91
(Malcolm Jefferson) *hld up in tch: outpcd 1/2-way: rallied over 2f out: kpt on fnl f: no imp* **7/2**[1]

6 *21* **Plexton** 5-11-4 0.. JamesReveley 70
(Karen McLintock) *cl up: lft in ld arnd 1/2-way: rdn and hdd over 2f out: sn wknd* **9/2**[2]

7 *88* **Italian Cousin (IRE)** 6-11-1 0............................ ColmMcCormack(3)
(George Charlton) *hld up: drvn and struggling 1/2-way: lost tch fr 6f out: t.o* **33/1**

8 *5* **Lucky Violet (IRE)** 4-9-11 0.............................. LorcanMurtagh(7)
(Hugh Burns) *hld up: stdy hdwy and in tch 1/2-way: wknd 4f out: t.o* **80/1**

4 **9** *99* **Callnineninenine**[174] 1817 5-11-1 0.............................. AdamNicol(3)
(John Weymes) *hld up: pushed along and outpcd after 7f: rallied: wknd over 5f out: virtually p.u fnl 3f* **40/1**

0 **10** *1* **Beyondtheflame**[20] 4559 6-10-4 0.............................. ThomasDowson(7)
(Jonathan Haynes) *t.k.h: hld up: struggling fr 1/2-way: no ch whn virtually p.u fr 3f out* **200/1**

P **Baracalu (FR)**[65] 5-11-4 0.. DannyCook
(Sandy Thomson) *t.k.h: led tl hung rt and hdd arnd 1/2-way: sn p.u* **7/1**

4m 25.2s (12.50) **Going Correction** +0.825s/f (Soft) **11 Ran SP% 114.4**
WFA 4 from 5yo+ 7lb
Speed ratings: **101,100,97,95,93 82,38,36, ,**
CSF £31.84 TOTE £7.10: £2.10, £1.40, £4.00; EX 51.40 Trifecta £635.20.
Owner Imperial Racing Partnership **Bred** Keith M Griffin **Trained** Naunton, Gloucs

FOCUS
This modest bumper was run at a muddling gallop. The runner-up sets the standard and the winner can rate higher. Race distance increased by 30yds.

T/Plt: £68.70 to a £1 stake. Pool: £90,536.84 - 961.58 winning units. T/Qpdt: £19.50 to a £1 stake. Pool: £7,005.33 - 265.60 winning units. **Richard Young**

4841 SOUTHWELL (L-H)
Tuesday, March 29

OFFICIAL GOING: Soft (good to soft in places; 6.7)
Wind: moderate 1/2 behind Weather: fine

5015 SOUTHWELL GOLF CLUB H'CAP CHASE (19 fncs) 2m 7f 209y
1:50 (1:50) (Class 4) (0-110,109) 5-Y-0+ **£5,325** (£1,653; £890)

Form RPR

3112 **1** **Global Dream**[28] 4423 6-11-8 **105**.. AdamPogson 119+
(Caroline Bailey) *chsd ldrs: led 9th: j.rt at times: styd on wl fr 3 out: v readily* **5/2**[3]

4315 **2** *4½* **Foot The Bill**[3] 4903 11-10-6 **92**.................................. JohnKington(3) 97
(Patrick Holmes) *chsd ldr: led after 2nd: hdd 9th: pushed along 14th: over 3 l down whn hit last: kpt on same pce* **85/40**[2]

53P4 **3** *64* **Abigail Lynch (IRE)**[16] 4647 8-11-7 **109**......................(t) JamieBargary(5) 74
(Nigel Twiston-Davies) *led tl after 2nd: chsd ldrs: drvn 13th: 3 l 2nd whn blnd 16th: sn lost pl and reminders: t.o next: heavily eased run-in: eventually completed* **15/8**[1]

P-P2 **F** **That's The Deal (IRE)**[11] 4776 12-10-0 **83** oh3........................ AdamWedge
(John Cornwall) *hld up in last: wl in tch whn fell 3rd* **11/1**

3033 **P** **Volcanic Jack (IRE)**[253] 1068 8-10-7 **97**.......................... GrahamCarson(7)
(Michael Chapman) *chsd ldrs: reminders 8th: sn drvn: bhd next: t.o 12th: sn p.u* **25/1**

7m 1.4s (38.40) **Going Correction** +1.70s/f (Heav) **5 Ran SP% 107.5**
Speed ratings: **104,102,81, ,**
CSF £8.06 TOTE £2.40: £1.30, £1.50; EX 5.90 Trifecta £13.30.
Owner Mrs Susan Carsberg **Bred** Mrs S Carsberg **Trained** Holdenby, Northants

FOCUS
The going was soft, good to soft in places. Fences and hurdles 5yds outside line raced on March 21. Both bends moved to provide fresh ground. A modest handicap chase to start, with the race only concerning the three market leaders on the final circuit. The winner is on the upgrade.

5016 SOUTHWELL GOLF AND RACING H'CAP CHASE (13 fncs) 1m 7f 153y
2:20 (2:20) (Class 5) (0-100,106) 5-Y-0+ **£3,249** (£954; £477; £238)

Form RPR

5P24 **1** **Edlomond (IRE)**[10] 4778 10-11-4 **97**..............................(t) JakeHodson(5) 109+
(Bill Turner) *chsd ldrs: hit 2nd: 6th and 9th: led appr 3 out: drvn out* **9/4**[2]

3P30 **2** *3¼* **Money For Nothing**[53] 3968 7-11-12 **100**......................(t) AdamWedge 106
(Harriet Bethell) *hld up in last but wl in tch: effrt and handy 3rd 3 out: sn drvn and hung lft: kpt on to take 2nd clsng stages* **7/2**[3]

6341 **3** *1* **Guaracha**[8] 4850 5-12-4 **106** 7ex..(v) RhysFlint 112
(Alexandra Dunn) *chsd ldrs: chal appr 3 out: kpt on one pce between last 2* **2/1**[1]

3564 **4** *4½* **Molko Jack (FR)**[12] 4741 12-10-0 **74** oh8......................(p) RichieMcLernon 76
(Michael Mullineaux) *chsd ldr: outpcd 3 out: kpt on run-in* **8/1**

4320 **P** **Mandy's Boy (IRE)**[8] 4850 6-11-6 **94**..............................(bt[1]) WillKennedy
(Sally Randell) *led: drvn 10th: hdd and lost pl bef next: wl bhd whn p.u bef 3 out* **8/1**

4m 29.8s (27.80) **Going Correction** +1.70s/f (Heav) **5 Ran SP% 108.5**
Speed ratings: **98,96,95,93,**
CSF £10.14 TOTE £3.10: £1.50, £1.80; EX 10.80 Trifecta £21.70.
Owner R A Bracken **Bred** Bernard Flynn **Trained** Sigwells, Somerset

FOCUS
A moderate chase run at an ordinary gallop and all five runners were still within a couple of lengths of each other turning for home.

5017 SOUTHWELL GOLF CLUB MEMBERSHIP H'CAP HURDLE (13 hdls) 2m 7f 209y
2:55 (2:55) (Class 4) (0-110,109) 4-Y-0+ **£3,898** (£1,144; £572; £286)

Form RPR

4532 **1** **Vinegar Hill**[23] 4504 7-10-3 **86**..............................(v[1]) AndrewTinkler 98+
(Anna Brooks) *w ldr: led 4th: reminders appr 2 out: rdn clr between last 2: styd on wl* **10/3**[1]

44 **2** *9* **San Pietro (FR)**[46] 4108 8-11-2 **102**.............................. HarryChalloner(3) 101
(Richard Ford) *hld up wl in tch: chsng ldrs whn hit 3 out: sn outpcd in 5th: styd on between last 2: tk modest 2nd last 100yds* **12/1**

002 **3** *2* **Giveitachance (IRE)**[47] 4069 9-11-12 **109**......................(t) BrendanPowell 105
(Claire Dyson) *led to 4th: drvn and clr 2nd appr 2 out: kpt on one pce* **9/2**[3]

2PP3 **4** *½* **Fresh By Nature (IRE)**[22] 4537 9-11-5 **105**.................. HarryBannister(3) 101
(Harriet Bethell) *trckd ldrs: pushed along 9th: outpcd 4th sn after 3 out: kpt on between last 2* **7/1**

P614 **5** *2¾* **Mondo Cane (IRE)**[8] 4846 9-11-10 **107**..............................(p) AdamPogson 102
(Charles Pogson) *t.k.h: trckd ldrs: pushed along 9th: 3rd and outpcd appr 2 out: hdwy between last 2: fdd clsng stages* **10/3**[1]

11-P **P** **Detour Ahead**[13] 4709 8-11-2 **99**..............................(p) LeightonAspell
(Clare Ellam) *trckd ldrs: t.k.h: drvn 10th: lost pl bef next: t.o whn p.u bef 2 out* **25/1**

3660 **P** **Presenting Streak (IRE)**[73] 3628 7-11-4 **108**..........................[1] MrWinks(7)
(Peter Winks) *racd in last: pushed along 5th: reminders 7th: sn bhd: t.o whn p.u bef 9th* **4/1**[2]

6m 56.2s (41.20) **Going Correction** +1.325s/f (Heav) **7 Ran SP% 108.4**
Speed ratings (Par 105): **84,81,80,80,79 , ,**
CSF £34.97 TOTE £6.20: £2.30, £4.20; EX 38.70 Trifecta £256.80.
Owner Theshouldhavehadabiggerbudgetgroup **Bred** Mrs J Thomason-Murphy **Trained** Alderton, Northants

FOCUS
A modest staying handicap hurdle and they dawdled through the early stages. The winner has been rated back to the best of last season's form.

5018 MEMBERSHIP AT SOUTHWELL GOLF CLUB NOVICES' HURDLE (11 hdls) 2m 4f 62y
3:30 (3:31) (Class 4) 4-Y-0+ **£3,898** (£1,144; £572; £286)

Form RPR

-13U **1** **Aqua Dude (IRE)**[30] 4388 6-11-7 130.................................. PaulMoloney 133+
(Evan Williams) *trckd ldrs: t.k.h: swtchd rt sn after 3 out: chsng wnr appr next: drvn and qcknd to ld between last 2: hung rt and idled run-in whn abt 6 l clr: drvn rt out* **11/4**[3]

-4PP **2** *3½* **Present View**[136] 2483 8-11-1 0.................................. BrendanPowell 123
(Jamie Snowden) *led: hdd between last 2: kpt on same pce* **7/4**[2]

0 **3** *14* **Bigpipenotobacee (IRE)**[46] 4102 5-11-1 0.......................... PaddyBrennan 110
(Tom George) *racd wd: hld up in rr: hdwy 8th: chsng ldr next: one pce appr 2 out* **25/1**

F14 **4** *6* **Churchtown Champ (IRE)**[38] 4248 6-11-7 130................ HarrySkelton 109
(Dan Skelton) *hld up in rr: taken wd and hdwy 7th: sn chsng ldrs: drvn appr 2 out: sn btn* **11/8**[1]

PP6 **5** *8* **Cab On Times (IRE)**[8] 4844 7-11-1 0.......................... JakeGreenall 94
(Mark Walford) *w ldr: lost pl bef 2 out* **200/1**

-P04 **6** *23* **Midnight Owle**[13] 4711 6-11-1 0..........................(t) JoshuaMoore 71
(Claire Dyson) *chsd ldrs: pushed along 7th: lost pl next: sn bhd: t.o bef 2 out* **200/1**

5m 36.9s (23.90) **Going Correction** +1.325s/f (Heav) **6** Ran SP% **110.0**
Speed ratings (Par 105): **105,103,98,95,92 83**
CSF £7.87 TOTE £3.40: £1.70, £1.20; EX 7.50 Trifecta £40.20.
Owner Mr & Mrs William Rucker **Bred** Cathal Ennis **Trained** Llancarfan, Vale Of Glamorgan

FOCUS
Quite an interesting novice hurdle despite a modest early pace.

5019 SOUTHWELL MARES' NOVICES' HURDLE (9 hdls) 1m 7f 153y
4:05 (4:05) (Class 4) 4-Y-0+ **£3,898** (£1,144; £572; £286)

Form RPR

1P21 **1** **My Little Cracker (IRE)**[12] 4737 6-11-6 120.................. BrianHarding 121+
(Iain Jardine) *trckd ldr: led to 1st: trckd ldr: led after 4th: hit 3 out: nt fluent next: wnt clr between last 2: v comf* **11/10**[1]

130- **2** *11* **Isla Fernandos (IRE)**[353] 5277 6-11-0 0........................ PaddyBrennan 102+
(Fergal O'Brien) *trckd ldrs: blnd 3rd: kpt on same pce fr 2 out: tk 2nd last 100yds: no imp* **4/1**[3]

504P **3** *1 3/4* **Alys Rock (IRE)**[67] 3729 7-11-0 97....................... JonathanEngland 97
(Michael Appleby) *trckd ldrs: 2nd 6th: kpt on same pce fr 2 out* **8/1**

02 **4** *14* **Regal Ways (IRE)**[20] 4555 4-10-2 0......................... CraigGallagher(5) 76
(Brian Ellison) *chsd ldrs: lost pl bef 2 out* **3/1**[2]

5 *32* **Kool Lady (IRE)**[72] 5-11-0 0............................. TrevorWhelan 51
(Des Donovan) *t.k.h: led 1st: hdd after 4th: lost pl sn bef 2 out: sn bhd: t.o* **18/1**

0- **6** *13* **Bron Fair**[393] 3143 7-10-11 0.................................. BenPoste(3) 38
(Edward Bevan) *in rr: hdwy 5th: drvn next: lost pl bef 2 out: sn bhd: t.o* **150/1**

P **Right Madam (IRE)**[45] 4-10-7 0................................ DaveCrosse
(Sarah Hollinshead) *t.k.h in rr: hdwy 5th: drvn next: hit 3 out: sn lost pl and bhd: t.o whn p.u bef next* **50/1**

4m 18.5s (21.50) **Going Correction** +1.325s/f (Heav)
WFA 4 from 5yo+ 7lb **7** Ran SP% **111.6**
Speed ratings (Par 105): **99,93,92,85,69 63,**
CSF £5.74 TOTE £1.70: £1.40, £2.50; EX 8.60 Trifecta £24.30.
Owner Paul & Clare Rooney **Bred** Martin Sheridan **Trained** Carrutherstown, D'fries & G'way

FOCUS
Not the most competitive of mares' novice hurdles and one-way traffic.

5020 PLAY GOLF BEFORE RACING AT SOUTHWELL "HANDS AND HEELS" H'CAP HURDLE (CONDITIONALS & AMATEURS) (11 hdls) 2m 4f 62y
4:40 (4:40) (Class 4) (0-105,106) 4-Y-0+ **£3,898** (£1,144; £572; £286)

Form RPR

3421 **1** **Riddlestown (IRE)**[8] 4845 9-11-6 **102** 7ex..................(b) MrJAndrews(5) 112+
(Caroline Fryer) *trckd ldrs gng wl: upsides fr 7th: led narrowly 2 out: pushed along between last 2: edgd lft run-in: fnd ex clsng stages* **7/5**[1]

PP-2 **2** *1 1/4* **Clara Peggotty**[22] 4538 9-10-5 **82**.......................(p) MrShaneQuinlan 89
(Tom Gretton) *t.k.h: w ldr: led 2nd: hit 5th: hdd 2 out: rallied and upsides last: kpt on same pce last 50yds* **3/1**[2]

35-U **3** *46* **Stonemadforspeed (IRE)**[23] 4504 8-11-3 **97**.................. HarryTeal(3) 58
(Roger Teal) *hld up in rr: hdwy to join ldrs 5th: drvn 3 out: lost pl bef next: sn bhd: t.o* **11/2**[3]

052F **4** *29* **Warsaw Pact (IRE)**[32] 4349 13-9-11 **79**................. MrBParis-Crofts(5) 11
(Steven Dixon) *led to 2nd: pushed along 4th: drvn 6th: lost pl bef next: bhd whn j.rt 3 out: sn t.o* **3/1**[2]

-000 **P** **Betty Borgia**[107] 3067 10-9-9 **77** oh8..................(t) MrGregoryWalters(5)
(Nicholas Pomfret) *t.k.h: trckd ldrs: drvn 4th: lost pl bef 7th: sn t.o: p.u after 3 out* **66/1**

5m 37.8s (24.80) **Going Correction** +1.325s/f (Heav) **5** Ran SP% **108.5**
Speed ratings (Par 105): **103,102,84,72,**
CSF £5.94 TOTE £2.10: £1.50, £1.60; EX 5.90 Trifecta £16.40.
Owner J Ward **Bred** Jeremiah O'Brien **Trained** Wymondham, Norfolk

FOCUS
An uncompetitive event and the front pair had the race to themselves from some way out, though they did provide a decent finish. The winner has been rated in line with his recent C&D win.

5021 NOTTINGHAMSHIRE STANDARD OPEN NATIONAL HUNT FLAT RACE 1m 7f 153y
5:15 (5:15) (Class 6) 4-6-Y-O **£1,949** (£572; £286; £143)

Form RPR

5 **1** **Wylde Magic (IRE)**[53] 3980 5-11-3 0........................ PaulMoloney 117+
(Evan Williams) *trckd ldrs: 2nd over 4f out: chal over 2f out: hung lft: led over 1f out: drvn clr* **15/8**[2]

2 *7* **Get Rhythm (IRE)**[304] 6-11-3 0............................ PaddyBrennan 110
(Tom George) *led after 2f: drvn over 2f out: hdd over 1f out: kpt on same pce* **5/4**[1]

0 **3** *42* **Snatchitback**[30] 4392 5-11-3 0................................ JamesDavies 68
(Tom Symonds) *hld up: hdwy to trck ldrs after 6f: reminders and drvn over 7f out: lost pl 6f out: sn bhd: t.o 3f out: remote 3rd last 150yds* **20/1**

3 **4** *2 1/4* **Focaccia (IRE)**[34] 4308 5-11-3 0.............................. HarrySkelton 66
(Dan Skelton) *hld up: hdwy to chse ldrs after 7f: 2nd 7f out: reminders over 4f out: sn lost pl and bhd: t.o over 2f out* **3/1**[3]

0 **5** *dist* **Nomadrush**[54] 3952 6-10-10 0................................ CharliePoste
(John Holt) *led 2f: pushed along after 7f: lost pl over 8f out: sn wl bhd: t.o 6f out: eventually completed* **200/1**

4m 9.4s (18.00) **Going Correction** +1.325s/f (Heav) **5** Ran SP% **109.5**
Speed ratings: **108,104,83,82,**
CSF £4.54 TOTE £2.60: £1.40, £1.20; EX 4.40 Trifecta £19.90.
Owner Mr & Mrs William Rucker **Bred** Edward Devereux **Trained** Llancarfan, Vale Of Glamorgan

FOCUS
An uncompetitive bumper, but despite the small field the pace was honest and the winner looks a nice sort.
T/Jkpt: Not won. T/Plt: £34.90 to a £1 stake. Pool: £59,492.23 - 1243.47 winning units. T/Qpdt: £11.40 to a £1 stake. Pool: £5,485.25 - 354.09 winning units. **Walter Glynn**

5022 - (Foreign Racing) - See Raceform Interactive

5001 FAIRYHOUSE (R-H)
Tuesday, March 29

OFFICIAL GOING: Yielding (yielding to soft in places on chase course)

5023a NORMANS GROVE CHASE (GRADE 2) (13 fncs) 2m 1f
3:55 (3:55) 5-Y-0+ **£18,437** (£5,937; £2,812; £1,250; £625)

RPR

1 **Top Gamble (IRE)**[45] 4114 8-11-10 159................... RichardJohnson 164+
(Kerry Lee) *w.w in rr: tk clsr order bef 2nd where j. sltly lft: 4th 1/2-way: wnt 3rd fr 7th and impr into 2nd gng wl into st: led 2 out and rdn clr bef last: comf* **5/4**[1]

2 *7* **Sizing Granite (IRE)**[13] 4718 8-11-12 152................................. JJBurke 159+
(C A Murphy, Ire) *chsd ldrs: wnt 3rd bef 5th: niggled along in 4th after 6 out and slt mstke next: rdn into 3rd fr 3 out: bad mstke next and wnt 2nd u.p bef last where mstke: no imp on wnr run-in: kpt on same pce* **6/1**

3 *10* **Days Hotel (IRE)**[37] 4281 11-11-10 153............................. DavyRussell 145
(Henry De Bromhead, Ire) *disp early tl settled bhd ldr fr 1st: j.sltly lft 2nd and at times after: disp and led narrowly bef 6 out: rdn and hdd 2 out: sn no imp on wnr and dropped to 3rd bef last where mstke: one pce run-in* **7/1**

4 *6* **Flemenstar (IRE)**[38] 4240 11-11-12 157.............................. AELynch 141
(Anthony Curran, Ire) *led bef 1st tl jnd and hdd narrowly bef 6 out: rdn and dropped to 3rd into st: wknd u.p in 4th fr 3 out* **10/3**[2]

5 *dist* **Ludo Et Emergo (IRE)**[122] 2794 9-11-4 135................... RobbieColgan
(Andrew Lee, Ire) *a bhd: last at 1/2-way: detached bef 6th and no imp t.o bef 5 out: nvr a factor* **100/1**

P **Twinlight (FR)**[37] 4281 9-11-12 153.................................... RWalsh
(W P Mullins, Ire) *disp early tl settled bhd ldrs fr 1st: slt mstke in 3rd at 4th and dropped to 5th bef next: detached bef 6th and no imp bef 5 out: t.o whn p.u bef 4 out* **11/2**[3]

4m 16.4s (-14.60) **Going Correction** -0.30s/f (Good) **6** Ran SP% **110.7**
Speed ratings: **122,118,114,111,**
CSF £9.06 TOTE £2.00: £1.02, £3.70; DF 9.50 Trifecta £49.50.
Owner Walters Plant Hire & James & Jean Potter **Bred** J D Cantillon **Trained** Byton, H'fords

FOCUS
A race run at a really concussive pace which suited the winner best as it turned out. The first two ran close to their marks.

5024a I.N.H. STALLION OWNERS EUROPEAN BREEDERS FUND NOVICE H'CAP HURDLE SERIES FINAL (GRADE B) (13 hdls) 3m
4:30 (4:30) 5-Y-0+ **£23,860** (£7,683; £3,639; £1,617; £808; £404)

RPR

1 **Coney Island (IRE)**[52] 4004 5-11-7 **130**.......................... BarryGeraghty 147+
(Edward P Harty, Ire) *mid-div: 6th 1/2-way: clsr in 4th bef 8th: gng wl in 3rd appr st and disp fr 2 out: led narrowly gng best between last 2: sn rdn clr and styd on wl* **9/1**

2 *2 3/4* **Stowaway Shark (IRE)**[15] 4689 7-10-10 **117**.......................(t) APHeskin 130
(John Joseph Hanlon, Ire) *cl up: 3rd 1/2-way: cl 2nd gng wl fr 3 out: disp briefly fr next where slt mstke tl hdd between last 2: sn no ch w wnr: kpt on wl in 2nd run-in* **7/1**[3]

3 *5 1/2* **Jury Duty (IRE)**[31] 4374 5-10-11 **120**........................ KevinSexton 126+
(Gordon Elliott, Ire) *hld up towards rr: rdn in 9th appr st and clsd u.p between horses 2 out: r.o wl in 7th between last 2 into 3rd run-in: nvr trbld ldrs* **14/1**

4 *1 3/4* **Space Cadet (IRE)**[30] 4393 6-11-0 **121**.....................(p) DavyRussell 129+
(Gordon Elliott, Ire) *chsd ldrs: 4th 1/2-way: gng wl bhd ldrs whn short of room and stmbld sltly between horses after 3 out: pushed along in 5th into st and disp 4th u.p after 2 out: no imp on ldrs and one pce run-in* **7/2**[1]

5 *1 1/2* **Road To Respect (IRE)**[33] 4332 5-11-5 **128**................. DavidMullins 130
(Eoin Griffin, Ire) *led: pressed clly fr 3 out: rdn and jnd 2 out: hdd u.p between last 2: no imp on ldrs whn swtchd lft in 3rd bef last: one pce in 5th fr after last* **16/1**

6 *1 1/2* **Positive Approach (IRE)**[33] 4334 8-11-7 **128**.............. PhillipEnright 131
(John J Walsh, Ire) *chsd ldrs: 5th 1/2-way: pushed along in cl 4th appr st: rdn on inner bef 2 out where nt fluent and no imp on ldrs disputing 4th bef last where sltly awkward and hmpd sltly: one pce in 6th run-in* **14/1**

7 *1/2* **Ah Littleluck (IRE)**[18] 4602 6-10-6 **113**............................ AELynch 115
(Thomas Gibney, Ire) *chsd ldrs early: sn settled in mid-div: rdn and no imp bef 2 out: one pce after* **33/1**

8 *nk* **Golan Lodge (IRE)**[38] 4259 7-10-11 **123**.................. DonaghMeyler(5) 125
(Paul Nolan, Ire) *in rr: pushed along after 5th: tk clsr order after 3 out: rdn in 7th bef 2 out and sn no imp on ldrs: one pce after* **16/1**

9 *59* **Dont Tell No One (IRE)**[40] 4215 8-11-5 **126**............................ JJBurke 69
(D K Weld, Ire) *a bhd: nt fluent 1st: slt mstkes 4th and 7th: rdn towards rr after 3 out and no imp bef st: wknd and eased bef 2 out: t.o* **9/1**

10 *1 1/4* **Ben Button (IRE)**[16] 4654 6-10-1 **113**...................(p) AndrewRing(5) 55
(P J Rothwell, Ire) *in rr of mid-div: 8th 1/2-way: wknd to rr after 8th: mstke 4 out and j.lft next: wknd and eased into st: t.o* **33/1**

P **Double Scores (IRE)**[17] 4627 7-11-0 **121**........................(t) LPDempsey
(Gordon Elliott, Ire) *towards rr early tl impr into 7th bef 1/2-way: tk clsr order bhd ldrs on outer 3 out: rdn in 6th appr st and wknd bef 2 out where slt mstke: p.u bef last* **20/1**

P **Kinnitty Castle (IRE)**[91] 3359 6-10-2 **109**..................... PaulTownend
(A J Martin, Ire) *mid-div: slt mstke 1st: sme hdwy after 8th to chse ldrs briefly bef next: rdn and no ex bef 3 out: wknd and t.o whn p.u bef 2 out* **11/2**[2]

P **Robin Thyme (IRE)**[41] 4191 6-11-7 **128**................................... RWalsh
(Gordon Elliott, Ire) *w ldrs: nt fluent in 2nd at 2nd and next: slt mstke 5th: mstke in 2nd 4 out: wknd qckly fr 3 out: sn eased and t.o whn p.u bef 2 out* **9/1**

P **Burgas (FR)**[23] 4516 5-11-8 **131**... BJCooper
(W P Mullins, Ire) *hld up: 7th 1/2-way: impr through narrow gap after 3 out: rdn in 6th into st and no ex on outer fr 2 out where sn wknd and eased: p.u bef last* **10/1**

6m 3.8s (-24.20) **Going Correction** -0.70s/f (Firm) **14** Ran SP% **124.9**
Speed ratings: **112,111,109,108,108 107,107,107,87,87 , , ,**
CSF £72.72 CT £894.73 TOTE £9.40: £2.80, £2.50, £4.20; DF 102.60 Trifecta £591.00.
Owner John P McManus **Bred** Pat Tobin **Trained** Curragh, Co Kildare

FOCUS
It looked a competitive handicap, but the winner was certainly coming in here somewhat under the radar and won like a good horse.

5025a FARMHOUSE FOODS H'CAP HURDLE (GRADE B) (10 hdls) 2m
5:05 (5:07) 4-Y-0+
£21,691 (£6,985; £3,308; £1,470; £735; £367)

RPR
1 **Clondaw Warrior (IRE)**[164] 96 9-10-9 **132** RWalsh 146+
(W P Mullins, Ire) *w.w towards rr: tk clsr order after 4 out: hdwy in 9th into st and impr on inner after 2 out gng wl: sn swtchd lft in 2nd and led fr last: drvn clr run-in and styd on wl* **9/2**[3]
2 3 **The Plan Man (IRE)**[72] 3650 6-10-8 **131** (t) DavidMullins 140
(A J Martin, Ire) *chsd ldrs: 3rd 1/2-way: tk clsr order bhd ldrs fr 4 out and disp after next: led bef 2 out: strly pressed and hdd fr last: no imp on wnr and kpt on same pce run-in* **28/1**
3 3/4 **Modem**[9] 4829 6-10-12 **135** (b) RobbiePower 143
(Mrs John Harrington, Ire) *chsd ldrs: t.k.h: slt mstkes 1st and 3rd: 5th 1/2-way: rdn in 6th bef 2 out and no imp on wnr in 4th at last: sn wnt 3rd and kpt on same pce run-in* **25/1**
4 1 **Desoto County**[72] 3650 7-10-7 **130** (t) BJCooper 137
(Gordon Elliott, Ire) *hld up in tch: 6th 1/2-way: hdwy bhd ldrs to chal in 2nd after 2 out: sn rdn and no imp on wnr u.p in 3rd bef last where slt mstke: sn dropped to 4th and one pce run-in* **3/1**[2]
5 3/4 **Art Of Payroll (GER)**[52] 4006 7-10-9 **132** (t) RogerLoughran 139
(Ms Sandra Hughes, Ire) *w.w towards rr: 9th 1/2-way: hdwy after 3 out: rdn in 4th briefly after 2 out and no imp on ldrs bef last: kpt on one pce in 5th run-in* **25/1**
6 8 1/2 **Anibale Fly (FR)**[30] 4394 6-10-13 **136** (t) BarryGeraghty 134
(A J Martin, Ire) *mid-div: 7th 1/2-way: rdn and no imp bef 2 out: mod 8th bef last: lft mod 6th after last and one pce run-in* **9/4**[1]
7 1 3/4 **Lilshane (IRE)**[16] 4660 8-9-5 **119** oh3 JonathanMoore(5) 115
(Thomas P O'Connor, Ire) *led: jnd and hdd 3 out: rdn in 3rd appr st and wknd fr 2 out* **16/1**
8 1 1/4 **Ted Veale (IRE)**[159] 2049 9-11-5 **147** DonaghMeyler(5) 142
(A J Martin, Ire) *hld up: last at 1/2-way: pushed along in 13th into st and no imp bef 2 out: one pce after* **33/1**
9 nse **Western Boy (IRE)**[170] 1175 7-10-7 **130** MarkWalsh 125
(P A Fahy, Ire) *in tch: 8th bef 1/2-way: mstke 5th: nt fluent 3 out and rdn: no imp bef next where slt mstke* **20/1**
10 1 **Princely Conn (IRE)**[72] 3650 7-10-4 **130** JodyMcGarvey(3) 124
(Thomas Mullins, Ire) *in rr of mid-div best: pushed along in 12th after 3 out and no imp bef next: one pce* **16/1**
11 3/4 **Riviera Sun (IRE)**[242] 1172 7-9-9 **125** DylanRobinson(7) 118
(Henry De Bromhead, Ire) *in rr early: tk clsr order bef 1/2-way: pushed along and no imp towards rr bef 2 out* **33/1**
12 7 1/2 **Mick Thonic (FR)**[88] 3431 6-10-0 **123** JJBurke 109
(C A Murphy, Ire) *chsd ldrs: 4th 1/2-way: hit 3 out: rdn in 4th bef st and sn no ex: wknd bef 2 out* **10/1**
13 51 **Whatsforuwontgobyu (IRE)**[72] 3650 6-10-3 **126** NiallPMadden 61
(A J Martin, Ire) *a bhd: pushed along in rr after 5th and no imp detached after 4 out: t.o* **20/1**
F **Officieux (FR)**[52] 4006 5-10-0 **123** SeanFlanagan 128
(Noel Meade, Ire) *chsd ldr: slt mstke in 2nd at 2nd: led narrowly fr 3 out tl sn jnd: rdn and hdd bef 2 out: sn no ex and wknd into 7th at last where fell* **66/1**
F **Ordinary World (IRE)**[30] 4394 6-9-13 **122** (t) AELynch 129
(Henry De Bromhead, Ire) *towards rr: 10th 1/2-way: prog in 11th bef 2 out to chse ldrs: n.m.r between horses and disp 4th briefly fr last where no imp on ldrs: stmbld and fell after last* **16/1**

4m 1.3s (-10.70) **Going Correction** -0.70s/f (Firm) **15 Ran SP% 128.7**
Speed ratings: **98,96,96,95,95 91,90,89,89,88 88,84,59,,**
CSF £132.69 CT £2918.24 TOTE £5.20: £1.90, £10.30, £4.30; DF 193.30 Trifecta £3239.20.
Owner Act D Wagg Syndicate **Bred** John & Miriam Murphy **Trained** Muine Beag, Co Carlow

FOCUS
A terrific ride from the champion jockey here on a very talented horse who ultimately stamped plenty of class over this contest. He improved to a rating of 112 on the Flat last year and looked well treated here.

5026-5028a (Foreign Racing) - See Raceform Interactive

4854 EXETER (R-H)
Wednesday, March 30

OFFICIAL GOING: Heavy (soft in places: chs 6.2, hdl 6.3) changing to soft after race 3 (3.05)
Wind: mild breeze behind Weather: sunny with cloudy periods Rails: Third fence in back straight omitted. All races used Hurdle bends. Adjusted race distances - Races 1 & 2 +30yds; Races 3 & 7 -55yds; Race 4 -95yds; Races 5 & 6 +45yds.

5029 OFF THE MARK TO FINLAKE PARK NOVICES' (S) HURDLE (10 hdls) 2m 2f 111y
2:00 (2:00) (Class 5) 4-Y-0+ £2,274 (£667; £333; £166)

Form RPR
P531 1 **Mother Meldrum (IRE)**[8] 4854 7-10-6 97 (tp) DavidPrichard(7) 101+
(Victor Dartnall) *trckd ldrs: led 5th: rdn clr bef 3 out: tending to hang lft but in n.d after* **5/4**[1]
550P 2 10 **Dainty Diva (IRE)**[22] 4541 8-10-8 104 NickScholfield 84
(Jeremy Scott) *trckd ldrs: wnt 2nd bef 3 out: rdn bef 2 out: no further imp* **8/1**
6533 3 11 **Romeo Is Bleeding (IRE)**[10] 4822 10-11-1 105 PaulMoloney 79
(David Rees) *hld up in last pair: struggling 6th: plenty to do 3 out: styd on fr last to snatch 3rd nring fin but nvr a danger to front pair* **4/1**[3]
2605 4 3/4 **Drummond**[4] 4919 7-10-8 74 MissPFuller(7) 80
(Katie Stephens) *chsd ldr tl rdn after 7th: hld in 3rd whn blnd 2 out: wknd run-in: lost 3rd nring fin* **40/1**
2510 P **Apache Outlaw (IRE)**[10] 4825 7-11-6 0 RichardJohnson
(Rebecca Curtis) *j.lft: led tl 5th: sn struggling: wknd after 7th: t.o whn p.u 3 out* **5/2**[2]
04F U **Pomicide**[10] 4821 6-10-12 0 LucyGardner(3)
(Sue Gardner) *nvr fluent in last: wnt rt whn uns rdr 3rd* **25/1**

4m 55.5s (12.80) **Going Correction** +0.75s/f (Soft) **6 Ran SP% 110.4**
Speed ratings (Par 103): **103,98,94,93,,**
CSF £11.54 TOTE £2.00: £1.30, £3.20; EX 9.80 Trifecta £27.60.No bid for the winner.
Owner G D Hake **Bred** John Bourke **Trained** Brayford, Devon

FOCUS
All races were run on the hurdles bend. The distance of this race was increased by 30yds. The ground wasn't quite as testing as first thought. A straightforward success for the favourite, with her main market rival flopping, though she has been rated below her recent course win.

5030 CITY OF EXETER CHALLENGE CUP H'CAP HURDLE (8 hdls) 2m 175y
2:30 (2:30) (Class 3) (0-125,125) 4-Y-0+ £5,523 (£1,621; £810; £405)

Form RPR
046- 1 **Twentytwo's Taken (IRE)**[340] 5541 8-11-7 **125** DavidNoonan(5) 127
(David Pipe) *mde all: kpt on wl: drvn out* **4/1**[3]
4424 2 1 1/4 **Catchin Time (IRE)**[27] 4447 8-10-5 **107** (t) KieronEdgar(3) 108
(Laura Hurley) *hld up in tch: rdn and hdwy 3 out: wnt 2nd next: ev ch last: kpt on but no ex nring fin* **12/1**
1441 3 3 3/4 **Canadian Diamond (IRE)**[40] 4229 9-11-1 **121** MikeyHamill(7) 118
(Richard Rowe) *hld up last: hdwy 3 out: sn drvn: wnt 3rd next: kpt on same pce fr next* **7/1**
41 4 2 **Space Oddity (FR)**[27] 4449 5-11-1 **114** NoelFehily 112+
(Harry Fry) *racd keenly in tch: taking clsr order whn sltly hmpd 3 out: blnd next: kpt on same pce fr last* **11/4**[1]
3F14 5 1/2 **Winning Spark (USA)**[67] 3748 9-11-8 **121** (t) JamesBest 117
(Jackie Du Plessis) *hld up in last pair: rdn and sme prog 3 out: hmpd 2 out: swtchd lft: styd on but nt pce to get involved* **7/1**
143 6 1/2 **Darwins Theory (IRE)**[31] 4384 8-10-8 **112** (t) MrMLegg(5) 106
(Fiona Shaw) *trckd ldrs: rdn appr 3 out: kpt on same pce fr 2 out* **8/1**
0542 7 16 **Steel City**[13] 4745 8-11-5 **118** (v) JeremiahMcGrath 108
(Seamus Mullins) *trckd ldrs: rdn whn wnt rt 3 out: blnd bdly next: wknd last* **7/2**[2]
50P6 8 25 **Phantom Prince (IRE)**[39] 4252 7-11-0 **120** MissBFrost(7) 73
(Jimmy Frost) *in tch tl dropped to rr after 5th: no threat fr next* **50/1**

4m 27.1s (11.60) **Going Correction** +0.75s/f (Soft) **8 Ran SP% 114.7**
Speed ratings (Par 107): **102,101,99,98,98 98,90,78**
CSF £48.28 CT £325.21 TOTE £5.50: £2.30, £4.70, £2.30; EX 54.50 Trifecta £350.30.
Owner K Alexander **Bred** Ms Siobhan Mackinnon **Trained** Nicholashayne, Devon

FOCUS
The distance of this race was increased by 30yds. A fair hurdle run at a steady early gallop courtesy of the winner who recorded a small personal best.

5031 FINAL FINLAKE FURLONG NOVICES' LIMITED H'CAP CHASE (14 fncs 1 omitted) 2m 3f 48y
3:05 (3:05) (Class 4) (0-120,120) 5-Y-0+ £6,498 (£1,908; £954)

Form RPR
2PP0 1 **An Poc Ar Buile (IRE)**[17] 4648 7-10-7 **106** oh1 PaulMoloney 110
(Sophie Leech) *chsd ldrs tl outpcd after 10th: 10 1/2 l down 4 out: 14 l down 2 out: hdwy into 7 l 3rd at the last: str run to ld towards fin: drvn out* **7/1**[3]
6305 2 2 1/4 **Doitforthevillage (IRE)**[32] 4352 7-10-7 **106** oh3 NickScholfield 111+
(Paul Henderson) *trckd ldr: hit 2nd: mstke 4th: chal 4 out: ldng whn wnt lft and broke fence next: drvn and idling fr 2 out: 3 1/2 l up last: hdd towards fin* **8/13**[1]
5F0F 3 4 1/2 **Lord Ballim (FR)**[25] 4491 6-10-7 **106** oh1 (t) JamesBest 106
(Nigel Hawke) *racd keenly: led: rdn whn jnd 4 out: hdd and hmpd next: 3 1/2 l down whn blnd bdly last: wknd* **2/1**[2]

5m 1.7s (4.40) **Going Correction** +0.325s/f (Yiel) **3 Ran SP% 107.8**
Speed ratings: **103,102,100**
CSF £12.06 TOTE £4.40; EX 11.50 Trifecta £5.90.
Owner Leech Racing Platinum Club **Bred** Liam Lane **Trained** Elton, Gloucs
■ Stewards' Enquiry : Nick Scholfield four-day ban: used whip above permitted level (Apr 13-16)

FOCUS
This was run over 55yds shorter than advertised. The open ditch in the back straight was omitted. Two key non-runners and it ultimately went to the outsider of the trio who has been a 124-rated horse at his best.

5032 FINLAKE DEVON'S PREMIER HOLIDAY RESORT H'CAP CHASE (14 fncs 4 omitted) 3m 54y
3:40 (3:40) (Class 4) (0-115,111) 5-Y-0+ £4,548 (£1,335; £667; £333)

Form RPR
0F64 1 **Brook (FR)**[11] 4803 5-11-5 **105** (bt) ConorO'Farrell 117+
(David Pipe) *travelled best: trckd ldrs: wnt 2nd 11th: led 2 out: rdn clr fr last* **9/1**
4504 2 7 **Umberto D'Olivate (FR)**[18] 4612 8-11-10 **109** TomCannon 115
(Robert Walford) *led: pushed along fr 10th: rdn and hdd 2 out: no ex fr last* **15/8**[2]
0532 3 14 **Mountain Of Mourne (IRE)**[6] 4884 7-11-12 **111** RichardJohnson 103
(Linda Blackford) *nvr that fluent or travelling: dropped to rr but in tch 7th: wnt btn 3rd appr 2 out: nvr any threat to front pair* **7/4**[1]
24-P 4 7 **Red Penny (IRE)**[104] 3122 9-11-2 **108** MissBFrost(7) 92
(Jimmy Frost) *trckd ldrs: rdn in cl 3rd after 11th tl wknd 2 out* **12/1**
5143 5 32 **Call The Detective (IRE)**[42] 4185 7-11-4 **108** (p) DavidNoonan(5) 60
(Ali Stronge) *trckd ldr: rdn along fr 10th: wknd bef 3 out: t.o* **4/1**[3]

6m 28.0s (18.70) **Going Correction** +0.325s/f (Yiel)
WFA 5 from 7yo+ 1lb **5 Ran SP% 108.8**
Speed ratings: **81,78,74,71,61**
CSF £26.26 TOTE £11.60: £3.80, £1.40; EX 26.10 Trifecta £75.30.
Owner Pipe - Dreaming Ladies **Bred** Philippe Hardy **Trained** Nicholashayne, Devon

FOCUS
This was run over 95yds shorter than advertised. Both the open ditch in the back straight and the third-last fence (damaged in the previous race) were omitted. Suspect form, with a few of these struggling from an early stage, although it was a tidy performance from the improved winner who has been rated in line with the best of his hurdle form.

5033 LUXURY LODGES FOR SALE AT FINLAKE RESORT H'CAP HURDLE (12 hdls) 2m 7f 25y
4:10 (4:10) (Class 4) (0-105,105) 4-Y-0+ £3,249 (£954; £477; £238)

Form RPR
6035 1 **Lunar Flow**[27] 4450 5-10-11 **90** BrendanPowell 95+
(Jamie Snowden) *trckd ldr: chal 3 out: rdn to take narrow advantage next: strly pressed fr last: hld on: all out* **7/1**
-35F 2 nk **Admiral Blake**[55] 3948 9-10-5 **84** RobertDunne 88
(Laura Young) *hld up: hdwy fr 7th: str chal fr 3 out: sn rdn: ev ch fr last: jst hld* **4/1**[3]
0521 3 5 **Shoofly Milly (IRE)**[36] 4290 7-11-12 **105** (b) MattGriffiths 106
(Jeremy Scott) *led: hit 6th: pushed along fr next: rdn and hdd 2 out: styd on same pce* **3/1**[2]

600 4 ½ **Titch Strider (IRE)**28 4438 11-11-8 **101**............ ConorO'Farrell 100
(John Panvert) *hld up: hdwy after 9th: wnt 4th next: sn rdn: styd on same pce fr 2 out* **25/1**

0404 5 19 **El Indio (IRE)**23 4528 9-9-9 **79** oh10............(vt) DanielHiskett(5) 59
(Claire Dyson) *in tch: pushed along after 5th: rdn after next: wknd 3 out* **20/1**

3432 6 17 **Storm Alert**13 4749 9-10-10 **92**............ LucyGardner(3) 65
(Sue Gardner) *chsd ldrs: rdn after 7th: lost pl after 9th: wknd 3 out: t.o* **13/8**1

P660 7 44 **Earcomesthedream (IRE)**13 4749 13-11-4 **100**.........(b) TomBellamy(3) 19
(Peter Pritchard) *sn drvn along: lost tch 5th: t.o* **20/1**

05P6 P **Karl Marx (IRE)**39 4250 6-10-3 **82**............(bt) TomCannon
(Mark Gillard) *chsd ldrs: rdn after 6th: wknd after 9th: t.o whn p.u 3 out* **12/1**

6m 14.4s (15.40) **Going Correction** +0.75s/f (Soft) **8** Ran SP% **116.7**
Speed ratings (Par 105): **103,102,101,100,94 88,73,**
CSF £35.01 CT £103.03 TOTE £7.00: £1.50, £1.50, £1.70; EX 43.00 Trifecta £315.80.
Owner L G Partnership **Bred** William Wallace **Trained** Lambourn, Berks
■ Stewards' Enquiry : Robert Dunne four-day ban: used whip above permitted level (Apr 13-16)

FOCUS
Race distance increased by 45yds. Moderate staying hurdles form, although it was run at a good pace and a step up from the winner.

5034 RACING UK IN GLORIOUS HD NOVICES' H'CAP HURDLE (11 hdls) 2m 5f 135y
4:45 (4:45) (Class 4) (0-105,105) 4-Y-O+ **£3,249** (£954; £477; £238)

Form RPR

546- 1 **Alderley Heights**538 1808 7-9-11 **79** oh5............ ConorShoemark(3) 93+
(Polly Gundry) *hld up: hdwy 8th: trcking ldrs 3 out: styd on strly* **33/1**

3P51 2 6 **Allchilledout**36 4291 7-11-5 **103**............(t) PaulO'Brien(5) 110
(Colin Tizzard) *trckd ldrs: pushed along after 6th: nt fluent whn ldng 3 out: sn rdn: hdd and hmpd next: styd on same pce* **4/1**3

-1P6 3 4 ½ **Brave Deed (IRE)**31 4384 10-11-7 **100**............ NickScholfield 103
(Jeremy Scott) *trckd ldrs tl dropped to last after 7th: rdn and hdwy after 8th: styd on same pce fr 2 out: wnt 3rd at the last* **13/2**

242F 4 2 ¾ **Dusk Till Dawn (IRE)**140 2441 7-11-5 **103**............ DavidNoonan(5) 103
(David Pipe) *disp tl after 4th: trckd ldr: rdn after 8th: styd on same pce fr next* **7/2**2

5522 5 1 **Craiganee (IRE)**39 4250 9-11-7 **103**............(t) KieronEdgar(3) 101
(Chris Down) *prom: led after 4th: nt fluent and hdd 3 out: sn rdn and hld: fdd run-in (dismntd)* **7/2**2

065P 6 36 **Bound Hill**26 4463 7-11-7 **105**............1 MrMLegg(5) 67
(Fiona Shaw) *disp ld tl after 4th: trckd ldr tl rdn after 6th: wknd 8th: t.o* **12/1**

U340 7 48 **Prince Mahler (IRE)**95 3223 6-11-12 **105**............ JamesBest 19
(Caroline Keevil) *chsd ldrs: rdn after 6th: wknd after 8th: t.o* **25/1**

P332 P **Trespassers Will (IRE)**61 3841 5-11-12 **105**............(t) PaddyBrennan
(Fergal O'Brien) *trckd ldrs: nudged along after 6th: rdn after 8th: wknd bef 3 out: nt fluent 2 out: p.u bef last* **3/1**1

5m 52.9s (19.90) **Going Correction** +0.75s/f (Soft) **8** Ran SP% **117.3**
Speed ratings (Par 105): **93,90,89,88,87 74,57,**
CSF £165.65 CT £995.79 TOTE £28.20: £6.50, £2.10, £1.90; EX 295.60 Trifecta £1733.30.
Owner Mrs E D Shepherd **Bred** Mrs E D Shepherd **Trained** Ottery St Mary, Devon

FOCUS
Race distance increased by 45yds. This went to the outside of the field, who was receiving tons of weight all round and also the only mare.

5035 TOTNES AND BRIDGETOWN OPEN HUNTERS' CHASE (15 fncs) 2m 3f 48y
5:15 (5:17) (Class 6) 5-Y-O+ **£1,247** (£387; £193; £96)

Form RPR

0-22 1 **Big Fella Thanks**28 4437 14-11-9 127............(t) MrNGeorge(7) 126+
(Tom George) *trckd ldrs: chal 3 out (usual 4 out): led 2 out: hit last: kpt on* **9/4**1

2011 2 1 ¾ **Delta Borget (FR)**19 4592 11-12-1 117............(p) MissJBuck(5) 127
(L Jefford) *trckd ldrs: led after 3 out: hdd next: sn rdn: kpt on but a being hld fr last* **5/2**2

0PP6 3 1 ½ **Midnight Appeal**19 4592 11-11-7 120............(t) MrRobertHawker(5) 119+
(Sophie Leech) *hld up: hdwy after 9th: styd on fr after 3 out (usual 4 out): wnt 3rd bef last: kpt on and clsng on front pair run-in* **10/1**

6P04 4 5 **Mr Moss (IRE)**17 4651 11-11-5 108............ MrJNailor(7) 113
(S Rea) *trckd ldr: led 7th tl after 9th: rdn and ev ch next: kpt on same pce fr 2 out* **10/1**

P3P/ 5 3 ¼ **Peterbrown (IRE)**17 8-11-5 0............ MrJakeBament(7) 109
(Mrs K Heard) *in tch: rdn appr 3 out (usual 4 out): chal for hld 3rd 2 out: no ex fr last* **9/1**

0-25 6 9 **Mr Satco (IRE)**305 557 8-11-11 110............1 MrMWoodward(5) 104
(Mrs Emma Oliver) *led tl 7th: pressed ldr: led after 9th: wnt lft u.p next: sn hdd: wknd bef last* **16/1**

1-33 P **Blinding Lights (IRE)**28 4437 11-11-9 104......(t) MrMatthewHampton(5)
(Mary Sanderson) *trckd ldrs tl after 6th: in tch: rdn appr 3 out (usual 4 out): wknd bef 2 out: p.u bef last* **5/1**3

1P3 P **Formal Bid (IRE)**25 9-11-13 115............(bt) MrJLThomas(7)
(Miss Lydia Svensson) *a towards rr: t.o 9th: p.u bef next* **33/1**

6P3- P **Presenting The Way**297 9-11-12 0............(p) MrMLegg
(G B Foot) *in tch whn p.u appr 7th* **40/1**

5m 9.8s (12.50) **Going Correction** +0.75s/f (Soft) **9** Ran SP% **115.5**
Speed ratings: **86,85,84,82,81 77,,,**
CSF £8.54 TOTE £3.30: £1.40, £1.20, £2.60; EX 8.20 Trifecta £51.00.
Owner T R George **Bred** R J Wilding **Trained** Slad, Gloucs

FOCUS
This was run over 55yds shorter than advertised. Both the open ditch in the back straight and third-last (damaged in an earlier race) were omitted. Ordinary hunter chase form, but a popular winner.

T/Jkpt: Not won. T/Plt: £458.50 to a £1 stake. Pool: £68,323.00 - 108.77 winning tickets. T/Qpdt: £60.90 to a £1 stake. Pool: £6,437.66 - 78.20 winning tickets. **Tim Mitchell**

5036 - 5041a (Foreign Racing) - See Raceform Interactive

4539 ENGHIEN (L-H)
Wednesday, March 30

OFFICIAL GOING: Turf: heavy

5042a PRIX DU MONT-DORE (HURDLE) (CONDITIONS) (5YO+) (TURF) 2m 3f
1:05 (12:00) 5-Y-O+ **£22,941** (£11,470; £6,691; £4,540; £2,150)

RPR

1 **Ozamo (FR)**23 9-11-3 0............ JacquesRicou 137
(P Peltier, France) **19/10**2

2 1 ½ **Captain Chaos (FR)**33 4339 5-10-8 0............ HarrySkelton 127
(Dan Skelton) *hld up in 2nd as ldr set stdy gallop: pce qcknd fr 3rd: remained in 2nd: awkward 5th: pressed for 2nd and shkn up 3 out: 2 l 2nd whn rdn 2 out: lft in front last: hdd sn after: kpt on at same pce u.p* **17/10**1

3 1 ¾ **Grinamix (FR)**14 5-10-10 0............ JonathanNattiez 127
(P Lenogue, France) **68/10**

4 20 **Nouma Jelois (FR)**23 4540 5-10-8 0............ KevinNabet 105
(Yannick Fouin, France) **17/2**

5 2 **Defile De Mode (FR)**264 11-11-0 0............ StephanePaillard 109
(Mme V Seignoux, France) **237/10**

F **Flight Zero (FR)**153 5-10-8 0............ AlexisAcker
(S Foucher, France) **39/10**3

5m 4.3s (304.30) **6** Ran SP% **119.3**
PARI-MUTUEL (all including 1 euro stake): WIN 2.90 PLACE: 1.60, 1.70 SF: 8.30.
Owner Mme Patrick Papot **Bred** J P J Dubois & M Montbroussous **Trained** France

4709 BANGOR-ON-DEE (L-H)
Thursday, March 31

OFFICIAL GOING: Soft (6.4)
Wind: Nil Weather: Fine

5043 HAMPTON VETERINARY CENTRE NOVICES' HURDLE (11 hdls) 2m 3f 123y
2:10 (2:10) (Class 4) 4-Y-O+ **£3,249** (£954; £477)

Form RPR

1 1 **Belami Des Pictons (FR)**18 4646 5-11-13 132............ AidanColeman 132+
(Venetia Williams) *mde all: shkn up to draw clr appr last: unchal* **10/11**1

P0 2 13 **Tjongejonge (FR)**118 2886 5-11-13 127............ RichardJohnson 117
(Charlie Longsdon) *chsd wnr: mstke 7th: nt fluent 3 out: rdn appr 2 out: unable to go w wnr and no ch bef last* **6/4**2

20 3 25 **Boatswain (IRE)**91 3388 5-11-1 0............ PaddyBrennan 85
(Henry Daly) *nt fluent: racd keenly in rr: lft wl bhd fr bef 4 out* **8/1**3

5m 0.6s (8.60) **Going Correction** +0.20s/f (Yiel) **3** Ran SP% **103.5**
Speed ratings (Par 105): **90,84,74**
CSF £2.47 TOTE £1.60; EX 2.30 Trifecta £2.20.
Owner Hills Of Ledbury (Aga) **Bred** S C E A Du Marais Des Pictons **Trained** Kings Caple, H'fords

FOCUS
All race distances as advertised. A disappointing turnout for this novices' hurdle which turned out to be a fairly uneventful affair. Bar the winner, the result serves to only raises more questions about the pair behind.

5044 STELLA ARTOIS SUPPORTING BANGOR-ON-DEE H'CAP CHASE (18 fncs) 3m 30y
2:40 (2:40) (Class 4) (0-110,110) 5-Y-O+ **£3,898** (£1,144; £572; £286)

Form RPR

6634 1 **Beauboreen (IRE)**18 4648 9-11-7 **105**............(b1) SeanQuinlan 122+
(Jennie Candlish) *lft in ld 2nd: mde rest: abt 5 l clr after 3 out: pressed fr 2 out tl styd on strly to go clr fnl 150yds: eased cl home* **2/1**2

54P4 2 6 **Thedrinkymeister (IRE)**57 3924 7-11-11 **109**............ DavidBass 119
(Kim Bailey) *trckd ldrs: wnt 2nd 5 out: rdn and outpcd abt 5 l down after 3 out: rallied to chal 2 out: no ex fnl 150yds* **7/4**1

04PP 3 26 **Qulinton (FR)**29 4433 12-11-6 **104**............ RichieMcLernon 87
(Johnny Farrelly) *lft in 2nd pl at 2nd: lost 2nd 5 out: wknd bef 3 out* **8/1**

024P 4 1 ¾ **Wellforth (IRE)**51 4047 12-11-12 **110**............(p) DavidEngland 91
(Clare Ellam) *in rr: j. slowly 3rd: lft bhd bef 6 out: plugged on to cl on 3rd plcd runner bef 2 out but no ch w front two* **28/1**

U205 F **Market Option (IRE)**29 4433 10-10-13 **97**............(p) LiamTreadwell
(Venetia Williams) *led tl fell 2nd* **7/2**3

6m 50.9s (31.10) **Going Correction** +1.375s/f (Heav) **5** Ran SP% **106.5**
Speed ratings: **103,101,92,91,**
CSF £5.72 TOTE £2.70: £1.40, £1.60; EX 6.50 Trifecta £21.10.
Owner Mrs R N C Hall **Bred** Richard Hall **Trained** Basford Green, Staffs

FOCUS
A modest little handicap chase which was dominated by the eventual winner who ran to a rating of 123 over fences last year.

5045 STELLA CIDRE H'CAP HURDLE (12 hdls) 2m 7f 32y
3:15 (3:19) (Class 3) (0-135,130) 4-Y-O+ **£6,498** (£1,908; £954; £477)

Form RPR

3135 1 **Weststreet (IRE)**63 3817 6-11-2 **120**............(p) LeightonAspell 127+
(Oliver Sherwood) *hld up in rr: clsd after 4 out: led after 3 out: drew clr appr last: styd on wl: comf* **7/2**2

2P34 2 6 **Shantou Tiger (IRE)**55 3970 7-10-11 **120**............(p) JamesCowley(5) 119
(Donald McCain) *chsd ldrs: led after 4 out tl after 3 out: rdn and no imp bef last* **9/1**

F-34 3 3 **Lower Hope Dandy**57 3923 9-11-3 **121**............ RichardJohnson 119
(Venetia Williams) *hld up: clsd and upsides 4 out: blnd 3 out: sn outpcd: kpt on same pce fr 2 out* **7/1**

2UPP 4 ¾ **Red Devil Lads (IRE)**12 4802 7-11-12 **130**............ AidanColeman 128
(Rebecca Curtis) *led: hdd after 4 out: mstke 3 out: sn outpcd: wl hld and keeping on same pce whn blnd last* **11/2**3

F032 5 18 **Saint John Henry (FR)**47 4127 6-10-13 **122**............(b) DavidNoonan(5) 102
(David Pipe) *chsd ldr: pushed along bef 8th: lost pl bef 4 out: bhd whn mstke 3 out: wl btn* **10/11**1

5m 57.2s (6.20) **Going Correction** +0.20s/f (Yiel) **5** Ran SP% **112.5**
Speed ratings (Par 107): **97,94,93,93,87**
CSF £29.11 TOTE £4.30: £1.70, £3.80; EX 30.20 Trifecta £82.40.
Owner Weststreet Partnership **Bred** Michael C Griffin **Trained** Upper Lambourn, Berks

FOCUS
Not the strongest 0-135 given the top weight was rated 5lb below the ceiling rating for the grade, and the race took less winning than it should have done with Saint John Henry, who brought the best recent form, bombing out.

5046 STELLA ARTOIS H'CAP CHASE (15 fncs) 2m 4f 72y
3:45 (3:47) (Class 3) (0-125,123) 5-Y-O+
£15,640 (£4,620; £2,310; £1,155; £577; £290)

Form RPR
1 **Mezendore (IRE)**[63] 3832 7-11-4 115 ....(b[1]) LeightonAspell 126+
(Rebecca Curtis) *led: rdn and hdd appr 2 out: continued to chal: led again last: styd on to draw clr fnl 150yds* 9/1

PPPF 2 2¾ **Tara Road**[55] 3979 8-11-4 115 ....(tp) AidanColeman 123
(Rebecca Curtis) *hld up: hdwy 9th: trckd ldrs appr 3 out: rdn to ld narrowly between last 2: mstke and hdd last: one pce fnl 150yds* 9/2[2]

1-30 3 3 **Russborough (FR)**[133] 2593 7-11-12 123 .... RichardJohnson 130
(Venetia Williams) *in tch: mstke and j.lft 6th: mstke 3 out and outpcd: rallied 2 out: j.lft last: styd on u.p to take 3rd run-in: no imp on front two* 14/1

3221 4 6 **I Am Colin**[30] 4422 7-11-6 120 ....(p) RyanHatch[(3)] 120
(Nigel Twiston-Davies) *in tch: big effrt 3 out: sn wnt 2nd: led appr 2 out: hdd between last 2: no ex run-in* 3/1[1]

3161 5 14 **Little Jimmy**[29] 4431 9-11-2 113 ....(tp) FelixDeGiles 101
(Tom Gretton) *hld up: blnd 3rd: struggling bef 3 out: nvr a threat* 7/1

1/-3 6 2 **Fear Glic (IRE)**[90] 3415 10-11-12 123 .... JamesBest 107
(Jackie Du Plessis) *prom: ev ch 3 out: rdn and outpcd bef 2 out: wknd between last 2* 7/1

5-1P 7 38 **Hughesie (IRE)**[26] 4487 7-11-12 123 .... PaulMoloney 67
(Evan Williams) *trckd ldrs: lost pl bef 10th: toiling bef 3 out* 15/2

P3B2 P **Supreme Asset (IRE)**[29] 4431 8-11-4 115 .... WayneHutchinson
(Donald McCain) *hld up: pushed along appr 4 out: wl bhd whn p.u bef last* 6/1[3]

5m 33.1s (24.00) **Going Correction** +1.375s/f (Heav) **8** Ran SP% **110.9**
Speed ratings: **107,105,104,102,96 95,80,**
CSF £46.84 CT £542.38 TOTE £11.00: £2.70, £1.90, £3.80; EX 58.20 Trifecta £473.50.
Owner G Costelloe **Bred** Mrs Liz O'Leary **Trained** Newport, Pembrokeshire

FOCUS
An open handicap chase on paper but a few of the leading players underperformed, notably Little Jimmy and Hughesie. This was a big step up from the winner.

5047 STELLA ARTOIS H'CAP HURDLE (9 hdls) 2m 145y
4:20 (4:20) (Class 4) (0-120,120) 4-Y-O+ £3,249 (£954; £477; £238)

Form RPR
P252 1 **Itshard To No (IRE)**[79] 3568 7-11-12 120 ....(t) RichardJohnson 131+
(Kerry Lee) *hld up: hdwy 5th: led 2 out: asserted bef last: styd on wl* 5/2[1]

5003 2 3¾ **Beau Bay (FR)**[114] 2961 5-10-12 106 .... RhysFlint 111
(Alan Jones) *racd keenly: led: rdn and hdd 2 out: kpt on same pce and unable to go w wnr after* 8/1

-355 3 8 **Cape Caster (IRE)**[33] 4366 5-11-11 119 .... PaulMoloney 119
(Evan Williams) *chsd ldrs: rdn after 2 out: one pce* 3/1[2]

111/ 4 9 **Professeur Emery (FR)**[973] 1175 9-11-9 117 ....(t) NoelFehily 107
(Warren Greatrex) *chsd ldr tl after 3 out: wknd bef 2 out* 7/1

3420 5 16 **Zarawi (IRE)**[160] 2058 5-11-5 113 .... AidanColeman 85
(Charlie Longsdon) *in tch: lft in detached last pl 4 out: wl bhd and struggling 3 out* 25/1

45-2 B **Ivanhoe**[25] 4506 6-11-6 114 .... NickScholfield
(Michael Blanshard) *in rr: struggling whn b.d 4 out* 7/1

3/P- F **Masquerade (IRE)**[487] 2839 7-11-4 112 .... GavinSheehan
(Warren Greatrex) *chsd ldrs: nt fluent 1st: nt fluent 4th: lost pl 5th: struggling whn fell 4 out* 5/1[3]

4m 11.5s (0.60) **Going Correction** +0.20s/f (Yiel) **7** Ran SP% **110.2**
Speed ratings (Par 105): **106,104,100,96,88 ,**
CSF £20.46 TOTE £2.30: £1.80, £6.30; EX 25.20 Trifecta £97.10.
Owner D E Edwards **Bred** Dr J F Dawson **Trained** Byton, H'fords

FOCUS
A trappy handicap hurdle on paper. The pace was sound and they finished well strung out, so the form looks fairly trustworthy. A step up from the winner switched to a left-handed track.

5048 "VOTE FOR REPEAL" "NATIONAL HUNT" NOVICES' HURDLE (9 hdls) 2m 145y
4:50 (4:52) (Class 4) 4-Y-O+ £3,249 (£954; £477; £238)

Form RPR
100 1 **Vive Le Roi (IRE)**[36] 4308 5-11-0 0 .... AidanColeman 119+
(Charlie Longsdon) *racd keenly: mde all: drew clr appr last: r.o strly: readily* 8/1

/13 2 10 **Matchaway (IRE)**[82] 3522 7-11-0 0 .... JakeGreenall 106
(Kerry Lee) *hld up in tch: effrt appr 2 out: wnt 2nd bef last: no ch w wnr* 15/8[2]

4353 3 1¾ **Officer Hoolihan**[26] 4494 6-11-0 0 ....(t) RichardJohnson 106
(Tim Vaughan) *hld up: nt fluent 4th: nt fluent 4 out: mstke 3 out: rdn and kpt on appr last: no ch w wnr* 7/4[1]

25 4 6 **The Pierre Lark (IRE)**[14] 4742 6-11-0 0 .... WayneHutchinson 98
(Donald McCain) *chsd wnr tl rdn appr 2 out: sn btn* 14/1

P3 5 1¼ **Ballycash (IRE)**[26] 4475 5-10-11 0 .... RyanHatch[(3)] 98
(Nigel Twiston-Davies) *in tch: wnt 2nd bef 2 out where j.lft: sn lost 2nd and wknd* 6/1[3]

240 6 5 **Diamond Rock**[15] 4714 5-11-0 0 .... JamesDavies 94
(Henry Oliver) *prom: rdn and lost pl bef 2 out where mstke: wknd after* 12/1

00-0 7 24 **Amber Gambler (GER)**[32] 4388 6-11-0 0 .... WillKennedy 68
(Ian Williams) *hld up: lft bhd after 4 out: nvr a threat* 33/1

4m 14.0s (3.10) **Going Correction** +0.20s/f (Yiel) **7** Ran SP% **113.8**
Speed ratings (Par 105): **100,95,94,91,91 88,77**
CSF £23.95 TOTE £8.20: £2.40, £2.20; EX 30.50 Trifecta £90.50.
Owner Thomas Richens **Bred** Anngrove Stud **Trained** Over Norton, Oxon

FOCUS
Quite an open little heat on paper, but the race was taken apart by a bold front-running display from a hurdles debutant.

5049 YORTON FARM STUD MARES' MAIDEN OPEN NATIONAL HUNT FLAT RACE 2m 145y
5:25 (5:25) (Class 6) 4-6-Y-O £2,053 (£598; £299)

Form RPR
1 **Ilovemints** 4-10-10 0 .... GavinSheehan 109+
(Warren Greatrex) *chsd ldr tl over 9f out: wnt 2nd again over 3f out: led on bit over 2f out: effrtlessly wnt clr over 1f out: v easily* 8/13[1]

4 2 15 **River Arrow**[40] 4242 5-11-3 0 .... RichardJohnson 94
(Susan Johnson) *chsd ldrs: racd in 2nd pl over 9f out tl over 3f out: rdn and outpcd over 2f out: wnt 2nd again wl over 1f out: no ch w wnr* 10/1

3 6 **More Than Two** 6-11-3 0 .... PaddyBrennan 88
(Fergal O'Brien) *hld up: rdn over 4f out: sn outpcd: tk mod 3rd ins fnl f: plugged on* 6/1[3]

02-4 4 4 **Missesgeejay**[44] 4168 6-11-0 0 .... HarryChalloner[(3)] 84
(Richard Ford) *led: rdn over 3f out: hdd over 2f out: wknd over 1f out* 16/1

5 46 **Maggie Rose** 4-10-10 0 .... WayneHutchinson 31
(Donald McCain) *hld up: rdn 5f out: lft bhd 4f out: t.o* 4/1[2]

4m 8.6s (3.30) **Going Correction** +0.20s/f (Yiel)
WFA 4 from 5yo+ 7lb **5** Ran SP% **111.2**
Speed ratings: **100,92,90,88,66**
CSF £7.84 TOTE £1.10: £1.10, £3.50; EX 8.00 Trifecta £16.30.
Owner P Mott **Bred** R D & Mrs J S Chugg **Trained** Upper Lambourn, Berks

FOCUS
A modest little mares' bumper, but it was lit up by the performance of the winner who could be another star for her talented trainer.
T/Plt: £492.00 to a £1 stake. Pool of £51756.78 - 76.79 winning tickets. T/Qpdt: £203.20 to a £1 stake. Pool of £4641.92 - 16.90 winning tickets. **Darren Owen**

4821 FFOS LAS (L-H)
Thursday, March 31

OFFICIAL GOING: Heavy (soft in places; 4.3)
Wind: fresh half against Weather: fine

5050 WEATHERBYS HAMILTON MAIDEN HURDLE (10 hdls) 2m 4f
2:20 (2:21) (Class 4) 4-Y-O+ £3,994 (£1,240; £667)

Form RPR
2620 1 **Ballypoint (IRE)**[19] 4620 5-11-1 122 .... SamTwiston-Davies 122+
(Nigel Twiston-Davies) *trckd ldrs: clsd 6th: led after next: drew clr between last 2: v easily* 1/4[1]

15 2 21 **Mac Gregory**[37] 4296 5-11-1 0 .... AdamWedge 101+
(Evan Williams) *hld up in last: clsd to go 2nd bef 3 out: 3 l down and stl gng wl 2 out: sn shkn up and hld: blnd bdly last: hld on for 2nd* 9/2[2]

3P0P 3 2 **Master Ally (IRE)**[29] 4430 6-11-1 0 ....(p) TrevorWhelan 92
(Rebecca Curtis) *led: j.rt: rdn and hdd after 7th: lost 2nd bef 3 out: no ch after: plugged on to press for 2nd flat* 16/1

05PU P **Over The Bridge**[8] 4874 6-10-8 0 .... MrJNixon[(7)]
(Steve Flook) *w ldr tl j.rt and lost pl 6th: bhd fr next: t.o whn p.u bef last* 200/1

303 P **Moontripper**[7] 4881 7-10-1 0 .... MrTGreatrex[(7)]
(Phillip Dando) *led part of way to post: chsd ldrs tl rdn and wknd after 7th: poor 4th whn p.u bef 3 out* 11/1[3]

5m 31.1s (331.10) **5** Ran SP% **112.9**
CSF £2.11 TOTE £1.20: £1.02, £2.10; EX 1.80 Trifecta £5.20.
Owner DJ Langdon & AW Morgan **Bred** Mrs S Cox **Trained** Naunton, Gloucs

FOCUS
Some starts have been moved at this track following remeasuring, so some races will not have speed figures until there is sufficient data to calculate updated median times. Both bends were railed out by 8 metres from the inner line. The movement added approximately 84yds to this race distance. It's doubtful that the market leader needed to run anywhere near his mark to take this.

5051 ROA/RACING POST OWNERS JACKPOT H'CAP HURDLE (12 hdls) 2m 7f 191y
2:50 (2:50) (Class 4) (0-115,110) 4-Y-O+ £3,249 (£954; £477; £238)

Form RPR
5303 1 **Highway Storm (IRE)**[19] 4614 6-11-9 107 ....(p) TrevorWhelan 110+
(Rebecca Curtis) *mde all: clr fr 2nd: 11 l up at 7th: much reduced ld after 9th: idled and rdn bef 3 out: styd on wl: drvn out flat* 4/1[3]

1U-5 2 2¼ **Obistar (FR)**[19] 4618 6-11-12 110 ....(b) ConorO'Farrell 111
(David Pipe) *trckd ldrs: chsd wnr 3 out to 2 out: rallied u.p to go 2nd again flat: kpt on* 9/4[2]

3U3- 3 2¾ **Frontier Vic**[489] 2778 9-11-3 101 .... SamTwiston-Davies 100
(Nigel Twiston-Davies) *hld up in last: j.rt and mstke 1st: stdy hdwy 3 out: wnt 2nd next: sn rdn: no ex flat* 11/2

4P32 4 13 **Rainbow Haze**[7] 4883 10-10-9 100 .... MrTGreatrex[(7)] 90
(Phillip Dando) *chsd ldr: lost 2nd after 9th: rallied u.p 3 out: keeping on same pce in 4th whn mstke 2 out: no ch after* 7/4[1]

1P56 5 4½ **Fishing Bridge (IRE)**[11] 4822 11-11-8 109 ....(vt) KieronEdgar[(3)] 93
(David Rees) *chsd ldrs: bmpd 1st: blnd bdly 8th: briefly wnt 2nd after next: hung lft and wknd qckly 3 out* 12/1

6m 42.0s (53.00) **Going Correction** +1.85s/f (Heav) **5** Ran SP% **110.2**
Speed ratings (Par 105): **85,84,83,79,77**
CSF £13.58 TOTE £6.00: £1.90, £1.10; EX 16.40 Trifecta £95.80.
Owner Carl Hinchy **Bred** Ian And Rosemary Shanahan **Trained** Newport, Pembrokeshire

FOCUS
Both bends were railed out by 8 metres from the inner line. The movement added approximately 98yds to this race distance. The winner, who is on the upgrade, was allowed to set his own fractions in front and did enough to hang on.

5052 WEATHERBYS BANK H'CAP CHASE (18 fncs) 2m 7f 177y
3:25 (3:27) (Class 4) (0-120,120) 5-Y-O+ £3,898 (£1,144; £572; £286)

Form RPR
6-40 1 **Alfie Spinner (IRE)**[145] 2348 11-11-10 118 ....(tp) JoshuaMoore 135+
(Kerry Lee) *hld up towards rr: hdwy to ld 10th: in command whn shkn up 2 out: rdn clr flat* 9/4[2]

3PU2 2 13 **Belmount (IRE)**[11] 4826 7-11-12 120 ....(p) SamTwiston-Davies 129
(Nigel Twiston-Davies) *cl up: led 6th to 10th: trckd wnr after: hit 13th: rdn 3 out: one pce and hld fr next* 5/4[1]

2666 3 30 **Strumble Head (IRE)**[154] 2149 11-11-7 115 ....(p) SeanBowen 89
(Peter Bowen) *cl up: led 3rd tl after 5th: trckd ldr after tl dropped to 3rd at 11th: wknd 4 out* 16/1

3510 4 3 3/4 **Barton Gift**[19] 4612 9-11-3 111 ....(p) NicodeBoinville 81
(John Spearing) *led to 3rd: led after 5th to 6th: dropped last of 4 remaining 9th and sn rdn along: lost tch 14th* **10/1**

-P5P P **Lovcen (GER)**[17] 4684 11-11-2 117 ....(t) MrRobertHawker(7)
(Sophie Leech) *hld up in last: tended to jump rt: reminder 4th: stmbld 8th: p.u bef next* **25/1**

30P3 U **Copper Birch (IRE)**[19] 4612 8-10-2 106 ....(p) CianMaher(10)
(Evan Williams) *towards rr whn mstke and uns rdr 3rd* **9/2[3]**

6m 41.9s (24.50) **Going Correction** +1.30s/f (Heav) **6 Ran SP% 112.2**
Speed ratings: **111,106,96,95,**
CSF £5.77 TOTE £3.60: £1.80, £1.20; EX 6.70 Trifecta £36.70.
Owner Alan Beard & Brian Beard **Bred** Andrew Jenkins **Trained** Byton, H'fords

FOCUS
Both bends were railed out by 8 metres from the inner line. The movement added approximately 112yds to this race. The field was down to four with a circuit remaining, but two pulled miles clear late on. The winner has been rated back to something like his best.

5053 WEATHERBYS H'CAP HURDLE (10 hdls) 2m 4f
3:55 (3:58) (Class 3) (0-130,130) 4-Y-0+ £6,498 (£1,908; £954; £477)

Form RPR

1166 1 **Arctic Gold (IRE)**[40] 4239 5-11-12 128 .... SamTwiston-Davies 136+
(Nigel Twiston-Davies) *trckd ldrs: wnt 2nd after 7th: led 2 out: drawing clr whn blnd last: drvn out* **7/2[2]**

3411 2 3 1/2 **Calculated Risk**[11] 4825 7-10-7 112 .... TomBellamy(3) 113
(Debra Hamer) *hld up in last: hdwy 7th: drvn in 3rd after 3 out: chsd wnr last: nt qckn flat* **5/2[1]**

-00P 3 4 1/2 **Rendl Beach (IRE)**[23] 4542 9-10-10 117 ....(tp) CiaranGethings(5) 114
(Robert Stephens) *led to 3rd: hit next: led 5th tl rdn and hdd 2 out: lost 2nd last: no ex* **10/1**

/2-0 4 1 **Zalgarry (FR)**[49] 4066 9-10-9 118 .... JoshWall(7) 114+
(Arthur Whitehead) *hld up: clsd 7th: nudged along in 4th fr 2 out and outpcd by ldrs: rdn and styd on flat* **33/1**

1232 5 53 **Pilgrims Bay (IRE)**[18] 4643 6-11-8 124 .... ConorO'Farrell 66
(David Pipe) *wnt to post early: hld up: clsd after 7th: rdn and wknd 3 out: t.o* **9/2[3]**

301 P **Driftashore (IRE)**[11] 4824 9-11-7 130 7ex .... MissBHampson(7)
(Sally Randell) *trckd ldr tl led 3rd: hdd and hit 5th: mstke and rdn next: lost 2nd after 7th: wkng whn p.u bef 3 out* **9/2[3]**

-353 P **Wabanaki (IRE)**[42] 4196 6-10-8 110 .... AdamWedge
(Evan Williams) *racd in 4th tl lost pl qckly appr 7th: t.o whn p.u bef 3 out* **5/1**

5m 30.3s (330.30) **7 Ran SP% 115.9**
CSF £13.42 TOTE £4.70: £2.20, £1.90; EX 15.30 Trifecta £84.40.
Owner Geoffrey & Donna Keeys **Bred** Ms Deidre Connolly **Trained** Naunton, Gloucs

FOCUS
Both bends were railed out by 8 metres from the inner line. The movement added approximately 84yds to this race. A decent contest run at a respectable gallop considering conditions. The winner is back on the upgrade.

5054 VICTORIAN HOUSE WINDOW GROUP NOVICES' HUNTERS' CHASE (17 fncs) 2m 4f 199y
4:30 (4:31) (Class 6) 5-Y-0+ £1,975 (£607; £303)

Form RPR

33-3 1 **Coeur De Fou (FR)**[43] 4180 11-11-5 103 ....(p) MrNGeorge(7) 111+
(Tom George) *mde all: several careful jumps: clr 2nd to 8th: drvn 3 out: nt fluent next: kpt on wl* **5/4[1]**

360/ 2 1 1/2 **Stony Road (IRE)**[18] 9-11-7 0 ....(p) MrBGibbs(5) 109
(Ian Prichard) *chsd wnr: mstke 1st: lost 2nd at 10th: bk in 2nd 3 out: hit next: kpt on same pce* **2/1[2]**

3P-4 3 2 1/4 **Churchtown Love (IRE)**[26] 8-10-12 95 .... MrWGordon(7) 99
(Miss A Griffiths) *racd in 3rd tl trckd wnr 10th: lost 2nd 3 out: rdn next: one pce* **4/1[3]**

4 18 **Northgeorge**[26] 8-11-12 0 .... MrBMoorcroft 92
(J W Tudor) *bucking and swishing tail as tapes rose: a in last: mstke 11th: cl enough whn nt fluent 4 out: sn outpcd: no ch fr 2 out* **9/1**

6m 14.3s (45.70) **Going Correction** +1.30s/f (Heav) **4 Ran SP% 107.8**
Speed ratings: **64,63,62,55**
CSF £4.19 TOTE £1.90; EX 3.60 Trifecta £4.70.
Owner T R George **Bred** Scea De La Fontaine **Trained** Slad, Gloucs

FOCUS
Both bends were railed out by 8 metres from the inner line. The movement added approximately 84yds to this contest. Weak form for the race type.

5055 FFOS LAS RACECOURSE INTERMEDIATE OPEN NATIONAL HUNT FLAT RACE 1m 7f 202y
5:00 (5:00) (Class 6) 4-5-Y-0 £1,949 (£572; £286; £143)

Form RPR

20 1 **Geordie Des Champs (IRE)**[15] 4721 5-11-0 0 .... TrevorWhelan 104
(Rebecca Curtis) *trckd ldr: led 3f out: drvn 2f out: wandered u.p: styd on* **4/6[1]**

4 2 1 1/4 **Eaton Hill (IRE)**[23] 4552 4-10-7 0 .... JoshuaMoore 96
(Kerry Lee) *hld up in last: rdn over 4f out: chsd wnr 2f out: hld ent fnl f: clsng nr fin* **13/2[3]**

3 5 **Hurricane Dylan (IRE)**[60] 5-11-0 0 .... NicodeBoinville 98
(Daniel Mark Loughnane) *trckd ldrs: rdn 3f out: one pce and sn lost 3rd: wnt 3rd again appr fnl f but no imp* **7/2[2]**

4 1 1/2 **Way Of The World (IRE)**[94] 3332 5-11-0 0 .... MarkQuinlan 97
(Sheila Lewis) *hld up in 4th: rdn over 3f out: in 3rd 2f out tl wknd appr fnl f* **25/1**

5 9 **West Torr (IRE)**[54] 5-11-0 0 .... SamTwiston-Davies 88
(Nigel Twiston-Davies) *led: rdn and hdd 3f out: grad wknd* **7/1**

4m 10.2s (27.30) **Going Correction** +1.85s/f (Heav) **5 Ran SP% 111.9**
WFA 4 from 5yo 7lb
Speed ratings: **105,104,101,101,96**
CSF £5.82 TOTE £1.60: £1.10, £3.30; EX 4.90 Trifecta £8.90.
Owner Trembath, Outhart, Moran & Costelloe **Bred** David Fenton **Trained** Newport, Pembrokeshire

FOCUS
Both bends were railed out by 8 metres from the inner line. The movement added approximately 56yds to this race. Just ordinary bumper form, with the winner the clear pick on RPRs though he didn't need to improve to win.
T/Plt: £17.00 to a £1 stake. Pool of £56923.63 - 2431.22 winning tickets. T/Qpdt: £6.30 to a £1 stake. Pool of £3956.35 - 460.35 winning tickets. **Richard Lowther**

5056 - 5062a (Foreign Racing) - See Raceform Interactive

4777 FONTWELL (L-H)
Friday, April 1

OFFICIAL GOING: Chase course - soft (good to soft in places); hurdle course - good to soft (soft in places; 6.4)
Wind: breezy Weather: some sun; 11 degrees

5063 MALCOLM "HAIRY" ROBERTS & PEPE RUFINO MEMORIAL NOVICES' HURDLE (10 hdls) 2m 3f 33y
1:40 (1:40) (Class 4) 4-Y-0+ £3,898 (£1,144; £572; £286)

Form RPR

413 1 **Champagne George (IRE)**[74] 3664 6-11-0 0 .... NoelFehily 116+
(Neil Mulholland) *tall rngy: j. sltly rt: a ldng pair: led 6th: jnd 2 out: rdn clr bef last: styd on wl* **11/4[2]**

5 2 2 1/2 **Laugharne**[18] 4681 5-11-0 0 .... LeightonAspell 115
(Luke Dace) *impeded s: settled towards rr: effrt 3 out: sn rdn: drvn upsides wnr briefly 2 out: kpt on same pce after: a wl hld flat but clr of rest* **13/2**

004 3 7 **Cocker**[14] 4771 4-10-0 96 .... MissTWorsley(7) 101
(Alan Blackmore) *pressed ldrs: rdn and outpcd home turn: styd on wl to pass two rivals fr last but nt rch ldrs* **100/1**

52-5 4 3/4 **It's A Steal (IRE)**[107] 3109 9-11-0 0 ....(t) PaulMoloney 109+
(Evan Williams) *impeded s: chsd ldrs: mstkes 3rd and 6th: wnt 2nd 3 out tl rdn bef next: one pce after: 7 l 3rd at last* **5/4[1]**

606 5 1 1/4 **Bramble Brook**[107] 3105 6-10-9 0 .... PaulO'Brien(5) 105
(Colin Tizzard) *tall scopey: chsd ldrs: rdn 3 out: last of five gng clr home turn: making no imp after but kpt plugging on steadily and ev ch of 3rd at last* **9/2[3]**

0/P4 6 28 **Mylittlemouse (IRE)**[24] 4546 8-10-2 0 .... ConorRing(5) 74
(Helen Nelmes) *v small: bhd: rdn 7th: lost tch next: t.o* **200/1**

06 7 3 3/4 **Seayoujimmy**[11] 4848 6-10-7 0 .... MrJPearce(7) 76
(Daniel O'Brien) *cl up: rdn 3 out: sn fdd: t.o* **200/1**

60 8 2 1/4 **Dragoon Guard (IRE)**[18] 4681 5-11-0 0 .... AidanColeman 74
(Anthony Honeyball) *midfield: 6th and outpcd home turn: racing w awkward hd carriage whn pushed along after 2 out: t.o* **14/1**

0305 9 18 **Manhattan Mead**[25] 4530 6-11-0 110 ....(b[1]) MarcGoldstein 58
(Michael Madgwick) *swvd lft s and lost 15 l: reluctant and travelled v awkwardly in rr: rdn at several stages: mstke 3rd: t.o after blunder 3 out* **20/1**

P03 10 41 **The Child (IRE)**[18] 4668 7-11-0 0 ....(t) AndrewThornton 21
(Anna Newton-Smith) *small: nt fluent 1st: led or w ldr tl 6th: dropped out rapidly bef 3 out where blnd: sn t.o* **200/1**

04P5 10 dht **Stoical Patient (IRE)**[28] 4457 7-10-7 0 .... MattGriffiths 14
(Mark Wall) *last pair: rdn and struggling after 6th: t.o 3 out* **200/1**

5m 5.8s (6.40) **Going Correction** +0.40s/f (Soft)
WFA 4 from 5yo+ 5lb **11 Ran SP% 117.0**
Speed ratings (Par 105): **102,100,98,97,97 85,83,82,75,58 58**
CSF £20.60 TOTE £3.00: £1.30, £1.90, £12.60; EX 19.80 Trifecta £622.10.
Owner 7Rus **Bred** J O'Donoghue **Trained** Limpley Stoke, Wilts

FOCUS
Better ground over hurdles than on the chase track. Rail movements meant that the opener was run over 108 yards more than the advertised distance. Manhattan Mead veered sharply to his left as the tape rose, hampering several opponents. The winner was building on the promise of his course bumper win.

5064 CHANCELLOROFTHEFORMCHECKER.NET H'CAP CHASE (13 fncs) 2m 1f 96y
2:15 (2:15) (Class 4) (0-115,112) 5-Y-0+ £4,659 (£1,446; £779)

Form RPR

3312 1 **Here I Am (IRE)**[36] 4321 9-11-8 108 .... MarcGoldstein 120+
(Diana Grissell) *jumping boldly thrght: rdn and hrd pressed bef 3 out: kpt finding a bit more and a in command fr next* **6/4[1]**

254U 2 5 **Guanciale**[16] 4713 9-10-10 96 .... RobertDunne 104
(Dai Burchell) *settled trcking ldrs: wnt 3rd at 8th and rdn to press wnr bef 3 out where out j.: a fighting a losing battle fr next* **7/1**

6566 3 14 **For Two (FR)**[33] 4380 7-11-9 109 ....(tp) TomCannon 103
(Chris Gordon) *tended to lack fluency: a 2nd or 3rd: drvn fr 1/2-way: ev ch tl fnd nil and fdd bef 3 out* **2/1[2]**

640 P **See It As It Is (IRE)**[68] 9-10-1 94 ....(p) MissTWorsley(7)
(Diana Grissell) *handy tl lost pl u.p 5th: sn t.o: p.u after 7th: b.b.v* **50/1**

F50 P **It's All An Act (IRE)**[137] 2540 8-11-12 112 .... MattieBatchelor
(Daniel O'Brien) *t.k.h: mstkes 1st and 2nd: detached last whn j. violently rt 3rd: t.o and p.u 4th* **20/1**

554- F **Stella's Fella**[528] 1987 8-11-5 110 .... ChrisWard(5)
(Giles Smyly) *t.k.h in 2nd or 3rd tl rdn 8th: last and losing tch whn fell next* **4/1[3]**

4m 42.1s (7.40) **Going Correction** +0.55s/f (Soft) **6 Ran SP% 112.6**
Speed ratings: **104,101,95, ,**
CSF £12.25 TOTE £2.40: £1.30, £2.60; EX 9.10 Trifecta £21.70.
Owner Nigel & Barbara Collison **Bred** M Conaghan **Trained** Brightling, E Sussex

FOCUS
Add 84 yards to advertised race distance. A weak race for the class, but it was run at a decent pace and the form should prove sound with the winner on the upgrade.

5065 "WINNER" TOM CANNON, FONTWELL'S CHAMPION JOCKEY H'CAP HURDLE (11 hdls) 2m 5f 139y
2:50 (2:50) (Class 4) (0-120,120) 4-Y-0+ £3,898 (£1,144; £572; £286)

Form RPR

053B 1 **Sartorial Elegance**[24] 4541 5-11-1 109 ....(b) PaddyBrennan 116+
(Colin Tizzard) *trckd ldrs: wnt 3rd at 5th: led after 3 out: sn in command: 4 l clr and rdn whn mstke last: styd on wl* **7/2[1]**

-432 2 2 3/4 **Laughton Park**[137] 2548 11-11-6 119 .... JackSherwood(5) 121
(Suzy Smith) *midfield: rdn 6th: drvn to chse wnr bef 2 out: no imp fr bef last* **12/1**

6446 3 6 **Occasionally Yours (IRE)**[14] 4774 12-10-5 106 .... MissTWorsley(7) 103
(Alan Blackmore) *a abt same pl: 4th and rdn home turn: kpt on gamely wout threatening after: lft 3rd at last* **16/1**

2PPP 4 1 **Handy Andy (IRE)**[69] 3748 10-11-2 115 ....(bt) PaulO'Brien(5) 113
(Colin Tizzard) *led or cl 2nd tl blnd 3 out: sn hdd: one pce and n.d fr next: lft 4th at last* **8/1[3]**

0PP5 5 11 **Lightentertainment (IRE)**[13] 4781 8-11-12 120 .... TomCannon 114+
(Chris Gordon) *rn in snatches: rdn fr 7th: brief effrt bef 3 out: no rspnse to press fr next: wl hld 3rd whn blnd last* **7/2[1]**

3250 **6** *8* **Romulus Du Donjon (IRE)**[130] 2687 5-11-9 **117**........... LeightonAspell 100
(Oliver Sherwood) *nt fluent 4th: led or cl 2nd tl rdn 3 out: nt run on: wl btn after next* **8/1**[3]

1445 **7** *3* **The Geegeez Geegee (IRE)**[30] 4438 7-11-5 **113**......(bt) AidanColeman 90
(Anthony Honeyball) *hld up towards rr: lost tch after 3 out* **6/1**[2]

P051 **8** *5* **Rior (IRE)**[18] 4674 9-10-11 **105**.................................... NickScholfield 77
(Paul Henderson) *pressed ldrs tl rdn 7th: sn dropped rt out* **16/1**

022U **9** *36* **Halling's Wish**[163] 2012 6-11-3 **111**.............................(bt) JoshuaMoore 50
(Gary Moore) *nt fluent 2nd: bhd: pushed along 7th: no rspnse: t.o 2 out: mstke last* **8/1**[3]

-34P **P** **Dollar Bill**[13] 4789 7-11-0 **108**..(p) JamesDavies
(Nick Gifford) *j.lft 1st: nt fluent 3rd: sn towards rr and nt travelling: last and drvn 7th: t.o next: p.u 2 out* **18/1**

5m 47.6s (5.10) **Going Correction** +0.40s/f (Soft) **10** Ran SP% **116.8**
Speed ratings (Par 105): **106,105,102,102,98 95,94,92,79,**
CSF £44.64 CT £597.54 TOTE £4.20: £1.90, £3.10, £5.50; EX 50.80 Trifecta £3147.20.
Owner R G Tizzard **Bred** W C Tincknell And Mrs A Tincknell **Trained** Milborne Port, Dorset

FOCUS
Add 132 yards to advertised race distance. A soundly run handicap hurdle and the winner is on the upgrade with more to come.

5066 CHANCELLOR OF THE FORMCHECKER H'CAP CHASE (16 fncs) 2m 5f 31y
3:25 (3:25) (Class 4) (0-120,114) 5-Y-0+ **£4,548** (£1,335; £667; £333)

Form RPR

3542 **1** **Venetian Lad**[33] 4380 11-11-3 **105**.................................. MarcGoldstein 107
(Lydia Richards) *j. soundly: chsd ldng pair: rdn fr 10th: 4 l 3rd bef 3 out: hrd drvn to chal last: styd on v gamely to ld fnl 100yds* **8/1**

1126 **2** *1* **Arquebusier (FR)**[55] 3994 6-11-2 **104**.............................(p) JamesBanks 104
(Emma Baker) *j.lft 5th: nt a too fluent: led or disp ld: rdn fr 3 out: hdd and no ex fnl 100yds* **7/1**

-405 **3** *9* **Money Talks**[49] 4098 6-11-11 **113**.................................(t) LeightonAspell 111+
(Michael Madgwick) *chsd ldrs: rdn fr 10th: impeded next: sn pressing ldr: upsides whn blnd 3 out: drvn and rallied and upsides 2 out tl last: floundered bdly fnl 150yds: eased cl home* **8/1**

/253 **4** *7* **Fountains Flypast**[59] 3916 12-11-9 **111**.........................(t) AidanColeman 98
(Anthony Honeyball) *a last: nt a fluent: outpcd and hit 10th: sn remote: styd on after last but no ch* **4/1**[3]

P343 **F** **Atlantic Roller (IRE)**[4] 4971 9-11-8 **110**.........................(p) TomCannon
(Chris Gordon) *led or disp ld tl 10th: cl 2nd whn fell next* **2/1**[1]

2-32 **U** **De Blacksmith (IRE)**[25] 4529 8-11-12 **114**....................(tp) JoshuaMoore
(Gary Moore) *sweating: handy tl blnd and uns rdr 9th* **7/2**[2]

5m 51.8s (8.80) **Going Correction** +0.55s/f (Soft) **6** Ran SP% **110.3**
Speed ratings: **105,104,101,98,**
CSF £54.80 TOTE £6.50: £2.40, £2.50; EX 68.30 Trifecta £206.10.
Owner The Venetian Lad Partnership **Bred** Mrs Lydia Richards **Trained** Funtington, W Sussex

FOCUS
Add 96 yards to advertised race distance. A soundly run handicap chase. The winner is on a good mark and can probably stiff improve on this.

5067 ALWAYS A CHANCE H'CAP HURDLE (9 hdls) 2m 1f 145y
4:00 (4:00) (Class 5) (0-100,100) 4-Y-0+ **£3,249** (£954; £477; £238)

Form RPR

6063 **1** **Royal Salute**[30] 4440 6-11-10 **98**.................................(t) AidanColeman 105+
(Anthony Honeyball) *settled trcking ldrs: effrt 3 out: rdn to ld bef 2 out: sn 3 l clr: gd jump last: kpt up to work but a holding chalr flat* **11/2**[2]

F002 **2** *4 ½* **Antiphony (IRE)**[11] 4846 5-11-7 **100**.......................... CiaranGethings(5) 104+
(Philip Hobbs) *hld up last: sltly impeded 3rd: stdy prog fr bef 3 out: wnt 2nd next: rdn and nt finding much whn awkward last: hung lft whn hld flat* **2/1**[1]

2UUU **3** *¾* **Highbury High (IRE)**[14] 4776 9-11-3 **91**.........................(tp) NoelFehily 91
(Neil Mulholland) *bhd: effrt 3 out: 5th and rdn next: plugged on in to 3rd after last: no ch w wnr* **16/1**

24 **4** *2 ¼* **Distant Sound (IRE)**[15] 4747 9-10-7 **86**........................(b) ConorRing(5) 84
(Grace Harris) *settled midfield: effrt in 4th bef 2 out: rdn and little rspnse whn hld bef last: edgd rt flat* **13/2**[3]

/P20 **5** *12* **Clonusker (IRE)**[26] 4504 8-11-0 **88**.........................(t) LeightonAspell 80
(Linda Jewell) *sn chsng ldrs: rdn to go 2nd briefly bef 2 out: one pce after: blnd last* **11/1**

4-65 **6** *8* **Ding Ding**[122] 2829 5-11-2 **90**.. MarcGoldstein 72
(Sheena West) *chsd ldrs: pushed along 6th: wknd wl bef 2 out* **7/1**

P-32 **7** *43* **Keppel Isle (IRE)**[151] 2253 7-11-7 **95**............................ TomCannon 37
(Laura Mongan) *sn 3rd or 4th: led narrowly 6th tl next: rdn and fdd rapidly bef 2 out: t.o and eased* **8/1**

-00P **8** *2 ½* **Nouailhas**[123] 2826 10-10-0 **74** oh5.............................(v) MattieBatchelor 13
(Daniel O'Brien) *t.k.h: led tl 6th: rdn and dropped out rapidly: t.o 2 out* **66/1**

U0 **9** *7* **Griesenau (IRE)**[11] 4845 10-10-7 **88**...........................(t[1]) MrGTreacy(7) 21
(Paul Henderson) *a bhd: struggling 6th: t.o 2 out* **100/1**

246P **10** *13* **Dancing Dik**[109] 3088 11-9-11 **78**.................................... MrJPearce(7)
(Steven Dixon) *blnd 2nd: t.o fr next* **25/1**

-040 **11** *20* **Comedy House**[16] 1596 8-10-0 **74** oh5.............................(p) PeterCarberry
(Michael Madgwick) *pressed ldr: shkn up 5th: rdn to ld 3 out: hdd bef next and dropped out v rapidly: t.o and virtually p.u flat* **33/1**

62/4 **F** **Cropley (IRE)**[30] 4440 7-11-0 **88**.................................... RobertDunne
(Dai Burchell) *pressing ldrs whn fell 3rd* **17/2**

4m 42.5s (8.20) **Going Correction** +0.40s/f (Soft) **12** Ran SP% **119.7**
Speed ratings (Par 103): **97,95,94,93,88 84,65,64,61,55 46,**
CSF £17.18 CT £171.19 TOTE £6.70: £2.30, £1.50, £4.00; EX 22.00 Trifecta £146.30.
Owner Anthony Honeyball Racing Club Ltd **Bred** Distillery Stud **Trained** Mosterton, Dorset

FOCUS
Add 108 yards to advertised race distance. Ordinary handicap hurdle form, but a step up from the winner with the second setting the level.

5068 CHANCELLOROFTHEFORMCHECKER THANKS MANDY AUSTEN H'CAP CHASE (15 fncs) 2m 3f 35y
4:35 (4:35) (Class 5) (0-100,100) 5-Y-0+ **£3,249** (£954; £477; £238)

Form RPR

-031 **1** **Bertenbar**[13] 4778 12-11-5 **93**.. AidanColeman 107+
(Lawney Hill) *sn 2nd: nt fluent 5th: led 6th: hit 10th: hdd 12th: hit next and rdn: u.p whn blnd last: swtchd lft and kpt trying and c through on ins of ldr fnl 100yds and outbattled him* **5/2**[1]

P1P4 **2** *1 ½* **Gowanauthat (IRE)**[25] 4531 8-10-10 **91**...............(tp) TommyDowling(7) 104+
(Charlie Mann) *3rd tl wnt 2nd at 9th: led 12th: 2 l clr and rdn last: wandered and looking arnd bdly after: hdd fnl 100yds and threw it away* **15/2**

5P64 **3** *15* **Humbel Ben (IRE)**[12] 4823 13-10-8 **82**............................(tp) RhysFlint 80
(John Flint) *mstke 4th: trckd ldrs: lft 3rd at 11th: 5 l 3rd and rdn bef 3 out: plugged on and n.d after* **9/1**

6535 **4** *1* **Matrow's Lady (IRE)**[12] 4823 9-10-8 **89**..............(bt) MrMartinMcIntyre(7) 83
(Neil Mulholland) *towards rr: shkn up 9th: rdn and struggling fr 12th* **15/2**

0P40 **5** *19* **George Nympton (IRE)**[18] 4686 10-9-8 **75**............(tp) MissBHampson(7) 50
(Zoe Davison) *tended to jump lft: a in last pair and nt gng wl: remote fr 11th* **25/1**

-P46 **6** *41* **Princesse Fleur**[34] 4356 8-11-2 **90**................................... RobertDunne 24
(Michael Scudamore) *towards rr: rdn and outpcd bef 12th: 12 l 4th bef 3 out: eased after next and continued t.o* **5/1**[3]

F3P3 **P** **Houseparty**[91] 3419 8-9-10 **77**... MissTWorsley(7)
(Diana Grissell) *mstke 3rd: in last pair: rdn and nt keen after 9th: clambered over next and t.o: p.u 12th* **16/1**

2/U3 **U** **Lost Arca (FR)**[13] 4778 10-10-2 **76**..................................... TomCannon
(David Bridgwater) *led tl 6th: 3rd and drvn at 9th: stl cl 3rd but nt really travelling whn blnd and uns rdr 11th* **3/1**[2]

5m 15.0s (7.70) **Going Correction** +0.55s/f (Soft) **8** Ran SP% **113.5**
Speed ratings: **105,104,98,97,89 72, ,**
CSF £21.21 CT £143.43 TOTE £3.10: £1.50, £2.40, £2.70; EX 20.00 Trifecta £118.50.
Owner Mrs C A Wyatt **Bred** T J Wyatt **Trained** Aston Rowant, Oxon

FOCUS
Add 84 yards to advertised race distance. The first two came clear in this moderate handicap chase and the winner looks as good as ever.

5069 INTRODUCING THE BARON TO CHANCELLOROFTHEFORMCHECKER STANDARD OPEN NATIONAL HUNT FLAT RACE 1m 5f 143y
5:10 (5:13) (Class 6) 4-6-Y-O **£1,559** (£457; £228; £114)

Form RPR

1 **Alfredo (IRE)** 4-10-12 **0**.. ConorO'Farrell 104+
(Seamus Durack) *str attractive: mde all: rdn clr 3f out: kpt up to work but nvr looked like being ct after* **8/1**

1 **2** *6* **London Prize**[300] 644 5-11-11 **0**.. AidanColeman 110+
(John Ferguson) *small: settled handy: rdn to chse wnr fnl 2f: no imp and a wl hld but kpt on gamely* **2/1**[1]

3 *4 ½* **The Mighty Don (IRE)** 4-10-12 **0**.................................... LeightonAspell 92
(Nick Gifford) *tall: midfield: 6th home turn: pushed along and kpt on steadily to go 3rd fnl f: nt rch ldrs* **20/1**

4 *8* **Capsis Desbois (FR)** 4-10-12 **0**...................................... JoshuaMoore 82
(Gary Moore) *tall unfurnished: chsd ldrs: 7th home turn: n.d after but plugged on steadily: decent debut* **5/1**[3]

5 *2 ¾* **Lillington (IRE)** 4-10-12 **0**... PaddyBrennan 80
(Colin Tizzard) *tall unfurnished: chsd ldrs: rdn to go 2nd briefly home turn: rn green and fdd 2f out: do bttr in time* **16/1**

6 *1 ½* **Camron De Chaillac (FR)** 4-10-12 **0**................................... JamesBest 77
(Nigel Hawke) *v small: midfield: btn over 2f out* **33/1**

7 *1* **Coyoacan (FR)** 4-10-12 **0**.. NoelFehily 76
(Warren Greatrex) *small: pressed wnr tl rdn and wknd qckly 3f out: t.o* **3/1**[2]

6 **8** *2 ¼* **Soulsaver**[91] 3409 4-10-12 **0**... NickScholfield 73
(Anthony Honeyball) *ly: nvr bttr than midfield: btn 3f out: t.o* **14/1**

0 **9** *1* **Sulamani The Late (FR)**[34] 4364 4-10-12 **0**.......................... IanPopham 72
(Dan Skelton) *small: wore earplugs: midfield: lost tch over 3f out: t.o* **12/1**

10 *15* **Pokari (FR)** 4-10-12 **0**.. PaulMoloney 54
(Alan Jones) *small: keen and pressed ldrs: wnt 3rd briefly and rdn home turn: sn dropped rt out: t.o* **66/1**

11 *41* **Flybridge** 4-10-12 **0**.. MarcGoldstein 5
(Lydia Richards) *burly: bhd: t.o fnl 4f* **100/1**

0 **12** *9* **Harvey (IRE)**[106] 3132 5-10-11 **0**.. TomCannon
(Laura Mongan) *small: cl up tl rdn and fdd 4f out: sddle slipped and hanging rt: t.o* **40/1**

13 *8* **Pomme Rouge** 6-11-4 **0**.. MarkQuinlan
(Neil Mulholland) *big rngy: unruly and tk off bef s: hld up in rr: rdn 1/2-way: t.o fnl 5f* **66/1**

0- **14** *54* **A Lasting Joy**[398] 4499 5-10-8 **0**............................ ConorShoemark(3)
(Jonathan Geake) *in last pair: t.o fr 1/2-way* **200/1**

3m 27.8s (-3.30) **14** Ran SP% **121.0**
CSF £23.67 TOTE £9.10: £2.50, £1.50, £4.60; EX 37.90 Trifecta £1047.20.
Owner Stephen Tucker & Keith McIntosh **Bred** Colin Kennedy **Trained** Upper Lambourn, Berkshire

FOCUS
Add 78 yards to advertised race distance. The first two in this bumper are above average, but not an easy race to put a figure on.
T/Plt: £117.80 to a £1 stake. Pool: £86,967.00 - 538.71 winning tickets T/Qpdt: £53.50 to a £1 stake. Pool: £8,125.18 - 112.28 winning tickets **Iain Mackenzie**

4482 NEWBURY (L-H)
Friday, April 1

OFFICIAL GOING: Good to soft (soft in places; chs 6.4, hdl 6.1)
Wind: quite strong across Weather: sunny periods

5070 AJC PREMIER NOVICES' HURDLE (10 hdls) 2m 4f 118y
1:50 (1:50) (Class 3) 4-Y-0+ **£5,848** (£1,717; £858; £429)

Form RPR

02 **1** **Bigbadjohn (IRE)**[24] 4544 7-11-0 **0**................................... TrevorWhelan 135+
(Rebecca Curtis) *mde all: awkward 2 out: shkn up bef last: styd on gamely to draw clr fnl 100yds: pushed out* **20/1**

31 **2** *9* **Hell's Kitchen**[28] 4463 5-11-7 **137**.................................. BarryGeraghty 137+
(Harry Fry) *trckd ldrs: mstke 6th: wnt 2nd 3 out: rdn whn hit next: nt fluent last: nt quite pce to mount chal: fdd fnl 100yds* **1/3**[1]

-151 **3** *28* **Dueling Banjos**[30] 4439 6-12-0 **137**............................... RichardJohnson 125
(Kim Bailey) *pressed wnr: awkward 2nd: rdn after 3 out: wknd next: eased last* **4/1**[2]

P **4** *20* **Crack On Tom (IRE)**[43] 4198 7-11-0 **0**................................ DenisO'Regan 85
(Emma Lavelle) *sn struggling and detached in last pair: wnt modest 4th 3 out: nvr on terms: t.o* **100/1**

10 **5** *¾* **Fly Du Charmil (FR)**[105] 3133 5-10-11 **0**........................... HarryBannister(3) 82
(Warren Greatrex) *sn struggling and detached in last pair: lost tch 3 out* **9/1**[3]

6- **P** **Granit (IRE)**[496] 2657 6-11-0 **0**... AndrewTinkler
(Nicky Henderson) *chsd ldng trio: hit 5th: wknd bef 3 out: t.o whn p.u bef last* **50/1**

5m 1.5s (-17.50) **Going Correction** -0.575s/f (Firm) **6** Ran SP% **112.7**
Speed ratings (Par 107): **110,106,95,88,88**
CSF £29.21 TOTE £15.80: £7.90, £1.02; EX 30.00 Trifecta £72.80.
Owner Nigel Morris **Bred** Godfrey Moylan **Trained** Newport, Pembrokeshire

FOCUS
The rail had been moved in on both courses and the distance of this race was increased by 10yds. The ground had dried to predominantly good to soft, with soft patches, and Trevor Whelan described it as "very dead". A decent novice, although a couple of them failed to run to their previous best, notably the heavy odds-on favourite in second. The winner looked to step up for the better surface.

5071 EQUINE PRODUCTIONS H'CAP CHASE (17 fncs) 2m 6f 93y
2:25 (2:25) (Class 3) (0-125,124) 5-Y-0 **£6,330** (£1,870; £935; £468; £234)

Form RPR
16P0 **1** **Bob Tucker (IRE)**[28] 4465 9-11-7 **119**........................ BrianHughes 128
(Charlie Longsdon) *trckd ldrs: rdn after 3 out: str chal after last: kpt on: won on nod* **11/2**
3355 **2** *nse* **Kings Cross (FR)**[6] 4910 6-10-12 **110**...................(p) LeeEdwards 120
(Tony Carroll) *hld up: tk clsr order 13th: chal 3 out: narrow advantage next: strly pressed run-in: kpt on: lost on nod* **15/2**
5-60 **3** *17* **Hindon Road (IRE)**[70] 3727 9-10-11 **109**.................. WayneHutchinson 107
(Alan King) *trckd ldrs: led after 3 out: nt fluent and hdd 2 out: 1 l down last: no ex run-in* **9/2**[3]
22-4 **4** *5* **Velator**[337] 29 9-11-12 **124**...................(p) SamTwiston-Davies 113
(Neil Mulholland) *j.lft: in tch: rdn in cl 5th appr 4 out: hld fr 3 out: snatched 4th towards fin* **8/1**
3354 **5** *1* **Bincombe**[112] 3014 8-11-11 **123**..............................(bt) RichardJohnson 112
(Philip Hobbs) *trckd ldrs: led 5th: rdn and hdd after 3 out: grad fdd: lost 4th towards fin* **4/1**[2]
0150 **6** *11* **Astigos (FR)**[13] 4787 9-11-10 **122**.............................. AlainCawley 105
(Venetia Williams) *nvr fluent: led tl 5th: struggling in last 8th: nvr bk on terms* **10/1**
0P-P **7** *18* **The Ould Lad (IRE)**[146] 2348 8-11-10 **122**..................(t) DenisO'Regan 84
(Neil Mulholland) *hld up in last pair: pushed along after 13th: rdn bef 4 out: nvr any imp: wknd 3 out* **3/1**[1]
5m 44.8s (-2.20) **Going Correction** -0.175s/f (Good) **7 Ran SP% 110.5**
Speed ratings: **97,96,90,88,88 84,78**
CSF £40.89 TOTE £5.00: £2.20, £2.90; EX 40.70 Trifecta £194.50.
Owner Nigel M Davies **Bred** Mrs Mary Mangan **Trained** Over Norton, Oxon

FOCUS
Distance as advertised. The front pair came clear in what was a fair chase and they have been rated in line with the best of this season's runs.

5072 SMITH & WILLIAMSON H'CAP HURDLE (12 hdls) 3m 52y
3:00 (3:00) (Class 4) (0-115,115) 4-Y-0+ **£4,548** (£1,335; £667; £333)

Form RPR
0543 **1** **City Supreme (IRE)**[29] 4450 6-10-11 **105**.................. HarryCobden(5) 113+
(Anthony Honeyball) *hld up: hdwy after 9th: rdn to chal 3 out: upsides whn lft wl clr 2 out: in n.d after* **13/2**[3]
02P2 **2** *18* **Bassarabad (FR)**[25] 4530 5-11-3 **106**........................ RichardJohnson 100
(Tim Vaughan) *trckd ldr: led 3 out: rdn and hdd bef next where lft 2nd: kpt on same pce* **10/1**
12UP **3** *10* **Ballyrath (IRE)**[19] 4649 6-11-12 **115**....................(p) SamTwiston-Davies 98
(Nigel Twiston-Davies) *chsd ldrs: ev ch 3 out: sn rdn: wl hld whn lft 3rd next* **9/1**
62F2 **4** *3 ½* **Fin D'Espere (IRE)**[28] 4466 5-11-8 **111**...................(t) DenisO'Regan 92
(Suzy Smith) *nvr travelling in last: plugged on home st: wnt btn 4th bef last: nvr any danger* **10/1**
P35 **5** *nk* **Barenice (FR)**[34] 4351 5-11-3 **109**..........................(t) KillianMoore(3) 88
(Alex Hales) *hld up: pushed along in last trio appr 3 out: nvr threatened ldrs* **10/1**
6P12 **6** *8* **Speredek (FR)**[10] 4860 5-11-12 **115**.......................(tp) SeanBowen 90
(Nigel Hawke) *j.rt: led: mstke 4th: nt fluent next: rdn and hdd 3 out: sn hld: wknd after next* **5/2**[1]
4P24 **7** *2 ¼* **Major Milborne**[42] 4226 8-11-2 **112**.............................. MissPFuller(7) 85
(Jamie Snowden) *chsd ldrs tl 7th: rdn in last after 9th: no threat after* **20/1**
636 **8** *nk* **Monetary Fund (USA)**[28] 4467 10-11-9 **112**.................. AlainCawley 82
(Venetia Williams) *chsd ldr: rdn after 9th: wknd next* **18/1**
0531 **U** **Roycano**[42] 4226 6-11-9 **115**.............................. HarryBannister(3) 128+
(Michael Easterby) *in tch: smooth hdwy 3 out: travelling best in narrow ld whn stmbld bdly and uns rdr 2 out: unlucky* **10/3**[2]
6m 1.1s (361.10) **9 Ran SP% 112.3**
CSF £65.57 CT £580.48 TOTE £8.50: £2.10, £2.80, £2.50; EX 71.10 Trifecta £575.80.
Owner San Siro Six **Bred** E Farrell **Trained** Mosterton, Dorset

FOCUS
Race distance increased by 20yds. Modest handicap form and the picture changed when the strong-travelling Roycano unseated two out, but the winner still looks on the upgrade.

5073 OAKLEY COACHBUILDERS NOVICES' LIMITED H'CAP CHASE (FOR THE BROWN CHAMBERLIN TROPHY) (18 fncs) 2m 7f 86y
3:35 (3:35) (Class 3) (0-140,135) 5-Y-0+ **£7,147** (£2,098; £1,049; £524)

Form RPR
P/UF **1** **Potters Cross**[20] 4612 9-10-3 **116** oh1.....................(t) TrevorWhelan 130+
(Rebecca Curtis) *trckd ldr: led appr 4 out: tended to edge lft sltly last 3: strly chal after last: hld on: all out* **11/4**[1]
2660 **2** *hd* **Viva Steve (IRE)**[17] 4700 8-10-13 **129**.................. HarryBannister(3) 139
(Mick Channon) *cl up: hdwy 11th: led after 13th tl 4 out: sn rdn: ev ch fr last: styd on wl: jst hld* **7/2**[2]
4130 **3** *9* **Cadoudoff (FR)**[21] 4596 6-11-4 **131**........................ BrianHughes 133
(Charlie Longsdon) *cl up: hdwy into 3rd after 15th: rdn after next: styd on same pce fr 2 out* **6/1**
P31P **4** *2* **Benenden (IRE)**[20] 4621 8-10-12 **125**........................ RichieMcLernon 126
(Michael Scudamore) *cl up: chalng for 3rd whn hit 3 out: sn rdn: styd on same pce fr next* **14/1**
-13P **5** *27* **Katgary (FR)**[17] 4701 6-11-8 **135**...................(b[1]) SamTwiston-Davies 115
(Paul Nicholls) *trckd ldrs: wnt cl 3rd after 15th: hit next: sn rdn: wknd after 3 out* **11/2**
2P5P **6** *27* **Dreamsoftheatre (IRE)**[93] 3373 8-11-1 **128**...............(t) BarryGeraghty 80
(Jonjo O'Neill) *trckd ldrs tl lost pl 14th: qckly struggling: wknd after next: t.o* **16/1**
F42P **P** **Vintage Vinnie (IRE)**[17] 4700 7-11-6 **133**........................ AdamWedge
(Rebecca Curtis) *led tl after 13th: sn pushed along: wknd bef 15th: t.o whn p.u bef 4 out* **5/1**[3]
5m 56.7s (-9.30) **Going Correction** -0.175s/f (Good) **7 Ran SP% 107.8**
Speed ratings: **109,108,105,105,95 86,**
CSF £11.62 TOTE £4.20: £3.70, £1.80; EX 13.30 Trifecta £43.40.
Owner Conyers, O'Reilly, Roddis, Zeffman **Bred** Shade Oak Stud **Trained** Newport, Pembrokeshire

FOCUS
Race distance as advertised. Solid form an the front pair came clear. The winner looks better than the bare result and has been rated in line with his hurdle mark.

5074 EVENTS BAR MANAGEMENT H'CAP HURDLE (8 hdls) 2m 69y
4:10 (4:10) (Class 2) (0-145,143) 4-Y-0+ **£9,747** (£2,862; £1,431; £715)

Form RPR
1601 **1** **Thunder Sheik (IRE)**[6] 4913 8-10-6 **126** 7ex..................(tp) RyanHatch(3) 133+
(Nigel Twiston-Davies) *trckd ldrs: chalng whn hit 2 out: rdn to ld bef last: styd on strly* **7/2**[2]
2111 **2** *3* **Gala Ball (IRE)**[27] 4484 6-11-12 **143**........................ MichealNolan 146+
(Philip Hobbs) *trckd ldrs: led appr 3 out where nt fluent: rdn and hdd bef last: styd on but nt pce of wnr* **15/8**[1]
4-0U **3** *10* **Montbazon (FR)**[14] 4765 9-11-7 **138**........................ WayneHutchinson 134
(Alan King) *nvr travelling and nt a fluent: last but in tch: reminders after 3rd: drvn along fr next: styd on into 3rd after 2 out but nt pce to get on terms w front pair* **7/2**[2]
43P- **4** *10* **Close Touch**[357] 5251 8-11-9 **140**........................ NicodeBoinville 123
(Nicky Henderson) *trckd ldrs effrt after 3 out: wknd bef last* **6/1**[3]
3306 **5** *nse* **Leviathan**[71] 3708 9-10-1 **118**........................ AlainCawley 101
(Venetia Williams) *chsd ldrs: chal after 5th: sn rdn: hld after next: wknd bef last* **16/1**
10 **6** *3 ¾* **Mr Fitzroy (IRE)**[69] 3733 6-10-3 **120**...................(tp) JeremiahMcGrath 100
(Jo Davis) *pressed ldr most of way tl rdn appr 3 out: sn outpcd: wknd bef last* **14/1**
413- **P** **Mollasses**[202] 4558 5-11-1 **132**........................ RichardJohnson
(Harry Whittington) *racd freely after hitting 1st: mde most tl hdd and squeezed up appr 3 out: appeared to lose action and sn p.u* **16/1**
3m 56.1s (-13.90) **Going Correction** -0.575s/f (Firm) **7 Ran SP% 111.9**
Speed ratings (Par 109): **111,109,104,99,99 97,**
CSF £10.37 TOTE £3.90: £1.80, £1.90; EX 12.00 Trifecta £43.70.
Owner R J Rexton **Bred** Janus Bloodstock Inc **Trained** Naunton, Gloucs

FOCUS
Race distance increased by 10yds. Rock-solid form with two bang in-form types dominating and this rates a step up from the winner.

5075 BJP INSURANCE BROKERS OPEN HUNTERS' CHASE (18 fncs) 2m 7f 86y
4:45 (4:45) (Class 6) 6-Y-0+ **£960** (£314; £169)

Form RPR
1 **Glint Of Steel (IRE)**[34] 10-11-5 0........................ MrCharlieMarshall(7) 119
(P G Hall) *trckd ldr: disp ld fr after 13th tl rdn appr 3 out: rallied to regain ld on landing last: styd on wl to assert run-in* **5/4**[2]
4650 **2** *3* **Twirling Magnet (IRE)**[14] 4768 10-11-13 127...........(bt) MrMWalton(7) 125
(Jonjo O'Neill) *trckd ldrs: disp ld after 13th: led after 4 out: nt fluent last 2 out: hdd on landing last: sn rdn and hld* **8/11**[1]
-5P0 **3** *19* **Trafalgar (FR)**[19] 4651 9-11-7 94...................(p) MrJMahot(5) 99
(Sarah-Jayne Davies) *led: jnd after 13th: rdn and hdd 4 out: sn hld: wknd after 2 out* **25/1**[3]
40/U **P** **Featherintheattic (IRE)**[33] 4383 11-11-9 103........................ MrJSole(3)
(A J S Phillips-Hill) *trckd ldr tl slow jump 9th: mstke next: nvr travelling after: lost tch after 13th: p.u bef 4 out* **66/1**
6m 15.6s (9.60) **Going Correction** -0.175s/f (Good) **4 Ran SP% 107.7**
Speed ratings: **76,74,68,**
CSF £2.61 TOTE £2.30; EX 2.40 Trifecta £4.50.
Owner Mrs P A Wilkins **Bred** B Cantwell **Trained** Eridge Green, Kent

FOCUS
Race distance as advertised. Only two mattered in the market and they duly dominated.

5076 1905 CLUB "HANDS AND HEELS" NOVICES' H'CAP HURDLE (CONDITIONAL/AMATEUR) (10 hdls) 2m 2f 183y
5:20 (5:20) (Class 4) (0-120,120) 4-Y-0+ **£4,548** (£1,335; £667; £333)

Form RPR
4431 **1** **Florrie Boy (IRE)**[8] 4882 5-11-1 **112** 7ex........................ MrJJSlevin(3) 120+
(Nigel Twiston-Davies) *trckd ldrs: led appr 3 out: r.o strly to draw clr fr last* **8/15**[1]
5P54 **2** *7* **Max The Minister**[26] 4504 6-10-1 **100**........................ MrGRoberts(5) 101
(Hughie Morrison) *hld up last pair: short of room on inner on bnd after 7th: hdwy 3 out: sn pushed along chal for 2nd at the last: edgd lft and nt gng pce of wnr run-in* **10/1**[3]
0213 **3** *4 ½* **McCabe Creek (IRE)**[34] 4362 6-11-9 **120**........................ JamieInsole(3) 119
(Alan King) *hld up: nt fluent 4th: hdwy 3 out: chal for 2nd fr next: kpt on same pce fr last* **5/1**[2]
4 *¾* **Orion's Might (IRE)**[162] 2048 6-11-0 **108**........................ MrStanSheppard 104
(Matt Sheppard) *led: hdd appr 3 out: shkn up whn disputing 2nd appr last: kpt on same pce* **20/1**
1504 **5** *3* **One Cool Scorpion (IRE)**[91] 3411 5-10-13 **110**............ MrSeanHoulihan(3) 106
(Philip Hobbs) *trckd ldrs: chal for 2nd fr 3 out tl wknd last* **11/1**
3124 **6** *1 ¼* **Royal Battalion**[182] 1734 5-11-0 **111**...................(p) GeorgeGorman(3) 103
(Gary Moore) *trckd ldrs: effrt after 3 out: one pce fr next* **20/1**
4m 40.2s (-7.80) **Going Correction** -0.575s/f (Firm) **6 Ran SP% 108.8**
Speed ratings (Par 105): **93,90,88,87,86 86**
CSF £6.21 TOTE £1.70: £1.10, £3.10; EX 7.50 Trifecta £22.20.
Owner Options O Syndicate **Bred** Laurence G Kennedy **Trained** Naunton, Gloucs

FOCUS
Race distance increased by 10yds. Modest form and, despite a steady gallop, the favourite duly won with a fair bit in hand. He was well in on his recent win and has been rated to a similar level.
T/Plt: £239.10 to a £1 stake. Pool: £62,044.15 - 189.42 winning tickets T/Qpdt: £34.10 to a £1 stake. Pool: £5,649.02 - 122.46 winning tickets **Tim Mitchell**

4861 WETHERBY (L-H)
Friday, April 1

OFFICIAL GOING: Soft (good to soft in places; hdl 6.0, chs 6.1)
Wind: overcast, breezy and very cool Weather: fresh 1/2 behind

5077 WEAR A HAT DAY SUPPORTING BRAINTUMOURRESEARCH.ORG CONDITIONAL JOCKEYS' NOVICES' HURDLE (9 hdls) 1m 7f 175y
2:05 (2:05) (Class 4) 4-Y-0+ **£3,249** (£954; £477; £238)

Form RPR
1 **Sioux Chieftain (IRE)**[328] 6-10-6 0........................ CharlieHammond(8) 119+
(Dr Richard Newland) *w ldr: 2nd 3rd: effrt 3 out: over 2 l down but styng on last: kpt on to ld last 50yds* **8/1**[3]

P532 **2** *1* **Bonne Question (FR)**[18] 4681 7-11-0 119.......................... TomBellamy 121+
(Venetia Williams) *t.k.h: hdwy to ld 2nd: pushed along 2 out: blnd last: hdd and no ex last 50yds* **6/4**[2]

0001 **3** *2 ½* **Iniciar (GER)**[12] 4819 6-11-3 111.................................... DavidNoonan(3) 122
(David Pipe) *chsd ldrs: 3rd and drvn 6th: outpcd bef 2 out: kpt on run-in* **10/11**[1]

34 **4** *8* **Misfits (IRE)**[24] 4548 5-10-11 0.................................... DerekFox(3) 107
(Lucinda Russell) *hld up in last: modest 5th and drvn 6th: 4th next: nvr a factor* **12/1**

45 **5** *14* **Notts So Blue**[9] 2808 5-10-2 0.................................... GrahamCarson(5) 88
(Shaun Harris) *led to 2nd: drvn 6th: lost pl bef next: sn bhd* **300/1**

4m 5.7s (245.70) **Going Correction** +0.175s/f (Yiel) 5 Ran SP% **111.5**
Speed ratings (Par 105): **82,81,80,76,69**
CSF £21.34 TOTE £9.60: £2.90, £1.10; EX 22.40 Trifecta £27.90.
Owner ValueRacingClub.co.uk **Bred** Newsells Park Stud **Trained** Claines, Worcs

FOCUS
Following a dry night the going remained soft, good to soft in places. The gallop was steady in the opening novices' hurdle and it developed into a sprint up the home straight.

5078 HIGH DEFINITION RACING UK H'CAP CHASE (18 fncs) 2m 5f 75y
2:40 (2:40) (Class 4) (0-120,120) 5-Y-0+ **£4,548** (£1,335; £667; £333)

Form RPR

U-F3 **1** **Double Whammy**[13] 4789 10-10-13 112.......................(b) ShaneShortall(5) 132+
(Iain Jardine) *hld up wl in tch: hdwy to trck ldrs 10th: led gng wl 3 out: rdn clr between last 2: v readily* **7/2**[3]

P55F **2** *13* **Wolf Sword (IRE)**[10] 4866 7-11-0 108.................................... DannyCook 115+
(Sue Smith) *t.k.h: trckd ldrs 10th: hit next: drvn 4 out: swtchd rt appr 2 out: 2nd last: no imp* **13/8**[1]

0331 **3** *1* **Voyage A New York (FR)**[19] 4637 7-11-12 120.......................(t) DerekFox 123
(Lucinda Russell) *led: hdd bef 4 out: 2nd 3 out: kpt on same pce* **9/2**

/4-5 **4** *½* **Total Submission**[27] 4482 11-11-10 118.................................... LiamHeard 121
(John Groucott) *chsd ldrs: 2nd 11th: led bef 4 out: hdd 3 out: kpt on same pce* **20/1**

-643 **P** **American World (FR)**[131] 2666 12-9-7 94 oh20.......... MissLBrooke(7)
(Lady Susan Brooke) *j.rt: in rr: hdwy to chse ldrs 4th: lost pl after 9th: t.o 11th: p.u bef last* **300/1**

12-F **P** **Tsar Alexandre (FR)**[31] 4425 9-11-9 117.......................(t) GavinSheehan
(Warren Greatrex) *chsd ldrs: upsides 9th: drvn 14th: sn lost pl: t.o whn p.u bef next* **3/1**[2]

5m 43.6s (6.60) **Going Correction** +0.475s/f (Soft) 6 Ran SP% **108.6**
Speed ratings: **106,101,100,100,**
CSF £9.41 TOTE £5.10: £2.40, £1.80; EX 10.60 Trifecta £40.30.
Owner Alex and Janet Card **Bred** R W Huggins **Trained** Carrutherstown, D'fries & G'way
■ Stewards' Enquiry : Liam Heard two-day ban: use of whip (15-16 Apr)

FOCUS
Race distance increased by 54yds. A fair handicap chase and the winner pulled well clear. It was a step up from him, even on the best of his old form.

5079 RACINGUK.COM H'CAP HURDLE (12 hdls) 2m 5f 38y
3:15 (3:15) (Class 4) (0-115,111) 4-Y-0+ **£3,736** (£1,097; £548; £274)

Form RPR

-403 **1** **Lowcarr Motion**[31] 4415 6-10-7 95.................................... JoeColliver(3) 103
(Micky Hammond) *in rr: drvn 3rd: hdwy 9th: sn chsng ldrs: cl 2nd next: led last: drvn out* **4/1**[1]

6P43 **2** *2 ¾* **Christmas Twenty (IRE)**[26] 4506 6-11-12 111.......................(p) BrendanPowell 117
(Stuart Edmunds) *chsd ldrs: hit 5th: led 3 out: hdd last: kpt on same pce* **11/2**[3]

3064 **3** *8* **Karisma King**[13] 4796 7-11-1 100.................................... DannyCook 96
(Sue Smith) *w ldrs: led 4th hdd 3 out: wknd appr last* **7/1**

-P42 **4** *1* **Mr Snoozy**[16] 4455 7-11-0 104.......................(p) JamieHamilton(5) 99
(Mark Walford) *w ldrs: led 2nd to 4th: drvn and outpcd appr 3 out: one pce and modest 4th fr 3 out* **4/1**[1]

622 **5** *¾* **Pennywell (IRE)**[35] 4337 6-11-6 105.................................... GavinSheehan 99
(Warren Greatrex) *rr-div: hdwy and modest 5th bef 3 out: one pce* **12/1**

3231 **6** *20* **Theatrical Style (IRE)**[30] 4429 7-11-12 111.......................(p) WillKennedy 88
(Donald McCain) *chsd ldrs: drvn 9th: lost pl bef next* **5/1**[2]

0045 **7** *3 ½* **Alchimix (FR)**[22] 4570 6-9-8 89.................................... BillyGarritty(10) 60
(Micky Hammond) *in rr: bhd fr 6th: t.o 3 out* **16/1**

FP40 **8** *8* **Expanding Universe (IRE)**[15] 4749 9-9-9 85 oh5.......... JamieBargary(5) 48
(Tony Carroll) *led to 2nd: chsd ldrs: reminders 4th: lost pl 8th: eased sn after next: t.o 3 out* **40/1**

5-16 **9** *11* **Heurtevent (FR)**[46] 612 7-9-10 86.................................... NickSlatter(5) 38
(Tony Carroll) *chsd ldrs: drvn 9th: lost pl bef next: sn bhd: t.o 2 out* **25/1**

4235 **10** *13* **Petrou (IRE)**[30] 4432 6-11-12 111.................................... CharliePoste 50
(Ben Case) *in rr: drvn 3rd: lost pl 8th: sn bhd: t.o 3 out* **12/1**

5m 27.8s (327.80) **Going Correction** +0.175s/f (Yiel) 10 Ran SP% **112.1**
Speed ratings (Par 105): **105,103,100,100,100 92,91,88,84,79**
CSF £25.54 CT £146.12 TOTE £5.30: £1.60, £2.20, £1.40; EX 29.30 Trifecta £203.00.
Owner Irv's Gang **Bred** Mark & Louis Massarella **Trained** Middleham, N Yorks

FOCUS
A fair, open-looking handicap in which first two pulled clear. The winner was on a fair mark and has been rated back to his best.

5080 DAVID THOMPSON/PRINCE NEARCO H'CAP CHASE (16 fncs) 2m 3f 85y
3:50 (3:51) (Class 4) (0-110,110) 5-Y-0+ **£4,548** (£1,335; £667; £333)

Form RPR

32-0 **1** **Crown And Glory (IRE)**[5] 4938 9-9-12 85.................................... AdamNicol(3) 100+
(Chris Fairhurst) *trckd ldrs: 2nd whn swtchd rt appr 2 out: shkn up to ld appr last: pushed clr run-in: eased towards fin* **15/2**

4122 **2** *12* **Brother Scott**[174] 1855 9-11-3 101.................................... DannyCook 101
(Sue Smith) *led to 2nd: led after 7th: drvn appr 4 out: hdd appr last: kpt on same pce* **11/4**[2]

13-5 **3** *3 ½* **Lord Of Drums (IRE)**[20] 4606 10-11-6 104.................................... DerekFox 103
(Lucinda Russell) *trckd ldrs: led 2nd: hdd after 7th: drvn 12th: sn outpcd and last: kpt on fr 2 out: tk modesr 3rd clsng stages* **7/2**[3]

4P-P **4** *¾* **Free World (FR)**[122] 2837 12-10-5 96.................................... MissLBrooke(7) 92
(Lady Susan Brooke) *chsd ldrs: 3rd 3 out: one pce: j.lft last* **20/1**

5601 **5** *10* **Ballyvaughn (IRE)**[27] 4491 6-11-3 101.................................... AdamPogson 92
(Caroline Bailey) *t.k.h: trckd ldrs: hit 4 out: wknd after next* **5/4**[1]

5m 19.4s (319.40) **Going Correction** +0.475s/f (Soft) 5 Ran SP% **109.9**
Speed ratings: **94,88,87,87,82**
CSF £27.89 TOTE £7.40: £2.70, £1.40; EX 30.60 Trifecta £44.00.
Owner Mr & Mrs W H Woods **Bred** Raymond Cahalane **Trained** Middleham, N Yorks

FOCUS
Race distance increased by 54yds. A modest handicap chase but a clear-cut winner who took a big step up.

5081 RACING UK IN GLORIOUS HD H'CAP HURDLE (9 hdls) 1m 7f 175y
4:25 (4:25) (Class 4) (0-110,110) 4-Y-0+ **£3,736** (£1,097; £548; £274)

Form RPR

P264 **1** **El Massivo (IRE)**[17] 3921 6-11-12 110.................................... DannyCook 121+
(Harriet Bethell) *hld up wl in tch: hdwy to chse ldrs appr 3 out: led 2 out: drvn clr appr last* **14/1**

0245 **2** *6* **Perseid (IRE)**[61] 3886 6-11-2 100.................................... SeanQuinlan 103
(Sue Smith) *led: drvn 6th: hdd 2 out: kpt on same pce* **5/1**[2]

2433 **3** *1 ¼* **Three Colours Red (IRE)**[9] 4871 4-11-2 106.......................(tp) GavinSheehan 101
(Warren Greatrex) *chsd ldrs: reminders after 5th: 3rd 3 out: sn rdn: kpt on one pce between last 2* **6/4**[1]

4664 **4** *½* **Cadore (IRE)**[24] 4550 8-10-11 98.......................(p) AdamNicol(3) 98
(Lucy Normile) *in rr: drvn 4th: hdwy 6th: sn chsng ldrs: one pce fr 2 out* **13/2**

00-0 **5** *16* **Magnolia Ridge (IRE)**[39] 3101 6-10-11 95.................................... JakeGreenall 79
(Mark Walford) *in rr but wl in tch: reminders sn after 3 out: sn lost pl and bhd* **40/1**

022F **6** *hd* **Astrum**[31] 4415 6-11-9 107.......................(b) WillKennedy 92
(Donald McCain) *chsd ldrs: drvn 6th: wknd 2 out: sn bhd* **6/1**[3]

0354 **7** *2* **Summer Storm**[120] 2869 6-11-2 103.......................(tp) TonyKelly(3) 85
(Rebecca Menzies) *chsd ldr: wknd appr 2 out: sn bhd* **17/2**

0FPR **R** **Arkaim**[8] 4891 8-11-7 110.................................... JamieBargary(5)
(Olly Williams) *reluctant to line up s: ref to r* **14/1**

3m 57.5s (237.50) **Going Correction** +0.175s/f (Yiel)
WFA 4 from 6yo+ 5lb 8 Ran SP% **110.6**
Speed ratings (Par 105): **102,99,98,98,90 90,89,**
CSF £77.18 CT £160.52 TOTE £20.10: £4.00, £1.90, £1.20; EX 105.90 Trifecta £272.10.
Owner W A Bethell **Bred** Laundry Cottage Stud Farm **Trained** Arnold, E Yorks

FOCUS
Only a modest handicap hurdle and the warm favourite ran below expectations. A hurdles personal best from the winner and in line with the best of his Flat form.

5082 RACING UK DAY PASS JUST £10.00 OPEN HUNTERS' CHASE (19 fncs) 3m 45y
5:00 (5:01) (Class 6) 5-Y-0+ **£987** (£303; £151)

Form RPR

2 **1** **Thetalkinghorse (IRE)**[31] 4426 8-11-1 0.................................... MrTAMcclorey(7) 113+
(G T H Bailey) *trckd ldrs: upsides 15th: drvn to ld appr next: edgd lft 2 out: drvn clr run-in* **6/5**[1]

U16 **2** *12* **Railway Dillon (IRE)**[37] 4307 11-11-11 111.................................... MissETodd(5) 110
(Mrs C Drury) *w ldr: led bef 14th: drvn between last 2: fdd last* **6/4**[2]

0-PU **3** *3 ¾* **Grouse Lodge (IRE)**[15] 4748 10-11-5 112.................................... MrWEasterby(5) 96
(Mrs Emma Clark) *chsd ldrs 6th: outpcd 13th: lost pl 15th* **6/1**[3]

/P0- **4** *49* **Code Blue**[33] 13-11-3 84.......................(v) MrRSmith(5) 47
(R Tate) *led: pushed along 10th: hdd bef 14th: sn lost pl and bhd: t.o 4 out* **25/1**

U **Wizadora**[33] 8-11-1 0.................................... MissJCoward
(Miss J M Coward) *in last: outpcd and lost pl after 10th: sn bhd: mstke and uns rdr 13th* **20/1**

6m 41.1s (-6.90) 5 Ran SP% **108.3**
CSF £3.40 TOTE £1.90: £1.10, £1.20; EX 4.10 Trifecta £7.30.
Owner Mrs M E Moody **Bred** L Mulryan **Trained** Holdenby, Northants

FOCUS
Race distance increased by 54yds. Little depth to this hunter chase and it proved a match between the two market leaders. The winner was building on his decent Leicester run.

5083 FAMILY FUN DAY - SUNDAY 17TH APRIL STANDARD OPEN NATIONAL HUNT FLAT RACE 1m 7f 175y
5:35 (5:35) (Class 6) 4-6-Y-0 **£1,949** (£572; £286; £143)

Form RPR

1 **1** **Betameche (FR)**[113] 2984 5-11-5 0.................................... BridgetAndrews(5) 128+
(Dan Skelton) *hld up: t.k.h: hdwy to trck ldrs 6f out: shkn up to ld over 1f out: drvn and styd on strly* **3/1**[2]

1 **2** *4 ½* **Sam Spinner**[46] 4156 4-11-1 0.................................... JoeColliver(3) 114
(Jedd O'Keeffe) *t.k.h: w ldrs: led briefly after 2f: led over 3f out: hdd over 1f out: kpt on same pce* **8/1**[3]

1 **3** *6* **Keeper Hill (IRE)**[134] 2597 5-11-10 0.................................... GavinSheehan 115
(Warren Greatrex) *led 1f: trckd ldrs: upsides and rdn 3f out: fdd over 1f out* **4/6**[1]

33 **4** *10* **Captain Moirette (FR)**[10] 4867 4-10-11 0.................................... DannyCook 91
(Sue Smith) *led after 1f: hdd briefly after 2f: hdd over 3f out: lost pl over 2f out* **12/1**

5 *4 ½* **Mortens Leam** 4-10-6 0.................................... JamieBargary(5) 87
(Pam Sly) *chsd ldrs: drvn over 5f out: lost pl over 2f out* **28/1**

6 *32* **Venturepredementia** 5-11-0 0.................................... JohnKington(3) 61
(Andrew Crook) *mid-div: drvn over 7f out: reminders and lost pl over 4f out: sn bhd: t.o 3f out* **125/1**

00-0 **7** *31* **Early Boy (FR)**[329] 187 5-11-3 0.................................... HenryBrooke 30
(Andrew Crook) *racd in last: drvn 7f out: sn bhd: t.o 4f out* **250/1**

3m 47.5s (227.50) **Going Correction** +0.175s/f (Yiel)
WFA 4 from 5yo 5lb 7 Ran SP% **108.4**
Speed ratings: **113,110,107,102,100 84,69**
CSF £23.10 TOTE £2.60: £1.20, £2.90; EX 23.70 Trifecta £36.50.
Owner Judy Craymer **Bred** Pascal Noue **Trained** Alcester, Warwicks

FOCUS
An interesting bumper, featuring three first-time-out winners, and the form looks solid. The winner was building on his debut win and looks a smart prospect.
T/Plt: £26.50 to a £1 stake. Pool: £46,676.78 - 1,283.56 winning tickets T/Qpdt: £8.80 to a £1 stake. Pool: £4,852.58 - 404.90 winning tickets **Walter Glynn**

[4835] **KELSO** (L-H)

Saturday, April 2

OFFICIAL GOING: Good to soft (good in places) changing to soft (good to soft in places) after race 4 (3.25)

Wind: Almost nil Weather: Overcast, showers

5084 BELHAVEN BEST NOVICES' H'CAP CHASE (16 fncs) 2m 5f 133y

1:45 (1:45) (Class 4) (0-120,120) 5-Y-O+ **£4,659** (£1,446; £779)

Form RPR

23P2 **1** **Lowanbehold (IRE)**[20] 4634 9-10-7 **106**.................. JamieHamilton(5) 114+
(Sandy Forster) *chsd ldr: nt fluent 11th: hdwy to ld 4 out: qcknd after next: 1 l up and rdn last: kpt on strly run-in* **3/1**[3]

-341 **2** 2 3/4 **Superior Command (IRE)**[20] 4634 7-11-3 **111**............. PeterBuchanan 117
(Lucinda Russell) *j.rt on occasions: in tch: hit 11th: hdwy to chse wnr 2 out: edgd lft and 1 l down last: kpt on same pce run-in* **11/4**[2]

5241 **3** 60 **Court Dismissed (IRE)**[32] 4420 6-11-7 **120**............... JamesCowley(5) 71
(Donald McCain) *led: rdn and hdd 4 out: wknd after next: sn lost tch: lft poor 3rd run-in* **11/4**[2]

4313 **P** **Gold Opera (IRE)**[20] 4634 7-11-10 **118**...........................(p) BrianHarding 112
(N W Alexander) *nt fluent on occasions: trckd ldrs: reminders after 8th: rallied: effrt and chsd wnr after 3 out: to next: wknd bef last: 3rd and hld whn p.u and dismntd run-in* **5/2**[1]

5m 53.1s (23.90) **Going Correction** +0.925s/f (Soft) **4 Ran SP% 106.9**
Speed ratings: **93,92,70,**
CSF £10.88 TOTE £4.40; EX 10.10 Trifecta £24.70.
Owner C Storey **Bred** John Kenny **Trained** Kirk Yetholm, Roxburghshire

FOCUS
The rail was moved out a further 2yds since the last meeting, making it 4yds from the innermost line. Race distance increased by 75yds. The ground was good, good to soft in places for the opener, a fair novices' handicap chase in which three of the four runners locked horns once more having filled the top three places at this course three weeks ago. The first two have been rated similar to that recent race.

5085 ISLE OF SKYE BLENDED SCOTCH WHISKY H'CAP HURDLE (13 hdls) 3m 1f 170y

2:20 (2:20) (Class 2) 4-Y-O+ **£12,996** (£3,816; £1,908; £954)

Form RPR

1243 **1** **Silsol (GER)**[42] 4244 7-11-7 **152**...........................(bt[1]) JackSherwood(5) 158+
(Paul Nicholls) *nt fluent on occasions: prom: hdwy to ld bef 2 out: rdn and styd on strly fr last* **5/2**[1]

311 **2** 1 1/2 **Shades Of Midnight**[21] 4610 6-11-1 **144**...................(t) CallumWhillans(3) 148
(Donald Whillans) *hld up: stdy hdwy whn nt fluent 3 out: effrt whn hit next: rdn and chsd wnr bef last: kpt on same pce run-in* **11/4**[2]

1332 **3** 3 3/4 **Isaacstown Lad (IRE)**[23] 4568 9-10-7 **133**..................... BrianHarding 132
(Nicky Richards) *t.k.h: hld up: smooth hdwy to press ldrs bef 2 out: sn rdn: kpt on same pce fr last* **17/2**

31P4 **4** 2 1/4 **Donna's Diamond (IRE)**[14] 4794 7-10-6 **135**.................... TonyKelly(3) 133
(Chris Grant) *pressed ldr: nt fluent 3 out: sn led: hdd bef next: wknd fr last* **13/2**

P322 **5** 7 **Central Flame**[35] 4370 8-10-6 **137**.......................... MissCWalton(5) 129
(James Walton) *bhd and nvr really travelling: hdwy after 4 out: pushed along and no imp bef 2 out* **17/2**

-24P **6** 2 3/4 **Knockara Beau (IRE)**[16] 4732 13-10-11 **140**.......... ColmMcCormack(3) 128
(George Charlton) *led: rdn and hdd after 3 out: wknd fr next* **14/1**

451F **7** 1 1/2 **Top Wood (FR)**[16] 4735 9-11-0 **140**...........................(bt) ConorO'Farrell 128
(David Pipe) *t.k.h early: trckd ldrs: hit 3 out: effrt and rdn bef next: wknd after 2 out* **11/2**[3]

6m 47.4s (7.40) **Going Correction** +0.625s/f (Soft) **7 Ran SP% 111.7**
Speed ratings (Par 109): **113,112,111,110,108 107,107**
CSF £9.60 TOTE £3.10: £1.50, £2.10; EX 9.50 Trifecta £50.10.
Owner Michelle And Dan MacDonald **Bred** Gestut Hof Iserneichen **Trained** Ditcheat, Somerset

FOCUS
The rail was moved out a further 2yds since the last meeting, making it 4yds from the innermost line. Race distance increased by 75yds. A quality handicap in which they went a good gallop from the outset. The winner has been rated back to his best.

5086 ASHLEYBANK INVESTMENTS REG & BETTY TWEEDIE H'CAP CHASE (12 fncs) 2m 1f 14y

2:50 (2:51) (Class 4) (0-120,116) 5-Y-O+ **£4,548** (£1,335; £667; £333)

Form RPR

5F-4 **1** **Some Lad (IRE)**[326] 256 11-9-12 **95**........................... MrTHamilton(7) 101
(Alison Hamilton) *pressed ldr: chal after 3 out: rdn and 3 l down whn lft in ld last: kpt on wl* **16/1**

3033 **2** 5 **Rupert Bear**[14] 4795 10-9-9 **90**.............................(p) MissCWalton(5) 101+
(James Walton) *led: jnd bef 3 out: shkn up and 3 l up whn blnd bdly: nrly uns rdr and hdd last: rdr rode wout irons run-in: nt rcvr* **9/1**

1U5P **3** 5 **Clan Chief**[14] 4795 7-10-1 **91**.................................. BrianHarding 91
(N W Alexander) *nt fluent on occasions in rr: hld up: hit 4th: stdy hdwy after 4 out: rdn and outpcd next: plugged on fr last: no imp* **4/1**[2]

155U **4** 4 1/2 **Quick Brew**[20] 4634 8-11-3 **112**...........................(t) DaraghBourke(5) 105
(Maurice Barnes) *hld up: stdy hdwy and prom 3 out: sn rdn: wknd bef last* **9/2**[3]

3241 **5** 9 **Trust Thomas**[46] 4166 8-11-7 **116**........................ JamieHamilton(5) 102
(Ann Hamilton) *trckd ldrs: rdn bef 3 out: wknd fr next* **5/2**[1]

5325 **6** 10 **Ballycool (IRE)**[114] 2979 9-11-5 **109**.............................(t) DerekFox 85
(Lucinda Russell) *hld up: struggling after 4 out: lost tch bef next* **5/1**

P440 **P** **Formidableopponent (IRE)**[46] 4166 9-10-5 **102**.......(b) SamColtherd(7)
(William Young Jnr) *nt fluent on occasions: prom: hit 7th: rdn and wknd bef 3 out: p.u bef next* **11/1**

11-U **P** **Have You Had Yours (IRE)**[322] 331 10-11-2 **106**........ PeterBuchanan
(Jane Walton) *in tch: outpcd after 7th: struggling fr next: t.o whn p.u bef 2 out* **8/1**

4m 33.1s (15.10) **Going Correction** +0.925s/f (Soft) **8 Ran SP% 118.7**
Speed ratings: **101,98,96,94,89 85, ,**
CSF £147.83 CT £697.81 TOTE £20.10: £3.20, £2.70, £3.00; EX 133.00 Trifecta £770.30.
Owner J P G Hamilton **Bred** W Tanner **Trained** Denholm, Borders

FOCUS
The rail was moved out a further 2yds since the last meeting, making it 4yds from the innermost line. Race distance increased by 60yds. A moderate handicap run at a sedate pace, which meant it proved difficult for those coming from behind and there was drama at the last. The winner and third set the level.

5087 LIZ ADAM MEMORIAL CHASE (12 fncs) 2m 1f 14y

3:25 (3:25) (Class 2) 5-Y-O+ **£32,490** (£9,540; £4,770; £2,385)

Form RPR

34P4 **1** **Savello (IRE)**[15] 4770 10-10-12 151..............................(t) BridgetAndrews 150+
(Dan Skelton) *t.k.h early: hld up: stdy hdwy 4 out: effrt whn lft 2nd 2 out: pushed along and led bef last: rdn clr run-in* **4/1**

2242 **2** 5 **Dormello Mo (FR)**[21] 4624 6-10-7 144...........................(t) NickScholfield 140
(Paul Nicholls) *prom: effrt and pushed along whn lft 3rd 2 out: chsd (clr) wnr run-in: no imp* **11/4**[2]

2626 **3** 2 1/4 **Just Cameron**[17] 4718 9-10-12 150..............................(t) JoeColliver 147+
(Micky Hammond) *led: j.rt 7th: jnd after 3 out: jst in front but keeping on whn blnd bdly and hdd 2 out: nt rcvr* **2/1**[1]

2P42 **4** 3 3/4 **Indian Voyage (IRE)**[12] 4838 8-10-12 131.....................(t) DaraghBourke 138
(Maurice Barnes) *pressed ldr: chal after 3 out: ev ch lft in ld next: rdn and hdd bef last: wknd run-in* **50/1**

0651 **5** 2 3/4 **Upsilon Bleu (FR)**[28] 4469 8-11-6 147........................ BrianHughes 145
(Pauline Robson) *trckd ldrs: nt fluent 3 out: rdn and wknd fr next* **11/1**

4253 **P** **Simply Ned (IRE)**[41] 4281 9-11-6 158........................... BrianHarding
(Nicky Richards) *t.k.h early: hld up: rdn and outpcd after 4 out: wknd next: lost tch and p.u bef 2 out* **7/2**[3]

4m 27.4s (9.40) **Going Correction** +0.925s/f (Soft) **6 Ran SP% 112.5**
Speed ratings: **114,111,110,108,107**
CSF £15.85 TOTE £5.40: £2.50, £1.90; EX 19.50 Trifecta £51.90.
Owner S Smith & S Campion **Bred** Anthony Walsh **Trained** Alcester, Warwicks

FOCUS
The rail was moved out a further 2yds since the last meeting, making it 4yds from the innermost line. Race distance increased by 60yds. The feature event attracted only one last-time-out winner, but it provided an exciting finish. The winenr didn't need to improve on his Festival run to win.

5088 G & H ANCRUM CELEBRATION H'CAP HURDLE (8 hdls) 2m 51y

4:00 (4:00) (Class 4) (0-120,120) 4-Y-O+ **£3,898** (£1,144; £572; £286)

Form RPR

6310 **1** **Jokers And Rogues (IRE)**[14] 4799 8-10-10 **104**...........(t) HenryBrooke 108+
(Kenneth Slack) *mde all: clr 2nd to bef 2 out: sn drvn along: hrd pressed between last 2: hld on gamely u.p run-in* **4/1**[1]

031 **2** 2 1/4 **Nine Altars (IRE)**[32] 4417 7-11-5 **113**........................... CraigNichol 114
(Ann Hamilton) *chsd wnr and clr of remainder to bef 2 out: effrt and ch 2 out: keeping on whn lft 2nd last: nt rch wnr* **16/1**

065 **3** 1 1/4 **Cactus Valley (IRE)**[92] 3397 7-10-10 **104**................(t) JakeGreenall 107+
(Michael Easterby) *hld up in tch: nt fluent 3rd: smooth hdwy after 3 out: shkn up and chal bef last: blnd and rdn last: nt rcvr* **14/1**

204 **4** 2 **Prince Khurram**[47] 4154 6-11-4 **112**...........................(t) WillKennedy 110
(Donald McCain) *chsd clr ldng pair: effrt and rdn after 3 out: kpt on fr next* **12/1**

1055 **5** 4 1/2 **Stoneham**[37] 4320 5-10-10 **109**............................. ShaneShortall(5) 103
(Iain Jardine) *hld up in midfield: rdn along after 4 out: plugged on fr 2 out: nvr able to chal* **9/1**[3]

33 **6** 42 **The Compeller (IRE)**[148] 2324 4-10-12 **112**.................. PeterBuchanan 57
(Lucinda Russell) *hld up: rdn along after 4 out: no imp fr next: btn fnl 2: t.o* **12/1**

3600 **7** 7 **Lochalsh (IRE)**[163] 2027 5-10-13 **112**...................... StephenMulqueen(5) 56
(Katie Scott) *hld up in midfield: drvn and outpcd bef 4 out: sn struggling: t.o* **40/1**

0650 **P** **Franciscan**[43] 4229 8-11-4 **112**..................................... AdrianLane
(Donald McCain) *bhd: struggling 1/2-way: nvr on terms: p.u bef 2 out* **22/1**

5551 **F** **Ash Park (IRE)**[23] 4570 8-10-9 **110**........................ SamColtherd(7) 105
(Stuart Coltherd) *hld up: pushed along bef 4 out: hdwy after 3 out: 10 l 5th and styng on steadily whn fell next* **6/1**[2]

24-1 **P** **Celtic Artisan (IRE)**[15] 489 5-10-1 **100**...............(p) BridgetAndrews(5)
(Rebecca Menzies) *hld up: drvn and struggling after 4 out: lost tch and p.u bef 2 out* **16/1**

6312 **P** **Quill Art**[29] 4460 4-10-8 **108**..................................... BrianHughes
(Richard Fahey) *prom: pushed along and struggling after 4 out: lost tch and p.u bef 2 out* **4/1**[1]

3120 **P** **So Satisfied**[35] 4366 5-11-5 **120**.............................. StevenFox(7)
(Sandy Thomson) *hld up: struggling 1/2-way: lost tch and p.u bef 2 out* **6/1**[2]

4m 13.3s (11.50) **Going Correction** +0.875s/f (Soft)
WFA 4 from 5yo+ 5lb **12 Ran SP% 119.2**
Speed ratings (Par 105): **106,104,104,103,101 80,76, , ,**
CSF £66.69 CT £827.62 TOTE £5.40: £2.10, £4.40, £4.10; EX 69.40 Trifecta £1744.50.
Owner A Slack **Bred** J P Russell **Trained** Hilton, Cumbria
■ Stewards' Enquiry : Henry Brooke two-day ban: used whip above permitted level (Apr 16-17)

FOCUS
The rail was moved out a further 2yds since the last meeting, making it 4yds from the innermost line. Race distance increased by 60yds. The going was given as soft, good to soft in places prior to this truly-run competitive handicap, which saw more drama at the last. The winner was well in on his Sedgefield win.

5089 KELSO EARLY BIRD H'CAP HURDLE (11 hdls) 2m 4f 189y

4:35 (4:35) (Class 4) (0-115,115) 4-Y-O+ **£3,898** (£1,144; £572; £286)

Form RPR

465P **1** **One For Hocky (IRE)**[22] 4583 8-11-2 **110**........................ RyanDay(5) 119+
(Nicky Richards) *hld up: smooth hdwy to chse ldr 4 out: led next: shkn up and kpt on strly fr 2 out* **11/1**

3-FP **2** 4 **Rowdy Rocher (IRE)**[67] 3792 10-11-3 **113**...................... StevenFox(7) 114
(Sandy Thomson) *hld up in midfield: shkn up bef 7th: rallied to press wnr 3 out: ev ch bef next: rdn and one pce between last 2* **9/1**

1111 **3** 1 3/4 **Marlee Massie (IRE)**[20] 4638 7-11-0 **110**.............. MrKitAlexander(7) 109
(N W Alexander) *chsd ldrs: drvn and outpcd bef 4 out: rallied to chse ldrs bef 2 out: kpt on same pce fr last* **4/1**[1]

3044 **4** 21 **Cruachan (IRE)**[20] 4638 7-10-5 **94**............................ JonathanEngland 75
(Lucy Normile) *hld up: rdn and outpcd 7th: rallied after next: wknd fr 2 out* **15/2**

0343 **5** 28 **Mondlicht (USA)**[122] 2843 6-11-3 **106**.......................... BrianHughes 56
(James Moffatt) *hld up: rdn 7th: rallied whn nt fluent 3 out: wknd bef next* **17/2**

F446 **6** 7 **Dutch Canyon (IRE)**[73] 3684 6-9-10 **90**..........(v) StephenMulqueen(5) 33
(N W Alexander) *led and clr to 4 out: hdd next: wknd bef 2 out* **7/1**[3]

32P2 **7** ¾ **Boruma (IRE)**[12] 4839 6-11-10 **113**........................ HenryBrooke 56
(Dianne Sayer) *in tch: struggling 7th: btn fr 3 out* **15/2**

-P0P **P** **Jewellery (IRE)**[199] 1551 9-10-5 **97**........................(t) JohnKington(3)
(Katie Scott) *chsd ldrs: drvn and struggling bef 7th: wknd bef next: t.o whn p.u bef 2 out* **33/1**

532F **P** **Tantamount**[91] 3437 7-11-12 **115**........................(t) DerekFox
(Lucinda Russell) *hld up: pushed along bef 4 out: rallied after next: wknd bef 2 out: no ch whn p.u appr last* **14/1**

POU0 **P** **George Fernbeck**[156] 2145 8-11-4 **110**........................(p) JoeColliver(3)
(Micky Hammond) *bhd: struggling fr 4th: t.o fnl circ: p.u bef 2 out* **33/1**

4312 **P** **Sean Ban (IRE)**[23] 4570 6-11-12 **115**........................ WillKennedy
(Donald McCain) *chsd clr ldr to 4 out: rdn and wknd after next: t.o whn p.u after 2 out* **6/1**[2]

05PP **P** **Wee Jock Elliot**[96] 3312 6-10-0 **89** oh3........................(p) CraigNichol
(Alistair Whillans) *bhd: struggling fnl circ: t.o whn p.u and dismntd bef 2 out* **25/1**

5m 32.6s (24.60) **Going Correction** +0.875s/f (Soft) **12** Ran SP% **115.6**
Speed ratings (Par 105): **88,86,85,77,67 64,64,, ,**
CSF £101.50 CT £464.36 TOTE £16.20: £4.30, £3.00, £1.90; EX 98.70 Trifecta £1373.80.
Owner Kingdom Taverns Ltd **Bred** John Sayers **Trained** Greystoke, Cumbria

FOCUS
The rail was moved out a further 2yds since the last meeting, making it 4yds from the innermost line. Race distance increased by 75yds. A fair handicap, in which an honest gallop was set. The winner is on a good mark, but this still rates a small personal best.

5090 LADS & VULTURES OPEN HUNTERS' CHASE (19 fncs) 3m 2f 39y
5:10 (5:10) (Class 5) 5-Y-0+ **£2,495** (£774; £386; £193)

Form RPR

-414 **1** **Durban Gold**[13] 4820 9-11-2 113........................ MissJWalton(5) 111+
(Mrs D Walton) *cl up: led 4 out: sn hrd pressed: kpt on strly to draw clr fr last* **14/1**

61-P **2** 5 **Beggar's Velvet (IRE)**[34] 10-11-9 112........................(p) MrRSmith(5) 114
(D Holmes) *hld up in tch: stdy hdwy bef 5 out: ev ch 3 out to last: kpt on same pce run-in* **9/2**[3]

113U **3** 8 **Cave Hunter (IRE)**[15] 4768 9-12-1 113........................(tp) MrTHamilton(3) 109
(Mrs Wendy Hamilton) *led to 6th: sn pushed along: reminders after 11th: drvn and struggling 5 out: kpt on fr 2 out: nt rch first two* **5/4**[1]

1220 **4** 1 **Pena Dorada (IRE)**[15] 4768 9-11-13 115........................ MissRMcDonald(5) 109
(Alan J Brown) *trckd ldrs: pushed along and outpcd 4 out: rallied after next: no imp fr 2 out* **4/1**[2]

-44P **5** 30 **Isla Pearl Fisher**[55] 4016 13-11-7 113........................(t) MrKitAlexander(3) 80
(N W Alexander) *cl up: led 6th to 4 out: rallied and ev ch next: wknd bef 2 out* **10/1**

06 **6** 63 **Havana Jack (IRE)**[44] 4207 6-11-5 0........................ MrNOrpwood(5) 7
(L Kerr) *prom tl rdn and wknd after 3 out: t.o* **66/1**

134- **P** **Dica (FR)**[34] 10-11-4 113 ow1........................ MrPCollins(7)
(Paul Collins) *bhd: hdwy and in tch 4 out: rdn and wknd after next: lost tch and p.u after 2 out* **7/1**

7m 24.7s (37.50) **Going Correction** +0.925s/f (Soft) **7** Ran SP% **112.4**
Speed ratings: **79,77,75,74,65 46,**
CSF £72.54 TOTE £16.50: £4.30, £2.40; EX 113.80 Trifecta £347.30.
Owner Mrs D Walton **Bred** R J And Mrs E M D Chugg **Trained** Chathill, Northumberland

FOCUS
The rail was moved out a further 2yds since the last meeting, making it 4yds from the innermost line. Race distance increased by 75yds. The finale was a fair little hunters' chase, in which they were closely grouped for most of the race. The first two set the level.
T/Plt: £1,036.70 to a £1 stake. Pool: £60,573.90 - 42.65 winning units. T/Qpdt: £82.00 to a £1 stake. Pool: £5,156.82 - 46.50 winning units. **Richard Young**

5070 NEWBURY (L-H)
Saturday, April 2

OFFICIAL GOING: Good (good to soft in places; chs 6.7, hdl 6.1)
Wind: Moderate, half behind Weather: Fine

5091 JOHN HAINE MEMORIAL NOVICES' HURDLE (8 hdls) 2m 69y
2:00 (2:01) (Class 4) 4-Y-0+ **£4,548** (£1,335; £667; £333)

Form RPR

31 **1** **Ozzie The Oscar (IRE)**[19] 4681 5-11-6 0........................ RichardJohnson 140+
(Philip Hobbs) *chsd ldrs: led 3 out: clr whn blnd last: comf* **6/4**[1]

4 **2** 4 **Herewego Herewego (IRE)**[49] 4111 5-11-0 0........................ BarryGeraghty 127+
(Alan King) *t.k.h in midfield: rdn and hdwy 3 out: 3rd whn mstke last: styd on to take 2nd run-in* **2/1**[2]

3 3¾ **No Heretic**[940] 8-11-0 0........................[1] NicodeBoinville 122+
(Nicky Henderson) *plld hrd in midfield: hdwy to chse ldr 3 out: mstke and hung rt next: no ex and lost 2nd run-in* **6/1**[3]

4 **4** 13 **Counterfeiter**[92] 3418 6-10-7 0........................ MrZBaker(7) 109
(Martin Bosley) *t.k.h: prom tl wknd 2 out* **50/1**

3-26 **5** 2¼ **Vaillant Nonantais (FR)**[35] 4364 5-11-0 0........................ AndrewTinkler 107+
(Nicky Henderson) *towards rr: effrt 3 out: nvr rchd ldrs* **20/1**

44 **6** 5 **Persian Breeze**[15] 4773 4-10-1 0........................ AidanColeman 88
(Lucy Wadham) *t.k.h: chsd ldrs tl wknd 2 out* **33/1**

3-26 **7** nk **Bilzic (FR)**[133] 2646 5-11-0 0........................(t) IanPopham 101
(Dan Skelton) *in tch: rdn 3 out: no imp* **33/1**

624 **8** 2¼ **Baraymi (FR)**[38] 4304 4-10-8 122........................(p) MichealNolan 92
(Jamie Snowden) *prom tl wknd 3 out* **25/1**

0321 **9** nk **Starving Marvin**[22] 4594 8-11-6 123........................ LeightonAspell 105
(Rod Millman) *led: j.rt 1st: hdd & wknd 3 out* **9/1**

04 **10** 12 **Vocaliser (IRE)**[29] 4462 4-10-8........................ CharliePoste 82
(Robin Dickin) *plld hrd towards rr on outer: hdwy appr 3 out: sn wknd* **50/1**

-3P0 **11** 8 **Jaslamour (FR)**[19] 4681 5-11-0 0........................ AdamWedge 78
(Alexandra Dunn) *a towards rr* **200/1**

000 **12** 2¼ **Actiondancer (IRE)**[9] 4888 5-11-0 0........................ JamesDavies 76
(Henry Oliver) *in tch tl rdn and wknd 5th* **250/1**

PP0 **13** 2¼ **Austin Friars**[33] 4409 4-10-8 0........................ JoshuaMoore 68
(Jim Best) *towards rr: mstke 2nd: hrd rdn 4th: sn lost tch* **200/1**

0- **14** 10 **Bit Of A Charlie**[463] 3282 7-11-0 0........................(t) AndrewThornton 64
(John Ryall) *bhd: mstke 2nd: no ch whn mstke 3 out* **250/1**

000 **15** 5 **Badger Run (IRE)**[28] 4494 5-10-7 0........................ MrTGreatrex(7) 59
(Pat Murphy) *a bhd* **250/1**

3m 57.3s (-12.70) **Going Correction** -0.75s/f (Firm)
WFA 4 from 5yo+ 5lb **15** Ran SP% **118.2**
Speed ratings (Par 105): **101,99,97,90,89 87,86,85,85,79 75,74,73,68,65**
CSF £4.26 TOTE £2.20: £1.10, £1.50, £2.00; EX 5.70 Trifecta £14.90.
Owner Bradley Partnership **Bred** William O'Keeffe **Trained** Withycombe, Somerset

FOCUS
Rail movements meant the hurdle course was set at 31yds further per circuit than official distances. It was a bright, drying day and no doubt the going was quicker than the previous afternoon. This should prove to be straightforward novice form, but the first two are both on the upgrade.

5092 BETFRED "FOLLOW US ON TWITTER" H'CAP CHASE (21 fncs) 3m 1f 214y
2:35 (2:36) (Class 3) (0-140,140) 5-Y-0+
£12,512 (£3,696; £1,848; £924; £462; £232)

Form RPR

P5P3 **1** **Benvolio (IRE)**[19] 4684 9-11-8 **136**........................(b) SamTwiston-Davies 152+
(Paul Nicholls) *prom: outpcd and rdn 16th: rallied and mstke next: chsd wnr 4 out: led appr last: drvn clr* **5/1**

60P5 **2** 11 **Ned Stark (IRE)**[50] 4101 8-11-5 **133**........................(p) DenisO'Regan 139
(Alan King) *led: rdn 4 out: hdd appr last: no ex run-in* **9/2**[3]

1-PU **3** 4 **Seebright**[50] 4101 9-11-2 **130**........................ IanPopham 134
(Victor Dartnall) *sn struggling towards rr: rdn 4 out: styd on fr 2 out* **9/1**

P441 **4** nk **Tour Des Champs (FR)**[6] 4935 9-11-3 **134** 7ex........................(p) RyanHatch(3) 137+
(Nigel Twiston-Davies) *bhd: rdn along fr 11th: styd on fr 3 out* **3/1**[1]

1104 **5** hd **Greenlaw**[227] 1288 10-10-11 **125**........................(t) AidanColeman 127
(Charlie Longsdon) *prom tl wknd 2 out* **20/1**

123P **6** 20 **Amidon (FR)**[5] 4971 6-10-10 **124**........................(b[1]) LeightonAspell 109
(Lucy Wadham) *prom: mstke 17th: wknd 4 out* **9/1**

6-15 **7** 2 **Ikorodu Road**[63] 3860 13-11-4 **132**........................(p) DavidBass 114
(Graeme McPherson) *nvr gng wl in rr: no ch fr 17th* **16/1**

332P **8** 5 **Fingal Bay (IRE)**[16] 4733 10-11-12 **140**........................(tp) RichardJohnson 119
(Philip Hobbs) *hld up: hdwy 11th: wknd 17th* **7/2**[2]

6m 30.2s (-15.80) **Going Correction** -0.30s/f (Good) **8** Ran SP% **112.7**
Speed ratings: **112,108,107,107,107 101,100,98**
CSF £27.39 CT £194.14 TOTE £5.20: £1.70, £1.90, £2.60; EX 19.80 Trifecta £167.90.
Owner Mrs D Thompson **Bred** Mrs Mary And Paul Motherway **Trained** Ditcheat, Somerset

FOCUS
A fair staying handicap, run at a fair gallop. The winner is on a good mark and has been rated back to his best.

5093 BETFRED "GOALS GALORE EXTRA" H'CAP CHASE (16 fncs) 2m 3f 187y
3:05 (3:07) (Class 2) (0-150,143) 5-Y-0+ **£12,660** (£3,740; £1,870; £936; £468)

Form RPR

3003 **1** **Thomas Crapper**[11] 4857 9-11-3 **134**........................(p) CharliePoste 142
(Robin Dickin) *prom: rdn to join ldr 3 out: led last: drvn out* **4/1**[2]

3000 **2** 1¾ **Fox Appeal (IRE)**[18] 4697 9-11-12 **143**........................ GavinSheehan 151
(Emma Lavelle) *in tch: effrt 4 out: drvn to chse ldng pair appr last: r.o to take 2nd nr fin* **4/1**[2]

03U **3** ½ **Art Of Logistics (IRE)**[96] 3320 8-11-9 **140**........................(p) RichardJohnson 146
(Philip Hobbs) *chsd ldr: led 12th: jnd by wnr 3 out: hdd last: kpt on* **9/2**[3]

-5P0 **4** 14 **Shantou Magic (IRE)**[112] 3031 9-11-2 **133**........................ AidanColeman 126
(Charlie Longsdon) *rdn and lost tch 8th: styd on fr 2 out* **11/2**

P0-P **5** ½ **Headly's Bridge (IRE)**[49] 4128 10-10-10 **127**........................ AndrewThornton 122
(Simon Earle) *t.k.h in 6th: rdn and no hdwy fr 4 out* **25/1**

3321 **6** 14 **Morning Reggie**[21] 4625 7-10-5 **122**........................(p) LeightonAspell 106
(Oliver Sherwood) *towards rr: mstke 7th: struggling fr 11th* **7/2**[1]

F3P5 **7** 26 **The Clock Leary (IRE)**[43] 4230 8-10-0 **117**........................(p) SamTwiston-Davies 73
(Venetia Williams) *led: mstke 10th: nt fluent and hdd 12th: sn wknd* **7/1**

4m 51.2s (-11.80) **Going Correction** -0.30s/f (Good) **7** Ran SP% **112.1**
Speed ratings: **111,110,110,104,104 98,88**
CSF £19.83 CT £72.66 TOTE £5.40: £2.70, £1.90; EX 22.70 Trifecta £62.30.
Owner apis.uk.com **Bred** Mrs J A Carr-Evans **Trained** Alcester, Warwicks

FOCUS
There was no hanging around in this fair handicap and the principals dominated the finish. The winner is on a fair mark and has been rated back to his best.

5094 EBF & TBA MARES' "NATIONAL HUNT" NOVICES' HURDLE FINALE (LIMITED H'CAP) (LISTED RACE) (10 hdls) 2m 4f 118y
3:40 (3:40) (Class 1) 4-Y-0+
£22,780 (£8,548; £4,280; £2,132; £1,072; £536)

Form RPR

1F41 **1** nse **Briery Queen**[29] 4457 7-11-0 **123**........................ BarryGeraghty 132+
(Noel Williams) *hld up in midfield: hdwy 3 out: disp ld fr 2 out: hmpd and rdr lost iron after last: hrd rdn: r.o wl: fin 2nd: awrdd the r* **11/4**[1]

-252 **2** **Lady Of Lamanver**[14] 4779 6-10-6 **115**........................(t) AidanColeman 124+
(Harry Fry) *prom: disp ld fr 2 out: edgd rt after last: all out: fin 1st: demoted to 2nd* **11/2**[2]

2U12 **3** 3½ **Antartica De Thaix (FR)**[31] 4435 6-10-13 **122**........................(t) SamTwiston-Davies 127
(Paul Nicholls) *hld up in rr: gd hdwy on bit appr 2 out: rdn appr last: unable qck* **8/1**

21P1 **4** 6 **At First Light**[98] 3217 7-10-11 **120**........................ GavinSheehan 120
(David Weston) *prom: hrd rdn 2 out: no ex run-in* **20/1**

312 **5** 12 **Timon's Tara**[45] 4186 7-10-4 **113** oh1........................ JackQuinlan 101
(Robin Dickin) *hld up in rr: hdwy 3 out: outpcd fr next* **16/1**

-2P3 **6** 3¾ **Avispa**[9] 4890 7-10-11 **120**........................ WayneHutchinson 105
(Alan King) *hld up towards rr: hdwy 3 out: wknd last* **8/1**

3112 **7** 4½ **Rene's Girl (IRE)**[25] 4546 6-11-0 **123**........................ IanPopham 104
(Dan Skelton) *bhd: sme hdwy 3 out: nvr able to chal* **7/1**[3]

3465 **8** shd **Miss Serious (IRE)**[14] 4779 6-11-2 **125**........................ JamesDavies 108
(Jeremy Scott) *in tch: rdn after 7th: sn wknd* **16/1**

2432 **9** 4½ **Kentford Myth**[21] 4616 6-9-13 **113** oh6........................ KevinJones(5) 91
(Seamus Mullins) *led: mstke 7th: hdd & wknd 2 out* **33/1**

1132 **10** 8 **Surtee Du Berlais (IRE)**[65] 3825 6-11-7 **130**........................ LeightonAspell 99
(Oliver Sherwood) *a towards rr* **9/1**

3P-3 **11** 17 **Hannah Just Hannah**[323] 314 7-10-8 **117**........................(t) JamesBanks 71
(Heather Main) *t.k.h: prom tl wknd 3 out* **25/1**

021P **12** 20 **Pulling Power**[30] 4445 6-10-7 **116**........................(t) DavidBass 52
(Kim Bailey) *towards rr: mstke 1st: hdwy 7th: wknd 3 out* **20/1**

1314 **P** **Ruby Rambler**[94] 3372 6-11-10 **133**........................ RichardJohnson
(Lucy Wadham) *in tch tl wknd 3 out: bhd whn j. slowly and p.u next* **12/1**

4m 53.9s (-25.10) **Going Correction** -0.75s/f (Firm) **13** Ran SP% **122.5**
Speed ratings (Par 111): **116,117,115,113,108 107,105,105,103,100 94,86,**
CSF £17.83 CT £112.69 TOTE £3.50: £1.70, £1.80, £2.40; EX 19.00 Trifecta £161.30.
Owner Helen Plumbly & Kathryn Leadbeater **Bred** Simon And Helen Plumbly **Trained** Blewbury, Oxon

FOCUS
Race distance increased by 36yds. A typically competitive edition of this well-established mares' handicap which saw a dramatic finish. The first three are on the upgrade in a solid renewal.

5095 DOOM BAR JUVENILE H'CAP HURDLE (10 hdls) 2m 2f 183y
4:15 (4:17) (Class 2) 4-Y-O £25,992 (£7,632; £3,816; £1,908)

Form RPR
1320 1 **Duke Street (IRE)**[17] 4720 4-11-3 125 AidanColeman 128+
(Dr Richard Newland) *hld up: smooth hdwy 3 out: led next: sn clr* 7/2[1]
5314 2 8 **Cobra De Mai (FR)**[39] 4294 4-10-10 118 IanPopham 111
(Dan Skelton) *hld up in rr: hdwy 3 out: chsd wnr next: no imp* 11/1
2141 3 6 **Culture De Sivola (FR)**[19] 4683 4-10-11 124 LizzieKelly(5) 113
(Nick Williams) *prom: led after 7th tl wknd 2 out* 5/1[2]
220 4 ½ **Pillard (FR)**[17] 4720 4-11-7 129 (p) RichieMcLernon 116
(Jonjo O'Neill) *prom tl wknd 2 out* 25/1
442 5 7 **Deebaj (IRE)**[28] 4489 4-10-13 121 LeightonAspell 103
(Richard Price) *hld up in midfield: hdwy appr 3 out: sn wknd* 12/1
1250 6 ½ **Duke Of Medina (IRE)**[17] 4720 4-11-2 134 (v[1]) HarryTeal(10) 114
(Harry Whittington) *prom: chalng whn mstke 3 out: sn wknd* 9/1
114 7 2 **Jaboltiski (SPA)**[84] 3519 4-11-8 130 RichardJohnson 108
(Philip Hobbs) *a towards rr* 5/1[2]
5 8 11 **Clic Work (FR)**[70] 3745 4-11-6 128 (t) SamTwiston-Davies 97
(Paul Nicholls) *a in rr* 7/1[3]
2115 F **Pemba (FR)**[36] 4338 4-10-12 120 WayneHutchinson
(Alan King) *mid-div tl fell 3rd* 8/1
611P P **Akavit (IRE)**[17] 4720 4-11-7 129 (p) DavidBass
(Ed de Giles) *led: j. slowly 1st: drvn along fr 4th: hdd & wknd after 7th: wl bhd whn p.u bef 2 out* 12/1

4m 29.1s (-18.90) **Going Correction** -0.75s/f (Firm) **10** Ran SP% **116.7**
Speed ratings: **109,105,103,102,99 99,98,94, ,**
CSF £41.50 CT £193.52 TOTE £4.00: £1.60, £4.30, £2.00; EX 43.60 Trifecta £337.80.
Owner Chris Stedman & Mark Albon **Bred** Mrs Joan Keaney **Trained** Claines, Worcs

FOCUS
Race distance increased by 31yds. A decent prize and it attracted a competitive field of juveniles. The winner was building on the promise of his Festival run, but is a potential 140-rated hurdler on his Flat form.

5096 DOOM BAR CHELMSFORD H'CAP CHASE (13 fncs) 2m 92y
4:50 (4:50) (Class 3) (0-130,129) 5-Y-0+ £6,498 (£1,908; £954; £477)

Form RPR
4015 1 **Ultragold (FR)**[28] 4485 8-11-7 129 (t) HarryCobden(5) 138+
(Colin Tizzard) *in tch: rdn 4 out: clsd on ldrs 2 out: styd on to ld fnl 75yds: won gng away* 9/4[1]
FP36 2 2¼ **Whispering Harry**[21] 4617 7-11-8 125 JamesDavies 131
(Henry Oliver) *prom: jnd ldrs 9th: ev ch run-in: outpcd by wnr fnl 75yds* 16/1
223U 3 1½ **Mr Muddle**[35] 4363 9-11-2 119 (p) MarcGoldstein 124
(Sheena West) *wnt prom 6th: outpcd 4 out: styd on run-in* 16/1
PP3P 4 hd **Starkie**[7] 4918 9-11-4 121 TomCannon 126
(Chris Gordon) *prom: led 5th tl 3 out: led again next: hdd and no ex fnl 75yds* 9/1
6552 5 2½ **Owen Na View (IRE)**[12] 4841 8-11-1 118 (t) PaddyBrennan 120
(Fergal O'Brien) *chsd ldrs: led and mstke 3 out: hdd next: wknd last* 5/2[2]
23-4 6 12 **Go Conquer (IRE)**[140] 2489 7-11-8 125 AidanColeman 119
(Jonjo O'Neill) *led tl 5th: mstke 4 out: wknd next* 7/2[3]
2561 7 23 **Sportsreport (IRE)**[19] 4670 8-10-9 112 (p) AndrewThornton 90
(Seamus Mullins) *hld up: hdwy on outer 9th: wknd 3 out* 14/1
0163 P **Cappielow Park**[26] 4529 7-11-1 118 (tp) GavinSheehan
(Ali Stronge) *nvr gng wl: sn bhd: t.o whn p.u bef 4 out* 25/1

4m 2.9s (-5.10) **Going Correction** -0.30s/f (Good) **8** Ran SP% **113.8**
Speed ratings: **100,98,98,96,96 90,79,**
CSF £34.29 CT £463.95 TOTE £3.10: £1.30, £2.20, £3.10; EX 25.20 Trifecta £176.50.
Owner Brocade Racing J P Romans Terry Warner **Bred** Gilles Chaignon **Trained** Milborne Port, Dorset

FOCUS
A modest handicap that saw a tight finish. The winner was nicely in on his Wincanton win and can probably rate higher.

5097 WEST BERKSHIRE RACING CLUB STANDARD OPEN NATIONAL HUNT FLAT RACE 2m 69y
5:25 (5:26) (Class 6) 4-6-Y-O £1,689 (£496; £248; £124)

Form RPR
1 **Jenkins (IRE)** 4-10-10 0 DavidBass 128+
(Nicky Henderson) *hld up in midfield on inner: n.m.r and lost pl 7f out: gd hdwy to hld on bit 2f out: qcknd clr over 1f out: impressive* 7/2[1]
2 9 **Cash Again (FR)**[146] 4-11-3 0 BarryGeraghty 124+
(Paul Nicholls) *in tch on inner: led briefly over 2f out: comf outpcd by wnr over 1f out* 7/2[1]
3 16 **Mankala (IRE)** 6-11-2 0 LeightonAspell 108
(Oliver Sherwood) *t.k.h in rr: hdwy on outer 6f out: rdn and btn 2f out* 8/1
4 4 ¾ **Le Dauphin (IRE)**[50] 4103 5-11-2 0 PeterCarberry 108
(Nicky Henderson) *in tch tl outpcd 3f out* 16/1
3 5 1½ **Reilly's Minor (IRE)**[65] 3827 5-11-2 0 GavinSheehan 106
(Warren Greatrex) *led tl over 2f out: sn outpcd* 12/1
6-33 6 1½ **The Poodle Faker**[130] 2702 5-11-2 0 TomO'Brien 105
(Hughie Morrison) *bhd tl styd on fnl 3f* 20/1
7 4½ **Drama King (IRE)** 5-10-11 0 (p) DavidNoonan(5) 101
(David Pipe) *towards rr: sme hdwy 6f out: wknd 4f out: btn whn hung lft 3f out* 16/1
8 1 **Summer Name (IRE)** 4-10-10 0 TrevorWhelan 94
(Rebecca Curtis) *t.k.h: prom tl wknd over 2f out* 7/1[2]
9 hd **Gulshanigans** 4-10-10 0 SamTwiston-Davies 94
(Nigel Twiston-Davies) *prom tl wknd over 2f out* 16/1
2 10 5 **Black Country Boy**[34] 4392 4-10-10 0 CharliePoste 89
(Robin Dickin) *towards rr on outer: hdwy 1/2-way: wknd over 4f out* 7/1[2]
11 2 **Clondaw Westie (IRE)**[111] 5-11-2 0 (t) JoshuaMoore 94
(Lawney Hill) *in tch on outer tl wknd over 3f out* 50/1
03 12 4 **Instingtive (IRE)**[57] 3980 5-11-2 0 (t) AidanColeman 90
(Harry Fry) *prom tl wknd 4f out* 15/2[3]
6 13 1 **Let's Tango (IRE)**[35] 4357 5-11-2 0 MichealNolan 89
(Caroline Keevil) *a towards rr* 80/1
4 14 46 **Brother Norphin**[120] 2882 4-10-10 0 (p) DenisO'Regan 42
(Simon Hodgson) *mid-div tl wknd 6f out* 100/1
15 99 **Valleyofthefox** 6-11-2 0 MarkQuinlan
(Malcolm Jones) *a bhd: t.o and virtually p.u 1/2-way* 100/1

3m 45.7s (-18.60) **Going Correction** -0.75s/f (Firm) **15** Ran SP% **127.6**
Speed ratings: **116,111,103,103,102 101,99,98,98,96 95,93,92,69,20**
CSF £14.43 TOTE £5.90: £2.10, £2.00, £4.10; EX 27.40 Trifecta £115.10.
Owner Pump & Plant Services Ltd **Bred** Mr And Mrs L & A Gleeson **Trained** Upper Lambourn, Berks

FOCUS
Race distance increased by 31yds. An interesting bumper in which the market leaders came to the fore around 2f out and the pair drew well clear. Both look well above average.
T/Plt: £47.20 to a £1 stake. Pool: £123,723.03 - 1912.42 winning units. T/Qpdt: £15.80 to a £1 stake. Pool: £7,604.89 - 355.50 winning units. **Lee McKenzie**

4798 UTTOXETER (L-H)
Saturday, April 2

OFFICIAL GOING: Heavy (5.9)
Wind: light 1/2 behind Weather: fine

5098 BETFRED TV CONDITIONAL JOCKEYS' TRAINING SERIES MAIDEN HURDLE (RACING EXCELLENCE INITIATIVE) (10 hdls) 2m 3f 207y
2:05 (2:06) (Class 4) 4-Y-0+ £3,898 (£1,144; £572; £286)

Form RPR
1 **Buckskin Boulta (IRE)**[125] 8-11-2 0 (t) ConorSmith 114
(Mark Michael McNiff, Ire) *t.k.h: led after 1st: jnd last: fnd ex nr fin* 11/1
324 2 nk **Marquis Of Carabas (IRE)**[148] 2318 6-11-2 117 GarethMalone 114+
(David Dennis) *t.k.h: wnt prom 3rd: stdd bef 6th: smooth hdwy and 2nd bef 3 out: upsides on bit last: shkn up last 100yds: hld nr line* 9/4[2]
32-3 3 11 **Aston Cantlow**[43] 4229 8-11-2 120 (t) CiaranGethings 103
(Philip Hobbs) *t.k.h: led tl after 1st: trckd ldrs: stdd bef 6th: 3rd bef 3 out: one pce fr 2 out* 1/1[1]
5 4 ½ **Nice Thoughts (IRE)**[30] 4449 4-10-9 0 (p) MichaelHeard 96
(David Pipe) *towards rr: wnt prom 6th: outpcd appr 2 out: one pce* 7/2[3]
5 8 **Bringewood Blue (IRE)** 9-10-4 0 GeorgeGorman(5) 88
(John Needham) *hld up in rr: hdwy 7th: wkndbetween last 2* 100/1
04 6 3¾ **Here Comes Love (IRE)**[22] 4580 6-10-11 0 (t) AdamShort(5) 94
(Patrick Griffin, Ire) *t.k.h: trckd ldrs: outpcd whn nt fluent 3 out: 4th and wl hld whn blnd next* 66/1
U 7 1 **Catch A Thief (IRE)**[19] 4681 5-10-13 0 LewisGordon(3) 90
(Evan Williams) *in rr: drvn 7th: lost pl next* 22/1
26PF 8 8 **Kendari King (IRE)**[20] 4646 5-11-2 0 WilliamFeatherstone 82
(Tim Vaughan) *chsd ldrs: lost pl bef 3 out: bhd whn wandered appr last* 50/1

5m 56.2s (53.00) **Going Correction** +1.65s/f (Heav)
WFA 4 from 5yo+ 6lb **8** Ran SP% **120.1**
Speed ratings (Par 105): **60,59,55,55,52 50,50,46**
CSF £38.24 TOTE £14.60: £3.30, £1.20, £1.02; EX 48.70 Trifecta £112.10.
Owner C & C Bloodstock Ltd **Bred** James Kearney **Trained** Coolaney, Co. Sligo

FOCUS
There were divided bends. The hurdles were moved out on to fresher ground, with the rail 6yds off inside. Chute Hurdle (1st in 2m hurdle race) omitted due to the flooding earlier in week. This race distance had approximately 50yds added to it. This seemed a fair contest considering the official marks of the two that headed the betting, but the early gallop was slow. The race has been rated through the runner-up.

5099 BETFRED BINGO H'CAP HURDLE (8 hdls 1 omitted) 1m 7f 168y
2:40 (2:40) (Class 5) (0-100,97) 4-Y-0+ £2,599 (£763; £381; £190)

Form RPR
2531 1 **Kayf Charmer**[9] 4886 6-10-9 86 ConorSmith(7) 90
(Linda Blackford) *chsd ldrs: cl 2nd 5th: led bef next: jnd last: hdd narrowly and briefly 100yds out: rallied gamely* 9/4[1]
000P 2 ¾ **Lough Derg Island (IRE)**[26] 4528 8-11-6 90 RhysFlint 93
(Alexandra Dunn) *mid-div: hdwy appr 3 out: 2nd 2 out: upsides last: led briefly and narrowly 100yds out: no ex in clsng stages* 9/1
6536 3 3¾ **Pink Tara**[21] 4616 5-11-12 96 AlainCawley 97+
(Venetia Williams) *led: nt fluent 1st: j.rt 2nd: hdd appr 3 out: kpt on same pce fr 2 out* 8/1
0604 4 11 **Moreece (IRE)**[138] 2547 7-11-3 92 AlanJohns(5) 81
(Tim Vaughan) *chsd ldrs: outpcd 3 out: wknd next* 5/2[2]
4344 5 4½ **Lean Burn (USA)**[93] 3376 10-10-9 84 (bt) CiaranGethings(5) 68
(Barry Leavy) *in rr: sme hdwy 3 out: modest 5th next: nvr a factor* 7/1[3]
06-3 6 5 **Garde Ville (FR)**[5] 4975 6-10-9 86 GrahamCarson(7) 65
(Lisa Williamson) *chsd ldrs: wknd appr 3 out* 16/1
0-0P 7 hd **Fine Jewellery**[296] 694 7-10-0 70 oh1 (t) TommyPhelan 48
(Tom Gretton) *t.k.h towards rr: hdwy 5th: wknd next* 40/1
40 8 21 **Hang Fire (IRE)**[28] 4494 6-11-8 92 LeeEdwards 49
(Tony Carroll) *chsd ldrs: drvn 5th: lost pl and bhd bef next* 20/1
04PP 9 25 **Beau Knight**[11] 4856 4-10-10 91 ConorRing(5) 17
(Alexandra Dunn) *in rr-div: sme hdwy and drvn 5th: sn lost pl and bhd: t.o* 33/1
5P00 10 10 **Diamond Reflection (IRE)**[17] 4714 4-11-7 97 (t) PaulMoloney 13
(Tom Weston) *hld up in last: t.k.h: bhd fr 5th: t.o* 25/1
P/5- P **Lisdonagh House (IRE)**[492] 2763 14-10-0 70 oh3 SeanQuinlan
(Lynn Siddall) *in rr: bhd fr 5th: t.o whn p.u bef last* 50/1

4m 21.2s (23.80) **Going Correction** +1.65s/f (Heav)
WFA 4 from 5yo+ 5lb **11** Ran SP% **114.8**
Speed ratings (Par 103): **106,105,103,98,96 93,93,82,70,65**
CSF £20.58 CT £137.99 TOTE £2.90: £1.50, £2.20, £2.30; EX 24.50 Trifecta £183.60.
Owner Mrs V W Jones **Bred** Brian & Gwen Griffiths **Trained** Rackenford, Devon
■ Stewards' Enquiry : Conor Smith two-day ban: used whip above permitted level (Apr 16-17)

FOCUS
There were divided bends. The hurdles were moved out on to fresher ground, with the rail 6yds off inside. Chute Hurdle (1st in 2m hurdle race) omitted due to the flooding earlier in week. This race distance had approximately 33yds added to it. A moderate contest, but the first three are on the upgrade.

5100 BETFRED 1400 SHOPS NATIONWIDE H'CAP HURDLE (12 hdls) 2m 7f 70y
3:10 (3:11) (Class 4) (0-120,119) 4-Y-0 £4,431 (£1,309; £654; £327; £163)

Form RPR
4323 1 **Ballywilliam (IRE)**[94] 3361 6-11-8 118 (p) KieronEdgar(3) 127+
(David Pipe) *hld up towards rr: t.k.h: hdwy to trck ldrs 9th: hit next: 2nd 2 out: sn rdn: led narrowly last: drvn rt out* 5/1[3]
4141 2 3½ **Transient Bay (IRE)**[22] 4581 6-10-10 103 (p) DannyCook 107
(Philip Kirby) *trckd ldr: led after 7th: drvn appr 2 out: hdd narrowly last: styd on same pce* 11/2

P6P0 3 4 **Mountain Tunes (IRE)**[42] 4246 7-11-12 **119** NoelFehily 119+
(Jonjo O'Neill) *hld up towards rr: hdwy to trck ldrs 9th: 2nd next: one pce fr 2 out: j.lft last* **9/1**

6244 4 42 **Another Frontier (IRE)**[21] 4618 5-11-3 **115** JamieBargary(5) 84
(Nigel Twiston-Davies) *chsd ldrs: drvn appr 3 out: wknd bef 2 out: sn bhd: t.o* **7/2**[1]

2651 5 18 **Georgieshore (IRE)**[26] 4530 8-10-9 **109** WilliamFeatherstone(7) 48
(Zoe Davison) *led: hdd after 7th: drvn 9th: sn reminders: lost pl bef next: sn bhd: t.o* **10/1**

2-21 P **Bangkok Pete (IRE)**[42] 4241 11-11-7 **114** MattieBatchelor
(Jamie Poulton) *chsd ldrs: blnd 7th: sn lost pl: bhd whn reminders next: t.o 3 out: p.u bef last* **9/2**[2]

3322 P **Zephyros Bleu (IRE)**[39] 4301 6-11-12 **119** (p) SeanBowen
(Harry Whittington) *chsd ldrs: drvn 9th: sn lost pl: bhd whn p.u bef 3 out* **7/2**[1]

6m 32.9s (34.10) **Going Correction** +1.65s/f (Heavy) **7 Ran SP% 113.8**
Speed ratings (Par 105): **106,104,103,88,82** ,
CSF £31.71 CT £238.89 TOTE £6.00: £3.20, £3.40; EX 32.40 Trifecta £253.20.
Owner Mrs Doone Hulse **Bred** Robert McCarthy **Trained** Nicholashayne, Devon

FOCUS
There were divided bends. The hurdles were moved out on to fresher ground, with the rail 6yds off inside. Chute Hurdle (1st in 2m hurdle race) omitted due to the flooding earlier in week. This race distance had approximately 66yds added to it. Probably just modest form, but a step up from the winner with the second confirming the merit of his Ayr win.

5101 BETFRED "GREAT VALUE EVERYDAY" NOVICES' LIMITED H'CAP CHASE (13 fncs 2 omitted) 2m 4f
3:45 (3:46) (Class 3) 5-Y-O+ **£8,157** (£2,805)

Form RPR

115P 1 **Kilfinichen Bay (IRE)**[16] 4730 8-11-4 **138** GrahamWatters(3) 146+
(Charlie Longsdon) *j. soundly: mde all: drvn clr 3 out (normal 4 out): lft virtually alone last* **11/2**[3]

3213 2 51 **Rothman (FR)**[12] 4852 6-10-6 **123** (t) SeanBowen 86
(Paul Nicholls) *chsd wnr: pushed along 7th: drvn to chse wnr briefly 10th: lost pl bef next: t.o 2 out: lft remote 2nd last: eventually completed* **7/4**[2]

2213 F **Oscar Sunset (IRE)**[35] 4355 9-11-8 **139** PaulMoloney 135
(Evan Williams) *nt fluent in last: hdwy to trck ldng pair 4th: 2nd 8th: regained 2nd appr 3 out (normal 4 out): wknd 2 out: 10 l 2nd and wl btn whn fell heavily last* **5/6**[1]

5m 30.5s (20.70) **Going Correction** +1.30s/f (Heav) **3 Ran SP% 106.3**
Speed ratings: **110,89,**
CSF £13.56 TOTE £5.00; EX 6.30 Trifecta £8.00.
Owner Cracker Syndicate **Bred** Brian Kearney **Trained** Over Norton, Oxon

FOCUS
Divided bends. The open ditch (third-last) was omitted on both circuits - ground under repair. This is an easy race to sum up as the winner got on with things in front and comfortably saw off his two rivals. He looks like being a better chaser than hurdler.

5102 BETFRED "BE PART OF THE ACTION" H'CAP HURDLE (10 hdls) 2m 3f 207y
4:20 (4:22) (Class 4) (0-120,115) 4-Y-O+ **£4,431** (£1,309; £654; £327; £163)

Form RPR

225P 1 **Deputy Commander (IRE)**[36] 4342 7-10-12 **106** (t) JamieBargary(5) 116+
(Nigel Twiston-Davies) *trckd ldrs: led 3 out: drvn clr next: 6 l clr last: kpt up to work* **10/3**[1]

6212 2 9 **Join The Navy**[20] 4648 11-11-2 **108** KieronEdgar(3) 111
(Kate Buckett) *dropped in detached last: bhd: hdwy 6th: 5th 3 out: 3rd 2 out: 2nd bef last: hit last: kpt on same pce* **14/1**

1311 3 9 **Loves Destination**[6] 4936 5-10-7 **99** ThomasGarner(3) 92
(Chris Gordon) *j.rt: chsd ldrs: led 3rd: hdd 3 out: wknd appr last* **10/3**[1]

2222 4 11 **Good Vibration (FR)**[62] 3884 5-11-7 **110** DannyCook 91
(Sue Smith) *j.rt: chsd ldrs: drvn 7th: wknd bef 2 out* **7/2**[2]

2534 5 19 **Hollywood All Star (IRE)**[19] 4685 7-11-1 **111** ArchieBellamy(7) 73
(Graeme McPherson) *chsd ldrs whn hit 3rd: drvn 7th: sn lost pl* **16/1**

0366 6 44 **Lochnagar (GER)**[39] 4294 7-11-7 **110** AlainCawley 28
(Venetia Williams) *chsd ldrs: drvn along 5th: bhd fr 7th: sn t.o* **16/1**

00F0 7 shd **Lava Lamp (GER)**[13] 4824 9-11-9 **112** PaulMoloney 30
(Evan Williams) *in rr: drvn along 5th: j. slowly next: sn bhd: t.o after 7th* **25/1**

31P6 P **Solidago (IRE)**[11] 4863 9-9-13 **93** CiaranGethings(5)
(Barry Leavy) *chsd ldrs: drvn 7th: lost pl bef next: t.o whn p.u bef 2 out* **25/1**

4312 P **Bryden Boy (IRE)**[13] 4815 6-11-12 **115** (p) SeanQuinlan
(Jennie Candlish) *nt fluent: led: blnd 2nd: hdd next: chsd ldr wknd qckly bef 2 out: t.o whn p.u bef last* **9/2**[3]

5m 32.9s (29.70) **Going Correction** +1.65s/f (Heav) **9 Ran SP% 112.7**
Speed ratings (Par 105): **106,102,98,94,86 69,69,** ,
CSF £45.83 CT £164.16 TOTE £4.80: £1.60, £2.60, £1.70; EX 57.10 Trifecta £244.70.
Owner Imperial Racing Partnership No 7 **Bred** James And Mrs Wickham **Trained** Naunton, Gloucs

FOCUS
There were divided bends. The hurdles were moved out on to fresher ground, with the rail 6yds off inside. Chute Hurdle (1st in 2m hurdle race) omitted due to the flooding earlier in week. This race distance had approximately 50yds added to it. Just modest form, but a step up from the winner in the tongue-tie and the runner-up is in the form of his life.

5103 BETFRED "RACING'S BIGGEST SUPPORTER" H'CAP CHASE (13 fncs 2 omitted) 2m 4f
4:55 (4:55) (Class 4) (0-115,115) 5-Y-O+ **£6,279** (£1,871; £947; £485; £254)

Form RPR

-452 1 **Ratify**[31] 4436 12-11-6 **109** RobertDunne 120+
(Dai Burchell) *led after 1st to next: w ldrs: led 7th: j.rt last 2: 5 l ahd last: drvn rt out* **10/1**

3541 2 3 **Special Wells**[14] 4803 7-11-10 **113** DannyCook 119
(Sue Smith) *chsd ldrs: drvn 10th: chsd wnr fr 2 out: kpt on same pce run-in* **13/8**[1]

3U43 3 3 ¼ **Crafty Roberto**[20] 4642 8-11-8 **111** (t) NoelFehily 115
(Alex Hales) *hld up towards rr: hdwy 7th: sn chsng ldrs: 3rd 2 out: one pce* **7/1**[3]

3142 4 1 ½ **Pret A Thou (FR)**[16] 4747 13-11-8 **114** HarryChalloner(3) 116
(John Groucott) *led 3rd to 7th: outpcd appr 2 out: kpt on one pce appr last* **9/1**

61F3 5 28 **Storming Strumpet**[9] 4889 6-11-1 **109** (t) JamieBargary(5) 90
(Tom George) *hld up towards rr: hdwy 7th: chsng ldrs 8th: disputing 2nd 3 out (normal 4 out): wknd qckly bef 2 out: sn bhd: mstke last: t.o* **11/2**[2]

52F4 P **Sean Airgead (IRE)**[141] 2477 11-11-12 **115** (t) PaulMoloney
(Mark Michael McNiff, Ire) *detached in last: drvn 5th: t.o whn j.lft 8th: sn p.u* **20/1**

1220 P **Capilla (IRE)**[70] 3731 8-11-2 **112** (t) MrConorOrr(7)
(Evan Williams) *led tl after 1st: mstke 2nd: lost pl and bhd whn p.u after 8th* **7/1**[3]

11PU P **Very Live (FR)**[22] 4595 7-10-12 **101** (p) JamesBest
(Paul Webber) *chsd ldrs 3rd: sn pushed along: hit 9th: lost pl 3 out: bhd whn p.u bef next* **8/1**

5m 37.7s (27.90) **Going Correction** +1.30s/f (Heav) **8 Ran SP% 113.4**
Speed ratings: **96,94,93,92,81** , ,
CSF £27.61 CT £124.06 TOTE £12.10: £1.80, £1.40, £2.40; EX 36.40 Trifecta £180.90.
Owner J J King **Bred** Mrs R Lyon **Trained** Briery Hill, Blaenau Gwent

FOCUS
Divided bends. The open ditch (third-last) was omitted on both circuits - ground under repair. Quite a well-run modest handicap. The winner was well in on the best of his 2014 form and has been rated back to that level.

5104 BETFRED MARES' STANDARD OPEN NATIONAL HUNT FLAT RACE 1m 7f 168y
5:30 (5:31) (Class 5) 4-6-Y-O **£2,599** (£763; £381; £190)

Form RPR

1 **Ms Parfois (IRE)**[111] 5-11-0 0 DarylJacob 115+
(Anthony Honeyball) *chsd ldr: upsides after 5f: led 8f out: sn drvn: reminders 2f out: forged clr over 1f out: styd on wl* **7/4**[2]

3 2 10 **Calling Des Blins (FR)**[42] 4242 4-11-1 0 NoelFehily 106
(Harry Fry) *hld up in last: t.k.h: wnt 2nd gng wl 5f out: effrt over 2f out: rdn and fnd little over 1f out* **8/11**[1]

0 3 12 **Sidbury Fair**[35] 4364 5-10-9 0 CiaranGethings(5) 93
(Victor Dartnall) *trckd ldrs: clr 3rd over 4f out: sn drvn: one pce* **16/1**

4 55 **Omg Western Bunny (IRE)** 5-10-7 0 MrConorOrr(7) 38
(Evan Williams) *led: hdd 8f out: lost pl over 4f out: sn bhd: t.o over 2f out* **9/1**[3]

4m 15.1s (23.30) **Going Correction** +1.65s/f (Heav) **4 Ran SP% 110.1**
Speed ratings: **107,102,96,68**
CSF £3.48 TOTE £2.70; EX 3.10 Trifecta £10.60.
Owner M R Chapman **Bred** William & Daryl Deacon **Trained** Mosterton, Dorset

FOCUS
This race distance had a approximately 33yds added to it. This can't be form to take overly serious considering the amount of runners, though the winner could be alright.
T/Plt: £106.00 to a £1 stake. Pool of £70321.36 - 483.92 winning tickets. T/Qpdt: £46.80 to a £1 stake. Pool of £3966.94 - 62.60 winning tickets. **Walter Glynn**

5105 - 5108a (Foreign Racing) - See Raceform Interactive

4659 NAVAN (L-H)
Saturday, April 2

OFFICIAL GOING: Soft changing to soft to heavy after race 1 (2.25)

5109a WEBSTER CUP CHASE (GRADE 2) (14 fncs) 2m 4f
4:40 (4:41) 5-Y-O+ **£18,437** (£5,937; £2,812; £1,250; £625)

RPR

1 **Smashing (FR)**[16] 4731 7-11-10 **158** JJBurke 166+
(Henry De Bromhead, Ire) *mde virtually all: jnd briefly 3 out: sn regained ld and extended advantage u.p bef last where nt fluent: strly pressed run-in and kpt on wl in clsng stages: all out* **9/4**[2]

2 ½ **Road To Riches (IRE)**[16] 4731 9-11-12 **165** DavyRussell 168+
(Noel Meade, Ire) *settled bhd ldr in 2nd: disp briefly 3 out: pushed along in cl 2nd bef 2 out where slt mstke: sn rdn and slt mstke last: kpt on wl run-in wout matching wnr: hld* **4/5**[1]

3 ¾ **Foxrock (IRE)**[56] 4007 8-11-5 **157** (bt) APHeskin 160+
(T M Walsh, Ire) *chsd ldrs in 3rd: mstke 3 out: sn rdn and no imp on ldrs bef next: r.o wl fr last: nrst fin* **7/2**[3]

4 35 **Smokey Joe Joe (IRE)**[37] 4331 10-11-5 **128** (t) GerFox 125
(S J Mahon, Ire) *hld up towards rr: nt fluent 10th: rdn in 4th after 3 out and no imp on ldrs: lost tch next: wknd* **100/1**

5 3 ½ **Strongpoint (IRE)**[70] 3740 12-11-5 **128** AELynch 121
(S R B Crawford, Ire) *in rr thrght: j. sltly rt 1st and at times after: detached in rr whn slow 7th: no imp bef 3 out* **100/1**

5m 47.9s (7.60) **5 Ran SP% 110.5**
CSF £4.73 TOTE £3.00: £1.90, £1.02; DF 4.20 Trifecta £7.10.
Owner Ann & Alan Potts Partnership **Bred** Jacques Seror **Trained** Knockeen, Co Waterford

FOCUS
A cracking and somewhat surprising showdown between three top-notch chasers given the time of year. The gallop was relentless from the outset and the winner dug very deep to fend off all challengers, recording another personal best.

5110 - 5114a (Foreign Racing) - See Raceform Interactive

4236 ASCOT (R-H)
Sunday, April 3

OFFICIAL GOING: Good to soft (soft in places) changing to good to soft after race 1 (2.00)
Wind: Light, across Weather: Cloudy

5115 DAVID BROWNLOW CHARITABLE FOUNDATION MAIDEN HURDLE (10 hdls) 2m 3f 58y
2:00 (2:01) (Class 4) 4-Y-O+ **£5,198** (£1,526; £763; £381)

Form RPR

3620 1 **Dark Flame (IRE)**[22] 4620 7-11-2 **125** AndrewGlassonbury 119+
(Richard Rowe) *trckd ldrs: urged along fr 3 out: drvn in 4th fr 2 out tl styd on wl fr last to ld fnl strides* **8/1**

0205 2 hd **Bold Runner**[21] 4648 5-11-2 **108** (p) JamesDavies 117
(Jose Santos) *prom: trckd ldr 5th: led 7th: drvn and hrd pressed fr 2 out: hdd flat: kpt on wl nr fin* **66/1**

4324 3 shd **Midnight Cowboy**[30] 4463 5-11-2 **117** WayneHutchinson 117
(Alan King) *trckd ldrs: cl up fr 3 out: rdn to chal fr 2 out: led flat: hdd fnl strides* **9/2**[2]

5 4 3 ¾ **Firsty (IRE)**[37] 4339 5-11-2 **128** SamTwiston-Davies 113
(Paul Nicholls) *mde most to 7th: styd pressing ldr: drvn and upsides fr 2 out: stl one of three in line last: no ex fnl 150yds* **7/1**

352 5 22 **What's The Scoop (IRE)**[23] 4594 6-11-2 0 NicodeBoinville 93
(Nicky Henderson) *nt a fluent: hld up in rr: stdy prog fr 5th: trckd ldrs fr 3 out: mstke 2 out: sn rdn and fnd nil: wl btn whn nt fluent last: hung bdly lft nr fin* **10/11**[1]

3526 **6** *23* **Bim Bam Boum (FR)**[32] 4438 5-11-2 125.............................. NoelFehily 68
(Harry Fry) *hld up wl in rr: prog 6th: in tch in ldng gp after 3 out: rdn whn nt fluent 2 out: wknd qckly: sltly hmpd last* **5/1**[3]

-005 **7** *28* **Teachmetobougie**[13] 4848 6-11-2 0.............................. RhysFlint 40
(Alexandra Dunn) *a in rr: struggling after 5th: t.o fr 7th* **200/1**

0- **8** *86* **Topamichi**[78] 3060 6-11-2 0.............................. RobertDunne
(Mark H Tompkins) *prom: trckd ldr 4th to 5th: wknd rapidly and j. slowly 7th: t.o and eased bef 2 out* **66/1**

0-4 **P** **Maigh Dara (IRE)**[305] 602 7-11-2 0.............................. MarcGoldstein
(Lydia Richards) *in tch: mstke 5th: sn wknd: t.o fr 7th: p.u bef last* **125/1**

00 **F** **Bellini Dubreau (FR)**[121] 2879 5-11-2 0.............................. JamesBest
(Nigel Hawke) *t.k.h: hld up: fell 1st* **200/1**

-032 **F** **Norman The Red**[45] 4198 6-11-2 110.............................. MattieBatchelor 88
(Jamie Poulton) *prom: lost pl bef 5th: struggling in rr fr 6th: rallied u.p bef 3 out: 10 l down in 6th and wl hld whn fell heavily last* **40/1**

05 **P** **Hopefordebest (IRE)**[15] 4798 6-11-2 0.............................. DarylJacob
(Ian Williams) *pressed ldr to 4th: lost pl fr next: styd in tch to 3 out: wknd and bhd in 7th whn p.u bef 2 out* **150/1**

PU4 **P** **Tango Unchained (IRE)**[38] 4322 7-10-13 0.............................. HarryBannister[(3)]
(Charlie Mann) *mstkes: wl in rr: drvn after 6th and brief effrt next: wknd bef 3 out: wl bhd in 8th whn p.u bef 2 out* **66/1**

4m 43.4s (-1.30) **Going Correction** 0.0s/f (Good) **13** Ran SP% **120.2**
Speed ratings (Par 105): **102,101,101,100,91 81,69,33, , ,**
CSF £359.26 TOTE £11.60: £3.00, £13.30, £1.80; EX 502.20 Trifecta £3375.50.
Owner The Encore Partnership III **Bred** Thomas Connolly **Trained** Sullington, W Sussex

FOCUS
The rail on the hurdle course was positioned 8yds out from its innermost position around Swinley Bottom. This race distance was approximately 18yds further than advertised. After the opener the going was altered to good to soft. This looked a reasonable maiden for the time of year, but there wasn't a lot of pace on early and the runner-up's effort, considering his official mark, holds the level down.

5116 COUTTS JUVENILE H'CAP HURDLE (8 hdls) 1m 7f 152y
2:35 (2:35) (Class 2) 4-Y-O
£25,024 (£7,392; £3,696; £1,848; £924; £464)

Form RPR

221 **1** **Adrien Du Pont (FR)**[85] 3519 4-11-12 **139**..........(t) SamTwiston-Davies 145+
(Paul Nicholls) *racd freely: led after 2nd and sn clr: abt 10 l up fr 1/2-way: flattened 5th: rdn 2 out: stl same ld whn blnd last: kpt on: unchal* **13/8**[1]

1144 **2** *6* **Oceane (FR)**[36] 4360 4-11-5 **132**.............................. WayneHutchinson 129
(Alan King) *hld up in chsng gp: reminders after 4th: rdn and prog 2 out: kpt on to take 2nd after last: nvr nr to chal* **12/1**

132 **3** *1 1/2* **Berland (IRE)**[60] 3926 4-10-13 **126**.............................. AidanColeman 122
(John Ferguson) *in tch in chsng gp: rdn to chse clr wnr bef 2 out: no imp: lost 2nd after last: kpt on* **8/1**[3]

116 **4** *6* **St Saviour**[36] 4358 4-11-4 **131**.............................. RichardJohnson 124
(Philip Hobbs) *in tch in chsng gp: hit 3 out: sn rdn: effrt u.p to press for 2nd pl 2 out tl wknd after last* **8/1**[3]

201 **5** *1/2* **Pinkie Brown (FR)**[68] 3790 4-10-11 **124**.............................. NoelFehily 115
(Neil Mulholland) *t.k.h: hld up in chsng gp: nt fluent 3rd: rdn and nt qckn bef 2 out: no ch after* **4/1**[2]

3124 **6** *3/4* **Impulsive American**[11] 4873 4-10-5 **123**..........(p) DavidNoonan[(5)] 113
(David Pipe) *hld up in rr: effrt and rdn after 3 out: no prog 2 out: hanging and wl btn bef last* **8/1**[3]

-323 **7** *13* **Swincombe Toby**[71] 3730 4-10-4 **122**.............................. LizzieKelly[(5)] 105
(Nick Williams) *led tl after 2nd: clr of rest in 2nd pl tl 5th: lost 2nd and wknd bef 2 out: clambered over last* **12/1**

235 **8** *5* **Consortium (IRE)**[32] 3039 4-10-3 **116**.............................. TrevorWhelan 89
(Neil King) *led chsng gp to 5th: lost pl and wknd fr next* **20/1**

3 **9** *10* **La Paimpolaise (FR)**[20] 4683 4-11-1 **128**.............................. JoshuaMoore 92
(Gary Moore) *prom in chsng gp tl wknd 5th: bhd after 3 out* **33/1**

3m 43.4s (-4.00) **Going Correction** 0.0s/f (Good) **9** Ran SP% **114.5**
Speed ratings: **110,107,106,103,103 102,96,93,88**
CSF £21.45 CT £122.96 TOTE £2.30: £1.30, £3.10, £2.40; EX 26.60 Trifecta £151.00.
Owner Mrs Johnny de la Hey **Bred** Thierry Cypres **Trained** Ditcheat, Somerset

FOCUS
The rail on the hurdle course was positioned 8yds out from its innermost position around Swinley Bottom. Race distance was approximately 18yds further than advertised. A really good handicap for juveniles, won last year by Lil Rockerfella, was taken apart by the favourite and this rates a step up from him.

5117 TINDLE NEWSPAPERS NOVICES' CHASE (17 fncs) 2m 5f 8y
3:10 (3:10) (Class 3) 5-Y-O+ **£9,747** (£2,862; £1,431)

Form RPR

PP25 **1** **Twelve Roses**[19] 4701 8-11-4 138..........................(p) RichardJohnson 116+
(Kim Bailey) *j. sltly lft: trckd ldr: led 12th: gng much bttr than other pair tl shkn up and drew clr fr 2 out: drvn out after last* **4/9**[1]

-41P **2** *3 3/4* **Nexius (IRE)**[31] 4444 7-11-4 132.............................. NickScholfield 113+
(Paul Nicholls) *trckd ldr: sloppy jumping fr 8th and dropped to last: shkn up 13th: tk 2nd bef last and styd on: no real threat to wnr* **15/8**[2]

6522 **3** *5* **Veauce De Sivola (FR)**[16] 4772 7-10-12 88..........................(t) TomCannon 102
(Mark Gillard) *j. slowly 1st: led: j.lft 9th: hdd 12th: drvn upsides wnr briefly bef 2 out: sn btn: lost 2nd bef last* **33/1**[3]

5m 29.6s (3.60) **Going Correction** 0.0s/f (Good) **3** Ran SP% **107.0**
Speed ratings: **93,91,89**
CSF £1.67 TOTE £1.40; EX 1.70 Trifecta £1.40.
Owner Jones Broughtons Wilson Weaver **Bred** Coln Valley Stud **Trained** Andoversford, Gloucs

FOCUS
The rail on the chase course was positioned 2yds out on the home straight and going down the hill. Race distances was approximately 6yds further than advertised. Only two had a chance on known form, but the outsider hung in for a long time so the front pair have been rated well below their best.

5118 WAITROSE NOVICES' H'CAP CHASE (13 fncs) 2m 192y
3:45 (3:45) (Class 2) 5-Y-O+ **£25,024** (£7,392; £3,696; £1,848; £924)

Form RPR

212P **1** **Big Jim**[22] 4617 7-11-3 **123**.............................. KielanWoods 136+
(Alex Hales) *pressed ldng pair: nt fluent 4th and 5th and dropped off them: clsd again fr 9th and tk 2nd after next (4 out): led bef 2 out and sn 3 l clr: drvn and hld on wl fr last* **9/2**[2]

P-14 **2** *1 1/2* **Orbasa (FR)**[15] 4787 5-11-12 **132**..........................(t) SamTwiston-Davies 144+
(Paul Nicholls) *hld up in last pair: nt fluent 7th: prog fr next: cl up 3 out: sn rdn and nt qckn: kpt on fr 2 out but nvr able to chal* **11/10**[1]

2056 **3** *18* **Purple 'n Gold (IRE)**[15] 4785 7-11-7 **132**..........................(p) DavidNoonan[(5)] 125
(David Pipe) *pressed ldr: led 8th and sn kicked for home: drvn and hdd bef 2 out: qckly btn* **7/1**

2614 **4** *13* **All Together (FR)**[22] 4617 5-11-12 **132**.............................. JamesBest 115
(Johnny Farrelly) *led: nt fluent and lost 8th: nt fluent next: lost 2nd and wknd after 4 out: hung rt after last* **9/2**[2]

115P **5** *10* **Vikekhal (FR)**[131] 2701 7-11-5 **125**..........................(b) JoshuaMoore 101
(Gary Moore) *nt fluent: a in last pair: rdn and struggling fr 8th: sn bhd* **6/1**[3]

4m 10.5s (-4.10) **Going Correction** 0.0s/f (Good) **5** Ran SP% **110.8**
Speed ratings: **109,108,99,93,89**
CSF £10.52 TOTE £3.80: £1.60, £1.20; EX 7.10 Trifecta £30.80.
Owner Gumbrills Racing Partnership **Bred** John S C And Mrs K A Fry **Trained** Edgcote, Northamptonshire

FOCUS
The rail on the chase course was positioned 2yds out on the home straight and going down the hill. Race distance was approximately 6yds further than advertised. It probably wasn't a strong race for the level, but the first two are on the upgrade.

5119 DAVIDSTOW VETERANS' H'CAP CHASE (QUALIFIER) (LEG 5 OF THE VETERANS' CHASE SERIES) (20 fncs) 2m 7f 180y
4:20 (4:20) (Class 2) (0-150,142)
10-Y-O+
£18,768 (£5,544; £2,772; £1,386; £693; £348)

Form RPR

-146 **1** **Forgotten Gold (IRE)**[113] 3038 10-11-2 **132**.............................. PaddyBrennan 147+
(Tom George) *jumping lacked zip early on: led chsng gp: clsd 14th: led after next: clr bef 2 out: styd on strly* **13/2**[2]

0-30 **2** *8* **Mon Parrain (FR)**[17] 4735 10-11-5 **142**..........(bt) MrDavidMaxwell[(7)] 150
(Paul Nicholls) *wl plcd in chsng gp: clsd 14th: wnt 2nd 4 out: urged along and kpt on but no ch w wnr bef last* **20/1**

6U41 **3** *9* **Shotavodka (IRE)**[29] 4483 10-11-9 **139**..........................(p) ConorO'Farrell 140
(David Pipe) *hld up wl in rr: stdy prog fr 13th: disp 2nd after 3 out and looked a threat: btn 2 out: wknd bef last but hld on for 3rd* **8/1**

-322 **4** *3/4* **Foundry Square (IRE)**[31] 4444 10-10-10 **126**.............................. PeterCarberry 124
(David Evans) *wl in rr: lost tch w main gp 14th: kpt on fr 3 out: styd on fr last: nrst fin* **33/1**

PP-0 **5** *1/2* **Loch Ba (IRE)**[127] 2780 10-10-10 **126**.............................. WayneHutchinson 125
(Mick Channon) *mstkes: mostly in last: wl bhd after 14th: stl only 10th 2 out: styd on wl fr last: nrst fin* **16/1**

1634 **6** *nk* **So Fine (IRE)**[29] 4483 10-10-9 **125**..........................(p) JamesBest 125
(Philip Hobbs) *j.lft: nt gng wl and shkn up in midfield after 4th: latched on to main gp 15th: one pce after 3 out* **12/1**

P-2P **7** *8* **Court By Surprise (IRE)**[64] 3860 11-11-8 **138**.............................. DarylJacob 129
(Emma Lavelle) *wl plcd in chsng gp: in tch 14th: wknd fr next* **16/1**

4/PP **8** *4 1/2* **Si C'Etait Vrai (FR)**[32] 4436 10-10-12 **128**..........(tp) DenisO'Regan 117
(Neil Mulholland) *blnd 1st: wl in rr: lost tch w main gp 14th: brief effrt whn blnd 4 out: no ch after* **33/1**

4-4P **9** *3/4* **Creevytennant (IRE)**[92] 3448 12-11-8 **141**..........(t) ConorShoemark[(3)] 127
(Fergal O'Brien) *alternated ld w one rival and wl clr of rest tl in 2nd pl fr 10th: mstke next: lost pl 15th: kpt on and stl disputing 2nd 4 out: wknd qckly after next* **8/1**

2422 **10** *10* **Pete The Feat (IRE)**[29] 4483 12-11-3 **133**..........................(t) RichardJohnson 112
(Charlie Longsdon) *alternated ld w one rival and wl clr of rest: def advantage 10th: c bk to field and mstke 14th: mstke next and hdd: wknd qckly after 4 out* **6/1**[1]

0420 **11** *23* **Grandads Horse**[17] 4735 10-11-6 **136**..........................(p) AidanColeman 92
(Charlie Longsdon) *in tch in chsng gp: cl enough 14th: wknd next: t.o* **8/1**

500P **U** **Theatrical Star**[120] 2907 10-10-12 **133**..........................(t) PaulO'Brien[(5)]
(Colin Tizzard) *mstke and uns rdr 1st* **9/1**

-5P2 **P** **Opening Batsman (IRE)**[36] 4361 10-11-11 **141**..........(bt) NoelFehily
(Harry Fry) *hld up wl in rr: no prog 14th and bhd fr next: t.o whn p.u bef 2 out* **7/1**[3]

0P02 **U** **Ardkilly Witness (IRE)**[23] 4595 10-10-7 **130**..........(t) MissPFuller[(7)]
(Jamie Snowden) *in tch in midfield whn uns rdr 10th* **12/1**

5m 59.1s (-4.40) **Going Correction** 0.0s/f (Good) **14** Ran SP% **121.2**
Speed ratings: **107,104,101,101,100 100,98,96,96,93 85, , ,**
CSF £127.40 CT £1060.33 TOTE £7.80: £2.70, £8.00, £3.10; EX 195.00 Trifecta £1608.70.
Owner Mr & Mrs R Cornock **Bred** Patrick Hayes **Trained** Slad, Gloucs

FOCUS
The rail on the chase course was positioned 2yds out on the home straight and going down the hill. Race distance was approximately 6yds further than advertised. A competitive race of its type, run at a strong gallop thanks to a couple of known front-runners. The winner has been rated back to his best.

5120 ROYAL MAIL 500 YEARS CONDITIONAL JOCKEYS' H'CAP HURDLE (11 hdls) 2m 7f 118y
4:55 (4:56) (Class 3) (0-140,137) 4-Y-O+ **£5,848** (£1,717; £858; £429)

Form RPR

-014 **1** **Taj Badalandabad (IRE)**[43] 4246 6-11-5 **133**..........(p) MichaelHeard[(3)] 139+
(David Pipe) *hld up wl in rr: gd prog fr 7th: swept through to ld 2 out: sn rdn and idled: drvn at least 2 l clr after last: idled again and nrly jnd 75yds out: fnd ex* **6/1**[1]

514P **2** *1* **Salmanazar**[15] 4786 8-11-2 **130**.............................. TomBellamy[(3)] 133
(Alan King) *t.k.h early: a.p: drvn after 3 out keeping on but looked hld after 2 out: styd on fnl 100yds to grab 2nd last stride* **20/1**

-5PP **3** *shd* **Return Spring (IRE)**[37] 4340 9-10-8 **122**..........(b) CiaranGethings[(3)] 125
(Philip Hobbs) *led: hdd and rdn 8th: responded and led again after 3 out: hdd 2 out: looked hld but lft w ev ch as wnr idled flat: kpt on but lost 2nd last stride* **16/1**

1304 **4** *1* **Max Forte (IRE)**[31] 4442 6-11-0 **125**.............................. KieronEdgar 127
(Chris Down) *prom: drvn after 3 out: looked wl hld 2 out: kpt on again flat to take 4th nr fin* **8/1**[2]

3314 **5** *nk* **Dolores Delightful (FR)**[15] 4779 6-10-11 **125**..........(t) LizzieKelly[(3)] 127
(Nick Williams) *wl in tch: chsd ldrs fr 8th: rdn after 3 out: kpt on fr last but nvr quite able to chal* **10/1**[3]

34FP **6** *10* **The Tourard Man (IRE)**[49] 4139 10-11-0 **135**.............................. KevinDowling[(10)] 128
(Alan King) *settled towards rr: prog 7th to chse ldrs next: cl 4th after 3 out: wknd 2 out* **14/1**

411P **7** *8* **The Boss's Dream (IRE)**[36] 4354 8-11-10 **135**..........(p) KillianMoore 123
(Neil King) *chsd ldr: nt fluent 4th: lost 2nd pl 7th: styd cl up: wl there but hld whn nt fluent 2 out: wknd* **12/1**

6/12 **8** *hd* **Spencer Lea**[23] 4596 8-11-0 **125**.............................. JeremiahMcGrath 113
(Henry Oliver) *j. 1st 3 bdly: hld up in last: sme prog fr 7th: last of ten w a ch after 3 out: no hdwy after* **6/1**[1]

602P **9** *3 1/4* **Easter Day (FR)**[49] 4141 8-11-4 **137**..........................(b[1]) JordanWilliams[(8)] 120
(Paul Nicholls) *hld up midfield pl 4th and sn in rr: lost tch w ldrs after 7th: wl bhd next: modest late prog* **8/1**[2]

32P6 **10** *1* **Norse Legend**[43] 4241 5-10-13 **124** MattGriffiths 108
(Chris Gordon) *hld up wl in rr: nt fluent 4th: mstke 7th and lost tch w ldng gp: nvr on terms after* **33/1**

F11P **11** *2 ¾* **Wade Harper (IRE)**[22] 4620 6-11-1 **132** (t) GarethMalone(6) 113
(David Dennis) *prom: trckd ldr 7th: led next gng strly: hdd after 3 out: cl up but hld whn blnd 2 out: wknd rapidly* **20/1**

-30P **12** *1 ¾* **Ballyheigue Bay (IRE)**[78] 3624 9-10-13 **124** (t) ThomasGarner 102
(Chris Gordon) *trckd ldrs on inner: lost pl and rdn 7th: struggling next: wl btn 11th after 3 out* **33/1**

/PPP **13** *1* **African Gold (IRE)**[111] 3079 8-11-3 **131** (tp) JamieBargary(3) 108
(Nigel Twiston-Davies) *chsd ldrs to 6th: struggling and u.str.p 8th: sn no ch* **10/1**[3]

-103 **14** *nse* **Optimistic Bias (IRE)**[35] 4389 7-10-6 **125** PatrickCowley(8) 102
(Jonjo O'Neill) *nvr beyond midfield: lost tch w ldng gp after 7th: wl bhd 3 out* **6/1**[1]

-00F **15** *8* **Seaviper (IRE)**[15] 4801 7-10-8 **122** DanielHiskett(3) 92
(Richard Phillips) *a towards rr: lost tch after 7th: t.o* **40/1**

-634 **F** **Kingfisher Creek**[31] 4452 6-10-9 **126** (p) PaulO'Brien(6) 126
(Colin Tizzard) *hld up in last trio: pushed along and prog fr 8th: rdn after 3 out: keeping on and disputing 7th whn a ch prospects whn unsighted and fell 2 out: fatally injured* **16/1**

5m 49.2s (-6.80) **Going Correction** 0.0s/f (Good) **16** Ran SP% **127.2**
Speed ratings (Par 107): **111,110,110,110,110 106,104,104,103,102 101,101,100,100,98**
CSF £130.20 CT £1868.26 TOTE £7.30: £2.30, £4.20, £4.40, £2.40; EX 136.20 Trifecta £5449.90.
Owner W Frewen **Bred** Patrick Kelly **Trained** Nicholashayne, Devon

FOCUS
The rail on the hurdle course was positioned 8yds out from its innermost position around Swinley Bottom. Race distance was approximately 36yds further than advertised. A wide-open race run at a sound gallop and a small personal best from the winner.

5121 ROYAL ASCOT RACING CLUB OPEN HUNTERS' CHASE (17 fncs) 2m 5f 8y
5:30 (5:32) (Class 5) 5-Y-O+ £2,807 (£870; £435; £217)

Form RPR

53-2 **1** **Polisky (FR)**[170] 1948 9-11-7 121 (tp) MissBFrost(5) 124+
(Paul Nicholls) *settled in rr cajoled along fr 11th but little imp on ldng pair: clsd fr 2 out as they tired: r.o to ld flat: sn clr* **3/1**[2]

1-31 **2** *2 ½* **Penmore Mill (IRE)**[33] 4424 11-11-13 127 MrHFNugent(7) 129
(F A Hutsby) *cl up: trckd ldr 8th: upsides fr 12th tl led 3 out: sn rdn 3 l clr: idled after 2 out: hdd and no ex flat* **5/4**[1]

34-4 **3** *nk* **Flaming Gorge (IRE)**[32] 4437 11-11-5 117 (t) MrJoeHill(7) 120
(Alan Hill) *led: jnd 12th: rdn and hdd 3 out: kpt on as ldr idled and ch again last: hung lft and no ex* **8/1**

-231 **4** *1 ¼* **Nowurhurlin (IRE)**[21] 4651 9-12-1 118 MrNOrpwood(5) 128
(Mrs S J Stilgoe) *in tch: rdn and no imp on ldng pair fr 13th tl clsd fr 2 out as they tired: ch last: fdd flat* **10/3**[3]

125/ **P** **Rumbury Grey**[441] 13-11-9 117 MrRJarrett(3)
(Steve Flook) *chsd ldr to 8th: mstke 10th: sn wknd: t.o whn blnd 3 out and p.u* **33/1**

4-6P **P** **Allerton (IRE)**[15] 9-11-5 99 MissLMPinchin(7)
(Fergal O'Brien) *chsd ldrs: struggling fr 12th: wknd 3 out: t.o whn p.u bef last* **25/1**

5m 26.0s **Going Correction** 0.0s/f (Good) **6** Ran SP% **110.4**
Speed ratings: **100,99,98,98,**
CSF £7.30 TOTE £3.70: £1.90, £1.50; EX 8.50 Trifecta £34.00.
Owner Mrs Johnny de la Hey **Bred** M L Bloodstock Limited **Trained** Ditcheat, Somerset
■ Stewards' Enquiry : Mr Joe Hill two-day ban: careless riding (tbn); two-day ban: used whip above permitted level (tbn)

FOCUS
The rail on the Chase course was positioned 2yds out on the home straight and going down the hill. Race distance was approximately 6yds further than advertised. This seemed a fair race of its type, run at a respectable pace, and the winner has been rated a 128 chaser at his best.
T/Plt: £141.30 to a £1 stake. Pool: £105,717.74 - 545.85 winning tickets. T/Qpdt: £15.20 to a £1 stake. Pool: £9,230.32 - 448.40 winning tickets. **Jonathan Neesom**

4902 CARLISLE (R-H)
Sunday, April 3

OFFICIAL GOING: Good to soft (good in places in home straight on chase course) changing to good to soft after race 2 (2.45)
Wind: Light, half against Weather: Cloudy

5122 APOLLOBET HOME OF CASHBACK OFFERS CONDITIONAL JOCKEYS' H'CAP HURDLE (11 hdls) 2m 3f 61y
2:10 (2:10) (Class 4) (0-110,109) 4-Y-0+ £3,898 (£1,144; £572; £286)

Form RPR

5453 **1** **Kilronan Castle**[30] 4455 5-11-6 **106** JamesCowley(3) 120+
(Donald McCain) *pressed ldr: clr of rest 3 out: led next: clr last: rdn out* **9/2**[1]

-650 **2** *8* **Wake Your Dreams (IRE)**[63] 3884 8-11-7 **109** (p) ConorWalsh(5) 117
(Jennie Candlish) *led at reasonable gallop: clr w wnr 3 out: hdd next: kpt on same pce bef last* **9/2**[1]

6324 **3** *14* **Landmeafortune (IRE)**[23] 4581 7-10-10 **93** (p) GrahamWatters 89
(Martin Todhunter) *hld up in midfield: drvn and outpcd 1/2-way: rallied to chse clr ldng pair bef 2 out: plugged on fr last: no imp* **9/1**

4462 **4** *7* **Marcus Antonius**[23] 4583 9-11-2 **102** DerekFox(3) 90
(Lucinda Russell) *hld up: pushed along after 4 out: hdwy on outside to dispute modest 3rd pl appr 2 out: wknd fr last* **8/1**[3]

6643 **5** *47* **Solway Prince**[24] 4570 7-10-11 **97** (p) CallumBewley(3) 43
(Lisa Harrison) *in tch: drvn and outpcd after 4 out: struggling fr next: n.d after* **13/2**[2]

4332 **6** *½* **Urban Kode (IRE)**[150] 2292 8-10-12 **98** (p) GrantCockburn(3) 43
(Lucinda Russell) *trckd ldrs tl rdn and wknd after 3 out: btn next* **14/1**

5000 **7** *1* **Gabriel Oats**[52] 4064 7-10-8 **99** ArchieBellamy(8) 43
(Graeme McPherson) *in tch: hit 6th: chsd clr ldng pair 3 out to bef next: sn wknd* **20/1**

-053 **8** *1 ¾* **Bibi D'Eole (FR)**[30] 4460 5-11-5 **102** RyanHatch 45
(Graeme McPherson) *hld up: stdy hdwy 1/2-way: chsd clr ldng pair after 3 out to bef next: sn wknd* **9/2**[1]

0503 **9** *hd* **Rhythm Of Sound (IRE)**[24] 4566 6-10-5 **91** JoeColliver(3) 33
(Micky Hammond) *hld up in midfield on outside: pushed along and struggling bef 3 out: sn wknd* **16/1**

4P6P **10** *7* **Bolton Blue (IRE)**[17] 4739 7-9-12 **86** (t) ThomasDowson(5) 22
(Katie Scott) *nt fluent: hld up: struggling whn hit 4 out: sn btn* **33/1**

600F **P** **Bold Henmie (IRE)**[12] 4863 5-10-10 **93** RyanDay
(Philip Kirby) *hld up: hit 4th: struggling after 4 out: sn btn: no ch whn p.u bef last* **22/1**

4m 58.3s (-10.50) **Going Correction** -0.45s/f (Good) **11** Ran SP% **113.6**
Speed ratings (Par 105): **104,100,94,91,72 71,71,70,70,67**
CSF £23.73 CT £172.64 TOTE £4.60: £2.10, £1.90, £2.90; EX 27.20 Trifecta £344.50.
Owner P J Byrne **Bred** Miss A Baker Cresswell **Trained** Cholmondeley, Cheshire

FOCUS
Rails changes increased race distance by 36yds. A modest conditional jockeys' handicap hurdle. They went a decent gallop on ground officially described as good to soft, good in places on the Chase course in the home straight.

5123 APOLLOBET DAILY RACING REFUNDS NOVICES' CHASE (12 fncs) 1m 7f 207y
2:45 (2:45) (Class 4) 5-Y-O+ £4,548 (£1,335; £667)

Form RPR

1624 **1** **Gurkha Brave (IRE)**[182] 1782 8-10-12 120 BrianHughes 132+
(Karen McLintock) *t.k.h early: pressed ldr: chal 4 out: shkn up next: led 2 out: pushed clr fr last* **5/1**[2]

1145 **2** *10* **Red Spinner (IRE)**[16] 4770 6-11-10 142 DavidBass 137+
(Kim Bailey) *j.lft on occasions: led: hit 5 out: jnd and rdn next: hdd 2 out: edgd lft bef last: outpcd run-in* **1/6**[1]

2105 **3** *29* **Stormbay Bomber (IRE)**[116] 2976 7-10-12 101 RichieMcLernon 102
(Patrick Holmes) *trckd ldrs: drvn and outpcd bef 4 out: btn fnl 2* **25/1**[3]

4m 16.7s (0.60) **Going Correction** -0.05s/f (Good) **3** Ran SP% **106.2**
Speed ratings: **96,91,76**
CSF £6.75 TOTE £4.90; EX 6.80 Trifecta £3.30.
Owner Alan Lamont **Bred** Miss Penny Downes **Trained** Ingoe, Northumberland

FOCUS
Rails changes increased race distance by 33yds. A fairly decent little novice chase. They went a respectable gallop at best. The chase course ground description became good to soft after this race.

5124 PAULINE PHIZACKLEA MEMORIAL "NATIONAL HUNT" NOVICES' HURDLE (10 hdls) 2m 1f
3:20 (3:20) (Class 4) 4-Y-O+ £3,898 (£1,144; £572; £286)

Form RPR

1 **1** **Mister Kit**[14] 4817 8-11-2 0 TonyKelly(3) 125+
(Chris Grant) *mde virtually all: shkn up and drew clr bef 2 out: easily* **11/10**[1]

6P02 **2** *26* **Improved (IRE)**[29] 4473 6-10-10 115 AdamNicol(3) 100
(Philip Kirby) *t.k.h: pressed wnr to 2nd: rdn and outpcd 4th: rallied to chse wnr bef 2 out: sn rdn and no ex: hld whn mstke last: hung lft and no imp* **3/1**[3]

-440 **3** *4* **Move To The Groove (IRE)**[18] 4714 6-10-13 0 WillKennedy 94
(Donald McCain) *in tch: drvn and outpcd after 3 out: lft modest 3rd whn nt fluent next: no ch whn edgd lft run-in* **28/1**

040 **4** *93* **Ping (IRE)**[26] 4548 5-10-8 0 RyanDay(5) 7
(Nicky Richards) *bhd: struggling sing fnl circ: t.o* **33/1**

04-1 **P** **Miami Present (IRE)**[158] 2136 6-11-5 115 DannyCook
(Harriet Bethell) *t.k.h: cl up: wnt 2nd 2nd: chal 4th to after 3 out: wknd and p.u bef next* **5/2**[2]

4m 24.7s (-4.50) **Going Correction** -0.45s/f (Good) **5** Ran SP% **107.6**
Speed ratings (Par 105): **92,79,77,34,**
CSF £4.62 TOTE £2.30: £1.10, £2.60; EX 4.10 Trifecta £25.00.
Owner Mrs H N Eubank **Bred** A Eubank **Trained** Newton Bewley, Co Durham

FOCUS
Rails changes increased race distance by 30yds. An ordinary novice hurdle. They went a respectable gallop at best.

5125 APOLLOBET BET THROUGH YOUR MOBILE NOVICES' H'CAP CHASE (18 fncs) 2m 4f 198y
3:55 (3:58) (Class 4) (0-105,103) 5-Y-O+ £4,548 (£1,335; £667; £333)

Form RPR

600 **1** **Nortonthorpelegend (IRE)**[63] 3883 6-11-1 **92** BrianHughes 109+
(John Wade) *cl up: led gng wl 3 out: shkn up and clr next: kpt on strly* **11/1**

2533 **2** *8* **Treliver Manor (IRE)**[17] 4741 8-9-9 **79** (tp) LorcanMurtagh(7) 89
(Rose Dobbin) *hld up in tch: stdy hdwy after 5 out: rdn to chse (clr) wnr 2 out: hung rt run-in: kpt on: no imp* **11/2**[2]

6000 **3** *6* **Whatsthestoryman (IRE)**[47] 4163 8-10-13 **90** (t) SeanQuinlan 95
(Katie Scott) *cl up: led 6th: rdn whn nt fluent and hdd 3 out: kpt on same pce fr next* **20/1**

F350 **4** *2 ½* **Seven Devils (IRE)**[26] 4550 6-11-9 **100** (t) DerekFox 101
(Lucinda Russell) *in tch: effrt and rdn bef 3 out: kpt on same pce fr next* **10/1**

3-P4 **5** *19* **Tambour Major (FR)**[14] 4816 9-11-4 **95** (tp) HenryBrooke 79
(Alison Hamilton) *prom: rdn and outpcd after 3 out: wknd fr next* **9/2**[1]

650U **6** *3* **Vayland**[46] 4177 7-11-11 **102** CraigNichol 85
(Micky Hammond) *hld up towards rr: stdy hdwy 13th: rdn and wknd after 3 out* **12/1**

3-03 **7** *4 ½* **Nefyn Bay**[25] 4556 7-11-12 **103** (t) WillKennedy 81
(Donald McCain) *hld up bhd ldng gp on ins: drvn after 5 out: struggling fr next* **7/1**[3]

0-PP **8** *3 ¼* **Wildest Dreams (IRE)**[148] 2343 7-10-6 **83** PeterBuchanan 58
(Jane Walton) *bhd: struggling 1/2-way: nvr on terms* **40/1**

6526 **9** *2* **Top Cat Dj (IRE)**[74] 3679 8-9-7 **77** oh3 (v) ThomasDowson(7) 51
(Chris Grant) *led: j.lft 2nd: hdd 6th: cl up tl outpcd bef 12th: struggling fr next* **11/1**

0-PP **10** *28* **The Perfect Crime (IRE)**[28] 4504 7-10-8 **85** (p) TomO'Brien 33
(Ian Williams) *hld up towards rr: mstke 2nd: struggling fr 1/2-way: t.o* **9/1**

0005 **11** *63* **Kilmainham (IRE)**[17] 4739 8-10-13 **90** (p) BrianHarding
(Martin Todhunter) *bhd: struggling fnl circ: t.o* **22/1**

1P/2 **F** **Brae On (IRE)**[25] 4557 8-10-13 **95** JonathonBewley(5)
(George Bewley) *hld up in last pl: fell 4th* **11/2**[2]

5m 41.19s (4.19) **Going Correction** -0.05s/f (Good) **12** Ran SP% **116.4**
Speed ratings: **90,86,84,83,76 75,73,72,71,60 36,**
CSF £68.95 CT £1204.62 TOTE £10.30: £3.10, £2.70, £6.20; EX 84.60 Trifecta £1358.20.
Owner Miss Maria D Myco **Bred** Sean Gorman **Trained** Mordon, Co Durham

FOCUS
Rails changes increase race distance 42yds. A modest novice handicap chase. They went a decent gallop.

5126 APOLLOBET WEEKLY GOLF REFUNDS H'CAP CHASE (16 fncs) 2m 4f
4:30 (4:30) (Class 4) (0-120,117) 5-Y-0+ **£6,498** (£1,908; £954; £477)

Form RPR
-PU2 1 **Ghost Of A Smile (IRE)**[29] 4491 8-10-1 92........ WillKennedy 100+
(Ian Williams) *hld up in tch: pushed along 5 out: hdwy to chse clr ldng pair bef next: effrt and chsd clr ldr 2 out: chalng whn bmpd and carried lft last 100yds: rdr sn dropped reins: kpt on wl to ld cl home* 11/4[2]
2133 2 *nse* **Rear Admiral (IRE)**[58] 3972 10-11-12 117........(t) JakeGreenall 126+
(Michael Easterby) *t.k.h: trckd ldrs: wnt 2nd 5 out: 3 l clr and gng wl whn hit last: sn pushed along: drvn and drifted lft last 100yds: hdd nr fin* 7/2
52UP 3 *16* **Pay The King (IRE)**[7] 4940 9-10-3 94........ HenryBrooke 88
(Micky Hammond) *hld up in tch: rdn and outpcd 5 out: rallied 2 out: tk modest 3rd after last: no ch w first two* 3/1[3]
11F2 4 *1 1/4* **The Backup Plan (IRE)**[128] 2753 7-11-3 108........ BrianHarding 101
(Donald McCain) *racd wd: cl up: led bef 8th: pushed along whn hit and hdd 3 out: lost 2nd next: sn wknd* 5/2[1]
1P22 5 *13* **Dystonia's Revenge (IRE)**[164] 2030 11-11-4 114...... JamieHamilton[(5)] 98
(Sheena Walton) *led to bef 8th: chsd ldr to 5 out: wknd bef next: hld whn mstke last* 9/1

5m 23.2s (-4.20) **Going Correction** -0.05s/f (Good) 5 Ran SP% **112.5**
Speed ratings: **106,105,99,99,93**
CSF £12.85 TOTE £4.40: £1.70, £2.00; EX 12.30 Trifecta £38.40.
Owner S J Cox **Bred** Kevin Talbot **Trained** Portway, Worcs
■ Stewards' Enquiry : Jake Greenall three-day ban: careless riding (Apr 17-19)

FOCUS
Rails changes increase race distance 42yds. The feature race was an ordinary handicap chase. They went an even gallop.

5127 APOLLOBET ONLINE CASINO AND GAMES STANDARD OPEN NATIONAL HUNT FLAT RACE 2m 1f
5:05 (5:05) (Class 5) 4-6-Y-0 **£2,599** (£763; £381; £190)

Form RPR
1 **Robintheaulad (IRE)**[322] 5-10-9 0........(t) StevenFox[(7)] 103
(Sandy Thomson) *trckd ldrs on outside: led over 4f out: pushed clr over 1f out: idled last 100yds: pushed out towards fin* 17/2
2 *2 1/4* **Chateau Robin (IRE)** 5-11-2 0........ TomO'Brien 101
(Seamus Mullins) *in tch on outside: stdy hdwy over 4f out: rdn and sltly outpcd over 2f out: rallied to chse (clr) wnr appr fnl f: one pce last 75yds* 8/1[3]
P 3 *2 1/4* **Baracalu (FR)**[5] 5014 5-11-2 0........ BrianHughes 99
(Sandy Thomson) *t.k.h: cl up: effrt and chsd wnr over 2f out to appr fnl f: kpt on same pce* 9/1
4 *6* **Alfie's Choice (IRE)** 4-10-10 0........ DavidBass 88
(Kim Bailey) *prom: drvn and outpcd over 4f out: rallied u.p over 2f out: no imp fr over 1f out* 7/4[1]
4 5 *13* **Oscar's Prospect (IRE)**[40] 4302 4-10-3 0........ BrianHarding 69
(Jedd O'Keeffe) *t.k.h early: w ldrs to over 4f out: rdn and wknd fr over 2f out* 20/1
6 *7* **Oishin** 4-10-3 0........ ThomasDowson[(7)] 70
(Maurice Barnes) *led to over 4f out: rallied: rdn and wknd over 2f out* 50/1
2 7 *1/2* **Strike West (IRE)**[28] 4515 4-10-10 0........ HenryBrooke 69
(Micky Hammond) *t.k.h in midfield: rdn over 4f out: struggling fr 2f out* 9/1
8 *21* **Big Oaks (IRE)** 4-10-10 0........ AndrewTinkler 50
(Tim Fitzgerald) *plld hrd early: hld up: rdn and outpcd over 4f out: sn struggling: no ch fnll 2f* 11/4[2]
0 9 *17* **Kalaharry (IRE)**[154] 2216 4-10-5 0........ CallumBewley[(5)] 35
(Katie Scott) *t.k.h: hld up on outside: hung lft and struggling 5f out: sn btn* 66/1
3 10 *6* **Shantou Theatre (IRE)**[28] 4515 6-10-13 0........ ColmMcCormack[(3)] 36
(George Charlton) *hld up on ins: drvn and struggling over 4f out: sn btn* 20/1

4m 26.4s (2.80) **Going Correction** -0.45s/f (Good)
WFA 4 from 5yo+ 5lb 10 Ran SP% **117.6**
Speed ratings: **75,73,72,70,63 60,60,50,42,39**
CSF £71.74 TOTE £11.90: £2.50, £1.90, £2.10; EX 104.80 Trifecta £1304.30.
Owner Mrs A M Thomson **Bred** Martin J Dibbs **Trained** Lambden, Berwicks

FOCUS
Rails changes increased race distance by 30yds. An ordinary bumper and they went a modest gallop.
T/Plt: £1,732.00 to a £1 stake. Pool: £55,047.32 - 23.20 winning tickets. T/Qpdt: £162.40 to a £1 stake. Pool: £5,376.88 - 24.50 winning tickets. **Richard Young**

5128 - 5131a (Foreign Racing) - See Raceform Interactive

4652 LIMERICK (R-H)
Sunday, April 3

OFFICIAL GOING: Heavy

5132a HUGH MCMAHON MEMORIAL NOVICE CHASE (GRADE 2) (16 fncs) 3m
4:10 (4:10) 5-Y-0+ **£18,437** (£5,937; £2,812; £1,250)

RPR
1 **Avant Tout (FR)**[18] 4717 6-11-3 144........ RWalsh 145+
(W P Mullins, Ire) *chsd ldr in 2nd: nt fluent 6 out: travelled wl to ld appr 2 out: styd on wl run-in* 8/15[1]
2 *2* **Lord Scoundrel (IRE)**[38] 4331 7-11-6 145........ BJCooper 145
(Gordon Elliott, Ire) *chsd ldrs in 3rd: bit clsr to press for 2nd after 3 out: pressed ldr 2 out in 2nd where pckd sltly: kpt on wl run-in: no imp on wnr cl home* 5/2[2]
3 *7* **The Housekeeper (IRE)**[222] 1359 9-10-10........ SeanFlanagan 129
(David Harry Kelly, Ire) *racd in rr: rdn and no imp 2 out: kpt on same pce into 3rd at last: nvr on terms* 40/1
4 *3* **Fine Theatre (IRE)**[29] 4499 6-11-3........(bt) PaulTownend 132
(Paul Nolan, Ire) *led: pushed along after 3 out: rdn and hdd bef 2 out where dropped to 3rd: sn no ex and dropped to rr at last* 6/1[3]

7m 12.3s (37.30) 4 Ran SP% **110.5**
CSF £2.45 TOTE £1.70; DF 1.80 Trifecta £12.10.
Owner Supreme Horse Racing Club & Brett T Graham **Bred** Yves De Soultrait **Trained** Muine Beag, Co Carlow

FOCUS
Hardly a deep race for a Grade 2, but the first two are Grade 2 horses and it was a good jumping test on really tough ground.

5133a (Foreign Racing) - See Raceform Interactive

5134a KEVIN MCMANUS BOOKMAKER CHAMPION (PRO/AM) INH FLAT RACE (LISTED RACE) 2m
5:20 (5:20) 4-Y-0 **£11,305** (£3,492; £1,654; £735)

RPR
1 **Without Limites (FR)**[46] 4195 4-11-6 0........ MrFMaguire 128+
(Miss Elizabeth Doyle, Ire) *led: extended advantage over 4f out: clr home turn: nt extended* 4/6[1]
2 *49* **Finula (IRE)** 4-11-2 0........ MsKWalsh 75+
(Edward U Hales, Ire) *racd in rr: wnt remote 3rd 4f out: plugged on one pce into remote 2nd ins fnl f* 14/1[3]
3 *14* **Chalonnial (FR)**[59] 3959 4-11-6 0........ MrSClements 69+
(Harry Fry) *trckd ldr in 2nd: rdn and nt qckn w wnr 4f out: weary 2nd fr home turn: dropped to 3rd ins fnl f* 6/4[2]
4 *78* **Belarusian (IRE)** 4-11-2 0........ MrJFO'Meara
(Denis Gerard Hogan, Ire) *settled in mod 3rd: dropped to rr 4f out and sn no ex: t.o* 33/1

4m 30.6s (270.60) 4 Ran SP% **109.6**
Tote aggregates: 2015:170,422.00, 2016: 118,514.00. CSF £9.91 TOTE £1.80; DF 7.50 Trifecta £10.40.
Owner Goliath Syndicate **Bred** S C E A Domaine De Montmoreau **Trained** Crossabeg, Co Wexford

FOCUS
Very little depth to a Listed bumper where the winning lengths are pretty revealing as to the state of conditions. This was a one-horse race.
T/Jkpt: @500.60. Pool of @715.13 - 1 winning unit. T/Plt: @234.80. Pool of @27,068.37 - 80.69 winning units. **Alan Hewison**

MORLAIX (L-H)
Sunday, April 3

OFFICIAL GOING: Turf: heavy

5135a PRIX DE PLOUESCAT (CHASE) (CONDITIONS) (5YO) (TURF) 2m 1f 110y
2:00 (12:00) 5-Y-0 **£4,588** (£2,294; £1,338; £908; £430)

RPR
1 **Saint Lino (FR)**[35] 4401 5-10-8 0........ StephanePaillard
(Nick Williams) 11/10[1]
2 *20* **Jemaben (FR)** 5-10-8 0........ KevinGuignon
(Christian Le Galliard, France)
3 *4* **Mister Du Mene (FR)**[230] 5-10-3 0........ CelineCrouzet[(5)]
(B Lefevre, France)
4 *7* **Whip Dancer (FR)**[64] 3876 5-10-8 0........ PACarberry
(Louisa Carberry, France)
5 *15* **Burmese Temple (FR)**[148] 2362 5-10-8 0........(p) JordanDuchene
(Patrice Quinton, France)
6 *dist* **Miss Protektor (FR)** 5-9-13 0........(b) ChristopherCouillaud[(4)]
(B Letourneux, France)
P **Dream's Burg (FR)**[406] 5-9-13 0........ RichardLeStang[(4)]
(X-L Le Stang, France)
P **Gwaien (FR)**[130] 5-10-3 0........ OlivierAuge
(L Viel, France)
F **Blague D'Oudairies (FR)** 5-10-3 0........ AlbanDesvaux
(J Follain, France)
P **Bine Des Salines (FR)** 5-10-3 0........ AnthonyGouard
(J Follain, France)

Owner French Gold **Bred** Ecurie Manuel Garcia **Trained** George Nympton, Devon
WIN (incl. 1 euro stake): 2.10. PLACES: 1.80, 3.20, 1.70. SF: 14.90

5136a PRIX LOUIS CRENN (CHASE) (CLAIMER) (5YO+) (TURF) 2m 3f 110y
3:00 (12:00) 5-Y-0+ **£3,882** (£1,941; £1,132; £768; £363)

RPR
1 **Twister Klass (FR)**[1025] 9-10-3 0........(b) YoannBriant[(9)]
(S Gouyette, France) 47/1
2 *3* **Starimperial (FR)**[179] 9-10-3 0........ KeneganDeniel[(9)]
(S Foucher, France)
3 *8* **Black Pearl Tavel (FR)**[145] 5-10-3 0........ SimonCossart[(9)]
(Jerome Zuliani, France)
4 *5 1/2* **Cadouma (FR)** 10-9-13 0........ GeoffreyDumont[(9)]
(P Mehat, France)
5 *1/2* **Blootender (FR)**[15] 9-10-3 0........ RichardLeStang[(9)]
(X-L Le Stang, France)
6 *dist* **Brise Coeur (FR)**[14] 4825 5-10-8 0........ StephanePaillard
(Nick Williams)
P **Eclair Gris (FR)**[35] 4400 7-10-8 0........(p) ChristopherCouillaud[(9)]
(Y Fertillet, France)
P **Alibaba Precieux (FR)**[341] 6-10-12 0........(p) AlbanDesvaux
(Mme M Desvaux, France)
P **Biskoazh (FR)**[357] 5-9-13 0........ CelineCrouzet[(9)]
(B Lefevre, France)
P **Swing Folish (FR)** 7-10-8 0........ AnthonyGouard[(9)]
(P Mehat, France)

PARI-MUTUEL (all including 1 euro stake): WIN 47.90 PLACE 9.60, 2.10, 3.20 SF 40.00
Owner Rene Guillerm **Bred** Mme B Nicco **Trained** France

4874 WARWICK (L-H)
Monday, April 4

OFFICIAL GOING: Soft (good to soft in places on chase course; chs 6.0, hdl 5.8)
Wind: Light behind Weather: Showers

5137 APOLLOBET BEST ODDS GUARANTEED MAIDEN HURDLE (11 hdls) 2m 5f
2:00 (2:00) (Class 5) 4-Y-0+ **£2,274** (£667; £333; £166)

Form RPR
-0F5 1 **Beggars Cross (IRE)**[31] 4463 6-11-0 0........ WillKennedy 120+
(Jonjo O'Neill) *a.p: led appr 2 out: clr whn blnd last: comf* 11/1

3-00 **2** *10* **Wicked Willy (IRE)**[15] 4827 5-10-7 0 MrZBaker(7) 107
(Nigel Twiston-Davies) *chsd ldrs: led appr 7th: mstke 3 out: rdn and hdd bef next: styd on same pce* **25/1**

-323 **3** *12* **Bacchanel (FR)**[37] 4357 5-11-0 0 RichardJohnson 98+
(Philip Hobbs) *hld up in tch: mstke 7th and next: sn rdn: wknd 3 out: wnt 3rd last* **15/8**[1]

-34P **4** *1 1/4* **Buttercup (FR)**[30] 4471 5-10-7 120 RobertDunne 87
(Venetia Williams) *chsd ldrs: ev ch 3 out: sn rdn: wkng whn mstke next* **13/2**

-4 **5** *43* **Denboy (IRE)**[174] 1895 6-11-0 0 (t) MichealNolan 50
(Jamie Snowden) *hld up: rdn appr 7th: wknd next* **10/1**

4 **6** *2 3/4* **Mercian King (IRE)**[73] 3725 5-11-0 116 (p) AidanColeman 47
(Charlie Longsdon) *led to 4th: remained handy tl rdn and wknd after 8th* **4/1**[2]

P **Opera Buff**[12] 7-11-0 0 (p) JamesDavies
(Jose Santos) *prom: rdn appr 7th: wknd next: bhd whn p.u bef 2 out* **50/1**

0 **P** **Restless Rebel**[70] 3775 7-11-0 0 WayneHutchinson
(Polly Gundry) *hld up: nt fluent 5th: rdn and wknd appr 7th: bhd whn p.u bef 2 out* **66/1**

P **Sail With Sultana**[20] 5-10-4 0 RyanHatch(3)
(Mark Rimell) *mid-div: nt fluent and lost pl 3rd: wknd appr 7th: bhd whn p.u bef 2 out* **100/1**

3624 **P** **Nobel Leader (IRE)**[22] 4639 6-11-0 0 (p) LeightonAspell
(James Evans) *chsd ldr tl led 4th: hdd appr 7th: wknd after next: bhd whn p.u bef 2 out* **6/1**[3]

-P03 **P** **Colmers Hill**[33] 4439 6-11-0 0 MattGriffiths
(Jeremy Scott) *hld up and a in rr: wknd after 6th: bhd whn p.u bef 2 out* **20/1**

00 **U** **Canton Massini**[40] 4309 5-11-0 0 CharliePoste
(John Holt) *hld up: rdn and wkng whn tried to refuse and uns rdr 7th* **200/1**

5m 21.7s (0.70) **Going Correction** +0.225s/f (Yiel) **12 Ran SP% 113.4**
Speed ratings (Par 103): **107,103,98,98,81 80,,,,**
CSF £233.57 TOTE £11.80: £3.10, £6.90, £1.20; EX 263.00 Trifecta £2235.30.
Owner Trevor Hemmings **Bred** Martin Donnellan **Trained** Cheltenham, Gloucs

FOCUS
All starts have been moved at this track following remeasuring, so there will be no speed figures here until there is sufficient data to calculate updated median times. The hurdle and bumper races were run on the inner hurdles course at standard distances. The Chase course rail was out by approx 12yds on the home turn. Richard Johnson described the ground as a mix of "soft and good to soft." They were on the stretch a fair way out in this ordinary maiden hurdle and only half the field finished. A big step up from the winner.

5138 APOLLOBET CASINO FREE £10 NOVICES H'CAP CHASE (18 fncs) 3m
2:30 (2:30) (Class 4) (0-105,101) 5-Y-0+ £3,768 (£1,106; £553; £276)

Form RPR

-6PU **1** **Maybe Plenty**[88] 3501 7-11-4 98 (p) CiaranGethings(5) 112+
(Giles Smyly) *a.p: chsd ldr 5th: led 10th: rdn clr appr 2 out* **8/1**

5051 **2** *7* **Midnight Jade (IRE)**[36] 4387 7-10-10 85 LeeEdwards 94
(John Groucott) *led: mstke 7th: hdd 10th: chsd wnr: ev ch whn mstke 4 out: sn rdn: styd on same pce fr 2 out* **9/2**[2]

0/25 **3** *10* **Sacre Malta (FR)**[18] 4747 10-11-1 97 ConorWalsh(7) 95
(Dominic Ffrench Davis) *hld up: hdwy 12th: rdn after 3 out: wknd last* **12/1**

250- **4** *6* **Broome Lane**[29] 7-10-7 82 RichardJohnson 73
(Tim Vaughan) *prom to 12th* **9/2**[2]

33P0 **5** *8* **Mrsrobin (IRE)**[13] 4859 6-11-11 100 (v[1]) AidanColeman 88+
(Emma Lavelle) *chsd ldrs: lost pl after 7th: rallied 9th: hit 13th: sn rdn: wknd next* **20/1**

-PP0 **P** **Vintage Vixon (IRE)**[16] 4804 9-9-11 75 oh3 (p) BenPoste(3)
(Adrian Wintle) *bhd whn nt fluent 1st: lost tch fr next: bhd whn p.u bef 11th* **50/1**

4222 **P** **Glendermot (IRE)**[38] 4346 7-11-6 95 DannyCook
(Paul Cowley) *hld up: hdwy and hit 10th: rdn and wknd 12th: bhd whn p.u bef 2 out* **2/1**[1]

P113 **P** **Some Finish (IRE)**[24] 4591 7-11-7 96 (v) CharliePoste
(Robin Dickin) *chsd ldr to 5th: remained handy: drvn and lost pl 10th: rallied appr 12th: wknd next: bhd whn j. slowly 3 out: p.u bef next* **5/1**[3]

6m 33.7s (-0.30) **Going Correction** +0.05s/f (Yiel) **8 Ran SP% 111.9**
Speed ratings: **102,99,96,94,91 ,,**
CSF £42.51 CT £425.91 TOTE £8.90: £2.60, £1.20, £3.20; EX 39.70 Trifecta £347.40.
Owner Nick Sutton & Adam Waugh **Bred** Adam Waugh **Trained** Wormington, Worcs

FOCUS
This was run over 62yds further than advertised. The rain had set in quite heavily prior to this race, a moderate handicap chase in which they finished strung out. The winner has been rated in line with the best of her hurlde form.

5139 LISTERS AUDI NOVICES' H'CAP HURDLE (8 hdls) 2m
3:00 (3:01) (Class 3) (0-130,123) 4-Y-0+ £6,498 (£1,908; £954; £477)

Form RPR

3100 **1** **Draytonian (IRE)**[37] 4366 6-11-11 122 RichardJohnson 134+
(Philip Hobbs) *hld up: hdwy 3 out: led appr last: drvn out* **8/1**

0210 **2** *3 3/4* **Clayton**[23] 4622 7-11-11 122 (t) JoshuaMoore 130+
(Gary Moore) *chsd ldr tl led after 3 out: mstke next: rdn and hdd bef last: styd on same pce* **5/1**[3]

3120 **3** *10* **Bold Duke**[9] 4913 8-11-3 117 BenPoste(3) 115
(Edward Bevan) *chsd ldrs: drvn along 5th: wkng whn j.lft last* **16/1**

115F **4** *7* **Pemba (FR)**[2] 5095 4-11-3 120 WayneHutchinson 104
(Alan King) *hld up: rdn 5th: hdwy next: rdn and wknd bef 2 out* **10/1**

2120 **5** *2 3/4* **Robin Of Locksley (IRE)**[23] 4620 6-11-12 123 RobertDunne 112
(Dan Skelton) *led: rdn and hdd after 3 out: wknd bef next* **7/2**[1]

2351 **6** *12* **Gin And Tonic**[7] 4970 6-10-11 108 7ex JackQuinlan 83
(Michael Wigham) *hld up: hdwy 3 out: sn rdn and wknd* **8/1**

0243 **7** *16* **Eddiemaurice (IRE)**[32] 4447 5-10-13 110 (b[1]) RhysFlint 69
(John Flint) *hld up: hdwy 4th: rdn and wknd after 3 out* **14/1**

3145 **P** **Template (IRE)**[43] 4273 5-11-12 123 (p) NoelFehily
(Harry Fry) *hld up: mstke 1st: nt fluent 3rd: rdn and wknd bef next: bhd whn p.u bef 2 out* **20/1**

0331 **P** **Instant Karma (IRE)**[17] 4774 5-11-6 122 JackSherwood(5)
(Michael Bell) *hld up: hdwy appr 4th: rdn and wknd after next: bhd whn p.u bef 2 out* **9/2**[2]

04 **P** **Distant Rain (IRE)**[23] 4613 6-10-7 104 JamesDavies
(Henry Oliver) *chsd ldrs: nt fluent 2nd: rdn and wknd 4th: bhd whn p.u bef 2 out* **10/1**

3m 59.5s (0.50) **Going Correction** +0.225s/f (Yiel)
WFA 4 from 5yo+ 5lb **10 Ran SP% 114.8**
Speed ratings (Par 107): **107,105,100,96,95 89,81,,,**
CSF £47.63 CT £626.89 TOTE £6.30: £2.70, £2.20, £3.80; EX 47.70 Trifecta £651.30.

Owner Mrs Diana L Whateley **Bred** Mrs C J Berry **Trained** Withycombe, Somerset

FOCUS
This competitive novice handicap was a strongly run affair and a proper test. A step up from the first two, and there's a case for rating the race 5lb higher through the third and fourth.

5140 APOLLOBET CASHBACK IF YOU FINISH 2ND "CONFINED" H'CAP CHASE (18 fncs) 3m
3:30 (3:30) (Class 3) (0-130,129) 5-Y-0+ £6,498 (£1,908; £954; £477)

Form RPR

3624 **1** **Beeves (IRE)**[49] 4155 9-11-11 128 (v) SeanQuinlan 138+
(Jennie Candlish) *plld hrd and prom: led appr 2nd: rdn clr whn nt fluent 2 out: eased flat* **7/2**[2]

U222 **2** *4* **Dawson City**[23] 4621 7-11-12 129 AndrewThornton 132+
(Polly Gundry) *chsd ldrs: lost pl 3rd: mstke 7th: pushed along after next: rdn and outpcd bef 12th: r.o u.p flat* **13/8**[1]

4633 **3** *13* **Drumshambo (USA)**[32] 4444 10-10-9 112 RobertDunne 101
(Venetia Williams) *chsd ldrs: rdn after 12th: wknd 14th* **13/2**

S5P3 **4** *2 1/4* **Shangani (USA)**[23] 4625 10-11-4 121 (bt) AidanColeman 108
(Venetia Williams) *s.i.s: hdwy after 2nd: chsd ldr 5th to 12th: rdn and wknd after 3 out* **6/1**

2256 **P** **St Johns Point (IRE)**[16] 4780 8-11-0 117 (p) RichardJohnson
(Charlie Longsdon) *led tl appr 2nd: led 13th: hdd bef 15th: rdn and wknd after 3 out: bhd whn p.u bef next* **4/1**[3]

6m 37.0s (3.00) **Going Correction** +0.325s/f (Yiel) **5 Ran SP% 107.9**
Speed ratings: **108,106,102,101,**
CSF £9.60 TOTE £4.20: £1.70, £1.50; EX 4.80 Trifecta £40.00.
Owner Paul & Clare Rooney **Bred** Donal O'Brien **Trained** Basford Green, Staffs

FOCUS
This took plenty of getting. Due to rail movements it was run over a distance 62yds further than advertised. The cosy winner was well in on the best of his novice form and has been rated back to that level.

5141 APOLLOBET CASHBACK SPECIALS H'CAP HURDLE (12 hdls) 3m 1f
4:00 (4:00) (Class 3) (0-130,130) 4-Y-0+ £6,498 (£1,908; £954; £477)

Form RPR

2144 **1** **Mustmeetalady (IRE)**[139] 2558 6-11-8 126 NoelFehily 131+
(Jonjo O'Neill) *hld up: hdwy after 7th: jnd ldrs appr 2 out: rdn to ld last: edgd rt flat: styd on u.p* **8/1**

105P **2** *1* **Atlantic Gold (IRE)**[17] 4766 6-11-12 130 AidanColeman 134
(Charlie Longsdon) *led: nt fluent 7th: rdn appr 2 out: hdd last: styd on same towards fin* **6/1**

5251 **3** *2 3/4* **You Say What (IRE)**[27] 4544 6-11-12 130 TrevorWhelan 131
(Neil King) *chsd ldrs: wnt 2nd 8th: ev ch 2 out: sn rdn: no ex flat* **3/1**[1]

/002 **4** *9* **Ballyrock (IRE)**[23] 4618 10-11-6 124 (t) RichardJohnson 116
(Tim Vaughan) *hld up: hdwy after 7th: lost pl bef next: rallied appr 3 out: sn rdn and wknd* **7/2**[2]

5611 **5** *17* **Touch Back (IRE)**[16] 4794 10-11-3 128 MrTommieMO'Brien(7) 106
(Chris Bealby) *prom: mstke 1st: lost pl 3rd: hdwy after 7th: rdn and wknd 3 out* **11/2**[3]

1P20 **6** *13* **Decimus (IRE)**[44] 4241 9-11-4 122 MattGriffiths 85
(Jeremy Scott) *hld up: hdwy after 7th: rdn and wknd after next* **25/1**

3034 **7** *1 3/4* **Sybarite (FR)**[44] 4241 10-11-2 123 (p) RyanHatch(3) 85
(Nigel Twiston-Davies) *hld up: hdwy 4th: nt fluent next: sn lost pl and drvn: bhd after next* **6/1**

3110 **8** *1 1/4* **Extreme Impact**[23] 4618 10-10-11 115 (v) KielanWoods 75
(Graeme McPherson) *rdn to chse ldr and mstke 1st: drvn along appr 7th: wknd next* **14/1**

6m 31.1s (391.10) **8 Ran SP% 112.8**
CSF £53.35 CT £175.93 TOTE £7.20: £2.50, £1.70, £1.90; EX 50.90 Trifecta £143.80.
Owner Ms Diane Carr **Bred** Clongiffin Stud **Trained** Cheltenham, Gloucs

FOCUS
This handicap was another race that proved a thorough test and the principals came clear. Sound form. Small steps up from the first two.

5142 APOLLOBET MASTERS GOLF H'CAP CHASE (12 fncs) 2m
4:30 (4:30) (Class 4) (0-110,107) 5-Y-0+ £3,898 (£1,144; £572; £286)

Form RPR

6323 **1** **Modeligo (IRE)**[38] 4346 7-10-13 94 (t) CharliePoste 109+
(Matt Sheppard) *chsd ldrs: wnt 2nd 8th: mstke next: led 3 out: sn pushed clr: eased nr fin* **13/8**[1]

56P3 **2** *4 1/2* **Too Scoops (IRE)**[32] 4453 9-11-11 106 (tp) ConorO'Farrell 108
(Richard Woollacott) *disp ld tl wnt on 6th: hdd 3 out: rrdn and hung lft bef next: styd on same pce* **3/1**[3]

2PPU **3** *17* **Bobble Boru (IRE)**[11] 4889 8-11-2 100 (p) CallumWhillans(3) 87
(Venetia Williams) *disp ld to 6th: sn rdn: wknd 3 out* **5/1**

2242 **4** *11* **Take The Crown**[24] 4587 7-11-7 102 (t) JamesDavies 76
(Henry Oliver) *prom to 7th* **11/4**[2]

4m 17.5s (7.50) **Going Correction** +0.60s/f (Soft) **4 Ran SP% 106.4**
Speed ratings: **105,102,94,88**
CSF £6.51 TOTE £2.60; EX 6.70 Trifecta £19.10.
Owner Simon Gegg **Bred** Edward And Joseph McCormack **Trained** Eastnor, H'fords

FOCUS
A moderate little handicap. This was run over 31yds further than advertised. A big step up from the winner, with the second to the level of his latest run.

5143 APOLLOBET FREE DOWNLOAD APP MAIDEN OPEN NATIONAL HUNT FLAT RACE (DIV I) 2m
5:00 (5:00) (Class 6) 4-6-Y-0 £1,624 (£477; £238; £119)

Form RPR

1 **Aintree My Dream (FR)**[64] 6-11-2 0 (t) RobertDunne 125+
(Dan Skelton) *a.p: chsd ldr over 6f out: led over 3f out: rdn out* **6/1**

42 **2** *1 1/2* **Misterton**[41] 4296 5-11-2 0 NoelFehily 122+
(Harry Fry) *hld up: hdwy over 4f out: rdn over 2f out: chsd wnr over 1f out: styd on* **5/1**

2 **3** *13* **River Of Intrigue (IRE)**[46] 4201 6-10-6 0 AlanDoyle(10) 109
(Nicky Henderson) *chsd ldrs: rdn over 2f out: wknd over 1f out* **9/2**[3]

4 **4** *nk* **Azzerti (FR)**[37] 4364 4-10-10 0 WayneHutchinson 103+
(Alan King) *hld up: hdwy over 4f out: chsd wnr over 2f out tl rdn over 1f out: wknd fnl f* **3/1**[1]

3 **5** *14* **Eamon An Cnoic (IRE)**[15] 4827 5-11-2 0 ConorO'Farrell 97
(David Pipe) *led and sn clr: c bk to the field 1/2-way: rdn and hdd over 3f out: wknd 2f out* **4/1**[2]

-0 **6** *9* **Tonganui (IRE)**[339] 67 5-11-2 0 AidanColeman 86
(Harry Fry) *hld up: rdn and wknd over 3f out* **28/1**

The Form Book Jumps 2015-16, Raceform Ltd, Newbury, RG14 5SJ

7 1 ½ **Templehills (IRE)**[37] 5-10-9 0....................[1] MrJJSlevin(7) 84
(Nigel Twiston-Davies) *hld up: hdwy over 5f out: rdn and wknd over 3f out* **14/1**

30 8 28 **Crazy Penguin (IRE)**[135] 2636 5-11-2 0....................(p) RichardJohnson 56
(Charlie Longsdon) *prom tl rdn and wknd over 5f out* **8/1**

9 99 **Baile Sheain (IRE)** 6-10-13 0.................... RyanHatch(3)
(Roy Brotherton) *hld up: wknd over 7f out* **100/1**

3m 57.7s (12.30) **Going Correction** +0.975s/f (Soft)
WFA 4 from 5yo+ 5lb 9 Ran SP% **116.4**
Speed ratings: **108,107,100,100,93 89,88,74,24**
CSF £36.34 TOTE £7.60: £2.50, £2.20, £1.80; EX 35.90 Trifecta £162.50.
Owner Malcolm Olden **Bred** Anne-Sophie Orriere & Didier Veillon **Trained** Alcester, Warwicks

FOCUS
Probably not a bad bumper in which two pulled well clear. The winner looks a smart prospect, while the third, fourth and fifth give the form a solid look, backed up by an okay time.

5144 APOLLOBET FREE DOWNLOAD APP MAIDEN OPEN NATIONAL HUNT FLAT RACE (DIV II) 2m

5:30 (5:30) (Class 6) 4-6-Y-O **£1,624** (£477; £238; £119)

Form RPR

22 1 **Crank Em Up (IRE)**[36] 4385 5-11-2 0.................... NoelFehily 114
(David Dennis) *mde all: rdn over 1f out: styd on wl* **9/2**[3]

2 2 1 ¾ **Nightfly**[38] 4350 5-10-9 0.................... AidanColeman 105
(Charlie Longsdon) *trckd ldr: rdn over 2f out: chsd wnr over 1f out: no imp ins fnl f* **11/10**[1]

3 10 **Longtown (IRE)** 5-11-2 0.................... RichardJohnson 102
(Philip Hobbs) *hld up: hdwy over 10f out: chsd wnr 3f out tl rdn over 1f out: wknd fnl f* **9/2**[3]

4 3 ¾ **Call Me Ben (IRE)**[317] 6-11-2 0.................... LeightonAspell 98
(James Evans) *chsd wnr tl rdn 3f out: wknd 2f out* **4/1**[2]

34 5 7 **Miss Yeats (IRE)**[53] 4075 5-10-9 0.................... JoshuaMoore 84
(Laura Mongan) *prom: rdn over 3f out: wknd over 2f out* **16/1**

6 6 25 **Silent Doctor (IRE)**[88] 3502 6-11-2 0.................... JamesBanks 66
(Roy Brotherton) *hld up: hdwy 11f out: rdn over 7f out: wknd over 4f out* **100/1**

7 3 ½ **Rien Du Tout (IRE)** 4-10-10 0.................... KielanWoods 57
(Mark Wall) *hld up: rdn and wknd 5f out* **50/1**

4m 5.2s (19.80) **Going Correction** +0.975s/f (Soft)
WFA 4 from 5yo+ 5lb 7 Ran SP% **112.8**
Speed ratings: **89,88,83,81,77 65,63**
CSF £9.59 TOTE £5.00: £2.20, £1.30; EX 12.50 Trifecta £41.30.
Owner Favourites Racing Ltd **Bred** Spencer Hawkins **Trained** Hanley Swan, Worcestershire

FOCUS
They went steadily in this second division of the bumper and two useful prospects dominated the finish. A step up from the winner, with the second setting the level.
T/Plt: £197.30 to a £1 stake. Pool: £81,562.38 - 301.66 winning units. T/Qpdt: £24.00 to a £1 stake. Pool: £6,801.28 - 209.10 winning units. **Colin Roberts**

4435 WINCANTON (R-H)

Monday, April 4

OFFICIAL GOING: Good (good to soft in places) changing to soft after race 3 (3.10)
Wind: mild breeze across Weather: rain, heavy at times

5145 TOM PERRETT 60TH BIRTHDAY MARES' NOVICES' HURDLE (11 hdls) 2m 5f 82y

2:10 (2:10) (Class 4) 4-Y-O+ **£3,249** (£954; £477; £238)

Form RPR

-222 1 **Via Volupta**[139] 2561 6-10-12 117.................... GavinSheehan 112+
(Warren Greatrex) *disp ld most of way tl clr ldr appr 2 out where wnt bdly lft: hdd between last 2: rallied gamely run-in to ld fnl 120yds: rdn out* **Evs**[2]

3120 2 ½ **Awesome Rosie**[18] 4734 5-11-2 118.................... TomBellamy(3) 119+
(Alan King) *trckd ldrs: carried lft 2 out: led between last 2: drvn after last: hdd fnl 120yds: no ex nring fin* **10/11**[1]

F/ 3 20 **Ziggerson Hill**[22] 9-10-12 0.................... JamesBest 94
(Jackie Du Plessis) *disp ld most of way tl rdn appr 2 out: wknd between last 2* **25/1**[3]

6 4 22 **Up Till Midnight**[38] 4350 7-10-12 0.................... MarcGoldstein 74
(Lydia Richards) *trckd ldrs: rdn after 3 out: sn wknd: t.o* **33/1**

P **Caniver Queen (IRE)**[172] 1934 6-10-12 0.................... LiamHeard
(Brian Barr) *hld up in last pair: struggling 8th: sn wknd: t.o whn p.u bef 2 out* **250/1**

000P P **Piccomore**[13] 4854 6-10-9 0....................(t) ConorShoemark(3)
(Polly Gundry) *hld up in last pair: stmbld 6th: sn struggling: wknd after next: tailing off whn p.u bef 8th* **250/1**

5m 30.0s (3.50) **Going Correction** +0.125s/f (Yiel) 6 Ran SP% **110.0**
Speed ratings (Par 105): **98,97,80,81,**
CSF £2.22 TOTE £2.10: £1.30, £1.10; EX 2.70 Trifecta £4.00.
Owner Equis **Bred** Mill House Stud (shropshire) Ltd **Trained** Upper Lambourn, Berks

FOCUS
Both courses had been moved in and they were racing on ground that hadn't been used since November. This was run over 18yds further than advertised. There was standing water on the track but the going was still initially given as good to soft, good in places. Gavin Sheehan called it "loose, winter good to soft." Only two of these mattered and they duly drew a long way clear. The first two have been rated to their marks.

5146 JIM MORGAN & RONNIE STEVENS MEMORIAL H'CAP HURDLE (11 hdls) 2m 5f 82y

2:40 (2:40) (Class 3) (0-125,125) 4-Y-O+ **£5,523** (£1,621; £810; £405)

Form RPR

3-42 1 **Fortunate George (IRE)**[14] 4848 6-11-3 116.................... DarylJacob 123+
(Emma Lavelle) *trckd ldrs: nudged along after 8th: hdwy appr 2 out: shkn up to ld last: styd on wl* **6/1**

-4P0 2 4 **Blue Atlantic (USA)**[37] 4362 5-11-9 122....................(p) GavinSheehan 126
(Warren Greatrex) *trckd ldrs: rdn after 3 out: styd on between last 2: wnt 2nd nring fin* **25/1**

P532 3 ½ **Batavir (FR)**[15] 4824 7-11-7 125....................(bt) MichaelHeard(5) 128
(David Pipe) *prom: led 7th: rdn after 2 out: hdd last: no ex* **5/2**[1]

2262 4 9 **Present Man (IRE)**[14] 4853 6-11-7 120....................(bt[1]) SamTwiston-Davies 117
(Paul Nicholls) *led: j.rt and hdd 7th: rdn after 3 out: styd on same pce fr next* **4/1**[3]

0351 5 10 **Who's Micky Brown (IRE)**[7] 4972 6-10-11 110 7ex.....(p) DenisO'Regan 98
(Neil Mulholland) *last and nudged along tl tk clsr order 5th: in tch: rdn after 3 out: styd on same pce fr next: nvr threatened* **7/2**[2]

-6F3 6 3 ½ **Kazlian (FR)**[21] 4685 8-11-8 121....................(p) AlainCawley 105
(Johnny Farrelly) *trckd ldrs: rdn after 3 out: wknd bef last* **16/1**

-F36 7 6 **Degooch (IRE)**[65] 3855 7-10-13 117....................(p) DavidNoonan(5) 95
(Johnny Farrelly) *in tch: rdn after 3 out: wknd bef last* **9/1**

1521 8 43 **Howaboutnever (IRE)**[30] 4482 8-11-4 124....................(p) HarryTeal(7) 63
(Roger Teal) *in tch: struggling in detached last 6th: t.o fr 3 out* **14/1**

6000 9 8 **Byron Blue (IRE)**[112] 3078 7-11-4 117.................... TomCannon 48
(Mark Gillard) *in last pair most of way: lost tch 3 out: t.o* **40/1**

5m 25.3s (-1.20) **Going Correction** +0.125s/f (Yiel) 9 Ran SP% **113.9**
Speed ratings (Par 107): **107,105,105,101,98 96,94,78,75**
CSF £124.36 CT £467.70 TOTE £7.10: £1.90, £5.00, £1.40; EX 128.40 Trifecta £815.90.
Owner The George Inn Racing Syndicate **Bred** Hugh Hazzard **Trained** Hatherden, Hants

FOCUS
Race run over 18yds further than advertised. The rain had really kicked in by this point. Modest handicap form but an improving winner. The first two are on the upgrade and there's a case for rating the race a couple of pounds higher through the third and fourth.

5147 APOLLOBET CASHBACK IF YOU FINISH 2ND H'CAP CHASE (17 fncs) 2m 4f 35y

3:10 (3:10) (Class 3) (0-125,124) 5-Y-O+ **£6,498** (£1,908; £954; £477)

Form RPR

3001 1 **Native Robin (IRE)**[66] 3834 6-10-12 110.................... NickScholfield 120
(Jeremy Scott) *trckd ldr tl 8th: cl up: led bef 3 out: sn rdn: narrowly hdd last: styd on: won on nod* **9/2**[3]

4032 2 nse **Ballinvarrig (IRE)**[24] 4584 9-11-8 120....................(b[1]) PaddyBrennan 132+
(Tom George) *trckd ldrs: hit 3rd: chal after 3 out: rdn to take narrow ld at the last: styd on: lost on nod* **11/4**[1]

PF34 3 8 **Sidbury Hill**[27] 4542 8-10-6 109.................... KevinJones(5) 114
(Seamus Mullins) *trckd ldrs: rdn after 11th: led after 13th: hdd appr 3 out: styd on same pce* **3/1**[2]

51-0 4 2 ¾ **Casino Markets (IRE)**[16] 4785 8-11-0 112.................... DarylJacob 113
(Emma Lavelle) *hld up in tch: hdwy fr 12th: wnt cl 4th after 4 out: hit next: sn rdn: styd on same pce* **15/2**

15P0 5 51 **Houston Dynimo (IRE)**[30] 4483 11-11-6 123..........(bt) MichaelHeard(5) 77
(David Pipe) *led: nt fluent 9th (water): hdd after 12th: sn hld: wknd 4 out: t.o* **16/1**

6215 P **The Brock Again**[24] 4597 6-11-11 123....................(tp) SamTwiston-Davies
(Paul Nicholls) *hld up in tch: rdn after 11th: wknd qckly: p.u bef 13th* **7/1**

11U2 P **Exmoor Mist**[30] 4487 8-11-12 124....................(t) IanPopham
(Victor Dartnall) *chsd ldrs: pushed along fr 10th: wknd after 4 out: p.u bef next* **13/2**

5m 24.2s (6.70) **Going Correction** +0.525s/f (Soft) 7 Ran SP% **113.3**
Speed ratings: **107,106,103,102,82 ,**
CSF £17.55 TOTE £5.00: £2.20, £2.20; EX 19.00 Trifecta £62.10.
Owner The Punchestown Syndicate **Bred** Barry O'Connor **Trained** Brompton Regis, Somerset

FOCUS
Race distance increased by 18yds. The front pair drew a few lengths clear in what was a fairly ordinary chase. The third and fourth have been rated close to their marks.

5148 APOLLOBET BEST ODSS GUARANTEED H'CAP HURDLE (8 hdls) 1m 7f 65y

3:40 (3:41) (Class 4) (0-115,115) 4-Y-O+ **£3,249** (£954; £477; £238)

Form RPR

5-54 1 **Dadsintrouble (IRE)**[327] 279 6-11-6 109.................... AlanJohns 116+
(Tim Vaughan) *chsd ldr: rdn to ld bef last: kpt on wl* **20/1**

22 2 2 ½ **Alberta (IRE)**[94] 3418 7-11-12 115.................... AndrewGlassonbury 118
(Jim Best) *trckd ldr: led 3 out: rdn and hdd bef last: kpt on same pce* **4/1**[3]

640P 3 11 **Westend Prince (IRE)**[106] 3174 5-10-13 102.................... PaddyBrennan 97
(Colin Tizzard) *hld up: mstke 3rd: rdn after 3 out: hdwy next: wnt 3rd between last 2: nt pce to get on terms w front pair* **9/2**

0-24 4 10 **Rafafie**[15] 4824 8-11-2 108.................... LucyGardner(3) 91
(Sue Gardner) *hld up bhd ldrs: hdwy into 3rd after 3 out: rdn bef next: wknd between last 2* **5/2**[1]

322P 5 6 **Deja Bougg**[21] 4672 5-11-7 110.................... MarkQuinlan 89
(Neil Mulholland) *hld up bhd ldrs: blnd bdly 2nd: hit 5th: wnt cl 4th after 3 out: sn rdn: wknd between last 2* **10/1**

-033 6 17 **Sandford Castle (IRE)**[81] 3592 6-11-12 115.................... AlainCawley 81
(Johnny Farrelly) *hld up bhd ldrs: rdn after 3 out: wknd next* **10/3**[2]

55P0 7 24 **Mr Lando**[26] 2734 7-11-9 112.................... TomCannon 63
(Alison Batchelor) *led: blnd 5th: hdd next: wknd bef 2 out* **14/1**

3m 49.25s (0.35) **Going Correction** +0.125s/f (Yiel) 7 Ran SP% **110.4**
Speed ratings (Par 105): **104,102,96,91,88 79,66**
CSF £91.33 CT £409.34 TOTE £19.80: £6.30, £2.10; EX 111.80 Trifecta £522.80.
Owner Paul Bowtell **Bred** B J Griffiths **Trained** Aberthin, Vale of Glamorgan

FOCUS
Race distance increased by 12yds. This went to the outsider of the field and the form looks modest. A big step up from the surprise winner, but the time was good and it looks believable.

5149 APOLLOBET MASTERS GOLF H'CAP CHASE (21 fncs) 3m 1f 30y

4:10 (4:10) (Class 4) (0-110,109) 5-Y-O+ **£4,992** (£1,550; £834)

Form RPR

2044 1 **Saint Raph (FR)**[24] 4589 8-11-7 109....................(t) PaulO'Brien(5) 126
(Robert Walford) *trckd ldrs: disp fr 9th: rdn and hdd after 4 out: rallied gamely to regain ld jst bef last: styd on wl: rdn out* **7/2**[2]

53P2 2 1 ¼ **Head Spin (IRE)**[21] 4673 8-10-1 84....................(bt) JeremiahMcGrath 100
(Seamus Mullins) *trckd ldrs: led appr 3 out: sn rdn: hdd jst bef last: no ex* **7/1**

-0PP 3 45 **Strollawaynow (IRE)**[53] 4062 9-11-11 108....................(tp) TomCannon 84
(David Arbuthnot) *nvr really travelling: pushed along to chse ldrs: wnt 4th u.p after 13th: lost tch after 17th: wnt 3rd next: t.o* **11/2**[3]

134P P **Kings Apollo**[44] 4255 7-11-3 107.................... MrJNixon(7)
(Tom Symonds) *led tl after 3rd: chsd ldrs: pushed along fr 12th: wknd after 16th: t.o whn p.u 4 out* **8/1**

205U P **Trillerin Minella (IRE)**[117] 2975 8-11-7 104.........(p) SamTwiston-Davies
(Graeme McPherson) *chsd ldrs: blnd 7th: sn struggling: lost tch 9th: sn p.u* **7/1**

P-04 P **Oliver's Hill (IRE)**[66] 3836 7-11-11 108....................(tp) NickScholfield
(Lawney Hill) *led after 3rd: jnd 9th: hit 16th: sn hdd: rdn after 17th: wknd next: p.u bef 3 out* **7/4**[1]

6m 56.2s (16.70) **Going Correction** +0.775s/f (Soft) 6 Ran SP% **110.1**
Speed ratings: **104,103,89, ,**
CSF £25.06 TOTE £4.00: £1.90, £2.20; EX 17.50 Trifecta £151.80.
Owner Mrs Christine M Hinks **Bred** Bernard Forges **Trained** Child Okeford, Dorset

FOCUS
Race distance increased by 24yds. The front pair drew a long way clear in what was a moderate handicap. Not form to be confident about but the first two had slipped to very good marks and have been rated back to something like their best.

5150 APOLLOBET FAIR PLAY MONEY BACK OPEN HUNTERS' CHASE (FOR THE JOHN DUFOSEE MEMORIAL TROPHY) (21 fncs) 3m 1f 30y
4:40 (4:41) (Class 6) 5-Y-O+ **£1,317** (£405; £202)

Form RPR
21-P **1** **Double Bank (IRE)**[11] [4887] 13-11-11 124 MrMWoodward(5) 123+
(Mrs Emma Oliver) *trckd ldr: led 17th: styd on wl and in command fr 3 out* **5/2**[2]
2355 **2** *16* **Best Boy Barney (IRE)**[162] [2089] 10-11-13 127 (bt) MissLScott(7) 117+
(Jeremy Scott) *led: reminders after 16th: hdd next: styd on same pce fr 3 out: blnd last* **11/8**[1]
1P-2 **3** *49* **Iron Chancellor (IRE)**[23] 11-11-7 115 (b) MrRobertHawker(5) 63
(Mrs Sue Popham) *trckd ldrs: rdn after 14th: mstke next: wknd 4 out: t.o* **8/1**
2-11 **F** **Cygnet**[36] 10-12-1 117 (t) MissJodieHughes(5)
(Mickey Bowen) *trcking ldrs whn fell 10th* **11/4**[3]
122- **P** **Crannaghmore Boy (IRE)**[7] 11-11-9 101 MissAGoschen(3)
(Mrs J Butler) *trckd ldrs: awkward 13th and rdr lost iron: lost tch after next: t.o whn p.u 3 out* **25/1**

7m 4.2s (24.70) **Going Correction** +0.775s/f (Soft) **5** Ran SP% **112.3**
Speed ratings: **91,85,70, ,**
CSF £6.83 TOTE £3.60: £1.80, £1.40; EX 7.20 Trifecta £29.40.
Owner J D Cole **Bred** Sean Hourigan **Trained** Teign Valley, Devon

FOCUS
A modest hunter chase, run at a respectable gallop. This was run over 24yds further than advertised. The winner is probably a better guide to the level than the second, who seems much happier on better ground.

5151 APOLLOBET CASINO & GAMES "NEWCOMERS" STANDARD OPEN NATIONAL HUNT FLAT RACE (DIV I) 1m 7f 65y
5:10 (5:12) (Class 6) 4-6-Y-O **£1,624** (£477; £238; £119)

Form RPR
1 **Touch Kick (IRE)** 5-11-4 0 (t) SamTwiston-Davies 111+
(Paul Nicholls) *hld up: hdwy 3f out: led over 1f out: styd on wl: rdn out* **8/1**
2 *1 ¼* **G For Ginger** 6-10-6 0 DavidNoonan(5) 102+
(Anthony Honeyball) *pressed ldr: led 4f out: rdn and hdd over 1f out: styd on fnl f: hld nring fin* **12/1**
3 *6* **Beni Light (FR)** 5-11-4 0 PaddyBrennan 104+
(Tom George) *trckd ldrs: rdn to chse ldr over 2f out tl over 1f out: styd on same pce* **8/1**
4 *2* **Djarkalin (FR)** 4-10-12 0 IanPopham 95
(Dan Skelton) *hld up: rdn 3f out: styd on fnl 2f but nt pce to get involved* **5/1**[3]
5 *1 ¾* **Count Meribel** 4-10-12 0 MarkGrant 93
(Nigel Twiston-Davies) *hld up: rdn 3f out: styd on fnl 2f but nt pce to get on terms* **16/1**
6 *7* **Dancing Conquest** 6-10-11 0 JeremiahMcGrath 85
(Seamus Mullins) *hld up: rdn over 3f out: nvr threatened* **25/1**
7 *23* **Major Davis (FR)** 4-10-12 0 GavinSheehan 63
(Warren Greatrex) *led: rdn and hdd 4f out: wknd 2f out* **2/1**[1]
8 *1 ¼* **Aspergillum** 4-10-12 0 NicodeBoinville 62
(Tom Lacey) *chsd ldrs: struggling 1/2-way: wknd over 4f out* **3/1**[2]

3m 50.3s (7.00) **Going Correction** +0.375s/f (Yiel) **8** Ran SP% **114.6**
Speed ratings: **96,95,92,91,90 86,74,73**
CSF £96.80 TOTE £6.30: £1.80, £2.40, £2.60; EX 47.20 Trifecta £369.30.
Owner Trevor Hemmings **Bred** Aaron Metcalfe **Trained** Ditcheat, Somerset

FOCUS
No previous form to go on but this looks a bumper to be positive about. This was run over 12yds further than the advertised distance.

5152 APOLLOBET CASINO & GAMES "NEWCOMERS" STANDARD OPEN NATIONAL HUNT FLAT RACE (DIV II) 1m 7f 65y
5:40 (5:40) (Class 6) 4-6-Y-O **£1,624** (£477; £238; £119)

Form RPR
1 **Winningtry (IRE)** 5-11-4 0 SamTwiston-Davies 102+
(Paul Nicholls) *trckd ldrs: chal 2f out: sn rdn: kpt on wl to ld ins fnl f: asserting towards fin* **7/2**[3]
2 *1 ¼* **Brunel Woods (IRE)** 4-10-12 0 DarylJacob 95
(David Dennis) *hld up: smooth hdwy 5f out: lft 2nd over 4f out: led over 2f out: rdn over 1f out: hdd ins fnl f: no ex nring fin* **16/1**
3 *5* **Waterloo Warrior (IRE)** 4-10-7 0 PaulO'Brien(5) 90
(Colin Tizzard) *disp ld for 5f: trckd ldrs: rdn and sltly outpcd 3f out: styd on fr over 1f out* **8/1**
4 *2 ½* **Present Destiny (IRE)** 4-10-7 0 KevinJones(5) 87
(Seamus Mullins) *t.k.h: hld up: rdn over 2f out: styd on but nt pce to get on terms* **12/1**
5 *2 ¼* **Hardrock Davis (FR)** 5-11-4 0 PaddyBrennan 91
(Tom George) *cl up: rdn over 2f out: styd on same pce* **3/1**[2]
6 *3 ½* **Spring Blossom** 6-10-11 0 IanPopham 81
(John Ryall) *disp ld for 5f: trcking ldr whn lft in ld over 4f out: rdn and hdd over 2f out: grad fdd* **50/1**
R **I'm A Game Changer (IRE)** 4-10-12 0 TomO'Brien
(Philip Hobbs) *trckd ldrs: led after 5f: rn out on bnd over 4f out* **15/8**[1]
R **Speedalong (IRE)** 5-11-4 0 NickScholfield
(Jeremy Scott) *trcking ldrs whn crashed into rails and uns rdr over 4f out* **16/1**

4m 12.6s (29.30) **Going Correction** +0.375s/f (Yiel) **8** Ran SP% **114.5**
Speed ratings: **36,35,32,31,30 28, ,**
CSF £56.12 TOTE £4.40: £1.80, £2.70, £2.10; EX 43.20 Trifecta £282.90.
Owner Trevor Hemmings **Bred** Robert McCarthy **Trained** Ditcheat, Somerset

FOCUS
This second division of the newcomers bumper was an eventful affair. The front pair locked horns from 2f out. This was run over 12yds further than the advertised distance.
T/Plt: £59.40 to a £1 stake. Pool: £70,066.41 - 860.49 winning units. T/Qpdt: £21.70 to a £1 stake. Pool: £4,878.82 - 165.70 winning units. **Tim Mitchell**

4888 LUDLOW (R-H)
Tuesday, April 5

OFFICIAL GOING: Hurdle course - good to soft (good in places); chase course - good (good to soft in places)
Weather: sunny spells

5153 ROGER GRIFFITHS MEMORIAL NOVICES' HURDLE (9 hdls) 1m 7f 169y
2:15 (2:15) (Class 4) 4-Y-O+ **£3,898** (£1,144; £572; £286)

Form RPR
3 **1** **Red Tornado (FR)**[31] [4489] 4-10-7 0 HarrySkelton 116+
(Dan Skelton) *chsd ldrs: wnt 2nd bef 3 out: led appr 2 out: wandered u.p between last 2: r.o* **10/1**
3231 **2** *2 ¾* **Baltic Storm (IRE)**[18] [4773] 5-10-6 123 TommyDowling(7) 120
(Charlie Mann) *chsd ldrs: nt fluent 5th: rdn after 3 out: swtchd rt appr last: kpt on: wnt 2nd nr fin* **11/4**[2]
P312 **3** *nk* **Beallandendall (IRE)**[12] [4888] 8-10-13 127 MrStanSheppard(7) 125
(Matt Sheppard) *racd keenly: chsd ldrs: nt fluent and rdn 3 out: ev ch next: edgd lft and one pce flat: lost 2nd nr fin* **9/2**[3]
12 **4** *½* **Imperial Presence (IRE)**[17] [4784] 5-11-6 130 RichardJohnson 127+
(Philip Hobbs) *t.k.h: led 1st: j.flt 3 out: sn hdd: one pce appr last* **6/4**[1]
3F **5** *8* **Haut Bages (FR)**[68] [3819] 4-10-7 0 DarylJacob 106
(Oliver Sherwood) *hld up towards rr: hdwy 6th: nudged along and outpcd by ldrs fr 3 out* **20/1**
6 **6** *12* **Zante (FR)**[32] [4462] 4-10-7 0 JoshuaMoore 97
(Gary Moore) *mid-div: hdwy after 5th: rdn 3 out: wkng whn mstke last* **28/1**
665P **7** *shd* **Ablazing (IRE)**[93] [3450] 5-10-10 0 KieronEdgar(3) 99
(Johnny Farrelly) *mid-div: rdn after 6th: kpt on steadily fr 3 out* **200/1**
44 **8** *½* **Hastrubal (FR)**[109] [3145] 6-10-13 0 JakeGreenall 100
(Henry Daly) *chsd ldrs: rdn appr 3 out: grad wknd* **40/1**
24 **9** *14* **Our Three Sons (IRE)**[138] [2597] 5-10-13 0 NickScholfield 86
(Jamie Snowden) *prom to 1st: sn in mid-div: in rr 5th: sme hdwy after next: nudged along and no imp fr 3 out* **40/1**
0P **10** *14* **Change Or Go (IRE)**[15] [4844] 4-10-2 0 JamieBargary(5) 68
(David Dennis) *chsd ldrs tl lost pl 5th: sn rdn along: wknd after 6th* **200/1**
P **11** *½* **Patronne (FR)**[50] [4157] 4-10-0 0 GavinSheehan 60
(Harry Whittington) *t.k.h: led to 1st: w ldr: lost 2nd appr 3 out: sn wknd* **16/1**
P **12** *1* **Recently Acquired**[31] [4489] 4-10-2 0 JackSherwood(5) 66
(David Loder) *hld up towards rr: sme hdwy after 6th: wknd 3 out* **66/1**
0 **13** *8* **Scot Daddy (USA)**[12] [4888] 4-10-7 0 TrevorWhelan 59
(David Dennis) *a in rr* **200/1**
6 **14** *10* **Hannington**[18] [4773] 5-10-13 0 JamesBanks 56
(Barry Brennan) *mid-div: rdn after 6th: sn wknd* **150/1**
06 **15** *19* **Shouting Hill (IRE)**[83] [3582] 6-10-13 0 RichieMcLernon 39
(Johnny Farrelly) *in rr: nt fluent 3rd: t.o fr 6th* **100/1**
0-PP **P** **No Bad News**[13] [4875] 6-10-13 0 (t) JamesDavies
(Henry Oliver) *in rr: mstke 5th: sn lost tch: p.u after 6th: b.b.v* **200/1**

3m 53.2s (3.70) **Going Correction** +0.50s/f (Soft)
WFA 4 from 5yo+ 5lb **16** Ran SP% **118.0**
Speed ratings (Par 105): **110,108,108,108,104 98,98,97,90,83 83,83,79,74,64**
CSF £36.31 TOTE £10.20: £2.90, £1.40, £1.70; EX 39.90 Trifecta £186.00.
Owner Notalotterry **Bred** Jean-Francois Gribomont **Trained** Alcester, Warwicks

FOCUS
Only three or four of these had proved themselves capable of better than a modest level of form over hurdles but there were some potential improvers in the line-up. The leaders set a strong pace and the field were soon strung out in a contest run over an extra 57.5 yards. Harry Skelton and Richard Johnson both felt the ground was good to soft, with Skelton adding it rode quite dead, and the winning time was more than 15 seconds slower than Racing Post standard. A big step up from the winner, with the second, third and fourth pretty much bang on their marks. Solid form that should produce winners.

5154 CORBETTSPORTS H'CAP CHASE (19 fncs) 2m 7f 171y
2:50 (2:50) (Class 3) (0-130,129) 5-Y-**£7,596** (£2,244; £1,122; £561; £280)

Form RPR
1P42 **1** **Toby Lerone (IRE)**[25] [4589] 9-11-7 **124** (b) HarrySkelton 136+
(Dan Skelton) *led to 3rd: w ldr tl led again 7th: rdn 4 out: drew clr fr 2 out: styd on wl* **11/2**[3]
15P **2** *5* **Double Silver**[116] [3025] 9-11-0 **117** PaddyBrennan 125+
(Fergal O'Brien) *hld up: mstke 8th: hdwy 10th: pushed along 12th: pckd next: one pce 4 out: styd on fr 2 out: tk 2nd flat* **10/1**
410U **3** *1* **Gone Too Far**[134] [2686] 8-11-12 **129** WayneHutchinson 134
(Alan King) *towards rr tl hdwy after 6th: wnt 2nd after 15th: j.flt last 4: one pce and hld by wnr fr 2 out: lost 2nd flat: b.b.v* **8/1**
223P **4** *2 ¼* **Alberobello (IRE)**[39] [4340] 8-11-6 **123** (t) MattGriffiths 124
(Jeremy Scott) *w ldr: led 3rd to 7th: lost 2nd after 15th: one pce fr 4 out* **9/2**[2]
0056 **5** *½* **Generous Ransom (IRE)**[31] [4485] 8-11-11 **128** (p) DarylJacob 130
(Nick Gifford) *chsd ldrs tl lost pl 8th: last by 11th: rallied 13th: rdn bef 4 out: mstke 3 out: wknd next* **4/1**[1]
4P36 **6** *10* **Orby's Man (IRE)**[17] [4789] 7-10-11 **114** (p) AndrewTinkler 105
(Charlie Longsdon) *chsd ldrs: lost pl 12th: mstke next: kpt on same pce fr 4 out* **15/2**
51P0 **7** *71* **Sonofagun (FR)**[41] [4306] 10-10-7 **117** TobyWheeler(7) 44
(Ian Williams) *towards rr: hdwy after 9th: rdn after 13th: wknd bef 4 out: t.o* **20/1**
42U2 **P** **Buck Mulligan**[37] [4386] 11-11-1 **118** PaulMoloney
(Evan Williams) *towards rr: sme hdwy 13th: wkng whn j. slowly 4 out: bhd whn p.u bef 2 out* **8/1**
15PU **P** **Dursey Sound (IRE)**[38] [4363] 8-11-8 **125** RichieMcLernon
(Jonjo O'Neill) *chsd ldrs tl lost pl rapidly 13th: t.o whn p.u bef 4 out* **16/1**
-1P4 **P** **Chicoria (IRE)**[110] [3129] 7-11-2 **119** (p) RichardJohnson
(Henry Daly) *hld up: mstke 10th: struggling 12th: t.o whn p.u bef 4 out: b.b.v* **9/1**

6m 17.8s (377.80) **10** Ran SP% **117.3**
CSF £58.71 CT £441.62 TOTE £5.50: £1.90, £3.20, £3.10; EX 55.50 Trifecta £732.60.
Owner Mrs Gill Duckworth & Mrs Pat Dry **Bred** M J Halligan **Trained** Alcester, Warwicks

FOCUS
Several with questions to answer in this handicap chase, which was run over an extra 90 yards, and few got into it up front. The winner has been rated close to his best, and the third and fourth close to their marks.

5155 CORBETTSPORTS MARES' NOVICES' HURDLE (11 hdls) 2m 5f 55y
3:25 (3:25) (Class 4) 4-Y-0+ **£3,898** (£1,144; £572; £286)

Form RPR
1132 1 **Unbuckled (IRE)**[12] 4890 6-11-5 112.................... TrevorWhelan 117+
(Neil King) *a.p: nt fluent 4th: mstke 8th: led and hit 2 out: sn rdn: styd on wl flat* **7/4**[2]
042 2 6 **Hollow Bay**[25] 4598 6-10-12 105.................... RichieMcLernon 102
(Paul Webber) *mid-div: clsd bef 3 out where nt fluent: sn rdn: swtchd lft and chsd wnr appr last: one pce and hld flat* **12/1**
-50P 3 2 ½ **Marvellous Monty (IRE)**[34] 4430 6-10-9 0.................... TomBellamy(3) 100
(Johnny Farrelly) *hld up towards rr: clsd after 8th: pushed along bef 2 out where mstke: jinked lft appr last: styd on to go 3rd flat* **100/1**
21 4 3 ¼ **Bagging Turf (IRE)**[25] 4598 6-11-5 112.................... JamieMoore 105
(Gary Moore) *chsd ldr: lost 2nd after 8th but styd prom: rdn 3 out: mstke next: 3rd and no ex whn nt fluent last* **8/1**[3]
50-0 5 6 **Wishing Wind**[66] 3862 6-10-12 0.................... NicodeBoinville 93
(Nicky Henderson) *chsd ldrs: rdn to chal whn mstke 3 out: sn one pce: wkng whn mstke last* **16/1**
U336 6 1 ¼ **Sahara Haze**[10] 4916 7-10-5 107.................... MrTGreatrex(7) 91
(Phillip Dando) *hld up in last pair: clsd after 8th: rdn bef 3 out: sn one pce and hld* **20/1**
0303 7 nk **Handpicked**[12] 4893 5-10-12 0.................... JakeGreenall 89
(Henry Daly) *chsd ldrs: wnt 2nd after 8th: rdn to ld bef 3 out: hit 2 out: wkng whn nt fluent last* **10/1**
6500 8 36 **Over To Midnight**[12] 4888 6-10-5 90.................... MissLBrooke(7) 57
(Lady Susan Brooke) *towards rr: clsd 5th: wknd bef 3 out: t.o* **125/1**
2323 P **Brise Vendeenne (FR)**[33] 4445 5-10-12 115..........(b[1]) RichardJohnson
(Philip Hobbs) *led: rdn after 8th: hdd bef 3 out: wknd qckly and p.u bef 2 out* **11/8**[1]
P0 P **Inspiring (IRE)**[12] 4888 5-10-9 0.................... KieronEdgar(3)
(Johnny Farrelly) *hld up in last pair: lost tch 7th: p.u after 8th* **150/1**

5m 23.5s (8.70) **Going Correction** +0.50s/f (Soft) **10 Ran SP% 119.5**
Speed ratings (Par 105): **103,100,99,98,96 95,95,81,,**
CSF £23.10 TOTE £3.00: £1.10, £2.80, £12.40; EX 24.00 Trifecta £572.40.
Owner Mrs J K Buckle **Bred** Mrs A S O'Brien **Trained** Barbury Castle, Wiltshire

FOCUS
Only half of these mares had proven themselves better than modest hurdlers ahead of this novice event, which was run over an extra 92.5 yards, and with the clear form choice palpably failing to run her race this is not form that is out of the ordinary. Small steps up from the first two, with the fourth helping to set the level.

5156 BET WITH CORBETTSPORTS H'CAP CHASE (12 fncs) 1m 7f 212y
4:00 (4:00) (Class 3) (0-140,128) 5-Y-0+ **£9,582** (£2,892; £1,490; £789)

Form RPR
P061 1 **Noche De Reyes (FR)**[12] 4891 7-11-3 **119**.................... PaddyBrennan 127+
(Tom George) *chsd ldng trio: clsd 8th: led 4 out: pushed clr fr 2 out: in command whn mstke last* **9/4**[1]
1312 2 6 **Tornado In Milan (IRE)**[24] 4617 10-11-11 **127**.................... PaulMoloney 131
(Evan Williams) *wnt to post early: t.k.h: trckd ldrs: wnt cl 2nd 4 out: hit next: sn outpcd by wnr: hld whn mstke last* **11/2**
6-24 3 27 **Such A Legend**[174] 1904 8-11-9 **125**.................... DavidBass 106
(Kim Bailey) *mainly trckd ldr: led after 9th: rdn and hdd 4 out: wknd next* **5/2**[2]
312P 4 35 **Hepijeu (FR)**[159] 2153 5-11-12 **128**..........(tp) RichardJohnson 72
(Charlie Longsdon) *led tl hdd after 9th: rdn and wknd bef 4 out: t.o* **7/1**
0136 B **Chestnut Ben (IRE)**[15] 4838 11-10-12 **121**.................... MrRWinks(7)
(Peter Winks) *qckly outpcd in rr: mod 6th whn b.d 6th* **16/1**
-PP0 P **Swift Arrow (IRE)**[60] 3972 10-11-6 **122**..........(p) WayneHutchinson
(Donald McCain) *qckly outpcd in rr: rdn after 5th: wl bhd whn p.u bef 7th: b.b.v* **33/1**
3222 F **Goohar (IRE)**[73] 3742 7-11-2 **118**..........(p) JakeGreenall
(Henry Daly) *chsd ldrs: 5th and rdn along to stay in tch whn fell 6th* **5/1**[3]

4m 8.5s (10.00) **Going Correction** +0.825s/f (Soft) **7 Ran SP% 112.7**
Speed ratings: **108,105,91,74,**
CSF £14.72 CT £31.74 TOTE £2.20: £1.80, £2.50; EX 17.10 Trifecta £39.20.
Owner David Rea & Express Contract Drying Ltd **Bred** Dr Vet R Y Simon & N Simon **Trained** Slad, Gloucs

FOCUS
The top-weight was 12lb below the ratings ceiling for this 0-140 and only a handful of these were in demonstrably good form ahead of a contest run over an extra 75 yards, and three of the field were gone by halfway. Three of the remaining quartet had helped to force a strong pace and that set things up perfectly for the winner. The second has been rated to his mark.

5157 CORBETTSPORTS FOR VALUE H'CAP HURDLE (11 hdls) 2m 5f 55y
4:35 (4:35) (Class 4) (0-120,120) 4-Y-0+ **£4,548** (£1,335; £667; £333)

Form RPR
1135 1 **Tanarpino**[24] 4620 5-11-12 **120**.................... PeterCarberry 125+
(Jennie Candlish) *cl up: led bef 3 out: hung lft and rdn next: j.lft last: all out* **7/1**
255 2 nk **Allbarnone**[67] 3837 8-10-13 **110**.................... ThomasGarner(3) 113
(William Kinsey) *hld up: hdwy 8th: rdn bef 3 out: styd on wl u.p flat: jst hld* **18/1**
25P1 3 nse **Deputy Commander (IRE)**[3] 5102 7-11-0 **113** 7ex....(t) JamieBargary(5) 116
(Nigel Twiston-Davies) *hld up towards rr: hdwy after 8th: rdn bef 3 out: stýd on to dispute 2nd last: jst hld* **9/4**[1]
4552 4 3 **Paddy The Deejay (IRE)**[17] 4782 7-11-9 **117**.................... JoshuaMoore 117
(Stuart Edmunds) *cl up: ev ch 3 out: sn rdn: no ex flat* **12/1**
P302 5 4 ½ **Rock On Rocky**[8] 4965 8-11-4 **119**..........(tp) MrStanSheppard(7) 116
(Matt Sheppard) *led in at s and s.i.s: sn led: hit 5th: hdd bef 3 out: kpt on same pce tl wknd flat* **6/1**[3]
5001 6 ½ **Drumlee Lad (IRE)**[32] 4455 6-11-6 **114**.................... DenisO'Regan 112
(Johnny Farrelly) *t.k.h in mid-div: clsd after 8th: mstke 3 out: sn shkn up and unable qck: wknd bef last* **5/1**[2]
6554 7 ½ **Kamool (GER)**[67] 3846 6-11-4 **112**.................... NoelFehily 107
(Jonjo O'Neill) *mid-div: hdwy 5th: rdn 3 out: grad wknd* **7/1**
-F03 8 42 **Kid Kalanisi (IRE)**[111] 3114 5-11-5 **113**.................... HarrySkelton 71
(Dan Skelton) *hld up: sme hdwy after 8th: rdn and wknd bef 3 out: t.o* **6/1**[3]
0P0P 9 8 **Arcamante (ITY)**[14] 4860 5-10-4 **105**..........(p) CharlieHammond(7) 55
(Mike Hammond) *t.k.h: prom tl dropped to mid-div 2nd: rdn 6th: mstke next: lost tch after 8th: t.o* **100/1**
1335 10 1 ½ **Iguacu**[21] 1549 12-10-8 **102**.................... RichardJohnson 51
(Richard Price) *hld up: rdn and wknd after 8th: t.o* **28/1**

5m 23.4s (8.60) **Going Correction** +0.50s/f (Soft) **10 Ran SP% 118.4**
Speed ratings (Par 105): **103,102,102,101,100 99,99,83,80,80**
CSF £119.56 CT £375.07 TOTE £6.50: £2.80, £4.00, £1.60; EX 113.90 Trifecta £438.70.
Owner P and Mrs G A Clarke **Bred** R W Huggins **Trained** Basford Green, Staffs
■ Stewards' Enquiry : Thomas Garner two-day ban: used whip above permitted level (Apr 19-20)

FOCUS
Several in-form hurdlers in the field for this handicap, which was run over an extra 92.5 yards, but the fact that most were still in contention going into the home turn owed plenty to the fact that they did not go a great pace. A small pb from the winner, with the second, third and fourth setting the level.

5158 MAGNUS-ALLCROFT MEMORIAL OPEN HUNTERS' CHASE (16 fncs) 2m 4f 11y
5:05 (5:06) (Class 5) 5-Y-0+ **£2,495** (£774; £386; £193)

Form RPR
11-4 1 **Tugboat (IRE)**[72] 8-11-13 118.................... MrJNixon(5) 130+
(G Slade-Jones) *j.lft at times: outpcd in last pair: hdwy 10th: chsd ldng trio 13th: sn rdn: wnt 3rd 2 out: led last: styd on wl* **6/1**[3]
4-03 2 1 **Hazy Tom (IRE)**[12] 4892 10-11-3 120.................... MrAWright(7) 122
(Gareth Thomas) *prom: trckd ldr 11th: rdn 4 out: chal next: led and hit 2 out: hdd last: kpt on u.p* **5/4**[1]
P5 3 4 ½ **Cooladerry King (IRE)**[35] 4426 8-11-7 0.................... MrPGerety(3) 118
(Mrs Sheila Crow) *mid-div: j.rt 3rd: hdwy 7th: rdn in 3rd after 13th: led narrowly 3 out: hdd and hit next: sn hung rt and one pce* **20/1**
6-34 4 7 **Grandioso (IRE)**[12] 4892 9-11-10 130..........(t) MissGAndrews 111
(S Flook) *trckd ldr tl rdn and hdd 3 out: wknd appr last* **7/2**[2]
3U-3 5 12 **Ballytober**[23] 10-11-3 118..........(tp) MissCPrichard(7) 102
(Ian Prichard) *in tch towards rr: struggling after 13th: no ch whn blnd 3 out* **7/1**
PP5P P **Sustainability (IRE)**[23] 4651 11-11-5 105..........(p) MissLBrooke(5)
(Miss B Eckley) *j.lft at times: chsd ldrs: losing pl whn reminder 9th: bhd fr 11th: t.o whn p.u bef 4 out* **50/1**
2-1P F **Neverownup (IRE)**[35] 4424 11-11-7 122.................... MrNLawton(7)
(M J Vanstone) *w ldr: jst lost 2nd whn fell 7th* **12/1**
P-3P P **Catch Tammy (IRE)**[35] 4424 10-11-3 105..........(p) MrJAndrews(7)
(Mrs I Barnett) *prom: chsd ldr 7th to 11th: sn wknd: t.o whn p.u bef 4 out* **33/1**
0-24 P **Troyan (IRE)**[51] 9-11-7 105..........(t) MrZBaker(3)
(G Slade-Jones) *sn outpcd in last pair: lost tch 9th: p.u bef next* **33/1**

5m 15.6s (11.20) **Going Correction** +0.825s/f (Soft) **9 Ran SP% 113.7**
Speed ratings: **110,109,107,105,100 ,,,**
CSF £14.02 TOTE £5.00: £1.30, £1.70, £3.50; EX 16.30 Trifecta £91.40.
Owner Neil Lewis & Mrs Gail Lewis **Bred** Airlie Stud & Miss K Rausing **Trained** Kington, Herefordshire

FOCUS
Several of these hunters had something to prove on recent efforts but they went a good pace in a race run over an extra 75 yards. A step up from the winner, with the fourth rated to his C&D mark.

5159 CORBETTSPORTS H'CAP HURDLE (9 hdls) 1m 7f 169y
5:40 (5:40) (Class 3) (0-130,127) 4-Y-0+ **£6,498** (£1,908; £954; £477)

Form RPR
F032 1 **King Muro**[31] 4486 6-10-13 **114**..........(t) PaddyBrennan 122+
(Fergal O'Brien) *hld up in rr: hdwy 5th: shkn up whn hit 2 out: sn wnt 2nd: nrly 3 l down last: r.o u.p to ld nr fin* **5/1**[2]
5310 2 ¾ **Herons Heir (IRE)**[37] 4384 8-10-9 **110**..........(t) HarrySkelton 116+
(Dan Skelton) *hld up towards rr: hdwy and nt fluent 5th: led bef 3 out: rdn 2 out: nrly 3 l up last: kpt on: hdd nr fin* **4/1**[1]
1413 3 10 **Polstar (FR)**[134] 2688 7-11-4 **119**.................... GavinSheehan 116
(Harry Whittington) *in rr: outpcd and detached 4th: rdn and styd on fr 3 out: wnt 3rd flat: no ch w ldng pair* **5/1**[2]
-PP0 4 2 ¾ **Forever Field (IRE)**[134] 2688 6-11-0 **115**.................... PeterCarberry 111
(Nicky Henderson) *chsd ldrs: ev ch 3 out: drvn whn hit next: wkng whn nt fluent last: lost 3rd flat* **8/1**
1263 5 8 **Qasser (IRE)**[18] 4774 7-10-13 **124**.................... HarryTeal(10) 111
(Harry Whittington) *chsd ldrs: rdn 3 out: sn one pce* **11/2**[3]
64U6 6 3 ½ **Rock N Rhythm (IRE)**[33] 4452 6-11-10 **125**.................... RichieMcLernon 109
(Jonjo O'Neill) *prom: reminder 5th: rdn and wknd 3 out* **20/1**
0405 7 1 **Ascendant**[33] 4452 10-11-7 **127**..........(b) ThomasCheesman(5) 110
(Johnny Farrelly) *w ldr tl rdn after 6th: wknd bef 3 out* **8/1**
35F 8 ¾ **Town Mouse**[115] 3036 6-11-6 **121**.................... TrevorWhelan 103
(Neil King) *wnt to post early: chsd ldrs to 6th: sn rdn along and lost tch* **20/1**
6133 9 6 **Marju's Quest (IRE)**[188] 1700 6-11-4 **119**.................... NoelFehily 96
(David Dennis) *led tl hdd bef 3 out: grad wknd* **10/1**
60P5 10 41 **Milestone (IRE)**[16] 4825 6-10-2 **103**..........(t[1]) PaulMoloney 43
(Evan Williams) *in rr: reminders bef 5th: lost tch next: t.o* **25/1**
P **Defining Year (IRE)**[228] 1313 8-11-0 **120**..........(t) ConorRing(5)
(Hugo Froud) *mid-div: wknd after 6th: wl bhd whn p.u bef 3 out* **22/1**

3m 54.1s (4.60) **Going Correction** +0.50s/f (Soft) **11 Ran SP% 117.7**
Speed ratings (Par 107): **108,107,102,101,97 95,95,94,91,71**
CSF £24.27 CT £106.37 TOTE £5.60: £1.70, £2.20, £2.40; EX 23.10 Trifecta £69.70.
Owner The General Asphalte Company Ltd **Bred** Stourbank Stud **Trained** Naunton, Gloucs

FOCUS
A really strong gallop for this handicap, which was run over an extra 57.5 yards, and two progressive hurdlers came from off the pace to pull well clear. The first four have all been rated close to their marks.
T/Jkpt: £144,441.40 to a £1 stake. Pool: £203,438.60 - 1 winning ticket. T/Plt: £88.50 to a £1 stake. Pool: £94,124.17 - 775.82 winning tickets. T/Qpdt: £15.60 to a £1 stake. Pool: £7,745.97 - 366.35 winning tickets. **Richard Lowther**

4916 NEWTON ABBOT (L-H)
Tuesday, April 5

OFFICIAL GOING: Soft (heavy in places; 4.7)
Wind: mild breeze across Weather: sunny with cloudy periods

5160 MARIE CURIE GREAT DAFFODIL APPEAL NOVICES' HURDLE (8 hdls) 2m 167y
1:50 (1:50) (Class 4) 4-Y-0+ **£4,548** (£1,335; £667; £333)

Form RPR
445 1 **Byron Flyer**[33] 4441 5-11-0 0.................... WillKennedy 106+
(Ian Williams) *trckd ldrs: disp 2nd fr 4th: rdn to chal whn nt fluent 2 out: renewed chal last: led sn after: rdn out* **15/8**[2]

-54F **2** *1 ¼* **Bleu Et Noir**[136] 2646 5-11-0 0.................................. TomO'Brien 104
(Tim Vaughan) *racd freely: led: rdn between last 2: hdd sn after last: no ex* **11/4**[3]

00P **3** *13* **Tactical Manoeuvre (IRE)**[51] 4137 5-11-0 0.................. AdamWedge 91
(Alexandra Dunn) *trckd ldrs: disp 2nd fr 4th tl rdn appr 2 out: sn one pce* **33/1**

6240 **4** *79* **Baraymi (FR)**[3] 5091 4-10-8 122.....................................(p) MichealNolan 6
(Jamie Snowden) *nvr travelling: chsd ldrs tl struggling and detached after 4th: lost tch fr next: t.o* **13/8**[1]

P **Gold Mountain (IRE)**[163] 6-11-0 0.. RhysFlint
(Alexandra Dunn) *chsd ldr tl 3rd: qckly lost tch: t.o whn p.u bef 5th* **12/1**

4m 22.7s (17.00) **Going Correction** +1.025s/f (Soft)
WFA 4 from 5yo+ 5lb **5 Ran SP% 110.2**
Speed ratings (Par 105): **101,100,94,57,**
CSF £7.57 TOTE £2.80: £1.20, £1.60; EX 7.50 Trifecta £68.30.
Owner Anchor Men **Bred** Barton Stud **Trained** Portway, Worcs

FOCUS
The course passed a morning inspection and it was demanding underfoot. This was an ordinary little novice event, run over a distance 95yds further than advertised due to rail movements, and it saw a slow-motion finish. A step up from the winner, with the second setting the level.

5161 ATTHERACES "NATIONAL HUNT" MAIDEN HURDLE (9 hdls) 2m 2f 110y
2:25 (2:25) (Class 4) 4-Y-O+ **£4,548** (£1,335; £667; £333)

Form RPR

42-3 **1** **Verni (FR)**[96] 3375 7-11-1 0.. TomO'Brien 108+
(Philip Hobbs) *travelled wl: trckd ldrs: led gng best 2 out: r.o strly: easily* **30/100**[1]

-060 **2** *7* **Quarryman**[22] 4681 5-10-10 0.. HarryCobden(5) 94
(Ron Hodges) *led: rdn and hdd appr 2 out: styd on to regain 2nd at the last: no ch w wnr* **33/1**

044 **3** *3 ¼* **Top And Drop**[25] 4598 5-10-8 0... AlainCawley 84
(Venetia Williams) *trckd ldr: led appr 2 out: sn rdn and hdd: no ex appr last* **6/1**[3]

3 **4** *8* **Winning Ticket (IRE)**[44] 4270 5-11-1 0................................... SeanBowen 83
(Paul Morgan) *trckd ldrs: wnt cl 4th after 3 out: rdn bef next: sn wknd* **3/1**[2]

405 **5** *15* **Glimpse Of Gold**[8] 4963 5-10-10 0...................................... AlanJohns(5) 68
(Tim Vaughan) *hld up: wnt 5th after 3 out: rdn bef next: nvr threatened: wknd between last 2* **20/1**

P **6** *8* **Relkwood (IRE)**[122] 2904 6-11-1 0.. RhysFlint 60
(Paul Morgan) *trckd ldrs: rdn after 3 out: sn wknd* **33/1**

04FU **7** *23* **Pomicide**[6] 5029 6-10-12 0.. LucyGardner(3) 37
(Sue Gardner) *nvr fluent: mainly towards rr: wknd 3 out: t.o* **40/1**

6P **P** **Monet Moor**[83] 3581 7-10-3 0... PaulO'Brien(5)
(Jimmy Frost) *racd keenly: trckd ldrs tl sddle slipped and p.u after 3rd* **40/1**

5m 9.7s (39.70) **Going Correction** +1.60s/f (Heav) **8 Ran SP% 131.7**
Speed ratings (Par 105): **80,77,75,72,66 62,52,**
CSF £23.93 TOTE £1.20: £1.02, £5.80, £2.00; EX 22.70 Trifecta £138.20.
Owner Paul & Clare Rooney **Bred** M Trinquet, E A R L Trinquet Et Al **Trained** Withycombe, Somerset

FOCUS
A modest maiden. Due to rail movement it was run over a distance 115yds further than advertised. The easy winner didn't need to be at his best to land the odds.

5162 SIS H'CAP CHASE (20 fncs) 3m 1f 170y
3:00 (3:00) (Class 3) (0-130,124) 5-Y-O+ **£7,346** (£2,217; £1,142; £605)

Form RPR

3P41 **1** **Millicent Silver**[34] 4433 7-11-2 117.................................(p) RyanHatch(3) 130+
(Nigel Twiston-Davies) *a.p: led 5th tl hit 12th: drvn upsides after 15th: hit 4 out: chsd ldr fr next: rallied between last 2: led towards fin: styd on wl: drvn out* **3/1**[2]

4P42 **2** *nk* **Sun Wild Life (FR)**[17] 4780 6-11-7 119...............................(p) SeanBowen 129
(Robert Walford) *a.p: j.w: led 12th: rdn between last 2: no ex whn hdd towards fin* **11/4**[1]

141P **3** *52* **Rocky Bender (IRE)**[23] 4649 11-11-7 119.............................. TomO'Brien 90
(Venetia Williams) *j.rt progively worse fnl circ: trckd ldrs: rdn after 16th: wknd and j. bdly rt fnl 3: t.o* **11/1**

-PP0 **4** *7* **Farbreaga (IRE)**[39] 4348 10-11-10 122..........................(p) JeremiahMcGrath 73
(Harry Whittington) *led tl hit 5th and reminders: prom: mstke 13th and dropped to last u.p: lost tch 16th: wnt modest 4th after 3 out: t.o* **10/3**[3]

-653 **P** **Minellahalfcentury (IRE)**[25] 4595 8-11-12 124..(tp) SamTwiston-Davies
(Paul Nicholls) *trckd ldrs: hit 3rd: carried lft 10th: pushed along tl travelling bttr 13th: rdn after 16th: wknd after next: p.u bef 2 out* **11/4**[1]

7m 8.0s (23.40) **Going Correction** +1.075s/f (Soft) **5 Ran SP% 109.7**
Speed ratings: **107,106,90,88,**
CSF £11.65 TOTE £4.40: £1.90, £1.70; EX 11.50 Trifecta £42.50.
Owner John Goodman **Bred** Owen Brennan / John Goodman **Trained** Naunton, Gloucs

FOCUS
Only two mattered from four out in this modest staying handicap. The second has been rated back to his best.

5163 ATTHERACES IN APP BETTING H'CAP HURDLE (8 hdls) 2m 167y
3:35 (3:35) (Class 5) (0-105,105) 4-Y-O+ **£3,898** (£1,144; £572; £286)

Form RPR

6-05 **1** **Wolftrap (IRE)**[14] 4855 7-10-10 89...[1] TomO'Brien 96+
(Philip Hobbs) *hld up: hdwy after 3 out: cl 3rd next: rdn to ld appr last: kpt on strly* **3/1**[2]

1231 **2** *3 ½* **Winged Express (IRE)**[38] 4356 7-11-8 101................................ IanPopham 105
(Alexandra Dunn) *trckd ldrs: chalng whn hit 2 out: sn rdn: kpt on but nt pce of wnr fr last* **11/4**[1]

0253 **3** *3 ¾* **Un Prophete (FR)**[25] 4593 5-11-12 105..................................... AlainCawley 105
(Venetia Williams) *led 1st: rdn and hdd between last 2: hld in 3rd whn nt fluent last* **10/3**[3]

1442 **4** *6* **Norse Light**[23] 4650 5-11-10 103......................(p) SamTwiston-Davies 97
(David Dennis) *hld up: nt clrest of runs after 3 out: rdn and hdwy bef next: nt pce to quite get on terms: no ex appr last* **9/2**

000 **5** *6* **Late Shipment**[15] 4849 5-11-1 99... ChrisWard(5) 86
(Nikki Evans) *led tl 1st: trckd ldrs: rdn after 5th: outpcd next* **9/1**

4000 **6** *42* **Worldor (FR)**[12] 4886 10-11-3 96..(t) RhysFlint 41
(Alexandra Dunn) *cl up: rdn 3 out: wknd qckly* **20/1**

PPPP **U** **Dont Call Me Oscar (IRE)**[34] 4440 9-10-10 96...................(t) MrTGillard(7)
(Mark Gillard) *trckd ldrs: pressed ldr fr 3rd tl wnt lft 3 out: sn wknd: bhd whn stmbld bdly and uns rdr 2 out* **25/1**

4m 31.4s (25.70) **Going Correction** +1.60s/f (Heav) **7 Ran SP% 111.5**
Speed ratings (Par 103): **103,101,99,96,93 74,**
CSF £11.38 CT £26.73 TOTE £4.00: £1.90, £2.00; EX 12.20 Trifecta £38.50.
Owner Mrs Sally White **Bred** Robert McCarthy **Trained** Withycombe, Somerset

FOCUS
A moderate handicap. The runner-up is a decent benchmark. Due to rail movement it was run over a distance 95yds further than advertised. The winner has been rated as improving in line with his bumper mark, while the second sets the level.

5164 NEWTONABBOTRACING.COM H'CAP CHASE (16 fncs) 2m 4f 216y
4:10 (4:10) (Class 4) (0-115,116) 5-Y-O+ **£4,873** (£1,431; £715; £357)

Form RPR

PP35 **1** **Cody Wyoming**[15] 4841 10-11-12 113......................(tp) SamTwiston-Davies 129+
(Charlie Mann) *mde all: j.rt bdly at times: rdn clr between last 2: hit last: eased towards fin* **9/2**

2F34 **2** *20* **Azert De Coeur (FR)**[32] 4456 6-11-9 110.............................. RobertDunne 108
(Venetia Williams) *trckd wnr thrght: rdn after 4 out: hld after next: tired whn awkward last* **7/2**[3]

1515 **3** *7* **Daliance (IRE)**[17] 4803 7-11-1 109..................(b) WilliamFeatherstone(7) 94
(Noel Williams) *trckd ldrs: hit 4th: mstke 9th: nvr travelling and detached fr next: no ch but clsd on wkng horses fr 2 out: wnt 3rd run-in* **5/2**[2]

P0UP **4** *3 ¼* **Paddy The Stout (IRE)**[32] 4464 11-10-13 100.....................(t) TomO'Brien 81
(Paul Henderson) *j.rt: trckd ldrs: rdn after 4 out: wknd 2 out* **10/1**

1324 **5** *3* **Long John**[12] 4884 9-11-5 106... JamesBest 83
(Jackie Du Plessis) *hld up 5th: wnt 3rd after 9th tl rdn 4 out: wknd 2 out* **9/4**[1]

5m 50.2s (28.80) **Going Correction** +1.50s/f (Heav) **5 Ran SP% 108.8**
Speed ratings: **105,97,94,93,92**
CSF £19.45 TOTE £3.80: £3.00, £1.50; EX 14.00 Trifecta £25.00.
Owner Charlie Mann Racing Club I **Bred** Spencer Bloodstock **Trained** Upper Lambourn, Berks

FOCUS
An ordinary handicap in which the winner got loose up front. The winner has been rated back to his best, with the third 7lb off.

5165 NEWTON ABBOT 150TH ANNIVERSARY H'CAP HURDLE (12 hdls) 3m 2f 105y
4:45 (4:48) (Class 4) (0-105,104) 4-Y-O+ **£4,548** (£1,335; £667; £333)

Form RPR

-1P3 **1** **Mogestic (IRE)**[10] 4920 7-11-0 97....................................... KevinJones(5) 109+
(Seamus Mullins) *mid-div: hdwy 9th: led 3 out: sn rdn: jockey dropped whip bef next: styd on wl whn chal fr last: pushed out* **9/1**

4 **2** *½* **Lilly Of The Moor**[20] 4709 8-11-6 101................................... RyanHatch(3) 110
(Ben Case) *trckd ldrs: rdn appr 9th: chsd wnr after 3 out: ev ch last: styd on* **8/1**

4P55 **3** *6* **Garde Fou (FR)**[16] 4822 10-11-8 100..................................(t) TomO'Brien 104
(Paul Henderson) *towards rr: stdy prog fr 9th: rdn after 3 out: wnt 3rd next: styd on same pce fr last* **16/1**

35F2 **4** *39* **Admiral Blake**[6] 5033 9-10-6 84... RobertDunne 70
(Laura Young) *mid-div: hdwy 9th: effrt in cl 3rd after 3 out: wknd bef next* **4/1**[2]

/PPP **P** **Kilrush (IRE)**[28] 4543 10-11-3 100..................................(t) DannyBurton(5)
(John Berwick) *sn in rr: struggling 4th: t.o whn p.u after 8th* **66/1**

P321 **P** **I'llhavealook (IRE)**[10] 4920 11-10-13 98........................(p) MissPFuller(7)
(Katie Stephens) *prom: rdn to chal appr 9th tl appr 3 out: sn wknd: p.u bef 2 out* **6/1**[3]

4326 **P** **Storm Alert**[6] 5033 9-10-11 92... LucyGardner(3)
(Sue Gardner) *chsd ldrs tl 6th: sn bhd: t.o whn p.u after 8th* **9/1**

00P3 **P** **Tales Of Milan (IRE)**[17] 4783 9-11-3 100............................(b) HarryCobden(5)
(Phil Middleton) *pressed ldr tl rdn after 8th: wknd 3 out: sn p.u* **7/2**[1]

6404 **P** **Comical Red**[22] 4682 8-10-4 82...(bt) TomCannon
(Mark Gillard) *led: rdn appr 9th: hdd 3 out: sn wknd: p.u bef next* **16/1**

-206 **P** **Zephyr**[14] 4860 5-11-5 104.. MrCWilliams(7)
(Nick Williams) *chsd ldrs tl 4th: sn struggling towards rr: t.o whn p.u bef 8th* **25/1**

5323 **P** **Precious Ground**[19] 4749 6-11-8 100.. JamesBest
(Kevin Bishop) *towards rr: reminders after 3rd: hdwy after 6th: drvn and wknd after 8th: p.u bef next* **7/1**

-P60 **P** **Doris De Silver**[12] 4881 7-9-12 81...(p) DavidNoonan(5)
(Jackie Du Plessis) *mid-div tl 4th: sn struggling in rr: t.o whn p.u after 6th* **40/1**

7m 22.3s (41.30) **Going Correction** +1.60s/f (Heav) **12 Ran SP% 119.7**
Speed ratings (Par 105): **100,99,98,86, , , , ,**
CSF £79.06 CT £1148.62 TOTE £9.90: £3.20, £3.10, £4.80; EX 99.50 Trifecta £1000.30.
Owner Andrew Cocks And Tara Johnson **Bred** Mick Berry **Trained** Wilsford-Cum-Lake, Wilts

FOCUS
A moderate staying handicap. There was a sound gallop on and it proved a war of attrition. Due to rail movement it was run over a distance 165yds further than advertised. A step up from the winner for the longer trip, with the third rated to his mark.

5166 INDEPENDENT RACECOURSES LTD, IRL OPEN HUNTERS' CHASE (20 fncs) 3m 1f 170y
5:15 (5:15) (Class 6) 5-Y-O+ **£1,317** (£405; £202)

Form RPR

0120 **1** **Impact Area (IRE)**[18] 4768 10-11-11 125...............(p) MrLouisMuspratt(5) 118+
(Mrs Harriet Waight) *j.rt virtually thrght bdly at times on 1st circ: led: mstke and hdd 4 out: sn drvn: led between last 2: styd on wl to assert towards fin* **4/5**[1]

UF-5 **2** *2* **Tony Star (FR)**[8] 9-12-1 130.. MrJamesKing(7) 120
(Mickey Bowen) *trckd ldrs: rdn after 3 out: chal 2 out: ev ch last: no ex towards fin* **3/1**[2]

-150 **3** *5* **Indiana Bay (IRE)**[18] 4768 9-11-13 118.............................. MrRobertHawker(5) 112
(Mrs Jill Dennis) *prom: led 4 out: rdn after next: hdd between last 2: no ex* **7/2**[3]

/P-3 **4** *15* **Batu Ferringhi (FR)**[31] 10-11-7 100.............................(p) MrSeanHoulihan(7) 94
(Mrs C Hitch) *trckd ldrs: rdn after 15th: nt pce to get on terms: wknd after 2 out* **28/1**

F21/ **5** *3 ¼* **Karinga Dandy (IRE)**[8] 10-11-7 0... MrSBurton(7) 88
(Miss R D Keeble) *nudged along in cl 5th: outpcd 15th: no threat after* **33/1**

7m 23.8s (39.20) **Going Correction** +1.50s/f (Heav) **5 Ran SP% 109.2**
Speed ratings: **99,98,96,92,91**
CSF £3.69 TOTE £1.70: £1.10, £1.60; EX 3.10 Trifecta £4.50.
Owner Mrs Harriet Waight **Bred** Hugh J Holohan **Trained** Enford, Wilts

FOCUS
A fair little hunter chase. It could be rated higher through the first three but the time was very slow compared with the earlier handicap and the fourth finished plenty close enough.
T/Plt: £122.90 to a £1 stake. Pool: £67,628.41 - 401.5 winning tickets. T/Qpdt: £62.90 to a £1 stake. Pool: £6,261.25 - 73.6 winning tickets. **Tim Mitchell**

5167 - 5173a (Foreign Racing) - See Raceform Interactive

2896
AINTREE (L-H)
Thursday, April 7

OFFICIAL GOING: National & hurdle courses - soft (good to soft in places; nat 4.8; hdl 5.3); mildmay course - good to soft (soft in places; 5.3)

Wind: fresh 1/2 behind Weather: fine but breezy and cold, shower race 2

5174 MERSEYRAIL MANIFESTO NOVICES' CHASE (GRADE 1) (16 fncs) 2m 3f 200y
1:40 (1:41) (Class 1) 5-Y-O+

£56,318 (£21,248; £10,658; £5,348; £2,708; £1,378)

Form — RPR

1132 **1** **Arzal (FR)**[68] 3856 6-11-4 151 .... GavinSheehan 164+
(Harry Whittington) *mde all: j. boldly: clr 5th: styd on wl: drvn out: unchal* **4/1**[3]

1123 **2** *8* **L'Ami Serge (IRE)**[21] 4729 6-11-4 153 .... DarylJacob 159
(Nicky Henderson) *trckd ldrs: 3rd whn j.lft 11th: chsd wnr sn after 12th: hit 2 out: swtchd rt appr last: kpt on: no imp* **9/2**

-122 **3** *16* **Sizing John**[23] 4696 6-11-4 151 .... JJBurke 144
(Henry De Bromhead, Ire) *trckd wnr: drvn bef 13th: wknd fr 2 out* **11/4**[1]

5152 **4** *2¾* **Bouvreuil (FR)**[23] 4701 5-11-4 147 ....(t) SamTwiston-Davies 141
(Paul Nicholls) *mid-div: hdwy 10th: drvn appr 3 out: one pce: hit last* **16/1**

-140 **5** *8* **Volnay De Thaix (FR)**[22] 4717 7-11-4 0 .... NicodeBoinville 134
(Nicky Henderson) *prom: pushed along 10th: outpcd 13th: sn btn* **12/1**

2135 **6** *25* **Aso (FR)**[23] 4696 6-11-4 145 .... AidanColeman 112
(Venetia Williams) *trckd wnr: hit 2nd: blnd 6th: lost pl 12th: wl bhd fr 3 out: t.o* **25/1**

5113 **7** *1* **Rock The World (IRE)**[20] 4770 8-11-4 149 ....(t) RobbiePower 113
(Mrs John Harrington, Ire) *t.k.h in rr: outpcd whn hit 12th: sn bhd: t.o 3 out* **14/1**

111F **F** **Garde La Victoire (FR)**[21] 4729 7-11-4 151 .... RichardJohnson
(Philip Hobbs) *nt fluent in rr: pushed along 9th: 7th and little imp whn fell 13th* **7/2**[2]

5m 8.2s (4.20) **Going Correction** +0.875s/f (Soft) 8 Ran SP% **111.2**
Speed ratings: **117,113,107,106,103 93,92,**
CSF £21.48 CT £54.27 TOTE £4.60: £1.60, £1.80, £1.40; EX 21.90 Trifecta £76.60.
Owner The Hennessy Six **Bred** Dominique Gouin & Mme Anna Racape **Trained** Sparsholt, Oxfordshire

FOCUS
This race had an additional 75yds added to the advertised distance. A really strong race to start off the Grand National meeting, with seven of the field last seen at Cheltenham about three weeks previously. The winner, a known pace-setter, was left alone to do his own thing in front and won with some authority. Daryl Jacob, who was on the second, described the ground on the chase course as 'a little on the soft side,' while Nico de Boinville said 'good to soft - soft and riding dead.' A step up from the winner, with the second rated to his Cheltenham mark.

5175 BETFRED ANNIVERSARY 4-Y-O JUVENILE HURDLE (GRADE 1) (9 hdls) 2m 209y
2:15 (2:18) (Class 1) 4-Y-O

£56,436 (£21,366; £10,776; £5,466; £2,826; £1,496)

Form — RPR

12 **1** **Apple's Jade (FR)**[20] 4764 4-10-7 145 .... BJCooper 164+
(W P Mullins, Ire) *wore ear plugs: trckd ldr: led appr 3 out: wl clr next: eased last 100yds: impressive* **3/1**[2]

41 **2** *41* **Ivanovich Gorbatov (IRE)**[20] 4764 4-11-0 154 ....(t) BarryGeraghty 131
(A P O'Brien, Ire) *trckd ldrs: effrt appr 3 out: 3rd whn hit 2 out: tk remote 2nd fnl 200yds* **7/4**[1]

52 **3** *½* **Azzuri**[40] 4358 4-11-0 0 ....(t) HarrySkelton 131
(Dan Skelton) *led: hit 3rd: hdd appr 3 out: kpt on same pce* **20/1**

1 **4** *4½* **Diego Du Charmil (FR)**[22] 4720 4-11-0 140 ....(t) SamTwiston-Davies 124
(Paul Nicholls) *hld up in mid-div: hdwy 5th: drvn appr 3 out: kpt on one pce* **10/1**

3252 **5** *2¾* **Romain De Senam (FR)**[22] 4720 4-11-0 141 ....(t) NickScholfield 125
(Paul Nicholls) *hld up in rr: nt fluent 1st: drvn appr 3 out: sn outpcd: blnd last* **16/1**

1110 **6** *2¼* **Sceau Royal (FR)**[20] 4764 4-11-0 141 .... DarylJacob 121
(Alan King) *chsd ldrs: effrt and hit 3 out: wknd 2 out* **16/1**

1115 **P** **Doubly Clever (IRE)**[22] 4720 4-11-0 135 .... NoelFehily
(Michael Blake) *in rr: bhd and outpcd 4th: mstke 6th: sn t.o: p.u bef next* **66/1**

313 **F** **Footpad (FR)**[20] 4764 4-11-0 150 .... RWalsh
(W P Mullins, Ire) *outpcd and lost pl 4th: in rr whn fell 6th* **7/2**[3]

3 **P** **Khezerabad (FR)**[40] 4358 4-11-0 0 .... NicodeBoinville
(Nicky Henderson) *chsd ldrs: drvn 5th: lost pl next: sn bhd: t.o whn p.u bef 3 out* **28/1**

4m 16.6s (2.90) **Going Correction** +0.65s/f (Soft) 9 Ran SP% **114.1**
Speed ratings: **119,99,99,97,96 95,,,**
CSF £8.65 CT £83.40 TOTE £3.60: £1.30, £1.30, £3.90; EX 8.40 Trifecta £137.10.
Owner Gigginstown House Stud **Bred** Ronny Coveliers **Trained** Muine Beag, Co Carlow

FOCUS
The bends and hurdles were on the outer lines, and were to be moved in after racing each day. This race had an additional 84yds added to the advertised distance. The ground on the hurdles course was viewed as being more testing than on the chase track. The first three from the Triumph and Fred Winter one-two squared off in what looked a strong edition of the race and it produced an extremely impressive winner, even taking into account the fact that the favourite was below par in second. A massive step up from the winner, and there's a case for rating her up to 3lb higher. As it is this is the joint-highest figure given to a juvenile in the history of RPRs. Throw in the mares' allowance and she looks Champion Hurdle material.

5176 BETFRED BOWL CHASE (GRADE 1) (19 fncs) 3m 210y
2:50 (2:51) (Class 1) 5-Y-O+

£84,655 (£32,050; £16,165; £8,200; £4,240; £2,245)

Form — RPR

111F **1** **Cue Card**[20] 4767 10-11-7 176 ....(t) PaddyBrennan 180+
(Colin Tizzard) *trckd ldrs: hit 9th: 3rd 13th: led 3 out: pushed clr sn after 2 out: 12 l ahd whn heavily eased last 75yds* **6/5**[1]

-113 **2** *9* **Don Poli (IRE)**[20] 4767 7-11-7 165 .... BJCooper 168
(W P Mullins, Ire) *led to 2nd: w ldr: drvn after 14th: upsides 3 out: styd on same pce fr next* **4/1**[3]

21F2 **3** *8* **Djakadam (FR)**[20] 4767 7-11-7 170 .... RWalsh 164+
(W P Mullins, Ire) *w ldrs: hmpd after 3rd: led next: hit 12th: hdd 3 out: kpt on same pce: stmbld landing last* **5/2**[2]

3020 **4** *5* **Dynaste (FR)**[21] 4731 10-11-7 155 ....(bt) TomScudamore 156
(David Pipe) *led 2nd: hit rogue running rail after next: hdd 4th: outpcd 15th: hit 3 out: lft modest 4th last* **33/1**

0-16 **5** *6* **Taquin Du Seuil (FR)**[21] 4731 9-11-7 156 .... NoelFehily 152
(Jonjo O'Neill) *in rr: hmpd after 3rd: hdwy 10th: outpcd 13th: lft modest 5th last* **22/1**

1556 **6** *16* **Saphir Du Rheu (FR)**[21] 4732 7-11-7 158 .... SamTwiston-Davies 138
(Paul Nicholls) *trckd ldrs: outpcd 13th: 4th whn hit 4 out: wknd 2 out: bhd whn hit last* **12/1**

0041 **P** **Houblon Des Obeaux (FR)**[54] 4113 9-11-7 158 ....(p) AidanColeman
(Venetia Williams) *in rr: drvn 3rd: mstke 5th: sn bhd: reminders after 11th: t.o whn p.u bef next* **33/1**

111P **P** **Wakanda (IRE)**[68] 3850 7-11-7 155 .... DannyCook
(Sue Smith) *in rr: hdwy 8th: drvn 12th: lost pl next: t.o 4 out: p.u bef last* **50/1**

55P5 **F** **Irish Cavalier (IRE)**[20] 4767 7-11-7 153 ....(b[1]) PaulTownend 157
(Rebecca Curtis) *hld up towards rr: hdwy 14th: modest 4th 2 out: fell last* **25/1**

6m 41.2s (11.20) **Going Correction** +0.875s/f (Soft) 9 Ran SP% **117.8**
Speed ratings: **117,114,111,109,108 102,,,**
CSF £6.38 CT £10.50 TOTE £1.90: £1.02, £1.80, £1.80; EX 7.10 Trifecta £12.20.
Owner Mrs Jean R Bishop **Bred** R T Crellin **Trained** Milborne Port, Dorset

FOCUS
This had an additional 100 yds added to the advertised distance. With the second and third in the Gold Cup, plus the unfortunate Cue Card, renewing rivalry here, this looked a well up to scratch renewal and it was run at a solid gallop. The first three in the betting strode away from the field heading towards the home bend for the final time, but only one mattered approaching the second-last. The impressive winner was value for further and he's been rated in line with his King George win.

5177 DOOM BAR AINTREE HURDLE (GRADE 1) (11 hdls) 2m 4f
3:25 (3:29) (Class 1) 4-Y-O- **£113,072** (£42,932; £21,752; £11,132; £5,852)

Form — RPR

F-11 **1** **Annie Power (IRE)**[23] 4698 8-11-0 162 .... RWalsh 170+
(W P Mullins, Ire) *trckd ldrs: 2nd 3rd: led after 5th: wnt wl clr on bit between last 2: v impressive* **4/9**[1]

23/2 **2** *18* **My Tent Or Yours (IRE)**[23] 4698 9-11-7 162 .... BarryGeraghty 160
(Nicky Henderson) *hld up: t.k.h: n.m.r bnd after 2nd: trckd ldrs 4th: 2nd bef 8th: drvn 3 out: wknd between last 2: 10 l 2nd and wl btn whn mstke last* **9/1**

1133 **3** *9* **Nichols Canyon**[23] 4698 6-11-7 162 .... PaulTownend 152
(W P Mullins, Ire) *j.rt: led tl after 5th: drvn and one pce 3 out* **11/2**[2]

0112 **4** *21* **Court Minstrel (IRE)**[75] 2634 9-11-7 157 .... PaulMoloney 128
(Evan Williams) *dropped in detached in last: wnt poor 4th bef 3 out: nvr on terms* **100/1**

U150 **5** *42* **Camping Ground (FR)**[23] 4698 6-11-7 160 ....(t) LeightonAspell 86
(Robert Walford) *trckd ldrs: t.k.h: pushed along 6th: nt fluent next: sn lost pl: bhd after 8th: t.o 2 out: eventually completed* **20/1**

1214 **F** **The New One (IRE)**[23] 4698 8-11-7 159 .... SamTwiston-Davies
(Nigel Twiston-Davies) *trckd ldrs: fell 5th* **8/1**[3]

5m 6.0s (5.30) **Going Correction** +0.65s/f (Soft) 6 Ran SP% **111.5**
Speed ratings (Par 117): **115,107,104,95,79**
CSF £5.41 TOTE £1.30: £1.10, £3.30; EX 4.30 Trifecta £11.50.
Owner Mrs S Ricci **Bred** Eamon Cleary **Trained** Muine Beag, Co Carlow

FOCUS
The bends and hurdles were on the outer lines, and were to be moved in after racing each day. This race had an additional 107yds added to the advertised distance. The first four from the Champion Hurdle reopposed over this longer trip and the outcome was the same, although the great mare was visually even more impressive with her rivals failing to perform to their best for one reason or another. A personal best from the winner for the step up in trip on softer ground. The second has been rated 7lb off his Festival mark.

5178 CRABBIE'S FOX HUNTERS' CHASE (18 fncs) 2m 5f 19y
4:05 (4:10) (Class 2) 6-Y-O+

£23,720 (£7,448; £3,724; £1,860; £932; £468)

Form — RPR

1-11 **1** **On The Fringe (IRE)**[20] 4768 11-12-0 147 .... MrJJCodd 148+
(E Bolger, Ire) *trckd ldrs: jnd ldrs 12th (Canal Turn): 2nd 3 out: led elbow: drvn clr* **15/8**[1]

0-22 **2** *8* **Dineur (FR)**[27] 4592 10-12-0 115 ....(t) MrJamesKing 140
(Mickey Bowen) *trckd ldrs: led 3 out: hdd elbow: kpt on same pce* **50/1**

-110 **3** *1¼* **Mendip Express (IRE)**[20] 4768 10-12-0 138 ....(t) MrDavidMaxwell 140
(Philip Hobbs) *chsd ldrs: hmpd 10th (Becher's): hit 14th: 3rd 3 out: kpt on same pce run-in* **11/1**

1124 **4** *16* **Current Event (FR)**[20] 4768 9-12-0 138 .... MsKWalsh 126
(Mrs Rose Loxton) *blnd 3rd (Chair): hdwy to chse ldrs 14th: wknd between last 2* **15/2**

3-33 **5** *10* **Doubledisdoubledat (IRE)**[16] 4866 9-12-0 99 .... MrTHamilton 114
(Stuart Coltherd) *w ldrs: led 3rd: hdd 5th: hit 11th (Foinavon): lft in ld sn after 12th (Canal Turn): blnd bdly 4 out: hdd next: wknd after 2 out* **80/1**

3U15 **6** *25* **Pacha Du Polder (FR)**[20] 4768 9-12-0 138 .... MrWBiddick 94
(Paul Nicholls) *led to 2nd: trckd ldrs: wknd bef 2 out: fin tired: t.o* **3/1**[2]

-13P **7** *16* **Monkey Kingdom**[35] 4446 8-12-0 133 ....(tp) MrDLQueally 82
(Rebecca Curtis) *led 2nd: hdd next: chsd ldrs: hit 11th (Foinavon): wknd 2 out: sn bhd: t.o* **25/1**

F-P2 **8** *41* **Ockey De Neulliac (FR)**[18] 4820 14-12-0 117 .... SamColtherd 30
(N Mechie) *prom: blnd 12th (Canal Turn): wknd 3 out: bhd whn blnd bdly last: virtually p.u: eventually completed* **33/1**

2-25 **P** **Fredo (IRE)**[25] 4651 12-12-0 116 ....(v) MrAlexFerguson
(Ian Williams) *nt jump wl in rr: bhd fr 5th: t.o 10th: p.u bef 12th (Canal Turn)* **50/1**

1P50 **U** **Major Malarkey (IRE)**[20] 4768 13-12-0 125 ....(v) MrSClements
(Nigel Twiston-Davies) *in rr: bhd fr 8th: t.o whn bdly hmpd and uns rdr 14th* **16/1**

4-23 **U** **Forge Valley**[29] 4558 12-12-0 100 ....(p) MrTGreenwood
(Miss G Walton) *in rr: bhd whn hit 5th: bdly hmpd and uns rdr next* **150/1**

41FP **P** **Night Alliance (IRE)**[14] 4892 11-12-0 119 ....(bt) MrJoeHill
(P R M Philips) *in rr: bhd fr 9th: t.o whn p.u bef 14th* **100/1**

55PP **P** **Fort George (IRE)**[301] 693 13-12-0 109 ....(p) MissBHampson
(Sally Randell) *in rr: bhd whn j.lft 7th: t.o whn p.u bef next* **100/1**

22P0 **U** **Richmond (FR)**[20] 4768 11-12-0 121 .... MissLMTurner
(P P C Turner) *in rr: bhd fr 7th: t.o whn blnd and uns rdr 13th* **100/1**

5-36 **U** **Bound For Glory (IRE)**[35] 4446 10-12-0 120 .... MissHLewis
(D M G Fitch-Peyton) *chsd ldrs: led 5th: rn wd: sddle slipped and uns rdr after 12th (Canal Turn)* **66/1**

26-0 **P** **Current Exchange (IRE)**[20] 4768 11-12-0 118........(tp) MrTimDonworth
(Gordon Elliott, Ire) *mid-div: bhd whn p.u bef 13th (Valentine's)* **66/1**

1P/ **P** **Marasonnien (FR)**[18] 10-12-0 131 MrPWMullins
(W P Mullins, Ire) *trckd ldrs: trckd ldrs and hit 8th: wknd and eased after 3 out: sn p.u: collapsed fatally* **7/1**[3]

662U **F** **Swallows Delight (IRE)**[27] 4592 11-12-0 108 MrDMansell
(Mrs Julie Mansell) *in rr: lost pl and mstke 6th: bhd whn fell 14th (Foinavon)* **100/1**

-401 **P** **Daymar Bay (IRE)**[35] 4446 10-12-0 120 MrAWright
(Gareth Thomas) *mid-div: hdwy 7th: lost pl 11th (Foinavon): sn bhd: t.o whn p.u bef 2 out* **40/1**

3P21 **P** **Clonbanan Lad (IRE)**[10] 4969 10-12-0 114 MrJSole
(Miss Louise Allan) *sn chsng ldrs: mstke 7th and 9th: j.lft 10th (Becher's): w ldrs whn hit 13th (Valentine's): eased and p.u bef next: collapsed fatally* **50/1**

2-1P **F** **Sam Cavallaro (IRE)**[14] 4892 10-12-0 111 MrJarrett
(Miss H Brookshaw) *mid-div: fell 6th* **100/1**

P-P0 **F** **Need To Know (IRE)**[20] 4768 8-12-0 109........(tp) MrBO'Neill
(John Paul Brennan, Ire) *in rr: fell 6th* **100/1**

5m 48.0s (11.00) **Going Correction** +0.85s/f (Soft) **22 Ran SP% 124.2**
Speed ratings: **113,109,109,103,99 90,83,68,, ,,,,, ,,,,, ,**
CSF £114.59 CT £888.82 TOTE £3.20: £1.50, £9.20, £3.30; EX 100.20 Trifecta £936.30.
Owner John P McManus **Bred** Pat Tobin **Trained** Bruree, Co Limerick
■ Stewards' Enquiry : Mr Alex Ferguson two-day ban: caused false start (2nd offence) (Apr 21-22)
Mr S Clements one-day ban: caused false start (Apr 21)
Sam Coltherd one-day ban: caused false start (Apr 21)
Ms K Walsh one-day ban: caused false start (Apr 21)
Mr T Hamilton one-day ban: caused false start (Apr 21)
Mr B O'Neill one-day ban: caused false start (Apr 21)
Mr D L Queally one-day ban: caused false start (Apr 21)

FOCUS
This race had an additional 10yds added to the advertised distance. The usual big field lined up for this well-established contest, but plenty of them were sent off at big odds and not many finished. The winner has been rated back to his best, with the third close to his mark.

5179 BETFRED RED RUM H'CAP CHASE (GRADE 3) (12 fncs) 1m 7f 176y
4:40 (4:47) (Class 1) 5-Y-0+
£56,270 (£21,200; £10,610; £5,300; £2,660; £1,330)

Form RPR

1223 **1** **Katachenko (IRE)**[18] 4816 7-10-10 **133** WayneHutchinson 139+
(Donald McCain) *w ldr: led bef 4th: mde rest: rdn bef 2 out: wandered between last 2: hit last: sn edgd lft: strly pressed fnl 110yds: fnd ex nr fin* **9/1**

12 **2** ½ **Dandridge**[20] 4770 7-11-5 **142**........(t) DavyRussell 146
(A L T Moore, Ire) *midfield: hdwy to trck ldrs 5th: nt fluent 2 out but wnt 2nd: sn rdn: chal strly run-in: kpt on: hld nr fin* **11/2**[2]

/0-3 **3** 1¼ **Viconte Du Noyer (FR)**[18] 4829 7-11-7 **144**........(t) JJBurke 149+
(Henry De Bromhead, Ire) *trckd ldng pair: rdn 3 out: ev ch whn nt fluent last: n.m.r on rail and hmpd 110yds out: btn in 3rd after* **8/1**[3]

1525 **4** 7 **Pearls Legend**[20] 4770 9-11-0 **137** NicodeBoinville 134
(John Spearing) *led narrowly: hdd bef 4th: remained prom: rdn after 3 out: hit last: wknd* **8/1**[3]

364F **5** 6 **Croco Bay (IRE)**[20] 4770 9-11-10 **147** KielanWoods 138
(Ben Case) *trckd ldng pair: rdn and outpcd 3 out: plugged on fr appr last* **16/1**

6424 **6** 4 **Going Concern (IRE)**[89] 3521 9-10-9 **132** PaulMoloney 120
(Evan Williams) *in tch: rdn and outpcd 3 out: plugged on fr appr last: no threat* **16/1**

2200 **7** 5 **Bright New Dawn (IRE)**[7] 5060 9-11-12 **150** 4ex........(t) BJCooper 134
(Gordon Elliott, Ire) *hld up in rr: mstke 8th: sme hdwy 4 out: rdn 3 out: wknd after 2 out* **11/1**

2630 **8** 3 **Workbench (FR)**[20] 4770 8-11-1 **138**........(t) HarrySkelton 119
(Dan Skelton) *hld up: rdn after 3 out: nvr threatened* **12/1**

00P0 **9** 13 **Surf And Turf (IRE)**[20] 4770 10-11-1 **138** BrianHughes 106
(Kevin Frost) *midfield: wknd bef 3 out* **16/1**

2551 **P** **Aye Well**[17] 4838 11-10-5 **128** DerekFox
(Stuart Coltherd) *hld up in midfield: mstke 6th: bit slow next: sn struggling: p.u bef last* **33/1**

4-P2 **P** **Fayette County (IRE)**[14] 4891 9-10-7 **130** BarryGeraghty
(Tim Vaughan) *unruly gng to s: midfield: effrt 4 out: sn wknd: p.u bef last* **11/2**[2]

3122 **P** **Minella Present (IRE)**[146] 2468 7-10-11 **134** NoelFehily
(Neil Mulholland) *hld up: nt fluent 7th: mstke 3 out: sn wknd: p.u bef last* **4/1**[1]

4m 9.0s (9.00) **Going Correction** +0.875s/f (Soft) **12 Ran SP% 119.6**
Speed ratings: **112,111,111,107,104 102,100,98,92, ,**
CSF £59.69 CT £421.57 TOTE £13.10: £3.50, £2.00, £2.80; EX 77.30 Trifecta £526.80.
Owner Trevor Hemmings **Bred** Charles Harte **Trained** Cholmondeley, Cheshire

FOCUS
This race had an additional 60yds added to the advertised distance. They didn't go the usual frantic gallop associated with this race and three came clear, with there being a bit of late trouble after the winner badly tightened up the third against the rail after the last. A small pb from the winner, with the second and third setting the level.

5180 GOFFS NICKEL COIN MARES' STANDARD OPEN NATIONAL HUNT FLAT RACE (GRADE 2) 2m 209y
5:15 (5:16) (Class 1) 4-6-Y-0
£22,508 (£8,480; £4,244; £2,120; £1,064; £532)

Form RPR

3-21 **1** **Kayf Grace**[10] 4974 6-11-0 109 NicodeBoinville 128+
(Nicky Henderson) *wore ear plugs: trckd ldng pair: rdn over 3f out: chal strly over 1f out: led narrowly 110yds out: styd on* **14/1**

10 **2** ½ **Augusta Kate**[22] 4721 5-11-0 129 RWalsh 128+
(W P Mullins, Ire) *in tch: rdn to chse ldrs over 3f out: led wl over 1f out: sn strly pressed: hdd narrowly 110yds out: hld nr fin* **15/8**[1]

3 5 **Shattered Love (IRE)**[32] 4522 5-11-0 BJCooper 123+
(Gordon Elliott, Ire) *trckd ldrs: dropped to midfield 12f out: pushed along over 4f out: hdwy to chse ldrs over 3f out: one pce in 3rd fr appr fnl f* **8/1**[3]

-116 **4** 7 **Copper Kay**[26] 4623 6-11-0 123 RichardJohnson 116
(Philip Hobbs) *hld up in midfield: rdn over 4f out: sme hdwy over 3f out: plugged on fnl 2f: nvr threatened ldrs* **8/1**[3]

1 **5** hd **Snow Leopardess**[43] 4309 4-10-8 114 AidanColeman 109
(Charlie Longsdon) *in tch: rdn over 3f out: wandered over 1f out: plugged on: nvr threatened ldrs* **20/1**

21 **6** nk **Little Miss Poet**[41] 4350 4-10-1 117 ConorSmith(7) 109
(Philip Hobbs) *trckd ldng pair: led over 3f out: sn rdn: hdd wl over 1f out: wknd fnl f* **33/1**

1-11 **7** 6 **La Bague Au Roi (FR)**[123] 2929 5-11-0 126 GavinSheehan 111
(Warren Greatrex) *trckd ldng pair: led over 4f out: sn rdn: hdd over 3f out: edgd lft 2f out: sn wknd* **2/1**[2]

1 **8** 4½ **Lastbutnotleast (IRE)**[32] 4515 6-11-0 106 AdrianLane 105
(Donald McCain) *w ldr: rdn 4f out: wknd over 2f out* **80/1**

13 **9** 7 **Lillian (IRE)**[38] 4414 5-10-9 103 KevinJones(5) 98
(Seamus Mullins) *hld up in rr: rdn along over 5f out: nvr threatened* **150/1**

2440 **10** 5 **Cajun Fiddle (IRE)**[26] 4623 5-11-0 111 BrendanPowell 93
(Alan King) *hld up: nvr threatened* **100/1**

32 **11** 6 **Theatre Territory (IRE)**[47] 4242 6-11-0 116 DavidBass 87
(Nicky Henderson) *in tch towards outside: rdn 4f out: sn wknd* **33/1**

1 **12** 5 **Bells On Sunday**[10] 4967 5-11-0 112 SamTwiston-Davies 82
(Tom Lacey) *midfield: rdn over 4f out: sn wknd* **40/1**

41 **13** 4 **Potters Lady Jane**[48] 4228 4-10-8 108 HarrySkelton 72
(Lucy Wadham) *hld up in midfield: rdn over 4f out: sn wknd* **100/1**

2 **14** 6 **Storm Patrol**[56] 4074 5-11-0 115........(t) DarylJacob 72
(Suzy Smith) *hld up in midfield: rdn over 4f out: sn wknd* **25/1**

21 **15** 55 **Miss Spent (IRE)**[68] 3862 6-11-0 115 LeightonAspell 17
(Lucy Wadham) *hld up: sme hdwy over 5f out: rdn 4f out: sn wknd* **66/1**

21 **16** nk **My Khaleesi**[56] 4074 5-11-0 117 WayneHutchinson 16
(Alan King) *hld up in midfield: rdn over 4f out: sn wknd* **33/1**

001 **17** 22 **Beyond Measure (IRE)**[56] 4075 5-11-0 114 [1] DenisO'Regan
(Don Cantillon) *led narrowly: hdd over 4f out: wknd* **100/1**

4m 17.26s (9.86) **Going Correction** +0.65s/f (Soft)
WFA 4 from 5yo+ 5lb **17 Ran SP% 123.2**
Speed ratings: **104,103,101,98,98 97,95,92,89,87 84,82,80,77,51 51,41**
CSF £38.04 CT £243.44 TOTE £17.10: £3.90, £1.50, £2.40; EX 54.90 Trifecta £295.00.
Owner James and Jean Potter **Bred** James & Jean Potter **Trained** Upper Lambourn, Berks

FOCUS
This race had an additional 84yds added to the advertised distance. Lots of fillies and mares with at least one win in their profile lined-up for some black type, making the race look really competitive, but the early gallop wasn't overly strong and many took a keen grip as a result. The first three look smart mares and it's been rated around the balance of the fourth, fifth, sixth, eighth and ninth.
T/Jkpt: Not won. T/Plt: £13.30 to a £1 stake. Pool: £521,544.60 - 28,467.99 winning units.
T/Qpdt: £7.70 to a £1 stake. Pool: £24,186.04 - 2318.88 winning units.
Walter Glynn & Andrew Sheret

4848 TAUNTON (R-H)
Thursday, April 7

OFFICIAL GOING: Good changing to good (good to firm in places) after race 2 (2.40)
Wind: quite strong across Weather: overcast

5181 EDDIE AND MARY DUNN MEMORIAL (S) H'CAP HURDLE (9 hdls) 2m 104y
2:05 (2:05) (Class 5) (0-100,100) 4-7-Y-0 **£3,898** (£1,144; £572; £286)

Form RPR

P00P **1** **Memory Of Light (IRE)**[50] 4184 7-9-11 **71**........(t[1]) BenPoste(3) 82+
(Sally Randell) *mid-div: hdwy 5th: rdn to chal after 3 out: led next: kpt on wl: rdn out* **5/1**[2]

P-P0 **2** 8 **Unify**[12] 4919 6-10-1 **75** HarryBannister(3) 80
(Grant Cann) *towards rr: pushed along after 4th: hdwy after 6th: rdn to chse ldrs after 3 out: lft cl 3rd next: styd on fr last: wnt 2nd fnl 120yds* **40/1**

5330 **3** 3¼ **Cahill (IRE)**[17] 4845 4-11-9 **100** AlainCawley 95
(Fergal O'Brien) *led 2nd: rdn whn hrd pressed after 3 out: hdd next: styd on same pce fr last* **15/2**

2P6P **4** ½ **Warrant Officer**[52] 4159 6-11-1 **86** MarcGoldstein 87
(Sheena West) *led tl 2nd: chsd ldrs: rdn after 3 out: lft cl 4th next: styd on same pce fr last* **8/1**

0654 **5** 6 **Little James (IRE)**[64] 3925 7-11-1 **89**........(p) RyanHatch(3) 84
(Nigel Twiston-Davies) *trckd ldrs: rdn after 3 out: wknd next* **4/1**[1]

44-P **6** 11 **Major Martin (IRE)**[117] 3042 7-10-7 **88** JasonNuttall(10) 73
(Gary Moore) *mid-div tl 5th: sn bhd* **8/1**

6054 **7** 8 **Drummond**[8] 5029 7-9-10 **72** DavidNoonan(5) 50
(Katie Stephens) *sn trcking ldrs: rdn after 5th: wknd after next* **11/2**[3]

4-P0 **8** 13 **Miss Siskin**[99] 3368 7-10-1 **79** MissBFrost(7) 45
(Jimmy Frost) *a bhd* **20/1**

50-0 **R** **Ginjo**[326] 361 6-10-7 **81**........(p) RobertWilliams(3)
(Bernard Llewellyn) *hld up towards rr of midfield: making hdwy whn rn out 5th* **25/1**

00P0 **P** **Culm Counsellor**[14] 4886 7-10-1 **72**........(b[1]) JamesDavies
(Chris Down) *racd keenly: trckd ldrs: rdn after 5th: wknd qckly: t.o whn p.u after 3 out* **33/1**

530P **C** **Marley Joe (IRE)**[130] 2810 5-11-12 **97** AndrewTinkler 95+
(Martin Keighley) *hld up: smooth hdwy 3 out: hmpd by loose horse whn attempting to mount chal fnl bnd: upsides but pushed along whn carried out 2 out* **6/1**

(-8.00) **Going Correction** -0.525s/f (Firm)
WFA 4 from 5yo+ 5lb **11 Ran SP% 114.3**
Speed ratings: **99,95,93,93,90 84,80,74, ,**
CSF £184.27 CT £1478.43 TOTE £4.70: £2.00, £9.50, £2.70; EX 206.20 Trifecta £1497.20 Part won..Cahill was bought by Mr L Corcoran for £6,000; Marley Joe was bought by Mrs Ali Stronge for £6,000
Owner Guy Sainsbury **Bred** J C Condon **Trained** Broad Hinton, Wilts

FOCUS
The going was good following a dry night, though it was felt that if the showers missed the course there would be some good to firm places in the home straight. The jockeys in the first felt that the ground rode as advertised. Divided bends with the rail positions increasing the distance of the opening race by 87yds. A moderate selling handicap hurdle to start, but plenty of drama at the penultimate flight. A hurdle pb from the runner-up.

5182 PORTER DODSON NOVICES' HURDLE (10 hdls) 2m 3f 1y
2:40 (2:40) (Class 4) 4-Y-0+ **£4,548** (£1,335; £667; £333)

Form RPR

-412 **1** **Emerging Talent (IRE)**[54] 4111 7-11-6 135........(t) SeanBowen 137+
(Paul Nicholls) *j. sltly rt: nt a fluent: mde all: rdn clr after last: readily* **1/4**[1]

400 **2** 3½ **Ebadani (IRE)**[42] 4317 6-11-0 119 MichealNolan 124
(Jamie Snowden) *trckd ldrs: chal 2 out: sn rdn: ev ch last: outpcd fnl 140yds* **8/1**[3]

61 **3** *26* **Mr Kite**[162] 783 5-10-9 0.. MrMLegg(5) 100
(Harry Fry) *racd keenly: trckd ldrs: rdn in cl 3rd appr 2 out: sn wknd* **4/1**[2]
4 *14* **Bestwork D'Olivate (FR)**[148] 5-10-7 0........................ LiamHeard 77
(Martin Hill) *towards rr: stdy prog fr 6th: wnt 4th 3 out: sn outpcd* **12/1**
400 **5** *14* **My Anchor**[76] 3725 5-10-7 103........................(t) TommyDowling(7) 70
(Charlie Mann) *towards rr: wnt modest 5th latter stages: nvr any threat* **14/1**
060 **6** *½* **Denny Kerrell**[19] 4784 5-11-0 0.................................... IanPopham 70
(Caroline Keevil) *mid-div tl wknd after 3 out* **80/1**
00 **7** *nk* **Starlit Night**[12] 4916 4-10-0 0.................................... JamesDavies 55
(Chris Down) *mid-div: rdn after 6th: wknd 3 out* **100/1**
8 *1 ½* **Sticking Point** 5-11-0 0..(t[1]) AndrewTinkler 68
(Martin Keighley) *trckd ldrs: rdn bef 3 out: wknd sn after* **22/1**
00 **9** *8* **Galice Du Ciel**[55] 4103 5-11-0 0................................ TomCannon 60
(Giles Smyly) *trckd ldrs: rdn after 3 out: sn wknd* **150/1**
6 **10** *29* **Nosper (FR)**[179] 1866 4-10-2 0.................................... AliceMills(5) 24
(Martin Hill) *struggling 6th: a towards rr: t.o* **80/1**
-5PP **11** *17* **Real Gone Kid**[63] 3949 5-10-11 0.........................(p) KillianMoore(3) 14
(Martin Keighley) *mid-div tl wknd after 7th: t.o* **66/1**
606 **P** **Goonjim (IRE)**[10] 4963 5-11-0 0.................................... RhysFlint
(Alexandra Dunn) *racd keenly: mid-div tl 5th: lost tch qckly bef next: t.o whn p.u after 3 out* **125/1**

4m 34.6s (-11.40) **Going Correction** -0.525s/f (Firm)
WFA 4 from 5yo+ 5lb **12 Ran SP% 136.2**
Speed ratings (Par 105): **103,101,90,84,78 78,78,77,74,62 55,**
CSF £5.01 TOTE £1.20: £1.02, £2.30, £1.30; EX 7.60 Trifecta £15.60.
Owner Mr & Mrs Paul Barber **Bred** T J Nagle **Trained** Ditcheat, Somerset

FOCUS
Race distance increased by 87yds. An uncompetitive novices' hurdle and the market leaders dominated throughout. The cosy winner has been rated close to his mark, with the third in line with his bumper form.

5183 C & D SOUTHWEST H'CAP HURDLE (12 hdls) 2m 7f 198y
3:15 (3:15) (Class 4) (0-120,119) 4-Y-0+ **£4,548** (£1,335; £667; £333)

Form RPR
0312 **1** **Horace Hazel**[279] 897 7-10-12 110.............................. DavidNoonan(5) 113+
(Anthony Honeyball) *in tch: trckd ldrs 8th: rdn to chse ldr after 3 out: looked hld whn nt fluent 2 out: 7 l down last: styd on wl to catch idling ldr towards fin* **6/1**[3]
1331 **2** *½* **Minellacelebration (IRE)**[17] 4853 6-11-3 117..................... MrJNixon(7) 125+
(Katy Price) *whipped rnd at tapes at standing s: steadily rcvrd to join ldr 5th: led 8th: 7 l clr last: hung lft and looked to be idling fnl 140yds: ct towards fin* **11/4**[1]
430P **3** *24* **Tokyo Javilex (FR)**[16] 4860 9-10-9 109.........................(t) MrLDrowne(7) 89
(Nigel Hawke) *trckd ldrs early: in rr and drvn fr 5th: no ch 3 out: 32 l 5th jumping 2 out: wnt modest 3rd towards fin* **25/1**
501 **4** *1* **Church Field (IRE)**[25] 4648 8-11-7 119........................(v) HarryCobden(5) 98
(Phil Middleton) *in tch: struggling after 8th: 5th and btn 3 out: wnt modest 3rd briefly run-in* **9/2**[2]
35-6 **5** *3* **Church Hall (IRE)**[18] 4824 8-11-4 111............................. JamesBanks 87
(Emma Baker) *in tch: hdwy 8th: rdn to chse ldng pair after 3 out: wknd next: lost 2 pls run-in* **7/1**
U2 **6** *22* **Lord Heathfield (IRE)**[25] 4651 10-11-1 115.....(p) MrTommieMO'Brien(7) 72
(Graeme McPherson) *trckd ldrs: rdn after 6th: lost pl after next: wknd after 8th: t.o* **25/1**
140 **7** *13* **Handsome Sam**[69] 3846 5-11-2 116.............. WilliamFeatherstone(7) 61
(Alan King) *in tch: rdn after 8th: wknd after next: t.o* **6/1**[3]
-FPP **8** *17* **Seranwen (IRE)**[18] 4823 9-10-8 104................................. RyanHatch(3) 34
(Nigel Twiston-Davies) *hld up: hdwy 8th: rdn in 4th after 3 out: sn wknd: t.o* **16/1**
413P **P** **Absolutlyfantastic**[202] 1579 9-11-10 117.........................(t) LiamHeard
(Martin Hill) *led tl hit 8th: wknd next: t.o whn p.u after 3 out* **20/1**
-020 **P** **Fivefortyfive**[15] 4874 8-11-0 107.................................(t) TomO'Brien
(Polly Gundry) *chsd ldr tl 5th: sn pushed along: last and drvn after 7th: lost tch fr next: p.u after 3 out* **9/1**

5m 52.3s (-11.70) **Going Correction** -0.525s/f (Firm) **10 Ran SP% 114.3**
Speed ratings (Par 105): **98,97,89,89,88 81,76,71, ,**
CSF £22.32 CT £377.24 TOTE £6.00: £2.30, £1.70, £4.20; EX 25.30 Trifecta £1353.20.
Owner T C Frost **Bred** T C Frost **Trained** Mosterton, Dorset

FOCUS
Race distance increased by 114yds. The ground was changed to good, good to firm in places before this fair staying handicap hurdle. It proved to be another dramatic event and a horror show for many in-running players, with the favourite being matched at 1.01 to decent money. The runners had to cope with a standing start. The second has been rated as running a pb, with the third in line with his Exeter run.

5184 RETREAT RESTAURANT ILMINSTER H'CAP CHASE (14 fncs) 2m 2f 40y
3:55 (3:57) (Class 3) (0-140,140) 5-Y-0+ **£8,431** (£2,633; £1,418)

Form RPR
1041 **1** **Carrigmorna King (IRE)**[173] 1976 10-11-12 140..........(t) MichealNolan 146
(Philip Hobbs) *trckd ldr: prom 8th: rdn to chse ldr after 3 out: keeping on strly and narrow advantage whn lft clr last* **5/1**[3]
0510 **2** *5* **Sew On Target (IRE)**[21] 4733 11-11-6 139..................(t) HarryCobden(5) 143+
(Colin Tizzard) *j.lft bdly at times: led tl 4 out: sn rdn: keeping on at same pce in hld 3rd whn lft 2nd at the last* **11/8**[1]
PB00 **3** *2* **Le Bacardy (FR)**[82] 3620 10-11-1 129............................. RobertDunne 130
(Dan Skelton) *trckd ldrs: rdn in cl 3rd after 3 out: no ex appr last where lft 3rd and sltly hmpd* **4/1**[2]
123P **U** **Easily Pleased (IRE)**[12] 4918 10-10-8 122.................. JeremiahMcGrath 128
(Martin Hill) *racd keenly: trckd ldrs: led 4 out: rdn whn chal after 2 out: narrowly hdd whn stmbld bdly and uns rdr last* **8/1**

4m 39.9s (-12.10) **Going Correction** -0.60s/f (Firm) **4 Ran SP% 89.9**
Speed ratings: **102,99,98,**
CSF £8.69 TOTE £3.70; EX 7.80 Trifecta £12.60.
Owner Robert & Janet Gibbs **Bred** Tom McCarthy **Trained** Withycombe, Somerset

FOCUS
Race distance increased by 48yds. A decent handicap chase despite the field being reduced to four and another race with a dramatic climax. The winner and unseater have been rated pretty much to their marks.

5185 DAVE CRIDDLE TRAVEL H'CAP HURDLE (10 hdls) 2m 3f 1y
4:30 (4:30) (Class 3) (0-140,139) 4-Y-0+ **£6,498** (£1,908; £954; £477)

Form RPR
5201 **1** **Here's Herbie**[24] 4685 8-10-12 128............................(t) LucyGardner(3) 130
(Sue Gardner) *mid-div: hdwy 7th: led appr 2 out: edgd lft run-in: hld on: all out* **12/1**
6020 **2** *shd* **Qualando (FR)**[20] 4769 5-11-7 139..............................(b[1]) HarryCobden(5) 141
(Paul Nicholls) *hld up towards rr: nudged along fr 6th: hdwy after 3 out: wnt 4th 2 out: rdn and str run fr last: chal fnl 75yds: jst hld* **10/3**[1]
3B30 **3** *2 ¾* **Gores Island (IRE)**[34] 4464 10-10-9 122.......................... JamieMoore 122
(Gary Moore) *mid-div: hdwy 6th: chal 2 out: rdn and ev ch fr last: no ex fnl 75yds* **16/1**
2425 **4** *12* **Heath Hunter (IRE)**[12] 4913 9-10-12 130....................(p) DavidNoonan(5) 120
(David Pipe) *mid-div: hdwy 6th: disp 7th: hit next: rdn and hdd bef 2 out: sn one pce* **6/1**
1030 **5** *3* **Cousin Khee**[33] 4482 9-11-0 127...................................... TomO'Brien 113
(Hughie Morrison) *nvr really travelling in rr: sme late prog: nvr a threat* **14/1**
2451 **6** *¾* **Eardisland**[30] 4546 6-10-0 113...(t) JamesBest 98
(Philip Hobbs) *trckd ldrs: rdn after 7th: one pce fr 2 out* **16/1**
2553 **7** *nk* **After Eight Sivola (FR)**[35] 4452 6-10-6 124........................ LizzieKelly(5) 110
(Nick Williams) *trckd ldrs: disp 7th tl rdn appr 2 out: sn one pce* **4/1**[3]
3414 **8** *24* **Crimson Ark (IRE)**[19] 4788 6-10-9 122............................. SeanBowen 85
(Emma Lavelle) *trckd ldr: disputing whn nt fluent 7th: sn hdd: wknd next: t.o* **7/2**[2]
FPPP **9** *10* **Kingscourt Native (IRE)**[40] 4362 8-10-12 130..............(t) PaulO'Brien(5) 84
(Colin Tizzard) *chsd ldrs tl 6th: sn bhd: t.o* **16/1**
-1P0 **10** *27* **Vif Argent (FR)**[40] 4362 7-10-1 114 ow1............................ TomCannon 44
(Andrew Reid) *trckd ldrs:disp 7th tl after rdn 3 out: wknd qckly: t.o* **33/1**
11 *3 ¼* **Theatre Mill (IRE)**[222] 990 8-10-13 126........................ RichieMcLernon 53
(Richenda Ford) *led tl after 6th: wknd after next: t.o* **50/1**

4m 33.2s (-12.80) **Going Correction** -0.525s/f (Firm) **11 Ran SP% 116.5**
Speed ratings (Par 107): **105,104,103,98,97 97,97,86,82,71 69**
CSF £52.47 CT £656.46 TOTE £13.30: £3.10, £2.30, £3.60; EX 63.60 Trifecta £1823.20.
Owner D V Gardner **Bred** D V Gardner Woodhayes Stud **Trained** Longdown, Devon

FOCUS
Race distance increased by 87yds. A decent handicap hurdle run at a fair pace and a thrilling battle between the front three up the run-in. A pb from the winner, with the second to his best and third similar to his recent hurdle form.

5186 PONTISPOOL EQUINE SPORTS CENTRE "GRASSROOTS' HUNTERS" CHASE (FOR THE MITFORD-SLADE CHALLENGE TROPHY) (17 fncs) 2m 7f 3y
5:05 (5:05) (Class 5) 6-Y-0+ **£2,305** (£709; £354)

Form RPR
3/3- **1** **Benedictus (IRE)**[18] 11-11-7 0............................ MrMartinMcIntyre(5) 127+
(Jack R Barber) *trckd ldrs: rdn in cl 4th after 4 out: wnt 2nd after next: str chal appr last: won on nod* **5/6**[1]
/23- **2** *shd* **Foynes Island (IRE)**[18] 10-11-5 100..........................(p) MrDAndrews(7) 126+
(Miss L J Cabble) *led: rdn after 3 out: narrow advantage whn hit last: styd on: lost on nod* **4/1**[3]
2-14 **3** *17* **Parkam Jack**[19] 10-11-9 111.. MrJLThomas(7) 114
(Mrs Kayley Woollacott) *trckd ldrs: chal 13th tl hit 4 out: sn rdn in cl 3rd: hld after next: wknd between last 2* **11/4**[2]
P5P **4** *22* **Triggywinkle (FR)**[37] 4426 7-10-12 0.........................(tp) MrNLawton(7) 79
(Roderick Chelton) *cl up: trckd ldr after 4 out: rdn next: sn hld: wknd between last 2* **33/1**
4U6- **P** **Lundy Sky**[12] 11-11-5 0.. MrJMorris(7)
(Miss L Luxton) *j.rt at times: prom: mstke 4th: nt fluent 11th: wknd 13th: hit 4 out: sn p.u* **12/1**

5m 52.5s (-23.50) **Going Correction** -0.60s/f (Firm) **5 Ran SP% 111.9**
Speed ratings: **109,108,103,95,**
CSF £4.90 TOTE £1.50: £1.10, £2.10; EX 3.90 Trifecta £5.20.
Owner The Benedictus Partnership **Bred** Mrs Eleanor Hadden **Trained** Crewkerne, Somerset

FOCUS
Race distance increased by 48yds. A fair hunter chase and another thrilling finish. The winner was a 130 chaser at his best and there's a case for rating this a bit higher. The second has been rated in line with the best of his form for Philip Hobbs.

5187 HIGOS INSURANCE STANDARD OPEN NATIONAL HUNT FLAT RACE (DIV I) 2m 104y
5:40 (5:40) (Class 5) 4-6-Y-O **£2,737** (£798; £399)

Form RPR
25 **1** **Show On The Road**[19] 4790 5-11-3 0.................................[1] MichealNolan 113+
(Philip Hobbs) *trckd ldr: led over 4f out: in command fr over 2f out: pushed out* **3/1**[2]
3 **2** *1 ¾* **Only For Love**[34] 4468 5-10-5 0................................ FreddieMitchell(5) 101
(Nicky Henderson) *trcking ldrs whn rn wd on bnd after 7f: sn pushed along in tch: rdn and hdwy fr 3f out: styd on fnl f but a being hld by wnr: wnt 2nd nring fin* **3/1**[2]
1 **3** *½* **Captain Buck's (FR)**[44] 4296 4-10-11 0..................(t) MrStanSheppard(7) 109
(Paul Nicholls) *cl up: wnt 2nd over 3f out: rdn to chse wnr over 2f out: styd on fnl f but a being hld: lost 2nd nring fin* **6/4**[1]
0 **4** *19* **Lady Ash (IRE)**[47] 4242 6-10-10 0.................................... SeanBowen 83
(Robert Walford) *chsd ldrs: rdn 4f out: wknd wl over 2f out* **25/1**
5 *11* **Deckers Delight** 5-10-10 0.. JamesBest 74
(Nigel Hawke) *in last pair: struggling and detached 1/2-way: nvr any threat* **25/1**
6 *9* **Executive Prince (IRE)**[320] 6-11-3 0............................ MattGriffiths 72
(Jeremy Scott) *racd freely: led tl over 4f out: wknd 3f out* **16/1**
7 *92* **Tigers Rock** 5-10-10 0.. JamesBanks
(Noel Williams) *a in last pair: lost tch 1/2-way: t.o* **12/1**[3]

3m 54.7s (-7.70) **Going Correction** -0.525s/f (Firm)
WFA 4 from 5yo+ 5lb **7 Ran SP% 111.3**
Speed ratings: **98,97,96,87,81 77,31**
CSF £11.73 TOTE £3.60: £1.50, £2.30; EX 12.20 Trifecta £21.60.
Owner R M Penny **Bred** Robin Mathew **Trained** Withycombe, Somerset

FOCUS
Race distance increased by 87yds. This looked the stronger of the two divisions and the pace was decent for a race of its type. The finish only involved the three at the head of the market, but not the result many would have expected. The second and third set the level.

5188 HIGOS INSURANCE STANDARD OPEN NATIONAL HUNT FLAT RACE (DIV II) 2m 104y
6:10 (6:10) (Class 5) 4-6-Y-O **£2,737** (£798; £399)

Form RPR
1 **Brahms De Clermont (FR)** 5-11-3 0................................ SeanBowen 119+
(Paul Nicholls) *cl up: led over 2f out: qcknd clr over 1f out: easily* **6/4**[1]
2 *16* **Flush Or Bust**[95] 6-11-3 0.. TomO'Brien 103
(Philip Hobbs) *racd wout declared tongue tie: trckd ldrs: rdn wl over 2f out: styd on into 2nd fnl f but no ch w wnr* **10/1**

6 **3** *5* **Baby Sherlock**[63] 3959 5-11-3 0.............................. ConorO'Farrell 98
(David Pipe) *led: drvn and hung lft over 2f out: sn hdd: outpcd by wnr over 1f out: no ex whn lost 2nd ins fnl f* **15/8**[2]

2 **4** *4* **Royal Plaza**[135] 2702 5-10-10 0.............................. WilliamFeatherstone[(7)] 94
(Alan King) *racd keenly: cl up: effrt over 2f out: wknd fnl f* **9/2**[3]

6 **5** *18* **Toosey**[43] 4308 5-11-3 0.............................. JamesDavies 76
(Tom Symonds) *chsd ldrs: rdn 4f out: sn wknd* **14/1**

P **P** **Lure Des Pres (IRE)**[40] 4357 4-10-11 0..............................(t) IanPopham
(Linda Blackford) *struggling 1/2-way: t.o whn p.u over 3f out* **40/1**

3m 57.2s (-5.20) **Going Correction** -0.525s/f (Firm)
WFA 4 from 5yo+ 5lb **6** Ran SP% **111.2**
Speed ratings: **92,84,81,79,70**
CSF £16.65 TOTE £2.60: £1.60, £1.90; EX 16.60 Trifecta £40.10.
Owner Paul Nicholls **Bred** Elevage De Clermont **Trained** Ditcheat, Somerset

FOCUS
Race distance increased by 87yds. They didn't go such a strong pace in this leg and the winning time was 2.5sec slower, but that's not to say the winner is not a very nice prospect. It's been rated around the balance of the third and fourth.
T/Plt: £59.10 to a £1 stake. Pool: £69,708.92 - 860.59 winning units. T/Qpdt: £14.60 to a £1 stake. Pool: £4,941.81 - 249.52 winning units. **Tim Mitchell**

5174 AINTREE (L-H)
Friday, April 8

OFFICIAL GOING: Hurdle & national course - soft (good to soft in places; hdl 5.3, ntl 4.8); mildmay course - good to soft (soft in places; mmy 5.3)
Wind: moderate 1/2 against Weather: fine and sunny

5189 ALDER HEY CHILDREN'S CHARITY H'CAP HURDLE (GRADE 3) (11 hdls) 2m 4f
1:40 (1:40) (Class 1) 4-Y-O+
£28,135 (£10,600; £5,305; £2,650; £1,330; £665)

Form RPR

6P-P **1** **Party Rock (IRE)**[20] 4801 9-10-8 **130**.............................. SeanQuinlan 140+
(Jennie Candlish) *led tl after 2nd: chsd ldrs: led 2 out: mstke last: edgd rt drvn out* **33/1**

1502 **2** *5* **Champagne At Tara**[20] 4801 7-10-11 **133**.............................. RichardJohnson 135
(Jonjo O'Neill) *hld up towards rr: hdwy 8th: chsng ldrs next: kpt on to take 2nd last 100yds* **14/1**

F-25 **3** *hd* **Starchitect (IRE)**[21] 4765 5-11-5 **141**..............................(bt) TomScudamore 145
(David Pipe) *chsd ldrs: 2nd whn blnd 2 out: kpt on same pce run-in* **7/1**[1]

6163 **4** *6* **Sky Khan**[21] 4769 7-11-4 **140**..............................(p) PeterBuchanan 136
(Lucinda Russell) *in rr-div: hdwy to chse ldrs 7th: kpt on one pce fr 2 out* **25/1**

111P **5** *shd* **Virgilio (FR)**[98] 3408 7-11-12 **148**..............................(t) HarrySkelton 145
(Dan Skelton) *in rr: hdwy appr 3 out: kpt on run-in* **8/1**[2]

5233 **6** *3 1/4* **San Benedeto (FR)**[40] 4381 5-11-3 **144**..............................(t) HarryCobden[(5)] 136
(Paul Nicholls) *t.k.h: trckd ldrs: lost pl after 7th: kpt on one pce fr 2 out* **16/1**

04 **7** *2 1/4* **Blazer (FR)**[23] 4717 5-11-6 **142**.............................. BarryGeraghty 133
(W P Mullins, Ire) *hld up in rr: hdwy 6th: trcking ldrs next: one pce appr 2 out* **8/1**[2]

2351 **8** *12* **Ibis Du Rheu (FR)**[21] 4769 5-11-6 **147**..............................(t) JackSherwood[(5)] 130+
(Paul Nicholls) *hld up in rr: sme hdwy 3 out: nvr a threat: hmpd last* **12/1**[3]

-3P0 **9** *1/2* **Theinval (FR)**[23] 4717 6-11-12 **148**.............................. JeremiahMcGrath 128
(Nicky Henderson) *hld up in rr: hdwy appr 3 out: nvr a factor: hmpd last* **20/1**

34P0 **10** *3/4* **Box Office (FR)**[22] 4730 5-10-11 **133**.............................. NoelFehily 111
(Jonjo O'Neill) *hld up in rr: hdwy 8th: effrt appr 3 out: wknd 2 out* **25/1**

50F0 **11** *11* **Buiseness Sivola (FR)**[21] 4769 5-11-0 **136**.............................. DarylJacob 102
(W P Mullins, Ire) *in rr: nvr a factor* **66/1**

1436 **12** *1* **Francis Of Assisi (IRE)**[21] 4765 6-10-10 **139**.............. MrAlexFerguson[(7)] 104
(John Ferguson) *mid-div: drvn bef 3 out: sn lost pl* **33/1**

2066 **13** *3 3/4* **Foxcub (IRE)**[48] 4244 8-11-5 **141**..............................(p) JamesDavies 102
(Tom Symonds) *chsd ldrs: reminders 5th: sn lost pl: bhd fr 8th* **50/1**

3205 **14** *48* **Cardinal Palace (IRE)**[35] 3765 6-11-2 **138**.............................. PaulTownend 51
(J A Nash, Ire) *mid-div: drvn bef 3 out: bhd whn heavily after sn after last: virtually p.u: walked last 100yds* **66/1**

00-4 **F** **Clondaw Kaempfer (IRE)**[46] 4287 8-10-12 **134**...(tp) WayneHutchinson
(Donald McCain) *in tch: outpcd whn fell 7th* **25/1**

3325 **P** **Melodic Rendezvous**[40] 4381 10-11-8 **144**..............................(p) NickScholfield
(Jeremy Scott) *in rr: reminders after 2nd: bhd next: t.o whn p.u bef 7th* **50/1**

3220 **B** **Qewy (IRE)**[23] 4717 6-11-6 **142**..............................(p) AidanColeman
(John Ferguson) *mid-div: outpcd whn b.d 7th* **25/1**

-111 **P** **Ma Du Fou (FR)**[57] 4072 6-11-3 **139**.............................. GavinSheehan
(Warren Greatrex) *trckd ldrs: j. path after 1st: j. path and lost pl after 6th: bhd whn eased and p.u bef last* **7/1**[1]

0200 **U** **Mad Jack Mytton (IRE)**[21] 4765 6-11-1 **137**.............. RichieMcLernon
(Jonjo O'Neill) *mid-div: hdwy to chse ldrs whn blnd and uns rdr 6th* **25/1**

4/32 **P** **Tycoon Prince (IRE)**[117] 3070 6-11-3 **139**..............................(t) BJCooper
(Gordon Elliott, Ire) *t.k.h: hdwy to ld after 2nd: hdd 4th: blnd and lost pl 8th: sn eased and bhd: p.u bef next: lame* **7/1**[1]

1211 **F** **Curious Carlos**[231] 1308 7-10-8 **130**.............................. SeanBowen 110
(Peter Bowen) *t.k.h: sn trcking ldrs: led 4th: hdd 2 out: 7th and wkng whn fell last* **18/1**

2245 **P** **Whiteout (GER)**[21] 4769 5-11-3 **139**.............................. RWalsh
(W P Mullins, Ire) *mid-div: lost pl 5th: sn bhd: t.o whn p.u bef next* **16/1**

5m 1.6s (0.90) **Going Correction** +0.375s/f (Yiel) **22** Ran SP% **127.9**
Speed ratings (Par 113): **113,111,110,108,108 107,106,101,101,100 96,96,94,75, , , , ,**
CSF £402.44 CT £3612.78 TOTE £33.60: £6.80, £3.40, £2.20, £6.80; EX 542.80 Trifecta £4619.60.
Owner Mrs Pam Beardmore **Bred** Daniel O'Keeffe **Trained** Basford Green, Staffs
■ Stewards' Enquiry : Sean Quinlan four-day ban; excessive use of whip (22nd, 28th-30th Apr)

FOCUS
Bends and hurdles had been moved in at least 3yds since the previous day. Still, this was run over 63yds further than advertised. Richard Johnson said of the ground "It's essentially good to soft". Jumping let down plenty of these in what was a wide-open and competitive handicap and it seemed an advantage to race handily. The winner is good round here and has been rated back to the level of his 2013 C&D win. The second and third have been rated in line with their good recent runs.

5190 IMAGINE CRUISING FIRST IN THE FRAME TOP NOVICES' HURDLE (GRADE 1) (9 hdls) 2m 103y
2:15 (2:15) (Class 1) 4-Y-O+
£42,202 (£15,900; £7,957; £3,975; £1,995; £997)

Form RPR

-113 **1** **Buveur D'Air (FR)**[24] 4695 5-11-4 152.............................. NoelFehily 154+
(Nicky Henderson) *wore ear plugs: hld up in midfield: hdwy after 6th: wnt 2nd 3 out: rdn to chal strly appr last: styd on wl: led towards fin* **11/4**[2]

-340 **2** *nk* **Petit Mouchoir (FR)**[24] 4695 5-11-4 144.............................. DavidMullins 154
(W P Mullins, Ire) *w ldr: led after 6th: rdn after 3 out: strly pressed appr last: styd on wl but hdd towards fin* **40/1**

11 **3** *8* **Limini (IRE)**[22] 4734 5-10-11 151.............................. RWalsh 140+
(W P Mullins, Ire) *racd keenly in midfield: smooth hdwy to trck ldrs 3 out: nt fluent 2 out: rdn and one pce* **11/10**[1]

2120 **4** *3/4* **North Hill Harvey**[24] 4695 5-11-4 140.............................. HarrySkelton 146
(Dan Skelton) *hld up: rdn after 3 out: wnt 4th last: kpt on same pce* **25/1**

-41F **5** *3/4* **Bleu Et Rouge (FR)**[21] 4766 5-11-4 149.............................. BarryGeraghty 144
(W P Mullins, Ire) *racd keenly in midfield: rdn after 3 out: one pce* **8/1**[3]

2131 **6** *1/2* **Agrapart (FR)**[55] 4115 5-11-4 150.............................. LizzieKelly 145
(Nick Williams) *trckd ldng pair: reminder after 5th: rdn and ev ch appr 3 out: hit 2 out: sn outpcd: plugged on run-in* **10/1**

-311 **7** *2 1/4* **Ball D'Arc (FR)**[47] 4280 5-11-4 146.............................. BJCooper 144
(Gordon Elliott, Ire) *hld up: hdwy bef 3 out: sn rdn: nt fluent last: wknd* **16/1**

21 **8** *26* **Three Stars (IRE)**[152] 2385 6-11-4 145.............................. JJBurke 118
(Henry De Bromhead, Ire) *chsd ldng pair on outer: rdn whn nt fluent 3 out: sn wknd* **50/1**

14P2 **U** **Altruism (IRE)**[16] 4869 6-11-4 133..............................[1] BrianHughes
(James Moffatt) *trckd ldng pair on inner: blnd and uns rdr 4th* **100/1**

1132 **P** **Marracudja (FR)**[41] 4360 5-11-4 140..............................(t) SamTwiston-Davies
(Paul Nicholls) *led narrowly: hdd after 6th: wknd appr 3 out: p.u bef last* **50/1**

611 **U** **Gwafa (IRE)**[43] 4317 5-11-4 140.............................. RichieMcLernon
(Paul Webber) *midfield on inner: bdly hmpd and uns rdr 4th* **16/1**

4m 4.5s (-1.70) **Going Correction** +0.375s/f (Yiel) **11** Ran SP% **117.4**
Speed ratings (Par 117): **119,118,114,114,114 113,112,99, ,**
CSF £107.47 CT £187.65 TOTE £3.60: £1.40, £6.40, £1.10; EX 82.40 Trifecta £227.80.
Owner Potensis Bloodstock Ltd & Chris Giles **Bred** Gerard Ferte **Trained** Upper Lambourn, Berks

FOCUS
Race run over 48 yards further than advertised. This intriguing edition of the Top Novices' Hurdle was run at a muddling gallop and they only got racing seriously from the third-last flight. The form looks rock-solid with the first two coming clear from a classy mare. The winner has been rated to his Supreme mark.

5191 BETFRED MILDMAY NOVICES' CHASE (GRADE 1) (19 fncs) 3m 210y
2:50 (2:50) (Class 1) 5-Y-O+
£56,318 (£21,248; £10,658; £5,348; £2,708; £1,378)

Form RPR

1332 **1** **Native River (IRE)**[24] 4700 6-11-4 149..............................(p) RichardJohnson 165+
(Colin Tizzard) *led to 2nd: led after 3rd: hit 12th: sn drvn: styd on gamely fr 3 out* **11/2**[3]

4U11 **2** *3* **Henri Parry Morgan**[20] 4800 8-11-4 149..............................(tp) SeanBowen 160
(Peter Bowen) *trckd ldrs: chsd wnr sn after 3 out: kpt on same pce between last 2* **10/1**

1211 **3** *3 3/4* **Blaklion**[23] 4716 7-11-4 154.............................. RyanHatch 158
(Nigel Twiston-Davies) *trckd ldrs: drvn 16th: 3rd 3 out: hung lft between last 2: kpt on one pce* **3/1**[2]

2241 **4** *7* **Un Temps Pour Tout (IRE)**[24] 4697 7-11-4 159......(bt) TomScudamore 152
(David Pipe) *w ldr: led 2nd tl after next: nt fluent 4th: drvn 3 out: wknd between last 2: lame* **6/4**[1]

62F1 **5** *8* **Ballyalton (IRE)**[24] 4701 9-11-4 149..............................(p) BrianHughes 145
(Ian Williams) *trckd ldrs: t.k.h: effrt appr 3 out: wknd appr 2 out* **20/1**

-616 **6** *21* **Roi Des Francs (FR)**[23] 4716 7-11-4 149..............................[1] BJCooper 127
(W P Mullins, Ire) *prom: blnd 5th: reminders 9th: lost pl 11th: bhd fr 4 out: t.o 2 out* **10/1**

3110 **7** *15* **Out Sam**[24] 4697 7-11-4 139.............................. GavinSheehan 121
(Warren Greatrex) *chsd ldrs to 6th: hdwy 11th: drvn 13th: outpcd and lost pl 15th: sn bhd: t.o 2 out: eased and run-in* **16/1**

2113 **P** **Otago Trail (IRE)**[76] 3738 8-11-4 154.............................. AidanColeman
(Venetia Williams) *chsd ldrs: drvn 13th: outpcd and lost pl whn blnd 15th: sn p.u* **20/1**

6m 27.6s (-2.40) **Going Correction** +0.40s/f (Soft) **8** Ran SP% **114.0**
Speed ratings: **119,118,116,114,112 105,100,**
CSF £55.44 CT £192.68 TOTE £6.60: £1.90, £2.30, £1.30; EX 60.00 Trifecta £182.50.
Owner Brocade Racing **Bred** Fred Mackey **Trained** Milborne Port, Dorset

FOCUS
Race run over 52yds further than advertised. Three winners from last month's Cheltenham Festival lined up for this but none of the trio reproduced their form and it was left to a thoroughly tough performer to gain a deserved first Grade 1 victory. They went a sound gallop but the form is questionable. A pb from the winner, with the third and fourth rated below their Festival winning marks.

5192 JLT MELLING CHASE (GRADE 1) (16 fncs) 2m 3f 200y
3:25 (3:25) (Class 1) 5-Y-O **£112,788** (£42,748; £21,628; £11,068; £5,828)

Form RPR

-324 **1** **God's Own (IRE)**[23] 4718 8-11-10 162.............................. PaddyBrennan 167+
(Tom George) *t.k.h: trckd ldrs 4th: cl 2nd 3 out: led sn after 2 out: 5 l clr whn j.rt last: drvn rt out* **10/1**[3]

-134 **2** *2 3/4* **Al Ferof (FR)**[22] 4731 11-11-10 162.............................. HarrySkelton 163
(Dan Skelton) *hdwy and handy 3rd 8th: lft 2nd next: led sn after 3 out: hdd after next: rallied last: styd on same pce* **15/2**[2]

2540 **3** *9* **Clarcam (FR)**[89] 3552 6-11-10 154..............................(t) BJCooper 155
(Gordon Elliott, Ire) *chsd ldr: lft in ld 9th: hdd after 3 out: one pce* **28/1**

2445 **4** *22* **Somersby (IRE)**[23] 4718 12-11-10 157..............................(p) BrianHughes 136
(Mick Channon) *chsd ldrs: pushed along 8th: lost pl after 12th: modest 4th bef 3 out: sn lft bhd* **28/1**

334F 5 5 **Vibrato Valtat (FR)**[22] 4731 7-11-10 161...............(t) SamTwiston-Davies 133
(Paul Nicholls) *chsd ldrs 4th: pushed along 11th: outpcd whn hit 13th: reminders and bhd appr next* **14/1**

-121 F **Vautour (FR)**[22] 4731 7-11-10 176............................ RWalsh
(W P Mullins, Ire) *led: travelling strly whn fell 9th* **1/5**[1]

5m 8.2s (4.20) **Going Correction** +0.40s/f (Soft) **6** Ran SP% **117.8**
Speed ratings: **107,105,102,93,91**
CSF £76.52 TOTE £7.90: £3.10, £2.60; EX 81.00 Trifecta £372.20.
Owner Crossed Fingers Partnership **Bred** Mrs Caroline O'Driscoll **Trained** Slad, Gloucs

FOCUS
Race run over 40 yards further than advertised. With Vautour sensationally coming to grief, this year's Melling Chase was blown wide open. The runner-up sets the standard. The winner has been rated a pound higher than his Arkle run, with the third in line with the best of this season's runs.

5193 CRABBIE'S TOPHAM CHASE (H'CAP) (GRADE 3) (18 fncs) 2m 5f 19y
4:05 (4:05) (Class 1) 5-Y-O+
£67,356 (£25,332; £12,660; £6,324; £3,180; £1,584)

Form RPR

P5P0 1 **Eastlake (IRE)**[21] 4770 10-10-11 **142**...............(tp) BarryGeraghty 151+
(Jonjo O'Neill) *mid-div: hdwy to trck ldrs 9th: 2nd bef 2 out: styd on to ld last 75yds* **22/1**

051P 2 4 **Fairy Rath (IRE)**[20] 4787 10-10-0 **131**...............(t) TomCannon 137
(Nick Gifford) *w ldrs: led 4th (water): hdd and no ex last 75yds* **25/1**

3665 3 9 **Third Intention (IRE)**[23] 4719 9-11-12 **157**...............(bt[1]) TomO'Brien 155
(Colin Tizzard) *mid-div: hdwy to join ldrs 7th: 3rd 2 out: kpt on one pce* **33/1**

3603 4 nk **Distime (IRE)**[53] 4155 10-10-0 **131** oh3............... JonathanEngland 129
(Sam Drake) *led to 2nd: lost pl 6th: hmpd next (Becher's): hdwy 3 out: styd on to chal for modest 3rd last 75yds* **50/1**

P1P4 5 7 **Gallery Exhibition (IRE)**[74] 3776 9-10-6 **137**...............(t) DavidBass 128
(Kim Bailey) *in rr: hmpd 10th (Becher's): styd on appr 2 out: nvr a factor* **66/1**

6PP1 6 ½ **Top Cat Henry (IRE)**[17] 4866 8-9-11 **131** oh4.....(vt) MrSWaley-Cohen(3) 120
(Dr Richard Newland) *mid-div: hdwy 5th: chsng ldrs whn mstke 13th (Valentine's): 4th 2 out: one pce* **18/1**

3F25 7 5 **As De Mee (FR)**[22] 4729 6-11-0 **145**............... SamTwiston-Davies 128
(Paul Nicholls) *chsd ldrs: 5th 2 out: grad wknd* **10/1**[2]

6351 8 1¾ **La Vaticane (FR)**[37] 4436 7-10-11 **142**...............(bt) ConorO'Farrell 123
(David Pipe) *wore ear plugs: in rr: hdwy 8th: chsng ldrs 15th: wknd 2nd out* **25/1**

P-13 9 8 **Mr Moonshine (IRE)**[19] 4818 12-10-6 **137**............... DannyCook 114
(Sue Smith) *chsd ldrs: outpcd and lost pl 14th* **11/1**[3]

113P 10 16 **Al Alfa**[126] 2877 9-10-0 **131** oh2............... JamesBest 88
(Philip Hobbs) *rr-div: bhd fr 15th* **100/1**

P-P4 11 7 **Pass The Hat**[69] 3860 9-10-4 **135**...............(t) JJBurke 85
(A L T Moore, Ire) *in mid-div: hmpd 10th (Becher's): bhd fr 15th* **25/1**

P132 12 1½ **Bennys Mist (IRE)**[34] 4485 10-11-1 **146**............... AidanColeman 95
(Venetia Williams) *prom: lost pl 12th (Canal Turn): sme hdwy 3 out: wknd next* **10/1**[2]

1110 13 4½ **Village Vic (IRE)**[22] 4731 9-11-11 **156**............... RichardJohnson 108
(Philip Hobbs) *blnd bdly and lost pl 3rd (Chair): sme hdwy whn hmpd 10th (Becher's): sn bhd* **10/1**[2]

15-0 14 3¾ **Ruben Cotter (IRE)**[41] 4361 10-10-5 **136**............... NickScholfield 80
(Paul Nicholls) *mid-div: wknd 3 out* **20/1**

P-62 15 1½ **Dare To Endeavour**[26] 4655 9-10-4 **135**............... PaulMoloney 74
(E McNamara, Ire) *in rr: bhd fr 8th* **25/1**

615P 16 4 **Rouge Et Blanc (FR)**[90] 3521 11-9-11 **131** oh3.......(p) ThomasGarner(3) 66
(Oliver Sherwood) *mid-div: hdwy 7th: mstke 9th: hmpd next (Becher's): chsng ldrs 15th: wknd appr 2 out: b.b.v* **66/1**

4P40 17 2 **Ballykan**[24] 4697 6-10-1 **135** ow2...............(t) RyanHatch(3) 66
(Nigel Twiston-Davies) *a towards rr: wl bhd fr 15th* **20/1**

3503 18 17 **Dromnea (IRE)**[83] 3624 9-10-3 **134**............... BrianO'Connell 50
(M F Morris, Ire) *chsd ldrs: hmpd 10th (Becher's): sn lost pl: bhd fr 15th* **16/1**

0220 19 4 **Killer Crow (IRE)**[11] 5005 7-10-5 **136**...............(t) BJCooper 48
(Gordon Elliott, Ire) *in rr: hmpd 10th (Becher's): sn bhd: b.b.v* **12/1**

00P1 U **Rathlin**[27] 4606 11-10-7 **138**...............(tp) DavyRussell
(Micky Hammond) *prom: outpcd whn blnd and uns rdr 14th* **14/1**

4506 P **Astracad (FR)**[22] 4733 10-9-12 **134**...............(t) JamieBargary(5)
(Nigel Twiston-Davies) *in rr: bhd fr 8th: blnd 14th: t.o 3 out: sn p.u* **40/1**

2/00 F **Gullinbursti (IRE)**[69] 3860 10-10-0 **131** oh2...............(v) GavinSheehan
(Emma Lavelle) *mid-div: hdwy 8th: chsng ldrs whn fell 10th (Becher's): fatally injured* **25/1**

325U U **Witness In Court (IRE)**[125] 2902 9-10-6 **137**............... WayneHutchinson
(Donald McCain) *led 2nd to 3rd: chsd ldrs: 10th: outpcd whn blnd and uns rdr 8th* **50/1**

F512 F **Minella Reception (IRE)**[27] 4625 10-10-4 **135**...............(t) AdamWedge
(Nigel Twiston-Davies) *chsd ldrs: fell 10th (Becher's): fatally injured* **20/1**

F-43 P **Turban (FR)**[48] 4260 9-11-5 **150**............... PaulTownend
(W P Mullins, Ire) *in rr: bhd fr 5th: t.o 14th: p.u bef 2 out: b.b.v* **25/1**

-15P F **Blood Cotil (FR)**[23] 4717 7-11-8 **153**............... RWalsh
(W P Mullins, Ire) *wore ear plugs: mid-div: hit 3rd (Chair): hdwy whn blnd 9th: smooth hdwy to trck ldrs whn fell 15th* **20/1**

-0P0 P **Corrin Wood (IRE)**[22] 4735 9-10-3 **134**...............(tp) WillKennedy
(Donald McCain) *sn detached in last: t.o 9th: p.u bef 3 out* **40/1**

1-10 F **Cocktails At Dawn**[146] 2483 8-11-8 **153**............... NicodeBoinville
(Nicky Henderson) *w ldrs: led 3rd (Chair): hdd next: w ldrs whn fell 16th* **16/1**

0011 U **Bishops Road (IRE)**[48] 4245 8-11-9 **154**............... JamieMoore
(Kerry Lee) *in rr: blnd and uns rdr 1st* **8/1**[1]

5m 34.9s (-2.10) **Going Correction** +0.325s/f (Yiel) **29** Ran SP% **141.2**
Speed ratings: **117,115,112,111,109 109,107,106,103,97 94,94,92,90,90 88,88,81,80, , , ,EM**
CSF £485.18 CT £16562.94 TOTE £30.20: £6.40, £6.80, £9.00, £20.40; EX 1042.40 Trifecta £11209.00 Part won..
Owner John P McManus **Bred** Mrs Eleanor Hadden **Trained** Cheltenham, Gloucs
■ Stewards' Enquiry : Danny Cook one-day ban; weighed out 2lb lower (22nd Apr)
Ryan Hatch one-day ban; weighed out 2lb lower (22nd Apr)

FOCUS
Race run over 5yds further than advertised. A classy edition of the race, with six of the runners rated 150-plus, and it looked as wide-open as ever, something which was born out in the result with outsiders dominating. Two horses with previous placed form in the race came to the fore. The winner has been rated back to the level of last year's Grand Annual second. The second has been rated to his mark and the third back to something like his best.

5194 DOOM BAR SEFTON NOVICES' HURDLE (GRADE 1) (13 hdls) 3m 149y
4:40 (4:41) (Class 1) 4-Y-O+
£56,270 (£21,200; £10,610; £5,300; £2,660; £1,330)

Form RPR

11 1 **Ballyoptic (IRE)**[20] 4798 6-11-4 138............... RyanHatch 154+
(Nigel Twiston-Davies) *midfield: hdwy to trck ldrs bef 8th: led 3 out: sn rdn: edgd towards rail after 2 out: hdd last: styd on wl to ld again towards fin* **9/1**

1130 2 nk **Bellshill (IRE)**[24] 4695 6-11-4 146............... MrPWMullins 155+
(W P Mullins, Ire) *hld up: stdy hdwy after 4 out: chal whn blnd 2 out: sn rdn: led last: drvn and hung rt flat: hdd towards fin* **11/2**[1]

2122 3 13 **Potters Legend**[27] 4620 6-11-4 138............... LeightonAspell 141
(Lucy Wadham) *in tch: rdn to chse ldrs 3 out: one pce in 3rd fr last* **16/1**

5 4 2½ **Balko Des Flos (FR)**[21] 4766 5-11-4 141............... BJCooper 138
(W P Mullins, Ire) *hld up: hdwy after 4 out: rdn after 3 out: one pce in 4th fr last* **12/1**

131P 5 10 **Yala Enki (FR)**[23] 4715 6-11-4 142............... AidanColeman 129
(Venetia Williams) *led: hdd after 7th: rdn and outpcd appr 3 out: plugged on again after 2 out* **25/1**

1213 6 2¾ **Duke Des Champs (IRE)**[48] 4248 6-11-4 142............... RichardJohnson 125
(Philip Hobbs) *trckd ldrs towards outer: rdn 3 out: wknd run-in* **9/1**

41 7 14 **Arkwrisht (FR)**[64] 3962 6-11-4 138............... DavidMullins 113
(W P Mullins, Ire) *trckd ldrs: led after 7th: hdd 3 out: sn rdn: wknd after 2 out* **25/1**

4223 8 13 **Ami Desbois (FR)**[69] 3859 6-11-4 130............... KielanWoods 98
(Graeme McPherson) *hld up in midfield: nt fluent 6th: short of room on rail after 7th: rdn 4 out: sn wknd* **100/1**

2112 9 19 **Ballydine (IRE)**[69] 3859 6-11-4 145............... BrianHughes 79
(Charlie Longsdon) *prom: rdn after 4 out: wknd appr 3 out* **6/1**[2]

10 P **Gangster (FR)**[21] 4766 6-11-4 147............... PaulTownend
(W P Mullins, Ire) *hld up: hit 8th: sme hdwy after 4 out: rdn 3 out: sn wknd: p.u bef last* **13/2**[3]

121 P **Mystical Knight**[26] 4662 7-11-4 130............... BarryGeraghty
(Rebecca Curtis) *midfield: rdn 4 out: sn wknd: p.u bef 3 out* **12/1**

-F20 P **Ghost River**[23] 4715 6-11-4 126............... SeanBowen
(Peter Bowen) *nt fluent: a in rr: p.u bef 3 out* **50/1**

1222 P **Vintage Clouds (IRE)**[48] 4248 6-11-4 137............... DannyCook
(Sue Smith) *prom: lost pl and pushed along after 7th: wknd after 4 out: p.u bef 3 out* **20/1**

1115 P **Baoulet Delaroque (FR)**[23] 4717 5-11-4 142......... SamTwiston-Davies
(Paul Nicholls) *hld up: hit 6th: sn pushed along: reminders after 7th: eased and p.u* **13/2**[3]

1111 P **Tomngerry (IRE)**[41] 4368 6-11-4 135............... WillKennedy
(Brian Ellison) *midfield: nt fluent 8th: sn pushed along: wknd after 4 out: p.u bef 2 out* **10/1**

6m 17.9s (1.60) **Going Correction** +0.375s/f (Yiel) **15** Ran SP% **122.1**
Speed ratings (Par 117): **112,111,107,106,103 102,98,94,88, , , ,**
CSF £56.19 CT £800.66 TOTE £10.60: £3.10, £2.30, £4.70; EX 66.10 Trifecta £1439.60.
Owner Mills & Mason Partnership **Bred** Roger Ryan **Trained** Naunton, Gloucs

FOCUS
Race run over 74yds further than advertised. A race won by Thistlecrack last season, who went on to take this year's World Hurdle. A few of these didn't run up to expectations but every reason to believe this was still good Grade 1 form, with two really promising types pulling clear. Another step forward from the winner and, along with the unlucky second, rates a high-class novice. The third and fourth help set the level.

5195 WEATHERBYS PRIVATE BANK CHAMPION STANDARD OPEN NATIONAL HUNT FLAT RACE (GRADE 2) 2m 209y
5:15 (5:15) (Class 1) 4-6-Y-O
£22,508 (£8,480; £4,244; £2,120; £1,064; £532)

Form RPR

3 1 **Bacardys (FR)**[23] 4721 5-11-4 131............... MrPWMullins 136
(W P Mullins, Ire) *midfield towards inner: stdy hdwy over 4f out: rdn to chse ldrs 3f out: led ins fnl f: kpt on* **15/2**

2 2 ½ **Battleford**[23] 4721 5-11-4 133............... PaulTownend 136
(W P Mullins, Ire) *trckd ldng pair: rdn to ld over 3f out: hdd ins fnl f: styd on* **7/2**[2]

3 1½ **The Minch (IRE)** 5-11-4 0............... DannyCook 134+
(Jim Goldie) *hld up: stl towards rr over 4f out: rdn and gd hdwy fr 3f out: wnt 3rd ins fnl f: styd on* **100/1**

1211 4 2½ **Ballyandy**[23] 4721 5-11-8 135............... SamTwiston-Davies 136
(Nigel Twiston-Davies) *trckd ldng pair: chal on bit 3f out: rdn wl over 1f out: edgd lft and wknd ins fnl f* **9/4**[1]

3-11 5 1 **Willoughby Court (IRE)**[120] 2998 5-11-4 116............... NicodeBoinville 131
(Ben Pauling) *midfield: hdwy and in tch over 3f out: rdn and outpcd over 2f out: styd on ins fnl f* **16/1**

0- 6 7 **Any Drama (IRE)**[72] 3814 5-11-4 120............... MsKWalsh 125
(Harry Fry) *led narrowly: rdn whn hdd over 3f out: wknd appr fnl f* **20/1**

2210 7 16 **Pride Of Lecale**[23] 4721 5-11-4 125...............(t) PaddyBrennan 108
(Fergal O'Brien) *trckd ldng pair: jnd ldr over 5f out: rdn over 3f out: wknd fnl 2f* **25/1**

12 8 1¼ **Manhattan Spring**[32] 4532 5-11-4 109............... AndrewThornton 106
(Seamus Mullins) *midfield on outer: rdn over 4f out: nvr threatened* **100/1**

3 9 16 **Zipple Back (IRE)**[70] 3847 4-10-12 116............... NoelFehily 92
(Alan King) *hld up: bit short of room 5f out: rdn over 3f out: nvr threatened* **28/1**

-521 10 2 **King Uther**[40] 4385 6-11-4 112............... TomCannon 88
(Chris Gordon) *hld up: pushed along in rr over 7f out: nvr threatened* **50/1**

21 11 7 **Rodneythetrotter**[150] 2414 4-10-12 107............... JoshuaMoore 75
(Pat Phelan) *hld up: rdn over 4f out: sn btn* **33/1**

21 12 14 **Atomix (GER)**[60] 4037 5-11-4 114............... BrianHughes 67
(Peter Niven) *hld up: rdn and sme hdwy 4f out: wknd fnl 2f* **40/1**

12 13 hd **Jam Session (IRE)**[98] 3409 4-10-12 112............... WillKennedy 61
(Ian Williams) *midfield: rdn over 4f out: sn wknd* **50/1**

1 14 1 **Utility (GER)**[122] 2965 5-11-4 124............... RichardJohnson 66
(Jonjo O'Neill) *in tch towards outer: rdn over 4f out: sn wknd* **4/1**[3]

1 15 44 **Bolving (IRE)**[41] 4364 5-11-4 116...............[1] NickScholfield 22
(Victor Dartnall) *a towards rr* **12/1**

10-5 **16** *41* **Red Six (IRE)**[19] 4827 5-11-4 120 ... SeanBowen
(Peter Bowen) *w ldr: lost pl 6f out: sn bhd: t.o fnl 4f* **50/1**
17 *dist* **Cheque En Blanc (FR)**[47] 4-10-12 0 ... JamesDavies
(Tom Symonds) *midfield: lost pl qckly and dropped to rr 7f out: t.o fnl 5f* **100/1**

4m 9.1s (1.70) **Going Correction** +0.375s/f (Yiel)
WFA 4 from 5yo+ 5lb **17** Ran SP% **124.6**
Speed ratings: **113,112,112,110,110 107,99,99,91,90 87,80,80,80,59 40,**
CSF £31.75 CT £2497.11 TOTE £8.60: £2.80, £1.70, £20.60; EX 38.40 Trifecta £3765.80.
Owner Shanakiel Racing Syndicate **Bred** Eric Vagne & Jose Da Silva **Trained** Muine Beag, Co Carlow

FOCUS
Race run over 48 yards further than advertised. With the 1-2-3 from the Champion Bumper renewing rivalry this was obviously a strong affair. It was run at an ordinary gallop and two Willie Mullins-trained inmates fought it out. The first two have been rated as improving on their Cheltenham marks, with the fourth pretty much to form.
T/Jkpt: Not won. T/Plt: £9,946.90 to a £1 stake. Pool: £51,8742.00 - 38.07 winning tickets
T/Qpdt: £1,167.00 to a £1 stake. Pool: £31,543.00 - 20.00 winning tickets
Walter Glynn & Andrew Sheret

4791 NEWCASTLE (L-H)
Friday, April 8

OFFICIAL GOING: Soft (5.2)
Wind: Breezy, half against Weather: Overcast, showers

5196 GIBSON & CO NOVICES' HURDLE (9 hdls 2 omitted) 2m 4f 133y
2:05 (2:05) (Class 4) 4-Y-0+ **£3,898** (£1,144; £572)

Form | | | | RPR
F114 **1** **Lake View Lad (IRE)**[26] 4636 6-11-7 136 ... StephenMulqueen(5) 115+
(N W Alexander) *nt fluent on occasions: trckd ldrs: smooth hdwy to ld bef 2 out: shkn up and qcknd clr fr last: readily* **1/14**[1]
05 **2** *7* **Broad Spectrum (IRE)**[18] 4835 5-11-0 0 ... (t) AdrianLane 90
(Donald McCain) *t.k.h: pressed ldr: chal and rdn bef 2 out: 2 l down whn nt fluent last: sn outpcd* **9/1**[2]
45P **3** *8* **Raymond Reddington (IRE)**[111] 3159 5-11-0 0 ... CraigNichol 81
(Chris Grant) *nt fluent on occasions: led at modest gallop: rdn and hdd bef 2 out: sn outpcd: btn last* **50/1**[3]

5m 28.2s (7.10) **Going Correction** +0.375s/f (Yiel) **3** Ran SP% **105.3**
Speed ratings (Par 105): **101,98,95**
CSF £1.32 TOTE £1.10; EX 1.40 Trifecta £1.40.
Owner Alistair Cochrane **Bred** Peter Magnier **Trained** Kinneston, Perth & Kinross

FOCUS
An uncompetitive novice hurdle run at a modest gallop and not a race from which to draw any firm conclusions. The winner didn't need to be anywhere near his best.

5197 LYCETTS H'CAP CHASE (13 fncs) 2m 75y
2:40 (2:40) (Class 5) (0-100,92) 5-Y-0+ **£3,573** (£1,049; £524; £262)

Form | | | | RPR
2324 **1** **Mumgos Debut (IRE)**[29] 4569 8-11-12 92 ... (t) DerekFox 104+
(Lucinda Russell) *trckd ldr to 3rd: niggled along next: rallied and lft 2 l 2nd 4 out: led after next: clr 2 out: easily* **13/8**[1]
2301 **2** *7* **Asuncion (FR)**[20] 4795 6-11-0 85 ... (b) JamieHamilton(5) 87
(Rebecca Menzies) *led: hdd and 2 l down whn lft 2 l in front 4 out: hdd after next: kpt on same pce fnl 2* **5/2**[2]
0PPP **3** *1 ½* **Bertielicious**[10] 5010 8-9-7 66 oh10 ... ThomasDowson(7) 68
(Jonathan Haynes) *bhd: hit 2nd: rallied after 5 out: effrt and disp 2nd pl 3 out: kpt on same pce fr next* **25/1**
5455 **4** *7* **Pamak D'Airy (FR)**[24] 4707 13-11-9 92 ... (p) TonyKelly(3) 89
(Henry Hogarth) *in tch: outpcd after 4th: effrt whn lft 3rd 4 out: sn rdn and outpcd* **6/1**
2410 **U** **Rosquero (FR)**[43] 4325 11-10-13 86 ... (b) MrWHRReed(7)
(Kenny Johnson) *cl up: led and 2 l up whn nt fluent and uns rdr 4 out* **3/1**[3]

4m 25.7s (4.60) **Going Correction** +0.375s/f (Yiel) **5** Ran SP% **109.8**
Speed ratings: **103,99,98,95,**
CSF £6.26 TOTE £2.30: £1.50, £1.20; EX 4.40 Trifecta £41.20.
Owner Mrs Suzy Brown & Peter R Brown **Bred** D Phelan **Trained** Arlary, Perth & Kinross

FOCUS
A moderate handicap chase with the top weight rated 92. The pace was reasonable and there's a case for rating the form a few pounds higher.

5198 UNITED CARLTON H'CAP HURDLE (DIV I) (9 hdls 2 omitted) 2m 4f 133y
3:15 (3:15) (Class 5) (0-100,100) 4-Y-0+ **£3,898** (£1,144; £572; £286)

Form | | | | RPR
040 **1** **Simmply Sam**[20] 4804 9-9-7 74 ... MrWEasterby(7) 83+
(Marjorie Fife) *trckd ldrs: effrt and wnt 2nd bef 2 out: shkn up and led bef last: pricked ears and drew clr run-in* **14/1**
335P **2** *5* **Turtle Cask (IRE)**[10] 5010 7-11-5 96 ... (p) ColmMcCormack(3) 100
(Dianne Sayer) *chsd ldrs: led 3 out (usual 4 out): rdn and hdd bef last: kpt on: nt pce of wnr* **17/2**
F2FP **3** *12* **Naburn**[28] 4581 8-11-7 100 ... RyanDay(5) 91
(Andrew Wilson) *hld up: stdy hdwy to trck ldrs after 3 out (usual 4 out): rdn and outpcd bef next* **13/2**[2]
1000 **4** *15* **Ardesia (IRE)**[38] 4415 12-9-9 74 oh2 ... JamieHamilton(5) 50
(Tina Jackson) *nt fluent on occasions: prom: lost pl bef 2nd: drvn and outpcd whn nt fluent 3 out (usual 4 out): btn next* **40/1**
4RP2 **5** *3 ½* **Cadgers Hole**[17] 4863 9-10-1 75 ... BrianHarding 48
(Lynn Siddall) *hld up: stdy hdwy after 3 out: sn rdn: wknd bef next* **9/1**
0050 **6** *17* **Kilmainham (IRE)**[5] 5125 8-10-4 81 ... JoeColliver(3) 37
(Martin Todhunter) *bhd: struggling fr 4th: nvr on terms* **7/1**[3]
154P **7** *4* **Tribal Dance (IRE)**[149] 2434 10-10-8 87 ... (p) DavidNoonan(5) 39
(John O'Shea) *led: rdn 4th: hdd 6th: rdn and wknd fr next* **12/1**
2304 **P** **Diamond D'Amour (IRE)**[39] 4404 10-11-6 99 ... JonathonBewley(5)
(George Bewley) *cl up: led 6th to next: sn rdn: wknd and p.u bef 2 out* **3/1**[1]
5400 **P** **High Fair**[59] 4047 10-10-12 93 ... (p) MrTHamilton(7)
(Sandy Forster) *prom: outpcd after 3rd: struggling fr next: t.o whn p.u bef 2 out* **12/1**
-2P2 **P** **Molly Milan**[20] 4796 8-11-1 89 ... HenryBrooke
(Jim Goldie) *hld up: stdy hdwy and prom 3 out (usual 4 out): wknd and p.u bef next* **3/1**[1]

5m 23.3s (2.20) **Going Correction** +0.375s/f (Yiel) **10** Ran SP% **120.8**
Speed ratings (Par 103): **110,108,103,97,96 90,88, , ,**
CSF £130.80 CT £862.76 TOTE £17.20: £4.00, £2.90, £2.40; EX 204.80 Trifecta £3012.60.
Owner Mrs S Barker **Bred** J W Barker **Trained** Stillington, N Yorks

FOCUS
An ordinary handicap hurdle but the pace was fair and they finished strung out. The winner was well in on last year's Ayr win and is rated back to that level.

5199 UNITED CARLTON H'CAP HURDLE (DIV II) (9 hdls 2 omitted) 2m 4f 133y
3:50 (3:50) (Class 5) (0-100,100) 4-Y-0+ **£3,898** (£1,144; £572; £286)

Form | | | | RPR
0P06 **1** **Tomahawk Wood**[59] 4047 7-10-3 80 ... CallumWhillans(3) 90+
(Donald Whillans) *hld up in tch: stdy hdwy 1/2-way: led gng wl bef 2 out: rdn and kpt on strly fr last* **9/2**[2]
P621 **2** *3 ½* **Man Of God (IRE)**[11] 4987 8-10-11 90 ... AlanJohns(5) 96
(Tim Vaughan) *in tch: stdy hdwy after 3 out (usual 4 out): effrt and chsd wnr bef last: kpt on: nt pce to chal* **2/1**[1]
5565 **3** *5* **Dalby Spook (IRE)**[13] 4904 6-9-12 75 ... HarryChalloner(3) 75
(Dianne Sayer) *hld up in tch: hdwy to press ldrs after 3 out: rdn and one pce fr last* **16/1**
3200 **4** *7* **Rock Relief (IRE)**[20] 4797 10-11-9 97 ... (be) CraigNichol 93
(Chris Grant) *nt fluent on occasions: cl up: rdn fr 1/2-way: rallied: outpcd after 2 out: 4th and hld whn nt fluent last* **9/1**
0-0P **5** *14* **Super Lunar (IRE)**[38] 4421 7-11-9 100 ... (t) TonyKelly(3) 79
(Henry Hogarth) *hld up: pushed along and sme hdwy bef 3 out (usual 4 out): wknd bef next* **50/1**
3004 **6** *4 ½* **Final Fling (IRE)**[50] 4202 5-11-5 96 ... AdamNicol(3) 70
(Rose Dobbin) *hld up: pushed along bef 4th: struggling 3 out (usual 4 out): nvr on terms* **5/1**[3]
5555 **7** *27* **Mrs Grass**[33] 4513 9-9-7 74 oh6 ... (vt) ThomasDowson(7) 21
(Jonathan Haynes) *disp ld tl rdn and wknd bef 2 out* **50/1**
1-5P **P** **See The Legend**[26] 4638 11-10-6 87 ... MissJWalton(7)
(Sandy Forster) *in tch: struggling bef 3 out (usual 4 out): p.u bef next* **20/1**
P3-P **P** **Needwood Park**[17] 4862 8-9-7 74 ... (p) LorcanMurtagh(7)
(Ray Craggs) *in tch: drvn bef 4th: struggling 6th: t.o whn p.u bef 2 out* **20/1**
5026 **P** **Titian Boy (IRE)**[31] 4547 7-10-6 83 ... JoeColliver(3)
(N W Alexander) *led to bef 2 out: sn rdn and wknd: p.u 2 out* **9/2**[2]

5m 25.8s (4.70) **Going Correction** +0.375s/f (Yiel) **10** Ran SP% **115.7**
Speed ratings (Par 103): **106,104,102,100,94 93,82, , ,**
CSF £13.67 CT £128.87 TOTE £5.10: £2.40, £1.20, £3.70; EX 15.50 Trifecta £142.40.
Owner The Enduria Partnership **Bred** Allan Gilchrist **Trained** Hawick, Borders

FOCUS
The second division of this 0-100 handicap hurdle and once again it was run at a fair gallop. The winner was back to the best of last season's form.

5200 PERCY HEDLEY H'CAP CHASE (16 fncs) 2m 4f 19y
4:25 (4:25) (Class 3) (0-140,138) 5-Y-0+ **£7,797** (£2,289; £1,144; £572)

Form | | | | RPR
411P **1** **Un Noble (FR)**[47] 4279 6-10-11 123 ... CraigNichol 135+
(Nicky Richards) *nt fluent on occasions: led to bef 3rd: pressed ldr: regained ld 8th: mde rest: clr 3 out: hit next: kpt on strly* **9/4**[2]
3UP2 **2** *1 ¾* **Silver Tassie (IRE)**[27] 4609 8-10-13 132 ... FinianO'Toole(7) 139
(Micky Hammond) *hld up in tch: stdy hdwy to chse ldrs bef 4 out: rdn and outpcd next: rallied to chse (clr) wnr 2 out: kpt on run-in* **10/3**[3]
303P **3** *6* **Presenting Junior (IRE)**[76] 3741 9-11-6 132 ... HenryBrooke 134
(Martin Todhunter) *in tch: stdy hdwy and wnt 2nd bef 5 out: effrt and rdn bef next: lost 2nd and one pce fr 2 out* **9/1**
3423 **4** *15* **King Of The Wolds (IRE)**[27] 4609 9-10-11 128 ... JamieHamilton(5) 114
(Malcolm Jefferson) *chsd ldrs: led bef 3rd to 8th: drvn and outpcd after 5 out: struggling fr next* **13/8**[1]
46PF **5** *5* **Alderbrook Lad (IRE)**[98] 3425 10-11-9 138 ... JoeColliver(3) 121
(Micky Hammond) *nt fluent on occasions: cl up: lost pl 1/2-way: struggling 6 out: btn 4 out* **14/1**

5m 29.6s (2.40) **Going Correction** +0.375s/f (Yiel) **5** Ran SP% **108.6**
Speed ratings: **110,109,106,100,98**
CSF £9.84 TOTE £3.00: £1.70, £1.80; EX 10.20 Trifecta £53.50.
Owner Mrs C A Torkington **Bred** Richard Godefroy **Trained** Greystoke, Cumbria

FOCUS
Quite a competitive handicap chase run at just an ordinary gallop. The winner is on the upgrade.

5201 BREWIN DOLPHIN H'CAP HURDLE (8 hdls 1 omitted) 2m 98y
5:00 (5:00) (Class 3) (0-140,136) 4-Y-0+ **£7,147** (£2,098; £1,049; £524)

Form | | | | RPR
1241 **1** **Nuts Well**[20] 4793 5-11-5 129 ... CraigNichol 133+
(Ann Hamilton) *trckd ldrs: nt fluent 4th: hit next: smooth hdwy to ld whn hrd pressed 2 out: rdn clr after last* **4/9**[1]
3-P0 **2** *7* **Ifandbutwhynot (IRE)**[69] 3857 10-11-12 136 ... BrianHarding 134
(Tim Easterby) *in tch: smooth hdwy to chal 2 out: ev ch whn blnd last: sn rdn: edgd rt and no ex run-in* **13/2**[3]
440P **3** *2 ½* **Brave Spartacus (IRE)**[20] 4793 10-10-7 120 ... TonyKelly(3) 113
(Keith Reveley) *t.k.h: pressed ldr: led 3 out (usual 4 out): hdd next: rdn and outpcd appr last* **9/2**[2]
620P **4** *17* **Swaledale Lad (IRE)**[205] 1553 9-10-12 125 ... HarryChalloner(3) 106
(Richard Ford) *led to 3 out (usual 4 out): rdn and wknd fr next* **9/1**

4m 14.2s (4.20) **Going Correction** +0.375s/f (Yiel) **4** Ran SP% **110.8**
Speed ratings (Par 107): **104,100,99,90**
CSF £3.98 TOTE £1.30; EX 3.80 Trifecta £4.80.
Owner Ian Hamilton **Bred** Chesters Stud Ltd **Trained** Great Bavington, Northumbland

FOCUS
Quite a valuable handicap hurdle but not particularly competitive and, with a dawdling pace, not a race from which to draw too many conclusions. The four were abreast jumping the second-last.

5202 MEDIAWORKS H'CAP CHASE (19 fncs) 2m 7f 91y
5:35 (5:35) (Class 4) (0-120,118) 5-Y-0+ **£4,548** (£1,335; £667; £333)

Form | | | | RPR
3U23 **1** **The Orange Rogue (IRE)**[31] 4549 9-10-5 102 ... StephenMulqueen(5) 111+
(N W Alexander) *nt fluent on occasions: pressed ldr: chal 13th: led 2 out: sn rdn along: kpt on wl fr next* **13/8**[2]
3411 **2** *1 ¼* **Veroce (FR)**[20] 4792 7-10-8 105 ... JamieHamilton(5) 112
(Mark Walford) *prom: hit 10th: rdn and outpcd after 5 out: rallied 3 out: chsd wnr bef last: kpt on run-in: hld last* **1/1**[1]
-PPP **3** *6* **Frank The Slink**[31] 4549 10-10-2 101 ... FinianO'Toole(7) 101
(Micky Hammond) *led at modest gallop: jnd 13th: hdd 2 out: outpcd bef last* **12/1**
31-4 **4** *23* **Abbey Storm (IRE)**[46] 4288 10-11-9 115 ... BrianHarding 91
(Micky Hammond) *in tch: blnd 5th: hdwy and cl up after 9th: rdn and wknd fr 4 out* **6/1**[3]

6m 39.0s (16.50) **Going Correction** +0.375s/f (Yiel) **4** Ran SP% **110.1**
Speed ratings: **86,85,83,75**
CSF £3.88 TOTE £2.50; EX 4.00 Trifecta £12.60.

Owner Mrs S Irwin **Bred** Patrick F Toole **Trained** Kinneston, Perth & Kinross
FOCUS
Just a fair handicap chase run at an ordinary gallop. The winner is rated 4lb off his best.

5203 ATLAS CLOUD CONDITIONAL JOCKEYS' NOVICES' H'CAP HURDLE (11 hdls 2 omitted) 3m 10y
6:05 (6:05) (Class 5) (0-100,100) 4-Y-0+ £3,249 (£954; £477; £238)

Form RPR
40P4 1 **Triumph Davis (IRE)**[12] 4942 7-10-7 **84**..........(p) JoeColliver(3) 90+
(Micky Hammond) *hld up: stdy hdwy after 3 out (usual 4 out): sn pushed along: led bef next: clr last: kpt on wl* 8/1
5026 2 6 **Tickanrun (IRE)**[38] 4421 6-11-6 **94**..........(v[1]) CraigNichol 93
(Chris Grant) *trckd ldrs: hdwy to chal bef 2 out: sn rdn: edgd rt u.p and kpt on same pce fr last* 9/1
526 3 29 **Diego Suarez (FR)**[18] 4845 6-10-12 **91**..........(p) TrevorRyan(5) 65
(Chris Bealby) *trckd ldrs: hit 5th: rdn and ev ch bef 2 out: sn wknd: fin 4th: plcd 3rd* 6/1[3]
-45P 4 3 3/4 **Raid Stane (IRE)**[46] 4289 10-10-8 **92**..........(p) RossTurner(10) 58
(Julia Brooke) *hld up in midfield: drvn along after 4 out (usual 5 out): wknd bef 2 out: fin 5th: plcd 4th* 8/1
005P 5 1/2 **Higgs Boson**[20] 4792 11-10-0 **74** oh3..........(b) DaleIrving 40
(Jim Goldie) *mde most tl rdn and hdd bef 2 out: sn wknd: fin sixth: plcd 5th* 20/1
066P 6 77 **Wayward Sun (IRE)**[30] 4557 5-9-10 **80**..........BillyGarritty(10)
(Micky Hammond) *hld up: hdwy to chse ldrs 1/2-way: rdn and wknd after 3 out (usual 4 out): t.o: fin seventh: plcd sixth* 16/1
61 D 1 **When In Roam (IRE)**[20] 4804 7-11-4 **92**..........(p) DavidNoonan 91
(John O'Shea) *in tch: drvn along 7th: rallied to chse ldrs bef 2 out: sddle slipped and lost weight cloth after last: kpt on: fin 3rd: disqualified and plcd last* 4/1[2]
P3PP P **Generous Chief (IRE)**[136] 2708 8-10-12 **89**..........FinianO'Toole(3)
(Chris Grant) *in tch: lost pl 5th: struggling fr 4 out (usual 5 out): p.u bef 2 out* 25/1
4P12 P **Sgt Bull Berry**[132] 2771 9-10-6 **80**..........JamieHamilton
(Peter Maddison) *pressed ldr tl wknd 3 out: p.u bef next* 10/1
4630 P **Smuggler's Stash (IRE)**[26] 4638 6-11-4 **100**..........(p) LorcanMurtagh(8)
(Rose Dobbin) *hld up: drvn along 1/2-way: rallied bef 3 out (usual 4 out): sn wknd: p.u bef next* 3/1[1]
4P54 P **Massini's Lady**[22] 4739 5-10-9 **86**..........StephenMulqueen(3)
(N W Alexander) *nt fluent in rr: nvr gng wl: lost tch and p.u 3 out* 12/1
6m 29.6s (15.60) **Going Correction** +0.375s/f (Yiel) 11 Ran SP% **122.8**
Speed ratings (Par 103): **89,87,77,75,75 49, ,86, ,**
CSF £81.22 CT £473.49 TOTE £9.70: £2.90, £3.00, £2.40; EX 74.40 Trifecta £807.50.
Owner M H O G **Bred** Mrs Miriam O'Donnell **Trained** Middleham, N Yorks
FOCUS
Just an ordinary staying novice handicap hurdle run at a medium gallop. The first three past the post finished a long way clear and the form is sound.
T/Plt: £55.10 to a £1 stake. Pool: £51,839.90 - 686.23 winning tickets T/Qpdt: £23.80 to a £1 stake. Pool: £3,779.36 - 117.10 winning tickets **Richard Young**

5204 - 5212a (Foreign Racing) - See Raceform Interactive

5189
AINTREE (L-H)
Saturday, April 9

OFFICIAL GOING: Hurdle & national course - soft (good to soft in places) changing to soft (heavy in places) after race 5 (4.20); mildmay course - good to soft changing
light 1/2 behindchangeable, heavy showers

5213 GASKELLS WASTE MANAGEMENT H'CAP HURDLE (GRADE 3) (13 hdls) 3m 149y
1:45 (1:47) (Class 1) 4-Y-0+
£28,135 (£10,600; £5,305; £2,650; £1,330; £665)

Form RPR
U423 1 **Ubak (FR)**[24] 4717 8-11-0 **146**..........JoshuaMoore 153+
(Gary Moore) *trckd ldrs: hmpd 1st: lost pl sltly after 4 out: rdn and hdwy after 3 out: chal 2 out: led last: styd on wl* 16/1
-P13 2 1 3/4 **If In Doubt (IRE)**[23] 4730 8-11-4 **150**..........BarryGeraghty 154
(Philip Hobbs) *midfield: pushed along after 4 out: bit short of room appr 3 out: rdn bef 2 out: stl only 7th last: styd on wl: wnt 2nd 100yds out* 9/2[1]
2431 3 3 1/4 **Silsol (GER)**[7] 5085 7-11-7 **158**..........(bt) JackSherwood(5) 159
(Paul Nicholls) *prom: hmpd 1st: rdn to ld narrowly 2 out: hdd last: one pce* 20/1
F331 4 1 1/2 **Murrayana (IRE)**[21] 4801 6-10-0 **132** oh2..........(t) PaddyBrennan 131
(Colin Tizzard) *prom: rdn 3 out: plugged on* 20/1
-24P 5 nse **At Fishers Cross (IRE)**[23] 4732 9-10-11 **148**..........(b) JonathanMoore(5) 147
(Rebecca Curtis) *prom: rdn after 3 out: ev ch whn j.rt 2 out: plugged on run-in* 16/1
0 6 1 1/4 **Squouateur (FR)**[22] 4769 5-10-9 **141**..........(t) MarkWalsh 139
(Gordon Elliott, Ire) *midfield towards inner: pushed along and hdwy after 3 out: swtchd rt appr 2 out: rdn and one pce* 8/1[2]
5320 7 nk **Join The Clan (IRE)**[23] 4730 7-10-7 **139**..........(b) AidanColeman 137
(Jonjo O'Neill) *midfield: rdn and sme hdwy after 3 out: one pce after 2 out* 25/1
3512 8 3 3/4 **Minella Daddy (IRE)**[33] 4535 6-10-0 **132** oh4..........(p) SeanBowen 128
(Peter Bowen) *hld up: hmpd 1st: rdn after 4 out: plugged on after 2 out: nvr threatened* 20/1
2P12 9 1/2 **Arpege D'Alene (FR)**[23] 4730 6-11-3 **149**..........(tp) SamTwiston-Davies 144
(Paul Nicholls) *in tch: rdn after 3 out: nt fluent 2 out and last: wknd run-in* 8/1[2]
3521 10 6 **Ballycross**[29] 4596 5-9-13 **134**..........RyanHatch(3) 124
(Nigel Twiston-Davies) *hld up: pushed along after 8th: rdn bef 3 out: nvr threatened* 12/1
2110 11 8 **Rock The Kasbah (IRE)**[24] 4717 6-11-6 **152**..........RichardJohnson 135
(Philip Hobbs) *led: rdn 3 out: hdd 2 out: wknd appr last* 11/1[3]
40 12 2 **Childrens List (IRE)**[22] 4769 6-10-7 **139**..........DavidMullins 118
(W P Mullins, Ire) *wore ear plugs: hld up: rdn after 4 out: nvr threatened* 20/1
2340 13 2 1/4 **Ruacana**[23] 4730 7-10-5 **144**..........MrAlexFerguson(7) 120
(John Ferguson) *in tch: lost pl and nt fluent 4 out: wknd bef 3 out* 66/1
30-4 14 6 **Tiger Roll (IRE)**[17] 71 6-10-13 **145**..........(bt) BJCooper 113
(Gordon Elliott, Ire) *hld up: sme hdwy on outside after 4 out: mstke 3 out: sn wknd* 20/1
1120 15 54 **Pinnacle Panda (IRE)**[21] 4794 5-9-11 **134**..........(b[1]) DavidNoonan(5) 48
(Tom Lacey) *midfield: pushed along and lost pl after 4 out: sn wknd: t.o after 2 out* 66/1
3-0 16 4 **Mydor (FR)**[12] 5003 6-10-1 **133**..........PaulTownend 43
(A J Martin, Ire) *midfield on outer: hdwy whn hmpd 3 out: sn wknd: eased after 2 out* 8/1[2]
-0P3 P **Kings Palace (IRE)**[23] 4733 8-10-10 **142**..........(tp) TomScudamore
(David Pipe) *hld up: p.u sharply bef 9th: lame* 8/1[2]
23P- F **Urban Hymn (FR)**[464] 3443 8-10-3 **135**..........BrianHughes
(Malcolm Jefferson) *w ldr: fell 1st* 16/1
/51P P **Saddlers Encore (IRE)**[23] 4730 7-10-2 **134**..........TomO'Brien
(Philip Hobbs) *hld up: sltly hmpd by faller 1st: pushed along bef 8th: sn bhd: t.o whn p.u bef last* 33/1
6m 25.6s (9.30) **Going Correction** +0.75s/f (Soft) 19 Ran SP% **129.9**
Speed ratings (Par 113): **115,114,113,112,112 112,112,111,111,109 106,105,105,103,86 84, , ,**
CSF £80.45 CT £1510.93 TOTE £22.60: £3.70, £1.80, £4.50, £4.80; EX 119.40 Trifecta £3506.30.
Owner Nick Peacock **Bred** P De Maleissye Melun Et Al **Trained** Lower Beeding, W Sussex
FOCUS
Bends and hurdles moved in at least 4yds since the previous day to nearly the innermost configuration. The opener was run over 30yds further than advertised and the actual race distance was 3m179yds. Following 7mm of overnight rain the going was changed to good to soft on the Mildmay Course and soft, good to soft in places on the National and hurdle courses. After riding in the opener Bryan Cooper said: "The ground is on the slow side" and Ryan Hatch said: "It is good to soft, soft in places" while Richard Johnson and Sam Twiston-Davies both called it "soft". A cracking staying handicap to begin proceedings, featuring several who ran well in defeat at Cheltenham. The early tempo was steady and they were well bunched before the pace began to increase heading out on the final circuit. Ubak is rated back to the level of his smart novice form.

5214 EZ TRADER MERSEY NOVICES' HURDLE (GRADE 1) (11 hdls) 2m 4f
2:25 (2:25) (Class 1) 4-Y-0+ £42,402 (£16,099; £8,157; £4,174; £2,194)

Form RPR
111 1 **Yorkhill (IRE)**[24] 4715 6-11-4 156..........PaulTownend 149+
(W P Mullins, Ire) *hld up in rr: t.k.h 2nd: sn trcking ldrs: led bef 7th: j.lft and nt fluent after: hung lft landing last: drvn out* 30/100[1]
1121 2 2 1/4 **Le Prezien (FR)**[27] 4636 5-11-4 142..........(t) SamTwiston-Davies 144
(Paul Nicholls) *hld up wl in tch: effrt appr 3 out: rdn to take 2nd last: styd on same pce last 75yds* 8/1[2]
5312 3 1 1/2 **Flying Angel (IRE)**[22] 4769 5-11-4 144..........RyanHatch 142
(Nigel Twiston-Davies) *trckd ldr: drvn 3 out: kpt on same pce appr last* 17/2[3]
4 4 nse **Bello Conti (FR)**[24] 4715 5-11-4 140..........BJCooper 141
(W P Mullins, Ire) *t.k.h: trckd ldrs: drvn 3 out: swtchd rt between last 2: kpt on same pce* 9/1
311 5 52 **Prince Of Steal (IRE)**[61] 4026 6-11-4 144..........LeightonAspell 101
(James Evans) *t.k.h: trckd ldrs: drvn bef 3 out: sn lost pl and bhd: t.o whn eased last 200yds: eventually completed* 33/1
212 P **The Dutchman (IRE)**[27] 4636 6-11-4 137..........NicodeBoinville
(Sandy Thomson) *led tl bef 7th: outpcd and lost pl 8th: sn bhd: t.o 6th whn p.u bef last: b.b.v* 20/1
5m 10.1s (9.40) **Going Correction** +0.75s/f (Soft) 6 Ran SP% **116.3**
Speed ratings (Par 117): **111,110,109,109,88**
CSF £4.07 TOTE £1.40: £1.10, £2.60; EX 3.20 Trifecta £8.70.
Owner Andrea & Graham Wylie **Bred** Patrick Keating **Trained** Muine Beag, Co Carlow
FOCUS
Race distance increased by 28yds. Under 4l between the front four at the line, but the story of the race was very much how the red-hot favourite did everything to throw it away and still proved good enough, albeit it wasn't pretty. Yorkhill is arted 9lb below his Festival mark. The early pace was a steady one.

5215 DOOM BAR MAGHULL NOVICES' CHASE (GRADE 1) (12 fncs) 1m 7f 176y
3:00 (3:02) (Class 1) 5-Y-0+ £56,270 (£21,200; £10,610; £5,300; £2,660)

Form RPR
-111 1 **Douvan (FR)**[25] 4696 6-11-4 161..........PaulTownend 176+
(W P Mullins, Ire) *trckd ldr: nt fluent 3rd: led sn after 9th: clr 2 out: v easily* 2/13[1]
1114 2 14 **The Game Changer (IRE)**[25] 4696 7-11-4 151..........(t) BJCooper 156
(Gordon Elliott, Ire) *trckd ldng pair: wnt modest 2nd appr 2 out: kpt on: no ch w wnr* 8/1[3]
2333 3 18 **Fox Norton (FR)**[25] 4696 6-11-4 146..........NoelFehily 140
(Neil Mulholland) *hld up off pce: kpt on to take poor 3rd between last 2* 14/1
3331 4 1 1/2 **Ballybolley (IRE)**[14] 4910 7-11-4 143..........(t) DarylJacob 139
(Nigel Twiston-Davies) *wore ear plugs: hld up off pce: hit 8th: tk poor 4th between last 2* 25/1
36- 5 21 **Alisier D'Irlande (FR)**[41] 4396 6-11-4 148..........(t) AELynch 130
(Henry De Bromhead, Ire) *t.k.h: led: j.lft: hit 9th: sn hdd: hit last 3: wknd 2 out: fin tired* 6/1[2]
3m 56.8s (-3.20) **Going Correction** +0.45s/f (Soft) 5 Ran SP% **122.6**
Speed ratings: **126,119,110,109,98**
CSF £3.41 TOTE £1.20: £1.10, £2.60; EX 2.60 Trifecta £10.90.
Owner Mrs S Ricci **Bred** S A R L Haras De La Faisanderie **Trained** Muine Beag, Co Carlow
FOCUS
A poor turnout largely due to the presence of Douvan, but they went a decent gallop and the short-priced favourite was in total control up the home straight. He became the third horse in recent years, joining Tidal Bay and Sprinter Sacre, to follow up in this race after taking the Arkle and confirmed his status as the season's leading novice chaser.

5216 LIVERPOOL STAYERS' HURDLE (GRADE 1) (13 hdls) 3m 149y
3:40 (3:44) (Class 1) 4-Y-0+
£84,405 (£31,800; £15,915; £7,950; £3,990; £1,995)

Form RPR
1111 1 **Thistlecrack**[23] 4732 8-11-7 174..........TomScudamore 171+
(Colin Tizzard) *set v stdy pce: t.k.h: qcknd gallop 8th: hit 2 out: sn wnt clr: v impressive* 2/7[1]
-342 2 7 **Shaneshill (IRE)**[24] 4716 7-11-7 154..........PaulTownend 155
(W P Mullins, Ire) *t.k.h: trckd ldrs: wnt modest 2nd 2 out: kpt on: no ch w wnr* 8/1[3]
5-11 3 5 **Prince Of Scars (IRE)**[103] 3322 6-11-7 159..........BJCooper 151
(Gordon Elliott, Ire) *hld up in rr: nt fluent 8th: hdwy 10th: effrt and hung lft after 3 out: 5th last: tk modest 3rd last 100yds* 10/1
20-0 4 2 1/4 **Serienschock (GER)**[34] 4525 8-11-7 144..........(t) LudovicPhilipperon 149
(Mlle A Rosa, France) *trckd ldrs: 2nd 3 out: one pce fr next* 66/1
11-1 5 2 **Different Gravey (IRE)**[49] 4239 6-11-7 160..........NicodeBoinville 148
(Nicky Henderson) *chsd wnr: pushed along 9th: one pce fr 2 out* 5/1[2]

-346 **6** *19* **Aqalim**[112] 3149 6-11-7 150.......................................(b) AidanColeman 128
(John Ferguson) *hld up in last: nt fluent 6th: pushed along 7th: hrd drvn 9th: reminders and lost tch next* **50/1**

6m 33.4s (17.10) **Going Correction** +0.75s/f (Soft) **6 Ran SP% 118.1**
Speed ratings (Par 117): **102,99,98,97,96 90**
CSF £4.23 TOTE £1.40: £1.10, £3.10; EX 4.40 Trifecta £12.60.
Owner John and Heather Snook **Bred** R F And S D Knipe **Trained** Milborne Port, Dorset

FOCUS
An excellent opportunity for Thistlecrack to supplement his World Hurdle success and he never looked in a moment's danger, making his own running at a slow pace. He didn't need to reproduce his festival figure to win easily.

5217 BETFRED H'CAP CHASE (LISTED RACE) (19 fncs) 3m 210y
4:20 (4:21) (Class 1) 5-Y-0+
£33,862 (£12,820; £6,466; £3,280; £1,696; £898)

Form RPR

1356 **1** **Maggio (FR)**[27] 4635 11-10-9 **140**.....................................(t) JamesReveley 156+
(Patrick Griffin, Ire) *hld up: gd hdwy after 4 out: wnt 2nd 3 out: led jst after 2 out: pushed clr appr last: kpt on* **50/1**

2220 **2** *12* **Virak (FR)**[42] 4361 7-11-7 **157**.....................................(p) HarryCobden(5) 159
(Paul Nicholls) *prom: led 4 out: rdn whn hdd jst after 2 out: one pce and sn no ch w wnr* **12/1**

-P00 **3** *1/2* **Al Co (FR)**[58] 4066 11-10-1 **132**.....................................(p) SeanBowen 137+
(Peter Bowen) *in tch towards outer: slow 6th: rdn bef 3 out: one pce in 3rd after 2 out: nt fluent last* **14/1**

21U0 **4** *12* **Thomas Brown**[25] 4701 7-10-8 **139**.....................................(b) NoelFehily 131
(Harry Fry) *midfield: sme hdwy whn nt fluent 3 out: sn rdn: mstke 2 out but sn 4th: no imp* **7/1[2]**

-530 **5** *2 1/4* **Band Of Blood (IRE)**[25] 4697 8-10-0 **131** oh2.............(bt) JoshuaMoore 123
(Dr Richard Newland) *trckd ldrs: hit 8th: nt fluent 13th and 14th: mstke 5 out: outpcd after 4 out: no threat after* **8/1[3]**

3135 **6** *5* **Cloudy Too (IRE)**[27] 4635 10-11-1 **146**..................................... DerekFox 129
(Sue Smith) *trckd ldrs: rdn bef 4 out: wknd after 2 out* **14/1**

00-6 **P** **No Secrets (IRE)**[55] 4147 12-10-5 **136**.....................................(t) DenisO'Regan
(A J Martin, Ire) *midfield: blnd 9th: lost pl and reminders after next: bhd whn blnd 5 out: p.u bef next* **33/1**

1511 **P** **Mystifiable**[36] 4465 8-10-3 **134**.....................................(t) SamTwiston-Davies
(Fergal O'Brien) *midfield on inner: hdwy to trck ldrs 4 out: rdn next: already wkng whn mstke 2 out: p.u bef last* **13/2[1]**

1P13 **P** **Roc D'Apsis (FR)**[42] 4361 7-10-5 **136**.....................................(p) PaddyBrennan
(Tom George) *midfield: hit 5th: nt fluent 13th and 14th: rdn after 5 out: wknd after 4 out: p.u bef 3 out* **7/1[2]**

14F4 **P** **Knock House (IRE)**[23] 4735 7-10-12 **143**.....................................(p) MsNCarberry
(Mick Channon) *hld up in rr: blnd 4th: rdn after 5 out: sn wknd: p.u bef 3 out* **8/1[3]**

51P0 **P** **Racing Pulse (IRE)**[25] 4701 7-10-8 **139**.....................................(tp) JJBurke
(Rebecca Curtis) *midfield: bit slow 13th: sn lost pl and bhd: p.u bef 5 out* **18/1**

00PF **P** **Little Jon**[23] 4733 8-10-6 **140**.....................................(p) RyanHatch(3)
(Nigel Twiston-Davies) *hld up: rdn bef 4 out: sn wknd: p.u bef last* **18/1**

3222 **P** **Coologue (IRE)**[36] 4458 7-10-10 **141**.....................................(t) RichardJohnson
(Charlie Longsdon) *led: hdd 4 out: sn wknd: p.u bef 2 out* **7/1[2]**

2122 **P** **Cernunnos (FR)**[21] 4787 6-10-4 **135**.....................................(tp) MarkWalsh
(Tom George) *hld up: nt fluent 13th and 14th: wknd after 4 out: p.u bef last* **17/2**

6m 39.5s (9.50) **Going Correction** +0.45s/f (Soft) **14 Ran SP% 120.0**
Speed ratings: **102,98,98,94,93 91,,,,,,,,**
CSF £567.10 CT £8594.89 TOTE £46.30: £11.40, £3.80, £4.80; EX 556.70 Trifecta £24476.10.
Owner D G Pryde/James Beaumont **Bred** Haras Du Reuilly **Trained** Oldtown, Co Dublin

FOCUS
After persistent rain during the afternoon the going was changed to soft on all three courses prior to this race. As usual a competitive renewal and they went a good clip in the conditions, which contributed to only six finishers. Maggio's 2014 Kelso win could be rated to this sort of level.

5218 CRABBIE'S GRAND NATIONAL CHASE (H'CAP) (GRADE 3) (30 fncs) 4m 2f 74y
5:15 (5:17) (Class 1) 7-Y-0+
£561,300 (£211,100; £105,500; £52,700; £26,500; £13,200)

Form RPR

2254 **1** **Rule The World**[34] 4517 9-10-7 **148**..................................... DavidMullins 164+
(M F Morris, Ire) *chsd ldrs: blnd 4 out: hdwy next: cl 3rd last: led last 150yds: styd on wl* **33/1**

-311 **2** *6* **The Last Samuri (IRE)**[35] 4472 8-10-8 **149**..................................... DavidBass 158
(Kim Bailey) *w ldrs: led 26th: hdd and no ex last 150yds* **8/1[1]**

05P6 **3** *8* **Vics Canvas (IRE)**[49] 4260 13-10-6 **147**.....................................(p) RobertDunne 153+
(Dermot Anthony McLoughlin, Ire) *mid-div: blnd bdly and lost pl 6th (1st Bechers): mstke next (1st Foinavon): hdwy to chse ldrs 16th (water): cl 2nd appr 2 out: upsides last: wknd last 100yds* **100/1**

3455 **4** *2* **Gilgamboa (IRE)**[23] 4731 8-11-1 **156**..................................... RobbiePower 154
(E Bolger, Ire) *prom: chsng ldrs 16th (water): one pce appr 2 out* **28/1**

-302 **5** *19* **Goonyella (IRE)**[34] 4521 9-10-8 **149**.....................................(tp) JJBurke 133
(J T R Dreaper, Ire) *rr-div: sme hdwy whn mstke and lost pl 18th: kpt on fr 3 out: nvr a threat* **12/1[3]**

623 **6** *1 3/4* **Ucello Conti (FR)**[79] 3715 8-10-8 **149**.....................................(t) DarylJacob 125
(Gordon Elliott, Ire) *in rr: hdwy 16th (water): chsng ldrs whn blnd 19th: hit 26th: one pce bef 2 out* **25/1**

1U26 **7** *11* **Vieux Lion Rouge (FR)**[25] 4700 7-10-5 **146**.....................................(p) JamesReveley 114
(David Pipe) *in rr: hdwy 18th: chsng ldrs 26th: wknd fr 2 out* **66/1**

/-24 **8** *14* **Morning Assembly (IRE)**[25] 4697 9-10-9 **150**..................................... DavyRussell 101
(P A Fahy, Ire) *racd wd: mid-div: hdwy to trck ldrs 20th: w ldrs 4 out: wknd appr 2 out* **16/1**

5-3P **9** *1/2* **Shutthefrontdoor (IRE)**[35] 4485 9-10-11 **152**.....................................(tp) BarryGeraghty 103
(Jonjo O'Neill) *chsd ldrs: wknd after 3 out* **12/1[3]**

0312 **10** *9* **Unioniste (FR)**[27] 4635 8-10-8 **149**..................................... NickScholfield 101
(Paul Nicholls) *mstkes: in rr: bhd fr 16th* **28/1**

2615 **11** *5* **Le Reve (IRE)**[42] 4361 8-10-8 **149**.....................................(b) HarrySkelton 86
(Lucy Wadham) *mid-div: hdwy to chse ldrs 12th: wknd after 3 out* **50/1**

3243 **12** *7* **Buywise (IRE)**[70] 3860 9-10-10 **151**..................................... PaulMoloney 81
(Evan Williams) *mid-div: hdwy to chse ldrs whn mstke 17th: lost pl 21st* **33/1**

5-15 **13** *dist* **Pendra (IRE)**[112] 3150 8-10-5 **146**.....................................(p) AidanColeman
(Charlie Longsdon) *in rr: hdwy 19th: blnd 24th (2nd Canal Turn): wknd 3 out: bhd whn heavily eased sn after last: eventually completed* **50/1**

3-15 **14** *14* **Triolo D'Alene (FR)**[49] 4240 9-11-0 **155**..................................... JeremiahMcGrath
(Nicky Henderson) *in rr: bhd fr 26th: heavily eased sn after last: t.o: eventually completed* **50/1**

-002 **15** *20* **Just A Par (IRE)**[18] 4858 9-10-6 **147**.....................................(b) SeanBowen
(Paul Nicholls) *in rr: bhd fr 4 out: t.o whn heavily eased sn after last: eventually completed* **40/1**

6221 **16** *1* **Many Clouds (IRE)**[27] 4635 9-11-10 **165**..................................... LeightonAspell
(Oliver Sherwood) *trckd ldrs: led 19th: hdd and blnd 26th: wknd after 3 out: virtually p.u sn after last: t.o and walked home fr elbow* **8/1[1]**

1200 **P** **Aachen**[35] 4483 12-10-10 **151**..................................... HenryBrooke
(Venetia Williams) *led: hmpd by loose horse bef 13th: hdd 15th (Chair): lost pl 19th: bhd whn p.u bef 22nd (2nd Bechers)* **50/1**

4020 **F** **On His Own (IRE)**[22] 4767 12-11-1 **156**.....................................(p) MrPWMullins
(W P Mullins, Ire) *in rr: mstke 2nd: fell heavily 15th (Chair)* **33/1**

432P **F** **First Lieutenant (IRE)**[63] 4007 11-11-4 **159**.....................................(p) BJCooper
(M F Morris, Ire) *prom: fell 2nd* **50/1**

50P1 **P** **Boston Bob (IRE)**[49] 4260 11-10-10 **151**..................................... PaulTownend
(W P Mullins, Ire) *mid-div: lost pl and bhd whn p.u bef 22nd (2nd Bechers): lame* **25/1**

-1U5 **U** **Gallant Oscar (IRE)**[34] 4521 10-10-8 **149**..................................... MarkWalsh
(A J Martin, Ire) *mid-div: blnd 9th (1st Valentines): sme hdwy whn blnd and eventually uns rdr 18th* **16/1**

0413 **P** **Soll**[51] 4205 11-10-11 **152**.....................................(bt) ConorO'Farrell
(David Pipe) *mstke 1st: hld up towards rr: pushed along 14th: bhd 17th: t.o whn p.u bef 21st* **40/1**

5PP0 **U** **Ballynagour (IRE)**[23] 4733 10-11-2 **157**.....................................(t) TomScudamore
(David Pipe) *mid-div: blnd 14th: hdwy whn blnd and uns rdr 19th* **50/1**

/150 **F** **Sir Des Champs (FR)**[63] 4007 10-10-13 **154**..................................... MsNCarberry
(W P Mullins, Ire) *in rr whn fell heavily 15th (Chair)* **20/1**

P-P0 **F** **Katenko (FR)**[25] 4697 10-10-6 **147**..................................... WillKennedy
(Venetia Williams) *hld up: hit 17th: sme hdwy into mid-div whn fell 22nd (2nd Bechers)* **40/1**

4500 **P** **Double Ross (IRE)**[25] 4697 10-10-9 **150**.....................................(tp) RyanHatch
(Nigel Twiston-Davies) *w ldrs: sddle slipped and lost pl 24th (2nd Canal Turn): j. next (2nd Valentines) w no irons: bhd whn p.u bef 26th* **80/1**

-601 **P** **Saint Are (FR)**[45] 4306 10-10-5 **146**.....................................(tp) PaddyBrennan
(Tom George) *mstkes: w ldrs: led 15th (Chair): hdd next (water): lost pl 3 out: sn bhd: t.o whn p.u bef last* **16/1**

22P1 **P** **Silviniaco Conti (FR)**[49] 4240 10-11-8 **163**.....................................(b) NoelFehily
(Paul Nicholls) *prom: hmpd 11th: hit next: mid-div: sn lost pl and eased: t.o whn p.u bef 14th* **12/1[3]**

-0U6 **P** **Black Thunder (FR)**[63] 3993 9-10-6 **147**.....................................(t) MrSWaley-Cohen
(Paul Nicholls) *hld up towards rr: hdwy and in tch whn blnd 16th (water): sn bhd: blnd 20th: t.o whn p.u bef next* **50/1**

2P40 **P** **Rocky Creek (IRE)**[42] 4361 10-10-13 **154**.....................................(t) AndrewThornton
(Paul Nicholls) *in rr: blnd bdly 11th: t.o whn p.u bef next* **66/1**

4035 **U** **Ballycasey (IRE)**[23] 4733 9-10-6 **147**.....................................(p) MsKWalsh
(W P Mullins, Ire) *mid-div: hit 17th: hdwy 25th (2nd Valentines): prom 4 out: wknd and modest 10th whn mstke and uns rdr 2 out* **50/1**

0P0- **P** **Home Farm (IRE)**[41] 4395 9-10-4 **145**.....................................(t) AELynch
(Henry De Bromhead, Ire) *in rr: blnd 7th: sn bhd: t.o whn p.u bef 21st* **50/1**

2-15 **P** **Kruzhlinin (GER)**[25] 4697 9-10-7 **148**..................................... RichardJohnson
(Philip Hobbs) *in rr: blnd 11th: bhd whn mstke 23rd (2nd Foinavon): t.o whn p.u bef 4 out* **33/1**

6P-0 **U** **Hadrian's Approach (IRE)**[42] 4361 9-10-6 **147**..................................... NicodeBoinville
(Nicky Henderson) *mid-div: blnd and uns rdr 1st* **50/1**

54P2 **F** **Holywell (IRE)**[25] 4697 9-10-12 **153**.....................................(b) RichieMcLernon
(Jonjo O'Neill) *mid-div: hit 1st: fell 2nd* **11/1[2]**

-662 **P** **The Druids Nephew (IRE)**[35] 4472 9-11-0 **155**.....................................(p) DenisO'Regan
(Neil Mulholland) *mstkes: mid-div: lost pl after 6th (1st Bechers): sn bhd: t.o whn p.u bef 21st* **16/1**

0F30 **U** **The Romford Pele (IRE)**[24] 4717 9-10-4 **145**.....................................(b) TrevorWhelan
(Rebecca Curtis) *chsd ldrs: blnd and uns rdr 8th (1st Canal Turn)* **33/1**

3P-2 **P** **Wonderful Charm (FR)**[120] 3016 8-11-3 **158**.....(tp) SamTwiston-Davies
(Paul Nicholls) *mid-div: lost pl after 16th (water): sn bhd: t.o whn p.u bef 21st* **40/1**

1225 **U** **Onenightinvienna (IRE)**[49] 4237 7-10-8 **149**..................................... TomO'Brien
(Philip Hobbs) *in rr: bhd whn bdly hmpd and uns rdr 22nd (2nd Bechers)* **33/1**

9m 29.0s (16.00) **Going Correction** +0.90s/f (Soft) **39 Ran SP% 148.7**
Speed ratings: **117,115,113,113,108 108,105,102,102,100 99,97,,, ,,,, ,EM**
CSF £255.07 CT £23181.66 TOTE £44.50: £9.20, £3.10, £18.90, £8.40; EX 667.60 Trifecta £57778.10 Part won..
Owner Gigginstown House Stud **Bred** Mrs P G Wilkins And R J McAlpine **Trained** Fethard, Co Tipperary

■ Stewards' Enquiry : David Bass 20-day ban (6 days deferred): 29 Apr-13 May (used whip above permitted level)

FOCUS
A top-quality edition of the race, with 19 of the 39 rated 150-plus, and they went a good gallop from the outset, soon being strung out. The rain had a significant effect on the race also, not suiting a fair few of the runners and obviously making it an even more thorough test of stamina. More of an old school National, 16 finished, with the first four well clear, and perhaps unsurprisingly the lower-weighted horses dominated. Remarkably it went to a horse who was a second-season novice and still a maiden over fences coming into the race. Rule The World is rated in line with his best hurdles form with only the first four really passing the stamina test.

5219 PINSENT MASONS H'CAP HURDLE (FOR CONDITIONAL JOCKEYS AND AMATEUR RIDERS) (9 hdls) 2m 103y
6:10 (6:11) (Class 2) 4-Y-0+
£30,950 (£9,190; £4,595; £2,290; £1,150; £580)

Form RPR

/000 **1** **Ivan Grozny (FR)**[22] 4765 6-11-9 **141**..................................... DavidMullins(3) 158+
(W P Mullins, Ire) *hld up: hdwy gng wl 2 out: led sn after: clr last: styd on wl: eased cl home* **16/1**

2 *8* **Automated**[21] 4809 5-10-10 **128**..................................... JackKennedy(3) 135+
(Gordon Elliott, Ire) *midfield: hdwy 3 out: wnt 2nd bef last: no imp on wnr* **7/1[2]**

2143 **3** *6* **Bigmartre (FR)**[21] 4781 5-10-8 **133**..................................... HarryTeal(10) 131
(Harry Whittington) *midfield: u.p appr 4 out: hdwy 2 out: edgd lft bef last: styd on to take 3rd cl home: no ch w front two* **10/1**

12-2 **4** *nk* **Boite (IRE)**[35] 4484 6-11-3 **135**..................................... HarryBannister(3) 135
(Warren Greatrex) *chsd ldrs: hit 2nd: led appr 3 out: rdn 2 out: sn hdd: kpt on u.p run-in but no ch w front two* **12/1**

5310 **5** *5* **Frodon (FR)**[22] 4764 4-10-13 **139**........................ HarryCobden(5) 126
(Paul Nicholls) *prom: ev ch 3 out: stl wl there 2 out: styd on same pce run-in* **9/2**[1]

2U61 **6** *2 1/4* **Nesterenko (GER)**[19] 4851 7-11-2 **131**........................ JeremiahMcGrath 122
(Nicky Henderson) *chsd ldrs: rdn bef 2 out: kpt on u.p run-in: nvr able to chal* **25/1**

350P **7** *1/2* **Dell' Arca (IRE)**[55] 4139 7-11-1 **135**........................(b) DavidNoonan(5) 128+
(David Pipe) *in tch: effrt appr 2 out: kpt on same pce run-in* **9/2**[1]

1313 **8** *1* **Sir Chauvelin**[62] 4012 4-9-13 **127**........................ FinianO'Toole(7) 110
(Jim Goldie) *racd keenly: hld up: kpt on run-in: nvr able to chal* **20/1**

1100 **9** *3/4* **Nabucco**[22] 4769 7-10-13 **135**........................ MrAlexFerguson(7) 124
(John Ferguson) *chsd ldrs: ev ch 2 out: one pce whn nt fluent last: wknd fnl 100yds* **20/1**

10 *4 1/2* **Mr Boss Man (IRE)**[17] 1140 8-10-4 **124**........................ JonathanMoore(5) 108
(Adrian McGuinness, Ire) *hld up: hdwy into midfield 2 out: nvr able to chal* **25/1**

0 **11** *4 1/2* **My Manekineko**[50] 2186 7-10-10 **125**........................ MsKWalsh 104
(J A Nash, Ire) *midfield: lost pl after 4 out: struggling after* **33/1**

1031 **12** *15* **Master Jake (IRE)**[13] 4937 8-10-10 **130**........................ BridgetAndrews(5) 94
(Dan Skelton) *hld up: rdn after 4 out: nvr a threat* **16/1**

-000 **13** *shd* **Sgt Reckless**[24] 4717 9-11-7 **136**........................ MsNCarberry 107
(Mick Channon) *hld up: no imp whn mstke 2 out: nvr a threat* **16/1**

1151 **14** *3* **Allee Bleue (IRE)**[12] 4976 6-11-1 **135**........................ CiaranGethings(5) 96
(Philip Hobbs) *w ldr: led after 3rd: hdd appr 3 out where nt fluent: wknd bef 2 out* **8/1**[3]

15 *8* **Madfuninthewest (IRE)**[109] 3208 5-10-11 **133**........................ GarethMalone(7) 86
(David Dennis) *in tch: rdn appr 3 out: wknd 2 out* **10/1**

/3 **16** *29* **Sir Ector (USA)**[14] 2278 9-10-10 **128**........................(bt) ThomasGarner(3) 52
(Miss Nicole McKenna, Ire) *in tch: lost pl bef 5th: u.p and bhd after: t.o* **25/1**

P36P **17** *4* **Chieftain's Choice (IRE)**[56] 4115 7-10-9 **127**...........(p) PatrickCorbett(3) 47
(Kevin Frost) *led: hdd after 3rd: remained prom tl wknd bef 3 out: eased: t.o* **50/1**

4m 12.2s (6.00) **Going Correction** +0.75s/f (Soft)
WFA 4 from 5yo+ 5lb **17** Ran SP% **129.5**
Speed ratings (Par 109): **115,111,108,107,105 104,103,103,103,100 98,91,91,89,85 71,69**
CSF £121.35 CT £1217.65 TOTE £16.60: £3.90, £2.30, £3.30, £3.30; EX 148.20 Trifecta £1695.80.
Owner Andrea & Graham Wylie **Bred** Mme Larissa Kneip **Trained** Muine Beag, Co Carlow
■ Stewards' Enquiry : Thomas Garner five-day ban; used whip when out of contention (23rd, 28th-30th Apr, 2nd May)

FOCUS
The finale was run over 21yds further than advertised and the actual race distance was 2m124yds. It was another competitive handicap hurdle, this time confined to conditional jockeys and amateur riders, in which they went a sensible early gallop before the pace increased going down the back straight. The form should work out. A big hurdles pb from the impressive winner but in line with his Flat form.
T/Jkpt: Not won. T/Plt: £697.10 to a £1 stake. Pool: £442,801.06 - 463.67 winning tickets. T/Qpdt: £113.90 to a £1 stake. Pool: £27,200.47 - 176.67 winning tickets.
W Glynn, A Sheret & D Owen

4961 **CHEPSTOW** (L-H)
Saturday, April 9
OFFICIAL GOING: Soft (good to soft in places; chs: 4.3, hdl: 4.7)
Wind: light, across Weather: dry, bright spells

5220 TOTESCOOP6 PLAY TODAY NOVICES' HURDLE (DIV I) (8 hdls) 2m 11y
2:15 (2:15) (Class 4) 4-Y-0+ **£3,898** (£1,144; £572; £286)

Form RPR

5 **1** **Satellite (IRE)**[86] 3590 5-10-13 0........................ TomCannon 111+
(Tim Vaughan) *chsd ldrs: effrt to chal 2 out: drvn to ld between last 2: dived last: styd on wl: drvn out* **11/4**[3]

342 **2** *1 3/4* **One Style (FR)**[35] 4494 6-10-13 115........................ AlainCawley 108
(Venetia Williams) *chsd ldrs: wnt cl 2nd 5th: led 2 out: drvn and hdd between last 2: styd on same pce u.p flat* **2/1**[2]

1 **3** *8* **Unison (IRE)**[65] 3955 6-11-5 0........................ MattGriffiths 108
(Jeremy Scott) *t.k.h: w ldr tl led after 1st: j.rt 5th: rdn and hdd 2 out: 3rd and outpcd between last 2: wknd flat* **15/8**[1]

51/ **4** *11* **Act Four (IRE)**[329] 8-10-6 0........................ MrStanSheppard(7) 90
(Matt Sheppard) *in tch in midfield: pushed along and outpcd whn j. slowly 5th: wl btn 4th 2 out: plugged on* **14/1**

0 **5** *8* **Whatsthatallabout (IRE)**[26] 4687 5-10-6 0........................ MarkQuinlan 77
(Neil Mulholland) *taken down early: chsd ldr after 1st tl lost 2nd and sltly hmpd 5th: wknd next* **25/1**

P4FU **6** *3 1/2* **Blackadder**[18] 4854 4-10-7 0........................ BrendanPowell 72
(Mark Gillard) *hld up in last pair: sme prog after 4th: hmpd and wnt lft next: sn wknd* **150/1**

-05P **7** *10* **Bestwork (FR)**[102] 3334 5-10-10 0........................[1] GrahamWatters(3) 68
(Charlie Longsdon) *t.k.h: led tl after 1st: blnd and lost pl 2nd: bhd and mstke 4th: lost tch and t.o next* **40/1**

5 **8** *10* **Common Practice (IRE)**[269] 1003 5-10-13 0........................ AndrewTinkler 58
(Jonjo O'Neill) *hld up in tch in midfield: 6th and rdn after 4th: btn next: wknd: t.o* **12/1**

9 *20* **Buffalo Sabre (FR)** 4-10-7 0........................(t) JamesBest 32
(Nigel Hawke) *rn green in rr: j. awkwardly 1st: rdn after 4th: lost tch and t.o next* **40/1**

4m 9.8s (-0.80) **Going Correction** +0.25s/f (Yiel)
WFA 4 from 5yo+ 5lb **9** Ran SP% **118.5**
Speed ratings (Par 105): **112,111,107,101,97 95,90,85,75**
CSF £9.09 TOTE £4.00: £1.20, £1.20, £1.20; EX 11.20 Trifecta £22.40.
Owner Paul & Louise Bowtell **Bred** Whisperview Trading Ltd **Trained** Aberthin, Vale of Glamorgan

FOCUS
After 5mm of overnight rain the ground was officially changed to soft from soft with good to soft places. The rails on the far bend were out by ten metres and the rails on the stable bend were out by four metres; This added the following distances - Races 1, 2, 4, 6, 7 & 8 - 40yds; Races 3 & 5 - 70yds. This opener lacked depth and revolved around only three of the runners. A big step up from the winner but he's entitled to rate a lot higher on Flat form.

5221 TOTESCOOP6 PLAY TODAY NOVICES' HURDLE (DIV II) (8 hdls) 2m 11y
2:50 (2:51) (Class 4) 4-Y-0+ **£3,898** (£1,144; £572; £286)

Form RPR

1-3 **1** **Mere Anarchy (IRE)**[17] 4869 5-10-13 0........................ GavinSheehan 115+
(Robert Stephens) *hld up in tch: hdwy to chse ldrs 2nd: led sn after 4th: gng clr w rival whn mstke and wnt lft next: drvn between last 2: forged ahd flat: kpt on: jst lasted home* **6/4**[1]

62 **2** *shd* **Bennys King (IRE)**[28] 4613 5-10-13 0........................ AlainCawley 115+
(Venetia Williams) *prom tl 3rd: bhd whn pushed along and outpcd after next: hdwy to pass btn rivals 5th: modest 3rd next: mstke 2 out:clsd and 6 l down last: styd on strly to go 2nd fnl 75yds: clsng qckly but nvr quite getting to* **4/1**[3]

201 **3** *3* **Nabhan**[36] 4462 4-10-10 135........................ RobertWilliams(3) 109
(Bernard Llewellyn) *chsd ldr tl jnd ldr 2nd: chsd wnr and gng clr whn carried lft 5th: drvn between last 2: stl ev ch last: no ex and styd on same pce flat* **2/1**[2]

-P56 **4** *15* **Rose Revived**[21] 4784 5-9-13 0........................ PatrickCowley(7) 87
(Jonjo O'Neill) *hld up in tch: rdn bef 5th: sn struggling and wl btn bef 3 out: plugged on* **12/1**

30 **5** *11* **El Tiburon (IRE)**[99] 3416 4-10-7 0........................ JamesBanks 77
(Sam Thomas) *hld up in tch: hdwy into midfield after 4th: 4th and outpcd whn blnd 5th: wl btn next* **50/1**

6-60 **6** *9* **Royal Roo**[17] 4875 7-10-6 0........................(t) KielanWoods 67
(Mark Rimell) *in tch: dropped to rr 3rd: lost tch bef 5th: t.o* **33/1**

44 **7** *20* **Sandgate**[123] 2954 4-10-7 0........................ MarkQuinlan 48
(Neil Mulholland) *t.k.h: led tl sn after 4th: 3rd and wkng whn mstke 3 out: fdd: t.o* **14/1**

P **Le Tigre De Bronze**[953] 6-10-10 0........................(t) BenPoste(3)
(Adrian Wintle) *hld up in tch: hdwy 4th: struggling and blnd 5th: wl btn and p.u next* **50/1**

4m 16.3s (5.70) **Going Correction** +0.25s/f (Yiel)
WFA 4 from 5yo+ 5lb **8** Ran SP% **114.6**
Speed ratings (Par 105): **95,94,93,85,80 75,65,**
CSF £8.13 TOTE £2.60: £1.10, £1.60, £1.30; EX 8.90 Trifecta £15.80.
Owner The Warriors **Bred** J Hanly & C Neilan **Trained** Penhow, Newport

FOCUS
As with the first division, few could be seriously fancied. It served up a dramatic finish as the favourite clung on to a fast-diminishing advantage from a big eyecatcher. The winner is rated similar to his Haydock run.

5222 TOTESCOOP6 THE MILLIONAIRE MAKER H'CAP CHASE (18 fncs) 2m 7f 131y
3:30 (3:32) (Class 4) (0-115,115) 5-Y-0+ **£4,548** (£1,335; £667; £333)

Form RPR

24PP **1** **Loughalder (IRE)**[27] 4649 10-11-3 **106**........................(bt) CharliePoste 118+
(Matt Sheppard) *mde all: mstke 8th: 3 l clr 2 out: styd on wl: rdn out* **16/1**

23P2 **2** *2 1/2* **Somerset Lias (IRE)**[18] 4859 8-10-11 **100**........................ LiamHeard 107
(Bob Buckler) *chsd wnr thrght: rdn after 3 out: 3 l down and styd on same pce fr next* **17/2**

U332 **3** *7* **Grove Silver (IRE)**[27] 4649 7-11-12 **115**........................(p) SeanQuinlan 120+
(Jennie Candlish) *chsd ldrs: blnd 9th: 3rd and u.p whn mstke 3 out: styd on same pce after* **11/4**[1]

3453 **4** *5* **Rosa Fleet (IRE)**[12] 4962 8-11-8 **111**........................ AlainCawley 109
(Venetia Williams) *off the pce in last pair: j.rt 4th: clsd after 7th: rdn and prog to chse clr ldng trio bef 14th: no imp whn blnd 3 out: plugged on* **25/1**

PP64 **P** **Boardwalk Empire (IRE)**[21] 4789 9-10-10 **106**(tp)
WilliamFeatherstone(7)
(Kate Buckett) *in tch: chsd ldrs 8th tl lost pl u.p 11th: lost tch after 13th: t.o whn p.u 15th* **7/1**

23PP **P** **Smart Exit (IRE)**[28] 4612 9-11-5 **108**........................(b[1]) BrendanPowell
(Stuart Edmunds) *chsd ldrs: mstke 5th: lost pl and toiling u.p 13th: lost tch and bhd whn p.u 14th* **14/1**

3P5P **U** **Heronshaw (IRE)**[48] 4267 9-11-12 **115**........................(b) JakeGreenall
(Henry Daly) *midfield: reminders after 3rd and after next: rdn after 7th: blnd and uns rdr 9th* **12/1**

-552 **P** **Heroes Or Ghosts (IRE)**[17] 4876 7-11-4 **107**...............(p) GavinSheehan
(Jo Davis) *in tch in midfield: 5th and rdn after 13th: sn struggling and btn next: bhd whn p.u 15th* **4/1**[2]

F641 **P** **Brook (FR)**[10] 5032 5-11-5 **113**........................(bt) MichaelHeard(5)
(David Pipe) *in tch in midfield: hdwy to chse ldrs 9th: rdn and btn after 13th: wknd next: wl bhd whn p.u 3 out* **5/1**[3]

02P1 **P** **What Larks (IRE)**[12] 4962 8-11-1 **109**........................ ConorRing(5)
(Hugo Froud) *sn detached in last and nvr travelling: mstke 6th: lost tch and t.o whn mstke 11th: p.u next* **10/1**

6m 27.3s (5.30) **Going Correction** +0.30s/f (Yiel) **10** Ran SP% **119.5**
Speed ratings: **103,102,99,98, , , ,**
CSF £146.60 CT £495.84 TOTE £23.50: £5.50, £3.30, £1.40; EX 243.90 Trifecta £2616.40 Part won. Pool: £3,488.63 - 0.66 winning tickets..
Owner Simon Gegg & Tony Scrivin **Bred** Tom Burns **Trained** Eastnor, H'fords

FOCUS
A fair handicap chase, in which they appeared to go a good gallop throughout. Only four completed. The winner was back to something like his best.

5223 TOTETRIFECTA NOVICES' H'CAP HURDLE (11 hdls) 2m 3f 100y
4:05 (4:06) (Class 5) (0-100,100) 4-Y-0+ **£2,599** (£763; £381; £190)

Form RPR

4555 **1** **Zara Hope (IRE)**[94] 3483 5-11-6 **97**........................ GrahamWatters(3) 105+
(Charlie Longsdon) *chsd ldrs tl rdn to ld 3 out: 2 l clr last: styd on wl: rdn out* **7/1**

P463 **2** *3* **Glenariff**[24] 4709 7-11-6 **99**........................(p) KevinJones(5) 103
(Seamus Mullins) *in tch in midfield: hdwy to chse ldrs whn dived and mstke 3 out: 3rd and drvn 2 out: swtchd lft flat: wnt 2nd and kpt on wl fnl 100yds: no threat to wnr* **5/1**[2]

2222 **3** *4 1/2* **Mr Mafia (IRE)**[125] 2930 7-11-10 **98**........................(t) LeeEdwards 98
(Tony Carroll) *hld up in tch in midfield: clsd to trck ldrs 8th: ev ch next: shkn up 2 out: drvn and unable qck between last 2: plugged on same pce and lost 2nd 100yds* **4/1**[1]

6235 **4** *8* **Mazovian (USA)**[36] 4460 8-11-1 **96**......................(tp) MrStanSheppard(7) 87
(Matt Sheppard) *t.k.h: wl in tch in midfield: rdn and outpcd after 8th: wl hld and plugged on same pce fr next* **6/1**[3]

5 *3 ¼* **Replacement Plan (IRE)**[186] 1800 7-11-3 **91**.................. MichealNolan 77
(Richard Woollacott) *hld up in tch in last quartet: clsd and wl in tch 8th: pushed along and mstke next: sn btn and wknd 2 out* **12/1**

F445 **6** *7* **Richardofdoccombe (IRE)**[14] 4917 10-11-6 **99**.............. AliceMills(5) 78
(Gail Haywood) *led tl hdd and rdn bef 8th: btn whn short of room and mstke 3out: wknd bef next* **14/1**

4356 **7** *12* **Stepover**[24] 4709 5-11-12 **100**.................................. KielanWoods 67
(Alex Hales) *chsd ldr tl led bef 8th: rdn and hdd 3 out: wkng whn mstke next: fdd: t.o* **9/1**

5460 **8** *1 ¼* **Cry Fury**[12] 4965 8-11-1 **96**.................................. MrRobertHawker(7) 62
(Sophie Leech) *hld up in tch in rr: clsd and in tch whn hmpd 8th: sn btn and wknd: t.o* **20/1**

00P0 **9** *18* **Up The Junction**[45] 4303 5-11-1 **89**.................................. JamesBest 37
(Tim Vaughan) *in tch in midfield: hdwy to chse ldrs after 7th: rdn bef next: wknd qckly bef 3 out: t.o* **14/1**

003/ **P** **Follow The Master**[735] 5177 10-11-5 **93**............................ CharliePoste
(Brian Forsey) *t.k.h: chsd ldrs: rdn and struggling whn blnd 8th: sn wknd: bhd whn p.u 2 out* **14/1**

05-0 **P** **Ta Ha (IRE)**[37] 4441 8-11-10 **98**.................................. MarkQuinlan
(Malcolm Jones) *in tch in midfield: dropped to last and nt fluent 6th: sn rdn and lost tch: t.o whn p.u 8th* **25/1**

5PF3 **P** **Rosygo (IRE)**[18] 4855 8-11-8 **99**.................................. BenPoste(3)
(Adrian Wintle) *hld up in tch in last pair: rdn and short lived effrt bef 8th: sn wknd: bhd whn p.u 2 out* **10/1**

0-44 **P** **Wojciech**[257] 1120 6-11-1 **89**.................................. LiamHeard
(Martin Hill) *hld up in tch in last quartet: rdn and short lived effrt after 7th: sn btn and bhd whn p.u next* **11/1**

5m 8.6s (6.80) **Going Correction** +0.25s/f (Yiel) **13** Ran SP% **127.2**
Speed ratings (Par 103): **95,93,91,88,87 84,79,78,71, , ,**
CSF £45.45 CT £166.67 TOTE £7.00: £1.90, £2.10, £2.10; EX 52.50 Trifecta £250.20.

Owner Mark E Smith **Bred** Richard And Marie Hennessy **Trained** Over Norton, Oxon

FOCUS
A competitive, if only moderate handicap hurdle. It was won comfortably by a potentially well-treated individual. A step up from the winner but it looks beleivable.

5224 TOTEPOOLLIVEINFO.COM NOVICES' LIMITED H'CAP CHASE (18 fncs) 2m 7f 131y
4:40 (4:41) (Class 3) (0-135,135) 5-Y-O+ **£7,797** (£2,289; £1,144)

Form RPR

123P **1** **Waldorf Salad**[25] 4700 8-11-4 **131**.................................. AlainCawley 140+
(Venetia Williams) *mounted on crse: mde all: rdn bef 14th: kpt on dourly u.p: asserted between last 2: rdn out* **2/1**[2]

314P **2** *2 ¾* **Alternatif (FR)**[23] 4735 6-11-3 **135**......................(b) MichaelHeard(5) 140
(David Pipe) *hld up in 3rd: j. slowly 1st: chsd wnr 14th: 1 l down 2 out: no ex u.p bef last: hld and one pce flat* **11/10**[1]

3FP3 **3** *8* **Vice Et Vertu (FR)**[35] 4493 7-10-3 **116** oh4...................(bt) AndrewTinkler 113
(Henry Daly) *travelled wl: chsd wnr: mstke 12th: dropped to 3rd 14th: sn rdn and little rspnse: wl hld and plugged on same pce fr 3 out* **5/2**[3]

6m 28.75s (6.75) **Going Correction** +0.30s/f (Yiel) **3** Ran SP% **109.5**
Speed ratings: **100,99,96**
CSF £4.65 TOTE £2.60; EX 5.00 Trifecta £3.60.

Owner Alan Parker **Bred** A Parker **Trained** Kings Caple, H'fords

FOCUS
This represented a significant drop in grade for the first two home, both of whom had been pulled up at the Cheltenham Festival last time. The winner is rated in line with his earlier Cheltenham second.

5225 TOTEWIN BEAT SP LAST 4 NATIONALS H'CAP HURDLE (8 hdls) 2m 11y
5:35 (5:38) (Class 4) (0-120,117) 4-Y-O+ **£3,898** (£1,144; £572; £286)

Form RPR

1440 **1** **Hill Fort**[37] 4447 6-11-0 **112**......................................(t) MrStanSheppard(7) 124+
(Matt Sheppard) *hld up in tch: clsd to trck ldrs 5th: upsides ldr 2 out: rdn to ld last: r.o strly: readily* **7/2**[1]

5005 **2** *8* **Tamarillo Grove (IRE)**[19] 4851 9-10-10 **104**..............(t) KillianMoore(3) 106
(Sophie Leech) *led: rdn bef 2 out: hdd last: sn outpcd and hld on for 2nd flat* **16/1**

3332 **3** *2* **Celestial Magic**[37] 4447 4-10-13 **115**........................ DanielHiskett(5) 110
(Richard Phillips) *t.k.h: chsd ldrs: wnt 2nd 3rd: ev ch and mstke 5th: 3rd and outpcd whn hung lft between last 2: kpt on same pce flat* **4/1**[2]

F506 **4** *½* **Red Devil Star (IRE)**[21] 4782 6-11-12 **117**..................(t) MichealNolan 118
(Suzy Smith) *chsd ldrs: nt fluent 4th: rdn bef next: j.lft 5th: kpt on same pce u.p fr 2 out* **4/1**[2]

63P0 **5** *2 ¾* **Dun Scaith (IRE)**[12] 4965 8-10-13 **104**........................ JamesDavies 101
(Sophie Leech) *hld up in tch in rr: effrt 5th: no imp and kpt on same pce fr 2 out* **12/1**

33P3 **6** *8* **Drumviredy (IRE)**[48] 4268 7-11-6 **111**.......................... AlainCawley 100
(Venetia Williams) *hld up in tch: 6th and rdn 5th: sn outpcd and wl hld 3 out: wknd between last 2* **14/1**

220 **7** *29* **Number One London (IRE)**[20] 4824 6-11-12 **117**.............. JamesBest 77
(Tim Vaughan) *hld up in tch in midfield: rdn and struggling bef 5th: wknd bef 3 out: t.o* **14/1**

4506 **8** *33* **Chief Brody**[12] 4965 5-10-10 **106**.................................. ConorRing(5) 33
(Grace Harris) *hld up in rr: rdn and struggling after 4th: lost tch 5th: t.o whn hmpd last* **10/1**

P **F** **Equity Swap (IRE)**[72] 3826 7-11-12 **117**........................ TomCannon
(Tim Vaughan) *pressed ldr tl 3rd: chsd ldrs tl lost pl bef 5th: bhd whn hmpd 3 out: t.o whn fell last* **14/1**

4242 **F** **Catchin Time (IRE)**[10] 5030 8-10-13 **111**..................(t) MikeyHamill(7)
(Laura Hurley) *hld up in tch in last trio: hdwy 5th: 5th and rdn whn dived and fell 3 out* **13/2**[3]

4m 11.07s (0.47) **Going Correction** +0.25s/f (Yiel)
WFA 4 from 5yo+ 5lb **10** Ran SP% **118.2**
Speed ratings (Par 105): **108,104,103,102,101 97,82,66, ,**
CSF £57.11 CT £236.57 TOTE £5.00: £2.50, £4.00, £1.80; EX 79.80 Trifecta £493.40.

Owner Tony Scrivin **Bred** Darley **Trained** Eastnor, H'fords

FOCUS
This looked competitive on paper but was won in some style by the gambled-on winner. The form makes sense.

5226 TOTEWIN BEAT SP 2015 H'CAP CHASE (16 fncs) 2m 3f 98y
6:05 (6:06) (Class 4) (0-120,119) 5-Y-O+ **£4,659** (£1,446; £779)

Form RPR

44F0 **1** **Long Lunch**[36] 4465 7-11-9 **119**................................(t) GrahamWatters(3) 129+
(Charlie Longsdon) *chsd ldr tl after 5th: jnd ldr again 7th: 3rd and rdn bef 12th: wnt 2nd and 4 l down whn lft clr 13th: styd on and drew wl clr 2 out: rdn out* **7/4**[1]

04/2 **2** *20* **Hit The Headlines (IRE)**[29] 4588 10-11-5 **112**..................(t) TomCannon 105
(Luke Dace) *hld up in tch in rr: nt fluent 4th: effrt bef 12th: lft 6 l 2nd and pckd 13th: no imp: wknd between last 2* **9/1**

PP **3** *10* **Didntitellya (IRE)**[58] 4062 7-10-12 **112**..................(tp) MikeyHamill(7) 95
(Kim Bailey) *led tl 11th: rdn and lost pl bef next: btn whn lft 3rd and hmpd 13th* **15/2**

3526 **F** **Iona Days (IRE)**[21] 4803 11-11-3 **110**...........................(p) MarkGrant
(Julian Smith) *hld up in tch in 4th: hdwy to chse ldr sn after 11th tl after 12th: 6 l down and looked btn whn fell 13th* **5/1**[3]

314P **U** **Calin Du Brizais (FR)**[32] 4542 5-11-0 **107**....................(t) JamesBest +
(Nigel Hawke) *chsd ldrs: wnt 2nd after 5th tl led 11th: rdn and wnt 4 l clr whn blnd and uns rdr 13th* **2/1**[2]

5m 21.1s (9.80) **Going Correction** +0.30s/f (Yiel) **5** Ran SP% **108.1**
Speed ratings: **91,82,78, ,**
CSF £14.72 TOTE £2.40: £1.50, £2.10; EX 12.40 Trifecta £26.90.

Owner Battersby, Birchall, Halsall & Vestey **Bred** Overbury Stallions Ltd **Trained** Over Norton, Oxon

FOCUS
There was no shortage of drama in this small-field handicap chase. The winner might have been fortunate.

5227 TOTEEXACTA STANDARD OPEN NATIONAL HUNT FLAT RACE 2m 11y
6:35 (6:35) (Class 6) 4-6-Y-O **£1,949** (£572; £286; £143)

Form RPR

1 **The Worlds End (IRE)**[153] 5-11-0 0.......................... WayneHutchinson 116+
(Tom George) *led for 2f: styd chsng ldrs: 4th and swtchd rt 4f out: rdn to ld over 1f out: styd on wl: readily* **4/1**[2]

2 *3* **Flints Legacy** 4-10-1 0.. JamesBest 98
(Nigel Hawke) *hld up in tch: hdwy to join ldrs 1/2-way: rdn over 3f out: chsd wnr but unable qck jst over 1f out: kpt on same pce after* **50/1**

120 **3** *3 ¼* **Ballymalin (IRE)**[24] 4721 6-11-2 0............................ JamieBargary(5) 115
(Nigel Twiston-Davies) *chsd ldrs tl led 10f out: rdn and hdd over 3f out: drvn and outpcd in 4th 2f out: kpt on same pce after: wnt 3rd ins fnl f* **7/4**[1]

4 *2 ¼* **Indy Five (IRE)**[504] 6-11-0 0.. JamesDavies 105
(David Dennis) *hld up in tch towards rr: hdwy to chse ldrs 5f out: led over 3f out: rdn and hdd over 1f out: no ex: wknd ins fnl f* **12/1**

4 **5** *nk* **Cinderfella**[68] 3907 5-11-0 0.. JamesBanks 105
(Noel Williams) *in tch in midfield: rdn and outpcd 4f out: rallied 2f out: no threat to wnr but kpt on ins fnl f* **25/1**

3 **6** *10* **Post War**[17] 4880 5-11-0 0.. AndrewTinkler 95
(Nicky Henderson) *hld up in tch in midfield: 5th and rdn 4f out: outpcd and btn over 2f out: wknd over 1f out* **5/1**

6-04 **7** *6* **Hoo Bally Diva (IRE)**[26] 4687 5-10-7 0.......................... LiamHeard 82
(Bob Buckler) *chsd ldrs tl clsd to join ldrs 1/2-way tl rdn and btn over 4f out: sn lost pl: wl btn fnl 2f* **33/1**

0 **8** *14* **Monthyne**[18] 4867 5-11-0 0.. GavinSheehan 75
(Warren Greatrex) *in tch: hdwy to join ldrs 1/2-way tl lost pl 5f out: sn wl btn and bhd fnl 3f: t.o* **20/1**

9 *9* **Resolution Bay** 4-10-8 0.. MichealNolan 60
(Philip Hobbs) *in tch in midfield: rdn and lost pl 5f out: bhd fnl 3f: t.o* **9/2**[3]

0 **10** *26* **Bueno Rica (FR)**[21] 4805 5-10-7 0.......................... MrJDrinkwater(7) 40
(Richard Hobson) *t.k.h: set off in rr: rapid hdwy to ld after 2f: hdd 10f out: lost pl 7f out: lost tch over 4f out: t.o fnl 3f* **100/1**

4 **11** *66* **Admiral's Secret**[46] 4296 5-10-7 0..........................(t) DavidPrichard(7)
(Victor Dartnall) *in tch in rr: rdn and lost tch 5f out: t.o fnl 4f* **16/1**

4m 6.75s (1.75) **Going Correction** +0.25s/f (Yiel)
WFA 4 from 5yo+ 5lb **11** Ran SP% **119.3**
Speed ratings: **105,103,101,100,100 95,92,85,81,68 35**
CSF £201.98 TOTE £5.60: £1.80, £10.10, £1.20; EX 200.20 Trifecta £2675.80 Part won. Pool: £3,567.86 - 0.70 winning tickets..

Owner McNeill Family **Bred** J Sheehan **Trained** Slad, Gloucs

FOCUS
An informative bumper, in which the favourite set a good standard. The winner looks a fair prospect.
T/Plt: £29.60 to a £1 stake. Pool: £83,747.96 - 2063.90 winning tickets T/Qpdt: £30.40 to a £1 stake. Pool: £3,758.11 - 91.45 winning tickets **Steve Payne**

4937 SEDGEFIELD (L-H)
Saturday, April 9

OFFICIAL GOING: Soft (5.7)
Wind: Light, half against Weather: Cloudy, bright

5228 BETFRED "TREBLE ODDS ON LUCKY 15'S" H'CAP CHASE (21 fncs) 3m 2f 59y
2:05 (2:06) (Class 4) (0-110,110) 5-Y-O+ **£3,898** (£1,144; £572; £286)

Form RPR

6333 **1** **Chanceofa Lifetime (IRE)**[13] 4940 9-11-2 **107**.............. ThomasDowson(7) 114
(Victor Thompson) *t.k.h: cl up: wnt 2nd 12th: led 14th: mde rest: hrd pressed fr 2 out: hld on wl fr last* **4/1**[3]

2132 **2** *hd* **Jonny Eager (IRE)**[23] 4740 7-11-12 **110**.......................... CraigNichol 119+
(Alistair Whillans) *prom: rdn after 4 out: rallied and ev ch fr 2 out: sn rdn and hung lft: kpt on fr last: jst hld* **2/1**[1]

/3-5 **3** *7* **Waltz Legend (IRE)**[10] 5040 10-11-1 **104**..................(b) ShaneShortall(5) 106
(Liam Lennon, Ire) *hld up: hit 12th: rdn and outpcd 4 out: rallied bef 2 out: kpt on: no imp* **9/1**

43P1 **4** *hd* **Bennys Well (IRE)**[12] 4985 10-10-8 **99**.......................... TrevorRyan(7) 101
(Sue Smith) *led to 14th: pressed ldr: ev ch 3 out: edgd lft and outpcd next: n.d after* **3/1**[2]

24P4 **P** **Wellforth (IRE)**[9] 5044 12-11-6 **104**............................(p) DavidEngland
(Clare Ellam) *chsd ldr to 12trh: drvn and outpcd 14th: lost tch and p.u 3 out* **25/1**

0P12 **P** **Notonebuttwo (IRE)**[21] 4792 9-10-1 **88**..........................(tp) TonyKelly(3)
(Chris Grant) *nt fluent on occasions: in tch on outside: struggling after 13th: lost tch fr next: p.u bef 4 out* **4/1**[3]

7m 13.8s (2.80) **Going Correction** +0.55s/f (Soft) **6** Ran SP% **112.2**
Speed ratings: **112,111,109,109,**
CSF £12.93 TOTE £5.80: £2.00, £1.40; EX 12.50 Trifecta £60.20.
Owner V Thompson **Bred** Mrs Maura T Furlong **Trained** Alnwick, Northumbria

FOCUS
All race distances as advertised. A fair staying handicap chase for the grade but the pace was only fair. Straightforward form.

5229 BETFRED "SUPPORTS JACK BERRY HOUSE" MARES' NOVICES' HURDLE (8 hdls) 2m 178y
2:40 (2:42) (Class 4) 4-Y-O+ **£3,378** (£992; £496; £248)

Form				RPR
13P2	**1**		**Mardale (IRE)**[17] 4868 6-11-9 **124**..........................(t) BrianHarding (Nicky Richards) *cl up in chsng gp: hdwy after 3 out: rdn bef next: rallied to ld between last 2: edgd rt last: drvn out* **2/5**[1]	110+
5052	**2**	*2 1/4*	**Theatre Act**[25] 4702 5-10-13 **105**.......................... TonyKelly(3) (Chris Grant) *led to 1st: chsd clr ldr: rdn after 3 out: outpcd bef next: rallied last: kpt on to take 2nd nr fin: nt rch wnr* **9/2**[3]	100
4	**3**	*nk*	**Harmonic Lady**[13] 4937 6-10-11 **0**.......................... RyanDay(5) (Mike Sowersby) *plld hrd: led 1st and clr to bef 2 out: jnd whn blnd bdly 2 out: hdd between last 2: rallied: kpt on fr last: lost 2nd nr fin* **66/1**	103
4U14	**4**	*6*	**Mo Chailin (IRE)**[16] 4893 5-11-4 **107**.......................... JamesCowley(5) (Donald McCain) *in tch chsng gp: hdwy after 3 out: ev ch and rdn next: one pce whn n.m.r appr last: sn outpcd* **4/1**[2]	102
00	**5**	*3 1/4*	**Little Miss Flossy**[70] 3861 7-10-13 **0**.......................... JohnKington(3) (Andrew Crook) *nt fluent in rr: pushed along and outpcd after 3 out: no imp fr next* **66/1**	90
00	**6**	*61*	**Knysna Bay**[61] 4037 5-11-2 **0**.......................... CraigNichol (Chris Grant) *hld up towards rr: drvn and struggling bef 3 out: sn lost tch: t.o* **66/1**	29

4m 26.3s (19.40) **Going Correction** +0.75s/f (Soft) **6** Ran SP% **114.1**
Speed ratings (Par 105): **84,82,82,79,78 49**
CSF £3.00 TOTE £1.30: £1.10, £2.10; EX 2.90 Trifecta £29.00.
Owner East To West Racing Club **Bred** Frank Motherway **Trained** Greystoke, Cumbria
■ Stewards' Enquiry : Brian Harding two-day ban; careless riding 28th-29th Apr)

FOCUS
An uncompetitive mares' novice hurdle in which they bet big prices bar three. However, it proved to be a rather muddling event and is perhaps not form to rely on. The race has been given a token rating through the second.

5230 BETFRED 1400 SHOPS NATIONWIDE MOBILE NOVICES' HURDLE 2m 3f 188y
3:20 (3:21) (Class 4) 4-Y-O+ **£3,768** (£1,106; £553; £276)

Form				RPR
1312	**1**		**Lamool (GER)**[204] 1576 9-11-12 **134**..........................(t) AlanJohns(5) (Tim Vaughan) *mde all: sn clr: shkn up bef 2 out: kpt on strly: unchal* **5/4**[2]	141+
-312	**2**	*14*	**Sakhee's City (FR)**[21] 4799 5-11-7 **123**.......................... AdamNicol(3) (Philip Kirby) *chsd (clr) wnr: effrt and clsd bef 2 out: rdn and outpcd between last 2: hld whn mstke last* **1/1**[1]	122
4225	**3**	*59*	**Rocky Two (IRE)**[163] 2142 6-10-12 **107**.......................... ShaneShortall(5) (Philip Kirby) *chsd clr ldng pair: rdn and outpcd 4 out: lost tch fr next* **7/1**[3]	53
06	**4**	*11*	**Ask Paddy (IRE)**[12] 4988 4-10-10 **0**.......................... JonathanEngland (Sam Drake) *bhd: struggling fr 1/2-way: nvr on terms* **66/1**	35
U/4	**5**	*8*	**Kyllachykov (IRE)**[16] 4861 8-11-3 **0**.......................... BrianHarding (Rebecca Bastiman) *hld up: struggling bef 4 out: nvr on terms* **50/1**	34
	P		**The Saskatoon** 7-10-12 **0**.......................... JamieHamilton(5) (Peter Maddison) *mstkes in rr: lost tch fr 6th: t.o whn p.u bef 3 out* **40/1**	

5m 7.1s (13.00) **Going Correction** +0.75s/f (Soft)
WFA 4 from 5yo+ 6lb **6** Ran SP% **112.8**
Speed ratings (Par 105): **104,98,74,70,67**
CSF £3.00 TOTE £2.10: £1.20, £1.10; EX 3.00 Trifecta £4.10.
Owner J H Frost **Bred** Frau M U W Lohmann **Trained** Aberthin, Vale of Glamorgan

FOCUS
An uncompetitive novice hurdle run at a sound pace in which few featured. Arguably a pb from the winner.

5231 BETFRED MOBILE NOVICES' H'CAP CHASE (13 fncs) 2m 77y
3:55 (3:56) (Class 4) (0-105,90) 5-Y-O+ **£3,898** (£1,144; £572; £286)

Form				RPR
2213	**1**		**Discoverie**[25] 4707 8-11-9 **90**..........................(b) ColmMcCormack(3) (Kenneth Slack) *cl up: led 4 out: rdn clr fr 2 out: eased nr fin* **2/1**[2]	105+
PPP3	**2**	*6*	**Bertielicious**[1] 5197 8-9-7 **64** oh8.......................... ThomasDowson(7) (Jonathan Haynes) *hld up: stdy hdwy 1/2-way: outpcd 4 out: rallied whn nt fluent 2 out: chsd (clr) wnr last: no imp* **9/1**	68
1523	**3**	*2*	**Captain Sharpe**[13] 4938 8-10-11 **80**..........................(b) JamieHamilton(5) (Kenny Johnson) *chsd ldrs: nt fluent 6th and next: outpcd 4 out: mstke next: plenty to do 2 out: kpt on wl fr last: nvr able to chal* **3/1**[3]	86
4221	**4**	*3/4*	**Duhallowcountry (IRE)**[25] 4707 10-10-13 **84**..........................(p) MissAWaugh(7) (Victor Thompson) *led to 4 out: chsd wnr: rdn bef 2 out: lost 2nd and outpcd last* **7/4**[1]	85
0PR-	**P**		**Khazium (IRE)**[366] 5247 7-11-0 **78**..........................(t[1]) IanPopham (Claire Dyson) *reluctant to s: bhd: hdwy 3rd: downed tools and drvn next: plld himself up after 5th* **18/1**	

4m 22.0s (8.00) **Going Correction** +0.55s/f (Soft) **5** Ran SP% **110.0**
Speed ratings: **102,99,98,97,**
CSF £17.07 TOTE £2.10: £1.70, £2.60; EX 19.60 Trifecta £43.10.
Owner A Slack **Bred** Ally And Les Mitchell **Trained** Hilton, Cumbria

FOCUS
An ordinary handicap chase but the pace was sound.

5232 BETFRED TV MARES' H'CAP HURDLE (8 hdls) 2m 178y
4:30 (4:31) (Class 3) (0-130,122) 4-Y-O+ **£6,498** (£1,908; £954; £477)

Form				RPR
5110	**1**		**Card Game (IRE)**[14] 4909 7-11-7 **122**.......................... JamieHamilton(5) (Malcolm Jefferson) *prom: outpcd bef 4th: rallied 3 out: led next: drew clr fr last* **2/1**[1]	134+
1111	**2**	*10*	**Beyondtemptation**[13] 4939 8-9-13 **102**..........................(t) ThomasDowson(7) (Jonathan Haynes) *j.w: led: rdn and hdd 2 out: kpt on same pce fr last* **9/2**	105
P211	**3**	*12*	**My Little Cracker (IRE)**[11] 5019 6-11-10 **120**.......................... BrianHarding (Iain Jardine) *t.k.h early: cl up: rdn after 3 out: outpcd fr next* **11/4**[2]	111
15P2	**4**	*13*	**Samedi Soir**[13] 4939 6-11-5 **120**.......................... MrJohnDawson(5) (Keith Reveley) *hld up in tch: hit 2nd: stdy hdwy after next: rdn and outpcd after 3 out: btn next* **7/2**[3]	100
3P-2	**P**		**Thankyou Very Much**[18] 4865 6-10-2 **101**..........................(p) JoeColliver(3) (James Bethell) *cl up: outpcd 4 out: lost tch next: btn whn p.u and dismntd bef 2 out* **15/2**	

4m 16.7s (9.80) **Going Correction** +0.75s/f (Soft) **5** Ran SP% **112.2**
Speed ratings (Par 107): **106,101,95,89,**
CSF £11.30 TOTE £2.90: £2.50, £2.60; EX 11.70 Trifecta £25.20.
Owner Messrs Hales Dodd Wood & Dickinson **Bred** David Connors **Trained** Norton, N Yorks
■ Stewards' Enquiry : Joe Colliver jockey said mare lost its action

FOCUS
This was quite a competitive mares' handicap hurdle run at a sound gallop. The winner was back on the upgrade.

5233 BETFRED "RACING'S BIGGEST SUPPORTER" H'CAP HURDLE (13 hdls) 3m 3f 9y
5:00 (5:00) (Class 5) (0-100,100) 4-Y-O+ **£2,599** (£763; £381; £190)

Form				RPR
2541	**1**		**Agent Louise**[13] 4942 8-10-11 **88**..........................(p) AdamNicol(3) (Mike Sowersby) *racd wd: hld up: stdy hdwy 4th: led gng wl bef 2 out: drvn out fr last* **9/4**[1]	94+
032P	**2**	*2*	**Moscow Presents (IRE)**[23] 4738 8-11-7 **100**..........(p) ShaneShortall(5) (Philip Kirby) *in tch: rdn and outpcd 3 out: rallied next: chsd wnr run-in: kpt on: nt pce to chal* **9/4**[1]	102
6P65	**3**	*1/2*	**Debt To Society (IRE)**[17] 4877 9-11-8 **99**..........(tp) HarryChalloner(3) (Richard Ford) *cl up: led 7th to 3 out: rdn and styd w ldr to bef next: kpt on same pce fr last* **9/1**	101
4045	**4**	*3 1/4*	**El Indio (IRE)**[10] 5033 9-10-0 **74** oh5..........................(vt) IanPopham (Claire Dyson) *led: nt fluent and hdd 7th: cl up: rdn 4 out: rallied: kpt on same pce fr 2 out* **10/1**	72
4FU5	**5**	*8*	**Latest Fashion (IRE)**[54] 4151 10-9-11 **74** oh10..(tp) ColmMcCormack(3) (Christopher Wilson) *in tch: stdy hdwy after 3 out: rdn and wknd fr next* **33/1**	66
453P	**P**		**Rocky Stone (IRE)**[24] 4713 8-11-0 **93**..........................(tp) JamesCowley(5) (Donald McCain) *t.k.h early: cl up: led and mstke 3 out: hdd bef next: sn wknd: p.u bef last* **5/1**[2]	
	P		**Mister To Mister (IRE)**[20] 4828 8-11-3 **96**.......................... DeanPratt(5) (Benjamin Arthey, Ire) *hld up in tch: awkward 3rd: rdn and outpcd bef 3 out: lost tch and p.u bef next* **6/1**[3]	

7m 27.2s (35.20) **Going Correction** +0.75s/f (Soft) **7** Ran SP% **114.5**
Speed ratings (Par 103): **77,76,76,75,72 ,**
CSF £8.06 TOTE £2.50: £1.30, £2.20; EX 7.70 Trifecta £35.80.
Owner M E Sowersby **Bred** Mrs C J Zetter-Wells **Trained** Goodmanham, E Yorks

FOCUS
A 0-100 staying handicap run at slow gallop with all seven in with a chance at the fourth-last. Another step up from the winner.

5234 BETFRED "LIKE US ON FACEBOOK" H'CAP CHASE (16 fncs) 2m 3f 65y
5:45 (5:45) (Class 5) (0-100,101) 5-Y-O+ **£2,599** (£763; £381; £190)

Form				RPR
4-P2	**1**		**Attimo (GER)**[13] 4938 7-11-13 **101**..........................(t) JonathanEngland (Sam Drake) *prom: smooth hdwy to ld 2 out: shkn up and clr appr last: kpt on strly* **1/1**[1]	117+
3634	**2**	*7*	**King Of The Dark (IRE)**[13] 4938 9-11-1 **96**.......................... ThomasDowson(7) (Victor Thompson) *cl up: led 3 out to next: plugged on fr last: no ch w wnr* **7/2**[2]	102
346-	**3**	*16*	**Personal Shopper**[10] 5039 9-10-5 **86**.......................... RachaelBlackmore(7) (H Smyth, Ire) *in tch: effrt after 3 out: rdn and wknd fr next* **9/1**[3]	77
6F45	**4**	*3*	**Court Of Law (IRE)**[44] 4325 8-11-2 **90**..........................(p) AdrianLane (Donald McCain) *led to 3 out: drvn and wknd fr next* **7/2**[2]	78
UPRP	**5**	*24*	**Hi Bob**[44] 4325 8-10-5 **84**.......................... DeanPratt(5) (Lucinda Egerton) *nt fluent in rr: struggling bef 1/2-way: t.o* **12/1**	45

5m 11.7s (8.70) **Going Correction** +0.55s/f (Soft) **5** Ran SP% **112.1**
Speed ratings: **103,100,93,92,81**
CSF £5.25 TOTE £2.00: £1.10, £1.80; EX 6.30 Trifecta £18.50.
Owner Mrs J Drake **Bred** Gestut Hof Ittlingen **Trained** Guiseley, West Yorkshire

FOCUS
A 0-100 handicap chase with not many coming into it in much form. The pace was an ordinary one. A step up from the winner compared with the second.
T/Plt: £14.90 to a £1 stake. Pool: £47,638.62 - 2,325.35 winning tickets T/Qpdt: £7.30 to a £1 stake. Pool: £2,580.62 - 259.76 winning tickets **Richard Young**

5050 FFOS LAS (L-H)
Sunday, April 10

OFFICIAL GOING: Soft (heavy in places; 4.3)
Wind: strong, behind Weather: very windy

5235 BET TOTEPLACEPOT NOVICES' HURDLE (10 hdls) 2m 4f
2:00 (2:01) (Class 4) 4-Y-O+ **£3,249** (£954; £477; £238)

Form				RPR
1326	**1**		**Potters Corner (IRE)**[29] 4620 6-11-10 **130**.......................... DenisO'Regan (Paul Morgan) *hld up in tch: hdwy into midfield after 4th: clsd to press ldr and travelling strly 2 out: led last: rdn and wnt clr flat: comf* **4/5**[1]	134+
1160	**2**	*3*	**Eminent Poet**[39] 4438 5-11-10 **123**.......................... AlainCawley (Venetia Williams) *chsd ldr: clsd and upsides after 7th: led next: rdn and jnd between last 2: hdd last: styd on same pce flat* **7/1**	128
F115	**3**	*7*	**Overtown Express (IRE)**[28] 4636 8-12-3 **134**.......................... NoelFehily (Harry Fry) *chsd ldrs 4th: wnt 2nd after 3 out tl 2 out: rdn and btn bef last: wknd flat* **5/2**[2]	128
R	**4**	*22*	**Sutter's Mill (IRE)**[27] 4681 5-10-10 **0**.......................... MrConorOrr(7) (Evan Williams) *chsd ldrs: wnt 3rd 2nd tl 4th: styd in tch in midfield: pushed along and outpcd bef 3 out: wl btn whn hit 2 out: plugged on to go modest 4th flat* **66/1**	94
4341	**5**	*3 3/4*	**Kilcullen Flem (IRE)**[25] 4711 6-11-10 **124**..........................(p) TrevorWhelan (Rebecca Curtis) *taken down early: led: clr tl after 4th: reminders 5th: rdn and jnd after 7th: hdd next: sn btn: wknd and wl btn 4th whn blnd last* **4/1**[3]	98
U0	**6**	*40*	**Catch A Thief (IRE)**[8] 5098 5-10-10 **0**.......................... LewisGordon(7) (Evan Williams) *chsd ldrs tl 2nd: lost pl but in tch in rr 4th: rdn after 7th: lost tch bef next: t.o* **66/1**	48
	7	*26*	**New Republic (IRE)** 5-10-12 **0**.......................... ConorRing(5) (Evan Williams) *in tch towards rr: rdn after 7th: sn lost tch: t.o* **50/1**	22
	P		**Thirty Bob (IRE)** 5-10-7 **0**.......................... CianMaher(10) (Evan Williams) *in tch in rr: pushed along after 5th: rdn and dropped out rapidly after next: t.o whn p.u next* **50/1**	

5m 39.0s (339.00) **8** Ran SP% **123.5**
CSF £8.59 TOTE £1.70: £1.02, £2.10, £1.20; EX 8.30 Trifecta £17.00.

Owner Walters Plant, Maule, Davies, Potter **Bred** Mrs P J O'Connor **Trained** Ystrad, Rhondda C Taff

FOCUS

Some starts have been moved at this track following remeasuring, so some races will not have speed figures until there is sufficient data to calculate updated median times. Allowing for rail movements, race distances were increased as follows: Races 1,3,5 & 6 +105yds; Races 2 & 7 +70yds and Race 4 +140yds. A solid opener, in which half the field had already won over hurdles and carried penalties. The four non winners in the race, all trained by Evan Williams, were sent off at huge prices. It was run in very blustery conditions.

5236 TOTEEXACTA H'CAP CHASE (13 fncs) 2m

2:30 (2:31) (Class 5) (0-100,100) 5-Y-0+ £2,469 (£725; £362; £181)

Form RPR

4513 **1** **Bredon Hill Lad**[40] 4423 9-11-9 **100**..........(p) LucyGardner(3) 112+
(Sue Gardner) *chsd ldr tl 6th: styd handy: 4th and rdn after 9th: rallied to chse ldr 3 out: 2 l down and styng on whn lft 8 l clr 2 out: styd on: rdn out* **10/3**[2]

3532 **2** *20* **Petit Ecuyer (FR)**[13] 4980 10-10-0 **74** oh3..........(p) JamesBanks 65
(Dai Williams) *in tch in rr: cl enough in 5th and rdn after 9th: no imp on ldrs whn lft 9 l 3rd 2 out: plugged on to go modest 2nd towards fin: no ch w wnr* **7/1**

P503 **3** *1* **Castletown (IRE)**[21] 4823 8-10-9 **83**..........(b) MarkQuinlan 75
(Sheila Lewis) *j.rt: led tl 8th: 3rd and drvn after next: struggling whn mstke 3 out: lft 8 l 2nd next: no ex and wl btn last: lost modest 2nd towards fin* **7/2**[3]

1346 **4** *9* **Entry To Evrywhere (IRE)**[27] 4686 8-10-10 **84**..........(t) RhysFlint 67
(Alexandra Dunn) *taken down early and led to post: t.k.h: chsd ldrs tl wnt 2nd 6th: bmpd next: led 8th tl sn after next: struggling u.p whn mstke 3 out: lft btn 4th next: wknd last* **11/2**

F345 **P** **Zero Visibility (IRE)**[22] 4778 9-10-1 **80**.......... DavidNoonan(5)
(Alexandra Dunn) *in tch: dropped to rr and drvn after 8th: little rspnse and btn 10th: wl bhd whn p.u 3 out* **6/1**

P546 **U** **Jaunty Inflight**[25] 4712 7-11-0 **95**.......... WilliamFeatherstone(7) 107+
(Brian Eckley) *in tch in midfield: hdwy to join ldrs 8th: led sn after next: clr 10th: rdn bef 3 out: 2 l clr whn blnd and uns rdr 2 out* **11/4**[1]

4m 28.3s (268.30) **6 Ran SP% 114.1**
CSF £25.47 TOTE £3.60: £1.50, £3.40; EX 17.80 Trifecta £68.80.
Owner R W & Mrs J M Mitchell **Bred** R W And Mrs Mitchell **Trained** Longdown, Devon

FOCUS

Only four points separated the six runners in the betting in this open handicap chase. It was run at a stern gallop in testing conditions. Rail movements added 70 yards to the distance.

5237 BET TOTEQUADPOT CONDITIONAL JOCKEYS' (S) HURDLE (10 hdls) 2m 4f

3:05 (3:05) (Class 5) 4-7-Y-0 £2,274 (£667; £333; £166)

Form RPR

3052 **1** **Filatore (IRE)**[21] 4825 7-10-11 109..........(tp) RobertWilliams(3) 114+
(Bernard Llewellyn) *mde all: set v stdy gallop tl after 7th: rdn after 3 out: drvn between last 2: styd on to assert flat: rdn out* **6/5**[1]

23FP **2** *3* **Air Glider (IRE)**[18] 4877 6-10-11 107..........(bt) BridgetAndrews(3) 111
(Dan Skelton) *hld up wl in tch: wnt 2nd bef 3 out: hit 3 out: mstke next: sn drvn: 1 l down last: no ex and btn 150yds out* **3/1**[2]

614 **3** *16* **Fuzzy Logic (IRE)**[129] 2858 7-10-13 110..........(b) JordanWilliams(5) 99
(Bernard Llewellyn) *trckd ldrs: wnt 2nd on inner after 7th tl bef next: sn rdn and outpcd: wl hld 2 out: wnt modest 3rd last* **5/1**[3]

22P6 **4** *½* **Bar A Mine (FR)**[21] 4825 7-10-11 105..........(v) JamieBargary(3) 95
(Nigel Twiston-Davies) *chsd wnr: nt fluent 2nd: mstke 4th: shkn up and dropped to 4th bef 8th: sn outpcd and wl hld 2 out: mstke and lost 3rd last* **3/1**[2]

5m 47.6s (347.60) **4 Ran SP% 112.1**
CSF £5.34 TOTE £2.00; EX 4.40 Trifecta £9.10.There was no bid for the winner.
Owner B J Llewellyn **Bred** Ballymacoll Stud Farm Ltd **Trained** Fochriw, Caerphilly

FOCUS

A weak selling hurdle. 105 yards were added to the race distance as a consequence of rail movements.

5238 TOTETRIFECTA H'CAP CHASE (18 fncs) 2m 7f 177y

3:40 (3:40) (Class 3) (0-135,132) 5-Y-0+ £7,147 (£2,098; £1,049; £524)

Form RPR

0253 **1** **Cloudy Copper (IRE)**[31] 4568 9-11-4 **124**..........(tp) NoelFehily 136+
(Jonjo O'Neill) *hld up in tch: clsd to trck ldrs 12th: upsides ldr 15th: led next: rdn between last 2: styd on and a doing enough flat: rdn out* **5/2**[2]

P115 **2** *1 ½* **As De Fer (FR)**[44] 4348 10-10-12 **123**..........(t) DavidNoonan(5) 133
(Anthony Honeyball) *led: jnd and rdn 3 out: kpt on gamely u.p: one pce and a hld flat* **9/2**[3]

43U0 **3** *5* **Allez Vic (IRE)**[43] 4354 10-11-0 **125**.......... ConorRing(5) 130
(Evan Williams) *chsd ldrs: j. into 2nd 2nd tl 7th: styd handy: wnt 2nd again 11th tl bef 15th: stl cl enough in 3rd and j.lft 2 out: sn rdn and styd on same pce after* **14/1**

4466 **4** *29* **West Of The Edge (IRE)**[15] 4906 8-10-0 **106** oh3..........(p) JamesBanks 82
(Dai Williams) *in tch: j.rt 8th: rdn 13th: struggling next: sn outpcd and wl btn 15th: t.o* **22/1**

2362 **5** *11* **Take The Mick**[29] 4612 9-10-11 **117**..........(p) AlainCawley 82
(Venetia Williams) *chsd ldr 2nd tl 3rd: styd handy: wnt 2nd again 7th tl 11th: lost pl next: bhd and lost tch after 14th: t.o* **8/1**

3PP1 **P** **Universal Soldier (IRE)**[15] 4914 11-11-12 **132**.......... SeanBowen
(Peter Bowen) *chsd ldr tl j. slowly and lost pl 1st: j. slowly next 3 and dropped to last and nvr travelling after: detached and no rspnse whn pushed along 1/2-way: p.u 11th* **9/4**[1]

PP4F **P** **Wilton Milan (IRE)**[19] 4858 8-11-2 **127**..........(t) JackSherwood(5)
(Dan Skelton) *hld up in tch: 4th and cl enough 13th: rdn after next: sn wknd: wl bhd whn mstke next: t.o whn p.u 3 out* **7/1**

6m 55.3s (37.90) **Going Correction** +2.00s/f (Heav) **7 Ran SP% 112.1**
Speed ratings: **109,108,106,97,93**
CSF £13.87 CT £125.43 TOTE £3.00: £1.50, £2.00; EX 13.20 Trifecta £106.70.
Owner Mrs Gay Smith **Bred** Donal Coffey **Trained** Cheltenham, Gloucs

FOCUS

A good feature handicap chase. Rail movements meant it was run over 140 yards further than officially described.

5239 TOTESWINGER H'CAP HURDLE (11 hdls) 2m 5f 192y

4:15 (4:15) (Class 3) (0-135,135) 4-Y-0+ £5,523 (£1,621; £810; £405)

Form RPR

6210 **1** **Driftwood Haze**[15] 4922 8-10-9 **125**.......... MrTGreatrex(7) 130
(Phillip Dando) *hld up in tch: clsd to join ldrs 3 out: drew clr w runner-up between last 2: led last: styd on wl* **8/1**

0135 **2** *1* **Suit Yourself (IRE)**[30] 4596 7-10-13 **122**..........(t) NoelFehily 126
(Jonjo O'Neill) *hld up in tch: clsd to join ldrs 3 out: led next and drew clr w wnr bef last: hdd last: kpt on u.p: edgd lft and no ex towards fin* **3/1**[1]

0540 **3** *6* **Little Boy Boru (IRE)**[30] 4596 8-10-4 **118**.......... JackSherwood(5) 116
(Suzy Smith) *chsd ldrs tl led 3 out: hdd and mstke next: outpcd by ldng pair between last 2: kpt on same pce after* **9/2**[3]

-512 **4** *6* **Pobbles Bay (IRE)**[85] 3622 6-11-5 **128**.......... DenisO'Regan 120
(Evan Williams) *hld up in tch in rr: effrt bef 3 out: outpcd 3 out and no imp in 5th 2 out: plugged on to go 4th flat: no ch w ldrs* **10/3**[2]

-564 **5** *2* **Hansupfordetroit (IRE)**[43] 4354 11-10-12 **124**.....(tp) RobertWilliams(3) 114
(Bernard Llewellyn) *hld up in tch in last pair: effrt 3 out: sn outpcd in 4th: wl hld and plugged on same pce between last 2* **5/1**

51PP **6** *28* **Rock Of Leon**[106] 3216 5-11-4 **127**..........(t) DavidEngland 89
(Dan Skelton) *chsd ldr tl lost pl jst bef 3 out: wknd qckly bef 2 out: t.o* **16/1**

P032 **7** *½* **Bishop Wulstan (IRE)**[21] 4822 5-10-0 **109** oh7..........(tp) SeanBowen 71
(Peter Bowen) *led: clr tl after 5th: hdd 3 out: sn wknd: t.o* **8/1**

6m 11.6s (51.60) **Going Correction** +2.35s/f (Heav) **7 Ran SP% 111.0**
Speed ratings (Par 107): **100,99,97,95,94 84,84**
CSF £30.86 CT £117.10 TOTE £8.20: £3.20, £2.30; EX 31.40 Trifecta £169.40.
Owner P Dando **Bred** Phillip C And Mrs Kathryn M Dando **Trained** Peterston-Super-Ely, S Glamorg

FOCUS

This was competitive, though, with the top weight rated 7lb below the ceiling of 135, it did not look up to the standard of last year's renewal. An additional 105 yards was covered due to rail movements. The first two pulled nicely clear.

5240 TOTEPOOLLIVEINFO.COM H'CAP CHASE (17 fncs) 2m 4f 199y

4:45 (4:48) (Class 4) (0-105,105) 5-Y-0+ £3,768 (£1,106; £553; £276)

Form RPR

P131 **1** **High Aspirations (IRE)**[15] 4921 8-10-10 **94**.......... HarryCobden(5) 110+
(Michael Blake) *trckd ldrs 5th: j. into ld 11th: clr and in command after 3 out: mstke last: easily* **2/1**[1]

0213 **2** *10* **Johns Luck (IRE)**[27] 4669 7-11-7 **105**..........(b) DavidNoonan(5) 107
(Neil Mulholland) *hld up in tch: hdwy 11th: chsd wnr 13th: effrt 3 out: rdn and btn bef next: plugged on* **5/1**

61U2 **3** *4 ½* **Try It Sometime (IRE)**[24] 4746 8-10-2 **88**..........(tp) MikeyHamill(7) 88
(Sheila Lewis) *w ldr tl led after 4th: outj. and hdd 11th: drvn after 13th: wnt 3rd but struggling next: blnd 3 out: wl btn after* **4/1**[3]

P34P **4** *4 ½* **Miss Oscarose (IRE)**[25] 4710 9-10-8 **87**..........(t) NickScholfield 81
(Paul Henderson) *nt a fluent: in tch: rdn and outpcd bef 14th: wl btn 3 out* **16/1**

P366 **5** *29* **Forgivienne**[13] 4962 9-11-1 **99**.......... ConorRing(5) 62
(Evan Williams) *led tl after 4th: styd pressing ldr tl 11th: rdn after next: struggling in 3rd whn blnd 14th: lost pl and bhd after: t.o* **10/1**

4221 **U** **Magical Man**[21] 4823 9-10-13 **92**..........(v) TrevorWhelan
(Debra Hamer) *hld up in tch: mstke and uns rdr 2nd* **11/4**[2]

6m 9.3s (40.70) **Going Correction** +2.00s/f (Heav) **6 Ran SP% 111.6**
Speed ratings: **102,98,96,94,83**
CSF £12.25 TOTE £2.70: £1.60, £2.30; EX 12.80 Trifecta £33.20.
Owner Mrs J M Haines **Bred** David Moran **Trained** Trowbridge, Wilts

FOCUS

Four of these brought recent winning form to the table. 105 yards was added to the original distance.

5241 BRITISH STALLION STUDS EBF MARES' INTERMEDIATE OPEN NATIONAL HUNT FLAT RACE 1m 7f 202y

5:15 (5:20) (Class 6) 4-6-Y-0 £1,984 (£578; £289)

Form RPR

33 **1** **Alice Pink (IRE)**[20] 4847 6-11-0 0.......... NickScholfield 105+
(Paul Henderson) *trckd rivals: swtchd rt 2f out: pushed into ld over 1f out: sn qcknd clr: eased towards fin: easily* **6/1**[3]

33 **2** *12* **What A Diva**[94] 3502 5-11-0 0..........(t) SeanBowen 89
(Peter Bowen) *led: rdn and hdd over 1f out: sn btn: b.b.v* **1/2**[1]

3 *6* **Pick Up Trix (IRE)** 4-10-3 0.......... JackSherwood(5) 75
(Seamus Mullins) *chsd ldr: clsd to join ldr 1/2-way: rdn 1/2-way: outpcd 2f out: wknd over 1f out* **3/1**[2]

4m 19.6s (36.70) **Going Correction** +2.35s/f (Heav)
WFA 4 from 5yo+ 5lb **3 Ran SP% 106.0**
Speed ratings: **102,96,93**
CSF £9.71 TOTE £3.60; EX 4.80 Trifecta £3.70.
Owner B C Harding **Bred** Eugene Condon **Trained** Whitsbury, Hants

FOCUS

A disappointing turn out for this bumper and hard to get overly excited about the form. Not for the first time, it went the way of the outsider of three.

T/Jkpt: £12,587.60 to a £1 stake. Pool: £132,967.87 - 7.50 winning units. T/Plt: £94.60 to a £1 stake. Pool: £85,434.98 - 658.79 winning units. T/Qpdt: £29.10 to a £1 stake. Pool: £5,667.79 - 143.82 winning units. **Steve Payne**

4982 MARKET RASEN (R-H)

Sunday, April 10

OFFICIAL GOING: Soft changing to soft (good to soft in places) after race 1 (2.15)

Wind: light 1/2 behind Weather: fine

5242 RACING UK DAY PASS JUST £10 NOVICES' HURDLE (8 hdls) 2m 148y

2:15 (2:18) (Class 4) 4-Y-0+ £3,249 (£954; £477; £238)

Form RPR

1 **Dream Berry (FR)**[171] 5-11-5 129..........(t) RichardJohnson 124+
(Jonjo O'Neill) *hld up in mid-div: smooth hdwy after 5th: led 2 out: 2 l ahd last: sn drvn: jst hld on: b.b.v* **7/4**[1]

4022 **2** *nse* **Ballycamp (IRE)**[194] 1693 7-10-13 117..........(t) AdamPogson 117
(Charles Pogson) *w ldr: led 2nd: hdd 2 out: rallied last 75yds: jst hld* **4/1**[3]

5220 **3** *15* **Colla Pier (IRE)**[84] 3650 7-11-4 128.......... RobertDunne 111
(Robert Alan Hennessy, Ire) *trckd ldrs: effrt appr 2 out: j.rt last: hung bdly lft: and one pce* **15/8**[2]

3 **4** *3* **Arabian Oasis**[252] 1177 4-10-4 0.......... AdamNicol(3) 96
(Philip Kirby) *chsd ldrs: mstke 3 out: lost pl and j.rt 2 out: sn bhd* **11/1**

606 **5** *30* **Breezemount (IRE)**[22] 4791 6-10-13 0.......... AdrianLane 69
(Donald McCain) *in rr: wnt distant 6th sn after 3 out: lft 5th next* **66/1**

0-00 **6** *1 ¾* **Amber Gambler (GER)**[10] 5048 6-10-13 0.......... WillKennedy 67
(Ian Williams) *in rr: reminders 3 out: sn bhd: lft distant 6th next* **28/1**

0500 **7** *19* **Trooper Royal**[19] 4863 6-10-13 77.......... SeanQuinlan 48
(Sue Smith) *chsd ldrs: lost pl and reminders 3 out: sn bhd: t.o* **100/1**

000 **8** *2 ½* **Sarazen Bridge**[45] 4317 5-10-13 0................................ RichieMcLernon 46
(Jonjo O'Neill) *t.k.h: led j. bdly lft: blnd and hdd 2 out: reminders after 5th: sn lost pl and bhd: t.o* **50/1**

9 *29* **Brooke's Bounty**[167] 6-10-13 0................................ HenryBrooke 17
(Hugh Burns) *in rr: bhd fr 3 out: t.o* **100/1**

F **Mariners Moon (IRE)**[53] 5-10-10 0................................ JohnKington(3)
(Patrick Holmes) *mid-div: hdwy to chse ldrs 3 out: wknd and remote 5th whn fell next* **66/1**

P **Nanamour (IRE)**[195] 5-10-6 0................................ SamTwiston-Davies
(Robert Alan Hennessy, Ire) *in rr: bhd whn reminders and j. slowly 4th: t.o next: p.u bef 2 out* **20/1**

4m 18.2s (11.50) **Going Correction** +0.775s/f (Soft)
WFA 4 from 5yo+ 5lb **11** Ran **SP% 114.6**
Speed ratings (Par 105): **103,102,95,94,80 79,70,69,55,**
CSF £8.74 TOTE £2.90: £2.70, £1.40, £1.10; EX 10.00 Trifecta £17.10.
Owner John P McManus **Bred** Mme Caroline Decazes **Trained** Cheltenham, Gloucs

FOCUS
After 4.5mm of rain the previous day the going was changed to soft all over. Rail movements meant this was run over 75yds further than advertised and the actual race distance was 2m1f3yds. Not many got into this uncompetitive novices' hurdle and the two principals pulled well clear.

5243 RACINGUK.COM MAIDEN HURDLE (10 hdls) 2m 4f 139y
2:45 (2:47) (Class 5) 4-Y-O+ **£2,737** (£798; £399)

Form RPR

23 **1** **Young Dillon (IRE)**[112] 3179 7-11-0 117................................ SamTwiston-Davies 119+
(Dr Richard Newland) *j.lft: led to 7th: hit next: led bef 2 out: forged clr run-in* **5/4**[1]

6/2- **2** *6* **Orchard Boy (IRE)**[487] 3018 8-11-0 0................................ JamesBest 115+
(Paul Webber) *trckd ldrs: handy 3rd 3 out: chal appr next: blnd bdly last: kpt on same pce* **4/1**[3]

3 *25* **Mr Bien (IRE)**[183] 1859 7-11-0 0................................ RobertDunne 85
(Robert Alan Hennessy, Ire) *hld up towards rr: outpcd 3 out: lft poor 5th bef next: tk 3rd clsng stages* **125/1**

-100 **4** *1 ¼* **Top Priority (FR)**[45] 4323 5-11-0 0................................ RichieMcLernon 84
(Jonjo O'Neill) *chsd ldrs: mstke 5th: pushed along next: outpcd 3 out: lft poor 3rd bef next: wknd clsng stages* **16/1**

5 *5* **Hey Bill (IRE)**[448] 6-11-0 0................................ KielanWoods 80
(Graeme McPherson) *in rr: bhd fr 7th: lft poor 4th bef 2 out* **25/1**

6 *2 ¼* **That Man Of Mine (IRE)**[358] 4-10-4 0................................ AdamNicol(3) 72
(Mike Sowersby) *t.k.h: trckd ldrs: lost pl bef 3 out: sn bhd* **100/1**

0- **7** *16* **Dark Diamond (IRE)**[3] 3659 6-10-7 0................................ GrahamCarson(7) 67
(Michael Chapman) *in rr: pushed along 4th: bhd 6th: t.o 3 out* **100/1**

P3 **8** *19* **Butney Island (IRE)**[14] 4930 6-11-0 0................................ ConorO'Farrell 42
(Nick Mitchell) *t.k.h: trckd ldrs: dropped to rr 5th: bhd 7th: t.o next* **10/1**

502 **P** **Minella Experience (IRE)**[20] 4844 5-11-0 114................................ HarrySkelton
(Dan Skelton) *w ldr: led 7th: hdd bef 2 out: wkng whn sn p.u: fatally injured* **5/2**[2]

5m 27.6s (18.80) **Going Correction** +0.775s/f (Soft)
WFA 4 from 5yo+ 6lb **9** Ran **SP% 114.6**
Speed ratings (Par 103): **95,92,83,82,80 79,73,66,**
CSF £6.74 TOTE £2.20: £1.10, £1.80, £18.40; EX 8.10 Trifecta £500.30.
Owner Canard Vert Racing Club **Bred** Tristan Voorspay **Trained** Claines, Worcs

FOCUS
Rail movements meant this was run over 105yds further than advertised and the actual race distance was 2m5f24yds. An ordinary maiden hurdle and they went sensible pace.

5244 FOLLOW @RACING_UK ON TWITTER H'CAP CHASE (12 fncs) 2m 1f 43y
3:20 (3:20) (Class 4) (0-120,112) 5-Y-O+ **£3,898** (£1,144; £572; £286)

Form RPR

6402 **1** **Discay**[17] 4889 7-11-12 112................................(p) SamTwiston-Davies 127+
(Dr Richard Newland) *t.k.h: mde all: hit 8th: hit 3 out: 8 l and whn blnd last: drvn clr* **9/4**[2]

6341 **2** *18* **Midnight Chorister**[20] 4841 8-11-11 111................................(t) KielanWoods 108+
(Alex Hales) *trckd ldrs: clr 2nd 7th: hit 2 out: hung rt and wknd run-in* **9/4**[2]

5333 **3** *7* **Coozan George**[13] 4984 7-11-2 102................................(t) HenryBrooke 87
(Malcolm Jefferson) *in rr: pushed along 5th: modest 3rd sn after 7th: reminders and outpcd bef 3 out: nvr a factor* **15/8**[1]

0/PF **4** *dist* **Sir Pitt**[38] 4453 9-11-7 107................................ RobertDunne
(Mark Brisbourne) *chsd wnr: blnd bdly and rdr briefly lost iron 1st: hit 7th: sn lost pl: bhd whn eased 9th: sn t.o: eventually completed* **7/1**[3]

4m 40.2s (5.20) **Going Correction** +0.475s/f (Soft) **4** Ran **SP% 108.8**
Speed ratings: **106,97,94,**
CSF £7.66 TOTE £2.50; EX 8.00 Trifecta £13.70.
Owner Foxtrot NH Racing Partnership VIII **Bred** C H And W A Greensit **Trained** Claines, Worcs

FOCUS
Rail movements meant this was run over 75yds further than advertised and the actual race distance was 2m1f118yds. A weak handicap for the grade and the winner made all the running.

5245 RACING UK NOW IN HD! CHASE (A NOVICES' LIMITED H'CAP) (14 fncs) 2m 5f 89y
3:55 (3:55) (Class 3) (0-135,129) 5-Y-O+ **£7,797** (£2,289; £1,144; £572)

Form RPR

4625 **1** **Under The Phone (IRE)**[18] 4876 7-10-0 110 oh3..(p) ConorShoemark(3) 116+
(Robin Dickin) *j.rt: w ldr: led 6th: edgd rt and drvn clr run-in* **5/2**[1]

0-0P **2** *6* **Western Jo (IRE)**[59] 4066 8-10-11 125................................ GLavery(7) 128+
(Alan Brown) *chsd ldrs: blnd 4th: mstke 9th: 2nd 11th: kpt on same pce fr 2 out* **12/1**

0310 **3** *1 ¾* **Raktiman (IRE)**[15] 4910 9-11-8 129................................(t) JonathanEngland 126
(Sam Drake) *j. slowly 1st: chsd ldrs 5th: one pce fr 3 out* **3/1**[3]

22PF **4** *12* **Mont Royale**[134] 2774 8-11-5 126................................ RichardJohnson 112
(Jonjo O'Neill) *chsd ldrs: drvn 3 out: wknd last: eased nr fin* **4/1**

224R **P** **Friendly Royal (IRE)**[48] 4286 7-10-12 119................................ DannyCook
(Sue Smith) *led to 6th: reminders next and 9th: lost pl 10th: bhd whn p.u bef next* **11/4**[2]

5m 56.4s (10.40) **Going Correction** +0.475s/f (Soft) **5** Ran **SP% 107.9**
Speed ratings: **99,96,96,91,**
CSF £23.63 TOTE £3.20: £1.10, £5.30; EX 29.70 Trifecta £104.10.
Owner The Tricksters **Bred** Sean Murphy **Trained** Alcester, Warwicks

FOCUS
Rail movements meant this was run over 105yds further than advertised and the actual race distance was 2m5f194yds. Not the strongest handicap for the grade, in which the top-weight was rated 6lb below the ceiling.

5246 RACINGUK.COM/DAYPASS H'CAP HURDLE (10 hdls) 2m 4f 139y
4:30 (4:31) (Class 4) (0-115,115) 4-Y-O+ **£3,249** (£954; £477; £238)

Form RPR

0044 **1** **Ten Trees**[14] 4939 6-10-8 97................................ PaulMoloney 102
(Alan Swinbank) *in rr: reminders 3 out: sn bhd: n.m.r on bnd bef 2 out: hdwy on ins between last 2: 6th last: str run to ld last 100yds* **13/2**

34U6 **2** *3 ¼* **Mwaleshi**[22] 4793 11-11-5 115................................ TrevorRyan(7) 118
(Sue Smith) *chsd ldrs: drvn 7th: outpcd appr 2 out: styd on to take 2nd last 75yds* **10/1**

0551 **3** *2 ½* **Quieto Sol (FR)**[19] 4856 5-11-11 114................................ RichardJohnson 115+
(Charlie Longsdon) *trckd ldrs: t.k.h: swtchd rt between last 2: led sn after last: hdd and no ex last 100yds* **5/1**[2]

222 **4** *¾* **Alberta (IRE)**[6] 5148 7-11-12 115................................ JamieMoore 114
(Jim Best) *chsd ldrs: drvn and clumsy 2 out: sn outpcd: kpt on wl run-in* **11/4**[1]

4000 **5** *6* **Crockery**[46] 4303 6-11-4 107................................ HarrySkelton 103
(Dan Skelton) *prom: jnd ldrs 3 out: 3rd whn blnd next: wknd fnl 150yds* **16/1**

042P **6** *3* **Malibu Sun**[113] 3148 9-11-12 115................................ NicodeBoinville 107
(Ben Pauling) *led: edgd lft between last 2: hit last: sn hdd & wknd* **10/1**

32P **7** *2* **Charlie Cook (IRE)**[28] 4648 7-11-9 112................................ KielanWoods 100
(Graeme McPherson) *trckd ldrs: t.k.h: drvn bef 2 out: wknd between last 2* **6/1**[3]

P0OP **8** *1 ½* **Wolf Shield (IRE)**[15] 4906 9-11-0 106................................(t) JohnKington(3) 93
(Patrick Holmes) *in rr: reminders and outpcd 3 out: kpt on appr last: nvr a factor* **25/1**

/P-5 **9** *5* **Max Milano (IRE)**[13] 4975 11-10-6 95................................ JackQuinlan 76
(Alan Jessop) *in rr: brief effrt 3 out: sn lost pl* **40/1**

420- **10** *17* **Pass Muster**[264] 2301 9-11-1 107................................ AdamNicol(3) 71
(Philip Kirby) *hld up in rr: brief effrt 3 out: sn lost pl: bhd whn heavily eased clsng stages* **22/1**

3F0- **11** *16* **Bajardo (IRE)**[423] 4179 8-11-6 109................................ RichieMcLernon 57
(Emma Baker) *in rr: sme hdwy 3 out: drvn and lost pl bef next: sn bhd: t.o* **50/1**

53F **P** **Menace**[148] 2490 5-11-0 103................................ WayneHutchinson
(Noel Williams) *trckd ldrs: t.k.h: drvn 3 out: sn lost pl: t.o whn p.u bef next* **12/1**

5m 34.2s (25.40) **Going Correction** +0.775s/f (Soft) **12** Ran **SP% 115.3**
Speed ratings (Par 105): **82,80,79,79,77 76,75,74,72,66 60,**
CSF £64.62 CT £352.15 TOTE £10.60: £3.10, £3.40, £1.90; EX 82.10 Trifecta £926.70.
Owner Spencer, Bradbury & Parsons **Bred** James Nelson **Trained** Melsonby, N Yorks

FOCUS
Race run over 105 yards further than advertised. A competitive handicap for the grade, in which they went a good gallop, and the complexion of the race changed dramatically on the run-in.

5247 RACING UK IN GLORIOUS HD H'CAP CHASE (17 fncs) 2m 7f 191y
5:00 (5:04) (Class 4) (0-120,120) 5-Y-O+ **£3,994** (£1,240; £667)

Form RPR

P44P **1** **Express Du Berlais (FR)**[106] 3236 7-11-7 115....(t) SamTwiston-Davies 133+
(Dr Richard Newland) *j.lft: racd wd: trckd ldrs: led bef 11th: hdd 13th: led appr 3 out: wnt clr after 2 out: coasted home: eased last 75yds* **2/1**[1]

P2U1 **2** *11* **Lily Little Legs (IRE)**[14] 4940 7-10-1 95 ow1................................ RyanDay(5) 103
(Mike Sowersby) *hld up in last wl in tch: hit 10th: handy 2nd appr 3 out: kpt on one pce* **8/1**

3F4P **3** *41* **Red Admirable (IRE)**[28] 4649 10-11-8 116................................(p) KielanWoods 77
(Graeme McPherson) *chsd ldrs: mstke and rdr briefly lost iron 10th: outpcd and lost pl 4 out: sn bhd: lft distant 3rd bef 2 out: t.o* **7/1**

32P2 **P** **Fine Parchment (IRE)**[18] 4872 13-11-4 115................................(tp) HarryBannister(3)
(Charlie Mann) *chsd ldrs: drvn and outpcd 11th: bhd 4 out: t.o bef next* **13/2**

20P2 **U** **Ultimatum Du Roy (FR)**[28] 4641 8-11-3 114................................(tp) KillianMoore(3)
(Alex Hales) *chsd ldrs: handy 3rd whn blnd and uns rdr 4 out* **11/2**[3]

PP46 **P** **Cowards Close (IRE)**[30] 4595 9-11-12 120................................ TomCannon
(Chris Gordon) *led: hdd bef 11th: drvn to ld 13th: hdd appr 3 out: sn wknd: distant 3rd whn p.u bef 2 out* **3/1**[2]

6m 40.9s (9.60) **Going Correction** +0.475s/f (Soft) **6** Ran **SP% 110.7**
Speed ratings: **103,99,85, ,**
CSF £16.69 TOTE £3.10: £2.00, £2.90; EX 18.40 Trifecta £93.40.
Owner Dr R D P Newland **Bred** Jean-Marc Lucas **Trained** Claines, Worcs

FOCUS
Race run over 105 yards further than advertised. A fair handicap chase but only three finished and they were well strung out.

5248 RACING UK PROFITS RETURNED TO RACING MAIDEN OPEN NATIONAL HUNT FLAT RACE 2m 148y
5:30 (5:31) (Class 6) 4-6-Y-O **£1,559** (£457; £228; £114)

Form RPR

1 **Mount Mews (IRE)** 5-11-0 0................................ HenryBrooke 104
(Malcolm Jefferson) *trckd ldrs: effrt on ins 2f out: led 1f out: styd on wl: readily* **10/1**

2 *2 ½* **Bally Gilbert (IRE)**[141] 5-11-0 0................................ NicodeBoinville 101
(Ben Pauling) *led: t.k.h: drvn over 3f out: hdd 1f out: kpt on same pce* **2/1**[1]

3 *4 ½* **Sierra Oscar (IRE)** 4-10-8 0................................ HarrySkelton 91
(Dan Skelton) *hld up wl in tch: hdwy to trck ldrs over 5f out: 2nd over 3f out: one pce fnl 2f* **9/2**[3]

0 **4** *3 ¾* **Brandenburg Gate (IRE)**[162] 2188 5-11-0 0................................ AidanColeman 93
(Charlie Longsdon) *wore ear plugs: hld up wl in tch: hdwy to chse ldrs over 3f out: rdn over 2f out: one pce* **11/2**

5 *4* **Just Minded (IRE)** 5-11-0 0................................ DannyCook 89
(Sue Smith) *trckd ldrs: dropped bk after 7f: outpcd over 5f out: kpt on fnl 2f* **12/1**

6 *28* **Codeshare** 4-10-8 0................................ PaulMoloney 55
(Alan Swinbank) *trckd ldrs: 2nd over 5f out: lost pl over 2f out: sn bhd: t.o* **7/2**[2]

6 **7** *nse* **New Providence (FR)**[318] 525 5-11-0 0................................ JeremiahMcGrath 61
(Nicky Henderson) *chsd ldr: edgd lft and lost pl 3f out: sn bhd: t.o* **12/1**

4m 18.9s (17.80) **Going Correction** +0.775s/f (Soft)
WFA 4 from 5yo+ 5lb **7** Ran **SP% 113.6**
Speed ratings: **89,87,85,83,82 68,68**
CSF £30.06 TOTE £12.80: £3.50, £2.80; EX 39.00 Trifecta £191.50.
Owner Trevor Hemmings **Bred** Kedrah House Stud **Trained** Norton, N Yorks

FOCUS
Race run over 75 yards further than advertised. This looked a good bumper and the form is worth noting.
T/Plt: £86.50 to a £1 stake. Pool: £97,529.50 - 822.91 winning units. T/Qpdt: £49.90 to a £1 stake. Pool: £5,462.45 - 80.90 winning units. **Walter Glynn**

5249 - 5255a (Foreign Racing) - Abandoned

5084 KELSO (L-H)
Monday, April 11

OFFICIAL GOING: Good to soft (good in places; 7.2)
Wind: Fresh, behind Weather: Overcast

5256 DUNCAN SINCLAIR MEMORIAL NOVICES' HURDLE (10 hdls) 2m 2f 25y
2:10 (2:10) (Class 4) 4-Y-0+ **£3,898** (£1,144; £572; £286)

Form RPR
U12F **1** **Sharp Rise (IRE)**[175] 1637 9-11-12 135 JamesReveley 140+
(Pauline Robson) *mde all: shkn up and clr bef last: kpt on strly: unchal* **9/4**[2]
3220 **2** *9* **Our Thomas (IRE)**[26] 4720 4-11-0 123 BrianHarding 118
(Tim Easterby) *trckd ldrs: wnt 2nd 3 out: effrt and pushed along next: one pce whn nt fluent last* **11/4**[3]
0 **3** *26* **Bako De La Saulaie (FR)**[172] 2031 5-10-13 0 CraigNichol 98+
(Rose Dobbin) *hld up bhd ldng gp: hmpd 6th: hdwy to chse ldrs bef 2 out: sn rdn: wknd between last 2* **40/1**
4000 **4** *6* **Heilan Rebel (IRE)**[34] 4548 6-10-8 0 StephenMulqueen(5) 87
(N W Alexander) *hld up in midfield: drvn and outpcd after 3 out: rallied next: sn rdn and btn* **100/1**
PF **5** *1¾* **Overtheedge (IRE)**[64] 4013 7-10-10 0 JohnKington(3) 89
(Simon West) *hld up: hmpd 6th: rdn after 3 out: outpcd bef next: sn btn* **100/1**
2 **6** *9* **Grexit (IRE)**[29] 4633 5-10-6 0 MrWHRReed(7) 78
(Lucinda Russell) *nt fluent on occasions: rdn and effrt 3 out: wknd bef next* **10/1**
6-55 **7** *11* **Red Mystique (IRE)**[53] 4202 7-10-8 79 (t) DaraghBourke(5) 73
(Maurice Barnes) *chsd wnr to 3 out: rdn and wknd bef next* **80/1**
PF **P** **Byronegetonefree**[29] 4633 5-10-6 0 SamColtherd(7)
(Stuart Coltherd) *nt fluent on occasions in rr: struggling bef 3 out: sn wknd: lost tch and p.u bef next* **100/1**
4121 **F** **Road To Gold (IRE)**[53] 4202 7-11-12 127 LucyAlexander
(N W Alexander) *nt fluent: t.k.h: trckd ldrs: fell 6th* **11/8**[1]
P **Nettlebush (IRE)**[43] 4393 6-10-13 0 (t) PeterBuchanan
(Benjamin Arthey, Ire) *trckd ldrs: lost pl 1/2-way: lost tch bef 4 out: t.o whn p.u bef 2 out* **40/1**
0P **P** **Anna Grey**[53] 4202 7-9-13 0 MissAWaugh(7)
(Simon Waugh) *prom tl rdn and wknd 3 out: lost tch and p.u bef next* **200/1**

4m 40.0s (13.00) **Going Correction** +0.95s/f (Soft)
WFA 4 from 5yo+ 5lb **11 Ran SP% 118.2**
Speed ratings (Par 105): **109,105,93,90,90 86,81, , ,**
CSF £9.21 TOTE £4.60: £2.10, £1.20, £8.00; EX 12.40 Trifecta £138.10.
Owner I Couldn't Switch Club **Bred** Mrs M Brophy **Trained** Kirkharle, Northumberland

FOCUS
The chase course rail, home bend and stands bend were all in innermost position. The club house bend and bottom bend moved out 4yds. They went a routine sort of gallop in this modest novice hurdle and got sorted out from the home turn. The runner-up is a good benchmark and has been rated to his mark. It was run over a distance 80yds further than advertised.

5257 MANNERS FW AWARD LE GARCON D'OR H'CAP CHASE (12 fncs) 2m 1f 14y
2:40 (2:40) (Class 4) (0-110,110) 5-Y-0+ **£5,198** (£1,526; £763; £381)

Form RPR
3P21 **1** **Lowanbehold (IRE)**[9] 5084 9-11-7 110 JamieHamilton(5) 125+
(Sandy Forster) *prom: pushed along and outpcd 5th: rallied 5 out: nt fluent 3 out: led after next: pushed clr fr last* **13/8**[1]
U5P3 **2** *8* **Clan Chief**[9] 5086 7-10-5 89 BrianHarding 94
(N W Alexander) *hld up: nt fluent 3rd: hdwy to press ldr 4th: led 6th: rdn and hdd between last 2: sn no ex* **4/1**[3]
U364 **3** *7* **Gin Cobbler**[27] 4707 10-10-1 92 ThomasDowson(7) 91
(Victor Thompson) *trckd ldrs: wnt 2nd 7th to bef 2 out: sn rdn and outpcd* **8/1**
540F **4** *11* **Kai Broon (IRE)**[192] 1743 9-11-9 107 (p) PeterBuchanan 98
(Lucinda Russell) *in tch: pushed along and outpcd bef 4 out: shortlived effrt after next: sn btn* **9/1**
224P **5** *8* **Uno Valoroso (FR)**[50] 4275 8-11-7 108 TonyKelly(3) 96
(Mark Walford) *mstkes: prom: lost pl after 4th: rdn and no imp fr 4 out* **7/2**[2]
2512 **U** **Carters Rest**[136] 2755 13-10-12 103 MissJWalton(7)
(Alison Hamilton) *nt fluent on occasions: led to 6th: struggling bef 4 out: last and no ch whn blnd and uns rdr 2 out* **10/1**

4m 24.8s (6.80) **Going Correction** +0.50s/f (Soft) **6 Ran SP% 110.5**
Speed ratings: **104,100,96,91,88**
CSF £8.49 TOTE £2.70: £1.30, £2.30; EX 8.20 Trifecta £46.00.
Owner C Storey **Bred** John Kenny **Trained** Kirk Yetholm, Roxburghshire

FOCUS
A moderate handicap, rated around the runner-up. It was run over a distance 10yds further than advertised. A small chase pb frmo the runner-up.

5258 BORDERS CARERS CENTRE BUCCLEUCH CUP (A MAIDEN HUNTERS' CHASE) (19 fncs) 3m 2f 39y
3:10 (3:10) (Class 4) 5-Y-0+ **£4,367** (£1,354; £676; £338)

Form RPR
P54- **1** **New Vic (IRE)**[30] 10-11-9 70 (t) MissRMcDonald(5) 107+
(Mrs A M Thomson) *hld up: pushed along after 5 out: rallied to chse ldrs bef 2 out: edgd lft and cl 2nd whn lft 3 l in front last: kpt on strly* **25/1**
P4 **2** *10* **Damiens Dilemma (IRE)**[30] 8-11-9 0 SamColtherd(5) 102+
(Mrs L A Coltherd) *mstkes: mde most tl blnd and hdd 2 out: one pce whn lft 3 l 2nd last: sn outpcd* **7/2**[3]
3505 **3** *24* **Senor Alco (FR)**[8] 10-11-11 78 (b) MrTDavidson(3) 83
(Victor Thompson) *t.k.h in midfield: effrt 3 out: outpcd bef next: lft 18 l 3rd whn mstke last* **28/1**
0/P- **4** *9* **Whiteabbey (IRE)**[8] 11-11-7 80 MissAWaugh(7) 67
(Mrs R Hewit) *hld up in tch on outside: stdy hdwy 1/2-way: outpcd bef 4 out: n.d after* **66/1**
0-U2 **5** *7* **Danehills Well (IRE)**[14] 8-11-11 98 MrTHamilton(3) 64
(J P G Hamilton) *cl up: rdn bef 3 out: wknd next: no ch whn lft 4th and blnd last* **8/1**
450/ **6** *12* **Farm Pixie (IRE)**[14] 10-11-7 84 MissCDun(7) 50
(Mrs K Weir) *racd wd: prom: struggling fr 12th: btn fnl 4* **50/1**
605- **7** *3½* **Fight Away Boys (IRE)**[30] 8-11-9 0 (t) MrNOrpwood(5) 47
(Mrs Caroline Crow) *hld up: struggling fr 13th: sn btn* **20/1**
6U54 **P** **Little Fritz (FR)**[23] 9-11-11 95 MrCDawson(3)
(L Kerr) *hld up in tch: stdy hdwy 1/2-way: wknd after 4 out: p.u bef 2 out* **25/1**
U **Ardea (IRE)**[14] 8-11-7 0 MrJoeWright(7) 107+
(Justin Landy) *early mstkes: hld up: hdwy and prom 5 out: led gng wl 2 out: shkn up and jst in front whn edgd rt and uns rdr last* **15/8**[1]
5-3F **P** **Dun Faw Good**[36] 9-12-0 0 MissCWalton
(Mrs C Walton) *prom: outpcd whn mstke 14th: sn btn: p.u bef 2 out* **10/3**[2]
U **S For Estuary (IRE)**[8] 7-11-11 0 (t) MrKitAlexander(3)
(Victor Thompson) *midfield: effrt bef 4 out: wknd next: 5th and btn whn blnd and uns rdr 2 out* **28/1**

7m 11.6s (24.40) **Going Correction** +0.50s/f (Soft) **11 Ran SP% 114.0**
Speed ratings: **82,78,71,68,66 62,61, , ,**
CSF £104.97 TOTE £28.70: £6.10, £1.60, £6.20; EX 184.00 Trifecta £5501.30.
Owner Peter K Dale **Bred** Peter K Dale **Trained** Duns, Berwicks

FOCUS
This was a competitive-looking maiden hunter chase. It was run at a fair gallop and only three mattered coming to the last. It was run over a distance 20yds further than advertised. A big step up from the winner, but the second and third give the form a believable look.

5259 EILDON HILL STABLES H'CAP CHASE (FOR THE HADDINGTON JUBILEE CUP) (19 fncs) 3m 2f 39y
3:40 (3:40) (Class 3) (0-130,125) 5-Y-0+ **£7,797** (£2,289; £1,144; £572)

Form RPR
64U2 **1** **Nakadam (FR)**[42] 4407 6-10-2 101 (tp) RichieMcLernon 115+
(R Mike Smith) *hld up: smooth hdwy on outside 13th: led gng wl 2 out: rdn bef last: edgd lft run-in: styd on wl* **9/4**[1]
25-1 **2** *2¼* **Fiddlers Reel**[19] 4872 13-11-6 119 PeterBuchanan 130
(Jane Clark) *prom: hdwy and ev ch 2 out: sn rdn: kpt on same pce fr last* **5/1**[3]
32PP **3** *9* **Harry The Viking**[22] 4818 11-11-5 125 (p) StevenFox(7) 128
(Sandy Thomson) *led to bef 4th: cl up: led after 5 out to 2 out: rdn and outpcd bef last* **7/1**
0P30 **4** *8* **Scotswell**[22] 4818 10-10-10 116 ThomasDowson(7) 112
(Harriet Graham) *cl up: led bef 4th to after 5 out: rdn and wknd fr 2 out* **15/2**
3423 **5** *21* **Tikkandemickey (IRE)**[21] 4836 10-10-11 115 CallumBewley(5) 95
(Raymond Shiels) *hld up: pushed along and outpcd 14th: n.d after* **14/1**
2232 **6** *6* **Carrigdhoun (IRE)**[16] 4907 11-11-7 125 (tp) DaraghBourke(5) 99
(Maurice Barnes) *cl up tl outpcd bef 5 out: btn bef 2 out* **11/4**[2]
050P **P** **Chicago Outfit (IRE)**[127] 2934 11-11-0 118 (p) JonathonBewley(5)
(George Bewley) *in tch: outpcd fr 3rd: struggling fnl circ: lost tch and p.u bef 4 out* **16/1**

6m 59.6s (12.40) **Going Correction** +0.50s/f (Soft) **7 Ran SP% 110.9**
Speed ratings: **100,99,96,94,87 85,**
CSF £13.25 CT £62.65 TOTE £3.10: £1.80, £2.60; EX 13.50 Trifecta £80.30.
Owner Smith & Spittal **Bred** Richard, Ange & Rose-Marie Corveller **Trained** Galston, E Ayrshire

FOCUS
A modest staying handicap. It was run over a distance 20yds further than advertised. A step up from the winner, with the second rated to his best.

5260 LANGDALE BLOODSTOCK H'CAP HURDLE (11 hdls) 2m 6f 151y
4:10 (4:10) (Class 4) (0-120,120) 4-Y-0+ **£3,898** (£1,144; £572; £286)

Form RPR
0031 **1** **Imperial Prince (IRE)**[23] 4796 7-10-11 112 StevenFox(7) 117+
(Sandy Thomson) *hld up: stdy hdwy to chse ldrs bef 3 out: wnt 2nd next: sn rdn: led run-in: drvn out* **8/1**[3]
2542 **2** *1½* **Maggie Blue (IRE)**[21] 4840 8-10-5 104 CallumBewley(5) 107
(Harriet Graham) *led: rdn 2 out: hdd run-in: kpt on towards fin* **12/1**
0453 **3** *4½* **Landecker (IRE)**[21] 4839 8-11-3 118 (p) MrKitAlexander(7) 121+
(N W Alexander) *hld up in tch: n.m.r and lost grnd bnd after 7th: rallied 3 out: sn rdn: chsng ldrs whn nt fluent last: one pce* **9/2**[2]
65P1 **4** *9* **One For Hocky (IRE)**[9] 5089 8-11-7 120 RyanDay(5) 111
(Nicky Richards) *prom: wnt 2nd bef 4 out: rdn bef 2 out: edgd rt and wknd appr last* **4/1**[1]
2P00 **5** *2* **Always Tipsy**[53] 4206 7-11-5 118 StephenMulqueen(5) 107
(N W Alexander) *hld up in midfield on ins: effrt after 3 out: rdn and wknd fr next* **12/1**
4160 **6** *4½* **Grey Monk (IRE)**[13] 5012 8-11-3 116 (t) NathanMoscrop(5) 101
(Sara Ender) *hld up: stdy hdwy bef 4 out: rdn after next: wknd bef 2 out* **33/1**
P4P3 **7** *9* **Snapping Turtle (IRE)**[21] 4840 11-10-7 104 CallumWhillans(3) 81
(Donald Whillans) *hld up: drvn bef 5 out: shortlived effrt bef 2 out: sn btn* **14/1**
6122 **8** *7* **Andhaar**[158] 2296 10-11-1 109 LucyAlexander 80
(N W Alexander) *hld up: outpcd bef 5 out: n.d after* **28/1**
3332 **9** *10* **Bollin Ace**[15] 4941 5-11-7 115 (bt) BrianHarding 77
(Tim Easterby) *in tch: effrt bef 3 out: wknd bef next* **4/1**[1]
5233 **10** *nk* **Bowdler's Magic**[23] 4793 9-11-6 117 AdamNicol(3) 78
(David Thompson) *prom: drvn and outpcd 4 out: btn bef 2 out* **14/1**
626P **11** *1½* **Bonzo Bing (IRE)**[41] 4420 8-11-2 110 HenryBrooke 70
(Martin Todhunter) *hld up in midfield: stdy hdwy bef 4 out: wknd bef next* **28/1**
3UP6 **12** *1* **Hellorboston (IRE)**[36] 4514 8-11-11 119 (p) AdrianLane 78
(Donald McCain) *pressed ldr: rdn whn bmpd 4 out: sn wknd* **66/1**
2235 **P** **Hunters Belt (IRE)**[21] 4840 12-10-5 104 (vt) JonathonBewley(5)
(George Bewley) *bhd: struggling fnl circ: lost tch and p.u bef 4 out* **18/1**
3013 **P** **Welcome Ben (IRE)**[190] 1776 7-11-4 115 TonyKelly(3)
(Jackie Stephen) *chsd ldrs: j.lft 4 out: rdn and wknd next: p.u bef 2 out* **28/1**

5m 59.1s (18.10) **Going Correction** +0.95s/f (Soft) **14 Ran SP% 118.1**
Speed ratings (Par 105): **106,105,103,100,100 98,95,92,89,89 88,88, ,**
CSF £92.23 CT £489.11 TOTE £8.00: £3.10, £4.10, £2.20; EX 130.60 Trifecta £956.20.
Owner MPACT **Bred** John Ryan **Trained** Lambden, Berwicks

FOCUS
A fair handicap for the class, rated around the third. It was run over a distance 90yds further than advertised. Another step up from the winner, with the second setting the level.

5261 ANDERSONS BUTCHERS & LYNTOUN TAXIS EAST LOTHIAN H'CAP CHASE (16 fncs) 2m 5f 133y

4:40 (4:40) (Class 4) (0-105,101) 5-Y-O+ **£4,548** (£1,335; £667; £333)

Form RPR
P6P1 **1** **Whats Up Woody (IRE)**[13] 5010 11-11-7 **101**........ JonathonBewley(5) 112+
(George Bewley) *cl up: led 9th: mde rest: styng on strly whn hung rt run-in* **7/2**[1]

0104 **2** 3 1/2 **Harleys Max**[13] 5010 7-10-0 **82**........ JamesCorbett(7) 89
(Susan Corbett) *hld up: hdwy to chse ldrs bef 10th: wnt 2nd 5 out: effrt and 1 l down bef 2 out: one pce fr last* **13/2**

6333 **3** 8 **Amilliontimes (IRE)**[158] 2293 8-11-6 **98**........(t) TonyKelly(3) 98
(Jackie Stephen) *hld up: hdwy and prom 4 out: rdn next: kpt on same pce fr 2 out* **18/1**

500 **4** 7 **Blueside Boy (IRE)**[16] 4903 8-9-7 **75** oh2........ ThomasDowson(7) 69
(Harriet Graham) *in tch: effrt and rdn after 3 out: outpcd fr next* **11/1**

3644 **5** 35 **What A Dream**[31] 4582 10-10-12 **92**........(tp) JamieHamilton(5) 54
(Alison Hamilton) *cl up: rdn after 4 out: wknd fr next* **16/1**

4-P5 **6** 1 3/4 **Major Ridge (IRE)**[32] 4569 7-10-12 **92**........(t) CallumBewley(5) 53
(Robert Bewley) *hld up in midfield: pushed along fr 11th: btn bef 3 out* **12/1**

42P6 **7** 4 **Kalastar (IRE)**[16] 4903 7-10-2 **84**........(b) MrTHamilton(7) 41
(Katie Scott) *led to 9th: drvn and struggling 11th: struggling fr 5 out* **11/2**[3]

35/- **8** 12 **Alexander Oats**[742] 5107 13-10-0 **75** oh13........(b) HenryBrooke 21
(Robert Goldie) *bhd: rdn 1/2-way: rallied bef 4 out: wknd fr next* **66/1**

3/PP **9** 14 **Moscow Menace (IRE)**[21] 4840 9-11-5 **94**........ SeanQuinlan 28
(Katie Scott) *hld up: rdn and outpcd 11th: sn struggling* **22/1**

3P33 **P** **Shady Sadie (IRE)**[126] 2950 9-9-7 **75** oh1........(t) LorcanMurtagh(7)
(Rose Dobbin) *hld up: hit 6th: drvn bef 5 out: struggling next: p.u after 2 out* **10/1**

0PP0 **P** **Stitched In Time (IRE)**[15] 4938 9-10-5 **85**........(t) NathanMoscrop(5)
(Sara Ender) *hld up towards rr: struggling 9th: lost tch and p.u next* **50/1**

-532 **P** **Westend Theatre (IRE)**[13] 5010 7-10-13 **88**........ PeterBuchanan
(Jane Walton) *in tch: outpcd 5 out: struggling next: p.u bef 2 out* **4/1**[2]

5m 44.1s (14.90) **Going Correction** +0.50s/f (Soft) **12 Ran SP% 115.0**
Speed ratings: **92,90,87,85,72 71,70,66,61, ,**
CSF £25.88 CT £356.92 TOTE £4.60: £1.70, £3.20, £3.80; EX 26.70 Trifecta £380.60.
Owner G T Bewley **Bred** Michael Hayes **Trained** Bonchester Bridge, Borders

FOCUS
A moderate handicap that proved a real test of the distance. It was run over a distance 20yds further than advertised. The winner and second pretty much reproduced their Hexham form, although there's a case for rating both a bit higher.

5262 GREEN TREE HOTEL PEEBLES CONDITIONAL JOCKEYS' H'CAP HURDLE (10 hdls) 2m 2f 25y

5:10 (5:10) (Class 4) (0-115,115) 4-Y-O+ **£3,249** (£954; £477; £238)

Form RPR
0411 **1** **Generous Pet (IRE)**[27] 4706 7-10-8 **97**........ JoeColliver 112+
(Kenneth Slack) *chsd clr ldrs: smooth hdwy to ld appr 2 out: v easily* **7/4**[1]

0555 **2** 14 **Stoneham**[9] 5088 5-11-4 **107**........ KieronEdgar 103
(Iain Jardine) *prom chsng gp: effrt and rdn after 3 out: one pce fr next: lft 16 l 2nd last* **7/1**[3]

5-32 **3** 3 3/4 **Kumbeshwar**[201] 1628 9-11-9 **115**........ DerekFox(3) 108
(Lucinda Russell) *prom: drvn and outpcd bef 3 out: rallied whn lft modest 4th last: kpt on: no imp* **16/1**

2324 **4** 1/2 **Veinard (FR)**[13] 5009 7-11-4 **107**........(t) CallumBewley 101
(Robert Bewley) *hld up: mstke 6th: stdy hdwy bef 3 out: 3rd and one pce whn stmbld next: hld whn lft 20 l 3rd last* **9/2**[2]

05-4 **5** 4 1/2 **Neville Woods**[341] 138 9-11-2 **105**........ DaleIrving 93
(George Charlton) *chsd clr ldng pair: rdn after 3 out: wknd fr next* **25/1**

4P-4 **6** 5 **Chain Of Beacons**[170] 2066 7-10-13 **108**........ StevenFox(6) 92
(Sandy Thomson) *hld up: drvn and outpcd after 4 out: btn bef 2 out* **15/2**

1614 **U** **Danceintothelight**[22] 4819 9-10-9 **108**........(t) CaiWilliams(10) 104
(Donald McCain) *led and wl clr to after 3 out: hdd appr next: 14 l 2nd and one pce whn nt fluent and uns rdr last* **8/1**

PF0 **P** **Telex Du Berlais (FR)**[71] 3886 7-10-11 **105**........(t[1]) ThomasDowson(5)
(Simon Waugh) *bhd: struggling bef 4 out: lost tch and p.u bef 2 out* **40/1**

-3F5 **P** **Galleons Way**[22] 4819 7-10-2 **91**........ StephenMulqueen
(Katie Scott) *hld up: stdy hdwy after 4 out: rdn and wknd next: p.u bef 2 out* **14/1**

P266 **P** **Archipeligo**[19] 4871 5-10-13 **102**........ GrantCockburn
(Iain Jardine) *hld up: struggling after 6th: t.o whn p.u bef 2 out* **12/1**

4m 47.0s (20.00) **Going Correction** +0.95s/f (Soft) **10 Ran SP% 116.4**
Speed ratings (Par 105): **93,86,85,84,82 80, , , ,**
CSF £14.97 CT £149.21 TOTE £2.90: £1.50, £2.30, £3.00; EX 14.00 Trifecta £207.30.
Owner Miss H P Tate **Bred** R J A McGaw **Trained** Hilton, Cumbria

FOCUS
Few got into this ordinary handicap for conditional riders, probably due to Danceintothelight going well clear early and stretching them. It was run over a distance 80yds further than advertised. The winner is improving at a rate of knots and there's a case for rating this a few pounds higher through the second and unseater.
T/Plt: £85.60 to a £1 stake. Pool: £84,376.18 - 718.87 winning units T/Qpdt: £25.40 to a £1 stake. Pool: £9,012.86 - 262.55 winning units **Richard Young**

5029 EXETER (R-H)
Tuesday, April 12

OFFICIAL GOING: Good to soft (good in places; chs 6.6, hdl 6.5)
Wind: mild breeze half behind Weather: sunny periods Rails: The third fence in the back straight (open ditch) will be omitted. All races will be run on hurdle bends.

5263 APOLLOBET BEST ODDS GUARANTEED NOVICES' HURDLE (11 hdls 1 omitted) 2m 7f 25y

1:50 (1:50) (Class 4) 4-Y-O+ **£3,249** (£954; £477; £238)

Form RPR
1 **Wotzizname (IRE)**[65] 6-11-1 0........(t) NoelFehily 130+
(Harry Fry) *hld up towards rr: stdy prog fr 6th: disp 8th tl outrt ldr after 9th: drew clr fr next: v easily* **9/1**[3]

0251 **2** 15 **Say My Name (IRE)**[46] 4342 5-11-7 130........(p) LiamHeard 114
(Bob Buckler) *led tl 7th: rdn to chse ldrs after next: dropped to hld 5th after 9th: hdwy after 2 out (usual 3 out): styd on fr last (usual 2 out) to go 2nd by-passing last: no ch w wnr* **9/4**[2]

3310 **3** hd **Aurillac (FR)**[25] 4766 6-11-7 133........(p) LeightonAspell 115
(Rebecca Curtis) *rn in snatches: towards rr after nt being fluent 1st 2: prom after 5th: led 7th tl next where drvn: dropped to btn 7th after 9th: hdwy between last 2 but no ch: styd on same pce fr last* **5/4**[1]

604 **4** 6 **Behind The Wire (IRE)**[22] 4844 5-11-1 0........ PaddyBrennan 103
(Tom George) *hld up towards rr: hdwy after 9th: rdn bef next: styd on same pce* **20/1**

5 7 **Whipcord (IRE)**[185] 5-11-1 0........(t) NickScholfield 98
(Paul Nicholls) *trckd ldrs: disp 7th tl after 9th: sn rdn: styd on same pce fr next* **10/1**

0 **6** 3 **Glengra (IRE)**[20] 4874 7-11-1 0........ AidanColeman 94
(Ian Williams) *hld up: hdwy fr 6th: rdn to chse wnr appr 2 out: nvr any threat: wknd on long run fr last (usual 2 out)* **66/1**

7 11 **Sugar Loaf Sholto (IRE)**[121] 5-11-1 0........ DavidBass 84
(Kim Bailey) *mid-div: rdn after 8th: sn in rr* **16/1**

00P **8** 1 3/4 **Hinxworth (IRE)**[35] 4544 7-11-1 0........(tp) DarylJacob 82
(Nick Mitchell) *mid-div: hdwy 8th: effrt after next: wknd 2 out (usual 3 out)* **125/1**

-0P **9** 14 **Morris The Miner**[41] 4439 6-11-1 0........ DenisO'Regan 69
(Neil Mulholland) *mid-div tl wknd after 9th* **150/1**

36 **P** **Clondaw Fonz (IRE)**[20] 4874 5-11-1 0........ WayneHutchinson
(Alan King) *mid-div: mstke 4th: wknd 7th: t.o whn p.u bef 3 out (usual 2 out)* **14/1**

0P **P** **Port Navas (IRE)**[17] 4917 5-11-1 0........(p) TomScudamore
(David Pipe) *trckd ldr tl 7th: wknd qckly after 9th: p.u bef next* **100/1**

06P6 **P** **Wun Destination**[24] 4777 7-10-8 0........ JamesBest
(John Panvert) *towards rr: wknd 7th: t.o whn p.u after 9th* **250/1**

5m 54.9s (-4.10) **Going Correction** -0.075s/f (Good) **12 Ran SP% 116.0**
Speed ratings (Par 105): **104,98,98,96,94 93,89,88,83, ,**
CSF £29.58 TOTE £8.70: £2.60, £1.30, £1.10; EX 30.70 Trifecta £148.60.
Owner C J S Horton **Bred** Raymond Murphy **Trained** Seaborough, Dorset

FOCUS
Rail movement resulted in this being run over 20yds further than advertised. Noel Fehily confirmed the ground to be riding "good to soft". Not a bad novice hurdle and it was won in quite taking fashion by one of the rules newcomers. There's a case for rating the race 10lb+ higher through the second and third, but not on time compared to the following handicap, and the fourth and eighth a probably a better guide to the level.

5264 APOLLOBET CASHBACK IF YOU FINISH 2ND H'CAP HURDLE (12 hdls) 2m 7f 25y

2:25 (2:25) (Class 3) (0-130,128) 4-Y-O+ **£5,848** (£1,717; £858; £429)

Form RPR
043 **1** **Valhalla (IRE)**[24] 4784 6-11-6 **122**........(t) RichardJohnson 132+
(Colin Tizzard) *hld up towards rr: hdwy after 7th: chal 3 out: nt fluent 2 out: led bef last: rdn clr: r.o wl* **4/1**[1]

F312 **2** 7 **Wild West Wind (IRE)**[32] 4586 7-11-7 **123**........(t) PaddyBrennan 123
(Tom George) *hld up towards rr: hdwy 6th: led appr 3 out: sn strly chal: hdd between last 2: no ex fr last* **4/1**[1]

5251 **3** 1/2 **A Plein Temps (FR)**[40] 4450 6-10-11 **113**........(tp) NoelFehily 113
(Harry Fry) *trckd ldr: rdn whn outpcd appr 3 out: styd on between last 2 but comf hld by wnr: clsng on 2nd at fin* **4/1**[1]

2230 **4** 4 1/2 **Tambura**[24] 4779 6-11-7 **123**........ TomCannon 122+
(G C Maundrell) *hld up towards rr: pushed along 7th: hdwy after 9th: sn rdn: wnt 4th next: styd on same pce* **33/1**

P360 **5** 3 1/2 **Kalmbeforethestorm**[116] 3137 8-10-6 **108**........(t) PaulMoloney 102
(Helen Nelmes) *hld up towards rr: hdwy after 9th: disp 4th 3 out: sn rdn: nt fluent next: sn no ex (fin lame)* **10/1**

1250 **6** 12 **Milord (GER)**[69] 3923 7-11-7 **123**........(p) DavidBass 106
(Kim Bailey) *mid-div: nt fluent 8th: rdn next: sn btn* **20/1**

PP11 **7** 3/4 **Tara Tavey (IRE)**[19] 4883 11-10-8 **117**........(t) ConorSmith(7) 98
(Kevin Bishop) *chsd ldrs tl 8th: sn rdn: nvr bk on terms* **16/1**

-40P **8** 24 **No No Mac (IRE)**[24] 4786 7-11-12 **128**........(p) AidanColeman 88
(Charlie Longsdon) *chsd ldr tl wknd appr 3 out: t.o* **33/1**

3216 **9** 3/4 **Millanisi Boy**[59] 4112 7-11-9 **125**........ DarylJacob 84
(Richard Woollacott) *mid-div: hdwy 9th: sn rdn: wknd bef next: t.o* **14/1**

P421 **P** **Toby Lerone (IRE)**[7] 5154 9-11-4 **120**........(b) HarrySkelton
(Dan Skelton) *led tl rdn appr 3 out: sn wknd: bhd whn p.u 2 out* **6/1**[2]

4S43 **P** **Brod Na Heireann (IRE)**[19] 4883 7-11-2 **118**........ WayneHutchinson
(Alan King) *mid-div tl wknd 7th: t.o whn p.u after 9th* **8/1**[3]

5m 52.9s (-6.10) **Going Correction** -0.075s/f (Good) **11 Ran SP% 117.7**
Speed ratings (Par 107): **107,104,104,102,101 97,97,88,88, ,**
CSF £20.25 CT £67.22 TOTE £5.90: £1.80, £2.30, £2.10; EX 21.50 Trifecta £61.40.
Owner J P Romans & Terry Warner **Bred** Ms N Metcalfe **Trained** Milborne Port, Dorset

FOCUS
Rail movement resulted in this being run over 20yds further than advertised. The right horses filled the places and the winner scored with loads in hand. The winner is on the upgrade, while the second, third and fourth have all been rated pretty close to their marks.

5265 EXETER AUDI STAYERS H'CAP CHASE (19 fncs 2 omitted) 3m 6f 153y

3:00 (3:00) (Class 3) (0-125,120) 5-Y-O+ **£7,596** (£2,244; £1,122; £561; £280)

Form RPR
5104 **1** **Barton Gift**[12] 5052 9-11-1 **109**........(b) NicodeBoinville 121
(John Spearing) *led tl 7th: trckd ldr: led after 15th: styd on wl fr 3 out: rdn out* **8/1**

PF53 **2** 2 1/4 **Nail 'M (IRE)**[20] 4879 8-10-12 **106**........(bt[1]) TomScudamore 115
(Nigel Hawke) *trckd ldrs: wnt cl 2nd after 15th: rdn bef next: styd on but a being hld fr 3 out* **10/3**[1]

5042 **3** 5 **Umberto D'Olivate (FR)**[13] 5032 8-11-0 **108**........ TomCannon 112
(Robert Walford) *prom: led 7th tl after 15th: sn drvn to chse ldng pair: styd on same pce fr 3 out* **4/1**[2]

0P3U **4** 12 **Copper Birch (IRE)**[12] 5052 8-10-12 **106**........ PaulMoloney 101
(Evan Williams) *mid-div: hdwy 14th: rdn to chse ldng trio appr 4 out: nvr quite threatened to get on terms: wknd bef last* **8/1**

5-4P **5** 7 **Upham Atom**[82] 3707 13-10-13 **110**........ KieronEdgar(3) 96
(Kate Buckett) *hld up: rdn along fr 14th: nvr threatened* **7/1**[3]

-152 **P** **Quinz (FR)**[130] 2887 12-11-12 **120**........ NickScholfield
(Lawney Hill) *hld up: cajoled along fr 9th: detached fr 12th: t.o whn p.u 15th* **7/1**[3]

-P5R **P** **Alpha Victor (IRE)**[46] 4340 11-11-9 **117**........(t) PeterBuchanan
(William Kinsey) *in tch: rdn along fr 10th: lost tch after 14th: t.o whn p.u after next* **9/1**

0543 **P** **Haughtons Bridge (IRE)**[17] 4921 8-9-10 **95**..........(t) AliceMills[(5)]
(Martin Hill) *hld up: v awkward 1st: hdwy whn mstke 14th: sn rdn: wknd after 4 out: p.u bef last* **20/1**

2PU5 **P** **Golden Milan (IRE)**[15] 4962 8-11-7 **115**..........(bt) LeightonAspell
(Rebecca Curtis) *trckd ldrs: rdn after 15th: wknd bef next: p.u bef 3 out* **14/1**

7m 48.1s (-0.50) **Going Correction** +0.15s/f (Yiel) **9** Ran SP% **111.7**
Speed ratings: **106,105,104,101,99** , , ,
CSF £34.42 CT £120.94 TOTE £8.20: £2.60, £1.30, £1.60; EX 40.50 Trifecta £133.20.
Owner Mercy Rimell & Kate Ive **Bred** Mrs Mercy Rimell **Trained** Kinnersley, Worcs

FOCUS
Race run over 140yds shorter than advertised. The front three came clear in what was a modest marathon chase. Little got into it. The second helps set the level.

5266 APOLLOBET CASINO FREE £10 H'CAP HURDLE (DIV I) (8 hdls) 2m 175y
3:35 (3:36) (Class 4) (0-115,115) 4-Y-0+ **£3,249** (£954; £477; £238)

Form RPR

01-5 **1** **Libeccio (FR)**[24] 4782 5-11-4 **113**..........(t) TommyDowling[(7)] 124+
(Charlie Mann) *hld up: hdwy fr 3rd: chalng whn hit 3 out: sn led: rdn clr* **7/1**

5416 **2** *9* **Grams And Ounces**[15] 4986 9-11-5 **114**.......... MikeyHamill[(7)] 118
(Grace Harris) *trckd ldr: led 5th: sn rdn: hdd bef 2 out where nt fluent: kpt on same pce* **9/1**

4P50 **3** *13* **Thatchers Gold (IRE)**[24] 4803 8-11-7 **109**..........(p) DenisO'Regan 103
(Henry Oliver) *led: pushed along fr 2nd: hdd 5th: sn rdn: one pce fr next* **12/1**

324 **4** *18* **Retro Valley (IRE)**[22] 4851 4-11-7 **115**..........(p) NoelFehily 83
(David Dennis) *j.lft at times: hld up: rdn after 5th: nvr any imp: wnt modest 4th bef last* **6/1**[3]

6024 **5** *3* **Jester Jet**[31] 4616 6-10-8 **96**.......... LeeEdwards 67
(Tony Carroll) *mid-div: rdn after 5th: wknd next* **12/1**

6PPF **6** *1 3/4* **Take A Break (FR)**[15] 4984 5-11-5 **114**..........(vt) ConorSmith[(7)] 84
(Nigel Hawke) *wnt lft 1st: chsd ldrs: drvn along fr 2nd: wknd 3 out: lft 4th briefly next* **3/1**[1]

4205 **P** **Zarawi (IRE)**[12] 5047 5-11-8 **110**.......... AidanColeman
(Charlie Longsdon) *a towards rr: lost tch 4th: p.u bef 3 out* **16/1**

0320 **P** **Rustamabad (FR)**[74] 3846 6-11-6 **108**..........(t) RichardJohnson
(Tim Vaughan) *racd keenly: trckd ldrs tl after 4th: sn wknd: t.o whn p.u bef 3 out* **9/2**[2]

0455 **F** **Scooby (IRE)**[39] 4455 5-11-4 **106**.......... KielanWoods 87
(Graeme McPherson) *mid-div: hdwy appr 3 out: sn rdn in 4th: hld whn fell 2 out* **8/1**

4m 11.3s (-4.20) **Going Correction** -0.075s/f (Good)
WFA 4 from 5yo+ 5lb **9** Ran SP% **112.3**
Speed ratings (Par 105): **106,101,95,87,85 84**, , ,
CSF £64.86 CT £736.94 TOTE £7.10: £2.40, £3.70, £3.40; EX 60.70 Trifecta £574.20.
Owner John Heron **Bred** Capricorn Stud Sa **Trained** Upper Lambourn, Berks

FOCUS
Race run over 10yds further than advertised. A couple of the leading fancies disappointed and the form looks ordinary. A big step up from the winner in the fastest of the four races over the trip, but this is in line with his Flat form and it looks believable. The second has been rated in line with his Towcester win.

5267 APOLLOBET CASINO FREE £10 H'CAP HURDLE (DIV II) (8 hdls) 2m 175y
4:10 (4:10) (Class 4) (0-115,114) 4-Y-0+ **£3,249** (£954; £477; £238)

Form RPR

3P-3 **1** **Miss Estela (IRE)**[51] 4272 6-11-7 **109**.......... GavinSheehan 119+
(Warren Greatrex) *mid-div: hdwy 3rd: chal 3 out: narrow ld whn awkward 2 out: in command whn wnt lft last: rdn out* **5/4**[1]

4001 **2** *4* **Fields Of Glory (FR)**[37] 4506 6-11-6 **108**.......... RichardJohnson 111
(Tim Vaughan) *hld up: hdwy fr 4th: led bef 3 out: rdn and hdd after 2 out: styd on same pce fr last* **6/1**

3434 **3** *3 3/4* **Jarlath**[22] 4849 5-11-3 **110**.......... KevinJones[(5)] 111
(Seamus Mullins) *mid-div: hit 2nd: hdwy after 5th: ev ch 3 out: sn rdn: kpt on same pce fr next* **8/1**

PP5P **4** *19* **Exiles Return (IRE)**[117] 3120 14-9-9 **88** oh24.......... AliceMills[(5)] 73
(Jackie Retter) *led tl appr 3 out: grad fdd* **250/1**

2-PP **5** *3 3/4* **Courtlands Prince**[123] 3023 7-11-4 **106**..........(t) NickScholfield 85
(Neil Mulholland) *trckd ldr: led v briefly appr 3 out: sn hung lft: wknd qckly* **20/1**

153- **6** *21* **Revaader**[356] 5478 8-11-3 **112**.......... MrTGillard[(7)] 82+
(Mark Gillard) *hld up: hdwy 5th: sn rdn and wknd: j.lft last 3: t.o* **28/1**

113P **P** **Billy Congo (IRE)**[302] 746 9-11-4 **113**..........(t) MrRobertHawker[(7)]
(Richard Hawker) *mid-div tl struggling in rr after 2nd: sn bhd: p.u bef 3 out* **40/1**

2543 **P** **Pied Du Roi (IRE)**[19] 4882 6-11-4 **106**..........(p) AidanColeman
(Charlie Longsdon) *chsd ldrs tl after 2nd: sn struggling in rr: bhd whn p.u 3 out* **11/2**[3]

0341 **U** **Justatenner**[24] 4799 5-11-12 **114**.......... TomScudamore
(Colin Tizzard) *uns rdr 1st* **4/1**[2]

4m 12.9s (-2.60) **Going Correction** -0.075s/f (Good) **9** Ran SP% **116.3**
Speed ratings (Par 105): **103,101,99,90,88 78**, , ,
CSF £9.27 CT £43.33 TOTE £2.20: £1.10, £2.90, £2.00; EX 9.20 Trifecta £58.30.
Owner R S Brookhouse **Bred** Mrs L Suenson-Taylor **Trained** Upper Lambourn, Berks

FOCUS
Race run over 10yds further than advertised. The front three came clear and the form is probably more solid than the first division. The race was made more winnable after Justatenner unseated at the first. A step up from the winner, with the second and third setting the level.

5268 APOLLOBET CASHBACK SPECIALS MAIDEN HURDLE (DIV I) (8 hdls) 2m 175y
4:45 (4:45) (Class 5) 4-Y-0+ **£2,599** (£763; £381; £190)

Form RPR

43 **1** **Brotherly Company (IRE)**[22] 4849 4-10-8 114.......... NoelFehily 107+
(Harry Fry) *cl up in chsng gp: chal 3 out: led 2 out: r.o wl* **9/2**[3]

0-UP **2** *1 3/4* **Ninepointsixthree**[24] 647 6-10-9 105.......... DavidNoonan[(5)] 109
(John O'Shea) *hld up towards rr: hdwy fr 3rd: cl 5th appr 3 out: wnt 2nd appr last: sn rdn: styd on but a being hld in run-in* **100/1**

4 **3** *5* **Whispering Storm (GER)**[24] 4790 6-11-0 0..........(t) SamTwiston-Davies 105
(Paul Nicholls) *led chsng gp: clsd on ldr 4th: ev ch 3 out: rdn after 2 out: kpt on same pce* **8/1**

6065 **4** *6* **Bramble Brook**[11] 5063 6-11-0 0.......... TomScudamore 98
(Colin Tizzard) *trckd ldr in chsng gp: led 3 out: rdn and hdd next: styd on same pce* **14/1**

1-2 **5** *23* **Star Trouper (IRE)**[138] 2731 6-11-0 0..........(t[1]) RichardJohnson 89+
(Philip Hobbs) *racd freely: led and sn clr: hdd 3 out: cl up but hld whn blnd bdly 2 out: wknd* **11/8**[1]

6 *2 1/4* **My King (FR)** 4-10-8 0.......... JamesBest 69
(Nigel Hawke) *hld up towards rr: wnt 6th bef 5th but nvr on terms w ldrs* **50/1**

0-40 **7** *1/2* **Kapgarde King (FR)**[47] 4317 5-11-0 0.......... BrendanPowell 75
(Jamie Snowden) *mid-div: rdn after 5th: wknd next* **100/1**

P6 **8** *42* **Relkwood (IRE)**[7] 5161 6-11-0 0.......... RhysFlint 37
(Paul Morgan) *chsd ldrs early: bhd fr 3rd: t.o* **100/1**

4FU0 **9** *nse* **Pomicide**[7] 5161 6-10-11 0.......... LucyGardner[(3)] 37
(Sue Gardner) *a bhd: t.o* **250/1**

224 **10** *3 3/4* **Pure Vision (IRE)**[38] 4488 5-11-0 0.......... BarryGeraghty 34
(Anthony Honeyball) *mid-div: struggling fr 2nd: sn bhd: t.o* **85/40**[2]

125 **11** *6* **Catcher On The Go (IRE)**[23] 4821 6-11-0 0.......... PaulMoloney 28
(Evan Williams) *mid-div: struggling after 3rd: sn bhd: t.o* **25/1**

12 *16* **Lir Flow** 7-10-7 0.......... NickScholfield 7
(Jess Westwood) *a towards rr: t.o* **250/1**

4m 13.9s (-1.60) **Going Correction** -0.075s/f (Good)
WFA 4 from 5yo+ 5lb **12** Ran SP% **119.6**
Speed ratings (Par 103): **100,99,96,94,83 82,81,62,62,60 57,49**
CSF £326.21 TOTE £5.00: £1.60, £7.50, £2.80; EX 132.10 Trifecta £1511.60.
Owner Brian & Sandy Lambert **Bred** Rabbah Bloodstock Limited **Trained** Seaborough, Dorset

FOCUS
Race run over 10yds further than advertised. With the favourite bolting and the second in the betting running no sort of race this was left looking a modest event and a 105-rated 100-1 shot chased the winner home. This could be rated higher but it was the slowest of the races over the trip and it's probably not one to get carried away with. The first three set the level.

5269 APOLLOBET CASHBACK SPECIALS MAIDEN HURDLE (DIV II) (8 hdls) 2m 175y
5:20 (5:20) (Class 5) 4-Y-0+ **£2,599** (£763; £381; £190)

Form RPR

14-3 **1** **Rainy City (IRE)**[74] 3839 6-11-0 0..........(t) SamTwiston-Davies 123+
(Paul Nicholls) *trckd ldrs: led 3 out: kpt on wl* **5/4**[1]

-243 **2** *5* **Lettheriverrundry (IRE)**[26] 4745 6-11-0 118.......... BarryGeraghty 119+
(Brendan Powell) *trckd ldrs: rdn after 2 out: wnt 2nd bef last: kpt on but a being hld by wnr* **7/4**[2]

-U05 **3** *2 1/4* **Mr Kit Cat**[78] 3772 6-11-0 0.......... PaulMoloney 114
(Evan Williams) *racd keenly: upsides ldr: rdn after 3 out: hld fr next: kpt on but no ex whn lost 2nd appr last* **10/1**

2042 **4** *11* **Viva Rafa (IRE)**[30] 4646 6-11-0 125.......... IanPopham 107
(Richard Phillips) *led tl 3 out: sn rdn: styd on same pce fr next* **7/1**[3]

036 **5** *1* **Cucklington**[31] 4614 5-11-0 0.......... AidanColeman 102
(Colin Tizzard) *in tch: struggling 4th: blnd next and lost pl: styd on again between last 2 but no threat to ldrs* **20/1**

4P **6** *nk* **Indian Brave (IRE)**[130] 2879 5-11-0 0.......... NoelFehily 102
(Neil Mulholland) *hld up towards rr: sme prog 3 out: styd on fr last but n.d to ldrs* **40/1**

63 **7** *1* **Carqalin (FR)**[16] 4934 4-10-3 0.......... DavidNoonan[(5)] 95
(David Pipe) *in tch: rdn to chse ldrs appr 3 out: wknd after 2 out* **20/1**

8 *10* **Thomas Blossom (IRE)**[34] 6-11-0 0..........(t) GavinSheehan 92
(Ali Stronge) *hit 2nd: a towards rr* **40/1**

9 *2* **Bermeo (IRE)**[149] 2522 5-11-0 0.......... LiamHeard 90
(Johnny Farrelly) *a towards rr* **100/1**

20 **10** *3 1/2* **Verygoodverygood (FR)**[178] 1966 5-11-0 0..........(t) DenisO'Regan 89
(Paul Morgan) *mid-div: rdn appr 3 out: nvr any imp: wknd bef 2 out* **50/1**

6PP **11** *43* **Monet Moor**[7] 5161 7-10-2 0.......... PaulO'Brien[(5)] 41
(Jimmy Frost) *a towards rr: t.o* **200/1**

4m 12.2s (-3.30) **Going Correction** -0.075s/f (Good)
WFA 4 from 5yo+ 5lb **11** Ran SP% **120.2**
Speed ratings (Par 103): **104,101,100,95,94 94,94,89,88,87 66**
CSF £3.61 TOTE £2.10: £1.10, £1.20, £2.70; EX 5.30 Trifecta £19.20.
Owner Sir A Ferguson,G Mason,R Wood & P Done **Bred** Kenilworth House Stud **Trained** Ditcheat, Somerset

FOCUS
Race run over 10yds further than advertised. More depth to the first division as it turned out and the favourite won readily. The cosy winner has been rated to his mark.

5270 APOLLOBET BET ON THE LOTTERIES NOVICES' HUNTERS' CHASE (16 fncs 2 omitted) 3m 54y
5:50 (5:51) (Class 6) 5-Y-0+ **£1,247** (£387; £193; £96)

Form RPR

1 **Dicky Bob**[9] 9-11-5 0.......... MissJBuck[(5)] 113+
(Miss V J Nicholls) *hld up: hdwy 3rd: prom 9th: led appr 4 out: styd on wl: pushed out* **7/2**[3]

2 *5* **Im All Set (IRE)**[23] 7-11-3 0.......... MrSeanHoulihan[(7)] 108+
(Mrs C Hitch) *in tch: trckd ldrs 11th: rdn appr 4 out: chsd wnr fr 3 out: styng on at same pce whn blnd last* **10/3**[2]

426- **3** *nk* **Blazing Whale**[17] 11-11-10 99..........(t) MrWBiddick 105
(E Walker) *hld up: hdwy 12th: rdn in cl 4th after 4 out: wnt 3rd after next: styd on to chal for 2nd run-in but no ch w wnr* **13/8**[1]

00/U **4** *19* **Sonoftheking (IRE)**[17] 8-11-10 80..........(t) MrDEdwards 93
(Miss Nicky Martin) *disp ld: rdn and hdd bef 4 out: wknd after 3 out* **16/1**

6 **5** *37* **Way Before Dawn**[51] 9-11-3 0..........(p) MissLeandaTickle[(7)] 55
(Mrs Sarah Tickle) *disp ld tl rdn after 12th: wknd bef 4 out: t.o* **33/1**

2/0- **P** **Bathwick Scanno (IRE)**[15] 8-11-5 84..........(t) MrMartinMcIntyre[(5)]
(Mrs Teresa Clark) *hld up in tch: struggling 10th: sn wknd: t.o whn p.u bef 4 out* **40/1**

5 **P** **Carry On Nando (IRE)**[23] 9-11-3 0.......... MrNLawton[(7)]
(G Chambers) *disp tl 3rd: trckd ldrs tl wknd 11th: t.o whn p.u bef 4 out* **40/1**

P **River Of Time (IRE)**[199] 1667 8-11-3 0..........(t) MrEDavid[(7)]
(K M Hanmer) *trckd ldrs: rdn after 12th: sn wknd: p.u bef 13th* **10/1**

P **In The Tub (IRE)**[30] 7-11-5 0..........(t) MrRobertHawker[(5)]
(Tom Malone) *disp tl 5th: chsd ldrs tl 11th: sn wknd: t.o whn p.u bef 4 out* **8/1**

6m 9.6s (0.30) **Going Correction** +0.15s/f (Yiel) **9** Ran SP% **117.3**
Speed ratings: **105,103,103,96,84** , , ,
CSF £16.25 TOTE £4.60: £1.70, £1.60, £1.20; EX 16.20 Trifecta £60.10.
Owner Miss V J Nicholls **Bred** Jethro Bloodstock **Trained** Yelverton, Devon

■ Stewards' Enquiry : Mr W Biddick one-day ban: cantered into start (Mar 27)
Mr Martin McIntyre one-day ban: cantered into start (Mar 27)
Mr N Lawton one-day ban: cantered into start (Mar 27)
Mr D Edwards one-day ban: cantered into start (Mar 27)
Miss Leanda Tickle one-day ban: cantered into start (Mar 27)
Mr E David one-day ban: cantered into start (Mar 27)

Mr Sean Houlihan one-day ban: cantered into start (Mar 27)
Miss J Buck one-day ban: cantered into start (Mar 27)
Mr Robert Hawker one-day ban: cantered into start (Mar 27)

FOCUS
They jumped off at the second attempt, following a false start, and the three market leaders finished a long way clear. Race run over 110yds shorter than advertised. The third sets the level.
T/Plt: £111.30 to a £1 stake. £78,941.19 - 517.51 winning units. T/Qpdt: £49.20 to a £1 stake. £6,488.89 - 97.50 winning units. **Tim Mitchell**

5271 - 5272a (Foreign Racing) - See Raceform Interactive

4764 CHELTENHAM (L-H)
Wednesday, April 13

OFFICIAL GOING: Good to soft (good in places) changing to good (good to soft in places) after race 5 (4.10)
Wind: almost nil Weather: sunny periods

5273 CITIPOST NOVICES' HURDLE (10 hdls) 2m 4f 56y
1:50 (1:50) (Class 2) 4-Y-0+
£10,009 (£2,956; £1,478; £739; £369; £185)

Form RPR
-116 **1** **Mister Miyagi (IRE)**[29] 4695 7-11-8 145 HarrySkelton 149+
(Dan Skelton) *hld up last but in tch: smooth hdwy after 2 out to ld bef last: r.o wl: readily* **13/8**[1]
1112 **2** 3 ½ **Solstice Star**[32] 4622 6-11-8 140 (t) KillianMoore 142
(Martin Keighley) *led tl 3rd: rdn after 2 out: led briefly bef last: kpt on but nt pce of wnr* **8/1**
2211 **3** *1* **Rock On Oscar (IRE)**[23] 4848 6-11-4 135 (t) SamTwiston-Davies 138
(Paul Nicholls) *hld up but wl in tch: hdwy after 2 out: rdn appr last: kpt on but nt quite pce to mount chal run-in* **9/2**[2]
123 **4** *5* **Whataknight**[36] 4544 7-11-4 140 (t) NoelFehily 133
(Harry Fry) *trckd ldrs: rdn after 2 out: ev ch appr last: no ex run-in* **5/1**[3]
1241 **5** *7* **Never Equalled (IRE)**[30] 4668 7-11-4 130 RobertWilliams 126
(Bernard Llewellyn) *prom: led 3rd: nt fluent 7th: rdn after 2 out: hdd bef last: fdd run-in* **25/1**
1110 **6** *1* **Holly Bush Henry (IRE)**[29] 4695 5-11-8 142 (t) KielanWoods 129
(Graeme McPherson) *trckd ldrs: rdn after 2 out: wknd last* **14/1**
-214 **7** *31* **Premier Bond**[53] 4236 6-11-4 136 (t) DavidBass 120
(Nicky Henderson) *hld up bhd ldrs: nt fluent 6th: stmbld next: nt travelling after: drvn after 2 out: sn wknd: no ch whn bdly hmpd last* **6/1**
131 **F** **Three Ways**[39] 4494 5-11-4 0 (t) BrendanPowell 115+
(Jamie Snowden) *hld up in last pair but in tch: rdn after 2 out: nt pce to get involved: disputing hld 6th whn fell last* **33/1**

4m 58.1s (0.70) **Going Correction** +0.225s/f (Yiel) **8 Ran SP% 111.8**
Speed ratings (Par 109): **107,105,105,103,100 100,87,**
CSF £14.84 TOTE £2.40: £1.20, £2.00, £1.60; EX 12.90 Trifecta £28.40.
Owner Ben Turner & Jay Tabb **Bred** Stephen Nolan **Trained** Alcester, Warwicks

FOCUS
New Course. Hurdles distances were as advertised, but the chase rail was dolled out 7yds, adding 42yds per circuit. A classy novice hurdle run at what looked an ordinary gallop. Winning jockey Harry Skelton thought the ground was riding good to soft, and the verdict of Sam Twiston-Davies was: "a mix of good and good to soft". The cosy winner has been rated similar to his Festival run, with the second and third pretty much to their marks.

5274 RACING UK NOW IN HD H'CAP CHASE (24 fncs) 3m 4f 21y
2:25 (2:27) (Class 3) (0-130,130) 5-Y-0+
£6,256 (£1,848; £924; £462; £231; £116)

Form RPR
4201 **1** **Any Currency (IRE)**[28] 4719 13-11-12 130 (p) AidanColeman 145+
(Martin Keighley) *a.p: led 16th tl 19th: led 3 out: rdn 5 l clr bef next: styd on gamely* **6/1**[2]
U111 **2** 2 ¾ **Conas Taoi (IRE)**[131] 2887 7-10-9 113 (p) DenisO'Regan 125+
(Paul Morgan) *towards rr of midfield: hdwy after 18th: wnt 4th 4 out: hit next: sn rdn: 5 l 2nd 2 out: styd on run-in but a being comf hld* **11/2**[1]
310P **3** *6* **Thomas Wild**[47] 4340 11-11-7 125 RichardJohnson 132+
(Philip Hobbs) *mid-div: u.p whn stmbld bdly 4 out: hdwy after next: styd on wl to go 3rd run-in but no threat to front pair* **12/1**
2PP3 **4** 1 ¼ **Finish The Story (IRE)**[17] 4935 10-10-8 112 (bt) BrendanPowell 116
(Johnny Farrelly) *trckd ldrs: led 19th: rdn and hdd whn hit 3 out: styd on same pce fr next* **16/1**
00P5 **5** *13* **Azure Fly (IRE)**[22] 4858 8-11-9 130 (tp) GrahamWatters(3) 123
(Charlie Longsdon) *trckd ldrs: rdn after 4 out: kpt chsng ldrs tl no ex between last 2* **25/1**
63P4 **6** *1* **Financial Climate (IRE)**[32] 4621 9-11-3 124 (v[1]) ThomasGarner(3) 114
(Oliver Sherwood) *hld up towards rr: hit 9th: rdn and stdy prog fr 4 out: styd on but nvr threatened to get involved* **14/1**
P351 **7** *6* **Morney Wing (IRE)**[16] 4971 7-11-2 123 (tp) HarryBannister(3) 109
(Charlie Mann) *hld up towards rr: pushed along briefly after 13th: rdn after 18th: hdwy after next: one pce 5th and hld fr 3 out* **14/1**
1314 **8** *nk* **Mysteree (IRE)**[46] 4367 8-10-12 121 GrantCockburn(5) 106
(Lucinda Russell) *in tch: losing pl whn rdn after 18th: no threat after* **6/1**[2]
P-1P **9** *9* **Ruapehu (IRE)**[124] 3024 10-10-10 119 (t) KevinJones(5) 96
(Charles Whittaker) *awkward 1st: led tl nt fluent 16th: rdn after next: wknd after 19th* **20/1**
0256 **10** *6* **Godsmejudge (IRE)**[22] 4858 10-11-6 124 (tp) WayneHutchinson 95
(David Dennis) *trckd ldrs: u.p whn pckd 4 out: wknd next* **12/1**
1PP4 **11** *6* **Whats Left (IRE)**[18] 4914 8-11-5 123 (tp) NoelFehily 89
(Neil Mulholland) *mid-div: cl 5th 4 out: sn rdn: wknd after next* **20/1**
P5U3 **12** 1 ½ **Bertie Boru (IRE)**[22] 4858 9-11-10 128 (p) TomO'Brien 96
(Philip Hobbs) *pushed along fr 10th: a towards rr* **9/1**[3]
6230 **13** *shd* **Hollow Blue Sky (FR)**[18] 4912 9-10-5 114 (tp) JamieBargary(5) 78
(Nigel Twiston-Davies) *mid-div: hit 2nd: hdwy 16th: rdn after 4 out: wknd after next* **20/1**
6604 **14** *4* **Rebeccas Choice (IRE)**[24] 4826 13-11-4 122 (p) PaulMoloney 83
(Dai Burchell) *a towards rr* **20/1**
156P **15** *12* **Woodford County**[18] 4914 9-11-4 127 (p) CiaranGethings(5) 77
(Philip Hobbs) *mid-div: hit 4th: pushed along fr 6th: lost pl 14th: towards rr and struggling after: nvr bk on terms* **20/1**
13PF **P** **Hi Vic (IRE)**[24] 4826 11-11-2 120 (p) SamTwiston-Davies
(David Loder) *mid-div: rdn after 20th: sn wknd: t.o whn p.u after 3 out* **33/1**

7m 23.2s (-1.80) **Going Correction** +0.225s/f (Yiel) **16 Ran SP% 119.2**
Speed ratings: **111,110,108,108,104 104,102,102,99,98 96,95,95,94,91**
CSF £34.11 CT £390.33 TOTE £6.50: £1.90, £2.00, £2.70, £4.10; EX 30.50 Trifecta £188.90.
Owner Cash Is King **Bred** Gerald Mitchell **Trained** Condicote, Gloucs

FOCUS
Actual race distance 3m4f105yds. They went a solid gallop in this competitive staying chase. The winner has been rated to the best of his form over regulation fences, and the third and fourth in line with their recent runs.

5275 GREG JAMES AFTER PARTY 27TH APRIL H'CAP HURDLE (10 hdls) 2m 4f 56y
3:00 (3:01) (Class 2) 4-Y-0+
£12,512 (£3,696; £1,848; £924; £462; £232)

Form RPR
2400 **1** **Matorico (IRE)**[26] 4769 5-10-12 134 (tp) AidanColeman 138
(Jonjo O'Neill) *mid-div: hdwy after 2 out: led sn after last: drifted rt: r.o wl: rdn out* **20/1**
-360 **2** *nk* **Zarib (IRE)**[60] 4115 5-10-11 133 (t) HarrySkelton 136
(Dan Skelton) *hld up towards rr: smooth hdwy after 2 out to chal last: sn rdn and hdd: kpt on wl* **10/1**
12UU **3** 2 ½ **Laurium**[26] 4769 6-11-2 138 DavidBass 140
(Nicky Henderson) *mid-div: hdwy after 3 out: cl up whn sltly hmpd next: rdn to ld bef last: hdd run-in: kpt on same pce* **14/1**
1-63 **4** *1* **Hedley Lamarr (IRE)**[126] 2977 6-10-4 126 RichieMcLernon 127
(Jonjo O'Neill) *trckd ldrs: hit 2 out: led narrowly sn after: rdn and hdd bef last: kpt on same pce* **33/1**
3301 **5** *hd* **Kerisper (FR)**[24] 4821 7-10-5 127 SamTwiston-Davies 127
(Nigel Twiston-Davies) *trckd ldrs: rdn and ch after 2 out: kpt on same pce fr last* **20/1**
3040 **6** 1 ¼ **Kayf Blanco**[26] 4765 7-11-1 137 KielanWoods 136
(Graeme McPherson) *mid-div: hdwy after 2 out: rdn in cl 6th last: kpt on same pce* **16/1**
1-51 **7** *hd* **Might Bite (IRE)**[25] 4786 7-11-12 148 NicodeBoinville 148
(Nicky Henderson) *mid-div: hdwy fnl bnd: drifted rt and rdn sn after: kpt on same pce fr last* **5/2**[1]
-122 **8** 1 ¼ **Vivant Poeme (FR)**[235] 1325 7-10-11 133 (t) NoelFehily 130
(Harry Fry) *hld up towards rr: sme prog after 2 out: styd on fr last but nt pce to get involved* **20/1**
U341 **9** *nk* **Drumlee Sunset (IRE)**[21] 4875 6-10-11 133 RichardJohnson 131
(Philip Hobbs) *in tch: hdwy on inner fnl bnd: rdn and ch sn after: no ex fr last* **8/1**
1F11 **10** *hd* **The Gipper (IRE)**[32] 4613 6-10-8 130 PaulMoloney 127
(Evan Williams) *led 2nd: rdn and hdd after 2 out: no ex* **16/1**
2P1B **11** ½ **Muhtaris (IRE)**[25] 4801 6-10-3 125 LiamTreadwell 122
(James Evans) *racd keenly: hld up towards rr: hdwy after 3 out: rdn after next: nt pce to get on terms* **25/1**
3115 **12** 2 ¾ **Theo's Charm (IRE)**[81] 3733 6-10-10 132 TomCannon 131+
(Nick Gifford) *slowly away: a towards rr: nvr any threat* **6/1**[2]
3221 **13** 2 ¼ **Double W's (IRE)**[21] 4869 6-10-4 126 HenryBrooke 119
(Malcolm Jefferson) *t.k.h early: trckd ldrs: rdn and ch after 2 out: wknd bef last* **7/1**[3]
040B **14** *4* **Bear's Affair (IRE)**[27] 4733 10-11-0 141 FreddieMitchell(5) 129
(Nicky Henderson) *mid-div: hdwy 2 out: sn rdn: wknd bef last* **33/1**
3150 **15** *29* **Masterplan (IRE)**[25] 4801 6-10-3 125 (t) TomScudamore 87
(Charlie Longsdon) *trckd ldr: chal briefly after 2 out: wknd qckly* **50/1**
123- **P** **Quinlandio (IRE)**[426] 4178 6-10-3 125 JamesBanks
(Richard Rowe) *hmpd s: towards rr: hit 5th: rdn whn hit 2 out: sn wknd: p.u bef last* **100/1**

4m 55.3s (-2.10) **Going Correction** +0.225s/f (Yiel) **16 Ran SP% 121.0**
Speed ratings (Par 109): **113,112,111,111,111 110,110,110,110,110 109,108,107,106,94**
CSF £191.80 CT £2904.38 TOTE £28.50: £4.70, £2.20, £2.90, £5.30; EX 263.30 Trifecta £6245.70 Part won..
Owner John P McManus **Bred** Cadran & Scea Des Bissons **Trained** Cheltenham, Gloucs

FOCUS
A good handicap hurdle. Most of these were in with some sort of a shout between the last two flights. Small personal bests from the first two, with the third, fourth and fifth setting the level.

5276 TEENAGE CANCER TRUST SILVER TROPHY CHASE (A LIMITED H'CAP) (GRADE 2) (17 fncs) 2m 4f 166y
3:35 (3:36) (Class 1) 5-Y-0+
£28,475 (£10,685; £5,350; £2,665; £1,340; £670)

Form RPR
1213 **1** **Voix D'Eau (FR)**[116] 3147 6-9-13 145 oh1 (t) MrMLegg(5) 155+
(Harry Fry) *travelled wl most of way: hld up in tch: tk clsr order 4 out: led 3 out: rdn after last: kpt on strly* **9/2**[3]
600P **2** 1 ½ **Art Mauresque (FR)**[27] 4733 6-10-4 145 oh3 SamTwiston-Davies 154+
(Paul Nicholls) *trckd ldrs: rdn after 2 out: chal last: kpt on but no ex* **4/1**[2]
064P **3** *8* **Johns Spirit (IRE)**[27] 4733 9-10-4 145 JoshuaMoore 147
(Jonjo O'Neill) *hld up in tch: hdwy 3 out: wnt 3rd bef next: sn rdn no ex fr last* **3/1**[1]
2340 **4** *7* **Cloud Creeper (IRE)**[151] 2483 9-10-8 149 TomO'Brien 145
(Philip Hobbs) *trckd ldrs: pckd 9th (water) and 4 out: sn rdn: wnt hld 4th between last 2: styd on same pce* **8/1**
322P **5** 1 ½ **Tenor Nivernais (FR)**[46] 4361 9-10-11 152 AidanColeman 145
(Venetia Williams) *led tl 3 out: sn rdn: one pce fr next* **15/2**
UP30 **6** *1* **Splash Of Ginge**[27] 4735 8-10-1 145 oh8 (v) RyanHatch(3) 138
(Nigel Twiston-Davies) *trckd ldr: chal after 13th: hit 4 out: rdn after 3 out: grad fdd* **15/2**
-232 **7** *11* **Wishfull Thinking**[95] 3526 13-11-10 165 (t) RichardJohnson 150
(Philip Hobbs) *hld up in tch: rdn after 3 out: wknd next* **12/1**
0000 **F** **Next Sensation (IRE)**[26] 4770 9-10-4 145 oh2 (t[1]) TomScudamore 138
(Michael Scudamore) *hld up: hdwy 5th: dropped to last 9th: hld in last pair after 3 out: fell last* **11/1**

5m 12.2s (-3.50) **Going Correction** +0.225s/f (Yiel) **8 Ran SP% 113.8**
Speed ratings: **115,114,111,108,108 107,103,**
CSF £23.19 CT £61.42 TOTE £5.00: £1.80, £1.80, £1.30; EX 26.10 Trifecta £114.30.
Owner Harry Fry Racing Club **Bred** Christophe Toussaint & Emmanuel Clayeux **Trained** Seaborough, Dorset

FOCUS
Actual race distance 2m4f208yds. A classy event, but most of these came having been below-par on their most recent outing. The finish was fought out by a pair of six-year-olds. A step up from the winner, with the second rated to his best.

5277 MESSIER-BUGATTI-DOWTY "CONFINED" H'CAP HURDLE (12 hdls) 2m 7f 213y
4:10 (4:11) (Class 3) (0-130,130) 4-Y-0+
£6,256 (£1,848; £924; £462; £231; £116)

Form RPR
4243 **1** **Altesse De Guye (FR)**[25] 4779 6-10-9 **113**.................. RichardJohnson 118+
(Martin Keighley) *travelled wl: hld up: hdwy after 2 out: mounting chal whn wnt bdly lft last: led sn after: kpt on wl: drvn out* **5/1**[3]

43P0 **2** ½ **Anteros (IRE)**[46] 4354 8-11-10 **128**..............................(t) PaulMoloney 133
(Sophie Leech) *travelled wl: mid-div: bdly hmpd 4th: hdwy appr 2 out: led appr last: rdn and hdd run-in: kpt on* **12/1**

00F2 **3** 3 ½ **Kentucky Star (FR)**[16] 4986 7-10-11 **115**.................. HarrySkelton 116+
(Dan Skelton) *hld up bhd: hdwy after 2 out: mounting chal whn hmpd last: sn rdn: kpt on same pce* **7/2**[1]

F20P **4** 2 **Fort Worth (IRE)**[49] 4305 7-11-11 **129**.................. PaddyBrennan 130+
(Jonjo O'Neill) *hld up: hmpd 4th: hdwy after 3 out: mounting chal whn quite bdly hmpd last: no ch after* **10/1**

5323 **5** 2 ¾ **Batavir (FR)**[9] 5146 7-11-2 **125**..........................(bt) MichaelHeard(5) 121
(David Pipe) *mid-div: hdwy after 3 out: rdn and ev ch appr last: one pce run-in* **9/2**[2]

552 **6** 2 ½ **Allbarnone**[8] 5157 8-10-3 **110**.................. ThomasGarner(3) 104
(William Kinsey) *mid-div: hdwy after 3 out: led after next: rdn and hdd whn short of room and mstke last: fdd* **7/1**

4000 **7** 8 **Horizontal Speed (IRE)**[25] 4786 8-11-12 **130**.....................(p) NoelFehily 117
(David Dennis) *racd keenly: trckd ldr: hit 3rd and 8th: led after 3 out: rdn and hdd after 2 out: wknd bef last where mstke* **16/1**

0340 **8** 6 **Sybarite (FR)**[9] 5141 10-11-5 **123**..............................(p) SamTwiston-Davies 104
(Nigel Twiston-Davies) *led: rdn and hdd after 3 out: wknd after next* **16/1**

000P **9** 11 **According To Trev (IRE)**[29] 4697 10-11-1 **124**..........(p[1]) JakeHodson(5) 95
(David Bridgwater) *trckd ldr tl rdn after 9th: wknd 2 out* **33/1**

4030 **10** 47 **While You Wait (IRE)**[45] 4384 7-10-3 **110**.................. LucyGardner(3) 39
(Sue Gardner) *hld up last: wknd after 2 out: t.o* **50/1**

3023 **F** **Billy Dutton**[18] 4911 10-11-10 **128**.............................. JamesDavies
(Chris Down) *trcking ldrs whn fell 4th* **15/2**

5m 59.5s (-1.50) **Going Correction** +0.225s/f (Yiel) **11 Ran SP% 114.8**
Speed ratings (Par 107): **111,110,109,109,108 107,104,102,98,83**
CSF £61.35 CT £236.17 TOTE £5.00: £2.00, £3.80, £2.00; EX 78.80 Trifecta £573.30.
Owner Daydream Believers **Bred** G A E C Delorme Gerard & Vincent **Trained** Condicote, Gloucs

FOCUS
The second in a series of races confined to horses that have run in at least four British handicap hurdles in the last year, but have not won during that period. The second has been rated back to his best.

5278 WEATHERITE NOVICES' CHASE (14 fncs) 2m 62y
4:45 (4:45) (Class 2) 5-Y-0+ **£12,512** (£3,696; £1,848; £924)

Form RPR
3333 **1** **Fox Norton (FR)**[4] 5215 6-11-8 146.................. RichardJohnson 151
(Neil Mulholland) *mde all: hit 1st: rchd for 5th: hit 3 out: kpt on wl fr last: drvn out* **8/11**[1]

2422 **2** 1 ¼ **Dormello Mo (FR)**[11] 5087 6-11-8 142..................(t) SamTwiston-Davies 150
(Paul Nicholls) *trckd wnr thrght: blnd 2nd: drvn between last 2: kpt on but a being hld fr last* **11/4**[2]

1015 **3** 12 **Presenting Arms (IRE)**[20] 4891 9-11-5 136..........................(t) NoelFehily 137
(Harry Fry) *trckd ldng pair: rdn after 3 out: nt pce to get on terms* **4/1**[3]

-014 **4** 39 **Agenor (GER)**[221] 1480 5-11-0 0..............................(t) BrendanPowell 101
(Jamie Snowden) *trckd ldrs tl outpcd after 4 out: t.o* **33/1**

4m 6.7s **Going Correction** +0.225s/f (Yiel) **4 Ran SP% 107.5**
Speed ratings: **109,108,102,82**
CSF £3.16 TOTE £1.50; EX 3.00 Trifecta £3.20.
Owner B Dunn **Bred** S A Scuderia Del Bargelo **Trained** Limpley Stoke, Wilts

FOCUS
Actual race distance 2m104yds. The order barely changed during this good little novice chase. The first three have been rated pretty much to their marks.

5279 CHELTENHAM PONY RACING AUTHORITY GRADUATES' H'CAP HURDLE (COND/AM THAT HAVE RIDDEN IN PRA RACES) (8 hdls) 2m 179y
5:20 (5:22) (Class 3) (0-140,134) 4-Y-0+
£6,256 (£1,848; £924; £462; £231; £116)

Form RPR
UFP3 **1** **Minellaforleisure (IRE)**[52] 4273 8-10-11 **122**.............. HarryBannister(3) 133+
(Alex Hales) *travelled wl in midfield: hdwy 2 out: upsides gng to last: rdn to ld run-in: kpt on wl: drvn out* **6/1**[3]

5-02 **2** ½ **Vosne Romanee**[316] 592 5-10-1 **119**..................(tp) CharlieHammond(10) 129
(Dr Richard Newland) *hld up: hdwy 2 out: led bef last: rdn and hdd run-in: kpt on but no ex nring fin* **14/1**

1346 **3** 10 **Simon Squirrel (IRE)**[66] 4010 6-11-7 **134**..................(t) HarryCobden(5) 134
(Paul Nicholls) *racd keenly: in tch: hdwy 2 out: rdn and ev ch after 2 out: hld bef last: kpt on same pce* **7/2**[1]

30P0 **4** 1 **Lough Kent**[26] 4770 7-10-13 **126**..................(p) ThomasCheesman(5) 125
(Nicky Henderson) *trckd ldr: chalng whn awkward 2 out: sn led: rdn and hdd bef last: no ex run-in* **9/1**

F040 **5** nse **Global Thrill**[27] 4745 7-9-13 **110**..................(t) RobertWilliams(3) 109
(Bernard Llewellyn) *hld up: struggling 5th: hdwy appr last: styd on wl run-in but no threat to ldrs* **20/1**

3123 **6** ¾ **Beallandendall (IRE)**[8] 5153 8-10-12 **127**.............. MrStanSheppard(7) 125
(Matt Sheppard) *hld up: hdwy 2 out: rdn to chse ldrs bef last: nt pce to threaten* **11/1**

240 **7** nk **Desert Recluse (IRE)**[96] 2617 9-10-7 **118**.............. MissGAndrews(3) 116
(Henry Oliver) *hld up: hdwy after 3 out: rdn after next: styd on same pce* **28/1**

2130 **8** nk **Divine Spear (IRE)**[32] 4620 5-10-12 **125**.............................. NedCurtis(5) 124
(Nicky Henderson) *trckd ldrs: hmpd 2 out: sn rdn w ev ch: fdd bef last* **11/2**[2]

F221 **9** 7 **Authorized Too**[17] 4934 5-10-7 **120**..................(p) JackSherwood(5) 116+
(Noel Williams) *racd keenly: mid-div: hit 2nd: dropped to last pair after 5th: nvr bk on terms* **8/1**

36-P **10** 7 **Jolly Roger (IRE)**[237] 442 9-9-7 **108**.............. JordanWilliams(7) 93
(Bernard Llewellyn) *mid-div: rdn after 3 out: sn btn* **66/1**

114P **11** 3 ¾ **Isaac Bell (IRE)**[25] 4799 8-10-5 **120**..................(t) ArchieBellamy(7) 102
(Alex Hales) *mid-div: rdn after 3 out: wknd bef last* **33/1**

535- **12** 6 **Castlemorris King**[19] 1592 8-11-4 **131**.................. LizzieKelly(5) 107
(Brian Barr) *trckd ldrs: rdn after 2 out: sn wknd* **50/1**

-P0P **13** 9 **Rathealy (IRE)**[17] 4933 5-10-11 **124**..................(bt[1]) MichaelHeard(5) 93
(David Pipe) *led: rdn and hdd sn after 2 out: wknd qckly* **25/1**

6011 **P** **Thunder Sheik (IRE)**[12] 5074 8-11-6 **133**..................(p) FreddieMitchell(5)
(Nigel Twiston-Davies) *in tch tl rdn after 3 out: sn btn: p.u bef last* **7/1**

4m 3.1s (-8.20) **Going Correction** -0.25s/f (Good) **14 Ran SP% 119.0**
Speed ratings (Par 107): **109,108,104,103,103 103,103,102,99,96 94,91,87,**
CSF £77.28 CT £342.08 TOTE £6.40: £2.60, £5.00, £1.80; EX 106.80 Trifecta £951.70.
Owner The Patient Partnership **Bred** Ballina Stud Ltd **Trained** Edgcote, Northamptonshire

FOCUS
The first two pulled clear in this fair handicap hurdle. The winner has been rated back to the level of his C&D form, and the runner-up has been rated as running a personal best.
T/Jkpt: Not won. T/Plt: £216.70 to a £1 stake. Pool: £169,668.95 - 571.55 winning units. T/Qpdt: £69.30 to a £1 stake. Pool: £9,620.63 - 102.59 winning units. **Tim Mitchell**

5273 CHELTENHAM (L-H)
Thursday, April 14

OFFICIAL GOING: Good (good to soft in places; 7.5)
Wind: mild breeze half across Weather: overcast with showers

5280 THOROUGHBRED BREEDERS' ASSOCIATION MARES' NOVICES' HURDLE (LISTED RACE) (10 hdls) 2m 4f 56y
1:50 (1:52) (Class 1) 4-Y-0+
£11,390 (£4,274; £2,140; £1,066; £536; £268)

Form RPR
-112 **1** **Katie Too (IRE)**[55] 4231 5-11-0 131.............................. WayneHutchinson 132
(Alan King) *trckd ldrs: outpcd and lost pl after 3 out: rallied after 2 out: lft w ev ch last: sn led: styd on: drvn out* **10/3**[1]

1130 **2** nk **Actinpieces**[28] 4734 5-11-0 130.............................. MissGAndrews 132
(Pam Sly) *trckd ldrs: mstke 4th: rdn after 2 out: lft w ev ch last: kpt on: hld nring fin* **8/1**

5111 **3** 2 **Sainte Ladylime (FR)**[24] 4837 5-11-0 130.................. DavidBass 129
(Kim Bailey) *led tl 4th: pressed ldr: rdn after 2 out: 3 l down whn lft in ld and mstke last: sn hdd: kpt on but no ex* **8/1**

2F25 **4** 6 **Bantam (IRE)**[28] 4734 6-11-0 130.............................. RichardJohnson 124
(Henry Daly) *hld up towards rr: hdwy after 3 out: disp 3rd after 2 out: sn rdn: fading whn lft 4th at the last* **8/1**

-031 **5** 2 ½ **Midnight Tour**[29] 4714 6-11-0 115.............................. SamTwiston-Davies 122
(David Loder) *hld up towards rr: outpcd appr 2 out: styd on bef last but nvr any ch* **50/1**

2-10 **6** 3 ¾ **Chocca Wocca**[28] 4734 6-11-0 0..............................(t) NicodeBoinville 118
(Nicky Henderson) *mid-div: hdwy after 2 out: sn rdn: wknd bef last* **9/1**

3114 **7** 4 **Yes I Did (IRE)**[40] 4471 6-11-0 128.............................. HarrySkelton 114
(Dan Skelton) *hld up towards rr: rdn after 2 out: little imp* **8/1**

1022 **8** 22 **Robinesse (IRE)**[51] 4293 5-11-0 115.............................. GavinSheehan 95
(Oliver Sherwood) *mid-div: rdn after 7th: wknd after 3 out* **33/1**

9 53 **Omessa Has (FR)**[159] 2359 4-10-12 138.............................. DarylJacob 45
(Nicky Henderson) *mid-div: losing pl whn short of room after 3 out: sn wknd: t.o* **13/2**[3]

1121 **F** **The Organist (IRE)**[40] 4471 5-11-5 135.............................. LeightonAspell 140+
(Oliver Sherwood) *prom: led 4th: pushed along after 2 out: 3 l up whn fell last* **9/2**[2]

4m 54.7s (-2.70) **Going Correction** -0.075s/f (Good)
WFA 4 from 5yo+ 6lb **10 Ran SP% 113.9**
Speed ratings (Par 111): **102,101,101,98,97 96,94,85,64,**
CSF £29.76 TOTE £3.90: £1.60, £3.30, £2.30; EX 33.50 Trifecta £319.00.
Owner Mr & Mrs Christopher Harris **Bred** Regina Anne Hennessy **Trained** Barbury Castle, Wilts

FOCUS
New course used. The hurdle rails were on the innermost line with distances as advertised. This looked a tight race both on BHA figures and RPRs. This Listed event was previously run over 2m1f, and three of these ran in the inaugural mares' novice hurdle over that trip at the festival. Afterwards Wayne Hutchinson said: "It's closer to good than anything else", while David Bass's verdict was: "It rode good ground". The first two have been rated to their marks, with the third close to her best.

5281 EBF/THOROUGHBRED BREEDERS' ASSOCIATION MARES' NOVICES' CHASE FINALE (A H'CAP) (LISTED RACE) (17 fncs) 2m 4f 166y
2:25 (2:26) (Class 1) 5-Y-0+
£22,508 (£8,480; £4,244; £2,120; £1,064; £532)

Form RPR
131 **1** **Indian Stream**[225] 1445 7-11-0 **125**..............................(t) NoelFehily 139+
(Neil Mulholland) *trckd ldrs: led 2 out: clr last: styd on wl: readily* **8/1**[3]

1FP3 **2** 8 **Kilronan High (IRE)**[49] 4319 7-11-2 **127**..................(t) SamTwiston-Davies 134
(Nigel Twiston-Davies) *a.p: lft w ev ch 2 out: sn drvn: styd on but nt pce of wnr* **16/1**

3F4P **3** 6 **Ebony Empress (IRE)**[106] 3373 7-10-10 **121**..................(p) MarkQuinlan 124
(Neil Mulholland) *in tch: disp 3rd 3 out: sn rdn: hld in 4th whn hmpd and lft 3rd 2 out: styd on same pce fr last* **10/1**

1123 **4** hd **Emerald Rose**[27] 4775 9-10-6 **117**..............................(p) MarkGrant 117
(Julian Smith) *in tch: hit 3 out: rdn whn mstke: hmpd and lft disputing 4th 2 out: styd on same pce* **33/1**

1F35 **5** 2 ¼ **Storming Strumpet**[12] 5103 6-10-0 **111** oh5..................(t) PaddyBrennan 110
(Tom George) *hld up: nt fluent 2nd: rdn after 3 out: lft disputing 4th whn sltly hmpd 2 out: styd on same pce* **25/1**

5223 **6** nk **Kayfleur**[32] 4647 7-10-13 **124**.............................. JakeGreenall 123
(Henry Daly) *mid-div: struggling in rr after 12th: styd on again fr 2 out but n.d* **9/1**

F1F3 **7** 2 **Kalane (IRE)**[83] 3726 7-11-10 **135**.............................. AidanColeman 134
(Charlie Longsdon) *chsd ldrs: pushed along after 11th: lost pl after 4 out: styd on fr 2 out but nvr gng pce to get bk on terms* **3/1**[1]

2154 **8** hd **Kassis**[49] 4319 7-10-0 **111** oh8.............................. BrendanPowell 109
(Jamie Snowden) *mid-div tl dropped in rr and struggling 10th: styd on but nvr gng pce to get bk involved fr 3 out* **25/1**

2221 **9** 14 **Bon Chic (IRE)**[27] 4772 7-11-0 **125**.............................. HarrySkelton 115
(Dan Skelton) *nvr that fluent: hld up: reminders after 7th: swtchd wd after next: drvn in midfield after 3 out: wknd between last 2* **3/1**[1]

1F2F **F** **Alder Mairi (IRE)**[32] 4647 9-10-9 **120**..................(p) AndrewThornton
(Seamus Mullins) *prom: led 8th: rdn and jst been hdd whn fell heavily 2 out* **33/1**

1322 **F** **Cresswell Breeze**[32] 4647 6-11-0 **130**........................(t) DavidNoonan[(5)]
(Anthony Honeyball) *led tl 8th: prom: nt fluent 8th: disputing ld and travelling wl enough whn fell 4 out* **5/1[2]**

5m 15.8s (0.10) **Going Correction** +0.325s/f (Yiel) **11** Ran SP% **116.3**
Speed ratings: **112,108,106,106,105 105,104,104,99,**
CSF £111.15 CT £1283.32 TOTE £7.50: £2.40, £4.90, £2.90; EX 172.30 Trifecta £2127.10.

Owner Mrs G Davies **Bred** A W Buller **Trained** Limpley Stoke, Wilts

FOCUS
The chase bends were dolled out seven yards. Actual race distance 2m 4f 108yds. A competitive mares' finale on paper, but not that many ever got into it. The winner is on the upgrade, while the runner-up's Southwell win could be rated to this sort of level.

5282 ARKELLS BREWERY MARES' H'CAP HURDLE (LISTED RACE) (10 hdls) 2m 4f 56y

3:00 (3:00) (Class 1) 4-Y-0+

£12,529 (£4,701; £2,354; £1,172; £589; £294)

Form RPR

0312 **1** **Briery Belle**[40] 4471 7-11-7 **129**........................ TomO'Brien 140+
(Henry Daly) *mid-div: hdwy 5th: led 2 out: pushed clr last: styd on strly: rdn out* **8/1[3]**

3-1F **2** *3* **Debdebdeb**[54] 4239 6-11-4 **126**........................ HarrySkelton 135
(Dan Skelton) *hld up towards rr: hdwy after 2 out: chsd wnr jst bef last: sn rdn: kpt on but nt pce to get on terms* **11/2[1]**

20 **3** *9* **Flementime (IRE)**[124] 3034 8-11-2 **124**........................(tp) AndrewTinkler 125
(Martin Keighley) *towards rr: reminders after 3rd: midfield next: hdwy u.p 2 out: disp 2nd bef last where mstke: styd on same pce run-in* **9/1**

1321 **4** *¾* **Unbuckled (IRE)**[9] 5155 6-10-10 **118** 6ex........................ TrevorWhelan 117
(Neil King) *mid-div: nudged along briefly after 5th: nt clr run appr 2 out: hdwy on inner fnl bnd: disp 2nd bef last: kpt on same pce run-in* **7/1[2]**

51 **5** *3 ¾* **Barnahash Rose (IRE)**[32] 4653 8-11-4 **131**.........(t) AmbroseMcCurtin[(5)] 128
(Jonathan Sweeney, Ire) *trckd ldrs: pressed ldr 3 out: upsides wnr 2 out: sn rdn: no ex and lost 3 pls appr last* **14/1**

3132 **6** *hd* **Theatre Goer**[41] 4467 7-10-9 **117**........................ JamesBanks 113
(Noel Williams) *chsd ldr: rdn whn outpcd after 3 out: styd on again appr last but n.d* **16/1**

U550 **7** *4 ½* **Blue Buttons (IRE)**[26] 4801 8-11-9 **131**........................(t) DarylJacob 123
(Emma Lavelle) *chsd ldrs: rdn after 3 out: one pce fr next* **25/1**

P11 **8** *2* **Treaty Girl (IRE)**[26] 4777 5-11-4 **126**........................ NicodeBoinville 117
(Ben Pauling) *trckd ldrs: rdn whn hit 2 out: wknd bef last* **10/1**

1440 **9** *2 ¾* **Promanco**[145] 2632 7-10-12 **120**........................(t) RichardJohnson 111+
(Charlie Longsdon) *hld up towards rr: hdwy 5th: trckd ldrs after 3 out: wnt 3rd turning in: sn rdn: wknd bef last* **16/1**

-566 **10** *4* **Loyaute (FR)**[48] 4338 9-10-9 **117**........................(t) JamesDavies 103
(Chris Down) *struggling 6th: a towards rr* **25/1**

6P21 **11** *38* **Lady Of Longstone (IRE)**[19] 4909 6-11-4 **131**.........(p) MichaelHeard[(5)] 81
(David Pipe) *led: drvn after 3 out: hdd next: sn wknd* **8/1[3]**

1P14 **P** **At First Light**[12] 5094 7-10-11 **119**........................ DavidBass
(David Weston) *mid-div tl dropped in rr after 4th: lost tch after 3 out: p.u after 2 out* **20/1**

-124 **P** **Robins Reef (IRE)**[28] 4734 6-11-5 **132**........................ FreddieMitchell[(5)]
(Nicky Henderson) *trcking ldrs whn blnd bdly 2nd and lost pl: nvr travelling or fluent after: drvn after 3 out: lost action whn p.u after 2 out* **11/2[1]**

4m 52.8s (-4.60) **Going Correction** -0.075s/f (Good) **13** Ran SP% **115.5**
Speed ratings (Par 111): **106,104,101,100,99 99,97,96,95,94 78, ,**
CSF £49.10 CT £401.69 TOTE £8.50: £3.00, £2.50, £3.90; EX 62.20 Trifecta £902.80.

Owner Mrs H Plumbly J Trafford K Deane S Holme **Bred** Simon And Helen Plumbly **Trained** Stanton Lacy, Shropshire

FOCUS
An ordinary edition of this Listed mares' handicap, run at a sound pace. A step up from the winner, with the third and fourth helping to set the level.

5283 LLEWELLYN HUMPHREYS H'CAP CHASE (21 fncs) 3m 2f

3:35 (3:36) (Class 2) (0-150,148) 5-Y-0+

£12,512 (£3,696; £1,848; £924; £462; £232)

Form RPR

2510 **1** **Perfect Candidate (IRE)**[28] 4735 9-11-3 **142**.........(t) ConorShoemark[(3)] 155+
(Fergal O'Brien) *hld up: hdwy 8th: rdn whn pckd 4 out: clsd on ldrs after next: led between last 2: styd on wl: rdn out* **11/1**

1461 **2** *1 ¾* **Forgotten Gold (IRE)**[11] 5119 10-11-3 **139** 7ex........................ PaddyBrennan 147
(Tom George) *trckd ldrs: mstke 10th: led 3 out: sn rdn: hdd between last 2: styd on but a being hld run-in* **9/2[2]**

121- **3** *12* **Warden Hill (IRE)**[368] 5296 8-10-12 **137**........................ HarryBannister[(3)] 133
(Mick Channon) *in tch: drvn along fr 18th: hdwy after 3 out: wnt 4th next: styd on into 3rd run-in: no threat to front pair* **9/2[2]**

540P **4** *2 ½* **Seventh Sky (GER)**[40] 4472 9-11-12 **148**........................(tp) GavinSheehan 145+
(Charlie Mann) *trckd ldrs: hit 9th: j.lft fr 17th: wnt 2nd 3 out: sn drvn: lost 2nd after next: no ex fr last* **25/1**

4-45 **5** *5* **Amigo (FR)**[28] 4735 9-10-7 **134**........................(bt) DavidNoonan[(5)] 125
(David Pipe) *prom tl 4th: chsd ldrs: rdn after 4 out: sltly hmpd next: one pce fr 2 out* **11/4[1]**

2-66 **6** *6* **Candide (IRE)**[33] 4618 9-10-0 **122** oh2........................(p) JamesBanks 109
(Sally Randell) *led: hit 13th: nt fluent next: pckd 4 out: sn rdn and hdd: wknd between last 2* **25/1**

PS20 **7** *24* **Sire Collonges (FR)**[29] 4719 10-10-12 **139**..............(b) JackSherwood[(5)] 101
(Paul Nicholls) *in tch: in last pair 8th: struggling 15th: sn detached: no threat fr 4 out: wknd after 2 out* **6/1**

5P31 **P** **Benvolio (IRE)**[12] 5092 9-11-9 **145**........................(b) SamTwiston-Davies
(Paul Nicholls) *in tch: dropped to last pair 8th: hit 10th and 13th: rdn 15th: outpcd and detached fr 17th: nvr threatened to get bk on terms: p.u bef last* **11/2[3]**

6m 46.3s (0.30) **Going Correction** +0.325s/f (Yiel) **8** Ran SP% **108.7**
Speed ratings: **112,111,107,107,105 103,96,**
CSF £54.82 CT £231.68 TOTE £10.60: £2.80, £2.00, £1.60; EX 39.10 Trifecta £247.00.

Owner ISL Recruitment **Bred** Hugh Suffern Bloodstock Ltd **Trained** Naunton, Gloucs

■ Stewards' Enquiry : Conor Shoemark two-day ban: used whip in incorrect place (Apr 28-29)

FOCUS
Actual race distance 3m 2f 84yds. A decent handicap chase which produced a likeable staying performance from the winner. The second sets the level.

5284 BARBURY INTERNATIONAL SUPPORTING THE IJF H'CAP HURDLE (12 hdls) 2m 7f 213y

4:10 (4:11) (Class 2) (0-145,145) 4-Y-0+

£10,009 (£2,956; £1,478; £739; £369; £185)

Form RPR

124P **1** **The Eaglehaslanded (IRE)**[60] 4139 6-10-6 **125**(bt[1])
SamTwiston-Davies 135+
(Paul Nicholls) *mid-div: hdwy after 3 out: wnt lft and bmpd next: led last: qcknd clr: readily* **8/1[2]**

5322 **2** *6* **Sir Ivan**[47] 4362 6-11-3 **136**........................(t) NoelFehily 139
(Harry Fry) *mid-div: hdwy after 3 out: hanging lft but ev ch last: sn outpcd by wnr but kpt on wl for 2nd* **14/1**

P641 **3** *2 ¼* **San Telm (IRE)**[32] 4643 11-10-3 **122**........................(p) JoshuaMoore 122
(Stuart Edmunds) *in tch: led 2 out: sn rdn: hdd last: styd on but no ex* **33/1**

2226 **4** *4 ½* **Southfield Vic (IRE)**[47] 4354 7-11-7 **145**........................(b) HarryCobden[(5)] 142
(Paul Nicholls) *trckd ldrs: led after 3 out tl next: sn rdn w ev ch tl last: styd on same pce* **14/1**

1U2 **5** *9* **Long House Hall (IRE)**[29] 4717 8-11-10 **143**........................(t) HarrySkelton 134
(Dan Skelton) *hld up towards rr: hdwy 6th: trckd ldrs 3 out: rdn after 2 out: fnd little: btn 5th whn sprawled on landing last* **10/3[1]**

1355 **6** *8* **Pull The Chord (IRE)**[26] 4786 6-11-0 **133**........................ TomO'Brien 115
(Philip Hobbs) *mid-div tl dropped in rr 4th: pushed along after 7th: prog into midfield 2 out: no further imp* **33/1**

-06U **7** *2 ¼* **Kingsmere**[153] 2471 11-10-6 **125**........................ AndrewTinkler 104
(Henry Daly) *hld up towards rr: hdwy after 3 out: rdn after next: nvr threatened: wknd bef last* **25/1**

4012 **8** *3* **Fingerontheswitch (IRE)**[19] 4911 6-11-0 **138**..........(p) DavidNoonan[(5)] 114
(Neil Mulholland) *mid-div: hit 6th: hdwy 2 out: sn rdn: nvr threatened: wknd bef last* **9/1[3]**

4P40 **9** *3 ¼* **Rolling Maul (IRE)**[28] 4730 8-11-0 **133**........................(bt) SeanBowen 108
(Peter Bowen) *sn struggling towards rr: nvr a factor* **14/1**

23FP **10** *2 ¼* **Souriyan (FR)**[71] 3929 5-10-10 **129**........................(b) MichealNolan 102
(Jamie Snowden) *chsd ldrs tl 3 out: sn btn* **66/1**

4254 **11** *12* **Goodbye Dancer (FR)**[26] 4786 5-10-6 **130**........................ JamieBargary[(5)] 93
(Nigel Twiston-Davies) *in tch tl rdn after 3 out: sn btn* **12/1**

-104 **12** *3 ½* **Bells 'N' Banjos (IRE)**[34] 4596 6-10-13 **132**........................ GavinSheehan 89
(Warren Greatrex) *mid-div: rdn after 8th: hdwy after 3 out: nvr threatened: wknd bef last* **66/1**

5332 **13** *1* **Ten Sixty (IRE)**[26] 4788 6-10-6 **125**........................ RichardJohnson 81
(Philip Hobbs) *hld up towards rr: hdwy into midfield appr 2 out: sn drvn: wknd bef last* **9/1[3]**

UP12 **14** *7* **Delgany Demon**[26] 4800 8-10-11 **130**........................ TrevorWhelan 80
(Neil King) *led tl rdn and hdd after 3 out: sn wknd* **25/1**

-601 **15** *10* **Sugar Baron (IRE)**[40] 4470 6-11-1 **134**........................ DavidBass 75
(Nicky Henderson) *nt fluent 1st 2: a towards rr* **8/1[2]**

-160 **16** *1* **Drum Valley**[67] 4017 8-11-5 **138**........................(b[1]) LeightonAspell 78
(Oliver Sherwood) *trckd ldr: rdn appr 2 out where hmpd: sn wknd* **40/1**

/32- **P** **Taigan (FR)**[511] 2621 9-10-6 **125**........................ DavidEngland
(Giles Smyly) *trckd ldrs tl wknd 3 out: t.o whn p.u bef last* **66/1**

P1P4 **P** **Royal Guardsman (IRE)**[40] 4487 9-10-10 **132**..............(p) RyanHatch[(3)]
(Ali Stronge) *a towards rr: t.o whn p.u bef last* **100/1**

-613 **P** **Ballyhenry (IRE)**[26] 4788 6-10-6 **125**........................(tp) NicodeBoinville
(Ben Pauling) *in tch tl wknd after 3 out: t.o whn p.u bef last* **14/1**

5m 52.6s (-8.40) **Going Correction** -0.075s/f (Good) **19** Ran SP% **121.1**
Speed ratings (Par 109): **111,109,108,106,103 101,100,99,98,97 93,92,92,89,86 86, , ,**
CSF £103.41 CT £3494.76 TOTE £8.00: £2.40, £3.00, £6.20, £3.50; EX 107.40 Trifecta £4425.90.

Owner Mrs Angela Tincknell & W Tincknell **Bred** Grange Stud **Trained** Ditcheat, Somerset

FOCUS
This well-contested handicap was run in a heavy downpour. The second and third have been rated to their marks.

5285 NICHOLSON HOLMAN NOVICES' LIMITED H'CAP CHASE (21 fncs) 3m 1f 56y

4:45 (4:47) (Class 3) (0-135,127) 5-Y-0+

£6,256 (£1,848; £924; £462; £231; £116)

Form RPR

6-61 **1** **Solstice Son**[26] 4780 7-10-13 **123**........................(bt) HarryCobden[(5)] 136+
(Anthony Honeyball) *trckd ldrs: led 2 out: styd on wl: rdn out* **5/1[2]**

5P13 **2** *4* **Get Involved (IRE)**[23] 4860 7-10-10 **115**........................ CharliePoste 124+
(Robin Dickin) *trckd ldr: led after 3 out: sn rdn: hdd next: styd on but hld whn mstke last* **10/1**

6-14 **3** *22* **Deadly Sting (IRE)**[22] 4870 7-11-8 **127**........................(tp) NoelFehily 120
(Neil Mulholland) *hld up: pushed along fr 16th: lft btn 6th 4 out: plugged on fr next: wnt wl hld 3rd run-in* **12/1**

1312 **4** *3 ½* **Troika Steppes**[17] 4977 8-10-9 **117**........................ ConorShoemark[(3)] 103
(Fergal O'Brien) *led: sn clr: nt fluent 3rd: rdn and hdd after 3 out: wknd between last 2* **14/1**

325 **5** *4* **Kilmurvy (IRE)**[140] 2733 8-11-8 **127**........................(tp) MattGriffiths 111
(Jeremy Scott) *towards rr: rdn along fr 14th: hmpd 4 out: wknd after next* **25/1**

1 **6** *2* **Mezendore (IRE)**[14] 5046 7-11-2 **121**........................(b) LeightonAspell 104
(Rebecca Curtis) *j.lft at times: trckd ldrs: blnd 2nd: hit 7th: disp 2nd 16th tl next: sn rdn: lft 4th 4 out: wknd bef 2 out: t.o* **10/1**

46U1 **7** *12* **Themanfrom Minella (IRE)**[37] 4542 7-10-9 **121**..(tp) MrMJPKendrick[(7)] 95
(Ben Case) *in tch: rdn along fr 16th: lft 5th whn mstke and bdly hmpd 4 out: sn wknd* **9/1[3]**

PP01 **8** *7* **An Poc Ar Buile (IRE)**[15] 5031 7-10-3 **108** oh3........................ JamesDavies 71
(Sophie Leech) *struggling 7th: a towards rr* **33/1**

U21F **U** **Vendredi Trois (FR)**[26] 4789 7-10-8 **113**........................ DarylJacob
(Emma Lavelle) *mid-div whn blnd bdly and uns rdr 6th* **25/1**

31P4 **P** **Benenden (IRE)**[13] 5073 8-11-5 **124**........................(t) RichieMcLernon
(Michael Scudamore) *hit 4th and reminders: a towards rr: t.o whn p.u 3 out* **20/1**

P-22 **F** **Lovely Job (IRE)**[97] 3507 6-11-3 **122**........................ PaddyBrennan
(Fergal O'Brien) *hld up: nt fluent 1st: making hdwy whn awkward 13th (water): 5th whn blnd bdly 17th: clsng in 4th whn fell 4 out* **3/1[1]**

F134 **P** **Wild Bill (IRE)**[47] 4352 7-11-2 **121**........................ PaulMoloney
(Evan Williams) *in tch tl 15th: sn bhd: t.o whn p.u 3 out* **5/1[2]**

6m 46.1s (7.90) **Going Correction** +0.525s/f (Soft) **12** Ran SP% **116.3**
Speed ratings: **108,106,99,98,97 96,92,90, , ,**
CSF £49.79 CT £570.83 TOTE £6.90: £2.90, £3.40, £3.30; EX 59.20 Trifecta £835.10.

Owner The Summer Solstice **Bred** R W Russell **Trained** Mosterton, Dorset

FOCUS

Actual race distance 3m 1f 140yds. Not many figured in this fair novice handicap, which was run in softening ground. The second has been rated as stepping up on his hurdle form.

5286 SPREADEX SPORTS AND FINANCIAL BETTING MARES' STANDARD OPEN NATIONAL HUNT FLAT RACE 2m 179y

5:20 (5:23) (Class 4) 4-6-Y-O £4,873 (£1,431; £715; £357)

Form RPR

1 **Hitherjacques Lady (IRE)** 4-10-8 0 LeightonAspell 92+
(Oliver Sherwood) *trckd ldr: led over 2f out: kpt on wl: rdn out* 4/1[2]

2 ½ **Midnight Glory** 4-10-8 0 JamesBest 92+
(Philip Hobbs) *in tch: rdn for str chal 2f out: looked hld ent fnl f: kpt on again cl home* 14/1

3 5 **Katy P** 4-10-3 0 MissKHarrington(5) 87
(Mrs John Harrington, Ire) *trckd ldrs: rdn 3f out: chsd ldng pair over 1f out: styd on but nt pce to chal* 11/4[1]

1 **4** 1½ **Meribel Millie**[139] 2750 5-11-7 0 (t) NoelFehily 99
(Harry Fry) *hld up towards rr: hdwy over 2f out: rdn in 4th over 1f out: no further imp tl styd on fnl 120yds* 4/1[2]

50 **5** 2½ **Miss Maiden Over (IRE)**[24] 4847 4-10-8 0 PaddyBrennan 84
(Fergal O'Brien) *hld up towards rr: hdwy fr 2f out: styd on wl fnl f wout threatening ldrs* 33/1

0 **6** 1 **Tara View**[40] 4488 5-11-0 0 WayneHutchinson 89
(Alan King) *in tch: rdn over 2f out: styd on same pce fnl f* 10/1[3]

164 **7** ½ **Westerbee (IRE)**[41] 4468 5-11-2 0 KevinJones(5) 95
(Seamus Mullins) *hld up towards rr: hdwy fr 2f out: styd on fnl f: nvr trbld ldrs* 33/1

6 **8** 7 **Kahaleesi**[101] 3469 4-10-8 0 RichardJohnson 76
(Philip Hobbs) *mid-div: effrt 3f out: nvr threatened: wknd fnl f* 10/1[3]

4 **9** 6 **Dalton Glance**[48] 4350 6-10-11 0 KillianMoore(3) 77
(Martin Keighley) *mid-div: outpcd 3f out: n.d after* 20/1

10 1½ **Pearlita** 4-10-8 0 JakeGreenall 69
(Henry Daly) *trckd ldr tl wknd 3f out* 50/1

11 1 **Roxy Belle** 6-11-0 0 GavinSheehan 74
(Mark Rimell) *nvr bttr than mid-div* 14/1

21 **12** 3½ **Water Willow**[161] 2304 4-11-1 0 AidanColeman 72
(Harry Fry) *led: rdn and hdd 2 out: wknd over 1f out* 12/1

40 **13** 25 **Bitter Virtue**[162] 2277 5-11-0 0 SamTwiston-Davies 49
(David Dennis) *trckd ldr tl 3f out* 33/1

14 55 **Blossom Again** 5-10-9 0 ThomasCheesman(5)
(Laura Young) *mid-div tl wknd 2f out* 100/1

P **Pacific Pearl (IRE)** 5-11-0 0 NicodeBoinville
(Sam Thomas) *v unruly on way to s and for 1st f of r itself: bhd: lost tch 1/2-way: t.o whn p.u 2f out* 66/1

4m 20.0s (14.30) **Going Correction** +0.975s/f (Soft)
WFA 4 from 5yo+ 5lb 15 Ran SP% 123.9
Speed ratings: **105,104,102,101,100 100,99,96,93,93 92,90,79,53,**
CSF £57.21 TOTE £5.80: £2.40, £4.10, £1.80; EX 82.80 Trifecta £421.90.
Owner A F Lousada **Bred** Niall Flynn **Trained** Upper Lambourn, Berks

FOCUS

The ground was officially soft by this stage. It paid to race prominently in this fair mares' bumper. This might need to go up, but it's not obviously strong form, rated round the fourth to the seventh for the time being.

T/Jkpt: Not won. T/Plt: £1,392.10 to a £1 stake. Pool of £139939.23 - 73.38 winning tickets. T/Qpdt: £207.70 to a £1 stake. Pool of £12183.23 - 43.40 winning tickets. **Tim Mitchell**

5287 - 5293a (Foreign Racing) - See Raceform Interactive

4605

AYR (L-H)

Friday, April 15

OFFICIAL GOING: Soft (good to soft in places; chs 7.2, hdl 7.5)

Wind: Light, half against Weather: Overcast

5294 WEST SOUND NOVICES' HURDLE (12 hdls) 2m 4f 100y

2:00 (2:00) (Class 3) 4-Y-O+ £6,498 (£1,908; £954)

Form RPR

1435 **1** **Welsh Shadow (IRE)**[30] 4715 6-11-10 140 HarrySkelton 138+
(Dan Skelton) *trckd ldr: led 7th: shkn up 2 out: kpt on wl fr last* 4/7[1]

-210 **2** 1¼ **Jetstream Jack (IRE)**[28] 4769 6-11-10 135 RichardJohnson 137+
(Gordon Elliott, Ire) *trckd ldrs: wnt 2nd 4 out: effrt after 2 out: jst over 1 l down and rdn last: kpt on: hld nr fin* 6/4[2]

U036 **3** 40 **Dubai Shen (IRE)**[20] 4902 5-11-0 0 CraigNichol 92
(Alistair Whillans) *nt fluent: led at ordinary gallop: rdn and hdd 7th: chsd wnr to 4 out: rdn and wknd fr next* 50/1[3]

5m 28.6s (328.60) 3 Ran SP% 105.6
CSF £1.76 TOTE £1.40; EX 1.80 Trifecta £1.90.
Owner Walters Plant Hire Ltd **Bred** Hugh O'Connor **Trained** Alcester, Warwicks

FOCUS

Hurdle rail out approximately 8yds and chase rail out 5yds. The opener was run over 72yds further than advertised and the actual race distance was 2m4f172yds. Following a dry morning the going was changed slightly to soft, good to soft in places. A poor turnout for a good prize and it was a tactical affair, which developed into a sprint for home. It's been given a token rating through the second.

5295 QTS H'CAP HURDLE (9 hdls) 2m

2:35 (2:35) (Class 3) (0-130,130) 4-Y-O+ £7,797 (£2,289; £1,144; £572)

Form RPR

0312 **1** **Nine Altars (IRE)**[13] 5088 7-10-11 115 CraigNichol 117+
(Ann Hamilton) *cl up: wnt 2nd 2nd: led bef 3 out: sn pushed along: hld on gamely u.p fr last* 11/2

0213 **2** ¾ **Apterix (FR)**[20] 4913 6-11-7 130 MeganCarberry(5) 131+
(Brian Ellison) *hld up in tch: smooth hdwy and ev ch bef 3 out: hit and rdn next: styd on u.p fr last: tk 2nd cl home* 11/4[1]

1200 **3** shd **Captain Brown**[105] 3426 8-11-3 121 SamTwiston-Davies 121
(James Moffatt) *hld up: stdy hdwy to trck ldrs bef 3 out: rdn and ev ch last: edgd lft run-in: kpt on: no ex and lost 2nd cl home* 18/1

661P **4** 24 **Wells De Lune (FR)**[41] 4484 5-11-7 125 (t) RichardJohnson 102
(Charlie Longsdon) *led at decent gallop: rdn and hdd bef 3 out: sn outpcd: 4th and hld whn mstke last* 4/1[2]

4-05 **5** 6 **Rockabilly Riot (IRE)**[194] 1773 6-10-1 105 HenryBrooke 74
(Martin Todhunter) *hld up: pushed along and outpcd 1/2-way: no imp bef 3 out* 25/1

53BP **6** 7 **Uriah Heep (FR)**[25] 4839 7-11-2 120 (p) RichieMcLernon 82
(R Mike Smith) *trckd ldrs: rdn after 4 out: wknd fr next* 25/1

31-5 **7** 1¼ **Rock A Doodle Doo (IRE)**[27] 4793 9-10-13 120 AdamNicol(3) 81
(Sally Hall) *j.lft in rr: detached after 3rd: nvr on terms* 14/1

F022 **P** **Craiganboy (IRE)**[13] 5106 7-11-0 118 BarryGeraghty
(S R B Crawford, Ire) *hld up in midfield: nt fluent and pushed along 5th: struggling next: btn and p.u bef 3 out* 11/2

1131 **P** **Clan Legend**[35] 4583 6-11-2 120 LucyAlexander
(N W Alexander) *chsd ldr to 2nd: lost grnd after next: struggling fr 5th: btn whn p.u bef 3 out* 9/2[3]

4m 1.7s (241.70) 9 Ran SP% 115.2
CSF £21.51 CT £249.31 TOTE £6.10: £1.60, £1.40, £4.00; EX 22.80 Trifecta £245.50.
Owner Ian Hamilton **Bred** Noel James **Trained** Great Bavington, Northumbland
■ Stewards' Enquiry : Megan Carberry two-day ban: used whip above permitted level (Apr 29-30)

FOCUS

The second race was run over 48yds further than advertised and the actual distance was 2m48yds. A decent handicap hurdle run at a strong gallop, in which the first three home pulled a long way clear of the rest. The winner's recent second could be rated to this level.

5296 ABBOTT RISK CONSULTING NOVICES' H'CAP HURDLE (12 hdls) 3m 70y

3:10 (3:10) (Class 3) (0-135,127) 4-Y-O+ £7,797 (£2,289; £1,144; £572)

Form RPR

2321 **1** **Gully's Edge**[17] 5011 6-11-6 126 (t) JamieHamilton(5) 132+
(Malcolm Jefferson) *prom: stdy hdwy 8th: rdn and outpcd bef 3 out: rallied and led next: drvn clr run-in* 9/2[2]

F214 **2** 5 **Caledonia**[20] 4911 9-11-7 122 HenryBrooke 124
(Jim Goldie) *cl up: led bef 3 out: rdn and hdd next: rallied: kpt on run-in: nt pce of wnr* 6/1[3]

531U **3** 4 **Roycano**[14] 5072 6-11-9 127 HarryBannister(3) 128
(Michael Easterby) *hld up: stdy hdwy and prom bef 3 out: effrt and rdn next: 3 l down whn hit last: sn outpcd* 7/1

221F **4** 8 **Sevenballs Of Fire (IRE)**[20] 4906 7-11-6 126 ShaneShortall(5) 118
(Iain Jardine) *hld up in tch: hit and lost grnd 7th: rallied u.p bef 3 out: no imp fr next* 9/2[2]

3125 **5** 1¼ **Timon's Tara**[13] 5094 7-10-11 112 JackQuinlan 103
(Robin Dickin) *hld up: stdy hdwy to trck ldrs bef 3 out: outpcd whn hit next: sn btn* 16/1

2141 **6** 3 **Takingrisks (IRE)**[20] 4906 7-11-7 127 RyanDay(5) 115
(Nicky Richards) *hld up: rdn after 4 out: hit next: nvr on terms* 4/1[1]

1303 **7** ¾ **Tradewinds (FR)**[27] 4794 8-11-7 127 GrantCockburn(5) 113
(Lucinda Russell) *led: hit 6th: hdd 8th: outpcd 4 out: struggling fr next* 11/1

2122 **8** 33 **Another Mattie (IRE)**[27] 4794 9-11-10 125 (t) LucyAlexander 82
(N W Alexander) *in tch on outside: lost grnd 7th: struggling fr next: eased whn no ch run-in* 20/1

6-32 **9** 3¾ **Birch Hill (IRE)**[23] 4873 6-11-11 126 AndrewTinkler 79
(Nicky Henderson) *pressed ldr: led 8th: hdd whn mstke 3 out: sn wknd: eased whn no ch run-in* 8/1

6m 24.8s (-7.00) **Going Correction** 0.0s/f (Good) 9 Ran SP% 113.2
Speed ratings (Par 107): **111,109,108,105,104 103,103,92,91**
CSF £31.20 CT £184.30 TOTE £5.20: £2.00, £2.20, £3.00; EX 30.60 Trifecta £268.20.
Owner Mrs K S Gaffney & Mrs Alix Stevenson **Bred** Mrs K S Gaffney & Mrs Alix Stevenson **Trained** Norton, N Yorks

FOCUS

The third race was run over 96yds further than advertised and the actual distance was 3m166yds.Not the strongest race for the grade, but it was competitive and they finished quite well strung out. The winner is on the upgrade.

5297 HILLHOUSE QUARRY H'CAP CHASE (LISTED RACE) (17 fncs) 2m 4f 110y

3:45 (3:45) (Class 1) 5-Y-O+

£25,627 (£9,616; £4,815; £2,398; £1,206; £603)

Form RPR

122F **1** **Definitly Red (IRE)**[31] 4700 7-11-1 137 DannyCook 148+
(Brian Ellison) *pressed ldr: led and pushed along 4 out: sn hrd pressed: kpt on gamely u.p fr last* 7/4[1]

-142 **2** 1 **Orbasa (FR)**[12] 5118 5-10-10 132 (t) SamTwiston-Davies 142
(Paul Nicholls) *trckd ldrs on outside: hdwy and ev ch whn hit 3 out: sn rdn: rallied and disp ld last: kpt on: hld nr fin* 13/2

01P4 **3** 3 **Full Shift (FR)**[29] 4733 7-10-13 135 BarryGeraghty 142
(Nicky Henderson) *in tch: pushed along bef 3 out: drvn and effrt after next: kpt on same pce run-in* 9/2[3]

03P3 **4** 1½ **Presenting Junior (IRE)**[7] 5200 9-10-10 132 HenryBrooke 138
(Martin Todhunter) *hld up: stdy hdwy after 5 out: rdn and outpcd bef 3 out: kpt on fr last: nt pce to chal* 20/1

2413 **5** 4½ **Double Shuffle (IRE)**[31] 4701 6-11-5 141 PaddyBrennan 144
(Tom George) *nt fluent on occasions: cl up: effrt and rdn bef 2 out: wknd bef last* 11/4[2]

6211 **6** 17 **Firth Of The Clyde**[26] 4818 11-11-12 148 (b) NoelFehily 133
(Malcolm Jefferson) *hld up: outpcd and rdn 10th: struggling fr next: nvr on terms* 14/1

-254 **P** **Fago (FR)**[132] 2902 8-11-11 147 (t) SeanBowen
(Paul Nicholls) *led to 4 out: sn wknd qckly: no ch whn p.u bef last* 16/1

5m 25.5s (325.50) 7 Ran SP% 111.9
CSF £13.04 TOTE £2.40: £1.40, £4.00; EX 12.70 Trifecta £49.40.
Owner P J Martin **Bred** James Keegan **Trained** Norton, N Yorks

FOCUS

The fourth race was run over 45yds further than advertised and the actual distance was 2m4f155yds. A competitive Listed handicap and smart form. The first two are rated close to their best.

5298 PORCELANOSA SCOTLAND NOVICES' LIMITED H'CAP CHASE (12 fncs) 1m 7f 112y

4:15 (4:15) (Class 3) (0-130,129) 5-Y-O+ £9,747 (£2,862; £1,431; £715)

Form RPR

102P **1** **Special Catch (IRE)**[20] 4910 9-11-8 129 JamesReveley 137+
(Keith Reveley) *pressed ldr: led 5th: hdd and pushed along 4 out: jst over 3 l down 2 out: styd on wl run-in to ld towards fin* 4/1

1122 **2** 1¼ **Monbeg River (IRE)**[34] 4606 7-11-6 127 HenryBrooke 135+
(Martin Todhunter) *trckd ldrs: led 4 out: rdn next: jst over 3 l in front 2 out: kpt on u.p run-in: hdd and no ex towards fin* 9/4[1]

2314 **3** 2 **Morning Royalty (IRE)**[33] 4634 9-11-4 125 RichardJohnson 129
(James Moffatt) *bhd and detached: rdn and hdwy 3 out: kpt on fr last: nt rch first two* 3/1[3]

2222 **4** 19 **Notnowsam**[27] 4785 5-11-4 125 (p) HarrySkelton 110
(Dan Skelton) *trckd ldrs: rdn and outpcd after 7th: rallied bef 4 out: edgd lft and wknd bef next* 11/4[2]

0223 **5** 3 ¾ **Silk Hall (UAE)**[138] 2803 11-10-7 **117**..........(vt) ColmMcCormack(3) 98
(Dianne Sayer) *led tl rdn and hdd 5th: struggling fr 7th: btn 4 out* **12/1**
3m 59.3s (-11.40) **Going Correction** -0.50s/f (Good) **5** Ran **SP% 110.1**
Speed ratings: **108,107,106,96,95**
CSF £13.65 TOTE £4.80: £1.80, £1.40; EX 14.00 Trifecta £43.10.
Owner Mike Browne & William McKeown **Bred** Thistletown Stud **Trained** Lingdale, Redcar & Cleveland

FOCUS
The fifth race was run over 30yds further than advertised and the actual distance was 1m7f142yds. A decent, open-looking novice handicap chase and they went an ordinary gallop. The first three are rated pretty much to their marks.

5299 CORAL.CO.UK MARES' H'CAP HURDLE (12 hdls) 3m 70y
4:45 (4:45) (Class 2) 4-Y-0+
£15,640 (£4,620; £2,310; £1,155; £577; £290)

Form RPR
2560 **1** **Rons Dream**[31] 4699 6-11-4 **137**.......... SeanBowen 142+
(Peter Bowen) *trckd ldrs: smooth hdwy to ld 3 out: sn hrd pressed: rdn clr fr last* **2/1**[1]
6-6P **2** 6 **Golden Sparkle (IRE)**[34] 4608 10-9-7 **119** oh5.......... MrTGreatrex(7) 119
(Ian Duncan) *nt fluent on occasions: t.k.h: hld up: hdwy to chse ldrs 3rd: hit and outpcd 4 out: rallied next: chsd (clr) wnr run-in: no imp* **40/1**
5210 **3** 2 ¾ **Girly Girl (IRE)**[29] 4734 7-10-3 **122**.......... HarrySkelton 120
(Dan Skelton) *hld up in tch: gd hdwy and chal 3 out to next: 3 l down whn hit last: sn outpcd* **9/2**[3]
1 **4** 1 **Valyssa Monterg (FR)**[109] 3320 7-11-5 **138**..........(t) PaulTownend 134
(W P Mullins, Ire) *t.k.h: hld up on ins: stdy hdwy bef 3 out: effrt and rdn bef next: sn no imp* **11/2**
6111 **5** 18 **W Six Times**[34] 4608 10-9-11 **119** oh4..........(p) CallumWhillans(3) 98
(Alistair Whillans) *led to 4 out: w ldr tl rdn and wknd appr next* **12/1**
2PP2 **6** 4 ½ **Run Ructions Run (IRE)**[20] 4905 7-10-13 **132**..........(b) JamesReveley 106
(Tim Easterby) *pressed ldr: led 4 out: hdd whn hit next: sn wknd* **4/1**[2]
1200 **7** 19 **Desert Queen**[31] 4699 8-11-12 **145**..........(t) NoelFehily 99
(Harry Fry) *t.k.h: hld up: rdn and outpcd whn hit 3 out: sn struggling* **5/1**
6m 25.2s (-6.60) **Going Correction** 0.0s/f (Good) **7** Ran **SP% 113.7**
Speed ratings (Par 109): **111,109,108,107,101 100,93**
CSF £53.90 CT £327.40 TOTE £3.00: £2.00, £6.60; EX 62.80 Trifecta £790.30.
Owner Mrs Tania Stepney **Bred** Peter E Clinton **Trained** Little Newcastle, Pembrokes

FOCUS
The sixth race run over 96yds further than advertised and the actual distance was 3m166yds. A good mares' handicap and a tough winner, who's rated back to the level of her Cheltenham second.

5300 SEKO LOGISTICS SCOTLAND H'CAP HURDLE (12 hdls) 3m 70y
5:15 (5:19) (Class 3) (0-125,120) 4-Y-0+ **£7,797** (£2,289; £1,144; £572)

Form RPR
5661 **1** **Arctic Court (IRE)**[86] 3684 12-11-2 **110**.......... SeanBowen 116+
(Jim Goldie) *hld up: hdwy after 4 out: lft 5 l 2nd and swvd to avoid faller next: led 2 out: clr last: rdn out* **14/1**
5621 **2** 4 ½ **Some Are Lucky (IRE)**[25] 4843 5-11-5 **120**.......... MrJJSlevin(7) 122
(Tom George) *nt fluent on occasions: midfield: hdwy and already led whn lft 5 l clr 3 out: hdd next: kpt on same pce fr last* **4/1**[2]
FP06 **3** 3 **Victor Hewgo**[27] 4794 11-11-7 **115**..........(b[1]) JamesReveley 112
(Keith Reveley) *prom: reminders 8th: outpcd next: rallied after 2 out: plugged on fr last: nt rch first two* **11/1**
4BP0 **4** 5 **Aigle De La See (FR)**[55] 4241 6-11-12 **120**.......... DarylJacob 114
(Nicky Henderson) *nt fluent: chsd ldrs: hit 4 out: lft disputing 3rd next: sn outpcd: no imp fr 2 out* **8/1**
3311 **5** 1 ½ **Ceann Sibheal (IRE)**[23] 4877 7-11-9 **117**..........(p) RichardJohnson 110
(Warren Greatrex) *led at decent gallop: already hdd whn lft disputing 3rd pl 3 out: rallied: wknd fr last* **3/1**[1]
6242 **6** 14 **Quel Elite (FR)**[55] 4246 12-11-8 **116**.......... HenryBrooke 94
(James Moffatt) *hld up: outpcd 1/2-way: short-lived effrt after 4 out: struggling fr next* **14/1**
4013 **7** 9 **Bertalus (IRE)**[34] 4607 7-11-7 **115**.......... LucyAlexander 84
(N W Alexander) *midfield: hit 5th: drvn and outpcd after next: struggling fr 4 out* **25/1**
/03- **P** **Wicklow Gold (FR)**[520] 2439 8-11-6 **119**.......... StephenMulqueen(5)
(N W Alexander) *sn towards rr: struggling after 3rd: lost tch and p.u after 6th* **40/1**
4321 **F** **General Mahler (IRE)**[19] 4941 6-11-12 **120**.......... RichieMcLernon
(Brian Ellison) *hld up: stdy hdwy 1/2-way: effrt and jst over 2 l 2nd whn fell 3 out* **9/2**[3]
0636 **P** **I Just Know (IRE)**[64] 4066 6-11-0 **108**.......... DannyCook
(Sue Smith) *chsd wnr to after 4 out: sn rdn and outpcd: wknd bef next: p.u bef 2 out* **5/1**
6m 28.0s (-3.80) **Going Correction** 0.0s/f (Good) **10** Ran **SP% 118.9**
Speed ratings (Par 107): **106,104,103,101,101 96,93, ,**
CSF £71.94 CT £657.21 TOTE £10.80: £3.10, £1.70, £3.70; EX 82.40 Trifecta £1121.30.
Owner Mr & Mrs Raymond Anderson Green **Bred** Paul Doyle **Trained** Uplawmoor, E Renfrews

FOCUS
The finale was run over 96yds further than advertised and the actual distance was 3m166yds. This wasn't the strongest of staying handicaps for the grade, but it was well contested. The winner was back to the level of his run in this race last year.
T/Jkpt: Not won. T/Plt: £60.00 to a £1 stake. Pool: £98,223.20 - 1,194.03 winning tickets. T/Qpdt: £23.70 to a £1 stake. Pool: £8,837.23 - 275.50 winning tickets. **Richard Young**

5063 FONTWELL (L-H)
Friday, April 15

OFFICIAL GOING: Good to soft (soft in places) changing to soft after race 1 (1.35) changing to heavy after race 3 (2.45)
Wind: breezy Weather: heavy rain; 11 degrees

5301 CHARLIE MILLINGTON 80 NOT OUT H'CAP HURDLE (9 hdls) 2m 1f 145y
1:35 (1:40) (Class 4) (0-120,120) 4-Y-0+ **£3,898** (£1,144; £572; £286)

Form RPR
5064 **1** **Red Devil Star (IRE)**[6] 5225 6-11-9 **117**..........(t) MichealNolan 123+
(Suzy Smith) *mde nrly all: drew 4 l clr home turn: in command after tl idled and rdn out fnl 75yds* **10/3**[2]
26-1 **2** 3 ¼ **Planetoid (IRE)**[14] 4411 8-11-10 **118**..........(b) JamieMoore 120
(Jim Best) *settled towards rr: effrt 3 out: 5 l 3rd home turn: sn u.p and nvr clsng after: disputing 2nd whn flattened last: plugged on* **11/2**[3]
53B1 **3** nk **Sartorial Elegance**[14] 5065 5-11-3 **116**..........(b) PaulO'Brien(5) 116
(Colin Tizzard) *a 2nd or 3rd: rdn bef 6th and nt travelling wl enough after: chsd wnr but a drvn and at least 4 l bhd fr bef 2 out which he hit tl last: lost 2nd nr fin* **6/4**[1]
-2P6 **4** 32 **Space Walker (IRE)**[71] 3956 5-11-10 **118**..........(b) DavidBass 86
(Ben Pauling) *midfield: hit 5th: effrt 3 out: 6 l 4th and drvn home turn: fdd bef 2 out* **7/1**
5 33 **Polished Rock (IRE)**[547] 1925 6-11-12 **120**.......... LeightonAspell 55
(Alison Batchelor) *towards rr but in tch tl rdn 3 out: dropped out rapidly bef next: sn t.o: eased flat* **66/1**
-206 **6** 67 **Needless Shouting (IRE)**[27] 4781 5-11-6 **114**..........(v) AndrewThornton
(Mick Channon) *led briefly and j.v.slowly 2nd: v awkward 3rd: handy tl dropped bk last after 6th: t.o next: fin a f bhd* **8/1**
020F **P** **Right Step**[29] 4745 9-10-13 **107**..........(t) JoshuaMoore
(Pat Phelan) *in tch tl drvn 5th: nt travelling after: t.o 3 out: p.u next* **14/1**
4m 42.7s (8.40) **Going Correction** +0.625s/f (Soft)
WFA 4 from 5yo+ 5lb **7** Ran **SP% 110.2**
Speed ratings (Par 105): **106,104,104,90,75 45,**
CSF £20.21 CT £34.56 TOTE £4.70: £2.80, £2.20; EX 23.40 Trifecta £54.30.
Owner Mrs V Palmer **Bred** Clare Kehoe & Bill Byrne **Trained** Lewes, E Sussex

FOCUS
Fences outer, Hurdles inner and all bends on the inner line. 4mm of overnight rain and a soggy lead up to racing saw the ground deteriorate markedly. This was a modest handicap, run at an average gallop. The winner is rated back to the level of his Sandown fall.

5302 DO IT THE RIVERVALE WAY NOVICES' CHASE (19 fncs) 3m 1f 106y
2:10 (2:15) (Class 4) 5-Y-0+ **£5,049** (£1,836)

Form RPR
F-1P **1** **Saint Roque (FR)**[77] 3838 10-11-4 139..........(t) ConorO'Farrell 141+
(Paul Nicholls) *hld up in last pair: wnt 2nd at 13th: lft w big ld 3 out: unchal* **5/4**[2]
0P **2** 27 **Restless Rebel**[11] 5137 7-10-12 0.......... DavidBass 115
(Polly Gundry) *last tl wnt 2nd 10th tl 13th: outpcd next: lft poor 2nd 3 out: plodded on: j.rt last* **33/1**
1-23 **U** **Lessons In Milan (IRE)**[24] 4864 8-10-12 134.......... PeterCarberry 130
(Nicky Henderson) *2nd tl lft in ld 9th: pushed along and jst over one l ahd whn blnd and uns rdr 3 out* **6/5**[1]
206 **P** **Don'tdropmein (IRE)**[140] 2763 6-10-12 108.......... MarkQuinlan
(Neil Mulholland) *j.lft and mstkes: blnd 4th and rdr lost iron briefly: led tl nrly fell 9th: struggling in last after: t.o 13th: p.u 15th* **13/2**[3]
7m 17.9s (16.80) **Going Correction** +0.925s/f (Soft) **4** Ran **SP% 106.2**
Speed ratings: **110,101, ,**
CSF £16.68 TOTE £1.80; EX 18.70 Trifecta £19.30.
Owner Ian J Fogg **Bred** Mme Genevieve Mongin **Trained** Ditcheat, Somerset

FOCUS
This novice chase saw plenty of mistakes and it was an unsatisfactory affair. It's been given a token rating through the winner.

5303 MILES COMMERCIAL NOVICES' HURDLE (11 hdls) 2m 5f 139y
2:45 (2:50) (Class 4) 4-Y-0+ **£3,898** (£1,144; £572; £286)

Form RPR
F03 **1** **Red Hanrahan (IRE)**[48] 4351 5-11-0 0..........(t) ConorO'Farrell 131+
(Paul Nicholls) *2nd tl led after 3rd: drew clr bef 2 out: 6 l ahd last and in full command: veered violently rt whn drvn over 100yds out: fnlly stened by rails and a gng to hold on* **5/2**[2]
1402 **2** 7 **Clondaw Cian (IRE)**[32] 4668 6-11-6 133.......... TomO'Brien 128
(Suzy Smith) *chsd ldrs: wnt 2nd bef 8th: 2 l 2nd and rdn and struggling to get on terms home turn: wl hld after but lft clsr by antics of wnr* **4/11**[1]
3 38 **Mad Moll (IRE)**[446] 8-10-2 0.......... LizzieKelly(5) 77
(Daniel Steele) *chsd ldrs: mstke 3rd: brief effrt 3 out: 12 l 3rd home turn: dropped out rapidly: remote 3rd* **20/1**
6PP5 **4** 22 **Sweet'N'Chic (IRE)**[27] 4777 6-10-7 0.......... AndrewGlassonbury 55
(Richard Rowe) *prom tl drvn and wknd bef 3 out: t.o next: lft v remote 4th nr fin* **40/1**
-0PP **5** 3 ½ **Leith Hill (IRE)**[185] 1895 6-11-0 0..........[1] TomCannon 59
(Laura Mongan) *led tl after 3rd: pressed wnr tl rdn bef 8th: slowed rapidly: bdly t.o next: veered bdly rt after last: nrly stopped and lost 4th* **100/1**
P0P **6** 9 **Kent Ragstone (USA)**[97] 3525 7-11-0 0..........[1] BrendanPowell 50
(Daniel Steele) *chsd ldrs: rdn and outpcd 3 out: t.o* **40/1**
0-4P **7** 8 **Maigh Dara (IRE)**[12] 5115 7-11-0 0.......... MarcGoldstein 42
(Lydia Richards) *bhd: rdn after 7th: bdly t.o fr 3 out* **14/1**
0 **P** **Tee It Up Tommo (IRE)**[100] 3083 7-10-9 0..........(t) FreddieMitchell(5)
(Daniel Steele) *a last: rdn 6th: reluctant and sn t.o: p.u after 7th* **33/1**
-5PP **F** **Evening Stanley (IRE)**[27] 4798 6-11-0 0.......... LeightonAspell
(Oliver Sherwood) *bhd: rdn 7th: last and toiling whn fell next* **8/1**[3]
6m 2.4s (19.90) **Going Correction** +1.20s/f (Heav) **9** Ran **SP% 133.2**
Speed ratings (Par 105): **111,108,94,86,85 82,79, ,**
CSF £4.51 TOTE £3.90: £1.10, £1.02, £5.50; EX 5.20 Trifecta £38.40.
Owner Mr And Mrs J D Cotton **Bred** Cathal Ennis **Trained** Ditcheat, Somerset

FOCUS
This uncompetitive novice event was predictably dominated by the two clear market leaders. The form could be 5lb out either way.

5304 NEIL MADGWICK MEMORIAL H'CAP CHASE (16 fncs) 2m 5f 31y
3:20 (3:27) (Class 3) (0-140,136) 5-Y-0+ **£6,388** (£1,928; £993; £526)

Form RPR
1-43 **1** **Dont Do Mondays (IRE)**[152] 2517 9-11-0 **124**..........(p) TomCannon 136+
(David Bridgwater) *towards rr: mstke 6th: rdn next: effrt 11th: led 13th: steadily drew clr fr next: 10 l ahd last: hrd drvn fnl 100yds: tired and all out but in n.d of being ct* **13/2**
FP44 **2** 13 **Howlongisafoot (IRE)**[24] 4858 7-11-7 **136**..........(p) HarryCobden(5) 132
(Paul Nicholls) *settled trcking ldrs: wnt 2nd at 13th: hrd drvn and chsd wnr after: in vain pursuit fr 2 out* **6/1**
1232 **3** ½ **Quite By Chance**[18] 4964 7-11-7 **136**.......... PaulO'Brien(5) 133
(Colin Tizzard) *trckd ldrs: 3rd and drvn 13th: sn last and wl hld: plugged on gamely flat to snatch modest 3rd and nrly ct 2nd* **9/2**[3]
1152 **4** ½ **As De Fer (FR)**[5] 5238 10-10-8 **123**..........(tp) DavidNoonan(5) 117
(Anthony Honeyball) *nt fluent 2nd: slt ld tl 3rd: w ldr tl slt advantage 8th tl 13th: sn hrd drvn: wknd next: lost mod 3rd nr fin* **11/4**[1]
/110 **P** **Dark Lover (GER)**[28] 4768 11-10-8 **123**..........(p) MissPFuller(7)
(Jamie Snowden) *detached in last: slow 5th: struggling 10th: sn t.o: p.u 3 out* **9/1**

0P1P **P** **Leo Luna**[20] 4912 7-11-8 **132**..............................(tp) JamieMoore
(Gary Moore) *mde most 4th tl 8th: ev ch tl mstke 11th and hrd drvn: dropped out tamely: t.o and p.u 13th* **3/1**[2]

6m 2.1s (19.10) **Going Correction** +1.15s/f (Heav) **6** Ran SP% **107.5**
Speed ratings: **109,104,103,103,**
CSF £38.67 TOTE £8.50: £3.50, £2.50; EX 36.40 Trifecta £203.30.
Owner F W K Griffin **Bred** Niall Radford **Trained** Icomb, Gloucs

FOCUS
The going was downgraded to heavy after the novice hurdle. This was run at a sound gallop and it therefore proved a thorough test. The winner is rated back to the level of his Stratford win.

5305 SALISBURY HARDWOOD FLOORING LTD H'CAP HURDLE (DIV I) (11 hdls) 2m 5f 139y
3:55 (4:00) (Class 5) (0-100,100) 4-Y-0+ **£2,924** (£858; £429; £214)

Form RPR
-664 **1** **Snippetydoodah**[19] 4936 8-10-9 **83**..............................(t[1]) TomO'Brien 90+
(Michael Roberts) *ldng pair: led fr 6th: 6 l clr 8th: rdn and pressed between last two: hit last: plugged on gamely u.p flat: all out* **16/1**

UUU3 **2** 3/4 **Highbury High (IRE)**[14] 5067 9-11-3 **91**..............................(tp) DenisO'Regan 98
(Neil Mulholland) *hld up in last pair tl stdy prog fr 7th: wnt 2nd 3 out: patiently rdn tl pushed along to chal between last two: ev ch whn nt fluent last: plodded on but a jst hld after* **5/1**[2]

043 **3** 44 **Leg Lock Luke (IRE)**[18] 4963 6-11-7 **100**.............................. HarryCobden(5) 67
(Colin Tizzard) *pressed ldrs tl wnt 2nd after 7th: 3rd and rdn 3 out: floundering bef next: t.o and v tired whn hung bdly rt flat* **5/4**[1]

350P **4** 28 **Minority Interest**[128] 2316 7-9-10 **77**..............................(b) MrJPearce(7) 11
(Daniel O'Brien) *towards rr: t.o fr 8th: plodded to completion* **22/1**

0335 **P** **Fifi L'Amour (IRE)**[19] 4936 10-10-0 **74** oh1.............................. BrendanPowell
(Linda Jewell) *j.rt: mde most tl 6th: rdn and dropped out rapidly next: t.o and p.u after 3 out* **16/1**

P260 **P** **Izzy Piccolina (IRE)**[76] 3868 8-11-8 **96**.............................. MarkGrant
(Geoffrey Deacon) *nt travelling in rr: rdn 6th: t.o and p.u after next* **50/1**

4536 **P** **Sir Hubert**[46] 4411 6-11-7 **95**.............................. LeightonAspell
(Richard Rowe) *dropped to rr after 5th: blnd next and reminders: t.o and p.u after 7th* **10/1**

0003 **P** **Song Of The Night (IRE)**[20] 4919 5-11-1 **89**..............................(tp) KielanWoods
(Charlie Longsdon) *midfield: rdn and struggling after 7th: t.o and p.u after 3 out* **8/1**[3]

P **Show's Over (IRE)**[231] 1397 5-11-0 **93**.............................. AlanJohns(5)
(Tim Vaughan) *t.k.h chsng ldrs: chalng for 2nd whn blnd and nrly fell 8th: lost all ch: t.o and p.u 2 out* **5/1**[2]

6m 11.8s (29.30) **Going Correction** +1.40s/f (Heav) **9** Ran SP% **116.1**
Speed ratings (Par 103): **102,101,85,75, , , ,**
CSF £95.17 CT £175.46 TOTE £11.30: £2.70, £1.70, £1.50; EX 44.50 Trifecta £104.90.
Owner Mike Roberts **Bred** E R Hanbury **Trained** Bodle Street Green, E Sussex

FOCUS
A very weak handicap in which most failed to handle the going. The form should be taken with a pinch of salt and it isn't an easy race to put a figure on.

5306 SALISBURY HARDWOOD FLOORING LTD H'CAP HURDLE (DIV II) (11 hdls) 2m 5f 139y
4:25 (4:31) (Class 5) (0-100,100) 4-Y-0+ **£2,995** (£930; £500)

Form RPR
0-P0 **1** **Frank N Fair**[30] 4709 8-9-9 **76**.............................. FrankiePenford(7) 86+
(Zoe Davison) *bhd: clsd qckly fr 8th: led 2 out as others floundered bdly: sn drew wl clr: tired whn wnt rt flat and rdr dropped reins 100yds out* **25/1**

42P6 **2** 54 **Surf In September (IRE)**[155] 2454 7-10-12 **93**........ BenFfrenchDavis(7) 50
(Dominic Ffrench Davis) *chsd ldrs: chal ldng pair after 7th: blnd 3 out: ev ch tl drvn and wknd bef next: scrapping for remote 2nd and hrd drvn after: fin v tired* **6/1**

P0-0 **3** 3/4 **Upham Running (IRE)**[141] 2730 8-10-10 **91**....... WilliamFeatherstone(7) 44
(Kate Buckett) *sn prom: led 7th: rdn and hdd bef 2 out: sn v tired: continued w ev ch of poor 2nd tl hit last and stmbld: lost duel for 2nd fnl 50yds* **11/2**

-P46 **P** **Baldadash (IRE)**[42] 4455 11-11-12 **100**..............................(p) JamesDavies
(Jose Santos) *nvr travelling: pushed along in rr after 3rd: racing awkwardly after: t.o and p.u after 3 out* **4/1**[3]

1P43 **P** **Hi Bronco**[120] 3125 9-10-0 **74**..............................(p) IanPopham
(John Ryall) *lost pl and rdn and mstke 4th: nvr travelling after: t.o and p.u after 7th* **3/1**[2]

4002 **P** **Ashkoun (FR)**[57] 4200 5-11-3 **96**..............................(t) AlanJohns(5)
(Tim Vaughan) *taken down early: led tl 7th: slowed qckly and t.o next: p.u after 3 out* **5/2**[1]

S042 **P** **Walk Of Gleams**[152] 2520 7-10-9 **83**.............................. AndrewThornton
(Anna Newton-Smith) *racd wd: prom: pushed along after 7th: ev ch tl rdn and fdd rapidly wl bef 2 out: v tired and t.o last whn p.u last* **16/1**

6m 12.3s (29.80) **Going Correction** +1.40s/f (Heav) **7** Ran SP% **113.0**
Speed ratings (Par 103): **101,81,81, , ,**
CSF £157.67 CT £955.67 TOTE £34.10: £8.70, £3.50; EX 189.90.
Owner The Secret Circle Racing Club **Bred** Mrs Janet M Sexton **Trained** Hammerwood, E Sussex
■ Frankie Penford's first winner.

FOCUS
The ground again played a big part in this second division of the weak 2m5f handicap as only three completed. The winner could be rated at least 10lb higher.

5307 RIVERVALE APPROVED USED VEHICLES H'CAP CHASE (13 fncs) 2m 1f 96y
5:00 (5:01) (Class 5) (0-100,100) 5-Y-0+ **£3,606** (£1,311)

Form RPR
0311 **1** **Bertenbar**[14] 5068 12-11-12 **100**.............................. AndrewThornton 110+
(Lawney Hill) *led after 1st: j. awkwardly next two: hit 6th: clumsy 9th: drew clr bef 3 out: v awkward next whn 10 l ahd: plugged on gallantly to hold dwindling advantage flat* **3/1**[3]

30-2 **2** 2 1/4 **Withy Mills**[27] 4778 11-10-6 **80**..............................(tp) JamesBest 84
(Kevin Bishop) *chsd ldrs: cajoled along 6th and nt really travelling: rdn after next: wnt 2nd bef 3 out: styd on to make 10 l fr last but nvr really looked like catching wnr* **9/4**[1]

00P0 **P** **Nouailhas**[14] 5067 10-10-2 **76**..............................(v) MattieBatchelor
(Daniel O'Brien) *a 3rd: blnd 3rd: nvr travelling: t.o and p.u 8th* **25/1**

163 **P** **Mr Bachster (IRE)**[35] 4587 11-11-10 **98**..............................(p) JamieMoore
(Kerry Lee) *led tl after 1st: pressed wnr tl v slow 8th and next: mstke and u.p 10th: hrd rdn and v tired tired 3 out: poor 3rd whn p.u next* **11/4**[2]

4F22 **P** **Treacy Hotels Boy (IRE)**[148] 2601 9-11-7 **95**.............................. TomO'Brien
(Paul Henderson) *towards rr: rdn after 7th: brief effrt 9th: floundering bef 3 out: v tired 3rd whn p.u last* **7/2**

5m 8.1s (33.40) **Going Correction** +2.025s/f (Heav) **5** Ran SP% **108.5**
Speed ratings: **102,100, , ,**
CSF £10.08 TOTE £3.40: £1.70, £1.20; EX 8.60 Trifecta £8.60.
Owner Mrs C A Wyatt **Bred** T J Wyatt **Trained** Aston Rowant, Oxon

FOCUS
This moderate handicap was run at a fair gallop. The winner rates better than the bare result.

5308 SIS LIVE STANDARD OPEN NATIONAL HUNT FLAT RACE 1m 5f 143y
5:30 (5:32) (Class 6) 4-6-Y-0 **£1,559** (£457; £228; £114)

Form RPR
0 **1** **Knightly Pleasure**[195] 1758 5-10-11 0.............................. JoshuaMoore 103+
(Gary Moore) *mde all: rdn over 2f out: in command after and styd on stoutly in gruelling conditions* **5/1**[3]

2 9 **Hahnenkam (IRE)**[502] 6-11-4 0.............................. ConorO'Farrell 98
(Seamus Durack) *narrow: t.k.h and pressed ldrs: rdn to go 2nd over 2f out: a wl hld by wnr after* **6/4**[1]

5 **3** 3 **Lillington (IRE)**[14] 5069 4-10-7 0.............................. PaulO'Brien(5) 88
(Colin Tizzard) *wnt 2nd at 1/2-way tl drvn over 2f out: one pce and making no imp after* **2/1**[2]

4 7 **Cassivellaunus (IRE)** 4-10-7 0.............................. FreddieMitchell(5) 79
(Daniel Steele) *small: pressed wnr tl 1/2-way: lost pl 5f out: plodded on in poor 4th fnl 3f* **25/1**

5 7 **Double Storm** 6-10-11 0.............................. PeterCarberry 69
(John Gallagher) *wl-mde: in tch: rdn 1/2-way: lost tch 4f out: t.o* **10/1**

6 21 **Hab Sab (IRE)** 4-10-12 0.............................. TomCannon 43
(Linda Jewell) *compact: chsd ldrs tl rdn 1/2-way: t.o fnl 5f* **33/1**

7 45 **Keepyourheadup** 5-10-13 0.............................. ConorRing(5)
(Helen Nelmes) *v small: pushed along in last: nt travelling: t.o fnl 6f* **16/1**

3m 39.4s (8.30) **7** Ran SP% **111.8**
CSF £12.34 TOTE £7.90: £3.60, £1.20; EX 16.20 Trifecta £35.70.
Owner The Knights Of Pleasure **Bred** Bryan Fry **Trained** Lower Beeding, W Sussex

FOCUS
This was hit by non-runners. They went steadily yet the form doesn't look bad, the third giving some sort of guide.
T/Plt: £479.80 to a £1 stake. Pool: £78,882.93 - 120 winning tickets. T/Qpdt: £53.90 to a £1 stake. Pool: £7,872.21 - 108.02 winning tickets. **Iain Mackenzie**

5015 SOUTHWELL (L-H)
Friday, April 15

OFFICIAL GOING: Good to soft changing to soft after race 1 (4.40)
Wind: almost nil Weather: raining

5309 HAMPSONS RECOVERY TO THE RESCUE H'CAP CHASE (16 fncs) 2m 4f 62y
4:40 (4:40) (Class 4) (0-105,108) 5-Y-0+ **£3,898** (£1,144; £572; £286)

Form RPR
-P21 **1** **Attimo (GER)**[6] 5234 7-12-2 **108** 7ex..............................(t) JonathanEngland 117+
(Sam Drake) *mde all: j.rt at times: jnd whn hit 2 out: fnd ex clsng stages* **7/4**[1]

6145 **2** 1 **Mondo Cane (IRE)**[17] 5017 9-11-12 **104**..............................(p) AdamPogson 111
(Charles Pogson) *swvd bdly rt s: t.k.h: jnd ldrs 9th: 2nd 4 out: upsides 2 out: hit last: no ex clsng stages* **9/2**[3]

/253 **3** 10 **Sacre Malta (FR)**[11] 5138 10-10-12 **97**..............................(p) ConorWalsh(7) 96
(Dominic Ffrench Davis) *in rr: hit 8th: chsd ldrs next: 3rd appr 3 out: one pce whn hit 3 out and 2 out: hung rt run-in* **14/1**

3043 **4** 10 **Odds On Dan (IRE)**[50] 4329 10-9-10 **79** oh7 ow1..........(t) DeanPratt(5) 68
(Lucinda Egerton) *hmpd s: in rr: hdwy to chse ldrs 9th: wknd appr 3 out* **22/1**

PP53 **5** 5 **Rock Of Ages**[35] 4588 7-10-2 **87**..............................(tp) MrJNixon(7) 72
(Steve Flook) *chsd ldrs: lost pl bef 3 out* **33/1**

-P2F **P** **That's The Deal (IRE)**[17] 5015 12-9-13 **80**.............................. BenPoste(3)
(John Cornwall) *chsd ldrs: lost pl and reminders next: sn bhd: t.o whn p.u bef 11th* **25/1**

P2P4 **P** **Midnight Charmer**[28] 4776 10-10-12 **90**..............................(t) JamesBanks
(Emma Baker) *w wnr: drvn 12th: lost pl bef 2 out: sn bhd: t.o whn p.u bef last* **16/1**

4211 **P** **Riddlestown (IRE)**[17] 5020 9-11-5 **97**..............................(b) AidanColeman
(Caroline Fryer) *chsd ldrs: lost pl 12th: sn bhd: t.o whn p.u bef 3 out* **15/8**[2]

5m 45.0s (28.00) **Going Correction** +1.50s/f (Heav) **8** Ran SP% **113.0**
Speed ratings: **104,103,99,95,93 , , ,**
CSF £9.99 CT £79.59 TOTE £2.50: £1.10, £1.10, £3.50; EX 11.20 Trifecta £59.10.
Owner Mrs J Drake **Bred** Gestut Hof Ittlingen **Trained** Guiseley, West Yorkshire

FOCUS
After some rain the going was changed to good to soft. The fences and hurdles were on the outside rail and the bend into the home straight was 4 yards outside its correct line. This increased the distance of races by around 24 yards, except for race 3 which was run over 36 yards further than advertised. There was a messy start in this minor handicap and the pace was steady, but the market leader battled well to score and the form looks solid enough for the grade. Starightforward form, the first three pretty much to their marks.

5310 HAPPY BIRTHDAY MARK COMEDIAN GLASSETT H'CAP CHASE (13 fncs) 1m 7f 153y
5:10 (5:10) (Class 4) (0-105,104) 5-Y-0+ **£3,898** (£1,144; £572; £286)

Form RPR
243P **1** **Trapper Peak (IRE)**[19] 4932 7-11-10 **102**..............................(b) RhysFlint 109+
(Alexandra Dunn) *trckd ldrs: pushed along 9th: 2nd appr 3 out: led between last 2: drvn out* **9/2**

51P1 **2** 2 1/4 **Chankillo**[33] 4642 7-11-12 **104**..............................(p) JamesBanks 107
(Sarah-Jayne Davies) *chsd ldrs: pushed along after 6th: led bef 3 out: hdd between last 2: over 1 l down last: kpt on same pce* **4/1**[3]

P241 **3** 1/2 **Edlomond (IRE)**[17] 5016 10-11-5 **102**..............................(t) JakeHodson(5) 104
(Bill Turner) *chsd ldrs: outpcd 10th: 3rd next: hit 2 out: kpt on same pce run-in* **7/2**[2]

1F36 **4** 3 3/4 **Bollin Line**[19] 4938 9-10-12 **95**.............................. DeanPratt(5) 95
(Lucinda Egerton) *j.rt in last: hdwy to chse ldrs 3 out: one pce* **4/1**[3]

63P3 **5** 1 3/4 **The Jugopolist (IRE)**[18] 4977 9-9-11 **78** oh20..................(b) BenPoste(3) 74
(John Cornwall) *led: hdd bef 3 out: one pce* **100/1**

1053 **P** **Stormbay Bomber (IRE)**[12] 5123 7-11-6 **101**.............................. JohnKington(3)
(Patrick Holmes) *w ldr: drvn 9th: lost pl next: sn bhd: p.u bef 3 out* **11/4**[1]

4m 27.8s (25.80) **Going Correction** +1.50s/f (Heav) **6** Ran SP% **108.1**
Speed ratings: **95,93,93,91,90**
CSF £20.91 TOTE £5.20: £2.60, £1.90; EX 22.30 Trifecta £82.30.

Owner David Gilbert **Bred** M Kelly **Trained** West Buckland, Somerset
FOCUS
Race distance increased by 24 yards. The going was changed to soft. They went a steady pace and there was not much separating the first five in this minor handicap. The winner is rated in line with his best chase figures.

5311 ADVERTISER MEDIA GROUP NOVICES' CHASE (19 fncs) 2m 7f 209y
5:40 (5:40) (Class 4) 5-Y-0+ £3,994 (£1,240; £667)

Form RPR
153P 1 **Capard King (IRE)**[29] 4735 7-11-5 136 AidanColeman 147+
(Jonjo O'Neill) *sat 3rd: trckd ldng pair 11th: 2nd 4 out: led 2 out: clr bef last: easily* 9/4[3]
1UFP 2 22 **Warrantor (IRE)**[31] 4700 7-11-5 138 (t) GavinSheehan 132
(Warren Greatrex) *w ldr: led after 2nd: reminders 13th: drvn 3 out: hdd next: eased whn wl btn last 100yds* 6/4[1]
25P1 3 25 **Spirit Of Shankly**[29] 4744 8-11-2 130 GrahamWatters(3) 99
(Charlie Longsdon) *j.rt: led tl after 2nd: reminders 7th: drvn 14th: lost pl bef 3 out: sn bhd: t.o* 7/4[2]
60/P P **Charming Grace (IRE)**[80] 3795 10-10-2 87 ow2 NathanMoscrop(5)
(Mark Campion) *hopelessly detached in last: t.o 3rd: blnd 8th: p.u bef next* 100/1
6m 55.1s (32.10) **Going Correction** +1.50s/f (Heav) 4 Ran SP% 108.1
Speed ratings: **106,98,90,**
CSF £6.16 TOTE £2.70; EX 5.60 Trifecta £9.40.
Owner J B Gilruth & G & P Barker Ltd **Bred** Mrs Annemarie Byrnes **Trained** Cheltenham, Gloucs
FOCUS
Race distance increased by 36 yards. There were not many runners but this was a fairly useful novice chase and the winner scored in good style from off the strong pace. The form could be 5lb out either way.

5312 NEWARKFESTIVAL.CO.UK OPEN HUNTERS' CHASE (16 fncs) 2m 4f 62y
6:10 (6:10) (Class 6) 5-Y-0+ £1,247 (£387; £193; £96)

Form RPR
1FPP 1 **Night Alliance (IRE)**[8] 5178 11-11-9 119 (bt) MrLeoMahon(7) 130+
(P R M Philips) *led tl after 1st: chsd clr ldr: upsides 7th: led bef 10th: hdd and hit 11th: led bef 4 out: sn wl clr: eased clsng stages* 8/1[3]
-001 2 22 **Klepht (IRE)**[27] 11-11-9 129 (t) MrDHolmes(7) 104
(D Holmes) *t.k.h: led after 1st: hit 4th: clr to 6th: hdd bef 10th: led and mstke 11th: hdd bef 4 out: sn btn* 7/4[2]
-PPP 3 14 **Chartreux (FR)**[33] 4651 11-11-9 114 (t) MissCVHart(3) 86
(Mrs Julie Marles) *sn bhd: sme hdwy 7th: outpcd 10th: mstke next: tk distant 3rd bef 3 out* 20/1
214/ 4 15 **Callhimwhatyouwant (IRE)**[13] 11-11-5 102 MissSLKlug(7) 71
(Miss S L Klug) *sn bhd: sme hdwy 7th: outpcd 10th: distant 3rd sn after 4 out: wknd next* 33/1
-140 P **Mr Mercurial (IRE)**[28] 4768 8-12-3 118 (t) MrPGerety(3)
(Mrs Sheila Crow) *j.lft: wnt modest 3rd 3rd: drvn 10th: sn outpcd: lost pl sn after 4 out: sn wl bhd: last whn p.u bef next* 4/5[1]
5m 56.0s (39.00) **Going Correction** +1.50s/f (Heav) 5 Ran SP% 110.7
Speed ratings: **82,73,67,61,**
CSF £23.19 TOTE £8.70: £3.30, £1.50; EX 21.10 Trifecta £94.80.
Owner P R M Philips **Bred** Mrs Mary Doyle And Peter Sherry **Trained** Claines, Worcestershire
FOCUS
Race distance increased by 24 yards. They finished well strung out in this hunters' chase and the odds-on favourite was disappointing. The form is a little suspect but the winner was a 139 chaser at his best.

5313 ALEA EAST MIDLANDS PREMIER ENTERTAINMENT VENUE H'CAP HURDLE (9 hdls) 1m 7f 153y
6:40 (6:40) (Class 4) (0-105,105) 4-Y-0+ £4,223 (£1,240; £620; £310)

Form RPR
603 1 **Lord Of The Island (IRE)**[34] 4613 8-11-12 105 JamesBanks 112+
(Sally Randell) *w ldrs: 2nd 3rd: led appr 2 out: forged clr between last 2: eased clsng stages* 9/1
3400 2 9 **Baraboy (IRE)**[26] 4819 6-11-0 100 LorcanMurtagh(7) 98
(Barry Murtagh) *in rr: hdwy 3 out: 4th 2 out: 3rd between last 2: kpt on same pce to take modest 2nd last 75yds* 12/1
5664 3 2¼ **Aza Run (IRE)**[27] 4797 6-10-10 89 WillKennedy 85
(Shaun Harris) *in rr: chsd ldrs 4th: 3rd 2 out: kpt on one pce* 13/2[3]
0040 4 hd **Whitstable Native**[150] 2559 8-10-7 86 (t) PaulMoloney 82
(Sophie Leech) *in rr: hdwy 6th: 5th 2 out: kpt on one pce: tk modest 4th nr fin* 33/1
0504 5 1½ **Social Climber (IRE)**[22] 4885 4-10-3 91 ConorShoemark(3) 81
(Fergal O'Brien) *trckd ldr: led 3rd: drvn sn after 3 out: wknd last 100yds* 7/1
6060 6 14 **Miss Fortywinks**[25] 4846 7-11-7 100 RyanMahon 84
(Seamus Mullins) *chsd ldrs 3rd: lost pl bef 2 out: sn bhd* 6/1[2]
00P2 7 15 **Lough Derg Island (IRE)**[13] 5099 8-11-3 96 RhysFlint 61
(Alexandra Dunn) *rr-div: chsd ldrs 4th: drvn 3 out: sn lost pl and bhd* 9/2[1]
04P3 P **Alys Rock (IRE)**[17] 5019 7-11-4 97 JonathanEngland
(Michael Appleby) *trckd ldrs: 3rd 4th: lost pl bef 2 out: bhd whn p.u bef last* 8/1
1FP- P **Danby's Legend**[583] 1516 9-9-11 81 (t) ThomasCheesman(5)
(Olly Williams) *t.k.h: led to 3rd: lost pl and bhd whn blnd 5th: t.o whn p.u bef next* 12/1
0244 P **Red Hott Robbie**[44] 4432 7-11-5 103 KevinJones(5)
(Giuseppe Fierro) *chsd ldrs 3rd: p.u after 5th: fatally injured* 9/2[1]
4m 23.2s (26.20) **Going Correction** +1.325s/f (Heav)
WFA 4 from 5yo+ 5lb 10 Ran SP% 115.9
Speed ratings (Par 105): **87,82,81,81,80 73,66,,,**
CSF £108.18 CT £752.51 TOTE £7.50: £2.80, £2.10, £2.40; EX 111.20 Trifecta £490.60.
Owner The 'Lord Of The Island' Syndicate **Bred** Noel Collins **Trained** Broad Hinton, Wilts
FOCUS
Race distance increased by 24 yards. Nothing really got involved from off the pace but an unexposed type scored with authority and the form could work out. A big step up from the winner.

5314 BEAUMOND HOUSE COMMUNITY HOSPICE NOVICES' H'CAP HURDLE (11 hdls) 2m 4f 62y
7:10 (7:10) (Class 4) (0-105,105) 4-Y-0+ £3,898 (£1,144; £572; £286)

Form RPR
P004 1 **Violoniste (FR)**[52] 4299 7-10-8 87 JonathanEngland 92+
(Sam Drake) *stdd s: hld up in rr: hdwy 2nd sn trcking ldrs: 2nd 8th: led appr 2 out: j.lft last 2: styd on wl run-in: drvn rt out* 11/2[3]
2524 2 2 **Twenty Eight Guns**[33] 4644 6-11-12 105 (p) LiamTreadwell 107
(Michael Scudamore) *chsd ldrs: 2nd appr 2 out: upsides between last 2: kpt on same pce last 150yds* 6/1
-P34 3 1½ **Pawn Star (IRE)**[57] 4198 6-11-12 105 AidanColeman 107
(Emma Lavelle) *chsd ldrs: 3rd appr 2 out: kpt on same pce between last 2* 9/4[1]
112P 4 45 **Showboater (IRE)**[33] 4642 7-11-10 103 (b[1]) NicodeBoinville 59
(Ben Pauling) *led: hdd appr 2 out: sn wknd: t.o* 4/1[2]
0005 5 24 **Just Like Dylan (IRE)**[31] 4703 5-9-12 84 LorcanMurtagh(7) 16
(Barry Murtagh) *in rr: bhd fr 8th: t.o 2 out: blnd bdly and rdr lost irons last* 40/1
P/PF P **Fuhgeddaboudit**[55] 4250 9-11-7 100 RyanMahon
(Seamus Mullins) *in rr: chsd ldrs 6th: drvn 3 out: sn wknd: poor 6th whn p.u bef 2 out* 25/1
060P P **Lawsons Thorns (IRE)**[109] 3312 7-10-11 90[1] SeanQuinlan
(Joanne Foster) *in rr: bhd and reminders 6th: t.o next: p.u sn after 3 out* 14/1
5P1B P **Perfect Poison (IRE)**[31] 4703 8-11-10 103 (p) WillKennedy
(Donald McCain) *chsd ldrs: drvn 6th: reminders next: lost pl bef 3 out: sn bhd: t.o whn p.u bef 2 out* 10/1
-605 P **Maybell**[41] 4494 5-11-1 94 JamesBanks
(Alex Hales) *chsd ldrs: hit 8th: drvn next: lost pl and poor 5th whn p.u bef 2 out* 7/1
5m 37.9s (24.90) **Going Correction** +1.325s/f (Heav) 9 Ran SP% 115.0
Speed ratings (Par 105): **103,102,101,83,74 , , ,**
CSF £38.45 CT £95.01 TOTE £6.00: £2.30, £2.00, £1.80; EX 38.90 Trifecta £140.30.
Owner Mrs J Drake **Bred** Bruno Vagne **Trained** Guiseley, West Yorkshire
FOCUS
Race distance increased by 24 yards. This was dominated by the market leaders and the first three pulled clear. The form is rated around the second.

5315 HALL-FAST.COM STANDARD NATIONAL HUNT FLAT RACE (COND' JOCKEYS & AMATEUR RIDERS) 1m 7f 153y
7:40 (7:40) (Class 6) 4-6-Y-O £1,949 (£572; £286; £143)

Form RPR
1 **First Drift**[34] 5-10-11 0 MrMJPKendrick(7) 109+
(Ben Case) *w ldr: led after 7f: drvn over 2f out: hung rt and styd on wl appr fnl f* 10/1
2 3 **Kalanisi Circle (IRE)** 4-10-9 0 MauriceLinehan(3) 100
(Ben Pauling) *t.k.h: led 7f: trckd wnr: drvn over 2f out: kpt on same pce fnl f* 9/4[1]
1 3 1 **Boyhood (IRE)**[58] 4181 5-11-4 0 MrNGeorge(7) 112
(Tom George) *trckd ldrs: drvn over 2f out: hung rt and kpt on same pce to take 3rd appr fnl f* 3/1[3]
4 7 **Steal My Thunder (IRE)**[82] 5-10-13 0 CiaranGethings(5) 98
(Philip Hobbs) *trckd ldrs: 3rd over 2f out: wknd fnl f* 5/2[2]
5 8 **Safe Harbour (IRE)** 4-10-9 0 ThomasGarner(3) 84
(Oliver Sherwood) *chsd ldrs: drvn over 2f out: wknd over 1f out* 5/1
6 21 **Bobba Benetta (IRE)** 6-10-4 0 MrAlexEdwards(7) 62
(Derek Shaw) *in rr: drvn and outpcd 7f out: chsd ldrs over 4f out: lost pl over 2f out* 33/1
0 7 4 **Sound The Bugle**[23] 4880 6-10-13 0 JakeHodson(5) 65
(Anthony Day) *t.k.h: trckd ldrs: drvn over 4f out: lost pl and bhd whn hung rt bnd 3f out* 100/1
8 88 **Rogue Planet (IRE)** 5-11-1 0 RyanHatch(3)
(Kevin Frost) *prom: drvn and outpcd after 7f: lost pl over 4f out: sn wl bhd: t.o 3f out* 33/1
4m 19.2s (27.80) **Going Correction** +1.325s/f (Heav)
WFA 4 from 5yo+ 5lb 8 Ran SP% 117.0
Speed ratings: **83,81,81,77,73 63,61,17**
CSF £33.51 TOTE £10.70: £2.00, £1.30, £1.70; EX 40.00 Trifecta £174.90.
Owner Mrs Carolyn Kendrick **Bred** A W Buller **Trained** Edgcote, Northants
FOCUS
Race distance increased by 24 yards. An interesting bumper. The winner was fairly impressive and there were some promising performances behind him. The third sets the level.
T/Plt: £544.30 to a £1 stake. Pool: £55,698.34 - 74.70 winning tickets. T/Qpdt: £64.70 to a £1 stake. Pool: £5,819.85 - 66.56 winning tickets **Walter Glynn**

5316 - 5322a (Foreign Racing) - See Raceform Interactive

5294
AYR (L-H)
Saturday, April 16

OFFICIAL GOING: Good to soft (soft in places; chs 7.4, hdl 7.5)
Wind: Breezy, half against Weather: Cloudy, bright

5323 WEATHERBYS PRIVATE BANK NOVICES' LIMITED H'CAP CHASE (19 fncs) 3m 67y
1:50 (1:50) (Class 2) 5-Y-0+ £16,245 (£4,770; £2,385; £1,192)

Form RPR
-151 1 **Vivaldi Collonges (FR)**[63] 4124 7-11-8 143 (t) SeanBowen 157+
(Paul Nicholls) *w ldr: hit 7th: led bef 5 out: rdn 2 out: kpt on strly to draw clr fr last* 9/4[1]
2221 2 5 **Kilbree Chief (IRE)**[47] 4407 8-10-4 125 DerekFox 131
(Lucinda Russell) *chsd ldrs: effrt and wnt 2nd bef 3 out: sn rdn and edgd lft: kpt on same pce bef last* 6/1
3524 3 21 **One For Arthur (IRE)**[35] 4609 7-10-8 129 PeterBuchanan 124
(Lucinda Russell) *hld up: outpcd 12th: 4th and no imp whn hmpd by faller 3 out: tk modest 3rd next: no ch w first two* 4/1[2]
F323 4 14 **Smooth Stepper**[28] 4800 7-10-8 129 DannyCook 116
(Sue Smith) *led: hit 12th: hdd bef 5 out: outpcd next: 8 l 3rd and hld whn mstke 2 out: sn btn* 5/1[3]
1263 P **Top Billing**[21] 4905 7-10-2 128 ow1 RyanDay(5)
(Nicky Richards) *hld up in tch: blnd and lost pl 4th: struggling fr 10th: lost tch and p.u bef 4 out* 13/2
21FP F **Cultram Abbey**[28] 4802 9-10-11 132 (p) BrianHarding
(Nicky Richards) *trckd ldrs: wnt 2nd after 5 out to bef 3 out: nrly four l down and one pce whn fell heavily 3 out* 12/1
1303 U **Cadoudoff (FR)**[15] 5073 6-10-9 130 TomO'Brien
(Charlie Longsdon) *nt fluent: hld up: hit and uns rdr 7th* 8/1
6m 23.2s (-26.70) **Going Correction** -0.85s/f (Firm) 7 Ran SP% 113.9
Speed ratings: **110,108,101,96,**
CSF £16.05 CT £50.16 TOTE £2.80: £1.90, £2.60; EX 15.00 Trifecta £40.20.
Owner The Gi Gi Syndicate **Bred** G A E C Delorme Freres **Trained** Ditcheat, Somerset

FOCUS
The rail was on the innermost line, and all distances were as advertised. The leaders appeared to go a respectable gallop in this staying handicap. The winner's latest wide-margin win could be rated at least this high.

5324 JORDAN ELECTRICS LTD FUTURE CHAMPION NOVICES' CHASE (GRADE 2) (17 fncs) 2m 4f 110y
2:25 (2:25) (Class 1) 5-Y-O+ **£26,283** (£10,056; £5,187; £2,739)

Form RPR
3P30 **1** **Le Mercurey (FR)**[31] 4716 6-11-7 147..................(bt[1]) SamTwiston-Davies 160+
(Paul Nicholls) *pressed ldrs: wnt 2nd 5th: led 10th to 13th: regained ld after 4 out: drvn and kpt on strly fr 2 out* **11/2**[2]
1112 **2** *7* **Bristol De Mai (FR)**[30] 4729 5-11-7 154.............................. DarylJacob 155+
(Nigel Twiston-Davies) *led to 10th: nt fluent 12th: regained ld next: hdd after 4 out: drvn next: mstke 2 out: kpt on same pce* **1/2**[1]
113P **3** *22* **Otago Trail (IRE)**[8] 5191 8-11-7 148.............................. AidanColeman 131
(Venetia Williams) *bhd: hdwy to chse clr ldng pair whn hit 5 out: drvn and no imp fr next* **9/1**
4410 **4** *1 1/2* **Killala Quay**[32] 4701 9-11-7 139..................................(p) RichardJohnson 130
(Charlie Longsdon) *pressed ldr to 5th: outpcd wkn hit 12th: hit next: struggling fr 4 out* **16/1**
3113 **F** **Pain Au Chocolat (FR)**[56] 4253 5-11-7 145.......................(t) HarrySkelton
(Dan Skelton) *prom: fell 4th* **13/2**[3]

5m 14.2s (314.20) **5 Ran SP% 111.3**
CSF £9.47 TOTE £6.60: £2.70, £1.10; EX 11.70 Trifecta £29.30.
Owner Colm Donlon & Chris Giles **Bred** S A R L Carion Emm **Trained** Ditcheat, Somerset

FOCUS
Despite a small field, this looked a strong race before the off but one of the leading candidates departed pretty early and the market leader ran below his season's best, so it may not be reliable form. However there's a case for rating the race higher.

5325 QTS SCOTTISH CHAMPION HURDLE (A LIMITED H'CAP) (GRADE 2) (8 hdls 1 omitted) 2m
3:00 (3:01) (Class 1) 4-Y-O+ **£57,519** (£21,583; £10,807; £5,383; £2,706; £1,353)

Form RPR
223 **1** **Ch'Tibello (FR)**[142] 2728 5-11-1 135.............................. HarrySkelton 144+
(Dan Skelton) *hld up in midfield: smooth hdwy to ld 2 out: mstke last: drvn out* **8/1**
1311 **2** *1 1/4* **Cloudy Dream (IRE)**[19] 4986 6-10-13 133.............................. NoelFehily 140+
(Malcolm Jefferson) *t.k.h: hld up: stdy hdwy whn nt fluent 2 out: nt clr run and swtchd rt bef last: rdn and edgd lft run-in: kpt on strly to take 2nd nr fin: nt rch wnr* **15/2**[3]
2-31 **3** *1 1/4* **Clondaw Warrior (IRE)**[18] 5025 9-11-10 144.............................. PaulTownend 149
(W P Mullins, Ire) *hld up: nt fluent 2nd: smooth hdwy bef 2 out: chsd wnr last: kpt on: no ex and lost 2nd nr fin* **7/2**[2]
-540 **4** *3/4* **Some Plan (IRE)**[29] 4765 8-11-5 144..............................(t) HarryCobden[(5)] 148
(Paul Nicholls) *t.k.h: in tch: effrt and cl up 2 out: rdn and kpt on same pce fr last* **14/1**
0001 **5** *nse* **Ivan Grozny (FR)**[7] 5219 6-11-7 146 5ex.............................. DavidMullins[(3)] 149
(W P Mullins, Ire) *nt fluent on occasions: hld up: smooth hdwy and prom 2 out: sn rdn: kpt on same pce fr last* **11/4**[1]
1-20 **6** *hd* **John Constable (IRE)**[29] 4765 5-11-3 137.............................. PaulMoloney 140
(Evan Williams) *trckd ldrs: effrt and ev ch 2 out: sn rdn: outpcd fr last* **14/1**
3441 **7** *3 1/2* **Zaidiyn (FR)**[49] 4366 6-11-8 142.............................. GavinSheehan 143
(Brian Ellison) *hld up: effrt and rdn bef 2 out: kpt on fr last: nvr able to chal* **16/1**
1F42 **8** *nk* **Always Resolute**[28] 4791 5-11-1 135.............................. DannyCook 135
(Brian Ellison) *t.k.h: prom tl rdn and outpcd 2 out: btn last* **40/1**
-340 **9** *1/2* **Zamdy Man**[29] 4765 7-11-10 144.............................. AidanColeman 145
(Venetia Williams) *disp ld: rdn bef omitted 3 out: wknd after 2 out* **25/1**
11P3 **10** *12* **Sternrubin (GER)**[29] 4765 5-11-8 142.............................. RichardJohnson 133
(Philip Hobbs) *led to 2 out: sn rdn and wknd* **8/1**
-210 **11** *1* **Connetable (FR)**[29] 4764 4-11-8 147.............................. SamTwiston-Davies 130
(Paul Nicholls) *sn lost prom position: hld up: shortlived effrt on outside bef omitted 3 out: wknd fr 2 out* **20/1**
1311 **12** *10* **Shrewd**[18] 4461 6-10-12 137.............................. ShaneShortall[(5)] 116
(Iain Jardine) *hld up: rdn bef omitted 3 out: wknd bef 2 out* **11/1**
-P02 **13** *15* **Ifandbutwhynot (IRE)**[8] 5201 10-11-2 136.............................. JamesReveley 101
(Tim Easterby) *in tch tl lost pl bef omitted 3 out: sn btn: eased whn no ch fr last* **40/1**

3m 51.5s (231.50)
WFA 4 from 5yo+ 5lb **13 Ran SP% 123.9**
CSF £67.12 CT £253.62 TOTE £9.60: £2.70, £2.40, £2.00; EX 66.60 Trifecta £365.80.
Owner The Can't Say No Partnership **Bred** Mme Elisabeth Cucheval **Trained** Alcester, Warwicks

FOCUS
Plenty of talented hurdlers lined up for this, but the pace wasn't overly strong and lots of them held a chance two out - the third-last was not jumped. The winner confirmed the merit of his Ascot second, and the next two are still on the upgrade.

5326 SCOTTY BRAND H'CAP CHASE (LISTED RACE) (12 fncs) 1m 7f 112y
3:35 (3:35) (Class 1) 5-Y-O+ **£28,475** (£10,685; £5,350; £2,665; £1,340; £670)

Form RPR
1050 **1** **De Faithesdream (IRE)**[28] 4787 10-10-3 128.............................. PaulMoloney 138+
(Evan Williams) *w ldr: lft in ld 1st: hdd 5th: pressed ldr: effrt after 3 out: rdn and led whn mstke last: edgd lft run-in: drvn out* **20/1**
0151 **2** *1 3/4* **Ultragold (FR)**[14] 5096 8-10-3 133..............................(t) HarryCobden[(5)] 140
(Colin Tizzard) *cl up: led 5th: rdn bef 2 out: hdd bef last: kpt on run-in: nt pce of wnr* **11/4**[2]
-3P1 **3** *6* **Solar Impulse (FR)**[29] 4770 6-11-10 149..............(bt) SamTwiston-Davies 150
(Paul Nicholls) *prom: stdy hdwy 4 out: effrt and rdn bef 2 out: kpt on same pce between last 2* **4/1**[3]
6515 **4** *1/2* **Upsilon Bleu (FR)**[14] 5087 8-11-7 146.............................. JamesReveley 146
(Pauline Robson) *hld up: stdy hdwy bef 3 out: rdn and effrt next: no imp fr last* **13/2**
31UP **5** *3/4* **Ubaltique (FR)**[19] 4964 8-10-2 127..............................(bt) AidanColeman 127
(Donald McCain) *hld up: stdy hdwy after 4 out: rdn next: no imp fr 2 out* **16/1**
1P23 **6** *24* **Grey Gold (IRE)**[19] 4964 11-11-12 151.............................. JamieMoore 134
(Kerry Lee) *trckd ldrs tl rdn and wknd fr 4 out* **15/2**
2411 **U** **Always On The Run (IRE)**[28] 4785 6-10-8 133.............................. PaddyBrennan
(Tom George) *t.k.h: led tl mstke and uns rdr 1st* **9/4**[1]

3m 52.1s (-18.60) **Going Correction** -0.85s/f (Firm) **7 Ran SP% 113.2**
Speed ratings: **112,111,108,107,107 95,**
CSF £74.91 TOTE £21.00: £7.60, £2.10; EX 85.10 Trifecta £603.70.
Owner R Abbott & M Stavrou **Bred** Pierce Whyte **Trained** Llancarfan, Vale Of Glamorgan

FOCUS
Some very useful 2m chasers took their chance for a decent prize, but the winner was almost impossible to find on recent efforts. The pace appeared to be sound throughout and the form looks solid.

5327 CORAL SCOTTISH GRAND NATIONAL H'CAP CHASE (GRADE 3) (27 fncs) 3m 7f 176y
4:10 (4:12) (Class 1) 5-Y-O+ **£119,595** (£44,877; £22,470; £11,193; £5,628; £2,814)

Form RPR
3145 **1** **Vicente (FR)**[32] 4700 7-11-3 146.............................. SamTwiston-Davies 159+
(Paul Nicholls) *hld up in midfield: smooth hdwy to trck ldrs 4 out: drvn 2 out: led last: kpt on strly* **14/1**
54-0 **2** *2 3/4* **Alvarado (IRE)**[42] 4483 11-10-6 135.............................. PaulMoloney 143
(Fergal O'Brien) *prom: rdn and outpcd 4 out: rallied 2 out: kpt on wl to take 2nd cl home: nt rch wnr* **25/1**
1110 **3** *hd* **Seeyouatmidnight**[31] 4716 8-11-1 149.............................. StevenFox[(5)] 158
(Sandy Thomson) *t.k.h: chsd ldrs: wnt 2nd 19th: led 4 out: rdn next: hdd whn hit last: kpt on same pce: lost 2nd cl home* **14/1**
0125 **4** *1 3/4* **Royale Knight**[56] 4241 10-10-13 142.............................. BrendanPowell 148
(Dr Richard Newland) *hld up in midfield: stdy hdwy and prom 4 out: effrt and ch next: kpt on same pce fr last* **20/1**
1215 **5** *5* **Vyta Du Roc (FR)**[31] 4716 7-11-2 145.............................. DarylJacob 148
(Nicky Henderson) *hld up: stdy hdwy and in tch bef 4 out: rdn next: outpcd fr 2 out* **8/1**[1]
42P4 **6** *7* **Sun Cloud (IRE)**[44] 4444 9-10-1 135..............................(t) JamieHamilton[(5)] 131
(Malcolm Jefferson) *bhd: pushed along fnl circ: pluged on fr 3 out: nvr able to chal* **40/1**
0002 **7** *5* **Milborough (IRE)**[27] 4818 10-10-5 137.............................. GrahamWatters[(3)] 131
(Ian Duncan) *hld up: pushed along and effrt 20th: drvn bef 4 out: no imp whn hmpd next: sn btn* **25/1**
P332 **8** *1* **Masters Hill (IRE)**[33] 4684 10-10-11 140..............................(tp) JamesReveley 132
(Colin Tizzard) *j.w: led to 4 out: rdn next: nt fluent and wknd 2 out* **28/1**
212 **9** *3* **Milansbar (IRE)**[28] 4802 9-11-2 145.............................. TrevorWhelan 132
(Neil King) *prom: wnt 2nd after 18th to next: outpcd 21st: rallied bef 4 out: sn wknd* **20/1**
532P **10** *14* **Shotgun Paddy (IRE)**[28] 4802 9-10-13 142..............................(p) NoelFehily 121
(Emma Lavelle) *nt fluent on occasions: hld up: rdn fr 19th: shortlived effrt after 5 out: wknd bef next* **20/1**
F1P0 **U** **Pineau De Re (FR)**[42] 4483 13-10-8 137..............................(p) NicodeBoinville 146
(Dr Richard Newland) *hld up: blnd 3rd: stdy hdwy and in tch bef 4 out: seventh and outpcd whn hit: stmbld and uns rdr next* **25/1**
41FF **P** **Golden Chieftain (IRE)**[28] 4802 11-10-10 139..............................(bt) TomO'Brien
(Colin Tizzard) *hld up: blnd 20th: stdy hdwy into midfield 1/2-way: wknd 4 out: p.u bef last: collapsed fatally* **14/1**
4210 **P** **Midnight Prayer**[30] 4735 11-10-12 141.............................. WayneHutchinson
(Alan King) *hld up: reminders after 13th: struggling 18th: p.u bef 21st* **25/1**
-300 **P** **Dolatulo (FR)**[31] 4719 9-11-2 145..............................(bt) HarrySkelton
(Warren Greatrex) *hld up in midfield on ins: struggling fr 19th: p.u after 6 out* **66/1**
1-1P **P** **Emperor's Choice (IRE)**[98] 3518 9-10-12 141.............................. AidanColeman
(Venetia Williams) *midfield: lost pl 10th: lost tch and p.u bef 19th* **40/1**
3034 **B** **Folsom Blue (IRE)**[19] 5005 9-10-3 137..............................(p) AndrewRing[(5)]
(M F Morris, Ire) *hld up: stdy hdwy whn hit 21st: prom but gng wl whn b.d 6 out* **16/1**
-021 **P** **Highland Lodge (IRE)**[133] 2899 10-10-8 137..............................(p) HenryBrooke
(James Moffatt) *in tch: drvn and outpcd fr 19th: lost tch and p.u bef 3 out* **16/1**
4414 **P** **Tour Des Champs (FR)**[14] 5092 9-10-4 136..............................(p) RyanHatch[(3)]
(Nigel Twiston-Davies) *bhd: nt fluent 5th: struggling and p.u after 9th* **22/1**
51F1 **P** **Ballyculla (IRE)**[25] 4864 9-10-7 136..............................(b[1]) GavinSheehan
(Warren Greatrex) *mstkes: chsd ldr to 18th: blnd and wknd next: p.u bef 21st* **25/1**
0051 **P** **Cause Of Causes (USA)**[30] 4735 8-11-12 155..............................(tp) BarryGeraghty
(Gordon Elliott, Ire) *nt fluent and nvr gng wl in rr: lost tch and p.u bef 21st* **10/1**[3]
51F0 **F** **Top Wood (FR)**[14] 5085 9-11-1 144..............................(bt) ConorO'Farrell
(David Pipe) *t.k.h: in tch: hdwy and disputing 5th pl whn fell 6 out* **50/1**
1000 **P** **Heathfield (IRE)**[14] 5108 9-10-7 136.............................. MarkWalsh
(A J Martin, Ire) *bhd: struggling fnl circ: p.u bef 3 out* **9/1**[2]
4111 **P** **Berea Boru (IRE)**[19] 4966 8-10-9 138..............................(tp) SeanBowen
(Peter Bowen) *nt fluent: sn towards rr: lost tch and p.u after 18th* **20/1**
2P11 **P** **Goodtoknow**[33] 4684 8-10-11 140..............................(p) JakeGreenall
(Kerry Lee) *prom: drvn and outpcd 6 out: wknd and p.u bef 3 out* **33/1**
-013 **F** **Measureofmydreams (IRE)**[32] 4700 8-11-3 146.............................. BJCooper
(W P Mullins, Ire) *hld up: hit 1st: fell 3rd* **8/1**[1]
4412 **P** **Straidnahanna (IRE)**[35] 4605 7-10-8 137.............................. DannyCook
(Sue Smith) *in tch: drvn and outpcd 19th: p.u after 6 out* **33/1**
1244 **P** **Spookydooky (IRE)**[28] 4802 8-10-10 139..............................(tp) RichardJohnson
(Jonjo O'Neill) *hld up: struggling fr 19th: wknd and p.u bef 4 out* **16/1**
3022 **P** **A Good Skin (IRE)**[30] 4735 7-10-10 139.............................. PaddyBrennan
(Tom George) *midfield: hdwy and prom 9th: wknd bef 6 out: p.u bef 3 out* **20/1**

8m 24.1s (-28.90) **Going Correction** -0.85s/f (Firm) **28 Ran SP% 144.0**
Speed ratings: **102,101,101,100,99 97,96,96,95,92 ,,,, ,,,,**
CSF £333.14 CT £5007.66 TOTE £16.30: £4.30, £6.20, £5.30, £5.20; EX 544.00 Trifecta £13470.00.
Owner Ian Fogg & John Hales **Bred** Thierry Cypres & Jean-Francois Naudin **Trained** Ditcheat, Somerset

FOCUS
Lots of these had some good form when last seen, whether it was recently or a few months previously, so this has the look of strong staying form. \bMasters Hill\p made sure it was run at a sound gallop, and being in midfield or close to the front proved to be a positive. The winner is rated back to the level of his Cheltenham win, with the form rated around the second to fourth.

5328 AYRSHIRE HOSPICE LAND O'BURNS STARLIGHT WALK H'CAP HURDLE (12 hdls) 2m 5f 91y
4:45 (4:47) (Class 2) (0-155,150) 4-Y-O+ **£12,996** (£3,816; £1,908; £954)

Form RPR
3234 **1** **Two Taffs (IRE)**[35] 4620 6-10-5 **129**.................. HarrySkelton 135+
(Dan Skelton) *hld up towards rr: hdwy 8th: trcking ldrs 3 out: led narrowly last: edgd lft: drvn clr last 100yds: won gng away* **5/2**[1]
3-1P **2** 3 **Missed Approach (IRE)**[30] 4730 6-11-5 **143**.................. GavinSheehan 147+
(Warren Greatrex) *clr ldr: nt fluent and pushed along 7th: hdd narrowly last: styd on same pce last 100yds* **10/1**
4-20 **3** 3¼ **Arbre De Vie (FR)**[31] 4717 6-11-12 **150**.................. PaulTownend 150
(W P Mullins, Ire) *trckd ldrs: upsides 2 out: kpt on same pce run-in* **3/1**[2]
0U-2 **4** 7 **Eshtiaal (USA)**[43] 1983 6-10-6 **130**..................(tp) BarryGeraghty 126
(Gordon Elliott, Ire) *mid-div: hdwy to chse ldrs 7th: one pce and modest 4th between last 2* **6/1**[3]
2P20 **5** 6 **Warriors Tale**[30] 4730 7-11-2 **140**.................. SamTwiston-Davies 129
(Paul Nicholls) *chsd ldrs: effrt appr 3 out: wknd between last 2* **8/1**
42P3 **6** 1½ **Forest Bihan (FR)**[42] 4484 5-11-1 **139**.................. RichieMcLernon 126
(Brian Ellison) *in rr: hdwy 6th: drvn appr 3 out: wknd between last 2* **11/1**
3323 **7** 4½ **Isaacstown Lad (IRE)**[14] 5085 9-10-9 **133**.................. CraigNichol 116
(Nicky Richards) *in rr: pushed along 8th: hdwy appr 3 out: wknd after next: j.rt last* **25/1**
-236 **8** ¾ **Reaping The Reward (IRE)**[52] 4306 12-9-9 **124** oh1(t) GrantCockburn(5) 110
(Lucinda Russell) *in rr: pushed along 8th: hdwy appr 3 out: wknd between last 2* **33/1**
0142 **9** 14 **Zeroeshadesofgrey (IRE)**[42] 4470 7-11-5 **143**.................. TrevorWhelan 113
(Neil King) *chsd ldr: hit 8th: lost pl appr 2 out: bhd whn eased in clsng stages* **10/1**
30 **10** 1¼ **Mango Cap (FR)**[69] 4014 5-9-9 **124**..................(t[1]) DavidNoonan(5) 93
(David Pipe) *chsd ldrs: drvn 9th: sn lost pl: bhd whn eased in clsng stages* **25/1**
2511 **11** 16 **Baby Bach (IRE)**[21] 4902 6-10-8 **132**.................. AELynch 86
(S R B Crawford, Ire) *hld up detached in last: drvn bef 3 out: nvr on terms: bhd whn heavily eased in clsng stages* **16/1**
5m 18.5s (318.50) **11 Ran SP% 122.0**
CSF £28.62 CT £81.51 TOTE £3.50: £1.50, £4.00, £1.60; EX 37.70 Trifecta £160.70.
Owner Walters Plant Hire & James & Jean Potter **Bred** Grange Stud **Trained** Alcester, Warwicks

FOCUS
A decent handicap over an intermediate distance, run at a sound pace. The winner provided Dan Skelton with his 100th domestic success of the season. Three pulled nicely clear. The winner looked well in on his unlucky Sandown run and is rated to a similar level.

5329 ORTUS HOMES RACING EXCELLENCE "HANDS AND HEELS" FINALE H'CAP HURDLE (CONDITIONALS/AMATEURS) (12 hdls) 2m 4f 100y
5:20 (5:20) (Class 3) (0-130,128) 4-Y-O+ **£7,797** (£2,289; £1,144; £572)

Form RPR
1246 **1** **Impulsive American**[13] 5116 4-10-12 **120**..................(b) DavidNoonan 123+
(David Pipe) *mid-div: chsd ldrs 9th: 2nd appr 2 out: led narrowly last: drvn clr* **8/1**[3]
4613 **2** 6 **Alcala (FR)**[35] 4620 6-11-11 **127**..................(t) HarryCobden 130
(Paul Nicholls) *t.k.h: w ldr: led 5th: qcknd pce next: hdd narrowly last: styd on same pce* **6/5**[1]
241 **3** 3¾ **Oldgrangewood**[47] 4403 5-11-1 **120**.................. MrJAndrews(3) 119
(Dan Skelton) *hld up in rr: hdwy 8th: trcking ldrs next: kpt on same pce appr last* **9/4**[2]
1255 **4** 1½ **Oh Land Abloom (IRE)**[34] 4643 6-11-12 **128**......(t) WilliamFeatherstone 126
(Neil King) *set stdy pce: hdd 5th: kpt on one pce fr 2 out* **10/1**
2/65 **5** 4½ **Now This Is It (IRE)**[162] 2326 12-11-3 **124**.................. WJBoyes(5) 117
(S R B Crawford, Ire) *nt fluent in last: bhd: t.k.h: sme hdwy 3 out: styd on between last 2: nvr a factor* **25/1**
0-04 **6** 1 **Nathans Pride (IRE)**[28] 4781 8-11-7 **126**.................. MrEDavid(3) 119
(Tim Vaughan) *t.k.h: trckd ldrs: 2nd 7th: hit 3 out: wknd appr next* **22/1**
3F2F **7** 1 **Knocklayde Sno Cat (IRE)**[35] 4608 7-10-0 **105**......(t) AdamShort(3) 96
(S R B Crawford, Ire) *chsd ldrs: lost pl bef 3 out* **16/1**
2111 **8** 8 **Amuse Me**[170] 2142 10-11-6 **122**.................. FinianO'Toole 106
(James Moffatt) *mid-div: drvn 9th: lost pl bef next* **12/1**
5m 28.5s (328.50)
WFA 4 from 5yo+ 6lb **8 Ran SP% 118.2**
CSF £19.40 CT £30.40 TOTE £8.50: £2.60, £1.20, £1.20; EX 22.00 Trifecta £62.40.
Owner Mrs Jo Tracey **Bred** D Brocklehurst **Trained** Nicholashayne, Devon

FOCUS
A well-run fair handicap in which whips were not allowed to be used. The finish was dominated by two trainers who had decent records in the contest. Heading into this, Paul Nicholls had three winners and a place from five he'd sent, while David Pipe had two placed from three he'd run. Improvemnt from the winner with the second to his mark.

5330 SKYFORM GROUP STANDARD OPEN NATIONAL HUNT FLAT RACE 2m
5:50 (5:50) (Class 3) 4-6-Y-0 **£6,498** (£1,908; £954; £477)

Form RPR
1 **Gibbes Bay (FR)** 4-10-10 0.................. SamTwiston-Davies 106+
(Paul Nicholls) *prom: stdy hdwy over 2f out: rdn to ld over 1f out: edgd lft ins fnl f: kpt on wl* **5/1**[3]
3 **2** 1¾ **Jimmy Breekie (IRE)**[17] 5041 6-11-1 0.................. AELynch 109
(S R B Crawford, Ire) *hld up: stdy hdwy over 2f out: drvn to chse wnr ins fnl f: kpt on* **12/1**
21 **3** 1½ **Reivers Lad**[37] 4572 5-11-8 0.................. DavidMullins(3) 118
(Nicky Richards) *hld up bhd ldng gp: stdy hdwy over 2f out: effrt and ev ch over 1f out: kpt on same pce ins fnl f* **10/3**[2]
65 **4** ½ **Cougar's Gold (IRE)**[52] 4308 5-11-1 0.................. SeanBowen 107
(Peter Bowen) *trckd ldrs: drvn and ev ch over 1f out: outpcd ins fnl f* **14/1**
5 **5** 1½ **Nicholas T**[21] 4915 4-10-10 0.................. HenryBrooke 102+
(Jim Goldie) *t.k.h: hld up: shkn up and swtchd lft 2f out: rdn and edgd lft over 1f out: kpt on ins fnl f: nvr able to chal* **20/1**
1 **6** 1½ **Mere Ironmonger**[28] 4790 4-11-3 0.................. BrendanPowell 106
(Brendan Powell) *led: rdn and hdd over 1f out: wknd ins fnl f* **5/2**[1]
2 **7** 1 **Man O'Words (IRE)**[52] 4308 5-11-1 0.................. RichardJohnson 103
(Tom Lacey) *hld up: hdwy on outside over 2f out: sn rdn: no imp fr over 1f out* **7/1**
3P **8** 14 **Brackenmoss Rory**[35] 4611 4-10-10 0.................. CraigNichol 84
(Alistair Whillans) *t.k.h: hld up in tch: struggling 4f out: n.d after* **33/1**
31 **9** 4½ **Ballycrystal (IRE)**[52] 4308 5-11-8 0.................. DannyCook 100
(Brian Ellison) *trckd ldrs: effrt and rdn over 2f out: wknd over 1f out* **11/2**
5 **10** 21 **Disturb**[25] 4867 4-10-7 0.................. JohnKington(3) 59
(Andrew Crook) *t.k.h: cl up tl wknd wl over 2f out: t.o* **33/1**
3m 55.8s (235.80)
WFA 4 from 5yo+ 5lb **10 Ran SP% 121.2**
CSF £64.08 TOTE £5.70: £2.10, £3.30, £1.20; EX 30.70 Trifecta £461.70.
Owner The Gi Gi Syndicate **Bred** Dominique Le Baron **Trained** Ditcheat, Somerset

FOCUS
This has often gone to a decent horse in the past decade, with Sprinter Sacre standing out by a mile as being the best. It went this year to an unraced runner from Paul Nicholls' stable who looks promising, but it's not hard to knock the form at this stage due to it being slowly run and the previous efforts of the runner-up and fourth. It will be interesting to see if it works out.
T/Jkpt: Not won. T/Plt: £142.80 to a £1 stake. Pool of £228821.22 - 1168.95 winning tickets.
T/Qpdt: £55.50 to a £1 stake. Pool of £16429.05 - 218.74 winning tickets.
Richard Young & Walter Glynn

5043 BANGOR-ON-DEE (L-H)
Saturday, April 16

OFFICIAL GOING: Heavy (4.5)
Wind: Moderate, half behind Weather: Fine but cold

5331 BANGORBET MAIDEN HURDLE (12 hdls) 2m 7f 32y
2:15 (2:16) (Class 5) 5-Y-O+ **£3,138** (£1,073)

Form RPR
243 **1** **Beware The Bear (IRE)**[24] 4873 6-11-2 120.................. JeremiahMcGrath 120+
(Nicky Henderson) *in rr: reminder after 8th: moved upsides after 4 out: lft in ld 3 out: sn drew clr: mstke last: eased down towards fin* **8/11**[1]
3-P3 **2** 29 **Mahler Lad (IRE)**[31] 4711 6-11-2 0.................. WillKennedy 90
(Donald McCain) *led: hdd 4 out: sn dropped to 3rd: lft 2nd 3 out: sn rdn and unable to go w wnr: no ch* **9/2**[3]
2 **F** **Powerful Symbol (IRE)**[37] 4572 6-11-2 0.................. JoshuaMoore
(Jonjo O'Neill) *w ldr: led 4 out: sn jnd: fell 3 out* **9/4**[2]
6m 25.7s (34.70) **Going Correction** +1.525s/f (Heav) **3 Ran SP% 106.9**
Speed ratings: **100,89,**
CSF £3.84 TOTE £1.90; EX 4.30 Trifecta £4.70.
Owner G B Barlow **Bred** Mrs Marilyn Syme **Trained** Upper Lambourn, Berks

FOCUS
All distances as advertised. Rain overnight left the ground pretty testing. This was an uncompetitive maiden hurdle, run at a slow pace. The race has been given a token rating throught the winner.

5332 EXCEL SIGNS H'CAP HURDLE (DIV I) (11 hdls) 2m 3f 123y
2:45 (2:45) (Class 5) (0-100,100) 4-Y-O+ **£3,249** (£954; £477; £238)

Form RPR
0643 **1** **Karisma King**[15] 5079 7-11-11 **99**.................. SeanQuinlan 104+
(Sue Smith) *led: hdd 4th: regained ld after 5th: rdn whn mstke 2 out: asserted appr last: drvn out abt 4 l clr fnl 110yds out: eased fnl strides* **3/1**[1]
4315 **2** ½ **Old Magic (IRE)**[23] 4885 11-10-8 **87**..................(t) BridgetAndrews(5) 87
(Sophie Leech) *midfield: hdwy 7th: sn chsd ldrs: rdn and outpcd after 3 out: rallied 2 out: wnt 2nd jst bef last: styd on and clsd on wnr nr fin: sltly flattered* **11/2**[3]
-P35 **3** 3¼ **Kavanaghs Corner (IRE)**[101] 3489 7-10-11 **85**.................. AndrewThornton 85
(Simon Earle) *hld up: hdwy appr 4 out: effrt whn cl up and mstke 2 out: disp 2nd last: no ex fnl 75yds* **4/1**[2]
0-00 **4** 5 **Ginjo**[9] 5181 6-10-4 **81**..................(p) RobertWilliams(3) 75
(Bernard Llewellyn) *trckd ldrs: hit 7th: wnt 2nd appr 4 out: rdn and ev ch 2 out: lost 2nd jst bef last: no ex* **25/1**
-500 **5** 3 **Bourne**[34] 4648 10-11-12 **100**..................(p) AdrianLane 89
(Donald McCain) *trckd ldrs: dropped to midfield 4th: rdn and lost pl appr 7th: struggling whn blnd 3 out: no ch after* **6/1**
6626 **6** 11 **L Frank Baum (IRE)**[30] 4747 9-10-9 **90**..................(p) JordanWilliams(7) 68
(Bernard Llewellyn) *prom tl rdn and lost pl after 6th: n.d after* **13/2**
5UU2 **7** 3½ **Lost In Newyork (IRE)**[19] 4987 9-9-11 **74**..................(v[1]) MauriceLinehan(3) 48
(Nick Kent) *hld up: sme hdwy 4 out: sn rdn: wknd 3 out* **13/2**
P000 **8** 7 **Diamond Reflection (IRE)**[14] 5099 4-10-10 **90**..................(t[1]) DenisO'Regan 55
(Tom Weston) *hld up: niggled along whn j. slowly 6th: hdwy 4 out: mstke 3 out: sn wknd* **20/1**
00/ **P** **Howya Buddy (IRE)**[1013] 925 11-10-8 **85**.................. BenPoste(3)
(Adrian Wintle) *racd keenly: prom: led 4th: hdd after 5th: wknd 4 out: t.o whn p.u bef 2 out* **25/1**
5m 31.2s (39.20) **Going Correction** +1.525s/f (Heav)
WFA 4 from 5yo+ 6lb **9 Ran SP% 113.8**
Speed ratings (Par 103): **82,81,80,78,77 72,71,68,**
CSF £19.16 CT £64.56 TOTE £4.30: £1.50, £2.00, £3.70; EX 18.60 Trifecta £45.50.
Owner Broadway Racing Club 15 **Bred** Mr & Mrs W Hodge **Trained** High Eldwick, W Yorks

FOCUS
A slow-motion finish to this modest handicap hurdle. A step up from the winner.

5333 EXCEL SIGNS H'CAP HURDLE (DIV II) (11 hdls) 2m 3f 123y
3:20 (3:20) (Class 5) (0-100,100) 4-Y-O+ **£3,249** (£954; £477; £238)

Form RPR
00F **1** **Normandy King (IRE)**[32] 4703 5-10-8 **87**.................. AlanJohns(5) 103+
(Tim Vaughan) *trckd ldrs: led after 3 out: mstke 2 out: drew clr bef last: comf* **9/2**[2]
U134 **2** 16 **Fiddler's Flight (IRE)**[32] 4703 10-10-8 **85**.................. ColmMcCormack(3) 84
(John Norton) *in rr: nt fluent 1st: mstke 4 out: effrt after 3 out: styd on u.p to take 2nd run-in: no ch w wnr* **11/2**
005/ **3** 1 **Desert Sting**[21] 7-10-1 **75**..................(bt) IanPopham 71
(Oliver Greenall) *hld up: hdwy appr 4 out: rdn bef 3 out: wnt 2nd bef 2 out: unable to go w wnr bef last: lost 2nd run-in: kpt on u.p* **7/2**[1]
3424 **4** ½ **Aaman (IRE)**[23] 4886 10-10-6 **83**..................(t) RobertWilliams(3) 80
(Bernard Llewellyn) *racd keenly: trckd ldrs: nt fluent 7th: led appr 3 out: hdd after flight: rdn and outpcd bef 2 out: kpt on u.p run-in: no ch w wnr* **6/1**
1-PP **5** ¾ **Detour Ahead**[18] 5017 8-11-6 **94**..................(p) DavidEngland 90
(Clare Ellam) *prom: led 2nd: hdd appr 3 out: rdn and outpce 2 out: kpt on u.p run-in: no ch w wnr* **20/1**
-PP3 **P** **Up Your Game (IRE)**[51] 4318 8-10-0 **74**..................(tp) JamesBanks
(Roy Brotherton) *prom: mstke 3 out: sn wknd: eased and p.u bef last* **8/1**

U51 **P** **Wymeswold**[141] 2745 9-10-9 **86**.. BenPoste(3)
(Michael Mullineaux) *midfield: rdn and lost pl after 6th: bhd whn p.u bef 4 out* **12/1**

P **P** **Time For Champers (IRE)**[45] 4439 6-11-7 **100**................ ChrisWard(5)
(Nikki Evans) *led: hdd 2nd: remained prom: pushed along and wknd qckly appr 4 out: bhd whn p.u bef next* **25/1**

0040 **P** **Leaving Las Vegas**[53] 4297 5-11-8 **96**.......................... DenisO'Regan
(William Kinsey) *hld up: rdn after 3 out: sn btn: eased and p.u bef last* **5/1**[3]

5m 27.8s (35.80) **Going Correction** +1.525s/f (Heav) **9** Ran SP% **114.2**
Speed ratings (Par 103): **89,82,82,82,81** , , ,
CSF £29.39 CT £95.45 TOTE £6.50: £2.50, £1.80, £1.70; EX 35.00 Trifecta £131.50.
Owner The 600 Club **Bred** Mrs Anthea Smyth **Trained** Aberthin, Vale of Glamorgan
■ Stewards' Enquiry : Robert Williams one-day ban: improper use of the whip (Apr 30)

FOCUS
Another weak handicap, but the quicker division by 3.4sec. The fourth sets the level.

5334 WREXHAM LAGER H'CAP CHASE (16 fncs 2 omitted) 3m 30y
3:55 (3:55) (Class 4) (0-120,119) 5-Y-O+ **£6,657** (£2,067; £1,113)

Form RPR

6341 **1** **Beauboreen (IRE)**[16] 5044 9-11-7 **114**........................(b) SeanQuinlan 125+
(Jennie Candlish) *prom: led 3rd: mstke 7th: j.lft 3 out: rdn clr bef 2 out: styd on gamely run-in* **4/1**[3]

P1-1 **2** *1 ½* **Wood Yer (IRE)**[35] 4612 10-11-7 **119**.......................(tp) JamieBargary(5) 126
(Nigel Twiston-Davies) *trckd ldrs: rdn appr 4 out: mstke 3 out: sn outpcd: rallied to take 2nd fnl 150yds: styd on but nt get to wnr* **10/3**[2]

4211 **3** *3* **Whiskey Chaser (IRE)**[31] 4710 8-11-5 **112**................. WillKennedy 115
(Donald McCain) *hld up: hdwy appr 11th: wnt 2nd 12th: rdn bef 2 out: no imp on wnr after last: lost 2nd fnl 150yds: one pce towards fin* **15/8**[1]

1104 **P** **Sunny Ledgend**[42] 4493 11-11-3 **117**........................... MrJMartin(7)
(Andrew J Martin) *led 2nd: hdd 3rd: remained prom: rdn 4 out: sn wknd and p.u* **16/1**

-0P0 **P** **Howard's Legacy (IRE)**[27] 4818 10-11-11 **118**.........(b[1]) LiamTreadwell
(Venetia Williams) *led: hdd 2nd: remained prom: lost pl 6th: rdn bef 10th: bhd whn p.u bef 4 out* **8/1**

441- **P** **Ballybough Andy (IRE)**[496] 2970 7-11-4 **111**................ LeightonAspell
(David Dennis) *hld up in tch: lost pl 12th: bhd whn p.u bef 3 out* **11/2**

6m 59.9s (40.10) **Going Correction** +1.825s/f (Heav) **6** Ran SP% **110.2**
Speed ratings: **106,105,104**, ,
CSF £17.23 CT £29.62 TOTE £3.80: £2.70, £1.90; EX 20.00 Trifecta £59.90.
Owner Mrs R N C Hall **Bred** Richard Hall **Trained** Basford Green, Staffs

FOCUS
A contested pace placed the emphasis on stamina in this fair staying handicap. Probably a chase best from the winner.

5335 WREXHAM LAGER BEER COMPANY H'CAP HURDLE (12 hdls) 2m 7f 32y
4:30 (4:31) (Class 4) (0-120,120) 4-Y-O+ **£5,848** (£1,717; £858; £429)

Form RPR

3441 **1** **Moidore**[19] 4983 7-11-12 **120**.. AdamPogson 132+
(Charles Pogson) *hld up in rr: hdwy appr 3 out: wnt 2nd travelling wl bef 2 out: led jst after flight: sn clr: easily* **11/1**

-343 **2** *15* **Lower Hope Dandy**[16] 5045 9-11-11 **119**...................... LiamTreadwell 119+
(Venetia Williams) *prom: hit 4th: led appr 6th: hdd bef 7th: led again 4 out: blnd and hdd 2 out: sn no ch w wnr* **8/1**

U-52 **3** *3 ½* **Obistar (FR)**[16] 5051 6-11-1 **112**..............................(b) KieronEdgar(3) 104
(David Pipe) *led: hit 4th: hdd appr 6th: led again bef 7th: blnd 8th: sn rdn: hdd 4 out: btn bef 2 out: mod 3rd bef last: plugged on but no ch* **9/2**[3]

F130 **4** *23* **Paddy's Field (IRE)**[35] 4620 6-11-12 **120**...................... DavidBass 87
(Ben Pauling) *chsd ldrs: rdn appr 3 out: sn wknd* **9/4**[1]

1402 **5** *hd* **Uncle Tone (IRE)**[42] 4492 7-11-7 **120**......................... AlanJohns(5) 86
(Tim Vaughan) *hld up: hdwy 8th: trckd ldrs appr 3 out: u.p bef 2 out: sn wknd* **10/1**

6P03 **P** **Mountain Tunes (IRE)**[14] 5100 7-11-11 **119**...............(tp) JoshuaMoore
(Jonjo O'Neill) *hld up in midfield: wknd 4 out: t.o whn p.u bef 2 out* **11/4**[2]

451 **P** **Too Many Chiefs (IRE)**[30] 4742 5-10-13 **112**.............. JamesCowley(5)
(Sharon Watt) *chsd ldrs: niggled along after 6th: rdn and lost pl 7th: bhd 4 out: t.o whn p.u 3 out* **18/1**

6m 31.2s (40.20) **Going Correction** +1.525s/f (Heav) **7** Ran SP% **109.4**
Speed ratings (Par 105): **91,85,84,76,76** , ,
CSF £82.52 CT £420.08 TOTE £6.70: £3.60, £2.90; EX 62.80 Trifecta £150.60.
Owner C T Pogson **Bred** The Queen **Trained** Farnsfield, Notts

FOCUS
An easy winner of this fair handicap hurdle. Probably not form to be confident in, though.

5336 WREXHAM LAGER EXPORT NOVICES' LIMITED H'CAP CHASE (14 fncs 1 omitted) 2m 4f 72y
5:05 (5:06) (Class 4) (0-120,120) 5-Y-O+ **£5,928** (£2,027)

Form RPR

442 **1** **San Pietro (FR)**[18] 5017 8-10-1 **102**........................... HarryChalloner(3) 115+
(Richard Ford) *hld up in rr: lft in ld 9th: drew clr appr last: easily* **5/2**[3]

PF35 **2** *29* **Globalisation (IRE)**[27] 4826 6-11-8 **120**...................(tp) LeightonAspell 113
(Rebecca Curtis) *led appr 2nd: hdd bef 4th: continued to chse ldr: dropped to 3rd briefly and lft 2nd 9th: nt fluent 2 out: sn rdn and btn: eased whn no ch run-in* **6/4**[1]

1121 **U** **Global Dream**[18] 5015 6-11-0 **112**................................. AdamPogson
(Caroline Bailey) *led: hdd appr 2nd: mstke 3rd: regained ld bef 4th: j.lft and uns rdr 9th* **13/8**[2]

5m 52.9s (43.80) **Going Correction** +1.825s/f (Heav) **3** Ran SP% **106.7**
Speed ratings: **85,73**,
CSF £6.23 TOTE £4.10; EX 6.70 Trifecta £5.40.
Owner Mrs C P Lees-Jones **Bred** S C E A Des Prairies Et Al **Trained** Garstang, Lancs

FOCUS
A small-field event which was reduced to two contenders six from home. Rather suspect form, with a case for rating the race up to 10lb higher.

5337 WREXHAM LAGER STANDARD NATIONAL HUNT FLAT RACE (CONDITIONALS & AMATEURS) 2m 145y
5:35 (5:37) (Class 6) 4-6-Y-O **£1,949** (£572; £286; £143)

Form RPR

1 **Our Dancing Dandy (IRE)**[125] 6-10-13 0......................... JamesCowley(5) 120+
(Donald McCain) *mde all: rdn over 2f out: sn clr: styd on wl: unchal* **5/2**[2]

0 **2** *20* **Twist On Ginge (IRE)**[42] 4488 4-10-6 0......................... MrJJSlevin(7) 95
(Nigel Twiston-Davies) *chsd ldrs: niggled along after 4f: rdn and lost pl 7f out: rdn and outpcd 4f out: kpt on to take 2nd over 1f out: no ch w wnr* **8/11**[1]

3 *7* **Badbad Leroy Brown**[21] 4-10-6 0......................... MrEGlassonbury(7) 88
(Oliver Greenall) *hld up: impr to take 2nd 7f out: outpcd by wnr over 2f out: no ch after: lost 2nd over 1f out* **7/1**[3]

4 *10* **Picknick Park** 4-10-10 0... ConorShoemark(3) 78
(Nick Kent) *racd keenly: hld up: trckd ldrs 7f out: rdn over 3f out: btn over 2f out* **25/1**

5 *dist* **Luca Brazi (IRE)** 4-10-6 0... TobyWheeler(7)
(Alan Phillips) *chsd wnr to 7f out: sn wknd and lft bhd: t.o* **16/1**

4m 25.6s (20.30) **Going Correction** +1.525s/f (Heav)
WFA 4 from 5yo+ 5lb **5** Ran SP% **108.7**
Speed ratings: **113,103,100,95**,
CSF £4.57 TOTE £2.80: £1.40, £1.60; EX 5.80 Trifecta £12.50.
Owner Deva Racing Scorpion Partnership **Bred** Leo Cahalane **Trained** Cholmondeley, Cheshire
■ Stewards' Enquiry : James Cowley two-day ban: used whip when clearly winning (Apr 30,May 2)

FOCUS
The winner set a fair pace considering the state of the ground. The winner could be decent.
T/Plt: £516.00 to a £1 stake. Pool of £56946.62 - 80.55 winning tickets. T/Qpdt: £119.00 to a £1 stake. Pool of £3195.32 - 19.86 winning tickets. **Darren Owen**

4489 STRATFORD (L-H)
Sunday, April 17
5338 Meeting Abandoned - waterlogged

5077 WETHERBY (L-H)
Sunday, April 17

OFFICIAL GOING: Soft (heavy in places; chs 5.0, hdl 5.3)
Wind: fresh behind Weather: fine

5345 NATIONAL FESTIVAL CIRCUS IS HERE TODAY CONDITIONAL JOCKEYS' H'CAP HURDLE (8 hdls 1 omitted) 1m 7f 193y
2:05 (2:10) (Class 4) (0-115,113) 4-Y-O+ **£3,249** (£954; £477; £238)

Form RPR

653 **1** **Cactus Valley (IRE)**[15] 5088 7-11-2 **106**..............(t) ThomasCheesman(3) 110+
(Michael Easterby) *hld up wl in tch: wnt handy 3rd bef 3 out: rdn after 2 out: 3rd last: styd on between horses to ld last 50yds* **15/8**[1]

553- **2** *1 ¼* **Celtic Agent**[472] 3435 8-11-3 **110**.................................. FinianO'Toole(6) 111
(Micky Hammond) *trckd ldng pair: t.k.h: cl 2nd bef 3 out: upsides last: sn led: hdd and no ex last 50yds* **15/8**[1]

0405 **3** *1 ¼* **Polarbrook (IRE)**[26] 4862 9-10-8 **95**................................(v) DerekFox 96
(Derek Shaw) *w ldr: led after 3rd: drvn 3 out: hdd sn after last: kpt on same pce last 50yds* **5/1**[2]

4056 **4** *18* **Boldbob (IRE)**[20] 4819 4-10-0 **102**................................ BillyGarritty(10) 81
(Micky Hammond) *led: hit 2nd: hdd after 3rd: drvn bef 3 out: lost pl bef 2 out: sn bhd* **10/1**

44P5 **5** *3* **Super Collider**[164] 2293 9-11-3 **112**..........................(t) JamesCorbett(8) 91
(Susan Corbett) *racd in last: shkn up after 5th: chsng ldrs briefly bef 3 out: sn outpcd and lost pl: sn bhd* **7/1**[3]

4m 7.0s (247.00) **Going Correction** +0.825s/f (Soft)
WFA 4 from 5yo+ 5lb **5** Ran SP% **107.8**
Speed ratings (Par 105): **105,104,103,94,93**
CSF £5.70 TOTE £2.30: £1.10, £2.10; EX 5.90 Trifecta £15.40.
Owner D Fielding, S Hollings & S Hull **Bred** Gerrardstown House Stud **Trained** Sheriff Hutton, N Yorks

FOCUS
Race 2 increased by 45yds, race 3 by 9yds, race 4 by 90yds and race 6 by 81yds. The meeting was given the green light after an early inspection and the ground was officially soft, heavy in places. There werr 21 non-runners on account of the ground. Due to isolated pockets of water on the course the last flight of hurdles down the back straight was omitted. The opener was a modest handicap and it produced a thrilling finish.

5346 RACINGUK.COM H'CAP CHASE (9 fncs 4 omitted) 1m 7f 36y
2:35 (2:41) (Class 4) (0-120,120) 5-Y-O+ **£4,548** (£1,335; £667)

Form RPR

2415 **1** **Trust Thomas**[15] 5086 8-11-2 **115**................................. JamieHamilton(5) 122+
(Ann Hamilton) *trckd ldrs: pushed along and upsides whn hit 3 out (normal 4 out): cl 2nd omitted 2 out: led narrowly last: forged clr* **5/4**[1]

1112 **2** *5* **Roxyfet (FR)**[33] 4705 6-11-0 **115**................................. FinianO'Toole(7) 116
(Micky Hammond) *trckd ldr: led omitted 2 out: hdd and hit last: wknd fnl 100yds* **11/8**[2]

P-P4 **3** *hd* **Free World (FR)**[16] 5080 12-9-8 **95** oh2 ow1............... MissLBrooke(7) 94
(Lady Susan Brooke) *j. soundly: led: hdd omitted 2 out: sn outpcd and 5 l down last: kpt on last 75yds* **7/2**[3]

4m 7.0s (11.20) **Going Correction** +0.875s/f (Soft) **3** Ran SP% **108.8**
Speed ratings: **105,102,102**
CSF £3.38 TOTE £2.10; EX 3.00 Trifecta £2.30.
Owner Ian Hamilton **Bred** Wood Farm Stud **Trained** Great Bavington, Northumbland

FOCUS
Race distance 45yds further than advertised. Due to isolated pockets of water on the course the second-last fence and the last two down the back straight were omitted. Just a fair handicap and all three runners had their chance.

5347 D M KEITH MARES' MAIDEN HURDLE 2m 3f 154y
3:10 (3:16) (Class 5) 4-Y-O+ **£3,249** (£954; £477)

Form RPR

2 **1** **Two Smokin Barrels**[20] 4961 7-11-2 0......................... LiamTreadwell 103
(Michael Scudamore) *wnt 2nd after 4th: upsides 5th: led bef 3 out: sn pushed along: hdd narrowly last 100yds: fnd ex to ld again clsng stages* **1/2**[1]

-33F **2** *½* **Angel Face**[110] 3333 5-11-2 108..........................(t) LeightonAspell 102
(Paul Morgan) *trckd ldr tl after 4th: cl 2nd bef 3 out: drvn upsides 2 out: led narrowly last 100yds: hdd and no ex clsng stages* **13/8**[2]

0F/ **3** *97* **Bygones For Coins (IRE)**[316] 506 8-10-9 0.......... ThomasDowson(7) 5
(Kenny Johnson) *led: clr tl after 2nd: hdd bef 3 out: sn lost pl and bhd: t.o 3 out: eventually completed: fin tired* **25/1**[3]

5m 10.1s (3.10) **3** Ran SP% **108.6**
CSF £1.74 TOTE £1.70; EX 1.70 Trifecta £1.50.
Owner Martin Jones **Bred** Richard R Evans **Trained** Bromsash, H'fords

FOCUS
Race distance 9yds further than advertised. A modest maiden hurdle, in which the two principals fought out a thrilling finish.

5348 WETHERBYRACING.CO.UK H'CAP CHASE (13 fncs 6 omitted) 3m 45y
3:45 (3:50) (Class 3) (0-130,130) 5-Y-O **£6,330** (£1,870; £935; £468; £234)

Form RPR

1F **1** **Streets Of Promise (IRE)**[35] 4649 7-11-12 **130**........(p) RichieMcLernon 139+
(Michael Scudamore) *mde all: drvn clr fr 3 out (normal 4 out): kpt up to work* **9/2**[3]

0034 **2** *6* **Barafundle (IRE)**[28] 4818 12-11-9 **127**..........................(bt) SeanQuinlan 131
(Jennie Candlish) *j. slowly at times: chsd wnr fr 2nd: drvn 10th: outpcd next: 10 l down last: kpt on* **3/1**[1]

3113 **3** *23* **Swing Hard (IRE)**[22] 4907 8-10-11 **115**.............................. DannyCook 95
(Sue Smith) *chsd ldng pair fr 4th: pushed along 8th: one pce fr 10th* **5/1**

-1P6 **4** *17* **Beforeall (IRE)**[28] 4826 8-11-9 **127**...............................(t) LeightonAspell 87
(Oliver Sherwood) *in rr: mstke and reminders 3rd: drvn 5th: bhd next: t.o 3 out (normal 4 out): tk distant 4th clsng stages* **9/1**

3121 **5** *1 1/4* **Oscar O'Scar (IRE)**[27] 4836 8-10-7 **118**.................. FinianO'Toole[(7)] 77
(Micky Hammond) *hld up towards rr: hdwy 7th: modest 4th 8th: drvn 10th: sn wknd: t.o* **7/2**[2]

U45/ **P** **Top Of The Range (IRE)**[764] 4806 9-10-11 **122**...............(t) MrBGibbs[(7)]
(Paul Morgan) *chsd ldrs 4th: wknd 8th: sn bhd: t.o whn p.u after 10th* **16/1**

-303 **P** **Russborough (FR)**[17] 5046 7-11-5 **123**.......................... LiamTreadwell
(Venetia Williams) *chsd ldrs: hit 1st: reminders 6th: lost pl and mstke 8th: sn bhd: t.o 10th: p.u bef omitted 2 out* **7/1**

6m 39.2s (-8.80) **7 Ran SP% 110.5**
CSF £17.63 CT £64.41 TOTE £5.40: £2.40, £2.80; EX 19.10 Trifecta £103.80.
Owner Gempro **Bred** Gareth Adair **Trained** Bromsash, H'fords

FOCUS
Race distance 90yds further than advertised. A decent staying handicap and the winner made all the running under topweight.

5349 BULLOUGHS CLEANING SERVICES NOVICES' HURDLE (8 hdls 1 omitted) 1m 7f 193y
4:20 (4:26) (Class 4) 4-Y-0+ **£3,898** (£1,144; £572; £286)

Form RPR

PF5 **1** **Overtheedge (IRE)**[6] 5256 7-10-9 0................................ JohnKington[(3)] 110
(Simon West) *trckd ldrs: 2nd 5th: upsides 3 out: led next: 3 l clr last: drvn out* **9/1**[2]

131F **2** *1 3/4* **Flashjack (IRE)**[36] 4620 6-11-12 130.............................. TomO'Brien 123
(Henry Daly) *nt fluent: trckd ldrs: led after 3rd: jnd and drvn 3 out: hdd next: styd on same pce run-in* **1/5**[1]

3 *35* **Falcon's Reign (FR)**[25] 7-10-12 0............................(p) JonathanEngland 73
(Michael Appleby) *chsd ldrs: 3rd fr 5th: outpcd appr next: grad wknd: t.o whn j.lft last* **12/1**

4665 **4** *11* **Captain Mowbray**[47] 4417 5-10-9 0.............................. TonyKelly[(3)] 62
(Rebecca Menzies) *stdd s: t.k.h: detached in last: bhd and drvn 5th: distant 5th bef 3 out: tk remote 4th last 100yds: t.o* **10/1**[3]

2000 **5** *2 3/4* **First Of Never (IRE)**[79] 3840 10-10-12 66.......................... SeanQuinlan 60
(Lynn Siddall) *hld up towards rr: sme hdwy 5th: lost pl bef next: sn bhd: t.o whn hung rt run-in* **50/1**

/F2- **6** *29* **Desert Nova (IRE)**[669] 724 14-10-5 92.............................. MissAWaugh[(7)] 31
(Mark Campion) *t.k.h: led: hdd after 3rd: lost pl after 5th: sn bhd: t.o* **50/1**

4m 5.3s (245.30) **Going Correction** +0.825s/f (Soft)
WFA 4 from 5yo+ 5lb **6 Ran SP% 114.0**
Speed ratings (Par 105): **109,108,90,85,83 69**
CSF £12.23 TOTE £9.00: £3.20, £1.10; EX 13.50 Trifecta £57.60.
Owner Paul Hothersall **Bred** Liam Walsh **Trained** Middleham Moor, N Yorks

FOCUS
An uncompetitive novice hurdle and a bit of a turn up, with the short-priced favourite failing to deliver.

5350 SUNDAY CAR BOOT FAIR EVERY WEEK H'CAP CHASE (12 fncs 6 omitted) 2m 5f 75y
4:50 (4:55) (Class 4) (0-120,112) 5-Y-0+ **£4,548** (£1,335; £667; £333)

Form RPR

4P42 **1** **Thedrinkymeister (IRE)**[17] 5044 7-11-9 **109**...................(p) DavidBass 122
(Kim Bailey) *mde all: j. soundly: drvn and styd on fr 2 out (normal 3 out): sn forged clr* **7/4**[1]

2UP3 **2** *10* **Pay The King (IRE)**[14] 5126 9-10-3 **92**.......................... JoeColliver[(3)] 98
(Micky Hammond) *chsd ldng pair: pushed along to chse wnr sn after 9th: hit 3 out (normal 4 out) and last: one pce* **7/2**[2]

2-01 **3** *17* **Crown And Glory (IRE)**[16] 5080 9-10-4 **93**...................... AdamNicol[(3)] 82
(Chris Fairhurst) *trckd ldng pair: handy 3rd sn after 9th: effrt bef next: wknd bef last: fin tired* **7/4**[1]

33B0 **4** *57* **Bonnet's Vino**[25] 4878 8-11-7 **112**............................... JamieBargary[(5)] 41
(Pam Sly) *j.rt: chsd wnr: drvn 9th: sn lost pl and bhd: t.o 2 out (normal 3 out): eventually completed* **7/1**[3]

5m 59.7s (22.70) **Going Correction** +0.875s/f (Soft) **4 Ran SP% 107.4**
Speed ratings: **91,87,80,59**
CSF £7.73 TOTE £3.10; EX 8.40 Trifecta £12.40.
Owner J Perriss **Bred** Mrs C J C Bailey **Trained** Andoversford, Gloucs

FOCUS
Race distance 81yds further than advertised. A modest handicap chase and not the strongest for the grade.

5351 ROYAL PIGEON RACING ASSOCIATION MARES' STANDARD OPEN NATIONAL HUNT FLAT RACE 1m 7f 193y
5:20 (5:25) (Class 5) 4-6-Y-0 **£2,599** (£763; £381; £190)

Form RPR

1 **Champagne To Go (IRE)**[71] 6-11-0 0.................................. DavidBass 104+
(Kim Bailey) *t.k.h: led 1f: w ldr: led over 3f out: drvn clr over 2f out: 10 l clr whn eased clsng stages* **5/2**[2]

1 **2** *6* **Kelka**[39] 4559 4-10-11 0... JamieHamilton[(5)] 96
(Malcolm Jefferson) *t.k.h: led after 1f: drvn and hdd over 3f out: kpt on same pce* **9/4**[1]

3 *28* **Banjo Girl (IRE)** 4-10-9 0... LeightonAspell 69
(Lucy Wadham) *trckd ldrs: drvn over 4f out: sn lost pl: t.o whn eased clsng stages* **9/4**[1]

4 *79* **Palm Valley**[29] 6-10-11 0....................................(t) JohnKington[(3)]
(Chris Grant) *trckd ldrs: pushed along over 7f out: sn lost pl and bhd: t.o 6f out: eventually completed* **33/1**

P **Reine Des Champs (IRE)** 5-11-0 0................................ JamesDavies
(Tom Symonds) *trckd ldrs: t.k.h: drvn and lost pl over 7f out: sn eased and t.o: p.u over 6f out: fatally injured* **6/1**[3]

4m 0.1s (240.10) **Going Correction** +0.825s/f (Soft)
WFA 4 from 5yo+ 5lb **5 Ran SP% 107.3**
Speed ratings: **108,105,91,51,**
CSF £8.05 TOTE £2.90: £1.80, £1.30; EX 6.30 Trifecta £8.40.
Owner J Perriss **Bred** Paul Gibbons & Mrs Lucy Gibbons **Trained** Andoversford, Gloucs

FOCUS
An ordinary bumper that went to an ex-pointer, who did it nicely.
T/Jkpt: Not won. T/Plt: £18.80 to a £1 stake. Pool: £74,385.92. 2,784.00 winning tickets. T/Qpdt: £8.90 to a £1 stake. Pool: £4,059.31. 334.02 winning tickets. **Walter Glynn**

5145 WINCANTON (R-H)
Sunday, April 17

OFFICIAL GOING: Good to soft (5.7)
Wind: mild breeze across Weather: sunny Rails: Hurdle on stable bend omitted due to a false patch of ground. Race distances; Races 1, 2, 6, 7 & 8 add about 24yds. Race 3 add about 18yds. Races 4 & 5 add about 36yds.

5352 CHILDREN'S TRUST CONDITIONAL JOCKEYS' H'CAP HURDLE (7 hdls 1 omitted) 1m 7f 65y
1:55 (1:55) (Class 4) (0-110,105) 4-Y-0+ **£3,249** (£954; £477; £238)

Form RPR

P66 **1** **Centreofexcellence (IRE)**[41] 4530 5-10-8 **95**........ GeorgeGorman[(8)] 94
(Gary Moore) *trckd ldrs: chal 2 out: sn drvn: 1 1/4 l 3rd whn lft in ld sn after last: kpt on: rdn out* **8/1**

0022 **2** *3* **Antiphony (IRE)**[16] 5067 5-11-5 **104**......................... ConorSmith[(6)] 105+
(Philip Hobbs) *hld up in tch: hdwy to ld 3rd where nt fluent: nt fluent next: rdn and hdd between last 2: stl ev ch whn nt fluent last: lft in ld briefly and hmpd sn after: no ex* **13/8**[1]

50R5 **3** *7* **Blue April (FR)**[25] 4871 5-11-9 **105**........................(p) MattGriffiths[(3)] 97
(Jeremy Scott) *disp ld tl 3rd: trckd ldr: rdn appr 2 out: sn one pce: lft 3rd at the last* **9/2**[3]

600 **4** *2 3/4* **Dragoon Guard (IRE)**[16] 5063 5-11-8 **101**........................ DavidNoonan 87
(Anthony Honeyball) *disp ld tl 3rd: trckd ldr: rdn appr 2 out: sn one pce: lft 4th at the last* **7/2**[2]

0-05 **5** *14* **Knight's Reward**[34] 4674 6-10-6 **88**................ WilliamFeatherstone[(3)] 60
(Tim Vaughan) *hld up but in tch: rdn after 3 out: sn btn* **9/1**

6500 **U** **Berry De Carjac (FR)**[129] 2987 5-11-9 **102**...............(t) TomBellamy 103
(Nigel Hawke) *trckd ldrs: chal 3 out: sn led: travelling best in 1 l ld whn stmbld v bdly on landing last and uns rdr* **8/1**

3m 51.8s (2.90) **Going Correction** -0.175s/f (Good) **6 Ran SP% 110.7**
Speed ratings (Par 105): **85,83,79,78,70**
CSF £21.57 CT £62.74 TOTE £10.20: £4.30, £1.10; EX 20.20 Trifecta £113.00.
Owner G L Moore **Bred** I McGrath & K McGrath **Trained** Lower Beeding, W Sussex

FOCUS
After the opener George Gorman described the ground as "a little bit dead" and Conor Smith said: "It's riding not far off good ground". A weak handicap which was run at a very steady pace, meaning it became rather a sprint from the home turn. Add 24 yards to advertised race distance.

5353 RIDGEWAY BMW NOVICES' HURDLE (7 hdls 1 omitted) 1m 7f 65y
2:25 (2:26) (Class 4) 4-Y-0+ **£3,249** (£954; £477; £238)

Form RPR

10 **1** **Zubayr (IRE)**[30] 4764 4-11-1 0..................................... NickScholfield 115+
(Paul Nicholls) *trckd ldr: led sn after 3 out: wl in command fr next: v easily* **1/8**[1]

445- **2** *8* **Alphabet Bay (IRE)**[361] 5467 6-11-0 108........................ GavinSheehan 99+
(Warren Greatrex) *led tl sn after 3 out: rdn in 3rd bef next: nt fluent last: styd on to go 2nd run-in: no ch w wnr* **5/1**[2]

3 *2* **Abertillery**[32] 4-10-9 0... MarkGrant 91
(Michael Blanshard) *trckd ldrs: hit 2nd: rdn to chse wnr whn nt fluent 2 out: sn no ch: no ex whn lost 2nd run-in* **25/1**[3]

4 *3 3/4* **Approaching Star (FR)**[25] 5-10-7 0.............................. RobertDunne 84
(Dai Burchell) *racd keenly: hld up in tch: wnt 4th after 3 out: rdn bef next: sn one pce* **40/1**

2240 **5** *3 3/4* **Pure Vision (IRE)**[5] 5268 5-11-0 0................................ AidanColeman 88
(Anthony Honeyball) *trckd ldrs: rdn appr 2 out: sn one pce* **5/1**[2]

0F-5 **6** *2 3/4* **Gifted Island (IRE)**[195] 1792 6-10-9 0........................ AlanJohns[(5)] 85
(Tim Vaughan) *t.k.h: trckd ldrs tl 3rd: in last pair: rdn appr 2 out: sn one pce* **33/1**

5UPP **7** *6* **Hawaian Rose**[46] 4435 6-10-2 0................................(b[1]) PaulO'Brien[(5)] 74
(Colin Tizzard) *hld up in tch: hmpd 1st: rdn appr 2 out: sn outpcd* **50/1**

U06 **8** *13* **Catch A Thief (IRE)**[7] 5235 5-10-7 0............................ LewisGordon[(7)] 66
(Evan Williams) *hld up: hmpd 1st: struggling 3rd: nvr threatened: wknd 2 out* **25/1**[3]

00P **U** **Yenston (IRE)**[36] 4614 5-11-0 0..................................(t) BrendanPowell
(Colin Tizzard) *trcking ldrs whn v green and uns rdr 1st* **33/1**

3m 50.7s (1.80) **Going Correction** -0.175s/f (Good) **9 Ran SP% 140.2**
Speed ratings (Par 105): **88,83,82,80,78 77,74,67,**
CSF £2.45 TOTE £1.10: £1.02, £1.30, £8.80; EX 2.50 Trifecta £29.30.
Owner P J Vogt **Bred** His Highness The Aga Khan's Studs S C **Trained** Ditcheat, Somerset

FOCUS
Add 24 yards to advertised race distance. The pace wasn't strong and the hot favourite clocked a time only around a second quicker than that of the earlier 0-110 handicap.

5354 YEOVIL RADIO CABS 426666 H'CAP CHASE (17 fncs) 2m 4f 35y
2:55 (2:55) (Class 3) (0-130,129) 5-Y-0+ **£6,498** (£1,908; £954; £477)

Form RPR

3-46 **1** **Go Conquer (IRE)**[15] 5096 7-11-5 **122**............................ AidanColeman 139+
(Jonjo O'Neill) *mde all: kpt on strly fr 2 out: rdn out* **7/1**[3]

P641 **2** *7* **Dusky Lark**[20] 4978 6-11-12 **129**................................(t) DarylJacob 140
(Colin Tizzard) *chsd wnr thrght: nt fluent 4th: rdn after 3 out: styd on but a being hld fr next* **5/2**[1]

4P52 **3** *5* **Somchine**[27] 4842 8-11-3 **120**..................................... AndrewThornton 125
(Seamus Mullins) *hld up: hdwy after 11th: disp 3rd 3 out: sn rdn: styd on same pce fr 2 out* **14/1**

2122 **4** *1* **Sonny The One**[40] 4542 6-11-1 **118**.......................... BrendanPowell 123
(Colin Tizzard) *trckd ldrs: nodded 6th: nt fluent 4 out: sn rdn: styd on same pce fr 2 out* **3/1**[2]

1121 **5** *1/2* **Ashcott Boy**[24] 4889 8-11-2 **124**................................ DavidNoonan[(5)] 130
(Neil Mulholland) *mid-div: hit 2nd: pushed along fr 11th: hdwy 4 out: disp cl 3rd next: styd on same pce fr 2 out* **12/1**

0-P5 **6** *11* **Headly's Bridge (IRE)**[15] 5093 10-11-7 **124**.................. PaddyBrennan 119
(Simon Earle) *hld up: nt pce to get involved: wknd bef 3 out* **7/1**[3]

214 **7** *3 1/2* **Miss Tenacious**[22] 4918 9-11-6 **128**.................. HarryCobden(5) 119
(Ron Hodges) *trckd ldrs: rdn after 13th: wknd after next* **25/1**

640P **8** *1* **Perfect Timing**[160] 2404 8-11-4 **121**..................(p) NoelFehily 110
(Neil Mulholland) *mid-div tl 13th: wknd next* **25/1**

2-54 **P** **It's A Steal (IRE)**[16] 5063 9-11-8 **125**..................(t) PaulMoloney
(Evan Williams) *hld up: lost tch fr 10th: t.o whn p.u 4 out* **7/1**[3]

-PF5 **P** **Dance Floor King (IRE)**[22] 4918 9-11-8 **125**.................. NickScholfield
(Nick Mitchell) *trckd ldrs tl after 13th: bhd whn p.u 3 out* **33/1**

5m 12.9s (-4.60) **Going Correction** -0.025s/f (Good) **10** Ran SP% **116.1**
Speed ratings: **108,105,103,102,102 98,96,96, ,**
CSF £25.25 CT £241.95 TOTE £12.00: £3.30, £1.60, £4.20; EX 31.90 Trifecta £302.20.
Owner Paul & Clare Rooney **Bred** Ben Furney **Trained** Cheltenham, Gloucs

FOCUS
Add 18 yards to advertised race distance. A decent handicap in which the winner set a fair pace.

5355 WESSEX WASTE H'CAP HURDLE (10 hdls 1 omitted) 2m 5f 82y
3:30 (3:30) (Class 4) (0-110,115) 4-Y-0+ **£3,249** (£954; £477; £238)

Form				RPR
2/4F	**1**		**Cropley (IRE)**[16] 5067 7-10-4 **88**.................. RobertDunne (Dai Burchell) *trckd ldr: led 3 out: rdn next: kpt on v gamely fr last where strly chal: drvn out* **16/1**	93+
2052	**2**	*1*	**Bold Runner**[14] 5115 5-11-10 **115**..................(p) ConorWalsh(7) (Jose Santos) *led tl 3 out: pressed wnr: sn rdn: ev ch fr last: kpt on gamely tl no ex nring fin* **13/2**[3]	118
6F24	**3**	*1 1/4*	**Tikkapick (IRE)**[29] 4783 6-10-8 **92**.................. PaddyBrennan (Colin Tizzard) *trckd ldrs: rdn after 3 out: styd on fr last but a being hld* **10/1**	95
52P2	**4**	*8*	**Bishops Court**[24] 4882 6-11-11 **109**..................(t) NoelFehily (Neil Mulholland) *hld up: midfield 5th: rdn after 3 out: styd on into 4th between last 2: nvr trbld ldrs* **7/1**	105
6225	**5**	*7*	**Pennywell (IRE)**[16] 5079 6-11-6 **104**.................. GavinSheehan (Warren Greatrex) *trckd ldrs: ev ch 3 out: styd on same pce fr next* **10/1**	94
0004	**6**	*1 1/4*	**Aka Doun (FR)**[40] 4543 5-11-3 **101**..................(v) DarylJacob (Emma Lavelle) *mid-div: hdwy after 7th: wnt cl 3rd after 3 out: sn rdn: wknd bef last* **12/1**	88
53/6	**7**	*6*	**Benzel (IRE)**[34] 4681 8-11-12 **110**.................. RichardJohnson (Jonjo O'Neill) *hld up towards rr: midfield u.p after 3 out: no further imp fr next* **9/2**[1]	96
4P46	**8**	*2 1/2*	**Kahdian (IRE)**[26] 4856 6-10-5 **89**..................(t) IanPopham (Helen Rees) *hld up: rdn and sme prog after 3 out: wknd between last 2* **66/1**	69
004	**9**	*1 1/2*	**Titch Strider (IRE)**[18] 5033 11-11-3 **101**.................. ConorO'Farrell (John Panvert) *a towards rr* **25/1**	79
2F26	**10**	*1 1/2*	**Bennachie (IRE)**[195] 1794 7-11-6 **109**..................(t) AlanJohns(5) (Tim Vaughan) *trckd ldrs tl 3 out: sn wknd* **10/1**	86
P553	**11**	*8*	**Garde Fou (FR)**[12] 5165 10-11-2 **100**..................(t) JamieMoore (Paul Henderson) *mid-div: rdn after 3 out: wknd bef next where nt fluent: nt fluent last* **16/1**	70
1P63	**12**	*72*	**Brave Deed (IRE)**[18] 5034 10-11-1 **99**.................. NickScholfield (Jeremy Scott) *mid-div tl after 5th: bhd fr next: t.o* **10/1**	4
5P33	**P**		**Lime Street (IRE)**[26] 4856 5-11-7 **105**.................. NicodeBoinville (Tom Symonds) *racd keenly: mid-div: sme hdwy 3 out: sn rdn: wknd bef next: t.o whn p.u bef last* **6/1**[2]	

5m 19.7s (-6.80) **Going Correction** -0.175s/f (Good) **13** Ran SP% **119.5**
Speed ratings (Par 105): **105,104,104,101,98 97,95,94,94,93 90,63,**
CSF £117.79 CT £1113.27 TOTE £19.10: £3.80, £2.50, £3.60; EX 154.70 Trifecta £1690.40.
Owner Miss Sarah Carter **Bred** Whisperview Trading Ltd **Trained** Briery Hill, Blaenau Gwent

FOCUS
Add 36 yards to advertised race distance. Not many got involved in this ordinary handicap hurdle.

5356 RACING UK PROFITS RETURNED TO RACING "NATIONAL HUNT" NOVICES HURDLE (9 hdls 1 omitted) 2m 3f 166y
4:05 (4:05) (Class 4) 4-Y-0+ **£3,573** (£1,049; £524; £262)

Form				RPR
4121	**1**		**Emerging Talent (IRE)**[10] 5182 7-11-7 135..................(t) HarryCobden(5) (Paul Nicholls) *trckd ldr: chalng whn nt fluent 2 out: led bef last: comf* **5/6**[1]	140+
-44U	**2**	*3*	**Kerrow (IRE)**[66] 4063 6-11-0 122.................. WayneHutchinson (Alan King) *trckd ldrs: rdn in 3rd whn rchd for 2 out: wnt 2nd at the last: styd on but a being comf hld* **9/2**[3]	122
1415	**3**	*20*	**Bun Doran (IRE)**[50] 4368 5-11-6 138..................(t) PaddyBrennan (Tom George) *led: rdn and hdd after 2 out: wknd last* **7/4**[2]	111
	4	*4*	**Sarah Marie**[365] 6-10-7 0.................. RichardJohnson (Philip Hobbs) *in tch: trckd ldrs 3 out: rdn bef next: wknd between last 2* **14/1**	96+
0-40	**5**	*19*	**Tudors Treasure**[25] 4874 5-11-0 0.................. MichealNolan (Robert Stephens) *hld up: nvr threatened: wknd after 3 out* **100/1**	79
030	**6**	*15*	**Instingtive (IRE)**[15] 5097 5-11-0 0..................(t) NoelFehily (Harry Fry) *mid-div tl wknd after 3 out: t.o* **16/1**	64
0	**7**	*90*	**New Republic (IRE)**[7] 5235 5-10-9 0.................. ConorRing(5) (Evan Williams) *struggling 3rd: sn lost tch: t.o 5th* **66/1**	
00F	**P**		**Bellini Dubreau (FR)**[14] 5115 5-10-11 0.................. TomBellamy(3) (Nigel Hawke) *trckd ldrs: pushed along fr 7th: wknd after 3 out: p.u bef next* **100/1**	

4m 53.1s (293.10) **8** Ran SP% **125.1**
CSF £6.39 TOTE £1.80: £1.02, £1.80, £1.30; EX 7.20 Trifecta £12.40.
Owner Mr & Mrs Paul Barber **Bred** T J Nagle **Trained** Ditcheat, Somerset

FOCUS
Add 36 yards to advertised race distance. The top two in the market set a useful standard.

5357 LANCER SCOTT NOVICES' H'CAP CHASE (21 fncs) 3m 1f 30y
4:40 (4:40) (Class 4) (0-105,102) 5-Y-0+ **£4,659** (£1,446; £779)

Form				RPR
1311	**1**		**High Aspirations (IRE)**[7] 5240 8-11-6 **101** 7ex.................. HarryCobden(5) (Michael Blake) *hld up: tk clsr order 17th: rdn and str chal 3 out where pckd: led between last 2: styd on: drvn out* **11/10**[1]	110
33P1	**2**	*1 1/4*	**Railway Storm (IRE)**[26] 4859 11-11-7 **102**.................. PaulO'Brien(5) (Jimmy Frost) *trckd ldrs: str chal fr 3 out: rdn next: ev ch between last 2: styd on but no ex* **4/1**[3]	109
3P05	**3**	*4*	**Mrsrobin (IRE)**[13] 5138 6-11-6 **96**..................(v) DarylJacob (Emma Lavelle) *trckd ldr: tended to follow ldr lft at his fences: hit 16th: led after 4 out: strly pressed and u.p next: hdd between last 2: no ex* **9/1**	101+
404P	**P**		**Comical Red**[12] 5165 8-10-0 **76** oh1..................(p) JamesBanks (Mark Gillard) *chsd ldrs tl slow jump 9th and dropped to last: struggling but remained in tch tl wknd 17th: p.u next* **14/1**	
5PB3	**P**		**Lawless Island (IRE)**[33] 4704 7-11-9 **99**.................. RichardJohnson (Tim Vaughan) *j.lft bdly at times: led tl rdn after 4 out: sn wknd: p.u next* **3/1**[2]	
0P-0	**P**		**Sisterbrooke (IRE)**[26] 4859 7-10-3 **79** ow3.................. ConorO'Farrell (John Panvert) *hld up: j.lft at times: struggling 13th: wknd after 4 out: t.o whn p.u 2 out* **40/1**	

6m 42.0s (2.50) **Going Correction** -0.025s/f (Good) **6** Ran SP% **111.7**
Speed ratings: **95,94,93, ,**
CSF £6.17 TOTE £2.10: £1.20, £2.10; EX 6.60 Trifecta £16.50.
Owner Mrs J M Haines **Bred** David Moran **Trained** Trowbridge, Wilts

FOCUS
Add 24 yards to advertised race distance. An ordinary novice handicap.

5358 COLLECTS POINTS, GO RACING WITH REWARDS4RACING STANDARD OPEN NATIONAL HUNT FLAT RACE (DIV I) 1m 7f 65y
5:10 (5:10) (Class 6) 4-6-Y-0 **£1,624** (£477; £238; £119)

Form				RPR
	1		**Movewiththetimes (IRE)** 5-11-3 0.................. SamTwiston-Davies (Paul Nicholls) *mid-div: hdwy over 2f out: led ent fnl f: styd on wl: pushed out* **11/4**[2]	107+
	2	*3/4*	**Cruiseaweigh (IRE)** 5-11-3 0.................. PaddyBrennan (Tom George) *trckd ldrs: led 2f out: sn rdn: hdd ent fnl f: drifted lft: styd on but no ex nring fin* **9/4**[1]	106+
0	**3**	*9*	**Louis' Vac Pouch (IRE)**[43] 4488 4-10-12 0.................. RichardJohnson (Philip Hobbs) *mid-div: rdn and hdwy over 2f out: styd on fnl f: wnt 3rd nring fin* **10/1**	92
0	**4**	*hd*	**Stealing Mix**[29] 4790 6-11-3 0..................(t) DenisO'Regan (Neil Mulholland) *trckd ldr: rdn and ev ch 2f out: kpt on same pce fr over 1f out* **25/1**	97
	5	*3/4*	**Notre Ami (IRE)** 5-11-3 0.................. TomCannon (Nick Gifford) *hld up: hdwy over 2f out: styd on nicely but no threat to ldrs* **25/1**	96
	6	*1*	**Melrose Boy (FR)** 4-10-12 0.................. NoelFehily (Harry Fry) *pressed ldr tl over 3f out: outpcd over 2f out* **7/2**[3]	90
	7	*nk*	**Burst Ya Bubble (IRE)** 4-10-12 0.................. AndrewThornton (Seamus Mullins) *hld up: styd on fnl 2f: nvr trbld ldrs* **16/1**	90
0	**8**	*5*	**Speedalong (IRE)**[13] 5152 5-11-3 0.................. NickScholfield (Jeremy Scott) *led tl over 2f out: wknd over 1f out* **40/1**	90
0	**9**	*2 1/2*	**Master Majic (IRE)**[29] 4790 5-11-3 0.................. PaulMoloney (Colin Tizzard) *trckd ldrs tl lost pl over 3f out: nvr bk on terms* **16/1**	87
	10	*20*	**Heluvagood** 4-10-12 0.................. IanPopham (Victor Dartnall) *mid-div tl wknd over 2f out* **33/1**	62
	11	*15*	**Brereton (IRE)** 5-11-3 0.................. DarylJacob (Richard Woollacott) *a towards rr* **25/1**	52

3m 39.1s (-4.20) **Going Correction** -0.175s/f (Good) **11** Ran SP% **117.4**
Speed ratings: **104,103,98,98,98 97,97,94,93,82 74**
CSF £8.68 TOTE £3.40: £1.90, £1.60, £2.00; EX 9.60 Trifecta £51.00.
Owner John P McManus **Bred** Raymond Egan **Trained** Ditcheat, Somerset

FOCUS
Add 24 yards to advertised race distance. A certain Thistlecrack won this bumper two years ago, and the first two, who pulled clear, look useful prospects. It was the slower division by 2.5sec.

5359 COLLECTS POINTS, GO RACING WITH REWARDS4RACING STANDARD OPEN NATIONAL HUNT FLAT RACE (DIV II) 1m 7f 65y
5:40 (5:41) (Class 6) 4-6-Y-0 **£1,624** (£477; £238; £119)

Form				RPR
2	**1**		**Capitaine (FR)**[129] 2991 4-10-12 0.................. SamTwiston-Davies (Paul Nicholls) *mid-div: smooth hdwy fr 4f out: cantering bhd ldr over 2f out: led sn after: cruised clr: impressive* **7/4**[1]	126+
	2	*13*	**Minella For Me (IRE)**[168] 6-11-3 0..................(t) PaddyBrennan (Tom George) *chsd ldrs: wnt 30 l 2nd 1/2-way: clsd on ldr fr 4f out to ld over 2f out: sn rdn and hdd: no ch w impressive wnr fnl f* **3/1**[2]	112+
05	**3**	*18*	**Lets Go Dutchess**[157] 2460 6-10-3 0.................. ConorSmith(7) (Kevin Bishop) *led: sn clr: 30 l clr 1/2-way: rdn and hdd over 2f out: sn hld: wknd jst over 1f out* **20/1**	88
	4	*5*	**Speronimo (FR)** 4-10-9 0..................(t) TomBellamy(3) (Nigel Hawke) *mid-div: hdwy fr 3f out: nvr threatened ldrs: wknd jst over 1f out* **33/1**	86
44	**5**	*1/2*	**Mr Fenton (IRE)**[79] 3847 5-11-3 0.................. DarylJacob (Emma Lavelle) *in tch: rdn 4f out: outpcd 3f out: hdwy 2f out: wknd jst over 1f out* **10/1**[3]	90
	6	*6*	**Jabbea (IRE)** 4-10-7 0.................. DavidNoonan(5) (Mary Sanderson) *chsd ldrs: rdn 3f out: wknd over 1f out* **50/1**	80
44	**7**	*18*	**Burton Boru (IRE)**[73] 3959 4-10-12 0.................. AidanColeman (Colin Tizzard) *chsd ldrs tl 1/2-way: sn bhd* **25/1**	64
0	**8**	*17*	**I'm A Game Changer (IRE)**[13] 5152 4-10-12 0.................. RichardJohnson (Philip Hobbs) *racd keenly in midfield: wknd 3f out* **3/1**[2]	48
	9	*25*	**Blue Sire (FR)** 5-11-3 0.................. JamieMoore (Gary Moore) *mid-div tl 5f out: sn t.o* **12/1**	31
	10	*1/2*	**Missmebutletmego** 6-11-3 0.................. NickScholfield (Alan Jones) *a towards rr: t.o 4f out* **100/1**	30
0	**11**	*6*	**Earth Legend**[179] 2020 5-11-3 0..................(t) NoelFehily (Neil Mulholland) *a towards rr: t.o 4f out* **50/1**	25

3m 36.6s (-6.70) **Going Correction** -0.175s/f (Good) **11** Ran SP% **119.6**
Speed ratings: **110,103,93,90,90 87,77,68,55,55 51**
CSF £6.74 TOTE £2.70: £1.30, £1.80, £5.20; EX 10.00 Trifecta £87.60.
Owner Martin Broughton & Friends 2 **Bred** S C E A Haras De Saint Voir **Trained** Ditcheat, Somerset

FOCUS
Add 24 yards to advertised race distance. This looked the slightly weaker division on paper, but it was 2.5sec quicker, with the third ensuring it was more of a stamina test than a lot of these races are.

T/Plt: £20.30 to a £1 stake. Pool: £89,799.68. 3,218.30 winning tickets. T/Qpdt: £11.60 to a £1 stake. Pool £6,408.99. 407.60 winning tickets. **Tim Mitchell**

5360 - 5362a (Foreign Racing) - See Raceform Interactive

5211
AUTEUIL (L-H)
Sunday, April 17

OFFICIAL GOING: Turf: very soft

5363a PRIX JEAN GRANEL (HURDLE) (LISTED RACE) (5YO+) (TURF) 2m 3f 110y
4:20 (12:00) 5-Y-O+ **£30,000** (£15,000; £8,750; £5,937; £2,812)

RPR
1 **Verdure Des Obeaux (FR)**[35] 7-10-8 0........................ ThomasBeaurain 144
(N Devilder, France) **13/5**[3]
2 6 **Vieux Morvan (FR)**[161] 2395 7-10-10 0..............................(b) KevinNabet 140
(G Cherel, France) **44/5**
3 nk **Fracafigura Has (FR)**[42] 4525 5-10-8 0.......................... JonathanNattiez 138
(P Lenogue, France) **73/10**
4 4 **Totalize**[23] 4070 7-10-10 0................................... ArnaudDuchene 136
(Brian Ellison) *w.w in middle of main gp wl adrift of clr ldr: disp 2nd 30 l off ldr bef 4 out: rdn and sltly outpcd fnl bnd bef 2 out: styd on u.p appr last: kpt on run-in but nt trble front three* **238/10**
5 12 **Pythagore**[43] 4485 11-11-0 0...................................... FelixDeGiles 128
(Emmanuel Clayeux, France) **23/10**[1]
6 1 **The Stomp (FR)**[42] 4525 6-11-3 0.............................. JacquesRicou 130
(Francois Nicolle, France) **12/5**[2]
P **Derwent (USA)**[336] 6-10-12 0....................................(p) JamesReveley
(J-P Gallorini, France) **17/1**

4m 53.09s (-1.91) **7 Ran SP% 119.3**
PARI-MUTUEL (all including 1 euro stake): WIN 3.60; PLACE 2.30, 3.30; SF 24.00.
Owner Mme Nicolas Devilder **Bred** N Devilder **Trained** France

985
LES LANDES
Sunday, April 17

OFFICIAL GOING: Turf: good
Wind: Moderate, against Weather: Cloudy early, sunny later

5364a GEORGE & LEONORA SULLIVAN PERPETUAL H'CAP HURDLE 2m
2:30 (2:30) 4-Y-0+ **£1,780** (£640; £380)

RPR
1 **Steely**[230] 8-9-3 0 oh2.............................(p) PhilipPrince 92
(K Kukk, Jersey) *mde all: sn 15 l clr: breather 1/2-way and 5 l ahd 3 out: sn qcknd clr again: unchal* **11/1**
2 12 **Rossetti**[230] 985 8-11-10 0.............................. MattieBatchelor 115
(Mrs A Malzard, Jersey) *chsd clr ldr: clsd 1/2-way: outpcd 3 out* **6/4**[2]
3 5 **Dalmo**[230] 7-9-3 0.......................................(p) AliceMills 75
(K Kukk, Jersey) *outpcd and bhd tl styd on fr 2 out* **9/1**[3]
4 6 **Fourni (IRE)**[230] 7-11-1 0...................................... MissMHooper 95
(Mrs A Malzard, Jersey) *outpcd and bhd: nvr rchd ldrs* **12/1**
5 4 **Master Burbidge**[53] 3077 5-10-8 0................................ MarkQuinlan 84
(Neil Mulholland) *hld up off the pce in 3rd: effrt 6th: wknd 3 out* **4/6**[1]

Owner Karl Kukk Racing **Bred** Mrs S E Barclay **Trained** Jersey

5009
HEXHAM (L-H)
Monday, April 18

OFFICIAL GOING: Heavy (3.7)
Wind: Fairly strong, half against Weather: Overcast

5365 WELCOME TO HEXHAM "NATIONAL HUNT" NOVICES' HURDLE (7 hdls 1 omitted) 2m 48y
2:00 (2:00) (Class 4) 4-Y-0+ **£4,174** (£1,216; £608)

Form RPR
0 1 **Newtown Lad (IRE)**[23] 4915 6-10-12 0.................................. DerekFox 112+
(Lucinda Russell) *chsd clr ldr: hdwy to ld bef 3 out: shkn up whn nt fluent last: kpt on strly to draw clr run-in* **17/2**[3]
004 2 7 **Motion To Strike (IRE)**[28] 4835 6-10-9 0.....................(t) TonyKelly(3) 104
(Rebecca Menzies) *cl up in chsng gp: wnt 2nd bef 3 out: ev ch after next to bef last: kpt on: nt pce of wnr* **12/1**
6241 3 1 1/2 **Very First Time**[41] 4548 4-11-0 0.............................. BrianHarding 105
(Tim Easterby) *hld up: stdy hdwy to trck ldrs whn j.lft 3 out: rdn along next: kpt on same pce bef last* **2/7**[1]
F35 4 25 **Wazowski**[23] 4902 7-10-7 108................................ JamesCowley(5) 83
(Donald McCain) *nt fluent on occasions: hld up: hit 3rd: hdwy and prom bef 2 out: rdn and wknd bef last* **6/1**[2]
4F0 5 10 **Flying Jack**[20] 5009 6-10-5 0............................ ThomasDowson(7) 68
(Maurice Barnes) *in tch chsng gp: rdn and outpcd after 3 out: sn struggling: btn next* **66/1**
60- 6 74 **Kev The Car (IRE)**[141] 6-10-5 0..............................[1] MrTimDonworth(7)
(Paul Cowley) *t.k.h: led and sn clr: hdd bef 3 out: sn wknd: t.o* **66/1**

4m 28.6s (11.20) **Going Correction** +0.80s/f (Soft) **6 Ran SP% 113.2**
Speed ratings (Par 105): **104,100,99,87,82 45**
CSF £87.68 TOTE £11.60: £2.80, £3.90; EX 92.10 Trifecta £97.60.
Owner John J Murray & Mrs Lynne MacLennan **Bred** Gerard Rochford **Trained** Arlary, Perth & Kinross

FOCUS
Due to ground conditions, the first two fences in the back straight and the first hurdle in the back straight are omitted.\n\x\x A modest novice hurdle. They went an honest gallop on heavy ground into a strong headwind. Not a bad time considering and the winner could be fairly useful.

5366 RAMSIDE EVENT CATERING H'CAP CHASE (10 fncs 2 omitted) 1m 7f 133y
2:30 (2:30) (Class 5) (0-100,99) 5-Y-0+ **£2,729** (£801; £400; £200)

Form RPR
0P12 1 **Suprise Vendor (IRE)**[13] 4741 10-11-5 99...................... SamColtherd(7) 111+
(Stuart Coltherd) *pressed ldr: led 3 out: shkn up bef last: rdn out run-in* **4/1**[1]
410U 2 3 **Rosquero (FR)**[10] 5197 11-10-6 86.......................(b) ThomasDowson(7) 94
(Kenny Johnson) *hld up: hdwy to trck ldrs 4 out: wnt 2nd next: drvn along between last 2: kpt on run-in: nt pce of wnr* **17/2**
3241 3 29 **Mumgos Debut (IRE)**[10] 5197 8-11-12 99........................(t) PeterBuchanan 81
(Lucinda Russell) *trckd ldrs: pushed along 3 out: effrt next: wkng whn hit last* **9/2**[2]
1233 4 10 **Oscar Lateen (IRE)**[30] 4792 8-11-6 98...........................(b) StevenFox(5) 68
(Sandy Thomson) *hld up in tch: effrt and pushed along whn hit and outpcd 3 out: struggling fr next* **6/1**[3]
00P0 5 6 **West Ship Master (IRE)**[13] 5172 12-10-5 83..........(v) JonathanMoore(5) 45
(Paul Stafford, Ire) *led to 4 out: drvn and sn outpcd: struggling fr next: sn btn* **9/2**[2]
2214 6 8 **Duhallowcountry (IRE)**[9] 5231 10-10-4 84.................(p) MissAWaugh(7) 41
(Victor Thompson) *cl up: led 4 out to next: rdn and wknd fr 2 out* **12/1**
36-5 7 13 **Runswick Days (IRE)**[22] 4938 9-11-1 88.............................(p) DannyCook 29
(John Wade) *hld up: niggled along 1/2-way: effrt after 4 out: rdn and wknd fr next: t.o* **6/1**[3]
3012 P **Asuncion (FR)**[10] 5197 6-10-6 84..................................(b) JamieHamilton(5)
(Rebecca Menzies) *a bhd: t.o fr 7th: p.u bef last* **8/1**

4m 20.4s (10.60) **Going Correction** +0.725s/f (Soft) **8 Ran SP% 114.3**
Speed ratings: **102,100,86,81,78 74,67,**
CSF £36.60 CT £157.86 TOTE £5.20: £2.00, £2.30, £1.20; EX 49.10 Trifecta £200.40.
Owner Aidan Gunning **Bred** P Travers **Trained** Selkirk, Borders

FOCUS
A modest handicap chase. They went a decent gallop and there's a case for rating the form a few pounds higher.

5367 THORNTON FIRKIN MAIDEN HURDLE (10 hdls 2 omitted) 2m 7f 63y
3:00 (3:00) (Class 5) 5-Y-O+ **£2,395** (£698; £349)

Form RPR
22 1 **Conquer Gold (IRE)**[90] 3666 6-10-7 0.................................... BrianHarding 107+
(Nicky Richards) *w ldr: led 6th: mde rest: hit 3 out: drew clr after 2 out: mstke last: kpt on* **11/4**[2]
U323 2 14 **Toarmandowithlove (IRE)**[30] 4796 8-10-0 87...........(t) JamesCorbett(7) 87
(Susan Corbett) *hld up: hdwy to trck ldrs 7th: effrt and disp ld appr 2 out: drvn and outpcd by wnr after 2 out: plugged on fr last: no imp* **14/1**[3]
23U3 3 1 **Ryedale Racer**[22] 4941 5-10-9 120............................. JamieHamilton(5) 93
(Malcolm Jefferson) *t.k.h: led 1st to 6th: pressed wnr tl rdn and outpcd appr 2 out: n.d after* **4/9**[1]
UP 4 72 **My Lady West (IRE)**[8] 7-10-0 0.................................. ThomasDowson(7) 46
(Victor Thompson) *prom: drvn along after 7th: lost tch fr 3 out: t.o* **66/1**
6366 P **Kilquiggan (IRE)**[28] 4840 8-10-9 92.................................(p) StevenFox(5)
(Sandy Thomson) *led to 1st: prom: outpcd bef 7th: lost tch bef 3 out: t.o whn p.u bef next* **18/1**
P **Miss Mix** 7-10-7 0...[1] PeterBuchanan
(Iain Jardine) *hld up: pushed along 5th: struggling whn veered rt after 7th: sn lost tch and p.u* **50/1**

6m 39.9s (30.90) **Going Correction** +1.25s/f (Heav) **6 Ran SP% 111.3**
Speed ratings: **96,91,90,65,**
CSF £33.27 TOTE £3.80: £1.60, £4.00; EX 18.60 Trifecta £36.70.
Owner Paul & Clare Rooney **Bred** Ben Furney **Trained** Greystoke, Cumbria

FOCUS
An ordinary maiden hurdle. The tempo increased before going out on the final circuit. The first two were close to their marks with the favourite 20lb+ off.

5368 HEXHAM AUCTION MART H'CAP HURDLE (8 hdls 2 omitted) 2m 4f 28y
3:30 (3:30) (Class 3) (0-125,122) 4-Y-0+ **£7,147** (£2,098; £1,049; £524)

Form RPR
1112 1 **Beyondtemptation**[9] 5232 8-9-11 100..........................(t) ThomasDowson(7) 112+
(Jonathan Haynes) *mde all: clr to 4th: qcknd clr bef 2 out: edgd lft run-in: pushed out: unchal* **7/1**
0635 2 17 **Rinnagree Rosie**[20] 5012 10-9-9 96 oh12..................(p) GrantCockburn(5) 88
(Lucy Normile) *chsd clr ldr: clsd 1/2-way: lost 2nd after 3 out: outpcd bef next: rallied to chse (clr) wnr bef last: plugged on: no imp* **18/1**
41 3 19 **Kid Valentine (IRE)**[20] 5009 6-11-10 120........................... DannyCook 93
(Michael Smith) *pressed ldrs: wnt 2nd after 3 out: rdn bef next: outpcd whn lost 2nd bef last: wknd run-in* **3/1**[2]
B32P 4 12 **Octagon**[23] 4911 6-11-12 122.. HenryBrooke 83
(Dianne Sayer) *hld up: stdy hdwy and in tch bef 2 out: sn rdn: wknd between last 2* **4/1**[3]
P642 5 22 **Manballandall (IRE)**[20] 5012 8-10-7 110...............(bt) JamesCorbett(7) 49
(Susan Corbett) *hld up: pushed along and hdwy after 4th: drvn and outpcd bef 3 out: btn next: t.o* **11/4**[1]
-PPP 6 3 1/4 **Silverton**[107] 3438 9-10-2 98....................................... AdrianLane 34
(Lucy Normile) *hld up in tch: hdwy and cl up 4th: rdn after 3 out: wknd bef next: t.o* **25/1**
1PP5 7 10 **Redkalani (IRE)**[30] 4796 8-10-6 105.......................... HarryChalloner(3) 31
(Keith Reveley) *trckd ldrs: lost pl 4th: struggling fr next: t.o* **7/1**
2223 P **Milly Baloo**[21] 4983 5-10-8 109.. RyanDay(5)
(Tim Easterby) *bhd: niggled along bef 3rd: struggling fr 5th: t.o whn p.u 2 out* **8/1**

5m 33.7s (21.20) **Going Correction** +1.25s/f (Heav) **8 Ran SP% 116.9**
Speed ratings (Par 107): **107,100,92,87,79 77,73,**
CSF £111.42 CT £459.68 TOTE £4.30: £1.10, £4.10, £1.80; EX 57.90 Trifecta £667.70.
Owner J C Haynes **Bred** J C Haynes **Trained** Low Row, Cumbria

FOCUS
The feature contest was a fair handicap hurdle. They went a decent gallop. Another step up from the winner.

5369 RACING TO SCHOOL H'CAP CHASE (15 fncs 4 omitted) 3m 41y
4:00 (4:03) (Class 5) (0-100,97) 5-Y-0+ **£2,729** (£801; £400; £200)

Form RPR
1012 1 **Flaming Thistle (IRE)**[20] 5013 12-11-1 91..............(p) GrantCockburn(5) 105+
(John Hodge) *cl up: led 4 out: rdn after 2 out: forged clr fr last* **9/2**[2]
6-PP 2 8 **Maz Majecc (IRE)**[32] 4738 7-10-4 78.......................... CallumWhillans(3) 85
(Jonathan Haynes) *t.k.h: trckd ldrs: led bef 5th: hdd appr 4 out: sn chsng wnr: rdn after 2 out: edgd lft appr last: sn no ex* **20/1**
-P56 3 20 **Major Ridge (IRE)**[7] 5261 7-11-2 92................................(t) CallumBewley(5) 78
(Robert Bewley) *trckd ldrs: reminders after 10th: rallied: drvn bef 3 out: wknd after next* **10/1**
4531 4 17 **Gibbstown (IRE)**[20] 5013 10-11-7 97.........................(p) JonathanMoore(5) 66
(Paul Stafford, Ire) *hld up: stdy hdwy and prom bef 4 out: rdn and outpcd bef next: sn struggling* **5/2**[1]
6342 5 14 **King Of The Dark (IRE)**[9] 5234 9-11-2 94...................... ThomasDowson(7) 49
(Victor Thompson) *led to bef 5th: w ldr: drvn and struggling after 4 out: btn fnl 2* **11/2**
6545 P **Joseph Mercer (IRE)**[32] 4738 9-10-2 80........................(p) FinianO'Toole(7)
(Tina Jackson) *hld up bhd ldng gp: struggling fr 9th: lost tch and p.u bef 4 out* **13/2**

P/2F **P** **Brae On (IRE)**[15] 5125 8-11-5 95 JonathonBewley(5)
(George Bewley) *bhd: struggling fr 7th: lost tch and p.u bef 4 out* **8/1**

3214 **P** **The Bishop (IRE)**[20] 5013 8-11-8 93 LucyAlexander
(N W Alexander) *in tch: drvn and outpcd 9th: wknd after 11th: p.u bef 4 out* **5/1**[3]

6m 59.1s (26.90) **Going Correction** +1.175s/f (Heav) **8** Ran SP% **117.1**
Speed ratings: **102,99,92,87,82 , ,**
CSF £76.79 CT £859.80 TOTE £4.90: £2.10, £3.50, £4.10; EX 92.20 Trifecta £1362.80.
Owner John Mc C Hodge **Bred** John Noonan **Trained** Cumnock, Ayrshire

FOCUS
Another modest handicap chase. There was a false start after the tape failed to rise. They went a decent gallop. A pb from the winner.

5370 FOLLOW HEXHAM ON FACEBOOK AND TWITTER OPEN HUNTERS' CHASE (15 fncs 4 omitted) 3m 41y
4:35 (4:35) (Class 6) 5-Y-0+ **£2,048** (£670; £361)

Form RPR
-P20 **1** **Ockey De Neulliac (FR)**[11] 5178 14-11-9 117 SamColtherd(5) 119+
(N Mechie) *mde all: qcknd clr 2 out: 8 l in front last: rdn last 200yds: edgd rt and wknd nr fin: jst hld on* **5/6**[1]

3U-2 **2** *nk* **Wicklow Lad**[8] 12-11-11 122 (v) MrKitAlexander(3) 117
(N W Alexander) *chsd wnr: ev ch briefly appr 3 out: sn outpcd: 8 l down whn nt fluent last: rpr on wl last 150yds: jst hld* **9/5**[2]

-PU3 **3** *18* **Grouse Lodge (IRE)**[17] 5082 10-11-11 108 MrWEasterby(3) 96
(Mrs Emma Clark) *trckd ldrs: drvn and outpcd bef 4 out: no imp fr next* **8/1**[3]

5P5- **P** **Tommysteel (IRE)**[8] 11-11-11 75 MrTDavidson(3)
(Victor Thompson) *hld up: nt fluent 5th: struggling fr 7th: lost tch and p.u bef 10th* **40/1**

0-43 **P** **Barachois Silver**[15] 12-11-2 94 MissRMcDonald(5)
(Mrs J M Hollands) *rn in snatches: hld up in tch: effrt after 11th: wknd fr next: sn btn: t.o whn p.u bef last* **16/1**

7m 3.1s (30.90) **Going Correction** +1.175s/f (Heav) **5** Ran SP% **109.7**
Speed ratings: **95,94,88, ,**
CSF £2.80 TOTE £1.60: £1.10, £1.40; EX 2.50 Trifecta £5.10.
Owner N Mechie **Bred** Michel J Collin **Trained** Thirsk, North Yorks

FOCUS
A fair little hunters' chase. They went a respectable gallop. The winner was below the level of his Carlisle second.

5371 HEART OF ALL ENGLAND NEXT MEETING STANDARD OPEN NATIONAL HUNT FLAT RACE 2m 48y
5:10 (5:11) (Class 6) 4-5-Y-O **£1,711** (£498; £249)

Form RPR
4 **1** **Knocklayde (IRE)**[49] 4408 4-10-7 0 StephenMulqueen(5) 70+
(Katie Scott) *trckd ldr: shkn up to ld over 2f out: pushed clr over 1f out: kpt on wl fnl f* **11/4**[3]

4 **2** *4 1/2* **Shy (CZE)**[34] 4708 4-10-2 0 ColmMcCormack(3) 58
(George Charlton) *trckd ldrs: effrt over 2f out: chsd (clr) wnr over 1f out: edgd lft: sn no imp* **11/8**[1]

3 *11* **Only A Tipple**[21] 5-10-10 0 MrTGillard(7) 59
(Donald McCain) *led at stdy pce: pushed along: hung rt and hdd over 2f out: sn outpcd: wknd ins fnl f* **6/4**[2]

4m 52.4s (39.70) **Going Correction** +1.25s/f (Heav)
WFA 4 from 5yo 5lb **3** Ran SP% **108.8**
Speed ratings: **50,47,42**
CSF £6.67 TOTE £3.40; EX 8.80 Trifecta £6.30.
Owner The Jackson Partnership **Bred** Philip Brady **Trained** Galasheils, Scottish Borders

FOCUS
A weak little bumper run in a slow time. They went a muddling gallop.
T/Plt: £227.00 to a £1 stake. Pool: £54,204.98 - 174.25 winning units. T/Qpdt: £25.30 to a £1 stake. Pool: £7,693.42 - 224.50 winning units. **Richard Young**

4975 HUNTINGDON (R-H)
Monday, April 18

OFFICIAL GOING: Good to soft (soft in places; chs 7.4; hdl 7.0)
Wind: breezy Weather: overcast; 11 degrees

5372 RACING UK NOW IN HD! "NATIONAL HUNT" NOVICES' HURDLE (10 hdls) 2m 4f 145y
5:05 (5:07) (Class 4) 4-Y-0+ **£3,898** (£1,144; £572; £286)

Form RPR
-1F6 **1** **Younevercall (IRE)**[67] 4065 5-11-8 126 DavidBass 133+
(Kim Bailey) *trckd ldrs: chal on bit 2 out: sn led: in command bef last: easily* **6/1**

511P **2** *5* **Will O'The West (IRE)**[37] 4620 5-11-8 125 RichardJohnson 125
(Henry Daly) *settled in midfield: effrt 3 out: rdn to ld bef 2 out and hit flight: drvn and hdd sn after 2 out: no match for wnr bef last* **4/1**[3]

0/0- **3** *2 1/4* **Global Bonus (IRE)**[451] 3840 7-11-2 0 HarrySkelton 117
(Caroline Bailey) *hld up last tl 6th: effrt 3 out where all field in tight bunch: sn drvn in 7th: styd on to go 3rd after hitting last: kpt on wl wout threatening* **150/1**

121 **4** *3* **Vinciaettis (FR)**[21] 4963 5-11-8 127 GavinSheehan 120
(Warren Greatrex) *racd keenly: disp 2nd tl led 3 out: rdn and hdd bef next: no ex bef last* **5/4**[1]

2341 **5** *3/4* **Board Of Trade**[53] 4322 5-11-8 132 WayneHutchinson 119
(Alan King) *settled chsng ldrs: effrt 3 out: 5th and rdn home turn: little rspnse: disputing btn 3rd whn hit last* **5/2**[2]

-034 **6** *14* **Classic Tune**[43] 4508 6-11-2 0 JoshuaMoore 104
(Claire Dyson) *in rr but in tch: brief effrt 3 out: rdn and btn whn mstke next: blnd bdly last* **50/1**

5-32 **7** *16* **Banny's Lad**[48] 4419 7-10-13 117 HarryBannister(3) 90
(Michael Easterby) *prom tl 4th and rdn home turn: fdd between last two* **14/1**

0P **8** *9* **Gustav (IRE)**[151] 2603 6-10-9 0 WilliamFeatherstone(7) 73
(Zoe Davison) *midfield: mstke 5th: wknd rapidly 3 out: t.o bef next* **150/1**

PP **9** *29* **King Of Milan (IRE)**[42] 4535 6-11-2 0 TrevorWhelan 44
(Des Donovan) *led at mod pce: mstke 6th: blnd bdly next: blnd and hdd 3 out: sn t.o* **150/1**

5m 7.4s (-3.20) **Going Correction** -0.05s/f (Good) **9** Ran SP% **117.9**
Speed ratings (Par 105): **104,102,101,100,99 94,88,84,73**
CSF £31.26 TOTE £8.70: £2.10, £1.60, £5.70; EX 41.40 Trifecta £2121.10.
Owner Youneverknow Partnership **Bred** Paddy Kennedy **Trained** Andoversford, Gloucs

FOCUS
All bends had been moved and this was run over 13yds further than advertised. A fair little novice and quite a taking winner. He had threatened this sort of rating when falling here.

5373 RACING UK DAY PASS JUST £10 MARES' MAIDEN HURDLE (8 hdls) 1m 7f 171y
5:40 (5:41) (Class 5) 4-Y-0+ **£2,274** (£667; £333; £166)

Form RPR
242 **1** **Late Night Lily**[43] 4507 5-11-2 108 HarrySkelton 112+
(Dan Skelton) *hld up in midfield: stdy prog bef 3 out: hrd drvn to ld bef last: sn forged clr despite hanging lft flat* **7/4**[1]

1- **2** *6* **Lets Hope So**[387] 5035 6-11-2 0 [1] WayneHutchinson 108+
(Emma Lavelle) *trckd ldrs: chal 3 out: slt ld and hit next: hrd drvn and looking awkward whn hmpd bef last where hdd and blnd: immediately outpcd by wnr* **9/1**

02P2 **3** *1/2* **Goldray**[25] 4881 10-11-2 104 JamieMoore 106
(Kerry Lee) *cl up: chal 3 out: 2nd and drvn home turn: disputing ld whn hung bdly lft bef last: sn hdd: kpt on same pce flat* **8/1**

-0F2 **4** *4 1/2* **Lapalala (IRE)**[23] 4916 5-11-2 0 RichardJohnson 105+
(Philip Hobbs) *settled in midfield: effrt 3 out: drvn to chal and blnd 2 out: nt rcvr* **11/4**[2]

446 **5** *1 3/4* **Persian Breeze**[16] 5091 4-10-11 104 LeightonAspell 94
(Lucy Wadham) *cl up: led and mstke 5th: hrd drvn and hdd 2 out: no ex bef last* **5/1**[3]

3 **6** *12* **My Mistress (IRE)**[43] 4502 4-10-11 0 JackQuinlan 80
(Phil McEntee) *cl up: last of six gng clr bef 2 out: rdn and sn wknd* **33/1**

P0 **7** *25* **Patronne (FR)**[13] 5153 4-10-11 0 GavinSheehan 72+
(Harry Whittington) *plld hrd in detached last: j. modly: mstke 4th: passed sme stragglers fr next: nvr nr front rnk: eased bef last: t.o* **14/1**

00/0 **8** *2 1/2* **Crazy Train**[25] 4881 7-11-2 0 JamesBanks 58
(Robert Walford) *racd freely: 2nd tl led briefly bef 5th: rdn and lost tch after next: eased bef last: t.o* **150/1**

9 *12* **Fair Comment**[47] 6-11-2 0 MarkGrant 46
(Michael Blanshard) *hld up in rr: short-lived effrt 5th: t.o bef 2 out* **33/1**

560 **10** *1 1/2* **Winola**[31] 4773 6-11-2 0 (t) JoshuaMoore 44
(Charlie Wallis) *bhd: t.o bef 2 out* **200/1**

/0-5 **11** *4* **Choral Bee**[307] 748 7-10-9 75 CharlieHammond(7) 40
(Alan Jessop) *mstkes: in rr and drvn after 3rd: t.o fr 5th* **100/1**

5 **12** *12* **Kool Lady (IRE)**[20] 5019 5-11-2 0 [1] TrevorWhelan 28
(Des Donovan) *led tl hdd bef 5th: t.o bef 2 out* **66/1**

000 **13** *24* **Heighnow**[53] 4322 5-11-2 0 AndrewTinkler 4
(Conrad Allen) *plld hrd and mstkes: w ldrs: blnd 3rd: wkng rapidly whn mstke 5th: bdly t.o after next* **200/1**

3m 51.1s (-3.80) **Going Correction** -0.05s/f (Good)
WFA 4 from 5yo+ 5lb **13** Ran SP% **117.5**
Speed ratings (Par 103): **107,104,103,101,100 94,82,80,74,74 72,66,54**
CSF £18.59 TOTE £2.70: £1.20, £3.10, £2.80; EX 19.70 Trifecta £89.80.
Owner Braybrooke Lodge Partnership **Bred** Martin Bates & Neil Jennings **Trained** Alcester, Warwicks

FOCUS
Race run over 13yds further than advertised. Modest form, although the right horses came to the fore and the pace was a decent one. A step up from the cosy winner.

5374 FOLLOW @RACING_UK ON TWITTER H'CAP HURDLE (8 hdls) 1m 7f 171y
6:10 (6:13) (Class 4) (0-105,105) 4-Y-0+ **£3,573** (£1,049; £524; £262)

Form RPR
660P **1** **King Simba (IRE)**[108] 3411 5-11-11 104 DavidBass 108
(Kim Bailey) *trckd ldrs: effrt 5th: wnt 2nd next: led 2 out: rdn and in command whn hung bdly lft flat* **20/1**

6550 **2** *1 3/4* **Quantum Of Solace**[26] 4878 6-11-4 97 [1] JamesBanks 99
(Noel Williams) *hld up: rdn and effrt bef 2 out: tried to chal last: no imp fnl 100yds* **16/1**

2336 **3** *1* **Tiradia (FR)**[114] 3223 9-11-6 104 MikeyEnnis(5) 105
(J R Jenkins) *hld up towards rr: styd on fr 2 out: drvn to snatch 3rd cl home: unable to chal* **10/1**

2150 **4** *nk* **Empty The Tank (IRE)**[28] 4846 6-11-12 105 LeightonAspell 106
(Jim Boyle) *cl up: led 3 out: sn drvn: hdd last: nt qckn and lost 3rd cl home* **20/1**

6P5 **5** *1/2* **Levelling**[43] 4502 4-11-0 98 (p) HarrySkelton 94
(Dan Skelton) *pressed ldrs: wnt 2nd and u.p home turn: ev ch nring last: hung lft and no ex flat* **22/1**

64-5 **6** *nse* **Nicholascopernicus (IRE)**[41] 4550 7-11-11 104 (tp) JamieMoore 106
(Kerry Lee) *hld up: rdn and effrt after 3 out: no imp and fnd little fr between last two* **9/4**[1]

4424 **7** *1/2* **Norse Light**[13] 5163 5-11-1 101 (p) GarethMalone(7) 101
(David Dennis) *towards rr: rdn and effrt 3 out: kpt on wout threatening fr last* **8/1**[3]

132- **8** *1 3/4* **One Cool Boy (IRE)**[416] 4465 7-11-2 98 BenPoste(3) 97
(Tracey Watkins) *plld hrd in rr div: effrt after 3 out: rdn and kpt on steadily wout threatening fr next* **22/1**

563 **9** *5* **Kayfton Pete**[21] 4985 10-11-8 101 AdamPogson 96
(Charles Pogson) *mulish in preliminaries: j. slowly 1st: w ldr tl led 3rd: mstke 4th: drvn and hdd 3 out: sn dropped out* **16/1**

003 **10** *2 1/2* **Sarpech (IRE)**[28] 4846 5-11-9 102 RichardJohnson 97
(Charlie Longsdon) *hld up and bhd: effrt on outside bef 3 out: sn hrd drvn: no imp fr next* **7/1**[2]

5P00 **11** *4* **Mr Lando**[14] 5148 7-11-5 105 HarryTeal(7) 94
(Alison Batchelor) *taken down early: t.k.h: tl 3rd: pressed ldr tl 5th: dropped out next* **20/1**

4F25 **12** *15* **Ogaritmo**[81] 3816 7-11-2 98 (t) KillianMoore(3) 73
(Alex Hales) *bhd: drvn 5th: nvr travelling and sn lost tch* **18/1**

4402 **13** *3/4* **Dylan's Storm (IRE)**[21] 4970 4-10-0 89 (t) JamieBargary(5) 58
(David Dennis) *chsd ldrs tl drvn 5th: sn btn* **16/1**

4P54 **14** *2* **Terra Firma**[43] 4502 6-11-5 98 BrendanPowell 70
(Claire Dyson) *cl up tl 5th: t.o* **22/1**

00-P **15** *52* **Bhakti (IRE)**[97] 3572 9-11-9 105 RyanHatch(3) 30
(Mark Rimell) *v reluctant and sn tailed himself off* **25/1**

3m 52.9s (-2.00) **Going Correction** -0.05s/f (Good)
WFA 4 from 5yo+ 5lb **15** Ran SP% **117.6**
Speed ratings (Par 105): **103,102,101,101,101 101,100,100,97,96 94,86,86,85,59**
CSF £269.89 CT £3370.27 TOTE £17.90: £5.40, £6.90, £2.90; EX 465.40 Trifecta £2949.30 Part won..
Owner GSTTKPA Charity Partnership **Bred** J Delaney **Trained** Andoversford, Gloucs

The Form Book Jumps 2015-16, Raceform Ltd, Newbury, RG14 5SJ

FOCUS
Race run over 13yds further than advertised. No hanging around yet a number held a chance in the straight. Straightforward form.

5375 WATCH RACING UK IN HD H'CAP CHASE (19 fncs) 2m 7f 129y
6:40 (6:40) (Class 4) (0-110,110) 5-Y-0+ **£3,898** (£1,144; £572; £286)

Form RPR
F213 **1** **The Mumper (IRE)**[41] 4545 9-11-11 **109**.................... WayneHutchinson 114
(Alan King) *trckd ldrs: wnt 3rd at 15th: stl 3 l 3rd at last: drvn and styd on gamely to pass ldng pair fnl 100yds and got up cl home* **7/2**[2]

5404 **2** *hd* **Ready Token (IRE)**[26] 4876 8-11-11 **109**....................(t) RichardJohnson 115
(Charlie Longsdon) *2nd tl lft in ld 13th: hdd 3 out: rdn and led again 2 out: r.o u.p flat tl collared fnl strides* **3/1**[1]

2221 **3** *4* **Basford Ben**[23] 4903 8-11-8 **106**..................................(b) SeanQuinlan 112+
(Jennie Candlish) *led tl downed tools suddenly and v slow 13th: sn dropped himself bk to poor 6th: rallied 2 out: racd awkwardly flat but fin strly and jst snatched 3rd* **9/2**

P13P **4** *hd* **Golanova**[22] 4935 8-11-12 **110**..(b) JamieMoore 111
(Gary Moore) *settled in midfield: wnt 4th at 15th: 6 l 4th home turn: drvn 2 out: no imp fr bef last and jst lost 3rd* **8/1**

52P1 **5** *shd* **Pandy Wells**[21] 4980 7-10-8 **92**.................................... KielanWoods 94
(Graeme McPherson) *trckd ldng pair: wnt 2nd at 15th: led and looked to be gng best 3 out: rdn and hdd next: fnd little: lost 2nd last 100yds out* **11/1**

/0P3 **6** *3 ½* **Silver Eagle (IRE)**[25] 4884 8-11-8 **106**................................(tp) DavidBass 107
(Kim Bailey) *towards rr: rdn 10th: nt travelling smoothly after: poor 6th home turn: drvn and plugged on* **4/1**[3]

P240 **7** *33* **Major Milborne**[17] 5072 8-11-5 **110**..................................(p) MissPFuller(7) 78
(Jamie Snowden) *in tch: dropped bk last at 16th: sn struggling: t.o bef 2 out* **14/1**

6P-F **P** **Steepleofcopper (IRE)**[31] 4772 10-10-0 **84** oh17............(t) JackQuinlan
(Alan Jessop) *pckd bdly 2nd and lost tch: mstkes: t.o and p.u 11th* **100/1**

6m 9.0s (-1.30) **Going Correction** +0.05s/f (Yiel) **8 Ran SP% 112.5**
Speed ratings: **104,103,102,102,102 101,90,**
CSF £14.49 CT £46.09 TOTE £4.30: £1.40, £1.60, £1.90; EX 18.80 Trifecta £72.10.
Owner The Weighed In Partnership **Bred** Patrick Day **Trained** Barbury Castle, Wilts
■ Stewards' Enquiry : Wayne Hutchinson four-day ban: used whip above permitted level (May 2-5)

FOCUS
Race run over 30yds further than advertised. Ordinary form, but it makes sense.

5376 RACINGUK.COM H'CAP HURDLE (12 hdls) 3m 1f 10y
7:10 (7:10) (Class 4) (0-115,115) 4-Y-0+ **£3,249** (£954; £477; £238)

Form RPR
-203 **1** **Bronco Billy (IRE)**[72] 3997 6-11-12 **115**.........................(t) RichardJohnson 121
(Jonjo O'Neill) *nt a fluent: trckd ldrs: wnt 2nd at 9th: hit 2 out: drvn fr last: kpt on steadily to ld cl home* **4/1**[3]

6502 **2** *1* **Wake Your Dreams (IRE)**[15] 5122 8-11-7 **110**...............(p) SeanQuinlan 115
(Jennie Candlish) *led: nrly 5 l clr 2 out: stl 3 l up but rdn after last w rdr looking rnd: edgd lft and jst ct* **9/4**[1]

2011 **3** *13* **Ganbei**[28] 4840 10-11-9 **115**.. HarryBannister(3) 107
(Michael Easterby) *sn pushed along in last pair: drvn after 7th: stl detached 5th bef 2 out: styd on after: 3rd at last: nvr nr ldng pair and no imp flat* **3/1**[2]

45/4 **4** *5* **Upthemsteps (IRE)**[21] 4975 11-10-9 **105**.....................(p) TobyWheeler(7) 94
(Ian Williams) *pressed ldr tl 9th: drvn and btn whn hit 2 out* **16/1**

P115 **5** *17* **Shinooki (IRE)**[21] 4983 9-11-12 **115**................................(p) KielanWoods 87
(Alex Hales) *towards rr: rdn 8th: struggling after* **20/1**

3304 **6** *13* **Road To Freedom**[21] 4983 7-11-9 **112**............................ LeightonAspell 82+
(Lucy Wadham) *midfield: effrt 9th: 3rd and drvn after 3 out: wl btn 5th whn blnd bdly next* **17/2**

023 **7** *9* **Giveitachance (IRE)**[20] 5017 9-11-6 **109**..........................(t) BrendanPowell 61
(Claire Dyson) *cl up tl lost pl and drvn bef 8th: qckly lost tch: t.o 3 out* **8/1**

5645 **P** **Dylanseoghan (IRE)**[30] 4788 7-11-0 **110**........... WilliamFeatherstone(7)
(Zoe Davison) *nrly a in rr: drvn 9th: sn dropped out: t.o and p.u 2 out* **25/1**

6m 22.3s (-0.60) **Going Correction** -0.05s/f (Good) **8 Ran SP% 111.9**
Speed ratings (Par 105): **98,97,93,91,86 82,79,**
CSF £13.21 CT £29.08 TOTE £5.00: £1.60, £1.50, £1.40; EX 14.10 Trifecta £36.80.
Owner Mrs John Magnier, D Smith & M Tabor **Bred** Miss Caroline Coonan **Trained** Cheltenham, Gloucs

FOCUS
Race run over 13yds further than advertised. The front pair finished clear in what was an ordinary handicap, although the winner could yet rate higher. The second sets the level.

5377 RACING UK PROFITS RETURNED TO RACING H'CAP CHASE (16 fncs) 2m 3f 189y
7:40 (7:40) (Class 5) (0-100,99) 5-Y-0+ **£2,599** (£763; £381; £190)

Form RPR
P310 **1** **Swizzler (IRE)**[26] 4876 7-11-11 **98**..................................... WillKennedy 106+
(Ian Williams) *settled towards rr: rdn 3 out: clsd on inner fr bef 2 out: led w ears pricked last: drvn and kpt on gamely* **8/1**

-203 **2** *1* **Zayfire Aramis**[42] 4527 7-11-8 **95**.................................... LiamTreadwell 103+
(Michael Scudamore) *mounted on crse: lacked fluency and j. and hung rt: last tl after 3 out where all hld a ch: began to stay on fr 2 out: drvn and str run to dispute 2nd fnl 100yds: nvr quite rchd wnr* **10/1**

05UP **3** *shd* **Trillerin Minella (IRE)**[14] 5149 8-11-9 **96**................... KielanWoods 102
(Graeme McPherson) *cl 2nd: hit 10th: rdn 3 out: stl ev ch bef last: nt qckn and edgd lft flat: duelled for 2nd fnl 100yds* **15/2**

U60U **4** *5* **Toast And Jam (IRE)**[21] 4980 7-10-0 **73** oh1...................(t) LeeEdwards 77
(Claire Dyson) *mstke 1st: t.k.h: pressed ldrs: mstke 8th: urged along and and ev ch whn wnt rt 2 out: hung and j. bdly rt last: no ch after* **14/1**

P-4P **5** *1 ¾* **Parting Way (IRE)**[61] 4187 8-11-10 **97**........................ RichardJohnson 96
(Tim Vaughan) *bhd: stl wl in tch tl rdn and no ex bef 2 out* **6/1**[2]

-444 **6** *1 ½* **Grand March**[46] 4453 7-11-12 **99**......................................(p) DavidBass 99
(Kim Bailey) *trckd ldrs: hit 10th: rdn 2 out: btn whn hmpd last* **4/1**[1]

2/3P **7** *1 ½* **Genstone Trail**[48] 4427 10-11-8 **95**............................... BrendanPowell 92
(Alan King) *midfield: rdn after 3 out: btn next* **10/1**

-34P **8** *5* **Copperfacejack (IRE)**[137] 2861 6-11-5 **92**.......................(p) CharliePoste 85
(Paul Webber) *t.k.h and led at brisk gallop: rdn after 3 out: sltly bmpd next and hdd: dropped out rapidly bef last and eased* **4/1**[1]

-234 **9** *25* **Halcyon Days**[28] 4836 7-10-9 **85**.....................................(p) TonyKelly(3) 55
(Rebecca Menzies) *chsd ldrs: cl 4th 3 out: rdn and wknd bef next* **7/1**[3]

5m 12.9s (7.60) **Going Correction** +0.05s/f (Yiel) **9 Ran SP% 114.5**
Speed ratings: **86,85,85,83,82 82,81,79,69**
CSF £81.25 CT £624.18 TOTE £8.00: £3.20, £2.50, £2.60; EX 90.70 Trifecta £766.90.
Owner Peter P Elliott **Bred** Mrs Kathleen Hoey **Trained** Portway, Worcs

FOCUS
Race run over 21yds further than advertised. Moderate stuff with virtually all the runners being in with some sort of chance coming to the last. A step up from the winner.
T/Plt: £740.20 to a £1 stake. Pool: £60,082.00 - 59.25 winning units. T/Qpdt: £47.50 to a £1 stake. Pool: £8,968.59 - 139.60 winning units. **Iain Mackenzie**

5160 NEWTON ABBOT (L-H)
Monday, April 18

OFFICIAL GOING: Soft (good to soft in places; 5.1)
Wind: almost nil Weather: overcast

5378 SIS MAIDEN HURDLE (9 hdls) 2m 2f 110y
1:50 (1:50) (Class 4) 4-Y-0+ **£3,898** (£1,144; £572; £286)

Form RPR
5 **1** **Meme's Horse (IRE)**[84] 3775 6-11-0 0.................................(t) NoelFehily 124+
(Harry Fry) *in tch: tk clsr order 4th: led after 3 out: wandered whn rdn after 2 out: kpt on wl* **11/4**[3]

3-20 **2** *3 ½* **Amanto (GER)**[40] 2725 6-11-0 122..................(b) SamTwiston-Davies 117
(Paul Nicholls) *chsd ldrs: rdn to chse wnr appr 2 out: kpt on same pce and a being hld* **6/4**[1]

6432 **3** *3 ¼* **Muffins For Tea**[23] 4917 6-11-0 115.................................... DarylJacob 116
(Colin Tizzard) *trckd ldr: led bef 6th: rdn and hdd after 3 out: styd on same pce fr next* **7/4**[2]

54 **4** *29* **Fille Des Champs (IRE)**[21] 4961 5-10-0 0.................. LewisGordon(7) 78
(Evan Williams) *hld up: lost tch after 5th: wnt modest 4th 2 out* **33/1**

6 **5** *14* **Executive Prince (IRE)**[11] 5187 6-11-0 0......................... NickScholfield 76
(Jeremy Scott) *j.lft thrght: led: sn clr: hdd bef 6th: wknd after 3 out: t.o* **20/1**

0 **6** *34* **Staunton**[45] 4468 5-10-2 0.. CiaranGethings(5) 30
(Susan Johnson) *in tch tl after 5th: sn t.o* **50/1**

FU00 **U** **Pomicide**[6] 5268 6-10-11 0.. LucyGardner(3)
(Sue Gardner) *lost tch 6th: t.o whn blnd and uns rdr 3 out* **100/1**

P **P** **Wallawallabingbang**[55] 4293 7-10-7 0.............................. IanPopham
(Alexandra Dunn) *lost tch after 5th: t.o whn p.u after 3 out* **125/1**

4m 46.1s (16.10) **Going Correction** +0.90s/f (Soft) **8 Ran SP% 114.5**
Speed ratings (Par 105): **102,100,99,86,81 66, ,**
CSF £7.38 TOTE £3.70: £1.10, £1.10, £1.10; EX 9.60 Trifecta £14.30.
Owner Masterson Holdings Limited **Bred** Donal & Pat Barnwell **Trained** Seaborough, Dorset

FOCUS
There was a fair gallop on in this maiden and it's straightforward form. The race distance was 122yds further than advertised due to rail movement. THE form looks solid enough.

5379 NEWTONABBOTRACING.COM H'CAP CHASE (13 fncs) 2m 75y
2:20 (2:20) (Class 4) (0-110,110) 5-Y-0+ **£4,873** (£1,431; £715; £357)

Form RPR
2413 **1** **Edlomond (IRE)**[3] 5310 10-10-13 **102**.....................(tp[1]) JakeHodson(5) 115+
(Bill Turner) *trckd ldrs: blnd 6th: led bef 2 out: kpt on wl: rdn out* **5/1**

512P **2** *4 ½* **Pembroke House**[47] 4431 9-11-5 **103**.................(p) SamTwiston-Davies 109
(Sarah-Jayne Davies) *trckd ldrs: rdn to chse wnr between last 2: kpt on but nt pce to chal* **7/2**[2]

220P **3** *8* **Capilla (IRE)**[16] 5103 8-11-12 **110**....................................(t) PaulMoloney 108
(Evan Williams) *disp ld: outrt ldr 8th: rdn and hdd appr 2 out: kpt on same pce* **13/2**

0UP4 **4** *3* **Paddy The Stout (IRE)**[13] 5164 11-10-11 **95**.....................(t) TomO'Brien 92
(Paul Henderson) *hld up: wnt cl 3rd 4 out: rdn after next: kpt on same pce fr 2 out* **10/1**

6P32 **5** *12* **Too Scoops (IRE)**[14] 5142 9-11-6 **104**..............................(tp) DarylJacob 88
(Richard Woollacott) *chsd ldrs: pushed along fr 7th: btn 4 out* **4/1**[3]

2F33 **6** *nk* **Val D'Arc (FR)**[109] 3380 7-11-11 **109**.................................. AlainCawley 93
(Richard Hobson) *disp ld tl 8th: rdn after 4 out: wknd next* **5/2**[1]

4m 16.4s (9.90) **Going Correction** +0.725s/f (Soft) **6 Ran SP% 109.9**
Speed ratings: **104,101,97,96,90 90**
CSF £21.88 TOTE £5.90: £2.70, £1.90; EX 24.70 Trifecta £52.60.
Owner R A Bracken **Bred** Bernard Flynn **Trained** Sigwells, Somerset

FOCUS
Race run over 18 yards further than advertised. An ordinary handicap, run at a routine gallop. The cosy winner was close to his best.

5380 NEWTONABBOTRACE ON TWITTER MARES' H'CAP HURDLE (8 hdls) 2m 167y
2:50 (2:50) (Class 4) (0-115,115) 4-Y-0+ **£4,548** (£1,335; £667; £333)

Form RPR
0243 **1** **Ayla's Emperor**[25] 4886 7-10-5 **94**..................................(p) RobertDunne 100+
(John Flint) *trckd ldr: blnd 4th: rdn after 3 out: led 2 out: hit last: kpt on: rdn out* **9/2**[3]

3051 **2** *3* **The Missus**[25] 4881 5-11-2 **108**.................................. MrSWaley-Cohen(3) 113+
(Warren Greatrex) *led: tried to run out on bnd after 4th and briefly hdd: hdd 2 out: sn rdn: kpt on same pce* **4/1**[2]

-205 **3** *10* **Giveagirlachance (IRE)**[54] 2418 7-10-11 **105**................ KevinJones(5) 95
(Seamus Mullins) *hld up: hdwy 4th: rdn after 3 out: wnt 3rd next: kpt on same pce* **11/1**

232P **4** *8* **Midnight Sapphire**[159] 2441 6-11-2 **105**........................(t) AndrewThornton 88
(Victor Dartnall) *hld up: rdn after 3 out: styd on fr next: wnt 4th at the last* **6/1**

0466 **5** *3 ¼* **Ice Tres**[130] 2987 7-10-7 **96**..(tp) JamesDavies 75
(Chris Down) *trckd ldrs: rdn after 3 out: wknd between last 2* **13/2**

3412 **6** *4 ½* **Definitely Better (IRE)**[33] 4709 8-10-11 **100**...............(p) PaddyBrennan 77
(Tom George) *hld up: hdwy after 5th: effrt disputing 3rd after 3 out: wknd after next* **3/1**[1]

50P2 **7** *22* **Dainty Diva (IRE)**[19] 5029 8-10-12 **101**.......................... NickScholfield 53
(Jeremy Scott) *chsd ldrs tl 4th: struggling in last next: wknd 3 out: t.o* **10/1**

PP **P** **Sureness (IRE)**[205] 1659 6-11-5 **115**......................(tp) TommyDowling(7)
(Charlie Mann) *trckd ldrs: rdn after 5th: stmbld next: sn wknd: p.u bef next* **18/1**

4m 18.6s (12.90) **Going Correction** +0.90s/f (Soft) **8 Ran SP% 113.5**
Speed ratings (Par 105): **105,103,98,95,93 91,81,**
CSF £22.85 CT £183.78 TOTE £6.00: £1.90, £1.50, £2.50; EX 25.40 Trifecta £215.20.
Owner L H & Mrs T Evans **Bred** Barry Walters Farms **Trained** Kenfig Hill, Bridgend

FOCUS
It paid to race prominently in this modest mares' handicap as the first pair dominated the finish. Both are better than the bare result. The race distance was 96yds further than advertised due to rail movement.

5381 HAPPY 96TH BIRTHDAY, LES BICKHAM NOVICES' CHASE (16 fncs) 2m 4f 216y

3:20 (3:20) (Class 3) 5-Y-O+ **£7,279** (£2,150; £1,075; £538)

Form RPR

1356 **1** **Aso (FR)**[11] 5174 6-10-12 143.......... AidanColeman 154+
(Venetia Williams) *trckd ldrs: hit 11th: shkn up after 3 out: led between last 2: comf* **6/4**[2]

231P **2** *10* **Fourth Act (IRE)**[34] 4701 7-10-12 137.......... (tp) PaddyBrennan 140
(Colin Tizzard) *led after 2nd: reminders after 9th: rdn after 4 out: hdd between last 2: no ex* **4/1**[3]

4222 **3** *10* **Dormello Mo (FR)**[5] 5278 6-10-12 142.......... (t) SamTwiston-Davies 132
(Paul Nicholls) *j.rt at times: led tl after 2nd: trckd ldr: rdn after 4 out: hld 2 out* **11/8**[1]

-244 **4** *5* **Union Saint (FR)**[27] 4857 8-10-5 128.......... MissBFrost(7) 126
(Jimmy Frost) *trckd ldng trio tl outpcd 12th: n.d after* **14/1**

5m 31.4s (10.00) **Going Correction** +0.725s/f (Soft) **4 Ran SP% 108.8**
Speed ratings: **109,105,101,99**
CSF £7.41 TOTE £2.40; EX 7.20 Trifecta £8.50.
Owner The Bellamy Partnership **Bred** I Pacault, A Pacault & M Pacault **Trained** Kings Caple, H'fords

FOCUS
Race run over 26 yards further than advertised. They went a sound gallop in this good little novice chase. The winner is rated back to his best.

5382 ST AUSTELL BREWERY H'CAP HURDLE (10 hdls) 2m 5f 122y

3:50 (3:50) (Class 4) (0-115,115) 4-Y-O+ **£4,548** (£1,335; £667; £333)

Form RPR

4-53 **1** **Carre Noir (FR)**[23] 4922 7-11-4 **107**.......... LiamHeard 113+
(Martin Hill) *hld up towards rr: hdwy 7th: rdn to chse ldrs after 3 out: led between last 2: r.o strly* **7/1**[3]

4212 **2** *3 ¼* **Talk Of The South (IRE)**[26] 4877 7-11-10 **113**.......... NickScholfield 115
(Paul Henderson) *hld up towards rr: rdn and hdwy after 3 out: styd on wl fr next: wnt 2nd run-in but no threat to wnr* **6/1**[2]

-0PP **3** *nk* **Tea Time Fred**[41] 4543 7-11-0 **106**.......... LucyGardner(3) 108
(Sue Gardner) *trckd ldrs: hmpd 3 out: sn led: rdn and hdd whn hit 2 out: kpt on same pce* **7/1**[3]

310 **4** *¾* **Kayf Willow**[158] 2455 7-11-7 **115**.......... CiaranGethings(5) 116
(Philip Hobbs) *mid-div: hdwy 7th: rdn to ld 2 out: hdd between last 2: no ex* **6/1**[2]

6-P4 **5** *2 ¾* **Welcome Bach (IRE)**[23] 4917 7-11-12 **115**.......... DarylJacob 114
(Liam Corcoran) *trckd ldrs: rdn and ev ch appr 2 out: no ex between last 2* **14/1**

3-F3 **6** *2 ¼* **Carry On Sydney**[148] 2667 6-11-2 **115**.......... HarrisonBeswick(10) 112
(Oliver Sherwood) *mid-div: rdn and hdwy after 3 out: chsd ldrs next: no ex appr last* **11/1**

P512 **7** *5* **Allchilledout**[19] 5034 7-10-11 **105**.......... (t) PaulO'Brien(5) 97
(Colin Tizzard) *mid-div: pushed along after 6th: hdwy after next: rdn to chse ldrs after 3 out: wknd between last 2* **5/1**[1]

4545 **8** *15* **Barton Rose**[23] 4922 7-10-13 **107**.......... (p) HarryCobden(5) 85
(Michael Blake) *mid-div: hdwy 7th: sn rdn: wknd after 3 out* **10/1**

5213 **9** *8* **Shoofly Milly (IRE)**[19] 5033 7-11-2 **105**.......... (b) MattGriffiths 73
(Jeremy Scott) *led: drvn and hdd after 3 out: sn wknd* **8/1**

040F **10** *10* **Present Times (IRE)**[25] 4882 5-11-1 **104**.......... PaulMoloney 62
(Evan Williams) *hld up towards rr: j.rt: sme prog after 3 out: wknd next* **40/1**

0-42 **11** *4 ½* **Bourdello**[159] 2444 7-10-13 **102**.......... RichieMcLernon 55
(Emma Baker) *trckd ldrs tl wknd after 3 out* **25/1**

0P60 **12** *4 ½* **Phantom Prince (IRE)**[19] 5030 7-11-5 **115**.......... MissBFrost(7) 64
(Jimmy Frost) *a towards rr* **80/1**

PP-6 **P** **Comte D'Anjou**[41] 4541 7-11-0 **103**.......... AidanColeman
(Johnny Farrelly) *trckd ldrs tl dropped to rr after 6th: sn struggling: losing tch whn p.u 3 out* **18/1**

5m 39.1s (18.90) **Going Correction** +0.90s/f (Soft) **13 Ran SP% 118.2**
Speed ratings (Par 105): **101,99,99,99,98 97,95,90,87,83 82,80,**
CSF £48.17 CT £309.48 TOTE £8.90: £3.10, £2.10, £3.50; EX 58.80 Trifecta £584.20.
Owner The Pi Eyed Squared **Bred** Claude Michel **Trained** Littlehempston, Devon

FOCUS
A wide-open looking handicap. The runner-up sets the level. The race distance was 155yds further than advertised due to rail movement. The second to fourth are the best guides.

5383 ATTHERACES MARES' STANDARD OPEN NATIONAL HUNT FLAT RACE 2m 167y

4:20 (4:20) (Class 6) 4-6-Y-O **£1,711** (£498; £249)

Form RPR

000 **1** **Lady Markby (IRE)**[67] 4074 5-10-12 0.......... DarylJacob 95+
(Emma Lavelle) *trckd ldrs: rdn over 2f out: str run ins fnl f: led fnl 100yds: drifted lft: drvn out* **20/1**

6 **2** *¾* **Theatre Rouge (IRE)**[35] 4687 4-10-7 0.......... MichealNolan 90+
(Philip Hobbs) *hld up towards rr: hdwy but nt clr run fr 5f out: swtchd rt and rdn wl over 2f out: c wd into st: styd on to ld ent fnl f: hdd fnl 100yds* **7/1**[3]

3 *¾* **Widow On The Run (IRE)**[351] 5-10-5 0.......... MikeyHamill(7) 94
(Kim Bailey) *hld up towards rr: hdwy fr 4f out: led over 2f out: sn rdn: hdd ent fnl f: kpt on but no ex* **5/1**[2]

5 **4** *1 ¾* **Pampanini**[45] 4468 5-10-12 0.......... (t) NoelFehily 92
(Harry Fry) *trckd ldrs: chal 4f out: led briefly over 2f out: sn rdn: styd on same pce fnl f* **7/2**[1]

5 *8* **Arctic Lady (IRE)**[339] 5-10-12 0.......... PaddyBrennan 85
(Tom George) *mid-div: hdwy fr 6f out: chal over 2f out: sn rdn: wknd over 1f out* **7/2**[1]

6 *5* **Braventara** 5-10-7 0.......... LizzieKelly(5) 79
(Nick Williams) *chsd ldrs tl outpcd over 3f out: n.d after* **12/1**

0 **7** *½* **Actlikeacountess**[35] 4687 5-10-12 0.......... DenisO'Regan 79
(Neil Mulholland) *led: rdn and hdd over 2f out: sn wknd* **66/1**

8 *20* **Magic Three** 5-10-12 0.......... SamTwiston-Davies 59
(Peter Croke, Ire) *mid-div: hdwy over 6f out: rdn over 3f out: wknd 2f out* **14/1**

6- **9** *2* **Miss Williams**[438] 4052 5-10-12 0.......... ConorO'Farrell 57
(David Pipe) *in tch tl wknd 3f out* **5/1**[2]

0 **10** *19* **Chicksgrove Sprite (IRE)**[35] 4687 5-10-12 0.......... MarkQuinlan 38
(Neil Mulholland) *pressed ldr: rdn over 4f out: wknd 3f out: t.o* **40/1**

11 *20* **Ruby Redhead** 6-10-12 0.......... RhysFlint 18
(Alexandra Dunn) *a towards rr: t.o* **66/1**

12 *¾* **Midnightmistress** 4-10-7 0.......... JamesDavies 12
(Jose Santos) *in tch tl wknd 1/2-way: t.o* **22/1**

13 *1 ½* **Kemicallie** 4-10-7 0.......... JamesBest 10
(Carroll Gray) *mid-div tl wknd over 7f out: t.o* **100/1**

14 *28* **Black Marble** 5-10-12 0.......... (t) AndrewGlassonbury
(Mark Shears) *a towards rr: t.o* **100/1**

15 *dist* **Russian's Legacy** 6-10-7 0.......... AliceMills(5)
(Gail Haywood) *sn struggling in detached last: t.o after 7f: virtually p.u* **40/1**

4m 17.2s (17.10) **Going Correction** +0.90s/f (Soft)
WFA 4 from 5yo+ 5lb **15 Ran SP% 123.6**
Speed ratings: **95,94,94,93,89 87,87,77,76,67 58,58,57,44,**
CSF £151.69 TOTE £28.50: £6.40, £2.00, £2.70; EX 273.90 Trifecta £3774.90 part won..
Owner Mrs Sarah Metcalfe **Bred** S McElroy **Trained** Hatherden, Hants

FOCUS
This well-contested but ordinary mares' bumper was run at a routine gallop. The winner and fourth are the best guides. The race distance was 96yds further than advertised due to rail movement.

5384 TOTNES AND BRIDGETOWN NOVICES' HUNTERS' CHASE (16 fncs) 2m 4f 216y

4:55 (5:00) (Class 6) 5-Y-O+ **£1,247** (£387; £193; £96)

Form RPR

/33- **1** **Steeltown (IRE)**[9] 11-11-5 105.......... MrJLThomas(7) 104+
(Mrs Kayley Woollacott) *led tl 6th: prom: led 4 out: rdn clr after next: styd on wl* **11/10**[1]

P5P4 **2** *14* **Triggywinkle (FR)**[11] 5186 7-11-0 67.......... (tp) MrMartinMcIntyre(5) 85
(Roderick Chelton) *trckd ldrs: wnt 2nd after 3 out: rdn next: styd on but no further imp on wnr* **20/1**

3 *12* **The Grey Celt (IRE)**[29] 8-11-5 0.......... MrNLawton(7) 81
(R G Chapman) *j.rt bdly at times: hld up in tch: hdwy 3 out: sn rdn: wnt 3rd next: styd on same pce* **14/1**

P-34 **4** *nk* **Batu Ferringhi (FR)**[13] 5166 10-11-5 95.......... (p) MrSeanHoulihan(7) 80
(Mrs C Hitch) *trckd ldrs: j.rt and awkward 1st: rdn after 4 out: styd on same pce fr next* **7/1**[3]

500/ **P** **Squinch**[736] 12-11-7 77.......... MrJMartin(5)
(Mrs David Plunkett) *trckd ldrs tl 6th: sn pushed along in last: wknd 11th: p.u bef 3 out* **18/1**

3-31 **U** **Coeur De Fou (FR)**[18] 5054 11-11-9 103.......... (p) MrNGeorge(7)
(Tom George) *hld up in tch: mstke and uns rdr 3rd* **2/1**[2]

2P4/ **P** **Flemensgael (IRE)**[23] 9-11-5 93.......... (t) MrCharlieDando(7)
(R J Harraway) *hld up in tch: wknd 10th: tailing off whn p.u after next* **33/1**

/44- **U** **Katie's Massini (IRE)**[329] 8-10-12 73.......... MrSEllicott(7)
(Mrs E Scott) *bdly hmpd and uns rdr 1st* **18/1**

-60P **P** **Thymeandthymeagain**[21] 7-10-12 77.......... MrPhilipThomas(7)
(Philip Thomas) *prom: led 6th tl mstke 4 out: wknd after next: p.u bef last* **150/1**

5m 44.1s (22.70) **Going Correction** +0.725s/f (Soft) **9 Ran SP% 119.0**
Speed ratings: **85,79,75,74, , , ,**
CSF £24.91 TOTE £2.00: £1.10, £5.50, £3.20; EX 23.80 Trifecta £297.80.
Owner J F Symes **Bred** William Hayes **Trained** South Molton, Devon

FOCUS
Race run over 26 yards further than advertised. An uncompetitive novice hunter chase that proved eventful. The easy winner set a fair standard.
T/Plt: £125.80 to a £1 stake. Pool: £67,633.52 - 392.40 winning units. T/Qpdt: £52.60 to a £1 stake. Pool: 35,252.95 - 73.90 winning units. **Tim Mitchell**

MESLAY-DU-MAINE
Monday, April 18

OFFICIAL GOING: Heavy

5385a PRIX PAPILLON - PRIX APGO REVERDY (CHASE) (CONDITIONS) (5YO) (TURF) 2m 5f

4:10 (12:00) 5-Y-O **£7,764** (£3,882; £2,264; £1,536; £727)

RPR

1 **Saint Lino (FR)**[15] 5135 5-11-3 0.......... StephanePaillard
(Nick Williams) *settled in midfield abt 25 l off the pce: stdy hdwy fr 9th: led travelling easily after 5 out: rdn whn pressed appr 2 out: hdd last: rallied u.p to regain ld 100yds out: drvn out* **9/5**[1]

2 *2* **Orange Karma (FR)** 5-10-8 0.......... (b[1]) OlivierJouin
(D Sourdeau De Beauregard, France) **149/10**

3 *15* **Call Hector (FR)**[50] 4401 5-11-0 0.......... ArthurBrunetti(5)
(G Chaignon, France) **61/10**

4 *15* **Bow Window (FR)**[22] 5-11-5 0.......... (b[1]) GeoffreyRe
(E Leray, France) **8/1**

5 *15* **Parc Monceau (FR)**[42] 5-11-3 0.......... (p) ReesMorganMurphy(4)
(Patrice Quinton, France) **16/5**[2]

6 *dist* **Craic (FR)**[327] 5-11-0 0.......... JoAudon
(P-J Fertillet, France) **168/10**

P **Opera Lyrique (FR)** 5-10-12 0.......... ThomasBeaurain
(J-L Guillochon, France) **28/1**

P **Newlight (FR)** 5-10-3 0.......... GuillaumeFabre(5)
(A Chaille-Chaille, France) **4/1**[3]

Owner French Gold **Bred** Ecurie Manuel Garcia **Trained** George Nympton, Devon
WIN (incl. 1 euro stake): 2.80. PLACES: 1.40, 3.20, 1.80. DF: 24.80. SF: 32.10

[4784]KEMPTON (R-H)

Tuesday, April 19

OFFICIAL GOING: Good (good to soft on lakeside bend on hurdle course; chs 7.8 hdl 7.3)

Wind: Light, half behind Weather: Fine

5386 POLYROOF PRODUCTS CONDITIONAL JOCKEYS' H'CAP HURDLE (8 hdls) 2m

2:00 (2:01) (Class 4) (0-120,120) 5-Y-0+ **£3,898** (£1,144; £572; £286)

Form RPR

3454 1 **Artifice Sivola (FR)**[26] 4891 6-11-6 **114**.......... DavidNoonan 118
(Lucy Wadham) *hld up in last quartet: prog fr 3 out: clsd on ldrs 2 out: rdn to chse ldr last: styd on to ld last 75yds* **5/1**[2]

6466 2 ½ **Threebarmymen (IRE)**[110] 3375 5-10-9 **106**.......... MattGriffiths[(3)] 109
(Jeremy Scott) *hld up in last quartet: prog fr 3 out: rdn to cl after 2 out: chal after last: nt qckn fnl 100yds* **10/1**[3]

3130 3 *nse* **Ladies Dancing**[195] 1810 10-10-5 **102**..........(b) GilesHawkins[(3)] 106+
(Chris Down) *wl in tch: rdn and prog to chse ldr after 3 out: nt fluent 2 out but sn led: 2 l ahd last: hung lft: idled and hdd 75yds out: styd on again nr fin but ch gone* **18/1**

5220 4 6 **Benbecula**[89] 3705 7-11-10 **118**..........(b) TomBellamy 116
(Richard Mitchell) *unable to ld: chsd ldr tl after 1st: clsd to ld 3 out: hdd sn after 2 out: lost 2nd and wknd last* **12/1**

43F0 5 10 **Noble Friend (IRE)**[171] 2182 8-11-0 **108**.......... ThomasGarner 98
(Chris Gordon) *hld up in last quartet: rdn and no prog after 3 out: kpt on past wkng rivals bef last* **12/1**

05P 6 1½ **Quebec**[115] 3238 5-10-12 **114**.......... TommyDowling[(8)] 103
(Charlie Mann) *trckd ldrs: hrd rdn and no rspnse after 3 out: hung lft and racd awkwardly fr 2 out: wknd* **5/1**[2]

040- 7 ½ **Classic Colori (IRE)**[458] 2226 9-10-4 **105**.......... TomHumphries[(7)] 92
(Martin Keighley) *t.k.h: trckd ldr after 1st tl jst bef 3 out: sn wknd* **50/1**

1330 8 2 **Marju's Quest (IRE)**[14] 5159 6-11-2 **116**.......... GarethMalone[(6)] 102
(David Dennis) *racd freely: led at gd pce: clr w one rival 4th: hdd 3 out: rdn and wknd bef 2 out* **12/1**

4025 9 9 **Smart Catch (IRE)**[39] 4593 10-10-8 **105**.......... NickSlatter[(3)] 84
(Tony Carroll) *hld up in last quartet: shkn up and no prog after 3 out: no ch fr next* **10/1**[3]

10 2¾ **Bambi Du Noyer (FR)**[198] 5-11-12 **120**.......... CallumBewley 94
(Simon Waugh) *wl in tch tl wknd 3 out: sn bhd* **25/1**

-164 F **Adrakhan (FR)**[143] 2773 5-11-5 **116**.......... BridgetAndrews[(3)]
(Dan Skelton) *t.k.h: hld up in last: stl last: pushed along and no prog whn fell 3 out* **5/2**[1]

3m 48.5s (-9.50) **Going Correction** -0.60s/f (Firm) **11** Ran SP% **114.2**
Speed ratings: **99,98,98,95,90 89,89,88,84,82**
CSF £52.46 CT £826.69 TOTE £5.60: £2.00, £3.50, £5.80; EX 57.40 Trifecta £842.50.
Owner R B Holt **Bred** Gilles Trapenard **Trained** Newmarket, Suffolk

FOCUS

All rails moved. The chase course was 3yds, and the winter hurdle course 4yds, out from their innermost configurations. As a result this race was run over 23yds further than advertised. David Noonan said of the ground: "It's lovely - good with a bit of sponge to it." Modest handicap form, but solid enough, with a big hurdles best from the winner.

5387 VELUX COMPANY LTD "NATIONAL HUNT" NOVICES' HURDLE (8 hdls) 2m

2:30 (2:30) (Class 4) 4-Y-0+ **£3,249** (£954; £477; £238)

Form RPR

322 1 **Swansea Mile (IRE)**[46] 4461 6-11-5 137.......... BridgetAndrews[(5)] 121+
(Dan Skelton) *t.k.h: trckd ldng pair: led 2 out gng strly: lft clr sn after last: pushed out* **2/1**[2]

244- 2 3¼ **Broughtons Rhythm**[375] 5262 7-10-12 0.......... LeightonAspell 107+
(Willie Musson) *hld up in 6th: prog after 3 out: chal fr 2 out: w wnr and shkn up whn stmbld sn after last: could nt rcvr* **20/1**

PU 3 2¼ **Cabernet D'Alene (FR)**[45] 4489 4-10-7 0.......... DarylJacob 99
(Nick Williams) *racd in 5th: pushed along and cl up 2 out: tk 3rd bef last: kpt on encouragingly* **12/1**

00-P 4 4½ **Le Capricieux (FR)**[89] 3710 5-10-12 0.......... JamieMoore 98
(Gary Moore) *hld up in last pair and off the pce: prog after 3 out: cl up 2 out: nudged along and outpcd sn after: shaped w promise* **100/1**

2130 5 ½ **Abbreviate (GER)**[88] 3724 5-11-4 125.......... DavidBass 106
(Kim Bailey) *t.k.h: nt a fluent: chsd ldr: mstke 4th: chal and upsides whn nt fluent 2 out: wknd qckly* **5/2**[3]

050 6 2½ **Twycross Warrior**[52] 4364 4-10-7 0.......... CharliePoste 91
(Robin Dickin) *hld up in 7th and wl off the pce: clsd on ldrs after 3 out: cl up 2 out: shkn up and outpcd and also green bef last: nt disgracd* **100/1**

124 7 2 **Imperial Presence (IRE)**[14] 5153 5-11-4 130..........[1] TomO'Brien 101
(Philip Hobbs) *racd freely: led and clr to 3rd: hdd 2 out: wknd qckly* **7/4**[1]

60 8 27 **Let's Tango (IRE)**[17] 5097 5-10-12 0.......... JamesBest 66
(Caroline Keevil) *chsd ldng trio tl nt fluent 5th: sn pushed along: wknd 3 out: t.o* **150/1**

10/ P **Peter The Horse**[1690] 1600 9-10-5 0.......... RomainClavreul[(7)]
(Joanne Thomason-Murphy) *hld up in last: nt fluent 2nd: lost tch 5th: bhd whn mstke 3 out and p.u* **100/1**

3m 52.1s (-5.90) **Going Correction** -0.60s/f (Firm)
WFA 4 from 5yo+ 5lb **9** Ran SP% **114.4**
Speed ratings (Par 105): **90,88,87,85,84 83,82,69,**
CSF £33.15 TOTE £2.40: £1.10, £3.50, £3.20; EX 36.10 Trifecta £203.80.
Owner Craig Buckingham **Bred** W Kane **Trained** Alcester, Warwicks

FOCUS

Race run over 23yds further than advertised. A couple of these failed to give their running, the favourite racing too freely in front, and the highest-rated runner won with a bit in hand. They bunched right up coming to two out and the form is questionable. The winner is rated below his best.

5388 SIKA ROOFING RAPID CHALLENGE NOVICES' H'CAP CHASE (16 fncs) 2m 4f 110y

3:00 (3:00) (Class 4) (0-105,105) 5-Y-0+ **£4,548** (£1,335; £667; £333)

Form RPR

35P0 1 **Ballycoe**[68] 4071 7-11-1 **94**..........(t) TomCannon 112+
(Chris Gordon) *hld up in rr: stdy prog after 10th to chse ldrs 4 out: rdn to ld 2 out: sn clr: 14 l ahd last: heavily eased* **7/1**

2220 2 7 **Very Intense (IRE)**[59] 4250 5-11-8 **101**.......... NoelFehily 105
(Tom Lacey) *hld up in rr: stdy prog fr 10th to trck ldng pair after 4 out: shkn up and nt qckn 3 out: kpt on to take 2nd after last* **5/1**[2]

430P 3 2 **What Happens Now (IRE)**[47] 4442 7-11-12 **105**.......... WayneHutchinson 106
(Donald McCain) *tended to jump lft: prom: blnd 8th: led after 11th to 2 out: sn btn: lost 2nd after last* **9/1**

1P42 4 11 **Gowanauthat (IRE)**[18] 5068 8-10-11 **97**..........(tp) TommyDowling[(7)] 93
(Charlie Mann) *trckd ldrs: effrt to press ldr 12th tl after 3 out: btn whn mstke 2 out: wknd* **8/1**

542 5 7 **Larteta (FR)**[60] 4222 7-10-7 **96**.......... RomainClavreul[(10)] 82
(Sarah Humphrey) *in tch: prog to press ldr 10th tl after next: sn dropped to midfield and struggling* **16/1**

2324 6 1 **Reyno**[37] 4645 8-11-11 **104**..........(bt) JoshuaMoore 90
(Stuart Edmunds) *pressed ldr to 3rd: lost pl qckly: in last pair whn mstke 7th: wl in rr whn blnd 4 out: passed stragglers fr next* **10/1**

5042 7 14 **Malanos (IRE)**[39] 4597 8-11-8 **101**.......... LeeEdwards 73
(Tony Carroll) *led to 4th: steadily lost pl fr 7th: last and wl bhd 4 out* **11/1**

-043 8 6 **Surging Seas (IRE)**[28] 4859 7-11-0 **93**..........(tp) SamTwiston-Davies 59
(Ali Stronge) *prog to ld 4th: hdd 10th and immediately dropped to midfield: struggling after* **13/2**[3]

5620 9 6 **Royal Chief (IRE)**[26] 4883 7-11-11 **104**..........(p) RhysFlint 67
(Alexandra Dunn) *stmbld 2nd and mstke 4th: a in rr: struggling fr 11th* **16/1**

PPP6 10 18 **Mor Brook**[28] 4859 8-11-9 **102**..........(vt[1]) DavidBass 62
(Kim Bailey) *sltly impeded 1st: sn prom: trckd ldr 7th: led 10th: nt fluent next: sn hdd and lost pl tamely: wknd 4 out* **9/2**[1]

13P F **Derryogue (IRE)**[45] 4491 11-10-5 **91**..........(tp) WilliamFeatherstone[(7)]
(Zoe Davison) *mstkes: a last: bhd whn fell 11th* **25/1**

5m 7.2s (-4.80) **Going Correction** -0.225s/f (Good) **11** Ran SP% **114.8**
Speed ratings: **100,97,96,92,89 89,84,81,79,72**
CSF £41.91 CT £318.71 TOTE £8.00: £2.60, £2.00, £3.30; EX 44.90 Trifecta £419.00.
Owner D S Dennis **Bred** J A And Mrs M A Knox **Trained** Morestead, Hampshire

FOCUS

Race run over 25yds further than advertised. Not a bad race for the level, it set up for the closers, and the race should produce winners. A big chase best from Ballycoe.

5389 BUILDING INNOVATION TAPERED CHASE MARES' NOVICES' HURDLE (10 hdls) 2m 5f

3:30 (3:30) (Class 4) 4-Y-0+ **£3,249** (£954; £477; £238)

Form RPR

1320 1 **Surtee Du Berlais (IRE)**[17] 5094 6-11-1 128.......... HarrisonBeswick[(10)] 121
(Oliver Sherwood) *chsd ldrs: pushed along fr 3rd and nvr gng that wl: 5 l bhd and no imp on ldng pair whn nt fluent 2 out: lft w ch last: drvn and styd on to ld fnl strides* **2/1**[1]

2221 2 *nk* **Via Volupta**[15] 5145 6-11-5 117.......... SamTwiston-Davies 115
(Warren Greatrex) *led: gng best 3 out: hanging lft and racd awkwardly bnd sn after: hdd bef 2 out: no imp on ldr whn lft in ld last: hdd fnl strides* **9/4**[2]

-041 3 2 **Morning Herald**[26] 4893 5-11-5 115.......... AndrewTinkler 117+
(Martin Keighley) *prom: trckd ldr 5th: rdn 3 out: clsd to ld bef 2 out: drvn and 3 l ahd whn blnd bdly last: hdd and nt rcvr* **11/4**[3]

P-P 4 5 **Buche De Noel (FR)**[88] 3726 5-11-1 132.......... GrahamCarson[(10)] 115
(Jamie Snowden) *chsd ldrs: pushed along after 7th: nt qckn and nvr able to get cl enough to chal* **10/1**

530 5 3¼ **Atlanta Ablaze**[38] 4623 5-10-13 0.......... TomO'Brien 101
(Henry Daly) *blnd 1st and often j.lft: chsd ldrs: drvn in 6th after 3 out: no imp fr next: one pce* **14/1**

06 6 1½ **Cottonwool Baby (IRE)**[26] 4881 5-10-10 0.......... ThomasGarner[(3)] 98
(Michael Scudamore) *hld up in rr: rdn in 7th and nt on terms 3 out: no ch after but plugged on fr 2 out* **100/1**

005 7 27 **Kaddys Dream**[26] 4881 5-10-13 0.......... CharliePoste 94+
(Robin Dickin) *hld up in rr: impeded 4th: prog into 5th 3 out and gng quite wl: wknd and mstke 2 out: heavily eased* **50/1**

64 8 8 **Up Till Midnight**[15] 5145 7-10-13 0.......... MarcGoldstein 67
(Lydia Richards) *chsd ldr to 5th: wknd 7th: t.o* **100/1**

0 9 *nk* **Bowberry**[26] 4881 5-10-10 0.......... RyanHatch[(3)] 67
(Ali Stronge) *a in rr: wknd 6th: t.o* **100/1**

5m 7.3s (-13.70) **Going Correction** -0.60s/f (Firm) **9** Ran SP% **111.5**
Speed ratings (Par 105): **102,101,101,99,97 97,87,84,83**
CSF £6.60 TOTE £3.00: £1.20, £1.20, £1.30; EX 9.60 Trifecta £19.50.
Owner Mrs Sue Griffiths **Bred** Mrs Kathryn Lillis **Trained** Upper Lambourn, Berks

FOCUS

Race run over 32yds further than advertised. The market leaders dominated, but the third was an unlucky loser. The winner was below the level of her soft-ground form.

5390 RECTICEL INSULATION PERFECT FINISH H'CAP CHASE (18 fncs) 3m

4:00 (4:00) (Class 3) (0-140,140) 5-Y-0+ **£6,498** (£1,908; £954; £477)

Form RPR

26U2 1 **Loose Chips**[60] 4234 10-11-4 **132**..........(b) NoelFehily 138
(Charlie Longsdon) *mde virtually all: jnd 3 out and next: fine jump last and take def advantage: drvn out and styd on wl* **9/1**

-136 2 1 **Port Melon (IRE)**[28] 4857 8-11-10 **138**.......... SamTwiston-Davies 144+
(Paul Nicholls) *mostly in midfield tl prog fr 14th: cl up 3 out: drvn 2 out: tk 2nd and chal last: styd on but a hld* **11/2**[2]

2316 3 ¾ **Cloudy Bob (IRE)**[24] 4910 9-10-10 **124**.......... LeightonAspell 128
(Pat Murphy) *taken patiently in rr: stdy prog fr 13th: cl up 3 out: tried to chal on outer fr 2 out: styd on u.p fr last* **14/1**

4520 4 1¾ **Valadom (FR)**[34] 4719 7-10-11 **125**..........(t) AlainCawley 130
(Richard Hobson) *prom: chsd wnr 6th: blnd 13th: chal and upsides 3 out and next: lost 2nd and one pce last* **12/1**

4PP2 5 41 **Present View**[21] 5018 8-11-12 **140**.......... BrendanPowell 106
(Jamie Snowden) *led in s: taken patiently in rr on outer: prog 12th: cl up 4 out: nt fluent 3 out and wknd rapidly: t.o* **9/1**

1335 6 11 **Border Breaker (IRE)**[159] 2459 7-10-9 **128**..........(tp) CallumBewley[(5)] 84
(Simon Waugh) *chsd wnr after 2nd to 6th: styd prom tl wknd rapidly after 4 out: t.o* **50/1**

P5-0 U **Representingceltic (IRE)**[191] 1871 11-10-7 **121**.......... JoshuaMoore
(Pat Phelan) *hld up in rr: blnd bdly and uns rdr 2nd* **33/1**

00PU F **Theatrical Star**[16] 5119 10-11-5 **133**..........(t) TomO'Brien
(Colin Tizzard) *chsd wnr tl fell 2nd* **9/1**

P-0P P **Pantxoa (FR)**[276] 1040 9-11-8 **136**.......... WayneHutchinson
(Alan King) *trckd ldrs: lost pl fr 9th: t.o in last whn blnd bdly 14th: p.u bef 3 out* **14/1**

-1F3 U **Harry's Farewell**[101] 3528 9-10-11 **132**.......... MrJoshuaNewman[(7)]
(Polly Gundry) *prom: disputing 3rd whn blnd bdly and uns rdr 5th* **6/1**[3]

5P04 **U** **Shantou Magic (IRE)**[17] 5093 9-11-2 **130**........................ AndrewTinkler
(Charlie Longsdon) *prog into midfield 8th: wl in tch in 5th whn blnd and uns rdr 12th* **11/1**

413P **U** **Fond Memory (IRE)**[60] 4234 8-10-2 **119**........................(t) RyanHatch[(3)]
(Nigel Twiston-Davies) *in tch towards rr: bdly hmpd and uns rdr 10th* **12/1**

P3P5 **F** **Wizards Bridge**[28] 4857 7-10-8 **127**........................(tp) HarryCobden[(5)]
(Colin Tizzard) *chsd ldrs: wl in tch whn fell 10th* **9/2**[1]

(-9.00) **Going Correction** -0.225s/f (Good) **13** Ran SP% **119.8**
Speed ratings: **106,105,105,104,91 87,, , , ,**
CSF £59.38 CT £702.11 TOTE £9.40: £3.40, £1.90, £4.80; EX 30.70 Trifecta £471.20.
Owner Barrels Of Courage **Bred** Peter Lamyman **Trained** Over Norton, Oxon

FOCUS
Race run over 31yds further than advertised. Poor jumping was the feature of this chase, less than half the field completing, but the winner deserves credit for a gutsy display. The winner is rated to his mark.

5391 PROTAN, AHEAD OF THE REST H'CAP HURDLE (10 hdls) 2m 5f
4:30 (4:30) (Class 3) (0-135,135) 4-Y-0+ **£5,393** (£1,583; £791; £395)

Form RPR

22 **1** **Cottersrock (IRE)**[54] 4323 6-11-2 **125**........................ AndrewTinkler 140+
(Martin Keighley) *trckd ldng pair: led 5th: rdn whn mstke 2 out: sn drew away: styd on strly* **9/1**

20F4 **2** *9* **Willem (FR)**[146] 2711 6-10-10 **124**........................(p) DavidNoonan[(5)] 128
(David Pipe) *hld up in tch: prog 6th: trckd wnr after 3 out and gng strly: rdn and ch after 2 out: sn lft bhd and btn* **33/1**

501 **3** *1 ½* **Chartbreaker (FR)**[31] 4788 5-11-3 **126**........................ SamTwiston-Davies 128+
(Paul Nicholls) *settled in midfield: effrt 3 out: sn rdn and no imp in 6th: kpt on fr 2 out to take 3rd after last* **7/2**[1]

P500 **4** *2 ½* **Shammick Boy (IRE)**[31] 4801 11-10-11 **125**..........(b) CiaranGethings[(5)] 125
(Victor Dartnall) *mostly in ldng trio: chsd wnr 6th tl after 3 out: one pce u.p* **33/1**

5223 **5** *3* **Mountain Eagle (IRE)**[46] 4466 7-10-9 **118**........................(t) NoelFehily 120+
(Harry Fry) *nt jump wl: hld up in last: stdy prog fr 7th: rch 4th on long run bef 2 out: no imp after: mstke last* **5/1**[2]

044P **6** *4* **Kings Lad (IRE)**[33] 4733 9-11-7 **135**........................(tp) PaulO'Brien[(5)] 128
(Colin Tizzard) *hld up wl in rr: pushed along and no prog 7th: 11th and no ch after 3 out: passed wkng rivals after: nrst fin* **33/1**

-614 **7** *2* **Clondaw Banker (IRE)**[152] 2594 7-11-1 **124**............ JeremiahMcGrath 115
(Nicky Henderson) *wl in tch in midfield: shkn up and no prog on long run after 3 out: one pce and n.d after* **6/1**[3]

6F64 **8** *22* **Political Quiz**[48] 4429 6-10-1 **113**........................ BenPoste[(3)] 85
(Tom Symonds) *a in rr: lost tch after 7th: mstke 3 out: wknd and sn t.o: mstke last* **20/1**

-020 **9** *4 ½* **Special Agent**[46] 4465 7-10-13 **122**........................ DavidBass 89
(Nicky Henderson) *trckd ldrs: pushed along and lost pl 7th: wl in rr whn mstke 3 out: t.o* **12/1**

301P **10** *2 ¼* **Driftashore (IRE)**[19] 5053 9-11-0 **130**........................ MissBHampson[(7)] 95
(Sally Randell) *led to 5th: sn urged along: wknd 7th: t.o whn j. bdly lft 3 out: blnd last* **33/1**

6140 **11** *11* **See The Rock (IRE)**[108] 3449 6-10-13 **122**........................ BarryGeraghty 78
(Jonjo O'Neill) *hld up early but prog to trck ldrs after 2nd: clsd gng strly after 7th: shkn up and wknd tamely sn after 3 out: eased* **6/1**[3]

P420 **12** *18* **Detroit Blues**[178] 2064 6-10-8 **117**........................(t) MichealNolan 56
(Jamie Snowden) *a wl in rr: lost tch 7th: t.o fr next* **50/1**

-0U3 **P** **Montbazon (FR)**[18] 5074 9-11-12 **135**....................(b[1]) WayneHutchinson
(Alan King) *in tch in rr tl wknd rapidly 5th: t.o whn p.u after next* **6/1**[3]

5210 **P** **Howaboutnever (IRE)**[15] 5146 8-10-8 **124**........................(p) HarryTeal[(7)]
(Roger Teal) *nvr gng wl: lost tch after 4th: t.o whn p.u after 6th* **50/1**

5m 2.1s (-18.90) **Going Correction** -0.60s/f (Firm) **14** Ran SP% **119.9**
Speed ratings (Par 107): **112,108,108,107,105 104,103,95,93,92 88,81, ,**
CSF £268.07 CT £1240.20 TOTE £9.40: £3.30, £9.30, £1.60; EX 275.70 Trifecta £3683.40 Part won. Pool: £4,911.24 - 0.48 winning units..
Owner Stuart Baikie **Bred** Alistair Corrigan **Trained** Condicote, Gloucs

FOCUS
Race run over 32yds further than advertised. A fair hurdle won by an unexposed type, with probably more to come from him.

5392 EGR NATURALLY THE BEST OPEN HUNTERS' CHASE (16 fncs) 2m 4f 110y
5:00 (5:00) (Class 5) 6-Y-0+ **£2,495** (£774; £386; £193)

Form RPR

-344 **1** **Grandioso (IRE)**[14] 5158 9-11-3 127........................(t) MrJamesKing[(7)] 128
(Steve Flook) *hld up in rr off str pce: prog 12th and sn cl up: led after 3 out: rdn and styd on wl fr last* **6/1**

6502 **2** *1 ½* **Twirling Magnet (IRE)**[18] 5075 10-11-11 127........................(bt) MrCHGDavies[(7)] 137
(Jonjo O'Neill) *trckd ldng trio fr 7th tl nt fluent 12th and dropped to 6th: effrt and chsd ldng pair after 3 out: nt fluent 2 out and rdr unbalanced briefly: tk 2nd last: styd on but nvr quite able to chal* **7/2**[1]

4-43 **3** *5* **Flaming Gorge (IRE)**[16] 5121 11-11-3 117........................(t) MrJoeHill[(7)] 125
(Alan Hill) *unable to ld: chsd ldr: clsd fr 12th: led after 4 out: drvn and hdd sn after 3 out: lost 2nd and blnd last* **9/2**[3]

3-21 **4** *15* **Polisky (FR)**[16] 5121 9-11-11 121........................(tp) MissBFrost[(3)] 113
(Paul Nicholls) *hld up in last trio: cajoled along fr 9th and nvr any rspnse: wl btn after 4 out* **4/1**[2]

11 **5** *1 ¾* **Drom**[24] 13-11-13 120........................ MissETodd[(5)] 116
(Mrs C Drury) *bking away as tape wnt up and unable to ld: chsd ldng pair: urged along 4 out: lost pl and btn bef 3 out* **8/1**

3552 **6** *1* **Best Boy Barney (IRE)**[15] 5150 10-11-11 121............(bt) MissLScott[(7)] 117
(Jeremy Scott) *unable to ld: chsd ldng trio to 7th: sn pushed along: nvr gng pce to threaten after: wl btn after 4 out: hmpd next* **6/1**

00PP **F** **Anquetta (IRE)**[243] 1296 12-11-10 125........................(p) MrSWaley-Cohen
(Robert Waley-Cohen) *set off at manic pce and sn clr: mstke 11th and c bk to rivals: hdd after 4 out: 5th and wkng rapidly whn fell 3 out* **14/1**

4-20 **P** **King Of Alcatraz (IRE)**[16] 10-11-3 109........................ MrJakeBament[(7)]
(R C Smith) *a in last: mstke 11th and lost tch: t.o whn hmpd 3 out: p.u bef last* **10/1**

5m 2.9s (-9.10) **Going Correction** -0.225s/f (Good) **8** Ran SP% **115.8**
Speed ratings: **108,107,105,99,99 98, ,**
CSF £28.45 TOTE £7.60: £2.30, £1.40, £2.10; EX 35.30 Trifecta £139.60.
Owner Foxhunters In Mind **Bred** Frank Barry **Trained** Leominster, Herefordshire

FOCUS
Race run over 25yds further than advertised. No hanging around in this decent hunter chase and the form should work out.
T/Plt: £256.10 to a £1 stake. Pool: £77,005.58 - 219.42 winning tickets. T/Qpdt: £22.00 to £1 stake. Pool: £7,536.41 - 253.10 winning tickets. **Jonathan Neesom**

5153 LUDLOW (R-H)
Tuesday, April 19

OFFICIAL GOING: Hurdle course - good to soft (good in places); chase course - good (good to soft in places)
Wind: almost nil Weather: fine

5393 FAMILY DAY ON 8TH MAY NOVICES' HURDLE (9 hdls) 1m 7f 169y
2:10 (2:10) (Class 4) 4-Y-0+ **£3,898** (£1,144; £572; £286)

Form RPR

311 **1** **Ozzie The Oscar (IRE)**[17] 5091 5-11-11 138........................ RichardJohnson 132+
(Philip Hobbs) *t.k.h: trckd ldrs tl led 3rd: gng clr whn mstke 5th: 15 l up after next: j.rt 3 out: 5 l up whn blnd next and shkn up: rdn out flat* **1/9**[1]

35 **2** *3 ¼* **Eamon An Cnoic (IRE)**[15] 5143 5-10-12 0........................ ConorO'Farrell 112
(David Pipe) *hld up in rr: hdwy after 6th: chsd wnr bef 3 out: rdn next: kpt on same pce* **7/2**[2]

3 *6* **Shininstar (IRE)**[352] 7-10-12 0........................ LiamHeard 106
(John Groucott) *chsd ldrs: wnt 3rd after 6th: shkn up 3 out: one pce and no imp fr next* **66/1**

4335 **4** *19* **Stickee Fingers**[27] 4868 5-10-5 0........................ GavinSheehan 80
(Warren Greatrex) *led to 3rd: styd in 2nd tl bef 3 out: grad wknd* **7/1**[3]

P **5** *3 ½* **Right Madam (IRE)**[21] 5019 4-10-0 0........................(p) JackQuinlan 72
(Sarah Hollinshead) *t.k.h towards rr: lost tch after 6th: kpt on steadily fr 3 out* **33/1**

0 **6** *10* **Pray For A Rainbow**[26] 4894 5-10-7 0........................ ConorRing[(5)] 77
(Evan Williams) *disp ld tl j. slowly 2nd: chsd ldrs after: slow 4th: pushed along next: wknd after 6th* **12/1**

50 **7** *25* **My Son Max**[26] 4888 8-10-9 0........................ RobertWilliams[(3)] 49
(Nikki Evans) *t.k.h: prom: rdn and wknd after 6th: mstke 3 out: t.o* **33/1**

P **Never To Be (USA)**[74] 5-10-7 0........................(t) ChrisWard[(5)]
(Nikki Evans) *t.k.h: a in rr: lost tch 6th: t.o whn p.u bef 3 out* **33/1**

3m 48.3s (-1.20) **Going Correction** -0.025s/f (Good)
WFA 4 from 5yo+ 5lb **8** Ran SP% **142.7**
Speed ratings (Par 105): **102,100,97,87,86 81,68,**
CSF £2.08 TOTE £1.10: £1.02, £1.30, £20.50; EX 2.00 Trifecta £76.30.
Owner Bradley Partnership **Bred** William O'Keeffe **Trained** Withycombe, Somerset

FOCUS
Rails moved to the inside and all the fences moved in the home straight to the outside by 5m. It was very much a drying day and the going looked on the lively side in the opener. This was all about the 138-rated winner, who ran some way below that mark. The second built on his bumper mark.

5394 WEATHERBYS HAMILTON "CONFINED" H'CAP CHASE (12 fncs) 1m 7f 212y
2:40 (2:40) (Class 3) (0-130,127) 5-Y-0+ **£7,797** (£2,289; £1,144; £572)

Form RPR

P446 **1** **Festive Affair (IRE)**[31] 4787 8-11-6 **121**........................(tp) RichardJohnson 130+
(Jonjo O'Neill) *cl up: j.rt at times: blnd 1st: led next and mde rest: shkn up 3 out: in command fr next: drvn out flat* **9/4**[1]

2544 **2** *4 ½* **Kitegen (IRE)**[199] 1755 10-10-2 **106**........................ ConorShoemark[(3)] 111
(Robin Dickin) *towards rr: hit 7th: clsd after 9th: chsng ldng trio and rdn 4 out: wnt 2nd 2 out: hld by wnr whn nt fluent last* **9/2**[3]

6UPP **3** *2 ¾* **Another Journey**[29] 4841 7-10-2 **103**........................ JamesBanks 105
(Sarah-Jayne Davies) *chsd ldrs: wnt 2nd bef 6th: rdn whn mstke 3 out: lost 2nd next: one pce* **25/1**

B003 **4** *3 ¾* **Le Bacardy (FR)**[12] 5184 10-11-12 **127**........................(p) RobertDunne 127
(Dan Skelton) *chsd ldrs: mstke 3rd: wnt 3rd at 9th: rdn 4 out: nt qckn: wknd 2 out* **9/2**[3]

3P3P **P** **Laser Hawk (IRE)**[45] 4485 9-11-9 **124**........................ PaulMoloney
(Evan Williams) *towards rr whn j. slowly 2nd: last and nvr gng after: lost tch 7th: p.u bef 9th* **3/1**[2]

35F0 **P** **Town Mouse**[14] 5159 6-11-5 **120**........................(p) TrevorWhelan
(Neil King) *wnt to post early: led to 2nd: lost 2nd bef 6th: wknd 9th: wl bhd whn p.u bef 2 out: lame* **11/2**

3m 58.2s (-0.30) **Going Correction** +0.20s/f (Yiel) **6** Ran SP% **111.4**
Speed ratings: **108,105,104,102,**
CSF £12.60 TOTE £3.60: £2.80, £2.20; EX 11.80 Trifecta £176.50.
Owner Four the Fun of It Partnership **Bred** Noel O'Brien **Trained** Cheltenham, Gloucs

FOCUS
A modest "confined" handicap, run at a routine gallop. The winner is rated back to the best of his novice form

5395 H R SMITH GROUP LTD H'CAP CHASE (19 fncs) 2m 7f 171y
3:10 (3:10) (Class 3) (0-125,124) 5-Y-0+
£11,260 (£3,326; £1,663; £831; £415; £208)

Form RPR

P414 **1** **Bucking The Trend**[22] 4971 8-11-5 **122**........................(p) AlanJohns[(5)] 136+
(Tim Vaughan) *mde all: drvn 2 out: styd on strly to draw clr flat* **10/1**

5563 **2** *6* **Lord Grantham (IRE)**[29] 4842 9-10-13 **111**........................ AndrewThornton 119
(Henry Daly) *hld up towards rr: tk clsr order 11th: disp 2nd 4 out: drvn 2 out: sn chsng wnr: kpt on same pce* **12/1**

P0P5 **3** *1 ¾* **Kilbree Kid (IRE)**[24] 4914 9-11-5 **117**........................(tp) PaddyBrennan 125
(Tom George) *a.p: chsd wnr after 15th tl appr last: one pce* **4/1**[2]

21 **4** *2* **Thoonavolla (IRE)**[29] 4842 8-10-0 **98**........................ SeanBowen 103
(Tom Weston) *chsd ldrs: rdn in 4th 4 out: kpt on same pce* **9/2**[3]

025F **5** *28* **Relentless Dreamer (IRE)**[52] 4352 7-11-7 **119**...........(tp) TrevorWhelan 99
(Rebecca Curtis) *cl up tl nt fluent 3rd: in mid-div after: wknd 15th* **16/1**

6663 **6** *10* **Strumble Head (IRE)**[19] 5052 11-11-0 **112**........................(p) RobertDunne 83
(Peter Bowen) *prom: chsd wnr 7th tl after 15th: wknd bef 4 out* **25/1**

0P2U **7** *shd* **Ultimatum Du Roy (FR)**[9] 5247 8-11-2 **114**........................(tp) KielanWoods 85
(Alex Hales) *hld up towards rr: reminder 10th: struggling fr 14th* **20/1**

P5P6 **8** *2 ¼* **Dreamsoftheatre (IRE)**[18] 5073 8-11-2 **124**................(t) JackSavage[(10)] 93
(Jonjo O'Neill) *towards rr: hdwy into mid-div 6th: lost pl and struggling fr 11th: no ch whn mstke 15th* **16/1**

PP63 **9** *40* **Midnight Appeal**[20] 5035 11-10-11 **116**................(t) MrRobertHawker[(7)] 49
(Sophie Leech) *a in rr: mstke 12th: t.o fr 14th* **16/1**

44P1 **P** **Express Du Berlais (FR)**[9] 5247 7-11-10 **122** 7ex.....(t) RichardJohnson
(Dr Richard Newland) *tended to jump lft: cl up tl nt fluent 2nd (water): in rr by 5th: struggling 11th: wl bhd whn p.u bef 14th* **5/2**[1]

53F1 **P** **Captain Flash (IRE)**[26] 4884 7-10-7 **105**........................(p) GavinSheehan
(Jo Davis) *j.lft: mainly trckd wnr to 7th: styd prom tl drvn and wknd 13th: t.o whn p.u bef 4 out* **12/1**

5m 59.1s (359.10) **11** Ran SP% **117.5**
CSF £120.70 CT £564.15 TOTE £12.20: £3.60, £5.80, £1.80; EX 168.30 Trifecta £692.80.
Owner The Marinades **Bred** Richard R Evans **Trained** Aberthin, Vale of Glamorgan

FOCUS
This competitive staying handicap was run at a fair gallop. Only four mattered from three out. The winner is rated back to his best.

5396 MICHAEL LUMSDEN MEMORIAL H'CAP HURDLE (FOR THE HENLEY HALL GOLD CUP) (12 hdls) 2m 7f 174y
3:40 (3:40) (Class 3) (0-130,132) 4-Y-O+ **£7,797** (£2,289; £1,144; £572)

Form RPR
-030 **1** **Alzammaar (USA)**[24] 4911 5-11-6 **122**........................(bt) GavinSheehan 131+
(Warren Greatrex) *led: j. sltly lft: rdn after 9th: sn hdd and disputing 3rd: rallied into 2nd appr last: r.o u.p to ld fnl 100yds* **6/1**[2]
3145 **2** *2 ¼* **Dolores Delightful (FR)**[16] 5120 6-11-4 **125**..................(t) LizzieKelly(5) 133
(Nick Williams) *chsd ldrs: led 3 out: hit next and rdn: wandered last: edgd lft u.p flat: hdd and unable qck 100yds out* **6/1**[2]
3224 **3** *9* **Foundry Square (IRE)**[16] 5119 10-10-10 **112**.................. PeterCarberry 113+
(David Evans) *prom to 3rd: mid-div after: rdn bef 3 out: styd on fr next: tk 3rd post* **8/1**
U413 **4** *hd* **Shotavodka (IRE)**[16] 5119 10-11-11 **127**.................(p) ConorO'Farrell 127
(David Pipe) *chsd ldr: led briefly appr 3 out: lost 2nd after 2 out: one pce: pipped for 3rd post* **8/1**
2101 **5** *¾* **Driftwood Haze**[9] 5239 8-11-9 **132** 7ex.............................. MrTGreatrex(7) 130
(Phillip Dando) *t.k.h towards rr: hdwy 4th: rdn and hld after 9th: styd on again fr 2 out* **16/1**
1415 **6** *1 ½* **Towering (IRE)**[156] 2513 7-11-6 **122**............................ NicodeBoinville 119
(Nicky Henderson) *prom: rdn bef 3 out: grad wknd* **9/2**[1]
P02 **7** *nk* **Tjongejonge (FR)**[19] 5043 5-11-4 **123**..................... GrahamWatters(3) 119
(Charlie Longsdon) *t.k.h towards rr: hdwy to trck ldrs after 6th: disp 3rd 3 out tl wknd next* **20/1**
445 **8** *12* **Minnie Milan (IRE)**[114] 3283 7-11-7 **123**........................ TrevorWhelan 111
(Neil King) *a towards rr* **25/1**
23P1 **9** *2 ¼* **Colin's Brother**[22] 4965 6-11-2 **123**............................ JamieBargary(5) 109
(Nigel Twiston-Davies) *mid-div: mstke 2nd: rdn 8th: wknd bef 3 out* **10/1**
2F01 **F** **Mighty Leader (IRE)**[47] 4442 8-10-9 **111**......................... JamesDavies
(Henry Oliver) *mid-div: rdn after 9th: hld in 7th whn fell 3 out* **12/1**
4650 **P** **Miss Serious (IRE)**[17] 5094 6-11-7 **123**............................(t) NickScholfield
(Jeremy Scott) *a in rr: mstke 7th: sn lost tch: p.u bef 9th* **14/1**
351 **P** **Royal Milan (IRE)**[49] 4419 6-11-12 **128**.........................(t) RichardJohnson
(Philip Hobbs) *sn towards rr: nt fluent 2nd: j.rt and reminder 6th: lost tch after 9th: t.o whn p.u bef 3 out* **15/2**[3]

5m 46.3s (-6.00) **Going Correction** -0.025s/f (Good) **12** Ran SP% **118.7**
Speed ratings (Par 107): **109,108,105,105,104 104,104,100,99, ,**
CSF £42.51 CT £294.19 TOTE £8.00: £3.00, £2.50, £3.10; EX 59.10 Trifecta £558.90.
Owner Riverdee Stable & ROA Arkle Partnership **Bred** Kirsten Rausing **Trained** Upper Lambourn, Berks

FOCUS
A wide-open looking staying handicap and it's fair, solid form.

5397 WEATHERBYS HAMILTON NOVICES' H'CAP HURDLE (DIV I) (11 hdls) 2m 5f 55y
4:10 (4:10) (Class 4) (0-110,109) 4-Y-O+ **£3,898** (£1,144; £572; £286)

Form RPR
PP3 **1** **Bobble Emerald (IRE)**[95] 3607 8-11-2 **102**....................(p) KillianMoore(3) 112+
(Martin Keighley) *got flyer in ragged s: mde all: clr to 3rd: dictated after: qcknd bef 3 out: hit next: sn shkn up: unchal* **5/1**[3]
4456 **2** *10* **North Hill (IRE)**[31] 4798 5-11-7 **104**............................ RichardJohnson 107+
(Ian Williams) *slowly away in ragged s: towards rr: n.m.r bef 3 out: sn chsng wnr: j.rt last 2: no real imp* **9/4**[1]
0P0 **3** *17* **Kaddys Girl**[98] 3568 6-10-5 **91**............................ ConorShoemark(3) 77
(Robin Dickin) *s.i.s in ragged s: sn chsng ldrs: wnt modest 3rd 3 out: kpt on same pce and nvr able to threaten ldng pair* **40/1**
0P60 **4** *½* **Midnight Folie**[62] 4183 6-11-0 **97**.............................. NicodeBoinville 84
(Ben Pauling) *standing sideways as tapes rose and v.s.a: in rr: rdn and struggling 7th: stl only 8th 2 out: styng on whn jinked last* **16/1**
2P03 **5** *4* **Midnight Gem**[29] 4845 6-11-0 **100**.............................. GrahamWatters(3) 82
(Charlie Longsdon) *slowly away in ragged s: sn chsng ldrs: rdn bef 3 out: grad wknd* **7/1**
0305 **6** *3* **Thyne For Gold (IRE)**[62] 4183 5-11-8 **105**......................... WillKennedy 83
(Donald McCain) *slowly away in ragged s: towards rr: rdn after 8th: no imp* **12/1**
1P60 **7** *12* **Bayley's Dream**[27] 4876 7-11-6 **103**..........................(b[1]) RichieMcLernon 68
(Paul Webber) *w.r.s: rcvrd to chse wnr after 1st: rdn after 8th: lost 2nd 3 out: grad wknd* **12/1**
0005 **8** *½* **Late Shipment**[14] 5163 5-10-6 **94**................................... ChrisWard(5) 59
(Nikki Evans) *led in s and slowly away: a in rr: mstke 4th: j. slowly 6th: struggling after* **14/1**
6400 **9** *29* **Movie Legend**[81] 3839 6-11-12 **109**..............................(t) KielanWoods 48
(Ben Case) *s.i.s in ragged s: in 2nd tl after 1st: chsd ldng pair tl rdn and wknd bef 3 out: t.o* **4/1**[2]
0P0/ **P** **Best Director (IRE)**[367] 8-10-4 **87**................................... LiamHeard
(John Groucott) *v.s.a in ragged s: towards rr: sme hdwy after 8th: sn wknd: bhd whn p.u bef 3 out* **25/1**

5m 13.4s (-1.40) **Going Correction** -0.025s/f (Good) **10** Ran SP% **114.2**
Speed ratings (Par 105): **101,97,90,90,89 87,83,83,72,**
CSF £16.70 CT £398.54 TOTE £5.20: £2.20, £1.50, £8.40; EX 17.20 Trifecta £1116.10.
Owner D Bishop, C Bowkley & M Parker **Bred** J S Bellingham **Trained** Condicote, Gloucs

FOCUS
A moderate novice handicap. There was a very messy start and the winner took full advantage of an easy lead. This still rates a step up.

5398 WEATHERBYS HAMILTON NOVICES' H'CAP HURDLE (DIV II) (11 hdls) 2m 5f 55y
4:40 (4:40) (Class 4) (0-110,106) 4-Y-O+ **£3,898** (£1,144; £572; £286)

Form RPR
2354 **1** **Mazovian (USA)**[10] 5223 8-10-7 **94**......................(tp) MrStanSheppard(7) 97+
(Matt Sheppard) *hld up: hdwy appr 3 out: swtchd rt next: chal last: sn led: drvn and r.o wl* **5/1**
603 **2** *2 ¼* **Coeur Tantre (IRE)**[29] 4848 5-11-6 **105**.......................... ConorRing(5) 108+
(Hugo Froud) *nt fluent: chsd ldng trio: clsd bef 3 out: rdn next: sn led: hdd and unable qck flat* **5/2**[1]
5000 **3** *6* **Over To Midnight**[14] 5155 6-10-3 **90**.............................. MissLBrooke(7) 85
(Lady Susan Brooke) *wnt to s early: disp 2nd: rdn after 3 out: one pce appr last* **40/1**
346P **4** *10* **Darnitnev**[131] 2997 6-10-12 **95**...............................(p) KillianMoore(3) 81
(Martin Keighley) *hld up: clsd 3 out: outpcd by ldrs fr next: tk modest 4th post* **7/2**[2]
F00 **5** *hd* **Definitly Grey (IRE)**[55] 4303 5-11-7 **104**..................... GrahamWatters(3) 91
(Charlie Longsdon) *led: hit 4th: hdd appr last: wknd flat: lost 4th post* **7/1**
6000 **6** *1 ½* **Better Days (IRE)**[28] 4855 5-10-13 **98**............................ JamieBargary(5) 84
(Nigel Twiston-Davies) *disp 2nd: rdn after 8th: ev ch 3 out: wknd after next* **9/1**
500 **7** *nk* **Golden Bird (IRE)**[31] 4782 5-10-13 **103**......................... RichardCondon(10) 89
(Brendan Powell) *hld up: mstke and dropped to last 5th: struggling fr 7th* **9/2**[3]

5m 18.4s (3.60) **Going Correction** -0.025s/f (Good) **7** Ran SP% **110.6**
Speed ratings (Par 105): **92,91,88,85,84 84,84**
CSF £17.13 CT £415.32 TOTE £4.80: £1.90, £2.20; EX 12.50 Trifecta £185.80.
Owner Lost In The Summer Wine **Bred** Darley **Trained** Eastnor, H'fords

FOCUS
This second division of the novice handicap was run at a fair gallop but was the slower time. The first two are rated to their marks.

5399 EDDIE MAPP MEMORIAL "GRASSROOTS" HUNTERS' CHASE (16 fncs) 2m 4f 11y
5:10 (5:14) (Class 5) 5-Y-O+ **£2,495** (£774; £386; £193)

Form RPR
U-35 **1** **Ballytober**[14] 5158 10-11-5 114...............................(vt[1]) MrBGibbs(5) 124+
(Ian Prichard) *mid-div: hdwy 9th: wnt 2nd after 13th: led bef 4 out: drew clr fr 3 out: easily* **7/1**[3]
/3-6 **2** *23* **Spock (FR)**[16] 11-11-5 107.....................................(b) MissLBrooke(5) 104
(Lady Susan Brooke) *led: mstkes 3rd and 5th: clr to 9th: hdd bef 4 out: no ch w wnr fr next: hld on to 2nd run-in* **50/1**
P53 **3** *¾* **Cooladerry King (IRE)**[14] 5158 8-11-7 116...................... MrPGerety(3) 102
(Mrs Sheila Crow) *towards rr: hdwy after 9th: rdn 13th: wnt mod 3rd 2 out: pressing for 2nd flat* **5/1**[2]
-2PP **4** *12* **Gentle Duke**[9] 9-11-3 102..(p) MrPBryan(7) 91
(Miss L Wallace) *prom: chsd ldr 12th tl after next: no ch fr 4 out: lost mod 3rd 2 out* **40/1**
-33P **5** *1* **Blinding Lights (IRE)**[20] 5035 11-11-7 104....(tp) MrMatthewHampton(5) 92
(Mary Sanderson) *chsd ldrs tl lost pl after 9th: no ch fr 13th* **14/1**
-1PF **6** *6* **Neverownup (IRE)**[14] 5158 11-11-7 122............... MrSeanHoulihan(7) 89
(M J Vanstone) *j.lft: chsd ldr to 12th: sn wknd* **20/1**
1-41 **7** *2* **Tugboat (IRE)**[14] 5158 8-11-13 129.................................. MrJNixon(5) 91
(G Slade-Jones) *j.lft and nt fluent: sn detached in last: rdn 12th: nvr any imp* **1/1**[1]
42F- **8** *1 ¼* **Comehomequietly (IRE)**[16] 12-11-3 104.............(t) MrMarkRobinson(7) 82
(Paul Hamer) *mid-div: hdwy 10th: wknd after 13th: wl bhd whn mstke 2 out* **20/1**
3F-0 **F** **Torran Sound**[24] 9-11-3 88.. MrWMaskill(7)
(Miss E Rodney) *a in rr: fell 10th* **100/1**
1P-P **P** **Grove Pride**[16] 11-12-1 122.................................. MrStanSheppard(3)
(Mrs D J Ralph) *towards rr: rdn along whn mstke 8th: lost tch 12th: t.o whn p.u bef 4 out* **5/1**[2]

5m 2.6s (-1.80) **Going Correction** +0.20s/f (Yiel) **10** Ran SP% **117.4**
Speed ratings: **111,101,101,96,96 93,93,92, ,**
CSF £275.53 TOTE £6.90: £3.00, £3.30, £3.00; EX 314.10 Trifecta £798.00.
Owner John Thomson and Matthew Paterson **Bred** Mrs C J Berry **Trained** Pontypridd, Rhondda C Taff

FOCUS
This modest hunter chase rather fell apart from the home turn. The winner is rated to the best of last season's form.

5400 LADIES DAY ON 8TH MAY INTERMEDIATE OPEN NATIONAL HUNT FLAT RACE 1m 7f 169y
5:45 (5:45) (Class 4) 4-6-Y-O **£3,249** (£954; £477; £238)

Form RPR
1 **Coup De Pinceau (FR)** 4-10-12 0.............................. NickScholfield 106+
(Paul Nicholls) *trckd ldrs: wnt 2nd over 2f out: led over 1f out: shkn up and easily c clr fnl f* **13/8**[1]
2 *9* **Smoking Dixie (IRE)** 5-11-3 0..................................... NicodeBoinville 102+
(Ben Pauling) *led: drvn and hdd over 1f out: rn green: hung rt and sn no ch w wnr* **2/1**[2]
0 **3** *1 ½* **Grand Coureur (FR)**[67] 4103 4-10-7 0............................ LizzieKelly(5) 95
(Nick Williams) *t.k.h early: trckd ldrs: rdn over 2f out: kpt on one pce* **4/1**[3]
4 *1 ¼* **Sue Be It (IRE)** 5-10-5 0..(t) ChrisWard(5) 92
(Nikki Evans) *trckd ldr: rdn over 2f out: sn lost 2nd: one pce* **66/1**
3-40 **5** *2 ¾* **Dothraki Raider**[115] 3226 5-11-3 0.................................. PaulMoloney 96
(Sophie Leech) *hld up in last: hdwy 5f out: shkn up and rn green 2f out: hld fnl f* **15/2**
00-3 **6** *18* **Kalaskadesemilley**[43] 4532 5-10-12 0...................... ThomasCheesman(5) 78
(Kevin Morgan) *mid-div: rdn over 4f out: sn wknd* **12/1**
0 **7** *24* **Middle Barn (IRE)**[30] 4827 6-11-3 0.................................. RobertDunne 54
(Sirrell Griffiths) *towards rr: rdn and wknd 5f out: t.o* **66/1**
0 **8** *3 ½* **Courting Harry**[52] 4357 5-11-3 0.................................... JamesBanks 51
(Sarah-Jayne Davies) *t.k.h: in rr: sme hdwy 5f out: wknd 3f out: hung lft over 2f out and again over 1f out: t.o* **66/1**

3m 42.2s (-1.70) **Going Correction** -0.025s/f (Good)
WFA 4 from 5yo+ 5lb **8** Ran SP% **115.4**
Speed ratings: **103,98,97,97,95 86,74,73**
CSF £5.16 TOTE £2.60: £1.50, £1.10, £1.50; EX 3.90 Trifecta £13.40.
Owner Colm Donlon **Bred** Emmanuel Clayeux **Trained** Ditcheat, Somerset

FOCUS
This proved a fair test and the winner looks very useful. The third and fifth are the best guides.
T/Plt: £65.20 to a £1 stake. Pool: £57,681.99 - 645.08 winning tickets. T/Qpdt: £19.30 to a £1 stake. Pool: £4,528.00 - 173.10 winning tickets. **Richard Lowther**

5228 SEDGEFIELD (L-H)
Tuesday, April 19

OFFICIAL GOING: Good to soft (6.0) changing to good to soft (good in places) after race 3 (6.05)
Wind: light 1/2 against Weather: fine and sunny

5401 EQUESTRIAN SURFACES LTD NOVICES' HURDLE (8 hdls) 2m 178y
5:05 (5:05) (Class 4) 4-Y-O+ **£3,508** (£1,030; £515; £257)

Form RPR
31 **1** **Red Tornado (FR)**[14] 5153 4-11-5 **126**............................ HarrySkelton 119+
(Dan Skelton) *trckd ldr: led sn after 2 out: drvn out* **1/1**[1]

5322 **2** *3 1/4* **Bonne Question (FR)**[18] [5077] 7-11-3 119...................... LiamTreadwell 115
(Venetia Williams) *led: qcknd pce 5th: drvn and hit 2 out: sn hdd: styd on same pce* **6/4**[2]

524 **3** *6* **Carthage (IRE)**[49] [4417] 5-11-3 0................................ DannyCook 109
(Brian Ellison) *hdwy to chse ldrs 4th: 3rd bef 2 out: kpt on one pce* **7/1**[3]

2253 **4** *9* **Rocky Two (IRE)**[10] [5230] 6-11-0 105............................ AdamNicol(3) 101
(Philip Kirby) *trckd ldrs: outpcd appr 2 out: modest 4th last* **16/1**

254 **5** *3 3/4* **The Pierre Lark (IRE)**[19] [5048] 6-11-3 0....................... AdrianLane 98
(Donald McCain) *trckd ldrs 4th: outpcd bef 2 out: wknd and mstke last* **33/1**

P00 **6** *30* **Scrutiny**[16] [4817] 5-11-3 0................................... SeanQuinlan 71
(Barry Murtagh) *hld up in rr: hdwy 4th: lost pl after 3 out: blnd next: t.o* **125/1**

4m 6.5s (-0.40) **Going Correction** -0.075s/f (Good) **6** Ran SP% **112.1**
Speed ratings (Par 105): **97,95,92,88,86 72**
CSF £2.87 TOTE £2.10: £1.30, £1.10; EX 3.50 Trifecta £5.10.
Owner Notalotterry **Bred** Jean-Francois Gribomont **Trained** Alcester, Warwicks

FOCUS
This was run over 52yds shorter than advertised. This was quite a competitive novice hurdle for the course but the pace wasn't strong. The third and fifth are perhaps the best guide.

5402 PHOENIX SECURITY H'CAP HURDLE (13 hdls) 3m 3f 9y
5:35 (5:35) (Class 4) (0-120,120) 4-Y-O+ **£3,378** (£992; £496; £248)

Form RPR

PP34 **1** **Fresh By Nature (IRE)**[21] [5017] 9-10-9 **103**...................... DannyCook 108
(Harriet Bethell) *in rr: hit 6th: chsng ldrs 9th: upsides 3 out: sn drvn led narrowly last: fnd ex clsng stages* **5/1**

32P2 **2** *1 3/4* **Moscow Presents (IRE)**[10] [5233] 8-10-6 **100**.................(p) HarrySkelton 103
(Philip Kirby) *trckd ldng pair: led narrowly bef 3 out: hdd last: kpt on same pce* **5/2**[1]

P305 **3** *24* **Bop Along (IRE)**[24] [4906] 9-10-13 **107**..........................(p) SeanQuinlan 89
(Alistair Whillans) *w ldr: drvn 6th: wknd bef 2 out: sn bhd* **6/1**

0U0P **4** *10* **George Fernbeck**[17] [5089] 8-10-13 **110**........................(b) JoeColliver(3) 84
(Micky Hammond) *in rr: sn pushed along: lost pl 5th: reminders next: t.o 9th: distant 4th appr 2 out* **20/1**

F4P5 **5** *19* **Warksburn Boy**[30] [4815] 6-9-9 **94** oh8........................ JamieHamilton(5) 48
(Sheena Walton) *chsd ldrs: lost pl bef 3 out: sn bhd* **20/1**

P342 **6** *7* **Shantou Tiger (IRE)**[19] [5045] 7-11-7 **120**...............(p) JamesCowley(5) 68
(Donald McCain) *led: reminders 10th: hdd bef next: sn lost pl and bhd* **3/1**[2]

5411 **P** **Agent Louise**[10] [5233] 8-9-11 **94** oh3...........................(p) AdamNicol(3)
(Mike Sowersby) *nt fluent in last: detached: nt fluent and reminders 3rd: j. slowly next: t.o 7th: p.u after next* **7/2**[3]

6m 45.6s (-6.40) **Going Correction** -0.075s/f (Good) **7** Ran SP% **116.3**
Speed ratings (Par 105): **106,105,98,95,89 87,**
CSF £18.95 CT £74.57 TOTE £7.00: £3.80, £1.90; EX 24.00 Trifecta £110.50.
Owner W A Bethell **Bred** Bridepark Stud **Trained** Arnold, E Yorks

FOCUS
This was run over 208yds shorter than advertised. They finished well strung out in this staying handicap hurdle after a fair gallop had been set. The form is unlikely to prove anything special, with the first two pretty much to their marks.

5403 ROA/RACING POST OWNERS JACKPOT H'CAP HURDLE 2m 3f 188y
6:05 (6:05) (Class 4) (0-120,120) 4-Y-O+ **£3,378** (£992; £496; £248)

Form RPR

4111 **1** **Generous Pet (IRE)**[8] [5262] 7-10-0 **97**......................... JoeColliver(3) 105+
(Kenneth Slack) *w ldr: nt fluent 1st: nt fluent and reminder 5th: pushed along to ld sn after 3 out: rdn between last 2: styd on run-in: won gng away* **2/11**[1]

5355 **2** *3 3/4* **De Boitron (FR)**[38] [4610] 12-11-12 **120**........................ DannyCook 121
(Sue Smith) *trckd ldng pair: pushed along and cl 2nd bef 2 out: kpt on same pce run-in* **10/1**[3]

202 **3** *10* **Snowed In (IRE)**[30] [4819] 7-10-2 **96**..........................(p) SeanQuinlan 90
(Barry Murtagh) *led: qcknd pce 6th: drvn 3 out: sn hdd wknd between last 2* **8/1**[2]

6P05 **4** *31* **Minella Hero (IRE)**[126] [3102] 8-10-6 **107**................. MissBeckySmith(7) 67
(Micky Hammond) *j.rt: detached whn j. slowly 1st: drvn 2nd: sme hdwy 5th: sn lost pl: t.o 7th* **25/1**

4m 56.4s (2.30) **Going Correction** -0.075s/f (Good) **4** Ran SP% **108.7**
Speed ratings (Par 105): **92,90,86,74**
CSF £2.87 TOTE £1.20; EX 2.80 Trifecta £3.60.
Owner Miss H P Tate **Bred** R J A McGaw **Trained** Hilton, Cumbria

FOCUS
This was run over 63yds shorter than advertised, but with only four runners and a long odds-on favourite, it wasn't particularly competitive. The winner was well in on his recent win but below that level here.

5404 JG PAXTONS H'CAP CHASE (11 fncs 10 omitted) 3m 2f 59y
6:35 (6:37) (Class 4) (0-120,114) 5-Y-O+ **£3,994** (£1,240; £667)

Form RPR

121 **1** **Auldthunder (IRE)**[44] [4511] 9-11-9 **113**........................ JoeColliver(3) 121+
(Micky Hammond) *jnd ldrs 3rd: led omitted 5 out: j.rt last 2: drvn out* **2/1**[1]

P26 **2** *7* **Feast Of Fire (IRE)**[21] [5013] 9-10-9 **96**.......................(p) SeanQuinlan 97
(Joanne Foster) *trckd ldrs: 2nd omitted 15th: kpt on same pce fr 2 out* **13/2**

P-PP **3** *44* **Tutchec (FR)**[50] [4407] 9-11-3 **104**.............................(v[1]) DannyCook 63
(Chris Grant) *led: hdd omitted 5 out: sn wknd: t.o 2 out: lft distant 3rd last* **9/2**[3]

3P45 **U** **Urban Gale (IRE)**[21] [5013] 11-10-5 **92**......................(p) HenryBrooke 90
(Joanne Foster) *j. slowly 1st (normal 3rd): lost pl 5th (normal 11th): lost pl w full circ to go: sme hdwy and modest 3rd whn hit 3 out: 6 l down in 3rd whn slt mstke and uns rdr last* **7/1**

P225 **P** **Dystonia's Revenge (IRE)**[16] [5126] 11-11-6 **112**............ JamieHamilton(5)
(Sheena Walton) *chsd ldrs: lost pl w full circ to go: sn reminders: t.o whn p.u bef 3 out* **11/1**

3331 **U** **Chanceofa Lifetime (IRE)**[10] [5228] 9-11-3 **111**............ ThomasDowson(7)
(Victor Thompson) *handy 3rd whn blnd and uns rdr 2nd (normal 4th)* **5/2**[2]

6m 56.2s (-14.80) **Going Correction** -0.425s/f (Good) **6** Ran SP% **114.3**
Speed ratings: **105,102,89,,**
CSF £15.30 TOTE £2.70: £1.80, £3.30; EX 17.20 Trifecta £71.70.
Owner The Rat Pack Racing Club **Bred** Miss Jill Farrell **Trained** Middleham, N Yorks

FOCUS
This was run over 102yds further than advertised but more importantly the four fences down the far side were omitted due to the low sun so only 11 of the intended 21 were jumped. The in-form winner is rated to his mark.

5405 JENNINGS FORD TRANSIT CENTRE H'CAP HURDLE (5 hdls 3 omitted) 2m 178y
7:05 (7:06) (Class 3) (0-130,130) 4-Y-O+ **£5,458** (£1,602; £801; £400)

Form RPR

40P3 **1** **Brave Spartacus (IRE)**[11] [5201] 10-10-10 **117**.......... HarryChalloner(3) 122
(Keith Reveley) *mde all: drvn appr 2 out: styd on wl* **7/1**

3102 **2** *2* **Herons Heir (IRE)**[14] [5159] 8-10-11 **115**....................(t) HarrySkelton 118
(Dan Skelton) *trckd ldrs: handy 2nd appr 2 out: kpt on same pce appr last* **11/10**[1]

0P-3 **3** *5* **Mcvicar**[27] [4550] 7-9-13 **110**.................................(p) FinianO'Toole(7) 111
(John Davies) *prom: pushed along omitted 3 out: one pce and 3rd whn hit last* **6/1**[3]

2216 **4** *4 1/2* **Teo Vivo (FR)**[24] [4913] 9-11-11 **129**..........................(b) BrianHarding 123
(Pauline Robson) *trckd wnr: one pce appr 2 out* **4/1**[2]

2063 **5** *3/4* **It's A Mans World**[16] [4771] 10-9-11 **106**...............(p) CraigGallagher(5) 100
(Brian Ellison) *chsd ldrs: pushed along w fuklk circ to go: one pce bef 2 out* **9/1**

4000 **6** *18* **Venue**[24] [4913] 6-11-2 **120**.....................................(t) HenryBrooke 103
(Donald McCain) *hld up in last wl in tch: brief effrt appr 2 out: sn wknd: wl bhd whn eased clsng stages* **10/1**

4m 4.4s (-2.50) **Going Correction** -0.075s/f (Good)
WFA 4 from 6yo+ 5lb **6** Ran SP% **113.5**
Speed ratings (Par 107): **102,101,98,96,96 87**
CSF £16.14 CT £49.21 TOTE £8.20: £2.10, £1.70; EX 18.20 Trifecta £69.00.
Owner Richard Collins **Bred** Dan O'Regan **Trained** Lingdale, Redcar & Cleveland

FOCUS
This was run over 52yds shorter than advertised. Quite a competitive handicap hurdle for the grade, but only five flights were jumped due to the low sun. The pace was ordinary. The winner was close to the best of last season's hurdles form.

5406 COLLINS SEAFOODS NOVICES' HURDLE 2m 3f 188y
7:35 (7:35) (Class 4) 4-Y-O+ **£3,508** (£1,030; £515; £257)

Form RPR

3153 **1** **Abricot De L'Oasis (FR)**[31] [4786] 6-12-2 127............... HarrySkelton 128+
(Dan Skelton) *led to 2nd (normal 3rd): led 5th (normal 6th): wnt clr after 2 out: eased last 75yds* **4/9**[1]

-2P4 **2** *16* **Huehuecoytle**[33] [4742] 6-11-2 0................................... CraigNichol 99
(Keith Dalgleish) *trckd ldng pair: mstke 4th (normal 5th): pushed along 3 out: reminders and chsd wnr appr 2 out: one pce* **7/1**[3]

6 **3** *49* **That Man Of Mine (IRE)**[9] [5243] 4-10-7 0..................... AdamNicol(3) 47
(Mike Sowersby) *sn poor 4th: t.o w full circ to go: lft dist 3rd 2 out* **100/1**

P **4** *16* **The Saskatoon**[10] [5230] 7-10-11 0........................ JamieHamilton(5) 39
(Peter Maddison) *s.s: detached in last: reminders 2nd (normal 3rd): t.o w full circ to go: lft remote 4th 2 out* **100/1**

FF35 **U** **Raise A Spark**[27] [4873] 6-10-6 110........................ RonanShort(10) 99
(Donald McCain) *t.k.h: trckd wnr: led 2nd (normal 3rd): hdd 5th (normal 6th): drvn 3 out: 2 l down in 3rd and wl hld whn blnd and uns rdr 2 out* **5/2**[2]

4m 51.6s (-2.50) **Going Correction** -0.075s/f (Good)
WFA 4 from 5yo+ 6lb **5** Ran SP% **112.3**
Speed ratings (Par 105): **102,95,76,69,**
CSF £4.73 TOTE £1.60: £1.10, £2.70; EX 4.90 Trifecta £27.20.
Owner Frank McAleavy **Bred** S Blanchais, N Blanchais Et Al **Trained** Alcester, Warwicks

FOCUS
One hurdle per circuit was omitted on account of the low sun. This was uncompetitive, with a long odds-on winner. He ran to his mark.

5407 WILLS PROPERTY SERVICES STANDARD OPEN NATIONAL HUNT FLAT RACE 2m 178y
8:05 (8:05) (Class 6) 4-6-Y-O **£1,559** (£457; £228; £114)

Form RPR

1 **Vanilla Run (IRE)** 5-10-7 0..................................... TonyKelly(3) 103+
(Chris Grant) *chsd ldrs: effrt over 4f out: outpcd 3f out: styd on to ld over 1f out: drvn clr last 100yds* **20/1**

052 **2** *6* **Desert Sensation (IRE)**[62] [4181] 4-10-12 0......................(t) BrianHarding 99
(Tracy Waggott) *led: drvn over 2f out: hdd over 1f out: kpt on same pce* **17/2**[2]

2 **3** *3/4* **Bandsman**[26] [4894] 5-11-3 0.................................... HarrySkelton 103
(Dan Skelton) *trckd ldrs: drvn over 2f out: kpt on one pce over 1f out* **1/6**[1]

4 *1 3/4* **Acdc (IRE)** 6-11-3 0.. CraigNichol 102
(Chris Grant) *trckd ldr: t.k.h: upsides 3f out: one pce over 1f out* **12/1**[3]

0 **5** *9* **Montydarkdestroyer**[28] [4867] 5-10-10 0.................. FinianO'Toole(7) 93
(John Davies) *chsd ldrs: drvn 3f out: lost pl over 1f out* **25/1**

40 **6** *64* **Callnineninenine**[21] [5014] 5-11-0 0...............................[1] AdamNicol(3) 29
(John Weymes) *chsd ldrs: drvn and lost pl after 6f: hdwy to chse ldrs 6f out: lost pl over 4f out: sn wl bhd: t.o 3f out: eventually completed* **50/1**

4m 6.4s (5.10) **Going Correction** -0.075s/f (Good)
WFA 4 from 5yo+ 5lb **6** Ran SP% **114.5**
Speed ratings: **85,82,81,81,76 46**
CSF £165.76 TOTE £14.10: £6.10, £2.50; EX 111.60 Trifecta £131.40.
Owner John Wade **Bred** Chesters Stud Ltd **Trained** Newton Bewley, Co Durham

FOCUS
This looked an uncompetitive bumper, with a long odds-on favourite, but it produced a surprise result. The gallop was ordinary. It was run over 52yds shorter than advertised. The form is rated around the second and third.
T/Plt: £5.20 to a £1 stake. Pool: £51,632.74 - 7,195.23 winning tickets. T/Qpdt: £2.40 to a £1 stake. Pool: £4,988.74 - 1,513.30 winning tickets. **Walter Glynn**

[1634] PERTH (R-H)

Wednesday, April 20

OFFICIAL GOING: Good (7.8)

Wind: Breezy, half against Weather: Sunny, warm

5408 ABERDEEN ASSET MANAGEMENT MAIDEN HURDLE (10 hdls) 2m 4f 35y

2:10 (2:10) (Class 4) 4-Y-O+ **£3,898** (£1,144; £572; £286)

Form RPR

364 **1** **Ballinvegga (IRE)**[25] 4902 6-10-11 0................................ TonyKelly(3) 104+
(Jackie Stephen) *led to 2nd: pressed ldr: led 4 out: rdn and clr last: kpt on strly run-in: eased nr fin* **10/1**

344 **2** *5* **Misfits (IRE)**[19] 5077 5-11-0 0................................ DerekFox 100
(Lucinda Russell) *t.k.h: hld up on ins: drvn and outpcd after 3 out: rallied bef last: chsd (clr) wnr run-in: styd on: no imp* **11/2[3]**

435U **3** *¾* **Badged**[167] 2293 7-11-0 110................................ BrianHarding 97
(Lucy Normile) *hld up: hdwy bef 3 out: rdn next: kpt on u.p fr last* **28/1**

0-63 **4** *shd* **This Thyne Jude**[34] 4736 8-10-2 85................................ GrantCockburn(5) 90
(Lucy Normile) *hld up: rdn and hdwy bef 2 out: kpt on fr last* **100/1**

34P4 **5** *1 ½* **Buttercup (FR)**[16] 5137 5-10-7 115................................ LiamTreadwell 92
(Venetia Williams) *hld up in tch: nt fluent 4 out: effrt and cl up whn mstke 2 out: edgd rt and outpcd fr last* **11/2[3]**

6 *¾* **The Jazz Singer**[18] 5106 5-11-0 0................................ RichieMcLernon 95
(C A McBratney, Ire) *chsd ldrs: rdn along 2 out: outpcd fr last* **22/1**

5 **7** *1 ¼* **Spifer (IRE)**[145] 2747 8-11-0 0................................ HenryBrooke 96
(Julia Brooke) *hld up: smooth hdwy bef 2 out: chsd wnr between last 2: drifted lft and lost 2nd run-in: sn btn* **25/1**

-002 **8** *4 ½* **Wicked Willy (IRE)**[16] 5137 5-10-7 0................................ MrZBaker(7) 93
(Nigel Twiston-Davies) *nt fluent on occasions: cl up: led 2nd: hit and hdd 4 out: ev ch to bef 2 out: wknd bef last* **11/4[1]**

2223 **9** *6* **Berkshire Downs**[38] 4633 6-10-4 110................................ AdamNicol(3) 78
(Lucy Normile) *hld up in tch: pushed along bef 2 out: sn wknd* **7/1**

-153 **10** *17* **Petapenko**[179] 2066 5-11-0 0................................(b) PaddyBrennan 69
(Malcolm Jefferson) *prom: nt fluent 1st: mstke 6th: rdn and wknd bef 2 out* **7/2[2]**

4m 53.6s (-8.40) **Going Correction** -0.475s/f (Good) **10 Ran SP% 113.9**

Speed ratings (Par 105): **97,95,94,94,94 93,93,91,89,82**

CSF £60.38 TOTE £13.20: £3.30, £1.20, £6.20; EX 95.90 Trifecta £1735.40.

Owner Mrs P Clark and Mrs J Stephen **Bred** B Murphy And Mrs Mary Devereaux **Trained** Inverurie, Aberdeens

FOCUS

The rails were on the innermost position and all distances were as advertised. Selective watering was done to maintain good ground all week, but after the first Brian Harding reported: "It's mainly good, but it is beginning to get quick down the far side and is likely to dry out as the afternoon goes on." Not a strong race considering the proximity of the fourth horse, and the winning time was just over four seconds slower than the 0-120 mares'-only handicap that followed. The winner and seventh help with the level.

5409 RONNIE THORBURN MEMORIAL MARES' H'CAP HURDLE (10 hdls) 2m 4f 35y

2:40 (2:40) (Class 4) (0-120,117) 4-Y-O+ **£4,548** (£1,335; £667; £333)

Form RPR

-05P **1** **Princess Tara (IRE)**[83] 3824 6-11-6 116................................ JamieHamilton(5) 122+
(Malcolm Jefferson) *prom: hdwy to ld 2 out: rdn out fr last* **3/1[1]**

0063 **2** *1 ¾* **Dubh Eile (IRE)**[28] 4878 8-11-9 114................................ RichardJohnson 118
(Tim Vaughan) *hld up: rdn and hdwy bef 2 out: chsd wnr run-in: kpt on u.p* **5/1[3]**

1240 **3** *3 ¼* **Carinena (IRE)**[25] 4909 7-11-8 113................................ CraigNichol 114
(Nicky Richards) *in tch: stdy hdwy whn hit 3 out: chal gng wl next: sn rdn: lost 2nd and one pce run-in* **14/1**

65R0 **4** *1* **Gold Chain (IRE)**[24] 4939 6-9-11 91................................(t) HarryChalloner(3) 91
(Dianne Sayer) *hld up in midfield: outpcd whn nt fluent and lost pl 6th: rallied bef 2 out: kpt on run-in: nvr able to chal* **33/1**

/6-5 **5** *7* **Degenerous (IRE)**[27] 4895 8-10-5 96................................ RichieMcLernon 92
(Sarah Dawson, Ire) *mstkes: led tl rdn and hdd 2 out: sn outpcd* **40/1**

3112 **6** *1* **Presenting Rose (IRE)**[39] 4608 6-11-4 114................................ StephenMulqueen(5) 109
(N W Alexander) *t.k.h: trckd ldr: nt fluent 3rd: rdn bef 2 out: hung lft and wknd between last 2* **14/1**

2113 **7** *2* **My Little Cracker (IRE)**[11] 5232 6-11-12 117................................ BrianHarding 109
(Iain Jardine) *hld up: smooth hdwy to chse ldrs on outside whn stmbld 2 out: sn outpcd and struggling: n.d after* **16/1**

0543 **8** *1 ½* **Daytripper**[22] 5009 5-10-11 107................................ GrantCockburn(5) 100
(Lucinda Russell) *hld up: hit and outpcd 4 out: sn rdn: no imp bef 2 out* **25/1**

1336 **9** *hd* **Lochnell (IRE)**[22] 5012 7-9-12 96................................ MrTGreatrex(7) 89
(Ian Duncan) *hld up: pushed along bef 3 out: nvr able to chal* **10/1**

-211 **10** *2 ¾* **Song Saa**[23] 4961 6-11-7 112................................ PaddyBrennan 101
(Tom George) *t.k.h: hld up: mstke 1st: rdn after 3 out: wknd bef next* **7/2[2]**

400P **11** *½* **High Fair**[12] 5198 10-10-0 91 oh2................................(p) DerekFox 78
(Sandy Forster) *chsd ldrs tl rdn and wknd bef 2 out* **28/1**

6P46 **12** *3 ½* **Whatdoesthefoxsay (IRE)**[25] 4909 7-11-5 110................................ WayneHutchinson 94
(Donald McCain) *prom: rdn bef 3 out: wknd bef next* **17/2**

4m 49.5s (-12.50) **Going Correction** -0.475s/f (Good) **12 Ran SP% 115.4**

Speed ratings (Par 105): **106,105,104,103,100 100,99,99,98,97 97,96**

CSF £17.37 CT £180.07 TOTE £3.70: £1.50, £1.80, £3.60; EX 23.20 Trifecta £296.50.

Owner Kate Perkins Chris Perkins & Toby Becton **Bred** Brendan Fitzpatrick & Timmy Hillman **Trained** Norton, N Yorks

FOCUS

Very much a modest event for mares. The early gallop didn't look overly strong. The winner should still be competitive when reassessed.

5410 BRITISH STALLIONS FUTURE CHAMPIONS EBF "NATIONAL HUNT" NOVICES' HURDLE (12 hdls) 2m 7f 207y

3:15 (3:15) (Class 2) 5-Y-O+ **£11,260** (£3,326; £1,663; £831)

Form RPR

314P **1** **Up For Review (IRE)**[33] 4766 7-11-6 145................................ PaulTownend 148+
(W P Mullins, Ire) *mde all: shkn up and clr 2 out: 4 l up whn j. sltly rt last: kpt on strly: unchal* **5/1**

322 **2** *8* **Nambour (GER)**[24] 4955 6-11-6 139................................(t) BJCooper 143
(W P Mullins, Ire) *chsd wnr: effrt and rdn bef 2 out: sn one pce: 4 l down and no imp whn hit last* **2/1[2]**

1141 **3** *6* **Barney Dwan (IRE)**[39] 4620 6-11-6 137................................ PaddyBrennan 137
(Fergal O'Brien) *chsd ldrs: hdwy to dispute 2nd pl 3 out: drvn and outpcd next: 9 l 3rd and no imp whn hit and stmbld last* **9/2[3]**

1122 **4** *10* **Fagan**[33] 4766 6-11-3 149................................ RichardJohnson 125
(Gordon Elliott, Ire) *hld up in tch: hit and outpcd 3 out: sn struggling: btn bef next* **11/8[1]**

5m 47.4s (-17.60) **Going Correction** -0.475s/f (Good) **4 Ran SP% 110.3**

Speed ratings: **110,107,105,102**

CSF £15.27 TOTE £7.60; EX 15.60 Trifecta £74.60.

Owner Andrea & Graham Wylie **Bred** Ms Colette O'Driscoll **Trained** Muine Beag, Co Carlow

FOCUS

Despite the small field, this looked a cracker of a race on paper but, as can often be the case in these scenarios, a decent horse was left alone in front and won comfortably, meaning this form is almost certainly not reliable. The winning time was just under four seconds faster than the 0-105 handicap later on the card. The third is rated 5lb off his Sandown mark.

5411 ABERDEEN ASSET MANAGEMENT H'CAP CHASE (18 fncs) 2m 7f 180y

3:50 (3:50) (Class 3) (0-140,137) 5-Y-O+ **£9,747** (£2,862; £1,431; £715)

Form RPR

0P21 **1** **No Duffer**[25] 4912 9-11-8 133................................(t) PaddyBrennan 144+
(Tom George) *trckd ldrs: wnt 2nd 4th: led 12th: hdd whn pckd bdly last: rcvrd and regained ld run-in: drvn out: gamely* **2/1[1]**

1305 **2** *1 ¾* **Presented (IRE)**[39] 4609 9-10-0 116................................ CallumBewley(5) 122
(Lisa Harrison) *trckd ldrs: drvn after 4 out: rallied next: led last: hdd run-in: kpt on same pce towards fin* **16/1**

UP22 **3** *1 ¾* **Silver Tassie (IRE)**[12] 5200 8-11-3 135................................ FinianO'Toole(7) 138
(Micky Hammond) *hld up: stdy hdwy 5 out: effrt and rdn 3 out: cl 3rd last: kpt on same pce run-in* **6/1**

15 **4** *9* **Topper Thornton (IRE)**[31] 4831 7-11-5 130................................ RichardJohnson 128
(C A McBratney, Ire) *hld up: stdy hdwy on outside 5 out: effrt and rdn 3 out: drifted rt and outpcd between last 2: sn no imp* **7/2[2]**

452P **5** *2 ¼* **Plus Jamais (FR)**[25] 4910 9-10-5 116................................ HenryBrooke 109+
(Jim Goldie) *hld up: drvn and outpcd 4 out: plenty to do next: kpt on wl fr last: nvr able to chal* **20/1**

3313 **6** *1 ¾* **Voyage A New York (FR)**[19] 5078 7-10-9 120................................(t) DerekFox 114
(Lucinda Russell) *trckd ldr to 4th: cl up: mstke 11th (water): drvn and outpcd bef 3 out: struggling fr next* **13/2**

P120 **7** *½* **Royal Macnab (IRE)**[32] 4787 8-10-8 122................................(t) TonyKelly(3) 113
(Rebecca Menzies) *led to 12th: pressed wnr to 2 out: sn rdn and wknd* **18/1**

2311 **F** **Jennys Surprise (IRE)**[40] 4595 8-10-13 127................................ ConorShoemark(3)
(Fergal O'Brien) *in tch: fell 2nd* **11/2[3]**

6m 0.2s (-3.80) **Going Correction** +0.075s/f (Yiel) **8 Ran SP% 114.5**

Speed ratings: **109,108,107,104,104 103,103,**

CSF £31.25 CT £166.27 TOTE £3.00: £1.10, £2.30, £2.40; EX 39.90 Trifecta £240.70.

Owner David Robey **Bred** Mrs R Crank **Trained** Slad, Gloucs

FOCUS

This had quite a competitive look to it for the level and it was run at a good tempo. A pb from the winner with the next three all close to their marks.

5412 BAILLIE GIFFORD LONG-TERM INVESTMENT PARTNERS AMATEUR RIDERS' H'CAP HURDLE (12 hdls) 2m 7f 207y

4:25 (4:25) (Class 4) (0-105,104) 4-Y-O+ **£3,119** (£967; £483; £242)

Form RPR

U3-3 **1** **Frontier Vic**[20] 5051 9-11-6 101................................ MrZBaker(3) 107+
(Nigel Twiston-Davies) *hld up: stdy hdwy 1/2-way: effrt and led appr 2 out: edgd rt and drvn out fr last* **7/2[1]**

P000 **2** *1 ¼* **Wyfield Rose**[110] 3427 7-9-9 78 oh3................................(p) MissKBryson(5) 84
(Alistair Whillans) *hld up: stdy hdwy 4th: effrt and wnt 2nd 4 out: ev ch whn hit next: disp ld bef 2 out: kpt on same pce run-in* **16/1**

6PPP **3** *1 ½* **Heart O Annandale (IRE)**[24] 4942 9-10-5 88................................(tp) MrWHRReed(5) 92
(Iain Jardine) *cl up: led after 2nd to 5th: rdn and outpcd 4 out: rallied 2 out: edgd lft and kpt on fr last: nt rch first two* **33/1**

3043 **4** *6* **Solway Sam**[25] 4903 13-10-11 94................................ MissRMcDonald(5) 95
(Lisa Harrison) *cl up: led 8th to appr 2 out: sn rdn and outpcd* **10/1**

05 **5** *¾* **Benarty Hill (IRE)**[15] 5170 6-11-1 98................................(t) MrTGreatrex(5) 95
(Liam Lennon, Ire) *hld up: nt fluent 2nd: hdwy and prom bef 3 out: rdn next: sn outpcd* **12/1**

6 *nk* **Boris Boru (IRE)**[21] 5038 5-10-9 92................................(p) MrHHunt(5) 89
(Sarah Dawson, Ire) *t.k.h: hld up: stdy hdwy 1/2-way: cl up whn stmbld bdly and lost grnd 3 out: rdn and wknd bef next* **12/1**

2020 **7** *2* **Bescot Springs (IRE)**[30] 4840 11-11-3 102................................(v) MrDDelahunt(7) 98
(Lucinda Russell) *hld up in midfield: stdy hdwy 4 out: drvn and outpcd after next: btn fnl 2* **16/1**

05P6 **8** *6* **Higgs Boson**[12] 5203 11-9-7 78 oh7................................(b) MrMEnnis(7) 68
(Jim Goldie) *bhd and nvr gng wl: struggling fnl circ: sme late hdwy: nvr on terms* **40/1**

2343 **9** *2* **More Madness (IRE)**[34] 4739 9-10-8 89................................(v) MrKitAlexander(3) 78
(N W Alexander) *cl up: led 1st to after next: outpcd after 7th: n.d after* **5/1[3]**

65PP **10** *1 ¼* **Darsi Dancer (IRE)**[71] 4047 8-10-10 93................................(p) SamColtherd(5) 81
(Stuart Coltherd) *led to 1st: chsd ldrs: lost pl bef 4th: n.d after* **9/1**

-5PP **11** *1 ¼* **See The Legend**[12] 5199 11-10-3 84................................ MissJWalton(3) 70
(Sandy Forster) *hld up: stdy hdwy bef 4 out: rdn and wknd after next* **25/1**

366P **12** *71* **Kilquiggan (IRE)**[2] 5367 8-10-11 92................................(tp) MrTHamilton(5) 14
(Sandy Thomson) *chsd ldrs: struggling after 4 out: lost tch fr next: t.o whn mstke last* **22/1**

2P32 **P** **Rolling Thunder (IRE)**[45] 4509 6-11-5 104................................ MrTGillard(7)
(Donald McCain) *t.k.h: cl up: led 5th to 8th: wknd after 4 out: lost tch and p.u bef 2 out* **4/1[2]**

5m 51.3s (-13.70) **Going Correction** -0.475s/f (Good) **13 Ran SP% 118.7**

Speed ratings (Par 105): **103,102,102,100,99 99,99,97,96,95 95,71,**

CSF £54.84 CT £1602.21 TOTE £4.80: £1.50, £5.70, £8.70; EX 57.20 Trifecta £1473.10.

Owner Jump For Fun Racing **Bred** B Mayoh, Eskdale Thoroughbreds **Trained** Naunton, Gloucs

FOCUS

They didn't appear to go any great pace early in what was a moderate event. Solid enough form at its level.

5413 BILL AND BUNNY CADOGAN MEMORIAL CHASE (NOVICES' LIMITED H'CAP) (FOR BILL & BUNNY CADOGAN TROPHY) (18 fncs) 2m 7f 180y

5:00 (5:00) (Class 3) (0-125,125) 5-Y-O+ **£7,797** (£2,289; £1,144; £572)

Form RPR

333- **1** **Ballyboker Breeze (IRE)**[403] 4769 8-11-8 125................................ BrianHarding 135+
(Nicky Richards) *pressed ldr: disp ld fr 3rd: rdn 2 out: ev ch whn hmpd run-in: styd on wl u.p to ld towards fin* **9/2[3]**

354P **2** *¾* **Florida Calling (IRE)**[46] 4487 7-10-10 113................................ PaddyBrennan 121+
(Tom George) *j.lft on occasions: led: rdn 2 out: hung lft run-in: kpt on u.p: hdd towards fin* **7/2[2]**

P211 **3** *9* **Lowanbehold (IRE)**[9] 5257 9-10-9 **117** 7ex................ JamieHamilton(5) 115
(Sandy Forster) *in tch: effrt and rdn 3 out: chsd clr ldng pair next: sn no imp* **9/4**[1]

3-12 **4** *10* **Mossies Well (IRE)**[137] 2918 7-10-12 **120**.......................(t) StevenFox(5) 111
(Sandy Thomson) *chsd ldrs: lost grnd 5th: rdn whn blnd and outpcd 4 out: sn n.d* **6/1**

P242 **5** *12* **Present Flight (IRE)**[30] 4836 7-11-3 **120**..............................(t) DerekFox 101
(Lucinda Russell) *trckd ldrs tl rdn and nt fluent 3 out: edgd rt and wknd fr next* **9/2**[3]

U132 **F** **Gallic Warrior (FR)**[38] 4642 9-10-7 **113**....................(t) ConorShoemark(3)
(Fergal O'Brien) *hld up: nt fluent 1st: fell next* **10/1**

6m 8.2s (4.20) **Going Correction** +0.075s/f (Yiel) **6** Ran SP% **112.7**
Speed ratings: **96,95,92,89,85**
CSF £20.83 TOTE £5.50: £3.40, £1.80; EX 21.20 Trifecta £71.50.
Owner Paul & Clare Rooney **Bred** Mrs Olivia Byrne **Trained** Greystoke, Cumbria

FOCUS
A fair race of its type run at an ordinary pace, which meant it paid to race handily. Those held up played no part. The first two produced steps up on thier hurdles form.

5414 ABERDEEN ASSET MANAGEMENT PLC H'CAP HURDLE (8 hdls) 2m 47y
5:30 (5:30) (Class 3) (0-135,128) 4-Y-0+ **£6,498** (£1,908; £954; £477)

Form RPR

1P22 **1** **Banyu (FR)**[30] 4849 5-11-8 **124**................................ RichardJohnson 134+
(Philip Hobbs) *t.k.h: mde all: set decent gallop tl stdd 1/2-way: qcknd clr 2 out: shkn up after last: unchal* **3/1**[1]

523- **2** *6* **Top Of The Glas (IRE)**[17] 5196 5-10-12 **114**...................... DannyCook 119
(Brian Ellison) *nt fluent on occasions: chsd wnr and clr of rest to 1/2-way: effrt and rdn bef 2 out: one pce whn hit last* **9/2**[2]

6053 **3** *7* **Jet Master (IRE)**[30] 4838 10-11-4 **120**......................(t) LucyAlexander 116
(N W Alexander) *hld up in chsng gp: stdy hdwy 4 out: rdn and outpcd after next: rallied and chsd clr ldng pair last: no imp* **11/1**

4304 **4** *3 3/4* **Baby King (IRE)**[46] 4484 7-11-12 **128**......................(t) PaddyBrennan 122
(Tom George) *prom chsng gp: hdwy to chse clr ldng pair 4th: clsd bef next: effrt and rdn bef 2 out: wknd fr last* **3/1**[1]

551F **5** *8* **Ash Park (IRE)**[18] 5088 8-10-0 **109**........................ SamColtherd(7) 95
(Stuart Coltherd) *hld up: drvn and outpcd bef 4 out: n.d after* **10/1**

4500 **6** *7* **Silver Duke (IRE)**[25] 4913 5-10-11 **113**............................ HenryBrooke 94
(Jim Goldie) *bhd: pushed along after 3rd: sme hdwy bef 3 out: sn rdn: btn next* **9/1**

0321 **7** *5* **King Muro**[15] 5159 6-10-11 **120**..........................(t) PhilipDonovan(7) 105
(Fergal O'Brien) *t.k.h: prom chsng gp: stdy hdwy 1/2-way: rdn and wknd bef 2 out* **6/1**[3]

5360 **8** *22* **Cool Baranca (GER)**[113] 3346 10-9-12 **103**.................... EmmaSayer(3) 65
(Dianne Sayer) *chsd clr ldng pair to 4th: struggling fr next: btn whn hit 2 out* **25/1**

3m 44.0s (224.00) **8** Ran SP% **113.7**
CSF £17.03 CT £127.72 TOTE £3.60: £1.30, £1.90, £3.40; EX 12.10 Trifecta £118.00.
Owner David Maxwell Racing & Barber Wadlow Ltd **Bred** Snig Elevage **Trained** Withycombe, Somerset

FOCUS
A wide range of ability was on show here, with the top weight officially rated 25lb higher than \bCool Baranca\p at the foot of the weight. One of the joint market leaders set a strong gallop early on and six of his rivals were well behind at one stage. There should be more to come from the winner.
T/Plt: £1,494.60 to a £1 stake. Pool: £65,497.47 - 31.99 winning tickets T/Qpdt: £139.90 to a £1 stake. Pool: £4,641.94 - 24.54 winning tickets **Richard Young**

5181 TAUNTON (R-H)
Wednesday, April 20

OFFICIAL GOING: Good (good to firm in places; 6.5)
Wind: quite strong against Weather: sunny Rails: Shared bends, effect on distances: Races 1, 2 & 4 adds approx 39yds; Races 3 & 5 adds approx 168yds; Race 6 adds approx 48yds. Hurdles on inside line.

5415 BATHWICK TYRES BATH MARES' NOVICES' HURDLE (10 hdls) 2m 3f 1y
5:35 (5:35) (Class 4) 4-Y-0+ **£4,873** (£1,431; £715; £357)

Form RPR

61 **1** **Rejaah**[27] 4888 4-10-8 0...(t) DavidNoonan(5) 118+
(Nigel Hawke) *trckd ldrs: led appr 2 out: r.o wl: rdn out* **6/1**[3]

U123 **2** *5* **Antartica De Thaix (FR)**[18] 5094 6-11-5 125.......(t) SamTwiston-Davies 120
(Paul Nicholls) *led: rdn and hdd appr 2 out: styd on same pce* **4/11**[1]

3641 **3** *11* **Western Sunrise (IRE)**[25] 4916 7-11-5 113..................... AlainCawley 111
(Johnny Farrelly) *trckd ldr: nt fluent 6th: rdn after 3 out: outpcd bef next* **11/2**[2]

5155 **4** *20* **Belcanto (IRE)**[161] 2444 6-10-12 0.............................. BrendanPowell 87
(Jamie Snowden) *chsd ldrs tl wknd after 3 out* **20/1**

4/0 **5** *43* **Truckers First**[55] 4322 8-10-12 0..................................... TomO'Brien 58
(Ian Williams) *nvr fluent: detached 5th: t.o after 3 out* **50/1**

0 **6** *117* **Lir Flow**[8] 5268 7-10-12 0.. NickScholfield
(Jess Westwood) *racd keenly: trckd ldrs tl dropped to last qckly after 3rd: t.o fr 5th* **250/1**

4m 29.3s (-16.70) **Going Correction** -0.925s/f (Hard)
WFA 4 from 6yo+ 5lb **6** Ran SP% **110.1**
Speed ratings (Par 105): **98,95,91,82,64**
CSF £8.83 TOTE £6.20: £2.70, £1.10; EX 8.10 Trifecta £23.00.
Owner Mrs K Hawke & W Simms **Bred** Rabbah Bloodstock Limited **Trained** Stoodleigh, Devon

FOCUS
Hurdles on the inside line, but shared bends which increased race distances throughout the card. 5mm of water was applied the previous day to ensure good ground, but after a drying day 'good to firm in places' was added to the going description. After the first both Sam Twiston-Davies and David Noonan were of the opinion that the ground was on the fast side of good. An uncompetitive mares' event, but the strong odds-on favourite was turned over. They went 39yds further than the official distance. The winner has the potential to rate a bit higher yet on Flat form.

5416 BATHWICK TYRES YEOVIL NOVICES' HURDLE (9 hdls) 2m 104y
6:05 (6:05) (Class 4) 4-Y-0+ **£4,873** (£1,431; £715; £357)

Form RPR

401 **1** **All Set To Go (IRE)**[30] 4849 5-11-7 125..................(t) HarryCobden(5) 134+
(Paul Nicholls) *trckd ldrs: chalng whn nt fluent 2 out: sn led: kpt on wl: readily* **4/5**[1]

1523 **2** *3 1/4* **General Ginger**[30] 4851 6-11-12 131..............................(t) NoelFehily 130
(Harry Fry) *led: nt a fluent: rdn and hdd between last 2: kpt on but nt pce of wnr* **2/1**[2]

14 **3** *10* **Great Hall**[176] 2123 6-11-6 127...................................... TrevorWhelan 114
(Kevin Frost) *trckd ldrs: disp 2nd after 3 out tl next: hld in 3rd whn mstke last: nt pce of front pair* **5/1**[3]

U **4** *11* **Cobham's Circus (IRE)**[136] 2928 5-11-0 0.......................... TomCannon 96
(Robert Walford) *in tch: rdn into 4th after 4 out: styd on same pce fr next* **50/1**

63 **5** *15* **Baby Sherlock**[13] 5188 5-11-0 0.................................. ConorO'Farrell 80
(David Pipe) *hld up: wnt rt 2nd: styd on past btn horses fr 2 out but nvr any ch* **14/1**

2 **6** *3 3/4* **Monsart (IRE)**[23] 4976 4-10-4 0................................ JamieBargary(5) 71
(Shaun Lycett) *in tch: awkward 3 out: sn drvn: wknd next* **33/1**

00P **7** *11* **Surfing The Stars (IRE)**[25] 4917 5-11-0 0......................... RobertDunne 65
(Laura Young) *trckd ldrs: rdn after 3 out: wknd bef next* **250/1**

0 **8** *1/2* **Bertie Barnes (IRE)**[28] 4875 5-11-0 0................................. IanPopham 65
(Richard Phillips) *hld up: rdn after 3 out: wknd bef next* **66/1**

P **Weld Arab (IRE)**[63] 5-11-0 0... NickScholfield
(Michael Blake) *nvr fluent: sn detached: wnt bdly lft 5th: sn p.u* **20/1**

3m 55.4s (-12.60) **Going Correction** -0.925s/f (Hard)
WFA 4 from 5yo+ 5lb **9** Ran SP% **123.8**
Speed ratings (Par 105): **94,92,87,81,74 72,67,66,**
CSF £2.96 TOTE £2.00: £1.10, £1.30, £1.70; EX 2.90 Trifecta £5.70.
Owner C G Roach **Bred** Mrs S M Rogers & Sir Thomas Pilkington **Trained** Ditcheat, Somerset

FOCUS
14-1 bar three in this typical novice hurdle, which took place over 39yds further than the official distance. The form is rated around the second and third.

5417 BATHWICK TYRES BRIDGWATER NOVICES' H'CAP CHASE (17 fncs) 2m 7f 3y
6:35 (6:35) (Class 4) (0-105,103) 5-Y-0+ **£5,523** (£1,621; £810; £405)

Form RPR

FP0 **1** **Fort Gabriel (FR)**[59] 5-10-7 **84**................................... TomMessenger 96+
(Fiona Kehoe) *in tch: trckd ldrs 12th: chalng whn nt fluent 3 out: led sn after 2 out: styd on: drvn out* **25/1**

3P22 **2** *1 3/4* **Somerset Lias (IRE)**[11] 5222 8-11-9 **100**............................ LiamHeard 108
(Bob Buckler) *led: rdn whn chal 3 out: hdd sn after next: styd on but a being jst hld fr last* **5/2**[1]

0425 **3** *5* **To Begin**[149] 2692 5-11-12 **103**..(t) NoelFehily 108
(Charlie Mann) *hld up: hdwy 4 out: rdn into 3rd after next: styd on same pce fr 2 out* **8/1**

-P14 **4** *7* **Minella Web (IRE)**[321] 612 7-11-12 **103**...................(t) ConorO'Farrell 102
(Richard Woollacott) *in tch: stmbld bdly 1st: trckd ldrs 10th: rdn after 4 out: styd on same pce fr next* **12/1**

5-P5 **5** *12* **Bedrock Fred**[196] 1813 10-10-4 **81**.................................. NicodeBoinville 67
(David Weston) *pressed ldr tl rdn after 4 out: wknd next* **11/2**

P64P **U** **Boardwalk Empire (IRE)**[11] 5222 9-11-5 **103**..(t) WilliamFeatherstone(7)
(Kate Buckett) *trckd ldrs: blnd bdly 3rd: rdn after 11th: sn btn: t.o whn awkward and uns rdr last* **5/1**[3]

-6F0 **P** **Well Rewarded (IRE)**[136] 2930 6-11-7 **98**.......................(p) DarylJacob
(Emma Lavelle) *in tch: shkn up after 7th: p.u after 10th (lame)* **11/4**[2]

5m 55.6s (-20.40) **Going Correction** -0.80s/f (Firm) **7** Ran SP% **109.9**
Speed ratings: **103,102,100,98,94** ,
CSF £83.05 CT £526.16 TOTE £22.30: £6.60, £2.20; EX 114.00 Trifecta £283.70.
Owner M Kehoe **Bred** Mme Henri Devin **Trained** Stewkley, Beds

FOCUS
A weak race, not even up to the standard of usual 0-105's. They went 168yds further than the official distance due to rail movement. The second and fourth set the level.

5418 BATHWICK TYRES TAUNTON H'CAP HURDLE (9 hdls) 2m 104y
7:05 (7:05) (Class 4) (0-115,115) 4-Y-0+ **£4,873** (£1,431; £715; £357)

Form RPR

F0RR **1** **Newton Geronimo**[40] 4593 7-11-6 **109**........................ NicodeBoinville 113+
(Ben Pauling) *bhd: hdwy fr 6th: wnt 5th 2 out: 2 1/2 l 4th at the last: edgd rt but r.o strly to ld fnl 75yds: pushed out* **50/1**

414 **2** *1/2* **Space Oddity (FR)**[21] 5030 5-11-11 **114**................................ NoelFehily 119
(Harry Fry) *hld up towards rr: mid-div 5th: hdwy after 3 out: disputing 4th whn rdn between last 2: r.o wl w wnr fr last: wnt 2nd fnl 75yds: a being jst hld* **9/2**[2]

3230 **3** *3/4* **Destiny's Gold (IRE)**[48] 4447 6-11-12 **115**........................ AndrewTinkler 118
(George Baker) *trckd ldrs: chal 3 out: rdn to take narrow advantage between last 2: kpt on but no ex whn hdd fnl 75yds* **25/1**

13 **4** *1 1/2* **Unison (IRE)**[11] 5220 6-11-11 **114**................................... MattGriffiths 116
(Jeremy Scott) *led: rdn after 3 out: hdd between last 2: ev ch tl no ex fnl 140yds* **14/1**

-236 **5** *2 1/2* **My Lord**[18] 3233 8-11-1 **104**.. RobertDunne 104
(David Evans) *mid-div: hdwy after 3 out: rdn and ev ch between last 2: hit last: no ex fnl 140yds* **12/1**

24-4 **6** *13* **Brother Bennett (FR)**[130] 3047 6-11-8 **111**.....................(t) JamieMoore 100
(Jim Best) *in tch: cl 4th after 3 out: sn rdn: wknd between last 2: nt fluent last* **14/1**

P012 **7** *3 3/4* **Goal (IRE)**[33] 4771 8-10-12 **108**...............................(vt) MissBHampson(7) 92
(Sally Randell) *a mid-div* **20/1**

0336 **8** *4 1/2* **Sandford Castle (IRE)**[16] 5148 6-11-9 **112**.................. BrendanPowell 92
(Johnny Farrelly) *hld up towards rr: rdn and stdy prog after 3 out but nt pce to get involved* **12/1**

341U **9** *1 1/2* **Justatenner**[8] 5267 5-11-11 **114**...................................... AidanColeman 93
(Colin Tizzard) *in tch: effrt after 3 out: wknd next* **9/1**[3]

PP5- **10** *1 3/4* **Moss Street**[408] 4683 6-11-1 **104**..(bt) RhysFlint 81
(John Flint) *racd keenly: trckd ldrs: ch 3 out: sn rdn: wknd bef next* **12/1**

654P **11** *2* **Frozen Over**[160] 2458 8-11-4 **107**...................................(t) JamesDavies 82
(Chris Down) *mid-div: rdn after 3 out: nvr any imp* **16/1**

P546 **12** *2 1/2* **Olympian Boy (IRE)**[25] 4922 12-11-0 **103**.........................(t) PaulMoloney 76
(Sophie Leech) *a towards rr* **33/1**

65P0 **13** *7* **Ablazing (IRE)**[15] 5153 5-11-3 **106**................................... AlainCawley 75
(Johnny Farrelly) *mstke 3 out: a bhd* **33/1**

4021 **14** *5* **Discay**[10] 5244 7-11-9 **112**................................(p) SamTwiston-Davies 74
(Dr Richard Newland) *trckd ldrs tl dropped to rr tamely after 6th* **2/1**[1]

2354 **15** *2* **Shadow Blue (IRE)**[37] 4681 7-11-2 **112**........................ MrGTreacy(7) 73
(Steven Dixon) *pressed ldr tl after 5th: wknd after 3 out* **16/1**

0/34 **16** *44* **Just When**[40] 4593 7-11-1 **104**..(v) DavidBass 25
(Patrick Chamings) *mid-div tl after 5th: sn bhd: t.o* **14/1**

3m 51.1s (-16.90) **Going Correction** -0.925s/f (Hard) **16** Ran SP% **132.8**
Speed ratings (Par 105): **105,104,104,103,102 95,94,91,91,90 89,87,84,81,80 58**
CSF £280.71 CT £5899.87 TOTE £58.90: £8.00, £2.20, £2.80, £2.20; EX 602.30 Trifecta £2857.10 Part won..
Owner J H And N J Foxon **Bred** J H And N J Foxon **Trained** Bourton-On-The-Water, Gloucs

FOCUS
They went a good pace in this modest handicap hurdle which totally changed complexion after the last with something of a surprise result. The official distance was extended by 39yds. The winner improved in line with his chase mark.

5419 BATHWICK TYRES H'CAP CHASE (17 fncs) 2m 7f 3y
7:35 (7:35) (Class 4) (0-115,115) 5-Y-O+ £5,523 (£1,621; £810; £405)

Form RPR
0441 1 **Saint Raph (FR)**[16] 5149 8-11-4 **112**.....................(t) HarryCobden(5) 126+
(Robert Walford) *trckd ldr: led on landing 3 out: rdn clr fr next: styd on strly: readily* **11/8**[1]
130B 2 14 **Georgie Lad (IRE)**[32] 4789 8-11-7 **115**.................... CiaranGethings(5) 118
(Philip Hobbs) *trckd ldrs: wnt 2nd after 3 out: sn rdn: hld whn nt fluent next: no ex fr last* **5/2**[2]
5PPP 3 3 **Fort George (IRE)**[13] 5178 13-10-9 **105**.................(p) MissBHampson(7) 105
(Sally Randell) *led: clr 3rd tl 8th: nt fluent 10th: wnt lft and hdd 3 out: sn rdn and hld* **9/1**
653F 4 49 **I'm In Charge**[153] 2598 10-11-5 **108**......................(t) NickScholfield 62
(Grant Cann) *a detached in last: nvr gng pce to get involved: wnt modest 4th run-in: t.o* **6/1**
252P 5 1 **Buckhorn Tom**[75] 3979 8-10-11 **105**......................(b) PaulO'Brien(5) 58
(Colin Tizzard) *chsd ldrs: reminders after 7th: nvr travelling and detached fr next: sme hdwy after 10th: wknd after 12th: t.o* **5/1**[3]
5m 54.4s (-21.60) **Going Correction** -0.80s/f (Firm) **5** Ran SP% **111.6**
Speed ratings: **105,100,99,82,81**
CSF £5.53 TOTE £2.00: £1.60, £1.80; EX 5.60 Trifecta £35.10.
Owner Mrs Christine M Hinks **Bred** Bernard Forges **Trained** Child Okeford, Dorset

FOCUS
The race was extended by 168yds due to rail movements. Only one of these came into the race with a completed start next to their name, that was the winner, and the form is modest at best. The winner is rated to form.

5420 BATHWICK TYRES MIDSOMER NORTON MARES' H'CAP HURDLE (12 hdls) 2m 7f 198y
8:05 (8:05) (Class 5) (0-100,100) 4-Y-O+ £4,223 (£1,240; £620; £310)

Form RPR
/02P 1 **Double Accord**[112] 3369 6-11-5 **98**.....................(t) DavidNoonan(5) 101+
(Anthony Honeyball) *trckd ldr: rdn to ld appr 2 out: styd on wl and a holding on* **5/1**[3]
-P02 2 3/4 **Unify**[13] 5181 6-10-2 **79**.............................. HarryBannister(3) 80
(Grant Cann) *racd keenly: hld up towards rr: hdwy after 3 out: sn rdn: styd on strly fr last: wnt 2nd fnl 150yds: clsng on wnr at fin* **12/1**
3P33 3 3 **Tara Mac**[57] 4290 7-11-5 **98**.............................. AlanJohns(5) 97
(Tim Vaughan) *mid-div: hdwy after 3 out: swtchd rt 2 out: hmpd whn lft 2nd briefly at the last: styd on same pce* **9/2**[2]
3P2- 4 3/4 **Ereyna**[380] 5191 7-11-6 **99**.............................. CiaranGethings(5) 100+
(Stuart Edmunds) *trckd ldrs: rdn after 3 out: chsd wnr next: styng on at same pce in hld 2nd whn mstke last: sn no ex* **3/1**[1]
0P5 5 14 **Ann Maries Reject (IRE)**[34] 4743 7-10-5 **84**.............. MichaelHeard(5) 71
(Brian Barr) *trckd ldrs: rdn after 3 out: one pce fr next* **50/1**
605 6 3/4 **Supreme Hope (IRE)**[35] 4709 7-11-3 **91**.....................(t) NoelFehily 75
(Neil Mulholland) *racd keenly: a mid-div* **7/1**
P060 7 3 **Weston Flame**[29] 4862 6-11-7 **95**.....................(t) DarylJacob 77
(Ben Case) *hld up towards rr: sme late prog u.p: nvr on terms* **16/1**
5-2P 8 5 **Penzflo (IRE)**[314] 695 10-11-10 **98**.............................. BrendanPowell 75
(Johnny Farrelly) *nvr bttr than mid-div* **33/1**
-44P 9 1 3/4 **Milly Malone (IRE)**[310] 741 10-11-2 **90**.....................(t) AidanColeman 66
(Adrian Wintle) *hld up towards rr: sme late prog: nvr on terms* **16/1**
4P66 10 3 **Diamond Gesture (IRE)**[69] 4068 8-10-0 **74**.....................(t) ConorO'Farrell 57
(Fergal O'Brien) *led: rdn and hdd appr 2 out: sn wknd* **14/1**
5405 11 3 3/4 **Oneforthenure (IRE)**[57] 4293 7-11-7 **95**.............................. TomO'Brien 65
(Richard Woollacott) *in tch tl rdn after 8th: no threat after* **25/1**
654P 12 1 3/4 **Meyrem Ana**[52] 4382 6-9-12 **79**.............................. MrWillPettis(7) 47
(Natalie Lloyd-Beavis) *a towards rr* **66/1**
4045 13 3 **Mari Me Oscar (IRE)**[23] 4961 6-10-7 **86**.............................. ChrisWard(5) 51
(Nikki Evans) *mid-div tl wknd after 3 out* **50/1**
-055 14 10 **Apple Pops**[25] 4916 6-10-12 **86**.............................. MarkQuinlan 42
(Neil Mulholland) *racd keenly in midfield: wknd 3 out* **16/1**
11P6 15 33 **Kentford Heiress**[28] 4878 6-11-7 **100**.............................. KevinJones(5) 27
(Seamus Mullins) *racd keenly in midfield: sddle slipped after 2nd: jockey kicked irons out 4th: nvr rcvrd: trckd ldrs 6th tl blnd bdly 9th and lost rein: sn bhd* **14/1**
-436 U **Buckboru (IRE)**[110] 3410 8-10-9 **83**.............................. RobertDunne 84
(Laura Young) *in tch: rdn after 3 out: wnt 3rd next: styng on at same pce in hld 3rd whn mstke and uns rdr last* **16/1**
5m 55.6s (-8.40) **Going Correction** -0.925s/f (Hard) **16** Ran SP% **129.1**
Speed ratings (Par 103): **77,76,75,75,70 70,69,67,67,66 65,64,63,60,49**
CSF £65.51 CT £302.73 TOTE £8.70: £2.10, £2.90, £3.60, £2.40; EX 78.70 Trifecta £464.80.
Owner R W Huggins & Atlantic Racing **Bred** R W Huggins **Trained** Mosterton, Dorset

FOCUS
A real moderate handicap hurdle for mares', but a fair few potential improvers lurked. The race took place over 48yds further than the official distance. A small pb from the winner with the second and the unseater to their marks.
T/Plt: £8.90 to a £1 stake. Pool: £63,060.45 - 5148.09 winning units. T/Qpdt: £8.10 to a £1 stake. Pool: £7,041.94 - 636.31 winning units. **Tim Mitchell**

5421 - 5427a (Foreign Racing) - See Raceform Interactive

5271 ENGHIEN (L-H)
Wednesday, April 20

OFFICIAL GOING: Turf: very soft

5428a PRIX DU CHER (HURDLE) (LISTED RACE) (5YO+) (TURF) 2m 3f
12:30 (12:00) 5-Y-O+ £30,000 (£15,000; £8,750; £5,937; £2,812)

RPR
1 **Shelford (IRE)**[44] 4540 7-10-12 0.............................. HarrySkelton 137
(Dan Skelton) *a cl up: rdn to chal whn nt fluent 2 out: drvn to ld bef last: wnt clr run-in: rdn out* **7/10**[1]
2 1 1/2 **Comas Sola (FR)**[28] 5-10-3 0.............................. AnthonyLecordier 127
(J-P Gallorini, France) **205/10**
3 1 3/4 **Ozamo (FR)**[21] 5042 9-11-3 0.............................. JacquesRicou 139
(P Peltier, France) **23/5**[2]
4 2 1/2 **Grinamix (FR)**[21] 5042 5-10-8 0.............................. JonathanNattiez 128
(P Lenogue, France) **36/5**
5 1 1/2 **Polygona (FR)**[143] 2821 6-10-10 0.............................. DavidCottin 128
(J-Y Artu, France) **47/10**[3]
6 7 **Fafintadenient**[24] 9-10-12 0.............................. JVanaJr 123
(Josef Vana, Czech Republic) **24/1**
7 6 **Golden Chop (FR)**[15] 8-11-0 0.............................. DavidGallon 119
(Francois Nicolle, France) **153/10**
4m 43.1s (283.10) **7** Ran SP% **121.2**
PARI-MUTUEL (all including 1 euro stake) WIN: 1.70 PLACE: 1.40, 5.10 SF: 19.90.
Owner Carl Hodgson **Bred** Brittas & Minch Bloodstock **Trained** Alcester, Warwicks

5429 - (Foreign Racing) - See Raceform Interactive

5263 EXETER (R-H)
Thursday, April 21

OFFICIAL GOING: Good (good to soft in places; chs: 7.0, hdl: 7.2)
Wind: almost nil Weather: cloudy

5430 RACING UK IN GLORIOUS HD NOVICES' HURDLE (12 hdls) 2m 7f 25y
4:55 (4:56) (Class 4) 4-Y-O+ £3,249 (£954; £477; £238)

Form RPR
1136 1 **Vieux Lille (IRE)**[39] 4636 6-11-5 137.............................. ConorSmith(7) 130+
(Philip Hobbs) *trckd ldr: awkward 8th: shkn up after 9th: led 3 out: hit next: kpt on wl: rdn out* **11/10**[1]
PP 2 3 1/4 **All Kings (IRE)**[156] 2558 7-10-9 0.....................(t) MrMLegg(5) 115+
(Harry Fry) *unruly s and slowly away: bhd: hdwy fr 6th: wnt 3rd after 9th: rdn bef 3 out: wnt 2nd between last 2: styd on same pce* **7/1**
3-P 3 10 **Boa Island (IRE)**[170] 2257 6-11-0 0.....................(t) NickScholfield 103
(Paul Nicholls) *led: rdn and hdd 3 out: no ex appr last* **3/1**[3]
0PP 4 21 **Port Navas (IRE)**[9] 5263 5-10-9 0.....................(p) MichaelHeard(5) 86
(David Pipe) *in tch: rdn in 3rd after 9th: wknd bef next* **40/1**
54 5 4 1/2 **Remember Forever (IRE)**[25] 4930 6-11-0 0.......... AndrewGlassonbury 80
(Richard Rowe) *hld up but in tch: rdn after 9th: wknd bef next* **50/1**
PP 6 dist **Shift It Franklin**[26] 4917 7-10-7 0.............................. MrNLawton(7)
(Philip Hobbs) *trckd ldr: rdn after 9th: wknd bef next: virtually p.u* **50/1**
3213 P **Chase End Charlie (IRE)**[70] 4063 5-11-6 129.............................. AidanColeman
(Tom Lacey) *trckd ldrs: drvn after 7th: wknd 9th: t.o whn p.u 3 out* **5/2**[2]
P P **Caniver Queen (IRE)**[17] 5145 6-10-7 0.............................. LiamHeard
(Brian Barr) *hld up but in tch: wknd after 8th: t.o whn p.u 3 out* **150/1**
5m 41.4s (-17.60) **Going Correction** -0.65s/f (Firm) **8** Ran SP% **120.7**
Speed ratings (Par 105): **104,102,99,92,90 , ,**
CSF £10.67 TOTE £1.90: £1.02, £2.60, £1.40; EX 10.30 Trifecta £26.70.
Owner Louisville Syndicate III **Bred** Park Athlete Partnership **Trained** Withycombe, Somerset

FOCUS
A fair novices' hurdle run at an even gallop. The winner set a high standard and is rated 10lb off his best.

5431 MANY HAPPY RETURNS HM THE QUEEN H'CAP HURDLE (12 hdls) 2m 7f 25y
5:30 (5:30) (Class 5) (0-100,100) 4-Y-O+ £2,274 (£667; £333; £166)

Form RPR
0504 1 **Motts Cross (IRE)**[30] 4860 5-11-6 **97**.....................(p) GilesHawkins(3) 102+
(Chris Down) *trckd ldrs: rdn after 9th: chal next: nt fluent 2 out: led sn after last: styd on: drvn out* **13/2**
563 2 1/2 **Easy Street (IRE)**[24] 4976 6-11-12 **100**.............................. AidanColeman 106+
(Jonjo O'Neill) *hld up: hdwy but nt clr run home bnd: wnt 4th and hit next: sn rdn: upsides whn nodded last: kpt on* **3/1**[1]
46-1 3 nk **Alderley Heights**[22] 5034 7-10-13 **90**.............................. ConorShoemark(3) 94
(Polly Gundry) *hld up: hdwy 9th: rdn appr 3 out: wnt 4th 2 out: styd on fr last: wnt 3rd nring fin* **9/2**[3]
P05P 4 1 1/2 **Follow The Tracks (IRE)**[35] 4746 8-10-9 **88**.............................. MichaelHeard(5) 90
(Brian Barr) *led: rdn appr 3 out: strly chal fr 3 out: hdd sn after last: no ex* **9/1**
PPPP 5 18 **Kilrush (IRE)**[16] 5165 10-11-2 **95**.....................(t) DannyBurton(5) 83
(John Berwick) *in tch: trckd ldrs 5th: rdn after 9th: wknd 2 out* **50/1**
PP15 6 14 **Flugzeug**[38] 4671 8-11-1 **94**.....................(p) KevinJones(5) 67
(Seamus Mullins) *mid-div: rdn appr 3 out: nvr threatened: wknd 2 out* **12/1**
P542 7 4 **Max The Minister**[20] 5076 6-11-12 **100**.............................. TomO'Brien 70
(Hughie Morrison) *mid-div: rdn after 9th: sn btn* **4/1**[2]
606P 8 8 **Up To Al (IRE)**[26] 4919 8-11-2 **90**.............................. LiamHeard 52
(Bob Buckler) *hld up: rdn after 9th: wknd next* **16/1**
-P40 9 2 3/4 **Kudu Shine**[61] 4250 10-11-1 **96**.....................(t) MrMatthewHampton(7) 56
(Richard Woollacott) *trckd ldrs: rdn after 9th: wknd 3 out* **10/1**
6000 P **Padova**[28] 4885 10-10-13 **87**.............................. TommyPhelan
(Dr Jeremy Naylor) *hld up: wknd after 7th: t.o whn p.u bef 3 out* **66/1**
P/00 P **Primo Milano**[89] 3745 7-11-1 **94**.............................. ConorRing(5)
(Evan Williams) *chsd ldrs: drvn along after 3rd: last at the 5th: lost tch after next: t.o whn p.u bef 3 out* **22/1**
5m 45.0s (-14.00) **Going Correction** -0.65s/f (Firm) **11** Ran SP% **117.0**
Speed ratings (Par 103): **98,97,97,97,90 86,84,81,80,**
CSF £26.46 CT £98.26 TOTE £7.50: £2.80, £1.40, £2.20; EX 35.10 Trifecta £214.70.
Owner Mrs S M Trump **Bred** K P O'Driscoll **Trained** Mutterton, Devon
■ Stewards' Enquiry : Giles Hawkins four-day ban: used whip above permitted level (May 5-8)

FOCUS
The gallop was steady for this open handicap. The front four finished clear and the form has a fairly solid look.

5432 HELEN TELLAM 50TH BIRTHDAY NOVICES' H'CAP CHASE (18 fncs) 3m 54y
6:00 (6:01) (Class 4) (0-120,120) 5-Y-O+ £5,198 (£1,526; £763; £381)

Form RPR
1435 1 **Call The Detective (IRE)**[22] 5032 7-10-10 **104**.....................(p) RobertDunne 113+
(Dai Burchell) *hld up: hdwy 13th: rdn to chse ldng pair after 4 out: chal last: led run-in: styd on: all out* **17/2**
2624 2 hd **Present Man (IRE)**[17] 5146 6-11-12 **120**.....................(t) NickScholfield 128
(Paul Nicholls) *j.w: led: rdn after 3 out: narrowly hdd run-in: kpt on: jst hld* **7/2**[2]
424P 3 8 **Dancing Shadow (IRE)**[44] 4542 7-11-12 **120**.........(p) WayneHutchinson 122
(Victor Dartnall) *trckd ldrs: sltly outpcd 14th: styd on fr 3 out: wnt 3rd towards fin but nt pce to get involved* **4/1**[3]
641P 4 1/2 **Brook (FR)**[12] 5222 5-11-2 **113**.....................(bt) KieronEdgar(3) 117
(David Pipe) *trckd ldrs: tried to chal on inner and short of room 11th and 12th where mstke: swtchd lft to renew chal next: rdn after 4 out: no ex appr last* **12/1**

F665 5 16 **Free Of Charge (IRE)**[30] 4859 7-10-6 **100** TomO'Brien 90
(Philip Hobbs) *trckd ldrs: pushed along after 11th: chal next tl mstke 13th: in tch but u.str.p tl wknd 3 out* **11/4**[1]

P4FP 6 ½ **Letemgo (IRE)**[91] 3705 8-11-11 **119** (p) TomCannon 105
(Giles Smyly) *hld up: detached 11th: nvr threatened to get involved* **18/1**

3251 7 12 **Like Sully (IRE)**[25] 4932 8-10-13 **107** AndrewGlassonbury 82
(Richard Rowe) *hld up: hdwy after 12th: chsd ldrs and rdn after 14th: wknd 3 out* **14/1**

0U 8 11 **Speed Demon (IRE)**[33] 4789 7-11-4 **112** IanPopham 77
(Richard Phillips) *racd keenly: mid-div: hdwy after 11th: cl 3rd turning in: sn rdn: wknd after next* **33/1**

2-3P P **Horsehill (IRE)**[113] 3371 7-11-6 **117** ThomasGarner(3)
(Oliver Sherwood) *hld up: mstke 2nd: hdwy 11th: losing pl whn stmbld 13th: wknd bef 4 out: p.u 3 out* **7/1**

5m 54.9s (-14.40) **Going Correction** -0.875s/f (Firm) 9 Ran SP% **114.5**
Speed ratings: **89,88,86,86,80 80,76,72,**
CSF £39.20 CT £138.51 TOTE £12.00: £3.10, £1.60, £1.60; EX 53.30 Trifecta £296.90.
Owner J J King **Bred** Rockvale Stud **Trained** Briery Hill, Blaenau Gwent
■ Stewards' Enquiry : Nick Scholfield nine-day ban: used whip above permitted level (May 5-13)

FOCUS
Due to rail movement the actual race distance was 2m7f149yds. A fair handicap run at an honest gallop. The winner was back to the level of his Fontwell win.

5433 WESTERLY BMW EXETER H'CAP HURDLE (8 hdls) 2m 175y
6:30 (6:30) (Class 4) (0-110,110) 4-Y-0+ **£3,249** (£954; £477; £238)

Form RPR

214 1 **Fort Carson (IRE)**[33] 4799 10-11-11 **109** TrevorWhelan 116+
(Neil King) *trckd ldrs: nt fluent 2nd: led after 5th: kpt on wl fr 3 out: nt fluent last: pushed out* **9/1**

3540 2 4 **Perspicace**[161] 2458 5-11-7 **108** (p) KieronEdgar(3) 110
(David Pipe) *mid-div: hdwy 5th: wnt 2nd and nt fluent 3 out: sn rdn: styd on but nvr threatened to get on terms w wnr* **7/1**[1]

4-3F 3 1¾ **Lamblord (IRE)**[340] 363 9-11-8 **106** IanPopham 106
(Robert Walford) *in tch: rdn to chse ldng pair 3 out: hit 2 out: styd on same pce* **8/1**[3]

3045 4 ½ **Elkstone**[31] 4846 5-11-4 **102** WayneHutchinson 101
(Alan King) *hld up towards rr: hdwy after 5th: rdn 3 out: styd on into 4th bef last but nt quite pce to get on terms* **9/1**

500U 5 ¾ **Berry De Carjac (FR)**[4] 5352 5-11-1 **102** (t) TomBellamy(3) 102
(Nigel Hawke) *mid-div: hdwy after 5th: wnt 4th 3 out: hung bdly lft u.p fr next: sn hld* **8/1**[3]

2334 6 ½ **Fred Le Macon (FR)**[141] 2855 7-10-9 **103** (p) KevinDowling(10) 102
(Alan King) *mid-div: hdwy 4th: rdn appr 3 out: styd on but nt pce to get involved* **10/1**

-500 7 7 **Tidestream**[48] 4455 6-11-2 **105** (t) AlanJohns(5) 98
(Tim Vaughan) *in tch: rdn after 5th: wknd next* **16/1**

40P3 8 7 **Westend Prince (IRE)**[17] 5148 5-11-4 **102** (t) TomO'Brien 87
(Colin Tizzard) *mid-div: rdn after 5th: wknd bef next* **8/1**[3]

063 9 6 **Blackfire (FR)**[24] 4979 4-11-6 **109** (p) AidanColeman 85
(Jonjo O'Neill) *mid-div: rdn after 5th: wknd bef next* **25/1**

6P/2 10 23 **Superman De La Rue (FR)**[30] 4856 10-11-7 **105** PaulMoloney 64
(Mary Evans) *led: nt fluent 1st: hdd whn hit 2nd: rdn after 5th: wknd next* **16/1**

0302 11 hd **Back By Midnight**[29] 4871 7-11-12 **110** (t) JamesBanks 69
(Emma Baker) *struggling after 4th: a towards rr* **20/1**

/13- 12 ½ **High Talk (IRE)**[115] 12-11-0 **105** (tp) MrZBaker(7) 64
(Barry Brennan) *lost tch 3rd: a towards rr* **66/1**

4P03 13 shd **Only Gorgeous (IRE)**[58] 4291 7-11-3 **104** LucyGardner(3) 62
(Sue Gardner) *a towards rr* **12/1**

14 5 **Zigger Zagger (IRE)**[209] 1652 7-11-11 **109** AndrewGlassonbury 63
(Richard Rowe) *led 2nd: hit next: rdn and hdd after 5th: wknd bef next* **33/1**

2-32 15 nk **Generous Jack (IRE)**[80] 3902 7-11-9 **107** AndrewThornton 61
(Jim Best) *hld up towards rr: hdwy on outer fnl bnd: sn rdn: hit next: wknd 2 out* **12/1**

P461 P **Alottarain (IRE)**[28] 4885 6-10-12 **101** KevinJones(5)
(Seamus Mullins) *a towards rr: struggling 5th: nvr any imp: p.u bef last* **15/2**[2]

4m 2.6s (-12.90) **Going Correction** -0.65s/f (Firm)
WFA 4 from 5yo+ 5lb 16 Ran SP% **126.9**
Speed ratings (Par 105): **104,102,101,101,100 100,97,93,91,80 80,79,79,77,77**
CSF £71.76 CT £544.25 TOTE £9.80: £2.30, £3.10, £2.90, £2.30; EX 71.10 Trifecta £1522.00.
Owner The Ridgeway Racing For Fun Partnership **Bred** Ronald O'Neill **Trained** Barbury Castle, Wiltshire

FOCUS
A competitive contest for the grade run at a decent gallop. The winner is rated similar to the level of his Market Rasen win.

5434 WILD BEER CO MAIDEN HURDLE (7 hdls 1 omitted) 2m 175y
7:00 (7:01) (Class 5) 4-Y-0+ **£2,599** (£763; £381; £190)

Form RPR

3 1 **Black Corton (FR)**[61] 4256 5-11-1 0 (t[1]) NickScholfield 123+
(Paul Nicholls) *trckd ldr: nt fluent 1st: led after 2 out: kpt on wl: pushed out* **6/4**[1]

5 2 4½ **Whipcord (IRE)**[9] 5263 5-10-10 0 (t) HarryCobden(5) 117+
(Paul Nicholls) *j.flt most of way tl home st: led: rdn appr 3 out: hdd after 2 out: styd on but no ex* **3/1**[2]

524 3 10 **Magic Music Man**[28] 4888 5-11-1 117 WayneHutchinson 106
(Alan King) *trckd ldrs: rdn to chse ldng pair appr 3 out: styd on same pce fr 2 out* **3/1**[2]

4P6 4 ½ **Indian Brave (IRE)**[9] 5269 5-11-1 0 AndrewThornton 108
(Neil Mulholland) *racd keenly: in tch: drvn into 3rd appr 3 out: styd on same pce fr 2 out* **20/1**

3F5 5 2¾ **Haut Bages (FR)**[16] 5153 4-10-10 115 DarylJacob 97
(Oliver Sherwood) *mid-div: hdwy after 5th: rdn next: sn one pce* **5/1**[3]

630 6 6 **Carqalin (FR)**[9] 5269 4-10-5 0 MichaelHeard(5) 91
(David Pipe) *hld up: sme minor prog 3 out: nvr threatened ldrs* **40/1**

50 7 6 **Common Practice (IRE)**[12] 5220 5-11-1 0 (b[1]) AidanColeman 90
(Jonjo O'Neill) *mid-div tl wknd 3 out* **40/1**

0 8 3¾ **Thomas Blossom (IRE)**[9] 5269 6-11-1 0 (t) TomO'Brien 87
(Ali Stronge) *racd keenly in mid-div: rdn after 5th: wknd next* **40/1**

00-4 9 7 **Scartare (IRE)**[268] 1139 5-10-12 0 [1] BenPoste(3) 80
(Rosemary Gasson) *a towards rr* **66/1**

00 10 31 **New Republic (IRE)**[4] 5356 5-10-10 0 ConorRing(5) 49
(Evan Williams) *mid-div tl after 4th* **250/1**

00P F **Primary Suspect (IRE)**[26] 4917 6-10-8 0 ConorSmith(7)
(Linda Blackford) *trckd ldr: chal after 5th: sn rdn: wkng whn fell 3 out: fatally injured* **200/1**

P P **Thirty Bob (IRE)**[11] 5235 5-10-5 0 (t) CianMaher(10)
(Evan Williams) *hld up: lost action and p.u after 3rd: fatally injured* **100/1**

4m 5.2s (-10.30) **Going Correction** -0.65s/f (Firm)
WFA 4 from 5yo+ 5lb 12 Ran SP% **122.1**
Speed ratings (Par 103): **98,95,91,90,89 86,84,82,78,64 ,**
CSF £6.44 TOTE £2.70: £1.40, £1.50, £1.50; EX 8.30 Trifecta £23.90.
Owner The Brooks, Kyle & Stewart Families **Bred** Dominique Guyon **Trained** Ditcheat, Somerset

FOCUS
A fair maiden hurdle run at a sound gallop. The slow time and the fourth are probably a better guide to the level.

5435 OTTER BREWERY 25 YEARS H'CAP CHASE (14 fncs 1 omitted) 2m 3f 48y
7:30 (7:31) (Class 5) (0-100,107) 5-Y-0+ **£2,924** (£858; £429; £214)

Form RPR

0-22 1 **Withy Mills**[6] 5307 11-10-6 **80** (tp) JamesBest 92+
(Kevin Bishop) *chsd ldrs: rdn after 4 out: chal next: led after 2 out: styd on wl* **5/1**[2]

3432 2 7 **Lamb's Cross**[26] 4921 10-10-2 **79** HarryBannister(3) 85
(Brian Barr) *trckd ldrs: pressed ldr 8th: led appr 4 out: hdd after 2 out: sn no ex* **4/1**[1]

-413 3 9 **Edeiff's Lad**[31] 4850 9-10-3 **84** MrJoshuaNewman(7) 82
(Polly Gundry) *mid-div: hdwy 8th: rdn to chse ldng pair after 4 out: styd on same pce* **17/2**

0000 4 1¾ **Sabroclair (FR)**[26] 4921 7-11-2 **90** (t) TomO'Brien 87
(Richard Woollacott) *hld up: rdn after 10th: styd on fr 4 out: chalng for 4th whn hit 2 out: chalng for 3rd whn mstke last: no ex* **12/1**

13P- 5 7 **Spanish Optimist (IRE)**[341] 10-11-6 **94** DarylJacob 83
(Sarah Robinson) *hld up: rdn appr 4 out: styd on fr 2 out: nvr threatened to get involved* **20/1**

6002 6 4 **Beauchamp Viking**[31] 4850 12-9-12 **77** (t) ConorRing(5) 64
(Hugo Froud) *led tl rdn appr 4 out: sn one pce* **16/1**

5P40 7 4 **Tinelyra (IRE)**[29] 4879 10-10-2 **79** (t) ConorShoemark(3) 64
(Fergal O'Brien) *towards rr: mstke 4th: nvr trbld ldrs* **8/1**

PPPU 8 ½ **Sylvan Legend**[31] 4850 8-10-4 **78** (tp) TrevorWhelan 59
(Matt Sheppard) *chsd ldrs: rdn after 10th: outpcd next* **7/1**[3]

P1P0 9 1½ **Taroum (IRE)**[30] 4855 9-11-8 **96** (bt) RobertDunne 77
(John Flint) *hld up: hdwy fr 9th: rdn in 3rd 4 out: wknd after 2 out* **28/1**

P255 10 3½ **Ballyegan (IRE)**[38] 4686 11-11-3 **91** LiamHeard 68
(Bob Buckler) *pressed ldr tl 8th: rdn after next: wknd bef 4 out* **14/1**

55U3 P **Ma'ire Rua (IRE)**[25] 4932 9-11-7 **95** NickScholfield
(Alan Jones) *a bhd: t.o whn v slow 7th: p.u 9th* **20/1**

P3PP P **Pursuitofhappiness (IRE)**[47] 4491 8-10-9 **83** (bt[1]) AndrewThornton
(Neil Mulholland) *chsd ldrs: rdn after 8th: sn in rr: t.o whn p.u bef 4 out* **7/1**[3]

4m 39.8s (-17.50) **Going Correction** -0.875s/f (Firm) 12 Ran SP% **116.5**
Speed ratings: **101,98,94,93,90 88,87,87,86,84 ,**
CSF £24.88 CT £167.28 TOTE £7.40: £2.90, £2.70, £2.20; EX 37.20 Trifecta £99.50.
Owner Slabs And Lucan **Bred** K Bishop **Trained** Spaxton, Somerset
■ Stewards' Enquiry : Robert Dunne one-day ban: disobeyed starter (May 5)
Liam Heard one-day ban: disobeyed starter (May 5), matter referred 4th offince in 12 mths
Daryl Jacob two-day ban: disobeyed starter (May 5-6) 2nd offence in 12 mths
James Best one-day ban: disobeyed starter (May 5)
Conor Shoemark one-day ban: disobeyed starter (May 5)
Nick Scholfield two-day ban: disobeyed starter (May 14-15) 2nd offence in 12 mths
Trevor Whelan two-day ban: disobeyed starter (May 5-6) 2nd offence in 12 mths
Mr Joshua Newman one-day ban: disobeyed starter (May 5)
Andrew Thornton one-day ban: disobeyed starter (May 5)

FOCUS
Due to rail movement the actual race distance was 2m2f188yds. The gallop was solid for this modest handicap. The form could be rated a few pounds higher through the second and third.

5436 GOFFS SPRING SALES P2P BUMPER (A MAIDEN NATIONAL HUNT FLAT RACE FOR AMATEUR RIDERS) 2m 175y
8:00 (8:00) (Class 4) 4-6-Y-0 **£3,165** (£935; £467; £234; £117)

Form RPR

1 **Fearless Fantasy (IRE)**[26] 5-11-5 0 MrBGibbs 95
(C Price) *trckd ldrs: led 6f out: rdn over 2f out: kpt on strly fnl f* **16/1**

2 1 **Boygojumping**[18] 4-11-0 0 MrGHiscock(7) 96
(Martin Peaty) *travelled wl in mid-div: hdwy over 3f out: rdn to press wnr over 2f out: kpt on tl no ex fnl f* **50/1**

3 2 **On Account (IRE)**[39] 4-11-0 0 MrLeoMahon(7) 94+
(Francesca Nimmo) *hld up: rdn and gd hdwy over 2f out: wnt 3rd jst over 1f out: styd on but nt pce to rch ldng pair* **17/2**[3]

4 4½ **Emperor Renard (IRE)**[46] 5-11-5 0 MrSeanHoulihan(7) 95
(Mrs Marie McGuinness) *mid-div: outpcd 3f out: hdwy over 1f out: styd on fnl f* **12/1**

5 shd **Irish Legionnaire (IRE)**[11] 5-11-7 0 MrMartinMcIntyre(5) 94
(Richard J Bandey) *hld up: rdn over 2f out: hdwy over 1f out: styd on fnl f* **20/1**

6 ½ **Bill And Barn (IRE)**[46] 5-11-12 0 MrWBiddick 94
(Paul Nicholls) *hld up bhd: trying to make hdwy whn nt clr run fnl bnd: rdn over 2f out: nvr gng pce to get on terms* **10/11**[1]

7 5 **Pyleigh Brae**[32] 5-10-12 0 (t) MrCBarber(7) 82
(P M Bryant) *racd keenly: trckd ldrs: rdn over 2f out: wknd over 1f out* **50/1**

8 1¾ **Thinking Out Loud (IRE)**[24] 5-11-9 0 MrTommieMO'Brien(3) 87
(Mrs Z Hammond) *in tch: rdn wl over 2f out: wknd over 1f out* **18/1**

9 3¼ **Arcs Abound**[18] 6-11-7 0 MrMatthewHampton(5) 84
(Miss L Gardner) *prom: rdn wl over 2f out: sn wknd* **33/1**

10 nk **Live For Today (IRE)**[26] 5-11-5 0 MrEDavid(7) 84
(N Williams) *mid-div tl wknd over 1f out* **16/1**

11 ½ **Super Charge**[19] 4-11-4 0 MrEGlassonbury(3) 78
(Edward Glassonbury) *mid-div: rdn over 2f out: wknd over 1f out* **25/1**

12 10 **It Just Aint Right**[18] 5-10-12 0 MrHFNugent(7) 66
(Mrs L Redman) *trckd ldrs: struggling 6f out: lost pl 4f out: wknd over 2f out* **33/1**

13 42 **Robin Longstride**[39] 6-11-9 0 MissBFrost(3) 31
(Mrs N Frost) *led tl 6f out: wknd 4f out* **40/1**

U **Triopas (IRE)**[67] 4-11-4 0 MrZBaker(3)
(Tom Lacey) *hld up: stmbld and uns rdr on bnd over 3f out* **5/1**[2]

4m 5.5s (-3.30) **Going Correction** -0.65s/f (Firm)
WFA 4 from 5yo+ 5lb 14 Ran SP% **123.7**
Speed ratings: **81,80,79,77,77 77,74,74,72,72 72,67,47,**
CSF £667.07 TOTE £18.00: £3.90, £8.60, £2.60; EX 797.20 Trifecta £3203.40.

Owner M Engel & Lord Lipsey **Bred** Edmond Coleman **Trained** Hay-On-Wye, Powys
FOCUS
A steadily run bumper for horses that have been placed in a maiden point this season. It paid to race handy.
T/Plt: £24.30 to a £1 stake. Pool of £61395.85 - 1838.50 winning tickets. T/Qpdt: £8.40 to a £1 stake. Pool of £6829.15 - 601.25 winning tickets. **Tim Mitchell**

5242 MARKET RASEN (R-H)
Thursday, April 21

OFFICIAL GOING: Good to soft (good in places; chs 7.7, hdl 7.6)
Wind: moderate 1/2 behind Weather: fine

5437 RACING UK DAY PASS JUST £10 "NATIONAL HUNT" NOVICES' HURDLE (8 hdls) 2m 148y
4:45 (4:46) (Class 4) 4-Y-0+ £3,249 (£954; £477; £238)

Form RPR
22 1 **Querry Horse (FR)**[49] 4441 4-10-11 135 JackSherwood(5) 122+
(Oliver Sherwood) *best away: drvn appr 2 out: fnd ex last 150yds* 5/4[1]
105 2 2 3/4 **Closest Friend**[150] 2688 7-11-2 123 (t) BridgetAndrews(5) 124+
(Dan Skelton) *trckd ldng pair: handy 2nd 2 out: almost upsides last: styd on same pce last 150yds* 5/2[2]
32 3 8 **Eyes Of A Tiger (IRE)**[25] 4937 5-11-2 117 CraigGallagher(5) 118+
(Brian Ellison) *t.k.h: trckd wnr: drvn appr 2 out: nt fluent 2 out: one pce between last 2* 5/2[2]
4-1P 4 3 3/4 **Miami Present (IRE)**[18] 5124 6-11-7 115 DannyCook 112
(Harriet Bethell) *hld up towards rr: hdwy and modest 4th 5th: drvn bef 2 out: kpt on one pce* 12/1[3]
0-PP 5 21 **Bold Prince Rupert (IRE)**[69] 4108 6-10-7 0 ThomasDowson(7) 84
(Sara Ender) *mid-div: nt fluent 1st: outpcd 5th: bhd fr next* 200/1
5-PP 6 5 **Tropical Sunshine (IRE)**[50] 4430 8-10-9 0 NickSlatter(5) 79
(Pippa Bickerton) *chsd ldng trio: outpcd 5th: lost pl next: sn bhd* 200/1
0 7 7 **Fieldsofsilk (IRE)**[26] 4915 4-10-9 0 PeterCarberry 67
(Jennie Candlish) *in rr: drvn 5th: bhd fr next* 100/1
4m 1.7s (-5.00) **Going Correction** -0.125s/f (Good)
WFA 4 from 5yo+ 5lb 7 Ran SP% 111.3
Speed ratings (Par 105): **106,104,100,99,89 86,83**
CSF £4.60 TOTE £2.00: £1.10, £3.30; EX 4.30 Trifecta £5.30.
Owner Luksonwood Partnership **Bred** P Duvignaud **Trained** Upper Lambourn, Berks
FOCUS
Allowing for rail movements, race distance increased 27yds. A fair novice hurdle. They went a respectable gallop on drying ground officially described as good to soft, good in places. The form is rated around the balance of the first four.

5438 RACINGUK.COM MARES' H'CAP HURDLE (8 hdls) 2m 148y
5:20 (5:22) (Class 4) (0-120,120) 4-Y-0+ £3,898 (£1,144; £572; £286)

Form RPR
3164 1 **Grimley Girl**[28] 4890 10-10-10 104 DannyCook 110+
(Henry Oliver) *led: hit 3 out: hdd wl bef 2 out: rallied appr last: styd on to ld last 150yds* 9/2[2]
1442 2 3/4 **Mystic Sky**[33] 4777 5-11-2 115 (b) JackSherwood(5) 119
(Lucy Wadham) *trckd ldrs: 2nd 3 out: led wl bef next: sn 8 l clr: 5 l ahd last: hdd and no ex last 150yds* 9/2[2]
4131 3 16 **Midtech Valentine**[28] 4890 5-10-5 106 TobyWheeler(7) 98
(Ian Williams) *trckd ldrs: j.lft and hit 5th: drvn next: modest 3rd bef 2 out: one pce* 9/4[1]
5-P3 4 9 **Quiet Candid (IRE)**[161] 2455 7-11-11 119 JeremiahMcGrath 101
(Nicky Henderson) *hld up towards rr: effrt 3 out: outpcd bef next* 5/1[3]
U652 5 nk **Roja Dove (IRE)**[24] 4736 7-10-10 107 (b) AdamNicol(3) 89
(David Thompson) *trckd ldrs: drvn 3 out: sn btn* 12/1
5133 6 4 **Superfection (IRE)**[37] 4702 7-11-1 109 WillKennedy 87
(Donald McCain) *chsd ldrs: reminders 3 out: sn modest 3rd: lost pl appr next* 11/1
-P3P F **Faerie Reel (FR)**[26] 4909 6-11-5 120 (p) MikeyHamill(7) 106
(Kim Bailey) *chsd ldrs: drvn 5th: outpcd next: poor 4th whn fell last* 15/2
4m 1.9s (-4.80) **Going Correction** -0.125s/f (Good) 7 Ran SP% 111.6
Speed ratings (Par 105): **106,105,98,93,93 91,**
CSF £23.80 TOTE £5.60: £2.50, £2.80; EX 37.80 Trifecta £146.30.
Owner R M Phillips **Bred** R M And Mrs Phillips **Trained** Abberley, Worcs
FOCUS
Allowing for rail movements, race distance increased 27yds. A fair mares' handicap hurdle run at a decent gallop. The first two are rated to their best.

5439 RACING UK PROFITS RETURNED TO RACING H'CAP CHASE (14 fncs) 2m 3f 34y
5:50 (5:52) (Class 4) (0-115,115) 5-Y-0+ £4,288 (£1,259; £629; £314)

Form RPR
26-P 1 **Lemon's Gent**[78] 3931 9-11-0 103 (bt[1]) GavinSheehan 118+
(Paul Webber) *j. soundly: mde all: styd on wl to draw clr sn after last: eased in clsng stages* 9/1
1P12 2 6 **Chankillo**[6] 5310 7-10-8 104 (p) CharlieHammond(7) 112
(Sarah-Jayne Davies) *chsd ldrs 4th: drvn 10th: 2nd appr next: 2 l down last: kpt on same pce* 8/1
153 3 7 **Allow Dallow (IRE)**[31] 4841 9-11-12 115 (b[1]) JoshuaMoore 118
(Jonjo O'Neill) *chsd ldrs 4th: hit 8th: 3rd and drvn 3 out: one pce* 7/2[2]
6251 4 shd **Under The Phone (IRE)**[11] 5245 7-11-6 114 7ex (p) ChrisWard(5) 116
(Robin Dickin) *chsd wnr tl 4th 3 out: one pce* 3/1[1]
P302 5 18 **Money For Nothing**[23] 5016 7-10-11 100 (t) DannyCook 85
(Harriet Bethell) *hld up: hdwy and modest 4th 4 out: drvn bef next: sn wknd: hung bdly lft run-in* 6/1[3]
1222 6 20 **Brother Scott**[20] 5080 9-10-11 100 SeanQuinlan 67
(Sue Smith) *chsd ldrs: outpcd whn hit 10th: bhd bef 3 out: t.o* 13/2
2333 P **Frizzo (FR)**[48] 4456 9-10-13 112 (b) HarryTeal(10)
(Harry Whittington) *in rr whn mstke 2nd: sn drvn along and nt jump wl: bhd and reminders 4th: t.o 7th: p.u bef 3 out* 13/2
033P P **Volcanic Jack (IRE)**[23] 5015 8-9-8 90 ow1 GrahamCarson(7)
(Michael Chapman) *chsd ldrs: drvn 6th: lost pl after next: sn bhd: t.o 8th: p.u bef 10th* 25/1
4m 55.3s (-10.40) **Going Correction** -0.40s/f (Good) 8 Ran SP% 113.1
Speed ratings: **105,102,99,99,91 83,**
CSF £74.23 CT £299.99 TOTE £10.40: £2.20, £2.10, £1.60; EX 68.80 Trifecta £709.70.
Owner R V Shaw **Bred** G R Waters **Trained** Mollington, Oxon
FOCUS
Allowing for rail movements, race distance increased 72yds. The feature contest was an ordinary handicap chase. They went a decent gallop. A pb from the winner.

5440 RACING UK NOW IN HD! H'CAP HURDLE (12 hdls) 2m 7f 16y
6:20 (6:21) (Class 4) (0-115,115) 4-Y-0+ £3,898 (£1,144; £572; £286)

Form RPR
/P-1 1 **Call It On (IRE)**[159] 2496 10-11-4 110 (tp) AdamNicol(3) 115
(Philip Kirby) *led 1st: drvn 3 out: 6 l ahd last: jst lasted home* 12/1
3666 2 1 **Echo Springs**[83] 3837 6-11-5 108 (t) GavinSheehan 113
(Christopher Kellett) *in rr: nt fluent and outpcd 9th: styd on appr 2 out: 4th last: tk 2nd last 100yds: keeping on at fin* 7/2[3]
0-32 3 1/2 **Buckontupence (IRE)**[39] 4645 8-10-5 101 WilliamFeatherstone(7) 105
(James Evans) *t.k.h in rr: hdwy to trck ldrs 6th: 2nd and drvn 3 out: kpt on in clsng stages* 10/3[2]
5153 4 7 **Quinto**[26] 4906 6-11-11 114 DannyCook 111
(John Quinn) *chsd ldrs: 2nd 8th: 3rd 2 out: wknd last* 11/4[1]
P032 5 9 **Phare Isle (IRE)**[24] 4983 11-11-3 113 (tp) MrMJPKendrick(7) 104
(Ben Case) *chsd ldrs: blnd 4th: wknd between last 2* 10/1
4U62 6 6 **Mwaleshi**[11] 5246 11-11-5 115 TrevorRyan(7) 99
(Sue Smith) *led to 1st: t.k.h: trckd ldrs: lost pl bef 2 out* 15/2
2506 7 1 1/4 **Romulus Du Donjon (IRE)**[20] 5065 5-11-6 114 (p) JackSherwood(5) 97
(Oliver Sherwood) *chsd ldrs: drvn 8th: lost pl 3 out: bhd whn stmbld bnd bef next* 8/1
5m 50.2s (-0.30) **Going Correction** -0.125s/f (Good) 7 Ran SP% 111.6
Speed ratings (Par 105): **95,94,94,92,88 86,86**
CSF £51.57 CT £170.96 TOTE £6.30: £3.10, £2.20; EX 70.00 Trifecta £334.50.
Owner The Green Oaks Partnership **Bred** Martyn J McEnery **Trained** East Appleton, N Yorks
FOCUS
Allowing for rail movements, race distance increased 36yds. An ordinary handicap hurdle. They went an even gallop. The winner has the potential to rate higher on Flat form.

5441 HIGH DEFINITION RACING UK H'CAP HURDLE (10 hdls) 2m 4f 139y
6:50 (6:52) (Class 5) (0-100,96) 4-Y-0+ £2,599 (£763; £381; £190)

Form RPR
0-PP 1 **Pass On The Mantle**[114] 3334 8-10-9 79 MarkGrant 82
(Julian Smith) *reluctant to join others s: t.k.h in rr: hdwy to trck ldrs 5th: led appr 2 out: blnd 2 out: kpt on wl run-in* 16/1
1254 2 2 **Running Wolf (IRE)**[31] 4845 5-11-12 96 (t) KielanWoods 97
(Alex Hales) *hld up towards rr: hdwy to trck ldrs 5th: 2nd 2 out: upsides whn j.lft last: styd on same pce last 150yds* 8/1
P/51 3 2 1/4 **Lombardy Boy (IRE)**[24] 4975 11-11-1 92 MrShaneQuinlan(7) 90
(Michael Banks) *chsd ldrs: drvn 3 out: 3rd last: kpt on one pce* 9/1
RP25 4 nk **Cadgers Hole**[13] 5198 9-10-5 75 SeanQuinlan 73
(Lynn Siddall) *in rr: hdwy to chse ldrs 5th: outpcd 3 out: hdwy between last 2: styd on wl fnl 200yds: tk 4th nr fin* 14/1
264 5 1 **Diego Suarez (FR)**[13] 5203 6-10-12 89 (p) TrevorRyan(7) 87
(Chris Bealby) *in rr: drvn 3 out: styd on between last 2: hit last: kpt on wl to take 5th nr fin* 9/2[1]
4562 6 1/2 **Icanmotor**[189] 1933 9-10-10 80 (tp) BrendanPowell 76
(Claire Dyson) *trckd ldrs: 2nd 3 out: 4th last: wknd last 75yds* 9/1
560P 7 4 1/2 **Strictly The One (IRE)**[152] 2649 6-10-1 74 AdamNicol(3) 66
(Mike Sowersby) *in rr: hdwy 2 out: nvr a factor* 25/1
00P 8 nse **Perfect Timing (FR)**[142] 2841 6-10-13 83 MarkQuinlan 75
(Paul Webber) *in rr: hdwy 6th: chsng ldrs 3 out: wknd appr last* 20/1
P-05 9 4 1/2 **Flamingo Beat**[24] 4987 6-10-3 73 JackQuinlan 61
(Christine Dunnett) *in rr: hdwy 6th: chsng ldrs and drvn 3 out: wknd between last 2* 33/1
PP5 10 1 1/2 **Hillview Lad (IRE)**[30] 4863 8-11-8 95 MauriceLinehan(3) 83
(Nick Kent) *trckd ldrs: t.k.h: led 4th: hdd appr 2 out: wkng whn mstke last* 13/2[2]
PP36 11 3/4 **Vodka Island (IRE)**[33] 4804 7-10-9 86 WilliamFeatherstone(7) 72
(Tim Vaughan) *led to 4th: upsides 3 out: wkng whn hit last* 17/2
-5PP P **Tomsk (FR)**[117] 3219 6-10-10 80 GavinSheehan
(Tim Vaughan) *nt fluent: chsd ldrs: lost pl after 3 out: eased and t.o whn p.u bef next* 7/1[3]
660- F **Birthday Guest (GER)**[274] 4761 7-10-4 79 NathanMoscrop(5)
(Philip Kirby) *in rr-div whn fell 2nd* 14/1
2PP0 P **Duc De Seville (IRE)**[29] 4645 4-9-8 77 (b[1]) GrahamCarson(7)
(Michael Chapman) *w ldr: lost pl after 4th: sn bhd: t.o 6th: p.u after 3 out* 66/1
5m 10.4s (1.60) **Going Correction** -0.125s/f (Good)
WFA 4 from 5yo+ 6lb 14 Ran SP% 117.9
Speed ratings (Par 103): **91,90,89,89,88 88,86,86,85,84 84, , ,**
CSF £131.73 CT £1237.17 TOTE £14.90: £5.90, £2.80, £2.30; EX 259.70 Trifecta £1380.20.
Owner Grand Jury Partnership **Bred** Grand Jury Partnership **Trained** Tirley, Gloucs
FOCUS
Allowing for rail movements, race distance increased 36yds. A modest handicap hurdle rated around the first three. They went a decent gallop.

5442 RACING UK IN GLORIOUS HD H'CAP CHASE (8 fncs 9 omitted) 2m 7f 191y
7:20 (7:23) (Class 5) (0-100,90) 5-Y-0+ £3,249 (£954; £477; £238)

Form RPR
4-00 1 nk **Dr Beaujolais (IRE)**[25] 4938 10-11-9 90 HarryChalloner(3) 99+
(Richard Ford) *hld up in rr: hdwy to trck ldrs after 4th (normal 7th): chsd wnr omitted 3 out: led narrowly appr omitted last: carried lft fnl f: hdd and n.m.r clsng stages: fin 2nd: plcd 1st* 16/1
000P 2 **Inchcolm (IRE)**[56] 4329 6-10-13 77 DannyCook 87+
(Micky Hammond) *chsd ldrs: led bef omitted 3 out: hdd appr omitted last: edgd lft fnl f: led narrowly last 50yds: all out: fin first: disqualified and plcd 2nd* 2/1[1]
U1F0 3 9 **It's Oscar (IRE)**[31] 4846 9-11-2 80 (p) MarkQuinlan 80
(James Evans) *in rr: hit 7th: hdwy to chse ldrs bef omitted 3 out: one pce fr 2 out* 9/1
PPP 4 3/4 **Castley Lane**[69] 4110 10-10-9 78 (tp) NathanMoscrop(5) 77
(Sara Ender) *w ldrs: led 3 out (normal 12th): hit last (normal 4 out): hdd bef omitted 3 out: one pce fr omitted 2 out* 33/1
5322 5 32 **Petit Ecuyer (FR)**[11] 5236 10-10-0 71 (p) MissPFuller(7) 40
(Dai Williams) *w ldrs: reminders 2 out (normal 13th): wknd last (normal 4 out): sn bhd: t.o* 15/2
P12P 6 4 **Sgt Bull Berry**[13] 5203 9-10-12 81 JamieHamilton(5) 47
(Peter Maddison) *led to 3 out (normal 12th): hung lft and lost pl omitted 2 out* 5/1[2]
113P P **Xenophon**[70] 4062 8-11-6 89 (b) ThomasCheesman(5)
(Olly Williams) *chsd ldrs: lost pl w full circ to go: sn t.o: hit 2 out (normal 13th): t.o whn p.u after last (normal 4 out)* 10/1

43PP **P** **Combustible Kate (IRE)**[144] 2811 10-10-7 **74**......... MauriceLinehan(3)
(Nick Kent) *t.k.h: trckd ldrs: j.rt 2nd (normal 5th): drvn and lost pl w full circ to go: t.o whn p.u bef 3 out (normal 12th)* **17/2**

555P **P** **Silver Dragon**[25] 4942 8-11-3 **84**.......................... AdamNicol(3)
(Mike Sowersby) *nt j.w in last: bhd and reminders 7th: t.o whn p.u bef 4 out (normal 11th)* **6/1**[3]

6m 12.7s (-18.60) **Going Correction** -0.775s/f (Firm) **9** Ran SP% **114.5**
Speed ratings: **99,100,96,96,85 84, , ,**
CSF £50.09 CT £317.76 TOTE £14.60: £4.40, £2.20; EX 71.60 Trifecta £1121.90.
Owner Winks Racing **Bred** Lillian Mahon **Trained** Garstang, Lancs
■ Stewards' Enquiry : Danny Cook three-day ban: careless riding (May 5-7)

FOCUS
Allowing for rail movements, race distance increased 126yds. The three fences in the home straight were omitted due to a low sun. A moderate handicap chase run at a respectable gallop. The first two past the post can probably rate higher over fences.

5443 RACING UK DAY PASS JUST £10 MARES' MAIDEN OPEN NATIONAL HUNT FLAT RACE 2m 148y
7:50 (7:50) (Class 6) 4-6-Y-O £1,559 (£457; £228; £114)

Form RPR

1 **Naranja** 4-10-12 0.......................... BrendanPowell 92+
(Jamie Snowden) *chsd ldrs: outpcd over 4f out: hdwy: 4th and swtchd rt over 1f out: styd on wl to ld last 50yds* **25/1**

2 *3/4* **Seelateralligator (IRE)** 4-10-12 0.................... HarrySkelton 91
(Dan Skelton) *hld up in rr: hdwy over 3f out: led over 1f out: hdd and no ex last 50yds* **6/4**[1]

6 **3** *2 3/4* **Tinted Rose**[28] 4894 4-10-12 0..................... WillKennedy 88
(Charlie Longsdon) *led 1f: chsd ldr: drvn over 2f out: kpt on one pce over 1f out* **10/1**

4 *4* **Ms Arsenal** 4-10-5 0.............................. MrMJPKendrick(7) 85+
(Giles Bravery) *t.k.h: led after 1f: clr tl 7f out: hdd over 1f out: fdd* **16/1**

5 *1 3/4* **Polly's Pursuit (IRE)** 4-10-12 0..................... DavidBass 83+
(Nicky Henderson) *t.k.h in rr: pushed along over 5f out: modest 4th over 2f out: hung lft and fdd* **9/4**[2]

05 **6** *1 1/2* **Daytime Ahead (IRE)**[31] 4847 5-10-12 0............... JackSherwood(5) 86
(Oliver Sherwood) *prom early: lost pl and pushed along over 5f out: one pce fnl 3f* **14/1**

0 **7** *1 3/4* **Waterberry**[169] 2277 5-11-3 0.......................... JoshuaMoore 84
(Lucy Wadham) *in rr: drvn 7f out: hdwy over 3f out: one pce* **40/1**

223 **8** *1 3/4* **Passmore**[96] 3632 4-10-12 0............................ GavinSheehan 77
(Alan King) *mid-div: effrt over 3f out: one pce* **9/1**[3]

2 **9** *1/2* **Indulgence**[24] 4974 4-10-12 0........................ KielanWoods 77
(Pam Sly) *chsd ldrs 3rd over 5f out: wknd over 1f out* **25/1**

10 *10* **Another Nudge (IRE)** 4-10-12 0......................... JamesDavies 67
(David Dennis) *mid-div: in rr and drvn after 6f: bhd fnl 6f* **33/1**

4m 1.8s (0.70) **Going Correction** -0.125s/f (Good)
WFA 4 from 5yo 5lb **10** Ran SP% **115.5**
Speed ratings: **93,92,91,89,88 87,87,86,86,81**
CSF £60.85 TOTE £17.50: £6.70, £1.30, £3.10; EX 121.70 Trifecta £1927.60.
Owner White Diamond Racing & Ms K J Austin **Bred** Bryan & Sandra Mayoh, Eskdale Stud **Trained** Lambourn, Berks

FOCUS
Allowing for rail movements, race distance increased 27yds. An ordinary mares' bumper in terms of form but some promising newcomers on show. They went a respectable gallop.
T/Plt: £513.50 to £1 stake. Pool of £47152.01 - 67.02 winning tickets. T/Qpdt: £145.90 to a £1 stake. Pool of £6310.04 - 32.0 winning tickets. **Walter Glynn**

5408 PERTH (R-H)
Thursday, April 21

OFFICIAL GOING: Good (8.4)
Wind: Breezy, half against Weather: Cloudy, bright

5444 CRABBIE'S ALCOHOLIC GINGER BEER NOVICES' HURDLE (8 hdls) 2m 47y
2:00 (2:00) (Class 4) 4-Y-O+ £3,898 (£1,144; £572; £286)

Form RPR

0 **1** **Townshend (GER)**[33] 4786 5-11-5 135...................... PaulTownend 121+
(W P Mullins, Ire) *mde all: nt fluent 4 out: shkn up and qckn clr after 2 out: nt fluent last: readily* **1/2**[1]

60 **2** *9* **Outlaw Josey Wales (IRE)**[110] 3442 5-10-12 0.......... RichieMcLernon 100
(R Mike Smith) *t.k.h: chsd ldrs: effrt and pushed along bef 2 out: chsd (clr) wnr bef last: kpt on run-in: no imp* **14/1**

3 *2 3/4* **Buyer Beware (IRE)**[22] 5036 4-11-0 120.............. RichardJohnson 100
(Gordon Elliott, Ire) *t.k.h: trckd ldrs: hit 4th: effrt and disp 2nd pl bef 2 out: rdn and hung lft between last 2: sn outpcd* **15/8**[2]

0P **4** *8* **Green Zone (IRE)**[37] 4817 5-10-7 0..................... CallumBewley(5) 90
(Lisa Harrison) *hld up: pushed along and outpcd 3 out: rallied last: plugged on: nvr able to chal* **66/1**

44-0 **5** *nse* **Arantes**[173] 2189 5-10-7 103.................(p) StephenMulqueen(5) 92
(R Mike Smith) *chsd wnr: rdn whn j.lft 2 out: outpcd whn j.lft and hit last: sn btn* **10/1**[3]

PFP **6** *4 1/2* **Byronegetonefree**[10] 5256 5-10-5 0................... SamColtherd(7) 85
(Stuart Coltherd) *nt fluent in rr: shortlived effrt after 4 out: struggling fr next* **80/1**

0 **7** *20* **Brooke's Bounty**[11] 5242 6-10-12 0...................... HenryBrooke 65
(Hugh Burns) *hld up towards rr: struggling after 3 out: sn btn: t.o* **100/1**

0-0P **P** **Shotofwine**[114] 3334 7-10-12 0........................ BrianHarding 75
(Nicky Richards) *nt fluent: hld up: struggling after 3 out: btn next: t.o whn p.u and dismntd run-in* **10/1**[3]

3m 49.4s (229.40)
WFA 4 from 5yo+ 5lb **8** Ran SP% **130.0**
CSF £12.91 TOTE £1.60: £1.02, £4.10, £1.10; EX 18.70 Trifecta £47.20.
Owner Mrs S Ricci **Bred** H -H Rodenburg **Trained** Muine Beag, Co Carlow

FOCUS
Rails were at innermost position and distances were as advertised. Richard Johnson said of the going: "It's good ground, beautiful." Little depth to this novice hurdle and the favourite won as he pleased. It was steadily run.,

5445 MACKIES OF SCOTLAND H'CAP HURDLE (FOR THE MARK BLACK MEMORIAL TROPHY) (8 hdls) 2m 47y
2:30 (2:30) (Class 5) (0-100,98) 4-Y-O+ £3,249 (£954; £477; £238)

Form RPR

0355 **1** **Abyaat (IRE)**[50] 4440 5-11-5 98.................(tp) DavidPrichard(7) 106+
(Victor Dartnall) *hld up: pushed along and hdwy 3 out: led next: rdn out fr last* **9/2**[2]

0-42 **2** *2* **Bring Back Charlie**[28] 4885 6-10-6 83.................. JamieBargary(5) 89
(Nigel Twiston-Davies) *in tch: hit 3rd: chsd ldrs: effrt bef 2 out: chsd wnr bef last: kpt on run-in* **7/2**[1]

005P **3** *6* **Celestino (FR)**[23] 5010 5-11-2 88.................(t) LucyAlexander 89
(N W Alexander) *bhd: hit 3rd: outpcd next: rallied 2 out: kpt on fr last: nt rch first two* **20/1**

3U60 **4** *1 1/2* **Great Demeanor (USA)**[44] 2292 6-9-11 72 oh3...........(vt) JoeColliver(3) 71
(Dianne Sayer) *t.k.h: trckd ldrs: led bef 4th to 3 out: led briefly appr next: outpcd bef last* **40/1**

3326 **5** *1 1/2* **Urban Kode (IRE)**[18] 5122 8-11-3 96...............(v) MrWHRReed(7) 93
(Lucinda Russell) *w ldr to 2nd: chsd ldrs: effrt and rdn bef 2 out: kpt on same pce* **12/1**

3540 **6** *1* **Summer Storm**[20] 5081 6-11-6 95......................... TonyKelly(3) 91
(Rebecca Menzies) *prom: rdn along bef 2 out: outpcd between last 2* **9/1**[3]

6644 **7** *3/4* **Cadore (IRE)**[20] 5081 8-11-6 97...............(p) GrantCockburn(5) 93
(Lucy Normile) *bhd: pushed along after 3 out: styd on fr last: nvr able to chal* **9/1**[3]

003- **8** *9* **Hopefull**[412] 4597 6-10-10 87.............................. StevenFox(5) 74
(R Mike Smith) *hld up: pushed along 1/2-way: effrt on outside whn hit 2 out: no imp fr last* **66/1**

0624 **9** *3/4* **Rioja Day (IRE)**[19] 4585 6-10-13 85...................(b) HenryBrooke 72
(Jim Goldie) *in tch: rdn after 3 out: wknd bef next* **14/1**

0566 **10** *hd* **Jebulani**[149] 2706 6-10-5 77............................. BrianHarding 64
(Barry Murtagh) *midfield: drvn along 3 out: sn no imp: btn next* **20/1**

0054 **11** *2 1/4* **Miss Mackie (IRE)**[26] 4904 5-10-12 89............... StephenMulqueen(5) 74
(R Mike Smith) *in tch: lost pl after 3rd: rdn bef 3 out: nvr rchd ldrs* **18/1**

0440 **12** *1/2* **Red Story**[41] 4581 5-11-9 95............................. CraigNichol 79
(Alistair Whillans) *hld up: pushed along after 3 out: sn btn* **12/1**

0404 **13** *3/4* **Ping (IRE)**[18] 5124 5-11-2 93.............................. RyanDay(5) 77
(Nicky Richards) *hld up in midfield: lost pl 4th: n.d after* **20/1**

5/-5 **14** *1* **Anitopia**[41] 4585 11-10-11 90........................... FinianO'Toole(7) 73
(Linda Perratt) *hld up in midfield: struggling 3 out: btn whn hit next* **16/1**

0P60 **15** *hd* **Norfolk Sound**[26] 4904 5-9-11 76......................... SamColtherd(7) 58
(Stuart Coltherd) *led to 2nd: cl up: led 3 out to appr next: sn wknd* **20/1**

-0F0 **16** *1/2* **Why But Why (USA)**[65] 4166 8-11-6 95............(b) GrahamWatters(3) 77
(Ian Duncan) *hld up: hdwy bef 3 out: rdn and wknd bef next* **28/1**

46P0 **17** *9* **Endeavor**[56] 4326 11-11-9 98...........................(p) EmmaSayer(3) 72
(Dianne Sayer) *t.k.h: cl up: led 2nd to bef 4th: cl up tl wknd appr 2 out* **20/1**

2PP- **18** *1 1/4* **Murtys Delight (IRE)**[365] 5463 9-11-6 97................ CallumBewley(5) 70
(Lisa Harrison) *hld up: stdy hdwy 3 out: rdn and wknd bef next* **40/1**

3m 49.4s (229.40) **18** Ran SP% **127.2**
CSF £18.48 CT £303.63 TOTE £5.30: £1.90, £1.60, £4.60, £13.30; EX 30.60 Trifecta £787.00.
Owner Mrs C Carter & V Dartnall **Bred** Malih Al Basti **Trained** Brayford, Devon

FOCUS
Race distance as advertised. The two at the head of the market dominated this moderate handicap. The winner is rated back to his best.

5446 LONMAR GLOBAL RISKS H'CAP HURDLE (10 hdls) 2m 4f 35y
3:00 (3:00) (Class 3) (0-140,140) 4-Y-O+ £7,797 (£2,289; £1,144; £572)

Form RPR

3216 **1** **Braavos**[33] 4801 5-10-5 119.............................. RichardJohnson 129+
(Philip Hobbs) *prom: hdwy to chse ldr 5th: led and hit 3 out: rdn next: clr whn rdr dropped whip run-in: styd on wl* **7/2**[3]

4311 **2** *8* **Florrie Boy (IRE)**[20] 5076 5-10-2 121.................. JamieBargary(5) 123
(Nigel Twiston-Davies) *hld up in tch: hdwy to chse wnr appr 2 out: kpt on same pce bef last* **11/4**[2]

1112 **3** *5* **Shear Rock (IRE)**[182] 2027 6-10-11 128............... GrahamWatters(3) 126
(Charlie Longsdon) *nt fluent on occasions: led: clr 2nd to 5th: hdd 3 out: rallied: rdn and outpcd fr next* **12/1**

121 **4** *16* **Sharpasaknife (IRE)**[29] 4873 6-11-3 131.................. PaddyBrennan 119
(Malcolm Jefferson) *nt fluent: hld up in tch: stdy hdwy 4 out: rdn and wknd bef 2 out* **7/4**[1]

6050 **5** *5* **Tap Night (USA)**[26] 4911 9-10-11 125................(p) RichieMcLernon 103
(Lucinda Russell) *chsd ldr to 5th: drvn and lost pl after 4 out: struggling fr next* **25/1**

P12P **6** *47* **One For Harry (IRE)**[36] 4717 8-11-12 140.................. BrianHarding 75
(Nicky Richards) *chsd ldrs: lost pl whn nt fluent 3rd: outpcd 1/2-way: lost tch fr 3 out: eased whn no ch* **12/1**

4533 **P** **Landecker (IRE)**[10] 5260 8-10-4 118...............(p) LucyAlexander
(N W Alexander) *w.r.s: t.o whn consented to jump off: p.u after 1st* **14/1**

4m 44.2s (-17.80) **Going Correction** -0.675s/f (Firm) **7** Ran SP% **110.1**
Speed ratings (Par 107): **108,104,102,96,94 75,**
CSF £12.83 TOTE £4.10: £1.60, £1.60; EX 17.10 Trifecta £133.10.
Owner Mrs Diana L Whateley **Bred** C R Mason **Trained** Withycombe, Somerset

FOCUS
Race distance as advertised. No hanging around here and the race produced a clear-cut winner. Sound form, despite the disappointing run of the favourite. The second is probably the best guide.

5447 PITCHCARE AND WATT FENCES GROUNDSTAFF MERIT AWARD CHASE (A NOVICES' LIMITED H'CAP) (12 fncs) 2m
3:30 (3:30) (Class 4) (0-120,120) 5-Y-O+ £7,147 (£2,098; £1,049; £524)

Form RPR

0653 **1** **Ink Master (IRE)**[33] 4785 6-11-3 115.................. RichardJohnson 128+
(Philip Hobbs) *t.k.h: led and mstke 1st: mde rest: hit 2 out: rdn and edgd rt run-in: drvn out* **13/8**[1]

2261 **2** *1* **Tomorrow's Legend**[32] 4816 6-11-0 115................. JohnKington(3) 122
(Patrick Holmes) *in tch: rdn along and outpcd after 3 out: rallied bef last: kpt on to take 2nd nr fin: nt rch wnr* **7/1**[3]

PPU3 **3** *1 1/4* **Bobble Boru (IRE)**[17] 5142 8-10-0 101 oh4............. CallumWhillans(3) 108
(Venetia Williams) *t.k.h: led to 1st: pressed wnr: nt fluent next: rdn 3 out: swtchd rt bef last: kpt on run-in: no ex and lost 2nd nr fin* **33/1**

3504 **4** *1* **Seven Devils (IRE)**[18] 5125 6-10-3 101 oh4..........(t) DerekFox 106
(Lucinda Russell) *hld up: outpcd bef 4 out: rallied 2 out: hung rt run-in: kpt on: nvr able to chal* **10/1**

1332 **5** *20* **Rear Admiral (IRE)**[18] 5126 10-11-8 120..............(t) JakeGreenall 109
(Michael Easterby) *hld up: rdn and outpcd bef 4 out: btn next: hld whn pckd last* **8/1**

3244 **P** **Quick Decisson (IRE)**[41] 4583 8-10-9 112............... GrantCockburn(5)
(Stuart Coltherd) *hld up in tch: outpcd 1/2-way: wknd 5 out: p.u bef next* **16/1**

3533 **P** **Valseur Du Granval (FR)**[33] 4803 7-10-8 106.........(t) PaddyBrennan
(Tom George) *mstkes: chsd ldrs: drvn along and outpcd bef 3 out: wknd and p.u after next* **3/1**[2]

The Form Book Jumps 2015-16, Raceform Ltd, Newbury, RG14 5SJ

-640 **P** **Drumhart (IRE)**[32] 4830 7-10-12 **110**..........................(t) RichieMcLernon
(C A McBratney, Ire) *chsd ldrs: rdn along whn mstke 5 out: wknd and p.u bef next* **20/1**
3m 49.8s (229.80) **8** Ran SP% **109.4**
CSF £12.47 CT £232.81 TOTE £2.30: £1.10, £2.00, £6.00; EX 10.50 Trifecta £187.80.
Owner Alan Peterson **Bred** Michael G Daly **Trained** Withycombe, Somerset
FOCUS
Race distance as advertised. Not a particularly strong event and the favourite did enough. The second and third set the level.

5448 LINDSAYS H'CAP CHASE (FOR THE KILMANY CHALLENGE CUP) (14 fncs 1 omitted) 2m 4f 20y
4:00 (4:00) (Class 2) (0-150,150) 5-Y-0+
£15,640 (£4,620; £2,310; £1,155; £577; £290)

Form RPR
25UU **1** **Witness In Court (IRE)**[13] 5193 9-10-13 **137**..................... HenryBrooke 147
(Donald McCain) *trckd ldrs: lft 2nd 2nd: led appr 4 out: rdn and kpt on strly fr 2 out* **12/1**
-P42 **2** *2 ¼* **Tennis Cap (FR)**[38] 4690 9-11-7 **145**.............................. PaulTownend 153
(W P Mullins, Ire) *hld up: hdwy to chse wnr bef 2 out: kpt on fr last: nt pce to chal* **7/2[2]**
6263 **3** *3 ¼* **Just Cameron**[19] 5087 9-11-9 **150**..........................(t) JoeColliver(3) 155
(Micky Hammond) *trckd ldrs: wnt 2nd 4 out to bef 2 out: drvn and kpt on same pce fr last* **9/2[3]**
30-0 **4** *½* **Shadows Lengthen**[174] 2171 10-10-8 **132**.......................... JakeGreenall 138
(Michael Easterby) *prom: rdn and outpcd whn blnd 2 out: kpt on fr last: no imp* **16/1**
-P10 **5** *1 ¼* **Dare Me (IRE)**[35] 4733 12-11-7 **145**.................................. AlainCawley 150
(Venetia Williams) *hld up in tch: nt fluent 5 out: pushed along next: rallied bef 3 out: rdn and one pce fr next* **20/1**
-33U **6** *3* **Saints And Sinners (IRE)**[111] 3425 8-10-8 **132**.............(t) BrianHarding 136
(Michael Easterby) *hld up: rdn and outpcd bef 4 out: no imp fr next* **10/1**
6PF5 **7** *nk* **Alderbrook Lad (IRE)**[13] 5200 10-10-4 **135**.................. FinianO'Toole(7) 136
(Micky Hammond) *pressed ldr: lft in ld 2nd: hdd 4 out: rdn and wknd bef 2 out* **25/1**
5213 **8** *50* **Gleann Na Ndochais (IRE)**[166] 2341 10-10-0 **124** oh3....... CraigNichol 80
(Alistair Whillans) *bhd: outpcd 1/2-way: lost tch fr 4 out: t.o* **33/1**
3-0F **U** **Filbert (IRE)**[161] 2459 10-10-10 **134**..............................(p) RichardJohnson
(Philip Hobbs) *hld up: stmbld bdly and uns rdr jst after 8th* **14/1**
12F1 **U** **Sharp Rise (IRE)**[10] 5256 9-10-3 **130**.................................. TonyKelly(3)
(Pauline Robson) *led: blnd and uns rdr 2nd* **2/1[1]**
4m 52.8s (-12.20) **Going Correction** -0.325s/f (Good) **10** Ran SP% **114.6**
Speed ratings: **111,110,108,108,108 106,106,86, ,**
CSF £53.33 CT £221.65 TOTE £12.50: £3.20, £1.60, £1.60; EX 63.20 Trifecta £257.90.
Owner T G Leslie **Bred** Michael Ronayne **Trained** Cholmondeley, Cheshire
FOCUS
Race distance as advertised. A good-quality handicap chase that saw last year's winner account for the two classiest runners in the race. The race was made easier when the favourite \bSharp Rise\p unseated at the second. The form is solid with Witness In Court related to last year's winning mark.

5449 FONAB CASTLE SPA OPEN HUNTERS' CHASE (FOR THE PERTH HUNT BALNAKEILY CUP) (18 fncs) 2m 7f 180y
4:30 (4:30) (Class 5) 5-Y-0+ **£3,119** (£967; £483; £242)

Form RPR
035- **1** **Monsieur Jourdain (IRE)**[18] 10-11-9 110.................(p) MrWEasterby(3) 99
(Mrs Sarah Easterby) *mde all: jnd and rdn 2 out: kpt on gamely fr last* **9/2[3]**
2314 **2** *2 ¼* **Nowurhurlin (IRE)**[18] 5121 9-12-1 120......................... MrNOrpwood(5) 106+
(Mrs S J Stilgoe) *trckd ldrs: n.m.r and lost pl bnd bef 3 out: rallied and chal 2 out to last: kpt on same pce run-in* **11/8[1]**
6P/0 **3** *1 ¾* **Molten Brown**[11] 11-11-9 83.................................(p) MissJWalton(3) 94
(Tony Hogarth) *prom: hdwy to chse wnr 4 out to appr 2 out: kpt on fr last* **25/1**
U162 **4** *shd* **Railway Dillon (IRE)**[20] 5082 11-12-1 111......................... MissETodd(5) 102
(Mrs C Drury) *in tch: effrt whn hit and outpcd 2 out: kpt on u.p fr last* **7/2[2]**
/P-1 **5** *42* **Probably George**[11] 9-11-9 88...................................... MissKBryson(5) 74
(Mrs K Lynn) *nt fluent in rr: outpcd bef 4 out: rallied on outside bef next: wknd bef 2 out* **12/1**
050- **F** **Rossini's Dancer**[18] 11-11-9 112.......................(p) MrKitAlexander(3)
(N W Alexander) *chsd wnr to 4 out: 2 l down and disputing 3rd pl whn fell heavily next* **13/2**
PP1/ **U** **Milans Well (IRE)**[11] 10-11-7 101... MrJDixon(5)
(William Young Jnr) *hld up: outpcd whn mstke 12th: rallied after 5 out: mstke and wknd next: no ch whn blnd and uns rdr last* **50/1**
6m 11.6s (7.60) **Going Correction** -0.325s/f (Good) **7** Ran SP% **109.3**
Speed ratings: **74,73,72,72,58**
CSF £10.67 TOTE £6.30: £3.20, £1.70; EX 13.40 Trifecta £136.20.
Owner Mrs Sarah Easterby **Bred** Jim McCormack **Trained** Malton, North Yorks
FOCUS
Race distance as advertised. Not a terribly strong hunter chase and little got into it. It's probably worth not taking the form too seriously.

5450 CRABBIE'S ALCOHOLIC GINGER BEER NOVICES' H'CAP HURDLE (10 hdls) 2m 4f 35y
5:05 (5:05) (Class 4) (0-120,120) 4-Y-0+ **£5,198** (£1,526; £763; £381)

Form RPR
2461 **1** **Impulsive American**[5] 5329 4-11-1 **120**...................(b) DavidNoonan(5) 121+
(David Pipe) *hld up in midfield: nt fluent 6th: smooth hdwy bef 2 out: led between last 2: sn pushed along and edgd rt: kpt on wl fr last* **15/8[1]**
5552 **2** *¾* **Stoneham**[10] 5262 5-10-8 **107**....................................... ShaneShortall(5) 113+
(Iain Jardine) *chsd ldrs: wnt 2nd 4 out: effrt and ev ch after 2 out: checked by loose horse appr last: kpt on run-in: hld nr fin* **18/1**
531 **3** *10* **Cactus Valley (IRE)**[4] 5345 7-10-12 **106**....................(t) JakeGreenall 102
(Michael Easterby) *t.k.h early: hld up: stdy hdwy 1/2-way: effrt and rdn bef 2 out: chsd clr ldng pair last: kpt on: no imp* **5/1[3]**
-603 **4** *hd* **Dimple (FR)**[132] 3022 5-11-5 **113**.. AlainCawley 111
(Pauline Robson) *hld up: nt fluent 6th: rdn and outpcd 3 out: rallied next: kpt on fr last: no imp* **18/1**
5256 **5** *1 ¼* **Ronaldinho (IRE)**[210] 1637 6-10-13 **110**.................(t) ColmMcCormack(3) 105
(Dianne Sayer) *chsd clr ldr to 4 out: cl up tl rdn and wknd bef 2 out* **66/1**
04 **6** *6* **Bright Prospect (IRE)**[111] 3424 7-11-5 **116**.......................... TonyKelly(3) 105
(Jackie Stephen) *in tch: drvn along after 3 out: wknd bef next* **14/1**
1502 **7** *nk* **Western Miller (IRE)**[26] 4922 5-11-11 **119**.................. RichardJohnson 108
(Charlie Longsdon) *hld up: rdn and outpcd 3 out: sn struggling: btn bef next* **3/1[2]**
4303 **8** *nk* **Jackofhearts**[166] 2338 8-10-6 **100**..................................... HenryBrooke 89
(Jean McGregor) *trckd ldrs: lost pl after 5th: struggling 4 out: n.d after* **33/1**
FFU1 **9** *½* **Benny's Secret (IRE)**[31] 4835 6-11-1 **109**...................... LucyAlexander 97
(N W Alexander) *nt fluent in rr: rdn along 3 out: nvr on terms* **10/1**
10 *nk* **Cuil Rogue (IRE)**[363] 5528 8-11-4 **112**............................... CraigNichol 102
(Nicky Richards) *t.k.h early: led and sn clr: rdn bef 2 out: hdd between last 2: sn wknd* **28/1**
6435 **U** **Solway Prince**[18] 5122 7-9-11 **96**..................................... CallumBewley(5)
(Lisa Harrison) *midfield on ins: blnd and uns rdr 1st* **14/1**
4m 51.5s (-10.50) **Going Correction** -0.675s/f (Firm)
WFA 4 from 5yo+ 6lb **11** Ran SP% **117.3**
Speed ratings (Par 105): **94,93,89,89,89 86,86,86,86,86**
CSF £34.77 CT £151.76 TOTE £2.80: £1.50, £3.90, £1.90; EX 37.80 Trifecta £228.30.
Owner Mrs Jo Tracey **Bred** D Brocklehurst **Trained** Nicholashayne, Devon
FOCUS
Race distance as advertised. The front pair came clear in what was a modest handicap. The winner was well in on his recent win and rated below that level here.
T/Jkpt: £41276.10. Pool of £87203.11 - 1.50 winning units. T/Plt: £15.90 to a £1 stake. Pool of £70106.24 - 3205.97 winning tickets. T/Qpdt: £9.40 to a £1 stake. Pool of £4922.43 - 386.55 winning tickets. **Richard Young**

5137 WARWICK (L-H)
Thursday, April 21

OFFICIAL GOING: Chase course: good (good to soft in places); hurdle course: good to soft (good in places) changing to good after race 1 (1.40)
Wind: Fresh against Weather: Fine

5451 CLOSE BROTHERS MAIDEN HURDLE (DIV I) (11 hdls) 2m 5f
1:40 (1:40) (Class 4) 4-Y-0+ **£3,249** (£954; £477; £238)

Form RPR
-2PP **1** **Holbrook Park**[63] 4198 6-11-0 0.................................... TrevorWhelan 114+
(Neil King) *chsd ldrs: lft 2nd 8th: led appr 2 out: clr last: easily* **13/2**
3 **2** *13* **Sporting Milan (IRE)**[148] 2715 5-11-0 0............................ GavinSheehan 100
(Harry Whittington) *prom: lost pl appr 5th: wnt handy again 7th: rdn appr 2 out: styd on same pce: wnt 2nd last* **6/1[3]**
4305 **3** *2* **Mr Banks (IRE)**[29] 4874 5-11-0 0..................................(p) CharliePoste 98
(Paul Webber) *hld up: hdwy after 5th: rdn bef 3 out: sn outpcd: styd on appr last* **22/1**
6 **4** *7* **A Bold Move (IRE)**[33] 4790 6-11-0 0................................. DenisO'Regan 94
(Paul Morgan) *hld up: nt fluent 5th: hdwy bef next: chsd ldr appr 7th: upsides whn lft in ld 8th: hdd bef 2 out: wknd last* **7/2[2]**
6000 **5** *15* **Good Man Hughie (IRE)**[29] 4875 7-10-7 0............(t) MissBHampson(7) 77
(Sally Randell) *prom: chsd ldr 3rd tl appr 7th: rdn and wknd after 3 out* **16/1**
0 **6** *20* **Sugar Loaf Sholto (IRE)**[9] 5263 5-11-0 0.............................. DavidBass 59
(Kim Bailey) *chsd ldr to 3rd: remained handy: rdn appr 7th: wknd next* **15/2**
2P42 **U** **Vaillant Creek (FR)**[49] 4442 7-11-0 115...........................(bt) KielanWoods
(Alex Hales) *led: nt fluent 5th: jnd whn blnd and uns rdr 8th* **9/4[1]**
4 **P** **Call Me Ben (IRE)**[17] 5144 6-11-0 0................................ LiamTreadwell
(James Evans) *nt fluent in rr: lost tch appr 6th: bhd whn p.u bef next* **9/1**
5m 6.4s (-14.60) **Going Correction** -0.625s/f (Firm) **8** Ran SP% **112.6**
Speed ratings (Par 105): **102,97,96,93,87 80, ,**
CSF £43.49 TOTE £8.40: £2.20, £1.70, £3.90; EX 41.20 Trifecta £944.60.
Owner Mrs C H N Chamberlain **Bred** G W Paul **Trained** Barbury Castle, Wiltshire
FOCUS
The hurdles and bumper were run on the inner track, and rail movements meant all races were run over further than advertised. The opener was run over 10 yards further than advertised. Drying ground, and the official description was changed to good all round after the opener. A weak maiden hurdle, especially once the favourite was out of the way. A big step up from the winner on his bumper form.

5452 CLOSE BROTHERS MAIDEN HURDLE (DIV II) (11 hdls) 2m 5f
2:10 (2:10) (Class 4) 4-Y-0+ **£3,249** (£954; £477; £238)

Form RPR
6-03 **1** **El Bandit (IRE)**[29] 4874 5-11-0 0.......................... SamTwiston-Davies 112+
(Paul Nicholls) *hld up: hdwy 8th: led 2 out: shkn up flat: styd on wl* **15/8[2]**
PPP **2** *4* **Thady Quil (IRE)**[168] 2299 6-11-0 0..........................(p) AndrewTinkler 106
(Martin Keighley) *led to 3rd: led again next: rdn and hdd 2 out: styd on same pce flat* **25/1**
5-55 **3** *4* **Ted's Lad**[31] 4843 6-10-11 0....................................(t) TomBellamy(3) 102
(Alan King) *hld up: hdwy 8th: rdn appr 2 out: no ex last* **11/1**
6 **4** *11* **What Kept You (IRE)**[44] 4552 4-10-8 0................................ NoelFehily 87
(David Dennis) *hld up: shkn up after 3 out: mstke next: nvr trbld ldrs* **25/1**
103/ **5** *½* **Il Presidente (GER)**[928] 1794 9-11-0 0............................ DenisO'Regan 93+
(Ian Williams) *hld up: hdwy 8th: ev ch after 3 out: wknd after next* **14/1**
4- **6** *6* **Peter Silver (FR)**[197] 5-11-0 135.. TomCannon 88
(Giles Smyly) *chsd ldrs: wnt 2nd bef 7th: ev ch 3 out: rdn and wknd bef next* **13/2[3]**
00 **7** *13* **Falcons Fall (IRE)**[33] 4805 5-11-0 0.................................... JamesDavies 75
(Tom Symonds) *hld up: rdn appr 7th: wknd next* **100/1**
3-36 **8** *43* **Robinsson (IRE)**[147] 2725 6-11-0 118.............................. LeightonAspell 36
(Oliver Sherwood) *prom: rdn appr 3 out: sn wknd* **6/4[1]**
040 **9** *9* **Magic Mustard (IRE)**[33] 4798 5-11-0 0.........................(p) KielanWoods 28
(Charlie Longsdon) *chsd ldr tl led 3rd: hdd next: remained in 2nd tl appr 7th: rdn and wknd after next* **40/1**
5m 6.1s (-14.90) **Going Correction** -0.625s/f (Firm)
WFA 4 from 5yo+ 6lb **9** Ran SP% **114.2**
Speed ratings (Par 105): **103,101,99,95,95 93,88,71,68**
CSF £46.33 TOTE £3.30: £1.10, £6.90, £2.60; EX 37.70 Trifecta £306.80.
Owner Colm Donlon, Barry Fulton & Richard Webb **Bred** Padhraic Doran **Trained** Ditcheat, Somerset

FOCUS
Race run over 10 yards further than advertised. The stronger division, and just the quicker. The third helps set the level.

5453 CLOSE BROTHERS H'CAP HURDLE (9 hdls) 2m 3f
2:40 (2:40) (Class 4) (0-120,118) 4-Y-0+ **£3,249** (£954; £477; £238)

Form | | | | RPR
1351 **1** **Zanstra (IRE)**[26] 4922 6-11-5 **116**.................. PaulO'Brien(5) 123
(Colin Tizzard) *chsd ldrs: rdn appr 2 out: led flat: styd on u.p* **6/1**[2]
2044 **2** 1 3/4 **Vivas (FR)**[90] 3724 5-11-4 **110**.................. SamTwiston-Davies 116
(Charlie Longsdon) *disp ld tl wnt on 5th: rdn appr last: hdd flat: no ex nr fin* **13/2**[3]
2400 **3** 2 **Benissimo (IRE)**[132] 3023 6-11-5 **111**.................. HarrySkelton 114
(Dan Skelton) *mid-div: hdwy after 4th: chsd ldr 6th: rdn appr last: no ex flat* **9/2**[1]
0413 **4** 1 **Tanit River (IRE)**[33] 4782 6-11-6 **117**.................. AlanJohns(5) 120
(Tim Vaughan) *chsd ldrs: rdn after 3 out: sn outpcd: styd on flat* **13/2**[3]
-104 **5** 10 **Dazinski**[48] 4466 10-11-10 **116**..................(t) JamesDavies 109
(Henry Oliver) *hld up: sme hdwy appr 3 out: n.d* **14/1**
13P **6** 3/4 **Que Sera (IRE)**[26] 4917 6-11-7 **118**..................(p) ThomasCheesman(5) 112
(Philip Hobbs) *mid-div: hdwy after 4th: rdn 3 out: wknd bef next* **20/1**
4560 **7** nk **Definite Future (IRE)**[150] 2694 7-10-13 **105**.................. JamieMoore 97
(Kerry Lee) *hld up: hdwy 6th: rdn and wknd after 3 out* **20/1**
124- **8** 5 **Paloma's Prince (IRE)**[520] 2566 7-10-12 **109**.................. DanielHiskett(5) 98
(Richard Phillips) *disp ld to 5th: chsd ldr tl rdn and wknd after 3 out* **40/1**
2056 **9** 3 1/4 **Give Him A Glance**[55] 4344 5-10-13 **105**.................. DenisO'Regan 90
(Alan King) *hld up: rdn 5th: sn wknd: bhd whn hung lft after 3 out* **16/1**
2122 **10** 8 **Join The Navy**[19] 5102 11-10-13 **108**.................. KieronEdgar(3) 86
(Kate Buckett) *hld up: pushed along 5th: a in rr* **12/1**
P000 **11** 19 **She's Late**[30] 4865 6-11-1 **107**..................(p) NoelFehily 68
(Jonjo O'Neill) *mid-div: pushed along 5th: wknd after next* **14/1**
5033 **12** 1 3/4 **Lord Golan**[30] 4865 8-11-4 **110**.................. AndrewTinkler 69
(Nick Kent) *prom: rdn appr 5th: wknd next* **20/1**
0016 **U** **Drumlee Lad (IRE)**[16] 5157 6-11-7 **113**.................. BrendanPowell
(Johnny Farrelly) *hld up: mstke and uns rdr 6th* **6/1**[2]

4m 31.2s (-14.80) **Going Correction** -0.625s/f (Firm) **13** Ran SP% **119.0**
Speed ratings (Par 105): **106,105,104,99 99,99,97,95,92 84,83,**
CSF £43.94 CT £194.94 TOTE £6.90: £2.50, £2.60, £2.80; EX 41.10 Trifecta £126.40.
Owner Moonrakers **Bred** Mrs Darina Kelly **Trained** Milborne Port, Dorset

FOCUS
Race run over 10 yards further than advertised. The principals were always prominent in this fair handicap hurdle and the form should work out.

5454 CLOSE BROTHERS FINANCE H'CAP HURDLE (12 hdls) 3m 1f
3:10 (3:11) (Class 3) (0-140,135) 4-Y-0+ **£7,147** (£2,098; £1,049; £524)

Form | | | | RPR
24P1 **1** **The Eaglehaslanded (IRE)**[7] 5284 6-11-9 **132** 7ex(bt)
SamTwiston-Davies 140+
(Paul Nicholls) *a.p: jnd ldr 3 out: led and nt fluent next: edgd rt flat: styd on wl* **1/1**[1]
5431 **2** 2 3/4 **City Supreme (IRE)**[20] 5072 6-9-11 **111**.................. HarryCobden(5) 113+
(Anthony Honeyball) *hld up in tch: outpcd after 3 out: rallied appr last: styd on* **5/1**[2]
1100 **3** 2 3/4 **For Good Measure (IRE)**[33] 4786 5-11-5 **128**.................. MichealNolan 128
(Philip Hobbs) *hld up: hdwy 3 out: styd on same pce last* **25/1**
02P0 **4** 4 **Easter Day (FR)**[18] 5120 8-11-10 **133**..................(b) ConorO'Farrell 129
(Paul Nicholls) *disp ld to 6th: remained handy: led 3 out: rdn and hdd next: wknd last* **14/1**
1PP5 **5** 1 1/4 **Grape Tree Flame**[68] 4125 8-11-8 **131**..................(p) SeanBowen 128
(Peter Bowen) *hld up: racd keenly: hdwy 5th: rdn appr 2 out: wkng whn hung lft flat* **28/1**
1441 **6** 4 1/2 **Mustmeetalady (IRE)**[17] 5141 6-11-9 **132**.................. NoelFehily 123
(Jonjo O'Neill) *hld up: racd keenly: pushed along appr 3 out: wknd bef next* **13/2**[3]
3025 **7** 7 **Rock On Rocky**[16] 5157 8-10-6 **122**..................(tp) MrStanSheppard(7) 108
(Matt Sheppard) *chsd ldrs tl led and j.lft 6th: mstke next: hdd 3 out: sn wknd* **12/1**
5PP3 **8** 13 **Return Spring (IRE)**[18] 5120 9-11-0 **123**..................(b) JamesBest 96
(Philip Hobbs) *disp ld to 6th: remained handy tl rdn appr 8th: wknd bef next* **14/1**
041P **P** **The Artful Cobbler**[70] 4066 5-10-11 **120**.................. AndrewTinkler
(Henry Daly) *hld up: pushed along 6th: mstke next: rdn and wknd after 3 out: bhd whn p.u bef next* **20/1**

6m 9.1s (369.10) **9** Ran SP% **113.1**
CSF £6.36 CT £71.43 TOTE £2.20: £1.40, £1.60, £3.10; EX 6.20 Trifecta £101.60.
Owner Mrs Angela Tincknell & W Tincknell **Bred** Grange Stud **Trained** Ditcheat, Somerset

FOCUS
Race run over 10 yards further than advertised. An ordinary race for the class, with a 1-2 for sons of Milan. Arguably another step up from thr winner.

5455 CLOSE BROTHERS NOVICES' LIMITED H'CAP CHASE (12 fncs) 2m
3:40 (3:40) (Class 2) 5-Y-0+ **£15,640** (£4,620; £2,310)

Form | | | | RPR
0124 **1** **Hollywoodien (FR)**[49] 4443 5-10-11 **131**.................. JamesDavies 141+
(Tom Symonds) *chsd ldr: mstke 2nd: wnt upsides 4th: led briefly next: led 6th to 8th: led again 9th: jnd after 3 out: sn rdn: nt fluent last: r.o u.p* **9/4**[2]
U220 **2** 3 1/2 **Jayo Time (IRE)**[37] 4701 7-10-10 **135**..................(p) CiaranGethings(5) 142
(Kerry Lee) *a.p: jnd wnr after 3 out: rdn and nt fluent next: styd on same pce last* **3/1**[3]
2F1F **3** 22 **Stilletto (IRE)**[35] 4733 7-11-8 **142**.................. SamTwiston-Davies 132
(Paul Nicholls) *led: hdd briefly 5th: lost the ld next: led again 8th to 9th: rdn and wknd after 3 out* **1/1**[1]

3m 52.6s (-17.40) **Going Correction** -0.80s/f (Firm) **3** Ran SP% **105.8**
Speed ratings: **111,109,98**
CSF £7.56 TOTE £3.10; EX 7.00 Trifecta £7.80.
Owner Sir Peter & Lady Gibbings **Bred** Mme Aliette Forien & Gilles Forien **Trained** Harewood End, H'fords

FOCUS
Race run over 60 yards further than advertised. A disappointing turnout considering the chunky prize on offer. The winner is probably still on the upgrade and should go on to rate higher.

5456 CLOSE BROTHERS H'CAP CHASE (22 fncs) 3m 5f
4:10 (4:10) (Class 3) (0-130,131) 5-Y-0+ **£6,498** (£1,908; £954; £477)

Form | | | | RPR
1112 **1** **Conas Taoi (IRE)**[8] 5274 7-10-13 **113**..................(p) DenisO'Regan 129+
(Paul Morgan) *hld up: hdwy 15th: chsd ldr bef next: led appr 3 out: sn pushed clr: comf* **15/8**[2]
/143 **2** 9 **Prideofthecastle (IRE)**[41] 4589 9-11-11 **125**.................. ConorO'Farrell 131
(David Pipe) *hld up: hdwy 16th: rdn after 3 out: sn outpcd: styd on to go 2nd last* **7/1**[3]
4133 **3** 8 **Arbeo (IRE)**[46] 4505 10-10-11 **111**.................. MarcGoldstein 110
(Diana Grissell) *chsd ldrs: wnt 2nd 15th tl rdn appr next: remained handy: drvn along 3 out: mstke and wknd last* **12/1**
5305 **4** 15 **Band Of Blood (IRE)**[12] 5217 8-11-12 **126**.........(bt) SamTwiston-Davies 113+
(Dr Richard Newland) *chsd ldr tl led 12th: hit 18th: hdd appr 3 out: rdn and wkng whn mstke next* **7/4**[1]
-23P **5** 13 **Orange Nassau (FR)**[132] 3024 10-11-5 **119**.................. AndrewTinkler 90
(Charlie Longsdon) *led to 12th: rdn and wknd 16th* **12/1**
23P6 **6** 50 **Amidon (FR)**[19] 5092 6-11-7 **121**..................(p) LeightonAspell 47
(Lucy Wadham) *hld up: pushed along 12th: mstke 14th: wknd after next* **17/2**

7m 30.9s (-25.10) **Going Correction** -0.80s/f (Firm) **6** Ran SP% **109.6**
Speed ratings: **102,99,97,93,89 75**
CSF £14.05 CT £108.54 TOTE £2.50: £1.70, £3.50; EX 11.10 Trifecta £48.80.
Owner All Stars Sports Racing **Bred** Martin McCaughey **Trained** Ystrad, Rhondda C Taff

FOCUS
Race run over 121 yards further than advertised. Not as competitive a staying chase as it might have been. Another pb from the winner.

5457 CLOSE BROTHERS STANDARD OPEN NATIONAL HUNT FLAT RACE 2m
4:40 (4:41) (Class 6) 4-6-Y-O **£1,624** (£477; £238; £119)

Form | | | | RPR
1 **Clondaw Cracker (IRE)**[151] 5-11-2 0.................. NoelFehily 110+
(Neil Mulholland) *led at stdy pce tl qcknd over 3f out: rdn over 1f out: jst hld on* **7/2**[3]
2 3/4 **Asum** 5-11-2 0.................. HarrySkelton 109+
(Dan Skelton) *hld up: hdwy and swtchd rt over 2f out: rdn over 1f out: r.o wl to go 2nd nr fin: too much to do* **5/2**[1]
3 hd **Brio Conti (FR)** 5-11-2 0.................. SamTwiston-Davies 109+
(Paul Nicholls) *hld up: hdwy 5f out: chsd wnr over 1f out: sn rdn: styd on* **5/1**
4 5 **Magic Bullet (IRE)** 5-11-2 0.................. NicodeBoinville 104
(Nicky Henderson) *trckd ldrs: racd keenly: rdn over 1f out: no ex ins fnl f* **10/3**[2]
5 3/4 **Yorgonnahearmeroar (IRE)** 5-11-2 0.................. JamesDavies 103
(Henry Oliver) *hld up: hdwy 7f out: rdn over 2f out: no ex fnl f* **33/1**
6 nk **Jaisalmer (IRE)** 4-10-11 0.................. SeanBowen 98
(Mark Bradstock) *chsd ldr: wnt upsides over 7f out: rdn over 2f out: lost 2nd over 1f out: no ex fnl f* **28/1**
4 **7** 3 3/4 **Yewlands (IRE)**[30] 4867 5-11-2 0.................. JamieMoore 99
(Jonjo O'Neill) *hld up: plld hrd: rdn over 4f out: nvr trbld ldrs* **14/1**
4 **8** hd **Molineaux (IRE)**[67] 4143 5-10-11 0.................. PaulO'Brien(5) 99
(Colin Tizzard) *trckd ldrs: racd keenly: rdn over 2f out: wknd over 1f out* **25/1**
9 1 1/2 **Game On (IRE)** 4-10-11 0.................. LeightonAspell 93
(Lucy Wadham) *hld up in tch: rdn over 3f out: wknd over 1f out* **22/1**
10 2 1/2 **Silent Encore (IRE)** 4-10-4 0.................. MrStanSheppard(7) 90
(Ben Case) *wnt rt s: hld up and a in rr* **66/1**
4 **11** 10 **Dreamingofrevelry**[277] 1057 5-10-9 0.................. MichealNolan 78
(David Dennis) *hld up: rdn over 4f out: sn wknd* **100/1**

3m 50.4s (5.00) **Going Correction** -0.625s/f (Firm)
WFA 4 from 5yo+ 5lb **11** Ran SP% **114.3**
Speed ratings: **62,61,61,59,58 58,56,56,55,54 49**
CSF £11.42 TOTE £4.70: £1.90, £1.20, £1.80; EX 17.70 Trifecta £66.50.
Owner R S Brookhouse **Bred** D Mitchell **Trained** Limpley Stoke, Wilts

FOCUS
Race run over 5 yards further than advertised. There were a number of absentees owing to the ground. It became rather a sprint from the home turn but the first three could all be decent and the race should produce winners.

5458 CLOSE BROTHERS CRUDWELL CUP HUNTERS' CHASE (FOR THE CRUDWELL CHALLENGE CUP) (20 fncs) 3m 1f 100y
5:15 (5:15) (Class 6) 5-Y-0+ **£1,434** (£445; £222; £111)

Form | | | | RPR
5301 **1** **On The Bridge (IRE)**[28] 4892 11-11-9 135..................(tp) MissVWade(7) 116+
(Jeremy Scott) *hld up: hdwy 7th: lost pl after 10th: hdwy appr 14th: led flat: shkn up and r.o wl* **10/11**[1]
0/1 **2** 3 3/4 **Mr Madeit (IRE)**[24] 4973 10-11-9 0.................. MrGGreenock(7) 110
(G T H Bailey) *chsd ldrs: nt fluent 13th: pushed along 16th: outpcd after 3 out: r.o to go 2nd post* **3/1**[2]
0-45 **3** nk **Shoreacres (IRE)**[28] 4892 13-11-9 110.................. MrJDrinkwater(7) 110
(Mrs Gillian Jones) *hld up: hdwy appr 14th: chsd wnr 3 out: ev ch last: no ex flat: rdr dropped hands and lost 2nd on post* **9/2**[3]
P/4- **4** 1 3/4 **Croan Rock (IRE)**[12] 11-11-9 93..................(t) MrAlexEdwards(3) 103
(R A Owen) *led to 6th: led again appr 9th: hdd 15th led again next: rdn bef last: hdd flat: wknd towards fin* **50/1**
00-0 **5** 16 **Our Mick**[24] 10-11-9 118..................(p) MrJJarrett(3) 89
(S Allwood) *chsd ldrs: lost pl 7th: hdwy after 10th: nt fluent next: lost pl appr 14th: sn bhd* **9/1**
P044 **6** 4 1/2 **Mr Moss (IRE)**[22] 5035 11-11-5 103.................. MrJNailor(7) 84
(S Rea) *chsd ldrs: led 6th tl appr 9th: led 15th to next: rdn and wknd bef 2 out* **20/1**

6m 41.2s (-17.80) **Going Correction** -0.80s/f (Firm) **6** Ran SP% **112.3**
Speed ratings: **96,94,94,94,89 87**
CSF £4.23 TOTE £1.90: £1.20, £1.90; EX 4.70 Trifecta £10.90.
Owner Kit James **Bred** J & D Melody **Trained** Brompton Regis, Somerset
■ Stewards' Enquiry : Mr J Drinkwater ten-day ban: failed to ride out for second (May 5,9-12,17,19,20,24,27)

FOCUS
Race run over 121 yards further than advertised. An ordinary hunter chase. There's a case for rating the race up to 8lb higher but the time was modest and the fourth was close enough.
T/Plt: £261.00 to a £1 stake. Pool of £58372.89 - 163.23 winning tickets. T/Qpdt: £19.30 to a £1 stake. Pool of £6381.15 - 244.05 winning tickets. **Colin Roberts**

5459 - 5461a (Foreign Racing) - See Raceform Interactive

[5220]CHEPSTOW (L-H)
Friday, April 22

OFFICIAL GOING: Good to firm (good in places) changing to good after race 1 (4.30)
Wind: breezy Weather: 10 degrees

5462 EVAN AND MEGAN BRACE MEMORIAL NOVICES' HURDLE (DIV I) (11 hdls) 2m 3f 100y
4:30 (4:30) (Class 4) 4-Y-O+ **£3,898** (£1,144; £572; £286)

Form RPR
3215 1 **Big Chief Benny (IRE)**[62] 4236 5-11-5 131 WayneHutchinson 126+
(Alan King) *cl up trcking ldrs: rdn 8th: outpcd briefly next: rallied and ev ch 2 out: cl 3rd at last: led u.p fnl 50yds: gamely* **11/10**[1]
1236 2 *hd* **Beallandendall (IRE)**[9] 5279 8-10-12 130 MrStanSheppard(7) 125
(Matt Sheppard) *t.k.h: led or disp ld tl led 8th: rdn 3 out: jnd by two rivals last: batteld on tl hdd 50yds out: jst hld* **7/2**[3]
4-31 3 *shd* **Rainy City (IRE)**[10] 5269 6-11-5 0 (t) SamTwiston-Davies 126+
(Paul Nicholls) *trckd ldng pair: rdn to chal 2 out: w ldr last: no ex fnl 50yds* **7/4**[2]
0606 4 30 **Denny Kerrell**[15] 5182 5-10-13 0 IanPopham 89
(Caroline Keevil) *nt fluent in rr: mstke 6th: t.o bef 2 out* **100/1**
P60 5 *shd* **Relkwood (IRE)**[10] 5268 6-10-13 0 (t) TomO'Brien 89
(Paul Morgan) *bhd: lost tch 8th: t.o bef 2 out: sddle slipped* **100/1**
0 6 2 **Kipuka**[27] 4916 4-10-0 0 (t) JamesBest 74
(Nigel Hawke) *racd keenly: led or w ldr tl rdn 3 out: wknd qckly: t.o* **66/1**

4m 47.1s (-14.70) **Going Correction** -1.00s/f (Hard)
WFA 4 from 5yo+ 5lb 6 Ran SP% 109.7
Speed ratings (Par 105): **90,89,89,77,77 76**
CSF £5.28 TOTE £1.80: £1.30, £2.80; EX 5.40 Trifecta £7.60.
Owner Oitavos Partnership **Bred** Brian And Mrs Bronagh Lawlor **Trained** Barbury Castle, Wilts

FOCUS
Following afternoon rain the going was changed to Good following this race. The rails on the bends were moved out, adding 31yds to the race distance. The first division of a decent novices' hurdle for the time of year, but weakened by withdrawals. The three market leaders came well clear in the straight and produced a tremendous close finish. The time was slow.

5463 EVAN AND MEGAN BRACE MEMORIAL NOVICES' HURDLE (DIV II) (11 hdls) 2m 3f 100y
5:00 (5:01) (Class 4) 4-Y-O+ **£3,898** (£1,144; £572; £286)

Form RPR
211F 1 **Curious Carlos**[14] 5189 7-11-11 129 [1] SeanBowen 129+
(Peter Bowen) *plld hrd: wnt cl up at 4th: tk 2nd between last two: nt yet asked for maximum effrt whn lft clr and hmpd last: in n.d after* **9/2**[3]
200 2 6 **Verygoodverygood (FR)**[10] 5269 5-10-13 0 (t) TomO'Brien 110
(Paul Morgan) *prom: 2nd and rdn 3 out: mstke 2 out: relegated 3rd between last two: lft wl hld 2nd at last* **100/1**
1103 3 15 **Ascotdeux Nellerie (FR)**[29] 4888 6-11-5 125 DavidBass 99
(Kim Bailey) *pressed ldrs: drvn 8th: wknd tamely next* **3/1**[2]
06 4 1 **Pray For A Rainbow**[3] 5393 5-10-8 0 ConorRing(5) 95
(Evan Williams) *mstkes but prom tl rdn and wknd and fluffed 3 out* **50/1**
105 5 38 **Fly Du Charmil (FR)**[21] 5070 5-10-10 0 HarryBannister(3) 54
(Warren Greatrex) *mstke 2nd: in rr and nt travelling after: lost tch bef 8th: t.o* **12/1**
5 6 *dist* **Bringewood Blue (IRE)**[20] 5098 9-10-6 0 PaulMoloney
(John Needham) *small: in last pair: mstke 7th: lost tch bef next: sn t.o: two hurdles bhd* **100/1**
3463 F **Simon Squirrel (IRE)**[9] 5279 6-11-5 134 (t) SamTwiston-Davies 123+
(Paul Nicholls) *led and j. boldly: rdn and 2 l ahd whn fell last: fatally injured* **5/6**[1]

4m 45.3s (-16.50) **Going Correction** -1.00s/f (Hard) 7 Ran SP% 109.4
Speed ratings (Par 105): **94,91,85,84,68** ,
CSF £183.04 TOTE £3.80: £1.80, £8.30; EX 126.30 Trifecta £207.00.
Owner Carl Pyne **Bred** Carl Pyne **Trained** Little Newcastle, Pembrokes

FOCUS
The rails on the bends were moved out adding 31yds to the race distance. The second leg of this novices' hurdle was run 1,8secs faster than the first division and produced drama at the last. There's a case for rating the form a lot higher through the faller and the third.

5464 SUN TRADE WINDOWS H'CAP HURDLE (8 hdls) 2m 11y
5:35 (5:35) (Class 4) (0-120,119) 4-Y-O+ **£3,898** (£1,144; £572; £286)

Form RPR
-022 1 **Vosne Romanee**[9] 5279 5-11-12 119 (tp) SamTwiston-Davies 127+
(Dr Richard Newland) *settled in midfield: smooth prog after 5th: wnt 2nd 2 out: led last: pushed out and styd on strly* **5/2**[1]
-051 2 1 1/4 **Wolftrap (IRE)**[17] 5163 7-10-5 98 LiamHeard 103
(Philip Hobbs) *hld up in rr tl prog gng wl after 5th: cl 3rd 2 out and 2nd at last: rdn and kpt on wl but wnr jst too str flat* **9/2**[2]
B050 3 1 1/2 **Midnight Shot**[34] 4782 6-11-9 116 AidanColeman 120
(Charlie Longsdon) *led tl 4th: rdn to ld again 3 out: drvn and racing awkwardly bef last where hdd: kpt on same pce flat* **5/1**[3]
4162 4 1/2 **Grams And Ounces**[10] 5266 9-11-0 114 MikeyHamill(7) 118
(Grace Harris) *trckd ldrs: mstke 5th: sn rdn: kpt on gamely fr 2 out but no imp after* **12/1**
4600 5 2 3/4 **Cry Fury**[13] 5223 8-10-0 93 JamesBest 94
(Sophie Leech) *hld up in last pair tl bef 5th: hdwy to chse ldrs between last two: sn rdn and no further imp but kpt gng steadily* **25/1**
6F36 6 10 **Kazlian (FR)**[18] 5146 8-11-10 117 (b[1]) BrendanPowell 109
(Johnny Farrelly) *pressed ldrs tl 5th: sn rdn and wknd* **11/2**
4130 7 6 **Fuse Wire**[29] 4882 9-9-7 93 oh2 MissJodieHughes(7) 79
(Dai Burchell) *planted in paddock: taken down early: hld up and bhd: n.d fr 5th* **16/1**
0450 8 2 1/2 **Mister Dick (FR)**[32] 4846 4-10-1 106 (bt[1]) PatrickCowley(7) 85
(Jonjo O'Neill) *midfield: btn after 5th* **20/1**
-5FF 9 3 1/4 **Kudu Country (IRE)**[58] 3107 10-11-3 115 (tp) ConorRing(5) 98
(Evan Williams) *cl 2nd tl led 4th: rdn next: hdd 3 out and dropped out rapidly* **16/1**
200 10 3/4 **Number One London (IRE)**[13] 5225 6-11-5 112 TomO'Brien 92
(Tim Vaughan) *midfield early: dropped to rr 4th: no ch fr next* **25/1**
464 11 57 **Kauto Riko (FR)**[84] 3835 5-10-10 103 JamesDavies 32
(Tom Gretton) *prom: rdn 4th: qckly dropped bk to last bef next: sn t.o* **12/1**

3m 52.1s (-18.50) **Going Correction** -1.00s/f (Hard)
WFA 4 from 5yo+ 5lb 11 Ran SP% 118.4
Speed ratings (Par 105): **106,105,104,104,103 98,95,93,92,91 63**
CSF £14.16 CT £51.31 TOTE £2.80: £1.20, £1.70, £1.50; EX 13.60 Trifecta £86.40.
Owner Foxtrot NH Racing Partnership VI **Bred** Mrs L M G Walsh **Trained** Claines, Worcs

FOCUS
The rails on the bends were moved out adding 31yds to the race distance. A modest handicap hurdle but victory for a well-in top weight.

5465 DUNRAVEN WINDOWS H'CAP CHASE (16 fncs) 2m 3f 98y
6:05 (6:07) (Class 3) (0-135,135) 5-Y-O+ **£7,797** (£2,289; £1,144; £572)

Form RPR
5-00 1 **Ruben Cotter (IRE)**[14] 5193 10-11-6 134 HarryCobden(5) 146+
(Paul Nicholls) *gng wl in 3rd or 4th tl led bef 3 out: 6 l clr and travelling strly last: easily* **7/2**[1]
0563 2 7 **Purple 'n Gold (IRE)**[19] 5118 7-11-2 130 (p) DavidNoonan(5) 133
(David Pipe) *hld up and bhd: stdy prog 11th: stl 6th 2 out: rdn and kpt on wl after: snatched 2nd but no match for wnr* **12/1**
2514 3 *nk* **No Likey (IRE)**[226] 1521 9-11-1 124 (tp) TomO'Brien 126
(Philip Hobbs) *midfield: effrt and cl up 11th: rdn to chse wnr bef 2 out: in vain pursuit tl wknd flat: jst lost 2nd* **16/1**
F6 4 7 **Cruchain (IRE)**[29] 4884 13-10-1 110 (p) RobertDunne 107
(Dai Burchell) *bhd: prog bef 12th: rdn in 3rd 2 out: kpt on gamely at one pce whn hld after* **33/1**
12P4 5 3 **Hepijeu (FR)**[17] 5156 5-10-13 125 (t) GrahamWatters(3) 120
(Charlie Longsdon) *t.k.h: prog bef 6th: chsd ldrs 12th: 4th and rdn and btn 2 out* **16/1**
P422 6 4 **Sun Wild Life (FR)**[17] 5162 6-10-10 119 (p) SeanBowen 109
(Robert Walford) *rn in snatches: lost pl bef 12th: styd on v strly after last: no ch w ldrs* **7/2**[1]
5-03 7 11 **Master Of The Game (IRE)**[297] 863 10-10-13 122 (t) NoelFehily 103
(David Dennis) *hld up and bhd: brief effrt wd bef 12th: nvr nr ldrs* **18/1**
4411 8 2 **Milgen Bay**[153] 2648 10-10-9 121 (p) ThomasGarner(3) 102
(Oliver Sherwood) *midfield: clsd qckly to 2nd at 10th: led 11th tl rdn and hdd bef 3 out: dropped out rapidly and heavily eased* **16/1**
3356 9 12 **Fair Dilemma (IRE)**[201] 1777 11-11-12 135 SamTwiston-Davies 102
(Chris Gordon) *prom tl 11th: dropped out rapidly: t.o* **20/1**
52FP 10 *shd* **Off The Ground (IRE)**[48] 4485 10-11-12 135 AidanColeman 103
(Charlie Longsdon) *led tl 2nd: pressed ldr tl 12th: dropped out rapidly: t.o* **10/1**
243- 11 8 **Trickaway (IRE)**[372] 5358 8-11-2 125 RichardJohnson 87
(Philip Hobbs) *plld hrd: led 2nd tl 11th: fdd rapidly bef next: eased and t.o* **11/2**[2]
2U1U 12 36 **Sandy Beach**[25] 4964 6-11-4 127 BrendanPowell 54
(Colin Tizzard) *in rr and rdn and nvr travelling: t.o 12th* **7/1**[3]
-P20 13 13 **Drumlang (IRE)**[156] 2577 10-11-0 123 LeeEdwards 39
(Kevin Frost) *chsd ldrs tl 1/2-way: t.o* **66/1**
3054 P **Lookslikerainted (IRE)**[31] 4855 9-10-9 118 (t) PaulMoloney
(Sophie Leech) *bhd: last whn mstke 6th: sn t.o: p.u 12th* **25/1**

4m 48.8s (-22.50) **Going Correction** -0.95s/f (Hard) 14 Ran SP% 125.1
Speed ratings: **109,106,105,102,101 100,95,94,89,89 86,70,65,**
CSF £45.32 CT £620.46 TOTE £4.40: £3.10, £3.50, £6.20; EX 58.50 Trifecta £864.90.
Owner C G Roach **Bred** Jerry Murphy **Trained** Ditcheat, Somerset

FOCUS
The rails on the bends were moved out adding 31yds to the race distance. The feature race and a competitive event on paper, but ultimately a decisive winner. He was well in on last year's Kempton win and is rated back to that sort of level.

5466 BRACEYS "THE FRIENDLY BUILDERS MERCHANT" H'CAP HURDLE (12 hdls) 2m 7f 131y
6:35 (6:37) (Class 4) (0-115,115) 4-Y-O+ **£3,898** (£1,144; £572; £286)

Form RPR
5045 1 **One Cool Scorpion (IRE)**[21] 5076 5-11-4 107 RichardJohnson 113+
(Philip Hobbs) *smooth prog 5th: 5th home turn: led bef 2 out: rdn 5 l clr last: kpt up to work whn in command flat* **6/1**[2]
4243 2 5 **Jully Les Buxy**[32] 4853 6-11-1 104 AidanColeman 106
(Robert Walford) *prom: rdn and lost pl after 8th: drvn and rallied 2 out: wnt 2nd after last but no ch w wnr* **7/1**[3]
F0F3 3 1 1/2 **Lord Ballim (FR)**[23] 5031 6-10-13 102 (t) JamesBest 103
(Nigel Hawke) *hld up in rr tl stdy prog bef 9th where mstke: rdn to chse wnr between last two: wl hld whn mstke last and lost 2nd: kpt on* **20/1**
30P3 4 *nk* **Tokyo Javilex (FR)**[15] 5183 9-10-13 109 (t) MrLDrowne(7) 109
(Nigel Hawke) *trckd ldrs: led after 8th: drvn and hdd bef 3 out: nt qckn fr next* **16/1**
42F4 5 *nk* **Dusk Till Dawn (IRE)**[23] 5034 7-10-7 101 (p) DavidNoonan(5) 100
(David Pipe) *2nd tl led 7th: rdn and hdd after next: continued to press ldrs: kpt on same pce fr between last two* **9/2**[1]
PPP4 6 8 **Handy Andy (IRE)**[21] 5065 10-11-5 113 (bt) PaulO'Brien(5) 106
(Colin Tizzard) *a abt same pl: rdn 9th: kpt on steadily at same pce fr 3 out* **6/1**[2]
00P3 7 9 **Rendl Beach (IRE)**[22] 5053 9-11-7 115 (tp) CiaranGethings(5) 99
(Robert Stephens) *trckd ldrs: wnt 4th home turn: led briefly 3 out: drvn and lost pl after next* **8/1**
P324 8 9 **Rainbow Haze**[22] 5051 10-10-7 103 MrTGreatrex(7) 79
(Phillip Dando) *mstke 4th: led tl 7th: sn rdn: wknd bef 9th* **8/1**
-00P 9 48 **Walk On Al (IRE)**[71] 4066 8-11-9 115 ThomasGarner(3) 47
(Sally Randell) *bhd: rdn 5th: t.o fr 9th* **33/1**
354/ 10 2 1/2 **Rocknrollrambo (IRE)**[1128] 4882 9-11-2 105 WillKennedy 35
(Ian Williams) *chsd ldrs tl 7th: t.o fr 9th* **7/1**[3]
13PP 11 14 **Billy Congo (IRE)**[10] 5267 9-11-3 113 (t) MrRobertHawker(7) 30
(Richard Hawker) *a in rr: t.o fr 9th* **33/1**
-544 P **Carn Rock**[30] 4877 8-11-0 103 PeterCarberry
(Michael Gates) *bhd: sme prog in 8th home turn: nvr rchd ldrs: p.u 3 out* **14/1**
5533 P **Appletree Lane**[27] 4904 6-10-10 99 JamesDavies
(Tom Gretton) *bhd early: midfield and drvn home turn: sn t.o: p.u 2 out* **20/1**

5m 55.7s (-6.50) **Going Correction** -0.375s/f (Good) 13 Ran SP% 121.9
Speed ratings (Par 105): **95,93,92,92,92 89,86,83,67,67 62, ,**
CSF £46.76 CT £799.06 TOTE £6.30: £2.30, £2.90, £6.50; EX 51.80 Trifecta £564.80 Part won..
Owner Louisville Syndicate II **Bred** F R Jarvey **Trained** Withycombe, Somerset

FOCUS
The rails on the bends were moved out adding 46yds to the race distance. A modest staying handicap hurdle but a decisive winner, who stepped up for the longer trip.

5467 DUNRAVEN BOWL NOVICES' HUNTERS' CHASE (FOR DUNRAVEN WINDOWS SOUTH AND WEST WALES P2P CHAMPIONSHIP) (18 fncs) 2m 7f 131y
7:05 (7:06) (Class 5) 5-Y-O+ **£3,119** (£967; £483; £242)

Form RPR

1 **My Coranna (IRE)**[12] 7-11-0 0 MrBGibbs(5) 105+
(D C Gibbs) *trckd ldrs in muddling r: led 14th: rdn 2 out: over 2 l clr last: styd on gamely and in command flat* **2/1**[1]

P5/2 **2** 3 **Repeat Business (IRE)**[12] 8-11-5 0 (p) MrRichardPatrick(7) 109+
(J W Tudor) *mstkes: lost several positions: blnd 4th: wnt 3rd at 14th: tk 2nd 3 out: rdn and mstke next: no imp after* **7/2**[2]

4- **3** 3 1/4 **Key People (IRE)**[12] 9-11-12 103 (p) MrWBiddick 104
(J Lean) *blnd 4th: led or prom at slow pce tl rdn 14th: chsd ldng pair vainly fr 3 out* **25/1**

4- **4** 2 1/2 **C Me In Oz (IRE)**[27] 9-11-5 0 MrJamesKing(7) 100
(S A Jones) *mstke 1st: cl up: 4th and rdn 3 out: kpt on same pce wout threatening fr next* **14/1**

5 1 **Captain Camelot (IRE)**[25] 7-11-12 0 (t) MrTomDavid 99
(Gareth Moore) *hld up in last pl: nt fluent 10th: effrt 14th: chsng ldrs 3 out: rdn and no imp after* **14/1**

6-50 **6** 8 **Withoutdefavourite (IRE)**[12] 8-11-9 102 MrJFMathias(3) 92
(Miss A Griffiths) *racd wd: pressed ldrs tl rdn 14th: btn 3 out* **6/1**[3]

7 1 **Bob The Butcher**[27] 7-11-12 0 MrBMoorcroft 90
(David Brace) *midfield: rdn and outpcd 14th: styng on after last* **16/1**

06P/ **8** 5 **Tiger Rag (FR)**[12] 8-11-5 0 MrEDavid(7) 87
(J W Tudor) *prom: 2nd and rdn 14th: sn lost pl* **25/1**

F **9** 3/4 **A Country Mile**[12] 8-11-7 0 MrMatthewBarber(5) 86
(Matthew Barber) *bhd: hit 7th: struggling 14th: mstke 2 out* **50/1**

UP0/ **10** 2 1/4 **Books Review**[40] 12-11-5 91 MrMarkRobinson(7) 82
(Paul Hamer) *led 8th tl after 13th: rdn and sn dropped out: lame* **8/1**

11 17 **Nicholasville (IRE)**[12] 7-11-5 0 (p) MrLWilliams(7) 65
(Mrs Lorna Williams) *t.k.h: midfield early: detached last after 13th: t.o* **50/1**

60/2 **12** 13 **Stony Road (IRE)**[22] 5054 9-11-5 0 (p) MrConorOrr(7) 52
(J W Tudor) *led briefly and hit 7th: rdn and dropped to rr and mstke 12th: t.o: b.b.v* **10/1**

6m 17.4s (-4.60) **Going Correction** -0.20s/f (Good) **12 Ran SP% 120.9**
Speed ratings: **99,98,96,96,95 93,92,91,90,90 84,80**
CSF £9.03 TOTE £2.60: £1.80, £1.90, £3.40; EX 13.30 Trifecta £67.00.
Owner Miss Claire Sherriff **Bred** Miss D And P Keating **Trained** Pontypridd, Rhondda C Taff

FOCUS
The rails on the bends were moved out adding 46yds to the race distance. Very few with experience over regulation fences in this novices' hunter chase. It's rated around the second and fourth.

5468 SUN TRADE WINDOWS H'CAP CHASE (22 fncs) 3m 2f 54y
7:35 (7:36) (Class 5) (0-100,100) 5-Y-O+ **£2,924** (£858; £429; £214)

Form RPR

50-4 **1** **Broome Lane**[18] 5138 7-10-5 79 [1] TomO'Brien 99+
(Tim Vaughan) *taken down early: j. boldly: cl up tl led after 11th: nvr less than 6 l clr and galloping strly fr 19th: unchal after* **10/1**

5UP3 **2** 9 **Trillerin Minella (IRE)**[4] 5377 8-11-8 96 KielanWoods 105
(Graeme McPherson) *led tl after 11th: 2nd or 3rd after: rdn and outpcd by him 19th: pckd sltly last but jst hung on to 2nd* **5/1**[2]

PPP/ **3** nse **Rockabilly (FR)**[425] 11-11-9 97 (t) PaulMoloney 108+
(Tom Weston) *bhd 3rd: mstke 8th and reminders: several positions: rdn and last of five gng clr 18th: contested 2nd fr 3 out: styd on wl flat but no match for wnr: nrly snatched 2nd* **25/1**

1U23 **4** 28 **Try It Sometime (IRE)**[12] 5240 8-10-7 88 (tp) MikeyHamill(7) 73
(Sheila Lewis) *prom: mstke 4th and reminders: 4th and drvn and reluctant whn mstke 18th: sn lost tch* **10/1**

5252 **5** 1 1/4 **Mist The Boat**[37] 4713 8-11-8 96 (v) JamesBest 81
(Tim Vaughan) *cl up: 4th whn blnd 13th: 3rd at 18th: rdn and dropped out tamely bef next* **11/1**

4421 **6** 4 1/2 **Mission Complete (IRE)**[30] 4879 10-11-1 99 (tp) JackSavage(10) 78
(Jonjo O'Neill) *hit 1st: bhd and nvr looked to be gng wl: hit 12th and struggling after: t.o* **3/1**[1]

221U **7** 1 1/2 **Magical Man**[12] 5240 9-11-4 92 (v) TrevorWhelan 68
(Debra Hamer) *midfield: 6th and drvn after 17th: struggling after: t.o* **8/1**

4305 **8** 9 **The Last Bridge**[30] 4879 9-11-0 88 (p) RichardJohnson 56
(Susan Johnson) *midfield: hit 11th and rdn: no ch after: t.o 19th* **6/1**[3]

63PP **9** 26 **Handsome Buddy (IRE)**[30] 4879 9-11-1 89 (b) SeanBowen 34
(Michael Gates) *bhd and gng in snatches: drvn 4th: t.o 17th* **11/1**

4PP3 **P** **Quilinton (FR)**[22] 5044 12-11-12 100 AidanColeman
(Johnny Farrelly) *midfield tl 1/2-way: steadily lost pl: t.o and p.u 18th* **8/1**

6m 55.3s (-6.70) **Going Correction** -0.20s/f (Good) **10 Ran SP% 116.9**
Speed ratings: **102,99,99,90,90 88,88,85,77,**
CSF £60.71 CT £1227.13 TOTE £10.70: £3.10, £2.50, £7.60; EX 85.30 Trifecta £830.00 Part won..
Owner Wayne Jones **Bred** R Johnson **Trained** Aberthin, Vale of Glamorgan

FOCUS
The rails on the bends were moved out adding 46yds to the race distance. A low-grade staying handicap chase and they finished strung out. Not an easy race to put a figure on.

5469 BRACEYS "THE FRIENDLY BUILDERS MERCHANT" "NATIONAL HUNT" MAIDEN HURDLE RACE (7 hdls 1 omitted) 2m 11y
8:05 (8:05) (Class 5) 4-Y-O+ **£2,599** (£763; £381; £190)

Form RPR

3P0 **1** **Celldomfed (IRE)**[70] 4097 6-11-0 0 NoelFehily 111+
(Jonjo O'Neill) *settled towards rr: stdy prog home turn: 3rd and chalng on bit whn lft clr last: stormed clr wout fuss* **7/1**

43 **2** 3 1/4 **Whispering Storm (GER)**[10] 5268 6-11-0 0 (t) SamTwiston-Davies 105
(Paul Nicholls) *a 2nd or 3rd: rdn and ev ch fr 2 out: w ldr whn blnd last: nt rcvr but wnr gng best anyway* **9/4**[1]

P-30 **3** 2 3/4 **Hannah Just Hannah**[20] 5094 7-10-7 113 (t) JamesBanks 97+
(Heather Main) *led tl bdly hmpd 4th and nrly put out of r: rallied in 3rd home turn: slt ld whn hit 3 out: rdn and hdd last: no ex but v plucky effrt* **13/2**[3]

/6-0 **4** 2 1/4 **Stafford Jo**[139] 2909 7-10-7 0 GrahamCarson(7) 98
(John O'Shea) *sn 2nd: lft in ld 4th: 6 l clr home turn: rdn and hdd 3 out: one pce fr next* **200/1**

34 **5** hd **Winning Ticket (IRE)**[17] 5161 5-11-0 0 (t) TomO'Brien 98
(Paul Morgan) *small: towards rr: effrt home turn: kpt on steadily wout threatening fr 3 out* **16/1**

51/4 **6** 2 3/4 **Act Four (IRE)**[13] 5220 8-10-7 0 MrStanSheppard(7) 96
(Matt Sheppard) *bdly hmpd 1st: chsd ldrs: rdn bef 3 out: no imp after* **16/1**

2160 **7** 1/2 **Tour De Ville (IRE)**[29] 4888 6-11-0 0 (t) ConorO'Farrell 95
(Seamus Durack) *last at 2nd: pushed along to pass btn horses fr 3 out: nvr threatened ldrs* **25/1**

-45 **8** 1/2 **Denboy (IRE)**[18] 5137 6-11-0 0 (t) BrendanPowell 94
(Jamie Snowden) *cl up tl rdn 3 out: btn next* **33/1**

05P0 **9** 5 **Bestwork (FR)**[13] 5220 5-10-11 0 GrahamWatters(3) 89
(Charlie Longsdon) *hmpd 1st: nvr bttr than midfield or dangerous* **100/1**

6- **10** 2 1/2 **Allelu Alleluia (GER)**[366] 5468 5-11-0 0 AidanColeman 89
(Jonjo O'Neill) *bhd: pushed along and wl btn bef 3 out* **40/1**

00 **11** 17 **Too Far Gone (IRE)**[34] 4790 5-11-0 0 WayneHutchinson 70
(Alan King) *chsd ldrs tl btn bef 3 out* **40/1**

4 **12** 1 1/4 **Drip Tray (IRE)**[61] 4266 6-11-0 0 (t) RobertDunne 68
(John Flint) *hmpd 1st: midfield: struggling 3 out* **100/1**

0000 **13** 2 1/4 **Badger Run (IRE)**[20] 5091 5-10-7 0 MrTGreatrex(7) 66
(Pat Murphy) *a bhd: t.o* **200/1**

2-33 **F** **Aston Cantlow**[20] 5098 8-11-0 120 (t) RichardJohnson 110+
(Philip Hobbs) *settled trcking ldrs: rdn and effrt in cl 4th whn fell 3 out* **11/4**[2]

03 **U** **Bigpipenotobacee (IRE)**[24] 5018 5-11-0 0 SeanBowen
(Tom George) *bdly hmpd and uns rdr 1st* **8/1**

-05U **U** **Sugar Mix**[32] 4843 5-11-0 0 (p) AndrewTinkler
(Martin Keighley) *j. violently lft and uns rdr 1st* **50/1**

4m 1.2s (-9.40) **Going Correction** -0.375s/f (Good) **16 Ran SP% 122.7**
Speed ratings (Par 103): **108,106,105,103,103 102,102,101,99,98 89,89,87, ,**
CSF £23.02 TOTE £7.90: £2.50, £1.70, £1.90; EX 24.40 Trifecta £138.80.
Owner Masterson Holdings Limited **Bred** William James **Trained** Cheltenham, Gloucs

FOCUS
The rails on the bends were moved out adding 31yds to the race distance. An ordinary maiden hurdle in which they finished in a heap behind the winner, who impressed.
T/Plt: £317.20 to a £1 stake. Pool: £61,673.86 - 141.9 winning units T/Qpdt: £18.40 to a £1 stake. Pool: £8,303.66 - 332.6 winning units **Iain Mackenzie**

5444 PERTH (R-H)
Friday, April 22

OFFICIAL GOING: Good (good to firm in places; 8.6)
Wind: Light, half against Weather: Overcast

5470 CRABBIE'S ALCOHOLIC GINGER BEER MARES' "NATIONAL HUNT" NOVICES' HURDLE (8 hdls) 2m 47y
2:00 (2:02) (Class 4) 4-Y-O+ **£3,798** (£1,122; £561; £280; £140)

Form RPR

3P21 **1** **Mardale (IRE)**[13] 5229 6-11-5 124 (t) RyanDay(5) 108
(Nicky Richards) *chsd ldr to bef 4th: cl up: rdn to ld bef last: kpt on wl run-in* **4/1**[3]

412P **2** nk **Myztique (IRE)**[26] 4954 6-11-4 0 (t) PaulTownend 102
(Gordon Elliott, Ire) *led: rdn along 2 out: hdd bef last: kpt on u.p towards fin* **11/8**[1]

064F **3** 1/2 **Sweet Holly**[45] 4548 5-10-7 103 GrantCockburn(5) 95
(Lucinda Russell) *hld up towards rr: stdy hdwy at 1/2-way: effrt and cl 4th 2 out: rdn and kpt on fr last* **22/1**

2-10 **4** 1 1/4 **Danielle's Journey**[36] 4734 6-10-11 124 (t) AdamShort(7) 100
(S R B Crawford, Ire) *prom: drvn along after 2 out: kpt on same pce run-in* **5/2**[2]

5066 **5** 8 **Cupid's Quest (IRE)**[44] 4559 4-10-0 0 (t[1]) JamesCorbett(7) 81
(Susan Corbett) *hld up: hdwy and in tch after 3 out: rdn and outpcd fr next* **200/1**

4F03 **6** 3 1/4 **Ethelwyn**[30] 4868 6-10-7 115 JamieHamilton(5) 89+
(Malcolm Jefferson) *prom: wnt 2nd bef 4th: effrt and cl 3rd whn stmbld and rdr lost iron briefly 2 out: sn outpcd: no imp whn stmbld after last* **11/2**

6-00 **7** 2 **Miss Blanche**[66] 4164 5-10-12 0 DerekFox 81
(Lucinda Russell) *hld up: rdn after 3 out: wknd fr next* **100/1**

535 **8** 57 **Supreme Gael**[27] 4908 5-10-7 0 ShaneShortall(5) 24
(Iain Jardine) *nt fluent on occasions: hld up: rdn after 4 out: lost tch bef 2 out: t.o* **66/1**

3m 56.7s (236.70)
WFA 4 from 5yo+ 5lb **8 Ran SP% 113.4**
CSF £10.13 TOTE £5.20: £1.30, £1.10, £4.00; EX 11.00 Trifecta £114.90.
Owner East To West Racing Club **Bred** Frank Motherway **Trained** Greystoke, Cumbria

FOCUS
Officially the ground was quicker than it had been on Thursday. After riding in the first Grant Cockburn said: "There's a bit of everything out there." This mares' event was steadily run and the first four finished in a heap. The third and fifth are probably the best guides. Actual race distance 2m 63yds.

5471 GLENEARN FLOORING H'CAP CHASE (12 fncs) 2m
2:30 (2:30) (Class 3) (0-140,135) 5-Y-O+ **£9,097** (£2,671; £1,335; £667)

Form RPR

5525 **1** **Owen Na View (IRE)**[20] 5096 8-10-7 116 (t) PaddyBrennan 127+
(Fergal O'Brien) *mde all: shkn up and qcknd clr after 3 out: drvn and kpt on wl fr last: eased towards fin* **5/2**[2]

2410 **2** 1 1/2 **Raven's Tower (USA)**[35] 4770 6-11-12 135 NicodeBoinville 141
(Ben Pauling) *t.k.h early: hld up: nt fluent 1st: hdwy on outside bef 2 out: lft 7 l 3rd last: rdn and chsd (clr) wnr run-in: kpt on: nt gng pce to chal* **11/4**[3]

P424 **3** 1 1/4 **Indian Voyage (IRE)**[20] 5087 8-11-5 133 (t) DaraghBourke(5) 138
(Maurice Barnes) *pressed wnr: rdn 3 out: kpt on same pce fr next: lost 2nd run-in* **7/1**

136B **4** 4 1/2 **Chestnut Ben (IRE)**[17] 5156 11-10-3 119 MrWinks(7) 123
(Peter Winks) *prom: nt fluent 7th: rdn and outpcd bef 2 out: lft disputing 3rd pl (7 l down) and hld whn hmpd last* **14/1**

1222 **F** **Monbeg River (IRE)**[7] 5298 7-11-4 127 HenryBrooke 134
(Martin Todhunter) *prom: rdn and outpcd after 3 out: rallied next: 6 l down and disputing 2nd pl whn fell last* **7/4**[1]

3m 56.2s (236.20) **5 Ran SP% 110.8**
CSF £9.97 TOTE £3.60: £1.50, £1.60; EX 10.30 Trifecta £46.30.
Owner The Yes No Wait Sorries **Bred** Brian Walsh **Trained** Naunton, Gloucs

The Form Book Jumps 2015-16, Raceform Ltd, Newbury, RG14 5SJ

FOCUS
Actual race distance 2m 7yds. Not the strongest race for the class. The idling winner was value for further.

5472 HEINEKEN PARTNERSHIP H'CAP HURDLE (10 hdls) 2m 4f 35y
3:05 (3:05) (Class 5) (0-100,100) 4-Y-0+ **£3,898** (£1,144; £572; £286)

Form RPR
5R04 1 **Gold Chain (IRE)**[2] 5409 6-11-0 **91**.........................(tp) HarryChalloner(3) 97
(Dianne Sayer) *hld up in midfield: effrt and rdn after 3 out: styd on wl to ld last 30yds: rdn out* **5/1**[3]
0053 2 1 ½ **Desert Island Dusk**[167] 2343 5-10-13 **92**.........................(t) DaraghBourke(5) 98
(Maurice Barnes) *hld up: hdwy to chse ldrs bef 3 out: stmbld on bnd bef next: chal fr 2 out: kpt on fr last: tk 2nd cl home* **16/1**
5630 3 shd **Bell Weir**[24] 5012 8-11-8 **99**.........................(t) EmmaSayer(3) 105
(Dianne Sayer) *prom: wnt 2nd 4 out: effrt and led 2 out: nt fluent last: kpt on: hdd last 30yds: hld and lost 2nd cl home* **10/1**
4466 4 4 **Dutch Canyon (IRE)**[20] 5089 6-10-13 **87**.........................(v) LucyAlexander 88
(N W Alexander) *prom: drvn and outpcd after 3 out: rallied bef last: kpt on: nt gng pce to chal* **10/1**
505 5 7 **Baysbrown (IRE)**[146] 2769 6-11-10 **98**......................... BrianHarding 93
(Nicky Richards) *midfield: effrt and rdn bef 2 out: outpcd between last 2* **7/2**[1]
6-55 6 ¾ **Degenerous (IRE)**[2] 5409 8-11-8 **96**......................... RichieMcLernon 92
(Sarah Dawson, Ire) *led: hit 5th: rdn and hdd whn blkd 2 out: wknd fr last* **16/1**
2FP3 7 hd **Naburn**[14] 5198 8-11-5 **98**......................... RyanDay(5) 92
(Andrew Wilson) *hld up: stdy hdwy 4 out: drvn along fr next: no imp fnl 2* **12/1**
1443 8 3 ¾ **Innis Shannon (IRE)**[24] 5012 6-11-7 **100**................. JonathonBewley(5) 95+
(George Bewley) *hld up on outside: blnd and rdr lost iron briefly 5th: nt fluent next: rdn after 3 out: outpcd fr next* **13/2**
4123 9 4 **Lord Landen (IRE)**[30] 4872 11-11-9 **97**.........................(t) PaddyBrennan 85
(Fergal O'Brien) *t.k.h: hld up: rdn along after 3 out: wknd bef next* **9/2**[2]
P6P0 10 2 ½ **Bolton Blue (IRE)**[19] 5122 7-10-0 **81**......................... ThomasDowson(7) 66
(Katie Scott) *hld up in midfield: drvn and outpcd 4 out: n.d after* **50/1**
0056 11 1 **Morning Time (IRE)**[42] 4585 10-10-7 **86**...............(tp) GrantCockburn(5) 70
(Lucinda Russell) *bhd: rdn along bef 3 out: nvr on terms* **25/1**
P4 12 7 **Hop 'n Pop (IRE)**[44] 4555 9-11-0 **88**......................... HenryBrooke 66
(Hugh Burns) *midfield: lost pl 6th: struggling fr next* **66/1**
P0PP 13 ½ **Jewellery (IRE)**[20] 5089 9-11-0 **91**.........................(t) JohnKington(3) 69
(Katie Scott) *cl up: wnt 2nd 6th to next: sn rdn and lost pl: btn bef 2 out* **50/1**
P31P 14 8 **Strobe**[228] 1492 12-10-4 **81**.........................(p) AdamNicol(3) 51
(Lucy Normile) *chsd ldr to 6th: drvn and wknd fr 3 out* **20/1**
4m 49.9s (-12.10) **Going Correction** -0.55s/f (Firm) 14 Ran SP% **122.1**
Speed ratings (Par 103): **102,101,101,99,96 96,96,95,93,92 92,89,89,85**
CSF £77.52 CT £787.03 TOTE £6.30: £2.30, £5.60, £3.30; EX 104.50 Trifecta £1291.90.
Owner Mrs Margaret Coppola **Bred** Sheikh Sultan Bin Khalifa Al Nahyan **Trained** Hackthorpe, Cumbria

FOCUS
Actual race distance 2m 4f 51yds. An ordinary but competitive handicap hurdle. The winner and third were very well in on the best of last season's form.

5473 MCCARTHY & STONE CHASE (A NOVICES' LIMITED H'CAP) (15 fncs) 2m 4f 20y
3:40 (3:40) (Class 3) (0-140,139) 5-Y-0+ **£9,097** (£2,671; £1,335; £667)

Form RPR
1 **Rolly Baby (FR)**[55] 4375 11-11-3 **134**......................... PaulTownend 146+
(W P Mullins, Ire) *trckd ldr: nt fluent 5 out: led gng wl after 3 out: drvn clr fr last* **2/1**[2]
452F 2 8 **Uhlan Bute (FR)**[27] 4910 8-10-4 **121**.........................(p) AlainCawley 127
(Venetia Williams) *led: rdn and hdd after 3 out: outpcd whn hung rt run-in* **5/1**
3414 3 23 **The Cobbler Swayne (IRE)**[27] 4910 7-10-5 **122**......... PeterBuchanan 111
(Lucinda Russell) *nt fluent on occasions: in tch: outpcd after 10th: rallied after 4 out: wknd bef 2 out* **15/8**[1]
2-11 4 21 **Pair Of Jacks (IRE)**[338] 395 8-11-8 **139**......................... PaddyBrennan 116
(Malcolm Jefferson) *mstkes: in tch: rdn bef 9th: rdn and outpcd bef 4 out: mstke and lost tch next* **10/3**[3]
4m 51.6s (-13.40) **Going Correction** -0.40s/f (Good) 4 Ran SP% **107.9**
Speed ratings: **110,106,97,89**
CSF £10.66 TOTE £2.50; EX 12.90 Trifecta £19.40.
Owner Teahon Consulting Limited **Bred** Bernard Guillossou **Trained** Muine Beag, Co Carlow

FOCUS
Actual race distance 2m 4f 27yds. The first two finished clear in this decent little novice handicap and the time was quick. A big step up from the unexposed winner.

5474 DEESIDE TIMBERFRAME HIGHLAND NATIONAL H'CAP CHASE (FOR JULIAN LLEWELYN PALMER MEMORIAL TROPHY) (23 fncs) 3m 6f 121y
4:15 (4:15) (Class 3) (0-125,125) 5-Y-0+ **£12,996** (£3,816; £1,908; £954)

Form RPR
-F31 1 **Double Whammy**[21] 5078 10-11-5 **123**.........................(b) ShaneShortall(5) 141+
(Iain Jardine) *hld up: nt fluent 15th and next: smooth hdwy bef 4 out: led gng wl 2 out: shkn up and qcknd clr run-in: readily* **9/2**[2]
3052 2 8 **Presented (IRE)**[2] 5411 9-10-12 **116**......................... CallumBewley(5) 122
(Lisa Harrison) *prom: hdwy 5 out: led 3 out to next: plugged on: no ch w ready wnr* **13/2**
2PP3 3 ¾ **Harry The Viking**[11] 5259 11-11-7 **125**.........................(p) StevenFox(5) 130
(Sandy Thomson) *prom: rdn and outpcd after 5 out: rallied bef 3 out: kpt on fr next: nt pce to chal* **17/2**
0432 4 5 **Mo Rouge (IRE)**[27] 4903 8-9-13 **101**.........................(p) TonyKelly(3) 106
(Jackie Stephen) *nt fluent early in rr: reminders after 9th: hdwy and in tch 16th: outpcd 18th: kpt on fr 2 out: no imp* **3/1**[1]
44P1 5 ½ **Bertie Milan (IRE)**[212] 1629 11-10-0 **99**.........................(p) LucyAlexander 99
(N W Alexander) *in tch: hdwy 3rd: chsd wnr 13th to 18th: rdn and outpcd fr 3 out* **10/1**
P0P1 6 nk **Itstimeforapint (IRE)**[36] 4740 8-10-12 **111**.........................(t) DerekFox 111
(Lucinda Russell) *in tch: rdn and outpcd after 4 out: n.d fr next* **8/1**
1055 7 ¾ **Settledoutofcourt (IRE)**[33] 4818 10-11-4 **117**......................... PeterBuchanan 117
(Lucinda Russell) *led to 7th: chsd ldr to 13th: wnt 2nd 18th to bef 4 out: outpcd 3 out: wknd and lost 3 pls last 50yds* **12/1**
PP40 8 14 **Winged Crusader (IRE)**[27] 4912 8-10-6 **110**............(v) JamieBargary(5) 101
(Nigel Twiston-Davies) *pressed ldr: led 7th: hit 4 out: hdd next: sn wknd* **11/2**[3]
P0P6 9 5 **William Money (IRE)**[27] 4914 9-10-13 **112**.........................(v[1]) HenryBrooke 99
(Chris Grant) *nt fluent in rr: outpcd fr 18th: btn bef 3 out* **14/1**
7m 49.2s (-0.80) **Going Correction** -0.40s/f (Good) 9 Ran SP% **117.0**
Speed ratings: **85,82,82,81,81 81,81,77,76**
CSF £34.48 CT £241.59 TOTE £4.50: £1.80, £2.80, £3.30; EX 37.80 Trifecta £284.60.
Owner Alex & Janet Card & Partner **Bred** R W Huggins **Trained** Carrutherstown, D'fries & G'way

FOCUS
Actual race distance 3m 6f 135yds. This marathon handicap looked competitive on paper but it didn't work out like that. Another big step forward from the easy winner.

5475 SALTIRE STABLES CONDITIONAL JOCKEYS' H'CAP HURDLE (FOR THE JAN WILSON MEMORIAL) (20 hdls) 3m 2f 127y
4:45 (4:45) (Class 3) (0-130,129) 4-Y-0+ **£6,498** (£1,908; £954; £477)

Form RPR
P5P4 1 **Iora Glas (IRE)**[24] 5011 7-10-0 **113**.........................(t) PhilipDonovan(10) 120+
(Fergal O'Brien) *trckd ldrs: wnt 2nd 4th: led 4 out: pushed clr fr 2 out* **5/1**[3]
533P 2 6 **Landecker (IRE)**[1] 5446 8-10-12 **118**.........................(p) StephenMulqueen(3) 119
(N W Alexander) *hld up in tch: hdwy to chse wnr 3 out: rdn next: kpt on same pce fnl last* **9/2**[2]
5110 3 8 **Maraweh (IRE)**[112] 3428 6-10-12 **118**.........................(p) DerekFox(3) 111
(Lucinda Russell) *led to 3rd: chsd ldrs: pushed along 4 out: effrt bef 2 out: sn no imp* **11/2**
1220 4 1 ¼ **Andhaar**[11] 5260 10-10-6 **109**......................... GrantCockburn 101
(N W Alexander) *hld up: pushed along after 3 out: no imp fr next* **18/1**
2340 5 5 **Seldom Inn**[34] 4794 8-11-6 **129**.........................(p) StevenFox(6) 118
(Sandy Thomson) *trckd ldrs: mstke 4 out: rdn and wknd fr 2 out* **3/1**[1]
3400 6 7 **Sybarite (FR)**[9] 5277 10-11-3 **123**.........................(p) JamieBargary(3) 104
(Nigel Twiston-Davies) *bhd: drvn along fr 6th: struggling bef 4 out: nvr on terms* **11/2**
33P- 7 7 **Blenheim Brook (IRE)**[401] 4848 11-9-9 **108**.........(t) AlexanderThorne(10) 84
(Lucinda Russell) *cl up: led 3rd: hdd 4 out: rdn and wknd bef 2 out* **25/1**
1350 8 6 **Johnny Go**[147] 2744 6-10-2 **108**......................... CallumBewley(3) 78
(Lisa Harrison) *nt fluent: hld up in tch: hit and struggling 4 out: wknd bef next* **9/2**[2]
6m 40.2s (-1.80) **Going Correction** -0.55s/f (Firm) 8 Ran SP% **117.9**
Speed ratings (Par 107): **80,78,75,75,74 71,69,68**
CSF £28.98 CT £129.69 TOTE £6.10: £1.70, £2.00, £1.50; EX 34.00 Trifecta £144.70.
Owner Imperial Racing Partnership **Bred** Mrs Mary Jane Roberts **Trained** Naunton, Gloucs

FOCUS
Actual race distance 3m 2f 189yds. Plenty of these arrived out of form and it was a steadily run race. A pb from the winner under a claimer.

5476 GS GROUP STANDARD OPEN NATIONAL HUNT FLAT RACE 2m 47y
5:15 (5:16) (Class 4) 4-6-Y-0 **£3,249** (£954; £477; £238)

Form RPR
1 **Tyrrell's Succes (FR)**[76] 5-11-0 0......................... PaulTownend 107
(C A McBratney, Ire) *mde all: rdn and edgd lft over 1f out: kpt on wl fnl f* **3/1**[2]
1 2 1 ¼ **Imperial Eloquence (IRE)**[24] 5014 4-10-13 0......... ConorShoemark(3) 107
(Fergal O'Brien) *prom: effrt and chsd wnr wl over 1f out: kpt on u.p ins fnl f* **2/1**[1]
3 ½ **Mr Monochrome** 5-10-9 0......................... JamieHamilton(5) 105
(Malcolm Jefferson) *trckd ldrs: effrt and wnt 2nd over 3f out to wl over 1f out: sn swtchd rt: kpt on ins fnl f* **2/1**[1]
3 4 ¾ **River Dun**[142] 2849 6-10-7 0......................... PeterBuchanan 97
(S R B Crawford, Ire) *prom: effrt and rdn over 2f out: kpt on same pce fnl f* **9/2**[3]
0 5 14 **Silver Trix (IRE)**[109] 3476 6-10-2 0.........................(t) JonathonBewley(5) 83
(George Bewley) *hld up: stdy hdwy over 5f out: rdn and outpcd over 2f out: sn btn* **20/1**
0 6 32 **Lucky Violet (IRE)**[24] 5014 4-9-9 0......................... LorcanMurtagh(7) 46
(Hugh Burns) *hld up: struggling over 3f out: sn wknd* **66/1**
3m 51.8s (231.80)
WFA 4 from 5yo+ 5lb 6 Ran SP% **116.1**
CSF £9.91 TOTE £4.40: £2.20, £2.10; EX 10.60 Trifecta £22.50.
Owner High Flying Hooves Syndicate **Bred** Damien Bellanger & Antoine Bellanger **Trained** Crossgar, Co. Down

FOCUS
Actual race distance 2m 63yds. Fair bumper form, the second and fourth helping with the level.
T/Plt: £436.40 to a £1 stake. Pool: £70,747.47 - 118.34 winning tickets T/Qpdt: £114.20 to a £1 stake. Pool: £5,967.46 - 38.65 winning tickets **Richard Young**

4930 PLUMPTON (L-H)
Friday, April 22

OFFICIAL GOING: Good (watered; chs: 7.8, hdl: 7.7)
Wind: light, half behind Weather: overcast

5477 CORAL.CO.UK MAIDEN HURDLE (9 hdls) 1m 7f 195y
4:50 (4:53) (Class 4) 4-Y-0+ **£3,249** (£954; £477; £238)

Form RPR
66 1 **Zante (FR)**[17] 5153 4-10-9 0......................... JoshuaMoore 98
(Gary Moore) *t.k.h: in tch in midfield: hdwy to chse ldrs and nt fluent 5th: ev ch 3 out: rdn to ld last: styd on wl: rdn out* **5/1**[3]
3-16 2 1 **Welluptoscratch (FR)**[139] 2910 5-11-0 0......................... TomCannon 102
(David Arbuthnot) *chsd ldrs: mstke 4th: rdn and effrt after 3 out: cl 4th last: kpt on u.p fnl 100yds: wnt 2nd cl home* **4/1**[2]
656 3 ½ **Lovely Bubbly**[29] 4888 5-10-9 ....(t) AlanJohns(5) 101
(Tim Vaughan) *hld up in tch towards rr: hdwy after 4th: chsd ldrs bef 3 out: rdn bef 2 out: cl 3rd last: chsd wnr flat: kpt on but lost 2nd cl home* **16/1**
240 4 ½ **Our Three Sons (IRE)**[17] 5153 5-11-0 0......................... MichealNolan 102
(Jamie Snowden) *chsd ldr 2nd: upsides and mstke 3 out: sn led and rdn bef next: hdd last: no ex and styd on same pce flat: lost 2 pls fnl 100yds* **14/1**
5 3 **Jamhoori**[21] 8-11-0 0......................... JamieMoore 100
(Jim Best) *hld up in tch in last trio: hdwy after 5th: chsd ldrs and rdn bef 2 out: no ex and styd on same pce between last 2* **5/1**[3]
5024 6 3 **Ourmanmassini (IRE)**[54] 4384 8-11-0 107.........................(t) GavinSheehan 98
(Suzy Smith) *led: blnd 3 out: sn hdd and lost pl u.p: plugged on same pce fr next: hdd 6th whn mstke last* **5/4**[1]
-P0P 7 17 **Velvet Edge**[29] 4893 7-10-5 0 ow3......................... JakeHodson(5) 76
(Anthony Day) *wl in tch in midfield: nt fluent 2nd: clsd and ev ch 3 out: rdn and lost pl bnd bef 2 out: wknd qckly between last 2* **200/1**

25/P **8** *23* **Sutton Sid**[26] 4934 6-10-7 **89**............(p) MissBHampson(7) 59
(Michelle Bryant) *a in rr: j.lft and bmpd rival 3rd: rdn and short-lived effrt after 6th: wknd wl bef 2 out: t.o* **80/1**

PP00 **9** *1 1/2* **Austin Friars**[20] 5091 4-10-9 0............ AndrewThornton 53
(Jim Best) *j. slowly 1st and 2nd: chsd ldr tl 2nd: reminders and lost pl after 5th: lost tch 3 out: t.o* **100/1**

00/ **10** *44* **Two Sugars**[133] 2564 8-11-0 0............ AndrewGlassonbury 18
(Gary Moore) *t.k.h: hld up in tch in midfield: rdn and struggling 6th: lost tch bef next: t.o* **33/1**

5/PP **P** **Generous June (IRE)**[159] 2519 8-10-7 0............(p) MarcGoldstein
(Paddy Butler) *a in rr: blnd 1st: bmpd 3rd: rdn and struggling after 5th: t.o bef 3 out: p.u 2 out* **200/1**

3m 54.95s (-5.85) **Going Correction** -0.275s/f (Good)
WFA 4 from 5yo+ 5lb **11 Ran SP% 116.5**
Speed ratings (Par 105): **103,102,102,102,100 99,90,79,78,56**
CSF £25.50 TOTE £4.10: £1.60, £2.20, £4.20; EX 31.40 Trifecta £298.10.
Owner Heart Of The South Racing **Bred** Mme Henri Devin **Trained** Lower Beeding, W Sussex

FOCUS
A modest maiden hurdle, rated around the winner and third. Due to rail movement the race distance was 60yds further than advertised.

5478 BET & WATCH AT CORAL.CO.UK CONDITIONAL JOCKEYS' H'CAP CHASE (14 fncs) 2m 3f 164y

5:20 (5:20) (Class 5) (0-100,101) 5-Y-O+ **£3,249** (£954; £477; £238)

Form RPR

5P01 **1** **Ballycoe**[3] 5388 7-12-5 **101** 7ex............(t) KillianMoore 116+
(Chris Gordon) *chsd ldr 3rd tl j. into ld 3 out: sn 3 l clr: mstke next: rdn and readily asserted between last 2: comf* **8/15[1]**

2402 **2** *10* **Bonds Conquest**[26] 4931 7-10-6 **74**............(v[1]) JeremiahMcGrath 78
(Seamus Mullins) *led tl hdd 3 out: sn u.p and unable qck: wl hld whn mstke last: wknd flat* **11/2[2]**

P2P2 **3** *5* **Kayflin (FR)**[26] 4936 8-10-9 **77**............(p) JackSherwood 74
(Linda Jewell) *hld up in rr: clsd and in tch 9th: sn outpcd again in 5th: pushed along 11th: wnt modest 3rd last: kpt on flat: no ch w wnr* **14/1[3]**

4-P6 **4** *2 1/2* **Major Martin (IRE)**[15] 5181 7-11-0 **90**............(b[1]) GeorgeGorman(8) 86
(Gary Moore) *in tch in midfield: 6 l 4th and rdn 11th: no imp and wl btn after 3 out: wnt modest 4th sn after last* **14/1[3]**

U2 **5** *5* **Carobello (IRE)**[183] 2037 9-11-2 **84**............(t) TomBellamy 74
(Martin Bosley) *chsd ldr tl 3rd: chsd ldng pair after: rdn and outpcd after 3 out: wl hld next: lost pls fr last* **16/1**

-PP0 **6** *131* **The Perfect Crime (IRE)**[19] 5125 7-10-4 **80**............(p) TobyWheeler(8)
(Ian Williams) *mstke 1st: in tch in midfield: mstke 9th: sn outpcd and bhd whn nt fluent next: sn lost tch: t.o* **20/1**

046- **P** **Our Georgie Girl**[646] 975 9-10-6 **74**............ ThomasCheesman
(Polly Gundry) *dropped to rr: 3rd: mstke 7th: rdn and lost tch after next: tailing off whn p.u bef 10th* **16/1**

5m 4.65s (-2.65) **Going Correction** -0.075s/f (Good) **7 Ran SP% 110.5**
Speed ratings: **102,98,96,95,93 ,**
CSF £4.00 TOTE £1.50: £1.50, £2.30; EX 4.40 Trifecta £20.20.
Owner D S Dennis **Bred** J A And Mrs M A Knox **Trained** Morestead, Hampshire

FOCUS
A weak handicap, confined to conditional riders. Due to rail movement the race distance was 60yds further than advertised. The winner is closing in on his best hurdles mark.

5479 CORAL.CO.UK BEST ODDS GUARANTEED ON RACING H'CAP HURDLE (12 hdls) 2m 4f 114y

5:50 (5:50) (Class 4) (0-115,120) 4-Y-O+ **£3,898** (£1,144; £572; £286)

Form RPR

1-51 **1** **Libeccio (FR)**[10] 5266 5-11-12 **120** 7ex............(t) TommyDowling(7) 124+
(Charlie Mann) *hld up in last pair: hmpd 3rd: clsd and in tch 6th: effrt in 4th after 3 out: chsd ldr sn after 2 out: upsides and bttr jump than rival last: sn led: r.o: pushed out* **13/8[1]**

-2P0 **2** *1/2* **Knight Bachelor**[155] 2595 6-11-12 **113**............(tp) GavinSheehan 117+
(Warren Greatrex) *chsd ldr tl led 2nd: rdn and 2 l clr after 3 out: hrd pressed and hit last: sn hdd: kpt on u.p but a jst hld flat* **11/4[2]**

4463 **3** *8* **Occasionally Yours (IRE)**[21] 5065 12-10-11 **105**............ MissTWorsley(7) 100
(Alan Blackmore) *chsd ldrs: rdn after 9th: 6th and outpcd after 3 out: rallied between last 2: wnt 3rd flat: kpt on but no threat to ldng pair* **17/2**

33 **4** *3 1/4* **Epsom Flyer**[58] 2256 6-11-1 **102** ow3............ JoshuaMoore 95
(Pat Phelan) *led tl 2nd: chsd ldrs after: wnt 2nd 3 out: sn rdn: lost 2nd and outpcd between last 2: lost 3rd and wknd flat* **9/1**

5153 **5** *1 1/4* **Daliance (IRE)**[17] 5164 7-11-4 **112**............(p) WilliamFeatherstone(7) 104
(Noel Williams) *pressed ldrs: mstke 9th: 3rd and u.p after next: outpcd and btn between last 2: wknd flat* **8/1[3]**

0062 **6** *3 1/2* **Kastani Beach (IRE)**[42] 4593 10-10-10 **104**............(v) MrDSansom(7) 93
(Seamus Mullins) *hld up in midfield: clsd and in tch 5th: effrt in 5th after 3 out: unable qck and btn next: wknd between last 2* **11/1**

250P **7** *14* **Sebs Sensei (IRE)**[53] 4411 5-11-2 **110**............ MrDGBurchell(7) 86
(Mark Hoad) *bhd: hmpd 3rd and detached in last after: mstke next: nvr on terms after* **40/1**

1P00 **F** **Vif Argent (FR)**[15] 5185 7-11-5 **109**............ BenPoste(3)
(Andrew Reid) *in tch in midfield tl fell 3rd* **20/1**

5m 7.9s (-9.10) **Going Correction** -0.275s/f (Good) **8 Ran SP% 111.9**
Speed ratings (Par 105): **106,105,102,101,101 99,94,**
CSF £6.45 CT £25.95 TOTE £2.60: £1.30, £1.40, £1.90; EX 7.30 Trifecta £40.10.
Owner John Heron **Bred** Capricorn Stud Sa **Trained** Upper Lambourn, Berks

FOCUS
A modest race in which the two market leaders came clear from two out. Straightforward form. Due to rail movement the race distance was 78 yds further than advertised.

5480 CORAL PROUD SUPPORTERS OF BRITISH RACING H'CAP CHASE (18 fncs) 3m 1f 152y

6:20 (6:20) (Class 5) (0-100,100) 5-Y-O+ **£3,249** (£954; £477; £238)

Form RPR

-44F **1** **Roparta Avenue**[39] 4673 9-10-2 **76**............ JoshuaMoore 93+
(Diana Grissell) *midfield: 6th and rdn 13th: no imp tl str run to cl after 3 out: led sn after 2 out: clr and mstke last: styd on wl* **4/1[2]**

0-24 **2** *8* **Spartilla**[39] 4669 7-10-8 **82**............ MattieBatchelor 91
(Daniel O'Brien) *t.k.h: j.rt: hld up in tch in midfield: effrt to chse ldr 3 out: sn led: hdd sn after 2 out: styd on same pce after* **7/1**

2226 **3** *7* **Bawden Rocks**[39] 4669 7-11-12 **100**............ TomCannon 106+
(David Bridgwater) *shied away as tape wnt up and slowly away: bhd: hdwy to chse ldrs 12th: led 15th: hdd and drvn sn after 3 out: 3rd and wknd between last 2* **13/2**

34P4 **4** *6* **Miss Oscarose (IRE)**[12] 5240 9-10-13 **87**............(t) NickScholfield 83
(Paul Henderson) *chsd ldr tl 3rd: styd prom: no ex u.p after next: wknd 2 out* **8/1**

22P3 **5** *3 1/2* **Burgess Dream (IRE)**[39] 4673 7-10-5 **79**............(p) AndrewThornton 73
(Anna Newton-Smith) *led: rdn after 14th: hdd next: no ex and wknd bef 2 out* **8/1**

141U **6** *3* **Ya Hafed**[118] 3218 8-11-1 **89**............ MarcGoldstein 79
(Sheena West) *a towards rr: 7th and rdn after 13th: no imp: wl btn after 3 out* **7/2[1]**

-22F **7** *4 1/2* **Charming Lad (IRE)**[332] 486 11-11-6 **99**............(bt) JakeHodson(5) 89
(Anthony Day) *chsd ldrs: wnt 2nd 3rd tl 7th: styd chsng ldrs: rdn after 13th: lost pl after next: wknd 3 out* **16/1**

PPP3 **8** *10* **Red Anchor (IRE)**[46] 4531 12-9-9 **74** oh6............(p) ThomasCheesman(5) 53
(Linda Jewell) *chsd ldrs: mstke 8th: rdn and lost pl after 12th: wl bhd whn j.rt 15th: t.o* **18/1**

P405 **9** *23* **George Nympton (IRE)**[21] 5068 10-9-7 **74** oh4............(tp) FrankiePenford(7) 31
(Zoe Davison) *j. awkwardly 1st: a in rr: lost tch after 13th: t.o* **40/1**

PP1P **P** **Toohighforme (IRE)**[118] 3214 7-10-2 **76**............(tp) LiamTreadwell
(Nick Gifford) *midfield: dropped to rr 8th: t.o whn p.u 11th* **6/1[3]**

6m 49.0s (-1.70) **Going Correction** -0.075s/f (Good) **10 Ran SP% 118.1**
Speed ratings: **99,96,94,92,91 90,89,86,79,**
CSF £33.02 CT £180.54 TOTE £4.80: £2.30, £3.30, £1.90; EX 40.70 Trifecta £255.10.
Owner Mrs D M Grissell **Bred** Mrs C A Bailey **Trained** Brightling, E Sussex

FOCUS
A weak staying handicap. The winner ran to the level of his 2014 C&D form. Due to rail movement the race distance was 90yds further than advertised.

5481 GRAEME MASON HOARE MEMORIAL H'CAP HURDLE (14 hdls) 3m 217y

6:50 (6:50) (Class 5) (0-100,100) 4-Y-O+ **£3,898** (£1,144; £572; £286)

Form RPR

-P01 **1** **Frank N Fair**[7] 5306 8-10-2 **83** 7ex............ WilliamFeatherstone(7) 88+
(Zoe Davison) *hld up in rr: hdwy to chse ldng pair 10th: effrt after 3 out: chsd clr ldr next: clsd and 1 l down last: led flat: styd on wl: rdn out* **8/1**

206P **2** *2* **Zephyr**[17] 5165 5-11-5 **100**............(b) MrCWilliams(7) 103+
(Nick Williams) *chsd ldrs 3rd: wnt 2nd 8th: steadily clsd and pressed ldr 3 out: sn pushed into ld: 4 l clr next: rdn between last 2: hdd and no ex flat* **14/1**

335P **3** *1 1/2* **Fifi L'Amour (IRE)**[7] 5305 10-9-7 **74** oh1............(p) TommyDowling(7) 77
(Linda Jewell) *hld up in last trio: rdn and hdwy after 11th: chsd ldng trio after 3 out: clsng and sltly hmpd 2 out: sn chsng ldng pair: styd on same pce flat* **20/1**

UUFP **4** *12* **Generous Helpings (IRE)**[31] 4860 7-11-12 **100**............(v[1]) JoshuaMoore 94
(Gary Moore) *mstkes: chsd ldr tl led 4th: clr and blnd 6th: hdd and rdn after 3 out: mstke next: wknd between last 2* **4/1[2]**

400P **5** *7* **Kerry's Lord (IRE)**[46] 4528 7-10-12 **86**............ JackQuinlan 71
(Joanne Thomason-Murphy) *hld up towards rr: hdwy into midfield after 7th: 4th and rdn after 10th: no imp: wknd bef 2 out* **33/1**

P603 **6** *1* **Flemi Two Toes (IRE)**[25] 4972 10-10-6 **90**............ RomainClavreul(10) 74
(Sarah Humphrey) *midfield: rdn after 9th: no imp and nvr on terms w ldrs: wl btn after 3 out* **16/1**

OPUP **7** *8* **Benability (IRE)**[39] 4682 6-10-13 **92**............ AlanJohns(5) 69
(Tim Vaughan) *hld up towards rr: hdwy into midfield and rdn after 9th: no imp: wl btn and mstke 2 out* **11/1**

2553 **8** *15* **Onwiththeparty**[39] 4671 7-11-10 **98**............(p) TomCannon 61
(Chris Gordon) *led tl 4th: chsd ldr tl 8th: steadily lost pl: bhd 11th: sn lost tch: t.o* **3/1[1]**

P00 **9** *6* **Acajou Des Bieffes (FR)**[80] 3915 6-11-12 **100**............(t) NickScholfield 58
(Anthony Honeyball) *midfield: sme hdwy but nt on terms w ldrs after 11th: effrt after 3 out: sn btn and wknd* **5/1[3]**

402P **P** **Whispering Speed (IRE)**[54] 4391 6-10-10 **84**............(p) LeightonAspell
(Lucy Wadham) *prom tl 2nd: steadily lost pl: bhd after 9th: lost tch after 11th: t.o whn p.u 2 out* **7/1**

6m 23.05s (-1.95) **Going Correction** -0.275s/f (Good) **10 Ran SP% 113.9**
Speed ratings (Par 103): **92,91,90,87,84 84,81,77,75,**
CSF £107.46 CT £2137.83 TOTE £11.00: £2.60, £5.10, £3.60; EX 120.30 Trifecta £1789.30 Part won..
Owner The Secret Circle Racing Club **Bred** Mrs Janet M Sexton **Trained** Hammerwood, E Sussex

FOCUS
An ordinary staying handicap, run at a sound gallop. The winner may still rate higher. Due to rail movement the race distance was 99yds further than advertised.

5482 CORAL RAISING FUNDS FOR CHILDREN WITH CANCER H'CAP CHASE (12 fncs) 2m 214y

7:20 (7:22) (Class 5) (0-100,93) 5-Y-O+ **£3,249** (£954; £477; £238)

Form RPR

12U **1** **Killabraher Cross (IRE)**[149] 2714 9-11-11 **92**............ MarcGoldstein 95+
(Paddy Butler) *led tl 5th: chsd ldr tl 7th: pushed along and rallied to join ldrs 9th: led 3 out: stmbld and hdd sn after: short of room on inner bnd bef 2 out: swtchd rt and rallied to chal 2 out: sn led: edgd lft styd on flat* **2/1[1]**

0P0P **2** *1 1/4* **Nouailhas**[7] 5307 10-10-6 **76**............(b[1]) BenPoste(3) 76
(Daniel O'Brien) *t.k.h: chsd ldr tl after 4th: wnt 2nd again 7th: ev ch 3 out: sn rdn and led wl bef next: hdd sn after 2 out: 1 l down last: swtchd rt and kpt on same pce flat* **7/1**

05-F **3** *10* **Edgar (GER)**[30] 524 6-11-7 **93**............(p) JakeHodson(5) 87
(David Bridgwater) *j.rt: hld up in tch: blnd 3rd: struggling and j.rt 3 out: sn outpcd and btn next: plugged on modest 3rd last: swtchd lft flat* **2/1[1]**

122- **4** *18* **Sitting Back (IRE)**[435] 4177 12-11-1 **89**............ MissTWorsley(7) 69
(Diana Grissell) *wl in tch: cl enough in 4th and mstke 3 out: 3rd and no imp on ldng pair next: lost 3rd and mstke 2 out: wknd flat* **5/1[2]**

5446 **5** *30* **Topthorn**[32] 4850 10-11-3 **84**............(b[1]) TomCannon 32
(Martin Bosley) *t.k.h: hld up in tch: hdwy to press ldrs 4th: led next: hdd and mstke 3 out: sn btn and dropped to last next: eased flat: t.o* **11/2[3]**

4m 25.9s (2.90) **Going Correction** -0.075s/f (Good) **5 Ran SP% 111.2**
Speed ratings: **90,89,84,76,62**
CSF £14.81 TOTE £2.90: £1.50, £3.50; EX 17.10 Trifecta £54.50.
Owner Homewoodgate Racing Club **Bred** Mr And Mrs J O'Sullivan **Trained** East Chiltington, E Sussex

FOCUS
The first pair had this weak handicap to themselves from three out. The winner is rated to his mark. Due to rail movement the race distance was 60yds further than advertised.

5483 CORAL DOWNLOAD THE APP H'CAP HURDLE (10 hdls) 2m 1f 164y
7:50 (7:50) (Class 5) (0-100,100) 4-Y-O+ £3,898 (£1,144; £572; £286)

Form RPR
-503 1 **Hermosa Vaquera (IRE)**[190] 1596 6-11-0 **88**..............(p) JoshuaMoore 93+
(Gary Moore) *trckd ldrs: jnd ldrs and travelling strly after 7th: led and wnt clr bnd bef 2 out: mstke last: r.o wl: comf* 3/1[1]
PP30 2 2 ¾ **Prince Of Thieves (IRE)**[71] 4068 6-10-9 **83**..............(t) NickScholfield 85+
(Anthony Honeyball) *j.lft: hld up in tch in rr: gd hdwy after 4 out: 4th and clsng next: chsd clr wnr and wnt lft last: kpt on u.p flat: no serious threat to wnr* 13/2[3]
5550 3 4 ½ **Thundering Home**[27] 4922 9-11-9 **100**..............(bt) TomBellamy[(3)] 97
(Richard Mitchell) *hld up in tch: hdwy 7th: chsd clr wnr and j.lft last: lost 2nd and styd on same pce fr last* 6/1[2]
-656 4 9 **Ding Ding**[21] 5067 5-10-13 **87**.............................. MarcGoldstein 76
(Sheena West) *hld up in tch in midfield: nt clrest of runs sn after 3 out: 6th and no imp u.p next: plugged on into 4th flat* 8/1
24P3 5 2 ½ **Directional**[39] 4674 4-10-6 **90**..............................(t) AlanJohns[(5)] 71
(Tim Vaughan) *hld up in tch: rdn after 7th: hdwy into 5th after 3 out: no imp fr 2 out* 9/1
/140 6 4 ½ **Sir Dylan**[31] 4856 7-11-9 **97**.............................. AndrewThornton 79
(Polly Gundry) *t.k.h: hld up wl in tch: jnd ldrs after 7th: led next: rdn and hdd bnd bef 2 out: outpcd and lost 2nd whn hmpd 2 out: wknd bef last* 16/1
P205 7 1 **Clonusker (IRE)**[21] 5067 8-10-12 **86**..............(t) LeightonAspell 67
(Linda Jewell) *chsd ldrs: lost pl 3 out: rdn and wknd bef next* 7/1
3652 8 2 ½ **Up Four It (IRE)**[39] 4674 8-10-0 **74**.............................. MattieBatchelor 54
(Jamie Poulton) *led tl after 6th: lost pl bef 3 out: wknd wl bef 2 out* 8/1
6F0 9 ¾ **Staff Sergeant**[53] 4409 9-10-12 **93**.............................. MrDGBurchell[(7)] 71
(Mark Hoad) *hld up in tch: hdwy into midfield 5th: j. slowly and lost pl 3 out: wknd and bhd next* 25/1
P P **Dutchesofrathmolyn (IRE)**[143] 2829 7-11-2 **90**.............................. TomCannon
(Alison Batchelor) *t.k.h: w ldr 2nd tl led after 6th: hdd 3 out: sn dropped out: bhd and p.u next* 66/1
0P36 P **Brise Coeur (FR)**[19] 5136 5-11-3 **98**.............................. MrCWilliams[(7)]
(Nick Williams) *a in rr: in tch: bmpd 3 out: lost tch and bhd whn p.u next* 9/1

4m 31.5s (0.60) **Going Correction** -0.275s/f (Good)
WFA 4 from 5yo+ 5lb 11 Ran SP% 118.6
Speed ratings (Par 103): **87,85,83,79,78 76,76,75,74,**
CSF £23.47 CT £112.10 TOTE £4.40: £2.30, £2.20, £2.10; EX 29.30 Trifecta £111.00.
Owner Michael Baldry **Bred** James Burns And A Moynan **Trained** Lower Beeding, W Sussex

FOCUS
Race distance increaded by 78 yards. This ordinary handicap was run at a routine gallop. Small pbs from the first two.
T/Plt: £407.80 to a £1 stake. Pool: £55,167.78 - 98.75 winning units T/Qpdt: £107.10 to a £1 stake. Pool: £7,259.02 - 50.12 winning units **Steve Payne**

5484 - 5490a (Foreign Racing) - See Raceform Interactive

4619 **SANDOWN** (R-H)
Saturday, April 23

OFFICIAL GOING: Good (good to soft in places; chs:7.4, hdl:7.1)
Wind: light, across Weather: light cloud

5491 BET365 JUVENILE H'CAP HURDLE (8 hdls) 1m 7f 216y
2:20 (2:20) (Class 2) 4-Y-O
£31,280 (£9,240; £4,620; £2,310; £1,155; £580)

Form RPR
116 1 **Wolf Of Windlesham (IRE)**[31] 3848 4-11-5 **137**.............................. JoshuaMoore 139+
(Stuart Edmunds) *hld up in tch: hdwy to chse ldrs after 3 out: c wd and ev ch whn mstke next: rdn and led bef last: drifted rt u.p flat: hld on gamely cl home* 7/1
F 2 ½ **Voix Du Reve (FR)**[38] 4720 4-11-9 **144**.............................. DavidMullins[(3)] 144+
(W P Mullins, Ire) *hld up in rr: clsd 4th: wl in tch in midfield after 3 out: effrt u.p bef next: hdwy after 2 out: cl 3rd last: styd on flat: pressing wnr towards fin: wnt 2nd last strides* 9/4[1]
210 3 hd **Tommy Silver (FR)**[36] 4764 4-11-6 **138**..............(t) SamTwiston-Davies 138
(Paul Nicholls) *hld up in midfield: clsd and wl in tch 4th: wnt 2nd after 3 out: led bef next: hit 3 out: sn drvn and hdd bef last: stl ev ch last: kpt on u.p: no ex cl home: lost 2nd last strides* 4/1[2]
3340 4 5 **Sikandar (IRE)**[49] 4486 4-10-0 **118** oh6..............(tp) GavinSheehan 115
(Brian Ellison) *hld up in rr: clsd and in tch 3 out: rdn and outpcd in 7th next: rallied last and styd on wl flat: snatched 4th last strides: no threat to ldrs* 33/1
3201 5 nk **Duke Street (IRE)**[21] 5095 4-11-5 **137**.............................. AidanColeman 134
(Dr Richard Newland) *prom in main gp: wnt 2nd after 2nd: clsd and trcking ldr 4th: ev ch and mstke 2 out: no ex last: outpcd flat: lost 4th last strides* 15/2
115P 6 ½ **Doubly Clever (IRE)**[16] 5175 4-10-12 **135**.............................. HarryCobden[(5)] 130
(Michael Blake) *chsd clr ldr tl after 2nd: styd prom tl rdn and outpcd bef 2 out: rallied last: kpt on u.p flat: no threat to ldrs* 12/1
2013 7 14 **Nabhan**[14] 5221 4-10-7 **128**.............................. RobertWilliams[(3)] 110
(Bernard Llewellyn) *midfield: clsd and wl in tch 4th: rdn and outpcd bef 2 out: struggling whn j. slowly 2 out: sn wknd* 25/1
4425 8 4 ½ **Deebaj (IRE)**[21] 5095 4-10-0 **118**.............................. ConorO'Farrell 96
(Richard Price) *a towards rr: effrt bef 2 out: sn struggling and outpcd: wknd 2 out* 28/1
1220 9 3 ½ **Big McIntosh (IRE)**[36] 4764 4-10-2 **120**.............................. MattieBatchelor 97
(John Ryan) *led and clr tl 4th: rdn and hdd bef 2 out: sn lost pl and btn 2 out: wknd wl bef last* 33/1
1532 10 20 **Darebin (GER)**[27] 4933 4-10-7 **125**..............(v[1]) JamieMoore 94
(Gary Moore) *hld up in midfield: clsd and wl in tch 4th: rdn and lost pl qckly bef 2 out: sn wknd: wl bhd and eased flat: t.o* 14/1
142 P **Ashoka (IRE)**[76] 4012 4-10-7 **125**..............(p) HarrySkelton
(Dan Skelton) *hld up in rr: p.u and dismntd 1st* 13/2[3]

3m 57.0s (-10.20) **Going Correction** -0.30s/f (Good) 11 Ran SP% 115.9
Speed ratings: **113,112,112,110,110 109,102,100,98,88**
CSF £22.53 CT £71.32 TOTE £6.80: £1.80, £1.50, £1.80; EX 18.30 Trifecta £66.90.
Owner M W Lawrence **Bred** Joe And Edel Banahan **Trained** Newport Pagnell, Bucks

FOCUS
All race distances as advertised. 4mm of rain the previous evening and a bit of light rain in the run up to racing would have kept some moisture in the ground and David Mullins described the ground as "good to soft". A good-quality juvenile handicap, although they didn't go that fast, ignoring the early leader. The winner is a decent juvenile and this rates a step up, with the next two to form.

5492 BET365 OAKSEY CHASE (GRADE 2) (21 fncs) 2m 6f 164y
2:55 (2:55) (Class 1) 5-Y-O+
£28,475 (£10,685; £5,350; £2,665; £1,340; £670)

Form RPR
1-P3 1 **Menorah (IRE)**[140] 2900 11-11-10 **165**.............................. RichardJohnson 170
(Philip Hobbs) *j.w: chsd ldrs: wnt 2nd 7th: upsides and slt mstke 17th: led next: rdn after 2 out: styd on gamely u.p and a doing enough flat: rdn out* 5/1[2]
2FU2 2 1 **Valseur Lido (FR)**[37] 4731 7-11-5 **162**.............................. BJCooper 165+
(W P Mullins, Ire) *in tch: mstke 1st: chsd ldng pair 14th: pushed along to chse wnr 3 out: rdn and chal between last 2: slt mstke last: kpt on u.p but nvr quite matching pce of wnr flat* 4/5[1]
P40P 3 10 **Rocky Creek (IRE)**[14] 5218 10-11-6 **147**.............................. SeanBowen 155
(Paul Nicholls) *chsd ldr tl 7th: pushed along 14th: rdn bef 3 out: outpcd in 4th after 3 out: no ch w ldng pair after: kpt on same pce u.p to take 3rd flat* 25/1
6653 4 1 ¼ **Third Intention (IRE)**[15] 5193 9-11-6 **155**..............(bt) TomO'Brien 157
(Colin Tizzard) *j.lft: led tl 18th: 3rd and no ex u.p 3 out: outpcd and btn whn j.lft and mstke next: mstke last: lost 3rd flat* 16/1
5566 5 1 ½ **Saphir Du Rheu (FR)**[16] 5176 7-11-10 **154**..............(b[1]) NickScholfield 159
(Paul Nicholls) *hld up in tch in last pair: effrt bef 3 out: 5th and outpcd after 3 out: wl hld and plugged on same pce fr 2 out* 8/1[3]
035U 6 ½ **Ballycasey (IRE)**[14] 5218 9-11-0 **145**..............(p) PaulTownend 148
(W P Mullins, Ire) *hld up in tch in last pair: mstke 4th (water) and 8th: shortlived effrt 3 out: 6th and wl hld next: plugged on and swtchd rt flat* 12/1
P-2P 7 29 **Wonderful Charm (FR)**[14] 5218 8-11-6 **154**.....(bt[1]) SamTwiston-Davies 138
(Paul Nicholls) *in tch in midfield: rdn after 18th: no rspnse and dropped to last next: wknd bef 2 out: wl bhd and eased flat: t.o* 10/1

5m 48.0s (-5.40) **Going Correction** -0.30s/f (Good) 7 Ran SP% 109.8
Speed ratings: **97,96,93,92,92 92,81**
CSF £9.18 TOTE £4.70: £2.50, £1.20; EX 8.50 Trifecta £135.80.
Owner Mrs Diana L Whateley **Bred** Mrs E Grant And Miss Anna Brislane **Trained** Withycombe, Somerset

FOCUS
Race distance as advertised. The two highest-rated runners dominated with the winner recording a third successive victory in the race. Menorah is a 172 horse at his best, while Valseur Lido was 3lb off his optimum.

5493 BET365 CELEBRATION CHASE (GRADE 1) (13 fncs) 1m 7f 119y
3:35 (3:35) (Class 1) 5-Y-O+
£71,187 (£26,712; £13,375; £6,662; £3,350; £1,675)

Form RPR
-111 1 **Sprinter Sacre (FR)**[38] 4718 10-11-7 **175**.............................. NicodeBoinville 176+
(Nicky Henderson) *trckd ldrs: clsd after 10th: upsides and gng strly whn led: mstke and lft in command 3 out: drew clr between last 2: r.o strly: rdn out* 11/10[1]
1F12 2 15 **Un De Sceaux (FR)**[38] 4718 8-11-7 **171**.............................. PaulTownend 167+
(W P Mullins, Ire) *led but a hassled: hdd 5th: styd w ldr: stood a long way off and mstke next: ev ch whn blnd bdly 3 out: 3rd and nvr looked like getting bk om terms w wnr after: mstke next: wnt 2nd last: kpt on same pce* 5/4[2]
1-20 3 1 **Dodging Bullets**[38] 4718 8-11-7 **166**..............(t) SamTwiston-Davies 162
(Paul Nicholls) *nt jump fluently and j.lft at several fences: off the pce in last pair: wnt modest 4th 7th: 15 l down 3 out: rdn and styd on flat: no ch w wnr* 12/1[3]
1220 4 7 **Sire De Grugy (FR)**[38] 4718 10-11-7 **168**.............................. JamieMoore 155
(Gary Moore) *w ldr tl led 5th: rdn and hdd 3 out: unable qck w wnr u.p bef next: wl hld and lost 2nd last: wknd flat* 12/1[3]
3P13 5 ½ **Solar Impulse (FR)**[7] 5326 6-11-7 **149**..............(bt) SeanBowen 156
(Paul Nicholls) *a off the pce in last pair: mstke 4th: n.d and wl bhd fr 7th* 50/1
P022 6 23 **Ulck Du Lin (FR)**[28] 4918 8-11-7 **143**..............(bt) NickScholfield 133
(Paul Nicholls) *chsd ldrs tl 4th: outpcd in 4th next: mstke 7th (water) dropped to last and t.o bef 3 out* 80/1

3m 47.0s (-14.80) **Going Correction** -0.30s/f (Good) 6 Ran SP% 110.6
Speed ratings: **125,117,117,113,113 101**
CSF £2.86 TOTE £2.10: £1.30, £1.20; EX 2.90 Trifecta £7.40.
Owner Mrs Caroline Mould **Bred** Christophe Masle **Trained** Upper Lambourn, Berks
■ Stewards' Enquiry : Nico de Boinville two-day ban: use of whip

FOCUS
Race distance as advertised. A few of these wanted to lead early and the race set up perfectly for Sprinter Sacre. He's rated right up to the level of his recent Champion Chase win. The time was good and the form has a solid look to it.

5494 BET365 GOLD CUP CHASE (H'CAP) (GRADE 3) (24 fncs) 3m 4f 166y
4:10 (4:14) (Class 1) 5-Y-O+
£84,405 (£31,800; £15,915; £7,950; £3,990; £1,995)

Form RPR
U463 1 **The Young Master**[39] 4697 7-10-12 **148**..............(p) MrSWaley-Cohen[(3)] 155
(Neil Mulholland) *t.k.h: chsd ldrs: wnt 2nd 17th tl 21st: styd chsng ldrs: led 3 out tl next: sn drvn: ev ch and mstke last: battled on gamely u.p: led last stride* 8/1[3]
0020 2 shd **Just A Par (IRE)**[14] 5218 9-10-10 **148**..............(b) HarryCobden[(5)] 156
(Paul Nicholls) *in tch towards rr of midfield: hdwy and sltly hmpd 19th: rdn and chsd ldrs 3 out: ev ch last: led flat: edgd lft u.p fnl 100yds: hdd last stride* 20/1
1214 3 2 ¼ **Sausalito Sunrise (IRE)**[41] 4635 8-11-12 **159**..........(p) RichardJohnson 166
(Philip Hobbs) *hld up in tch towards rr: hdwy into midfield 10th: j.rt and mstke 21st: clsd to chse ldrs 3 out: led next: drvn bef last: hdd and no ex flat: outpcd towards fin* 20/1
-34B 4 4 **Southfield Theatre (IRE)**[39] 4697 8-11-3 **150**.............................. SamTwiston-Davies 152
(Paul Nicholls) *in tch in midfield: sltly hmpd 19th: chsd ldrs next: rdn and pressing ldrs 2 out: 4th and no ex last: styd on same pce flat* 8/1[3]
662P 5 1 ¼ **The Druids Nephew (IRE)**[14] 5218 9-11-6 **153**..............(p) DenisO'Regan 155
(Neil Mulholland) *hld up in tch towards rr: sltly hmpd 19th: hdwy 3 out: 7th and swtchd rt between last 2: kpt on flat: no threat to ldrs* 16/1

P-0U **6** *1* **Hadrian's Approach (IRE)**[14] 5218 9-10-11 **144**.......... NicodeBoinville 143
(Nicky Henderson) *chsd ldrs: rdn and 3 out: no ex and outpcd between last 2: 5th and hld last: kpt on same pce flat* **10/1**

-100 **7** *6* **Oscar Rock (IRE)**[37] 4731 8-11-6 **153**..........................(b) JoshuaMoore 150+
(Malcolm Jefferson) *hld up in tch towards rr: sme hdwy after 3 out: mstke and pckd next: hdwy and passed btn horses between last 2: no imp last* **25/1**

231F **8** *2 1/4* **Theatre Guide (IRE)**[39] 4697 9-11-3 **150**......................(tp) PaddyBrennan 144
(Colin Tizzard) *in tch in midfield: mstke 4th: hdwy to chse ldrs 14th: ev ch 3 out: struggling to qckn and mstke next: 7th and btn last: wknd flat* **11/1**

0204 **9** *3/4* **Dynaste (FR)**[16] 5176 10-11-8 **155**............................(bt) TomScudamore 147
(David Pipe) *wl in tch in midfield: chsd ldrs 18th: wnt 2nd 21st tl bef 3 out: mstke 3 out: wknd between last 2* **20/1**

601P **10** *4 1/2* **Saint Are (FR)**[14] 5218 10-11-3 **150**.......................(tp) WayneHutchinson 139
(Tom George) *led tl hdd and nt fluent 3 out: lost pl and btn whn mstke next: wknd between last 2* **25/1**

-51P **11** *nse* **Carole's Destrier**[39] 4697 8-11-4 **151**............................ NoelFehily 138
(Neil Mulholland) *in tch in midfield: effrt bef 3 out: no imp bef 2 out: wknd between last 2* **12/1**

013F **12** *5* **Measureofmydreams (IRE)**[7] 5327 8-10-13 **146**.................. BJCooper 131
(W P Mullins, Ire) *hld up in tch in midfield: rdn and hdwy after 21st: cl enough 3 out: no imp and mstke next: wknd bef last* **15/2**[2]

40P4 **13** *13* **Seventh Sky (GER)**[9] 5283 9-11-1 **148**.......................(tp) GavinSheehan 119
(Charlie Mann) *j. a in rr but wl in tch: effrt after 21st: sn struggling: wknd after next: t.o* **50/1**

000U **14** *2 3/4* **Spring Heeled (IRE)**[39] 4697 9-10-12 **145**..................(p) BrianO'Connell 113
(J H Culloty, Ire) *a towards rr but wl in tch: rdn 15th: struggling and btn bef 3 out: no ch whn carried lft and sltly hmpd bef last* **20/1**

1150 **15** *2* **Drop Out Joe**[32] 4858 8-10-13 **146**...............................(p) AidanColeman 113
(Charlie Longsdon) *chsd ldr: mstke 12th: lost 2nd 17th: lost pl and towards rr 19th: wknd bef 3 out: t.o* **33/1**

3410 **16** *8* **Gold Futures (IRE)**[41] 4635 7-10-11 **144**........................ BrianHarding 103
(Nicky Richards) *in tch in midfield: lost pl and pushed along 18th: bhd after 3 out: sn lost tch: t.o* **25/1**

150F **P** **Sir Des Champs (FR)**[14] 5218 10-11-4 **154**................(p) DavidMullins(3)
(W P Mullins, Ire) *a towards rr but in tch: pushed along 14th: effrt after 21st: no real imp and wl btn after 3 out: p.u last* **20/1**

U112 **U** **Henri Parry Morgan**[15] 5191 8-11-2 **149**...................(tp) SeanBowen
(Peter Bowen) *wl in tch in midfield: nt fluent 7th: blnd and uns rdr 19th* **5/1**[1]

6150 **P** **Le Reve (IRE)**[14] 5218 8-11-1 **148**.............................(b) HarrySkelton
(Lucy Wadham) *wl in tch in midfield: cl 6th and blnd 20th: lost pl qckly after next: wl btn and p.u 3 out* **16/1**

011U **F** **Bishops Road (IRE)**[15] 5193 8-11-7 **154**............................ JamieMoore
(Kerry Lee) *fell 1st* **20/1**

7m 25.65s (-18.35) **Going Correction** -0.30s/f (Good) **20** Ran SP% **132.5**
Speed ratings: **113,112,112,111,110 110,108,108,108,106 106,105,101,101,100 98, , , ,**
CSF £161.94 CT £3144.51 TOTE £9.40: £2.70, £6.30, £4.70, £2.70; EX 243.60 Trifecta £5753.50.
Owner Dajam & The Old Masters **Bred** Brendan Boyle **Trained** Limpley Stoke, Wilts
■ Stewards' Enquiry : Harry Cobden four-day ban: use of whip (7-10 May)

FOCUS
Race distance as advertised. A typically competitive edition of the race, they didn't go a mad gallop and the winner was well placed throughout, although plenty did come through from the rear. At least ten were still in with a chance at the Pond Fence. Good handicap form in a strong renewal, with a step up from The Young Master for the marathon trip. The second was possibly unlucky.

5495 BET365 SELECT HURDLE (LISTED RACE) (11 hdls) 2m 5f 110y
4:45 (4:47) (Class 1) 4-Y-0+

£28,475 (£10,685; £5,350; £2,665; £1,340; £670)

Form RPR

2FU2 **1** **Ptit Zig (FR)**[84] 3853 7-11-0 153............................... SamTwiston-Davies 157+
(Paul Nicholls) *trckd ldrs: nt clrest of runs bef bef 2 out: gap opened and effrt in 3rd 2 out: led and j.rt last: styd on strly: rdn out* **7/4**[1]

4313 **2** *1 3/4* **Silsol (GER)**[14] 5213 7-11-0 158...............................(bt) JackSherwood 154
(Paul Nicholls) *mde most tl after 3 out: rdn and ev ch bef next: chsd wnr and kpt on same pce flat* **9/2**[3]

121U **3** *1 1/2* **Vaniteux (FR)**[39] 4696 7-11-0 150.............................. NicodeBoinville 153
(Nicky Henderson) *hld up in tch: clsd and trckd ldrs 8th: smooth hdwy to ld bef 2 out: rdn between last 2: hdd last: no ex and styd on same pce after: lost 2nd flat* **9/4**[2]

4231 **4** *3* **Ubak (FR)**[14] 5213 8-11-4 151.................................. JoshuaMoore 153
(Gary Moore) *wl in tch in midfield: clsd and trckd ldrs 8th: rdn and c wd bef 2 out: outpcd 2 out: kpt on same pce after* **5/1**

2336 **5** *12* **San Benedeto (FR)**[15] 5189 5-11-0 142..........................(t) NickScholfield 140
(Paul Nicholls) *w ldr: led on inner after 3 out: hdd bef next and mstke 2 out: wknd between last 2* **20/1**

1124 **6** *27* **Court Minstrel (IRE)**[16] 5177 9-11-4 154.......................... PaulMoloney 125
(Evan Williams) *hld up in rr: rdn and short-lived effrt after 3 out: wl btn next: wknd* **16/1**

5m 22.7s (0.20) **Going Correction** -0.30s/f (Good) **6** Ran SP% **112.6**
Speed ratings (Par 111): **87,86,85,84,80 70**
CSF £10.27 TOTE £2.40: £1.50, £2.60; EX 9.50 Trifecta £25.70.
Owner Barry Fulton, Chris Giles & Richard Webb **Bred** Jean-Francois Vermand **Trained** Ditcheat, Somerset

FOCUS
Race distance as advertised. This was made much more winnable with Vroum Vroum Mag being taken out and they didn't go much of a gallop. Ptit Zig is a 160 hurdler at best and may still be capable of matching that, with the next three close to their marks.

5496 BET365 JOSH GIFFORD NOVICES' H'CAP CHASE (17 fncs) 2m 4f 10y
5:20 (5:20) (Class 2) 5-Y-0+

£18,768 (£5,544; £2,772; £1,386; £693; £348)

Form RPR

-115 **1** **Junction Fourteen (IRE)**[127] 3136 7-11-8 **141**..................(t) DarylJacob 151+
(Emma Lavelle) *mde all: stl travelling strly 3 out: rdn and fnd ex between last 2: styd on wl: rdn out* **11/2**[3]

1405 **2** *1 1/4* **Volnay De Thaix (FR)**[16] 5174 7-11-12 **145**.................. NicodeBoinville 154+
(Nicky Henderson) *chsd ldrs: wnt 2nd 8th: rdn after 3 out: unable qck w wnr between last 2: rallied and styd on wl u.p flat* **7/1**

01P5 **3** *5* **Antony (FR)**[35] 4785 6-10-6 **125**.............................. JamieMoore 129
(Gary Moore) *in tch in midfield: effrt 2 out: kpt on same pce u.p flat: wnt 3rd last strides* **12/1**

0031 **4** *nk* **Thomas Crapper**[21] 5093 9-11-4 **137**...........................(p) CharliePoste 142
(Robin Dickin) *j.rt at times: chsd wnr tl 8th: styd prom: rdn bef 3 out: unable qck u.p between last 2: styd on same pce flat: lost 3rd last strides* **9/1**

6602 **5** *2* **Viva Steve (IRE)**[22] 5073 8-10-11 **133**...................... HarryBannister(3) 135
(Mick Channon) *chsd ldrs: carried rt 1st: mstke 5th: lost pl next but stl in tch: effrt bef 3 out: styd on same pce fr 2 out* **8/1**

-6P1 **6** *3/4* **Some Buckle (IRE)**[31] 4870 7-11-7 **140**......................(t) NickScholfield 146+
(Paul Nicholls) *hld up in rr: mstke 2nd: hdwy 11th: blnd 14th: midfield and blnd 2 out: styd on to pass btn horses flat: no threat to ldrs* **7/1**

3113 **7** *1 1/2* **Daveron (IRE)**[31] 4870 8-10-10 **129**........................... AidanColeman 129
(Jeremy Scott) *hld up in tch: in rr of main gp and rdn after 14th: no imp after 3 out: wl hld and plugged on same pce fr next* **33/1**

-133 **8** *3/4* **Calipto (FR)**[141] 2881 6-11-7 **140**.......................(t) SamTwiston-Davies 141
(Paul Nicholls) *in tch in midfield: effrt bef 3 out: no imp u.p bef 2 out: wknd bef last* **9/2**[2]

F250 **9** *hd* **As De Mee (FR)**[15] 5193 6-11-9 **142**.........................(b[1]) SeanBowen 141
(Paul Nicholls) *trckd ldrs: stl travelling strly 3 out: nt clr run bnd bef next: effrt and little rspnse 2 out: sn btn: wknd last* **4/1**[1]

0125 **10** *57* **Blandfords Gunner**[26] 4964 7-10-9 **128**...................... LeightonAspell 76
(Evan Williams) *dropped to rr after 3rd: detached and struggling fr 8th: lost tch after 14th: t.o* **25/1**

4433 **P** **Gentleman Jon**[63] 4254 8-10-3 **122**...........................(t) PaddyBrennan
(Colin Tizzard) *chsd ldrs after 6th: mstke 13th: lost pl bef 3 out: bhd whn p.u last* **33/1**

5m 6.6s (-11.80) **Going Correction** -0.30s/f (Good) **11** Ran SP% **117.1**
Speed ratings: **111,110,108,108,107 107,106,106,106,83**
CSF £43.10 CT £441.26 TOTE £7.10: £2.90, £2.60, £2.90; EX 47.70 Trifecta £663.80.
Owner Martin St Quinton & Tim Syder **Bred** John And Iris Lunny **Trained** Hatherden, Hants
■ Emma Lavelle's first winner from her new yard at Marlborough.

FOCUS
Race distance as advertised. They went pretty slowly here and it paid to race handily, the winner making all. The winner was well handicapped on his Wincanton win and is rated back to that level.

5497 BET365 H'CAP HURDLE (9 hdls) 2m 3f 173y
5:55 (5:57) (Class 2) (0-145,145) 4-Y-0+

£18,768 (£5,544; £2,772; £1,386; £693; £348)

Form RPR

56U4 **1** **McKinley**[27] 4956 6-11-2 **135**...................................(p) BJCooper 142
(W P Mullins, Ire) *wl in tch in midfield: pushed along bef 3 out: hdwy and ev ch 2 out: led last: forged ahd flat: drvn out* **16/1**

1510 **2** *1 1/4* **Gioia Di Vita**[203] 1754 6-10-1 **130**........................ CharlieHammond(10) 136
(Dr Richard Newland) *t.k.h: pressed ldr tl led bef 2 out: drvn between last 2: hdd last: no ex and one pce flat* **16/1**

4001 **3** *1 3/4* **Matorico (IRE)**[10] 5275 5-11-5 **138**.........................(tp) BarryGeraghty 141
(Jonjo O'Neill) *hld up in tch towards rr: pushed along and hdwy on outer bef 2 out: rdn to chse ldrs last: drifted rt and kpt on u.p flat* **15/2**[3]

50P0 **4** *1/2* **Dell' Arca (IRE)**[14] 5219 7-11-2 **135**.........................(b) TomScudamore 139
(David Pipe) *chsd ldrs: rdn and ev ch 2 out: unable qck and j.lft last: styd on same pce flat* **12/1**

200U **5** *2 3/4* **Mad Jack Mytton (IRE)**[15] 5189 6-11-2 **135**.................. RichardJohnson 138+
(Jonjo O'Neill) *hld up in tch towards rr: hdwy after 3rd: chsd ldrs 3 out: nt clr run bnd bef next: rdn and hit next: unable qck between last 2: btn whn squeezed for room flat: styd on same pce after* **5/1**[1]

111P **6** *3 1/2* **Ma Du Fou (FR)**[15] 5189 6-11-6 **139**............................ GavinSheehan 137
(Warren Greatrex) *in tch in midfield: chsd ldrs after 3 out: rdn and hit 2 out: outpcd between last 2: 6th and btn last: plugged on* **12/1**

1123 **7** *2* **Bon Enfant (FR)**[43] 4596 5-10-6 **128**....................... HarryBannister(3) 124
(Warren Greatrex) *chsd ldrs: rdn and lost pl after 3 out: rallied bef next: styd on same pce between last 2* **20/1**

0- **8** *1/2* **Bellow Mome (FR)**[20] 5130 5-10-10 **129**...................... PaulTownend 124
(W P Mullins, Ire) *hld up in tch in rr: hdwy bef 3 out: cl enough in 8th 2 out: sn rdn and no imp: wknd last* **7/1**[2]

1-F6 **9** *3/4* **Kilcrea Vale (IRE)**[91] 3733 6-11-12 **145**.................. JeremiahMcGrath 139
(Nicky Henderson) *in tch in midfield: rdn bef 2 out: outpcd and btn 2 out: plugged on flat* **8/1**

4611 **10** *5* **Royal Vacation (IRE)**[27] 4930 6-10-11 **130**.................(tp) PaddyBrennan 121
(Colin Tizzard) *in tch in midfield: rdn after 3 out: no imp: outpcd and btn bef next: wknd 2 out* **16/1**

-100 **11** *1* **Hunters Hoof (IRE)**[38] 4717 7-11-5 **138**.................... NicodeBoinville 127
(Nicky Henderson) *hld up in tch in rr: rdn and hdwy after 3 out: no imp and btn 2 out: wknd* **16/1**

F54/ **12** *7* **Wilde Blue Yonder (IRE)**[749] 5167 7-11-6 **139**............ WayneHutchinson 121
(Alan King) *hld up in tch towards rr: shkn up 2 out: sn btn: no ch whn hit last* **20/1**

1-P6 **13** *5* **Gold Present (IRE)**[35] 4786 6-11-2 **135**........................ DavidBass 113
(Nicky Henderson) *in tch in midfield: rdn after 3 out: lost pl and bhd next: wknd* **25/1**

3P-4 **14** *1/2* **Close Touch**[22] 5074 8-11-2 **135**.............................. PeterCarberry 112
(Nicky Henderson) *in tch in midfield: mstke 3 out: rdn and lost pl bef next: wknd 2 out* **25/1**

0202 **15** *2* **Qualando (FR)**[16] 5185 5-11-5 **143**.........................(b) HarryCobden(5) 119
(Paul Nicholls) *a towards rr: in tch: u.p bef 3 out: wknd bef next* **14/1**

P-P1 **16** *11* **Party Rock (IRE)**[15] 5189 9-11-4 **137**.......................... SeanQuinlan 103
(Jennie Candlish) *led tl bef 2 out: sn lost pl and wkng whn mstke 2 out: t.o* **16/1**

F031 **P** **Red Hanrahan (IRE)**[8] 5303 5-10-11 **130**..........(t) SamTwiston-Davies
(Paul Nicholls) *in tch towards rr: mstke 4th: rdn and btn after 3 out: bhd next: p.u last* **10/1**

4m 52.6s (-7.00) **Going Correction** -0.30s/f (Good) **17** Ran SP% **129.8**
Speed ratings (Par 109): **102,101,100,100,99 98,97,97,96,94 94,91,89,89,88 84,**
CSF £249.43 CT £2100.24 TOTE £21.00: £4.30, £5.90, £2.50, £2.60; EX 550.70 Trifecta £3621.30.
Owner Gigginstown House Stud **Bred** The Priera Menta Partnership **Trained** Muine Beag, Co Carlow

FOCUS
Race distance as advertised. This looked wide-open and plenty had their chance. The winner's best result since his Naas Grade 1 win, with the pb from the winner.

T/Jkpt: £3550.00 to a £1 stake. Pool of £10000.00 - 2.00 winning units. T/Plt: £24.00 to a £1 stake. Pool of £212547.02 - 6460.81 winning tickets. T/Qpdt: £18.60 to a £1 stake. Pool of £10401.90 - 413.64 winning tickets. **Steve Payne**

COMPIEGNE (L-H)

Saturday, April 23

OFFICIAL GOING: Turf: very soft

5498a PRIX DU CARNOIS (HURDLE) (CONDITIONS) (3YO) (TURF) — 2m 1f

4:00 (12:00) 3-Y-O **£7,764** (£3,882; £2,264; £1,536; £727)

RPR

1 **Flying Tiger (IRE)** 3-10-9 0 ow1 ... DavidCottin
(Nick Williams) *hld up: stl plenty to do appr 2 out: gd hdwy on run to last: rdn to chal flat and sn led: styd on strly and forged clr: readily* **3/1**[2]

2 *4* **Burrows Saint (FR)**[35] 3-10-8 0 ... JamesReveley
(G Macaire, France) **9/5**[1]

3 *1 3/4* **Topissime (FR)** 3-10-12 0 ... (p) ArnaudDuchene
(G Macaire, France) **19/5**[3]

4 *7* **Valentine Spring (FR)** 3-10-3 0 ... AlexisAcker
(M Rolland, France) **9/1**

5 *1 1/4* **Lou Tango (FR)** 3-10-8 0 ... (p) ClementLefebvre
(G Cherel, France) **20/1**

6 *1/2* **Fils Prodige (FR)**[18] 3-10-8 0 ... MorganRegairaz
(D Bressou, France) **27/1**

7 *nk* **Lucky Ruby (FR)** 3-10-8 0 ... ErvanChazelle
(Robert Collet, France) **10/1**

8 *8* **Laurenzio (FR)**[15] 3-10-8 0 ... GeoffreyRe
(G Cherel, France) **14/1**

9 *10* **Detroit De Baune (FR)** 3-10-8 0 ... DamienMescam
(F-M Cottin, France) **71/1**

10 *4* **Auteuil Oliverie (FR)** 3-10-3 0 ... LudovicSolignac
(A Le Clerc, France) **77/1**

11 *2* **De D'Or Esqua (FR)** 3-10-3 0 ... (p) MaximilienFarcinade(5)
(O Regley, France) **75/1**

Owner The Macaroni Beach Society **Bred** Patrick Chedeville **Trained** George Nympton, Devon
WIN (incl. 1 euro stake): 4.00. PLACES: 1.80, 1.30, 1.60. DF: 5.50. SF: 14.70.

5499a PRIX D'AUMALE (HURDLE) (CONDITIONS) (5YO+ MARES) (TURF) — 2m 2f

7:00 (12:00) 5-Y-O+ **£7,764** (£3,882; £2,264; £1,536; £727)

RPR

1 **Amazone Du Lemo (FR)**[177] 6-10-8 0 ... LudovicSolignac
(A Le Clerc, France) **42/10**[2]

2 *2* **Norse Wave (FR)**[11] 5-10-10 0 ... (p) SelimAgbal(4)
(H Billot, France) **45/1**

3 *7* **Belle Du Chenet (FR)**[521] 5-10-6 0 ... DylanUbeda(4)
(M Rolland, France) **12/1**

4 *hd* **Amour D'Or**[185] [2022] 5-10-10 0 ... JamesReveley
(Nick Williams) *prom bhd clr ldr: rdn 2 out: styd on same pce and nt able to chal: jst lost out for 3rd* **5/2**[1]

5 *1 1/4* **Suffisante (FR)**[313] 6-10-6 0 ... RegisSchmidlin
(F-M Cottin, France) **12/1**

6 *1 1/2* **Liberalis (FR)**[691] 6-10-1 0 ... MlleLauraPoggionovo(5)
(Yannick Fouin, France) **8/1**

7 *nse* **Bravarde (FR)**[27] 5-10-10 0 ... MorganRegairaz
(G Elbaz, France) **83/10**

8 *6* **Tinaka (FR)** 5-10-6 0 ... RomainBonnet
(G Lassaussaye, France) **83/1**

9 *nse* **Carnival Flag (FR)**[465] [3675] 7-10-12 0 ... DavidCottin
(N Bertran De Balanda, France) **73/10**[3]

10 *6* **Antioches (FR)**[729] 6-10-6 0 ... ThomasMessina(4)
(Mlle M-L Mortier, France) **73/10**[3]

F **Early Flower (FR)**[118] 5-10-8 0 ... BenjaminGelhay
(P Chatelain, France) **16/1**

P **Hard Run (FR)**[689] 6-10-2 0 ow1 ... AnthonyLeJoncour(5)
(M Blanchard-Jacquet, France) **118/1**

WIN (incl. 1 euro stake): 5.20. PLACES: 1.80, 8.20, 3.90. DF 138.20. SF: 134.00

Owner Maurice Le Floch **Bred** M Le Floch **Trained** France

Index to meetings Jumps 2015/16

*AW bumper meeting
† Abandoned
(M) Mixed meeting

INDEX TO STEEPLECHASING & HURDLE RACING

Figure underneath the horse's name indicates its age. The figures following the pedigree refer to the numbers of the races (steeplechases are in bold) in which the horse has run; parentheses () indicate a win; superscript figures denote other placings. Foreign races are denoted by the suffix 'a'. Horses withdrawn (not under orders) are shown with the suffix 'w'. The figures within arrows indicate Raceform Private Handicap MASTER ratings. The ratings are based on a scale of 0-175. The following symbols are used: 'h' hurdle rating, 'c' chase rating, '+' on the upgrade, 'd' disappointing, '?' questionable form. 't' tentative rating based on time.

Aachen *Venetia Williams* 142h 153c
11 b g Rainbow Quest(USA) Anna Of Saxony (Ela-Mana-Mou)
2374[4] (2872) (3016) 3448[2] 3860[11] 4483[9] 5218[P]

Aalim *John Ferguson* 133h 122c
5 b g Nayef(USA) Anna Palariva (IRE) (Caerleon (USA))
701[3] **779[2]** (916)

Aaly *Lydia Richards* 79h
8 b g Milan Leyaaly (Night Shift (USA))
451[8] 966[5] 1756[3] 2649[3]

Aaman (IRE) *Bernard Llewellyn* 80h
9 gr g Dubai Destination(USA) Amellnaa (IRE) (Sadler's Wells (USA))
2363[5] 2564[9] 2850[8] 3368[4] 3925[3] 4161[4] 4390[2] 4886[4] 5333[4]

Abba Des Genievres (FR) *E Vagne*
5 gr m Antarctique(IRE) Lobelie (FR) (Round Sovereign (FR))
2536a[13]

Abbey Storm (IRE) *Micky Hammond* 93h 103c
9 br g Presenting Bobbies Storm (IRE) (Bob Back (USA))
4288[4] 5202[4]

Abbeyview (IRE) *Mrs Sheila Crow* 99c
8 b g Misternando Castle Spirit (IRE) (Clearly Bust)
506[3]

Abbreviate (GER) *Kim Bailey* 133h
4 b g Authorized(IRE) Azalee (GER) (Lando (GER))
1718[2] (2407) ◆ 2972[3] 3724[7] 5387[5]

Abertillery *Michael Blanshard* 91h
3 b g Shamardal(USA) Nantyglo (Mark Of Esteem (IRE))
5353[3]

Abidjan (FR) *Paul Nicholls* 140h
5 b g Alberto Giacometti(IRE) Kundera (FR) (Kadalko (FR))
(1822) (2007) 3027[5]

Abigail Lynch (IRE) *Nigel Twiston-Davies* 102h 113c
7 b m Oscar(IRE) Tanit Lady (IRE) (Presenting)
259[5] 3155[3] 3709[P] 4647[4] 5015[3]

Abijoe *Pam Sly* 83h
6 b m Fair Mix(IRE) Casewick Mist (Primitive Rising (USA))
56[7] 421[DSQ]

Abitofbob *Emma Lavelle* 42h
6 b g Enrique My World (FR) (Lost World (IRE))
279[9]

Ablazing (IRE) *Johnny Farrelly* 99h
4 b g Mastercraftsman(IRE) Moore's Melody (IRE) (Marju (IRE))
761[6] 1644[6] 2091[6] 2217[5] 3450[P] 5153[7] 5418[13]

A Bold Move (IRE) *Paul Morgan* 94h
5 b g Shantou(USA) Sprint For Gold (USA) (Slew O'Gold (USA))
4790[6] 5451[4]

Abolitionist (IRE) *John Joseph Hanlon* 131h 134c
7 b g Flemensfirth(USA) All The Roses (IRE) (Roselier (FR))
50a[9] 1184a[6] **1235[2] 1417[2]**

Above Board (IRE) *Jonjo O'Neill* 113b
4 br g Mahler Blackwater Babe (IRE) (Arctic Lord (IRE))
(1872)

Abracadabra Sivola (FR) *David Pipe* 133h 138c
5 b g Le Fou(IRE) Pierrebrune (FR) (Cadoudal (FR))
1867[2] 2260[2] 2780[7] 2963[3] (4425) 4800[F]

Abricot De L'Oasis (FR) *Dan Skelton* 128h 127c
5 b g Al Namix(FR) La Normandie (FR) (Beyssac (FR))
(35) 315[4] 568[F] (2085) 2647[3] (3846) 4354[5] 4786[3] (5406)

Absolute (IRE) *Sue Smith* 103h
4 b g Danehill Dancer(IRE) Beyond Belief (IRE) (Sadler's Wells (USA))
1886[3] 2123[7] ◆ 2474[2] 4865[6] 4941[P]

Absolute Angel *Peter Niven* 86b
4 b m Primo Valentino(IRE) Send Me An Angel (IRE) (Lycius (USA))
(1688)

Absolutely Bygones (IRE) *Jackie Du Plessis* 112h
7 b g Alderbrook Majella (IRE) (Fourstars Allstar (USA))
2658[P]

Absolutlyfantastic *Martin Hill* 120h 121c
8 b g Alhaarth(IRE) Persian Walk (FR) (Persian Bold)
162[5] 751[4] 895[4] (1055) 1119[3] 1579[P] 5183[P]

Abuelo (FR) *Zoe Davison* 80b
5 bl g Califet(FR) Quolcevyta (FR) (Ungaro (GER))
61[P]

Abundantly *Venetia Williams* 110h
6 b m Sakhee(USA) Composing (IRE) (Noverre (USA))
2314[4]

Abyaat (IRE) *Victor Dartnall* 106h
4 b g Halling(USA) Why Dubai (USA) (Kris S (USA))
2458[11] 2734[13] 2987[3] 4096[5] 4440[5] (5445)

Academy (IRE) *N W Alexander* 62h
7 br g Montjeu(IRE) Rock The Casbah (FR) (Lavirco (GER))
1892[9] 2292[P] 3672[7]

Academy General (IRE) *Patricia Shaw* 94h 116c
9 b g Beneficial Discerning Air (Ezzoud (IRE))
534[F] 718[6] 1292[8] 1547[P] 1675[4]

Acadian (FR) *Nigel Hawke* 83h
5 b g Sulamani(IRE) Acarina (IRE) (Desert Story (IRE))
2730[7] 3256[P] 4882[5]

Acajou Des Bieffes (FR) *Anthony Honeyball* 89h
5 bb g Millennium Bio(JPN) Pietragella (FR) (Baryshnikov (AUS))
601[3] 1843[6] 2457[7] 2723[U] 3117[P] 3745[13] 3915[9] 5481[9]

Acapella Bourgeois (FR) *Ms Sandra Hughes* 145h
5 ch g Network(GER) Jasmine (FR) (Valanjou I (FR))
3765a[2] ◆ (4332a) (4955a)

Acapulco Bay *Dai Burchell* 97h
11 b g Pursuit Of Love Lapu-Lapu (Prince Sabo)
237[3] 3932[P] 4390[11] 4885[7]

Accessallareas (IRE) *Sarah-Jayne Davies* 84h 104c
10 ch g Swift Gulliver(IRE) Arushofgold (IRE) (Alphabatim (USA))
42[4] (161) 258[7] 514[8] 828[11] **914[5] 972[P] 1045[3] 1133[5] 1422[4] 1489[3] 1548[3] 1703[5] 1796[6]**

According To Harry (IRE) *Philip Hobbs* 111h
6 b g Old Vic Cassilis (IRE) (Persian Bold)
2443[3] 2986[F] 3124[4] 4853[5]

According To Sarah (IRE) *Philip Hobbs* 100h 115c
7 ch m Golan(IRE) Miss Accordion (IRE) (Accordion)
750[6] 1007[3] 1306[2] 1523[3]

According To Trev (IRE) *David Bridgwater* 130h 138c
9 ch g Accordion Autumn Sky (IRE) (Roselier (FR))
2089[P] 3018[2] 3407[12] 3622[7] 4389[8] **4697[P]** 5277[9]

Acdc (IRE) *Chris Grant* 102b
5 b g King's Theatre(IRE) Always Alert (IRE) (Slip Anchor)
5407[4]

Ace Fighter Pilot *Jim Best* 110b
9 b g Silver Patriarch(IRE) Vedra (IRE) (Carlingford Castle)
3867[P]

Ace High *Mrs Janet Ackner* 100b 114c
11 b g Kayf Tara Celtic Native (IRE) (Be My Native (USA))
17[F] 295[3] 4249[2]

Ace Of Marmalade (IRE) *Brian Ellison* 88h
3 b g Duke Of Marmalade(IRE) Pharapache (USA) (Lyphard (USA))
636[4] 778[3] 975[4]

Acertain Circus *Pam Sly* 124h
5 ch g Definite Article Circus Rose (Most Welcome)
216[4] 418[4]

Aces Over Eights (IRE) *Kerry Lee* 106h
6 b m Old Vic Conjure Up (IRE) (Jurado (USA))
2314[2] 2812[7] 3498[P] 3930[6] **4647[P]**

Achemenes (FR) *Daniel Steele* 83h
6 gr g Bonbon Rose(FR) Aimessa Du Berlais (FR) (Nikos)
65[8] 2000[P]

Achille (FR) *Venetia Williams* 128c
5 gr g Dom Alco(FR) Hase (FR) (Video Rock (FR))
2616[5]

Achimota (IRE) *Graeme McPherson* 105h 127c
9 b g Double Eclipse(IRE) Tullyfoyle (IRE) (Montelimar (USA))
2436[4] 3038[3] 3837[9] **4348[3] 4914[F]**

Achour (FR) *F-M Cottin* 129h 126c
4 b g Limnos(JPN) Jolie Menthe (FR) (Bateau Rouge)
1882a[5]

Ackertac (IRE) *Tim Vaughan* 113h 133c
10 ch g Anshan Clonsingle Native (IRE) (Be My Native (USA))
431[4] 1288[P]

Acordingtoscript (IRE) *Martin Todhunter* 102h 77c
9 ch g Accordion Jane Jones (IRE) (Beau Sher)
453[7] (Dead)

A Cor Et A Cri (FR) *Harry Fry* 113h 89c
5 b g Alberto Giacometti(IRE) Millesimee (FR) (Video Rock (FR))
102[2] 1242[P] 1269[P]

A Country Mile *Matthew Barber* 90h 86c
7 ch g Alflora(IRE) Country House (Town And Country)
292[F] 5467[9]

Acrai Rua (IRE) *Tim Fitzgerald* 86h 86c
12 ch g Rock Hopper Dontbelieveaword (IRE) (Be My Native (USA))
133[6] 1069[5]

Across The Bay (IRE) *Donald McCain* 86h 149c
11 b g Bob's Return(IRE) The Southern (IRE) (Glacial Storm (USA))
318[U]

Act Four (IRE) *Matt Sheppard* 96h
7 b g Old Vic Quadrennial (IRE) (Un Desperado (FR))
5220[4] 5469[6]

Actinpieces *Pam Sly* 135h
4 gr m Act One Bonnet's Pieces (Alderbrook)
334[2] (2494) (2847) (3420) 4231[3] 4734[8] 5280[2]

Actiondancer (IRE) *Henry Oliver* 76h
4 b g Craigsteel Sudden Action (IRE) (Shardari)
2636[9] 4441[15] 4888[12] 5091[12]

Action Du Manoir (FR) *A Sannier* 10b
5 b m Cachet Noir(USA) Neptune Du Manoir (FR) (Dress Parade)
2536a[12]

Action Master *Charlie Mann* 82h 106c
9 b g Domedriver(IRE) All Is Fair (Selkirk (USA))
141[6] 458[9] 2687[8] 2985[13]

Activial (FR) *Harry Fry* 152h 154c
5 gr g Lord Du Sud(FR) Kissmirial (FR) (Smadoun (FR))
4a[4] 663a[9] **2760[2] (3415)** ◆ **4116[3]**

Actlikeacountess *Neil Mulholland* 79b
4 gr m Act One Countess Point (Karinga Bay)
4687[11] 5383[7]

Act Now *Anthony Honeyball* 92h
6 br m Act One Lady Turk (FR) (Baby Turk)
2075 1837[8]

Act Of Supremacy (IRE) *Warren Greatrex* 102h
5 b g Presenting Supreme Touch (IRE) (Supreme Leader)
2136[3] 2823[7]

Actonetaketwo *Ron Hodges* 73h
5 b m Act One Temple Dancer (Magic Ring (IRE))
2258[10] 2604[8]

Adadream *Claire Dyson* 1b
6 b g Abzu Madam Ross (Ardross)
341[12] 2808[P] 3064[P] 4430[P]

Adam Du Breteau (FR) *Jonjo O'Neill* 103h 117c
5 ch g Network(GER) Odelie De Fric (FR) (April Night (FR))
56[4] 1522[4] **1753[U]** ◆ **2243[3]**

A Decent Excuse (IRE) *Eugene M O'Sullivan* 113h 129c
8 b g Fruits Of Love(USA) Brave Thistle (IRE) (Bravefoot)
2228a[P]

Adeenne De Sevres (FR) *Tom Lacey* 81h
5 ch g Network(GER) Gelee Royale (FR) (Royal Charter (FR))
2169[6] 2840[10] 3568[6] 4391[P]

Adelar (GER) *Venetia Williams* 59h
10 b g Samum(GER) Arpista (GER) (Chief Singer)
3584[P] 3932[13]

Adept Approach (IRE) *P G Hall* 120c
9 b g Milan Musical Approach (IRE) (Dry Dock)
295[F]

Ad Idem *Mrs Pauline Gavin* 95h 130c
11 b g Kayf Tara Major Hoolihan (Soldier Rose)
4521a[7]

A Dieu Vat (FR) *A Adeline De Boisbrunet* 101h 117c
5 b g Presenting Montanara Paris (FR) (Turgeon (USA))
436a[5]

Adios Alonso (IRE) *Rosemary Gasson* 97h 102c
9 b g Saffron Walden(FR) Rosy Rockford (IRE) (Beneficial)
524[U] (752) 934[3] 1080[3] 1298[F] 1785[P] 1933[4]

Adman Sam (IRE) *Ian Williams* 87h
4 b g Black Sam Bellamy(IRE) Koral Bay (FR) (Cadoudal (FR))
1973[3] 3226[4] 3835[9]

Admiral Barton (IRE) *Paul W Flynn* 114b 96c
9 b g Flemensfirth(USA) Ashanti Dancer (IRE) (Dancing Dissident (USA))
1287[5] 1298[P]

Admiral Blake *Laura Young* 90h 64c
8 b g Witness Box(USA) Brenda Bella (FR) (Linamix (FR))
2661[3] **3803[5] 3948[F]** 5033[2] 5165[4]

Admiral Kid (IRE) *Neil Mulholland* 110b
4 b g Mythical Kid(USA) English Clover (Tina's Pet)
(4201)

Admiral Miller *Nicky Henderson* 62h
5 b g Multiplex Millers Action (Fearless Action (USA))
279[8]

Admiral's Secret *Victor Dartnall* 98b
4 b g Kayf Tara Bobs Bay (IRE) (Bob's Return (IRE))
4296[4] 5227[11]

Adrakhan (FR) *Dan Skelton* 113h
4 b g Martaline Annee De La Femme (IRE) (Common Grounds)
(1967) 2472[6] 2773[4] 5386[F]

Adrenalin Flight (IRE) *Seamus Mullins* 101h 134c
9 b g Dr Massini(IRE) Chapel Queen (IRE) (Jolly Jake (NZ))
92a[8] (448) 855[3] 1699[5] **2008[6]**

Adrien Du Pont (FR) *Paul Nicholls* 145h
3 b g Califet(FR) Santariyka (FR) (Saint Des Saints (FR))
(1866) 3028[2] (3519) (5116) ◆

Aengus (IRE) *Noel Meade* 126h 58c
5 b g Robin Des Champs(FR) Which Thistle (IRE) (Saddlers' Hall (IRE))
50a[18] 2676a[11]

Aerial (FR) *Paul Nicholls* 108h 137c
9 b g Turgeon(USA) Fille Formidable (USA) (Trempolino (USA))
660[F]

Aerlite Supreme (IRE) *Evan Williams* 133h 135c
8 b g Gold Well Supreme Evening (IRE) (Supreme Leader)
2186[9] 2639[2] 3156[7] 3254[7] ◆ **3735[6] 4485[3]**

Affaire D'Honneur (FR) *Harry Whittington* 133h
4 ch g Shirocco(GER) Affaire De Moeurs (FR) (Kaldounevees (FR))
3284[2] ◆ 4115[4] ◆ 4622[4]

Aficionado *Dr Richard Newland* 126h
5 ch g Halling(USA) Prithee (Barathea (IRE))
645[2] 812[2] 876[2] 1035[6]

African Gold (IRE) *Nigel Twiston-Davies* 108h 100c
7 b g King's Theatre(IRE) Mrs Dempsey (IRE) (Presenting)
2153[P] 2727[P] 3079[P] 5120[13]

Afterclass (IRE) *N W Alexander* 109h 57c
7 b g Stowaway Afsana (IRE) (Bluebird (USA))
143[P] 2320[3] 2786[8] 2983[5]

After Eight Sivola (FR) *Nick Williams* 128h
5 b g Shaanmer(IRE) Eva De Chalamont (FR) (Iron Duke (FR))
(1754) 2438[2] 3284[5] 4070[5] 4452[3] 5185[7]

After Hours (IRE) *Henry Oliver* 119h
6 b g Milan Supreme Singer (IRE) (Supreme Leader)
1909[3] 2265[5] 2763[5] (3152) 3917[4] 4484[6]

After Rain (FR) *J R Barry* 132h
5 br g Al Namix(FR) La Lorelei (FR) (Passing Sale (FR))
3650a[11]

Agapanthus (GER) *Neil Mulholland* 106h 105c
10 b g Tiger Hill(IRE) Astilbe (GER) (Monsun (GER))
170[F] (284) (740a) 844a[2] **1353[5]**

Agenor (GER) *Jamie Snowden* 122h 101c
4 b g Medicean Acerba (GER) (Monsun (GER))
1234[7] (1305) 1480[4] **5278[4]**

Agentleman (IRE) *Tim Easterby* 89h 97c
5 b g Trans Island Silvine (IRE) (Shernazar)
2106[4] 2498[3] 2890[4] **3345[P] 3845[2] 3968[7] 4985[P]**

Agent Louise *Mike Sowersby* 94h
7 b m Alflora(IRE) Oso Special (Teenoso (USA))
398[P] 522[8] 758[3] 838[P] 939[P] 1972[7] 3067[8] 3378[2] 4557[5] 4804[4] (4942) (5233) 5402[P]

Age Of Discovery *Dan Skelton* 94h
4 b g Nayef(USA) Magic Tree (UAE) (Timber Country (USA))
171[3] 396[2] 776[8]

Age Of Glory *Barry Murtagh* 112h
6 b g Zamindar(USA) Fleeting Moon (Fleetwood (IRE))
82[4] 780[5] 4055[5]

Agesilas (FR) *Andrew Crook* 64h
7 gr g Ultimately Lucky(IRE) Aimessa Du Berlais (FR) (Nikos)
153[P] 3161[3] 3840[8] 4297[8] 4536[2] 4797[7]

Agha Des Mottes (FR) *Ian Williams* 98h
5 b g Mister Sacha(FR) Java Des Mottes (FR) (Passing Sale (FR))
433[5] 2888[5]

Agincourt Reef (IRE) *Gary Moore* 118h 118c
6 b g Gold Well Hillside Native (IRE) (Be My Native (USA))
2957[4] 3931[4] 4197[2] (4453) 4670[2]

Aglaja *Steph Hollinshead*
6 b m Tiger Cafe(JPN) Undovica (Primo Dominie)
361[P]

A Good Skin (IRE) *Tom George* 122h 143c
6 b g Presenting Trixskin (IRE) (Buckskin (FR))
2055[5] 2348[3] 3406[9] 4101[2] 4735[2] 5327[P]

Agrapart (FR) *Nick Williams* 151h
4 bb g Martaline Afragha (IRE) (Darshaan)
1909[5] 2363[2] (2898) 3447[3] (4115) 5190[6]

Agreement (IRE) *Nikki Evans* 117h
5 b g Galileo(IRE) Cozzene's Angel (USA) (Cozzene (USA))
2906[8] 3978[7]

Agricultural *Lucy Normile* 59h 98c
9 b g Daylami(IRE) Rustic (IRE) (Grand Lodge (USA))
872[9] **1330[9] 1496[5] 1629[U] 1853[P]**

Aguicheuse (FR) *Francois Nicolle* 117h 115c
5 b m Lavirco(GER) Nouvelle Vague (FR) (Ragmar (FR))
350a[11]

A Hairy Koala (FR) *David Pipe* 105h
5 ch g Dom Alco(FR) Kandy De Vonnas (FR) (Cadoudal (FR))
1100[6] 1264[10] 1819[8] 1951[8]

A Hare Breath (IRE) *Ben Pauling* 138h
7 b g Alkaadhem Lady Willmurt (IRE) (Mandalus)
(2472) 3015[4] (3775) 4786[P]

Ahhdehken *Alistair Whillans* 84h
10 b g Cloudings(IRE) Swazi Princess (IRE) (Brush Aside (USA))
291[4]

Ah Littleluck (IRE) *Thomas Gibney* 121h
5 b g Mahler Star Of Hope (IRE) (Turtle Island (IRE))
5024a[7]

Ahzana (FR) *L Viel* 113h
4 b m Voix Du Nord(FR) Quela De Casmar (FR) (Smadoun (FR))
2362a[2]

Aiaam Al Namoos *John Wade* 117h
6 b g Teofilo(IRE) Deveron (USA) (Cozzene (USA))
319[4] 705[P]

Aigle De La See (FR) *Nicky Henderson* 130h 105c
5 gr g Al Namix(FR) Janita De La See (FR) (Useful (FR))
2897[4] 3348[B] 3818[P] 4241[12] 5300[4]

Aigrette De Loire (FR) *G Cherel* 127h 127c
5 ch m Network(GER) Gribiche (FR) (Montorselli)
350a[5]

Ainsi Fideles (FR) *David Pipe* 101h 151c
5 ch g Dream Well(FR) Loya Lescribaa (FR) (Robin Des Champs (FR))
198[3] 855[P]

Aintree My Dream (FR) *Dan Skelton* 125b
5 bb g Saint Des Saints(FR) Pretty Melodie (FR) (Lesotho (USA))
(5143) ◆

Air Chief *Andrew Crook* 97h 92c
10 ch g Dr Fong(USA) Fly For Fame (Shaadi (USA))
3307[P] 3628[P]

Airebridge (IRE) *Michael Easterby* 56h
4 b g Publisher(USA) Old Society (IRE) (Dr Devious (IRE))
2597[9] 2917[P] 3063[7]

Air Glider (IRE) *Dan Skelton* 111h
5 b g Mountain High(IRE) California Blue (FR) (Pebble (FR))
852[2] 1044[3] 4152[F] 4877[P] 5237[2]
Air Horse One *Harry Fry* 122h
4 gr g Mountain High(IRE) Whisky Rose (IRE) (Old Vic)
(124) 2065[2] 2683[7] 3745[2] 4594[U] 4798[3]
Air Of Glory (IRE) *Martin Bosley* 101h
5 ch g Shamardal(USA) Balloura (USA) (Swain (IRE))
1453[2] 1676[3] 2253[P]
Airpur Desbois (FR) *Charlie Mann* 105h
5 b g Canyon Creek(IRE) Hero's Dancer (FR) (Hero's Honor (USA))
865[7] 1122[5] 1290[3] 1507[3] 1699[4] 2658[4] 3174[6] 4860[P]
Aka Doun (FR) *Emma Lavelle* 93h
4 b g Smadoun(FR) Akar Baby (Akarad (FR))
1648[10] 2154[8] 2995[8] 4543[4] 5355[6]
Akavit (IRE) *Ed de Giles* 122h
3 b g Vale Of York(IRE) Along Came Molly (Dr Fong (USA))
2273[6] (2718) (3988) 4720[P] 5095[P]
A Keen Sense (GER) *David Dennis* 89h 82c
6 b g Sholokhov(IRE) All Our Luck (GER) (Spectrum (IRE))
1080[10] 1237[4] (1326)
Akinspirit (IRE) *Nikki Evans* 107h 97c
11 b g Invincible Spirit(IRE) Akebia (USA) (Trempolino (USA))
1376[3] 2449[6] 2851[3] 3108[3] 3932[10]
Akula (IRE) *Barry Leavy* 116h 88c
8 ch g Soviet Star(USA) Danielli (IRE) (Danehill (USA))
465[6] 2218[2] 2540[4] 2961[2] 3238[7] 3784[2] 4129[5] 4448[5]
Alabama Le Dun (FR) *J-P Gallorini* 119h 113c
5 bl g Network(GER) Silvazeyra (FR) (Sheyrann (IRE))
437a[7]
Aladdins Cave *R K Watson* 128h 119c
11 b g Rainbow Quest(USA) Flight Of Fancy (Sadler's Wells (USA))
2206a[F]
Alajmal (USA) *Janet E Elliot* 114h
7 b g First Samurai(USA) Alattrah (USA) (Shadeed (USA))
1983a[7]
Al Alfa *Philip Hobbs* 125h 134c
8 ch g Alflora(IRE) Two For Joy (IRE) (Mandalus)
(1382) (1576) 2153[3] 2877[P] 5193[10]
Alamein (IRE) *M F Morris* 130h
5 b g Beneficial Lady Of Appeal (IRE) (Lord Of Appeal)
53a[7]
Alanjou (FR) *Henry Tett* 64h 116c
5 b g Maresca Sorrento(FR) Partie Time (FR) (Nononito (FR))
3146[8] 4027[3] 4450[P]
A Lasting Joy *Jonathan Geake*
4 b m Refuse To Bend(IRE) Sir Kyffin's Folly (Dansili)
5069[14]
Albahar (FR) *Chris Gordon* 109h
4 gr g Dark Angel(IRE) Downland (USA) (El Prado (IRE))
3777[6] 4411[2]
Alba King (IRE) *Sue Smith* 27h 81c
9 b g Beauchamp King Alba Dancer (Gran Alba (USA))
1080[7] 1367[4] 1569[4] 1744[4]
Albatros De Guye (FR) *Anna Newton-Smith* 30h 90c
5 ch g Maille Pistol(FR) Balibirds (FR) (Bricassar (USA))
1999[4] (2416) 2698[4] 3834[P] (4073) 4503[2]
Alberobello (IRE) *Jeremy Scott* 128h 129c
7 b g Old Vic Tourist Attraction (IRE) (Pollerton)
169[2] 553[2] 3978[3] ◆ 4340[P] 5154[4]
Alberta (IRE) *Jim Best* 118h
6 ch g Choisir(AUS) Akita (IRE) (Foxhound (USA))
2699[2] 3418[2] 5148[2] 5246[4]
Albert D'Olivate (FR) *Robert Walford* 115h 73c
5 bb g Alberto Giacometti(IRE) Komunion (FR) (Luchiroverte (IRE))
2456[7] 3705[3] 4099[2] 4342[2] (4618)
Albert Herring *Jonathan Portman* 94h
3 b g Tobougg(IRE) Balsamita (FR) (Midyan (USA))
1732[3] 2092[2] 2273[4] 2954[3]
Alberto's Dream *Tom Symonds* 102h 110c
6 b g Fantastic Spain(USA) Molly's Folly (My Lamb)
3384[P] 3867[P] 4073[2] (4503) 4978[3]
Alcala (FR) *Paul Nicholls* 130h
5 gr g Turgeon(USA) Pail Mel (FR) (Sleeping Car (FR))
(2024) 2470[4] 2641[4] ◆ 3254[6] (4196) 4620[3] ◆ 5329[2]
Alchimix (FR) *Micky Hammond* 106h
5 b g Al Namix(FR) Julie Noire (FR) (Agent Bleu (FR))
2196[U] 2498[7] 2801[9] 3398[10] 3973[4] 4570[5] 5079[7]
Al Co (FR) *Peter Bowen* 111h 137c
10 ch g Dom Alco(FR) Carama (FR) (Tip Moss (FR))
2783[P] 3404[7] 4066[7] 5217[3] ◆
Alco Sivola (FR) *Fergal O'Brien* 109h
5 gr g Dom Alco(FR) Oeuvre Vive (FR) (Robin Des Champs (FR))
999[P] 1647[6] ◆ 2042[P] (Dead)
Aldeburgh *Nigel Twiston-Davies* 108h
6 b g Oasis Dream Orford Ness (Selkirk (USA))
3022[2] 4506[6] ◆
Alderbrook Lad (IRE) *Micky Hammond* 136h 146c
9 ch g Alderbrook Alone Tabankulu (IRE) (Phardante (FR))
184[10] (470) (849) 1268[2] 1417[4] 2335[6] 2935[P] 3425[F] 5200[5] 5448[7]

Alderley Heights *Polly Gundry* 94h
6 b m Windsor Heights Alderley Girl (Footloose Esquire)
(5034) 5431[3]
Alder Mairi (IRE) *Seamus Mullins* 129h 128c
8 ch m Alderbrook Amari Queen (Nicholas Bill)
107[3] (2601) (3044) 3706[F] 4158[2] 4647[F] 5281[F]
Alderwood (IRE) *Thomas Mullins* 139h 156c
11 b g Alderbrook Clamit Falls (IRE) (Homo Sapien)
1152a[4]
Alefou D'Airy (FR) *Jimmy Frost* 30h 97c
5 b g Anzillero(GER) Lafolie D'Airy (FR) (Oblat (FR))
27[P] 390[4] 2989[11] 3466[P]
Aleksandar *Jim Goldie* 82h
6 ch g Medicean Alexander Celebre (FR) (Peintre Celebre (USA))
2189[9] 2428[P]
Alelchi Inois (FR) *W P Mullins* 142h 152c
7 b g Night Tango(GER) Witness Gama (FR) (Take Risks (FR))
1152a[6] 1556a[F] 1763a[2] 2232a[4]
Alert *Jonathan Portman* 66h
3 b f Zamindar(USA) Tereshkina (IRE) (Sadler's Wells (USA))
2537[7]
Alexander Oats *Robert Goldie* 71b 21c
12 b g Insan(USA) Easter Oats (Oats)
5261[8]
Alexander The Grey *Graeme McPherson* 96b
4 gr g Fair Mix(IRE) Cadourova (FR) (Cadoudal (FR))
2842[4]
Alex Girl (IRE) *W McCreery* 85b
4 b m Nayef(USA) Rise And Fall (USA) (Quiet American (USA))
11a[13]
Al Fatih (IRE) *Steve Flook* 79h
4 b g Montjeu(IRE) Sky High Flyer (Anabaa (USA))
3021[12] 4441[13]
Al Ferof (FR) *Dan Skelton* 153h 171c
10 gr g Dom Alco(FR) Maralta (FR) (Altayan)
(2927) 3231[3] 4731[4] 5192[2]
Alfiboy *Paul Webber* 107h
5 b g Alflora(IRE) Cloudy Pearl (Cloudings (IRE))
98[2]
Alfie's Choice (IRE) *Kim Bailey* 88b
3 b g Shantou(USA) Bally Bolshoi (IRE) (Bob Back (USA))
5127[4]
Alfie Spinner (IRE) *Kerry Lee* 124h 135c
10 b g Alflora(IRE) Little Red Spider (Bustino)
1871[4] 2348[8] (5052)
Alfloreda *Nick Gifford* 44b
6 b g Alflora(IRE) Hi Breda (IRE) (Camden Town)
242[10]
Alf 'N' Dor (IRE) *Peter Bowen* 120b
4 ch g Flemensfirth(USA) Greenflag Princess (IRE) (Executive Perk)
188[5] 1797[3] (3573) 3980[2]
Alfredo (IRE) *Seamus Durack* 104b
3 ch g Arcano(IRE) Western Sky (Barathea (IRE))
(5069) ◆
Alfred Oats *Robert Goldie* 95c
11 b g Alflora(IRE) Easter Oats (Oats)
2430[5] 2786[6]
Alf The Audacious *Sue Smith* 60h 103c
9 gr g Alflora(IRE) Rua Ros (IRE) (Roselier (FR))
1370[7] 2147[U]
Alf Wright (IRE) *Tracey L Bailey* 116h 121c
9 bb g King's Theatre(IRE) Bobby Dolphin (IRE) (Bob Back (USA))
1381[5] 1661[5] 1818[9] 2168[3] 3585[P]
Algernon Pazham (IRE) *Nigel Twiston-Davies* 129h 145c
6 b g Milan Kitty Star (IRE) (Montelimar (USA))
2436[2] ◆ 2899[U] 3624[F] 3741[P] 4697[6]
Al Guwair (IRE) *Mark Hoad* 69h
5 b g Shirocco(GER) Katariya (IRE) (Barathea (IRE))
451[9] 599[P] 1245[3] 1427[5] 1756[9] 2015[2] 2256[8]
Alhamareer (IRE) *Paul Webber* 102h
3 ch g Teofilo(IRE) Ribot's Guest (IRE) (Be My Guest (USA))
2992[7] 4038[3] 4304[3] 4619[2]
Alianca (IRE) *Lawney Hill* 73h
4 ch m Heliostatic(IRE) Midris (IRE) (Namid)
1506[7]
Aliandy (IRE) *Kim Bailey* 108h
4 b g Presenting Water Rock (El Conquistador)
341[5] 1929[2] 2163[P] 2581[3] 3398[3]
Alibaba Precieux (FR) *Mme M Desvaux* 105h
5 gr g Al Namix(FR) Kalikrates (FR) (Cyborg (FR))
5136a[P]
Alibi De Sivola (FR) *Paul Nicholls* 122h
5 bb g Shaanmer(IRE) Neva De Sivola (FR) (Blushing Flame (USA))
2267[2] (2801)
Alice Pink (IRE) *Paul Henderson* 105b
5 b m Milan That's The Goose (IRE) (Be My Native (USA))
4201[3] 4847[3] (5241)
Alisier D'Irlande (FR) *Henry De Bromhead* 120h 151c
5 bb g Kapgarde(FR) Isati'S (FR) (Chamberlin (FR))
5215[5]
A Little Bit Dusty *Conor Dore* 121h
7 ch g Needwood Blade Dusty Dazzler (IRE) (Titus Livius (FR))
186[2] 354[4] (1376) (2150) 2218[5] 2808[4] 3417[P]
A Little Magic (IRE) *Jonjo O'Neill* 116h
4 b g Kayf Tara Debut (IRE) (Presenting)
1519[6] 1613[2] (1929)
Alizee De Janeiro (FR) *Lucinda Russell* 114h
5 b m Network(GER) Katana (GER) (Funambule (USA))
(2069) 2343[2] (2933) 3346[2] 4272[4] 4909[9]
Alizee Javilex (FR) *Lucy Wadham* 101h
5 b m Le Fou(FR) Etoile Du Lion (FR) (New Target)
67[U] 594[10] (1811) 2929[3] 3485[2]

Al Jaz (CZE) *Jan Blecha* 135c
9 ch g Moonjaz Arani (SWI) (Law Society (USA))
1885a[F]
Alkia D'Oudairies (FR) *A Le Clerc* 86b
5 b m Svedov(FR) Pythie D'Oudairies (FR) (Grand Tresor (FR))
2536a[2]
Allanard (IRE) *Martin Todhunter* 90h 121c
11 b g Oscar(IRE) Allatrim (IRE) (Montelimar (USA))
420[5]
Alla Svelta (IRE) *Brendan Powell* 105h 108c
9 b g Milan Miss Greinton (GER) (Greinton)
170[U] 449[6] 669[5] 776[9] 1012[5] 1237[2] ◆ 1487[F]
Allbarnone *William Kinsey* 113h
7 b g Alflora(IRE) What A Gem (Karinga Bay)
468[2] 833[5] 3837[5] ◆ 5157[2] 5277[6]
Allblak Des Places (FR) *W P Mullins* 139h
3 bb g Full Of Gold(FR) Amiraute (FR) (Septieme Ciel (USA))
4002a[2]
All But Grey *Carroll Gray* 105h 107c
9 gr g Baryshnikov(AUS) Butleigh Rose (Nicholas Bill)
(170) 514[4] 2552[4] 3257[P]
Allchilledout *Colin Tizzard* 110h
6 b g Alflora(IRE) Miss Chinchilla (Perpendicular)
1998[6] 2563[3] 2871[P] 3586[5] (4291) 5034[2] 5382[7]
Allee Bleue (IRE) *Philip Hobbs* 134h
5 ch g Mount Nelson Murrieta (Docksider (USA))
2221[P] 2723[5] 3114[6] (3484) (3745) ◆ 4622[5] (4976) 5219[14]
Allegri (IRE) *Alan Coogan* 45h
6 b g Key Of Luck(USA) Bermuxa (FR) (Linamix (FR))
3418[11]
Allelu Alleluia (GER) *Jonjo O'Neill* 89h
4 b g Doyen(IRE) Anna Spectra (IRE) (Spectrum (IRE))
5469[10]
Allerford Jack *Richard Woollacott* 69h 83c
11 br g Overbury(IRE) Jiggiwithit (Distant Relative)
266[P] (Dead)
Allerton (IRE) *Fergal O'Brien* 89b 110c
8 b g Flemensfirth(USA) Bonny Hall (IRE) (Saddlers' Hall (IRE))
90[6] 3585[P] 5121[P]
Allez Cool (IRE) *John Wade* 104h
6 ch g Flemensfirth(USA) La Fisarmonica (IRE) (Accordion)
2802[8]
Allez Encore (IRE) *Kim Bailey* 126h
6 b m Turtle Island(IRE) Glebe Beauty (IRE) (Good Thyne (USA))
2199[4] 2852[3]
Allez Sea (IRE) *James Leavy* 91b
3 b g Sea The Stars(IRE) Alizaya (IRE) (Highest Honor (FR))
2368[3]
Allez Vic (IRE) *Evan Williams* 125h 133c
9 b g Old Vic Newgate Fairy (IRE) (Flair Path)
1809[P] 2367[4] 2908[3] 3518[U] 4354[14] 5238[3]
All Fired Up (IRE) *Evan Williams* 81h 110c
8 b g Mr Combustible(IRE) Hannah's Retreat (IRE) (Houmayoun (FR))
771[5]
All Force Majeure (FR) *David Pipe* 100h
5 gr g Dom Alco(FR) Naiade Du Moulin (FR) (Ragmar (FR))
265[4] 716[3]
All For Lily *Charles Pogson* 88b
6 b m Alflora(IRE) Who Let The Foxout (Saddlers' Hall (IRE))
679[P]
All Hell Let Loose (IRE) *Ms Sandra Hughes* 142h 136c
6 b g Shantou(USA) Gan Ainm (IRE) (Mujadil (USA))
4730[16]
All In Favour (IRE) *Jonjo O'Neill* 72h
4 b g Mahler Tisindabreedin (IRE) (Zaffaran (USA))
1826[6]
All Kings (IRE) *Harry Fry* 115h
6 b g Milan Rilmount (IRE) (Roselier (FR))
2257[P] 2558[P] 5430[2] ◆
Allnecessaryforce (FR) *Alex Hales* 104h
5 gr g Verglas(IRE) Kosmic View (USA) (Distant View (USA))
1898[7] 2287[4] 2694[6]
Allow Dallow (IRE) *Jonjo O'Neill* 118h 123c
8 b g Gold Well Russland (GER) (Surumu (GER))
(2645) ◆ 3115[5] 4841[3] 5439[3]
All Riled Up *Harry Chisman* 91h
7 b m Dr Massini(IRE) Martha Reilly (IRE) (Rainbows For Life (CAN))
675[7] (977) 1297[6] 1716[5] 1816[2] 2015[4]
All Set To Go (IRE) *Paul Nicholls* 134h
4 gr g Verglas(IRE) Firecrest (IRE) (Darshaan)
(2840) ◆ 3135[4] 3708[10] (4849) (5416)
Allstar Vinnie (IRE) *Tom Lacey*
5 ch g Vinnie Roe(IRE) Inniscarra Lass (IRE) (Fourstars Allstar (USA))
3570[P]
All That Remains (IRE) *Susan Corbett* 116h 102c
10 b g King's Theatre(IRE) Morning Breeze (IRE) (Bigstone (IRE))
802[6]
All The Answers *A P O'Brien* 117h
4 br g Kayf Tara Shatabdi (IRE) (Mtoto)
4280a[5]
Allthedollars (IRE) *Joanne Foster* 73h
5 ch g Stowaway Pamsy Wamsy (IRE) (Taipan (IRE))
1888[P] 2707[P]
Allthegear No Idea (IRE) *Nigel Twiston-Davies* 122h
8 b g Sayarshan(FR) All The Gear (IRE) (Nashamaa)
404[4]
Allthekingshorses (IRE) *Philip Hobbs* 133h 129c
9 b g King's Theatre(IRE) Penny Brae (IRE) (Montelimar (USA))
1616[5] 1807[10] 2471[10]

All The Winds (GER) *Shaun Lycett* 105h
10 ch g Samum(GER) All Our Luck (GER) (Spectrum (IRE))
1801[1]
All Together (FR) *Johnny Farrelly* 110h 135c
4 ch g Zambezi Sun Mareha (IRE) (Cadeaux Genereux)
207[3] 566[2] ◆ 2019[3] (2765) 3134[2] 3620[6] (4210) 4617[4] 5118[4]
All Together (USA) *David Jacobson* 132h
10 b g Danzig(USA) Unify (USA) (Farma Way (USA))
1983a[4]
Allycat *Chris Grant* 79h
5 b g Beat All(USA) Alikat (IRE) (Alhaarth (IRE))
(257) 590[P] 730[P] 933[6] 1030[6] 1329[10] 1400[8]
All You Need (FR) *Alan Fleming* 133h 132c
5 b m Crillon(FR) Californie (FR) (Mistigri)
3071a[5]
All Yours (FR) *Paul Nicholls* 145h
4 ch g Halling(USA) Fontaine Riant (FR) (Josr Algarhoud (IRE))
2350[5] 4765[12]
Allysson Monterg (FR) *Richard Hobson* 135h
5 b g Network(GER) Mellyssa (FR) (Panoramic)
2860[2] 3403[2] ◆ (3920) 4766[6]
Almaas (USA) *Kevin Bishop* 94h
6 ch g Hard Spun(USA) Summer Dream Girl (USA) (Unbridled (USA))
119[5] 360[5] 860[4]
Almagest *Robert Stephens* 96h
7 br g Galileo(IRE) Arabesque (Zafonic (USA))
893[4] 999[4] 1117[3] 1295[2] 1721[F] 1819[6]
Almahoy *Andrew Crook* 78b
4 b m Martaline Tokahy (FR) (Kahyasi)
1926[6]
Almost Gemini (IRE) *Kenneth Slack* 119h 65c
6 gr g Dylan Thomas(IRE) Streetcar (IRE) (In The Wings)
(2426) 3344[4] (3680) 4035[2] ◆ (4328) 4801[5]
Al Musheer (FR) *Donald McCain* 85h
4 gr h Verglas(IRE) Canzonetta (FR) (Kahyasi)
1571[0]
Along Came Theo (IRE) *Andrew Crook* 98h
5 b g Vertical Speed(FR) Kachina (IRE) (Mandalus)
3056[3] 3626[7]
Alongthewatchtower (IRE) *Barry Brennan* 75h
7 b g Heron Island(IRE) Manesbil (IRE) (Fourstars Allstar (USA))
378[P] 1990[6]
Aloomomo (FR) *Warren Greatrex* 136h 144c
5 b g Tirwanako(FR) Kayola (FR) (Royal Charter (FR))
(2168) (2276) (2780) ◆ 4236[3] 4701[6]
Alottarain (IRE) *Seamus Mullins* 102h
5 b m Zerpour(IRE) Alottalady (IRE) (Mandalus)
268[2] ◆ 714[3] 1009[4] 2088[P] 2604[4] 3089[6] (4885) 5433[P]
A Lovable Rogue *R Mike Smith*
3 b g Dutch Art Dance Card (Cape Cross (IRE))
2324[P]
Alphabet Bay (IRE) *Warren Greatrex* 105h
5 b g Kalanisi(IRE) A And Bs Gift (IRE) (Mr Combustible (IRE))
5353[2]
Alpha Des Obeaux (FR) *M F Morris* 170h
5 b g Saddler Maker(IRE) Omega Des Obeaux (FR) (Saint Preuil (FR))
72a[2] 2815a[2] 3322a[2] (3713a) 4732[2]
Alpha Native *Alan Hill* 78c
11 b g Alflora(IRE) Cassia (Be My Native (USA))
292[6]
Alpha Victor (IRE) *William Kinsey* 114h 116c
10 b g Old Vic Harvest View (IRE) (Good Thyne (USA))
2431[P] 3999[5] 4340[R] 5265[P]
Alpine Secret (IRE) *Ben Pauling* 87b
3 br g Stowaway Squaw Valley (IRE) (Saddlers' Hall (IRE))
4880[8]
Al Reesha (IRE) *Dan Skelton* 113b
4 b m Kayf Tara Simply Kitty (IRE) (Simply Great (FR))
2277[6] 3847[5] (4168)
Alright Benny (IRE) *Paul Henderson* 90h 102c
12 ch g Beneficial Flashey Thyne (IRE) (Good Thyne (USA))
(126) 280[5]
Alskamatic *Richard J Bandey* 120c
9 b g Systematic Alska (FR) (Leading Counsel (USA))
17[2] 4768[10]
Alta Rock (IRE) *Sue Smith* 112h 101c
10 b g Luso Princess Lulu (IRE) (Carroll House (IRE))
934[7] (1462) 1930[2] 2173[P] 2297[6]
Alternatif (FR) *David Pipe* 135h 145c
5 b g Shaanmer(IRE) Katerinette (FR) (Video Rock (FR))
196[2] 505[2] 2473[3] (2955) 3404[4] ◆ 4735[P] 5224[2]
Alterno (IRE) *Desmond McDonogh* 104h
3 b g Fastnet Rock(AUS) Altarejos (IRE) (Vettori (IRE))
5001a[5]
Altesse De Guye (FR) *Martin Keighley* 118h
5 ch m Dom Alco(FR) Mascotte De Guye (FR) (Video Rock (FR))
2268[4] ◆ 2632[2] 4186[4] 4779[3] (5277)
Altiepix (FR) *Gordon Elliott* 129h 129c
5 ch g Fragrant Mix(IRE) Naltiepy (FR) (Dom Alco (FR))
2225a[4] 4663a[U]
Altior (IRE) *Nicky Henderson* 163h
5 b g High Chaparral(IRE) Monte Solaro (IRE) (Key Of Luck (USA))
23[6] (1844) (2183) (2509) (3227) ◆ (4695) ◆
Alto Des Mottes (FR) *Henry Hogarth* 111h 134c
5 b g Dream Well(FR) Omance (FR) (Video Rock (FR))
(201) 2026[4] 2400[5] 2848[3] (3160) 3591[2] 4286[P] 4914[3]

Alto Esqua (FR) *C Byrnes* 118h
5 br g Network(GER) Kemia (FR) (Beyssac (FR))
4955a[7]

Alton Bay (IRE) *Peter Fahey* 130h
7 b g Pushkin(IRE) Miss Chapman (IRE) (Imperial Ballet (IRE))
73a[5]

Altruism (IRE) *James Moffatt* 130h
5 b g Authorized(IRE) Bold Assumption (Observatory (USA))
(1065) ◆ (1399) 2626[4] 4010[P] 4869[2] ◆ 5190[U]

Alvarado (IRE) *Fergal O'Brien* 125h 143c
10 ch g Goldmark(USA) Mrs Jones (IRE) (Roselier (FR))
4483[8] 5327[2]

Alwareed *John Wade* 82b
3 ch g Makfi Sinduda (Anabaa (USA))
2923[6] 3165[P]

Always Archie *Robert Stephens* 124h
8 b g Silver Patriarch(IRE) Angel Dust (FR) (Cadoudal (FR))
967[7]

Always Bold (IRE) *Martin Keighley* 110h 109c
10 ch g King's Best(USA) Tarakana (USA) (Shahrastani (USA))
926[7] 1114[P]

Always Lion (IRE) *Ben Pauling* 125h
5 b g Let The Lion Roar Addie's Choice (IRE) (Norwich)
2023[2] (2450)

Always Managing *Warren Greatrex* 107h
6 b m Oscar(IRE) Sunshine Rays (Alflora (IRE))
938[3] (1236) 1490[3]

Always On The Run (IRE) *Tom George* 116h 141c
5 br g Robin Des Pres(FR) Kerrys Cottage (IRE) (Leading Counsel (USA))
330[4] (648) 834[2] 1030[2] **3384[4] (4098) (4785)** ◆ **5326[U]**

Alwaysrecommended (IRE) *Jane Walton* 77h
6 ch g Gamut(IRE) Awbeg Beauty (IRE) (Supreme Leader)
328[2] 1683[8] 1920[6] 2937[P]

Always Resolute *Brian Ellison* 135h
4 b g Refuse To Bend(IRE) Mad Annie (USA) (Anabaa (USA))
(3309) 3590[F] 4010[4] 4791[2] 5325[8]

Alwaystheoptimist *Shaun Lycett* 118h 128c
12 b g Muhtarram(USA) Miss Optimist (Relkino)
556[5] 862[3] (1100) **1296[3]** 1549[3] **1617[5]**

Always Tipsy *N W Alexander* 123h
6 b g Dushyantor(USA) French Pick (USA) (Johannesburg (USA))
2190[2] 3018[P] 3428[9] 4206[8] 5260[5]

Alyasan (IRE) *Seamus Durack* 98h
4 ch g Sea The Stars(IRE) Alaya (IRE) (Ela-Mana-Mou)
(865) ◆ (1300) 1898[6] 2056[5] 3019[7]

Alys Rock (IRE) *Michael Appleby* 100h
6 gr m Medaaly Rock Slide (IRE) (Bob Back (USA))
366[5] 860[7] 1094[5] 1179[7] 1427[4] 1683[5] 1974[7] 2559[4] 3729[P] 5019[3] 5313[P]

Alzammaar (USA) *Warren Greatrex* 131h
4 b g Birdstone(USA) Alma Mater (Sadler's Wells (USA))
2513[7] 3027[3] 4911[8] (5396)

Amalfi Doug (FR) *Michael Blanshard* 95b
5 gr g Network(GER) Queissa (FR) (Saint Preuil (FR))
2044[6] *3200[5]*

Amanto (GER) *Paul Nicholls* 124h
5 b g Medicean Amore (GER) (Lando (GER))
2458[2] 2725[7] 5378[2]

Amaragon (CZE) *Pavel Poles*
10 b g Rainbows For Life(CAN) Amadara (CZE) (Dara Monarch)
1885a[F]

Amazing D'Azy (IRE) *Kim Bailey* 115h 84c
7 br m Presenting Shuil Mavourneen (IRE) (Welsh Term)
382[6] 756[P] 1007[F] 1490[8]

Amazone Du Lemo (FR) *A Le Clerc* 87h 108c
5 b m Roli Abi(FR) Iris De La Nuit (FR) (Gaspard De La Nuit (FR))
(5499a)

Amazone Mome (FR) *J Delaunay* 49b
5 b m Honolulu(IRE) Iphanie (FR) (Panoramic)
2536a[8]

Amber Alert *Anthony Honeyball* 103b
5 b m Vitus Imperial Amber (Emperor Fountain)
152[8] 2929[10] 4687[5]

Amber Flush *Martin Smith* 104h 110c
6 b m Sir Harry Lewis(USA) Sari Rose (FR) (Vertical Speed (FR))
808[2] 913[4] 1134[3] 1272[4] 1547[5] (1771) 1897[4] 4804[5]

Amber Gambler (GER) *Ian Williams* 83h
5 b g Doyen(IRE) Auenglocke (GER) (Surumu (GER))
4388[7] 5048[7] 5242[6]

Amber Spyglass *David Bridgwater* 107b
5 ch g Act One Northern Bows (Bertolini (USA))
1484[2] 1998[0]

Ambion Lane (IRE) *Victor Dartnall* 104h
5 b g Scorpion(IRE) Thrilling Prospect (IRE) (King's Ride)
3258[3] 3920[P] 4137[4] 4614[4]

Ambion Wood (IRE) *Victor Dartnall* 111h 85c
9 b g Oscar(IRE) Dorans Grove (Gildoran)
2669[P] 3254[10] 3705[9] 4342[P]

Ambitious Pursuit (IRE) *Mrs L Glanville* 104c
7 b g Cloudings(IRE) Gladriels Jem (IRE) (Mister Lord (USA))
4295[4] 4437[P]

Ambre Des Marais (FR) *Alison Batchelor* 88h
5 ch m Network(GER) Fee Des Marais (FR) (Chamberlin (FR))
1816[8]

Ame En Peine (FR) *Christian Le Galliard* 91b
5 b m Saint Des Saints(FR) Haldiana (FR) (Garde Royale)
2536a[3]

American (FR) *Harry Fry* 138h
5 b g Malinas(GER) Grande Sultane (FR) (Garde Royale)
2080[3] (2630) 4955a[6]

American Gigolo *Sally Hall* 75b
3 b g Azamour(IRE) Sadie Thompson (IRE) (King's Best (USA))
2216[5] 3165[4]

American Legend (IRE) *Jonjo O'Neill* 112h 125c
7 b g Presenting Coole Eile (IRE) (King's Ride)
523[P] 760[3] (1007) 1288[2] 1722[3] 3339[U]

American Life (FR) *Sophie Leech* 122h
8 bb g American Post Poplife (FR) (Zino)
1911[8] 2125[P] 2367[7] 2694[11] 2924[7] (3361) 3383[3] 3498[3] 3904[3] 4127[5] 4467[3] 4596[6]

American Spin *Luke Dace* 92h 115c
11 ch g Groom Dancer(USA) Sea Vixen (Machiavellian (USA))
448[5] 681[6]

American World (FR) *Lady Susan Brooke* 77h 77c
11 bb g Lost World(IRE) Rose Laura (FR) (Rose Laurel)
527[6] **698[4] 2666[3] 5078[P]**

Amethyst Rose (IRE) *Stuart Coltherd* 60h 116c
8 ch m Beneficial Cap The Rose (IRE) (Roselier (FR))
202[2] 2342[4] 2805[P] 3343[6] 3937[F] 4406[6]

Ami Desbois (FR) *Graeme McPherson* 129h
5 b g Dream Well(FR) Baroya (FR) (Garde Royale)
2493[4] ◆ 3037[2] 3509[2] 3859[3] 5194[8]

Amidon (FR) *Lucy Wadham* 125h 126c
5 b g Dom Alco(FR) Immage (FR) (Bad Conduct (USA))
2182[8] 2558[P] **(2957) 3349[2] 3818[3] 4971[P] 5092[6] 5456[6]**

Amigo (FR) *David Pipe* 107h 137c
8 b g Ballingarry(IRE) Allez Y (FR) (Pistolet Bleu (IRE))
532[4] **4735[5] 5283[5]**

Amilliontimes (IRE) *Jackie Stephen* 103h 98c
7 b g Olden Times Miss Million (IRE) (Roselier (FR))
508[7] 661[6] 872[6] **1630[3] 1853[3] 2293[3] 5261[3]**

Aminabad (FR) *W P Mullins* 140h 115c
5 b g Singspiel(IRE) Amenapinga (FR) (Spinning World (USA))
73a[6] 1163a[14] 3071a[8]

Amiral Collonges (FR) *James Evans* 126h 113c
5 ch g Dom Alco(FR) Idole Collonges (FR) (Brezzo (FR))
2591[3] (3146) 3844[P] 4389[4]

Amirli (IRE) *Donald McCain* 81h
4 ch g Medicean Amenapinga (FR) (Spinning World (USA))
489[P] 1786[P]

Amir Pasha (UAE) *Micky Hammond* 93h 78c
10 br g Halling(USA) Clarinda (IRE) (Lomond (USA))
34[6] 137[4] **256[6] 504[5] 728[6]**

Amirr (IRE) *John Ferguson* 119b
5 b g New Approach(IRE) Dress Uniform (USA) (Red Ransom (USA))
(753) (963) 1246[2]

Amore Alato *Johnny Farrelly* 140h 150c
6 b g Winged Love(IRE) Sardagna (FR) (Medaaly)
2222[4] 2846[2] 3136[U] 3738[2] 4240[4] 4701[9]

Amour Collonges (FR) *Chris Grant* 75h
5 b g Lavirco(GER) Kapucine Collonges (FR) (Dom Alco (FR))
132[P] 621[5] 966[6]

Amour D'Or *Nick Williams* 104h
4 b m Winged Love(IRE) Diletia (Dilum (USA))
111[5] 433[2] 813[2] (1231a) 1841[5] 2022[3] 5499a[4]

Amtired *Marjorie Fife* 102h
9 gr g Beauchamp King Rising Talisker (Primitive Rising (USA))
252[4]

Amuse Me *James Moffatt* 119h 118c
9 gr g Daylami(IRE) Have Fun (Indian Ridge)
704[8] **874[2] (1080)** 1171[4] **1298[3] 1444[2]** (1887) (2029) (2142) 5329[8]

Amys Choice (IRE) *Rose Dobbin* 67h
5 b m Craigsteel Tanya Thyne (IRE) (Good Thyne (USA))
4369[5] 4837[4]

Anaking (FR) *Emmanuel Clayeux* 119h 134c
5 b g Astarabad(USA) Toutevoie (FR) (Sillery (USA))
664a[6]

Analifet (FR) *W P Mullins* 146h
5 b m Califet(FR) Viana (FR) (Signe Divin (USA))
93a[2] 350a[2]

Anatol (FR) *Paul Nicholls* 141c
5 b g Apsis Teresa Moriniere (FR) (Saint Cyrien (FR))
2184[3]

Anay Turge (FR) *Nigel Hawke* 127h 141c
10 gr g Turgeon(USA) Anayette (FR) (Vaguely Pleasant (FR))
(184) 4818[8]

An Capall Mor (IRE) *Gordon Elliott* 108h 101c
9 b g Flemensfirth(USA) Corravilla (IRE) (Yashgan)
(870)

Ancient Sands (IRE) *John E Kiely* 130h 115c
7 b g Footstepsinthesand Antiguan Wells (IRE) (Sadler's Wells (USA))
3650a[14]

Anda De Grissay (FR) *Anthony Honeyball* 123h
5 b m Network(GER) Karima II (FR) (Luchiroverte (IRE))
89[3] 597[3] (2520) 2661[2] (3198) 3217[3] 3921[3] 4338[4] 4616[5]

Anddante (IRE) *Miss G T Lee*
7 b g Antonius Pius(USA) Lady Digby (IRE) (Petorius (IRE))
80[P]

Andhaar *N W Alexander* 109h
9 b g Bahri(USA) Deraasaat (Nashwan (USA))
886[7] 1633[6] (2071) 2102[2] 2296[2] 5260[8] 5475[4]

Andi'Amu (FR) *Warren Greatrex* 116h 109c
5 b g Walk In The Park(IRE) Sainte Parfaite (FR) (Septieme Ciel (USA))
365[3] 672[5]

Andy Kelly (IRE) *Emma Lavelle* 113h 138c
6 ch g Flemensfirth(USA) Fae Taylor (IRE) (Desert Style (IRE))
(2001) ◆

Anemos (FR) *B Duchemin* 126h
8 b g Okawango(USA) Kallithea (FR) (Esprit Du Nord (USA))
836a[4]

Ange Des Malberaux (FR) *James Ewart* 89h
5 b g Michel Georges Petite Baie (FR) (Alamo Bay (USA))
145[7] 4031[10] 4403[6] 4633[4]

Ange D'Or Javilex (FR) *J R Barry* 124h
5 b g Puit D'Or(IRE) Ixia De Menil (FR) (Port Etienne (FR))
19a[21]

Ange Du Lemo (FR) *A Le Clerc* 102c
8 gr g Maille Pistol(FR) Kiswa (FR) (Top Waltz (FR))
1223a[U]

Angel Face *Paul Morgan* 102h
4 b m Kayf Tara Safari Run (IRE) (Supreme Leader)
2252[3] 2644[3] 3333[F] 5347[2]

Anginola (IRE) *David Dennis* 81h
6 b m Kodiac Lady Montekin (Montekin)
167[7] 1941[5] 3233[2] 3307[7]

Anglingforcharlie *Miss Beth Childs* 10h 94c
6 b g Catcher In The Rye(IRE) Annies Valentine (My Best Valentine)
293[3] ◆ **4295[F]**

Anglo Paddy (IRE) *Neil Mulholland* 15h
6 ch m Mountain High(IRE) Hazel Sylph (IRE) (Executive Perk)
2730[12]

Angrove Fatrascal *Micky Hammond*
3 sk g Angrove Spottedick Marshal Plat Club (Monsieur Bond (IRE))
1899[F] 2718[P]

Angus Glens *David Dennis* 121h
5 gr g Dalakhani(IRE) Clara Bow (IRE) (Sadler's Wells (USA))
119[U] (263) ◆ 452[2] 710[3] 1822[2] 2035[2]

Anibale Fly (FR) *A J Martin* 149h
5 b g Assessor(IRE) Nouba Fly (FR) (Chamberlin (FR))
3459a[3] 5025a[6]

Aniknam (FR) *Philip Kirby* 120h
5 b g Nickname(FR) Kelle Home (FR) (Useful (FR))
436a[8] 1905[6] 2426[2]

Anis Des Malberaux (FR) *Nigel Hawke*
5 b g Reste Tranquille(FR) Scavenger (FR) (Nashamaa)
621[P]

Anitopia *Linda Perratt* 73h
10 gr g Alflora(IRE) The Whirlie Weevil (Scallywag)
4585[5] 5445[14]

Annacotty (IRE) *Alan King* 127h 159c
7 b g Beneficial Mini Moo Min (Ardross)
(2483) 3031[6] (3851) 4731[11]

Annagh Haven (IRE) *Michael Mulvany* 112h
5 ch m Indian Haven Avicia (Vettori (IRE))
1150a[13]

Anna Grey *Simon Waugh*
6 gr m Fair Mix(IRE) Little Flora (Alflora (IRE))
3971[11] 4202[P] 5256[P]

Annakrista (GER) *Zoe Davison* 99h
7 b m Kallisto(GER) Annabelle (GER) (Esclavo (FR))
2162[8] 2565[P] 3177[8] 3376[7]

Annaluna (IRE) *David Evans* 104h
6 b m Whipper(USA) Annaletta (Belmez (USA))
1808[7]

Annamatopoeia (IRE) *Brian Jordan* 121h 107c
7 b m Luso Endless Melody (IRE) (Carroll House (IRE))
52a[7] **3604a[4] 4656a[5]**

Annamult (IRE) *Alan Phillips* 89h 84c
7 ch m Beneficial Summer Smile (IRE) (Hollow Hand)
808[4] 1004[5] 1118[6]

Annaroe (IRE) *Alexandra Dunn* 85h
6 b m Beneficial Dun Belle Magic (IRE) (Darazari (IRE))
(864) 1085[3] 1293[9]

Anne Of Brittany (FR) *Henry Spiller* 89b
3 b f King's Best(USA) Abyaan (IRE) (Ela-Mana-Mou)
1772[3] ◆ 2304[4] *3048[5]*

Annie Confidential (IRE) *M J Jackson* 60h 63c
12 b m Turtle Island(IRE) Black Ivor (USA) (Sir Ivor (USA))
297[3]

Annie Hughes (IRE) *Adrian Wintle* 60b
6 b m Golan(IRE) Broadfield Cruiser (IRE) (Shujan (USA))
3381[9] 4350[10]

Annie Oakley (IRE) *Mrs John Harrington* 120h 127c
7 bb m Westerner Gaye Artiste (IRE) (Commanche Run)
70a[5]

Annie Power (IRE) *W P Mullins* 170h
7 ch m Shirocco(GER) Anno Luce (Old Vic)
(93a) (4698) (5177)

Annie'sboydave *Peter Pritchard* 54b
5 b g Passing Glance Earcomesannie (IRE) (Anshan)
558[12] 2250[9] 3952[11]

Annies Idea *Mandy Rowland* 87b
6 ch m Yoshka Danum Diva (IRE) (Danehill Dancer (IRE))
178[P]

Ann Maries Reject (IRE) *Brian Barr* 71h
6 br m Sendawar(IRE) Charlestown Lass (Bob Back (USA))
3773[9] 3947[P] 4743[5] 5420[5]

Announcement *Ronald Thompson* 112h
4 ch m Proclamation(IRE) Anapola (GER) (Polish Precedent (USA))
1036[4] 1793[3] 1974[6] 2974[P]

Annskert Lady (IRE) *Anthony McCann* 91h
5 b m Robin Des Pres(FR) Lady Henrietta (IRE) (Simply Great (FR))
1109[5]

Ann's Lottery *Tim Dennis* 100h
9 ch m Old Vic Vallingale (IRE) (Strong Gale)
30[3] 513[6]

Anomaly *John Ferguson* 128h
6 ch g Pivotal Anna Palariva (IRE) (Caerleon (USA))
(1234) ◆ 1660[2] 2221[4]

Anoosou (FR) *Barry John Murphy* 118h 99c
11 ch g Cyborg(FR) Anoosha (IRE) (Ahonoora)
3323a[12]

Another (IRE) *David C Griffiths* 53b
3 b f Lawman(FR) Enchanting Muse (USA) (Fusaichi Pegasus (USA))
2923[5] 3632[6]

Another Bill (IRE) *Nicky Richards* 121h
5 ch g Beneficial Glacier Lilly (IRE) (Glacial Storm (USA))
2189[2] 2787[4]

Another Bygones (IRE) *Karen McLintock* 96h
6 b g High-Rise(IRE) Little Chartridge (Anshan)
452[3] 727[3] 960[6] 1265[14] 1493[5] 1744[F] 2948[8]

Another Cobbler (FR) *Henry Daly* 84h
5 gr m Fragrant Mix(IRE) Qualine Du Maquis (FR) (Video Rock (FR))
2302[12] 3363[7] 3928[8] 4460[8]

Another Dimension (IRE) *Rose Dobbin* 107h 88c
9 b g Overbury(IRE) Freshwater (IRE) (Commanche Run)
421[4]

Another Dragon (FR) *Yannick Fouin* 111h
5 b g Enrique Nathalie Blue (FR) (Epervier Bleu)
436a[3]

Another Flutter (IRE) *Matt Sheppard* 105h 141c
11 b g Lahib(USA) Golden Fizz (Carroll House (IRE))
218[7] (555) 974[6] 1135[5] 1344[6]

Another For Joe *Jim Goldie* 76h
7 b g Lomitas Anna Kalinka (GER) (Lion Cavern (USA))
2069[9]

Another Frontier (IRE) *Nigel Twiston-Davies* 114h
4 b g Darsi(FR) Scent With Love (IRE) (Winged Love (IRE))
2126[12] 2807[6] 3570[2] 4063[4] 4618[4] 5100[4]

Another Hero (IRE) *Jonjo O'Neill* 129h 140c
6 b g Kalanisi(IRE) Storm Front (IRE) (Strong Gale)
(2631) (3929) 5005a[F]

Another Job (IRE) *Nicky Richards* 80b
5 b g Gold Well Itsonlyraheen (IRE) (Mister Lord (USA))
4591[0]

Another Journey *Sarah-Jayne Davies* 118h 105c
6 b g Rail Link Singasongosixpence (Singspiel (IRE))
(59) 556[8] 1905[9] **2857[6] 3362[U] 3466[P] 4841[P] 5394[3]**

Anotherlady (IRE) *J P Dempsey* 105h
7 b m Gamut(IRE) Leinster Lady (IRE) (Lord Chancellor (USA))
1150a[12]

Another Mattie (IRE) *N W Alexander* 126h 94c
8 b g Zagreb(USA) Silver Tassie (FR) (Kaldounevees (FR))
2069[7] (2429) ◆ 2978[2] (3344) 3999[2] 4794[2] 5296[8]

Another Nudge (IRE) *David Dennis* 67b
3 b f Getaway(GER) Another Shot (IRE) (Master Willie)
5443[10]

Another Sunshine *Warren Greatrex* 86b
4 b m Kayf Tara Sunshine Rays (Alflora (IRE))
2856[7]

An Poc Ar Buile (IRE) *Sophie Leech* 110h 124c
6 ch g Mountain High(IRE) Miniconjou (IRE) (Be My Native (USA))
355[2] 553[P] 798[2] 3824[P] **4352[P]** 4648[9] **(5031) 5285[8]**

Anquetta (IRE) *Robert Waley-Cohen* 80h 108c
11 b g Anshan Quetta (IRE) (Alphabatim (USA))
184[12] 555[7] 809[P] 1296[P] 5392[F]

An Tarbh Og (IRE) *Caroline Keevil* 107h
7 b g Fruits Of Love(USA) Finnuala Supreme (IRE) (Supreme Leader)
1597[5] 2262[8]

Antartica De Thaix (FR) *Paul Nicholls* 127h
5 gr m Dom Alco(FR) Nouca De Thaix (FR) (Subotica (FR))
2875[2] 3252[U] (4293) 4435[2] 5094[3] 5415[2]

Anteros (IRE) *Sophie Leech* 133h 108c
7 b g Milan Sovereign Star (IRE) (Taufan (USA))
2415[3] **2963[4]** 3407[3] 3992[P] 4354[10] 5277[2]

Anti Cool (IRE) *Robin Dickin* 94b
6 b g Heron Island(IRE) Youngborogal (IRE) (Anshan)
242[3] 590[P] 3483[P] 4063[P]

Antilope Du Seuil (FR) *Gordon Elliott* 121h
5 b m Alberto Giacometti(IRE) Sweet Laly (FR) (Marchand De Sable (USA))
(299) (656)

Antioches (FR) *Mlle M-L Mortier*
5 gr m Fragrant Mix(IRE) Oudette (FR) (Apple Tree (FR))
5499a[10]

Antiphony (IRE) *Philip Hobbs* 105h
4 b g Royal Anthem(USA) Hazel's Glory (IRE) (Mister Lord (USA))
2258[4] 2879[F] 3483[8] 3777[12] 4846[2] ◆ 5067[2] 5352[2]

Anton Dolin (IRE) *Michael Mullineaux* 106h
7 ch g Danehill Dancer(IRE) Ski For Gold (Shirley Heights)
180[2] 529[5] 751[F] 1166[3] 1265[3] 1421[3] 1508[4] 1647[9] 2043[7] 2492[9] 3932[3]

Antonio Joli (IRE) *Jo Hughes* 96b
3 b g Arcano(IRE) Snowtime (IRE) (Galileo (IRE))
2882[2]

Antony (FR) *Gary Moore* 121h 130c
5 b g Walk In The Park(IRE) Melanie Du Chenet (FR) (Nikos)
(669) 780[3] 1240[2] 1485[2] 1754[3] 2182[12] **(2885) ◆ 3228[P] 4785[5] 5496[3]**

Anwyl House *Jo Hughes* 86b
5 gr g Auction House(USA) Amwell Star (USA) (Silver Buck (USA))
83[P]

Any Currency (IRE) *Martin Keighley* 123h 155c
12 b g Moscow Society(USA) Native Bavard (IRE) (Be My Native (USA))
313a[3] 2082[4] 2471[2] 3017[8] (4719) (5274)

Any Destination (IRE) *Andy Turnell* 54b
4 b g Dubai Destination(USA) Cutting Glance (USA) (Woodman (USA))
558[11]

Any Drama (IRE) *Harry Fry* 125b
4 b g Gamut(IRE) Oak Lodge (IRE) (Roselier (FR))
9a[11] 5195[6]

Anythingmayhappen (IRE) *Jeremy Scott* 99b
4 b g Publisher(USA) Wild Coast (IRE) (Gothland (FR))
2991[5] 4827[11]

Apache Blue (IRE) *Kenneth Slack* 73h 12c
11 b g Presenting La Eile (IRE) (Brief Truce (USA))
842[7] 2751[9] **3310[P]**

Apachee Prince (IRE) *Alistair Whillans* 117h
6 b g Indian Danehill(IRE) Wheredidthemoneygo (IRE) (Anshan)
456[2] 799[6] 1038[F] 1331[4] 2949[11]

Apache Outlaw (IRE) *Rebecca Curtis* 111h
6 b g Westerner Bermuda Bay (IRE) (Be My Native (USA))
3012[2] 4264[5] (4448) 4825[7] 5029[P]

Apache Pearl (IRE) *Warren Greatrex* 44h
4 br g Indian Danehill(IRE) Pearl Buttons (Alflora (IRE))
407[8] 2562[7] 3927[8]

Apache Pilot *Maurice Barnes* 71h 95c
7 br g Indian Danehill(IRE) Annie-Jo (Presenting)
1890[9] **2147[4] 2708[6] 3310[5] 4032[5] 4175[4] 4940[5]**

Apache Stronghold (IRE) *Noel Meade* 149h 162c
7 b g Milan First Battle (IRE) (Un Desperado (FR))
10a[3]

A Plein Temps (FR) *Harry Fry* 113h
5 b g Alberto Giacometti(IRE) Flower Des Champs (FR) (Robin Des Champs (FR))
2275[5] 3124[2] 3580[5] (4450) 5264[3]

Applaus (GER) *Micky Hammond* 99b
3 b g Tiger Hill(IRE) All About Love (GER) (Winged Love (IRE))
2216[3] (2923) ◆ 3165[3] 4371[3]

Applejack Lad *Michael Smith* 99h
4 ch g Three Valleys(USA) Fittonia (FR) (Ashkalani (IRE))
3022[13] 3471[6] 4033[6]

Apple Of Our Eye *Charlie Longsdon* 114h
5 b g Passing Glance Apple Anthem (True Song)
105[5] (2690) 3334[4]

Apple Pops *Neil Mulholland* 65h
5 b m Apple Tree(FR) Rio Pops (Broadsword (USA))
2258[8] 4435[5] 4916[5] 5420[14]

Applesandpierres (IRE) *Dan Skelton* 118h
7 b g Pierre Cluain Chaoin (IRE) (Phardante (FR))
(834)

Apples And Trees (IRE) *Donald McCain* 84h
6 b g Oscar(IRE) Native Bramble (IRE) (Be My Native (USA))
3397[F] (Dead)

Apple's Jade (FR) *W P Mullins* 164h
3 b f Saddler Maker(IRE) Apple's For Ever (FR) (Nikos)
(3268a) 4764[2] (5175)

Appletree Lane *Tom Gretton* 91h
5 b m Croco Rouge(IRE) Emmasflora (Alflora (IRE))
2665[5] 3252[5] 3785[3] 4904[3] 5466[P]

Approaching Star (FR) *Dai Burchell* 84h
4 ch m New Approach(IRE) Madame Arcati (IRE) (Sinndar (IRE))
5353[4]

Appropriate (FR) *Paul Henderson* 50h 58c
5 b m Kapgarde(FR) Oreli (FR) (Robin Des Pres (FR))
120[6] 1136[8] **1326[P] 1595[5] 1757[4] 2521[F]** 2713[7] 3256[5]

April Dusk (IRE) *Warren Greatrex* 132h 138c
6 b g Turtle Island(IRE) Rabble Run (IRE) (Zaffaran (USA))
(2488) **(2963) 3922[F]** 4368[2] **4800[P]**

Apterix (FR) *Brian Ellison* 131h
5 b g Day Flight Ohe Les Aulmes (FR) (Lute Antique (FR))
3487[10] 4273[2] (4447) 4913[3] 5295[2]

Aqalim *John Ferguson* 150h
5 b g Raven's Pass(USA) Aviacion (BRZ) (Know Heights (IRE))
2198[3] 2782[4] 3149[6] 5216[6]

Aqua Dude (IRE) *Evan Williams* 133h
5 br g Flemensfirth(USA) Miss Cozzene (FR) (Solid Illusion (USA))
(2406) ◆ 3135[3] 4388[U] (5018) ◆

Aquitania (FR) *C Gourdain*
4 b m Early March Saga Du Souvestre (FR) (Sagamix (FR))
3815a[P]

Arabian Oasis *Philip Kirby* 96h
3 b g Oasis Dream Love Divine (Diesis)
1177[3] 5242[4]

Arabian Revolution *John Ferguson* 133h
4 gr g Dalakhani(IRE) Mont Etoile (IRE) (Montjeu (IRE))
2064[13]

Araldur (FR) *Alan King* 128h 134c
11 ch g Spadoun(FR) Aimessa (FR) (Tropular)
2436[5] 2809[3] 3448[8] 4347[3]

Aramadyh *Jim Best* 92h
4 gr m Authorized(IRE) Swift Dispersal (Shareef Dancer (USA))
3902[P] 4157[3] 4409[8] 4672[P]

Aranhill Chief (IRE) *S J Mahon* 97h 129c
8 b g Blueprint(IRE) Aran Jewel (IRE) (Brief Truce (USA))
1185a[5] 1938a[4]

Arantes *R Mike Smith* 100h
4 b g Sixties Icon Black Opal (Machiavellian (USA))
2189[7] 5444[5]

Arbeo (IRE) *Diana Grissell* 93h 118c
9 b g Brian Boru Don't Waste It (IRE) (Mister Lord (USA))
149[4] 2616[P] 3349[4] (3609) 4234[3] 4505[3] 5456[3]

Arbre De Vie (FR) *W P Mullins* 155h 140c
5 b g Antarctique(IRE) Nouvelle Recrue (FR) (Ragmar (FR))
96a[2] 4717[10] 5328[3]

Arcadiana (IRE) *John Gallagher*
5 b m Arcadio(GER) Sovana (FR) (Kadounor (FR))
4974[P]

Arcamante (ITY) *Mike Hammond* 109h
4 b g High Chaparral(IRE) Caractere (IRE) (Indian Ridge)
2543[3] 2754[8] 3902[P] 4233[7] 4860[P] 5157[9]

Arcanciel Val (FR) *X-L Le Stang*
4 b g Le Balafre(FR) Zenita Des Brosses (FR) (Nononito (FR))
3815a[P]

Arch Duchess (FR) *M Rolland* 118h
5 b m Arch(USA) Jacira (FR) (Sillery (USA))
2821a[P]

Archie Boy (IRE) *Sophie Leech* 88h 110c
13 b g Basanta(IRE) Darial Mill (IRE) (Salluceva (IRE))
18[6] 260[3] 514[5] 677[3] 827[5]

Archie Meade (IRE) *Daniel John Howard* 137h 131c
10 b g Beneficial Polar Charm (IRE) (Supreme Leader)
95a[2]

Archie Rice (USA) *Jimmy Frost* 106h
9 b g Arch(USA) Gold Bowl (USA) (Seeking The Gold (USA))
(675) (828) 1046[5] 1675[5] 2087[9] 2850[6] 3125[P]

Archipeligo *Iain Jardine* 102h
4 b g Archipenko(USA) Red Slew (Red Ransom (USA))
960[P] 3470[2] 4416[6] 4871[6] 5262[P]

Archive (FR) *Eoin Griffin* 136h
5 b g Sulamani(IRE) Royale Dorothy (FR) (Smadoun (FR))
2385a[4] 2814a[5] 3650a[13]

Arco (IRE) *Philip Kirby* 55b
4 b m Flemensfirth(USA) Babygotback (IRE) (Amilynx (FR))
1858[6]

Arcs Abound *Miss L Gardner* 84b
5 b g Rainbow High Winter Scene (IRE) (Oscar (IRE))
5436[9]

Arctic Ben (IRE) *Henry Daly* 101h 130c
11 gr g Beneficial Hurst Flyer (Neltino)
4269[P] 4651[6]

Arctic Court (IRE) *Jim Goldie* 116h
11 b g Arctic Lord(IRE) Polls Joy (Pollerton)
798[F] 1291[7] 1628[P] 1903[P] 2296[5] ◆ 2948[6] 3428[6] (3684) (5300)

Arctic Destination (IRE) *Donald McCain* 110b
4 b g Dubai Destination(USA) Arctic Scale (IRE) (Strong Gale)
4915[4]

Arctic Dixie *Rob Summers* 104h
7 ch m Desideratum Arctic Oats (Oats)
462[4] 757[4] 939[5]

Arctic Fire (GER) *W P Mullins* 168h
6 b g Soldier Hollow Adelma (GER) (Sternkoenig (IRE))
71a[2] (2386a) (2815a) 3322a[4] 3768a[2]

Arctic Gold (IRE) *Nigel Twiston-Davies* 136h
4 b g Gold Well Arctic Warrior (IRE) (Arctic Lord (IRE))
213[11] 1634[5] (1979) (2768) (3465) ◆ 3622[6] 4239[6] (5053)

Arctic Lady (IRE) *Tom George* 85b
4 b m Milan Arctic Rose (IRE) (Jamesmead)
5383[5]

Arctic Skipper (IRE) *Vincent Laurence Halley* 125h 133c
6 b g Flemensfirth(USA) Coco Opera (IRE) (Lafontaine I (USA))
21a[8] **4517a[3] 4949a[3]**

Ard Agus Fada (IRE) *Joanne Foster* 94c
12 ch g Anshan Whispering Dawn (Then Again)
1069[P]

Ardamir (FR) *Alan King* 120h
3 b g Deportivo Kiss And Cry (FR) (Nikos)
2757[5] 3112[P] (4304) 4720[P]

Ardea (IRE) *Justin Landy* 110c
7 b g Millenary Dark Dame (IRE) (Norwich)
5258[U]

Ardesia (IRE) *Tina Jackson* 78h
11 b g Red Sunset Lowtown (Camden Town)
502[5] 805[5] 918[3] (1071) 1405[7] 2982[11] 4415[8] 5198[4]

Ardkilly Witness (IRE) *Jamie Snowden* 98h 134c
9 b g Witness Box(USA) Ardkilly Angel (IRE) (Yashgan)
2064[14] **2899[P] 3282[10] 4595[2] 5119[U]**

Ardmay (IRE) *Kevin Ryan* 113h
6 b g Strategic Prince Right After Moyne (IRE) (Imperial Ballet (IRE))
(1684) 2893[P] 4941[8]

Aregra (FR) *Peter Niven* 73h 91c
5 gr g Fragrant Mix(IRE) Elisa De Mai (FR) (Video Rock (FR))
777[5] 1098[6] 1272[5] **1687[2] (2844) 2866[3]**

Are They Your Own (IRE) *Fergal O'Brien* 123h
7 b g Exit To Nowhere(USA) Carioca Dream (USA) (Diesis)
(214) 511[5] (1000) 1308[5] 1480[3] 1590[4] 2058[2] 2472[9]

Areuwitmenow (IRE) *Jennie Candlish*
10 b g Beneficial Clonartic (IRE) (Be My Native (USA))
1569[P]

Argante (FR) *Nicky Henderson* 124h
6 bb g Singspiel(IRE) Abyaan (IRE) (Ela-Mana-Mou)
4111[3] ◆

Argentino (FR) *W P Mullins* 134h
5 b g Sinndar(IRE) Syssiss (FR) (River Bay (USA))
1175a[2]

Argocat (IRE) *Nicky Henderson* 132h 143c
7 b g Montjeu(IRE) Spirit Of South (AUS) (Giant's Causeway (USA))
4112[8]

Argot *Charlie Longsdon* 118h
4 b g Three Valleys(USA) Tarot Card (Fasliyev (USA))
(1590) 1814[2] 2472[13] 2888[8] 3238[10] 3607[2] (3865)

Arian (IRE) *John Flint* 73b
3 b f King's Theatre(IRE) Brave Betsy (IRE) (Pistolet Bleu (IRE))
3952[6]

Aristocracy *Sally Randell* 105h
4 b g Royal Applause Pure Speculation (Salse (USA))
2490[P] 2880[6] 3098[4] 4291[8] 4490[6]

Aristo Du Plessis (FR) *James Ewart* 148h
5 b g Voix Du Nord(FR) J'Aime (FR) (Royal Charter (FR))
1905[F] (2194) (2328) ◆ (3426) 4014[6]

Arkaim *Olly Williams* 103h 137c
7 b g Oasis Dream Habariya (IRE) (Perugino (USA))
218[9] (1989) 2635[7] 3107[F] 3318[P] **4891[RR]** 5081[RR]

Arkwrisht (FR) *W P Mullins* 138h
5 b g Lavirco(GER) Latitude (FR) (Kadalko (FR))
25a[4] (3962a) 5194[7]

Ar Mad (FR) *Gary Moore* 124h 164c
5 b g Tiger Groom Omelia (FR) (April Night (FR))
2001[6] (2370) (2913) (3280) (4158)

Armarissis (IRE) *Alex Hales* 69b
8 b g Oscar(IRE) Corcomohide (IRE) (Homo Sapien)
4711[P]

Armchair Theatre (IRE) *Evan Williams* 114h
5 b g King's Theatre(IRE) Oh Susannah (FR) (Turgeon (USA))
2363[3] 2689[3]

Armedanddangerous (IRE) *Tom Gretton* 104h 113c
10 b g Kris Kin(USA) Lucky Fountain (IRE) (Lafontaine I (USA))
2598[4] (3144) (3792) 4340[F]

Armement (FR) *James Grassick*
4 b g Smadoun(FR) Apparemment (IRE) (Anabaa (USA))
2650[10] 4357[9]

Armistice Day (IRE) *John Joseph Hanlon* 86h
3 b f Azamour(IRE) Announcing Peace (Danehill (USA))
1631[6]

Aroma Baie (FR) *M Postic* 86h 113c
5 b m Crillon(FR) Ysalla (FR) (Nikos)
2822a[F]

Aroseforoscar *Chris Down* 100h
6 b m Oscar(IRE) Made For A King (Roselier (FR))
2298[P]

Around A Pound (IRE) *Nick Kent* 88h 100c
10 b g Old Vic Mary Ellen Best (IRE) (Danehill (USA))
44[4] 211[5] (Dead)

Arpege D'Alene (FR) *Paul Nicholls* 151h 140c
5 gr g Dom Alco(FR) Joliette D'Alene (FR) (Garde Royale)
2347[2] 3116[P] (4354) 4730[2] 5213[9]

Arquebusier (FR) *Emma Baker* 107h 104c
5 bl g Discover D'Auteuil(FR) Djurjura (FR) (Akarad (FR))
1933[P] 2263[7] (2713) (2862) 3498[2] 3994[6] **5066[2]**

Arroyeau (FR) *Nick Gifford*
5 ch g Nidor(FR) Miss Lamour (FR) (Valanour (IRE))
2375[8] 4317[P] 4409[P] 4773[P]

Arryzona *Christine Dunnett* 73h
4 b g Phoenix Reach(IRE) Southwarknewsflash (Danetime (IRE))
2409[7] 3418[9]

Arsenale (GER) *Michael Appleby* 42h
4 b m Nicaron(GER) Alte Rose (GER) (Monsun (GER))
3612[P]

Art Deco Marsal (FR) *Robert Walford* 71h
5 b g Passing Sale(FR) Guiguite Du Pots (FR) (Marasali)
2260[P]

Arthamint *Dan Skelton* 105h 110c
7 b g Passing Glance Araminta (Carlingford Castle)
1613[7] 1810[6] 2165[2] **2420[DSQ] (2582) 3224[4] 4160[2] 4387[2] 4534[2]**

Arthur Burrell *Jackie Du Plessis* 97h
6 ch g With The Flow(USA) Kingsmill Quay (Noble Imp)
(1122) 1843[5] 2443[4]

Arthur Mc Bride (IRE) *Nigel Twiston-Davies* 103h
6 bb g Royal Anthem(USA) Lucky Diverse (IRE) (Lucky Guest)
86[P] 2301[5] 2833[2] 3841[5]

Arthur's Gift (IRE) *Nigel Twiston-Davies* 107h
4 b g Presenting Uncertain Affair (IRE) (Darshaan)
1698[5] 2762[8]

Arthur's Oak *Venetia Williams* 120h 154c
7 b g Kayf Tara Myumi (Charmer (IRE))
(3155) ◆ 3446[2] ◆ (3990) (4355) 4770[16]

Arthur's Queen (FR) *Carroll Gray* 90h
4 b m Soldier Of Fortune(IRE) Tintagel (Oasis Dream)
1009[7] 1117[6] 1234[U] 1384[8] 2876[4] 3125[P]

Arthur's Secret (FR) *Nigel Twiston-Davies* 111h 119c
5 bb g Secret Singer(FR) Luna Park (FR) (Cyborg (FR))
177[6]

Arthurs Secret *John Quinn* 126h
5 ch g Sakhee's Secret Angry Bark (USA) (Woodman (USA))
2499[4] 4865[4]

Articulum (IRE) *Terence O'Brien* 120b
5 b g Definite Article Lugante (IRE) (Luso)
25a[3]

Artifice Sivola (FR) *Lucy Wadham* 118h 133c
5 gr g Dom Alco(FR) Kerrana (FR) (Cadoudal (FR))
107[4] (2138) 2691[2] 2884[3] 3843[4] 4464[5] 4891[4] (5386)

Artiste Du Gouet (FR) *Heather Dalton* 90h
5 bb g Lavirco(GER) Newhaven (FR) (Subotica (FR))
2440[6] 2612[8] 2928[13] 4441[12]

Art Libre (FR) *Gary Moore* 66h
4 b g Librettist(USA) Peinture Parfaite (FR) (Peintre Celebre (USA))
279[7] 447[P] 3484[13]

Art Lord (IRE) *Karl Thornton* 112h 121c
9 b g Lord Americo Oilpainting (IRE) (Welsh Term)
2947[3] 3472[F] (3671) 4406[P] 4521a[P]

Art Mauresque (FR) *Paul Nicholls* 136h 154c
5 b g Policy Maker(IRE) Modeva (FR) (Valanour (IRE))
(99) 1840[3] (2063) 2483[6] 3031[7] 4485[7] 4733[P] 5276[2]

Art Of Logistics (IRE) *Philip Hobbs* 142h 146c
7 b g Exit To Nowhere(USA) Sanadja (IRE) (Slip Anchor)
24a[12] 603a[3] 2902[U] 5093[3] ◆

Art Of Payroll (GER) *Ms Sandra Hughes* 139h 129c
6 b g Shirocco(GER) Anna Maria (GER) (Night Shift (USA))
5025a[5]

Art Of Swing (IRE) *Gary Moore* 81b
3 b g Excellent Art Shahmina (IRE) (Danehill (USA))
2414[5] *3048[7]*

Art Of Synergy (IRE) *Ms Sandra Hughes* 114h
4 b g Yeats(IRE) Elizabeth Tudor (IRE) (Supreme Leader)
9a[10]

Art Of War (IRE) *David Pipe*
4 b g Invincible Spirit(IRE) Chica Roca (USA) (Woodman (USA))
1234[P]

Arty Bella *Jimmy Frost* 68h
4 b m Overbury(IRE) Gertrude Webb (Central Park (IRE))
2444[7] 2879[9] 3119[7] 3410[P]

Arty Campbell (IRE) *Bernard Llewellyn* 108h
5 b g Dylan Thomas(IRE) Kincob (USA) (Kingmambo (USA))
1324[2] 2244[2]

Arzal (FR) *Harry Whittington* 131h 164c
5 bb g Vendangeur(IRE) Ghostaline (FR) (Ghost Buster'S (FR))
1978[8] **(2034) (2779) 3280[3] 3856[2] (5174)**

As A Dream (IRE) *Nikki Evans*
3 b f Azamour(IRE) Wedding Dream (Oasis Dream)
3464[P]

Ascendant *Johnny Farrelly* 132h
9 ch g Medicean Ascendancy (Sadler's Wells (USA))
2247[3] 3015[12] 3584[4] 3844[7] 4452[5] 5159[7]

Ascot De Bruyere (FR) *James Ewart* 115h 109c
5 bb g Kapgarde(FR) Quid De Neuville (FR) (Le Balafre (FR))
(4031) 4799[8]

Ascotdeux Nellerie (FR) *Kim Bailey* 124h
5 ch g Network(GER) Jumper Nellerie (FR) (Panoramic)
(220) (2035) ◆ 2772[7] 4888[3] 5463[3]

As De Fer (FR) *Anthony Honeyball* 95h 135c
9 b g Passing Sale(FR) Miss Hollywood (FR) (True Brave (USA))
149[5] 2366[2] 2878[P] (3823) (3957) 4348[5] 5238[2] 5304[4]

As De Mee (FR) *Paul Nicholls* 132h 153c
5 bb g Kapgarde(FR) Koeur De Mee (FR) (Video Rock (FR))
1846[2] 2469[2] 2913[3] 3229[F] 3991[2] 4729[5] 5193[7] 5496[9]

A Shade Of Bay *Kim Bailey* 124h
7 b m Midnight Legend Pulling Strings (IRE) (Accordion)
3394[4] ◆ 1808[4]

Ashanti Moon (IRE) *Diana Grissell* 95c
9 br g Great Palm(USA) Toasted Oats (IRE) (Be My Native (USA))
598[P]

Ashbrittle *Neil King* 122h 69c
8 b g Rainbow Quest(USA) Caesarea (GER) (Generous (IRE))
(210) 2202[8] 2669[U] 3705[P] **4327[4]**

Ashcott Boy *Neil Mulholland* 106h 130c
7 ch g Lahib(USA) Last Ambition (IRE) (Cadeaux Genereux)
1595[4] (1825) (1888) (2546) 4533[2] (4889) 5354[5]

Ashes Corner (IRE) *Julia Brooke* 98b
5 b g Marienbard(IRE) Up Thyne Girl (IRE) (Good Thyne (USA))
419[P] 3022[RR] 3340[5] 4108[7]

Ashes Of Love (IRE) *Mrs John Harrington* 102h
5 b m Fruits Of Love(USA) Brave Thistle (IRE) (Bravefoot)
4653a[P]

Ashford Wood (IRE) *Tim Vaughan* 124h 98c
7 b g Stowaway Shambala (IRE) (Imperial Ballet (IRE))
3348[5] 4267[P]

Ashjar (FR) *C A McBratney* 115h
5 b g Oasis Dream Asharna (IRE) (Darshaan)
872[5]

Ashkoun (FR) *Tim Vaughan* 100h
4 b g Sinndar(IRE) Ashalina (FR) (Linamix (FR))
43[0] 449[4] 776[4] 1054[4] 2956[8] 3376[9] 4200[2] 5306[P]

Ashoka (IRE) *Dan Skelton* 120h
3 gr g Azamour(IRE) Jinskys Gift (IRE) (Cadeaux Genereux)
(2992) 3279[4] 4012[2] 5491[P]

Ash Park (IRE) *Stuart Coltherd* 108h
7 b g Milan Distant Gale (IRE) (Strong Gale)
3240[5] 3668[5] 3883[5] (4570) 5088[F] 5414[5]

Ashtown (IRE) *Malcolm Jones* 100h
8 b g Westerner Christmas River (IRE) (Be My Native (USA))
1519[5] 1909[4]

Asian Ali (IRE) *Richard Lee* 42h
6 b g Asian Heights Ali Fortuna (IRE) (Ali-Royal (IRE))
525[7] 823[8]

Ask A Bank (IRE) *David Dennis* 93h
5 b g Presenting Highness Lady (GER) (Cagliostro (GER))
1598[7] 1812[3]

Askamore Darsi (IRE) *Donald McCain* 120h 126c
6 b g Darsi(FR) Galamear (Strong Gale)
355[4] (2865) 3160[2] (3507) (3885) 4153[3] 4511[4]

Asker (IRE) *Zoe Davison* 79h
7 b g High Chaparral(IRE) Pay The Bank (High Top)
2520[P] 2958[3] 3219[5] 3665[P]

Asknotwhat (IRE) *David Bridgwater* 117h
4 ch g Dylan Thomas(IRE) Princess Roseburg (USA) (Johannesburg (USA))
221[3]

Ask Paddy (IRE) *Sam Drake* 35h
3 ch g Ask Dalzenia (FR) (Cadoudal (FR))
4392[9] 4988[6] 5230[4]

Ask Vic (IRE) *W P Mullins* 137h
6 b m Old Vic No Dunce (IRE) (Nordance (USA))
96a[10]

Aso (FR) *Venetia Williams* 136h 154c
5 bb g Goldneyev(USA) Odyssee Du Cellier (FR) (Dear Doctor (FR))
2274[2] ◆ 2779[2] 3153[2] (3726) 4100[3] 4696[5] 5174[6] (5381)

Asockastar (IRE) *Tim Vaughan* 105h 94c
7 b g Milan Baie Barbara (IRE) (Heron Island (IRE))
1661[7] 1977[P] 4965[5]

Aspasius (GER) *Charlie Mann* 71h
3 b g Desert Prince(IRE) Aspasia Lunata (GER) (Tiger Hill (IRE))
1768[4]

Aspecialpresent (IRE) *Adrian Wintle* 84b
5 b g Presenting Escrea (IRE) (Oscar (IRE))
644[7] 875[2]

Aspergillum *Tom Lacey* 62b
3 b g Midnight Legend Rosita Bay (Hernando (FR))
5151[8]

Astaroland (FR) *Jennie Candlish* 118h
5 b g Astarabad(USA) Orlandaise (FR) (Goldneyev (USA))
153[4] 529[6] 776[2] (1048) (1166)

Aster's Approval *Grant Cann*
5 b g With Approval(CAN) Aster (IRE) (Danehill (USA))
4849[11] 4874[P]

Asthuria (FR) *W P Mullins* 129h
4 b m Sagacity(FR) Baturia (FR) (Turgeon (USA))
4954a[3]

Astigos (FR) *Venetia Williams* 120h 137c
8 bb g Trempolino(USA) Astonishing (BRZ) (Vacilante (ARG))
2184[4] 2631[3] 3253[2] 3849[7] (4106) 4469[5] 4787[8] 5071[6]

Aston Cantlow *Philip Hobbs* 120h
7 b g Hurricane Run(IRE) Princess Caraboo (IRE) (Alzao (USA))
4229[3] ◆ 5098[3] 5469[F]

Astracad (FR) *Nigel Twiston-Davies* 134h 141c
9 br g Cadoudal(FR) Astre Eria (FR) (Garde Royale)
(1869) 2059[4] 2468[5] 3030[7] 4733[6] 5193[P]

Astre De La Cour (FR) *Robert Walford* 144h 112c
5 bb g Khalkevi(IRE) Gracieuse Delacour (FR) (Port Etienne (FR))
7a[18] **2166[4]**

Astre Rose (FR) *Victor Dartnall* 67h
5 bb g Al Namix(FR) Quetcha D'Isigny (FR) (Silver Rainbow)
26[3] 434[3]

Astrowolf *Mark H Tompkins* 94h
4 b g Halling(USA) Optimistic (Reprimand)
61[7] 494[4] 999[P]

Astrum *Donald McCain* 115h
5 gr g Haafhd Vax Star (Petong)
200[2] 481[7] 2843[4] 3223[10] 3807[2] 4025[2] 4415[F] 5081[6]

Asum *Dan Skelton* 109b
4 b g Kayf Tara Candy Creek (IRE) (Definite Article)
5457[2] ◆

Asuncion (FR) *Rebecca Menzies* 95h 92c
5 b m Antarctique(IRE) Liesse De Marbeuf (FR) (Cyborg (FR))
2143[P] 2707[6] 3059[4] 3683[2] 4034[3] 4329[7] (4795) 5197[2] 5366[P]

Ata Boy (IRE) *Richard Phillips* 76h 83c
9 br g Key Of Luck(USA) Atalina (FR) (Linamix (FR))
44[5]

At First Light *David Weston* 120h
6 b m Echo Of Light Bisaat (USA) (Bahri (USA))
(835) 892[2] (1012) 1239[2] (1290) 2911[P] (3217) 5094[4] 5282[P]

At Fishers Cross (IRE) *Rebecca Curtis* 147h
8 b g Oscar(IRE) Fermoy Supreme (IRE) (Supreme Leader)
3713a[2] 4244[4] 4732[P] 5213[5]

Athou Du Nord (FR) *Richard Hobson* 115h
5 b g Voix Du Nord(FR) Orathou Du Plaid (FR) (Lute Antique (FR))
2487[2] 2890[5] 3375[P] (4968)

Atirelarigo (FR) *Philip Hobbs* 121h 69c
5 b g Puit D'Or(IRE) Ouchka (FR) (April Night (FR))
4097[3] ◆ **4787[10]**

Atlanta Ablaze *Henry Daly* 101h
4 b m Kayf Tara Rocheflamme (FR) (Snurge)
3132[5] 3861[3] 4623[12] 5389[5]

Atlantic Gold (IRE) *Charlie Longsdon* 134h
5 bb g Robin Des Pres(FR) Marys Isle (IRE) (Erins Isle)
185[2] (1723) (2062) 2484[12] 3037[5] 4766[P] 5141[2]

Atlantic Roller (IRE) *Chris Gordon* 115h 130c
8 b g Old Vic Tourist Attraction (IRE) (Pollerton)
430[2] 715[2] 2832[P] 3113[P] 3776[P] 4251[3] 4436[4] 4971[3] 5066[F]

A Toi Phil (FR) *W P Mullins* 152h
5 b g Day Flight Lucidrile (FR) (Beyssac (FR))
(3765a) 4715[7]

Atomix (GER) *Peter Niven* 109b
4 b g Doyen(IRE) Aloe (GER) (Lomitas)
3104[2] ◆ (4037) 5195[12]

A Touch Of Sass (IRE) *John Spearing* 82h
5 b m Mahler Lwitikila (Denel (FR))
970[4] 1289[9] 1908[7] 3126[5] 3500[3]

A Tout Propos (FR) *M De Montfort*
4 ch g Limnos(JPN) Adrede (FR) (Pistolet Bleu (IRE))
4401a[P]

Attention Please (IRE) *Rose Dobbin* 92h 72c
5 b g Kalanisi(IRE) Dangerous Dolly (IRE) (Jurado (USA))
1552[5] 1887[3] 2174[5] 2745[7] **4034[P] 4325[6]**

Attention Seaker *Tim Easterby* 120h
5 b m Bollin Eric Pay Attention (Revoque (IRE))
1854[5] 3342[3] 3592[8] (4512) 4909[8] 4939[3]

At The Doubble (IRE) *Warren Greatrex* 120h
6 b g Oscar(IRE) Glebe Melody (IRE) (Supreme Leader)
(2210)

At The Top (FR) *Dan Skelton* 89h
5 b m Network(GER) Quaiou (FR) (Robin Des Champs (FR))
2406[4] 2840[4] **3845[P]**

Attila De Sivola (FR) *Y-M Porzier* 131h 131c
5 ch g Kapgarde(FR) Wild Rose Bloom (FR) (Kaldounevees (FR))
663a[8]

Attimo (GER) *Sam Drake* 102h 117c
6 ch g Nayef(USA) Alanda (GER) (Lando (GER))
4569[P] 4938[2] (5234) (5309)

Attonburn (IRE) *George Charlton* 70b
8 b g Lahib(USA) Ash (Salse (USA))
201[P]

Attractive Liason (IRE) *Neil Mulholland* 67h
5 b m Scorpion(IRE) Sounds Attractive (IRE) (Rudimentary (USA))
2252[5]

Attribution *Henry De Bromhead* 142h
5 ch g Alhaarth(IRE) Competa (Hernando (FR))
3539a[2] 4516a[5] 5002a[7]

Atuvuedenuo (FR) *Guy Denuault* 139h 128c
5 b m Assessor(IRE) Paresca (FR) (Maresca Sorrento (FR))
2821a[5]

Aubusson (FR) *Nick Williams* 150h 145c
6 b g Ballingarry(IRE) Katioucha (FR) (Mansonnien (FR))
1883a[7] 2361a[2] **(2960)** ◆ **3405[P]**

Auckland De Re (FR) *Neil Mulholland* 110h
5 bb g Network(GER) Osee De Re (FR) (April Night (FR))
2239[7] 2603[4] 3414[P] 4855[6]

Audacious Plan (IRE) *Rebecca Curtis* 122h 133c
6 b g Old Vic North Star Poly (IRE) (Presenting)
92a[2] 1849[6] 2061[4] 2482[P] 4354[13] **4697[F]**

Auenwirbel (GER) *Laura Young* 126h 106c
4 b g Sholokhov(IRE) Auentime (GER) (Dashing Blade)
2781[7] 3015[11] 3196[P] 4824[8]

Aughcarra (IRE) *Harry Chisman* 71h
10 b g High Chaparral(IRE) Pearly Brooks (Efisio)
1051[5] 1299[6]

Augusta Kate *W P Mullins* 130b
4 b m Yeats(IRE) Feathard Lady (IRE) (Accordion)
(2677a) 4721[7] 5180[2]

Auld Fyffee (IRE) *Tom Gretton* 84h
3 b f Haatef(USA) Lucky Fountain (IRE) (Lafontaine I (USA))
690[C] 891[3] 1111[3] 1294[2] 1384[5] 1732[4] 2137[3]

Auldthunder (IRE) *Micky Hammond* 105h 121c
8 b g Oscar(IRE) Jill's Girl (IRE) (Be My Native (USA))
35[P] 2400[P] 2844[9] (3803) (3969) 4110[2] **(4511) (5404)**

Auntie Annie (IRE) *Mrs Gillian Callaghan* 81h
4 b m Kalanisi(IRE) Billythefilly (IRE) (Exit To Nowhere (USA))
846[4]

Aunt Nora (IRE) *P A Fahy* 111h 125c
8 b m Kayf Tara Niat Supreme (IRE) (Supreme Leader)
(3604a)

Aupcharlie (IRE) *Henry De Bromhead* 112h 142c
9 b g Daliapour(IRE) Lirfa (USA) (Lear Fan (USA))
95a[P] 4768[6]

Au Quart De Tour (FR) *W P Mullins* 133h
5 b g Robin Des Champs(FR) Qualite Controlee (FR) (Poliglote)
23a[10] 4280a[4]

Aurillac (FR) *Rebecca Curtis* 132h
5 gr g Martaline Ombrelle (FR) (Octagonal (NZ))
(2065) 2514[3] 3974[3] (4351) 4766[10] 5263[3]

Aurora Bell (IRE) *John M Burke* 116h 132c
7 b g Beneficial Fair Choice (IRE) (Zaffaran (USA))
2675a[4] 4397a[5]

Aurore D'Estruval (FR) *Rebecca Curtis* 147h
5 ch m Nickname(FR) Option D'Estruval (FR) (Epervier Bleu)
3408[4] 3732[9] 4699[15]

Aussie Berry (IRE) *Donald McCain*
3 gr g Aussie Rules(USA) Berry Baby (IRE) (Rainbow Quest (USA))
1712[P]

Austin Friars *Jim Best* 68h
3 b g New Approach(IRE) My Luigia (IRE) (High Estate)
3790[P] 3988[P] 4409[11] 5091[13] 5477[9]

Australasia (IRE) *Karen McLintock* 14h
5 b g Zerpour(IRE) Leachestown (IRE) (Insatiable (IRE))
732[2] 3159[4]

Australia Day (IRE) *Paul Webber* 139h 154c
12 gr g Key Of Luck(USA) Atalina (FR) (Linamix (FR))
184[U] 1180[2] 1263[4] **1735[4]**

Auteuil Oliverie (FR) *A Le Clerc*
2 ch f Coastal Path My Belle Du Rheu (FR) (Fill My Hopes (FR))
5498a[10]

Authinger (IRE) *Barry Murtagh* 78h 108c
7 b g Sadler's Wells(USA) Ange Bleu (USA) (Alleged (USA))
304[4] 470[8] 1493[6] 2322[9] 2946[6]

Authorative (IRE) *Anthony McCann* 101h
5 b g Refuse To Bend(IRE) Reasonably Devout (CAN) (St Jovite (USA))
1115[2] 1544[3]

Authorized Too *Noel Williams* 123h
4 b g Authorized(IRE) Audaz (Oasis Dream)
2544[2] 3083[F] 3375[2] 3773[2] (4934) 5279[9]

Auto Mac *Mike Sowersby* 83h
7 b g Auction House(USA) Charlottevalentina (IRE) (Perugino (USA))
34[8] 252[3] 399[4] 694[7] (937) 1096[4]

Automated *Gordon Elliott* 135h
4 b g Authorized(IRE) Red Blooded Woman (USA) (Red Ransom (USA))
5219[2] ◆

Auvergnat (FR) *Jonjo O'Neill* 123h 127c
5 b g Della Francesca(USA) Hesmeralda (FR) (Royal Charter (FR))
199[4] 1970[2] 2878[U] 3008[4] 3824[P]

Aux Ptits Soins (FR) *Paul Nicholls* 146h
5 gr g Saint Des Saints(FR) Reflexion Faite (FR) (Turgeon (USA))
4732[5]

Avant Tout (FR) *W P Mullins* 145h 156c
5 ch g Agent Bleu(FR) Quiwfty (FR) (Dark Moondancer)
(50a) **3301a[2] 3830a[F]** 4717[9] ◆ **(5132a)**

Avellino (IRE) *Dermot Anthony McLoughlin* 125b
4 b m Muhtathir Alliata (USA) (Southern Halo (USA))
4623[5] ◆

Avel Parc Leur (FR) *E Mahe* 16b
5 b m Tiger Groom Kerivel (FR) (Dadarissime (FR))
2536a[11]

Avel Vor (IRE) *Nigel Hawke* 107h 69c
4 ch g Green Tune(USA) High Perfection (IRE) (High Chaparral (IRE))
701[5] 895[5] **1047[7] 1233[4]** 2093[8] 2458[8] 2833[3] 3368[12]

Avenir D'Une Vie (FR) *W P Mullins* 136b
5 gr g Lavirco(GER) Par Bonheur (FR) (Robin Des Champs (FR))
4721[12]

Aviador (GER) *Lucy Wadham* 104h
9 b g Paolini(GER) Albarana (GER) (Sure Blade (USA))
2687[5] 3220[5] 3662[P] 4184[3] 4671[4]

Aviator (GER) *James Eustace* 125h
7 br g Motivator Amore (GER) (Lando (GER))
63[4] (621) 916[2] 1325[4] 4066[11]

Avidity *James Ewart* 136h
6 b g Passing Glance Epicurean (Pursuit Of Love)
418[3] 2194[2] 2639[P]

Avispa *Alan King* 120h
6 b m Kayf Tara Ladylliat (FR) (Simon Du Desert (FR))
2021[2] 2314[P] 4890[3] 5094[6]

A Vos Gardes (FR) *Charlie Longsdon* 134h
5 br g Kapgarde(FR) Miscia Nera (FR) (Panoramic)
2083[5] 2411[5] 2767[2] 3407[P] 4354[7]

Away For Slates (IRE) *Keith Dalgleish* 126h
5 b g Arcadio(GER) Rumi (Nishapour (FR))
2100[6] 2318[5] 2945[2] 3242[4] (3424) 3728[P] 4389[5] (4705)

Away In May *John Spearing* 54b
4 gr m Proclamation(IRE) Loch Shiel (IRE) (Selkirk (USA))
2650[7] 3132[12]

Awaywiththegreys (IRE) *Peter Bowen* 130h 108c
8 gr g Whipper(USA) Silver Sash (GER) (Mark Of Esteem (IRE))
2906[7] (3517) 4354[11] **4826[F]**

Awesome Rosie *Alan King* 119h
4 b m Midnight Legend Awesome Aunt (IRE) (Vestris Abu)
152[2] (432) 2561[3] (3252) 4271[2] 4734[15] 5145[2]

Ayalor (FR) *Harry Fry* 127h
5 b g Khalkevi(IRE) Physicienne (FR) (Bonnet Rouge (FR))
3978[2] ◆ 4596[10]

Aye Well *Stuart Coltherd* 111h 133c
10 b g Overbury(IRE) Squeeze Box (IRE) (Accordion)
2193[P] 2719[5] 3475[2] 3806[5] 4011[5] (4838) ◆ **5179[P]**

Ayla's Emperor *John Flint* 103h
6 b m Holy Roman Emperor(IRE) Ayla (IRE) (Daylami (IRE))
3077[8] 3516[10] 4157[2] 4435[4] 4886[3] (5380)

Aza Run (IRE) *Shaun Harris* 101h
5 b g Hurricane Run(IRE) Aza Wish (IRE) (Mujadil (USA))
852[6] 1137[5] 3784[6] 4460[6] 4797[4] 5313[3]

Azastar (FR) *F-M Cottin* 91c
4 b g Walk In The Park(IRE) Malrose (FR) (Apeldoorn (FR))
3815a[F]

Azerodegree (IRE) *Harriet Graham* 92h 80c
6 b g Azamour(IRE) Fairy (USA) (Gulch (USA))
1402[7] 1857[4] 2321[P] 2844[8]

Azert De Coeur (FR) *Venetia Williams* 123c
5 b g Tiger Groom Eden De Coeur (FR) (Lampon (FR))
2438[P] **3466[4] 3631[2] 3794[F] 4042[3] 4456[4] 5164[2]**

Azorian (IRE) *Gordon Elliott* 126h 142c
7 b g Westerner Eliane Di Rupette (Cosmonaut)
69a[5] 2063[4] 2232a[3]

Azure Fly (IRE) *Charlie Longsdon* 125h 139c
7 br g Blueprint(IRE) Lady Delight (IRE) (Be My Native (USA))
(1807) 2061[7] 2482[11] 3109[P] 4858[5] 5274[5]

Azure Glamour (IRE) *Kenneth Slack* 98h
6 br g Golan(IRE) Mirazur (IRE) (Good Thyne (USA))
421[5] 3242[P] 4049[P] (4703) (4943)

Azyaan (IRE) *Kevin Ryan* 41h
3 gr f Mastercraftsman(IRE) Hidden Heart (USA) (Kingmambo (USA))
1415[5]

Azzerti (FR) *Alan King* 104b
3 b g Voix Du Nord(FR) Zalagarry (FR) (Ballingarry (IRE))
4364[4] 5143[4] ◆

Azzuri *Dan Skelton* 134h
3 b g Azamour(IRE) Folly Lodge (Grand Lodge (USA))
4010[5] 4358[2] 5175[3]

Babbling Stream *W P Mullins* 128h
4 b g Authorized(IRE) Elasouna (IRE) (Rainbow Quest (USA))
5002a[5]

Babeny Bridge (IRE) *Nick Williams* 107h 93c
6 b g Exit To Nowhere(USA) Rose Of Clare (Bob Back (USA))
219[3]

Baby Bach (IRE) *S R B Crawford* 131h
5 gr g Bach(IRE) Anns Island (IRE) (Turtle Island (IRE))
(2791) 3156[2] ◆ 3739[5] (4567) (4902) 5328[11]

Baby Bee Jay *Nigel Twiston-Davies* 50h
4 b m King's Theatre(IRE) Belle Magello (FR) (Exit To Nowhere (USA))
334[4] 3119[P] 4893[8]

Baby Cat Delaroque (FR) *J Merienne*
4 b m Nickname(FR) La Valliere (FR) (Anabaa (USA))
4401a[6]

Baby Jake (IRE) *John Joseph Hanlon* 118h
6 b g Morozov(USA) Potters Dawn (IRE) (Talkin Man (CAN))
(1347) 1459[2]

Baby King (IRE) *Tom George* 129h
6 b g Ivan Denisovich(IRE) Burn Baby Burn (IRE) (King's Theatre (IRE))
(2637) 3156[4] 3708[3] 4115[14] 4484[4] 5414[4]

Babylone Colombe (FR) *Tom Symonds* 35h
4 b m Coastal Path Ruse De Guerre (FR) (Cadoudal (FR))
2856[16] 3105[14] 4388[P]

Baby Mix (FR) *Warren Greatrex* 139h 147c
7 gr g Al Namix(FR) Douchka (FR) (Fijar Tango (FR))
24a[2] 362[2] 1040[2] 2185[3]

Baby Sherlock *David Pipe* 80h
4 ch g Shirocco(GER) Lady Cricket (FR) (Cricket Ball (USA))
3959[6] 5188[3] 5416[5]

Baby Shine (IRE) *Lucy Wadham* 130h 139c
9 b m King's Theatre(IRE) Brambleshine (IRE) (Phardante (FR))
2724[F] (3046)

Baby Ticker *Donald Whillans* 90h
6 ch m Endoli(USA) Baby Gee (King Among Kings)
3060[4] 4284[7] 4509[4] 4835[3] ◆

Bacardys (FR) *W P Mullins* 136b
4 b g Coastal Path Oasice (FR) (Robin Des Champs (FR))
4721[3] ◆ (5195)

Bacchanel (FR) *Philip Hobbs* 98h
4 b g Vendangeur(IRE) Pardielle (FR) (Robin Des Champs (FR))
2493[3] ◆ 3416[2] 4357[3] 5137[3]

Bachasson (FR) *W P Mullins* 148h
4 gr g Voix Du Nord(FR) Belledonne (FR) (Shafoun (FR))
(1788a) 2814a[2] 3294a[8] 4766[U]

Bach To Before (IRE) *Graeme McPherson* 83h 74c
7 b g Bach(IRE) Fairfield Mist (IRE) (Mandalus)
155[P] 416[5] 527[7] **2861[U] 3062[5]**

Back By Midnight *Emma Baker* 109h
6 ch g Midnight Legend Roberta Back (IRE) (Bob Back (USA))
(1931) 2734[3] 2987[13] 3619[3] 4129[8] 4871[2] 5433[11]

Back Door Johnny (IRE) *Paul Nolan* 67c
4 b g Westerner Nolagh Supreme (IRE) (Supreme Leader)
3716a[6]

Backhomeinderry (IRE) *Dominic Ffrench Davis* 72b
10 b g Oscar(IRE) Foyle Wanderer (IRE) (Supreme Leader)
811[P] 977[P]

Back In June *Paul Henderson* 101h 110c
7 b g Bach(IRE) Bathwick June (IRE) (Supreme Leader)
388[2] 670[4]

Back Off Mate (IRE) *A L T Moore* 106h 128c
7 b g Old Vic Flyhalf (IRE) (Be My Native (USA))
2236a[8]

Backoftherock *David Rees* 64b
6 b g Scorpion(IRE) Oscars Vision (IRE) (Oscar Schindler (IRE))
875[4] 1011[P]

Back To Balloo (IRE) *C A McBratney* 117h 113c
9 gr g Jimble(FR) Fleur Du Chenet (FR) (Northern Fashion (USA))
657[7]

Back To Bracka (IRE) *Lucinda Russell* 107h 139c
8 b g Rudimentary(USA) Martha's Glimpse (IRE) (Tidaro (USA))
198[4] (2192) 2615[P] 3155[2]

Badbad Leroy Brown *Oliver Greenall* 88b
3 b g Lucarno(USA) Leroy's Sister (FR) (Phantom Breeze)
5337[3]

Bad Boy Du Pouldu (FR) *Gary Moore*
4 b g Loup Solitaire(USA) Wild Flush (USA) (Pine Bluff (USA))
4594^{P}

Baden (FR) *Nicky Henderson* 134h
4 gr g Martaline Ma Sonate (USA) (Val De L'Orne (FR))
3019^{2} 3852^{5} ◆

Badged *Lucy Normile* 111h 81c
6 b g High Chaparral(IRE) Meshhed (USA) (Gulch (USA))
285^{4} **659^{3} 885^{5} 2293^{U}** 5408^{3}

Badger Run (IRE) *Pat Murphy* 66h
4 gr g Acambaro(GER) Charannah (IRE) (Red Sunset)
1843^{8} 2597^{10} 4494^{9} 5091^{15} 5469^{13}

Badgers Cove (IRE) *Robin Dickin* 99h 87c
11 b g Witness Box(USA) Celestial Rose (IRE) (Roselier (FR))
4466^{5} **4879^{P}** (Dead)

Badgers Retreat *Nick Mitchell* 99h 103c
9 b g Elusive City(USA) Heuston Station (IRE) (Fairy King (USA))
1121^{P} 1298^{4} 1614^{2} (1720) 1978^{P}

Badger Wood *Giles Smyly* 96h 108c
6 b g Overbury(IRE) Parlour Game (Petoski)
3256^{3} **(3746) 4185^{P} 4780^{P}**

Badilou (FR) *Martin Hill* 96h
4 bb g Ballingarry(IRE) Doumia (FR) (Dounba (FR))
2262^{P} 2880^{4} 3108^{8}

Bagad Bihoue (FR) *Paul Nicholls* 82b
4 b g Nickname(FR) Lann Bihouee (FR) (Video Rock (FR))
3258^{7}

Bagging Turf (IRE) *Gary Moore* 105h
5 b m Scorpion(IRE) Monica's Story (Arzanni)
3947^{2} (4598) 5155^{4}

Bags Groove (IRE) *Harry Fry* 124b
4 b g Oscar(IRE) Golden Moment (IRE) (Roselier (FR))
2636^{2} (3847) 4488^{2}

Baguette D'Or (FR) *Gabriel Leenders*
4 b m Nidor(FR) Arche's Manor (FR) (Wagon Master (FR))
1231a^{5}

Baie Des Iles (FR) *Ross O'Sullivan* 132h 134c
4 gr m Barastraight Malownia (FR) (Smadoun (FR))
2676a^{7} **3894a^{2} 4260a^{4} 5005a^{6}**

Baile Sheain (IRE) *Roy Brotherton*
5 b g Zagreb(USA) Gathabawn Lass (IRE) (Norwich)
5143^{9}

Baileys Concerto (IRE) *Dianne Sayer* 122h 143c
9 b g Bach(IRE) None The Wiser (IRE) (Dr Massini (IRE))
1035^{16} **1417^{5} 2335^{4} 3038^{P} 4306^{3}**

Baily Cloud (IRE) *M F Morris* 136h
5 ch g Touch Of Land(FR) Cap The Rose (IRE) (Roselier (FR))
2814a^{4} 3294a^{7}

Baily Green (IRE) *M F Morris* 107h 157c
9 b g King's Theatre(IRE) Dream On Boys (IRE) (Anshan)
8a^{2} 1152a^{16} 3552a^{P} 4733^{10}

Baily Moon (IRE) *M F Morris* 104h
4 b g Milan Givehertime (IRE) (Commanche Run)
11a^{21}

Bajan Blu *David Brace* 113h
7 b g Generous(IRE) Bajan Girl (FR) (Emperor Jones (USA))
529^{P}

Bajardo (IRE) *Emma Baker* 113h 76c
7 b g Jammaal Bit Of Peace (IRE) (Le Bavard (FR))
5246^{11}

Bako De La Saulaie (FR) *Rose Dobbin* 98h
4 b g Balko(FR) Krickette (FR) (Passing Sale (FR))
2031^{7} 5256^{3} ◆

Baku Bay (IRE) *Ali Stronge* 125h 125c
7 b g Flemensfirth(USA) The Girlfriend (IRE) (Glacial Storm (USA))
2064^{S} **2631^{4} 3836^{3} 4465^{2} 4912^{4}**

Balade Mail (FR) *Shaun Lycett* 60b
4 b m Walk In The Park(IRE) Boisy Deauville (FR) (Pistolet Bleu (IRE))
1378^{6}

Baldadash (IRE) *Jose Santos* 107h 103c
10 b g Beneficial Balda Girl (IRE) (Mandalus)
3662^{P} 4250^{4} 4455^{6} 5306^{P}

Balding Banker (IRE) *Rebecca Menzies* 97h 123c
9 b g Accordion What A Breeze (IRE) (Naheez (USA))
1114^{P} (1332)

Baler Boy *Des Donovan* 47h
3 b g Sakhee(USA) Olindera (GER) (Lomitas)
2439^{4} 2718^{10}

Balgarry (FR) *David Pipe* 137h 142c
8 ch g Ballingarry(IRE) Marie de Motreff (FR) (Kendor (FR))
2412^{3} 2779^{4} (2990) 3351^{U} 3524^{5}

Balinas D'Airy (FR) *J Ortet*
4 b g Legolas(JPN) Dalina D'Airy (FR) (Marasali)
3876a^{P}

Balinderry (IRE) *Nick Kent* 63h 92c
8 b g Flemensfirth(USA) Erins Love (IRE) (Double Bed (FR))
340^{P}

Balinroab (IRE) *Mark Bradstock* 100h 112c
8 b g Milan Gentle Eyre (IRE) (Aristocracy (IRE))
750^{2} 1987^{P}

Balisha (FR) *S Foucher* 97c
4 ch m Honolulu(IRE) Fetuque Du Moulin (FR) (Royal Charter (FR))
3876a^{6}

Balkato Des Bois (FR) *Tom Lacey* 68b
4 b g Balko(FR) Equatoriale (FR) (Saint Estephe (FR))
783^{5}

Balkevie (FR) *J Provost* 40b
4 b m Khalkevi(IRE) Linattendue (FR) (Passing Sale (FR))
2536a^{10}

Balko Des Flos (FR) *W P Mullins* 138h
4 ch g Balko(FR) Royale Marie (FR) (Garde Royale)
4766^{5} 5194^{4}

Ballagh (IRE) *Ben Case* 139h
6 b g Shantou(USA) Go Along (IRE) (Saddlers' Hall (IRE))
2910^{3} 3623^{P}

Ballalough *Chris Grant* 96h
5 b g Lucarno(USA) Cerise Bleue (FR) (Port Lyautey (FR))
33^{3}

Ball D'Arc (FR) *Gordon Elliott* 144h
4 b g Network(GER) Pretty Moon (FR) (Moon Madness)
9a^{12} 3539a^{3} (3890a) (4280a) 5190^{7}

Ball Hopper (IRE) *Richenda Ford* 93c
11 ch g Rock Hopper Lady Vic (IRE) (Old Vic)
(2255) 2447^{2} 3088^{P} 4422^{P}

Ballinalacken (IRE) *Clare Ellam* 106h
7 b g Fruits Of Love(USA) Miss Daisy (Daylami (IRE))
2042^{13} 2490^{5} 2694^{9} 2839^{P} 2997^{5} (3223) 3607^{4} 3837^{13} 4301^{5} 4706^{3} 4749^{5}

Ballinure (IRE) *Nicky Henderson* 112h
5 b g Alkaadhem Christy's Pride (IRE) (Kambalda)
(407) 1898^{2} ◆ 2239^{3} 3420^{P}

Ballinvarrig (IRE) *Tom George* 108h 132c
8 b g Beneficial Leos Holiday (IRE) (Commanche Run)
2615^{4} 3282^{9} 3706^{3} 4584^{2} 5147^{2}

Ballinvegga (IRE) *Jackie Stephen* 104h
5 gr g Royal Anthem(USA) Gill's Honey (IRE) (Celio Rufo)
1640^{3} 2031^{6} 4902^{4} (5408)

Ballochmyle (IRE) *Caroline Fryer* 85h
5 b g Milan Not So Green (IRE) (Roselier (FR))
127^{4} 494^{6} 2223^{3} 2649^{P} 3128^{2} 3489^{3} 3946^{4} 4349^{5}

Ballotin (FR) *G Macaire* 138h 130c
4 b g Enrique Orphee De Vonnas (FR) (Jimble (FR))
1882a^{7}

Ballyadam Approach (IRE) *Terence O'Brien* 125h 141c
10 b g Bob Back(USA) Timely Approach (IRE) (Good Thyne (USA))
(24a) 4397a^{7} 5005a^{3}

Ballyadeen (IRE) *Dai Williams* 97h 135c
7 b g King's Theatre(IRE) Akilara (IRE) (Kahyasi)
2733^{P} 3081^{F} (3235) 3794^{6} (4042) ◆ 4465^{10} 4775^{U} (Dead)

Ballyallia Man (IRE) *Mrs N Sheppard* 85h 133c
10 b g Flemensfirth(USA) Hatch Away (IRE) (Lord Americo)
3585^{4} 4651^{8} 4892^{P}

Ballyalton (IRE) *Ian Williams* 149h 153c
8 b g Pierre Almilto (IRE) (Mandalus)
2274^{U} ◆ 2469^{6} 3726^{2} 4237^{F} (4701) 5191^{5}

Ballyandrew (IRE) *Nigel Twiston-Davies* 70b
4 b g Westerner Royale Acadou (FR) (Cadoudal (FR))
1817^{5}

Ballyandy *Nigel Twiston-Davies* 137b
4 b g Kayf Tara Megalex (Karinga Bay)
(2020) (2514) 3138^{2} (4117) (4721) ◆ 5195^{4}

Ballyarthur (IRE) *Nigel Twiston-Davies* 116h
5 b g Kayf Tara Ariels Serenade (IRE) (Presenting)
1895^{2}

Ballybane (IRE) *Rebecca Curtis* 122h
5 gr g Acambaro(GER) Madam Sophie (IRE) (Moscow Society (USA))
1829^{4} 3516^{3}

Bally Beaufort (IRE) *Nigel Twiston-Davies* 130h 146c
7 b g Old Vic Miss Compliance (IRE) (Broken Hearted)
(2332) (2897) 3229^{6} 3621^{P} 4238^{5} 4700^{P}

Ballyben (IRE) *Lucinda Russell* 103h 125c
7 ch g Beneficial I'm Maggy (NZ) (Danseur Etoile (FR))
(458) 707^{8} 1632^{4} 2068^{3} 3024^{5} 3472^{P}

Ballybogey (IRE) *Charles Pogson* 130h 123c
9 b g Definite Article Beenaround (IRE) (King's Ride)
338^{4} (677) 1005^{3} 1690^{2}

Ballyboker Breeze (IRE) *Nicky Richards* 129h 135c
7 b g Gold Well Ballyboker Lady (IRE) (Rashar (USA))
(5413)

Ballyboker Bridge (IRE) *Peter Maher* 98h 132c
8 b g Gold Well Ballyboker Lady (IRE) (Rashar (USA))
48a^{F} 3017^{3} 4719^{6}

Ballybolley (IRE) *Nigel Twiston-Davies* 136h 148c
6 b g Kayf Tara Gales Hill (IRE) (Beau Sher)
2274^{3} 2691^{7} 3134^{4} 3611^{3} ◆ 3794^{3} 4787^{3} (4910) 5215^{4}

Ballybough Andy (IRE) *David Dennis* 94b 115c
6 ch g City Honours(USA) Princess Ruth (IRE) (Weld)
5334^{P}

Ballybough Gorta (IRE) *Nick Mitchell* 60h 126c
8 b g Indian Danehill(IRE) Eyelet (IRE) (Satco (FR))
169^{4} 448^{2}

Ballybough Pat (IRE) *David Dennis* 93h 138c
8 b g Waky Nao Princess Ruth (IRE) (Weld)
(282) (358) 707^{3}

Ballybrowneybridge (IRE) *Sam Thomas* 92h
5 b m Kalanisi(IRE) Ballybrowney Hall (IRE) (Saddlers' Hall (IRE))
2856^{6} 3485^{4} 4151^{P}

Ballycamp (IRE) *Charles Pogson* 117h
6 br g Kayf Tara All Our Blessings (IRE) (Statoblest)
83^{2} 397^{2} 780^{4} 1002^{7} 1425^{2} 1693^{2} 5242^{2}

Ballycasey (IRE) *W P Mullins* 142h 154c
8 gr g Presenting Pink Mist (IRE) (Montelimar (USA))
95a^{4} 3715a^{9} 4131a^{3} 4733^{5} 5218^{U} 5492^{6}

Ballycash (IRE) *Nigel Twiston-Davies* 98h
4 b g Kalanisi(IRE) Waterlily (IRE) (Revoque (IRE))
3827^{P} 4475^{3} 5048^{5}

Ballychorus (IRE) *Ms Margaret Mullins* 133h 143c
6 b m King's Theatre(IRE) Royal Rosy (IRE) (Dominion Royale)
2675a^{F} 3296a^{F} 4700^{U}

Ballycoe *Chris Gordon* 119h 117c
6 b g Norse Dancer(IRE) Lizzy Lamb (Bustino)
1821^{3} 2872^{5} 3253^{P} 4071^{7} (5388) (5478) ◆

Ballycool (IRE) *Lucinda Russell* 94h 119c
8 b g Helissio(FR) Carnoustie (USA) (Ezzoud (IRE))
202^{5} 1738^{3} 2104^{2} 2979^{5} 5086^{6}

Ballycross *Nigel Twiston-Davies* 129h
4 b g King's Theatre(IRE) Ninna Nanna (FR) (Garde Royale)
1648^{6} 2275^{3} ◆ 3032^{5} 3316^{2} (4596) ◆ 5213^{10}

Ballycrystal (IRE) *Brian Ellison* 106b
4 b g Oscar(IRE) Musical Madam (IRE) (Musical Pursuit)
4037^{3} (4308) 5330^{9}

Ballyculla (IRE) *Warren Greatrex* 136h 143c
8 b g Westerner Someone Told Me (IRE) (Saddlers' Hall (IRE))
95a^{5} (3008) ◆ 4367^{F} (4864) 5327^{P}

Ballydague Lady (IRE) *Neil Mulholland* 91h 117c
8 b m Luso Cottstown Belle (IRE) (Flemensfirth (USA))
2022^{4} **2346^{2} 2551^{2} 3007^{4} 3972^{2} 4545^{4} 4985^{2}**

Ballydine (IRE) *Charlie Longsdon* 143h
5 ch g Stowaway Bealaha Essie (IRE) (Denel (FR))
1829^{2} (2152) (2787) 3859^{2} 5194^{9}

Ballyegan (IRE) *Bob Buckler* 91h 100c
10 b g Saddlers' Hall(IRE) Knapping Princess (IRE) (Prince Of Birds (USA))
161^{4} 2447^{4} 2735^{3} (3131) 3977^{P} 4187^{2} 4453^{5} 4686^{5} 5435^{10}

Ballygarvey (FR) *Philip Hobbs* 120h 144c
9 b g Laveron Vollore (FR) (Cadoudal (FR))
1869^{6} 2335^{2}

Bally Gilbert (IRE) *Ben Pauling* 101b
4 ch g Stowaway Reedsbuck (FR) (Cyborg (FR))
5248^{2}

Ballyglasheen (IRE) *Evan Williams* 139h
5 ch g Galileo(IRE) Luas Line (IRE) (Danehill (USA))
1974 812^{8} 1119^{2} 1325^{7} 1591^{3} 1868^{6} 4353^{F}

Ballygrooby Bertie (IRE) *S R B Crawford* 72h 109c
7 b g King's Theatre(IRE) Vigna Maggio (FR) (Starborough)
958^{8} 2190^{7}

Ballyheigue Bay (IRE) *Chris Gordon* 102h 136c
8 b g Rudimentary(USA) Terinka (IRE) (Erins Isle)
2916^{3} 3282^{8} 3624^{P} 5120^{12}

Ballyhenry (IRE) *Ben Pauling* 120h
5 br g Presenting Afarka (IRE) (Kahyasi)
2762^{6} (4097) 4788^{3} 5284^{P}

Ballyhill (FR) *Nigel Twiston-Davies* 108b
4 bb g Al Namix(FR) Laly Light (FR) (Start Fast (FR))
1872^{2} 2562^{4} 4894^{7}

Ballykan *Nigel Twiston-Davies* 116h 140c
5 b g Presenting La Marianne (Supreme Leader)
219^{2} (518) **(1520) ◆ (1701) 2055^{4} 2790^{P} 4361^{4} 4697^{10} 5193^{17}**

Ballyknock Lad (IRE) *Kim Bailey* 120h
6 b g Bach(IRE) Ballyknock Lass (IRE) (Electric)
1699^{2} **2456^{P}** 2744^{9}

Bally Lagan (IRE) *Robin Dickin* 79h 86c
7 gr g Kalanisi(IRE) Rose Palma (FR) (Great Palm (USA))
2542^{6} 2811^{2}

Bally Legend *Caroline Keevil* 124h 142c
10 b g Midnight Legend Bally Lira (Lir)
1736^{6}

Bally Longford (IRE) *Henry De Bromhead* 106h 135c
7 b g Gold Well Stay On Line (IRE) (Over The River (FR))
96a^{19} **(1186a)**

Ballymalin (IRE) *Nigel Twiston-Davies* 118b
5 b g Presenting Murrurundi (IRE) (Old Vic)
(3522) 3952^{2} 4721^{20} 5227^{3}

Ballymoat *Sue Smith* 108h 125c
8 b g Grape Tree Road Frosty Mistress (Arctic Lord (IRE))
2837^{4}

Ballymorris (IRE) *Kenny Johnson* 18c
6 b g Courteous Lady Phoenix (IRE) (Erins Isle)
452^{7} **635^{7}** 798^{P}

Ballynagour (IRE) *David Pipe* 149h 167c
9 b g Shantou(USA) Simply Deep (IRE) (Simply Great (FR))
22a^{F} (349a) 663a^{5} **2200^{3} ◆ 2642^{5} 3231^{P} 4113^{P} 4733^{7} 5218^{U}**

Ballyoliver *Venetia Williams* 95h 135c
11 b g Kayf Tara Macklette (IRE) (Buckskin (FR))
2213^{9} 3918^{3} 4109^{4} 4684^{5}

Ballyoptic (IRE) *Nigel Twiston-Davies* 154h
5 b g Old Vic Lambourne Lace (IRE) (Un Desperado (FR))
(4264) (4798) (5194)

Ballypoint (IRE) *Nigel Twiston-Davies* 127h
4 b g Mahler Angel Trix (IRE) (Un Desperado (FR))
2842^{8} 3130^{2} 3739^{6} 4344^{2} 4620^{11} (5050)

Ballyrath (IRE) *Nigel Twiston-Davies* 119h 126c
5 b g Flemensfirth(USA) Rose Wee (IRE) (Roselier (FR))
1600^{4} **2365^{3} 2996^{5} (3788) 3924^{2} 4505^{U} 4649^{P}** 5072^{3}

Ballyrock (FR) *Y-M Porzier* 124h 131c
6 b g Ballingarry(IRE) Rochambelle (FR) (Truculent (USA))
374a^{7}

Ballyrock (IRE) *Tim Vaughan* 126h
9 b g Milan Ardent Love (IRE) (Ardross)
2268^{12} 3517^{8} 4618^{2} 5141^{4}

Ballyroe Rambler (IRE) *J A Berry* 116h 116c
8 br g Lahib(USA) Victoria's Rose (IRE) (Be My Native (USA))
2530a^{4} 4663a^{R}

Bally Sands (IRE) *Robin Mathew* 104c
11 b g Luso Sandwell Old Rose (IRE) (Roselier (FR))
3826^{P}

Ballythomas *David Thompson* 101h 86c
8 b g Kayf Tara Gregale (Gildoran)
261^{6} 398^{2} ◆ **959^{6}**

Ballytober *Ian Prichard* 124h 124c
9 b g Kahyasi Full Of Birds (FR) (Epervier Bleu)
393^{3} 5158^{5} (5399)

Ballyvaughn (IRE) *Caroline Bailey* 89h 102c
5 bb g Robin Des Pres(FR) Countessdee (IRE) (Arctic Lord (IRE))
2023^{5} 2407^{6} 2807^{7} **(4491) 5080^{5}**

Ballyvoneen (IRE) *Neil King* 88h 108c
10 b g Stowaway Miss Ira Zarad (IRE) (Darazari (IRE))
471^{U} 1592^{5} 1733^{3} 1850^{U} (Dead)

Ballyvoque (IRE) *George Charlton* 112h 119c
9 b g Revoque(IRE) Timissa (IRE) (Kahyasi)
802^{2} **1068^{4} 2846^{4}**

Ballywilliam (IRE) *David Pipe* 127h
5 b g Mahler Henrietta Howard (IRE) (King's Ride)
1635^{4} 2265^{3} 2903^{2} 3361^{3} (5100)

Balmoral Prince *Shaun Lycett* 69b
4 b g Multiplex Balmoral Princess (Thethingaboutitis (USA))
2991^{8} 3502^{7}

Balmusette *Keith Reveley* 132h
6 b m Halling(USA) Tcherina (IRE) (Danehill Dancer (IRE))
2637^{8} 3027^{4} ◆ 3336^{6} 4066^{15}

Balnaslow (IRE) *W P Mullins* 53h 139c
8 b g Presenting Noble Choice (Dahar (USA))
1185a^{6}

Balthazar King (IRE) *Philip Hobbs* 98b
11 b g King's Theatre(IRE) Afdala (IRE) (Hernando (FR))
4719^{F}

Baltic Blue *B Dowling* 93c
8 b g Beat All(USA) Laced Up (IRE) (The Parson)
129^{4} 531^{5} 4227^{U}

Baltic Pathfinder (IRE) *Martin Smith* 80h 110c
11 b g Alflora(IRE) Boro Bow (IRE) (Buckskin (FR))
674^{F}

Baltic Storm (IRE) *Charlie Mann* 121h
4 b g Kandahar Run Born Wild (GER) (Sadler's Wells (USA))
1895^{3} 2251^{2} 2747^{3} (4773) 5153^{2}

Baltimore Rock (IRE) *Neil Mulholland* 143h 149c
6 b g Tiger Hill(IRE) La Vita E Bella (IRE) (Definite Article)
(3335) 3975^{2} 4696^{F}

Bamako Moriviere (FR) *W P Mullins* 142h
4 b g Califet(FR) Halladine (FR) (Passing Sale (FR))
3650a^{P}

Bambi Du Noyer (FR) *Simon Waugh* 120h 82c
4 bb g Sageburg(IRE) Zouk Wood (USA) (Woodman (USA))
5386^{10}

Bambys Boy *Keith Reveley* 110b
4 b g Lucarno(USA) Bamby (IRE) (Glacial Storm (USA))
(2344) ◆ 2984^{3}

Banco (FR) *R-M Dupuis* 93h
4 b g Marathon(USA) Mega'T'Hop (FR) (Alesso (USA))
2362a^{P}

Banderitos *Anna Brooks* 40h
6 b g Revoque(IRE) Orchid (Orchestra)
2299^{P}

Bandit Country (IRE) *Jonjo O'Neill* 118h 132c
6 b g Flemensfirth(USA) Calomeria (Groom Dancer (USA))
611^{5} 1167^{12} 1262^{3}

Bandito Conti (FR) *G Macaire* 124h 137c
4 b g Saint Des Saints(FR) Orne Saosnoise (FR) (Pistolet Bleu (IRE))
1882a^{4}

Band Of Blood (IRE) *Dr Richard Newland* 138h 138c
7 b g King's Theatre(IRE) Cherry Falls (IRE) (Ali-Royal (IRE))
4128^{5} 4472^{3} 4697^{8} 5217^{5} 5456^{4}

Band Of Thunder *Mark H Tompkins* 87h
7 ch g Shirocco(GER) Black Opal (Machiavellian (USA))
(222) 398^{4}

Bandon Roc *Kim Bailey* 100h
4 b g Shirocco(GER) Azur (IRE) (Brief Truce (USA))
2995^{7} 3568^{9} 4317^{11} 4650^{4}

Bandsman *Dan Skelton* 110b
4 b g Bandmaster(USA) Soleil Sauvage (Loup Sauvage (USA))
4894^{2} ◆ 5407^{3}

Bangkok Pete (IRE) *Jamie Poulton* 114h 73c
10 b g Alflora(IRE) Kinnegads Pride (IRE) (Be My Native (USA))
3142^{2} ◆ (4241) 5100^{P}

Bang On Time (IRE) *Richard Woollacott* 122c
9 b g Chevalier(IRE) Dysart Lady (IRE) (King's Ride)
163^{2} (390) 510^{P}

Banjo Girl (IRE) *Lucy Wadham* 69b
3 ch f Presenting Oh Susannah (FR) (Turgeon (USA))
5351^{3}

Bank Bonus *Gordon Elliott* 126h
6 b g Motivator Small Fortune (Anabaa (USA))
(886)

Banksandditches (IRE) *Clare Hobson* 88b 98c
9 b g Dilshaan Ardbess (Balla Cove)
(488) 3222^{P}

Banks O' Houxty *Karen McLintock* 113b
5 b g Generous(IRE) Border Mist (IRE) (Mull Of Kintyre (USA))
(459)

Banks Road (IRE) *Geoffrey Deacon* 86h
10 b g Beneficial Cecelia's Charm (IRE) (Mister Lord (USA))
2316^{4} 3128^{7}

Bannow Storm (IRE) *George Bewley* 91b
4 b m Presenting Bannow Girl (IRE) (Glacial Storm (USA))
4908^2

Banny's Lad *Michael Easterby* 110h 58c
6 ch g Osorio(GER) Skytrial (USA) (Sky Classic (CAN))
3971^3 4419^2 5372^7

Bantam (IRE) *Henry Daly* 132h
5 b m Teofilo(IRE) Firecrest (IRE) (Darshaan)
(268) ◆ 591^4 (1271) 1574^2 1974^2 2199^F 4064^2 4734^5 5280^4

Banyu (FR) *Philip Hobbs* 140h
4 b g Dylan Thomas(IRE) Banyu Dewi (GER) (Poliglote)
(2689) 3353^P 3915^2 4849^2 (5414)

Baoulet Delaroque (FR) *Paul Nicholls* 143h
4 b g Ungaro(GER) Opale De La Roque (FR) (Bricassar (USA))
2265^4 (3508) (3956) (4070) 4717^5 5194^P

Baraboy (IRE) *Barry Murtagh* 107h
5 b g Barathea(IRE) Irina (IRE) (Polar Falcon (USA))
(137) (336) ◆ (804) 851^2 962^3 2069^3 2893^4 3398^7 4819^7 5313^2

Baracalu (FR) *Sandy Thomson* 99b
4 gr g Califet(FR) Myragentry (FR) (Myrakalu (FR))
5014^P 5127^3

Barachois Silver *Mrs J M Hollands* 94c
11 gr m Silver Patriarch(IRE) Barachois Princess (USA) (Barachois (CAN))
4207^4 4820^3 5370^P

Baradari (IRE) *Dan Skelton* 152h
5 br g Manduro(GER) Behra (IRE) (Grand Lodge (USA))
(2641) (Dead)

Barafundle (IRE) *Jennie Candlish* 120h 134c
11 ch g Flemensfirth(USA) Different Dee (IRE) (Beau Sher)
2399^P 2641^P 3058^6 3737^7 4066^{14} **4286^3 4818^4 5348^2**

Baraka De Thaix (FR) *David Pipe* 119h
4 gr g Dom Alco(FR) Jaka De Thaix (FR) (Kadalko (FR))
2472^F 3077^3 3570^4 4342^4 4566^2 4815^6

Bar A Mine (FR) *Nigel Twiston-Davies* 108h
6 b g Martaline Treekle Toffee (FR) (Cadoudal (FR))
1629^P 1827^2 2223^8 2855^3 3314^2 3921^2 4127^P 4825^6 5237^4

Baratineur (FR) *Dan Skelton* 130h
4 ch g Vendangeur(IRE) Olmantina (FR) (Ragmar (FR))
1898^4 2628^2 3152^2 ◆ 3743^3 (4409) 4933^P

Baraymi (FR) *Jamie Snowden* 109h
3 b g Makfi Brusca (USA) (Grindstone (USA))
3112^6 3790^2 ◆ 4304^4 5091^8 5160^4

Baraza (FR) *Tom George* 93h
4 gr g Smadoun(FR) Gerbora (FR) (Art Bleu I)
2437^4 3021^8 3375^9

Bardd (IRE) *Nicky Henderson* 95b
3 b g Dylan Thomas(IRE) Zarawa (IRE) (Kahyasi)
4981^2

Bar De Ligne (FR) *Brian Ellison* 132h 134c
9 b g Martaline Treekle Toffee (FR) (Cadoudal (FR))
184^9 660^5 (781) 1040^8

Barel Of Laughs (IRE) *Philip Rowley* 119h 132c
9 b g Milan Danette (GER) (Exit To Nowhere (USA))
3826^P 4307^4

Bare Necessities (IRE) *Shaun Lycett* 113h
5 b g Sandmason Marquante (IRE) (Brief Truce (USA))
865^5 1117^9 1425^3 1780^2

Barenger (IRE) *Ali Stronge* 92h 97c
8 b g Indian Danehill(IRE) Build A Dream (USA) (Runaway Groom (CAN))
165^5

Barenice (FR) *Alex Hales* 112h
4 b g Denham Red(FR) Delice Du Soleil (FR) (Altayan)
2299^P 3626^3 4351^5 5072^5

Bargain (FR) *M Postic*
4 b g Goldneyev(USA) Medanik (FR) (Medaaly)
$4401a^0$

Barista (IRE) *Brian Forsey* 98h
7 b g Titus Livius(FR) Cappuccino (IRE) (Mujadil (USA))
2730^4 (3143) 3376^P

Barizan (IRE) *Brendan Powell* 138h 135c
9 b g Kalanisi(IRE) Behra (IRE) (Grand Lodge (USA))
197^2

Barlow (IRE) *Miss Chloe Roddick* 97h 100c
8 br g Beneficial Carrigeen Kerria (IRE) (Kemal (FR))
4887^5

Barman (FR) *Nicky Henderson* 95h
4 b g Racinger(FR) Koscina (FR) (Dress Parade)
3819^P

Barnahash Rose (IRE) *Jonathan Sweeney* 128h
7 ch m Exit To Nowhere(USA) Shean Bracken (IRE) (Le Moss)
$2677a^5$ (4653a) 5282^5

Barneby (FR) *David Pipe* 75h
4 ro g Dom Alco(FR) Jimanji (FR) (Kadalko (FR))
1599^6 2413^6

Barney Dwan (IRE) *Fergal O'Brien* 142h
5 b g Vinnie Roe(IRE) Kapricia Speed (FR) (Vertical Speed (FR))
1555^5 2258^3 (2591) (3239) ◆ 3744^4 (4620) 5410^3

Barney Rubble *Richard Lee* 88h
6 b g Medicean Jade Chequer (Green Desert (USA))
435^9

Barneys Honour (IRE) *Andy Turnell* 123h 112c
11 b g City Honours(USA) Ballyburn Lady (IRE) (Needle Gun (IRE))
(125) (416) 527^5

Baron Alco (FR) *Gary Moore* 142h
4 ch g Dom Alco(FR) Paula (FR) (Network (GER))
(1977) (2516) (3232) 3733^2 4717^{12}

Baron De Ligniere (FR) *Paul Nicholls* 102b
4 b g Balko(FR) Madame La Comtesse (FR) (Adieu Au Roi (IRE))
213^5 1873^6 3085^P

Baron Du Plessis (FR) *Ian Williams* 105h
4 b g Network(GER) Larme A L'Oeil (FR) (Luchiroverte (IRE))
2729^{10} 4103^{12} 4848^4

Baron Du Seuil (FR) *F-M Cottin* 99h 124c
4 bl g Network(GER) Nistabelle (FR) (Lights Out (FR))
$3876a^3$

Barrakilla (IRE) *Evan Williams* 129h 143c
8 b g Milan Kigali (IRE) (Torus)
2990^2 3446^4 3776^3

Barranco Valley *Nick Williams* 120h
4 b g Midnight Legend Shali San (FR) (Saint Des Saints (FR))
1837^2 ◆

Barra Rotha (IRE) *Laura Hurley* 91h
8 ch g Perugino(USA) That's Magic (IRE) (Lord Americo)
852^7 1082^6 2287^5 **2861^P 3131^P 4412^P** 4877^P

Barren Brook *Michael Easterby* 49h 62c
8 b g Beat Hollow Carinthia (IRE) (Tirol)
2026^6

Barrick's Hill (IRE) *Mrs Sarah J Bosley* 115c
10 b g Oscar(IRE) Lisnacunna Lord (IRE) (Mister Lord (USA))
14^3

Barters Hill (IRE) *Ben Pauling* 153h
5 b g Kalanisi(IRE) Circle The Wagons (IRE) (Commanche Run)
(2221) (3350) ◆ (3859) 4766^4

Barton Antix *Neil Mulholland* 119h
6 b g Fair Mix(IRE) Barton Dante (Phardante (FR))
465^9 935^9 1297^5 1510^2 (1812) (1951) ◆ 2087^2

Barton Gift *John Spearing* 99h 121c
8 b g Alflora(IRE) Marina Bird (Julio Mariner)
2272^4 2878^P 3236^3 3591^5 (4255) 4612^7 5052^4 (5265)

Barton Rose *Michael Blake* 118h 114c
6 b m Midnight Legend Barton Flower (Danzero (AUS))
1971^4 2150^2 2911^4 3217^5 4268^4 4922^5 5382^8

Basford Ben *Jennie Candlish* 103h 113c
7 b g Trade Fair Moly (FR) (Anabaa (USA))
156^4 2213^5 2566^P 2848^5 3144^P 3609^2 3948^2 4276^2 4591^2 (4903) 5375^3

Bashful Beauty (IRE) *Norman Lee* 122h 127c
8 gr g High-Rise(IRE) Killaloonty Rose (IRE) (Roselier (FR))
$1790a^4$ $2675a^P$

Basilic D'Alene (FR) *Nick Williams* 94b
4 gr g Fragrant Mix(IRE) Haifa Du Noyer (FR) (Video Rock (FR))
1826^P 2136^P (Dead)

Bassarabad (FR) *Tim Vaughan* 110h
4 b g Astarabad(USA) Grivette (FR) (Antarctique (IRE))
1455^4 2085^8 2569^2 3662^P 4530^2 5072^2

Bastien (FR) *Alan King* 106b
4 bb g Panoramic Que Du Charmil (FR) (Grand Seigneur (FR))
4880^4

Batavir (FR) *David Pipe* 133h
6 ch g Muhtathir Elsie (GER) (Barathea (IRE))
2484^9 2641^3 3407^P 4112^5 4354^3 4824^2 5146^3 5277^5

Bathilde (FR) *D Bressou* 112h 124c
4 b m Nickname(FR) Nantilde (FR) (Cadoudal (FR))
$350a^8$

Baths Well (IRE) *Ben Pauling* 116h
5 br g Beat All(USA) Bathsheba (Overbury (IRE))
449^2 529^2 775^8 917^2 1100^2 1238^{10}

Bathwick Man *David Pipe* 115h
10 b g Mark Of Esteem(IRE) Local Abbey (IRE) (Primo Dominie)
380^P 645^F (Dead)

Bathwick Scanno (IRE) *Mrs Teresa Clark*
7 b g Aptitude(USA) Hundred Year Flood (USA) (Giant's Causeway (USA))
5270^P

Battle Bridge (IRE) *Mrs H M Tory*
10 br g Amilynx(FR) Hells Angel (IRE) (Kambalda)
3958^P

Battlecat *Evan Williams* 116h 113c
8 b g Tiger Hill(IRE) Applecross (Glint Of Gold)
217^7 442^2 810^7 973^7 1347^4 **1504^3 1595^2 1703^3 2248^2 2692^9**

Battle Dust (IRE) *Kim Bailey* 122h
6 b g Portrait Gallery(IRE) Katie O'Toole (IRE) (Commanche Run)
2558^2 ◆ (2903) 3383^2 3824^5 4544^4

Battleford *W P Mullins* 136b
4 b g Midnight Legend Well Maid (Saddlers' Hall (IRE))
4721^2 ◆ 5195^2 ◆

Battle Master *Michael Mullineaux* 84b
5 b g Starcraft(NZ) Jig Time (Sadler's Wells (USA))
220^4 526^4 2126^{14} 2493^{14}

Battle Of Shiloh (IRE) *Tom George* 125h
6 b g Shantou(USA) Realt Na Ruise (IRE) (Soviet Star (USA))
(3570)

Battleship Boy (IRE) *Sarah-Jayne Davies* 66h
7 b g Kaieteur(USA) Battle On (Blakeney)
57^P

Battling Boru (IRE) *Anthony Mullins* 120h 119c
9 b g Brian Boru Dance Rhythm (IRE) (Dancing Dissident (USA))
$1515a^4$ 2513^P (Dead)

Batu Ferringhi (FR) *Mrs C Hitch* 115h 94c
9 b g Numerous(USA) Dara (IRE) (Danehill (USA))
166^3 5166^4 5384^4

Bawden Rocks *David Bridgwater* 106h 111c
6 b g Anabaa(USA) Late Night (GER) (Groom Dancer (USA))
3195^2 4106^2 4527^2 4669^6 5480^3

Bawnogues Bahri (IRE) *Paul Stafford* 82h
6 b m Bahri(USA) Carhue Journey (IRE) (Barathea (IRE))
960^4 1165^8

Bayan (IRE) *Gordon Elliott* 150h
6 b g Danehill Dancer(IRE) Kindling (Dr Fong (USA))
$1163a^9$

Bayfirth (IRE) *Andrew Hamilton* 57h 84c
12 b g Flemensfirth(USA) Baylough Lady (IRE) (Lancastrian)
842^8 1068^5 (1402) 1462^6 1775^5 4741^P

Bay Fortuna *Mark Usher* 101h
6 b g Old Vic East Rose (Keen)
262^3 615^4 1098^7

Bayley's Dream *Paul Webber* 108h 95c
6 b g Presenting Swaythe (USA) (Swain (IRE))
380^4 746^5 (1721) 2125^P 2687^6 **4876^7** 5397^7

Bay Of Freedom (IRE) *Peter Fahey* 124h
6 b g Heron Island(IRE) Kate Gale (IRE) (Strong Gale)
$23a^7$

Baysbrown (IRE) *Nicky Richards* 95h
5 b g Fruits Of Love(USA) Whenever Wherever (IRE) (Saddlers' Hall (IRE))
459^6 1886^5 2066^8 2769^5 5472^5

Bay Sly (IRE) *Seamus Durack* 110h
8 b g Stowaway On A Mission (IRE) (Dolphin Street (FR))
3927^2 4441^3

Bay To Go (IRE) *Mrs H M Kemp* 58h 110c
9 b g Moscow Society(USA) Lily Langtry (IRE) (Duky)
12^6 270^6 536^5

Baywing (IRE) *Nicky Richards* 135h
6 br g Winged Love(IRE) Cerise De Totes (FR) (Champ Libre (FR))
(2396) ◆ (2962) (3142) (3737) 4248^P

Be A Dreamer *Sue Smith* 88h 96c
7 ch g Dreams End Miss Fahrenheit (IRE) (Oscar (IRE))
134^2 2143^P 2500^U 2889^2 3312^5

Beallandendall (IRE) *Matt Sheppard* 125h
7 b g Beneficial Railstown Lady (IRE) (Supreme Leader)
3571^P 3928^3 (4441) 4888^2 5153^3 5279^6 5462^2

Bear Island Flint *Patrick Holmes* 81b
7 br g Overbury(IRE) Chippewa (FR) (Cricket Ball (USA))
330^P

Bearly Legal (IRE) *Karl Thornton* 118h 134c
9 b g Court Cave(IRE) Fair Size (IRE) (Jurado (USA))
657^4 $4397a^9$ $5005a^5$

Bear's Affair (IRE) *Nicky Henderson* 142h 152c
9 br g Presenting Gladtogetit (Green Shoon)
(318) 855^{10} 2083^4 3018^{12} **4733^B** 5275^{14}

Bearskin (IRE) *Donald Whillans* 96h
4 br g Kodiac Dark Arts (USA) (Royal Anthem (USA))
1178^5 2931^5 3471^8

Bears Rails *Colin Tizzard* 102h 118c
5 b g Flemensfirth(USA) Clandestine (Saddlers' Hall (IRE))
2121^4 **(3178) 3823^3 4352^2 (4545) 4962^4**

Beast Of Burden (IRE) *Rebecca Curtis* 105h 146c
6 ch g Flemensfirth(USA) Nuit Des Chartreux (FR) (Villez (USA))
1867^U 2726^F 4717^P

Beatabout The Bush (IRE) *Henry Oliver* 123h
4 bb g Bushranger(IRE) Queen Of Fibres (IRE) (Scenic (IRE))
1905^7 2170^8 2926^9 4447^5 4774^{12}

Beat The Tide *Tim Vaughan* 106h
5 b g Black Sam Bellamy(IRE) Sablonne (USA) (Silver Hawk (USA))
852^5 1116^3 1290^2 2880^2 3592^2 4429^3

Beatu (IRE) *Donald McCain* 113h
6 b g Beat All(USA) Auntie Bob (Overbury (IRE))
3928^5 4416^3 (4871)

Beau Bay (FR) *Alan Jones* 111h
4 b g Bernebeau(FR) Slew Bay (FR) (Beaudelaire (USA))
1602^5 1818^7 2087^{10} 2961^3 5047^2

Beauboreen (IRE) *Jennie Candlish* 101h 125c
8 b g Revoque(IRE) Roseboreen (IRE) (Roselier (FR))
2490^6 2919^6 4069^3 4648^4 **(5044) (5334)**

Beauchamp Bella *John Ryall*
5 b m Manduro(GER) Baharah (USA) (Elusive Quality (USA))
1574^P

Beauchamp Eagle *Jamie Snowden*
3 ch g Compton Admiral Ashford Castle (USA) (Bates Motel (USA))
3907^P

Beauchamp Viking *Hugo Froud* 68h 83c
11 b g Compton Admiral Beauchamp Jade (Kalaglow)
(42) 379^6 699^7 4686^7 4850^2 5435^6

Beau Dandy (IRE) *Chris Grant* 81h 104c
10 b g Exit To Nowhere(USA) Northern Dandy (The Parson)
(38) 471^P

Beau Du Brizais (FR) *Philip Hobbs* 99h
3 gr g Kapgarde(FR) Belle Du Brizais (FR) (Turgeon (USA))
4880^7

Beau Et Sublime (FR) *A J Martin* 119h
5 b g Saddler Maker(IRE) Jolie Jouvencelle (FR) (Sandhurst Prince)
$53a^8$

Beaujolais Bob *Richard Hawker* 66h 92c
7 gr g Grape Tree Road Charliebob (Nomadic Way (USA))
31^3 388^6 (4590) 4669^2 4823^F

Beau Knight *Alexandra Dunn* 62h
3 b g Sir Percy Nicola Bella (IRE) (Sadler's Wells (USA))
3418^{12} 3745^{10} 4138^4 4439^P 4856^P 5099^9

Beau Lake (IRE) *Suzy Smith* 116h
11 b g Heron Island(IRE) Brennan For Audits (IRE) (Creative Plan (USA))
2637^7 2961^6 3216^4 4129^9

Beau Marsh *Barry Murtagh* 31h
6 ro m Fair Mix(IRE) Heron Marsh (IRE) (Heron Island (IRE))
3681^{12} 4050^P 4737^P

Beaumont's Party (IRE) *Chris Grant* 99h
8 b g High Chaparral(IRE) Miss Champagne (FR) (Bering)
(2706) 2982^6 3398^8

Beau Phil (FR) *Paul Nicholls* 111h
4 ch g Cachet Noir(USA) Neyrianne (FR) (Sheyrann (IRE))
3710^{12} 4449^2 4917^3

Beau Star (FR) *M Rolland* 107h
4 b g Khalkevi(IRE) Rose Star (FR) (Passing Sale (FR))
$2362a^7$

Beautiful Gem (FR) *Dan Skelton* 92h
5 ch m Muhtathir Hunorisk (FR) (Mansonnien (FR))
2302^{10} 2898^4

Beautiful King's (FR) *G Taupin*
4 b g King's Best(USA) Beautiful Note (USA) (Red Ransom (USA))
$3815a^P$

Beautiful People (FR) *Richard Phillips* 89h
4 bb m Early March Night Fever (FR) (Garde Royale)
2421^5 3381^{10} 4881^9

Bebinn (IRE) *Ben Case* 103h 112c
8 b m Brian Boru Windmill Star (IRE) (Orchestra)
211^4 1813^7 2269^2 3222^3 (3663) (3906) 4185^4 4879^2

Be Bop Boru (IRE) *Tim Vaughan* 127h
8 b g Brian Boru Henrietta Howard (IRE) (King's Ride)
85^4 (614) ◆

Becauseicouldntsee (IRE) *N F Glynn* 122b 48c
12 ch g Beneficial Ath Dara (Duky)
$48a^R$

Becauseshesaidso (IRE) *Venetia Williams* 112h
7 b g Winged Love(IRE) Huit De Coeur (FR) (Cadoudal (FR))
2210^4

Bedale *John Ferguson* 106h
4 b g Cape Cross(IRE) Beta (Selkirk (USA))
1240^3 1379^3

Bedale Lane (IRE) *Nicky Richards* 108b
6 b m Kayf Tara Misleain (IRE) (Un Desperado (FR))
2494^P

Be Daring (FR) *Paul Nicholls* 110h
4 gr g Dom Alco(FR) Quinine (FR) (Network (GER))
3104^4

Bedouin Bay *Johnny Farrelly* 112h 25c
8 b g Dubai Destination(USA) Sahara Sonnet (USA) (Stravinsky (USA))
704^2 ◆ 1055^6 1170^{11} 1236^{14}

Bedrock Fred *David Weston* 92b 95c
9 ch g Monsieur Bond(IRE) Sea Mist (IRE) (Shalford (IRE))
610^P 1813^5 5417^5

Beechroad Ally (IRE) *Sandy Thomson* 100h
6 b m Danroad(AUS) Knock Bridge (IRE) (Rossini (USA))
1550^6 1774^4 2069^5

Beedee *Tim Vaughan* 85h
5 b g Beat Hollow Dawnus (IRE) (Night Shift (USA))
912^6 1081^7 1178^P (Dead)

Been Decided (IRE) *N W Alexander* 75h
5 b g Flemensfirth(USA) Laboc (Rymer)
2344^4 2984^7 4050^8 4548^9 5009^8

Beer Goggles (IRE) *Micky Hammond* 118h
4 br g Oscar(IRE) Tynelucy (IRE) (Good Thyne (USA))
1684^5 1886^6 2169^4 2843^7 3474^{13} 4163^7 (4510) (4739)

Beeves (IRE) *Jennie Candlish* 133h 138c
8 b g Portrait Gallery(IRE) Camas North (IRE) (Muharib (USA))
458^3 800^6 3024^2 4155^4 (5140)

Beforeall (IRE) *Oliver Sherwood* 101h 135c
7 b g Spadoun(FR) Maggie Howard (IRE) (Good Thyne (USA))
(3818) 4367^P 4826^6 5348^4

Beggars Cross (IRE) *Jonjo O'Neill* 120h
5 b g Presenting Ballygill Heights (IRE) (Symboli Heights (FR))
3334^{11} 3971^F 4463^5 (5137)

Beggar's Velvet (IRE) *D Holmes* 84h 114c
9 b g Dr Massini(IRE) Lakelough (IRE) (Mandalus)
457^P 5090^2

Beggar's Wishes (IRE) *Peter Bowen* 100b
4 b g Oscar(IRE) Strong Wishes (IRE) (Strong Gale)
1645^5 2965^4 4270^2

Beg To Differ (IRE) *Jonjo O'Neill* 134h 147c
5 ch g Flemensfirth(USA) Blossom Trix (IRE) (Saddlers' Hall (IRE))
2197^3 2960^3 3404^2 (4234) 4697^U

Be Here Now *Jo Davis* 3b
4 b m Rainbow High Bright Spangle (IRE) (General Monash (USA))
4074^{11}

Behind The Scenes (IRE) *A Coveney* 76h 85c
13 br g Presenting Run For Cover (IRE) (Lafontaine I (USA))
292^5

Behind The Wire (IRE) *Tom George* 103h
4 b g Mahler Mujavail (IRE) (Mujadil (USA))
2636^6 3839^9 4844^4 5263^4

Behind Time (IRE) *Harry Fry* 108h
4 b g Stowaway She's Got To Go (IRE) (Glacial Storm (USA))
2763^8 3744^5 4339^3 ◆

Beidh Tine Anseo (IRE) *Lucinda Russell* 106h 106c
9 b g Rock Of Gibraltar(IRE) Siamsa (USA) (Quest For Fame)
(455) 871[6] 962[6]
Being Global (FR) *Caroline Bailey* 111h
4 b g Epalo(GER) Haida IV (FR) (Passing Sale (FR))
105[4] 494[3] 2271[9] 2924[6] 3223[3] (4846)
Bekkensfirth *Dan Skelton* 107h 135c
6 b g Flemensfirth(USA) Bekkaria (FR) (Clafouti (FR))
1826[3] 2182[9] **(2973) 3228[2]**
Belak Chop (FR) *F Cellier* 82h
4 b g Deportivo Black Smith (FR) (Indian Rocket)
3876a[P]
Belami Des Pictons (FR) *Venetia Williams* 132h
4 b g Khalkevi(IRE) Nina Des Pictons (FR) (Denham Red (FR))
(4646) (5043)
Bel Ami Rich *Sally Randell* 93h
5 b g Black Sam Bellamy(IRE) Granny Rich (Ardross)
2986[5] 3580[8] 3976[10]
Belarusian (IRE) *Denis Gerard Hogan* 77b
3 b g Cape Cross(IRE) Russian Society (Darshaan)
5134a[4]
Belcami (FR) *C Lotoux* 58b
4 b m Vatori(FR) Pannick Du Faou (FR) (Port Lyautey (FR))
2536a[7]
Belcanto (IRE) *Jamie Snowden* 99h
5 b m Bach(IRE) Love Divided (IRE) (King's Ride)
594[3] 970[5] (1491) 1960[5] 2444[5] 5415[4]
Belize *Tim Vaughan* 110h
4 b g Rail Link Costa Rica (IRE) (Sadler's Wells (USA))
1893[9] 3619[10] (4919)
Bella (FR) *David Pipe* 118h
4 bb m Johann Quatz(FR) Hasta Manana (FR) (Useful (FR))
(405) 744[5] 938[P] (2852) (4157) 4512[3] 4909[7]
Bella Bourgeoise (FR) *J-D Marion* 71b
4 ch m Storm Trooper(GER) Jasmine (FR) (Valanjou I (FR))
2536a[6]
Belladone (FR) *L Cadot*
4 b m Traditionally(USA) De Couleur The (FR) (Fly To The Stars)
3815a[5]
Bella Girino *Dan Skelton* 26b
3 b f Yeats(IRE) Dancingwithbubbles (IRE) (Supreme Leader)
4392[10]
Bellas Rock (IRE) *Gordon Elliott* 85b
4 ch g Rock Of Gibraltar(IRE) Hopeful Isabella (IRE) (Grand Lodge (USA))
963[4]
Bellator (FR) *Nicky Henderson*
4 gr g Network(GER) Onysia (FR) (April Night (FR))
4430[P] 4874[P]
Bel La Vie (FR) *G Macaire* 135h 143c
9 b g Lavirco(GER) Bibelle (FR) (Le Balafre (FR))
375a[P] (664a) 1477a[4]
Bellecoat (FR) *F Foucher* 82b
4 b m Axxos(GER) Pepita D'Armor (FR) (Start Fast (FR))
(2536a)
Belle Du Chenet (FR) *M Rolland* 89h
4 b m Poliglote Orthence (FR) (Epervier Bleu)
5499a[3]
Belle Ile (FR) *P Peltier*
4 b m Linda's Lad Quamiland (FR) (Lost World (IRE))
1231a[F]
Bellemady Monterg (FR) *Alain Couetil* 74b
4 b m Maresca Sorrento(FR) Melody D'Herodiere (FR) (Assessor (IRE))
2536a[5]
Bellenos (FR) *Dan Skelton* 107h 142c
7 b g Apsis Palmeria (FR) (Great Palm (USA))
103[5] 2185[P]
Belle Peinture (FR) *Alan Lockwood*
4 ch m Peintre Celebre(USA) Grosgrain (USA) (Diesis)
4417[P]
Bellini Dubreau (FR) *Nigel Hawke* 75h
4 ch g Anzillero(GER) Lonita D'Airy (FR) (Oblat (FR))
2270[14] 2879[10] 5115[F] 5356[P]
Bello Conti (FR) *W P Mullins* 141h
4 b g Coastal Path Posterite (FR) (Video Rock (FR))
4715[4] 5214[4]
Bellow Mome (FR) *W P Mullins* 132h
4 b g Honolulu(IRE) Oll Mighty Fellow (FR) (Ungaro (GER))
5497[8]
Bellshill (IRE) *W P Mullins* 155h
5 b g King's Theatre(IRE) Fairy Native (IRE) (Be My Native (USA))
(23a) (3070a) (3459a) 4004a[3] 4695[13] 5194[2]
Bells 'N' Banjos (IRE) *Warren Greatrex* 135h
5 b g Indian River(FR) Beechill Dancer (IRE) (Darnay)
(2711) 3232[11] 4596[4] 5284[12]
Bells Of Ailsworth (IRE) *Tim Vaughan* 110h
5 b g Kayf Tara Volverta (FR) (Green Tune (USA))
353[3] 647[2] (893) 3855[12] 4450[2] 4972[P]
Bells Of Castor (IRE) *Tim Vaughan* 70h
5 ch g Golan(IRE) Tocane (FR) (Phantom Breeze)
1299[9] 1786[P]
Bells On Sunday *Tom Lacey* 111b
4 br m Black Sam Bellamy(IRE) Lago D'Oro (Slip Anchor)
(4967) 5180[12]
Bell Weir *Dianne Sayer* 126h
7 gr g Tobougg(IRE) Belly Dancer (IRE) (Danehill Dancer (IRE))
1419[6] 3361[5] 3970[6] 4712[3] 5012[10] 5472[3]

Belmont Park (FR) *David Bridgwater* 87b
4 bb g Al Namix(FR) Goldoulyssa (FR) (Cadoudal (FR))
4102[10] 4385[3]
Belmount (IRE) *Nigel Twiston-Davies* 116h 135c
6 b g Westerner Artist's Jewel (Le Moss)
(215) 1616[2] 2261[P] 2724[3] 3349[P] 3929[U] 4826[2] 5052[2]
Beltor *Robert Stephens* 140h
4 b g Authorized(IRE) Carahill (AUS) (Danehill (USA))
2789[7]
Be My Witness (IRE) *Robin Dickin* 96h 73c
6 b m Witness Box(USA) Smokey Firth (IRE) (Flemensfirth (USA))
130[6] 759[4] **1056[4] 1614[5]**
Benability (IRE) *Tim Vaughan* 95h
5 b g Beneficial Whataliability (IRE) (Leading Counsel (USA))
65[9] 2256[0] **2851[P] 4387[U]** 4682[P] 5481[7]
Ben Akram (IRE) *Lucinda Russell* 99b
7 b g Beneficial Ring Four (IRE) (Supreme Leader)
2745[P]
Benarty Hill (IRE) *Liam Lennon* 96h
5 b g September Storm(GER) Crossmacahilly (IRE) (Executive Perk)
837[7] 3667[5] 5412[5]
Benbane Head (USA) *Martin Keighley* 77h 85c
11 ch g Giant's Causeway(USA) Prospectress (USA) (Mining (USA))
855[13]
Benbecula *Richard Mitchell* 120h
6 b g Motivator Isle Of Flame (Shirley Heights)
(63) 556[13] 1754[9] 2093[5] 2600[2] 3120[2] 3705[13] 5386[4]
Benbens (IRE) *Nigel Twiston-Davies* 119h 146c
10 ch g Beneficial Millicent Bridge (IRE) (Over The River (FR))
1871[7] (2082) 2783[10] 3448[5] 4306[8]
Ben Button (IRE) *P J Rothwell* 123h
5 b g Double Eclipse(IRE) Lady Coldunell (Deploy)
2225a[2] 3393a[4] 5024a[10]
Ben Cee Pee M (IRE) *Brian Ellison* 116h
10 ch g Beneficial Supreme Magical (Supreme Leader)
1661[3] 2042[2] 2426[5] 3238[8] 3884[6] 4328[5]
Bendomingo (IRE) *Nigel Twiston-Davies* 111h
4 b g Beneficial Bobbies Storm (IRE) (Bob Back (USA))
525[2] 2450[9] 3835[14] 4875[3]
Benedictus (IRE) *Jack R Barber* 127c
10 ch g Alderbrook Dante's Thatch (IRE) (Phardante (FR))
(5186)
Beneficial Joe (IRE) *Graeme McPherson* 90h
5 bb g Beneficial Joleen (IRE) (Bob's Return (IRE))
3334[6] 4843[7]
Benefit Cut (IRE) *Stuart Edmunds* 108h 137c
9 b g Beneficial I'm Maggy (NZ) (Danseur Etoile (FR))
318[6] 568[U] 1643[2] ◆ 2404[3] 2897[F] (Dead)
Benefit In Kind (IRE) *Katie Scott* 73h 98c
7 b g Beneficial She's So Beautiful (IRE) (Bluebird (USA))
1855[4] 2297[2] 2950[5] 3472[3] 3679[P]
Benefitofhindsight *Hywel Evans* 22h
6 ch g Sir Harry Lewis(USA) Aoninch (Inchinor)
615[8] 704[P]
Benefit Of Youth (IRE) *Tim Vaughan* 62h
8 b g Beneficial Persian Avenue (IRE) (Persian Mews)
2081[6]
Benefits Well (IRE) *Warren Greatrex* 109h
8 b g Beneficial Farran Lady (IRE) (The Parson)
1100[3] ◆ 1350[3]
Benemeade (IRE) *Noel Meade* 128h 133c
7 b g Beneficial Millicent Bridge (IRE) (Over The River (FR))
69a[P]
Benenden (IRE) *Michael Scudamore* 117h 130c
7 b g Moscow Society(USA) Ashanti Dancer (IRE) (Dancing Dissident (USA))
177[P] **2973[3] (3472) 4621[P] 5073[4] 5285[P]**
Benevolent (IRE) *Chris Bealby* 123h 128c
8 ch g Beneficial Bobs Lass (IRE) (Bob's Return (IRE))
(568) 1970[F] (Dead)
Bengali (IRE) *Patrick Griffin* 108h 84c
6 br m Beneficial Kigali (IRE) (Torus)
613[3] ◆ 846[P]
Benie Des Dieux (FR) *Mlle I Gallorini* 118h
4 b m Great Pretender(IRE) Cana (FR) (Robin Des Champs (FR))
2821a[3]
Beni Light (FR) *Tom George* 104b
4 b g Crossharbour Or Light (FR) (Sleeping Car (FR))
5151[3] ◆
Benissimo (IRE) *Dan Skelton* 120h
5 b g Beneficial Fennor Rose (IRE) (Kotashaan (FR))
(207) 401[2] 1752[4] 2472[15] 3023[8] 5453[3]
Benjamin Bogle (IRE) *Rose Dobbin* 64h
4 b g Yeats(IRE) Zalama (FR) (Red Ransom (USA))
2423[4]
Benjamin Tree (IRE) *Rose Dobbin* 91h
4 ch g Beneficial Lady Millie (IRE) (Milan)
2709[6] 4031[5]
Bennachie (IRE) *Tim Vaughan* 109h
6 b g Milan Stormy Lady (IRE) (Glacial Storm (USA))
(106) (262) 399[2] 1055[F] 1493[2] 1794[6] 5355[10]
Bennylicious (IRE) *Rose Dobbin* 105h 94c
6 b g Beneficial Railstown Lady (IRE) (Supreme Leader)
2143[6] 2844[5] 3968[5] 4329[P]
Bennys King (IRE) *Venetia Williams* 120h
4 b g Beneficial Hellofafaithful (IRE) (Oscar (IRE))
4256[6] 4613[2] ◆ 5221[2] ◆

Bennys Mist (IRE) *Venetia Williams* 119h 152c
9 b g Beneficial Dark Mist (IRE) (Mister Lord (USA))
2187[P] 2483[P] (2902) 3735[3] 4485[2] 5193[12]
Benny's Secret (IRE) *N W Alexander* 110h
5 br g Beneficial Greenhall Rambler (IRE) (Anshan)
144[5] 2101[4] 2791[4] 3346[F] 4152[F] 4581[U] (4835) 5450[9]
Bennys Well (IRE) *Sue Smith* 61h 112c
9 b g Beneficial Alure (IRE) (Carroll House (IRE))
38[2] 2030[8] 2491[3] 2668[4] 4046[3] ◆ 4792[P] (4985) 5228[4]
Ben's Folly (IRE) *R A Owen* 101b 100c
10 ch g Beneficial Daddy's Folly (Le Moss)
17[P]
Bentelimar (IRE) *J R Barry* 148h
6 ch g Beneficial Montel Girl (IRE) (Montelimar (USA))
3071a[2] 3650a[6] 4133a[2] 4765[19]
Bentons Lad *George Moore* 97h
4 br g Bollin Eric Spirit Of Ecstacy (Val Royal (FR))
419[3] 746[F] 1740[4] 2042[11] 3023[11]
Bentworth Boy *Patrick Chamings* 74h
4 b g Archipenko(USA) Maria Di Scozia (Selkirk (USA))
(1873) 2514[12] 3138[8] 4784[9]
Benvardin (IRE) *Andrew Hamilton* 85b
5 ch g Beneficial Ramona Style (IRE) (Duky)
1776[P] 2100[P]
Benvolio (IRE) *Paul Nicholls* 136h 152c
8 b g Beneficial Coumeenoole Lady (The Parson)
2348[P] 2907[5] 3518[P] 4684[3] (5092) 5283[P]
Benzanno (IRE) *Donald McCain* 118h
6 b g Refuse To Bend(IRE) Crossanza (IRE) (Cape Cross (IRE))
110[4]
Benzel (IRE) *Jonjo O'Neill* 110h 114c
7 b g Beneficial Jezel (IRE) (Accordion)
4681[6] 5355[7]
Be On Time (FR) *Jamie Snowden* 72h 114c
4 b g Linda's Lad One More Time (FR) (Le Balafre (FR))
(1907) ◆ 2138[2] 2645[P] 3061[P]
Berce (FR) *Nicky Henderson* 92b
4 b g Peer Gynt(JPN) Fauconnerie (FR) (Franc Parler)
4364[11]
Berea Boru (IRE) *Peter Bowen* 124h 145c
7 b g Brian Boru Wayward Venture (IRE) (Mister Mat (FR))
774[3] 2367[6] **2905[4] 3520[4] (3979) (4267) (4966) 5327[P]**
Berea Venture (IRE) *Peter Bowen* 121h
7 b g Indian Danehill(IRE) Ballinard Lady (IRE) (Phardante (FR))
(335) 441[2]
Bering Upsun *James Ewart* 84b
4 b g And Beyond(IRE) Bering Up (IRE) (Bering)
4001[5] 4408[2] 4805[10]
Berkeley Barron (IRE) *Richard Phillips* 135h 116c
7 b g Subtle Power(IRE) Roseabel (IRE) (Roselier (FR))
1867[6] 2701[P] 3348[4]
Berkshire Downs *Lucy Normile* 108h
5 b m Tiger Hill(IRE) Cut Corn (King's Theatre (IRE))
2031[2] 2428[4] 3054[2] 3342[2] 4050[2] 4633[3] 5408[9]
Berland (IRE) *John Ferguson* 122h
3 b g Cape Cross(IRE) Ballantrae (IRE) (Diktat)
(3099) 3279[3] 3926[2] 5116[3]
Bermeo (IRE) *Johnny Farrelly* 90h
4 b g Definite Article Miss Blueyes (IRE) (Dushyantor (USA))
5269[9]
Bermuda Boy (FR) *Steve Flook* 104h 108c
10 b g Anabaa Blue Fast Reema (IRE) (Fast Topaze (USA))
393[8] 527[P]
Bernardelli (IRE) *Nicky Richards* 118h 143c
7 b g Golan(IRE) Beautiful Blue (IRE) (Xaar)
2192[5] 2766[2] (3162) 3735[0] (4167) 4609[P]
Bernisdale *John Flint* 86h
7 ch m Bertolini(USA) Carradale (Pursuit Of Love)
2565[P] 4223[3]
Berry De Carjac (FR) *Nigel Hawke* 103h
4 ch g Epalo(GER) Miria Galanda (FR) (Chef De Clan (FR))
1379[6] 2154[5] 2457[11] 2987[10] 5352[U] 5433[5]
Bertalus (IRE) *N W Alexander* 110h
6 b g City Honours(USA) Deep Dalus (IRE) (Mandalus)
2189[5] 2716[4] 3667[7] (4165) 4607[3] 5300[7]
Bertenbar *Lawney Hill* 87h 110c
11 b g Bertolini(USA) Ardenbar (Ardross)
2453[7] **3497[3] (4778) (5068) (5307)**
Bertie Barnes (IRE) *Richard Phillips* 96h
4 b g Craigsteel Mahon Rose (IRE) (Roselier (FR))
4875[7] 5416[8]
Bertie Boru (IRE) *Philip Hobbs* 119h 139c
8 b g Brian Boru Sleeven Lady (Crash Course)
2348[6] 2916[4] 3518[P] 4234[5] 4621[U] 4858[3] 5274[12]
Bertielicious *Jonathan Haynes* 80h 68c
7 b g And Beyond(IRE) Pennepoint (Pennekamp (USA))
33[5] 200[P] **485[U] 639[U] 728[7]** 1368[P] 1740[8] **1857[U]** 2148[P] 2474[4] 2716[P] 2891[3] 3161[6] 3307[9] 3883[9] 4045[P] 4547[P] **5010[P] 5197[3] 5231[2]**
Bertie Lugg *Henry Oliver* 96h
7 b g Beat All(USA) Flakey Dove (Oats)
219[7] 4068[2] (4536) 4862[8]
Bertie Milan (IRE) *N W Alexander* 99h 106c
10 b g Milan Miss Bertaine (IRE) (Denel (FR))
289[4] 867[4] 1332[P] (1629) 5474[5]
Bertie Moon *Keith Dalgleish* 103h
5 b g Bertolini(USA) Fleeting Moon (Fleetwood (IRE))
(34) ◆ 1048[6] 1324[10] 1677[7] 4326[7] (4550)
Bertie's Desire *Oliver Sherwood* 99h 116c
7 b g King's Theatre(IRE) Temptation (FR) (Lando (GER))
62[4] 523[4] 1767[6] 2008[4]

Berwin (IRE) *Sarah Robinson* 72h
6 b m Lawman(FR) Topiary (IRE) (Selkirk (USA))
860[12] 3119[P] 4916[4]
Bescot Springs (IRE) *Lucinda Russell* 104h 93c
10 b g Saddlers' Hall(IRE) Silver Glen (IRE) (Roselier (FR))
287[3] 303[3] 484[6] (1573) ◆ **1778[6]** 2432[4] 2800[2] 3344[2] 4035[9] 4581[2] 4840[7] 5412[7]
Be Seeing You *Gordon Elliott* 118h
4 ch g Medicean Oshiponga (Barathea (IRE))
1637[4]
Bespoke Lady (IRE) *Micky Hammond* 101b
6 ch m Presenting Coole Alainn (IRE) (Glacial Storm (USA))
4420[P]
Best Boy Barney (IRE) *Jeremy Scott* 104h 137c
9 b g Rashar(USA) Graigue Lass (IRE) (Phardante (FR))
101[2] 1288[3] 1807[5] 2089[5] 5150[2] 5392[6]
Best Director (IRE) *John Groucott* 97b
7 b g Oscar(IRE) Taneys Leader (IRE) (Supreme Leader)
5397[P]
Bestiarius (IRE) *Keith Reveley* 105b
3 b g Vinnie Roe(IRE) Chione (IRE) (Mandalus)
(4552) ◆
Best Kept Secret (IRE) *A P O'Brien* 108h
3 b g Duke Of Marmalade(IRE) Rawabi (Sadler's Wells (USA))
4002a[P]
Best Of Company *Chris Grant*
4 b m Denounce Gemgaballou (IRE) (Luso)
1858[P] (Dead)
Bestwork (FR) *Charlie Longsdon* 89h
4 bl g Network(GER) Harmony (FR) (Lute Antique (FR))
187[8] 1717[5] 3334[P] 5220[7] 5469[9]
Bestwork D'Olivate (FR) *Martin Hill* 77h
4 bb m Network(GER) Komunion (FR) (Luchiroverte (IRE))
5182[4]
Betameche (FR) *Dan Skelton* 128b
4 gr g Kapgarde(FR) Kaldona (FR) (Kaldoun (FR))
(2984) (5083) ◆
Bete A Bon Dieu (FR) *A Lacombe* 115h 116c
4 gr m Saint Des Saints(FR) Griffee (FR) (Royal Charter (FR))
2821a[4]
Bethellie Pride *Lynn Siddall*
5 b m Misu Bond(IRE) Sunset Lady (IRE) (Red Sunset)
2721[10]
Betsy Boo Boo *Michael Roberts* 80h
6 b m King's Theatre(IRE) Quark Top (FR) (Perrault)
227[7] 2252[4] 2519[7] 2952[P] 3821[6] 4783[5]
Better Back Bracka (IRE) *Noel C Kelly* 96b
4 b m Flemensfirth(USA) Merrill Gaye (IRE) (Roselier (FR))
2433[3]
Better B Quick (IRE) *Paul Stafford* 70h 110c
9 b g Overbury(IRE) Snow Shine (IRE) (Rainbows For Life (CAN))
202[3] 331[4] 2947[5] 3474[14]
Better Days (IRE) *Nigel Twiston-Davies* 87h
4 gr g Daylami(IRE) Miss Edgehill (IRE) (Idris (IRE))
2131[2] 2154[6] 2928[11] 4233[8] 4855[7] 5398[6]
Better Getalong (IRE) *Nicky Richards* 111b
4 b g Gold Well Arequipa (IRE) (Turtle Island (IRE))
3226[2] ◆
Betterthanalright (IRE) *Liam Casey* 117h 117c
9 b g Cloudings(IRE) Garden Heaven (IRE) (Roselier (FR))
2228a[6]
Betty Borgia *Nicholas Pomfret* 46h
6 ch m Killer Instinct Bellefleur (Alflora (IRE))
2401[2] 2453[11] 3067[9] 5020[P]
Beware The Bear (IRE) *Nicky Henderson* 122h
5 b g Shantou(USA) Native Bid (IRE) (Be My Native (USA))
2163[2] 2995[4] 4873[3] (5331)
Beyond Measure (IRE) *Don Cantillon* 111b
4 ch m Flemensfirth(USA) Faucon (Polar Falcon (USA))
159[7] 2929[7] (4075) 5180[17]
Beyondtemptation *Jonathan Haynes* 112h
7 ch m And Beyond(IRE) Tempted (IRE) (Invited (USA))
205[4] 507[P] 1572[8] 1892[10] 2148[8] 2427[2] 2706[4] 2980[4] 3163[2] 3888[6] (4297) (4415) (4736) (4939) 5232[2] (5368) ◆
Beyondtheflame *Jonathan Haynes* 54b
5 b m And Beyond(IRE) Flame Of Zara (Blushing Flame (USA))
4559[8] 5014[10]
Beyond The Glen *Chris Grant* 64b
5 b m And Beyond(IRE) Calabria (Neltino)
2895[7] 3593[5]
Bhakti (IRE) *Mark Rimell* 72h
8 b g Rakti Royal Bossi (IRE) (Spectrum (IRE))
3572[P] 5374[15]
Bibi D'Eole (FR) *Graeme McPherson* 101h
4 ch g Storm Trooper(GER) Bibi Star (FR) (Sinjar (FR))
2840[8] 3484[5] 4460[3] 5122[8]
Bidourey (FR) *David Pipe* 130h
4 b g Voix Du Nord(FR) Love Wisky (FR) (Mansonnien (FR))
2512[12] 3151[P]
Bien Faire (IRE) *Anthony Honeyball* 51h
5 ch g Bienamado(USA) Fairpark (IRE) (Shardari)
335[P]
Bien Well (IRE) *Edmond Daniel Linehan* 88b
4 b m Bienamado(USA) Mrs Masters (IRE) (Un Desperado (FR))
3082[5]
Big Bad Dude (IRE) *Tom George* 14b
6 ch g Blueprint(IRE) Cathedral Ave (IRE) (Darazari (IRE))
2965[6]

Bigbadjohn (IRE) *Rebecca Curtis* 135h
6 br g Vinnie Roe(IRE) Celtic Serenade (IRE) (Yashgan)
2762^{10} 4544^{2} ◆ (5070)

Bigbury Bay (IRE) *Warren Greatrex* 53b
4 b m Stowaway Clamper (IRE) (Ala Hounak)
2721^{7}

Big Casino *Nigel Twiston-Davies* 125h 132c
9 b g Court Cave(IRE) Migsy Malone (Afzal)
(198) 2061^{9} 2780^{6} 3148^{8} 4444^{P}

Big Chief Benny (IRE) *Alan King* 138h
4 ch g Beneficial Be Airlie (IRE) (Lord Americo)
2351^{2} 2763^{3} 3117^{2} (3839) 4236^{5} (5462)

Big Fella Thanks *Tom George* 113h 131c
13 b g Primitive Rising(USA) Nunsdream (Derrylin)
4000^{2} 4437^{2} (5035)

Big Generator *Caroline Bailey* 126h 119c
9 ch g Generous(IRE) Frizzball (IRE) (Orchestra)
(1291) (1448) 1784^{P} 2775^{7}

Big Georgie (IRE) *J M Ridley* 111c
8 b g Exit To Nowhere(USA) Afreen (IRE) (Entrepreneur)
3958^{2} 4213^{4}

Bigindie (IRE) *John Weymes* 115h
5 ch g Indian Haven Graceful Air (IRE) (Danzero (AUS))
2634 (592) ◆ 1156^{4} 1602^{4} 1814^{3} 2027^{4}

Bigironhiship (IRE) *Rose Dobbin* 122h
4 b g Beneficial Portobello Lady (IRE) (Broken Hearted)
(3436) 3997^{2} ◆ 4368^{3}

Big Jim *Alex Hales* 121h 136c
6 b g Revoque(IRE) Chilly Squaw (IRE) (Commanche Run)
2289^{P} 2668^{3} 3141^{2} (3620) 4300^{2} 4617^{P} (5118)

Bigmartre (FR) *Harry Whittington* 134h
4 b g Montmartre(FR) Oh La Miss (FR) (Le Balafre (FR))
(2011) 2710^{2} (3363) 3739^{4} 4781^{3} 5219^{3}

Big McIntosh (IRE) *John Ryan* 114h
3 b g Bushranger(IRE) Three Decades (IRE) (Invincible Spirit (IRE))
1452^{6} (1768) 1984^{2} 2324^{2} 4764^{15} 5491^{9}

Big Meadow (IRE) *Neil King* 126b
4 br g Marienbard(IRE) Lakyle Lady (IRE) (Bob Back (USA))
(4357) 4805^{2}

Big Night Out *Laura Hurley* 91h 81c
9 b m Midnight Legend Big Decision (Arzanni)
8134 **2976^{8} 3951^{P}** 4878^{P}

Big Oaks (IRE) *Tim Fitzgerald* 50b
3 b g Westerner Cobblers Hall (IRE) (Saddlers' Hall (IRE))
5127^{8}

Big Occasion (IRE) *David Pipe*
8 b g Sadler's Wells(USA) Asnieres (USA) (Spend A Buck (USA))
2517^{P}

Bigpipenotobacee (IRE) *Tom George* 110h
4 bb g King's Theatre(IRE) Another Dollar (IRE) (Supreme Leader)
4102^{9} 5018^{3} ◆ 5469^{U}

Big River (IRE) *Lucinda Russell* 111h
5 b g Milan Call Kate (IRE) (Lord Americo)
(2066)

Big Smile (IRE) *John Groucott* 14b
7 b g Zagreb(USA) Pretty Buckskin (IRE) (Supreme Leader)
2850^{P} 3126^{P}

Big Society (IRE) *Harry Whittington* 129h 132c
9 b g Flemensfirth(USA) Choice Of Kings (IRE) (King's Ride)
2261^{P} (2566) 3349^{3} 3707^{P} 4267^{3} 4826^{P}

Big Sound *Mark Walford* 103h 119c
8 b g Supreme Sound Tarbolton Moss (Le Moss)
81^{2} (693) 967^{6} **1309^{7} 1458^{5} 1571^{3} 1783^{5} 1970^{8} 2288^{3} 4792^{4}**

Big Thunder *Micky Hammond* 91h
5 gr g Dalakhani(IRE) Charlotte O Fraise (IRE) (Beat Hollow)
3835^{7}

Big Time Frank (IRE) *Alex Hales* 86b
4 b g Bienamado(USA) Pure Spirit (IRE) (Hubbly Bubbly (USA))
4188^{3} 4805^{9}

Big Touch (FR) *Paul Morgan* 77b
4 b g Network(GER) Etoile D'Or II (FR) (Lute Antique (FR))
444^{7} 1966^{8}

Big Water (IRE) *Alan Swinbank* 115h 142c
7 ch g Saffron Walden(FR) Magic Feeling (IRE) (Magical Wonder (USA))
1976^{P} 2214^{13} **2935^{P}**

Big Windmill (IRE) *Tom George* 92b
4 b g Stowaway Neighbours Wager (IRE) (Darazari (IRE))
3111^{4}

Bilbrook Blaze *Philip Hobbs* 117h 120c
5 b g Kayf Tara Za Beau (IRE) (Beneficial)
2182^{3} **2885^{F} 3123^{P} 4852^{2}**

Bilko's Back (IRE) *Warren Greatrex* 97b
3 b g Big Bad Bob(IRE) Chica Roca (USA) (Woodman (USA))
2368^{2}

Bill And Barn (IRE) *Paul Nicholls* 94b
4 br g Presenting Forgotten Star (IRE) (Don't Forget Me)
5436^{6}

Billbushay (IRE) *Sean Byrne* 125h
6 b g Westerner Oscareen (IRE) (Oscar (IRE))
2385a^{5}

Bill D'Aron (FR) *James Ewart* 31h
4 ch g Dom Alco(FR) Nobless D'Aron (FR) (Ragmar (FR))
4403^{7} 4835^{P}

Billfromthebar (IRE) *Donald McCain* 117b
8 b g Morozov(USA) Eden Breeze (IRE) (Insan (USA))
1632^{P} 3465^{P}

Billy Billy (IRE) *S R B Crawford* 121h
5 b m Darsi(FR) Mrs Gordi (Classic Cliche (IRE))
(3060) (4605) 5011^{P}

Billy Biscuit (IRE) *Alan King* 71h
7 b g Presenting Native Novel (IRE) (Be My Native (USA))
2744^{12}

Billy Bronco *Debra Hamer* 115b
4 ch g Central Park(IRE) Nan (Buckley)
(3502)

Billy Congo (IRE) *Richard Hawker* 113h
8 bb g Zagreb(USA) Delicate Child (IRE) (Son Of Sharp Shot (IRE))
(55) (363) 445^{3} 746^{P} 5267^{P} 5466^{11}

Billy Dutton *Chris Down* 128h 106c
9 ch g Sir Harry Lewis(USA) Tinoforty (FR) (Saint Estephe (FR))
2268^{3} ◆ 3018^{3} 3407^{9} 4241^{2} 4911^{3} 5277^{F}

Billy Merriott (IRE) *Harry Fry* 123h 128c
9 b g Dr Massini(IRE) Hurricane Bella (IRE) (Taipan (IRE))
99^{U} 2240^{8} 2774^{U}

Billy My Boy *Chris Down* 106h
6 b g Volochine(IRE) Key West (FR) (Highest Honor (FR))
(164) 465^{2} 718^{2} 895^{3} 1951^{6}

Billy No Name (IRE) *Colin Tizzard* 132h 114c
7 b g Westerner Just Little (Mtoto)
(2202) 2759^{2} 3232^{7} (4159) 4933^{5}

Billy's Hope (IRE) *Mrs John Harrington* 113h
4 b m King's Theatre(IRE) Lady Bellingham (IRE) (Montelimar (USA))
2677a^{3} 4954a^{6}

Bilzic (FR) *Dan Skelton* 101h
4 bb g Axxos(GER) Izellane (FR) (Funny Baby (FR))
2044^{2} 2646^{6} 5091^{7}

Bim Bam Boum (FR) *Harry Fry* 124h
4 b g Crossharbour Quobalt (FR) (Ragmar (FR))
2091^{3} 2731^{5} ◆ 3370^{2} ◆ 4438^{6} 5115^{6}

Bincombe *Philip Hobbs* 105h 131c
7 gr g Indian Danehill(IRE) Siroyalta (FR) (Royal Charter (FR))
199^{3} 2335^{3} 2758^{5} 3014^{4} 5071^{5}

Bindon Mill *Victor Dartnall* 108h
6 b g Tamure(IRE) Singing Cottage (Greensmith)
392^{2} 2317^{5} 3413^{3} 3976^{6} 4339^{2}

Bine Des Salines (FR) *J Follain*
4 b m Nickname(FR) Ikeya Des Salines (FR) (Le Nain Jaune (FR))
5135a^{P}

Binge Drinker (IRE) *Rebecca Curtis* 145h
6 b g Spadoun(FR) Our Honey (IRE) (Old Vic)
21a^{9}

Bingo Conti (FR) *C A Murphy* 98b
4 b g Coastal Path Regina Conti (FR) (Lavirco (GER))
9a^{9}

Bingo D'Olivate (FR) *Noel Williams* 123h
4 b g Laverock(IRE) Ombrelle De L'Orme (FR) (Marchand De Sable (USA))
2646^{F} 3411^{6} 3608^{F} 4026^{3} (4486)

Binowagh Bay (IRE) *Brian M McMahon* 105h
7 b m Flemensfirth(USA) Sarah O'Malley (IRE) (Bob Back (USA))
(1420) 1547^{P}

Bipolaire (FR) *Francois Nicolle* 115h 127c
4 gr g Fragrant Mix(IRE) Kenna (FR) (Epervier Bleu)
2820a^{4}

Birch Hill (IRE) *Nicky Henderson* 125h
5 b g Kalanisi(IRE) Miss Compliance (IRE) (Broken Hearted)
3994^{3} 4873^{2} 5296^{9}

Bird D'Estruval (FR) *David Pipe*
4 ch g Vatori(FR) Onde D'Estruval (FR) (Art Bleu I)
2437^{P}

Biretta *Harry Fry* 94h
4 ch m Kirkwall Burqa (Nashwan (USA))
1843^{4} 2302^{7} 4435^{P}

Birthday Guest (GER) *Philip Kirby* 98h
6 ch g Areion(GER) Birthday Spectrum (GER) (Spectrum (IRE))
5441^{F}

Bishophill Jack (IRE) *Caroline Bailey* 59h 65c
9 b g Tikkanen(USA) Kerrys Cross (IRE) (Phardante (FR))
1930^{P}

Bishop Of Ruscombe *Jamie Snowden* 61h
4 b g Mount Nelson Pain Perdu (IRE) (Waajib (IRE))
491^{6} 932^{11}

Bishops Court *Neil Mulholland* 109h
5 b g Helissio(FR) Island Of Memories (IRE) (Beneficial)
3201^{2} 1844^{4} 2091^{4} 2345^{8} 2564^{5} 3919^{2} ◆ 4099^{P} 4882^{2} 5355^{4}

Bishopslough (IRE) *Alan Fleming* 122h 136c
7 b g Fruits Of Love(USA) Maid In Blue (IRE) (Bluebird (USA))
3650a^{7}

Bishops Road (IRE) *Kerry Lee* 130h 157c
7 b g Heron Island(IRE) Nice Resemblance (IRE) (Shernazar)
69a^{8} 1175a^{12} **(3445) (4245) 5193^{U} 5494^{F}**

Bishopstone Girl (IRE) *Paul Cowley* 47b
4 b m Westerner Katies Pet (IRE) (Glacial Storm (USA))
152^{9} 831^{9}

Bishop Wulstan (IRE) *Peter Bowen* 118h
4 b g Oratorio(IRE) Laurentine (USA) (Private Account (USA))
1699^{9} 2291^{6} 2694^{12} 3080^{3} 3498^{5} 3662^{P} 4028^{7} 4266^{3} 4822^{2} 5239^{7}

Biskoazh (FR) *B Lefevre*
4 b m Trempolino(USA) First Elorn (FR) (Funny Baby (FR))
5136a^{P}

Bison Grass *Giles Bravery*
5 b g Halling(USA) Secret Blend (Pivotal)
528^{P}

Bit Of A Charlie *John Ryall* 64h
6 b g Emperor Fountain Win A Hand (Nearly A Hand)
5091^{14}

Bit Of A Jig (IRE) *Adrian Wintle* 75h 95c
8 ch g Alderbrook Ardower (IRE) (Montelimar (USA))
705^{P} 869^{P} 1692^{6} **2028^{P}**

Bitofapuzzle *Harry Fry* 147h 147c
7 b m Tamure(IRE) Gaelic Gold (IRE) (Good Thyne (USA))
(3122) 3604a^{U} 3998^{P} 4699^{17}

Bitter Virtue *David Dennis* 95h
4 b m Lucarno(USA) Avoine (IRE) (Saddlers' Hall (IRE))
432^{4} 2277^{15} 5286^{13}

Bivouac (FR) *Nicky Henderson* 139h
4 b g Califet(FR) Pazadena (FR) (Ragmar (FR))
1847^{11} (2411) 3527^{P} 4769^{P}

Bjornlucky (IRE) *Caroline Fryer* 95h
5 b g Key Of Luck(USA) Super Trouper (FR) (Nashwan (USA))
40^{9} 399^{P} 626^{P}

Blackadder *Mark Gillard* 72h
3 b g Myboycharlie(IRE) Famcred (Inchinor)
2662^{P} 3076^{4} 3926^{F} 4854^{U} 5220^{6}

Blackandamber Vic (IRE) *Norman Lee* 103h
8 ch m Old Vic Lady Of Gortmerron (IRE) (Orchestra)
1150a^{7}

Black Benny (IRE) *J P Broderick* 67h 135c
10 br g Close Conflict(USA) Treen (IRE) (Charnwood Forest (IRE))
50a^{15} **2061^{12}**

Black Corton (FR) *Paul Nicholls* 125h
4 br g Laverock(IRE) Pour Le Meilleur (FR) (Video Rock (FR))
4256^{3} (5434) ◆

Black Country Boy *Robin Dickin* 98b
3 b g Black Sam Bellamy(IRE) Simple Glory (IRE) (Simply Great (FR))
4392^{2} 5097^{10}

Blackdown Babe *Kevin Bishop* 50h
7 b m Weld Blackdown Beauty (Deltic (USA))
2267^{11} 2563^{F} 3125^{P}

Blackdown Hills *Mark Bradstock* 95b
5 b m Presenting Lady Prunella (IRE) (Supreme Leader)
(526) 4198^{P}

Blackfire (FR) *Jonjo O'Neill* 103h
3 br g Kingsalsa(USA) Sister Celestine (Bishop Of Cashel)
3318^{9} 4486^{6} 4979^{3} 5433^{9}

Black Hawk (IRE) *Henry Oliver* 81h
6 b g Craigsteel Coolharbour Lady (IRE) (Lord Americo)
2689^{9}

Black Hercules (IRE) *W P Mullins* 118h 164c
6 b g Heron Island(IRE) Annalecky (IRE) (Bob's Return (IRE))
(3621) ◆ **4148a^{F} (4729)**

Black Iceman *Lydia Pearce* 104h
7 gr g Iceman Slite (Mind Games)
(702) 1081^{4} 1346^{5} 2139^{P}

Black Ink *Michael Smith* 104b
4 b g Black Sam Bellamy(IRE) Incony (Daggers Drawn (USA))
2344^{2} 2756^{2} 3476^{8} 4867^{14}

Black Ivory *Malcolm Jefferson* 97b
3 b g Revoque(IRE) Annie's Gift (IRE) (Presenting)
4552^{3} ◆ 4988^{4}

Black Jack Rover (IRE) *Donald McCain* 115h
6 b g Vinnie Roe(IRE) Kilgefin Tina (IRE) (City Honours (USA))
(251) 518^{2} 877^{2}

Black Kettle (IRE) *Ronald Thompson* 85h
5 b g Robin Des Pres(FR) Whistful Suzie (IRE) (Eurobus)
1122^{6} 1345^{4} 1449^{3} 1723^{4} 2025^{6} 2169^{5}

Black Kit (FR) *J-D Marion* 140h
7 b g Black Sam Bellamy(IRE) Kitara (GER) (Camp David (GER))
4a^{10}

Black Lily (IRE) *Chris Bealby* 94h 28c
7 b m Quws Sandaluna (IRE) (Desert King (IRE))
89^{P} 1972^{5} 2223^{7} 2554^{3} 2868^{2} ◆ 4391^{5}

Black Marble *Mark Shears*
4 br m Passing Glance Pinegar Lady (Montjoy (USA))
5383^{14}

Black Mischief *Harry Fry* 112b
3 b g Black Sam Bellamy(IRE) Miss Mitch (IRE) (King's Theatre (IRE))
4805^{3}

Black Narcissus (IRE) *Alexandra Dunn* 103h 104c
6 b m Westerner Arcanum (IRE) (Presenting)
2698^{3} (3088) (3501) (3789) **4199^{F}** 4822^{P}

Black Pearl Tavel (FR) *Jerome Zuliani* 109c
4 gr m Al Namix(FR) Quiza (FR) (Ungaro (GER))
5136a^{3}

Black River (FR) *Paul Nicholls* 131h 140c
6 b g Secret Singer(FR) Love River (FR) (Epervier Bleu)
2459^{3}

Black Sam The Man *John Joseph Hanlon* 113h
5 b g Black Sam Bellamy(IRE) Sonda (IRE) (Dolphin Street (FR))
1648^{3}

Blackthirteen (IRE) *Michael B Jones*
11 br g Key Of Luck(USA) Jenny May (IRE) (Orchestra)
521^{P}

Black Thunder (FR) *Paul Nicholls* 142h 157c
8 bl g Malinas(GER) Blackmika (FR) (Subotica (FR))
2482^{12} 3518^{U} 3993^{6} 5218^{P}

Black Vale (IRE) *Ralph J Smith* 37h
4 b g Moss Vale(IRE) Limit (IRE) (Barathea (IRE))
703^{7}

Blackwater King (IRE) *Johnny Farrelly* 112h 109c
7 bb g Beneficial Accordian Lady (IRE) (Accordion)
2458^{P} 2667^{2} ◆ **2833^{F}**

Blackwell Synergy (FR) *John Upson* 109h 77c
9 b g Antarctique(IRE) Pyu (GER) (Surumu (GER))
398^{P} (757) 939^{2} (1113) 2839^{4}

Blackwood Rover (IRE) *J R Jenkins* 37h 94c
7 b g Turtle Island(IRE) Lady Of Fleet (IRE) (Buckskin (FR))
533^{P} 877^{7} 1159^{3} 1243^{3} 1373^{3} 1894^{2}

Black Zero (IRE) *Michael J McDonagh* 113h 116c
7 br g Blueprint(IRE) My Native Glen (IRE) (Be My Native (USA))
3302a^{5}

Blades Lad *Peter Niven* 115h 116c
6 ch g Haafhd Blades Girl (Bertolini (USA))
1888^{2} ◆ (2755) 3134^{8} 3475^{6} 4386^{5}

Bladoun (FR) *David Pipe* 115h
7 gr g Smadoun(FR) Blabliramic (FR) (Panoramic)
2540^{12} 2831^{4} 4384^{5} (4541) 4706^{4}

Blague D'Oudairies (FR) *J Follain*
4 b m Sleeping Car(FR) Forlane V (FR) (Quart De Vin (FR))
5135a^{F}

Blair Perrone (IRE) *A J Martin* 140h 150c
6 b g Rudimentary(USA) Stonehallqueen (IRE) (King's Ride)
6a^{3} **3652a^{2} 4005a^{5} 4956a^{3}**

Blake Dean *Sue Smith* 100h
7 b g Halling(USA) Antediluvian (Air Express (IRE))
2492^{12} 2893^{3} 3102^{2} 3402^{4} 3791^{5}

Blakemount (IRE) *Sue Smith* 140h 140c
7 br g Presenting Smashing Leader (IRE) (Supreme Leader)
2067^{3} 2399^{3} 4370^{5} (4905)

Blakerigg (IRE) *Nicky Richards* 109b
4 b g Presenting Azalea (IRE) (Marju (IRE))
4552^{2} ◆

Blaklion *Nigel Twiston-Davies* 134h 162c
6 b g Kayf Tara Franciscaine (FR) (Legend Of France (USA))
1846^{4} 2481^{F} (3013) 3405^{2} (3998) (4716) 5191^{3}

Blameitalonmyroots (IRE) *Oliver Sherwood* 124h 136c
5 b m Turtle Island(IRE) Makingyourmindup (IRE) (Good Thyne (USA))
(2764) 3113^{5} (3866) 4800^{U} 4935^{4}

Blandfords Gunner *Evan Williams* 114h 131c
6 b g Needle Gun(IRE) Miss Millbrook (Meadowbrook)
26^{2} **2266^{7} (2857) 4230^{2} ◆ 4964^{5} 5496^{10}**

Blast Martha (IRE) *Michael Smith* 76h
6 b m Definite Article Calendula (Be My Guest (USA))
37^{3} **454^{P}**

Blast Of Koeman (IRE) *Robert Tyner* 106h
4 ch g Shantou(USA) Erintante (IRE) (Denel (FR))
9a^{6}

Blayney Queen (IRE) *S R B Crawford* 107h
6 gr m Desert King(IRE) Lady Blayney (IRE) (Mazaad)
1334^{3} 2325^{3}

Blazer (FR) *W P Mullins* 144h 121c
4 ch g Network(GER) Juppelongue (FR) (Trebrook (FR))
4115^{9} 4717^{4} ◆ 5189^{7}

Blazing Whale *E Walker* 105c
10 b g Classic Cliche(IRE) Baby Whale (IRE) (Supreme Leader)
5270^{3}

Blenheim Brook (IRE) *Lucinda Russell* 84h 81c
10 br g Alderbrook Blenheim Blinder (IRE) (Mandalus)
5475^{7}

Blessed King (IRE) *Gordon Elliott* 120h
5 b g Desert King(IRE) Lady Max (IRE) (Mandalus)
662^{2}

Bless The Wings (IRE) *Gordon Elliott* 129h 148c
10 b g Winged Love(IRE) Silva Venture (IRE) (Mandalus)
95a^{3} 660^{3} 868^{3} 2228a^{4} 2471^{3} 3017^{4} 4719^{3} 5005a^{2}

Bletchley Castle (IRE) *Seamus Durack* 103h
6 b g Dylan Thomas(IRE) Zaafran (Singspiel (IRE))
330^{3} 680^{4} ◆ 754^{2} 858^{3}

Bleu Astral (FR) *Alexandra Dunn*
3 b g Astronomer Royal(USA) Passion Bleue (In The Wings)
690^{4}

Bleu Berry (FR) *W P Mullins* 124h
4 b g Special Kaldoun(IRE) Somosierra (FR) (Blushing Flame (USA))
4117^{7}

Bleu Et Noir *Tim Vaughan* 109h
4 b g Enrique Gastina (FR) (Pistolet Bleu (IRE))
392^{5} 1967^{4} 2646^{F} 5160^{2}

Bleu Et Or (FR) *Donald McCain* 88h
4 b g Maresca Sorrento(FR) Panoplie (FR) (Arnaqueur (USA))
680^{3}

Bleu Et Rouge (FR) *W P Mullins* 151h
4 gr g Charming Groom(FR) Lady Du Renom (FR) (Art Francais (USA))
3294a^{4} (4004a) 4766^{F} 5190^{5}

Blinding Lights (IRE) *Mary Sanderson* 109c
10 b g Snurge Tender Return (IRE) (Strong Gale)
123^{3} 4437^{3} 5035^{P} 5399^{5}

Bling Noir (IRE) *Tony Coyle* 71h
5 b m High Chaparral(IRE) Tribal Princess (IRE) (Namaqualand (USA))
1797^{4} 1968^{4} 2287^{7} 2498^{6}

Blondymarie (FR) *J-L Delaplace* 45b
4 b m Le Balafre(FR) Micamarie (FR) (Epervier Bleu)
2536a^{9}

Blood Cotil (FR) *W P Mullins* 144h 154c
6 b g Enrique Move Along (FR) (Northern Crystal)
(69a) 3651a^{5} 4717^{P} **5193^{F}**

Blood Crazed Tiger (IRE) *P M J Doyle* 112b
4 b g King's Theatre(IRE) Mardi Roberta (IRE) (Bob Back (USA))
11a^{10}

Bloody Mary (FR) *Nicky Henderson* 139h
4 gr m Fragrant Mix(IRE) Sacade (FR) (Robin Des Champs (FR))
(3915) 4734^{3}

Blootender (FR) *X-L Le Stang* 88h
8 b g Great Pretender(IRE) Bloom (FR) (Nononito (FR))
5136a[5]

Blossom Again *Laura Young*
4 b m Apple Tree(FR) Millkom Elegance (Millkom)
5286[14]

Blown Cover *Emma Lavelle* 114h
6 b g Kayf Tara Cullen Bay (IRE) (Supreme Leader)
2489[P] 2996[P]

Blu Cavalier *Alexandra Dunn* 110b
5 b g Kayf Tara Blue Ride (IRE) (King's Ride)
392[4] (2460) 4894[4]

Blue April (FR) *Jeremy Scott* 103h
4 b g Blue Bresil(FR) Royale Little (FR) (Garde Royale)
2136[2] 2710[5] 3114[7] 4447[RR] 4871[5] 5352[3]

Blue Atlantic (USA) *Warren Greatrex* 126h
4 b g Stormy Atlantic(USA) Bluemamba (USA) (Kingmambo (USA))
73a[4] 418[P] 4362[8] 5146[2]

Blue Bear (IRE) *Diana Grissell* 124h
4 b g Blueprint(IRE) In For It (IRE) (Tale Quale)
225[5] 2700[3] 4070[8] **4379[F]**

Blue Buttons (IRE) *Emma Lavelle* 133h
7 b m King's Theatre(IRE) Babet (IRE) (Mujadil (USA))
(2199) **2602[U]** 3034[5] 3748[5] 4801[7] 5282[7]

Blue Cannon (IRE) *S R B Crawford* 108h 94c
7 b g High Chaparral(IRE) Blushing Barada (USA) (Blushing Groom (FR))
1503[5]

Blue Comet *Richard Phillips* 91b
4 b g Blueprint(IRE) Be My Valentine (IRE) (Be My Native (USA))
2138[8] 2270[9]

Blue Court (IRE) *Evan Williams* 73h
4 b m Court Cave(IRE) Bobazure (IRE) (Bob's Return (IRE))
4961[3]

Blue Cove *Lynn Siddall* 73h
10 ch g Karinga Bay Meadow Blue (Northern State (USA))
136[2] 2488[4] 3503[2] 3793[P] 4047[4] 4391[8] 4557[4] 4942[P]

Blue Dragon (FR) *G Cherel* 154h
4 b g Califet(FR) Nathalie Blue (FR) (Epervier Bleu)
(665a)

Blue Fashion (IRE) *Nicky Henderson* 140h 63c
6 b g Scorpion(IRE) Moon Glow (FR) (Solar One (FR))
3147[P] 4067[6]

Blue Hell (FR) *Alan Fleming* 140h
5 b g Russian Blue(IRE) Art Fair (FR) (Fairy King (USA))
4765[22]

Blue Is The Colour (IRE) *Nicky Henderson* 35b
5 b g Dalakhani(IRE) Coyote (Indian Ridge)
1966[9] 2375[9]

Blue Kascade (IRE) *Sandy Thomson* 99h 118c
8 ch g Kaieteur(USA) Lydia Blue (IRE) (Eve's Error)
(2173) 3671[3]

Blue Prairie *Dan Skelton* 78h
4 b g Tobougg(IRE) Prairie Sun (GER) (Law Society (USA))
1873[7] 2221[9] 2581[10] 3130[9] 3841[4]

Blue Rambler *John Ferguson* 127h
5 b g Monsun(GER) La Nuit Rose (FR) (Rainbow Quest (USA))
3306[3] 4033[2] ◆ 4317[2] 4986[5]

Blue Sea Of Ibrox (IRE) *Alan Brown* 78h 62c
7 gr m Subtle Power(IRE) Jerpoint Rose (IRE) (Roselier (FR))
57[5] 258[P]

Blueside Boy (IRE) *Harriet Graham* 79h 72c
7 b g Blueprint(IRE) Asidewager (IRE) (Brush Aside (USA))
2191[5] 4163[10] **4903[7] 5261[4]**

Blue Sire (FR) *Gary Moore* 31b
4 bb g Day Flight Hirlish (FR) (Passing Sale (FR))
5359[9]

Blue Talisman (IRE) *Peter Bowen* 94h
4 ch g Alhaarth(IRE) Amaniy (USA) (Dayjur (USA))
106[P]

Blue Top *Dai Burchell* 84h
6 b g Millkom Pompey Blue (Abou Zouz (USA))
616[5] 2264[2] 4886[5]

Blu Passione *Oliver Sherwood* 74b
4 gr m Halling(USA) Dissolve (Sharrood (USA))
594[6] 970[10]

Blurred Lines (IRE) *Trevor Wall* 102h
6 ch m Shantou(USA) Balda Girl (IRE) (Mandalus)
503[5] 1165[3] 1293[P] 4391[P]

Boa Island (IRE) *Paul Nicholls* 103h
5 b g Trans Island Eskimo Kiss (IRE) (Distinctly North (USA))
2257[6] 5430[3]

Board Of Trade *Alan King* 132h
4 ch g Black Sam Bellamy(IRE) Realms Of Gold (USA) (Gulch (USA))
2011[2] 2762[3] 3370[4] (4322) 5372[5]

Boardwalk Empire (IRE) *Kate Buckett* 119h 110c
8 b g Overbury(IRE) Mighty Mandy (IRE) (Mandalus)
2733[P] 3197[P] 4465[6] 4789[4] 5222[P] 5417[U]

Boatswain (IRE) *Henry Daly* 85h
4 b g Flemensfirth(USA) Royale Laguna (FR) (Cadoudal (FR))
2965[2] 3388[9] 5043[3]

Bobba Benetta (IRE) *Derek Shaw* 62b
5 gr m Beneficial Boberelle (IRE) (Bob Back (USA))
5315[6]

Bobbits Way *Alan Jones* 91h 99c
10 b g Overbury(IRE) Bit Of A Chick (Henbit (USA))
2659[P] 4410[3]

Bobble Boru (IRE) *Venetia Williams* 107h 112c
7 b m Brian Boru Balreask Lady (IRE) (Shardari)
57[4] 331[3] (2364) 2837[P] 3141[F] 3337[4] 3501[2] 3866[P] 4432[P] **4889[U] 5142[3] 5447[3]**

Bobble Emerald (IRE) *Martin Keighley* 112h
7 ch g Rudimentary(USA) Aunt Emeralds (IRE) (Roselier (FR))
147[3] (460) 833[6] 1292[7] **1520[P]** 2985[P] 3607[3] (5397)

Bobby Benton (IRE) *Jim Best* 69h
4 b g Invincible Spirit(IRE) Remarkable Story (Mark Of Esteem (IRE))
3418[6] 3772[P] 3902[P] 4111[P] 4409[9] 4849[10]

Bobby Dove *Bernard Llewellyn* 93h 98c
8 b g Fraam Flakey Dove (Oats)
1786[4] 1933[6]

Bobcatbilly (IRE) *Ian Williams* 96h 138c
9 b g Overbury(IRE) Cush Jewel (IRE) (Executive Perk)
100[4] **4207[7] 4592[3]**

Bob Ford (IRE) *Rebecca Curtis* 130h 148c
8 b g Vinnie Roe(IRE) Polar Lamb (IRE) (Brush Aside (USA))
2436[P] (3079) 3518[F] 4113[P] 4802[P]

Bob Lewis *Stuart Kittow* 103h 101c
9 b g Sir Harry Lewis(USA) Teelyna (Teenoso (USA))
1293[2] **1546[2] 1978[2]**

Bobo Mac (IRE) *Michael Hourigan* 103h
4 gb g Whitmore's Conn(USA) Blazing Love (IRE) (Fruits Of Love (USA))
11a[4]

Bobonyx *Dai Williams* 68h 52c
5 b g Phoenix Reach(IRE) Twist The Facts (IRE) (Un Desperado (FR))
811[9] 878[7] 1010[6] 1158[7] 1244[9] **1343[4] 1401[5] 1489[P]**

Bobowen (IRE) *Dr Richard Newland* 101h 113c
9 b g Bob Back(USA) Opus One (Slip Anchor)
77[5]

Bob's Call (IRE) *Tony Coyle* 97h 90c
6 b g Scorpion(IRE) Whizz (Salse (USA))
758[7] **1004[P]** 1272[P] **1687[3] 1796[4]**

Bob's Dream (IRE) *Alison Hamilton* 93b
13 b g Bob's Return(IRE) Back In Kansas (IRE) (Mister Lord (USA))
2705[P]

Bobs Lady Tamure *Maurice Barnes* 129h
8 b m Tamure(IRE) Bob Back's Lady (IRE) (Bob Back (USA))
2773[P] 2921[6] 3440[F] 4125[6] 4366[2] 4608[U]

Bob's Legend (IRE) *Jamie Snowden* 95h 89c
9 b g Bob's Return(IRE) Pepsi Starlet (IRE) (Heavenly Manna)
34[3] 252[5] 507[7] 634[2] 804[4] **1373[5] 1489[4]** 1578[10] 1691[6]

Bobs Worth (IRE) *Nicky Henderson* 153h 157c
10 b g Bob Back(USA) Fashionista (IRE) (King's Theatre (IRE))
(2334) **2783[6]** 3408[6] 4732[3]

Bob The Butcher *David Brace* 90c
6 b g Needle Gun(IRE) Brydferth Ddu (IRE) (Supreme Leader)
5467[7]

Bob Tucker (IRE) *Charlie Longsdon* 119h 138c
8 b g Brian Boru Acumen (IRE) (Phardante (FR))
109[3] (1906) 2616[6] 4232[P] 4465[9] (5071)

Bob Will (IRE) *John Flint* 62h 77c
10 b g Bob's Return(IRE) Mini Moo Min (Ardross)
31[4] 438[P] 3946[P]

Bodega *Ian Williams* 115h 128c
7 b g Grape Tree Road Gurleigh (IRE) (Pivotal)
2271[F] 2540[2] **3134[3] 3384[3] 4230[F] 4420[2]** ◆ **(4493) 4800[B] 4912[6]**

Bodekin Point (IRE) *Charlie Longsdon* 16b
4 br g Robin Des Pres(FR) Countessdee (IRE) (Arctic Lord (IRE))
4790[16]

Bogoss Du Perret (FR) *Jimmy Frost* 96h
4 bb g Malinas(GER) Lady De Paques (FR) (Lights Out (FR))
511[3] 823[7] 2258[6] 2871[P] 3414[P] 4917[P]

Boheme (FR) *Emmanuel Clayeux* 104h 84c
4 gr m Dom Alco(FR) Jonquiere (FR) (Trebrook (FR))
350a[12]

Bohemian Rhapsody (IRE) *Joseph Tuite* 123h
6 b g Galileo(IRE) Quiet Mouse (USA) (Quiet American (USA))
(261) 2513[17]

Boher Lad (IRE) *Alan Phillips* 75h
8 b g Gold Well Shindeeshamick (IRE) (Roselier (FR))
1120[2] 1323[4] 1423[3]

Boherna Lady (IRE) *Denis Gerard Hogan* 115h
7 ch m Shantou(USA) Bally Bolshoi (IRE) (Bob Back (USA))
1771[3] (1816)

Boite (IRE) *Warren Greatrex* 135h
5 b g Authorized(IRE) Albiatra (USA) (Dixieland Band (USA))
4484[2] 5219[4]

Bol D'Air (FR) *Paul Nicholls* 88h
4 b g Blue Bresil(FR) Holding (FR) (Useful (FR))
2351[5] 3772[7] 4875[9]

Bold Bachelor (IRE) *Dr Richard Newland* 94h 120c
6 b g Bachelor Duke(USA) Bold Nora (IRE) (Persian Bold)
3199[2] (3419) 3731[P]

Boldbob (IRE) *Micky Hammond* 99h
3 gr g Verglas(IRE) Special Park (USA) (Trempolino (USA))
1177[5] (1415) 2863[4] 3423[4] 3590[8] 4154[5] 4819[6] 5345[4]

Bold Conquest (IRE) *Stuart Edmunds* 117h 119c
7 b g Oscar(IRE) Massappeal Supreme (IRE) (Supreme Leader)
(85) 363[4] 1615[3] **2018[5]** 2268[6] 2744[2] 3336[4] **4780[5]**

Bold Duke *Edward Bevan* 120h
7 b g Sulamani(IRE) Dominant Duchess (Old Vic)
880[4] 2694[5] 3374[3] (3619) 4353[2] 4913[9] 5139[3]

Bold Henmie (IRE) *Philip Kirby* 102h
4 b g Henrythenavigator(USA) Seminole Lass (USA) (Indian Charlie (USA))
1568[9] 1898[3] 2294[6] 2933[8] 3628[9] 4863[F] 5122[P]

Bold Henry *Philip Hobbs* 127h 143c
9 b g Kayf Tara Madam Min (Overbury (IRE))
47a[7] 3030[8] (3446) 3990[4] 4770[F]

Bold Prince Rupert (IRE) *Sara Ender* 84h
5 br g Royal Anthem(USA) Fortune And Favour (IRE) (Homo Sapien)
2591[P] 4108[P] 5437[5]

Bold Runner *Jose Santos* 118h
4 ch g Mount Nelson Music In Exile (USA) (Diesis)
1234[9] 3664[2] 4097[7] 4648[5] 5115[2] 5355[2]

Bold Sir Brian (IRE) *Lucinda Russell* 121h 142c
9 b g Brian Boru Black Queen (IRE) (Bob Back (USA))
2641[9] 3737[F] 4165[5] (4607)

Bolero Collonges (FR) *Simon Waugh* 63h
4 gr g Fragrant Mix(IRE) Katy Collonges (FR) (Lute Antique (FR))
3473[11] 3807[P] **4327[P]**

Bolister (FR) *Gary Moore* 98h
4 b g Le Balafre(FR) Girlish (FR) (Passing Sale (FR))
2188[6] 2544[10] 3450[6] 3660[3] 3994[9] 4674[P]

Bollihope *Richard Guest*
3 ch g Medicean Hazy Dancer (Oasis Dream)
2718[P]

Bollin Ace *Tim Easterby* 117h
4 b g Bollin Eric Bollin Annabel (King's Theatre (IRE))
2169[2] 2498[2] 2801[3] 3240[3] 4108[3] 4941[2] 5260[9]

Bollin Beauty *Malcolm Jefferson* 98h
6 br m Bollin Eric Miss Danbys (Charmer (IRE))
400[3] 640[2] 970[7] 1165[5] 1374[4]

Bollin Fiona *Donald Whillans* 99h 85c
11 ch m Silver Patriarch(IRE) Bollin Nellie (Rock Hopper)
958[6]

Bollin Line *Lucinda Egerton* 91h 101c
8 b g Bollin Eric Leading Line (Leading Man)
2143[5] 2844[2] 3103[2] 3308[4] (3968) 4177[F] 4418[3] 4938[6] 5310[4]

Bolton Blue (IRE) *Katie Scott* 77h
6 b g Blueprint(IRE) Ebony Countess (IRE) (Phardante (FR))
3056[4] 3340[P] 3668[6] 4739[P] 5122[10] 5472[10]

Bolving (IRE) *Victor Dartnall* 119b
4 b g Stowaway Kiniohio (FR) (Script Ohio (USA))
(4364) 5195[15]

Bon Chic (IRE) *Dan Skelton* 131h 126c
6 b m Presenting Homebird (IRE) (Be My Native (USA))
2613[2] 2925[2] 3317[2] (4772) 5281[9]

Bondi Mist (IRE) *Jonathan Geake* 103h
6 gr m Aussie Rules(USA) Akoya (IRE) (Anabaa (USA))
268[3] 2349[8] 3108[P] 4936[P]

Bonds Conquest *Seamus Mullins* 78h 78c
6 ch g Monsieur Bond(IRE) Another Conquest (El Conquistador)
2269[P] 2712[2] 3195[4] 4356[8] 4931[2] 5478[2]

Bond Starprincess *George Moore* 65h
3 ch f Monsieur Bond(IRE) Presidium Star (Presidium)
1631[9] 1899[10] 2718[5] 3587[7] 3791[P]

Bonelli's Warbler *Stuart Edmunds* 15b
5 ch m Notnowcato Cetti's Warbler (Sir Harry Lewis (USA))
2644[P]

Bon Enfant (FR) *Warren Greatrex* 128h
4 gr g Saint Des Saints(FR) Montanara Paris (FR) (Turgeon (USA))
9a[20] (2312) (2917) 3994[2] 4596[3] 5497[7]

Bon Genre (IRE) *Robert Stephens* 101b
4 b g Fruits Of Love(USA) Cobblers Hall (IRE) (Saddlers' Hall (IRE))
2849[6]

Bonito Du Berlais (FR) *A Chaille-Chaille* 150h 139c
4 b g Trempolino(USA) Chica Du Berlais (FR) (Cadoudal (FR))
665a[4]

Bonjour Bonsoir (FR) *Emmanuel Clayeux* 102h
4 b g Laverock(IRE) Esprit Live (FR) (Dark Moondancer)
2362a[4]

Bonne Fee *Kim Bailey* 127h 104c
8 b m Karinga Bay Jolika (FR) (Grand Tresor (FR))
216[8] **1479[4] 1821[F]**

Bonne Question (FR) *Venetia Williams* 122h
6 gr g Tagula(IRE) Amonita (GER) (Medaaly)
2437[P] 3724[5] 4317[3] 4681[2] 5077[2] 5401[2]

Bonnet's Vino *Pam Sly* 112h 106c
7 b m Grape Tree Road Bonnet's Pieces (Alderbrook)
(2812) 3174[2] **3486[3] 3866[3]** 4492[B] 4878[7] **5350[4]**

Bonnie Black Rose *Arthur Whiting* 15b
5 b m Black Sam Bellamy(IRE) Fragrant Rose (Alflora (IRE))
334[10]

Bonnie Lizzie *Dianne Sayer*
4 ch m Alflora(IRE) Caitlin Ash (Karinga Bay)
4408[6]

Bonny Kate (IRE) *Noel Meade* 126h 138c
5 ch m Beneficial Peppardstown (IRE) (Old Vic)
(3894a) (4656a) 5005a[P]

Bonobo (IRE) *Evan Williams* 110h 115c
8 b g Quws Better Folly (IRE) (Rhoman Rule (USA))
2577[7] 4482[3] 4822[4]

Bonvilston Boy *Tim Vaughan* 101h
4 b g Martaline Lisa Du Chenet (FR) (Garde Royale)
188[8] 3105[8] 3927[5] 4351[6] 4970[3]

Bonzo Bing (IRE) *Martin Todhunter* 70h 112c
7 b g Gold Well She's A Dreamer (IRE) (Safety Catch (USA))
1741[4] 1902[5] 2788[6] 3937[2] 4166[6] 4420[P] 5260[11]

Boogangoo (IRE) *Grace Harris* 99h
4 b m Acclamation Spice World (IRE) (Spinning World (USA))
1979[F] (Dead)

Boogie In The Barn (IRE) *Charlie Longsdon* 121h
7 b g Milan Presenting Mist (IRE) (Presenting)
2202[F] (Dead)

Boogie Life *Jim Goldie* 105b
4 b m Tobougg(IRE) Life Is Life (FR) (Mansonnien (FR))
(159) 459[3]

Book At Bedtime *Keith Reveley* 104b
4 b m Midnight Legend Northern Native (IRE) (Be My Native (USA))
4847[2] ◆

Book'em Danno (IRE) *Laura Hurley* 96h 99c
9 ch g Moscow Society(USA) Rifada (Ela-Mana-Mou)
358[P]

Book Of Excuses (IRE) *Donald McCain* 114h 119c
7 b g Brian Boru Out Of Danger (IRE) (Darnay)
693[P] 873[2]

Books Review *Paul Hamer* 65h 82c
11 b g Karinga Bay In A Whirl (USA) (Island Whirl (USA))
5467[10]

Boolavard King (IRE) *Kim Bailey* 102h
6 b g Winged Love(IRE) Eastender (Opening Verse (USA))
2840[2] 3928[6] 4784[P]

Boondooma (IRE) *Dr Richard Newland* 135h 156c
8 b g Westerner Kissantell (IRE) (Broken Hearted)
(2059) 2483[P]

Booted Eagle (IRE) *Anabel K Murphy* 49b
5 b g Oscar(IRE) Warmley's Gem (IRE) (Phardante (FR))
4188[5]

Bop Along (IRE) *Alistair Whillans* 109h
8 b g Double Eclipse(IRE) Bob Girl (IRE) (Bob Back (USA))
2933[7] 3346[P] 4035[3] 4638[8] 4906[5] 5402[3]

Borak (IRE) *Bernard Llewellyn* 115h
3 b g Kodiac Right After Moyne (IRE) (Imperial Ballet (IRE))
1928[3] (3076) 3519[6] 3926[3]

Border Breaker (IRE) *Simon Waugh* 123h 133c
6 br g Indian Danehill(IRE) Flying Answer (IRE) (Anshan)
625[2] **808[3] (1502)** ◆ **1632[3] 2008[3] 2459[5] 5390[6]**

Bordini (FR) *W P Mullins* 132b
5 b g Martaline Didinas (FR) (Kaldou Star)
23a[11]

Bored Or Bad (IRE) *David Dennis* 80h
3 b g Oscar(IRE) Siberiansdaughter (IRE) (Strong Gale)
4303[12] 4843[6]

Boric *Simon Waugh* 67h 113c
7 b g Grape Tree Road Petrea (St Ninian)
2477[P] (2788) 3162[B]

Boris Boru (IRE) *Sarah Dawson* 94h
4 b g Brian Boru Gaye Roberta (IRE) (Bob Back (USA))
5412[6]

Born Survivor (IRE) *Dan Skelton* 140h
4 b g King's Theatre(IRE) Bob's Flame (IRE) (Bob Back (USA))
(2995) 3623[4] (4299)

Born To Be Free *Diana Grissell* 14h
6 b m Phoenix Reach(IRE) Charlie's Angel (Rakaposhi King)
2004[P] 2649[P]

Born To Benefit (IRE) *Fergal O'Brien* 94h 86c
9 b m Beneficial Sister Superior (IRE) (Supreme Leader)
178[4] 466[5] **934[P] 1133[P]**

Born To Succeed (IRE) *Ben Pauling* 98h
5 b g Robin Des Pres(FR) Born To Win (IRE) (Torus)
600[F]

Boruma (IRE) *Dianne Sayer* 117h 107c
5 b g Brian Boru Itlallendintears (IRE) (Lil's Boy (USA))
85[9] 356[8] 780[6] 2027[3] ◆ 2775[3] ◆ 3027[2] 3344[P] 4839[2] 5089[7]

Boru's Brook (IRE) *Jim Best* 125h 141c
7 b g Brian Boru Collybrook Lady (IRE) (Mandalus)
(2495) 3738[P]

Boscraie (FR) *Emmanuel Clayeux* 105h 110c
4 b m Martaline Iconea (FR) (Lights Out (FR))
350a[P] 2821a[P]

Bo's Return *Tim Vaughan* 43h
5 b g Tobougg(IRE) Lamp's Return (Bob's Return (IRE))
1158[P]

Bossa Nova (FR) *F-M Cottin* 123h 129c
4 b m Network(GER) Gamine Royale (FR) (Garde Royale)
1882a[2]

Boss Des Mottes (FR) *Dan Skelton* 130h
4 b g Califet(FR) Puszta Des Mottes (FR) (Useful (FR))
1847[4] 2516[3] 4774[4]

Bosseur (FR) *G Cherel* 142h
4 b g Coastal Path Suite (FR) (Octagonal (NZ))
665a[2]

Boss In Boots (IRE) *Seamus Mullins* 109h 121c
7 gr g King's Theatre(IRE) Grey Mo (IRE) (Roselier (FR))
402[5] 672[4] 1451[2] 1690[4] 2019[U] 2419[6] 2884[10]

Bostin (IRE) *Daniel O'Brien* 106h
7 ch g Busy Flight Bustingoutallover (USA) (Trempolino (USA))
283[7] 669[9]

Boston Blue *Tony Carroll* 107h 87c
8 b g Halling(USA) City Of Gold (IRE) (Sadler's Wells (USA))
2688[11] 2788[2] 3314[4] **4588[4]**

Boston Bob (IRE) *W P Mullins* 146h 163c
10 b g Bob Back(USA) Bavaway (Le Bavard (FR))
22a[5] 1152a[13] 3715a[P] (4260a) 5218[P]

Boston De La Roche (FR) *David Loder* 111h
4 b g Malinas(GER) Quesland De La Roche (FR) (Amaqueur (USA))
2748[5] 3019[6] 4869[4]

Bothair Clei (IRE) *Daniel G Murphy* 91h 126c
10 b g Snurge Gentle Leader (IRE) (Supreme Leader)
92a[5] 3894a[4] 4521a[8]

Botney Bay (IRE) *Robert Walford*
5 b g September Storm(GER) Sword Lady (Broadsword (USA))
1044[P]

Boudry (FR) *Warren Greatrex* 116b
4 b g Crossharbour Lavande (FR) (Iris Noir (FR))
2460[2] 3952[3] (4371) 4488[6]

Bouggietopieces *Gordon Elliott* 73b 114c
5 b g Tobougg(IRE) Bonnet's Pieces (Alderbrook)
57[U] 280[4] 871[2] 959[5] 1400[4] **(1492) 1629[2] 1795[2]**

Boum Boum (FR) *M Seror* 96h
2 b g Buck's Boum(FR) Victory Ball (FR) (Ballingarry (IRE))
4539a[P]

Bound For Glory (IRE) *D M G Fitch-Peyton* 110h 126c
9 b g Witness Box(USA) Musical View (IRE) (Orchestra)
534[3] 4446[6] 5178[U]

Bound Hill *Fiona Shaw* 98h
6 b g Kayf Tara Ardent Bride (Ardross)
213[7] 3710[6] 4137[5] 4463[P] 5034[6]

Bountiful Bess *Pam Sly* 90h
5 ch m Bahamian Bounty Saida Lenasera (FR) (Fasliyev (USA))
2840[11] 3177[5] 3307[5]

Bountiful Sin *Oliver Sherwood* 90h
4 ch g Sinndar(IRE) Tropical Barth (IRE) (Peintre Celebre (USA))
2544[7] 3047[5] 3777[7]

Bourbondi *Conrad Allen* 49h
4 b g Sakhee(USA) Lake Diva (Docksider (USA))
125[5]

Bourbon Prince *Sam Drake* 89h
4 ch g Aqlaam Good Enough (FR) (Mukaddamah (USA))
3840[3]

Bourdello *Emma Baker* 95h
6 b m Milan Haudello (FR) (Marignan (USA))
1845[4] 2444[2] 5382[11]

Bourne *Donald McCain* 114h
9 gr g Linamix(FR) L'Affaire Monique (Machiavellian (USA))
1455[5] 1897[9] 4648[7] 5332[5]

Bouvreuil (FR) *Paul Nicholls* 135h 151c
4 b g Saddler Maker(IRE) Madame Lys (FR) (Sheyrann (IRE))
2512[15] **2913[5] (3504) 3856[5] 4701[2] 5174[4]**

Bowberry *Ali Stronge* 67h
4 b m Cockney Rebel(IRE) Blaeberry (Kirkwall)
4881[10] 5389[9]

Bowdler's Magic *David Thompson* 121h
8 b g Hernando(FR) Slew The Moon (ARG) (Kitwood (USA))
661[F] 1774[2] (2139) (2498) 2901[5] 3420[2] 4107[3] 4793[3] 5260[10]

Bowie (IRE) *Nick Kent* 120h
8 br g Pelder(IRE) La Fenice (IRE) (Krayyan)
356[3] 624[2] 1903[9]

Bow Window (FR) *E Leray* 99c
4 gr g Fairly Ransom(USA) Petite Perruche (FR) (Shaindy (FR))
5385a[4]

Boxatrix *Paul Phillips* 72h
7 ch g Arkadian Hero(USA) Mardereil (IRE) (Moscow Society (USA))
1576[4] 1829[7] 2005[6]

Boxing Along (IRE) *Vincent Laurence Halley* 102h 116c
11 b g Witness Box(USA) Ballybeg Rose (IRE) (Roselier (FR))
48a[5] 4949a[4]

Box Office (FR) *Jonjo O'Neill* 137h
4 b g Great Pretender(IRE) Quelle Mome (FR) (Video Rock (FR))
1847[6] 2083[3] 2912[4] 4246[P] 4730[12] 5189[10]

Boyfromnowhere (IRE) *Neil Mulholland* 102b 121c
8 br g Old Vic Eist Do Gale (IRE) (Strong Gale)
2566[P]

Boygojumping *Martin Peaty* 96b
3 ch g Midnight Legend Maisie Malone Vii (Damsire Unregistered)
5436[2]

Boyhood (IRE) *Tom George* 112b
4 b g Oscar(IRE) Glen Dubh (IRE) (Supreme Leader)
(4181) 5315[3]

Boy In A Bentley (IRE) *Kim Bailey* 118h
5 b g Kayf Tara All Our Blessings (IRE) (Statoblest)
242[2] 4322[2] 4711[2]

Boy Of Boru (IRE) *Miss Rose Grissell* 110b
8 b g Brian Boru Don't Waste It (IRE) (Mister Lord (USA))
292[P]

Braavos *Philip Hobbs* 129h
4 br g Presenting Tatanka (IRE) (Lear Fan (USA))
124[5] (1973) 2407[3] 2898[2] (3414) 4801[6] (5446)

Bracing *N W Alexander* 90h
6 ch m Alflora(IRE) Sports Express (Then Again)
2103[2] ◆ 2751[4] ◆ 3474[2]

Bracken Brae *Mark H Tompkins* 93h
3 b f Champs Elysees Azure Mist (Bahamian Bounty)
2537[3] 2896[7]

Brackenmoss Rory *Alistair Whillans* 84b
3 b g Overbury(IRE) Thorterdykes Lass (IRE) (Zaffaran (USA))
4208[3] 4611[P] 5330[8]

Brackloon High (IRE) *M Kehoe* 88h 95c
10 b g Bob Back(USA) Homebird (IRE) (Be My Native (USA))
15[4] 4768[14]

Bradbury (IRE) *Julia Brooke*
7 ch g Redback Simonaventura (IRE) (Dr Devious (IRE))
2843[P] (Dead)

Bradford Bridge (IRE) *Philip Hobbs* 88b
3 b g Milan Isis Du Berlais (FR) (Cadoudal (FR))
3959[5]

Bradley Brook (IRE) *Miss Nicky Martin* 115c
9 ch g Alderbrook Mazza (Mazilier (USA))
17[7]

Brae On (IRE) *George Bewley* 95h
7 ch g Presenting Raphuca (IRE) (Be My Native (USA))
4557[2] **5125[F] 5369[P]**

Braepark (IRE) *D J Dickenson* 43b
6 b g Oscar(IRE) Phecda (FR) (Ocean Of Wisdom (USA))
320[19]

Brahms De Clermont (FR) *Paul Nicholls* 119b
4 b g Califet(FR) Colline De Clermon (FR) (Vertical Speed (FR))
(5188) ◆

Brain Power (IRE) *Nicky Henderson* 144h
4 b g Kalanisi(IRE) Blonde Ambition (IRE) (Old Vic)
(2683) 4010[2] (4784)

Brake Hill *Mrs Julie Marles* 97b
6 b g Passing Glance Red Karinga (Karinga Bay)
320[5]

Bramble Brook *Colin Tizzard* 105h
5 b g Kayf Tara Briery Ann (Anshan)
2351[6] 2729[11] 3105[6] 5063[5] 5268[4]

Brandenburg Gate (IRE) *Charlie Longsdon* 99h
4 b g Germany(USA) Miss Anchor (IRE) (Slip Anchor)
2188[8] 5248[4]

Brannoc (IRE) *Gail Haywood* 89b
10 b g Pilsudski(IRE) Ned's Choice (IRE) (Montelimar (USA))
163[P] 1120[P] **1237[P]**

Braqueur D'Or (FR) *Rebecca Curtis* 92b
4 b g Epalo(GER) Hot D'Or (FR) (Shafoun (FR))
4894[9]

Brass Monkey (IRE) *Neil King* 111h 95c
8 b g Craigsteel Saltee Great (IRE) (Fourstars Allstar (USA))
(451) 593[3]

Brass Tax (IRE) *Ben Case* 97h 114c
9 b g Morozov(USA) Cry Before Dawn (IRE) (Roselier (FR))
101[5] 1167[10]

Bravarde (FR) *G Elbaz* 108h 105c
4 b m Kapgarde(FR) Brave D'Honneur (FR) (Baroud D'Honneur (FR))
5499a[7]

Brave Buck *Henry Daly* 72h 108c
7 b g Bollin Eric Silken Pearls (Leading Counsel (USA))
2500[6] 3144[P] 4276[P]

Brave Cupid *Michael Roberts* 73h
5 ch m Black Sam Bellamy(IRE) Newport (FR) (Hawker's News (IRE))
2549[6] 2829[6] 3043[4] 3817[P]

Brave Deed (IRE) *Jeremy Scott* 105h
9 b g Kadeed(IRE) Merlins Return (IRE) (Torenaga)
(2263) **2712[P]** 4384[6] 5034[3] 5355[12]

Brave Helios *Richard Phillips* 126h 119c
5 b g High Chaparral(IRE) Renowned (IRE) (Darshaan)
210[2] (705) 1035[11] 2513[15] 3318[3] 3923[6]

Brave Jaq (FR) *Paul Nicholls* 110h
4 ch g Network(GER) Galaxie (FR) (Useful (FR))
1844[8] 2544[3]

Braventara *Nick Williams* 79b
4 b m Kayf Tara L'Aventure (FR) (Cyborg (FR))
5383[6]

Brave Richard (IRE) *J R Jenkins* 108h
4 b g Jeremy(USA) Certainly Brave (Indian Ridge)
(188) (682) ◆ 1101[2] 2406[5] 2614[3] 2910[5]

Brave Spartacus (IRE) *Keith Reveley* 122h 148c
9 b g Spartacus(IRE) Peaches Polly (Slip Anchor)
184[3] 850[3] **(1040)** 1448[4] **2084[4]** 2594[8] 4793[P] 5201[3] (5405)

Bravo Riquet (FR) *Robin Mathew* 69h 76c
9 br g Laveron Jeroline (FR) (Cadoudal (FR))
2441[4] **3977[P] 4380[8]** 4747[9]

Breakdown Cover (IRE) *S R B Crawford* 99b
4 b g Robin Des Pres(FR) Lady Malka (IRE) (Supreme Leader)
2330[5] 4611[4] 5014[3]

Breaking Bits (IRE) *Jamie Snowden* 115h
8 br g Oscar(IRE) Lantern Lark (IRE) (Be My Native (USA))
1602[3] 1893[2] 2038[5] 3015[13]

Breaking The Bank *Ben Case* 103h 124c
6 ch g Medicean Russian Dance (USA) (Nureyev (USA))
241[4] 643[2] 857[4] 1169[6] 1424[3] 1769[6] 2090[6] 2577[11]

Brean Splash Susie *Bill Turner* 58h
4 b m Tobougg(IRE) Straight As A Die (Pyramus (USA))
1117[P] 1506[10]

Breath Of Blighty (FR) *Paul Webber* 119h
4 bb g Policy Maker(IRE) Nosika D'Airy (FR) (Oblat (FR))
2126[7] 2690[4] 3227[7] 3842[2] 4875[6]

Breath Of Life *Mark Rimell* 73b
5 b m Zafeen(FR) Pretty Lady Rose (Perpendicular)
682[6] *2421[10]*

Breddy Du Desert (FR) *J Planque*
4 b g Nickname(FR) Mamounia Bay (FR) (Alamo Bay (USA))
4401a[F]

Bredon Hill Lad *Sue Gardner* 101h 112c
8 ch g Kirkwall Persian Clover (Abutammam)
2262[6] **2446[4] (2666) 2830[2] 3412[4] 3746[5] (4187) 4423[3] (5236)**

Bredon Hill Poppy *Sue Gardner* 70b
6 b m Kayf Tara Persian Clover (Abutammam)
2270[12]

Breeze Along *Sue Gardner* 75b
5 ch g Denounce Briery Breeze (IRE) (Anshan)
2460[10] 3416[5]

Breezemount (IRE) *Donald McCain* 79h
5 b g Flemensfirth(USA) Hep To The Jive (FR) (Bahri (USA))
4050[6] 4388[11] 4791[6] 5242[5]

Breezy Kin (IRE) *Andy Turnell* 91h 99c
7 ch g Kris Kin(USA) Presentbreeze (IRE) (Presenting)
40[3] 569[5] **600[3] 741[2] 926[U] 1004[10] 1243[4] (1546)**

Brelan D'As (FR) *Paul Nicholls* 123h
4 b g Crillon(FR) Las De La Croix (FR) (Grand Tresor (FR))
4137[P]

Brenda De Ronceray (FR) *David Pipe* 87h
4 b m Al Namix(FR) Landza De Ronceray (FR) (Chamberlin (FR))
831[6] 1050[3] 1506[9] 1694[4]

Brereton (IRE) *Richard Woollacott* 52b
4 b g Kalanisi(IRE) Westgrove Berry (IRE) (Presenting)
5358[11]

Briac (FR) *Jim Best* 100h
4 b g Kapgarde(FR) Jarwin Do (FR) (Grand Tresor (FR))
2317[3] *3200[3]* 3502[4] 3819[5] 4097[11] 4233[9]

Brian Boranha (IRE) *Peter Niven* 108h
4 b g Brian Boru Tapneiram (IRE) (Kahyasi)
2756[9] 3835[3] 4303[9] 4639[2]

Briar Hill (IRE) *W P Mullins* 152h
7 b g Shantou(USA) Backaway (IRE) (Bob Back (USA))
3713a[4]

Bricbracsmate *Michael Mullineaux* 44h
7 b g Revoque(IRE) Blissphilly (Primo Dominie)
754[8]

Bridal Suite (IRE) *Charlie Mann* 93h
6 b g Craigsteel Selinda Spectrum (IRE) (Spectrum (IRE))
222[6] 1972[6] 3067[6] 3220[7] **4160[P]**

Bridgets Pet (IRE) *Alan Fleming* 144h 146c
8 ch g Arakan(USA) Classy Act (Lycius (USA))
1556a[P] 4701[4]

Briery Belle *Henry Daly* 140h
6 b m King's Theatre(IRE) Briery Ann (Anshan)
2472[8] 3034[3] (3612) 4471[2] (5282)

Briery Queen *Noel Williams* 132h
6 b m King's Theatre(IRE) Briery Gale (Strong Gale)
(2776) 3154[F] 3787[4] (4457) (5094)

Brigadier Miller *Nicky Henderson* 122h
8 gr g Act One Tread Carefully (Sharpo)
2170[7] 2472[U]

Brigadoon *Michael Appleby* 113h
8 b g Compton Place Briggsmaid (Elegant Air)
1041[2] 1178[3] 1425[6] 1549[4] 1686[3] 1977[P]

Bright Eyes *Nicky Henderson* 69b
4 b m Hernando(FR) Chomba Womba (IRE) (Fourstars Allstar (USA))
4075[6]

Bright Light *Dan Skelton* 66h 61c
8 ch m Exit To Nowhere(USA) Lamp's Return (Bob's Return (IRE))
1678[8] **752[4]**

Bright New Dawn (IRE) *Gordon Elliott* 139h 157c
8 br g Presenting Shuil Dorcha (IRE) (Bob Back (USA))
24a[8] 1938a[F] 2388a[U] 2464a[2] 3092a[2] 3552a[7] 4770[18] 5179[7]

Bright Prospect (IRE) *Jackie Stephen* 120h
6 b g Kutub(IRE) Bright Future (IRE) (Satco (FR))
2949[9] 3424[4] 5450[6]

Bright Sunshine *Anthony Honeyball* 83b
6 ch m Loup Sauvage(USA) Bright Lady (Sunyboy)
432[8]

Bright Tomorrow (IRE) *Mrs John Harrington* 103b
4 b g Robin Des Pres(FR) Gweedara (IRE) (Saddlers' Hall (IRE))
11a[5]

Brin D'Avoine (FR) *Neil Mulholland* 79h
4 b g Califet(FR) Nemenchka (FR) (Turgeon (USA))
2991[7] 3411[14] 3581[7] 3710[10] 3955[7] 4886[6]

Brindor Des Iles (FR) *M Nicolau*
4 ch g Le Triton(USA) Lumiere Sacree (FR) (Commendable (IRE))
3876a[P]

Brinestine (USA) *Emma Baker* 109h
6 b g Bernstein(USA) Miss Zafonic (FR) (Zafonic (USA))
32[U] 186[3] 556[14] 1893[5] 2093[10] 2869[3] ◆ 3368[6] 3816[3] 4885[3]

Bring Back Charlie *Nigel Twiston-Davies* 89h
5 b g Green Card(USA) Nafertiti (IRE) (Bob Back (USA))
4343[4] 4885[2] 5445[2]

Bringewood Belle *John Needham* 96b 87c
12 b m Kayf Tara Carlingford Belle (Carlingford Castle)
58[P] 1237[P] 1355[U]

Bringewood Blue (IRE) *John Needham* 88h
8 br m Blueprint(IRE) Carramore (IRE) (Topanoora)
5098[5] 5463[6]

Bringithomeminty *David Evans* 95h
6 gr g Presenting Rosie Redman (IRE) (Roselier (FR))
999[U]

Brio Conti (FR) *Paul Nicholls* 109b
4 gr g Dom Alco(FR) Cadoulie Wood (FR) (Cadoudal (FR))
5457[3]

Brise Coeur (FR) *Nick Williams* 98h
4 b g Daramsar(FR) Rose Bombon (FR) (Cadoudal (FR))
2024[3] 2362a[11] 2997[6] 3586[3] 3815a[8] **4400a[P]** 4825[3] **5136a[6]** 5483[P]

Brise D'Allier (FR) *Guy Denuault*
4 b m Crossharbour Peur Bleue (FR) (Agent Bleu (FR))
1231a[4]

Brise Vendeenne (FR) *Philip Hobbs* 115h
4 gr m Dom Alco(FR) Naiade Mag (FR) (Kadalko (FR))
1845[2] 2325[2] 2911[3] 3953[2] 4445[3] 5155[P]

Bristol De Mai (FR) *Nigel Twiston-Davies* 138h 161c
4 gr g Saddler Maker(IRE) La Bole Night (FR) (April Night (FR))
2166[2] (2580) ◆ 2913[2] (3317) ◆ (3738) (3991) 4729[2] 5324[2]

Britanio Bello (FR) *Gary Moore* 121h
4 b g Irish Wells(FR) Tchi Tchi Bang Bang (FR) (Perrault)
2183[7] 2417[5] 3608[3] (3928)

Broad Spectrum (IRE) *Donald McCain* 90h
4 b g Gamut(IRE) Knock Na Brona (IRE) (Oscar (IRE))
3442[8] 4835[5] 5196[2]

Broadway Belle *Chris Grant* 84h
5 b m Lucarno(USA) Theatre Belle (King's Theatre (IRE))
415[4]

Broadway Buffalo (IRE) *David Pipe* 146h 151c
7 ch g Broadway Flyer(USA) Benbradagh Vard (IRE) (Le Bavard (FR))
2361a[5] **4245[2]**

Brod Na Heireann (IRE) *Alan King* 121h
6 b g Westerner Diaconate (IRE) (Cape Cross (IRE))
2152[4] 2513[13] (3126) 3525[4] 4241[5] 4438[4] 4883[3] 5264[P]

Brody Bleu (FR) *Robert Walford* 111h 133c
8 b g Kotky Bleu(FR) Brodie Blue (FR) (Agent Bleu (FR))
(121) 715[4] 3731[F] 3957[6] 4212[3] 4436[P] 4966[P]

Broken Eagle (USA) *Alan Hill* 96h 118c
7 b g Broken Vow(USA) Tricky Bird (USA) (Storm Bird (CAN))
298[P]

Broken Soul (IRE) *P M J Doyle* 116h
4 b g Beneficial Alicia's Charm (IRE) (Executive Perk)
9a[18]

Brokethegate *Chris Grant* 76h 91c
10 b g Presenting Briery Ann (Anshan)
140[4] 4180[F]

Bronco Billy (IRE) *Jonjo O'Neill* 121h
5 b g Flemensfirth(USA) La Fisarmonica (IRE) (Accordion)
3056[2] 3316[7] 3997[3] (5376)

Bron Fair *Edward Bevan* 38h
6 b m Multiplex Spectacular Hope (Marju (IRE))
5019[6]

Bronwydd *Debra Hamer* 70h
5 br m Needle Gun(IRE) Talkingstick (IRE) (Bob Back (USA))
1506[8] 1960[8] 2454[11]

Brook (FR) *David Pipe* 117h 117c
4 ch g Kandidate Ninon De Re (FR) (Denham Red (FR))
2513[P] 2989[9] 3705[12] **4153[F] 4352[6] 4803[4] (5032) 5222[P] 5432[4]**

Brooke's Bounty *Hugh Burns* 65h
5 ch g Bahamian Bounty Choysia (Pivotal)
5242[9] 5444[7]

Broome Lane *Tim Vaughan* 82h 99c
6 b m Kayf Tara Aranga (IRE) (Supreme Leader)
5138[4] (5468)

Brother Bennett (FR) *Jim Best* 100h
5 gr g Martaline La Gaminerie (FR) (Cadoudal (FR))
3047[4] 5418[6]

Brotherly Company (IRE) *Harry Fry* 117h
3 b g Fast Company(IRE) Good Lady (IRE) (Barathea (IRE))
3926[4] 4849[3] (5268)

Brother Norphin *Simon Hodgson* 88b
3 b g Norse Dancer(IRE) Orphina (IRE) (Orpen (USA))
2882[4] 5097[14]

Brother Scott *Sue Smith* 91h 106c
8 b g Kirkwall Crimson Shower (Dowsing (USA))
78[7] 454[2] 676[F] 1079[P] 1372[4] (1569) 1741[2] 1855[2] 5080[2] 5439[6]

Brother Tedd *Philip Hobbs* 152h
6 gr g Kayf Tara Neltina (Neltino)
(2241) 2634[3] 3527[4] 4717[7]

Broughton (GER) *John Ferguson* 137h 137c
5 b g Teofilo(IRE) Boccassini (GER) (Artan (IRE))
638[7] **(1157) 1343[2]** (1482) 1657[4] (1868)

Broughton Green (IRE) *P G Hall* 108b
14 b g Shernazar Lucy Walters (IRE) (King's Ride)
292[P]

Broughtons Bandit *Gordon Elliott* 108h 118c
8 b g Kyllachy Broughton Bounty (Bahamian Bounty)
(883) **2057[9]**

Broughtons Rhythm *Willie Musson* 107h
6 b g Araafa(IRE) Broughton Singer (IRE) (Common Grounds)
5387[2]

Brown Bear (IRE) *Nick Gifford* 86h
4 b g Yeats(IRE) Moray Firth (UAE) (Halling (USA))
67[5] 2267[8] 3114[9] 3483[9] 4096[9] 4856[P]

Brownville *Nigel Twiston-Davies* 112h 122c
6 b g Kayf Tara Cool Spice (Karinga Bay)
216[5] **1906[4] 2566[P] 4443[5] 4876[6]**

Broxbourne (IRE) *Nicky Henderson* 140h
6 b m Refuse To Bend(IRE) Rafting (IRE) (Darshaan)
(2333) 3034[6] 3283[3] 4730[7]

Bruce Almighty (IRE) *Donald McCain* 121h
4 b g Yeats(IRE) Lady Rolfe (IRE) (Alzao (USA))
(1927) (2174) 2323[2] 3361[6] (4815)

Bruce Of Crionaich (IRE) *John Ferguson* 101b
5 b g Flemensfirth(USA) Sommer Sonnet (IRE) (Taipan (IRE))
761[5]

Brunello *Michael Smith* 95h 104c
7 b g Leporello(IRE) Lydia Maria (Dancing Brave (USA))
153[6] **2500[U] 2708[P]** 2980[P] 3973[9]

Brunel Woods (IRE) *David Dennis* 95b
3 b g Oscar(IRE) Golden Bay (Karinga Bay)
5152[2] ◆

Brunette'sonly (IRE) *Seamus Mullins* 81h 90c
10 ch m Flemensfirth(USA) Pride Of St Gallen (IRE) (Orchestra)
66[6] 223[7]

Brunswick Gold (IRE) *Miss Rose Grissell* 98h 105c
10 ch g Moscow Society(USA) Tranbu (IRE) (Buckskin (FR))
151[4]

Bryden Boy (IRE) *Jennie Candlish* 117h
5 b g Craigsteel Cailin Vic Mo Cri (IRE) (Old Vic)
146[3] 463[3] 837[4] 3588[3] (4430) 4815[2] 5102[P]

Buachaill Alainn (IRE) *Peter Bowen* 144h 139c
8 b g Oscar(IRE) Bottle A Knock (IRE) (Le Moss)
611[3] 1033[2] (1288) 1849[2] 2638[5] 2899[P] 4234[7]

Buachaill Beag *Fergal O'Brien* 79b
4 gr g And Beyond(IRE) Bon Enfant (IRE) (Roselier (FR))
2250[8] 4434[4]

Bubbly Breeze (IRE) *Alastair Ralph* 70h 76c
10 br g Hubbly Bubbly(USA) Belon Breeze (IRE) (Strong Gale)
17[8]

Buche De Noel (FR) *Jamie Snowden* 118h 103c
4 ch m Coastal Path Kyrie (FR) (Lute Antique (FR))
3726[P] 5389[4]

Buckboru (IRE) *Laura Young* 95h
7 b m Brian Boru Buckland Filleigh (IRE) (Buckskin (FR))
2263[4] 2876[3] 3410[6] 5420[U]

Buck Dancing (IRE) *Edward P Harty* 115h 115c
6 b g King's Theatre(IRE) Polly Anthus (Kahyasi)
2236a[4] 2676a[9]

Buckers Bridge (IRE) *Henry De Bromhead* 138h 141c
9 b g Pelder(IRE) La Fiere Dame (IRE) (Lafontaine I (USA))
3073a[5] 3715a[6] 4733[12]

Buckhorn Timothy *Colin Tizzard* 130h 137c
6 b g Tamure(IRE) Waimea Bay (Karinga Bay)
2001[3] (2518) 2905[2] 3228[F] (3611) 4800[5]

Buckhorn Tom *Colin Tizzard* 111h 114c
7 b g Tamure(IRE) Waimea Bay (Karinga Bay)
2447[6] 3086[2] 3412[5] 3788[2] 3979[P] 5419[5]

Bucking The Trend *Tim Vaughan* 122h 136c
7 b g Kayf Tara Macklette (IRE) (Buckskin (FR))
1944[3] 3046[P] 3818[4] (4641) 4971[4] (5395)

Buckled *Sandy Thomson* 104h
5 b g Midnight Legend Mulberry Wine (Benny The Dip (USA))
285[10] 2294[7] 2791[5] 3023[3] ◆ 3438[6] 4815[P]

Buck Magic (IRE) *Neil Mulholland* 113h 126c
9 b g Albano(IRE) Green Sea (Groom Dancer (USA))
102[4] 389[5]

Buck Mulligan *Evan Williams* 121h 132c
10 b g Robellino(USA) Music Park (IRE) (Common Grounds)
362[3] 568[2] 1053[2] 1268[6] 1481[F] 1601[4] 2036[2] 2746[U] 4386[2] 5154[P]

Buckontupence (IRE) *James Evans* 107h
7 b g Brian Boru Miss Od (IRE) (Good Thyne (USA))
4235[3] 4645[2] 5440[3]

Buck's Bank (FR) *Yannick Fouin* 130h 138c
7 b g Trempolino(USA) Buck's (FR) (Le Glorieux)
1477a[3]

Buck's Broker (FR) *E Lecoiffier* 95h
5 ch g Nickname(FR) Buck's Beauty (FR) (Lyphard's Wish (FR))
436a[9]

Buckshot Robert (IRE) *Noel C Kelly* 32b
4 ch m Flemensfirth(USA) Go Katie (Gunner B)
2752[P]

Buckskin Boulta (IRE) *Mark Michael McNiff* 114h
7 b g Vertical Speed(FR) Ballymartin Trix (IRE) (Buckskin (FR))
(5098)

Buckstruther (IRE) *Paul O J Hosgood* 47b 107c
13 ch g Anshan Immediate Action (Roselier (FR))
166[P]

Buckwheat *John Ferguson* 143h
5 b g Manduro(GER) Russian Snows (IRE) (Sadler's Wells (USA))
(708) 1039[9] 2350[7]

Budapest (IRE) *Josef Vana*
10 b g Montjeu(IRE) Run To Jane (IRE) (Doyoun)
1672a[P]

Buddy Love *Nigel Twiston-Davies* 90h 111c
8 gr m Silver Patriarch(IRE) O My Love (Idiots Delight)
458[2]

Bueno Rica (FR) *Richard Hobson* 40b
4 bl g Califet(FR) Infante De Rica (FR) (Garde Royale)
4805[8] 5227[10]

Buffalo Sabre (FR) *Nigel Hawke* 32h
3 b g Turgeon(USA) Kerry Rose (FR) (Tel Quel (FR))
5220[9]

Bugsie Malone (IRE) *Paul Nicholls* 119h
5 b g Mahler The Irish Whip (Presenting)
3037[3] 4439[4]

Buiseness Sivola (FR) *W P Mullins* 139h
4 b g Archange D'Or(IRE) Louve Orientale (Red Ransom (USA))
94a[2] 665a[5] 3650a[22] 4115[F] 4769[18] 5189[11]

Bulletproof (IRE) *Ken Cunningham-Brown* 110h 62c
9 b g Wareed(IRE) Laura's Native (IRE) (Be My Native (USA))
172[6] 675[4] 856[5] 1010[2] 1244[4] (1578) (1677) (1823) ◆ 2006[4]

Bullet Street (IRE) *Evan Williams* 119h 132c
7 ch g Arakan(USA) Play A Tune (IRE) (Fayruz)
(218) 2185[4] 2635[9] 3257[U] 3749[F]

Bumble Bay *Robert Stephens* 105h
5 b g Trade Fair Avriel (IRE) (Averti (IRE))
702[5] 971[5] 1081[6] 1525[5] 1677[2]

Bunclody *Barry Brennan* 101h 108c
10 b g Overbury(IRE) Wahiba Reason (IRE) (Robellino (USA))
43[4] 237[7] 695[5] 870[2] **(884) 961[4]**

Bun Doran (IRE) *Tom George* 140h
4 b g Shantou(USA) Village Queen (IRE) (King's Theatre (IRE))
(2270) ◆ 2763[4] (3743) 4368[5] 5356[3]

Burgas (FR) *W P Mullins* 136h 112c
4 b g Protektor(GER) Tyrolienne Bleue (FR) (Sunshack)
4516a[3] 5024a[P]

Burgess Dream (IRE) *Anna Newton-Smith* 94h 95c
6 b g Spadoun(FR) Ennel Lady (IRE) (Erin's Hope)
62[P] 2015[P] 2515[2] **2827[2]** 3087[6] **3663[2] 3906[2] 4346[P] 4673[3] 5480[5]**

Burgundy Betty (IRE) *Ben Pauling* 88h
5 b m Presenting Lady Meribel (Kahyasi)
28[4] 2223[5] 3128[P] 3771[11] 4783[6]

Burlington Bert (FR) *Warren Greatrex* 113b
4 b g Califet(FR) Melhi Sun (FR) (Mansonnien (FR))
(213) 3138[5] 4001[3]

Burma (FR) *Paul Webber* 89h
4 bb m Charming Groom(FR) Tadorna (FR) (Maresca Sorrento (FR))
1613[9] 2536a[4] 3066[4] 4784[8]

Burmese Temple (FR) *Patrice Quinton* 112h
4 b g Sulamani(IRE) Goldarvor (FR) (Beat Hollow)
(2362a) **5135a[5]**

Burn And Turn (IRE) *Mrs John Harrington* 134h 141c
9 b m Flemensfirth(USA) Pescetto Lady (IRE) (Toulon)
70a[3]

Burner (IRE) *Olly Williams* 83h
3 b g High Chaparral(IRE) Breathe (FR) (Ocean Of Wisdom (USA))
2863[8] 3443[4] 3610[4] 3840[5]

Burning Desire (IRE) *Richard Hughes* 103h
4 b g Galileo(IRE) Flames (Blushing Flame (USA))
2723[4] 3773[5] 4111[5]

Burnt Sienna (IRE) *Noel C Kelly* 91h
5 ch m Papal Bull Lucky Achievement (USA) (St Jovite (USA))
482[4] 1400[5] 1572[5] 1887[5] 2071[5]

Burrows Lane (FR) *Miss Elizabeth Doyle* 98b
4 b g Astarabad(USA) Condoleezza (FR) (Mansonnien (FR))
11a[16]

Burrows Saint (FR) *G Macaire* 110h
2 b c Saint Des Saints(FR) La Bombonera (FR) (Mansonnien (FR))
5498a[2]

Burst Ya Bubble (IRE) *Seamus Mullins* 90b
3 b g Spadoun(FR) Accordian Lady (IRE) (Accordion)
5358[7]

Burton Boru (IRE) *Colin Tizzard* 88b
3 b g Brian Boru Tiffiny Gale (IRE) (Glacial Storm (USA))
3416[4] 3959[4] 5359[7]

Burtredgipandgump (IRE) *Malcolm Jefferson* 100b
6 br g Blueprint(IRE) Always Proud (IRE) (Supreme Leader)
257[2]

Bushel (USA) *Tony Newcombe* 27h
5 b g Street Cry(IRE) Melhor Ainda (USA) (Pulpit (USA))
4384[9]

Businessmoney Judi *Martin Hill* 104h
9 ch m Kirkwall Cloverjay (Lir)
265[8] 513[3] 759[3] 977[P] (Dead)

Bus Named Desire *Matt Sheppard* 93h 94c
7 b m Alflora(IRE) Arctic Ring (Karinga Bay)
361[2] (466) 537[6] 864[6] 1010[5] 1310[6] 1509[2] 1599[2] 1910[6] **2249[3]** ◆ **2539[7] (2735) 3144[2] 3609[P]**

Buster Dan Dan (IRE) *Terence O'Brien* 137h
7 b g Buster King Ms Monroe (IRE) (Oscar (IRE))
2236a[3]

Busty Brown (IRE) *M O Cullinane* 125h 129c
9 b g Mr Combustible(IRE) Misty Brown (IRE) (Aristocracy (IRE))
3716a[8]

Busy Baro (IRE) *Paul Cowley* 94h
5 ch g Acambaro(GER) Miss Busy Lizzy (IRE) (Supreme Leader)
3130[5] 3506[4] 3949[5]

Busy Lilly *Charles Pogson* 36b
6 b m Bollin Eric Princess Derry (Derrylin)
4228[7]

Busy Street *Alan Swinbank* 76b
3 b g Champs Elysees Allegro Viva (USA) (Distant View (USA))
2216[4]

Butlergrove King (IRE) *Dai Burchell* 96h 121c
6 b g King's Theatre(IRE) Sanadja (IRE) (Slip Anchor)
634[3] 877[5] 1011[5] **1235[P] 1796[2] (1824) (2036) 2988[4] 4492[3] 4800[4] 4962[2]**

Butney Island (IRE) *Nick Mitchell* 105h
5 b g Trans Island Tash McGarry (IRE) (Publisher (USA))
4439[P] 4930[3] 5243[8]

Buttercup (FR) *Venetia Williams* 121h 108c
4 b m Limnos(JPN) Paranoia (FR) (Esprit Du Nord (USA))
3825[3] 4039[4] 4471[P] 5137[4] 5408[5]

Buveur D'Air (FR) *Nicky Henderson* 154h
4 b g Crillon(FR) History (FR) (Alesso (USA))
(2763) ◆ (3842) 4695[3] ◆ (5190) ◆

Buy Back Bob (IRE) *Tim Vaughan* 120h 75c
8 b g Big Bad Bob(IRE) Abeyr (Unfuwain (USA))
(171) 491[2] **4098[7]**

Buyer Beware (IRE) *Gordon Elliott* 113h
3 br g Big Bad Bob(IRE) Adoring (IRE) (One Cool Cat (USA))
5444[3]

Buy Me Out *Grace Harris* 102h
5 gr m Fair Mix(IRE) Maid Equal (Pragmatic)
392[8] 700[4] 834[7] 1234[4] 1379[2] 1618[U] 1698[4]

Buywise (IRE) *Evan Williams* 135h 158c
8 b g Tikkanen(USA) Greenogue Princess (IRE) (Rainbows For Life (CAN))
2084[3] 2483[2] 3031[4] 3860[3] 5218[12]

Byerley Babe (IRE) *Robert Tyner* 122h 139c
8 b m Beneficial I Can Imagine (IRE) (Husyan (USA))
2525a[P]

Bygones For Coins (IRE) *Kenny Johnson* 89h
7 ch m Danroad(AUS) Reservation (IRE) (Common Grounds)
5347[3]

Byron Blue (IRE) *Mark Gillard* 125h
6 br g Dylan Thomas(IRE) High Society (IRE) (Key Of Luck (USA))
876[5] 1046[2] 1270[2] 1488[7] 1949[6] 2350[8] 2600[8] 3078[7] 5146[9]

Byronegetonefree *Stuart Coltherd* 85h
4 b g Byron Lefty's Dollbaby (USA) (Brocco (USA))
2474[P] 4633[F] 5256[P] 5444[6]

Byron Flyer *Ian Williams* 106h
4 b g Byron Nursling (IRE) (Kahyasi)
188[4] 4233[4] ◆ 4441[5] ◆ (5160)

By The Boardwalk (IRE) *Kim Bailey* 115h 134c
7 br g Presenting Peripheral Vision (IRE) (Saddlers' Hall (IRE))
173[2] (239) ◆ **(381)** ◆ **490[F] (1632) 1924[3] 2240[F] 2733[6] 4443[P]**

Cabaret Girl *John O'Neill* 100h 109c
8 ch m Karinga Bay Little Miss Prim (Gildoran)
183[4]

Cabernet D'Alene (FR) *Nick Williams* 99h
3 b g Day Flight Haifa Du Noyer (FR) (Video Rock (FR))
3279[P] 4489[U] 5387[3]

Cabin Fever *Tom Lacey* 87h
4 ch m Medicean Folly Lodge (Grand Lodge (USA))
853[4] 1000[4] 1109[3] 1299[8]

Cable *John Joseph Hanlon* 77b
3 b g Champs Elysees Talkative (Oasis Dream)
3409[8]

Cab On Times (IRE) *Mark Walford* 94h
6 b g Indian Danehill(IRE) Evening Fashion (IRE) (Strong Gale)
4213[P] 4426[P] 4844[6] 5018[5]

Cactus Valley (IRE) *Michael Easterby* 110h
6 b g Lawman(FR) Beech Gardens (Sadler's Wells (USA))
2748[6] 3022[10] 3309[6] 3397[5] 5088[3] (5345) 5450[3]

Cadellin *George Moore* 72b
4 b g Black Sam Bellamy(IRE) Clotted Cream (USA) (Eagle Eyed (USA))
2895[5]

Cadgers Hole *Lynn Siddall* 81h
8 b g Helissio(FR) Not So Prim (Primitive Rising (USA))
148[4] 466[3] 3791[4] 4045[RR] 4184[P] 4863[2] 5198[5] 5441[4]

Cadmium *Micky Hammond* 17h
4 b m Major Cadeaux Miss Mirasol (Sheikh Albadou)
2752[8]

Cadore (IRE) *Lucy Normile* 99h
7 b g Hurricane Run(IRE) Mansiya (Vettori (IRE))
142[4] 2426[6] 2933[6] 4550[4] 5081[4] ◆ 5445[7]

Cadoudoff (FR) *Charlie Longsdon* 128h 137c
5 gr g Davidoff(GER) Hera Du Berlais (FR) (Cadoudal (FR))
2001[2] 2545[4] 3046[4] (3843) 4252[3] 4596[8] **5073[3] 5323[U]**

Cadouma (FR) *P Mehat*
9 b m Panoramic Ascotte Royale (FR) (Cadoudal (FR))
5136a[4]

Caged Lightning (IRE) *Steve Gollings* 111h
5 b g Haatef(USA) Rainbow Melody (IRE) (Rainbows For Life (CAN))
3309[2] 3509[4] 4324[3] 4643[3]

Cahill (IRE) *Fergal O'Brien* 95h
3 b g Lawman(FR) Malaspina (IRE) (Whipper (USA))
1656[5] 1768[3] 2092[3] 4845[7] 5181[3]

Cailin Annamh (IRE) *Mrs John Harrington* 142h 143c
7 b m Definite Article Prairie Bell (IRE) (Sadler's Wells (USA))
(1185a) (1763a) 1938a[3]

Cailleach Annie (IRE) *Jackie Du Plessis* 108h
6 b m Blueprint(IRE) Graineuaile (IRE) (Orchestra)
3119[3] 3413[2] ◆ (4860)

Cairde Aris (IRE) *John E Kiely* 118h 115c
6 b g Definite Article Avitta (IRE) (Pennekamp (USA))
2236a[15] 2525a[5]

Cairnshill (IRE) *Mark Michael McNiff* 71h
4 gr g Tikkanen(USA) Ilikeyou (IRE) (Lord Americo)
640[6]

Caitys Joy (GER) *Warren Greatrex* 121h
5 b m Malinas(GER) Cassilera (GER) (Anzillero (GER))
3612[2] ◆ (3947)

Caius Marcius (IRE) *Nicky Richards* 117h
4 b g King's Theatre(IRE) Ain't Misbehavin (IRE) (Trempolino (USA))
(2195) 2514[5] 4548[3]

Cajun Fiddle (IRE) *Alan King* 106b
4 b m Robin Des Champs(FR) Silk Style (Polish Precedent (USA))
2721[2] ◆ 3132[4] 3861[4] 4623[7] 5180[10]

Calcite (FR) *G Mousnier*
4 gr m Sulamani(IRE) Jaillissante (FR) (Verglas (IRE))
1231a[F]

Calculated Risk *Debra Hamer* 117h 105c
6 ch g Motivator Glen Rosie (IRE) (Mujtahid (USA))
2411[7] 2808[3] 4105[4] (4266) (4825) 5053[2]

Caldey *Ian Williams* 54h
6 b m Overbury(IRE) Barfleur (IRE) (Anshan)
3506[6] 4349[P]

Caledon Craic (IRE) *Lady Jane Gillespie* 118h 102c
8 b g Oscar(IRE) Supremely Deep (IRE) (Supreme Leader)
869[2]

Caledonia *Jim Goldie* 124h
8 b g Sulamani(IRE) Vanessa Bell (IRE) (Lahib (USA))
2100[2] 2428[F] 3440[2] (4405) 4911[4] 5296[2]

Ca Le Ferra (FR) *James Ewart* 101b
5 b g Turgeon(USA) Branceilles (FR) (Satin Wood)
4835[F]

Calin Des Ongrais (FR) *Gordon Elliott* 98h
3 b g Elasos(FR) Nympheas (FR) (Video Rock (FR))
5001a[7]

Calin Du Brizais (FR) *Nigel Hawke* 110h
4 b g Loup Solitaire(USA) Caline Du Brizais (FR) (Turgeon (USA))
181[3] 2139[3] (2595) 2989[4] **4542[P] 5226[U]**

Calipto (FR) *Paul Nicholls* 140h 149c
5 b g Califet(FR) Peutiot (FR) (Valanour (IRE))
(2012) ◆ **2510[3] 2881[3] 5496[8]**

Calisto *Ben Pauling* 66b
5 b g Josr Algarhoud(IRE) Kentucky Blue Nova (Ra Nova)
2460[12] 2986[P]

Calivigny (IRE) *N W Alexander* 126h
6 b g Gold Well Summer Holiday (IRE) (Kambalda)
299[2] (2100) (2432) ◆ 2787[7] 4015[4] 4405[P] 5011[3]

Call At Midnight *Sarah Humphrey* 19h 27c
10 b m Midnight Legend Second Call (Kind Of Hush)
3067[10]

Call Hector (FR) *G Chaignon* 85h
4 b g Speedmaster(GER) Free Girl (FR) (Le Balafre (FR))
2362a[F] **4401a[P] 5385a[3]**

Callhimwhatyouwant (IRE) *Miss S L Klug* 52h 71c
10 b g Old Vic Jaynes Supreme (IRE) (Supreme Leader)
5312[4]

Calling Des Blins (FR) *Harry Fry* 115b
3 b f Konig Turf(GER) Quelye Des Blins (FR) (Silver Rainbow)
4242[3] 5104[2]

Call It On (IRE) *Philip Kirby* 115h 115c
9 ch g Raise A Grand(IRE) Birthday Present (Cadeaux Genereux)
(2496) (5440)

Call Me Ben (IRE) *James Evans* 98b
5 ch g Beneficial Good Foundation (IRE) (Buckskin (FR))
5144[4] 5451[P]

Call Me Kate *Henry Daly* 86h
5 b m Kalanisi(IRE) Last Of Her Line (Silver Patriarch (IRE))
89[5] 443[5] 757[10] 1264[6] 1547[9]

Call Me Mulligan (IRE) *Ms Jackie Williamson* 47h 97c
11 ch g Bach(IRE) They Call Me Molly (CAN) (Charlie Barley (USA))
(743) 842[3] 4820[6]

Callmenewtown (IRE) *Katie Stephens* 115h
8 b g Cloudings(IRE) Clonleigh Lady (IRE) (Moscow Society (USA))
146[4] 468[P] **770[P]** 1048[9]

Call Me Vic (IRE) *Tom George* 129h 139c
8 b g Old Vic Call Me Dara (IRE) (Arapahos (FR))
215[2] (861) (965) 2018[6]

Call Me Win (IRE) *Paul Henderson* 33h 77c
6 gr g Fleetwood(IRE) Betseale (IRE) (Step Together I (USA))
27[U]

Callnineninenine *John Weymes* 71b
4 b g Dr Massini(IRE) Scarlet Target (IRE) (Anshan)
1817[4] 5014[9] 5407[6]

Call Of Duty (IRE) *Dianne Sayer* 85h 9c
10 br g Storming Home Blushing Barada (USA) (Blushing Groom (FR))
1501[4] **1630[6]**

Call The Cops (IRE) *Nicky Henderson* 149h
6 b g Presenting Ballygill Heights (IRE) (Symboli Heights (FR))
4017[8] 4717[17]

Call The Detective (IRE) *Dai Burchell* 109h 113c
6 b g Winged Love(IRE) Aneeza (IRE) (Charnwood Forest (IRE))
2930[5] (3218) 3788[4] 4185[3] 5032[5] (5432)

Call To Order *Jonjo O'Neill* 111h
5 b g Presenting Theatre Girl (King's Theatre (IRE))
213[2] ◆ 2493[2] 3021[3] ◆

Calton Entry (IRE) *Katie Scott* 112h 102c
6 b g Bahri(USA) Gaybrook (IRE) (Shernazar)
1333[7] 1501[3] ◆ 1773[7] **2293[6] 2755[P] 4329[U] 4707[6]**

Calypso Storm (IRE) *Rebecca Menzies* 97b
4 b g Trans Island Valin Thyne (IRE) (Good Thyne (USA))
2479[3] 3442[5]

Camachoice (IRE) *Joanne Foster* 120h
5 b g Camacho Nouvelle Reve (GER) (Acatenango (GER))
125[U] 176[5] 1714[9] 2142[6]

Camakasi (IRE) *Ali Stronge* 91h
4 b g Camacho Innocence (Unfuwain (USA))
3114[14] 3835[8] 4441[14] 4849[6]

Camborne *John Ferguson* 96h
7 b g Doyen(IRE) Dumnoni (Titus Livius (FR))
2409[3]

Camden (IRE) *Mrs Sarah Easterby* 108b
9 b g Old Vic Electric View (IRE) (Electric)
4768[P]

Camillas Wish (IRE) *J T R Draper* 91h 90c
6 b m Presenting Take Ine (FR) (Take Risks (FR))
383[2] **2147[2] 2708[P]** 3437[3] 4184[7] 4804[2]

Camlann (IRE) *John Joseph Hanlon* 105h
4 b g Cape Cross(IRE) Elle Galante (GER) (Galileo (IRE))
11a[12] 3323a[5]

Campeador (FR) *Gordon Elliott* 143h
3 gr g Gris De Gris(IRE) Royale Video (FR) (Video Rock (FR))
3268a^{4} 4720^{F}

Camping Ground (FR) *Robert Walford* 163h 155c
5 b g Goldneyev(USA) Camomille (GER) (Pennekamp (USA))
2927^{U} (3408) 3853^{5} 4698^{9} 5177^{5}

Camron De Chaillac (FR) *Nigel Hawke* 77b
3 bl g Laverock(IRE) Hadeel (Polish Precedent (USA))
5069^{6}

Canadian Diamond (IRE) *Richard Rowe* 118h
8 ch g Halling(USA) Six Nations (USA) (Danzig (USA))
2540^{6} (2987) 3284^{4} 3777^{4} (4229) 5030^{3}

Canarbino Girl *Caroline Keevil* 84h
8 b m Beat All(USA) Peasedown Tofana (Teenoso (USA))
40^{2} 222^{4} 569^{7} 1599^{9} 1816^{4} 2004^{5} 2298^{8}

Candelita *Clare Ellam* 72h 74c
8 b m Trade Fair Gramada (IRE) (Cape Cross (IRE))
217^{4} 515^{9} 1420^{P} 1525^{7} 2559^{10} 3108^{10}

Candide (IRE) *Sally Randell* 94h 109c
8 ch g Albano(IRE) Sweet Cicely (IRE) (Darshaan)
707^{6} 4618^{6} **5283^{6}**

Canicallyouback *Evan Williams* 123h 89c
7 b g Auction House(USA) Island Colony (USA) (Pleasant Colony (USA))
440^{2} 613^{2} ◆ 932^{4} (1139) 1612^{2} (1718) **2518^{R} 3106^{9}**

Caniver Queen (IRE) *Brian Barr* 35h
5 ch m Sendawar(IRE) Sharp Dancer (Danehill Dancer (IRE))
5145^{P} 5430^{P}

Can Mestret (IRE) *S R Andrews* 103b 120c
8 b g Millenary River Anita (IRE) (Riverhead (USA))
(296) ◆ 536^{P} 4227^{3} 4592^{P}

Cannon Fodder *Sheena West* 131h
8 b m Nomadic Way(USA) Grace Dieu (Commanche Run)
1594^{F} 1736^{2} 2002^{4} 2825^{2} (3283) 3732^{3} 4159^{3} 4779^{6}

Canny Tom (IRE) *S Donohoe* 99h
5 b g Jimble(FR) Tombazaan (IRE) (Good Thyne (USA))
2756^{11}

Canoodle *Hughie Morrison* 98b
3 b f Stimulation(IRE) Flirtatious (Generous (IRE))
(4468)

Canova (IRE) *Gordon Elliott* 95h
4 ch g Art Connoisseur(IRE) Rain Dancer (IRE) (Sadler's Wells (USA))
882^{2}

Canshetrain (IRE) *J W Tudor* 100c
8 b g Westerner Nahla (Wassl)
12^{10}

Can't Be Done (IRE) *W F Treacy* 113h
4 ch g Royal Anthem(USA) Melissa's Pet (IRE) (Presenting)
9a^{21}

Cantilien (IRE) *Y-M Porzier* 133h
5 b g Tot Ou Tard(IRE) Simin (TUR) (Down The Flag (USA))
437a^{6}

Cantlow (IRE) *E Bolger* 116h 139c
10 b g Kayf Tara Winnowing (IRE) (Strong Gale)
1175a^{14} **1556a^{F} 2187^{5} 3296a^{R} 4719^{11} 5005a^{11}**

Canton Massini *John Holt* 50b
4 b g Dr Massini(IRE) Mandarin Star (Weld)
3625^{7} 4309^{8} 5137^{U}

Canton Prince (IRE) *Tim Vaughan* 95b
5 b g Shantou(USA) Hasainm (IRE) (Grand Lodge (USA))
1797^{2} 3522^{4} 4894^{8}

Cantor *Daniel O'Brien* 79h
7 b g Iceman Choir Mistress (Chief Singer)
2251^{8} 2699^{7} 2823^{9} 3089^{5}

Capard King (IRE) *Jonjo O'Neill* 131h 147c
6 b g Beneficial Capard Lady (IRE) (Supreme Leader)
(2557) ◆ 3439^{5} 4247^{3} 4735^{P} (5311)

Capatosta (USA) *Charlie Mann* 40h
3 ch g Flashy Bull(USA) Da River Hoss (USA) (River Special (USA))
1866^{P} 2371^{5}

Cape Arrow *Barry Murtagh* 83h
4 b g Cape Cross(IRE) Aiming (Highest Honor (FR))
2429^{6}

Cape Caster (IRE) *Evan Williams* 122h
4 br g Cape Cross(IRE) Playboy Mansion (IRE) (Grand Lodge (USA))
2373^{3} 3015^{5} 4366^{5} 5047^{3}

Cape Glory (IRE) *Gordon Elliott* 135h
5 b g Cape Cross(IRE) Array Of Stars (IRE) (Barathea (IRE))
1175a^{15}

Capeland (FR) *Paul Nicholls* 105b
3 b g Poliglote Neiland (FR) (Cyborg (FR))
(3409)

Cape York *Malcolm Jefferson* 109h 116c
7 ch g Revoque(IRE) Altogether Now (IRE) (Step Together I (USA))
134^{3} 420^{6} 756^{5} 1369^{6}

Capilla (IRE) *Evan Williams* 98h 123c
7 gr g Beneficial Cap The Rose (IRE) (Roselier (FR))
2364^{3} (2834) (2874) 2994^{2} 3380^{2} 3731^{7} 5103^{P} 5379^{3}

Capisci (IRE) *Sarah-Jayne Davies* 50h 114c
10 br g Tikkanen(USA) Dolce Notte (IRE) (Strong Gale)
175^{F} 284^{3} 490^{4} 976^{P} 1043^{4} 1422^{5} 1604^{6}

Capitaine (FR) *Paul Nicholls* 126b
3 gr g Montmartre(FR) Patte De Velour (FR) (Mansonnien (FR))
2991^{2} ◆ (5359)

Cappielow Park *Ali Stronge* 116h 120c
6 b g Exceed And Excel(AUS) Barakat (Bustino)
3015^{10} **(3379) 4098^{6} 4529^{3} 5096^{P}**

Caprice De Nuit (FR) *P Chevillard* 88h
4 b g Bachir(IRE) Dame Caprice (IRE) (Bering)
(3815a)

Capsis Desbois (FR) *Gary Moore* 82b
3 b g Apsis Gesse Parade (FR) (Dress Parade)
5069^{4}

Captain Bocelli (IRE) *Philip Hobbs* 111h
6 b g Kayf Tara Beautiful Tune (FR) (Green Tune (USA))
(187) 1662^{5} 3101^{2}

Captain Brown *James Moffatt* 125h 109c
7 b g Lomitas Nicola Bella (IRE) (Sadler's Wells (USA))
508^{3} 850^{7} 1035^{5} (1404) 1554^{2} 2214^{8} 3426^{8} 5295^{3}

Captain Buck's (FR) *Paul Nicholls* 109b
3 b g Buck's Boum(FR) Ombre Jaune (FR) (Brier Creek (USA))
(4296) 5187^{3}

Captain Camelot (IRE) *Gareth Moore* 99c
6 b g Urban Ocean(FR) Harneyspet (IRE) (Sharifabad (IRE))
5467^{5}

Captain Canada *Katie Stephens* 81h 78c
8 br g Tamayaz(CAN) Hattie (Sylvan Express)
19a^{15} 2262^{5} 2658^{5} 2985^{12}

Captain Chaos (IRE) *Dan Skelton* 141h
4 ch g Golan(IRE) Times Have Changed (IRE) (Safety Catch (USA))
(2487) 2886^{2} ◆ 3403^{7} (4339) 5042a^{2}

Captain Conan (FR) *Nicky Henderson* 128h 137c
8 b g Kingsalsa(USA) Lavandou (Sadler's Wells (USA))
3740^{4} **4114^{3} 4731^{12}**

Captain Crackers (IRE) *Linda Jewell* 70h 68c
11 b g King's Theatre(IRE) Love The Lord (IRE) (Mister Lord (USA))
674^{7}

Captain Flash (IRE) *Jo Davis* 94h 106c
6 b g Indian River(FR) Westgate Run (Emperor Jones (USA))
407^{6} 671^{3} 2163^{3} 3377^{5} 3572^{3} **4346^{F} (4884) 5395^{P}**

Captain Hox (IRE) *Patrick Griffin* 126h 127c
6 b g Danehill Dancer(IRE) Shangri La (IRE) (Sadler's Wells (USA))
3153^{3} 3652a^{F} 3935^{2} (4402) 4816^{2} 4905^{4}

Captain Kelly (IRE) *Dan Skelton* 100b
8 b g Oscar(IRE) Tri Folene (FR) (Nebos (GER))
3728^{P} 4041^{F}

Captain Knock (IRE) *Polly Gundry* 88c
12 bb g Busy Flight Alien Jane (IRE) (Weavers Web)
31^{6} 674^{10} 806^{P} (Dead)

Captain McGinley (IRE) *Rebecca Curtis* 114h
5 bl g Robin Des Pres(FR) Rocella (GER) (Goofalik (USA))
2024^{2} 2275^{7} 3452^{4} 4342^{5} 4822^{7}

Captain Moirette (FR) *Sue Smith* 105b
3 gr g Kap Rock(FR) Rahana Moirette (FR) (Dom Alco (FR))
4156^{3} ◆ 4867^{3} 5083^{4}

Captain Mowbray *Rebecca Menzies* 90h
4 ch g Shami Some Like It Hot (Ashkalani (IRE))
2344^{3} 2951^{4} 4064^{6} 4324^{6} 4417^{5} 5349^{4}

Captainofindustry (IRE) *Mark Pitman* 116h
6 b g Definite Article Talk Of Rain (FR) (Turgeon (USA))
1964^{2} 2262^{4} (2732) 3078^{2} 3517^{5} 4241^{7}

Captainofthefleet (IRE) *Eamonn O'Connell* 143h
8 ch g Refuse To Bend(IRE) Darabaka (IRE) (Doyoun)
49a^{9}

Captain Redbeard (IRE) *Stuart Coltherd* 138h
6 ch g Bach(IRE) Diesel Dancer (IRE) (Toulon)
2319^{4} 2716^{3} 2945^{3} 3152^{3} ◆ 3398^{6} (3884) 4055^{4} (4566) (4839) ◆

Captain Sam *Malcolm Jefferson* 105b
3 b g Black Sam Bellamy(IRE) Grande Terre (IRE) (Grand Lodge (USA))
2777^{2}

Captain Sharpe *Kenny Johnson* 122h 86c
7 ch g Tobougg(IRE) Helen Sharp (Pivotal)
801^{6} 966^{P} 2148^{13} 2559^{11} 2703^{P} 2982^{9} **3241^{4}** 3807^{5} **(4048) 4329^{5} 4707^{2} 4938^{3} 5231^{3}**

Captain Starlight (IRE) *Aytach Sadik* 64h
5 b g Captain Marvelous(IRE) Jewell In The Sky (IRE) (Sinndar (IRE))
360^{P} 703^{6} 811^{11} 1154^{6} 1781^{7}

Captain Swift (IRE) *John Mackie* 110h
4 br g Captain Rio Grannys Reluctance (IRE) (Anita's Prince)
(131) 620^{4} 853^{5} 1000^{F} 2540^{13}

Captain Von Trappe (IRE) *Gordon Elliott* 123h 139c
6 b g Germany(USA) Culmore Native (IRE) (Be My Native (USA))
2531a^{2} 2817a^{6} 3296a^{P} 3894a^{5} 4279a^{3} 4521a^{9} 5005a^{P}

Cara Carlotta *Philip Hobbs* 87h
6 br m Presenting Dara's Pride (IRE) (Darazari (IRE))
813^{6}

Caracci Apache (IRE) *Nicky Henderson* 116h 124c
5 b g High Chaparral(IRE) Campanella (GER) (Lomitas)
2332^{3}

Cara Court (IRE) *Joanne Foster* 58h 102c
9 b g Court Cave(IRE) Tarasandy (IRE) (Arapahos (FR))
133^{2} 743^{3} 841^{5} 1402^{5} 1796^{5} 2173^{5} 2500^{2} 2771^{4} 3062^{6} 3803^{P}

Caraline (FR) *Micky Hammond* 88h 123c
4 b m Martaline Vie Ta Vie (FR) (Villez (USA))
153^{8} 487^{3} 694^{9} 805^{9} **(2786) (2891) ◆ (3343) (3631) 4551^{P}**

Caramba (IRE) *Brendan Powell* 44h
3 b f Lord Shanakill(USA) Known Class (USA) (Known Fact (USA))
1593^{3}

Carbon Emission (IRE) *John Needham* 45h
12 ch g City Honours(USA) Aupora (IRE) (Bob Back (USA))
877^{6}

Card Game (IRE) *Malcolm Jefferson* 134h
6 b m Scorpion(IRE) Cardona (Dashing Blade)
159^{4} 516^{3} 679^{3} 3242^{5} (3886) ◆ (4272) 4909^{11} (5232)

Cardinal Palace (IRE) *J A Nash* 137h
5 b g Papal Bull Heat (King's Best (USA))
6a^{4} (706) 1788a^{3} 1870^{2} 3449^{10} 3765a^{5} 5189^{14}

Cardinal Rose *Mark Wall* 97h 106c
8 ch g Karinga Bay Miniature Rose (Anshan)
403^{2} (741) 1098^{4} **2451^{3} (2930)**

Cardinal Walter (IRE) *Nicky Henderson* 141h
6 bb g Cape Cross(IRE) Sheer Spirit (IRE) (Caerleon (USA))
4014^{3} ◆ 4765^{10}

Carhue (IRE) *Sheila Lewis* 69h 69c
8 b g Luso Awtaar (USA) (Lyphard (USA))
30^{6} 265^{7} **2692^{8} 3081^{4} 3948^{P}**

Carhue Princess (IRE) *Tom Symonds* 93h 95c
9 b m Desert Prince(IRE) Carhue Journey (IRE) (Barathea (IRE))
1816^{3} **2551^{3} 3131^{3} 3497^{4}** 3789^{8}

Carinena (IRE) *Nicky Richards* 114h
6 b m Shantou(USA) Dinny Kenn (IRE) (Phardante (FR))
662^{3} 963^{2} (1334) 1627^{2} (2325) ◆ 2644^{2} 3065^{4} 4909^{10} 5409^{3} ◆

Carlingford Lough (IRE) *John E Kiely* 148h 170c
9 b g King's Theatre(IRE) Baden (IRE) (Furry Glen)
2386a^{4} **3324a^{6} (4007a) 4767^{4}**

Carlo Rocks (IRE) *Caroline Bailey* 112h
5 b g Carlo Bank(IRE) Rock Garden (IRE) (Bigstone (IRE))
2408^{2} ◆ (2839) ◆ 3146^{6} 3884^{4} 4537^{2}

Carlos Fandango (IRE) *Martin Todhunter* 110h 110c
9 gr g Silver Patriarch(IRE) Elegant City (Scallywag)
78^{10}

Carlton Ryan (IRE) *Mrs Stephanie Easterby* 118c
7 b g Morozov(USA) Dante's Arrow (IRE) (Phardante (FR))
(4213) (4558)

Carnaross *Julia Brooke* 102h 102c
6 b g Norse Dancer(IRE) Miss Lewis (Sir Harry Lewis (USA))
1166^{9} 1182^{4} (1405) ◆ 1461^{2} **2339^{3}**

Carnglave Cat (IRE) *T D B Underwood* 75h 94c
9 ch g Moscow Society(USA) Time O' Day (IRE) (Tale Quale)
298^{4} 531^{P}

Carningli (IRE) *Rebecca Curtis* 136h 127c
6 b g Old Vic Name For Fame (USA) (Quest For Fame)
1848^{14} **3929^{4}**

Carnival Flag (FR) *N Bertran De Balanda* 113h
6 ch m Ballingarry(IRE) Run For Laborie (FR) (Lesotho (USA))
5499a^{9}

Carn Rock *Michael Gates* 105h 96c
7 b g Tamure(IRE) Solent Sunbeam (Sovereign Water (FR))
1906^{5} 2081^{4} 4877^{4} 5466^{P}

Carobello (IRE) *Martin Bosley* 81h 88c
8 b g Luso Vic's Queen (IRE) (Old Vic)
379^{U} 2037^{2} 5478^{5}

Carole's Destrier *Neil Mulholland* 130h 157c
7 b g Kayf Tara Barton May (Midnight Legend)
2348^{5} (2916) 4697^{P} 5494^{11}

Carole's Vigilante (IRE) *Neil Mulholland* 113b
4 ch g Flemensfirth(USA) Gotta Goa (IRE) (Publisher (USA))
2401^{2}

Carqalin (FR) *David Pipe* 95h
3 gr g Martaline Mica Doree (FR) (Video Rock (FR))
3907^{6} 4934^{3} 5269^{7} 5434^{6}

Carre Noir (FR) *Martin Hill* 113h
6 bb g Clety(FR) Luella (FR) (Bois Mineau (FR))
2732^{5} 4922^{3} ◆ (5382) ◆

Carriganog (IRE) *A P O'Brien* 129h 137c
6 ch g Shantou(USA) Penny Fiction (IRE) (Welsh Term)
3296a^{U}

Carrigdhoun (IRE) *Maurice Barnes* 122h 142c
10 gr g Goldmark(USA) Pet Tomjammar (IRE) (Accordion)
318^{P} 1902^{6} 2213^{8} 3162^{2} 4203^{2} 4635^{3} 4907^{2} 5259^{6}

Carrigeen Lantana (IRE) *Donald McCain* 93h
6 b m Beneficial Carrigeen Lily (IRE) (Supreme Leader)
(383) 694^{6} 1066^{4} 1310^{8}

Carrigkerry (IRE) *Mrs R Fuller* 96c
8 br g Pilsudski(IRE) Lady Lorraine (IRE) (Oscar (IRE))
13^{P}

Carrigmoorna Rock (IRE) *Robert Tyner* 134h 127c
7 b m King's Theatre(IRE) Carrigmorna Flyer (IRE) (Bob Back (USA))
1748a^{5} **4019a^{F}** (Dead)

Carrigmorna King (IRE) *Philip Hobbs* 130h 146c
9 b g King's Theatre(IRE) Carrigmorna Flyer (IRE) (Bob Back (USA))
121^{3} (362) 1040^{11} 1715^{4} (1976) (5184)

Carrowbeg (IRE) *Lawney Hill* 90h
7 b g Cape Cross(IRE) Love And Affection (USA) (Exclusive Era (USA))
125^{3} 929^{4}

Carry On Nando (IRE) *G Chambers* 82c
8 b g Misternando Carry On Pierre (IRE) (Pierre)
123^{5} 5270^{P}

Carry On Sydney *Oliver Sherwood* 117h
5 ch g Notnowcato River Fantasy (USA) (Irish River (FR))
283^{F} 2667^{3} 5382^{6}

Carters Rest *Alison Hamilton* 101h 108c
12 gr g Rock City Yemaail (IRE) (Shaadi (USA))
256^{2} (504) 848^{2} 2104^{5} (2290) 2755^{2} 5257^{U}

Carthage (IRE) *Brian Ellison* 109h
4 b g Mastercraftsman(IRE) Pitrizzia (Lando (GER))
3101^{5} 3471^{2} 4417^{4} 5401^{3} ◆

Carvers Hill *Pat Murphy*
4 b g Assertive Illustre Inconnue (USA) (Septieme Ciel (USA))
1873^{P}

Cascavel (GER) *Yannick Fouin* 124h
6 b g Dansili Casanga (IRE) (Rainbow Quest (USA))
4540a^{P}

Cash Again (FR) *Paul Nicholls* 124b
3 br g Great Pretender(IRE) Jeu De Lune (FR) (Useful (FR))
5097^{2} ◆

Cash And Go (IRE) *Venetia Williams* 143h 141c
8 b g Sulamani(IRE) Calcida (GER) (Konigsstuhl (GER))
99^{2} 3121^{3} 3446^{3} 3749^{F}

Cashanova (IRE) *Nick Gifford* 105h
4 b g Arcadio(GER) Starshade (IRE) (Oscar (IRE))
2250^{2} 3227^{8} 3608^{6}

Cashelard Lady (IRE) *Shane Crawley* 130h
5 b m Key Of Luck(USA) Volcano Snow (Zilzal (USA))
2677a^{2} 3873a^{2} 4954a^{4}

Cash Injection *Richard Woollacott* 112h
6 b g Halling(USA) Cape Siren (Warning)
122^{6} **1504^{P}**

Cash Is King *Kenny Johnson* 82h
5 b g Bahamian Bounty Age Of Chivalry (IRE) (Invincible Spirit (IRE))
634^{8} 1261^{P} 1366^{4} 1550^{7} 1683^{P} 1892^{13}

Casino Markets (IRE) *Emma Lavelle* 120h 114c
7 br g Fruits Of Love(USA) Vals Dream (IRE) (Pierre)
4785^{7} 5147^{4}

Casper King (IRE) *Philip Hobbs* 121h
4 b g Scorpion(IRE) Princess Supreme (IRE) (Supreme Leader)
187^{2} 2375^{2} 3105^{2} 3710^{2}

Caspian Piper (IRE) *Tim Vaughan* 112h 105c
8 b g Millenary Pepsi Starlet (IRE) (Heavenly Manna)
(340) (612) ◆ 770^{3} 1370^{2}

Cassells Rock (IRE) *A J Martin* 131h
5 br g Rock Of Gibraltar(IRE) Se La Vie (FR) (Highest Honor (FR))
19a^{2}

Cassie *Ben Pauling* 93h
5 b m Refuse To Bend(IRE) Strictly Cool (USA) (Bering)
2689^{7} 3215^{2} 3835^{11} 4184^{P}

Cassivellaunus (IRE) *Daniel Steele* 79b
3 b g Danehill Dancer(IRE) Celtic Heroine (IRE) (Hernando (FR))
5308^{4}

Castarnie *Robert Walford* 83h 109c
7 b g Alflora(IRE) Just Jenny (IRE) (King's Ride)
2566^{6} 3823^{P}

Castello Sforza (IRE) *W P Mullins* 130b
4 b g Milan Young Elodie (FR) (Freedom Cry)
4721^{4} ◆

Castle Cavalier *Robert Stephens* 67b
3 b g Nayef(USA) Jardin (Sinndar (IRE))
2009^{6} 2629^{6}

Castle Cheetah (IRE) *Ben Pauling* 118h 127c
7 br g Presenting Castle Crystal (IRE) (Beneficial)
2039^{2} ◆ 4071^{P} 4789^{2}

Castle Conflict (IRE) *Henry Daly* 108h 120c
10 b g Close Conflict(USA) Renty (IRE) (Carlingford Castle)
85^{5} 614^{2} 774^{5} **2451^{P}** 2839^{P}

Castle Goer (IRE) *Benjamin Arthey* 13h 72c
6 b m Helissio(FR) Hill Of Light (IRE) (Luso)
253^{4}

Castlelawn (IRE) *Lucinda Russell* 92h 113c
8 b g Runyon(IRE) Pure Magic (IRE) (Flemensfirth (USA))
2104^{3} 2755^{3} 3343^{P} 4795^{5}

Castlemorris King *Brian Barr* 107h
7 br g And Beyond(IRE) Brookshield Baby (IRE) (Sadler's Wells (USA))
5279^{12}

Castletown (IRE) *Sheila Lewis* 93h 88c
7 b g Oscar(IRE) Closing Thyne (IRE) (Good Thyne (USA))
3572^{P} **3951^{5} 4356^{9} 4823^{3} 5236^{3}**

Castley Lane *Sara Ender* 89h 77c
9 b g Dapper Holly (Skyliner)
484^{P} 798^{P} 4110^{P} **5442^{4}**

Castor Solaire (FR) *Mlle I Gallorini* 74h
4 ch m Zambezi Sun Cykapri (FR) (Cyborg (FR))
3876a^{9}

Casual Approach (IRE) *Gordon Elliott* 129h 126c
6 b g Scorpion(IRE) Lead'Er Inn (IRE) (Supreme Leader)
2052^{6}

Casual Cavalier (IRE) *John Wade* 100h 103c
7 br g Presenting Asklynn (IRE) (Beau Sher)
3968^{4} 4556^{4}

Catcharose (IRE) *Jennifer Mason* 92h
5 b m Catcher In The Rye(IRE) Persian Flower (Persian Heights)
267^{5} 673^{6} 892^{5} 1084^{12}

Catch A Thief (IRE) *Evan Williams* 90h
4 b g Darsi(FR) Geray Lady (IRE) (Roselier (FR))
4681^{U} 5098^{7} 5235^{6} 5353^{8}

Catcher On The Go (IRE) *Evan Williams* 106h
5 b g Catcher In The Rye(IRE) Suspicious Minds (Anabaa (USA))
(444) 1234^{2} 4821^{5} 5268^{11}

Catching On (IRE) *Jonjo O'Neill* 121h 141c
7 b g Milan Miracle Lady (Bob's Return (IRE))
2436^{P}

Catching Shadows (IRE) *James Ewart* 101h
6 b g Catcher In The Rye(IRE) Castletown Girl (Bob Back (USA))
144^{3} 656^{4}

Catchin Time (IRE) *Laura Hurley* 108h
7 b g Chineur(FR) Lady Dane (IRE) (Danetime (IRE))
43[8] 2121[6] 2547[8] 3011[3] (3376) 3498[4] 3784[4] 4129[2] 4447[4] 5030[2] 5225[F]

Catch Tammy (IRE) *Mrs I Barnett* 109h 110c
9 br g Tamayaz(CAN) Bramble Orchard (IRE) (Orchestra)
536[3] 4424[P] 5158[P]

Catch The Magic (IRE) *John Joseph Hanlon* 88b
6 b m Catcher In The Rye(IRE) That's Magic (IRE) (Lord Americo)
1688[3]

Catchthemoonlight *Lucinda Russell* 94h
7 b m Generous(IRE) Moon Catcher (Kahyasi)
487[5] 805[4]

Catena Alta (IRE) *Martin Keighley* 69b
4 br g Kalanisi(IRE) Solar Quest (IRE) (King's Ride)
4103[13]

Catherines Well *Philip Hobbs* 127h
6 b m Kayf Tara Dudeen (IRE) (Anshan)
2252[2] ◆ 2812[2] (3333)

Catimini (IRE) *Sean Byrne* 121h
7 ch m Golan(IRE) Oscareen (IRE) (Oscar (IRE))
1150a[F]

Catkin Copse *Richard Phillips* 97h
7 b m Alflora(IRE) Run Tiger (IRE) (Commanche Run)
90[3] 597[5] 879[P] 1427[2] 1598[2]

Catmoves (FR) *J-P Gallorini* 136h 135c
8 ch m Medicean Cattiva Generosa (Cadeaux Genereux)
349a[5]

Catwalk Babe (IRE) *Dan Skelton* 67h
5 br m Presenting Supreme Dreamer (IRE) (Supreme Leader)
181[6]

Caulfields Venture (IRE) *Emma Lavelle* 103h 135c
9 b g Catcher In The Rye(IRE) Saddlers' Venture (IRE) (Saddlers' Hall (IRE))
101[P] 448[3] 1053[P] (2008) 2616[P]

Caulkin (IRE) *David Kemp* 90h 102c
12 b g King's Theatre(IRE) Alice Brennan (IRE) (Good Thyne (USA))
12[9] 296[4]

Cause Of Causes (USA) *Gordon Elliott* 151h 156c
7 b g Dynaformer(USA) Angel In My Heart (FR) (Rainbow Quest (USA))
3296a[12] 3651a[10] 4281a[5] (4735) 5327[P]

Cave Hunter (IRE) *Mrs Wendy Hamilton* 121c
8 b g Court Cave(IRE) Beasty Maxx (GER) (Keen)
(80) (457) 4307[3] 4768[U] 5090[3]

Cayman Islands *John Ferguson* 128h 127c
7 b g Shirocco(GER) Barbuda (Rainbow Quest (USA))
857[5] 1008[F] 1330[2] 1504[4] 1639[3] (1896) 2593[8] 3176[4]

Ceann Sibheal (IRE) *Warren Greatrex* 118h
6 b g Flemensfirth(USA) Imperial Award (IRE) (Oscar (IRE))
2299[8] 2762[9] 3126[6] 3946[3] 4349[3] ◆ (4528) (4877) 5300[5]

Cearys (IRE) *Martin Keighley* 81h
7 br m Zagreb(USA) Quel Bleu (IRE) (Tel Quel (FR))
238[P] 591[5] 1009[P] 1506[4] 1931[P]

Ceasar Milan (IRE) *Paul Nicholls* 133h 140c
7 br g Milan Standfast (IRE) (Supreme Leader)
1976[P] 2780[9] 2990[5]

Cecile De Volanges *Michael Hawker* 33h 85c
7 ch m Kheleyf(USA) Fyvie (Grand Lodge (USA))
1044[5] **1134[4] 4887[6]**

Ceithre Delta (IRE) *S R B Crawford* 74h 90c
10 b m Samraan(USA) Wissey (IRE) (Florida Son)
300[2] 656[7]

Celestial Magic *Richard Phillips* 110h
3 b g Black Sam Bellamy(IRE) Mighty Merlin (Royal Applause)
1928[4] 2448[3] 2992[3] 3464[3] 4447[2] 5225[3]

Celestino (FR) *N W Alexander* 97h 97c
4 b g Leeds(IRE) Evamoon (FR) (River Bay (USA))
107[2] 2212[7] **2753[6]** 2933[9] 4036[7] 4404[5] **5010[P]** 5445[3]

Celldomfed (IRE) *Jonjo O'Neill* 111h
5 b g Beneficial Eyebright (IRE) (Zaffaran (USA))
2628[3] 3126[P] 4097[10] ◆ (5469) ◆

Celtic Abbey *Joanne Foster* 114h
8 br g Overbury(IRE) Celtic Native (IRE) (Be My Native (USA))
2843[8]

Celtic Agent *Micky Hammond* 111h
7 b g Kayf Tara Poor Celt (Impecunious)
5345[2]

Celtic Artisan (IRE) *Rebecca Menzies* 98h
4 ch g Dylan Thomas(IRE) Perfectly Clear (USA) (Woodman (USA))
(489) 5088[P]

Celtic Fella (IRE) *Debra Hamer* 43h 78c
8 gr g Kahtan Mens Business (IRE) (Buckskin (FR))
612[5] 698[3] 1326[P] 1950[3]

Celtic Flames (IRE) *Lucinda Russell* 107h
5 gr g Celtic Swing Don't Forget Shoka (IRE) (Don't Forget Me)
1640[2] 1852[3]

Celtic Intrigue (IRE) *David Bridgwater* 90h 119c
8 b g Celtic Swing Macca Luna (IRE) (Kahyasi)
(610) ◆ (717) (1049) 3569[4] 4027[4]

Celtic Monarch (IRE) *Mark Michael McNiff* 112h
6 b g Celtic Swing Trim (IRE) (Ela-Mana-Mou)
(634) 798[3] 1742[4]

Celtic Thunder (IRE) *R K Watson* 103c
6 b g Definite Article Clash Princess (IRE) (Supreme Leader)
4549[P]

Celtic Tune (FR) *Jonjo O'Neill* 106h
4 b g Green Tune(USA) Kerry Rose (FR) (Tel Quel (FR))
4064[4] 4875[5]

Centasia *Neil Mulholland* 130h 130c
8 b m Presenting Cent Prime (Hernando (FR))
394[3] (4647)

Central Flame *James Walton* 132h 138c
7 ch g Central Park(IRE) More Flair (Alflora (IRE))
3100[P] 3627[3] 3936[2] 4370[2] 5085[5]

Centre Haafhd *Barry Murtagh* 81h
4 b g Haafhd Deira Dubai (Green Desert (USA))
1634[P] 1774[7] 1886[10] 2292[P]

Centreofexcellence (IRE) *Gary Moore* 94h
4 b g Oscar(IRE) Calm Approach (IRE) (Anshan)
3608[P] 4409[6] 4530[6] (5352)

Centurius *Venetia Williams* 112h
5 ch g New Approach(IRE) Questina (FR) (Rainbow Quest (USA))
2183[6] 3773[3] 4233[3] (4502)

Cerca Trova (IRE) *J T R Dreaper* 104h 89c
9 b m Brian Boru Aran Dawn (IRE) (Phardante (FR))
2705[7]

Cernunnos (FR) *Tom George* 142c
5 b g Della Francesca(USA) Jackette (USA) (Mr Greeley (USA))
1989[4] 3020[2] (3924) 4363[2] 4787[2] 5217[P]

Cest Notre Gris (IRE) *Miss Elizabeth Doyle* 116h
5 gr g Verglas(IRE) Alikhlas (Lahib (USA))
231a[11]

Chac Du Cadran (FR) *Chris Bealby* 58h 104c
9 b g Passing Sale(FR) L'Indienne (FR) (Le Nain Jaune (FR))
403[P]

Chain Gang *Alan Fleming* 126h
4 b g Midnight Legend Gaspaisie (FR) (Beyssac (FR))
3765a[4]

Chain Of Beacons *Sandy Thomson* 104h
6 b g Midnight Legend Millennium Girl (Skyliner)
2066[4] 5262[6]

Chakisto (FR) *Tim Vaughan* 109h
7 b g Discover D'Auteuil(FR) Chattawakie (FR) (Nikos)
1818[8] 2006[8] 2736[11] 3586[4] 4712[5]

Chalk It Down (IRE) *Warren Greatrex* 143h
6 b g Milan Feedthegoodmare (IRE) (Heron Island (IRE))
(418) ◆

Chalonnial (FR) *Harry Fry* 105b
3 ch g Protektor(GER) Kissmirial (FR) (Smadoun (FR))
(3959) 5134a[3]

Chambord Du Loir (FR) *Sarah Humphrey* 38h
5 b g Ange Gabriel(FR) Etoile De Loir (FR) (Lost World (IRE))
3047[P] 4865[9]

Chambray Dancer (IRE) *Simon Hodgson* 56h
7 b m Darsi(FR) Cotton Gale (Strong Gale)
28[6] 1084[P]

Champagne Agent (IRE) *Donald Whillans* 117h 92c
9 b g Smadoun(FR) Madame Jean (FR) (Cricket Ball (USA))
303[4] 639[5] 871[5] 1370[4] 1492[5] (1891) 2143[P] 2950[P]

Champagne At Tara *Jonjo O'Neill* 135h
6 gr g Kayf Tara Champagne Lil (Terimon)
2202[5] 2564[2] (3306) 3854[5] 4115[8] 4801[2] 5189[2]

Champagne Chaser *Tim Vaughan* 117h
5 b g Tobougg(IRE) Champagne Lil (Terimon)
1518[9] 1661[8] 2093[6] (4504) 4645[3]

Champagne Express *Nicky Henderson* 133h
5 b g Kalanisi(IRE) Marvellous Dream (FR) (Muhtathir)
2485[4] 4070[P] 4786[P]

Champagne Fever (IRE) *W P Mullins* 164h 166c
8 gr g Stowaway Forever Bubbles (IRE) (Roselier (FR))
8a[5]

Champagne George (IRE) *Neil Mulholland* 116h
5 gr g Acambaro(GER) Charannah (IRE) (Red Sunset)
2317[4] (2715) 3664[3] (5063)

Champagne James (IRE) *T M Walsh* 116h 137c
7 b g Stowaway Champagne Lady (IRE) (Turtle Island (IRE))
4246[5]

Champagne Present (IRE) *Jonjo O'Neill* 128h
5 br g Presenting My Name's Not Bin (IRE) (Good Thyne (USA))
1448[6] 1521[3] 1736[5]

Champagne Ransom (FR) *Micky Hammond* 86h
3 rg f Mastercraftsman(IRE) Linorova (USA) (Trempolino (USA))
1294[4] 1452[3] 1928[8] 4415[9] 4943[P]

Champagne To Go (IRE) *Kim Bailey* 104b
5 b m Beneficial Terre D'Orient (FR) (Kabool)
(5351)

Champagne West (IRE) *Philip Hobbs* 143h 162c
7 b g Westerner Wyndham Sweetmarie (IRE) (Mister Lord (USA))
3031[2] 3851[P] 4361[F] 4731[P]

Champ De Bataille (FR) *F-M Cottin* 141h 120c
4 gr g Dream Well(FR) La Champmesle (FR) (Turgeon (USA))
665a[7]

Champers On Ice (IRE) *David Pipe* 147h
5 gr g Robin Des Champs(FR) Miss Nova (Ra Nova)
(25a) 2470[2] (2762) (3403) 3852[3] 4766[3]

Champion Court (IRE) *Martin Keighley* 148h 159c
10 b g Court Cave(IRE) Mooneys Hill (IRE) (Supreme Leader)
(101) (812) **(1112) 2061[8] 2471[7]**

Chance Du Roy (FR) *K J Parker* 57h 146c
11 ch g Morespeed La Chance Au Roy (FR) (Rex Magna (FR))
3585[5] 4887[7]

Chanceofa Lifetime (IRE) *Victor Thompson* 107h 116c
8 ch g Beneficial Bounty Queen (IRE) (King's Ride)
(143) (290) 457[F] 2753[4] 3160[4] 3341[4] 3671[6] 4177[3] 4327[3] 4940[3] (5228) 5404[U]

Chance Taken *Noel Williams* 101h
7 b m Overbury(IRE) New Dawn (Rakaposhi King)
108[8] 451[4]

Chandos (IRE) *Sandy Thomson* 64h 38c
7 b g Heron Island(IRE) Park Belle (IRE) (Strong Gale)
290[4]

Changeofluck (IRE) *Lawney Hill* 113h 79c
7 b g Gold Well Sotattie (Teenoso (USA))
283[6] 1615[7] **2090[5] 2410[P]**

Change Or Go (IRE) *David Dennis* 68h
3 b g Kalanisi(IRE) Teffia Rose (IRE) (Old Vic)
4303[13] 4844[P] 5153[10]

Changing The Guard *Barry Brennan* 117h 129c
9 b g King's Best(USA) Our Queen Of Kings (Arazi (USA))
1261[3] 1376[2] 1554[3] 1945[4] (4771)

Chankillo *Sarah-Jayne Davies* 92h 112c
6 ch g Observatory(USA) Seasonal Blossom (IRE) (Fairy King (USA))
515[3] 712[4] 811[7] **1133[2] 1373[4] 1603[2] 1689[F] (1796) 2124[2] 2249[5] (3237) 3497[P] (4642) 5310[2] 5439[2]**

Chantara Rose *Neil Mulholland* 114h
6 br m Kayf Tara Fragrant Rose (Alflora (IRE))
28[2] 1675[7] 2595[3] 3025[2] 3837[11] (4878)

Chantecler *Neil Mulholland* 68h
4 b g Authorized(IRE) Snow Goose (Polar Falcon (USA))
2258[P] 2543[10] 3077[P]

Chap *Dan Skelton* 78h
5 ch g Midnight Legend Silver Solace (Silver Patriarch (IRE))
(320) 2514[10] 3334[9]

Chapoturgeon (FR) *Jack R Barber* 93h 131c
11 gr g Turgeon(USA) Chapohio (FR) (Script Ohio (USA))
4768[F]

Charbel (IRE) *Kim Bailey* 150h
4 b g Iffraaj Eoz (IRE) (Sadler's Wells (USA))
23a[4] (2154) ◆ 2748[2] 3135[2] (4010) ◆ 4695[5]

Charging Indian (IRE) *Paul Henderson* 95h
9 b g Chevalier(IRE) Kathy Tolfa (IRE) (Sri Pekan (USA))
858[P] 1048[10]

Charles Bruce (IRE) *A Campbell* 109c
12 br g Lord Americo Lissanuhig (Le Bavard (FR))
17[U] 429[3] 4748[P]

Charlie Breekie (IRE) *Ben Pauling* 110h
6 b g Alkaadhem Highland Breeze (IRE) (Kotashaan (FR))
102[F]

Charlie Cook (IRE) *Graeme McPherson* 111h
6 b g Royal Anthem(USA) Supreme Baloo (IRE) (Supreme Leader)
2182[14] 2624[5] 3238[3] 3855[2] 4648[P] 5246[7]

Charlie's Oscar (IRE) *Dan Skelton* 102h
5 b g Oscar(IRE) Blue Gallery (IRE) (Bluebird (USA))
1943[5]

Charlie Wingnut (IRE) *Sue Smith* 98h
8 br g Westerner Back To Stay (IRE) (Supreme Leader)
4045[2] 4328[2] 4906[4]

Charming Grace (IRE) *Mark Campion* 61b
9 b m Flemensfirth(USA) Lady Laureate (Sir Harry Lewis (USA))
3795[P] **5311[P]**

Charming Lad (IRE) *Anthony Day* 98h 104c
10 b g Dushyantor(USA) Glens Lady (IRE) (Mister Lord (USA))
66[2] 223[2] 486[F] 5480[7]

Charminster (IRE) *Cyril Murphy* 127h 136c
9 b g Broadway Flyer(USA) Monteleena (IRE) (Montelimar (USA))
1983a[6]

Charmix (FR) *Harry Fry* 144h
5 bb g Laveron Open Up (FR) (Fabulous Don (SPA))
320[13] (2196) 2723[2] (3117) 3852[P]

Charm Park *Geoffrey Harker* 77b
5 b g Desideratum Queen's Lodge (IRE) (Grand Lodge (USA))
359[5]

Chartbreaker (FR) *Paul Nicholls* 128h
4 b g Shirocco(GER) Caucasienne (FR) (Galileo (IRE))
2183[5] 2762[7] (4788) 5391[3]

Chartreux (FR) *Mrs Julie Marles* 75h 86c
10 gr g Colonel Collins(USA) Ruaha River (FR) (Villez (USA))
95a[P] 4249[P] 4651[P] 5312[3]

Chase End Charlie (IRE) *Tom Lacey* 130h
4 b g Scorpion(IRE) Artist's Muse (IRE) (Cape Cross (IRE))
444[3] 2126[3] 2750[2] (3509) 4063[3] 5430[P]

Chase The Spud *Fergal O'Brien* 122h 141c
7 b g Alflora(IRE) Trial Trip (Le Moss)
2701[2] 3518[P] (4141) 4966[3]

Chase The Wind (IRE) *Joanne Foster* 127h 129c
6 ch g Spadoun(FR) Asfreeasthewind (IRE) (Moscow Society (USA))
329[6] 641[2] 861[2] 2010[2] 2846[5] 4864[2]

Chasing Fairies *Alexandra Dunn* 62b
4 gr m Fair Mix(IRE) Trial Trip (Le Moss)
4201[4] 4893[P]

Chasing The Light (IRE) *Jonjo O'Neill* 78h
5 b g King's Theatre(IRE) Starry Lady (IRE) (Marju (IRE))
703[4] 834[8]

Chasma *Michael Easterby* 93h
5 b m Kayf Tara Luneray (FR) (Poplar Bluff)
33[7] (2670) 3402[5] (4045) 4862[2]

Chasse En Mer (FR) *Caroline Bailey* 104h
5 b m Protektor(GER) Cybertina (FR) (Cyborg (FR))
130[3] 482[2]

Chateau Robin (IRE) *Seamus Mullins* 101b
4 b g Robin Des Pres(FR) Bella With A Zee (IRE) (Persian Bold)
5127[2]

Chavoy (FR) *Rebecca Menzies* 94h 126c
10 br g Saint Des Saints(FR) Dictania (FR) (Iron Duke (FR))
2431[5] 2934[U] 3341[3] 3671[P] 4407[5] 4840[8]

Chaz Michaels (IRE) *Lucinda Russell* 94h
5 ch g Bach(IRE) Breanletter (IRE) (Ala Hounak)
960[2] 1328[8] 3470[4]

Cheat The Cheater (IRE) *Claire Dyson* 118h 106c
8 b g Flemensfirth(USA) Ballyclough Gale (IRE) (Strong Gale)
2582[3] (2830) 3062[2] 3236[4] 3663[3] (3948) (4346) 4738[4]

Chebsey Beau *John Quinn* 129h
5 b g Multiplex Chebsey Belle (IRE) (Karinga Bay)
(1170) 1404[2] 2202[7]

Chef D'Oeuvre (FR) *Warren Greatrex* 143h
4 b g Martaline Kostroma (FR) (Lost World (IRE))
2375[3] (3043) 3852[4] (4198) 4801[10]

Cheiliuradh (IRE) *David Harry Kelly* 107h
4 b m Oscar(IRE) Ballycleary (IRE) (Phardante (FR))
2225a[F] 3169a[5] 4653a[6]

Chelsea Flyer (IRE) *Emma Lavelle* 119b
4 b g Westerner Aktress (IRE) (Oscar (IRE))
2351[3] ◆ 3258[2] 4790[2]

Cheltenam De Vaige (FR) *Giles Smyly* 89b
3 b g Forestier(FR) Ratina De Vaige (FR) (April Night (FR))
3625[3] 4102[12]

Cheltenian (FR) *Philip Hobbs* 153h 140c
9 b g Astarabad(USA) Salamaite (FR) (Mansonnien (FR))
197[6] 3033[5] 3854[2] 4115[7] 4381[4] 4765[15]

Chemistry Master *Alexandra Dunn* 46h
7 b g Doyen(IRE) Elemental (Rudimentary (USA))
2151[P]

Cheque En Blanc (FR) *Tom Symonds*
3 bb g Bernebeau(FR) Necossaise (FR) (Michel Georges)
5195[17]

Cherry Bomb (IRE) *S R B Crawford* 93h
4 b m Robin Des Pres(FR) Cherry Tart (IRE) (Persian Mews)
4052[2]

Cherry Princess *Barbara Butterworth* 83h
5 gr m Act One Francia (Legend Of France (USA))
155[4] 503[6] 727[4] 845[9] 1066[5] 2148[10]

Cherry Tiger *Graeme McPherson* 86h
5 b g Tiger Hill(IRE) Lolla's Spirit (IRE) (Montjeu (IRE))
489[5]

Cheshire Prince *Neil King* 107h
11 br g Desert Prince(IRE) Bundle Up (USA) (Miner's Mark (USA))
520[8]

Chesterfieldavenue (IRE) *C Roche* 122h
4 br g Presenting Fashionista (IRE) (King's Theatre (IRE))
3070a[3]

Chestnut Ben (IRE) *Peter Winks* 76h 130c
10 ch g Ridgewood Ben Betseale (IRE) (Step Together I (USA))
315[5] 469[6] 2765[4] 3237[4] (3475) 3857[8] (4011) 4597[3] 4838[6] 5156[B] 5471[4]

Cheyanwe (IRE) *David Kemp* 90b 81c
11 ch m Subtle Power(IRE) Not A Bother Tohim (IRE) (Abednego)
297[2]

Chiaromonte (FR) *Ilenia Nero* 121h
6 b g Domedriver(IRE) Charlotte Alix (Celestial Storm (USA))
1671a[3]

Chicago Outfit (IRE) *George Bewley* 94h 130c
10 b g Old Vic Lambourne Lace (IRE) (Un Desperado (FR))
140[3] (486) (637) (800) 1033[7] (1571) 1856[11] **2068[5] 2213[10] 2934[P] 5259[P]**

Chicksgrove Sprite (IRE) *Neil Mulholland* 65b
4 b m Scorpion(IRE) Homebird (IRE) (Be My Native (USA))
4687[9] 5383[10]

Chic Name (FR) *Richard Hobson* 132h
3 b g Nickname(FR) Vuelta Al Ruedo (FR) (Ballingarry (IRE))
778[6] 1452[2] 1712[3] 1928[2] (2273) 2371[4] 3028[3] 3519[2] 4204[3] 4720[15]

Chicoria (IRE) *Henry Daly* 108h 128c
6 ch g Presenting Coco Girl (Mystiko (USA))
(2592) 2973[P] 3129[4] 5154[P]

Chic Theatre (IRE) *David Pipe* 120h
5 gr g King's Theatre(IRE) La Reine Chic (FR) (Balleroy (USA))
2065[8] 2972[4] 4182[2] (4303) 4620[9]

Chief Brody *Grace Harris* 109h
4 b g Phoenix Reach(IRE) Cherry Plum (Medicean)
1817[3] 2563[U] 2731[4] 3077[9] 3745[4] 4235[5] 4782[11] 4965[6] 5225[8]

Chief Spirit *James Eustace* 80h
3 b g Norse Dancer(IRE) Indian Angel (Indian Ridge)
4462[8] 4773[5]

Chieftain's Choice (IRE) *Kevin Frost* 110h
6 b g King's Theatre(IRE) Fairy Native (IRE) (Be My Native (USA))
2438[P] 3041[3] 3352[6] 4115[P] 5219[17]

Childrens List (IRE) *W P Mullins* 143h
5 b g Presenting Snipe Hunt (IRE) (Stalker)
2676a[4] 4769[17] 5213[12]

Chill (IRE) *Zoe Davison*
7 b g Diamond Green(FR) Time To Relax (IRE) (Orpen (USA))
512[5] 1099[5] 4096[P]

Chill Factor (IRE) *Anthony Honeyball* 122h 138c
6 b g Oscar(IRE) Glacial Princess (IRE) (Glacial Storm (USA))
(29) 4158[3]

Chilli Romance (IRE) *Fergal O'Brien* 101b
4 b m Flemensfirth(USA) Blue Romance (IRE) (Bob Back (USA))
3132[3] 4074[3]

Chilly Miss *Malcolm Jefferson* 116h
6 b m Iceman Fairlie (Halling (USA))
415[5] 591[3] ◆ 846[2] (1036) 1170[7] 1404[5]

Chimere Du Berlais (FR) *Robert Collet* 136h
3 b f Martaline Shinca (FR) (Port Lyautey (FR))
1881a[2]

Chinatown Boy (IRE) *Charles Whittaker* 119h 122c
7 ch g Presenting Asian Maze (IRE) (Anshan)
269[2]

Chitu (IRE) *S R B Crawford* 121h
5 b g Desert King(IRE) Polly's Joy (IRE) (Oscar (IRE))
(662) (2754) 3765a[6]

Chocca Wocca *Nicky Henderson* 118h
5 b m Kayf Tara Chomba Womba (IRE) (Fourstars Allstar (USA))
(4271) 4734[10] 5280[6]

Choochoobugaloo *Tom Symonds* 64b
3 b f Rail Link Charmante Femme (Bin Ajwaad (IRE))
3118[7] 4075[5]

Choral Bee *Alan Jessop* 40h
6 b m Oratorio(IRE) Chief Bee (Chief's Crown (USA))
748[5] 5373[11]

Chorlton House *Ian Williams* 78h
3 ch g Compton Place Really Ransom (Red Ransom (USA))
4976[P]

Chosen Destiny (IRE) *Dan Skelton* 94b
5 b m Well Chosen Despute (IRE) (Be My Native (USA))
1057[6]

Chosen Milan (IRE) *R E Luke* 88b 132c
8 b m Milan Grey Mistral (Terimon)
(16) 535[P]

Chosen Well (IRE) *Alan King* 134h 124c
6 b g Well Chosen Killmaleary Cross (IRE) (Needle Gun (IRE))
2727[4] ◆

Chou Du Mathan (FR) *Christian Le Galliard*
7 b g Nononito(FR) Very Happy (FR) (Tip Moss (FR))
4400a[P]

Chris Pea Green *Gary Moore* 137h 148c
6 b g Proclamation(IRE) Another Secret (Efisio)
1735[U] 3990[3] 4770[P]

Christmas Twenty (IRE) *Stuart Edmunds* 117h
5 br g Zagreb(USA) Celestial Gale (IRE) (Presenting)
1449[6] 1718[P] 2154[2] 2928[6] 3420[P] 3949[4] 4506[3] 5079[2]

Ch'Tibello (FR) *Dan Skelton* 144h
4 b g Sageburg(IRE) Neicha (FR) (Neverneyev (USA))
1946[2] 2183[2] 2728[3] (5325)

Church Field (IRE) *Phil Middleton* 122h
7 b g Heron Island(IRE) Dante's Thatch (IRE) (Phardante (FR))
177[10] 747[5] 1181[2] (1350) 1699[U] (1827) 3465[5] 3846[7] (4648) 5183[4]

Church Gallery (IRE) *S Rea* 34h 9c
8 gr g Portrait Gallery(IRE) Mill Afrique (Mtoto)
14[5] 429[P]

Church Hall (IRE) *Emma Baker* 121h
7 b g Craigsteel Island Religion (IRE) (Religiously (USA))
4824[6] 5183[5]

Church Leap (IRE) *Patrick Chamings* 107h
4 gr g High Chaparral(IRE) Alambic (Cozzene (USA))
2683[5] 3114[4]

Churchtown Champ (IRE) *Dan Skelton* 132h
5 b g Robin Des Champs(FR) Annagh Lady (IRE) (Dr Massini (IRE))
3316[F] (3580) 4248[4] 5018[4]

Churchtown Love (IRE) *Miss A Griffiths* 113h 102c
7 b m Beneficial Katie Murphy (IRE) (Over The River (FR))
4269[4] 5054[3]

Ciceron (IRE) *Neil King* 107h 104c
9 b g Pivotal Aiglonne (USA) (Silver Hawk (USA))
390[3] 1965[5] 2138[4] 2994[P] 3225[P]

Cinderfella *Noel Williams* 105b
4 gr g Sagamix(FR) Firecracker Lady (IRE) (Supreme Leader)
3907[4] 5227[5] ◆

Cinder Rua (IRE) *J J Lambe* 109h 109c
8 ch m Carroll House(IRE) Scree (IRE) (Broken Hearted)
1420[6] **2430[3]** (3666)

Cinevator (IRE) *Richard Woollacott* 97h 94c
8 b g Dr Massini(IRE) Hurricane Bella (IRE) (Taipan (IRE))
827[7] 1049[6]

Circus Star (USA) *John Dixon* 118h
7 b g Borrego(USA) Picadilly Circus (USA) (Fantastic Fellow (USA))
301[6] 2194[7] 2921[3] 3152[11] 4285[4]

Ciro Vincenti (IRE) *R Romano*
7 b g Clodovil(IRE) Lucy Liu (IRE) (Grand Lodge (USA))
1672a[P]

Citizenship *Venetia Williams* 118h 127c
9 b g Beat Hollow Three More (USA) (Sanglamore (USA))
177[P]

City Dreams (IRE) *Michael Blake* 79h
5 b m Rakti Attymon Lill (IRE) (Marju (IRE))
1781[5]

City Slicker (IRE) *Jonjo O'Neill* 121b
7 b g King's Theatre(IRE) Donna's Princess (IRE) (Supreme Leader)
2166[P]

City Supreme (IRE) *Anthony Honeyball* 113h
5 b g Milan Run Supreme (IRE) (Supreme Leader)
63[5] 2262[10] 2713[5] 3855[4] 4450[3] (5072) 5454[2]

Civil Unrest (IRE) *James Ewart* 106h 113c
9 ch g Blueprint(IRE) Yore (IRE) (Ore)
417[5]

Claire Pet (IRE) *Dr Richard Newland* 114h 90c
8 b g Pierre Babs Girld (IRE) (Cataldi)
4200[5]

Clan Chief *N W Alexander* 99h 94c
6 ch g Generous(IRE) Harrietfield (Nicholas Bill)
2707[U] (3161) **3938[U] 4166[5] 4795[P] 5086[3] 5257[2]**

Clancy's Cross (IRE) *Kevin Frost* 119h
6 b g Oscar(IRE) Murphys Lady (IRE) (Over The River (FR))
(212) 1648[7]

Clan Des Obeaux (FR) *Paul Nicholls* 139h
3 bb g Kapgarde(FR) Nausicaa Des Obeaux (FR) (April Night (FR))
(3112) ◆ 3848[2] 4764[6]

Clan Legend *N W Alexander* 122h
5 ch g Midnight Legend Harrietfield (Nicholas Bill)
(2343) (2982) (3438) 3865[3] (4583) 5295[P]

Clanville Lass *Ali Stronge* 85b
3 b f Tobougg(IRE) Mulberry Wine (Benny The Dip (USA))
2583[3] 3118[5]

Clan William (IRE) *Sue Smith* 106h 121c
7 b g Antonius Pius(USA) Celebrated Smile (IRE) (Cadeaux Genereux)
2042[9] **2477[2] (2920) 3155[P]** (Dead)

Claragh Native (IRE) *Martin Todhunter* 109h 118c
10 ch g Beneficial Susy In The Summer (IRE) (Be My Native (USA))
35[4] (417) 709[2] 1169[8] 1416[4] 1494[4] 1904[5] 2755[P]

Clara Peggotty *Tom Gretton* 89h
8 b m Beat All(USA) Clair Valley (Ardross)
4538[2] 5020[2]

Clarcam (FR) *Gordon Elliott* 139h 159c
5 b g Califet(FR) Rose Beryl (FR) (Lost World (IRE))
1763a[3] 2206a[2] 2941a[5] 3293a[4] 3552a[8] 5192[3]

Claret Cloak (IRE) *Emma Lavelle* 103h 158c
8 b g Vinnie Roe(IRE) Bewildered (IRE) (Prince Sabo)
(103) 556[12] **1322[4] 1658[2]** (Dead)

Clar Na Mionn (IRE) *V T O'Brien* 124h 128c
8 b g Witness Box(USA) Playtime Girl (IRE) (Commanche Run)
2228a[2]

Classic Colori (IRE) *Martin Keighley* 92h
8 b g Le Vie Dei Colori Beryl (Bering)
5386[7]

Classic Palace (IRE) *J J Lambe* 110h 100c
6 b m Classic Cliche(IRE) Winconjon (IRE) (Oscar (IRE))
503[3] (730) (1030) 1414[3] 2025[4] **2805[5]**

Classic Tune *Claire Dyson* 104h
5 b g Scorpion(IRE) Classic Fantasy (Classic Cliche (IRE))
2337[7] 3012[3] 4508[4] 5372[6]

Classi Massini *Peter Bowen* 65b
4 b m Dr Massini(IRE) Classi Maureen (Among Men (USA))
2086[7]

Classinaglass *Michael Easterby* 118c
8 b g Grape Tree Road Sounds Familiar (IRE) (Orchestra)
35[3] 2342[5] 4073[5]

Claude Carter *Alistair Whillans* 107h
11 b g Elmaamul(USA) Cruz Santa (Lord Bud)
962[5] 1261[5] 1369[4] 2069[2] 2326[4] 2843[2] 3424[6] 3682[8] 4036[3]

Clayton *Gary Moore* 130h
6 b g Peintre Celebre(USA) Blossom (Warning)
2614[2] ◆ 2928[9] 3450[2] (3902) 4622[11] 5139[2] ◆

Clean Sheet (IRE) *Nicky Henderson* 133h
6 b g Oscar(IRE) High Park Lady (IRE) (Phardante (FR))
3854[7] 4362[6]

Cleetons Turn *Alan Hollingsworth* 25h
8 b g Alflora(IRE) Indyana Run (Commanche Run)
212[P]

Cleeve Hill Lad *Tom Lacey* 105h
7 b g Overbury(IRE) Lady Prunella (IRE) (Supreme Leader)
212[5]

Clemency *Nicky Henderson* 111h
4 b m Halling(USA) China Tea (USA) (High Chaparral (IRE))
1612[F] (1960) (3485) 4272[P]

Clenagh Castle (IRE) *Chris Grant* 46h
5 b g King's Theatre(IRE) Orwell's Marble (IRE) (Definite Article)
1890[11] 2937[P] **4034[P]**

Cleni Wells (FR) *Martin Hill* 104h
4 b g Poliglote Kailasa (FR) (R B Chesne)
4466[10] 4917[P]

Clerk's Choice (IRE) *Michael Banks* 55h
9 b g Bachelor Duke(USA) Credit Crunch (IRE) (Caerleon (USA))
4470[5]

Cleve Cottage *Philip Kirby* 95h
7 ch g Presenting Reverse Swing (Charmer (IRE))
2720[P] 2937[P] 3503[F] 3793[3] 4289[2] ◆

Clic Work (FR) *Paul Nicholls* 97h
3 b g Network(GER) Qape Noir (FR) (Subotica (FR))
3745[5] 5095[8]

Cliff House (IRE) *John J Walsh* 141h
5 b g Mustameet(USA) Babble On (IRE) (Anita's Prince)
7a[12] 3650a[9]

Clock On Tom *Denis Quinn* 114h
5 b g Trade Fair Night Owl (Night Shift (USA))
1154[2] 1261[8] 1346[2] 1421[7] 1781[2] (2217) (2538)

Cloggy Powell (IRE) *Kevin Hunter* 59h
8 ch g Classic Cliche(IRE) Ann's Delight (IRE) (Imperial Ballet (IRE))
502[8] 838[9] 1065[7]

Clonbanan Lad (IRE) *Miss Louise Allan* 118h 123c
9 b g Rudimentary(USA) Flute Orchestra (IRE) (Deep Run)
19a[7] **3826[3] 4232[P] 4424[2] (4969) 5178[P]** (Dead)

Clondaw Banker (IRE) *Nicky Henderson* 126h
6 b g Court Cave(IRE) Freya Alex (Makbul)
2058[6] (2369) 2594[4] 5391[7]

Clondaw Bisto (IRE) *Suzy Smith* 116b
4 b g September Storm(GER) Solo Venture (IRE) (Abednego)
(3907) 4414[2]

Clondaw Cian (IRE) *Suzy Smith* 135h
5 br g Gold Well Cocktail Bar (IRE) (Hubbly Bubbly (USA))
1843[2] (2317) (2710) 2886[4] 3852[7] 4668[2] 5303[2]

Clondaw Court (IRE) *W P Mullins* 143h
8 br g Court Cave(IRE) Secret Can't Say (IRE) (Jurado (USA))
2815a[6]

Clondaw Cracker (IRE) *Neil Mulholland* 110b
4 b g Court Cave(IRE) Twelve Pence (IRE) (Bob Back (USA))
(5457)

Clondaw Fonz (IRE) *Alan King* 119h
4 b g Court Cave(IRE) Sweetasanu (IRE) (Sri Pekan (USA))
4323[3] 4874[6] 5263[P]

Clondaw Kaempfer (IRE) *Donald McCain* 123h 112c
7 b g Oscar(IRE) Gra-Bri (IRE) (Rashar (USA))
4287[4] 5189[F]

Clondaw Warrior (IRE) *W P Mullins* 149h
8 br g Overbury(IRE) Thespian (IRE) (Tiraaz (USA))
96a[3] (5025a) 5325[3]

Clondaw Westie (IRE) *Lawney Hill* 94b
4 b g Westerner You're A Native (IRE) (Saddlers' Hall (IRE))
5097[11]

Clonleney (IRE) *Alison Hamilton* 97h 77c
9 ch g Broadway Flyer(USA) Most Effective (IRE) (Lancastrian)
455[3] 871[P]

Clonusker (IRE) *Linda Jewell* 87h
7 b g Fasliyev(USA) Tamburello (IRE) (Roi Danzig (USA))
2826[P] 4161[2] 4504[7] 5067[5] 5483[7]

Cloonacool (IRE) *Stuart Edmunds* 136h 147c
6 b g Beneficial Newhall (IRE) (Shernazar)
(1657) 2186[5] 2617[7] **3084[2] (3466)** ◆ **4359[3] 4891[3]**

Close Escape (IRE) *Nicky Henderson* 57b
4 b g Robin Des Pres(FR) Music School (IRE) (Saddlers' Hall (IRE))
2065[P] 2729[7]

Closer To Home (IRE) *David Pipe* 100h
3 b g Soldier Of Fortune(IRE) Maid For Music (IRE) (Dubai Destination (USA))
3112[7] 3955[5] 4183[8] (4855) 4882[9]

Closest Friend *Dan Skelton* 124h
6 b g Kayf Tara Princess Of War (Warrshan (USA))
1480[2] (1792) 2186[10] 2688[5] 5437[2] ◆

Close Touch *Nicky Henderson* 123h 128c
7 ch g Generous(IRE) Romantic Dream (Bustino)
5074[4] 5497[14]

Closing Ceremony (IRE) *Emma Lavelle* 150h
6 b g Flemensfirth(USA) Supreme Von Pres (IRE) (Presenting)
2198[5] 2641[6] **3774[3]**

Cloudburst *Oliver Sherwood* 55b
4 gr m Authorized(IRE) Secret Night (Dansili)
334[9]

Cloud Creeper (IRE) *Philip Hobbs* 123h 153c
8 b g Cloudings(IRE) First Of April (IRE) (Presenting)
198[2] 1658[3] 1840[4] 2483[13] 5276[4]

Cloudy Beach (IRE) *Venetia Williams* 108h 125c
8 gr g Cloudings(IRE) Niki Beach (IRE) (Needle Gun (IRE))
2885[6] (4197) 4431[4] (4615)

Cloudy Bob (IRE) *Pat Murphy* 122h 130c
8 gr g Cloudings(IRE) Keen Supreme (IRE) (Bob Back (USA))
1641[3] 1970[4] 2593[6] 2975[3] 3315[F] 3499[2] 3731[2] 4363[3] (4789) 4910[6] 5390[3]

Cloudy Copper (IRE) *Jonjo O'Neill* 113h 136c
8 gr g Cloudings(IRE) Copper Supreme (IRE) (Supreme Leader)
1867[3] 2442[7] 3079[2] 3349[5] 4568[3] **(5238)** ◆

Cloudy Dream (IRE) *Malcolm Jefferson* 140h
5 gr g Cloudings(IRE) Run Away Dream (IRE) (Acceglio)
(1926) 2318[3] (2772) (4986) 5325[2] ◆

Cloudy Joker (IRE) *Donald McCain* 108h 131c
7 gr g Cloudings(IRE) Rosa View (IRE) (Roselier (FR))
1570[F] 1792[RR] 1909[2] 2041[4] **2425[6] 2884[5] (3401) (3589)** ◆ **3972[F] 4464[8]**

Cloudy Lady *Caroline Keevil* 72h
7 gr m Alflora(IRE) Cirrious (Cloudings (IRE))
267[7]

Cloudy Too (IRE) *Sue Smith* 116h 154c
9 b g Cloudings(IRE) Curra Citizen (IRE) (Phardante (FR))
2194[9] **2436[P] 2790[8] 3157[3] (3741) 4245[3] 4635[5] 5217[6]**

Cloughernagh Boy (IRE) *David Pipe* 112b
7 ch g Flemensfirth(USA) Windy Bee (IRE) (Aristocracy (IRE))
3006[F]

Clovis Du Berlais (FR) *Robert Collet* 133h 114c
4 b h King's Theatre(IRE) Kenza Du Berlais (FR) (Kahyasi)
665a[6]

Clubs Are Trumps (IRE) *Jonjo O'Neill* 93h 119c
6 b g Flemensfirth(USA) Pairtree (Double Trigger (IRE))
388[4] (771) (1079) (1450) 1783[4]

Clues And Arrows (IRE) *John Wade* 95h 106c
7 b g Clerkenwell(USA) Ballela Girl (IRE) (Mandalus)
729[4] **1068[2] 1401[3]**

Clyne *Evan Williams* 134h
5 b g Hernando(FR) Lauderdale (GER) (Nebos (GER))
2445[3] (3080) (4129)

C Me In Oz (IRE) *S A Jones* 100c
8 b g Zagreb(USA) Tell Me Princess (IRE) (Insan (USA))
5467[4]

Coachie Bear *Katie Scott* 77h
4 ch g Grape Tree Road Gentle Approach (Rakaposhi King)
145[9] 4208[5] 4633[6] 4835[P]

Cobajayisland (IRE) *Lucinda Russell* 103h 121c
7 b g Heron Island(IRE) Shinora (IRE) (Black Minstrel)
2017[2] (2295) 3671[P] 4406[3] 4907[5]

Cobham's Circus (IRE) *Robert Walford* 96h
4 ch g Hernando(FR) Protectorate (Hector Protector (USA))
2928[U] 5416[4]

Cobh National (IRE) *Victor Thompson* 40h
7 b g Millenary Not A Bother Tohim (IRE) (Abednego)
419[U] 481[P] 634[7] 1739[P] 2319[P]

Cobra De Mai (FR) *Dan Skelton* 111h
3 b g Great Pretender(IRE) Miria Galanda (FR) (Chef De Clan (FR))
2273[5] 3112[3] (4104) 4294[4] 5095[2]

Cochinillo (IRE) *Ben Case* 112h
6 b g Shantou(USA) Nut Touluze (IRE) (Toulon)
680[2] ◆ 930[2] (2667)

Cocker *Alan Blackmore* 101h
3 b g Shirocco(GER) Treble Heights (IRE) (Unfuwain (USA))
3418[7] 4317[14] 4771[4] 5063[3]

Cocktails At Dawn *Nicky Henderson* 130h 155c
7 b g Fair Mix(IRE) Fond Farewell (IRE) (Phardante (FR))
(1846) 2483[14] 5193[F]

Coco Des Champs (IRE) *Oliver Sherwood* 116h
5 br m Robin Des Champs(FR) American Chick (IRE) (Lord Americo)
1960[4] 2911[2] 4231[5]

Coco Flower (FR) *Alex Hales* 42h
3 ch f Born King(JPN) La Fleur Du Roy (FR) (Sleeping Car (FR))
2304[6] 2583[4] 3842[7] 4271[8] 4489[6] 4714[12]

Coco Shambhala *Oliver Sherwood* 102h
7 b m Indian Danehill(IRE) Kohinor (Supreme Leader)
2579[3] 2952[4]

Code Blue *R Tate* 107h 76c
12 b g Sir Harry Lewis(USA) Nevermind Hey (Teenoso (USA))
5082[4]

Codeshare *Alan Swinbank* 55b
3 b g Dansili Clepsydra (Sadler's Wells (USA))
5248[6]

Cody Wyoming *Charlie Mann* 115h 129c
9 b g Passing Glance Tenderfoot (Be My Chief (USA))
1989[2] 2153[P] 2497[P] 2758[P] 4106[3] 4841[5] (5164)

Coeur Blimey (IRE) *Sue Gardner* 131b
4 bb g Winged Love(IRE) Eastender (Opening Verse (USA))
(3138) 4721[11]

Coeur Brule (FR) *David Turner* 96h 94c
9 b g Polish Summer Sally's Cry (FR) (Freedom Cry)
298[2] 488[3]

Coeur De Fou (FR) *Tom George* 105h 112c
10 ch g Limnos(JPN) Folly Lady (FR) (Saint Estephe (FR))
4180[3] (5054) 5384[U]

Coeur Joyeux (IRE) *Ms Sandra Hughes* 125h
4 ch g Beneficial Hayabusa (Sir Harry Lewis (USA))
11a[2]

Coeur Tantre (IRE) *Hugo Froud* 108h
4 ch g Fruits Of Love(USA) Ding Dong Belle (Minster Son)
3370[6] 3710[8] 4848[3] 5398[2] ◆

Coffee (IRE) *E Bolger* 123h 55c
8 bb g Beneficial Boro Cruise (IRE) (Accordion)
1175a[11]

Cogry *Nigel Twiston-Davies* 120h 141c
6 b g King's Theatre(IRE) Wyldello (Supreme Leader)
2482[4] ◆ **3518[P] 4128[3] 4802[3]**

Cogryhill (IRE) *Gordon Elliott* 125h
5 b g Presenting Rare Gesture (IRE) (Shalford (IRE))
2672a[5] 3169a[3] 3393a[6]

Cold Knight *Tom Weston* 106h 109c
9 b g Sir Harry Lewis(USA) Arctic Chick (Henbit (USA))
260[2] 531[4]

Cold March (FR) *Venetia Williams* 112h 153c
5 bb g Early March Tumultueuse (FR) (Bering)
(2185) 2635[3] 3030[6] 3735[0] 4360[5]

Coldstonesober (IRE) *J R Finn* 127h 123c
9 ch g Great Palm(USA) You Can Dance (IRE) (King's Theatre (IRE))
1186a[15]

Cole Harden (IRE) *Warren Greatrex* 168h
6 b g Westerner Nosie Betty (IRE) (Alphabatim (USA))
2782[3] 3408[3] 4732[4]

Colin's Brother *Nigel Twiston-Davies* 124h 124c
5 b g Overbury(IRE) Dd's Glenalla (IRE) (Be My Native (USA))
2151[2] 2758[3] 4493[P] (4965) 5396[9]

Colin's Sister *Fergal O'Brien* 120b
4 b m Central Park(IRE) Dd's Glenalla (IRE) (Be My Native (USA))
152[4] 2065[4] 2486[5] 2929[5] 4623[2] ◆

Colla Pier (IRE) *Robert Alan Hennessy* 128h
6 b m Hawk Wing(USA) Medalha Milagrosa (USA) (Miner's Mark (USA))
1150a[5] 2176a[2] 2778[2] 3650a[10] 5242[3]

Collen Beag (IRE) *David M O'Brien* 128h
5 b m Mountain High(IRE) Well Water (IRE) (Old Vic)
1748a[3]

Colley Row (IRE) *Tim Vaughan* 100h
7 b g Vinnie Roe(IRE) Sliabhin Hall (IRE) (Saddlers' Hall (IRE))
530[10] (1010) 1426[6] 2453[9]

Collodi (GER) *David Bridgwater* 127h
6 b g Konigstiger(GER) Codera (GER) (Zilzal (USA))
84[F] 406[7] 556[15] 751[2] 826[7] 1039[10]

Colmers Hill *Jeremy Scott* 89h
5 b g Crosspeace(IRE) My Dancing Kin (Baryshnikov (AUS))
2265^{P} 2986^{7} 4439^{3} 5137^{P}

Colms Dream (IRE) *Karl Thornton* 116h 145c
6 ch g Beneficial African Waters (IRE) (Be My Native (USA))
3425^{F} (4397a)

Colonel Ali *Denis Quinn* 44b
4 b g Halling(USA) Preceder (Polish Precedent (USA))
1758^{10}

Colonial Style (IRE) *George Moore* 73h
5 b g Gamut(IRE) The Dukes Pert (IRE) (Revoque (IRE))
33^{6} 518^{P} 1368^{P}

Colorado Kid (IRE) *John Hellens* 88b
9 b g Presenting Silent Orders (IRE) (Bob Back (USA))
472^{P}

Colour Squadron (IRE) *E Bolger* 126h 147c
9 b g Old Vic That's The Goose (IRE) (Be My Native (USA))
1152a^{F} 1185a^{3} 1556a^{7}

Colrockin *Russell Ross*
4 b g Great Palm(USA) Suetsu (IRE) (Toulon)
4552^{8}

Columbanus (IRE) *Kenneth Slack* 77h
4 b g Jeremy(USA) Shamah (Unfuwain (USA))
1115^{P} 1702^{P} 1980^{6} 2604^{2} 2730^{5} 3256^{P} 3368^{F} 4797^{5}

Comas Sola (FR) *J-P Gallorini* 127h 115c
4 gr m Lord Du Sud(FR) Moon Glow (FR) (Solar One (FR))
2821a^{7} 4540a^{5} 5428a^{2}

Combe Breeze *Bob Buckler* 67b
3 b f Multiplex Flawspar (Montjoy (USA))
2583^{5}

Combustible Kate (IRE) *Nick Kent* 105h 85c
9 b m Mr Combustible(IRE) Aussie Hope (Gran Alba (USA))
183^{3} 493^{3} 782^{2} 1813^{4} 1972^{3} **2303^{P} 2811^{P} 5442^{P}**

Comedinewithme *I M Mason* 109h 109c
7 b m Milan Skipcarl (IRE) (Carlingford Castle)
4558^{2}

Comedy House *Michael Madgwick* 76h
7 b g Auction House(USA) Kyle Akin (Vettori (IRE))
451^{11} 673^{4} 1596^{9} 5067^{11}

Comehomequietly (IRE) *Paul Hamer* 69h 82c
11 bb g King's Theatre(IRE) Windswept Lady (IRE) (Strong Gale)
5399^{8}

Come On Annie *Alexandra Dunn* 118h 119c
9 b m Karinga Bay Irish Ferry (Overbury (IRE))
162^{2}

Comeonbonny *Katie Scott* 84b
6 ch m Common World(USA) Burnaby Belle (IRE) (Elnadim (USA))
1591^{0}

Comeonginger (IRE) *Chris Gordon* 114h 130c
8 b g King's Theatre(IRE) Miss Poutine (FR) (Chamberlin (FR))
1755^{6} 2153^{P} 3014^{2} 3524^{4} 4363^{P} 4625^{4}

Come On Harriet *Alex Hales* 94h
6 b m Kayf Tara Royal Musical (Royal Abjar (USA))
130^{4} **524^{P}**

Come On Laurie (IRE) *Oliver Sherwood* 106h 123c
7 b g Oscar(IRE) Megan's Magic (Blue Ocean (USA))
2001^{4} 2853^{6}

Come On Sunshine *Brian Ellison* 104h
4 b g Authorized(IRE) Tagula Sunrise (IRE) (Tagula (IRE))
1369^{7} 1600^{P} 1794^{7} 2595^{P}

Come On You (IRE) *N Pearce* 97c
7 ch g Presenting Dreamy Run (IRE) (Commanche Run)
13^{P}

Come To The Party (IRE) *Harry Chisman* 100b
12 b g Taipan(IRE) Iron Mariner (IRE) (Mandalus)
2081^{P} 2658^{P} 2833^{P}

Come Up And See Me *J R Jenkins*
3 b g Cockney Rebel(IRE) Sakhacity (Sakhee (USA))
1984^{4}

Comical Red *Mark Gillard* 92h 52c
7 ch g Sulamani(IRE) Sellette (IRE) (Selkirk (USA))
148^{P} 2454^{12} 3369^{6} 3914^{4} 4349^{8} 4682^{4} 5165^{P} **5357^{P}**

Commissioned (IRE) *John Ferguson* 154h
5 b g Authorized(IRE) Zelda (IRE) (Caerleon (USA))
(850) 1039^{7} 1333^{2} 1657^{P} 2334^{3} 4717^{13}

Commitment *Neil Mulholland* 124h 125c
6 b g Motivator Courting (Pursuit Of Love)
430^{3} ◆ (829) 1112^{4} 1268^{7} 1701^{P}

Common Practice (IRE) *Jonjo O'Neill* 90h
4 b g Gold Well Satalda (IRE) (Satco (FR))
1003^{5} 5220^{8} 5434^{7}

Compadre (IRE) *Jonjo O'Neill* 116b
4 b g Yeats(IRE) Jolivia (FR) (Dernier Empereur (USA))
(2440) 4721^{17}

Company Of Ring (IRE) *P Favero* 112c
4 b g Windsor Knot(IRE) Diamond Soles (IRE) (Danetime (IRE))
1672a^{6}

Competition *Brian Rothwell* 97b
3 b g Multiplex Compolina (Compton Place)
4867^{2}

Competitive Edge (IRE) *Conor O'Dwyer* 124h 138c
8 b g Presenting Sanghasta (IRE) (Un Desperado (FR))
2236a^{13}

Comragh (IRE) *Jeremy Scott* 104h
5 br m Desert King(IRE) Akica (IRE) (Oscar (IRE))
(2428) 4320^{7}

Comte D'Anjou *Johnny Farrelly* 73h
6 b g Desert King(IRE) Delayed (FR) (Fijar Tango (FR))
4541^{6} 5382^{P}

Conas Taoi (IRE) *Paul Morgan* 90h 129c
6 b g Exit To Nowhere(USA) Zudika (IRE) (Ezzoud (IRE))
209^{4} 569^{3} **(807) 1326^{4} (1678) (1813) 2057^{U} (2272) (2366) (2887) 5274^{2} (5456)**

Coney Choice (IRE) *Lady Jane Gillespie* 107h 65c
7 br g Strategic Choice(USA) Coney Ficial (IRE) (Beneficial)
872^{4}

Coneygree *Mark Bradstock* 148h 178c
8 b g Karinga Bay Plaid Maid (IRE) (Executive Perk)
(2372)

Coney Island (IRE) *Edward P Harty* 148h
4 b g Flemensfirth(USA) Millys Gesture (IRE) (Milan)
4004a^{5} (5024a)

Conigre *G E Burton* 84b
8 b g Selkirk(USA) Mystify (Batshoof)
298^{P}

Coniston Cold *Michael Easterby* 71h
3 b g Captain Rio Returning (Bob's Return (IRE))
4417^{6}

Connetable (FR) *Paul Nicholls* 135h
3 b g Saint Des Saints(FR) Montbresia (FR) (Video Rock (FR))
3730^{2} (3989) 4764^{11} 5325^{11}

Connies Cross (IRE) *Mrs Sheila Crow* 129c
8 b g Windsor Castle Rock-On Beauty (IRE) (Mister Lord (USA))
17^{3} 533^{2} 4249^{P}

Conquer Gold (IRE) *Nicky Richards* 107h
5 b m Gold Well Ballinamona Wish (IRE) (Kotashaan (FR))
3060^{2} 3666^{2} (5367)

Conquisto *Brian Ellison* 138h 150c
10 ch g Hernando(FR) Seal Indigo (IRE) (Glenstal (USA))
1040^{9} 1185a^{4} 1481^{3} ◆ 1658^{P}

Conserve (IRE) *Neil King* 74h
5 b m Duke Of Marmalade(IRE) Minor Point (Selkirk (USA))
222^{9}

Consortium (IRE) *Neil King* 102h
3 b g Teofilo(IRE) Wish List (IRE) (Mujadil (USA))
1732^{2} 1768^{2} 2371^{3} 3039^{5} 5116^{8}

Consul De Thaix (FR) *Nicky Henderson* 131h
3 b g Loxias(FR) Mange De Thaix (FR) (Mont Basile (FR))
3848^{3} 4764^{10}

Consult *Alan Phillips* 4h
8 ch g Dr Fong(USA) Merle (Selkirk (USA))
1656

Contempt Of Court (IRE) *Mark Pitman* 97h
6 b g Milan Moss Artiste (IRE) (Beneficial)
1873^{5} 2257^{P} 2699^{5} 2995^{P} 3664^{P}

Cooking Fat *Dianne Sayer* 119h
4 ch g Tobougg(IRE) Ostfanni (IRE) (Spectrum (IRE))
1369^{5} 1776^{2} 2027^{6} 2594^{9} 2949^{6}

Cooladerry King (IRE) *Mrs Sheila Crow* 106b 118c
7 b g King Cheetah(USA) Daly Lady (IRE) (Lord Of Appeal)
60^{P} 4426^{5} 5158^{3} 5399^{3}

Coolanure (IRE) *Kenny Johnson* 93h 79c
6 b m Portrait Gallery(IRE) Aiguille (IRE) (Lancastrian)
454^{5} 639^{U} 731^{8}

Cool Baranca (GER) *Dianne Sayer* 111h
9 b m Beat Hollow Cool Storm (IRE) (Rainbow Quest (USA))
3024 (711) 1034^{3} 1638^{5} 2326^{3} 3065^{6} 3346^{9} 5414^{8}

Cool Bob (IRE) *Matt Sheppard* 78h 90c
12 b g Bob Back(USA) Rosie Jaques (Doyoun)
1306^{9} 1825^{3} (2037)

Cool Chief *Alan Blackmore* 28h
6 b g Sleeping Indian Be Bop Aloha (Most Welcome)
125^{P}

Coole Charmer (IRE) *Nicky Henderson* 75h
6 ch g Flemensfirth(USA) Ericas Charm (Alderbrook)
2514^{11} 3403^{9} 4463^{6}

Cool Fusion *Anthony Day* 71h
6 b m Beat All(USA) Fusion Of Tunes (Mr Confusion (IRE))
61^{P} 238^{8} 462^{8} 1691^{P}

Cool George *Jackie Du Plessis* 111b
7 b g Pastoral Pursuits Magic Valentine (Magic Ring (IRE))
2988^{P}

Coolking *Chris Gordon* 115h 117c
8 b g King's Theatre(IRE) Osocool (Teenoso (USA))
2149^{7} 2955^{P} 3349^{P} 3771^{8} (4349) (4783) **4935^{P}**

Cool Macavity (IRE) *Nicky Henderson* 133h
7 b g One Cool Cat(USA) Cause Celebre (IRE) (Peintre Celebre (USA))
7a^{24} 1482^{3} (1591)

Coolmill (IRE) *D F O'Shea* 129h
8 b g Cloudings(IRE) Beneverse (IRE) (Beneficial)
2525a^{P}

Coologue (IRE) *Charlie Longsdon* 122h 145c
6 b g Helissio(FR) Scolboa (IRE) (Bob's Return (IRE))
(2122) 2774^{3} 3040^{2} 3860^{2} 4458^{2} 5217^{P}

Cool Runnings (IRE) *Tim Fitzgerald* 95h
5 gr g Dalakhani(IRE) Aguinaga (IRE) (Machiavellian (USA))
181^{4}

Cool Sky *Ian Williams* 122h
6 b g Millkom Intersky High (USA) (Royal Anthem (USA))
1868^{3}

Cool Star (IRE) *Maurice Barnes* 43h 116c
9 b g One Cool Cat(USA) Pack Ice (USA) (Wekiva Springs (USA))
78^{U} (731) (841) 1032^{6} 1329^{9} **1496^{P}**

Coombe Hill *Chris Honour* 120c
14 b g Prince Daniel(USA) Betty Ann Pit VII (Damsire Unregistered)
15^{P}

Cooper *Kevin Ryan* 107h
3 b g Sir Percy Blossom (Warning)
(1456) 1656^{4} (2170) 2921^{U}

Cooper's Friend (IRE) *Charlie Longsdon* 113h 114c
6 b g Kayf Tara Graphic Lady (IRE) (Phardante (FR))
590^{2} ◆ (1597) 1925^{5} 2548^{4} 3146^{P}

Coo Star Sivola (FR) *Nick Williams* 133h
3 b g Assessor(IRE) Santorine (FR) (Della Francesca (USA))
2480^{2} ◆ 3519^{3} ◆ 4720^{3}

Cootamundra (IRE) *J A Berry* 128h 129c
12 ch g Broken Hearted Sigginstown (Kambalda)
95a^{7}

Coote Street (IRE) *Iain Jardine*
7 b g Winged Love(IRE) Unknown Quality (Sabrehill (USA))
1011^{P} **2067^{P}**

Coozan George *Malcolm Jefferson* 99h 109c
6 b g Bollin Eric Pasja (IRE) (Posen (USA))
2558^{5} 2841^{3} **3834^{3} ◆ 4984^{3} 5244^{3}**

Copain De Classe (FR) *Paul Nicholls* 72h
3 b g Enrique Toque Rouge (FR) (Loup Solitaire (USA))
2757^{F}

Coppelia (IRE) *Nicky Richards* 77h
7 gr m Baryshnikov(AUS) Jerusala (IRE) (Religiously (USA))
656^{10} 799^{9} 960^{7} 1171^{5} 1420^{5}

Copper Birch (IRE) *Evan Williams* 118h 113c
7 ch g Beneficial Givehertime (IRE) (Commanche Run)
439^{5} 553^{5} 2366^{3} 2638^{7} 4267^{P} 4612^{3} 5052^{U} 5265^{4}

Copperfacejack (IRE) *Paul Webber* 96h 96c
5 b g Robin Des Pres(FR) Leone Des Pres (FR) (Tip Moss (FR))
1824^{3} 2410^{4} 2861^{P} 5377^{8}

Copper Kay *Philip Hobbs* 118b
5 b m Kayf Tara Presenting Copper (IRE) (Presenting)
(1843) ◆ (2486) 4623^{6} 5180^{4}

Coppice Lad *Ken Wingrove*
6 b g Thethingaboutitis(USA) Coppice Lane (Sula Bula)
3388^{P}

Copt Hill *Tracy Waggott* 86h
7 b g Avonbridge Lalique (IRE) (Lahib (USA))
2982^{10} 3244^{3} 3807^{3} 4049^{3} 4297^{4} 4513^{2} 4943^{4}

Coral Queen *Peter Niven* 71b
4 b m Desideratum Queen's Lodge (IRE) (Grand Lodge (USA))
970^{9}

Cordey Warrior *Victor Dartnall* 72b
5 b g Tobougg(IRE) Aquavita (Kalaglow)
2493^{11} 3111^{5}

Cork Citizen *David Pipe* 132c
7 b g Overbury(IRE) Peach Of A Citizen (IRE) (Anshan)
3918^{2} ◆ 4367^{U} 4684^{4}

Cornas (NZ) *Nick Williams* 79h 117c
12 b g Prized(USA) Duvessa (NZ) (Sound Reason (CAN))
1223a^{7}

Cornborough *Mark Walford* 116h
4 ch g Sir Percy Emirates First (IRE) (In The Wings)
(2189) 2931^{3}

Corner Creek (IRE) *Michael Scudamore* 104h
5 b g Presenting No Moore Bills (Nicholas Bill)
2023^{4}

Cornish Beau (IRE) *Dr Richard Newland* 94h
8 ch g Pearl Of Love(IRE) Marimar (IRE) (Grand Lodge (USA))
537^{5} 695^{4} (918) 977^{U} 1182^{5} 1244^{5} 1524^{8}

Cornish Warrior (IRE) *Rebecca Curtis* 62b
4 b g Oscar(IRE) Ballylooby Moss (IRE) (Supreme Leader)
2351^{8}

Correlate *John Wade* 48b
5 ch g Zamindar(USA) Snow Blossom (Beat Hollow)
257^{P} 459^{11}

Corrin Wood (IRE) *Donald McCain* 107h 146c
8 gr g Garuda(IRE) Allstar Rose (IRE) (Fourstars Allstar (USA))
3737^{8} **4205^{P} 4735^{11} 5193^{P}**

Corscia (FR) *G Macaire* 130h 130c
4 b m Nickname(FR) Cardamine (FR) (Garde Royale)
4960a^{5}

Cor Wot An Apple *Colin Tizzard* 97h
4 b g Apple Tree(FR) Chipewyas (FR) (Bering)
67^{7} 644^{4} 2460^{9} 3085^{P} 3450^{P} 4409^{4} 4917^{6}

Cosmic Diamond *Paul Webber* 77h
5 b m Multiplex Lucy Glitters (Ardross)
2302^{14} 2776^{7} 3066^{6} 4878^{10}

Cosmic King (FR) *Richard Phillips* 84b
3 b g Kingsalsa(USA) Kikinda (FR) (Daliapour (IRE))
4488^{13}

Cosmic Statesman *Richard Fahey* 104h
3 ch g Halling(USA) Cosmic Case (Casteddu)
2718^{2} ◆ 3099^{3}

Cosmic Tigress *John Quinn* 97h
4 b m Tiger Hill(IRE) Cosmic Case (Casteddu)
1334^{4} 1684^{3} ◆ 2066^{6} (2752)

Costante Via (IRE) *Dominic Ffrench Davis* 98b
4 b m Milan Spirit Rock (IRE) (Rock Hopper)
3907^{3} 4687^{3}

Cosway Spirit (IRE) *Ben Pauling* 83h 107c
8 ch g Shantou(USA) Annalisa (IRE) (Rhoman Rule (USA))
239^{2} 1813^{P}

Cotillion *Ian Williams* 131h
9 b g Sadler's Wells(USA) Riberac (Efisio)
(3314) (3417) 3728^{2} (4105) (4273)

Cotswold Road *Colin Tizzard* 108h
5 b g Flemensfirth(USA) Crystal Ballerina (IRE) (Sadler's Wells (USA))
2650^{3} 2986^{3} 3413^{4} 4096^{10} 4860^{8}

Cottage Oak (IRE) *J J O'Shea* 119b 119c
12 ch g Flemensfirth(USA) Native Thistle (IRE) (Ovac (ITY))
18^{2}

Cottersrock (IRE) *Martin Keighley* 140h
5 b g Robin Des Pres(FR) Toasted Oats (IRE) (Be My Native (USA))
3839^{2} ◆ 4323^{2} (5391)

Cotton King *Graham Mays* 79h
8 b g Dubawi(IRE) Spinning The Yarn (Barathea (IRE))
61^{8} 401^{4} 671^{7}

Cottonwool Baby (IRE) *Michael Scudamore* 98h
4 b m Gold Well Golden Steppes (IRE) (Titus Livius (FR))
831^{7} 4881^{6} 5389^{6}

Cottstown Fox (IRE) *Neil Mulholland* 96h
6 ch g Bandari(IRE) Cottstown Belle (IRE) (Flemensfirth (USA))
2731^{7} 3117^{4}

Cougar Kid (IRE) *Philip Hide* 106h
4 b g Yeats(IRE) Western Skylark (IRE) (Westerner)
601^{6} 2065^{10} 2683^{6} 3083^{8} 3660^{9} 3915^{7}

Cougar's Gold (IRE) *Peter Bowen* 107b
4 b g Oscar(IRE) Top Her Up (IRE) (Beneficial)
3522^{6} 4308^{5} 5330^{4}

Counterfeiter *Martin Bosley* 109h
5 b g Singspiel(IRE) Grain Of Truth (Gulch (USA))
3418^{4} 5091^{4}

Countersign *Charles Pogson* 113h
6 b g Authorized(IRE) Circle Of Love (Sakhee (USA))
(353) 620^{6} 1308^{0} 1660^{4}

Count Guido Deiro (IRE) *Nigel Twiston-Davies* 135h 137c
8 b g Accordion Ivy Lane (IRE) (Be My Native (USA))
2367^{2} **2916^{P}** (4112) **4802^{F}**

Count Meribel *Nigel Twiston-Davies* 93b
3 ch c Three Valleys(USA) Bakhtawar (IRE) (Lomitas)
5151^{5}

Country'N'Western (FR) *David Elsworth* 108b
3 b g Samum(GER) Cracking Melody (Shamardal (USA))
(2216)

Count Salazar (IRE) *Andy Turnell* 128h 124c
10 b g Revoque(IRE) Cherry Sent (IRE) (Presenting)
358^{5} 1002^{8} (1181) (1264) **1332^{2}** 1503^{3}

Coup De Grace (IRE) *Pat Phelan* 119h 49c
6 b g Elusive City(USA) No Way (IRE) (Rainbows For Life (CAN))
2485^{9} **3042^{5}** 3994^{5} 4782^{9}

Coup De Pinceau (FR) *Paul Nicholls* 106b
3 b g Buck's Boum(FR) Castagnette III (FR) (Tin Soldier I (FR))
(5400) ◆

Court Baloo (IRE) *Alistair Whillans* 84h
4 b g Court Cave(IRE) Tremplin (IRE) (Tremblant)
206^{5} 459^{8} 753^{3} 2931^{6} 3436^{5} 3668^{8}

Court By Surprise (IRE) *Emma Lavelle* 125h 145c
10 b g Beneficial Garryduff Princess (IRE) (Husyan (USA))
1871^{2} 3860^{P} 5119^{7}

Court Challenge (IRE) *Shane Crawley* 120h
6 b m Court Cave(IRE) Legal Challenge (IRE) (Strong Gale)
4653a^{3}

Court Dismissed (IRE) *Donald McCain* 116h 122c
5 b g Court Cave(IRE) Carramanagh Lady (IRE) (Anshan)
332^{2} **1922^{4} 2293^{2} 2857^{5} 3235^{2} 4046^{4} (4420) 5084^{3}**

Court Finale *Peter Purdy*
14 ch g One Voice(USA) Tudor Sunset (Sunyboy)
595^{P}

Courting Harry *Sarah-Jayne Davies* 51b
4 b g Lucarno(USA) Harry's Bride (Sir Harry Lewis (USA))
4357^{7} 5040^{8}

Court Jester (IRE) *S Wilson* 111h
9 b g Pushkin(IRE) Noeleens Delight (IRE) (Le Bavard (FR))
4943^{P}

Court King (IRE) *Peter Bowen* 97h
4 b g Indian River(FR) Eliza Everett (IRE) (Meneval (USA))
4445 2317^{9} 2904^{6} 3077^{5} 3516^{9} 4030^{P}

Courtlands Prince *Neil Mulholland* 85h
6 b g Presenting Bathwick Annie (Sula Bula)
2396^{P} 3023^{P} 5267^{5}

Court Minstrel (IRE) *Evan Williams* 155h 155c
8 b g Court Cave(IRE) Theatral (Orchestra)
850^{9} 1039^{16} (1333) (1848) 2634^{2} 5177^{4} 5495^{6}

Courtncatcher (IRE) *Patrick J Duffy* 142h 122c
8 b g Catcher In The Rye(IRE) Tapneiram (IRE) (Kahyasi)
96a^{22} 231a^{12}

Court Of Law (IRE) *Donald McCain* 105h 102c
7 b g Court Cave(IRE) Divine Dancer (IRE) (Carmelite House (USA))
726^{8} 1086^{7} **1380^{3} 1496^{2} (1614) 1891^{2} 2037^{U} 2297^{5} 2844^{3}** 3140^{6} **3683^{F} 4034^{4} 4325^{5} 5234^{4}**

Courtown Oscar (IRE) *Philip Kirby* 119h 134c
6 b g Oscar(IRE) Courtown Bowe VII (Damsire Unregistered)
(150) 2028^{P} (2800) **(2922) ◆ 3520^{P} 4054^{3} (4286) ◆ 4802^{P}**

Court Red Handed (IRE) *Mrs S Case* 92b 120c
10 ch g Flemensfirth(USA) Desert Gail (IRE) (Desert Style (IRE))
295^{R}

Cousin Guillaume (FR) *Donald McCain* 103h 111c
6 bb g Kapgarde(FR) Tante Zoe (FR) (Danzero (AUS))
1054^{3} 1139^{2} 1307^{7}

Cousin Khee *Hughie Morrison* 132h 128c
8 b g Sakhee(USA) Cugina (Distant Relative)
(1549) (1602) 1848^{15} **2684^{3}** 4482^{7} 5185^{5}

Cove Lodge *Richard Woollacott* 72b
5 b g Sakhee's Secret Limonia (GER) (Perugino (USA))
2875[4] 4296[8]

Cover Story (FR) *L Godard*
8 b m Okawango(USA) Julia's Dance (IRE) (Alhaarth (IRE))
1223a[3]

Cowards Close (IRE) *Chris Gordon* 119h 133c
8 br g Presenting Parsee (IRE) (Persian Mews)
1849[4] 2089[P] 2899[P] 4232[4] 4595[6] 5247[P]

Cowslip *George Moore* 125h
6 b m Tobougg(IRE) Forsythia (Most Welcome)
319[3] 705[2] 1856[5] 2081[7] 2624[11] 3025[P]

Coxwell Crofter *Jimmy Fox*
7 b g Kirkwall Coxwell Quick Step (Balinger)
378[P]

Coyoacan (FR) *Warren Greatrex* 76b
3 b g Al Namix(FR) Jetty Dancer (FR) (Smadoun (FR))
5069[7]

Crack Away Jack *Emma Lavelle* 135h 124c
11 ch g Gold Away(IRE) Jolly Harbour (Rudimentary (USA))
681[2]

Crackdeloust (FR) *Brian Ellison* 103b
3 b g Daramsar(FR) Magic Rose (FR) (Manninamix)
2629[2]

Cracked Rear View (IRE) *Kim Bailey* 112h
5 gr g Portrait Gallery(IRE) Trip To Knock (Be My Chief (USA))
2978[3] (4473) 4839[P]

Cracking Find (IRE) *Henry Daly* 84b
4 b g Robin Des Pres(FR) Crack The Kicker (IRE) (Anshan)
341[9]

Crack Of Thunder (IRE) *Charlie Longsdon* 110h 107c
6 b g September Storm(GER) Keep Hunting (IRE) (Nestor)
(108) **2039[4] 2566[P]** 3220[P] **4879[4]**

Crack On Tom (IRE) *Emma Lavelle* 85h
6 ch g Great Exhibition(USA) Nordic Cloud (IRE) (Lure (USA))
4198[P] 5070[4]

Craftybird *Denis Quinn* 85h
4 ch m Mastercraftsman(IRE) Tobaranama (IRE) (Sadler's Wells (USA))
3417[P]

Crafty Power (IRE) *Sabrina J Harty* 130h
4 gr g Mastercraftsman(IRE) Gali Gal (IRE) (Galileo (IRE))
4955a[8]

Crafty Roberto *Alex Hales* 120h 121c
7 ch g Intikhab(USA) Mowazana (IRE) (Galileo (IRE))
2151[4] 2648[4] 3042[3] 3589[U] 3742[4] 4642[3] 5103[3]

Craic (FR) *P-J Fertillet*
4 b g Creachadoir(IRE) Rockette (FR) (Ange Gabriel (FR))
5385a[6]

Craiganboy (IRE) *S R B Crawford* 120h
6 b g Zagreb(USA) Barnish River (IRE) (Riverhead (USA))
285[9] 3436[F] 3743[7] 4403[2] 4580[2] 5295[P]

Craiganee (IRE) *Chris Down* 106h
8 b g Craigsteel Hows She Going (IRE) (Strong Statement (USA))
1819[4] 2087[5] 2871[5] 3414[2] 4250[2] 5034[5]

Craigdancer (IRE) *Joanne Foster* 89h
6 b g Craigsteel Green Sea (Groom Dancer (USA))
(522) 838[2] 1067[P] (1368) 1683[3] 2296[P]

Crank Em Up (IRE) *David Dennis* 114b
4 b g Royal Anthem(USA) Carrawaystick (IRE) (Old Vic)
3959[2] 4385[2] (5144)

Crannaghmore Boy (IRE) *Mrs J Butler* 111b
10 b g Pilsudski(IRE) Glencairn Mist (IRE) (Roselier (FR))
5150[P]

Crashing Thew Life *Sheena West* 69h
5 b g Tobougg(IRE) Kalmina (USA) (Rahy (USA))
749[4] 3083[9]

Crazy (GER) *David Dennis* 74h
6 b m Nicaron(GER) Chato's Girl (GER) (Chato (USA))
3930[7] 4538[3]

Crazy Diamond *Miss J Mckie* 99c
11 b g Silver Patriarch(IRE) Your Punishment (IRE) (Montelimar (USA))
80[9]

Crazy Jack (IRE) *Kim Bailey* 125h 128c
7 b g Royal Anthem(USA) Cindy's Fancy (IRE) (Shernazar)
(1648) 1903[3] 2513[9] 3137[10] 3465[2] 4824[P]

Crazy Jane (IRE) *Tom Gretton* 62h 49c
6 br m Definite Article Blue Romance (IRE) (Bob Back (USA))
3382[P]

Crazy Penguin (IRE) *Charlie Longsdon* 95b
4 b g Milan Lady Appeal (IRE) (Phardante (FR))
2020[3] ◆ 2636[7] 5143[8]

Crazy Queen *Anthony Carson* 68b
3 ch f Le Fou(IRE) Queen Of Norway (USA) (Woodman (USA))
3118[3]

Crazy Train *Robert Walford* 70h
6 ch m Sir Harry Lewis(USA) Vent D'Aout (IRE) (Imp Society (USA))
4881[7] 5373[8]

Createur (IRE) *Tim Vaughan* 107h
4 b g Muhtathir Cracovie (Caerleon (USA))
566[4] 1065[3] 1305[5] 1823[2] 2253[6]

Credit Crunched (IRE) *Miss L Thomas*
10 ch g Humbel(USA) Owenageera (IRE) (Riot Helmet)
14[P]

Creepy (IRE) *Martin Keighley* 114h 147c
7 b g Westerner Prowler (IRE) (Old Vic)
1617[3] 2341[P]

Creevytennant (IRE) *Fergal O'Brien* 151c
11 b g Bob's Return(IRE) Northwood May (Teenoso (USA))
2809[4] 3448[P] 5119[9]

Cresswell Breeze *Anthony Honeyball* 130h 137c
5 b m Midnight Legend Cresswell Willow (IRE) (Witness Box (USA))
2313[2] (2602) 3122[3] 4251[2] 4647[2] 5281[F]

Cresswell Prince (IRE) *Claire Dyson* 102b
5 b g Bienamado(USA) Faraday Lady (IRE) (Lord Americo)
3226[8]

Crest *Gordon Elliott* 114h
4 b g Kayf Tara Maiden Voyage (Slip Anchor)
4955a[10]

Crickel Wood (FR) *Charlie Longsdon* 121h
5 b g Muhtathir Tanguista (FR) (War Chant (USA))
1612[3] 1979[4] (2271) 2617[F] 4875[2]

Crimson Ark (IRE) *Emma Lavelle* 119h
5 b g Arcadio(GER) Crimson Flower (IRE) (Soviet Lad (USA))
1484[3] 1645[4] (1968) 4788[4] 5185[8]

Crin Au Vent (FR) *Paul Nicholls* 110h
3 b g Laveron Tentative (FR) (Blushing Flame (USA))
3955[4]

Crinkle Crags (IRE) *Nicky Richards* 102h
5 ch g Trans Island Ashanti Dancer (IRE) (Dancing Dissident (USA))
456[4] 2029[10] 2649[5] 3474[11] 4178[11]

Criq Rock (FR) *Alan King* 123b
4 ch g Kap Rock(FR) Criquetot (FR) (Epervier Bleu)
(2126) (2636) 4364[5] 4721[14]

Croan Rock (IRE) *R A Owen* 107h 103c
11 b g Milan Fiddlers Bar (IRE) (Un Desperado (FR))
5458[4]

Crockery *Dan Skelton* 103h
5 b m Croco Rouge(IRE) Always Forgiving (Commanche Run)
2270[4] 2644[7] 4097[8] 4303[11] 5246[5]

Crockett *Noel Wilson* 62h
4 b g Rail Link Tarocchi (USA) (Affirmed (USA))
3470[9]

Croco Bay (IRE) *Ben Case* 118h 161c
8 b g Croco Rouge(IRE) April Thistle (IRE) (Alphabatim (USA))
1777[3] 2511[6] 4204[4] **4770[F] 5179[5]**

Croco Mister (IRE) *Rosemary Gasson* 95c
6 ch g Croco Rouge(IRE) Nimrods Dream (IRE) (Orchestra)
(806) 1053[3] 1155[3] 1978[4]

Cro Easy (USA) *P Dubois*
4 gr g Rock Hard Ten(USA) Pahlmuhree (USA) (Gone West (USA))
4401a[4]

Crofton Trail (IRE) *Patrick Griffin* 55h
6 b m Heron Island(IRE) Raishah (GER) (Motley (USA))
957[F] 1165[7]

Crookofdevon *Jean McGregor* 1b
6 b g Desideratum Blue Morning (Balnibarbi)
2106[8]

Crookstown (IRE) *Ben Case* 124h 139c
6 b g Rudimentary(USA) Millview Lass (IRE) (Jurado (USA))
1847 2373[4] 2775[2] 3045[4] 3487[8] 4353[6] 4913[7]

Cropley (IRE) *Dai Burchell* 93h
6 gr g Galileo(IRE) Niyla (IRE) (Darshaan)
4440[4] 5067[F] (5355)

Cross Appeal (IRE) *Noel Meade* 121h 127c
9 b g Cape Cross(IRE) Hadeb (Unfuwain (USA))
92a[P]

Crosshare *Lawney Hill*
4 b g Crosspeace(IRE) Perecapa (IRE) (Archway (IRE))
4880[18]

Crosslanes (IRE) *Chris Bealby* 71h
4 b m Brian Boru Threecrossmammies (IRE) (Be My Native (USA))
834[6] 932[8] 1109[7] 1374[8]

Crosspark *Caroline Bailey* 123h
5 b g Midnight Legend Blue Shannon (IRE) (Be My Native (USA))
(2558) 2838[3] 3728[P] 4305[6]

Cross To Boston (IRE) *Sue Smith* 84h 89c
9 b g Oscar(IRE) Collopy's Cross (Pragmatic)
2040[3] 2402[3] 4419[4]

Crowd Control (IRE) *Lady Susan Brooke* 102h
6 b g Oscar(IRE) Apollo Lady (Alflora (IRE))
3467[7] 3570[5] 4264[P] 4442[7]

Crown And Glory (IRE) *Chris Fairhurst* 83h 100c
8 b g Turtle Island(IRE) Monteleena (IRE) (Montelimar (USA))
4938[10] (5080) 5350[3]

Crown Theatre (IRE) *Henry De Bromhead* 119h 134c
6 b g King's Theatre(IRE) Palesa's Legacy (IRE) (Montelimar (USA))
2635[4]

Cruachan (IRE) *Lucy Normile* 97h
6 b g Authorized(IRE) Calico Moon (USA) (Seeking The Gold (USA))
2429[3] ◆ 2980[7] 4163[4] 4638[4] 5089[4]

Cruchain (IRE) *Dai Burchell* 117h 121c
12 ch g Shernazar Mack Tack (IRE) (Shardari)
470[4] 750[P] (1070) 1418[4] 1641[5] 4493[F] 4884[6] 5465[4]

Cruiseaweigh (IRE) *Tom George* 106b
4 b g Oscar(IRE) Triptoshan (IRE) (Anshan)
5358[2] ◆

Cruise In Style (IRE) *Kevin Bishop* 106h 106c
9 b m Definite Article Henrietta Street (IRE) (Royal Academy (USA))
383[3] (515) 718[U] 1048[4] (1323) 1454[2] (1525) 1647[4] (2006) **2168[5]** 2734[17]

Cruising Bye *Gary Hanmer* 67h 108c
9 b g Alflora(IRE) Althrey Flame (IRE) (Torus)
4713[3]

Cry Fury *Sophie Leech* 105h
7 b g Beat Hollow Cantanta (Top Ville (IRE))
1234[5] 1379[4] ◆ 4650[6] 4965[8] 5223[8] 5464[5]

Crystal Earth (IRE) *Peter Fahey* 122h
8 b m Muhtarram(USA) Dochas (IRE) (King's Theatre (IRE))
1150a[2]

Cucklington *Colin Tizzard* 102h
4 b g Kayf Tara Ardrom (Ardross)
1872[8] 4296[3] 4614[6] 5269[5]

Cue Card *Colin Tizzard* 152h 180c
9 b g King's Theatre(IRE) Wicked Crack (IRE) (King's Ride)
22a[4] (2200) (2642) (3231) 4767[F] (5176)

Cuil Rogue (IRE) *Nicky Richards* 102h
7 b g Presenting Coolshamrock (IRE) (Buckskin (FR))
5450[10]

Cul Dealga (IRE) *Chris Bealby* 101h
6 b m Kalanisi(IRE) Yes Boss (IRE) (Carlingford Castle)
212[3] 1971[5] **2749[U] 3864[P]**

Cully Mac (IRE) *Andrew Wilson* 56h
4 b g Coroner(IRE) Catch Those Kisses (Deploy)
4208[6]

Culm Counsellor *Chris Down* 78h
6 ch g Erhaab(USA) Miss Counsel (Leading Counsel (USA))
1822[4] 2091[8] 2258[9] 4343[P] 4886[10] 5181[P]

Cultivator *Nicky Henderson* 109b
4 b g Alflora(IRE) Angie Marinie (Sabrehill (USA))
(2188) 4488[10]

Cultram Abbey *Nicky Richards* 123h 140c
8 br g Fair Mix(IRE) Kansas City (FR) (Lute Antique (FR))
2211[2] 2785[7] 3439[2] (3794) ◆ 4367[F] 4802[P] 5323[F]

Culture De Sivola (FR) *Nick Williams* 113h
3 b f Assessor(IRE) Neva De Sivola (FR) (Blushing Flame (USA))
1772[4] ◆ 2137[2] (2537) 2896[4] (4683) 5095[3]

Culworth Boy (IRE) *Sophie Leech* 52h
5 b g Tajraasi(USA) Cadre Idris (IRE) (College Chapel)
2035[6] 2267[12] 2689[13] 3221[P] 3816[P]

Cumbrian Farmer *Kenneth Slack* 79h
8 ch g Alflora(IRE) Quark Top (FR) (Perrault)
78[P] 522[4] 661[7] 870[3] 1400[6] 2703[P] (3402) 4415[4] 4557[3] 4942[5]

Cupachai *Dan Skelton* 57h
4 b g Indian Danehill(IRE) Chai (Lando (GER))
1797[5] 2091[7]

Cup Final (IRE) *Nicky Henderson* 146h
6 ch g Presenting Asian Maze (IRE) (Anshan)
(4017) ◆ 4730[P]

Cupid's Quest (IRE) *Susan Corbett* 81h
5 b f Jeremy(USA) Lovers Nest (Groom Dancer (USA))
3632[5] 4037[8] 4371[6] 4559[6] 5470[5]

Curious Carlos *Peter Bowen* 132h
6 b g Overbury(IRE) Classi Maureen (Among Men (USA))
(147) 316[2] (440) (1308) 5189[F] (5463)

Curragh Na Gold (IRE) *David Harry Kelly* 119h 119c
6 b m Gold Well Kirktonmoor Katie (IRE) (Rich Charlie)
3093a[6]

Curraigflemens (IRE) *David Kemp* 40b
7 b g Flemensfirth(USA) Curraig Monashee (IRE) (Monashee Mountain (USA))
293[P]

Current Event (FR) *Mrs Rose Loxton* 118h 132c
8 b g Muhtathir La Curamalal (IRE) (Rainbow Quest (USA))
(18) ◆ (393) 534[2] 4768[4] 5178[4]

Current Exchange (IRE) *Gordon Elliott* 119c
10 ch g Beneficial Musical Millie (IRE) (Orchestra)
4768[9] 5178[P]

Cushcapple (IRE) *Noel C Kelly* 77h
8 gr m Tikkanen(USA) Maccarrons Run (IRE) (Riberetto)
484[8]

Cusheen Bridge (IRE) *Charles Pogson* 130h
7 b g Oscar(IRE) One Hell Ofa Woman (IRE) (Fourstars Allstar (USA))
1100[8] (1377) 1719[8] (2042) 2485[3] 2926[7] 4070[P]

Cut The Corner (IRE) *Dr Richard Newland* 122h 134c
7 br g Vinnie Roe(IRE) Snipe Victory (IRE) (Old Vic)
(110) 418[2] ◆ 520[5] 701[2] 917[3] 1138[2] 1270[3] **1450[2] 1601[3] (1690) ◆ 1809[3]**

Cyclop (IRE) *David Dennis* 111h 133c
4 b g King's Theatre(IRE) Tasmani (FR) (Turgeon (USA))
2151[6] 2434[3] 2865[F] ◆ (2996) 3364[4] 3885[4] 4341[P] 4914[2]

Cygnet *Mickey Bowen* 116c
6 b g Dansili Ballet Princess (Muhtarram (USA))
(294) ◆ (506) 5150[F]

Cypress Grove (IRE) *John Ryall* 92h 59c
12 b g Windsor Castle Grecian Queen (Fairy King (USA))
66[7]

Cyrien Star *Henry Daly* 128h 123c
8 b g Bollin Eric Sainte Etoile (FR) (Saint Cyrien (FR))
(2149) (2848) 3836[7] 4649[P]

Cyril The Squirrel *Lawney Hill*
11 b g Cyrano De Bergerac All Done (Northern State (USA))
2409[P]

Cyrius Moriviere (FR) *Ben Pauling* 129h
5 b g Vendangeur(IRE) Sagesse Moriviere (FR) (Vaguely Pleasant (FR))
2152[P] 2646[2] (2928) 3447[P] (3835)

Cyrus Darius *Malcolm Jefferson* 153h 130c
6 b g Overbury(IRE) Barton Belle (Barathea (IRE))
(1636)

Dabadiyan (IRE) *Gary Moore* 61h
5 b g Zamindar(USA) Dabista (IRE) (Highest Honor (FR))
1425[P]

Dabinett Moon *Charlie Longsdon* 119c
7 b m Midnight Legend Miss Crabapple (Sunyboy)
(531) 1713[3] 2036[P] 2749[5]

Dabuki (FR) *Evan Williams* 56h
5 b g Desert Style(IRE) Semenova (FR) (Green Tune (USA))
554[7] 755[P]

Daddy's Favourite *Bill Turner* 14b
3 b g Hellvelyn Wavet (Pursuit Of Love)
3082[7]

Dadsintrouble (IRE) *Tim Vaughan* 116h
5 b g Presenting Gemini Lucy (IRE) (Glacial Storm (USA))
100[5] 279[4] (5148)

Daidaidai (FR) *Gary Moore* 92h
5 b g Lando(GER) Noble World (GER) (Winged Love (IRE))
104[7] 449[9]

Dainty Diva (IRE) *Jeremy Scott* 103h
7 b m Indian Danehill(IRE) She's So Dainty (IRE) (Great Commotion (USA))
237[5] 597[U] (2015) 2139[5] 2956[5] 3784[8] 4541[P] 5029[2] 5380[7]

Dais Return (IRE) *John Coombe* 109h 101c
11 b g Lahib(USA) Bayazida (Bustino)
774[8] 1113[P] 1375[P]

Daisy Back *Barry Brennan* 55h
7 b m Pasternak Ban Dubh (Syrtos)
111[P] 433[6]

Daisy's Gift (IRE) *W P Mullins* 140h
8 b m Presenting Daizinni (Dr Massini (IRE))
(1748a)

Daizy (IRE) *Hilary Parrott* 94h
6 ch g Presenting I Remember It Well (IRE) (Don't Forget Me)
451[6] (968) 1310[3]

Dakota Grey *Micky Hammond* 123h
4 gr g Fair Mix(IRE) Miss Sassi (Terimon)
2917[2] ◆ 3340[3] (4050) 4567[2] 4817[2]

Dalaki (IRE) *Des Donovan* 125h
4 b g Dalakhani(IRE) Lunda (IRE) (Soviet Star (USA))
3021[15] (3418) 3660[7]

Dalaman (IRE) *Tim Vaughan* 65h
4 b g Duke Of Marmalade(IRE) Crimphill (IRE) (Sadler's Wells (USA))
2417[P] 4108[5] 4821[6]

Dalby Spook (IRE) *Dianne Sayer* 82h
5 b m Jeremy(USA) Lamassu (IRE) (Entrepreneur)
843[5] 1683[4] 1892[5] 2427[6] 2670[5] 4297[5] 4513[6] 4904[5] 5199[3]

Daliance (IRE) *Noel Williams* 111h 101c
6 ch g Dalakhani(IRE) Everlasting Love (Pursuit Of Love)
2560[4] 2997[4] (3607) 3846[5] (4028) **4803[5] 5164[3]** 5479[5]

Dalia Pour Moi (FR) *Philip Hobbs* 123h
6 gr g Daliapour(IRE) Khariyada (FR) (Akarad (FR))
1901[2] ◆ 2450[5]

Dalkadam (FR) *J R Jenkins* 103h 112c
4 gr g Martaline Cadoudame (FR) (Cadoudal (FR))
3508[3] 4026[4] **4321[P] 4789[9] 4971[P]**

Dallas Cowboy (IRE) *Gordon Elliott* 126h 80c
5 b g Beneficial Watson River (IRE) (Presenting)
2672a[F]

Dalmo *K Kukk* 98h 80c
6 b g Dalakhani(IRE) Morina (USA) (Lyphard (USA))
236a[3] 740a[4] 844a[3] 985a[P] 5364a[3]

Dalstontosiloth (IRE) *Barry Murtagh* 87h
7 b g Gamut(IRE) The Boss's Dance (USA) (Sword Dance)
882[5] 1095[7] 1461[8]

Dalton Glance *Martin Keighley* 96b
5 b m Passing Glance Catzybaby (IRE) (Darazari (IRE))
4350[4] 5286[9]

Dame Doris *Lawney Hill* 55b
5 b m Westerner Ethel Smyth (Singspiel (IRE))
1758[9] 2277[16]

Damefirth (IRE) *Henry De Bromhead* 125h 121c
6 ch m Flemensfirth(USA) Dame Foraine (FR) (Raintrap)
1150a[3] 2058[3]

Damiens Dilemma (IRE) *Mrs L A Coltherd* 104c
7 b g Wareed(IRE) Olympos Belle (IRE) (Shahrastani (USA))
4016[P] 4180[4] 5258[2]

Damut (IRE) *Joseph Dullea* 137h
7 b g Gamut(IRE) Society Hunter (IRE) (Moscow Society (USA))
(2525a) 3169a[4]

Danandy (IRE) *Philip Hobbs* 120h 132c
8 b g Cloudings(IRE) Tower Princess (IRE) (King's Ride)
(1053) 2008[2]

Danby's Legend *Olly Williams*
8 b g Midnight Legend Miss Danbys (Charmer (IRE))
5313[P]

Dance *Rod Millman* 90h
6 b m Erhaab(USA) Shi Shi (Alnasr Alwasheek)
828[U] 892[7] 1823[8]

Dance And Romance *Tim Easterby* 77h
3 b f Kayf Tara Sweetheart (Sinndar (IRE))
3632[4] 3861[8] 4104[4] 4509[5] 4737[3]

Dance Floor King (IRE) *Nick Mitchell* 71h 136c
8 b g Generous(IRE) Strawberry Fool (FR) (Tel Quel (FR))
4355[P] 4787[F] 4918[5] 5354[P]

Dance In The Dust (IRE) *Jonjo O'Neill* 96h
4 b g Scorpion(IRE) Samotracia (IRE) (Rock Of Gibraltar (IRE))
4880[11]

Danceintothelight *Donald McCain* 110h 89c
8 gr g Dansili Kali (Linamix (FR))
(37) 522[U] 695[2] 802[4] **1370[F]** 1686[6] 1739[4] 1890[8] 2142[3] 2453[2] (3098) 3932[6] (4178) 4819[4] 5262[U]

Dance With Me (IRE) *Jonathan Geake* 12h
6 b g Danehill Dancer(IRE) Perpetual Time (Sadler's Wells (USA))
511[6]

Dancing Admiral *Anthony Carson* 62b
4 b g Kyllachy Dream Dance (Diesis)
753^{4}

Dancing Conquest *Seamus Mullins* 85b
5 bb m Imperial Dancer Another Conquest (El Conquistador)
5151^{6}

Dancing Dik *Steven Dixon* 97h 94c
10 b g Diktat Maureena (IRE) (Grand Lodge (USA))
31^{F} 450^{3} 752^{P} 1049^{4} 1236^{15} (1595) 1999^{2} 2255^{4} 2546^{6} 3088^{P} 5067^{10}

Dancing Dude (IRE) *Barry Leavy* 118h 94c
8 ch g Danehill Dancer(IRE) Wadud (Nashwan (USA))
86^{5} 340^{P}

Dancing Ecco (IRE) *Evan Williams* 75h 82c
6 b g Elnadim(USA) Ecco Mi (IRE) (Priolo (USA))
588^{7} ◆ 964^{P}

Dancing Meadows (IRE) *Gordon Elliott* 125h 89c
5 ch m Alhaarth(IRE) Kylebeg Dancer (IRE) (General Monash (USA))
881^{2} 2064^{4} 2176a^{4}

Dancing Shadow (IRE) *Victor Dartnall* 121h 124c
6 br g Craigsteel Be My Shadow (IRE) (Torus)
2442^{4} 2885^{2} 4234^{4} 4542^{P} 5432^{3}

Dandan (IRE) *Miss Francesca Moller* 107c
7 b g Zagreb(USA) Temporary Setback (IRE) (Moonax (IRE))
531^{P}

Dandridge *A L T Moore* 124h 147c
6 ch g Doyen(IRE) Arantxa (Sharpo)
(3857) 4770^{2} 5179^{2}

Dandy Duke (IRE) *Tom George* 111h
4 b g Duke Of Marmalade(IRE) Quest For Eternity (IRE) (Sadler's Wells (USA))
2559^{6} 2964^{2} ◆ (3489)

Danehills Well (IRE) *J P G Hamilton* 106h 64c
7 b g Indian Danehill(IRE) Collatrim Choice (IRE) (Saddlers' Hall (IRE))
421^{U} 726^{2} 5258^{5}

Daneking *W P Mullins* 142h 131c
6 b g Dylan Thomas(IRE) Sadie Thompson (IRE) (King's Best (USA))
96a^{9}

Dan Emmett (USA) *Michael Scudamore* 131h
5 ch g Flower Alley(USA) Singing Dixie (USA) (Dixieland Band (USA))
2275^{2} (2906) 3407^{7} 3824^{4} 4354^{2} 4794^{5}

Danielle's Journey *S R B Crawford* 115h
5 b m Presenting Harringay (Sir Harry Lewis (USA))
(4164) 4734^{12} 5470^{4}

Danimix (IRE) *Peter Bowen* 122h 140c
10 b g Dr Massini(IRE) Spring Blend (IRE) (Persian Mews)
1417^{3} (1733) (1871) 2082^{6} 2907^{P}

Danmurphysdoor (IRE) *Tim Vaughan* 95h
6 b g Definite Article Needle Doll (IRE) (Needle Gun (IRE))
145^{3} 397^{3} 1295^{3} 1405^{8} 2003^{P}

Dannanceys Hill (IRE) *Miss A Waugh* 101b
8 b g Revoque(IRE) Some Orchestra (IRE) (Orchestra)
457^{F}

Danny O'Ruairc (IRE) *James Moffatt* 71h
3 b c Fast Company(IRE) Tawoos (FR) (Rainbow Quest (USA))
1631^{8} 1899^{9} 2845^{8}

Danny The Dancer *Micky Hammond* 66b
5 ch g Indian Haven Invincible (Slip Anchor)
39^{6} 640^{4}

Dan's Quest *Robin Dickin* 91h
5 b g Kalanisi(IRE) Piedmont (UAE) (Jade Robbery (USA))
646^{6}

Dante's Way (IRE) *Malcolm Jefferson* 106h
6 b g Scorpion(IRE) Benedicta Rose (IRE) (Beneficial)
(145) 2401^{3} 4844^{3}

Danvinnie *Oliver Sherwood* 111h
6 b g Midnight Legend Top Gale (IRE) (Topanoora)
2312^{2} 3194^{P} 3863^{2} 4821^{4}

Daphiglote (FR) *Eugene Stanford* 86h
6 b g Poliglote Daphnee (FR) (Baryshnikov (AUS))
4028^{4}

Dardanella *Hugo Froud* 110h
8 b m Alflora(IRE) Ella Falls (IRE) (Dancing Dissident (USA))
711^{4} 1897^{P} 2455^{9} 2987^{15} 3198^{3} 3498^{P} 3665^{5}

Darebin (GER) *Gary Moore* 115h
3 ch g It's Gino(GER) Delightful Sofie (GER) (Grand Lodge (USA))
1732^{6} (2371) 2757^{P} (2954) 3279^{5} 3610^{3} 4933^{2} 5491^{10}

Dare Me (IRE) *Venetia Williams* 134h 150c
11 b g Bob Back(USA) Gaye Chatelaine (IRE) (Castle Keep)
2436^{P} (3735) 4733^{9} 5448^{5}

Dare To Achieve *Tom George* 116h
5 b g Galileo(IRE) Mussoorie (FR) (Linamix (FR))
706^{3} 1052^{P}

Dare To Endeavour *E McNamara* 108h 140c
8 b g Alflora(IRE) Miss Chinchilla (Perpendicular)
1556a^{6} 2899^{2} 5193^{15}

Daring Article (IRE) *Robert Tyner* 109h 111c
9 bb g Definite Article Daring Hen (IRE) (Henbit (USA))
95a^{P}

Daring Exit *Robert Bewley* 85h 100c
6 b g Exit To Nowhere(USA) Aberdare (Overbury (IRE))
291^{6} 421^{6} 635^{5}

Daring Indian *Roger Teal* 101h
7 ch g Zamindar(USA) Anasazi (IRE) (Sadler's Wells (USA))
167^{6} 864^{11} 2974^{3} 3368^{11}

Dark And Dangerous (IRE) *Simon Waugh* 91h 76c
7 b g Cacique(IRE) Gilah (IRE) (Saddlers' Hall (IRE))
2148^{5} 2322^{7} 2844^{7}

Dark Diamond (IRE) *Michael Chapman* 98h
5 b g Dark Angel(IRE) Moon Diamond (Unfuwain (USA))
5243^{7}

Darkening Night *Sarah-Jayne Davies*
3 b g Cape Cross(IRE) Garanciere (FR) (Anabaa (USA))
3076^{F} 4345^{P}

Darkestbeforedawn (IRE) *Caroline Keevil* 102h 105c
8 br g Dr Massini(IRE) Camden Dolphin (IRE) (Camden Town)
2985^{9} 3220^{6} 3662^{4} 3977^{6} 4160^{U}

Dark Flame (IRE) *Richard Rowe* 129h
6 b g Gold Well Glorys Flame (IRE) (Flemensfirth (USA))
1990^{3} 2886^{6} 3452^{2} 4620^{7} (5115)

Dark Glacier (IRE) *Peter Bowen* 88h 131c
10 b g Flemensfirth(USA) Glacier Lilly (IRE) (Glacial Storm (USA))
156^{P} 707^{7} 3079^{P}

Dark Justice (IRE) *Michael Madgwick* 46h
5 b m Lawman(FR) Dark Raider (IRE) (Definite Article)
1485^{5} 1590^{9}

Dark Lover (GER) *Jamie Snowden* 141h 131c
10 b g Zinaad Dark Lady (GER) (Lagunas)
(3585) (4043) 4768^{18} 5304^{P}

Dark Music *Jo Davis* 45b
4 br m Misu Bond(IRE) Tender Moments (Tomba)
432^{11}

Dark Spirit (IRE) *Evan Williams* 144h 110c
7 b m Whipper(USA) Dark Raider (IRE) (Definite Article)
(2054) 2484^{7} 3122^{4} 3732^{4}

Darna *Kim Bailey* 125h 148c
9 b g Alflora(IRE) Dutch Dyane (Midyan (USA))
2483^{P} 4733^{F}

Darnborough (IRE) *Mark Shears* 29h 39c
9 b g Darnay Princesse Sharpo (USA) (Trempolino (USA))
699^{4} 874^{P}

Darnitnev *Martin Keighley* 101h
5 b g Darnay Lavender Della (IRE) (Shernazar)
337^{2} 1324^{7} 1599^{3} 1812^{4} 2569^{6} 2997^{P} 5398^{4}

Darsi Dancer (IRE) *Stuart Coltherd* 97h 95c
7 b g Darsi(FR) Jaystara (IRE) (Jurado (USA))
80^{P} 143^{3} (1890) 2323^{6} 2806^{5} 3402^{P} 4047^{P} 5412^{10}

Dartford Warbler (IRE) *Sue Smith* 118h 128c
8 bb g Overbury(IRE) Stony View (IRE) (Tirol)
1404^{7} (1600) 1784^{2} 2435^{2} (2593) 3148^{7} 3794^{2} 4910^{3}

Darwins Fox (FR) *Henry De Bromhead* 145h 148c
9 bb g Kahyasi Parcelle De Sou (FR) (Ajdayt (USA))
603a^{2} 954a^{5}

Darwins Theory (IRE) *Fiona Shaw* 114h 96c
7 b g Montjeu(IRE) Thrift (IRE) (Green Desert (USA))
64^{4} 510^{P} (2880) 4096^{4} 4384^{3} 5030^{6}

Dashaway (IRE) *Jeremy Scott* 126h
6 ch g Shantou(USA) Backaway (IRE) (Bob Back (USA))
2268^{8}

Dashing Oscar (IRE) *Harry Fry* 112h
5 b g Oscar(IRE) Be My Leader (IRE) (Supreme Leader)
2123^{2} 3835^{17}

Dashul (IRE) *Jeremy Scott* 78h
6 b m Generous(IRE) Midway (IRE) (Warcraft (USA))
120^{8} 387^{4} 1673^{6} 1910^{9}

Daulys Anthem (IRE) *David Dennis* 94h
7 br g Royal Anthem(USA) Over Dubai (Overbury (IRE))
1829^{5} 2023^{6} 2152^{P} 2406^{3} 2869^{7} 3374^{8} 4099^{P}

Daveron (IRE) *Jeremy Scott* 114h 133c
7 b g Winged Love(IRE) Double Doc (IRE) (Moonax (IRE))
1977^{6} 2513^{18} 3379^{3} (3709) (4443) 4870^{3} 5496^{7}

Dave The Rave (IRE) *Ronald Thompson*
5 b g Craigsteel Coolharbour Lady (IRE) (Lord Americo)
4156^{11}

David John *Dai Burchell* 103h
4 b g Overbury(IRE) Molly's Secret (Minshaanshu Amad (USA))
56^{8} 1647^{5} (1892) 2271^{3} 2924^{8}

Dawalan (FR) *Cyril Murphy* 150h
5 rg g Azamour(IRE) Daltawa (IRE) (Miswaki (USA))
(1983a)

Dawerann (IRE) *Michael Hourigan* 117h 102c
6 b g Medicean Dawera (IRE) (Spinning World (USA))
1184a^{8}

Dawlish *Noel Wilson* 12b
4 b g Rail Link Pnyka (IRE) (Montjeu (IRE))
1449^{12}

Dawn Commander (GER) *Stuart Edmunds* 143h 125c
8 gr g Mamool(IRE) Dark Lady (GER) (Lagunas)
196^{6} 681^{3} 916^{4} 1138^{7}

Dawnieriver (IRE) *Michael Scudamore* 86h 95c
5 br m Indian River(FR) In Sin (IRE) (Insan (USA))
167^{5} 443^{6} 1326^{8} 1785^{2} 2303^{U} 2735^{2} 3222^{4}

Dawson City *Polly Gundry* 122h 137c
6 b g Midnight Legend Running For Annie (Gunner B)
2660^{3} 2905^{U} 3707^{2} 4124^{2} 4621^{2} 5140^{2}

Daydreamer *Alan King* 100h
4 b g Duke Of Marmalade(IRE) Storyland (USA) (Menifee (USA))
263^{P} 912^{4} 1425^{P}

Daymar Bay (IRE) *Gareth Thomas* 110h 130c
9 b g Oscar(IRE) Sunset View (IRE) (Good Thyne (USA))
121^{4} 772^{7} (4446) 5178^{P}

Day Of Roses (IRE) *Jeremy Scott* 50h
6 b g Acambaro(GER) Dan's Choice (IRE) (Spanish Place (USA))
3775^{8} 4137^{7} 4339^{7}

Days Ahead (IRE) *Richenda Ford* 118h 122c
8 ch g Kheleyf(USA) Hushaby (IRE) (Eurobus)
266^{3} (1674) 2019^{4}

Days Hotel (IRE) *Henry De Bromhead* 133h 157c
10 b g Oscar(IRE) Call Catherine (IRE) (Strong Gale)
2388a^{2} 3092a^{4} 3552a^{5} 3892a^{4} (4281a) 5023a^{3}

Days Like These *Adrian Wintle*
6 b m Westerner One Of Those Days (Soviet Lad (USA))
4264^{P} 4614^{P}

Days Of Heaven (FR) *Nicky Henderson* 134h 136c
5 bb g Saint Des Saints(FR) Daramour (FR) (Anabaa Blue)
2512^{16} 4014^{7} 4717^{23}

Daytime Ahead (IRE) *Oliver Sherwood* 102b
4 gr m Daylami(IRE) Bright Times Ahead (IRE) (Rainbows For Life (CAN))
4102^{8} 4847^{5} 5443^{6}

Daytripper *Lucinda Russell* 102h
4 gr m Daylami(IRE) Stravaigin (Primitive Rising (USA))
159^{8} 4033^{5} 4403^{4} 5009^{3} 5409^{8}

Dazinski *Henry Oliver* 118h
9 ch g Sulamani(IRE) Shuheb (Nashwan (USA))
(2577) 2734^{10} 4466^{4} 5453^{5}

Dazzling Rita *Sophie Leech* 58h
9 b m Midnight Legend Pytchley Dawn (Welsh Captain)
44^{P}

Dazzling Susie (IRE) *John F Phelan* 127h 127c
10 b m Stowaway Aunt Sue (IRE) (Shahanndeh (IRE))
70a^{8} 1150a^{6}

Deadly Approach *Sarah-Jayne Davies* 108h
4 b g New Approach(IRE) Speirbhean (IRE) (Danehill (USA))
2747^{2} 4065^{4} 4773^{2}

Deadly Move (IRE) *Peter Bowen* 108h
6 b g Scorpion(IRE) Sounds Attractive (IRE) (Rudimentary (USA))
1519^{P} 2437^{P} 3927^{3} 4473^{3}

Deadly Sting (IRE) *Neil Mulholland* 127h 132c
6 b g Scorpion(IRE) Gaza Strip (IRE) (Hamas (IRE))
(430) 4870^{4} 5285^{3}

Dead Or Alive (IRE) *Miss Rose Grissell* 83h 100c
12 b g Exit To Nowhere(USA) Avro Avian (Ardross)
4595^{7}

Dead Ringa *Mrs E J Clark*
10 ch g Karinga Bay Deadly Dove (Little Wolf)
472^{F}

Deal Done (FR) *Richard Drake* 115h 119c
11 b g Vertical Speed(FR) Five Rivers (FR) (Cadoudal (FR))
471^{P}

Dear Darling *Colin Tizzard* 105h
5 b m Midnight Legend Easibrook Jane (Alderbrook)
648^{3} 893^{5}

Dear Lottie (FR) *Gary Moore* 36h
4 b m Nickname(FR) Vuelta Al Ruedo (FR) (Ballingarry (IRE))
601^{4} 1845^{F} 2252^{P} 2829^{8}

Dear Sire (FR) *S R B Crawford* 95b
3 gr g Al Namix(FR) Polismith (FR) (Poliglote)
4552^{5}

Deauville Dame *Sir Mark Prescott Bt* 82b
3 b f Alflora(IRE) Hispalis (IRE) (Barathea (IRE))
3048^{6} 3469^{3} 4074^{8}

Deauville Dancer (IRE) *David Dennis* 113h
4 b g Tamayuz Mathool (IRE) (Alhaarth (IRE))
3021^{2} ◆ 3306^{5}

Debdebdeb *Dan Skelton* 135h
5 b m Teofilo(IRE) Windmill (Ezzoud (IRE))
(3777) 4239^{F} 5282^{2}

Debece *Tim Vaughan* 112h
4 b g Kayf Tara Dalamine (FR) (Sillery (USA))
341^{4} 1873^{4} (4988)

De Bee Keeper (IRE) *Russell Ross* 59h 6c
7 b g Milan Festival Leader (IRE) (Supreme Leader)
4163^{8}

De Bene Esse (IRE) *Evan Williams* 43h 135c
5 br g Scorpion(IRE) Benedicta Rose (IRE) (Beneficial)
2801^{8} 3411^{8} 3580^{P} (4142) 4816^{5}

De Blacksmith (IRE) *Gary Moore* 115h 120c
7 b g Brian Boru Gift Of The Gab (IRE) (Orchestra)
62^{3} 4529^{2} ◆ 5066^{U}

De Boitron (FR) *Sue Smith* 133h 124c
11 b g Sassanian(USA) Pondiki (FR) (Sicyos (USA))
2335^{5} 2637^{3} 3156^{5} 4610^{5} 5403^{2}

Debt To Society (IRE) *Richard Ford* 101h 108c
8 ch g Moscow Society(USA) Nobody's Darling (IRE) (Supreme Leader)
38^{P} 798^{6} 3803^{P} 4105^{6} 4877^{5} 5233^{3}

Decade Player (IRE) *Miss Kelly Morgan* 93h 98c
7 b g Gamut(IRE) Ballindante (IRE) (Phardante (FR))
4295^{3}

Deciding Moment (IRE) *Ben De Haan* 101h 127c
9 b g Zagreb(USA) Fontaine Jewel (IRE) (Lafontaine I (USA))
707^{U} 2853^{5}

Decimus (IRE) *Jeremy Scott* 122h 118c
8 b g Bienamado(USA) Catch Me Dreaming (IRE) (Safety Catch (USA))
(897) 1419^{P} 2711^{2} 4241^{9} 5141^{6}

Deckers Delight *Nigel Hawke* 74b
4 b m Tobougg(IRE) Oleana (IRE) (Alzao (USA))
5187^{5}

Decoy Daddy (IRE) *Cyril Murphy* 130h 134c
13 ch g Lord Of Appeal Young Bebe (IRE) (M Double M (USA))
1983a^{5}

Dedigout (IRE) *A J Martin* 158h 150c
9 b g Bob Back(USA) Dainty Daisy (IRE) (Buckskin (FR))
4146a^{3} 5004a^{3}

De D'Or Esqua (FR) *O Regley*
2 ch g Grand Couturier Taquineuse Esqua (FR) (Nononito (FR))
5498a^{11}

Deebaj (IRE) *Richard Price* 108h
3 br g Authorized(IRE) Athreyaa (Singspiel (IRE))
3822^{4} 4243^{4} 4489^{2} ◆ 5095^{5} 5491^{8}

Deep Resolve (IRE) *Alan Swinbank* 108h
4 b g Intense Focus(USA) I'll Be Waiting (Vettori (IRE))
2933^{5}

Deepsand (IRE) *Ali Stronge* 111h
6 br g Footstepsinthesand Sinamay (USA) (Saint Ballado (CAN))
2926^{8} 4096^{11}

Deep Trouble (IRE) *Ben Case* 133h 147c
8 b g Shantou(USA) Out Of Trouble (IRE) (Mandalus)
2914^{P} 3527^{6} 3786^{2} 4274^{U} 4347^{P}

De Faoithesdream (IRE) *Evan Williams* 117h 138c
9 br g Balakheri(IRE) Cutteen Lass (IRE) (Tremblant)
103^{6} 2059^{11} (2659) 2884^{9} 3917^{5} 4787^{9} (5326)

Defiant Dazzler (IRE) *Lady Susan Brooke* 66h
6 b g Kadeed(IRE) Over The Wonder (Overbury (IRE))
220^{5} 526^{7} 834^{P} 929^{6}

Defi D'Anjou (FR) *L Viel* 138h 121c
7 b g Saint Des Saints(FR) Rosane (FR) (Sheyrann (IRE))
349a^{8} 663a^{P}

Defile De Mode (FR) *Mme V Seignoux* 109h
10 b g Ultimately Lucky(IRE) Naomie (FR) (Pistolet Bleu (IRE))
5042a^{5}

Definately Vinnie *Jane Mathias* 78h
5 ch g Vinnie Roe(IRE) Sohapara (Arapahos (FR))
271^{5} 558^{5} 2731^{11} 3105^{11} 3568^{8} 4439^{5}

Defining Year (IRE) *Hugo Froud* 126h
7 b g Hawk Wing(USA) Tajaathub (USA) (Aljabr (USA))
5159^{P}

Definite Dream (IRE) *Evan Williams* 79h 131c
8 b g Definite Article Brooks Chariot (IRE) (Electric)
131^{4}

Definite Earl (IRE) *D Broad* 122h
7 b g Definite Article Line Sigune (FR) (Kadalko (FR))
3323a^{9}

Definite Future (IRE) *Kerry Lee* 97h 107c
6 b g Definite Article Miss Marilyn (IRE) (Welsh Term)
177^{4} 691^{F} 936^{4} 1504^{5} 1600^{6} 2694^{8} 5453^{7}

Definitely Better (IRE) *Tom George* 107h 97c
7 ch m Definite Article Chevet Girl (IRE) (Roselier (FR))
88^{P} 524^{P} 2022^{P} 2263^{6} 2812^{5} 3680^{3} 4178^{4} (4538) 4709^{2} 5380^{6}

Definitely Glad (IRE) *Susan Corbett* 95h 83c
8 b m Definite Article Gladys May (IRE) (Moscow Society (USA))
3471^{4} 3681^{3} 3839^{P} 4036^{9} 4904^{11}

Definite Outcome (IRE) *Rebecca Curtis* 133h
6 b g Definite Article Magical Theatre (IRE) (King's Theatre (IRE))
1870^{3} (2331) 3623^{3} ◆ 4766^{P}

Definite Ruby (IRE) *Gordon Elliott* 119h 133c
7 br m Definite Article Sunset Queen (IRE) (King's Theatre (IRE))
849^{2} 2057^{2} 2473^{8}

Definite Soldier (IRE) *P J Rothwell* 91h 111c
6 b g Definite Article Loadsofability (IRE) (Supreme Leader)
2513^{14} 4663a^{P}

Definitly Grey (IRE) *Charlie Longsdon* 102h
4 gr g Daylami(IRE) Caroline Fontenail (IRE) (Kaldounevees (FR))
1990^{7} 2519^{F} 3021^{9} 4303^{8} 5398^{5}

Definitly Red (IRE) *Brian Ellison* 147h 150c
6 ch g Definite Article The Red Wench (IRE) (Aahsaylad)
2641^{2} ◆ (3399) 3621^{2} 3998^{2} 4700^{F} (5297)

De Forgotten Man (IRE) *Philip Rowley* 92h 112c
10 b g Commander Collins(IRE) Jrred Up (IRE) (Jurado (USA))
4446^{7}

Degenerous (IRE) *Sarah Dawson* 99h 28c
7 b m Generous(IRE) Brescia (FR) (Monsun (GER))
869^{5} 5409^{5} 5472^{6}

Degooch (IRE) *Johnny Farrelly* 113h 126c
6 ch g Gamut(IRE) Blonde Ambition (IRE) (Old Vic)
255^{F} 2711^{3} 3855^{6} 5146^{7}

Deja Bougg *Neil Mulholland* 110h
4 b m Tobougg(IRE) La Riveraine (USA) (Riverman (USA))
2959^{3} 3252^{2} 4320^{2} 4672^{P} 5148^{5}

De Kerry Man (IRE) *David Bridgwater* 97h 132c
7 b g Westerner Fishy Fishy (IRE) (Mull Of Kintyre (USA))
3404^{U} 3624^{F} 4363^{8} (4529)

Delagoa Bay (IRE) *Sylvester Kirk*
7 b m Encosta De Lago(AUS) Amory (GER) (Goofalik (USA))
1845^{P}

Delegate *Gordon Elliott* 117h
5 ch g Robin Des Champs(FR) As You Leave (FR) (Kaldounevees (FR))
1875a^{F}

Delgany Demon *Neil King* 131h 136c
7 b g Kayf Tara Little Twig (IRE) (Good Thyne (USA))
461^{3} 2261^{2} 2631^{2} 3113^{U} 3591^{P} (4389) 4800^{2} 5284^{14}

Delgardo (IRE) *John David Riches* 8b
6 b g Mountain High(IRE) Mistery Girl (Mister Mat (FR))
206^{6} 1030^{P}

Dell' Arca (IRE) *David Pipe* 154h 150c
6 b g Sholokhov(IRE) Daisy Belle (GER) (Acatenango (GER))
71a[3] **(461) 2469[3] 2760[5]** 3527[8] 4139[P] 5219[7] 5497[4]

Della Sun (FR) *Arthur Whitehead* 119h
9 b g Della Francesca(USA) Algarve Sunrise (IRE) (Highest Honor (FR))
1347[5] 1600[7]

Dellbuoy *Pat Phelan* 102h
6 b g Acclamation Ruthie (Pursuit Of Love)
2712[P] 4098[F]

Delta Borget (FR) *L Jefford* 130c
10 b g Kapgarde(FR) L'Oceane (FR) (Epervier Bleu)
12[2] 393[7] (4295) (4592) 5035[2]

Delusionofgrandeur (IRE) *Sue Smith* 140h
5 b g Mahler Olivia Rose (IRE) (Mujadil (USA))
1923[2] (2319) 2787[3] (3400) 4015[3] 4368[4]

Demographic (USA) *Emma Lavelle* 107h
6 b g Aptitude(USA) Private Line (USA) (Private Account (USA))
493[6] 1545[5] 1951[3]

Demon Magic (CZE) *Cestmir Olehla* 113c
9 br g Jape(USA) Diva Bara (CZE) (Sectori (USA))
1672a[7]

Demonstrative (USA) *Richard L Valentine* 134h
8 b g Elusive Quality(USA) Loving Pride (USA) (Quiet American (USA))
1983a[9]

Denala *Michael Appleby* 58b
4 ch m Denounce Fuwala (Unfuwain (USA))
2562[8]

Denali Highway (IRE) *Caroline Bailey* 90h 122c
8 ch g Governor Brown(USA) Amaretto Flame (IRE) (First Trump)
2648[2] 2996[3] 3843[5] 4348[7] 4842[4]

Denboy (IRE) *Jamie Snowden* 94h
5 b g King's Theatre(IRE) Miss Denman (IRE) (Presenting)
1895[4] 5137[5] 5469[8]

Denny Kerrell *Caroline Keevil* 89h
4 b g Midnight Legend Tilla (Bin Ajwaad (IRE))
2991[9] 3416[6] 4784[7] 5182[6] 5462[4]

Denton Carnival (IRE) *Michael Dods* 81h
3 ch g Captain Rio Be My Lover (Pursuit Of Love)
2286[3] 2718[9]

Deny *Henry Hogarth* 88h
7 ch g Mr Greeley(USA) Sulk (IRE) (Selkirk (USA))
3807[P] 4553[6]

De Plotting Shed (IRE) *Gordon Elliott* 132h
5 b g Beneficial Lady Willmurt (IRE) (Mandalus)
3138[4]

Deportation *John Norton* 75h
8 b g Deportivo Kyle Rhea (In The Wings)
2868[5] 3128[6] 4047[P]

Deputy Commander (IRE) *Nigel Twiston-Davies* 116h
6 b g Shantou(USA) Artic Native (IRE) (Be My Native (USA))
2904[2] 3159[2] 3855[5] ◆ 4342[P] (5102) 5157[3]

Deputy Dan (IRE) *Oliver Sherwood* 151h 145c
7 b g Westerner Louisas Dream (IRE) (Supreme Leader)
2399[F] 2782[2] 3149[3] 4244[5] (Dead)

Deputy Marshall (IRE) *Peter Fahey* 114h
6 b g Pushkin(IRE) Posh Kidd (IRE) (Semillon)
3323a[10]

Derksen (IRE) *Nicky Henderson* 98h
5 b g Robin Des Champs(FR) Anns Present (IRE) (Presenting)
3839[14] 4322[6] 4874[11]

Derrick D'Anjou (IRE) *Graeme McPherson* 97b
4 b g Double Eclipse(IRE) Belle D'Anjou (FR) (Saint Cyrien (FR))
4915[6]

Derrintogher Bliss (IRE) *Kim Bailey* 127h 131c
6 b g Arcadio(GER) His Fair Lady (IRE) (In The Wings)
1701[2] ◆

Derrydoon *Karen McLintock* 88b
5 b g Multiplex Wahiba Reason (IRE) (Robellino (USA))
3476[4]

Derryfadda (IRE) *Richard Ford* 94h 112c
6 b g Scorpion(IRE) San Diego (IRE) (Leading Counsel (USA))
1371[2] **1775[2] 2039[3] (2297)**

Derrymix *Matt Sheppard*
7 gr g Fair Mix(IRE) Princess Derry (Derrylin)
1698[P]

Derryogue (IRE) *Zoe Davison* 96c
10 b g Tikkanen(USA) Snugville Sally (Derrylin)
126[5] (2811) 2994[3] 4491[P] 5388[F]

Derwent (USA) *J-P Gallorini* 125h
5 b g Mizzen Mast(USA) Skiable (IRE) (Niniski (USA))
5363a[P]

Descaro (USA) *Fergal O'Brien* 99h 54c
9 gr g Dr Fong(USA) Miarixa (FR) (Linamix (FR))
125[2] 776[6] 1085[P] 1299[4] 1405[5]

Descartes (GER) *G Macaire* 138h
6 ch g Sholokhov(IRE) Dynamica (GER) (Dashing Blade)
2183[4]

Desert Cry (IRE) *Donald McCain* 131h 146c
9 bb g Desert Prince(IRE) Hataana (USA) (Robellino (USA))
3030[11] 3440[4] 3804[4] 4839[4]

Desert Island Dusk *Maurice Barnes* 98h
4 b g Superior Premium Desert Island Disc (Turtle Island (IRE))
155[7] 1892[7] 2100[5] 2343[3] 5472[2] ◆

Desert Joe (IRE) *Alan King* 124h 129c
9 b g Anshan Wide Country (IRE) (Good Thyne (USA))
1970[P] 2616[4] 3024[7] 4621[5]

Desertmore Hill (IRE) *Peter Bowen* 110h
5 b g Beneficial Youngborogal (IRE) (Anshan)
(1662) 1844[F] 2265[10] 3506[2] 3855[8]

Desertmore View (IRE) *Marc Barber* 99h 120c
7 b g Fruits Of Love(USA) The Iron Lady (IRE) (Polish Patriot (USA))
296[U]

Desert Nova (IRE) *Mark Campion* 31h
13 ch g Desert King(IRE) Assafiyah (IRE) (Kris)
5349[6]

Desert Queen *Harry Fry* 146h
7 b m Desert King(IRE) Priscilla (Teenoso (USA))
2349[P] (2632) 3283[2] 3732[7] 4699[7] 5299[7]

Desert Recluse (IRE) *Henry Oliver* 125h
8 ch g Redback Desert Design (Desert King (IRE))
1381[2] 1719[4] 2617[9] 5279[7]

Desert Retreat (IRE) *Philip Hobbs* 113b
4 b g Sandmason Suny House (Carroll House (IRE))
1704[2] ◆ 2270[2] 3980[4] 4915[2]

Desert Sensation (IRE) *Tracy Waggott* 99b
3 b g Authorized(IRE) Awwal Malika (USA) (Kingmambo (USA))
2777[9] 3165[5] 4181[2] 5407[2]

Desert Sting *Oliver Greenall* 71h
6 b g Scorpion(IRE) Skipcarl (IRE) (Carlingford Castle)
5333[3]

Deshan (GER) *Tim Vaughan* 100b
4 b g Soldier Hollow Desimona (GER) (Monsun (GER))
526[2]

Desilvano *James Evans* 133h
6 b g Desideratum Cruz Santa (Lord Bud)
2484[15]

Desinvolte (FR) *P Leblanc* 122h
2 b c Early March Omarie (FR) (Johann Quatz (FR))
4539a[6]

Desoto County *Gordon Elliott* 137h
6 gr g Hernando(FR) Kaldounya (Kaldoun (FR))
3650a[3] 5025a[4]

Despearado *Richard Phillips*
4 b g Virtual Princess Raya (Act One)
3012[7]

Desroches (GER) *Robin Dickin* 70h
7 b m Royal Dragon(USA) Dadrala (IRE) (Be My Guest (USA))
361[8] 1374[6] 2150[P] 2850[10]

Destiny Awaits (IRE) *Keith Pollock* 99h
6 b g Dubai Destination(USA) Mellow Jazz (Lycius (USA))
79[3] 288[5] 481[2] 845[6] 935[5] 1329[4] 1779[2] (2103) 2323[P]

Destiny's Gold (IRE) *George Baker* 118h
5 b g Millenary Knockhouse Rose (IRE) (Roselier (FR))
32[3] 279[2] 745[3] 4447[9] 5418[3]

Detour Ahead *Clare Ellam* 90h 82c
7 ch m Needwood Blade My Tern (IRE) (Glacial Storm (USA))
4709[P] 5017[P] 5333[5]

Detroit Blues *Jamie Snowden* 118h
5 ch g Tobougg(IRE) Blue Missy (USA) (Swain (IRE))
147[2] (447) 671[P] 1290[4] 1521[2] 2064[9] 5391[12]

Detroit De Baune (FR) *F-M Cottin* 79h
2 ch c Evasive Suradana (FR) (Dr Fong (USA))
5498a[9]

Device (FR) *G Macaire* 150h
3 b g Poliglote Westonne (FR) (Mansonnien (FR))
(1881a)

Devil Inside (FR) *L Viel* 134h 125c
6 b g Numerous(USA) Une Nonantaise (FR) (Kaldounevees (FR))
437a[5]

Devilment *John Ferguson* 150h
4 b g Cape Cross(IRE) Mischief Making (USA) (Lemon Drop Kid (USA))
(2060) 2512[6] 2914[2] 3151[8] 4765[13]

Devils Bride (IRE) *W P Mullins* 144h 150c
8 b g Helissio(FR) Rigorous (Generous (IRE))
1763a[6] (2232a)

Devil To Pay *Alan King* 128h 124c
9 b g Red Ransom(USA) My Way (IRE) (Marju (IRE))
2857[F] 4098[F]

Devon Mead *Andrew Quick*
10 ch g Generous(IRE) Devon Peasant (Deploy)
3585[P] 4295[RR]

Devon River (FR) *Simon Waugh* 87h 84c
5 gr g Stormy River(FR) Devon House (USA) (Chester House (USA))
1684[6] 1967[7] 2294[4] **3968[8] 4325[7]**

De Vous A Moi (FR) *Sue Smith* 107h 143c
7 b g Sinndar(IRE) Dzinigane (FR) (Exit To Nowhere (USA))
2192[2] (2497) (4551) ◆

Dewberry *Geoffrey Deacon* 69b
4 br m Lucarno(USA) Elderberry (Bin Ajwaad (IRE))
602[5] 4242[7]

Dexcite (FR) *Tom George* 127h
4 bb g Authorized(IRE) Belle Alicia (FR) (Smadoun (FR))
1847[3] 2512[11] 3019[4] 4026[P]

Dexter Benjamin (IRE) *Nick Gifford* 98h
6 b g Milan Just Stunning (IRE) (Presenting)
65[7] 451[12]

Dhaular Dhar (IRE) *Jim Goldie* 89h
13 b g Indian Ridge Pescara (IRE) (Common Grounds)
2292[7]

Diakali (FR) *W P Mullins* 160h
6 gr g Sinndar(IRE) Diasilixa (FR) (Linamix (FR))
(954a) 1163a[13]

Diamant Catalan (FR) *P Peltier* 126c
4 ch g Balko(FR) Catalane (FR) (Alleged (USA))
2820a[6]

Diamond D'Amour (IRE) *George Bewley* 107h
9 gr g Danehill Dancer(IRE) Diamond Line (FR) (Linamix (FR))
2720[2] ◆ 3438[3] 4055[7] 4404[4] 5198[P]

Diamond Gesture (IRE) *Fergal O'Brien* 86h
7 ch m Presenting Rare Gesture (IRE) (Shalford (IRE))
383[4] 694[P] 882[6] 4068[6] 5420[10]

Diamond Joel *Tom Lacey* 81h
3 b g Youmzain(IRE) Miss Lacroix (Picea)
1928[5] 2032[7]

Diamond King (IRE) *Gordon Elliott* 154h
7 b g King's Theatre(IRE) Georgia On My Mind (FR) (Belmez (USA))
(4717)

Diamond Life *Mark Pitman* 107h 104c
9 b g Silver Patriarch(IRE) Myrrh (Salse (USA))
2253[10] 2958[7] **4211[2]** ◆ **4527[P]**

Diamond Reflection (IRE) *Tom Weston* 63h
3 b g Oasis Dream Briolette (IRE) (Sadler's Wells (USA))
3610[5] 3790[P] 4441[9] 4714[9] 5099[10] 5332[8]

Diamond Reign (IRE) *Bob Buckler* 77h
9 b m Double Eclipse(IRE) Solo Venture (IRE) (Abednego)
647[6] 824[8] 878[6]

Diamond Rock *Henry Oliver* 94h
4 b g Kayf Tara Crystal Princess (IRE) (Definite Article)
3573[2] 4441[4] 4714[7] 5048[6]

Dibble Bridge *Philip Kirby* 82h
4 ch g Spirit One(FR) Willows World (Agnes World (USA))
1740[7] 1886[9] 2318[10] 2550[P]

Dica (FR) *Paul Collins*
9 ch g Kapgarde(FR) Easy World (FR) (Lost World (IRE))
5090[P]

Dick Dundee *Paul Nolan* 123h 139c
10 b g King's Theatre(IRE) Bayariyka (IRE) (Slip Anchor)
47a[U]

Dicky Bob *Miss V J Nicholls* 113c
8 gr g Exit To Nowhere(USA) She's A Gift (Bob's Return (IRE))
(5270)

Dicosimo (FR) *W P Mullins* 150h
4 b g Laveron Coralisse Royale (FR) (Tip Moss (FR))
4115[F] 4765[F]

Diddypurptoon *Jackie Du Plessis* 63h
9 b m Lucky Story(USA) Dafne (Nashwan (USA))
828[10] 1675[8]

Didntitellya (IRE) *Kim Bailey* 69h 95c
6 b g Presenting Beauty Star (IRE) (Shalford (IRE))
2975[P] 4062[P] 5226[3]

Did You Ever (IRE) *Jamie Poulton*
9 gr g Environment Friend Did You Know (IRE) (Balinger)
716[P]

Diego Du Charmil (FR) *Paul Nicholls* 135h
3 b g Ballingarry(IRE) Daramour (FR) (Anabaa Blue)
(4720) ◆ 5175[4]

Diego Suarez (FR) *Chris Bealby* 93h
5 b g Astarabad(USA) Shabada (FR) (Cadoudal (FR))
90[5] 3973[2] 4845[6] 5203[3] 5441[5]

Different Gravey (IRE) *Nicky Henderson* 164h
5 b g High Chaparral(IRE) Newtown Dancer (IRE) (Danehill Dancer (IRE))
(4239) 5216[5]

Dig Deeper *Caroline Bailey* 132c
6 b g Overbury(IRE) Tickle The Tiller (IRE) (Strong Gale)
2495[2] 2960[2]

Dimple (FR) *Pauline Robson* 111h
4 gr g Montmartre(FR) Dynella (FR) (Sillery (USA))
2318[6] 2791[8] 3022[3] ◆ 5450[4]

Dineur (FR) *Mickey Bowen* 122h 140c
9 ch g Discover D'Auteuil(FR) Sky Rocket (FR) (Sky Lawyer (FR))
4269[2] 4592[2] 5178[2]

Ding Ding *Sheena West* 83h
4 ch m Winker Watson Five Bells (IRE) (Rock Of Gibraltar (IRE))
2544[6] 2829[5] 5067[6] 5483[4]

Dinky Challenger *Mark Gillard* 66h
7 bb g Midnight Legend Crusty Lily (Whittingham (IRE))
2457[12] 2986[P] 3411[P] 4849[7]

Dinky Dave *Richard Drake*
4 b g Josr Algarhoud(IRE) Festive Chimes (IRE) (Efisio)
1365[P] 1568[P]

Dino Mite *Jamie Snowden* 116h 81c
10 b m Doctor Dino(FR) Compose (Anabaa (USA))
913[2] 1180[4]

Dipity Doo Dah *Peter Bowen* 94h 78c
11 b m Slip Anchor Lyra I (Blakeney)
615[3] **770[5]** 966[P]

Direct Flo (IRE) *Rob Summers* 89h 79c
8 b m Mr Combustible(IRE) Direct Pursuit (IRE) (Hubbly Bubbly (USA))
530[7] 864[5]

Directional *Tim Vaughan* 90h
3 b g Raven's Pass(USA) Rose Street (USA) (Street Cry (IRE))
690[2] 3523[4] 3925[P] 4674[3] ◆ 5483[5]

Dire Straits (IRE) *Neil King* 116h
4 b g Teofilo(IRE) Kalagold (IRE) (Magical Strike (USA))
335[3] 467[3] 912[2] (1041) 1457[4]

Discay *Dr Richard Newland* 115h 127c
6 b g Distant Music(USA) Caysue (Cayman Kai (IRE))
1868[8] 2247[4] 2977[6] **3311[4]** 4447[8] **4889[2] (5244)** 5418[14]

Discoverie *Kenneth Slack* 91h 118c
7 b g Runyon(IRE) Sri (IRE) (Sri Pekan (USA))
287[2] 454[P] 841[P] 845[10] 1067[5] 3244[2] 3398[2] 3672[5] **3968[2] 4325[2] (4556) 4707[3] (5231)**

Disko (FR) *Noel Meade* 134h
4 gr g Martaline Nikos Royale (FR) (Nikos)
23a[2]

Dispour (IRE) *Donald McCain* 133h
5 ch g Monsun(GER) Dalataya (IRE) (Sadler's Wells (USA))
406[P] 1459[6] 1770[5]

Disputed (IRE) *Chris Gordon* 129h
5 b g Westerner Pearly Princess (IRE) (Definite Article)
1734[2] 3015[7] 3216[5] 4096[2] 4381[6] 4782[U] (4933)

Distant Rain (IRE) *Henry Oliver* 100h
5 b g Robin Des Champs(FR) Lala Nova (IRE) (Zaffaran (USA))
4344[9] 4613[4] 5139[P]

Distant Sound (IRE) *Grace Harris* 87h
8 b g Luso Distant Dreams (IRE) (Saddlers' Hall (IRE))
646[9] 879[8] 1293[13] 1744[2] ◆ 1927[4] 3946[2] 4184[8] 4343[2] 4747[4] 5067[4]

Distime (IRE) *Sam Drake* 124h 133c
9 b g Flemensfirth(USA) Technohead (IRE) (Distinctly North (USA))
1902[8] (2425) 2902[3] 3425[6] 3860[10] 4155[3] 5193[4]

Distracted (IRE) *Robert Stephens* 28h 116c
7 b m Publisher(USA) Richmond Usa (IRE) (Insan (USA))
1118[3] (1842) 2403[2] (2598)

District Attorney (IRE) *Chris Fairhurst* 87h 63c
6 b g Lawman(FR) Mood Indigo (IRE) (Indian Ridge)
34[10] 1368[3] 1552[6] **1775[6]** 1887[10]

Disturb *Andrew Crook* 95b
3 ch g Halling(USA) Ataraxy (Zamindar (USA))
4867[5] 5330[10]

Divine Folly (IRE) *Lawney Hill* 106b
10 b g Kotashaan(FR) Jennys Grove (IRE) (Strong Gale)
610[P]

Divine Intavention (IRE) *Miss Francesca Moller* 102b 122c
11 b g Exit To Nowhere(USA) Merrill Gaye (IRE) (Roselier (FR))
270[3] 535[P]

Divine Port (USA) *Alan Swinbank* 119h
5 b g Arch(USA) Out Of Reach (Warning)
(2802) (3242) 3630[5] 3886[6] 4566[5]

Divine Spear (IRE) *Nicky Henderson* 124h
4 b g Oscar(IRE) Testaway (IRE) (Commanche Run)
(242) 3508[2] ◆ (3927) 4303[3] 4620[10] 5279[8]

Dixie Bull (IRE) *Tom Symonds* 122h 98c
10 br g Milan Calora (USA) (Private Account (USA))
3062[P] 3488[4]

Dizoard *Ollie Pears* 84h
5 b m Desideratum Riviere (Meadowbrook)
1371[P]

Djagble (FR) *J Bertran De Balanda* 114h 135c
4 b g Astarabad(USA) Three Well (FR) (Sicyos (USA))
1882a[9] 2820a[2] 4540a[3]

Djakadam (FR) *W P Mullins* 136h 177c
6 b g Saint Des Saints(FR) Rainbow Crest (FR) (Baryshnikov (AUS))
22a[2] (2941a) 3850[F] 4767[2] 5176[3]

Djarkalin (FR) *Dan Skelton* 95b
3 b g Martaline Djarissime (FR) (Dadarissime (FR))
5151[4]

Dj Gerry *Nick Kent* 64h
4 b g Cockney Rebel(IRE) Lady Trish (Red Ransom (USA))
491[P] 620[P]

Doasuwouldbedoneby (IRE) *David Arbuthnot* 67h
4 b g Robin Des Champs(FR) Sarah Princess (IRE) (Presenting)
3907[5] 4322[10] 4874[P]

Doctor Harper (IRE) *David Pipe* 120h 147c
7 b g Presenting Supreme Dreamer (IRE) (Supreme Leader)
2912[9] **3451[2]** ◆ **3571[2]** ◆ **(3786) 4735[U]**

Doctor Henry (IRE) *Richard Mathias* 116b
9 b g Dr Massini(IRE) Russian Ballerina (IRE) (Moscow Society (USA))
60[P]

Doctor Kingsley *Mrs Pauline Harkin* 127c
13 ch g Classic Cliche(IRE) Query Line (High Line)
15[6] 295[2]

Doctor Look Here (IRE) *Sue Gardner* 117h
5 b g Dr Massini(IRE) Eye Vision (IRE) (Taipan (IRE))
119[2] 433[4] 2263[2] (2989) 4596[9]

Doctor Phoenix (IRE) *David Dennis* 131h 143c
7 br g Dr Massini(IRE) Lowroad Cross (IRE) (Anshan)
2018[7] (2419) (2625) 3031[8] 3425[5]

Dodging Bullets *Paul Nicholls* 141h 173c
7 b g Dubawi(IRE) Nova Cyngi (USA) (Kris S (USA))
4114[2] 4718[7] 5493[3]

Dogora (FR) *W P Mullins* 135h 134c
6 gr g Robin Des Pres(FR) Garde De Nuit (FR) (Courtroom (FR))
48a[F] 2471[F] 3296a[P]

Doing Fine (IRE) *Rebecca Curtis* 114h 140c
7 b g Presenting Howaya Pet (IRE) (Montelimar (USA))
69a[11] 1849[3] 2348[P] 4697[F]

Doitforthevillage (IRE) *Paul Henderson* 110h 111c
6 b g Turtle Island(IRE) Last Chance Lady (IRE) (Mister Lord (USA))
2312[F] 2519[6] 2903[3] ◆ 3146[11] **4352[5] 5031[2]**

Do It Tomorrow (IRE) *J R Jenkins* 71b
3 b f Daylami(IRE) Seminova (Cape Cross (IRE))
2414[8] *3048[8]*

Doktor Glaz (FR) *Rose Dobbin* 110h 104c
5 b g Mount Nelson Deviolina (IRE) (Dr Devious (IRE))
2190[4] **2749[4]**

Dolatulo (FR) *Warren Greatrex* 140h 150c
8 ch g Le Fou(FR) La Perspective (FR) (Beyssac (FR))
2899[3] 3860[7] 4719[9] 5327[P]

Dollar And A Dream (IRE) *A J Martin* 123h
6 b g Fruits Of Love(USA) Gorgeous Georgina (IRE) (Tirol)
1565a[4] 2472[4]

Dollar Bill *Nick Gifford* 111h 98c
6 ch g Medicean Jardin (Sinndar (IRE))
3451[3] 4098[4] 4789[P] 5065[P]

Dolly Diamond *Graeme McPherson* 99h
6 b m Erhaab(USA) Solid Land (FR) (Solid Illusion (USA))
55[P] 2298[4] 2661[5] 3930[2]

Dolores Delightful (FR) *Nick Williams* 133h 123c
5 b m Saint Des Saints(FR) Us Et Coutumes (FR) (Shining Steel)
1906[6] 2365[2] 3122[P] 3956[3] 4186[3] ◆ (4445) 4779[4] 5120[5] 5396[2]

Domesday Book (USA) *Henry De Bromhead* 126h 140c
5 b g Street Cry(IRE) Film Script (Unfuwain (USA))
3766a[3] 4701[11]

Dominada (IRE) *Brian Ellison* 98h
3 b g Mastercraftsman(IRE) Red Blossom (USA) (Silver Hawk (USA))
(690) 778[2] 2292[4]

Domtaline (FR) *Peter Winks* 125h 133c
8 gr g Martaline Domna Noune (FR) (Dom Pasquini (FR))
402[4] 863[2] 1296[4] 1755[8] 3238[2] 3682[7] 4774[2]

Donapollo *Rose Dobbin* 86h 106c
7 b g Kayf Tara Star Of Wonder (FR) (The Wonder (FR))
1500[3] (1778) 2173[P] 2950[P]

Don Cossack (GER) *Gordon Elliott* 146h 182c
8 br g Sholokhov(IRE) Depeche Toi (GER) (Konigsstuhl (GER))
(22a) (1938a) (2207a) 3231[F] (3603a) (4767)

Done A Runner (IRE) *Alan Hill* 105c
9 b g Alderbrook Last Wager (IRE) (Strong Gale)
13[P]

Don Hugues Pipard (FR) *A Chaille-Chaille* 90h
4 b h Desert Style(IRE) Nouvelle Reine (GER) (Konigsstuhl (GER))
2362a[10]

Donna's Delight (IRE) *Chris Grant* 88b
4 b g Portrait Gallery(IRE) Hot Lips (IRE) (Good Thyne (USA))
2984[6]

Donna's Diamond (IRE) *Chris Grant* 133h
6 gr g Cloudings(IRE) Inish Bofin (IRE) (Glacial Storm (USA))
2340[3] 3058[3] (3428) 3992[P] 4794[4] 5085[4]

Donna's Pride *Keith Reveley* 109h
6 b m Beat All(USA) Pennys Pride (IRE) (Pips Pride)
2949[3] 3333[2] 3505[3] 3858[7] 4272[7] 4909[12]

Don Padeja *Jonjo O'Neill* 119h
5 br g Dansili La Leuze (IRE) (Caerleon (USA))
973[6] 1156[2] 1263[5] 1661[F] 2042[8]

Don Poli (IRE) *W P Mullins* 153h 168c
6 b g Poliglote Dalamine (FR) (Sillery (USA))
10a[5] (2900) ◆ (3324a) 4767[3] 5176[2]

Don't Be Late (IRE) *Jonjo O'Neill* 104h 40c
7 b g Court Cave(IRE) Sylvella (Lear Fan (USA))
84[7] 461[P] 715[P] 1038[6]

Dont Call Me Doris *Jess Westwood* 53b
5 b m Franklins Gardens Grove Dancer (Reprimand)
1574[P]

Dont Call Me Oscar (IRE) *Mark Gillard* 103h
8 b g Oscar(IRE) Coolrua (IRE) (Commanche Run)
828[P] 2458[P] 2987[P] 4440[P] 5163[U]

Dont Do Mondays (IRE) *David Bridgwater* 114h 136c
8 b g Rashar(USA) Bit Of A Chance (Lord Ha Ha)
2089[4] 2517[3] (5304)

Dont Do That *Richard Rowe* 50h
7 ch m Double Trigger(IRE) Poles Pitch (Colonel Collins (USA))
120[7] 671[8]

Don'tdropmein (IRE) *Neil Mulholland* 106h
5 b g Stowaway Real Tempest (IRE) (Phardante (FR))
1921[2] 2265[8] 2763[6] 5302[P]

Don't Hang About *Gary Hanmer* 78h 106c
10 ch g Alflora(IRE) Althrey Flame (IRE) (Torus)
(60) 3144[4] 4710[P]

Dont Tell No One (IRE) *D K Weld* 130h
7 b g Westerner Kings Rose (IRE) (King's Ride)
3962a[3] 5024a[9]

Donttellthemissis (IRE) *Gary Hanmer* 94b
4 b m Flemensfirth(USA) Blue Gale (IRE) (Be My Native (USA))
970[3]

Don't Touch It (IRE) *Mrs John Harrington* 149h
5 b g Scorpion(IRE) Shandora (IRE) (Supreme Leader)
4280a[3]

Dontupsettherhythm (IRE) *Michael Chapman* 91h
10 bb g Anshan Whatalady (IRE) (Executive Perk)
468[7] 779[P]

Dorabaloo *Tim Easterby* 80b
4 b m Desideratum Bellabaloo (Seymour Hicks (FR))
39[5]

Doris De Silver *Jackie Du Plessis* 65h
6 gr m Silver Patriarch(IRE) Magic Valentine (Magic Ring (IRE))
4137[P] 4546[6] 4881[11] 5165[P]

Dormello Mo (FR) *Paul Nicholls* 137h 150c
5 b g Conillon(GER) Neogel (USA) (Theatrical (IRE))
(512) (825) ◆ 1047[2] 1322[U] (1575) 1838[2] 2053[2] 2510[4] 4624[2] ◆ 5087[2] 5278[2] 5381[3]

Dormouse *Anabel K Murphy* 118h
10 b g Medicean Black Fighter (USA) (Secretariat (USA))
1719[5] 1977[8] 2271[7] 2577[F] (3047) (3196) 3529[4] 4129[7]

Dorry K (IRE) *Jim Best* 93h
6 b m Ad Valorem(USA) Ashtaroute (USA) (Holy Bull (USA))
224[7]

Dos'Ntsuitme (IRE) *Tom Weston*
6 b g Acambaro(GER) Divine Rapture (IRE) (Buckskin (FR))
2972[P]

Dos Santos (FR) *Emmanuel Clayeux* 145h 132c
5 ch g Smadoun(FR) Sainte Astrid (FR) (Saint Cyrien (FR))
349a[3] 663a[4] 1883a[8]

Dot Dash Dot *Christopher Kellett*
3 b f Rainbow High Never Lost (Golden Snake (USA))
2219[P] 2863[P]

Dothraki Raider *Sophie Leech* 96b
4 b g Kayf Tara French Spice (Cadeaux Genereux)
2849[4] 3226[7] 5400[5]

Dotties Dilema (IRE) *Lucinda Russell* 108h 106c
7 b g Pierre Tellarue (IRE) (Rhoman Rule (USA))
661[8]

Dottore (FR) *E Leenders* 113h
3 b g Doctor Dino(FR) Turbotiere (FR) (Turgeon (USA))
4959a[3]

Double Accord *Anthony Honeyball* 101h
5 ch m Double Trigger(IRE) Got Tune (FR) (Green Tune (USA))
2164[7] 2736[2] 3369[P] (5420)

Double Bank (IRE) *Mrs Emma Oliver* 108h 125c
12 b g Double Trigger(IRE) Misty Silks (Scottish Reel I (IRE))
4887[P] (5150)

Double Chocolate *Martin Keighley* 85h 95c
12 b g Doubletour(USA) Matching Green (Green Ruby (USA))
(1930) 2539[2] 2735[U]

Double Cool *Matt Sheppard* 34h
6 b m Double Trigger(IRE) Chillout Polly (Baron Blakeney)
83[8]

Double Court (IRE) *Nigel Twiston-Davies* 72h
4 b g Court Cave(IRE) Miss Top (IRE) (Tremblant)
335[U] 441[4] 613[7] 1829[U] 1979[10] 2408[5] 3128[P] 4504[3] 4936[3]

Double Dan (IRE) *Alexandra Dunn* 88h 75c
6 b g Danroad(AUS) Brilliant Trees (IRE) (Spectrum (IRE))
1295[6] 1647[13] 1824[P] 2402[4] 2714[2]

Doubledisdoubledat (IRE) *Stuart Coltherd* 82h 114c
8 ch g Vinnie Roe(IRE) Castle Graigue (IRE) (Aylesfield)
4043[3] 4866[3] 5178[5]

Double Double (FR) *Peter Bowen* 130h
9 b g Sakhee(USA) Queen Sceptre (IRE) (Fairy King (USA))
416[3]

Double Handful (GER) *Lawney Hill* 122h 120c
9 bl g Pentire Durania (GER) (Surumu (GER))
282[2] 760[2] 1042[7]

Double Miss *Robert Stephens*
4 b m Double Trigger(IRE) Ladyalder (Alderbrook)
3980[8]

Double Ross (IRE) *Nigel Twiston-Davies* 141h 159c
9 ch g Double Eclipse(IRE) Kinross (Nearly A Hand)
2187[2] 2483[4] 2902[5] 3860[9] 4697[9] 5218[P]

Double Scores (IRE) *Gordon Elliott* 114h
6 br g Kalanisi(IRE) Izntitgreat (IRE) (Montelimar (USA))
5024a[P]

Double Shuffle (IRE) *Tom George* 134h 145c
5 b g Milan Fiddlers Bar (IRE) (Un Desperado (FR))
2063[2] 2469[4] (3106) ◆ 4701[3] 5297[5]

Double Silver *Fergal O'Brien* 120h 125c
8 gr m Silver Patriarch(IRE) Shadows Of Silver (Carwhite)
(216) 2349[5] 3025[P] 5154[2]

Double Storm *John Gallagher* 69b
5 b m Double Trigger(IRE) Storm Kitten (IRE) (Catrail (USA))
5308[5]

Double Treasure *Jamie Snowden* 30h
4 b g King's Theatre(IRE) Double Red (IRE) (Thatching)
3258[6] 4714[11]

Double Whammy *Iain Jardine* 116h 141c
9 b g Systematic Honor Rouge (IRE) (Highest Honor (FR))
3339[F] 4789[3] ◆ (5078) (5474)

Double W's (IRE) *Malcolm Jefferson* 125h
5 ch g Fruits Of Love(USA) Zaffre (IRE) (Mtoto)
1660[3] 2101[2] 2472[3] ◆ 2773[2] 3971[2] ◆ (4869) 5275[13]

Doubly Clever (IRE) *Michael Blake* 131h
3 ch g Iffraaj Smartest (IRE) (Exceed And Excel (AUS))
(891) (1111) (1321) 4720[5] 5175[P] 5491[6]

Douchkirk (FR) *Kevin Bishop* 93h
8 b g Prince Kirk(FR) Douchka (FR) (Fijar Tango (FR))
364[P]

Dougalstar (FR) *Jennie Candlish* 93h 79c
6 b g Layman(USA) Concert House (IRE) (Entrepreneur)
88[5] 258[3] 588[5] 806[5] 934[10] 3131[P]

Douglas Julian *Katie Scott* 76h 118c
13 br g Overbury(IRE) Swing Quartet (IRE) (Orchestra)
81[P] 470[7]

Dounya's Boy *Christopher Kellett* 60h
6 ch g Sakhee(USA) Dounya (USA) (Caro)
353[6] 2024[P] 3484[11] 3840[15]

Douvan (FR) *W P Mullins* 159h 176c
5 b g Walk In The Park(IRE) Star Face (FR) (Saint Des Saints (FR))
(6a) (3271a) (3766a) (4696) (5215)

Dover The Moon (IRE) *Tom Gretton* 72h 61c
4 b g Bushranger(IRE) Gold Script (FR) (Script Ohio (USA))
360[7] 745[6] 1182[F] 1461[9] 1687[4] 2124[P]

Dovils Date *Tim Vaughan* 130h
6 gr g Clodovil(IRE) Lucky Date (IRE) (Halling (USA))
708[5]

Do We Like Him (IRE) *Chris Gordon* 109h
5 b g Beneficial Pattern Queen (IRE) (Alderbrook)
61[5] (1819) 2182[15]

Down The Line (IRE) *Alan Swinbank* 82h
5 b g Celtic Swing Aweigh (Polar Falcon (USA))
145[6] 2210[6] 2591[9] 3397[P] 4388[8] 4871[P]

Down Time (USA) *Brian Ellison* 108h 110c
5 b g Harlan's Holiday(USA) Frappay (USA) (Deputy Minister (CAN))
(1237) 1500[4] 1629[3] 2592[5] 3243[3] 4035[4] 4326[4] 4415[2]

Downtown Boy (IRE) *Ray Craggs* 105h
7 br g Kheleyf(USA) Uptown (IRE) (Be My Guest (USA))
1180[3] 1459[5] 1686[RR] 1887[8] 3398[P] 4863[7]

Down Under (IRE) *F Flood* 114h 126c
8 b g Milan She's All That (IRE) (Bob Back (USA))
3894a[7]

Doyly Carte *Donald McCain* 114h 121c
7 b m Doyen(IRE) Generous Diana (Generous (IRE))
418[6]

Draco *A P O'Brien* 140h
6 ch g Hernando(FR) Easibrook Jane (Alderbrook)
1565a[6] 4765[11]

Draco's Code *Gary Moore* 118h
4 b g Galileo(IRE) Lady Karr (Mark Of Esteem (IRE))
2409[4] 3083[2]

Dragon City *Charlie Mann* 92h
5 b g Elusive City(USA) Oulianovsk (IRE) (Peintre Celebre (USA))
1519[P] 1613[6] 1898[10] (2256) 2745[3]

Dragon De La Tour (FR) *Dan Skelton* 88h
4 b g Royal Dragon(USA) Turga De La Tour (FR) (Turgeon (USA))
2519[5] 3842[6] 4183[9]

Dragon Fei (IRE) *Dermot Anthony McLoughlin* 122h
5 b m Jeremy(USA) Wallonia (IRE) (Barathea (IRE))
2176a[5]

Dragon's Den (IRE) *Chris Down* 130h 132c
8 b g Antonius Pius(USA) Tallassee (Indian Ridge)
1754[2] (2010) 2347[5]

Dragonstone (FR) *D De Watrigant*
4 b g Muhtathir Solar Crystal (IRE) (Alzao (USA))
3876a[P]

Dragoon Guard (IRE) *Anthony Honeyball* 94h
4 b g Jeremy(USA) Elouges (IRE) (Dalakhani (IRE))
4449[6] 4681[7] 5063[8] 5352[4]

Drama King (IRE) *David Pipe* 101b
4 b g King's Theatre(IRE) Miss Arteea (IRE) (Flemensfirth (USA))
5097[7]

Dr Anubis (IRE) *Miss Hannah Taylor* 96h 89c
10 ch g Beneficial Gaelic (IRE) (Strong Gale)
12[U] 429[2] 699[3] 1894[5] 2057[4] 4295[P]

Draycott Place (IRE) *John Patrick Ryan* 123h 131c
6 b g Oscar(IRE) Power Again (GER) (Dashing Blade)
3552a[6] 3892a[6] 4397a[11]

Draytonian (IRE) *Philip Hobbs* 134h
5 br g King's Theatre(IRE) Full Of Birds (FR) (Epervier Bleu)
2196[3] (2716) 3284[12] 4366[8] (5139) ◆

Dr Beaujolais (IRE) *Richard Ford* 103h 99c
9 b g Dr Massini(IRE) Satlin (IRE) (Satco (FR))
3680[12] 4938[8] (5442)

Dr Cuddles (IRE) *David Bridgwater* 111h
7 b g Dr Massini(IRE) Native Emigrant (IRE) (Be My Native (USA))
2287[3]

Dr Dalwhinny *Donald McCain* 108h
6 ch g Dr Fong(USA) Snow Polina (USA) (Trempolino (USA))
843[6] 1010[P]

Dr Dreamy (IRE) *Claire Dyson* 61h 84c
8 b g Dr Massini(IRE) Proud Aldi (IRE) (Cataldi)
66[P] 333[3] 741[4] 926[4] 1004[8] (1287)

Dreambaby (IRE) *W P Mullins* 102b
4 b m Yeats(IRE) Monumental Gesture (IRE) (Head For Heights)
2486[13]

Dream Berry (FR) *Jonjo O'Neill* 124h
4 gr g Dream Well(FR) Kalberry (FR) (Kaldounevees (FR))
(5242)

Dream Bolt (IRE) *David Rees* 108h 119c
7 ch g Urban Ocean(FR) Riviera Dream (IRE) (Over The River (FR))
698[6] 976[3] (1121) 1241[F] 1455[3] (1577) (1647)

Dream Deal *Jeremy Scott* 121h
7 b g Presenting Rowlands Dream (IRE) (Accordion)
122[P] 1906[P]

Dream Flyer (IRE) *Michael Smith* 81h 120c
8 ch g Moscow Society(USA) Bright Choice (IRE) (The Parson)
2400[6] 3341[P]

Dreamingofrevelry *David Dennis* 81b
4 b m Kalanisi(IRE) Clandestine (Saddlers' Hall (IRE))
1057[4] 5457[11]

Dreamisi (IRE) *Ben Pauling* 90h
6 b g Kalanisi(IRE) Marvellous Dream (FR) (Muhtathir)
599[5] 858[P] 935[4] 1084[7]

Dream N (IRE) *Sean Curran* 98h 50c
7 b m Flemensfirth(USA) Roses Niece (IRE) (Jeu De Paille (FR))
90[P] 238[6]

Dream Place *Barry Murtagh*
4 b m Multiplex Globe Dream (IRE) (Eagle Eyed (USA))
257[6] 3476[12]

Dream's Burg (FR) *X-L Le Stang* 100h
4 b m Sageburg(IRE) Dream's Pegasus (AUS) (Fusaichi Pegasus (USA))
5135a[P]

Dreams Of Milan (IRE) *Peter Bowen* 108h 109c
7 b g Milan Joe's Dream Catch (IRE) (Safety Catch (USA))
2663[2] 3235[F]

Dreamsoftheatre (IRE) *Jonjo O'Neill* 85h 134c
7 gr g King's Theatre(IRE) Caroline Fontenail (IRE) (Kaldounevees (FR))
(1309) (1417) 1807[2] 2240[P] 2905[5] 3373[P] 5073[6] 5395[8]

Dresden (IRE) *Henry Oliver* 125h 151c
7 b g Diamond Green(FR) So Precious (IRE) (Batshoof)
1382[3] 1643[3] 1868[5] (2336) (2635) 3857[6] 4355[4] 4770[7]

Dressedtothenines (IRE) *Edward P Harty* 142h 121c
8 b m Oscar(IRE) Regal Holly (Gildoran)
3073a[7] 4397a[P] 5006a[4]

Driftashore (IRE) *Sally Randell* 130h
8 b g Jackson's Drift(USA) Your Cheatin Heart (IRE) (Broken Hearted)
127[3] 3804[3] 4389[7] (4824) 5053[P] 5391[10]

Drifter (IRE) *Harry Whittington* 116h
4 b g Footstepsinthesand Bright Bank (IRE) (Sadler's Wells (USA))
281[3] 835[3] 1012[4] 1166[11] (1493) (1686) 2006[3]

Driftwood Haze *Phillip Dando* 130h 34c
7 b g Nomadic Way(USA) Kristal Haze (Krisinsky (USA))
3570[6] 3745[8] 4339[6] 4614[2] (4822) 4922[7] (5239) 5396[5]

Drip Tray (IRE) *John Flint* 68h
5 b g Gamut(IRE) Superior Dawn (IRE) (Mandalus)
4266[4] 5469[12]

Dr Irv *Micky Hammond* 109h
6 ch g Dr Fong(USA) Grateful (Generous (IRE))
1260[4] 1661[4] 1903[11]

Drive On Locky (IRE) *Johnny Farrelly* 95h
8 b g Milan Husyans Beauty (IRE) (Husyan (USA))
4291[9] 4845[8]

Driving Well (IRE) *Arthur Whiting* 89h 47c
7 b g Oscar(IRE) Polly Anthus (Kahyasi)
388[7] 698[U] 782[P] 878[4] 972[4] 1287[8] 1509[8]

Dr Izzymoo (IRE) *Jennie Candlish* 79b
6 b g Dr Massini(IRE) Izzymoo (IRE) (Shahrastani (USA))
1378[5] 1693[P] 1895[P]

Dr Moloney (IRE) *S R B Crawford* 113h 115c
8 b g Dr Massini(IRE) Solal Queen (Homo Sapien)
483[2] 2105[6] 2788[3] 4053[2] 4582[3]

Drom *Mrs C Drury* 64h 118c
12 b g Gildoran Sabre Drom (Broadsword (USA))
(260) (521) 5392[5]

Drombeg West *Anna Brooks* 106h
8 b m Westerner Quinag (Tina's Pet)
(43) 283[U] 625[7] 2301[P] 2867[U] 3223[2] 3846[6] 4320[6] 4745[6]

Dromnea (IRE) *M F Morris* 121h 137c
8 bb g Presenting Fifth Imp (IRE) (Commanche Run)
69a[3] 2675a[5] 3296a[7] 3624[3] 5193[18]

Drop A Gear (IRE) *Lucinda Russell* 101h
5 b g Presenting Indian Love (FR) (Indian Danehill (IRE))
881[8] 1328[6] 1498[4] 1741[F] 2174[3] 2751[3]

Drop In The Ocean *Jonjo O'Neill* 70h
5 b g Kayf Tara Teenero (Teenoso (USA))
1290[6]

Drop Out Joe *Charlie Longsdon* 131h 153c
7 ch g Generous(IRE) La Feuillarde (FR) (Nikos)
318[4] (1849) (2348) 4472[5] 4858[7] 5494[15]

Dropzone (USA) *Brian Forsey* 88h 80c
6 b g Smart Strike(CAN) Dalisay (IRE) (Sadler's Wells (USA))
391[3] 675[2] 859[3] 1084[2] 1293[10] 1579[P]

Dr Paddy (IRE) *Lucy Normile* 51h
8 b g Dr Massini(IRE) Tina Torus (IRE) (Torus)
883[P]

Dr Robin (IRE) *Peter Bowen* 122h
5 b g Robin Des Pres(FR) Inter Alia (IRE) (Dr Massini (IRE))
837[2] (967) 1181[P] (1292) 1615[4]

Druid's Folly (IRE) *Rebecca Curtis* 116b
5 b g Beneficial Sweet Vale (IRE) (Supreme Leader)
2729[6] 3522[2] (4270)

Druids Lodge *Don Cantillon* 106b
4 ch g Tiger Hill(IRE) Mimiteh (USA) (Maria's Mon (USA))
188[7] 444[6] 2330[3] 3952[4]

Drumacoo (IRE) *Ben Pauling* 142h 155c
6 b g Oscar(IRE) My Native (IRE) (Be My Native (USA))
(3486) 4237[4]

Drumcliff (IRE) *Harry Fry* 122h
4 b g Presenting Dusty Too (Terimon)
(2991) ◆ 4364[3] 5002a[8]

Drumhart (IRE) *C A McBratney* 103h 105c
6 ch g Beneficial Nancylu (IRE) (Luso)
656[6] 881[4] 1330[7] 5447[P]

Drumlang (IRE) *Kevin Frost* 111h 134c
9 b g Soviet Star(USA) Sherekiya (IRE) (Lycius (USA))
642[P] 2121[2] 2577[9] 5465[13]

Drumlee Lad (IRE) *Johnny Farrelly* 119h
5 b g Millenary Rockport Rosa (IRE) (Roselier (FR))
1699[7] 1911[5] 2271[12] 3035[10] (4455) 5157[6] 5453[U]

Drumlee Sunset (IRE) *Philip Hobbs* 134h
5 br g Royal Anthem(USA) Be My Sunset (IRE) (Bob Back (USA))
2056[2] 2509[U] 3019[3] 3403[4] (4875) 5275[9]

Drumlister (IRE) *Dianne Sayer* 96h 108c
9 b g Luso Murrurundi (IRE) (Old Vic)
519[2] ◆ 847[3] 2950[2] 3310[P]

Drummond *Katie Stephens* 80h
6 b g Zamindar(USA) Alrisha (IRE) (Persian Bold)
1356[F] 1478[7] 1578[7] 1702[3] 1980[2] 2264[6] 4291[7] 4919[5] 5029[4] 5181[7]

Drumshambo (USA) *Venetia Williams* 86h 134c
9 b g Dynaformer(USA) Gossamer (USA) (Seattle Slew (USA))
2758^{4} 3109^{6} 3979^{3} 4444^{3} 5140^{3}
Drum Valley *Oliver Sherwood* 140h 132c
7 b g Beat Hollow Euippe (Air Express (IRE))
(2013) 3018^{6} 4017^{10} 5284^{16}
Drumviredy (IRE) *Venetia Williams* 108h
6 b m Flemensfirth(USA) Leitrim Bridge (IRE) (Earl Of Barking (IRE))
(2444) 2952^{3} 3252^{3} 3953^{P} 4268^{3} 5225^{6}
Dr West (IRE) *George Bewley* 103b
4 b g Westerner Contessa Messina (IRE) (Dr Massini (IRE))
4552^{U} 5014^{4}
Dry Ol'Party *Philip Hobbs* 113h
5 ch m Tobougg(IRE) Emergence (FR) (Poliglote)
511^{2} 714^{5} 1009^{3} 1352^{2} (1574) 1949^{3} ◆ 2093^{4}
Dubai Angel (IRE) *Malcolm Jefferson* 118b
4 b g Dubai Destination(USA) Just Another Penny (IRE) (Terimon)
1555^{2} 1973^{2}
Dubai Celebrity *John Wade* 90h
3 b g Sakhee(USA) Aljana (IRE) (Exceed And Excel (AUS))
4050^{3} 4633^{5} 4937^{P}
Dubai Devils (IRE) *Paul Stafford* 114h
4 b g Dubai Destination(USA) Saddlers Leader (IRE) (Saddlers' Hall (IRE))
2951^{3} 4031^{2} 4430^{2} 5012^{4}
Dubai Prince (IRE) *John Ferguson* 149h 147c
7 b g Shamardal(USA) Desert Frolic (IRE) (Persian Bold)
556^{3} (826) ◆ **(1047) (1266)** ◆ **1575^{2}**
Dubai Shen (IRE) *Alistair Whillans* 101h
4 b g Dubai Destination(USA) Graineuaile (IRE) (Orchestra)
257^{U} 2756^{8} 4181^{3} 4902^{6} 5294^{3}
Dubai Star (IRE) *John Ferguson* 76h
4 b g Dubawi(IRE) Tango Tonic (IRE) (Trans Island)
702^{8}
Dubawi Island (FR) *Venetia Williams* 135h
6 b g Dubawi(IRE) Housa Dancer (FR) (Fabulous Dancer (USA))
(2247) 2781^{8} 3254^{2} 3733^{10} 4730^{P}
Dubh Eile (IRE) *Tim Vaughan* 118h
7 br m Definite Article Aine Dubh (IRE) (Bob Back (USA))
(30) (314) 812^{3} 1038^{7} 3232^{12} 4466^{6} 4878^{3} 5409^{2}
Duc De Seville (IRE) *Michael Chapman* 69h
3 b g Duke Of Marmalade(IRE) Splendid (IRE) (Mujtahid (USA))
2863^{7} 3139^{2} 3724^{P} 3946^{P} 4645^{7} 5441^{P}
Dude Alert (IRE) *Gary Moore* 82h
5 b g Windsor Knot(IRE) Policy (Nashwan (USA))
2826^{4}
Due East *Micky Hammond* 84b
5 b m Bollin Eric Poor Celt (Impecunious)
1449^{5} 1688^{4} 2479^{5}
Dueling Banjos *Kim Bailey* 134h
5 rg g Proclamation(IRE) Kayf Lady (Kayf Tara)
(2239) 2787^{5} (4439) 5070^{3}
Due South (IRE) *Linda Jewell* 23h
4 b g City Honours(USA) Lady Shackleton (IRE) (Zaffaran (USA))
2710^{7}
Duhallowcountry (IRE) *Victor Thompson* 112h 89c
9 b g Beneficial Milltown Lass (IRE) (Mister Lord (USA))
77^{3} 254^{3} 288^{P} 487^{P} 1365^{5} 1570^{4} **1687^{6} 1857^{6} 2026^{5} 2320^{P} 2705^{2} 2981^{4} 3164^{4} 3243^{5} 3670^{4} 4329^{2} 4556^{2} (4707) 5231^{4} 5366^{6}**
Duke Arcadio (IRE) *Oliver Sherwood* 120h
6 b g Arcadio(GER) Kildowney Duchess (IRE) (Jurado (USA))
2898^{P} 4097^{9} 4323^{4}
Duke Des Champs (IRE) *Philip Hobbs* 142h
5 b g Robin Des Champs(FR) Ballycowan Lady (IRE) (Accordion)
2257^{2} (2864) 3137^{2} (3736) 4248^{3} 5194^{6}
Duke Of Medina (IRE) *Harry Whittington* 124h
3 br g Rock Of Gibraltar(IRE) Daruliyya (IRE) (Highest Honor (FR))
1805^{2} (2286) 3279^{2} 3848^{5} 4720^{14} 5095^{6}
Duke Of Monmouth (IRE) *Tom Symonds* 96h 98c
8 b g Presenting Hayley Cometh (IRE) (Supreme Leader)
55^{F}
Duke Of Navan (IRE) *Nicky Richards* 148h 153c
7 bb g Presenting Greenfieldflyer (IRE) (Alphabatim (USA))
103^{4} 2084^{5}
Duke Of North (IRE) *Jim Boyle*
3 b g Danehill Dancer(IRE) Althea Rose (IRE) (Green Desert (USA))
4784^{P}
Duke Of Sonning *Alan King* 113h
3 ch g Duke Of Marmalade(IRE) Moonshadow (Diesis)
(1928) 2219^{2}
Duke's Affair *Jeremy Scott* 105h
7 b g Fair Mix(IRE) Dunsfold Duchess (IRE) (Bustino)
(1383) 1598^{8} (1933) (2599) 2855^{2}
Dukes Den *Charlie Mann* 104h
4 b g Duke Of Marmalade(IRE) Green Room (FR) (In The Wings)
2710^{4} 3467^{4} 3837^{P} 4069^{P}
Duke Street (IRE) *Dr Richard Newland* 134h
3 b g Duke Of Marmalade(IRE) Act Of The Pace (IRE) (King's Theatre (IRE))
1656^{3} (1805) 2219^{3} 2371^{2} 4720^{9} (5095) 5491^{5}
Dulce Leo (FR) *J-P Gallorini* 145h 138c
9 b g Priolo(USA) Danissima (FR) (Fabulous Dancer (USA))
4a^{8} 349a^{9} 1883a^{12} 2361a^{8}
Dumbarton (IRE) *James Moffatt* 112h
7 br h Danehill Dancer(IRE) Scottish Stage (IRE) (Selkirk (USA))
502^{2}
Dun Bay Creek *Alan King* 87h
4 b g Dubai Destination(USA) Over It (Overbury (IRE))
3085^{4} 3525^{P}
Duncomplaining (IRE) *William Kinsey* 90h
6 b g Milan Notcomplainingbut (IRE) (Supreme Leader)
2428^{3}
Dundee Blue (IRE) *Henry Hogarth* 81h 91c
7 gr g Cloudings(IRE) Eurolucy (IRE) (Shardari)
135^{2} 2321^{R} 2705^{P} 3103^{8} 4048^{5} 4325^{4} 4704^{5}
Dun Faw Good *Mrs C Walton* 101c
8 br g Grape Tree Road Dun Rose (Roscoe Blake)
80^{3} 531^{F} 5258^{P}
Dunmallet Belle *Tom Symonds* 91h
6 b m Kayf Tara Magic Mistress (Magic Ring (IRE))
1618^{6} 2263^{8}
Dunnicks Boris *Sue Gardner* 74b
6 gr g Baryshnikov(AUS) Dunnicks Country (Town And Country)
4137^{P}
Dunnicks Delia *Sue Gardner* 74b
6 b m Crosspeace(IRE) Dunnicks Chance (Greensmith)
4321^{0}
Dunowen Point (IRE) *Donald McCain* 107h 123c
9 b g Old Vic Esbeggi (Sabrehill (USA))
338^{P}
Dunraven Storm (IRE) *Philip Hobbs* 143h 152c
10 br g Presenting Foxfire (Lord Americo)
103^{3} 1777^{4} 2059^{3} 2259^{4} 2635^{2} 3121^{2} 4770^{13}
Dun Scaith (IRE) *Sophie Leech* 114h 106c
7 b g Vinnie Roe(IRE) Scathach (IRE) (Nestor)
(328) 678^{3} 1046^{4} 1238^{6} 1366^{3} 4648^{P} 4965^{7} 5225^{5}
Durban Gold *Mrs D Walton* 95h 113c
8 ch m Flemensfirth(USA) Kohinor (Supreme Leader)
143^{4} (4207) 4820^{4} (5090)
Duroob *Anthony McCann* 85h 92c
13 b g Bahhare(USA) Amaniy (USA) (Dayjur (USA))
1462^{2} 1547^{3} 1890^{F}
Dursey Sound (IRE) *Jonjo O'Neill* 125h 131c
7 b g Milan Glendante (IRE) (Phardante (FR))
101^{6} 3954 642^{7} 1418^{3} (1616) 2008^{5} 2853^{P} 4363^{U} 5154^{P}
Dushrembrandt (IRE) *Robert Tyner* 133h 127c
9 b g Dushyantor(USA) Sue's A Lady (Le Moss)
2228a^{P} 3296a^{16}
Dusk Till Dawn (IRE) *David Pipe* 103h
6 b g King's Theatre(IRE) Savu Sea (IRE) (Slip Anchor)
928^{2} 1519^{4} 1912^{2} 2441^{F} 5034^{4} 5466^{5}
Dusky Bob (IRE) *Brian Ellison* 97h 102c
10 br g Bob Back(USA) Sunsets Girl (IRE) (The Parson)
203^{4} (2323) 2800^{7} 3312^{P} 4510^{3}
Dusky Lark *Colin Tizzard* 127h 140c
5 b g Nayef(USA) Snow Goose (Polar Falcon (USA))
2885^{3} 3134^{P} 3843^{6} 4363^{4} ◆ **(4978) 5354^{2}**
Dusky Legend *Alan King* 134h
5 b m Midnight Legend Tinagoodnight (FR) (Sleeping Car (FR))
2852^{2} 4734^{2}
Du Soleil (FR) *Venetia Williams* 106b
3 ch g Zambezi Sun Cykapri (FR) (Cyborg (FR))
(2629)
Dutch Canyon (IRE) *N W Alexander* 94h
5 b g Craigsteel Chitabe (IRE) (Lord Of Appeal)
139^{6} 2029^{F} 2322^{4} 2720^{4} 3684^{6} 5089^{6} 5472^{4}
Dutchesofrathmolyn (IRE) *Alison Batchelor* 87h
6 b m Kutub(IRE) Greenfieldflyer (IRE) (Alphabatim (USA))
2829^{P} 5483^{P}
Dye Of A Needle (IRE) *Evan Williams* 104h
5 ch g Lakeshore Road(USA) Laskine (IRE) (Charnwood Forest (IRE))
2413^{P} 3807^{P}
Dylanseoghan (IRE) *Zoe Davison* 112h
6 b g Pierre Sabbatical (IRE) (Jurado (USA))
3522^{5} 3775^{6} 4097^{4} 4788^{5} 5376^{P}
Dylan's Storm (IRE) *David Dennis* 87h
3 b g Zebedee Storm Lady (IRE) (Alhaarth (IRE))
1452^{4} 1486^{4} 1805^{4} 2000^{7} 4970^{2} 5374^{13}
Dynamic Drive (IRE) *Maurice Barnes* 119h 100c
8 b g Motivator Biriyani (IRE) (Danehill (USA))
345 **154^{4} 728^{9}** 805^{6} 872^{2} 1071^{6} 1182^{2} 1461^{3} 1501^{2} (1572) ◆ (1773) 1920^{2} 2170^{5}
Dynamic Idol (USA) *Johnny Farrelly* 95h 108c
8 bb g Dynaformer(USA) El Nafis (USA) (Kingmambo (USA))
569^{2} 824^{4} 878^{P}
Dynamic Ranger (USA) *Gary Moore* 112h
4 b g US Ranger(USA) Dynamous (USA) (Dynaformer (USA))
1425^{4} 1590^{3} 1998^{4} 2538^{2}
Dynamo (IRE) *Dan Skelton* 99h 99c
4 b g Galileo(IRE) Trading Places (Dansili)
131^{2} 353^{2} 624^{7} **1008^{3} 1169^{5} 1367^{U}**
Dynaste (FR) *David Pipe* 135h 161c
9 gr g Martaline Bellissima De Mai (FR) (Pistolet Bleu (IRE))
1883a^{9} **2200^{2} 2642^{3}** 3149^{8} **4240^{2} 4731^{7} 5176^{4} 5494^{9}**
Dysios (IRE) *Denis W Cullen* 103h 135c
7 b g Invincible Spirit(IRE) Hataana (USA) (Robellino (USA))
7a^{21}
Dystonia's Revenge (IRE) *Sheena West* 125h 117c
10 b g Woods Of Windsor(USA) Lady Isaac (IRE) (Le Bavard (FR))
800^{P} (1032) 1332^{P} 1743^{2} 2030^{2} 5126^{5} 5404^{P}
Eagle De L'Aube (FR) *E Lecoiffier*
4 b g Royal Dragon(USA) Cri De Coeur (FR) (Vettori (IRE))
4401a^{3}
Eamon An Cnoic (IRE) *David Pipe* 112h
4 b g Westerner Nutmeg Tune (IRE) (Accordion)
4827^{3} 5143^{5} 5393^{2} ◆
Earcomesthedream (IRE) *Peter Pritchard* 108h 44c
12 b g Marignan(USA) Play It By Ear (IRE) (Be My Native (USA))
(148) 377^{4} 758^{5} 2405^{P} (3128) 3220^{P} 3824^{6} 4127^{6} 4749^{7} 5033^{7}
Eardisland *Philip Hobbs* 113h
5 b m Kayf Tara Aranga (IRE) (Supreme Leader)
528^{2} 2452^{4} 3119^{5} (4546) 5185^{6}
Earls Quarter (IRE) *Ian Williams* 123h 111c
9 b g Shantou(USA) Par Street (IRE) (Dolphin Street (FR))
624^{5} 1051^{P} (Dead)
Early Boy (FR) *Andrew Crook* 67b
4 b g Early March Eclat De Rose (FR) (Scribe I (IRE))
187^{9} 5083^{7}
Early Flower (FR) *P Chatelain*
4 gr m Early March Fleur D'Irlande (IRE) (Kenmare (FR))
5499a^{F}
Early Retirement (IRE) *Caroline Bailey* 87h
3 b g Daylami(IRE) Deep Lilly (Glacial Storm (USA))
2992^{6} 4843^{U}
Earth Legend *Neil Mulholland* 25b
4 b g Helissio(FR) Maori Legend (Midnight Legend)
2020^{9} 5359^{11}
Earthmoves (FR) *Paul Nicholls* 130h
5 b g Antarctique(IRE) Red Rym (FR) (Denham Red (FR))
1848^{P}
Earth Shaker *Michael Easterby* 68b
3 b g Poseidon Adventure(IRE) Upton Seas (Josr Algarhoud (IRE))
2777^{12}
Earthwindorfire *Geoffrey Deacon* 86b
4 br g High Chaparral(IRE) Elemental (Rudimentary (USA))
67^{6} 341^{10} 2828^{5}
Easily Pleased (IRE) *Martin Hill* 107h 130c
9 b g Beneficial Bro Ella (IRE) (Cataldi)
121^{2} 218^{3} 669^{2} **(896) (1327) 1577^{2} 1735^{3} 4918^{P} 5184^{U}**
Easter Day (FR) *Paul Nicholls* 134h 152c
7 b g Malinas(GER) Sainte Lea (FR) (Sirk)
2242^{P} 2484^{6} 2759^{9} **3583^{2} 4141^{P}** 5120^{9} 5454^{4}
Easter Hunt (IRE) *Sara Ender* 109h 113c
6 br g Kalanisi(IRE) Easter Day (IRE) (Simply Great (FR))
2595^{8}
Eastern Calm *Oliver Sherwood* 101h
6 b m Kayf Tara New Dawn (Rakaposhi King)
108^{F} 746^{4}
Eastern Magic *Ben Case* 104h
8 b g Observatory(USA) Inchtina (Inchinor)
2221^{5} 2543^{8}
Eastern Witness (IRE) *Venetia Williams* 97h 82c
8 b g Witness Box(USA) Eastertide (IRE) (Alphabatim (USA))
2300^{P} 2827^{4}
East Hill *Colin Tizzard* 88h
5 b g Lucarno(USA) Sunnyland (Sovereign Water (FR))
1677^{P} (1947) 2087^{4} 3256^{8}
Eastlake (IRE) *Jonjo O'Neill* 126h 152c
9 b g Beneficial Guigone (FR) (Esprit Du Nord (USA))
2059^{P} 2784^{5} 3030^{P} 4770^{9} (5193)
Eastview Boy *Philip Kirby* 119h
4 ch g Iktibas Eastview Princess (J B Quick)
2984^{4} 3245^{3} 4001^{4} 4303^{7} 4548^{2} ◆ (4791)
Easy Beesy *Warren Greatrex* 114h 108c
7 b g Kalanisi(IRE) Queen Of The Bees (IRE) (Bob Back (USA))
210^{3} 445^{5}
Easydoesit (IRE) *Tony Carroll* 80h
7 b g Iffraaj Fawaayid (USA) (Vaguely Noble (IRE))
2038^{7} 2550^{RR}
Easyontheeye (IRE) *Linda Jewell* 52b
4 br m Kalanisi(IRE) Lady Bernie (IRE) (Supreme Leader)
2549^{9}
Easy Street (IRE) *Jonjo O'Neill* 106h
5 b g High Chaparral(IRE) Victorine (IRE) (Un Desperado (FR))
3413^{5} 4063^{6} 4976^{3} 5431^{2} ◆
Easy To Find (IRE) *Denis Gerard Hogan* 96h
5 b m High Chaparral(IRE) Stashedaway (IRE) (Treasure Hunter)
3474^{4} ◆
Eaton Hill (IRE) *Kerry Lee* 96b
3 b g Yeats(IRE) Guilt Less (FR) (Useful (FR))
4552^{4} 5055^{2}
Eaton Rock (IRE) *Tom Symonds* 108h 103c
6 b g Rocamadour Duchess Of Kinsale (IRE) (Montelimar (USA))
(2420) 3387^{4} 3746^{4} 4803^{P}
Ebadani (IRE) *Jamie Snowden* 124h
5 ch g Halling(USA) Ebatana (IRE) (Rainbow Quest (USA))
2928^{4} 3411^{9} 4317^{7} 5182^{2} ◆
Ebazan (USA) *Brian Ellison* 118h
6 ch g Lemon Drop Kid(USA) Ebaza (IRE) (Sinndar (IRE))
(747)
Ebony Empress (IRE) *Neil Mulholland* 126h 130c
6 br m Kris Kin(USA) Auditing Empress (IRE) (Accordion)
339^{2} ◆ **1932^{3}** ◆ **2313^{F} 2805^{4} 3373^{P} 5281^{3}**
Ebony Express *Dr Richard Newland* 136h
6 bl g Superior Premium Coffee Ice (Primo Dominie)
2512^{13} 2914^{7} 3449^{6} 3733^{13} 4622^{P}
Echo Brava *Jim Best* 99h
5 gr g Proclamation(IRE) Snake Skin (Golden Snake (USA))
3083^{5}
Echo Springs *Christopher Kellett* 113h
5 b g Kayf Tara Mrs Malt (IRE) (Presenting)
2080^{4} 2331^{3} 2744^{6} 3344^{6} 3837^{6} 5440^{2}
Eclair Gris (FR) *Y Fertillet* 93h 94c
6 gr g Fairly Ransom(USA) Rose Candy (FR) (Roli Abi (FR))
4400a^{3} 5136a^{P}
Eclectica Girl *Kevin Frost*
4 b m Multiplex Evelith Abbey (IRE) (Presenting)
3827^{6} 4188^{6}
Eco Warrior *Venetia Williams* 111h
5 b g Echo Of Light Kryssa (Kris)
2212^{4} 2472^{12} 2888^{4} **3362^{P} 3788^{P}** 4200^{4} 4712^{2}
Eddiemaurice (IRE) *John Flint* 111h
4 ch g Captain Rio Annals (Lujain (USA))
2093^{9} 2540^{10} 3318^{2} 3708^{4} 4447^{3} 5139^{7}
Eddy *John Panvert* 92h
6 b g Exit To Nowhere(USA) Sharway Lady (Shareef Dancer (USA))
167^{10} 435^{5} 712^{2} 858^{2} 1158^{6} 1236^{4}
Edeiff's Lad *Polly Gundry* 75h 86c
8 ch g Loup Sauvage(USA) Ede'Iff (Tragic Role (USA))
4291^{4} **(4686) 4850^{3} 5435^{3}**
Ede's The Business *Ken Wingrove* 81h
4 ch m Halling(USA) My Amalie (IRE) (Galileo (IRE))
1975^{4} 2218^{7}
Edeymi (IRE) *A J Martin* 137h 130c
7 b g Barathea(IRE) Edabiya (IRE) (Rainbow Quest (USA))
196^{8} (Dead)
Edgar (GER) *David Bridgwater* 97h 89c
5 b g Big Shuffle(USA) Estella (GER) (Acatenango (GER))
524^{F} 5482^{3}
Edgardo Sol (FR) *Emma Lavelle* 139h 151c
8 ch g Kapgarde(FR) Tikiti Dancer (FR) (Fabulous Dancer (USA))
1658^{8} 1976^{6}
Edlomond (IRE) *Bill Turner* 106h 115c
9 gr g Great Palm(USA) Samardana (IRE) (Hernando (FR))
2987^{5} 3314^{P} **3951^{2} 4778^{4} (5016) 5310^{3} (5379)**
Edmund (IRE) *Ann Hamilton* 104h 122c
8 b g Indian River(FR) Awomansdream (IRE) (Beneficial)
4046^{P} 4418^{6} 4551^{3} 4907^{7}
Edward Elgar *Caroline Bailey* 113h
4 ch g Avonbridge Scooby Dooby Do (Atraf)
(2808) (2974) 3725^{6} 4774^{P}
Edwulf *A P O'Brien* 128h 131c
6 b g Kayf Tara Valentines Lady (IRE) (Zaffaran (USA))
25a^{7} 4332a^{F}
Egmont *George Moore* 92h
3 b g Notnowcato Salutare (IRE) (Sadler's Wells (USA))
(636) 1111^{2} 1294^{3} 1456^{3} 2029^{7} 3804^{P}
Egon Spenglar *Donald Whillans* 32b
7 b g River Falls Wee Willow (Minster Son)
2338^{P}
Egret (IRE) *Lucinda Russell* 97h
5 b g Definite Article Bright Sprite (IRE) (Beneficial)
2479^{2} 2801^{4} 3340^{4} 3839^{12}
Egyptian Warrior (IRE) *A P O'Brien* 129h
6 bb g Galileo(IRE) Beltisaal (FR) (Belmez (USA))
19a^{F}
Egypt Mill Rebel *Tom George* 87h
5 b g Cockney Rebel(IRE) Beauchamp Jade (Kalaglow)
4915^{10}
Eightfold *Mrs A Corson* 77h 56c
6 b g Cadeaux Genereux Nirvana (Marju (IRE))
985a^{4}
Eight Till Late (IRE) *Peter Casey* 134h 83c
7 ch g Desert King(IRE) Princess Lek (IRE) (Bob Back (USA))
19a^{9} 1175a^{6}
Eiri Na Casca (IRE) *Denis Gerard Hogan* 98h 101c
6 b g Spadoun(FR) Lady Of Fleet (IRE) (Buckskin (FR))
3472^{2}
El Bandit (IRE) *Paul Nicholls* 112h
4 bb g Milan Bonnie Parker (IRE) (Un Desperado (FR))
4449^{8} 4874^{3} ◆ (5452)
El Beau (IRE) *John Quinn* 126h
4 ch g Camacho River Beau (IRE) (Galileo (IRE))
4179^{4} 4913^{8}
El Duque *Bill Turner*
4 b g Byron Royal Tavira Girl (IRE) (Orpen (USA))
1001^{U}
Electric Mayhem *Nick Mitchell* 99h 83c
8 b g Alflora(IRE) She's No Muppet (Teenoso (USA))
3222^{P}
Element Quartet (IRE) *Brendan Powell* 83h
6 b m Brian Boru Glendante (IRE) (Phardante (FR))
28^{5} 398^{5} 966^{7} 1509^{5} 2515^{3} 3087^{F} 3489^{P}
Elenika (FR) *Venetia Williams* 99h 127c
7 gr g Martaline Nika Glitters (FR) (Nikos)
2497^{F} (2908) 3365^{3} 3731^{4} 4234^{8} 4866^{5}
Elgin *Alan King* 107b
3 b g Duke Of Marmalade(IRE) China Tea (USA) (High Chaparral (IRE))
4392^{5} ◆ (4915)
El Indio (IRE) *Claire Dyson* 77h
8 b g Flemensfirth(USA) Final Bond (IRE) (Supreme Leader)
2410^{P} 2649^{6} 3220^{8} 3489^{4} 4349^{7} 4528^{4} 5033^{5} 5233^{4}
Elishpour (IRE) *A J Martin* 134h
5 b g Oasis Dream Elbasana (IRE) (Indian Ridge)
231a^{6} 1175a^{18}
Elkstone *Alan King* 103h
4 b g Midnight Legend Samandara (FR) (Kris)
98^{3} 2987^{11} 4460^{4} 4846^{5} 5433^{4} ◆
Ella's Promise *Martin Hill* 74b
6 ch m Doyen(IRE) Sweet N' Twenty (High Top)
4435^{U} 4916^{P}
Ellerslie Joe *Tom Tate* 16b
3 b g Captain Gerrard(IRE) Madam Bijou (Atraf)
4392^{12}

Ellie's Choice (IRE) *Des Donovan* 73h
6 b m Mountain High(IRE) Dolly Dove (Gran Alba (USA))
1781[6]

Ellistrin Belle *Donald Whillans* 91h
7 b m Helissio(FR) Hannah Park (IRE) (Lycius (USA))
(2427) 3473[9] 3888[P]

Ellusivance (IRE) *Nick Kent* 64h
5 b g Elusive Quality(USA) Germance (USA) (Silver Hawk (USA))
2972[P]

El Massivo (IRE) *Harriet Bethell* 121h
5 bb g Authorized(IRE) Umthoulah (IRE) (Unfuwain (USA))
(860) 973[5] 1261[7] 1945[P] 2808[2] 3318[6] 3921[4] (5081)

Elmore Back (IRE) *Charlie Mann* 125h 123c
6 b g Wareed(IRE) Katie Buckers (IRE) (Yashgan)
2774[4] 3235[P] 4465[P] 4876[P]

El Namoose *John Ferguson* 123h 137c
6 b g Authorized(IRE) Hashimiya (USA) (Gone West (USA))
2222[2] 2613[4]

Eloped *Ben Pauling* 84b
4 b m Midnight Legend Southern Exit (Poliglote)
4894[10]

Elsafeer (IRE) *D Russell* 85b
10 b g Sakhee(USA) Nabadhaat (USA) (Mr Prospector (USA))
260[P]

Elsie (IRE) *Thomas Mullins* 131h 115c
8 b m Milan Notcomplainingbut (IRE) (Supreme Leader)
70a[7]

El Tiburon (IRE) *Sam Thomas* 77h
3 b g Court Cave(IRE) Rongo's Last (IRE) (Little Bighorn)
2882[3] 3416[7] 5221[5]

El Toreros (USA) *Lawney Hill* 95h 99c
7 b g El Prado(IRE) Soul Reason (USA) (Seeking The Gold (USA))
713[6] 859[5] 1244[3]

Elusive Ivy (IRE) *Gavin Cromwell* 126h
5 b m Elusive City(USA) Just Like Ivy (CAN) (Street Cry (IRE))
3323a[4]

Ely Brown (IRE) *Charlie Longsdon* 104b
10 b g Sunshine Street(USA) Browneyed Daughter (IRE) (Broken Hearted)
2082[P]

Embracing Change (IRE) *Robert Tyner* 72h 135c
10 b g Anshan Temple Heather (Faustus (USA))
92a[3] 3894a[6]

Emcon (IRE) *W J Austin* 129h 131c
6 b m Vinnie Roe(IRE) So Supreme (IRE) (Supreme Leader)
1748a[4] **2465a[4] 3093a[3] 3604a[F] 4656a[3] 5006a[5]**

Emdale Ruby (IRE) *Sarah Dawson* 37b
5 ch m Generous(IRE) Bonny Rathlin (IRE) (Beauchamp King)
887[4]

Emerald Rose *Julian Smith* 115h 123c
8 b m Sir Harry Lewis(USA) Swiss Rose (Michelozzo (USA))
(128) (2551) 3176[2] 4775[3] 5281[4]

Emerging Force (IRE) *Harry Whittington* 148h
5 b g Milan Danette (GER) (Exit To Nowhere (USA))
(2519) 3117[3] (4066) 4911[U]

Emerging Talent (IRE) *Paul Nicholls* 140h
6 b g Golan(IRE) Elviria (IRE) (Insan (USA))
1870[4] (3411) 4111[2] (5182) (5356)

Emilio Largo *Mark Pitman*
7 b g Cadeaux Genereux Gloved Hand (Royal Applause)
3114[P]

Emily Gray (IRE) *Kim Bailey* 136h 150c
7 b m Flemensfirth(USA) Rose Island (Jupiter Island)
(2313) (2805) 3337[2] 3621[3] (4319) (5006a)

Eminent Poet *Venetia Williams* 128h
4 b g Montjeu(IRE) Contare (Shirley Heights)
2182[10] 3047[3] (3374) (3498) 3844[6] 4438[7] 5235[2]

Emkae (IRE) *J P G Hamilton* 74h 92c
7 b g Milan Hindi (FR) (Cadoudal (FR))
78[9] 453[4] 637[8] 1775[F] 1853[5] 4180[6]

Emma Lee *Peter Winks* 68b
5 b m Lucarno(USA) Marsh Run (Presenting)
359[6] 1057[7]

Emma Soda *Paul Davies* 103h 112c
10 b m Milan Ms Trude (IRE) (Montelimar (USA))
3385[P] 3979[2] (4185) 4649[4]

Emmy Lou (IRE) *Denis Gerard Hogan* 104h
7 ch m Presenting Ardnacrusha (IRE) (Electric)
2135[5]

Emperor Commodos *David Bridgwater* 121h
8 b g Midnight Legend Theme Arena (Tragic Role (USA))
2748[3] 3284[P]

Emperor Renard (IRE) *Mrs Marie McGuinness* 95b
4 b g Scorpion(IRE) Lirfox (FR) (Foxhound (USA))
5436[4]

Emperor Sakhee *Karen McLintock* 113b
5 ch g Sakhee(USA) Pochard (Inchinor)
(640) 3839[F]

Emperor's Choice (IRE) *Venetia Williams* 118h 143c
8 b g Flemensfirth(USA) House-Of-Hearts (IRE) (Broken Hearted)
(2638) 3518[P] 5327[P]

Empire Builder (IRE) *G T H Bailey* 111h 109c
9 b g Brian Boru Fair Draw (IRE) (Mister Mat (FR))
13[3] ◆ 533[6]

Empire Of Dirt (IRE) *C A Murphy* 144h 154c
8 b g Westerner Rose Of Inchiquin (IRE) (Roselier (FR))
2675a[F] 3296a[P] (3651a) (4733)

Empresario (IRE) *Matthew J Smith* 125h 130c
6 ch g Hurricane Run(IRE) La Stravaganza (USA) (Rainbow Quest (USA))
2329[3]

Empty Marmalades (FR) *Gary Moore* 83h
4 b g Poliglote Arvicaya (Kahyasi)
61[9] 279[5]

Empty The Tank (IRE) *Jim Boyle* 106h
5 b g Lawman(FR) Asian Alliance (IRE) (Soviet Star (USA))
180[10] (1095) (1446) 1524[2] (1596) 1810[5] 4846[10] 5374[4]

Empyrean (USA) *Mrs Annabel Wheatley* 59c
7 b m Aptitude(USA) Eternity (Suave Dancer (USA))
296[P]

Emral Silk *Sue Smith* 126h
7 b g Revoque(IRE) Silk Stockings (FR) (Trempolino (USA))
259[F] (Dead)

Enchanted Garden *Malcolm Jefferson* 19h 148c
7 ch g Sulamani(IRE) Calachuchi (Martinmas)
253[2] 635[3] (913) 1502[F] (1924) 2746[F] (Dead)

Encouraging (IRE) *Mike Sowersby*
6 ch g Rock Of Gibraltar(IRE) Unreachable Star (Halling (USA))
755[P]

Endeavor *Dianne Sayer* 103h 107c
10 ch g Selkirk(USA) Midnight Mambo (USA) (Kingmambo (USA))
508[4] 851[4] 1071[2] **(1416) 1639[6]** 1773[3] (1920) 2292[3] **2755[4] 2947[6] 3343[P]** 4326[8] 5445[17]

Endless Credit (IRE) *Micky Hammond* 126h
5 bb g High Chaparral(IRE) Pay The Bank (High Top)
1905[8]

Energica (FR) *D Windrif* 111h 122c
4 gr m Anabaa Blue Milonga (IRE) (Barathea (IRE))
2821a[8]

Engrossing *Peter Niven* 119h 109c
6 b g Tiger Hill(IRE) Pan Galactic (USA) (Lear Fan (USA))
2475[P] 2846[7] 3311[6]

Enjoy Responsibly (IRE) *Sam Thomas* 79h 140c
6 b g Flemensfirth(USA) Spice Patrol (IRE) (Mandalus)
47a[10] 3446[7] 3749[4] 4436[P]

Ennisnag (IRE) *Paul Henderson* 102h 80c
10 b m Bach(IRE) Ask Mother (IRE) (Buckskin (FR))
1086[2] 1293[7] 1509[3] 1756[5] 1951[4] 2139[4] 2548[5] **3903[P] 4412[3]**

Ennistown *John Ferguson* 132h
5 b g Authorized(IRE) Saoirse Abu (USA) (Mr Greeley (USA))
554[2] (932) (1081) 2196[2] 2594[2] 3032[4]

En Passe (IRE) *Charlie Longsdon* 40h
6 b m Flemensfirth(USA) Asklynn (IRE) (Beau Sher)
2164[9] 3612[P]

Entry To Evrywhere (IRE) *Alexandra Dunn* 83h 95c
7 b g Exit To Nowhere(USA) Killowen Pam (IRE) (Arctic Lord (IRE))
2712[3] 3089[4] 3586[8] **(4029) 4211[3] 4527[4] 4686[6] 5236[4]**

Ephraim *Charlie Mann* 125h
4 b g Rail Link Enrica (Niniski (USA))
2630[3] (3037) 3859[P]

Epic Ethel *Philip Hobbs* 88b
4 b m Midnight Legend Violet Elizabeth (Overbury (IRE))
(831)

Epic Warrior (IRE) *David Pipe* 126h 125c
6 b g Brian Boru Deise Dreamer (IRE) (Beneficial)
700[3] 1349[2] (1447) 1633[5] 1963[4] 2906[3] **3348[3] 4109[5] 4542[P] (4876)**

Episode *Philip Kirby* 61h
4 bb g Lucky Story(USA) Epicurean (Pursuit Of Love)
39[2] 706[5]

Epsom Flyer *Pat Phelan* 97h
5 ch g Haafhd River Cara (USA) (Irish River (FR))
449[3] 2256[3] 5479[4]

Equity Swap (IRE) *Tim Vaughan* 121h 73c
6 ch g Strategic Prince Medicean Star (IRE) (Galileo (IRE))
3826[P] 5225[F]

Ereyna *Stuart Edmunds* 104h
6 gr m Erhaab(USA) Tereyna (Terimon)
5420[4]

Erica Starprincess *George Moore* 80h
5 b m Bollin Eric Presidium Star (Presidium)
503[U] 679[5] 837[8] 1066[8] 1400[P]

Ericht (IRE) *Nicky Henderson* 132h 142c
9 b g Alderbrook Lady Orla (IRE) (Satco (FR))
24a[9] 420[2] 2473[4] 2780[U] 3776[5] (4363) 4735[P]

Erlkonig (GER) *Anthony Mullins* 135h
5 gr g Sternkoenig(IRE) Elora (GER) (Alkalde (GER))
1175a[9] 2485[5]

Ermyn's Edith *Pat Phelan* 69b
4 b m Fair Mix(IRE) Ivy Edith (Blakeney)
4103[10]

Ermyn's Emerald *Pat Phelan* 82b
3 bb g Alflora(IRE) Emerald Project (IRE) (Project Manager)
4414[4] 4790[13]

Eshtiaal (USA) *Gordon Elliott* 134h
5 b g Dynaformer(USA) Enfiraaj (USA) (Kingmambo (USA))
1983a[2] 5328[4]

Essteepee *Tim Vaughan* 99h
6 b g Double Trigger(IRE) Lamper's Light (Idiots Delight)
398[P]

Etania *Ian Williams* 101h 101c
7 b m King's Theatre(IRE) Linnet (GER) (Dr Fong (USA))
827[2] (873) 1306[4] (1598) **1930[6] 2539[5]**

Ethan (IRE) *Sheena Walton* 88h
6 b g Beneficial Timissa (IRE) (Kahyasi)
1774[6] 2025[7] 2791[10] 3474[9] 4035[8] 4815[P] (Dead)

Ethelred (IRE) *Jamie Snowden* 96h 96c
7 b g Alflora(IRE) Navale (FR) (Baryshnikov (AUS))
1842[U] 2598[P]

Ethelwyn *Malcolm Jefferson* 102h
5 ch m Alflora(IRE) Our Ethel (Be My Chief (USA))
334[3] 590[4] ◆ 1499[F] 2776[9] 4868[3] 5470[6]

Etheridge Annie *Hugo Froud* 91h
6 b m Leander Lady Harriet (Sir Harry Lewis (USA))
391[8]

Evening Stanley (IRE) *Oliver Sherwood* 101b
5 b g Stowaway Suzy Q (IRE) (King's Ride)
187[5] 4409[P] 4798[P] 5303[F]

Everaard (USA) *Micky Hammond* 114h 123c
9 ch g Lion Heart(USA) Via Gras (USA) (Montbrook (USA))
693[P]

Everlasting Spring (IRE) *Johnny Farrelly* 82h
7 b g High Chaparral(IRE) Lady Marshall (FR) (Octagonal (NZ))
360[6] 554[8] 1153[7]

Ever So Much (IRE) *Ben Haslam* 111h 114c
6 b g Westerner Beautiful World (IRE) (Saddlers' Hall (IRE))
157[7] 520[9] 1100[7] (1310) 1600[2] 1686[2] **2425[4] 2746[F] 3806[6] 4795[4]**

Everylasting (IRE) *Rose Dobbin* 79h 90c
8 b g Millenary All French (IRE) (Lepanto (GER))
78[2] (519) 842[4] 1551[4] 1857[5] 2191[P]

Exactly What *Donald McCain* 88h
6 b g Multiplex Heathyards Tipple (IRE) (Marju (IRE))
2401[4] 2895[4] 3397[U] 3509[6] 3971[7]

Exclusive Tara *Tim Easterby* 27h
5 b g Kayf Tara Exclusive Davis (USA) (Our Native (USA))
2169[12] 2716[7]

Executive Benefit (IRE) *J J O'Shea* 77h 105c
8 b m Beneficial Executive Dream (IRE) (Executive Perk)
16[3] 151[5]

Executive Order *Martin Smith* 1b
6 b g Overbury(IRE) Maiden Aunt (IRE) (Distant Relative)
3388[7]

Executive Prince (IRE) *Jeremy Scott* 93h
5 bl g Presenting Callanagh Pride (IRE) (Executive Perk)
5187[6] 5378[5]

Exemplary *Johnny Farrelly* 107h
8 b g Sulamani(IRE) Epitome (IRE) (Nashwan (USA))
283[4] 747[7] 1002[9] 1113[10] 1238[9] 2458[6] (2730) 2862[4] 3374[5] 3919[6] **4292[F]** 4922[10]

Exiles Return (IRE) *Jackie Retter* 73h
13 b g Needle Gun(IRE) Moores Girl (IRE) (Mandalus)
391[P] 527[P] 2454[P] 2661[P] 2880[5] 3120[P] 5267[4]

Exitas (IRE) *Phil Middleton* 124h 130c
7 b g Exit To Nowhere(USA) Suntas (IRE) (Riberetto)
2184[P] 2541[3] 2824[2] 3284[11] 3529[5] 3708[5] 4781[P]

Exit To Freedom *John Wainwright* 66h
9 ch g Exit To Nowhere(USA) Bobanvi (Timeless Times (USA))
522[11] 1273[P] **1370[F]** 1691[4] 2139[P] 4391[P] 4645[6]

Exmoor Challenge *Neil King* 72h 81c
6 b g Thank Heavens Bullys Maid (Button Bright (USA))
2410[U] 2771[3] 3062[P] 4783[7]

Exmoor Mist *Victor Dartnall* 108h 126c
7 gr g Kayf Tara Chita's Flora (Alflora (IRE))
2266[3] (2859) ◆ (3115) ◆ 4098[U] 4487[2] 5147[P]

Expanding Universe (IRE) *Tony Carroll* 84h 104c
8 b g Galileo(IRE) Uliana (USA) (Darshaan)
2811[3] 3199[F] 3218[P] 4214[4] 4749[8] 5079[8]

Expedite (IRE) *Charlie Mann* 111h
4 b g Brian Boru Angelica Garnett (Desert Story (IRE))
2807[5] (3221) ◆ 3736[P] 4224[P]

Expensive Taste (IRE) *Phil McEntee*
4 b g Moss Vale(IRE) Priceoflove (IRE) (Inchinor)
1766[F]

Experimentalist *Tim Vaughan* 103h 100c
7 b g Monsieur Bond(IRE) Floppie (FR) (Law Society (USA))
283[P] **772[4] 934[P]** 1137[2]

Explained (IRE) *Tim Vaughan* 114h 120c
8 b g Exit To Nowhere(USA) All Told (IRE) (Valanjou I (FR))
3931[2] 4642[P]

Express Du Berlais (FR) *Dr Richard Newland* 123h 133c
6 b g Saint Des Saints(FR) Euil Eagle (FR) (Saint Preuil (FR))
(62) 318[5] 532[P] **2517[4] 2766[4] 3236[P] (5247) 5395[P]**

Extreme Appeal (IRE) *Warren Greatrex* 92h
3 b g Excellent Art Silk Mascara (IRE) (Barathea (IRE))
2757[6] 2954[2]

Extreme Impact *Graeme McPherson* 117h 71c
9 b g Rock Of Gibraltar(IRE) Soviet Moon (IRE) (Sadler's Wells (USA))
2548[8] (2997) 3142[3] (3662) (4127) 4618[7] 5141[8]

Exxaro (IRE) *Henry De Bromhead* 136h
5 b g Presenting Mandys Gold (IRE) (Mandalus)
2052[5]

Eyes Of A Tiger (IRE) *Brian Ellison* 118h
4 ch g Golan(IRE) Backtothekingsnest (IRE) (King's Theatre (IRE))
4639[3] 4937[2] 5437[3]

Ezetiger *Pat Eddery* 86b
5 b g Tiger Hill(IRE) Guilty Secret (IRE) (Kris)
1817[7]

Face To Face *Mark Pitman* 99b
6 b g Kayf Tara Monsignorita (IRE) (Classic Cliche (IRE))
2188[5]

Face Value *Adrian McGuinness* 124h
7 b g Tobougg(IRE) Zia (GER) (Grand Lodge (USA))
2064[5] 2484[13]

Fact Of Life *Anthony Honeyball* 59b
3 b f Black Sam Bellamy(IRE) Fact Not Fiction (Erhaab (USA))
3862[10]

Fact Of The Matter (IRE) *Jamie Snowden* 110h
5 b g Brian Boru Womanofthemountain (IRE) (Presenting)
(1704) 1909[U] ◆ 2591[6] 4798[4]

Factor Fifty (IRE) *Philip Kirby* 120h 96c
6 b g Definite Article Sun Screen (Caerleon (USA))
622[5] 917[5] 1181[7] 1270[5] 1770[3] 2042[5]

Faerie Reel (FR) *Kim Bailey* 122h
5 b m Country Reel(USA) Final Whistle (IRE) (Rossini (USA))
2314[P] 4459[3] 4909[P] 5438[F]

Fafintadenient *Josef Vana* 123h 127c
8 b g Sakhee(USA) Sentee (IRE) (Montjeu (IRE))
(1671a) 5428a[6]

Fagan *Gordon Elliott* 147h
5 ro g Fair Mix(IRE) Northwood May (Teenoso (USA))
(1640) ◆ (2106) (2945) 4015[2] 4766[2] 5410[4]

Fago (FR) *Paul Nicholls* 108h 153c
7 bb g Balko(FR) Merciki (FR) (Villez (USA))
2171[2] 2635[5] 2902[4] 5297[P]

Faheem *Lydia Richards* 99b
4 b g Halling(USA) White Star (IRE) (Darshaan)
4102[7]

Fair Comment *Michael Blanshard* 46h
5 b m Tamayuz Cliche (IRE) (Diktat)
5373[9]

Fair Dilemma (IRE) *Chris Gordon* 79h 141c
10 b g Dr Massini(IRE) Midnight Dilemma (IRE) (Eagle Eyed (USA))
830[3] 974[3] 1482[5] **1777[6] 5465[9]**

Fairlee Grace *George Charlton* 67h
8 b m Fair Mix(IRE) Halo Flora (Alflora (IRE))
2721[9] 3476[10] 4052[4] 4369[6] 4702[4]

Fairlee Grey *Nicky Henderson* 109h
6 gr g Fair Mix(IRE) Halo Flora (Alflora (IRE))
378[F]

Fair Loch *Brian Ellison* 120h
7 gr g Fair Mix(IRE) Ardentinny (Ardross)
(1261) 1661[6] (2218) 3318[5] 3886[3] (4553) 4774[9]

Fair Lucky *Gary Moore*
6 gr g Fair Mix(IRE) Sunley Shines (Komaite (USA))
671[9]

Fair To Middling *Peter Bowen* 95h
5 gr g Fair Mix(IRE) Mtilly (Mtoto)
181[F] 1792[3] 2287[8] 3592[P]

Fair Wind *Conor O'Dwyer* 89b
4 b g High Chaparral(IRE) Night Teeny (Platini (GER))
11a[15]

Fairy Alisha *Trevor Wall* 106h
7 ch m Doyen(IRE) Regal Fairy (IRE) (Desert King (IRE))
217[3] 465[4] 1166[7] 1384[U] 1454[3] 1647[3]

Fairyinthewind (IRE) *Brendan Powell* 118h 125c
6 ch m Indian Haven Blue Daze (Danzero (AUS))
1135[7] (1344) 1451[4] 1643[5] 2468[8] 2784[7]

Fairy Princess *Mark Hoad* 68h
6 b m Volochine(IRE) Queen Of Cologne (IRE) (Brief Truce (USA))
100[7] 673[5]

Fairy Rath (IRE) *Nick Gifford* 113h 137c
9 ch g Accordion Killoughey Fairy (IRE) (Torus)
1976[P] 2615[3] 3036[2] 3445[7] 3731[5] (4230) 4787[P] 5193[2]

Fairytale Theatre (IRE) *Dan Skelton* 136h
8 b m King's Theatre(IRE) Bay Dove (Alderbrook)
2685[3] 3444[3] 3732[8] **4402[F]** 4699[16]

Fairy Theatre (IRE) *Iain Jardine* 102h
4 b m King's Theatre(IRE) Fairy Native (IRE) (Be My Native (USA))
459[5] 1555[7] 1852[2] 2428[P]

Faithful Mount *Ian Williams* 122h
6 b g Shirocco(GER) Lady Lindsay (IRE) (Danehill Dancer (IRE))
105[3] 621[4] 2516[F]

Faith Jicaro (IRE) *David Bridgwater* 109h 108c
8 b m One Cool Cat(USA) Wings To Soar (USA) (Woodman (USA))
170[5] 589[4] 806[3] 976[2] 1159[2] 1458[6] 1595[6]

Falcarragh (IRE) *Tim Vaughan* 112h 132c
8 ch g Alderbrook Magheraregh Lady (IRE) (Old Vic)
709[3] 927[3] 1418[5] 1714[8] 2867[3] 3884[3]

Falcon Crest (IRE) *C Roche* 142h
5 b g Milan One By One (IRE) (Topanoora)
(2672a) 3294a[5]

Falconettei (GER) *P Vovcenko* 120h
6 bb g Desert Prince(IRE) Fortezza (GER) (Law Society (USA))
1671a[6]

Falcons Fall (IRE) *Tom Symonds* 75h
4 ch g Vertical Speed(FR) Ellie Park (IRE) (Presenting)
2493[7] 4805[7] 5452[7]

Falcon's Legend *John Weymes* 76b
5 ch m Midnight Legend Bling Noir (FR) (Moscow Society (USA))
1094[P] 1447[P]

Falcon's Reign (FR) *Michael Appleby* 73h
6 ch g Haafhd Al Badeya (IRE) (Pivotal)
5349[3]

False Accusation (IRE) *Nigel Twiston-Davies* 50h
6 b g Artan(IRE) Annadot (IRE) (Roselier (FR))
242[5] 554[9]

Family Motto *Chris Gordon* 108h 86c
6 b g Tobougg(IRE) Be My Mot (IRE) (Be My Native (USA))
450[P] 675[P]

Fanny Fantastic *Miss Imogen Pickard*
6 b m Alflora(IRE) Court Champagne (Batshoof)
176[P]

Fantasy King *James Moffatt* 117h 128c
9 b g Acclamation Fantasy Ridge (Indian Ridge)
186[4] **(469) 830[U]** 1404[4] **1418[2] 1553[F] 1922[3]**

Farang Ber Song *Declan Carroll*
4 b g Selkirk(USA) Dazzle (Gone West (USA))
783[7]

Faraway Mountain (IRE) *Gordon Elliott* 19h
7 ch g Indian Haven Muschana (Deploy)
2428[6]

Farbreaga (IRE) *Harry Whittington* 88h 134c
9 b g Shernazar Gleann Alainn (Teenoso (USA))
3046[P] 3373[P] 4348[9] 5162[4]

Farewelltocheyenne (IRE) *N W Alexander* 91h
7 b g Zagreb(USA) Valerie Ellen (IRE) (Accordion)
285[7] 3667[10] 4403[5] 5009[6]

Far From Defeat (IRE) *Michael Scudamore* 105h
5 b g Robin Des Pres(FR) Clonsingle Native (IRE) (Be My Native (USA))
1852[P] 2995[P] 3817[P] 4351[4] 4883[P]

Farmer Matt (IRE) *Fergal O'Brien* 111h 124c
9 bb g Zagreb(USA) Ashville Native (IRE) (Be My Native (USA))
141[P] 4043[2] 4651[P]

Farm Pixie (IRE) *Mrs K Weir* 54h 56c
9 b g Snurge Blue Bobby (IRE) (Flemensfirth (USA))
5258[6]

Farragon (IRE) *Lucinda Russell* 91h
5 b g Marienbard(IRE) Oath Of Allegiance (IRE) (Supreme Leader)
2102[4]

Farrells Destiny *Chris Bealby* 73b
3 gr g Proclamation(IRE) Hello Hello (Helissio (FR))
3048[9]

Fashion Icon (FR) *Nigel Hawke* 79h
4 b m Arvico(FR) Royale Sulawesie (FR) (Jimble (FR))
119[3] 383[P] 658[8] 1120[P] 1261[U] 1823[P]

Fast Exit (IRE) *Neil Mulholland* 104h 100c
8 b g Exit To Nowhere(USA) Gift Token (Batshoof)
450[2] 698[P] 1079[7] 1287[P]

Fast Scat (USA) *Steve Flook* 91h
3 ch f Scat Daddy(USA) Furusato (USA) (Sendawar (IRE))
690[3] 778[4] 1805[3] 2032[2] 4799[9]

Fatcatinthehat *Harry Whittington* 117h
6 b g Authorized(IRE) Fin (Groom Dancer (USA))
3152[5] 4129[P]

Father Edward (IRE) *John Ferguson* 123h 123c
6 b g Flemensfirth(USA) Native Side (IRE) (Be My Native (USA))
494[2] (647) 957[3] (1082) 1179[3] **2289[2] 2691[5] 3024[9]**

Father Probus *Michael Appleby* 93h 100c
9 ch g Fleetwood(IRE) Nearly At Sea (Nearly A Hand)
2839[3] **3727[P] 4073[P]**

Faugheen (IRE) *W P Mullins* 177h
7 b g Germany(USA) Miss Pickering (IRE) (Accordion)
(71a) 2532a[2] (3230) ◆ (3768a)

Faustina Pius (IRE) *Matt Sheppard* 95h 121c
7 b m Antonius Pius(USA) Out In The Sun (USA) (It's Freezing (USA))
712[F] **1056[2] (1159) (1298) 1715[3] 2149[3] 2451[P]**

Fauve (IRE) *Richard Hawker* 102h
4 b g Montjeu(IRE) Simaat (USA) (Mr Prospector (USA))
702[3] 932[3] 1153[10] 2271[16] 3619[14]

Favorite Girl (GER) *Michael Appleby* 124h 43c
7 b m Shirocco(GER) Favorite (GER) (Montjeu (IRE))
2186[7] **2774[U] 3335[5]** 4459[2] 4986[7]

Favorito Buck's (FR) *Paul Nicholls* 121h
3 b g Buck's Boum(FR) Sangrilla (FR) (Sanglamore (USA))
3279[P] 4462[3]

Favoured Nation (IRE) *Jonjo O'Neill* 89h 125c
8 b g Milan Bless Of Honour (IRE) (Shardari)
553[4]

Fayette County (IRE) *Tim Vaughan* 130h 139c
8 b g Golden Lariat(USA) Midsyn Lady (IRE) (Sharp Victor (USA))
3521[P] 4891[2] 5179[P]

Fazakerley (IRE) *Paul Nicholls* 24b
4 b g Robin Des Pres(FR) Vita (Northern Park (USA))
2351[11]

Fazenda's Girl *Ian Williams* 81h
3 b f Stimulation(IRE) Goes A Treat (IRE) (Common Grounds)
1486[3]

Fearachain (IRE) *Anthony Mullins* 129h
7 b g Craigsteel Amerfontaine (IRE) (Lord Americo)
2485[8]

Fear Glic (IRE) *Jackie Du Plessis* 127h 107c
9 b g Dr Massini(IRE) Graineuaile (IRE) (Orchestra)
3415[3] 5046[6]

Fearless Fantasy (IRE) *C Price* 95b
4 b m Oscar(IRE) Pharlen's Dream (IRE) (Phardante (FR))
(5436)

Fearsome Fred *Caroline Bailey* 95h
6 b g Emperor Fountain Ryewater Dream (Touching Wood (USA))
1447[5]

Feast Of Fire (IRE) *Joanne Foster* 108h 103c
8 ch g St Jovite(USA) Bellagrana (Belmez (USA))
81[4] 967[5] 1113[8] 1264[8] 1615[6] **(1783) 1970[7] 3024[8] 3310[P] 4514[2] 5013[6] 5404[2]**

Featherintheattic (IRE) *A J S Phillips-Hill* 105b
10 b g Bahri(USA) Silk Feather (USA) (Silver Hawk (USA))
4383[U] 5075[P]

Feather Lane (IRE) *Donald McCain* 80h
5 br g Court Cave(IRE) Laffan's Bridge (IRE) (Mandalus)
2769[P] 4817[4]

Federici *E Bolger* 128h 134c
6 b g Overbury(IRE) Vado Via (Ardross)
2236a[9] 2525a[2] **4397a[6]**

Feeling Peckish (USA) *Michael Chapman* 44h 45c
11 ch g Point Given(USA) Sunday Bazaar (USA) (Nureyev (USA))
1273[P]

Feel The Air (IRE) *Mark Michael McNiff* 114h
5 br m Papal Bull Zephyr Lilly (IRE) (Alhaarth (IRE))
1854[7] 4939[6]

Feisty Girl *Michael Mullineaux* 40h
5 ch m Erhaab(USA) Dolly Duff (Alflora (IRE))
528[U] 813[P] 1165[9]

Felice (IRE) *Scott Dixon*
5 b m Papal Bull Tarabaya (IRE) (Warning)
3947[P] 4473[4]

Felix Yonger (IRE) *W P Mullins* 138h 165c
9 b g Oscar(IRE) Marble Sound (IRE) (Be My Native (USA))
(8a) 2464a[3] (3092a) (3892a) 4718[P]

Fella *Gary Moore* 91b
3 b g Sagamix(FR) Encore Du Cristal (USA) (Quiet American (USA))
3048[3] 3847[10]

Fell Runner *Nicky Henderson* 12b
4 b g High Chaparral(IRE) Firoza (FR) (King's Best (USA))
187[P] 4102[15]

Fenlon's Hill (IRE) *Paul Stafford* 98h
4 b g Court Cave(IRE) Eva's Lass (IRE) (Flemensfirth (USA))
3476[2] 4037[7]

Fennis Moll (IRE) *John Joseph Hanlon* 101h 110c
6 b m Presenting No Moore Bills (Nicholas Bill)
(1978)

Fergall (IRE) *Seamus Mullins* 137h 101c
8 br g Norwich Gaybrook Girl (IRE) (Alderbrook)
1977

Fergal Mael Duin *David Bridgwater* 115h 132c
7 gr g Tikkanen(USA) Fad Amach (IRE) (Flemensfirth (USA))
(2014) 2436[6] 3235[F]

Ferngrove (USA) *Warren Greatrex* 79h
4 gr g Rockport Harbor(USA) Lucky Pipit (Key Of Luck (USA))
1693[7]

Festive Affair (IRE) *Jonjo O'Neill* 130c
7 b g Presenting Merry Batim (IRE) (Alphabatim (USA))
2336[P] 2884[4] 4464[4] 4787[6] (5394)

Fethard Player (IRE) *W F Treacy* 155h
8 b g King's Theatre(IRE) Sly Empress (IRE) (Supreme Leader)
7a[8] 1787a[2] 4765[2]

Fever Pitch (IRE) *A L T Moore* 124h 129c
9 b g Dushyantor(USA) Stormey Tune (IRE) (Glacial Storm (USA))
3073a[2] 3651a[8]

Fiasco *A Campbell* 68c
6 b g Presenting Deep Sunset (IRE) (Supreme Leader)
3585[P]

Fibre Optic *Rose Dobbin* 98h
3 b g Rip Van Winkle(IRE) Wind Surf (USA) (Lil's Lad (USA))
2324[P] 4104[3] 4324[5]

Fiddler's Flight (IRE) *John Norton* 90h
9 b g Convinced Carole's Dove (Manhal)
2492[6] 2982[5] (3244) 3807[U] (4049) 4513[3] 4703[4] 5333[2]

Fiddlers Reel *Jane Clark* 115h 130c
12 ch g Karinga Bay Festival Fancy (Le Coq D'Or)
(4872) 5259[2]

Fidelity *Jonathan Geake* 48h
3 b g Halling(USA) Sir Kyffin's Folly (Dansili)
2273[9] 2578[3] 2992[9] 4454[8]

Fields Of Glory (FR) *Tim Vaughan* 111h
5 b g King's Best(USA) Lavandou (Sadler's Wells (USA))
400[2] ◆ 1544[6] 1781[4] 2123[8] 3487[7] (4506) 5267[2]

Fieldsofsilk (IRE) *Jennie Candlish* 67h
3 b g Robin Des Champs(FR) Silk Style (Polish Precedent (USA))
4915[12] 5437[7]

Fifi L'Amour (IRE) *Linda Jewell* 77h
9 ch m Flemensfirth(USA) Supreme Adventure (IRE) (Supreme Leader)
597[8] 4025[3] 4528[3] 4936[5] 5305[P] 5481[3]

Fifteen Kings (IRE) *Lucinda Russell* 90h
5 b g King's Theatre(IRE) Mistletoeandwine (IRE) (Un Desperado (FR))
2101[F] 2318[8] 2474[5]

Figaro *Tim Vaughan* 125h 105c
7 ch g Medicean Chorist (Pivotal)
259[4] 623[P] 677[P] 1043[P]

Fight Away Boys (IRE) *Mrs Caroline Crow* 103h 47c
7 ch g Vertical Speed(FR) Say Ya Love Me (IRE) (Presenting)
5258[7]

Fight Commander (IRE) *Oliver Sherwood* 109h 125c
6 b g Oscar(IRE) Creidim (IRE) (Erins Isle)
2222[7] (4071) 4451[2] 4780[4]

Fighter Jet *John Mackie* 127h
7 b g Oasis Dream Totality (Dancing Brave (USA))
461[P] 681[4] 1002[2] 2054[6] 2624[9] 2744[13]

Fighting Back *Henry Hogarth* 73h
4 b g Galileo(IRE) Maroochydore (IRE) (Danehill (USA))
3021[16]

Filament Of Gold (USA) *Roy Brotherton* 53h
4 b g Street Cry(IRE) Raw Silk (USA) (Malibu Moon (USA))
860[10] 1452[7]

Filatore (IRE) *Bernard Llewellyn* 119h
6 ch g Teofilo(IRE) Dragnet (IRE) (Rainbow Quest (USA))
2369[7] 2873[5] 3078[6] 3517[3] 3978[8] 4537[5] 4825[2] (5237)

Filbert (IRE) *Philip Hobbs* 119h 143c
9 b g Oscar(IRE) Coca's Well (IRE) (Religiously (USA))
1869[8] 2459[F] 5448[U]

Filbert Fox (IRE) *Ms Samantha Burns* 29h 80c
9 b g Snurge Shean Storm (IRE) (Glacial Storm (USA))
80[7]

Fille Des Champs (IRE) *Evan Williams* 78h
4 b m Robin Des Champs(FR) South Queen Lady (IRE) (King's Ride)
4270[5] 4961[4] 5378[4]

Fill The Power (IRE) *Sue Smith* 126h 140c
9 b g Subtle Power(IRE) Our Alma (IRE) (Be My Native (USA))
(156)

Fillydelphia (IRE) *Patrick Holmes* 81h
4 b m Strategic Prince Lady Fonic (Zafonic (USA))
2325[6]

Film Director (IRE) *Brian Ellison* 115h
7 b g Tiger Hill(IRE) Stage Manner (In The Wings)
1967[2]

Fils Prodige (FR) *D Bressou*
2 b g Naaqoos Lulu Rouge (FR) (Astarabad (USA))
5498a[6]

Finaghy Ayr (IRE) *Ian Duncan* 102h 41c
7 ch g Lahib(USA) Ali Ankah (IRE) (Insan (USA))
2103[3] 2432[3] (2806)

Final Assault (IRE) *Lucinda Russell* 116h 149c
6 bb g Beneficial Last Campaign (IRE) (Saddlers' Hall (IRE))
1902[3] ◆ (2431) ◆ 2790[4] 3157[U] 3851[5] 4370[4] 4912[P]

Final Countdown *John Quinn* 111h
4 ch g Selkirk(USA) Culture Queen (King's Best (USA))
1979[5]

Final Fling (IRE) *Rose Dobbin* 89h
4 b g Milan Supreme Singer (IRE) (Supreme Leader)
1926[3] 2895[3] 3668[7] 4031[7] 4202[4] 5199[6]

Final Flow *Colin Tizzard*
6 ch g With The Flow(USA) The Final One (Nearly A Hand)
4256[P] 4848[P]

Final Nudge (IRE) *David Dennis* 138h
6 b g Kayf Tara Another Shot (IRE) (Master Willie)
2287[2] (2603) (2769) 3032[2] 3623[5] 4072[3] (4535) ◆

Final Say *Simon Hodgson*
5 b m Alflora(IRE) En Vacances (IRE) (Old Vic)
4687[13]

Financial Climate (IRE) *Oliver Sherwood* 116h 137c
8 b g Exit To Nowhere(USA) Claudia's Pearl (Deploy)
2616[7] 2899[6] ◆ 3404[3] 4101[P] 4621[4] 5274[6]

Finch Flyer (IRE) *Aytach Sadik* 95h 74c
8 ch g Indian Ridge Imelda (USA) (Manila (USA))
258[5] 806[7] 3932[P]

Fin D'Espere (IRE) *Suzy Smith* 113h
4 b g Zagreb(USA) Rapsan (IRE) (Insan (USA))
1973[5] 2239[6] 3085[2] 3775[F] 4466[2] 5072[4]

Finding Your Feet (IRE) *Jonjo O'Neill* 115h 111c
7 bb g Heron Island(IRE) Silvretta (IRE) (Tirol)
1837 239[P] (698) 1372[5]

Findlay's Find (IRE) *Mrs Myfanwy Miles* 112c
9 ch g Medicean Lady Pahia (IRE) (Pivotal)
17[4] 393[4] 535[P]

Finea (IRE) *R K Watson* 81h 121c
8 b g Exit To Nowhere(USA) Annies Carmen (IRE) (Zaffaran (USA))
2177a[7] **2206a[5] 4166[4] (4177) 4327[2] 4517a[5]**

Fine Jewellery *Tom Gretton* 71h
6 b g Epalo(GER) Lola Lolita (FR) (Dom Alco (FR))
1801[3] 694[P] 5099[7]

Fine Parchment (IRE) *Charlie Mann* 87h 123c
12 b g Presenting Run For Cover (IRE) (Lafontaine I (USA))
2374[5] 2766[6] 3373[3] 4027[2] 4255[P] 4872[2] 5247[P]

Fine Resolve *Andrew Leyshon* 104c
6 b g Refuse To Bend(IRE) Papillon De Bronze (IRE) (Marju (IRE))
13[8] 393[5]

Fine Rightly (IRE) *S R B Crawford* 114h 150c
7 b g Alflora(IRE) Bealtaine (IRE) (Zaffaran (USA))
2676a[10] **(3073a) 3651a[4] 4007a[3] (4949a)**

Fine Theatre (IRE) *Paul Nolan* 124h 132c
5 b g King's Theatre(IRE) Finemar Lady (IRE) (Montelimar (USA))
2676a[P] **5132a[4]**

Fine Tune (IRE) *Linda Jewell* 95h
4 b g Medicean Phillippa (IRE) (Galileo (IRE))
2251[6] 2928[12] 3450[3] 4028[5]

Fingal Bay (IRE) *Philip Hobbs* 153h 147c
9 b g King's Theatre(IRE) Lady Marguerrite (Blakeney)
2242[2] 2783[4] 3150[3] 3741[3] 4141[2] 4733[P] 5092[8]

Fingerontheswitch (IRE) *Neil Mulholland* 138h
5 b g Beneficial Houseoftherisinsun (IRE) (Fourstars Allstar (USA))
1550[2] (1829) 2513[4] 3018[9] (4305) 4911[2] 5284[8]

Fingers Crossed (IRE) *Paul Webber* 108h
5 b g Bach(IRE) Awesome Miracle (IRE) (Supreme Leader)
3628[4] 4229[7]

Fingertips (FR) *David Pipe* 125h
3 gr g Martaline Deesse D'Arabie (FR) (Trempolino (USA))
2480[5] (2883) 3988[F] 4239[2] 4470[3]

Finish The Story (IRE) *Johnny Farrelly* 100h 121c
9 b g Court Cave(IRE) Lady Of Grange (IRE) (Phardante (FR))
363[6] 716[4] 897[4] **1007[6] 1114[3]** 1375[8] 1890[3] **2146[3] 2517[2] 2934[P] 4340[P] 4935[3] 5274[4]**

Finnegan's Garden (IRE) *Zoe Davison* 80h 27c
6 b g Definite Article Tri Folene (FR) (Nebos (GER))
401[3] 595[7] 2312[6] **3178[4]**

Fintan *Sheena West* 100h
12 ch g Generous(IRE) Seeker (Rainbow Quest (USA))
2599[P]

Finula (IRE) *Edward U Hales* 92b
3 bb g Robin Des Champs(FR) Glens Ruby (IRE) (Presenting)
5134a[2]

Fionn Mac Cul (IRE) *Venetia Williams* 120h
4 b g Oscar(IRE) No Moore Bills (Nicholas Bill)
2331[6] (3581) 3795[3] (4284)

Fire (IRE) *Chris Bealby* 91h
5 ch g Royal Anthem(USA) Patsy's Choice (IRE) (Eurobus)
1829[6] 2221[7] 2487[7] 3234[8] **4556[P]**

Firebird Flyer (IRE) *Evan Williams* 117h 144c
8 b g Winged Love(IRE) Kiora Lady (IRE) (King's Ride)
2643[P] 2907[3] 3518[2] (4802)

Fire In Soul (IRE) *W P Mullins* 144h
4 br g Robin Des Champs(FR) Cherry Black (IRE) (Roselier (FR))
4955a[9]

Fire Rock (IRE) *Nicky Richards* 73h
4 b g Scorpion(IRE) Cooline Jana (IRE) (Presenting)
2101[6] 2318[11] 2704[7] 4403[8]

Fire Ship *Brendan Powell* 95h
6 b g Firebreak Mays Dream (Josr Algarhoud (IRE))
3114[5] 3484[9]

Fire Tower *Richard Phillips* 109h
7 ch m Firebreak Lamper's Light (Idiots Delight)
(337) ◆ 747[2]

Firm Order (IRE) *Paul Webber* 103h 134c
10 b g Winged Love(IRE) Fairylodge Scarlet (IRE) (Mister Lord (USA))
1807[P] 2473[10] 2887[3] 4062[U] 4789[P]

Firmount Beech (IRE) *Mrs E Scott* 74b
11 b g Anshan Tinkers Lady (IRE) (Sheer Grit)
4295[U]

First Avenue *Laura Mongan* 131h
10 b g Montjeu(IRE) Marciala (IRE) (Machiavellian (USA))
701[7] 2415[7] 3045[2] 4159[5]

First Bag (FR) *Anthony Clement*
4 b h Rashbag Drop Dead Gorgeous (IRE) (Bering)
3815a[7]

First Drift *Ben Case* 109b
4 ch g Generous(IRE) Supreme Cove (Supreme Leader)
(5315)

First Du Charmil (FR) *Tom Lacey* 91b
3 ch g Ballingarry(IRE) Famous Member (FR) (Peintre Celebre (USA))
4392[4]

First Fandango *Tim Vaughan* 136h 136c
8 b g Hernando(FR) First Fantasy (Be My Chief (USA))
448[9] 681[5] 916[P] 1138[5]

First Figaro (GER) *D K Weld* 128b
5 ch g Silvano(GER) Felina (GER) (Acatenango (GER))
25a[2] 4721[9] ◆

First Lieutenant (IRE) *M F Morris* 125h 161c
10 ch g Presenting Fourstargale (IRE) (Fourstars Allstar (USA))
95a[8] 2464a[4] 2783[3] 3324a[2] 4007a[P] 5218[F]

First Moon (FR) *Y Fertillet* 111h 101c
4 gr m Nombre Premier October Moon (FR) (Octagonal (NZ))
3815a[2]

First Of Never (IRE) *Lynn Siddall* 73h
9 b g Systematic Never Promise (FR) (Cadeaux Genereux)
137[2] 2492[13] 2745[10] 3840[12] 5349[5]

First Post (IRE) *Adrian McGuinness* 118h
8 b g Celtic Swing Consignia (IRE) (Definite Article)
3323a[8] 4179[9]

First Sargeant *Lawrence Mullaney*
5 gr g Dutch Art Princess Raya (Act One)
4065[P]

First To Boogie (IRE) *Aidan Anthony Howard* 108h 113c
7 b g Tobougg(IRE) Evening Scent (Ardkinglass)
3017[F]

Firsty (IRE) *Paul Nicholls* 113h
4 b g Flemensfirth(USA) Loughaderra Dame (IRE) (King's Theatre (IRE))
4339[5] 5115[4]

Firth Of The Clyde *Malcolm Jefferson* 111h 151c
10 b g Flemensfirth(USA) Miss Nel (Denel (FR))
2171[6] 2935[2] (3887) (4818) ◆ 5297[6]

Fiscal Focus (IRE) *Desmond McDonogh* 144h
4 b g Intense Focus(USA) Elida (IRE) (Royal Academy (USA))
94a[10]

Fisherman Frank *Natalie Lloyd-Beavis* 97b
4 b g Rail Link Ribbons And Bows (IRE) (Dr Devious (IRE))
1289[2] 2842[6]

Fishing Bridge (IRE) *David Rees* 110h 99c
10 ch g Definite Article Rith Ar Aghaidh (IRE) (Phardante (FR))
2367[5] 3078[5] (3572) 3978[P] 4543[5] 4822[6] 5051[5]

Fishy Story *David Pipe* 97b
5 b m Midnight Legend Zolotaya (Kayf Tara)
1491[2] 1688[5]

Fit The Brief *Tom George* 100b
5 b m Kayf Tara Tulipa (POL) (Jape (USA))
4074[6] 4687[2]

Fitzwilliam *Mick Channon* 95h
3 ch g Sixties Icon Canadian Capers (Ballacashtal (CAN))
2757[4] 3112[4] 3213[3]

Fitzwilly *Mick Channon* 103h
5 b g Sixties Icon Canadian Capers (Ballacashtal (CAN))
2415[6] 2781[6]

Five For Fifteen (IRE) *Donald McCain* 86b
6 b g Craigsteel Gentle Eyre (IRE) (Aristocracy (IRE))
2597[8]

Fivefortyfive *Polly Gundry* 95h
7 ch g Erhaab(USA) Golden Mile (IRE) (King's Ride)
2986[8] 4439[2] 4874[9] 5183[P]

Five In A Row (IRE) *Brian Ellison* 128h 143c
7 ch g Blueprint(IRE) Ela Plaisir (IRE) (Grand Plaisir (IRE))
(1856) 3428[13] **(4013) (4370) 4701[13] 4910[2]**

Five O'clock Tea (FR) *A J Martin* 80h 93c
8 b g Martillo(GER) Sally's Cry (FR) (Freedom Cry)
936[2]
Five Star Wilsham (IRE) *Nigel Twiston-Davies* 92h 130c
11 b g Bob's Return(IRE) Riverpauper (IRE) (Over The River (FR))
1632[6] 2057[6] 2451[P]
Fixe Le Kap (FR) *Nicky Henderson* 142h
3 gr g Kapgarde(FR) Lady Fix (FR) (Turgeon (USA))
(3347) (3822) ◆ 4243[2] 4720[8]
Fizzlestix (FR) *Dan Skelton* 85h
3 b g Bonbon Rose(FR) Skipnight (Ashkalani (IRE))
2219[5] 2845[5] 3213[P]
Fizzy Dancer *Kim Bailey* 105h
5 ch m Norse Dancer(IRE) Mrs Fizziwig (Petoski)
1811[3] 2033[4] 4546[3] 4868[4]
Flabello (IRE) *David Pipe* 88h 74c
5 br g Publisher(USA) Uptodate (IRE) (Gothland (FR))
880[6] 1086[P] **1157[3]**
Flamenco Flyer *Tracey Barfoot-Saunt*
6 b g Fantastic Spain(USA) Magical Gift (Groom Dancer (USA))
2062[9] 2450[11]
Flamenco Lad *Martin Hill* 114h
5 b g Tamure(IRE) Monda (Danzig Connection (USA))
1837[6] 2345[2] ◆ 3105[P] (Dead)
Flaming Gorge (IRE) *Alan Hill* 113h 125c
10 ch g Alderbrook Solmus (IRE) (Sexton Blake)
4437[4] 5121[3] 5392[3]
Flamingo Beat *Christine Dunnett* 61h
5 ch g Beat Hollow Flamingo Flower (USA) (Diesis)
4502[7] 4987[5] 5441[9]
Flaming Thistle (IRE) *John Hodge* 85h 105c
11 b g Flemensfirth(USA) Native Thistle (IRE) (Ovac (ITY))
(204) 3679[10] (4741) 5013[2] (5369)
Flapjack (FR) *C Scandella* 120h
2 b g Soldier Of Fortune(IRE) Prima Ballerina (FR) (Tot Ou Tard (IRE))
4539a[2]
Flash Crash *Barry Brennan* 114h 112c
6 b g Val Royal(FR) Tessara (GER) (Big Shuffle (USA))
176[4] 1518[4] **1741[P]** 1912[5] 2150[3] **2364[2] 2698[P]**
3081[2] 3362[P] 3619[13]
Flash Garden (IRE) *J M B Cookson* 117c
7 b g Heron Island(IRE) Latin Lady (IRE) (Dr Massini (IRE))
531[2]
Flashjack (IRE) *Henry Daly* 130h
5 br g Soapy Danger Open Miss (Dracula (AUS))
2543[6] (2860) 3363[3] (3949) 4620[F] 5349[2]
Flashman *Gary Moore* 110h
6 ch g Doyen(IRE) Si Si Si (Lomitas)
237[P] 1770[4] (2253) 4781[7]
Flash Tommie (IRE) *Michael Appleby* 102h 107c
7 b g City Honours(USA) African Keys (IRE) (Quws)
150[4] (365) 519[9] 863[P] 1042[8]
Flashyfrank *Tim Fitzgerald* 86h
6 b g Franklins Gardens White Flash (Sure Blade (USA))
335[4]
Flavin (FR) *Mme P Butel* 115h 126c
4 ch g Pomellato(GER) Some Other Spring (FR) (Majorien)
2362a[3]
Fled Or Pled (IRE) *David Dennis* 33h
6 b g Shantou(USA) Desert Gail (IRE) (Desert Style (IRE))
3927[9] 4304[6] 4848[F] 4874[12]
Fleet Dawn *John Wainwright* 118h 110c
9 b g Polish Precedent(USA) Wychnor Dawn (IRE) (Broken Hearted)
(177) **691[3]** 1661[9] 1903[12] 2217[7] 2667[P]
Flemensbay *Richard Phillips* 109h 102c
7 b m Flemensfirth(USA) Mandys Native (IRE) (Be My Native (USA))
(89) 339[6] (758) ◆ 939[6] 3025[5] 4069[9] **4859[P]**
Flemensfirthleader *Keith Dalgleish* 121h
6 b m Flemensfirth(USA) National Leader (IRE) (Supreme Leader)
3340[F] (4234) 4555[3] 4737[2]
Flemensgael (IRE) *R J Harraway* 97b
8 b g Flemensfirth(USA) Rosarium (IRE) (Silver Kite (USA))
5384[P]
Flemensmix *Kim Bailey* 121h
7 gr g Flemensfirth(USA) Perfect Mix (FR) (Sagamix (FR))
(2413) (3023) ◆
Flemenstar (IRE) *Anthony Curran* 126h 162c
10 b g Flemensfirth(USA) Different Dee (IRE) (Beau Sher)
8a[7] 2388a[3] 2941a[4] (3293a) 3892a[2] 4240[6]
5023a[4]
Flementime (IRE) *Martin Keighley* 125h 101c
7 ch m Flemensfirth(USA) Funny Times (Silver Patriarch (IRE))
2415[2] 3034[7] 5282[3]
Flemerina (IRE) *Sue Smith* 90h
6 b m Flemensfirth(USA) Ballerina Laura (IRE) (Riot Helmet)
159[6] 682[4] 799[8] 1109[4] 1271[4] (3888) ◆ 4421[4]
Flemi Two Toes (IRE) *Sarah Humphrey* 95h 84c
9 b g Flemensfirth(USA) Silva Venture (IRE) (Mandalus)
2223[2] 2649[4] 3087[5] (3220) 3662[P] 4069[6] 4349[9]
4972[3] 5481[6]
Fletchers Flyer (IRE) *Harry Fry* 145h 154c
7 b g Winged Love(IRE) Crystal Chord (IRE) (Accordion)
21a[P] **2660[2] 3013[3] 3486[2]**
Flichity (IRE) *John Cornwall* 86h 70c
10 br g Turtle Island(IRE) Chancy Gal (Al Sirat I)
2556[3] 2836[4] 3816[7]

Flicka's Witness (IRE) *Ms J Johnston* 103h 62c
10 b g Witness Box(USA) Ballinard Sarah (IRE) (Phardante (FR))
531[7]
Flick Knife (IRE) *Mark Wall* 29h
6 b g Bach(IRE) River Clyde (IRE) (Presenting)
865[8] 1101[7] 1178[7]
Flight Control (IRE) *Peter Croke* 63h 31c
10 b g Lahib(USA) Theredandthegreen (IRE) (Bob Back (USA))
1166[10] **1237[P]**
Flights *Robert Walford* 55b
4 b m King's Theatre(IRE) Motcombe (IRE) (Carroll House (IRE))
4075[7]
Flight Zero (FR) *S Foucher* 116h
4 b g Zero Problemo(FR) Kaillila River (FR) (River Mist (USA))
5042a[F]
Flintham *Mark Bradstock* 144h
6 b g Kayf Tara Plaid Maid (IRE) (Executive Perk)
2260[P] 3018[11] (3622) 4730[18]
Flints Legacy *Nigel Hawke* 98b
3 gr f Sagamix(FR) Luneray (FR) (Poplar Bluff)
5227[2]
Flobury *Barry Leavy* 83h
7 b m Overbury(IRE) Miss Flora (Alflora (IRE))
4297[3] 4706[P]
Flora Aurora *Nigel Hawke* 31b
7 ch g Alflora(IRE) Dawn Spinner (Arctic Lord (IRE))
3037[P]
Floral Spinner *Bill Turner* 117h 79c
8 b m Alflora(IRE) Dawn Spinner (Arctic Lord (IRE))
2002[5] 2262[9] 3465[3] 3622[P] 3930[P]
Floramoss *Keith Reveley* 90b
4 b m Alflora(IRE) Brackenmoss (IRE) (Supreme Leader)
3862[6] 4559[4] 4908[3]
Floresco (GER) *Richard Woollacott* 124h
5 ch g Santiago(GER) Fiori (GER) (Chief Singer)
2734[2] (3708) 4353[5] 4913[4]
Florida Calling (IRE) *Tom George* 114h 121c
6 ch g Presenting Miami Nights (GER) (Tertullian (USA))
1829[3] 2299[5] 2986[4] **4487[P] 5413[2]**
Florrie Boy (IRE) *Nigel Twiston-Davies* 123h
4 b g Milan Second Best (IRE) (Supreme Leader)
341[6] 1544[4] 1826[4] 2560[3] ◆ (4882) (5076) 5446[2]
Flowalong (IRE) *Bruce Mactaggart*
5 b m Flemensfirth(USA) Water Stratford (IRE) (Jurado (USA))
1591[2] 3060[5] 4572[6]
Flower Power *Tony Coyle* 110h
4 br m Bollin Eric Floral Rhapsody (Alflora (IRE))
1593[3] 754[4] (1094) 1374[3] 1716[2] 1854[11] 2776[8]
Flugzeug *Seamus Mullins* 95h 90c
7 gr g Silver Patriarch(IRE) Telmar Flyer (Neltino)
222[2] 599[8] **1842[5] 2521[P]** 3087[P] (3771) 4671[5]
5431[6]
Flush Or Bust *Philip Hobbs* 103b
5 b g Trade Fair Polly Flinders (Polar Falcon (USA))
5188[2]
Flute Bowl *Gary Moore* 139h
5 b m Black Sam Bellamy(IRE) Queen's Dancer (Groom Dancer (USA))
(2314) 2647[4] (2911) 3444[6] (4125) 4699[11]
Flybridge *Lydia Richards* 5b
3 b g Avonbridge Baytown Flyer (Whittingham (IRE))
5069[11]
Fly Du Charmil (FR) *Warren Greatrex* 82h
4 b g Saint Des Saints(FR) Famous Member (FR) (Peintre Celebre (USA))
(2729) ◆ 3133[10] 5070[5] 5463[5]
Fly Home Harry *Alan Swinbank* 102h 95c
6 b g Sir Harry Lewis(USA) Fly Home (Skyliner)
2143[3] (2596) 4569[P]
Flyinga De Liaf (FR) *C Pautier*
4 b m Marathon(USA) Flying Fast (FR) (Sendawar (IRE))
3876a[P]
Flying Angel (IRE) *Nigel Twiston-Davies* 145h
4 gr g Arcadio(GER) Gypsy Kelly (IRE) (Roselier (FR))
(1909) ◆ 2331[2] 2898[3] 3232[5] 4115[3] ◆ (4622)
◆ 4769[2] 5214[3]
Flying Eagle (IRE) *Peter Bowen* 120h 123c
7 b g Oscar(IRE) Fille D'Argent (IRE) (Desert Style (IRE))
1701[4]
Flying Jack *Maurice Barnes* 85h
5 b g Rob Roy(USA) Milladella (FR) (Nureyev (USA))
2709[4] 4001[F] 5009[7] 5365[5]
Flying Light (IRE) *Graeme McPherson* 127h 110c
9 b g Chevalier(IRE) Light-Flight (IRE) (Brief Truce (USA))
87[3] 463[2] (645)
Flying Native (IRE) *George Bewley* 50h
6 b g Winged Love(IRE) Native Success (IRE) (Be My Native (USA))
3471[10] 4033[P]
Flying Phoenix *Michael Blake* 85h
7 b m Phoenix Reach(IRE) Rasmalai (Sadler's Wells (USA))
2816 616[5]
Flying Tiger (IRE) *Nick Williams*
2 b g Soldier Of Fortune(IRE) Ma Preference (FR) (American Post)
(5498a)
Focaccia (IRE) *Dan Skelton* 87b
4 b g Milan Dantes Term (IRE) (Phardante (FR))
4308[3] 5021[4]
Focal Point *Sue Smith* 98b
5 ch g Pivotal Centreofattention (AUS) (Danehill (USA))
2031[5] 2401[5]
Focusing *Stuart Edmunds* 100b
5 ch m Central Park(IRE) Spot The Dot (Silver Patriarch (IRE))
2856[9] 4228[4]

Foildubh (IRE) *John Patrick Ryan* 151h 154c
11 b g Woods Of Windsor(USA) Bushey Glen (IRE) (Roselier (FR))
24a[5] 603a[5] 1152a[F]
Following Dreams (IRE) *Alastair Ralph* 130c
8 b g Beneficial Follow Mama (IRE) (Saddlers' Hall (IRE))
14[2] 533[3]
Followmeuptocarlow (IRE) *Thomas Foley* 132h 139c
12 b g Tiraaz(USA) Cush Na Mhan (IRE) (Supreme Leader)
69a[4]
Followmybuttons (IRE) *David Arbuthnot* 88h
5 br g Kalanisi(IRE) Clondalee (IRE) (Presenting)
3772[8]
Follow The Master *Brian Forsey* 79b
9 b g Alflora(IRE) Daisy May (In The Wings)
5223[P]
Follow The Sign (IRE) *Oliver McKiernan* 136h 83c
7 b g Old Vic Conjure Up (IRE) (Jurado (USA))
50a[P]
Follow The Tracks (IRE) *Brian Barr* 100h 57c
7 bb g Milan Charming Mo (IRE) (Callernish)
398[P] 2454[8] 2985[8] **3178[P]** 3771[12] **4346[5] 4746[P]**
5431[4]
Folsom Blue (IRE) *M F Morris* 150h 141c
8 b g Old Vic Spirit Leader (IRE) (Supreme Leader)
3296a[3] 3715a[11] 3894a[3] 5005a[4] 5327[8]
Fond Memory (IRE) *Nigel Twiston-Davies* 115h 122c
7 b g Dr Massini(IRE) Glacier Lilly (IRE) (Glacial Storm (USA))
(174) 523[3] 1617[4] (1987) 2872[3] 4234[P] 5390[U]
Footpad (FR) *W P Mullins* 145h
3 b g Creachadoir(IRE) Willamina (IRE) (Sadler's Wells (USA))
3268a[3] (4002a) 4764[3] 5175[F]
Footstepsintherain (IRE) *David Dennis* 96h
5 b g Footstepsinthesand Champagne Toni (IRE) (Second Empire (IRE))
171[4] 440[4] 1054[8] 1307[5] 1461[10]
Foot The Bill *Patrick Holmes* 87h 99c
10 b g Generous(IRE) Proudfoot (IRE) (Shareef Dancer (USA))
334[4] 519[6] 2844[8] 3102[4] **4032[3]** ◆ **(4534) 4903[5]**
5015[2]
Forest Bihan (FR) *Brian Ellison* 143h
4 ch g Forestier(FR) Katell Bihan (FR) (Funny Baby (FR))
2194[3] 2617[6] 3041[4] 3804[2] 4115[P] 4484[3] 5328[6]
Forestside (IRE) *Barry Murtagh* 77h 79c
10 br g Zagreb(USA) Silver Sunset (Arzanni)
78[6] 485[2] 728[2] 871[3] 1031[2] 1370[5] 1569[5]
Foreverbest (IRE) *Roger Ingram* 30b
6 b m Kalanisi(IRE) Clerhane Belle (IRE) (Astarabad (USA))
4934[P]
Forever Field (IRE) *Nicky Henderson* 119h
5 b g Beneficial Sarahs Reprive (IRE) (Yashgan)
56[P] 554[P] 2688[7] 5159[4]
Forever Gold (IRE) *Edward Cawley* 136h 131c
8 b g Gold Well Clonbrook Lass (IRE) (Lord Americo)
92a[P] 4521a[4]
Forever My Friend (IRE) *Peter Bowen* 92h 122c
8 b g King's Theatre(IRE) Kazan Lady (IRE) (Petardia)
598[5] 873[P] 1114[4] (1418) (1659) 1965[4] 2346[3]
2648[5]
Forget And Forgive (IRE) *Sophie Leech* 77h 96c
7 b g Clouseau(DEN) Mollunde (IRE) (Un Desperado (FR))
695[P] **972[3] 1237[P] 1306[8] 1546[P] 1595[P]**
Forge Valley *Miss G Walton* 77b 107c
11 b g Bollin William Scalby Clipper (Sir Mago)
506[2] 4558[3] 5178[U]
Forgivienne *Evan Williams* 108h 103c
8 b m Alflora(IRE) Always Forgiving (Commanche Run)
85[11] **2988[P] 3977[3] 4612[6] 4962[6] 5240[5]**
Forgiving Glance *Alan King* 112h
3 gr f Passing Glance Giving (Generous (IRE))
2537[2] ◆ 2896[2] ◆ 3519[5] (4345) 4683[2]
For Good Measure (IRE) *Philip Hobbs* 130h
4 b g King's Theatre(IRE) Afdala (IRE) (Hernando (FR))
2123[6] 2409[6] ◆ 2683[8] (2961) ◆ (3120) 4622[12]
4786[10] 5454[3]
For Goodness Sake (IRE) *Warren Greatrex* 101h
3 b f Yeats(IRE) Muschana (Deploy)
2992[2] 3790[4] 4271[3] ◆ 4489[4]
Forgotten Gold (IRE) *Tom George* 134h 147c
9 b g Dr Massini(IRE) Ardnataggle (IRE) (Aristocracy (IRE))
(2089) 2348[4] 3038[6] (5119) 5283[2]
Forgotten Hero (IRE) *Kim Bailey* 119h
6 b g High Chaparral(IRE) Sundown (Polish Precedent (USA))
3022[P]
For Instance (IRE) *Jonjo O'Neill* 123h
5 b g Milan Justamemory (IRE) (Zaffaran (USA))
407[2] 2299[2] ◆
Formal Bid (IRE) *Miss Lydia Svensson* 105h 121c
8 b g Oratorio(IRE) Sharamaine (IRE) (King Charlemagne (USA))
338[P] 465[7] 872[3] **(1043) 1241[P] 1494[3] 5035[P]**
Formidableopponent (IRE) *William Young Jnr* 113h 110c
8 b g Arakan(USA) Sliding (Formidable I (USA))
2104[6] 2193[P] 2755[7] 2947[7] 3343[P] 3475[4] 4106[4]
4166[7] 5086[P]
For 'N' Against (IRE) *David Pipe* 122h 118c
6 br g Presenting Cut 'N' Run (IRE) (Mister Mat (FR))
(1242) 1292[4] **1450[5] 1821[2]** 2005[2] **2272[3]**
Fornebello (FR) *X-L Le Stang*
5 b g Tiger Groom La Pecardiere (FR) (Balleroy (USA))
4400a[P]
Foresters Folly *Claire Dyson* 108h 101c
9 b g Bollin Eric Miss Wyandotte (Henbit (USA))
280[7] 676[3] 874[7] 1080[P]

Fort Belvedere *Micky Hammond* 17h
7 ch g King's Best(USA) Sweet Folly (IRE) (Singspiel (IRE))
1684[9]
Fort Carson (IRE) *Neil King* 117h
9 b g Stowaway The Red One (IRE) (Camden Town)
4541[2] (4645) 4799[4] (5433)
Fort Gabriel (FR) *Fiona Kehoe* 76h 96c
4 ch g Ange Gabriel(FR) Forge Neuve (FR) (Tel Quel (FR))
41[F] 378[P] 1082[9] **(5417)**
Fort George (IRE) *Sally Randell* 99h 121c
12 b g King's Theatre(IRE) Barrack Village (IRE) (Montelimar (USA))
18[5] 294[5] 557[P] 693[P] 5178[P] 5419[3]
Forthefunofit (IRE) *Jonjo O'Neill* 131h
6 b g Flemensfirth(USA) Sommer Sonnet (IRE) (Taipan (IRE))
2411[6] 2759[4]
Fort Smith (IRE) *Sam Thomas* 132h 130c
6 b g Presenting Land Of Honour (Supreme Leader)
285[3] 2901[3] ◆ **3397[3]** 3923[8] 4466[7]
Fortuna Glas (IRE) *Donald McCain* 63h
3 gr g Verglas(IRE) Fortuna Limit (Linamix (FR))
636[5] 1294[5] 1456[4]
Fortunata Fashions *Ben Case* 105h
5 b m Kayf Tara Aniston (IRE) (Eurodeal (IRE))
2257[3] 2778[6] 3386[P]
Fortunate George (IRE) *Emma Lavelle* 123h
5 b g Oscar(IRE) Fine Fortune (IRE) (Bob Back (USA))
2239[4] 4848[2] (5146)
For Two (FR) *Chris Gordon* 116h 119c
6 gr g Act One Forcat (FR) (Bering)
2211[5] 2779[6] 3106[5] 3776[6] 4380[6] 5064[3]
Fort Worth (IRE) *Jonjo O'Neill* 131h
6 b g Presenting Victorine (IRE) (Un Desperado (FR))
876[4] 1138[F] 2485[2] 2901[7] 4305[P] 5277[4]
Forty Crown (IRE) *John Wade* 107h 110c
9 b g Court Cave(IRE) Forty Quid (IRE) (Exhibitioner)
2029[9] **2320[P]** 2919[5] 3344[8]
Forty Foot Tom *Daniel Miley* 112h 128c
10 b g King's Theatre(IRE) Gardana (FR) (Garde Royale)
24a[P]
Forty Something (IRE) *Stuart Coltherd* 37h
10 b g Moothyeb(USA) Drumquin Girl (IRE) (Brush Aside (USA))
3056[5] 3340[P] 3684[P]
Forward Flight (IRE) *Sue Smith* 118h 121c
9 b g Dilshaan Too Advanced (USA) (Nijinsky (CAN))
2475[2] ◆ **2719[6]**
Fosters Cross (IRE) *Thomas Mullins* 137h 142c
13 b g Dr Massini(IRE) Francie's Treble (Quayside)
47a[U] 1186a[9]
Fouburg (FR) *Dan Skelton* 112h
3 b g Sageburg(IRE) Folie Lointaine (FR) (Poliglote)
2448[2] ◆ 3039[4] 4784[4]
Fou Et Sage (FR) *Dan Skelton* 144h
4 b g Sageburg(IRE) Folie Lointaine (FR) (Poliglote)
2060[8] 2640[4] 3740[6]
Foundation Man (IRE) *Jonjo O'Neill* 85h 135c
8 b g Presenting Function Dream (IRE) (Strong Gale)
642[4] 927[4] 1902[4] 2261[P] 2648[6]
Foundry Square (IRE) *David Evans* 113h 124c
9 br g Oscar(IRE) Moon Approach (IRE) (Shernazar)
18[3] 294[2] 4444[2] 5119[4] 5396[3]
Fountains Blossom *Anthony Honeyball* 107h
6 b m Passing Glance Fountain Crumble (Dr Massini (IRE))
83[5] 1837[7] 2732[2] 3505[2] 4159[P]
Fountains Cider *Anthony Honeyball* 87h
7 b g Pasternak Fountain Crumble (Dr Massini (IRE))
878[P]
Fountains Flypast *Anthony Honeyball* 114h 111c
11 b g Broadway Flyer(USA) Miss Flower Girl (Petoski)
87[2] 614[5] **3916[3] 5066[4]**
Fountains Windfall *Anthony Honeyball* 127h
5 b g Passing Glance Fountain Crumble (Dr Massini (IRE))
(602) 2065[6] 2549[4] 3745[3] ◆ 4256[2] ◆
Fourni (IRE) *Mrs A Malzard* 106h
6 ch m Rakti Eckbeag (USA) (Trempolino (USA))
5364a[4]
Fourovakind *Harry Whittington* 136h 140c
10 b g Sir Harry Lewis(USA) Four M'S (Majestic Maharaj)
2701[3] 3518[P] (4340) 4802[P]
Four Plus *Hugo Froud* 22h
4 b m Multiplex Four Thyme (Idiots Delight)
865[10] 1052[8]
Four Shuck Men (IRE) *Sarah-Jayne Davies* 99h 38c
7 b g Spartacus(IRE) Shed (Halling (USA))
2698[P] 2976[11] 3199[P]
Foursquare Funtime *Trevor Wall*
6 b g Common World(USA) Farina (IRE) (Golan (IRE))
5288 2035[P]
Fourstar River (IRE) *S W Reddaway*
10 ch g Fourstars Allstar(USA) Merry River (Over The River (FR))
123[P]
Fourth Act (IRE) *Colin Tizzard* 118h 141c
6 b g King's Theatre(IRE) Erintante (IRE) (Denel (FR))
(1952) 2093[3] **(2400)** ◆ **2727[F] 3106[2] 3521[3]**
(4251) 4701[P] 5381[2]
Fourth Estate (IRE) *John Wade* 122h
9 b g Fantastic Light(USA) Papering (IRE) (Shaadi (USA))
2921[7]

Fox Appeal (IRE) *Emma Lavelle* 148h 158c
8 b g Brian Boru Lady Appeal (IRE) (Phardante (FR))
2061[3] 2187[3] 3150[11] 4361[9] 4697[11] 5093[2]

Foxbridge (IRE) *Nigel Twiston-Davies* 115h 136c
9 b g King's Theatre(IRE) Fairy Native (IRE) (Be My Native (USA))
2473[2] 3282[4] 3624[U]

Foxcub (IRE) *Tom Symonds* 144h 98c
7 b g Bahri(USA) Foxglove (Hernando (FR))
1754[7] (2438) 2912[2] 3407[11] 3748[6] 4244[6] 5189[13]

Foxes Bridge *Nick Mitchell* 104h 113c
7 b g Tamure(IRE) Risky May (Petoski)
782[P] (926) (1118) 1450[3]

Fox Norton (FR) *Neil Mulholland* 143h 152c
5 b g Lando(GER) Natt Musik (FR) (Kendor (FR))
(492) (1969) 2510[2] 3856[3] 4126[3] 4696[3] 5215[3] (5278)

Foxrock (IRE) *T M Walsh* 127h 164c
7 b g Flemensfirth(USA) Midnight Light (IRE) (Roselier (FR))
2676a[8] **2941a[6] 3324a[3] 4007a[4] 5109a[3]**

Foxtail Hill (IRE) *Nigel Twiston-Davies* 129h 117c
6 b g Dr Massini(IRE) Flynn's Girl (IRE) (Mandalus)
556[6] **1047[4] 1809[P]**

Foxy Act *Chris Down* 73b
4 ch m Act One Brown Fox (FR) (Polar Falcon (USA))
2270[11]

Foxy Mistress *Ali Stronge* 61b
5 b m Kayf Tara Frosty Mistress (Arctic Lord (IRE))
644[9]

Foynes Island (IRE) *Miss L J Cabble* 109h 126c
9 b g Presenting Lucy Lodge (IRE) (Moscow Society (USA))
5186[2]

Fozy Moss *Sheena Walton*
9 b g And Beyond(IRE) Peggy Sioux (IRE) (Little Bighorn)
2478[P] 2800[P] **3308[P]**

Fracafigura Has (FR) *P Lenogue* 145h
4 ro m Artiste Royal(IRE) Fragante Royale (FR) (Fragrant Mix (IRE))
5363a[3]

Frampton (IRE) *Charlie Longsdon* 123h 130c
6 b g Presenting Drumavish Lass (IRE) (Oscar (IRE))
99[3] 622[4] 1783[2] 2240[3]

Franche Alliance (FR) *A De Watrigant* 138h
6 gr m Poliglote Alliance Royale (FR) (Turgeon (USA))
836a[8]

Franciscan *Donald McCain* 114h
7 b g Medicean Frangy (Sadler's Wells (USA))
317[P] 1333[8] 1554[6] 1814[5] 4229[8] 5088[P]

Francis Of Assisi (IRE) *John Ferguson* 140h
5 b g Danehill Dancer(IRE) Queen Cleopatra (IRE) (Kingmambo (USA))
(1480) (1693) ◆ (1946) 2350[4] 2886[3] 4765[6] 5189[12]

Francophile (FR) *David Loder* 14b
3 ch g Sea The Stars(IRE) Empress of France (USA) (Storm Cat (USA))
4357[8]

Frankie's Promise (IRE) *N W Alexander* 108h 114c
7 ch g Fruits Of Love(USA) According To Molly (IRE) (Accordion)
2430[U] 2788[4] 3345[P] 4154[8] 4796[7]

Frankly Speaking *Tom Symonds* 106b
5 ch g Flemensfirth(USA) No More Money (Alflora (IRE))
4309[3] 4981[5]

Frank N Fair *Zoe Davison* 88h
7 br m Trade Fair Frankfurt (GER) (Celtic Swing)
4413[P] 4709[8] (5306) (5481)

Frank The Slink *Micky Hammond* 63h 101c
9 b g Central Park(IRE) Kadari (Commanche Run)
3310[P] 3934[P] 4549[P] 5202[3]

Fraser Canyon *Tim Vaughan*
3 b g Halling(USA) Valley Of Gold (FR) (Shirley Heights)
4304[P]

Freckle Face *Bill Turner* 91h 128c
8 br g Septieme Ciel(USA) Wavet (Pursuit Of Love)
184[5] 431[U] 568[F]

Freddies Portrait (IRE) *Donald McCain* 105h
6 gr g Portrait Gallery(IRE) Phara (IRE) (Lord Americo)
2398[2] 2628[5] 2804[3] 3102[3]

Freddy Fox (IRE) *Ben Case* 90h 27c
5 ch g Shantou(USA) Ballyquinn (IRE) (Anshan)
493[8] **741[6]** 1086[P] 1158[9]

Frederic *Micky Hammond* 113h
4 b g Zamindar(USA) Frangy (Sadler's Wells (USA))
3426[7] 3682[6]

Frederic Chopin *James Moffatt* 108h
4 ch g Tamayuz Eliza Gilbert (Noverre (USA))
1634[3] (1921)

Fred Le Macon (FR) *Alan King* 105h
6 b g Passing Sale(FR) Princess Leyla (Teenoso (USA))
692[3] 977[4] 1297[2] 1545[4] 1818[2] 2121[3] 2418[3] 2855[4] 5433[6]

Fredo (IRE) *Ian Williams* 123h 125c
11 ch g Lomitas Felina (GER) (Acatenango (GER))
4180[2] 4651[5] 5178[P]

Free Expression (IRE) *Gordon Elliott* 144h 146c
6 b g Germany(USA) Create A Storm (IRE) (Bob Back (USA))
2817a[3] 3301a[3]

Free Of Charge (IRE) *Philip Hobbs* 112h 108c
6 ch g Stowaway Sweetasanu (IRE) (Sri Pekan (USA))
1906[F] 2272[6] 2749[6] 4859[5] 5432[5]

Free Stone Hill (IRE) *Dan Skelton* 106b
5 b g Beneficial Claramanda (IRE) (Mandalus)
4385[4]

Free World (FR) *Lady Susan Brooke* 66h 94c
11 b g Lost World(IRE) Fautine (FR) (Fast Topaze (USA))
2837[P] 5080[4] 5346[3]

French Canadian (FR) *Heather Dalton* 84h 13c
9 b g Spadoun(FR) Floresca (FR) (Hellios (USA))
57[7]

French Opera *Nicky Henderson* 134h 155c
12 b g Bering On Fair Stage (IRE) (Sadler's Wells (USA))
603a[6] 2809[2] 3448[P] 4306[9]

French Seventyfive *Keith Reveley* 96h 88c
8 b g Pursuit Of Love Miss Tun (Komaite (USA))
(966) 1272[3] 1375[5] **1569[3]**

Fresh By Nature (IRE) *Harriet Bethell* 111h 101c
8 b m Flemensfirth(USA) Star Alert (IRE) (Darazari (IRE))
635[U] 917[8] 1113[2] 1615[10] 1856[6] (2405) 2839[2] 3999[P] 4186[P] 4537[3] 5017[4] (5402)

Friendly Royal (IRE) *Sue Smith* 99h 128c
6 b g Royal Anthem(USA) Friendly Girl (IRE) (King's Ride)
(1853) 2424[5] (2668) 2963[2] 3365[2] 3996[4] 4286[R] 5245[P]

Friendly Society (IRE) *Noel Williams* 112h 122c
10 ch g Moscow Society(USA) Friendly Breeze (Strong Gale)
62[2] 557[P] 1659[6] 2014[U] 2262[11] 4504[8]

Frightened Rabbit (USA) *Keith Dalgleish* 107h
3 b g Hard Spun(USA) Champagne Ending (USA) (Precise End (USA))
3724[2] ◆ 4791[4] 5009[5]

Frizzo (FR) *Harry Whittington* 126h 123c
8 ch g Ballingarry(IRE) Floridene (FR) (Saumarez)
2014[2] 2837[3] 3931[3] 4456[3] 5439[P]

Frodon (FR) *Paul Nicholls* 136h 136c
3 b g Nickname(FR) Miss Country (FR) (Country Reel (USA))
1881a[5] 3854[3] ◆ (4243) 4764[8] 5219[5]

Frolon (FR) *P Favero* 83h 127c
10 b g Lavirco(GER) Fourmille (FR) (Rose Laurel)
1672a[4]

Fromdusktilldawn (IRE) *Graeme McPherson* 96b
5 ch g Mahler Lady Transcend (IRE) (Aristocracy (IRE))
2838[P]

From Frost *Gordon Elliott* 118h
4 b g Nayef(USA) Salutare (IRE) (Sadler's Wells (USA))
839[2]

Fromthetop (IRE) *G Slade-Jones* 85c
9 b g Windsor Castle Rose Of Solway (IRE) (Derring Rose)
148[2] **4446[P]**

Frontier Spirit (IRE) *Nigel Twiston-Davies* 89h 127c
11 b g New Frontier(IRE) Psalmist (Mystiko (USA))
109[P]

Frontier Vic *Nigel Twiston-Davies* 107h 92c
8 b g Old Vic Right On Target (IRE) (Presenting)
5051[3] (5412)

Frontline (IRE) *Paul Cowley* 130h 124c
7 b g King's Theatre(IRE) Thunder Road (IRE) (Mtoto)
7a[10] **4274[3]**

Frosty Steel (IRE) *Tom George* 97h
5 b g Craigsteel Smiths Lady (IRE) (Anshan)
1826[5] 2267[4] 2860[5] ◆ **3379[U]**

Frozen Over *Chris Down* 112h
7 b g Iceman Pearly River (Elegant Air)
(217) 406[3] 826[6] 1156[5] 1676[4] 2458[P] 5418[11]

Fruity O'Rooney *Gary Moore* 118h 132c
12 b g Kahyasi Recipe (Bustino)
169[3] 448[8] 2008[7] 2517[P] (2616) 3046[3] 3818[P]

Fuhgeddaboudit *Seamus Mullins* 78b
8 ch g Generous(IRE) Serraval (FR) (Sanglamore (USA))
3846[P] 4250[F] 5314[P]

Full Blast (FR) *Chris Gordon* 113h
4 b g Khalkevi(IRE) La Troussardiere (FR) (Maresca Sorrento (FR))
1673[2] 1949[4] 2373[P] 2989[8] 3487[14] 3777[9]

Full Irish (IRE) *Emma Lavelle* 122b
4 b g Flemensfirth(USA) Miss Kettlewell (IRE) (Saddlers' Hall (IRE))
(2375) 3138[3] 4117[6]

Full Jack (FR) *Pauline Robson* 115h 140c
8 b g Kahyasi Full Contact (FR) (Cadoudal (FR))
458[5] (4907)

Full Ov Beans *Michael Gates* 93h 117c
11 ch g Midnight Legend Scarlet Baroness (Baron Blakeney)
1721[6] 1941[6]

Full Shift (FR) *Nicky Henderson* 128h 142c
6 b g Ballingarry(IRE) Dansia (GER) (Lavirco (GER))
96a[7] **2779[8] (3228) 4011[P] 4733[4] 5297[3]**

Full Trottle (IRE) *Miss L Thomas* 96c
6 ch g Vertical Speed(FR) Keerou Lady (IRE) (Be My Native (USA))
(298)

Fullwak (IRE) *J J Lambe* 58h
8 b g Waky Nao Lognafulla (IRE) (Warcraft (USA))
2428[P]

Funny Irish (FR) *Fiona Kehoe* 65h
4 b g Irish Wells(FR) Funny Miss (FR) (Bering)
4323[8]

Furas (IRE) *Ruth Carr*
4 br g Shamardal(USA) Albaraari (Green Desert (USA))
1178[P]

Fureys Bar (IRE) *J Teal* 74c
7 b g Golan(IRE) Geray Lady (IRE) (Roselier (FR))
4558[6]

Furrows *Oliver Sherwood* 113h 125c
10 b g Alflora(IRE) See More Furrows (Seymour Hicks (FR))
109[4] 338[3] (742) 830[5] 1327[F] 2246[4]

Fuse Wire *Dai Burchell* 93h 97c
8 b g Tamayaz(CAN) Zaffaranni (IRE) (Zaffaran (USA))
537[4] (712) 828[3] 4882[8] 5464[7]

Fusionforce (IRE) *Gary Hanmer* 100b
8 b g Overbury(IRE) Seviot (Seymour Hicks (FR))
2363[P]

Fu's Island (IRE) *P Meany* 113h
5 b m Turtle Island(IRE) Fu's Legend (IRE) (Pistolet Bleu (IRE))
1875a[4]

Futuramic (IRE) *Andrew Lynch* 118h 126c
8 b g Shantou(USA) Backaway (IRE) (Bob Back (USA))
3296a[8] 4521a[3] 5005a[P]

Future Security (IRE) *William Kinsey* 118h
6 ch g Dalakhani(IRE) Schust Madame (IRE) (Second Set (IRE))
59[4] 219[4] 1035[8]

Fuzzy Logic (IRE) *Bernard Llewellyn* 115h 115c
6 b g Dylan Thomas(IRE) Gates Of Eden (USA) (Kingmambo (USA))
176[2] **825[3] 1110[3] 1479[6]** (1700) 2858[4] 5237[3]

Gabrial The Boss (USA) *Michael Mullineaux*
5 ch g Street Boss(USA) Bacinella (USA) (El Gran Senor (USA))
1967[P]

Gabrial The Great (IRE) *David Pipe* 118h
6 b g Montjeu(IRE) Bayourida (USA) (Slew O'Gold (USA))
2873[4] ◆ 4484[P]

Gabriel Brandy (IRE) *Robert Alan Hennessy* 89h
7 ch g Urban Ocean(FR) Right Style (IRE) (Right Win (IRE))
2292[6]

Gabriella Rose *Alan King* 125h
5 b m Kayf Tara Elaine Tully (IRE) (Persian Bold)
2632[5]

Gabriel Oats *Graeme McPherson* 88h
6 ch g Grape Tree Road Winnow (Oats)
2562[5] 3483[10] 3819[9] 4064[7] 5122[7]

Gaelic Joy (FR) *G Taupin* 110h 69c
5 ch m Turgeon(USA) Gaelic Jane (FR) (Hero's Honor (USA))
1477a[12]

Gaelic Myth *Kim Bailey* 122h
5 b g Midnight Legend Shannon Native (IRE) (Be My Native (USA))
3777[11] 4096[12]

Gaelic O'Reagan *Robert Eddery*
4 b g Refuse To Bend(IRE) Gaelic Roulette (IRE) (Turtle Island (IRE))
2218[P] (Dead)

Gainsborough's Art (IRE) *Harry Chisman* 78h 72c
10 ch g Desert Prince(IRE) Cathy Garcia (IRE) (Be My Guest (USA))
379[P]

Gala Ball (IRE) *Philip Hobbs* 146h
5 b g Flemensfirth(USA) Nuit Des Chartreux (FR) (Villez (USA))
2257[F] 2603[6] 3411[2] ◆ (3710) (4256) (4484) 5074[2]

Galactic Power (IRE) *Robin Dickin* 91h
5 ch g Gamut(IRE) Celtic Peace (IRE) (Deploy)
164[2] 435[3] 626[2]

Gale Force Oscar (IRE) *Sean Curran* 95c
10 br g Oscar(IRE) Distant Gale (IRE) (Strong Gale)
17[6] 567[U] 698[P] 1069[9] 1118[P]

Galice Du Ciel *Giles Smyly* 60h
4 br g Septieme Ciel(USA) Galice Du Soleil (FR) (Royal Charter (FR))
2351[9] 4103[14] 5182[9]

Galizzi (USA) *John Ferguson* 129h
4 b g Dansili Dancing Abbie (USA) (Theatrical (IRE))
799[2] (960) 2472[2] 3151[11]

Gallaflynn (IRE) *Marc Barber* 31c
10 b g Winged Love(IRE) Cockney Rainbow (IRE) (Rainbows For Life (CAN))
298[P]

Gallant Oscar (IRE) *A J Martin* 136h 156c
9 b g Oscar(IRE) Park Wave (IRE) (Supreme Leader)
(95a) 3296a[U] 4521a[5] 5218[U]

Galleons Way *Katie Scott* 96h
6 gr g Generous(IRE) Yemaail (IRE) (Shaadi (USA))
3672[3] 4404[F] 4819[5] 5262[P]

Gallery Artist (IRE) *Dai Burchell*
5 gr m Portrait Gallery(IRE) Distinctly Flo Jo (IRE) (Distinctly North (USA))
2056[P]

Gallery Exhibition (IRE) *Kim Bailey* 100h 140c
8 b g Portrait Gallery(IRE) Good Hearted (IRE) (Broken Hearted)
101[8] 1722[P] (2686) 3109[P] 3776[4] 5193[5]

Gallic Destiny (IRE) *Jo Davis* 111h
4 b g Champs Elysees Cross Your Fingers (USA) (Woodman (USA))
528[5] (671) 1870[6] 2301[6] 4070[P]

Gallic Warrior (FR) *Fergal O'Brien* 117h 117c
8 b g Nononito(FR) Rosa Gallica (Sula Bula)
2249[4] 2851[2] 3412[U] (3916) 4209[3] 4642[2] 5413[F]

Galuppi *J R Jenkins* 110h
4 b g Galileo(IRE) La Leuze (IRE) (Caerleon (USA))
1898[8] 1946[3] 2238[6] (2555) 2823[10]

Galveston (IRE) *Fergal O'Brien* 101h
6 ch g Presenting Rare Gesture (IRE) (Shalford (IRE))
761[2] 1966[4] 4063[P] 4844[5]

Galway Jack (IRE) *Caroline Bailey* 140c
10 b g Witness Box(USA) Cooldalus (IRE) (Mandalus)
184[4] 3524[2] 3776[2] 4128[4] 4444[F]

Gamain (IRE) *Ben Case* 114h 118c
6 b g Gamut(IRE) Glass Curtain (IRE) (Old Vic)
2435[6] 3127[2] 3385[3] 3836[6] (4225) 4775[F] 4971[2] ◆

Gambol (FR) *Ian Williams* 112h 112c
5 ch g New Approach(IRE) Guardia (GER) (Monsun (GER))
214[2] 440[3] 1425[5] 1518[3] 1828[4] 2170[9] 2734[8] 3146[10] **4067[5] 4803[P]**

Game As A Pheasant *Mrs C A Coward* 71b
5 ch g Supreme Sound Burnaby Belle (IRE) (Elnadim (USA))
320[15]

Game On (IRE) *Lucy Wadham* 93b
3 b g Gamut(IRE) Dar Dar Supreme (Overbury (IRE))
5457[9]

Ganbei *Michael Easterby* 116h 123c
9 ch g Lomitas Native Ring (FR) (Bering)
3064[2] 3684[7] (4069) (4840) ◆ 5376[3]

Gangster (FR) *W P Mullins* 147h
5 ch g Green Tune(USA) Dahlia's Krissy (USA) (Kris S (USA))
(3169a) 4766[7] 5194[P]

Ganndar (FR) *P Cottin*
4 b g Acclamation Grand Vadla (FR) (Grand Lodge (USA))
3876a[5]

Gardefort (FR) *Venetia Williams* 110h 144c
6 bb g Agent Bleu(FR) La Fresnaie (FR) (Exit To Nowhere (USA))
2784[P] (3629) 3857[3] 4254[2] 4770[F]

Garde Fou (FR) *Paul Henderson* 118h 89c
9 b g Kapgarde(FR) Harpyes (FR) (Quart De Vin (FR))
2268[9] 2906[5] 3383[4] **3746[P]** 4467[5] 4822[5] 5165[3] 5355[11]

Garde Freinet (IRE) *Steve Flook* 67h
6 br m High Chaparral(IRE) Cradle Of Love (USA) (Roberto (USA))
328[7] 518[3]

Garde La Victoire (FR) *Philip Hobbs* 152h 157c
6 b g Kapgarde(FR) Next Victory (FR) (Akarad (FR))
(2166) (2510) (3571) 4729[F] 5174[F]

Garde Ville (FR) *Lisa Williamson* 73h
5 ch g Kapgarde(FR) Ville Eagle (FR) (Villez (USA))
4975[3] 5099[6]

Gardiners Hill (IRE) *David Rees* 73h
5 br g Stowaway Mysterious Lass (IRE) (Satco (FR))
702[9] 2024[P] 2267[10] 2563[8]

Garnock (IRE) *David Bridgwater* 119h 102c
7 b m Craigsteel Sister Stephanie (IRE) (Phardante (FR))
1006[3] 1134[P]

Garrahalish (IRE) *Robin Dickin* 115h 129c
7 b g Presenting Savu Sea (IRE) (Slip Anchor)
1616[3] 1849[P] 2615[2] 3014[U] 3445[4]

Garryduff Cross (IRE) *Helen Nelmes* 23b
5 b g Stowaway Cooleycall (IRE) (Scribano)
392[11] 2715[6] 2986[P]

Gars Bar Dine (FR) *Mrs S A Bramall* 124h
4 b g Martaline Treekle Toffee (FR) (Cadoudal (FR))
3539a[4]

Gas Line Boy (IRE) *Jim Best* 122h 147c
9 b g Blueprint(IRE) Jervia (Affirmed (USA))
3741[U] 4245[P]

Gasoline (IRE) *Ian Williams*
3 b g Mahler Judelle De Thou (FR) (Trebrook (FR))
4805[11]

Gassin Golf *Kerry Lee* 143h
6 b g Montjeu(IRE) Miss Riviera Golf (Hernando (FR))
1848[P]

Gather Round *Mrs K Lawther*
8 b g Kayf Tara Tickle The Tiller (IRE) (Strong Gale)
12[P]

Gauner Danon (GER) *Frantisek Holcak* 107c
9 bb g Royal Dragon(USA) Gaunerin (GER) (Goofalik (USA))
1885a[U]

Gauvain (GER) *Miss V Collins*
13 b g Sternkoenig(IRE) Gamina (GER) (Dominion)
18[P] 4437[U]

Gayebury *Tom Symonds* 118b
5 b g Overbury(IRE) Gaye Sophie (Environment Friend)
3082[2] (3416) ◆ 4117[3]

Gaye Memories *Dan Skelton* 108h
7 b m Overbury(IRE) Gaye Memory (IRE) (Buckskin (FR))
339[7]

Gee Hi (IRE) *Warren Greatrex* 115h 125c
9 b g Milan Curzon Street (Night Shift (USA))
959[2] 1372[3] (2124) 2300[5]

Gemini Ahhs (IRE) *Mrs S M McPherson* 57h 70c
12 b g Broken Hearted Madam Madcap (Furry Glen)
151[7]

General Brook (IRE) *John O'Shea* 91h
5 b g Westerner Danse Grecque (IRE) (Sadler's Wells (USA))
214[F] 613[5]

General Bux *Suzy Smith* 107b
4 b g Lucarno(USA) Cadoutene (FR) (Cadoudal (FR))
2375[5]

General Ginger *Harry Fry* 130h
5 ch g Generous(IRE) Nuzzle (Salse (USA))
98[6] (279) (1673) 2011[5] 2457[2] 4851[3] 5416[2]

General Girling *Caroline Keevil* 95h
8 b g General Gambul Gold Charm (Imperial Fling (USA))
123[9] (2316) (2515)

General Mahler (IRE) *Brian Ellison* 121h
5 b g Mahler High Dough (IRE) (High Roller (IRE))
3476[5] 3883[4] ◆ 4033[3] 4416[2] (4941) 5300[F]

General Montgomery (IRE) *Neil Mulholland* 101h
6 b g Desert King(IRE) Supreme Course (IRE) (Supreme Leader)
678[6] 1100[9]

General Principle (IRE) *Gordon Elliott* 126h
6 b g Gold Well How Provincial (IRE) (Be My Native (USA))
4662a[2] 5002a[6]

General Ross (IRE) *Adrian Wintle* 55h 61c
8 b g Generous(IRE) Rossmore Girl (IRE) (Scenic (IRE))
180[12] 615[P]
Generous Chief (IRE) *Chris Grant* 96h 101c
7 b g Generous(IRE) Yosna (FR) (Sicyos (USA))
38[3] 458[7] 676[P] 803[6] 842[6] 1069[2] 1403[P] 1778[3] 2173[P] 2708[P] 5203[P]
Generous Helpings (IRE) *Gary Moore* 94h
6 ch g Generous(IRE) Saffron Pride (IRE) (Be My Native (USA))
3042[U] 3834[U] 4160[F] 4860[P] 5481[4]
Generous Jack (IRE) *Jim Best* 103h
6 ch g Generous(IRE) Yosna (FR) (Sicyos (USA))
3130[3] 3902[2] 5433[15]
Generous June (IRE) *Paddy Butler* 80b
7 ch m Generous(IRE) Outo'Theblue (IRE) (Grand Lodge (USA))
2252[P] 2519[P] 5477[P]
Generous Past *Michael Mullineaux* 49b
5 ch g Generous(IRE) Majestic Past (IRE) (Pasternak)
1101[11] 1973[8]
Generous Pet (IRE) *Kenneth Slack* 112h 69c
6 ch g Generous(IRE) Sarahs Music (IRE) (Orchestra)
1082[10] 1453[4] 1648[11] 2582[4] (4547) (4706) (5262) ◆ (5403)
Generous Ransom (IRE) *Nick Gifford* 109h 145c
7 ch g Generous(IRE) Penneyrose Bay (Karinga Bay)
2064[11] 2483[15] 3038[5] 4485[6] 5154[5]
Genstone Trail *Alan King* 97h 92c
9 b m Generous(IRE) Stoney Path (Petoski)
4073[3] ◆ 4427[P] 5377[7]
Gentle Duke *Miss L Wallace* 105c
8 b g Kayf Tara Hopperdante (IRE) (Phardante (FR))
4213[2] 4748[P] 4892[P] 5399[4]
Gentleman Anshan (IRE) *Rosemary Gasson*
11 b g Anshan Second Violin (IRE) (Cataldi)
863[P]
Gentleman Duke (IRE) *A L T Moore* 117h 129c
7 b g Bachelor Duke(USA) Housekeeping (Dansili)
1565a[5]
Gentleman Jon *Colin Tizzard* 121h 131c
7 b g Beat All(USA) Sudden Spirit (FR) (Esprit Du Nord (USA))
(1948) 2347[F] 2733[4] 3113[4] 3786[3] 4254[3] 5496[P]
Gentle Mel (IRE) *Anabel K Murphy* 62h
7 b m King's Theatre(IRE) Miss Ellora (IRE) (Aahsaylad)
1718[8] 1979[11] 2252[6] 2554[P]
Gentle Nature *John Flint* 59b
4 b g Dr Massini(IRE) Eagle's Landing (Eagle Eyed (USA))
928[0] 1484[8] 1704[6]
Geordie Des Champs (IRE) *Rebecca Curtis* 112b
4 br g Robin Des Champs(FR) Kilcoleman Lady (IRE) (Presenting)
4357[2] 4721[18] (5055)
George Fernbeck *Micky Hammond* 84h 87c
7 ch g Java Gold(USA) Burmese Days (Montjeu (IRE))
203[P] 1571[7] 1924[U] 2145[8] 5089[P] 5402[4]
George Nympton (IRE) *Zoe Davison* 69h 90c
9 br g Alderbrook Countess Camilla (Bob's Return (IRE))
256[P] 2859[7] 4073[P] 4410[4] 4686[8] 5068[5] 5480[9]
Georges Conn (IRE) *Gordon Elliott* 116h 128c
7 b g Whitmore's Conn(USA) Georges Girl (IRE) (Montelimar (USA))
2675a[2]
Georgian Firebird *Barry Leavy* 111h
5 b m Firebreak Skovshoved (IRE) (Danetime (IRE))
3375[8] 3863[U] (4183) ◆
Georgian King *Martin Keighley* 113h 118c
12 b g Overbury(IRE) Roslin (Roscoe Blake)
403[4] 760[5] 939[3] 1138[4] 1288[5] 1850[3] 2272[U] 2566[3] 3127[4] 3948[5]
Georgie *M O Cullinane* 94h 103c
11 b g Best Of The Bests(IRE) Silver Peak (FR) (Sillery (USA))
1186a[13]
Georgie Lad (IRE) *Philip Hobbs* 125h 120c
7 b g Gold Well Top Step (IRE) (Step Together I (USA))
(2125) 2663[3] ◆ 2996[8] 4789[B] 5419[2]
Georgieshore (IRE) *Zoe Davison* 113h
7 b g Turtle Island(IRE) Pride Of St Gallen (IRE) (Orchestra)
2862[2] 3143[2] 3619[6] 3950[5] (4530) 5100[5]
Georgies Pip *Brendan Powell* 47h
4 b m Apple Tree(FR) Lady Kay (Kayf Tara)
602[7] 3215[3] 4382[6]
Germany Calling (IRE) *Charlie Longsdon* 130h 145c
6 b g Germany(USA) Markir (IRE) (Flemensfirth (USA))
(84) 461[2] (1922) ◆ 2336[4] 4770[17]
Getaway Driver (IRE) *Mrs Janet Ackner* 93b 103c
8 br g Zagreb(USA) Catch The Mouse (IRE) (Stalker)
12[8] 4446[P]
Get Home Now *Peter Bowen* 122h
7 b g Diktat Swiftly (Cadeaux Genereux)
87[7] 356[5] 625[F] 812[9] 1002[6]
Get Involved (IRE) *Robin Dickin* 114h 124c
6 b g Milan Strong Red (Strong Gale)
212[P] 397[4] 2839[5] 3146[P] (4467) 4860[3] 5285[2]
Getmeouthedoldrums *Mark Wall* 47h 57c
10 b g Dolpour(IRE) Ruby Laser (Bustino)
897[P] 1181[P] 1326[9] 1462[P]
Geton Xmoor (IRE) *Richard Woollacott* 119h
8 b g Heron Island(IRE) Get On With It (IRE) (Old Vic)
3371[F] 3705[P]
Getoutwhenyoucan (IRE) *Augustine Leahy* 122h 86c
6 br g Beneficial Ballycleary (IRE) (Phardante (FR))
2676a[13]

Get Ready Freddy *Nick Mitchell* 86h
5 b g Sixties Icon Summer Shades (Green Desert (USA))
2345[5] 3077[P] 3194[2] 3619[8] 3905[4]
Get Rhythm (IRE) *Tom George* 110b
5 b g Kayf Tara Ninna Nanna (FR) (Garde Royale)
5021[2]
Gevrey Chambertin (FR) *David Pipe* 149h 128c
7 gr g Dom Alco(FR) Fee Magic (FR) (Phantom Breeze)
1477a[9] 1839[5] 2484[8] 2759[7] (3045) 3517[9] 4112[7] 4354[9] (4568)
G For Ginger *Anthony Honeyball* 102b
5 ch m Lucarno(USA) Kaream (Karinga Bay)
5151[2] ◆
Ghost Of A Smile (IRE) *Ian Williams* 92h 100c
7 b g Oscar(IRE) Dix Huit Brumaire (FR) (General Assembly (USA))
2491[P] 3569[U] 4491[2] (5126)
Ghost River *Peter Bowen* 125h
5 ch g Flemensfirth(USA) Cresswell Native (IRE) (Be My Native (USA))
4138[F] 4351[2] ◆ 4715[9] 5194[P]
Ghost Runner (IRE) *Mark Shears* 70h
5 b g Tagula(IRE) Ball Cat (FR) (Cricket Ball (USA))
1822[P]
Giant O Murchu (IRE) *John Upson* 96h 104c
11 b g Carroll House(IRE) Centralspires Best (Nishapour (FR))
1099[4] 1703[P] 1767[8]
Gibbes Bay (FR) *Paul Nicholls* 106b
3 gr g Al Namix(FR) Nouvelle Donne (FR) (Sleeping Car (FR))
(5330) ◆
Gibbstown (IRE) *Paul Stafford* 93h 102c
9 b m Bob Back(USA) Kitty Maher (IRE) (Posen (USA))
141[4] 2950[4] 4185[5] 4433[3] (5013) 5369[4]
Gibralfaro (IRE) *Alan King* 136h
3 b g Dalakhani(IRE) Ronda (Bluebird (USA))
(3279) ◆ (3730) 4358[4] 4764[9]
Gifted Island (IRE) *Tim Vaughan* 85h
5 b g Turtle Island(IRE) Life Support (IRE) (High Estate)
1792[5] 5353[6]
Gifted Rose *Christopher Kellett* 58b
4 b m Presenting Santia (Kahyasi)
188[9] 5941[2]
Gild Master *Alan King* 101h
3 b g Excellent Art Nirvana (Marju (IRE))
3523[3]
Gilgamboa (IRE) *E Bolger* 143h 165c
7 b g Westerner Hi Native (IRE) (Be My Native (USA))
2941a[3] 3296a[4] 4007a[5] 4731[5] 5218[4]
Gilmer (IRE) *Laura Young* 76h
4 b g Exceed And Excel(AUS) Cherokee Rose (IRE) (Dancing Brave (USA))
1234[10] 1453[5] 1544[8] 2043[P]
Gilzean (IRE) *Alex Hales* 108h
9 b g Flemensfirth(USA) Sheknowso (Teenoso (USA))
2135[3] 2496[3] 2919[3] 3220[3]
Gin And Tonic *Michael Wigham* 109h
5 ch g Phoenix Reach(IRE) Arctic Queen (Linamix (FR))
1095[6] 1307[2] (1604) 1786[7] (1945) 2647[2] 3177[3] 4774[5] (4970) 5139[6]
Gin Cobbler *Victor Thompson* 99h 106c
9 b g Beneficial Cassia (Be My Native (USA))
36[U] 256[5] 417[2] (485) 639[6] (728) 848[5] 1639[F] 1738[5] 1891[3] 2292[9] 2755[0] 2979[4] 3589[F] 3938[U] 4048[3] ◆ 4329[6] 4707[4] 5257[3]
Ginger Fizz *Ben Case* 110h
8 ch m Haafhd Valagalore (Generous (IRE))
314[5] 744[2] 938[6] 1166[2] 1454[5]
Gingili *Rose Dobbin* 110h
5 b g Beat All(USA) Gentian (Generous (IRE))
(254) 2949[8] ◆ 3424[10]
Ginjo *Bernard Llewellyn* 86h
5 b m Sakhee(USA) Gulshan (Batshoof)
361[7] 5181[0] 5332[4]
Ginny's Tonic (IRE) *Suzy Smith* 100h
6 b m Oscar(IRE) Golden Bay (Karinga Bay)
2952[5] 3904[P] 4413[P]
Gino Trail (IRE) *David Bridgwater* 127h 134c
8 br g Perugino(USA) Borough Trail (IRE) (Woodborough (USA))
3571[3] 3954[P]
Gioia Di Vita *Dr Richard Newland* 136h
5 b g Sakhee(USA) Dhuyoof (IRE) (Sinndar (IRE))
(528) 671[2] (930) 1039[5] (1485) 1754[8] 5497[2]
Girly Girl (IRE) *Dan Skelton* 120h
6 b m Golan(IRE) Clan Music (IRE) (Accordion)
(1908) (2252) ◆ 3372[5] 3817[2] (4337) 4734[9] 5299[3]
Gitane Du Berlais (FR) *W P Mullins* 140h 153c
5 b m Balko(FR) Boheme Du Berlais (FR) (Simon Du Desert (FR))
349a[7] 2805[2] 3444[4] (4019a) 4319[2] 4699[5]
Giveagirlachance (IRE) *Seamus Mullins* 101h
6 b m Iffraaj Farewell To Love (IRE) (Darshaan)
(179) 1893[7] 2418[5] 5380[3]
Give Her Bach (IRE) *Patrick Cronin* 122h 119c
6 b m Bach(IRE) Thebigtwelve (IRE) (Phardante (FR))
1150a[4] 1679a[4] 4656a[4] 5006a[6]
Give Him A Glance *Alan King* 97h
4 rg g Passing Glance Giving (Generous (IRE))
2562[2] 3130[7] 3835[5] 4344[6] 5453[9]
Give Him Time *Nick Gifford* 38h
4 b g Kalanisi(IRE) Delayed (FR) (Fijar Tango (FR))
3484[12]
Giveimachance (IRE) *Claire Dyson* 81h
7 b g Exit To Nowhere(USA) Native Lisa (IRE) (Be My Native (USA))
1599[P]
Giveitachance (IRE) *Claire Dyson* 109h
8 b g Clerkenwell(USA) Native Lisa (IRE) (Be My Native (USA))
1897[11] (2223) 2687[10] 3837[8] 4069[2] 5017[3] 5376[7]

Give Me A Break (IRE) *Michael Hourigan* 125h 114c
6 br m Scorpion(IRE) Love And Porter (IRE) (Sheer Grit)
50a[7]
Give Us A Hand (IRE) *J A Berry* 102h 60c
13 br g Anshan Desperado Dawn (IRE) (Un Desperado (FR))
4662a[4]
Gizzit (IRE) *Seamus Mullins* 101h 101c
9 b g Son Of Sharp Shot(IRE) Suez Canal (FR) (Exit To Nowhere (USA))
450[4]
Glacial Rock (IRE) *Alistair Whillans* 117h 101c
9 b g Sonus(IRE) Glacial Princess (IRE) (Glacial Storm (USA))
285[2] 2429[5] 3055[4] 3345[4] 3834[12] 4569[8]
Gladiator King (IRE) *A J Martin* 132h
6 b g Dylan Thomas(IRE) Sheer Bliss (IRE) (Sadler's Wells (USA))
3650a[21]
Glance Back *Emma Baker* 87b
4 b g Passing Glance Roberta Back (IRE) (Bob Back (USA))
1758[6]
Gleann Na Ndochais (IRE) *Alistair Whillans* 106h 126c
9 b g Zagreb(USA) Nissereen (USA) (Septieme Ciel (USA))
315[2] 707[5] 961[3] 1332[5] 1639[2] (2030) 2341[3] 5448[8]
Glenariff *Seamus Mullins* 103h
6 b m Kayf Tara Lady Racquet (IRE) (Glacial Storm (USA))
447[4] 813[P] 2911[P] 3374[4] 3841[6] 4709[3] ◆ 5223[2]
Glenarm *Seamus Mullins* 109h
6 b m Kayf Tara Rumbled (Halling (USA))
2298[9] (2876) 3729[4]
Glenbank King (IRE) *R K Watson* 79h
7 b g Desert King(IRE) Miss Glenbank (IRE) (Over The River (FR))
4548[5]
Glen Countess (IRE) *Sue Smith* 103h 127c
8 b m Pilsudski(IRE) Countessdee (IRE) (Arctic Lord (IRE))
(199) 470[P] 3367[4] 4109[P] 4512[2]
Glendermot (IRE) *Paul Cowley* 96h 104c
6 b g Portrait Gallery(IRE) Native Bandit (IRE) (Un Desperado (FR))
3067[4] 3489[2] 3914[2] 4346[2] 5138[P]
Glengra (IRE) *Ian Williams* 98h
6 gr g Beneficial Zaraza (IRE) (Darshaan)
4874[8] 5263[6]
Glen Gyle (IRE) *Liam Lennon* 101h 81c
8 b g Exit To Nowhere(USA) Fionnuala (Royal Vulcan)
3670[F]
Glenlyon *Paul Webber* 57b
3 b g Thewayyouare(USA) Helena (Helissio (FR))
4894[12]
Glenquest (IRE) *S R B Crawford* 115h 127c
12 b g Turtle Island(IRE) Solar Quest (IRE) (King's Ride)
3071a[11] 3428[10] 4367[5]
Glenwood For Ever (IRE) *Paul John Gilligan* 83h 97c
7 b g King's Theatre(IRE) Decent Preacher (Decent Fellow)
395[3] 3421[F] 3820[4] 4131a[4] 4281a[6]
Glenwood Prince (IRE) *Kevin Hunter* 57h 65c
9 b g King's Theatre(IRE) Moll Bawn (IRE) (Presenting)
133[P] 486[5] 637[P]
Glenwood Star (IRE) *Rebecca Curtis* 121h
7 b g Oscar(IRE) Shuil Ar Aghaidh (The Parson)
2125[7] 3129[F] 4443[P]
Glevum Acrobatis *Hugo Froud* 71b
4 b m Kayf Tara Top Of The Dee (Rakaposhi King)
3469[5]
Glimmer Of Hope *Mark Hoad*
4 b g Tiger Hill(IRE) Fontaine House (Pyramus (USA))
4409[U] 4934[P]
Glimpse Of Gold *Tim Vaughan* 81h
4 b g Passing Glance Tizzy Blue (IRE) (Oscar (IRE))
1378[4] 4441[7] 4963[5] 5161[5]
Glingerburn (IRE) *Nicky Richards* 152h
7 b g King's Theatre(IRE) Wychnor Dawn (IRE) (Broken Hearted)
2194[F]
Glint Of Steel (IRE) *P G Hall* 97b 119c
9 b g Craigsteel Shining Spear (Commanche Run)
(5075)
Global Bonus (IRE) *Caroline Bailey* 117h
6 b g Heron Island(IRE) That's The Bonus (IRE) (Executive Perk)
5372[3]
Global Domination *Caroline Bailey* 86h 99c
7 b g Alflora(IRE) Lucia Forte (Neltino)
2410[2] ◆ (2836) (3421)
Global Dream *Caroline Bailey* 98h 119c
5 ch g Lucarno(USA) Global Girl (Shambo)
2649[2] 2964[4] 3422[3] (3925) (4211) 4423[2] (5015) 5336[U]
Globalisation (IRE) *Rebecca Curtis* 106h 125c
5 b g Tikkanen(USA) On A Mission (IRE) (Dolphin Street (FR))
(2365) ◆ 2727[P] 3836[F] 4443[3] 4826[5] 5336[2]
Global Thrill *Bernard Llewellyn* 120h
6 b g Big Shuffle(USA) Goonda (Darshaan)
2688[10] 3080[F] 3708[11] 4353[4] 4745[7] 5279[5]
Glory For Rory (IRE) *Jonjo O'Neill* 43h
4 b g Beneficial Baldrica (FR) (Lost World (IRE))
400[4] 2163[6] 2407[P]
Goal (IRE) *Sally Randell* 116h 116c
7 b g Mujadil(USA) Classic Lin (FR) (Linamix (FR))
1239[7] 1377[5] 1501[6] 2271[11] 2458[4] 2987[4] 3108[4] 3242[P] 3586[11] (4390) 4771[2] 5418[7]
Go Conquer (IRE) *Jonjo O'Neill* 126h 139c
6 b g Arcadio(GER) Ballinamona Wish (IRE) (Kotashaan (FR))
2489[4] 5096[6] (5354)

Godsmejudge (IRE) *David Dennis* 108h 139c
9 b g Witness Box(USA) Eliza Everett (IRE) (Meneval (USA))
2482[15] 2916[13] 3339[2] ◆ 4306[5] 4858[6] 5274[10]
God's Own (IRE) *Tom George* 135h 170c
7 b g Oscar(IRE) Dantes Term (IRE) (Phardante (FR))
2259[3] 4100[2] 4718[4] (5192)
Going Concern (IRE) *Evan Williams* 112h 137c
8 b g Overbury(IRE) Scorpio Girl (Scorpio (FR))
2059[6] 2468[4] 3030[2] 3521[4] 5179[6]
Goingforamooch *Katie Stephens* 37b
4 b m Primo Valentino(IRE) Emmasflora (Alflora (IRE))
4687[12]
Going For Broke (IRE) *Rebecca Curtis* 116h
5 b g Gold Well Kokopelli Star (Hernando (FR))
1837[5] 2080[5] 4442[6]
Going Nowhere Fast (IRE) *Bernard Llewellyn* 95h 106c
10 b g Exit To Nowhere(USA) Sister Gabrielle (IRE) (Buckskin (FR))
180[8] 336[6] 616[3] ◆ 713[4] 1373[2] (1548) (1603) 1703[4] 2040[4]
Golan Dancer (IRE) *David Bridgwater* 110h 112c
7 b g Golan(IRE) Seductive Dance (Groom Dancer (USA))
2039[F] 2456[6] 3129[6] 3903[3]
Golan Lodge (IRE) *Paul Nolan* 130h
6 b g Golan(IRE) Fontaine Lodge (IRE) (Lafontaine I (USA))
5024a[8]
Golanova *Gary Moore* 113h 118c
7 b g Golan(IRE) Larkbarrow (Kahyasi)
170[4] 1767[7] (2539) 3836[P] (4199) 4380[3] 4935[P] 5375[4]
Golans Choice (IRE) *Rose Dobbin* 111h 85c
6 b g Golan(IRE) Sea Voyager (IRE) (High Roller (IRE))
291[7] 2429[8] 3344[5] 3933[3] 4289[P]
Golantilla (IRE) *Alan Fleming* 132h 126c
7 br g Golan(IRE) Scintilla (Sir Harry Lewis (USA))
4517a[P]
Goldan Jess (IRE) *Philip Kirby* 136h
11 b g Golan(IRE) Bendis (GER) (Danehill (USA))
1035[12] (1419) 2198[P]
Gold Bonne Raine (IRE) *Evan Williams* 83h
4 b m Gold Well Be My Bonne (Be My Native (USA))
2164[10] 2665[6] 3119[8]
Goldboy (IRE) *Jonjo O'Neill* 78h
7 b g Gold Well Woodbinesandroses (IRE) (Roselier (FR))
2768[5] 3063[5] 3366[5]
Gold Bullet (IRE) *T J Taaffe* 119h 143c
7 gr g Generous(IRE) Glenmoss Rosy (IRE) (Zaffaran (USA))
24a[P] 603a[8]
Gold Carrot *Gary Moore* 89h 102c
7 b g Beat All(USA) Emma-Lyne (Emarati (USA))
3903[F] 4356[5] (4527) 4778[6]
Gold Chain (IRE) *Dianne Sayer* 99h
5 b m Authorized(IRE) Mountain Chain (USA) (Royal Academy (USA))
301[4] 1036[6] 3065[5] 3424[R] 4939[7] 5409[4] (5472)
Gold Class *Robert Alan Hennessy* 99h
4 ch g Firebreak Silken Dalliance (Rambo Dancer (CAN))
1170[9]
Golden Bird (IRE) *Brendan Powell* 107h
4 b g Sinndar(IRE) Khamsin (USA) (Mr Prospector (USA))
2088[5] 2221[3] 2630[5] 3220[9] 4782[7] 5398[7]
Golden Birthday (FR) *Harry Fry* 110b
4 b g Poliglote Gold Or Silver (FR) (Glint Of Gold)
4103[3] 4790[3]
Golden Boot (IRE) *Oliver McKiernan* 120h 121c
6 b g Westerner Siberiansdaughter (IRE) (Strong Gale)
19a[17]
Golden Chieftain (IRE) *Colin Tizzard* 138h 149c
10 b g Tikkanen(USA) Golden Flower (GER) (Highland Chieftain)
(2517) 3057[2] 3448[4] (3707) 4140[F] 4802[F] 5327[P] (Dead)
Golden Chop (FR) *Francois Nicolle* 140h 128c
7 b g Muhaymin(USA) Vaubecourt (FR) (Courtroom (FR))
5428a[7]
Golden Doyen (GER) *Philip Hobbs* 129h 139c
4 b g Doyen(IRE) Goldsamt (GER) (Rienzi (EG))
1969[2] 2370[2] 2881[4] 4857[2]
Golden Feet *Tim Vaughan* 65b
4 b g Dubawi(IRE) One So Marvellous (Nashwan (USA))
1003[6] 1717[F]
Golden Games (IRE) *Daniel O'Brien* 94h
9 b m Montjeu(IRE) Ski For Gold (Shirley Heights)
65[F]
Golden Gate Bridge (GER) *Mark Pitman* 99h
3 br g Kamsin(GER) Galla Placidia (GER) (Kaldounevees (FR))
1772[6] (2009) (2368) 3409[7] 3523[2]
Golden Heritage *John Ferguson* 111h
4 b g Halling(USA) Summertime Legacy (Darshaan)
1453[F] 1684[4] 2035[3]
Golden Investment (IRE) *Donald McCain* 109h
6 b g Gold Well Mangan Pet (IRE) (Over The River (FR))
2337[2] 2791[6] 3802[3] 4430[4]
Golden Milan (IRE) *Rebecca Curtis* 119h 108c
7 b g Milan Belle Provence (FR) (Phantom Breeze)
3010[2] 4127[P] 4615[U] 4962[5] 5265[P]
Golden Sandstorm (IRE) *Daniel Mark Loughnane* 85b
6 ch g Golden Tornado(IRE) Killoughey Fairy (IRE) (Torus)
2562[6]
Golden Sparkle (IRE) *Ian Duncan* 119h 122c
9 ch m Samraan(USA) Bye For Now (Abednego)
4405[6] 4608[P] 5299[2]

Golden Thread *Neil King* 91b
5 ch g Singspiel(IRE) Alpenrot (IRE) (Barathea (IRE))
1003[2] 1449[8] 1797[6]

Golden Wonder (IRE) *Ms Sandra Hughes* 110h 122c
9 b g Goldmark(USA) Polyploid (IRE) (Pollerton)
4521a[P]

Gold Futures (IRE) *Nicky Richards* 133h 146c
6 b g Gold Well Don't Discount Her (IRE) (Millfontaine)
329[4] (635) 801[2] (1167) ◆ 1322[3] 1658[4] (2068) 4635[7] 5494[16]

Goldie Horn *Nigel Twiston-Davies* 106h 94c
7 ch m Where Or When(IRE) Gulshan (Batshoof)
589[P] 770[6] 874[5] 1056[5] 1346[3] 1478[9]

Goldie Lynch (IRE) *Richard Phillips*
6 b g High-Rise(IRE) Reapers Present (IRE) (Presenting)
3226[P]

Gold Ingot *Caroline Bailey* 107h 123c
8 ch g Best Of The Bests(IRE) Realms Of Gold (USA) (Gulch (USA))
1970[5] 2168[6] 2975[5] 3313[2] 3727[3] 4209[2] 4866[2]

Gold Man (IRE) *Kim Bailey* 97h 94c
6 ch g Presenting Mama Jaffa (IRE) (In The Wings)
1824[U] 2017[U] 2140[3]

Gold Medal (IRE) *Jonjo O'Neill* 94h
5 b g Dylan Thomas(IRE) Sogno Verde (IRE) (Green Desert (USA))
104[6] 757[8]

Gold Mountain (IRE) *Alexandra Dunn*
5 b g Gold Well La Belle De Serk (IRE) (Shernazar)
5160[P]

Gold Opera (IRE) *N W Alexander* 109h 122c
6 b g Gold Well Flute Opera (IRE) (Sharifabad (IRE))
2475[3] (3164) 3669[4] 4203[3] (4582) 4634[3] 5084[P]

Gold Present (IRE) *Nicky Henderson* 133h
5 br g Presenting Ouro Preto (Definite Article)
2438[P] 4786[5] 5497[13]

Goldray *Kerry Lee* 106h
9 ch m Central Park(IRE) Go Mary (Raga Navarro (ITY))
938[7] 1165[2] **4298[P]** 4881[2] 5373[3]

Goldslinger (FR) *Dean Ivory* 92h
3 b g Gold Away(IRE) Singaporette (FR) (Sagacity (FR))
1984[3] 2718[8]

Gold Thief (IRE) *Laura Young* 59b
5 b g Gold Well Mullaghcloga (IRE) (Glacial Storm (USA))
1003[7] 3952[8]

Go Long (IRE) *Evan Williams* 133h
5 b g Hurricane Run(IRE) Monumental Gesture (IRE) (Head For Heights)
(2748) 3334[2]

Gonalston Cloud (IRE) *Nick Kent* 98h 132c
8 gr g Cloudings(IRE) Roseoengus (IRE) (Roselier (FR))
13[P] (3310) (3836) (4153) ◆ 4912[2]

Gone Forever *Brian Ellison* 128h
5 b g Quest For Fame Erudite (Generous (IRE))
185[P] 2081[5] 2594[5]

Gone Too Far *Alan King* 124h 139c
7 b g Kayf Tara Major Hoolihan (Soldier Rose)
(691) 894[4] (1617) ◆ 2001[7] 2686[U] 5154[3]

Gone Viral (IRE) *George Baker* 102h
4 ch g Virtual Dorinda Gray (IRE) (Docksider (USA))
3375[7] 3773[6] 4317[6] 4784[5]

Gontdevon *R J Harraway*
10 b g Sea Freedom Arctic Affair (IRE) (Glacial Storm (USA))
429[P]

Goodacres Garden (IRE) *Shaun Lycett* 69h
8 b g Oscar(IRE) Living A Dream (IRE) (Heavenly Manna)
434[2] 695[6] 824[U]

Good As Gold *P A Fahy* 124h
7 gr m Beneficial Poppet (Terimon)
3650a[5]

Goodbye Dancer (FR) *Nigel Twiston-Davies* 132h
4 b g Dragon Dancer Maribia Bella (FR) (Urban Ocean (FR))
1657[U] 1847[10] 2513[10] (2977) 3010[F] 3137[4] 3737[2] 4139[5] 4786[4] 5284[11]

Go Odee Go (IRE) *Dan Skelton* 123h
7 b g Alkaadhem Go Franky (IRE) (Hollow Hand)
(419) 812[7] 1038[5] 1234[3]

Good Egg (IRE) *Miss Sarah Rippon* 110c
12 b g Exit To Nowhere(USA) Full Of Surprises (IRE) (Be My Native (USA))
4227[2] 4383[U] 4892[6]

Good Idea (IRE) *Nicky Henderson* 93b
4 b g Arcadio(GER) Aunt Annie (IRE) (Synefos (USA))
4532[5]

Good Man Hughie (IRE) *Sally Randell* 85h
6 ch g Flemensfirth(USA) Good Dawn (IRE) (Good Thyne (USA))
2909[5] 4182[6] 4441[11] 4784[10] 4875[10] 5451[5]

Goodnight Vienna (IRE) *Mrs L Redman* 90c
9 b g High Roller(IRE) Curragh Bridge (Pitpan)
13[5] 4748[3]

Good Of Luck *Warren Greatrex* 128h
6 b g Authorized(IRE) Oops Pettie (Machiavellian (USA))
(332) 708[4] (973) 1381[4]

Goodoldhonkytonk (IRE) *James Evans* 100h 84c
7 b m Oscar(IRE) Pharfetched (Phardante (FR))
1067[7] **2290[U]** 2694[7] 3067[3] 3312[P] 3930[P]

Good Order *E Turner* 9h 37c
10 b g Alflora(IRE) Twinnings Grove (IRE) (Lord Americo)
129[P] 4973[3]

Good Rhythm *Neil King* 89b
5 b g Beat Hollow Silken Act (CAN) (Theatrical (IRE))
1122[8] 1300[4] 1662[6]

Goodtoknow *Kerry Lee* 111h 145c
7 b g Presenting Atlantic Jane (Tamure (IRE))
2853[2] 3109[P] (4109) ◆ (4684) 5327[P]

Good Value *David Pipe* 92h
4 ch g Champs Elysees Change Course (Sadler's Wells (USA))
106[2] 466[2] 712[5] 828[P]

Good Vibration (FR) *Sue Smith* 113h
4 gr g Saddler Maker(IRE) Queenhood (FR) (Linamix (FR))
2041[5] 2423[2] 2791[2] 3240[2] 3884[2] 5102[4]

Goodwood Mirage (IRE) *Jonjo O'Neill* 138h
5 b g Jeremy(USA) Phantom Waters (Pharly (FR))
2512[9] 3336[7] 4769[19]

Goohar (IRE) *Henry Daly* 121h 125c
6 b g Street Cry(IRE) Reem Three (Mark Of Esteem (IRE))
2151[3] 2765[2] 3466[2] 3742[2] 5156[F]

Go On Henry (IRE) *Philip Hobbs* 116c
7 bb g Golan(IRE) The Millers Tale (IRE) (Rashar (USA))
1097[3] 1520[3]

Goonjim (IRE) *Alexandra Dunn* 40h
4 ch g Beneficial Clogga Native (IRE) (Good Thyne (USA))
749[6] 853[8] 4963[6] 5182[P]

Goonyella (IRE) *J T R Dreaper* 122h 152c
8 br g Presenting Miss Fresher (FR) (Pampabird)
2225a[3] **2899[9] 4521a[2] 5218[5]**

Go Paddy Go (IRE) *James Grace* 127h
9 b g Flemensfirth(USA) Blue Bouquet (Cure The Blues (USA))
3071a[7]

Gores Island (IRE) *Gary Moore* 122h 133c
9 b g Beneficial Just Leader (IRE) (Supreme Leader)
1989[3] 2419[3] 2990[3] 3148[3] 3706[8] 3957[3] 4464[7] 5185[3]

Gorey Lane (IRE) *John Norton* 96h 83c
9 b g Oscar(IRE) Supremely Deep (IRE) (Supreme Leader)
2964[P] (3378) 3793[8] 4648[6]

Gorgehous Lliege (FR) *Venetia Williams* 83h 123c
9 b g Lavirco(GER) Charme D'Estruval (FR) (Mistigri)
2517[P] 2878[P] 3591[3]

Goring One (IRE) *Anna Newton-Smith* 65h 90c
10 b g Broadway Flyer(USA) Brigette's Secret (Good Thyne (USA))
2546[P]

Goring Two (IRE) *Anna Newton-Smith* 58h 96c
10 br g Needle Gun(IRE) Kam Slave (Kambalda)
2255[3] 2521[P] 3088[U] (3661) 4197[P] 4529[P] 4670[3] 4931[3]

Gorman (FR) *Evan Williams* 90h
4 ch g King's Best(USA) Gerone (FR) (Saumarez)
207[6] 465[F] 776[10] 3376[F]

Gorsky Island *Tom George* 114h 142c
7 b g Turtle Island(IRE) Belle Magello (FR) (Exit To Nowhere (USA))
2275[4] **3109[3]**

Gorvino (FR) *G Macaire* 109h
2 b g Lucarno(USA) Rolandale (FR) (Mansonnien (FR))
4539a[5]

Gotcha *N W Alexander*
4 gr m Fair Mix(IRE) Shazana (Key Of Luck (USA))
1499[P]

Go Teescomponents *Keith Reveley* 31h 76c
8 b g Septieme Ciel(USA) Linea-G (Keen)
588[4] ◆ 841[7] 934[8] 1373[P]

Gotoyourplay (IRE) *Mrs Dawn Woolf* 34h 131c
11 ch g Definite Article Johnston's Flyer (IRE) (Orchestra)
15[8]

Got The Nac (IRE) *Keith Dalgleish* 122h 128c
6 br g Beneficial Hey Jude (IRE) (Mandalus)
(2981) ◆ 4011[6]

Goudevivre (FR) *Frau S Weis* 108h
3 b f Gentlewave(IRE) Goudeluxe (FR) (Trempolino (USA))
4959a[P]

Gowanauthat (IRE) *Charlie Mann* 85h 106c
7 ch g Golan(IRE) Coolrua (IRE) (Commanche Run)
1824[2] 2037[U] 2364[6] 2714[3] 2953[P] (3468) 3864[P] 4531[4] 5068[2] 5388[4]

Gowell (IRE) *Seamus Mullins* 103h
4 b m Gold Well Glen Supreme (IRE) (Supreme Leader)
4777[4]

Go West Young Man (IRE) *Henry Daly* 125h
7 b g Westerner Last Of Her Line (Silver Patriarch (IRE))
2412[U] 4183[2] 4430[6]

Graasten (GER) *Gary Moore* 114h
3 ch g Sholokhov(IRE) Golden Time (GER) (Surumu (GER))
4409[2] ◆

Graceful Legend *Ben Case* 100h
4 b m Midnight Legend Clover Green (IRE) (Presenting)
3132[2] 3381[3] 3947[3] 4471[5]

Grammar *David Thompson* 89h
6 b g Rail Link Comma (USA) (Kingmambo (USA))
1886[7] 2422[5] 4943[P]

Grams And Ounces *Grace Harris* 118h 118c
8 b g Royal Applause Ashdown Princess (IRE) (King's Theatre (IRE))
59[6] 615[9] 776[3] 937[P] 1115[4] (1299) (1369) (1810) 3932[9] 4252[5] 4411[4] (4745) 4986[6] 5266[2] 5464[4]

Grandads Horse *Charlie Longsdon* 139h 144c
9 bb g Bollin Eric Solid Land (FR) (Solid Illusion (USA))
2916[12] 3528[4] 4306[2] 4735[14] 5119[11]

Grand Article (IRE) *Paul Cowley* 99h 87c
11 ch g Definite Article Grand Morning (IRE) (King Of Clubs)
42[3] 466[P]

Grandasowt (IRE) *Evan Williams* 107h
6 b g Darsi(FR) Cooksgrove Rosie (IRE) (Mandalus)
3077[6] 4526[2]

Grand Coureur (FR) *Nick Williams* 95b
3 bb g Grand Couturier Iris Du Berlais (FR) (Bonnet Rouge (FR))
4103[7] 5400[3]

Grand Diamond (IRE) *Jim Goldie* 68h
11 b g Grand Lodge(USA) Winona (IRE) (Alzao (USA))
870[4]

Grand Enterprise *Tom George* 100h
5 b g Fair Mix(IRE) Miss Chinchilla (Perpendicular)
1484[4] 2564[10] 3105[7] 3239[6]

Grand Fella (IRE) *Ken Wingrove*
10 ch g Raise A Grand(IRE) Mummys Best (Bustino)
1133[P]

Grand Introduction (IRE) *Fergal O'Brien* 110h
5 b g Robin Des Pres(FR) What A Breeze (IRE) (Naheez (USA))
264[3] 2044[3] 2450[10] 2838[5] 3582[2] 4241[10]

Grandioso (IRE) *Steve Flook* 96h 128c
8 b g Westerner Champagne Warrior (IRE) (Waajib (IRE))
4446[3] 4892[4] 5158[4] (5392)

Grand Jesture (IRE) *Henry De Bromhead* 121h 150c
7 b g Gold Well Four Moons (IRE) (Cardinal Flower)
3296a[R]

Grand March *Kim Bailey* 106h 107c
6 b g Beat All(USA) Bora Bora (Bairn (USA))
2300[4] 2976[4] 4453[4] 5377[6]

Grandmaster George (IRE) *Seamus Mullins* 103h
6 ch g Generous(IRE) Merewood Lodge (IRE) (Grand Lodge (USA))
(264) 2879[6] 3353[8] 3773[7] 4856[4]

Grand Moss (FR) *S Foucher* 88h 103c
4 b g Astarabad(USA) Mossita (FR) (Tip Moss (FR))
2820a[P] 4400a[2]

Grand Turina *Venetia Williams* 110b
4 b m Kayf Tara Cesana (IRE) (Desert Prince (IRE))
4242[6] 4967[4]

Grand Vintage (IRE) *Kenneth Slack* 108h
9 gr g Basanta(IRE) Rivers Town Rosie (IRE) (Roselier (FR))
34[2] (468) 839[4] 1034[8]

Grange Hall (IRE) *Paul Stafford* 111h 68c
8 b m Flemensfirth(USA) Odeeka (IRE) (Posen (USA))
52a[8] 200[3]

Granit (IRE) *Nicky Henderson* 94b
5 b g Arcadio(GER) Can't Stop (GER) (Lando (GER))
5070[P]

Gran Maestro (USA) *Dr Richard Newland* 130h
6 ch g Medicean Red Slippers (USA) (Nureyev (USA))
(1039) 1657[6]

Gran Torino (IRE) *Mary Evans* 81h 88c
10 b g Milan Miss Greinton (GER) (Greinton)
88[3] 717[P]

Grape Tree Flame *Peter Bowen* 134h
7 ch m Grape Tree Road Althrey Flame (IRE) (Torus)
(404) 2759[P] 3336[P] 4125[5] 5454[5]

Grate Fella (IRE) *Sue Smith* 113h 139c
7 b g King's Best(USA) Moonlight Paradise (USA) (Irish River (FR))
2193[4] 2425[2]

Grayhawk (IRE) *Diana Grissell* 11h
5 b g Kalanisi(IRE) Saddler Regal (IRE) (Saddlers' Hall (IRE))
2710[9]

Gray Hession (IRE) *Jonjo O'Neill* 113h 142c
8 b g Vinnie Roe(IRE) Little Paddle (IRE) (Remainder Man)
(259) ◆ (1268) 1658[5]

Grays Choice (IRE) *George Bewley* 117b
6 b g Well Chosen Pennyworth (IRE) (Zaffaran (USA))
2756[4] 4037[4] 4408[U] (4611)

Gray Wolf River *Richard Harper* 75h
4 gr m Fair Mix(IRE) Inkpen (Overbury (IRE))
4182[7] 4507[4] 4743[4]

Great Anticipation (IRE) *Lynsey Kendall* 62h
6 b g Ashkalani(IRE) La Bekkah (FR) (Nononito (FR))
1366[5] 1570[5] 2025[8]

Great Choice (IRE) *David Pipe* 128h
6 b g Westerner Granuale (IRE) (Seamanship)
2301[P]

Great Demeanor (USA) *Dianne Sayer* 71h 86c
5 b g Bernstein(USA) Hangin Withmy Buds (USA) (Roar (USA))
286[F] 455[2] 1031[3] 1630[U] 1888[6] 2292[8] 5445[4]

Great Field (FR) *W P Mullins* 148h
4 b g Great Pretender(IRE) Eaton Lass (IRE) (Definite Article)
4765[P]

Great Fighter *John Ferguson* 128h
5 b g Street Cry(IRE) Evil Empire (GER) (Acatenango (GER))
1290[F] ◆ 1485[3] (1568) 1977[3] 2926[2]

Great Hall *Kevin Frost* 114h
5 b g Halling(USA) L'Affaire Monique (Machiavellian (USA))
(1898) 2123[4] 5416[3]

Great Link *Dan Skelton* 112h 130c
6 b g Rail Link The Strand (Gone West (USA))
(623) 2897[2] 3315[4] 3728[3]

Greek Islands (IRE) *Neil Mulholland*
7 b g Oasis Dream Serisia (FR) (Exit To Nowhere (USA))
1544[9]

Green And White (ITY) *Dave Roberts* 93h
5 b g Denon(USA) Sequita (GER) (Lomitas)
176[6] 440[7] 673[2] 843[7] 1166[8] 2408[P]

Green Bank (IRE) *Charlie Longsdon* 104h 115c
9 b g Morozov(USA) Queen Polly (IRE) (Pollerton)
670[5] 760[6] 1114[2] 1309[P] 1592[2]

Green Du Ciel (FR) *Carroll Gray* 97h 74c
10 gr g Smadoun(FR) Sucre Blanc (FR) (Green Tune (USA))
3369[P] **4850[4]**

Greenlaw *Charlie Longsdon* 120h 132c
9 b g Helissio(FR) Juris Prudence (IRE) (Law Society (USA))
215[3] (523) (760) 1040[12] 1288[4] 5092[5]

Green Wizard (IRE) *Sue Smith* 99h 115c
9 b g Wizard King Ajo Green (IRE) (Moscow Society (USA))
81[6] 358[4] 800[2] 1033[6] 1114[7] 1571[2] 1783[F]

Greenworldsolution *Jennie Candlish* 83b
3 b g Lucarno(USA) Basford Lady (IRE) (Accordion)
2777[7] 3165[6]

Green Zone (IRE) *Lisa Harrison* 90h
4 b g Bushranger(IRE) Incense (Unfuwain (USA))
1568[7] 4817[P] 5444[4]

Grexit (IRE) *Lucinda Russell* 112h
4 b g Oratorio(IRE) Baboosh (IRE) (Marju (IRE))
4633[2] 5256[6]

Greybougg *Nigel Hawke* 133h 114c
6 gr g Tobougg(IRE) Kildee Lass (Morpeth)
382[5] 622[3]

Grey Gold (IRE) *Kerry Lee* 133h 155c
10 gr g Strategic Choice(USA) Grouse-N-Heather (Grey Desire)
47a[P] (2784) 3446[P] 4355[2] 4964[3] 5326[6]

Grey Life *Malcolm Jefferson* 109h 129c
9 gr g Terimon More To Life (Northern Tempest (USA))
(36) 2719[2] ◆ 2920[6] 3589[3] 4328[3] ◆

Grey Messenger (IRE) *Emma Baker* 80h
6 gr g Heron Island(IRE) Turlututu (FR) (Turgeon (USA))
1844[U] 1909[7] 2408[P]

Grey Monk (IRE) *Sara Ender* 123h 33c
7 gr g Alderbrook Thats The Bother (IRE) (Roselier (FR))
1261[4] (1646) 2145[6] 5012[8] 5260[6]

Grey Storm (IRE) *Rose Dobbin*
9 gr g September Storm(GER) Lady Blayney (IRE) (Mazaad)
2398[P]

Greywell Boy *Nick Williams* 103h 126c
8 gr g Fair Mix(IRE) Rakajack (Rakaposhi King)
109[P]

Griesenau (IRE) *Paul Henderson* 27h 14c
9 b g Luso Persian Wonder (IRE) (Persian Mews)
4295[U] 4845[12] 5067[9]

Grimley Girl *Henry Oliver* 110h 118c
9 b m Sir Harry Lewis(USA) Grimley Gale (IRE) (Strong Gale)
1793[5] **2449[3] (3931) 4443[6]** 4890[4] (5438)

Grinamix (FR) *P Lenogue* 128h
4 gr g Verglas(IRE) Courageuse (FR) (Linamix (FR))
5042a[3] 5428a[4]

Grisedenuit (FR) *Trevor Wall* 90h
3 bb f Gris De Gris(IRE) Ambacity (FR) (Sagacity (FR))
2537[P] 3338[2] 4489[5] 4846[9]

Grissom (FR) *Jimmy Frost* 95h 89c
7 ch g Sabrehill(USA) Nuit De Chine (FR) (Valanour (IRE))
160[2] **1047[6]**

Groody Hill (IRE) *C Roche* 123h 137c
9 gr g Alderbrook Secret Leave (Long Leave)
92a[P]

Groomed (IRE) *Sue Smith* 72h 120c
7 b g Acclamation Enamoured (Groom Dancer (USA))
82[7] **395[F]** 681[8] 802[7] **1267[4] 1458[2]**

Groove (FR) *Francois Nicolle* 110h 130c
6 b g Mister Sacha(FR) Dallas Des Mottes (FR) (Maresca Sorrento (FR))
1882a[6] 2820a[3]

Groundbreaking *John Ferguson*
5 b g New Approach(IRE) Ladeena (IRE) (Dubai Millennium)
3221[P]

Groundunderrepair (IRE) *Warren Greatrex* 107b
4 b g Milan Discerning Air (Ezzoud (IRE))
1926[2] 4309[5]

Grouse Lodge (IRE) *Mrs Emma Clark* 89h 96c
9 b g Well Chosen Arctic Jane (IRE) (Dayeem (USA))
523[P] 4748[U] 5082[3] 5370[3]

Grove Pride *Mrs D J Ralph* 81h 130c
10 b g Double Trigger(IRE) Dara's Pride (IRE) (Darazari (IRE))
4249[P] 5399[P]

Grove Silver (IRE) *Jennie Candlish* 117h 120c
6 gr g Gamut(IRE) Cobbler's Well (IRE) (Wood Chanter)
2727[7] 2963[6] 3362[4] 3836[U] 4062[3] ◆ 4352[3] 4649[2] 5222[3]

Grow Nasa Grow (IRE) *Peter Winks* 66h
4 ch g Mahler Dereenavurrig (IRE) (Lancastrian)
558[3] 2750[5] 4156[8]

Grumeti *Alan King* 149h 107c
7 b g Sakhee(USA) Tetravella (IRE) (Groom Dancer (USA))
2198[4] 2634[5] 4381[7]

Grumpy Jackie *Chris Down*
3 ch f Grape Tree Road Hayley's Flower (IRE) (Night Shift (USA))
3118[9]

Guadeloupe (IRE) *David Loder* 39b
6 b g Refuse To Bend(IRE) Cantaloupe (Priolo (USA))
2337[8] 2493[13]

Guanciale *Dai Burchell* 94h 107c
8 b g Exit To Nowhere(USA) Thenford Lass (IRE) (Anshan)
1931[10] 2264[4] 2736[3] **3224[2] 3931[5] 4321[4] 4713[U] 5064[2]**

Guantoshol (IRE) *Venetia Williams* 98h
4 ch g Sholokhov(IRE) Glicine (GER) (Tiger Hill (IRE))
3484[8] 3772[9] 3955[2] 4447[6]

Guaracha *Alexandra Dunn* 106h 112c
4 ch g Halling(USA) Pachanga (Inchinor)
2251[8] 2689[6] 2850[2] 3108[9] 3417[3] (3665) 3816[6]
4491[3] 4712[4] **(4850) 5016[3]**

Guard of Honour (IRE) *Rebecca Curtis* 119h
4 b g Galileo(IRE) Queen Of France (USA) (Danehill (USA))
360[3]

Guards Chapel *Gary Moore* 113h 99c
7 b g Motivator Intaaj (IRE) (Machiavellian (USA))
449[12] 2577[3] 2924[2] 4466[8] 4782[4]

Gud Day (IRE) *Conor Dore* 82h 85c
7 gr g Aussie Rules(USA) Queen Al Andalous (IRE) (King's Best (USA))
186[8] 2291[7] 2560[P] 2841[6] 3140[3] 3233[3] 3925[5] 4184[9] 4390[P] 4553[2] 4747[3] 4987[4]

Guiding George (IRE) *Dan Skelton* 123h 132c
7 b g Flemensfirth(USA) Shatani (IRE) (Shahrastani (USA))
523[2] 1167[3]

Guitar Pete (IRE) *Ms Sandra Hughes* 105h 137c
5 gr g Dark Angel(IRE) Innishmore (IRE) (Lear Fan (USA))
3552a[3] 3853[7]

Guiting Power *Nigel Twiston-Davies* 67h
4 b g Lucarno(USA) Sparkling Jewel (Bijou D'Inde)
2023[7] 2904[8] 3221[8] 3771[P]

Gullinbursti (IRE) *Emma Lavelle* 119h 126c
9 b g Milan D'Ygrande (IRE) (Good Thyne (USA))
3150[7] 3860[8] 5193[F] (Dead)

Gully's Edge *Malcolm Jefferson* 132h
5 b g Kayf Tara Shuildante (IRE) (Phardante (FR))
144[2] 2031[3] 3588[2] (5011) ◆ (5296)

Gulshanigans *Nigel Twiston-Davies* 94b
3 b c Sakhee(USA) Gulshan (Batshoof)
5097[9]

Gunna Be A Devil (IRE) *Jeremy Scott* 120h 125c
11 b g Alflora(IRE) Gunna Be Precious (Gunner B)
471[5] (Dead)

Gunner Fifteen (IRE) *Harry Fry* 119h
7 b g Westerner Grandy Hall (IRE) (Saddlers' Hall (IRE))
2639[5] 3232[10] **3922[U]**

Gunner Gotya *Ben Pauling*
6 ch h Double Trigger(IRE) Gunner Getya (Gunner B)
1082[P]

Gunner Lindley (IRE) *Stuart Coltherd* 93h
8 ch g Medicean Lasso (Indian Ridge)
1892[3] 2148[2] 2322[2] 2891[2] 2946[4] 3244[4] 3807[4] 4326[3] 4550[9]

Gunnery Sergeant (IRE) *Noel Meade* 135h
4 bb g Presenting Dame Foraine (FR) (Raintrap)
2814a[3]

Gun Shy (IRE) *Gary Moore* 123h 138c
7 b g Norwich Debbies Scud (IRE) (Roselier (FR))
(241) 596[5] 2184[6]

Gurkha Brave (IRE) *Karen McLintock* 122h 132c
7 b g Old Vic Honeyed (IRE) (Persian Mews)
508[2] (638) 850[6] 1263[2] **1782[4] (5123)** ◆

Gurteen (IRE) *Robert Tyner* 128h
5 b g Golan(IRE) Aussieannie (IRE) (Arapahos (FR))
4516a[4]

Gus Macrae (IRE) *Rebecca Curtis* 83h 96c
11 b g Accordion Full Of Surprises (IRE) (Be My Native (USA))
1641[4] 1965[6] 2434[P]

Gustav (IRE) *Zoe Davison* 97h
5 b g Mahler Pakaradyssa (FR) (Roakarad)
2044[10] 2603[P] 5372[8]

Gusty Rocky (IRE) *Patrick J Flynn* 126h
6 b g King's Theatre(IRE) Liss A Paoraigh (IRE) (Husyan (USA))
1175a[4]

Gwafa (IRE) *Paul Webber* 140h
4 gr g Tamayuz Atalina (FR) (Linamix (FR))
3227[6] (3819) ◆ (4317) 5190[U]

Gwaien (FR) *L Viel*
4 b m Astarabad(USA) Kiluti (FR) (Solid Illusion (USA))
5135a[P]

Gwencily Berbas (FR) *Alan Fleming* 147h
4 b g Nickname(FR) Lesorial (FR) (Lesotho (USA))
(2353a) 2815a[3] 5004a[6]

Gwili Spar *Laura Hurley* 80h 46c
7 ch g Generosity Lady Of Mine (Cruise Missile)
106[8] 337[4] 704[3] 1010[9]

Haatefina *Mark Usher* 107h
5 b m Haatef(USA) Felona (Caerleon (USA))
1793[6] 1974[5] 2538[3] 2974[F]

Habbie Simpson *Pauline Robson* 127h 127c
10 b g Elmaamul(USA) Hamanaka (USA) (Conquistador Cielo (USA))
199[2] 657[6] 2477[P]

Hab Sab (IRE) *Linda Jewell* 43b
3 b g Papal Bull Tamburello (IRE) (Roi Danzig (USA))
5308[6]

Hada Men (USA) *Rebecca Menzies* 100h 95c
10 b g Dynaformer(USA) Catchy (USA) (Storm Cat (USA))
198[5] 2802[7] 3428[14] 3837[12] 5012[9]

Hadfield (IRE) *John Ferguson* 112h
3 b g Sea The Stars(IRE) Rezyana (AUS) (Redoute's Choice (AUS))
(1452) 1631[2] (2027) 2170[4]

Hadrian's Approach (IRE) *Nicky Henderson* 123h 147c
8 b g High Chaparral(IRE) Gifted Approach (IRE) (Roselier (FR))
4361[7] 5218[U] 5494[6]

Hag Stone *Tom Lacey* 74b
4 b g Kayf Tara Caoba (Hernando (FR))
2842[9]

Hahnenkam (IRE) *Seamus Durack* 98b
5 b g Stowaway Bahnasa (IRE) (Shardari)
5308[2] ◆

Hail The Brave (IRE) *Michael Smith* 104h
6 ch g Lahib(USA) Parverb (IRE) (Parliament)
2142[P] 2948[9] 3346[6] 3592[P] 4797[9]

Hainan (FR) *Sue Smith* 120h
4 gr g Laveron Honor Smytzer (Highest Honor (FR))
2499[7] 2962[4] 3367[2] ◆ (3970) 4911[5]

Hairy O'Malley (IRE) *Evan Williams* 105h
6 b g Oscar(IRE) Ballilaurenkadolly (IRE) (Shernazar)
110[9] 332[P]

Halcyon Days *Rebecca Menzies* 70h 91c
6 b g Generous(IRE) Indian Empress (Emperor Jones (USA))
3805[2] 4325[3] 4836[4] 5377[9]

Haleo *Laura Young* 89h
4 ch g Halling(USA) Oatey (Master Willie)
466[P]

Hallingham *Chris Gordon* 68h
5 b g Halling(USA) In Luck (In The Wings)
2011[8] 2898[5] 3114[12] 3619[9] 4161[6] 4440[7]

Hallings Comet *Adrian Wintle* 90h 136c
6 ch g Halling(USA) Landinium (ITY) (Lando (GER))
87[P] 1911[6]

Halling's Wish *Gary Moore* 118h 117c
5 br g Halling(USA) Fair View (GER) (Dashing Blade)
99[4] 598[3] 1350[7] 1591[2] **1769[2] 2012[U]** 5065[9]

Hall Kelly (IRE) *Mrs C Banks* 56h 82c
10 b g Saddlers' Hall(IRE) Native Monk (IRE) (Be My Native (USA))
429[U]

Hallssio *P Lenogue* 114h 87c
7 b g Halling(USA) Elayoon (USA) (Danzig (USA))
437a[10]

Hallstatt (IRE) *John Mackie* 96h
9 ch g Halling(USA) Last Resort (Lahib (USA))
2162[4]

Halo Moon *Neil Mulholland* 107h 125c
7 br g Kayf Tara Fragrant Rose (Alflora (IRE))
2420[2] 2698[2] 2930[3] 3421[8] (3820) (3937) (4027) ◆

Hameldown Tor *E Walker* 70h 117c
11 b g Kayf Tara Priscilla (Teenoso (USA))
15[5]

Hammersly Lake (FR) *Nicky Henderson* 145h
7 b g Kapgarde(FR) Loin De Moi (FR) (Loup Solitaire (USA))
96a[6] 1039[2] **1942[F]**

Handazan (IRE) *Ben Case* 74h 65c
6 b g Nayef(USA) Handaza (IRE) (Be My Guest (USA))
208[2] **2197[P] 2885[8]**

Handittolewi *Dianne Sayer* 93b
4 b g Lucarno(USA) Foxglove (Hernando (FR))
1926[5] 2330[4]

Handiwork *Steve Gollings* 139h
5 ch g Motivator Spinning Top (Alzao (USA))
1979 2594[3] 2901[6] 4769[13]

Handmaid *Peter Bowen* 119h
6 b m King's Theatre(IRE) Hand Inn Glove (Alflora (IRE))
839[5] 1113[3] 1264[2] 1419[3] 1808[9] **2592[P]**

Hand On Bach (IRE) *Tim Vaughan* 97h
7 b g Bach(IRE) Deise Blues (IRE) (Flemensfirth (USA))
31[P] 1086[9]

Handpicked *Henry Daly* 94h
4 b m King's Theatre(IRE) Hand Inn Glove (Alflora (IRE))
220[2] 2086[9] 3573[3] 4317[9] 4893[3] 5155[7]

Handsome Buddy (IRE) *Michael Gates* 87h 102c
8 br g Presenting Moya's Magic (IRE) (Phardante (FR))
1720[2] 1850[6] 2276[3] 2996[F] 4879[P] 5468[9]

Handsome Dan (IRE) *Sarah Hollinshead* 122h 121c
9 b g Busy Flight Beautiful City (IRE) (Jurado (USA))
1264[3] (1661) 1949[8]

Handsome Horace (IRE) *Philip Hobbs* 99h 100c
5 b g Presenting Paumafi (IRE) (Shardari)
30[2] **388[3] 827[3]** ◆

Handsome Sam *Alan King* 110h
4 ch g Black Sam Bellamy(IRE) Rose Marine (Handsome Sailor)
(2972) ◆ 3316[4] 3846[8] 5183[7]

Handy Andy (IRE) *Colin Tizzard* 113h 128c
9 b g Beneficial Maslam (IRE) (Robellino (USA))
1849[P] 2089[2] 2955[P] 3109[P] 3748[P] 5065[4] 5466[8]

Hang Fire (IRE) *Tony Carroll* 84h
5 ch m Shirocco(GER) Ambrosine (Nashwan (USA))
3920[4] 4494[7] 5099[8]

Hank Williams *Kristin Stubbs* 60b
3 b g Schiaparelli(GER) Jezadil (IRE) (Mujadil (USA))
1772[10]

Hannah Just Hannah *Heather Main* 97h
6 gr m Proclamation(IRE) Evaporate (Insan (USA))
314[3] 5094[11] 5469[3]

Hannah's Princess (IRE) *Warren Greatrex* 133h
6 b m Kalanisi(IRE) Donna's Princess (IRE) (Supreme Leader)
52a[6] 2775[4] (4338) ◆ 4909[5]

Hannibal The Great (IRE) *Charlie Longsdon* 119h
7 b g Milan Town Gossip (IRE) (Indian Ridge)
4362[P]

Hannington *Barry Brennan* 77h
4 ch g Firebreak Manderina (Mind Games)
4773[6] 5153[14]

Hansupfordetroit (IRE) *Bernard Llewellyn* 131h 136c
10 b g Zagreb(USA) Golden Needle (IRE) (Prince Of Birds (USA))
2809[5] 3517[6] 4354[4] 5239[5]

Ha'penny Woods (IRE) *Chris Grant* 106h
5 b g Wareed(IRE) Muriel's Pride (IRE) (Mister Lord (USA))
2070[4] 2432[6]

Happy Diva (IRE) *Kerry Lee* 110h
4 b m King's Theatre(IRE) Megans Joy (IRE) (Supreme Leader)
2302[2] 2697[F] 3500[2]

Happy Hollow *Alan Swinbank* 111b
3 b g Beat Hollow Dombeya (IRE) (Danehill (USA))
(4392) (4867)

Happy Jack (IRE) *Michael Wigham* 83h
4 b g Elusive City(USA) Miss Pelling (IRE) (Danehill Dancer (IRE))
1780[6] 2217[8]

Harangue (IRE) *Paul John Gilligan* 112h 127c
7 br g Street Cry(IRE) Splendeur (FR) (Desert King (IRE))
855[4] 1184a[2]

Harbour Court *Alan Hill* 127c
9 ch g Karinga Bay Royal Squeeze (IRE) (King's Ride)
(14)

Hard As A Rock (FR) *Emma Lavelle* 99b
4 b g Network(GER) Fany Noune (FR) (Reste Tranquille (FR))
2875[3]

Hardrock Davis (FR) *Tom George* 91b
4 bb g Saint Des Saints(FR) Trumpet Davis (FR) (Rose Laurel)
5152[5]

Hard Run (FR) *M Blanchard-Jacquet*
5 b m Le Fou(IRE) Bairgaine (FR) (Cardoun (FR))
5499a[P]

Hard Toffee (IRE) *Conrad Allen* 92b
4 b g Teofilo(IRE) Speciale (USA) (War Chant (USA))
1484[6] *4532[6]*

Hardtorock (IRE) *Liam Corcoran* 66h
6 b g Mountain High(IRE) Permissal (IRE) (Dr Massini (IRE))
2065[9] 2519[8] 2879[P] 4494[6] 4920[P]

Hard To Swallow (IRE) *Tom Weston* 65h 118c
9 b g Snurge Nicat's Daughter (IRE) (Oscar (IRE))
4226[5] **4352[P]**

Hargam (FR) *Nicky Henderson* 159h
4 gr g Sinndar(IRE) Horasana (FR) (Galileo (IRE))
2060[4] 3033[3] 3230[3] 4698[10]

Harley Rebel *Neil Mulholland* 128h
3 br g Cockney Rebel(IRE) Al Kahina (Mark Of Esteem (IRE))
1899[7] ◆ 2032[4] (3213) 3777[2] (3978) (4619) ◆ 4720[12]

Harleys Max *Susan Corbett* 81h 89c
6 b g Winged Love(IRE) Researcher (Cosmonaut)
201[2] **1853[P] 2708[P] 2983[2]** 3503[5] **(3683) 3834[8] (4034) 4569[7] 5010[4] 5261[2]**

Harmonic Lady *Mike Sowersby* 103h
5 ch m Trade Fair First Harmony (First Trump)
4937[4] 5229[3]

Harriet's Ark *Julian Smith* 79h
8 ch m Sir Harry Lewis(USA) Brush The Ark (Brush Aside (USA))
328[4] 552[4] 2670[6] 3234[6] 4804[9]

Harris (IRE) *Alan Brown* 108h 111c
8 b g Beneficial Porter Tastes Nice (IRE) (Dry Dock)
58[P] 1795[P] 1889[P] 2405[P] 2919[P]

Harristown *Charlie Longsdon* 136h 117c
5 ch g Bering New Abbey (Sadler's Wells (USA))
319[6] **2012[3] 2593[U] 2727[6] 4775[P]**

Harry Hunt *Graeme McPherson* 120h 119c
8 b g Bertolini(USA) Qasirah (IRE) (Machiavellian (USA))
2125[3] 2496[5] (2744) 3428[2] 4066[13] 4911[10]

Harry's Farewell *Polly Gundry* 121h 140c
8 b g Sir Harry Lewis(USA) Golden Mile (IRE) (King's Ride)
(2724) 3282[F] 3528[3] 5390[U]

Harry's Summer (USA) *Gordon Elliott* 83h
4 bb g Roman Ruler(USA) Magnificent Lady (USA) (Cherokee Run (USA))
962[P]

Harrys Whim *Maurice Barnes* 102h 117c
10 b m Sir Harry Lewis(USA) Whimbrel (Dara Monarch)
781[2] ◆ **868[4]** 1181[8] **1458[4] (1738) 2104[F]**

Harry The Viking *Sandy Thomson* 111h 134c
10 ch g Sir Harry Lewis(USA) Viking Flame (Viking (USA))
2068[F] 2638[3] 3057[3] 3364[2] 4245[P] 4818[P] 5259[3] 5474[3]

Hartforth *Donald Whillans* 118h
7 ch g Haafhd St Edith (IRE) (Desert King (IRE))
2033[5] 2802[3] 3058[7] 3970[F] 4405[P]

Hartside (GER) *Peter Winks* 119h
6 b g Montjeu(IRE) Helvellyn (USA) (Gone West (USA))
43[3] (157) 237[4] 2499[6] 2810[4] 2921[2] 3035[7] 4055[3] (4154) (4865)

Harvey (IRE) *Laura Mongan* 93b
4 br m Presenting One Swoop (IRE) (Be My Native (USA))
3132[9] 5069[12]

Harvey Logan (IRE) *Noel Meade* 130h
6 b g Saffron Walden(FR) Baie Barbara (IRE) (Heron Island (IRE))
3071a[9]

Harvey's Hope *Keith Reveley* 116h
9 b g Sinndar(IRE) Ancara (Dancing Brave (USA))
82[2] 802[3] 969[3] 1270[4] 2775[8] 3035[9] 3592[6] **3834[F]** 4066[9]

Hash Brown (IRE) *Michael Hourigan* 138h 128c
6 ch g Vinnie Roe(IRE) Keralba (USA) (Sheikh Albadou)
96a[20] **3651a[6]**

Hasiteasy (IRE) *Peter Croke* 82b
4 b m Kalanisi(IRE) Hasainiya (IRE) (Top Ville (IRE))
206[7]

Hassadin *Michael Blake* 102h
9 ch g Reset(AUS) Crocolat (Croco Rouge (IRE))
859[2] 1098[P] 1383[2] 1771[2] 1961[4] 2316[3] (3219) (3821) 3946[5]

Hassle (IRE) *Clive Cox* 118h
6 b g Montjeu(IRE) Canterbury Lace (USA) (Danehill (USA))
1977[7]

Hastrubal (FR) *Henry Daly* 100h
5 br g Discover D'Auteuil(FR) Miss Montrose (Tina's Pet)
2440[4] 3145[4] 5153[8]

Hatters River (IRE) *Ali Stronge* 109h 119c
8 b g Milan Curzon Ridge (IRE) (Indian Ridge)
1987[3] 2243[P]

Hattons Hill (IRE) *Henry Hogarth* 66h
6 b g Pierre Cluain Chaoin (IRE) (Phardante (FR))
2169[8] 2889[3]

Hatton Springs (IRE) *Stuart Coltherd* 95h
4 b m Jeremy(USA) Oopsadaisy (IRE) (High Chaparral (IRE))
157[6] 1887[6] 2144[3] 2343[5] 2427[5] (3672) 3888[5] 4404[3] 4581[7]

Haughtons Bridge (IRE) *Martin Hill* 85h 88c
7 gr g Cloudings(IRE) Miss Badsworth (IRE) (Gunner B)
293[P] 1236[7] 1383[5] **1546[4] 4921[3]** ◆ **5265[P]**

Haut Bages (FR) *Oliver Sherwood* 106h
3 b g Archange D'Or(IRE) Rotina (FR) (Crystal Glitters (USA))
2439[3] 3819[F] 5153[5] 5434[5]

Havana Dancer (IRE) *Anthony John Black* 104h
6 b m Flemensfirth(USA) Senorita Rumbalita (Alflora (IRE))
1150a[16]

Havana Jack (IRE) *L Kerr* 69b 38c
5 b g Westerner Hackler Poitin (IRE) (Little Bighorn)
320[16] **4207[6] 5090[6]**

Have One For Me (IRE) *Victor Thompson* 102h
8 b g Sonus(IRE) Dunmanogue (IRE) (Supreme Leader)
251[3] 299[3] 397[5]

Haverstock *Caroline Keevil* 96h
5 b g New Approach(IRE) Endorsement (Warning)
1702[4] 2000[5] 2263[P]

Have You Had Yours (IRE) *Jane Walton* 82h 111c
9 br g Whitmore's Conn(USA) Mandys Moynavely (IRE) (Semillon)
331[U] 5086[P]

Hawaian Rose *Colin Tizzard* 74h
5 b m Helissio(FR) Waimea Bay (Karinga Bay)
2875[5] 3258[U] 3825[P] 4435[P] 5353[7]

Hawaii Five Nil (IRE) *Jonjo O'Neill* 118h 121c
7 b g Gold Well Polish Rhythm (IRE) (Polish Patriot (USA))
177[5] (810) **1008[U] 1327[4] 1483[2] 1641[P]**

Hawdyerwheesht *David Dennis* 123h 98c
7 b g Librettist(USA) Rapsgate (IRE) (Mozart (IRE))
157[3] 718[5] 835[2] (931) 1012[2] 1156[3] **1343[3]** 1549[2] 1719[3] 1945[3] 2217[3]

Hawk Gold (IRE) *Michelle Bryant* 77h
11 ch g Tendulkar(USA) Heiress Of Meath (IRE) (Imperial Frontier (USA))
224[6] 675[6] 918[6] 1423[6] 1596[7] 2004[8] 2253[4] 2547[7]

Hawk High (IRE) *Tim Easterby* 140h
5 b g High Chaparral(IRE) Septembers Hawk (IRE) (Machiavellian (USA))
4014[5] ◆ 4765[9]

Hawkhurst (IRE) *Paul Nicholls* 130h
5 b g Flemensfirth(USA) Silaoce (FR) (Nikos)
2152[2] 3064[U] 3403[6] 4821[F]

Hayjack *Martin Keighley* 119h 123c
10 b g Karinga Bay Celtic Native (IRE) (Be My Native (USA))
2451[4] 3014[F] (Dead)

Haymount (IRE) *W P Mullins* 134h
6 ch g Presenting Ali's Dipper (IRE) (Orchestra)
4955a[4]

Hazy Tom (IRE) *Gareth Thomas* 114h 127c
9 b g Heron Island(IRE) The Wounded Cook (IRE) (Muroto)
317[8] **4892[3] 5158[2]**

Hazzaat (IRE) *Fergal O'Brien* 111h 91c
5 ch g Iffraaj Hurricane Irene (IRE) (Green Desert (USA))
1055[7] (1137) 1291[4]

Heading To First *Jim Best* 97h
8 b g Sulamani(IRE) Bahirah (Ashkalani (IRE))
172[4] (267) 489[2] 811[4] 918[8]

Headly's Bridge (IRE) *Simon Earle* 108h 136c
9 b g Tillerman Brockton Flame (Emarati (USA))
4128[P] 5093[5] 5354[6]

Heads Or Tails (IRE) *S R Andrews* 80h 109c
8 b g Milan She's A Gamble (IRE) (Teenoso (USA))
292[3]

Head Spin (IRE) *Seamus Mullins* 93h 106c
7 b g Beneficial Who Tells Jan (Royal Fountain)
31[2] 403[3] 670[F] 2416[5] 2874[5] 3088[3] 3661[P] 4673[2] 5149[2]

Head To The Stars *Henry Daly* 62h
4 br g Kayf Tara Sail By The Stars (Celtic Cone)
2909[6] 3221[12]

Heartening *Paul Phillips* 71h
7 b m Wace(USA) Heartleys Quest (IRE) (Broken Hearted)
1574[7] 2302[15] 2603[10]

Hear The Chimes *Shaun Harris* 117h
6 b g Midnight Legend Severn Air (Alderbrook)
2042[12] 2540[5] 2810[P] 3398[4] (3932) 4411[3] 4793[4]

Heart O Annandale (IRE) *Iain Jardine* 100h 64c
8 b g Winged Love(IRE) She's All Heart (Broken Hearted)
(136) 730[3] **803[P]** 869[6] 4047[P] 4421[P] 4942[P] 5412[3]

Heathfield (IRE) *A J Martin* 136h 138c
8 ch g Definite Article Famous Lady (IRE) (Presenting)
(92a) 2672a[8] **3296a[9] 3651a[9] 5327[P]**

Heath Hunter (IRE) *David Pipe* 132h 110c
8 b g Shantou(USA) Deep Supreme (IRE) (Supreme Leader)
2446[3] 2781[4] 3080[2] 3529[10] 3917[2] 4366[4] 4793[2] 4913[5] 5185[4]

Heavenly Brook (IRE) *Alexandra Dunn* 85h 119c
11 b g Alderbrook Heavenly Mandy (IRE) (Mandalus)
2405[4]

Heavenly Magic *Bernard Llewellyn* 37b
6 gr g Septieme Ciel(USA) Magical Wonderland (Thowra (FR))
124^{11}

Heckley Herbert *James Walton*
8 b g Helissio(FR) Heckley Spark (Electric)
143^{P}

Heck Thomas (IRE) *Noel Meade* 125h 103c
7 b g Oscar(IRE) Good Heighway (IRE) (Good Thyne (USA))
50a^{P}

Hector's Chance *Heather Main*
6 ch g Byron Fleur A Lay (USA) (Mr Greeley (USA))
1234^{P}

Hedge End (IRE) *Jimmy Fox* 52h
4 gr m Verglas(IRE) Trilemma (Slip Anchor)
1485^{4}

Hedley Lamarr (IRE) *Jonjo O'Neill* 130h
5 b g Gold Well Donna's Tarquin (IRE) (Husyan (USA))
2485^{6} 2977^{3} 5275^{4}

Heighnow *Conrad Allen* 27h
4 b m Indian Danehill(IRE) Mooreheigh (Sir Harry Lewis (USA))
761^{7} 2277^{17} 4322^{11} 5373^{13}

Heilan Rebel (IRE) *N W Alexander* 87h
5 b g Where Or When(IRE) Nordice Equity (IRE) (Project Manager)
2709^{3} 3442^{3} 3668^{9} 4176^{7} 4548^{7} 5256^{4}

Heist (IRE) *Patrick Griffin* 113h 114c
5 b g Galileo(IRE) Matikanehanafubuki (IRE) (Caerleon (USA))
332^{5} 1170^{5} **(1460) 1738^{2}**

Helamis *Barry Leavy* 90h
5 b m Shirocco(GER) Alnoor (USA) (Danzig (USA))
(2565) 2812^{6} 3011^{4} 3789^{5}

Helenpark (IRE) *Paul Henderson* 68b
6 b m Westerner Celestial Rose (IRE) (Roselier (FR))
271^{8}

He Likes Tobouggie *Neil King* 75b
4 ch g Tobougg(IRE) Tamise (USA) (Time For A Change (USA))
4308^{9} 4894^{13} 4981^{4}

Helium (FR) *Alexandra Dunn* 134h 135c
10 b g Dream Well(FR) Sure Harbour (SWI) (Surumu (GER))
1907^{2} (2019) (2246) (2449) 2854^{3} 3153^{4} 3749^{3} 4230^{3} 4624^{3}

He'llberemembered (IRE) *P G Fahey* 147h 146c
12 ch g Blue Ocean(USA) Remember Rob (IRE) (Deep Society)
3634a^{3}

Hello George (IRE) *Philip Hobbs* 130h
6 b g Westerner Top Ar Aghaidh (IRE) (Topanoora)
(1776)

Hello Jazz *John Ryall* 83h
5 b m Helissio(FR) Just Jasmine (Nicholas Bill)
271^{2} ◆ 1872^{5} 2486^{10} 3119^{4}

Hello Pretty Ladys *Les Eyre*
4 b g Revoque(IRE) Staff Nurse (IRE) (Night Shift (USA))
39^{7}

Hellorboston (IRE) *Donald McCain* 125h 110c
7 b g Court Cave(IRE) Helorhiwater (IRE) (Aristocracy (IRE))
2766^{3} 3224^{3} 3669^{U} 3969^{P} 4514^{6} 5260^{12}

Hell's Kitchen *Harry Fry* 137h
4 b g Robin Des Champs(FR) Mille Et Une (FR) (Trempolino (USA))
3772^{3} (4463) ◆ 5070^{2}

Helmsley Lad *Malcolm Jefferson* 101b
4 gr g Fair Mix(IRE) Wuchowsen (IRE) (King's Ride)
2750^{4}

Heluvagood *Victor Dartnall* 62b
3 b g Helissio(FR) Cape Siren (Warning)
5358^{10}

Henllan Harri (IRE) *Peter Bowen* 135h 131c
7 br g King's Theatre(IRE) Told You So (IRE) (Glacial Storm (USA))
(87) 319^{5} 833^{2} **965^{2} (1235) 1962^{2} 3349^{P}** 4305^{10}

Henri De Boistron (FR) *Tom George* 81h 99c
5 b g Enrique Highness Royale (FR) (Garde Royale)
180^{P}

Henri Parry Morgan *Peter Bowen* 128h 160c
7 b g Brian Boru Queen Of Thedaises (Over The River (FR))
85^{3} 404^{2} (681) 1594^{4} 2333^{6} **2764^{4} 3348^{U} (4352) (4800) ◆ 5191^{2} 5494^{U}**

Henrybrowneyes (IRE) *Ian Williams* 37h
6 ch g Goldmark(USA) The Vine Browne (IRE) (Torus)
2188^{4} 2581^{11} 4063^{U} 4303^{F}

Henry Higgins (IRE) *Charles O'Brien* 145h
5 b g Jeremy(USA) Moonchild (GER) (Acatenango (GER))
7a^{15} 231a^{F} (3650a) 4765^{21}

Henry Oliver (IRE) *John O'Shea* 95h
7 b g Hasten To Add(USA) Lisnabrin (IRE) (Witness Box (USA))
167^{2} 515^{2} **1824^{P}** 3140^{5} 3665^{7} 4223^{4}

Henryville *Harry Fry* 121h 150c
7 b g Generous(IRE) Aquavita (Kalaglow)
(1737) 1840^{2} (4857)

Hepijeu (FR) *Charlie Longsdon* 119h 126c
4 b g Palace Episode(USA) Helenjeu (Montjeu (IRE))
316^{3} 703^{2} 832^{3} **1008^{2}** (1153) 1308^{3} **(1479) 1809^{2} 2153^{P} 5156^{4} 5465^{5}**

Herbert Park (IRE) *David Pipe* 133h
5 b g Shantou(USA) Traluide (FR) (Tropular)
2485^{U} 3254^{9} 3824^{P}

Herdsman (IRE) *D J Dickenson* 122b 139c
10 b g Flemensfirth(USA) My Sunny South (Strong Gale)
4000^{P}

Herdwick Holloa (IRE) *Neil King* 82b
4 ch g Marienbard(IRE) Cash A Lawn (IRE) (Executive Perk)
4102^{11}

Here Comes Love (IRE) *Patrick Griffin* 94h 49c
5 b g Winged Love(IRE) Heres McGoogan (IRE) (Shaamit (IRE))
4050^{7} 4580^{4} 5098^{6}

Here Comes Molly (IRE) *John Joseph Hanlon* 92h
4 ch m Stowaway Grange Melody (IRE) (Presenting)
1499^{6} 1980^{9}

Herecomesnelson (IRE) *Katie Scott* 108h
6 b g Morozov(USA) Undesperado View (IRE) (Un Desperado (FR))
144^{8} 2066^{5} 2189^{13} 2804^{2} 3346^{7} 3667^{3} 4055^{8}

Herecomesthetruth (IRE) *Chris Gordon* 96h 104c
13 ch g Presenting Beagan Rose (IRE) (Roselier (FR))
280^{3} (490) 674^{4} 926^{6} 1244^{2} **(1487) 1757^{2} 1999^{5}**

Here I Am (IRE) *Diana Grissell* 97h 120c
8 br g Presenting The Last Bank (IRE) (Phardante (FR))
293^{4} 596^{3} 672^{3} (1767) 4321^{2} (5064)

Here's Herbie *Sue Gardner* 130h
7 b g Classic Cliche(IRE) Tyre Hill Lilly (Jupiter Island)
1719^{6} 2064^{3} 2247^{2} ◆ **3176^{F}** 3584^{5} 3748^{2} 4241^{11} (4685) (5185)

Heresmynumber (IRE) *Ali Stronge* 93h
5 b g Kalanisi(IRE) Broken Rein (IRE) (Orchestra)
2136^{5} 2612^{6} 2995^{9} 4972^{2}

Herewego Herewego (IRE) *Alan King* 127h
4 b g Kalanisi(IRE) Downtown Train (IRE) (Glacial Storm (USA))
4111^{4} 5091^{2} ◆

Heritage Way *Henry Hogarth* 87h
6 b g Tamayaz(CAN) Morning Caller (IRE) (Zaffaran (USA))
2791^{11} 3239^{9} 3509^{8}

Herminator (FR) *W P Mullins* 130h 125c
5 br g Night Tango(GER) Roannaise (FR) (Octagonal (NZ))
3323a^{6}

Hermosa Vaquera (IRE) *Gary Moore* 93h
5 b m High Chaparral(IRE) Sundown (Polish Precedent (USA))
224^{5} 856^{7} 1596^{3} (5483) ◆

He Rock's (IRE) *S J Mahon* 29h 115c
6 ch g Beneficial Rubys Shadow (IRE) (Supreme Leader)
2675a^{P}

Herod The Great *Richard Phillips*
5 ch g Sakhee's Secret Pella (Hector Protector (USA))
3487^{P}

Heroes Or Ghosts (IRE) *Jo Davis* 109h 109c
6 br g Indian River(FR) Awomansdream (IRE) (Beneficial)
380^{5} **4071^{5} 4876^{2} 5222^{P}**

Heronshaw (IRE) *Henry Daly* 131h 126c
8 b g Heron Island(IRE) Cool Merenda (IRE) (Glacial Storm (USA))
2442^{3} 2878^{P} 3520^{5} 4267^{P} 5222^{U}

Herons Heir (IRE) *Dan Skelton* 118h 127c
7 b g Heron Island(IRE) Kyle Lamp (IRE) (Miner's Lamp)
2409^{5} 3009^{3} (3725) ◆ 4384^{8} 5159^{2} 5405^{2}

Heron's Mill (IRE) *James Ewart* 106h 48c
7 b g Heron Island(IRE) Princess Vic (IRE) (Old Vic)
2103^{4} **2892^{4}**

He's A Bully (IRE) *Philip Hobbs* 101h 118c
6 b g Westerner Kitty Maher (IRE) (Posen (USA))
86^{2} 510^{3} 1298^{6} 1659^{4} 1820^{2} (1950) 2456^{2}

He's A Charmer (IRE) *Harry Fry* 113h
5 gr g Mahler Sunny South East (IRE) (Gothland (FR))
2188^{2} 2612^{2} 3133^{P} 4788^{F}

He's A Hawker (IRE) *Michael Mullineaux* 48h 18c
10 ch g Fourstars Allstar(USA) Dromin Deel (IRE) (Lanfranco)
1602^{6} 1933^{P} 2121^{5} **2666^{P}** 4045^{P}

Hester Flemen (IRE) *Nicky Richards* 127h 137c
7 ch m Flemensfirth(USA) Hester Hall (IRE) (Saddlers' Hall (IRE))
(3100) ◆

He's The Daddy *Nigel Twiston-Davies* 110h 101c
8 b g Generous(IRE) Brambly Hedge (Teenoso (USA))
210^{4} 614^{P}

Heurtevent (FR) *Tony Carroll* 87h 103c
6 bb g Hold That Tiger(USA) Sybilia (GER) (Spectrum (IRE))
(379) 612^{6} 5079^{9}

Hey Bill (IRE) *Graeme McPherson* 80h
5 b g Indian Danehill(IRE) Grange More (IRE) (Ridgewood Ben)
5243^{5}

Hey Bob (IRE) *Chris Grant* 88h
3 br g Big Bad Bob(IRE) Bounty Star (IRE) (Fasliyev (USA))
1456^{0} 1899^{8} 2845^{4} 3099^{7} 3628^{5} 3886^{7} 4154^{9} 4553^{4} 4943^{3}

Hey Up Ashey *Michael Mullineaux* 87b
5 b g Black Sam Bellamy(IRE) Miss Holly (Makbul)
341^{11} 2044^{9} 2597^{5} 3724^{P} 4324^{P} (Dead)

Hi Bob *Lucinda Egerton* 27h 94c
7 b g Bollin Eric Leading Line (Leading Man)
2191^{U} 2866^{P} 3419^{R} 4325^{P} 5234^{5}

Hi Bronco *John Ryall* 77h
8 b g Emperor Fountain Win A Hand (Nearly A Hand)
(65) 552^{P} 2661^{4} 3125^{3} 5306^{P}

Hi Dancer *Ben Haslam* 93h 81c
12 b g Medicean Sea Music (Inchinor)
137^{3} 1461^{5} 1892^{4} 2720^{7} 4049^{P} 4297^{10} 4797^{6}

Hidden Cyclone (IRE) *John Joseph Hanlon* 141h 162c
10 b g Stowaway Hurricane Debbie (IRE) (Shahanndeh (IRE))
8a^{3} 1163a^{4} **(2388a) 2941a^{U} 3092a^{3} 3293a^{3}**

Hidden Future (IRE) *Mrs S J Stilgoe* 105h 111c
6 b g Akbar(IRE) Lisheen Lady (IRE) (Broken Hearted)
151^{P} 521^{5}

Hidden Justice (IRE) *John Quinn* 119h
6 b g Lawman(FR) Uncharted Haven (Turtle Island (IRE))
2624^{8} 3027^{6} 3420^{P}

Higgs Boson *Jim Goldie* 104h 72c
10 b g Overbury(IRE) Evening Splash (IRE) (Royal Fountain)
2983^{4} 3427^{P} 3672^{8} 4163^{11} 4581^{5} **4792^{P}** 5203^{5} 5412^{8}

High Aspirations (IRE) *Michael Blake* 86h 110c
7 b g Dr Massini(IRE) Divining (IRE) (Dowsing (USA))
2836^{P} 3421^{P} (3951) 4265^{3} (4921) (5240) (5357)

High Bridge *John Ferguson* 130b
4 b g Monsun(GER) Ameerat (Mark Of Esteem (IRE))
2065^{3} (2650) (3104) 4721^{6}

Highbury High (IRE) *Neil Mulholland* 98h 110c
8 gr g Salford Express(IRE) Betseale (IRE) (Step Together I (USA))
2515^{4} **2953^{2} 3214^{U} 3661^{U} 4776^{U}** 5067^{3} 5305^{2}

High Counsel (IRE) *Gary Hanmer* 125h
6 br g Presenting The Bench (IRE) (Leading Counsel (USA))
1521^{5} 2367^{8}

Highest Red *Natalie Lloyd-Beavis*
6 ch g Byron Honor Rouge (IRE) (Highest Honor (FR))
3955^{P} 4854^{P}

High Fair *Sandy Forster* 98h
9 b m Grape Tree Road Miss Tango (Batshoof)
482^{5} 869^{4} 3684^{9} 4047^{7} 5198^{P} 5409^{11}

High Hopper (IRE) *Malcolm Jefferson* 115h
5 b g Mountain High(IRE) Stormy Moment (IRE) (Glacial Storm (USA))
187^{7} 3037^{4} 3743^{4} 4419^{3}

High Kite (IRE) *T D B Underwood* 93b 114c
9 bb g High-Rise(IRE) Sister Rose (IRE) (Roselier (FR))
239^{P} 439^{7} (676) 847^{4} 4232^{P}

Highlander Ted *Mark Walford* 90h 95c
7 b g Midnight Legend Half Each (Weld)
637^{5}

Highland Life *Steve Flook* 83h
5 b m Trans Island High Life (Kayf Tara)
56^{5} 219^{5} 2033^{5}

Highland Lodge (IRE) *James Moffatt* 127h 140c
9 b g Flemensfirth(USA) Supreme Von Pres (IRE) (Presenting)
1616^{7} 1889^{2} (2899) 5327^{P}

Highland River *Dave Roberts* 60h 65c
9 b g Indian Creek Bee One (IRE) (Catrail (USA))
695^{3}

High Policy (FR) *Stephen Ramsay* 113h
7 b g Policy Maker(IRE) Hoping High (ITY) (High Estate)
836a^{6}

Highpower (IRE) *Jonjo O'Neill* 128h 117c
6 b g Flemensfirth(USA) Holly Grove Lass (Le Moss)
(463) **756^{4}** 1292^{2} (1414) **2451^{P}**

Highridge Princess (IRE) *Johnny Farrelly* 81h
7 b m Lord Americo End Of The Rainbow (IRE) (Rainbows For Life (CAN))
1234^{P} 1271^{P} 1574^{5} 2457^{9} 2876^{P}

High Ron *Caroline Bailey* 90h 131c
10 b g Rainbow High Sunny Heights (Golden Heights)
395^{2} 693^{2} 760^{P} (1114)

Highsalvia Cosmos *Mark Hoad* 109h
4 b g High Chaparral(IRE) Salvia (Pivotal)
2544^{8} 2823^{4} ◆ 3216^{3}

High Stratos *Mrs John Harrington* 136h
6 b g Montjeu(IRE) Hyabella (Shirley Heights)
21a^{7}

High Talk (IRE) *Barry Brennan* 64h 55c
11 b g Craigsteel Ponka (IRE) (Sir Mordred)
5433^{12}

Highway Code (USA) *Kerry Lee* 120h 122c
9 b g Street Cry(IRE) Fairy Heights (IRE) (Fairy King (USA))
1005^{6} 1167^{4} ◆ 1309^{P} 1807^{7} 1987^{P}

Highway Storm (IRE) *Rebecca Curtis* 110h
5 b g Stowaway Snow In Summer (IRE) (Glacial Storm (USA))
2440^{5} 3124^{3} 3580^{7} 4614^{3} (5051)

Hija *Gail Haywood* 94h
4 b m Avonbridge Pantita (Polish Precedent (USA))
360^{4} 828^{P} 1109^{6} 1841^{7} 2007^{3} 2455^{7}

Hill Fort *Matt Sheppard* 124h
5 ch g Pivotal Cairns (UAE) (Cadeaux Genereux)
702^{4} 1048^{7} 2038^{4} 2492^{3} 2876^{5} (3108) 3318^{4} 3932^{4} 4447^{7} (5225)

Hill Forts Gypse (IRE) *Seamus Mullins* 51h
4 b g Bienamado(USA) Whistling Gypse (IRE) (Good Thyne (USA))
168^{U} 509^{5} 2519^{P} **2881^{P}** 3582^{7} 4291^{P} **4932^{P}**

Hill Of Gold (IRE) *David Kemp* 94c
7 ch g Beneficial Cap The Waves (IRE) (Roselier (FR))
488^{2}

Hillview Lad (IRE) *Nick Kent* 97h
7 b g Vinnie Roe(IRE) Kabale (IRE) (Ikdam)
56^{2} 1901^{6} 2490^{P} 4455^{P} 4863^{5} 5441^{10}

Hilton Du Berlais (FR) *A Chaille-Chaille* 135h 107c
5 b m Saint Des Saints(FR) Anais Du Berlais (FR) (Dom Pasquini (FR))
4a^{5} 349a^{10}

Himalayan Express *Mrs David Plunkett* 48h 102c
11 b g Rakaposhi King Street Magic (IRE) (Jolly Jake (NZ))
270^{5}

Hindon Road (IRE) *Alan King* 116h 107c
8 b g Antonius Pius(USA) Filoli Gardens (Sanglamore (USA))
2973^{6} 3727^{7} 5071^{3}

Hi Note *Sheena West* 117h 110c
7 b m Acclamation Top Tune (Victory Note (USA))
669^{3} 1242^{3} 1350^{4}

Hinton Indiana *Dan Skelton* 121h 114c
10 b g Kayf Tara Hinton Grace (Vital Season)
471^{2} 1049^{2} 1309^{4}

Hinxworth (IRE) *Nick Mitchell* 85h
6 b g Milan Open Cry (IRE) (Montelimar (USA))
2062^{8} 4097^{12} 4544^{P} 5263^{8}

Hipo Jape (CZE) *Josef Vana*
9 b g Jape(USA) Hipozetta (POL) (Who Knows I (IRE))
1885a^{P}

Hippiart *David Bridgwater* 64b
3 ch g Dutch Art Hippogator (USA) (Dixieland Band (USA))
4880^{15}

Hippomene (FR) *J-P Gallorini* 148h 124c
5 b g Dream Well(FR) Dindounas (FR) (Astarabad (USA))
4a^{3} 1883a^{4} 2361a^{3}

Hisaabaat (IRE) *D K Weld* 137h
7 b g Dubawi(IRE) Phariseek (IRE) (Rainbow Quest (USA))
1163a^{16}

His Excellency (IRE) *M N Dawson* 117h 144c
7 ch g King's Best(USA) Road Harbour (USA) (Rodrigo De Triano (USA))
534^{5}

Hitherjacques Lady (IRE) *Oliver Sherwood* 92b
3 br f Robin Des Champs(FR) Crackin' Liss (IRE) (Bob Back (USA))
(5286)

Hi Tide (IRE) *J R Jenkins* 96h 96c
11 br g Idris(IRE) High Glider (High Top)
177^{9} 592^{5} 810^{6} 931^{7} 1083^{5} 1446^{5} 1691^{P} 2043^{6}

Hitman Hearns (IRE) *Keith Dalgleish* 116h
6 b g Milan Desirable Asset (IRE) (Zagreb (USA))
1499^{3} 1568^{4} (3398) ◆

Hit The Headlines (IRE) *Luke Dace* 100h 105c
9 b g Flemensfirth(USA) Heather Breeze (IRE) (Lord Americo)
4588^{2} 5226^{2}

Hit The Highway (IRE) *Giles Smyly* 133h
6 b g Pierre Highway Belle (IRE) (Germany (USA))
2519^{2} ◆ (3316) ◆ (3787) 4766^{P}

Hi Vic (IRE) *David Loder* 127c
10 ch g Old Vic Tully Bridge (IRE) (Heavenly Manna)
(2491) 3008^{3} 4348^{P} 4826^{F} 5274^{P}

Hogan's Alley (IRE) *M F Morris* 97h
4 ch g Presenting Enniscoffey (IRE) (Old Vic)
11a^{17}

Ho Good Lord Has (FR) *J-P Gallorini* 112h 128c
5 gr m Lord Du Sud(FR) Horta (FR) (Assessor (IRE))
436a^{2}

Hoist The Colours (IRE) *Robert Walford* 103h
4 b g Sea The Stars(IRE) Multicolour Wave (IRE) (Rainbow Quest (USA))
61^{P} 449^{13} 669^{10} 3919^{9}

Hoke Colburn (IRE) *Harry Whittington* 95b
3 br g Beneficial Ravaleen (IRE) (Executive Perk)
4880^{6}

Holbrook Park *Neil King* 114h
5 b g Midnight Legend Viciana (Sir Harry Lewis (USA))
3388^{2} 3664^{P} 4198^{P} (5451)

Hold Court (IRE) *Evan Williams* 114h 129c
8 br g Court Cave(IRE) Tipsy Miss (IRE) (Orchestra)
87^{6} 449^{5} 775^{3} 969^{4} 1170^{13} 1238^{11}

Hold Hands *Brendan Powell* 66b
4 b m Lawman(FR) Tiponi (IRE) (Traditionally (USA))
4075^{10}

Hold The Bucks (USA) *Sheena West*
9 b g Hold That Tiger(USA) Buck's Lady (USA) (Alleged (USA))
2957^{P} 3196^{P}

Hold The Fort (IRE) *Johnny Farrelly* 98h
8 b g Brian Boru Go Katie (Gunner B)
745^{5} 1120^{3} 1244^{7} 1604^{3} 1677^{3}

Ho Lee Moses (IRE) *Evan Williams* 93h
5 bl g Kalanisi(IRE) Tipsy Miss (IRE) (Orchestra)
330^{5} 440^{8} 832^{5} 931^{8} 1236^{P}

Holeinthewall Bar (IRE) *Michael Hourigan* 118h 109c
7 b g Westerner Cockpit Lady (IRE) (Commanche Run)
1186a^{12}

Hollies Pearl *Peter Bowen* 128h
5 b m Black Sam Bellamy(IRE) Posh Pearl (Rakaposhi King)
(1845) 2579^{2} 4026^{2} 4471^{3} (4868)

Hollins Hill *Sam Drake* 80h
5 b g Lucarno(USA) Bonnie Buttons (Lord Bud)
4001^{9} 4791^{5}

Hollow Bay *Paul Webber* 102h
5 ch m Beat Hollow Cavernista (Lion Cavern (USA))
2277^{9} 3608^{4} 4598^{2} 5155^{2}

Hollow Blue Sky (FR) *Nigel Twiston-Davies* 101h 129c
8 gr g Turgeon(USA) Run For Laborie (FR) (Lesotho (USA))
318^{P} 855^{P} 3157^{5} 3404^{6} 3836^{2} ◆ 4321^{3} 4912^{8} 5274^{13}

Hollow Penny *Alan King* 120h 146c
7 b g Beat Hollow Lomapamar (Nashwan (USA))
1040^{5}

Holly Bush Henry (IRE) *Graeme McPherson* 139h
4 b g Yeats(IRE) Maslam (IRE) (Robellino (USA))
263^{2} ◆ 1260^{6} (2747) (3035) (3682) 4695^{11} 5273^{6}

Hollywood All Star (IRE) *Graeme McPherson* 116h
6 b g Kheleyf(USA) Camassina (IRE) (Taufan (USA))
2664[5] (3011) (3140) 3529[2] 3777[5] 4129[3] 4685[4] 5102[5]

Hollywoodien (FR) *Tom Symonds* 92h 141c
4 gr g Martaline Incorrigible (FR) (Septieme Ciel (USA))
2499[10] **(3134) 4067[2] 4443[4] (5455)**

Holstmaker (FR) *P Peltier* 109h 116c
5 b g Saddler Maker(IRE) Miss Holst (FR) (Holst (USA))
(4400a)

Holy Cross (IRE) *Rebecca Curtis* 87b
4 b g Yeats(IRE) Bleu Ciel Et Blanc (FR) (Pistolet Bleu (IRE))
1644[7] 2126[9]

Holy Dancer *Chris Bealby* 59h
5 b m Norse Dancer(IRE) Litany (Colonel Collins (USA))
2498[4]

Holywell (IRE) *Jonjo O'Neill* 156h 170c
8 b g Gold Well Hillcrest (IRE) (Thatching)
2200[5] 2642[4] 3860[P] 4697[2] 5218[F]

Home Farm (IRE) *Henry De Bromhead* 124h 123c
8 b g Presenting Tynelucy (IRE) (Good Thyne (USA))
5218[P]

Home For Tea *Keith Dalgleish* 84h 93c
6 b g Westerner Wolnai (Cloudings (IRE))
841[P] 3683[F] 3938[F] 4178[6] 4703[2] 4943[P]

Homers Odyssey *Simon Hodgson* 56b
5 b g Overbury(IRE) Aikaterine (Kris)
4880[16]

Honey Badger *Eugene Stanford*
4 bb g Pastoral Pursuits Taminoula (IRE) (Tagula (IRE))
3819[P]

Honey Brown *Tom Lacey* 84h
4 b m Scorpion(IRE) Phar Breeze (IRE) (Phardante (FR))
831[5] 970[8] 1094[7]

Honeychile Ryder *Dianne Sayer* 56h
4 ch m Black Sam Bellamy(IRE) Dusky Dante (IRE) (Phardante (FR))
1066[6]

Honey'N'Spice *George Margarson* 44b
6 b m Silver Patriarch(IRE) Honey's Gift (Terimon)
671[3] 5941[1]

Honey Pound (IRE) *Tim Vaughan* 125h 117c
7 b g Big Bad Bob(IRE) Moon Review (USA) (Irish River (FR))
854[5] 973[U] (1238) 1404[6] 1977[4] **2518[2] 3351[U] 4852[F]**

Honkytonktennessee (IRE) *Hugo Froud* 110h
6 b g Scorpion(IRE) Polly Platinum (IRE) (Phardante (FR))
(892) 1166[F] 1508[7] 4506[7]

Honourable Exit (IRE) *Alexandra Dunn* 77h
8 b g Exit To Nowhere(USA) Honor Love (FR) (Pursuit Of Love)
832[7] 2904[P] 3905[F] 4291[P]

Honourable Gent *Rose Dobbin* 112h 119c
7 b g Gentleman's Deal(IRE) Gudasmum (Primitive Rising (USA))
(154) 338[5] 884[2] 1330[5] 1572[2]

Honour A Promise *Paul Webber* 104h 65c
7 b m Norse Dancer(IRE) Motcombe (IRE) (Carroll House (IRE))
43[2] ◆ 466[6] **934[9]** 1910[10] 2565[P]

Hoo Bally Diva (IRE) *Bob Buckler* 93b
4 b m Scorpion(IRE) Dr Sandra (IRE) (Dr Massini (IRE))
4103[9] 4687[4] 5227[7]

Hooghly River (IRE) *Jennifer Mason* 84b
5 b g Indian River(FR) Mrs Woman (IRE) (Oscar (IRE))
2715[4] 3145[6] 4344[P]

Hooks Lane *Shaun Harris* 13b
3 ch g Bertolini(USA) Zaville (Zafonic (USA))
2195[9]

Hooley Time (IRE) *Olly Williams*
3 b f Rugby(USA) Rahelly Lady (IRE) (Kheleyf (USA))
4228[9]

Hooray Hebe *Mark Wall*
8 b m Lahib(USA) North End Lady (Faustus (USA))
1094[P]

Hopeand *Charles Pogson* 87h 107c
10 b m King's Theatre(IRE) Land Of Glory (Supreme Leader)
588[P]

Hopefordebest (IRE) *Ian Williams* 95h
5 b g Zagreb(USA) Rapsan (IRE) (Insan (USA))
3221[7] 4798[5] 5115[P]

Hope For Glory *Maurice Barnes* 70h
6 b g Proclamation(IRE) Aissa (Dr Devious (IRE))
1065[6] 2025[9]

Hopefull *R Mike Smith* 74h
5 bl m Overbury(IRE) Maryscross (IRE) (Presenting)
5445[8]

Hope's Wishes *Barry Brennan* 125h
5 b m Kayf Tara Otarie (FR) (Lute Antique (FR))
238[3] 704[9] (1384) (2604) 2778[7] 3223[4] 3950[2] (4320) (4672)

Hop 'n Pop (IRE) *Hugh Burns* 66h 15c
8 b m Millenary Rivita Princess (IRE) (Riverhead (USA))
4176[P] 4555[4] 5472[12]

Hoponandsee *George Baker* 69h
4 b m Nomadic Way(USA) Jago's Girl (Bob's Return (IRE))
1908[3] 2561[P] 3927[7]

Hopstrings *Tom Lacey* 116h 105c
7 ch m Sulamani(IRE) Hop Fair (Gildoran)
438[4] 698[P]

Horace Hazel *Anthony Honeyball* 117h
6 b g Sir Harry Lewis(USA) Karеam (Karinga Bay)
557[7] 377[3] (716) 897[2] (5183)

Horatio Hornblower (IRE) *Nick Williams* 132h 135c
7 bb g Presenting Countess Camilla (Bob's Return (IRE))
1722[2] 4267[5] (4826)

Horendus Hulabaloo (IRE) *M F Morris* 117h 137c
6 b g Beneficial Renvyle Society (IRE) (Moscow Society (USA))
50a[12] **1556a[F] 2227a[4]**

Horizontal Speed (IRE) *David Dennis* 136h 123c
7 b g Vertical Speed(FR) Rockababy (IRE) (King's Ride)
2242[4] 3147[F] 3407[4] 3737[9] 4246[8] 4786[9] 5277[7]

Horse Force One (IRE) *Philip Hobbs* 95b
4 b g Kalanisi(IRE) Oilpainting (IRE) (Welsh Term)
124[7]

Horseguardsparade *Nigel Twiston-Davies* 32b
4 b g Montjeu(IRE) Honorlina (FR) (Linamix (FR))
2020[8] 2729[12]

Horsehill (IRE) *Oliver Sherwood* 111h 119c
6 b g Flemensfirth(USA) Maid For Adventure (IRE) (Strong Gale)
2456[3] 3371[P] 5432[P]

Horsted Valley *Warren Greatrex* 117h
5 gr g Fair Mix(IRE) Kullu Valley (Turgeon (USA))
(445) 1925[P] 2687[12] 3837[2] 4883[8]

Hortense Mancini *Mark Bradstock* 77h
6 ch m King's Best(USA) Have Fun (Indian Ridge)
2004[P] 2298[P]

Hostile Fire (IRE) *Gordon Elliott* 124h
4 b g Iffraaj Royal Esteem (Mark Of Esteem (IRE))
2353a[F]

Hotgrove Boy *Stuart Coltherd* 86h 112c
8 b g Tobougg(IRE) Tanwir (Unfuwain (USA))
36[2] 417[4] 848[7]

Hot Madras (IRE) *Trevor Wall* 32h
7 b m Milan Hot Fudge (IRE) (Roselier (FR))
179[P] 434[4] 877[8] 1171[7] 1598[11]

Houblon Des Obeaux (FR) *Venetia Williams* 145h 164c
8 b g Panoramic Harkosa (FR) (Nikos)
2187[9] 2783[9] 3150[8] 3624[4] (4113) 5176[P]

Houndscourt (IRE) *Joanne Foster* 121h 115c
8 b g Court Cave(IRE) Broken Rein (IRE) (Orchestra)
(134) 693[3] 1032[9] 1902[7] 2975[P] 3401[5] 3969[3] 4940[4]

Houseparty *Diana Grissell* 109h 88c
7 b g Invincible Spirit(IRE) Amusing Time (IRE) (Sadler's Wells (USA))
150[R] (446) **674[9] 1999[F] 2315[3] 2712[P] 3419[3] 5068[P]**

Housewives Choice *James Bethell* 83h
4 ch m Black Sam Bellamy(IRE) Maid Of Perth (Mark Of Esteem (IRE))
1094[6] 1328[0] 1774[RR]

Houston Dynimo (IRE) *David Pipe* 114h 132c
10 b g Rock Of Gibraltar(IRE) Quiet Mouse (USA) (Quiet American (USA))
122[4] **611[4]** ◆ **772[3] 1112[6] 1871[6] 1948[3] 2057[11] 2243[2] (2346) 2659[4] (2809)** 3174[5] **3448[P] 4483[10] 5147[5]**

How About It (IRE) *Rebecca Curtis* 114h 131c
6 b g Kayf Tara Midnight Gift (IRE) (Presenting)
(1821) ◆ **2332[5] 3106[3] 3228[P] 4267[P] 4700[P]**

Howaboutnever (IRE) *Roger Teal* 119h
7 b g Shantou(USA) Sarah's Cottage (IRE) (Topanoora)
933[5] 1139[3] (1427) 1686[7] 2490[3] 2919[2] ◆ (3383) 3622[5] 4284[2] (4482) 5146[8] 5391[P]

Howaboutnow (IRE) *Ian Williams* 117h 85c
8 ch g Shantou(USA) Sarah's Cottage (IRE) (Topanoora)
2157 2922[P] 3837[10]

Howard's Legacy (IRE) *Venetia Williams* 83h 100c
9 b g Generous(IRE) Ismene (FR) (Bad Conduct (USA))
2853[9] 4140[P] 4818[10] 5334[P]

Howlongisafoot (IRE) *Paul Nicholls* 128h 141c
6 b g Beneficial Miss Vic (IRE) (Old Vic)
1869[5] (2459) 2761[F] 3282[P] 4347[4] 4858[4] 5304[2]

How's Vienna (IRE) *David Dennis* 83h
5 b g Westerner Plant A Smacker (IRE) (Goldmark (USA))
2406[7]

Howwrongcanyoube *Alan King* 110h
6 b g Kayf Tara Diva (Exit To Nowhere (USA))
261[P] 774[6]

Howya Buddy (IRE) *Adrian Wintle*
10 b g Heron Island(IRE) Boccachera (IRE) (Phardante (FR))
5332[P]

Hoy Hoy (IRE) *Alexandra Dunn* 12h
4 b g Iffraaj Luxie (IRE) (Acclamation)
702[10]

Hubal (POL) *George Charlton* 94h
3 b g Safety Wire(IRE) Hebra (POL) (Who Knows I (IRE))
3099[5] 3967[4]

Huehuecoytle *Keith Dalgleish* 99h
5 br g Turgeon(USA) Azturk (FR) (Baby Turk)
2890[2] 3436[P] 4742[4] 5406[2]

Huff And Puff *Venetia Williams* 121h 96c
8 b g Azamour(IRE) Coyote (Indian Ridge)
196[7] **3106[8]**

Hughesie (IRE) *Evan Williams* 118h 125c
6 b g Indian Danehill(IRE) Collatrim Choice (IRE) (Saddlers' Hall (IRE))
(2424) 4487[P] 5046[7]

Hugh's Secret (IRE) *Philip Kirby* 12h
3 b g Yeats(IRE) Walkyrie (FR) (Sleeping Car (FR))
3099[P] 3306[11] 3590[10] 3863[7]

Humbel Ben (IRE) *John Flint* 93h 93c
12 br g Humbel(USA) Donegans Daughter (Auction Ring (USA))
161[2] 1306[6] 1685[3] 2364[5] 3088[P] 3314[6] **4823[4] 5068[3]**

Humbie (IRE) *Pauline Robson* 116h 125c
11 b g Karinga Bay South Queen Lady (IRE) (King's Ride)
3425[4] 4370[8]

Humphrey Bee (IRE) *N W Alexander* 114c
12 br g Oscar Schindler(IRE) Gladriels Jem (IRE) (Mister Lord (USA))
885[P]

Hunt Ball (IRE) *Nicky Henderson* 134h 156c
10 b g Winged Love(IRE) La Fandango (IRE) (Taufan (USA))
(127) ◆ (434) (1507) 1983a[8]

Hunters Belt (IRE) *George Bewley* 115h 76c
11 b g Intikhab(USA) Three Stars (Star Appeal)
82[6] 520[6] 638[8] 802[5] 1572[4] ◆ 1887[14] 2492[2] 2933[3] 3346[4] 4178[2] 4421[2] 4638[3] 4840[5] 5260[P]

Hunters Hoof (IRE) *Nicky Henderson* 139h
6 b g Flemensfirth(USA) Madgehil (IRE) (Anshan)
(2083) 2639[8] 4717[16] 5497[11]

Hunters Vision (IRE) *Denis Gerard Hogan* 84h
6 ch g Hawk Wing(USA) Stashedaway (IRE) (Treasure Hunter)
3470[6]

Hurricancrys (FR) *J Boisnard*
4 b g Hurricane Cat(USA) Crystivoli (FR) (Northern Crystal)
(4401a)

Hurricane Dylan (IRE) *Daniel Mark Loughnane* 98b
4 b g Brian Boru Definetly Sarah (IRE) (Definite Article)
5055[3]

Hurricane Fly (IRE) *W P Mullins* 170h
11 b g Montjeu(IRE) Scandisk (IRE) (Kenmare (FR))
49a[2] 663a[6]

Hurricane Higgins (IRE) *Nicky Henderson* 120h
7 br g Hurricane Run(IRE) Mare Aux Fees (Kenmare (FR))
(316)

Hurricane Hollow *Dan Skelton* 140h
5 b g Beat Hollow Veenwouden (Desert Prince (IRE))
1039[8] 1848[3] 3151[9]

Hurricane Ivan (IRE) *S Wilson* 104h 95c
7 b g Golden Tornado(IRE) Woodram Delight (Idiots Delight)
4938[7]

Hurricane Ridge (IRE) *Jimmy Frost* 42h 41c
6 b g Hurricane Run(IRE) Warrior Wings (Indian Ridge)
19a[20] **1185a[8] 2990[8]** 4855[P]

Hurricane Rita (FR) *Stuart Coltherd* 109h
5 gr m Sagamix(FR) Madonna Da Rossi (Mtoto)
139[2] 468[3]

Hurricane Vic *Alan King* 108h 68c
5 b g Mount Nelson Fountains Abbey (USA) (Giant's Causeway (USA))
2408[4] **2861[5]**

Hurricane Volta (IRE) *Ralph J Smith*
4 ch g Hurricane Run(IRE) Haute Volta (FR) (Grape Tree Road)
2519[P]

Hurry Henry (IRE) *Henry De Bromhead* 126h
6 b g Blueprint(IRE) Tower Princess (IRE) (King's Ride)
4280a[8]

Hustle (IRE) *Clare Hobson* 51h
10 ch g Choisir(AUS) Granny Kelly (USA) (Irish River (FR))
1153[8] 1376[P] 1425[P]

Hydrant *Richard Guest* 68h
9 b g Haafhd Spring (Sadler's Wells (USA))
4297[6] 4460[7]

Hyperlink (IRE) *Heather Dalton* 73h 89c
6 b g Cape Cross(IRE) Surf The Web (IRE) (Ela-Mana-Mou)
281[10] **492[5] 699[5]**

I Am Colin *Nigel Twiston-Davies* 107h 126c
6 b g Zafeen(FR) Dd's Glenalla (IRE) (Be My Native (USA))
2410[3] 2692[2] 3387[2] ◆ **(4422) 5046[4]**

Ibetellingyoualie (IRE) *Terence O'Brien* 123c
9 b g Turtle Island(IRE) My Kit (IRE) (Be My Native (USA))
4521a[6]

Ibis Du Rheu (FR) *Paul Nicholls* 146h
4 b g Blue Bresil(FR) Dona Du Rheu (FR) (Dom Pasquini (FR))
2781[2] ◆ 3527[3] 3992[5] (4769) 5189[8]

Ibsen (IRE) *Gordon Elliott* 124h
6 b g Dubawi(IRE) Really (IRE) (Entrepreneur)
1175a[16]

Icancan *Alan Hollingsworth*
7 b g Alflora(IRE) Shadowgraff (Scorpio (FR))
105[P] 460[P]

Icanmotor *Claire Dyson* 78h
8 b m Midnight Legend Lochnagold (Lochnager)
337[6] 759[5] 935[7] 1084[4] 1310[5] 1598[6] 1933[2] 5441[6] ◆

Ice Konig (FR) *Jimmy Frost* 98h
6 gr g Epalo(GER) Isarwelle (GER) (Sternkoenig (IRE))
32[5] 515[6] (824) 2263[11] 4922[P]

Ice Tres *Chris Down* 100h
6 br m Iceman Tup Tim (Emperor Jones (USA))
162[6] 1841[9] 2093[7] 2455[4] 2730[6] 2987[6] 5380[5]

Icing On The Cake (IRE) *Oliver Sherwood* 118h
5 b g Spadoun(FR) Honeyed (IRE) (Persian Mews)
2646[5] 3353[3] ◆

Iconic Star *Philip Hobbs* 99h
5 b m Sixties Icon Cullen Bay (IRE) (Supreme Leader)
2141[3] 2579[4] 3110[3]

Icthec (IRE) *Jennifer Mason* 98h 31c
8 gr g Norwich Miss McCormick (IRE) (Roselier (FR))
741[5] 874[P]

Identity Thief (IRE) *Henry De Bromhead* 164h
5 b g Kayf Tara Miss Arteea (IRE) (Flemensfirth (USA))
(2177a) (2789) 3358a[2] 4698[6]

Idle Talker (IRE) *Jose Santos* 64h
3 b g Dandy Man(IRE) Special Pearl (IRE) (Alhaarth (IRE))
1232[4]

Idlewild *Mark Michael McNiff* 112h
5 b g Papal Bull Singe (Pivotal)
1154[4]

I'dliketheoption (IRE) *Jonjo O'Neill* 125h
4 bb g Presenting Supreme Dreamer (IRE) (Supreme Leader)
558[4] (754) 1168[5] (1240) 2182[6] (2773) 3284[10]

Ifan (IRE) *Tim Vaughan* 92h
7 b g Ivan Denisovich(IRE) Montana Miss (IRE) (Earl Of Barking (IRE))
1612[6]

Ifandbutwhynot (IRE) *Tim Easterby* 141h 94c
9 b g Raise A Grand(IRE) Cockney Ground (IRE) (Common Grounds)
3041[P] **3857[10]** 5201[2] 5325[13]

Iffjack (IRE) *Gordon Elliott* 106h 109c
5 b g Iffraaj Last Cry (FR) (Peintre Celebre (USA))
960[3] **1630[2]**

If In Doubt (IRE) *Philip Hobbs* 155h 159c
7 b g Heron Island(IRE) Catchers Day (IRE) (Catcher In The Rye (IRE))
2783[P] (3254) 4730[3] 5213[2]

If It Be Your Will *Dan Skelton* 80h 99c
5 gr g Kadastrof(FR) My Beautiful Loser (IRE) (Silver Patriarch (IRE))
1159[7] 1287[P]

Ifits A Fiddle *Richard Phillips* 82h
6 b m Kalanisi(IRE) Fiddling Again (Hernando (FR))
759[P]

Ifonlyalfie *C H G Davies* 84c
10 b g Alflora(IRE) Ifni Du Luc (FR) (Chamberlin (FR))
166[R]

Iftiraaq (IRE) *Seamus Durack* 121h
4 b g Muhtathir Alzaroof (USA) (Kingmambo (USA))
(2543) ◆ 2860[3] 3487[4]

Ifyousayso (IRE) *David Bridgwater* 104h 119c
8 ch g Definite Article Rosato (IRE) (Roselier (FR))
239[P] 553[P]

Iguacu *Richard Price* 108h
11 b g Desert Prince(IRE) Gay Gallanta (USA) (Woodman (USA))
177[8] (537) 751[3] 1055[3] 1549[5] 5157[10]

I Just Know (IRE) *Sue Smith* 106h
5 b g Robin Des Pres(FR) Desperado Queen (IRE) (Un Desperado (FR))
2169[3] 2628[7] 3021[6] 3366[3] 4066[6] 5300[P]

Ikorodu Road *Graeme McPherson* 119h 136c
12 b g Double Trigger(IRE) Cerisier (IRE) (Roselier (FR))
(3024) 3860[5] 5092[7]

Ikrapol (FR) *David Pipe* 107h
3 gr g Poliglote Ikra (FR) (Simon Du Desert (FR))
2662[U] 4104[2] 4486[4] 4745[5]

Iktiview *Matt Sheppard* 90h
7 ch g Iktibas Eastview Princess (J B Quick)
435[2] 695[F] 977[U] 1086[3] 1293[6] 1509[7]

Ilewin For Hannah *Gary Moore* 94h 100c
8 b g Generous(IRE) Ilewin Janine (IRE) (Soughaan (USA))
2953[P]

Ilewin Geez *Gary Moore* 104b
5 ch g Generous(IRE) Ilewin Janine (IRE) (Soughaan (USA))
(67) 227[3]

I'llhavealook (IRE) *Katie Stephens* 99h
10 b g Milan Kelly's Native (IRE) (Be My Native (USA))
893[6] 1116[4] 1234[6] 1579[7] 3125[8] 3914[P] 4250[3] 4682[2] (4920) 5165[P]

Illusionary Star *Julian Smith* 62h
7 b m Sir Harry Lewis(USA) Tirley Pop Eye (Cruise Missile)
207[RR]

Ilovemints *Warren Greatrex* 109b
3 b f Kayf Tara La Harde (FR) (Valanour (IRE))
(5049) ◆

Il Presidente (GER) *Ian Williams* 93h
8 ch g Royal Dragon(USA) Independent Miss (GER) (Polar Falcon (USA))
5452[5]

Imada (IRE) *Nicky Richards* 114h
5 br g Arcadio(GER) Anck Su Namun (IRE) (Supreme Leader)
(2101) ◆ 3221[4] 4817[3]

I'm A Game Changer (IRE) *Philip Hobbs* 48b
3 b g Arcadio(GER) Drinadaly (IRE) (Oscar (IRE))
5152[0] 5359[8]

Imagine The Chat *Rebecca Curtis* 116h 133c
6 b g Kayf Tara Be My Bird (Be My Chief (USA))
2266[8] (3348) 3849[P] 4341[P] 4663a[3]

Imahustler Baby (IRE) *Andrew Hamilton* 53h
4 b g Robin Des Pres(FR) A Winters Eve (IRE) (Saddlers' Hall (IRE))
2474[6] 2754[P] 3470[10]

I'm A Joker *Sarah Humphrey* 83h 93c
6 ch g Erhaab(USA) Yota (FR) (Galetto (FR))
622[6]

Im All Set (IRE) *Mrs C Hitch* 108c
6 b g Darsi(FR) Gathabawn Lass (IRE) (Norwich)
5270[2]

I'm All You Need (IRE) *Paul Nolan* 119h 130c
5 b m King's Theatre(IRE) Jolie Landaise (FR) (Beaudelaire (USA))
1150a[15] **3093a[P] 3604a[F] 4019a[2]**

Iman (GER) *Sophie Leech* 61h
5 bb g Dansili Ioannina (Rainbow Quest (USA))
3306[9] 3819[8] 4064[8]

I'm Foxy Too *Neil Mulholland*
4 ch m Notnowcato Starlight Express (FR) (Air Express (IRE))
2650[9]

I'm In Charge *Grant Cann* 99h 112c
9 b g Rakaposhi King Cloudy Pearl (Cloudings (IRE))
(66) ◆ **266[2] 1820[6]** 1951[5] 2454[3] **2598[F] 5419[4]**

Imjoeking (IRE) *Lucinda Russell* 119h 135c
8 b g Amilynx(FR) Go Franky (IRE) (Hollow Hand)
2193[3]

I'm Lucy (IRE) *Linda Jewell* 50h
4 b m Papal Bull Melaaya (USA) (Aljabr (USA))
222[11]

I'm Oscar (IRE) *Jeremy Scott* 99h
5 b g Oscar(IRE) I'm Maggy (NZ) (Danseur Etoile (FR))
2152[P] 2879[5] 3413[P]

Impact Area (IRE) *Mrs Harriet Waight* 119c
9 gr g Portrait Gallery(IRE) Walk On (IRE) (Welsh Term)
13[7] (292) 4383[2] 4768[11] (5166)

Impeccability *John Mackie* 101h
5 b m Lucky Story(USA) Impeccable Guest (IRE) (Orpen (USA))
41[4] 361[F] 1716[3] 1971[6] 2559[3] 2745[9] 3307[8]

Imperial Eloquence (IRE) *Fergal O'Brien* 107b
3 b g Kalanisi(IRE) Babble On (IRE) (Anita's Prince)
(5014) 5476[2]

Imperial Glance *Nick Williams* 82h
5 br g Passing Glance Juno Mint (Sula Bula)
1613[5] 2007[4]

Imperial Leader (IRE) *Nigel Twiston-Davies* 80h
7 b g Flemensfirth(USA) Glamorous Leader (IRE) (Supreme Leader)
2905[U] 3160[P] 4062[P]

Imperial Plan (IRE) *Jamie Snowden* 108h 89c
5 b g Antonius Pius(USA) White Paper (IRE) (Marignan (USA))
175[4] 588[9] 918[2] 1182[8]

Imperial Presence (IRE) *Philip Hobbs* 128h
4 ch g Presenting Penneyrose Bay (Karinga Bay)
(2238) 4784[2] 5153[4] 5387[7]

Imperial Prince (IRE) *Sandy Thomson* 117h
6 b g Subtle Power(IRE) Satco Rose (IRE) (Satco (FR))
2189[8] 2791[9] 4178[3] (4796) (5260) ◆

Imperial Vic (IRE) *Harriet Bethell* 95h 111c
10 bb g Old Vic Satco Rose (IRE) (Satco (FR))
358[P] 676[P] 1403[5]

Improved (IRE) *Philip Kirby* 106h
5 ch g Rainwatch Show Potential (IRE) (Glacial Storm (USA))
(1003) 2750[6] 3508[P] 4322[9] 4473[2] 5124[2]

Improver (IRE) *J T Gorman* 107h
4 b g Ad Valorem(USA) Titus Wonder (IRE) (Titus Livius (FR))
11a[7]

Improvisation (IRE) *John Ferguson* 135h
5 b g Teofilo(IRE) Dance Troupe (Rainbow Quest (USA))
(491) (866)

Impulse *Philip Hobbs* 61b
5 b m Kayf Tara Mrs Philip (Puissance)
4687[10]

Impulsive American *David Pipe* 123h
3 b g American Post Impulsive Decision (IRE) (Nomination)
1631[4] 1712[2] 1893[F] 2038[2] 2093[2] 2516[4] 4010[3] (4176) 4452[2] 4873[4] 5116[6] (5329) (5450)

Incentivise (IRE) *Kerry Lee* 79h 122c
12 ch g Snurge Festive Isle (IRE) (Erins Isle)
2366[U] 2996[6] 3385[2] (4649)

Inchcolm (IRE) *Micky Hammond* 79h 87c
5 br g Presenting Rose Of Inchiquin (IRE) (Roselier (FR))
1740[6] 1901[8] 2169[10] 3834[13] 4329[P] 5442[2]

Inchiquin All Star (IRE) *Tim Vaughan* 89h
5 b g Definite Article Inchiquin Princess (IRE) (Bob Back (USA))
1718[7] 1844[F]

Inch Wing (IRE) *Jim Best* 56b
7 b m Winged Love(IRE) Incharder (IRE) (Slip Anchor)
3194[P]

Indalo Return (IRE) *Philip Kirby* 100h 87c
9 ch g Bob's Return(IRE) Daiquiri (IRE) (Houmayoun (FR))
35[5] 486[3] 731[5]

Indepub *Lisa Harrison* 91h
6 b g Indesatchel(IRE) Champenoise (Forzando)
153[9] 291[5] 502[4] 2029[5] 2751[13]

Indevan *W P Mullins* 137h 147c
7 b g Indesatchel(IRE) Be Most Welcome (Most Welcome)
603a[7] 1152a[F] 1185a[7] 1556a[8] 1763a[4]

Indiana Bay (IRE) *Mrs Jill Dennis* 120c
8 ch g Indian River(FR) Easter Saturday (IRE) (Grand Plaisir (IRE))
(166) 533[5] 4768[13] 5166[3]

Indiana Oscar *Carroll Gray* 70h
7 b g Oscar(IRE) Indian Miss (Idiots Delight)
391[P] 1044[P]

Indian Brave (IRE) *Neil Mulholland* 108h
4 b g Definite Article Fridays Folly (IRE) (Flemensfirth (USA))
2020[4] 2879[P] 5269[6] 5434[4] ◆

Indian Castle (IRE) *Ian Williams* 129h 146c
7 b g Dr Massini(IRE) Indian Legend (IRE) (Phardante (FR))
2643[4] 3038[P] 3404[5] 4735[6]

Indian Dancer (IRE) *Katie Stephens*
8 b g Indian River(FR) Lisselan Lass (IRE) (Lancastrian)
1044[P]

Indian Daudaie (FR) *Sarah Humphrey* 82h 77c
8 ch g Nicobar Aldounia (FR) (Kaldoun (FR))
2648[P] 3046[P] 3420[3] 3607[6] 4223[U] 4390[6] 4968[4]

Indian Fairy (IRE) *Eoin Doyle* 128h 126c
7 bb m Indian Danehill(IRE) Fairy Castle (Exit To Nowhere (USA))
70a[4]

Indian Icon (FR) *Ms Sandra Hughes* 126h
5 b g Indian Rocket Playing Star (FR) (Starborough)
7a[17]

Indian Jack (IRE) *Seamus Mullins* 77h
7 ch g Indian Haven Almaviva (IRE) (Grand Lodge (USA))
515[P]

Indian Leader (IRE) *Peter Bowen* 96b
6 b g Indian Danehill(IRE) Supreme Fivestar (IRE) (Supreme Leader)
601[5]

Indian Print (IRE) *Victor Thompson* 91c
11 ch g Blueprint(IRE) Commanche Glen (IRE) (Commanche Run)
290[3] 506[5] 803[P]

Indian Road Runner (IRE) *Shane Crawley* 106h
7 b g Indian Creek Volcano Snow (Zilzal (USA))
1964[7]

Indian Secret (IRE) *Jim Best* 56b
5 ch m Indian River(FR) Secret Leave (Long Leave)
3625[6]

Indian Stream *Neil Mulholland* 119h 139c
6 ch m Generous(IRE) Zaffarimbi (IRE) (Zaffaran (USA))
314[P] 593[2] 810[2] (1008) 1266[3] (1445) (5281)

Indian Temple (IRE) *W T Reed* 97h 132c
6 b g Indian River(FR) Ballycraggan (IRE) (Beneficial)
2497[2] 2947[2] (3425) 4370[3]

Indian Voyage (IRE) *Maurice Barnes* 94h 138c
7 b g Indian Haven Voyage Of Dreams (USA) (Riverman (USA))
156[P] 315[P] 1904[7] 2192[U] (2342) (2719) ◆ 2920[2] 3996[P] 4606[4] 4838[2] 5087[4] 5471[3]

Indiefront *Jo Davis* 88h 76c
6 b m Indesatchel(IRE) Jonchee (FR) (Le Thuit Signol (FR))
571[6] 770[P] 807[F] 1373[P]

Indigo Island (IRE) *R A Owen* 75b
6 b g Trans Island Go Indigo (IRE) (Cyrano De Bergerac)
80[P]

Indimoon *David Bridgwater* 76b
5 b g Indesatchel(IRE) Moonfleet (IRE) (Entrepreneur)
1484[7] 1644[9]

Indubitably *Roger Teal* 24h
9 b g Tobougg(IRE) Margaret's Gift (Beveled (USA))
240[10]

Indulgence *Pam Sly* 77b
3 b f Sir Percy Kaloni (IRE) (Kalanisi (IRE))
4974[2] 5443[9]

Indy Five (IRE) *David Dennis* 105b
5 b g Vertical Speed(FR) Beesplease (IRE) (Snurge)
5227[4]

I Need Gold (IRE) *Donald McCain* 138h 135c
7 b g Gold Well Coola Cross (IRE) (Be My Native (USA))
2341[P]

Infinityandbeyond (IRE) *Neil King* 79h
4 gr g Medaaly Ten Dollar Bill (IRE) (Accordion)
2597[6] 2998[2] 3334[13] 3997[4] 4798[7]

Informationisking (IRE) *Alan King* 113b
4 b g Flemensfirth(USA) Leading Lady (Fraam)
3388[3] (3952)

Infrontofthejudge (IRE) *J J Lambe* 101h
6 b g Clerkenwell(USA) Judicial Audience (IRE) (Thatching)
3667[6]

Iniciar (GER) *David Pipe* 122h
5 b g Galileo(IRE) Iota (GER) (Tiger Hill (IRE))
2457[5] 2747[7] 3411[11] 3484[7] (4819) ◆ 5077[3]

Iniesta (IRE) *Gary Moore* 109h
4 b h Galileo(IRE) Red Evie (IRE) (Intikhab (USA))
2011[7] 2244[3] 2688[9]

Ink Master (IRE) *Philip Hobbs* 123h 128c
5 b g Whitmore's Conn(USA) Welsh Connection (IRE) (Welsh Term)
(1828) 2472[7] 3134[6] 3466[5] 4785[3] (5447)

Inner Drive (IRE) *Alan King* 137h 112c
7 b g Heron Island(IRE) Hingis (IRE) (Shernazar)
2545[5]

Inner Loop *Robert Stephens* 89b
3 b f Rail Link Sailing Days (Kris)
2009[3] 2583[2]

Innis Shannon (IRE) *George Bewley* 98h
5 br m Stowaway Put On Hold (IRE) (Lord Americo)
1627[5] 1854[10] 2210[5] (2476) 2936[4] 4608[4] 5012[3] 5472[8]

Innocent Touch (IRE) *Richard Fahey* 110h
4 bl g Intense Focus(USA) Guajira (FR) (Mtoto)
(2294) 2747[4]

Innoko (FR) *Tony Carroll* 104h
5 gr g Carlotamix(FR) Chalana (Ashkalani (IRE))
180[3] (856)

Innovate (FR) *Paul Webber* 79b
3 ch f Full Of Gold(FR) Ryde (FR) (Sillery (USA))
3861[7]

Innox Park *Kevin Bishop* 78h
5 b g Helissio(FR) Redgrave Bay (Karinga Bay)
124[8] 511[U] 832[8] 932[10] 1120[U] 1293[14] 1604[5]

In On The Act *Evan Williams* 125h
5 b g Act One Pequenita (Rudimentary (USA))
(613) ◆ (971) 1482[4] 1806[3] 4965[9]

Inspiring (IRE) *Johnny Farrelly* 8h
4 br m Waky Nao Newtown Dancer (IRE) (Danehill Dancer (IRE))
4137[P] 4888[11] 5155[P]

Instant Karma (IRE) *Michael Bell* 123h
4 b g Peintre Celebre(USA) Kotdiji (Mtoto)
2928[7] 3418[3] 3819[3] ◆ (4774) 5139[P]

Instinctual *Charlie Longsdon* 47h
5 ch g Observatory(USA) Be Glad (Selkirk (USA))
2694[13] 2976[U]

Instingtive (IRE) *Harry Fry* 75h
4 b g Scorpion(IRE) Fully Focused (IRE) (Rudimentary (USA))
558[8] 3980[3] 5097[12] 5356[6]

Intense Tango *K R Burke* 136h
4 b m Mastercraftsman(IRE) Cover Look (SAF) (Fort Wood (USA))
2199[2] ◆ 2789[5] 3858[6]

Intercooler Turbo (IRE) *Dan Skelton* 60h
6 gr g Dr Massini(IRE) Moigh Endeavour (IRE) (Ala Hounak)
893[P] 1001[4]

Interior Minister *Warren Greatrex* 91h
5 b g Nayef(USA) Sister Maria (USA) (Kingmambo (USA))
537[11]

Interpleader *Sheila Lewis* 99h 101c
10 b g Luso Braceys Girl (IRE) (Be My Native (USA))
(44) 333[2] 717[4] 879[7] 926[9] 1813[3] 1930[9]

In The Crowd (IRE) *Roy Brotherton* 102h
6 ch g Haafhd Eliza Gilbert (Noverre (USA))
(435) 704[6] 864[7] 1084[9] 2413[4] 2730[8] 3586[2] 3925[2] 4855[8]

In The Hold (IRE) *Evan Williams* 96h
5 b g Stowaway Carrigeen Kerria (IRE) (Kemal (FR))
2265[12] 2769[3] 3581[4] 4198[3] 4615[3]

Inthenicoftime *Jess Westwood* 20b
5 b g With The Flow(USA) Rose Lir (Lir)
3959[9] 4449[P]

In The Rough (IRE) *Jonjo O'Neill* 136h 118c
6 b g Scorpion(IRE) Sounds Charming (IRE) (Presenting)
394[2]

In The Tub (IRE) *Tom Malone*
6 b g Kutub(IRE) County Classic (Noble Patriarch)
5270[P]

Invicta Lake (IRE) *Suzy Smith* 124h 103c
8 b g Dr Massini(IRE) Classic Material (Classic Cliche (IRE))
2002[3] 2484[10] 3113[6] 3844[4] 3992[P]

Invictus (GER) *Micky Hammond* 102h
3 b g Exceed And Excel(AUS) Ivowen (USA) (Theatrical (IRE))
3967[3] 4324[4]

Invisible Man (FR) *Mrs D J Ralph* 99h 125c
10 ch g Mansonnien(FR) J'y Reste (FR) (Freedom Cry)
534[U] 4446[2]

Iona Days (IRE) *Julian Smith* 97h 118c
10 br g Epistolaire(IRE) Miss Best (FR) (Grand Tresor (FR))
470[3] 2668[5] 3061[2] 4803[6] 5226[F]

Iora Glas (IRE) *Fergal O'Brien* 120h 84c
6 gr g Court Cave(IRE) Crossdrumrosie (IRE) (Roselier (FR))
139[3] (380) 1638[7] 2145[3] 2785[P] 3129[5] 3904[P] 5011[4] (5475)

Irish Cavalier (IRE) *Rebecca Curtis* 133h 164c
6 rg g Aussie Rules(USA) Tracker (Bustino)
10a[4] 69a[2] (1840) ◆ 2483[5] 3231[5] 3851[P] 4767[5] 5176[F]

Irish Legionnaire (IRE) *Richard J Bandey* 94b
4 b g Kalanisi(IRE) Harifana (FR) (Kahyasi)
5436[5]

Irish Octave (IRE) *Rosemary Gasson* 83h
5 b g Gamut(IRE) Fairytaleofnewyork (IRE) (Zaffaran (USA))
337[5] 1158[4] 2841[7] 3382[4] 3503[5]

Irish Ranger (IRE) *Rosemary Gasson* 74b
4 b g Gamut(IRE) Erins Emblem (IRE) (Erins Isle)
1101[8]

Irish Rebel (IRE) *Clare Hobson* 86c
11 b g Tel Quel(FR) Never On Sunday (IRE) (Religiously (USA))
292[P]

Irish Thistle (IRE) *Dai Williams* 111h 126c
8 b g Luso Which Thistle (IRE) (Saddlers' Hall (IRE))
3073a[8] 3552a[F] 4011[7] 4232[5] (4597) 4907[4]

Irmao Joao Has (FR) *J-P Gallorini* 138h 107c
3 b g Ballingarry(IRE) Irostare (FR) (Astarabad (USA))
1881a[4]

Iron Butterfly *James Eustace* 123h
6 b m Shirocco(GER) Coh Sho No (Old Vic)
2139[2] (3025) (3505) 3970[2]

Iron Chancellor (IRE) *Mrs Sue Popham* 48h 63c
10 b g Alderbrook Masriyna (IRE) (Shahrastani (USA))
166[2] 5150[3]

Irondale Express *Barry Brennan* 102h
4 b m Myboycharlie(IRE) Olindera (GER) (Lomitas)
745[4] 846[3] 1009[2] 1271[2] 1454[7] 2164[3] 2494[6] 3816[4]

Iroufícar Has (FR) *J-P Gallorini* 134h 122c
5 b g Dream Well(FR) Irostare (FR) (Astarabad (USA))
664a[F] 1477a[2] 1884a[P]

Irving *Paul Nicholls* 158h
7 b g Singspiel(IRE) Indigo Girl (GER) (Sternkoenig (IRE))
(2350) (2640) 2789[6] 4253[4]

Isaac Bell (IRE) *Alex Hales* 122h
7 b g Fruits Of Love(USA) Oso Well (IRE) (Oscar (IRE))
(1893) (2810) 3352[4] 4799[P] 5279[11]

Isaacstown Lad (IRE) *Nicky Richards* 132h 99c
8 b g Milan Friends Of Friends (IRE) (Phardante (FR))
(139) ◆ (291) (2340) 3058[F] (3158) ◆ 3622[3] 4246[3] 4568[2] 5085[3] 5328[7]

Isabellesprincess (IRE) *Mike Hammond* 110h
7 b m Westerner Perkaway (IRE) (Oscar (IRE))
1841[8] 2167[P]

Isdaal *Kevin Morgan* 84h
8 ch m Dubawi(IRE) Faydah (USA) (Bahri (USA))
180[4]

Is Herself About (IRE) *David M O'Brien* 126h 124c
8 b m Flemensfirth(USA) Alpha Style (GER) (Saddlers' Hall (IRE))
47a[11]

I Shot The Sheriff (IRE) *A J Martin* 146h
8 b g Westerner Sherin (GER) (Surumu (GER))
49a[11]

Ishusharella *Clare Hobson* 93h
6 b m Doyen(IRE) Emily-Mou (IRE) (Cadeaux Genereux)
41[2] 262[P]

Isla Di Milano (IRE) *Tim Vaughan* 72h
4 b g Milan Monagee Island (IRE) (Fourstars Allstar (USA))
1966[6] 2591[8] 4441[10] 4613[7]

Isla Fernandos (IRE) *Fergal O'Brien* 102h
5 ch m Flemensfirth(USA) Kon Tiky (FR) (Perrault)
5019[2]

Island Confusion (IRE) *Lucinda Russell* 107h 122c
7 b g Heron Island(IRE) Anshan Gail (IRE) (Anshan)
3164[2] 3742[5]

Island Heights (IRE) *Lucinda Russell* 132h 128c
6 b g Heron Island(IRE) La Reina (IRE) (Executive Perk)
(2190) (2624) 3058[5] 3737[4]

Island Rendezvous (IRE) *Jeremy Scott* 98b
5 b g Trans Island Verlaya (FR) (Vertical Speed (FR))
2270[8]

Island Villa (IRE) *Denis Gerard Hogan* 100h 110c
6 b g Turtle Island(IRE) Violet Ville (IRE) (Toulon)
1630[5] 1975[2]

Isla Pearl Fisher *N W Alexander* 98h 127c
12 br g Supreme Sound Salem Beach (Strong Gale)
1889[4] 2192[4] 4016[P] 5090[5]

Isle Of Ewe *Tom Lacey* 99b
4 b m Kayf Tara Apple Town (Warning)
4242[5] 5014[2]

Isthereadifference (IRE) *Neil Mulholland* 100h 112c
8 gr g Amilynx(FR) Jennys Grove (IRE) (Strong Gale)
490[3] (827) 1005[8] 1424[4] 1551[3] 1965[3] 2346[P] 4545[6]

Istimraar (IRE) *Dan Skelton* 119h 104c
4 b g Dansili Manayer (IRE) (Sadler's Wells (USA))
1754[5] 1945[2] ◆ 2645[4] 3156[6]

Italian Cousin (IRE) *George Charlton*
5 b g Milan Cousin Kizzy (IRE) (Toulon)
5014[7]

It Came To Pass (IRE) *J H Culloty* 121c
5 b g Brian Boru Satellite Dancer (IRE) (Satco (FR))
4768[F]

It Is I (IRE) *Don Cantillon* 107h
5 b g Presenting Nivalf (Gildoran)
83[9] 829[3] 1082[2]

It Is What It Is (IRE) *Jonjo O'Neill* 66h 107c
8 b g Presenting Valley (IRE) (Flemensfirth (USA))
(333)

It Just Aint Right *Mrs L Redman* 66b
4 gr m Dr Massini(IRE) Dawn Spinner (Arctic Lord (IRE))
5436[12]

It'll Be Grand *David Pipe* 96h
6 b g Beat All(USA) Everything's Rosy (Ardross)
212[4]

Itoldyou (IRE) *Linda Jewell* 102h 121c
9 ch g Salford Express(IRE) Adisadel (IRE) (Petardia)
2724[7] 3176[6] 3823[4] 4380[7] 4935[P]

Itsaboutime (IRE) *Helen Nelmes* 101h
5 gr g Whitmore's Conn(USA) Blazing Love (IRE) (Fruits Of Love (USA))
447[5] 2710[3] 3133[11] 4200[3] 4922[9]

It's A Close Call (IRE) *Paul Nicholls* 132h 141c
6 br g Scorpion(IRE) Sherin (GER) (Surumu (GER))
(1867) 3040[F]

Its A Dizzy Life *Peter Hedger* 77h
5 b g Amber Life Dizzy Massini (Dr Massini (IRE))
860[8]

Its'afreebee (IRE) *Dan Skelton* 146h
5 b g Danroad(AUS) Aphra Benn (IRE) (In The Wings)
(2437) (3366) (3739) 4715[3]

It's A Gimme (IRE) *Jonjo O'Neill* 138h 146c
8 b g Beneficial Sorcera (GER) (Zilzal (USA))
198[6] 555[2] 1040[6] 1152a[9]

It's All About Me (IRE) *Micky Hammond* 23b
3 b f King's Theatre(IRE) Annie Spectrim (IRE) (Spectrum (IRE))
4708[6]

It's All An Act (IRE) *Daniel O'Brien* 110h 117c
7 br g Presenting Royal Lucy (IRE) (King's Ride)
1233[F] 1494[5] 2540[9] 5064[P]

Its All Or Nothing *Miss C Rowe* 104c
6 gr g Terimon Little Vera (Carlingford Castle)
531[3]

Its A Long Road *Tim Dennis* 105h
7 b g Grape Tree Road Blue Shannon (IRE) (Be My Native (USA))
2664[3] 2962[5] 3705[8] 4250[P] 4342[P]

It's A Mans World *Brian Ellison* 118h 110c
9 b g Kyllachy Exhibitor (USA) (Royal Academy (USA))
332[6] 2217[2] 2499[8] 4154[6] 4771[3] 5405[5]

It's A Steal (IRE) *Evan Williams* 109h 136c
8 b g Craigsteel Mimosa Rose (IRE) (Be My Native (USA))
3109[5] 5063[4] 5354[P]

Its A Sting (IRE) *Oliver Sherwood* 117h 76c
6 b g Scorpion(IRE) Wyndham Sweetmarie (IRE) (Mister Lord (USA))
2151[P] 2973[P] 4321[5]

Its A Story *Mairi Wilson*
8 ch m Lucky Story(USA) Inchmore (Captain Maverick (USA))
263[P] 620[P]

Itshard To No (IRE) *Kerry Lee* 131h
6 b g Helissio(FR) Miniballist (IRE) (Tragic Role (USA))
1521[P] 2437[2] 2961[5] 3568[2] (5047)

Itsnoteasyted (IRE) *C A McBratney* 103h 100c
8 b g Dr Massini(IRE) Darvina (IRE) (Grand Plaisir (IRE))
3679[3]

Itsnowcato *Ben Pauling* 113h
4 b g Notnowcato Blaenavon (Cadeaux Genereux)
(2251) ◆ 2544[4] 2989[C] 3238[P] 4486[5]

It's Oscar (IRE) *James Evans* 100h 90c
8 b g Oscar(IRE) Lady Bramble (IRE) (Be My Native (USA))
2692[P] 2976[7] 3222[6] 3497[U] (3816) 4029[F] 4846[11] 5442[3]

Itstimeforapint (IRE) *Lucinda Russell* 99h 118c
7 b g Portrait Gallery(IRE) Executive Pearl (IRE) (Executive Perk)
2173[4] 2500[3] (2950) 3472[P] 3684[8] 4177[P] (4740) 5474[6]

Itsuptoyou (IRE) *Arthur Whiting* 112h 125c
11 b g Dr Massini(IRE) I Blame Theparents (Celtic Cone)
357^5 642^3 781^4

Ittirad (USA) *John Ferguson* 148h 152c
7 b g Dubai Destination(USA) Noushkey (Polish Precedent (USA))
(854) (1119) 1333^3 **(1505) (1838) ◆ 3280^4 4013^3**

It Was All A Dream (IRE) *Adrian Wintle* 7b
5 b m Indian River(FR) La Carlota (Starborough)
152^{11}

It Was Me *N R W Wright*
10 b g Bollin Eric Lady Confess (Backchat (USA))
4973^U

Ivan Grozny (FR) *W P Mullins* 158h
5 b g Turtle Bowl(IRE) Behnesa (IRE) (Suave Dancer (USA))
3650a1^5 4115^{16} 4765^8 (5219) 5325^5

Ivanhoe *Michael Blanshard* 116h
5 b g Haafhd Marysienka (Primo Dominie)
4506^2 5047^B

Ivanovich Gorbatov (IRE) *A P O'Brien* 152h
3 b g Montjeu(IRE) Northern Gulch (USA) (Gulch (USA))
4002a^4 (4764) 5175^2

Ivans Back (IRE) *Nick Kent* 101h 101c
10 b g Soviet Star(USA) Better Back Off (IRE) (Bob Back (USA))
42^U 623^3 914^3 (2866) 3308^P 4042^P

Ivebeenthinking *Tom Symonds* 86h
7 b m One More Tiger Moonlight Saunter (USA) (Woodman (USA))
(759)

Ivor's Queen (IRE) *Harry Fry* 88h
6 b m King's Theatre(IRE) Sonnerschien (IRE) (Be My Native (USA))
4881^4

Ivy Gate (IRE) *Jonjo O'Neill* 117h 122c
7 b g Westerner Key Partner (Law Society (USA))
1701^U 3445^6 3929^U 4352^7 4643^4 (4861)

Iwanabebobbiesgirl *Debra Hamer* 66h
5 b m Mahler Bajan Girl (FR) (Emperor Jones (USA))
1052^5 1153^9 1544^U

Izbushka (IRE) *David Thompson* 90h
4 b g Bushranger(IRE) Zaynaba (IRE) (Traditionally (USA))
37^P 262^6 399^P (569) 838^3 1400^{10} 1599^7 2478^P (3422) 4030^3 4421^P 4942^P

Izzy Piccolina (IRE) *Geoffrey Deacon* 94h
7 b m Morozov(USA) Chloara (IRE) (Flemensfirth (USA))
597^P 1384^2 1816^6 3868^7 5305^P

Jabbea (IRE) *Mary Sanderson* 80b
3 b g Robin Des Pres(FR) Welsh Bea (IRE) (Welsh Term)
5359^6

Jaboltiski (SPA) *Philip Hobbs* 120h
3 b g Delfos(IRE) Sonic Sea (IRE) (Zafonic (USA))
(2219) (2662) 3519^4 5095^7

Jack Albert (IRE) *Dianne Sayer* 110h 113c
8 gr g Cloudings(IRE) Lisdoylelady (IRE) (Glacial Storm (USA))
302^2 **(453)** 705^7 **781^6** 2948^2

Jackblack *Patrick Chamings* 69b
3 b g Crosspeace(IRE) Saharan Royal (Val Royal (FR))
2020^5 2414^7

Jack By The Hedge *Caroline Keevil* 112h 94c
6 b g Overbury(IRE) Bluebell Path (Classic Cliche (IRE))
1675^6 **2957^3 3224^6**

Jackfield *Robin Dickin* 67h
5 b g Norse Dancer(IRE) Small Amount (Sir Harry Lewis (USA))
262^7 1812^7 2453^3 2693^3 3771^6 4391^P

Jack Henri (FR) *Ian Williams* 107h
4 ch g Kapgarde(FR) Luba (FR) (Mansonnien (FR))
2909^7 3522^8 3839^6 4344^8 ◆

Jackies Solitaire *Peter Bowen* 119h 118c
7 ch m Generous(IRE) Bond Solitaire (Atraf)
711^2 1035^{10}

Jack Lamb *Sally Hall* 92b
3 gr g Sulamani(IRE) Charlotte Lamb (Pharly (FR))
2923^3 4308^4 4867^7

Jackofhearts *Jean McGregor* 104h
7 b g Beat Hollow Boutique (Selkirk (USA))
288^3 658^5 883^3 1329^5 1497^4 1637^3 2085^{11} 2338^3 5450^8

Jacksey's Well (IRE) *Edmond Daniel Linehan* 82h
4 b g Arcadio(GER) Nylon (GER) (Law Society (USA))
3012^4

Jacks Last Hope *Chris Grant* 119h
6 b g King's Theatre(IRE) Ninna Nanna (FR) (Garde Royale)
3027^{10} 4839^5

Jack Snipe *Jeremy Scott* 90h
6 b g Kirkwall Sea Snipe (King Luthier)
2731^9 3370^P 3568^3 4250^P 4919^6

Jacksonslady (IRE) *J P Dempsey* 133h 147c
10 b m Jackson's Drift(USA) Leinster Lady (IRE) (Lord Chancellor (USA))
(47a) 1152a^{17}

Jack Steel (IRE) *Lucinda Russell* 113h 129c
5 b g Craigsteel Wake Me Gently (IRE) (Be My Native (USA))
1638^2 **(2105) ◆ 2774^7 3475^7 4109^6 4912^P**

Jack The Gent (IRE) *George Moore* 111h 115c
11 b g Anshan Asidewager (IRE) (Brush Aside (USA))
742^2 1032^7 (1169) 1267^F 1553^4 1904^6

Jackthejourneyman (IRE) *Tom Gretton* 102h 110c
6 b g Beneficial Maslam (IRE) (Robellino (USA))
914^4 (1422) 1720^4 2449^P

Jac The Legend *Brian Ellison* 111h 126c
6 b g Midnight Legend Sky Burst (Gunner B)
(2145) 2669^R **3310^2 3591^F 3887^2 4155^2 4511^2 4912^2**

Jaguy De Cimbre (FR) *L Viel*
11 b g Homme De Loi(IRE) Belle De Liziere (FR) (Bojador (FR))
1477a^P

Jaisalmer (IRE) *Mark Bradstock* 98b
3 b g Jeremy(USA) Shara (IRE) (Kahyasi)
5457^6

Jajamcool (IRE) *Caroline Keevil* 123h
5 b g Marienbard(IRE) Scarlete (FR) (Cyborg (FR))
2904^3 3353^5 3660^2 4235^F (Dead)

Jaleo (GER) *John Ferguson* 133h
3 ch g New Approach(IRE) Jambalaya (GER) (Samum (GER))
(2845) 3112^2 (3967) 4720^{10}

Jalingo (IRE) *John Ferguson* 128h
4 b g Cape Cross(IRE) Just Special (Cadeaux Genereux)
745^2 (881) 973^2 1035^2

Jambul Tree *Robert Walford* 93b
5 ch m Apple Tree(FR) Jambles (Muhtarram (USA))
2952^P

Jamhoori *Jim Best* 100h
7 b h Tiger Hill(IRE) Tanasie (Cadeaux Genereux)
5477^5

Jamrham (IRE) *Sam Thomas* 82c
8 b g Great Palm(USA) Appleway (IRE) (Lord Americo)
3316^P **4073^U 4356^3 4686^4 4921^8**

Jam Session (IRE) *Ian Williams* 105h
3 ch g Duke Of Marmalade(IRE) Night Dhu (Montjeu (IRE))
(2777) 3409^2 5195^{13}

Jane's Fantasy (IRE) *N W Alexander* 19h
5 br m Robin Des Pres(FR) Trendy Attire (IRE) (Luso)
305^8 2752^7 3342^P

Janesmerlin *Kevin Bishop* 69b
3 b g Jelani(IRE) Janes Allweather (Rebelsway)
2009^8 2368^4

Jansboy *N Dooly* 121h 124c
8 b g Alflora(IRE) M N L Lady (Polar Falcon (USA))
2513^8

Jarlath *Seamus Mullins* 111h 110c
4 b g Norse Dancer(IRE) Blue Lullaby (IRE) (Fasliyev (USA))
98^4 554^6 (703) 933^4 1377^3 1693^4 1766^3 4849^4 5267^3

Jarob *Andrew Lynch* 143h 129c
8 br g Beat All(USA) Wishy (IRE) (Leading Counsel (USA))
5005a^P

Jasani *Alan Brown* 93h
7 b g Gentleman's Deal(IRE) Bred For Pleasure (Niniski (USA))
3795^8 4108^6 (4863)

Jaslamour (FR) *Alexandra Dunn* 78h
4 ch g Valanour(IRE) Jasla (FR) (Highest Honor (FR))
682^3 4351^P 4681^{11} 5091^{11}

Jaune Et Bleue (FR) *David Dennis* 105h
3 gr f Al Namix(FR) Jaune De Beaufai (FR) (Ultimately Lucky (IRE))
4734^{14}

Jaunty Inflight *Brian Eckley* 100h 107c
6 b g Busy Flight Jaunty Walk (Overbury (IRE))
3011^5 **3379^2 3867^P 3916^5 4356^4** 4712^6 **5236^U**

Jaunty Journey *P Foster* 103h 103c
12 ch g Karinga Bay Jaunty June (Primitive Rising (USA))
4000^3 4249^P

Jaunty Thor *Brian Eckley* 99h
5 b g Norse Dancer(IRE) Jaunty Walk (Overbury (IRE))
3375^5 3863^5 4264^7 4714^5

Java Rose *Charlie Longsdon* 115h
6 b m Ishiguru(USA) Mighty Splash (Cape Cross (IRE))
463^6 938^4 1170^2 1348^4

Javert (IRE) *Emma Lavelle* 116h 145c
6 b g Kayf Tara Royalrova (FR) (Garde Royale)
(2266) ◆ 2779^U (3036) 4701^U

Jawahal Du Mathan (FR) *Arthur Whitehead*
7 b g Smadoun(FR) Stone's Glow (USA) (Arctic Tern (USA))
4885^P

Jayandbee (IRE) *Philip Hobbs* 88h 102c
8 b g Presenting Christines Gale (IRE) (Strong Gale)
1592^7 1842^4 2036^3

Jay Are (IRE) *Gary Moore* 96h 132c
6 b g Heron Island(IRE) Vulpalm (IRE) (Great Palm (USA))
402^3

Jayo Time (IRE) *Kerry Lee* 114h 142c
6 b g Morozov(USA) Billythefilly (IRE) (Exit To Nowhere (USA))
225^4 463^5 718^3 (755) (929) **1042^6 1169^3** 1291^3 **(1523) 1601^2 (1809) 2153^6 (2691) 2854^U 3107^2 4210^2 4701^{12} 5455^2**

Jazz In Montreux (FR) *Francois Nicolle* 127h
2 b g Rip Van Winkle(IRE) Back The Winner (IRE) (Entrepreneur)
4539a^3

Jazz Thyme (IRE) *Robert Stephens* 98h
6 b m Helissio(FR) Thyne Square (IRE) (Good Thyne (USA))
1057^2 1374^5 1718^4 1960^6

Jazzy Lady (IRE) *Jim Best* 98h
4 b m Intikhab(USA) Lock's Heath (CAN) (Topsider (USA))
4411^8 4970^P

Jean Fleming (IRE) *Jamie Snowden* 117h 111c
8 b m Flemensfirth(USA) Dromhale Lady (IRE) (Roselier (FR))
1808^2 2314^3 3025^6 4186^5 4878^2

Jeanpascal (FR) *Venetia Williams* 122h
4 b g Muhaymin(USA) Miss Karad (FR) (Akarad (FR))
2373^P

Jeans Lady *Martin Keighley* 93h
6 b m Milan Indian Miss (Idiots Delight)
648^4 860^9 1384^3 1618^U 2924^P

Jebril (FR) *Chris Gordon* 132h
5 b g Astronomer Royal(USA) Happy Clapper (Royal Applause)
7a^4

Jebs Gamble (IRE) *Nick Gifford* 87b
4 b g Dubai Destination(USA) Gentle Caribou (IRE) (Dushyantor (USA))
2317^8 2828^4

Jebulani *Barry Murtagh* 82h
5 b g Jelani(IRE) Susan's Dowry (Efisio)
34^4 487^6 694^5 843^{11} 1368^5 2148^6 2706^6 5445^{10}

Jellied Eel Jack (IRE) *Donald McCain* 99h
6 b g Scorpion(IRE) Melodic Tune (IRE) (Roselier (FR))
2716^5 3009^6 3316^P 4862^3

Jemaben (FR) *Christian Le Galliard*
4 b g Axxos(GER) Salsepareille (FR) (Leeds (IRE))
5135a^2

Jemy Baie (FR) *M Postic* 142h 145c
6 b g Crillon(FR) Jemycienne (FR) (Mansonnien (FR))
375a^U 1884a^3 2822a^2

Jenkins (IRE) *Nicky Henderson* 128b
3 b g Azamour(IRE) Aladiyna (IRE) (Indian Danehill (IRE))
(5097) ◆

Jennies Jewel (IRE) *Jarlath P Fahey* 144h 134c
8 b m Flemensfirth(USA) Fishin Joella (IRE) (Gone Fishin)
93a^5 3732^2 4125^3

Jennifer Eccles *Suzy Smith* 109h
5 b m Midnight Legend Cherrygayle (IRE) (Strong Gale)
(1758) *4532^4*

Jennys Surprise (IRE) *Fergal O'Brien* 125h 132c
7 b m Hawk Wing(USA) Winning Jenny (IRE) (Leading Counsel (USA))
404^3 **2805^3 3197^2 3520^3 ◆ (4232) (4595) 5411^F**

Jersey Bull (IRE) *Michael Madgwick* 94h
3 b g Clodovil(IRE) Chaguaramas (IRE) (Mujadil (USA))
1486^2 1732^5

Jer's Girl (IRE) *Gavin Cromwell* 143h
3 b f Jeremy(USA) African Scene (IRE) (Scenic (IRE))
(2896) 3268a^2 4002a^5 (4954a)

Jessber's Dream (IRE) *Harry Fry* 143h
5 b m Milan Maddy's Supreme (IRE) (Supreme Leader)
2086^4 (2697) (3119) 3372^2 4125^2 ◆ (4231) 4954a^2

Jessie Pinkman *Philip Kirby* 85b
4 b g Duke Of Marmalade(IRE) My Dream Castles (USA) (Woodman (USA))
400^5

Jessie Webster (IRE) *Rebecca Curtis* 101b
6 b m Kayf Tara Blueberry Bramble (IRE) (Pistolet Bleu (IRE))
2086^5

Jester Jet *Tony Carroll* 93h
5 br m Overbury(IRE) Hendre Hotshot (Exit To Nowhere (USA))
1845^6 2452^7 2959^2 4616^4 5266^5

Je T'Aime Encore *Gay Kelleway* 59h
3 b g Acclamation Mimisel (Selkirk (USA))
4771^6

Jethro (IRE) *Brian Ellison* 105h
4 b g Craigsteel Wee Mo (IRE) (Zaffaran (USA))
1555^4 1792^2 2041^6 2196^4 3242^P 4773^3

Jet Master (IRE) *N W Alexander* 125h 137c
9 b g Brian Boru Whats The Reason (IRE) (Strong Gale)
(1638) ◆ 2194^5 2639^6 3682^9 **4167^5 4838^3** 5414^3

Jetson (IRE) *Mrs John Harrington* 156h 130c
10 b g Oscar(IRE) La Noire (IRE) (Phardante (FR))
49a^6

Jetstream Jack (IRE) *Gordon Elliott* 137h
5 b g Beneficial Westgrove Berry (IRE) (Presenting)
3393a^2 (4033) 4769^9 5294^2

Jett (IRE) *Mrs John Harrington* 132h
4 b g Flemensfirth(USA) La Noire (IRE) (Phardante (FR))
5002a^4

Jewellery (IRE) *Katie Scott* 93h 118c
8 bb m King's Best(USA) Eilean Shona (Suave Dancer (USA))
141^P 482^7 **1551^P** 5089^P 5472^{13}

Jezki (IRE) *Mrs John Harrington* 171h
7 b g Milan La Noire (IRE) (Phardante (FR))
(49a)

Jigsaw Financial (IRE) *Laura Young* 102h
9 b g Brian Boru Ardcolm Cailin (IRE) (Beneficial)
529^{11} 828^4 1269^6 1579^4 (1675) 2042^{10}

Jimbill (IRE) *Tim Vaughan* 123h 124c
9 br g Flying Legend(USA) Ah Gowan (IRE) (High Estate)
260^P

Jim Job Jones *Wyn Morris* 76b 93c
11 b g Tipsy Creek(USA) Sulapuff (Sula Bula)
17^P

Jimmie Brown (USA) *Andrew Crook* 69h 52c
7 b g Street Cry(IRE) Vid Kid (CAN) (Pleasant Colony (USA))
34^{11} **519^P 731^P 1857^8** 3098^3 4415^5 4645^5

Jimmy Breekie (IRE) *S R B Crawford* 109b
5 b g Alkaadhem Highland Breeze (IRE) (Kotashaan (FR))
4408^3 ◆ 5330^2

Jimmy Crackle (IRE) *Brian Ellison* 82h
4 b g Intense Focus(USA) Slieve (Selkirk (USA))
727^6 853^P 1041^5

Jimmy Shan (IRE) *Tim Vaughan* 108h 96c
7 b g Milan Divine Prospect (IRE) (Namaqualand (USA))
1447^3 1692^2 **1795^4 4710^P**

Jimmy Two Times (IRE) *B R Hamilton* 140h
6 b g Shantou(USA) Shedan (IRE) (Perpendicular)
96a^5 3071a^3

Jimsneverright *Ian Brown* 35b
7 b g Iktibas Lady Lexie (Cape Cross (IRE))
4937^P

Jinsha Lake (IRE) *Evan Williams* 93h
3 b c Galileo(IRE) Al Ihsas (IRE) (Danehill (USA))
2888^3 3730^5 3822^P 4038^5

Jock Des Mottes (FR) *Ms Sarah-Jayne Weaver* 45b
8 b g Maresca Sorrento(FR) Jolie Redaely (FR) (Diamond Prospect (USA))
429^U

Jodies Miss (IRE) *P M Lynch* 111h
6 b m Winged Love(IRE) Dansana (IRE) (Insan (USA))
3873a^5

Joe Farrell (IRE) *John Ferguson* 120b
6 b g Presenting Luck Of The Deise (IRE) (Old Vic)
(875)

Joe The Rogue (IRE) *David Phelan*
8 gr g Amilynx(FR) Roco-Bridge (IRE) (Lord Americo)
294^P

Johanos (FR) *Nigel Hawke* 97b
4 ch g Limnos(JPN) Madame Johann (FR) (Johann Quatz (FR))
4988^2

John Biscuit (IRE) *Jo Davis* 85h
7 ch g Hawk Wing(USA) Princess Magdalena (Pennekamp (USA))
98^9 569^P 2604^3 **2851^F** 4440^6 4885^6

John Constable (IRE) *Evan Williams* 141h
4 b h Montjeu(IRE) Dance Parade (USA) (Gone West (USA))
2728^2 4765^{17} 5325^6

John Daniell *Mrs O Bush* 98c
10 b g Overbury(IRE) Hottentot (Sula Bula)
292^4

John Dory (IRE) *Alan Swinbank* 93b
4 b g Excellent Art Elauyun (IRE) (Muhtarram (USA))
39^P (Dead)

John Louis *Venetia Williams* 115h 127c
7 ch g Bertolini(USA) Native Ring (FR) (Bering)
1642^6 (2435) 3709^5 4288^3

John Monash *Gordon Elliott* 108h
4 b g Kayf Tara Miss Invincible (Invincible Spirit (IRE))
2100^3 2429^4

Johnny Go *Lisa Harrison* 109h
5 b g Bollin Eric Waverbeck (IRE) (Accordion)
206^3 481^6 656^8 799^7 962^2 1067^3 1329^2 (1400) 1493^4 (1637) 1856^3 2340^5 2744^7 5475^8

Johnny Og *Martin Keighley* 109h 134c
6 b g Flemensfirth(USA) Mrs Roberts (Bob Back (USA))
1349^4 **(1483)** 1647^7 **(2151) 2779^5 3148^6 (3731) 3849^P (4487) 4700^F**

Johnnys Legacy (IRE) *Ken Wingrove* 62h 44c
8 b g Ecton Park(USA) Lexy May (USA) (Lear Fan (USA))
2037^6 4536^3

Johns Luck (IRE) *Neil Mulholland* 108h 108c
6 b g Turtle Island(IRE) Jemima Yorke (Be My Guest (USA))
1351^3 1842^3 2269^5 2692^7 3081^S 3419^2 3746^7 4265^2 (4533) 4669^3 5240^2

Johns Spirit (IRE) *Jonjo O'Neill* 125h 162c
8 b g Gold Well Gilt Ridden (IRE) (Heron Island (IRE))
2084^P 2483^9 3031^9 3406^6 3851^4 4733^P 5276^3

John Williams (IRE) *Sandy Thomson* 95h
6 b g Presenting Duhallow Park (IRE) (Flemensfirth (USA))
155^3 2070^5 2804^6 3474^{10}

Join The Clan (IRE) *Jonjo O'Neill* 141h 134c
6 b g Milan Millicent Bridge (IRE) (Over The River (FR))
2333^5 **3317^3** 3992^2 4730^{10} 5213^7

Join The Navy *Kate Buckett* 111h 98c
10 b g Sea Freedom Join The Parade (Elmaamul (USA))
2713^6 3374^2 (3919) 4648^2 5102^2 5453^{10}

Join Together (IRE) *Mrs Rose Loxton* 107h 124c
10 b g Old Vic Open Cry (IRE) (Montelimar (USA))
3585^3 (3958) 4383^U 4887^4

Joker Choker (IRE) *Miss Nicky Martin* 137h 122c
10 b g Oscar(IRE) Stormy Lady (IRE) (Glacial Storm (USA))
536^2

Jokers And Rogues (IRE) *Kenneth Slack* 114h 76c
7 b g Beneficial Ashfield Girl (IRE) (Beau Sher)
2339^7 2705^6 4152^3 (4326) 4799^7 (5088)

Jolila (FR) *G Lassaussaye*
4 b m Layman(USA) Jorbalan (FR) (Danehill Dancer (IRE))
1231a^2

Jolly Boys Outing (IRE) *Rosemary Gasson* 90c
12 b g Glacial Storm(USA) St Carol (IRE) (Orchestra)
2394 1813^6 2303^5 3131^6 3948^3 4746^4

Jolly Roger (IRE) *Bernard Llewellyn* 112h 105c
8 b g Oratorio(IRE) Chalice Wells (Sadler's Wells (USA))
442^P 5279^{10}

Jolly's Cracked It (FR) *Harry Fry* 147h
6 b g Astarabad(USA) Jolly Harbour (Rudimentary (USA))
2186^3 (3151)

Jonnie Skull (IRE) *Phil McEntee* 99h 117c
9 b g Pyrus(USA) Sovereign Touch (IRE) (Pennine Walk)
570^2

Jonniesofa (IRE) *Rose Dobbin* 140h
5 b g Well Made(GER) Lucky Sarah (IRE) (Aahsaylad)
2025^3 (2338) 2787^2 (3159) 3400^2 (4248) 4766^9

Jonny Delta *Jim Goldie* 108h
8 ch g Sulamani(IRE) Send Me An Angel (IRE) (Lycius (USA))
2949[10] 3424[7] 4036[2] ◆ 4179[2] 4913[F]

Jonny Eager (IRE) *Alistair Whillans* 103h 119c
6 b g Craigsteel Dishy (IRE) (Jurado (USA))
2806[3] 3402[6] 3793[2] **(4051)** ◆ **4407[3] 4740[2] 5228[2]**

Jopaan (IRE) *Brian Barr* 72h
8 ch g Pierre No Precedent (IRE) (Be My Native (USA))
1590[10] 1952[5] 2299[10] 3946[6] 4184[6] 4920[2]

Joseph Mercer (IRE) *Tina Jackson* 108h 102c
8 b g Court Cave(IRE) Vikki's Dream (IRE) (Kahyasi)
2496[9] **2922[2] 3507[6] 3937[5] 4387[4] 4738[5] 5369[P]**

Josie Jump *Paul Henderson* 91b
6 b m Crosspeace(IRE) Chipewyas (FR) (Bering)
1122[2]

Josies Orders (IRE) *E Bolger* 126h 153c
7 b g Milan Silent Orders (IRE) (Bob Back (USA))
48a[U] (2471) (3017) 4719[2]

Josses Hill (IRE) *Nicky Henderson* 150h 161c
7 b g Winged Love(IRE) Credora Storm (IRE) (Glacial Storm (USA))
2915[F] (4100) 4731[8]

Jot'em Down (IRE) *David Bridgwater* 111b
4 b g Kalanisi(IRE) Shuil A Hocht (IRE) (Mohaajir (USA))
3952[5] (4414) 4721[19]

Jovial Joey (IRE) *Maurice Barnes* 112h
4 b g St Jovite(USA) Like A Bird (IRE) (Topanoora)
4902[2]

Joyful Motive *Brian Ellison* 67h 74c
6 ch g Motivator Triple Joy (Most Welcome)
779[3] 1004[P] 1370[3] 1603[5]

Jully Les Buxy *Robert Walford* 106h
5 b m Black Sam Bellamy(IRE) Jadidh (Touching Wood (USA))
2444[4] 2870[2] 3919[4] 4853[3] 5466[2]

Jumbo John (IRE) *Mrs Lorna Fowler* 104h
9 b g Presenting Hazel's Glory (IRE) (Mister Lord (USA))
4581[P]

Jumeirah Liberty *Zoe Davison* 83h 93c
7 ch g Proclamation(IRE) Gleam Of Light (IRE) (Danehill (USA))
104[P] 1980[4] **3084[5]**

Jump And Jump (IRE) *Robin Dickin* 65b
5 br m Oscar(IRE) My Twist (IRE) (Flemensfirth (USA))
696[7] 4880[13]

Jumpandtravel (IRE) *Micky Hammond* 101h 67c
6 b m Millenary Youbetido (IRE) (Eurobus)
1271[3] ◆ 1365[3] 1744[P] 2396[3] (2550) 2812[F] **3178[3]** 3312[2] 3503[3] 3821[4]

Jumps Road *Colin Tizzard* 126h 119c
8 b g Clerkenwell(USA) Diletia (Dilum (USA))
3120[3] 3529[7] 3708[7] 4159[4]

Junction Fourteen (IRE) *Emma Lavelle* 139h 151c
6 b g King's Theatre(IRE) Chevet Girl (IRE) (Roselier (FR))
(1932) ◆ **(2347) 3136[5] (5496)**

June French (FR) *Neil Mulholland* 74h 87c
7 b m Jimble(FR) Sunbelt Broker (Lahib (USA))
524[F] 807[P] 1595[P] 2542[5] 2861[6]

Junior Package *David Pipe* 59h
4 gr g Kayf Tara Shirley Cricket (Linamix (FR))
783[4] 1122[4] 1345[2] 1449[3] 2731[12] 3105[12] 3581[9] 3710[11] 4454[7]

Jupiter Storm *Gary Moore* 104h
6 ch g Galileo(IRE) Exciting Times (FR) (Jeune Homme (USA))
98[5]

Jury Duty (IRE) *Gordon Elliott* 128h
4 b g Well Chosen Swan Heart (IRE) (Broken Hearted)
5024a[3]

Just Acting (IRE) *Paul Nicholls*
5 b g Presenting Azalea (IRE) (Marju (IRE))
3920[P]

Just A Feeling *Paul Webber* 97h
5 ch m Flemensfirth(USA) Precious Lady (Exit To Nowhere (USA))
45[2] 2033[P] 3386[P] 4893[2]

Just Annie *Lucy Normile* 77b
7 b m Revoque(IRE) Carbery Spirit (IRE) (Glacial Storm (USA))
2338[P] 2936[P]

Just A Normal Day (IRE) *Dan Skelton* 121h
5 b g High Chaparral(IRE) Thats Luck (IRE) (Posen (USA))
(590) (775) 1035[3] 1839[4] 2333[4]

Justanother Muddle *Sheena West* 126h
6 gr g Kayf Tara Spatham Rose (Environment Friend)
(2417) 3032[P] 4072[4]

Just A Par (IRE) *Paul Nicholls* 145h 156c
8 b g Island House(IRE) Thebrownhen (IRE) (Henbit (USA))
2482[13] 2916[9] 4858[2] 5218[15] 5494[2]

Justatenner *Colin Tizzard* 113h
4 b g Northern Legend Shelayly (IRE) (Zaffaran (USA))
242[4] 2351[4] 2904[10] 3582[3] 4449[4] ◆ (4799) 5267[U] 5418[9]

Just Awake *Sandy Thomson* 95h 110c
8 b g Prince Daniel(USA) Katinka (Rymer)
(287) 453[F] (871) 883[5]

Just Bee (IRE) *Katie Scott* 62h
6 b m Zerpour(IRE) Miss Jamielou (IRE) (Be My Native (USA))
77[4] 487[7] 870[P]

Just Bill (IRE) *Evan Williams* 106h
7 b g Blueprint(IRE) Husdale (IRE) (Husyan (USA))
2903[P] 3976[3] ◆ 4530[3]

Just Brooke *N W Alexander* 41b
5 ch m Black Sam Bellamy(IRE) Sports Express (Then Again)
4611[5]

Just Cameron *Micky Hammond* 133h 155c
8 b g Kayf Tara Miss Fencote (Phardante (FR))
51a[2] 3446[6] 3857[2] 4718[6] 5087[3] 5448[3]

Justforthebuzz (IRE) *Chris Gordon*
10 ch g Dernier Empereur(USA) Island-Bay (IRE) (Executive Perk)
292[P]

Just Georgie *Sue Smith* 113h
5 b g Kayf Tara Just Kate (Bob's Return (IRE))
2066[2] 2331[3] 3239[2] 3971[4] 4299[2] 4941[4]

Justice Is Done *Shaun Lycett*
5 b h Siren's Missile Heckley Clare Glen (Dancing High)
1484[9]

Just Lewis *Nikki Evans* 64h
8 ch g Sir Harry Lewis(USA) Mcmahon's River (Over The River (FR))
1379[P] 1597[6] 1780[5] 1961[6] 2693[P]

Just Like Beth *Giuseppe Fierro* 14h
7 b m Proclamation(IRE) Just Beth (Carlingford Castle)
3366[6] 4123[4]

Just Like Dylan (IRE) *Barry Murtagh* 53h
4 b g Brian Boru Fainne Oir (IRE) (Montelimar (USA))
3309[11] 3971[8] 4403[9] 4703[5] 5314[5]

Just Minded (IRE) *Sue Smith* 89b
4 b g Kayf Tara Georgia On My Mind (FR) (Belmez (USA))
5248[5]

Just My Luke *Susan Corbett* 66h
6 b g Ferrule(IRE) Briar Rose (IRE) (Roselier (FR))
33[8] 1852[7] 2071[6] 2323[P] 2751[12] 2937[P]

Just Nobby *Jennie Candlish* 56b
4 b g Rainbow High Trinny Blue (IRE) (Blueprint (IRE))
1645[9] 1926[8]

Just Skittles *Richard Harper* 63h
7 b g Storming Home Miss Roberto (IRE) (Don Roberto (USA))
808[P] 1812[6] 1972[4] 2245[5]

Just So Cool (IRE) *David Dennis* 114h
4 gr g Acambaro(GER) Lauras Dote (IRE) (Muroto)
2126[10] 2581[8] 3105[10] 3467[3] 3865[2] 4226[2] 4648[3]

Just Talking (IRE) *Sara Ender* 40h 52c
13 br g Windsor Castle Fam-E Fam-E (IRE) (King's Ride)
803[9] 1080[P]

Just The Way It Is *Nicky Henderson* 68b
5 b m Presenting Storm In Front (IRE) (Fourstars Allstar (USA))
45[6]

Just When *Patrick Chamings* 100h
6 b g Dalakhani(IRE) Cape Grace (IRE) (Priolo (USA))
2831[3] 4593[4] 5418[16]

Kabjoy (IRE) *Mrs John Harrington* 118h
4 b m Intikhab(USA) Lunar Love (IRE) (In The Wings)
52a[4]

Kadalkin (FR) *Nigel Hawke* 107h 114c
9 b g Robin Des Champs(FR) Kadalma (FR) (Cadoudal (FR))
642[6] 857[P] 1265[10]

Kaddys Dream *Robin Dickin* 102h
4 b m Kadastrof(FR) Symbiosis (Bien Bien (USA))
3111[7] 3862[11] 4881[5] 5389[7]

Kaddys Girl *Robin Dickin* 77h
5 ch m Kadastrof(FR) Dickies Girl (Saxon Farm)
45[3] 432[5] 970[14] 2302[P] 3110[7] 3386[P] 3568[11] 5397[3]

Kafella *Dan Skelton* 104b
3 gr g Kayf Tara Sisella (IRE) (Bob Back (USA))
2777[3] 4508[3]

Kahaleesi *Philip Hobbs* 76b
3 b f Shirocco(GER) Maiden Voyage (Slip Anchor)
3469[6] 5286[8]

Kahdian (IRE) *Helen Rees* 102h
5 br g Rock Of Gibraltar(IRE) Katiykha (IRE) (Darshaan)
164[4] 3369[P] 4099[4] 4856[6] 5355[8]

Kahyadam (FR) *A Chaille-Chaille* 122h 127c
7 b g Kahyasi Cadoudame (FR) (Cadoudal (FR))
1477a[7]

Kai Broon (IRE) *Lucinda Russell* 99h 119c
8 b g Marju(IRE) Restiv Star (FR) (Soviet Star (USA))
(78) 331[5] 885[4] 1332[7] 1743[F] 5257[4]

Kaki De La Pree (FR) *Tom Symonds* 135h 144c
8 b g Kapgarde(FR) Kica (FR) (Noir Et Or)
2717[2]

Kala Brandy (IRE) *Timothy Townend* 122h 102c
7 bb m Kalanisi(IRE) Wild Spell (IRE) (Oscar (IRE))
4653a[7]

Kalaharry (IRE) *Katie Scott* 35b
3 b g Kalanisi(IRE) Full Imperatrice (FR) (Dernier Empereur (USA))
2216[7] 5127[9]

Kalane (IRE) *Charlie Longsdon* 132h 144c
6 b m Kalanisi(IRE) Fairy Lane (IRE) (Old Vic)
93a[3] 2349[F] **(2925)** ◆ **3337[F] 3726[3] 5281[7]**

Kalanisi Circle (IRE) *Ben Pauling* 100b
3 b g Kalanisi(IRE) Circle The Wagons (IRE) (Commanche Run)
5315[2]

Kalanisi Glen (IRE) *Kim Bailey* 108h
5 br g Kalanisi(IRE) Glen Ten (IRE) (Mandalus)
2630[7] 4535[3]

Kalaniti (IRE) *Chris Grant* 105b
4 b m Kalanisi(IRE) Miss Twinkletoes (IRE) (Zafonic (USA))
144[4] 2086[2] (2756) ◆ 3862[5] 4623[10]

Kalann (IRE) *Sabrina J Harty* 126h
8 b g Barathea(IRE) Karkiyla (IRE) (Darshaan)
1787a[6]

Kalasaya (IRE) *Philip Rowley* 79b
4 b g Kalanisi(IRE) Agasaya (IRE) (Invincible Spirit (IRE))
320[10]

Kalaskadesemilley *Kevin Morgan* 95b
4 b g Myboycharlie(IRE) Congressional (IRE) (Grand Lodge (USA))
4532[3] 5400[6]

Kalastar (IRE) *Katie Scott* 102c
6 b g Kalanisi(IRE) Katsura (Alflora (IRE))
80[2] 457[4] 2320[2] 3671[P] 4903[6] 5261[7]

Kalifourchon (FR) *David Pipe* 124h
4 gr g Martaline Kaly Flight (FR) (Great Palm (USA))
(811) 856[2] (1269) ◆ (1521) 2369[U] 3027[7] 3708[9]

Kalimantan (IRE) *Tim Vaughan* 114h
5 b g Azamour(IRE) Kalamba (IRE) (Green Dancer (USA))
216[3]

Kalkir (FR) *W P Mullins* 146h
4 gr g Montmartre(FR) Kakira (FR) (Cadoudal (FR))
3650a[2] 4115[6]

Kalmbeforethestorm *Helen Nelmes* 112h
7 ch g Storming Home Miss Honeypenny (IRE) (Old Vic)
102[P] 1579[3] 1839[6] 3137[8] 5264[5]

Kalmonto (FR) *R J Alford* 122h 123c
9 b g Kalanisi(IRE) Tramonto (Sri Pekan (USA))
3826[P]

Kalondra (IRE) *Neil Mulholland* 115h
4 b g Spadoun(FR) Mystic Vic (IRE) (Old Vic)
1926[4] 2407[F] 2768[2] 3179[4] ◆

Kalopsia (IRE) *A P O'Brien* 64h
4 b m Flemensfirth(USA) Lunar Beauty (IRE) (Milan)
2677a[6]

Kamaloka (IRE) *Patrice Quinton* 115h 115c
3 b f King's Theatre(IRE) Palapa (Pursuit Of Love)
2896[5]

Kamelie (FR) *Michal Lisek*
8 b m Martaline Kandis (FR) (Northern Treat (USA))
1672a[P]

Kamool (GER) *Jonjo O'Neill* 113h
5 ch g Mamool(IRE) Kiss Me Lips (GER) (Dashing Blade)
210[6] 2271[5] 2595[5] 3846[4] 5157[7]

Kansas City Chief (IRE) *Miss Mary Louise Hallahan* 100h 116c
6 b g Westerner Badawi Street (Thowra (FR))
3716a[5]

Kanturk Bank (IRE) *Rebecca Curtis* 94h
5 b g Carlo Bank(IRE) Kanturk Belle (IRE) (King's Ride)
1645[8] 2265[11] 3580[4]

Kap Call (USA) *Francois Nicolle* 112h
5 b m Kapgarde(FR) Call Me Blue (FR) (Pistolet Bleu (IRE))
2821a[10]

Kapgarde King (FR) *Jamie Snowden* 90h
4 ch g Kapgarde(FR) Cybertina (FR) (Cyborg (FR))
3568[4] 4317[12] 5268[7]

Kap Jazz (FR) *Venetia Williams* 114h 116c
5 b g Kapgarde(FR) Jazz And Liquer (FR) (Kahyasi)
2154[9] 2519[4] (2871) 3146[7] 3705[5] **4071[2]** 4543[P]

Kapko (FR) *J-D Marion* 91h
4 b g Kapgarde(FR) Chamberkoe (FR) (Chamberlin (FR))
2362a[9]

Kapricorne (FR) *Sophie Leech* 101h 100c
8 b g Kapgarde(FR) Colombe Royale (FR) (Passing Sale (FR))
1720[5] 1978[5] 2521[2] 3081[5] 3222[2] 3864[P] 4346[4] 4673[P] 4749[4] ◆

Kapstadt (FR) *Ian Williams* 128h
5 bb g Country Reel(USA) King's Parody (IRE) (King's Best (USA))
(751) (1676) ◆ 2170[2] 2728[6]

Kapville (FR) *E Leenders* 124c
8 b g Kapgarde(FR) Ville Eagle (FR) (Villez (USA))
313a[2]

Kap West (FR) *Laura Young* 83c
10 b g Kapgarde(FR) Themis Eria (FR) (Signe Divin (USA))
173[3]

Kara Tara *Lawrence Mullaney* 102h
5 b m Kayf Tara Matilda Too (IRE) (Definite Article)
187[6] 2591[7] 3022[9] 3508[4] 3888[3] 4902[3]

Karelcytic (FR) *F-M Cottin* 127h 140c
4 ch g High Rock(IRE) Saturnienne (FR) (Freedom Cry)
1882a[3] 2820a[F]

Karens Lad (IRE) *Nick Gifford* 98h
5 b g Kalanisi(IRE) Aremebooksready (IRE) (Good Thyne (USA))
3452[P] 3902[3]

Karezak (IRE) *Alan King* 147h 131c
4 b g Azamour(IRE) Karawana (IRE) (King's Best (USA))
1847[2] 2060[2] **2580[2]** 3149[4]

Karinga Dancer *Harry Fry* 141h 144c
9 b g Karinga Bay Miss Flora (Alflora (IRE))
2901[9] (4781)

Karinga Dandy (IRE) *Miss R D Keeble* 107h 88c
9 b g Karinga Bay Well Then Now Then (IRE) (Supreme Leader)
5166[5]

Karingo *Lucy Normile* 93h
8 ch g Karinga Bay Wild Happening (GER) (Mondrian (GER))
886[6] **1330[P] 1492[F]**

Karisma King *Sue Smith* 104h
6 br g Supreme Sound Hollybush (IRE) (Ali-Royal (IRE))
2196[5] 2487[5] 2890[3] 3242[8] 4326[6] 4796[4] 5079[3] (5332)

Karl Marx (IRE) *Mark Gillard* 93h
5 b g Red Clubs(IRE) Brillano (FR) (Desert King (IRE))
(265) 704[5] 1085[7] 2880[7] 3125[5] 3914[P] 4250[6] 5033[P]

Kasakh Noir (FR) *Dan Skelton* 134h
3 ch g Redback Vale Of Honor (FR) (Singspiel (IRE))
(2757) ◆ 3347[3] (4038) 4720[6] ◆

Kasbadali (FR) *Oliver Sherwood* 132h 126c
10 b g Kahyasi Nikalie (FR) (Nikos)
660[4] 1820[5]

Kashmir Peak (IRE) *John Quinn* 134h
6 b g Tiger Hill(IRE) Elhareer (IRE) (Selkirk (USA))
1905[U] 2194[4] 3027[F]

Kashstaree *Lisa Harrison* 94h
4 b m Sakhee(USA) Celestial Welcome (Most Welcome)
1887[12] 3233[8] 3505[4] 3672[4] 4163[P] 4547[P] 4904[P]

Kasim (CZE) *Premek Kejzlar* 118c
10 b g Magnus(POL) Kasira (CZE) (Paico (IRE))
1885a[6]

Kassis *Jamie Snowden* 103h 113c
6 b m Kalanisi(IRE) Gastina (FR) (Pistolet Bleu (IRE))
2300[2] (3007) 3727[5] 4319[4] 5281[8]

Kastani Beach (IRE) *Seamus Mullins* 104h 110c
9 br g Alderbrook Atomic View (IRE) (Old Vic)
529[13] 2548[9] 2956[6] 4593[2] 5479[6]

Katachenko (IRE) *Donald McCain* 131h 139c
6 b g Kutub(IRE) Karalee (IRE) (Arokar (FR))
138[2] ◆ **(2201) 2774[2] 3335[2] 4816[3] (5179)**

Katara Bay *Venetia Williams* 72b
4 b g Kayf Tara De Blanc (IRE) (Revoque (IRE))
3827[5]

Katarrhini *Mark Bradstock* 88h
6 b m Kayf Tara Dedrunknmunky (IRE) (Rashar (USA))
4413[5]

Katenko (FR) *Venetia Williams* 71h 109c
9 b g Laveron Katiana (FR) (Villez (USA))
3150[P] 4697[13] 5218[F]

Kates Benefit (IRE) *David Kenneth Budds* 130h 125c
9 b m Beneficial Greenflag Princess (IRE) (Executive Perk)
47a[12] 1186a[11]

Katgary (FR) *Paul Nicholls* 139h 139c
5 b g Ballingarry(IRE) Kotkira (FR) (Subotica (FR))
(1942) 3026[3] 4701[P] 5073[5]

Kathlatino *Micky Hammond* 77h
8 b m Danbird(AUS) Silver Rhythm (Silver Patriarch (IRE))
1071[5]

Katie Do (IRE) *Colin Bowe* 101b 115c
9 b m Milan Polar Crash (IRE) (Crash Course)
2057[7]

Katies Choice (IRE) *R Mike Smith* 89b
7 gr g Croco Rouge(IRE) Rosetown Girl (IRE) (Roselier (FR))
1634[P]

Katie's Massini (IRE) *Mrs E Scott* 86b
7 b m Dr Massini(IRE) Our Lucky Supreme (IRE) (Supreme Leader)
5384[U]

Katie T (IRE) *Kevin Prendergast* 141h
6 b m Beneficial Long Acre (Mark Of Esteem (IRE))
93a[4]

Katie Too (IRE) *Alan King* 132h
4 b m King's Theatre(IRE) Shivermetimber (IRE) (Arctic Lord (IRE))
(2952) (3386) ◆ 4231[2] (5280)

Katkeau (FR) *David Pipe* 136h 154c
8 b g Kotky Bleu(FR) Levine (FR) (Luynes (USA))
437a[3] 836a[5] **(2553) (3109) 3996[3] 4802[P]**

Katnap (FR) *John Laurence Cullen* 118h 126c
8 br g Sleeping Car(FR) Kittygale (IRE) (Strong Gale)
95a[9]

Katy P *Mrs John Harrington* 87b
3 b f Ask Kingara (Karinga Bay)
5286[3]

Kauto Riko (FR) *Tom Gretton* 99h
4 b g Ballingarry(IRE) Kauto Relstar (FR) (Art Bleu I)
467[4] 3363[6] 3835[4] 5464[11]

Kauto Stone (FR) *Ben Pauling*
9 ch g With The Flow(USA) Kauto Relka (FR) (Port Etienne (FR))
1902[U] 2153[F] (Dead)

Kauto Sweety (FR) *Giuseppe Satalia* 102h 127c
8 ch g Bonbon Rose(FR) Kauto Relstar (FR) (Art Bleu I)
1672a[8]

Kavanaghs Corner (IRE) *Simon Earle* 85h 89c
6 b g Coroner(IRE) Annacarney (IRE) (Moscow Society (USA))
2408[P] 3128[3] ◆ 3489[5] 5332[3]

Kavestorm *Polly Gundry* 65h
9 br m Kayf Tara Tudor Gale (IRE) (Strong Gale)
675[8]

Kayf Blanco *Graeme McPherson* 141h
6 b g Kayf Tara Land Of Glory (Supreme Leader)
317[6] 2170[3] (2499) 3015[3] 3449[8] 3989[4] 4765[7] 5275[6]

Kayf Charmer *Linda Blackford* 92h
5 b m Kayf Tara Silver Charmer (Charmer (IRE))
1823[5] 2876[2] 3368[5] 3789[3] (4886) (5099)

Kayf Grace *Nicky Henderson* 128b
5 b m Kayf Tara Potter's Gale (IRE) (Strong Gale)
3861[2] (4974) ◆ (5180)

Kayfleur *Henry Daly* 116h 127c
6 b m Kayf Tara Combe Florey (Alflora (IRE))
2313[3] 2685[5] **3122[2] 4247[2] 4647[3] 5281[6]**

Kayflin (FR) *Linda Jewell* 90h 74c
7 b m Kayf Tara Flinders (Henbit (USA))
280[8] 597[9] 673[F] 977[P] 3905[2] 4413[P] 4936[2] **5478[3]**

Kayf Moss *John Flint* 131h 139c
7 b g Kayf Tara Madam Mosso (Le Moss)
209[2] 2660[5] 3197[4] 3517[7] **4267[2] 4966[2]**

Kayf Tiger *Robin Dickin* 20h
6 b g Kayf Tara La Marette (Karinga Bay)
1101[9] 1379[P] 1844[5] 2299[11]

Kayfton Pete *Charles Pogson* 103h 111c
9 b g Kayf Tara Jonchee (FR) (Le Thuit Signol (FR))
284[2] 623[F] 742[4] 1043[5] 1376[6] **(1894) 2288[4]** 2924[5] 4028[6] **4985[3]** 5374[9]

Kayf Willow *Philip Hobbs* 116h
6 b m Kayf Tara Mrs Philip (Puissance)
(415) ◆ 748[2] 1012[3] (1841) ◆ 2455[8] 5382[4]

Kayla *Stuart Edmunds* 108h
5 b m Kayf Tara Palila (Petoski)
(45) 1506[2] (1694) 1910[2]

Kaylan's Rose *Dianne Sayer* 77h
5 b m Kayf Tara Ostfanni (IRE) (Spectrum (IRE))
1414[P]

Kaysersberg (FR) *Warren Greatrex* 135h 141c
8 b g Khalkevi(IRE) Alliance Royale (FR) (Turgeon (USA))
2241[4] **3116[P]** 4389[6]

Kazlian (FR) *Johnny Farrelly* 116h 102c
7 b g Sinndar(IRE) Quiet Splendor (USA) (Unbridled (USA))
2545[6] 4225[F] 4685[3] 5146[6] 5464[6]

Kazzio (GER) *P Vovcenko* 130c
7 b g Konigstiger(GER) Kalata (GER) (Lando (GER))
(1672a)

Kealigolane (IRE) *Barry Murtagh* 62h 127c
11 gr g Beneficial Leone Des Pres (FR) (Tip Moss (FR))
142[7]

Keel Haul (IRE) *Henry Oliver* 125h 136c
7 br g Classic Cliche(IRE) Tara Hall (Saddlers' Hall (IRE))
2153[5] (2468) 3030[4] 3446[8] 4254[4] 4918[3]

Keep Calm *John Mackie* 105h
5 b g War Chant(USA) Mayaar (USA) (Grand Slam (USA))
353[4] ◆ 620[5] 852[3] 1260[5] (1519) 2085[10] 3023[5]

Keeper Hill (IRE) *Warren Greatrex* 115b
4 b g Westerner You Take Care (IRE) (Definite Article)
(2597) 5083[3] ◆

Keep On Track (IRE) *I R Ferguson* 98h 126c
8 ch g Rudimentary(USA) Corries Rein (IRE) (Anshan)
48a[3]

Keep On Walking (IRE) *Peter Croke* 72h
4 b g Rock Of Gibraltar(IRE) Matikanehamatidori (JPN) (Sunday Silence (USA))
933[7] 1168[P]

Keep 'r Lit *Miss Imogen Pickard*
3 b f Multiplex Cashel Dancer (Bishop Of Cashel)
3464[P]

Keep To The Beat *Kevin Ryan* 111h
4 b m Beat Hollow Cadeau Speciale (Cadeaux Genereux)
415[2] ◆ 711[3] (843) 1454[4] 1618[7] 1887[2]

Keep Up (GER) *Philip Kirby* 96h
3 b g Monsun(GER) Katy Carr (Machiavellian (USA))
2718[F] 3099[4] 3309[3]

Keep Up Keira (IRE) *Neil Mulholland* 86h
4 b m Scorpion(IRE) Perspex Queen (IRE) (Presenting)
1908[5] 2856[4] 4435[6] 4893[7]

Keepyourheadup *Helen Nelmes*
4 b g Sir Percy Sweet Lemon (IRE) (Oratorio (IRE))
5308[7]

Keki Buku (FR) *I M Mason* 109b
12 b g Kadalko(FR) Bigouden (What A Guest)
521[P]

Kelforest (FR) *Gabriel Leenders* 108h
3 ch g Forestier(FR) Kelseurat Du Casse (FR) (Seurat)
4959a[5]

Kelka *Malcolm Jefferson* 96b
3 b f Exit To Nowhere(USA) Scarvagh Diamond (IRE) (Zaffaran (USA))
(4559) 5351[2]

Kellys Brow (IRE) *Ben Pauling* 110h 77c
8 b g Golan(IRE) Eyebright (IRE) (Zaffaran (USA))
463[4]

Kelpie Blaze (IRE) *Seamus Durack* 95b
4 b g Aussie Rules(USA) Woodsia (Woodman (USA))
3200[4]

Kelsey (IRE) *Tom Lacey* 102h
5 ch g Robin Des Champs(FR) Lady Mariah (IRE) (Moonax (IRE))
1698[8] 2417[P] 2904[4] 3378[5] (4184) 4349[6] 4747[P]

Keltic Rhythm (IRE) *Neil King* 114h 80c
8 b g Milan Ballinaroone Girl (IRE) (Carroll House (IRE))
283[3] **2975[P] 3339[P] 4789[7]**

Keltus (FR) *Paul Nicholls* 132h 137c
5 gr g Keltos(FR) Regina D'Orthe (FR) (R B Chesne)
2912[6] 3232[3] 4112[3] 4786[U]

Kelvingrove (IRE) *Jonjo O'Neill* 128h
5 b g Hurricane Run(IRE) Silversword (FR) (Highest Honor (FR))
916[5]

Kemicallie *Carroll Gray* 10b
3 b f Passing Glance Jenny From Brean (Commanche Run)
5383[13]

Kendari King (IRE) *Tim Vaughan* 82h
4 b g Misternando Native Mistress (IRE) (Be My Native (USA))
783[2] 1050[6] 1153[P] 4646[F] 5098[8]

Kenobe Star (IRE) *Jamie Snowden* 90h
3 b g Clodovil(IRE) Maimana (IRE) (Desert King (IRE))
2219[4] 2662[3] 3464[4]

Kentford Heiress *Seamus Mullins* 104h
5 b m Midnight Legend Kentford Duchess (Jupiter Island)
30[5] 383[F] 597[4] 759[8] 937[7] (1120) 1236[2] 3198[P] 4878[6] 5420[15]

Kentford Myth *Seamus Mullins* 105h
5 b m Midnight Legend Quistaquay (El Conquistador)
(172) 513[2] 2825[4] 3953[3] 4616[2] 5094[9]

Kent Ragstone (USA) *Daniel Steele* 76h
6 ch g Stonesider(USA) Sweet Charity (USA) (A.P. Indy (USA))
3194[P] 3483[11] 3525[P] 5303[6]

Kentucky Star (FR) *Dan Skelton* 124h
6 ch g Kentucky Dynamite(USA) La Gloria (Halling (USA))
1977[9] 2499[9] 4492[F] 4986[2] 5277[3]

Keppel Isle (IRE) *Laura Mongan* 96h
6 b g Heron Island(IRE) Wadi Khaled (FR) (Bering)
1893[3] 2253[2] 5067[7]

Keppols Queen (IRE) *Mrs John Harrington* 140h
7 br m Indian River(FR) Keppols Princess (IRE) (Soviet Lad (USA))
2525a[7] (3356a) 4699[6]

Kerisper (FR) *Nigel Twiston-Davies* 128h
6 b g Robin Des Champs(FR) Tina Rederie (FR) (Cadoudal (FR))
1635[P] 2406[2] ◆ 2995[3] 3336[3] 3844[8] (4821) 5275[5]

Kerrieonvic (IRE) *C Byrnes* 134h
8 b g Old Vic Naughty Executive (IRE) (Executive Perk)
2525a[3]

Kerrow (IRE) *Alan King* 122h
5 b g Mahler Olives Hall (IRE) (Saddlers' Hall (IRE))
2450[4] 3133[4] 4063[U] 5356[2]

Kerryhead Storm (IRE) *Matt Sheppard* 109h 119c
10 b g Glacial Storm(USA) Kerryhead Girl (IRE) (Be My Native (USA))
338[7] 2246[3] 2691[8] 3313[4] 3931[7] (4587) 4852[5]

Kerry Maur *Chris Gordon* 65h
6 b g Kayf Tara Eau De Vie (Terimon)
1243[F] 2004[P]

Kerry Mganga *Robert Stephens*
9 gr g M'Bebe Kerry Veil (Aspect (USA))
1134[P]

Kerry's Lord (IRE) *Joanne Thomason-Murphy* 71h
6 br g Lend A Hand Tesses Express (IRE) (Flemensfirth (USA))
2141[7] 3063[6] 3588[4] 3976[9] 4391[7] 4528[P] 5481[5]

Kettle *Donald Whillans*
4 b m Beat Hollow Eiszeit (GER) (Java Gold (USA))
662[6]

Kev The Car (IRE) *Paul Cowley* 95b
5 br g Gamut(IRE) Dancing Baloo (IRE) (Broken Hearted)
5365[6]

Key Account (IRE) *L Byrne* 106h 99c
7 b g Key Of Luck(USA) Messina (IRE) (Sadler's Wells (USA))
1686[5]

Keychain (IRE) *Brendan Powell* 101h 104c
5 b g Key Of Luck(USA) Sarifa (IRE) (Kahyasi)
64[5] 381[P] 835[5] 977[3] 1245[2] 1356[2] **1894[3] 2124[4] 2220[5]**

Key People (IRE) *J Lean* 113h 104c
8 b g Alderbrook Diamond Forever (Teenoso (USA))
5467[3]

Key To Milan *Chris Down* 111h
9 b g Milan Key West (FR) (Highest Honor (FR))
828[6] 1048[2] 1238[5] 1545[7] 2458[10]

Key To The West (IRE) *Matt Sheppard* 127h 130c
8 b g Westerner Monte Solaro (IRE) (Key Of Luck (USA))
2153[2] 2468[F] 2659[3] 3257[F]

Khazium (IRE) *Claire Dyson* 87c
6 br g Kheleyf(USA) Hazium (IRE) (In The Wings)
5231[P]

Kheskianto (IRE) *Michael Chapman* 76h
9 b m Kheleyf(USA) Gently (IRE) (Darshaan)
1261[9] 1384[9] 1793[7] 1941[4] 2217[6] 2554[P]

Khezerabad (FR) *Nicky Henderson* 133h
3 ch g Dalakhani(IRE) Khelwa (FR) (Traditionally (USA))
4358[3] 5175[P]

Kiama Bay (IRE) *Jim Best* 137h 115c
9 b g Fraam La Panthere (USA) (Pine Bluff (USA))
2981[3] 3975[4] 4353[7]

Kicking Lily *Ann Hamilton* 74b
5 b m Great Palm(USA) Miss Royello (Royal Fountain)
1688[6] 1923[P]

Kick On (FR) *P Cottin* 108h 132c
6 b g Poliglote Kilda (IRE) (Night Shift (USA))
(313a)

Kid Kalanisi (IRE) *Dan Skelton* 104h
4 b g Kalanisi(IRE) Nut Touluze (IRE) (Toulon)
1844[F] 2763[10] 3114[3] 5157[8]

Kid Valentine (IRE) *Michael Smith* 116h
5 b g Scorpion(IRE) Supreme Nova (Supreme Leader)
1901[4] ◆ (5009) ◆ 5368[3]

Kie (IRE) *David Pipe* 124h 148c
7 b g Old Vic Asura (GER) (Surumu (GER))
1039[13] 1325[6] **(1481) 1976[5] 2061[11]**

Kilas Girl (IRE) *John Quinn* 102h
5 b m Millenary Ballybeg Dusty (IRE) (Beneficial)
4151[2] 4644[5]

Kilbree Chief (IRE) *Lucinda Russell* 126h 131c
7 b g Dr Massini(IRE) Lame Excuse (IRE) (Presenting)
3345[2] 3669[2] 4054[2] (4407) 5323[2]

Kilbree Kid (IRE) *Tom George* 113h 136c
8 b g Cloudings(IRE) Bustingoutallover (USA) (Trempolino (USA))
(660) 868[2] 1616[4] 1944[5] 2471[8] 3017[P] 4101[8] 4444[P] 4914[5] 5395[3]

Kilcascan *Rosemary Gasson* 98c
11 b g Alflora(IRE) Peasedown Tofana (Teenoso (USA))
340[5] 698[2] 926[3] 1079[2] 1287[9] 1930[3] 2402[2] 2836[3] (3062) 3222[P] 4534[3]

Kilcooley (IRE) *Charlie Longsdon* 167h
6 b g Stowaway Bealaha Essie (IRE) (Denel (FR))
(2198) ◆ 4732[P]

Kilcrea Vale (IRE) *Nicky Henderson* 144h
5 b g Beneficial Inflation (FR) (Port Etienne (FR))
2614[F] 3733[6] 5497[9]

Kilcross Boy (IRE) *Neil Mulholland* 100h 81c
10 b g Snurge Sumtinforaweekend (IRE) (Supreme Leader)
864[2] **1004[9]** 1236[3]

Kilcullen Article (IRE) *Michael Scudamore* 93h
7 b g Definite Article Mood I'm In (GER) (Saddlers' Hall (IRE))
136[P] 758[P]

Kilcullen Flem (IRE) *Rebecca Curtis* 120h
5 ch g Flemensfirth(USA) Cansalrun (IRE) (Anshan)
1648[4] 4123[3] 4467[4] (4711) 5235[5]

Kilcullen Lady (IRE) *Henry Hogarth* 59b
5 b m Scorpion(IRE) Glittering Star (IRE) (Good Thyne (USA))
970[11]

Kilda Six (FR) *D Bressou* 109h 100c
4 gr g Martaline Kilda (IRE) (Night Shift (USA))
2362a[P] **4401a[2]**

Kilfinichen Bay (IRE) *Charlie Longsdon* 136h 146c
7 b g Westerner Cailin Deas (IRE) (Pistolet Bleu (IRE))
(625) (774) (1035) (1594) 2054[5] 4730[P] **(5101)**

Kilford (IRE) *Leonard Whitmore* 105h 133c
9 ch g Snurge African Waters (IRE) (Be My Native (USA))
(4663a) 5005a[P]

Kilgefin Star (IRE) *Michael Smith* 129h 137c
7 b g Saddlers' Hall(IRE) High Church Annie (IRE) (Bustomi)
329[3] 1900[3] (2341) 2932[F]

Kilkishen (IRE) *John Joseph Hanlon* 128h
5 b g Oscar(IRE) Coming Home (FR) (Exit To Nowhere (USA))
1837[4]

Killabraher Cross (IRE) *Paddy Butler* 87h 95c
8 gr g Kasmayo Enoughrose (IRE) (Roselier (FR))
(1999) 2255[2] 2714[U] (5482)

Killala Quay *Charlie Longsdon* 149h 151c
8 b g Karinga Bay Madam Bijou (Atraf)
(1782) 2726[4] 3136[4] (4359) 4701[14] 5324[4]

Killer Crow (IRE) *Gordon Elliott* 127h 137c
6 ch g Presenting Rivervail (IRE) (River Falls)
50a[19] **3302a[2] 3651a[2] 5005a[7] 5193[19]**

Killer Miller (IRE) *Noel Meade* 117h 139c
6 b g Flemensfirth(USA) Miss Brandywell (IRE) (Sadler's Wells (USA))
2531a[3]

Killfinnan Castle (IRE) *Violet M Jordan* 47h 76c
12 br g Arctic Lord(IRE) Golden Seekers (Manado)
589[P]

Killiecrankie *Kenneth Slack* 100h
7 b g Kayf Tara Bella Macrae (Bustino)
1399[7] 2210[9] 3239[5] 4550[P]

Killimordaly (IRE) *Andy Turnell* 89h 104c
6 bb g Indian River(FR) Bramblehill Fairy (IRE) (Toulon)
610[2] ◆ 1079[P] 1309[P] 1462[P] 1646[4]

Killone (IRE) *Stuart Coltherd*
6 gr g Flemensfirth(USA) Ceol Tire (IRE) (Roselier (FR))
3153[P] 3883[P]

Killshannon (IRE) *David Bridgwater* 86h 89c
6 ch g Royal Anthem(USA) Fortune And Favour (IRE) (Homo Sapien)
752[P] 861[3]

Killultagh Vic (IRE) *W P Mullins* 157h 156c
6 b g Old Vic Killultagh Dawn (IRE) (Phardante (FR))
(21a) **(3652a)**

Kilmacallogue Bay *C T Dawson* 77h 79c
9 b g Karinga Bay Wahiba Reason (IRE) (Robellino (USA))
472[4]

Kilmainham (IRE) *Martin Todhunter* 121h 96c
7 b g Celtic Swing Newhall (IRE) (Shernazar)
1330[6] 1496[4] 1853[U] 2191[3] 2320[U] 3669[P] 3973[8] 4163[12] 4415[7] 4739[5] **5125[11]** 5198[6]

Kilmurvy (IRE) *Jeremy Scott* 115h 129c
7 b g Shantou(USA) Spagna (IRE) (Definite Article)
(86) 1701[3] 2240[2] 2733[5] 5285[5]

Kilquiggan (IRE) *Sandy Thomson* 93h
7 gr g Vinnie Roe(IRE) Irene's Call (IRE) (Cardinal Flower)
299[4] 2102[6] 2937[3] 4638[6] 4840[6] 5367[P] 5412[12]

Kilronan Castle *Donald McCain* 120h
4 ch g Indian River(FR) Greatest Friend (IRE) (Mandalus)
1717[4] 2100[7] 2754[5] 3009[4] 3398[5] 4455[3] (5122)

Kilronan High (IRE) *Nigel Twiston-Davies* 119h 134c
6 b m Mountain High(IRE) Broadcast (Broadsword (USA))
1642[5] 1904[8] (2837) 3014[F] 3849[P] 4319[3] 5281[2]

Kilrush (IRE) *John Berwick* 83h 69c
9 gr g Dilshaan Pride Of Passion (IRE) (Daylami (IRE))
3415[P] 3977[P] 4543[P] 5165[P] 5431[5]

Kilty Caul (IRE) *Kim Bailey* 106h
6 b m Beneficial Gale Johnston (IRE) (Strong Gale)
152[12] 1716[7] 1960[2] 2302[4] 2632[4] 3333[3]

Kimora (IRE) *Debra Hamer* 79h 101c
9 b m Bach(IRE) Blue Gale (IRE) (Be My Native (USA))
(297) 1118[7]

Kinari (IRE) *Peter Bowen* 100h 95c
5 b g Captain Rio Baraza (IRE) (Kalanisi (IRE))
773[3] **1450[4] 2269[P] 2827[5] 3663[4]**

Kincora Fort (IRE) *Noel Williams* 115h
6 b g Brian Boru Glenview Rose (IRE) (Roselier (FR))
(283)

Kind Of Easy (IRE) *Alistair Whillans* 107h 117c
9 b g Kalanisi(IRE) Specifiedrisk (IRE) (Turtle Island (IRE))
2800[4] 3344[3] 3855[14] 4206[2] 4586[3] 4840[P]

King Alfonso *Dai Burchell* 128h 123c
6 br g Desert King(IRE) Satire (Terimon)
406[4] **697[3] 830[4] 1643[9] 1809[4] 1962[3] 2184[7] 2266[9]**

King Boru (IRE) *Dan Skelton* 126h 97c
7 b g Brian Boru Final Instalment (IRE) (Insan (USA))
523[P] 1615[2] 2054[B]

King Charlie (IRE) *Suzy Smith* 50h
5 b g Chevalier(IRE) Desert Treat (IRE) (Desert Prince (IRE))
4102[13] 4382[P] 4930[5]

King Cool *Gary Moore* 117h
4 b g King's Theatre(IRE) Cool Spice (Karinga Bay)
3949[6] (4382) 4526[F] 4930[2]

Kingcora (FR) *Venetia Williams* 133h 129c
7 b g King's Theatre(IRE) Coralisse Royale (FR) (Tip Moss (FR))
149[P] 448[7]

Kingdom (IRE) *Gary Moore* 108h
5 b g Montjeu(IRE) Shadow Song (IRE) (Pennekamp (USA))
554[4]

Kingfisher Creek *Colin Tizzard* 126h 115c
5 b g Kayf Tara Symbiosis (Bien Bien (USA))
2122[6] 2545[3] 4452[4] 5120[F] (Dead)

King Fontaine (IRE) *Lawney Hill* 92h 118c
12 b g King's Theatre(IRE) Kerfontaine (Lafontaine I (USA))
1007[4] 1309[P] (1592) 1820[4] 2028[5]

King Kayf *Noel Williams* 122h
6 b g Kayf Tara Firecracker Lady (IRE) (Supreme Leader)
2807[2] ◆ 3133[2] 3736[P] 4362[5] 4788[P]

King Leon (IRE) *A P O'Brien* 129h 122c
6 b g Mountain High(IRE) None The Wiser (IRE) (Dr Massini (IRE))
2228a[P]

King Massini (IRE) *Evan Williams* 113h 127c
9 b g Dr Massini(IRE) King's Linnet (IRE) (King's Ride)
149[3] 1807[4] (2451) ◆ 2853[4] 4912[5]

King Muro *Fergal O'Brien* 122h
5 b g Halling(USA) Ushindi (IRE) (Montjeu (IRE))
172[5] 354[5] 1001[3] 1095[2] (1307) (1508) 1591[4] 2472[F] 3015[8] 3487[3] 4486[2] (5159) 5414[7]

King Of Alcatraz (IRE) *R C Smith*
9 gr g Great Palm(USA) Foxy Flame (IRE) (Tremblant)
393[2] 536[8] 5392[P]

King Of All Kings (IRE) *Peter Bowen* 92h
5 b g Craigsteel Back The Queen (IRE) (Bob Back (USA))
440[5] 613[8] 1001[P]

King Of Fashion (IRE) *Ian Duncan* 90h
5 ch g Desert King(IRE) French Fashion (IRE) (Jamesmead)
732[5] 887[3] 1399[4]

King Of Glory *Venetia Williams* 109h 118c
7 b g Kayf Tara Glory Be (Gunner B)
2346[4] 2668[P] (3384)

King Of Milan (IRE) *Des Donovan* 44h
5 b g Milan Opera Mask (IRE) (Moscow Society (USA))
4322[P] 4535[P] 5372[9]

King Of Strings (IRE) *Mark Walford* 107h
6 b g Desert King(IRE) Lemon Cello (IRE) (Accordion)
(77) (205) 354[3] 593[4]

King Of The Dark (IRE) *Victor Thompson* 89h 106c
8 b g Zagreb(USA) Dark Bird (IRE) (Lashkari)
135[4] 253[F] 453[3] 635[6] 3159[3] **4938[4] 5234[2] 5369[5]**

King Of The Picts (IRE) *John Patrick Shanahan* 140h 131c
6 ch g Rock Of Gibraltar(IRE) Belle Rebelle (IRE) (In The Wings)
96a[15] 1333[4] **1679a[3] 2232a[5] 3301a[4]** 3768a[4] 4133a[4]

King Of The Wolds (IRE) *Malcolm Jefferson* 128h 136c
8 b g Presenting Azaban (IRE) (Be My Native (USA))
1632[2] 2213[3] 2638[4] 4109[2] 4609[3] 5200[4]

King Rolfe (IRE) *Tim Vaughan* 98h 126c
7 b g King's Theatre(IRE) Lady Rolfe (IRE) (Alzao (USA))
109[P]

Kings Apollo *Tom Symonds* 94h 113c
6 b g King's Theatre(IRE) Temple Dancer (Magic Ring (IRE))
2724[F] 2872[6] (3373) 3788[3] 4062[4] 4255[P] 5149[P]

Kings Bandit (IRE) *Oliver Sherwood* 135h 123c
7 b g King's Theatre(IRE) Gentle Lady (IRE) (Strong Gale)
2201[U] 2746[4]

Kings Bayonet *Alan King* 131h
8 ch g Needwood Blade Retaliator (Rudimentary (USA))
917[6] 2926[3] (3487) 4484[8] 4913[2]

King's Chorister *Barry Murtagh* 98h 88c
9 ch g King's Best(USA) Chorist (Pivotal)
504[3] 731[6] 1405[2] 1887[7] 2982[4] 3244[5] 4049[2] 4326[5] 4404[8] 4797[2]

Kingscombe (USA) *Linda Jewell* 59h
6 rg g Mizzen Mast(USA) Gombeen (USA) (Private Account (USA))
65[6] 451[7] 3177[7] 3489[P]

Kingscourt Native (IRE) *Colin Tizzard* 137h
7 b g King's Theatre(IRE) Freydis (IRE) (Supreme Leader)
2397[F] 2660[P] 3622[P] 4362[P] 5185[9]

Kings Cross (FR) *Tony Carroll* 96h 120c
5 bb g King's Theatre(IRE) Ladies Choice (FR) (Turgeon (USA))
2182[11] 2472[14] **(2832) 3044[2] 3499[5] 3731[3] 4225[3] 4545[5] 4910[5] 5071[2]**

Kingsfold Flare *W Russell* 81b
8 ch m Central Park(IRE) Kingsfold Blaze (Mazilier (USA))
297[P]

Kings Folly (IRE) *Lucinda Russell* 104h
7 b g Dushyantor(USA) Beltane Queen (IRE) (Strong Gale)
2754[4] ◆ 3424[P]

Kings Grey (IRE) *Philip Kirby* 109h 135c
11 gr g King's Theatre(IRE) Grey Mo (IRE) (Roselier (FR))
(709) 968[P] **1186a[P] 4207[P] 4651[P]**

King Simba (IRE) *Kim Bailey* 108h
4 b g Let The Lion Roar Anaaween (USA) (Diesis)
188[11] 2406[6] 2747[6] 3019[8] 3411[P] (5374)

Kings Lad (IRE) *Colin Tizzard* 128h 147c
8 b g King's Theatre(IRE) Festival Leader (IRE) (Supreme Leader)
2242[3] 2625[2] 2761[7] 3147[4] 4100[4] 4733[P] 5391[6]

King's Legacy (IRE) *Lawney Hill* 116h 119c
11 b g King's Theatre(IRE) Kotton (FR) (Cyborg (FR))
781[3] 1167[9] 1500[F] 1767[5] 1987[2]

Kingsmere *Henry Daly* 128h 139c
10 b g King's Theatre(IRE) Lady Emily (Alflora (IRE))
319[7] 1963[6] **2471[U]** 5284[7]

King's Odyssey (IRE) *Evan Williams* 125h 155c
6 b g King's Theatre(IRE) Ma Furie (FR) (Balleroy (USA))
2557[3] (3255) (3849)

King's Opus (IRE) *Kim Bailey* 77h
6 b g King's Theatre(IRE) Kahysera (Kahyasi)
1525[P]

Kings Palace (IRE) *David Pipe* 151h 154c
7 b g King's Theatre(IRE) Sarahs Quay (IRE) (Witness Box (USA))
2483[11] 4354[P] **4733[3]** 5213[P] (Dead)

King's Realm (IRE) *Tina Jackson* 102h 55c
8 ch g King's Best(USA) Sweet Home Alabama (IRE) (Desert Prince (IRE))
520[4] ◆ 747[6] **913[5]**

King's Request (IRE) *Laura Mongan* 116h
5 ch g New Approach(IRE) Palace Weekend (USA) (Seattle Dancer (USA))
283[5]

Kings River (FR) *Venetia Williams* 92h 102c
6 bb g Lost World(IRE) Si Parfaite (FR) (Solon (GER))
2162[2] 2453[8] **(2698) 3412[P] 3977[7]**

King's Road *Anabel K Murphy* 105h
10 ch g King's Best(USA) Saphire (College Chapel)
354[P] 2253[8] 2550[4] 3233[7]

King's Song (FR) *David Dennis* 97h 112c
5 b g King's Theatre(IRE) Chanson Indienne (FR) (Indian River (FR))
(1510) 1573[7] 1819[7] 1961[2] 2245[4] **(2692) 2861[4]**

Kingston Mimosa *Mark Gillard* 84h
3 b g Kheleyf(USA) Derartu (AUS) (Last Tycoon)
2757[P] 2954[5] 3347[6] 4849[8]

Kings Walk (IRE) *Colin Tizzard* 93b
4 b g King's Theatre(IRE) Shuil Sionnach (IRE) (Mandalus)
67[4] 4790[8]

Kingswell Theatre *Michael Scudamore* 125h 137c
6 b g King's Theatre(IRE) Cresswell Native (IRE) (Be My Native (USA))
(2289) (2905) 3364[6] 3998[P] 4341[3] 4800[P]

Kingussie *Ben Pauling* 96h
7 b g Diktat Highland Gait (Most Welcome)
3130[4] 3839[13] 4233[5] 4856[P]

King Uther *Chris Gordon* 120b
5 b g Master Blade Cadbury Castle (Midyan (USA))
3502[5] 3907[2] (4385) 5195[10]

King Vuvuzela (IRE) *Paul Nolan* 120h 134c
8 b g Flemensfirth(USA) Coolgavney Girl (IRE) (Good Thyne (USA))
24a[P]

Kinnitty Castle (IRE) *A J Martin* 104h
5 b g Beneficial Jendam (IRE) (Fourstars Allstar (USA))
73a[P] 5024a[P]

Kipuka *Nigel Hawke* 74h
3 b f Authorized(IRE) Rakata (USA) (Quiet American (USA))
4916[8] 5462[6]

Kir Royal *Alan King* 102b
4 ch m Lucarno(USA) Priscilla (Teenoso (USA))
2729[3] ◆ 3862[4]

Kisha Lad (IRE) *Richard Woollacott* 67h
8 b g Luso Baile An Droichid (IRE) (King's Ride)
1117[12]

Kisumu *Micky Hammond* 102h
3 b g High Chaparral(IRE) Arum Lily (USA) (Woodman (USA))
2718[3] 3099[6] 3790[3] 4416[4]

Kit Casey (IRE) *Rebecca Curtis* 117h
5 b g Robin Des Pres(FR) An Culainn Beag (IRE) (Supreme Leader)
3467[6] (4614)

Kitchapoly (FR) *Donald McCain* 119h 119c
5 b g Poliglote Kotkicha (FR) (Mansonnien (FR))
557[3] 677[P] 1043[3] 1416[2] ◆ 1738[4]

Kitegen (IRE) *Robin Dickin* 110h 118c
9 b g Milan Keen Gale (IRE) (Strong Gale)
331[6] 623[2] 857[2] 1424[5] 1577[4] 1755[4] 5394[2] ◆

Kitty Power (IRE) *Nigel Twiston-Davies* 75b
6 b m Presenting Hannigan's Lodger (IRE) (Be My Native (USA))
45[5]

Kk Lexion (IRE) *Tom George* 108h
4 b g Flemensfirth(USA) Kiloradante (IRE) (Phardante (FR))
3839[8] 4303[6]

Klaazia (FR) *Jeremy Gask* 94b
4 gr m Sinndar(IRE) Kritzia (Daylami (IRE))
159[2] 928[3]

Klaus (POL) *Cestmir Olehla* 122c
10 b g Jape(USA) Klara (POL) (Who Knows I (IRE))
1885a[11]

Kleitomachos (IRE) *Stuart Kittow* 112h
7 b g Barathea(IRE) Theben (GER) (Monsun (GER))
(2736) 2985[3] 3607[P] 4882[7]

Klepht (IRE) *D Holmes* 108h 120c
10 b g Great Palm(USA) What A Mewsment (IRE) (Persian Mews)
24a[11] 1186a[10] (4180) 5312[2]

Knight Bachelor *Warren Greatrex* 117h
5 ch g Midnight Legend Fenney Spring (Polish Precedent (USA))
380[2] 593[P] 2595[9] 5479[2] ◆

Knight In Purple *John Mackie* 119h
11 b g Sir Harry Lewis(USA) Cerise Bleue (FR) (Port Lyautey (FR))
520[2] 751[7] 2170[10]

Knightly Escapade *Brian Ellison* 101h
7 ch g Sakhee(USA) Queen Of Iceni (Erhaab (USA))
1260[8]

Knightly Pleasure *Gary Moore* 103b
4 b m Kayf Tara Kim Fontenail (FR) (Kaldounevees (FR))
1758[7] (5308)

Knight Of Pleasure *Gary Moore* 107h 119c
6 ch g Exit To Nowhere(USA) Kim Fontenail (FR) (Kaldounevees (FR))
2600[5]

Knight ofthe Realm *Caroline Keevil* 112h
6 b g Kayf Tara Flow (Over The River (FR))
2087[8] (2658) 2732[4] 3146[2] 3824[P] 4543[6]

Knight Pass (IRE) *Jimmy Frost* 128b
9 b g Accordion Toulon Pass (IRE) (Toulon)
894[P]

Knight's Parade (IRE) *Sarah Humphrey* 101h 100c
5 b g Dark Angel(IRE) Toy Show (IRE) (Danehill (USA))
1175a[17] 1633[P] 2150[4] 4774[13]

Knight's Reward *Tim Vaughan* 95h
5 b g Sir Percy Wardeh (Zafonic (USA))
4291[10] 4674[5] 5352[5]

Knight To Open (IRE) *Rebecca Curtis* 79b
5 b g Oscar(IRE) Sunset View (IRE) (Good Thyne (USA))
2317[7]

Knight Watchman (IRE) *Harry Fry*
5 b g Brian Boru Final Instalment (IRE) (Insan (USA))
2088[P]

Knock A Hand (IRE) *Kerry Lee* 135h 135c
10 br g Lend A Hand Knockcross (IRE) (Lake Coniston (IRE))
95a[P] 2436[P] 3057[4] 3448[P] 4568[4]

Knockalongi *Dominic Ffrench Davis* 109h 117c
9 b g Fair Mix(IRE) Understudy (In The Wings)
2985[10] 4069[8] **4380[5] 4789[8]**

Knockanarrigan (IRE) *Ms Sandra Hughes* 115h 123c
7 b g Shantou(USA) Ruby Thewes (IRE) (Anshan)
2675a[8] 3296a[11]

Knockanrawley (IRE) *Kim Bailey* 129h 143c
7 gr g Portrait Gallery(IRE) Hot Lips (IRE) (Good Thyne (USA))
2482[3]

Knockara Beau (IRE) *George Charlton* 144h 148c
12 b g Leading Counsel(USA) Clairabell (IRE) (Buckskin (FR))
3407[2] 3853[4] 4732[P] 5085[6]

Knockgraffon (IRE) *Dan Skelton* 137h
5 b g Flemensfirth(USA) Gleaming Spire (Overbury (IRE))
2080[2] (2807) ◆ 3787[2] 4622[7] (4917)

Knock House (IRE) *Mick Channon* 131h 151c
6 ch g Old Vic Lady's Gesture (IRE) (Anshan)
1944[2] (2473) 3016[4] 3993[F] 4735[4] 5217[P]

Knocklayde (IRE) *Katie Scott* 70b
3 b g Mountain High(IRE) Foret Noire (IRE) (Barathea (IRE))
4408[4] (5371)

Knocklayde Sno Cat (IRE) *S R B Crawford* 100h
6 b m King's Theatre(IRE) Sno-Cat Lady (IRE) (Executive Perk)
5034 3666[3] 4052[F] 4369[2] 4608[F] 5329[7]

Knocklong (IRE) *Ben Haslam* 114h 121c
7 b g Milan Banningham Blaze (Averti (IRE))
203[P] 1522[9] 1692[4]

Knockyoursocksoff (IRE) *Gary Moore* 82h 100c
5 b g Tikkanen(USA) Didn't You Know (FR) (Trempolino (USA))
674[2] ◆ 752[2] 1287[3]

Know The Rules (IRE) *Mrs G Smith* 94h 84c
10 b g Presenting Gift Token (Batshoof)
80[P] 521[4]

Knysna Bay *Chris Grant* 29h
4 b m Millkom Knysna Belle (Royal Fountain)
1688[7] 4037[11] 5229[6]

Kobrouk (FR) *G Macaire* 124h 149c
4 b g Saint Des Saints(FR) Kotkira (FR) (Subotica (FR))
(1882a) 2820a[5]

Kodicil (IRE) *Mark Walford* 113h 130c
7 b g Kodiac Miss Caoimhe (IRE) (Barathea (IRE))
624[4] (1601) 2329[F]

K O Kenny *Andrew Crook* 97b
4 b g Apple Tree(FR) Cool Island (IRE) (Turtle Island (IRE))
4371[4]

Kokomo *Noel Williams* 71b
4 b m Shirocco(GER) Kohiba (IRE) (Rock Of Gibraltar (IRE))
4074[9] 4974[3]

Kolaphos *Martin Brassil* 126h
7 b g Kayf Tara Devon Peasant (Deploy)
50a[11] (Dead)

Konig Dax (GER) *David Pipe* 50h
5 b g Saddex Konigin Shuttle (GER) (Big Shuffle (USA))
4685[F]

Konnos Bay *Brendan Powell* 26h
3 b g Phoenix Reach(IRE) Rasmalai (Sadler's Wells (USA))
1593[4] 1732[P]

Koolala (IRE) *Paul Webber* 118h
7 b m Kayf Tara Squaw Talk (USA) (Gulch (USA))
2925[P] 3866[P]

Kool Lady (IRE) *Des Donovan* 51h
4 b m Brian Boru Sarogini (IRE) (Executive Perk)
5019[5] 5373[12]

Korfou De Maspie (FR) *S Foucher* 132h 136c
6 gr g Fairly Ransom(USA) Vagueline De Maspi (FR) (Vaguely Pleasant (FR))
437a[2] 4540a[8]

Koultas King (IRE) *Tim Vaughan* 108h 108c
8 b g Exit To Nowhere(USA) Carrigmoorna Style (IRE) (Dr Massini (IRE))
939[9] 1113[11] **1380[2]** 1573[2] ◆ **1987[P]**

Koup De Kanon (FR) *Donald McCain* 127h 84c
9 b g Robin Des Pres(FR) Coup De Sabre (FR) (Sabrehill (USA))
1110[5] 1494[F] 1720[3]

Krackatoa King *Noel Williams* 129h 125c
7 b g Kayf Tara Firecracker Lady (IRE) (Supreme Leader)
2442[8] 3707[3] 4649[3] ◆ 4935[2] ◆

Krafty One *Michael Scudamore*
3 ch f Mastercraftsman(IRE) Wonderful Desert (Green Desert (USA))
3338[P]

Kris Cross (IRE) *Lucinda Russell* 118h 123c
8 ch g Kris Kin(USA) Perfidia (Perpendicular)
3428[5] 4206[9] 4911[P]

Kris Spin (IRE) *Kerry Lee* 147h 96c
7 br g Kris Kin(USA) Auditing Empress (IRE) (Accordion)
3197[3]

Kristal Star *Alex Hales* 43b
3 b f Midnight Legend Royal Musical (Royal Abjar (USA))
3847[12]

Krugermac (IRE) *Gary Moore* 123h
4 bb g Kalanisi(IRE) Vindonissa (IRE) (Definite Article)
(2612) ◆ 3043[2]

Kruzhlinin (GER) *Philip Hobbs* 134h 153c
8 ch g Sholokhov(IRE) Karuma (GER) (Surumu (GER))
(3528) 4697[5] 5218[P]

Kublai (FR) *Philip Hobbs* 123h
5 b g Laveron Java Dawn (IRE) (Fleetwood (IRE))
1579[9] (2694) 4362[11]

Kuda Huraa (IRE) *Harriet Bethell* 121h 110c
7 b g Montjeu(IRE) Healing Music (FR) (Bering)
63[2] 638[6] 2042[4] 2499[5] 3035[3] 3238[6] 4152[2] 4861[2]

Kudu Country (IRE) *Evan Williams* 117h 132c
9 gr g Captain Rio Nirvavita (FR) (Highest Honor (FR))
2516[5] **2854[F] 3107[F]** 5464[9]

Kudu Shine *Richard Woollacott* 104h 98c
9 b g Karinga Bay Flora Bright (Alflora (IRE))
108[P] 3410[4] 4250[8] 5431[9]

Kumbeshwar *Lucinda Russell* 116h 130c
8 b g Doyen(IRE) Camp Fire (IRE) (Lahib (USA))
1331[3] 1628[2] 5262[3]

Kylecrue (IRE) *John Patrick Ryan* 128h 128c
8 b g Gold Well Sher's Adamant (IRE) (Shernazar)
95a[P] 2228a[3] 2675a[3] 3302a[P] 4397a[3]

Kylemore Lough *Kerry Lee* 131h 162c
6 b g Revoque(IRE) One Of The Last (Supreme Leader)
1782[3] (2489) (3121) (4247) (4624) ◆ (4956a)

Kyles Faith (IRE) *Martin Keighley* 105h 111c
7 b g Court Cave(IRE) Littleton Liberty (Royal Applause)
239[5] 758[6] 917[4] 1010[4] 1137[3] 1181[5] **1298[5]** 1478[6] 1646[5] **1820[3] 2057[10]** 2453[6] **2542[4]**

Kylestyle (IRE) *F Flood* 129h 120c
6 b g Oscar(IRE) Bobs Star (IRE) (Bob Back (USA))
19a[16]

Kylie's Kenny *Derek Shaw*
5 b g Deportivo Haunt The Zoo (Komaite (USA))
3847[13]

Kyllachykov (IRE) *Rebecca Bastiman* 89h
7 ch g Kyllachy Dance On (Caerleon (USA))
4861[4] 5230[5]

Laajooj (IRE) *John Ferguson* 87h
7 b g Azamour(IRE) Flanders (IRE) (Common Grounds)
1499[4]

La Baghera (FR) *E Leray*
4 b m Forestier(FR) La Dauvilla (FR) (Seattle Dancer (USA))
1231a[3]

La Bague Au Roi (FR) *Warren Greatrex* 126b
4 b m Doctor Dino(FR) Alliance Royale (FR) (Turgeon (USA))
(2086) (2929) ◆ 5180[7]

Label Des Obeaux (FR) *Alan King* 138h
4 b g Saddler Maker(IRE) La Bessiere (FR) (Loup Solitaire (USA))
2630[2] (2886) ◆ 3350[3] 4097[2] 4769[12]

Lacerta *Micky Hammond* 68h
4 b g Astronomer Royal(USA) Rubber (IRE) (Namid)
2498[5] 2804[4] 3054[P] (Dead)

Lachlan Bridge (GER) *A Chaille-Chaille* 140h 143c
7 b g Dubawi(IRE) Lady Zorreghuietta (FR) (Anabaa (USA))
664a[4] 2822a[RR]

Lachlan Mor *Stuart Coltherd* 72b 17c
6 b g Josr Algarhoud(IRE) Miss Campanella (Bal Harbour)
4180[U]

Lackamon *Sue Smith* 119h 136c
10 b g Fleetwood(IRE) Pearlossa (Teenoso (USA))
471[3] 1903[8] **2146[2] 2638[2] 3024[4] (3591) 4367[9]** 4794[7]

Lac Leman (GER) *Pauline Robson* 120h
4 b g Doyen(IRE) Learned Lady (JPN) (Fuji Kiseki (JPN))
2928[5] 3083[4] (3470) 4010[P]

Lac Sacre (FR) *John Flint* 112h 123c
6 b g Bering Lady Glorieuse (FR) (Le Glorieux)
2404[5] 2663[P] 2858[5] 3080[4] 4266[2] 4448[4] 4825[4]

La Dama De Hierro *Malcolm Jefferson* 105h
5 gr m Proclamation(IRE) Altogether Now (IRE) (Step Together I (USA))
1627[3] 1854[6] 2287[6] (2936) 3344[7]

Ladfromhighworth *Jeremy Scott* 124c
10 b g Kier Park(IRE) Cavisoir (Afzal)
598[2] ◆ 827[4] 1007[2] (1267) 1523[4] 1641[2] 1965[2] 2404[2]

Ladies Dancing *Chris Down* 107h 81c
9 b g Royal Applause Queen Of Dance (IRE) (Sadler's Wells (USA))
281[4] 515[4] 810[3] 835[4] 1048[3] (1083) 1508[3] 1810[8] 5386[3]

Lady A *Chris Gordon* 90h
5 ch m Apple Tree(FR) Lady Kay (Kayf Tara)
1756[7] 4290[P] 4783[P]

Lady Ash (IRE) *Robert Walford* 83b
5 gr m Scorpion(IRE) La Fiamma (FR) (General Assembly (USA))
4242[8] 5187[4]

Lady Beaufort *John Quinn* 101b
4 ch m Shirocco(GER) Kadassa (IRE) (Shardari)
(4208)

Lady Bella *Seamus Mullins* 15b
6 b m Beat All(USA) Bromley Supreme (IRE) (Supreme Leader)
1758[11]

Ladybird Blue *Martin Hill*
4 b m Captain Gerrard(IRE) Pacifiste (IRE) (Anabaa (USA))
3111[S]

Lady Brienne (IRE) *Simon West* 65b
6 b m Flemensfirth(USA) Spirit Rock (IRE) (Rock Hopper)
3508[P]

Lady Broome *John David Riches* 31b
4 ch m Erhaab(USA) Minnesinger (Fraam)
4001[P] 4708[7]

Lady Busanda *George Moore* 79h
5 b m Fair Mix(IRE) Spirit Of Ecstacy (Val Royal (FR))
679[6] 1892[6] **2143[F]** 2720[P]

Lady Cardinal (IRE) *Mark Usher* 73b
4 ch m Papal Bull St Finan's Bay (IRE) (Ashkalani (IRE))
1704[5]

Lady Clitico (IRE) *Rebecca Menzies* 108h
4 b m Bushranger(IRE) Villa Nova (IRE) (Petardia)
1328[4] 1499[2] 1684[F] 4036[8] 4871[4]

Lady From Geneva *Brendan Powell* 98h 98c
8 ch m Generous(IRE) Schizo-Phonic (Gildoran)
1490[8] **1546[P]** 1756[2] 1951[2] **(2521)** 2958[2] **3218[2]**

Lady From Milan (IRE) *Ian Duncan* 39b
6 b m Milan Lady Bramble (IRE) (Be My Native (USA))
963[6]

Lady Helissio *Neil Mulholland* 59h
5 b m Helissio(FR) Barton Dante (Phardante (FR))
2021[5] 2345[7] 3119[6] 3382[P]

Lady Knight (IRE) *Andy Turnell* 78h
4 b m Champs Elysees Knight's Place (IRE) (Hamas (IRE))
530[P] 2550[5]

Lady Longshot *Jeremy Scott* 83b
4 b m Needle Gun(IRE) So Long (Nomadic Way (USA))
3861[9]

Lady Markby (IRE) *Emma Lavelle* 95b
4 b m Oscar(IRE) Leitrim Bridge (IRE) (Earl Of Barking (IRE))
2277[14] 3132[8] 4074[7] (5383)

Lady Of Lamanver *Harry Fry* 124h
5 b m Lucarno(USA) Lamanver Homerun (Relief Pitcher)
2164[2] 2455[5] 4779[2] ◆ 5094[2]

Lady Of Llanarmon *Kim Bailey* 102b
4 b m Yeats(IRE) One Gulp (Hernando (FR))
2086[8] 2856[2] 4559[7]

Lady Of Longstone (IRE) *David Pipe* 135h
5 ch m Beneficial Christdalo (IRE) (Glacial Storm (USA))
240[7] (443) 615[2] 759[7] 878[2] 1085[5] 1236[9] 1547[6] 1841[2] (1910) (2022) 2167[P] 2349[2] (2687) 2911[6] 4139[P] 4445[2] (4909) 5282[11]

Lady Percy (IRE) *Mark Usher* 54h
6 b m Sir Percy Genuinely (IRE) (Entrepreneur)
2543[11]

Lady Persephone (FR) *Alan King* 99h
4 br m Sir Percy Acenanga (GER) (Acatenango (GER))
2164[4] 2778[5] 3947[P] 4893[6]

Lady Ra (IRE) *Lucinda Egerton* 75h
6 br m Beneficial Thethirstyscholars (IRE) (Be My Native (USA))
383[5] 507[P]

Lady Vivona *Lisa Harrison* 64h
7 gr m Overbury(IRE) Ladylliat (FR) (Simon Du Desert (FR))
155[5] 466[P] 2323[5] 2868[4] 3234[5] 3503[8]

Lady Yeats *George Moore* 111h
4 b m Yeats(IRE) Oblique (IRE) (Giant's Causeway (USA))
1854[3] (2123) 2626[5] (3397)

Lagostovegas (IRE) *David Harry Kelly* 117h
3 b f Footstepsinthesand Reine De Coeur (IRE) (Montjeu (IRE))
4002a[P]

L'Aigle Royal (GER) *John Quinn* 129h
4 b g Sholokhov(IRE) Laren (GER) (Monsun (GER))
1903[2] ◆ 2214[7] 3465[4] 4839[7]

Laird Of Monksford (IRE) *Donald McCain* 91h
6 b g Shantou(USA) Back Log (IRE) (Bob Back (USA))
337[P]

Lake Champlain (IRE) *Mrs John Harrington* 119h
3 b g Manduro(GER) Fantasy Girl (IRE) (Marju (IRE))
5001a[8]

Lake Chapala (IRE) *Tim Vaughan* 96h
6 b g Shantou(USA) Rathcolman Queen (IRE) (Radical)
2736[12] 3108[2] 3816[2] 4025[4]

Lakeshore Lady (IRE) *David Bridgwater* 104h
5 b m Lakeshore Road(USA) Chiminee Chime (IRE) (Lord Americo)
2302[5] 2697[4] 3126[2] 4186[P] 4672[4] 4975[2]

Lake View Lad (IRE) *N W Alexander* 138h
5 gr g Oscar(IRE) Missy O'Brien (IRE) (Supreme Leader)
(2479) ◆ 2804[F] 3436[F] (3668) (4108) ◆ 4636[4] (5196)

La Madonnina (IRE) *Caroline Keevil* 88h 92c
7 b m Milan Supreme Nova (Supreme Leader)
(450) 567[F] 674[8] 1049[P]

Lamanver Alchemy *Tom Lacey* 98h
4 b m Lucarno(USA) Lamanver Homerun (Relief Pitcher)
1811^{5} (2277) 2721^{4} 3386^{2} 3795^{4} 4672^{3}

Lamanver Odyssey *Tom Lacey* 92b
3 b f Lucarno(USA) Lamanver Homerun (Relief Pitcher)
4350^{3} (4687)

Lamblord (IRE) *Robert Walford* 106h
8 b g Brian Boru Princess Symphony (IRE) (Lashkari)
177^{3} 363^{F} 5433^{3}

Lamboro Lad (IRE) *Peter Bowen* 99h 107c
10 b g Milan Orchard Spray (IRE) (Supreme Leader)
1616^{6}

Lamb's Cross *Brian Barr* 86h 93c
9 b g Rainbow High Angie Marinie (Sabrehill (USA))
31^{5} 2346^{P} 2601^{P} 2834^{2} 3199^{U} 3951^{3} 4187^{4} 4686^{3} 4921^{2} 5435^{2}

Lamego (FR) *Mme P Butel* 142h 117c
8 b g Ski Chief(USA) Bal De Foire (FR) (Always Fair (USA))
663a^{F} 1883a^{11} 4540a^{7}

L'Ami Serge (IRE) *Nicky Henderson* 154h 159c
5 b g King's Theatre(IRE) La Zingarella (IRE) (Phardante (FR))
(3451) (3627) 4126^{2} 4729^{3} 5174^{2}

Lamool (GER) *Tim Vaughan* 141h 139c
8 b g Mamool(IRE) Linara (GER) (Windwurf (GER))
318^{3} (710) (1116) 1325^{3} (1457) 1576^{2} (5230)

Lamps *Michael Blake* 127h 61c
8 b g Dynaformer(USA) Conspiring (USA) (Grand Slam (USA))
2405^{RR}

Lanceur (FR) *Lucy Wadham* 120h 120c
6 b g Rail Link Lanciana (IRE) (Acatenango (GER))
2993^{3} 3620^{7} 4098^{F}

Landau (IRE) *Gordon Elliott* 121h
5 gr g Aussie Rules(USA) Before The Storm (Sadler's Wells (USA))
19a^{13}

Landecker (IRE) *N W Alexander* 126h 91c
7 br g Craigsteel Winsome Breeze (IRE) (Glacial Storm (USA))
2067^{6} 2949^{7} 3428^{4} 4206^{5} 4839^{3} 5260^{3} 5446^{P} 5475^{2}

Landmeafortune (IRE) *Martin Todhunter* 95h
6 gr g Touch Of Land(FR) Mayrich (IRE) (Roselier (FR))
1570^{3} 1740^{5} 1852^{P} 1923^{4} 2322^{6} 2706^{3} 3672^{2} ◆ 4581^{4} 5122^{3}

Landscape (FR) *Sheena West* 94h
7 b g Lando(GER) Universelle (USA) (Miswaki (USA))
2600^{9} 3196^{P} 3487^{13}

Lanta's Legacy *Jeremy Scott* 76h
5 ch m Central Park(IRE) Purple Patch (Afzal)
30^{P}

La Paimpolaise (FR) *Gary Moore* 110h
3 b f Linda's Lad Medievale (FR) (Lost World (IRE))
4683^{3} 5116^{9}

Lapalala (IRE) *Philip Hobbs* 111h
4 b m Oscar(IRE) Lala Nova (IRE) (Zaffaran (USA))
67^{10} 4337^{F} 4916^{2} 5373^{4}

La Premiere Dame (FR) *Emma Lavelle*
4 b m Poliglote Sentosa (FR) (Kaldounevees (FR))
1644^{P}

La Pyle (FR) *Philip Hobbs* 83h
4 b m Le Havre(IRE) Lidana (IRE) (King's Best (USA))
2021^{3} 2689^{11} 2959^{5} 3215^{4}

Laraghcon Boy (IRE) *Tony Carroll* 52h
6 ch g Stowaway Hannah Mooney (IRE) (Shahanndeh (IRE))
2581^{12} 2772^{9} 3316^{9}

Largy Girl (IRE) *S R B Crawford* 88b
4 br m Kalanisi(IRE) Sumability (IRE) (Oscar (IRE))
2195^{3} 4908^{7}

Larkhall *Mike Sowersby* 74h 83c
8 b g Saddlers' Hall(IRE) Larkbarrow (Kahyasi)
521^{6} 743^{2} 841^{2} 934^{5} 1273^{5} **1603^{4} 1689^{2} (2040) 2290^{3} (2542) 2976^{6}**

Larks Rising *Caroline Keevil* 110b
7 b g Relief Pitcher Black A Brook (IRE) (Good Thyne (USA))
1673^{F}

Larmor (FR) *Micky Hammond* 97h
4 bl g Green Tune(USA) Mia's Baby (USA) (Rahy (USA))
33^{2} 254^{4}

Larteta (FR) *Sarah Humphrey* 96h 108c
6 b g Enrique Ariel (IRE) (Caerleon (USA))
464^{2} 1005^{7} 2552^{5} 2711^{5} 3422^{4} **4222^{2} 5388^{5}**

Laser Blazer *Alan King* 133h
7 b g Zafeen(FR) Sashay (Bishop Of Cashel)
854^{6} 973^{8} 1661^{2} 1949^{2}

Laser Hawk (IRE) *Evan Williams* 129h 130c
8 b g Rashar(USA) Alphablend (IRE) (Alphabatim (USA))
2779^{3} ◆ 3620^{P} 3747^{3} 4485^{P} 5394^{P}

Laser Light (IRE) *Alan King* 118b
4 b g Kutub(IRE) Sioux Falls (IRE) (Monashee Mountain (USA))
(4188) ◆

Lastbutnotleast (IRE) *Donald McCain* 105b
5 ch m Flemensfirth(USA) Lakil Princess (IRE) (Bering)
(4515) 5180^{8}

Last Echo (IRE) *Tom Symonds* 78h
4 b m Whipper(USA) Priory Rock (IRE) (Rock Of Gibraltar (IRE))
2022^{P} 2565^{4}

Last Encounter (IRE) *Ms Margaret Mullins* 137h
5 b g Beneficial Last Campaign (IRE) (Saddlers' Hall (IRE))
2672a^{3} 3169a^{2} 3459a^{2} 3962a^{5} 4955a^{P}

Last Goodbye (IRE) *Miss Elizabeth Doyle* 143h
4 b g Millenary Welsh Ana (IRE) (Welsh Term)
9a^{8}

Last Pick (IRE) *Barry Murtagh*
5 b g Gamut(IRE) Polyzar (IRE) (Shernazar)
2849^{7}

Last Shot (FR) *Venetia Williams* 95h 126c
8 b g Le Fou(IRE) Lucky Shot (FR) (Corporate Report (USA))
2246^{5}

Last Summer *John Ferguson* 108b
4 ch g New Approach(IRE) Evil Empire (GER) (Acatenango (GER))
(525)

Last Supper *James Bethell* 129h
6 b m Echo Of Light Scotland The Brave (Zilzal (USA))
197^{U} 2199^{5} 2901^{4} 3529^{9}

Last To Leave *Stuart Edmunds* 58b
4 ch g Midnight Legend Time For A Glass (Timeless Times (USA))
4392^{11} 4915^{11}

Last Wish (IRE) *Richard Guest* 95b
4 b g Raven's Pass(USA) Quiet Dream (USA) (Seattle Slew (USA))
682^{7} 1101^{5}

Late For Supper (IRE) *Richard Ford* 79h
6 ch g Kahtan Tillery (IRE) (Peintre Celebre (USA))
1552^{9} 1744^{3}

Late Night Lily *Dan Skelton* 112h
4 b m Midnight Legend Ready To Crown (USA) (More Than Ready (USA))
(2016) 2486^{14} 3221^{2} ◆ 3819^{4} 4507^{2} (5373)

Late Shipment *Nikki Evans* 89h
4 b g Authorized(IRE) Time Over (Mark Of Esteem (IRE))
3570^{7} 4449^{7} 4849^{9} 5163^{5} 5397^{8}

Latest Fashion (IRE) *Christopher Wilson* 83h
9 ch m Ashkalani(IRE) Musical Bramble (IRE) (Accordion)
37^{7} 481^{4} **635^{F} 803^{U}** 4151^{5} 5233^{5}

Latin Rebel (IRE) *Jim Goldie* 88h
8 b g Spartacus(IRE) Dance To The Beat (Batshoof)
2754^{9} 3471^{9} 4033^{7}

Latyle (FR) *D Windrif* 110h 107c
5 ch m Balko(FR) Calamity I (FR) (Exactly Sharp (USA))
350a^{9}

Laudatory *Nicky Henderson* 142h 88c
9 b g Royal Applause Copy-Cat (Lion Cavern (USA))
556^{2} 812^{P} 1039^{4} 1482^{2} 1657^{7}

Laugharne *Luke Dace* 115h
4 b g Authorized(IRE) Corsican Sunset (USA) (Thunder Gulch (USA))
4681^{5} 5063^{2} ◆

Laughingalltheway *Martin Keighley* 54h
4 b g Darnay Smilingatstrangers (Macmillion)
219^{F} 647^{7} 1295^{5} 1702^{5}

Laughton Park *Suzy Smith* 121h
10 ch g Karinga Bay Brass Castle (IRE) (Carlingford Castle)
389^{4} 2013^{3} 2548^{2} 5065^{2}

Laurenzio (FR) *G Cherel* 99h
2 b g Lauro(GER) Blue Risk (FR) (Take Risks (FR))
5498a^{8}

Laurium *Nicky Henderson* 140h
5 ch g Gold Away(IRE) Silver Peak (FR) (Sillery (USA))
105^{2} (441) 2052^{2} 2781^{U} 4769^{U} 5275^{3}

Lava Lamp (GER) *Evan Williams* 117h 103c
8 b g Shamardal(USA) La Felicita (Shareef Dancer (USA))
216^{2} 645^{3} 774^{4} (1046) 1119^{5} 1419^{4} 1699^{8} 3137^{7} 3978^{F} 4824^{7} 5102^{7}

Laval Noir (FR) *Kim Bailey* 108b
4 b g Laveron Vale Of Honor (FR) (Singspiel (IRE))
(4981)

La Vaticane (FR) *David Pipe* 134h 143c
6 gr m Turgeon(USA) Taking Off (FR) (Kahyasi)
2468^{6} 2780^{3} 3148^{5} (4436) 5193^{8}

La Vien Zen (IRE) *Jim Goldie*
3 b f Dylan Thomas(IRE) Se La Vie (FR) (Highest Honor (FR))
1177^{P}

La Voix (FR) *Jimmy Frost* 58h
3 b f Voix Du Nord(FR) Loupaline (FR) (Loup Solitaire (USA))
1232^{3} 1321^{4} 2164^{11}

Lawless Island (IRE) *Tim Vaughan* 99h 78c
6 b g Heron Island(IRE) Nylon (GER) (Law Society (USA))
251^{2} 595^{6} 1693^{5} **3864^{P} 4177^{8} 4704^{3} 5357^{P}**

Lawsons Thorns (IRE) *Joanne Foster* 104h
6 b g Presenting Ardnurcher (IRE) (King's Ride)
364^{3} 625^{4} ◆ 780^{7} 969^{6} 1273^{7} 3312^{P} 5314^{P}

Layerthorpe (IRE) *Debra Hamer* 91h
3 b g Vale Of York(IRE) Strobinia (IRE) (Soviet Star (USA))
1294^{6} 1452^{5} 1866^{4} 3108^{P}

Lazarus Bell *Alan Brown* 65h
5 ch g Bahamian Bounty Snake's Head (Golden Snake (USA))
1967^{8}

Leaderofthedance *Nicky Henderson* 115h
6 b m Norse Dancer(IRE) Glenda Lough (IRE) (Supreme Leader)
(2033) 2247^{P}

Leading Score (IRE) *James Ewart* 109h
5 b g Scorpion(IRE) Leading Rank (IRE) (Supreme Leader)
2101^{3} 2754^{3} 3471^{5} 4416^{5} 4742^{P}

League Of His Own (IRE) *Claire Dyson* 60h
6 ch g Beneficial Miss Eastwood (IRE) (Commanche Run)
90^{P} 3285 552^{3} 811^{8} 935^{10} 1098^{8} **1445^{U} 2402^{P}** 2693^{P} 3234^{4} 3841^{8} 4490^{4} 4845^{11}

Lean Burn (USA) *Barry Leavy* 85h
9 b g Johannesburg(USA) Anthelion (USA) (Stop The Music (USA))
465^{5} 858^{5} 2492^{4} 2862^{3} 3233^{4} 3376^{4} 5099^{5}

Leanna Ban *Tristan Davidson* 111h 124c
8 b g Alflora(IRE) Gurleigh (IRE) (Pivotal)
(158) (454) 2917^{3} **3507^{F} 3792^{2} 4153^{2} 4420^{3} 4870^{P}**

Leap Dearg (IRE) *Robert Tyner* 135c
7 b g Beneficial Wee Red Roo (IRE) (Supreme Leader)
3302a^{4}

Leath Acra Mor (IRE) *Ian Williams* 108h 106c
9 b g King's Theatre(IRE) Happy Native (IRE) (Be My Native (USA))
1055^{P} 2405^{P} 2744^{3} 3220^{2} 4853^{6}

Leave At Dawn (IRE) *C Byrnes* 136h
5 ch g Presenting Hannigan's Lodger (IRE) (Be My Native (USA))
(2485) 4730^{9}

Leavethelighton (IRE) *Eoin Doyle* 136h 138c
8 b g Oscar(IRE) Royale Boja (FR) (Kadalko (FR))
3073a^{4} 3302a^{3} 3715a^{8}

Leaving Las Vegas *William Kinsey* 86h
4 b g Layman(USA) Woven Silk (USA) (Danzig (USA))
3009^{7} 3363^{8} 3863^{4} 4297^{7} 5333^{P}

Le Bacardy (FR) *Dan Skelton* 128h 139c
9 b g Bahhare(USA) La Balagna (Kris)
184^{2} (357) 2084^{6} 2468^{P} 2746^{8} 3036^{7} 3620^{8} 5184^{3} 5394^{4}

Le Bel Anjou (FR) *F-M Cottin* 137h 135c
7 b g Malinas(GER) Epsibelle (IRE) (Darshaan)
836a^{P}

Le Boizelo (FR) *Robert Walford* 125h
4 b g Irish Wells(FR) Bois Tendre (FR) (Murmure (FR))
3978^{4} (4235) 4596^{U}

Le Capricieux (FR) *Gary Moore* 101h
4 b g Alberto Giacometti(IRE) Eria Flore (FR) (Hero's Honor (USA))
3710^{P} 5387^{4}

Le Chateau (FR) *C Scandella* 144h
6 b g Enrique La Remigeasse (FR) (Poliglote)
4a^{7} 349a^{4} 663a^{7} 1883a^{5}

Le Coeur Net (FR) *Anthony Honeyball* 89b
3 ch g Network(GER) Silverwood (FR) (Garde Royale)
3409^{5} 4827^{6}

Le Curieux (FR) *Francois Nicolle* 125h
3 b g Lauro(GER) La Curieuse (FR) (Robin Des Champs (FR))
4720^{16}

Le Dauphin (IRE) *Nicky Henderson* 108b
4 b g Robin Des Champs(FR) Miss Denman (IRE) (Presenting)
4103^{4} 5097^{4}

Lee Side Lady (IRE) *Neil Mulholland* 100h
5 ch m Mountain High(IRE) Vicante (IRE) (Old Vic)
1052^{4} 1116^{5} 1240^{5} (1356) 1509^{4} 4028^{2} (4200)

Le Fin Bois (FR) *Richard Hobson* 123h 125c
5 b g Poliglote La Mache (FR) (Morespeed)
1769^{2} 2184^{8} 2897^{5} 3313^{U} (Dead)

Legacy Gold (IRE) *S R B Crawford* 140h
7 b m Gold Well Durgams Delight (IRE) (Durgam (USA))
4699^{3}

Legal Exit (IRE) *Tom Lacey* 121h 123c
8 ch g Exit To Nowhere(USA) New Legislation (IRE) (Dominion Royale)
3504^{4} 4230^{6}

Legal Legend *Christopher Henn* 103b 107c
8 b g Midnight Legend Calamintha (Mtoto)
13^{4} 4748^{4}

Legendara *Charlie Longsdon* 15b
3 b f Midnight Legend Samandara (FR) (Kris)
4488^{14}

Legend Lady *Oliver Sherwood* 112h
4 b m Midnight Legend Aoninch (Inchinor)
2136^{4} (3773)

Legion D'Honneur (UAE) *Chris Down* 101h 101c
10 b g Halling(USA) Renowned (IRE) (Darshaan)
530^{8} 824^{6} 1086^{6} 1236^{6} (2447) 2664^{4}

Leg Iron (IRE) *Sheena West* 108h 121c
10 b g Snurge Southern Skies (IRE) (Dr Massini (IRE))
670^{P} (3086) 4505^{2}

Leg Lock Luke (IRE) *Colin Tizzard* 99h
5 b g Indian River(FR) Delirious Tantrum (IRE) (Taufan (USA))
3710^{7} 4224^{4} 4963^{3} 5305^{3}

Le Grand Chene (FR) *Gordon Elliott* 102h 103c
9 b g Turgeon(USA) Faitiche D'Aubry (FR) (Le Nain Jaune (FR))
958^{2}

Leith Hill (IRE) *Laura Mongan* 59h
5 b g Mountain High(IRE) Ballinacariga Rose (IRE) (Revoque (IRE))
1246^{7} 1752^{P} 1895^{P} 5303^{5}

Leith Hill Lad *Charlie Longsdon* 109h
5 b g Kayf Tara Leith Hill Star (Comme L'Etoile)
320^{7} 2995^{5}

Leith Hill Legasi *Charlie Longsdon* 89h 100c
6 b m Kahyasi Leith Hill Star (Comme L'Etoile)
(2269) (2827) 3385^{P} 3663^{5} 4185^{2} 4879^{P}

Le Legro (IRE) *Charlie Mann* 101h
5 b g Mountain High(IRE) Good To Travel (IRE) (Night Shift (USA))
1752^{2} 1968^{3} 3855^{9} 4226^{P}

Le Mercurey (FR) *Paul Nicholls* 141h 160c
5 b g Nickname(FR) Feroe (FR) (Bulington (FR))
(2545) (3136) 3405^{3} 3860^{P} 4237^{3} 4716^{8} (5324)

Lemon's Gent *Paul Webber* 108h 118c
8 br g Generous(IRE) Lemon's Mill (USA) (Roberto (USA))
3931^{P} (5439)

Lemony Bay *Oliver Sherwood* 117h 120c
6 b g Overbury(IRE) Lemon's Mill (USA) (Roberto (USA))
492^{4} 894^{2} 1110^{2} (1372) 1807^{8}

Lemtara Bay *Oliver Sherwood* 101h
4 b m Kayf Tara Lemon's Mill (USA) (Roberto (USA))
696^{3} 2549^{5} 4743^{2}

Leney Cottage (IRE) *Maurice Barnes* 98h 114c
8 b g Witness Box(USA) Fleur De Tal (Primitive Rising (USA))
4047^{3} ◆ 4421^{7} **(4569) 4741^{R}**

Len's Legacy (IRE) *Tim Easterby*
3 ch g Fruits Of Love(USA) Manucrin (Zafonic (USA))
4001^{8}

Leo Luna *Gary Moore* 130h 145c
6 b g Galileo(IRE) Eva Luna (USA) (Alleged (USA))
2187^{P} 2916^{10} 3707^{P} (4348) 4912^{P} 5304^{P}

Leoncavallo (IRE) *John Ferguson* 138h
3 br g Cape Cross(IRE) Nafura (Dubawi (IRE))
(975) (1232) (1294) (1656) (2172) 3028^{U} 4764^{5}

Le Prezien (FR) *Paul Nicholls* 144h
4 br g Blue Bresil(FR) Abu Dhabi (FR) (Saint Cyrien (FR))
2581^{2} ◆ (3105) ◆ (3506) 3739^{2} (4636) 5214^{2}

Le Reve (IRE) *Lucy Wadham* 133h 154c
7 br g Milan Open Cry (IRE) (Montelimar (USA))
2187^{P} 2482^{10} 3528^{2} 3860^{6} (3993) 4361^{5} 5218^{11} 5494^{P}

Le Sacre Coeur (GER) *C Cheminaud*
4 b g Samum(GER) L'Heure Bleue (IRE) (Kendor (FR))
3815a^{4}

Le Saumon (IRE) *Sarah Humphrey* 63h
5 b g Milan Super Size (IRE) (Shernazar)
2275^{P} 3085^{P} 4861^{6}

Les Beaufs (FR) *Mme V Seignoux* 131h
6 b g Apsis Yeomanry (FR) (Saumarez)
349a^{12}

L'Es Fremantle (FR) *Michael Chapman* 54h
4 b g Orpen(USA) Grand Design (Danzero (AUS))
1260^{10} 1379^{7} 2043^{9} **2222^{P}**

Lessons In Milan (IRE) *Nicky Henderson* 135h 130c
7 b g Milan Lessons Lass (IRE) (Doyoun)
3922^{2} 4864^{3} 5302^{U}

Less Time (IRE) *Jonjo O'Neill* 105h 120c
6 br g Oscar(IRE) Woodville Princess (IRE) (Torus)
677^{P} 1424^{P} 1444^{F}

Letbeso (IRE) *Peter Bowen* 118h 128c
7 ch g Vinnie Roe(IRE) Go Hunting (IRE) (Abednego)
2517^{P} 3707^{P} 4127^{3}

Letemgo (IRE) *Giles Smyly* 122h 120c
7 b g Brian Boru Leteminletemout (IRE) (Be My Native (USA))
319^{P} **2149^{4} 3253^{F}** 3705^{P} **5432^{6}**

Lethegoodtimesroll (IRE) *Brian Ellison*
4 ch m Mahler Little Pearl (IRE) (Bigstone (IRE))
4908^{P}

Le Tigre De Bronze *Adrian Wintle*
5 b g Tiger Hill(IRE) Papillon De Bronze (IRE) (Marju (IRE))
5221^{P}

Let Me Alone (FR) *G Chaignon* 90h
5 b g Malinas(GER) Salsa Rock (FR) (Matahawk)
436a^{6}

Let's Dance (FR) *W P Mullins* 132h
3 b f Poliglote Baraka Du Berlais (FR) (Bonnet Rouge (FR))
4002a^{3} 4764^{4}

Lets Get Cracking (FR) *Alan Jones* 67h
11 gr g Anabaa Blue Queenhood (FR) (Linamix (FR))
712^{P} 1117^{8} 1323^{U}

Lets Get Serious (IRE) *Dai Williams* 126h 130c
9 b g Overbury(IRE) Vendimia (Dominion)
(295) ◆ 535^{6} 774^{7}

Lets Go Dutchess *Kevin Bishop* 93b
5 b m Helissio(FR) Lets Go Dutch (Nicholas Bill)
1249 2460^{5} 5359^{3}

Lets Hope So *Emma Lavelle* 108h
5 b m Generous(IRE) Baily Mist (IRE) (Zaffaran (USA))
5373^{2}

Let's Tango (IRE) *Caroline Keevil* 66h
4 ch g Mahler Miss Ogan (IRE) (Supreme Leader)
4357^{6} 5097^{13} 5387^{8}

Letter Exit (IRE) *Lucy Wadham* 103h
5 b g Exit To Nowhere(USA) Letterwoman (IRE) (Fourstars Allstar (USA))
2039^{P}

Letter Of Credit (IRE) *James Joseph Mangan* 126h 145c
10 br g Bob Back(USA) Common Verse (IRE) (Common Grounds)
1152a^{10} 2606a^{4} 3715a^{12}

Lettheriverrundry (IRE) *Brendan Powell* 120h
5 br g Diamond Green(FR) Dissitation (IRE) (Spectrum (IRE))
2238^{2} 2683^{4} 4745^{3} 5269^{2}

Lettre De Cachet *Noel Meade* 124h
4 gr m Authorized(IRE) Regrette Rien (USA) (Unbridled's Song (USA))
94a^{9}

Le Vagabond (FR) *E J O'Grady* 120h
3 b g Footstepsinthesand Miryale (FR) (Anabaa (USA))
2813a^{3} 3268a^{6}

Levelling *Dan Skelton* 94h
3 ch f Pivotal Lane County (USA) (Rahy (USA))
3835^{6} 4345^{P} 4502^{5} 5374^{5}

Leviathan *Venetia Williams* 128h
8 b g Dubawi(IRE) Gipsy Moth (Efisio)
2617^{3} 2873^{3} 3449^{7} 3708^{6} 5074^{5}

Lewis *Tom Symonds* 116h 42c
6 b g Kayf Tara Island Of Memories (IRE) (Beneficial)
2963^{7} 3709^{R} 4843^{F} (Dead)

Lexicon Lad (IRE) *Heather Dalton* 109h 128c
10 ch g Presenting Hazel's Glory (IRE) (Mister Lord (USA))
315^{3}

Lexi Lou (IRE) *David Thompson* 56b
5 ch m Sendawar(IRE) Fleeting Arrow (IRE) (Commanche Run)
1378^{7}

Lexington Bay (IRE) *Philip Kirby* 90h
7 b g High Chaparral(IRE) Schust Madame (IRE) (Second Set (IRE))
468^{6}

Lexi's Boy (IRE) *Donald McCain* 122h
7 gr g Verglas(IRE) Jazan (IRE) (Danehill (USA))
197^{P} 2214^{15} 4482^{6} 4705^{3}

Ley Lady Grey *Jamie Snowden* 59h
5 gr m With Approval(CAN) Prospectress (USA) (Mining (USA))
120^{5} 566^{F}

L Frank Baum (IRE) *Bernard Llewellyn* 101h
8 b g Sinndar(IRE) Rainbow City (IRE) (Rainbow Quest (USA))
2520^{3} 3374^{6} 3978^{6} 4318^{2} 4747^{6} 5332^{6}

Liannastarr (IRE) *J J Lambe* 87h
5 ch m Fruits Of Love(USA) Lanastarr (IRE) (Beneficial)
4164^{4}

Liars Poker (IRE) *Oliver Sherwood* 98h 89c
8 b g Beneficial Strong Willed (Strong Gale)
258^{6}

Libby Mae (IRE) *Micky Hammond* 110h
5 b m High Chaparral(IRE) Empty Pocket (Danehill Dancer (IRE))
(2704) ◆ 3883^{2}

Libeccio (FR) *Charlie Mann* 124h
4 b g Shirocco(GER) Francais (Mark Of Esteem (IRE))
4782^{5} (5266) (5479)

Liberalis (FR) *Yannick Fouin* 111h 108c
5 ch m Muhtathir Ethelinda (Indian Ridge)
5499a^{6}

Liberty One (IRE) *Richard Woollacott* 125h 130c
9 b g Milan Same Old Story (IRE) (Welsh Term)
2057^{8} 2513^{P} **3371^{P}**

Lickpenny Larry *Tom Gretton* 80b
4 gr g Sagamix(FR) Myriah (IRE) (Strong Gale)
4392^{7} 4880^{17}

Lie Forrit (IRE) *Lucinda Russell* 152h 150c
11 b g Subtle Power(IRE) Ben Roseler (IRE) (Beneficial)
2082^{P} 3448^{7}

Lieutenant Colonel *Ms Sandra Hughes* 159h 110c
6 br g Kayf Tara Agnese (Abou Zouz (USA))
49a^{4} 4146a^{2} 4732^{P}

Lieutenant Gruber (IRE) *Henry Daly* 96b
4 b g Scorpion(IRE) Tanit Lady (IRE) (Presenting)
4889^{5}

Life And Soul (IRE) *Donald McCain* 120h 102c
8 b g Azamour(IRE) Way For Life (GER) (Platini (GER))
643^{P} 931^{P}

Lifeboat Mona *Paul Nicholls* 127h
5 b m Kayf Tara Astar Love (FR) (Astarabad (USA))
(2870) 3372^{P} (3953)

Life Of A Luso (IRE) *Paul Henderson* 76h 99c
11 b g Luso Life Of A Lady (IRE) (Insan (USA))
448^{P} 897^{6} 1426^{P}

Lifetime (IRE) *Neil Mulholland* 105h
7 b g Shamardal(USA) La Vita E Bella (IRE) (Definite Article)
1067 165^{2}

Lift The Latch (IRE) *A J Martin* 145h
5 b g Beneficial Queen Astrid (IRE) (Revoque (IRE))
4955a^{5}

Lift The Lid (IRE) *Neil Mulholland* 92h
5 b g Robin Des Pres(FR) Kindly Light (IRE) (Supreme Leader)
3593 3411^{15} 3582^{5} 3744^{7} 3915^{6}

Light Breaks (IRE) *Nigel Twiston-Davies* 72h
3 b g Dylan Thomas(IRE) Anywaysmile (IRE) (Indian Ridge)
2273^{12} 2448^{6} 2992^{P} 3464^{P}

Lightening Rod *Michael Easterby* 136h 130c
10 b g Storming Home Bolero (Rainbow Quest (USA))
2194^{6} **2854^{4} 3107^{4} 3475^{3} 4838^{4}**

Lightentertainment (IRE) *Chris Gordon* 130h
7 b g King's Theatre(IRE) Dochas Supreme (IRE) (Supreme Leader)
2013^{2} 2912^{10} 3748^{P} 4070^{P} 4781^{5} 5065^{5}

Lights Of Broadway (IRE) *Bernard Llewellyn* 108h 99c
9 b m Broadway Flyer(USA) Supreme Call (IRE) (Supreme Leader)
4616^{7}

Light The City (IRE) *Ruth Carr* 108h 110c
8 b g Fantastic Light(USA) Marine City (JPN) (Carnegie (IRE))
2142^{7}

Light Well (IRE) *Gary Moore* 116h
7 b g Sadler's Wells(USA) L'Ancresse (IRE) (Darshaan)
3196^{P} 3705^{4} (3921)

Like Sully (IRE) *Richard Rowe* 97h 111c
7 bb g Presenting Swing Into Action (IRE) (Be My Native (USA))
2415^{4} **2885^{5} 3129^{3} 3903^{2} 4669^{5} (4932) 5432^{7}**

Lilac Tree *John Ferguson* 127h
5 b g Dubawi(IRE) Kalidasa (USA) (Nureyev (USA))
933^{2} (1117) 1308^{2} (1381) 1676^{2}

Lilbourne Legacy *David Pipe* 90h
4 b g Kyllachy Gold And Blue (IRE) (Bluebird (USA))
1289^{8} 1518^{8} 1576^{F} 1673^{4} 1964^{8} 2005^{5}

Lillian (IRE) *Seamus Mullins* 103b
4 bb m Milan Kay Tully (Kahyasi)
(601) 4414^{3} 5180^{9}

Lillington (IRE) *Colin Tizzard* 88b
3 br g Westerner Kind Word (IRE) (Yashgan)
5069^{5} 5308^{3}

Lilly Of The Moor *Ben Case* 110h
7 b m Flemensfirth(USA) Serenique (Good Thyne (USA))
4709^{4} 5165^{2}

Lilly's Legend *Mark Walford* 82h
5 ch m Midnight Legend Dalticia (FR) (Cadoudal (FR))
90^{2} (421) 759^{6} 966^{P} 2323^{4}

Lilly The Lioness (IRE) *Garrett James Power* 121h 115c
8 b m Welsh Lion(IRE) Norwer (IRE) (Norwich)
(1150a) 1565a^{2}

Lil Rockerfeller (USA) *Neil King* 156h
4 ch g Hard Spun(USA) Layounne (USA) (Mt. Livermore (USA))
2060^{3} 2411^{3} (2914) 3408^{2} 3733^{3} (4381) 4698^{7}

Lilshane (IRE) *Thomas P O'Connor* 122h
7 ch g Beneficial Liagry Road Lass (IRE) (Old Vic)
231a^{8} 5025a^{7}

Lily Little Legs (IRE) *Mike Sowersby* 101h 106c
6 gr m Westerner Silvers Promise (IRE) (Presenting)
226^{4} 874^{4} 976^{P} 1426^{2} 1618^{F} 1971^{2} 2595^{7} 3025^{P} **4298^{2} 4554^{U} (4940) 5247^{2}**

Lily Marie *Mike Hammond*
6 b m Overbury(IRE) Rose Marie (IRE) (Executive Perk)
1345^{6}

Lily Mars (IRE) *Neil Mulholland* 45h
8 br m Presenting Tiffany Jazz (IRE) (Good Thyne (USA))
2693^{6} ◆ 3125^{7}

Lily Waugh (IRE) *Anthony Honeyball* 142h 137c
8 b m King's Theatre(IRE) Killultagh Dawn (IRE) (Phardante (FR))
70a^{9} 1445^{F} 1808^{6} (2349) (2455) (3034) 3858^{2} 4699^{14}

Lilywhite Gesture (IRE) *Fergal O'Brien* 93h
6 b m Presenting Loyal Gesture (IRE) (Darazari (IRE))
2644^{6} 3234^{7} 3930^{3} 4413^{2} 4804^{3}

Lime Street (IRE) *Tom Symonds* 101h
4 b g Presenting Specifiedrisk (IRE) (Turtle Island (IRE))
2270^{5} 3009^{5} 3411^{P} 4064^{3} 4856^{3} 5355^{P}

Limini (IRE) *W P Mullins* 148h
4 ch m Peintre Celebre(USA) Her Grace (IRE) (Spectrum (IRE))
(3873a) (4734) ◆ 5190^{3}

Limos (GER) *James Ewart* 102b
5 br g Sholokhov(IRE) La Prima (GER) (Surumu (GER))
145^{4}

Limpopo Tom (IRE) *David Rees* 115h 122c
8 ch g Saffron Walden(FR) Sharpe (FR) (Dr Devious (IRE))
218^{6} 701^{6} **974^{5}** 1051^{3} 1239^{8} **1641^{6}**

Lincoln County *John Ferguson* 105h
4 b g Authorized(IRE) Lane County (USA) (Rahy (USA))
865^{6} (1050) 1792^{4} 1923^{3}

Linda's Charm (FR) *Mlle T Puitg* 124h
5 ch m Linda's Lad Rylara Des Brosses (FR) (Rapid Man (USA))
350a^{3}

Lindenhurst (IRE) *John C McConnell* 113h
5 b g Captain Marvelous(IRE) Royal Jubilee (IRE) (King's Theatre (IRE))
3634a^{4}

Lindsay's Dream *Zoe Davison* 89h 84c
9 b m Montjeu(IRE) Lady Lindsay (IRE) (Danehill Dancer (IRE))
224^{2} 2264^{8} 4712^{P}

Line D'Aois (IRE) *Michael Scudamore* 91h 107c
7 b g Craigsteel Old Line (IRE) (Old Vic)
2556^{4} 2830^{3}

Lined With Silver (IRE) *Dai Burchell* 95h
6 gr g Cloudings(IRE) Tinkers Lady (IRE) (Sheer Grit)
1979^{P} 2062^{7} 2299^{6} 2563^{4} 2841^{P}

Lineman *Sarah Hollinshead* 36h
5 b g Rail Link Shamana (USA) (Woodman (USA))
105^{6}

Linguine (FR) *Seamus Durack* 116h
5 ch g Linngari(IRE) Amerissage (USA) (Rahy (USA))
1544^{5} 2007^{2} 2409^{2} 2888^{7} 3664^{4}

Lions Charge (USA) *Neil Mulholland* 94h
8 ch g Lion Heart(USA) Fellwaati (USA) (Alydar (USA))
267^{3} 616^{4} 3256^{4}

Lipstickandpowder (IRE) *Dianne Sayer* 34h
3 gr f Mastercraftsman(IRE) Raphimix (FR) (Linamix (FR))
3099^{12} 3306^{10} 4104^{5}

Lir Flow *Jess Westwood* 7h
6 b m With The Flow(USA) Rose Lir (Lir)
5268^{12} 5415^{6}

Lisbon (IRE) *Patrick Griffin* 123h 125c
7 b g Cape Cross(IRE) Caraiyma (IRE) (Shahrastani (USA))
329^{P} 801^{4} 936^{3} 1169^{2} (1233) 1554^{4} **1777^{5}**

Lisdonagh House (IRE) *Lynn Siddall* 69h
13 b g Little Bighorn Lifinsa Barina (IRE) (Un Desperado (FR))
5099^{P}

Lisheen Prince (IRE) *Philip Hobbs* 103b
4 b g Oscar(IRE) Dino's Monkey (IRE) (Mr Dinos (IRE))
2514^{8}

Listen And Learn (IRE) *Jonjo O'Neill* 127h
7 b g Presenting Loyal Gesture (IRE) (Darazari (IRE))
774^{2} 1594^{3} 2002^{2} 2624^{10} 3158^{P}

Listen Boy (IRE) *Nigel Twiston-Davies* 114h 129c
9 ch g Presenting Buckalong (IRE) (Buckskin (FR))
2832^{3} 3364^{3} ◆ 3818^{5} 4872^{5}

Listen Dear (IRE) *W P Mullins* 140h
5 b m Robin Des Champs(FR) Crescendor (FR) (Lavirco (GER))
(2176a)

Listen To The Man (IRE) *Dan Skelton* 118b
5 b m Court Cave(IRE) Badia Dream (IRE) (Old Vic)
(4302) 4623^{3} ◆

Lithic (IRE) *Jonjo O'Neill* 116b
4 b g Westerner Acoola (IRE) (Flemensfirth (USA))
(2842) 4117^{5}

Little Acorn *Harry Fry* 88b
4 b m Presenting Whiteoak (IRE) (Oscar (IRE))
3862^{7}

Little Big Town (IRE) *Julia Brooke* 44h
5 br g Westerner My Kinda Girl (IRE) (Supreme Leader)
2748^{7}

Little Boy Boru (IRE) *Suzy Smith* 129h 109c
7 b g Brian Boru How Is Things (IRE) (Norwich)
2369^{4} 2669^{F} 3254^{8} 3527^{5} 3992^{4} 4596^{7} 5239^{3}

Little Bruce (IRE) *Philip Kirby* 100h
3 b g Yeats(IRE) Lady Rolfe (IRE) (Alzao (USA))
4567^{6} 4791^{3}

Little Buxted (USA) *Jim Best* 92h
5 bb g Mr Greeley(USA) Mo Cheoil Thu (IRE) (In The Wings)
3450^{P} 3660^{8} 3819^{7} 3902^{5}

Little Dotty *Giuseppe Fierro*
6 br m Erhaab(USA) Marsh Marigold (Tina's Pet)
3388^{8}

Little Dream (IRE) *Evan Williams* 89h
8 b m Beneficial Miss Franco (IRE) (Lanfranco)
1308^{6} 1506^{5} 1694^{3} 2167^{P}

Little Fritz (FR) *L Kerr* 110h 106c
8 gr g Turgeon(USA) Hunorisk (FR) (Mansonnien (FR))
80^{6} 4016^{U} 4180^{5} 4558^{4} 5258^{P}

Little Glenshee (IRE) *N W Alexander* 121h 124c
9 gr m Terimon Harrietfield (Nicholas Bill)
2400^{4} 2935^{4} 3631^{5} 3934^{2} (4406) 4584^{3}

Little James (IRE) *Nigel Twiston-Davies* 84h
6 b g Craigsteel Brymar Lass (IRE) (Homo Sapien)
2407^{8} 2838^{6} 3382^{5} 3925^{4} 5181^{5}

Little Jimmy *Tom Gretton* 68h 123c
8 br g Passing Glance Sementina (USA) (Silver Charm (USA))
2834^{3} (3380) 3742^{6} (4431) 5046^{5}

Little Jon *Nigel Twiston-Davies* 129h 147c
7 b g Pasternak Jowoody (Gunner B)
1976^{4} (2761) 3031^{10} 3406^{11} 4485^{P} 4733^{F} 5217^{P}

Little Miss Flossy *Andrew Crook* 90h
6 b m Kayf Tara The Ginger Whinger (Sir Harry Lewis (USA))
159^{11} 3861^{11} 5229^{5}

Little Miss Poet *Philip Hobbs* 110b
3 b f Yeats(IRE) R De Rien Sivola (FR) (Robin Des Champs (FR))
3118^{2} ◆ (4350) 5180^{6} ◆

Little Missserious (IRE) *J J Lambe* 85b
4 b m Kalanisi(IRE) Burnt Out (IRE) (Anshan)
4168^{3}

Littlemissylennon *Kenny Johnson*
4 b m Ferrule(IRE) Lorna Lennon (IRE) (Carroll House (IRE))
257^{P}

Little Mitch (IRE) *Yvonne Latta* 121h
6 br m Westerner Party Woman (IRE) (Sexton Blake)
1875a^{3}

Little Mix *Emma Lavelle* 98h
4 gr g Sagamix(FR) Folie Dancer (Exit To Nowhere (USA))
(378) 773^{8}

Little Pop *Nigel Twiston-Davies* 113h 100c
7 b g Pasternak Flagship Daisy May (IRE) (Kahyasi)
(776) 931^{5} **1460^{4} 1630^{4}**

Little Roxy (IRE) *Anna Newton-Smith* 83h
10 b m Dilshaan Brunswick (Warning)
2004^{6} 2547^{6}

Little Vic *Eugene Stanford* 67b
4 br g Overbury(IRE) Vicky Bee (Alflora (IRE))
3226^{9}

Little Windmill (IRE) *Neil King* 104h 99c
5 ch g Mahler Ennismore Queen (IRE) (Glacial Storm (USA))
999^{3} 1153^{5} 1179^{6} 1447^{4} 1692^{7} 1897^{10} 2223^{6} **2592^{3} 3020^{U} 3225^{3} 3421^{F}**

Little Wren *Chris Grant* 86b
6 b m Iktibas Ouzel (IRE) (Mandalus)
516^{P}

Live For Today (IRE) *N Williams* 84b
4 b g Alflora(IRE) Uppermost (Montjeu (IRE))
5436^{10}

Livelovelaugh (IRE) *W P Mullins* 138h
5 b g Beneficial Another Evening (IRE) (Saddlers' Hall (IRE))
23a^{8}

Live Miracle (USA) *Venetia Williams* 78h
3 b f Falco(USA) Zaragoza Girl (BRZ) (Trempolino (USA))
3822^{P} 4345^{5} 4683^{6}

Living Next Door (IRE) *A J Martin* 105h 148c
9 b g Beneficial Except Alice (IRE) (Orchestra)
5005a^{P}

Lizzie Langton *Robert Walford* 90b
4 b m Kayf Tara Madam Flora (Alflora (IRE))
2277^{7}

Llancillo Lord (IRE) *Thomas Mullins* 115b
5 b g Beneficial Llancillo Lady (IRE) (Be My Native (USA))
25a^{10}

Llantara *Tom Symonds* 100b
4 b m Kayf Tara Lady Llancillo (IRE) (Alflora (IRE))
3132^{6} 4228^{3} 4967^{5}

Local Celebrity (IRE) *Sally Randell* 63h 109c
11 b g Bach(IRE) Shanks Design (IRE) (Broken Hearted)
847^{P} 1269^{P} 4105^{5} **4424^{P} 4859^{P}**

Local Present (IRE) *Denis Quinn* 77h 90c
12 ch g Presenting Local Issue (IRE) (Phardante (FR))
1287^{6} 1569^{2} 1785^{P}

Local Show (IRE) *Ben Pauling* 126h 152c
7 br g Oscar(IRE) Loughaderra Rose (IRE) (Roselier (FR))
(3113) (3774) 4700^{7}

Lochalsh (IRE) *Katie Scott* 116h
4 ch g Duke Of Marmalade(IRE) Kylemore (IRE) (Sadler's Wells (USA))
(41) 556^{4} 749^{3} 1046^{6} 1238^{8} 2027^{7} 5088^{7}

Loch Ard (IRE) *Miss S L Gould* 142h 93c
7 b g Pivotal My Giddy Aunt (IRE) (Danehill (USA))
12^{11}

Loch Ba (IRE) *Mick Channon* 88h 129c
9 b g Craigsteel Lenmore Lisa (IRE) (Phardante (FR))
2780^{8} 5119^{5}

Loch Garman (FR) *Nigel Hawke* 108h
4 gr g Maresca Sorrento(FR) Ballade Nordique (FR) (Royal Charter (FR))
160^{6} 528^{6} 1698^{6} 1947^{4} 2734^{6}

Loch Garman Aris (IRE) *Gary Hanmer* 114b
5 b g Jammaal See Em Aime (IRE) (Little Bighorn)
(1717) 3145^{2}

Loch Linnhe *Mark Walford* 74h
3 b g Tobougg(IRE) Quistaquay (El Conquistador)
2923^{2} 3593^{3} 3971^{5}

Lochnagar (GER) *Venetia Williams* 120h
6 b g Sholokhov(IRE) Lindenblute (Surumu (GER))
3449^{11} 3917^{3} 4229^{6} 4294^{6} 5102^{6}

Lochnell (IRE) *Ian Duncan* 109h
6 br m Winged Love(IRE) Nothing For Ever (IRE) (Tikkanen (USA))
2429^{12} 3163^{3} (3437) 4165^{3} 4608^{3} 5012^{6} 5409^{9}

Lochore (IRE) *Jean McGregor* 70h 18c
9 b g Morozov(USA) Fulgina (FR) (Double Bed (FR))
287^{P} 454^{4} 867^{P} 1371^{P}

Lochwell Lad (IRE) *Rebecca Menzies* 67b
6 b g Portrait Gallery(IRE) Mill Afrique (Mtoto)
1101^{10}

Locked Inthepocket (IRE) *Mrs Anthea Morshead* 100b 97c
11 b g Beneficial Ruby Rubenstein (IRE) (Camden Town)
4043^{P}

Lockedoutaheaven (IRE) *Maurice Barnes* 97h
4 ch g Rock Of Gibraltar(IRE) Second Burst (IRE) (Sadler's Wells (USA))
799^{3} 882^{U}

Lockstockandbarrel (IRE) *Jonjo O'Neill* 133h 145c
6 b g Flemensfirth(USA) Omas Lady (IRE) (Be My Native (USA))
3975^{3} ◆ (4274) ◆ 4425^{2}

Lock Towers (IRE) *Ben Pauling* 105h 107c
6 b g Classic Cliche(IRE) Katieella (IRE) (King's Theatre (IRE))
641^{4} 782^{6} 873^{4} 1659^{3} 1795^{5}

Lockydor (FR) *S Foucher* 96c
4 b g Ballingarry(IRE) Khazana (FR) (Saumarez)
4401a^{U}

Lolli (IRE) *Nicky Henderson* 110h
5 b m High Chaparral(IRE) Unicamp (Royal Academy (USA))
178^{3} 462^{2} 679^{2} (1009)

Lombardy Boy (IRE) *Michael Banks* 90h
10 b g Milan Horner Water (IRE) (Over The River (FR))
4504^{5} (4975) 5441^{3}

Londonia *Graeme McPherson* 60h
3 gr g Paco Boy(IRE) Snowdrops (Gulch (USA))
891^{4} 1037^{3} 1177^{7}

London Prize *John Ferguson* 110b
4 b g Teofilo(IRE) Zibet (Kris)
(644) 5069^{2}

Long Dog *W P Mullins* 151h
5 b g Notnowcato Latanazul (Sakhee (USA))
(1875a) (2814a) (3294a) 4766^{U} (Dead)

Long House Hall (IRE) *Dan Skelton* 144h 150c
7 b g Saddlers' Hall(IRE) Brackenvale (IRE) (Strong Gale)
(329) 2063^{U} 4717^{2} **5284^{5}**

Long John *Jackie Du Plessis* 104h 113c
8 gr g Silver Patriarch(IRE) Magic Valentine (Magic Ring (IRE))
514^{9} (3123) 3412^{3} 3867^{2} 4884^{4} 5164^{5}

Long Lunch *Charlie Longsdon* 127h 136c
6 b g Kayf Tara Royal Keel (Long Leave)
2637^{4} **2885^{4} 3335^{F} 4465^{8} (5226)**

Long Run (FR) *Robert Waley-Cohen* 72h 111c
10 bb g Cadoudal(FR) Libertina (FR) (Balsamo (FR))
4820^{5}

Long Strand (IRE) *Miss Evanna McCutcheon* 90h 110c
11 b g Saddlers' Hall(IRE) Oh So Breezy (IRE) (Be My Native (USA))
48a^{6}

Longtown (IRE) *Philip Hobbs* 102b
4 b g Scorpion(IRE) Desirable Asset (IRE) (Zagreb (USA))
5144^{3}

Longueville Flier (IRE) *Micky Hammond* 100c
6 b g Definite Article Talk The Talk (Terimon)
801^{5} 1462^{3} ◆ 1571^{5} 1775^{3} 2030^{6} 2173^{2} (2500) 3792^{4} 4051^{P} 4740^{3}

Longuivy De La Mer (FR) *Patrice Quinton* 100h
2 ch g Martaline Millessima (FR) (Bering)
4539a^{P}

Looking For Mick *Chris Down* 90h
6 ch g Milk It Mick Seeker (Rainbow Quest (USA))
1576^{5} 1673^{5} 1837^{9} 2087^{11}

Looking On *Edward Bevan*
7 b g Observatory(USA) Dove Tree (FR) (Charnwood Forest (IRE))
3318^{P}

Looking Well (IRE) *Nicky Richards* 125h 130c
6 b g Gold Well Different Level (IRE) (Topanoora)
319^{3} **2803^{4} 3399^{2} 4155^{F}**

Looks Like Magic *Neil King* 97h
6 gr g Fair Mix(IRE) Cirrious (Cloudings (IRE))
569^{6}

Looks Like Power (IRE) *Debra Hamer* 113h
5 ch g Spadoun(FR) Martovic (IRE) (Old Vic)
177^{P} 2182^{7} 2694^{3} 3078^{4}

Lookslikerainted (IRE) *Sophie Leech* 112h 108c
8 b g Milan Kilcrea Gale (IRE) (Strong Gale)
19a^{P} 701^{4} 1002^{3} 1265^{8} **1382^{5}** 4855^{4} **5465^{P}**

Looksnowtlikebrian (IRE) *Tim Vaughan* 96h
4 b g Brian Boru Sheebadiva (IRE) (Norwich)
2044^{4} 3508^{5} 3974^{4} 4264^{6} 4685^{5}

Loom Of Life (IRE) *Richard Fahey* 78h
3 b g Rip Van Winkle(IRE) Feeling Wonderful (IRE) (Fruits Of Love (USA))
975^{5}

Loose Chips *Charlie Longsdon* 144h 139c
9 b g Sir Harry Lewis(USA) Worlaby Rose (Afif)
1924[2] 2471[U] 2616[2] 3282[6] 3624[U] 4234[2] (5390)

Lorain (CZE) *Stepanka Myskova* 109c
8 ch g Rainbows For Life(CAN) Lodgia (IRE) (Grand Lodge (USA))
1885a[7]

Lord Adare (IRE) *Nikki Evans* 93h 87c
7 b g Moscow Society(USA) Gonearethedays (IRE) (Be My Native (USA))
2906[P] 3584[9]

Lord Aldervale (IRE) *Luke Dace* 71h
8 br g Alderbrook Monavale (IRE) (Strong Gale)
89[2] 222[7]

Lord Ballim (FR) *Nigel Hawke* 103h 110c
5 ch g Balko(FR) Lady Pauline (FR) (Hamas (IRE))
2267[5] 2560[F] 3592[9] 4491[F] 5031[3] 5466[3]

Lord Ben (IRE) *Henry De Bromhead* 126h 137c
10 b g Beneficial Lady Bluebell (IRE) (Mister Lord (USA))
2084[7]

Lord Brantwood *Tim Vaughan* 72h
4 b g Sir Percy Diddymu (IRE) (Revoque (IRE))
1182[7]

Lord Brendy *Kenny Johnson* 114h 124c
7 gr g Portrait Gallery(IRE) Hervey Bay (Primitive Rising (USA))
458[4] 707[4]

Lord Bryan (IRE) *Peter Bowen* 90b
4 b g Brian Boru Run Cat (IRE) (Lord Americo)
407[4] 4162[2]

Lord De Beaufai (FR) *Georgios Pakidis* 103h
7 b g Epalo(GER) Perle De Beaufai (FR) (Epervier Bleu)
25a[14]

Lord Emerson *David Dennis*
7 ch g Pursuit Of Love Lady Emm (Emarati (USA))
105[P] 263[P]

Lord Fingal (IRE) *J T R Dreaper* 129c
7 b g Brian Boru Line Jade (FR) (Luchiroverte (IRE))
(533)

Lord Fox (IRE) *Shaun Harris* 67h 97c
8 b g Alflora(IRE) Foxfire (Lord Americo)
1402[3] 1629[5] 1978[F]

Lord Golan *Nick Kent* 109h
7 b g Singspiel(IRE) Lady Golan (IRE) (Golan (IRE))
3309[5] 3839[11] 4065[3] 4865[3] 5453[12]

Lord Grantham (IRE) *Henry Daly* 126h 122c
8 b g Definite Article Last Of Her Line (Silver Patriarch (IRE))
215[5] 750[4] 1042[5] 2774[5] 4071[6] 4842[3] 5395[2]

Lord Heathfield (IRE) *Graeme McPherson* 92h 105c
9 br g Classic Cliche(IRE) Garryduff Bridge (IRE) (Taipan (IRE))
4043[U] 4651[2] 5183[6]

Lord Landen (IRE) *Fergal O'Brien* 98h 114c
10 br g Beneficial Agua Caliente (IRE) (Old Vic)
174[5] 1812[P] 2057[5] 2724[4] (3014) 4422[2] 4872[3] 5472[9]

Lord Lir (IRE) *Tim Vaughan* 38h 108c
9 b g Oscar Schindler(IRE) Milford Woman (IRE) (Taipan (IRE))
280[2] 446[5] 713[2] (1031) (1133) 1985[3] 2220[3] 4230[P]

Lord Of Drums (IRE) *Lucinda Russell* 80h 103c
9 b g Beat Of Drums Treat A Lady (IRE) (Lord Americo)
4606[5] 5080[3]

Lord Of The Dunes *Jamie Snowden* 94h 95c
7 b g Desert King(IRE) Dame Fonteyn (Suave Dancer (USA))
567[5] 806[2] 874[3] 1159[6] 1243[6]

Lord Of The Hosts *Nick Williams*
4 gr g Saint Des Saints(FR) Telmar Flyer (Neltino)
2879[8] 3314[P]

Lord Of The Island (IRE) *Sally Randell* 112h
7 b g Heron Island(IRE) Miss Morose (IRE) (Arctic Lord (IRE))
4183[6] 4388[10] 4613[3] (5313)

Lord Of Words (IRE) *Patrick Holmes* 68h
3 b g Thousand Words Dame Laura (IRE) (Royal Academy (USA))
1899[12] 2324[P]

Lord Redsgirth (IRE) *Lucy Normile* 97h 102c
10 ch g Flemensfirth(USA) Wisebuy (IRE) (Mister Lord (USA))
519[P]

Lord Scoundrel (IRE) *Gordon Elliott* 136h 145c
6 b g Presenting Noble Choice (Dahar (USA))
(2227a) 2530a[2] 3069a[2] 3652a[3] 5132a[2]

Lordship (IRE) *Tom Gretton* 45h 27c
11 b g King's Best(USA) Rahika Rose (Unfuwain (USA))
3840[14] 4390[9] 4854[P]

Lords Park Star (IRE) *Nicholas Pomfret* 100h
6 bb g Presenting Mary's View (IRE) (Phardante (FR))
2044[12] 2646[3] 3022[14] 3221[9]

Lord Usher (IRE) *George Charlton* 101h 106c
8 b g Lord Americo Beet Five (IRE) (Seclude (USA))
139[4] 1572[P] 2707[3] 3243[F] 3884[5] 4638[5]

Lord Valentine *Mark Bradstock* 105b
7 b g Overbury(IRE) Lady Fleur (Alflora (IRE))
2995[P]

Lord Westy (IRE) *Jamie Snowden* 85b
4 b g Westerner Smile Later (IRE) (Arctic Lord (IRE))
2044[8] 3388[4]

Lord Wishes (IRE) *James Ewart* 128h 132c
8 b g Milan Strong Wishes (IRE) (Strong Gale)
319[8] (1903) 2214[5] 3020[F] (3345) 3936[P] 4839[6]

L'Orfeo *John Ferguson*
5 ch g Singspiel(IRE) Limeira (Bertolini (USA))
1065[P]

Los Amigos (IRE) *Dermot Anthony McLoughlin* 129h 140c
8 b g Overbury(IRE) Lady Shackleton (IRE) (Zaffaran (USA))
3296a[10] 3651a[7]

Los Banderos (FR) *F-X De Chevigny* 107h 118c
6 b g Sinndar(IRE) La Bandera (Bahhare (USA))
1477a[11]

Los Nadis (GER) *Jim Goldie* 106h 83c
11 ch g Hernando(FR) La Estrella (GER) (Desert King (IRE))
661[2] 869[3] 958[4] 1181[9] (1331)

Lost Arca (FR) *David Bridgwater* 95h 75c
9 b g Lost World(IRE) Luarca (Robellino (USA))
4423[U] 4778[3] 5068[U]

Lost Book (IRE) *S J Mahon* 106h
7 b m Oscar(IRE) Borrismore Lass (IRE) (Presenting)
1150a[8]

Lost In Newyork (IRE) *Nick Kent* 86h 84c
8 b g Arakan(USA) Lace Flower (Old Vic)
57[3] 258[2] 588[6] 807[3] 934[4] 1080[4] 1614[4] 1785[3] 1930[8] 2542[2] 2862[5] 3419[U] 3951[U] 4987[2] 5332[7]

Lost Legend (IRE) *Jonjo O'Neill* 112h 153c
8 b g Winged Love(IRE) Well Orchestrated (IRE) (King's Ride)
1040[7] 1322[10] (1715) ◆ 2187[8] 2761[4] 3406[4] 3851[3] 4735[F]

Lots Of Memories (IRE) *P G Fahey* 137h 144c
8 b g Jammaal Remember Rob (IRE) (Deep Society)
49a[10] 1556a[F] (Dead)

Loud And Clear *Iain Jardine* 96b
4 b g Dalakhani(IRE) Whispering Blues (IRE) (Sadler's Wells (USA))
4037[10]

Loughalder (IRE) *Matt Sheppard* 88h 118c
9 ch g Alderbrook Lough Lein Leader (IRE) (Supreme Leader)
(149) 2491[2] 2878[4] 3385[P] 4649[P] (5222) ◆

Lough Derg Cruise (IRE) *Sandy Thomson* 92h
5 b m Beneficial Present Your Own (IRE) (Presenting)
257[4] 1498[3] 1568[5]

Lough Derg Island (IRE) *Alexandra Dunn* 93h
7 b g Court Cave(IRE) Clondalee Fred (IRE) (Jurado (USA))
2152[P] 2564[7] 2904[9] 3368[8] 3586[10] 4528[P] 5099[2] 5313[7]

Lough Kent *Nicky Henderson* 130h 147c
6 b g Barathea(IRE) King's Doll (IRE) (King's Best (USA))
(402) ◆ 431[3] 2468[7] 2784[P] 4770[10] 5279[4]

Lough Salt (IRE) *Mark Walford* 101h
4 b g Brian Boru Castlehill Lady (IRE) (Supreme Leader)
2842[5] 3397[4] 3626[9] 4299[3]

Louis Ludwig (IRE) *Tim Vaughan* 69h 55c
10 b g Mull Of Kintyre(USA) Fantastic Bid (USA) (Auction Ring (USA))
828[8] 918[9] 1071[8]

Louis Phillipe (IRE) *Linda Blackford* 85h 89c
8 ch g Croco Rouge(IRE) Presenting's Wager (IRE) (Presenting)
(31) 438[2] 612[2] ◆ 972[2] 1237[3]

Louis' Vac Pouch (IRE) *Philip Hobbs* 92b
3 b g Oscar(IRE) Coming Home (FR) (Exit To Nowhere (USA))
4488[12] 5358[3]

Loukhaar (IRE) *Jonathan Geake* 94h
7 b g Westerner Gold Air (Sri Pekan (USA))
102[P] 2604[P] 4932[U]

Louloumills *Maurice Barnes* 86h
5 b m Rob Roy(USA) Etching (USA) (Groom Dancer (USA))
1065[5] 1179[4] 1457[3] 1550[U] 1887[9] 2476[2] 3888[4] 4045[4]

Lou Tango (FR) *G Cherel*
2 ro g Martaline Green Emerald (Warning)
5498a[5]

Lou Vert (FR) *Paul Nicholls* 115h
3 b g Vertigineux(FR) Lourinha (FR) (Loup Solitaire (USA))
3915[4] ◆ 4304[5]

Lovcen (GER) *Sophie Leech* 99h 74c
10 b g Tiger Hill(IRE) Lady Hawk (GER) (Grand Lodge (USA))
2700[P] 2887[5] 4684[P] 5052[P]

Love Anthem (IRE) *Denis Gerard Hogan* 84h
6 b m Royal Anthem(USA) Rita's Charm (IRE) (Arctic Lord (IRE))
2487[8]

Lovefromabove (IRE) *Dan Skelton* 74h
4 b m Flemensfirth(USA) Good Looking Woman (IRE) (Oscar (IRE))
928[5] 4039[6] 4164[7] 4344[13] 4845[5]

Lovely Bubbly *Tim Vaughan* 101h
4 gr g Kayf Tara Champagne Lil (Terimon)
602[6] 1968[5] 4888[6] 5477[3]

Lovely Job (IRE) *Fergal O'Brien* 120h 131c
5 ch g Touch Of Land(FR) Wyckoff Queen (IRE) (Carefree Dancer (USA))
2973[2] 3507[2] 5285[F]

Love Marmalade (IRE) *Alistair Whillans* 73h
5 ch g Duke Of Marmalade(IRE) Green Castle (IRE) (Indian Ridge)
1773[9]

Love Over Heels *Richard Price* 77h
6 b m Overbury(IRE) Love Supreme (IRE) (Supreme Leader)
178[6]

Love Rory (IRE) *E Bolger* 116h 128c
7 b g Winged Love(IRE) Lonely Teardrop (IRE) (Spanish Place (USA))
2236a[10] 3017[U] 4719[P]

Loves Destination *Chris Gordon* 107h
4 b m Dubai Destination(USA) Bijou Love (IRE) (Winged Love (IRE))
2252[7] 2958[4] 3219[2] 3789[2] (3905) 4413[3] (4593) (4936) 5102[3]

Love The Leader (IRE) *Johnny Farrelly* 114h 110c
7 b g Fruits Of Love(USA) Suelena (IRE) (Supreme Leader)
281[7] 892[6] 1427[6] 1599[10] (1972) (2004) (2102) (2143) 2456[F]

Lowanbehold (IRE) *Sandy Forster* 107h 125c
8 gr g Cloudings(IRE) Marble Quest (IRE) (Roselier (FR))
730[2] 866[3] 1067[P] 4634[2] (5084) (5257) 5413[3]

Lowcarr Motion *Micky Hammond* 103h
5 b g Rainbow High Royalty (IRE) (Fairy King (USA))
2174[4] 2745[8] 4415[3] ◆ (5079)

Lower Hope Dandy *Venetia Williams* 127h
8 gr g Karinga Bay Cheeky Mare (Derrylin)
3352[3] 3923[4] 5045[3] 5335[2]

Low Key (IRE) *David Pipe* 136h
8 b g Pentire La Capilla (Machiavellian (USA))
1119[4] (1379) (1488) 2241[3] 2641[10]

Loyaute (FR) *Chris Down* 120h 111c
8 ch m Green Tune(USA) Iles Marquises (IRE) (Unfuwain (USA))
1808[5] 2247[6] 4338[6] 5282[10]

L Stig *John O'Shea* 99h
5 b g Striking Ambition Look Here's May (Revoque (IRE))
180[5] 5074 1156[F] 1297[7] 1478[8] 1604[7]

Luca Brazi (IRE) *Alan Phillips*
3 b g Mahler Carriacou (Mark Of Esteem (IRE))
5337[5]

Lucarno Dancer *Raymond Shiels* 82h
5 b m Lucarno(USA) Sing And Dance (Rambo Dancer (CAN))
2318[9] 2847[6]

Luccombe Down *Donald McCain* 100h
5 b g Primo Valentino(IRE) Flaming Rose (IRE) (Roselier (FR))
155[2] 730[4]

Lucematic *Chris Grant* 110h 117c
9 b m Systematic Soldier's Song (Infantry I)
158[3] 2785[3] 3885[5] 4203[4]

Lucie Rie (IRE) *K R Burke* 86h
3 b f Excellent Art Farthingale (IRE) (Nashwan (USA))
1928[6] 2537[6] 3587[5]

Lucky Bridle (IRE) *Chris Grant* 147h
6 b g Dylan Thomas(IRE) Auction Room (USA) (Chester House (USA))
7a[23] 850[11] 1333[6] 1922[U] 1969[P] 2293[F]

Lucky Buttons (IRE) *S R B Crawford* 101h
7 b m Winged Love(IRE) Cute N'Shy (IRE) (Shy Groom (USA))
881[7]

Luckydom (FR) *E Leray*
4 bb g Domedriver(IRE) Kindara (IRE) (Sinndar (IRE))
3815a[P]

Lucky Dottie *Pat Phelan* 95h
4 bb m Lucky Story(USA) Auntie Dot Com (Tagula (IRE))
104[3]

Lucky Dreamer *Chris Bealby* 61h
4 ch m Lucarno(USA) Arcady (Slip Anchor)
2494[5]

Lucky Gal *Martin Hill* 94b
5 b m Overbury(IRE) Lucky Arrow (Indian Ridge)
387[P]

Lucky Jim *David Dennis* 124h 121c
4 b g Lucky Story(USA) Lateralle (IRE) (Unfuwain (USA))
162[4] 1847[9] 2266[8] 4465[5] 4984[2]

Lucky Landing (IRE) *Tony Coyle* 114h 135c
9 bb g Well Chosen Melville Rose (IRE) (Phardante (FR))
(315) 709[4] 917[7]

Lucky Ruby (FR) *Robert Collet*
2 ch g Soldier Of Fortune(IRE) Rubilite (FR) (Indian River (FR))
5498a[7]

Lucky Touch (IRE) *Hugh Burns* 39b
4 b m Duke Of Marmalade(IRE) Sabindra (Magic Ring (IRE))
459[12]

Lucky Violet (IRE) *Hugh Burns* 46b
3 b f Dandy Man(IRE) Rashida (King's Best (USA))
5014[8] 5476[6]

Lucydoli *Stuart Coltherd* 24h
6 b m Endoli(USA) Kariba Dream (Hatim (USA))
2070[6]

Lucy Lane *Phillip Dando*
5 ch m Lucarno(USA) Herballistic (Rolfe (USA))
4687[14]

Lucy Mc (IRE) *Gordon Elliott* 72b
4 gr m Tikkanen(USA) Careless Abandon (IRE) (Mull Of Kintyre (USA))
1334[5]

Lucy Milan (IRE) *Andrew Crook* 84h
6 b m Milan Katty Barry (IRE) (Alderbrook)
33[4] 251[F] (Dead)

Luddsdenene (IRE) *Alexandra Dunn* 117h 124c
10 b g Beneficial Kilcowan (IRE) (Beau Sher)
125[4] 718[9] 835[9]

Ludo Et Emergo (IRE) *Andrew Lee* 61h 142c
8 b g Needle Gun(IRE) Brook Forte (Alderbrook)
47a[F] 5023a[5]

Lukeys Luck *Jennie Candlish* 76b
9 b g Cape Town(IRE) Vitelucy (Vettori (IRE))
859[P]

Lukie *Peter Niven* 57h
7 ch g Revoque(IRE) Subtle Blush (Nashwan (USA))
132[6]

Luna Nuova (IRE) *Chris Bealby* 41h
5 b m Milan Perfect Prospect (IRE) (Golan (IRE))
1898[13] 2561[7]

Lunar Flow *Jamie Snowden* 95h
4 b g With The Flow(USA) Misty Move (IRE) (Saddlers' Hall (IRE))
227[6] 601[7] 2299[P] 2699[6] 3077[10] 3914[3] 4450[5] (5033)

Lundy Sky *Miss L Luxton* 106b
10 b g Zaha(CAN) Rosina Mae (Rousillon (USA))
5186[P]

L'Unique (FR) *Alan King* 138h 135c
6 br m Reefscape Sans Tune (FR) (Green Tune (USA))
1848[13] 2347[3] ◆ 2760[3] 3229[4] ◆ 3611[P]

Lupita (IRE) *Derrick Scott* 22h 11c
11 ch m Intikhab(USA) Sarah (IRE) (Hernando (FR))
269[P] 4859[P]

Lure Des Pres (IRE) *Linda Blackford*
3 b g Robin Des Pres(FR) Pinkeen Lady (IRE) (Presenting)
4357[P] 5188[P]

Luso's Way (IRE) *Tim Vaughan* 94h
7 b m Stowaway Coccinella (IRE) (Luso)
443[7] 811[P]

Lutece *Venetia Williams* 114h
3 b f Cape Cross(IRE) Loutka (FR) (Trempolino (USA))
4462[2]

Lybowler *James Ewart* 90b
5 b g Lyphento(USA) Bowling On (Gildoran)
144[7]

Lycidas (GER) *James Ewart* 62h
6 b g Zamindar(USA) La Felicita (Shareef Dancer (USA))
4033[4]

Lynda's Boy *Dan Skelton* 23h
4 b g Rainbow High Braybrooke Lady (IRE) (Presenting)
2750[9] 3835[18]

Lyreen Legend (IRE) *Ms Sandra Hughes* 130h 136c
8 b g Saint Des Saints(FR) Bint Bladi (FR) (Garde Royale)
2606a[3] 3894a[8]

Lyrical Theatre (IRE) *W P Mullins* 133h
6 b m King's Theatre(IRE) Shuil Dorcha (IRE) (Bob Back (USA))
52a[3]

Lyric Street (IRE) *Donald McCain* 120h 121c
7 b g Hurricane Run(IRE) Elle Danzig (GER) (Roi Danzig (USA))
1505[2] 2034[4] 2424[F] 2765[P] 3346[P]

Lysino (GER) *Dr Richard Newland* 113h 125c
6 ch g Medicean Lysuna (GER) (Monsun (GER))
198[U]

Lyssio (GER) *Mark Hoad* 107h
8 b g Motivator Lysuna (GER) (Monsun (GER))
675[5] 1244[6] 1423[5] 1734[3] 2004[F]

Mab Dab (IRE) *Linda Jewell* 95b
4 b g Papal Bull Pret A Porter (UAE) (Jade Robbery (USA))
3200[6]

Macarthur *David Rees* 117h 110c
11 b g Montjeu(IRE) Out West (USA) (Gone West (USA))
527[4] 697[4] 1008[5] 1169[4] 1296[F] 1483[5] 1674[6]

Mac Bertie *Evan Williams* 110h 83c
6 b g Beat All(USA) Macnance (IRE) (Mandalus)
(615) 776[5] 1054[2] 1269[2] 1377[2] 1701[6] 1965[P]

Maccabees *Linda Jewell* 81h
6 b g Motivator Takarna (IRE) (Mark Of Esteem (IRE))
222[3] 2004[4] 2316[2] (3087) 3771[5]

Mac Gregory *Evan Williams* 101h
4 b g Multiplex Macnance (IRE) (Mandalus)
(2250) 4296[5] 5050[2]

Mackerye End (IRE) *Jonjo O'Neill* 125h
6 b g Milan Great Outlook (IRE) (Simply Great (FR))
2268[11]

Mackeys Forge (IRE) *P E Froud* 85h 117c
11 b g Mr Combustible(IRE) Lucy Walters (IRE) (King's Ride)
4969[4]

Mac Le Couteau *Evan Williams* 93h 103c
7 b g Overbury(IRE) Macnance (IRE) (Mandalus)
439[P]

Mac N Cheese (IRE) *Rose Dobbin* 103h
5 b g Milan Fox Burrow (IRE) (Supreme Leader)
1572[7] 2029[6] (2720) ◆

Macnicholson (IRE) *Mrs John Harrington* 104h 120c
6 b g Definite Article Heroic Performer (IRE) (Royal Applause)
7a[2] 1163a[7]

Mac's Grey (IRE) *Ian Williams* 72h 86c
8 gr g Great Palm(USA) Gypsy Kelly (IRE) (Roselier (FR))
446[4] (914) 964[2] 1133[P]

Mac's Superstar (FR) *Alan Coogan*
5 b g Elusive City(USA) Diamond Light (USA) (Fantastic Light (USA))
221[U]

Mad About The Boy *Robert Walford* 98h 106c
5 b g Robin Des Pres(FR) Dalamine (FR) (Sillery (USA))
212[2] 2630[P] 3133[9] 3516[6] 3916[4] 4255[P]

Madaboy Cross (IRE) *Thomas P O'Connor* 100h
5 ch m Beneficial Liagry Road Lass (IRE) (Old Vic)
1150a[14]

Madam Be *Brian Barr* 89h 23c
5 b m Kayf Tara Mrs Be (IRE) (Be My Native (USA))
30[P] 1004[12]

Madame Allsorts *Willie Musson* 96h
10 b m Double Trigger(IRE) Always A Pleasure (Chauve Souris)
291[3]

Madame De Guise (FR) *Laura Mongan* 110h 122c
6 b m Le Balafre(FR) Paradana (FR) (Dress Parade)
(431)

Madame Evelyn *Suzy Smith*
4 gr m Beat All(USA) Madam Blaze (Overbury (IRE))
671[P]

Madame Trigger *Dan Skelton* 111h
7 b m Double Trigger(IRE) Marathea (FR) (Marathon (USA))
2164[6] 2476[3]

Madam Lilibet (IRE) *Sharon Watt* 108h
6 b m Authorized(IRE) Foxilla (IRE) (Foxhound (USA))
1925[P] 2432[5] 2800[R] 3503[R]

Mad Brian (IRE) *Mrs Gillian Callaghan* 124h 133c
9 b g Brian Boru Needle Doll (IRE) (Needle Gun (IRE))
4802[P]

Mad For Road (IRE) *Ben Haslam* 101h
6 b g Galileo(IRE) Potion (Pivotal)
34[F] 843[3] 1098[9]

Madfuninthewest (IRE) *David Dennis* 124h
4 b g Jeremy(USA) Gaybrook (IRE) (Shernazar)
5219[15]

Mad Jack Mytton (IRE) *Jonjo O'Neill* 139h
5 b g Arcadio(GER) Gilt Ridden (IRE) (Heron Island (IRE))
1905[2] ◆ 2512[14] 3015[2] 4115[17] 4765[14] 5189[U] 5497[5]

Mad Moll (IRE) *Daniel Steele* 77h
7 b m Heron Island(IRE) Rose Gold (IRE) (Nucleon (USA))
5303[3]

Mad Money (IRE) *Sophie Leech* 92c
9 b g Alderbrook Merry Gladness (IRE) (King's Ride)
713[3] 1182[3] 1446[7]

Madrasa (IRE) *Tony Forbes* 104h
7 b g High Chaparral(IRE) Shir Dar (FR) (Lead On Time (USA))
1522[8]

Ma Du Fou (FR) *Warren Greatrex* 140h
5 bb g Le Fou(IRE) Belle Du Ma (FR) (Zamindar (USA))
(2363) (3009) (4072) 5189[P] 5497[6]

Maestro Royal *Nicky Henderson* 124h
6 b g Doyen(IRE) Close Harmony (Bustino)
3854[P] 4070[7] 4781[2]

Maetrufel Annie *Paul Webber*
6 b m Flemensfirth(USA) Materiality (Karinga Bay)
3500[P]

Ma Filleule (FR) *Nicky Henderson* 136h 162c
7 gr m Turgeon(USA) Kadaina (FR) (Kadalko (FR))
2199[6] 2781[3] 3150[10] (3337) 4240[P]

Maggie Blue (IRE) *Harriet Graham* 107h 70c
7 b m Beneficial Top Ar Aghaidh (IRE) (Topanoora)
845[8] 1067[2] 1420[7] (1925) 3025[4] 3437[2] 3970[5] 4510[4] 4840[2] 5260[2]

Maggie Rose *Donald McCain* 31b
3 b f King's Theatre(IRE) Holme Rose (Bob Back (USA))
5049[5]

Maggio (FR) *Patrick Griffin* 135h 156c
10 b g Trempolino(USA) La Musardiere (FR) (Cadoudal (FR))
(868) 2082[3] 2606a[5] 4635[6] (5217)

Magheral Express (IRE) *Jonjo O'Neill* 117h 89c
6 b g Gold Well Patzanni (IRE) (Arzanni)
614[P] 1011[2] 2456[5] 2749[P]

Magical Man *Debra Hamer* 72h 95c
8 bb g Lahib(USA) Majestic Di (IRE) (Zaffaran (USA))
438[5] 2364[4] 2836[2] 3468[2] (4823) 5240[U] 5468[7]

Magic Bullet (IRE) *Nicky Henderson* 104b
4 b g Flemensfirth(USA) Some Bob Back (IRE) (Bob Back (USA))
5457[4]

Magic Dancer *Charlie Longsdon* 110h
3 b g Norse Dancer(IRE) King's Siren (IRE) (King's Best (USA))
2992[5] 3423[2] 3819[2] 4979[2]

Magic Haze *Sally Hall*
9 b g Makbul Turn Back (Pivotal)
4326[P]

Magic Magnolia (IRE) *Dan Skelton* 102h
4 b m Azamour(IRE) Royal Aly (USA) (Royal Academy (USA))
405[4] 621[3] (748) 938[8]

Magic Money *Kim Bailey* 113h
7 b m Midnight Legend Sticky Money (Relkino)
130[F] 1618[2] 2167[P] 2812[4] 3930[4] (4709)

Magic Music Man *Alan King* 110h
4 b g Authorized(IRE) Magic Music (IRE) (Magic Ring (IRE))
2238[5] 2689[2] 4888[4] 5434[3]

Magic Mustard (IRE) *Charlie Longsdon* 85h
4 ch g Stowaway Honey Mustard (IRE) (Roselier (FR))
341[8] 2299[4] 4798[8] 5452[9]

Magic Present *Sarah-Jayne Davies* 104h
8 b g Presenting Magic Bloom (Full Of Hope)
55[P] 262[8]

Magic Three *Peter Croke* 59b
4 bb m Three Valleys(USA) Magic Number (Dansili)
5383[8]

Magna Cartor *Ronald Thompson* 73h
5 b g Motivator Hora (Hernando (FR))
1101[3] 1300[2] 1453[U] 1590[8] 1826[F] 1967[P]

Magnimity (IRE) *Nicky Henderson* 74h
5 b g Generous(IRE) Strawberry Fool (FR) (Tel Quel (FR))
181[5] 648[P]

Magnolia Ridge (IRE) *Mark Walford* 79h
5 b g Galileo(IRE) Treasure The Lady (IRE) (Indian Ridge)
3101[7] 5081[5]

Magnus Romeo *Gail Haywood*
4 b g Manduro(GER) Chili Dip (Alhaarth (IRE))
1781[0]

Mahayogin (USA) *Sarah-Jayne Davies* 99h 71c
7 bb g Dixie Union(USA) Shiva (JPN) (Hector Protector (USA))
489[7] 777[4] 843[8] 977[P] 1159[5] 1373[P]

Mahler And Me (IRE) *Alistair Whillans* 112h
5 ch g Mahler Tisindabreedin (IRE) (Zaffaran (USA))
(2978) 3400[P] 5011[5]

Mahler Bay (IRE) *Michael Smith* 87h
5 b g Mahler Belalzao (IRE) (Alzao (USA))
3104[6] 4031[8] 4835[7]

Mahlerdramatic (IRE) *Brian Ellison* 116b
5 br g Mahler Image Of Vermont (IRE) (Accordion)
1449[4] (1797) (2337)

Mahler Lad (IRE) *Donald McCain* 113h
5 b g Mahler Sister Merenda (IRE) (Dr Massini (IRE))
3340[P] 4711[3] 5331[2]

Mahlers Spirit (IRE) *Sarah Humphrey* 64h
5 ch g Mahler Belle Dame (IRE) (Executive Perk)
2141[4] 2549[7] 3221[10] 3817[P]

Mahlers Star (IRE) *David Bridgwater* 115h
5 ch g Mahler Celestial Rose (IRE) (Roselier (FR))
3949[2] 4409[5] 4976[4]

Maid Of Milan (IRE) *Charlie Mann* 108h
4 br m Milan Joes Lady (IRE) (Win Quick (IRE))
2702[6] 4457[2] ◆ 4777[3]

Maid Of Silk (IRE) *Mrs K Lee* 29h 31c
9 b m Blueprint(IRE) Silk Style (Polish Precedent (USA))
536[11]

Maid Of Tuscany (IRE) *Neil Mulholland* 110h
4 b m Manduro(GER) Tuscania (USA) (Woodman (USA))
405[5] 694[8] 892[4] 1095[3] 1299[F] (1941) 2043[2] 4970[4]

Maigh Dara (IRE) *Lydia Richards* 42h
6 br g Cacique(IRE) Dara Diva (IRE) (Barathea (IRE))
602[4] 5115[P] 5303[7]

Ma'ire Rua (IRE) *Alan Jones* 97h 66c
8 ch g Presenting Long Acre (Mark Of Esteem (IRE))
2091[5] 2604[5] 4379[U] 4932[3] 5435[P]

Maizy Missile (IRE) *Mary Evans* 94h 94c
13 b m Executive Perk Landsker Missile (Cruise Missile)
514[3] 1045[2] 1603[3] 1703[2]

Majala (FR) *Tom George* 96h 117c
9 b g Lavirco(GER) Majae (FR) (Dom Pasquini (FR))
2468[12] 2780[P] 3957[8] 4370[6]

Majestic Sun (IRE) *Jim Boyle* 97h
4 b g King's Best(USA) Shining Vale (USA) (Twilight Agenda (USA))
2000[6]

Majestic Touch (IRE) *Tracey L Bailey* 93b
4 br g Kalanisi(IRE) Alexander Divine (Halling (USA))
444[2] 4867[12]

Major Davis (FR) *Warren Greatrex* 63b
3 b g Vision D'Etat(FR) Majorica Sancta (FR) (Saint Des Saints (FR))
5151[7]

Major Decision (IRE) *Miss J Wickens* 99h 99c
13 bb g Saddlers' Hall(IRE) Real Prospect (IRE) (Henbit (USA))
294[4]

Major Ivan (IRE) *Malcolm Jefferson* 129h 129c
6 b g Fruits Of Love(USA) Martinstown Queen (IRE) (Saddlers' Hall (IRE))
132[2] 1635[3] 2070[3] 2624[2] 3158[4] 3805[F]

Major Mac *Hughie Morrison* 100h
3 ch g Shirocco(GER) Spring Fashion (IRE) (Galileo (IRE))
2757[3] 3519[P]

Major Malarkey (IRE) *Nigel Twiston-Davies* 108h 129c
12 b g Supreme Leader Valley (IRE) (Flemensfirth (USA))
(17) 535[P] 4307[5] 4768[7] 5178[U]

Major Martin (IRE) *Gary Moore* 79h 86c
6 b g Flemensfirth(USA) Miss Emer (IRE) (Be My Native (USA))
3042[P] 5181[6] 5478[4]

Major Milborne *Jamie Snowden* 112h 124c
7 ch g Exit To Nowhere(USA) Motown Melody (IRE) (Detroit Sam (FR))
2168[4] 2758[P] 3662[2] 4226[4] 5072[7] 5375[7]

Major Ridge (IRE) *Robert Bewley* 89h 91c
6 b g Indian Danehill(IRE) Native Novel (IRE) (Be My Native (USA))
2983[P] 4569[5] 5261[6] 5369[3]

Makadamia *Robert Waley-Cohen* 109h 112c
6 b m Kahyasi Makounji (FR) (Tip Moss (FR))
557[P]

Makbullet *Michael Smith* 104h 89c
8 gr g Makbul Gold Belt (IRE) (Bellypha)
2499[P] 2949[4] 3473[13]

Make A Track (IRE) *Gordon Elliott* 137h 149c
9 ch g Hernando(FR) Tracker (Bustino)
1152a[U]

Make It Happen (IRE) *Lucinda Russell* 106h
6 b g Saffron Walden(FR) Kelpie (IRE) (Kahyasi)
(456)

Make Me A Fortune (IRE) *Steve Gollings* 130h 86c
7 bb g Heron Island(IRE) Biora Queen (IRE) (Old Vic)
4801[11] 4986[4]

Makethedifference (IRE) *Tim Vaughan* 117h 118c
7 b g Shantou(USA) La Panthere (USA) (Pine Bluff (USA))
776[7] 1265[4] (1501) ◆ (1554) 1868[2] 2038[3] 3216[F]

Makler (CZE) *Michal Lisek* 120h
8 b g Ballingarry(IRE) Magical Millie (Muhtarram (USA))
1671a[5]

Mala Beach (IRE) *Gordon Elliott* 156h 157c
7 b g Beneficial Peppardstown (IRE) (Old Vic)
2606a[F] 3147[2] 3715a[2] 4260a[F] 5005a[P]

Malanos (IRE) *Tony Carroll* 111h 107c
7 bb g Lord Of England(GER) Majorata (GER) (Acatenango (GER))
104[2] 2810[3] ◆ 3216[5] 3784[7] 4211[4] 4597[2] ◆ 5388[7]

Malapie (IRE) *Caroline Bailey*
7 b g Westerner Victorian Lady (Old Vic)
177[B]

Maldivian Reef (IRE) *Alan King* 87h
7 ch g Reefscape Spirited Soul (IRE) (Luso)
460[3] 757[7]

Malibu Rock *Chris Gordon* 110h
7 b g Tiger Hill(IRE) High Straits (Bering)
(4099) 4972[4]

Malibu Sun *Ben Pauling* 114h 133c
8 ch g Needwood Blade Lambadora (Suave Dancer (USA))
315[P] 2042[7] 2301[4] 2884[2] 3148[P] 5246[6] ◆

Malin Bay (IRE) *Nicky Richards* 125h
10 b g Milan Mirror Of Flowers (Artaius (USA))
2190[3] 2744[10]

Mallards In Flight (IRE) *Gavin Cromwell* 103h 119c
9 b m Well Chosen Lasracha Mairead (IRE) (Case Law)
(70a)

Mall Dini (IRE) *Patrick G Kelly* 144h
5 b g Milan Winsome Breeze (IRE) (Glacial Storm (USA))
(4730)

Maller Tree *David Dennis* 115h 108c
8 b g Karinga Bay Annaberg (IRE) (Tirol)
380[P] 678[4] 839[11] 1079[3] 1287[11] 1545[6]

Mallowney (IRE) *Timothy Doyle* 145h 161c
9 br g Oscar(IRE) Silkaway (IRE) (Buckskin (FR))
8a[4] 2464a[5]

Maltese Doll *Nick Kent* 88b
5 ch m Primo Valentino(IRE) Farmer's Pet (Sharrood (USA))
359[4]

Malt Gem (IRE) *Miss Mary Louise Hallahan* 120h 138c
7 b g Germany(USA) Maltesse (IRE) (Never So Bold)
3715a[R] 4397a[12] 4949a[U]

Manballandall (IRE) *Susan Corbett* 128h 113c
7 b g Flemensfirth(USA) Omas Lady (IRE) (Be My Native (USA))
(203) 473[6] 1633[4] 1856[4] 2932[4] 3162[4] 3507[4] 3837[P] 4206[6] 4566[4] 5012[2] 5368[5]

Mandy's Boy (IRE) *Sally Randell* 103h 100c
5 b g Kyllachy African Queen (IRE) (Cadeaux Genereux)
1239[6] 1421[2] 1524[3] 2869[8] 3103[4] 3845[3] 4029[2] 4850[7] 5016[P]

Man From Mars *Nick Williams* 92b
3 b g Schiaparelli(GER) Diletia (Dilum (USA))
4143[2] ◆ 4880[10]

Man From Seville *Fergal O'Brien* 116h
5 ch g Duke Of Marmalade(IRE) Basanti (USA) (Galileo (IRE))
3509[7] (4388) 4869[6]

Mangans Turn *Miss Karen A Williams* 78b 56c
8 b g Generous(IRE) Little Feat (Terimon)
4269[7]

Manger Hanagment (IRE) *Barry Brennan* 104h 110c
10 br g Heron Island(IRE) Island Religion (IRE) (Religiously (USA))
914[6] 1492[2] ◆ 1548[P] 1743[3]

Mango Cap (FR) *David Pipe* 113h
4 b g Zambezi Sun Medjai (FR) (Kendor (FR))
3054[3] 4014[10] 5328[10]

Manhattan Mead *Michael Madgwick* 112h
5 ch g Central Park(IRE) Honey Nut (Entrepreneur)
2417[6] 2823[2] 3133[7] 3452[3] 3994[7] 4530[5] 5063[9]

Manhattan Spring *Seamus Mullins* 106b
4 b g Central Park(IRE) Risky May (Petoski)
(3200) 4532[2] 5195[8]

Manhattan Swing (IRE) *Brian Ellison* 138h
5 b g Invincible Spirit(IRE) Bluebell Park (USA) (Gulch (USA))
1039[3] (1263) 1657[5]

Mankala (IRE) *Oliver Sherwood* 108b
5 b g Flemensfirth(USA) Maracana (IRE) (Glacial Storm (USA))
5097[3]

Man Of Conquest (IRE) *Desmond McDonogh* 109b
4 b g Teofilo(IRE) My Girl Sophie (USA) (Danzig (USA))
11a[6]

Man Of God (IRE) *Tim Vaughan* 96h
7 b g Sadler's Wells(USA) Jude (Darshaan)
1297[9] 1933[5] 3108[P] 3665[6] 4291[2] (4987) 5199[2]

Man Of Leisure *Anthony Honeyball* 126h
11 b g Karinga Bay Girl Of Pleasure (IRE) (Namaqualand (USA))
356[2] 527[3] 798[4] (1051) 1291[2]

Man Of Steel (IRE) *Alan Hill* 107h 119c
6 b g Craigsteel Knappogue Honey (IRE) (Anshan)
(4426) 4969[2]

Man O'Words (IRE) *Tom Lacey* 103b
4 b g Scorpion(IRE) Mrs Malt (IRE) (Presenting)
4308[2] 5330[7]

Mansonien L'As (FR) *Donald McCain* 66h 91c
9 b g Mansonnien(FR) Star Des As (FR) (Kaldou Star)
1355[P] 2173[P] 3059[2] 3222[P] 3948[P] 4433[P]

Mansuri *Warren Greatrex*
4 ch g Piccolo Antonia's Choice (Music Boy)
98[P]

Manton Boy *Michael Mullineaux* 79b
6 b g Revoque(IRE) Got On A Lucky One (IRE) (Shernazar)
2126[8] 2440[7] 3568[P]

Mantou (IRE) *John Ferguson* 129h
4 ch g Teofilo(IRE) Shadow Roll (IRE) (Mark Of Esteem (IRE))
1488[2] 1848[6] 2058[7] 4066[12]

Man With Van (IRE) *S R B Crawford* 136h 136c
9 b g Milan Delibonne (IRE) (Erdelistan (FR))
92a[6] 2790[P] 3439[4] 3741[U]

Many Clouds (IRE) *Oliver Sherwood* 139h 170c
8 br g Cloudings(IRE) Bobbing Back (IRE) (Bob Back (USA))
2200[6] 2900[2] 3850[2] (4635) ◆ 5218[16]

Maoi Chinn Tire (IRE) *Jennie Candlish* 100h 93c
8 b g Mull Of Kintyre(USA) Primrose And Rose (Primo Dominie)
1170[8] 1714[7]

Maputo *John Ferguson* 150h
5 b g Cape Cross(IRE) Insijaam (USA) (Secretariat (USA))
(1328) (1544) (1766) (1986) 2509[2] (Dead)

Marakoush (IRE) *Alan Fleming* 130h
4 b g Danehill Dancer(IRE) Mouramara (IRE) (Kahyasi)
3459a[4] 4280a[6]

Marasonnien (FR) *W P Mullins* 141h 128c
9 b g Mansonnien(FR) Maracay (FR) (Subotica (FR))
5178[P] (Dead)

Maraweh (IRE) *Lucinda Russell* 118h
5 b g Muhtathir Itqaan (USA) (Danzig (USA))
661[5] 883[6] (1329) (1497) 1637[5] (2296) (2948) 3428[15] 5475[3]

Marchese Marconi (IRE) *A P O'Brien* 150h 130c
6 b g Galileo(IRE) Charroux (IRE) (Darshaan)
1163a[5] 5004a[2]

Marcilhac (FR) *Venetia Williams* 123h 121c
6 b g Smadoun(FR) One Way I (FR) (Exit To Nowhere (USA))
3148[9] 4128[6]

Marcus Antonius *Lucinda Russell* 104h 103c
8 b g Mark Of Esteem(IRE) Star Of The Course (USA) (Theatrical (IRE))
3035[4] ◆ 3473[4] 4179[6] 4583[2] 5122[4]

Mardale (IRE) *Nicky Richards* 120h
5 b m Robin Des Champs(FR) Lizzy Langtry (IRE) (King's Theatre (IRE))
1555[3] (1854) 2626[3] 3154[P] 4868[2] (5229) (5470)

Marden Court (IRE) *Colin Tizzard* 112h 117c
5 b g Tikkanen(USA) Shilling Hill (IRE) (Supreme Leader)
61[4] 2240[5] 2659[2] 2874[3] 3253[3] 3709[2] 4225[F] (Dead)

Marey (IRE) *Ms N M Hugo*
6 b m Fruits Of Love(USA) Mill Thyme (Thowra (FR))
3226[P]

Margaret's Rose (IRE) *Nigel Twiston-Davies* 84h
5 b m Millenary Alannah Rose (IRE) (Roselier (FR))
462[7] 1845[7]

Maria's Choice (IRE) *Jim Best* 104h
6 b g Oratorio(IRE) Amathusia (Selkirk (USA))
(2547) 3011[P]

Marie Des Anges (FR) *Anthony Honeyball* 114h 126c
7 b m Ballingarry(IRE) No Coincidence (IRE) (Indian Ridge)
(64) 357[U] 431[2] 672[2] 927[5] (1241) 1327[3]

Mariet *Suzy Smith* 95h
6 ch m Dr Fong(USA) Medway (IRE) (Shernazar)
(4413)

Mari Me Oscar (IRE) *Nikki Evans* 71h
5 b m Oscar(IRE) Nostra (FR) (Limnos (JPN))
432[7] 2770[4] 3110[10] 4293[4] 4961[5] 5420[13]

Marina Bay *Christopher Kellett* 60h
10 b m Karinga Bay Marina Bird (Julio Mariner)
40[8] 240[13]

Marinas (GER) *G Macaire* 128c
8 b g Sholokhov(IRE) Majorata (GER) (Acatenango (GER))
(374a) 1672a[2]

Marinero (IRE) *A J Martin* 142h 122c
6 b g Presenting Peggy Maddock (IRE) (Oscar (IRE))
3716a[7]

Mariners Moon (IRE) *Patrick Holmes*
4 ch g Mount Nelson Dusty Moon (Dr Fong (USA))
5242[F]

Marito (GER) *C A McBratney* 145h 152c
9 b g Alkalde(GER) Maratea (USA) (Fast Play (USA))
1152a[11] 4768[2]

Marju's Quest (IRE) *David Dennis* 130h 110c
5 b g Marju(IRE) Queen's Quest (Rainbow Quest (USA))
492[3] 830[6] 1038[8] 1180[6] (1346) 1646[3] 1700[3] 5159[9] 5386[8]

Markami (FR) *Johnny Farrelly* 55h
5 ch g Medicean Marque Royale (Royal Academy (USA))
537[13]

Market Option (IRE) *Venetia Williams* 100h 109c
9 b g Lord Americo Ticklepenny (IRE) (In The Wings)
1850[U] 2149[5] 2598[2] 3127[U] 3572[2] 4069[7] 4433[5] 5044[F]

Marky Bob (IRE) *Hugo Froud* 100h 107c
10 b g Turtle Island(IRE) Bobomy (IRE) (Bob Back (USA))
1169[9] 1233[2] 1353[P] (2552) 4386[RR] 4670[4]

Marlbrook (IRE) *C A Murphy* 134h 146c
7 b g Beneficial Drinadaly (IRE) (Oscar (IRE))
(4279a)

Marlee Massie (IRE) *N W Alexander* 109h
6 b g Dr Massini(IRE) Meadstown Miss (IRE) (Flemensfirth (USA))
288[4] 658[6] 1400[2] 1779[U] (2937) (2980) (3868) (4638) 5089[3]

Marlee Mourinho (IRE) *N W Alexander* 81h 89c
9 br g Pushkin(IRE) Spur Of The Moment (Montelimar (USA))
303[6] 1891[P] 2191[P]

Marley Joe (IRE) *Martin Keighley* 95h
4 b g Arcadio(GER) Tuscarora (IRE) (Revoque (IRE))
1289[6] 1612[5] 1844[3] 2163[11] 2810[P] 5181[C]

Marlpit Oak *Seamus Mullins* 87h 68c
10 b m Midnight Legend Lonicera (Sulaafah (USA))
893[3] 1245[6] 1509[6] 1756[4] 2004[2]

Marmalade Man *Seamus Mullins* 94h
9 ch g Karinga Bay Kentford Duchess (Jupiter Island)
530[9]

Marquis Of Carabas (IRE) *David Dennis* 121h
5 bb g Hurricane Run(IRE) Miss Otis Regrets (IRE) (Bob Back (USA))
525[3] 2041[2] 2318[4] 5098[2]

Marracudja (FR) *Paul Nicholls* 140h
4 b g Martaline Memorial (FR) (Homme De Loi (IRE))
(2091) (2345) ◆ 3227[3] 4360[2] 5190[P]

Marrakech Trader (NZ) *Rose Dobbin* 87h
7 ch g Pentire Eastern Bazaar (IRE) (King Persian)
2071[3] 3402[7]

Marshgate Lane (USA) *Neil Mulholland* 97h
6 b g Medaglia d'Oro(USA) Louvain (IRE) (Sinndar (IRE))
1117[P] 1886[4] 2689[12] 4773[7]

Martalette (FR) *Yannick Fouin* 136h 132c
5 b m Martaline Cousette (FR) (Polish Precedent (USA))
350a[6] (2821a)

Martalin (FR) *Patrice Quinton* 103h 119c
9 b g Martaline Stanelme (FR) (Kashtan (FR))
3017[6]

Martello Tower (IRE) *Ms Margaret Mullins* 154h
7 b g Milan Johnsalice (IRE) (Zaffaran (USA))
3322a[3] 3713a[3] 4732[7]
Martha's Benefit (IRE) *Mike Sowersby* 90b
6 b m Beneficial Trajectus (Homo Sapien)
594[5] 696[5] 852[F]
Mart Lane (IRE) *Sophie Leech* 100h 133c
10 br g Stowaway Western Whisper (IRE) (Supreme Leader)
362[4] 642[8] 857[6]
Marvellous Moment (IRE) *J H Culloty* 108h 116c
6 b g Turtle Island(IRE) Sunshine Leader (IRE) (Supreme Leader)
4279a[5]
Marvellous Monty (IRE) *Johnny Farrelly* 100h
5 br m Oscar(IRE) Montys Miss (IRE) (Presenting)
2493[5] 3862[9] 4430[P] 5155[3]
Marygale Bridge (IRE) *John J Walsh* 120h
6 ch m Beneficial Cream Gorse (Alflora (IRE))
4653a[5]
Mary May *Susan Corbett*
7 b m Ferrule(IRE) Leighten Lass (IRE) (Henbit (USA))
3306[P]
Masirann (IRE) *Micky Hammond* 103b
7 b g Tiger Hill(IRE) Masilia (IRE) (Kahyasi)
2717[P]
Mason Hindmarsh *Karen McLintock* 128h 129c
8 ch g Dr Fong(USA) Sierra Virgen (USA) (Stack (USA))
(253) 469[3] 801[3] 961[P]
Masquerade (IRE) *Warren Greatrex* 102b
6 b g Fruits Of Love(USA) Beechill Dancer (IRE) (Darnay)
5047[F]
Massachusetts *Rob Summers* 77h
8 ch g Singspiel(IRE) Royal Passion (Ahonoora)
807[P] 977[5] 1119[6] 1383[8]
Massini's Lady *N W Alexander* 67h
4 b m Dr Massini(IRE) Lady Du Bost (FR) (Royal Charter (FR))
2025[5] 2398[4] 2936[P] 4163[5] 4739[4] 5203[P]
Massini's Trap (IRE) *J A Nash* 134h
6 b g Dr Massini(IRE) Sparrow's Trap (IRE) (Magical Wonder (USA))
231a[13] 1175a[3] 2236a[7] 3634a[2]
Master Ally (IRE) *Rebecca Curtis* 92h
5 gr g Flemensfirth(USA) Ally Rose (IRE) (Roselier (FR))
1873[3] 2152[P] 3976[7] 4430[P] 5050[3]
Master Benjamin *Jeremy Scott* 114h
8 b g Fair Mix(IRE) Morning Flight (IRE) (Supreme Leader)
1023 2152[5]
Master Burbidge *Neil Mulholland* 88h
4 b g Pasternak Silver Sequel (Silver Patriarch (IRE))
2183[9] 2768[6] 3077[7] 5364a[5]
Master Butcher (IRE) *N W Alexander* 83h 107c
8 b g Court Cave(IRE) Carleen Gold (Carlingford Castle)
883[P]
Master Cardor Visa (IRE) *Emma Baker* 84h
10 br g Alderbrook Princess Moodyshoe (Jalmood (USA))
65[2] ◆ 552[5] 879[6]
Master Dan *Kim Bailey* 96h
4 b g Mastercraftsman(IRE) Danella (IRE) (Platini (GER))
182[3]
Master Dee (IRE) *Donald McCain* 120h 99c
6 b g King's Theatre(IRE) Miss Lauren Dee (IRE) (Montelimar (USA))
253[3]
Masterful Act (USA) *Dan Skelton* 123h
8 ch g Pleasantly Perfect(USA) Catnip (USA) (Flying Paster (USA))
225[7] **691[P]** 1051[2]
Master Jake (IRE) *Dan Skelton* 130h
7 b g Pyrus(USA) Whitegate Way (Greensmith)
(2474) ◆ (2699) 3630[10] 4526[3] (4937) 5219[12]
Master Majic (IRE) *Colin Tizzard* 91b
4 b g Flemensfirth(USA) Majic Times Ahead (Weld)
4790[9] 5358[9]
Master Murphy (IRE) *Jane Walton* 78h 19c
10 b g Flemensfirth(USA) Awbeg Beauty (IRE) (Supreme Leader)
136[5] **486[P]** 1925[P] 4110[5] 4289[4] 4739[P]
Master Neo (FR) *Nigel Hawke* 55h 127c
9 gr g Turgeon(USA) Really Royale (FR) (Garde Royale)
760[4] 1659[2] 1783[F] **2288[P] 3253[P]**
Masterofdeception (IRE) *Dr Richard Newland* 127h
7 b g Darsi(FR) Sherberry (IRE) (Shernazar)
(319)
Master Of Speed (IRE) *Gary Moore* 111h
3 ch g Mastercraftsman(IRE) Mango Groove (IRE) (Unfuwain (USA))
3443[3]
Master Of The Game (IRE) *David Dennis* 108h 125c
9 ch g Bob's Return(IRE) Lady Monilousha (IRE) (Montelimar (USA))
469[7] 863[3] 5465[7]
Master Of The Hall (IRE) *Micky Hammond* 127h 123c
11 b g Saddlers' Hall(IRE) Frankly Native (IRE) (Be My Native (USA))
185[3] **358[3]** (729) **800[4] 915[3] 1033[3] 1267[3]**
Masterplan (IRE) *Charlie Longsdon* 123h
5 b g Spadoun(FR) Eurolucy (IRE) (Shardari)
378[P] 1911[2] (2182) 2725[3] (3137) 3736[5] 4801[13] 5275[15]
Master Rajeem (USA) *Neil King* 100h 115c
6 bb g Street Cry(IRE) Rajeem (Diktat)
448[4] 625[6] **2425[8] 2701[4] 3024[3] 3339[5] 4641[3]**
Master Red (IRE) *David Pipe* 109b
6 b g Red Clubs(IRE) Glory Days (GER) (Tiger Hill (IRE))
3917[P]
Master Ruffit (IRE) *Neil McKnight* 120h
7 ch g Blueprint(IRE) Miss Ruffit (IRE) (Phardante (FR))
(3667) 4165[2] 4605[3]
Masters Hill (IRE) *Colin Tizzard* 136h 150c
9 gr g Tikkanen(USA) Leitrim Bridge (IRE) (Earl Of Barking (IRE))
2399[2] ◆ **2790[P] 3518[P] 4141[3] 4483[3] 4684[2] 5327[8]**
Master Workman (IRE) *David Kemp* 119c
9 b g Posidonas Bobbie Magee (IRE) (Buckskin (FR))
129[U] 4973[2]
Matchaway (IRE) *Kerry Lee* 115h
6 b g Milan Hatch Away (IRE) (Lord Americo)
(3012) 3522[3] 5048[2]
Matorico (IRE) *Jonjo O'Neill* 141h
4 gr g Mastercraftsman(IRE) Hashbrown (GER) (Big Shuffle (USA))
94a[8] (2409) 2864[2] 3232[4] 4115[15] 4769[11] (5275) 5497[3]
Matrow's Lady (IRE) *Neil Mulholland* 122h 97c
8 b m Cloudings(IRE) I'm Maggy (NZ) (Danseur Etoile (FR))
1121[3] 2269[3] (2714) 2874[4] 3195[6] 3977[5] 4197[3] 4823[5] 5068[4]
Maura Lily (IRE) *Ian Duncan* 76h
6 br m Lahib(USA) Ali Ankah (IRE) (Insan (USA))
2433[6] 2752[5]
Mausefalle (IRE) *D Summersby* 91c
8 b g Kasmayo Euro Spirit (IRE) (Fourstars Allstar (USA))
123[7]
Mawaqeet (USA) *Michael Appleby* 115h
6 b g Dynaformer(USA) Lady Ilsley (USA) (Trempolino (USA))
1269[4] 1794[3] 2744[4]
Maxanisi (IRE) *Evan Williams* 127h
5 br g Kalanisi(IRE) Maxis Girl (IRE) (Mister Mat (FR))
(2564) 3516[4] 4963[2]
Maxdelas (FR) *Roy Brotherton* 78h
9 ch g Sabrehill(USA) Quendora (FR) (Kendor (FR))
537[12]
Max Dynamite (FR) *W P Mullins* 147h
5 b g Great Journey(JPN) Mascara (GER) (Monsun (GER))
73a[7] 1163a[2]
Max Dynamo *Jim Wilson* 83b
5 b g Midnight Legend Vivante (IRE) (Toulon)
4981[3]
Max Forte (IRE) *Chris Down* 129h
5 br g Indian River(FR) Brook Forte (Alderbrook)
(2088) 2450[3] 3232[8] 4442[4] 5120[4]
Maxie T *Micky Hammond* 136h
4 b g Dalakhani(IRE) Ballet Ballon (USA) (Rahy (USA))
87[8] 2933[4] ◆ (3346) 3630[4] 4107[2] 4287[2] ◆ 4640[2] 4937[3]
Maximiser (IRE) *Simon West* 140h 147c
7 gr g Helissio(FR) Clydeside (IRE) (General Ironside (IRE))
2397[2] ◆ **2760[F]** 4960a[2]
Maximo Meridio (FR) *Mme L Audon* 108h
4 b g Mr. Sidney(USA) Maria De La Luz (Machiavellian (USA))
2362a[6]
Max Milano (IRE) *Alan Jessop* 84h
10 b g Milan Stellissima (IRE) (Persian Bold)
4975[5] 5246[9]
Max The Minister *Hughie Morrison* 101h
5 bl g Pastoral Pursuits Franciscaine (FR) (Legend Of France (USA))
1872[6] 2612[5] 3117[P] 3608[5] 4504[4] ◆ 5076[2] 5431[7]
Maxximus (IRE) *Sarah Humphrey* 66h
5 ch g Insatiable(IRE) Rose Gallery (FR) (Gallery Of Zurich (IRE))
1827[4] 2150[P]
Maybe Enough *Phil McEntee* 75b
4 b m Authorized(IRE) Never Enough (GER) (Monsun (GER))
2842[10]
Maybe I Wont *James Moffatt* 108h
10 b g Kyllachy Surprise Surprise (Robellino (USA))
4733 839[7] 1067[4] 1400[3] 1890[7] 2980[2] 4105[2] 4607[4]
Maybell *Alex Hales* 85h
4 b m Black Sam Bellamy(IRE) Chilly Squaw (IRE) (Commanche Run)
3819[6] 4317[8] 4494[5] 5314[P]
Maybe Plenty *Giles Smyly* 114h 112c
6 b m Overbury(IRE) Mays Delight (IRE) (Glacial Storm (USA))
2167[6] **2865[P] 3501[U] (5138)**
May Be Some Time *Stuart Kittow* 115h
7 ch g Iceman Let Alone (Warning)
4685[2]
Mayden Massini *Tony Carroll* 2b
4 gr g Dr Massini(IRE) Miss Tehente (FR) (Tehente (FR))
761[10]
May Hay *Anthony Carson* 115h
5 b m Dubai Destination(USA) Trounce (Barathea (IRE))
2810[5] (3163) 4320[3] 4672[2]
May Mist *Trevor Wall* 68b
3 b f Nayef(USA) Midnight Mist (IRE) (Green Desert (USA))
4392[6]
Mayo Star (IRE) *Kevin Ryan* 92b
3 b g Stowaway Western Whisper (IRE) (Supreme Leader)
4867[6]
Maypole Lass *Clare Hobson* 73h
5 ch m Halling(USA) Maigold Lass (Mark Of Esteem (IRE))
3393 ◆ 757[6] 967[3] 1165[4] 3220[P] 4069[P]
May's Boy *James Moffatt* 109h
7 gr g Proclamation(IRE) Sweet Portia (IRE) (Pennekamp (USA))
851[3] 1034[4] 1404[U] 3680[10]
May's Sister *Anthony Carson* 70b
4 b m Tiger Hill(IRE) Trounce (Barathea (IRE))
264[4]
Mayze Bell *Alistair Whillans* 64b
6 br m And Beyond(IRE) Eleanor May (Crofthall)
662[4] 1328[U]
Maz Majecc (IRE) *Jonathan Haynes* 75h 85c
6 b g Robert Emmet(IRE) Madam Elsa (IRE) (Lycius (USA))
3864[P] 4738[P] 5369[2]
Mazovian (USA) *Matt Sheppard* 97h
7 b g E Dubai(USA) Polish Style (USA) (Danzig (USA))
171[5] 621[6] 3840[2] 3973[3] 4460[5] 5223[4] (5398)
Mazurati (IRE) *Ben Case* 104h
6 b g Definite Article Mazuma (IRE) (Mazaad)
364[8] 646[4] 879[P] 2453[10] 2745[P]
McCabe Creek (IRE) *Alan King* 121h
5 b g Robin Des Pres(FR) Kick And Run (IRE) (Presenting)
281[5] 2087[3] 2577[8] ◆ 2989[2] ◆ (3855) 4362[3] 5076[3]
Mcginty's Dream (IRE) *N W Alexander* 49b
4 br g Flemensfirth(USA) Laboc (Rymer)
2106[7] 2984[8] 4403[P]
Mcgregor's Cottage (IRE) *Malcolm Jefferson* 105b
4 b m Brian Boru Dewasentah (IRE) (Supreme Leader)
(2895) ◆ 3861[6] 4371[2] 4847[8]
Mckenzie's Friend (IRE) *Oliver Sherwood* 122h
4 b g Flemensfirth(USA) Escrea (IRE) (Oscar (IRE))
213[3] (2544) (3085) 3623[P] 4224[2]
McKinley *W P Mullins* 142h 137c
5 b g Kheleyf(USA) Priera Menta (IRE) (Montjeu (IRE))
72a[5] **4005a[6] 4701[U] 4956a[4]** (5497)
Mcvicar *John Davies* 111h 97c
6 b g Tobougg(IRE) Aries (GER) (Big Shuffle (USA))
4550[3] 5405[3]
Meadowcroft Boy *Alistair Whillans* 134h
6 b g Kayf Tara Blackbriery Thyne (IRE) (Good Thyne (USA))
3179 2328[3] ◆
Meadow Cross (IRE) *Denis Gerard Hogan* 77h
3 b f Cape Cross(IRE) Hovering (IRE) (In The Wings)
2137[4] 2492[7]
Measureofmydreams (IRE) *W P Mullins* 142h 153c
7 b g Shantou(USA) Le Bavellen (IRE) (Le Bavard (FR))
96a[16] **(4148a) 4700[3]** ◆ **5327[F] 5494[12]**
Medicine Hat *George Moore* 126h
4 b g Multiplex Blushing Heart (Observatory (USA))
2202[4] 2594[P] 3027[8] 3630[9]
Medieval Bishop (IRE) *Tony Forbes* 104h
6 b g Bachelor Duke(USA) On The Backfoot (IRE) (Bob Back (USA))
1597[3] 1780[3] 2080[6] 2490[U] 2962[P]
Medinah Gold (IRE) *Peter Fahey* 111h
6 b g Gold Well Grande Solitaire (FR) (Loup Solitaire (USA))
1184a[3]
Medinas (FR) *Alan King* 156h
8 bb g Malinas(GER) Medicis (FR) (Sicyos (USA))
3992[P] 4381[8]
Meet The Legend *Dan Skelton* 139h
4 b g Midnight Legend Combe Florey (Alflora (IRE))
(1555) ◆ 2106[2] ◆ 3227[5] (4111) 4636[3]
Megan Mint *Matt Sheppard*
5 b m Passing Glance Tizzy Blue (IRE) (Oscar (IRE))
2493[10]
Megansfield *Kenny Johnson* 25h
6 b m Dapper Ceresfield (NZ) (Westminster (NZ))
799[12]
Melbourne Lady *P Fegan* 132h 128c
7 b m Hawkeye(IRE) Red Barons Lady (IRE) (Electric)
52a[5] **3093a[5] 3604a[3]** 4699[18]
Melodic Rendezvous *Jeremy Scott* 147h 126c
9 ch g Where Or When(IRE) Vic Melody (FR) (Old Vic)
51a[5] 2350[2] 2640[3] 3033[4] 3449[3] 3740[3] 4253[2] 4381[5] 5189[P]
Melrose Boy (FR) *Harry Fry* 90b
3 b g Saint Des Saints(FR) Pollypink (FR) (Poliglote)
5358[6]
Melt The Silver *Mrs D J Ralph* 106c
9 ch g Karinga Bay Ms Trude (IRE) (Montelimar (USA))
4426[3]
Meme's Horse (IRE) *Harry Fry* 124h
5 b g Scorpion(IRE) Alittlebitofheaven (Cape Cross (IRE))
3775[5] (5378)
Memory Cloth *Brian Ellison* 55h
8 b g Cape Cross(IRE) Gossamer (Sadler's Wells (USA))
2647[6]
Memory Of Light (IRE) *Sally Randell* 82h
6 gr g Westerner Be Thankfull (IRE) (Linamix (FR))
2408[P] 2732[P] 3369[7] 3946[7] 4184[P] (5181)
Memphis Magic (GER) *Brendan Powell* 94h
5 b g Tertullian(USA) Maltage (USA) (Affirmed (USA))
4498 811[10] **1595[P]** 1975[5]
Menace *Noel Williams* 101h
4 ch g Papal Bull Wishfully Tropical (IRE) (Desert Prince (IRE))
928[6] 1246[3] 1425[7] 1590[5] 1822[3] 2490[F] 5246[P]
Mendip Express (IRE) *Philip Hobbs* 129h 154c
9 bb g King's Theatre(IRE) Mulberry (IRE) (Denel (FR))
(3826) ◆ **(4383) 4768[8] 5178[3]**
Menorah (IRE) *Philip Hobbs* 163h 171c
10 b g King's Theatre(IRE) Maid For Adventure (IRE) (Strong Gale)
2200[P] 2900[3] (5492)
Mercers Court (IRE) *Neil King* 126h 130c
7 b g Court Cave(IRE) Vikki's Dream (IRE) (Kahyasi)
185[4] 225[3] 595[3] 773[4] (1752) 2013[6] 2775[5] 3137[12] **3507[5]** 4474[2] **(4977)**
Merchant Of Dubai *Jim Goldie* 113h
10 b g Dubai Destination(USA) Chameleon (Green Desert (USA))
3023[P]
Merchant Of Milan *John Flint* 95h 107c
7 b g Milan Repunzel (Carlingford Castle)
(3387) 3709[4] 4422[3] 4823[F] (Dead)
Mercian King (IRE) *Charlie Longsdon* 99h
4 b g Robin Des Pres(FR) Mariah Rollins (IRE) (Over The River (FR))
3725[4] 5137[6]
Mercoeur (FR) *Warren Greatrex* 118h
4 gr g Archange D'Or(IRE) Erivia (FR) (Kendor (FR))
727[2]
Mercury *Kevin Ryan* 38h
3 ch g Showcasing Miss Rimex (IRE) (Ezzoud (IRE))
2845[9]
Mere Anarchy (IRE) *Robert Stephens* 115h
4 b g Yeats(IRE) Maracana (IRE) (Glacial Storm (USA))
4869[3] (5221)
Mere Ironmonger *Brendan Powell* 113b
3 ch g Galileo(IRE) Kindling (Dr Fong (USA))
(4790) ◆ 5330[6]
Meribel Millie *Harry Fry* 99b
4 b m Kayf Tara Ede'Iff (Tragic Role (USA))
(2750) 5286[4]
Merlin's Wish *Martin Keighley* 110c
10 gr g Terimon Sendai (Le Moss)
3792[5] 4340[8] 4649[P]
Merrydown Vintage (IRE) *Ray Fielder*
8 ch g Ballingarry(IRE) Cure The Blues (IRE) (Phardante (FR))
531[P]
Merry Mast (USA) *Paul Henderson* 59h
6 b g Mizzen Mast(USA) Dancing Shoes (IRE) (Danehill (USA))
671[11] 834[9] 893[P] 1044[9] 1323[P] 2604[6] 3089[7]
Messery (FR) *Tim Vaughan* 33h
4 b g Poliglote Iris Du Berlais (FR) (Bonnet Rouge (FR))
2265[13]
Messina Straights *George Bewley* 18h
7 br g Blueprint(IRE) Calabria (Neltino)
1852[9] 2103[5] 4047[P]
Messire Des Obeaux (FR) *Alan King* 126h
3 b g Saddler Maker(IRE) Madame Lys (FR) (Sheyrann (IRE))
4243[3] ◆ 4720[7]
Messire Fontenail (FR) *C Aubert* 105h 120c
8 ch g Maresca Sorrento(FR) Rose Fontenailles (FR) (Kaldounevees (FR))
375a[8]
Mesut (FR) *Sarah Humphrey* 58h 79c
4 bl g Early March Alicesprings (FR) (Pelder (IRE))
1737[U] 1942[4] 2136[8] 3608[P]
Me Voila (FR) *Nick Williams* 96h
3 b g Turgeon(USA) Saintenitouche (FR) (Saint Des Saints (FR))
3347[4] 3926[P] 4183[4] 4846[6]
Mexican Border (GER) *Martin Hill* 101h
6 b g Sholokhov(IRE) Moricana (GER) (Konigsstuhl (GER))
391[6] 1823[P] 2263[5] 2730[2] 4920[S]
Meyrem Ana *Natalie Lloyd-Beavis* 60h
5 b m Beat All(USA) Champagne Lou Lou (Supreme Leader)
526[6] 3825[5] 4196[4] 4382[P] 5420[12]
Mezendore (IRE) *Rebecca Curtis* 126c
6 ch g Bach(IRE) Ballinard Lady (IRE) (Phardante (FR))
(5046) 5285[6]
Mia Matriarch *Stuart Coltherd* 88h 73c
9 ch m Silver Patriarch(IRE) Youandi (Silver Season)
1853[6] 2321[P] 2771[6] 4514[4] 4903[9]
Miami Present (IRE) *Harriet Bethell* 112h
5 bb g Presenting Miami Nights (GER) (Tertullian (USA))
(2136) 5124[P] 5437[4]
Mia's Anthem (IRE) *Noel C Kelly* 105h 134c
7 ch g Royal Anthem(USA) Windmill View (IRE) (Glacial Storm (USA))
486[2] 803[4] (1069) 1573[3] (1743) (1889) 2473[12]
Mia's Storm (IRE) *Alan King* 108h
5 b m September Storm(GER) Letitia's Gain (IRE) (Zaffaran (USA))
2929[2] ◆ 3825[4] ◆ 4231[P]
Mia's Vic (IRE) *Tim Vaughan*
10 b g Old Vic Mill Lane Flyer (IRE) (Un Desperado (FR))
824[P] (Dead)
Mica Mika (IRE) *Richard Fahey* 100h
7 ch g Needwood Blade Happy Talk (IRE) (Hamas (IRE))
2540[7]
Michigan Assassin (IRE) *Debra Hamer* 81h 98c
13 b g King's Theatre(IRE) Shuil Ar Aghaidh (The Parson)
1298[P] 1894[4] 2037[3] 2248[4]
Mickieblueeyes (IRE) *Diana Grissell* 83b
3 b g Dilshaan Killerig Park (I'm Supposin (IRE))
(4162)
Mick Jazz (FR) *Harry Fry* 121h
4 b g Blue Bresil(FR) Mick Maya (FR) (Siam (USA))
2512[P]
Micklegate Run *Alan Swinbank* 110b
4 b g Tiger Hill(IRE) Mamoura (IRE) (Lomond (USA))
(144) ◆ (732)
Micks Lad (IRE) *Dan Skelton* 108h
5 b g Beneficial Floreen (IRE) (Shardari)
4322[5] 4875[4]

Mick Thonic (FR) *C A Murphy* 130h 114c
5 gr g Maresca Sorrento(FR) Mick Madona (FR) (Dadarissime (FR))
5025a[12]

Micquus (IRE) *Jonathan Geake* 71h
6 b g High Chaparral(IRE) My Potters (USA) (Irish River (FR))
977[P] 4454[3] 4682[P]

Micras *Tim Vaughan* 99h
4 b m Medicean Purple Heather (USA) (Rahy (USA))
813[5] 853[6] 932[7] 1120[7] 1383[7]

Middle Barn (IRE) *Sirrell Griffiths* 54b
5 b g Scorpion(IRE) Shed (Halling (USA))
4827[9] 5400[7]

Midnight Appeal *Sophie Leech* 118h 139c
10 b g Midnight Legend Lac Marmot (FR) (Marju (IRE))
855[12] 1033[4] 1167[5] 1322[8] 4113[P] 4424[P] 4592[6] 5035[3] 5395[9]

Midnight Belle *Tom Symonds* 124h 132c
8 b m Midnight Legend Cherry Alley (IRE) (Persian Mews)
2215[3] 2632[8] 2911[7] **3365[P]** 3978[5]

Midnight Cataria *Alan King* 117h 110c
6 b m Midnight Legend Calamintha (Mtoto)
2824 693[P] 1987[DSQ] ◆ 2288[P] 2975[P]

Midnight Charmer *Emma Baker* 55h 99c
9 b g Midnight Legend Dickies Girl (Saxon Farm)
1850[P] 2140[P] 3820[2] 4214[P] 4776[4] 5309[P]

Midnight Chorister *Alex Hales* 95h 118c
7 b g Midnight Legend Royal Musical (Royal Abjar (USA))
1907[5] 2138[6] 2648[3] 2859[4] (4841) 5244[2]

Midnight Cowboy *Alan King* 117h
4 gr g Midnight Legend Kali (Linamix (FR))
2375[4] 2928[3] 3775[2] 4463[4] 5115[3]

Midnight Dove *Andrew Price* 91h 85c
10 ch g Karinga Bay Flighty Dove (Cruise Missile)
211[P] 333[5]

Midnight Folie *Ben Pauling* 87h
5 b m Midnight Legend Lady Racquet (IRE) (Glacial Storm (USA))
602[3] 2299[7] 2690[P] 3947[6] 4183[7] 5397[4]

Midnight Game *Brian Ellison* 129h 124c
8 b g Montjeu(IRE) Midnight Angel (GER) (Acatenango (GER))
638[5] 1038[4] **1186a[5] 1266[4] 1479[3] 1904[P]** 2202[6]

Midnight Gem *Charlie Longsdon* 103h
5 b m Midnight Legend Barton Flower (Danzero (AUS))
334[5] 696[2] 1716[6] 1845[5] 2033[2] 2413[P] 3930[9] 4845[3] 5397[5]

Midnight Glory *Philip Hobbs* 92b
3 b f Midnight Legend Land Of Glory (Supreme Leader)
5286[2]

Midnight Gypsy *Stuart Kittow* 83h
5 b m Midnight Legend Romany Dream (Nomadic Way (USA))
644[3] 831[2] 1009[8] 1234[P] 1574[4]

Midnight Hop *Nick Ayliffe*
8 b m Midnight Legend Hopping Mad (Puget (USA))
2444[8] 3124[P]

Midnight Jade (IRE) *John Groucott* 68h 94c
6 b m King's Theatre(IRE) Hurricane Dawn (IRE) (Strong Gale)
2856[12] 3467[5] 3570[8] 3787[5] **(4387) ◆ 5138[2]**

Midnight Jazz *Ben Case* 134h
5 b m Midnight Legend Ring Back (IRE) (Bob Back (USA))
2199[3] 3034[4] 4338[2] 4909[2]

Midnight Jitterbug *Noel Williams* 96b
3 b g Midnight Legend Heebie Jeebie (Overbury (IRE))
3847[6] 4309[4]

Midnight King *Mrs J M Mann* 105h 103c
9 b g Midnight Legend Phar Breeze (IRE) (Phardante (FR))
14[U] 298[5]

Midnight Lira *Caroline Keevil* 93h 127c
8 ch m Midnight Legend Bally Lira (Lir)
1755[2] 2261[5] 2877[4]

Midnight Maestro *Alan King* 109b
3 b g Midnight Legend Calamintha (Mtoto)
(4475)

Midnight Memories *Steph Hollinshead* 82h
5 ch m Midnight Legend Bajan Blue (Lycius (USA))
679[P] 852[4] 1094[8] 1599[8] 1816[9]

Midnight Merlot *Noel Williams* 92b
3 b g Midnight Legend Peel Me A Grape (Gunner B)
4103[8] 4790[12]

Midnight Mint *Jeremy Scott* 113h
5 b m Midnight Legend Calamintha (Mtoto)
100[3] 462[3] 823[4] (1618)

Midnightmistress *Jose Santos* 12b
3 b f Midnight Legend Mistress Nell (Thethingaboutitis (USA))
5383[12]

Midnight Monty *Keith Reveley* 111h 123c
5 ch g Midnight Legend Marello (Supreme Leader)
4067[4] (4456) 4978[2]

Midnight Mustang *Andrew J Martin* 87h 87c
8 b g Midnight Legend Mustang Molly (Soldier Rose)
6461[0]

Midnight Oscar (IRE) *Kim Bailey* 129h 127c
8 br g Oscar(IRE) Midnight Light (IRE) (Roselier (FR))
169[P]

Midnight Owle *Claire Dyson* 71h
5 ch g Midnight Legend Owlesbury Dream (IRE) (Luso)
56[P] 4323[9] 4711[4] 5018[6]

Midnight Prayer *Alan King* 118h 143c
10 b g Midnight Legend Onawing Andaprayer (Energist)
2780[4] ◆ 3624[2] (4140) 4735[7] 5327[P]

Midnight Request *Nigel Hawke* 98h 119c
6 b g Midnight Legend Friendly Request (Environment Friend)
174[4] 1820[7]

Midnight Sapphire *Victor Dartnall* 107h
5 ch m Midnight Legend Norton Sapphire (Karinga Bay)
(513) 597[6] 1055[2] 1545[2] 1841[3] 2167[2] 2441[P] 5380[4]

Midnight Sequel *Neil Mulholland* 105h
6 b m Midnight Legend Silver Sequel (Silver Patriarch (IRE))
65[3] 443[2] 513[F] 1085[2] 1158[2] 1375[6] 1910[4] 2454[7]

Midnight Shot *Charlie Longsdon* 123h
5 b g Midnight Legend Suave Shot (Suave Dancer (USA))
(83) (396) 1986[5] 2472[8] 3487[11] 3728[5] 4782[8] 5464[3]

Midnight Silver *Jamie Snowden* 115h
5 gr m Midnight Legend Ruggtah (Daylami (IRE))
2302[3] ◆ 2697[3] 3217[4] 3612[4] (4268) 4616[3]

Midnight Target *John Groucott* 97h
5 b m Midnight Legend Right On Target (IRE) (Presenting)
334[7] 2856[5] 3381[4] 3570[P] 4430[5] 4714[3]

Midnight Thomas *Martin Keighley* 82h 90c
6 b g Midnight Legend Vivacious Lass (IRE) (Common Grounds)
161[P] 435[7] 918[P] **1133[6]** 4068[8] **4686[P]**

Midnight Tour *David Loder* 122h
5 b m Midnight Legend Uppermost (Montjeu (IRE))
2929[11] 4039[3] ◆ (4714) 5280[5]

Midnight Tune *Anthony Honeyball* 92b
4 b m Midnight Legend Harmonic Motion (IRE) (Bob Back (USA))
2016[2] (2828) 4623[11]

Midnight Velvet *Philip Hobbs* 105b
5 b m Midnight Legend Tamergale (IRE) (Strong Gale)
2086[3]

Midnight Whisper *Richard Woollacott* 107h 64c
9 ch g Midnight Legend Spread The Word (Deploy)
864[10] 1236[13] **1326[7] 1546[5] 1678[5]**

Midnight Wishes *Peter Hiatt* 47c
10 gr m Midnight Legend Star Control (IRE) (Phardante (FR))
329[7] 492[6]

Midtech Star (IRE) *Ian Williams* 81h
3 b g Kodiac Royal Rival (IRE) (Marju (IRE))
1928[7] 2273[8] 2448[5] 3023[7] 3234[9]

Midtech Valentine *Ian Williams* 107h
4 b m Act One Eveon (IRE) (Synefos (USA))
2131[5] 558[2] 2689[8] 3021[7] 3418[5] 4320[4] (4650) 4799[3] (4890) 5438[3]

Might Bite (IRE) *Nicky Henderson* 150h 139c
6 b g Scorpion(IRE) Knotted Midge (IRE) (Presenting)
2469[5] (4786) ◆ 5275[7]

Mighty Concorde (IRE) *J H Culloty* 121h
5 br g Arcadio(GER) Shy (FR) (Signe Divin (USA))
3323a[2]

Mighty Leader (IRE) *Henry Oliver* 112h
7 b g Milan Madam Leader (IRE) (Supreme Leader)
754[3] 931[4] ◆ (1084) 1455[2] 1522[2] **1824[F]** 2085[7] (4442) 5396[F]

Mighty Mambo *P Favero* 95h 45c
8 b g Fantastic Light(USA) Mambo's Melody (Kingmambo (USA))
489[4] **1672a[P]**

Mighty Minnie *Henry Daly* 116h
6 b m Sir Harry Lewis(USA) Vanina II (FR) (Italic (FR))
339[5] 1490[9] 1615[11]

Mighty Missile (IRE) *Warren Greatrex* 123h
4 ch g Majestic Missile(IRE) Magdalene (FR) (College Chapel)
182[2] (554) 749[2] (1168)

Mighty Mobb (IRE) *Seamus Mullins* 112h 121c
8 b g Accordion Dusty Lane (IRE) (Electric)
169[R] 445[2]

Mighty Mustang *Andrew J Martin* 37b
5 b g Passing Glance Mustang Molly (Soldier Rose)
2514[13]

Mighty Snazy *Alexandra Dunn* 105b
11 b g Overbury(IRE) Come To Tea (IRE) (Be My Guest (USA))
810[P] 1010[P]

Mighty Thor *Lydia Richards* 77h
5 b g Norse Dancer(IRE) Leyaaly (Night Shift (USA))
451[10]

Mighty Whitey (IRE) *Noel C Kelly* 116h 98c
9 b g Sesaro(USA) Deeco Valley (IRE) (Satco (FR))
(1459) 1773[2] 2069[4] 2893[6]

Mijhaar *John Ferguson* 141h
7 b g Shirocco(GER) Jathaabeh (Nashwan (USA))
2054[3] 2641[P]

Milan Bound (IRE) *Jonjo O'Neill* 132h 92c
7 b g Milan Bonnie And Bright (IRE) (Topanoora)
196[10] (1839) 2484[P] **2963[5]**

Milan Dancer (IRE) *Noel C Kelly* 91h
4 b m Milan Pawnee Trail (IRE) (Taipan (IRE))
4164[3] 4742[2]

Milanese Queen *Warren Greatrex* 63b
4 b m Milan Kaydee Queen (IRE) (Bob's Return (IRE))
4075[11]

Milan Flyer (IRE) *Noel C Kelly* 103h 111c
9 b g Milan Flying Jennie (Burslem)
4407[U]

Milan Hart (IRE) *Chris Down* 88b
5 b m Milan Queen Of Harts (IRE) (Phardante (FR))
305[4] 2277[11]

Milan Lady (IRE) *Chris Grant* 94h
4 b m Milan Terre D'Orient (FR) (Kabool)
2936[P] 3681[2]

Milan Of Crystal (IRE) *Robert Stephens* 91h
6 b m Milan Native Crystal (IRE) (Be My Native (USA))
513[5] 712[6] 1236[12] (1975) 4541[P]

Milan Royale *Kevin Hunter* 84h 92c
10 b g Milan Siroyalta (FR) (Royal Charter (FR))
78[8] 485[6]

Milansbar (IRE) *Neil King* 142h 151c
8 b g Milan Ardenbar (Ardross)
2717[3] ◆ 2960[4] 4116[2] (4341) ◆ 4802[2] 5327[9]

Milans Well (IRE) *William Young Jnr*
9 b g Milan Panoora Queen (IRE) (Topanoora)
5449[U]

Milborough (IRE) *Ian Duncan* 127h 142c
9 b g Milan Fox Burrow (IRE) (Supreme Leader)
92a[10] 2214[9] **2790[7] 4367[7] 4818[2] 5327[7]**

Milburn *Gail Haywood*
9 ch g First Trump Baroness Rose (Roselier (FR))
1116[P]

Mildmay Arms *Simon Hodgson*
3 b g Kheleyf(USA) Akathea (Barathea (IRE))
4854[P]

Mile House (IRE) *Robert Stephens* 133h 113c
7 b g Close Conflict(USA) Clogheen Lass (IRE) (Capricorn Line)
645[5] (876) 1038[3] **1351[2] 1520[U] 1642[F]** 1754[6] 2064[2]

Miles To Memphis (IRE) *Alan King* 123h
6 b g Old Vic Phillis Hill (Karinga Bay)
2600[7]

Miles To Milan (IRE) *Philip Hobbs* 127h
5 b g Milan Princesse Rooney (FR) (Baby Turk)
2457[3] (3370) 3744[3] 4786[11]

Milestone (IRE) *Evan Williams* 106h
5 b g Galileo(IRE) Cassydora (Darshaan)
214[5] 441[3] (773) 1594[6] 2989[10] 3919[P] 4825[5] 5159[10]

Miley Shah (IRE) *S J Kenny* 139h 111c
10 b g City Honours(USA) Mazovia (FR) (Taufan (USA))
2236a[6] 2525a[6]

Milgen Bay *Oliver Sherwood* 114h 123c
9 br g Generous(IRE) Lemon's Mill (USA) (Roberto (USA))
282[3] 1114[P] 1444[4] 1767[4] (2140) (2648) 5465[8]

Miliair *David Bridgwater* 86b
5 ch m Muhtathir Miliana (IRE) (Polar Falcon (USA))
1300[3]

Millanisi Boy *Richard Woollacott* 126h
6 b g Kalanisi(IRE) Millennium Rose (IRE) (Roselier (FR))
2262[3] 2725[2] (3516) 4112[6] 5264[9]

Mille Nautique (FR) *Alan King* 76h
4 b g Panis(USA) Anoush (USA) (Giant's Causeway (USA))
2163[P] 2725[8] 4455[P]

Millen Dollar Man (IRE) *Karl Thornton* 88h
6 b g Millenary Rare Dollar (IRE) (Bob's Return (IRE))
1572[P]

Miller Of Glanmire (IRE) *Charlie Mann* 72h 81c
7 b g Oscar(IRE) Instant Queen (IRE) (Executive Perk)
64[U] 226[5]

Miller's Maverick *Grant Cann* 52h 58c
7 b g Millkom Gables Girl (Sousa)
4921[6]

Millicent Silver *Nigel Twiston-Davies* 118h 130c
6 gr m Overbury(IRE) Common Girl (IRE) (Roselier (FR))
(2167) 2825[3] **3348[P] 4071[4] (4433) (5162)**

Millksheikh *Raymond York* 79h
8 b g Millkom Shelayly (IRE) (Zaffaran (USA))
1291[6] 1447[7] 1829[8] 2004[7]

Milly Baloo *Tim Easterby* 110h
4 b m Desideratum Tarabaloo (Kayf Tara)
132[4] 2169[7] 2494[3] 2847[5] (3234) 3729[2] 4041[2] ◆ 4644[2] 4983[3] 5368[P]

Milly Malone (IRE) *Adrian Wintle* 92h 107c
9 b m Milan Sharp Single (IRE) (Supreme Leader)
86[4] 443[4] **741[P]** 5420[9]

Milord (GER) *Kim Bailey* 125h
6 br g Monsun(GER) Montserrat (GER) (Zilzal (USA))
1818[5] (2301) 2977[2] 3336[5] 3923[7] 5264[6]

Milord Thomas (FR) *D Bressou* 141h 160c
6 b g Kapgarde(FR) Star D'Avril (FR) (Phantom Breeze)
(375a) (1477a) **1884a[2]**

Min (FR) *W P Mullins* 157h
4 b g Walk In The Park(IRE) Phemyka (FR) (Saint Estephe (FR))
(3539a) 4695[2]

Minden March *Peter Maddison* 75h
10 b m Baryshnikov(AUS) Minden Rose (Lord Bud)
1927[7] 2322[8] 2427[3] 2745[4] 3177[4] 3503[P]

Minella Aris (IRE) *Tom George* 126h
4 b g King's Theatre(IRE) Liss Rua (IRE) (Bob Back (USA))
4580[3]

Minella Awards (IRE) *Nicky Henderson* 135h
4 b g Oscar(IRE) Montys Miss (IRE) (Presenting)
2762[2] ◆ 4072[5]

Minella Bliss (IRE) *James Evans* 102h 89c
10 gr g Old Vic Carraigrose (IRE) (Roselier (FR))
530[5] 757[5] 1067[6] 1426[4] 1547[4] 1890[5] 1972[2] (2245) 2454[4] 3220[10] **3820[5]** 4030[4] 4467[F]

Minellacelebration (IRE) *Katy Price* 125h
5 b g King's Theatre(IRE) Knocktartan (IRE) (King's Ride)
2005[3] 2257[4] (2661) (2855) 3146[3] 4442[3] (4853) 5183[2]

Minella Charmer (IRE) *Alan King* 141h
4 b g King's Theatre(IRE) Kim Hong (IRE) (Charnwood Forest (IRE))
2460[8] 2995[2] (3452) ◆ 3859[5]

Minella Daddy (IRE) *Peter Bowen* 129h
5 b g Flemensfirth(USA) Old Moon (IRE) (Old Vic)
2998[3] 3516[5] (3817) 4535[2] 5213[8]

Minella Definitely (IRE) *Neil Mulholland* 121h 134c
8 br g Definite Article West Along (IRE) (Crash Course)
2185[P] 2691[4] 3257[4] 4230[4]

Minella Experience (IRE) *Dan Skelton* 113h
4 br g Westerner Southern Skies (IRE) (Dr Massini (IRE))
3842[5] 4344[10] 4844[2] 5243[P] (Dead)

Minella Forfitness (IRE) *Charles Pogson* 147h 135c
8 b g Westerner Ring Of Water (USA) (Northern Baby (CAN))
1942[2] 2335[7] 2746[5] 3176[F]

Minellaforleisure (IRE) *Alex Hales* 133h 108c
7 br g King's Theatre(IRE) Dame Foraine (FR) (Raintrap)
2412[6] 2686[U] 2846[F] 3232[P] 4273[3] (5279)

Minellaforlunch (IRE) *Henry Oliver* 111h 100c
8 b g King's Theatre(IRE) Loughaderra (IRE) (Strong Gale)
2168[2] 2666[2] 3224[5]

Minella For Me (IRE) *Tom George* 112b
5 b g King's Theatre(IRE) Irish Mystics (IRE) (Ali-Royal (IRE))
5359[2]

Minella For Party (IRE) *Miss V Collins* 45h 106c
8 b g Flemensfirth(USA) Dame Foraine (FR) (Raintrap)
13[9]

Minella Foru (IRE) *Edward P Harty* 142h 145c
6 b g King's Theatre(IRE) Shannon Rose (IRE) (Topanoora)
(3296a)

Minellahalfcentury (IRE) *Paul Nicholls* 119h 129c
7 b g Westerner Shanakill River (IRE) (Anshan)
2473[6] 3918[5] 4595[3] 5162[P]

Minella Hero (IRE) *Micky Hammond* 116h
7 b g Old Vic Shannon Rose (IRE) (Topanoora)
(421) (726) 1925[6] **2424[P]** 2744[14] 3102[5] 5403[4]

Minella On Line (IRE) *Rebecca Curtis* 120h 140c
6 b g King's Theatre(IRE) Bally Bolshoi (IRE) (Bob Back (USA))
1963[2] 2367[3] **3113[3] 4245[P] 4542[3] 4966[4]**

Minella Present (IRE) *Neil Mulholland* 110h 140c
6 b g Presenting Dabaya (IRE) (In The Wings)
512[3] (596) 1815[2] 2468[2] 5179[P]

Minella Reception (IRE) *Nigel Twiston-Davies* 126h 147c
9 b g King's Theatre(IRE) Cadourova (FR) (Cadoudal (FR))
3365[F] 3735[5] (4347) 4625[2] 5193[F] (Dead)

Minella Rocco (IRE) *Jonjo O'Neill* 146h 160c
5 b g Shirocco(GER) Petralona (USA) (Alleged (USA))
2627[3] ◆ 3013[P] 3405[6] 4237[2] (4700) ◆

Minella Web (IRE) *Richard Woollacott* 93h 103c
6 b g King's Theatre(IRE) Azalea (IRE) (Marju (IRE))
13[P] (524) 612[4] 5417[4]

Mine Now (IRE) *Peter Fahey* 129h
7 b g Heron Island(IRE) Aisjem (IRE) (Anshan)
50a[5] 3071a[10]

Miner's Lamp (IRE) *John Ferguson* 120h
4 b g Shamardal(USA) Truly Mine (IRE) (Rock Of Gibraltar (IRE))
(749) 1041[3] 1168[2]

Mini Frank *Chris Grant*
3 b g Josr Algarhoud(IRE) Micklow Magic (Farfelu)
3165[8] 4156[10]

Mini Muck *Nigel Twiston-Davies* 112h
9 b m Kayf Tara Madam Muck (Gunner B)
1985[F] 2447[P] 2577[4] 2812[3] 3198[4] 3930[8] 4878[5]

Ministerofinterior *Barry Leavy* 112h
10 b g Nayef(USA) Maureen's Hope (USA) (Northern Baby (CAN))
2405[P] (2858) 2962[3] 4105[3] 4448[2] 4968[2]

Minkie Moon (IRE) *Mark Campion* 64h 68c
7 b g Danehill Dancer(IRE) Minkova (IRE) (Sadler's Wells (USA))
804[5]

Minmore Grey (IRE) *Nick Lampard* 76h
6 gr g Primary(USA) Hopeful Memory (IRE) (Roselier (FR))
1704[7] 1952[3] 2275[8] 3043[5] 3946[P]

Minneapolis *Sophie Leech*
10 b g Sadler's Wells(USA) Teggiano (IRE) (Mujtahid (USA))
828[P]

Minnie Milan (IRE) *Neil King* 125h
6 b m Milan Shiminnie (IRE) (Bob Back (USA))
(339) (493) (1002) 1181[4] 2685[4] 3283[5] 5396[8]

Minority Interest *Daniel O'Brien* 88h
6 ch g Galileo(IRE) Minority (Generous (IRE))
240[5] 675[3] 878[5] 2015[7] 2316[P] 5305[4]

Minstrel Royal *Nicky Henderson* 118h
5 b g Kayf Tara Close Harmony (Bustino)
2636[3] 3133[3] ◆ 3736[6] 4323[5]

Minstrels Gallery (IRE) *Lucy Wadham* 130h
6 ch g Refuse To Bend(IRE) Lilakiya (IRE) (Dr Fong (USA))
2415[5] 2700[4] (3041) 3449[4] 3733[12] (4107) 4366[6] 4986[3]

Miracle Cure (IRE) *Venetia Williams* 110h
6 b g Whipper(USA) Bring Back Matron (IRE) (Rock Of Gibraltar (IRE))
110[5]

Mirkat *Alan King* 67h
5 b g Kalanisi(IRE) Miracle (Ezzoud (IRE))
2239[9] 4788[P]

Misfits (IRE) *Lucinda Russell* 107h
4 b g Beneficial Park Rose (IRE) (Roselier (FR))
3476[3] 4548[4] 5077[4] 5408[2]

Miss Barbossa (IRE) *Martin Todhunter* 72h
4 b m Gold Well Queens Quay (Grand Lodge (USA))
3593[6] 3995[P] 4416[8] 4817[5]

Miss Biscotti *Martin Bosley* 95h 97c
7 ch m Emperor Fountain Bellacaccia (IRE) (Beau Sher)
57[2] 438[3]

Miss Blanche *Lucinda Russell* 81h
4 b m King's Theatre(IRE) Keys Pride (IRE) (Bob Back (USA))
3681[10] 4164[9] 5470[7]

Miss Chatterbox *Chris Grant* 84h 77c
10 b m Dapper Clohamon Gossip (IRE) (Lord Americo)
416[4] 759[9] 837[6]

Miss Conway *Mark Walford* 77h 79c
4 br m Midnight Legend Miss Pross (Bob's Return (IRE))
415[6] 679[4] 2148[9] 3098[U] **3968[6] 4329[8]**

Miss Crick *Alan King* 108h
4 b m Midnight Legend Kwaheri (Efisio)
2016[5] 2452[3] ◆ 3110[5] 4457[3]

Miss Dimples (IRE) *Sarah-Jayne Davies* 67h 84c
6 gr m Tikkanen(USA) Scolboa House (IRE) (Bob's Return (IRE))
2551[P] 2692[4] 3007[5] (4776)

Miss Dinamic (IRE) *Gordon Elliott* 130h 131c
6 b m Kutub(IRE) Royal Molly (IRE) (Phardante (FR))
(846) (1627) **1937a[3] 2465a[2] 3093a[4]** 3356a[6]

Miss Dixie (FR) *A Lamotte D'Argy* 123h 123c
5 b m Smadoun(FR) Miss Divine (FR) (Signe Divin (USA))
350a[7]

Missed Approach (IRE) *Warren Greatrex* 147h
5 b g Golan(IRE) Polly's Dream (IRE) (Beau Sher)
(2759) ◆ 4730[P] 5328[2]

Missesgeejay *Richard Ford* 99b
5 br m Beat All(USA) Riverbank Rainbow (Overbury (IRE))
4168[4] 5049[4]

Miss Estela (IRE) *Warren Greatrex* 119h
5 b m Tobougg(IRE) Simply Divine (IRE) (Be My Native (USA))
4272[3] (5267)

Miss Excellence *Caroline Fryer*
3 b f Exceed And Excel(AUS) Hunter's Fortune (USA) (Charismatic (USA))
2137[P]

Miss Eyelash (IRE) *Peter Bowen* 56b
5 b m Kayf Tara Glacial Missile (IRE) (Glacial Storm (USA))
1449[11]

Miss Feistypants *Seamus Mullins* 76b
3 ch f Virtual Fu Wa (USA) (Distant View (USA))
1772[5] 2304[5]

Miss Fleming *David Loder* 98b
3 b f Flemensfirth(USA) Uppermost (Montjeu (IRE))
(2583) 3409[9] 4847[7]

Miss Fortywinks *Seamus Mullins* 111h
6 gr m Act One Andromache (Hector Protector (USA))
32[4] 462[9] (745) 1054[6] 2271[13] 2888[6] 4846[8] 5313[6]

Miss Giselle *Sam Thomas* 58h
6 b m Desideratum Pride Of The Oaks (Faustus (USA))
2770[2] 3381[6] 3947[P]

Miss Gotaway *David Pipe* 96h
6 b m Midnight Legend Strollaway (IRE) (Jurado (USA))
16[P] 3580[3] 4151[4]

Miss High Time (IRE) *Lucinda Russell*
4 b m Kalanisi(IRE) Windsor Dancer (IRE) (Woods Of Windsor (USA))
887[5]

Miss H Lewiss *Steve Flook* 90h
7 b m Sir Harry Lewis(USA) Broadbrook Lass (Broadsword (USA))
55[P] 361[6] 516[4] 755[4]

Missile Man (IRE) *Jim Best* 80h
5 b g Winged Love(IRE) Miss Ondee (FR) (Dress Parade)
2823[8] 3103[13]

Missionaire (USA) *Tony Carroll* 87h 89c
8 bb g El Corredor(USA) Fapindy (USA) (A.P. Indy (USA))
135[F]

Mission Complete (IRE) *Jonjo O'Neill* 96h 116c
9 b g Milan Kilmington Breeze (IRE) (Roselier (FR))
58[2] 403[5] 676[2] 873[7] 1264[9] **1403[3] 2402[U] 2771[F] 3062[4]** 3312[4] 4391[2] **(4879) 5468[6]**

Miss Joeking (IRE) *Lucinda Russell* 92h
4 b m Alkaadhem Go Franky (IRE) (Hollow Hand)
305[6] 846[U] 866[4] 1568[6] 1627[4] 1779[3] (2322) 2670[3] 3234[3]

Miss Lamorna (IRE) *Sue Gardner* 78h
6 br m Presenting Paumafi (IRE) (Shardari)
1677[5] 1816[7]

Miss Lillian *John Quinn* 67b
5 gr m Rob Roy(USA) Thorn Of The Rose (IRE) (Terimon)
2721[6]

Miss Lucarno *Evan Williams* 42h
5 ch m Lucarno(USA) She's Our Native (IRE) (Be My Native (USA))
753[0] 1290[P] 1374[9] 1574[8]

Miss Mackie (IRE) *R Mike Smith* 83h
4 b m Mr Combustible(IRE) Grannys Kitchen (IRE) (Flemensfirth (USA))
305[7] 2752[6] 3470[7] 3681[8] 4036[5] 4904[4] 5445[11]

Miss Macnamara (IRE) *Martin Todhunter* 109h
6 b m Dylan Thomas(IRE) Kincob (USA) (Kingmambo (USA))
157[2] 522[2] ◆ 805[3] (1165) 1404[3] (1742) 1856[9]

Miss Maiden Over (IRE) *Fergal O'Brien* 84b
3 br f Carlo Bank(IRE) Rock Garden (IRE) (Bigstone (IRE))
3625[5] 4847[11] 5286[5]

Miss Mash *Henry Daly* 93h
4 b m Multiplex Shanxi Girl (Overbury (IRE))
1811[7] 2164[8] 2689[5] 3500[4]

Miss Mayfair (IRE) *Lawney Hill* 94h
8 b m Indian Danehill(IRE) Cocktail Party (USA) (Arctic Tern (USA))
966[8] 1158[5] (1426) 1771[4] 2554[2] 3087[2]

Missmebutletmego *Alan Jones* 30b
5 b g With The Flow(USA) Bay Bianca (IRE) (Law Society (USA))
5359[10]

Miss Me Now (IRE) *W P Mullins* 118h
5 b m Presenting Miss Toulon (IRE) (Toulon)
4954a[P]

Miss Minx *Alan King* 78h
4 b m Tobougg(IRE) Victory Flip (IRE) (Victory Note (USA))
2302[13] 4881[8]

Miss Mix *Iain Jardine*
6 gr m Fair Mix(IRE) Miss Nel (Denel (FR))
5367[P]

Miss Mobot *Philip Hobbs* 61h
5 b m Midnight Legend Fleur De Nikos (FR) (Nikos)
2486[6] 2929[3] 3744[6]

Miss Moppet *Clare Hobson*
4 b m Nayef(USA) So Blissful (IRE) (Cape Cross (IRE))
263[P] 813[P]

Miss North Light (IRE) *Gordon Elliott* 102h
6 ch m North Light(IRE) Damask Rose (IRE) (Dr Devious (IRE))
1638[4]

Miss Oscarose (IRE) *Paul Henderson* 93h 91c
8 b m Oscar(IRE) Private Rose (IRE) (Roselier (FR))
2403[5] 2871[4] 3369[P] **3609[3] ◆ 4380[4] 4710[P] 5240[4] 5480[4]**

Miss Protektor (FR) *B Letourneux*
4 gr m Protektor(GER) Ruyu River (FR) (Nikos)
5135a[6]

Miss Ranger (IRE) *Brian Ellison* 95h
3 gr f Bushranger(IRE) Remiss (IRE) (Indian Ridge)
3099[2] ◆ 3587[2] 4271[4]

Miss Sassypants *Seamus Mullins* 116h
6 ch m Hernando(FR) Serraval (FR) (Sanglamore (USA))
380[3] (744) 938[2] 1269[3] 1793[2] 2349[7]

Miss Serious (IRE) *Jeremy Scott* 128h
5 br m Kalanisi(IRE) Burnt Out (IRE) (Anshan)
(28) (387) (1270) ◆ 1325[5] 1808[3] 2062[4] 2632[6] 4779[5] 5094[8] 5396[P]

Miss Siskin *Jimmy Frost* 48h
6 b m Morpeth Miss Grace (Atticus (USA))
2730[P] 3368[9] 5181[8]

Miss Spent (IRE) *Lucy Wadham* 31h
5 b m Presenting Cash And New (IRE) (Supreme Leader)
3469[2] ◆ (3862) 5180[15]

Miss Tenacious *Ron Hodges* 117h 130c
8 b m Refuse To Bend(IRE) Very Speed (USA) (Silver Hawk (USA))
555[3] 715[3] 830[2] 974[2] 1344[2] (1451) 4918[4] 5354[7]

Miss Tiger Lily *Jamie Snowden* 111h
5 b m Tiger Hill(IRE) Waitingonacloud (In The Wings)
1506[3] ◆ (1716) 4272[P]

Miss Tiggy (IRE) *Lucinda Russell* 99h
5 b m Milan Rockwell College (IRE) (Supreme Leader)
2936[2] 4052[P] 4837[3]

Miss Tilly Oscar (IRE) *Steve Flook* 102h 85c
9 b m Oscar(IRE) Whisky Chaser (Never So Bold)
60[U] 215[6] 517[3] 698[5] 808[5]

Miss Tongabezi *Paul Webber* 94h
6 b m Overbury(IRE) Shiwa (Bustino)
1179[4] 3386[4] 3612[5] 4413[4] 4878[4]

Miss U Peanuts *Mike Hammond* 14b
6 b m Norse Dancer(IRE) Rock N Role Vii (Damsire Unregistered)
2856[15]

Miss Williams *David Pipe* 91b
4 b m Kayf Tara Wee Dinns (IRE) (Marju (IRE))
5383[9]

Miss Xian (IRE) *F Flood* 131h 132c
8 b m Milan Beech Lodge (IRE) (Supreme Leader)
92a[P]

Miss Yeats (IRE) *Laura Mongan* 94b
4 b m Yeats(IRE) Mrs Wallensky (IRE) (Roselier (FR))
2721[3] ◆ 4075[4] 5144[5]

Missy Myrtle *Peter Niven* 46b
4 b m Indian Danehill(IRE) She Likes To Boogy (IRE) (Luso)
4908[6]

Missy Tata (FR) *Gordon Elliott* 140h
3 b f Astarabad(USA) Queen Running (FR) (Cadoudal (FR))
2813a[2] 4720[4]

Misteray *Bill Turner* 91h
5 ch g Singspiel(IRE) Hannda (IRE) (Dr Devious (IRE))
89[6] 552[7] 935[8] 1010[7]

Mister Chairman (IRE) *Rebecca Curtis* 75h
7 b g Shantou(USA) Out Of Trouble (IRE) (Mandalus)
262[5] 1961[7] 3369[P]

Mister D (IRE) *George Bewley* 98h 100c
9 ch g Anshan Eleanors Joy (Sheer Grit)
143[2] 472[3] 871[4] 1032[2] 1330[8] 1492[4]

Mister Dick (FR) *Jonjo O'Neill* 97h
3 b g Great Journey(JPN) Lyric Melody (FR) (Lyphard's Wish (FR))
1928[9] 2992[4] 3822[5] 4846[7] 5464[8]

Mister Don (IRE) *Rose Dobbin* 95h 64c
5 br g Presenting Spring Flower (IRE) (Beneficial)
1852[8] 2189[10] 2474[3] 3067[7] 3684[11] **4051[6]**

Mister Du Mene (FR) *B Lefevre*
4 ch g Jarn Miss Nono (FR) (Rajpoute (FR))
5135a[3]

Mister First (FR) *Robert Alan Hennessy* 115h 123c
9 b g Trempolino(USA) Queen Running (FR) (Cadoudal (FR))
289[2] (304) 657[5]

Mister Fizz *Miss Imogen Pickard* 144h
7 b g Sulamani(IRE) Court Champagne (Batshoof)
1035[4] (1325) 2241[5] 4717[21]

Mister Green (FR) *David Flood* 13h
9 b g Green Desert(USA) Summertime Legacy (Darshaan)
1051[P]

Mister Gregorium (IRE) *P Cottin*
4 b g Acclamation City Queen (Indian Ridge)
3876a[P]

Mister Hendre *Susan Corbett* 81h
7 gr g Fair Mix(IRE) Bonne Anniversaire (Alflora (IRE))
1570[P] 1683[10] 1923[5] 2751[U] 2937[P] 3161[2] 3473[5] 3840[9] 4297[2] 4513[4] (4797)

Mister Hotelier (IRE) *C A Murphy* 133h 135c
8 b g Beneficial Accordian Lady (IRE) (Accordion)
69a[6] 1186a[7]

Mister Jones *Sue Smith* 88h
7 b g Val Royal(FR) Madame Jones (IRE) (Lycius (USA))
37[6] 263[5] 487[4] 798[5]

Mister Kalanisi (IRE) *Dan Skelton* 105h
6 b g Kalanisi(IRE) Maxis Girl (IRE) (Mister Mat (FR))
2440[3] 3021[5] 3976[4] 4494[4]

Mister Kit *Chris Grant* 125h
7 gr g Tikkanen(USA) Rosie Mist (Missed Flight)
(4817) ◆ (5124)

Mister Marker (IRE) *Nicky Richards* 96h 128c
11 ch g Beneficial Bavards Girl (IRE) (Le Bavard (FR))
156[P] 4207[3]

Mister Miyagi (IRE) *Dan Skelton* 150h
6 b g Zagreb(USA) Muckle Flugga (IRE) (Karinga Bay)
(2056) (2731) 4695[6] (5273)

Mister Philson (IRE) *Mrs L Pomfret* 49h 66c
10 b g Saddlers' Hall(IRE) Molo River (IRE) (Fourstars Allstar (USA))
4000[5]

Mister Teddy *F A Hutsby* 101b 105c
10 b g Tamure(IRE) Thamesdown Tootsie (Comedy Star (USA))
4213[3] 4426[4]

Mister To Mister (IRE) *Benjamin Arthey* 88h 94c
7 br g Posidonas Gothic Shadow (IRE) (Mandalus)
5233[P]

Misterton *Harry Fry* 122b
4 gr g Sagamix(FR) Mighty Splash (Cape Cross (IRE))
2460[4] 4296[2] 5143[2]

Mister Uno (IRE) *Carroll Gray*
4 b h Tamayuz Starlight Smile (USA) (Green Dancer (USA))
4849[P]

Mister Wall Street (FR) *Rebecca Menzies* 87h 100c
10 br g Take Risks(FR) Miss Breezy (FR) (Sicyos (USA))
639[2] 731[2] 859[4] **976[4]**

Mister Wiseman *Nigel Hawke* 112h 110c
13 gr g Bal Harbour Genie Spirit (Nishapour (FR))
623[5]

Mist One (IRE) *J J Lambe* 102h
7 gr g Deploy Clifton Mist (Lyphento (USA))
139[P]

Mistress Mole (IRE) *Gordon Elliott* 105h
6 br m Definite Article Emmylou Du Berlais (FR) (Kadalko (FR))
1420[3] 1618[4]

Mist The Boat *Tim Vaughan* 99h 103c
7 b g Generous(IRE) Baily Mist (IRE) (Zaffaran (USA))
1598[10] 1819[5] 2245[2] 2567[5] **4713[2] 5468[5]**

Misty Lady (IRE) *John Laurence Cullen* 136h
6 b m Oscar(IRE) Lady Sam (IRE) (Topanoora)
231a[4] (1565a) 2676a[6] 3071a[6] 3650a[17]

Mitcd (IRE) *Martin Todhunter* 75h
4 gr m Mastercraftsman(IRE) Halicardia (Halling (USA))
1461[7] 1572[6] 2148[12]

Mitebeall Forluck *A L T Moore* 58h 120c
7 b g Westerner Iborga (FR) (Cyborg (FR))
1186a[U]

Mixboy (FR) *Keith Dalgleish* 122h
5 gr g Fragrant Mix(IRE) Leston Girl (FR) (Lesotho (USA))
(2893) ◆ 3886[2] 4285[2]

Mixchievous *Venetia Williams* 93h
4 gr g Fair Mix(IRE) Cheeky Mare (Derrylin)
2563[5] 3483[4] 4317[10] 4963[4]

Mixelle Days *Martin Hill* 70b
4 gr m Sagamix(FR) One Of Those Days (Soviet Lad (USA))
2351[7]

Mixit *Henry Daly* 20b
6 b g Fair Mix(IRE) Always Hope (Bob's Return (IRE))
928[7]

Mix N Match *Laura Young* 75h
11 b g Royal Applause South Wind (Tina's Pet)
489[3] 692[5] 856[8] 977[2] 1084[B] 1120[6] 1323[2] 1423[2] 1510[3] 1677[9]

Mixologist *James Evans* 60h
8 gr g Fair Mix(IRE) Matchboard Again (IRE) (Supreme Leader)
2775[9]

Moabit (GER) *Paul Nicholls* 111h
3 b g Azamour(IRE) Moonlight Danceuse (IRE) (Bering)
3835[2]

Mocalacato Has (FR) *J-P Gallorini* 140h 125c
3 b g Poliglote Monika (FR) (Dernier Empereur (USA))
1881a[3]

Mo Chailin (IRE) *Donald McCain* 108h
4 b m Milan Consultation (IRE) (Camden Town)
2849[2] 3469[4] 3681[4] ◆ 4052[U] (4555) 4893[4] 5229[4]

Modeligo (IRE) *Matt Sheppard* 102h 109c
6 b g Indian Danehill(IRE) Glens Lady (IRE) (Mister Lord (USA))
530[3] (692) (1115) 1324[6] 1647[8] **2435[F] 2692[6] 3141[3] 3977[2] ◆ 4346[3] (5142)**

Modem *Mrs John Harrington* 143h
5 b g Motivator Alashaan (Darshaan)
2177a[3] 5025a[3]

Modena (CZE) *Stanislav Popelka Jr* 95c
8 b m Jape(USA) Mest (RUS) (Mistnik)
1885a[8]

Modern Society *Andrew Reid*
5 sk h I Was Framed(USA) Artzola (IRE) (Alzao (USA))
221[U]

Modus *Paul Nicholls* 139h
5 ch g Motivator Alessandra (Generous (IRE))
23a[3] (2457) (2723) 3370[3] 4115[13] 4765[23]

Mogestic (IRE) *Seamus Mullins* 116h
6 b g Morozov(USA) Crosschild (IRE) (Buckskin (FR))
(3125) 3904[P] 4920[3] (5165)

Moidore *Charles Pogson* 132h
6 b g Galileo(IRE) Flash Of Gold (Darshaan)
263[3] 2540[3] 2961[7] 3509[3] 3839[4] 4388[4] (4983) (5335)

Mojawiz *John Ferguson* 91h
3 b g Dubawi(IRE) Zayn Zen (Singspiel (IRE))
636[2] 891[2]

Molineaux (IRE) *Colin Tizzard* 99b
4 b g King's Theatre(IRE) Steel Grey Lady (IRE) (Roselier (FR))
4143[4] 5457[8]

Molivias Lad *David Thompson* 4b
4 b g Monsieur Bond(IRE) Mississippi Millie (IRE) (Tagula (IRE))
257[5]

Molko Jack (FR) *Michael Mullineaux* 110h 100c
11 bb g Lavirco(GER) Line As (FR) (Cadoudal (FR))
88[4] 1422[6] 1603[6] 2290[4] 3241[5] 3376[3] 3729[5] **4048[6] 4741[4] 5016[4]**

Mollasses *Harry Whittington* 117h
4 b m Authorized(IRE) Muscovado (USA) (Mr Greeley (USA))
5074[P]

Mollyanna (IRE) *Jamie Snowden* 111h
5 b m Oscar(IRE) Baywatch Star (IRE) (Supreme Leader)
1136[5]

Mollylikestoboogie *Linda Blackford* 73b
5 b m Tobougg(IRE) Two Aye Em (Double Trigger (IRE))
1050[4] 1300[5]

Molly Milan *Jim Goldie* 94h
7 b m Milan Dolly Sparks (IRE) (Electric)
3438[2] ◆ 4163[P] 4796[2] 5198[P]

Molly Oscar (IRE) *Johnny Farrelly* 98h 88c
9 b m Oscar(IRE) Bishop's Folly (Weld)
388[5] 610[P] 3218[P] 4160[P] (4673) 4746[3] 4921[5]

Molly's A Diva *Kim Bailey* 140h 70c
8 ch m Midnight Legend Smokey Diva (IRE) (Orchestra)
(2367) 2759[10] **3197[P]** 3732[P]

Molten Brown *Tony Hogarth* 94c
10 b g Needle Gun(IRE) Molten (Ore)
4180[7] 5449[3]

Momkinzain (USA) *Lucinda Russell* 98h
8 b g Rahy(USA) Fait Accompli (USA) (Louis Quatorze (USA))
634[5]

Monbeg Charmer (IRE) *Charlie Longsdon* 120b
4 br g Daylami(IRE) Charming Present (IRE) (Presenting)
(2031) 3138[7]

Monbeg Dolly (IRE) *Alistair Whillans* 103h
5 ch m Flemensfirth(USA) Laughing Lesa (IRE) (Bob Back (USA))
(4702)

Monbeg Gold (IRE) *Jonjo O'Neill* 131h
5 b g Gold Well Little Hand (IRE) (Carroll House (IRE))
330[2] 1597[2] (2262) (2441) 3018[8] 3407[8]

Monbeg River (IRE) *Martin Todhunter* 101h 135c
6 bb g Indian River(FR) So Pretty (IRE) (Presenting)
(1630) (2104) ◆ 2193[2] 4606[2] ◆ 5298[2] 5471[F]

Monbeg Rose (IRE) *W P Mullins* 121h
5 gr m Beneficial Roses And Wine (IRE) (Roselier (FR))
3890a[3] 4653a[4] 4954a[5]

Monbeg Theatre (IRE) *Jamie Snowden* 130h 116c
6 b g King's Theatre(IRE) Amberina (IRE) (Bob Back (USA))
2881[U] 3504[3]

Mon Bonbon (FR) *J-C Bertin* 73h
6 ch g Bonbon Rose(FR) La Campanella (FR) (Mistigri)
349a[14]

Moncarno *David Pipe* 61h
5 b g Lucarno(USA) Sparkling Jewel (Bijou D'Inde)
30[P] 451[P] 1171[P]

Mon Chevalier (IRE) *Carroll Gray* 79h 110c
12 b g Montjeu(IRE) Kumta (IRE) (Priolo (USA))
1825[2]

Mondello (GER) *Richard Woollacott* 94h
4 b g Soldier Hollow Mandrella (GER) (Surumu (GER))
2564[6] 3370[9] 3745[9] 3915[5] 4250[P]

Monderon (FR) *Henry Oliver* 101h 108c
8 bb g Laveron Lomonde (FR) (Great Lakes)
1931[7] **2861[2] 3129[U]**

Mondlicht (USA) *James Moffatt* 112h
5 b g Malibu Moon(USA) Moonlight Cruise (USA) (Silver Deputy (CAN))
481[3] 669[4] 751[5] 895[8] 2212[3] 2396[4] 2843[3] 5089[5]

Mondo Cane (IRE) *Charles Pogson* 111h 111c
8 b g Beneficial La Vita E Bella (FR) (Le Nain Jaune (FR))
2560[5] **2837[2] 3236[P]** 3628[6] (3950) 4846[4] 5017[5] **5309[2]**

Monetaire (FR) *David Pipe* 127h 146c
9 bb g Anabaa(USA) Monitrice (FR) (Groom Dancer (USA))
96a[8] **2483[8] 2761[6]**

Monetary Fund (USA) *Venetia Williams* 112h 97c
9 b g Montjeu(IRE) Maddie G (USA) (Blush Rambler (USA))
2125[6] 2687[3] 4467[6] 5072[8]

Monet Moor *Jimmy Frost* 59h
6 b m Morpeth Miracle Monarch (Elegant Monarch)
2870[6] 3581[P] 5161[P] 5269[11]

Money For Nothing *Harriet Bethell* 99h 106c
6 b g Kayf Tara Top Of The Dee (Rakaposhi King)
2138[P] 2765[3] 3237[P] 3806[3] 3968[9] 5016[2] 5439[5]

Money Maid (IRE) *Graeme McPherson* 104h
7 ch m Blueprint(IRE) Maid Of Music (IRE) (Orchestra)
2841[2] 3234[2]

Money Talks *Michael Madgwick* 127h 111c
5 br g Motivator Movie Mogul (Sakhee (USA))
2012[4] 2885[7] 4098[5] 5066[3]

Monfass (IRE) *Rose Dobbin* 99b
4 b g Trans Island Ajo Green (IRE) (Moscow Society (USA))
4037[6] 4867[9]

Mon Garcon Frankie *Steve Flook*
3 ch g Sulamani(IRE) Rhetorique (FR) (Smadoun (FR))
2020[10]

Monkerty Tunkerty *Jess Westwood* 115h 139c
12 b g Silver Patriarch(IRE) Orphan Annie (Gunner B)
2374[P] 2558[3] 2838[4] **3707[P]**

Monkey Kingdom *Rebecca Curtis* 118h 138c
7 b g King's Theatre(IRE) Blast Freeze (IRE) (Lafontaine I (USA))
(209) 4269[3] 4446[P] 5178[7]

Monkey Rum *Brendan Powell* 82h
5 b g Araafa(IRE) Cephalonia (Slip Anchor)
271[3] 4256[7] 4382[3] ◆ 4646[4]

Monkhouse (IRE) *Kim Bailey* 109h
5 b g Scorpion(IRE) Gold Shot (Polish Precedent (USA))
3105[3] 4843[2]

Monksgold (IRE) *David Bridgwater* 108h
7 b g Gold Well Opium (Polish Precedent (USA))
83[7] 396[4]

Monksland (IRE) *Noel Meade* 153h 152c
8 b g Beneficial Cush Jewel (IRE) (Executive Perk)
2386a[2] **2817a[2] 3357a[3] 4005a[2]**

Mon Parrain (FR) *Paul Nicholls* 150c
9 b g Trempolino(USA) Kadaina (FR) (Kadalko (FR))
3016[3] 4735[15] 5119[2]

Mon Petit Ange (FR) *David Bridgwater* 64h
4 b g Ultimately Lucky(IRE) Line Tzigane (FR) (Bonnet Rouge (FR))
4184[P]

Monroe Park (IRE) *Alan Blackmore* 89h 85c
10 b g Spectrum(IRE) Paloma Bay (IRE) (Alzao (USA))
240[P] 571[U]

Monsamou (IRE) *P Chevillard* 135h 128c
6 b g Bienamado(USA) Alphadite (IRE) (Alphabatim (USA))
1883a[F] 4960a[6]

Monsart (IRE) *Shaun Lycett* 81h
3 gr g Echo Of Light Monet's Lady (IRE) (Daylami (IRE))
4976[2] 5416[6]

Monsieur Darsi (IRE) *Martin Hill* 98b
5 b g Darsi(FR) Durgams Delight (IRE) (Durgam (USA))
2270[7]

Monsieur Gibraltar (FR) *Paul Nicholls* 130h 130c
4 ch g Spirit One(FR) Palabras De Amor (FR) (Rock Of Gibraltar (IRE))
1847[P] 3284[6] 3733[P]

Monsieur Jourdain (IRE) *Mrs Sarah Easterby* 94h 111c
9 b g Royal Applause Palwina (FR) (Unfuwain (USA))
(5449)

Monsieur Murphy (IRE) *Neil Mulholland*
5 b g Presenting Mistress Cara (Terimon)
2257[P] 4439[P]

Monsieur Oliver (FR) *E Leray* 97c
4 b g Palace Episode(USA) Samarkand (USA) (Saarland (USA))
3815a[6]

Monsieur Valentine *Tony Carroll* 35h
3 ch g Monsieur Bond(IRE) Minnina (IRE) (In The Wings)
3347[7]

Mon Successeur (FR) *Paul Nicholls* 115h 142c
4 ch g Forestier(FR) Sainte Lea (FR) (Sirk)
2201[2] 2472[10] **2758[2] 2877[2] (3148) 3406[7] 4359[F]** (Dead)

Montana Belle (IRE) *S R B Crawford* 122b
5 b m High Chaparral(IRE) Stiletta (Dancing Brave (USA))
23a[13]

Montbazon (FR) *Alan King* 134h
8 bb g Alberto Giacometti(IRE) Duchesse Pierji (FR) (Cadoudal (FR))
4115[10] 4765[U] 5074[3] 5391[P]

Mont Choisy (FR) *Nigel Twiston-Davies* 134h
5 b g Vic Toto(FR) Rhapsodie St Eloi (FR) (Ragmar (FR))
(700) 1044[2] (1349) 1507[2] (1911) 2062[2] 2903[4]

Montdragon (FR) *Jonjo O'Neill* 135h
5 b g Turtle Bowl(IRE) Bonne Gargotte (FR) (Poliglote)
(105) (3156) ◆ 4239[3] 4769[P] (Dead)

Montecito (FR) *Chris Gordon* 70h
5 bb g Falco(USA) Bealli (IRE) (Bering)
1758[8] 2251[11] 2823[12] 3083[12] 4099[P]

Monte Wildhorn (IRE) *David Bridgwater* 116h
7 b g Old Vic Miss Lloyds (IRE) (Take Risks (FR))
(718) 810[4] 971[4] 1346[4] 1508[9]

Monthyne *Warren Greatrex* 96b
4 ch g Nomadic Way(USA) Captivating Tyna (IRE) (Presenting)
4867[8] 5227[8]

Mont Lachaux (FR) *Dan Skelton* 132h
2 b c Astarabad(USA) Belle Yepa (FR) (Mansonnien (FR))
(4539a)

Montoya's Son (IRE) *Keith Dalgleish* 114h 137c
10 ch g Flemensfirth(USA) Over The Grand (IRE) (Over The River (FR))
1268[10]

Mont Royale *Jonjo O'Neill* 121h 134c
7 b g Hurricane Run(IRE) Wild Academy (IRE) (Royal Academy (USA))
102[5] (593) ◆ 775[2] **1042[2] 1481[2] 1617[2] 2184[P] 2774[F] 5245[4]**

Montydarkdestroyer *John Davies* 94b
4 b g Lucarno(USA) Markila (FR) (Mark Of Esteem (IRE))
4867[11] 5407[5]

Montys Meadow (IRE) *James Joseph Mangan* 113h 136c
7 b g Oscar(IRE) Montys Miss (IRE) (Presenting)
4517a[F]

Monty's Revenge (IRE) *Martin Keighley* 58h 90c
10 b g Bob's Return(IRE) Native Bavard (IRE) (Be My Native (USA))
1293[12] **1813[8] (2303) 2811[6] 3131[5]** 3946[9]

Monyjean (FR) *Evan Williams* 102h 95c
4 b g Califet(FR) Rose Beryl (FR) (Lost World (IRE))
2412[7] 3335[4] 4273[6] 4685[P]

Monzino (USA) *Michael Chapman* 78h 72c
7 bb g More Than Ready(USA) Tasso's Magic Roo (USA) (Tasso (USA))
912[7] 1030[4] 1158[8] 1272[P] 1692[P] **1815[4] 2040[6] 2143[P]** 2550[P] 3233[9] 4773[9]

Moojaned (IRE) *David Evans* 88h
4 b g Raven's Pass(USA) Mufradat (IRE) (Desert Prince (IRE))
1810[7]

Moon Arc (IRE) *Keith Dalgleish* 85h
3 b g Arcano(IRE) Moon Unit (IRE) (Intikhab (USA))
1631[5] 2324[5] 2845[7] 3729[U]

Moon Jet (IRE) *John Mackie* 98b
3 b g Ask Playwaki (USA) (Miswaki (USA))
2777[4] 4309[6] 4915[8]

Moonlight Boy (IRE) *Ben Haslam* 126h 116c
8 bb g Saffron Walden(FR) High Gain (Puissance)
1769[P]

Moonlight Maggie *Tom George* 73h 93c
8 b m Pasternak Moyliscar (Terimon)
379[2] (588) ◆ 884[3] 2811[F] (Dead)

Moonlone Lane (IRE) *Paul Stafford* 112h 101c
8 b g Oscar(IRE) Shandarr (IRE) (John French)
(2946) 3473[2]

Moonman (IRE) *Gordon Elliott* 106b
5 b g Pelder(IRE) Mazalunna (FR) (Sillery (USA))
4037[2] ◆

Moonmeister (IRE) *A J Martin* 129h
4 b g Mastercraftsman(IRE) Moon Unit (IRE) (Intikhab (USA))
1788a[4]

Moon Melody (GER) *Mike Sowersby* 88h
12 b g Montjeu(IRE) Midnight Fever (IRE) (Sure Blade (USA))
966[P] 1098[P] 1272[P] 1371[P]

Moon Over Germany (IRE) *Edward P Harty* 141h
4 ch g Germany(USA) Elea Moon (IRE) (Moonax (IRE))
11a[8] 4280a[2] 5002a[3]

Moon Over Rio (IRE) *Ben Haslam* 64h
4 b m Captain Rio Moonchild (GER) (Acatenango (GER))
2427[P]

Moonshine Ridge (IRE) *Alan Swinbank* 96b
4 b m Duke Of Marmalade(IRE) Dreams Come True (FR) (Zafonic (USA))
(2330) 2895[2]

Moontime *John Ferguson* 96h
4 b g Sea The Stars(IRE) Time On (Sadler's Wells (USA))
1305[3]

Moon Trip *Geoffrey Deacon* 102h
6 b g Cape Cross(IRE) Fading Light (King's Best (USA))
2253[5] 2567[2] 3087[4] 3771[7]

Moontripper *Phillip Dando* 90h
6 b m Doyen(IRE) Moon Spinner (Elmaamul (USA))
1289[3] 4681[9] 4881[3] 5050[P]

Moorlands George *Jeremy Scott* 82h 106c
7 b g Grape Tree Road Sandford Springs (USA) (Robellino (USA))
(211) 600[2] (1155) 1326[3] 1678[3] 2402[P]

Moorlands Jack *Jeremy Scott* 104h 125c
10 b g Cloudings(IRE) Sandford Springs (USA) (Robellino (USA))
109[2] 510[2] (772) 1112[3] 1268[9] 1601[6] (2243) 3315[P]

Moorlands Mist *Evan Williams* 129h 94c
8 gr g Fair Mix(IRE) Sandford Springs (USA) (Robellino (USA))
2268[5] 2906[2] 3517[2] **3979[4]** 4911[P]

Moorstone *Giles Bravery* 84b
3 b f Manduro(GER) Pan Galactic (USA) (Lear Fan (USA))
4847[10]

Moorstown (IRE) *Lucinda Russell* 77h
5 b g Oscar(IRE) Glacial Princess (IRE) (Glacial Storm (USA))
2628[6] 3436[4]

Mootabar (IRE) *Chris Fairhurst* 57h
8 gr g Verglas(IRE) Melanzane (Arazi (USA))
3973[P] 4301[4]

Mor Brook *Kim Bailey* 98h 112c
7 b g Kayf Tara Miss Quickly (IRE) (Anshan)
(57) 331[P] 1850[P] 2994[P] 4859[6] 5388[10]

More Buck's (IRE) *Paul Nicholls* 114h 120c
5 ch g Presenting Buck's Blue (FR) (Epervier Bleu)
122[3] (509) **894[3]**

Moreece (IRE) *Tim Vaughan* 117h
6 b g Chevalier(IRE) Jumbo Romance (IRE) (Tagula (IRE))
832[6] 1034[9] 1156[6] 1323[8] 2547[4] 5099[4]

Morello Royale (IRE) *Colin Tizzard* 142h
5 b m King's Theatre(IRE) Mystic Cherry (IRE) (Alderbrook)
2064[F] 2349[4] (2685) 3444[8] 4699[13]

More Madness (IRE) *N W Alexander* 89h 104c
8 b g Dr Massini(IRE) Angelic Angel (IRE) (Phardante (FR))
92a[11] 2192[6] 2477[3] 2934[U] 3341[5] 3671[2] 4032[3] 4407[4] 4739[3] 5412[9]

More More More *Scott Dixon* 60b
5 b g Milk It Mick Snowmore (Glacial Storm (USA))
3952[9] 4475[5]

More Of That (IRE) *Jonjo O'Neill* 172h 162c
7 b g Beneficial Guigone (FR) (Esprit Du Nord (USA))
(2469) (3029) 4716[3]

More Play *George Moore* 59b
4 b m Multiplex For More (FR) (Sanglamore (USA))
2849[5] 3626[P]

Morestead Screamer *Chris Gordon* 107h
6 b m Imperial Dancer The Screamer (IRE) (Insan (USA))
225[6] 880[3] 1242[4] 1490[6] 1736[4] 2002[6] 4250[P]

More Than Two *Fergal O'Brien* 88b
5 b m Kayf Tara Sweet Stormy (IRE) (Bluebird (USA))
5049[3]

Morga (IRE) *Desmond McDonogh* 134h
5 b m Whipper(USA) Langfuhrina (USA) (Langfuhr (CAN))
7a[13]

Morgan's Bay *Laura Mongan* 16h 124c
10 b g Karinga Bay Dubai Dolly (IRE) (Law Society (USA))
2419[4] 2884[6] 4321[P]

Morito Du Berlais (FR) *Paul Nicholls* 144h
6 b g Turgeon(USA) Chica Du Berlais (FR) (Cadoudal (FR))
1839[7] 2484[3]

Morney Wing (IRE) *Charlie Mann* 114h 129c
6 b g Antonius Pius(USA) Tillan Fuwain (FR) (Unfuwain (USA))
1970[6] 2434[4] (3365) 3583[P] 4232[3] 4589[5] (4971) 5274[7]

Morning Assembly (IRE) *P A Fahy* 151h 156c
8 b g Shantou(USA) Barrack Village (IRE) (Montelimar (USA))
4131a[2] 4697[4] 5218[8]

Morning Herald *Martin Keighley* 120h
4 br m Lucky Story(USA) Wakeful (Kayf Tara)
2486[11] 3110[4] (4893) 5389[3]

Morning Reggie *Oliver Sherwood* 110h 130c
6 gr g Turgeon(USA) Nile Cristale (FR) (Northern Crystal)
128[2] ◆ 2780[U] 2897[3] 3257[3] 3620[2] (4625) 5093[6]

Morning Royalty (IRE) *James Moffatt* 120h 130c
8 b g King's Theatre(IRE) Portryan Native (IRE) (Be My Native (USA))
505[4] (840) 2211[4] 3055[2] 3362[2] 3742[3] (4053) 4634[4] 5298[3]

Morning Run (IRE) *W P Mullins* 143h
6 b m King's Theatre(IRE) Portryan Native (IRE) (Be My Native (USA))
3356a[3] 3858[3]

Morning Symphony (IRE) *Warren Greatrex* 116h
6 b g Vinnie Roe(IRE) Heart N Hope (IRE) (Fourstars Allstar (USA))
1179[2] 1912[U]

Morning Time (IRE) *Lucinda Russell* 88h 90c
9 b g Hawk Wing(USA) Desert Trail (IRE) (Desert Style (IRE))
205[5] **485[4] 2755[8]** 3473[10] 4178[5] 4585[6] 5472[11]

Morning With Ivan (IRE) *Martin Todhunter* 101h 99c
5 b m Ivan Denisovich(IRE) Grinneas (IRE) (Barathea (IRE))
34[7] (508) 711[5] 851[7] 1036[5] 1071[3] ◆ 1170[6] 1400[7] **1888[3] 2143[4] 3103[5] 3308[6]** 4328[4] 4550[6] 4736[4] 4904[9]

Moroman (IRE) *David Kemp* 140c
8 b g Morozov(USA) Emma's Love (IRE) (Witness Box (USA))
15[2] (535)

Mo Rouge (IRE) *Jackie Stephen* 103h 113c
7 b g Croco Rouge(IRE) Just A Mo (IRE) (Supreme Leader)
458[8] 1264[11] **2028[4] 2327[3] 4903[2] 5474[4]**

Morris The Miner *Neil Mulholland* 69h
5 b g Apple Tree(FR) Miner Yours (Miner's Lamp)
2351[10] 4439[P] 5263[9]

Mortens Leam *Pam Sly* 87b
3 b g Sulamani(IRE) Bonnet's Pieces (Alderbrook)
5083[5]

Morthanalegend *Brendan Powell* 116h
6 b g Midnight Legend Morwenna (IRE) (Zaffaran (USA))
(928) 2457[6] 2879[2] 3581[3] 4620[P]

Mortlestown (IRE) *Martin Keighley* 106h 124c
7 b g Milan Pima (IRE) (Commanche Run)
610[4] ◆ (894) (1005) 1701[P] 2342[U]

Moscow Blaze (IRE) *Mrs R Fuller* 114c
9 ch g Moscow Society(USA) Nobody's Darling (IRE) (Supreme Leader)
533[P]

Moscow Calling (IRE) *Nicky Richards* 63b
4 b g Morozov(USA) Bubble Bann (IRE) (Hubbly Bubbly (USA))
4515[4]

Moscow Me (IRE) *Henry Oliver* 107h 117c
8 b g Moscow Society(USA) Just Trust Me (IRE) (Warcraft (USA))
1647[10] **(2300) 2857[2] (3313) 4053[3] 4533[P]**

Moscow Menace (IRE) *Katie Scott* 28c
8 b g Moscow Society(USA) Sky Flagship (FR) (Sky Lawyer (FR))
2321[P] 4840[P] **5261[9]**

Moscow Presents (IRE) *Philip Kirby* 103h
7 b g Presenting Moscow Madame (IRE) (Moscow Society (USA))
2839[P] 3142[P] 3628[8] 3855[13] 4301[3] ◆ 4510[2] **4738[P]** 5233[2] 5402[2]

Mossies Well (IRE) *Sandy Thomson* 117h 121c
6 b g Morozov(USA) Kidora (IRE) (Broadsword (USA))
(2475) ◆ 2918[2] 5413[4]

Moss On The Mill *Tom George* 113h 120c
7 br g Overbury(IRE) Mimis Bonnet (FR) (Bonnet Rouge (FR))
2694[4] 3383[5] (4492)

Mosspark (IRE) *Emma Lavelle* 141h 141c
7 b g Flemensfirth(USA) Patio Rose (Petoski)
2780[5] (4621)

Moss Street *John Flint* 86h 73c
5 b g Moss Vale(IRE) Street Style (IRE) (Rock Of Gibraltar (IRE))
5418[10]

Most Honourable *John Joseph Hanlon* 108h
5 b g Halling(USA) Her Ladyship (Polish Precedent (USA))
484[P] 1405[4]

Mostly Bob (IRE) *Sophie Leech* 59h 74c
12 b g Bob Back(USA) Town Gossip (IRE) (Indian Ridge)
151[6] 471[U] 847[P] 1545[P] **1720[7] 2269[6] 2735[4] 3387[5]**

Mother Meldrum (IRE) *Victor Dartnall* 106h
6 b m Milan Europet (IRE) (Fourstars Allstar (USA))
2582[F] 2985[7] 3414[P] 4184[5] 4541[3] (4854) (5029)

Motion To Strike (IRE) *Rebecca Menzies* 104h
5 b g Beneficial Comeragh Girl (IRE) (Imperial Ballet (IRE))
4037[9] 4371[7] 4835[4] 5365[2]

Motts Cross (IRE) *Chris Down* 102h
4 b g Scorpion(IRE) Rainy Season (IRE) (Sulamani (IRE))
124[6] 2257[P] 2603[7] 3124[5] 3705[11] 4860[4] (5431)

Moulin Rouge (DEN) *Ian Williams* 85h
4 ch m Zambezi Sun Embattle (FR) (Dernier Empereur (USA))
554[3] 714[6]

Mountain Eagle (IRE) *Harry Fry* 127h
6 b g Mountain High(IRE) Ceart Go Leor (IRE) (Montelimar (USA))
1872[4] 2239[5] 2603[5] 3063[2] 3744[2] 4466[3] 5391[5]

Mountain Fighter *John Ferguson* 123h
4 b g Dubawi(IRE) River Pearl (GER) (Turfkonig (GER))
(566) 1590[2] 1949[5] 2472[11] 2949[2]

Mountain King *Philip Hobbs* 137h 142c
6 b g Definite Article Belle Magello (FR) (Exit To Nowhere (USA))
184[6] 2171[4] 2784[4] 3148[2] 3731[6]

Mountain Of Angels *Mary Evans* 44h
6 b m Midnight Legend Landsker Missile (Cruise Missile)
90[P]

Mountain Of Mourne (IRE) *Linda Blackford* 118h 115c
6 ch g Mountain High(IRE) Katies Native (IRE) (Be My Native (USA))
(2569) 2904[5] 3705[10] **3975[5] 4427[3] 4884[2] 5032[3]**

Mountainous (IRE) *Kerry Lee* 127h 147c
10 b g Milan Mullaghcloga (IRE) (Glacial Storm (USA))
1871[5] 2374[3] 2916[6] (3518) 4245[P]

Mountainside *Lucinda Egerton* 114h
3 ch g Dubawi(IRE) Maids Causeway (IRE) (Giant's Causeway (USA))
(778) 1321[2] (1486) 4640[4]

Mountain Tunes (IRE) *Jonjo O'Neill* 119h 98c
6 b g Mountain High(IRE) Art Lover (IRE) (Over The River (FR))
2442[P] 3348[6] 3843[P] 4246[9] 5100[3] 5335[P]

Mount Beckham (IRE) *Miss Clare Louise Cannon* 114h
6 b g Desert King(IRE) Nowhere Like Home (IRE) (Exit To Nowhere (USA))
3436[3]

Mount Colah (IRE) *J G Cosgrave* 136h 158c
9 b g Beneficial Lady Newmill (IRE) (Taipan (IRE))
47a[9] 3603a[4] 4281a[4]

Mount Gunnery *P A Fahy* 121h 129c
7 b g Kayf Tara Bobs Bay (IRE) (Bob's Return (IRE))
3716a[2] 4729[6]

Mount Haven (IRE) *David Pipe* 124h
5 b g Mountain High(IRE) Castlehaven (IRE) (Erins Isle)
(3467) 4305[9] 4537[4]

Mount Mews (IRE) *Malcolm Jefferson* 104b
4 b g Presenting Kneeland Lass (IRE) (Bob Back (USA))
(5248)

Mount Mizooka *Brian Ellison* 86b
4 b m Mount Nelson Mizooka (Tobougg (IRE))
1688[2] 4708[3]

Mount Prospex (IRE) *Tim Dennis* 91h 93c
6 ch g Golan(IRE) No Blues (IRE) (Orchestra)
3410[3] 3746[8] 4343[P] **4859[4]**

Mount Shamsan *Gary Moore* 96h
5 b g Danehill Dancer(IRE) Shamaiel (IRE) (Lycius (USA))
3083[6] 3660[6] 4390[7] 4854[5]

Mount Vesuvius (IRE) *Paul Henderson* 92h 88c
7 b g Spartacus(IRE) Parker's Cove (USA) (Woodman (USA))
267[2] 435[6] 515[5] 856[P] 1299[2] 1421[4] 1510[4] 1596[6] **1825[5] 2003[3]**

Mountyfirth *Nick Williams* 86b
5 b g Flemensfirth(USA) Valleyofthedolls (King's Theatre (IRE))
1003[4]

Mouskersize (IRE) *John C McConnell* 96h
4 b m Lawman(FR) Sesenta (IRE) (King's Theatre (IRE))
2176a[7]

Moveable Asset (IRE) *Henry Tett* 103h 104c
7 b g Trans Island Mica Male (ITY) (Law Society (USA))
669[8] 931[3] 1012[6] **1505[3] 1985[5] 2552[3] 2834[P]**

Move To The Groove (IRE) *Donald McCain* 94h
5 b g Catcher In The Rye(IRE) Valley Of Love (IRE) (Lure (USA))
3593[4] 4208[4] 4714[10] 5124[3]

Movewiththetimes (IRE) *Paul Nicholls* 107b
4 ch g Presenting Dare To Venture (IRE) (Darazari (IRE))
(5358)

Movie Legend *Ben Case* 106h
5 b g Midnight Legend Cyd Charisse (Kayf Tara)
1973[6] 2487[4] 2928[8] 3839[7] 5397[9]

Moving Waves (IRE) *Johnny Farrelly* 88h
4 b m Intense Focus(USA) Kimola (IRE) (King's Theatre (IRE))
1182[9] 1524[9] 3219[P] 4161[P] 4747[P]

Moylisha Tim (IRE) *R P Rath* 132h
5 b g Alkaadhem Moylisha Red (IRE) (Oscar (IRE))
(2225a) 2672a[2] 3393a[5] 4955a[P]

Moyode Wood *Brian Ellison* 102h 106c
10 b g Overbury(IRE) Country Choice (IRE) (Paean)
1082[5] 1264[5] **1571[4] 1659[5] 1855[6] 3934[4] 4276[P]**

Mozo *David Pipe* 104h
4 b m Milan Haudello (FR) (Marignan (USA))
(152) 2829[2] 3110[8] 3947[7]

Mozoltov *W P Mullins* 145h 154c
9 b g Kayf Tara Fairmead Princess (Rudimentary (USA))
3031[P] 3552a[2] 3892a[3]

Mr Bachster (IRE) *Kerry Lee* 95h 104c
10 b g Bach(IRE) Warrior Princess (IRE) (Mister Lord (USA))
(2315) 2416[F] 2855[P] **(3497) 3951[6] 4587[3] 5307[P]**

Mr Banks (IRE) *Paul Webber* 98h
4 br g Kalanisi(IRE) She's Supersonic (IRE) (Accordion)
2650[4] 3226[3] 4494[8] 4874[5] 5451[3]

Mr Beatle *Kim Bailey* 79h
6 br g Beat All(USA) Northern Native (IRE) (Be My Native (USA))
2860[6] 3334[P]

Mr Bennett (IRE) *Peter Bull* 106h 98c
12 b g Mister Mat(FR) Miss Bobby Bennett (Kings Lake (USA))
295[4]

Mr Bien (IRE) *Robert Alan Hennessy* 85h
6 b g Bienamado(USA) Aboulia (IRE) (Presenting)
5243[3]

Mr Big Shot (IRE) *David Pipe* 127b
4 br g Flemensfirth(USA) Une Etoile (IRE) (Un Desperado (FR))
(4805)

Mr Blue Nose *Simon Waugh* 117h
5 b g Tobougg(IRE) Cape Siren (Warning)
4206[P]

Mr Boss Man (IRE) *Adrian McGuinness* 122h
7 b g Beneficial Sarah Massini (IRE) (Dr Massini (IRE))
5219[10]

Mr Burbidge *Neil Mulholland* 120h 131c
7 b g Midnight Legend Twin Time (Syrtos)
442[5] **1838[5] 2266[4] 3115[2] ◆ 3589[F]** (Dead)

Mr Burgees (IRE) *Donald McCain* 127h 119c
6 b g Westerner My Kinda Girl (IRE) (Supreme Leader)
82[F] **697[2] (1068) 1460[3] 1741[3]**

Mr Caffrey *Robert Stephens* 101h
3 b g Duke Of Marmalade(IRE) Quest For Eternity (IRE) (Sadler's Wells (USA))
3213[4] 4854[2]

Mr Cardle (IRE) *Oliver Sherwood* 102h
6 b g Golan(IRE) Leave Me Be (IRE) (Be My Native (USA))
265[5] 493[2] 939[4]

Mr Cracker (IRE) *Tim Vaughan* 93b
10 ch g Anshan Sesame Cracker (Derrylin)
1296[P] 1522[P]

Mr Diablo (IRE) *J P Dempsey* 136h 136c
6 br g Presenting Aremebooksready (IRE) (Good Thyne (USA))
7a[19] **4279a[P]**

Mr Elevator (IRE) *Charles Pogson* 43h
5 br g Sandmason Greenwood Lady (IRE) (Roselier (FR))
2406[P] 3037[7] 3179[7]

Mr Fenton (IRE) *Emma Lavelle* 102b
4 b g Trans Island Carnagh Girl (IRE) (Saddlers' Hall (IRE))
2909[4] 3847[4] 5359[5]

Mr Fickle (IRE) *Gary Moore* 122h
6 b g Jeremy(USA) Mamara Reef (Salse (USA))
(281) 2418[2] (2888) 3216[P]

Mr Fiftyone (IRE) *Mrs John Harrington* 133h 136c
6 b g Jeremy(USA) Maka (USA) (Diesis)
69a[9] 1186a[3]

Mr Fitzroy (IRE) *Jo Davis* 122h
5 ch g Kyllachy Reputable (Medicean)
2516[2] 2831[5] (3529) 3733[14] 5074[6]

Mr Gillespie *Simon Waugh* 82b
5 gr g Desideratum Silivri (Silver Patriarch (IRE))
459[9] 2756[12]

Mr Hopeful (IRE) *Donald McCain* 102h
6 b g Helissio(FR) Lisadian Lady (IRE) (Erdelistan (FR))
139[P] 421[U] 1171[8]

Mr Jalfrazy (IRE) *Tom Weston* 81h
6 b g Pierre Brushaside Spa (IRE) (Brush Aside (USA))
2850[11] 2974[4] 3130[8] 3791[P]

Mr K (IRE) *Paul Webber* 92h
4 b g Kheleyf(USA) Undertone (IRE) (Noverre (USA))
3316[P] 3626[P]

Mr Kit Cat *Evan Williams* 114h
5 ch g Lucarno(USA) Makeabreak (IRE) (Anshan)
2056[U] 2747[8] 3772[5] 5269[3]

Mr Kite *Harry Fry* 102h
4 b g Sixties Icon Mar Blue (FR) (Marju (IRE))
644[6] (783) 5182[3]

Mr Lando *Alison Batchelor* 122h 79c
6 b g Shirocco(GER) Capitana (GER) (Lando (GER))
(104) 217[2] 406[5] **1047[5]** 1988[5] 2244[P] 2734[15] 5148[7] 5374[11]

Mr Madeit (IRE) *G T H Bailey* 25h 121c
9 b g Brian Boru Henrietta Howard (IRE) (King's Ride)
(4973) 5458[2]

Mr Mafia (IRE) *Tony Carroll* 106h 111c
6 b g Zerpour(IRE) Wizzy (IRE) (Presenting)
106[9] **697[5] (934) 1056[3]** 1293[3] **1504[2]** 1812[2] **2249[2] 2930[2]** 5223[3]

Mr McGregor (IRE) *Heather Dalton* 91h 99c
7 ch g Beneficial Our Idol (IRE) (Mandalus)
2827[3] 3144[3] 3793[5] **3948[P]**

Mr McGuiness (IRE) *Rosemary Gasson* 104h
5 b g Kalanisi(IRE) Maig Mandy (IRE) (Mandalus)
702[6] 932[6] 1153[3] 1549[6] 1786[3] 2043[3]

Mr Medic *Robert Walford* 90h
4 b g Dr Massini(IRE) Danse Slave (FR) (Broadway Flyer (USA))
2636[10] 3370[10] 3581[6] 4137[P] 4882[6]

Mr Mercurial (IRE) *Mrs Sheila Crow* 102b 109c
7 b g Westerner Arcanum (IRE) (Presenting)
(13) 533[4] 4768[12] 5312[P]

Mr Mix (FR) *Paul Nicholls* 143h
4 gr g Al Namix(FR) Royale Surabaya (FR) (Turgeon (USA))
2154[3] 2879[3] (3744) ◆ 4236[2] 4769[F]

Mr Mole (IRE) *Paul Nicholls* 148h 168c
7 br g Great Pretender(IRE) Emmylou Du Berlais (FR) (Kadalko (FR))
2511[5] 2915[5] 3406[10]

Mr Monochrome *Malcolm Jefferson* 105b
4 br g Indian Danehill(IRE) Our Ethel (Be My Chief (USA))
5476[3] ◆

Mr Moonshine (IRE) *Sue Smith* 139h 143c
11 b g Double Eclipse(IRE) Kinross (Nearly A Hand)
(4246) **4818[3] 5193[9]**

Mr Morocco *Giles Bravery* 77h
3 b g Shirocco(GER) Moxby (Efisio)
3099[10]

Mr Moss (IRE) *S Rea* 86h 127c
10 b g Moscow Society(USA) Yesterdays Gorby (IRE) (Strong Gale)
219[6] **611[6] 927[2] 1167[7] 1288[6] 3585[P] 4307[7] 4651[4] 5035[4] 5458[6]**

Mr Mountain (IRE) *Emma Lavelle* 67h
5 b g Mountain High(IRE) Not Mine (IRE) (Oscar (IRE))
3200[2] ◆ *4532[8]*

Mr Muddle *Sheena West* 113h 124c
8 gr g Imperial Dancer Spatham Rose (Environment Friend)
2546[2] 3445[2] 3843[3] 4363[U] 5096[3]

Mr Ooosh *Tom Symonds* 35h
5 b g Midnight Legend Blackbriery Thyne (IRE) (Good Thyne (USA))
1612[7]

Mr Robinson (FR) *Rob Summers* 80h 86c
8 b g Robin Des Pres(FR) Alberade (FR) (Un Desperado (FR))
(88) 340[3] 972[P] 1306[10] (1785) 1978[3] 2539[6]

Mr Satco (IRE) *Mrs Emma Oliver* 102h 118c
7 b g Mr Combustible(IRE) Satlin (IRE) (Satco (FR))
270[2] 557[5] 5035[6]

Mrs Burbidge *Neil Mulholland* 72h 56c
5 b m Pasternak Twin Time (Syrtos)
1084[5] 1384[6]

Mr Selby *Philip Kirby* 111h
6 b g Terimon Bee-A-Scally (Scallywag)
1178[4] (1260)

Mrs Grass *Jonathan Haynes* 80h
8 ch m And Beyond(IRE) Tempted (IRE) (Invited (USA))
37[9] 153[5] 502[6] 1573[P] 1744[5] 2322[5] 2703[5] 4513[5] 5199[7]

Mr Shahady (IRE) *Victor Thompson* 111h 61c
10 b g Xaar Shunaire (USA) (Woodman (USA))
143[P] 286[3] 399[P]

Mr Shantu (IRE) *Jonjo O'Neill* 143h
6 b g Shantou(USA) Close To Shore (IRE) (Bob Back (USA))
261[9] (833) (1615) 2054[2] ◆ 2767[5]

Mrs Jordan (IRE) *Sophie Leech* 101h 105c
7 b m King's Theatre(IRE) Regents Dancer (IRE) (Flemensfirth (USA))
503[2] **803[P] 926[P]** 1094[3] 1262[2] 1545[8]

Mrs Mac Veale (IRE) *Gavin Dower* 140h 115c
10 b m Karinga Bay Carrigmorna Flyer (IRE) (Bob Back (USA))
7a[20] 231a[2] 954a[3] (2236a) 3071a[13]

Mr Snoozy *Mark Walford* 109h
6 b g Pursuit Of Love Hard To Follow (Dilum (USA))
3724[P] 4152[4] 4455[2] 5079[4]

Mrsrobin (IRE) *Emma Lavelle* 95h 101c
5 b m Robin Des Pres(FR) Regents Dancer (IRE) (Flemensfirth (USA))
2444[6] 2870[3] 3386[3] 4250[P] **4859[8] 5138[5] 5357[3]**

Mr Steadfast (IRE) *Gordon Elliott* 119h 89c
5 bb g Kalanisi(IRE) Lady Of The Mill (IRE) (Woods Of Windsor (USA))
1328[2] 1498[2] 1634[4]

Mr Supreme (IRE) *Keith Reveley* 85b
10 b g Beneficial Ardfallon (IRE) (Supreme Leader)
3472[F] (Dead)

Mrs Winchester (IRE) *Caroline Keevil* 59h
6 b m Scorpion(IRE) Supreme Nova (Supreme Leader)
4157[5] 4435[7]

Mr Syntax (IRE) *Chris Grant* 87h 124c
11 b g King's Theatre(IRE) Smile Awhile (USA) (Woodman (USA))
3996[P] 4872[4]

Mr Witmore (IRE) *Michael Smith* 85h
5 b g Whitmore's Conn(USA) Bright Future (IRE) (Satco (FR))
39[3] 2951[2] 3971[6]

Ms Arsenal *Giles Bravery* 85b
3 b f Mount Nelson Magical Dancer (IRE) (Magical Wonder (USA))
5443[4]

Ms Parfois (IRE) *Anthony Honeyball* 115b
4 ch m Mahler Dolly Lewis (Sir Harry Lewis (USA))
(5104)

Mtada Supreme (IRE) *Peter Maher* 120c
10 b g Bishop Of Cashel Tullabards Leader (IRE) (Supreme Leader)
3017[7]

Mubrook (USA) *John David Riches* 58h
10 b g Alhaarth(IRE) Zomaradah (Deploy)
2843[P] 3307[10] 3791[P]

Muckle Roe (IRE) *Nigel Twiston-Davies* 91h 119c
6 b g Westerner Island Crest (Jupiter Island)
461[4] 1601[7] (2017) 2149[F] 2975[2] 3384[2] 4465[3] 4789[5]

Muffins For Tea *Colin Tizzard* 117h
5 ch g With The Flow(USA) Countess Point (Karinga Bay)
3980[6] 4357[4] 4681[3] 4917[2] ◆ 5378[3]

Mugs Money (IRE) *Garrett James Power*
7 ch g Bach(IRE) Miss Inga Leg (Welsh Captain)
25a[15]

Muhtaris (IRE) *James Evans* 127h
5 b g Teofilo(IRE) Fann (USA) (Diesis)
2202[2] 4241[P] (4466) 4801[B] 5275[11]

Mullaghanoe River (IRE) *Noel Meade* 121b
7 b g Beneficial Wahiba Hall (IRE) (Saddlers' Hall (IRE))
2675a[F]

Mulligan's Man (IRE) *Clare Ellam* 108h 98c
8 b g Morozov(USA) Rashmulligan (IRE) (Rashar (USA))
1071[10] 1525[3] 1927[5] 2165[3] (2492) 2667[4]

Mullinavat (IRE) *Jennie Candlish* 95h
6 b g Beneficial Kilfane (IRE) (Hollow Hand)
732[3] 912[5] 1000[5] 1168[6] 1375[9] 1691[5] 1890[10]

Multi Grain *Micky Hammond* 88h
3 b f Sir Percy Grain Only (Machiavellian (USA))
2324[4] 2845[3] 3309[4] 3587[4]

Multimedia *David Pipe* 100h
5 b g Multiplex Sunday News'N'Echo (USA) (Trempolino (USA))
108[3] 529[10]

Multipede *James Ewart* 89b
3 b g Multiplex Playful Lady (Theatrical Charmer)
2777[5] 4037[5] 4408[5]

Multiview *Tom Symonds* 88h
6 b m Multiplex Lacounsel (FR) (Leading Counsel (USA))
336[4] ◆ 597[2] 864[4]

Mumgos Debut (IRE) *Lucinda Russell* 99h 104c
7 b g Royal Anthem(USA) Black Queen (IRE) (Bob Back (USA))
2430[2] 2786[2] 3441[3] 4034[2] 4569[4] (5197) 5366[3]

Murchu (IRE) *Tim Vaughan* 97h 84c
9 b g Oscar(IRE) Bottle A Knock (IRE) (Le Moss)
1522[5] 2223[9]

Murifield *Anthony Honeyball* 83b
5 b g Tobougg(IRE) Kiwi Katie (Kayf Tara)
124[10]

Murphys Filly (IRE) *Colin Bowe* 90c
7 bb m Flemensfirth(USA) Desperately Hoping (IRE) (Un Desperado (FR))
48a[U]

Murrayana (IRE) *Colin Tizzard* 131h 128c
5 b g King's Theatre(IRE) Royalrova (FR) (Garde Royale)
2034[2] 2580[3] 2908[F] 3583[3] 4438[3] (4801) 5213[4]

Murray Mount (IRE) *Charlie Mann* 105h
5 b g Trans Island Ash (Salse (USA))
1648[9] 1844[2] (2121) 2577[12]

Murtys Delight (IRE) *Lisa Harrison* 70h 69c
8 b g Bach(IRE) Valley Supreme (IRE) (Supreme Leader)
5445[18]

Musical Wedge *Claire Dyson* 70h 89c
11 ch g Sir Harry Lewis(USA) Wedge Musical (What A Guest)
58[4] 1850[P] 2303[2]

Music Hall (FR) *Shaun Harris* 66h
5 gr g Stormy River(FR) Aaliyah (GER) (Anabaa (USA))
1898[12] 2218[P]

Mustadrik (USA) *Gordon Elliott* 122h 122c
4 b g Jazil(USA) Uroobah (USA) (Dynaformer (USA))
1635[2]

Mustang On *Nick Kent* 92b
5 b g Croco Rouge(IRE) More To Life (Northern Tempest (USA))
4309[7] 4988[3]

Mustmeetalady (IRE) *Jonjo O'Neill* 131h
5 b g Mustameet(USA) Ladymcgrath (IRE) (Jamesmead)
146[2] 1648[2] (1901) 2214[4] 2558[4] (5141) 5454[6]

Must Meet Mrsgrath (IRE) *Robin Dickin* 55b
4 b m Mustameet(USA) Ladymcgrath (IRE) (Jamesmead)
3861[10]

Mutawaasel *Sue Smith* 63b
3 b g Teofilo(IRE) Muwakleh (Machiavellian (USA))
4552[7] 4988[5]

Mutdula (IRE) *Alan Swinbank* 98b
5 b g Gamut(IRE) Calendula (Be My Guest (USA))
2756[7] 3104[7]

Muthabir (IRE) *Richard Phillips* 118h
5 b g Nayef(USA) Northern Melody (IRE) (Singspiel (IRE))
761[4] 2267[7] 2748[4] 3483[2] (4065) 4486[3]

Muwalla *Lisa Harrison* 103h 115c
8 b g Bahri(USA) Easy Sunshine (IRE) (Sadler's Wells (USA))
1494[2] 1553[2] 1773[6] **1904[3]** 2069[6] **2329[4] 2755[6]**

Mwaleshi *Sue Smith* 118h 140c
10 b g Oscar(IRE) Roxy River (Ardross)
318[7] 2082[5] 2329[5] 2902[F] 3629[3] 3887[4] 4511[U] 4793[6] 5246[2] 5440[6]

Mwangaza (FR) *Pauline Robson* 90h 100c
5 gr m Martaline Saloria (FR) (Ecologist)
455[5] 804[8] 1773[10]

My Anchor *Charlie Mann* 105h
4 b g Mount Nelson War Shanty (Warrshan (USA))
2238[4] 2614[4] 3023[12] 3725[7] 5182[5]

My Betty (IRE) *Peter Croke* 109h 115c
7 b m Definite Article Banusal (IRE) (Lord Americo)
2293[4]

Mybrotherjohnny *John E Long* 83b
4 b g Tiger Hill(IRE) Montjeu's Melody (IRE) (Montjeu (IRE))
2835[4]

My Brother Sylvest *David Pipe* 102h 142c
9 b g Bach(IRE) Senna Da Silva (Prince Of Birds (USA))
103[2] 218[2] 357[2] 555[6] 974[4] 1135[2] 1268[8] 1344[3] 2635[8] 2854[F] 3107[5] 3584[7] **4011[P] (4852)**

My Coranna (IRE) *D C Gibbs* 105c
6 b m Craigsteel Tara's Pride (IRE) (Montelimar (USA))
(5467)

My Cousin Rachel (IRE) *Kim Bailey* 81b
4 br m Presenting Countess Camilla (Bob's Return (IRE))
2998[4] 4468[8]

My Diamond (IRE) *Laura Young* 86h
4 b g Brian Boru Our Idol (IRE) (Mandalus)
526[3] 2257[P] 2457[10] 2986[9] 4454[5] 4920[P]

My Direction *John Ferguson* 124h 126c
5 ch g Singspiel(IRE) Ejlaal (IRE) (Caerleon (USA))
812[P]

Mydor (FR) *A J Martin* 139h 119c
5 ch g Stormy River(FR) Fabulousday (USA) (Diesis)
96a[12] 5213[16]

My Escapade (IRE) *Simon Waugh* 98h
4 ch m Tamayuz Highly Respected (IRE) (High Estate)
79[4] 415[3] 804[3] 1552[10] 2148[3] 2706[5] 4904[2]

My Flora *Miss V Collins*
11 b m Alflora(IRE) Bishop's Folly (Weld)
16[F]

My Friend George *Kenneth Slack* 82h 112c
9 ch g Alflora(IRE) Snowgirl (IRE) (Mazaad)
(140) 519[5] 841[4] 2102[5] **(3243) 3671[5] (4046) 4418[2] 4554[2] 4940[2]**

My Hometown (IRE) *E Bolger* 116h 129c
5 b g Presenting Amathea (FR) (Exit To Nowhere (USA))
2530a[3]

My Idea *Maurice Barnes* 104h 108c
9 b g Golan(IRE) Ghana (GER) (Bigstone (IRE))
134[6] 731[P]

My Khaleesi *Alan King* 112b
4 b m Kayf Tara Katess (IRE) (Spectrum (IRE))
2277[2] (4074) 5180[16]

My King (FR) *Nigel Hawke* 69h
3 b g Kingsalsa(USA) My Belle (FR) (Smadoun (FR))
5268[6]

My Lad Percy *Martin Keighley* 113h 114c
7 b g Central Park(IRE) Only Millie (Prince Daniel (USA))
1641[P] 2054[8]

My Lady West (IRE) *Victor Thompson* 46h
6 b m Westerner River Action (IRE) (Saddlers' Hall (IRE))
635[U] 730[P] 5367[4]

My Legal Lady *Stuart Howe* 115h 107c
10 b m Sir Harry Lewis(USA) Clifton Mist (Lyphento (USA))
389[3] **825[2] 894[5] 1235[P]**

My Liege (IRE) *Evan Williams* 109b
4 b g Marienbard(IRE) Smashing Leader (IRE) (Supreme Leader)
(3258) 4143[3]

My Little Cracker (IRE) *Iain Jardine* 121h
5 b m Scorpion(IRE) Cailin Gruaig Dubh (IRE) (Danehill Dancer (IRE))
(2433) ◆ 2936[P] 4164[2] (4737) (5019) 5232[3] 5409[7]

Mylittlemouse (IRE) *Helen Nelmes* 75h
7 b m Turtle Island(IRE) Ballybeg Rose (IRE) (Roselier (FR))
3953[P] 4546[4] 5063[6]

My Lord *David Evans* 109h
7 br g Ishiguru(USA) Lady Smith (Greensmith)
2826[2] 3089[3] 3233[6] 5418[5]

My Manekineko *J A Nash* 125h
6 b g Authorized(IRE) Echo River (USA) (Irish River (FR))
2186[11] 5219[11]

My Miss Lucy *Richard Phillips* 86h
9 b m Alflora(IRE) Corn Lily (Aragon)
3498[P] 4186[U] **4491[P] 4778[P]**

My Mistress (IRE) *Phil McEntee* 80h
3 ch f Mastercraftsman(IRE) Majestic Eviction (IRE) (King's Theatre (IRE))
4502[3] 5373[6]

My Murphy (IRE) *W J Burke* 142h 151c
9 b g Presenting Fine De Claire (Teenoso (USA))
3073a[3] 3296a[P] (3715a) 5005a[P]

My My My Diliza *Mlle M Henry*
4 br m Sakhee's Secret Diliza (Dilum (USA))
3876a[F]

My Nosy Rosy *Ben Case* 98h 103c
7 b m Alflora(IRE) Quiz Night (Kayf Tara)
383[P] **699[F] 874[6] 1080[8] 1422[2] 1548[2] (1703) 1825[F] 2220[2]**

Myoran Oscar (IRE) *Zoe Davison* 22c
7 b g Oscar(IRE) Miss Bertaine (IRE) (Denel (FR))
2824[3]

My Painter (IRE) *Denis Gerard Hogan* 101h
4 b m Jeremy(USA) Last Cry (FR) (Peintre Celebre (USA))
(3471)

My Renaissance *Ben Case* 73h
5 bb g Medicean Lebenstanz (Singspiel (IRE))
1297[P] 1446[4] 2165[4] 2559[7]

Myroundorurs (IRE) *Robin Dickin* 87h
5 b g Arakan(USA) Six Bob (IRE) (Anshan)
105[P] 2299[9] 2581[5] 3382[P] 4885[10]

Myrtle Drive (IRE) *Donald McCain* 99h
4 b m Kalanisi(IRE) Miss Fara (FR) (Galetto (FR))
334[6] 640[5] 2452[6] 2752[2] 4417[3]

My Scat Daddy (USA) *Daniel Steele* 68h
6 b g Scat Daddy(USA) Will Be A Bates (USA) (Bates Motel (USA))
360[P]

My Silver Cloud (IRE) *Paddy Butler* 13h 87c
8 gr g Cloudings(IRE) Royal Patrol (IRE) (Phardante (FR))
126[4] 674[5] (Dead)

My Simon (IRE) *Peter Croke* 88h
6 b g Scorpion(IRE) Banusal (IRE) (Lord Americo)
2106[6]

Myska (IRE) *W P Mullins* 136h
5 br m Presenting Zenaide (IRE) (Zaffaran (USA))
(3372) 3890a[5] 4954a[P]

My Son Max *Nikki Evans* 84h
7 b g Avonbridge Pendulum (Pursuit Of Love)
2035[5] 4888[10] 5393[7]

Mysteree (IRE) *Lucinda Russell* 124h 131c
7 b g Gold Well Hillside Native (IRE) (Be My Native (USA))
(2918) 3507[3] (3933) 4367[4] 5274[8]

Mystery Code *Alan King* 106h
3 b f Tobougg(IRE) Mystery Lot (IRE) (Revoque (IRE))
(2137) 2896[3] 3822[3] 4459[5]

Mystery Drama *Alexandra Dunn* 88h
5 b m Hernando(FR) Mystery Lot (IRE) (Revoque (IRE))
2170[11] 2445[6] 2734[16] 2956[7] 3498[P]

Mystical Knight *Rebecca Curtis* 123h
6 b g Kayf Tara Dark Diva (Royal Fountain)
(3388) ◆ 4123[2] (4662a) 5194[P]

Mystic Princess (IRE) *Mark Michael McNiff* 103h
4 ch m Manduro(GER) Granny Kelly (USA) (Irish River (FR))
3473[6]

Mystic Sky *Lucy Wadham* 119h
4 b m Midnight Legend Kentucky Sky (Cloudings (IRE))
2421[4] 2776[3] (3175) 3842[4] 4459[4] 4777[2] 5438[2]

Mystifiable *Fergal O'Brien* 115h 138c
7 gr g Kayf Tara Royal Keel (Long Leave)
(1818) 2472[5] **(3315)** ◆ **(4465)** ◆ **5217[P]**

Mystified (IRE) *Alan Berry* 79c
12 b g Raise A Grand(IRE) Sunrise (IRE) (Sri Pekan (USA))
1401[P]

My Teescomponents *Keith Reveley* 51b
5 b m Fair Mix(IRE) Our Tees Component (IRE) (Saddlers' Hall (IRE))
970[12]

My Tent Or Yours (IRE) *Nicky Henderson* 167h
8 b g Desert Prince(IRE) Spartan Girl (IRE) (Ela-Mana-Mou)
4698[2] 5177[2]

Mythical Legend *Emma Lavelle* 99b
4 ch m Midnight Legend Materiality (Karinga Bay)
4847[6]

My Vicky (IRE) *Peter Croke* 51b
4 b m Alhaarth(IRE) Banusal (IRE) (Lord Americo)
2330[6]

Myztique (IRE) *Gordon Elliott* 121h
5 b m High Chaparral(IRE) Lady Rene (IRE) (Leading Counsel (USA))
2677a[4] (2951) 4653a[2] 4954a[P] 5470[2]

Nabateo *Philip Kirby* 93b
4 ch g Sea The Stars(IRE) Rosa Del Dubai (IRE) (Dubai Destination (USA))
1378[3]

Nabhan *Bernard Llewellyn* 126h
3 b g Youmzain(IRE) Danidh Dubai (IRE) (Noverre (USA))
3076[2] ◆ 3519[7] (4462) 5221[3] 5491[7]

Nabucco *John Ferguson* 137h
6 b g Dansili Cape Verdi (IRE) (Caerleon (USA))
706[2] (912) (1895) (2186) 2512[8] 4769[14] 5219[9]

Naburn *Andrew Wilson* 101h
7 b g Cape Cross(IRE) Allespagne (USA) (Trempolino (USA))
452[5] 881[6] 1307[6] 1552[4] 1683[7] 2103[F] 3791[2] ◆ 4163[F] 4581[P] 5198[3] 5472[7]

Nafaath (IRE) *Donald McCain* 112h 113c
9 ch g Nayef(USA) Alshakr (Bahri (USA))
1166[5] 1421[5] 1920[4] 2165[7] (2703) 3108[5] 3680[4] 4326[2] 4566[6]

Nailer (IRE) *Tristan Davidson* 53b
5 b g Coroner(IRE) Celtic Serenade (IRE) (Yashgan)
2401[6]

Nail 'M (IRE) *Nigel Hawke* 98h 116c
7 b g Milan Honor Kicks (FR) (Highest Honor (FR))
2566[4] 2878[2] 3591[P] 4340[F] 4612[5] 4879[3] 5265[2]

Nakadam (FR) *R Mike Smith* 89h 115c
5 b g Nickname(FR) Cadoudame (FR) (Cadoudal (FR))
2190[5] 2806[6] 3437[4] **3937[U] 4407[2]** ◆ **(5259)**

Nalim (IRE) *Harriet Bethell* 83h 94c
9 b g Milan Hati Roy (IRE) (Lafontaine I (USA))
204[2] 2173[3] 2836[P] 3948[4] 4433[4] 5013[3]

Nambour (GER) *W P Mullins* 143h
5 b g Sholokhov(IRE) Nanouska (GER) (Dashing Blade)
3393a[3] 4332a[2] 4955a[2] 5410[2]

Nam Hai (IRE) *Kim Bailey* 103h
4 b g Fastnet Rock(AUS) Bowstring (IRE) (Sadler's Wells (USA))
2840[5] 3397[2] 3863[3]

Nampararoo *David Bridgwater* 85b
6 b m Kayf Tara Silk Stockings (FR) (Trempolino (USA))
1717[3]

Nanamour (IRE) *Robert Alan Hennessy*
4 b m Azamour(IRE) Tequise (IRE) (Victory Note (USA))
5242[P]

Nancy's Trix (IRE) *David Loder* 95h
6 br m Presenting Murrurundi (IRE) (Old Vic)
2277[10] 2776[4] 3110[6] 4151[3] 4877[F]

Nando (FR) *Alex Taber* 138h 126c
5 b g Hernando(FR) Hespera (Danehill (USA))
4a[11] 663a[P] **1672a[5]**

Nansaroy *Evan Williams* 122h
5 br g Indian River(FR) Jurado Park (IRE) (Jurado (USA))
(2563) 3366[U] 4646[3]

Naranja *Jamie Snowden* 92b
3 ch f Black Sam Bellamy(IRE) Full Of Fruit (FR) (Apple Tree (FR))
(5443)

Narcissist (IRE) *Michael Easterby* 105h 119c
6 b g Dylan Thomas(IRE) Gabare (FR) (Galileo (IRE))
158[2]

Nashville (IRE) *Andrew Crook* 81h
6 b g Galileo(IRE) Brown Eyes (Danehill (USA))
2190[P]

Nataraja *Conrad Allen* 52b
6 b g Norse Dancer(IRE) Floral Rhapsody (Alflora (IRE))
188[10]

Nathans Pride (IRE) *Tim Vaughan* 119h 68c
7 ch g Definite Article Tricias Pride (IRE) (Broken Hearted)
2184[9] 4781[4] 5329[6]

Native Brian (IRE) *Andrew Hamilton* 66h 82c
9 b g Brian Boru Gentle Native (IRE) (Be My Native (USA))
77[6] 288[6] **453[F] 637[4]**

Native Display (IRE) *Nicky Henderson* 108h
5 b g Presenting Native Shore (IRE) (Be My Native (USA))
83[4] 1305[F] 1613[4] (2000) 2253[3]

Native Gallery (IRE) *Ben De Haan*
10 gr g Portrait Gallery(IRE) Native Bev (IRE) (Be My Native (USA))
2977[P]

Native Optimist (IRE) *Sheena Walton* 118h
8 b g Broadway Flyer(USA) Native Orchid (IRE) (Be My Native (USA))
201[P] (484) 726[2] 838[4] (1744) 1856[7] (2478) (2919) 3058[4]

Native Pride (IRE) *Ms J Johnston* 33c
7 b g Vertical Speed(FR) Nativefort (IRE) (Be My Native (USA))
488[4]

Native Princess *Stuart Edmunds* 104h
5 b m Tobougg(IRE) Forest Pride (IRE) (Be My Native (USA))
(594) (1352) 1716[DSQ]

Native Que (IRE) *J T R Dreaper* 92c
8 b g Revoque(IRE) Tullynaskeagh Lady (IRE) (Be My Native (USA))
2708[2]

Native River (IRE) *Colin Tizzard* 100h 165c
5 ch g Indian River(FR) Native Mo (IRE) (Be My Native (USA))
1846[3] (2260) (2726) ◆ **3229[3] 3998[3] 4700[2] (5191)**

Native Robin (IRE) *Jeremy Scott* 102h 120c
5 br g Robin Des Pres(FR) Homebird (IRE) (Be My Native (USA))
1246[5] 1518[6] 1576[3] 1752[3] 2087[7] 2987[16] **(3834) (5147)**

Nautical Nitwit (IRE) *Philip Kirby* 120h
6 b g Let The Lion Roar Mrs Pugwash (IRE) (Un Desperado (FR))
1184a[12] 2042[3] 2333[F] 2744[5] 3400[4]

Nautical Twilight *Malcolm Jefferson* 94h 129c
5 gr m Proclamation(IRE) Anabranch (Kind Of Hush)
2143[2] 2424[4] (2979) (3311) 3806[2] 4370[F] 4606[3]

Naval Action *Sandy Thomson* 36h
3 b g Lawman(FR) Dance Of The Sea (IRE) (Sinndar (IRE))
1111[4]

Navanman (IRE) *David Pipe* 117h
6 b g Well Chosen Teamplin (IRE) (Flemensfirth (USA))
2734[14] 3011[7] (3946) ◆ (4030) ◆ (4110)

Nearest The Pin (IRE) *Dai Williams* 97h 138c
10 b g Court Cave(IRE) Carnbelle (IRE) (Electric)
1344[4] 1502[4] 1643[4] 1989[5] 4016[P] 4307[8] 4852[4] 4978[P]

Nearly Nama'd (IRE) *Ms Sandra Hughes* 105h 145c
7 b g Millenary Coca's Well (IRE) (Religiously (USA))
(3552a) 3830a[3]

Near To Tears (IRE) *Lucinda Russell* 89h
5 br m Robin Des Pres(FR) Tears Of Jade (IRE) (Presenting)
2325[4] 2752[3] 3163[4] 4036[4]

Nebrius (POL) *Pavlina Surova*
7 ch g Belenus(GER) Nobila (POL) (Saphir I (GER))
1885a[F]

Nebula Storm (IRE) *Michael Blake* 109h
8 b g Galileo(IRE) Epping (Charnwood Forest (IRE))
1596[2] 1941[2] 2217[4] (2559) 2869[2] 3628[3] 4411[7]

Neck Or Nothing (GER) *Neil Mulholland* 123b
6 b g Intikhab(USA) Nova (GER) (Winged Love (IRE))
4984[P]

Ned Buntline *Noel Meade* 126h 150c
7 b g Refuse To Bend(IRE) Intrum Morshaan (IRE) (Darshaan)
47a[3]

Ned Stark (IRE) *Alan King* 111h 139c
7 b g Wolfe Tone(IRE) Last Moon (IRE) (Montelimar (USA))
2187[6] 2783[8] 3282[P] 4101[5] 5092[2]

Needless Shouting (IRE) *Mick Channon* 111h
4 b g Footstepsinthesand Ring The Relatives (Bering)
3216[2] 3708[8] 4781[6] 5301[6]

Need To Know (IRE) *John Paul Brennan* 115c
7 b g Definite Article Desperado Queen (IRE) (Un Desperado (FR))
75a[P] 4768[20] 5178[F]

Needwood Park *Ray Craggs* 79h
7 br g Needwood Blade Waterpark (Namaqualand (USA))
4862[P] 5199[P]

Neetside (IRE) *Tim Dennis* 57b
3 b f Getaway(GER) Lady Wagtail (IRE) (Milan)
4687[8]

Nefyn Bay *Donald McCain* 112h 96c
6 b g Overbury(IRE) So Cloudy (Cloudings (IRE))
354[7] **4556[3] 5125[7]**

Nellies Quest *Brendan Powell* 101h
6 b m Rainbow High Dream Seeker (IRE) (Kahyasi)
179[2]

Nellie The Elegant *Tim Vaughan* 92h
4 b m Mount Nelson Mexican Hawk (USA) (Silver Hawk (USA))
937[P] 1446[3] 1578[P] 1786[5] 1941[3] 2427[4]

Nelly La Rue (IRE) *Victor Thompson* 43h
8 b m Flemensfirth(USA) Desperately Hoping (IRE) (Un Desperado (FR))
1627[7]

Nelson's Victory *Diana Grissell*
5 b g Green Horizon First Class Girl (Charmer (IRE))
4385[5]

Nendrum (IRE) *S R B Crawford* 109h
6 br g Westerner Westgrove Berry (IRE) (Presenting)
3668[2] 4548[6]

Neofito (FR) *P Cottin*
7 b g Great Pretender(IRE) Nakille (FR) (Sillery (USA))
(1223a)

Neptune Equester *Sandy Thomson* 122h 138c
12 b g Sovereign Water(FR) All Things Nice (Sweet Monday)
2340[2] **(2934) 4205[2]** (Dead)

Nervous Nineties *Fergal O'Brien* 60h
6 gr g Proclamation(IRE) Born To Dream (IRE) (Supreme Leader)
43[F]

Neshikot (IRE) *Jonathan Portman* 32b
4 gr g Oscar(IRE) Winter Daydream (IRE) (Soviet Star (USA))
360[P]

Nesterenko (GER) *Nicky Henderson* 133h
6 b g Doyen(IRE) Nordwahl (GER) (Waajib (IRE))
1347[2] ◆ 1977[2] 2617[U] 2914[6] (4851) 5219[6]

Net D'Ecosse (FR) *W P Mullins* 126h 135c
5 ch g Network(GER) Ecossette (FR) (Ecossais (FR))
3229[5]

Netherby *Gary Moore* 92b
9 b g Fair Mix(IRE) Lissadell (IRE) (Zaffaran (USA))
3709[F] 4386[F] (Dead)

Nether Stream (IRE) *David Dennis* 100h 100c
11 b g Blueprint(IRE) Shuil Ub (Le Moss)
173[F]

Nettlebush (IRE) *Benjamin Arthey* 62h
5 br g Kalanisi(IRE) Amber Gale (IRE) (Glacial Storm (USA))
5256[P]

Net Work Rouge (FR) *Kim Bailey* 134h 40c
6 b g Network(GER) Lychee De La Roque (FR) (Officiel (FR))
107[P] 1642[7] (1912) (2275) 3032[P] 5011[2]

Neumond (GER) *Nicky Henderson* 109h
4 b g Sholokhov(IRE) Natalis (GER) (Law Society (USA))
2630[6] 4322[7] 4874[10]

Never Complain (IRE) *Mrs F Marshall* 110h 128c
7 ch g Beneficial Polly Native (IRE) (Be My Native (USA))
4437[P]

Never Equalled (IRE) *Bernard Llewellyn* 130h
6 br g Brian Boru Broken Thought (IRE) (Broken Hearted)
2363[4] 2563[2] (3077) 3516[2] 4264[4] (4668) 5273[5]

Never Learn (IRE) *Colin Tizzard* 99h
4 b g King's Theatre(IRE) Hamari Gold (IRE) (Priolo (USA))
392[9] 2791[7] 3117[P]

Never Never (IRE) *Iain Jardine* 115h
5 b g Jeremy(USA) Argus Gal (IRE) (Alzao (USA))
3424[8] 4819[3]

Neverownup (IRE) *M J Vanstone* 64h 130c
10 b g Quws Cobble (IRE) (Bigstone (IRE))
(129) 4424[P] 5158[F] 5399[6]

Never Said That (IRE) *Edward Cawley* 121h 78c
7 b g Gold Well Clonbrook Lass (IRE) (Lord Americo)
50a[4] 1184a[11]

Never Says Never *Anthony Honeyball* 120h
7 b g Tamure(IRE) Quick Exit (Exit To Nowhere (USA))
529[P] (2664) (2831) 2880[F] 4824[5]

Never To Be (USA) *Nikki Evans*
4 b g Thewayyouare(USA) Kitty Foille (USA) (Black Minnaloushe (USA))
5393[P]

Never Up (GER) *George Moore* 109h 101c
4 b g Danehill Dancer(IRE) Never Green (IRE) (Halling (USA))
254[2] (467) 710[5] **2495[4] 3164[3]**

Neverushacon (IRE) *Mrs John Harrington* 128h
4 b g Echo Of Light Lily Beth (IRE) (Desert King (IRE))
2353a[3]

Neville *Philip Hobbs* 118h 98c
7 b g Revoque(IRE) Dudeen (IRE) (Anshan)
1349[P]

Neville Woods *George Charlton* 93h 96c
8 b g Alflora(IRE) Angie Marinie (Sabrehill (USA))
138[4] 5262[5]

New Academy *John Wade* 99h 73c
7 ch g Zamindar(USA) New Abbey (Sadler's Wells (USA))
3161[4] **3968[10]**

Newberry New (IRE) *Mrs John Harrington* 125h
3 br g Kodiac Sunblush (UAE) (Timber Country (USA))
2813a[8] 5001a[3]

New Decade *Milton Bradley* 52h
6 ch g Pivotal Irresistible (Cadeaux Genereux)
860[11] 932[13]

New Horizons (IRE) *Caroline Fryer* 114h
5 b g Presenting Namloc (IRE) (Phardante (FR))
283[2] (746)

Newlight (FR) *A Chaille-Chaille*
4 b g Califet(FR) Yellow Light (FR) (Lightning (FR))
5385a[P]

New Member (IRE) *Nicky Henderson* 102b
4 b g Alhaarth(IRE) Sincere (IRE) (Bahhare (USA))
4894[3]

Newnham Flyer (IRE) *Sarah Robinson*
13 gr m Exit To Nowhere(USA) Paper Flight (Petong)
513[P]

Neworld (FR) *Richard Hobson* 107h
6 gr g Lost World(IRE) Crusch Alva (FR) (Unfuwain (USA))
2162[3] 2492[8] 2850[4] (3177) 3473[8] **3845[P]** 4223[2] 4970[P]

New Providence (FR) *Nicky Henderson* 83b
4 bb g Le Fou(IRE) Bahamas (FR) (Pistolet Bleu (IRE))
525[6] 5248[7]

New Reaction *Alexandra Dunn*
4 b g New Approach(IRE) Intaaj (IRE) (Machiavellian (USA))
1822[P]

New Republic (IRE) *Evan Williams* 49h
4 b g Morozov(USA) Saltee Great (IRE) (Fourstars Allstar (USA))
5235[7] 5356[7] 5434[10]

Newspage (IRE) *John Wade* 32h 95c
9 b g Blueprint(IRE) Newlineview (IRE) (Saddlers' Hall (IRE))
80[4] 472[2] 2707[P] 3308[5]

New Street (IRE) *Jim Best* 117h
4 gr h Acclamation New Deal (Rainbow Quest (USA))
2123[5] 2637[5] 2831[P]

Newsworthy (IRE) *Nicky Henderson* 128h
5 br g Presenting Cousin Jen (IRE) (Oscar (IRE))
53a[5] 2056[4] 4063[2] ◆

New Tarabela *Tony Carroll* 103h
4 ch g New Approach(IRE) Tarabela (CHI) (Hussonet (USA))
110[6] 354[8] 1927[6] 2555[3]

Newton Geronimo *Ben Pauling* 113h 114c
6 bb g Brian Boru Newton Commanche (IRE) (Commanche Run)
648[6] 832[4] 932[2] 1083[6] **1753[3] 2246[F]** 3487[12] 3950[RR] 4593[RR] (5418)

Newton Martini *Ben Pauling* 82h
6 b m Brian Boru Wedidthat (IRE) (Moscow Society (USA))
1085[P] 1293[5] 1426[P] 1510[7]

Newton Thistle *Ben Pauling* 102h 124c
8 b g Erhaab(USA) Newton Venture (Petoski)
2269[F] (3127) **3823[P] 4232[2]** 4749[P]

New To This Town (IRE) *Mrs John Harrington* 123b
4 b g Milan Jade River (FR) (Indian River (FR))
4721[21]

Newtown Lad (IRE) *Lucinda Russell* 112h
5 b g Craigsteel Rocher Lady (IRE) (Phardante (FR))
4915[7] (5365) ◆

New Vennture (FR) *Harry Fry* 93h
3 b f Kapgarde(FR) Polyandry (IRE) (Pennekamp (USA))
2537[5] ◆ 2896[6]

New Vic (IRE) *Mrs A M Thomson* 74h 107c
9 ch g Old Vic Innovate (IRE) (Posen (USA))
(5258)

Newyearsresolution (IRE) *Simon Waugh* 85h 81c
11 b g Mr Combustible(IRE) That's Magic (IRE) (Lord Americo)
2478[2] **2707[7]** 2980[8] (3793) 4289[5] 4739[2]

New Youmzain (FR) *Lucy Normile* 84h
6 b g Sinndar(IRE) Luna Sacra (FR) (Sadler's Wells (USA))
37[4] 522[5] 883[7]

Nexius (IRE) *Paul Nicholls* 142h 140c
6 b g Catcher In The Rye(IRE) Nicolaia (GER) (Alkalde (GER))
2122[4] (4067) 4444[P] 5117[2]

Next Bend (IRE) *Thomas Gibney* 113h
4 b g Azamour(IRE) Polite Reply (IRE) (Be My Guest (USA))
3323a[U]

Next Exit (IRE) *John Cornwall* 77h 74c
10 b g Exit To Nowhere(USA) Pilgrim Star (IRE) (Marju (IRE))
126[6] 258[4] 567[P] 741[3] 964[4] 1159[P]

Next Lot *Richard Phillips* 71h
5 b g Mountain High(IRE) Martha Reilly (IRE) (Rainbows For Life (CAN))
4296[6]

Next Sensation (IRE) *Michael Scudamore* 88h 138c
8 b g Brian Boru Road Trip (IRE) (Anshan)
2059[9] 2483[10] 2761[8] 3030[10] 4770[14] 5276[F]

Next Surprise (IRE) *Mrs Teresa Clark* 66b
6 b g Mountain High(IRE) Paperwork Lady (IRE) (Jurado (USA))
320[18]

Nicely Indeed (IRE) *Seamus Durack* 125h
5 b g Marienbard(IRE) Rare Dollar (IRE) (Bob's Return (IRE))
(1246) (1484) 3019[5]

Nice N Easy (IRE) *Paul Nicholls*
5 b g Presenting Miss Brandywell (IRE) (Sadler's Wells (USA))
4463[F]

Niceonefrankie *Venetia Williams* 105h 145c
9 b g Ishiguru(USA) Chesnut Ripple (Cosmonaut)
2761[P] 4128[2] 4733[F] (Dead)

Nice Thoughts (IRE) *David Pipe* 96h
3 b g Shamardal(USA) Zacheta (Polish Precedent (USA))
4449[5] 5098[4]

Nice Vintage (IRE) *Adrian Paul Keatley* 105h
3 bb f Big Bad Bob(IRE) High Vintage (IRE) (High Chaparral (IRE))
3268a[8]

Nicholascopernicus (IRE) *Kerry Lee* 106h
6 ch g Medicean Ascendancy (Sadler's Wells (USA))
4550[5] 5374[6]

Nicholas T *Jim Goldie* 102b
3 b g Rail Link Thorntoun Piccolo (Groom Dancer (USA))
4915[5] 5330[5]

Nicholasville (IRE) *Mrs Lorna Williams* 65c
6 b g Flemensfirth(USA) Cansalrun (IRE) (Anshan)
5467[11]

Nichols Canyon *W P Mullins* 168h
5 b g Authorized(IRE) Zam Zoom (IRE) (Dalakhani (IRE))
(72a) (2532a) (3358a) 3768a[3] 4698[3] ◆ 5177[3]

Nicki's Nipper *Sam Drake* 82h
7 b m Denounce Mistress Star (Soldier Rose)
65[P] 4390[5] 4703[3] 4862[4] ◆

Nickname Exit (FR) *Gordon Elliott* 127h 139c
5 b g Nickname(FR) Exit To Fire (FR) (Exit To Nowhere (USA))
19a[19] 2236a[12] **3715a[P] 4521a[10]**

Nicknos (FR) *Mlle I Gallorini* 121h 121c
4 b g Nickname(FR) Dindounas (FR) (Astarabad (USA))
665a[P]

Nicky Nutjob (GER) *John O'Shea* 62h
9 b g Fasliyev(USA) Natalie Too (USA) (Irish River (FR))
55[6] 240[6] 421[U] 599[7] **1824[P]** (Dead)

Nicolas Chauvin (IRE) *Nicky Henderson* 124h 136c
7 b g Saffron Walden(FR) Kenzie (IRE) (Presenting)
1575[3] ◆ 1838[3]

Nifty Kier *Phil McEntee*
6 b g Kier Park(IRE) Yeldham Lady (Mujahid (USA))
566[P]

Night Alliance (IRE) *P R M Philips* 115h 130c
10 ch g Pierre Next Venture (IRE) (Zaffaran (USA))
3826[4] (4269) 4424[F] 4892[P] 5178[P] (5312)

Nightfly *Charlie Longsdon* 105b
4 br m Midnight Legend Whichway Girl (Jupiter Island)
4350[2] ◆ 5144[2] ◆

Night In London (IRE) *Keith Reveley*
5 b m Vinnie Roe(IRE) Chione (IRE) (Mandalus)
3593[8] 3839[P] 3995[P] 4151[P]

Night In Milan (IRE) *Keith Reveley* 130h 149c
9 b g Milan Chione (IRE) (Mandalus)
2145[7] 2340[6] 2744[8] **3038[7]** 3428[3] (3837) **4306[F]** (Dead)

Nightline *Charlie Longsdon* 125h
5 b g Midnight Legend Whichway Girl (Jupiter Island)
2125[2] 4305[4] ◆ 4883[5]

Nightswift *James Evans* 61b
3 b g Midnight Legend Sharbasia (IRE) (King's Best (USA))
2777[13]

Nikas (CZE) *Stanislav Popelka Jr* 131c
10 b g Scater(POL) Nika (CZE) (Chiavari (IRE))
(1885a)

Nikos Extra (FR) *Alexandra Dunn* 113h 130c
11 b g Nikos Madame Extra (FR) (Sir Brink (FR))
751[8] **974[RR]**

Nimbus Gale (IRE) *Charlie Mann* 103h 79c
6 b g Cloudings(IRE) Barton Gale (IRE) (Strong Gale)
1906[7]

Nimdani (IRE) *Mrs Y Dunleavy* 107h 110c
6 gr g Dalakhani(IRE) Narmina (IRE) (Alhaarth (IRE))
4556[5]

Nine Altars (IRE) *Ann Hamilton* 117h
6 b g Heron Island(IRE) Tawny Owl (IRE) (Be My Native (USA))
2401[7] 4044[3] (4417) 5088[2] (5295)

Ninepointsixthree *John O'Shea* 110h
5 b g Bertolini(USA) Armada Grove (Fleetwood (IRE))
456[U] 647[P] 5268[2]

Ninety Seconds (IRE) *T J Taaffe* 57b
4 b m Presenting Myown (IRE) (Le Bavard (FR))
2677a[14]

Ninny Noodle *Miss Imogen Pickard* 14h
5 b m Proclamation(IRE) Court Champagne (Batshoof)
2164[P] 2850[12] 3375[P]

Nishay (IRE) *David Rees* 82h 61c
8 bb g Classic Cliche(IRE) Winged Victory (IRE) (Dancing Brave (USA))
536[9] 828[9] 1086[4]

Nitrogen (IRE) *Harry Fry* 118h 123c
8 b g Old Vic Katday (FR) (Miller's Mate)
2727[3] ◆ 4465[4]

No Bad News *Henry Oliver* 28b
5 b g Beat All(USA) Emma's Dream (Karinga Bay)
3608[P] 4875[P] 5153[P]

Nobel Leader (IRE) *James Evans* 110h
5 b g Alflora(IRE) Ben Roseler (IRE) (Beneficial)
2597[3] 3226[6] 4388[2] 4639[4] 5137[P]

Noble Air *Tony Coyle*
5 b g Tamure(IRE) Royal Czarina (Czaravich (USA))
783[6]

Noble Ben (IRE) *J M Ridley* 70h 76c
13 ch g Beneficial I'm Happy Now (IRE) (Torus)
12[12]

Noble Emperor (IRE) *A J Martin* 142h 145c
7 b g Spadoun(FR) Cherry Tops (IRE) (Top Of The World)
3302a[F] 3713a[5]

Noble Endeavor (IRE) *Gordon Elliott* 134h 146c
6 b g Flemensfirth(USA) Old Moon (IRE) (Old Vic)
4148a[2] 4700[F]

Noble Friend (IRE) *Chris Gordon* 109h 127c
7 b g Presenting Laragh (IRE) (Oscar (IRE))
(672) (863) ◆ 1042[3] 1240[4] 1488[3] **1735[F]** 2182[13] 5386[5]

Noble Galileo (GER) *Tim Vaughan* 82h
5 b g Galileo(IRE) Nordtanzerin (GER) (Danehill Dancer (IRE))
3865[5] 4432[3] ◆

Noble Inn (FR) *W P Mullins* 134h
5 b g Sinndar(IRE) Nataliana (Surumu (GER))
3151[18]

Noble Legend *Caroline Bailey* 136c
8 b g Midnight Legend Elmside Katie (Lord David S (USA))
199[P] 2832[5] (3176) ◆ 3315[5] 3887[6] 4212[5] 4775[2] 4971[5]

Noble Ned *Harry Fry* 99h
6 b g Kayf Tara Leachbrook Lady (Alderbrook)
3775[4] 4439[P]

Noble Prince (GER) *Paul Nolan* 120h 135c
11 b g Montjeu(IRE) Noble Pearl (GER) (Dashing Blade)
75a[2]

Noble Reach *Lawrence Mullaney* 86h
4 b m Phoenix Reach(IRE) Comtesse Noire (CAN) (Woodman (USA))
1967[5] 2752[F] 2959[4]

Noble Witness (IRE) *Charles Pogson* 83h 108c
12 b g Witness Box(USA) Jennas Pride (IRE) (Kambalda)
88[0] 340[2] 743[5] 926[8]

Nobunaga *Andrew Hamilton* 69h 82c
10 ch g Beat Hollow Absolute Precision (USA) (Irish River (FR))
134[P] 519[P]

No Buts *David Bridgwater* 115h 146c
7 b g Kayf Tara Wontcostalotbut (Nicholas Bill)
2187[P] 3282[7]

No Ceiling (IRE) *Ian Williams* 110h
5 b g Turtle Island(IRE) Pyrexie (FR) (Pistolet Bleu (IRE))
3619[4] (4068) ◆ 4178[8]

Noche De Reyes (FR) *Tom George* 109h 127c
6 bb g Early March Cochinchine (IRE) (Namaqualand (USA))
1451[5] 1643[7] 2246[2] 2691[P] 2884[8] 4464[6] (4891) (5156)

No Comment *Philip Hobbs* 128h
4 br g Kayf Tara Dizzy Frizzy (Loup Sauvage (USA))
3111[2] ◆ 3795[2] ◆

No Deal (IRE) *Lucinda Russell* 119h 124c
9 b g Revoque(IRE) Noble Choice (Dahar (USA))
2638[P] 3162[F]

No Duffer *Tom George* 108h 144c
8 ch g Karinga Bay Dolly Duff (Alflora (IRE))
2473[11] 2887[P] 4348[2] (4912) (5411)

No Heretic *Nicky Henderson* 122h
7 b g Galileo(IRE) Intrigued (Darshaan)
5091[3]

Noir Girl *Zoe Davison* 38h
6 b m Beat All(USA) Forever Shineing (Glint Of Gold)
130[5] 2004[P] 4318[P]

Nolecce *Tony Forbes* 87h
8 ch g Reset(AUS) Ghassanah (Pas De Seul)
2162[5] 2492[11]

No Likey (IRE) *Philip Hobbs* 111h 126c
8 b g Helissio(FR) Money Galore (IRE) (Monksfield)
109[6] 642[2] 809[2] 1112[5] (1296) 1521[4] **5465[3]** ◆

No Loose Change (IRE) *Mrs Kim Smyly* 130c
10 b g Bob Back(USA) Quit The Noise (IRE) (Un Desperado (FR))
4016[P] 4892[P]

Nomadic Lad *Sarah Hollinshead* 30h
5 b g Nomadic Way(USA) Lysways (Gildoran)
2807[8]

Nomadic Warrior *Diana Grissell*
10 b g Nomadic Way(USA) Jesmund (Bishop Of Cashel)
450[P]

Nomadrush *John Holt*
5 b m Nomadic Way(USA) Tanguero (IRE) (Mister Lord (USA))
3952[10] 5021[5]

No More Heroes (IRE) *Gordon Elliott* 154h 163c
6 br g Presenting What A Breeze (IRE) (Naheez (USA))
21a[5] **(2817a) (3357a) 4716[4]** (Dead)

No No Cardinal (IRE) *Mark Gillard* 65h 90c
6 ch g Touch Of Land(FR) Four Moons (IRE) (Cardinal Flower)
170[2] (514) 713[5] 1045[5] 1299[10]

No No Mac (IRE) *Charlie Longsdon* 133h 103c
6 b g Oscar(IRE) Whatdoyouthinkmac (IRE) (Supreme Leader)
2289[4] 2733[7] 4786[P] 5264[8]

No Planning *Sue Smith* 142h 146c
8 b g Kayf Tara Poor Celt (Impecunious)
(196) 2198[P] **2643[3] 2899[U] 3860[P] (4609) 4802[5]**

No Principles *Julian Smith* 94h 99c
12 b g Overbury(IRE) Selective Rose (Derring Rose)
567[3] 743[4] 3419[P]

Nordical (IRE) *Evan Williams* 100h
5 b g Beneficial Nordic Abu (IRE) (Nordico (USA))
613[4] ◆ 1305[4] 3117[P] 3619[12] 3777[P]

Norfolk Sound *Stuart Coltherd* 78h
4 b m Pastoral Pursuits Cayman Sound (Turtle Island (IRE))
2189[14] 2494[4] 3342[6] 3681[7] 4049[P] 4404[6] 4904[8] 5445[15]

Norma (SPA) *T Callejo-Solana*
4 ch m Palamoss(IRE) Falaris (SPA) (Humool (USA))
3876a[8]

Normally *Hywel Evans*
11 b g Tobougg(IRE) Constant Delight (Never So Bold)
3914[P] 4822[P]

Normandy King (IRE) *Tim Vaughan* 103h
4 b g King's Theatre(IRE) Clairefontaine (Alflora (IRE))
601[2] 1979[9] 2251[12] 2772[10] 3368[7] 4703[F] (5333)

Norman The Red *Jamie Poulton* 100h
5 ch g Tobougg(IRE) Linden Lime (Double Trigger (IRE))
242[9] 3043[3] 4198[2] 5115[F] ◆

Norphin *Simon Hodgson* 38h
5 b g Norse Dancer(IRE) Orphina (IRE) (Orpen (USA))
2880[8] 3256[11]

Norse Da *Helen Nelmes* 65b
5 b g Norse Dancer(IRE) End Of An Error (Charmer (IRE))
392[10]

Norse Legend *Chris Gordon* 125h
4 b g Norse Dancer(IRE) Methodical (Lujain (USA))
3045[3] 3584[2] 3956[P] 4241[6] 5120[10]

Norse Light *David Dennis* 102h
4 ch g Norse Dancer(IRE) Dimelight (Fantastic Light (USA))
1893[6] 2121[P] 2418[6] 3140[2] 3368[2] (3784) 4129[4] 4541[4] 4650[2] 5163[4] 5374[7]

Norse Wave (FR) *H Billot* 105h
4 b m Norse Dancer(IRE) Wave Goodbye (FR) (Linamix (FR))
5499a[2]

Northandsouth (IRE) *Nigel Twiston-Davies* 97h
5 ch g Spadoun(FR) Ennel Lady (IRE) (Erin's Hope)
1826[7] 2581[7] (4460) 4799[5]

Northern Executive (IRE) *Karen McLintock* 103h 89c
7 b g Milan Letterwoman (IRE) (Fourstars Allstar (USA))
486[6] 637[3] 1287[7] 1496[3]

Northern Meeting (IRE) *Robert Stephens* 110h
5 b m Dylan Thomas(IRE) Scottish Stage (IRE) (Selkirk (USA))
592[3] ◆ 1352[3] (1506) 1618[5] (1974) 2852[6]

Northern Oscar (IRE) *Charles Pogson* 106h
7 b g Oscar(IRE) Cailin's Princess (IRE) (Luso)
777[F] 1096[6]

Northgeorge *J W Tudor* 92c
7 b g Overbury(IRE) River Treasure (IRE) (Over The River (FR))
5054[4]

North Hill (IRE) *Ian Williams* 107h
4 b g Westerner Hill Fairy (Monsun (GER))
2636[8] 3258[4] 3927[4] 4317[5] 4798[6] 5397[2] ◆

North Hill Harvey *Dan Skelton* 146h
4 b g Kayf Tara Ellina (Robellino (USA))
2221[2] ◆ (3019) 4072[2] 4695[9] 5190[4]

North London *Jimmy Frost* 57h 61c
8 b g Morpeth Miss Grace (Atticus (USA))
1121[P] 1236[8]

Northside Prince (IRE) *Alan Swinbank* 113h
9 b g Desert Prince(IRE) Spartan Girl (IRE) (Ela-Mana-Mou)
729[3] 1628[4]

Nortonthorpelegend (IRE) *John Wade* 91h 109c
5 b g Midnight Legend Tanit (Xaar)
3101[6] 3239[8] 3883[8] **(5125)** ◆

No Rum (IRE) *Olly Williams* 86h
3 b g Alfred Nobel(IRE) Common Rumpus (IRE) (Common Grounds)
1656[7] 1899[3]

No Secrets (IRE) *A J Martin* 123h 134c
11 b g King's Theatre(IRE) Happy Native (IRE) (Be My Native (USA))
50a[6] **5217[P]**

Nosey Box (IRE) *Noel C Kelly* 112h 117c
9 b m Witness Box(USA) Cautious Leader (Supreme Leader)
81[5] 2922[3] 3866[P] 4740[4]

Nosper (FR) *Martin Hill* 74h
3 b g Whipper(USA) Nostaltir (FR) (Muhtathir)
1866[6] 5182[10]

No Such Number *Sandy Forster* 115h 94c
7 b g King's Best(USA) Return (USA) (Sadler's Wells (USA))
455[6] 2296[6] 2751[8] **4034[P]**

Not A Bother Boy (IRE) *Sue Smith* 109h 123c
7 b g Flemensfirth(USA) Cab In The Storm (IRE) (Glacial Storm (USA))
1920[9] **2147[3] (2708) (2892)** (3067) **3236[2] 3885[2]**

Not Another Muddle *Sheena West* 105b
4 b g Kayf Tara Spatham Rose (Environment Friend)
2715[2]

Notebook *Martin Smith* 106h
4 b g Invincible Spirit(IRE) Love Everlasting (Pursuit Of Love)
1898[11] 2251[10] 3043[P] (3307) (3807) 3950[RR] 4068[3] 4506[4]

Not For You (IRE) *C Byrnes* 120h 105c
7 b g Beneficial Bonnie Thynes (IRE) (Good Thyne (USA))
1703[F] 4356[2] 4431[3]

No Through Road *Michael Scudamore* 90h 122c
8 b g Grape Tree Road Pendil's Delight (Scorpio (FR))
1855[3] 2366[4] 3086[P] 4046[5] 4803[2]

Notnowsam *Dan Skelton* 101h 131c
4 ch g Notnowcato First Fantasy (Be My Chief (USA))
(107) 261[4] **1904[2] 2412[2] 2993[2] 4785[2] ◆ 5298[4]**

Notonebuttwo (IRE) *Chris Grant* 90h 90c
8 b g Dushyantor(USA) Daiquiri (IRE) (Houmayoun (FR))
2478[P] **2950[U]** 3474[7] 3793[P] **(4514) 4792[2] 5228[P]**

Notre Ami (IRE) *Nick Gifford* 96b
4 br g Kalanisi(IRE) Shuilan (IRE) (Good Thyne (USA))
5358[5]

Notts So Blue *Shaun Harris* 88h
4 b m Pastoral Pursuits Blue Nile (IRE) (Bluebird (USA))
2538[4] 2808[5] 5077[5]

Nouailhas *Daniel O'Brien* 87h 76c
9 b g Mark Of Esteem(IRE) Barachois Princess (USA) (Barachois (CAN))
240[8] 2253[9] 2826[P] 5067[8] **5307[P] 5482[2]**

Nouma Jelois (FR) *Yannick Fouin* 123h 122c
4 b m Hannouma(IRE) Estephanie (FR) (Saint Estephe (FR))
350a[10] 4540a[6] 5042a[4]

Novel Dancer *Lydia Richards* 96h
7 b g Dansili Fictitious (Machiavellian (USA))
968[P]

No Win No Fee *Dr Richard Newland* 105h
5 b g Firebreak Milliscent (Primo Dominie)
1052[2] 1117[7]

Nowreyna *Kenny Johnson* 31b
4 gr m Notnowcato Kryena (Kris)
799[P]

Now This Is It (IRE) *S R B Crawford* 117h 96c
11 ch g Accordion Leitrim Bridge (IRE) (Earl Of Barking (IRE))
1903[6] 2326[5] 5329[5]

Nowurhurlin (IRE) *Mrs S J Stilgoe* 115h 128c
8 b g Saddlers' Hall(IRE) Pint Taken (IRE) (Needle Gun (IRE))
457[2] 4016[3] (4651) 5121[4] 5449[2]

Number One London (IRE) *Tim Vaughan* 121h
5 b g Invincible Spirit(IRE) Vadorga (Grand Lodge (USA))
214[4] (823) 1000[2] 1570[2] 4824[9] 5225[7] 5464[10]

Nutcracker Prince *Shaun Lycett* 91h
4 b g Rail Link Plum Fairy (Sadler's Wells (USA))
2024[4] 3483[7] 3745[12]

Nuts Well *Ann Hamilton* 133h
4 b g Dylan Thomas(IRE) Renada (Sinndar (IRE))
145[2] 459[4] 1740[2] (2318) 2931[2] 3240[4] (4793) (5201)

Nyanza (GER) *Alan King* 127h
4 b m Dai Jin Nouvelle Fortune (IRE) (Alzao (USA))
405[3]

Nyetimber (USA) *Sean Curran* 69h
9 ch g Forest Wildcat(USA) Once Around (CAN) (You And I (USA))
595[P] 749[5] 930[8] 1158[U]

Oakbank (USA) *Brett Johnson*
4 b g Empire Maker(USA) Summer Shower (Sadler's Wells (USA))
3418[P]

Oak Vintage (IRE) *Ann Hamilton* 109h
5 b g Fruits Of Love(USA) Brandam Supreme (IRE) (Supreme Leader)
2895[6] 3883[6] 4284[5] (4509) 4941[P]

Obistar (FR) *David Pipe* 114h
5 b g Astarabad(USA) Vallee Du Luy (FR) (Oblat (FR))
4618[5] 5051[2] 5335[3]

Occasionally Yours (IRE) *Alan Blackmore* 107h
11 b g Moscow Society(USA) Kristina's Lady (IRE) (Lafontaine (USA))
40[4] (399) (571) (1770) 2135[4] 2548[6] 2924[4] 3417[4] 4774[6] 5065[3] 5479[3]

Oceane (FR) *Alan King* 129h
3 b g Kentucky Dynamite(USA) Zahrana (FR) (Zamindar (USA))
(1732) (1984) ◆ 2480[4] 4360[4] 5116[2] ◆

Oceans Glory *John Ryan* 77b
3 b g Humbel(USA) Tamara Moon (IRE) (Acclamation)
1772[7]

Ocean Venture (IRE) *Graeme McPherson* 124h 82c
7 ch g Urban Ocean(FR) Starventure (IRE) (Insan (USA))
2906[6] **3486[4]**

Ochiltree Lady *Nick Kent*
9 b m Yoshka Mrs Poppyford (Mistertopogigo (IRE))
2488[P]

Ockey De Neulliac (FR) *N Mechie* 108h 129c
13 ch g Cyborg(FR) Graine De Neulliac (FR) (Le Nain Jaune (FR))
4424[P] 4820[2] 5178[8] (5370)

Octagon *Dianne Sayer* 122h
5 b g Overbury(IRE) Dusky Dante (IRE) (Phardante (FR))
83[6] (200) 710[4] 2214[3] ◆ 2802[B] 3367[3] 4405[2] 4911[P] 5368[4]

Oculist *Ben De Haan* 118h
7 b g Dr Fong(USA) Eyes Wide Open (Fraam)
710[2] (852)

Odds On Dan (IRE) *Lucinda Egerton* 86c
9 b g Oscar(IRE) Grange Classic (IRE) (Jurado (USA))
78[5] (256) 379[3] 2191[P] 2786[7] 3103[3] 3308[7] 4048[4] 4329[3] 5309[4]

O'Faolains Boy (IRE) *Rebecca Curtis* 124h 163c
8 b g Oscar(IRE) Lisa's Storm (IRE) (Glacial Storm (USA))
2633[P] (3116) 3850[P] 4354[8] **4767[7]**

Ofcoursewecan (USA) *Mark Gillard* 89h
5 b g Elusive Quality(USA) Valid Warning (USA) (Valid Appeal (USA))
168[5] 509[3] 1010[P]

Officer Cadet *Karen McLintock* 114h 112c
6 b g Kayf Tara Miss Invincible (Invincible Spirit (IRE))
3164[P]

Officer Drivel (IRE) *Jim Best* 116h 123c
4 b g Captain Rio Spiritville (IRE) (Invincible Spirit (IRE))
3084[4] 3466[3] 4774[7]

Officer Hoolihan *Tim Vaughan* 106h
5 b g Kayf Tara Major Hoolihan (Soldier Rose)
525[4] 3111[3] 4176[5] 4494[3] 5048[3]

Officer Sydney (IRE) *Gordon Elliott* 109h
3 b g Lawman(FR) Morena Park (Pivotal)
(1495) 3268a[7]

Officieux (FR) *Noel Meade* 132h
4 ch g Discover D'Auteuil(FR) Souri Des Champs (FR) (Robin Des Champs (FR))
2177a[5] 2525a[P] 5025a[F]

Off The Cuff *Donald McCain* 46b
4 b h Zamindar(USA) Comment (Sadler's Wells (USA))
1797[7]

Off The Ground (IRE) *Charlie Longsdon* 114h 138c
9 b g Oscar(IRE) Kaysel (IRE) (Torus)
1722[F] 2171[5] 2746[2] 3036[F] 4485[P] 5465[10]

Oficial Ben (IRE) *Jonjo O'Neill* 100h 117c
6 b g Beneficial Up A Dee (IRE) (Executive Perk)
2865[P] 3311[2] 4889[F]

Ogaritmo *Alex Hales* 103h
6 ch m Manduro(GER) Querida (Rainbow Quest (USA))
465[3] 744[4] 2559[F] 3177[2] 3816[5] 5374[12]

Ogwen Valley Girl *Michael Mullineaux* 39b
4 b m Indian Danehill(IRE) Lucky Find (IRE) (Key Of Luck (USA))
4309[9]

Oh Land Abloom (IRE) *Neil King* 133h
5 b g King's Theatre(IRE) Talinas Rose (IRE) (Definite Article)
181[2] 621[2] (1794) 1968[2] 2759[5] 4643[5] 5329[4]

Ohms Law *Anthony Day* 54h 58c
10 b g Overbury(IRE) Polly Live Wire (El Conquistador)
1961[8] 4845[9]

Oh Right (IRE) *Dianne Sayer* 77h 102c
11 b g Zagreb(USA) Conna Bride Lady (IRE) (Phardante (FR))
471[F] 842[5] 1069[8]

Oh So Fruity *Gary Moore* 103h
5 b g Midnight Legend Recipe (Bustino)
4099[F]

Oh So Gigolo (IRE) *Nicky Henderson* 48h
5 b g Milan Oh So Breezy (IRE) (Be My Native (USA))
865[4] 1246[4] 1644[5] 3353[9]

Oil Burner *Stuart Coltherd* 81h 104c
10 b g Sir Harry Lewis(USA) Quick Quote (Oats)
2500[5] 3671[4] 3937[4] 4175[6] 4637[4]

Oir Ion (IRE) *Mark Michael McNiff* 56b
3 ch g Court Masterpiece Cymbeline (IRE) (Dolphin Street (FR))
2195[7]

Oishin *Maurice Barnes* 84b
3 b g Paco Boy(IRE) Roshina (IRE) (Chevalier (IRE))
5127[6]

Okay Senam (FR) *G Macaire* 116h
2 b g Saint Des Saints(FR) Salvatrixe (FR) (Housamix (FR))
4539a[4]

Ok Corral (IRE) *Nicky Henderson* 131b
5 b g Mahler Acoola (IRE) (Flemensfirth (USA))
53a[2]

Okotoks (IRE) *A J Martin* 118h
5 b g Gamut(IRE) Whats Another One (IRE) (King's Theatre (IRE))
2672a[4]

Old Fashion *Neil King* 66h
3 b f Shirocco(GER) Oriental Dance (Fantastic Light (USA))
2137[5] 2537[P] 3039[P] 3338[U]

Oldgrangewood *Dan Skelton* 123h
4 b g Central Park(IRE) Top Of The Class (IRE) (Rudimentary (USA))
2591[2] ◆ 3353[4] (4403) 5329[3]

Old Guard *Paul Nicholls* 159h
4 b g Notnowcato Dolma (FR) (Marchand De Sable (USA))
(2058) (2512) (3033) 3230[4]

Old Magic (IRE) *Sophie Leech* 89h
10 b g Old Vic Maeve's Magic (IRE) (Mandalus)
2982[3] 3219[4] 3868[4] 4343[3] (4712) 4885[5] 5332[2]

Old Pride (IRE) *David Loder* 119h 110c
7 ch g Old Vic Feel The Pride (IRE) (Persian Bold)
2244[4] 2694[2] 3420[P] **4889[P]**

Old Storm (IRE) *Brian Ellison* 94h 100c
6 b g Old Vic Sissinghurst Storm (IRE) (Good Thyne (USA))
1501[5] **2645[3]**

Ole Companero (GER) *G Macaire* 111h 128c
9 b g Sholokhov(IRE) Orsina (IRE) (Glow (USA))
1672a[3]

Oliver's Gold *Mark Walford* 127h 140c
7 b g Danehill Dancer(IRE) Gemini Gold (IRE) (King's Best (USA))
854[3] 973[3] **1460[2]** 1554[5] **(1904) (2193) 2774[6]**

Oliver's Hill (IRE) *Lawney Hill* 122h 115c
6 b g Shantou(USA) River Rouge (IRE) (Croco Rouge (IRE))
2973[7] 3836[4] 5149[P]

Olivia Joan *Alistair Whillans* 37b
4 ch m Grape Tree Road Thorterdykes Lass (IRE) (Zaffaran (USA))
159[9]

Olofi (FR) *Tom George* 141h 118c
9 gr g Slickly(FR) Dona Bella (FR) (Highest Honor (FR))
437a[11] 2350[6] 2512[10] 3015[9] 3854[6] 4482[4]

Olymnia *Gary Moore* 80h
4 b m Teofilo(IRE) Diotima (High Estate)
281[8] 1084[F] 1816[P]

Olympiad (IRE) *Martin Todhunter* 81h
7 b g Galileo(IRE) Caumshinaun (IRE) (Indian Ridge)
710[6]

Olympian Boy (IRE) *Sophie Leech* 106h 103c
11 b g Flemensfirth(USA) Notanissue (IRE) (Buckskin (FR))
161[3] (3586) **3951[P] 4197[5] 4597[4]** 4922[6] 5418[12]

O Maonlai (IRE) *Tom George* 131h 143c
7 b g Oscar(IRE) Another Gaye (IRE) (Classic Cliche (IRE))
2780[2] 3157[P] 4697[12]

Omessa Has (FR) *Nicky Henderson* 123h 116c
3 gr f Martaline Ombre Folle (Celtic Swing)
5280[9]

Omgnotanother (IRE) *Evan Williams* 89h
4 b m Scorpion(IRE) Hot Bunny (IRE) (Distinctly North (USA))
152[5] 1716[8] 1960[7] 2665[4] 3011[6] 4290[P]

Omg Western Bunny (IRE) *Evan Williams* 38b
4 b m Westerner My Magic (IRE) (Saddlers' Hall (IRE))
5104[4]

Omid *Kenneth Slack* 105h
7 b g Dubawi(IRE) Mille Couleurs (FR) (Spectrum (IRE))
502[10] (1371) 1925[2] 3684[3] 3970[7] 4840[P]

On Account (IRE) *Francesca Nimmo* 94b
3 b g Scorpion(IRE) Derriana (IRE) (Snurge)
5436[3] ◆

On Alberts Head (IRE) *Laura Young* 105h 91c
5 b g Mountain High(IRE) Dear Money (IRE) (Buckskin (FR))
32[6]

On Demand *Simon Hodgson* 88h
4 ch m Teofilo(IRE) Mimisel (Selkirk (USA))
2699[4] 3114[13] 3252[6] 4343[P]

Onderun (IRE) *Emma Lavelle* 116h 117c
6 b g Flemensfirth(USA) Warts And All (IRE) (Commanche Run)
2442[6] 3046[2] ◆ 3707[P]

One Big Love *Harry Fry* 115h
7 b m Tamure(IRE) Sound Appeal (Robellino (USA))
100[2] 387[2]

One Cool Boy (IRE) *Tracey Watkins* 97h
6 bb g One Cool Cat(USA) Pipewell (IRE) (Lake Coniston (IRE))
5374[8]

One Cool Clarkson *Neil McKnight* 95c
8 b g Clerkenwell(USA) Decent Dime (IRE) (Insan (USA))
4569[3]

One Cool Scorpion (IRE) *Philip Hobbs* 113h
4 b g Scorpion(IRE) One Cool Kate (IRE) (Definite Article)
(392) 2331[5] 2928[10] 3411[4] 5076[5] (5466) ◆

One Day Like This (IRE) *Tim Vaughan* 53h
5 ch g Robin Des Champs(FR) Glebe Dream (IRE) (Be My Native (USA))
460[5] 773[9]

Onefitzall (IRE) *Philip Hobbs* 131h
5 b g Indian Danehill(IRE) Company Credit (IRE) (Anshan)
(2163) 2807[3] 4040[4]

One For Arthur (IRE) *Lucinda Russell* 133h 142c
6 b g Milan Nonnetia (FR) (Trempolino (USA))
(2067) 2481[3] 2932[3] 3849[5] 4286[2] ◆ 4609[4] 5323[3]

One For Harry (IRE) *Nicky Richards* 142h
7 b g Generous(IRE) Strawberry Fool (FR) (Tel Quel (FR))
(2214) 2641[P] (3630) 4204[2] 4717[P] 5446[6]

One For Hocky (IRE) *Nicky Richards* 119h 114c
7 b g Brian Boru Wire Lady (IRE) (Second Set (IRE))
356[4] **691[2] 959[4]** 1181[6] 2948[5] 4583[P] (5089) 5260[4]

One For The Boss (IRE) *Dai Burchell* 86h 114c
8 b g Garuda(IRE) Tell Nothing (IRE) (Classic Secret (USA))
2569[P] **4427[2] 4803[7]**

One For The Guv'Nr (IRE) *Nicky Henderson* 135h
6 b g Oscar(IRE) Wintry Day (IRE) (Presenting)
4070[U] ◆

Oneforthenure (IRE) *Richard Woollacott* 87h
6 b m Court Cave(IRE) Shining Willow (Strong Gale)
928[4] 1057[5] 2870[4] 3581[8] 4293[5] 5420[11]

Oneida Tribe (IRE) *Venetia Williams* 98h
6 b g Turtle Island(IRE) Glory Queen (IRE) (Taipan (IRE))
3775[3] 4344[7] 4614[7]

One Last Dream *Ron Hodges* 70h
6 ch g Resplendent Glory(IRE) Pip's Dream (Glint Of Gold)
2563[7] 2850[9] 2986[10]

One More Go (IRE) *Dr Richard Newland* 90h
4 b g Papal Bull Enchanted Wood (IRE) (Hawk Wing (USA))
2840[6]

One More Tune (IRE) *Philip Rowley* 113h 116c
7 b g Luso Strong Gale Pigeon (IRE) (Strong Gale)
4307[2]

Onenightinvienna (IRE) *Philip Hobbs* 139h 157c
6 b g Oscar(IRE) Be My Granny (Needle Gun (IRE))
(2660) 3013[2] 3774[2] 4237[5] 5218[U]

Oneofapear (IRE) *Mike Sowersby* 102h
9 b g Pyrus(USA) Whitegate Way (Greensmith)
416[2] 626[3] 777[3] 918[4] 968[2]

One Of Us *Nick Williams* 101b
3 b g Presenting One Gulp (Hernando (FR))
3409[3] ◆ 4117[4]

One Style (FR) *Venetia Williams* 108h 111c
5 b g Desert Style(IRE) Arieta (FR) (Pistolet Bleu (IRE))
3570[3] 4235[4] 4494[2] 5220[2]

One Term (IRE) *Rebecca Curtis* 129h 136c
8 b g Beneficial One Edge (IRE) (Welsh Term)
47a[6] 362[5]

One Track Mind (IRE) *Warren Greatrex* 154h
5 b g Flemensfirth(USA) Lady Petit (IRE) (Beneficial)
3018[5] (3352) 4244[2] ◆

Ongenstown Lad (IRE) *Mrs Gillian Callaghan* 127h 94c
11 b g Bach(IRE) Lantern Logic (IRE) (Royal Fountain)
839[3] (1963) 2484[11]

On His Own (IRE) *W P Mullins* 137h 168c
11 b g Presenting Shuil Na Mhuire (IRE) (Roselier (FR))
22a[P] 375a[7] 664a[9] 3017[U] 3324a[4] 4007a[8] 4260a[2] 4767[8] 5218[F]

Only A Tipple *Donald McCain* 59b
4 b g Multiplex Heathyards Tipple (IRE) (Marju (IRE))
5371[3]

Onlyfoolsownhorses (IRE) *Micky Hammond* 20h
4 br g Presenting Lizzy Langtry (IRE) (King's Theatre (IRE))
3839[P] 4417[7]

Only For Love *Nicky Henderson* 101b
4 br m Kalanisi(IRE) Sardagna (FR) (Medaaly)
4468[3] ◆ 5187[2] ◆

Only Gorgeous (IRE) *Sue Gardner* 106h 87c
6 b g Vertical Speed(FR) Pure Beautiful (IRE) (Un Desperado (FR))
320[9] 595[4] 837[U] 893[2] ◆ 1181[10] 1324[8] 1721[5] 2006[2] **2456[4]** 3414[P] 3919[8] 4291[3] 5433[13]

Only Orsenfoolsies *Micky Hammond* 133h 127c
6 b g Trade Fair Desert Gold (IRE) (Desert Prince (IRE))
2846[U] 3055[3] 3627[4] 3806[P]

Only Orvieto (IRE) *Malcolm Jefferson* 108b
4 b m Kayf Tara Vigna Maggio (FR) (Starborough)
(4708)

Onsaijamais (FR) *G Macaire* 125h
4 b g Kap Rock(FR) Romantique Cotte (FR) (Robin Des Champs (FR))
4540a[2]

On The Bridge (IRE) *Jeremy Scott* 135h 140c
10 b g Milan Bay Dove (Alderbrook)
404[5] 833[3] (1138) 1325[8] 1594[5] 1839[3] 2054[7] **(4892) (5458)**

On The Case *Tom George* 63h 95c
7 ch g Generous(IRE) Tulipa (POL) (Jape (USA))
450[P] 2542[3] 3241[3] 3683[U] 4029[P]

On The Couch (IRE) *Sam Thomas* 76h
6 bb m Heron Island(IRE) Miss Serenade (FR) (Saint Cyrien (FR))
3947[4] 4293[3] 4546[5]

On The Fringe (IRE) *E Bolger* 148c
10 b g Exit To Nowhere(USA) Love And Porter (IRE) (Sheer Grit)
(75a) (4768) (5178)

On The Move *Fiona Shaw* 94h
7 b m Sir Harry Lewis(USA) What A Mover (Jupiter Island)
265[P]

On The Raz *Jackie Retter* 57b
8 b m Rakaposhi King Trillow (Pitpan)
647[P]

On The Right Path *Barry Leavy* 102h
8 b g Pursuit Of Love Glen Falls (Commanche Run)
2667[5] 3314[3]

On The Road (IRE) *Evan Williams* 94h
5 b g Stowaway B Greenhill (Gunner B)
2409[9] 3009[8] 3256[10] (4343) (4454)

Onthewesternfront (IRE) *Jonjo O'Neill* 119b
5 b g Robin Des Champs(FR) Asian Maze (IRE) (Anshan)
2729[4] 4103[2] 4721[16]

On Tour (IRE) *Evan Williams* 117h 145c
7 b g Croco Rouge(IRE) Galant Tour (IRE) (Riberetto)
(2446) (2803) 3857[9] 4701[8]

On Trend (IRE) *Nick Gifford* 110h 127c
9 b g Jammaal Comrun (IRE) (Commanche Run)
239[3] 3086[P]

Onurbike *John O'Neill* 36h
7 b g Exit To Nowhere(USA) Lay It Off (IRE) (Strong Gale)
3316[8] 4097[P] 4535[4]

Onwiththeparty *Chris Gordon* 103h 53c
6 b g Sir Harry Lewis(USA) Kentford Fern (El Conquistador)
2420[3] 3137[13] 3369[2] 3662[5] 4069[5] 4671[3] 5481[8]

On Your Max *Raymond York* 96h
7 b g Tobougg(IRE) Maxilla (IRE) (Lahib (USA))
1290[5] 1590[7] 2000[9]

Onzo Mor (IRE) *J T R Dreaper* 109b
11 gr g Sonus(IRE) Buckners Girl (Weld)
75a[P]

O O Seven (IRE) *Nicky Henderson* 148h
5 b g Flemensfirth(USA) Kestral Heights (IRE) (Eagle Eyed (USA))
(2646) (2910) 3447[2] (4015) 4715[8]

Opechee (IRE) *David Bridgwater* 94h
4 b g Robin Des Champs(FR) Falcons Gift (IRE) (Zaffaran (USA))
2188[7] 2650[8] 3130[12] 3450[P] 4441[6]

Open Eagle (IRE) *W P Mullins* 142h
6 b g Montjeu(IRE) Princesse De Viane (FR) (Kaldoun (FR))
3227[2] 3623[2] (4123) 4766[8]

Open Hearted *Dan Skelton* 73h 147c
8 b g Generous(IRE) Romantic Dream (Bustino)
1715[2] ◆ (1944) 2759[11] **3282[P]**

Opening Batsman (IRE) *Harry Fry* 120h 147c
9 b g Morozov(USA) Jolly Signal (IRE) (Torus)
3282[5] 3776[P] 4361[2] 5119[P]

Opera Buff *Jose Santos*
6 b g Oratorio(IRE) Opera Glass (Barathea (IRE))
5137[P]

Opera Lyrique (FR) *J-L Guillochon*
4 b g Librettist(USA) Operam (Kris)
5385a[P]

Opera Og (IRE) *Sean Murray* 68h 127c
9 b g Oscar(IRE) Maspaloma (IRE) (Camden Town)
521[2]

Opera Rock (FR) *Venetia Williams* 102b
4 b g Kap Rock(FR) Open Up (FR) (Fabulous Don (SPA))
3625[2]

Operateur (IRE) *Ben Haslam* 97h
7 b g Oratorio(IRE) Kassariya (IRE) (Be My Guest (USA))
1524[6]

Operating (IRE) *Gordon Elliott* 111h 122c
8 b g Milan Seymourswift (Seymour Hicks (FR))
3296a[P]

Optical High *Sue Smith* 93h 64c
6 b g Rainbow High Forsweets (Forzando)
1110[6] 1370[6] 1692[5] 1890[4] 2323[3] (2868) 3793[6] 4047[2] 4510[5] 4942[P]

Optimistic Bias (IRE) *Jonjo O'Neill* 128h
6 b g Sayarshan(FR) Dashers Folly (IRE) (Dr Massini (IRE))
(2081) 2624[7] 4389[3] 5120[14]

Orangeaday *Ben Case* 122h 96c
8 b g Kayf Tara One Of Those Days (Soviet Lad (USA))
2513[P] **2973[8]**

Orange Karma (FR) *D Sourdeau De Beauregard*
4 ro g Martaline Vilaya (FR) (Cadoudal (FR))
5385a[2]

Orange Nassau (FR) *Charlie Longsdon* 97h 126c
9 gr g Martaline Vilaya (FR) (Cadoudal (FR))
156[2] 2028[3] 3024[P] 5456[5]

Oranger (FR) *Andrew J Martin* 52h 91c
13 b g Antarctique(IRE) True Beauty (Sun Prince)
536[P]

Orang Outan (FR) *Mrs R Hurley* 53h 53c
13 b g Baby Turk Ellapampa (FR) (Pampabird)
18[10] 536[10]

Orbasa (FR) *Paul Nicholls* 112h 144c
4 b g Full Of Gold(FR) Ierbasa De Kerpaul (FR) (Cadoubel (FR))
(4379) ◆ 4787[4] 5118[2] 5297[2]

Orbit Light (IRE) *Nicky Henderson* 74h
4 b m Echo Of Light Niobe (Pivotal)
1811[9] 2154[P] 2452[9]

Orby's Man (IRE) *Charlie Longsdon* 119h 119c
6 b g Arcadio(GER) Gleann Oisin (IRE) (Le Bavard (FR))
85[2] **430[4] 693[P] 873[3] 4789[6] 5154[6]**

Orchard Boy (IRE) *Paul Webber* 123h
7 b g Oscar(IRE) Beech Lodge (IRE) (Supreme Leader)
5243[2]

Orchard Park (IRE) *Jamie Snowden* 91h
4 b g Milan Tough As Leather (IRE) (Flemensfirth (USA))
2991[4] (4434)

Orchard Road (USA) *Tristan Davidson* 110h
8 b g Street Cry(IRE) Aunt Mottz (USA) (Honey Jay (USA))
2893[5] 3307[3] 3438[4] 3886[4] 4390[3] 4797[3]

Ordensritter (GER) *Chris Down* 90h
7 ch g Samum(GER) Dramraire Mist (Darshaan)
1677[6] 2245[3] 2693[2] 3369[P]

Ordinary World (IRE) *Henry De Bromhead* 129h
5 br g Milan Saucy Present (IRE) (Presenting)
5025a[F]

Oregon Gift *Brian Ellison* 60h
3 b g Major Cadeaux Dayville (USA) (Dayjur (USA))
3470[8]

Orfeo Conti (FR) *Diana Grissell* 59h 87c
13 ch g Bulington(FR) Gazelle Lulu (FR) (Altayan)
295[5] 670[3] 1355[3]

Organisedconfusion (IRE) *C A McBratney* 121h 54c
10 b g Laveron Histologie (FR) (Quart De Vin (FR))
868[P]

Organ Morgan *Richard Phillips* 71b
5 b g Dylan Thomas(IRE) Abide (FR) (Pivotal)
407[7]

Orioninverness (IRE) *Lucinda Russell* 101h
4 b g Brian Boru Woodville Leader (IRE) (Supreme Leader)
2195[6] 3442[7] 3667[4] 4403[3] 4796[6]

Orion's Might (IRE) *Matt Sheppard* 108h
5 b g Antonius Pius(USA) Imperial Conquest (IRE) (Imperial Ballet (IRE))
5076[4]

Orix (CZE) *Lenka Horakova*
8 b g Mill Pond(FR) Orega (CZE) (Regulus (CZE))
1885a[P]

Orpheus Valley (IRE) *Thomas Gibney* 86h 133c
12 ch g Beneficial Native Mo (IRE) (Be My Native (USA))
24a[P]

Orsippus (USA) *Michael Smith* 119h 127c
9 bb g Sunday Break(JPN) Mirror Dancing (USA) (Caveat (USA))
154[2]

Orsm *Laura Mongan* 81h
8 b g Erhaab(USA) Royal Roulette (Risk Me (FR))
1272[7] 1756[11] 1897[7]

Or So (USA) *Phil Middleton* 70h
3 ch g Rock Slide(USA) Miss Santa Anita (CAN) (Ide (USA))
1805[5]

Orthodox Lad *Grace Harris* 110h
7 ch g Monsieur Bond(IRE) Ashantiana (Ashkalani (IRE))
1714[5] 2271[2] 2734[7] 2974[2]

Oscara Dara (IRE) *Neil Mulholland* 147h 125c
10 b g Oscar(IRE) Lisa's Storm (IRE) (Glacial Storm (USA))
(1134)

Oscar Baby (IRE) *Diana Grissell* 75h 35c
9 b m Oscar(IRE) Snowbaby (IRE) (Be My Native (USA))
597[7] **782[P] 1243[P]** 1490[10] 1771[P]

Oscar Blue (IRE) *Brian Ellison* 125h
5 gr g Oscar(IRE) Blossom Rose (IRE) (Roselier (FR))
(1852) (2070) 2624[4] 3158[2] 4017[9] 4405[3] 4911[P]

Oscar Bravo (IRE) *Heather Dalton* 89b
4 br g Oscar(IRE) Brave Commitment (IRE) (Henbit (USA))
3417

Oscar Delta (IRE) *C Price* 96c
12 b g Oscar(IRE) Timerry (IRE) (Alphabatim (USA))
4269[6]

Oscar Fiain (IRE) *Tim Vaughan* 118h 109c
7 b g Oscar(IRE) Produzione (FR) (Baby Turk)
1419[P]

Oscar Fortune (IRE) *Jonjo O'Neill* 129h 137c
7 b g Oscar(IRE) Platin Run (IRE) (Strong Gale)
1849[P]

Oscargo (IRE) *Mrs Sue Popham* 93c
11 b g Oscar(IRE) Broken Rein (IRE) (Orchestra)
270[P]

Oscar Hill (IRE) *David Bridgwater* 133h 145c
9 b g Oscar(IRE) Elizabeth Tudor (IRE) (Supreme Leader)
8a[F]

Oscar Jane (IRE) *Johnny Farrelly* 105h
8 b m Oscar(IRE) Turrill House (Charmer (IRE))
435[8] 759[P] 1120[P] 1578[3] 1702[F] 2000[2] ◆ (2298) (2454) 2554[4] 3256[6] (3914) 4290[2] (4682)

Oscar Knight (IRE) *Thomas Mullins* 120h 111c
6 b g Oscar(IRE) Cool Supreme (IRE) (Supreme Leader)
19a[8] **4663a[2]**

Oscar Lantern (IRE) *C Byrnes* 127h
6 b g Milan Handy Cash (IRE) (Flemensfirth (USA))
4662a[3]

Oscar Lateen (IRE) *Sandy Thomson* 89h 104c
7 b g Oscar(IRE) Storm Call (Celestial Storm (USA))
2191[2] (2983) 4177[2] 4637[3] 4792[3] 5366[4]

Oscar Leney (IRE) *J T R Draper* 71h 64c
9 b g Oscar(IRE) Sound Case (IRE) (Husyan (USA))
537[8] 939[8]

Oscar Magic (IRE) *Nigel Twiston-Davies* 130h 114c
8 bb g Oscar(IRE) Just An Illusion (IRE) (Shernazar)
2489[2] 3044[5] 4803[8]

Oscar O'Scar (IRE) *Micky Hammond* 100h 121c
7 b g Oscar(IRE) Shining Lights (IRE) (Moscow Society (USA))
2937[2] 3791[3] 3968[3] (4325) 4456[2] (4836) 5348[5]

Oscar Prairie (IRE) *Warren Greatrex* 112h 100c
10 b g Oscar(IRE) Silver Prairie (IRE) (Common Grounds)
377[2] 726[4] 2664[2] 2956[4]

Oscar Robin (IRE) *Ken Wingrove*
6 b m Oscar(IRE) Bryan's Pet (IRE) (Lafontaine I (USA))
3388[P]

Oscar Rock (IRE) *Malcolm Jefferson* 141h 155c
7 b g Oscar(IRE) Cash And New (IRE) (Supreme Leader)
(1658) ◆ 2483[12] 4731[10] 5494[7]

Oscar Sam (IRE) *Mrs John Harrington* 139h
6 br g Oscar(IRE) Good Thyne Jenny (IRE) (Good Thyne (USA))
4730[17]

Oscar's Prospect (IRE) *Jedd O'Keeffe* 72b
3 b f Oscar(IRE) Divine Prospect (IRE) (Namaqualand (USA))
4302[4] 5127[5]

Oscar Sunset (IRE) *Evan Williams* 142h 147c
8 b g Oscar(IRE) Derravarra Sunset (IRE) (Supreme Leader)
2881[2] ◆ 3415[2] (3975) 4355[3] 5101[F]

Oscars Way (IRE) *Tom Symonds* 104h
7 b g Oscar(IRE) Derrigra Sublime (IRE) (Flemensfirth (USA))
4877[P]

Oscarteea (IRE) *Neil Mulholland* 132h
6 b g Oscar(IRE) Miss Arteea (IRE) (Flemensfirth (USA))
2639[4] 3018[10] 4252[2]

Oscatara (IRE) *Donald McCain* 120h 121c
8 bb g Oscar(IRE) Nethertara (Netherkelly)
691[P]

Osgood *Gary Moore* 107h
8 b g Danehill Dancer(IRE) Sabreon (Caerleon (USA))
104[P] 449[11] 669[11] 931[6] (1244)

Oskar's Eva (IRE) *Tim Vaughan* 90h
5 gr m Black Sam Bellamy(IRE) Sardagna (FR) (Medaaly)
2250[7] 2776[P] 3516[7] 4893[5]

Osorios Trial *Kevin Frost* 96h 82c
8 ch g Osorio(GER) Skytrial (USA) (Sky Classic (CAN))
694[3] 937[5] 1096[F]

Ossie's Dancer *Martin Smith* 126h
6 ch g Osorio(GER) Nina Ballerina (Kahyasi)
(225) 812[5] 1035[9]

Otago Trail (IRE) *Venetia Williams* 114h 157c
7 b g Heron Island(IRE) Cool Chic (IRE) (Roselier (FR))
2446[2] ◆ (2877) (3521) 3738[3] 5191[P] 5324[3]

Otto The Great (FR) *J H Henderson*
7 gr g Turgeon(USA) Hunorisk (FR) (Mansonnien (FR))
3958[P]

Ouest Ocean (FR) *Victor Dartnall* 71b
4 b g Early March Kalistina (FR) (Sillery (USA))
2731[P]

Oulamayo (FR) *Dan Skelton* 104h
4 b g Solon(GER) La Titie Du Perche (FR) (Rochesson (FR))
1758[4] 2251[3] 2543[7]

Our Boy Ben *Malcolm Jefferson* 85h 72c
6 b g Revoque(IRE) Magic Bloom (Full Of Hope)
(135) 728[8]

Our Boy Boru (IRE) *J Woods* 102h
4 b g Brian Boru She's My Aunt (IRE) (Beneficial)
11a[14]

Our Cat (IRE) *Fergal O'Brien* 81h 121c
7 b m Royal Anthem(USA) Run Cat (IRE) (Lord Americo)
2243[P] 3123[P] 4422[P]

Our Chief (IRE) *David Pipe* 101h
6 b g Old Vic Torsha (IRE) (Torus)
102[6] 758[4] 859[7]

Our Dancing Dandy (IRE) *Donald McCain* 120b
5 b g Scorpion(IRE) Woodsia (Woodman (USA))
(5337)

Our Duke (IRE) *Mrs John Harrington* 136h
5 b g Oscar(IRE) Good Thyne Jenny (IRE) (Good Thyne (USA))
4332a[P] 4955a[3]

Our Folly *Stuart Kittow* 103h
7 b g Sakhee(USA) Regent's Folly (IRE) (Touching Wood (USA))
(1545) 1819[2] 2732[6] 4922[4]

Our Georgie Girl *Polly Gundry*
8 ch m Zafeen(FR) Rosina May (IRE) (Danehill Dancer (IRE))
5478[P]

Our Island (IRE) *Hugo Froud* 65h 69c
10 b g Turtle Island(IRE) Linda's Leader (IRE) (Supreme Leader)
4185[6] 4433[6]

Our Jerry (IRE) *Miss Evanna McCutcheon* 89h
4 b g Jeremy(USA) Sonic Night (IRE) (Night Shift (USA))
11a[18]

Our Kaempfer (IRE) *Charlie Longsdon* 143h
6 b g Oscar(IRE) Gra-Bri (IRE) (Rashar (USA))
1848[4] 2333[2] 2641[B] 4730[5] ◆

Our Kylie (IRE) *Brian Ellison* 95h
3 b f Jeremy(USA) Prakara (IRE) (Indian Ridge)
1177[2] 1415[3] 1712[4] 2896[P] 3587[3] 4068[4] (4904)

Ourlittle Senorita *Miss Imogen Pickard*
3 b f Fantastic Spain(USA) Our Little Missy (Sadler's Way)
1452[P]

Ourmanmassini (IRE) *Suzy Smith* 120h 94c
7 b g Dr Massini(IRE) Aunty Dawn (IRE) (Strong Gale)
63[6] 2734[5] 2987[8] 3725[2] 4384[4] 5477[6]

Our Mick *S Allwood* 64h 89c
9 gr g Karinga Bay Dawn's Della (Scottish Reel I (IRE))
85[7] 5458[5]

Our Morris (IRE) *George Bewley* 92b
4 b g Milan Broken Gale (IRE) (Broken Hearted)
3442[4] 4572[3]

Ourniamheen (IRE) *Matt Sheppard* 59b
5 b m Papal Bull Still As Sweet (IRE) (Fairy King (USA))
2856[11]

Our Nipper *Chris Gordon*
3 ch g Grape Tree Road Lady Kay (Kayf Tara)
1732[P]

Our Phylli Vera (IRE) *Joanne Foster* 105h 71c
6 b m Motivator With Colour (Rainbow Quest (USA))
1892[12] 2144[4] 3311[7] 3834[11] 4298[3] 4861[3]

Our Reward (IRE) *Jamie Snowden* 119h
5 b g Morozov(USA) Paddyeoin (IRE) (Insan (USA))
1843[3] 3012[6]

Our Savannah (IRE) *J R Jenkins*
3 b f High Chaparral(IRE) Alinea (USA) (Kingmambo (USA))
4228[8]

Our Sox (IRE) *A J Martin* 112h 112c
6 b g September Storm(GER) Winning Sally (IRE) (Lancastrian)
1184a[16] 2473[9]

Our Thomas (IRE) *Tim Easterby* 118h
3 b g Dylan Thomas(IRE) Sinamay (USA) (Saint Ballado (CAN))
(1899) 2172[3] 3967[2] 4304[2] 4720[17] 5256[2]

Our Three Sons (IRE) *Jamie Snowden* 102h
4 b g Shantou(USA) Ballyquinn (IRE) (Anshan)
602[2] 2597[4] 5153[9] 5477[4]

Outlander (IRE) *W P Mullins* 147h 156c
7 b g Stowaway Western Whisper (IRE) (Supreme Leader)
72a[3] (3301a) (4005a) 4729[F] 4956a[2]

Outlaw Josey Wales (IRE) *R Mike Smith* 100h
4 b g Jeremy(USA) Trinity Scholar (IRE) (Invincible Spirit (IRE))
2756[6] 3442[10] 5444[2]

Out Now (IRE) *Mrs Kim Smyly* 94h 130c
11 br g Muroto Raven Night (IRE) (Mandalus)
4651[3]

Out Of Range *Mrs Pauline Harkin* 60b 94c
8 b g High-Rise(IRE) Sight'n Sound (Chief Singer)
13[P] (293) 531[6]

Out Of The Mist (IRE) *Emma Lavelle* 111h
6 b m Flemensfirth(USA) Mistinguett (IRE) (Doyoun)
(2164) 3154[4]

Outrageous Romana (IRE) *Graeme McPherson* 88b
4 b m Mahler South West Nine (IRE) (Oscar (IRE))
4559[5]

Outrath (IRE) *Jim Best* 109h
5 b g Captain Rio Silver Grouse (IRE) (Zagreb (USA))
2136[6] 2544[5] 2823[3]

Out Sam *Warren Greatrex* 139h 153c
6 b g Multiplex Tintera (IRE) (King's Theatre (IRE))
2214[6] 3136[3] (3805) (4116) 4697[7] 5191[7]

Outtilallhours (IRE) *Joanne Foster* 84h
7 br g Dr Massini(IRE) Cherry Vale (IRE) (Anshan)
620[7]

Over And Above (IRE) *Henry Hogarth* 102h 95c
9 b g Overbury(IRE) Rose Gold (IRE) (Nucleon (USA))
(133) 421[3] ◆ (842) 1069[3] 1462[5] 2708[4] 3803[P] 3969[P]

Overawed *Stuart Coltherd* 66b
4 b m Overbury(IRE) Alleged To Rhyme (IRE) (Leading Counsel (USA))
2344[5] 3476[11]

Overbury Queen *Alan Swinbank*
5 b m Overbury(IRE) Oscar's Lady (IRE) (Oscar (IRE))
1334[9]

Overdo *Seamus Mullins* 63h
4 br m Overbury(IRE) Shuil Do (IRE) (Be My Native (USA))
111[7]

Overlay *Lawney Hill* 77h
11 br m Overbury(IRE) Lay It Off (IRE) (Strong Gale)
1086[F]

Overlord *Mark Rimell* 25h
3 b g Lawman(FR) Hip (Pivotal)
2448[7]

Over My Head *Claire Dyson* 85h 89c
7 gr g Overbury(IRE) Altesse De Sou (FR) (Saint Preuil (FR))
3067[2] 3378[3] 3864[P] 4710[P]

Over The Air *John Spearing* 112h
7 br m Overbury(IRE) Moonlight Air (Bold Owl)
529[3] 876[3] 1292[3] (1455) 1721[4] 1911[3] 2042[6] 2560[U]

Over The Bridge *Steve Flook* 58b
5 b g Multiplex Do It On Dani (Weld)
2909[10] 3573[5] 4430[P] 4874[U] 5050[P]

Overtheedge (IRE) *Simon West* 110h
6 b g Morozov(USA) Ballyroe Hill (IRE) (Over The River (FR))
3504[P] 4013[F] 5256[5] (5349)

Over To Midnight *Lady Susan Brooke* 85h
5 b m Midnight Legend Makeover (Priolo (USA))
3469[7] 3573[6] 4266[5] 4441[16] 4888[8] 5155[8] 5398[3]

Overtown Express (IRE) *Harry Fry* 131h
7 br g Overbury(IRE) Black Secret (Gildoran)
2581[F] (4137) (4526) 4636[5] 5235[3]

Overtoyoulou *Chris Grant* 86h
7 b m Overbury(IRE) Champagne Lou Lou (Supreme Leader)
136[6]

Ovilia (IRE) *Donald McCain* 83h
6 gr m Clodovil(IRE) Five Of Wands (Caerleon (USA))
1096[3] 1384[P]

Owega Star (IRE) *Peter Fahey* 120h 111c
8 br g Basanta(IRE) Los Monteros (IRE) (College Chapel)
95a[P] 1556a[B]

Owen Glendower (IRE) *Sophie Leech* 108h 123c
10 br g Anshan Native Success (IRE) (Be My Native (USA))
(151) 331[2] 750[3] 961[2] 1053[F] 1268[5] 1332[U] 2057[U] 2593[3] 4965[3]

Owen Na View (IRE) *Fergal O'Brien* 126h 135c
7 bb g Presenting Lady Zephyr (IRE) (Toulon)
259[2] 430[5] (659) (799) 1178[2] 1268[3] 1343[U] 1658[7] 2059[8] 2468[10] 2784[6] 3030[5] 3620[5] 4841[2] ◆ 5096[5] (5471)

Owner Occupier *Chris Gordon* 66h 92c
10 ch g Foxhound(USA) Miss Beverley (Beveled (USA))
446[2] 571[P] 806[4] 1086[5] 1245[4] 1353[2] (1489) 2015[6]

Owners Day *Neil Mulholland* 76b
5 gr m Fair Mix(IRE) Charmeille (FR) (Exit To Nowhere (USA))
2421[11] 4468[6]

Oxalido (FR) *Hugh Burns* 95h 97c
13 b g Brier Creek(USA) Galene De Saisy (FR) (Montorselli)
140[9] 1552[7] 1691[11] 2751[P]

Oxwich Bay (IRE) *Evan Williams* 97b
3 b g Westerner Rose De Beaufai (FR) (Solon (GER))
4488[9]

Oyster Shell *Oliver Greenall* 71h 132c
8 br g Bollin Eric Pearly-B (IRE) (Gunner B)
406[6] 556[9] 826[5] 1046[8] 4592[5]

Ozamo (FR) *P Peltier* 140h 134c
8 b g Alamo Bay(USA) Ozee (FR) (Robin Des Champs (FR))
(5042a) 5428a[3]

Ozzie The Oscar (IRE) *Philip Hobbs* 140h
4 b g Oscar(IRE) Private Official (IRE) (Beneficial)
2991[3] (4681) (5091) (5393)

Ozzy Thomas (IRE) *Henry Oliver* 123h 130c
5 b g Gold Well Bramble Leader (IRE) (Supreme Leader)
2058[5] 2266[2] 2854[2] 3134[5] 4622[P]

Pacha Du Polder (FR) *Paul Nicholls* 123h 147c
8 b g Muhtathir Ambri Piotta (FR) (Caerwent)
535[3] 4227[U] (4437) 4768[5] 5178[6]

Pacific Pearl (IRE) *Sam Thomas*
4 b m Westerner Claudia's Pearl (Deploy)
5286[P]

Pack The Punch (IRE) *Desmond McDonogh* 118h
5 b g Teofilo(IRE) Zavaleta (IRE) (Kahyasi)
19a[12]

Paddling (FR) *Micky Hammond* 92b
4 b g Walk In The Park(IRE) Sea Mamaille (FR) (Sea Full (FR))
3104[5] 4572[5]

Paddocks Lounge (IRE) *Sophie Leech* 105h
8 b g Oscar(IRE) Sister Rosza (IRE) (Roselier (FR))
647[4] 999[2]

Paddy Mulligan (IRE) *John Ferguson* 97h 106c
6 b g Presenting Laragh (IRE) (Oscar (IRE))
695[7] 777[U] 914[2] 1080[6]

Paddy's Field (IRE) *Ben Pauling* 124h
5 bb g Flemensfirth(USA) Kittys Oscar (IRE) (Oscar (IRE))
213[4] 2163[F] (3724) 4344[3] 4620[8] 5335[4]

Paddys Runner *Alan King* 114h
3 gr g Sir Percy Frosty Welcome (USA) (With Approval (CAN))
975[2] (1593) (1712) 2688[2] 4720[P]

Paddy's Yarn (IRE) *Valerie Jackson* 90h
5 ch g Houmayoun(FR) Deidamia (USA) (Dayjur (USA))
963[3] 2343[4]

Paddy The Deejay (IRE) *Stuart Edmunds* 118h 115c
6 b g Fruits Of Love(USA) Sue Pickering (IRE) (Tremblant)
1986[4] 2266[5] 2973[5] 4782[2] 5157[4]

Paddy The Oscar (IRE) *Grace Harris* 101h 123c
12 b g Oscar(IRE) Parsonage (The Parson)
2272[5] 2566[5] 2996[2] (3385) 3583[F] 3823[5]

Paddy The Stout (IRE) *Paul Henderson* 115h 112c
10 b g Oscar Schindler(IRE) Misty Silks (Scottish Reel I (IRE))
163[4] 2568[P] 2884[7] 3257[U] 4464[P] 5164[4] 5379[4]

Padge (IRE) *Evan Williams* 134h 146c
6 b g Flemensfirth(USA) Mona Vic (IRE) (Old Vic)
(2184) 3029[U] 3774[U] 4139[3] ◆ 4730[15]

Padova *Dr Jeremy Naylor* 86h
9 b g Shahrastani(USA) My Song Of Songs (Norwick (USA))
749[7] 2267[6] 2713[8] 3256[9] 4885[8] 5431[P]

Padraig's Joy (IRE) *David Harry Kelly* 118h 127c
7 b m Vinnie Roe(IRE) Mattys Joy (IRE) (Beneficial)
2227a[3]

Padre Tito (IRE) *Emma Lavelle* 74h
7 b g Milan Augusta Brook (IRE) (Over The River (FR))
363[P] 647[3] 1055[4] 1642[P]

Page Turner (IRE) *John J Walsh* 132h 146c
10 b g Bishop Of Cashel I'm A Character (Tragic Role (USA))
3302a[P]

Pagham Belle *Nigel Hawke* 92h 95c
7 b m Brian Boru Sambara (IRE) (Shardari)
183[5] 646[5]

Pain Au Chocolat (FR) *Dan Skelton* 145h 150c
4 b g Enrique Clair Chene (FR) (Solido (FR))
94a[5] 1969[3] (3153) (3935) ◆ 4253[3] 5324[F]

Painters Lad (IRE) *Alison Hamilton* 65b
4 b g Fruits Of Love(USA) Great Cullen (IRE) (Simply Great (FR))
2195[8]

Paint The Clouds *Warren Greatrex* 131h 144c
10 b g Muhtarram(USA) Preening (Persian Bold)
535[2] (4307) 4768[3]

Pairofbrowneyes (IRE) *Barry John Murphy* 128h 136c
6 b g Luso Frankly Native (IRE) (Be My Native (USA))
(3302a)

Pair Of Jacks (IRE) *Malcolm Jefferson* 124h 134c
7 ch g Presenting Halona (Pollerton)
(138) (395) ◆ 5473[4]

Paladin (IRE) *Dominic Ffrench Davis*
6 b g Dubawi(IRE) Palwina (FR) (Unfuwain (USA))
1975[P]

Palermo Don *Donald McCain* 92h
5 b g Beat Hollow Kristal Bridge (Kris)
1718[5] 2066[12]

Palfrey Boy *Chris Down*
9 b g Tamure(IRE) Fresh Gale (Gildoran)
2660[P]

Palmaria *Caroline Keevil* 95h
5 b m Kayf Tara Ollejess (Scallywag)
45[4] 1574[6] 1752[5] 2444[3] 2812[8] 3950[6]

Palmello *Ann Hamilton* 69h
4 gr g Great Palm(USA) Miss Royello (Royal Fountain)
1683[9] 2806[R]

Palmerino (FR) *E Leenders* 96h
4 b g Doctor Dino(FR) Palmeriade (FR) (Kouroun (FR))
2362a[8]

Palmers Bridge *Linda Blackford* 63b
6 b g With The Flow(USA) Exit (Exbourne (USA))
392[12] 644[10] 1843[9] 2351[13]

Palm Grey (IRE) *Sue Smith* 117h 98c
7 gr g Great Palm(USA) Lucy Cooper (IRE) (Roselier (FR))
356[6] (2867) 3235[3] 3728[4] (4301) 4801[9]

Palm Valley *Chris Grant*
5 gr m Great Palm(USA) Ashworth Valley (Primitive Rising (USA))
5351[4]

Paloma's Prince (IRE) *Richard Phillips* 98h
6 ch g Nayef(USA) Ma Paloma (FR) (Highest Honor (FR))
5453[8]

Palus San Marco (IRE) *Jennie Candlish* 41h
6 b g Holy Roman Emperor(IRE) Kylemore (IRE) (Sadler's Wells (USA))
843[10]

Palypso De Creek (FR) *M N Dawson* 117h 134c
12 b g Brier Creek(USA) Belgheera (FR) (Vorias (USA))
(4000)

Pamak D'Airy (FR) *Henry Hogarth* 105h 112c
12 b g Cadoubel(FR) Gamaska D'Airy (FR) (Marasali)
36[3] 2788[5] 2979[2] 3441[5] 3938[4] 4300[5] 4707[5] 5197[4]

Pampanini *Harry Fry* 92b
4 b m Milan Loxhill Lady (Supreme Leader)
4468[5] 5383[4]

Pandorica *Bernard Llewellyn* 111h
7 b m Indesatchel(IRE) Hope Chest (Kris)
178[2] (714) 2852[5] 3080[5] 3932[11] 4390[4] 4538[F] (Dead)

Pandy Wells *Graeme McPherson* 78h 94c
6 b m Kayf Tara Alina Rheinberg (GER) (Waky Nao)
40[F] 2298[5] 2855[5] (3224) ◆ 3834[5] 4275[2] 4491[P] (4980) 5375[5]

Panis Angelicus (FR) *Tim Vaughan* 116h
6 b g Panis(USA) Pyu (GER) (Surumu (GER))
834[4] 1153[2] (1295) 1419[5] (2087) 4965[4]

Panopticon *Giles Bravery* 77b
4 ch m Lucky Story(USA) Barnacla (IRE) (Bluebird (USA))
558[6] 865[9]

Pantoloni *Richard Harper*
4 b g Dansili Short Skirt (Diktat)
2299[U] 2488[F] 3227[P]

Pantxoa (FR) *Alan King* 106h 147c
8 b g Daliapour(IRE) Palmeria (FR) (Great Palm (USA))
916[7] 1040[P] 5390[P]

Pao De Acuca (IRE) *Jose Santos* 85h
3 b g Rip Van Winkle(IRE) Splendeur (FR) (Desert King (IRE))
4875[8]

Paolozzi (IRE) *Seamus Durack* 127h
6 b g Oscar(IRE) Miss Eurolink (Touching Wood (USA))
(680) (832) 971[2] 1448[5]

Paper Lady (IRE) *Jimmy Frost* 71h
7 b m Beneficial Strong Craft (Warcraft (USA))
713[P]

Paper Roses (IRE) *Donald Whillans* 104b
4 b m Gamut(IRE) Rose Vic (IRE) (Old Vic)
2756[3] 4708[2]

Papradon *Nigel Twiston-Davies* 40h 124c
11 b g Tobougg(IRE) Salvezza (IRE) (Superpower)
557[4] 873[P] 1298[P]

Paradis Blanc (FR) *Nigel Twiston-Davies* 67h
4 b g Early March Mont Paradis (FR) (Baryshnikov (AUS))
2493[8] 3316[P] 3949[7]

Paradise Valley (IRE) *Mick Channon* 126h 120c
6 b g Presenting Native Wood (IRE) (Be My Native (USA))
84[3] 329[5]

Parc Des Princes (USA) *Nicky Richards* 106h
9 bb g Ten Most Wanted(USA) Miss Orah (Unfuwain (USA))
2069[10] 2751[2] 3223[7]

Parc Monceau (FR) *Patrice Quinton* 119h 116c
4 b g Trempolino(USA) Where Is Fleur (FR) (Exit To Nowhere (USA))
5385a[5]

Pareto (CZE) *Cestmir Olehla* 102c
8 ch g Rainbows For Life(CAN) Pulnoc (CZE) (Shy Groom (USA))
1885a[B]

Pariah (IRE) *M F O'Dowd* 98b
6 b m Hurricane Run(IRE) Multaka (USA) (Gone West (USA))
2677a[7]

Parish Business (IRE) *Emma Lavelle* 134h 131c
7 bb g Fruits Of Love(USA) Parkality (IRE) (Good Thyne (USA))
1520[U] 1642[3] 2240[4] 2631[P]

Parisian Star *J R Jenkins* 72b
3 ch f Champs Elysees Cavallo Da Corsa (Galileo (IRE))
3118[6] 4075[3] 4974[4]

Paris Snow *Ian Williams* 113h
5 b g Montjeu(IRE) Snow Key (USA) (Cozzene (USA))
2519[9] 2860[13] 2995[10] 3316[5] 3508[6] (4782) ◆

Pariyan (FR) *Donald McCain* 82h
3 ch c Sinndar(IRE) Pink And Red (USA) (Red Ransom (USA))
1495[3] 3967[5]

Parkam Jack *Mrs Kayley Woollacott* 102h 119c
9 b g Grape Tree Road Rakajack (Rakaposhi King)
(270) 3958[4] 5186[3]

Park House *Ray Craggs* 89h
6 b g Tillerman Rasin Luck (Primitive Rising (USA))
132[5] 522[7] 1368[2]

Parkie Boy *Nicky Richards* 72h
4 b g Central Park(IRE) Parlour Game (Petoski)
79[7] 452[U]

Park Light (FR) *B Lefevre* 146h
5 b g Walk In The Park(IRE) Yellow Light (FR) (Lightning (FR))
(4960a)

Park Place *John Quinn* 103h
5 b g Beat Hollow Blend (Zafonic (USA))
3022[4] 3309[P]

Parles Pond (IRE) *Martin Todhunter* 94h
6 b g Presenting Madam Newmill (IRE) (Taipan (IRE))
153[3] 726[5] 845[7]

Parlour Games *John Ferguson* 148h 137c
7 ch g Monsun(GER) Petrushka (IRE) (Unfuwain (USA))
2063[3]

Parlour Of Dreams (IRE) *Andrew Hamilton* 91h 54c
8 ch g Definite Article Wyndham Miss Sally (IRE) (Flemensfirth (USA))
1774[8] 2025[P] 2189[6] **2475[4] 2753[F] 2947[P] 3683[F]**

Parsnip Pete *Tom George* 109h 132c
9 b g Pasternak Bella Coola (Northern State (USA))
103[7] 2784[P] 3030[12]

Part And Parcel (IRE) *Alan Phillips* 102h
7 b g Zerpour(IRE) Carriacou (Mark Of Esteem (IRE))
877[3] 1044[4] 1292[6]

Parthian Empire *Seamus Mullins* 62h 56c
9 b g Parthian Springs Dudeen (IRE) (Anshan)
151[P] 429[4] 752[5]

Par Three (IRE) *Tony Carroll* 58h
4 bb g Azamour(IRE) Little Whisper (IRE) (Be My Guest (USA))
2196[7]

Parting Way (IRE) *Tim Vaughan* 108h 104c
7 b g Golan(IRE) Best Mother (IRE) (King's Theatre (IRE))
3379[4] 4187[P] 5377[5]

Party Palace *Stuart Howe* 105h
11 b m Auction House(USA) Lady-Love (Pursuit Of Love)
162[3] ◆ 718[7] 775[6] 826[4] 1046[7] 1238[4] 1490[7] 1618[6] 2006[7]

Party Rock (IRE) *Jennie Candlish* 140h
8 b g Vinnie Roe(IRE) Garryduff Eile (IRE) (Oscar (IRE))
4801[P] (5189) 5497[16]

Pasquini Rouge (FR) *Patrice Quinton* 79h 111c
7 b g Passing Sale(FR) Scevollia (FR) (Dom Pasquini (FR))
1885a[10]

Passato (GER) *Jo Davis* 103h 127c
11 b g Lando(GER) Passata (FR) (Polar Falcon (USA))
362[6] 568[3] 863[5] 1350[6]

Passing Du Moulin (FR) *Harry Whittington* 53b
4 gr g Passing Sale(FR) Ruaha River (FR) (Villez (USA))
4162[4]

Passing Fiesta *Sarah-Jayne Davies* 87h 90c
6 b m Passing Glance Clarice Starling (Saddlers' Hall (IRE))
383[P] 2565[P] **3834[9] 4275[3] 4686[2] 4850[5]**

Passing Lore (FR) *Yannick Fouin* 121h
4 b m Passing Sale(FR) Fille Fidele (FR) (Lost World (IRE))
2362a[13]

Passmore *Alan King* 94b
3 b f Passing Glance Call Me A Legend (Midnight Legend)
1772[2] ◆ 2304[2] 3632[3] 5443[8]

Pass Muster *Philip Kirby* 86h
8 b g Theatrical(IRE) Morning Pride (IRE) (Machiavellian (USA))
5246[10]

Pass On The Mantle *Julian Smith* 82h
7 b g Bollin Eric Swiss Rose (Michelozzo (USA))
26[P] 3334[P] (5441)

Pass The Hat *A L T Moore* 124h 147c
8 ch g Karinga Bay Moor Spring (Primitive Rising (USA))
24a[P] 3860[4] 5193[11]

Pass The Time *Neil Mulholland* 141h 122c
6 b m Passing Glance Twin Time (Syrtos)
93a[7] **2602[2]** 3034[P] 3858[4] 4699[4]

Password (FR) *Mlle T Puitg* 140h
6 b g Poliglote Maia Eria (FR) (Volochine (IRE))
836a[2]

Patavium (IRE) *Edwin Tuer* 79h
12 b g Titus Livius(FR) Arcevia (IRE) (Archway (IRE))
1887[13]

Patience Tony (IRE) *Alan Swinbank* 108b
4 b g Windsor Knot(IRE) Johar Jamal (IRE) (Chevalier (IRE))
2984[5] 4156[5]

Patricktom Boru (IRE) *Evan Williams* 99h 110c
8 b g Brian Boru Brehon Law (IRE) (Alphabatim (USA))
(438) (552) **610[3]** (879) **926[2] 1079[4] 1287[2]**

Patronne (FR) *Harry Whittington* 72h
3 b f Solon(GER) Parla (GER) (Lagunas)
4157[P] 5153[11] 5373[7]

Pattara *Noel Williams* 94h
6 b m Kayf Tara Fortunes Course (IRE) (Crash Course)
864[P] 1084[8] (1423) 1691[9] 2298[2]

Paul (FR) *Rebecca Curtis* 35b
4 b g Boris De Deauville(IRE) Bartjack (FR) (Lost World (IRE))
4827[8]

Pauls Conn (IRE) *Mary Sanderson* 92h
6 ch g Whitmore's Conn(USA) Toute Aplomb (IRE) (Toulon)
160[4] 509[4] 716[5] 823[5]

Pawn Star (IRE) *Emma Lavelle* 107h
5 b g Beneficial Missindependence (IRE) (Executive Perk)
2257[P] 3736[3] 4198[4] 5314[3]

Pay The King (IRE) *Micky Hammond* 97h 100c
8 b g King's Theatre(IRE) Knocktartan (IRE) (King's Ride)
2749[7] 3427[6] 3792[6] ◆ **4514[5] 4571[2] 4866[U] 4940[P] 5126[3] 5350[2]**

Pay Your Way (IRE) *David Rees* 93h
7 gr g Cloudings(IRE) Supreme Bond (IRE) (Supreme Leader)
2004[F] (2165) 2987[12]

Peace And Co (FR) *Nicky Henderson* 159h
4 b g Falco(USA) Peace Lina (FR) (Linamix (FR))
3033[6] 3989[3] 4698[P]

Peaceful Gardens *Jeremy Scott* 73h
6 b m Franklins Gardens So Peaceful (Prince Of Peace)
824[2] ◆ 1599[5] 1756[10] 1961[5] 2245[7]

Peachey Moment (USA) *Nicky Richards* 80h 114c
10 bb g Stormin Fever(USA) Given Moment (USA) (Diesis)
885[2]

Peak Seasons (IRE) *Michael Chapman* 62h 63c
12 ch g Raise A Grand(IRE) Teresian Girl (IRE) (Glenstal (USA))
841[6] 1069[4]

Peak Storm *John O'Shea* 86h
6 b g Sleeping Indian Jitterbug (IRE) (Marju (IRE))
1702[6]

Peal Of Bells *Henry Daly* 85h
4 b m Martaline Tambourine Ridge (IRE) (Tamure (IRE))
4074[10] 4468[7] 4743[3]

Pearl Castle (IRE) *K R Burke* 138h
5 b g Montjeu(IRE) Ghurra (USA) (War Chant (USA))
3426[2] 4014[9]

Pearlita *Henry Daly* 69b
3 b f Milan Pearl Buttons (Alflora (IRE))
5286[10]

Pearls Legend *John Spearing* 122h 143c
8 b g Midnight Legend Pearl's Choice (IRE) (Deep Run)
2185[2] 2468[3] 2784[3] (3030) 3446[5] 4469[2] 4770[5] 5179[4]

Pearl Swan (FR) *Peter Bowen* 136h 134c
7 b g Gentlewave(IRE) Swanson (USA) (Diesis)
196[4] 1846[6] 2055[6]

Pearlysteps *Henry Daly* 114h 138c
12 ch g Alflora(IRE) Pearly-B (IRE) (Gunner B)
75a[3] 3585[U] (4249) (4748) 4892[2]

Peckhamecho (IRE) *Sophie Leech* 120h 114c
9 b g Beneficial Nolans Pride (IRE) (Good Thyne (USA))
1070[5]

Pecuchet (FR) *T Civel*
2 gr g Stormy River(FR) Chene De Coeur (FR) (Comrade In Arms)
4539a[P]

Pegasus Walk (IRE) *Rose Dobbin* 87h
6 b g Beneficial Porter Tastes Nice (IRE) (Dry Dock)
139[5] 522[6]

Peggies Venture *Nick Gifford* 94b
4 b m Presenting Peggies Run (Kayf Tara)
(4532)

Peggy Do (IRE) *Nicky Henderson* 53h
7 b m Pierre So Marvellous (IRE) (Luso)
387[3]

Peintre Abstrait (IRE) *Radek Holcak*
9 ch g Peintre Celebre(USA) Prairie Runner (IRE) (Arazi (USA))
1885a[F]

Pekanheim (IRE) *Martin Todhunter* 102h 105c
7 b g Putra Pekan Delheim (IRE) (Un Desperado (FR))
76[F] 200[4] (487) **(639) 800[3] 1639[5] 1855[5] 2030[5] 2475[P] 3670[F] 3938[3] 4288[5]** 4570[4] 4815[3] ◆

Pemba (FR) *Alan King* 110h
3 ch f Zanzibari(USA) Ayaam (IRE) (Danehill (USA))
2273[2] (3338) (3587) 4338[5] 5095[F] 5139[4]

Pembridge *Adrian Wintle* 75h
6 b m Kayf Tara Supreme Gem (IRE) (Supreme Leader)
89[P] 1478[3] 1910[7] 2264[3] ◆ 2565[5]

Pembroke House *Sarah-Jayne Davies* 109h 109c
8 gr g Terimon Bon Coeur (Gunner B)
43[5] **2596[2] 2859[5] (3195) 4042[2] 4431[P] 5379[2]**

Pena Dorada (IRE) *Alan J Brown* 112h 123c
8 b g Key Of Luck(USA) Uluwatu (IRE) (Unfuwain (USA))
(847) (1033) 1309[2] 4016[2] ◆ **4768[15] 5090[4]**

Pencilhimin (IRE) *Norman Cassidy* 135h 113c
10 b g Presenting Una Juna (IRE) (Good Thyne (USA))
2676a[12]

Pendra (IRE) *Charlie Longsdon* 140h 149c
7 ch g Old Vic Mariah Rollins (IRE) (Over The River (FR))
(2187) 3150[5] 5218[13]

Penglai Pavilion (USA) *John Ferguson* 146h
5 bb g Monsun(GER) Maiden Tower (Groom Dancer (USA))
(727) (1052) (2052) 2470[3] 4695[12]

Pengo's Boy *Stuart Kittow* 112h
6 gr g Proclamation(IRE) Homeoftheclassics (Tate Gallery (USA))
119[6] 2457[4] 2989[7]

Penmore Mill (IRE) *F A Hutsby* 131c
10 b g Shernazar Stephens Street (IRE) (Kahyasi)
12[3] (4424) 5121[2]

Pennant Dancer *Debra Hamer* 102h
8 b g Grape Tree Road Pennant Princess (Alflora (IRE))
(40) (530) 615[8] 1375[P] 1897[P]

Pennant Lady *Debra Hamer* 54b
5 bb m Black Sam Bellamy(IRE) Pennant Princess (Alflora (IRE))
971[U] 1082[P] 1574[P]

Pennies And Pounds *Julian Smith* 87h
8 b m Sir Harry Lewis(USA) Sense Of Value (Trojan Fen)
55[5] 569[8] 2841[P] **3421[U]**

Pennine Panther *Sam Thomas* 50h
4 b g Notnowcato Kozmina (IRE) (Sadler's Wells (USA))
2860[10] 3842[8]

Penn Lane (IRE) *Warren Greatrex* 126h
4 b g Scorpion(IRE) Belsalsa (FR) (Kingsalsa (USA))
(2493) 3063[3] 4323[F]

Penny Boo (IRE) *Brian Ellison*
3 b f Acclamation Daqtora (Dr Devious (IRE))
1037[4]

Penny Option (IRE) *Robert Stephens* 70b
6 b m Gamut(IRE) Ticklepenny (IRE) (In The Wings)
152[6] 594[8] 3570[P] 3953[P]

Pennywell (IRE) *Warren Greatrex* 106h
5 b m Gold Well Boyne Bridge (IRE) (Lord Americo)
2697[6] 4039[2] 4337[2] 5079[5] 5355[5]

Pentiffic (NZ) *P P C Turner* 126c
11 br g Pentire Sailing High (NZ) (Yachtie (AUS))
17[5] 535[P] 4651[U] (4887)

Penzflo (IRE) *Johnny Farrelly* 81h
9 b m Luso Penzita (IRE) (The Bart (USA))
120[2] 695[P] 5420[8]

Pepite Rose (FR) *Venetia Williams* 113h 158c
8 bb m Bonbon Rose(FR) Sambre (FR) (Turgeon (USA))
(2335) 2927[2] 3337[F]

Pepito Collonges (FR) *Laura Mongan* 35h 13c
12 b g Brier Creek(USA) Berceuse Collonges (FR) (Vorias (USA))
675[11] 1545[P]

Peppay Le Pugh (IRE) *Nicky Henderson* 108b
4 b g Arakan(USA) Pinaflore (FR) (Formidable I (USA))
188[2] 4102[4]

Perceus *James Eustace* 115h
3 b g Sir Percy Lady Hestia (USA) (Belong To Me (USA))
2863[2] (3139) 3610[2] 3994[4] 4799[6]

Percys Choice (IRE) *Matt Sheppard* 97h
7 b g Choisir(AUS) Solemn Promise (IRE) (Entrepreneur)
1702[8] 1980[3] **2151[P]**

Perennial *Philip Kirby* 107h
6 ch g Motivator Arum Lily (USA) (Woodman (USA))
843[4] 2550[2] 2948[4]

Perfect Candidate (IRE) *Fergal O'Brien* 120h 155c
8 b g Winged Love(IRE) Dansana (IRE) (Insan (USA))
2061[2] 2482[5] (3404) 4735[10] (5283)

Perfect Gentleman (IRE) *W P Mullins* 140h 140c
10 b g King's Theatre(IRE) Millennium Lilly (IRE) (Mujadil (USA))
374a[4] 664a[U] 1152a[7] 1672a[F]

Perfect Poison (IRE) *Donald McCain* 104h
7 b g Vinnie Roe(IRE) Noddys Confusion (IRE) (Supreme Leader)
2291[4] 2745[5] 2964[P] (3973) 4703[8] 5314[P]

Perfect Promise (IRE) *James Joseph Mangan* 104b 133c
7 b m Presenting Snape (IRE) (Strong Gale)
70a[6] 2465a[3] 3296a[P] 5006a[3]

Perfect Summer (IRE) *Ian Williams* 102h
5 b m High Chaparral(IRE) Power Of Future (GER) (Definite Article)
3777[8] 4490[2] 4854[3]

Perfect Swing (IRE) *Jonjo O'Neill* 65h
4 b g Milan Lakil Princess (IRE) (Bering)
4344[11] 4788[P]

Perfect Timing (FR) *Paul Webber* 75h
5 b m Sassanian(USA) Royale Sulawesie (FR) (Jimble (FR))
1898[9] 2452[8] 2841[P] 5441[8]

Perfect Timing *Neil Mulholland* 93h 132c
7 b g Shantou(USA) Winnetka Gal (IRE) (Phardante (FR))
(510) 598[4] (915) 1040[P] 1322[6] 1722[4] 2057[12] 2404[P] 5354[8]

Perfect Woman (IRE) *Michael Winters* 124h 126c
7 b m Blueprint(IRE) Garrisker (IRE) (King's Ride)
3093a[2] 3604a[5]

Perform (IRE) *Philip Hobbs* 136h
6 b g King's Theatre(IRE) Famous Lady (IRE) (Presenting)
(2080)

Periquest *Alex Hales* 103h
6 b g Overbury(IRE) Rippling Brook (Phardante (FR))
2560[2] (2924)

Perseid (IRE) *Sue Smith* 103h
5 br g Robin Des Pres(FR) Cowanstown Miss (IRE) (Presenting)
937[8] 1084[3] 1273[2] 1375[7] (1599) (1683) 1856[8] 2142[2] 2595[4] 3886[5] 5081[2]

Pershing *Robert Alan Hennessy* 112h
4 gr g Mount Nelson La Gandilie (FR) (Highest Honor (FR))
866[2] 1168[3]

Persian Breeze *Lucy Wadham* 95h
3 b f Pivotal Persian Jasmine (Dynaformer (USA))
4317[4] 4773[4] 5091[6] 5373[5]

Persian Fashion (IRE) *Ian Duncan*
6 b m Lahib(USA) Kiera's Gale (IRE) (Strong Gale)
656[P] 727[10] 2100[P]

Persian Herald *Dianne Sayer* 104h 103c
7 gr g Proclamation(IRE) Persian Fortune (Forzando)
205[3] **504[7]** 851[5]

Persian Steel (IRE) *Brian Ellison* 73b
3 ch g Lucarno(USA) Persian Walk (FR) (Persian Bold)
4156[7]

Persiflage *Gordon Elliott* 98h
3 b f Sir Percy Emirates First (IRE) (In The Wings)
(1631)

Personable *John Ferguson* 112h
5 b g Cape Cross(IRE) Likeable (Dalakhani (IRE))
860[2] ◆

Personal Shopper *H Smyth* 94h 87c
8 b m King's Theatre(IRE) Island Hopper (Be My Native (USA))
5234[3]

Perspicace *David Pipe* 114h
4 b g Sir Percy Cassique Lady (IRE) (Langfuhr (CAN))
645[6] 1100[4] 1239[5] 1347[3] 1579[5] 1818[4] 2458[9] 5433[2] ◆

Petapenko *Malcolm Jefferson* 107h
4 b g Archipenko(USA) Tricoteuse (Kris)
(39) 1640[5] 2066[3] 5408[10]

Peterbrown (IRE) *Mrs K Heard* 107h 109c
7 b g Shantou(USA) Grove Juliet (IRE) (Moscow Society (USA))
5035[5]

Petergate *Nigel Hawke* 76h
4 b g Alhaarth(IRE) Shamayel (Pivotal)
3368[13] 4490[3]

Peterpanopirateman (IRE) *Ben Case* 98h
6 b g Kalanisi(IRE) Year'Fthehorse (IRE) (Zaffaran (USA))
2720[3]

Peters Grey (IRE) *R Mike Smith* 115h
5 gr g Aussie Rules(USA) Aliyshan (IRE) (Darshaan)
142[2] 301[5] 520[3]

Peter Silver (FR) *Giles Smyly* 126h 95c
4 b g Silver Cross(FR) Sainte Mante (FR) (Saint Des Saints (FR))
5452[6]

Peter The Horse *Joanne Thomason-Murphy* 88b
8 b g Groom Dancer(USA) Broughton Melody (Alhijaz)
5387[P]

Peter The Mayo Man (IRE) *Neil Mulholland* 115h
5 ch g Dylan Thomas(IRE) Mommkin (Royal Academy (USA))
4303[4] 4714[4]

Pete The Feat (IRE) *Charlie Longsdon* 83h 140c
11 b g King's Theatre(IRE) Tourist Attraction (IRE) (Pollerton)
2517[6] 2955[2] 3591[4] 3993[2] 4483[2] 5119[10]

Petethepear (IRE) *Stuart Edmunds* 129h
5 br g Pierre Rockababy (IRE) (King's Ride)
1704[3] 2265[2] 3133[5] 3626[5] 4241[3] (4911)

Petilucky (FR) *L Viel* 85h
4 b g Ultimately Lucky(IRE) La Petite Angevine (FR) (Sandhurst Prince)
2362a[12]

Petit Ecuyer (FR) *Dai Williams* 77h 74c
9 b g Equerry(USA) Petite Majeste (FR) (Riverquest (FR))
211[P] 2255[5] 2666[4] 2735[P] 3088[2] 3131[4] 3199[3] 3468[5] 4776[3] 4980[2] 5236[2] 5442[5]

Petite Fantasie *Mark Gillard* 84h
6 b m Flemensfirth(USA) Rowlands Dream (IRE) (Accordion)
222[10] 2263[12] 2567[P] 3410[2] 3789[7] 4138[3]

Petite Gold (IRE) *Gordon Elliott* 81b
4 b g Gold Well Petite Mielle (IRE) (Pasternak)
11a[20]

Petite Madame (IRE) *David Thompson* 43h
4 b m Champs Elysees Seeking The Fun (USA) (Alhaarth (IRE))
846[6]

Petite Parisienne (FR) *W P Mullins* 143h
4 gr m Montmartre(FR) Ejina (FR) (Highest Honor (FR))
(94a) 665a[9] 2353a[2] 3444[7] 4125[4]

Petite Power (IRE) *Ali Stronge* 108h
6 b g Subtle Power(IRE) Little Serena (Primitive Rising (USA))
320[4] 644[5] 2972[2] ◆ 3580[6] 4097[6] 4883[6]

Petit Mouchoir (FR) *W P Mullins* 154h
4 gr g Al Namix(FR) Arnette (FR) (Denham Red (FR))
(9a) 3294a[3] 4004a[4] 4695[8] 5190[2]

Petre' Island (IRE) *Katie Scott* 64h
6 b m Pierre Bannow Island (IRE) (Heron Island (IRE))
136[P] 2071[7] 2323[P] 2706[P]

Petrify *Bernard Llewellyn* 59h
5 b g Rock Of Gibraltar(IRE) Frigid (Indian Ridge)
2150[5] 2363[6] 2538[6]

Petrou (IRE) *Ben Case* 109h
5 b g Mountain High(IRE) Evnelu (IRE) (Old Vic)
2221[6] 2581[4] 3009[2] 4041[3] 4432[5] 5079[10]

Pettal *Sarah-Jayne Davies* 19b
4 b m Indian Danehill(IRE) Fields Of Home (IRE) (Synefos (USA))
3381[7] 3863[6] 4344[P]

Petuna (IRE) *M Phelan* 101b
5 b m Aussie Rules(USA) Sue N Win (IRE) (Beneficial)
2677a^{11}

Phakos (FR) *P Cottin* 119c
12 b g Robin Des Champs(FR) Tipperary II (FR) (Chamberlin (FR))
313a^F

Phangio (USA) *Colin Bowe* 112h 108c
6 ch g Invasor(ARG) Muneera (USA) (Green Dancer (USA))
1184a^{17}

Phantom Prince (IRE) *Jimmy Frost* 134h 47c
6 b g Jeremy(USA) Phantom Waters (Pharly (FR))
19a^5 1175a^{10} 3956^P 4252^6 5030^8 5382^{12}

Pharawaydante (IRE) *Norman Sanderson*
7 gr g Cloudings(IRE) Waydante (IRE) (Phardante (FR))
4016^P

Phar Away Island (IRE) *John Berwick* 45h
7 br g Heron Island(IRE) Phar From Men (IRE) (Phardante (FR))
3369^5 4682^P

Phare Isle (IRE) *Ben Case* 122h 120c
10 b g Turtle Island(IRE) Pharenna (IRE) (Phardante (FR))
50a^{20} 625^3 916^6 2912^8 3728^P 4305^7 4543^3 4983^2 5440^5

Phar Island (IRE) *Thomas Mullins* 108h
4 b g Trans Island Queen Of Harts (IRE) (Phardante (FR))
9a^{13}

Phase Shift *Harriet Bethell* 114h 74c
7 b m Iceman Silent Waters (Polish Precedent (USA))
137^5

Philba *Michael Appleby* 43h
3 b g Cockney Rebel(IRE) Hisaronu (IRE) (Stravinsky (USA))
1768^5 1928^P

Philharmonic Hall *Peter Hiatt* 94h
7 b g Victory Note(USA) Lambast (Relkino)
2413^P 2703^2 ◆

Phil's Magic (IRE) *Ms Sandra Hughes* 133h 130c
5 bb g Fruits Of Love(USA) Inch Rose (IRE) (Eurobus)
72a^6

Phil The Flyer (IRE) *Ray Hackett* 137h
8 b g Broadway Flyer(USA) Graigueheshia (IRE) (Strong Gale)
2236a^{14}

Phobiaphiliac (IRE) *Nicky Henderson* 104b
4 b g Beneficial Denys Eyre (IRE) (Eurobus)
4102^6 4880^5

Phoeniciana *Lucy Wadham* 99b
4 b m Phoenix Reach(IRE) Viciana (Sir Harry Lewis (USA))
4074^5

Phoenix Des Mottes (FR) *John Cornwall* 56h 79c
12 b g Useful(FR) Camille Des Mottes (FR) (Abdonski (FR))
88^P

Phone Home (IRE) *Nick Mitchell* 120h 133c
8 bb g Heron Island(IRE) Ancestral Voices (IRE) (Strong Gale)
2404^6 2780^F (Dead)

Pibrac (FR) *C Scandella* 126h 131c
11 ch g Spadoun(FR) Palissandre (FR) (Phantom Breeze)
437a^P

Picasso Do Brasil (FR) *P Chevillard* 101h 78c
4 b g Chichi Creasy(FR) Margie's Gold (GER) (Java Gold (USA))
3815a^P

Piccolino (FR) *P Peltier*
5 gr g Falco(USA) Peace Lina (FR) (Linamix (FR))
4540a^P

Piccomore *Polly Gundry* 13h
5 b m Morpeth Ivorsagoodun (Piccolo)
2016^7 3573^8 4681^{12} 4854^P 5145^P

Pickamix *Rebecca Curtis* 98b
4 gr g Sagamix(FR) Star Of Wonder (FR) (The Wonder (FR))
2250^3

Pickle And Tickle (IRE) *George Bewley* 77b
5 ch g Shirocco(GER) Cream Of Society (IRE) (Selkirk (USA))
1555^8 1852^P

Picknick Park *Nick Kent* 78b
3 b g Sulamani(IRE) Eva's Edge (IRE) (Good Thyne (USA))
5337^4

Pick Up Trix (IRE) *Seamus Mullins* 75b
3 b f Flemensfirth(USA) Blossom Trix (IRE) (Saddlers' Hall (IRE))
5241^3

Picodean *Robert Stephens* 94b
7 b g Tikkanen(USA) Gipsy Girl (Motivate I)
146^6

Pied Du Roi (IRE) *Charlie Longsdon* 114h 77c
5 b g Robin Des Pres(FR) Long Acre (Mark Of Esteem (IRE))
(237) 1647^{12} 2029^2 2577^5 4455^4 4882^3 5267^P

Pigeon Island *Nigel Twiston-Davies* 131h 127c
12 gr g Daylami(IRE) Morina (USA) (Lyphard (USA))
(439) 553^6 1114^5

Pikarnia *John Wade* 88b
5 b g Authorized(IRE) Kartuzy (JPN) (Polish Precedent (USA))
257^3 640^3

Pikes Peak (IRE) *Chris Grant* 84h
6 br g Kutub(IRE) Accordionline (IRE) (Accordion)
1852^5 2210^P 3997^P

Pilansberg *Paul Nicholls* 118h
3 b c Rail Link Posteritas (USA) (Lear Fan (USA))
4358^7

Pilgrims Bay (IRE) *David Pipe* 123h
5 b g Turtle Island(IRE) Lady Ariadna (IRE) (Supreme Leader)
227^4 761^3 2265^6 2763^7 3411^5 (3705) 3923^2 ◆ 4206^3 4643^2 ◆ 5053^5

Pilgrims Lane (IRE) *Anthony Middleton* 99b
11 b g Dr Massini(IRE) Miss Mylette (IRE) (Torus)
109^P

Pilgrims Rest (IRE) *George Baker* 106h
6 ch g Rock Of Gibraltar(IRE) Holly Blue (Bluebird (USA))
2437^3 ◆ 2823^5 3077^4

Pillard (FR) *Jonjo O'Neill* 116h
3 b g Muhaymin(USA) Ultime Moment (IRE) (Anabaa (USA))
3443^2 4345^2 4720^{13} 5095^4

Pindar (GER) *Joanne Foster* 79h 87c
11 b g Tertullian(USA) Pierette (GER) (Local Suitor (USA))
256^3 504^4 841^8 964^P 1891^6

Pindare (FR) *J-P Gallorini* 127h 138c
6 b g Ballingarry(IRE) Orcantara (FR) (Villez (USA))
375a^U 664a^7 1884a^7 2822a^6

Pineau De Re (FR) *Dr Richard Newland* 142h 146c
12 b g Maresca Sorrento(FR) Elfe Du Perche (FR) (Abdonski (FR))
1871^8 2374^2 2899^F (3058) 4354^P **4483^7 5327^U**

Pine Creek *John Ferguson* 130h 140c
7 b g Doyen(IRE) Valley Of Gold (FR) (Shirley Heights)
2083^6 **2541^2 3026^2 ◆ 4067^3**

Pinerolo *Joanne Foster* 95h 126c
9 b g Milan Hollybush (IRE) (Ali-Royal (IRE))
(81) 2146^P 2471^{11} 2766^P 3127^5 3591^P 4866^4

Pine Warbler *Stuart Edmunds* 118h
6 b g Pilsudski(IRE) Cetti's Warbler (Sir Harry Lewis (USA))
2972^F 3316^3 3787^3

Ping (IRE) *Nicky Richards* 77h
4 b g Mahler Corravilla (IRE) (Yashgan)
727^9 3590^4 4548^8 5124^4 5445^{13}

Pink Coat *Ms Sandra Hughes* 124h 116c
8 gr g Alhaarth(IRE) In The Pink (IRE) (Indian Ridge)
7a^{16}

Pink Gin *Nigel Twiston-Davies* 79h
7 ch g Alflora(IRE) Miss Mailmit (Rakaposhi King)
3846^P 4301^7 4749^6

Pinkie Brown (FR) *Neil Mulholland* 118h
3 gr g Gentlewave(IRE) Natt Musik (FR) (Kendor (FR))
1656^2 1881a^7 (3790) 5116^5

Pink Play (IRE) *Harry Whittington* 122h
4 b m King's Theatre(IRE) Strawberry Fool (FR) (Tel Quel (FR))
1908^2 2452^2 (3066) (3995)

Pink Tara *Venetia Williams* 97h
4 b m Kayf Tara Red And White (IRE) (Red Ransom (USA))
2302^8 2769^4 3743^6 3930^5 4338^3 4616^6 5099^3

Pinnacle Panda (IRE) *Tom Lacey* 133h
4 b g Scorpion(IRE) Scartara (FR) (Linamix (FR))
320^3 1758^5 2807^4 (3375) (3994) 4305^2 4794^9 5213^{15}

Pinotage *Peter Niven* 94h
7 br g Danbird(AUS) Keen Melody (USA) (Sharpen Up)
1892^3 2291^5 2843^6

Pinson Du Rheu (FR) *G Cherel* 116h 139c
4 b g Al Namix(FR) Venus Du Rheu (FR) (Bricassar (USA))
2820a^7

Pirate's Penny (IRE) *Hugh Burns*
4 ch g Duke Of Marmalade(IRE) Sweet Wind Music (Zamindar (USA))
960^P

Pires *A J Martin* 120h 144c
11 br g Generous(IRE) Kaydee Queen (IRE) (Bob's Return (IRE))
47a^8 1186a^6

Pistol (IRE) *John Dixon* 124h 99c
6 b g High Chaparral(IRE) Alinea (USA) (Kingmambo (USA))
157^4 473^5 2190^6 2720^U 2802^2 3346^5 (4055) (4287) 4568^U

Pistol Basc (FR) *Rebecca Menzies* 94c
11 ch g Maille Pistol(FR) Moldane (FR) (Sicyos (USA))
140^6 519^3 841^3 (972) 1155^4 1402^6

Pithivier (FR) *Ben Pauling* 124h
5 b g Poliglote Kelbelange (FR) (Ganges (USA))
(2560) ◆ 3137^9

Piton Pete (IRE) *Oliver Sherwood* 102b
4 b g Westerner Glenair Lucy (IRE) (Luso)
2460^3 4508^2

Pivot Bridge *Adrian McGuinness* 129h 97c
7 ch g Pivotal Specifically (USA) (Sky Classic (CAN))
7a^6 231a^3

Pixie Cut (IRE) *Alistair Whillans* 97h
5 b m Chineur(FR) Fantastic Cee (IRE) (Noverre (USA))
1066^2 1420^4

Pixiepot *Peter Niven* 99h
5 b m Alflora(IRE) Folly Foster (Relkino)
594^9 846^5 1041^4 1178^6 1683^2 1971^3 2396^2 2867^2 3333^4

Plan Again (IRE) *Donald McCain* 123h 127c
8 b g Gamut(IRE) Niamh's Leader (IRE) (Supreme Leader)
154^5

Planetoid (IRE) *Jim Best* 120h
7 b g Galileo(IRE) Palmeraie (USA) (Lear Fan (USA))
(4411) 5301^2

Platinum Proof (USA) *John Berry*
5 bb g Smart Strike(CAN) Keeper Hill (USA) (Deputy Minister (CAN))
1943^P

Playhara (IRE) *Martin Todhunter* 111h
6 b m King's Theatre(IRE) Harringay (Sir Harry Lewis (USA))
314^4 482^8 1920^7 2142^P

Playing The Field (IRE) *Jonjo O'Neill* 96h 99c
10 b g Deploy Gaelic Buccaneer (IRE) (Un Desperado (FR))
2017^4 2539^P 2848^P

Play Practice *James Walton* 67h
5 b m Josr Algarhoud(IRE) More Flair (Alflora (IRE))
144^{10} 2804^P 3101^9 3342^5

Play The Ace (IRE) *A Pennock* 80b 87c
6 bb g Scorpion(IRE) Henris Blaze (IRE) (Be My Native (USA))
320^{11}

Play The Market (IRE) *Stuart Morris* 124h 67c
8 b g King's Theatre(IRE) Market Lass (IRE) (Orchestra)
260^6

Pleasant Company (IRE) *W P Mullins* 137h 145c
7 b g Presenting Katie Flame (IRE) (Alderbrook)
50a^3 96a^4 **4148a^3 4700^P**

Plettenburg Bay (IRE) *Sean Curran* 87b
10 b g Oscar Schindler(IRE) Fairyfort Queen (IRE) (Lord Americo)
968^P

Plexton *Karen McLintock* 70b
4 b g Multiplex Barichara (FR) (Exit To Nowhere (USA))
5014^6

Plinth (IRE) *A P O'Brien* 148h
5 b g Montjeu(IRE) Crazy Volume (IRE) (Machiavellian (USA))
1163a^{10} (1787a) 2386a^F 2532a^5 3358a^3 3768a^5 5004a^5

Plumeur (FR) *G Chaignon* 143h
8 b g Great Pretender(IRE) Plume Rose (FR) (Rose Laurel)
1883a^6 2361a^7 4540a^P 4960a^3

Plus Jamais (FR) *Jim Goldie* 111h 121c
8 b g Caballo Raptor(CAN) Branceilles (FR) (Satin Wood)
2192^3 2431^2 3157^4 3794^5 4167^2 4910^P 5411^5

Pobbles Bay (IRE) *Evan Williams* 124h
5 b g Oscar(IRE) Rose De Beaufai (FR) (Solon (GER))
2569^5 (3078) 3622^2 5239^4

Poetic Lord *Rebecca Menzies* 120h
6 b g Byron Jumairah Sun (IRE) (Scenic (IRE))
4553^5 4865^7

Poetic Presence (IRE) *Adrian Wintle* 62h
5 b m Presenting Johnston's Crest (IRE) (Be My Native (USA))
648^5 864^8 1098^{10} 1910^P 2565^2 2876^P 4490^5 4682^P

Poetic Verse *John Quinn* 126h
5 gr m Byron Nina Fontenail (FR) (Kaldounevees (FR))
(1180) 1974^4

Poet Mark (IRE) *Tim Easterby* 82h
3 b g Vale Of York(IRE) Attanagh (IRE) (Darnay)
1899^6 2286^2 2718^6 3099^9 3791^8 4943^P

Poetry Emotion (IRE) *Nicky Henderson* 87b
4 b g Gamut(IRE) Vivre Aimer Rire (FR) (Cyborg (FR))
213^9 2998^6

Poets Day *Katie Stephens* 57b
5 ch m Apple Tree(FR) Lady Blade (IRE) (Daggers Drawn (USA))
1843^7 2879^P

Pointillism *J J Lambe* 57h
3 b g Manduro(GER) Impressionism (IRE) (Elusive Quality (USA))
3423^5

Point The Way (IRE) *Brian Ellison* 136h
4 br g Brian Boru Caslain Og (IRE) (Supreme Leader)
1662^3 (1858) 2514^6 (3240) (3802) (4040) ◆ 4620^P

Poisoned Berry (IRE) *Fergal O'Brien* 95b
3 b f Scorpion(IRE) Prunelle (GER) (Waky Nao)
3632^2 ◆ 4468^2

Pokari (FR) *Alan Jones* 54b
3 ch g Bonbon Rose(FR) Pokara (FR) (Kutub (IRE))
5069^{10}

Poker School (IRE) *Ian Williams* 125h
5 b g Gold Well Broken Pockets (IRE) (Broken Hearted)
208^4 463^7 **2449^U** 3846^2 (4362) 4801^4

Polamco (IRE) *Harry Fry* 126h
6 b g Old Vic Shanesia (IRE) (Erins Isle)
2054^4

Polarbrook (IRE) *Derek Shaw* 106h 112c
8 br g Alderbrook Frozen Cello (IRE) (Arctic Lord (IRE))
1600^P 1931^8 2142^4 (2408) 2745^2 3023^2 3855^{18} 4041^4 4455^8 4862^5 5345^3 ◆

Polarisation *John Ferguson* 114h
3 b g Echo Of Light Concordia (Pivotal)
2883^2

Policy Breach (IRE) *Kim Bailey* 118h
4 b g Kayf Tara Just Stunning (IRE) (Presenting)
9a^2 2690^0 3063^4

Polished Rock (IRE) *Alison Batchelor* 55h
5 ch g Rock Of Gibraltar(IRE) Where We Left Off (Dr Devious (IRE))
5301^5

Polisky (FR) *Paul Nicholls* 131h 128c
8 b g Poliglote Dusky Royale (FR) (Double Bed (FR))
1948^2 (5121) 5392^4

Politeness (FR) *Rose Dobbin* 118h
6 b g Poliglote Martiniquaise (FR) (Anabaa (USA))
142^5 (520) (872) 1034^2 1331^2 1638^6

Political Quiz *Tom Symonds* 116h
5 b g Lucarno(USA) Quiz Night (Kayf Tara)
(2041) 2581^6 3117^F 3221^6 4429^4 5391^8

Politikar (FR) *G Macaire* 138h 134c
3 b g Poliglote Kitara (GER) (Camp David (GER))
1881a^6

Politologue (FR) *Paul Nicholls* 141h
4 gr g Poliglote Scarlet Row (FR) (Turgeon (USA))
3019^U 3350^2 (4138) 4717^{20}

Pollyogan (IRE) *Harry Fry* 86b
5 br m Oscar(IRE) Marlogan (IRE) (Presenting)
392^6 2016^3

Polly Peachum (IRE) *Nicky Henderson* 152h
7 b m Shantou(USA) Miss Denman (IRE) (Presenting)
2685^2 (3444) 4699^{10}

Polly's Pursuit (IRE) *Nicky Henderson* 83b
3 br f Westerner Miss Denman (IRE) (Presenting)
5443^5

Polo (GER) *Venetia Williams* 99h
5 ch g Sholokhov(IRE) Poule D'Essai (GER) (Dashing Blade)
3619^{11}

Polo Springs *Graeme McPherson*
8 gr m Baryshnikov(AUS) Cristal Springs (Dance Of Life (USA))
3223^P

Polo The Mumm (FR) *Jimmy Frost* 92h
5 b g Great Journey(JPN) Maido (FR) (French Glory)
1044^6 1117^5 1324^9 1980^P

Polstar (FR) *Harry Whittington* 120h 77c
6 b g Poliglote Star Dancing (Danehill Dancer (IRE))
43^6 399^3 (616) ◆ 692^6 1048^F 1265^6 (1421) 1714^4 (2093) 2688^3 5159^3

Polygona (FR) *J-Y Artu* 131h 129c
5 b m Poliglote Dona Rez (FR) (Trempolino (USA))
2821a^2 5428a^5

Pomander (IRE) *J Moon* 82h
12 b m Bob's Return(IRE) Pheisty (Faustus (USA))
236a^2 740a^3 985a^5

Pomicide *Sue Gardner* 37h
5 ch g With The Flow(USA) The Swan (Old Vic)
3959^7 4188^4 4821^F 5029^U 5161^7 5268^9 5378^U

Pomme *Nigel Hawke* 102h
4 b m Observatory(USA) Mirthful (USA) (Miswaki (USA))
3021^4

Pomme Rouge *Neil Mulholland*
5 ch g Apple Tree(FR) Lavender Dancer (Tragic Role (USA))
5069^{13}

Pont Alexandre (GER) *W P Mullins* 156h 152c
7 b g Dai Jin Panzella (FR) (Kahyasi)
3635a^2 4005a^3 4700^P (Dead)

Ponte Fortune (FR) *Francois Nicolle* 112h
3 b f Soldier Of Fortune(IRE) Panzella (FR) (Kahyasi)
4959a^4

Poole Master *David Pipe* 119h 152c
10 ch g Fleetwood(IRE) Juste Belle (FR) (Mansonnien (FR))
2643^6 2902^7 3528^P 4347^5

Popaway *Mrs Pauline Harkin* 116c
10 b m Nomadic Way(USA) Sea Poppy (Baron Blakeney)
12^7 260^4

Popelys Gull (IRE) *Pam Sly* 87b
3 ch g Recharge(IRE) Circus Rose (Most Welcome)
4308^{10} 4867^{10}

Poppies Milan (IRE) *Rebecca Menzies* 93h
6 b g Milan Second Best (IRE) (Supreme Leader)
805^2 883^4

Popping Along *Jeremy Scott* 113h
6 ch m Volochine(IRE) So Long (Nomadic Way (USA))
(462) 714^4 1136^4 (1354) 1841^4 2455^6 2989^6

Poppy Kay *Philip Hobbs* 112b
5 b m Kayf Tara Double Red (IRE) (Thatching)
(2856)

Poprock Du Berlais (FR) *Robert Collet* 116h 104c
4 b m Martaline Populonia (FR) (Polish Precedent (USA))
350a^{13}

Popular Opinion (IRE) *Harry Fry* 87b
5 b m Oscar(IRE) Jeu De Dame (Perugino (USA))
432^6

Port And Ward (IRE) *John O'Shea* 63b
6 ch m Captain Rio Gold Stamp (Golden Act (USA))
2856^{13}

Porters War (IRE) *Jeremy Scott* 118h 126c
13 ch g Flemensfirth(USA) Grainne Geal (General Ironside (IRE))
557^2 863^4 1053^6 1309^3 1755^5 2017^6

Port Melon (IRE) *Paul Nicholls* 122h 144c
7 br g Presenting Omyn Supreme (IRE) (Supreme Leader)
(2240) 2726^3 4857^6 5390^2

Port Navas (IRE) *David Pipe* 86h
4 b g Court Cave(IRE) Mrs Quigley (IRE) (Mandalus)
3980^7 4917^P 5263^P 5430^4

Portrait King (IRE) *Patrick Griffin* 128h 140c
10 gr g Portrait Gallery(IRE) Storm Queen (IRE) (Le Bavard (FR))
92a^{12} 2436^P 2899^F 3518^6 4367^3 5005a^{12}

Portway Flyer (IRE) *Ian Williams* 132h 131c
7 br g King's Theatre(IRE) Next Best Thing (IRE) (Taipan (IRE))
3106^7 3466^P (4787) ◆

Posh Trip *Lady Blandford* 72c
10 b g Rakaposhi King Trial Trip (Le Moss)
536^P

Posilox (FR) *W Menuet* 123c
9 b g Loxias(FR) Positronique (FR) (Pigeon Voyageur (IRE))
313a^6

Positano Sud (FR) *M Rolland* 120h 121c
5 ch g Linda's Lad Amalfitana (FR) (Pistolet Bleu (IRE))
436a^P

Positive Approach (IRE) *John J Walsh* 131h
7 b g Aboo Hom Toureen Star (IRE) (Shardari)
5024a^6

Positively Dylan *Evan Williams* 124b
4 b g Multiplex Wou Oodd (Barathea (IRE))
(2909) 4117^2 ◆

Positive Vibes *Richard Woollacott* 92h 78c
6 ch g Nayef(USA) Steeple (Selkirk (USA))
170^3 514^P 2263^P 2599^6

Postbridge (IRE) *Warren Greatrex* 106b
4 br m Robin Des Pres(FR) Dartmeet (IRE) (Presenting)
2141^2 4228^2 4967^2

Post War *Nicky Henderson* 107b
4 b g Nayef(USA) Antebellum (FR) (Anabaa (USA))
4880[3] ◆ 5227[6]

Potters Corner (IRE) *Paul Morgan* 134h
5 b g Indian Danehill(IRE) Woodford Beauty (IRE) (Phardante (FR))
(1698) ◆ 1901[3] 4264[2] ◆ 4620[6] (5235) ◆

Potters Cross *Rebecca Curtis* 130h 130c
8 b g Alflora(IRE) Teeno Nell (Teenoso (USA))
4352[U] 4612[F] (5073)

Potters Lady Jane *Lucy Wadham* 94b
3 b f Sir Percy Arabescato (UAE) (Gone West (USA))
3118[4] (4228) 5180[13]

Potters Legend *Lucy Wadham* 141h
5 b g Midnight Legend Loose Morals (IRE) (Luso)
(2141) 2514[2] 3114[2] ◆ (3483) 3920[2] 4620[2] ◆ 5194[3]

Potters Midnight *Lucy Wadham* 116h
5 b m Midnight Legend Craughwell Suas (IRE) (Turtle Island (IRE))
152[7] (400) ◆ 748[4] 2561[4] 3179[5] 3612[3]

Pottinger (IRE) *Lucinda Russell* 69b
4 b g Zagreb(USA) Drumderry (IRE) (Shernazar)
3104[8]

Pougne Bobbi (FR) *Nicky Henderson* 139h
4 bb g Protektor(GER) Amicus (Xaar)
407[3] (3974) ◆ 4798[2]

Poulanassy (IRE) *Evan Williams* 119h
5 b g Tikkanen(USA) Winsome Mary (IRE) (Synefos (USA))
1979[7] (2423) (3101) 3804[F] (Dead)

Powderonthebonnet (IRE) *Richard Phillips* 106h
7 b g Definite Article Zuhal (Busted)
643[P] 746[6] 1098[2] (1171) 2271[14] 2577[13] 2997[10] 3223[9] 3784[5] 4184[P]

Powerful Blue (FR) *F-M Cottin* 109h
4 ch m Anabaa Blue Powerfull Pegasus (USA) (Fusaichi Pegasus (USA))
3815a[P]

Powerful Symbol (IRE) *Jonjo O'Neill* 101b
5 b g Robin Des Champs(FR) Be My Rainbow (IRE) (Be My Native (USA))
4572[2] 5331[F]

Prairie Hawk (USA) *Adrian Wintle* 71h
10 b g Hawk Wing(USA) Lady Carla (Caerleon (USA))
703[8] 977[F] 1084[6] 1297[P] 1691[P] 2256[5] 3143[6]

Prairie Lad *Sandy Thomson* 102h
7 b g Alflora(IRE) An Bothar Dubh (Strong Gale)
2806[4] 3793[P]

Prairie Town (IRE) *Tony Carroll* 129h
4 b g High Chaparral(IRE) Lake Baino (Highest Honor (FR))
1847[5] (2373) 2775[6] 3196[2] 3318[7] 3854[4] 4622[9]

Pray For A Rainbow *Evan Williams* 95h
4 b g Rainbow High Blackchurch Lass (IRE) (Taum Go Leor (IRE))
4894[11] 5393[6] 5463[4]

Precious Ground *Kevin Bishop* 98h
5 b g Helissio(FR) Wild Ground (IRE) (Simply Great (FR))
2263[3] 2567[3] (3410) ◆ 3919[5] 4342[3] 4543[2] 4749[3] 5165[P]

Precision Five *Alan King* 105h
6 b m Proclamation(IRE) Sashay (Bishop Of Cashel)
1574[3] 2123[U]

Premier Bond *Nicky Henderson* 138h
5 b g Kayf Tara Celtic Native (IRE) (Be My Native (USA))
2910[2] (3353) ◆ 4236[4] 5273[7]

Premier Jack's *Nikki Evans*
4 b g Tobougg(IRE) Arabellas Homer (Mark Of Esteem (IRE))
2850[P]

Premier Rose (IRE) *Katy Price* 21h
6 b m Westerner Alltoplayfor (IRE) (Broken Hearted)
2337[6] 3388[6] 3500[5]

Preseli Rock (IRE) *Rebecca Curtis* 127h
5 ch g Flemensfirth(USA) Chantoue Royale (FR) (Cadoudal (FR))
2270[3] 3077[2] 3403[3] 4264[3] 4821[2]

Preseli Star (IRE) *George Baker* 91h
5 b g Scorpion(IRE) Horner Hill (IRE) (Oscar (IRE))
1644[3] 1929[4] 4784[11]

Presence Felt (IRE) *Jonjo O'Neill* 122h 114c
7 br g Heron Island(IRE) Faeroe Isle (IRE) (Erins Isle)
108[P] 878[3] (1085) 1375[2] (1897) 2687[2]

Present Accord (IRE) *Michael Mullineaux* 27b
6 br m Presenting Supreme Accord (IRE) (Accordion)
761[9]

Present Destiny (IRE) *Seamus Mullins* 87b
3 b g Dubai Destination(USA) Anns Present (IRE) (Presenting)
5152[4]

Presented (IRE) *Lisa Harrison* 93h 123c
8 ch g Presenting Rustic Court (IRE) (Quayside)
883[8] 958[7] **1332[4] (1500) 1632[5] 1783[3]** 1925[4] **2028[2] 2213[2] 2431[3] 2934[2] (3439) 3934[3] 4367[11] 4609[5] 5411[2] 5474[2]**

Present Flight (IRE) *Lucinda Russell* 91h 127c
6 ch g Presenting Grangeclare Flight (IRE) (Old Vic)
(1775) 1853[2] (2327) ◆ 2749[P] 3341[2] 3936[4] 4836[2] 5413[5]

Presenting Arms (IRE) *Harry Fry* 134h 139c
8 b g Presenting Banningham Blaze (Averti (IRE))
(2688) (2873) 3151[19] **(4458) 4891[5] 5278[3]**

Presenting Junior (IRE) *Martin Todhunter* 92h 140c
8 b g Presenting Dr Alice (IRE) (Dr Massini (IRE))
470[2] 849[3] 2319[3] 2787[8] **3439[3] 3741[P] 5200[3] 5297[4]**

Presenting Lisa (IRE) *Alan King* 111h
6 b m Presenting Miss Esther (GER) (Alkalde (GER))
(1971) 2687[9]

Presenting Rose (IRE) *N W Alexander* 111h
5 b m Presenting Berkeley House (IRE) (Beneficial)
305[3] 2476[P] 2936[3] (3342) (4369) 4608[2] ◆ 5409[6]

Presenting Streak (IRE) *Peter Winks* 111h
6 b g Presenting Kuwalla (IRE) (New Frontier (IRE))
783[3] 1052[3] 1153[4] 1260[3] 1447[2] 1545[3] 2085[6] 2496[6] 3628[7] 5017[P]

Presenting The Way *G B Foot* 107b
8 ch g Presenting Euphorie (GER) (Feenpark (GER))
5035[P]

Present Lodger (IRE) *Lucinda Russell* 99h 121c
7 b g Presenting Hannigan's Lodger (IRE) (Be My Native (USA))
(1855) 2341[2] 3836[P]

Presently Tipsy *N W Alexander* 60h
6 b m Presenting Great Jane (FR) (Great Palm (USA))
288[P] 804[10]

Present Man (IRE) *Paul Nicholls* 121h 128c
5 b g Presenting Glen's Gale (IRE) (Strong Gale)
2088[2] 2603[2] 3705[6] 4853[2] 5146[4] **5432[2]**

Present Times (IRE) *Evan Williams* 89h
4 b g Kalanisi(IRE) Beguiling (IRE) (Dr Massini (IRE))
2683[9] 3582[4] 3915[10] 4882[F] 5382[10]

Present Trend (IRE) *Richard Ford* 82b
6 br m Presenting Trendy Attire (IRE) (Luso)
3888[P]

Present View *Jamie Snowden* 123h 148c
7 b g Presenting Carry Me (IRE) (Lafontaine I (USA))
1869[4] 2187[P] 2483[P] 5018[2] **5390[5]**

Pressurize (IRE) *Venetia Williams* 98h 138c
9 b g Witness Box(USA) Cockpit Rose (IRE) (Be My Native (USA))
2450[8] **3006[3] (3747) ◆ (3954) 4617[5] (4964)**

Preswell Lad (IRE) *Michael Butler* 98h 109c
12 b g Presenting Wayward Words (IRE) (Architect (USA))
1155[7]

Pret A Thou (FR) *John Groucott* 102h 119c
12 ch g Funny Baby(FR) Va Thou Line (FR) (El Badr)
2962[P] 3376[2] 3868[3] **(4209) 4386[4]** 4747[2] **5103[4]**

Prettyasapicture *Alan King* 108h
6 b m King's Theatre(IRE) Fortune's Girl (Ardross)
593[F] 775[5] 1454[6] 1618[P] 1823[6]

Pretty Miss Mahler (IRE) *Martin Todhunter* 91h
4 b m Mahler So Pretty (IRE) (Presenting)
3397[F] 3971[9] 4164[5] 4284[6]

Pretty Mobile (FR) *Paul Webber* 77h
4 gr m Al Namix(FR) Gobeline (FR) (Robin Des Champs (FR))
2022[P] 2862[7]

Pretty Rose (IRE) *Ben Case* 93h
5 b m King's Theatre(IRE) Rosies All The Way (Robellino (USA))
970[6] 1094[4] 1374[7] 1506[6] 1618[3] 1816[5]

Pride In Battle (IRE) *Alan King* 112h
10 b g Chevalier(IRE) Afasara (IRE) (Shardari)
283[P]

Pride Of Lecale *Fergal O'Brien* 130b
4 b g Multiplex Rock Gossip (IRE) (Inchinor)
2909[2] 3502[2] (3980) 4721[13] 5195[7]

Pride Of The Braid (IRE) *John E Kiely* 114h
5 b m Kayf Tara Debut (IRE) (Presenting)
2677a[10] 4653a[P]

Prideofthecastle (IRE) *David Pipe* 132h 131c
8 b g Waky Nao Park's Pet (IRE) (Bob Back (USA))
(3922) ◆ 4212[4] 4589[3] 5456[2]

Primary Suspect (IRE) *Linda Blackford* 38b
5 bg g Primary(USA) Charismatique (GER) (Greinton)
2875[7] 3416[8] 4917[P] 5434[F]

Prime Venture (IRE) *Evan Williams* 113b
4 br g Primary(USA) Next Venture (IRE) (Zaffaran (USA))
(3082) 4488[8]

Primo Blue *Noel Williams* 46h
5 b g Primo Valentino(IRE) Flintwood (Gunner B)
2904[7]

Primo Capitano (IRE) *Martin Keighley* 113h
7 b g Milan Miss Mayberry (IRE) (Bob Back (USA))
614[4] 897[7] 1447[P]

Primo Milano *Evan Williams* 73h
6 b g Milan She's Our Native (IRE) (Be My Native (USA))
3114[11] 3745[14] 5431[P]

Primo Rossi *Tom Gretton* 74h
5 b g Primo Valentino(IRE) Flaming Rose (IRE) (Roselier (FR))
262[P] 692[9] 1310[4] 1524[5] 1933[3]

Primo Time *Michael Appleby* 80b
4 b g Primo Valentino(IRE) Eva's Edge (IRE) (Good Thyne (USA))
3847[11] 4156[9]

Primrose Brown *Conrad Allen* 84b
4 b m Indian Danehill(IRE) Royal Tango (Petoski)
1817[2] 2044[11] *2421[9]*

Primrose Court (IRE) *Shaun Lycett* 96b
5 ch m Golan(IRE) Sugar Kane Kowa (IRE) (Flemensfirth (USA))
1491[3] 4350[5] 4847[12]

Prince Blackthorn (IRE) *Barry Murtagh* 82h 90c
9 b g Desert Prince(IRE) Notable Dear (ITY) (Last Tycoon)
287[U] 639[3] 803[8] 1069[P] 1492[6] 1685[4] 1857[7]

Prince Des Marais (FR) *Caroline Bailey* 99h 125c
12 bb g Network(GER) Djeba Royale (FR) (El Badr)
(109) (403)

Prince Khurram *Donald McCain* 114h
5 b g Nayef(USA) Saree (Barathea (IRE))
(33) 862[2] 1083[4] 1168[4] 1308[4] (1366) 1714[3] 2085[9] 3242[2] 3592[7] 4154[4] 5088[4]

Prince Kup (IRE) *E J O'Grady* 119h
4 ch g High Rock(IRE) Lockup (IRE) (Inchinor)
3323a[7]

Princely Conn (IRE) *Thomas Mullins* 134h
6 b g Whitmore's Conn(USA) High Priestess (IRE) (Priolo (USA))
96a[18] 2177a[4] 3071a[14] 3650a[18] 5025a[10]

Princely Hero (IRE) *R Cummings* 100c
11 b g Royal Applause Dalu (IRE) (Dancing Brave (USA))
15[P]

Prince Mahler (IRE) *Caroline Keevil* 102h
5 b g Mahler Strokestown Queen (IRE) (Presenting)
1698[10] 1998[U] 2267[3] 2564[4] 3223[8] 5034[7]

Prince Of Cardamom (IRE) *Jonathan Geake*
3 b g Nayef(USA) Tiger Spice (Royal Applause)
2273[11] 2578[4]

Prince Of Milan (IRE) *Andrew Slattery* 104h 116c
10 b g Milan Lough Gur (IRE) (Religiously (USA))
48a[P]

Prince Of Pirates (IRE) *Ben Haslam* 100h 124c
10 b g Milan Call Kate (IRE) (Lord Americo)
153[7] 522[3]

Prince Of Poets *David Pipe* 102h
4 gr g Byron Princess Maud (USA) (Irish River (FR))
187[4] 703[3] 1117[4] 1265[9] 1324[5] 1510[6] 1578[4] 1823[3] 2006[5]

Prince Of Scars (IRE) *Gordon Elliott* 163h
5 b g Flemensfirth(USA) Spirit Leader (IRE) (Supreme Leader)
(2676a) (3322a) 5216[3]

Prince Of Silver *Andy Turnell* 84h
9 gr g Helissio(FR) Fittleworth (IRE) (Bijou D'Inde)
932[9] 1081[8] 1240[7] 1691[8] **1950[P]**

Prince Of Steal (IRE) *James Evans* 136h
5 b g Craigsteel Princess Gloria (IRE) (Prince Rupert (FR))
2842[3] (3179) (4026) 5214[5]

Prince Of Thieves (IRE) *Anthony Honeyball* 85h
5 b g Robin Des Pres(FR) Sly Empress (IRE) (Supreme Leader)
90[P] 2263[P] 2730[3] 4068[7] 5483[2] ◆

Prince Oscar (IRE) *Ian Williams* 100b
6 b g Oscar(IRE) Athy Princess (IRE) (Over The River (FR))
227[2] ◆

Prince Philippe (FR) *P Bourgeais* 140h 130c
5 b g Denham Red(FR) Coquine D'Anjou (FR) (Saint Cyrien (FR))
(836a)

Prince Pippin (IRE) *Lucy Jones* 100h
9 b g King Charlemagne(USA) Staploy (Deploy)
240[3] 615[7]

Prince Rudi (IRE) *S T Nolan* 142h 127c
13 b g Rudimentary(USA) Ware Princess (Crash Course)
1175a[13]

Princess Annabelle *Rod Millman* 67h
6 ch m Sworn In(USA) Marybelle (Double Trigger (IRE))
30[P] 391[7] 513[4]

Princesse Fleur *Michael Scudamore* 76h 88c
7 b m Grape Tree Road Princesse Grec (FR) (Grand Tresor (FR))
3387[P] 3951[4] 4356[6] 5068[6]

Princess Roania (IRE) *Peter Bowen* 104h
4 b m Dubai Destination(USA) Lady Roania (IRE) (Saddlers' Hall (IRE))
594[2] 970[2] 1094[2]

Princess Tara (IRE) *Malcolm Jefferson* 126h
5 b m Kayf Tara Oscars Vision (IRE) (Oscar Schindler (IRE))
2268[7] 2825[5] 3824[P] (5409)

Princess Tiana (IRE) *Jonjo O'Neill* 71h
4 b m Yeats(IRE) Ar Muin Na Muice (IRE) (Executive Perk)
2561[6] 3947[5] 4388[9]

Prince Tom *Alexandra Dunn* 56h 140c
11 b g King's Theatre(IRE) Cresswell Native (IRE) (Be My Native (USA))
833[7]

Princeton Royale (IRE) *Neil King* 136h
6 br g Royal Anthem(USA) Shelikesitstraight (IRE) (Rising)
146[F] 671[5] 1054[5] 1350[5] (1375) (1522) 1594[2] (1784) 1963[3]

Printing Blue (IRE) *Chris Gordon*
7 b g Blueprint(IRE) Buckners Girl (Weld)
292[F]

Private Jones *Miss Imogen Pickard* 94h 61c
6 br g Trade Fair Dafne (Nashwan (USA))
1095[4] 1446[6] 1525[6] **1687[U] 1907[6]**

Private Malone (IRE) *Emma Lavelle* 134h 138c
6 b g Darsi(FR) Native Artist (IRE) (Be My Native (USA))
2627[2] 3013[5]

Probably George *Mrs K Lynn* 46h 97c
8 gr g Silver Patriarch(IRE) Java Dawn (IRE) (Fleetwood (IRE))
(472) 5449[5]

Problema Tic (FR) *Jackie Stephen* 112h 124c
9 b g Kapgarde(FR) Atreide (FR) (Son Of Silver)
800[5] 868[5] 1033[5] 2295[P]

Professeur Emery (FR) *Warren Greatrex* 107h 115c
8 b g Officiel(FR) Karmadeine (FR) (Kaldoun (FR))
5047[4] ◆

Professor Plum (IRE) *Rose Dobbin* 105h
5 b g Kalanisi(IRE) Miss Plum (Ardross)
1550[3]

Profit Commission (IRE) *Harry Fry* 120h
5 b g Presenting Silver Pursuit (Rainbow Quest (USA))
168[2] 773[5] 1011[6]

Progress Drive (IRE) *Nicky Richards* 98b
4 b g Stowaway Dolphins View (IRE) (Dolphin Street (FR))
3442[DSQ] (4408)

Promanco *Charlie Longsdon* 122h
6 b m Kayf Tara Shelayly (IRE) (Zaffaran (USA))
(219) (516) 1754[4] 2013[4] 2632[7] 5282[9] ◆

Proofreader *Neil Mulholland* 123h
6 b g Authorized(IRE) Blixen (USA) (Gone West (USA))
171[2] 528[4] 2238[3] (2734) 2888[3]

Protek Des Flos (FR) *Nicky Henderson* 135h
3 b g Protektor(GER) Flore De Chantenay (FR) (Smadoun (FR))
(3848) (4233) 4959a[2]

Proud Gamble (IRE) *Rose Dobbin* 90h 86c
6 b g Brian Boru Sister Anna (Gildoran)
139[8] **3427[F] 3679[7] 4032[2] (4175) 4637[P] 5010[P]**

Proud Times (USA) *Ali Stronge* 105h 114c
9 bb g Proud Citizen(USA) Laura's Pistolette (USA) (Big Pistol (USA))
2826[3] 3125[6] 3376[8] 4747[8] 4968[3]

Prouts Pub (IRE) *Nick Gifford* 131h 95c
6 b g Catcher In The Rye(IRE) A Woman In Love (Muhtarram (USA))
2001[P] 2266[11] (3216) 3854[8] 4159[P] 4786[8]

Provincial Pride (IRE) *Mike Hammond* 107h 106c
8 b g Whitmore's Conn(USA) Soraleda (IRE) (Toulon)
85[10] 529[9] 704[4] **770[4] 1155[2]**

Prussian Eagle (IRE) *Charles O'Brien* 133h
4 b g Jeremy(USA) Absolutely Cool (IRE) (Indian Ridge)
94a[6]

Ptit Zig (FR) *Paul Nicholls* 157h 168c
6 b g Great Pretender(IRE) Red Rym (FR) (Denham Red (FR))
(2206a) 2633[2] 2927[F] 3526[U] 3853[2] (5495)

Puddle Jumper (IRE) *Micky Hammond* 105b
4 br g Craigsteel Koko Kabana (IRE) (Glacial Storm (USA))
1858[2] 2984[2]

Pulling Power *Kim Bailey* 111h
5 br m Erhaab(USA) Pulling Strings (IRE) (Accordion)
124[2] 432[2] 2486[7] 3110[2] (3500) 4445[P] 5094[12]

Pull The Chord (IRE) *Philip Hobbs* 140h
5 b g St Jovite(USA) Gold Chord (IRE) (Accordion)
(2445) 3584[3] 4239[5] 4786[5] 5284[6]

Pulpitarian (USA) *Lucinda Russell* 108h
7 b g Pulpit(USA) Bedanken (USA) (Geri (USA))
468[5]

Pumaflor (IRE) *Richard Guest*
3 b g Aussie Rules(USA) Krasotka (IRE) (Soviet Star (USA))
2718[P]

Pumped Up Kicks (IRE) *Dan Skelton* 129h 142c
8 b m Flemensfirth(USA) Beauty Star (IRE) (Shalford (IRE))
1040[4] 2171[8] 2459[P] 4787[5]

Purcell's Bridge (FR) *Rose Dobbin* 118h 126c
8 b g Trempolino(USA) Theatrical Lady (USA) (Theatrical (IRE))
458[6] 2295[2]

Pure Poteen (IRE) *Neil Mulholland* 105h 122c
7 ch g Flemensfirth(USA) Taking My Time (IRE) (High Roller (IRE))
589[F] 676[P] (1850) 2272[2] 3507[F] 3979[P] 4876[3]

Pure Science (IRE) *Sue Smith* 127h 131c
7 ch g Galileo(IRE) Rebelline (IRE) (Robellino (USA))
2426[4] (2669)

Pure Vision (IRE) *Anthony Honeyball* 96h
4 b g Milan Distillery Lane (IRE) (Exit To Nowhere (USA))
1873[2] 2729[2] ◆ 4488[4] 5268[10] 5353[5]

Purple Bay (IRE) *John Ferguson* 160h
6 b g Dubawi(IRE) Velvet Lady (Nashwan (USA))
2334[4] 2789[4]

Purple Genie (GR) *Patrick Chamings* 90b
3 ch f Tiantai(USA) Purple Way (GR) (Apotheosis (USA))
2009[5] 2304[3] 3118[8] 4337[P]

Purple 'n Gold (IRE) *David Pipe* 125h 142c
6 b g Strategic Prince Golden Dew (IRE) (Montjeu (IRE))
708[3] 826[3] 973[4] 1039[15] **(1343) 1553[3] (1643) 1735[2] 2059[10] 2185[5] 4785[6] 5118[3] 5465[2]**

Pur Sang D'Or (FR) *Mlle S Sine* 111h
4 b g Ballingarry(IRE) Red Gardenia (FR) (Victory Note (USA))
2362a[P]

Pursuitofhappiness (IRE) *Neil Mulholland* 92h 64c
7 b g Classic Cliche(IRE) Lake Tour (IRE) (Aristocracy (IRE))
2612[7] **2881[P] 3255[3]** 3516[P] **4491[P] 5435[P]**

Push Ahead (IRE) *Gary Hanmer* 105b
6 br g Flemensfirth(USA) Candle Massini (IRE) (Dr Massini (IRE))
320[2]

Push Me (IRE) *Iain Jardine* 104h
8 gr m Verglas(IRE) Gilda Lilly (USA) (War Chant (USA))
1459[3] 1773[4] 1920[P]

Put The Boot In (IRE) *Barry Brennan* 79h
3 ch g Duke Of Marmalade(IRE) Mubkera (IRE) (Nashwan (USA))
2032[5] 2439[P] 4888[F]

Puyol (IRE) *Patricia Rigby* 118h 79c
13 bb g Zaffaran(USA) Star Mover (Move Off)
60[4] 506[6]

Pyjama Game (IRE) *Rose Dobbin* 96h 106c
9 b g Hernando(FR) Princess Claudia (IRE) (Kahyasi)
133[5] 486[4] 803[3]

Pyleigh Brae *P M Bryant* 82b
4 b m Alflora(IRE) Lady Callernish (Callernish)
5436[7]

Pylonthepressure (IRE) *W P Mullins* 130h
5 b g Darsi(FR) Minnie O'Grady (IRE) (Welsh Term)
23a[5]

Pyromaniac (IRE) *A J Martin* 138h
5 b g Invincible Spirit(IRE) Silly Goose (IRE) (Sadler's Wells (USA))
73a[2] 1175a[7]

Pyrshan (IRE) *Graeme McPherson* 118h
6 b g Pyrus(USA) Runshangale (IRE) (Anshan)
2152[P] 2687[4] 3146[4] 4389[2] 4860[F]

Pyrus Gold Wind (IRE) *S J Mahon* 132h
8 b g Pyrus(USA) Gold Wind (IRE) (Marju (IRE))
2525a[P]

Pythagore *Emmanuel Clayeux* 150h 151c
10 b g Kahyasi Peony Girl (FR) (Phantom Breeze)
(2822a) 4485[4] 5363a[5]

Qasser (IRE) *Harry Whittington* 128h
6 b g Intikhab(USA) Surrender To Me (USA) (Royal Anthem (USA))
(2458) 3035[2] 3487[6] 4774[3] ◆ 5159[5]

Qatea (IRE) *Donald McCain* 81h
3 ch g Duke Of Marmalade(IRE) Taking Liberties (IRE) (Royal Academy (USA))
2439[P] 3099[8] 3309[10] 3840[10] 4068[5] 4943[P]

Qewy (IRE) *John Ferguson* 144h 141c
5 b g Street Cry(IRE) Princess Nada (Barathea (IRE))
2053[3] 2684[2] 3041[2] 4717[11] 5189[B]

Qrackers (FR) *Miss V Collins*
11 b g Lahint(USA) Babolna (FR) (Tropular)
4446[P]

Q Twenty Girl (IRE) *John Norton* 46h
3 b f Fast Company(IRE) Extravagance (IRE) (King's Best (USA))
3587[8] 4271[9]

Quadriller (FR) *Philip Hobbs* 108h 117c
8 b g Lando(GER) Tabachines (FR) (Art Francais (USA))
828[2] ◆ 1051[4] **(1353) 1483[3]**

Quadriviae (FR) *D Sourdeau De Beauregard*
4 b m Kapgarde(FR) Qualvie (FR) (Port Etienne (FR))
1231a[F]

Qualando (FR) *Paul Nicholls* 142h
4 b g Lando(GER) Qualite Controlee (FR) (Poliglote)
94a[7] 2060[6] 2901[8] 4294[2] 4769[16] 5185[2] 5497[15]

Quality John (FR) *Christian Le Galliard*
11 b g Sleeping Car(FR) La Biche Du Pont (FR) (Abdonski (FR))
1223a[5]

Quantitativeeasing (IRE) *E Bolger* 106h 146c
10 ch g Anshan Mazuma (IRE) (Mazaad)
48a[2] 4719[4]

Quantum Of Solace *Noel Williams* 99h
5 b m Kayf Tara Fashion House (Homo Sapien)
1909[6] 2644[5] 2772[5] 4878[8] 5374[2]

Quarenta (FR) *Jonjo O'Neill* 97b
3 bb g Voix Du Nord(FR) Negresse De Cuta (FR) (Baroud D'Honneur (FR))
2414[3] *(3048)*

Quarryman *Ron Hodges* 94h
4 ch g Act One Bluebell Path (Classic Cliche (IRE))
124[11] 3111[6] 4681[10] 5161[2]

Quarrymount *E J Farrant*
14 b g Polar Falcon(USA) Quilt (Terimon)
296[P]

Quart De Lino (FR) *P Peltier* 101h 116c
10 b g Trempolino(USA) Wells Vision (GER) (Monsun (GER))
313a[4]

Quat'Car (FR) *G Chaignon* 116h 119c
11 b g Sleeping Car(FR) Djamena (FR) (Neustrien (FR))
437a[8]

Quebec *Charlie Mann* 122h
4 b g Dansili Milford Sound (Barathea (IRE))
214[3] 1814[4] 2058[10] 2328[5] 3238[P] 5386[6]

Queen Alphabet (IRE) *Peter Fahey* 135h
6 b m King's Theatre(IRE) A-To-Z (IRE) (Ahonoora)
1657[2] 1748a[6] 2177a[6]

Queen Matilda (IRE) *Donal Kinsella* 97h
4 b m Azamour(IRE) Maria Luisa (IRE) (King's Best (USA))
1150a[10]

Queen Odessa (IRE) *Harry Fry* 109b
4 b m King's Theatre(IRE) Ma Furie (FR) (Balleroy (USA))
2421[3] (3861)

Queen Of The Stage (IRE) *Nick Williams* 126h
5 b m King's Theatre(IRE) Supreme Du Casse (IRE) (Supreme Leader)
3444[5] 4252[4]

Queen Olivia *Oliver Sherwood* 115h 104c
7 b m King's Theatre(IRE) Queen's Leader (Supreme Leader)
107[5] 2449[2] ◆

Queen Spud *Henry Daly* 109h 107c
6 b m Multiplex Hurtebise (FR) (Groom Dancer (USA))
(130) ◆ 314[7] 747[8] 938[9] 2022[2] **2435[4]**

Queens Wild (IRE) *Edward P Harty* 120h 127c
5 b m Westerner Pepsi Starlet (IRE) (Heavenly Manna)
50a[10] **(3093a) 3604a[2] 4019a[3] 4279a[6]**

Quel Elite (FR) *James Moffatt* 117h
11 b g Subotica(FR) Jeenly (FR) (Kadalko (FR))
203[2] 2624[6] 3058[2] 3999[4] 4246[2] 5300[6]

Quelle Miss (FR) *D Sourdeau De Beauregard* 113h 113c
5 b m Poliglote Missy Wata (FR) (Trempolino (USA))
436a[4]

Quench Tara *Michael Scudamore* 95h
8 b m Kayf Tara Madam Min (Overbury (IRE))
178[7] 648[F] 813[3] 3105[13]

Querry Horse (FR) *Oliver Sherwood* 122h
3 b g Equerry(USA) La Richelandiere (FR) (Garde Royale)
3772[2] 4441[2] (5437) ◆

Que Sera (IRE) *Philip Hobbs* 117h
5 b g Rakti Mitsina (Fantastic Light (USA))
(3130) 4183[3] 4917[P] 5453[6]

Question Of Faith *Martin Todhunter* 93h
4 b m Yeats(IRE) Anastasia Storm (Mozart (IRE))
159[5] 1921[P] 2101[7] 3239[7] 3672[10] 3888[2] (4404) 4585[3]

Quest Magic (IRE) *George Bewley* 105h
9 ch g Fantastic Quest(IRE) Magic Sign (IRE) (The Parson)
37[F] 507[2] 658[3] 882[F]

Quick Brew *Maurice Barnes* 112h 112c
7 b g Denounce Darjeeling (IRE) (Presenting)
154[3] (1740) 2027[5] 4179[5] **4634[U] 5086[4]**

Quick Decisson (IRE) *Stuart Coltherd* 112h 126c
7 b g Azamour(IRE) Fleet River (USA) (Riverman (USA))
(162) ◆ **2342[3]** 2637[6] **3441[2] 3670[2] 3935[3] 4166[2] 4300[4]** 4583[4] **5447[P]**

Quick Eleven (FR) *Mlle S Delaroche* 81h 72c
4 b m Saint Des Saints(FR) Quick Ville (FR) (Villez (USA))
4401a[5]

Quick Jack (IRE) *A J Martin* 152h
6 ch g Footstepsinthesand Miss Polaris (Polar Falcon (USA))
(1163a)

Quick N' Easy (IRE) *Sue Gardner* 74h
5 ch g Vertical Speed(FR) Tarmons Duchess (IRE) (The Parson)
893[P] 1044[7] 1117[11] 1179[5]

Quiet Candid (IRE) *Nicky Henderson* 122h
6 b m Beneficial Lady Of Appeal (IRE) (Lord Of Appeal)
1974[P] 2455[3] 5438[4]

Quietly (IRE) *Sue Smith* 80b
4 b g Oscar(IRE) Gimme Peace (IRE) (Aristocracy (IRE))
4915[9]

Quieto Sol (FR) *Charlie Longsdon* 115h
4 ch g Loup Solitaire(USA) First Wonder (FR) (Mansonnien (FR))
188[6] 2317[6] 2791[12] 3022[5] 3450[5] (4856) 5246[3]

Quill Art *Richard Fahey* 98h
3 b g Excellent Art Featherweight (IRE) (Fantastic Light (USA))
1899[4] 2286[4] 2863[6] 3473[3] (3840) ◆ 4460[2] 5088[P]

Quincy Des Pictons (FR) *Alan Jones* 111h 149c
11 b g Kadalko(FR) Izabel Des Pictons (FR) (Bayolidaan (FR))
1857 389[6] **660[P] 3521[P]** 4432[2] **4733[F]**

Quincy Magoo (IRE) *Neil King* 106h
6 ch g Mountain High(IRE) Vicky's Lodge (IRE) (Daggers Drawn (USA))
146[5] 1990[4]

Quinlandio (IRE) *Richard Rowe* 121h
5 b g Thousand Words La Shalak (IRE) (Shalford (IRE))
5275[P]

Quintano (GER) *Heather Dalton* 86h
7 ch g Black Sam Bellamy(IRE) Quintana (GER) (Fantastic Light (USA))
150[P] 527[P]

Quinto *John Quinn* 113h
5 ch g Desideratum Cruz Santa (Lord Bud)
320[6] 2210[3] 2801[5] (3588) 4066[5] 4906[3] 5440[4]

Quinz (FR) *Lawney Hill* 110h 127c
11 b g Robin Des Champs(FR) Altesse Du Mou (FR) (Tin Soldier I (FR))
(15) 535[5] 2887[2] 5265[P]

Quite By Chance *Colin Tizzard* 117h 138c
6 b g Midnight Legend Hop Fair (Gildoran)
2261[P] 2568[2] 2877[3] (3257) (3706) 3957[2] 4436[3] 4964[2] 5304[3]

Quite Sparky *Lucinda Egerton* 66h
8 b g Lucky Story(USA) Imperialistic (IRE) (Imperial Ballet (IRE))
3973[7]

Quito Du Tresor (FR) *Lucinda Russell* 102h 124c
11 b g Jeune Homme(USA) Itiga (FR) (Djarvis (FR))
304[3] 1444[3] 1639[4] 2030[4] 2329[2] 2947[4] 3425[3] 4011[3] 4872[6]

Qulinton (FR) *Johnny Farrelly* 88h 101c
11 b g Bulington(FR) Klef Du Bonheur (FR) (Lights Out (FR))
553[7] 771[4] 2517[P] 4433[P] 5044[3] 5468[P]

Raajih *Richard Woollacott* 114h 143c
7 gr g Dalakhani(IRE) Thakafaat (IRE) (Unfuwain (USA))
389[7] **1322[9] 2089[P]**

Rabbit Well *Josef Vana* 116c
9 ch g Dream Well(FR) Celinda (FR) (Bering)
1885a[5]

Race To Glory (FR) *David Pipe* 92h
4 b g Montjeu(IRE) Cawett (IRE) (Danehill Dancer (IRE))
32[2] 673[3] 880[7]

Rachael's Ruby *Roger Teal* 67h
8 b m Joe Bear(IRE) Fajjoura (IRE) (Fairy King (USA))
2000[P] 2244[5] 2604[7]

Racing Europe (IRE) *Brian Ellison* 127h 135c
6 b g Kayf Tara Titanic Quarter (IRE) (Turgeon (USA))
1903[4] **2067[5] 3100[2] 3885[3]** ◆

Racing Pulse (IRE) *Rebecca Curtis* 142h 142c
6 b g Garuda(IRE) Jacks Sister (IRE) (Entitled (IRE))
1846[7] 2122[5] (3520) 4124[P] 4701[10] 5217[P]

Racing Spirit *John Quinn* 84h
3 ch g Sir Percy Suertuda (Domedriver (IRE))
975[3]

Racy Lady *Caroline Bailey* 13b
5 b m Rob Roy(USA) Elmside Katie (Lord David S (USA))
2835[5]

Radsoc De Sivola (FR) *John Cornwall* 64h 66c
10 bl g Video Rock(FR) Kerrana (FR) (Cadoudal (FR))
570[3] 779[RR]

Raduis Bleu (FR) *Lady Susan Brooke* 62h 65c
10 gr g Dadarissime(FR) Regence Bleue (FR) (Porto Rafti (FR))
2694[P] 2997[7] **3385[4] 3569[3] 4879[6]**

Rae's Creek *Mrs John Harrington* 134h
5 ch g New Approach(IRE) All's Forgotten (USA) (Darshaan)
1163a[P]

Rafafie *Sue Gardner* 109h
7 b g Kayf Tara Florie (Alflora (IRE))
3708[2] 4824[4] 5148[4]

Raffa *R Mitford-Slade* 87c
8 b g Milan Westbourne (IRE) (King's Ride)
13[6]

Ragdollianna *Mark Hoad* 99h
11 b m Kayf Tara Jupiters Princess (Jupiter Island)
2000[4] 2547[5]

Ragtime Lady *Steven Dixon*
7 b m General Gambul Pink Lady (El Conquistador)
268[4] 714[7]

Rahealty (IRE) *Dai Williams* 5h
9 ro g Pilsudski(IRE) Another Sparkle (Bustino)
100[8]

Raid Stane (IRE) *Julia Brooke* 99h 92c
9 b g Morozov(USA) Rashhattan (IRE) (Rashar (USA))
569[4] 838[5] 4289[P] 5203[4]

Raifteiri (IRE) *William Young Jnr* 84h 45c
8 b g Galileo(IRE) Naziriya (FR) (Darshaan)
157[5] 502[9] 804[6] 872[8] 1071[7] 1400[9] 1573[6] 1776[7]

Railway Benefit (IRE) *Adrian Wintle* 87h 86c
7 b g Beneficial Sorcera (GER) (Zilzal (USA))
2851[4]

Railway Dillon (IRE) *Mrs C Drury* 92h 123c
10 b g Witness Box(USA) Laura's Native (IRE) (Be My Native (USA))
506[U] (4016) 4307[6] 5082[2] 5449[4]

Railway Pearl (IRE) *Peter Fahey* 82h
5 b m Royal Anthem(USA) Colbinstown Pearl (IRE) (Broken Hearted)
25a[11]

Railway Storm (IRE) *Jimmy Frost* 11h 109c
10 ch g Snurge Stormy Bee (IRE) (Glacial Storm (USA))
827[6] 1118[2] 1326[2] 1842[2] 2017[3] 2447[3] 2878[3] 3412[P] (4859) 5357[2]

Railway Tommy (IRE) *Peter Fahey* 125h
7 b g Artan(IRE) Colbinstown Pearl (IRE) (Broken Hearted)
19a[8] 2676a[5]

Railway Vic (IRE) *Jimmy Frost* 70h 9c
8 b g Old Vic Penny Apples (IRE) (Jolly Jake (NZ))
165[3] 1323[7] 1578[8]

Rain Artist's (FR) *G Taupin* 117h
4 b m Montmartre(FR) Rain Lily (FR) (Priolo (USA))
2821a[9]

Rainbow Haze *Phillip Dando* 104h
9 b g Rainbow High Kristal Haze (Krisinsky (USA))
(1293) 1615[5] 2454[5] (2567) 2985[6] 3572[4] 4342[P] 4618[3] 4883[2] 5051[4] 5466[8]

Rainbow Lollipop *Tom Gretton* 49h
4 b m Dubawi(IRE) Cross Section (USA) (Cape Cross (IRE))
748[6] 1297[P]

Rainman (IRE) *Jonjo O'Neill* 98h
5 b g Craigsteel Trolly Dolly (IRE) (The Parson)
43[7] 529[7]

Rainy City (IRE) *Paul Nicholls* 126h
5 b g Kalanisi(IRE) Erintante (IRE) (Denel (FR))
3839[3] ◆ (5269) 5462[3]

Raise A Spark *Donald McCain* 113h
5 b g Multiplex Reem Two (Mtoto)
83[3] 433[3] 1365[2] 1684[0] 1967[6] 2212[2] 2704[2] (2889) 3240[F] 3743[F] 4224[3] 4873[5] 5406[U]

Raise A Tail (IRE) *Mrs John Harrington* 88b
5 ch g Definite Article Fillmein (IRE) (Gone Fishin)
25a[6]

Raised On Grazeon *John Quinn* 108b
4 ch m Lucky Story(USA) Graze On And On (Elmaamul (USA))
3862[2] 4156[2] 4847[4]

Raise Hell (IRE) *Sandy Thomson* 95b
8 b g Presenting Markiza (IRE) (Broken Hearted)
3164[P]

Rajdhani Express *Nicky Henderson* 134h 164c
8 br g Presenting Violet Express (FR) (Cadoudal (FR))
2084[P] (Dead)

Raknruin (IRE) *Joanne Foster* 62h
5 ch g Rakti Barrell Rose (IRE) (Definite Article)
518[P] 2890[P] 3590[P]

Raktiman (IRE) *Sam Drake* 130h 138c
8 ch g Rakti Wish List (IRE) (Mujadil (USA))
875 **1969[4] 2289[3]** 2594[7] **2846[3] (3972) 4910[7] 5245[3]**

Rally *Nigel Twiston-Davies* 126h 127c
6 b g Rail Link Waki Music (USA) (Miswaki (USA))
319[11] **517[2] 808[P]**

Ralphy Lad (IRE) *Alan Swinbank* 81h
4 b g Iffraaj Hawattef (IRE) (Mujtahid (USA))
1979[8]

Rambling Rosie (IRE) *J J Lambe* 13h
6 ch m Basanta(IRE) Rivers Town Rosie (IRE) (Roselier (FR))
2433[7]

Rameur (FR) *Louisa Carberry* 120h
10 b g Shaanmer(IRE) Imola II (FR) (Video Rock (FR))
663a[P]

Randy Pike (IRE) *Nicky Richards* 105b
5 b g Mahler Niamh's Leader (IRE) (Supreme Leader)
4208[2] 4611[3]

Ranjaan (FR) *S Wilson* 108h
7 b g Dubai Destination(USA) Ridafa (IRE) (Darshaan)
96a[21]

Rare Coincidence *Alan Berry* 28h
14 ch g Atraf Green Seed (IRE) (Lead On Time (USA))
502[P]

Rashaan (IRE) *Colin Kidd* 133h
3 ch g Manduro(GER) Rayyana (IRE) (Rainbow Quest (USA))
(2813a) 3268a[5] 4002a[6] 5001a[2]

Rasique (FR) *C Scandella* 134h 134c
5 b g Enrique Rasia (FR) (Pistolet Bleu (IRE))
664a[5] 1884a[8]

Rathealy (IRE) *David Pipe* 123h
4 b g Baltic King Baltic Belle (IRE) (Redback)
197[P] 4484[9] 4933[P] 5279[13]

Rather Be (IRE) *Nicky Henderson* 128b
4 b g Oscar(IRE) Irish Wedding (IRE) (Bob Back (USA))
220[U] (3111) ◆ 4309[2] 4721[9]

Rather Curious (IRE) *David Phelan* 80h 76c
11 b g Corrouge(USA) Imlistening (IRE) (Tremblant)
292[7]

Rathlin *Micky Hammond* 131h 145c
10 b g Kayf Tara Princess Timon (Terimon)
24a[6] 1152a[15] 2902[8] 3425[7] 3996[P] ◆ **(4606) 5193[U]**

Rathlin Rose (IRE) *David Pipe* 133h 139c
7 b g Bonbon Rose(FR) A Plus Ma Puce (FR) (Turgeon (USA))
(517)

Rathmuck Native (IRE) *Peter Fahey* 116h
7 b m Definite Article Fern Fields (IRE) (Be My Native (USA))
2176a[3]

Rathpatrick (IRE) *Eoin Griffin* 136h 55c
7 b g Oscar(IRE) Rua Lass (IRE) (Beau Sher)
50a[P] 4730[6]

Ratify *Dai Burchell* 95h 120c
11 br g Rakaposhi King Sea Sky (Oats)
2490[4] 3223[5] ◆ **4436[2] (5103)**

Ravens Brook (IRE) *Neil King* 58h 107c
9 br g Alderbrook Triple Triumph (IRE) (Welsh Term)
771[6] 2668[P] 2996[P] 3061[P] 3419[4] 3663[P] 4027[P]

Ravens Nest *Lawney Hill* 91h
5 b g Piccolo Emouna (Cadeaux Genereux)
1120[P] 1297[10]

Raven's Tower (USA) *Ben Pauling* 126h 141c
5 b g Raven's Pass(USA) Tizdubai (USA) (Cee's Tizzy (USA))
329[2] 596[4] (2412) 4770[11] 5471[2]

Ravished (IRE) *M F Morris* 128h 139c
7 b g Oscar(IRE) Fair Present (IRE) (Presenting)
1184a[9] **1556a[P]**

Raw Condition (IRE) *Julia Brooke* 23h
7 b g Zagreb(USA) Castlebanny Jenny (IRE) (Beneficial)
957[5]

Rawnaq (IRE) *Cyril Murphy* 147h 146c
8 b g Azamour(IRE) Sharemata (IRE) (Doyoun)
1163a[U] 1983a[3]

Rayadour (IRE) *Micky Hammond* 100h
6 b g Azamour(IRE) Rayyana (IRE) (Rainbow Quest (USA))
2496[7] 2720[8]

Raya Hope (IRE) *Alan King* 84b
4 b m Robin Des Champs(FR) Garden City (IRE) (Shernazar)
2421[8]

Rayak (IRE) *Jonjo O'Neill* 121h 56c
5 b g Invincible Spirit(IRE) Rayyana (IRE) (Rainbow Quest (USA))
1504[6]

Raydari (FR) *R K Watson* 99h 119c
7 b g Desert Style(IRE) Ridakiya (IRE) (Desert King (IRE))
2206a[6]

Ray Diamond *Jackie Du Plessis* 119c
10 ch g Medicean Musical Twist (USA) (Woodman (USA))
163[3] 750[5] 4424[P]

Raymond Reddington (IRE) *Chris Grant* 81h
4 b g Spadoun(FR) Martovic (IRE) (Old Vic)
2479[4] 2951[5] 3159[P] 5196[3]

Rayvin Black *Oliver Sherwood* 153h
6 b g Halling(USA) Optimistic (Reprimand)
197[12] 1988[3] 2617[2] 3151[16] (3449) 3740[2] 3989[2] (4253) 4622[6]

Raz De Maree (FR) *Gavin Cromwell* 92h 143c
10 ch g Shaanmer(IRE) Diyala III (FR) (Quart De Vin (FR))
5005a[13]

Razzle Dazzle 'Em *Shaun Harris* 87h
6 b g Phoenix Reach(IRE) Rasmani (Medicean)
1691[7] 1931[4] 2492[10] (4223) 4390[8]

Ready Token (IRE) *Charlie Longsdon* 117h 124c
7 gr g Flemensfirth(USA) Ceol Tire (IRE) (Roselier (FR))
58[6] (600) 771[3] (1795) 2288[2] 2766[5] 3371[4] 4352[8] 4876[4] 5375[2]

Real Gone Kid *Martin Keighley* 14h
4 b g Kalanisi(IRE) Karmest (Best Of The Bests (IRE))
2250[5] 2928[P] 3949[P] 5182[11]

Really Unique (IRE) *John J Walsh* 123h 8c
10 b g Witness Box(USA) Miss Od (IRE) (Good Thyne (USA))
50a[21]

Real Milan (IRE) *Anabel K Murphy* 91h 93c
10 b g Milan The Real Athlete (IRE) (Presenting)
108[P]

Real Steel (IRE) *M F Morris* 147h 148c
7 br g Old Vic Grangeclare Dancer (IRE) (Top Of The World)
51a[4] 603a[F] (Dead)

Realt Ag Leimt (IRE) *D Peters* 109h 108c
9 b g Beneficial Edwarda (Safawan)
12[5] 260[5]

Realt Mor (IRE) *Gordon Elliott* 98h 154c
10 b g Beneficial Suez Canal (FR) (Exit To Nowhere (USA))
603a[4]

Reaping The Reward (IRE) *Lucinda Russell* 110h 136c
11 b g Sylvan Express Zamaine (IRE) (Zaffaran (USA))
3038[2] 3448[3] 4306[6] 5328[8]

Rear Admiral (IRE) *Michael Easterby* 106h 126c
9 b g Dushyantor(USA) Ciaras Charm (IRE) (Phardante (FR))
2424[2] (2753) 3401[3] 3972[3] 5126[2] 5447[5]

Rebeccas Choice (IRE) *Dai Burchell* 100h 120c
12 b g Religiously(USA) Carolin Lass (IRE) (Carlingford Castle)
2600[6] **2907[6]** 4354[12] **4826[4] 5274[14]**

Rebekah Rabbit (IRE) *Tom Lacey* 89h
5 ch m Robin Des Champs(FR) Granny Grouse (IRE) (Rudimentary (USA))
179[6] 1648[12] 2670[2] 3382[2] 3789[6] 4538[P]

Rebel Beat *David Dennis* 106b
4 b g Lucarno(USA) Callitwhatyalike (Tamure (IRE))
2337[3] 2998[7] 3573[4]

Rebel Benefit (IRE) *David Dennis* 101h 112c
7 b g Craigsteel Tourmaline Girl (IRE) (Toulon)
590[3] 834[3] 2988[5] 3310[P] 3746[U] 3864[P]

Rebel Collins (IRE) *David Evans* 103b
4 gr g Jeremy(USA) Million All Day (IRE) (Daylami (IRE))
1449[2] 1644[2]

Rebel Fitz (FR) *Michael Winters* 152h 157c
10 b g Agent Bleu(FR) Gesse Parade (FR) (Dress Parade)
1185a[2]

Rebel High (IRE) *Derek Frankland* 78h 80c
11 ch g Hymns On High Celia's Fountain (IRE) (Royal Fountain)
88[P] 1999[3] 2303[4] 3313[5]

Rebel Island (IRE) *John Panvert* 66h
6 b m Heron Island(IRE) Rebel Rebel (FR) (Pebble (FR))
387[P]

Rebel Roger *Tina Jackson*
6 b g Revoque(IRE) Sally Scally (Scallywag)
2498[8] 2791[P] 3306[P]

Rebel Yell *Richard Price*
3 b g Shamardal(USA) Solaia (USA) (Miswaki (USA))
4345[P]

Reblis (FR) *Gary Moore* 107h 117c
10 b g Assessor(IRE) Silbere (FR) (Silver Rainbow)
2517[P] 2700[2] 3086[3] 3662[3] 4412[2] 4671[2]

Recently Acquired *David Loder* 66h
3 b g Beat Hollow Acquisition (Dansili)
4489[P] 5153[12]

Rectitude *Henry Tett* 35h
4 b m Virtual Evasive Quality (FR) (Highest Honor (FR))
2251[13] 2689[P]

Recway Lass *Hannah James* 92h
7 ch m Doyen(IRE) Zarma (FR) (Machiavellian (USA))
3925[P]

Recycle Rob *David Thompson*
6 b g Killer Instinct Bowdlane Barb (Commanche Run)
662[5]

Red Admirable (IRE) *Graeme McPherson* 120h 130c
9 b g Shantou(USA) Eimears Pet (IRE) (Lord Americo)
156[3] 2295[F] 3339[4] 4649[P] 5247[3]

Red Anchor (IRE) *Linda Jewell* 53h 89c
11 ch g Snurge Clonartic (IRE) (Be My Native (USA))
66[3] 223[6] 2416[4] 2827[P] 3218[P] 3906[P] 4531[3] 5480[8]

Redanna (IRE) *Robert Walford* 69h
6 b m Presenting Ask June (IRE) (Shernazar)
2022[5] 2316[P] 2670[P]

Redclue (IRE) *Mrs Gillian Callaghan* 123h 86c
6 br g Red Clubs(IRE) Stratospheric (Slip Anchor)
(838) (845) 1184a[4]

Red Danaher (IRE) *Sue Smith* 118h 107c
8 ch g Shantou(USA) Red Rover (Infantry I)
2039[5] 2865[2] 3243[2] 3631[6] 3969[4]

Red Devil Boys (IRE) *John Ferguson* 138h 132c
8 b g Oscar(IRE) Lohort Castle (IRE) (Presenting)
(2775) (3027) ◆ 3336[8]

Red Devil Lads (IRE) *Rebecca Curtis* 128h 143c
6 b g Beneficial Welsh Sitara (IRE) (Welsh Term)
3109[2] ◆ 3518[U] 3624[P] 4802[P] 5045[4]

Red Devil Star (IRE) *Suzy Smith* 123h
5 b g Beneficial Gortbofearna (IRE) (Accordion)
2011[3] 2373[F] 2926[5] 4484[7] 4782[6] 5225[4] (5301)

Redera (IRE) *A J Martin* 130h 102c
9 b g Chevalier(IRE) Lady Redera (IRE) (Inzar (USA))
2512[7]

Red Four *George Baker* 117h
5 ch m Singspiel(IRE) Protectorate (Hector Protector (USA))
(236a) 1150a[P]

Red Giant (IRE) *Noel Meade* 104b
4 ch g Beneficial Barrack Star (IRE) (Overbury (IRE))
9a[4]

Red Hammer *Nicky Henderson* 108h
3 b g Falco(USA) Voie De Printemps (FR) (Della Francesca (USA))
2032[3] 4502[2] (4979)

Red Hanrahan (IRE) *Paul Nicholls* 131h
4 b g Yeats(IRE) Monty's Sister (IRE) (Montelimar (USA))
2169[F] 2630[8] 4351[3] (5303) 5497[P]

Red Hott Robbie *Giuseppe Fierro* 107h
6 b g Revoque(IRE) Abbiejo (IRE) (Blues Traveller (IRE))
2840[7] 3363[10] 3619[2] 3865[4] 4432[4] 5313[P] (Dead)

Red Indian *Chris Bealby* 107b
3 b g Sulamani(IRE) Rafiya (Halling (USA))
(3165)

Red Infantry (IRE) *Ian Williams* 119h
5 ch g Indian River(FR) Red Rover (Infantry I)
2729[5] 3827[4] 4344[4] 4874[2]

Redkalani (IRE) *Keith Reveley* 106h
7 b g Ashkalani(IRE) La Femme En Rouge (Slip Anchor)
2980[5] (3503) 3933[P] 4203[P] 4796[5] 5368[7]

Red Lectra *Peter Bowen* 14b
5 b g Beat All(USA) Coronation Queen (Pivotal)
1966[10]

Redmond (IRE) *Venetia Williams* 108h
5 b g Tikkanen(USA) Medal Quest (FR) (Medaaly)
4264[P] 4463[P]

Red Mystique (IRE) *Maurice Barnes* 92h
6 b g Red Clubs(IRE) Sacred Love (IRE) (Barathea (IRE))
3054[5] 4202[5] 5256[7]

Red Orator *Jim Best* 97h
6 ch g Osorio(GER) Red Roses Story (FR) (Pink I (FR))
3083[7] 3227[9] 3660[4]

Redpender (IRE) *James Moffatt* 88h 89c
9 gr g Great Palm(USA) Josie Murphy (IRE) (Orchestra)
134[5] 470[P] 847[F] 1069[P] 1405[3] 2982[7] 3672[6]

Red Penny (IRE) *Jimmy Frost* 108h 92c
8 b m Definite Article Hurricane Dawn (IRE) (Strong Gale)
3122[P] 5032[4]

Red Piano *Andrew Hamilton* 80h 79c
6 ch g Flemensfirth(USA) Gavotte Du Cochet (FR) (Urbain Minotiere (FR))
3436[5] 4031[9] 4176[6] 4581[6] ◆ 4738[U] 4903[4]

Red Red Rover (IRE) *Nigel Hawke* 100h
5 ch g Royal Anthem(USA) Ithastobedone (IRE) (Be My Native (USA))
3582[U] 3744[F] 4339[4] 4614[5] 4882[4]

Red Riverman *Nigel Twiston-Davies* 116h 112c
7 b g Haafhd Mocca (IRE) (Sri Pekan (USA))
402[6] 1988[4] 2989[U] 3123[2]

Red Rosso *Rob Summers* 90h 86c
10 ch g Executive Perk Secret Whisper (Infantry I)
588[3] ◆ 976[P] 1133[4] 1422[3] 1689[3] 2040[2] 2220[4]

Red Rust *Robert Stephens* 40h
6 ch g Proclamation(IRE) Angel Dust (FR) (Cadoudal (FR))
644[8] 852[8]

Red Seventy *Sarah Humphrey* 119h 127c
6 b g Sakhee(USA) Dimakya (USA) (Dayjur (USA))
84[4] 338[2] ◆ (570) (974) 1135[4] 1382[P]

Red Six (IRE) *Peter Bowen* 109b
4 ch g Flemensfirth(USA) Glacial Missile (IRE) (Glacial Storm (USA))
4827[5] 5195[16]

Red Skipper (IRE) *John O'Shea* 122h 114c
10 ch g Captain Rio Speed To Lead (IRE) (Darshaan)
217[6] 442[4] (713) 896[2]

Red Spinner (IRE) *Kim Bailey* 128h 148c
5 b g Redback Massalia (IRE) (Montjeu (IRE))
(2541) (2993) 3857[4] 4770[5] 5123[2]

Red Story *Alistair Whillans* 85h
4 b g Kayf Tara Marabunta (SPA) (Exit To Nowhere (USA))
144[9] 2931[4] 4050[4] ◆ 4581[8] 5445[12]

Red Tornado (FR) *Dan Skelton* 119h
3 ch g Dr Fong(USA) Encircle (USA) (Spinning World (USA))
4489[3] (5153) (5401)

Red Tortue (IRE) *Charlie Longsdon* 115h 101c
6 b g Turtle Island(IRE) Howrwedoin (IRE) (Flemensfirth (USA))
1896[4] 2301[P]

Red Touch (USA) *Dave Roberts* 47h
3 bb g Bluegrass Cat(USA) Touchnow (CAN) (Pleasant Tap (USA))
2273[10]

Red Whisper *Rob Summers* 67h 100c
11 ch g Midnight Legend Secret Whisper (Infantry I)
42[2] 379[F] 699[6] 1603[7] 2124[5] 2315[P]

Reeflex *Jennie Candlish*
4 b g Multiplex Reem Two (Mtoto)
727[11]

Regal D'Estruval (FR) *Matt Sheppard* 96h 103c
10 b g Panoramic Haie D'Estruval (FR) (Cyborg (FR))
175[3] 514[6] 750[F] (Dead)

Regal Diamond (IRE) *Peter Bowen* 123h
7 b g Vinnie Roe(IRE) Paper Money (IRE) (Supreme Leader)
705[5] (999)

Regal Encore (IRE) *Anthony Honeyball* 140h 144c
7 b g King's Theatre(IRE) Go On Eileen (IRE) (Bob Back (USA))
1846[5] 2166[3] 2684[F] (3084) 3735[P] 3849[P] 4697[P]

Regal Flow *Caroline Keevil* 93h 131c
8 b g Erhaab(USA) Flow (Over The River (FR))
1699[6] (2057) 2517[5] 3445[5] 3818[2]

Regal One (IRE) *David Bridgwater* 107h 109c
7 b g Antonius Pius(USA) Regal Dancer (IRE) (Dancing Dissident (USA))
828[5] 929[2] 1137[4] 1154[5] 1261[6]

Regal Park (IRE) *Dr Richard Newland* 89h 91c
8 b g Montjeu(IRE) Classic Park (Robellino (USA))
(935) ◆ (1004)

Regal Ways (IRE) *Brian Ellison* 95h
3 bb f Royal Applause Step This Way (USA) (Giant's Causeway (USA))
3681[11] 4555[2] 5019[4]

Regent's Rock *Peter Niven* 56b
3 b f Shirocco(GER) Tiger's Gene (GER) (Perugino (USA))
2923[4] ◆ 3165[7]

Reglis Brunel (FR) *E Lecoiffier* 120h 137c
10 b g Ungaro(GER) Lady Du Rocher (FR) (Goldneyev (USA))
375a[U] 664a[2] 1477a[6]

Regulation (IRE) *Neil King* 134h
6 br g Danehill Dancer(IRE) Source Of Life (IRE) (Fasliyev (USA))
(186) 406[2] (933) 1039[6] 1263[3] (1612) 1766[2] (1949) 2058[9] 3041[6]

Reilly's Minor (IRE) *Warren Greatrex* 106b
4 b g Westerner Ringzar (IRE) (Shernazar)
3827[3] 5097[5]

Reine Des Champs (IRE) *Tom Symonds*
4 ch m Robin Des Champs(FR) Town Gossip (IRE) (Indian Ridge)
5351[P] (Dead)

Reivers Lad *Nicky Richards* 118b
4 b g Alflora(IRE) Reivers Moon (Midnight Legend)
3442[2] (4572) 5330[3]

Rejaah *Nigel Hawke* 118h
3 b f Authorized(IRE) Dhan Dhana (IRE) (Dubawi (IRE))
2137[6] (4888) (5415)

Reland (FR) *Jackie Stephen* 91b
10 ch g Shaanmer(IRE) Falkland III (FR) (Video Rock (FR))
870[P]

Relax (FR) *Venetia Williams* 144c
10 b g Fragrant Mix(IRE) Magik (FR) (Kadalko (FR))
2916[11] 3448[P] 4483[U] 4621[3]

Relentless Dreamer (IRE) *Rebecca Curtis* 125h 129c
6 br g Kayf Tara Full Of Elegance (FR) (Cadoudal (FR))
50a[16] 2018[2] 2631[5] 4352[F] 5395[5]

Relentless Pursuit (IRE) *Warren Greatrex* 105h
4 b g Kodiac Dancing Debut (Polar Falcon (USA))
186[9]

Reliable Richie (IRE) *R G Chapman* 57c
9 b g Sunshine Street(USA) Chance Eile (IRE) (Camden Town)
17[P]

Relic Rock (IRE) *Brian Ellison* 121h 124c
7 b g Bienamado(USA) Nighty Bless (IRE) (Executive Perk)
1922[2] 2201[P]

Relight The Fire *Denis Quinn* 97b
4 ch g Firebreak Alula (In The Wings)
2562[3] 2828[3] 4414[5]

Relkwood (IRE) *Paul Morgan* 89h
5 gr g Beneficial Rose Wood (Derring Rose)
2904[P] 5161[6] 5268[8] 5462[5]

Remarkable Man (IRE) *J P Owen*
9 b g Moscow Society(USA) Arctic Scale (IRE) (Strong Gale)
13[P] 293[P]

Remember Forever (IRE) *Richard Rowe* 80h
5 b g Indian River(FR) Running Wild (IRE) (Anshan)
4162[5] 4930[4] 5430[5]

Remind Me Later (IRE) *Gary Moore* 127h 132c
6 b g Zerpour(IRE) Two T'Three Weeks (Silver Patriarch (IRE))
317[U] 2613[3]

Renaissance Red *Brendan Powell* 88b
3 ch g Medicean Special Moment (IRE) (Sadler's Wells (USA))
2629[3] 2882[5] 3822[P]

Renard (FR) *Venetia Williams* 143c
10 bb g Discover D'Auteuil(FR) Kirmelia (FR) (Chamberlin (FR))
3057[5] 3448[P] 3706[4] 3996[2] ◆ 4347[2] 4545[2]

Rendl Beach (IRE) *Robert Stephens* 125h 113c
8 b g Milan Erins Emblem (IRE) (Erins Isle)
3705[7] 4066[8] 4542[P] 5053[3] 5466[7]

Rene's Girl (IRE) *Dan Skelton* 122h
5 b m Presenting Brogella (IRE) (King's Theatre (IRE))
1845[3] (2579) (3110) 4546[2] 5094[7]

Renfrew (IRE) *Tim Vaughan* 43b
5 b g Robin Des Pres(FR) Allstar Rose (IRE) (Fourstars Allstar (USA))
220[8] 2267[13]

Renneti (FR) *W P Mullins* 151h
6 b g Irish Wells(FR) Caprice Meill (FR) (French Glory)
2512[4] ◆ 3151[3]

Renoyr (FR) *Malcolm Jefferson* 110h
10 b g Kalmoss(FR) Idee De Valeur (FR) (Roi De Rome (USA))
1376[5] 2291[2] (2869) 3346[3] 3725[5]

Repeal *S Allwood* 25b
5 b g Revoque(IRE) Capania (IRE) (Cape Cross (IRE))
320[20]

Repeat Business (IRE) *J W Tudor* 94h 109c
7 b g Croco Rouge(IRE) Bay Pearl (FR) (Broadway Flyer (USA))
13[2] ◆ 5467[2]

Repeat The Feat (FR) *Charlie Longsdon* 62h
4 bb g Kingsalsa(USA) Sharon Du Berlais (FR) (Lute Antique (FR))
400[6] 2312[5] 2772[11] 3370[P]

Replacement Plan (IRE) *Richard Woollacott* 93h 90c
6 b g Flemensfirth(USA) Shannon Pearl (IRE) (Oscar (IRE))
5223[5]

Representingceltic (IRE) *Pat Phelan* 104h 126c
10 ch g Presenting Nobull (IRE) (Torus)
1871[9] 5390[U]

Residence And Spa (IRE) *Helen Rees* 59h 88c
7 b g Dubai Destination(USA) Toffee Nosed (Selkirk (USA))
2454[9] 3746[2]

Resolute Reformer (IRE) *Stuart Coltherd* 91h 104c
6 b g Arcadio(GER) Booking Note (IRE) (Brush Aside (USA))
141[7] 2400[7] 2788[8] 3472[4] 4032[P]

Resolution Bay *Philip Hobbs* 60b
3 b g Presenting Parthenia (IRE) (Night Shift (USA))
5227[9]

Rest And Be (IRE) *Alan Jones* 105h
8 bb m Vinnie Roe(IRE) Bobs Star (IRE) (Bob Back (USA))
714[2] ◆ 1960[3]

Rest Easy *Seamus Mullins* 84h
3 b f Rip Van Winkle(IRE) Early Evening (Daylami (IRE))
2137[7] 2883[U] 3213[F] 4683[5]

Restless Harry *Henry Oliver* 144h 140c
11 b g Sir Harry Lewis(USA) Restless Native (IRE) (Be My Native (USA))
2436[3] 2916[8] 3364[5] 4483[5] 4818[6]

Restless Rebel *Polly Gundry* 63h 115c
6 b g Rocamadour Restless Native (IRE) (Be My Native (USA))
3775[7] 5137[P] 5302[2]

Restraint Of Trade (IRE) *Jennie Candlish* 120h
5 br g Authorized(IRE) Zivania (IRE) (Shernazar)
638[4] (851) 1039[14]

Retrieve The Stick *Malcolm Jefferson* 102h 120c
6 b m Revoque(IRE) Anabranch (Kind Of Hush)
205[2] 2105[2] 2400[3] (2707) 3343[5] 3938[2] (4300)

Retro Valley (IRE) *David Dennis* 106h
3 b g Vale Of York(IRE) Retrato (USA) (Fusaichi Pegasus (USA))
(1037) (1177) 1321[3] 1456[2] 4851[4] 5266[4]

Return Flight *Micky Hammond* 103h
4 b g Kayf Tara Molly Flight (FR) (Saint Cyrien (FR))
2337[4] 2716[F] 3101[4] 3626[4] 4055[6] 4863[4]

Return Spring (IRE) *Philip Hobbs* 125h 134c
8 b g Vinnie Roe(IRE) Bettys Daughter (IRE) (Supreme Leader)
2473[5] 3518[P] 4340[P] 5120[3] 5454[8]

Revaader *Mark Gillard* 115h 78c
7 b m Revoque(IRE) Wave Rider (Zaffaran (USA))
5267[6]

Reve De Sivola (FR) *Nick Williams* 165h 123c
10 b g Assessor(IRE) Eva De Chalamont (FR) (Iron Duke (FR))
2361a[6] 3149[2] 3741[5] (4244)

Reventful (FR) *E Leray* 104c
10 b g Useful(FR) Serga Kan (FR) (Chamberlin (FR))
1223a[U]

Reverant Cust (IRE) *Peter Atkinson* 87b
4 gr g Daylami(IRE) Flame Supreme (IRE) (Saddlers' Hall (IRE))
3593[7] 4156[6]

Reverse The Charge (IRE) *Jane Walton* 40h 79c
8 b g Bishop Of Cashel Academy Jane (IRE) (Satco (FR))
453[6] 842[P] 1778[4] 1857[3] 2191[4] 3683[3] 4032[6]

Rev It Up (IRE) *Mrs K Lawther*
9 b g Revoque(IRE) Von Carty (IRE) (Supreme Leader)
122[7] 4748[F]

Revocation *Lucinda Russell* 115h 110c
7 b g Revoque(IRE) Fenella (Phardante (FR))
141[3] ◆

Revolutionary Road *Rebecca Menzies* 90h 112c
7 b g Shirocco(GER) Emilion (Fantastic Light (USA))
1170[12]

Revoque Dokey *Brian Eckley* 36b
4 b m Revoque(IRE) Somethingaboutmary (IRE) (Fayruz)
334[11]

Rev Up Ruby *George Bewley* 117h 109c
7 b m Revoque(IRE) Kingennie (Dunbeath (USA))
76[4] 483[4] 867[U] 958[3] (1067)

Rey Nacarado (IRE) *David Phelan* 55h 77c
10 b g Posidonas Ice Pearl (Flatbush)
295[P]

Reyno *Stuart Edmunds* 107h 90c
7 b g Sleeping Indian Tereyna (Terimon)
1647[2] 1931[3] 3932[2] 4645[4] 5388[6]

Rezorbi (FR) *Jonjo O'Neill* 115h 143c
4 b g Zafeen(FR) Reve De Nuit (FR) (Deploy)
3849[F] 4701[F] (Dead)

Rhialco (FR) *Emmanuel Clayeux* 139h 143c
10 b g Dom Alco(FR) Fhilida (FR) (Zelphi (USA))
4960a[4]

Rhianna *Kim Bailey* 82b
4 b m Robin Des Champs(FR) La Harde (FR) (Valanour (IRE))
242[6] 2856[10] 4790[10]

Rhymers Stone *Harriet Graham* 101h
7 b g Desideratum Salu (Ardross)
4154[3]

Rhythm Of Sound (IRE) *Micky Hammond* 84h
5 ch g Mahler Oscarvail (IRE) (Oscar (IRE))
3397[7] 3795[7] 4050[5] 4297[9] 4566[3] 5122[9]

Rhythm Star *Jamie Snowden* 114h 98c
5 b m Beat All(USA) Star Award (IRE) (Oscar (IRE))
2455[10] 2925[3] 4772[F]

Ribelino (FR) *Stanislav Kovar* 127c
7 b g Truth Or Dare I Rilabella (FR) (Roi De Rome (USA))
1885a[2]

Richardofdoccombe (IRE) *Gail Haywood* 87h 89c
9 b g Heron Island(IRE) Strike Again (IRE) (Phardante (FR))
(160) 3747[P] 3954[F] 4209[4] 4292[4] 4917[5] 5223[6]

Rich Coast *Noel Meade* 144h 113c
7 b g King's Best(USA) Costa Rica (IRE) (Sadler's Wells (USA))
6a[P] 1163a[15]

Richmond (FR) *P P C Turner* 115h 135c
10 b g Assessor(IRE) Hirondel De Serley (FR) (Royal Charter (FR))
3585[2] 3826[2] 4249[P] 4768[16] 5178[U]

Riddlestown (IRE) *Caroline Fryer* 112h 105c
8 b g Cloudings(IRE) Gandi's Dream (IRE) (Commanche Run)
44[3] (258) 381[2] 571[5] 677[P] 2140[P] 2408[3] 2556[2] (2841) 3131[2] 4187[3] 4391[4] 4590[2] (4845) (5020) 5309[P]

Ride On Time (IRE) *Ben Pauling* 103h 104c
5 b g Presenting Polly Anthus (Kahyasi)
237[P] 1824[5] 2290[2] 2596[4] 3771[P]

Ridgeway Flyer *Harry Fry* 111b
4 b g Tobougg(IRE) Running For Annie (Gunner B)
4102[2] (4894)

Rien Du Tout (IRE) *Mark Wall* 57b
3 b g Curtain Time(IRE) Back In Debt (IRE) (Bob Back (USA))
5144[7]

Rigadin De Beauchene (FR) *Venetia Williams* 92h 139c
10 bb g Visionary(FR) Chipie D'Angron (FR) (Grand Tresor (FR))
2482[9] 2907[4] (3364) 3624[F] 4245[P]

Rightback Atya (IRE) *P J Rothwell* 112h 105c
7 ch g Nazar(IRE) Marilyn's Rose (IRE) (Roselier (FR))
2525a[P]

Rightdownthemiddle (IRE) *Michael Mulvany* 130h 134c
7 b g Oscar(IRE) Alternative Route (IRE) (Needle Gun (IRE))
1937a^{4} 2227a^{2} 2531a^{4} 2817a^{P}

Right Madam (IRE) *Sarah Hollinshead* 72h
3 b f Jeremy(USA) Mawaared (Machiavellian (USA))
5019^{P} 5393^{5}

Right On Roy *Martin Keighley* 7h
5 b g Double Trigger(IRE) One Wild Night (Rakaposhi King)
1698^{11} 2152^{P}

Right Royals Day *John Needham* 4b
6 b m Beneficial Just For A Laugh (Idiots Delight)
2965^{7}

Right Step *Pat Phelan* 111h
8 b g Xaar Maid To Dance (Pyramus (USA))
2688^{8} 2956^{2} 3777^{10} 4745^{F} 5301^{P}

Rightville Boy (IRE) *Patrick Neville* 126h 119c
7 b g Cloudings(IRE) Journey Home (IRE) (Supreme Leader)
3302a^{6}

Rigolo Ville (FR) *Richard Hobson* 101h
10 gr g Visionary(FR) Imperatrice Ville (FR) (Seurat)
148^{P}

Rinnagree Rosie *Lucy Normile* 88h
9 gr m Silver Patriarch(IRE) Gretton (Terimon)
2429^{9} 2980^{6} 4581^{3} ◆ 5012^{5} 5368^{2}

Rio Bravo (IRE) *Graeme McPherson* 90b
4 b g Westerner Diaconate (IRE) (Cape Cross (IRE))
4434^{3}

Rio De Sivola (FR) *Miss V J Nicholls* 43h 112c
6 bl g Caballo Raptor(CAN) Pierrebrune (FR) (Cadoudal (FR))
4295^{6}

Rio Falls (IRE) *Jennie Candlish* 38h
3 b g Captain Rio Swallow Falls (IRE) (Lake Coniston (IRE))
2172^{5} 2439^{P} 2718^{F}

Rioja Day (IRE) *Jim Goldie* 86h
5 b g Red Clubs(IRE) Dai E Dai (USA) (Seattle Dancer (USA))
2189^{11} 2428^{P} 2754^{7} 2946^{5} 3473^{7} 3680^{7} 4036^{6} 4404^{2} 4585^{4} 5445^{9}

Rio Milan (IRE) *Fergal O'Brien* 113h 123c
9 b g Milan Lady Medina (IRE) (Be My Native (USA))
1807^{3} 2593^{5} 2853^{8}

Rior (IRE) *Paul Henderson* 105h
8 b g King's Theatre(IRE) Sara's Gold (IRE) (Ashkalani (IRE))
363^{2} 716^{2} 897^{5} 1547^{8} 2262^{P} 2736^{4} **3178^{P}** 3905^{7} 4291^{5} (4674) 5065^{8}

Ripasso *Jean McGregor* 14h
6 gr g Proclamation(IRE) Kompete (Komaite (USA))
459^{13} 656^{11} 881^{P}

Rising Breeze (FR) *Tom George* 86h
4 b g Shirocco(GER) Moon Tree (FR) (Groom Dancer (USA))
98^{10} 2271^{15}

Risk A Fine (IRE) *Philip Hobbs* 126h 139c
6 ch g Saffron Walden(FR) Portanob (IRE) (Be My Native (USA))
122^{2} **(622) (1006) 2686^{2}**

Risk It All (IRE) *Thomas James* 59b
4 b m King's Theatre(IRE) Stateable Case (IRE) (Be My Native (USA))
2677a^{13}

Ritual Of Senses (IRE) *Warren Greatrex* 106b
5 b g Milan Nonnetia (FR) (Trempolino (USA))
3847^{8}

Rivabodiva (IRE) *Lucinda Russell* 107h
5 ch m Flemensfirth(USA) Sheebadiva (IRE) (Norwich)
1854^{4} 2787^{6} 3342^{4} 4164^{8}

Rivage D'Or (FR) *A J Martin* 88h 139c
10 b g Visionary(FR) Deesse D'Allier (FR) (Pure Hasard (FR))
48a^{P} 2471^{9} 3017^{9} 3651a^{U} 4719^{12}

Rival D'Estruval (FR) *Pauline Robson* 125h 95c
10 b g Khalkevi(IRE) Kermesse d'Estruval (FR) (Cadoudal (FR))
1903^{5} 2340^{4} **3036^{6}** 3428^{8} 3630^{6} 4405^{P}

River Arrow *Susan Johnson* 96b
4 b m Kayf Tara Supreme Gem (IRE) (Supreme Leader)
4242^{4} 5049^{2}

River Bollin *Tim Easterby* 97h
5 b g Bollin Eric Bollin Roberta (Bob's Return (IRE))
3161^{P}

River Dancing (IRE) *Anthony Honeyball* 82h
8 b g Muhtarram(USA) Peacefull River (IRE) (Over The River (FR))
65^{5} **524^{P} 717^{P}** 824^{P}

River Deep (IRE) *Philip Hobbs* 125h 106c
6 ch g Mountain High(IRE) Testaway (IRE) (Commanche Run)
365^{4} 693^{P}

River Dun *S R B Crawford* 97b
5 br m Indian River(FR) Sight'n Sound (Chief Singer)
2849^{3} 5476^{4}

River Haze *Phillip Dando* 7b
5 b g Lucarno(USA) Kristal Haze (Krisinsky (USA))
4827^{10}

River Maigue (IRE) *Sophie Leech* 120h 130c
8 b g Zagreb(USA) Minor Tantrum (IRE) (Executive Perk)
3173 **(505) (808)** 2634^{6} **3040^{P}**

Rivermouth *Laura Mongan* 72h 84c
10 ch g Karinga Bay Rippling Brook (Phardante (FR))
66^{P}

River Of Intrigue (IRE) *Nicky Henderson* 109b
5 b g Indian River(FR) Molly Hussey (IRE) (Flemensfirth (USA))
4201^{2} 5143^{3}

River Of Time (IRE) *K M Hanmer* 58c
7 br g Oscar(IRE) Murrosie (IRE) (Anshan)
5270^{P}

River Purple *John Mackie* 27h 119c
8 b g Bollin Eric Cerise Bleue (FR) (Port Lyautey (FR))
331^{7} (464) 1005^{2} 1267^{5} 1523^{5} 1601^{8} 2168^{7}

Riversbridge *Johnny Farrelly*
6 b g Desert King(IRE) Kinsford Water (Then Again)
3081^{P} 3387^{P}

Riverside City (IRE) *Gordon Elliott* 117h 124c
6 ch g Presenting Blazing Sky (IRE) (Beneficial)
2228a^{5} (2675a) 3296a^{6} 3894a^{P} 4397a^{10} 5005a^{P}

River Wye *Anthony Honeyball* 74b
4 b m With The Flow(USA) Orange Princess (Cruise Missile)
696^{6}

River Wylde (IRE) *Nicky Henderson* 111b
4 b g Oscar(IRE) Clarin River (IRE) (Mandalus)
4915^{3}

Riviera Sun (IRE) *Henry De Bromhead* 128h
6 b g Milan Riviera Sands (IRE) (Mister Lord (USA))
19a^{6} 5025a^{11}

Roadie Joe (IRE) *Evan Williams* 136h
6 b g Golan(IRE) Granny Clampett (IRE) (Be My Native (USA))
(1289) ◆ (1453) (1613) (1870) 2886^{5} 4239^{8} 4769^{F}

Road To Freedom *Lucy Wadham* 118h 124c
6 b g Revoque(IRE) Go Classic (Classic Cliche (IRE))
57^{P} (397) **2140^{2} 2686^{4} 2975^{F} 3348^{U}** 3817^{3} 4066^{3} 4389^{9} 4983^{4} 5376^{6}

Road To Gold (IRE) *N W Alexander* 129h
6 bb g Gold Well Haut De Gamme (IRE) (Carmelite House (USA))
2189^{4} (2931) 3626^{2} (4202) 5256^{F}

Road To Respect (IRE) *Eoin Griffin* 130h
4 ch g Gamut(IRE) Lora Lady (IRE) (Lord Americo)
4332a^{3} 5024a^{5}

Road To Riches (IRE) *Noel Meade* 137h 173c
8 b g Gamut(IRE) Bellora (IRE) (Over The River (FR))
22a^{3} (2464a) 4007a^{2} 4731^{3} 5109a^{2}

Road To Rome (IRE) *William Kinsey* 110h
5 b g Choisir(AUS) Tibbie (Slip Anchor)
2965^{5} 4714^{2}

Road West (IRE) *Mrs C J Robinson* 83b
6 b g Westerner Gentian Blue (IRE) (Tirol)
531^{P}

Roalco De Farges (FR) *Philip Hobbs* 123h 140c
10 gr g Dom Alco(FR) Vonaria (FR) (Vorias (USA))
2061^{10} 2374^{6}

Robben *John Mackie* 83h
3 b g Dutch Art Little Greenbird (Ardkinglass)
1037^{2} 1177^{4} 2212^{5} 2869^{6}

Robbie *Keith Reveley* 117h 148c
11 b g Robellino(USA) Corn Lily (Aragon)
4424^{3} (4820)

Robbie Rabbit (IRE) *Nigel Hawke* 132h
5 b g Flemensfirth(USA) Leading Lady (Fraam) (146)

Robbing The Prey (IRE) *Nick Kent* 108b
4 b g Robin Des Pres(FR) Derravarra Lady (IRE) (Flemensfirth (USA))
2031^{4} 2709^{5}

Roberto Pegasus (USA) *Alan King* 114h 120c
9 bb g Fusaichi Pegasus(USA) Louju (USA) (Silver Hawk (USA))
2404^{4} 3014^{7} 4363^{7}

Robert's Star (IRE) *Mark Bradstock* 103h
5 b g Oscar(IRE) Halona (Pollerton)
2265^{9} 4874^{4}

Robertstown (IRE) *John Ferguson* 113h
3 b g Raven's Pass(USA) Sogno Verde (IRE) (Green Desert (USA))
3039^{2} (Dead)

Robin Des People (IRE) *Barry John Murphy* 109h 105c
5 br g Robin Des Pres(FR) Zelea (IRE) (Be My Guest (USA))
3716a^{4}

Robinesse (IRE) *Oliver Sherwood* 114h
4 ch m Robin Des Champs(FR) Jennifers Diary (IRE) (Supreme Leader)
(341) ◆ 2486^{9} 3119^{2} ◆ 4293^{2} 5280^{8}

Robin Longstride *Mrs N Frost* 31b
5 b g Morpeth Definite Lynn (IRE) (Definite Article)
5436^{13}

Robin Of Locksley (IRE) *Dan Skelton* 134h
5 b g Robin Des Pres(FR) Duggary Dancer (IRE) (Saddlers' Hall (IRE))
2052^{4} ◆ 2450^{2} ◆ (3063) 3974^{2} 4620^{12} 5139^{5}

Robin Roe (IRE) *Dan Skelton* 113b
4 b g Robin Des Champs(FR) Talktothetail (IRE) (Flemensfirth (USA))
(4880) ◆

Robin's Command (IRE) *Rose Dobbin* 109h 138c
8 gr g Tikkanen(USA) Marian's Wish (IRE) (Phardante (FR))
417^{3} 1328^{3} **(1494) (1553) ◆ 1777^{2} 2193^{P}**

Robinshill (IRE) *Nigel Twiston-Davies* 107h
4 ch g Robin Des Champs(FR) I Remember It Well (IRE) (Don't Forget Me)
1901^{9} 3366^{2} 3743^{F} 4843^{3}

Robins Reef (IRE) *Nicky Henderson* 133h
5 br m Robin Des Champs(FR) Tropical Ocean (IRE) (Anshan)
(2452) ◆ 2776^{2} 4734^{4} 5282^{P} (Dead)

Robinsson (IRE) *Oliver Sherwood* 120h
5 b g Robin Des Champs(FR) Silver Proverb (Silver Patriarch (IRE))
2299^{3} 2725^{6} 5452^{8}

Robintheaulad (IRE) *Sandy Thomson* 103b
4 b g Robin Des Champs(FR) Brotenstown (IRE) (Presenting)
(5127)

Robin Thyme (IRE) *Gordon Elliott* 126h
5 b g Robin Des Champs(FR) Boragh Thyme (IRE) (Simply Great (FR))
5024a^{P}

Robin Will (FR) *Miss G E J Anderson* 63h 77c
10 bl g Dark Moondancer Gleep Will (FR) (Laniste)
4000^{4} 4820^{P}

Rob Robin (IRE) *Chris Gordon* 37h
5 b g Robin Des Champs(FR) Ashwell Lady (IRE) (Presenting)
2460^{6} 3101^{8} 4196^{P}

Roby De Cimbre (FR) *S Robinson* 88h 105c
12 gr g Myrakalu(FR) Belle De Liziere (FR) (Bojador (FR))
129^{2} 260^{P}

Roc D'Apsis (FR) *Tom George* 116h 142c
6 gr g Apsis Rocapina (FR) (Solon (GER))
710^{7} **(2153) 2761^{P} (3776) 4361^{3} 5217^{P}**

Roc De Guye (FR) *James Evans* 19h 118c
10 b g Video Rock(FR) Kasibelle De Guye (FR) (Scooter Bleu (IRE))
2149^{P} 2693^{P}

Roc De Prince *James Ewart* 72h 111c
6 b g Shirocco(GER) Louella (USA) (El Gran Senor (USA))
728^{5} (1857) 2339^{6} 2948^{10} 3680^{9}

Roches Cross (IRE) *Josef Vana*
7 b h Whipper(USA) Danemarque (AUS) (Danehill (USA))
4960a^{P}

Rockabilly (FR) *Tom Weston* 93h 108c
10 ch g Robin Des Champs(FR) Massada I (FR) (Kashtan (FR))
5468^{3}

Rockabilly Riot (IRE) *Martin Todhunter* 107h
5 br g Footstepsinthesand Zawariq (IRE) (Marju (IRE))
638^{10} 1773^{5} 5295^{5}

Rock A Doodle Doo (IRE) *Sally Hall* 120h
8 b g Oratorio(IRE) Nousaiyra (IRE) (Be My Guest (USA))
4793^{5} 5295^{7}

Rockawango (FR) *James Ewart* 117h 130c
9 b g Okawango(USA) Janou La Belle (FR) (Shining Steel)
638^{11} 1905^{4} **2342^{F}** 3035^{6} **3475^{P}**

Rock Chick Supremo (IRE) *Dan Skelton* 81h
4 b m Scorpion(IRE) Ballerina Queen (IRE) (Be My Native (USA))
2086^{6} 2847^{3} 3819^{P} 4039^{5} 4323^{6}

Rock Des Champs (IRE) *Jonjo O'Neill* 102h 93c
5 b g Robin Des Champs(FR) Zaffaran Blends (IRE) (Zaffaran (USA))
1824^{4}

Rocket Punch (IRE) *Gordon Elliott* 76h
3 b g Makfi Crystal Reef (King's Best (USA))
2813a^{6}

Rock Gone (IRE) *Dr Richard Newland* 128h
7 b g Winged Love(IRE) Guillem (USA) (Nijinsky (CAN))
4159^{2} 4482^{F}

Rocking Blues (FR) *Rose Dobbin* 112h 147c
10 b g Lavirco(GER) Herbe De La Roque (FR) (Courtroom (FR))
2400^{2} ◆ 3014^{6} 3671^{F} (3934) ◆ (4203) (4367)

Rockiteer (IRE) *Henry Daly* 114h 129c
12 b g Rudimentary(USA) Party Woman (IRE) (Sexton Blake)
18^{4} 457^{P} 1807^{6} 2451^{2}

Rocklander (IRE) *Eoin Griffin* 105h
6 b g Oscar(IRE) Rua Lass (IRE) (Beau Sher)
25a^{5}

Rocklim (FR) *James Ewart* 109h
5 b g Laverock(IRE) Stille Baroque (FR) (Cyborg (FR))
2101^{5} 2754^{6} 3470^{3} (4035) ◆ 4474^{U} 4840^{4}

Rockmount River (IRE) *David Bridgwater* 107h 113c
6 b g Rock Of Gibraltar(IRE) Littlefeather (IRE) (Indian Ridge)
241^{2}

Rock N Rhythm (IRE) *Jonjo O'Neill* 126h 122c
5 b g Rock Of Gibraltar(IRE) Dark Rosaleen (IRE) (Darshaan)
(98) **2412^{5} 2691^{6} 3228^{4} 4225^{U}** 4452^{6} 5159^{6}

Rocknrobin (IRE) *Chris Gordon* 91h 104c
4 br g Robin Des Pres(FR) Our Presenting (IRE) (Presenting)
3085^{5} 3452^{5} 3915^{11} 4200^{P} **(4669) 4931^{P}**

Rocknrollrambo (IRE) *Ian Williams* 35h
8 b g Winged Love(IRE) Lady Padivor (IRE) (Zaffaran (USA))
5466^{10}

Rock Of Ages *Steve Flook* 110h 87c
6 ch g Pivotal Magic Peak (IRE) (Danehill (USA))
210^{F} 460^{4} 2838^{P} 3570^{P} 3868^{5} **4588^{3} 5309^{5}**

Rock Of Leon *Dan Skelton* 126h
4 b g Rock Of Gibraltar(IRE) Leonica (Lion Cavern (USA))
1977^{5} (2415) 2700^{P} 3216^{P} 5239^{6}

Rock On Bollinski *Brian Ellison* 59h
5 b g Bollin Eric Bred For Pleasure (Niniski (USA))
4509^{6}

Rock On Oscar (IRE) *Paul Nicholls* 138h
5 b g Oscar(IRE) Brogeen Lady (IRE) (Phardante (FR))
2239^{2} 2986^{2} (4063) ◆ (4848) 5273^{3}

Rock On Rocky *Matt Sheppard* 134h 99c
7 b g Overbury(IRE) Tachometer (IRE) (Jurado (USA))
1868^{7} 2438^{3} **2779^{7}** 3407^{P} 3923^{3} 4801^{8} 4965^{2} 5157^{5} 5454^{7}

Rock On Rosie (IRE) *Adrian Brendan Joyce* 113h
6 b m Gamut(IRE) Macs Goose (Kayf Tara)
2176a^{F}

Rock On Ruby (IRE) *Harry Fry* 160h 141c
10 b g Oscar(IRE) Stony View (IRE) (Tirol)
2198^{2} (2634)

Rock On The Moor (IRE) *Mrs John Harrington* 140h
7 b m Flemensfirth(USA) Home At Last (IRE) (Mandalus)
93a^{6} 3356a^{2} 3858^{5} 4699^{2}

Rockozal (FR) *P Chevillard* 91h
4 b m Rock Of Gibraltar(IRE) Corrozal (GER) (Cape Cross (IRE))
3815a^{3}

Rock Relief (IRE) *Chris Grant* 109h
9 gr g Daylami(IRE) Sheer Bliss (IRE) (Sadler's Wells (USA))
302^{5} 2429^{10} 2980^{3} 3361^{2} 4206^{7} 4797^{8} 5199^{4}

Rock The Kasbah (IRE) *Philip Hobbs* 152h
5 ch g Shirocco(GER) Impudent (IRE) (In The Wings)
1848^{2} (2639) (3733) 4717^{22} 5213^{11}

Rock The World (IRE) *Mrs John Harrington* 141h 156c
7 b g Orpen(USA) Sue N Win (IRE) (Beneficial)
231a^{5} **(1515a) (2053) 4770^{3} 5174^{7}**

Rocku *Russell Ross* 84b
5 b g Great Palm(USA) Suetsu (IRE) (Toulon)
4867^{13}

Rockweiller *Shaun Harris* 79h
8 b g Rock Of Gibraltar(IRE) Ballerina Suprema (IRE) (Sadler's Wells (USA))
180^{9} 2559^{9} 3067^{11}

Rocky Bender (IRE) *Venetia Williams* 108h 121c
10 b g Saddlers' Hall(IRE) Silver Spirit (IRE) (Parliament)
2701^{F} (3412) 3707^{4} (4505) 4649^{P} 5162^{3}

Rocky Court (IRE) *S J Mahon* 121h 106c
6 b g Court Cave(IRE) Easter Bee (IRE) (Phardante (FR))
1788a^{5}

Rocky Creek (IRE) *Paul Nicholls* 137h 165c
9 b g Dr Massini(IRE) Kissantell (IRE) (Broken Hearted)
2207a^{2} 2902^{P} 4113^{4} 4361^{10} 5218^{P} 5492^{3}

Rocky Island (IRE) *T H Messenger*
7 b g Heron Island(IRE) Loury The Louse (IRE) (Hollow Hand)
488^{P}

Rocky Rebel *Michael Blake* 113h 98c
7 b g Norse Dancer(IRE) Gulchina (USA) (Gulch (USA))
261^{3}

Rocky Stone (IRE) *Donald McCain* 99h 96c
7 b g Cloudings(IRE) Crandon Park (Sir Harry Lewis (USA))
2800^{3} 3402^{3} 3793^{4} 4047^{5} **4387^{3} 4713^{P}** 5233^{P}

Rocky Two (IRE) *Philip Kirby* 106h
5 ch g Rock Of Gibraltar(IRE) Toorah Laura La (USA) (Black Minnaloushe (USA))
634^{4} 799^{4} 1457^{2} 1684^{2} 2142^{5} 5230^{3} 5401^{4}

Roderick Random *Johnny Farrelly* 85h
5 b g Kayf Tara Clotted Cream (USA) (Eagle Eyed (USA))
119^{4} 3606 615^{P}

Rodneythetrotter *Pat Phelan* 92b
3 b g Royal Applause Ruthie (Pursuit Of Love)
2020^{2} (2414) 5195^{11}

Roger Beantown (IRE) *Zoe Davison* 78h 129c
10 b g Indian Danehill(IRE) Best Wait (IRE) (Insan (USA))
431^{P}

Rogue Angel (IRE) *M F Morris* 135h 150c
7 b g Presenting Carrigeen Kohleria (IRE) (Luso)
92a^{P} (1556a) 2228a^{F} 4397a^{4} (5005a)

Rogue Dancer (FR) *Michael Banks* 54h 97c
10 b g Dark Moondancer Esperanza IV (FR) (Quart De Vin (FR))
40^{6}

Rogue Planet (IRE) *Kevin Frost*
4 ch g St Jovite(USA) Shabra Lady (IRE) (Un Desperado (FR))
5315^{8}

Rogue Trader (IRE) *T J Taaffe* 137h 137c
6 b g Milan Bonnie Parker (IRE) (Un Desperado (FR))
50a^{2}

Roi Des Francs (FR) *W P Mullins* 145h 151c
6 b g Poliglote Grande Souveraine (FR) (Sillery (USA))
21a^{6} **(3635a) 4716^{6} 5191^{6}**

Roi Du Mee (FR) *Gordon Elliott* 142h 161c
10 b g Lavirco(GER) British Nellerie (FR) (Le Pontet (FR))
1938a^{2} 2207a^{3}

Roja Dove (IRE) *David Thompson* 119h
6 b m Jeremy(USA) Knight's Place (IRE) (Hamas (IRE))
(1001) 1154^{3} 1261^{2} 1376^{4} 2199^{U} 4272^{6} 4512^{5} 4736^{2} 5438^{5}

Rokbaan *Mark Usher*
3 b g Camacho Salinia (IRE) (Rainbow Quest (USA))
690^{F}

Rolling Dough (IRE) *Diana Grissell* 82h
7 b m Indian Danehill(IRE) High Dough (IRE) (High Roller (IRE))
106^{4} 507^{6} 2713^{4} 3089^{8} 4318^{5} 4674^{4}

Rolling Dylan (IRE) *Philip Hobbs* 124h
4 ch g Indian River(FR) Easter Saturday (IRE) (Grand Plaisir (IRE))
(2875) 3581^{2} 4137^{2} 4801^{3}

Rolling Maul (IRE) *Peter Bowen* 140h 87c
7 b g Oscar(IRE) Water Sports (IRE) (Marju (IRE))
2332^{P} 2660^{4} 2960^{P} 3622^{4} 4730^{13} 5284^{9}

Rolling Thunder (IRE) *Donald McCain* 100h
5 gr g Cloudings(IRE) Peazar (IRE) (Inzar (USA))
3245^{2} 3626^{P} 4176^{3} 4509^{2} 5412^{P}

Roll It Out (IRE) *Gordon Elliott* 138h
6 b g Kayf Tara Liss A Chroi (IRE) (Exit To Nowhere (USA))
50a^{13} 2236a^{2} 2676a^{3}

Roll Of Thunder *James Walton* 92h
6 b g Antonius Pius(USA) Ischia (Lion Cavern (USA))
157^{9} (805) 882^{3} 1329^{8} 1552^{2} 2029^{3} 4178^{9} 4815^{4}

Roll On Has (FR) *J-P Gallorini* 139h 111c
5 b m Policy Maker(IRE) Royale Lombok (FR) (Villez (USA))
4a^{6} 349a^{13} 1883a^{3} 2361a^{4}

Rollo's Reflection (IRE) *Ben Case* 90b
5 b g Shantou(USA) Lola's Reflection (Presenting)
700^{2}

Roll The Dice (IRE) *Philip Hobbs* 105h 116c
9 b g Oscar(IRE) Sallowglen Gale (IRE) (Strong Gale)
58[P]

Roll The Dough (IRE) *Philip Hobbs* 120h
6 b g Definite Article High Dough (IRE) (High Roller (IRE))
(2023) (2443)

Rolly Baby (FR) *W P Mullins* 135h 146c
10 b g Funny Baby(FR) Vancia (FR) (Top Dancer I (FR))
(5473)

Romain De Senam (FR) *Paul Nicholls* 139h
3 b g Saint Des Saints(FR) Salvatrixe (FR) (Housamix (FR))
(2092) 2480[3] 2845[2] 3449[5] 4720[2] 5175[5]

Romanee Vivant *Neil King* 64h
5 b m Multiplex Mrs Oh (IRE) (Arctic Lord (IRE))
2016[6] *2421[7]* *2702[4]* 3334[12]

Roman Flight (IRE) *David Dennis* 145h 122c
7 b g Antonius Pius(USA) Flight Sequence (Polar Falcon (USA))
(556) 850[2] 1039[12] **(1110)**

Roman Gold (IRE) *Gordon Elliott* 130h
5 ch g Beneficial Another Burden (Alflora (IRE))
3962a[P]

Romann Angel *Michael Mullineaux* 101b
6 b m Sir Harry Lewis(USA) Roman Gospel (Roi De Rome (USA))
3381[11] 4350[8]

Roman Numeral (IRE) *David Thompson* 118h 108c
7 b g King's Best(USA) Trespass (Entrepreneur)
1638[8] 3242[6] 3592[5] 3884[P]

Romany Ryme *Gordon Elliott* 115h 117c
9 ch g Nomadic Way(USA) Rakaposhi Ryme (IRE) (Rakaposhi King)
1418 (869) **1032[3] 1332[6] (1551)**

Romeo Americo (IRE) *Seamus Mullins* 112h 105c
8 b g Lord Americo Crazy Falcon (IRE) (Polar Falcon (USA))
395[U] 697[6] 876[7] 2734[9] 3414[P] 3950[4] 4411[5]

Romeo Is Bleeding (IRE) *David Rees* 107h
9 b g Carroll House(IRE) Ean Eile (IRE) (Callernish)
216[6] 3572[5] 4448[3] 4822[3] 5029[3]

Romulus Du Donjon (IRE) *Oliver Sherwood* 123h
4 gr g Stormy River(FR) Spring Stroll (USA) (Skywalker (USA))
61[2] (182) 467[2] 1082[3] 1943[2] 2182[5] 2687[11] 5065[6] 5440[7]

Ronaldinho (IRE) *Dianne Sayer* 119h
5 b g Jeremy(USA) Spring Glory (Dr Fong (USA))
221[U] 837[5] 1065[2] 1499[5] 1637[6] 5450[5]

Ron Hegarty (IRE) *Seamus Durack* 76b
4 b g Gamut(IRE) Financial Heiress (IRE) (Oscar (IRE))
671[1] 875[3]

Rons Dream *Peter Bowen* 142h
5 b m Kayf Tara Empress Of Light (Emperor Jones (USA))
1848[5] (2484) 3034[2] 3407[5] 3732[6] 4699[9] (5299)

Rooster Byron (IRE) *Paul Nolan* 127h
4 b g Oscar(IRE) Our Song (Classic Cliche (IRE))
9a[14]

Roparta Avenue *Diana Grissell* 84h 93c
8 b g Nomadic Way(USA) Miss Fizz (Charmer (IRE))
223[4] 2830[4] 4673[F] (5480)

Rory O'Moore (IRE) *Ronald O'Neill* 123h 114c
10 b g Stowaway Champagne Lady (IRE) (Turtle Island (IRE))
4133a[3]

Rory's Valentine (IRE) *J Larkin* 88b
4 br m Windsor Knot(IRE) Housekeeping (Dansili)
9a[15]

Rosabi (FR) *H Paysan* 103c
8 b g Roli Abi(FR) Rose De Hoc (FR) (Rose Laurel)
1223a[6]

Rosa Fleet (IRE) *Venetia Williams* 117h 122c
7 b m Alflora(IRE) Crimond (IRE) (Zaffaran (USA))
382[4] (2403) ◆ 3007[3] ◆ 3499[4] 4319[5] 4962[3] 5222[4]

Roseini (IRE) *Rob Summers* 2h
9 b m Dr Massini(IRE) Deise Rose (IRE) (Glacial Storm (USA))
704[11]

Roselaine (FR) *G Chaignon* 109c
10 b m Sleeping Car(FR) Solaine (FR) (Pot D'Or (FR))
313a[5]

Roseneath (IRE) *Alex Hales* 64h 97c
11 b g Saddlers' Hall(IRE) Vital Approach (IRE) (Mandalus)
66[5] 743[P]

Rose Of The Moon (IRE) *Ben Haslam* 99h 110c
9 b g Moonax(IRE) Little Rose (IRE) (Roselier (FR))
48a[4] 471[4] 2471[5] 3336[9]

Rose Red *Rob Summers* 88h
8 ch m Weld Secret Whisper (Infantry I)
811[3] 937[2] 1095[5] 1384[7] 1931[6] 2964[P] 3143[5]

Rose Revived *Jonjo O'Neill* 87h
4 b m Midnight Legend Miniature Rose (Anshan)
3927[P] 4388[5] 4784[6] 5221[4]

Rosette *Alan Swinbank* 69b
3 b f Archipenko(USA) Roses (Muhtarram (USA))
2195[4]

Rosetub (IRE) *T J Corcoran* 55h
7 b m Kutub(IRE) Bucktainey Rose (IRE) (Lafontaine I (USA))
25a[13]

Roseville Cottage (IRE) *John Wade* 98h 104c
8 b g Kris Kin(USA) Johnny's Idea (IRE) (Woodborough (USA))
255[2] 519[8] 841[P]

Roseyroo (IRE) *Miss L J Cabble* 118c
8 b m Brian Boru Rose Island (Jupiter Island)
16[2]

Rosie Alice (IRE) *C Byrnes* 120h
4 ch m Beneficial Caltra Royale (IRE) (Moscow Society (USA))
3873a[7]

Rosie Hall (IRE) *John Wainwright* 23h
5 ch m Lion Heart(USA) Baltic Dip (IRE) (Benny The Dip (USA))
1660[6] 1886[11]

Rosie Revenue *Gordon Elliott* 101h
5 b m Beneficial Returning (Bob's Return (IRE))
28[3] 238[4] 1329[3] 1497[3]

Rosies Peacock *D H Llewellyn* 60b 112c
12 b g Peacock Jewel Final Rose (Derring Rose)
15[7]

Roskeen Boy (IRE) *W M Wanless*
10 b g Oscar(IRE) Peptic Lady (IRE) (Royal Fountain)
151[P]

Roskilly (IRE) *Donald McCain* 90h
4 ch g Hurricane Run(IRE) Party Feet (IRE) (Noverre (USA))
336[8]

Rosquero (FR) *Kenny Johnson* 86h 94c
10 ch g Blushing Flame(USA) Kingsgirl (FR) (Dom Alco (FR))
2339[4] 2705[5] 2981[6] 3308[2] 3683[4] (3938) 4325[6] 5197[U] 5366[2]

Rossetti *Mrs A Malzard* 115h
7 gr g Dansili Snowdrops (Gulch (USA))
740a[F] (844a) (985a) 5364a[2]

Rosshaven Lady (IRE) *A P O'Brien* 105b
5 ch m Stowaway Penny Haven (IRE) (Camden Town)
2677a[8]

Rossington *John Wainwright* 67h
6 b g Gentleman's Deal(IRE) Ettrbee (IRE) (Lujain (USA))
353[5] 620[8]

Rossini's Dancer *N W Alexander* 116c
10 b g Rossini(USA) Bint Alhabib (Nashwan (USA))
5449[F]

Rosskerrig (IRE) *Dan Skelton* 78b
5 b g Flemensfirth(USA) Ryazhenka (IRE) (Soviet Star (USA))
1645[6]

Rossvoss *T M Walsh* 137h 133c
7 b g Medicean Dixielake (IRE) (Lake Coniston (IRE))
(3071a) **3296a[15] 4719[P]**

Rosygo (IRE) *Adrian Wintle* 104h
7 b m Oscar(IRE) Sharp Single (IRE) (Supreme Leader)
2697[5] 2985[P] 4454[F] 4855[3] 5223[P]

Rothman (FR) *Paul Nicholls* 103h 127c
5 b g Michel Georges Bravecentadj (FR) (True Brave (USA))
641[3] 1006[2] (1351) 4852[3] 5101[2]

Rouge Devils (IRE) *Paul Nicholls* 83b
4 b g Scorpion(IRE) Penny's Dream (IRE) (Saddlers' Hall (IRE))
1872[7]

Rouge Et Blanc (FR) *Oliver Sherwood* 105h 136c
10 ch g Mansonnien(FR) Fidelety (FR) (Villez (USA))
151[2] 470[6] (2758) 2877[5] 3521[P] 5193[16]

Rough Justice (IRE) *Alan Brown* 128h 130c
7 b g Beneficial Ringzar (IRE) (Shernazar)
2404[P] 3339[P]

Rough King (IRE) *Jennie Candlish* 105h
6 b g King's Theatre(IRE) Ringzar (IRE) (Shernazar)
158[P]

Round Robin (IRE) *Henry Daly* 81h
4 b g Robin Des Pres(FR) Another Whiparound (IRE) (Saddlers' Hall (IRE))
220[3] 2690[2]

Round Tower (IRE) *Karl Thornton* 123h
6 br g Presenting Cash Customer (IRE) (Bob Back (USA))
2754[2]

Rouquine Sauvage *Anthony Honeyball* 101h 115c
7 ch m Loup Sauvage(USA) No Need For Alarm (Romany Rye)
2365[F] 3042[2] 3379[6] 3977[4] 4647[5]

Routine Procedure (IRE) *Robin Dickin* 95h
5 b g Arcadio(GER) Wayward Bride (IRE) (Shernazar)
524[P]

Roving Lad (IRE) *Paul John Gilligan* 51h 51c
8 b g Vinnie Roe(IRE) Pellerossa (IRE) (Good Thyne (USA))
394[4]

Rowdy Rocher (IRE) *Sandy Thomson* 114h 122c
9 br g Winged Love(IRE) Madam Rocher (IRE) (Roselier (FR))
3425[F] 3792[P] 5089[2]

Roxy Belle *Mark Rimell* 74b
5 b m Black Sam Bellamy(IRE) Royal Roxy (IRE) (Exit To Nowhere (USA))
5286[11]

Roxyfet (FR) *Micky Hammond* 111h 117c
5 b g Califet(FR) Roxalamour (FR) (Valanour (IRE))
485[7] 731[7] 848[3] 1031[4] 1367[5] 1685[5] 1891[5] (2705) 2844[4] 2894[3] (3241) 3401[4] 4048[2] (4329) (4513) **(4554)** 4705[2] **5346[2]**

Roxy The Rebel *Simon Waugh* 75h
5 b m Bollin Eric Petrea (St Ninian)
3802[6] 4299[P] 4835[6]

Royal Astarania (FR) *P Peltier* 140h 138c
6 b g Astarabad(USA) Royale Cazoumaille (FR) (Villez (USA))
375a[9] 1884a[9]

Royal Battalion *Gary Moore* 110h
4 b g Sea The Stars(IRE) Yummy Mummy (Montjeu (IRE))
98[8] 491[4] ◆ 671[4] 930[3] (1239) 1354[2] 1734[4] 5076[6]

Royal Boy (FR) *Rebecca Curtis* 94h 53c
8 bb g Lavirco(GER) Quintanilla (FR) (Royal Charter (FR))
2334[F] 2438[4]

Royal Captain (IRE) *Ben Case* 107b
6 br g Presenting Dunahall Queen (IRE) (Saddlers' Hall (IRE))
2122[P]

Royal Caviar (IRE) *W P Mullins* 142h
7 b g Vinnie Roe(IRE) Blackwater Babe (IRE) (Arctic Lord (IRE))
3890a[2] 4516a[2] 5002a[2]

Royal Charm (FR) *Alexandra Dunn* 116h 117c
10 bl g Cadoudal(FR) Victoria Royale (FR) (Garde Royale)
4342[P]

Royal Chatelier (FR) *N W Alexander* 96h 109c
10 b g Video Rock(FR) Attualita (FR) (Master Thatch)
290[2]

Royal Chief (IRE) *Alexandra Dunn* 106h 110c
6 gr g Royal Anthem(USA) Help Yourself (IRE) (Roselier (FR))
2090[3] 2447[5] 2664[6] 2985[2] ◆ 4883[7] **5388[9]**

Royal Craftsman (IRE) *Peter Bowen* 92h
5 b g Robin Des Pres(FR) Crafty Women (IRE) (Warcraft (USA))
441[U] 613[6] 773[6] 1055[9] 1375[10]

Royal Debutante (IRE) *Paul Webber* 109b
4 b m Presenting Chinatownqueen (IRE) (Westerner)
(3469) 4074[4] 4623[8]

Royale Django (IRE) *Tim Vaughan* 128h 138c
6 b g Kayf Tara Royale Boja (FR) (Kadalko (FR))
(394) (641) 1138[6] **3929[3] 4451[F] 4887[3]**

Royale Flag (FR) *F-M Cottin* 125h 138c
5 ch m Nickname(FR) Royale Surabaya (FR) (Turgeon (USA))
664a[10]

Royale Knight *Dr Richard Newland* 123h 148c
9 b g King's Theatre(IRE) Gardana (FR) (Garde Royale)
1736[7] **(2146)** 3904[2] 4241[5] **5327[4]**

Royale's Legacy *Anthony Honeyball* 98h
6 bl g Fair Mix(IRE) Royale De Vassy (FR) (Royal Charter (FR))
595[5]

Royal Etiquette (IRE) *Lawney Hill* 91h
8 b g Royal Applause Alpine Gold (IRE) (Montjeu (IRE))
571[4]

Royal Guardsman (IRE) *Ali Stronge* 131h 129c
8 bb g King's Theatre(IRE) Lisa Du Chenet (FR) (Garde Royale)
197[P] (2781) 3733[P] **4487[4]** 5284[P]

Royal Irish Hussar (IRE) *Nicky Henderson* 138h
5 b g Galileo(IRE) Adjalisa (IRE) (Darshaan)
317[4] 1381[3]

Royal Macnab (IRE) *Rebecca Menzies* 108h 126c
7 b g Beneficial Tina McBride (IRE) (Oscar (IRE))
304[5] 2329[6] 2648[P] (2947) 3425[2] 4787[7] 5411[7]

Royal Milan (IRE) *Philip Hobbs* 121h
5 b g Milan Aimees Princess (IRE) (Good Thyne (USA))
3334[3] 3839[5] (4419) 5396[P]

Royal Moll (IRE) *Warren Greatrex* 118h
8 b m King's Theatre(IRE) Moll Bawn (IRE) (Presenting)
85[8]

Royal Native (IRE) *Anthony Honeyball* 120h 121c
7 b g King's Theatre(IRE) Hollygrove Native (IRE) (Be My Native (USA))
174[3] 4066[4]

Royal Palladium (FR) *Venetia Williams* 102h 132c
7 gr g King's Theatre(IRE) Dent Sucree (FR) (Turgeon (USA))
2348[2] 2643[5] 3079[P] 3707[5] 4444[P]

Royal Player *Philip Hobbs* 131h 149c
6 b g King's Theatre(IRE) Kaydee Queen (IRE) (Bob's Return (IRE))
2187[P]

Royal Plaza *Alan King* 98b
4 b g King's Theatre(IRE) Friendly Craic (IRE) (Mister Lord (USA))
2702[2] 5188[4]

Royalracket (IRE) *Paul Webber* 85h 102c
7 b g Royal Anthem(USA) Allaracket (IRE) (The Parson)
44[2] 490[2] 782[5]

Royalraise (IRE) *Oliver Sherwood* 124h 124c
6 b g Royal Anthem(USA) Raise The Issue (IRE) (Galileo (IRE))
(181) 595[2] **2733[2] 4744[2]**

Royal Regatta (IRE) *Philip Hobbs* 132h 161c
7 b g King's Theatre(IRE) Friendly Craic (IRE) (Mister Lord (USA))
2185[6] 2761[5] (3147) 3735[2] 4240[3]

Royal Roo *Mark Rimell* 67h
6 b m Overbury(IRE) Royal Roxy (IRE) (Exit To Nowhere (USA))
279[6] 4875[11] 5221[6]

Royal Salute *Anthony Honeyball* 105h 95c
5 br g Flemensfirth(USA) Loxhill Lady (Supreme Leader)
2258[5] 2563[6] 2763[12] 3955[6] 4440[3] (5067)

Royal Sea (IRE) *Michael Mullineaux* 108h
6 b g Refuse To Bend(IRE) Janayen (USA) (Zafonic (USA))
(1780) 2163[8] 3835[13] 4152[U] 4871[7]

Royal Skies (IRE) *John Ferguson* 120h
5 b g Dubawi(IRE) Kalana (FR) (Rainbow Quest (USA))
810[5] 895[2] 931[2] 1083[3] 1239[4]

Royal Street *Warren Greatrex*
3 b g Street Cry(IRE) Touch My Soul (FR) (Tiger Hill (IRE))
690[P]

Royal Supreme (IRE) *Alex Hales* 84h
5 br g Royal Anthem(USA) Supreme Baloo (IRE) (Supreme Leader)
106[P] 1310[7]

Royal Supremo (IRE) *Kim Bailey* 109b
4 b g Beneficial Slaney Athlete (IRE) (Warcraft (USA))
4880[2]

Royal Vacation (IRE) *Colin Tizzard* 131h
5 b g King's Theatre(IRE) Summer Break (IRE) (Foxhound (USA))
(2169) 2762[4] 3852[6] (4294) (4930) 5497[10]

Royalzaro (FR) *Harry Fry* 102b
5 gr g Laveron Royale Wheeler (FR) (Rusticaro (FR))
2126[2] 2729[13]

Royaume Bleu (FR) *Alex Hales* 60h 82c
10 ch g Kapgarde(FR) Dear Blue (FR) (Cyborg (FR))
211[7] 567[2] 926[10]

Roycano *Michael Easterby* 128h
5 ch g Lucarno(USA) Royal Distant (USA) (Distant View (USA))
2840[9] 3680[5] 3855[3] (4226) ◆ 5072[U] 5296[3]

Rozener (IRE) *Mike Sowersby* 92h
9 b g Moscow Society(USA) David's Lass (IRE) (Arctic Lord (IRE))
37[P]

Roztoc (IRE) *S R B Crawford* 66b
5 b m Desert King(IRE) Leitrim Bridge (IRE) (Earl Of Barking (IRE))
334[8]

Ruacana *John Ferguson* 147h 125c
6 b g Cape Cross(IRE) Farrfesheena (USA) (Rahy (USA))
2411[2] 2912[3] 3254[4] 4730[14] 5213[13]

Ruapehu (IRE) *Charles Whittaker* 122c
9 b g Presenting Silver Prayer (IRE) (Roselier (FR))
(266) 3024[P] 5274[9]

Ruaraidh Hugh (IRE) *Chris Bealby* 124h
6 b g Craigsteel Decent Shower (Decent Fellow)
(240) (626) (780) (969) 1856[P]

Ruben Cotter (IRE) *Paul Nicholls* 129h 146c
9 b g Beneficial Bonnie Thynes (IRE) (Good Thyne (USA))
4361[12] 5193[14] (5465) ◆

Rubi Light (FR) *Robert Alan Hennessy* 125h 155c
10 b g Network(GER) Genny Lights (FR) (Lights Out (FR))
24a[7] 2606a[2] 3603a[3]

Ruby Rambler *Lucy Wadham* 135h
5 b m Notnowcato Arruhan (IRE) (Mujtahid (USA))
(2302) ◆ 2778[3] (3065) 3372[4] 5094[P]

Ruby Redhead *Alexandra Dunn* 18b
5 b m Distant Peak(IRE) Redhead (IRE) (Redback)
5383[11]

Rubys Star (IRE) *Jeremy Scott* 81h
8 b m Exit To Nowhere(USA) Thyne And Shine (IRE) (Good Thyne (USA))
2870[5]

Ruby Susie *Seamus Mullins* 58b
4 b m Victory Note(USA) Ruby Too (El Conquistador)
2697[P]

Ruby Valentine (FR) *Jim Wilson* 77h 58c
12 b m Kayf Tara A Ma Valentine (FR) (Caerwent)
1671[1] 5371[4]

Ruby Vodka *Sharon Watt* 70b
4 b m Oscar(IRE) Auntie Kathleen (Terimon)
1858[7]

Ruby Wilde (IRE) *Graeme McPherson* 96b
4 b m Oscar(IRE) Hazel Grove (IRE) (Definite Article)
4847[9]

Ruby Yeats *Harry Fry* 51h
4 b m Yeats(IRE) Newbay Lady (Terimon)
2579[5]

Ruddy Article (IRE) *Paul Nicholls* 115h 89c
7 ch g Definite Article Cherry Tart (IRE) (Persian Mews)
531[P] 823[3] (1044) **1235[3]**

Rude And Crude (IRE) *Chris Gordon* 113h
6 b g Rudimentary(USA) Sorry Sarah (IRE) (Good Thyne (USA))
3117[P] 3487[5] 4129[P]

Ruggero *Roy Brotherton*
5 b g Tiger Hill(IRE) Bergamask (USA) (Kingmambo (USA))
1612[P]

Ruler Of All (IRE) *Peter Winks* 133h 101c
9 b g Sadler's Wells(USA) Shabby Chic (USA) (Red Ransom (USA))
208[3] 418[P] 854[2] 1263[U] (Dead)

Rule The World *M F Morris* 163h 164c
8 b g Sulamani(IRE) Elaine Tully (IRE) (Persian Bold)
95a[6] 1152a[S] 1556a[3] 1790a[2] 3357a[2] 3715a[5] 4517a[4] (5218)

Rum And Butter (IRE) *Jonjo O'Neill* 128h 138c
7 b g Milan Silent Valley (Forzando)
184[11] 812[6] 1046[3] 1325[9]

Rumble Of Thunder (IRE) *Philip Kirby* 127h
9 b g Fath(USA) Honey Storm (IRE) (Mujadil (USA))
645[7] 973[F] 1448[3] 3728[P]

Rumbury Grey *Steve Flook*
12 gr g Overbury(IRE) Polly Buckrum (Buckley)
5121[P]

Rumour Has It *Mark Rimell* 40b
4 b m Beat All(USA) Top Gale (IRE) (Topanoora)
4075[9]

Run Bob Run *John Flint* 77h
4 b g Beat All(USA) Rash-Gale (IRE) (Rashar (USA))
1484[5] 1704[4] 2152[P] 3077[12] 3516[12] 3914[P]

Run For Firth (IRE) *Kieran Purcell* 120h 99c
8 b g Dushyantor(USA) Run For Help (IRE) (Flemensfirth (USA))
3716a[P]

Run Hurricane (IRE) *John O'Shea* 100h
7 ch g Hurricane Run(IRE) Dame's Violet (IRE) (Groom Dancer (USA))
1480[F] 1604[8] 4223[F] 4854[P]

Running Brook (IRE) *R Mike Smith* 101h
8 b g Alderbrook May As Well (Kemal (FR))
285[6] (452) 727[5] 799[5] 957[4] 1638[P] 2069[8]

Running In Heels (IRE) *David Phelan* 51c
6 br m September Storm(GER) Ceo Draiochta (IRE) (Erins Isle)
297[4]

Running Wolf (IRE) *Alex Hales* 97h
4 b g Amadeus Wolf Monet's Lady (IRE) (Daylami (IRE))
2139[P] (2843) 3098[2] 3821[5] 4845[4] 5441[2]

Run Of The Mill (IRE) *Chris Bealby*
5 ch g Definite Article Stephens Street (IRE) (Kahyasi)
852[P] 1011[P]

Run On Sterling *Paul Webber* 107h
6 b g Dr Fong(USA) Dansara (Dancing Brave (USA))
678[P]

Run Ructions Run (IRE) *Tim Easterby* 137h 139c
6 b m Westerner Perfect Prospect (IRE) (Golan (IRE))
2411[4] (2717) ◆ 3337[3] 3627[2] 3998[P] 4800[P] 4905[2] 5299[6]

Runswick Days (IRE) *John Wade* 80h 95c
8 b g Presenting Miss Lauren Dee (IRE) (Montelimar (USA))
4938[5] ◆ 5366[7]

Runswick Relax *Kenneth Slack* 103h 104c
9 ch g Generous(IRE) Zany Lady (Arzanni)
2706[2] ◆ 2844[F] (3308) 3679[2] 3969[2] 4569[6] (4704) (4938)

Runswick Royal (IRE) *Ann Hamilton* 144h 153c
6 ch g Excellent Art Renada (Sinndar (IRE))
660[2]

Run To The Rhythm *Michael Easterby* 33h
5 gr g Erhaab(USA) Grace Dieu (Commanche Run)
799[11]

Run With The Wind (IRE) *S R B Crawford* 138h 134c
9 b g Sadler's Wells(USA) Race The Wild Wind (USA) (Sunny's Halo (CAN))
(961) 1502[3] 1904[P] 2329[P]

Ruperra Tom *Sophie Leech* 90h
7 b g Kayf Tara Cathy's Dream (IRE) (Husyan (USA))
4235[2] 4650[3]

Rupert Bear *James Walton* 105h 101c
9 b g Rambling Bear Glittering Stone (Dancing High)
1738[P] 2069[P] 2786[3] 2983[3] 3343[3] 4048[7] 4300[3] ◆ 4795[3] 5086[2]

Rupert Lamb *W P Mullins* 138h 148c
9 gr g Central Park(IRE) Charlotte Lamb (Pharly (FR))
7a[7]

Rush House (IRE) *Jeremy Scott* 38h
7 ch m Kris Kin(USA) Saucy Nun (IRE) (Orchestra)
1011[8]

Rushvale (IRE) *Ben Case* 112h
6 b g Moss Vale(IRE) Evidence (Machiavellian (USA))
528[3] 1826[P] 2041[3] 2488[2] 2871[3] 3238[4] 3795[5] 4235[P]

Russborough (FR) *Venetia Williams* 116h 130c
6 b g Turgeon(USA) Heritage River (FR) (Kaldounevees (FR))
2336[3] 2593[7] 5046[3] 5348[P]

Russe Blanc (FR) *Kerry Lee* 105h 138c
8 wh g Machiavellian Tsar(FR) Fleur De Mad (FR) (Maiymad)
2261[6] 2724[2] 3008[5] (3624) 4367[U] 5005a[P]

Russian Approval *William Knight* 84b
3 b f Authorized(IRE) Russian Rhapsody (Cosmonaut)
2009[4] 2777[8]

Russian Bill (IRE) *Noel Meade* 137h
5 b g Kalanisi(IRE) Littleton Liberty (Royal Applause)
19a[4] 2236a[5] 2676a[2] 3071a[4]

Russian Bolero (GER) *David Bridgwater* 112h 106c
4 ch g Tertullian(USA) Russian Samba (IRE) (Laroche (GER))
1047[3] 1479[5]

Russian Breeze (IRE) *Julia Brooke*
3 b g Shirocco(GER) Kirov (Darshaan)
4791[F]

Russian Link *John Berry* 99h
5 b m Rail Link Zathonia (Zafonic (USA))
2150[P] 2538[5]

Russian Regent (IRE) *Gordon Elliott* 118h 135c
11 b g Moscow Society(USA) Micro Villa (IRE) (Electric)
(289) 304[2] 657[2] (885) 961[5] 1502[2] 2082[2]

Russian Royale *Micky Hammond* 117h
5 b m Royal Applause Russian Ruby (FR) (Vettori (IRE))
487[U] (658) (777) 1036[2] 1180[5] 1369[3] (1793) 2144[2] 3152[7]

Russian's Legacy *Gail Haywood*
5 b m Kayf Tara Ruby Star (IRE) (Grand Plaisir (IRE))
5383[15]

Rustamabad (FR) *Tim Vaughan* 108h
5 ch g Dylan Thomas(IRE) Rosawa (FR) (Linamix (FR))
1289[7] 1693[3] ◆ 1952[2] 3846[10] 5266[P]

Rusty Nail (IRE) *Jimmy Frost* 58h 94c
10 b g Tikkanen(USA) Aoki (IRE) (Roselier (FR))
674[3] 806[P] 1237[6] (1355) 1978[F] 3468[P]

Ruzeiz (USA) *Peter Hedger* 66h
6 b g Muhtathir Saraama (USA) (Bahri (USA))
3083[10]

Ryalex (IRE) *Lucinda Russell* 110h
4 b g Arcadio(GER) Lady Ramona (IRE) (Lord Americo)
4835[2]

Rydon Pynes *Martin Hill* 129h 128c
7 b g Beat All(USA) Persian Smoke (Persian Bold)
1839[2] 2442[5] 2733[3]

Ryedale Racer *Malcolm Jefferson* 117h
4 b g Indian Danehill(IRE) Jontys'Lass (Tamure (IRE))
(206) 2319[2] 2704[3] 4509[U] 4941[3] 5367[3]

Rye House (IRE) *Tim Vaughan* 100h
6 b g Dansili Threefold (USA) (Gulch (USA))
440[6] 554[5] 828[7] 1115[5] 1810[2] 1931[2] 2555[4]

Ryeolliean *Gary Moore* 119h
4 ch g Haafhd Brave Mave (Daylami (IRE))
(221) 556[10] 1847[7] 2373[P] 2873[2] 3284[8]

Ryton Runner (IRE) *Lucinda Russell* 107h 84c
7 b g Sadler's Wells(USA) Love For Ever (IRE) (Darshaan)
291[9] 1331[P]

Ryvalo Des Brosses (FR) *Jean-Paul Gasnier* 94c
10 b g Passing Sale(FR) Idole Des Brosses (FR) (Port Etienne (FR))
1223a[4]

Sabroclair (FR) *Richard Woollacott* 100h 100c
6 b g Robin Des Champs(FR) Malicka Madrik (FR) (Volochine (IRE))
2300[3] 2736[7] 3368[10] 4356[10] 4921[7] 5435[4]

Sackett *Dianne Sayer* 76h
4 b g Midnight Legend Gloriana (Formidable I (USA))
1365[4] 1634[7] 1684[8]

Sacred Square (GER) *Conor Dore* 110h
5 ch g Peintre Celebre(USA) Square The Circle (Second Empire (IRE))
1305[2] 1568[3] 1740[3] 2294[3] 2850[3] 3177[6]

Sacred Summit (IRE) *Tim Vaughan* 62b
4 ch g Mountain High(IRE) D'Ygrande (IRE) (Good Thyne (USA))
2020[7]

Sacre Malta (FR) *Dominic Ffrench Davis* 109h 96c
9 ch g Discover D'Auteuil(FR) Neira Malta (FR) (Cardoun (FR))
4528[2] 4747[5] 5138[3] 5309[3]

Sacre Tsar (FR) *Mlle I Gallorini* 109h
4 gr g Stormy River(FR) Sartene (FR) (Bakharoff (USA))
3876a[7]

Saddle Pack (IRE) *James Walton* 47h 82c
12 b g Saddlers' Hall(IRE) Zuhal (Busted)
140[7] 485[3] 728[4] 884[5]

Saddlers Deal (IRE) *Brian Ellison* 98h 111c
10 b g Saddlers' Hall(IRE) Native Deal (IRE) (Be My Native (USA))
202[4] (331) 589[6]

Saddlers Encore (IRE) *Philip Hobbs* 135h
6 br g Presenting Saddlers Leader (IRE) (Saddlers' Hall (IRE))
3254[5] ◆ (3992) 4730[P] 5213[P]

Saddlers' Secret (IRE) *Mark Campion* 71b
10 b m Saddlers' Hall(IRE) Birdless Bush (IRE) (Be My Native (USA))
3791[P]

Sadiks Boy (IRE) *Aytach Sadik* 34b
6 b g Robert Emmet(IRE) Lough N Uisce (IRE) (Boyne Valley)
366[6] 644[11] 700[5] 2850[U] 3863[P]

Sadler's Risk (IRE) *Henry De Bromhead* 140h 154c
7 b g Sadler's Wells(USA) Riskaverse (USA) (Dynaformer (USA))
1152a[3]

Sadma *Nick Lampard* 110h
6 gr g Street Cry(IRE) Blue Dress (USA) (Danzig (USA))
241[P] (1702) 2000[3] 2418[4] (3256)

Safari Journey (USA) *Lucinda Egerton* 86h 114c
11 ch g Johannesburg(USA) Alvernia (USA) (Alydar (USA))
255[3] 381[3] 2788[7] 3225[2] 4275[P] 4418[5]

Safe Harbour (IRE) *Oliver Sherwood* 84b
3 b g Stowaway Beharista (FR) (Sendawar (IRE))
5315[5]

Saffron Prince *David Bridgwater* 112h 116c
7 b g Kayf Tara Jan's Dream (IRE) (Executive Perk)
2449[5] 4098[3] 4410[2] 4841[4]

Saffron's Song (IRE) *Harry Whittington* 72b
6 b m Saffron Walden(FR) Singhana (IRE) (Mouktar)
594[7]

Saffron Wells (IRE) *Neil King* 135h 130c
7 b g Saffron Walden(FR) Angel's Folly (Wesaam (USA))
1848[10] 2064[7] 2222[5] 2686[3]

Safran De Cotte (FR) *Henry Daly* 65h 116c
9 gr g Dom Alco(FR) Vanille De Cotte (FR) (Italic (FR))
2566[U] 2766[P] 3220[11] 3914[5]

Sagafor (FR) *P Leblanc* 90c
4 b g Forestier(FR) Sagacine De France (FR) (Dabistan (IRE))
4400a[4]

Sage Grouse *Stuart Edmunds* 43b
6 ch m Norse Dancer(IRE) Hazel Grouse (Absalom)
2856[14] 3386[P]

Sahara Haze *Phillip Dando* 108h
6 b m Rainbow High Gypsy Haze (Romany Rye)
2460[13] 2856[8] 3744[U] 4337[3] 4821[3] 4916[6] 5155[6]

Sail And Return *Phil Middleton* 123h 122c
11 b g Kayf Tara Maidwell (Broadsword (USA))
(589) ◆ (750) 855[7] 1053[4]

Sail By The Sea (IRE) *Neil Mulholland* 133c
7 b g Heron Island(IRE) Trajectus (Homo Sapien)
4254[P]

Sailors Legend *Michael Scudamore* 48b
6 b m Midnight Legend Jungle Way (Nomadic Way (USA))
970[13]

Sailors Warn (IRE) *Ronald Thompson* 128h
8 b g Redback Coral Dawn (IRE) (Trempolino (USA))
1459[4] 1591[6] 2170[6] 2577[F] 2893[2] ◆ 3725[3] ◆ 4152[7]

Sail With Sultana *Mark Rimell*
4 ch m Black Sam Bellamy(IRE) Strathtay (Pivotal)
5137[P]

Sainglend *Sean Curran*
10 b g Galileo(IRE) Verbal Intrigue (USA) (Dahar (USA))
363[P]

Saint Are (FR) *Tom George* 147h 155c
9 bb g Network(GER) Fortanea (FR) (Video Rock (FR))
2471[6] 2899[7] (4306) 5218[P] 5494[10]

Saint Breiz (FR) *Carroll Gray* 115h 110c
9 bb g Saint Des Saints(FR) Balladina (FR) (Saint Cyrien (FR))
109[F] 2568[5] 2874[2] 3371[P] 3709[6] 4453[2] 4884[5]

Saint Brieuc (FR) *Simon West* 89h
6 bb g Saint Des Saints(FR) Merci Alkmene (FR) (Exit To Nowhere (USA))
1182[P] 1368[4] 1497[5] 1552[8]

Saint Charles (FR) *Nicky Henderson* 135h
5 b g Manduro(GER) Tropical Barth (IRE) (Peintre Celebre (USA))
4484[5]

Sainte Ladylime (FR) *Kim Bailey* 132h
4 b m Saint Des Saints(FR) Lady Pauline (FR) (Hamas (IRE))
152[3] 3861[5] (4435) (4743) (4837) ◆ 5280[3]

Saint Elm (FR) *Richard Woollacott* 83h 98c
5 b g Poliglote Place D'Armes (IRE) (Spinning World (USA))
330[U] 799[10] 1166[6] 1501[7] 4886[8]

Saint Firmin (FR) *Robert Collet* 148h 127c
6 bb g Saint Des Saints(FR) Fleur Des Villes (FR) (Villez (USA))
4a[2] 349a[11] (1883a) 2361a[F]

Saint Goustan Blue (FR) *G Macaire* 134h 128c
3 b g Blue Bresil(FR) Les Saintes Glaces (FR) (Baryshnikov (AUS))
(4959a)

Saint John Henry (FR) *David Pipe* 126h
5 b g Saint Des Saints(FR) Noceane (FR) (Pistolet Bleu (IRE))
2054[F] 2759[8] 3078[3] 4127[2] 5045[5]

Saint Lino (FR) *Nick Williams* 121h
4 bb g Saint Des Saints(FR) Dona Rez (FR) (Trempolino (USA))
3467[2] ◆ 3876a[2] 4401a[U] (5135a) (5385a)

Saint Lucy *Jonjo O'Neill* 110h
4 b m Selkirk(USA) Sister Maria (USA) (Kingmambo (USA))
179[P]

Saint Palois (FR) *Emmanuel Clayeux* 118h 143c
7 b g Saint Des Saints(FR) Toutevoie (FR) (Sillery (USA))
1884a[4] 2822a[3]

Saint Pierrot *Francois Nicolle*
2 b g Della Francesca(USA) Soif D'Aimer (FR) (Robin Des Champs (FR))
4539a[7]

Saint Pistol (FR) *L Viel* 130h 140c
7 b g Saint Des Saints(FR) Miss Pistol (FR) (Pistolet Bleu (IRE))
375a[3] 1884a[6]

Saint Raph (FR) *Robert Walford* 114h 126c
7 gr g Saint Des Saints(FR) Speed Padoline (FR) (Saint Preuil (FR))
2153[4] 2832[2] 3046[5] 3521[2] 3957[7] 4251[4] 4589[4] (5149) (5419)

Saint Roque (FR) *Paul Nicholls* 146h 141c
9 b g Lavirco(GER) Moody Cloud (FR) (Cyborg (FR))
(2733) 3838[P] (5302)

Saints And Sinners (IRE) *Michael Easterby* 122h 140c
7 b g Gold Well How Provincial (IRE) (Be My Native (USA))
2425[3] ◆ 3036[3] 3425[U] 5448[6]

Sakhalin Star (IRE) *Richard Guest*
4 ch g Footstepsinthesand Quela (GER) (Acatenango (GER))
2840[P]

Sakhee's City (FR) *Philip Kirby* 123h
4 b g Sakhee(USA) A Lulu Ofa Menifee (USA) (Menifee (USA))
3724[3] (4416) 4799[2] 5230[2]

Salmanazar *Alan King* 135h 115c
7 b g Classic Cliche(IRE) Leroy's Sister (FR) (Phantom Breeze)
2977[5] (3728) 4139[4] 4786[P] 5120[2]

Salsa Sensation (IRE) *T M Walsh* 118h 113c
6 b g Luso Dance Rhythm (IRE) (Dancing Dissident (USA))
4279a[P]

Salto Chisco (IRE) *Oliver Sherwood* 115h 114c
7 b g Presenting Dato Fairy (IRE) (Accordion)
4782[10]

Salubrious (IRE) *Paul Nicholls* 155h 144c
8 b g Beneficial Who Tells Jan (Royal Fountain)
(2399) ◆ 3150[6] 3735[4] 3851[6] 4733[11]

Salut Honore (FR) *Alex Hales* 77h 91c
9 b g Lost World(IRE) Kadalkote (FR) (Kadalko (FR))
2303[3] 3062[3] 3468[3] 3820[3] 4276[3]

Samarinta *Nicholas Pomfret* 26b
6 ch m Samraan(USA) Araminta (Carlingford Castle)
2131[6] 3066[P]

Sambremont (FR) *W P Mullins* 119h 137c
5 b g Saint Des Saints(FR) Rainbow Crest (FR) (Baryshnikov (AUS))
50a[F] (4145a) 4735[8]

Sambulando (FR) *Richard Hobson* 96h 97c
12 gr g Kouroun(FR) Somnambula (IRE) (Petoski)
336[3] (465)

Sam Cavallaro (IRE) *Miss H Brookshaw* 94h 125c
9 b g Oscar Schindler(IRE) Gaelic Holly (IRE) (Scenic (IRE))
(12) 4892[P] 5178[F]

Samdibien (FR) *Sam Thomas* 31h
3 b g Day Flight Sambirane (FR) (Apeldoorn (FR))
4162[3] 4489[7]

Same Difference (IRE) *Warren Greatrex*
9 b g Mr Combustible(IRE) Sarahs Reprive (IRE) (Yashgan)
3373[P] 4483[P]

Samedi Soir *Keith Reveley* 123h
5 b m Black Sam Bellamy(IRE) Bonne Anniversaire (Alflora (IRE))
(482) 938[5] 1420[2] (1570) ◆ 1870[5] 4471[P] 4939[2] 5232[4]

Same Ole Trix (IRE) *Kim Bailey* 78h
5 gr g King's Theatre(IRE) Reklame's Gorl (GER) (Neshad (USA))
2221[8] 2646[8] 3021[11] 3484[10] 4650[U]

Sametegal (FR) *Paul Nicholls* 149h 154c
6 b g Saint Des Saints(FR) Loya Lescribaa (FR) (Robin Des Champs (FR))
(2222) 2760[U] 3029[2] 4013[2] (4485)

Sam Fairyann *Peter Niven* 84b
4 b g Black Sam Bellamy(IRE) Folly Foster (Relkino)
3476[6]

Samiesosa (IRE) *G A Kingston* 66h
6 b g Lend A Hand Delsy Flyer (IRE) (Grand Plaisir (IRE))
25a[8]

Samingarry (FR) *Nigel Hawke* 108h 147c
8 ch g Ballingarry(IRE) Samansonnienne (FR) (Mansonnien (FR))
318[2] 855[P]

Samizdat (FR) *John O'Neill* 71h
12 b g Soviet Star(USA) Secret Account (FR) (Bering)
104[8] 421[7] 571[P]

Sam Lord *James Moffatt* 107h 113c
11 ch g Observatory(USA) My Mariam (Salse (USA))
136[3] 502[F]

Sammy B *Lucinda Russell* 106b
5 br g Overbury(IRE) This Thyne (Good Thyne (USA))
2756[5] (3476) 4611[2]

Sammy Black (GER) *Alan Fleming* 113h 122c
7 br g Black Sam Bellamy(IRE) Sunshine Story (IRE) (Desert Story (IRE))
2236a[11]

Samoset *Graeme McPherson* 109h
5 b g Sir Percy Great Quest (IRE) (Montjeu (IRE))
354[2] 592[P] 860[3] 1714[6] 1893[4] 2291[3]

Sam Red (FR) *Alan Fleming* 133h
4 b g Denham Red(FR) Call Me Nana (FR) (Call Me Sam (FR))
2525a[4]

Sam's Adventure *Brian Ellison* 116b
3 b g Black Sam Bellamy(IRE) My Adventure (IRE) (Strong Gale)
(4001) (4488)

Samson *Hughie Morrison* 93b
4 ch g Black Sam Bellamy(IRE) Riverine (Risk Me (FR))
(1817)

Samson Collonges (FR) *Rebecca Menzies* 82c
9 gr g Fragrant Mix(IRE) Idole Collonges (FR) (Brezzo (FR))
2321[P] 3059[U] 3803[P]

Sam Spinner *Jedd O'Keeffe* 114b
3 b g Black Sam Bellamy(IRE) Dawn Spinner (Arctic Lord (IRE))
(4156) 5083[2] ◆

Samtheman *Pam Ford* 74h 93c
10 b g Dancing Spree(USA) Sisterly (Brotherly (USA))
296[2] 536[U] 1825[U] 2037[4] 2248[P] 2453[4]

Samtu (IRE) *Dan Skelton* 123h
4 b g Teofilo(IRE) Samdaniya (Machiavellian (USA))
(1518) 1806[2] 4324[2] 4941[5]

Sam Whiskey (GER) *Diana Grissell*
12 b g Tiger Hill(IRE) Schlenderaca (FR) (Monsun (GER))
599[P]

Sam Winner (FR) *Paul Nicholls* 144h 166c
8 b g Okawango(USA) Noche (IRE) (Night Shift (USA))
2200[4] 3850[5]

Sanaija *Nicky Henderson* 94h
4 ch m Pivotal Sanjida (IRE) (Polish Precedent (USA))
2164[5]

San Benedeto (FR) *Paul Nicholls* 147h
4 ch g Layman(USA) Cinco Baidy (FR) (Lure (USA))
(360) 1986[3] (2600) 2728[5] 3352[2] 4070[3] 4381[3] 5189[6] 5495[5]

Sand Artist (IRE) *Gordon Elliott* 76h 81c
7 b g Sandmason Belon Breeze (IRE) (Strong Gale)
303[2] 1287[4] 1380[6]

Sand Blast *Brian Ellison* 104b
4 b g Oasis Dream New Orchid (USA) (Quest For Fame)
2330[2] 2597[7]

Sandford Castle (IRE) *Johnny Farrelly* 114h
5 b g Norwich Pegs Polly (IRE) (Phardante (FR))
3105[15] 3411[3] 3592[3] 5148[6] 5418[8]

Sandgate *Neil Mulholland* 94h
3 ch g Compton Place Jump Ship (Night Shift (USA))
2448[4] 2954[4] 5221[7]

Sands Cove (IRE) *James Evans* 125h 130c
8 b g Flemensfirth(USA) Lillies Bordello (IRE) (Danehill Dancer (IRE))
121[5] 464[4] (2288) 2616[3] 3282[3] 4234[6] 4912[P]

Sandy Beach *Colin Tizzard* 114h 131c
5 b g Notnowcato Picacho (IRE) (Sinndar (IRE))
2013[7] 2262[7] 2458[7] (2988) 3348[2] 3747[2] 4451[U] (4617) 4964[U] 5465[12]

Sandygate (IRE) *Philip Hobbs* 116h
5 b g Golan(IRE) Wet And Windy (Cloudings (IRE))
61[3] 2312[3] 3152[9] 3846[P] 4843[4]

Sandy Grey (IRE) *Paul Stafford* 46b
6 gr m Sendawar(IRE) Sandy Road (IRE) (Supreme Leader)
963[5]

Sandymount Duke (IRE) *Mrs John Harrington* 146h
6 b g Hernando(FR) Joleah (IRE) (Ela-Mana-Mou)
53a[4] 2052[3]

Sandynow (IRE) *Peter Bowen* 113h 112c
10 ch g Old Vic Kasterlee (FR) (Stay For Lunch (USA))
108[2] 445[4] 1079[5] 1306[3] ◆ 1500[2] 1592[3] 2017[5] 3142[4]

Sangfroid *Andrew Quick*
11 gr g With Approval(CAN) Affaire D'Amour (Hernando (FR))
3585[P] 4295[F]

Sangram (IRE) *Jimmy Frost* 68h
8 b g Blueprint(IRE) Margeno's Fountain (IRE) (Royal Fountain)
30[8] 4854[7]

Sanok (POL) *Paul Cowley*
3 b g Jape(USA) Sun Queen (POL) (Don Corleone)
4345^P

San Pietro (FR) *Richard Ford* 101h 117c
7 b g Poliglote Sainte Berinne (FR) (Bering)
3802^4 4108^4 5017^2 **(5336)**

Santa's Secret (IRE) *Oliver Sherwood* 110h 124c
7 b g Basanta(IRE) Rivers Town Rosie (IRE) (Roselier (FR))
2266^10 2837^P (4386) 4842^6

San Telm (IRE) *Stuart Edmunds* 122h 124c
10 b g Oscar(IRE) Magical Mist (IRE) (Be My Native (USA))
1784^3 2669^P 3137^6 3837^4 (4643) 5284^3

Saphir Du Rheu (FR) *Paul Nicholls* 139h 168c
6 gr g Al Namix(FR) Dona Du Rheu (FR) (Dom Pasquini (FR))
(2215) ◆ 2783^5 3149^5 4732^6 **5176^6 5492^5**

Sapphire Moon *Richard Phillips* 71h
8 b m Alflora(IRE) Be My Valentine (IRE) (Be My Native (USA))
552^8 757^11

Sarafina *David Thompson* 70h
3 b f Mullionmileanhour(IRE) Nala (USA) (Lion Heart (USA))
1415^4 1631^10 1899^11

Sarah Marie *Philip Hobbs* 96h
5 b m Apple Tree(FR) Not Now Nellie (Saddlers' Hall (IRE))
5356^4

Sarazen Bridge *Jonjo O'Neill* 80h
4 b g Yeats(IRE) Strictly Cool (USA) (Bering)
3363^9 3835^15 4317^13 5242^8

Sarenice (FR) *Jimmy Frost* 41h
9 gr g April Night(FR) Delice Du Soleil (FR) (Altayan)
2263^9 2661^7 2880^P

Saroque (IRE) *Venetia Williams* 116h 134c
8 b g Revoque(IRE) Sarakin (IRE) (Buckskin (FR))
(2261) 2790^5 3518^4 3993^4 4340^2 4935^P

Sarpech (IRE) *Charlie Longsdon* 103h
4 b g Sea The Stars(IRE) Sadima (IRE) (Sadler's Wells (USA))
2543^9 2748^U 2823^11 3484^14 4846^3 ◆ 5374^10

Sartorial Elegance *Colin Tizzard* 116h
4 b g Kayf Tara Blue Ride (IRE) (King's Ride)
2126^4 2549^2 2879^7 3743^5 4137^3 4541^8 (5065) 5301^3

Saruni (IRE) *Jennifer Mason* 81b
4 b g September Storm(GER) Bathsheba (Overbury (IRE))
2875^P 2998^5

Sa Suffit (FR) *James Ewart* 139h 141c
12 b g Dolpour(IRE) Branceilles (FR) (Satin Wood)
2921^4 3440^3 3737^5 **3887^3** 4287^3 4610^2

Satanic Beat (IRE) *Phil Middleton* 132h
6 br g Dark Angel(IRE) Slow Jazz (USA) (Chief's Crown (USA))
638^9 (1719) 2186^8 2914^8

Satellite (IRE) *Tim Vaughan* 111h
4 b g Danehill Dancer(IRE) Perihelion (IRE) (Galileo (IRE))
3590^5 (5220)

Satin And Lace (IRE) *Michael Madgwick* 55h
3 b f Mawatheeq(USA) Katayeb (IRE) (Machiavellian (USA))
2954^6 3213^5 3523^5

Satin Waters *Christine Dunnett*
4 b m Halling(USA) Velvet Waters (Unfuwain (USA))
3537^7 566^P

Satu (IRE) *Lady Susan Brooke* 66h 65c
11 b g Marju(IRE) Magic Touch (Fairy King (USA))
2765^F 3108^11 **4431^P**

Saucysioux *Michael Roberts* 100h
5 b m Tobougg(IRE) Mohican Pass (Commanche Run)
3194^P (3664) 4382^7 4671^6

Sausalito Sunrise (IRE) *Philip Hobbs* 143h 166c
7 b g Gold Well Villaflor (IRE) (Religiously (USA))
1849^P (2482) 3116^2 (4238) 4635^4 5494^3

Savello (IRE) *Dan Skelton* 139h 161c
9 ch g Anshan Fontaine Frances (IRE) (Lafontaine I (USA))
8a^P (603a) 1152a^8 2058^4 **2511^3** 2914^4 **4240^P 4770^4 (5087)**

Saver *Nigel Twiston-Davies* 92h
6 b g Darnay Lifeguard (IRE) (Desert Prince (IRE))
522^9

Save The Bees *Declan Carroll* 107h
7 b g Royal Applause Rock Concert (Bishop Of Cashel)
2056^3 2398^3 2810^6 3035^5

Savingforvegas (IRE) *Stuart Edmunds* 117h
5 ch m Beneficial Peggy Cullen (IRE) (Presenting)
(2721) 3175^2 (3825)

Savoy Court (IRE) *Warren Greatrex* 120b
4 b g Robin Des Champs(FR) North Star Poly (IRE) (Presenting)
124^4 (4827)

Sawwala *J R Jenkins* 78h
5 b m Sakhee(USA) Jawwala (USA) (Green Dancer (USA))
179^7 591^7 1694^5 4025^P

Say My Name (IRE) *Bob Buckler* 127h
4 ch g Fleetwood(IRE) River Reine (IRE) (Lahib (USA))
2262^2 3146^9 3580^2 3976^5 (4342) 5263^2

Say When *Alan King* 97h
7 b g Fair Mix(IRE) Miss Wyandotte (Henbit (USA))
776^11 1085^8

Scales (IRE) *Kerry Lee* 110h 87c
9 b g Bob Back(USA) Mrs Avery (IRE) (Supreme Leader)
(2453) 2694^F 2997^2 3108^6 3932^8 4648^8

Scarlet Fire (IRE) *Nicky Richards* 121h 116c
8 b g Helissio(FR) Ross Dana (IRE) (Topanoora)
81^3 (483)

Scarlett Lady *Ali Stronge* 89h
7 bb m Kayf Tara Frosty Mistress (Arctic Lord (IRE))
120^4 462^6

Scarlett Peak (IRE) *Michael Easterby* 97b
4 b g Scorpion(IRE) Tabita (IRE) (Alzao (USA))
187^3

Scarper (IRE) *Harry Whittington* 80b
3 ch g Getaway(GER) Whats Anothershuil (IRE) (Bach (IRE))
4532^7

Scartare (IRE) *Rosemary Gasson* 94h
4 br g Trans Island La Speziana (IRE) (Perugino (USA))
1139^4 5434^9

Scarteen (IRE) *John Ferguson* 110b
5 b g Robin Des Champs(FR) Downsouth (IRE) (Supreme Leader)
2597^2

Sceau Royal (FR) *Alan King* 137h
3 b g Doctor Dino(FR) Sandside (FR) (Marchand De Sable (USA))
1866^2 2172^2 (2578) (3028) (3610) 4764^12 5175^6

School For Scandal (IRE) *Jimmy Frost* 93h 57c
7 b g Pivotal Sensation (Soviet Star (USA))
1238^12 1478^5 **1575^4 2698^P 2976^10**

Scimon Templar (FR) *Rose Dobbin* 113h 105c
7 b g Saint Des Saints(FR) Made In Law (FR) (Northern Crystal)
2342^P 2788^9 3441^4 3670^P 3886^P

Scoglio *Dave Roberts* 111h
7 b g Monsieur Bond(IRE) Ex Mill Lady (Bishop Of Cashel)
624^3 ◆

Scooby (IRE) *Graeme McPherson* 105h
4 b g Dubai Destination(USA) Maggie Howard (IRE) (Good Thyne (USA))
2750^7 3508^7 3773^4 4065^5 ◆ 4455^5 5266^F

Scooping (IRE) *E D Delany* 115h
4 b m Dylan Thomas(IRE) Meseta (Lion Cavern (USA))
52a^F

Scoop The Pot (IRE) *Philip Hobbs* 126h
5 b g Mahler Miss Brecknell (IRE) (Supreme Leader)
2513^3 ◆ 4139^P

Scootaloo (IRE) *Alistair Whillans* 45b
3 ch g Tagula(IRE) Just Tallulah (Tomba)
2923^7

Scooter Boy *Alex Hales* 114h
6 b g Revoque(IRE) Always Forgiving (Commanche Run)
2270^10 3130^6 (3608) 4344^5 4745^4

Scoppio Del Carro *Charles Pogson* 110h
4 b g Medicean Sadie Thompson (IRE) (King's Best (USA))
1967^3 2218^4 (2850) 3238^9 3855^11

Score Card (IRE) *Alastair Ralph* 112h
5 b g Scorpion(IRE) Auditing Empress (IRE) (Accordion)
4063^P 4888^5

Scoresheet (IRE) *Philip Hobbs*
4 br g Scorpion(IRE) Tocane (FR) (Phantom Breeze)
4874^P (Dead)

Scorpion Princess (IRE) *Charlie Longsdon* 107b
4 b m Scorpion(IRE) Cailin's Princess (IRE) (Luso)
67^3 1662^2 ◆ 2929^9 (4847)

Scorpions Sting (IRE) *James Ewart* 110h 110c
6 b g Scorpion(IRE) Strong Wishes (IRE) (Strong Gale)
(252) **455^4 1853^4 2753^3 3441^P**

Scorpy (IRE) *David Harry Kelly* 44b
3 gr f Scorpion(IRE) Passiflora (FR) (April Night (FR))
4653a^P

Scot Daddy (USA) *David Dennis* 59h
3 ch g Scat Daddy(USA) Flor De Oro (USA) (Out Of Place (USA))
4888^9 5153^13

Scotsbrook Legend *Shaun Lycett* 115h
7 b m Midnight Legend Scots Brook Terror (Terimon)
508^P

Scots Gaelic (IRE) *Chris McSharry* 95h 75c
8 ch g Tomba Harmonic I (USA) (Shadeed (USA))
4558^5

Scotswell *Harriet Graham* 116h 130c
9 b g Endoli(USA) Tofino Swell (Primitive Rising (USA))
3440^7 **4155^P 4511^3 4818^9 5259^4**

Scrafton *John Quinn* 122h
4 b g Leporello(IRE) Some Diva (Dr Fong (USA))
(1178) 1399^2

Screaming Rose (IRE) *W P Mullins* 111b
4 b m Darsi(FR) Screaming Witness (IRE) (Shernazar)
2929^4

Scripturist *Bernard Llewellyn* 19h
6 b g Oratorio(IRE) Lambroza (IRE) (Grand Lodge (USA))
824^9

Scrum V *Mrs N Naughton* 92h 97c
11 b g Sonus(IRE) Miss The Post (Bustino)
290^U

Scrutiny *Barry Murtagh* 71h
4 b g Aqlaam Aunty Mary (Common Grounds)
4202^P 4416^9 4817^7 5401^6

Seabass (IRE) *T M Walsh* 136h 140c
12 b g Turtle Island(IRE) Muscovy Duck (IRE) (Moscow Society (USA))
3651a^3

Sea Beat *A L T Moore* 117h 98c
5 ch g Beat Hollow Maritima (Darshaan)
19a^14

Seacon Beg (IRE) *Nikki Evans* 109h
6 b g Generous(IRE) Moon Storm (IRE) (Strong Gale)
524^P 811^5 1010^P 1323^DSQ 1478^2 2987^14

Seahorse (FR) *S Jousselin*
5 b g Falco(USA) Sea Paint (IRE) (Peintre Celebre (USA))
437a^P

Sea Lion *Tony Coyle* 24b
4 ch g Sea The Stars(IRE) Bourbonella (Rainbow Quest (USA))
264^5

Sea Lord (IRE) *John Ferguson* 152h
8 b g Cape Cross(IRE) First Fleet (USA) (Woodman (USA))
317^2 **659^F** (1038) 1325^10 2634^4

Sealous Scout (IRE) *Donald McCain* 125h 75c
7 b g Old Vic Hirayna (Doyoun)
319^10 (473) 1035^15 1292^5 (1633) 2145^5

Seamus Mor (IRE) *Henry Oliver* 105h 117c
7 b g Shantou(USA) Kublai (IRE) (Presenting)
(3628) **3916^F 4595^5**

Sean Airgead (IRE) *Mark Michael McNiff* 110h 117c
10 ch g Scribano Ryleen Lady (IRE) (Lashkari)
202^6 1291^5 1739^2 **1855^F 2477^4 5103^P**

Sean Ban (IRE) *Donald McCain* 114h
5 b g Flemensfirth(USA) Galingale (IRE) (Galileo (IRE))
3054^4 3363^4 ◆ 3784^3 (4285) 4570^2 5089^P

Seano (IRE) *Raymond Hurley*
4 b g Daylami(IRE) Topathistle (IRE) (Broadway Flyer (USA))
9a^22

Searching (IRE) *Gary Moore* 105h
3 ro g Mastercraftsman(IRE) Miracolia (IRE) (Montjeu (IRE))
3213^2 ◆ 3988^3 4619^4

Sea Scout *R A Ross* 59c
12 b g Lomitas Deeply (IRE) (Darshaan)
80^5

Sea Serpent (FR) *Gary Moore* 90h
3 b g Great Journey(JPN) Serpolette (FR) (Dear Doctor (FR))
3347^5 3730^4 4462^5 4784^12

Seas Of Green *Paul Cowley* 109h
8 ch m Karinga Bay Emerald Project (IRE) (Project Manager)
2812^P 4492^4 4648^P

Sea The Springs (FR) *Dan Skelton* 96h
4 gr g Slickly(FR) Cristal Springs (FR) (Loup Solitaire (USA))
106^3 678^F

Seaviper (IRE) *Richard Phillips* 125h
6 b g Presenting Priority Post (IRE) (Needle Gun (IRE))
2064^10 3027^9 4801^F 5120^15

Sea Wall (FR) *Chris Gordon* 132h 129c
7 b g Turgeon(USA) Si Parfaite (FR) (Solon (GER))
2151^5 (3042) 3351^F 3747^U (3917) 4294^5 4622^10 4933^4

Seayoujimmy *Daniel O'Brien* 76h
5 b g Primitive Academy Sea You Madame (Sea Raven (IRE))
1590^11 4848^6 5063^7

Sebadee (IRE) *Denis W Cullen* 115h 113c
11 b g Cape Cross(IRE) Phyllode (Pharly (FR))
75a^6

Sebastian Beach (IRE) *Jonjo O'Neill* 120h
4 b g Yeats(IRE) Night Club (Mozart (IRE))
2906^4 3137^11 3837^3

Sebs Sensei (IRE) *Mark Hoad* 101h
4 ch g Art Connoisseur(IRE) Capetown Girl (Danzero (AUS))
221^2 1998^5 2415^8 4411^P 5479^7

Secret Act (IRE) *N W Alexander* 53h
6 b g Milan Rose Of Salome (IRE) (Roselier (FR))
2931^P 4031^11 4835^P

Secret Dancer (IRE) *Alan Jones* 100h
10 b g Sadler's Wells(USA) Discreet Brief (IRE) (Darshaan)
1310^2 3015^14 3314^P

Secret Door (IRE) *Harry Fry* 113h
4 b m Stowaway Cellar Door (IRE) (Saddlers' Hall (IRE))
2277^3 3066^2 3995^2 4272^2 4909^3

Secretsista *Jennie Candlish* 46b
3 b f Presenting Princess Rainbow (FR) (Raintrap)
2777^14 3118^10

Secrets Safe (IRE) *John Joseph Hanlon* 98h
3 b g Arcano(IRE) Keritana (FR) (One Cool Cat (USA))
1232^2 1415^2

Sedgemoor Express (IRE) *Nigel Hawke* 116h 135c
7 bb g Presenting Pretty Native (IRE) (Be My Native (USA))
101^3 (420) 707^2 855^11

Seeanythingyoulike (IRE) *Jeremy Scott* 95h
4 b g Fruits Of Love(USA) California Dreamin (Slip Anchor)
1519^F 1698^U 2023^U 2563^F 3568^10 3772^4

Seebright *Victor Dartnall* 121h 134c
8 b g Milan Aranga (IRE) (Supreme Leader)
3232^P **4101^U 5092^3**

See Double You (IRE) *Ronan M P McNally* 121h 117c
12 b g Saddlers' Hall(IRE) Mandy's Treasure (IRE) (Mandalus)
4583^3 4607^2 ◆ 4638^2 (5012)

Seefood (IRE) *Dr Richard Newland* 130h 149c
8 b g Kahyasi Anne Theatre (Saddlers' Hall (IRE))
3528^F

See It As It Is (IRE) *Diana Grissell* 30h 24c
8 b g Shantou(USA) Opus One (Slip Anchor)
776^6 **1351^4 1546^7 5064^P**

Seeking Susan (IRE) *Miss Elizabeth Doyle* 88h
7 bb m Court Cave(IRE) Another Darling (IRE) (Un Desperado (FR))
2677a^15

Seelateralligator (IRE) *Dan Skelton* 91b
3 b f Getaway(GER) Charming Present (IRE) (Presenting)
5443^2

See The Legend *Sandy Forster* 91h
10 b m Midnight Legend Amys Delight (Idiots Delight)
4045^5 4638^P 5199^P 5412^11

See The Rock (IRE) *Jonjo O'Neill* 115h
5 b g Shirocco(GER) Samara (IRE) (Polish Patriot (USA))
1590^6 (2287) 2860^4 3449^9 5391^11

See The World *Emma Lavelle* 106h
5 b g Kayf Tara My World (FR) (Lost World (IRE))
2723^3 3839^P

Seeyouallincoppers (IRE) *Gordon Elliott* 127h
5 b g Saffron Walden(FR) Millenium Love (IRE) (Great Commotion (USA))
301^2 2513^6

Seeyouatmidnight *Sandy Thomson* 157h 161c
7 b g Midnight Legend Morsky Baloo (Morpeth)
2397^3 (2932) ◆ (3405) 4716^7 5327^3

See You Jack *Caroline Fryer* 79h 93c
10 b g Dolpour(IRE) Layston Pinzal (Afzal)
129^3 567^P

Sego Success (IRE) *Alan King* 123h 147c
7 b g Beneficial The West Road (IRE) (Mister Lord (USA))
1849^5 2482^14 (3038) 3624^F 4472^4

Seldom Inn *Sandy Thomson* 129h 140c
7 ch g Double Trigger(IRE) Portland Row (IRE) (Zaffaran (USA))
2067^2 2557^2 3100^3 4017^4 4794^8 5475^5

Selkirk's Island *Lucinda Russell* 94b
4 b m Yeats(IRE) Classic Gale (USA) (Classic Cliche (IRE))
2195^2 3060^3 4181^5

Semper Invicta (IRE) *Paul Nicholls* 113h
4 ch g Shantou(USA) Statim (Marju (IRE))
2636^4 3133^6 4614^P

Sempre Medici (FR) *W P Mullins* 158h
5 b g Medicean Sambala (IRE) (Danehill Dancer (IRE))
72a^4 3033^2 (3634a) (4133a) 4698^P

Send For Katie (IRE) *Chris Bealby* 87h
7 b m Kayf Tara Katsura (Alflora (IRE))
695^P

Sendiym (FR) *Dianne Sayer* 91h 95c
8 b g Rainbow Quest(USA) Seraya (FR) (Danehill (USA))
507^3 845^4 **1032^5 1367^2 1551^5 1685^2 1891^4** 2148^4 **2755^5** 2946^3 3307^4 4178^12 4404^9 **4938^9**

Senor Alco (FR) *Victor Thompson* 99h 83c
9 gr g Dom Alco(FR) Alconea (FR) (Brezzo (FR))
38^4 300^3 394^5 726^7 **803^5 5258^3**

Senor George (IRE) *Simon Hodgson* 66h
8 b g Traditionally(USA) Mrs St George (IRE) (Orpen (USA))
1234^8

Separate Shadows (FR) *Donald McCain* 109h 56c
7 ch g Bernebeau(FR) Chagrin D'Amour (IRE) (Last Tycoon)
1532^6 962^4 **1056^6**

September Blaze *Paul Webber* 104h 108c
8 b m Exit To Nowhere(USA) Mid Day Chaser (IRE) (Homo Sapien)
3007^2 3501^3

September Son (IRE) *Ian Duncan* 23h
5 b g September Storm(GER) Regal Pageant (IRE) (Welsh Term)
2106^5 2801^10 3436^P 4403^P

Seraffimo *Sharon Watt* 55h
3 ch g Monsieur Bond(IRE) Hula Ballew (Weldnaas (USA))
1415^6 3306^7 3590^9 3840^11 4045^P

Seranwen (IRE) *Nigel Twiston-Davies* 34h
8 b g Old Vic Glenarb Molly (IRE) (Phardante (FR))
3916^F 4209^P 4823^P 5183^8

Serenity Now (IRE) *Brian Ellison* 123h
7 b g Key Of Luck(USA) Imdina (IRE) (Soviet Star (USA))
(802) 1742^3 (1814) 2326^2 4014^11 4179^3 4913^F

Sergeant Dick (IRE) *Andy Turnell* 103h 121c
10 b g Lord Of Appeal Darawadda (IRE) (Kasmayo)
174^2 390^2 2276^P 2548^10

Sergeant Pink (IRE) *Dianne Sayer* 109h 117c
9 b g Fasliyev(USA) Ring Pink (USA) (Bering)
357^4 469^5 848^4 1070^R

Sergeant Thunder *Paul Nicholls* 123h 127c
6 ch g Halling(USA) Dissolve (Sharrood (USA))
(643) 1577^3

Serienschock (GER) *Mlle A Rosa* 149h 122c
7 b g Sholokhov(IRE) Saldenehre (GER) (Highest Honor (FR))
196^9 5216^4

Seskinane (IRE) *Brian M McMahon* 129h 108c
9 b g Imperial Ballet(IRE) Three For The Road (IRE) (Buckskin (FR))
19a^10 1184a^10

Set In My Ways (IRE) *Jonjo O'Neill* 118h
4 b g Presenting Kerry's Girl (IRE) (Flemensfirth (USA))
9a^5 2154^7 3334^7 3928^2 4883^4

Set List (IRE) *Emma Lavelle* 116h 129c
6 b g Heron Island(IRE) Copper Magic (IRE) (Zaffaran (USA))
335^2 ◆ 648^2 1002^5 **(1504) 1701^5 1970^3**

Set The Trend *David Dennis* 139h
9 br g Reset(AUS) Masrora (USA) (Woodman (USA))
360^2 (620)

Settledoutofcourt (IRE) *Lucinda Russell* [illegible]1h 124c
9 b g Court Cave(IRE) Ardagh Princess (Proverb)
289^3 1571^U (2028) 2213^7 3236^5 4818^5 5474^7

Sevenballs Of Fire (IRE) *Iain Jardine* 123h
6 b g Milan Leadamurraydance (IRE) (Supreme Leader)
3340^2 3667^2 (4586) ◆ 4906^F 5296^4

Seven Devils (IRE) *Lucinda Russell* 105h 106c
5 b g Definite Article Top Lot (IRE) (Topanoora)
144^6 1634^6 2189^F 2791^3 3367^5 4550^7 **5125^4 5447^4**

Seven Kingdoms (IRE) *David Dennis* 120h
3 b g Yeats(IRE) Valrhona (IRE) (Spectrum (IRE))
(3523) 3988^2 4462^7

Sevenoaks *Bill Turner*
4 b g Sakhee's Secret Treble Seven (USA) (Fusaichi Pegasus (USA))
3082^8

Seventeen Black (IRE) *Stuart Coltherd* 85h 85c
7 b g Subtle Power(IRE) Snowbaby (IRE) (Be My Native (USA))
77[7] (288) 487[2] ◆ 658[4] **2339[8] 2705[4] 2786[4]** 2982[8] 3438[5] 4045[3] **4329[4]** 4547[5]

Seventh Hussar *Alison Batchelor* 64h 77c
9 b g Alflora(IRE) Shuil Do (IRE) (Be My Native (USA))
2834[4] 3044[3] 3387[6]

Seventh Sky (GER) *Charlie Mann* 130h 156c
8 b g King's Best(USA) Sacarina (Old Vic)
1840[P] 2372[2] 2633[4] 2902[2] (3157) 3406[5] 3741[4] 3993[7] 4472[P] 5283[4] 5494[13]

Sew On Target (IRE) *Colin Tizzard* 113h 146c
10 b g Needle Gun(IRE) Ballykea (IRE) (Montelimar (USA))
357[3] 2059[7] 2468[9] 2686[5] (3996) 4733[8] 5184[2]

Seymour Eric *Martin Keighley* 104h 92c
10 b g Bollin Eric Seymour Chance (Seymour Hicks (FR))
3377[P] 3950[3] 4421[3]

Seymour Legend *Jim Wilson* 89h 46c
9 b g Midnight Legend Rosehall (Ardross)
364[2] 2736[9]

Seymour Star *Alastair Ralph* 106h
7 b g Alflora(IRE) Seymour Chance (Seymour Hicks (FR))
4430[3]

S For Estuary (IRE) *Victor Thompson* 74c
6 b g Milan Princess Supreme (IRE) (Supreme Leader)
5258[U]

Sgt Bull Berry *Peter Maddison* 79h 84c
8 b g Alflora(IRE) Cede Nullis (Primitive Rising (USA))
1004[P] (1272) (1380) 1775[4] 1930[4] 2500[P] (2556) 2771[2] 5203[P] **5442[6]**

Sgt Reckless *Mick Channon* 127h 148c
8 b g Imperial Dancer Lakaam (Danzero (AUS))
2185[7] 3151[17] 4717[19] 5219[13]

Shabach (IRE) *Mark Walford*
8 b g Bach(IRE) Jercost (IRE) (Shardari)
1739[P] **1900[P] 2197[P]**

Shabraque (IRE) *David Loder* 66h
3 b g Azamour(IRE) Teide Lady (Nashwan (USA))
2777[11] 3076[3] 3139[P]

Shadarpour (IRE) *Alan King* 126h
6 b g Dr Fong(USA) Shamadara (IRE) (Kahyasi)
1721[2] 2513[2] 3137[5] 4066[10]

Shaddaii (FR) *Robert Walford* 86h
9 gr g April Night(FR) Gypsie D'Artois (FR) (Mistigri)
(4318) 4886[2]

Shades Of Autumn (IRE) *Linda Blackford* 58h 94c
10 ch g Anshan Be Right (IRE) (Be My Native (USA))
1614[3]

Shades Of Midnight *Donald Whillans* 148h
5 b g Midnight Legend Hannah Park (IRE) (Lycius (USA))
2214[10] 2624[3] 3737[3] (4206) (4610) ◆ 5085[2]

Shadesofnavy *Peter Pritchard* 59b
9 ch g Fleetwood(IRE) Safe Arrival (USA) (Shadeed (USA))
2245[R] 2693[P] **2861[P]**

Shadow Blue (IRE) *Steven Dixon* 115h
6 br g Blueprint(IRE) Rosie Belle (IRE) (Roselier (FR))
2734[4] 2987[2] 3710[3] 4256[5] 4681[4] 5418[15]

Shadow Catcher *Gordon Elliott* 136h 139c
7 ch g Haafhd Unchain My Heart (Pursuit Of Love)
1636[2] 2206a[3] 3069a[3]

Shadow Play (IRE) *Paul Nolan* 118h 111c
5 b g Kalanisi(IRE) Lindas Present (IRE) (Presenting)
50a[17]

Shadows Lengthen *Michael Easterby* 127h 140c
9 b g Dansili Bay Shade (USA) (Sharpen Up)
2171[7] 5448[4]

Shady Glen (IRE) *Graeme McPherson* 85h 91c
6 br g Dr Massini(IRE) Poppins (IRE) (Invited (USA))
377[P] 646[3] 879[5] **1004[4] 1462[4] 1614[F] 1689[F]**

Shady Grey *Kevin Bishop* 28b
5 gr m Helissio(FR) Compton Amica (IRE) (High Estate)
2875[8] 4337[P]

Shady Lane *Dan Skelton* 111h 115c
8 b m Alflora(IRE) Stoney Path (Petoski)
135[3] (699) 744[3] 1036[3]

Shady Sadie (IRE) *Rose Dobbin* 82h 87c
8 b m Dushyantor(USA) Beltane Queen (IRE) (Strong Gale)
519[4] 731[3] 867[3] 1629[P] 2297[3] 2950[3] 5261[P]

Shah Of Persia *Warren Greatrex* 113h 124c
8 b g Fair Mix(IRE) Queen Soraya (Persian Bold)
447[3] 823[2] 1011[3] **1642[4] (2039) 2557[5] 3113[7]**

Shaiyzar (IRE) *David Thompson* 105h 96c
6 b g Azamour(IRE) Shaiyzima (IRE) (Polish Precedent (USA))
1604[4] 1691[2] 2043[4] 2560[6] 3474[5] 4301[6]

Shakalakaboomboom (IRE) *Nicky Henderson* 98h 122c
11 b g Anshan Tia Maria (IRE) (Supreme Leader)
439[6]

Shake Devaney (IRE) *Fergal O'Brien* 99h
5 b g Rakti Ediyrna (IRE) (Doyoun)
1758[3] 2345[6] 2646[4] 3902[6]

Shaky Gift (IRE) *Neil Mulholland* 116h
6 b m Milan Free Lift (Cadeaux Genereux)
1505[4] 1673[3] 2298[3] ◆ (2554) 2670[4] (3174)

Shalambar (IRE) *Tony Carroll* 110h
9 gr g Dalakhani(IRE) Shalama (IRE) (Kahyasi)
110[2] 354[6] 4774[10]

Shalamzar (FR) *Micky Hammond* 69h
6 ch g Selkirk(USA) Shamalana (IRE) (Sinndar (IRE))
3398[9] 3680[13] 3855[15] 4154[7] 4297[12]

Shales Rock *Mrs C J Robinson* 87c
9 b g Karinga Bay Home Talk (IRE) (Euphemism)
4651[7]

Shalianzi (IRE) *Gary Moore* 102h
5 b g Azamour(IRE) Shalama (IRE) (Kahyasi)
(1245) (1297) 1819[3] 2015[5] 2713[2] 2958[5]

Shambougg *Philip Hobbs* 108b
4 b g Tobougg(IRE) More Likely (Shambo)
3104[3] (3827) 4371[5]

Shamiran (IRE) *S T Nolan* 129h 125c
10 br g Polish Precedent(USA) Sharemata (IRE) (Doyoun)
(19a)

Shammick Boy (IRE) *Victor Dartnall* 139h 128c
10 b g Craigsteel Dulcet Music (IRE) (Topanoora)
2517[P] 2877[P] 3956[5] 4362[10] 4801[12] 5391[4]

Shanahan's Turn (IRE) *Henry De Bromhead* 140h 154c
7 b g Indian Danehill(IRE) Chanson Indienne (FR) (Indian River (FR))
69a[F] (1152a) 1763a[7] 2206a[4] 4697[14]

Shanandoa *Brian Barr* 90h
4 b m Shamardal(USA) Divisa (GER) (Lomitas)
2421[2] (2835) 3175[4] 4111[P] 4435[3] 4890[5]

Shaneshill (IRE) *W P Mullins* 155h 162c
6 b g King's Theatre(IRE) Darabaka (IRE) (Doyoun)
21a[3] **3856[4] 4716[2]** 5216[2]

Shangani (USA) *Venetia Williams* 111h 140c
9 b g Giant's Causeway(USA) Tanzania (IRE) (Alzao (USA))
2459[2] 2780[U] 3282[S] 3528[5] 4140[P] 4625[3] 5140[4]

Shanks A Bunch *Miss A Griffiths* 64c
7 b g Overbury(IRE) Florida Fact (Factual (USA))
18[9]

Shanksforamillion *David Rees* 76h
6 b g Needle Gun(IRE) Cool Connie (IRE) (Commanche Run)
1961[3] 2245[6] 2736[8]

Shannon Rock (FR) *J-P Gallorini* 133h 157c
9 b g Turgeon(USA) Shannondore (FR) (Nashamaa)
375a[2] 1884a[5]

Shannon Silver *Mrs Anthea Morshead*
6 b g Grape Tree Road Pinch Me Silver (Silver Patriarch (IRE))
80[P]

Shannon Smacker (IRE) *Joshua Pearce* 78c
10 ch g Windsor Castle Shannon Knock (Tumble Gold)
292[8]

Shanpallas (IRE) *C Byrnes* 130h 146c
7 b g Golan(IRE) Evnelu (IRE) (Old Vic)
603a[P] 1152a[5] 2483[P]

Shanroe Society (IRE) *J J Lambe* 106h
9 b g Definite Article Wensum Dancer (Shareef Dancer (USA))
142[6] 805[8]

Shanroe Street (IRE) *Lucinda Russell* 121h
5 b g Mustameet(USA) Zaffran Lady (IRE) (Zaffaran (USA))
3442[6] 4176[4] (4580)

Shan't Agree (IRE) *Henry Daly* 87b
4 b g Shantou(USA) Termsconditonsaply (IRE) (Lord Americo)
4075 2842[7]

Shantou Bob (IRE) *Warren Greatrex* 143h
7 b g Shantou(USA) Bobset Leader (IRE) (Bob Back (USA))
2641[P]

Shantou Ed (IRE) *P A Fahy* 135h 101c
6 ch g Shantou(USA) Fair Maid Marion (IRE) (Executive Perk)
96a[11]

Shantou Flyer (IRE) *Colin Bowe* 136h 146c
5 b g Shantou(USA) Carrigmorna Flyer (IRE) (Bob Back (USA))
(2055) (2531a) 2817a[5] 4148a[P] 4700[F]

Shantou Magic (IRE) *Charlie Longsdon* 129h 146c
8 b g Shantou(USA) Supreme Magical (Supreme Leader)
1840[5] 2436[P] 3031[11] 5093[4] ◆ 5390[U]

Shantou Theatre (IRE) *George Charlton* 90b
5 ch g Shantou(USA) As Lathair (IRE) (King's Theatre (IRE))
4515[3] 5127[10]

Shantou Tiger (IRE) *Donald McCain* 119h 124c
6 b g Shantou(USA) Opus One (Slip Anchor)
681[7] **1006[4] 1134[2] 1520[2] 1733[2] 2039[P] 3399[3]** 3970[4] 5045[2] 5402[6]

Shantou Village (IRE) *Neil Mulholland* 147h
5 b g Shantou(USA) Village Queen (IRE) (King's Theatre (IRE))
(1923) (2470) ◆ 3852[2] 4766[P]

Shareni (IRE) *Zoe Davison* 89h
6 b g Azamour(IRE) Sharesha (IRE) (Ashkalani (IRE))
3772[6] 4099[P] 4490[P]

Sharivarry (FR) *Victor Thompson* 73h 19c
9 ch g Ballingarry(IRE) Sharsala (IRE) (Shahrastani (USA))
2554 398[P] 484[5] **639[U]** 798[7] 2296[7] 2478[P]

Sharpasaknife (IRE) *Malcolm Jefferson* 131h
5 b g Flemensfirth(USA) Omas Lady (IRE) (Be My Native (USA))
(3626) ◆ 4040[2] ◆ (4873) 5446[4]

Sharp Rise (IRE) *Pauline Robson* 140h 140c
8 b g Croco Rouge(IRE) Missusan (IRE) (King's Ride)
(132) **(255) 470[U]** (957) 1414[2] 1637[F] (5256) **5448[U]**

Sharp Sword (IRE) *Neil Mulholland* 64h
4 ch g King's Best(USA) Pictavia (IRE) (Sinndar (IRE))
1052[6] 1117[13] 1240[8]

Shattered Love (IRE) *Gordon Elliott* 123b
4 b m Yeats(IRE) Tracker (Bustino)
5180[3]

Sheamus (IRE) *Ms Sandra Hughes* 144h
6 ch g Definite Article She's A Venture (IRE) (Supreme Leader)
5004a[8]

Shear Rock (IRE) *Charlie Longsdon* 126h
5 b g Spadoun(FR) Sleeping Diva (FR) (Sleeping Car (FR))
87[4] (330) (624) (1734) 2027[2] 5446[3]

Shecaughtmyeye *Polly Gundry*
7 b m Blueprint(IRE) Emerald Project (IRE) (Project Manager)
1234[P]

Sheer Poetry (IRE) *Richard Woollacott* 96h
4 b m Yeats(IRE) Sassari (IRE) (Darshaan)
178[5] 511[4] ◆ 712[3] 2263[P] 2455[F] 2730[U] 3256[7] 3919[7]

Shelford (IRE) *Dan Skelton* 140h
6 b g Galileo(IRE) Lyrical (Shirley Heights)
(4540a) (5428a)

Shepherd's Call (IRE) *Andrew Nicholls*
7 b g Winged Love(IRE) Little Bo Peep (IRE) (Roselier (FR))
472[P]

Sherardo (CZE) *Lenka Syslova* 102c
11 b g Security Risk I(USA) Shercana (CZE) (Arcane (USA))
1885a[F]

Sheriff's Star (IRE) *J J Lambe* 94h
4 gr g Lawman(FR) Silver Bandana (USA) (Silver Buck (USA))
732[7] 1399[8]

She's A Leader (IRE) *Robert Honner* 128h 89c
8 b m Viking Ruler(AUS) Pedros Pet (IRE) (Good Thyne (USA))
1748a[7]

Shesaportrait (IRE) *Patrick Neville* 108h 132c
7 gr m Portrait Gallery(IRE) Shesnotthelast (IRE) (Mandalus)
1556a[5]

She's Late *Jonjo O'Neill* 122h 108c
5 ch g Pivotal Courting (Pursuit Of Love)
930[4] 1507[4] **1932[5] 2288[5] 2593[9] 2973[P]** 3855[10] 4096[8] 4865[8] 5453[11]

Shift It Franklin *Philip Hobbs*
6 b g Franklins Gardens Shifty Over (Overbury (IRE))
2603[P] 4917[P] 5430[6]

Shimba Hills *Lawney Hill* 103h
4 b g Sixties Icon Search Party (Rainbow Quest (USA))
1893[8] 4846[P]

Shimla Dawn (IRE) *Mark Walford* 135h 137c
7 b g Indian Danehill(IRE) Tina Thyne (IRE) (Good Thyne (USA))
(2211) 2785[6] 3036[4] 4155[5] 4870[2]

Shine A Diamond (IRE) *Lucinda Russell* 94h 99c
7 gr g St Jovite(USA) Mossy Grey (IRE) (Step Together I (USA))
728[3] 882[4] **1492[3] 1857[2]**

Shine Away (IRE) *Sue Smith* 101h
5 b m Robin Des Pres(FR) Bramble Bree (IRE) (Rashar (USA))
2494[2] 2665[3] 2847[2] 3626[8] 4939[F]

Shining Grace *Sarah Robinson*
6 gr m Proclamation(IRE) Shining Oasis (IRE) (Mujtahid (USA))
178[P]

Shining Romeo *Denis Quinn* 86b
3 b g Royal Applause Silver Pivotal (IRE) (Pivotal)
2414[2] 2777[10] 3847[9]

Shininstar (IRE) *John Groucott* 106h
6 b g Westerner Shiny Button (Bob's Return (IRE))
5393[3]

Shinooki (IRE) *Alex Hales* 117h 116c
8 br g Blueprint(IRE) Rapid Response (IRE) (Be My Native (USA))
2848[P] 3310[P] (4391) (4557) 4983[5] 5376[5]

Shintori (FR) *Richard Woollacott* 98h
3 b g Enrique La Masai (FR) (Bernebeau (FR))
3112[5] 3464[5] 4619[3]

Shivsingh *Laura Young* 50h
6 b g Montjeu(IRE) Vistaria (USA) (Distant View (USA))
2880[9] 3807[7]

Shockingtimes (IRE) *Jamie Snowden* 107h 128c
8 b g Wareed(IRE) Jolly Lady (IRE) (Jolly Jake (NZ))
1424[2] ◆ 1767[3] 2149[2] 2593[2] 2975[4] (3253) 3707[P]

Shoofly Milly (IRE) *Jeremy Scott* 107h
6 b m Milan Jacksister (IRE) (Flemensfirth (USA))
108[5] 2441[3] 2985[11] 3410[5] 3771[2] (4290) 5033[3] 5382[9]

Shooters Wood (IRE) *David Pearson* 77h 116c
11 b g Needle Gun(IRE) Talbot's Hollow (IRE) (Strong Statement (USA))
338[6]

Shoot Themessenger *Mark Gillard* 9b
6 b m Double Trigger(IRE) Millie Boon (Petoski)
2351[12]

Shoreacres (IRE) *Mrs Gillian Jones* 118h 118c
12 b g Turtle Island(IRE) Call Me Dara (IRE) (Arapahos (FR))
4446[4] 4892[5] 5458[3]

Short Takes (USA) *Donald McCain* 112h 61c
7 ch g Lemon Drop Kid(USA) Gabriellina Giof (Ashkalani (IRE))
59[3] 508[6] 835[6] 929[3] 1405[6] 1478[4] **1687[5]**

Shotavodka (IRE) *David Pipe* 140h 146c
9 ch g Alderbrook Another Vodka (IRE) (Moscow Society (USA))
2214[2] **2790[6]** 3352[5] 3737[6] **4140[U] 4306[4] (4483) 5119[3]** 5396[4]

Shotgun Paddy (IRE) *Emma Lavelle* 133h 155c
8 b g Brian Boru Awesome Miracle (IRE) (Supreme Leader)
2482[5] 3518[3] 4367[2] 4802[P] 5327[10]

Shot In The Dark (IRE) *Jonathan Geake* 102h
6 ch g Dr Fong(USA) Highland Shot (Selkirk (USA))
240[4] 537[2] (704) 1055[5] 2599[7] 3223[P]

Shotofwine *Nicky Richards* 79h
6 b g Grape Tree Road Icy Gunner (Gunner B)
3021[14] 3334[P] 5444[P]

Shouldavboughtgold (IRE) *William Kinsey* 92h 127c
8 b g Classic Cliche(IRE) Sancta Miria (IRE) (Toulon)
2275[6]

Should I Stay (FR) *Alan Brown* 94h 74c
7 b g Muhtathir Dusky Royale (FR) (Double Bed (FR))
2843[5]

Shouting Hill (IRE) *Johnny Farrelly* 71h
5 b g Golan(IRE) Brook Queen (IRE) (Lafontaine I (USA))
3077[11] 3582[6] 5153[15]

Shout It Aloud *Tim Vaughan* 108h
6 b g Proclamation(IRE) Party Charmer (Charmer (IRE))
271[6] 853[3] 1117[2] 1324[3] 1549[P] 3886[P]

Showbiz Floozy *John O'Neill* 49h
6 b m Beat All(USA) Laced Up (IRE) (The Parson)
2298[P] 3386[P]

Showboater (IRE) *Ben Pauling* 88h 114c
6 b g Milan Dazala (IRE) (Mazaad)
30[P] **(2712) (3214) 4199[2] 4642[P]** 5314[4]

Showem Silver (IRE) *Noel Meade* 99b
4 b g Winged Love(IRE) Swap Shop (IRE) (Lord Americo)
11a[9]

Showman (IRE) *M S Dilworth*
12 ch g Carroll House(IRE) Bettys The Act (IRE) (Mister Lord (USA))
295[P]

Show On The Road *Philip Hobbs* 113b
4 b g Flemensfirth(USA) Roses Of Picardy (IRE) (Roselier (FR))
459[2] 4790[5] (5187)

Show's Over (IRE) *Tim Vaughan* 84h
4 b g Curtain Time(IRE) Sailors Run (IRE) (Roselier (FR))
5305[P]

Shrapnel (IRE) *Brian Ellison* 113h 109c
9 bb g Flemensfirth(USA) Victoria Theatre (IRE) (Old Vic)
357[6] 742[3] 848[6] 2893[P] **3243[P]**

Shrewd *Iain Jardine* 132h
5 b g Street Sense(USA) Cala (FR) (Desert Prince (IRE))
(3473) 3682[3] (4014) ◆ (4461) 5325[12]

Shrewd Investment *Miss L Thomas* 101h 123c
9 ch g Beauchamp King Zaffarimbi (IRE) (Zaffaran (USA))
260[P] 536[P] (Dead)

Shrewd Tactics (IRE) *Evan Williams* 105b
4 ch g Broadway Flyer(USA) Taking My Time (IRE) (High Roller (IRE))
3827[2] ◆

Shubaat *John Ferguson* 141h 130c
8 ch g Monsun(GER) Zaynaat (Unfuwain (USA))
1867[4] 2067[4]

Shuil Royale (IRE) *Harry Fry* 129h 143c
10 b g King's Theatre(IRE) Shuil Na Lee (IRE) (Phardante (FR))
101[4] (855) 2600[4] **3016[5] 4101[6] 4483[6]**

Shutthefrontdoor (IRE) *Jonjo O'Neill* 144h 157c
8 bb g Accordion Hurricane Girl (IRE) (Strong Gale)
2333[3] **4485[P] 5218[9]**

Shwaiman (IRE) *William Jarvis* 127h
5 br g Authorized(IRE) Blue Lightning (Machiavellian (USA))
1272[2] (494)

Shy (CZE) *George Charlton* 58b
3 br f Tiger Cafe(JPN) Solinka (CZE) (Monarch)
4708[4] 5371[2]

Shy John *Jennifer Mason* 124c
9 b g Kier Park(IRE) Shy Lizzie (Buzzards Bay)
266[F] 2451[6] 2872[U] 3086[4] 3572[P]

Siam De La Roque (FR) *Jerome Zuliani* 92h 87c
9 gr g Maille Pistol(FR) Corthalina (FR) (Saint Preuil (FR))
4400a[5]

Siberian Vixen (IRE) *Edmond Kent* 118h
5 b m Flemensfirth(USA) Siberiansdaughter (IRE) (Strong Gale)
2677a[12] 4653a[P]

Si C'Etait Vrai (FR) *Neil Mulholland* 117h 117c
9 b g Robin Des Champs(FR) Bleu Perle (FR) (Pistolet Bleu (IRE))
2780[P] 4436[P] 5119[8]

Sidbury Fair *Victor Dartnall* 95b
4 br m Fair Mix(IRE) Manque Pas D'Air (FR) (Kadalko (FR))
4364[9] 5104[3]

Sidbury Hill *Seamus Mullins* 117h 115c
7 ch g Midnight Legend Flora Macdonald (Alflora (IRE))
2727[P] 2988[F] 3709[3] 4542[4] 5147[3]

Side Saddle (IRE) *Ms Sandra Hughes* 113h
5 b m King's Theatre(IRE) Steel Grey Lady (IRE) (Roselier (FR))
3962a[P]

Sidi Bouknadel (FR) *J-L Guillochon* 134h 143c
7 gr g Blackdoun(FR) Essaouira (FR) (Solid Illusion (USA))
375a[4]

Sidsteel (IRE) *John Groucott* 59b
4 b g Craigsteel Clare Hogan (IRE) (Moscow Society (USA))
4894[14]

Siena Bouquet (FR) *S R B Crawford* 95b
4 bb m Saint Des Saints(FR) Sheyrinca (FR) (Sheyrann (IRE))
2433[4]

Sierra Nevada (FR) *Mlle S Delaroche* 112h 112c
5 ch m Ultimately Lucky(IRE) Quick Ville (FR) (Villez (USA))
2821a[6]

Sierra Oscar (IRE) *Dan Skelton* 91b
3 b g Robin Des Champs(FR) John's Eliza (IRE) (Dr Massini (IRE))
5248[3]

Signed Request (IRE) *Henry Oliver* 111h
8 b g Fantastic Quest(IRE) Magic Sign (IRE) (The Parson)
102[P]

Significant Move *Dr Richard Newland* 89h
8 b g Motivator Strike Lightly (Rainbow Quest (USA))
336[5] 856[3] 937[3] 1115[3] 1166[4] 1245[5] 1446[P]

Sign Manual *Donald McCain* 119h
6 b g Motivator New Assembly (IRE) (Machiavellian (USA))
(56) 419[2] 1648[8] 1921[3] 3101[3] 3588[P] (4152) 4328[8]

Sign Of A Victory (IRE) *Nicky Henderson* 156h
6 b g Kayf Tara Irish Wedding (IRE) (Bob Back (USA))
2186[4] 3230[5] 4698[8]

Sikandar (IRE) *Brian Ellison* 115h
3 ch g Medicean Siniyya (IRE) (Grand Lodge (USA))
1656[6] (2439) 2863[3] 3423[3] 4012[4] 4486[7] 5491[4]

Silent Cliche (IRE) *Ms N M Hugo* 98h 100c
11 b g Classic Cliche(IRE) Mini Moo Min (Ardross)
66[4]

Silent Doctor (IRE) *Roy Brotherton* 69b
5 br g Dr Massini(IRE) Wild Noble (IRE) (Aristocracy (IRE))
3502[6] 5144[6]

Silent Encore (IRE) *Ben Case* 90b
3 ch g Curtain Time(IRE) What Can I Say (IRE) (Mister Lord (USA))
5457[10]

Silent Knight (IRE) *Warren Greatrex* 117h
6 b g Pierre Aristocracy Lass (IRE) (Aristocracy (IRE))
750[U]

Silent Movie (IRE) *John Ferguson* 113h
5 gr g Cape Cross(IRE) Screen Star (IRE) (Tobougg (IRE))
853[2] 1000[3]

Silent Snow (IRE) *W T Reed* 71h 74c
10 ch g Moscow Society(USA) Miss Ogan (IRE) (Supreme Leader)
140[5] 519[10] 639[4] 731[4]

Silent Warrior *Charlie Longsdon* 64h
3 br g Yeats(IRE) Zariyka (IRE) (Kalanisi (IRE))
4880[12]

Silk Hall (UAE) *Dianne Sayer* 130h 123c
10 b g Halling(USA) Velour (Mtoto)
138[3] 505[P] 729[2] 1035[7] **1401[2] 2026[2] 2803[3] 5298[5]**

Silmi *Sophie Leech* 99h 106c
11 gr g Daylami(IRE) Intimaa (IRE) (Caerleon (USA))
470[5] 2843[P]

Silsol (GER) *Paul Nicholls* 159h 154c
6 b g Soldier Hollow Silveria (GER) (Groom Dancer (USA))
349a[6] **(2397) (2627) 2932[2] 3621[4]** 4244[3] (5085) 5213[3] 5495[2]

Silva Samourai *Susan Corbett* 51b
6 gr g Proclamation(IRE) Ladykirk (Slip Anchor)
1640[9]

Silver Concorde *D K Weld* 135h
7 b g Dansili Sacred Pearl (IRE) (Daylami (IRE))
4695[14]

Silver Dixie (USA) *Peter Hedger* 107h
5 br g Dixie Union(USA) More Silver (USA) (Silver Hawk (USA))
1612[4] 1822[5] 2251[7]

Silver Djebel *Jamie Snowden* 67b
4 gr m Tobougg(IRE) Navale (FR) (Baryshnikov (AUS))
45[7] 591[P]

Silver Dragon *Mike Sowersby* 104h 96c
7 gr g Silver Patriarch(IRE) Gotogeton (Le Moss)
2500[4] 2666[5] 2865[P] 2892[3] 3067[5] **3488[5] 4534[5]** 4942[P] **5442[P]**

Silver Duke (IRE) *Jim Goldie* 117h
4 gr g Papal Bull Dumaani's Dream (USA) (Dumaani (USA))
1039[11] 2328[4] 3041[5] 3426[4] 3682[5] 4179[8] 4913[12] 5414[6]

Silver Eagle (IRE) *Kim Bailey* 136h 107c
7 gr g Presenting Lady Lincon (IRE) (Great Palm (USA))
2749[8] 3727[P] 4884[3] 5375[6]

Silver Gent (IRE) *Donald McCain* 112h 93c
7 gr g Milan All's Rosey (IRE) (Roselier (FR))
2707[F]

Silver Glaze (IRE) *Brian Ellison* 12b
3 gr g Verglas(IRE) Tullawadgeen (IRE) (Sinndar (IRE))
2216[6] 3967[P]

Silvergrove *Ben Pauling* 103h 141c
7 b g Old Vic Classic Gale (USA) (Classic Cliche (IRE))
2887[U] ◆ (3349) (4101) 4735[3]

Silverhow (IRE) *Nicky Henderson* 107b
4 br g Yeats(IRE) Monte Solaro (IRE) (Key Of Luck (USA))
3847[2]

Silver Kayf *Kim Bailey* 104b
3 gr g Kayf Tara Silver Spinner (Silver Patriarch (IRE))
4488[5]

Silver Man *Jo Hughes* 145c
8 gr g Silver Patriarch(IRE) Another Mans Cause (FR) (Highest Honor (FR))
(355) (707) 855[2] 1713[2] 2061[6] 2916[F] 3038[F]

Silver O'Reilly *Mrs K M Diggle* 50c
9 ch g Silver Patriarch(IRE) Martha Reilly (IRE) (Rainbows For Life (CAN))
521[7]

Silver Roque (FR) *Fergal O'Brien* 106h 148c
9 b g Laveron Bible Gun (FR) (Pistolet Bleu (IRE))
184[8] 2468[11] 2902[U] 4212[P]

Silver Shuffle (IRE) *Dianne Sayer* 116h 75c
8 ch g Big Shuffle(USA) Silvetta (Lando (GER))
456[5] 2085[2] 2595[6] 2949[5] 3242[3] 4509[3] 4941[7]

Silver Story *Tim Vaughan* 70h 90c
12 gr g Silver Patriarch(IRE) Tall Story (Arzanni)
536[7] 771[7] 926[P] 1080[9] 1355[P]

Silver Tassie (IRE) *Micky Hammond* 132h 140c
7 b g Shantou(USA) Silver Castor (IRE) (Indian Ridge)
69a[U] 1175a[8] **2935[3] 3439[U] 3591[P] 4609[2] ◆ 5200[2] 5411[3]**

Silver Ticket (IRE) *Laura Mongan* 55h
4 gr f Tikkanen(USA) Windmill View (IRE) (Glacial Storm (USA))
227[8] 3133[P] 4323[P]

Silverton *Lucy Normile* 34h 58c
8 gr m Silver Patriarch(IRE) Gretton (Terimon)
304[P] 2400[P] 3438[P] 5368[6]

Silver Trix (IRE) *George Bewley* 83b
5 gr m Mahler Sika Trix (IRE) (Try Prospect (USA))
3476[9] 5476[5]

Silviniaco Conti (FR) *Paul Nicholls* 156h 176c
9 ch g Dom Alco(FR) Gazelle Lulu (FR) (Altayan)
2241[2] **2642[2] 3231[P] (4240) 5218[P]**

Simarthur *Lucinda Russell* 105h 88c
8 gr g Erhaab(USA) Dusty Too (Terimon)
1925[3] **2297[7]** 2806[7] (3474) 3684[4]

Simba De Teillee (FR) *E Leenders* 100c
4 b g Poliglote Lady De Mai (FR) (Michel Georges)
3815a[P]

Simmply Sam *Marjorie Fife* 85h 12c
8 b m Nomadic Way(USA) Priceless Sam (Silly Prices)
3791[7] 4110[4] 4804[8] (5198)

Simonsig *Nicky Henderson* 151h 166c
9 gr g Fair Mix(IRE) Dusty Too (Terimon)
2334[2]

Simon Squirrel (IRE) *Paul Nicholls* 136h
5 b g Robin Des Champs(FR) Misty Heather (IRE) (Oscar (IRE))
(1837) ◆ 2509[3] 3227[4] 4010[6] 5279[3] 5463[F]

Simple Assignment (IRE) *Warren Greatrex* 106h
6 br g Westerner Marlogan (IRE) (Presenting)
237[2]

Simple Joys *Mrs Denise Foster* 94h 83c
5 b m Singspiel(IRE) Chance Dance (IRE) (Danehill Dancer (IRE))
3716a[F]

Simplified *Michael Chapman* 67h
12 b m Lend A Hand Houston Heiress (USA) (Houston (USA))
591[P] 777[7] 918[7] 1271[P]

Simply A Legend *Alan King* 137h
6 b g Midnight Legend Disco Danehill (IRE) (Danehill Dancer (IRE))
2369[3] (2912) 3232[2] 3733[4] 4786[2]

Simply Lucky (IRE) *W T Reed* 62h 42c
6 b g Flemensfirth(USA) Derrygowna Court (IRE) (Rakaposhi King)
3474[12] **4051[F] 4569[F] 4905[5]**

Simply Ned (IRE) *Nicky Richards* 135h 164c
8 ch g Fruits Of Love(USA) Bishops Lass (IRE) (Marju (IRE))
(1777) 2511[4] 3293a[2] 3734[5] 4281a[3] 5087[P]

Simply Rouge *Peter Niven* 107b
5 b m Croco Rouge(IRE) Simply Mystic (Simply Great (FR))
(359)

Simply The West (IRE) *Charlie Longsdon* 125h 128c
6 b g Westerner Back To Stay (IRE) (Supreme Leader)
382[2] ◆ 1932[4] 2451[P] 2988[3] 3348[P]

Simply Wings (IRE) *Kerry Lee* 118h 135c
11 b g Winged Love(IRE) Simply Deep (IRE) (Simply Great (FR))
24a[P] (2404) 2780[F] 3339[P] 4212[2]

Sinakar (IRE) *David O'Meara* 107h
4 br g Manduro(GER) Siniyya (IRE) (Grand Lodge (USA))
4417[2] ◆

Sinbad The Sailor *George Baker* 114h
10 b g Cape Cross(IRE) Sinead (USA) (Irish River (FR))
1184a[P] 1522[6] 1794[5] 2125[4] 3837[7]

Sin Bin (IRE) *Paul Nicholls* 122h 126c
9 b g Presenting Navaro (IRE) (Be My Native (USA))
29[2]

Sindarban (IRE) *Donald McCain* 106h
4 ch g Teofilo(IRE) Sinndiya (IRE) (Pharly (FR))
353[F] 702[2] 960[5] (1774)

Singapore Sling (FR) *A Bonin* 140h 140c
6 ch g Muhtathir Spinning Secretary (USA) (Spinning World (USA))
4a[9] 836a[7] 4540a[9]

Singing Hinnie *Mark H Tompkins* 67b
4 b m Halling(USA) Tawny Way (Polar Falcon (USA))
1645[7] 2044[13]

Singlefarmpayment *Tom Lacey* 129h
5 b g Milan Crevamoy (IRE) (Shardari)
177[2] 2182[2] (2838) (3407) 3844[P]

Sinndar's Man *Michael Blake* 104h
4 b g Sinndar(IRE) Relish (IRE) (Sadler's Wells (USA))
895[7] 1100[5] 1269[7] 1964[9]

Siobhans Beauty (IRE) *Jamie Snowden* 103h 28c
7 gr g Cloudings(IRE) Farrangalway Lass (IRE) (King's Ride)
57[6] 514[10]

Sioux Chieftain (IRE) *Dr Richard Newland* 119h
5 b g Mount Nelson Lady Gin (USA) (Saint Ballado (CAN))
(5077)

Sirabad (FR) *Paul Nicholls* 137h 131c
5 b g Astarabad(USA) Maille Sissi (FR) (Dernier Empereur (USA))
2370[P] 2803[2] 3228[3] 4239[7] **4785[4]**

Sir Albie *Sally Randell* 83b
3 b g Sir Percy Hazel Bank Lass (IRE) (Insan (USA))
2414[4] 2629[4]

Sir Antony Browne *Alan King* 115b
3 ch g Black Sam Bellamy(IRE) Shayaza (Generous (IRE))
(4102) 4488[3]

Sir Bentley *Caroline Bailey* 81h
5 b g Flemensfirth(USA) Silk Rope (IRE) (Presenting)
335[5] 3418[8] 3787[P]

Sir Chauvelin *Jim Goldie* 120h
3 b g Authorized(IRE) Jabbara (IRE) (Kingmambo (USA))
(2324) 3039[3] (3423) 4012[3] 5219[8]

Sir Des Champs (FR) *W P Mullins* 129h 158c
9 b g Robin Des Champs(FR) Liste En Tete (FR) (Video Rock (FR))
(2606a) 3324a[5] 4007a[7] 5218[F] 5494[P]

Sir Du Bearn (FR) *Mickey Bowen* 76c
9 bb g Passing Sale(FR) Girl Du Bearn (FR) (Sarpedon I (FR))
535[U]

Sir Dylan *Polly Gundry* 100h
6 b g Dylan Thomas(IRE) Monteleone (IRE) (Montjeu (IRE))
(167) 364[4] 4856[7] 5483[6]

Sire Collonges (FR) *Paul Nicholls* 127h 149c
9 gr g Dom Alco(FR) Idylle Collonges (FR) (Quart De Vin (FR))
375a[P] 2471[S] 3017[2] 4719[8] 5283[7]

Sir Ector (USA) *Miss Nicole McKenna* 131h 110c
8 br g Dynaformer(USA) Beyond The Waves (USA) (Ocean Crest (USA))
19a[3] 5219[16]

Sire De Grugy (FR) *Gary Moore* 146h 171c
9 ch g My Risk(FR) Hirlish (FR) (Passing Sale (FR))
2259[5] (2915) 3281[2] 3734[2] 4718[8] 5493[4]

Sir Frank Morgan (IRE) *David Pipe* 113h
5 b g Montjeu(IRE) Woodland Orchid (IRE) (Woodman (USA))
669[6] 967[8]

Sir Hubert *Richard Rowe* 90h
5 b g Multiplex Lacounsel (FR) (Leading Counsel (USA))
2544[9] 3450[4] 3660[5] 3905[3] 4411[6] 5305[P]

Sirius Star *Brian Rothwell* 96h
6 b g Beat All(USA) Miss Sirius (Royal Vulcan)
2169[P] 2772[6] 4982[3]

Sir Ivan *Harry Fry* 139h
5 b g Midnight Legend Tisho (Sir Harry Lewis (USA))
2202[3] 2781[5] 3254[3] 3956[2] 4362[2] 5284[2]

Sir Lynx (IRE) *Chris Bealby* 116h 100c
8 gr g Amilynx(FR) Minilus (IRE) (Luso)
211[6]

Sir Mangan (IRE) *Dan Skelton* 138h 127c
7 b g Darsi(FR) Lady Pep (IRE) (Cajetano (USA))
(1736) 2484[2] 2912[5]

Sir Mattie (IRE) *David Rees* 109h 118c
10 bb g Moscow Society(USA) Manhattan Catch (IRE) (Safety Catch (USA))
439[4] 611[2] 873[5] 1167[6] 1309[5]

Sir Note (FR) *James Eustace* 94h 110c
5 gr g Victory Note(USA) Niangara (FR) (Baby Turk)
(180) 435[4] (694) 1096[P] **(3845) (4984)**

Siro Demur (FR) *Philip Rowley* 101c
9 ch g Murmure(FR) Journeuit (FR) (Chamberlin (FR))
4592[4]

Sirop De Menthe (FR) *Sue Gardner* 136h
5 ch g Discover D'Auteuil(FR) Jolie Menthe (FR) (Bateau Rouge)
1579[8] 2445[2] (2647) (2700) 2831[2] 3449[2] 4239[4] 4622[8]

Sirpertan *Marjorie Fife* 103h
4 b g Sir Percy Tanwir (Unfuwain (USA))
2148[7] 2946[2]

Sir Pitt *Mark Brisbourne* 139h 110c
8 b g Tiger Hill(IRE) Rebecca Sharp (Machiavellian (USA))
2435[P] 4453[F] 5244[4]

Sirrah Star (IRE) *Neil Mulholland* 89h
7 gr m Great Palm(USA) Simply Deep (IRE) (Simply Great (FR))
265[P]

Sir Safir *Peter Niven* 120h
5 b g Croco Rouge(IRE) Angela's Ashes (Common Grounds)
2499[3]

Sir Scorpion (IRE) *Thomas Mullins* 125h
6 b g Scorpion(IRE) Lady Goldilocks (IRE) (Mister Lord (USA))
3650a[20]

Sir Valentino (FR) *Tom George* 134h 148c
6 b g Early March Valentine (FR) (Double Bed (FR))
218[5] 2058[8] (2540) ◆ **(2854) (3107) 3281[5] 3629[2] 3857[5]**

Sir Vinnie (IRE) *R K Watson* 84c
6 b g Vinnie Roe(IRE) De Lissa (IRE) (Zaffaran (USA))
2206a[P]

Sir Vinski (IRE) *Nicky Richards* 132h
6 ch g Vinnie Roe(IRE) Mill Emerald (Old Vic)
2767[3] 3428[7] (3999) 4911[P]

Sir Will (IRE) *Peter Bowen* 113h
4 b g Yeats(IRE) Tinopasa (FR) (No Pass No Sale)
2270[6] 3509[5]

Sisterbrooke (IRE) *John Panvert* 66h 19c
6 ch m Trans Island Cool Merenda (IRE) (Glacial Storm (USA))
4859[7] 5357[P]

Sister Sibyl (IRE) *Hughie Morrison* 103b
4 b m King's Theatre(IRE) Rose Of The Erne (IRE) (Presenting)
(3132) 4623[9]

Sitting Back (IRE) *Diana Grissell* 71h 94c
11 b g Flying Legend(USA) Double Pearl (IRE) (Doubletour (USA))
5482[4]

Six One Away (IRE) *Paul Webber* 90h 85c
6 gr g Tikkanen(USA) Surfing France (FR) (Art Francais (USA))
1888[5]

Sizing Coal (IRE) *J T R Dreaper* 124h 144c
7 b g Presenting Hollygrove Cezanne (IRE) (King's Ride)
92a[P] 4802[P]

Sizing Codelco (IRE) *Henry De Bromhead* 144h 145c
6 b g Flemensfirth(USA) La Zingarella (IRE) (Phardante (FR))
7a[5] **2913[U] 4770[U]**

Sizing Granite (IRE) *C A Murphy* 132h 159c
7 br g Milan Hazel's Tisrara (IRE) (Mandalus)
2232a[2] 3293a[5] 4718[P] 5023a[2]

Sizing John *Henry De Bromhead* 149h 156c
5 b g Midnight Legend La Perrotine (FR) (Northern Crystal)
6a[2] **(2530a) 3271a[2] 4696[2] 5174[3]**

Sizing Platinum (IRE) *Henry De Bromhead* 124h 142c
7 b g Definite Article Quest Of Passion (FR) (Saumarez)
1679a[2] 1937a[2] 4956a[U]

Sizing Sahara *Paul Henderson* 100h 90c
7 gr g Shirocco(GER) Aristocratique (Cadeaux Genereux)
3176[5] 3727[4] 4225[4]

Sizing Solution (IRE) *J T R Dreaper* 111h 129c
7 b g King's Theatre(IRE) Toulon Rouge (IRE) (Toulon)
1186a[8]

Sizing Tennessee (IRE) *Henry De Bromhead* 137h
7 ch g Robin Des Champs(FR) Jolivia (FR) (Dernier Empereur (USA))
4133a[F] 4765[20]

Skating Home (IRE) *Richard Hawker* 68h 41c
9 b g Luso Wintry Day (IRE) (Presenting)
932[12] 971[6] **1118[P] 1287[10] 1678[4] 1813[U]** 2005[4] 3128[5] 3369[4]

Skiddaw Poppy *Maurice Barnes* 54b
4 b m Byron Skiddaw Wolf (Wolfhound (USA))
1334[8] 1688[8]

Skint *Ali Stronge* 109h 95c
9 b g King's Theatre(IRE) No More Money (Alflora (IRE))
645[8] **915[5]** 1242[2] **1458[3]** 1964[3] 2924[3] 4972[P]

Skipthecuddles (IRE) *Graeme McPherson* 80b
4 b g Westerner Autumn Sky (IRE) (Roselier (FR))
4805[5]

Skyfire *Nick Kent* 92h
8 ch g Storm Cat(USA) Sunray Superstar (Nashwan (USA))
186[7] 1377[6] 1892[11] 2869[5] 3233[5] 3840[7]

Sky Full Of Stars (IRE) *James Ewart* 92h
5 b g Mahler Gold Flo (IRE) (Fourstars Allstar (USA))
452[6] 2945[5] 3471[7] 3680[8] 4035[5]

Sky Khan *Lucinda Russell* 141h
6 b g Cape Cross(IRE) Starlit Sky (Galileo (IRE))
(356) 1633[2] 2064[6] (2594) 4017[6] 4769[3] 5189[4]

Skylander (IRE) *David Pipe* 122h 135c
6 b g Flemensfirth(USA) Cat Burglar (IRE) (Robellino (USA))
854[4] 969[5] 1238[3] 1503[2] (1579) **(1741) ◆ 1932[2] 2018[4]** 2513[11] **2853[3] 3106[4]**

Sky Lino (FR) *Nick Williams* 104h
3 b g Martaline Sky Dance I (FR) (Sky Lawyer (FR))
1866[3] 2439[2] 3028[4] 4096[6]

Sky Rose *Alexandra Dunn* 89h
3 b f Sakhee(USA) Intersky High (USA) (Royal Anthem (USA))
2537[4]

Sky Watch (IRE) *Brian Barr* 111h 111c
8 b g Flemensfirth(USA) The Shining Force (IRE) (Strong Gale)
1136[3] 1349[3] **1592[4] 2254[2] 2692[3]** 3662[P]

Slaney Star (IRE) *Jean McGregor* 66h
7 b g Cloudings(IRE) Slaney Rose (IRE) (Roselier (FR))
1552[11] 1776[6] 2296[P]

Sleep Easy *Neil Mulholland* 114h
3 b g Rip Van Winkle(IRE) Strictly Lambada (Red Ransom (USA))
(4489)

Sleep In First (FR) *James Ewart* 119h 116c
9 bb g Sleeping Car(FR) First Union (FR) (Shafoun (FR))
36[4] 508[5] 708[2] **1099[3] 1367[3]** 1773[8] 2326[6]

Sleeping City (FR) *Victor Dartnall* 112h
8 bb g Sleeping Car(FR) City Prospect (FR) (Diamond Prospect (USA))
281[2] 718[4] 856[9] (1096) (1324) 1591[5] ◆

Sleepy Haven (IRE) *Jennie Candlish* 138h 126c
5 b g Indian Haven High Society Girl (IRE) (Key Of Luck (USA))
197[11] **2412[4] 2580[4] 2920[3] 3365[4] 3589[F]** 4273[4]

Slidecheck (IRE) *Alexandra Dunn* 96h 105c
8 b g Dushyantor(USA) Stormey Tune (IRE) (Glacial Storm (USA))
293[2] 3419[F] 3661[2] 3821[3] **4265[4]** (4440) **(4713) (4931)**

Slide Show *David Thompson* 81h
7 b m Galileo(IRE) First Exhibit (Machiavellian (USA))
1774[5] 2325[5] 2847[4] 3244[P]

Slim Pickens (IRE) *Dr Richard Newland* 130h
7 b g Craigsteel Couleurs d'Automne (FR) (Galant Vert (FR))
2064[8] 2369[2] 2767[6]

Slipper Satin (IRE) *Simon West* 106h
5 b m Excellent Art In The Ribbons (In The Wings)
37[5] 482[6] 845[2] (1066) 2029[8]

Slowmotion (FR) *A P O'Brien* 138h
3 bb f Soldier Of Fortune(IRE) Second Emotion (FR) (Medaaly)
(5001a)

Slygufftou (IRE) *Michael McCullagh* 119h
6 gr g Shantou(USA) Slyguff Annie (IRE) (Oscar (IRE))
(1184a)

Smad Place (FR) *Alan King* 161h 173c
8 gr g Smadoun(FR) Bienna Star (FR) (Village Star (FR))
(2242) (2783) 3231[4] (3850) 4767[6]

Smadynium (FR) *Julia Brooke* 119h 125c
7 gr g Smadoun(FR) Sea Music (FR) (Bering)
2933[2] 3855[16] 5012[7]

Smart Boy (IRE) *Tim Easterby* 86h
4 b g Mahler Supreme Style (IRE) (Supreme Leader)
4001[7] 4742[3]

Smart Catch (IRE) *Tony Carroll* 112h 111c
9 b g Pivotal Zafaraniya (IRE) (Doyoun)
134[4] 2810[7] 4229[2] 4593[5] 5386[9]

Smart Exit (IRE) *Stuart Edmunds* 107h 122c
8 b g Exit To Nowhere(USA) Navaro (IRE) (Be My Native (USA))
1850[2] 2566[2] 3127[3] 3823[P] 4612[P] 5222[P]

Smartmax (FR) *Caroline Bailey* 84h 106c
6 ch g Until Sundown(USA) Quendora (FR) (Kendor (FR))
2582[2] ◆ 3061[3] 4980[U]

Smart Ruler (IRE) *James Moffatt* 124h
9 ch g Viking Ruler(AUS) Celebrated Smile (IRE) (Cadeaux Genereux)
850[5] 1034[5]

Smart Talk (IRE) *Brian Ellison* 145h
5 b m Hubbly Bubbly(USA) Belon Breeze (IRE) (Strong Gale)
206[2] 1854[2] (2021) (2422) ◆ 2632[3] (3154) (3858) 4734[13]

Smart Thinking (IRE) *Jonjo O'Neill* 35h
4 b g Kayf Tara Dame D'Asie (FR) (Kahyasi)
3411[10]

Smashing (FR) *Henry De Bromhead* 145h 166c
6 gr g Smadoun(FR) Faragreen (FR) (Green Tune (USA))
(3830a) (4131a) 4731[P] (5109a)

Smiley Miley (IRE) *Dai Burchell* 46h
7 ch m Danroad(AUS) Music Teacher (Piccolo)
853[7] 929[7]

Smirfy's Silver *Michael Mullineaux* 86h
11 b g Desert Prince(IRE) Goodwood Blizzard (Inchinor)
489[6]

Smokey Joe Joe (IRE) *S J Mahon* 112h 127c
9 b g Snurge Goldens Monkey (Monksfield)
3073a[9] 5109a[4]

Smoking Dixie (IRE) *Ben Pauling* 102b
4 ch g Beneficial Jacksister (IRE) (Flemensfirth (USA))
5400[2]

Smoking Jacket (IRE) *Tom George* 110h 105c
5 b g Beneficial Unalaska (IRE) (High Estate)
177[F] 2085[13] 2857[4]

Smoky Hill (IRE) *Tony Carroll* 89h
6 gr g Galileo(IRE) Danaskaya (IRE) (Danehill (USA))
2555[P]

Smooth River (IRE) *S R B Crawford* 100b
5 b m Desert King(IRE) River Rhyme (IRE) (Riverhead (USA))
3442[9]

Smooth Stepper *Sue Smith* 120h 135c
6 b g Alflora(IRE) Jazzy Refrain (IRE) (Jareer (USA))
2122[2] (2785) 3040[F] 3849[3] ◆ 4365[2] 4800[3] 5323[4]

Smugglers Lane (IRE) *David Evans* 75h
3 b g Bushranger(IRE) Finty (IRE) (Entrepreneur)
690[U] 778[5]

Smuggler's Stash (IRE) *Rose Dobbin* 97h
5 ch g Stowaway Sweetasanu (IRE) (Sri Pekan (USA))
2189[12] 2931[7] 3239[4] 3795[6] 4163[3] 4638[7] 5203[P]

Snag List (IRE) *W P Mullins* 108b
4 b m Shantou(USA) Back Log (IRE) (Bob Back (USA))
2486[4] 2929[6]

Snake Eyes (IRE) *Nicky Henderson* 118h
7 b g Oscar(IRE) Be My Belle (IRE) (Be My Native (USA))
(73a) 1163a[17]

Snapping Turtle (IRE) *Donald Whillans* 114h 107c
10 b g Turtle Island(IRE) Rachael's Dawn (Rakaposhi King)
291[2] 2145[2] 2496[2] 3428[11] 3999[P] 4165[4] 4510[P] 4840[3] 5260[7]

Snatchitback *Tom Symonds* 73b
4 b g Overbury(IRE) Talk The Talk (Terimon)
4392[8] 5021[3]

Sneaking Budge *Stuart Edmunds* 111h
3 b g Nayef(USA) Ikat (IRE) (Pivotal)
2992[8] (3443)

Snippetydoodah *Michael Roberts* 90h
7 b m King's Theatre(IRE) Kimpour (FR) (Hawker's News (IRE))
671[6] 930[6] 4936[4] (5305)

Snooze (FR) *John Laurence Cullen* 124c
9 br g Sleeping Car(FR) Kittygale (IRE) (Strong Gale)
48a[U]

Snowball (IRE) *David Arbuthnot* 92h
8 gr g Alderbrook Rosafi (IRE) (Roselier (FR))
1756[8] 2413[2] (2649) (3369) 3771[4] 3904[4] 4450[4]

Snowed In (IRE) *Barry Murtagh* 106h
6 gr g Dark Angel(IRE) Spinning Gold (Spinning World (USA))
157[8] 507[9] 1071[9] 1552[3] 2703[3] 3244[P] 3680[2] 4178[7] 4819[2] 5403[3]

Snowell (IRE) *Emma Baker* 100h 113c
8 b g Well Chosen Snow Water (IRE) (Jolly Jake (NZ))
2138[3] 2659[5]

Snow Falcon (IRE) *Noel Meade* 150h
5 b g Presenting Flocon De Neige (IRE) (Kahyasi)
2815a[5] 3322a[F] (4146a)

Snow Leopardess *Charlie Longsdon* 109b
3 gr f Martaline Queen Soraya (Persian Bold)
(4309) ◆ 5180[5]

Snowmane (IRE) *Kim Bailey*
4 b g Galileo(IRE) Tree Tops (Grand Lodge (USA))
1723[P]

Snow Prince *Steve Gollings* 55h
4 gr g Royal Applause Snowdrops (Gulch (USA))
3306[8] 3724[P]

Snuker *James Ewart* 91h 104c
8 b g Snurge Briar Rose (IRE) (Roselier (FR))
2800[6] 3144[5] (4047) 4740[P]

So Bazaar (IRE) *Andrew Wilson* 68h 77c
8 b g Xaar Nature Girl (USA) (Green Dancer (USA))
507[P] 870[5] 1461[6] (1687) 1888[P] (Dead)

Social Climber (IRE) *Fergal O'Brien* 99h
3 b g Strategic Prince Ivy Queen (IRE) (Green Desert (USA))
1631[7] 1866[5] 4490[7] 4885[4] 5313[5]

Soeur De Rois (IRE) *Philip Kirby* 67h
5 br m King's Theatre(IRE) Soeur Ti (FR) (Kaldoun (FR))
200[5] 415[P] (Dead)

So Fine (IRE) *Philip Hobbs* 131h 125c
9 b g Definite Article Not So Green (IRE) (Roselier (FR))
2484[14] (3018) 3407[6] 3844[3] 4483[4] 5119[6]

So French (FR) *G Macaire* 121h 151c
4 b g Poliglote Westonne (FR) (Mansonnien (FR))
(2820a)

Softly She Treads (IRE) *Pat Phelan* 56h
4 b m Azamour(IRE) Lady Lucre (IRE) (Last Tycoon)
281[9]

So It Begins (IRE) *John Flint*
5 b m Trans Island Sabang (Sabrehill (USA))
4825[P]

Sokol (CAN) *Michal Lisek*
8 rg g Perfect Soul(IRE) Silver Nithi (CAN) (Numerous (USA))
1885a[F]

Solar Impulse (FR) *Paul Nicholls* 131h 156c
5 b g Westerner Moon Glow (FR) (Solar One (FR))
2625[3] 3121[P] (4770) 5326[3] 5493[5]

Solatentif (FR) *Henry De Bromhead* 130h
5 b g Solon(GER) Indian Mist (FR) (River Mist (USA))
53a[6] 1875a[2]

Soleil D'Avril (FR) *Mrs Sarah Easterby* 107h 114c
9 bb g Laveron Melanie Du Chenet (FR) (Nikos)
4043[4]

Solidago (IRE) *Barry Leavy* 97h
8 b g Vinnie Roe(IRE) Native Belle (IRE) (Be My Native (USA))
2165[6] 2850[5] 3143[3] (3382) 4184[P] 4863[6] 5102[P]

Sol Invictus (ITY) *P Favero* 122h
7 b g King Charlemagne(USA) Sine Alia (IRE) (Lycius (USA))
1671a[2]

Solita (IRE) *Paul Nolan* 132h 135c
6 b m King's Theatre(IRE) Wind Over Water (IRE) (Erins Isle)
231a[7] 3093a[P]

Soll *David Pipe* 116h 152c
10 ch g Presenting Montelfolene (IRE) (Montelimar (USA))
2482[16] 2899[4] (3448) 4205[3] 5218[P]

Solomn Grundy (IRE) *Neil Mulholland* 121h
5 b g Westerner Marika's King (IRE) (King's Ride)
2879[4] 3375[4] 4668[F] (4982)

Solstalla *David Weston* 87h
3 b f Halling(USA) Solstice (Dubawi (IRE))
975[P] 4345[4] 4683[4]

Solstice Dawn *Peter Winks* 84h
7 b m Lyphento(USA) Ryders Hill (Zaffaran (USA))
4538[4]

Solstice Son *Anthony Honeyball* 117h 136c
6 b g Haafhd Karasta (IRE) (Lake Coniston (IRE))
4062[6] (4780) ◆ (5285)

Solstice Star *Martin Keighley* 142h
5 b g Kayf Tara Clover Green (IRE) (Presenting)
858[4] 1113[9] (2264) ◆ (2418) (2833) (3015) (3854) 4622[2] 5273[2]

Solway (FR) *G Cherel* 136h 135c
4 b g Califet(FR) Solveigh (GER) (Tiger Hill (IRE))
1882a[8]

Solway Bay *Lisa Harrison* 92h 100c
13 b g Cloudings(IRE) No Problem Jac (Safawan)
333[6] 842[2] 1069[7] 1171[6] 1272[2] 1332[3] 1503[4] 1551[2] ◆ 1778[2] 1930[5] 2297[4] 2751[11] 3472[U] (3679) 4175[5] 4872[P]

Solway Berry *Lisa Harrison* 67b
4 b m Overbury(IRE) Solway Rose (Minster Son)
1334[6]

Solway Dandy *Lisa Harrison* 125h
8 b g Danroad(AUS) Solway Rose (Minster Son)
(302) 886[2] 957[2]

Solway Dornal *Lisa Harrison* 83h 98c
10 b g Alflora(IRE) Solway Donal (IRE) (Celio Rufo)
35[6]

Solway Lark *Lisa Harrison* 94b
4 b g Beat All(USA) Solway Larkin (IRE) (Supreme Leader)
1640[6]

Solway Legend *Lisa Harrison* 81h 110c
8 ch g And Beyond(IRE) Spicey Cut (Cut Above)
78[4] (303) 637[2] (803) 959[3] 1330[4] 1403[4] (1496) 1629[4] 1853[F] 2030[3] 2320[P] 2749[3] 3235[P] 3684[P]

Solway Prince *Lisa Harrison* 105h
6 ch g Double Trigger(IRE) Solway Rose (Minster Son)
79[6] 288[2] 468[4] 661[4] 883[2] (939) 1113[4] 1264[7] 1329[7] 1637[2] 1784[5] 2296[4] 2429[7] 3428[12] 3680[6] 4035[6] 4547[4] 4570[3] 5122[5] 5450[U]

Solway Sam *Lisa Harrison* 100h 85c
12 b g Double Trigger(IRE) Some Gale (Strong Gale)
291[8] 484[3] 803[7] (958) 1264[12] 1426[3] 2432[2] 2948[3] 3474[3] 3684[10] 4051[4] 4903[3] 5412[4]

Solway Storm (IRE) *Lisa Harrison* 100b
5 gr g Indian River(FR) The Grey Lady (IRE) (Roselier (FR))
1858[3]

Solway Sunrise *Lisa Harrison* 86b
4 br m Overbury(IRE) Solway Sunset (Primitive Rising (USA))
1640[8] 2433[5]

Solway Trigger *Lisa Harrison* 78h
6 b g Double Trigger(IRE) Double Flight (Mtoto)
460[P] 634[6] 798[8] 935[6] 1098[3] 1273[4] 1427[3] 1497[2] 1573[4] 1890[6]

Somchine *Seamus Mullins* 110h 126c
7 b g Volochine(IRE) Seem Of Gold (Gold Dust)
2243[4] 3794[P] 4251[5] 4842[2] 5354[3]

Some Are Lucky (IRE) *Tom George* 122h
4 b g Gold Well Foreign Estates (IRE) (Be My Native (USA))
2065[5] 2450[6] 4176[2] ◆ (4843) 5300[2]

Some Article (IRE) *Thomas Mullins* 135h
7 ch g Definite Article Ahead Of My Time (IRE) (Royal Fountain)
(7a) 1175a[5]

Some Buckle (IRE) *Paul Nicholls* 134h 146c
6 b g Milan Miss Moppit (IRE) (Torus)
3015[6] 3747[P] (4870) 5496[6]

Some Finish (IRE) *Robin Dickin* 73h 101c
6 b g Kayf Tara Kylie Kaprice (GER) (Big Shuffle (USA))
2763[11] 2995[11] 3316[6] 3746[P] 3864[P] (4214) (4423) 4591[3] 5138[P]

Some Kinda Lama (IRE) *Charlie Mann* 116h
4 gr g Daylami(IRE) Last Sunrise (IRE) (Shahanndeh (IRE))
2772[4] 4463[3]

Some Lad (IRE) *Alison Hamilton* 94h 101c
10 b g Beneficial Some News (IRE) (Be My Native (USA))
256[4] (5086)

Somemothersdohavem *Venetia Williams* 123h 111c
6 ch g Avonbridge Show Off (Efisio)
108[4] 216[7]

Some Plan (IRE) *Paul Nicholls* 148h
7 b g Winged Love(IRE) Lough Hyne (Classic Cliche (IRE))
2914[5] 3151[4] 4765[16] 5325[4]

Somerby (IRE) *Richenda Ford* 86c
12 b g Sadler's Wells(USA) Oriental Mystique (Kris)
2269[4] 3412[6] (4531)

Somersby (IRE) *Mick Channon* 145h 167c
11 b g Second Empire(IRE) Back To Roost (IRE) (Presenting)
2511[2] 2915[4] 3281[4] 4718[5] 5192[4]

Somerset Jem *Kevin Bishop* 105h
6 b g Sir Harry Lewis(USA) Monger Lane (Karinga Bay)
2443[P] 2879[11] 3413[P] (4250) 4438[2] 4860[7]

Somerset Lias (IRE) *Bob Buckler* 98h 109c
7 b g Golan(IRE) Presenting Gayle (IRE) (Presenting)
1906[2] 2598[3] 2988[6] 3412[2] 3746[3] 4185[P] 4859[2] 5222[2] 5417[2]

Song Light *Seamus Mullins* 133h
5 b g Echo Of Light Blue Lullaby (IRE) (Fasliyev (USA))
197[3] 2728[7] 3151[5]

Song Of The Night (IRE) *Charlie Longsdon* 73h
4 b g Mahler Pollys Attic (IRE) (Rashar (USA))
1966[5] 2407[7] 2860[11] 3221[11] 4919[3] 5305[P]

Song Saa *Tom George* 111h
5 b m Midnight Legend Mystere (IRE) (Montelimar (USA))
4075[2] (4507) (4961) 5409[10]

Songsmith *Lucy Wadham* 127h
7 b g Librettist(USA) Venus Rising (Observatory (USA))
59[5] 1448[2] 2373[2]

Sonneofpresenting (IRE) *Kim Bailey* 101h
5 bb g Presenting Sonne Cinq (IRE) (Old Vic)
3221[3] ◆ 4063[5] 4303[10] 4840[P]

Sonny B (IRE) *John J Walsh* 140h 103c
8 b g Spadoun(FR) Miss Ell (IRE) (Houmayoun (FR))
3302a[P]

Sonny The One *Colin Tizzard* 112h 127c
5 ch g Tobougg(IRE) Annie Fleetwood (Anshan)
2090[2] 2546[4] 3371[2] (3918) 4292[2] 4542[2] 5354[4]

Sonofagun (FR) *Ian Williams* 95h 120c
9 b g Turgeon(USA) Detonante (FR) (Cardoun (FR))
218[8] 464[3] 2854[5] (3225) ◆ 3843[P] 4306[7] 5154[7]

Son Of Feyan (IRE) *Lucy Normile* 79h
4 ch g Nayef(USA) Miss Penton (Primo Dominie)
883[P]

Son Of Flicka *C Rae* 111h 128c
11 b g Groom Dancer(USA) Calendula (Be My Guest (USA))
521[3]

Son Of Suzie *Fergal O'Brien* 120h 124c
7 gr g Midnight Legend Suzie Cream Cheese (IRE) (Royal Charter (FR))
2213[4] 3014[5] 3499[3] 4433[2] 4740[P]

Sonoftheking (IRE) *Miss Nicky Martin* 93h 108c
7 b g King's Theatre(IRE) Nikadora (FR) (Nikos)
298[U] 5270[4]

So Oscar (IRE) *Fergal O'Brien* 103b
7 b g Oscar(IRE) So Proper (IRE) (Topanoora)
1911[P] 4487[P] 4859[P]

Sort It Out (IRE) *Edward P Harty* 148h
6 bb g Milan Snowbelle (IRE) (Flemensfirth (USA))
(96a) 3151[14] 5004a[4]

Sory *Tina Jackson* 76h
8 b g Sakhee(USA) Rule Britannia (Night Shift (USA))
200[P] 3309[8] 3791[P] 3973[5]

So Satisfied *Sandy Thomson* 122h
4 b g Aqlaam Pirouetting (Pivotal)
452[4] 656[5] 881[5] 3424[3] ◆ (4036) ◆ 4154[2] 4366[7] 5088[P]

Soudain (FR) *Brian Ellison* 111h 132c
9 ch g Dom Alco(FR) Ebene D'Avril (FR) (Video Rock (FR))
3236[P]

Soulsaver *Anthony Honeyball* 87b
3 ch g Recharge(IRE) Lapina (IRE) (Fath (USA))
3409[6] 5069[8]

Sound Investment (IRE) *Paul Nicholls* 141h 166c
7 b g Dr Massini(IRE) Drumcay Polly (IRE) (Le Bavard (FR))
1848[8] (2084) 2483[3] 3031[5]

Sound Money *E J O'Grady* 112h
3 b g Zamindar(USA) Alpensinfonie (IRE) (Montjeu (IRE))
5001a[6]

Sound The Bugle *Anthony Day* 71b
5 b g Overbury(IRE) Fusion Of Tunes (Mr Confusion (IRE))
4880[14] 5315[7]

Soupy Soups (IRE) *Neil Mulholland* 108h
4 ch g Stowaway Near Dunleer (IRE) (Soviet Lad (USA))
(1966) 2519[3]

Souriyan (FR) *Jamie Snowden* 126h 131c
4 b g Alhaarth(IRE) Serasana (Red Ransom (USA))
1782[2] 2211[3] 3255[F] 3929[P] 5284[10]

Southern Cross *Dai Williams* 68h
4 ch m Mount Nelson Bread Of Heaven (Machiavellian (USA))
179[P] 361[5] 832[9] 929[5] 1009[9] 1086[8] 1297[8]

Southerner (IRE) *William Cronin* 82b
5 b g Westerner Material Leader (Supreme Leader)
25a[12]

Southfield Fairy *Charles Whittaker* 42h
4 b m Victory Note(USA) Laureldean Belle (IRE) (Supreme Leader)
2452[11]

Southfield Royale *Neil Mulholland* 136h 158c
5 b g Presenting Chamoss Royale (FR) (Garde Royale)
1900[2] ◆ (2197) ◆ (3040) 3229[2] ◆ 4700[4]

Southfield Theatre (IRE) *Paul Nicholls* 145h 159c
7 b g King's Theatre(IRE) Chamoss Royale (FR) (Garde Royale)
2372[3] 2900[4] 4697[B] 5494[4]

Southfield Vic (IRE) *Paul Nicholls* 148h 140c
6 ch g Old Vic Chamoss Royale (FR) (Garde Royale)
2553[2] 3255[2] 4142[2] 4354[6] 5284[4]

Southsea Island (IRE) *S R B Crawford* 112h
7 b g Heron Island(IRE) Southsea Lady (IRE) (Kemal (FR))
2189[3]

Sovinnie (IRE) *Jane Mathias* 88h
6 ch g Vinnie Roe(IRE) Sohapara (Arapahos (FR))
773[7] 1082[7] 1136[7] 1293[4] 1599[4]

Space Cadet (IRE) *Gordon Elliott* 134h
5 b g Flemensfirth(USA) Shuil A Hocht (IRE) (Mohaajir (USA))
5024a[4]

Space Oddity (FR) *Harry Fry* 119h
4 bb g Al Namix(FR) Schoune (FR) (Majorien)
3928[4] (4449) 5030[4] 5418[2]

Space Ship *Robert Alan Hennessy* 127h
5 ch g Galileo(IRE) Angara (Alzao (USA))
2328[2]

Space Walker (IRE) *Ben Pauling* 119h
4 b g Astronomer Royal(USA) Hot Property (USA) (Thunder Gulch (USA))
2577[2] ◆ 2977[P] 3956[6] 5301[4]

Spa Hill (IRE) *Richard Woollacott* 90h
6 b g Fruits Of Love(USA) Calistoga (IRE) (Mujadil (USA))
2713[3]

Spanish Arch (IRE) *Martin Keighley* 103h 107c
8 b g Westerner Piepowder (In The Wings)
211[P]

Spanish Danser (IRE) *Jo Davis*
3 ch f Lord Shanakill(USA) Highwater Dancer (IRE) (Sadler's Wells (USA))
4157[P]

Spanish Fleet *John Wade* 134h 106c
7 b g Cadeaux Genereux Santisima Trinidad (IRE) (Definite Article)
3630[8] 3936[5] 4568[5]

Spanish Fork (IRE) *Sheena West* 91h
6 br g Trans Island Wings Awarded (Shareef Dancer (USA))
222[5] 493[4] 599[6] 1426[5] 1756[6]

Spanish Optimist (IRE) *Sarah Robinson* 98h 83c
9 b g Indian Danehill(IRE) La Traviata (Spectrum (IRE))
5435[5]

Spanish Treasure (GER) *Sophie Leech* 123b
9 b g Black Sam Bellamy(IRE) Santa Zinaada (GER) (Zinaad)
2418[P]

Sparkling Ice (IRE) *Laura Young* 90h
4 gr m Verglas(IRE) Sand Crystal (IRE) (Singspiel (IRE))
647[5]

Spartilla *Daniel O'Brien* 91h 91c
6 b g Teofilo(IRE) Wunders Dream (IRE) (Averti (IRE))
3421[2] 4669[4] 5480[2] ◆

Spa's Dancer (IRE) *James Eustace* 105h
8 b g Danehill Dancer(IRE) Spa (Sadler's Wells (USA))
1613[3] 1893[B] 2689[4] 3619[7] 4774[8]

Special Agent *Nicky Henderson* 123h 128c
6 b g Invincible Spirit(IRE) Flight Of Fancy (Sadler's Wells (USA))
2727[8] 3843[2] 4465[7] 5391[9]

Special Catch (IRE) *Keith Reveley* 137h 137c
8 b g Catcher In The Rye(IRE) Top Quality (Simply Great (FR))
2774[P] 2981[2] (3936) 4370[7] 4551[2] 4910[P] (5298)

Special Portrait (IRE) *Mark Hughes* 117c
11 rg g Portrait Gallery(IRE) Goin Home (IRE) (Warcraft (USA))
17[U] 290[U] 506[U]

Special Report (IRE) *Neil Mulholland* 103h
5 b g Mujadil(USA) Ellistown Lady (IRE) (Red Sunset)
43[P] (Dead)

Special Tiara *Henry De Bromhead* 122h 170c
8 b g Kayf Tara Special Choice (IRE) (Bob Back (USA))
2388a[4] 2915[2] 4718[3]

Special Wells *Sue Smith* 117h 119c
6 ch g Alflora(IRE) Oso Special (Teenoso (USA))
2026[3] 2211[6] 2922[P] 3362[3] 3972[5] 4420[4] (4803) 5103[2]

Speckled Wood (IRE) *C Roche* 134h 126c
7 b m High Chaparral(IRE) Like-A-Butterfly (IRE) (Montelimar (USA))
70a[2]

Speedalong (IRE) *Jeremy Scott* 90b
4 b g Vertical Speed(FR) Emily's Bracelet (IRE) (Priolo (USA))
5152[0] 5358[8]

Speed Check (IRE) *Don Cantillon* 93h
8 ch g Kris Kin(USA) Zaola (IRE) (Alzao (USA))
918[5]

Speed Demon (IRE) *Richard Phillips* 127h 112c
6 b g Beneficial Brierfield Lady (IRE) (Montelimar (USA))
3846[9] **4789[U] 5432[8]**

Speed Master (IRE) *Nigel Twiston-Davies* 129h 132c
9 b g King's Theatre(IRE) Handy Lass (Nicholas Bill)
(532) **855[5]** 1963[5]

Speed Rock (FR) *P Cottin* 121h
3 b g Sagacity(FR) Ebene Rock (FR) (Lost World (IRE))
4959a[P]

Speedy Bruere (FR) *David Bridgwater* 105h 120c
9 gr g Turgeon(USA) Divine Bruere (FR) (Son Of Silver)
226[3] 677[2] ◆ **809[4] 1007[5]**

Speedy Tunes (IRE) *Simon Waugh* 123h 101c
8 b g Heron Island(IRE) Art Lover (IRE) (Over The River (FR))
677[4] 867[P]

Spencer Lea *Henry Oliver* 125h
7 b g Overbury(IRE) Castanet (Pennekamp (USA))
(4041) ◆ 4596[2] ◆ 5120[8]

Spendajennie (IRE) *Nick Kent* 88h
6 b m Old Vic American Jennie (IRE) (Lord Americo)
2407[5] 2838[7] 3334[5]

Spending Time *David Pipe* 108h 120c
6 b g King's Theatre(IRE) Karello Bay (Kahyasi)
858[6] 1236[11] 1383[3] (1547) 1897[6] **(2410) 2872[2] 2988[P] 3836[F] 4427[P]**

Speranza *Susan Corbett* 58b
3 b f Bahri(USA) Toarmandowithlove (IRE) (Choisir (AUS))
4208[7] 4572[4]

Speredek (FR) *Nigel Hawke* 119h
4 bb g Kapgarde(FR) Sendamagic (FR) (Sendawar (IRE))
2163[4] 2591[4] 3023[6] 3662[P] (4543) 4860[2] 5072[6]

Speronimo (FR) *Nigel Hawke* 86b
3 b g Diamond Green(FR) Spepita (FR) (Marathon (USA))
5359[4]

Spice Fair *Mark Usher* 131h
8 ch g Trade Fair Focosa (ITY) (In The Wings)
2569[3] 2888[2] (3238) 3748[3] 4482[2] 4622[3]

Spicy Fruity (IRE) *Gordon Elliott* 106h
5 b g Fruits Of Love(USA) Rocksham (IRE) (Bluebird (USA))
837[3]

Spifer (IRE) *Julia Brooke* 96h
7 gr g Motivator Zarawa (IRE) (Kahyasi)
2747[5] 5408[7]

Spiker The Biker (IRE) *Nigel Thomas Slevin* 91h 91c
11 b g New Frontier(IRE) Hollies Promise (IRE) (Good Thyne (USA))
4942[2]

Spin Cast *Laura Young* 104h
7 b g Marju(IRE) Some Diva (Dr Fong (USA))
616[2] 892[3] 1120[5] 1578[9] 2599[P]

Spinning Away *N W Alexander* 92h
7 ch m Alflora(IRE) Minora (IRE) (Cataldi)
4404[P]

Spinning Scooter *Maurice Barnes* 74b
5 b g Sleeping Indian Spinning Coin (Mujahid (USA))
732[6]

Spirit Dame (IRE) *Rose Dobbin* 56h
4 ch m Beneficial Dramatic Chick (Riverwise (USA))
1854[12] 4369[7] 4837[P]

Spirit Ness (FR) *J-P Daireaux* 103h
4 ch g Spirit One(FR) Infusion (Efisio)
(3876a)

Spiritofchartwell *Raymond York* 93h 87c
7 ch g Clerkenwell(USA) Rollin Rock (Rock Hopper)
293[P] 1082[8] 1293[11] **1489[2] 1595[3]** ◆

Spirit Of Hale (IRE) *Jennie Candlish* 73b
4 ch g Stowaway Roseboreen (IRE) (Roselier (FR))
3012[5] 4001[6] 4805[6]

Spirit Of Kayf *Sandy Thomson* 110b
4 b g Kayf Tara Over Sixty (Overbury (IRE))
2106[3] (3442) ◆ 4001[2] 4721[22]

Spirit Of Shankly *Charlie Longsdon* 138h 138c
7 ch g Sulamani(IRE) Lago D'Oro (Slip Anchor)
1900[5] 2332[2] 2785[5] 3157[P] (4744) 5311[3]

Spirit Oscar (IRE) *Lucinda Russell* 112h 123c
7 b m Oscar(IRE) Grange Classic (IRE) (Jurado (USA))
483[5]

Spirit River (FR) *Dave Roberts* 124h 107c
10 b g Poliglote Love River (FR) (Epervier Bleu)
670[B] 839[8] **1167[11]**

Spitfire Ace (IRE) *Oliver Greenall* 76h 80c
7 b g Zagreb(USA) Coolafancy (IRE) (Accordion)
472[5]

Spitz (FR) *Rose Dobbin* 112h
7 b g Enrique Spezzia (FR) (Snurge)
886[3] 1170[4] 3023[10]

Splash Of Ginge *Nigel Twiston-Davies* 139h 146c
7 b g Oscar(IRE) Land Of Honour (Supreme Leader)
2198[7] **2483[7] 2783[U] 3741[P] 4113[3] 4735[12] 5276[6]**

Spock (FR) *Lady Susan Brooke* 74h 104c
10 b g Lost World(IRE) Quark Top (FR) (Perrault)
1043[6] 5399[2]

Spoils Of War (IRE) *Lucinda Russell* 111h
6 b g Craigsteel Mooreshill Lady (IRE) (King's Ride)
139[P]

Spoilt Rotten *Mark Pitman* 106b
6 b g Kayf Tara Rosita Bay (Hernando (FR))
1872[3] 2154[P] 3117[P]

Spookydooky (IRE) *Jonjo O'Neill* 136h 143c
7 b g Winged Love(IRE) Kiora Lady (IRE) (King's Ride)
2332[4] (2727) ◆ **3157[2] 4238[4] 4802[4]** ◆ **5327[P]**

Sporting Boy (IRE) *Johnny Farrelly* 126h 130c
7 b g Barathea(IRE) Sportsticketing (IRE) (Spectrum (IRE))
365[2] (557) (715) ◆ **1053[5]**

Sporting Milan (IRE) *Harry Whittington* 100h
4 b g Milan Sports Leader (IRE) (Supreme Leader)
2715[3] 5451[2]

Sports Barrow (IRE) *Ms Sandra Hughes* 107h
3 b g Windsor Knot(IRE) Liberty Grace (IRE) (Statue Of Liberty (USA))
2813a[7]

Sportsreport (IRE) *Seamus Mullins* 74h 115c
7 b g Coroner(IRE) Goforthetape (IRE) (Gothland (FR))
175[2] 2138[5] 2859[6] (4670) 5096[7]

Spot The Pro (IRE) *Rebecca Menzies* 96h
6 b g Barathea(IRE) Truly Precious (IRE) (Pennekamp (USA))
1404[P]

Spring Back *Edwin Tuer* 54h
7 b m Silver Patriarch(IRE) Danceback (IRE) (Bob Back (USA))
1066[P]

Spring Blossom *John Ryall* 81b
5 b m Apple Tree(FR) Spring Grass (Pardigras)
5152[6]

Springboks (IRE) *Alan King* 88h
5 b g Flemensfirth(USA) Roaming (IRE) (Be My Native (USA))
210[7]

Spring Heeled (IRE) *J H Culloty* 135h 151c
8 b g Old Vic Central Arch (Dilum (USA))
1152a[12] 2482[8] 3296a[13] 4697[U] 5494[14]

Spring Hill (IRE) *Chris Bealby* 50b
3 b g Stowaway Miss The Post (Bustino)
4475[4]

Springhill Lad *Geoffrey Deacon* 104h
8 b g Kayf Tara Anouska (Interrex (CAN))
2997[3] 4877[3]

Spring Over (IRE) *Ian Duncan* 97h 92c
9 ch m Samraan(USA) Superswap (IRE) (Gone Fishin)
3427[4] 4051[5] 4738[2] 5013[F]

Spring Steel (IRE) *Alexandra Dunn* 111h 111c
6 b g Dushyantor(USA) Fieldtown (IRE) (Anshan)
283[P] 780[2] 880[5] **1266[2]** 1911[7] **2153[P] 2568[P] 3141[P]**

Spring Wolf *John Ryall* 19h
7 br g Loup Sauvage(USA) Spring Grass (Pardigras)
2710[8] 4917[P]

Sprinter Sacre (FR) *Nicky Henderson* 137h 176c
9 bb g Network(GER) Fatima III (FR) (Bayolidaan (FR))
(2511) (3281) (4718) (5493)

Sprogzilla *Hannah James* 19b
6 gr m Fair Mix(IRE) Gentle Approach (Rakaposhi King)
3381[8] 3921[P]

Spurned Girl *Robin Dickin* 73h
5 b m Passing Glance Highlight Girl (Forzando)
106[P] 748[3] 1816[P] 1980[8] 2162[6] 4886[P]

Squeeze Me *Gary Hanmer* 66h
8 b m Grape Tree Road Ask Me Not (IRE) (Shernazar)
4069[P] 4709[7]

Squinch *Mrs David Plunkett* 94b
11 b g Kayf Tara Alta (Arctic Lord (IRE))
5384[P]

Squire Trelawney *Dan Skelton* 114h 116c
9 b g Domedriver(IRE) Crockadore (USA) (Nijinsky (CAN))
(2090) 2615[5] 4071[P]

Squouateur (FR) *Gordon Elliott* 140h
4 gr g Martaline Samansonnienne (FR) (Mansonnien (FR))
4769[7] 5213[6]

Stadium Of Light (IRE) *Christopher Kellett*
8 b g Fantastic Light(USA) Treble Seven (USA) (Fusaichi Pegasus (USA))
1423[P]

Stafford Charlie *John O'Shea* 89h 74c
9 ch g Silver Patriarch(IRE) Miss Roberto (IRE) (Don Roberto (USA))
173[4] 446[P] 1080[5] 1237[5] 1703[6] 1825[6] 1978[P]

Stafford Jo *John O'Shea* 98h
6 ch g Silver Patriarch(IRE) Miss Roberto (IRE) (Don Roberto (USA))
2909[9] 5469[4]

Staff Sergeant *Mark Hoad* 99h
8 b g Dubawi(IRE) Miss Particular (IRE) (Sadler's Wells (USA))
712[7] 811[6] 1941[F] 4409[7] 5483[9]

Stage One (IRE) *Dan Skelton* 111h
4 b g King's Theatre(IRE) Tara Tara (IRE) (Fayruz)
2772[3]

Stage Twenty (IRE) *Jamie Snowden* 74h
5 b m King's Theatre(IRE) Last Century (IRE) (Glacial Storm (USA))
28[P] 178[P]

Stags Leap (IRE) *Julia Brooke* 109h
8 b g Refuse To Bend(IRE) Swingsky (IRE) (Indian Ridge)
(502) (839)

Staigue Fort *Emma Lavelle* 102h
7 b g Kirkwall Mulberry Wine (Benny The Dip (USA))
701[8]

Staker Wallace (IRE) *E Bolger* 116h
4 b g King's Theatre(IRE) Honeybunch (IRE) (Supreme Leader)
3890a[4]

Stamp Your Feet (IRE) *Tom George* 114b
3 b g Galileo(IRE) Nausicaa (USA) (Diesis)
4392[3]

Stand Aside (IRE) *Jonjo O'Neill* 95h
5 b g Golan(IRE) Lady Accord (IRE) (Accordion)
364[7] 879[4] 1598[13]

Stand By Me (FR) *Alan Jones* 97b
5 b g Dream Well(FR) In Love New (FR) (Perrault)
392[3]

Stand Clear *Chris Grant* 87h 78c
10 b m Sir Harry Lewis(USA) Clair Valley (Ardross)
805[7] 966[3] 1066[7] 1552[12] 1744[P]

Standing Ovation (IRE) *David Pipe* 130h 137c
8 b g Presenting Glittering Star (IRE) (Good Thyne (USA))
1113[7] (1262) **(1322)** 1522[3] **1849[8] 2089[3] 4802[P]**

Stand To Reason (IRE) *Tony Carroll* 110h
7 ch g Danehill Dancer(IRE) Ho Hi The Moon (IRE) (Be My Guest (USA))
755[2] (1156) 2271[8] 2688[4] 3238[F]

Stanley (GER) *Donald McCain* 102h
4 bl g Pivotal Sky Dancing (IRE) (Exit To Nowhere (USA))
1399[3]

Stanley Bridge *Barry Murtagh* 93h
8 b g Avonbridge Antonia's Folly (Music Boy)
252[6] 507[5] 845[P] 1071[4]

Star Ascending (IRE) *Jennie Candlish* 25h
3 ch g Thousand Words Sakaka (Tobougg (IRE))
3464[6]

Star Benefit (IRE) *Adrian Wintle* 82h
5 b g Beneficial Beautiful Night (FR) (Sleeping Car (FR))
56[9] 2840[P] 4886[9]

Starchitect (IRE) *David Pipe* 146h
4 b g Sea The Stars(IRE) Humilis (IRE) (Sadler's Wells (USA))
4115[2] ◆ 4765[5] 5189[3]

Star Date (IRE) *Lucinda Russell* 111h
6 b g Galileo(IRE) Play Misty For Me (IRE) (Danehill Dancer (IRE))
658[P]

Star De La Prise (FR) *S Dory* 105c
9 gr g Smadoun(FR) Girl Royale (FR) (Cyborg (FR))
313a[7]

Star Foot (IRE) *Jo Davis* 120h
4 b g Soviet Star(USA) On The Backfoot (IRE) (Bob Back (USA))
1979[2] 2183[8] 2731[3] (4639)

Starimperial (FR) *S Foucher* 85h 92c
8 ch g Starborough L'Imperialis (FR) (Apeldoorn (FR))
5136a[2]

Starkhov (FR) *G Macaire*
2 b g Sholokhov(IRE) Free Sky (FR) (Ungaro (GER))
4539a[P]

Starkie *Chris Gordon* 127h 130c
8 b g Putra Sandhurst(IRE) Lysways (Gildoran)
3524[P] 3957[P] 4464[3] 4918[P] 5096[4]

Starlight Court (IRE) *Dan Skelton* 84b
4 b g Court Cave(IRE) Marie The (FR) (Exit To Nowhere (USA))
4357[5]

Starlight Sonata *Emma Lavelle* 6h
5 b m Tagula(IRE) Starlight Express (FR) (Air Express (IRE))
1574[9]

Starlit Night *Chris Down* 75h
3 b f Nayef(USA) Perfect Night (Danzig Connection (USA))
4683[7] 4916[7] 5182[7]

Starluck (IRE) *David Arbuthnot* 139h 121c
10 gr g Key Of Luck(USA) Sarifa (IRE) (Kahyasi)
1848[9] 2617[5] 3284[7]

Star Of Massini (IRE) *N W Padfield* 89h 91c
8 b g Dr Massini(IRE) Star Of The Orient (IRE) (Moscow Society (USA))
298[3] 533[P]

Star Of Salford *Warren Greatrex* 96h
6 b m Hernando(FR) City Of Angels (Woodman (USA))
558[7] 1009[5] 1262[P]

Star Presenter (IRE) *Sam Drake* 102h 114c
7 b g Presenting Star Councel (IRE) (Leading Counsel (USA))
446[3] 1596[8] **2705[3] (3103)** ◆ **(3806)**

Star Rise (IRE) *Marc Barber*
6 ch g Mountain High(IRE) Golden Jorden (IRE) (Cadeaux Genereux)
298[P]

Stars Over The Sea (USA) *David Pipe* 135h
4 b g Sea The Stars(IRE) Exciting Times (FR) (Jeune Homme (USA))
94a[4] 1847[8] 2060[7] 3529[6]

Stars Royale (IRE) *Nick Gifford* 111h 110c
6 b g King's Best(USA) Open Your Heart (IRE) (Soviet Star (USA))
61[10] **2003[2] 2300[P] 4073[P] 4410[5]** 4749[P]

Startinfromscratch (IRE) *Jonjo O'Neill* 27h
4 b g Yeats(IRE) Stony View (IRE) (Tirol)
11a[19]

Start Me Up (IRE) *Conor Dore* 73h 70c
11 b g Winged Love(IRE) Go And Tell (Kemal (FR))
1615[9]

Star Trouper (IRE) *Philip Hobbs* 112h
5 b g King's Theatre(IRE) Wyndham Sweetmarie (IRE) (Mister Lord (USA))
2731[2] 5268[5]

Start Royal (FR) *Alan Hill* 119c
11 b g Starborough Marie Des Epeires (FR) (Rose Laurel)
295[P]

Starving Marvin *Rod Millman* 122h
7 b g Hawk Wing(USA) Oleana (IRE) (Alzao (USA))
2860[12] 3484[3] 4233[2] (4594) 5091[9]

State Sovereignty *Michael Scudamore* 81b
3 b f Authorized(IRE) Sovereign's Honour (USA) (Kingmambo (USA))
4302[3]

Staunton *Susan Johnson* 30h
4 b m Kayf Tara Aranga (IRE) (Supreme Leader)
4468[9] 5378[6]

Stay In My Heart (IRE) *Susan Corbett* 95h
6 ch m Medicean Christmas Cracker (FR) (Alhaarth (IRE))
552[2] 864[3] 1490[4] 1771[5] 1897[5] 4178[10] 4837[2]

Stay Tuned (IRE) *Alexandra Dunn* 96h
7 ch m Saffron Walden(FR) Just A Song (IRE) (Sharifabad (IRE))
361[4] 615[10]

St Dominick (IRE) *Jackie Du Plessis* 109h 131c
8 b g Oscar(IRE) Kilcrea Breeze (IRE) (Fresh Breeze (USA))
389[2] ◆ **2442[2] (2663) 2878[5] 3583[P] 4621[6]**

Steady Eddie *Steve Flook* 68b
5 b g Zafeen(FR) Indian Girl (Erhaab (USA))
2840[P] 3022[U]

Steady Progress (IRE) *Richard Ford* 58h 85c
7 b g Flemensfirth(USA) Creaking Step (IRE) (Shernazar)
552[6] **803[P] 934[11]**

Stealing Mix *Neil Mulholland* 97b
5 b g Fair Mix(IRE) Minimum (Terimon)
4790[11] 5358[4]

Steal My Thunder (IRE) *Philip Hobbs* 98b
4 gr g Craigsteel Party Woman (IRE) (Sexton Blake)
5315[4]

Steel A Tune *Nick Mitchell* 22h
6 gr g Proclamation(IRE) Skip 'N' Tune (IRE) (Mandalus)
3081[F] 3609[P] 3977[U]

Steel City *Seamus Mullins* 121h
7 gr g Act One Serraval (FR) (Sanglamore (USA))
3487[9] 3923[5] 4229[4] 4745[2] 5030[7]

Steel Express (IRE) *Linda Blackford* 100b
3 b g Craigsteel Assidua (IRE) (Anshan)
(2882) 3959[3]

Steel Gold (IRE) *John Upson* 85h 7c
9 b g Craigsteel It Time To Run (IRE) (Buckskin (FR))
340[P] 646[7] 935[2] 966[2] (1098) 1273[6] 1897[P]

Steel King (IRE) *Paul W Flynn* 126h
6 b g Kalanisi(IRE) Prairie Bell (IRE) (Sadler's Wells (USA))
1184a[P]

Steel Summit (IRE) *David Dennis* 129h 141c
6 b g Craigsteel B Greenhill (Gunner B)
(169) (611) ◆

Steeltown (IRE) *Mrs Kayley Woollacott* 119h 108c
10 b g Craigsteel Black Sniper (IRE) (Random Shot)
(5384)

Steely *K Kukk* 92h
7 b g Librettist(USA) No Comebacks (Last Tycoon)
985a[3] (5364a)

Steepleofcopper (IRE) *Alan Jessop*
9 ch g Classic Cliche(IRE) Tanya Thyne (IRE) (Good Thyne (USA))
4772[F] 5375[P]

Stellar Notion (IRE) *Paul Nicholls* 96h 145c
7 bb g Presenting Green Star (FR) (Green Tune (USA))
2784[P] 3776[7]

Stella's Fella *Giles Smyly* 78b
7 b g Septieme Ciel(USA) Gaspaisie (FR) (Beyssac (FR))
5064[F]

Stentorian (IRE) *Linda Perratt* 101h
7 ch g Street Cry(IRE) Nomistakeaboutit (CAN) (Affirmed (USA))
142[F] 520[F]

Stephanie Frances (IRE) *Dan Skelton* 140h 134c
7 b m King's Theatre(IRE) Brownlow Castle (IRE) (Supreme Leader)
1163a[8] 1988[2] **2541[F] 2684[F]** 4699[8]

Stephen Hero (IRE) *Brian Barr* 130h 126c
5 br g Celtic Swing Albaiyda (IRE) (Brief Truce (USA))
622[2] (697) 809[3] 1296[5] 1949[7] 2301[2] 2989[5]

Stepover *Alex Hales* 99h
4 b m Midnight Legend Ring Back (IRE) (Bob Back (USA))
2131[4] 2277[5] 2644[4] 3175[3] 4272[5] 4709[6] 5223[7]

Steps And Stairs (IRE) *Jonjo O'Neill* 101h
5 b g Robin Des Pres(FR) Be Mine Tonight (IRE) (Carroll House (IRE))
262[4] 530[2] 758[2] (1273) 1426[P] 1972[F]

Sterling Gent (IRE) *Liam Corcoran* 91h 76c
8 gr g Cloudings(IRE) Company Credit (IRE) (Anshan)
30[4] **610[5]**

Sternrubin (GER) *Philip Hobbs* 144h
4 b g Authorized(IRE) Sworn Mum (GER) (Samum (GER))
(119) (2728) (3151) 4115[P] 4765[3] 5325[10]

Steuben (GER) *Des Donovan* 69h
9 ch g Monsun(GER) Schwarzach (GER) (Grand Lodge (USA))
2163[9] 2409[8]

Sthenic (FR) *Micky Hammond* 56h
3 b g Fastnet Rock(AUS) Ela's Giant (Giant's Causeway (USA))
3590[7]

Stickee Fingers *Warren Greatrex* 88h
4 b m Fair Mix(IRE) Sticky Money (Relkino)
594[4] ◆ 2856[3] 3995[3] 4868[5] 5393[4] ◆

Stickers *Alan Jessop*
8 b g Generous(IRE) Dunsfold Duchess (IRE) (Bustino)
4877[P]

Sticking Point *Martin Keighley* 68h
4 b g Needle Gun(IRE) Blue Plaid (Clantime)
5182[8]

Stickleback *Micky Hammond* 90h
6 ch m Manduro(GER) The Stick (Singspiel (IRE))
2478[P] 2806[2]

Stiff Upper Lip (IRE) *Oliver Sherwood* 101h
5 b g Sakhee's Secret Just In Love (FR) (Highest Honor (FR))
2369[6] 3045[5] 3978[9] 4824[3]

Still Believing (IRE) *Evan Williams* 118h 120c
7 ch m Blueprint(IRE) Im A Believer (IRE) (Erins Isle)
86^{3} 215^{4} 614^{3} **772^{2}** 967^{4} 1348^{3} (1808) **2403^{3} (3569) 3929^{2} 4826^{P}**

Stilletto (IRE) *Paul Nicholls* 132h 150c
6 b g Westerner Eastertide (IRE) (Alphabatim (USA))
2639^{3} **(2846) 3351^{2} 3957^{F} (4212) ◆ 4733^{F} 5455^{3}**

Still Together (IRE) *David Pipe* 97h
5 b g Alkaadhem All-Together (IRE) (Step Together I (USA))
1645^{3} 1926^{7} 3022^{7} 3411^{12} 3483^{6} 4069^{4} ◆ 4541^{7} (Dead)

Stilo Blue Native (IRE) *John Wade* 104h 115c
7 gr g Blueprint(IRE) Reconciliation (IRE) (Be My Native (USA))
1852^{4} 3592^{4} ◆ **4053^{4} 4795^{2} 4940^{U}**

Sting Jet (IRE) *Seamus Mullins* 74h
6 b g Ashkalani(IRE) Pharrambling (IRE) (Phardante (FR))
2860^{7}

Stitched In Time (IRE) *Sara Ender* 59h 65c
8 b g Needle Gun(IRE) Broken Pockets (IRE) (Broken Hearted)
1084^{P} 1265^{12} 1573^{P} 1691^{P} **4938^{11} 5261^{P}**

St Johns Point (IRE) *Charlie Longsdon* 119h 127c
7 b g Darsi(FR) Dunsford Belle (IRE) (Insan (USA))
2018^{3} 2592^{2} 3129^{2} 4062^{5} 4780^{6} 5140^{P}

St Lewis *Jennie Candlish* 89h
5 b g Erhaab(USA) Miss Lewis (Sir Harry Lewis (USA))
761^{8} 3506^{7} 3835^{12} 4065^{7} 4388^{6}

St Maxime (IRE) *Gavin Cromwell* 112h 120c
7 ch m Alhaarth(IRE) Estivau (USA) (Lear Fan (USA))
(867) (959) 1184a^{7}

Stoical Patient (IRE) *Mark Wall* 27h
6 b m Shantou(USA) Dust Gale (IRE) (Strong Gale)
3132^{10} 3785^{4} 4157^{P} 4457^{5} 5063^{10}

Stonebrook (IRE) *Donald McCain* 130h
7 b g Flemensfirth(USA) Boberelle (IRE) (Bob Back (USA))
96a^{13}

Stonecutter (IRE) *Brendan Powell* 93h
4 gr g Mastercraftsman(IRE) Sparkle Of Stones (FR) (Sadler's Wells (USA))
3353^{6}

Stonegate *Gary Moore* 98h
5 b g Kayf Tara Megalex (Karinga Bay)
2251^{4}

Stoneham *Iain Jardine* 113h
4 b m Sixties Icon Cibenze (Owington)
405^{2} (813) (2144) 3034^{8} 3681^{5} 4320^{5} 5088^{5} 5262^{2} 5450^{2}

Stone Hard (IRE) *W P Mullins* 135h
5 b g Robin Des Champs(FR) Amber Light (IRE) (Anshan)
3070a^{U} 3459a^{P} 3962a^{4}

Stonemadforspeed (IRE) *Roger Teal* 58h
7 b g Fruits Of Love(USA) Diamond Forever (Teenoso (USA))
4504^{U} 5020^{3}

Stoney (IRE) *Victor Thompson* 82h 95c
8 b g Stowaway Classical Rachel (IRE) (Shahanndeh (IRE))
141^{5} 303^{5} 506^{P}

Stony Road (IRE) *J W Tudor* 106h 109c
8 b g Hubbly Bubbly(USA) Laur's Melody (IRE) (Meneval (USA))
5054^{2} 5467^{12}

Stopped Out *Philip Kirby* 139h 142c
10 gr g Montjoy(USA) Kiomi (Niniski (USA))
2921^{5} 3407^{P}

Stop The Press *Mark Pitman* 110h
6 b g Halling(USA) Ryde On (Petoski)
3258^{5} (3582) 3976^{8} 4449^{3}

Storm Alert *Sue Gardner* 94h 51c
8 ch g Karinga Bay Rash-Gale (IRE) (Rashar (USA))
599^{3} 838^{7} 845^{3} 1293^{8} 1699^{3} 2125^{5} 2441^{2} 3174^{3} 3771^{3} 4349^{4} 4682^{3} 4749^{2} 5033^{6} 5165^{P}

Storm Away (IRE) *Patrick J Flynn* 130h
6 b m Kalanisi(IRE) Dance Up A Storm (USA) (Storm Bird (CAN))
52a^{9}

Stormbay Bomber (IRE) *Patrick Holmes* 94h 102c
6 b g September Storm(GER) Top Tottie (IRE) (Alzao (USA))
747^{4} 935^{11} 1171^{P} 1446^{2} (1714) 2043^{8} **2976^{5} 5123^{3} 5310^{P}**

Storm Forecast (IRE) *Malcolm Jefferson* 111h
4 b g September Storm(GER) Katie Kelly (IRE) (Deploy)
1858^{4} (2709) 3245^{4} 5009^{2} ◆

Storming Strumpet *Tom George* 115h 111c
5 b m Kayf Tara Rosita Bay (Hernando (FR))
1111^{3} 2302^{6} (3681) **4292^{F} 4889^{3} 5103^{5} 5281^{5}**

Stormin Tom (IRE) *Tim Easterby* 83h
3 b g Dylan Thomas(IRE) She Storm (IRE) (Rainbow Quest (USA))
1899^{5} 2286^{5}

Storm Lantern *Robert Waley-Cohen* 85b
6 b g King's Theatre(IRE) Katoune (FR) (Snurge)
808^{P}

Storm Of Swords (IRE) *Dan Skelton* 134h 121c
7 ch g Beneficial Crossbar Lady (IRE) (Flemensfirth (USA))
218^{P} (433) 620^{3} 854^{F}

Stormont Bridge *Maurice Barnes* 79h
7 b g Avonbridge Stormont Castle (USA) (Irish River (FR))
1399^{6} 1568^{8} 1683^{6} 1739^{5} 2704^{6}

Storm Patrol *Suzy Smith* 110b
4 b m Shirocco(GER) Material World (Karinga Bay)
4074^{2} 5180^{14}

Storm Run (IRE) *Roger Teal* 92b
4 ch m Hurricane Run(IRE) Jabroot (IRE) (Alhaarth (IRE))
1908^{8} 2141^{6} *3200^{7}*

Storm To Pass *Caroline Fryer* 93h
7 b g Overbury(IRE) Silver Peak (FR) (Sillery (USA))
398^{P} 571^{P} 755^{3}

Stout Cortez *Malcolm Jefferson* 93h
4 b g Hernando(FR) Zooming (IRE) (Indian Ridge)
2543^{F} 2864^{3}

Stow *Lucinda Egerton* 23h
10 ch g Selkirk(USA) Spry (Suave Dancer (USA))
527^{2} 726^{6} 4328^{9}

Stowaway Magic (IRE) *Nicky Henderson* 121b
4 b g Stowaway Irish Mystics (IRE) (Ali-Royal (IRE))
(4103) 4805^{4}

Stowaway Shark (IRE) *John Joseph Hanlon* 130h
6 b g Stowaway Anno Mundi (USA) (Red Ransom (USA))
5024a^{2}

St Paul's Square (IRE) *Chris Gordon*
3 b g Amadeus Wolf Swynford Lady (IRE) (Invincible Spirit (IRE))
975^{P}

St Quintin *David Brown* 105h
5 b g Act One Gloriana (Formidable I (USA))
525^{5} 1260^{7} 1519^{3} 1550^{4} 2296^{3} 2744^{P}

Straidnahanna (IRE) *Sue Smith* 109h 139c
6 gr g Medaaly Sue's Song (Alflora (IRE))
2068^{2} 2643^{F} 3038^{4} 3726^{4} (4155) 4605^{2} **5327^{P}**

Strait Of Magellan (IRE) *Nicky Richards* 75h
3 ch g Captain Rio Golden (FR) (Sanglamore (USA))
3470^{5}

Strait Run (IRE) *Micky Hammond* 85h
4 ch g Rock Of Gibraltar(IRE) Gentlemen's Guest (USA) (Gentlemen (ARG))
2196^{6} 2422^{4} 2804^{7} 3098^{5} 3307^{2} 3628^{10} 3807^{6} 4049^{4} 4326^{9} 4943^{2}

Strange Bird (IRE) *Richard Rowe* 93h 95c
10 b m Revoque(IRE) Ethel's Bay (IRE) (Strong Gale)
2416^{2} 2825^{P} 3198^{P} **4531^{P}**

Strangelittlegirl *Giles Bravery*
7 b m Shirocco(GER) Cephalonia (Slip Anchor)
130^{P} 569^{P}

Stratford Stroller (IRE) *Alastair Ralph* 102h 103c
11 b g Beneficial Kemchee (Kemal (FR))
60^{2} (429)

Strawberry Hill (IRE) *Caroline Keevil* 71h 114c
9 b g Winged Love(IRE) Icydora (FR) (Cyborg (FR))
2276^{5} 2658^{P} 3771^{9}

Streele (USA) *Ken Wingrove* 58h
5 gr m Thunder Gulch(USA) Crown Capers (USA) (Chief's Crown (USA))
1693^{6} 1975^{6} 2217^{9} 2670^{P}

Street Entertainer (IRE) *David Pipe* 136h 125c
8 br g Danehill Dancer(IRE) Opera Ridge (FR) (Indian Ridge)
(301) 442^{3} (701) **829^{2}** ◆ 1034^{7} **1157^{2}** 1419^{2} (1628)

Street Name (FR) *G Cherel* 144h 132c
5 b g Al Namix(FR) Acland Street (FR) (Zabeel (NZ))
1883a^{10}

Streets Of Promise (IRE) *Michael Scudamore* 131h 139c
6 b m Westerner Miracle Lady (Bob's Return (IRE))
1856^{P} **2557^{4}** 2825^{P} **3866^{2}** (4186) **(4549)** ◆ **4649^{F} (5348)** ◆

Strictly Glitz (IRE) *Mike Sowersby* 65h
4 b m Kodiac Dancing Steps (Zafonic (USA))
254^{5} 516^{6} 856^{P} 3378^{P}

Strictly The One (IRE) *Mike Sowersby* 66h
5 b g Robin Des Pres(FR) Rita's Charm (IRE) (Arctic Lord (IRE))
615^{5} 1368^{6} 1598^{12} 2649^{P} 5441^{7}

Strike Fast (IRE) *William Kinsey* 110h 93c
10 gr g Portrait Gallery(IRE) Street Rose (IRE) (Roselier (FR))
133^{3}

Strike West (IRE) *Micky Hammond* 87b
3 b g Westerner Fuel Queen (IRE) (Flemensfirth (USA))
4515^{2} 5127^{7}

Striking Nigella *Michael Chapman*
5 b m Striking Ambition Fiona Fox (Foxhound (USA))
4847^{13}

Strobe *Lucy Normile* 51h 99c
11 ch g Fantastic Light(USA) Sadaka (USA) (Kingmambo (USA))
315^{F} 885^{3} (1306) 1492^{P} 5472^{14}

Strollawaynow (IRE) *David Arbuthnot* 116h 122c
8 b g Oscar(IRE) Rose Of Salome (IRE) (Roselier (FR))
2996^{7} 3707^{P} 4062^{P} 5149^{3}

Strongly Suggested *Jonjo O'Neill* 111h 130c
8 b g Kayf Tara Branston Lily (Cadeaux Genereux)
(175) (338) ◆ **(1135)** 1322^{U} **1643^{6} 2185^{8} 2746^{6} 3155^{5} 3972^{6} 4464^{9} 4866^{6}**

Strongpoint (IRE) *S R B Crawford* 136h 140c
11 br g Bob Back(USA) Ceo Draiochta (IRE) (Erins Isle)
24a^{3} 657^{3} 3036^{B} 3426^{5} 3740^{5} **5109a^{5}**

Strumble Head (IRE) *Peter Bowen* 115h 124c
10 b g Anshan Milan Moss (Le Moss)
625 439^{3} 670^{2} 1167^{2} 1309^{6} 1571^{6} 2149^{6} 5052^{3} ◆ **5395^{6}**

St Saviour *Philip Hobbs* 125h
3 b g Danehill Dancer(IRE) Titivation (Montjeu (IRE))
(3464) (3926) 4358^{6} 5116^{4}

St Stephens Green (IRE) *W P Mullins* 115h
4 b g Diamond Green(FR) Lily Shing Shang (Spectrum (IRE))
9a^{7}

Sturdy Dawn *Michael Mullineaux* 65h
5 br m Striking Ambition Lucky Find (IRE) (Key Of Luck (USA))
491^{5} 706^{4} 937^{9}

Sturmwind (GER) *Alison Batchelor* 82h
4 b g Samum(GER) Suave (IRE) (Sadler's Wells (USA))
834^{5} 1044^{8} 1240^{6} 1427^{7}

Stylish Chap (IRE) *Lucinda Russell* 113h
5 b g New South Wales Curragh Bawn Lass (IRE) (Supreme Leader)
473^{2}

Sub Lieutenant (IRE) *Ms Sandra Hughes* 141h 148c
6 b g Brian Boru Satellite Dancer (IRE) (Satco (FR))
21a^{4} **2817a^{4} 3635a^{3} 4148a^{4} (4517a) 5005a^{P}**

Sublime Talent (IRE) *Evan Williams* 122h 118c
9 b g Sadler's Wells(USA) Summer Trysting (USA) (Alleged (USA))
555^{8} 772^{6} 1099^{2} 1233^{3} 1327^{2} 1416^{5} 1674^{5}

Subordinate (GER) *Emma Lavelle* 80h
6 b g Echo Of Light Suborneuse (USA) (Diesis)
1973^{4} 2460^{11} 4494^{P} 4849^{5}

Subtle Approach (IRE) *Emma Baker* 48h
10 b g Subtle Power(IRE) Rotoruasprings (IRE) (Jurado (USA))
3369^{P} 3771^{P} 3946^{8} 4391^{P}

Subtle Ben (IRE) *Miss Elizabeth Doyle* 77h 123c
8 b g Subtle Power(IRE) Benfrasea (IRE) (Beneficial)
50a^{14}

Subtle Grey (IRE) *Donald McCain* 130h 144c
6 gr g Subtle Power(IRE) Milltown Rose (IRE) (Roselier (FR))
2764^{3} (3055) 3520^{2} (4054) 4802^{P}

Such A Legend *Kim Bailey* 126h 132c
7 ch g Midnight Legend Mrs Fizziwig (Petoski)
84^{2} 1904^{4} 5156^{3}

Sudden Wish (IRE) *Gary Moore* 107h
6 b m Jeremy(USA) Fun Time (Fraam)
(361)

Sudski Star (IRE) *Harriet Graham* 87h 126c
7 br g Pilsudski(IRE) Mogen's Star (IRE) (Be My Native (USA))
849^{4} 1418^{6}

Sue Be It (IRE) *Nikki Evans* 92b
4 b m Presenting Runaround Sue (IRE) (Among Men (USA))
5400^{4}

Suffice (IRE) *Laura Young* 78h
6 b g Iffraaj Shallat (IRE) (Pennekamp (USA))
2024^{P} 2162^{7} 3368^{P}

Suffisante (FR) *F-M Cottin* 94h 103c
5 gr m Smadoun(FR) Salve D'Honneur (FR) (Baroud D'Honneur (FR))
5499a^{5}

Sugar Baron (IRE) *Nicky Henderson* 133h
5 b g Presenting Shuil Oilean (IRE) (Be My Native (USA))
3232^{6} 3733^{11} (4470) 5284^{15}

Sugar Loaf Sholto (IRE) *Kim Bailey* 84h
4 ch g Presenting Queensland Bay (Primitive Rising (USA))
5263^{7} 5451^{6}

Sugar Mix *Martin Keighley* 52h
4 gr g Sagamix(FR) Bruley (Weld)
2131^{3} 3388^{5} 4843^{U} 5469^{U}

Suit Yourself (IRE) *Jonjo O'Neill* 126h
6 b g Flemensfirth(USA) Corbetstown Queen (IRE) (Oscar (IRE))
2163^{10} (3054) 3949^{3} 4596^{5} 5239^{2}

Sukiyaki (IRE) *Charlie Longsdon* 111h
6 b g Dubawi(IRE) Sukeena (IRE) (Brief Truce (USA))
(364) 529^{8} 1055^{8}

Sulamani The Late (FR) *Dan Skelton* 97b
3 b g Sulamani(IRE) Delayed (FR) (Fijar Tango (FR))
4364^{8} 5069^{9}

Sultana Belle (IRE) *R Mike Smith* 81h 91c
7 b m Black Sam Bellamy(IRE) Sultana (GER) (Law Society (USA))
482^{3} 4036^{10} 4328^{7} 4581^{9} 4904^{7}

Sultan's Dancer *Brendan Powell* 31h
6 ch m Norse Dancer(IRE) Peel Me A Grape (Gunner B)
831^{8} 1295^{4} 1845^{P}

Summerhill Boy (IRE) *Nigel Twiston-Davies* 91b
4 b g Morozov(USA) Dante's Arrow (IRE) (Phardante (FR))
4880^{9}

Summer Name (IRE) *Rebecca Curtis* 94b
3 b g Duke Of Marmalade(IRE) Summer's Eve (Singspiel (IRE))
5097^{8}

Summer Sounds (IRE) *Tom Symonds* 103h
6 bb g Definite Article Marble Sound (IRE) (Be My Native (USA))
3023^{4} 3841^{3} 4226^{3}

Summer Storm *Rebecca Menzies* 106h
5 b g Lucarno(USA) Midsummer Magic (Muhtarram (USA))
1568^{2} 1774^{3} 2085^{12} 2423^{3} 2647^{5} 2869^{4} 5081^{7} 5445^{6}

Summery Justice (IRE) *Venetia Williams* 115h 140c
11 b g Witness Box(USA) Kinsella's Rose (IRE) (Roselier (FR))
2916^{2} 3993^{5} 4367^{10}

Sumos Novios (IRE) *W J Burke* 118h 139c
7 b g Flemensfirth(USA) Gaelic Million (IRE) (Strong Gale)
3296a^{8}

Sunblazer (IRE) *Kim Bailey* 104h
5 gr g Dark Angel(IRE) Damask Rose (IRE) (Dr Devious (IRE))
(32) 1044 835^{8} 2038^{6}

Sun Cloud (IRE) *Malcolm Jefferson* 121h 142c
8 b g Cloudings(IRE) Miss Melrose (Bob Back (USA))
1633^{3} **2146^{4} 2643^{2} 3157^{P} 4444^{4} 5327^{6}**

Sundance Boy *Giuseppe Fierro* 59b
6 gr g Proclamation(IRE) Just Beth (Carlingford Castle)
2493^{12} 2842^{11} 3145^{5}

Sunday Cerisy (FR) *F Foucher* 113h
4 ch g Sunday Break(JPN) Midalisy (FR) (Medaaly)
2362a^{5}

Sungai Long *Michael Scudamore* 94b
3 b g Lawman(FR) Ammo (IRE) (Sadler's Wells (USA))
2991^{6} 3593^{2} 4103^{5}

Sunken Secret (IRE) *Mrs L Glanville* 18c
10 b g Accordion Giolldante (IRE) (Phardante (FR))
123^{8}

Sunley Spirit *Chris Gordon* 71h
5 b m Lucarno(USA) Sunley Shines (Komaite (USA))
2317^{10} 2829^{7} 3252^{P} 4157^{P}

Sunny Bank *Alan Coogan* 90h
6 b g Notnowcato Sweet Mandolin (Soviet Star (USA))
566^{3} 860^{5} 1001^{P} 1261^{10} 1427^{8}

Sunny Ledgend *Andrew J Martin* 118h 120c
10 b g Midnight Legend Swordella (Broadsword (USA))
3123^{3} (3499) (3727) 4230^{7} 4493^{4} 5334^{P}

Sunny Purchase (IRE) *John C McConnell* 83h
3 b g Lord Shanakill(USA) Lucky Us (IRE) (Fayruz)
1495^{2}

Sunny West (IRE) *Sue Smith* 116h
6 b g Westerner Lunar Beauty (IRE) (Milan)
2070^{2} 2422^{2}

Sun Quest *Steven Dixon* 81h
11 b g Groom Dancer(USA) Icaressa (Anabaa (USA))
167^{9} 515^{8} 675^{12} 1980^{5} 2599^{4} 2730^{9} 3932^{12} 4291^{6} 4454^{4}

Sunsetstorise (IRE) *F Flood* 120h 117c
7 b g Millenary Otorum (IRE) (Muroto)
4663a^{P}

Sunshine Buddy *Chris Down* 95h
8 b m Reel Buddy(USA) Bullion (Sabrehill (USA))
240^{2} 2298^{10} 2565^{3}

Sunshine Corner (IRE) *Lucy Wadham* 135h
4 b m King's Theatre(IRE) Coolgreaney (IRE) (Bob Back (USA))
2486^{12} (2829) 3154^{2} (3660) 4231^{4} (4779)

Suntiep (FR) *W P Mullins* 102b
9 b g Ungaro(GER) Galostiepy (FR) (Laostic (FR))
3715a^{P}

Sun Wild Life (FR) *Robert Walford* 117h 130c
5 b g Antarctique(IRE) Nidelia (FR) (Sleeping Car (FR))
2261^{4} 2955^{P} 4101^{4} 4780^{2} 5162^{2} 5465^{6}

Supapowers (IRE) *Robert Stephens* 98h 112c
9 ch m Subtle Power(IRE) Hi Sheree (IRE) (Beau Sher)
840^{2} 1004^{3} 1371^{4} **1678^{2} 1950^{2}**

Supasundae *Henry De Bromhead* 150h
5 b g Galileo(IRE) Distinctive Look (IRE) (Danehill (USA))
23a^{9} 4695^{7}

Superb Story (IRE) *Dan Skelton* 148h
4 b g Duke Of Marmalade(IRE) Yes My Love (FR) (Anabaa (USA))
(1905) ◆ 2512^{2} (4765)

Super Charge *Edward Glassonbury* 78b
3 ch g Recharge(IRE) Arctic Ring (Karinga Bay)
5436^{11}

Superciliary *Chris Gordon* 118h
6 b g Dansili Supereva (IRE) (Sadler's Wells (USA))
1734^{5} 2244^{6} (2956) 3196^{3}

Super Collider *Susan Corbett* 110h 120c
8 b g Montjeu(IRE) Astorg (USA) (Lear Fan (USA))
76^{2} (202) 469^{4} 635^{4} 800^{P} 2293^{5} 5345^{5}

Super Duty (IRE) *Ian Williams* 130h 130c
9 b g Shantou(USA) Sarah's Cottage (IRE) (Topanoora)
2473^{7} 2916^{5}

Superfection (IRE) *Donald McCain* 112h
6 b m Shantou(USA) Sarah's Cottage (IRE) (Topanoora)
2770^{5} (4039) 4369^{3} 4702^{3} 5438^{6}

Superior Command (IRE) *Lucinda Russell* 104h 117c
6 b g Lahib(USA) Decent Dime (IRE) (Insan (USA))
3471^{3} 3668^{4} **(4634) 5084^{2}**

Superior Fire (IRE) *Charlie Longsdon* 102h
5 b g Arcadio(GER) Take Aim (Gunner B)
57^{P}

Super Lunar (IRE) *Henry Hogarth* 79h
6 b g Super Celebre(FR) Kapricia Speed (FR) (Vertical Speed (FR))
2174^{7} 4421^{P} 5199^{5}

Superman De La Rue (FR) *Mary Evans* 102h 74c
9 b g Akhdari(USA) Impala De La Rue (FR) (Brugnon (FR))
4856^{2} 5433^{10}

Supernoverre (IRE) *Alan Jones* 87h
9 b g Noverre(USA) Caviare (Cadeaux Genereux)
336^{2} ◆ 692^{2} 1524^{4} 1578^{6} 1786^{6}

Super Scorpion (IRE) *Debra Hamer* 114h
5 b g Scorpion(IRE) Nolagh Supreme (IRE) (Supreme Leader)
1648^{5} 1826^{2} 3105^{4} 4466^{9}

Supply And Demand (IRE) *Jonjo O'Neill* 95h
4 br g Scorpion(IRE) Native Fashion (IRE) (Be My Native (USA))
2487^{6}

Supreme Asset (IRE) *Donald McCain* 109h 129c
7 b g Beneficial Hollygrove Supreme (IRE) (Supreme Leader)
2497^{P} 3313^{3} 3670^{8} 4431^{2} 5046^{P}

Supreme Bob (IRE) *Debra Hamer* 119h 112c
9 b g Bob's Return(IRE) Supremememories (IRE) (Supreme Leader)
(3081) 3834^{7} (4265) 4615^{2}

Supreme Danehill (IRE) *Gordon Edwards* 98c
7 b g Indian Danehill(IRE) Monte Rosa (IRE) (Supreme Leader)
13^{P} 388^{P}

Supreme Gael *Iain Jardine* 24h
4 br m Supreme Sound Italstar (IRE) (Galileo (IRE))
4168[5] 4559[3] 4908[5] 5470[8]

Supreme Hope (IRE) *Neil Mulholland* 89h
6 b m Definite Article Dochas Supreme (IRE) (Supreme Leader)
1943[6] 2267[9] 4709[5] 5420[6]

Supreme Regime (IRE) *Miss G E J Anderson*
9 b g Old Vic Shampooed (IRE) (Law Society (USA))
80[P]

Supreme Vic (IRE) *Norman Lee* 123h 94c
9 b m Old Vic Supreme Argument (IRE) (Supreme Leader)
1150a[11]

Suprise Vendor (IRE) *Stuart Coltherd* 111h 111c
9 ch g Fath(USA) Dispol Jazz (Alhijaz)
142[3] **1855[F] 2477[P] 2765[P]** 3346[8] **3938[P]** (4585) ◆ **4741[2] (5366)**

Sureness (IRE) *Charlie Mann* 113h 121c
5 ch m Hurricane Run(IRE) Silk Dress (IRE) (Gulch (USA))
84[5] 854[7] **1042[4] 1267[U] 1372[P] 1659[P]** 5380[P]

Surf And Turf (IRE) *Kevin Frost* 123h 143c
9 ch g Beneficial Clear Top Waltz (IRE) (Topanoora)
555[4] (830) 1039[17] **2084[8] 2185[P] 4770[15] 5179[9]**

Surfing The Stars (IRE) *Laura Young* 65h
4 b g Brian Boru Golden Jorden (IRE) (Cadeaux Genereux)
2493[9] 4357[10] 4917[P] 5416[7]

Surf In September (IRE) *Dominic Ffrench Davis* 96h
6 b m September Storm(GER) Juno Beach (Jupiter Island)
1153[6] 1297[4] 1490[2] 2167[P] 2454[6] 5306[2]

Surging Seas (IRE) *Ali Stronge* 91h 96c
6 b g Tiger Hill(IRE) Musardiere (Montjeu (IRE))
2015[8] 3840[4] **4859[3] 5388[8]**

Surprise Choice (IRE) *William Stone* 78b
4 b m Thousand Words Common Cause (Polish Patriot (USA))
2141[5] *2835[3]*

Surprise Us *Mark Gillard* 57h 59c
8 b g Indian Ridge Pingus (Polish Precedent (USA))
699[P] 1509[9] 1677[8] **2040[5]** 3586[13] **4686[P]**

Surtee Du Berlais (IRE) *Oliver Sherwood* 125h
5 b m High Chaparral(IRE) Marina Du Berlais (FR) (Mister Sicy (FR))
(111) (2665) 3372[3] 3825[2] ◆ 5094[10] (5389)

Susie Sheep *David Pipe* 110h 122c
5 ch m Robin Des Champs(FR) Haudello (FR) (Marignan (USA))
238[2] 462[5] **756[2]** ◆ **1005[4]**

Susquehanna River (IRE) *Nigel Twiston-Davies* 106h 117c
8 b g Indian River(FR) Calistoga (IRE) (Mujadil (USA))
420[4] 771[2] 1049[5]

Sussex Road (IRE) *Aytach Sadik* 81h
5 b g Mahler Rose Island (Jupiter Island)
3143[4] 3586[14] 3868[6]

Sustainability (IRE) *Miss B Eckley* 98h 113c
10 ch g Old Vic Over The Glen (IRE) (Over The River (FR))
3585[P] 3826[F] 4446[5] 4651[P] 5158[P]

Sutter's Mill (IRE) *Evan Williams* 94h
4 b g Gold Well Shamriyna (IRE) (Darshaan)
4681[R] 5235[4]

Sutton Place (IRE) *Gordon Elliott* 144h
4 b g Mahler Glebe Beauty (IRE) (Good Thyne (USA))
(4516a) (5002a)

Sutton Sid *Michelle Bryant* 59h
5 ch g Dutch Art Drastic Measure (Pivotal)
4934[P] 5477[8]

Sutton Storm *John Ryall* 75h
10 b g Emperor Fountain Rock Rose (Arctic Lord (IRE))
1236[5] 1383[6]

Suzy's Music (IRE) *S R B Crawford* 80h 96c
7 b m Gamut(IRE) Vicky's Music (IRE) (Old Vic)
481[5] 503[7] 656[9] 3672[9] 4163[6] **(4298)** ◆ **4637[2]**

Swaledale Lad (IRE) *Richard Ford* 130h 137c
8 b g Arakan(USA) Tadjnama (USA) (Exceller (USA))
708[6] **1070[2]** 1459[7] **1553[P]** 5201[4]

Swallows Delight (IRE) *Mrs Julie Mansell* 113c
10 br g Tamayaz(CAN) Windmill Star (IRE) (Orchestra)
12[4] 393[6] 536[6] 4295[2] 4592[U] 5178[F]

Swampfire (IRE) *Barry Brennan* 114h
7 b g Anabaa(USA) Moonfire (Sadler's Wells (USA))
267[6] (962) 1001[2] (1154)

Swanage Bay (IRE) *Sophie Leech* 64h
8 b g Dilshaan Special Mention (IRE) (Nashwan (USA))
3902[7]

Swansea Mile (IRE) *Dan Skelton* 138h
5 b g Dylan Thomas(IRE) Hurry Up Helen (IRE) (In The Wings)
1657[3] 1986[2] 4461[2] (5387)

Swantykay (IRE) *Gordon Elliott* 123h 115c
6 b g Darsi(FR) Glamorous Leader (IRE) (Supreme Leader)
659[2]

Sweeping Rock (IRE) *John Spearing* 117h
5 b g Rock Of Gibraltar(IRE) Sweeping Story (USA) (End Sweep (USA))
2271[10] 2734[12]

Sweet Company (IRE) *Miss Elizabeth Anne Lalor* 94h 101c
4 b g Kalanisi(IRE) Almost Twilight (USA) (Silver Hawk (USA))
11a[11]

Sweet Holly *Lucinda Russell* 95h
4 b m Kayf Tara Presuming (Mtoto)
2756[10] 3681[6] 4031[4] 4548[F] 5470[3]

Sweetlittlekitty (IRE) *Rebecca Curtis* 99b
5 b m Robin Des Champs(FR) Alcrea (IRE) (Commander Collins (IRE))
3132[11] 4967[3]

Sweet Midnight *John Holt* 82h
3 b f Mawatheeq(USA) Sweet Reply (Opening Verse (USA))
2164[12] 2537[8] 2863[5] 3143[7] 4390[P] 4987[3]

Sweet'N'Chic (IRE) *Richard Rowe* 78h
5 b m Midnight Legend Sweetbitter (FR) (Turgeon (USA))
2016[4] 2828[6] 4157[P] 4526[P] 4777[5] 5303[4]

Sweet Summer *John Holt* 76h
4 ch m Sakhee(USA) Sweet Reply (Opening Verse (USA))
106[6] 466[4]

Sweettoothtommy (IRE) *David Pipe* 46h
5 b g Definite Article My Linda (IRE) (Bob Back (USA))
3124[6]

Sweet World *Bernard Llewellyn* 102h
11 b g Agnes World(USA) Douce Maison (IRE) (Fools Holme (USA))
895[6] 1356[3] 1525[2] 1578[2] 1786[2] 1931[5] 2264[7]

Swift Arrow (IRE) *Donald McCain* 3h 39c
9 b g Overbury(IRE) Clover Run (IRE) (Deep Run)
1553[P] 1902[P] 3972[7] 5156[P]

Swiftly Beyond *Brian Storey* 7h
7 b g And Beyond(IRE) Swiftly Supreme (IRE) (Supreme Leader)
1740[9] 1886[12]

Swincombe Stone *Robert Walford* 84h 35c
8 ch g Best Of The Bests(IRE) Soloism (Sulaafah (USA))
1054[7]

Swincombe Toby *Nick Williams* 108h
3 b g Tobougg(IRE) Soloism (Sulaafah (USA))
2273[3] 2662[2] 3730[3] 5116[7]

Swing Folish (FR) *P Mehat*
6 ch m Priolo(USA) Girl Folish (FR) (Lesotho (USA))
5136a[P]

Swing Hard (IRE) *Sue Smith* 107h 119c
7 br g Zagreb(USA) Hurricane Jane (IRE) (Strong Gale)
1690[3] 1889[3] 2295[3] 2788[U] 3310[3] ◆ **(4288) (4571) 4907[3] 5348[3]**

Swinton Diamond (IRE) *Ian Williams* 105h
4 b g Dubai Destination(USA) Absent Beauty (IRE) (Dancing Dissident (USA))
1973[7] 2493[6] 4461[3]

Swivel *Mark Wall* 115h
4 ch g Shirocco(GER) Pivotal Drive (IRE) (Pivotal)
1153[U] 1260[2] 1455[6] 3855[17] 4855[P]

Swizzler (IRE) *Ian Williams* 98b 106c
6 b g Scorpion(IRE) Arch Hall Lady (IRE) (Luso)
2080[F] 2558[P] 3736[P] **4458[3] (4588) 4876[8] (5377)**

Swnymor (IRE) *Kevin Frost* 121h
6 b g Dylan Thomas(IRE) Propaganda (IRE) (Sadler's Wells (USA))
2926[6] 3232[9] 3630[7]

Sword Fish (IRE) *C Roche* 131c
9 b g Sadler's Wells(USA) Lyrical (Shirley Heights)
92a[P] 2228a[P]

Sword Of The Lord *Nigel Twiston-Davies* 113h
5 b g Kheleyf(USA) Blue Echo (Kyllachy)
217[5] 1638[3] 2271[6] 2810[2] 2987[9] 3318[8]

Sybarite (FR) *Nigel Twiston-Davies* 125h 123c
9 bb g Dark Moondancer Haida III (FR) (Video Rock (FR))
196[5] **1807[9] 2638[6] 2878[P]** 3158[3] 3407[10] 3824[3] 4241[4] 5141[7] 5277[8] 5475[6]

Sybil Grey *George Bewley* 47h
6 gr m Fair Mix(IRE) Gimme Shelter (IRE) (Glacial Storm (USA))
2721[8] 3802[5] 3971[10]

Sydney De Baune (FR) *Robert Walford* 84h
4 b g Califet(FR) Perle De Baune (FR) (En Calcat (FR))
3625[4] 4351[7] 4613[5]

Sykes (IRE) *Philip Hobbs* 129h
6 b g Mountain High(IRE) Our Trick (IRE) (Flemensfirth (USA))
1675[2] ◆ (2081) (2268) 2759[3] 3517[4] 4112[2] ◆ 4911[7]

Sylvan Legend *Matt Sheppard* 75h 87c
7 b g Midnight Legend Sylvan Warbler (USA) (Blushing Groom (FR))
391[5] 695[P] **934[2] 1045[4] (1243) 1380[P] 1757[U] 2037[5] 2248[3] 2521[4] 3468[P]** 4184[P] **4356[P] 4850[U] 5435[8]**

Symphony Of Pearls *Dai Burchell* 87h
4 b m Lucarno(USA) Echostar (Observatory (USA))
180[6] 361[3] 694[2] 856[4] 2492[5] 2850[7] (4490) 4712[F] (Dead)

Synchronicity (IRE) *C Byrnes*
6 b g High Chaparral(IRE) Sea Of Time (USA) (Gilded Time (USA))
1700[5]

Table Bluff (IRE) *John Spearing* 93h 103c
6 ch g Indian Haven Double Deal (Keen)
379[4] 588[2] ◆ **964[3]**

Tachbury *Tim Vaughan* 76h 92c
11 br g Overbury(IRE) Tachometer (IRE) (Jurado (USA))
(674) 807[2] 879[3] 1158[3] **4590[3] 4921[4]**

Tactical Manoeuvre (IRE) *Alexandra Dunn* 91h
4 b g Marienbard(IRE) Pride O'Fleet (IRE) (Bob's Return (IRE))
3582[8] 3773[8] 4137[P] 5160[3] ◆

Taglietelle *Gordon Elliott* 157h
6 b g Tagula(IRE) Averami (Averti (IRE))
954a[4] 2386a[3] 2815a[4] 3149[7] 4017[3] ◆ 4730[4] 5004a[7]

Tagrita (IRE) *Paul Nicholls* 136h
7 b m King's Theatre(IRE) Double Dream (IRE) (Double Eclipse (IRE))
3283[6] (4252) (4438) 4779[7]

Ta Ha (IRE) *Malcolm Jones* 72h
7 br g Posidonas Euro Dancer (IRE) (Eurobus)
4441[8] 5223[P]

Tahira (GER) *Kevin Frost* 116h
5 ch m Doyen(IRE) Tennessee Queen (GER) (Big Shuffle (USA))
1109[2] 1716[4]

Tahiti Pearl (IRE) *Sue Smith* 83h 125c
11 b g Winged Love(IRE) Clara's Dream (IRE) (Phardante (FR))
35[2] (Dead)

Taigan (FR) *Giles Smyly* 128h
8 b g Panoramic Lazary (FR) (Bobinski)
5284[P]

Taj Badalandabad (IRE) *David Pipe* 139h
5 ch g Shantou(USA) Last Chance Lady (IRE) (Mister Lord (USA))
2912[7] (3844) 4246[4] (5120)

Takaatuf (IRE) *Tina Jackson* 68h 59c
9 b g Dubai Destination(USA) Karlaka (IRE) (Barathea (IRE))
416[6] **519[P]** 798[P]

Take A Bow *Lawney Hill* 116h 118c
6 b g Norse Dancer(IRE) Madame Illusion (FR) (Solid Illusion (USA))
756[3] 1372[2]

Take A Break (FR) *Nigel Hawke* 116h 121c
4 bb g Sunday Break(JPN) Popee (FR) (Take Risks (FR))
(26) 2011[4] 2247[5] 2688[6] **4487[P] 4889[P] 4984[F]** 5266[6]

Takeitfromalady (IRE) *Lee Carter* 103h
6 b g Intikhab(USA) Pinheiros (IRE) (Rock Of Gibraltar (IRE))
1998[3] 2251[5] 2544[11]

Take The Cash (IRE) *Donald McCain* 117h 117c
6 b g Cloudings(IRE) Taking My Time (IRE) (High Roller (IRE))
76[3] 2435[3]

Take The Crown *Henry Oliver* 100h 109c
6 gr g Fair Mix(IRE) Miss Wizadora (Gildoran)
1907[4] 2434[2] 2859[2] 3225[4] 4587[2] 5142[4]

Take The Mick *Venetia Williams* 95h 126c
8 b g Ishiguru(USA) Michaelmas Daizy (Michelozzo (USA))
2451[5] 3008[2] 3569[2] 3792[3] 4348[6] 4612[2] 5238[5]

Takingrisks (IRE) *Nicky Richards* 125h
6 b g Golden Tornado(IRE) Downtown Rosie (IRE) (Good Thyne (USA))
2100[4] ◆ 2801[2] ◆ (3340) 4405[4] (4906) 5296[6]

Tales Of Milan (IRE) *Phil Middleton* 101h 125c
8 b g Milan The Millers Tale (IRE) (Rashar (USA))
1522[7] 1615[8] **1722[P]** 1897[8] **2916[7] 3707[P]** 4783[3] 5165[P]

Talkin Thomas (IRE) *S Croft* 76h 80c
9 b g Talkin Man(CAN) Keerou Lady (IRE) (Be My Native (USA))
1508[8] 1686[4] **4969[3]**

Talk Of The South (IRE) *Paul Henderson* 115h
6 b g Milan Smalltowntalk (IRE) (Carroll House (IRE))
2886[8] 3353[7] 3902[4] 4382[2] (4671) ◆ 4877[2] 5382[2]

Talk Will (FR) *H De Lageneste* 117c
8 b g Poliglote New Will (FR) (Cadoudal (FR))
374a[5]

Tamarillo Grove (IRE) *Sophie Leech* 106h
8 b g Cape Cross(IRE) Tamarillo (Daylami (IRE))
2445[5] 2688[12] 3035[8] 4851[5] 5225[2]

Tambalong *Caroline Keevil* 54b
7 b m Tamure(IRE) Baie D'Along (FR) (Tel Quel (FR))
1574[P]

Tambour Major (FR) *Alison Hamilton* 86h 104c
8 b g Myrakalu(FR) Joaillere (FR) (Silver Rainbow)
2937[P] **4816[4] 5125[5]**

Tambura *G C Maundrell* 126h
5 b m Tamure(IRE) Singing Cottage (Greensmith)
2167[3] 2548[7] (2825) 3025[3] 3217[2] 3824[2] 3970[3] 4779[8] 5264[4]

Tanarpino *Jennie Candlish* 125h
4 ch g Tobougg(IRE) Got Tune (FR) (Green Tune (USA))
1717[2] 2126[6] 2628[4] 2860[9] 3114[8] (3592) ◆ (3729) 4040[3] 4620[5] ◆ (5157)

Tandem *D K Weld* 133h
6 b g Dansili Light Ballet (Sadler's Wells (USA))
73a[3]

Tandori *Paul Phillips* 84h 92c
13 b m El Conquistador Leatan (Leander I)
16[4] 533[P]

Tanerko Emery (FR) *Andy Turnell* 140h 131c
9 b g Lavirco(GER) Frequence (FR) (Panoramic)
317[7] (527) 916[P]

Tango De Juilley (FR) *Venetia Williams* 133h 153c
7 b g Lesotho(USA) Lasalsa De Juilley (FR) (Le Balafre (FR))
4733[2]

Tangolan (IRE) *Fergal O'Brien* 118h 131c
7 ch g Golan(IRE) Classic Note (IRE) (Classic Secret (USA))
658[2] 872[7] **(1042)** (1179) **(1424)** 1544[2] **1767[2] 1948[4]** 2247[7]

Tango Lima (FR) *J-P Gallorini* 131h 132c
7 bb m Turgeon(USA) Tres Passing (FR) (Medaaly)
836a[3]

Tango Unchained (IRE) *Charlie Mann* 107h
6 b g Golan(IRE) Crimson Bow (GER) (Night Shift (USA))
2842[P] 3839[U] 4322[4] 5115[P]

Tang Royal (FR) *Richard Rowe* 57h
8 ch g Epalo(GER) Bea De Forme (FR) (Sleeping Car (FR))
1244[8]

Taniokey (IRE) *Oliver Sherwood* 124h
5 b m Scorpion(IRE) Creation (IRE) (Definite Article)
2313[P]

Tanit River (IRE) *Tim Vaughan* 120h
5 br g Indian River(FR) Tanit Lady (IRE) (Presenting)
2182[4] 2694[10] 3377[4] (4432) 4782[3] 5453[4]

Tanner Bet *Polly Gundry* 56b
7 b m Thank Heavens Vercheny (Petoski)
671[10] 823[P]

Tanner Hill (IRE) *James Evans* 72h 94c
7 b g Milan Carlingford Leader (IRE) (Supreme Leader)
207[7] 2841[5] **3178[2] (3488) 4276[P] 4746[F]**

Tantalized *Dave Roberts* 80h
6 b m Authorized(IRE) Tarabela (CHI) (Hussonet (USA))
179[5] 443[3] 646[8] 759[2] 858[7]

Tantamount *Lucinda Russell* 119h
6 b g Observatory(USA) Cantanta (Top Ville (IRE))
1742[5] 2081[3] 2429[2] 3437[F] 5089[P]

Tapaculo *Philip Hobbs* 130h
4 b g Kayf Tara Aniston (IRE) (Eurodeal (IRE))
124[3] (2265) ◆ (2904) 3525[2]

Tap Night (USA) *Lucinda Russell* 129h 117c
8 ch g Pleasant Tap(USA) Day Mate (USA) (Dayjur (USA))
2214[12] (2949) 3440[6] 4017[7] 4405[5] 4911[9] 5446[5]

Taquin Du Seuil (FR) *Jonjo O'Neill* 151h 164c
8 bb g Voix Du Nord(FR) Sweet Laly (FR) (Marchand De Sable (USA))
(4128) 4731[6] 5176[5]

Tarabiyn (IRE) *W P Mullins* 124h
4 gr g Sinndar(IRE) Timabiyra (IRE) (Linamix (FR))
19a[11]

Tara Bridge *Chris Gordon* 120h
7 b g Kayf Tara Annie Greenlaw (Petoski)
3047[2] 3529[8] 3994[8] 4409[3] 4934[2]

Tara Dove *Alison Batchelor* 98h 82c
7 gr m Kayf Tara Kildee Lass (Morpeth)
167[13] **643[4]** 1245[P] **1373[U]**

Taradrewe *Anthony Honeyball* 127h
8 b m Kayf Tara Kaream (Karinga Bay)
1113[5] (1348) (1490) 2013[5]

Tara Flow *Venetia Williams* 133h
5 b m Kayf Tara Poppet (Terimon)
2665[2] (2959) (3318) 3487[2] (3785) 4231[6]

Tara Mac *Tim Vaughan* 106h
6 b m Kayf Tara Macklette (IRE) (Buckskin (FR))
(153) 775[7] 2880[3] 3217[P] 4028[3] 4290[3] 5420[3]

Tara Mactwo *Keith Dalgleish* 92b
5 b m Kayf Tara Macklette (IRE) (Buckskin (FR))
305[2]

Tara Mist *Henry Daly* 122h
6 gr m Kayf Tara Island Mist (Jupiter Island)
2349[3] 2852[4] 3283[4]

Tara Point *Paul Nicholls* 131h
6 gr m Kayf Tara Poppet (Terimon)
4699[12]

Tara Potter *Dan Skelton* 90b
5 b m Kayf Tara Lily Potter (Karinga Bay)
1289[4] 1491[4]

Tara Road *Rebecca Curtis* 117h 131c
7 b g Kayf Tara Sparkling Jewel (Bijou D'Inde)
1869[7] 2153[P] 2335[P] 3735[P] 3979[F] 5046[2] ◆

Tara's Honour *Emma Lavelle* 94b
5 b m Kayf Tara Prophets Honor (FR) (Highest Honor (FR))
1811[4] 3386[F]

Tara's Rainbow *Kim Bailey* 88h
5 b m Kayf Tara Nile Cristale (FR) (Northern Crystal)
120[3] 462[P] 2021[4] 2298[7] 2745[6] 4804[10]

Tara Tavey (IRE) *Kevin Bishop* 118h 84c
10 gr m Kayf Tara Slieve League (IRE) (Roselier (FR))
122[5] **388[P]** 2658[P] 3824[P] 4342[P] (4749) (4883) 5264[7]

Tara The Tiger *Tim Easterby* 112h
4 b m Kayf Tara El Tigress (GER) (Tiger Hill (IRE))
2716[2] 3054[6] 3626[6] (4052)

Tara Time *Philip Kirby* 97b
4 b m Kayf Tara Prophets Honor (FR) (Highest Honor (FR))
1334[2] 4708[5]

Tara View *Alan King* 89b
4 b m Kayf Tara Temptation (FR) (Lando (GER))
4488[11] 5286[6]

Tara Well (IRE) *Robin Dickin* 95h
5 b m Kayf Tara Miss Baden (IRE) (Supreme Leader)
1817[6] 2277[8] 3381[2] 3952[7] 4530[4] 4598[3] 4878[9]

Taroum (IRE) *John Flint* 98h 77c
8 b g Refuse To Bend(IRE) Taraza (IRE) (Darshaan)
1673[3] **524[P]** (695) 3498[P] 4855[9] **5435[9]**

Tarquinius (FR) *Miss K Frisby*
12 gr g Turgeon(USA) Shannon Bells (FR) (Nashamaa)
17[P]

Tarraco (FR) *Venetia Williams* 91h 122c
8 b g Sassanian(USA) Marie Esther (FR) (Chamberlin (FR))
2663[4] 3046[P]

Tarvini (IRE) *Jonjo O'Neill* 112h 103c
10 b g Kalanisi(IRE) Tarwila (IRE) (In The Wings)
363[5] 746[2]

Taste The Wine (IRE) *Bernard Llewellyn* 110h
9 gr g Verglas(IRE) Azia (IRE) (Desert Story (IRE))
449[7] 1048[5] 1600[3] 1702[2] 1927[3] 2264[9] 2599[P]

Tataniano (FR) *B A Sanderson* 115h 134c
11 b g Sassanian(USA) Rosa Carola (FR) (Rose Laurel)
536[4]

Taupin Rochelais (FR) *Patrice Quinton* 121h 106c
8 b g Al Namix(FR) Katia Rochelaise (FR) (Panoramic)
1671a[4]

Tawan *Brian Rothwell* 59h
4 b g Tiger Hill(IRE) Lady Netbetsports (IRE) (In The Wings)
4417[P] 4640[3]

Taweyla (IRE) *Pam Sly* 124h
4 b m Teofilo(IRE) Qasirah (IRE) (Machiavellian (USA))
(178) 491[3] (4096) (4459) 4909[F]

Tayarat (IRE) *Michael Chapman* 118h 108c
10 b g Noverre(USA) Sincere (IRE) (Bahhare (USA))
839[9] **915[P]**

Taylor (IRE) *Micky Hammond* 113h
6 b m Presenting Britway Lady (IRE) (Norwich)
(120) 463[8] 1488[6] 1675[3] 2167[4] 2802[6] 3505[5] 3970[8] 4939[5]

Tea Caddy *Jamie Snowden* 106h 113c
9 b m Kadastrof(FR) Little Tern (IRE) (Terimon)
1910[8] **2403[4] 3127[F] 3214[F] (3977)**

Teachmetobougie *Alexandra Dunn* 94h
5 ch g Tobougg(IRE) Teachmetotango (Mister Baileys)
2909[8] 3745[7] 4848[5] 5115[7]

Tea For Two *Nick Williams* 152h 161c
6 b g Kayf Tara One For Me (Tragic Role (USA))
1848[6] 2641[7] **(2881) (3229) ◆ 3991[3]**

Tea In Transvaal (IRE) *Evan Williams* 138h
4 b m Teofilo(IRE) Mpumalanga (Observatory (USA))
(591) ◆ (895) ◆ (1109) (1847) 2060[5] (2778) 4734[7]

Teak (IRE) *Ian Williams* 131h 122c
8 b g Barathea(IRE) Szabo (IRE) (Anabaa (USA))
916[3]

Teals Lad *Michael Easterby* 92b
6 b g Kayf Tara Derry Ann (Derrylin)
1101[6] 1449[10]

Tears From Heaven (USA) *Chris Grant* 66h 62c
9 bb g Street Cry(IRE) Heavenly Aura (USA) (St Jovite (USA))
3472[P] 3679[9] 4032[P] 4175[7] 4903[P]

Tearsofclewbay *Philip Hobbs* 120b
4 b m Kayf Tara Fenney Spring (Polish Precedent (USA))
(3381) (4242) 4623[4]

Tea Time Fred *Sue Gardner* 115h
6 b g Kayf Tara Darjeeling (IRE) (Presenting)
2268[10] 2667[P] 4543[P] 5382[3]

Ted Dolly (IRE) *Tom Symonds* 109h 111c
11 bb g Bob's Return(IRE) Little Pearl (IRE) (Bigstone (IRE))
110[P] 442[6] 692[8] 1115[6]

Teddy's Reflection (IRE) *Harriet Bethell* 106h 104c
12 b g Beneficial Regal Pursuit (IRE) (Roi Danzig (USA))
589[2] ◆

Teddy Tee (IRE) *Nicky Richards* 120h 130c
6 b g Mountain High(IRE) Knocksouna Lady (IRE) (Oscar (IRE))
2764[2] ◆ 4206[4] 4586[4]

Ted's Lad *Alan King* 102h
5 b g Kayf Tara Stravsea (Handsome Sailor)
2044[5] 4843[5] 5452[3]

Ted Spread *Suzy Smith* 129h 129c
8 b g Beat Hollow Highbrook (USA) (Alphabatim (USA))
1838[4]

Ted Veale (IRE) *A J Martin* 151h 149c
8 b g Revoque(IRE) Rose Tanner (IRE) (Roselier (FR))
51a[3] 1163a[3] 5025a[8]

Tee It Up Tommo (IRE) *Daniel Steele* 57h
6 gr g Clodovil(IRE) Lamh Eile (IRE) (Lend A Hand)
3083[11] 5303[P]

Teenage Dream (IRE) *Brian Ellison* 83h 113c
7 b g Antonius Pius(USA) Lucayan Star (IRE) (First Trump)
1643[8] 2425[5] ◆

Teescomponents Max *Keith Reveley* 86h 86c
6 b g Grape Tree Road Our Tees Component (IRE) (Saddlers' Hall (IRE))
507[10] 804[7] 937[4]

Tekthelot (IRE) *Keith Reveley* 116h
9 b g Shantou(USA) Bryna (IRE) (Ezzoud (IRE))
59[2] 638[3] 802[F] 2214[14] 2802[P] 3424[5] 3855[7] 4152[5] 4455[7]

Telex Du Berlais (FR) *Simon Waugh* 45h 20c
6 bb g Irish Wells(FR) Textos (FR) (Kaldounevees (FR))
1855[P] 2495[F] 3886[8] 5262[P]

Tell Tony (IRE) *Tim Dennis* 80h
5 b g Mahler Heather's Perk (IRE) (Executive Perk)
1673[7] 4339[8] 4449[9] 4919[4]

Tell Us More (IRE) *W P Mullins* 140h 145c
6 b g Scorpion(IRE) Zara's Victory (IRE) (Old Vic)
(3716a) 4145a[F] 4517a[2]

Tel Sleepin (FR) *D Retif*
5 bb g Sleeping Car(FR) Tel Muze (FR) (Tel Quel (FR))
436a[P]

Teme Trixie *Miss Imogen Pickard* 53b
5 b m Needwood Blade Castanet (Pennekamp (USA))
220[7] 831[10] 3921[P]

Templar (CZE) *Antonin Novak* 86c
8 b g Varadero(CZE) Terezie (CZE) (Ludovico (GER))
1885a[9]

Template (IRE) *Harry Fry* 124h
4 ch g Iffraaj Sagaing (Machiavellian (USA))
(2291) 2458[3] (2926) 3196[4] 4273[5] 5139[P]

Temple Grandin (IRE) *Philip Rowley* 69c
8 b g Presenting Bolly (IRE) (Jolly Jake (NZ))
15[3] 535[P] 4768[19]

Templehills (IRE) *Nigel Twiston-Davies* 84b
4 bb g Kalanisi(IRE) Sissinghurst Storm (IRE) (Good Thyne (USA))
5143[7]

Temple Lord (FR) *Jonjo O'Neill* 104h 105c
9 gr g Califet(FR) Temple Queen (GER) (Local Suitor (USA))
381[4] 589[3] ◆ 772[5] 966[4] (1086) 1375[11]

Templemills (IRE) *Thomas Cleary*
10 b g Iron Mask(USA) High Return (Last Tycoon)
75a[P]

Templeross (IRE) *Nigel Twiston-Davies* 123b
4 bb g Presenting Dame O'Neill (IRE) (Dr Massini (IRE))
1966[2] 2650[2] (3145) 4364[2]

Temple Tiger *James Turner* 92h
5 b g Tamure(IRE) Filey Flyer (Weldnaas (USA))
206[4] 3021[13] 3309[9] 3506[5] (4862) ◆

Tempo Mac (IRE) *Gordon Elliott* 139h
5 b g Antonius Pius(USA) Quecha (IRE) (Indian Ridge)
(1034) (1499)

Tempuran *David Bridgwater* 105h 103c
6 rg g Unbridled's Song(USA) Tenderly (IRE) (Danehill (USA))
588[P]

Tenby Jewel (IRE) *Mark Gillard* 81h 95c
10 ch g Pilsudski(IRE) Supreme Delight (IRE) (Supreme Leader)
718[8] 895[9] 1010[8] 1323[5] 1578[5] 1823[4] 2264[5] 2599[5] **3195[5] 4029[3] 4356[P]**

Tengri *John Ryan* 48b
3 b g Aqlaam Jackie's Opera (FR) (Indian Ridge)
4201[5]

Tennessee Bird *Mike Sowersby* 99h
7 b g Danbird(AUS) Tennessee Star (Teenoso (USA))
37[P] 522[10] 692[4] 777[2] (859) 935[3] 1265[7] 1598[4] (1691) 1927[2] 2085[4] 2560[P] 3023[9]

Tennis Cap (FR) *W P Mullins* 143h 153c
8 b g Snow Cap(FR) Jijie (FR) (Africanus (FR))
69a[P] 3552a[4] 3830a[2] 5448[2]

Tenor Nivernais (FR) *Venetia Williams* 142h 156c
8 b g Shaanmer(IRE) Hosanna II (FR) (Marasali)
(2615) 3031[3] 3406[2] 3851[2] 4361[P] 5276[5]

Ten Sixty (IRE) *Philip Hobbs* 123h
5 br g Presenting Senora Snoopy (IRE) (Un Desperado (FR))
2762[5] 3842[3] 4322[3] 4788[2] 5284[13]

Ten Times Better (IRE) *P A Fahy* 130h
5 ch m Beneficial Allaboveboard (IRE) (Alphabatim (USA))
2672a[6] 3873a[4] 4954a[7]

Ten Trees *Alan Swinbank* 102h
5 b m Millkom Island Path (IRE) (Jupiter Island)
2433[2] 2801[7] 3397[8] 3883[7] 4567[4] 4939[4] (5246)

Teochew (IRE) *Mark Shears* 103h 118c
7 b m Shantou(USA) Papal Princess (IRE) (Revoque (IRE))
1618[U] 1739[3] **(2147)** 2858[P] **3160[5] 3866[P] 4340[P]**

Teo Vivo (FR) *Pauline Robson* 127h 107c
8 gr g Great Pretender(IRE) Ifranne (FR) (April Night (FR))
1905[5] 2194[8] 3424[2] 3682[2] (4179) 4913[6] 5405[4]

Tercel (IRE) *Paul Nicholls* 114h
4 b g Monsun(GER) Kitty Hawk (Danehill Dancer (IRE))
(511) 832[2]

Ter Mill (CZE) *Antonin Novak*
9 ro g Mill Pond(FR) Tereza (CZE) (Ludovico (GER))
1885a[U]

Terminal (FR) *Anthony Day* 126h 90c
8 b g Passing Sale(FR) Durendal (FR) (Clafouti (FR))
532[3] 916[8] 1138[3] 1270[6] **1481[4] 1616[P] 1849[P]** 2405[2] **2878[P]** 3174[4]

Terra Bleu (IRE) *W Smith* 83c
8 b g Azamour(IRE) Pinaflore (FR) (Formidable I (USA))
294[P]

Terra Firma *Claire Dyson* 91h
5 b g Lucarno(USA) Solid Land (FR) (Solid Illusion (USA))
271[4] 3842[P] 4182[5] 4502[4] 5374[14]

Tesseract (IRE) *A P O'Brien* 101h
4 b g Trans Island Ballinagar Lady (IRE) (Fruits Of Love (USA))
9a[3]

Testing (FR) *David Thompson*
4 gr m New Approach(IRE) Testama (FR) (Testa Rossa (AUS))
2561[P]

Teviot Prince (IRE) *Martin Bosley* 111h
5 ch g Strategic Prince Nashville Skyline (Nashwan (USA))
1518[2] **2449[U]** 2754[P]

Texas Forever (IRE) *Kim Bailey* 91h
6 b g Heron Island(IRE) Gravinis (FR) (Grape Tree Road)
3467[P] 4064[5] 4869[5]

Texas Jack (IRE) *Noel Meade* 115h 159c
9 b g Curtain Time(IRE) Sailors Run (IRE) (Roselier (FR))
1152a[14] 1763a[5] 2207a[4] 3031[P]

Thackeray *Chris Fairhurst* 78h
8 b g Fasliyev(USA) Chinon (IRE) (Entrepreneur)
4050[B] 4416[7] 4817[6]

Thady Quil (IRE) *Martin Keighley* 106h
5 ch g Stowaway Aunt Sue (IRE) (Shahanndeh (IRE))
160[P] 590[P] 2299[P] 5452[2]

Thanks For Tea (IRE) *Edmond Kent* 127h
6 ch m Shantou(USA) Papal Princess (IRE) (Revoque (IRE))
3356a[P]

Thankyou Very Much *James Bethell* 101h
5 b m Lucky Story(USA) Maid Of Perth (Mark Of Esteem (IRE))
4865[2] 5232[P]

That Be Grand *Shaun Harris*
4 b m Firebreak Manila Selection (USA) (Manila (USA))
2748[P]

Thatchers Gold (IRE) *Henry Oliver* 111h 82c
7 b g Gold Well Chesterfield Lady (IRE) (Taipan (IRE))
(2490) 2977[4] **3384[P] 3979[5] 4803[9]** 5266[3]

Thate Hiana Juelli *William Knight* 68b
4 b g Sakhee(USA) Penlanfeigan (Abutammam)
1345[5]

Thatildee (IRE) *Chris Grant* 91h 92c
7 b g Heron Island(IRE) Good Thyne Mary (IRE) (Good Thyne (USA))
78[3] 2143[P] (2320) 2892[2] 3803[F] (Dead)

That Man Of Mine (IRE) *Mike Sowersby* 72h
3 ch g Thewayyouare(USA) Do The Deal (IRE) (Halling (USA))
5243[6] 5406[3]

Thats Ben (IRE) *Tom Gretton* 83c
10 b g Beneficial Classy Dancer (IRE) (Alphabatim (USA))
126[P] 698[P] 972[5]

Thats Digby *David Thompson* 84b
5 ch g Cayman Kai(IRE) Jupiter's Fancy (Jupiter Island)
1858[5]

That's Gonna Sting (IRE) *Jeremy Scott* 88b
4 b g Scorpion(IRE) Creme D'Arblay (IRE) (Singspiel (IRE))
1003[3] 3775[P]

Thatshowhedidit (IRE) *Mrs Gillian Callaghan* 117h
6 ch g Kutub(IRE) Last Hope (IRE) (Jurado (USA))
(837)

Thats My Rabbit (IRE) *Jim Best* 121h
6 b g Heron Island(IRE) Minnie Turbo (IRE) (General View)
(3377)

That's The Deal (IRE) *John Cornwall* 58h 85c
11 bb g Turtle Island(IRE) Sister Swing (Arctic Lord (IRE))
3820[P] 4776[2] 5015[F] 5309[P]

Thats Yer Man (IRE) *Linda Blackford* 84h 81c
7 ch g Marignan(USA) Glengarra Princess (Cardinal Flower)
173[5]

That Will Do *Helen Nelmes* 64b
5 ch g Desert King(IRE) Dusty Shoes (Shareef Dancer (USA))
3959[8] 4385[P]

The Absent Mare *Gordon Elliott* 89h 87c
7 gr m Fair Mix(IRE) Precious Lucy (FR) (Kadrou (FR))
286[2] 504[6] 843[2] (882)

The Artful Cobbler *Henry Daly* 120h
4 gr g Saint Des Saints(FR) Serhaaphim (Erhaab (USA))
213[10] 2437[6] 2879[8] 3484[4] (3923) ◆ 4066[P] 5454[P]

Theatre Act *Chris Grant* 102h
4 ch m Act One Theatre Belle (King's Theatre (IRE))
316[5] 3681[9] 4271[5] 4702[2] 5229[2]

Theatre Evening (IRE) *Mrs Frances Bishop* 111h 100c
7 b g King's Theatre(IRE) Waydale Hill (Minster Son)
270[4]

Theatre Flame (IRE) *David Bridgwater* 126h
5 b g King's Theatre(IRE) Bob's Flame (IRE) (Bob Back (USA))
(853) 1082[4] 4070[6] (4353)

Theatre Goer *Noel Williams* 117h
6 b m King's Theatre(IRE) Clover Green (IRE) (Presenting)
1116[2] 1576[U] 1723[3] 2088[3] 2658[3] (2985) 4305[3] 4467[2] 5282[6]

Theatre Guide (IRE) *Colin Tizzard* 127h 154c
8 b g King's Theatre(IRE) Erintante (IRE) (Denel (FR))
2171[3] 2783[2] 3850[3] (4361) 4697[F] 5494[8]

Theatre Mill (IRE) *Richenda Ford* 126h 113c
7 b g King's Theatre(IRE) River Mill (IRE) (Supreme Leader)
5185[11]

Theatre Rouge (IRE) *Philip Hobbs* 90b
3 b f King's Theatre(IRE) Toulon Rouge (IRE) (Toulon)
4687[6] 5383[2]

Theatre Territory (IRE) *Nicky Henderson* 113b
5 b m King's Theatre(IRE) Specifiedrisk (IRE) (Turtle Island (IRE))
2486[3] 4242[2] 5180[11]

Theatrical Star *Colin Tizzard* 70h 146c
9 b g King's Theatre(IRE) Lucy Glitters (Ardross)
2061[5] 2348[7] 2643[7] 2907[P] 5119[U] 5390[F]

Theatrical Style (IRE) *Donald McCain* 112h
6 b g Alhaarth(IRE) Little Theatre (IRE) (Old Vic)
1550[5] 1780[4] 2768[3] 3011[2] 4031[3] (4429) 5079[6]

The Backup Plan (IRE) *Donald McCain* 99h 113c
6 ch g Presenting Jay Lo (IRE) (Glacial Storm (USA))
328[8] **(1370) (1685) 2327[F] 2753[2] 5126[4]**

The Banastoir (IRE) *Rebecca Menzies* 106h
6 bb g Presenting Kimouna (FR) (Round Sovereign (FR))
76[U] 302[6]

The Bank Manager *David Pipe* 68h
4 b g Overbury(IRE) Alikat (IRE) (Alhaarth (IRE))
242[8] 558[9] 1698[9] 1909[8]

The Banshee *Liam Grassick*
9 b m Beat All(USA) Miniture Melody (IRE) (Kemal (FR))
648[P] 813[P]

The Barbury Queen (IRE) *Alan King* 100h
5 br m Milan Royal Shares (IRE) (Royal Fountain)
1662[4] 1908[6] 2302[11] 2952[6] 3485[3] 4644[3]

The Bay Bandit *Neil Mulholland* 104h 112c
8 b g Highest Honor(FR) Pescara (IRE) (Common Grounds)
514[2] 857[3] 985a[2] **(1367) 1674[3] 1907[3] 2449[7]**

The Big Dipper *David Dennis* 106h
6 b g Alflora(IRE) Pougatcheva (FR) (Epervier Bleu)
1453[3] (1692) 2085[3] 2577[6] 2773[3]

The Big Mare *Laura Young* 81h
6 b m Doyen(IRE) Fizzy Lady (Efisio)
2564[8] 3745[11] 3915[8] 4290[4] 4845[10]

The Bishop (IRE) *N W Alexander* 100h 99c
7 b g Winged Love(IRE) Charlie's Mary (IRE) (Daar Alzamaan (IRE))
2105[5] 2430[4] 2950[P] 3668[3] **4051[2] (4738) 5013[4] 5369[P]**

The Blue Bomber *Mick Channon* 103b
3 b g Stimulation(IRE) Mar Blue (FR) (Marju (IRE))
3048[2] 3409[3] 4364[7]

The Boss's Dream (IRE) *Neil King* 140h
7 b g Luso Mrs Kick (IRE) (Supreme Leader)
(2002) 2630[4] (3525) (3824) ◆ 4354[P] 5120[7]

The Brig At Ayr *S J Leadbetter* 20h 90c
11 gr g Terimon Rosie O'Keeffe (IRE) (Royal Fountain)
80[8]

The Brock Again *Paul Nicholls* 110h 130c
5 ch g Muhtathir Half Past Twelve (USA) (Cozzene (USA))
3584[6] **◆ 3954[2] (4292) 4597[5] 5147[P]**

The Brock Inn (IRE) *John W Nicholson* 128h
4 b m Stowaway She's Wonderful (IRE) (Magical Wonder (USA))
3356a[5] 3873a[6]

The Bugler (IRE) *Evan Williams* 102h
8 ch g Rock Of Gibraltar(IRE) Purple Spirit (IRE) (Sadler's Wells (USA))
1307[3] 1596[5] 2559[5] **◆ 2851[P]** 3586[12]

The Cat's Away (IRE) *Richenda Ford* 79h 79c
7 ch g Alderbrook Mrs Jack Russell (IRE) (Broken Hearted)
223[3] 1326[6] 1757[3] 2521[3] 2834[6]

The Child (IRE) *Anna Newton-Smith* 46h
6 b g Vertical Speed(FR) Chancy Hall (IRE) (Saddlers' Hall (IRE))
3902[P] 4409[10] 4668[3] 5063[10]

The Chuckmeister (IRE) *Chris Gordon*
6 b g Germany(USA) Lady Florian (Roselier (FR))
266[F] 4255[F]

The Cider Maker *Colin Tizzard* 104h 133c
5 b g Kayf Tara Dame Fonteyn (Suave Dancer (USA))
108[6] 1947[2] **2254[3] (4160) (4412) 4780[3]**

The Clock Leary (IRE) *Venetia Williams* 106h 121c
7 b g Helissio(FR) Kiwi Babe (Karinga Bay)
2468[P] 2686[F] 3524[3] 3843[P] 4230[5] 5093[7]

The Clonlisk Bug (IRE) *Kevin Frost* 104h
5 b g Scorpion(IRE) Apollo Lady (Alflora (IRE))
1101[4] 1289[5] 1519[2] 1597[4] 2174[6]

The Cobbler Swayne (IRE) *Lucinda Russell* 105h 129c
6 b g Milan Turtle Lamp (IRE) (Turtle Island (IRE))
2029[U] **(2293) 3014[3] 3972[4] (4584) ◆ 4910[4] 5473[3]**

The Coffee Hunter (FR) *Nick Williams* 100h
3 gr g Doctor Dino(FR) Mama Mia (FR) (Linamix (FR))
2092[4] 2757[2] 3464[2] 4447[10]

The Compeller (IRE) *Lucinda Russell* 98h
3 b g Lawman(FR) Mark Too (IRE) (Mark Of Esteem (IRE))
1631[3] 2324[3] 5088[6]

The Conn (IRE) *Chris Grant* 82h
5 b g Milan Grandy Invader (IRE) (Presenting)
2319[P] 3724[P] 4902[7]

Thecorruptor (IRE) *Paul Webber* 108h
5 bb g Robin Des Pres(FR) Cappard View (IRE) (Rudimentary (USA))
2244[7]

The Crafty Butcher (IRE) *Michael Hourigan* 133h 139c
8 b g Vinnie Roe(IRE) Ivy Queen (IRE) (Green Desert (USA))
95a[P] 3071a[12]

The Dark Duchess *C Brader* 67b
5 b m Bollin Eric Duchess Account (Mesleh)
320[14]

The Darling Boy *David Pipe* 105h 120c
10 b g Medicean Silver Top Hat (USA) (Silver Hawk (USA))
174[P]

The Doom Bar (IRE) *Philip Hobbs* 86h
6 ch g Beneficial The Sceardeen (IRE) (Lancastrian)
702[7] 935[12]

The Draconian (IRE) *David Pipe* 85b
4 b g Kalanisi(IRE) Lucky Hand (IRE) (Shernazar)
2270[13]

Thedrinkymeister (IRE) *Kim Bailey* 119h 122c
6 b g Heron Island(IRE) Keel Row (Relkino)
2727[5] ◆ 3079[4] 3384[P] 3924[4] 5044[2] (5350)

The Drone (IRE) *Liam Lennon* 80h
4 bb g Mahler Liberess (IRE) (Saddlers' Hall (IRE))
366[4]

The Druids Nephew (IRE) *Neil Mulholland* 139h 158c
8 b g King's Theatre(IRE) Gifted (Shareef Dancer (USA))
2198[6] **3016[6] 4472[2] 5218[P] 5494[5]**

The Dutchman (IRE) *Sandy Thomson* 137h
5 b g King's Theatre(IRE) Shivermetimber (IRE) (Arctic Lord (IRE))
3436[2] (3795) ◆ 4636[2] 5214[P]

The Eaglehaslanded (IRE) *Paul Nicholls* 140h
5 b g Milan Vallee Doree (FR) (Neverneyev (USA))
(2005) 2268[2] 3018[4] 4139[P] (5284) (5454)

The Ferbane Man (IRE) *Mike Hammond* 104b
11 b g Dr Massini(IRE) Hi Up There (IRE) (Homo Sapien)
676[P]

The Finger Post (IRE) *Helen Nelmes* 97b
8 b g Zagreb(USA) Mystic Madam (IRE) (Lafontaine I (USA))
449[F]

The Flaming Matron (IRE) *N W Alexander* 100h 95c
9 b m Flemensfirth(USA) The Mighty Matron (IRE) (Montelimar (USA))
287[4] 870[P]

Theflyingportrait (IRE) *Jennie Candlish* 98h 104c
6 gr g Portrait Gallery(IRE) Skule Hill Lass (IRE) (Close Conflict (USA))
56[6] 465[8] 1307[P] 2212[6] **2707[4] 2976[3] 3241[2] 3834[4] ◆ 4214[2] 4704[2]**

The Fresh Prince (IRE) *Oliver Sherwood* 121h
5 b g Robin Des Pres(FR) Hayley Cometh (IRE) (Supreme Leader)
2337[5] 3370[5] 3710[4] ◆ 4196[2] (4633)

Thefriendlygremlin *John Upson* 80h
7 b g Vinnie Roe(IRE) Queen's Fantasy (Grand Lodge (USA))
40[7] (858) 1598[9] 1927[P] 2520[4]

The Frugal Star *Caroline Bailey*
7 ch g Fraam Star Of Heaven (Bold Edge)
396[P]

The Fugitive (IRE) *Charlie Longsdon* 104h
4 b g Flemensfirth(USA) Alleygrove Lass (IRE) (Alderbrook)
2650[6] 3083[3] ◆

The Game Changer (IRE) *Gordon Elliott* 150h 156c
6 b g Arcadio(GER) Gilt Ridden (IRE) (Heron Island (IRE))
7a[3] 1163a[12] **1515a[2] (1679a) (1790a) (1937a) 4696[4] 5215[2]**

The Game Is A Foot (IRE) *Gary Moore* 103h
8 b g Oscar(IRE) Cooksgrove Rosie (IRE) (Mandalus)
225[2] ◆ 529[4]

The Geegeez Geegee (IRE) *Anthony Honeyball* 114h 99c
6 b g Beneficial Shanann Lady (IRE) (Anshan)
177[0] 261[2] 1964[4] (2548) 2867[4] 3956[4] 4438[5] 5065[7]

The Giant Bolster *David Bridgwater* 125h 161c
10 b g Black Sam Bellamy(IRE) Divisa (GER) (Lomitas)
22a[F] 2783[7] 3150[9] 3850[4] 4113[2] 4735[13]

The Gipper (IRE) *Evan Williams* 130h
5 b g King's Theatre(IRE) Merrill Gaye (IRE) (Roselier (FR))
444[4] (2267) 2904[F] (3568) (4613) ◆ 5275[10]

The Golden Hour (IRE) *Zoe Davison* 87b
5 b m Gold Well Kirktonmoor Katie (IRE) (Rich Charlie)
227[5] 601[8]

The Governess *Dr Richard Newland* 145h
6 b m Kayf Tara Just Kate (Bob's Return (IRE))
196[3] 3034[F] 3444[2] 3732[5] 4699[F] (Dead)

Thegreendalerocket (IRE) *Jimmy Frost* 111h
6 b g Oscar(IRE) Classy Society (IRE) (Moscow Society (USA))
2163[7] 2443[2] 2731[6] 2985[4] **3371[F]** 4860[5]

The Green Ogre *Gary Moore* 113h 122c
5 b g Dubai Destination(USA) Takegawa (Giant's Causeway (USA))
1985[2] 2546[3] 2857[3] (4410)

The Grey Celt (IRE) *R G Chapman* 98h 81c
7 gr g Verglas(IRE) Helen Wells (IRE) (Sadler's Wells (USA))
5384[3]

The Grey Taylor (IRE) *Brian Ellison* 127h 138c
6 gr g Royal Anthem(USA) Penny Tan (IRE) (Roselier (FR))
1900[4] (2026) 3335[3] 4011[4] 4838[7]

The Happy Warrior *C Price* 81b 107c
7 b g Luso Martomick (Montelimar (USA))
(163) 403[P] 523[P] 4269[P]

Thehill Ofthe Rock (IRE) *Jim Best* 75h
5 ch g Indian River(FR) Ballyburn Lady (IRE) (Needle Gun (IRE))
98[11] 2693[4] 3087[P]

The Hon Mackinlay (IRE) *Ben Pauling* 100h
6 ch g Bold Fact(USA) Khadija (Kadastrof (FR))
2543[5] 3022[6] 3607[P]

Thehoodlum *Jean McGregor* 37h
8 b g Fraam Trilby (In The Wings)
656[12] 1498[5] 1550[8]

Thehossbehind (IRE) *Ian Williams* 87b
4 ch g Mahler Bayloughbess (IRE) (Lancastrian)
644[2]

The Housekeeper (IRE) *David Harry Kelly* 104h 131c
8 b m Heron Island(IRE) The Wounded Cook (IRE) (Muroto)
70a[F] 5132a[3]

The Ice Factor *Alison Hamilton* 98h 90c
7 b g Iceman Kiruna (Northern Park (USA))
77[2] 537[10] 804[2] 872[P] 2071[8] 2322[3] 2703[4] 4861[5]

The Informant *Seamus Mullins* 84h 90c
9 gr g Central Park(IRE) Belle Rose (IRE) (Roselier (FR))
446[6] 1825[4] 2315[4] 2834[5]

Theinval (FR) *Nicky Henderson* 149h 128c
5 b g Smadoun(FR) Kinevees (FR) (Hard Leaf (FR))
2122[3] 3733[P] 4717[14] ◆ 5189[9]

Theionlady (IRE) *Richard Woollacott* 82h
5 gr m Presenting Valleya (FR) (Linamix (FR))
164[3] 515[7] 1158[P] 1323[6]

The Italian Yob (IRE) *Nick Williams* 112h 130c
7 b g Milan The Rebel Lady (IRE) (Mister Lord (USA))
(1965) 2459[4] 3315[3] 3957[5] 4225[2] 4910[F]

The Jazz Singer *C A McBratney* 101h
4 ch g Tobougg(IRE) Ridgeway Jazz (Kalanisi (IRE))
5408[6]

The Job Is Right *Michael Hourigan* 144h 143c
7 gr g With Approval(CAN) Common Request (USA) (Lear Fan (USA))
95a[P] 2484[5] **3296a[5] 3715a[4] 4735[U]**

The Jugopolist (IRE) *John Cornwall* 113h 74c
8 b g Oscar(IRE) Chance My Native (IRE) (Be My Native (USA))
128[4] 589[P] 678[5] 747[9] **965[4] 1155[P]** 2841[8] 3376[6] **4533[3] 4772[P] 4977[3] 5310[5]**

The King Of Brega (IRE) *Patrick Downey* 126h 128c
8 b g Court Cave(IRE) Heather Darling (IRE) (Be My Native (USA))
69a[P]

The Kings Assassin (IRE) *Chris Gordon* 99h
7 bb g King's Theatre(IRE) Assidua (IRE) (Anshan)
222[8] (599) 897[3] **1155[F]** 1547[P] 1897[3]

The Kvilleken *Martin Keighley* 105h 49c
7 b g Fair Mix(IRE) Wannaplantatree (Niniski (USA))
172[3] 237[6] **524[2]** 740a[2] (1054) (1182) 1383[4] 1524[7] 1818[3] 1947[3]

The Lampo Genie *K R Burke* 98h
3 b g Champs Elysees Samar Qand (Selkirk (USA))
1899[2] ◆ 2172[4]

The Last Bar *Dan Skelton* 110h
5 b m Kayf Tara Ardenbar (Ardross)
2776[6] 3724[6] 4065[2] 4878[F]

The Last Bridge *Susan Johnson* 76h 94c
8 b g Milan Celtic Bridge (Celtic Cone)
148[3] 599[4] 3369[3] 3771[10] **4879[5] 5468[8]**

The Last Leg (IRE) *Karen McLintock* 99h
6 b g Old Vic Raphuca (IRE) (Be My Native (USA))
845[3] 1181[3]

The Last Melon *James Bennett* 20b
3 ch g Sir Percy Step Fast (USA) (Giant's Causeway (USA))
4143[5]

The Last Samuri (IRE) *Kim Bailey* 134h 160c
7 ch g Flemensfirth(USA) Howaboutthis (IRE) (Oscar (IRE))
2790[3] (3282) (4472) ◆ 5218[2]

The Late Shift *Barry Murtagh* 88h
5 b g Midnight Legend Ashnaya (FR) (Ashkalani (IRE))
79[5] 337[3] 2029[P] 2751[7] 3402[P] 3973[6] 4863[3]

Theligny (FR) *Tim Vaughan* 112h
4 gr g Martaline Romilly (FR) (Subotica (FR))
1998[2] 2543[2]

The Linksman (IRE) *Brian Ellison* 64b
3 b g Westerner Lost Link (IRE) (Shernazar)
2020[6]

The Lion Man (IRE) *Robin Dickin* 99h
5 b g Let The Lion Roar Just Smart (IRE) (Anshan)
207[4] 1929[3] **2300[P]** 2855[P] 3841[7]

The Liquidator *David Pipe* 145h
7 b g Overbury(IRE) Alikat (IRE) (Alhaarth (IRE))
1848[12]

The Little Red Fox *Chris Down* 81b
5 ch m Volochine(IRE) Brown Fox (FR) (Polar Falcon (USA))
1811[8]

The Lizard King (IRE) *Charlie Longsdon* 65h
6 b g Indian River(FR) Norwich Breeze (IRE) (Norwich)
1912[4] 2275[P]

Thelobstercatcher *P A Fahy* 128h 122c
11 gr g Silver Patriarch(IRE) Everything's Rosy (Ardross)
92a[P]

The Mad Well (IRE) *Edmond Daniel Linehan* 113h
6 b g Milan Silverfortprincess (IRE) (Mull Of Kintyre (USA))
3010[3]

Themanfrom Minella (IRE) *Ben Case* 125h 128c
6 b g Shantou(USA) Bobomy (IRE) (Bob Back (USA))
382[3] 2489[P] 2996[4] 3236[6] 3823[U] (4542) 5285[7]

The Masters Choice (IRE) *Mark Campion* 44b
3 b g High Chaparral(IRE) Final Legacy (USA) (Boston Harbor (USA))
2923[8]

The Mighty Don (IRE) *Nick Gifford* 92b
3 ch g Shantou(USA) Flying Answer (IRE) (Anshan)
5069[3] ◆

The Minch (IRE) *Jim Goldie* 134b
4 b g Flemensfirth(USA) Akayid (Old Vic)
5195[3] ◆

The Minkle (IRE) *David Pipe* 85h
4 ch g Flemensfirth(USA) Impudent (IRE) (In The Wings)
2731[10] 3114[10] 3411[13] 3568[7]

The Missus *Warren Greatrex* 113h
4 b m Presenting Violet Express (FR) (Cadoudal (FR))
2750[3] 3334[10] 4303[5] (4881) 5380[2]

The Model County (IRE) *Alan Phillips* 73h
5 b m Robin Des Champs(FR) Ware It Vic (IRE) (Old Vic)
2486[15] 2909[3] 3132[7] 3516[11] 3787[P] 4449[10] 4798[P]

The Mooch (IRE) *Paul Nolan* 118h 127c
7 b g Bach(IRE) Bonne Inagh (IRE) (Broken Hearted)
4397a[2]

The Mumper (IRE) *Alan King* 114h 114c
8 br g Craigsteel Na Moilltear (IRE) (Miner's Lamp)
2957[F] 3834[2] (4275) 4545[3] (5375)

The Mustang *Nick Williams*
8 gr g Silver Patriarch(IRE) Phar Too Touchy (Mister Lord (USA))
1349[P]

The Mythologist (IRE) *Tim Vaughan* 95h
7 ch g Motivator Dilemma (Generous (IRE))
1379[5] 1544[7] 1718[6]

The Name's Bond *Keith Reveley* 85h
3 ch g Monsieur Bond(IRE) Fairlie (Halling (USA))
636[3] 2845[6] 3099[11]

The New One (IRE) *Nigel Twiston-Davies* 164h
7 b g King's Theatre(IRE) Thuringe (FR) (Turgeon (USA))
(1988) 3230[2] (3740) 4698[4] 5177[F]

The New Trick (IRE) *Sophie Leech*
5 b g Oscar(IRE) Mandyslady (IRE) (Husyan (USA))
3226[P]

The Nipper (IRE) *Warren Greatrex* 125b
4 b m Scorpion(IRE) Sharp Single (IRE) (Supreme Leader)
(334) (2770) (4623)

The Nutcracker (IRE) *Thomas Gibney* 120h
5 b m Antonius Pius(USA) Katies Crown (IRE) (Royal Abjar (USA))
1150a[9] 1565a[3]

Theo (IRE) *S Donohoe* 101h
5 b g Westerner Jemima Jay (IRE) (Supreme Leader)
487[8]

The Omen *Tim Vaughan* 80h 94c
9 b g Sir Harry Lewis(USA) High Sturt (Petoski)
806[6] 914[7] 1045[6] 1402[2] 1796[3] 2416[3] 4356[7] 4823[P]

Theophrastus (IRE) *J D Sole* 101h 101c
13 b g Overbury(IRE) Over The Glen (IRE) (Over The River (FR))
18[7] 294[3]

The Orange Rogue (IRE) *N W Alexander* 110h 115c
8 br g Alderbrook Classic Enough (Classic Cliche (IRE))
2788[2] 3160[3] 3669[U] 3933[2] 4549[3] (5202)

The Organist (IRE) *Oliver Sherwood* 140h
4 b m Alkaadhem Go On Eileen (IRE) (Bob Back (USA))
(305) (2644) (3215) ◆ 3785[2] (4471) 5280[F]

Theo's Charm (IRE) *Nick Gifford* 133h
5 b g Presenting Kates Charm (IRE) (Glacial Storm (USA))
2683[3] ◆ (3083) (3450) 3733[5] 5275[12]

The Ould Lad (IRE) *Neil Mulholland* 54h 139c
7 b g Heron Island(IRE) Badger Hammel (IRE) (Insan (USA))
2348[P] 5071[7]

The Outlaw (IRE) *Paul Nicholls* 112h
5 b g Presenting Bonnie Parker (IRE) (Un Desperado (FR))
2731[F]

The Package *David Pipe* 137h 151c
12 br g Kayf Tara Ardent Bride (Ardross)
855[8]

The Panama Kid (IRE) *Malcolm Jefferson* 109h 129c
11 b g Presenting Mrs Jodi (Yaheeb (USA))
156[5]

The Paparrazi Kid (IRE) *W P Mullins* 138h 146c
8 b g Milan Banbury Cross (IRE) (Supreme Leader)
1152a[2] 1556a[4]

Thepartysover *Paul Henderson* 110h 110c
10 gr g Cloudings(IRE) Just A Tipple (IRE) (Roselier (FR))
104[5] 451[3] **750[7]** 2599[3] (2958) 3125[4] **4197[4]** 4384[2] **4587[4]**

The Perfect Crime (IRE) *Ian Williams* 94h 33c
6 b g Oscar(IRE) Gimme Peace (IRE) (Aristocracy (IRE))
3572[P] 4504[P] **5125[10] 5478[6]**

The Phantom (FR) *Dianne Sayer* 89b
3 b g Apsis Idee Recue (FR) (Sicyos (USA))
2216[2]

The Pier (IRE) *Martin Keighley* 110h
9 ch g Alhaarth(IRE) Cois Cuain (IRE) (Night Shift (USA))
2043[P]

The Pierre Lark (IRE) *Donald McCain* 98h
5 b g Pierre Kyle Lark (IRE) (Miner's Lamp)
4434[2] 4742[5] 5048[4] 5401[5]

The Pine Martin (IRE) *Denis Gerard Hogan* 94h
5 bb g Kalanisi(IRE) Regal Holly (Gildoran)
2136[7]

The Plan Man (IRE) *A J Martin* 140h
5 b g Jeremy(USA) Sanfrancullinan (IRE) (Bluebird (USA))
7a[U] 197[5] 3650a[12] 5025a[2]

The Poodle Faker *Hughie Morrison* 105b
4 b g Pastoral Pursuits Flirtatious (Generous (IRE))
2188[3] *2702[3]* 5097[6]

The Purchaser (IRE) *Chris Bealby* 86h 100c
7 b g Definite Article Cash Customer (IRE) (Bob Back (USA))
(183) 782[3] 1004[6] 1287[12] 1785[4] 1825[U]

The Racing Duke (IRE) *Graeme McPherson* 90b
3 b g Duke Of Marmalade(IRE) Wrong Key (IRE) (Key Of Luck (USA))
3048[4] 4103[15]

The Ramblin Kid *Micky Hammond* 125h 120c
7 b g Westerner Disallowed (IRE) (Distinctly North (USA))
2211[7] 2785[4] 3162[F] 3507[P]

Theredballoon *Conrad Allen* 103h
9 ch g Sulamani(IRE) Sovana (FR) (Kadounor (FR))
1691[3] (2043) 2559[2]

There Is No Point (IRE) *Jonjo O'Neill* 116h
6 b m Galileo(IRE) Akilana (IRE) (Mark Of Esteem (IRE))
332[3]

The Road Ahead *Peter Bowen* 123h
8 b m Grape Tree Road Althrey Flame (IRE) (Torus)
(185) 314[2]

Theroadtogorey (IRE) *Sarah Robinson* 86b
9 b g Revoque(IRE) Shannon Mor (IRE) (Zaffaran (USA))
31[P] (Dead)

The Romford Pele (IRE) *Rebecca Curtis* 148h 149c
8 b g Accordion Back And Fore (IRE) (Bob Back (USA))
1849[7] 2482[7] 3016[F] 3853[3] 4717[8] **5218[U]**

The Saint James (FR) *Jonjo O'Neill* 138h 138c
4 b g Saint Des Saints(FR) Aimela (FR) (Sagamix (FR))
96a[14] **3006[2] 3280[5] 4359[F] 4770[P]**

The Saskatoon *Peter Maddison* 39h
6 b g Desideratum Skewsby Girl (Kayf Tara)
5230[P] 5406[4]

The Scarlett Woman *Kim Bailey* 87h
6 b m Kayf Tara Double Red (IRE) (Thatching)
2022[P]

The Scourge (IRE) *Sarah Humphrey* 105h
4 b g Whipper(USA) House Rebel (IRE) (Spartacus (IRE))
1628[3] **1636[3]** 4771[5]

The Selector *Chris Gordon* 82h
6 b m Crosspeace(IRE) Lojo (Pivotal)
65[4] 451[5]

The Shepherd King (IRE) *R K Watson* 110h 104c
11 b g Marignan(USA) Boolavogue (IRE) (Torus)
4166[8] 4550[8] **4554[3]**

The Shrimp (IRE) *Sandy Thomson* 56h 75c
8 gr g Indian Danehill(IRE) Rheban Lass (IRE) (Eurobus)
204[3] 303[7]

The Shropshire Lad *Dan Skelton* 80h 94c
5 gr g Fair Mix(IRE) Shropshire Girl (Cloudings (IRE))
1110[4] 1306[5] 1888[4] 1980[P]

The Sneezer (IRE) *Nikki Evans* 67h 103c
12 br g Topanoora Bel Azur (IRE) (Electric)
2601[3] 2908[P] 3586[7] **3977[P] 4187[P]**

The Society Man (IRE) *Michael Chapman* 59h 104c
8 ch g Moscow Society(USA) Redruth (IRE) (Sri Pekan (USA))
183[6] 504[2] 567[4] 782[4] 847[2] 1032[4] 1403[6] 1659[P] 1795[3] 1942[3] 2147[5] 2469[7] 3236[P] 4423[4] 4641[4] 4772[3] 4980[3]

The Squinty Bridge *Lucinda Russell* 90h
7 b g Heron Island(IRE) The Storm Bell (IRE) (Glacial Storm (USA))
2478[3] 2937[P] 4163[P]

The Stomp (FR) *Francois Nicolle* 139h
5 b g Layman(USA) Version Originale I (FR) (Poliglote)
(436a) 5363a[6]

The Sweetener (IRE) *Richard Woollacott* 81h
6 b g Kris Kin(USA) Sheila's Pet (IRE) (Welsh Term)
165[4]

The Tailgater (IRE) *Jonjo O'Neill* 92h
4 b g Oscar(IRE) Zaffaran Express (IRE) (Zaffaran (USA))
(2849) 3221[5]

Thetalkinghorse (IRE) *G T H Bailey* 113c
7 b g Presenting Praisethepreacher (IRE) (Sharifabad (IRE))
4426[2] (5082)

The Tall Blonde *Peter Purdy*
6 ch m Mutazayid(IRE) Tudor Blonde (Pablond)
2460[P]

The Toft *Lucinda Russell* 93h
6 b m Kayf Tara Gretton (Terimon)
1854[8] 2318[7] 2428[2] **2922[P]** 3666[4]

The Tourard Man (IRE) *Alan King* 142h 130c
9 b g Shantou(USA) Small Iron (General Ironside (IRE))
1848[11] **2260[3] 3109[4] 3838[F]** 4139[P] 5120[6]

Theturnofthesun (IRE) *Matthew J Smith* 113h
6 ch g Galileo(IRE) Something Mon (USA) (Maria's Mon (USA))
3323a[3]

The Unit (IRE) *Alan King* 120h
4 b g Gold Well Sovana (FR) (Kadounor (FR))
2514[7] 3608[2] 4303[2]

The Venerable Bede (IRE) *Paul Webber* 87h
4 b g Kalanisi(IRE) Feedthegoodmare (IRE) (Heron Island (IRE))
4233[6] 4714[8]

The Village (IRE) *Lucinda Russell* 59h 83c
6 b g Lahib(USA) Melisande (Slip Anchor)
286[RR] 455[7] 884[6]

The Wallace Line (IRE) *Tim Vaughan* 129h
4 b g Mastercraftsman(IRE) Surval (IRE) (Sadler's Wells (USA))
4107[4]

The Wealerdealer (IRE) *I Chanin* 114c
8 b g Vinnie Roe(IRE) Lantern Liz (IRE) (Montelimar (USA))
(123) 4295[F]

The Wee Barra (IRE) *Kevin Ryan* 18h
3 b f Rock Of Gibraltar(IRE) Gamra (IRE) (Green Desert (USA))
2137[8]

The Wee Midget *Arthur Whiting* 91h 90c
10 b g Mtoto Fragrant Rose (Alflora (IRE))
55[3] 599[2] **926[5] 1049[3] 1243[2] 1355[2] 1678[P]**

The Westener Boy (IRE) *C A Murphy* 133h 113c
8 b g Westerner Designer Lady (IRE) (Buckskin (FR))
2672a[7]

The Western Force (IRE) *Dan Skelton* 91h
5 b g Westerner Park Belle (IRE) (Strong Gale)
1081[5] 1240[9] 1887[11]

The Wexfordian (IRE) *Martin Keighley* 80h 106c
6 b g Shantou(USA) Going My Way (Henbit (USA))
3146[P] **4418[4]**

The White Duke (IRE) *Nick Kent* 95b
6 ch g Pelder(IRE) Concinna (FR) (Esprit Du Nord (USA))
1449[7]

The Winking Prawn (IRE) *Graeme McPherson* 110h 93c
8 b g Beneficial Rocamadoura (Roi Danzig (USA))
365[F] 589[5] 807[4] 1004[7] (1158) 1375[3] 1579[2]

The Worlds End (IRE) *Tom George* 116b
4 b g Stowaway Bright Sprite (IRE) (Beneficial)
(5227)

The Yank *David Bridgwater* 87h 111c
6 b g Trade Fair Silver Gyre (IRE) (Silver Hawk (USA))
626[4] 1096[2] **(1373) 1460[F] 1674[2] (2003)**

The Young Master *Neil Mulholland* 116h 155c
6 b g Echo Of Light Fine Frenzy (IRE) (Great Commotion (USA))
2215[2] 2783[U] 3150[4] ◆ 3853[6] **4697[3] (5494)**

Thiepval *Jason Ward*
3 ch g Kyllachy Lady Broughton (IRE) (Grand Lodge (USA))
2216[8]

Thinger Licht (FR) *Dan Skelton* 101h 129c
6 b g Clety(FR) Family Saga (FR) (Caerwent)
(173) ◆ 211[2] (280) (917) **961[P] 3727[2] ◆ (4380) 4493[2] 4912[P]**

Things Change (IRE) *John Quinn* 113h 125c
7 b g Old Vic Northwood May (Teenoso (USA))
76[5]

Thinking Out Loud (IRE) *Mrs Z Hammond* 87b
4 ch g Spadoun(FR) Hollygrove (IRE) (Commander Collins (IRE))
5436[8]

Think Of Me (IRE) *Fergal O'Brien* 98h
6 b m Germany(USA) Kate's Lass (IRE) (Montelimar (USA))
1384[4] 1910[3] 2298[6]

Third Act (IRE) *Colin Tizzard* 112h 115c
6 b g King's Theatre(IRE) Starry Lady (IRE) (Marju (IRE))
110[8] **596[2] 896[3] 3042[4] 3977[U]**

Third Chance (IRE) *Miss S L Gould* 104b 112c
8 b g Witness Box(USA) Princess Isle (Deep Run)
123[2]

Third Intention (IRE) *Colin Tizzard* 151h 164c
8 b g Azamour(IRE) Third Dimension (FR) (Suave Dancer (USA))
1869[2] 2259[2] 2633[3] 2915[6] 3741[6] 4719[5] 5193[3] 5492[4]

Third Of The Third *Gary Hanmer* 110b 107c
8 bb g Presenting Gavotte Du Cochet (FR) (Urbain Minotiere (FR))
506[F]

Thirty Bob (IRE) *Evan Williams*
4 b g Brian Boru The Rebel Lady (IRE) (Mister Lord (USA))
5235[P] 5434[P]

Thisonetime (IRE) *John Quinn* 108b
4 b g Kalanisi(IRE) Dizzy's Whisper (IRE) (Supreme Leader)
(3625)

This Thyne Jude *Lucy Normile* 90h
7 gr m Silver Patriarch(IRE) This Thyne (Good Thyne (USA))
4031[6] 4736[3] 5408[4]

Thistlecrack *Colin Tizzard* 178h
7 b g Kayf Tara Ardstown (Ardross)
21a[2] (2782) ◆ (3149) (3853) ◆ (4732) ◆ (5216)

Thisulldaeus *Jim Goldie* 87b
4 b g Black Sam Bellamy(IRE) I Got Rhythm (Lycius (USA))
145[8]

Thomas Blossom (IRE) *Ali Stronge* 92h
5 b g Dylan Thomas(IRE) Woman Secret (IRE) (Sadler's Wells (USA))
5269[8] 5434[8]

Thomas Brown *Harry Fry* 118h 147c
6 b g Sir Harry Lewis(USA) Tentsmuir (Arctic Lord (IRE))
(2613) ◆ 3136[2] (3838) 4361[U] 4701[7] 5217[4]

Thomas Campbell *Nicky Henderson* 89b
3 b g Yeats(IRE) Hora (Hernando (FR))
3847[7]

Thomas Crapper *Robin Dickin* 112h 142c
8 b g Tamure(IRE) Mollycarrs Gambul (General Gambul)
69a[7] 1815[3] 2064[12] **3406[6] 4857[3] (5093) 5496[4]**

Thomas Edison (IRE) *A J Martin* 155h
8 b g Danehill Dancer(IRE) Bright Bank (IRE) (Sadler's Wells (USA))
231a[10] 1163a[F] 1787a[3] 2532a[4] 2815a[7]

Thomas Hobson *W P Mullins* 148h
5 b g Halling(USA) La Spezia (IRE) (Danehill Dancer (IRE))
2385a[2] (3623) 4715[P]

Thomas Junior (FR) *Paul Morgan* 114h 44c
6 b g Dylan Thomas(IRE) Smiling (Sadler's Wells (USA))
364[6] 615[11]

Thomas Shelby (IRE) *Alan King* 104b
4 b g Witness Box(USA) Deemiss (IRE) (Buckskin (FR))
4102[5] ◆ 4790[7]

Thomas Wild *Philip Hobbs* 105h 132c
10 ch g Muhtarram(USA) Bisque (Inchinor)
29[3] (553) 855[9] 4340[P] 5274[3]

Thom Thumb (IRE) *Paul Webber* 78h 86c
9 ch g Flemensfirth(USA) Ardlea Dawn (IRE) (Glacial Storm (USA))
379[5]

Thoonavolla (IRE) *Tom Weston* 98h 103c
7 ch g Beneficial Another Partner (Le Bavard (FR))
2976[2] ◆ (4842) ◆ 5395[4] ◆

Thoresby (IRE) *Ben Case* 103h 110c
9 b g Milan I Remember It Well (IRE) (Don't Forget Me)
183[2] 782[P] (Dead)

Thorpe (IRE) *Lucinda Russell* 129h
5 b g Danehill Dancer(IRE) Minkova (IRE) (Sadler's Wells (USA))
301[3] 1776[4] 2513[12]

Thousand Stars (FR) *W P Mullins* 154h
11 gr g Grey Risk(FR) Livaniana (FR) (Saint Estephe (FR))
49a[7] 663a[2] 954a[2] 1163a[6] 1671a[7] 1787a[5] (2361a)

Threapwood *Oliver Greenall* 95c
8 b g Sulamani(IRE) Akathea (Barathea (IRE))
60[3] 506[4]

Threebarmymen (IRE) *Jeremy Scott* 109h
4 b g Winged Love(IRE) Midnight Susie (IRE) (Supreme Leader)
2011[6] 2312[4] 2710[6] 3375[6] 5386[2]

Three Colours Red (IRE) *Warren Greatrex* 101h
3 b g Camacho Colour's Red (IRE) (Red Ransom (USA))
3822[2] 4038[4] 4345[3] 4871[3] 5081[3]

Three Faces West (IRE) *Philip Hobbs* 128h 139c
7 b g Dr Massini(IRE) Ardnataggle (IRE) (Aristocracy (IRE))
3156[3] **3611[2] ◆ 4341[2] (4858)**

Three Kingdoms (IRE) *John Ferguson* 140h 134c
6 ch g Street Cry(IRE) Chan Tong (BRZ) (Hampstead (URU))
2617[4] 3151[13] 4717[18]

Three Musketeers (IRE) *Dan Skelton* 143h 158c
5 b g Flemensfirth(USA) Friendly Craic (IRE) (Mister Lord (USA))
2222[3] (2760) ◆ 3405[5] 4729[4]

Three Of A Kind (IRE) *Fergal O'Brien* 111h
6 b g Helissio(FR) Monadore (IRE) (Oscar Schindler (IRE))
2062[6] 2879[P] 3920[3] (4640)

Three Stars (IRE) *Henry De Bromhead* 140h
5 b g Westerner Hapeney (IRE) (Saddlers' Hall (IRE))
1788a[2] (2385a) 5190[8]

Three Ways *Jamie Snowden* 115h
4 b g Flemensfirth(USA) Serenique (Good Thyne (USA))
(2401) 3145[3] (4494) 5273[F]

Thrilling Moments *John Panvert* 53b
4 b m Lucarno(USA) Dont Bug Me Baby (Kayf Tara)
1050[7]

Throckley *John Davies* 97b
4 b g Passing Glance Porcelain (IRE) (Peintre Celebre (USA))
1378[2] 1555[6] 2650[5]

Throthethatch (IRE) *Lucinda Russell* 100h 120c
6 b g Beneficial Castletownroche (IRE) (Saddlers' Hall (IRE))
(286) (2339) 2753[5] (3362) ◆ 3794[4] 4247[4] 4582[2]

Thunder And Roses (IRE) *Ms Sandra Hughes* 114h 150c
7 bb g Presenting Glen Empress (IRE) (Lancastrian)
2899[P] 3715a[10] 4260a[5] 5005a[P]

Thundering Home *Richard Mitchell* 107h
8 gr g Storming Home Citrine Spirit (IRE) (Soviet Star (USA))
1325[P] 2445[4] 3708[P] 4096[7] 4229[5] 4541[5] 4856[5] 4922[8] 5483[3]

Thunder Sheik (IRE) *Nigel Twiston-Davies* 133h 98c
7 b g Green Tune(USA) Realy Queen (USA) (Thunder Gulch (USA))
(2244) 2831[6] 4362[7] (4913) (5074) 5279[P]

Thunder Zone *Gordon Elliott* 137h
4 gr g Shamardal(USA) Mussoorie (FR) (Linamix (FR))
94a[3]

Thymeandthymeagain *Philip Thomas* 67h
6 b m Alflora(IRE) Four Thyme (Idiots Delight)
171[6] 528[7] 1384[P] **5384[P]**

Thyne For Gold (IRE) *Donald McCain* 97h
4 b g Robin Des Pres(FR) My Name's Not Bin (IRE) (Good Thyne (USA))
2126[13] 3105[9] 3590[3] 3835[10] 4183[5] 5397[6]

Thyne River (IRE) *Robert Stephens* 59b
5 b m Indian River(FR) Thyne Square (IRE) (Good Thyne (USA))
526[5]

Thywillbedone (IRE) *Paul Hennessy* 103h
3 b f Holy Roman Emperor(IRE) Spare The Air (IRE) (Trans Island)
2813a[5]

Ticinese *Heather Main* 86h
5 b g Lucarno(USA) Maidwell (Broadsword (USA))
397[P]

Tickanrun (IRE) *Chris Grant* 93h
5 gr g Tikkanen(USA) Dusty Lane (IRE) (Electric)
145[5] 1886[8] 2066[11] 2422[3] 2751[5] 3503[7] 3684[2] 4421[6] 5203[2]

Tickatack (IRE) *Graeme McPherson* 74h 74c
10 gr g Tikkanen(USA) Theflyingcannister (IRE) (Little Bighorn)
4387[5]

Tickenwolf (IRE) *George Moore* 112h
5 gr g Tikkanen(USA) Emma's Choice (IRE) (Indian Danehill (IRE))
132[3] (481) 839[6] 2025[2] 2704[4] 3400[P]

Tickity Bleue *Alan King* 106h
7 gr m Tikkanen(USA) Cerise Bleue (FR) (Port Lyautey (FR))
2956[3]

Tidal Dance (IRE) *Venetia Williams* 130h 76c
8 b g Craigsteel Musical Waves (IRE) (Orchestra)
2905[U] 3348[7] 3823[P] 4342[P]

Tidal Way (IRE) *Charlie Longsdon* 107h 74c
6 gr g Red Clubs(IRE) Taatof (IRE) (Lahib (USA))
261[8]

Tidestream *Tim Vaughan* 104h
5 b g Galileo(IRE) Sweet Stream (ITY) (Shantou (USA))
2085[5] 3374[7] 4455[9] 5433[7]

Tiermore (IRE) *Ian Cobb* 91c
11 br g Bob's Return(IRE) Billmar (Kambalda)
296[P]

Tiger D'Oust (FR) *Chris Down* 53h
6 b g Tiger Groom Boleene (FR) (Funny Baby (FR))
976[P] 1237[P] 1823[7] 1951[P]

Tiger Feat *Ali Stronge* 87h
5 b g Tiger Hill(IRE) Hannah's Dream (IRE) (King's Best (USA))
224[4] 1084[10] **1243[P]**

Tiger Mountain (IRE) *Malcolm Jefferson* 91b
4 b g Mountain High(IRE) Our Trick (IRE) (Flemensfirth (USA))
5014[5]

Tiger O'Toole (IRE) *Henry Oliver* 118h 118c
10 gr g King's Theatre(IRE) Memsahib Ofesteem (Neltino)
356[7] 4482[P]

Tiger Rag (FR) *J W Tudor* 44h 87c
7 ch g Dano-Mast New Illusion (FR) (Solid Illusion (USA))
5467[8]

Tiger Roll (IRE) *Gordon Elliott* 139h
5 b g Authorized(IRE) Swiss Roll (IRE) (Entrepreneur)
71a[4] 5213[14]

Tigers Rock *Noel Williams*
4 b m Tiger Hill(IRE) Alexandra S (IRE) (Sadler's Wells (USA))
5187[7]

Tiger Twenty Two *Brian Rothwell* 115h
4 b g Authorized(IRE) Collette's Choice (Royal Applause)
620[2] ◆ 912[3] ◆ 1041[F] 1459[8] 1660[5]

Tigris River (IRE) *A P O'Brien* 138h
4 b g Montjeu(IRE) Hula Angel (USA) (Woodman (USA))
3650a[4]

Tijori (IRE) *Bernard Llewellyn* 114h
7 b g Kyllachy Polish Belle (Polish Precedent (USA))
1354[3] 1700[2] 1827[3] 2150[S] 2858[3] 3078[8] 4448[6] 4822[P]

Tikkandemickey (IRE) *Raymond Shiels* 115h 125c
9 gr g Tikkanen(USA) Miss Vikki (IRE) (Needle Gun (IRE))
825 **(300) 483[U] 2030[7] (2477) 2934[3] 3936[3] 4286[4] 4549[2] 4836[3] 5259[5]**

Tikkapick (IRE) *Colin Tizzard* 95h 98c
5 b g Tikkanen(USA) Takeanotherpick (IRE) (Winged Love (IRE))
240[11] **2582[F] 3746[6] 4255[F] ◆** 4454[2] 4783[4] 5355[3]

Tikketoride *Peter Pritchard* 51b
7 gr g Tikkanen(USA) Safe Arrival (USA) (Shadeed (USA))
460[U] 647[U] 877[P] 1011[P] 1599[11]

Tikkskinned (IRE) *Benjamin Arthey* 20b
4 b m Tikkanen(USA) Bucks Ploy (IRE) (Deploy)
4052[P]

Tilinisi (IRE) *Phil Middleton* 99h
5 b m Kalanisi(IRE) Montanara (IRE) (Montelimar (USA))
753[2] ◆ (970) 1057[3] 1518[5] 1781[3] 1912[3] 2256[6] 2515[P]

Tiliver (FR) *Alan Fleming* 111h
3 b g Muhaymin(USA) Springtale (FR) (Panis (USA))
2813a[4]

Tilstarr (IRE) *Roger Teal* 75h
5 b m Shamardal(USA) Vampire Queen (IRE) (General Monash (USA))
2614[5] 3130[14]

Tilsworth Phyllis *J R Jenkins* 40b
3 b f Schiaparelli(GER) Subtle One (IRE) (Polish Patriot (USA))
4228[6]

Time And Again (FR) *Tim Vaughan* 106h
5 b g Sassanian(USA) Petillante Royale (FR) (Vertical Speed (FR))
447[2] 680[5]

Time For Champers (IRE) *Nikki Evans* 87h
5 b m Robin Des Champs(FR) Someone Told Me (IRE) (Saddlers' Hall (IRE))
4439[P] 5333[P]

Timeforfirth (IRE) *Jennie Candlish* 22h
5 b m Flemensfirth(USA) Don't Be Upset (IRE) (Exit To Nowhere (USA))
2476[4] 3110[9]

Time Is Money *Emma Lavelle* 90h
6 b m Presenting No More Money (Alflora (IRE))
(271) 831[4] 1806[4]

Time Is Tickin *Diana Grissell* 84h 104c
9 b g Alflora(IRE) Miss Chinchilla (Perpendicular)
292[2] 600[5] 1353[3] 1487[P] 1592[6] 2254[4]

Time On Your Hands (IRE) *Tim Vaughan*
5 b g Beneficial Zalda (Zilzal (USA))
56[P]

Times Of Trouble *Fiona Shaw* 59b
5 b g Tobougg(IRE) Let It Be (Entrepreneur)
2991[10]

Time Wise *Richard Phillips* 90b
5 b m Kayf Tara Ceoperk (IRE) (Executive Perk)
4350[7] 4967[6]

Timing'severything (IRE) *P Twomey* 122h
4 b g Court Cave(IRE) Glen Eile (IRE) (Jurado (USA))
(11a)

Timon's Tara *Robin Dickin* 113h
6 br m Kayf Tara Princess Timon (Terimon)
111[6] 591[6] 679[7] 2452[5] 2725[5] 3065[3] 3377[3] (3930) 4186[2] 5094[5] 5296[5]

Tinaka (FR) *G Lassaussaye*
4 b m
5499a[8]

Tinctoria *Adrian Wintle* 20h
5 b m Oratorio(IRE) Blue Indigo (FR) (Pistolet Bleu (IRE))
755[5]

Tindaro (FR) *Paul Webber* 124h 140c
8 gr g Kingsalsa(USA) Star's Mixa (FR) (Linamix (FR))
915[2] 1268[4]

Tinelyra (IRE) *Fergal O'Brien* 85h 81c
9 b g Mr Combustible(IRE) Ladyogan (IRE) (Torus)
18[6] 2811[5] 3131[P] 3468[4] 4879[7] 5435[7]

Tingo In The Tale (IRE) *David Arbuthnot* 113h
6 b g Oratorio(IRE) Sunlit Skies (Selkirk (USA))
2006[6]

Tinkers Hill Tommy (IRE) *Tom Lacey* 75h
4 b g King's Theatre(IRE) Satco Street (IRE) (Satco (FR))
1246[6] 1447[6]

Tinker Time (IRE) *Bob Buckler* 123h 137c
7 b g Turtle Island(IRE) Gypsys Girl (IRE) (Husyan (USA))
2261[P] (2853) 4101[7]

Tinseltown *Harriet Bethell* 102h 47c
9 b g Sadler's Wells(USA) Peony (Lion Cavern (USA))
507[8] 678[2] 1272[6] 4553[3]

Tin Soldier (FR) *M Seror* 128h
4 b g Soldier Of Fortune(IRE) Everlast (FR) (Anabaa (USA))
665a[8]

Tinted Rose *Charlie Longsdon* 88b
3 ch f Black Sam Bellamy(IRE) Miniature Rose (Anshan)
4894[6] 5443[3]

Tiny Dancer (IRE) *Chris Grant* 97h 102c
7 b g Darsi(FR) Taipans Girl (IRE) (Taipan (IRE))
2173[U] 2848[4] ◆ 3243[4] 3727[6] 3937[7] 4706[2] ◆

Tiot Cas (FR) *P Chemin* 96h 132c
8 b g Dark Moondancer Legende Sacree (FR) (Hawker's News (IRE))
664a[F]

Tipperairy (IRE) *Dan Skelton* 99h
4 b g Flemensfirth(USA) Bambootcha (IRE) (Saddlers' Hall (IRE))
2636[5] 3839[10] 4182[3] 4382[8]

Tippmanboy (IRE) *Dr Richard Newland* 127h
5 b g Beneficial Ballys Baby (IRE) (Bob Back (USA))
2417[2] 2769[2] 3306[2] 3608[F]

Tipsy Dara (IRE) *N W Alexander* 57h 105c
11 gr m Dushyantor(USA) Tara The Grey (IRE) (Supreme Leader)
3341[P] 3937[3] 4288[2] 4571[4]

Tipsy Gypsy (IRE) *Nick Gifford* 96h 77c
8 b g Milan Montanara (IRE) (Montelimar (USA))
782[7] 1422[7]

Tiquer (FR) *Alan Jones* 14h 103c
7 b g Equerry(USA) Tirenna (FR) (Sleeping Car (FR))
623[4] 3380[4]

Tiradia (FR) *J R Jenkins* 107h
8 bb g Without Connexion(IRE) Jimanji (FR) (Kadalko (FR))
1421[6] 1508[5] 1591[7] 1770[2] 2218[3] 2413[3] 3223[6] 5374[3]

Tir Dubh (IRE) *Robert Stephens* 106h
6 br m Sandmason Turbine Hill (IRE) (Hubbly Bubbly (USA))
460[2] 1011[4] 1264[4] 1490[F] 1547[7] 1694[2]

Tisfreetdream (IRE) *Peter Pritchard* 81h 70c
14 b g Oscar(IRE) Gayley Gale (IRE) (Strong Gale)
530[4] 757[P] 2693[5] 2858[7] 3771[14] 3946[P]

Tish Hall (IRE) *S R B Crawford* 65h
5 b m Desert King(IRE) Sultana (GER) (Law Society (USA))
881[9] 960[8] 1499[7] 2292[5]

Titans Approach (IRE) *Graeme McPherson* 98h 97c
6 b g High Chaparral(IRE) Armelles Approach (IRE) (Definite Article)
89[4] 2174[2] 2520[U] **2930[4] 4859[F]**

Titch Strider (IRE) *John Panvert* 104h
10 b m Milan Just Little (Mtoto)
65[F] 265[3] (597) 1350[2] 1490[5] 1841[6] 2087[6] 2349[6] 3283[7] 4438[8] 5033[4] ◆ 5355[9]

Titian Boy (IRE) *N W Alexander* 76h
6 ch g Spadoun(FR) Leodotcom (IRE) (Safety Catch (USA))
2428[5] 3667[9] 4163[2] 4547[6] 5199[P]

Tito Dela Barriere (FR) *E Lecoiffier* 119h 134c
8 b g April Night(FR) Road Movie (FR) (Exit To Nowhere (USA))
2822a[4]

Tjongejonge (FR) *Charlie Longsdon* 119h
4 b g Blue Bresil(FR) Vavea (FR) (Saint Des Saints (FR))
2485[P] 2886[7] 5043[2] 5396[7]

Toarmandowithlove (IRE) *Susan Corbett* 87h
7 ch m Choisir(AUS) Deadly Buzz (IRE) (Darshaan)
1627[6] 1854[P] 2294[5] 2706[7] 3307[6] 3684[5] 4110[U] 4289[3] 4547[2] 4796[3] 5367[2] ◆

Toast And Jam (IRE) *Claire Dyson* 74h 77c
6 b g Clerkenwell(USA) Summittotalkabout (IRE) (Lahib (USA))
55[4] 364[5] 537[7] 704[7] **934[6] 1079[6] 2735[U]** 3771[15] 4318[U] 4504[6] 4747[7] **4980[U] 5377[4]**

Tobacco Road (IRE) *Tim Vaughan* 87h
5 b g Westerner Virginias Best (King's Best (USA))
1979[6]

Tobefair *Debra Hamer* 117h
5 bb g Central Park(IRE) Nan (Buckley)
(646) (878) (1699) ◆

To Begin *Charlie Mann* 107h 108c
4 b g Tobougg(IRE) Sagina (Shernazar)
61[6] (401) 671[12] 930[5] 1260[9] 1794[4] **2327[2] 2692[5] 5417[3]**

Toboggan's Gift *Ann Duffield* 49h
3 b f Major Cadeaux Toboggan Lady (Tobougg (IRE))
1177[6] 2718[P]

Tobouggaloo *Stuart Kittow* 119b
4 ch m Tobougg(IRE) Let Alone (Warning)
2486[8]

Toby Lerone (IRE) *Dan Skelton* 122h 138c
8 b g Old Vic Dawn's Double (IRE) (King's Ride)
(2299) **2643[P]** 3126[4] **4589[2] (5154)** 5264[P]

Tocororo (IRE) *Gordon Elliott* 119h
3 b f Teofilo(IRE) Firecrest (IRE) (Darshaan)
5001a[4]

Today Please (IRE) *Jonjo O'Neill* 91h
5 b g Westerner Casiana (GER) (Acatenango (GER))
108[P] 529[12]

Toe To Toe (IRE) *John Flint* 83h 73c
7 br g Presenting Tavildara (IRE) (Kahyasi)
30[7] 537[3] **806[P]** 937[6] **1133[3] 1548[4] 2124[3]**

Tokyo Brown (USA) *James Moffatt* 89h
6 b g Marquetry(USA) Miasma (USA) (Lear Fan (USA))
131[3] 468[8] 837[9] 1030[5] 1065[4] 1399[5] 1414[4] 2322[10]

Tokyo Javilex (FR) *Nigel Hawke* 111h 115c
8 b g Sleeping Car(FR) Etoile Du Lion (FR) (New Target)
1085[6] 1273[3] 1375[4] 1598[3] (1756) 1890[2] (1961) (2135) 2223[4] 2732[3] 4543[7] 4860[P] 5183[3] 5466[4]

Toledo Gold (IRE) *Maurice Barnes* 104h 126c
9 ch g Needwood Blade Eman's Joy (Lion Cavern (USA))
(848) 1070[4] 1553[5]

Tolethorpe *Harry Whittington* 114b
4 ch g Halling(USA) Tcherina (IRE) (Danehill Dancer (IRE))
(4508)

Tolkeins Tango (IRE) *Victor Dartnall* 107h 128c
7 ch g Beneficial Aule (FR) (Vaguely Pleasant (FR))
2568[3] 3123[P] 4545[P]

Tomahawk Wood *Donald Whillans* 90h
6 ch g Courteous Meda's Song (Master Willie)
2212[8] 2937[P] 3474[8] 4047[6] (5199)

Tom Bach (IRE) *Hywel Evans* 74c
11 ch g Bach(IRE) Fiovefontaine (IRE) (Lafontaine I (USA))
438[P] 771[P] 1850[4] 2366[5] 3977[P] 4823[P]

Tombstone (IRE) *Gordon Elliott* 150h
5 ch g Robin Des Champs(FR) Connaught Hall (IRE) (Un Desperado (FR))
3294a[2] 4004a[2] 4695[4]

Tomcat De Kerser (FR) *Patrice Quinton*
8 b g Kapgarde(FR) Riuscita (FR) (Vacarme (USA))
1672a[P]

Tom Hall *Neil King* 51h
5 b g Pastoral Pursuits Villarosi (IRE) (Rossini (USA))
3021[17] 3590[P]

Tomkevi (FR) *Rebecca Menzies* 121h 115c
4 b g Khalkevi(IRE) Tamsna (FR) (Smadoun (FR))
2425[7] 2802[4] (3367) (3804)

Tom Lamb *Jonjo O'Neill* 106b
5 ch g Central Park(IRE) Lucinda Lamb (Kayf Tara)
1518[P]

Tommy Dylon (IRE) *Martin Todhunter*
5 b g Dylan Thomas(IRE) Love Of The Game (IRE) (Croco Rouge (IRE))
2474[7]

Tommy Rapper (IRE) *Dan Skelton* 117b
4 b g Milan Supreme Evening (IRE) (Supreme Leader)
2842[2] ◆ 4827[2]

Tommy Silver (FR) *Paul Nicholls* 138h
3 b g Silver Cross(FR) Sainte Mante (FR) (Saint Des Saints (FR))
3347[2] ◆ (4012) ◆ 4764[7] 5491[3] ◆

Tommysteel (IRE) *Victor Thompson*
10 br g Craigsteel Sarahs Music (IRE) (Orchestra)
5370[P]

Tommy The Rascal *Jennie Candlish* 77h
5 b g Multiplex Tina Gee (Orchestra)
2804[5] 3130[11] 3239[P] 4318[P] 4862[6]

Tomnbill (IRE) *Paul Henderson* 84b
6 b g Soviet Star(USA) Rocksham (IRE) (Bluebird (USA))
271[7] 1050[5]

Tom Neary (IRE) *Robert Walford* 109h 130c
8 b g Atraf La Fandango (IRE) (Taufan (USA))
2459[F] 2990[7] 4363[6]

Tomngerry (IRE) *Brian Ellison* 134h
5 b g Craigsteel Lady Vic (IRE) (Old Vic)
(3245) (3593) (3997) (4368) 5194[P]

Tomorrow's Legend *Patrick Holmes* 93h 122c
5 b g Midnight Legend Colvada (North Col (IRE))
1887[4] 2339[2] 2707[2] 3103[6] (4816) ◆ 5447[2]

Tompatpeg (IRE) *David Phelan* 86c
8 b g Luso River Grove (IRE) (Over The River (FR))
298[P] 488[P]

Tom's Article (IRE) *Gordon Elliott* 112h
6 b g Definite Article Carrownisky Lass (IRE) (Saddlers' Hall (IRE))
1068[P]

Tomsk (FR) *Tim Vaughan* 77h
5 ch g Priolo(USA) Kauto Relstar (FR) (Art Bleu I)
396[5] 2263[P] 3219[P] 5441[P]

Tonganui (IRE) *Harry Fry* 86b
4 ch g Stowaway Murrosie (IRE) (Anshan)
67[8] 5143[6]

Tongie (IRE) *P A Fahy* 120h
5 b g Beneficial Montagues Lady (IRE) (Montelimar (USA))
3539a[5]

Tonto's Spirit *Kenneth Slack*
3 b g Authorized(IRE) Desert Royalty (IRE) (Alhaarth (IRE))
5009[P]

Tony (IRE) *Ken Wingrove* 50c
8 ch g High Roller(IRE) Plucky Hart (IRE) (Taipan (IRE))
697[7] 808[U] 965[3]

Tony Star (FR) *Mickey Bowen* 118h 120c
8 b g Lone Bid(FR) Effet De Star (FR) (Grand Tresor (FR))
4424[5] 5166[2] ◆

Tonythetarmacker (IRE) *Ali Stronge* 37b
4 b g Westerner Dianeme (Primo Dominie)
2549[10] 4102[14]

Too Cool To Fool (IRE) *Jim Goldie* 103h 117c
12 b g Bob Back(USA) Mandysway (IRE) (Mandalus)
2104[4] 2429[11] 3441[6] 4166[P] 4406[2] 4584[4]

Too Far Gone (IRE) *Alan King* 70h
4 br g Jeremy(USA) Rockahoolababy (IRE) (Kalanisi (IRE))
4103[11] 4790[15] 5469[11]

Toohighforme (IRE) *Nick Gifford* 69h 74c
6 b g Mountain High(IRE) Summertime Girl (IRE) (Glacial Storm (USA))
100[6] 600[P] 2303[P] (2953) 3214[P] 5480[P]

Toola Boola *George Moore* 88h
5 b m Tobougg(IRE) Forsythia (Most Welcome)
34[9] 516[5] 1461[4] 1920[8] (2148)

Too Many Chiefs (IRE) *Sharon Watt* 104h
4 br g Indian River(FR) Wahiba Hall (IRE) (Saddlers' Hall (IRE))
4284[4] 4567[5] (4742) 5335[P]

Too Much Too Soon (IRE) *Paul Webber* 112h 107c
6 b g Craigsteel Zara Rose (IRE) (Zaffaran (USA))
2412[U] 2645[5] 3134[7] 3631[7]

Toon River (IRE) *Miss Mary Louise Hallahan* 91h 147c
10 b g Witness Box(USA) Melody Thyne (IRE) (Good Thyne (USA))
95a[U] 4949a[2]

Too Scoops (IRE) *Richard Woollacott* 117h 122c
8 ch g Alderbrook Accordion To Bob (IRE) (Accordion)
162[P] 332[4] 512[4] 1577[5] 2990[6] 3709[P] 4453[3] 5142[2] 5379[5]

Toosey *Tom Symonds* 82b
4 b g Lucarno(USA) Quiz Night (Kayf Tara)
4308[6] 5188[5]

Too Trigger Happy *Dr Jeremy Naylor* 80b
6 b m Double Trigger(IRE) Hilarious (IRE) (Petorius (IRE))
893[P]

Toowoomba (IRE) *Philip Hobbs* 108h 123c
7 b g Milan Lillies Bordello (IRE) (Danehill Dancer (IRE))
2568[4] (2994) 3445[9] 3706[6] 4251[6] 4842[5]

Topamichi *Mark H Tompkins*
5 b g Beat Hollow Topatori (IRE) (Topanoora)
5115[8]

Top And Drop *Venetia Williams* 84h
4 b m Kayf Tara Ismene (FR) (Bad Conduct (USA))
3522[7] 4157[4] 4598[4] 5161[3]

Topaze Collonges (FR) *Mrs Emma Clark* 83h 109c
8 gr g Dom Alco(FR) Flicka Collonges (FR) (Trebrook (FR))
151[3]

Top Benefit (IRE) *Richard Harper* 71h 67c
13 gr g Beneficial Cottage Lass (IRE) (Roselier (FR))
44[6] 1813[P] 2315[P]

Top Billing *Nicky Richards* 136h 130c
6 br g Monsun(GER) La Gandilie (FR) (Highest Honor (FR))
(2767) ◆ 3336[2] 4246[6] 4905[3] 5323[P]

Top Cat Dj (IRE) *Chris Grant* 74h 90c
7 ch g St Jovite(USA) Lady Coldunell (Deploy)
133[U] 453[5] 1853[P] 2147[6] 2771[5] 3427[2] 3679[6] 5125[9]

Top Cat Henry (IRE) *Dr Richard Newland* 118h 133c
7 b g Dr Massini(IRE) Bells Chance (IRE) (Needle Gun (IRE))
(1755) 1976[2] 2057[3] 2902[6] 3235[P] 4443[P] (4866) 5193[6]

Top Chief *Anthony Honeyball* 102h 100c
7 b g Doyen(IRE) For More (FR) (Sanglamore (USA))
1004[2] 1118[5] 1380[5] 1487[2]

Top Dancer (FR) *Warren Greatrex* 109h 122c
8 b g Dark Moondancer Latitude (FR) (Kadalko (FR))
92a[9] 439[2] 2724[6]

Top Gamble (IRE) *Kerry Lee* 130h 165c
7 ch g Presenting Zeferina (IRE) (Sadler's Wells (USA))
1869[P] 2761[3] 3406[3] ◆ (4114) (5023a)

Topissime (FR) *G Macaire*
2 b g Khalkevi(IRE) Lhotse (FR) (Sarhoob (USA))
5498a[3]

Top Man Marty (IRE) *Sarah Humphrey* 107h
6 b g Westerner Tribal Princess (IRE) (Namaqualand (USA))
3045[6] 3422[6]

Top Man Tim (IRE) *M O Cullinane* 47h
8 b g Flemensfirth(USA) Wont Change (IRE) (Luso)
4557[6]

Top Notch (FR) *Nicky Henderson* 162h
4 b g Poliglote Topira (FR) (Pistolet Bleu (IRE))
2640[2] 2789[2] ◆ 3408[5] (4204) 4698[5]

Top Of The Glas (IRE) *Brian Ellison* 119h
4 gr g Verglas(IRE) Fury Dance (USA) (Cryptoclearance (USA))
5414[2]

Top Of The Range (IRE) *Paul Morgan* 99b
8 br g Presenting Brenny's Pearl (IRE) (Good Thyne (USA))
5348[P]

Top Of The Town (IRE) *C Byrnes* 114h
7 b g Craigsteel Hil Rhapsody (Anshan)
1184a[5]

Topolski (IRE) *David Arbuthnot* 105h
9 b g Peintre Celebre(USA) Witching Hour (IRE) (Alzao (USA))
625[5]

Topper Thornton (IRE) *C A McBratney* 114h 128c
6 ch g Double Eclipse(IRE) Gailybay Ellen (IRE) (Supreme Leader)
(661) 886[5] 5411[4]

Top Priority (FR) *Jonjo O'Neill* 99h
4 b g Solon(GER) Firstote (FR) (Tot Ou Tard (IRE))
(366) 3022[8] 4323[7] 5243[4]

Top Set (IRE) *Richard Phillips* 86h
5 ch g Tamayuz Pray (IRE) (Priolo (USA))
1998[F] 2238[7] 3021[10] 3221[13] 4885[9]

Top Spin (IRE) *Jonjo O'Neill* 123h
8 bb g Cape Cross(IRE) Beguine (USA) (Green Dancer (USA))
1184a[15] 1265[2] 1721[3] 1964[6]

Toptempo *Ali Stronge* 83h
6 ch m Halling(USA) Topatoo (Bahamian Bounty)
1700[4] 1975[3] 2218[6] 2550[3]

Topthorn *Martin Bosley* 84b 65c
9 gr g Silver Patriarch(IRE) Miss Traxdata (Absalom)
175[P] 2859[P] 3225[5] 3661[4] 4029[4] 4850[6] 5482[5]

Top Wood (FR) *David Pipe* 128h 145c
8 ch g Kotky Bleu(FR) Heure Bleu (FR) (Grand Tresor (FR))
2907[2] 3583[4] 3887[5] (4444) 4735[F] 5085[7] 5327[F]

Toquickly *Harriet Graham* 77b
3 b f Tobougg(IRE) Miss Quickly (IRE) (Anshan)
2195[5] 4908[4]

Torero *Gary Moore* 92h
6 b g Hernando(FR) After You (Pursuit Of Love)
(3089) 3219[3] 3665[2] 4161[3]

Torhousemuir *Sam Thomas* 92b
4 b g Sagamix(FR) Royal Musical (Royal Abjar (USA))
3226[5]

Tornade Precieuse (FR) *Mme M Desvaux* 118h 131c
8 b m Network(GER) Kerfournoise (FR) (Funny Baby (FR))
375a[5]

Tornado In Milan (IRE) *Evan Williams* 137h 131c
9 b g Milan Julika (GER) (Nebos (GER))
2336[2] 2691[3] 3584[8] (3748) 4294[3] (4452) 4617[2] 5156[2]

Torn Asunder (IRE) *Gary Hanmer* 131h 122c
8 b g Presenting Shuil Mavourneen (IRE) (Welsh Term)
(536)

Torran Sound *Miss E Rodney*
8 b g Tobougg(IRE) Velvet Waters (Unfuwain (USA))
493[7] 5399[F]

Tortueuse (IRE) *Dermot Anthony McLoughlin* 98h
8 b m Indian Danehill(IRE) Taffety (Last Tycoon)
1165[6]

Total Assets *Simon Waugh* 92h 117c
7 b m Alflora(IRE) Maid Equal (Pragmatic)
1856[10] 2029[U] 2424[3] 2894[2] ◆ (3341) 3934[P] 4549[P]

Totalize *Brian Ellison* 136h
6 b g Authorized(IRE) You Too (Monsun (GER))
2512[5] 4070[4] 5363a[4]

Total Submission *John Groucott* 121h 121c
10 gr g Kayf Tara Ardentinny (Ardross)
4482[5] 5078[4]

Toubaloo (IRE) *Andrew Lee* 115h 137c
7 b g Shantou(USA) Stone Baloo (IRE) (Rising)
4949a[F]

Touch A Million (IRE) *Gordon Elliott* 100b
5 b g Green Tune(USA) Janistra (USA) (Grand Slam (USA))
887[2]

Touch Back (IRE) *Chris Bealby* 130h 108c
9 b g Shantou(USA) Back Log (IRE) (Bob Back (USA))
185[5] 2405[3] 2962[2] 3238[5] 4328[6] (4537) ◆ (4794) 5141[5]

Touch Kick (IRE) *Paul Nicholls* 111b
4 b g Presenting Bay Pearl (FR) (Broadway Flyer (USA))
(5151)

Touch Of Steel (IRE) *James Ewart* 102h
6 b g Craigsteel Tourmaline Girl (IRE) (Toulon)
481[8] 727[8] 843[9] (1552) (1779) 2102[3] (2751) 3474[6]

Tour D'Argent (FR) *Donald McCain* 120h 119c
8 b g Martaline Keep Well (FR) (Agent Bleu (FR))
1008[4] 1169[7] 1330[3]

Tour Des Champs (FR) *Nigel Twiston-Davies* 129h 146c
8 bb g Robin Des Champs(FR) Massada I (FR) (Kashtan (FR))
(2907) 3518[P] 3918[4] 4267[4] (4935) 5092[4] 5327[P]

Tour De Ville (IRE) *Seamus Durack* 95h
5 b g Beneficial Galant Tour (IRE) (Riberetto)
682[5] 1050[2] (1345) 2375[6] 4888[7] 5469[7]

Toutancarmont (FR) *Mme I Pacault* 105h 140c
8 gr g Al Namix(FR) Furie De Carmont (FR) (Carmont (FR))
313a[F]

Toviere (IRE) *Oliver Sherwood* 117h
4 ch g Presenting Aventia (IRE) (Bob Back (USA))
67[2] 2250[4]

Towerburn (IRE) *Alison Hamilton* 100h
6 b g Cloudings(IRE) Lady Newmill (IRE) (Taipan (IRE))
79[2] 2066[7] 3680[11] 4404[7] 4835[P]

Towering (IRE) *Nicky Henderson* 125h
6 b g Catcher In The Rye(IRE) Bobs Article (IRE) (Definite Article)
(61) 509[2] (877) 1262[4] (2064) 2513[5] 5396[6]

Tower Of Allen (IRE) *Nicky Henderson* 55b
4 b g Beneficial Baile An Droichid (IRE) (King's Ride)
2729[8] 4790[P]

Town Mouse *Neil King* 103h 124c
5 ch g Sakhee(USA) Megdale (IRE) (Waajib (IRE))
241[3] 492[2] 570[F] 936[5] 1043[2] 1296[2] 1755[3] 2001[5] 3036[F] 5159[8] 5394[P]

Townshend (GER) *W P Mullins* 133h
4 b g Lord Of England(GER) Trikolore (GER) (Konigsstuhl (GER))
4786[12] (5444)

Trackmate *James Evans* 103b
9 b g Muhtarram(USA) Cruz Santa (Lord Bud)
3336[P]

Trader Jack *David Flood* 106h
6 b g Trade Fair Azeema (IRE) (Averti (IRE))
1081[3]

Tradewinds (FR) *Lucinda Russell* 127h
7 b g Kapgarde(FR) Royale Floriane (FR) (Cyborg (FR))
(1635) 2062[3] 4246[7] 4794[3] 5296[7]

Trafalgar (FR) *Sarah-Jayne Davies* 90h 99c
8 b g Laveron Dzaoudzie (FR) (El Badr)
282[5] 4446[P] 4651[9] 5075[3]

Traffic Fluide (FR) *Gary Moore* 165c
5 b g Astarabad(USA) Petale Rouge (FR) (Bonnet Rouge (FR))
3734[3]

Trafficker (IRE) *Dr Richard Newland* 109h 115c
8 b g Flemensfirth(USA) Sulawesi (IRE) (In The Wings)
(58) 757[3] 873[6]

Trakeur (FR) *Simon Hodgson* 87h 72c
8 b g Myrakalu(FR) Nataly (FR) (Ragmar (FR))
168[4] 674[6] 1085[4] 1235[P] 1510[5] 1952[4]

Trans Express (IRE) *Sue Gardner* 98h
5 br g Trans Island Hazel Fastrack (Shambo)
2126[5] 2250[6] *2702*[5] 2904[P] 3135[5] 3411[7] 3710[5] ◆ 4138[2]

Transfer *Tom Symonds* 86h
10 br g Trans Island Sankaty Light (USA) (Summer Squall (USA))
966[9]

Transient Bay (IRE) *Philip Kirby* 107h
5 b g Trans Island Boarding Pass (IRE) (Accordion)
(2964) 3140[4] (3791) ◆ 4184[4] (4581) 5100[2]

Trapper Peak (IRE) *Alexandra Dunn* 103h 110c
6 b g Westerner Banningham Blaze (Averti (IRE))
261[7] 1906[3] 2434[5] 2749[P] 3417[2] 4073[4] 4386[3] 4932[P] (5310)

Travertine (IRE) *Alan King* 109h
5 b g Danehill Dancer(IRE) Mer De Corail (IRE) (Sadler's Wells (USA))
3484[2] 3724[P]

Treacy Hotels Boy (IRE) *Paul Henderson* 103h 99c
8 br g Overbury(IRE) Bridgehotel Rose (IRE) (Synefos (USA))
1424[6] 1674[4] ◆ 2140[F] 2315[2] 2601[2] 5307[P]

Treaty Girl (IRE) *Ben Pauling* 124h
4 b m Milan Back To Cloghoge (IRE) (Bob Back (USA))
3825[P] (4323) (4777) 5282[8]

Treat Yourself (IRE) *A L T Moore* 121h 126c
8 b g Beat Hollow Cartesian (Shirley Heights)
47a[5]

Tregaro (FR) *Mike Sowersby* 87h 111c
9 b g Phantom Breeze Touques (FR) (Tip Moss (FR))
781[5] 915[4] 1005[5] 1267[2] (1444) 1601[9] 2648[P]

Trehan Cross *Jackie Du Plessis* 58h
6 b m Bandmaster(USA) Halton Quay (Lir)
2603[9] 2870[7] 3124[7] 3746[F]

Treliver Manor (IRE) *Rose Dobbin* 85h 89c
7 b g Flemensfirth(USA) Loch Lomond (IRE) (Dry Dock)
2937[4] 3427[5] 3803[2] 3969[5] 4514[3] 4741[3] 5125[2]

Trendsetter (IRE) *John Quinn* 105h
4 b g Mastercraftsman(IRE) Fashion Trade (Dansili)
2472[S]

Tresor De Bontee (FR) *Kerry Lee* 82h 97c
8 b g Grand Seigneur(FR) Bontee (FR) (Le Pontet (FR))
2419[5] 3115[P] 3367[6] 4593[7]

Tresor De La Vie (FR) *Victor Dartnall* 59h 65c
8 gr g Epalo(GER) Joie De La Vie (FR) (Quart De Vin (FR))
1576[P] 4919[2]

Trespassers Will (IRE) *Fergal O'Brien* 108h
4 b g Scorpion(IRE) Drum Majorette (Infantry I)
1640[4] 2152[P] 3085[3] 3483[3] 3841[2] 5034[P]

Tribal Dance (IRE) *John O'Shea* 98h 91c
9 br g Flemensfirth(USA) Native Sparkle (IRE) (Be My Native (USA))
58[5] 454[3] 1155[5] 1380[4] (1757) 1850[5] 1950[4] 2434[P] 5198[7]

Trickaway (IRE) *Philip Hobbs* 100h 133c
7 b g Stowaway Rosie's Trix (IRE) (Luso)
5465[11]

Tricky (IRE) *Philip Hobbs* 107h
6 br g Indian Danehill(IRE) Amelia Island (IRE) (Supreme Leader)
160[5] 703[5] 932[5] 1324[4]

Tried And Tested (IRE) *Jonjo O'Neill* 115h
4 b g Beneficial Shean Alainn (IRE) (Le Moss)
1698[2] ◆

Trigger Point *Hughie Morrison* 87h
5 ch m Double Trigger(IRE) Flirtatious (Generous (IRE))
238[5]

Triggers Ginger *Paul Cowley* 83h 88c
10 ch m Double Trigger(IRE) New Dawn (Rakaposhi King)
2997[P] 3488[2] 4276[U]

Triggitas *Oliver Sherwood* 58h
5 b g Double Trigger(IRE) Suntas (IRE) (Riberetto)
242[7] 933[8]

Triggywinkle (FR) *Roderick Chelton* 85c
6 b m Le Triton(USA) Periwinkle (FR) (Perrault)
297[P] 4295[5] 4426[P] 5186[4] 5384[2]

Trillerin Minella (IRE) *Graeme McPherson* 105h 113c
7 b g King's Theatre(IRE) Eva Fay (IRE) (Fayruz)
358[2] 519[7] 2346[5] 2975[U] 5149[P] 5377[3] 5468[2]

Trillion Stars (FR) *E Moullec* 82h
4 b g Poliglote Triclaria (GER) (Surumu (GER))
2362a[14]

Tri Nations (UAE) *Harriet Bethell* 109h 98c
10 ch g Halling(USA) Six Nations (USA) (Danzig (USA))
588[P] 914[8] 1133[P]

Triolo D'Alene (FR) *Nicky Henderson* 100h 160c
8 ch g Epalo(GER) Joliette D'Alene (FR) (Garde Royale)
(3526) 4240[5] 5218[14]

Triopas (IRE) *Tom Lacey*
3 b g Stowaway Aine Dubh (IRE) (Bob Back (USA))
5436[U]

Triple Chief (IRE) *Chris Down* 100h 103c
4 bb g High Chaparral(IRE) Trebles (IRE) (Kenmare (FR))
1676[5] 2093[11] 2987[7] 3368[3] 3586[6] (4161) 4343[5] 4932[2]

Triple Eight (IRE) *Philip Kirby* 97h
7 b g Royal Applause Hidden Charm (IRE) (Big Shuffle (USA))
(1478) 1604[2] 1714[2] 1920[5] (2292) 2946[7]

Triumph Davis (IRE) *Micky Hammond* 100h
6 b m Flemensfirth(USA) Bodhran Davis (FR) (Cadoudal (FR))
838[6] 1329[6] 1920[10] 2148[11] 2800[5] 3161[5] 3402[2] ◆ 3503[4] 3793[7] 4421[P] 4942[4] (5203)

Triumvirate *Venetia Williams* 95h
5 b m Rail Link Strike Lightly (Rainbow Quest (USA))
3398[P] 3947[P]

Troika Steppes *Fergal O'Brien* 91h 130c
7 b g Pasternak Killerton Clover (High Season)
2435[5] (2861) 3924[3] (4427) 4977[2] 5285[4]

Trojan Star (IRE) *Kim Bailey* 99h 118c
5 b g Tikkanen(USA) Mystical Queen (IRE) (Dr Devious (IRE))
98[7] 279[3] 1518[7] 1647[11] 1769[5] 2645[2] 2859[3] 4098[2] 4487[3]

Trojan Sun *Tom Symonds* 83h 94c
9 bb g Kayf Tara Sun Dante (IRE) (Phardante (FR))
398[P]

Trooper Royal *Sue Smith* 63h
5 b g Zafeen(FR) Faithful Beauty (IRE) (Last Tycoon)
1684[7] 1929[5] 2169[11] 4863[8] 5242[7]

Tropical Bachelor (IRE) *Pippa Bickerton* 14h
9 b g Bachelor Duke(USA) Tropical Coral (IRE) (Pennekamp (USA))
328[9]

Tropical Sunshine (IRE) *Pippa Bickerton* 79h
7 b g Bachelor Duke(USA) Tropical Coral (IRE) (Pennekamp (USA))
3839[P] 4430[P] 5437[6]

Troubled (IRE) *Aytach Sadik* 109h 87c
8 b g Vinnie Roe(IRE) Tart Of Tipp (IRE) (Saddlers' Hall (IRE))
126[3] (567) 803[2] 1004[11] 1403[2] 1785[P] (Dead)

Troubled Soul (IRE) *Denis Gerard Hogan* 112h
6 ch m Definite Article Dorrha Lass (IRE) (Fourstars Allstar (USA))
1974[3]

Troubled Waters *Chris Fairhurst* 68h
6 b m Kayf Tara Air Of Affection (Air Express (IRE))
3098[6]

Trouble In Paris (IRE) *Barry Murtagh* 93h 83c
8 ch g Great Palm(USA) Ten Dollar Bill (IRE) (Accordion)
2321[2] 2786[5] 3308[3] 3679[5] 4738[3] 5010[P]

Troyan (IRE) *G Slade-Jones* 103h 58c
8 b g King's Theatre(IRE) Talk The Talk (Terimon)
773[2] 877[4] 5158[P]

Truckers First *Ian Williams* 89h
7 b m Kayf Tara Cheeky Trucker (Atraf)
4322[8] 5415[5]

Truckers Highway (IRE) *John Groucott* 88h 128c
6 b g Rudimentary(USA) Countessdee (IRE) (Arctic Lord (IRE))
1812[8] **2249[F] (2851) (2976) (3141) 3311[3] (3867) ◆ 4210[3] 4443[R]**

Truckin All Night (IRE) *Don Cantillon* 120h 110c
9 b g Snurge Bun Doite (IRE) (Old Vic)
514[7] 857[7]

Trucking Along (IRE) *S R B Crawford* 125h 89c
9 br g Zagreb(USA) Pegus Gold (Strong Gale)
850[10] 1333[5] 4165[P] **4406[5] 4582[5]**

Trueflyingcolours (IRE) *S Penny* 50c
9 b g Dushyantor(USA) Prize Lady (IRE) (Cashel Court)
534[4]

Trust Thomas *Ann Hamilton* 108h 124c
7 ch g Erhaab(USA) Yota (FR) (Galetto (FR))
2477[P] 2979[3] 3162[3] 3343[2] 3631[4] (4166) 5086[5] (5346)

Try Catch Me (IRE) *Alison Batchelor* 87h 109c
10 b g Commander Collins(IRE) Misty River (IRE) (Over The River (FR))
1136[6] **1241[2] 1353[4] 1720[6] 1894[6]** 2004[3]

Try It Sometime (IRE) *Sheila Lewis* 92h 107c
7 b g Milan Lead'Er Inn (IRE) (Supreme Leader)
2249[6] 3081[U] 3572[6] **(3864) 4265[U] 4746[2] 5240[3] 5468[4]**

Tsar Alexandre (FR) *Warren Greatrex* 123c
8 b g Robin Des Champs(FR) Bertrange (FR) (Torvay (FR))
4425[F] 5078[P]

Ttebbob (IRE) *Mrs John Harrington* 148h 151c
6 b g Milan Our Dream (IRE) (Bob Back (USA))
49a[5] **(3069a) 3271a[P] 4145a[2]**

Tudor City (IRE) *A J Martin* 104h
3 b g Yeats(IRE) She's Our Mare (IRE) (Commanche Run)
2718[4]

Tudors Treasure *Robert Stephens* 80h
4 b g Dr Massini(IRE) Rude Health (Rudimentary (USA))
4270[4] 4874[7] 5356[5]

Tuffatthetop (IRE) *Jonjo O'Neill* 55h
4 br g Kalanisi(IRE) Anshabella (IRE) (Anshan)
4463[P]

Tuffstuff *Brian Barr* 99h
7 b g Generous(IRE) Life Line (Exit To Nowhere (USA))
160[3] 669[7] 2262[P] 2841[4] 3125[F] 3665[3]

Tugboat (IRE) *G Slade-Jones* 134h 130c
7 b g Galileo(IRE) Alleluia (Caerleon (USA))
14[4] (5158) 5399[7]

Tullamore Dew (IRE) *Micky Hammond* 132h 140c
13 ch g Pistolet Bleu(IRE) Heather Point (Pollerton)
(471) 2213[6] (3057) 3448[6] 4818[7]

Tullow Tonic (IRE) *Charlie Longsdon* 92h
4 b m Beneficial Annalecky (IRE) (Bob's Return (IRE))
682[2] ◆ 1811[6] 2302[9] 2561[5] 2823[6] 3619[5]

Tully East (IRE) *Alan Fleming* 140h
5 b g Shantou(USA) Ghillie's Bay (IRE) (King's Ride)
1788a[6] 3294a[6] 4769[4]

Tullyraine (IRE) *Dean Coleman* 108h 104c
11 b g Winged Love(IRE) Struell Princess (Avocat)
3958[3] 4269[5]

Tulsa Jack (IRE) *Noel Meade* 127h 136c
6 b g Urban Ocean(FR) Jessica's Pet (IRE) (King's Ride)
(2228a) 2675a[P] 5005a[8]

Tundridge *John Spearing* 74h
6 b g Authorized(IRE) Salanka (IRE) (Persian Heights)
105[U] 745[7] 930[7] 1095[9]

Turban (FR) *W P Mullins* 141h 155c
8 b g Dom Alco(FR) Indianabelle (FR) (Useful (FR))
24a[4] 4260a[3] 5193[P]

Turbo Charged (IRE) *Bill Turner* 49b
3 b g Jeremy(USA) House Rebel (IRE) (Spartacus (IRE))
2009[7]

Turcagua (FR) *W P Mullins* 119b
5 gr g Turgeon(USA) Acancagua (FR) (Subotica (FR))
4721[15]

Turn In Grey (FR) *Louis Baudron* 130h
5 gr m Martaline Miss Cotta (USA) (Dynaformer (USA))
350a[4]

Turnover (FR) *Alan Phillips*
7 b g Turgeon(USA) Sainte Innocence (FR) (Akarad (FR))
1134[P]

Turn Over Sivola (FR) *Alan King* 120h 145c
8 b g Assessor(IRE) Notting Hill (FR) (Garde Royale)
2059[5] 3031[12] 3857[7]

Turteene (FR) *Y-M Porzier* 142h
5 gr m Turgeon(USA) Manson Teene (FR) (Mansonnien (FR))
(350a)

Turtle Cask (IRE) *Dianne Sayer* 100h
6 b g Turtle Island(IRE) Sayce (IRE) (Supreme Leader)
502[P] 2029[4] 2426[3] 2720[5] (3102) 3312[3] 4110[3] 4421[5] **5010[P]** 5198[2]

Turtleplex *Maurice Barnes* 59b
4 b m Multiplex Turtle Bay (Dr Fong (USA))
144[11] 3054[P] 3995[P]

Turtle Watch *Jim Goldie* 122h
7 b g Where Or When(IRE) Cita Verda (FR) (Take Risks (FR))
(142)

Tutchec (FR) *Chris Grant* 27h 63c
8 gr g Turgeon(USA) Pocahontas (FR) (Nikos)
3792[P] 4407[P] 5404[3]

Tweedo Paradiso (NZ) *Rose Dobbin* 88h 89c
7 br g Golan(IRE) Buzz (NZ) (Dedicated Rullah (USA))
485[5] 804[9]

Tweedys Choice (IRE) *T O M Greenwood* 92c
10 b g Atraf Annotate (Groom Dancer (USA))
472[6]

Twelve Roses *Kim Bailey* 142h 142c
7 ch g Midnight Legend Miniature Rose (Anshan)
(1900) 2481[P] 2726[P] 4359[2] 4701[5] (5117)

Twelve Strings (IRE) *Venetia Williams* 110h
6 b g Iffraaj Favoritely (USA) (Favorite Trick (USA))
177[7] 378[2]

Twenty Eight Guns *Michael Scudamore* 107h
5 b m Black Sam Bellamy(IRE) Glory Be (Gunner B)
1854[9] 2697[2] 2952[2] 3198[2] 3904[5] 4268[2] 4644[4] 5314[2]

Twentytwo's Taken (IRE) *David Pipe* 127h
7 b m King's Theatre(IRE) Persian Desert (IRE) (Persian Mews)
(5030)

Twice Lucky *Sue Smith* 80h 100c
11 b g Mtoto Foehn Gale (IRE) (Strong Gale)
486[7]

Twin Barrels *Sarah-Jayne Davies* 111h
8 ch g Double Trigger(IRE) Caballe (USA) (Opening Verse (USA))
4099[P] 4429[2]

Twinkletoes (IRE) *Mrs John Harrington* 47h
4 gr m Daylami(IRE) Cool N Calm (Arctic Lord (IRE))
9a[19]

Twinlight (FR) *W P Mullins* 143h 166c
8 b g Muhtathir Fairlight (GER) (Big Shuffle (USA))
8a[6] 2388a[P] 3092a[P] 3892a[5] 4281a[2] 5023a[P]

Twirling Magnet (IRE) *Jonjo O'Neill* 114h 138c
9 b g Imperial Ballet(IRE) Molly Maguire (IRE) (Supreme Leader)
535[4] 855[6] 2146[5] 4768[17] 5075[2] 5392[2]

Twister Klass (FR) *S Gouyette*
8 b g Assessor(IRE) Marbela (FR) (Dom Alco (FR))
(5136a)

Twister Mix *J M Ridley* 62b
4 gr g Fair Mix(IRE) Reverse Swing (Charmer (IRE))
320[17]

Twist On Ginge (IRE) *Nigel Twiston-Davies* 103b
3 b g Craigsteel Miss Top (IRE) (Tremblant)
4488[7] 5337[2]

Two B'S *Tim Easterby* 106h
4 b g Bollin Eric Bollin Nellie (Rock Hopper)
3152[10]

Two Jabs *Michael Appleby* 101b
5 b g Teofilo(IRE) Red Bravo (USA) (Red Ransom (USA))
3724[P]

Twojayslad *Ian Williams* 109h 118c
6 b g Kayf Tara Fulwell Hill (Anshan)
261[P] **(782) 2276[4]**

Two Many Words (IRE) *Bill Turner*
3 b g Thousand Words Three Days In May (Cadeaux Genereux)
3573[7]

Two Smokin Barrels *Michael Scudamore* 103h
6 b m Kayf Tara Coldabri (IRE) (Husyan (USA))
4961[2] (5347)

Twosons *Malcolm Jefferson*
5 b g Iktibas Lady Lexie (Cape Cross (IRE))
783[8]

Two Sugars *Gary Moore* 18h
7 b g Val Royal(FR) Princess Galadriel (Magic Ring (IRE))
5477[10]

Two Taffs (IRE) *Dan Skelton* 135h
5 b g Flemensfirth(USA) Richs Mermaid (IRE) (Saddlers' Hall (IRE))
2123[3] 2683[2] 3284[3] ◆ 4620[4] (5328)

Twycross Warrior *Robin Dickin* 91h
3 b g Cockney Rebel(IRE) Gaelic Roulette (IRE) (Turtle Island (IRE))
1772[9] 2629[5] 4364[10] 5387[6]

Twyford *Laura Young*
8 b g Bach(IRE) Commanche Token (IRE) (Commanche Run)
2017[F] 2601[U] 4541[P]

Tycoon Prince (IRE) *Gordon Elliott* 135h
5 b g Trans Island Downtown Train (IRE) (Glacial Storm (USA))
2385a[3] 3070a[2] 5189[P]

Typical Oscar (IRE) *Michael Blake* 102c
8 b g Oscar(IRE) Kachina (IRE) (Mandalus)
1785[5] 2402[P]

Tyre Hill (IRE) *David Dennis* 101h
6 b g Catcher In The Rye(IRE) Stay At Home (IRE) (Blueprint (IRE))
108[7]

Tyre Hill Lady *David Dennis* 102h
6 b m Midnight Legend Springbrook Girl (Alderbrook)
1910[5]

Tyrrell's Succes (FR) *C A McBratney* 107b
4 br g Forestier(FR) Irish Succes (FR) (Turgeon (USA))
(5476)

Ubak (FR) *Gary Moore* 153h 150c
7 b g Kapgarde(FR) Gesse Parade (FR) (Dress Parade)
2760[4] 3611[U] 3991[4] 4381[2] 4717[3] (5213) 5495[4]

Ubaldo Des Menhies (FR) *Jonjo O'Neill* 124h 93c
7 bb g Network(GER) Ker Marie (FR) (Esprit Du Nord (USA))
(678) 969[2] 1100[10] 1508[P] **1962[4]**

Ubaltique (FR) *Donald McCain* 135h 133c
7 b g Balko(FR) Ode Antique (FR) (Subotica (FR))
2659[P] 2979[6] 3237[3] (3742) 4167[3] (4418) 4606[U] 4964[P] 5326[5]

Ucello Conti (FR) *Gordon Elliott* 124h 149c
7 b g Martaline Gazelle Lulu (FR) (Altayan)
3073a[6] 3296a[2] 3715a[3] 5218[6]

Ueueteotl (FR) *James Ewart* 109h 125c
7 gr g Tikkanen(USA) Azturk (FR) (Baby Turk)
(76) 483[3] 2105[F] 2749[2] 3024[6] 4153[4] 4836[P]

Ugly Bug *Tony Carroll* 117h 63c
9 b g Runyon(IRE) Mutual Decision (IRE) (Supreme Leader)
210[5] 2658[2] 3158[F]

Uhlan Bute (FR) *Venetia Williams* 127h 130c
7 ch g Brier Creek(USA) Jonquiere (FR) (Trebrook (FR))
58[3] 403[P] (2434) 2592[4] 3929[5] 4443[2] 4910[F] 5473[2]

Ujagar (IRE) *Graeme McPherson* 18h
4 gr g Dalakhani(IRE) No Secrets (USA) (El Corredor (USA))
823[9]

Ulanda (IRE) *Paul John Gilligan* 32h
3 b f Le Cadre Noir(IRE) Hataana (USA) (Robellino (USA))
3418[10]

Ulck Du Lin (FR) *Paul Nicholls* 125h 147c
7 b g Sassanian(USA) Miss Fast (FR) (Prince Fast (FR))
2185[P] 3030[9] 3990[2] 4918[2] 5493[6]

Ulis De Vassy (FR) *Dan Skelton* 114h 134c
7 b g Voix Du Nord(FR) Helathou (FR) (Video Rock (FR))
(857) (936) 1112[2] 1268[F] 1344[5] 4469[4]

Ullswater (IRE) *Gordon Elliott* 102h
7 b g Singspiel(IRE) Uluwatu (IRE) (Unfuwain (USA))
692[7] 835[7] (1786)

Ulodene (FR) *P Cottin* 71h 113c
7 b m Denham Red(FR) Hulotte Du Buard (FR) (April Night (FR))
313a[F]

Ultiep (FR) *Karen McLintock* 39h
7 gr g Ragmar(FR) Naltiepy (FR) (Dom Alco (FR))
140[P]

Ultimate Dream (FR) *Jonjo O'Neill* 78h
4 b g Ultimately Lucky(IRE) Carazia (FR) (Labus (FR))
2581[9] 2860[8] 3130[10] 3840[6] 4318[4]

Ultimatum Du Roy (FR) *Alex Hales* 96h 124c
7 b g Brier Creek(USA) La Fleur Du Roy (FR) (Sleeping Car (FR))
149[2] 2668[2] 3236[7] 3818[P] 4641[2] 5247[U] 5395[7]

Ultragold (FR) *Colin Tizzard* 97h 140c
7 bb g Kapgarde(FR) Hot D'Or (FR) (Shafoun (FR))
3014[F] 3148[4] 3445[8] (4254) 4485[5] (5096) 5326[2]

Ultranet (FR) *G Chaignon* 93h 111c
7 b g Network(GER) First Union (FR) (Shafoun (FR))
374a[6]

Ulysse Des Pictons (FR) *Yannick Fouin* 124h 115c
7 b g Passing Sale(FR) Nina Des Pictons (FR) (Denham Red (FR))
437a[4]

Ulysse De Touzaine (FR) *A Le Clerc* 105c
7 b g Voix Du Nord(FR) Domitia (FR) (El Badr)
1223a[2]

Umberto D'Olivate (FR) *Robert Walford* 104h 126c
7 b g Alberto Giacometti(IRE) Komunion (FR) (Luchiroverte (IRE))
2261[3] 2887[4] 3253[4] 3706[5] 4348[8] 4612[4] 5032[2] 5265[3]

Umoristic (FR) *Matt Sheppard* 80h
7 gr g Baroud D'Honneur(FR) Canlastou (FR) (Tanlas (FR))
537[9] 811[2] 1096[5] 1299[7]

Un Ace (FR) *Kim Bailey* 145h 150c
7 b g Voix Du Nord(FR) First Ball (FR) (Beyssac (FR))
2484[4] 2901[2] ◆ 3527[7] 3844[5] 4730[8]

U Name It (IRE) *R Mike Smith* 126h
7 b g Gold Well Bypharthebest (IRE) (Phardante (FR))
2067[U] 2397[P] 2785[P] 3440[5]

Unanimite (FR) *David Pipe* 136h
4 ch g Kentucky Dynamite(USA) Dame Blanche (USA) (Cherokee Run (USA))
418[5] 2186[2] 3151[10] 3733[8] 4017[5]

Un Anjou (FR) *David Dennis* 115h 129c
7 bb g Panoramic Idee D'Estruval (FR) (Port Etienne (FR))
218[4] 402[2] 456[3] **1135[6]** 1238[7] **1327[5]**

Un Beau Roman (FR) *Paul Henderson* 121h 144c
7 bl g Roman Saddle(IRE) Koukie (FR) (Lute Antique (FR))
1186a[2] 1556a[9] 3284[9] **(3524) 3851[P] 4114[4] 4485[P] 4787[P]**

Unbuckled (IRE) *Neil King* 117h
5 b m Presenting Una Kasala (GER) (Law Society (USA))
(2421) (3022) ◆ 3506[3] 4890[2] (5155) 5282[4]

Uncle Bernie (IRE) *Sarah Hollinshead* 88h
5 gr g Aussie Rules(USA) Alwiyda (USA) (Trempolino (USA))
860[6] 1000[6]

Uncle Chizza *Sean Curran* 70b
6 b g Avonbridge Sparkling Jewel (Bijou D'Inde)
558[10] 1117[14]

Uncle Junior (IRE) *W P Mullins* 114h 148c
14 b g Saddlers' Hall(IRE) Caslain Nua (Seymour Hicks (FR))
(48a) 2471[S] 3017[P] 4719[10]

Uncle Monty (IRE) *Donald McCain* 86h 59c
6 b g Milan She's A Gamble (IRE) (Teenoso (USA))
56[3] 2768[4] 3378[P] 4391[6] **4704[4]**

Uncle Muf (USA) *Ali Stronge* 13b
5 b g Curlin(USA) Peak Maria's Way (USA) (Pyramid Peak (USA))
263[P]

Uncle Tone (IRE) *Tim Vaughan* 125h
6 b g Pelder(IRE) Daisy A Day (IRE) (Asir)
730[F] 754[5] (1011) 1136[2] ◆ 1615[P] (1806) 2088[4] 2513[16] 4492[2] 5335[5]

Under The Phone (IRE) *Robin Dickin* 99h 116c
6 b g Heron Island(IRE) Theo On The Bench (IRE) (Mister Lord (USA))
1985[4] 2449[4] 2973[4] 3834[6] 4062[2] 4876[5] (5245) 5439[4]

Under The Red Sky (IRE) *Kenny Johnson* 83c
8 ch g Insatiable(IRE) Official Secret (Polish Patriot (USA))
2197[P] 2846[8] 2981[5] 3399[4] 3679[4] 3937[0] 4051[P] 4569[2] 5010[3]

Underwood (FR) *Michael Roberts* 91h
7 b g Assessor(IRE) Attualita (FR) (Master Thatch)
451[P]

Un De Sceaux (FR) *W P Mullins* 164h 172c
7 b g Denham Red(FR) Hotesse De Sceaux (FR) (April Night (FR))
(51a) 3293a[F] (3734) 4718[2] 5493[2]

Undisputed (IRE) *S R B Crawford* 99b
4 b m King's Theatre(IRE) Gleanntan (IRE) (Lil's Boy (USA))
2677a[9] 4168[2] 4559[2]

Unefille De Guye (FR) *Victor Dartnall* 80h
7 bb m Voix Du Nord(FR) Mascotte De Guye (FR) (Video Rock (FR))
824[3] 1236[10] 2298[P] 3125[P]

Une Lapin Rouge (IRE) *Emmanuel Clayeux*
5 ch m Martaline Rosy De Cyborg (FR) (Cyborg (FR))
2821a[P]

Unex Modigliani (IRE) *Derek Shaw* 104h
6 ch g Hurricane Run(IRE) Chronicle (Observatory (USA))
2543[4] 3487[16] 4506[5]

Unex Picasso *Barry Murtagh* 55h
7 b g Galileo(IRE) Ruff Shod (USA) (Storm Boot (USA))
505[P] 838[8]

Unic De Bersy (FR) *Gordon Elliott* 110h 139c
7 b g Nononito(FR) Caliostra De Bersy (FR) (Le Pontet (FR))
2531a[5] 3715a[P] 5005a[U]

Unidexter (IRE) *Richard Ford* 96h
5 br g Footstepsinthesand Run To Jane (IRE) (Doyoun)
2162[9] 2703[P]

Unify *Grant Cann* 80h
5 b m Midnight Legend Holy Smoke (Statoblest)
2997[P] 4919[7] 5181[2] 5420[2]

Unioniste (FR) *Paul Nicholls* 111h 161c
7 gr g Dom Alco(FR) Gleep Will (FR) (Laniste)
2899[8] 3150[12] 3993[3] (4205) 4635[2] ◆ 5218[10]

Union Jack D'Ycy (FR) *Venetia Williams* 104h 130c
7 b g Bonnet Rouge(FR) Jacady (FR) (Fill My Hopes (FR))
(2766) 2955[P] 3373[2] 3583[P]

Union Saint (FR) *Jimmy Frost* 130h 131c
7 b g Saint Des Saints(FR) Us Et Coutumes (FR) (Shining Steel)
512[2] 3415[4] 4857[4] 5381[4]

Unique De Cotte (FR) *David Pipe* 143h 146c
7 b g Voix Du Nord(FR) Kadalka De Cotte (FR) (Kadalko (FR))
2759[6] **3228[U] 3957[4]**

Unison (IRE) *Jeremy Scott* 116h
5 b g Jeremy(USA) Easter Song (USA) (Rubiano (USA))
(3955) 5220[3] 5418[4]

United Park (FR) *G Macaire* 124c
7 b g Antarctique(IRE) Goldoulyssa (FR) (Cadoudal (FR))
374a[3]

Universal Soldier (IRE) *Peter Bowen* 145h 143c
10 b g Winged Love(IRE) Waterland Gale (IRE) (Fourstars Allstar (USA))
553[3] 855[P] 3741[P] (4914) 5238[P]

Universe Of Gracie (GER) *Jiri Kousek* 121c
10 b g Pentire Ulanowa (GER) (Kamiros (IRE))
1885a[4]

Unknown Legend (IRE) *Sarah Humphrey* 110h 110c
8 b g Heron Island(IRE) Late Call (IRE) (Callernish)
109[5] (398) **568[U]**

Un Noble (FR) *Nicky Richards* 114h 135c
5 gr g Near Honor(GER) Noble Gary (FR) (Loup Solitaire (USA))
2105[3] ◆ 2431[4] (3061) (3669) ◆ 4279a[P] (5200)

Unoccupied *Eoghan O'Grady* 125h 127c
9 b g Old Vic Cesaria (FR) (Highest Honor (FR))
2228a[P]

Uno Valoroso (FR) *Mark Walford* 89h 118c
7 b g Voix Du Nord(FR) Danse D'Avril (FR) (Quart De Vin (FR))
2342[P] 2920[5] 3401[2] 3589[2] 3806[4] 4275[P] 5257[5]

Unowhatimeanharry *Harry Fry* 149h
7 b g Sir Harry Lewis(USA) Red Nose Lady (Teenoso (USA))
(2513) (2725) (3032) (4139) ◆ (4766)

Un Prophete (FR) *Venetia Williams* 107h
4 gr g Carlotamix(FR) Pollita (FR) (Nombre Premier)
2689[10] 3590[2] 3932[5] 4593[3] 5163[3]

Un Regard (FR) *Guy Denuault* 103h 117c
7 b g Bonnet Rouge(FR) Je Te Garde (FR) (Useful (FR))
1477a[10]

Un Temps Pour Tout (IRE) *David Pipe* 164h 164c
6 b g Robin Des Champs(FR) Rougedespoir (FR) (Bonnet Rouge (FR))
(663a) **2481[2] 2726[2] 3849[4] (4697) 5191[4]**

Until Forever (IRE) *Dan Skelton* 90h
5 b m Robin Des Champs(FR) Sugar Island (IRE) (Oscar (IRE))
(168)

Until The Man (IRE) *Barry Brennan* 74h
8 b g Tillerman Canoe Cove (IRE) (Grand Lodge (USA))
1182[6] 1299[5] 1423[4]

Until Winning (FR) *Tom George* 106h 132c
7 b g Kapgarde(FR) Fripperie (FR) (Bojador (FR))
1943[4] **2459[6] 2853[7]**

Unwanted Gift (IRE) *Alan Phillips* 73h 31c
10 b g Tendulkar(USA) Slievenue (IRE) (Zieten (USA))
704[10]

Unzing (FR) *Mrs S A Bramall* 109h 119c
7 b g Voix Du Nord(FR) Magik (FR) (Kadalko (FR))
3302a7
Unzo Du Bara (FR) *Francois Nicolle* 130c
7 b g Network(GER) Full Of Wisky (FR) (Useful (FR))
374aU
Up And Go (FR) *Donald McCain* 110h 115c
7 ch g Martaline Santoria (FR) (Limnos (JPN))
208P 27674 33614 3884P
Upazo (FR) *W P Mullins* 145h 142c
7 b g Enrique Honey (FR) (Highlanders (FR))
47a2 1515a3
Upbeat Cobbler (FR) *Henry Daly* 102h 110c
7 gr m Brier Creek(USA) Jade De Chalamont (FR) (Royal Charter (FR))
(2248) 29306 32225 (4746)
Upepito (FR) *Dan Skelton* 119h 136c
7 b g Khalkevi(IRE) Friandise II (FR) (Mistigri)
19022 2335U 27612
Up For An Oscar (IRE) *Peter Bowen* 107h 128c
8 b g Oscar(IRE) Queen Of Harts (IRE) (Phardante (FR))
856 363P **25934 2996P 3236P**
Up For Review (IRE) *W P Mullins* 151h
6 br g Presenting Coolsilver (IRE) (Good Thyne (USA))
53a3 (3393a) 38594 4766P (5410) ◆
Up Four It (IRE) *Jamie Poulton* 78h
7 b g Luso Newgate Beauty (IRE) (Beau Sher)
2214 4945 7128 25473 32196 41615 46742 54838
Upham Atom *Kate Buckett* 94h 128c
12 b g Silver Patriarch(IRE) Upham Lady (Bustino)
28724 3707P 52655
Upham Running (IRE) *Kate Buckett* 98h
7 b g Definite Article Tara Brooch (IRE) (Supreme Leader)
273011 53063
Uplifted (IRE) *Martin Todhunter* 89h
4 b g Jeremy(USA) Misty Peak (IRE) (Sri Pekan (USA))
192011 2343P
Up North (IRE) *Micky Hammond* 80b
3 b g Dylan Thomas(IRE) Difiya (IRE) (Cadeaux Genereux)
41814
Upsanddowns (IRE) *Evan Williams* 129h 24c
7 b g Definite Article Courtain (USA) (Diesis)
848 809P
Upsilon Bleu (FR) *Pauline Robson* 134h 153c
7 b g Panoramic Glycine Bleue (FR) (Le Nain Jaune (FR))
27619 34266 **36295 (4469) 50875 53264**
Upswing (IRE) *Jonjo O'Neill* 133h 143c
7 b g Beneficial Native Country (IRE) (Be My Native (USA))
16422 (2018) 24822 ◆ 3518P 47359
Uptendownone (IRE) *Gary Moore* 115h
6 b g Oscar(IRE) Lady Meribel (Kahyasi)
1488F
Up The Bees *Philip Kirby* 68h
5 b g Kayf Tara West River (USA) (Gone West (USA))
1556
Up The Junction *Tim Vaughan* 81h
4 b g New Approach(IRE) Hyabella (Shirley Heights)
16448 22587 3370P 430314 52239
Upthemsteps (IRE) *Ian Williams* 94h 100c
10 br g Beneficial Carrigloss (IRE) (Roselier (FR))
49754 53764
Up Till Midnight *Lydia Richards* 74h
6 ch m Midnight Legend Uplift (Bustino)
43506 51454 53898
Up To Al (IRE) *Bob Buckler* 91h
7 b g Heron Island(IRE) Pretonic (Precocious)
24578 29866 33708 44546 4919P 54318
Upton Wood *Chris Down* 110h 58c
9 ch g Fleetwood(IRE) Miss Counsel (Leading Counsel (USA))
2652 ◆ (391) ◆ 2732P 48552
Up Your Game (IRE) *Roy Brotherton* 74h
7 b g Milan Katie Snurge (IRE) (Snurge)
2851P 3951P 43183 5333P
Uranna (FR) *W P Mullins* 134h 138c
7 gr m Panoramic Irresistible Anna (FR) (Dom Pasquini (FR))
52a2 **4656a2 5006a2**
Urano (FR) *W P Mullins* 135h 144c
7 b g Enrique Neiland (FR) (Cyborg (FR))
92a4 1556a2 278311 3296a14 3715a7 47696
Uranox (FR) *Michael Roberts* 72h
7 b g Special Kaldoun(IRE) Judelle (FR) (Agent Bleu (FR))
6759 22562 29586
Urban Dusk (IRE) *Mark Michael McNiff* 107h
6 b m Golan(IRE) South West Nine (IRE) (Oscar (IRE))
10663
Urban Gale (IRE) *Joanne Foster* 117h 102c
10 b g City Honours(USA) Margale (IRE) (Strong Gale)
1364 10696 (1403) 19307 (2402) 27083 3310P 38033 4047P **45344 50135 5404U**
Urban Hymn (FR) *Malcolm Jefferson* 120b
7 b g Robin Des Champs(FR) Betty Brune (FR) (Dark Stone (FR))
5213F
Urban Kode (IRE) *Lucinda Russell* 99h
7 b g Kodiac Urbanize (USA) (Chester House (USA))
3023 6613 8864 14933 19203 22922 51226 54455
Urban Moon (IRE) *Jonjo O'Neill*
4 b g Galileo(IRE) Velouette (Darshaan)
449410
Urban Storm (IRE) *Ben Pauling* 101h
5 b g Urban Ocean(FR) Jessaway (IRE) (Dr Massini (IRE))
3983 18125 ◆ **2410P**
Urcalin (FR) *David Arbuthnot* 128h 137c
7 b g Network(GER) Caline So (FR) (Port Etienne (FR))
(102) 3192 **(756) 14452 (1722) 2240F**
Uriah Heep (FR) *R Mike Smith* 123h 124c
6 b g Danehill Dancer(IRE) Canasita (Zafonic (USA))
6425 19053 21948 4839P 52956
Usa (IRE) *S J Mahon* 131h 132c
8 b g Bertolini(USA) Varnay (Machiavellian (USA))
47a4 1186a14 1787a4
Usher Du Lys (FR) *J-L Guillochon*
4 b g Saint Des Saints(FR) Malika Du Lys (FR) (Chichicastenango (FR))
2362aP
Ustica (IRE) *Jonjo O'Neill* 130h
5 b g Trans Island Shady's Wish (IRE) (Lancastrian)
(389)
Utah De La Coquais (FR) *E Leray* 132c
7 b g Nidor(FR) Noblevie (FR) (Noblequest (FR))
4719P
Utility (GER) *Jonjo O'Neill* 121b
4 b g Yeats(IRE) Ungarin (GER) (Goofalik (USA))
(2965) ◆ 519514
Ut Majeur Aulmes (FR) *Victor Dartnall* 123h 139c
7 ch g Northern Park(USA) My Wish Aulmes (FR) (Lyphard's Wish (FR))
29904 32572 37492 (4464) (4918)
Vabinsaru (FR) *Jonjo O'Neill*
4 b g Enrique Yolaine (FR) (Astarabad (USA))
526P 853P
Vaihau (FR) *Jonjo O'Neill* 121h
6 br g Lavirco(GER) Niponne (FR) (Funny Baby (FR))
1866 (377) 4734 10024 ◆ 16005 19114 21454
Vaillant Creek (FR) *Alex Hales* 118h
6 b g Brier Creek(USA) Ker Marie (FR) (Esprit Du Nord (USA))
210P 23013 25952 3607P 38174 44422 5451U
Vaillant Nonantais (FR) *Nicky Henderson* 107h
4 b g My Risk(FR) Sweet Life (FR) (Villez (USA))
3662 43646 50915
Valadom (FR) *Richard Hobson* 132c
6 gr g Dadarissime(FR) Laurana (FR) (Badolato (USA))
15232 (1641) 17156 24714 30175 33152 47197 53904
Valantino Oyster (IRE) *Ali Stronge* 28h
8 b g Pearl Of Love(IRE) Mishor (Slip Anchor)
19417
Valco De Touzaine (FR) *Paul Nicholls* 133h 148c
6 gr g Dom Alco(FR) Narcisse De Touzaine (FR) (Roi De Rome (USA))
6454 **(809) 10403 13222 16586**
Val D'Arc (FR) *Richard Hobson* 113h 120c
6 b g Le Balafre(FR) Lextrienne (FR) (Neustrien (FR))
20192 22762 ◆ 2546F 31153 33803 53796
Val De Ferbet (FR) *W P Mullins* 144h 147c
6 bb g Voix Du Nord(FR) Intrigue Deferbet (FR) (Lights Out (FR))
69aP 349a2 663aP
Valentine Spring (FR) *M Rolland*
2 ch f Nombre Premier Spring Baby (FR) (Turgeon (USA))
5498a4
Valhalla (IRE) *Colin Tizzard* 132h
5 b g Scorpion(IRE) Fox Theatre (IRE) (King's Theatre (IRE))
31338 42564 47843 ◆ (5264)
Valid Point (IRE) *Nigel Twiston-Davies* 121h 130c
9 b g Val Royal(FR) Ricadonna (Kris)
2513P **(2975) 3339U 4212P 49076**
Valkyri Colombe (FR) *P Peltier* 136h 107c
6 gr g Dom Alco(FR) Krysaore Colombe (FR) (Royal Charter (FR))
(437a)
Valleyofmilan (IRE) *Donald McCain* 121h 129c
8 b g Milan Ikdam Valley (IRE) (Ikdam)
(927) 11678 14176 17844 **20684 22954 24882 (3312) 3591U 38365**
Valleyofthefox *Malcolm Jones*
5 b g Petrovich(USA) Ruby Dante (IRE) (Ajraas (USA))
509715
Valnamixe Du Mee (FR) *Kenny Johnson* 91h
6 b g Al Namix(FR) Kateline Du Mee (FR) (Panoramic)
206610 2319P 279113
Valours Minion (IRE) *V T O'Brien* 98h 120c
12 b g Corrouge(USA) Fiovefontaine (IRE) (Lafontaine I (USA))
1186a4
Valseur Du Granval (FR) *Tom George* 108h 112c
6 b g Della Francesca(USA) La Grande Vallee (FR) (Chef De Clan (FR))
17183 24375 **42923 48033 5447P**
Valseur Lido (FR) *W P Mullins* 147h 168c
6 b g Anzillero(GER) Libido Rock (FR) (Video Rock (FR))
(10a) 2941a2 3231F 4007aU 47312 54922
Valtor (FR) *E Leray* 119h 125c
6 b g Nidor(FR) Jossca (FR) (Badolato (USA))
4540a10
Value At Risk *Dan Skelton* 151h
6 b g Kayf Tara Miss Orchestra (IRE) (Orchestra)
2726F 3486F 37339 40702 (5004a)
Valyssa Monterg (FR) *W P Mullins* 138h 104c
6 b m Network(GER) Mellyssa (FR) (Panoramic)
(1175a) 52994
Vancouverite *John Ferguson* 129h
5 b g Dansili Villarrica (USA) (Selkirk (USA))
(1425) 16342 (1886) 21833
Vandross (IRE) *Neil King* 126h
5 b g Iffraaj Mrs Kanning (Distant View (USA))
1856 4046 755F 897P
Vanilla Run (IRE) *Chris Grant* 103b
4 b m Hurricane Run(IRE) Vanilla Delight (IRE) (Orpen (USA))
(5407)
Vanishing *Alexandra Dunn*
3 b f Sir Percy Valoria (Hernando (FR))
4683U 49169
Vaniteux (FR) *Nicky Henderson* 153h 162c
6 br g Voix Du Nord(FR) Expoville (FR) (Video Rock (FR))
(2684) 32802 (3856) 4696U 54953
Van Mildert (IRE) *Kenneth Slack* 80h
6 b m Observatory(USA) Vanilla Delight (IRE) (Orpen (USA))
(507) 45137
Vanvidd (FR) *Remy Nerbonne*
4 gr g Verglas(IRE) Magic Spin (USA) (Lord Avie (USA))
3876aP
Varabad Du Buisson (FR) *M Postic* 132c
6 b g Astarabad(USA) Diane Du Buisson (FR) (Pot D'Or (FR))
664a8
Varom (FR) *Paul Nicholls* 103h
6 gr g Charming Groom(FR) Morava (FR) (Perrault)
257710 28712 31465
Vasco Du Mee (FR) *Martin Weston* 121h 133c
6 b g Goldneyev(USA) British Nellerie (FR) (Le Pontet (FR))
92a7 (4227) 47482
Vasco D'Ycy (FR) *Julia Brooke* 114h 116c
6 b g Equerry(USA) Ingrid Des Mottes (FR) (Useful (FR))
9366
Vasco Pierji (FR) *Donald McCain* 93h
6 b g Sleeping Car(FR) Angelina (FR) (Brezzo (FR))
3286
Vauban Du Seuil (FR) *Alex Hales*
6 b g Epalo(GER) Parika Du Seuil (FR) (Blushing Flame (USA))
150P 524P
Vautour (FR) *W P Mullins* 158h 180c
6 b g Robin Des Champs(FR) Gazelle De Mai (FR) (Dom Pasquini (FR))
(2633) 32312 (4731) 5192F
Vayland *Micky Hammond* 116h 106c
6 ch g Generous(IRE) Dotandadash (IRE) (Clerkenwell (USA))
812F 13662 **2026P 28466 33455 36318 4177U 51256**
Vazaro Delafayette (FR) *David Pipe* 113h 131c
6 bl g Robin Des Champs(FR) Etoile Du Merze (FR) (If De Merze (FR))
40713 (4321) (4451)
Veauce De Sivola (FR) *Mark Gillard* 125h 102c
6 b g Assessor(IRE) Eva De Chalamont (FR) (Iron Duke (FR))
272 1283 2693 5676 8254 25533 30813 36094 36636 42655 45312 47722 51173
Vedani (IRE) *Tony Carroll* 72h
6 b g Dalakhani(IRE) Velandia (IRE) (Sadler's Wells (USA))
29618 477411
Vedettariat (FR) *W P Mullins* 128h 142c
6 bl g Lavirco(GER) Platine (FR) (Network (GER))
4956a5
Veinard (FR) *Robert Bewley* 107h
6 ch g Shaanmer(IRE) Ombline (FR) (Subotica (FR))
2858 28016 33664 36282 40552 42853 45502 ◆ 50094 52624
Velator *Neil Mulholland* 100h 133c
8 b g Old Vic Jupiter's Message (Jupiter Island)
294 50714
Velocity Boy (IRE) *William P Murphy* 136h
6 b g Westerner Sambre (FR) (Turgeon (USA))
6a5
Velvet Cognac *Warren Greatrex* 117h
7 b g Grape Tree Road Scandalous Affair (Alflora (IRE))
1683
Velvet Edge *Anthony Day* 76h
6 b m Central Park(IRE) Velvet Leaf (Rakaposhi King)
2164P 245210 4893P 54777
Velvet Maker (FR) *Alan Fleming* 132h 144c
6 b g Policy Maker(IRE) Evasion De L'Orne (FR) (Beyssac (FR))
3271a3 3766a2 477012
Vendor (FR) *Sue Smith* 141h 118c
7 gr g Kendor(FR) Village Rainbow (FR) (Village Star (FR))
221411 24992 26397 (2921) ◆ 36303 40142 43663 491310
Vendredi Trois (FR) *Emma Lavelle* 108h 115c
6 b g Shaanmer(IRE) Legende Sacree (FR) (Hawker's News (IRE))
15472 1615U 18972 **(2456) 4789F 5285U**
Venetian Lad *Lydia Richards* 97h 115c
10 ro g Midnight Legend Henrietta Holmes (IRE) (Persian Bold)
(226) (598) 17557 20143 25465 31154 43802 (5066)
Venez Horace (FR) *Giles Smyly* 15h 105c
6 b g Polish Summer Fripperie (FR) (Bojador (FR))
1642P 22226
Vengeur De Guye (FR) *Lucinda Russell* 115h 131c
6 b g Dom Alco(FR) Mascotte De Guye (FR) (Video Rock (FR))
4692 7095 1904F 23422 27193
Venitien De Mai (FR) *J T R Draper* 117h 138c
6 b g Network(GER) Meylba (FR) (Grand Tresor (FR))
(4521a) 5005a9
Vent Nivernais (FR) *James Evans* 88h 90c
6 ch g Shaanmer(IRE) Lobella (FR) (Hawker's News (FR))
18947 2248P 25963 38212 (4025) **4776U**
Vent Sombre (FR) *G Cherel* 129h 140c
6 b g Network(GER) Ode Rock (FR) (Video Rock (FR))
664a3 1884aP 2822a5
Ventura Castle *Jamie Snowden* 45h
3 b g Paco Boy(IRE) Bisaat (USA) (Bahri (USA))
6906 8915 20926 25387
Venture Lagertha (IRE) *Brian Barr* 80h
6 ch m Fruits Of Love(USA) Millmounts Tara (IRE) (Kayf Tara)
43509 46818 49163
Venturepredementia *Andrew Crook* 61b
4 b g Indian Danehill(IRE) Sounds Familiar (IRE) (Orchestra)
50836
Venue *Donald McCain* 123h
5 b g Beat Hollow Shirley Valentine (Shirley Heights)
(79) 3164 7277 41797 491311 54056
Verano (GER) *Dan Skelton* 119h 117c
6 ch g Lord Of England(GER) Vive La Vie (GER) (Big Shuffle (USA))
2593 18963 25483 29614
Verax *Raymond York* 60b
4 ch m Central Park(IRE) Veredus (Alderbrook)
14915
Vercingetorix (IRE) *Gordon Elliott* 128h 111c
4 b g Dylan Thomas(IRE) Great Artist (FR) (Desert Prince (IRE))
31517 47867
Verdure Des Obeaux (FR) *N Devilder* 144h 134c
6 m Saddler Maker(IRE) Herbe D'Estruval (FR) (Dom Pasquini (FR))
(5363a)
Vering (FR) *Carroll Gray* 77h 80c
9 b g Bering Forcia (FR) (Homme De Loi (IRE))
318 11214 12335 1489P 245410 26616 27365 32562 35869 44402 48546
Verko (FR) *Micky Hammond* 81h 114c
6 br g Lavirco(GER) Lady Vernizy (FR) (Video Rock (FR))
4842 93910 13713 15735 **(2321) (2894) (3059) 33104 40462 (4327) 45713**
Verni (FR) *Philip Hobbs* 118h
6 ch g Sabrehill(USA) Nobless D'Aron (FR) (Ragmar (FR))
33753 (5161)
Veroce (FR) *Mark Walford* 112c
6 bb g Assessor(IRE) Pyvoine (FR) (Video Rock (FR))
846 4615 23974 27085 30593 38034 (4276) (4792) 52022
Verona Opera (IRE) *S R B Crawford* 96h
4 b m King's Theatre(IRE) Timissa (IRE) (Kahyasi)
27524 41646 45852 49046
Vertical Venture (IRE) *Conor O'Dwyer* 90h
5 b g Vertical Speed(FR) Lady Kamando (Hernando (FR))
25a9
Vertueux (FR) *Tony Carroll* 86h 56c
10 gr g Verglas(IRE) Shahrazad (FR) (Bering)
19319 (3233) 42238 46505
Verve Argent (FR) *Paul Webber* 48h
6 gr g Fragrant Mix(IRE) Devise II (FR) (Djarvis (FR))
20245 2275P
Very Extravagant (IRE) *Neil Mulholland* 107h
6 ch m Touch Of Land(FR) Raveleen Rose (IRE) (Norwich)
27784 32524 ◆ 35168 3930P 48534
Very First Time *Tim Easterby* 109h
3 b g Champs Elysees Like A Virgin (IRE) (Iron Mask (USA))
17728 27776 31652 41564 (4548) 53653
Verygoodverygood (FR) *Paul Morgan* 110h
4 b g Yeats(IRE) Rose D'Or (IRE) (Polish Precedent (USA))
2642 ◆ 19667 526910 54632
Very Intense (IRE) *Tom Lacey* 106h 105c
4 b g Intense Focus(USA) Astralai (IRE) (Galileo (IRE))
2674 18103 20435 24542 25992 34222 42507 **53882**
Very Live (FR) *Paul Webber* 83h 108c
6 b g Secret Singer(FR) Iona Will (FR) (Kadalko (FR))
89P **28613 (3199) (3903) 4232P 4595U 5103P**
Very Much So (IRE) *W P Mullins* 128b
5 b g Scorpion(IRE) Lady Apprentice (IRE) (Phardante (FR))
47218
Very Noble (FR) *Chris Gordon* 113h 117c
6 b g Martaline Isati'S (FR) (Chamberlin (FR))
642 17534 22435 2418P **31156 3257P** 40963 43847
Vesperal Dream (FR) *Paul Nicholls* 131h 139c
6 bl g Network(GER) Pampanilla (FR) (April Night (FR))
(657) 13227
Vesuvhill (FR) *Ben Case* 110h 106c
6 ch g Sabrehill(USA) L'Orchidee (FR) (Gunboat Diplomacy (FR))
3553 2140P 25393
Vexillum (IRE) *Neil Mulholland* 106h
6 br g Mujadil(USA) Common Cause (Polish Patriot (USA))
1722 8566 12993 (1461) 16774 (1980)
Vezelay (FR) *Emmanuel Clayeux* 142h 146c
6 b g Dom Alco(FR) Outre Mer (FR) (Sleeping Car (FR))
(1884a)
Viaduct Jack (IRE) *Kim Bailey* 113h
6 b g King's Theatre(IRE) Back Market Lass (IRE) (Bob Back (USA))
20233 ◆ 24507 30376 4860P
Via Volupta *Warren Greatrex* 115h
5 b m Kayf Tara Via Ferrata (FR) (Nikos)
1112 5912 ◆ 25612 (5145) 53892
Vibrato Valtat (FR) *Paul Nicholls* 144h 164c
6 gr g Voix Du Nord(FR) La Tosca Valtat (FR) (Dom Alco (FR))
(2259) 29153 32813 37344 4731F 51925
Vicangelome (FR) *Robert Tyner* 127h 124c
6 b g Laveron Medicis (FR) (Sicyos (USA))
4279a2
Vic De Touzaine (FR) *Venetia Williams* 110h 135c
6 gr g Dom Alco(FR) Diana De Vonnas (FR) (El Badr)
22657 25643 **29572 34453 ◆ 39162 4436U (4589)**

Vice Et Vertu (FR) *Henry Daly* 122h 113c
6 b g Network(GER) Duchesse Du Cochet (FR) (Native Guile (USA))
2489^3 2905^3 3348^F 3824^P 4493^3 5224^3

Vicente (FR) *Paul Nicholls* 144h 159c
6 b g Dom Alco(FR) Ireland (FR) (Kadalko (FR))
(27) (269) 2055^3 (2481) 3013^4 4700^5 (5327)

Vicenzo Mio (FR) *Paul Nicholls* 130h
5 b g Corri Piano(FR) Sweet Valrose (FR) (Cadoudal (FR))
2369^5 2914^3 3151^{12} 4362^4 4851^2 4933^3

Vicky's Charm (IRE) *Barry Brennan* 110h
6 b m Old Vic Sweet Charm (IRE) (Glacial Storm (USA))
111^4 (2162) 2555^2 3377^2 3865^6 (4616)

Vicomte Du Seuil (FR) *Emmanuel Clayeux* 120h 131c
6 b g Special Kaldoun(IRE) Marie Du Seuil (FR) (Video Rock (FR))
4485^F

Viconte Du Noyer (FR) *Henry De Bromhead* 131h 149c
6 gr g Martaline Zouk Wood (USA) (Woodman (USA))
7a^{11} **1790a^3 5179^3**

Vics Canvas (IRE) *Dermot Anthony McLoughlin* 98h 153c
12 b g Old Vic Oilpainting (IRE) (Welsh Term)
2641^8 **2899^5 3715a^P 4260a^6 5218^3**

Vic's Last Stand (IRE) *Keith Reveley* 88h
5 b m Old Vic Misleain (IRE) (Un Desperado (FR))
3476^7 3835^{16} 4271^7 4369^4

Victor Hewgo *Keith Reveley* 112h 123c
10 b g Old Vic Pennys Pride (IRE) (Pips Pride)
3036^5 3339^F 3999^P 4305^{11} 4794^5 5300^3 ◆

Victorian Teo (FR) *Tom Symonds* 83h
5 b g Teofilo(IRE) Chalouchi (USA) (Mt. Livermore (USA))
436a^7 2312^7

Victoria Oats *Robert Goldie* 55h
9 b m Old Vic Easter Oats (Oats)
2428^P

Victor Leudorum (IRE) *Charlie Mann* 108h 102c
8 b g Wareed(IRE) Rock Garden (IRE) (Bigstone (IRE))
1784^6 **2036^4** 2744^{11}

Victors Serenade (IRE) *Anthony Honeyball* 88h 114c
10 b g Old Vic Dantes Serenade (IRE) (Phardante (FR))
2907^7 4140^P 4826^3

Victory Rich (IRE) *Henry Tett* 87h
4 b g Kheleyf(USA) Imperial Graf (USA) (Blushing John (USA))
41^3 263^P 2555^P 3256^P

Viel Gluck (IRE) *Lawney Hill*
12 b g Supreme Leader Discerning Air (Ezzoud (IRE))
1085^P

Viens Chercher (IRE) *Brian Ellison* 132h
4 b g Milan La Zingarella (IRE) (Phardante (FR))
(1365) (1660) 2509^4 2626^2 3623^P 4014^8

Vieux Lille (IRE) *Philip Hobbs* 140h
5 b g Robin Des Champs(FR) Park Athlete (IRE) (Supreme Leader)
(2351) (2879) (3413) 3739^3 4636^6 (5430)

Vieux Lion Rouge (FR) *David Pipe* 122h 150c
6 ch g Sabiango(GER) Indecise (FR) (Cyborg (FR))
(382) (779) (2643) ◆ 3016^U 4238^2 4700^6 5218^7

Vieux Morvan (FR) *G Cherel* 140h 140c
6 b g Voix Du Nord(FR) Moskoville (FR) (Kadalko (FR))
375a^6 1884a^F 5363a^2

Vif Argent (FR) *Andrew Reid* 120h 82c
6 b g Dom Alco(FR) Formosa (FR) (Royal Charter (FR))
(176) 3846^P 4362^9 5185^{10} 5479^F

Vigil (IRE) *D K Weld* 141h
6 b g Dansili Magnolia Lane (IRE) (Sadler's Wells (USA))
4715^6

Vikekhal (FR) *Gary Moore* 111h 130c
6 b g Khalkevi(IRE) Gesse Parade (FR) (Dress Parade)
226^2 523^5 (670) (1753) 2184^5 2701^P 5118^5

Viking Blond (FR) *Dafydd Jones* 92b 114c
10 ch g Varese(FR) Sweet Jaune (FR) (Le Nain Jaune (FR))
3585^P

Viking De Balme (FR) *Francois Nicolle* 102h 132c
6 ch g Cachet Noir(USA) Jonquille De Balme (FR) (Mansonnien (FR))
374a^2

Viking Mistress *Martin Keighley* 61h
7 b m Bollin Eric Mistress Caramore (IRE) (Moscow Society (USA))
3386^5 3570^9

Viking Queen *Paul Webber* 97b
4 b m Presenting Swaythe (USA) (Swain (IRE))
2421^6 3862^3

Viking Rebel (IRE) *W T Reed* 107h 100c
13 b g Taipan(IRE) Clodagh's Dream (Whistling Deer)
141^2 4407^P 4903^8

Viking Ridge (IRE) *Miss S L Klug* 34h 118c
8 gr g Cloudings(IRE) Lady Newmill (IRE) (Taipan (IRE))
521^8

Viking Warrior (IRE) *Shaun Harris* 72h
8 ch g Halling(USA) Powder Paint (Mark Of Esteem (IRE))
851^6

Viky Du Reponet (FR) *S Foucher* 134h 129c
6 b m Voix Du Nord(FR) Opale Du Moulin (FR) (Robin Des Champs (FR))
1477a^8 4540a^4

Village Vic (IRE) *Philip Hobbs* 136h 160c
8 b g Old Vic Etoile Margot (FR) (Garde Royale)
(1902) (2329) (3031) (3406) 4731^9 5193^{13}

Vilman (IRE) *Simon West*
3 b g Mastercraftsman(IRE) Velandia (IRE) (Sadler's Wells (USA))
2324^P

Vinaigrette *Richard Phillips* 74h
6 b m Kayf Tara What A Vintage (IRE) (Un Desperado (FR))
864^P

Vinceson (IRE) *Jess Westwood* 93h
7 b g Vinnie Roe(IRE) Velvet Huxley (IRE) (Fourstars Allstar (USA))
167^{12} 493^9 **934^P 1079^P 1243^P**

Vinciaettis (FR) *Warren Greatrex* 134h
4 b g Enrique Over The Sea (FR) (Urban Ocean (FR))
(2549) 3802^2 (4963) 5372^4

Vincitore (FR) *Miss C V Hart* 105h 123c
9 b g Starborough Viva Vodka (FR) (Crystal Glitters (USA))
4887^2

Vinegar Hill *Anna Brooks* 98h
6 b g Kayf Tara Broughton Melody (Alhijaz)
90^4 2413^5 2868^3 4504^2 (5017)

Vinnie My Boy (IRE) *Heather Dalton* 128h 92c
7 ch g Vinnie Roe(IRE) Copper Magic (IRE) (Zaffaran (USA))
108^P 493^P

Vinniespride (IRE) *Mark Michael McNiff* 109h 36c
8 b g Waky Nao L'Accolade (IRE) (Seattle Dancer (USA))
3473^{12}

Vinnie The Fish (IRE) *Dai Burchell* 121h 115c
7 br g Vinnie Roe(IRE) Darwin Angel (IRE) (Presenting)
643^3 1070^3 1416^3 1896^2 2090^4 4448^7

Vinnie Trenta (IRE) *Alan Phillips* 94h
7 b g Vinnie Roe(IRE) Proud Trenta (IRE) (King's Ride)
1010^3 1098^5

Vinniewhitefoot *Gary Hanmer* 88h
8 ch g Grape Tree Road Mistress Return (Bob's Return (IRE))
4072^6

Vinny Gambini (IRE) *Rose Dobbin* 116h 115c
8 b g Vinnie Roe(IRE) Red Velvet (So Factual (USA))
3343^4 3669^3 4051^3 4420^5

Vino Griego (FR) *Gary Moore* 132h 150c
10 b g Kahyasi Vie De Reine (FR) (Mansonnien (FR))
101^P (2374)

Vintage Clouds (IRE) *Sue Smith* 140h
5 gr g Cloudings(IRE) Rare Vintage (IRE) (Germany (USA))
2210^2 (2628) 3363^2 ◆ 3743^2 4248^2 5194^P

Vintage Star (IRE) *Sue Smith* 128h 146c
9 b g Presenting Rare Vintage (IRE) (Germany (USA))
(2213)

Vintage Vinnie (IRE) *Rebecca Curtis* 124h 143c
6 b g Vinnie Roe(IRE) Bobby's Jet (IRE) (Bob's Return (IRE))
(1642) 2055^F 2481^4 3838^2 4700^P 5073^P

Vintage Vixon (IRE) *Adrian Wintle* 45h
8 b m Moscow Society(USA) Bar Un'que (IRE) (Un Desperado (FR))
2841^P 3378^P 4804^7 **5138^P**

Violet Dancer *Gary Moore* 140h 157c
5 b g Bertolini(USA) Another Secret (Efisio)
(1815) 2545^2 (2824) (3351) (4126)

Violets Girl *Warren Greatrex* 100b
5 b m Black Sam Bellamy(IRE) Sunshine Rays (Alflora (IRE))
831^3 (1057)

Violoniste (FR) *Sam Drake* 92h
6 b g Epalo(GER) Parade (FR) (Robin Des Champs (FR))
3375^P 3795^9 4108^8 4299^4 (5314)

Virak (FR) *Paul Nicholls* 148h 164c
6 b g Bernebeau(FR) Nosika D'Airy (FR) (Oblat (FR))
2187^7 2790^2 3150^2 3741^2 4361^{11} 5217^2

Virgile De Gene (FR) *Nick Ayliffe* 75b
6 b g Le Fou(IRE) Dame De Gene (FR) (Le Pontet (FR))
392^7 511^P

Virgilio (FR) *Dan Skelton* 148h
6 b g Denham Red(FR) Liesse De Marbeuf (FR) (Cyborg (FR))
(208) ◆ (317) (2901) 3408^P 5189^5

Virnon *Alan Swinbank* 118h
4 b g Virtual Freedom Song (Singspiel (IRE))
(2398) (2804) 3152^4

Virtuose Du Chenet (FR) *Venetia Williams* 62h 97c
6 b g Irish Wells(FR) Lili Bleue (FR) (Epervier Bleu)
3379^5 3661^3 4214^P 4503^3

Visible Light (IRE) *Stuart Edmunds* 110h
7 b g Shantou(USA) Strand Lady (IRE) (Pistolet Bleu (IRE))
(4747) 4845^2

Vision De La Vie (FR) *Pauline Robson* 99h 101c
5 ch g Sin Kiang(FR) Vidahermosa (FR) (Kahyasi)
453^2 637^6 3427^3 (4032) 4175^P

Vision Des Champs (FR) *Gary Moore* 103h 124c
6 b g Saint Des Saints(FR) Manita Des Champs (FR) (Fabulous Dancer (USA))
64^3 (2220) 2758^6 (2884)

Vital Evidence (USA) *Donald McCain* 97h
5 b g Empire Maker(USA) Promising Lead (Danehill (USA))
452^F

Vital Plot (USA) *Liam Kenny* 137h 129c
7 b g Theatrical(IRE) First Breeze (USA) (Woodman (USA))
75a^5

Vitarra *Jim Wilson* 54b
6 b m Kayf Tara Vivante (IRE) (Toulon)
1057^8 2126^{11}

Vivaccio (FR) *Venetia Williams* 105h 130c
6 b g Antarctique(IRE) Cybelle (FR) (Saint Cyrien (FR))
2854^U 3107^3 3620^4 4964^4

Vivacissimo (IRE) *Dan Skelton* 108h 117c
8 ch g Muhtathir Valley Orchard (FR) (Zilzal (USA))
747^3 (862) 1034^6 **1298^P** (Dead)

Vivaldi Collonges (FR) *Paul Nicholls* 135h 157c
6 b g Dom Alco(FR) Diane Collonges (FR) (El Badr)
(2935) 3624^5 (4124) (5323)

Vivant Poeme (FR) *Harry Fry* 132h
5 b g Early March Hasta Manana (FR) (Useful (FR))
(595) 1038^2 1325^2 5275^8

Viva Rafa (IRE) *Richard Phillips* 116h
5 b g Scorpion(IRE) Back To Stay (IRE) (Supreme Leader)
242^U 865^2 3370^7 4182^4 4646^2 ◆ 5269^4

Vivas (FR) *Charlie Longsdon* 116h
4 bb g Davidoff(GER) Lavircas (FR) (Lavirco (GER))
1758^2 2065^7 2612^4 3724^4 5453^2

Viva Star *Michael Easterby* 68h
4 gr m Verglas(IRE) Jazan (IRE) (Danehill (USA))
252^7

Viva Steve (IRE) *Mick Channon* 124h 139c
7 b g Flemensfirth(USA) Eluna (Unfuwain (USA))
(1970) 3282^2 ◆ 3849^6 4361^6 4700^8 5073^2 5496^5

Vive La France (FR) *Alan Fleming* 136h 112c
6 b g Westerner Millesimee (FR) (Video Rock (FR))
3650a^{19}

Vive Le Roi (IRE) *Charlie Longsdon* 121h
4 b g Robin Des Pres(FR) Cappard View (IRE) (Rudimentary (USA))
(1644) 2514^9 4308^8 (5048)

Vizzy's Thunder *Tony Carroll* 43h
7 gr g Fair Mix(IRE) Vizulize (Robellino (USA))
146^P

Vladimir (FR) *P Peltier* 125h 137c
6 b g Saint Des Saints(FR) Haida III (FR) (Video Rock (FR))
1477a^5

Vocaliser (IRE) *Robin Dickin* 98h
3 b c Vocalised(USA) Bring Back Matron (IRE) (Rock Of Gibraltar (IRE))
2273^7 4462^4 5091^{10}

Vodka Island (IRE) *Tim Vaughan* 87h
6 b m Turtle Island(IRE) From Russia With Love (Moscow Society (USA))
1613^8 1845^8 (2693) 2868^P 3369^P 4391^3 4804^6 5441^{11}

Vodka Moon *Sharon Watt* 81h
6 gr g Beat All(USA) Auntie Kathleen (Terimon)
79^P 484^P

Vodka 'n Tonic (IRE) *Nicky Henderson* 116h
6 b g Presenting Ballagh Dawn (IRE) (Buckskin (FR))
261^5 1377^4

Vodka Red (IRE) *Kenny Johnson* 91h
7 b g Ivan Denisovich(IRE) Begine (IRE) (Germany (USA))
2142^P 2560^P 2706^8 2982^2 4547^3

Vodka Wells (FR) *Micky Hammond* 131h 131c
5 b g Irish Wells(FR) Kahipiroska (FR) (Mansonnien (FR))
(82) 197^{10} 638^2 **(801) 1922^5 2201^3 2495^3 3155^4 3475^5 3589^P**

Voiladenuo (FR) *Guy Denuault* 147h 133c
6 b h Network(GER) Paresca (FR) (Maresca Sorrento (FR))
(4a) 663a^P 1883a^2 2361a^9

Voix D'Eau (FR) *Harry Fry* 119h 155c
5 b g Voix Du Nord(FR) Eau De Chesne (FR) (R B Chesne)
1479^2 (1962) 2184^2 (2746) 3147^3 (5276)

Voix Du Reve (FR) *W P Mullins* 144h
3 br g Voix Du Nord(FR) Pommbelle (FR) (Apple Tree (FR))
4720^F 5491^2

Volcanic (FR) *Donald McCain* 128h 128c
6 br g Al Namix(FR) Queen Of Rock (FR) (Video Rock (FR))
505^3 635^2 840^3 1097^2 (1401) 1701^7 2105^4
(3010) 3622^P 4305^8 4911^6

Volcanic Jack (IRE) *Michael Chapman* 101h 103c
7 b g Kodiac Rosaria Panatta (IRE) (Mujtahid (USA))
502^3 571^3 850^8 **913^3 1068^3 5015^P 5439^P**

Volio Vincente (FR) *Lydia Richards* 62h 81c
8 bb g Corri Piano(FR) Vollore (FR) (Cadoudal (FR))
211^3 717^3

Volnay De Thaix (FR) *Nicky Henderson* 154h 154c
6 ch g Secret Singer(FR) Mange De Thaix (FR) (Mont Basile (FR))
(3026) ◆ 3405^4 4717^{15} **5174^5 5496^2**

Von Trappe (IRE) *Alan Phillips* 61b
6 ch g Well Made(GER) Hawkshaws Bridge (IRE) (Good Thyne (USA))
220^6 558^{13}

Vosne Romanee *Dr Richard Newland* 129h
4 ch g Arakan(USA) Vento Del Oreno (FR) (Lando (GER))
162^7 592^2 5279^2 (5464)

Voyage A New York (FR) *Lucinda Russell* 119h 123c
6 b g Kapgarde(FR) Pennsylvanie (FR) (Dadarissime (FR))
2497^P 3364^8 3631^3 4109^3 (4627) 5078^3 5411^6

Vroum Vroum Mag (FR) *W P Mullins* 157h 151c
6 b m Voix Du Nord(FR) Naiade Mag (FR) (Kadalko (FR))
(2465a) (3732) (4699)

Vujiyama (FR) *Jonjo O'Neill* 99h 109c
6 br g Voix Du Nord(FR) Ili Dancer (FR) (Missolonghi (USA))
173^U 340^P

Vulcanite (IRE) *Charlie Longsdon* 139h 145c
8 b g Dubawi(IRE) Daraliya (IRE) (Kahyasi)
96a^{17} 317^5 556^{11} 812^4

Vyta Du Roc (FR) *Nicky Henderson* 143h 151c
6 gr g Lion Noir Dolce Vyta (FR) (Grand Tresor (FR))
(3006) 3504^2 (4237) 4716^5 5327^5

Wabanaki (IRE) *Evan Williams* 105h
5 b g Indian River(FR) Treasure Island (Rainbow Quest (USA))
2699^3 ◆ 3363^5 4196^3 5053^P

Waddingtown Hero (IRE) *Andy Turnell* 68h 110c
8 b g Subtle Power(IRE) Miss Liz (IRE) (Beneficial)
88^2 126^2 (770) 1306^7

Wade Harper (IRE) *David Dennis* 123h
5 b g Westerner Nosie Betty (IRE) (Alphabatim (USA))
23a^{12} 1837^3 ◆ 2091^2 2628^F (3334) (3971) 4620^P 5120^{11}

Wadswick Court (IRE) *Neil Mulholland* 131h 131c
7 b g Court Cave(IRE) Tarasandy (IRE) (Arapahos (FR))
2012^2 ◆ 2779^F 3106^6 3706^7

Wagstaff (IRE) *Mick Channon* 26h
3 b g Rip Van Winkle(IRE) Ride A Rainbow (Rainbow Quest (USA))
1177^8

Wait A Second (IRE) *Jonjo O'Neill* 117h
5 b g Scorpion(IRE) Fast Time (IRE) (Be My Native (USA))
207^2 (880) 1113^6 1269^5 3146^P

Wait For Me (FR) *Philip Hobbs* 142h
5 b g Saint Des Saints(FR) Aulne River (FR) (River Mist (USA))
2763^2 (3114) ◆ (3772) 4765^4

Waiting Patiently (IRE) *Keith Reveley* 123h
4 b g Flemensfirth(USA) Rossavon (IRE) (Beneficial)
2318^2 2772^2 (3883) ◆

Wait No More (IRE) *R Gurney* 23h 44c
10 ch g Strategic Choice(USA) Tearaway Lady (IRE) (Tidaro (USA))
294^6

Wakanda (IRE) *Sue Smith* 122h 157c
6 b g Westerner Chanson Indienne (FR) (Indian River (FR))
(2171) (2790) ◆ (3150) 3850^P 5176^P

Wak A Turtle (IRE) *Richard Woollacott* 76h 106c
7 b g Turtle Island(IRE) Playwaki (USA) (Miswaki (USA))
699^2 (874) 1084^P

Wake Your Dreams (IRE) *Jennie Candlish* 117h 115c
7 b g Oscar(IRE) Rose Karanja (Terimon)
2962^6 3607^5 3884^7 5122^2 5376^2

Wakhan (IRE) *Sandy Thomson* 88h 96c
7 b g Dalakhani(IRE) Wrapitraise (USA) (Raise A Man (USA))
2707^5 2844^U (3427) 3679^8 4175^3

Walden Prince (IRE) *David Bridgwater* 123h 129c
8 b g Saffron Walden(FR) Kahyasi Princess (IRE) (Kahyasi)
(964) ◆ (1045) (1099) 1344^P 1451^3 (1769) 2518^3

Waldorf Salad *Venetia Williams* 128h 140c
7 b g Millenary Ismene (FR) (Bad Conduct (USA))
(3129) (3371) 3849^2 4238^3 4700^P (5224)

Walkabout Creek (IRE) *Derek Frankland* 99h 106c
8 b g Alderbrook La Mouette (USA) (Hawkster (USA))
102^7 529^P 1927^P 2405^5 2858^6 3314^5 **4491^P**

Walkami (FR) *Jonjo O'Neill* 104h
4 b g Walk In The Park(IRE) Ominneha (FR) (Exit To Nowhere (USA))
341^2 ◆ 2460^7 2840^3 ◆ 4344^{12} 4982^2

Walking In The Air (IRE) *Dan Skelton* 132h
5 b g Flemensfirth(USA) Rossavon (IRE) (Beneficial)
2257^5 4108^2 ◆ 4463^2 ◆ (4874)

Walk In The Mill (FR) *Robert Walford* 125c
5 b g Walk In The Park(IRE) Libre Amour (FR) (Lost World (IRE))
2419^2 2908^2 3620^3 3924^5 4464^2

Walk Of Gleams *Anna Newton-Smith* 81h
6 b m Gleaming(IRE) Harlequin Walk (IRE) (Pennine Walk)
1618^S 1910^{11} 2256^4 2520^2 5306^P

Walk Of Shame *Phil McEntee* 21h
4 b g Muhtathir Joshua's Princess (Danehill (USA))
67^9

Walk On Al (IRE) *Sally Randell* 105h 87c
7 b g Alflora(IRE) Wave Back (IRE) (Bob Back (USA))
1903^7 2687^7 4066^F 5466^9

Walk To Freedom (IRE) *Mrs John Harrington* 145h 136c
5 br g Arcadio(GER) Carryonharriet (IRE) (Norwich)
3652a^4

Walk Waterford *Jonjo O'Neill* 88b
4 bl g Fair Mix(IRE) Woore Lass (IRE) (Persian Bold)
2750^8

Wallawallabingbang *Alexandra Dunn*
6 b m Midnight Legend Suzie Cream Cheese (IRE) (Royal Charter (FR))
4293^P 5378^P

Wally's Wisdom *Lee Carter*
3 b g Dutch Art Faldal (Falbrav (IRE))
2219^P

Walpole (IRE) *Hugo Palmer* 100b
3 b g Rock Of Gibraltar(IRE) Serena's Storm (IRE) (Statue Of Liberty (USA))
(1772) ◆

Walser (IRE) *John Wade* 106h
8 b g Milan Brass Neck (IRE) (Supreme Leader)
82^3 520^7 3628^F 3886^P

Walt (IRE) *Nicky Henderson* 106h
4 b g King's Theatre(IRE) Allee Sarthoise (FR) (Pampabird)
2835^2 4103^6 4790^{14}

Walter De La Mare (IRE) *Anabel K Murphy* 98h
8 b g Barathea(IRE) Banutan (IRE) (Charnwood Forest (IRE))
106^5 399^F (Dead)

Walter White (IRE) *Philip Hobbs* 107h
5 b g Dark Angel(IRE) Fun Time (Fraam)
1818^F 2458^5 2734^{11}

Waltz Darling (IRE) *Keith Reveley* 123h 126c
7 b g Iffraaj Aljafliyah (Halling (USA))
2746^3 (3020)

Waltzing Tornado (IRE) *Liam Grassick* 80h 93c
11 ch g Golden Tornado(IRE) Lady Dante (IRE) (Phardante (FR))
530^P 646^P

Waltz Legend (IRE) *Liam Lennon* 106h 106c
9 b m Flying Legend(USA) Vienna Waltz (IRE) (Orchestra)
3666^5 **5228^3**

Wanaba (FR) *Mme P Butel* 108h 125c
6 b g Anabaa(USA) Willamina (IRE) (Sadler's Wells (USA))
437a^9

Wannabe King *Ian Brown*
9 b g King's Best(USA) Wannabe Grand (IRE) (Danehill (USA))
4417^U

War And Contrition (IRE) *Charlie Longsdon* 104h
6 br g Presenting Sweet Second (IRE) (Second Set (IRE))
1964^5 2263^P 2862^6 2997^9

Warden Hill (IRE) *Mick Channon* 128h 143c
7 br g Presenting Moon Storm (IRE) (Strong Gale)
5283^3

Warksburn Boy *Sheena Walton* 94h
5 b g Kayf Tara Bonchester Bridge (Shambo)
837^{10} 1030^7 1328^7 1779^4 2802^F 2978^4 4547^P 4815^5 5402^5

War Lord (IRE) *George Moore*
5 b g Aussie Rules(USA) Carn Lady (IRE) (Woodman (USA))
416^P

Warne (IRE) *Robert Waley-Cohen* 69b 128c
11 b g Bob Back(USA) Dusky Diva (IRE) (Be My Native (USA))
75a^4 4424^P

War On (IRE) *Victor Thompson* 73h 75c
8 br g Presenting Alannico (Overbury (IRE))
140^P 287^5 416^7

War On The Rocks (IRE) *Fergal O'Brien* 110h
6 b g Wareed(IRE) Rock Garden (IRE) (Bigstone (IRE))
865^3 1979^3 2154^4

Warrant Officer *Sheena West* 96h
5 gr g Misu Bond(IRE) Kilmovee (Inchinor)
224^3 449^{10} 751^6 1297^3 1596^4 2000^8 2253^7 2547^2 3089^2 3665^P 3905^6 4159^P 5181^4

Warrantor (IRE) *Warren Greatrex* 139h 139c
6 b g Turtle Island(IRE) Pixie Dust (IRE) (Desert King (IRE))
2347^4 (3197) 4155^U 4286^F 4700^P 5311^2

Warrigal (IRE) *Tim Vaughan* 39h
5 ch g Mount Nelson Waldblume (GER) (Halling (USA))
440^9 613^P

Warriors Tale *Paul Nicholls* 139h 143c
6 b g Midnight Legend Samandara (FR) (Kris)
2727^2 ◆ 3100^P 4017^2 4730^{11} 5328^5

Warsaw Pact (IRE) *Steven Dixon* 82h 52c
12 b g Polish Precedent(USA) Always Friendly (High Line)
40^5 265^6 451^2 675^{10} 1951^7 2453^5 3125^2 4349^F 5020^4

War Singer (USA) *Johnny Farrelly* 130h
8 b g War Chant(USA) Sister Marilyn (USA) (Saint Ballado (CAN))
(406) 2617^8 2926^4 3529^3 3917^6

War Sound *Philip Hobbs* 147h
6 b g Kayf Tara Come The Dawn (Gunner B)
(197) 4115^{12}

Washed Ashore (IRE) *Jonjo O'Neill* 102b
4 ch g Presenting Give It Time (Kayf Tara)
188^3

Watchmego *Maurice Barnes* 73h
7 b m Supreme Sound One Stop (Silly Prices)
77^8 251^4

Watchmetail (IRE) *John Panvert* 71h
9 bb g Amilynx(FR) Ellie Anna (IRE) (Bravefoot)
859^6 1323^3 1691^{10} 1952^6 2015^3 2256^7 2599^P 2736^6 4920^4

Waterberry *Lucy Wadham* 84b
4 gr m Sagamix(FR) Eneeymeenymineeymo (IRE) (Pistolet Bleu (IRE))
2277^{12} 5443^7

Waterclock (IRE) *Micky Hammond* 129h
6 ch g Notnowcato Waterfall One (Nashwan (USA))
1369^2 (1550) 1776^5 3630^2 3999^3 ◆ 4470^4

Water For Life *Martin Smith*
4 ch m Mount Nelson Echo River (USA) (Irish River (FR))
3175^P 3921^P

Waterloo Warrior (IRE) *Colin Tizzard* 90b
3 b g Kalanisi(IRE) Vindonissa (IRE) (Definite Article)
5152^3

Waterlord *John Ferguson* 121h
4 b g Cape Cross(IRE) Shell Garland (USA) (Sadler's Wells (USA))
(558) (887) (1101) 2514^4 ◆ 2928^2

Water Rail *Simon Earle* 74h
6 b g Manipulator(IRE) Madame Mozaik (USA) (Sandpit (BRZ))
4343^P

Water Sprite (IRE) *Gordon Elliott* 127h
4 b m Papal Bull Wish Upon A Star (IRE) (Russian Revival (USA))
4202^3 4734^6

Water Willow *Harry Fry* 95b
3 b f Tobougg(IRE) Water Flower (Environment Friend)
2009^2 (2304) 5286^{12}

Watt Broderick (IRE) *Ian Williams* 113h
6 ch g Hawk Wing(USA) Kingsridge (IRE) (King's Theatre (IRE))
63^3 110^3 332^7 592^4 751^F 1265^5 1508^2 1719^2 (2038) 2540^8 3152^8 3487^{15}

Waxies Dargle *Noel Meade* 144h
6 b g Sakhee(USA) Cup Of Love (USA) (Behrens (USA))
7a^9 (231a) 2512^3 3151^P 3650a^{16} 4115^5 4717^6

Way Before Dawn *Mrs Sarah Tickle* 71c
8 ch g Nomadic Way(USA) Isis Dawn (Rakaposhi King)
123^6 5270^5

Waydownsouth (IRE) *Patrick J Flynn* 121h
8 b g Chevalier(IRE) Ruffit (IRE) (Revoque (IRE))
19a^F

Way Of The World (IRE) *Sheila Lewis* 97b
4 b g Flemensfirth(USA) Night Heron (IRE) (St Jovite (USA))
5055^4

Way Up In The Air (IRE) *Robert Tyner* 122h 125c
8 ch m Rock Of Gibraltar(IRE) Gold Flair (Tap On Wood)
70a^P

Wayupinthesky (IRE) *J P G Hamilton* 115h 121c
8 gr g Cloudings(IRE) Riancoir Alainn (Strong Gale)
533^7 4000^P 4207^5

Wayward Frolic *Jim Best* 106h 99c
9 br g Fair Mix(IRE) Mighty Frolic (Oats)
3906^3 4214^3 4343^P **4531^P**

Wayward Sun (IRE) *Micky Hammond* 67h
4 b g Double Eclipse(IRE) Mahonrun (IRE) (King Charlemagne (USA))
1901^7 2169^9 2716^6 3791^6 4557^P 5203^6

Wazowski *Donald McCain* 104h
6 b g Overbury(IRE) Malay (Karinga Bay)
4050^F 4567^3 4902^5 5365^4

Weapon Of Choice (IRE) *Dianne Sayer* 110h
7 b g Iffraaj Tullawadgeen (IRE) (Sinndar (IRE))
4865^5

Weather Babe *David Pipe* 134h 135c
7 b m Storming Home Bathwick Babe (IRE) (Sri Pekan (USA))
(122) 532^2 833^4 **(1097) (1713) 2055^2 3040^3**

Webbswood (IRE) *Sean Curran* 108h 96c
6 b g Catcher In The Rye(IRE) Victory Run (IRE) (Old Vic)
209^3 752^3

Wee Holio (IRE) *Marjorie Fife* 76b
4 b g Tikkanen(USA) Eskimo Kiss (IRE) (Distinctly North (USA))
4108^P 4419^P

Wee Jock Elliot *Alistair Whillans* 76h
5 b g Overbury(IRE) Caitlin Ash (Karinga Bay)
2210^8 2704^5 2937^P 3312^P 5089^P

Wee Man (IRE) *Nicky Richards* 101b
5 b g Milan Newcastlebeauty (IRE) (Luso)
359^2

Weet In Nerja *Ken Wingrove* 51h
9 b g Captain Rio Persian Fortune (Forzando)
937^{10} 1051^6

Welcome Bach (IRE) *Liam Corcoran* 119h
6 ch g Bach(IRE) Massini's Daughter (IRE) (Dr Massini (IRE))
4494^P 4917^4 5382^5 ◆

Welcome Ben (IRE) *Jackie Stephen* 113h
6 b g High Roller(IRE) Bramble Cottage (IRE) (Eurobus)
285^5 656^2 881^3 1265^{13} (1498) 1776^3 5260^P

Welcometothejungle *Harry Fry* 119h
7 b m Lucky Story(USA) Kasamba (Salse (USA))
(938) 1238^2 (1374) 1488^5

Weld Arab (IRE) *Michael Blake* 58h
4 b g Shamardal(USA) Itqaan (USA) (Danzig (USA))
5416^P

Wellforth (IRE) *Clare Ellam* 95h 101c
11 b g New Frontier(IRE) Faitch's Lady (IRE) (Dock Leaf)
2125^8 2669^2 3378^4 4047^P **5044^4 5228^P**

Well I Never *Ray Craggs* 62h
3 b g Josr Algarhoud(IRE) Tour D'Amour (IRE) (Fruits Of Love (USA))
1456^5

Well Rewarded (IRE) *Emma Lavelle* 99h 105c
5 b g Beneficial Lady Fancy (IRE) (Taipan (IRE))
1579^6 **1950^F 2930^7 5417^P**

Wells De Lune (FR) *Charlie Longsdon* 129h 117c
4 b g Irish Wells(FR) Pepite De Lune (FR) (Mansonnien (FR))
2914^9 3152^6 4129^6 (4384) 4484^P 5295^4

Welluptoscratch (FR) *David Arbuthnot* 102h
4 bb g Irish Wells(FR) Aulne River (FR) (River Mist (USA))
(227) 2910^6 5477^2 ◆

Welsh Bard (IRE) *Donald McCain* 116h 122c
6 ch g Dylan Thomas(IRE) Delphinium (IRE) (Dr Massini (IRE))
1032^8 (1458)

Welsh Shadow (IRE) *Dan Skelton* 142h
5 b g Robin Des Champs(FR) What A Mewsment (IRE) (Persian Mews)
2258^2 ◆ (2626) 3447^4 4360^3 4715^5 (5294)

We Never Give Up (IRE) *Mrs Pauline Harkin* 62c
9 b m Mull Of Kintyre(USA) Parker's Cove (USA) (Woodman (USA))
16^P 298^P

Wenyerreadyfreddie (IRE) *John Ferguson* 110b
4 ch g Beneficial Ware It Vic (IRE) (Old Vic)
4475^2

Werenearlyoutofit (IRE) *Graeme McPherson* 119h
7 b g Asian Heights Ballerina Laura (IRE) (Riot Helmet)
(1136)

West Approach *Colin Tizzard* 125h
5 b g Westerner Ardstown (Ardross)
2763^9 3032^3 3403^5 4139^2 4766^{11}

Westbrooke Warrior (IRE) *David Pipe* 80b
4 b g Robin Des Champs(FR) Tango Lady (IRE) (King's Theatre (IRE))
3082^6

West Cork Flash (IRE) *Paul Henderson* 89b 103c
11 ch g Windsor Castle Galley Flash (IRE) (Phardante (FR))
1114^P

West End (IRE) *Kim Bailey* 111h 122c
8 b g Westerner Brown Bess (IRE) (Definite Article)
108^9 493^5 757^2 967^2 **1114^6 1298^2 1487^3 (1639)**

Westend Prince (IRE) *Colin Tizzard* 97h
4 gr g King's Theatre(IRE) Caltra Princess (IRE) (Traditionally (USA))
2088^6 2345^4 2731^8 3174^P 5148^3 5433^8

Westend Star (IRE) *Gordon Elliott* 138h
6 b g Old Vic Camlin Rose (IRE) (Roselier (FR))
3962a^2 4769^{15}

Westend Story (IRE) *Philip Hobbs* 130b
4 b g Westerner Sarahall (IRE) (Saddlers' Hall (IRE))
(3226) ◆ (4143) ◆ 4721^5 ◆

Westend Theatre (IRE) *Jane Walton* 87h 97c
6 b g Darsi(FR) Ballyvelig Lady (IRE) (Project Manager)
2339^5 4365^3 5010^2 5261^P

Westerbee (IRE) *Seamus Mullins* 95b
4 b m Westerner Pass The Honey (IRE) (Snurge)
(2702) 3138^6 4468^4 5286^7

Westerly *John Mackie* 54h
4 b m Rail Link Humility (Polar Falcon (USA))
1597^7 2543^{12}

Westerly Breeze (IRE) *Edward Bevan* 105h
7 b g Westerner Sup A Whiskey (IRE) (Commanche Run)
55^2 530^6 646^2 879^2 1011^7

Western Boy (IRE) *P A Fahy* 143h 84c
6 b g Antonius Pius(USA) Skala (IRE) (Hernando (FR))
7a^{22} 231a^9 1175a^P 5025a^9

Western Breeze (IRE) *Mark Walford* 115h
6 b m Westerner Winsome Breeze (IRE) (Glacial Storm (USA))
516^2 (679) ◆ 2144^U 2490^2 3065^2

Western Cape (IRE) *Seamus Mullins* 126h
4 b g Westerner Simons Girl (IRE) (Grand Plaisir (IRE))
(2044) 2417^4 (3133) 3736^2 4620^{13}

Western Diva (IRE) *David Pipe* 117h
6 b m Westerner Duck 'N' Dive (IRE) (Accordion)
556^7 775^4 1170^{10} 1348^F 1828^P

Western Dream *Dai Burchell* 45b
7 b g Westerner Simiola (Shaamit (IRE))
2062^P

Westerners Son (IRE) *Dermot Anthony McLoughlin* 132h 132c
7 b g Westerner Perfect Prospect (IRE) (Golan (IRE))
19a^{18}

Western Goose (IRE) *Heather Dalton* 105h
8 bb m Westerner That's The Goose (IRE) (Be My Native (USA))
1171^3 (1509) 1598^5

Western Home (IRE) *Gordon Elliott* 98h 96c
5 br m Kalanisi(IRE) Western Road (GER) (King's Theatre (IRE))
305^5 (503) 1030^3

Western Jo (IRE) *Alan Brown* 102h 128c
7 b g Westerner Jenny's Jewel (IRE) (Be My Native (USA))
1903^{10} 4066^P **5245^2**

Western Miller (IRE) *Charlie Longsdon* 119h
4 b g Westerner Definite Miller (IRE) (Definite Article)
1645^2 (2025) 2591^5 3403^8 4922^2 5450^7

Western Rules (IRE) *Nicky Richards* 123h
5 b g Westerner Ryehill Lady (IRE) (Accordion)
2338^2 (3056) 3883^3 4202^2 4610^4

Western Sunrise (IRE) *Johnny Farrelly* 111h
6 b m Westerner Presenting Gayle (IRE) (Presenting)
432^3 696^4 2549^3 2770^3 4137^6 4457^4 (4916) 5415^3

Western Wave (FR) *David Loder* 95b
3 b g Westerner Kaprissima (FR) (Epervier Bleu)
4188^2 ◆ 4827^4

Western Way (IRE) *Don Cantillon* 132h
6 b g Westerner Faucon (Polar Falcon (USA))
263^6 566^5 971^3 1117^{10} (1265) (1503) ◆ 1736^3 1990^2 (2326) 2485^7

Western Xpress (IRE) *Peter Bowen* 117h
7 b g Westerner Lockersleybay (IRE) (Orchestra)
1698^3

West Hill Legend *Richard Woollacott* 84h
4 b m Midnight Legend Bajan Blue (Lycius (USA))
2770^6 4854^4

West Montan (IRE) *David Harry Kelly* 113h 108c
5 b m Westerner Reine De Coeur (IRE) (Montjeu (IRE))
52a^{10} 1565a^7

West Of The Edge (IRE) *Dai Williams* 110h 109c
7 b g Westerner Bermuda Bay (IRE) (Be My Native (USA))
340^4 448^6 637^7 2567^4 2730^{10} 3087^3 **(3236) 3591^P** (3904) 4127^4 **4412^4** 4593^6 4906^6 **5238^4**

Weston Flame *Ben Case* 89h
5 b m Westerner Rocheflamme (FR) (Snurge)
3612^P 3928^7 4271^6 4862^7 5420^7

Weston Super Mare *Alexandra Dunn* 27h
5 br m Scorpion(IRE) Proby Lady (IRE) (Insan (USA))
361^P

Westren Warrior (IRE) *Dr Richard Newland* 138h
6 b g Westerner Charming Leader (IRE) (Supreme Leader)
2257^P 2838^2 (3194) 3527^2 3844^2 4730^{19}

West Ship Master (IRE) *Paul Stafford* 91h 100c
11 b g Oscar(IRE) Lady Of Aherlow (Le Bavard (FR))
140^8 333^7 2708^P 4032^7 5366^5

Weststreet (IRE) *Oliver Sherwood* 127h
5 b g Westerner Klipperstreet (IRE) (Supreme Leader)
2417^3 (3064) 3525^3 3817^5 (5045)

West Torr (IRE) *Nigel Twiston-Davies* 88b
4 br g Scorpion(IRE) Native Craft (IRE) (Be My Native (USA))
5055^5

Westward Point *Warren Greatrex* 123h 126c
8 ch g Karinga Bay Hottentot (Sula Bula)
2832^4 3339^P

Westwire Toby (IRE) *Lynn Siddall* 79h 58c
13 ch g Anshan Ware It Well (IRE) (Torus)
133^4

West Wizard (FR) *Nigel Twiston-Davies* 134h 118c
6 bb g King's Theatre(IRE) Queen's Diamond (GER) (Konigsstuhl (GER))
(100) **3228^F 4363^5**

Weybridge Light *David Thompson* 104h
10 b g Fantastic Light(USA) Nuryana (Nureyev (USA))
571^2 746^3 839^{10} 1692^3 2135^2 3422^5

Weyburn (IRE) *Martin Keighley* 113h
4 gr g September Storm(GER) Saffron Pride (IRE) (Be My Native (USA))
11a^3 2044^7 2338^4 3568^5 3795^P (4844)

What About Molly (IRE) *Heather Dalton* 73h
5 ch m Stowaway Great Legacy (IRE) (Great Palm (USA))
2249^P

What About Will (IRE) *N Harris* 93c
6 ch g Pierre Dinah B (IRE) (Yashgan)
123^4

What A Diva *Peter Bowen* 94b
4 b m Kayf Tara Land Of Glory (Supreme Leader)
3082^3 3502^3 5241^2

What A Dream *Alison Hamilton* 99h 99c
9 ch g Supreme Sound Ben Roseler (IRE) (Beneficial)
(2191) (2430) 3345^3 3937^6 4406^4 4582^4 5261^5

What A Game (IRE) *Tim Easterby* 96h
4 ch g Milan Moscow Mo Chuisle (IRE) (Moscow Society (USA))
2917^4 3397^6 3626^U 4152^6 4942^3

What A Good Night (IRE) *Dan Skelton* 93h 132c
7 br g Westerner Southern Skies (IRE) (Dr Massini (IRE))
2149^F (2436) 3624^P 4348^P

What A Jewel (IRE) *Eoin Doyle* 116h 109c
5 ch m Presenting Borleagh Blonde (IRE) (Zaffaran (USA))
(238) 1374^2

Whataknight *Harry Fry* 142h
6 b g Midnight Legend What A Mover (Jupiter Island)
2603^3 (2986) 4066^2 ◆ 4544^3 5273^4

What A Lark (IRE) *Tony Coyle* 91b
4 b m Kalanisi(IRE) Grangeclare Lark (IRE) (Old Vic)
(1378)

What A Laugh *Gary Hanmer* 115h 131c
10 b g Kayf Tara Just For A Laugh (Idiots Delight)
(534) 1828^2 **1976^3**

What A Moment (IRE) *David Pipe* 118h
5 b g Milan Cuiloge Lady (IRE) (Beneficial)
2910^4 3179^2 3736^4 4241^8

What A Scorcher *Oliver Sherwood* 108h
4 b m Authorized(IRE) Street Fire (IRE) (Street Cry (IRE))
179^3 3066^3 4429^P

What A Steel (IRE) *Alistair Whillans* 112h
11 b g Craigsteel Sonya's Pearl (IRE) (Conquering Hero (USA))
705^3 (798) 958^5 1264^{13} (1739) 1856^2 2340^P 2948^7

What A Tempest *Richard Phillips* 80h
5 b m Kayf Tara What A Vintage (IRE) (Un Desperado (FR))
2644^8 3022^{11} 3484^6

Whatatub (IRE) *Chris Grant* 55b
4 b g Kutub(IRE) County Classic (Noble Patriarch)
2344^6

What A Warrior (IRE) *Dan Skelton* 117h 141c
8 b g Westerner Be Right (IRE) (Be My Native (USA))
2187^4 3109^7

Whatdoesthefoxsay (IRE) *Donald McCain* 119h
6 ch m Vinnie Roe(IRE) She's The One (IRE) (Good Thyne (USA))
314^6 711^6 3333^P 4512^4 4909^6 5409^{12}

What Happens Now (IRE) *Donald McCain* 106h 106c
6 b g Dr Massini(IRE) Euro Burden (IRE) (Good Thyne (USA))
2709^2 2945^4 3239^3 4035^7 4442^P **5388^3** ◆

Whatiknownow *Charlie Wallis* 41b
4 b m Lucarno(USA) Wolnai (Cloudings (IRE))
67^{12}

What Kept You (IRE) *David Dennis* 87h
3 br g Kalanisi(IRE) Eluna (Unfuwain (USA))
4552^6 5452^4

What Larks (IRE) *Hugo Froud* 102h 114c
7 b g Pierre Bint Rosie (Exit To Nowhere (USA))
2263^{10} **2988^2 3746^P (4962) 5222^P**

What's For Tea *Paddy Butler* 57h 61c
10 b m Beat All(USA) Come To Tea (IRE) (Be My Guest (USA))
223^5 674^P

Whatsforuwontgobyu (IRE) *A J Martin* 132h
5 b g Well Chosen Meadstown Miss (IRE) (Flemensfirth (USA))
1565a^8 (3323a) 3650a^8 5025a^{13}

Whats Happening (IRE) *Tom George* 135h 143c
8 b g Lahib(USA) Rebeccas Star (IRE) (Camden Town)
(2061)

Whats Left (IRE) *Neil Mulholland* 114h 134c
7 b g Darsi(FR) Dynamic Venture (IRE) (King's Ride)
1372^P (1820) 2261^P 3113^P 4914^4 5274^{11}

Whatsthatallabout (IRE) *Neil Mulholland* 86h
4 b m Milan Peinture Francaise (FR) (Pistolet Bleu (IRE))
4687^7 5220^5

What's The Scoop (IRE) *Nicky Henderson* 130h
5 ch g Presenting Dame D'Harvard (USA) (Quest For Fame)
2612[3] 4097[5] 4594[2] 5115[5]

Whatsthestoryman (IRE) *Katie Scott* 94h 95c
7 b g Alderbrook Express Way Lady (IRE) (Camden Town)
1852[6] 2066[9] 2210[7] 4163[9] **5125[3]** ◆

Whatsupjack (IRE) *Shaun Harris* 82h
8 b g Catcher In The Rye(IRE) Riverstown Girl (IRE) (Buckskin (FR))
37[2] 262[P] 502[7] **2596[U]** 2868[P] 3821[7] 4645[P]

Whats Up Woody (IRE) *George Bewley* 103h 112c
10 b g Beneficial Lady Noellel (IRE) (Step Together I (USA))
2491[P] 3310[6] 3969[P] (5010) (5261)

Whatthebutlersaw (IRE) *Dominic Ffrench Davis* 104h
6 br g Arcadio(GER) Phar From Men (IRE) (Phardante (FR))
176[3] 463[U]

Wheelavit (IRE) *Claire Dyson* 69h
12 b g Elnadim(USA) Storm River (USA) (Riverman (USA))
1084[11] 1423[7]

When In Roam (IRE) *John O'Shea* 107h
6 b m Flemensfirth(USA) Roaming (IRE) (Be My Native (USA))
238[7] 552[U] 2964[3] 4415[6] (4804) 5203[DSQ]

Whenskiesareblue (IRE) *William Kinsey* 56b
4 b m Presenting Blue Gallery (IRE) (Bluebird (USA))
3381[5]

Where'd Ya Hide It (IRE) *Paul Henderson* 73h 87c
9 b g Old Vic Stashedaway (IRE) (Treasure Hunter)
280[6] 717[2] 1118[4] 1243[5] 1326[5]

Where's Cherry (IRE) *Fergal O'Brien* 77b
4 b m King's Theatre(IRE) I'm Grand (IRE) (Raise A Grand (IRE))
2277[13] 2486[16]

Where's Malachy (IRE) *Rose Dobbin* 91h
7 ch g Muhtarram(USA) County Classic (Noble Patriarch)
454[P] 728[U]

Where's Tiger *Lucinda Russell* 116h
4 b g Tiger Hill(IRE) Where's Broughton (Cadeaux Genereux)
1328[5] 1499[F] (1634) 1886[2] 3035[11] 3424[9]

Which One Is Which *Jonjo O'Neill* 112b
4 br m King's Theatre(IRE) Presenting Copper (IRE) (Presenting)
(696) ◆ 2486[2]

While You Wait (IRE) *Sue Gardner* 113h
6 b g Whipper(USA) Azra (IRE) (Danehill (USA))
1602[2] 1828[3] 2271[4] 2490[7] 3777[3] 4384[10] 5277[10]

Whimsical Notion *Nigel Hawke* 82h
5 b g Midnight Legend Friendly Request (Environment Friend)
419[4] 754[6] 2265[P] 4920[P]

Whipcord (IRE) *Paul Nicholls* 117h
4 gr g Tikkanen(USA) Dapples (IRE) (Accordion)
5263[5] 5434[2]

Whipcrackaway (IRE) *Peter Hedger* 84h
6 b g Whipper(USA) Former Drama (USA) (Dynaformer (USA))
391[4] 864[9]

Whip Dancer (FR) *Louisa Carberry*
4 b g Whipper(USA) Danse D'Amour (Dansili)
3876a[4] **5135a[4]**

Whiskey Chaser (IRE) *Donald McCain* 96h 126c
7 br g Flemensfirth(USA) Cregane Lass (IRE) (Oscar (IRE))
2894[4] 4175[2] (4591) (4710) 5334[3]

Whiskey John *Laura Young* 95h
5 b g Westerner Cherry Lane (Buckley)
2163[5] 2567[F] 2964[P] 4250[P]

Whiskey Ridge (IRE) *Sue Smith* 84b
9 b g High-Rise(IRE) Little Chartridge (Anshan)
4872[P]

Whisky Marmalade (IRE) *Ben Haslam* 99h
3 b f Duke Of Marmalade(IRE) Nashatara (USA) (Nashwan (USA))
778[U] 1768[U] 2718[7]

Whisper (FR) *Nicky Henderson* 165h 137c
7 b g Astarabad(USA) Belle Yepa (FR) (Mansonnien (FR))
2782[5] 3408[P] 4732[8]

Whispering Harry *Henry Oliver* 113h 131c
6 b g Sir Harry Lewis(USA) Welsh Whisper (Overbury (IRE))
2540[11] **2784[2] 3155[F] 3629[P]** 4353[3] **4617[6] 5096[2]**

Whispering Speed (IRE) *Lucy Wadham* 79h
5 ch g Vertical Speed(FR) Midnight Lover (Beveled (USA))
1990[5] 2239[8] 2772[8] 3128[4] 3771[13] 4030[2] ◆ 4391[P] 5481[P]

Whispering Storm (GER) *Paul Nicholls* 105h
5 b g Samum(GER) Wind In Her Hair (GER) (Turtle Island (IRE))
4790[4] 5268[3] 5469[2]

Whistle Dixie (IRE) *Gordon Elliott* 124h
5 b m Kayf Tara Fairy Blaze (IRE) (Good Thyne (USA))
3873a[3] 4734[11] 4954a[P]

Whistler Mountain *Mark Gillard* 25h
3 b g Oasis Dream Canda (USA) (Storm Cat (USA))
1232[P] 1294[7] 1452[7]

Whiteabbey (IRE) *Mrs R Hewit* 87h 67c
10 b g Luso Frantesa (Red Sunset)
5258[4]

White Arm (FR) *A J Martin* 112c
6 b g Turgeon(USA) White Consel (FR) (Leading Counsel (USA))
4663a[P]

Whiteout (GER) *W P Mullins* 147h
4 b m Samum(GER) Wassiliki (IRE) (Night Shift (USA))
(52a) 1748a[2] 2177a[2] 3356a[4] 4769[5] 5189[P]

Whitstable Native *Sophie Leech* 85h
7 b g Bertolini(USA) Break Of Dawn (USA) (Mt. Livermore (USA))
1544[10] 1693[8] 2035[4] 2559[8] 5313[4]

Whitsundays (IRE) *Donald McCain* 98h
6 b g Kutub(IRE) Urdite's Vic (IRE) (Old Vic)
2690[3] (2890) 3377[6] 4421[P]

Who Am I *Debra Hamer* 105h 106c
9 bb g Tamayaz(CAN) Short Fuse (IRE) (Zaffaran (USA))
173[F] 614[6] **1080[2] 1159[4] 1373[F] 1641[P]**

Who Dares Wins (IRE) *Alan King* 135h
3 b g Jeremy(USA) Savignano (Polish Precedent (USA))
(2448) ◆ (3039) 3848[4] 4764[14]

Wholestone (IRE) *Nigel Twiston-Davies* 121h
4 br g Craigsteel Last Theatre (IRE) (King's Theatre (IRE))
(1645) 2152[3] 2787[F]

Who Owns Me (IRE) *Michael Easterby* 120h 94c
9 b g Milan Top Lassie (IRE) (Topanoora)
2919[4]

Whos De Baby (IRE) *Sarah-Jayne Davies* 103h 95c
7 gr g Bienamado(USA) Beaus Rose (IRE) (Roselier (FR))
2995[6] 3467[P] 3927[6] 4714[6]

Whoshotwho (IRE) *Nicky Henderson* 110b
4 br g Beneficial Inishbeg House (IRE) (Glacial Storm (USA))
4102[3]

Who's Micky Brown (IRE) *Neil Mulholland* 120h
5 b g Turtle Island(IRE) Ginger Crunch (IRE) (Moonax (IRE))
2828[2] 3194[3] 3590[6] 3710[9] 3955[3] 4250[5] (4972) ◆ 5146[5]

Who You For (IRE) *Sarah Humphrey* 113h
5 b g Craigsteel Knappogue Honey (IRE) (Anshan)
(1449) ◆ 1723[2] 1943[3] ◆ 2496[4] 2839[P]

Why But Why (USA) *Ian Duncan* 101h 103c
7 b g Whywhywhy(USA) Miss Orah (Unfuwain (USA))
2755[9] 3438[F] **4166[9]** 5445[16]

Why Wait (FR) *J-Y Artu*
3 gr f Montmartre(FR) Our Beautiful (FR) (Sinndar (IRE))
4734P

Wicked Games (IRE) *Rose Dobbin* 97h
4 br m Flemensfirth(USA) Tariana (IRE) (Revoque (IRE))
3667[8] 4052[3] 4284[2] 4904[10]

Wicked Spice (IRE) *Nicky Richards* 128h 98c
6 b g Old Vic Afdala (IRE) (Hernando (FR))
50a[8] **2932[P] 3838[3]**

Wicked Willy (IRE) *Nigel Twiston-Davies* 107h
4 br g Arcadio(GER) How Provincial (IRE) (Be My Native (USA))
1640[7] 4827[7] 5137[2] 5408[8]

Wicklewood *Mark Gillard* 72h 112c
9 b g Mujahid(USA) Pinini (Pivotal)
240[9] **381[P] 676[P]** 2736[10] **3951[F] 4187[P] 4686[P] 4921[P]**

Wicklow Brave *W P Mullins* 163h
6 b g Beat Hollow Moraine (Rainbow Quest (USA))
1163a[11] 2532a[3] 2789[3]

Wicklow Gold (FR) *N W Alexander* 109b
7 b g Robin Des Champs(FR) Gamine D'Ici (FR) (Cadoudal (FR))
5300[P]

Wicklow Lad *N W Alexander* 114h 124c
11 gr g Silver Patriarch(IRE) Marina Bird (Julio Mariner)
4207[2] 5370[2]

Widow On The Run (IRE) *Kim Bailey* 94b
4 b m Milan O Mio My (IRE) (Roselier (FR))
5383[3]

Wiesentraum (GER) *Lucy Wadham* 116h 143c
9 ch g Next Desert(IRE) Wiesenblute (GER) (Big Shuffle (USA))
1658[9] 1944[4]

Wiffy Chatsby (IRE) *Dafydd Jones* 71h 100c
8 br g Presenting Star Child (GER) (Neshad (USA))
4227[4] 4887[P]

Wilberdragon *Charlie Longsdon* 129h
5 b g Kayf Tara Swaythe (USA) (Swain (IRE))
2186[6] 2728[4] 4781[P]

Wild Bill (IRE) *Evan Williams* 117h 129c
6 b g Westerner Sarahall (IRE) (Saddlers' Hall (IRE))
2365[F] ◆ **(2749) 3339[3] 4352[4] 5285[P]**

Wildcatted (GER) *Michael J McDonagh* 116h 119c
6 b g Shirocco(GER) Wildspiel (GER) (Singspiel (IRE))
3716a[9]

Wild Desert (FR) *Jennie Candlish*
10 bb g Desert Prince(IRE) Sallivera (IRE) (Sillery (USA))
1933[P]

Wilde And Willing (IRE) *Seamus Mullins* 42h
7 b g Oscar(IRE) Turtlena (IRE) (Turtle Island (IRE))
524[P]

Wilde Blue Yonder (IRE) *Alan King* 121h
6 b g Oscar(IRE) Blue Gallery (IRE) (Bluebird (USA))
5497[12]

Wildehearted Woman (IRE) *Jamie Snowden* 93b
4 b m Oscar(IRE) Burrator (Topanoora)
2715[5] 4302[2] (4908)

Wilde Oak (IRE) *Anthony Honeyball* 105b
5 b g Oscar(IRE) Tree Oaks (IRE) (Be My Native (USA))
1122[3] 1345[3]

Wildest Dreams (IRE) *Jane Walton* 88h 58c
6 b g Flemensfirth(USA) Suspicious Minds (Anabaa (USA))
251[P] 2343[P] **5125[8]**

Wild Fern (IRE) *Seamus Fahey* 116h
6 b m Beneficial Crossbar Lady (IRE) (Flemensfirth (USA))
2176a[6]

Wild Ginger *Jonjo O'Neill* 84h
4 ch g Presenting Diamant Noir (Sir Harry Lewis (USA))
3334[8]

Wildmoor Boy *Robin Dickin* 82h
4 b g Midnight Legend Simple Glory (IRE) (Simply Great (FR))
330[P] 396[3] 680[P] 3403[P]

Wild Rover (IRE) *Rebecca Curtis* 123h 107c
6 b g Scorpion(IRE) Pandalute (IRE) (Indian Danehill (IRE))
(1964) 2725[4] ◆ **3371[3] 4465[F]**

Wild West Wind (IRE) *Tom George* 127h
6 b g Westerner Mhuire Na Gale (IRE) (Norwich)
2440[2] 2903[F] ◆ 3400[3] (3976) 4586[2] 5264[2]

Willaldoo *Henry Daly* 55b
4 b m Black Sam Bellamy(IRE) Ella Falls (IRE) (Dancing Dissident (USA))
4075[8]

Willem (FR) *David Pipe* 128h
5 b g Turtle Bowl(IRE) Zita Blues (IRE) (Zieten (USA))
208[5] 826[2] 1035[13] 1742[2] 2054[9] 2513[F] 2711[4] 5391[2]

William H Bonney *Alan King* 136h
4 b g Midnight Legend Calamintha (Mtoto)
2317[2] (2823) 3353[2] (4182) ◆ 4695[10]

William Hunter *Alan King* 72b
3 b g Mawatheeq(USA) Cosmea (Compton Place)
2414[6] 4308[7]

William Money (IRE) *Chris Grant* 61h 99c
8 b g Cloudings(IRE) All Of A Kind (IRE) (Orchestra)
2068[6] 2790[F] 2934[P] 3364[7] 4367[P] 4914[6] 5474[9]

William Of Orange *Donald McCain* 114h
4 b g Duke Of Marmalade(IRE) Critical Acclaim (Peintre Celebre (USA))
3306[4] (3590) 4044[2] 4941[6]

Willie Hall *Lisa Harrison* 92h 101c
11 b g Alflora(IRE) G'Ime A Buzz (Electric)
37[8] **204[P]** 484[7] 2071[2] **2321[P] 2866[2] 3237[2]** ◆ **(3441) (3670) 3938[5] 4166[3]**

Willie Whistle *Maurice Barnes* 74h
6 b g Supreme Sound Zahara Joy (Cayman Kai (IRE))
251[5]

Will O'The West (IRE) *Henry Daly* 129h
6 b g Westerner Simply Divine (IRE) (Be My Native (USA))
213[6] 2487[3] 3105[5] (3863) (4344) 4620[P] 5372[2]

Willoughby Court (IRE) *Ben Pauling* 131b
4 br g Court Cave(IRE) Willoughby Sue (IRE) (Dabali (IRE))
(2562) (2998) 5195[5]

Willoughby Hedge *Alan King* 127h 131c
8 b g King's Theatre(IRE) Mini Mandy (Petoski)
3348[F] 3823[2] (4062) ◆

Willow Island (IRE) *Sophie Leech* 77h
6 b g Dark Angel(IRE) Cidaris (IRE) (Persian Bold)
110[7] 364[9] 824[7]

Willow's Saviour *Dan Skelton* 142h 144c
8 ch g Septieme Ciel(USA) Willow Gale (Strong Gale)
(2274) 2913[4] (4222) 4701[F]

Willshebetrying *Jim Best* 98h
4 b m Act One Precedence (IRE) (Polish Precedent (USA))
595[F] 2829[3] 3665[4] 3905[5]

Will Take Charge (IRE) *Jonjo O'Neill* 64h
4 b g Beneficial Corraig Lady (IRE) (Zaffaran (USA))
1644[4] 3309[7]

Willy Brennan (IRE) *Jo Davis* 100h
4 br g Bushranger(IRE) Miss Assertive (Zafonic (USA))
1898[5]

Wilton Milan (IRE) *Dan Skelton* 124h 137c
7 b g Milan Biondo (IRE) (College Chapel)
1869[3] 2348[P] (2701) 3157[6] 3748[P] **4155[P] 4595[4] 4858[F] 5238[P]**

Wily Fox *James Eustace* 112h
8 ch g Observatory(USA) Kamkova (USA) (Northern Dancer (CAN))
363[3] 705[4] 1794[2] ◆ 2135[6]

Wind Of Hope (IRE) *Alan J Brown* 115h 93c
6 b g September Storm(GER) Ciara's Run (IRE) (Topanoora)
(285) 656[3] **959[7]** 1646[2] **4180[U]**

Windsor Park (IRE) *D K Weld* 152h
6 b g Galileo(IRE) Blissful (USA) (Mr Prospector (USA))
3358a[4]

Windy Writer (IRE) *Shaun Lycett* 110h
5 bb g Rudimentary(USA) Hardabout (IRE) (Alderbrook)
2065[11] 2603[8] 3179[6] 4388[3]

Winged Crusader (IRE) *Nigel Twiston-Davies* 116h 121c
7 b g Winged Love(IRE) Reine Berengere (FR) (Esprit Du Nord (USA))
(141) 289[P] 2663[P] 4348[4] 4912[7] 5474[8]

Winged Express (IRE) *Alexandra Dunn* 105h 105c
6 b g Winged Love(IRE) Zaffaran Express (IRE) (Zaffaran (USA))
262[2] ◆ 391[2] **1838[P] 2254[P]** (3368) **3497[2]** 3919[3] **(4356)** 5163[2]

Wing Mira (IRE) *Venetia Williams* 87h 67c
7 b g Winged Love(IRE) Miraflores (IRE) (Montelimar (USA))
150[3] 450[P]

Wingoldandwearit (IRE) *Ms Sandra Hughes* 90h
4 bb g Definite Article Connemara Rose (IRE) (Desert King (IRE))
9a[16]

Wings Attract (IRE) *Chris Bealby* 118h 136c
6 b g Winged Love(IRE) Huncheon Siss (IRE) (Phardante (FR))
(1943) 2407[4] **(2774)** ◆ **3176[3] 4274[2] (4775)**

Wings Of Smoke (IRE) *Tim Vaughan* 117h 139c
10 gr g King's Theatre(IRE) Grey Mo (IRE) (Roselier (FR))
101[7] (642) 1040[10] 1382[4] (3749) 4424[U] 4964[6]

Winner Massagot (FR) *Alan King* 132h
4 ch g Muhaymin(USA) Winnor (FR) (Lesotho (USA))
(2617) ◆ 3151[15] 4273[P]

Winner Saulaie (FR) *G Cherel*
2 ch g Kentucky Dynamite(USA) Zurs (GER) (Lando (GER))
4539a[F]

Winning Spark (USA) *Jackie Du Plessis* 121h
8 b g Theatrical(IRE) Spark Sept (FR) (Septieme Ciel (USA))
2600[3] 2989[3] 3414[F] (3584) 3748[4] 5030[5]

Winning Ticket (IRE) *Paul Morgan* 98h
4 b g Kalanisi(IRE) Saddlers' Venture (IRE) (Saddlers' Hall (IRE))
4270[3] 5161[4] 5469[5]

Winningtry (IRE) *Paul Nicholls* 102b
4 br g Flemensfirth(USA) Jeruflo (IRE) (Glacial Storm (USA))
(5152)

Winola *Charlie Wallis* 72h
5 ch m Lucarno(USA) Wolnai (Cloudings (IRE))
4228[5] 4502[6] 4773[8] 5373[10]

Winsome Bucks (IRE) *T Hogan* 112b
5 b g Chevalier(IRE) Winsome Lady (IRE) (Buckskin (FR))
4721[23]

Winston Churchill (IRE) *Sophie Leech* 112h 110c
9 b g Presenting Star Councel (IRE) (Leading Counsel (USA))
(2568) 3044[4] 3867[P] 4255[2]

Winter Alchemy (IRE) *Nicky Richards* 92h 97c
10 b g Fruits Of Love(USA) Native Land (Be My Native (USA))
140[2] 486[P] 842[P] 1171[2] **1778[5]** 2071[4] 2751[6] 3220[4]

Wintered Well (IRE) *Jennie Candlish* 120h
7 b g Milan Stratosphere (Selkirk (USA))
2802[5] 3242[7] 3846[3] (4421) (4474) 4906[2]

Winter Escape (IRE) *Alan King* 140h
4 b g Robin Des Pres(FR) Saddleeruppat (IRE) (Saddlers' Hall (IRE))
(3021) (4064) ◆ (4360)

Winterfell (FR) *Dan Skelton* 123h
3 b g Voix Du Nord(FR) Goldville (FR) (Gold And Steel (FR))
2578[2]

Winter Garden (IRE) *R G Chapman* 96b
6 b g Dushyantor(USA) Flower Drum (FR) (Celtic Swing)
320[8]

Winter Link *Sandy Forster* 21b
5 b m Rail Link Winter Bloom (USA) (Aptitude (USA))
4208[8]

Winter Lion (IRE) *Matthew J Smith* 115h
5 ch g Galileo(IRE) Hill Of Snow (Reference Point)
2294[2] 3323a[11]

Winterlude (IRE) *Jennie Candlish* 77h
5 b g Street Cry(IRE) New Morning (IRE) (Sadler's Wells (USA))
1698[7]

Winter Soldier *Richard Woollacott* 112b
5 b g Apple Tree(FR) Primitive Quest (Commanche Run)
341[2] ◆ (761)

Wintour Leap *Robert Stephens* 112h
4 b m Nayef(USA) Mountain Leap (IRE) (Sadler's Wells (USA))
823[6] 1009[6] 1081[2] 1348[2] (1454) 1793[4] 2033[3]

Wishfull Dreaming *Philip Hobbs* 116h
4 ch g Alflora(IRE) Poussetiere Deux (FR) (Garde Royale)
(1826) 2345[3]

Wishfull Thinking *Philip Hobbs* 142h 170c
12 ch g Alflora(IRE) Poussetiere Deux (FR) (Garde Royale)
2084[2] 2927[3] 3526[2] 5276[7]

Wish In A Well (IRE) *Ben Case* 105h 89c
6 b g Gamut(IRE) Lady Bellingham (IRE) (Montelimar (USA))
2844 524[P] 2811[4] 3387[3] 3834[10] 4276[4] 4710[2]

Wishing And Hoping (IRE) *Alan King* 120h
5 b g Beneficial Desperately Hoping (IRE) (Un Desperado (FR))
(1998) (2614) 3623[U]

Wishing Well *Micky Hammond* 66h
3 b f Bahri(USA) Amourallis (IRE) (Dushyantor (USA))
3587[6] 3995[4]

Wishing Wind *Nicky Henderson* 93h
5 b m Kayf Tara Romantic Dream (Bustino)
3862[8] 5155[5]

Wistari Rocks (IRE) *Tim Vaughan* 97h
6 b g Heron Island(IRE) Hi Honey (IRE) (Persian Mews)
754[7] 933[3] 1168[P] 1421[8]

Witch's Hat (IRE) *R Gurney* 89b 90c
12 br g Hubbly Bubbly(USA) Bold Shilling (IRE) (Meneval (USA))
295[P]

Wither Yenot (IRE) *Ben Case* 114h 44c
8 b g Tikkanen(USA) Acacia Bloom (IRE) (Old Vic)
760[7] 873[8] 1375[P]

Withoutdefavourite (IRE) *Miss A Griffiths* 84h 113c
7 b g Oscar(IRE) Camden Confusion (IRE) (Camden Town)
1601[5] 1906[8] 5467[6]

Without Limites (FR) *Miss Elizabeth Doyle* 128b
3 gr g Martaline Sans Limites (FR) (Nikos)
(5134a)

Without Wings (IRE) *Liam Lennon*
7 b m Winged Love(IRE) Drumee (IRE) (Satco (FR))
840[P]

Withy Mills *Kevin Bishop* 99h 92c
10 gr m Baryshnikov(AUS) Gipsy Rose (Nicholas Bill)
4778[2] 5307[2] (5435)

Witness In Court (IRE) *Donald McCain* 131h 147c
8 b g Witness Box(USA) Inter Alia (IRE) (Dr Massini (IRE))
555[5] 849[5] 1135[3] 1382[2] 1715[5] 2902[U] 5193[U] (5448)

Wizadora *Miss J M Coward*
7 b m Alflora(IRE) Moor Spring (Primitive Rising (USA))
5082[U]

Wizards Bridge *Colin Tizzard* 123h 133c
6 b g Alflora(IRE) Island Hopper (Be My Native (USA))
1867[5] (2442) 2785[2] 3520[P] 4101[3] 4340[P] 4857[5] 5390[F]

Wojciech *Martin Hill* 93h
5 b m Lucarno(USA) Pondimari (FR) (Marignan (USA))
167[4] 1120[4] 5223[P]

Wolfcatcher (IRE) *John Ferguson* 130h
3 b g King's Best(USA) Miss Particular (IRE) (Sadler's Wells (USA))
(2863) ◆ 4038[2] 4358[5] 4720[11]

Wolf Hall (IRE) *Violet M Jordan* 116h 72c
8 br g Presenting Water Rock (El Conquistador)
588[8]

Wolf Of Windlesham (IRE) *Stuart Edmunds* 139h
3 ch g Mastercraftsman(IRE) Al Amlah (USA) (Riverman (USA))
(2032) (2480) 3848[6] (5491)

Wolf Shield (IRE) *Patrick Holmes* 93h 108c
8 b g King's Theatre(IRE) Garlucy (IRE) (Un Desperado (FR))
420[3] 707[P] 1113[P] 2496[8] 3837[14] 4906[P] 5246[8]

Wolf Sword (IRE) *Sue Smith* 108h 121c
6 b g Flemensfirth(USA) Dame O'Neill (IRE) (Dr Massini (IRE))
(155) 1901[5] **2645[P] 3311[5] 3669[5] 4866[F] 5078[2]**

Wolftrap (IRE) *Philip Hobbs* 103h
6 b g Mountain High(IRE) Dear Money (IRE) (Buckskin (FR))
180[7] 4855[5] (5163) 5464[2]

Wonderful Charm (FR) *Paul Nicholls* 143h 165c
7 b g Poliglote Victoria Royale (FR) (Garde Royale)
3016[2] 5218[P] 5492[7]

Woodford County *Philip Hobbs* 122h 134c
8 b g Sonus(IRE) Moylena (IRE) (Bustomi)
2146[6] (2878) 3518[5] 4367[6] 4914[P] 5274[15]

Woodford Island (IRE) *Gordon Elliott* 126h
4 bb g Trans Island Toulon Breeze (IRE) (Toulon)
3137[3] 4246[P]

Woodland Opera (IRE) *Mrs John Harrington* 143h
5 br g Robin Des Champs(FR) Opera Hat (IRE) (Strong Gale)
3294a[9] 3765a[3]

Woodland Walk *Emma Lavelle* 125h
7 ch m Generous(IRE) Duchess Of Kinsale (IRE) (Montelimar (USA))
1808[8] 2167[5] 2455[2] 2911[5] 4909[4]

Woodlark Island (IRE) *A Campbell* 68h 72c
9 b g Tagula(IRE) Be My Lover (Pursuit Of Love)
151[8] 296[3] 536[U]

Woodpole Academy (IRE) *Philip Kirby* 100b
8 b g Beneficial Midday Caller (IRE) (Miner's Lamp)
2105[F] 2342[P] 2921[P]

Woodstock (IRE) *Ann Hamilton* 97h
5 b g High Chaparral(IRE) Woodwin (IRE) (Woodman (USA))
1892[8] (2212)

Wood Yer (IRE) *Nigel Twiston-Davies* 95h 126c
9 ch g Anshan Glenasheen (IRE) (Presenting)
(4612) 5334[2]

Woofie (IRE) *Laura Mongan* 41h
3 b g Duke Of Marmalade(IRE) Violet Ballerina (IRE) (Namid)
2092[5]

Woolstone One *Harry Whittington* 120b
3 b f Authorized(IRE) Saralea (FR) (Sillery (USA))
(3118) ◆ (3632) 4623[13]

Wootsteps (IRE) *John Upson* 15b
7 ch g Shantou(USA) Mandyslady (IRE) (Husyan (USA))
105[P] 1011[P]

Worcester Pearmain *Rose Dobbin* 38h
5 b m Beat All(USA) Granoski Gala (Petoski)
1334[7] 2325[7]

Wordy's Boy *Charles Pogson* 112h
10 b g Kayf Tara Wordy's Wonder (Welsh Captain)
592[P]

Workbench (FR) *Dan Skelton* 114h 142c
7 b g Network(GER) Danhelis (FR) (Hellios (USA))
1170[3] 1322[5] (1735) 2059[2] 2635[6] 3030[3] ◆ **4770[8] 5179[8]**

Work In Progress (IRE) *Dan Skelton* 143h
5 b g Westerner Parsons Term (IRE) (The Parson)
(1990) ◆ 2083[2] 2594[6] (4224) 4769[8]

Worldor (FR) *Alexandra Dunn* 102h 100c
9 b g Lost World(IRE) Karenzed (FR) (Synefos (USA))
616[7] 856[10] 1048[8] (1524) 1572[3] 1810[4] 3932[7] 4390[10] 4886[7] 5163[6]

Worthy Award (IRE) *Jonjo O'Neill* 110h 124c
7 b g Presenting Take Ine (FR) (Take Risks (FR))
174[6]

Wot A Shot (IRE) *Nicky Richards* 97h 101c
6 b g Refuse To Bend(IRE) Ashdali (IRE) (Grand Lodge (USA))
658[7] **884[4]** 2706[9]

Wotzizname (IRE) *Harry Fry* 130h
5 b g Fruits Of Love(USA) Native Beau (IRE) (Be My Native (USA))
(5263)

Wounded Warrior (IRE) *Noel Meade* 134h 160c
6 b g Shantou(USA) Sparkling Sword (Broadsword (USA))
10a[2] 3603a[2] 4007a[6]

Wrath Of Titans (IRE) *Ms Sandra Hughes* 133h 134c
6 b g Oscar(IRE) Glen Empress (IRE) (Lancastrian)
2531a[6] 3357a[4] 4279a[4] 5005a[10]

W Six Times *Alistair Whillans* 111h
9 b m Double Trigger(IRE) Be My Mot (IRE) (Be My Native (USA))
148[P] 2720[6] (4163) (4289) (4608) 5299[5]

Wuff (IRE) *Paul Nicholls* 130h 139c
7 b g Beneficial Dummy Run (IRE) (Glacial Storm (USA))
69a[10] 2724[5] 3113[2] 3706[2]

Wun Destination *John Panvert* 75h
6 b m Dubai Destination(USA) Mourir D'Aimer (USA) (Trempolino (USA))
2421[12] 2875[6] 4439[P] 4777[6] 5263[P]

Wurring (IRE) *Michael Wigham*
7 b g Alamshar(IRE) Numeramang (IRE) (Euphemism)
2646[P]

Wyatt (IRE) *Philip Mitchell* 63b
3 b g Lawman(FR) Umlilo (Mtoto)
4532[9]

Wychwoods Brook *Evan Williams* 131h 142c
9 b g Midnight Legend Miss Millbrook (Meadowbrook)
2641[F] **3079[3] (3583) 3918[P]**

Wyck Hill (IRE) *David Bridgwater* 82h 109c
11 b g Pierre Willow Rose (IRE) (Roselier (FR))
4367[8] 4966[5]

Wyfield Rose *Alistair Whillans* 102h 18c
6 b m Kayf Tara Miniature Rose (Anshan)
139[7] 484[4] 845[P] 2212[9] 2751[10] **3427[7]** 5412[2]

Wylde Magic (IRE) *Evan Williams* 117b
4 b g Oscar(IRE) Voodoo Magic (GER) (Platini (GER))
3980[5] (5021) ◆

Wymeswold *Michael Mullineaux* 87h
8 b m Alflora(IRE) Dominie Breeze (Primo Dominie)
252[2] 694[4] 1307[4] 1525[8] 1786[U] 2165[5] (2745) 5333[P]

Wy Worry (IRE) *Mark Wall* 59b
5 b g Millenary Don't Fall (IRE) (Castle Keep)
1122[7]

Xaarcet (IRE) *Gordon Elliott* 101b 121c
8 b g Xaar Anoukit (Green Desert (USA))
867[2] 1184a[13] **(1330) 1632[7]**

Xclusive *Ronald Harris* 71h
5 b g Pivotal Dance A Daydream (Daylami (IRE))
703[F]

Xenophon *Olly Williams* 108h 100c
7 b g Phoenix Reach(IRE) Comtesse Noire (CAN) (Woodman (USA))
1155[6] 1265[11] **1402[4] 1546[3] 1813[2] 2303[P] 2539[4] (2771) (3222) 3488[3] 4062[P] 5442[P]**

Xsquared (IRE) *Sabrina J Harty* 137h 95c
7 b g Exceed And Excel(AUS) Jemalina (USA) (Trempolino (USA))
7a[14]

Yabadabadoo *Emma Lavelle* 109h 120c
7 b g Doyen(IRE) Kabayil (Dancing Brave (USA))
241[5] 643[P] 1769[4] (1985) 2246[P]

Y A Bon (IRE) *Aytach Sadik* 91h 63c
7 b g Black Sam Bellamy(IRE) Tarte Fine (FR) (Goldneyev (USA))
(165) 824[5] 1158[10] **1401[4]** 1827[P]

Ya Hafed *Sheena West* 101h 97c
7 ch g Haafhd Rule Britannia (Night Shift (USA))
(223) 600[4] (2254) 3218[U] 5480[6]

Yala Enki (FR) *Venetia Williams* 147h 121c
5 bb g Nickname(FR) Cadiane (FR) (Cadoudal (FR))
(2257) 2641[5] (3527) 3992[3] (4236) 4715[P] 5194[5]

Yanmare (IRE) *Nigel Twiston-Davies*
5 b g Soapy Danger Bell Walks Caroll (IRE) (Carroll House (IRE))
2417[P] 3736[P] **4425[U] 4744[P]**

Yanworth *Alan King* 160h
5 ch g Norse Dancer(IRE) Yota (FR) (Galetto (FR))
(2258) (2581) (3135) (3852) ◆ 4715[2]

Yasir (USA) *Sophie Leech* 93h
7 b g Dynaformer(USA) Khazayin (USA) (Bahri (USA))
3108[7] 3376[5] 3729[3] 4184[P]

Yenston (IRE) *Colin Tizzard* 67b
4 b g Ashkalani(IRE) Stylish Type (IRE) (Taipan (IRE))
2549[8] 4296[7] 4614[P] 5353[U]

Yes Daddy (IRE) *Robert Stephens* 119h
7 b g Golan(IRE) Hollygrove Samba (IRE) (Accordion)
186[5] 1083[2] 1868[4]

Yes I Did (IRE) *Dan Skelton* 129h
5 b m Craigsteel Younevertoldme (IRE) (Simply Great (FR))
1811[2] (2561) ◆ 3154[3] (4044) ◆ (4151) 4471[4] 5280[7]

Yes I Will *Linda Jewell* 81h 45c
6 b g Kahyasi Flinders (Henbit (USA))
451[U] 1245[P] **1546[6] 1757[F] 2254[F]**

Yes Sir Brian (IRE) *Garrett James Power* 126h
6 b g Brian Boru Ochto Lass (IRE) (King's Ride)
4280a[7]

Yes Tom (IRE) *S R B Crawford* 129h 147c
10 gr g Tikkanen(USA) Ammieanne (IRE) (Zaffaran (USA))
95a[P] 660[P] (3440) **4167[4]** 4610[3]

Yesyoucan (IRE) *Neil Mulholland* 122h 116c
10 b g Beneficial Except Alice (IRE) (Orchestra)
261[P] (449) 624[6] 1448[7]

Yewlands (IRE) *Jonjo O'Neill* 102b
4 b g Scorpion(IRE) Calimesa (IRE) (Desert Prince (IRE))
4867[4] 5457[7]

Yoko (FR) *J-P Gallorini* 135h 137c
4 b g Android(USA) Varangevilloise (FR) (Cosmopolitan (FR))
665a[3]

Yorgonnahearmeroar (IRE) *Henry Oliver* 103b
4 b g Scorpion(IRE) Etoile Margot (FR) (Garde Royale)
5457[5]

Yorkhill (IRE) *W P Mullins* 158h
5 ch g Presenting Lightning Breeze (IRE) (Saddlers' Hall (IRE))
(53a) (3447) (4715) (5214)

Yorkist (IRE) *Micky Hammond* 130h 147c
7 ch g Urban Ocean(FR) Kilbarry Demon (IRE) (Bob's Return (IRE))
2336[5] 2719[4] 2920[4] 3629[4] 4011[2] ◆ **4469[3] 4838[5]**

Youllneverrunalone *Richard Price* 72b
4 b m Blueprint(IRE) Miss Phoebe (IRE) (Catcher In The Rye (IRE))
432[9]

Youmaysee *Matt Sheppard*
5 b m Authorized(IRE) Purple Vision (Rainbow Quest (USA))
1506[P]

Youm Jamil (USA) *Tony Carroll* 74h 82c
8 gr g Mizzen Mast(USA) Millie's Choice (IRE) (Taufan (USA))
1095[8] 1525[4] **(1689)** 1980[7] **2552[2]** ◆ **2976[9] 3214[U]**

You Must Know Me (IRE) *Henry De Bromhead* 118h 137c
9 ch g Snurge Waterloo Park (IRE) (Alphabatim (USA))
24a[10] (Dead)

Younevercall (IRE) *Kim Bailey* 133h
4 b g Yeats(IRE) Afarka (IRE) (Kahyasi)
(1781) 2409[F] 4065[6] (5372)

Young Cheddar (IRE) *Polly Gundry* 95h 118c
8 b m Croco Rouge(IRE) Sin Ceist Eile (IRE) (Simply Great (FR))
150[2] (388) ◆

Young Dillon (IRE) *Dr Richard Newland* 119h
6 b g Vinnie Roe(IRE) Rongai (IRE) (Commanche Run)
2407[2] 3179[3] (5243)

Youngdocgallagher (IRE) *Michael Mullineaux* 110h
6 b g Zagreb(USA) Too Back (IRE) (Toulon)
(90) 705[6] 939[7] 2997[8]

Young Finnegan (IRE) *Robert Tyner* 128h 135c
9 b g Portrait Gallery(IRE) Lady Maria (IRE) (King's Ride)
3716a[3]

Young Hurricane (IRE) *G C Brewer* 98h 119c
9 b g Oscar(IRE) Georgia On My Mind (FR) (Belmez (USA))
457[3]

Young Lou *Robin Dickin* 92h
6 b m Kadastrof(FR) Wanna Shout (Missed Flight)
148[5] 328[3] 757[9] 3382[3] 3789[4] 4184[2] 4349[2] (4644) 4783[2]

Young Palm (IRE) *S R B Crawford* 105h 106c
8 gr g Great Palm(USA) Young Amelie (FR) (Garde Royale)
3020[3] 3670[3] 4166[F] 4300[6]

Your Busy (IRE) *J A Nash* 133h 141c
12 b g Anshan Springfort Society (IRE) (Moscow Society (USA))
1184a[14] **1556a[P] 1871[3] 3448[P] 4397a[8]**

Yourholidayisover (IRE) *Patrick Holmes* 105h 87c
8 ch g Sulamani(IRE) Whitehaven (Top Ville (IRE))
77[9]

You Say What (IRE) *Neil King* 131h
5 b g Milan Wave Back (IRE) (Bob Back (USA))
1966[3] 2375[7] 2965[3] (3124) 3400[5] 3976[2] 4305[5] (4544) 5141[3]

You Too Pet (IRE) *P W Mason* 80h 108c
7 b g Norwich Pollys Pet (IRE) (Little Bighorn)
4424[4]

You've Been Mowed *Neil King* 101h
9 ch m Ishiguru(USA) Sandblaster (Most Welcome)
130[2]

Yul Finegold (IRE) *Conor Dore* 106h
5 b g Invincible Spirit(IRE) Mascara (Mtoto)
1421[P]

Yur Next (IRE) *Alison Batchelor* 80h
7 br m Definite Article Listen Up (Good Thyne (USA))
3902[P] 4382[4] 4507[3]

Zabalee (IRE) *Andrew Wilson* 77h
5 b m Robin Des Pres(FR) Ballinapierce Lady (IRE) (Glacial Storm (USA))
503[P] (Dead)

Zabana (IRE) *Andrew Lynch* 155h 155c
6 ch g Halling(USA) Gandia (IRE) (Danehill (USA))
49a[3] **4005a[4] 4729[U]**

Zabeel Star (IRE) *Graeme McPherson* 83h
3 ch g Arcano(IRE) Deep Winter (Pivotal)
1593[2] 2032[6]

Zadok *Jamie Snowden* 70h
5 b g Nayef(USA) Panna (Polish Precedent (USA))
3082[4] 4382[5] 4613[6]

Zagelle (IRE) *Henry De Bromhead* 102h
5 b g Milan Mollys Present (IRE) (Presenting)
9a[17]

Zaidiyn (FR) *Brian Ellison* 144h 116c
6 b g Zamindar(USA) Zainta (IRE) (Kahyasi)
1969[F] 2637[2] 3426[3] 3682[4] 4014[4] (4366) 5325[7]

Zaidpour (FR) *W P Mullins* 160h
9 b g Red Ransom(USA) Zainta (IRE) (Kahyasi)
49a[8]

Zakety Zak *James Turner* 76h
4 b g Overbury(IRE) Jeanne D'Arc (Highest Honor (FR))
39[4] 459[7] 2747[9] 3022[12] 3306[6] 3628[11] 3840[13] 4943[5]

Zakharyina (IRE) *Steve Spice*
10 ch m High Roller(IRE) Tsarevna (IRE) (Moscow Society (USA))
297[P]

Zakti (IRE) *Jamie Snowden* 54b
5 gr m Shirocco(GER) Inner Strength (FR) (Take Risks (FR))
152[10] 1050[8]

Zalgarry (FR) *Arthur Whitehead* 121h
8 b g Ballingarry(IRE) Spleen (FR) (Sillery (USA))
4066[16] 5053[4] ◆

Zama Zama *Evan Williams* 125h 111c
8 b g Sakhee(USA) Insinuation (IRE) (Danehill (USA))
612[3] 770[2] (976) (1056) 1121[2] 1483[4] 1690[5] 2034[3] (2249) 3931[8] 4823[2]

Zamdy Man *Venetia Williams* 145h 138c
6 b g Authorized(IRE) Lauderdale (GER) (Nebos (GER))
3084[3] ◆ **3738[4]** 4765[18] 5325[9]

Zammia (FR) *David Dennis* 59b
3 b g Kingsalsa(USA) Aisyacall (FR) (Kahyasi)
3416[3]

Zandino (FR) *Warren Greatrex* 96b
4 b g Doctor Dino(FR) Belle Des Champs (Be My Chief (USA))
366[3] 732[4]

Zanstra (IRE) *Colin Tizzard* 123h
5 b g Morozov(USA) Enistar (IRE) (Synefos (USA))
2062[5] 2569[4] 2985[5] 3414[3] (3841) 4099[3] 4442[5] (4922) (5453)

Zante (FR) *Gary Moore* 98h
3 ch g Zanzibari(USA) Calling All Angels (FR) (Ange Gabriel (FR))
4462[6] 5153[6] (5477)

Zara Hope (IRE) *Charlie Longsdon* 105h
4 b m Stowaway Agua Caliente (IRE) (Old Vic)
1908[4] 2277[4] 2776[5] 3066[5] 3483[5] (5223)

Zarawi (IRE) *Charlie Longsdon* 112h 108c
4 b g Marju(IRE) Zarwala (IRE) (Polish Precedent (USA))
(224) 336[7] (673) 862[4] 1239[3] 1488[4] **1753[2]** 2058[11] 5047[5] 5266[P]

Zarib (IRE) *Dan Skelton* 136h
4 b g Azamour(IRE) Zariziyna (IRE) (Dalakhani (IRE))
2350[3] ◆ 3151[6] 4115[11] 5275[2]

Zarif (IRE) *Josef Vana Jr* 124c
8 ch g Observatory(USA) Zariliya (IRE) (Darshaan)
1885a[3]

Zarkandar (IRE) *Paul Nicholls* 165h
8 b g Azamour(IRE) Zarkasha (IRE) (Kahyasi)
663a[3]

Zarliman (IRE) *Neil Mulholland* 79h
5 ch g Zamindar(USA) Zarlana (IRE) (Darshaan)
2123[9] 4712[P]

Zarosa (IRE) *John Berry* 87h
6 b m Barathea(IRE) Shantalla Peak (IRE) (Darshaan)
2829[4] 3221[P] 3947[P] 4200[P]

Zarzal (IRE) *Evan Williams* 125h 139c
7 b g Dr Fong(USA) Zarwala (IRE) (Polish Precedent (USA))
(354) (442) (529) 850[4] 1035[14] 1719[7] **4617[3] 4891[6]**

Zayfire Aramis *Michael Scudamore* 100h 103c
6 ch g Zafeen(FR) Kaylifa Aramis (Kayf Tara)
3868[2] ◆ 4297[11] **4527[3] 5377[2]**

Zazamix (FR) *Andrew Crook* 56h 57c
10 b g Sagamix(FR) Ombre Bleue (FR) (Agent Bleu (FR))
2290[R] 3103[7] 3308[P] 4325[P] 4534[P]

Zeldina *Brian Ellison* 83b
5 ch m Mount Nelson Tetravella (IRE) (Groom Dancer (USA))
2721[5]

Zephyr *Nick Williams* 103h
4 ch g Shirocco(GER) Pelagia (IRE) (Lycius (USA))
880[2] 1238[13] 4860[6] 5165[P] 5481[2]

Zephyros Bleu (IRE) *Harry Whittington* 116h
5 b g Westerner Quel Bleu (IRE) (Tel Quel (FR))
2488[3] ◆ 3126[3] 3705[2] 4301[2] 5100[P]

Zermatt (IRE) *John Quinn* 99h
6 ch g Strategic Prince Await (IRE) (Peintre Celebre (USA))
139[P]

Zeroeshadesofgrey (IRE) *Neil King* 142h 128c
6 gr g Portrait Gallery(IRE) Hazy Rose (IRE) (Roselier (FR))
2197[2] 3018[7] (3336) 4112[4] 4470[2] 5328[9]

Zero Grand (IRE) *Johnny Farrelly* 111h
4 b g Thousand Words Ellistown Lady (IRE) (Red Sunset)
2272[9] 3581[5] 3745[6] 3915[3] ◆

Zero Visibility (IRE) *Alexandra Dunn* 90h 90c
8 b g Classic Cliche(IRE) Jessica's Pet (IRE) (King's Ride)
(2826) **2953[F] 3195[3] 3903[4] 4778[5] 5236[P]**

Ziga Boy (FR) *Alan King* 114h 144c
6 gr g Califet(FR) Our Ziga (FR) (Linamix (FR))
2261[P] 2955[3] (3339) (3860) 4361[8]

Ziggerson Hill *Jackie Du Plessis* 94h
8 ch m Kadastrof(FR) Tregale (Chukaroo)
5145[3]

Zigger Zagger (IRE) *Richard Rowe* 115h 73c
6 b g Mountain High(IRE) Main Suspect (IRE) (Be My Native (USA))
5433[14]

Ziggie (IRE) *P Ponting* 106b
8 b g Dilshaan Like A Caterpillar (IRE) (Supreme Leader)
4437[P]

Zipple Back (IRE) *Alan King* 93b
3 b g Sendawar(IRE) With Conviction (IRE) (Barathea (IRE))
3847[3] 5195[9]

Zip Top (IRE) *John Ferguson* 130h
6 b g Smart Strike(CAN) Zofzig (USA) (Danzig (USA))
876[6] 1046[P]

Zip Wire (IRE) *Donald McCain* 98h
6 b g Oratorio(IRE) Jaya (USA) (Ela-Mana-Mou)
1508[6] 1828[5]

Zruda *David Thompson* 36b
4 b m Observatory(USA) Pagan Princess (Mujtahid (USA))
2847[U] 3054[P]

Zubayr (IRE) *Paul Nicholls* 139h
3 b g Authorized(IRE) Zaziyra (IRE) (Dalakhani (IRE))
(4358) 4764[13] (5353)

Zuccotti Park (IRE) *Tom Lacey* 110h 110c
7 b g Flemensfirth(USA) Warts And All (IRE) (Commanche Run)
85[12]

Zulu Oscar *Harry Fry* 138h
6 b g Oscar(IRE) Loxhill Lady (Supreme Leader)
2773[F] (3284) 3733[7] 4769[10]

Season Statistics Trainers - British Jumps 2015-2016

NAME	WINS–RUNS	%	2ND	3RD	4TH	WIN PRIZE	TOTAL PRIZE	£1 STAKE
Paul Nicholls	122–568	21%	104	74	45	£1,505,434	£2,439,560	-73.23
W P Mullins	27–159	17%	24	13	14	£1,412,457	£2,341,735	-58.18
Nicky Henderson	81–414	20%	54	49	34	£1,066,035	£1,614,348	-101.03
Colin Tizzard	50–323	15%	39	52	39	£1,147,233	£1,442,083	-46.75
Philip Hobbs	113–523	22%	82	81	47	£909,949	£1,386,468	-64.73
Dan Skelton	104–529	20%	88	70	61	£732,806	£1,255,804	-156.34
Nigel Twiston-Davies	72–482	15%	62	45	48	£822,890	£1,205,966	-79.80
David Pipe	80–571	14%	77	68	71	£653,453	£1,151,789	-111.92
Alan King	68–403	17%	60	52	51	£742,259	£1,043,914	-120.54
Venetia Williams	56–419	13%	56	63	44	£612,960	£983,247	-104.92
Jonjo O'Neill	81–560	14%	72	44	67	£534,423	£845,767	-114.49
Evan Williams	70–448	16%	52	61	46	£492,638	£809,087	+12.95
Gordon Elliott	28–147	19%	34	22	20	£507,209	£737,993	-55.35
Harry Fry	54–240	23%	53	32	18	£521,342	£720,052	-15.36
M F Morris	1–8	13%	1	2	0	£561,300	£653,391	+26.00
Gary Moore	54–294	18%	39	41	32	£445,273	£653,159	+80.84
Neil Mulholland	60–427	14%	58	43	60	£397,072	£637,619	-145.57
Charlie Longsdon	62–416	15%	59	34	47	£423,775	£624,005	-105.15
Kim Bailey	43–275	16%	37	34	26	£277,775	£612,450	-77.93
Tom George	38–225	17%	32	28	25	£421,616	£587,022	-30.06
John Ferguson	71–251	28%	58	34	23	£385,192	£583,805	-67.02
Sue Smith	44–312	14%	63	42	38	£383,973	£576,199	-66.35
Brian Ellison	48–250	19%	37	34	32	£298,368	£453,584	-11.23
Warren Greatrex	53–254	21%	45	40	23	£267,715	£434,342	-58.89
Donald McCain	53–497	11%	60	73	67	£289,228	£430,725	-138.27
Lucinda Russell	48–376	13%	47	64	55	£243,126	£409,673	-44.21
Kerry Lee	23–110	21%	19	9	5	£313,559	£377,508	+39.06
Oliver Sherwood	32–207	15%	34	25	24	£212,975	£365,526	-50.61
Fergal O'Brien	33–237	14%	35	33	24	£218,002	£355,615	-5.50
Neil King	34–217	16%	30	30	24	£205,423	£328,386	-36.19
Peter Bowen	33–236	14%	34	28	20	£217,709	£326,520	-84.96
Nick Williams	12–112	11%	23	20	14	£209,601	£323,952	-52.20
Micky Hammond	43–347	12%	39	45	51	£193,743	£313,990	-122.72
Malcolm Jefferson	37–167	22%	31	37	17	£194,807	£297,934	+16.72
Dr Richard Newland	28–146	19%	29	17	9	£187,006	£294,437	-9.76
Nicky Richards	40–188	21%	29	20	23	£207,902	£288,940	-13.53
Tim Vaughan	42–449	9%	56	50	44	£164,980	£277,786	-225.75
Emma Lavelle	19–163	12%	18	20	20	£131,943	£246,013	-40.42
Rebecca Curtis	24–194	12%	15	26	15	£144,306	£245,319	-34.31
Martin Keighley	26–179	15%	11	19	23	£187,918	£240,886	+27.04
Ian Williams	28–225	12%	27	22	25	£169,509	£234,371	-77.60
Harry Whittington	21–91	23%	12	19	7	£155,810	£215,762	+20.36
Anthony Honeyball	28–170	16%	27	20	13	£150,338	£212,801	-29.53
Jeremy Scott	27–192	14%	23	28	14	£104,591	£211,804	-19.51
David Dennis	27–220	12%	32	32	26	£125,968	£204,358	-81.39
Lucy Wadham	21–119	18%	16	13	20	£119,665	£203,806	+28.58
Henry De Bromhead	1–23	4%	2	4	1	£63,585	£200,992	-16.00
Ben Pauling	26–155	17%	23	7	19	£147,259	£198,601	+58.12
Henry Oliver	15–119	13%	17	10	14	£136,837	£189,229	-13.53

Season Statistics Jockeys - British Jumps 2015-2016

NAME	WINS–RUNS	%	2ND	3RD	4TH	WIN PRIZE	TOTAL PRIZE	£1 STAKE
Richard Johnson	235–1044	23%	186	155	120	£1,591,005	£2,339,364	-180.10
Aidan Coleman	130–741	18%	112	103	81	£916,643	£1,375,705	-205.48
Sam Twiston-Davies	128–741	17%	118	89	81	£1,238,193	£1,941,441	-165.32
Noel Fehily	122–663	18%	106	85	78	£976,041	£1,531,260	-125.14
Brian Hughes	103–735	14%	131	113	92	£558,995	£988,219	-103.00
Harry Skelton	101–452	22%	79	57	52	£718,074	£1,190,865	+3.40
Tom Scudamore	85–536	16%	70	67	80	£988,441	£1,392,504	-146.00
Paddy Brennan	75–463	16%	70	55	61	£1,078,325	£1,366,226	-45.65
Gavin Sheehan	72–440	16%	64	51	56	£459,824	£747,679	-51.84
Nico de Boinville	69–327	21%	34	34	24	£910,496	£1,069,140	+105.75
Leighton Aspell	60–428	14%	55	59	51	£343,911	£580,168	-65.42
Sean Bowen	58–358	16%	42	46	38	£364,909	£552,523	-77.36
Wayne Hutchinson	56–388	14%	55	58	48	£480,026	£726,531	-102.31
Paul Moloney	54–366	15%	27	54	37	£298,015	£527,501	-28.28
David Bass	54–311	17%	43	31	29	£386,722	£783,128	-37.31
Daryl Jacob	50–384	13%	53	48	38	£362,104	£708,602	-178.96
Tom O'Brien	49–465	11%	59	61	53	£269,208	£500,986	-201.38
Danny Cook	48–295	16%	59	41	43	£424,038	£644,818	-37.09
Will Kennedy	47–350	13%	53	49	32	£241,035	£392,863	-37.87
Nick Scholfield	44–330	13%	44	32	27	£359,498	£548,353	-40.55
Henry Brooke	42–456	9%	50	46	44	£256,966	£373,900	-164.59
Brian Harding	42–350	12%	43	31	39	£197,034	£318,565	-147.63
David Noonan	41–253	16%	34	24	25	£219,026	£311,427	-3.28
Trevor Whelan	40–307	13%	35	34	31	£227,977	£360,926	-36.73
Tom Cannon	38–384	10%	29	44	32	£165,571	£290,612	-102.61
Craig Nichol	36–292	12%	34	34	29	£167,887	£240,821	-94.58
Adam Wedge	36–284	13%	31	37	36	£228,890	£363,959	-67.10
Jamie Moore	36–282	13%	33	30	29	£415,451	£588,792	-31.22
Andrew Tinkler	36–276	13%	25	28	30	£170,649	£261,234	-76.96
Brendan Powell	35–382	9%	35	45	48	£243,695	£389,555	-28.79
Joshua Moore	34–215	16%	24	27	22	£297,575	£448,250	+4.39
Richie McLernon	32–312	10%	30	19	30	£151,182	£262,580	-72.54
Barry Geraghty	30–198	15%	30	21	22	£491,229	£930,183	-82.12
Harry Cobden	30–138	22%	30	18	13	£190,675	£381,605	+5.45
James Reveley	28–188	15%	22	25	18	£191,532	£262,964	-13.16
Derek Fox	26–205	13%	22	25	35	£149,003	£230,683	-48.17
Joe Colliver	26–166	16%	21	15	16	£118,302	£175,352	-32.38
Kielan Woods	25–261	10%	30	30	36	£135,543	£221,561	-65.75
Denis O'Regan	25–240	10%	35	23	29	£103,961	£196,977	-113.53
James Banks	24–265	9%	34	35	19	£96,725	£167,351	-16.25
Adam Nicol	23–218	11%	25	19	24	£81,918	£125,046	-18.40
Ryan Hatch	22–170	13%	14	24	11	£337,237	£490,468	-45.90
Liam Treadwell	21–300	7%	35	37	37	£203,050	£389,414	-154.75
James Davies	21–299	7%	27	33	31	£175,135	£261,462	-140.17
Peter Buchanan	21–210	10%	24	30	38	£116,321	£207,699	-55.67
Jamie Hamilton	21–157	13%	17	26	21	£88,679	£138,345	+20.38
Sean Quinlan	20–246	8%	40	28	28	£125,948	£214,857	-105.46
Jake Greenall	20–189	11%	16	18	19	£93,274	£145,619	-54.13
Jeremiah McGrath	20–151	13%	20	13	19	£96,294	£148,696	+9.93

Season Statistics Owners - British Jumps 2015-2016

NAME	WINS–RUNS	%	2ND	3RD	4TH	WIN PRIZE	TOTAL PRIZE
Gigginstown House Stud	7–68	10%	8	8	7	£1,107,282	£1,572,907
John P McManus	82–493	17%	63	43	45	£834,953	£1,438,736
Mrs S Ricci	12–44	27%	4	4	3	£930,347	£1,210,314
Paul & Clare Rooney	42–223	19%	35	29	23	£272,613	£603,694
Bloomfields	71–251	28%	58	34	23	£385,192	£583,805
Andrea & Graham Wylie	12–60	20%	8	9	7	£340,248	£576,458
Simon Munir & Isaac Souede	27–145	19%	27	21	12	£243,624	£538,293
Mrs Jean R Bishop	10–24	42%	2	2	2	£455,234	£516,923
Mrs Caroline Mould	8–26	31%	0	1	5	£407,103	£415,218
John and Heather Snook	5–23	22%	1	1	1	£372,003	£379,105
Mrs Diana L Whateley	19–60	32%	10	6	4	£255,200	£342,930
S Such & Cg Paletta	7–23	30%	2	1	5	£200,903	£267,021
P J Martin	22–106	21%	23	14	12	£142,430	£250,418
Trevor Hemmings	19–100	19%	22	17	7	£149,662	£245,737
J Hales	4–23	17%	4	3	2	£101,915	£225,726
Brocade Racing	11–76	14%	7	9	5	£156,058	£219,334
Mrs Peter Andrews	5–11	45%	0	0	2	£193,536	£212,582
Potensis B'stock Ltd & C Giles	5–16	31%	4	1	0	£143,873	£205,981
Mrs Johnny de la Hey	8–35	23%	6	6	3	£125,292	£176,983
Crossed Fingers Partnership	4–23	17%	2	5	6	£129,618	£176,039
Harry Fry Racing Club	9–17	53%	1	1	1	£168,376	£174,885
A Brooks	6–46	13%	6	5	4	£106,501	£163,606
Mrs Peter Prowting	4–25	16%	2	1	5	£141,701	£158,018
The Brooks, Kyle & Stewart Families	4–8	50%	0	2	1	£139,840	£146,220
E O'Connell	1–4	25%	1	0	0	£71,188	£145,983
Ian Fogg & John Hales	3–6	50%	0	1	1	£138,178	£143,482
R J Rexton	7–20	35%	2	3	0	£102,758	£143,206
Options O Syndicate	6–26	23%	4	1	5	£89,605	£137,801
The Preston Family & Friends Ltd	1–7	14%	2	0	1	£85,425	£137,571
R S Brookhouse	10–82	12%	8	6	9	£48,640	£134,541
Mrs S Smith	15–131	11%	27	11	19	£68,871	£131,686
Mr & Mrs William Rucker	11–62	18%	6	10	7	£62,260	£129,600
M B Scholey & R H Scholey	4–25	16%	6	3	4	£114,579	£128,048
Potensis Bloodstock Limited	9–48	19%	10	6	5	£79,828	£127,936
R E R Williams	4–40	10%	6	6	5	£90,002	£127,664
Mrs Janet Davies	11–52	21%	6	6	8	£75,789	£127,002
Mrs J A Martin	15–49	31%	1	7	7	£109,339	£125,921
Alan Peterson	6–16	38%	1	1	1	£120,119	£122,942
R A Bartlett	4–13	31%	6	1	1	£38,943	£121,295
Hills Of Ledbury (Aga)	5–16	31%	4	1	0	£50,441	£118,426
Terry Warner	4–29	14%	3	5	3	£94,005	£115,937
Professor C Tisdall & B Drew	3–18	17%	5	3	4	£69,704	£113,849
Mrs Patricia Pugh	5–6	83%	1	0	0	£109,019	£109,477
Bodeen Bandits Partnership	0–3	—	0	1	0	£0	£109,226
T P Radford	4–30	13%	4	2	6	£31,486	£103,978
Gascoigne Brookes P'Ship III	2–6	33%	1	1	0	£94,552	£101,624
Dajam & The Old Masters	1–5	20%	0	1	1	£84,405	£101,239
Axom XLIX	2–4	50%	0	0	1	£96,070	£100,771
Davies Smith Govier & Brown	2–7	29%	1	3	0	£79,730	£99,172

Raceform Ratings - Jumps 2015-2016

RPR	HORSE	AGE	SEX	SIRE	CNTRY	TRAINER
182	Don Cossack	8	g	Sholokhov	IRE	Gordon Elliott
180	Cue Card	9	g	King's Theatre	GB	Colin Tizzard
180	Vautour	6	g	Robin Des Champs	IRE	W P Mullins
178	Thistlecrack	7	g	Kayf Tara	GB	Colin Tizzard
177	Djakadam	6	g	Saint Des Saints	IRE	W P Mullins
177	Faugheen	7	g	Germany	IRE	W P Mullins
176	Sprinter Sacre	9	g	Network	GB	Nicky Henderson
175	Coneygree	8	g	Karinga Bay	GB	Mark Bradstock
175	Silviniaco Conti	9	g	Dom Alco	GB	Paul Nicholls
173	Douvan	5	g	Walk In The Park	IRE	W P Mullins
173	Smad Place	8	g	Smadoun	GB	Alan King
172	Un De Sceaux	7	g	Denham Red	IRE	W P Mullins
171	Al Ferof	10	g	Dom Alco	GB	Dan Skelton
171	Sire De Grugy	9	g	My Risk	GB	Gary Moore
170	Alpha Des Obeaux	5	g	Saddler Maker	IRE	M F Morris
170	Annie Power	7	m	Shirocco	IRE	W P Mullins
170	Carlingford Lough	9	g	King's Theatre	IRE	John E Kiely
170	Menorah	10	g	King's Theatre	GB	Philip Hobbs
170	Special Tiara	8	g	Kayf Tara	IRE	Henry De Bromhead
169	Road To Riches	8	g	Gamut	IRE	Noel Meade
168	Don Poli	6	g	Poliglote	IRE	W P Mullins
168	Many Clouds	8	g	Cloudings	GB	Oliver Sherwood
168	Nichols Canyon	5	g	Authorized	IRE	W P Mullins
168	Ptit Zig	6	g	Great Pretender	GB	Paul Nicholls
168	Valseur Lido	6	g	Anzillero	IRE	W P Mullins
168	Wishfull Thinking	12	g	Alflora	GB	Philip Hobbs
167	God's Own	7	g	Oscar	GB	Tom George
167	Kilcooley	6	g	Stowaway	GB	Charlie Longsdon
167	My Tent Or Yours	8	g	Desert Prince	GB	Nicky Henderson
166	Sausalito Sunrise	7	g	Gold Well	GB	Philip Hobbs
166	Smashing	6	g	Smadoun	IRE	Henry De Bromhead
166	Sound Investment	7	g	Dr Massini	GB	Paul Nicholls
165	Felix Yonger	9	g	Oscar	IRE	W P Mullins
165	Gilgamboa	7	g	Westerner	IRE	E Bolger
165	Jezki	7	g	Milan	IRE	Mrs John Harrington
165	Native River	5	g	Indian River	GB	Colin Tizzard
165	Top Gamble	7	g	Presenting	GB	Kerry Lee
165	Traffic Fluide	5	g	Astarabad	GB	Gary Moore
164	Apple's Jade	3	f	Saddler Maker	IRE	W P Mullins
164	Ar Mad	5	g	Tiger Groom	GB	Gary Moore
164	Arzal	5	g	Vendangeur	GB	Harry Whittington
164	Black Hercules	6	g	Heron Island	IRE	W P Mullins
164	Different Gravey	5	g	High Chaparral	GB	Nicky Henderson
164	Holywell	8	g	Gold Well	GB	Jonjo O'Neill
164	Houblon Des Obeaux	8	g	Panoramic	GB	Venetia Williams
164	Identity Thief	5	g	Kayf Tara	IRE	Henry De Bromhead
164	Rule The World	8	g	Sulamani	IRE	M F Morris
164	Saphir Du Rheu	6	g	Al Namix	GB	Paul Nicholls

Raceform Jumps Record Times 2015-16

AINTREE

Distance	Time	Age	Weight	Going	Horse	Date
1m 7f 176y C	3m 45.30	9	10-7	Firm	Nohalmdun	Apr 7 1990
2m 103y H	3m 44.80	6	10-7	Firm	Spinning I	Apr 3 1993
2m 209y H	4m 4.30	5	10-12	Good	Gabrial The Great (IRE)	May 16 2014
2m 209y H	4m 4.30	4	11-10	Good	Hawk High	Oct 25 2014
2m 3f 200y C	4m 46.60	8	11-6	Good To Firm	Wind Force	Apr 2 1993
2m 4f H	4m 37.10	5	10-11	Good To Firm	Gallateen	Apr 2 1993
2m 5f 19y C	5m 19.30	10	10-4	Good	Always Waining	Apr 8 2011
3m 149y H	5m 50.70	6	10-2	Good To Firm	Andrew's First	Apr 1 1993
3m 210y C	6m 3.40	7	11-3	Good To Firm	Cab On Target	Apr 2 1993
3m 1f 188y C	6m 46.60	10	11-7	Good	Eurotrek	Nov 19 2006
4m 2f 74y C	9m 9.90	11	10-6	Good To Soft	Pineau De Re (FR)	Apr 5 2014

ASCOT

Distance	Time	Age	Weight	Going	Horse	Date
1m 7f 152y H	3m 33.30	4	10-8	Good	Brampour	Oct 29 2011
2m 192y C	4m 2.20	6	9-13	Good	Ulck Du Lin (FR)	Nov 1 2014
2m 2f 175y C	4m 34.10	6	10-3	Good	The Clock Leary	Nov 1 2014
2m 3f 58y H	4m 30.80	7	11-0	Good	Overturn	Nov 19 2011
2m 5f 8y C	5m 12.60	9	10-13	Good	Kew Jumper (IRE)	Apr 11 2008
2m 5f 141y H	5m 10.90	6	10-11	Good	Emmaslegend	Nov 19 2011
2m 7f 118y H	5m 34.10	6	11-2	Good	Heronry	Mar 30 2014
2m 7f 180y C	5m 49.60	9	10-10	Good	Exmoor Ranger	Oct 29 2011
3m 97y H	5m 57.30	7	11-7	Good To Firm	Lough Derg (FR)	Dec 22 2007

AYR

Distance	Time	Age	Weight	Going	Horse	Date
1m 7f 112y C	3m 38.60	6	11-0	Good To Firm	Clay County	Oct 12 1991
2m H	3m 27.40	6	10-7	Firm	Secret Ballot	Apr 19 1980
2m 5f 110y C	5m 10.20	6	11-5	Good To Firm	Star To The North	May 9 2001
2m 5f 110y H	5m 4.70	7	10-13	Good	Cucumber Run	Apr 21 2012
3m 67y C	5m 57.70	9	11-0	Good To Firm	Top 'N' Tale	May 12 1982
3m 70y H	5m 42.00	13	10-11	Firm	Nautical Lad I	Apr 6 1964
3m 2f 110y H	6m 26.90	13	10-0	Good	Meditator	Apr 18 1997
3m 2f 197y C	6m 50.20	5	10-12	Good	Joaaci	Apr 15 2005
3m 7f 176y C	7m 55.10	8	9-9	Good To Firm	Hot Weld	Apr 21 2007

BANGOR-ON-DEE

Distance	Time	Age	Weight	Going	Horse	Date
2m 145y H	3m 44.50	9	10-2	Firm	Andy Rew	Apr 24 1982
2m 1f 77y C	4m 3.50	11	10-8	Good	Jack The Gent	Jly 31 2015
2m 3f 123y H	4m 34.10	5	11-3	Good To Firm	Smithy's Choice	Apr 25 1987
2m 4f 72y C	4m 49.70	8	10-12	Good	The Disengager (IRE)	Jly 24 2012
2m 7f 32y H	5m 34.00	5	11-2	Good To Firm	General Pershing	Apr 20 1991
3m 30y C	5m 50.60	8	11-3	Good To Firm	He's The Gaffer (IRE)	Aug 16 2008
3m 5f 142y C	7m 34.10	6	12-0	Good	Kaki Crazy	May 23 2001

CARLISLE

Distance	Time	Age	Weight	Going	Horse	Date
1m 7f 207y C	3m 53.70	6	11-8	Good	Germany Calling	Oct 15 2015
2m 1f H	4m 10.90	6	11-5	Good	Houston Dynimo (IRE)	Oct 7 2011
2m 1f 33y H	4m 2.60	9	11-3	Firm	Supertop	Oct 25 1997
2m 3f 61y H	4m 45.10	5	11-11	Good	Nexius	Apr 19 2014
2m 4f C	5m 0.40	6	11-2	Good	New Alco (FR)	Nov 12 2007
2m 4f 8y H	4m 50.60	9	11-8	Firm	Gods Law	Sep 29 1990
2m 4f 198y C	5m 24.10	6	10-13	Good To Soft	Frank The Slink	Mar 22 2012
3m 110y C	6m 0.70	8	10-13	Good To Firm	Ripalong Lad	Oct 9 2009
3m 110y H	5m 46.50	8	11-2	Firm	Kinda Groovy	Oct 25 1997
3m 123y H	6m 2.30	7	9-8	Good	Maggie Blue	Oct 15 2015
3m 2f 34y C	6m 40.40	8	11-3	Good	Lady Of Gortmerron (IRE)	Oct 6 2000

CARTMEL

Distance	Time	Age	Weight	Going	Horse	Date
2m 1f 46y H	3m 56.20	5	10-9	Good To Firm	Lisbon	May 25 2013
2m 1f 61y C	4m 7.50	12	11-13	Hard	Clever Folly	May 27 1992
2m 5f 34y C	5m 6.50	10	10-10	Firm	Corrarder	May 30 1994
2m 6f 31y H	5m 10.40	5	10-12	Good	Shantou Tiger	Jly 19 2014
3m 1f 83y H	5m 58.00	10	11-3	Firm	Portonia	May 30 1994
3m 1f 107y C	6m 13.40	13	12-0	Good	Better Times Ahead I	Aug 28 1999
3m 5f 80y C	7m 12.00	10	11-4	Good	Chabrimal Minster	May 26 2007

CATTERICK

Distance	Time	Age	Weight	Going	Horse	Date
1m 7f 145y C	3m 44.60	6	10-0	Firm	Preston Deal	Dec 18 1971
1m 7f 156y H	3m 36.50	7	11-3	Firm	Lunar Wind	Apr 22 1982
2m 3f C	4m 38.50	5	11-0	Good	Hi George	Dec 4 2013
2m 3f 66y H	4m 31.50	5	11-6	Good	Smadynium (FR)	Dec 4 2013
3m 1f 54y C	6m 14.00	10	10-1	Good To Firm	Clever General	Nov 7 1981
3m 1f 71y H	6m 3.80	6	10-9	Good To Firm	Seamus O'Flynn	Nov 7 1981
3m 6f C	7m 41.80	10	10-11	Good To Soft	General Hardi	Jan 13 2011

CHELTENHAM

Distance	Time	Age	Weight	Going	Horse	Date
1m 7f 199y C	3m 44.70	8	12-0	Good	Edredon Bleu	Mar 15 2000
2m 62y C	3m 52.40	7	10-11	Good To Firm	Samakaan (IRE)	Mar 16 2000
2m 87y H	3m 45.10	8	11-3	Good To Soft	Annie Power	Mar 15 2016
2m 179y H	3m 51.20	5	11-2	Good To Firm	Moody Man	Mar 15 1990
2m 179y H	3m 51.20	4	11-0	Good	Detroit City (USA)	Mar 17 2006
2m 4f C	4m 43.32	6	11-12	Good To Firm	Poquelin (FR)	Oct 17 2009
2m 4f 78y C	4m 49.60	9	10-3	Good	Dark Stranger (FR)	Mar 15 2000
2m 4f 110y H	4m 45.00	6	10-4	Good To Firm	Sir Dante (IRE)	Apr 15 1997
2m 4f 110y H	4m 45.00	5	11-3	Good To Firm	Gospel	Apr 20 1994
2m 5f C	5m 1.10	7	11-10	Good	Uxizandre	Mar 12 2015
2m 5f C	5m 5.90	7	11-2	Good To Firm	Tri Folene	Sep 29 1993
2m 5f C	5m 5.90	8	11-1	Good To Firm	Lusty Light	Sep 29 1994
2m 5f 26y H	4m 52.00	6	11-7	Good	Monsignor (IRE)	Mar 15 2000
2m 5f 103y H	4m 53.60	4	10-9	Good	Fashion House I	Sep 19 1968
2m 7f 208y H	5m 46.96	7	11-4	Good	Trackmate	Oct 18 2013
2m 7f 213y H	5m 36.60	6	11-10	Good To Firm	Bacchanal (IRE)	Mar 16 2000
3m 80y C	5m 59.70	8	10-3	Good	Marlborough (IRE)	Mar 14 2000
3m 1f C	6m 59.30	10	11-8	Soft	Linden's Lotto (IRE)	Jan 1 1999
3m 1f 56y C	6m 13.40	9	10-11	Good To Firm	Bigsun	Mar 15 1990
3m 1f 67y H	6m 3.40	9	11-2	Good	Rubhahunish (IRE)	Mar 14 2000
3m 2f C	6m 20.60	11	10-9	Firm	The Pooka	Sep 26 1973
3m 2f 70y C	6m 29.70	6	11-10	Good	Long Run (FR)	Mar 18 2011
3m 3f 71y C	7m 1.00	6	10-2	Good	Shardam	Nov 15 2003
3m 4f 21y C	7m 14.50	8	11-12	Good	Gentle Ranger (IRE)	Apr 16 2010
3m 6f 37y C	7m 51.70	8	10-9	Good To Firm	Balthazar King (IRE)	Mar 13 2012
3m 7f 170y C	8m 0.60	8	12-0	Good	Relaxation (IRE)	Mar 15 2000
4m 120y C	8m 33.20	7	11-11	Good	Hot Weld	Mar 16 2006

CHEPSTOW

Distance	Time	Age	Weight	Going	Horse	Date
2m 11y H	3m 43.20	4	10-1	Firm	Tingle Bell	Oct 4 1986
2m 11y C	3m 54.10	8	12-0	Firm	Panto Prince	May 9 1989
2m 3f 98y C	4m 42.50	5	11-4	Good	Balder Succes (FR)	Oct 12 2013
2m 3f 100y H	4m 38.80	8	9-10	Firm	Court Appeal	May 8 1990
2m 7f 131y C	5m 47.90	9	11-10	Firm	Broadheath	Oct 4 1986
2m 7f 131y H	5m 33.60	10	10-0	Firm	Chucklestone	May 11 1993
3m 2f 54y C	6m 39.40	7	12-0	Firm	Jaunty Jane	May 26 1975
3m 4f 198y C	7m 24.00	9	10-5	Hard	Creeola II	Apr 27 1957

DONCASTER

Distance	Time	Age	Weight	Going	Horse	Date
2m 90y C	3m 51.90	12	10-9	Good To Firm	Itsgottabealright	Jan 28 1989
2m 140y H	3m 46.60	6	10-0	Firm	Good For A Loan	Feb 24 1993
2m 3f 44y C	4m 36.90	7	11-0	Good	Off The Ground (IRE)	Nov 29 2013
2m 3f 110y C	4m 45.40	8	10-0	Firm	Powder Horn	Feb 25 1985
2m 3f 120y H	4m 33.00	4	10-12	Good	Bobby Ewing	Dec 11 2009
3m 6y C	5m 52.40	7	11-7	Good	Beneficial Reform	Mar 3 2012
3m 6y C	5m 52.40	8	10-9	Good	Dalkey Sound	Jan 26 1991
3m 96y H	5m 43.20	6	11-10	Good	Allthekingshorses	Feb 22 2012
3m 2f 14y C	6m 11.80	9	10-10	Good	Always Right	Mar 5 2011

EXETER

Distance	Time	Age	Weight	Going	Horse	Date
2m 175y H	3m 49.20	6	11-0	Good To Firm	Remind Me Later	Apr 21 2015
2m 1f 109y C	3m 58.10	7	11-7	Firm	Bushwacker	May 3 2011
2m 2f 111y H	4m 14.70	5	10-13	Firm	My Brother Sylvest	Oct 18 2011
2m 3f 48y C	4m 27.90	8	11-11	Good To Firm	West With The Wind	May 7 2013
2m 5f 135y H	5m 5.70	7	10-6	Good To Firm	Cruising Bye	Oct 10 2013
2m 7f 25y H	5m 26.20	8	10-11	Good To Firm	Very Cool	May 4 2010
3m 54y C	5m 42.80	8	10-5	Good To Firm	Dennis The Legend	May 13 2009
3m 6f 153y C	7m 14.70	10	10-13	Good To Firm	Thomas Wild	Apr 14 2015
4m C	8m 9.30	10	11-5	Good	Major Malarkey	Dec 6 2013

FAKENHAM

Distance	Time	Age	Weight	Going	Horse	Date
2m H	3m 45.70	5	10-9	Good To Firm	Cobbet (CZE)	May 9 2001
2m 3y H	3m 47.80	5	11-10	Good To Firm	Tom Clapton	May 25 1992
2m 59y C	3m 44.90	11	12-4	Firm	Cheekio Ora	Apr 23 1984
2m 4f H	4m 41.20	4	10-3	Good To Firm	Ayem (IRE)	May 16 1999
2m 5f 44y C	5m 10.30	13	12-2	Good To Firm	Skipping Tim	May 25 1992
2m 7f 110y H	5m 37.10	6	11-3	Good	Laughing Gas (IRE)	May 20 1995
3m 38y C	5m 56.90	7	11-1	Good To Firm	Specialize	May 16 1999

FFOS LAS

Distance	Time	Age	Weight	Going	Horse	Date
1m 7f 202y H	3m 33.60	6	10-11	Good	Valain (IRE)	Aug 28 2009
2m C	3m 45.25	6	11-12	Good To Firm	West With The Wind	Aug 25 2011
2m 3f 83y C	4m 37.34	7	10-12	Firm	Cold Harbour	May 31 2011
2m 4f H	4m 39.40	6	10-9	Good	Plunkett (IRE)	Jun 18 2009
2m 4f 199y C	5m 9.70	8	11-11	Good To Firm	Putney Bridge	Jun 17 2010
2m 5f 192y H	5m 15.40	6	11-0	Good	Koultas King	Aug 22 2013
2m 7f 177y C	5m 49.60	7	11-7	Good	Sea Wall	Jun 18 2009
2m 7f 191y H	5m 39.00	5	11-8	Good	Chill Factor	Aug 21 2014
3m 1f 60y C	6m 7.10	7	10-1	Good	Backstage (FR)	Aug 28 2009

FONTWELL

Distance	Time	Age	Weight	Going	Horse	Date
2m 1f 96y C	4m 14.50	12	10-1	Good To Firm	A Thousand Dreams	Jun 3 2002
2m 1f 145y H	4m 6.80	7	10-2	Good To Firm	Hyperion Du Moulin II)	Jun 3 2002
2m 2f H	4m 5.90	4	10-13	Hard	Fighting Days	Aug 14 1990
2m 3f 33y H	4m 30.50	8	10-7	Good To Firm	Hillswick	Aug 27 1999
2m 3f 35y C	4m 38.10	6	11-0	Good To Firm	Chalcedony	Jun 3 2002
2m 5f 31y C	5m 13.90	10	10-0	Good To Firm	Contes (IRE)	Jun 3 2002
2m 5f 139y H	5m 6.70	7	10-1	Good To Firm	Mister Pickwick (IRE)	Jun 3 2002
2m 6f H	5m 3.00	5	11-8	Firm	Doualago	May 29 1995
3m 1f 106y C	6m 24.30	5	10-2	Good To Firm	Il Capitano	May 6 2002
3m 1f 142y H	6m 14.00	7	11-2	Good	Sir Mangan	Oct 2 2015
3m 2f 110y H	6m 14.80	10	10-0	Firm	Punch's Hotel	Apr 27 1995
3m 3f 45y C	7m 11.10	8	10-6	Good	Strolling Vagabond	Mar 18 2007

HAYDOCK

Distance	Time	Age	Weight	Going	Horse	Date
1m 7f 144y H	3m 32.30	6	10-0	Good	She's Our Mare (IRE)	May 1 1999
1m 7f 157y C	3m 52.30	7	11-7	Good	Witness In Court (IRE)	Apr 19 2014
2m H	3m 44.30	5	11-5	Good	Perpetually (IRE)	Oct 26 2011
2m 2f 191y H	4m 32.10	6	11-12	Good	Horizontal Speed	Apr 19 2014
2m 2f 191y H	4m 33.00	7	10-11	Good	Carlton Jack	Apr 19 2014
2m 2f 211y C	4m 49.90	6	11-7	Good	Etxalar (FR)	Oct 28 2009
2m 4f H	4m 33.10	5	11-2	Good	My Brother Sylvest	Oct 26 2011
2m 6f 177y H	5m 37.60	5	10-13	Good To Soft	Dynaste (FR)	Nov 19 2011
2m 6f 204y C	5m 41.50	7	10-6	Good	No Planning	Apr 19 2014
3m H	5m 33.70	8	10-9	Good	Liberate	May 7 2011
3m 3f 57y C	7m 7.70	9	10-8	Good	Blenheim Brook	Apr 19 2014

HEXHAM

Distance	Time	Age	Weight	Going	Horse	Date
1m 7f 133y C	3m 52.80	7	10-12	Good	Imjoeking	Jun 22 2014
2m 48y H	3m 57.80	8	11-7	Good To Firm	Francies Fancy (IRE)	Jun 19 2005
2m 4f 15y C	4m 55.40	8	9-11	Firm	Mr Laggan	Sep 14 2003
2m 4f 28y H	4m 31.50	6	11-0	Good To Firm	Pappa Charlie (USA)	May 27 1997
2m 7f 63y H	5m 45.50	7	9-9	Firm	Fingers Crossed	Apr 29 1991
3m 41y C	6m 7.60	9	9-11	Good To Firm	Silent Snipe	Jun 1 2002
3m 7f 199y C	8m 34.00	10	10-12	Good	Simply Smashing	Mar 18 2010

HUNTINGDON

Distance	Time	Age	Weight	Going	Horse	Date
1m 7f 171y H	3m 32.70	5	11-11	Good To Firm	Weather Front	Aug 31 2009
2m 104y C	3m 53.30	5	10-0	Good To Firm	No Greater Love (FR)	May 23 2007
2m 3f 137y H	4m 30.20	6	11-10	Good To Firm	Sabre Hongrois (FR)	Oct 4 2009
2m 3f 189y C	4m 46.40	10	10-13	Good To Firm	Peccadillo	Sep 26 2004
2m 4f 145y H	4m 45.80	6	11-5	Firm	Sound of Laughter	Apr 14 1984
2m 7f 129y C	5m 44.40	7	11-2	Good To Firm	Ozzie Jones	Sep 18 1998
3m 1f 10y H	5m 50.20	8	11-12	Good To Firm	Orchard King	Aug 31 2009
3m 6f 162y C	8m 2.70	9	10-4	Good To Soft	Kinnahalla (IRE)	Nov 24 2001

KELSO

Distance	Time	Age	Weight	Going	Horse	Date
2m 51y H	3m 38.90	6	11-12	Good To Firm	Life And Soul	May 26 2013
2m 1f C	4m 2.40	8	11-9	Firm	Mr Coggy	May 2 1984
2m 2f 25y H	4m 8.70	6	11-7	Good To Firm	Croco Bay	May 26 2013
2m 6f 110y C	5m 29.60	10	10-13	Good	Bas De Laine (FR)	Nov 13 1996
2m 6f 151y H	5m 12.20	4	11-3	Firm	Hit The Canvas (USA)	Sep 30 1995
3m 1f 170y H	6m 10.10	8	10-13	Good To Firm	Dook's Delight (IRE)	May 19 1999

KEMPTON

Distance	Time	Age	Weight	Going	Horse	Date
2m H	3m 40.40	7	11-8	Good	Australia Day (IRE)	Oct 17 2010
2m C	3m 43.60	11	11-3	Good	Australia Day	May 5 2014
2m 4f 110y C	5m 1.50	6	11-0	Good	Rum And Butter	May 5 2014
2m 5f H	4m 58.20	6	11-0	Good	Chilworth Screamer	May 5 2014
3m C	5m 54.20	10	11-7	Good	American Spin	May 5 2014
3m 110y H	6m 6.50	5	11-9	Good	Dreamsoftheatre	Nov 25 2013

LEICESTER

Distance	Time	Age	Weight	Going	Horse	Date
1m 7f 201y C	3m 54.50	5	11-7	Good	William's Wishes (IRE)	Nov 15 2010
2m H	3m 39.60	6	10-11	Good To Firm	Ryde Again	Nov 20 1989
2m 4f 45y C	5m 0.60	9	9-6	Firm	Prairie Minstrel	Dec 4 2003
2m 4f 110y H	4m 45.50	4	11-7	Good To Firm	Prince of Rheims	Dec 5 1989
2m 6f 151y C	5m 44.80	6	11-10	Good To Firm	Little Chip	Dec 11 2013

LINGFIELD

Distance	Time	Age	Weight	Going	Horse	Date
2m C	3m 48.70	9	11-2	Good To Firm	Rapide Plaisir	Sep 28 2007
2m 3f 110y H	4m 37.30	6	10-3	Firm	Bellezza	Mar 20 1993
2m 7f H	5m 31.90	8	11-6	Good To Firm	Herecomestanley	Sep 28 2007
3m C	5m 58.40	6	11-3	Firm	Mighty Frolic	Mar 19 1993

LUDLOW

Distance	Time	Age	Weight	Going	Horse	Date
1m 7f 169y H	3m 35.70	7	11-4	Good	Frozen Over	May 10 2015
1m 7f 212y C	3m 47.30	5	11-7	Good To Firm	Pearl King (IRE)	Apr 5 2007
1m 7f 212y C	3m 47.30	7	11-0	Good	Bullet Street	May 10 2015
2m 4f 11y C	4m 47.30	10	11-8	Good To Firm	Handy Money	Apr 5 2007
2m 5f 55y H	4m 58.00	8	11-0	Good To Firm	Willy Willy	Oct 11 2001
2m 7f 174y H	5m 33.30	5	9-11	Good	Dark Spirit	Oct 9 2013
3m C	5m 47.20	8	11-4	Good	Kilbree Kid	Apr 21 2015
3m 1f 125y C	6m 17.30	12	11-4	Good To Firm	Moving Earth	May 12 2005

MARKET RASEN

Distance	Time	Age	Weight	Going	Horse	Date
2m 148y H	3m 57.40	7	11-5	Good	Australia Day (IRE)	Jly 17 2010
2m 1f 43y C	4m 13.60	11	10-2	Good To Firm	Mister Wiseman	Jly 7 2013
2m 2f 140y H	4m 26.10	6	11-9	Good To Soft	Attaglance	Feb 19 2012
2m 3f 34y C	4m 41.40	8	11-1	Good	Bocciani	May 10 2013
2m 4f 139y H	5m 3.70	7	11-3	Good To Soft	Fiulin	Feb 19 2012
2m 5f 89y C	5m 18.30	8	10-12	Good To Firm	Paddy The Hare (IRE)	Jly 7 2013
2m 7f 16y H	5m 38.80	6	12-5	Firm	Trustful	May 21 1977
2m 7f 191y C	6m 1.00	7	11-8	Good To Firm	Allerlea	Jun 1 1985
3m 3f 123y C	7m 26.10	8	11-1	Good To Soft	Carli King	Dec 26 2014

MUSSELBURGH

Distance	Time	Age	Weight	Going	Horse	Date
1m 7f 124y H	3m 35.90	3	10-7	Good To Firm	Joe Bumpas	Dec 11 1989
1m 7f 182y C	3m 48.10	8	10-12	Good To Firm	Sonsie Mo	Dec 6 1993
2m 3f 81y H	4m 34.70	9	11-7	Good	Strongpoint (IRE)	Dec 9 2013
2m 3f 193y C	4m 44.50	7	11-9	Good To Firm	Bohemian Spirit (IRE)	Dec 18 2005
2m 7f 170y C	5m 47.70	7	11-10	Firm	Snowy (IRE)	Dec 18 2005
3m H	5m 39.10	8	11-5	Firm	Supertop	Dec 17 1996
3m 110y H	5m 36.20	6	11-1	Soft	Seeyouatmidnight	Feb 2 2014

NEWBURY

Distance	Time	Age	Weight	Going	Horse	Date
2m 69y H	3m 45.20	5	10-2	Good To Firm	Dhofar	Oct 25 1985
2m 92y C	3m 57.34	6	11-5	Good	Valdez	Nov 30 2013
2m 2f 64y C	4m 31.87	7	11-9	Good To Soft	Highway Code (USA)	Nov 29 2013
2m 2f 183y H	4m 26.70	4	11-0	Good	Songsmith	Mar 24 2012
2m 3f 187y C	4m 47.90	8	11-12	Good To Firm	Espy I	Oct 25 1991
2m 4f 118y H	4m 48.63	6	11-0	Good	Argento Luna	Mar 21 2009
2m 6f 93y C	5m 28.93	5	11-10	Good	Pepite Rose (FR)	Mar 24 2012
2m 7f 86y C	5m 42.53	7	11-10	Good To Soft	Long Run (FR)	Feb 17 2012
3m 52y H	5m 45.40	8	10-9	Good	Lansdowne	Oct 25 1996
3m 1f 214y C	6m 22.86	9	10-8	Good	Ikorodu Road	Mar 24 2012

NEWCASTLE

Distance	Time	Age	Weight	Going	Horse	Date
2m 75y C	3m 56.70	7	11-12	Firm	Greenheart	May 7 1990
2m 98y H	3m 40.70	7	10-10	Good	Padre Mio	Nov 25 1995
2m 110y H	3m 49.40	6	11-2	Firm	Mr Woodcock	Oct 23 1991
2m 4f 19y C	4m 46.70	7	9-13	Firm	Snow Blessed	May 19 1984
2m 4f 133y H	4m 42.00	4	10-10	Hard	Mils Mij	May 13 1989
2m 6f H	5m 24.90	6	10-12	Good To Soft	Bygones Of Brid (IRE)	Nov 28 2009
2m 7f 91y C	5m 48.10	-2	10-4	Firm	Even Swell	Oct 30 1975
3m 10y H	5m 40.10	4	10-5	Good	Withy Bank	Nov 29 1986
4m 122y C	8m 30.40	7	10-0	Good	Domaine De Pron (FR)	Feb 21 1998

NEWTON ABBOT

Distance	Time	Age	Weight	Going	Horse	Date
2m 75y C	3m 49.80	6	11-10	Good To Firm	Bullet Street	Aug 13 2014
2m 167y H	3m 45.00	5	11-0	Firm	Windbound Lass	Aug 1 1988
2m 2f 110y H	4m 15.20	5	10-8	Good To Firm	Rum And Butter	Aug 22 2013
2m 4f 216y C	5m 2.10	7	11-0	Good	Mhilu	Jly 13 2009
2m 5f 122y H	4m 55.40	7	10-0	Firm	Virbian	Jly 30 1983
3m 1f 170y C	6m 9.50	8	11-7	Good To Firm	No Loose Change	Jly 8 2013
3m 2f 105y H	6m 16.70	8	10-13	Good To Firm	Celebrity Call	Jun 4 2009

PERTH

Distance	Time	Age	Weight	Going	Horse	Date
2m C	3m 44.50	7	10-4	Good	Robin's Command	Jly 3 2014
2m 110y H	3m 38.20	5	11-6	Good To Firm	Lisbon (IRE)	Jly 3 2013
2m 4f 20y C	4m 48.20	9	10-7	Good To Firm	Strobe	Jly 14 2013
2m 4f 35y H	4m 41.20	8	10-2	Firm	Valiant Dash	May 19 1994
2m 7f 180y C	5m 46.20	7	10-12	Good To Firm	Problema Tic	Jun 9 2013
2m 7f 207y H	5m 41.60	10	11-1	Good To Firm	Imtihan	Jly 2 2009
3m 2f 127y H	6m 37.20	5	10-11	Good To Firm	Noir Et Vert (FR)	Apr 28 2006
3m 6f 121y C	7m 43.70	8	11-6	Good	Laertes	Apr 24 2009

PLUMPTON

Distance	Time	Age	Weight	Going	Horse	Date
1m 7f 195y H	3m 31.00	3	11-1	Firm	Royal Derbi	Sep 19 1988
2m 214y C	4m 5.00	7	11-12	Good	Gauvain	Apr 13 2009
2m 1f 164y H	4m 10.50	5	10-12	Good To Firm	Golanova	Sep 22 2013
2m 3f 164y C	4m 42.80	6	11-0	Good To Firm	Dead Or Alive	May 10 2009
2m 4f 114y H	4m 46.80	4	11-2	Good To Firm	Urban Warrior	Sep 21 2008
3m 217y H	5m 53.00	7	11-4	Good To Firm	Teak	Sep 21 2014
3m 1f 152y C	6m 23.50	9	9-7	Good To Firm	Sunday Habits	Apr 19 2003
3m 4f 102y C	7m 19.80	6	11-7	Good To Firm	Ecuyer Du Roi (FR)	Apr 15 2002

SANDOWN

Distance	Time	Age	Weight	Going	Horse	Date
1m 7f 119y C	3m 43.40	9	11-6	Good To Firm	Dempsey (IRE)	Apr 28 2007
1m 7f 216y H	3m 42.00	6	10-0	Firm	Olympian	Mar 13 1993
2m 3f 173y H	4m 35.70	5	11-3	Good To Firm	Oslot (FR)	Apr 28 2007
2m 4f 10y C	4m 57.10	8	11-7	Good	Coulton	Apr 29 1995
2m 6f H	5m 5.60	8	11-3	Firm	Kintbury I	Nov 5 1983
2m 7f 98y H	5m 39.10	6	11-5	Good To Firm	Rostropovich	Apr 26 2003
3m 37y C	5m 59.00	8	12-7	Good To Firm	Arkle	Nov 6 1965
3m 4f 166y C	7m 9.10	9	10-1	Good	Cache Fleur	Apr 29 1995

SEDGEFIELD

Distance	Time	Age	Weight	Going	Horse	Date
2m 77y C	3m 53.60	7	10-7	Good To Firm	Suas Leat (IRE)	Sep 16 1997
2m 178y H	3m 45.70	6	10-5	Good To Firm	Country Orchid	Sep 5 1997
2m 1f C	4m 0.40	8	10-10	Firm	Stay Awake	May 18 1994
2m 3f 34y H	4m 38.30	7	11-4	Good To Firm	Ad Murum (IRE)	Aug 11 2006
2m 3f 65y C	4m 44.20	6	11-12	Good	The Backup Plan	Sep 29 2015
2m 5f 34y H	4m 46.30	7	10-0	Good To Firm	Palm House	Sep 4 1992
3m 2f 59y C	6m 29.30	6	10-2	Good To Firm	The Gallopin'Major	Sep 14 1996
3m 3f 9y H	6m 19.70	7	9-13	Firm	Pikestaff (USA)	Jly 25 2005

SOUTHWELL

Distance	Time	Age	Weight	Going	Horse	Date
1m 7f 153y C	3m 54.60	6	11-7	Good	Memorabilia	Mar 17 2014
1m 7f 153y H	3m 44.30	7	10-8	Good	Dealing River	Jly 22 2014
2m 4f 62y C	5m 6.60	7	10-13	Good	Gentleman Anshan	May 17 2011
2m 4f 62y H	4m 57.30	8	11-3	Good	Red Not Blue (IRE)	May 17 2011
2m 7f 209y C	6m 10.10	8	11-2	Good	Best Boy Barney	Jly 22 2014
2m 7f 209y H	5m 55.40	10	11-7	Good	Jawaab	Jly 22 2014

STRATFORD

Distance	Time	Age	Weight	Going	Horse	Date
2m 70y H	3m 40.40	6	11-12	Hard	Chusan	May 7 1956
2m 213y C	3m 56.70	8	11-0	Good To Firm	Professeur Emery	Aug 1 2013
2m 2f 148y H	4m 18.30	11	11-12	Good	Man Of Leisure	Jly 19 2015
2m 3f 98y C	4m 35.40	9	10-0	Good To Soft	Gentleman Anshan	May 19 2013
2m 4f 205y C	4m 56.50	6	9-10	Good To Firm	Spare Change (IRE)	Sep 16 2007
2m 6f 7y H	5m 6.80	6	11-0	Firm	Broken Wing	May 31 1986
2m 6f 125y C	5m 22.80	8	11-0	Good	Danandy	Jly 19 2015
3m 2f 83y H	6m 13.10	7	10-8	Good To Firm	Burren Moonshine (IRE)	Jun 11 2006
3m 3f 119y C	6m 38.30	10	12-0	Good	Mossey Joe (IRE)	Jun 7 2013

TAUNTON

Distance	Time	Age	Weight	Going	Horse	Date
2m 12y C	3m 49.50	8	10-9	Firm	I Have Him	Apr 28 1995
2m 104y H	3m 39.40	4	12-0	Hard	Indian Jockey	Oct 3 1996
2m 2f 40y C	4m 24.90	7	11-3	Firm	Wait No More	Mar 28 2012
2m 3f 1y H	4m 19.70	5	10-6	Firm	Prairie Spirit	Apr 2 2009
2m 7f 3y C	5m 39.80	7	11-10	Firm	Glacial Delight (IRE)	Apr 24 2006
2m 7f 198y H	5m 30.20	7	10-4	Firm	On My Toes	Oct 15 1998

TOWCESTER

Distance	Time	Age	Weight	Going	Horse	Date
1m 7f 181y H	3m 39.50	4	11-0	Firm	Naskracker	May 22 1987
2m 70y C	3m 52.40	12	10-3	Good	Crack At Dawn	May 21 2013
2m 3f 34y H	4m 31.50	6	11-4	Good	Ballygrooby Bertie	May 19 2014
2m 3f 179y C	4m 53.50	6	11-0	Good To Firm	Home	May 20 2011
2m 4f 217y H	5m 0.90	7	11-2	Firm	Mailcom	May 3 1993
2m 5f 153y C	5m 15.60	7	10-12	Good	Top Wood	May 19 2014
2m 7f 211y H	5m 44.00	9	9-10	Firm	Dropshot I	May 25 1984
3m 102y C	5m 52.60	10	10-13	Good To Firm	Lucky Luk	May 29 2009

UTTOXETER

Distance	Time	Age	Weight	Going	Horse	Date
2m C	3m 41.50	6	11-0	Good	Tapageur	Aug 8 1991
2m H	3m 28.20	4	10-10	Firm	Mill De Lease	Sep 21 1989
2m 3f 207y H	4m 39.10	8	10-9	Good To Firm	Chicago's Best	Jun 11 1995
2m 4f C	4m 42.60	7	12-0	Good To Firm	Bertone (IRE)	Oct 5 1996
2m 5f C	4m 54.20	8	11-8	Firm	McKenzie	Apr 27 1974
2m 6f 105y C	5m 35.60	6	11-0	Good	Brassick	Jly 26 2013
3m C	5m 56.80	6	11-2	Good	Always Waining (IRE)	May 5 2007
3m H	5m 32.30	8	10-12	Good To Firm	Painted Sky	Oct 2 2011
3m 2f C	6m 17.60	7	11-5	Good	The Romford Pele	Jun 29 2014
4m 1f 92y C	8m 41.30	8	10-3	Good To Soft	Goulanes (IRE)	Mar 15 2014

WARWICK

Distance	Time	Age	Weight	Going	Horse	Date
2m C	3m 48.88	6	10-3	Good To Firm	Lake Imperial (IRE)	Nov 5 2007
2m H	3m 30.80	5	11-7	Firm	High Knowl	Sep 17 1988
2m 3f H	4m 15.00	6	11-7	Good To Firm	Runaway Pete (USA)	Nov 2 1996
2m 4f C	4m 56.20	8	11-8	Good	Dictum (IRE)	Nov 2 1999
2m 4f 110y C	4m 53.30	9	9-12	Good To Firm	Dudie I	May 16 1987
2m 4f 110y H	4m 43.00	7	10-0	Firm	Carrymore	Sep 19 1970
2m 5f H	4m 43.60	5	10-10	Firm	Three Eagles (USA)	May 11 2002
3m 110y C	6m 0.20	7	11-8	Good	Shining Gale (IRE)	Mar 18 2009
3m 1f H	5m 53.50	7	11-0	Good To Firm	City Poser	Apr 2 2002
3m 2f C	6m 16.10	12	10-12	Firm	Castle Warden	May 6 1989
3m 5f C	7m 12.09	12	11-7	Good	Arnold Layne	Mar 23 2011

WETHERBY

Distance	Time	Age	Weight	Going	Horse	Date
1m 7f 36y C	3m 41.60	7	11-2	Good	Oliver's Gold	Oct 14 2015
2m H	3m 43.20	9	11-5	Good	Lightening Rod	Oct 31 2014
2m 3f 85y C	4m 47.80	7	10-12	Good	Drever Route	Oct 13 2010
2m 3f 85y C	4m 44.80	8	11-3	Good	Village Vic (IRE)	Oct 14 2015
2m 4f H	4m 39.40	5	10-12	Good	Fort Worth (IRE)	Oct 15 2014
2m 5f 56y H	5m 2.10	7	11-9	Good	Kaysersberg (FR)	Oct 15 2014
2m 5f 75y C	5m 24.90	6	11-3	Good	Pistol Basc	Oct 13 2010
3m 26y H	5m 46.30	7	11-3	Good	Minella Hero	May 21 2015
3m 26y H	5m 46.30	5	9-7	Good	Lilly's Legend	May 21 2015
3m 1f C	5m 51.60	11	11-9	Good	Garleton	May 24 2012

WINCANTON

Distance	Time	Age	Weight	Going	Horse	Date
1m 7f 65y H	3m 25.80	6	10-5	Good	Nearby	Nov 6 2010
1m 7f 149y C	3m 37.90	6	11-11	Good	Kie	Apr 13 2014
2m 4f H	4m 29.46	7	10-4	Good To Firm	Uffa Fox	Oct 14 2010
2m 5f C	4m 59.20	11	11-10	Firm	Edredon Bleu (FR)	Oct 26 2003
2m 5f 82y H	4m 54.70	7	11-10	Good To Firm	Urcalin	Apr 19 2015
3m 1f 30y C	6m 9.70	7	11-6	Good To Firm	Swansea Bay	Nov 8 2003
3m 2f 162y C	6m 37.20	7	11-8	Good	Gullible Gordon (Ire)	Oct 24 2010

WORCESTER

Distance	Time	Age	Weight	Going	Horse	Date
2m H	3m 33.40	10	11-5	Good	Chilbury Hill	Aug 28 2013
2m C	3m 41.46	7	10-10	Good	Fit to Drive	Sep 25 2009
2m 110y C	3m 51.40	6	11-1	Good To Firm	Sedgemoor Express	Jly 29 2014
2m 4f C	4m 38.20	8	10-5	Good	Moorlands Jack	Sep 10 2013
2m 4f H	4m 28.70	7	10-4	Good To Firm	Jigsaw Financial	Jly 17 2013
2m 7f H	5m 23.50	7	11-5	Good	Saticon	Jun 27 2012
2m 7f C	5m 29.70	6	10-2	Good	Whistling Senator	Aug 28 2013

SPLIT SECOND SPEED RATINGS

The following lists the fastest performances of chasers, hurdlers & bumper horses which have recorded a speed figure of 90 or over during the 2015-16 season. Additional information in the parentheses following the speed figure shows the distance of the race in furlongs, course, state of going and the date on which the figurewas achieved.

CHASING

A Good Skin 108 *(25f,Wcn,S,Nov 7)*
A Keen Sense 98 *(26f,Nab,GS,Aug 22)*
Aachen 104 *(26f,Chl,S,Dec 11)*
Aalim 96 *(19f,Mar,G,Jun 19)*
Abbey Storm 90 *(20f,Crl,HY,Feb 22)*
Abigail Lynch 96 *(16f,Hay,HY,Dec 19)*
Abolitionist 110 *(25½f,Crt,G,Aug 31)*
Abracadabra Sivola 111 *(23f,Lei,HY,Mar 1)*
Abricot De L'Oasis 101 *(20f,Ain,G,May 15)*
Accessallareas 105 *(16½f,Nab,S,May 7)*
According To Sarah 97 *(20½f,Ban,G,Aug 21)*
Achille 96 *(24f,Asc,S,Nov 20)*
Achimota 107 *(24f,Ban,S,Nov 11)*
Acrai Rua 93 *(26f,Sed,S,May 5)*
Activial 112 *(19f,Exe,HY,Jan 1)*
Adam Du Breteau 104 *(20½f,Kem,G,Nov 2)*
Adams Wood 102 *(21½f,Fai,HY,Jan 30)*
Adios Alonso 108 *(21f,Str,G,Jun 16)*
Admiral Barton 93 *(23f,Wor,G,Aug 19)*
Admiral Blake 90 *(25f,Cat,S,Jan 27)*
Adrenalin Flight 109 *(26f,Utt,G,Jun 28)*
Aerlite Supreme 111 *(20f,Nby,S,Mar 5)*
Agapanthus 93 *(16f,Kem,G,May 13)*
Agentleman 92 *(16f,Cat,GS,Feb 5)*
Agincourt Reef 104 *(18f,Tau,S,Mar 3)*
Aigle De La See 93 *(20f,Ain,GS,Dec 5)*
Ainsi Fideles 106 *(21f,Hay,GS,May 9)*
Al Alfa 110 *(19½f,Str,G,Aug 27)*
Al Co 98 *(25f,Ain,S,Apr 9)*
Al Ferof 115 *(20f,Hun,GS,Dec 6)*
Alanjou 91 *(21f,Fak,S,Feb 8)*
Alba King 95 *(20f,Wor,GF,Jly 23)*
Albatros De Guye 91 *(20f,Lin,S,Nov 10)*
Alberobello 105 *(25f,Wcn,G,May 7)*
Alder Mairi 109 *(20f,Plu,HY,Feb 15)*
Alderbrook Lad 111 *(21f,Crt,G,Jun 28)*
Alfie Spinner 111 *(24f,Ffo,HY,Mar 31)*
Algernon Pazham 110 *(24f,Ban,S,Nov 11)*
Alisier D'Irlande 111 *(17f,Leo,S,Feb 28)*
All But Grey 97 *(16½f,Nab,G,May 27)*
All The Chimneys 90 *(20f,Pun,HY,Jan 9)*
All The Way Home 98 *(21½f,Fai,HY,Jan 30)*
All Together 114 *(17f,Asc,S,Dec 18)*
Allez Vic 106 *(24f,Ffo,S,Apr 10)*
Allow Dallow 103 *(16f,Sth,G,Mar 21)*
Allthekingshorses 98 *(25½f,War,G,Sep 22)*
Aloomomo 107 *(20½f,Chl,GS,Mar 15)*
Alright Benny 102 *(21f,Fak,G,May 5)*
Alta Rock 102 *(26f,Sed,GF,Sep 3)*
Alternatif 108 *(21f,Crt,G,May 27)*
Altiepix 104 *(24f,Fai,SH,Jan 20)*
Alto Des Mottes 104 *(25f,Cat,GS,Dec 2)*
Alvarado 101 *(32f,Ayr,GS,Apr 16)*
Always On The Run 98 *(20f,War,HY,Dec 31)*
Alwaystheoptimist 108 *(19½f,Str,G,Aug 20)*
Amazing D'Azy 94 *(22f,Tow,GS,May 18)*
Amber Flush 99 *(23f,Wor,G,Jun 21)*
American Legend 106 *(24f,War,G,Oct 1)*
American Spin 100 *(25½f,Fon,G,May 24)*
American World 95 *(20f,Utt,S,Nov 22)*
Amethyst Rose 101 *(15½f,Hex,HY,May 9)*
Amidon 104 *(24f,Fak,S,Jan 28)*
Amigo 105 *(26f,Chl,G,Apr 14)*
Amilliontimes 102 *(20f,Mus,G,Nov 5)*
Amir Pasha 96 *(16½f,Sed,G,May 12)*
Amore Alato 109 *(21f,Asc,S,Feb 20)*
Amuse Me 105 *(20f,Sth,G,Sep 2)*
An Poc Ar Buile 105 *(24f,Mar,G,May 17)*
Anatol 100 *(19f,Asc,G,Oct 31)*
Anay Turge 111 *(19f,Mar,G,May 8)*
Andi'Amu 97 *(19½f,Str,GF,May 17)*
Andy Kelly 104 *(20f,Plu,G,Oct 19)*
Annacotty 114 *(20½f,Chl,GS,Nov 14)*
Annamatopoeia 99 *(19f,Leo,HY,Dec 28)*
Annie Oakley 101 *(21f,Pun,GY,May 1)*
Another Flutter 99 *(17f,Str,G,May 30)*
Another Hero 90 *(24f,Asc,GS,Nov 21)*
Another Journey 104 *(16f,Lud,G,Apr 19)*
Anteros 94 *(20f,Utt,HY,Dec 8)*
Antony 113 *(20f,San,GS,Dec 4)*
Any Currency 113 *(30f,Chl,G,Mar 16)*
Apache Pilot 98 *(24f,Mus,S,Feb 8)*
Apache Stronghold 112 *(25f,Pun,GY,Apr 28)*
April Dusk 109 *(20f,Utt,HY,Dec 8)*
Ar Mad 121 *(15½f,San,GS,Dec 5)*
Araldur 104 *(24f,Ban,S,Nov 11)*
Arbeo 103 *(24f,San,S,Feb 19)*
Archie Boy 104 *(20f,Sth,G,Jun 9)*
Archie Meade 109 *(25f,Pun,S,May 2)*
Arctic Skipper 106 *(20f,Pun,HY,Jan 9)*
Ard Cregg 98 *(20f,Pun,HY,Jan 9)*
Ardkilly Witness 100 *(24f,San,S,Mar 11)*
Aregra 104 *(16½f,Sed,G,Sep 29)*
Arkaim 109 *(16f,Kem,G,Oct 18)*
Armedanddangerous 90 *(27f,Wcn,HY,Nov 19)*
Around A Pound 96 *(22f,Tow,GF,Apr 30)*
Arpege D'Alene 119 *(20f,Wcn,S,Nov 7)*
Arquebusier 104 *(21f,Fon,S,Apr 1)*
Art Lord 104 *(20f,Mus,S,Dec 7)*
Art Mauresque 120 *(20f,Chl,G,Oct 24)*
Art Of Logistics 110 *(20f,Nby,G,Apr 2)*
Arthamint 103 *(20f,Lin,S,Nov 10)*
Arthur's Oak 113 *(16f,Chp,S,Feb 27)*
Artifice Sivola 107 *(16f,Lud,GS,Nov 23)*
Arzal 117 *(20f,Ain,GS,Apr 7)*
As De Fer 108 *(24f,Ffo,S,Apr 10)*
As De Mee 115 *(20f,San,GS,Feb 6)*
As De Pique 106 *(25f,Pun,G,May 16)*
Ashcott Boy 103 *(16f,Sth,HY,Mar 7)*
Ashford Wood 91 *(22½f,Nby,S,Dec 29)*
Askamore Darsi 108 *(26f,Sed,GS,Jan 31)*
Aso 117 *(16f,Hay,HY,Dec 19)*
Astigos 100 *(25f,Wcn,S,Dec 26)*
Astracad 116 *(19½f,Chp,G,Oct 11)*
Asuncion 101 *(20f,Mus,S,Jan 20)*
Ata Boy 95 *(22f,Tow,GF,Apr 30)*
Atlantic Roller 106 *(21f,Nab,G,Jun 12)*
Attimo 104 *(20f,Sth,GS,Apr 15)*
Audacious Plan 105 *(23½f,Chp,G,Oct 10)*
Auldthunder 107 *(26f,Sed,S,Mar 6)*
Aurora Bell 105 *(21f,Leo,S,Feb 28)*
Authinger 96 *(20f,Per,S,May 14)*
Auvergnat 106 *(24f,Mar,G,Oct 17)*
Aye Well 102 *(17f,Kel,GS,Mar 21)*
Azerodegree 101 *(15½f,Hex,GS,Oct 10)*
Azert De Coeur 99 *(16f,Lud,HY,Jan 4)*
Azorian 115 *(20f,Chl,G,Oct 24)*
Azure Fly 107 *(27½f,Chl,GS,Nov 14)*

Baby Mix 109 *(19½f,Str,G,May 17)*
Baby Shine 108 *(23½f,Lin,HY,Dec 12)*
Back In June 102 *(26f,Nab,GS,May 19)*
Back To Bracka 106 *(21f,Hay,GS,May 9)*
Badger Wood 105 *(23f,Tau,HY,Jan 23)*
Badgers Retreat 94 *(20f,War,G,Sep 22)*
Baie Des Iles 113 *(25f,Fai,HY,Feb 20)*
Baileys Concerto 110 *(24f,Don,G,Feb 24)*
Baily Green 114 *(16f,Pun,GY,Apr 28)*
Baku Bay 107 *(24f,Hay,G,Mar 26)*
Balbir Du Mathan 105 *(19f,Leo,HY,Dec 28)*
Balding Banker 94 *(24f,Per,G,Aug 22)*
Balgarry 103 *(18f,Tau,GS,Dec 10)*
Balinroab 105 *(22½f,Str,G,Jun 16)*
Ball Hopper 103 *(19f,Exe,S,Nov 11)*
Ballinvarrig 106 *(21f,Asc,S,Nov 20)*
Bally Beaufort 109 *(20f,Ain,GS,Dec 5)*
Ballyadam Approach 110 *(29f,Fai,YS,Mar 28)*
Ballyadeen 107 *(21½f,Mar,S,Dec 26)*
Ballyalton 112 *(25f,Ain,GS,Apr 8)*
Ballyben 101 *(24f,Per,GS,Sep 23)*
Ballybogey 105 *(20f,Sth,G,Jun 9)*
Ballyboker Breeze 96 *(24f,Per,G,Apr 20)*
Ballyboker Bridge 109 *(30f,Chl,GS,Dec 11)*
Ballybolley 109 *(20½f,Kem,G,Mar 19)*
Ballybough Gorta 106 *(25½f,Fon,G,May 24)*
Ballybough Pat 110 *(21½f,Mar,G,May 17)*
Ballycasey 107 *(25f,Pun,S,May 2)*
Ballycoe 102 *(20f,Plu,G,Apr 22)*
Ballycool 102 *(15½f,Ayr,G,Oct 26)*
Ballyculla 105 *(25f,Pun,S,May 2)*
Ballydague Lady 108 *(20f,Wcn,S,Nov 7)*
Ballyegan 97 *(19f,Exe,S,Nov 11)*
Ballygarvey 111 *(19½f,Chp,G,Oct 11)*
Ballyheigue Bay 100 *(24f,Kem,GS,Dec 27)*
Ballykan 109 *(24f,Kem,GS,Feb 27)*
Ballymoat 91 *(20f,Sth,S,Dec 1)*
Ballynagour 97 *(21f,Chl,G,Mar 17)*
Ballyoliver 108 *(23f,Tau,HY,Feb 2)*
Ballyrath 103 *(20f,Lei,S,Feb 3)*
Ballyvaughn 97 *(21f,Str,S,Mar 5)*
Ballyvoneen 97 *(25½f,Fon,G,Oct 2)*
Ballyvoque 91 *(21f,Crt,GS,Jly 20)*
Balnagon Boy 110 *(20f,Fai,HY,Jan 10)*
Baltimore Rock 110 *(16½f,Don,GS,Dec 29)*
Band Of Blood 113 *(26f,Don,S,Mar 5)*
Bandit Country 97 *(24f,Ban,G,Jly 31)*
Bang On Time 103 *(21f,Nab,S,May 7)*
Bar De Ligne 100 *(19f,Mar,G,May 8)*
Barafundle 104 *(24½f,Crl,HY,Feb 22)*
Barrakilla 108 *(20½f,Kem,S,Jan 25)*
Barton Gift 106 *(31f,Exe,GS,Apr 12)*
Basford Ben 102 *(23½f,Hun,GS,Apr 18)*
Battlecat 102 *(20f,Wor,GF,Sep 8)*
Bawden Rocks 104 *(16f,Lin,HY,Mar 7)*
Bayfirth 99 *(21f,Crt,GS,Aug 29)*
Bayley's Dream 95 *(24f,War,G,Mar 23)*
Be A Dreamer 92 *(21f,Sed,S,May 5)*
Be On Time 96 *(16f,Fak,GS,Oct 28)*
Bear's Affair 111 *(25f,Ain,G,May 15)*
Bearly Legal 108 *(29f,Fai,YS,Mar 28)*
Bears Rails 106 *(19f,Exe,GS,Mar 8)*
Beau Dandy 105 *(26f,Sed,GF,Apr 30)*
Beauboreen 106 *(24f,Ban,HY,Apr 16)*
Beauchamp Viking 96 *(16f,Tau,G,Mar 21)*
Beaujolais Bob 104 *(20f,Plu,S,Mar 14)*
Bebinn 99 *(26f,Plu,HY,Feb 1)*
Bedrock Fred 94 *(23f,Tau,G,Apr 20)*
Beeves 108 *(24f,War,S,Apr 4)*
Beforeall 107 *(24f,Fak,S,Jan 28)*
Beg To Differ 109 *(24f,San,S,Feb 19)*
Bekkensfirth 112 *(20f,Lei,GS,Dec 9)*
Bellenos 101 *(16f,Kem,G,May 4)*
Belmount 108 *(25½f,War,G,Sep 22)*
Benbane Head 92 *(26f,Utt,G,Jun 28)*
Benbens 112 *(25f,Ain,G,Oct 25)*
Benefit Cut 105 *(25f,Ain,G,May 15)*
Benefit In Kind 98 *(20f,Hex,GS,Oct 10)*
Benenden 105 *(24f,Mus,GS,Jan 4)*
Benevolent 103 *(21f,Fak,G,May 31)*
Bennylicious 96 *(16f,Cat,GS,Feb 5)*
Bennys Mist 114 *(21f,Ain,S,Dec 5)*
Bennys Well 109 *(26f,Sed,S,Apr 9)*
Benvolio 112 *(26f,Nby,G,Apr 2)*
Berea Boru 108 *(24f,Ffo,HY,Feb 21)*
Berkeley Barron 95 *(22½f,Nby,S,Dec 29)*
Bernardelli 104 *(24f,Ban,HY,Nov 28)*
Bertenbar 105 *(19f,Fon,S,Apr 1)*
Bertie Boru 102 *(24f,San,S,Feb 19)*
Bertie Milan 106 *(24f,Per,GS,Sep 23)*
Bertie's Desire 106 *(24f,Exe,GF,Oct 20)*
Bertielicious 99 *(16½f,Sed,S,Apr 9)*
Best Boy Barney 108 *(24f,Kem,G,May 4)*
Better B Quick 100 *(15½f,Hex,HY,May 9)*
Betterthanalright 90 *(21½f,Fai,SH,Apr 5)*
Big Casino 112 *(21f,Hay,GS,May 9)*
Big Jim 109 *(17f,Asc,GS,Apr 3)*
Big Society 105 *(23½f,Chp,HY,Nov 18)*
Big Sound 106 *(24f,Utt,G,Jun 11)*
Bilbrook Blaze 100 *(18f,Tau,G,Mar 21)*
Bincombe 107 *(20f,Ain,S,Nov 7)*
Bishops Road 108 *(20f,San,HY,Jan 2)*
Bishopslough 103 *(17f,Fai,Y,Mar 27)*
Bitofapuzzle 117 *(19f,Exe,HY,Dec 17)*
Black Hercules 117 *(20f,Chl,G,Mar 17)*
Black Narcissus 108 *(20f,Tow,HY,Jan 7)*
Black Thunder 106 *(27½f,Chl,GS,Nov 14)*
Blackwood Rover 97 *(19½f,Str,G,Jly 30)*
Blades Lad 93 *(16f,Mus,GS,Nov 27)*
Blair Perrone 112 *(19f,Leo,S,Jan 17)*
Blakemount 107 *(23½f,Kel,G,Oct 24)*
Blaklion 117 *(24½f,Chl,G,Mar 16)*
Blameitalonmyroots 99 *(23½f,Nby,S,Dec 16)*
Blandfords Gunner 107 *(15½f,San,S,Feb 19)*
Blazer 91 *(19f,Leo,HY,Dec 28)*
Bless The Wings 112 *(30f,Chl,G,Mar 16)*
Blood Cotil 112 *(21f,Pun,GY,May 1)*
Boardwalk Empire 94 *(22½f,Nby,GS,Mar 4)*
Bob Ford 109 *(25f,Ffo,HY,Dec 14)*
Bob Lewis 101 *(22½f,Str,GS,Sep 14)*
Bob Tucker 106 *(23f,Wor,G,Oct 14)*
Bob's Call 100 *(16½f,Sed,G,Sep 29)*
Bob's Legend 93 *(16f,Sth,G,Aug 27)*
Bobbie's Diamond 90 *(17f,Fai,Y,Mar 29)*
Bobbits Way 97 *(17f,Plu,GS,Feb 29)*
Bobble Boru 103 *(20f,Tow,HY,Jan 7)*
Bobs Worth 107 *(26f,Nby,S,Nov 28)*
Bodega 112 *(17f,Asc,S,Dec 18)*
Boher Call 101 *(17f,Leo,S,Jan 24)*
Bold Bachelor 91 *(21f,Fak,S,Jan 1)*
Bold Conquest 103 *(23f,Wor,GS,Oct 21)*
Bold Henry 112 *(15½f,San,HY,Jan 2)*
Bollin Line 104 *(16f,Cat,GS,Mar 1)*
Bon Chic 105 *(24f,Fak,G,Mar 18)*
Bonds Conquest 98 *(20f,Plu,G,Apr 22)*
Bonne Fee 100 *(19½f,Str,GS,Sep 5)*
Bonnet's Vino 92 *(23½f,Hun,S,Jan 6)*
Bonzo Bing 98 *(19½f,Wet,G,Oct 14)*
Book Of Excuses 94 *(23f,Wor,GF,Jly 1)*
Boondooma 107 *(16f,Chl,G,Oct 24)*
Border Breaker 110 *(20f,Per,G,Sep 8)*
Boric 104 *(20f,Ncs,S,Nov 28)*
Boru's Brook 111 *(15f,Wet,S,Nov 14)*
Boss Croaker 102 *(25f,Pun,G,May 16)*
Boss In Boots 100 *(16½f,Wor,GS,Sep 2)*
Boston Bob 116 *(25f,Fai,HY,Feb 20)*
Bouggietopieces 104 *(24f,Per,GS,Sep 23)*
Bouvreuil 110 *(20½f,Chl,GS,Mar 15)*
Brass Tax 98 *(24f,Kem,G,May 4)*
Brave Spartacus 109 *(19f,Mar,G,May 8)*
Bravo Riquet 90 *(21f,Fon,GS,Feb 28)*
Breaking The Bank 104 *(20f,Hun,GS,Aug 31)*
Bredon Hill Lad 101 *(20f,Utt,S,Nov 22)*
Breezy Kin 102 *(22½f,Str,GS,Sep 14)*
Bridgets Pet 111 *(21½f,Fai,HY,Jan 30)*
Bright Light 94 *(21f,Str,G,Jun 16)*
Bright New Dawn 100 *(16f,Ain,GS,Apr 7)*
Bristol De Mai 118 *(20f,San,GS,Feb 6)*
Broadway Buffalo 99 *(28½f,Hay,HY,Feb 20)*
Brody Bleu 109 *(19f,Exe,G,May 5)*
Brokethegate 100 *(23½f,Kel,GS,May 6)*
Broome Lane 102 *(26f,Chp,G,Apr 22)*
Brother Scott 104 *(20f,Hex,GS,Oct 10)*
Broughton 109 *(16½f,Wor,GS,Aug 23)*
Broughtons Bandit 90 *(25f,Chl,G,Oct 23)*
Brownville 104 *(20f,Lud,S,Mar 3)*
Buachaill Alainn 112 *(23½f,Chp,G,Oct 10)*
Buck Mulligan 106 *(19½f,Str,G,May 17)*
Buckhorn Timothy 110 *(20f,Hun,HY,Jan 15)*
Buckhorn Tom 96 *(26f,Plu,S,Dec 14)*
Bucking The Trend 105 *(24f,Mar,S,Mar 13)*
Bullet Street 104 *(17f,Asc,G,Oct 31)*
Bunclody 94 *(20f,Per,G,Jly 12)*
Burgess Dream 92 *(26f,Plu,HY,Jan 18)*
Burn And Turn 102 *(21f,Pun,GY,May 1)*
Burren River 102 *(21½f,Fai,HY,Jan 30)*
Bus Named Desire 95 *(23f,Lei,GF,Nov 16)*
Butlergrove King 106 *(23f,Tau,GS,Dec 10)*
Buywise 113 *(20½f,Chl,GS,Nov 14)*
By The Boardwalk 110 *(24½f,Tow,G,May 11)*

Cabaret Girl 90 *(21½f,Mar,G,May 8)*
Cadoudoff 107 *(20f,Hun,S,Jan 29)*
Calipto 107 *(19f,Fon,GS,Oct 21)*
Call Me Mulligan 104 *(24f,Sth,GS,Jun 15)*
Call Me Vic 106 *(24f,Lud,G,May 10)*
Call The Detective 102 *(25½f,Fon,HY,Dec 26)*
Canaly 104 *(21½f,Fai,HY,Jan 30)*
Candide 103 *(26f,Chl,G,Apr 14)*
Cantlow 104 *(29f,Fai,YS,Mar 28)*
Caolaneoin 106 *(17f,Fai,Y,Mar 27)*
Capard King 109 *(24f,Sth,S,Nov 17)*
Capilla 114 *(16f,Lin,HY,Dec 1)*
Capisci 92 *(16½f,Hun,GS,Aug 31)*
Cappielow Park 103 *(16f,Utt,HY,Dec 31)*
Captain Conan 99 *(21f,Chl,G,Mar 17)*
Captain Flash 99 *(23½f,Chp,G,Mar 24)*
Captain Hox 111 *(16f,Hay,HY,Dec 19)*
Captain Sharpe 103 *(16½f,Sed,S,Feb 9)*
Captain Von Trappe 98 *(20f,Fai,SH,Nov 29)*
Cara Court 105 *(26f,Sed,S,May 5)*
Cara's Oscar 108 *(25f,Fai,Y,Mar 29)*
Caracci Apache 98 *(25f,Ain,S,Nov 7)*
Caraline 105 *(17f,Kel,HY,Dec 29)*
Cardinal Rose 105 *(24f,Sth,G,Jun 15)*
Carhue Princess 90 *(21f,Fak,GS,Nov 17)*
Carlingford Lough 116 *(26½f,Chl,G,Mar 18)*
Carn Rock 100 *(23f,Wor,G,Oct 14)*
Carnaross 100 *(17f,Kel,S,Nov 7)*
Carobello 95 *(20f,Lud,G,Oct 22)*
Carole's Destrier 106 *(29f,San,G,Apr 23)*
Carrigdhoun 111 *(23½f,Kel,S,Mar 13)*
Carrigmorna King 111 *(21f,Str,G,Oct 17)*
Carters Rest 100 *(16½f,Sed,G,May 12)*
Cash And Go 104 *(15½f,San,HY,Jan 2)*
Casino Markets 102 *(20f,Wcn,G,Apr 4)*
Caspian Piper 103 *(22½f,Utt,G,May 16)*
Castarnie 90 *(23½f,Chp,HY,Nov 18)*
Castle Cheetah 103 *(24f,Sth,G,Oct 22)*
Castlelawn 98 *(15½f,Ayr,G,Oct 26)*
Castley Lane 96 *(24f,Mar,GS,Apr 21)*
Casual Cavalier 98 *(16f,Cat,GS,Feb 5)*
Caulfields Venture 109 *(24f,Exe,GF,Oct 20)*
Cause Of Causes 102 *(26f,Chl,G,Mar 17)*
Cayman Islands 106 *(20f,Hun,G,Oct 13)*
Ceasar Milan 93 *(18f,Tau,GS,Dec 10)*
Celestino 103 *(16f,War,GS,May 4)*
Celtic Fella 93 *(23f,Wor,GF,Jun 11)*
Celtic Intrigue 104 *(24f,Ffo,G,Jun 4)*
Centasia 106 *(24f,Sth,G,May 20)*
Central Flame 107 *(20f,Ncs,S,Feb 3)*
Cernunnos 109 *(20½f,Kem,G,Mar 19)*
Champagne Agent 97 *(19f,Sed,GF,Aug 27)*
Champagne Fever 99 *(16f,Pun,GY,Apr 28)*
Champagne West 113 *(21f,Chl,S,Dec 12)*
Champion Court 112 *(20f,Utt,S,Jly 26)*
Chanceofa Lifetime 112 *(26f,Sed,S,Apr 9)*
Change The Rules 105 *(21½f,Fai,SH,Apr 5)*
Chankillo 107 *(17f,Mar,S,Dec 26)*
Charming Lad 101 *(26f,Plu,G,May 10)*
Chase The Spud 108 *(23½f,Lin,HY,Nov 24)*
Chase The Wind 96 *(17½f,Exe,GF,Oct 20)*
Chavoy 91 *(27f,Ayr,S,Feb 29)*
Cheat The Cheater 101 *(27½f,Mar,S,Dec 26)*
Cherryantor 96 *(25f,Pun,G,May 16)*
Chestnut Ben 109 *(16f,Mus,S,Feb 7)*
Chicago Outfit 108 *(24f,Hex,G,Jun 21)*
Chicoria 106 *(21½f,Mar,S,Nov 19)*
Chill 96 *(16f,Utt,G,Jly 24)*
Chill Factor 107 *(26f,Nab,GF,Apr 30)*
Chinatown Boy 99 *(25f,Wcn,GF,May 12)*
Chris Pea Green 100 *(15½f,San,GS,Feb 6)*
Churchfield Champ 101 *(17f,Leo,S,Jan 24)*
Ciceron 96 *(21f,Ffo,G,Oct 17)*
Cinevator 91 *(21f,Nab,G,Jun 23)*
Civil Unrest 90 *(15f,Wet,G,May 21)*
Clan Chief 102 *(15½f,Ayr,HY,Feb 16)*
Clan William 109 *(15f,Wet,S,Dec 5)*
Clar Na Mionn 107 *(21f,Leo,HY,Dec 29)*
Claragh Native 106 *(15f,Wet,G,May 21)*
Clarcam 108 *(20f,Pun,HY,Dec 6)*
Claret Cloak 111 *(21½f,Mar,G,Sep 26)*

Classic Jewel 91 (21½f,Fai,HY,Jan 30)
Classic Palace 91 (20f,Crl,HY,Nov 29)
Classinaglass 96 (19f,Sed,GF,Apr 30)
Clondaw Dude 91 (21½f,Fai,SH,Apr 5)
Cloonacool 109 (17f,Plu,S,Dec 14)
Cloud Creeper 111 (21f,Nab,GS,Oct 9)
Cloudy Beach 102 (17½f,Fon,HY,Feb 18)
Cloudy Bob 106 (24f,Mar,G,Oct 17)
Cloudy Copper 109 (24f,Ffo,S,Apr 10)
Cloudy Joker 109 (16f,Cat,S,Jan 14)
Cloudy Too 114 (24f,Hay,HY,Jan 23)
Clubs Are Trumps 106 (23f,Wor,GS,Sep 2)
Clues And Arrows 98 (21f,Crt,GS,Jly 20)
Cobajayisland 102 (24f,Mus,G,Nov 5)
Cocktails At Dawn 115 (19½f,Chp,G,Oct 10)
Cody Wyoming 108 (16f,Kem,G,Oct 18)
Cogry 112 (27½f,Chl,GS,Nov 14)
Cold March 112 (17f,Asc,G,Oct 31)
Colin's Brother 103 (17f,Str,S,Oct 29)
Colms Dream 110 (21f,Leo,S,Feb 28)
Combustible Kate 101 (24f,Mar,G,Jun 19)
Come On Laurie 99 (20f,Plu,G,Oct 19)
Comeonginger 94 (20f,San,S,Mar 12)
Commitment 111 (20f,Wor,GF,Jun 24)
Competitive Edge 107 (21½f,Fai,HY,Jan 30)
Conas Taoi 110 (28f,Chl,GS,Apr 13)
Coneygree 119 (24f,San,GS,Nov 8)
Conquisto 106 (22½f,Str,GS,Sep 5)
Cool Bob 97 (20f,Lud,G,Oct 22)
Cool Star 105 (21f,Crt,G,Jun 26)
Coolking 95 (22½f,Str,GS,Oct 29)
Coolnagorna Giggs 106 (25f,Fai,Y,Mar 29)
Coologue 112 (24f,Don,G,Jan 30)
Cootamundra 96 (25f,Pun,S,May 2)
Coozan George 105 (17f,Mar,S,Mar 28)
Copper Birch 101 (31f,Exe,GS,Apr 12)
Copperfacejack 97 (20f,Wor,G,Oct 8)
Cork Citizen 108 (23f,Tau,HY,Feb 2)
Corporate Box 99 (21f,Leo,HY,Dec 29)
Cosway Spirit 106 (24½f,Tow,G,May 11)
Count Salazar 93 (24f,Per,G,Aug 22)
Court By Surprise 103 (23½f,Chp,G,Oct 11)
Court Dismissed 106 (20f,Mus,G,Nov 5)
Court Frontier 104 (21f,Leo,HY,Dec 29)
Court Of Law 95 (20f,War,G,Sep 22)
Courtown Oscar 110 (24½f,Crl,HY,Feb 22)
Cowards Close 107 (23½f,Chp,G,Oct 10)
Crack Of Thunder 99 (24f,Sth,G,Oct 22)
Crafty Roberto 102 (20f,Hun,GS,Nov 21)
Creepy 98 (20f,War,G,Sep 22)
Creevytennant 96 (24f,Asc,GS,Apr 3)
Cresswell Breeze 110 (21f,Fon,S,Nov 6)
Croco Bay 111 (17f,Kel,GF,Oct 4)
Croco Mister 102 (20f,Wor,G,Jun 21)
Crookstown 101 (19f,Mar,G,May 8)
Cross To Boston 90 (24f,Sth,GS,Nov 9)
Crowded Room 105 (21½f,Fai,HY,Jan 30)
Crown And Glory 94 (19½f,Wet,S,Apr 1)
Crown Theatre 110 (17f,Asc,GS,Nov 21)
Cruchain 109 (17f,Crt,GS,Jly 20)
Cue Card 124 (24f,Hay,S,Nov 21)
Cultram Abbey 108 (20f,Crl,G,Nov 1)
Cut The Corner 106 (20f,Sth,G,Sep 29)
Cyclop 107 (24f,War,S,Dec 10)
Cyrien Star 106 (25f,Cat,GS,Dec 2)
Cyrus Darius 109 (20f,Per,GS,Sep 24)

Dabinett Moon 103 (24f,Ban,G,Oct 1)
Daliance 94 (21f,Nab,S,Apr 5)
Danandy 108 (22½f,Str,G,Jly 19)
Dance Floor King 92 (16½f,Nab,GS,Mar 26)
Dancing Dude 98 (24f,Utt,G,May 2)
Dancing Ecco 98 (16f,Sth,G,Jun 2)
Dancing Shadow 109 (20f,San,GS,Dec 4)
Dandridge 111 (16f,Chl,G,Mar 18)
Daneking 104 (16f,Pun,G,May 16)
Danimix 110 (25½f,Crt,G,Aug 31)
Dare Me 112 (21f,Asc,S,Jan 23)
Dare To Endeavour 103 (26f,Ain,S,Dec 5)
Dark Spirit 105 (19f,Exe,HY,Dec 17)
Darkestbeforedawn 95 (19½f,Chp,HY,Feb 5)
Dartford Warbler 107 (21½f,Mar,S,Nov 19)
Daveron 108 (20f,Lud,S,Mar 3)
Dawnieriver 96 (23½f,Hun,S,Dec 26)
Dawson City 107 (24f,San,S,Mar 12)
Daymar Bay 100 (19f,Exe,G,May 5)
Days Ahead 104 (16½f,Nab,G,Sep 28)
Days Hotel 114 (17f,Fai,Y,Mar 29)
Dazzling Susie 92 (21f,Pun,GY,May 1)
De Bene Esse 111 (19f,Exe,HY,Feb 14)
De Blacksmith 104 (16f,Lin,HY,Mar 7)
De Boitron 104 (20f,Ain,S,Nov 7)
De Faoithesdream 112 (15½f,Ayr,GS,Apr 16)
De Kerry Man 106 (16f,Lin,HY,Mar 7)
De Vous A Moi 108 (20f,Ncs,HY,Mar 8)
Dead Or Alive 91 (24f,San,S,Mar 11)
Deadly Sting 103 (23f,Wor,G,May 22)
Deciding Moment 90 (25½f,Lud,S,Dec 2)
Deep Trouble 106 (16f,Lei,S,Jan 26)
Definite Ruby 109 (21f,Crt,G,Jun 28)
Definitly Red 115 (24f,War,HY,Jan 16)
Delgany Demon 105 (24f,Utt,S,Mar 19)
Dell' Arca 111 (20½f,Chl,G,Nov 13)
Denali Highway 103 (20f,Hun,GS,Nov 21)
Derrintogher Bliss 107 (23½f,Chp,G,Sep 30)
Derryfadda 100 (24f,Sth,G,Oct 22)
Desert Cry 94 (16f,Chl,S,Dec 12)
Desert Joe 100 (24f,San,S,Mar 12)
Devon River 90 (16f,Cat,GS,Feb 5)
Dig Deeper 103 (15f,Wet,S,Nov 14)
Dino Mite 96 (19f,Mar,G,Jly 5)
Discay 106 (17f,Mar,S,Apr 10)
Discoverie 103 (16f,Cat,S,Mar 9)
Distime 111 (21f,Ain,S,Apr 8)
Distracted 104 (27f,Wcn,HY,Nov 19)
Djakadam 121 (26½f,Chl,G,Mar 18)
Doctor Harper 109 (16f,Lei,S,Jan 26)
Doctor Phoenix 109 (16f,Lin,S,Nov 10)
Dodging Bullets 117 (15½f,San,G,Apr 23)
Doing Fine 111 (23½f,Chp,G,Oct 10)
Doitforthevillage 102 (19f,Exe,HY,Mar 30)
Doktor Glaz 101 (24f,Don,G,Nov 27)
Dolatulo 104 (24f,Don,G,Jan 30)
Dolores Delightful 98 (23f,Wor,G,Oct 14)
Domesday Book 104 (17f,Leo,S,Jan 24)
Domtaline 107 (19½f,Str,G,Aug 20)
Don Cossack 123 (26½f,Chl,G,Mar 18)
Don Poli 118 (26½f,Chl,G,Mar 18)
Donapollo 96 (23½f,Kel,GF,Oct 4)
Dont Do Mondays 109 (21f,Fon,HY,Apr 15)
Dormello Mo 111 (16½f,Nab,G,Sep 18)
Double Chocolate 103 (23f,Lei,GF,Nov 16)
Double Dan 92 (19f,Fon,S,Nov 25)
Double Handful 105 (24f,Kem,G,May 13)
Double Ross 112 (20½f,Chl,GS,Nov 14)
Double Shuffle 116 (20f,Chl,G,Oct 24)
Double Whammy 106 (21½f,Wet,S,Apr 1)
Doubledisdoubledat 102 (21½f,Wet,GS,Mar 22)
Dougalstar 99 (20f,Sth,G,May 12)
Douvan 126 (16f,Ain,GS,Apr 9)
Dover The Moon 94 (16½f,Sed,G,Sep 29)
Down Time 102 (24f,Per,GS,Sep 23)
Down Under 103 (21f,Leo,HY,Dec 29)
Dr Anubis 100 (16½f,Wor,GF,Jun 11)
Dr Beaujolais 99 (24f,Mar,GS,Apr 21)
Dr Dreamy 98 (23f,Wor,G,Aug 19)
Dr Duckett 96 (21½f,Fai,SH,Apr 5)
Dr Moloney 101 (16f,Crl,HY,Feb 10)
Dragon's Den 103 (17½f,Exe,GF,Oct 20)
Draycott Place 101 (17f,Fai,HY,Jan 10)
Dream Bolt 100 (16½f,Nab,G,Sep 18)
Dreams Of Milan 100 (24f,Exe,HY,Nov 22)
Dreamsoftheatre 112 (24f,Ban,GS,Aug 21)
Dresden 113 (17f,Asc,GS,Nov 21)
Dressedtothenines 92 (20f,Fai,YS,Mar 28)
Drishogue Boy 93 (20f,Pun,HY,Jan 9)
Dromnea 109 (21f,Pun,GY,May 1)
Drop Out Joe 113 (23½f,Chp,G,Oct 10)
Drumacoo 113 (23½f,Hun,S,Jan 6)
Drumlister 102 (21½f,Wet,G,May 28)
Drumshambo 102 (24f,War,S,Apr 4)
Dubai Prince 107 (16½f,Nab,G,Sep 18)
Duhallowcountry 103 (16½f,Sed,S,Nov 24)
Duke Of Navan 104 (20f,Ain,G,Oct 25)
Dundee Blue 101 (16½f,Sed,S,May 5)
Dunraven Storm 111 (17f,Asc,GS,Nov 21)
Duroob 101 (26f,Sed,GF,Sep 3)
Dursey Sound 109 (25½f,War,G,Sep 22)
Dusky Lark 109 (20f,San,GS,Dec 4)
Dynamic Drive 97 (16f,Crl,G,May 7)
Dynamo 97 (16½f,Wor,G,Jly 15)
Dynaste 117 (24f,Hay,S,Nov 21)
Dysios 106 (17f,Leo,S,Feb 28)
Dystonia's Revenge 105 (20f,Crl,G,Oct 22)

Easily Pleased 108 (19f,Exe,G,May 5)
Easter Day 108 (23f,Tau,HY,Jan 13)
Eastlake 117 (21f,Ain,S,Apr 8)
Eaton Rock 102 (20f,Lin,S,Nov 10)
Ebony Empress 106 (21f,Chl,G,Apr 14)
Edeiff's Lad 101 (16f,Tau,GS,Mar 14)
Edgardo Sol 106 (21f,Str,G,Oct 17)
Edlomond 104 (16½f,Nab,S,Apr 18)
Edmund 104 (20f,Ncs,HY,Mar 8)
Eiri Na Casca 101 (24f,Mus,GS,Jan 4)
El Namoose 110 (20f,Hun,GS,Nov 1)
Elenika 108 (19½f,Chp,HY,Dec 5)
Elmore Back 104 (19f,Don,G,Nov 28)
Elsie 94 (21f,Pun,GY,May 1)
Emcon 91 (20f,Fai,YS,Mar 28)
Emerald Rose 106 (21f,Chl,G,Apr 14)
Emily Gray 113 (20f,Crl,HY,Nov 29)
Emma Soda 104 (24½f,Tow,S,Feb 17)
Empire Of Dirt 103 (21f,Chl,G,Mar 17)
Empresario 105 (20f,Mus,G,Nov 6)
Enchanted Garden 101 (24½f,Crl,G,Oct 15)
Endeavor 94 (20f,Mus,S,Dec 7)
Enjoy Responsibly 92 (16f,Pun,Y,Apr 30)
Ennisnag 93 (26f,Plu,GS,Feb 29)
Entry To Evrywhere 101 (16f,Fak,S,Feb 8)
Epic Warrior 105 (24f,War,G,Mar 23)
Ericht 104 (20½f,Kem,S,Jan 25)
Etania 104 (21f,Nab,G,Jun 23)
Ever So Much 103 (19f,Sed,GS,Nov 10)
Everylasting 103 (21½f,Wet,G,May 28)
Exitas 99 (17f,Plu,S,Nov 30)
Exmoor Challenge 94 (24f,Don,G,Nov 28)
Exmoor Mist 102 (16f,Chp,S,Nov 4)
Experimentalist 92 (19½f,Ffo,GF,Jun 18)
Explained 103 (16f,Lud,S,Feb 3)
Express Du Berlais 106 (25f,Ain,G,May 15)

Factor Fifty 97 (21½f,Mar,G,Jun 5)
Fago 100 (19½f,Wet,S,Oct 30)
Fair Dilemma 105 (16½f,Wor,GF,Jun 24)
Fairy Rath 115 (21f,Ain,S,Apr 8)
Fairyinthewind 110 (16½f,Wor,GS,Aug 23)
Faith Jicaro 101 (20f,Wor,G,Jun 21)
Falcarragh 98 (21f,Crt,G,Aug 31)
Fantasy King 108 (21f,Crt,G,Aug 31)
Farbreaga 97 (24f,War,S,Feb 26)
Father Edward 104 (21½f,Mar,S,Nov 5)
Faustina Pius 104 (20½f,Ban,G,Oct 1)
Favoured Nation 100 (27½f,Str,G,May 30)
Fayette County 104 (16f,Lud,G,Mar 24)
Fear Glic 95 (20½f,Ban,S,Mar 31)
Feast Of Fire 102 (26f,Sed,GS,Apr 19)
Federici 105 (21f,Leo,S,Feb 28)
Felix Yonger 115 (16f,Pun,GY,Apr 28)
Fergal Mael Duin 105 (21f,Fon,S,Oct 21)
Fergiethelegend 104 (25f,Fai,Y,Mar 29)
Festive Affair 108 (16f,Lud,G,Apr 19)
Fever Pitch 93 (21f,Leo,S,Jan 17)
Fiddlers Reel 106 (23f,Hay,G,Mar 23)
Figaro 101 (20f,Sth,G,May 12)
Fight Commander 106 (23½f,Hun,S,Feb 11)
Filbert 107 (19½f,Chp,G,Oct 11)
Fill The Power 105 (26f,Crl,G,May 7)
Final Assault 110 (23½f,Ncs,S,Nov 28)
Final Gift 98 (20f,Pun,HY,Jan 9)
Financial Climate 104 (28f,Chl,GS,Apr 13)
Finch Flyer 91 (20f,Sth,G,May 12)
Finding Your Feet 100 (23f,Wor,GF,Jun 11)
Fine Article 95 (17f,Leo,S,Feb 28)
Fine Parchment 105 (23f,Hay,G,Mar 23)
Fine Rightly 99 (21f,Leo,S,Jan 17)
Finea 105 (17f,Leo,S,Jan 24)
Fingal Bay 115 (20½f,Kem,G,Nov 2)
Finish The Story 108 (27f,Fon,S,Nov 15)
Firebird Flyer 112 (29½f,Chp,HY,Jan 9)
Firm Order 100 (24f,San,GS,Dec 4)
First Lieutenant 115 (24f,Leo,HY,Dec 28)
Firth Of The Clyde 111 (24½f,Crl,GS,Mar 20)
Five In A Row 105 (20f,Mus,S,Feb 7)
Five O'clock Tea 96 (16f,Utt,GF,Jly 7)
Five Star Wilsham 94 (24f,Per,GS,Sep 23)
Flaming Thistle 102 (24f,Hex,HY,May 9)
Flash Tommie 103 (19½f,Str,GF,May 17)
Fleet Dawn 90 (20f,Utt,G,Jun 11)
Flemenstar 116 (17f,Leo,HY,Dec 27)
Flemenstorm 104 (20f,Pun,HY,Jan 9)
Fletchers Flyer 115 (24f,Exe,HY,Nov 22)
Florida Calling 95 (24f,Per,G,Apr 20)
Fly Home Harry 93 (19f,Sed,S,Oct 29)
Flying Eagle 105 (23½f,Chp,G,Sep 30)
Foildubh 109 (16f,Pun,G,May 16)
Followmeuptocarlow 107 (21f,Pun,GY,May 1)
Folsom Blue 110 (29f,Fai,YS,Mar 28)
Fond Memory 107 (24f,Kem,G,Oct 18)
Foot The Bill 102 (24f,Sth,S,Mar 29)
For 'N' Against 98 (25½f,War,GS,Nov 4)
For Two 103 (20f,Crl,G,Nov 1)
Forestside 100 (15½f,Hex,G,Jun 13)
Forever My Friend 110 (21f,Crt,G,Aug 31)
Forget And Forgive 91 (22½f,Str,G,Jly 12)
Forgivienne 99 (19½f,Chp,HY,Feb 5)
Forgotten Gold 111 (26f,Chl,G,Apr 14)
Formidableopponent 98 (16f,Pun,G,May 16)
Fort Gabriel 103 (23f,Tau,G,Apr 20)
Fort George 99 (23f,Tau,G,Apr 20)
Forty Foot Tom 106 (17f,Leo,S,Jan 24)
Forward Flight 105 (15½f,Hex,HY,Nov 13)
Fosters Cross 99 (16f,Pun,G,May 16)
Foundation Man 103 (19½f,Wet,G,Oct 14)
Foundry Square 101 (24f,Asc,GS,Apr 3)
Fountains Flypast 98 (21f,Fon,S,Apr 1)
Fourovakind 104 (23½f,Lin,HY,Nov 24)
Fourth Act 105 (21f,Nab,S,Apr 18)
Fox Appeal 110 (20f,Nby,G,Apr 2)
Fox Norton 117 (16f,Chl,GS,Mar 15)
Foxbridge 105 (24f,Kem,GS,Dec 27)
Foxes Bridge 104 (23f,Wor,GS,Sep 2)
Foxrock 115 (24f,Leo,HY,Dec 28)
Foxtail Hill 93 (16½f,Nab,G,Jly 19)
Fr Humphrey 107 (25f,Pun,G,May 16)
Frampton 107 (24f,Kem,G,Nov 2)
Frankie's Promise 95 (20f,Ncs,S,Nov 28)
Freckle Face 103 (19f,Mar,G,May 8)
Free Expression 108 (20f,Fai,SH,Nov 29)
Free Of Charge 99 (24f,Don,G,Nov 27)
Free World 102 (15f,Wet,S,Apr 17)
French Opera 111 (23f,Lei,G,Nov 29)
Friendly Royal 108 (20f,Utt,HY,Dec 8)
Friendly Society 95 (21f,Fon,G,May 1)
Frizzo 103 (21f,Fon,S,Oct 21)
Fruity O'Rooney 105 (25f,Wcn,G,May 7)
Full Jack 107 (20f,Crl,G,Mar 26)
Full Shift 110 (20½f,Kem,GS,Dec 26)
Furrows 106 (16f,Sth,GS,Jun 15)
Futuramic 107 (24½f,Leo,HY,Dec 27)
Fuzzy Logic 103 (21f,Nab,G,Jun 23)
Gallant Oscar 112 (25f,Pun,S,May 2)
Gallery Exhibition 109 (20½f,Kem,GS,Nov 23)
Gallic Warrior 103 (18f,Tau,HY,Feb 2)
Galway Jack 109 (19f,Mar,G,May 8)
Gamain 107 (21f,Fak,S,Feb 19)
Gambol 100 (19f,Don,GS,Feb 11)
Garde La Victoire 113 (16f,Utt,S,Oct 30)
Gardefort 111 (15f,Wet,HY,Jan 16)
Garnock 101 (20f,Wor,G,Jly 15)
Garrahalish 108 (21f,Asc,S,Nov 20)
Gee Hi 92 (24f,Sth,G,Aug 27)
Generous Chief 101 (26f,Sed,GF,Apr 30)
Generous Ransom 104 (24f,Don,S,Dec 12)
Gentleman Jon 107 (20f,Wcn,GF,Oct 16)
George Fernbeck 91 (24f,Hex,G,Sep 18)
George Nympton 92 (17f,Plu,GS,Feb 29)
Georges Conn 94 (24f,Fai,HY,Dec 19)
Georgian King 100 (24½f,War,GS,May 20)
Georgie Lad 100 (23f,Tau,G,Apr 20)
Germany Calling 115 (16f,Utt,G,May 2)
Get Involved 106 (25f,Chl,G,Apr 14)
Ghost Of A Smile 106 (20f,Crl,GS,Apr 3)
Giant O Murchu 97 (16f,Utt,G,Jly 24)
Gibbstown 94 (30f,Ban,HY,Mar 2)
Gilgamboa 114 (21f,Chl,G,Mar 17)
Gin Cobbler 105 (15f,Wet,G,May 21)
Gino Trail 102 (16f,Lud,HY,Jan 12)
Gitane Du Berlais 112 (20f,Crl,HY,Nov 29)
Gleann Na Ndochais 106 (20f,Ain,G,May 15)
Glen Countess 109 (19f,Hay,GS,May 9)
Glen Gyle 92 (21½f,Fai,HY,Jan 30)
Glendermot 98 (24f,War,S,Feb 26)
Glenquest 106 (32½f,Ncs,GS,Feb 27)
Glenwood For Ever 91 (20f,Sth,G,May 20)
Glenwood Prince 91 (24f,Hex,G,May 26)
Global Domination 102 (21f,Fak,S,Jan 1)
Global Dream 104 (24f,Sth,S,Mar 29)
Globalisation 106 (20f,Lud,S,Mar 3)
Go Conquer 108 (20f,Wcn,GS,Apr 17)
Go On Henry 100 (22½f,Utt,G,Jly 24)
Go Teescomponents 100 (16f,Sth,G,Jun 2)
God's Own 114 (16f,Chl,G,Mar 16)
Godsmejudge 107 (24f,Don,GS,Dec 29)
Going Concern 112 (16f,Chl,S,Dec 12)
Going Nowhere Fast 101 (17f,Str,GS,Sep 14)
Golan Dancer 101 (17f,Plu,HY,Feb 1)
Golanova 107 (23f,Lei,GF,Nov 16)
Gold Carrot 107 (16f,Lin,HY,Mar 7)
Gold Futures 109 (21f,Nab,GS,Aug 22)
Gold Ingot 104 (16f,Lei,S,Dec 28)
Gold Man 97 (21f,Fak,GS,Oct 28)
Gold Opera 106 (16½f,Ncs,HY,Dec 19)
Golden Chieftain 109 (27f,Fon,S,Nov 15)
Golden Doyen 115 (17f,Mar,G,Oct 31)
Goldie Horn 95 (20f,Wor,GF,Jly 1)
Gonalston Cloud 107 (24f,Hay,G,Mar 26)
Gone Too Far 107 (20f,War,G,Sep 22)
Goodtoknow 108 (24f,Wet,HY,Feb 12)
Goohar 107 (16f,Lud,HY,Jan 4)
Goonyella 108 (34½f,Ain,S,Apr 9)
Gores Island 102 (16f,Lin,S,Nov 10)
Goring Two 102 (17f,Plu,HY,Jan 18)
Got The Nac 112 (16½f,Ncs,HY,Dec 10)
Goulane Chosen 107 (20f,Fai,HY,Jan 10)
Gowanauthat 104 (19f,Fon,S,Apr 1)
Gran Torino 98 (21f,Utt,G,May 2)
Grand March 96 (16f,Lei,GS,Dec 9)
Grandads Horse 111 (24f,Don,G,Feb 24)
Grate Fella 107 (19f,Sed,GS,Nov 10)
Gray Hession 110 (20f,Sth,GF,Aug 16)
Great Link 105 (19f,Mar,G,Jun 5)
Green Wizard 107 (24f,Hex,G,Jun 21)
Greenlaw 107 (26f,Nby,G,Apr 2)
Grey Gold 110 (16f,Chp,S,Feb 27)
Grey Life 109 (15f,Wet,HY,Nov 25)
Greybougg 103 (21½f,Mar,G,Jun 5)
Grimley Girl 105 (16f,Lud,S,Feb 3)
Grove Silver 106 (29f,War,S,Mar 13)
Guanciale 101 (17½f,Fon,S,Apr 1)
Guaracha 99 (16f,Tau,G,Mar 21)
Guiding George 105 (24f,Ban,G,Jly 31)
Guitar Pete 110 (17f,Fai,HY,Jan 10)
Gullinbursti 102 (24f,Don,G,Jan 30)
Gun Shy 99 (16½f,Tow,G,May 11)
Gurkha Brave 96 (16f,Crl,GS,Apr 3)
Gus Macrae 93 (20f,Wor,G,Sep 25)

Habbie Simpson 106 (19f,Hay,GS,May 9)
Hada Men 105 (21f,Hay,GS,May 9)
Hadrian's Approach 110 (29f,San,G,Apr 23)
Halcyon Days 91 (19f,Sed,GS,Feb 25)
Halling's Wish 103 (16½f,Hun,G,Oct 4)
Halo Moon 106 (21f,Fak,S,Feb 8)
Handsome Horace 104 (21f,Nab,G,Jun 23)
Handy Andy 108 (27f,Wcn,G,Oct 25)
Hansupfordetroit 92 (23f,Lei,G,Nov 29)
Harangue 109 (26f,Utt,G,Jun 28)
Harleys Max 102 (20f,Mus,S,Jan 20)
Harristown 96 (19f,Fon,GS,Oct 21)
Harry The Viking 106 (24½f,Crl,HY,Dec 13)
Harry's Farewell 109 (24f,Kem,S,Jan 9)
Harrys Whim 105 (15½f,Hex,G,Oct 2)

Hash Brown 96 *(21f,Leo,S,Jan 17)*
Hatters River 99 *(24f,Kem,G,Oct 18)*
Haughtons Bridge 91 *(21f,Nab,S,Mar 26)*
Hawaii Five Nil 96 *(17f,Str,GS,Sep 5)*
Hayjack 96 *(25½f,Lud,GS,Nov 12)*
He Rock's 104 *(25f,Fai,Y,Mar 29)*
He's A Bully 105 *(24f,Exe,G,Oct 8)*
Head Spin 103 *(25f,Wcn,S,Apr 4)*
Headly's Bridge 104 *(20f,Nby,G,Apr 2)*
Heathfield 105 *(24½f,Leo,HY,Dec 27)*
Heist 103 *(15½f,Hex,G,Oct 2)*
Helium 107 *(15½f,San,S,Feb 19)*
Hellorboston 100 *(24f,Ban,HY,Nov 28)*
Henllan Harri 106 *(26f,Nab,GS,Aug 12)*
Henri Parry Morgan 118 *(25f,Ain,GS,Apr 8)*
Henryville 112 *(21f,Nab,GS,Oct 9)*
Hepijeu 114 *(19½f,Str,GS,Sep 5)*
Here I Am 104 *(17½f,Fon,S,Apr 1)*
Herecomesthetruth 104 *(21f,Fon,G,Sep 6)*
Heroes Or Ghosts 104 *(24f,War,G,Mar 23)*
Heronshaw 104 *(23½f,Chp,HY,Jan 9)*
Hester Flemen 110 *(25f,Cat,S,Dec 15)*
Heurtevent 99 *(16½f,Tow,GS,May 18)*
Hi Vic 100 *(24f,Ban,HY,Dec 11)*
Hidden Cyclone 106 *(16f,Pun,GY,Apr 28)*
High Aspirations 102 *(21f,Ffo,S,Apr 10)*
High Kite 102 *(24f,Sth,G,Jun 9)*
High Ron 104 *(24f,Utt,G,Jun 11)*
Highland Lodge 105 *(26f,Sed,GS,Oct 12)*
Highlander Ted 93 *(24f,Hex,G,Jun 6)*
Highpower 99 *(22½f,Utt,G,Jun 17)*
Highway Code 105 *(24f,Ban,G,Jly 31)*
Hindon Road 93 *(20f,Lei,GS,Dec 9)*
Hinton Indiana 105 *(24f,Ban,GS,Aug 21)*
Hollow Blue Sky 103 *(24f,Don,GS,Jan 29)*
Hollywoodien 116 *(17f,Asc,S,Dec 18)*
Holywell 113 *(24f,Hay,S,Nov 21)*
Honourable Gent 110 *(16f,Crl,G,May 7)*
Horatio Hornblower 108 *(24f,Ffo,GS,Mar 20)*
Horizontal Speed 93 *(20½f,Kem,G,Nov 2)*
Horsehill 104 *(23f,Tau,G,Nov 12)*
Hotgrove Boy 101 *(16½f,Sed,GF,Apr 30)*
Houblon Des Obeaux 112 *(23½f,Nby,S,Feb 13)*
Houndscourt 97 *(25f,Cat,GS,Feb 5)*
Houston Dynimo 112 *(23f,Lei,G,Nov 29)*
How About It 98 *(24f,Exe,G,Oct 8)*
Howlongisafoot 112 *(19½f,Chp,G,Oct 11)*
Hughesie 104 *(19f,Sed,GS,Nov 10)*
Humbel Ben 102 *(16½f,Nab,S,May 7)*
Humbie 106 *(20f,Mus,GS,Jan 1)*
Hurricane Ivan 93 *(19f,Sed,S,Mar 27)*
Hurricane Vic 90 *(23f,Lei,G,Dec 3)*
Hyperlink 93 *(16½f,Hun,G,May 26)*

I Am Colin 104 *(23f,Lei,HY,Mar 1)*
I'm A Joker 96 *(21½f,Mar,G,Jun 5)*
I'm All You Need 106 *(17f,Leo,S,Feb 28)*
I'm In Charge 105 *(25f,Wcn,G,May 12)*
Ikorodu Road 108 *(26f,Don,GS,Dec 11)*
Imagine The Chat 107 *(22½f,Nby,S,Dec 29)*
Imjoeking 97 *(15½f,Ayr,GS,Oct 31)*
Imperial Plan 90 *(16½f,Wor,GS,May 7)*
In The Rough 110 *(24f,Sth,G,May 20)*
Incentivise 107 *(29f,War,S,Mar 13)*
Inchcolm 100 *(24f,Mar,GS,Apr 21)*
Indalo Return 93 *(24f,Hex,G,May 26)*
Indian Castle 101 *(24f,Hay,S,Nov 21)*
Indian Fairy 101 *(21f,Pun,GY,May 1)*
Indian Stream 112 *(21f,Chl,G,Apr 14)*
Indian Temple 110 *(20f,Mus,GS,Jan 1)*
Indian Voyage 110 *(15f,Wet,HY,Nov 25)*
Ink Master 102 *(17f,Asc,S,Dec 18)*
Inner Drive 97 *(20f,Plu,S,Nov 16)*
Interpleader 111 *(22f,Tow,GF,Apr 30)*
Invicta Lake 96 *(23½f,Nby,S,Dec 16)*
Iona Days 104 *(20f,Sth,S,Dec 13)*
Iora Glas 90 *(22f,Tow,S,Dec 17)*
Irish Cavalier 116 *(26½f,Chl,G,Mar 18)*
Irish Thistle 107 *(15½f,San,S,Mar 11)*
Is Herself About 92 *(16f,Pun,G,May 16)*
Isla Pearl Fisher 100 *(26f,Sed,GS,Oct 12)*
Island Confusion 105 *(16½f,Ncs,HY,Dec 19)*
Isthereadifference 105 *(21f,Nab,G,Jun 23)*
Istimraar 92 *(16½f,Hun,GS,Nov 21)*
It Is What It Is 102 *(24f,Ban,G,May 16)*
It's A Close Call 100 *(23½f,Chp,G,Oct 11)*
It's A Gimme 98 *(17f,Str,G,May 30)*
It's Oscar 96 *(24f,Mar,GS,Apr 21)*
Itoldyou 95 *(25½f,War,S,Jan 28)*
Itsnoteasyted 95 *(24f,Mus,S,Jan 20)*
Itstimeforapint 104 *(32f,Hex,HY,Mar 17)*
Itsuptoyou 107 *(17f,Mar,G,May 17)*
Ittirad 111 *(16f,Kem,GS,Dec 27)*
Ivans Back 101 *(19f,Mar,G,Jun 5)*
Ivy Gate 98 *(20f,San,HY,Jan 2)*

Jac The Legend 109 *(25f,Cat,S,Feb 15)*
Jack Steel 91 *(24f,Wet,HY,Feb 12)*
Jack The Gent 106 *(17½f,Ban,G,Jly 31)*
Jacksonslady 109 *(16f,Pun,Y,Apr 30)*
Jackthejourneyman 107 *(16½f,Hun,GS,Aug 31)*
Jamrham 93 *(16f,Tau,GS,Mar 14)*
Jaunty Inflight 102 *(16f,Utt,HY,Dec 31)*
Javert 107 *(16f,Chp,S,Nov 4)*
Jay Are 105 *(16f,War,GS,May 20)*
Jayo Time 109 *(16f,Lud,GS,Nov 23)*
Jennys Surprise 108 *(23½f,Chp,HY,Jan 9)*
Jet Master 96 *(17f,Kel,GS,Mar 21)*
Jimmy Shan 92 *(24f,Mar,G,Oct 5)*
John Louis 90 *(20f,Crl,HY,Feb 22)*
Johnny Og 106 *(17f,Str,S,Oct 29)*
Johns Luck 106 *(16f,Sth,HY,Mar 7)*
Johns Spirit 111 *(21f,Chl,GS,Apr 13)*
Join The Clan 93 *(20f,Lei,S,Dec 28)*
Jolly Boys Outing 105 *(24½f,Tow,G,May 11)*
Jonnie Skull 104 *(16f,Fak,G,May 31)*
Jonny Eager 111 *(26f,Sed,S,Apr 9)*
Joseph Mercer 93 *(24f,Hex,HY,Mar 17)*
Josies Orders 113 *(30f,Chl,G,Nov 13)*
Josses Hill 115 *(20½f,Kem,S,Feb 12)*
Joyful Motive 98 *(19f,Sed,GF,Aug 27)*
Jumeirah Liberty 98 *(17f,Plu,S,Dec 14)*
Junction Fourteen 121 *(20f,Wcn,S,Nov 7)*
Just A Par 112 *(29f,San,G,Apr 23)*
Just Awake 93 *(20f,Per,S,May 13)*
Just Cameron 119 *(16f,Pun,Y,Apr 30)*
Just Get Cracking 107 *(17f,Fai,Y,Mar 27)*

Kadalkin 101 *(20f,Wor,GF,Jun 6)*
Kai Broon 101 *(20f,Hex,G,May 2)*
Kalane 104 *(21f,Chl,G,Apr 14)*
Kalastar 95 *(24f,Hex,GS,Nov 6)*
Kap Jazz 104 *(23½f,Hun,S,Feb 11)*
Kapricorne 99 *(23½f,Hun,S,Dec 26)*
Karezak 102 *(16f,War,GS,Nov 18)*
Kasbadali 97 *(24f,Exe,G,Oct 8)*
Kassis 104 *(20f,Hun,S,Feb 25)*
Katachenko 112 *(16f,Ain,GS,Apr 7)*
Katenko 94 *(25f,Chl,GS,Mar 15)*
Katgary 95 *(21f,Fak,G,Oct 16)*
Katie Do 90 *(25f,Chl,G,Oct 23)*
Katkeau 93 *(19½f,Wet,S,Feb 6)*
Katnap 94 *(25f,Pun,S,May 2)*
Kayf Moss 107 *(24f,Ffo,HY,Feb 21)*
Kayf Supreme 107 *(19f,Leo,HY,Dec 28)*
Kayfleur 112 *(19f,Exe,HY,Dec 17)*
Kayflin 96 *(20f,Plu,G,Apr 22)*
Kayfton Pete 93 *(16f,Sth,GS,Jun 15)*
Kazlian 92 *(20f,Plu,S,Nov 16)*
Keel Haul 105 *(16f,Chl,G,Nov 13)*
Kerryhead Storm 103 *(16f,Lud,G,Nov 2)*
Key To The West 102 *(19½f,Str,S,Oct 29)*
Kiama Bay 104 *(16½f,Ncs,HY,Dec 10)*
Kie 110 *(22½f,Str,GS,Sep 5)*
Kilbree Chief 108 *(24f,Ayr,GS,Apr 16)*
Kilbree Kid 109 *(24f,Per,G,Jly 1)*
Kilcascan 101 *(24f,Sth,GS,Nov 9)*
Kilcrea 98 *(21f,Leo,HY,Dec 29)*
Kilfinichen Bay 110 *(20f,Utt,HY,Apr 2)*
Kilford 102 *(21f,Leo,HY,Dec 29)*
Kilgefin Star 109 *(23½f,Kel,S,Nov 7)*
Killabraher Cross 94 *(20f,Plu,G,Nov 2)*
Killala Quay 110 *(20f,Utt,G,Oct 4)*
Killer Crow 106 *(29f,Fai,YS,Mar 28)*
Killimordaly 101 *(24f,Ffo,G,Jun 4)*
Killultagh Vic 113 *(16f,Fai,HY,Dec 19)*
Kilmurvy 108 *(24f,Kem,G,Nov 2)*
Kilronan High 108 *(21f,Chl,G,Apr 14)*
Kinari 98 *(23f,Wor,GS,Sep 2)*
King Alfonso 103 *(16½f,Wor,GF,Jun 24)*
King Blue 99 *(20f,Pun,HY,Jan 9)*
King Fontaine 99 *(24f,Exe,G,Oct 8)*
King Massini 103 *(26f,Utt,HY,May 6)*
King Of Glory 106 *(20f,War,HY,Dec 31)*
King Of The Dark 100 *(19f,Sed,S,Apr 9)*
King Of The Wolds 105 *(24f,Per,GS,Sep 23)*
King's Legacy 105 *(24f,Kem,G,Oct 18)*
King's Odyssey 112 *(21f,Chl,HY,Jan 30)*
King's Song 92 *(23f,Lei,G,Dec 3)*
Kingcora 96 *(25½f,Fon,G,May 24)*
Kingfisher Creek 99 *(20f,Plu,S,Nov 16)*
Kings Apollo 108 *(23f,Tau,HY,Dec 30)*
Kings Bandit 91 *(19f,Don,G,Nov 27)*
Kings Cross 97 *(19f,Asc,S,Jan 23)*
Kings Grey 90 *(16f,Ain,G,Jun 12)*
Kings Lad 114 *(20½f,Kem,G,Nov 2)*
Kings Palace 102 *(20½f,Chl,GS,Nov 14)*
Kings River 90 *(19½f,Chp,HY,Feb 5)*
Kingswell Theatre 109 *(21½f,Mar,S,Nov 5)*
Kitchapoly 99 *(21f,Str,G,May 30)*
Kitegen 105 *(16f,Lud,G,Apr 19)*
Knock A Hand 105 *(24½f,Crl,HY,Dec 13)*
Knock House 109 *(24f,Fak,G,Oct 16)*
Knockalongi 101 *(21f,Fon,GS,Feb 28)*
Knockanarrigan 103 *(24½f,Leo,HY,Dec 27)*
Knockanrawley 112 *(27½f,Chl,GS,Nov 14)*
Knockyoursocksoff 105 *(21f,Str,G,Jun 16)*
Kodicil 106 *(20f,Utt,G,Sep 20)*
Krackatoa King 106 *(29f,War,S,Mar 13)*
Kruzhlinin 112 *(24f,Kem,S,Jan 9)*
Kylecrue 106 *(21f,Leo,S,Feb 28)*
Kylemore Lough 109 *(20f,Utt,S,Nov 14)*
Kyles Faith 100 *(24f,Exe,G,Oct 8)*
L'Ami Serge 115 *(20f,Chl,G,Mar 17)*
L'Unique 105 *(20f,Wcn,S,Nov 7)*
La Vaticane 109 *(20f,Wcn,S,Mar 2)*
Lackamon 109 *(29f,Sed,S,Oct 29)*
Ladfromhighworth 104 *(21f,Fon,GS,Jun 3)*
Lady From Geneva 93 *(25½f,Fon,HY,Dec 26)*
Lamb's Cross 101 *(16f,Lin,HY,Dec 1)*
Lamboro Lad 97 *(25½f,War,G,Sep 22)*
Lamool 110 *(25f,Ain,G,May 15)*
Larkhall 103 *(24f,Sth,GS,Jun 15)*
Larteta 99 *(20f,Utt,G,Jly 15)*
Laser Hawk 101 *(16f,Tau,HY,Jan 23)*
Last Shot 93 *(16f,Lud,G,Nov 2)*
Lawless Island 91 *(19f,Sed,S,Mar 15)*
Le Bacardy 110 *(19f,Mar,G,May 8)*
Le Fin Bois 103 *(16½f,Hun,G,Oct 4)*
Le Grand Chene 101 *(25f,Pun,G,May 16)*
Le Mercurey 113 *(21f,Asc,S,Dec 18)*
Le Reve 113 *(24f,San,GS,Feb 6)*
Leanna Ban 104 *(20f,Crl,G,May 7)*
Leg Iron 105 *(31f,Hun,S,Mar 6)*
Legal Exit 95 *(15½f,San,S,Feb 19)*
Legion D'Honneur 104 *(19f,Exe,S,Nov 11)*
Leith Hill Legasi 101 *(24½f,Tow,S,Feb 17)*
Lemon's Gent 105 *(19f,Mar,GS,Apr 21)*
Lemony Bay 106 *(24f,Sth,G,Aug 27)*
Leney Cottage 106 *(21f,Crl,S,Mar 10)*
Leo Luna 108 *(24f,War,S,Feb 26)*
Letemgo 98 *(22½f,Str,GS,Oct 29)*
Lexicon Lad 105 *(20f,Ain,G,May 15)*
Liars Poker 90 *(20f,Sth,G,May 12)*
Liberty One 90 *(25f,Chl,G,Oct 23)*
Lightening Rod 99 *(16f,Lud,S,Dec 2)*
Like Sully 105 *(17f,Plu,S,Mar 27)*
Lily Little Legs 101 *(21f,Sed,S,Mar 27)*
Limpopo Tom 98 *(17f,Str,G,Jly 12)*
Lisbon 102 *(17½f,Ban,G,Jly 31)*
Listen Boy 95 *(24f,Fak,S,Jan 28)*
Little Glenshee 100 *(23½f,Ncs,S,Feb 3)*
Little Jimmy 105 *(16f,Utt,HY,Dec 31)*
Little Jon 107 *(21f,Str,G,Oct 17)*
Little Windmill 101 *(21½f,Mar,S,Nov 19)*
Local Show 116 *(24f,Kem,S,Jan 25)*
Loch Ba 100 *(24f,Asc,GS,Apr 3)*
Lock Towers 93 *(21½f,Mar,G,Sep 26)*
Lockstockandbarrel 110 *(23f,Lei,HY,Mar 1)*
Long House Hall 112 *(17½f,Ban,G,May 16)*
Long John 97 *(20f,Utt,HY,Jan 30)*
Long Lunch 107 *(20f,San,GS,Dec 4)*
Longueville Flier 101 *(26f,Sed,GF,Sep 3)*
Looking Well 107 *(25f,Cat,S,Jan 1)*
Lookslikerainted 98 *(19½f,Str,G,Aug 27)*
Loose Chips 107 *(24f,San,S,Feb 19)*
Lord Ballim 100 *(19f,Exe,HY,Mar 30)*
Lord Ben 102 *(20f,Ain,G,Oct 25)*
Lord Brendy 99 *(25f,Ain,G,Jun 12)*
Lord Fox 97 *(24f,Per,GS,Sep 23)*
Lord Grantham 104 *(22½f,Str,G,Jun 16)*
Lord Landen 100 *(23f,Lei,HY,Mar 1)*
Lord Lir 103 *(16½f,Nab,G,Jun 12)*
Lord Of Drums 101 *(15½f,Ayr,HY,Mar 12)*
Lord Of The Dunes 101 *(20f,Wor,G,Jun 21)*
Lord Scoundrel 111 *(16f,Pun,SH,Nov 15)*
Lord Usher 98 *(19f,Sed,S,Nov 24)*
Los Amigos 104 *(24½f,Leo,HY,Dec 27)*
Lost In Newyork 102 *(20f,Utt,GF,Jly 7)*
Lost Legend 110 *(20½f,Ban,G,Oct 1)*
Lough Kent 115 *(16f,War,GS,May 20)*
Loughalder 106 *(26f,Utt,HY,May 6)*
Louis Phillipe 101 *(22½f,Str,G,Jly 12)*
Love The Leader 97 *(19f,Sed,S,Oct 29)*
Lovely Job 106 *(20f,Lei,GS,Dec 9)*
Lowanbehold 104 *(17f,Kel,GS,Apr 11)*
Lucematic 111 *(23½f,Ncs,S,Nov 28)*
Lucky Jim 105 *(17f,Mar,S,Mar 28)*
Lucky Landing 107 *(20f,Ain,G,May 15)*

Ma Filleule 102 *(20½f,Don,GS,Dec 29)*
Mac Bertie 95 *(23½f,Chp,G,Sep 30)*
Mac's Grey 103 *(17f,Mar,G,Jly 5)*
Macarthur 98 *(17½f,Ban,G,Jly 31)*
Macnicholson 97 *(16f,Pun,G,May 16)*
Mad About The Boy 95 *(18f,Tau,HY,Feb 2)*
Mad Money 102 *(16½f,Nab,G,Jun 12)*
Madame De Guise 107 *(20f,Wor,G,May 22)*
Maggio 110 *(24f,Per,G,Jly 1)*
Magheral Express 93 *(23f,Tau,G,Nov 12)*
Magical Man 96 *(21f,Ffo,GS,Mar 20)*
Mahayogin 93 *(19½f,Str,G,Jly 30)*
Maizy Missile 101 *(16f,Chp,G,Sep 30)*
Major Martin 95 *(20f,Plu,G,Apr 22)*
Major Milborne 90 *(23½f,Hun,GS,Apr 18)*
Major Ridge 99 *(21f,Crl,S,Mar 10)*
Mala Beach 112 *(21f,Asc,GS,Dec 19)*
Malanos 106 *(15½f,San,S,Mar 11)*
Malibu Sun 107 *(15½f,San,GS,Dec 4)*
Mallards In Flight 106 *(21f,Pun,GY,May 1)*
Maller Tree 94 *(23f,Wor,GF,Jly 23)*
Mallowney 106 *(16f,Pun,GY,Apr 28)*
Manger Hanagment 101 *(20f,Per,GF,Sep 7)*
Mansonien L'As 99 *(20f,Crl,HY,Dec 13)*
Many Clouds 121 *(25f,Chl,HY,Jan 30)*
Marchese Marconi 106 *(17f,Leo,S,Feb 28)*
Marcilhac 98 *(20f,War,S,Feb 13)*
Marden Court 102 *(17½f,Exe,HY,Nov 22)*
Marie Des Anges 106 *(20f,Wor,G,May 22)*
Marju's Quest 100 *(16½f,Hun,G,May 26)*
Market Option 102 *(27f,Wcn,HY,Nov 19)*
Marlbrook 112 *(20f,Fai,HY,Jan 10)*
Marshim 91 *(16f,Pun,G,May 16)*
Mart Lane 99 *(19½f,Str,G,May 17)*
Martalin 104 *(30f,Chl,GS,Dec 11)*
Marvellous Moment 93 *(21f,Leo,HY,Dec 29)*
Mason Hindmarsh 106 *(15½f,Hex,G,Jun 21)*
Master Neo 93 *(21½f,Mar,G,Sep 26)*
Master Of The Game 100 *(19½f,Str,G,Jun 30)*
Master Of The Hall 106 *(21½f,Mar,G,May 17)*
Master Rajeem 103 *(23½f,Lin,HY,Nov 24)*
Masters Hill 102 *(24½f,Crl,HY,Nov 9)*
Matrow's Lady 100 *(20f,Wcn,S,Dec 3)*
Maximiser 113 *(20f,Crl,HY,Nov 9)*
Maybe Plenty 102 *(24f,War,S,Apr 4)*
Maz Majecc 99 *(24f,Hex,HY,Apr 18)*
McKinley 108 *(17f,Fai,HY,Jan 10)*
Measureofmydreams 109 *(20f,Pun,HY,Jan 9)*
Melodic Rendezvous 106 *(16f,Pun,Y,Apr 30)*
Menorah 105 *(25f,Ain,S,Dec 5)*
Mercers Court 108 *(23½f,Hun,S,Mar 28)*
Merchant Of Milan 103 *(20f,War,HY,Dec 31)*
Mezendore 107 *(20½f,Ban,S,Mar 31)*
Mia's Anthem 107 *(26f,Sed,GS,Oct 12)*
Michigan Assassin 94 *(20f,Lud,G,Oct 22)*
Midnight Appeal 105 *(24f,Ban,G,Jly 31)*
Midnight Belle 92 *(20f,Crl,GS,Nov 1)*
Midnight Cataria 106 *(24f,Kem,G,Oct 18)*
Midnight Chorister 105 *(16f,Sth,G,Mar 21)*
Midnight Dove 92 *(24f,Ban,G,May 16)*
Midnight Game 101 *(19½f,Str,GS,Sep 5)*
Midnight Jade 99 *(24f,War,S,Apr 4)*
Midnight Lira 106 *(21f,Fon,G,Oct 3)*
Midnight Monty 105 *(19f,Don,S,Mar 4)*
Midnight Prayer 103 *(29f,War,HY,Jan 16)*
Midnight Request 96 *(24f,Exe,G,Oct 8)*
Midnight Whisper 91 *(26f,Nab,G,Sep 28)*
Might Bite 108 *(20½f,Chl,G,Nov 13)*
Milansbar 111 *(24f,Exe,S,Feb 26)*
Milborough 110 *(24½f,Crl,GS,Mar 20)*
Mile House 102 *(21f,Fon,S,Aug 25)*
Milgen Bay 106 *(21f,Fak,GS,Oct 28)*
Millicent Silver 109 *(30f,Ban,HY,Mar 2)*
Milly Malone 102 *(24f,Utt,G,May 2)*
Minella Definitely 106 *(15½f,San,S,Feb 19)*
Minella Forfitness 97 *(20f,Ain,S,Nov 7)*
Minella Foru 111 *(24½f,Leo,HY,Dec 27)*
Minella On Line 102 *(23½f,Nby,S,Dec 16)*
Minella Present 105 *(16½f,Tow,GF,Oct 7)*
Minella Reception 109 *(20f,San,S,Mar 12)*
Minella Rocco 110 *(24f,Asc,S,Feb 20)*
Minella Web 98 *(23f,Tau,G,Apr 20)*
Minellaforleisure 95 *(16½f,Hun,S,Nov 10)*
Minellaforlunch 100 *(20f,Utt,S,Nov 22)*
Minellahalfcentury 100 *(24f,San,S,Mar 11)*
Miss Biscotti 98 *(20½f,Ban,G,May 1)*
Miss Conway 93 *(16f,Cat,GS,Feb 5)*
Miss Dimples 92 *(21f,Fak,G,Mar 18)*
Miss Oscarose 102 *(21f,Fon,GS,Feb 28)*
Miss Speedy 91 *(24f,Fai,SH,Jan 20)*
Miss Tenacious 108 *(16½f,Wor,GS,Aug 23)*
Miss Tilly Oscar 93 *(24f,Lud,G,May 10)*
Mission Complete 103 *(24f,Ban,G,May 1)*
Missyspet 105 *(17f,Fai,HY,Jan 10)*
Mist The Boat 91 *(20½f,Ban,S,Mar 16)*
Mister D 100 *(21f,Crt,G,Jly 18)*
Mister First 106 *(20f,Per,S,May 14)*
Mister Hotelier 109 *(16f,Pun,G,May 16)*
Mister Wall Street 98 *(19½f,Str,G,Jly 12)*
Mo Rouge 95 *(26f,Crl,G,Mar 26)*
Modeligo 105 *(16f,War,S,Apr 4)*
Molko Jack 97 *(21f,Utt,G,May 2)*
Molly Oscar 102 *(26f,Plu,S,Mar 14)*
Mon Parrain 104 *(24f,Asc,GS,Apr 3)*
Mon Successeur 108 *(15f,Wet,S,Oct 31)*
Monbeg River 108 *(15½f,Ayr,GS,Oct 31)*
Monbeg Theatre 96 *(19f,Don,S,Jan 8)*
Monderon 105 *(23f,Lei,G,Dec 3)*
Mondo Cane 103 *(20f,Sth,GS,Apr 15)*
Monetaire 106 *(20½f,Chl,GS,Nov 14)*
Money For Nothing 101 *(16f,Cat,S,Jan 27)*
Money Talks 101 *(21f,Fon,S,Apr 1)*
Monkey Kingdom 97 *(20½f,War,S,May 9)*
Monksland 112 *(20f,Fai,SH,Nov 29)*
Mont Royale 107 *(22½f,Str,GS,Sep 5)*
Montoya's Son 91 *(20f,Sth,GF,Aug 16)*
Monty's Revenge 99 *(22f,Tow,S,Nov 5)*
Montys Meadow 90 *(22f,Pun,HY,Dec 6)*
Moonlight Maggie 102 *(16f,Sth,G,Jun 2)*
Moorlands George 102 *(22½f,Str,G,Jly 30)*
Moorlands Jack 109 *(20f,Utt,S,Jly 26)*
Mor Brook 100 *(20½f,Ban,G,May 1)*
More Buck's 101 *(21f,Sth,GS,Jly 3)*
More Madness 99 *(27f,Ayr,S,Feb 29)*
More Of That 114 *(20½f,Chl,G,Nov 13)*
Morgan's Bay 97 *(15½f,San,GS,Dec 4)*
Morney Wing 107 *(24f,Fak,S,Mar 28)*
Morning Assembly 110 *(21½f,Fai,HY,Jan 30)*
Morning Reggie 110 *(20f,San,S,Mar 12)*
Morning Royalty 107 *(25½f,Crl,G,Jun 26)*
Morning With Ivan 91 *(19f,Sed,S,Oct 29)*
Mortlestown 107 *(21f,Nab,GS,Jly 3)*

Moscow Me 106 *(16f,Lei,S,Dec 28)*
Mossies Well 106 *(15½f,Hex,HY,Nov 13)*
Mosspark 109 *(24f,San,S,Mar 12)*
Mount Colah 96 *(16f,Pun,Y,Apr 30)*
Mount Gunnery 100 *(20f,Chl,G,Mar 17)*
Mountain King 105 *(19½f,Wet,S,Oct 30)*
Mountain Of Mourne 98 *(23½f,Chp,G,Mar 24)*
Mountain Tunes 91 *(22½f,Nby,S,Dec 29)*
Mountainous 113 *(29½f,Chp,HY,Jan 9)*
Moyode Wood 97 *(24f,Hex,G,Sep 18)*
Mozoltov 111 *(16f,Pun,SH,Jan 31)*
Mr Bachster 99 *(16½f,Tow,HY,Jan 7)*
Mr Burbidge 99 *(16f,Chp,S,Nov 4)*
Mr Burgees 100 *(21f,Crt,GS,Jly 20)*
Mr Diablo 108 *(20f,Pun,HY,Jan 9)*
Mr Fiftyone 97 *(21f,Pun,GY,May 1)*
Mr Goodenough 95 *(21½f,Fai,HY,Jan 30)*
Mr Mafia 106 *(20f,Utt,GF,Jly 7)*
Mr Mole 109 *(16f,Chl,GS,Nov 15)*
Mr Moonshine 109 *(24½f,Crl,GS,Mar 20)*
Mr Moss 103 *(24f,Ban,G,Jly 31)*
Mr Muddle 101 *(20f,San,HY,Jan 2)*
Mr Picotee 99 *(16f,Pun,G,May 16)*
Mr Robinson 104 *(21f,Utt,G,May 1)*
Mr Syntax 95 *(23f,Hay,G,Mar 23)*
Mrsrobin 93 *(25f,Wcn,GS,Apr 17)*
Mtada Supreme 100 *(30f,Chl,GS,Dec 11)*
Muckle Roe 104 *(20f,War,HY,Dec 31)*
Mumgos Debut 103 *(15½f,Ayr,HY,Jan 2)*
Murphys Filly 97 *(25f,Pun,G,May 16)*
Murrayana 105 *(16f,Lud,G,Oct 22)*
Musical Wedge 99 *(24f,Ban,G,May 1)*
Muwalla 105 *(17f,Kel,GF,Sep 16)*
Mwaleshi 104 *(25f,Ain,G,Oct 25)*
My Betty 100 *(20f,Mus,G,Nov 5)*
My Brother Sylvest 108 *(17f,Mar,G,May 17)*
My Friend George 106 *(21f,Sed,S,Feb 9)*
My Hometown 97 *(16f,Pun,SH,Nov 15)*
My Legal Lady 105 *(21f,Nab,G,Jun 23)*
My Nosy Rosy 105 *(16½f,Hun,GS,Aug 31)*
Mysteree 109 *(32½f,Ncs,GS,Feb 27)*
Mystifiable 108 *(20f,Lei,S,Dec 28)*

Nail 'M 105 *(31f,Exe,GS,Apr 12)*
Nakadam 105 *(27f,Ayr,S,Feb 29)*
Nalim 101 *(24f,Hex,HY,May 9)*
Narcissist 98 *(20f,Crl,G,May 7)*
Native Brian 98 *(24f,Hex,G,Jun 6)*
Native Que 98 *(26f,Sed,S,Nov 24)*
Native River 119 *(25f,Ain,GS,Apr 8)*
Native Robin 107 *(20f,Wcn,G,Apr 4)*
Nautical Twilight 106 *(16f,Cat,S,Jan 27)*
Nearest The Pin 105 *(16½f,Wor,GS,Aug 23)*
Nearly Nama'd 113 *(17f,Fai,HY,Jan 10)*
Ned Buntline 105 *(16f,Pun,Y,Apr 30)*
Ned Stark 108 *(26f,Nby,G,Apr 2)*
Nefyn Bay 90 *(16f,Cat,S,Mar 9)*
Neptune Equester 108 *(32½f,Kel,HY,Dec 6)*
Net D'Ecosse 95 *(24f,Kem,GS,Dec 26)*
Never Enough Time 101 *(17f,Fai,HY,Jan 10)*
Never Up 96 *(16½f,Ncs,HY,Dec 19)*
Neville Woods 96 *(17f,Kel,GS,May 6)*
Newton Geronimo 98 *(19f,Fon,G,Oct 3)*
Newton Thistle 104 *(24½f,Tow,S,Dec 17)*
Nexius 112 *(19f,Don,GS,Feb 11)*
Next Exit 91 *(20f,Sth,G,May 12)*
Next Sensation 103 *(16f,Chl,G,Mar 18)*
Niceonefrankie 110 *(20f,War,S,Feb 13)*
Nicolas Chauvin 106 *(16½f,Nab,GS,Oct 9)*
Night In Milan 99 *(24f,Don,S,Dec 12)*
Nimbus Gale 93 *(23f,Wor,G,Oct 14)*
Nitrogen 102 *(22½f,Nby,GS,Mar 4)*
No Buts 100 *(24f,Kem,GS,Dec 27)*
No Duffer 109 *(24f,Hay,G,Mar 26)*
No Likey 111 *(19½f,Str,G,Aug 20)*
No More Heroes 113 *(20f,Fai,SH,Nov 29)*
No No Cardinal 101 *(16½f,Nab,G,May 27)*
No No Mac 97 *(23f,Tau,GS,Nov 26)*
No Planning 106 *(24f,Ayr,HY,Mar 12)*
No Principles 97 *(24f,Fak,G,May 31)*
No Through Road 98 *(20f,Hex,GS,Oct 10)*
Noble Friend 107 *(19½f,Str,G,Jun 30)*
Noble Legend 108 *(21f,Fak,GS,Dec 20)*
Noble Witness 98 *(22½f,Utt,G,May 16)*
Noche De Reyes 108 *(16f,Lud,G,Apr 5)*
Northern Executive 98 *(24f,Hex,G,Jun 6)*
Nortonthorpelegend 90 *(21f,Crl,GS,Apr 3)*
Nosey Box 98 *(32f,Hex,HY,Mar 17)*
Not A Bother Boy 107 *(26f,Sed,GS,Jan 31)*
Not For You 101 *(17½f,Ban,HY,Mar 2)*
Notnowsam 106 *(16f,War,GS,May 4)*
Notonebuttwo 102 *(23½f,Ncs,HY,Mar 19)*

O Maonlai 99 *(22½f,Nby,S,Nov 28)*
O'Donoghue's Opera 104 *(17f,Leo,S,Jan 24)*
O'Faolains Boy 112 *(23½f,Nby,S,Dec 16)*
Odds On Dan 101 *(16½f,Sed,G,May 12)*
Off The Ground 102 *(19½f,Wet,S,Oct 30)*
Officer Drivel 107 *(17f,Plu,S,Dec 14)*
Oficial Ben 95 *(16f,Cat,S,Dec 28)*
Oil Burner 94 *(20f,Ncs,S,Feb 3)*
Old Castletown 100 *(25f,Pun,G,May 16)*
Old Storm 92 *(16½f,Hun,GS,Nov 21)*
Oliver's Gold 109 *(15½f,Ayr,GS,Oct 31)*
Oliver's Hill 102 *(24f,Don,GS,Jan 29)*
Olympian Boy 105 *(15½f,San,S,Mar 11)*
On His Own 115 *(25f,Fai,HY,Feb 20)*
On The Case 96 *(16½f,Sed,HY,Dec 26)*
On The Shannon 98 *(21f,Leo,HY,Dec 29)*
On Tour 103 *(20½f,Chl,GS,Mar 15)*
On Trend 105 *(24½f,Tow,G,May 11)*
Onderun 105 *(23½f,Lin,HY,Dec 12)*
One Cool Clarkson 102 *(21f,Crl,S,Mar 10)*
One For Arthur 109 *(23½f,Kel,G,Oct 24)*
One For Hocky 96 *(20f,Utt,G,Jun 11)*
One Term 98 *(16f,Pun,Y,Apr 30)*
Onenightinvienna 116 *(24f,Exe,HY,Nov 22)*
Only Gorgeous 94 *(23f,Tau,G,Nov 12)*
Open Hearted 110 *(24f,Fak,G,Oct 16)*
Opening Batsman 110 *(24f,Kem,GS,Feb 27)*
Orange Nassau 102 *(26f,Crl,G,May 7)*
Orangeaday 92 *(20f,Lei,GS,Dec 9)*
Orbasa 108 *(17f,Asc,GS,Apr 3)*
Orby's Man 94 *(23f,Wor,G,May 22)*
Orfeo Conti 99 *(25½f,Fon,G,Jun 9)*
Orsippus 106 *(16f,Crl,G,May 7)*
Oscar Knight 100 *(25f,Fai,Y,Mar 29)*
Oscar Lateen 91 *(20f,Ncs,HY,Dec 10)*
Oscar Magic 102 *(20f,Utt,S,Nov 14)*
Oscar O'Scar 106 *(23½f,Kel,GS,Mar 21)*
Oscar Rock 113 *(21½f,Mar,G,Sep 26)*
Oscar Sunset 111 *(16f,Chp,HY,Feb 5)*
Oscara Dara 93 *(23f,Wor,G,Jly 28)*
Otago Trail 109 *(19f,Exe,HY,Dec 4)*
Our Boy Ben 102 *(16½f,Sed,S,May 5)*
Our Vinnie 91 *(24f,Fai,HY,Dec 19)*
Out Sam 108 *(21f,Asc,S,Dec 18)*
Outlander 103 *(20f,Fai,Y,Mar 27)*
Over And Above 109 *(26f,Sed,S,May 5)*
Owen Glendower 95 *(22½f,Str,G,Jun 16)*
Owen Na View 107 *(20f,Sth,G,May 12)*
Owner Occupier 98 *(20f,Wor,G,Jun 21)*
Ozzy Thomas 108 *(16f,Lud,S,Dec 2)*

Paddy Mulligan 102 *(17f,Mar,G,Jly 5)*
Paddy The Deejay 98 *(16f,Chp,S,Nov 4)*
Paddy The Oscar 106 *(24f,War,HY,Dec 31)*
Paddy The Stout 96 *(16½f,Nab,S,Apr 18)*
Padge 102 *(19f,Asc,G,Oct 31)*
Pain Au Chocolat 118 *(16f,Hay,HY,Dec 19)*
Pair Of Jacks 108 *(17f,Kel,GS,May 6)*
Palm Grey 90 *(21½f,Mar,S,Dec 26)*
Pamak D'Airy 102 *(16½f,Ncs,HY,Dec 10)*
Pandy Wells 102 *(23½f,Hun,GS,Apr 18)*
Paradise Valley 105 *(16f,Utt,G,May 2)*
Parish Business 105 *(24f,Kem,G,Nov 2)*
Parlour Games 116 *(20f,Chl,G,Oct 24)*
Parsnip Pete 93 *(16f,Chl,S,Dec 12)*
Parting Way 98 *(16f,Utt,HY,Dec 31)*
Pass The Hat 110 *(24f,Don,G,Jan 30)*
Pass The Time 95 *(20f,Wcn,HY,Nov 19)*
Passato 95 *(21f,Fak,G,May 31)*
Passing Fiesta 100 *(16f,Tau,GS,Mar 14)*
Patricktom Boru 101 *(21f,Ffo,G,May 23)*
Pay The King 105 *(20f,Crl,S,Mar 10)*
Peachey Moment 97 *(20f,Per,G,Jly 2)*
Peak Seasons 90 *(25½f,Crt,GS,Jly 20)*
Pearl Swan 108 *(19½f,Chp,G,Oct 10)*
Pearls Legend 113 *(16f,Chl,S,Dec 12)*
Peckhamecho 94 *(17f,Crt,GS,Jly 20)*
Pekanheim 100 *(16½f,Ncs,S,Feb 3)*
Pembroke House 102 *(16f,Lin,HY,Dec 21)*
Pena Dorada 109 *(24f,Ban,GS,Aug 21)*
Pendra 103 *(24f,Asc,G,Oct 31)*
Pepite Rose 112 *(20f,Ain,S,Nov 7)*
Perfect Candidate 112 *(26f,Chl,G,Apr 14)*
Perfect Promise 100 *(21f,Pun,GY,May 1)*
Perfect Timing 106 *(21f,Nab,G,May 27)*
Personal Shopper 93 *(19f,Sed,S,Apr 9)*
Pete The Feat 112 *(24f,San,GS,Feb 6)*
Peter From Paris 105 *(20f,Pun,HY,Jan 9)*
Petit Ecuyer 90 *(21f,Fak,G,Mar 18)*
Phil's Magic 104 *(16f,Fai,HY,Dec 19)*
Pigeon Island 97 *(24f,Ffo,G,May 23)*
Pindar 99 *(16½f,Sed,G,May 12)*
Pine Creek 108 *(19f,Don,GS,Feb 11)*
Pineau De Re 108 *(24f,San,GS,Nov 8)*
Pinerolo 106 *(24f,Hex,G,May 2)*
Pires 96 *(16f,Pun,Y,Apr 30)*
Pistol Basc 102 *(22½f,Str,G,Jly 12)*
Playing The Field 92 *(23f,Wor,GS,Oct 21)*
Plus Jamais 104 *(24f,Per,G,Apr 20)*
Polisky 105 *(20f,Wcn,GF,Oct 16)*
Pont Alexandre 95 *(22f,Pun,HY,Dec 6)*
Poole Master 96 *(24f,Hay,S,Nov 21)*
Port Melon 109 *(24f,Kem,G,Nov 2)*
Porters War 105 *(21f,Str,G,May 30)*
Portrait King 109 *(32½f,Ncs,GS,Feb 27)*
Portway Flyer 112 *(20½f,Kem,G,Mar 19)*
Potters Cross 109 *(23½f,Nby,GS,Apr 1)*
Present Flight 105 *(23½f,Kel,GS,Mar 21)*
Present Lodger 106 *(20f,Hex,GS,Oct 10)*
Present View 112 *(19½f,Chp,G,Oct 11)*
Presented 108 *(24f,Per,G,Apr 20)*
Presenting Arms 112 *(19f,Don,S,Mar 4)*
Presenting Junior 108 *(21f,Crt,G,Jun 28)*
Pressurize 113 *(19½f,Chp,HY,Mar 28)*
Pret A Thou 102 *(16f,Lei,HY,Feb 18)*
Prideofthecastle 112 *(23f,Lei,S,Feb 3)*
Prince Des Marais 105 *(24½f,War,GS,May 20)*
Private Malone 104 *(25f,Chl,S,Dec 11)*
Problema Tic 99 *(24f,Per,G,Jly 1)*
Proud Gamble 99 *(24f,Mus,S,Feb 8)*
Provincial Pride 101 *(22½f,Str,G,Jly 30)*
Ptit Zig 121 *(21f,Asc,GS,Nov 21)*
Pumped Up Kicks 100 *(20½f,Kem,G,Mar 19)*
Purcell's Bridge 101 *(24f,Mus,G,Nov 5)*
Pure Poteen 104 *(25½f,War,GS,Nov 4)*
Purple 'n Gold 110 *(16½f,Wor,GS,Aug 23)*
Pyjama Game 97 *(26f,Sed,S,May 5)*
Pythagore 109 *(20f,Nby,S,Mar 5)*

Qewy 110 *(16f,Chl,G,Oct 23)*
Quadriller 94 *(17f,Str,GS,Sep 5)*
Quantitativeeasing 111 *(30f,Chl,G,Mar 16)*
Queen Olivia 100 *(16f,Lud,GS,Nov 12)*
Quick Brew 99 *(16f,Crl,G,May 7)*
Quick Decisson 104 *(15½f,Ayr,HY,Feb 16)*
Quinz 101 *(24f,San,GS,Dec 4)*
Quite By Chance 111 *(19½f,Chp,HY,Mar 28)*
Quito Du Tresor 107 *(20f,Mus,G,Nov 6)*
Qulinton 96 *(24f,Ffo,GF,Jun 18)*

Raajih 96 *(21f,Nab,GS,Aug 22)*
Racing Europe 108 *(25f,Cat,S,Dec 15)*
Racing Pulse 111 *(23½f,Chp,HY,Jan 9)*
Raduis Bleu 90 *(24f,War,HY,Dec 31)*
Railway Storm 101 *(21f,Nab,G,Jun 23)*
Raktiman 102 *(21½f,Mar,S,Nov 5)*
Rare Legend 93 *(20f,Pun,HY,Jan 9)*
Rathlin 109 *(15½f,Ayr,HY,Mar 12)*
Ratify 99 *(20f,Wcn,S,Mar 2)*
Raven's Tower 111 *(16½f,Hun,S,Nov 10)*
Ray Diamond 99 *(21f,Nab,S,May 7)*
Raz De Maree 96 *(29f,Fai,YS,Mar 28)*
Ready Token 103 *(25½f,Fon,GS,Jun 3)*
Real Steel 116 *(16f,Pun,Y,Apr 30)*
Reaping The Reward 109 *(24f,Don,S,Dec 12)*
Rear Admiral 105 *(20f,Mus,GS,Nov 27)*
Rebeccas Choice 99 *(24f,Ffo,GS,Mar 20)*
Rebel Benefit 106 *(23f,Tau,GS,Dec 10)*
Reblis 101 *(26f,Plu,GS,Feb 29)*
Red Admirable 99 *(24f,Don,GS,Dec 29)*
Red Anchor 99 *(25½f,Fon,G,May 1)*
Red Danaher 99 *(19f,Sed,HY,Dec 26)*
Red Piano 91 *(26f,Crl,G,Mar 26)*
Red Riverman 91 *(16f,War,GS,May 20)*
Red Rosso 100 *(16f,Sth,G,Jun 2)*
Red Seventy 108 *(17f,Str,G,Jly 12)*
Red Skipper 106 *(16½f,Nab,G,Jun 12)*
Red Spinner 109 *(16f,War,S,Dec 10)*
Red Tortue 91 *(20f,Hun,G,Oct 13)*
Red Whisper 94 *(16½f,Tow,GF,Apr 30)*
Regal D'Estruval 101 *(16½f,Wor,GS,May 7)*
Regal Encore 112 *(17f,Plu,S,Dec 14)*
Regal Flow 106 *(24f,Fak,S,Jan 28)*
Relax 106 *(24f,San,S,Mar 12)*
Relentless Dreamer 106 *(23f,Wor,GS,Oct 21)*
Relic Rock 107 *(16f,Crl,G,Oct 15)*
Renard 105 *(19f,Exe,GS,Mar 8)*
Representingceltic 91 *(23½f,Chp,G,Oct 11)*
Residence And Spa 104 *(23f,Tau,HY,Jan 23)*
Resolute Reformer 94 *(24f,Mus,GS,Jan 4)*
Restless Harry 107 *(24f,Ban,S,Nov 11)*
Restless Rebel 101 *(25½f,Fon,S,Apr 15)*
Retrieve The Stick 106 *(15f,Wet,S,Feb 23)*
Reve De Sivola 99 *(24f,Hay,HY,Jan 23)*
Reverse The Charge 102 *(15½f,Hex,GS,Oct 10)*
Riddlestown 102 *(20f,Sth,G,May 12)*
Ride On Time 92 *(19f,Mar,S,Nov 5)*
Rigadin De Beauchene 110 *(27½f,Chl,GS,Nov 14)*
Rio Milan 98 *(25½f,Lud,G,Oct 7)*
Risk A Fine 115 *(21½f,Mar,G,Jun 5)*
Rivage D'Or 94 *(30f,Chl,G,Nov 13)*
River Deep 91 *(19½f,Str,GF,May 17)*
River Maigue 109 *(21f,Crt,G,May 27)*
River Purple 105 *(20f,Utt,G,Jly 15)*
Riverside City 108 *(24½f,Leo,HY,Dec 27)*
Road To Freedom 105 *(21f,Fak,GS,Oct 28)*
Road To Riches 115 *(21f,Chl,G,Mar 17)*
Roalco De Farges 93 *(24f,San,GS,Nov 8)*
Roberto Pegasus 94 *(20f,Sth,S,Nov 9)*
Robin's Command 111 *(17f,Kel,GF,Oct 4)*
Roc D'Apsis 110 *(20½f,Kem,S,Jan 25)*
Roc De Prince 107 *(15½f,Hex,GS,Oct 10)*
Rock Des Champs 97 *(20f,Wor,G,Oct 8)*
Rock N Rhythm 98 *(16½f,Hun,S,Nov 10)*
Rock Of Ages 93 *(20f,Sth,GS,Apr 15)*
Rock The World 112 *(16f,Chl,G,Oct 23)*
Rockabilly 99 *(26f,Chp,G,Apr 22)*
Rocking Blues 112 *(32½f,Ncs,GS,Feb 27)*
Rockiteer 97 *(25½f,Lud,GS,Nov 12)*
Rockmount River 95 *(16½f,Tow,G,May 11)*
Rocknrobin 105 *(20f,Plu,S,Mar 14)*
Rocky Bender 106 *(31f,Hun,S,Mar 6)*
Rocky Creek 106 *(24f,Kem,GS,Feb 27)*
Rocky Stone 91 *(25½f,Sth,GS,Feb 28)*
Rogue Angel 112 *(29f,Fai,YS,Mar 28)*
Roi Des Francs 110 *(24½f,Chl,G,Mar 16)*
Rolling Maul 93 *(24f,Exe,HY,Nov 22)*
Rolly Baby 110 *(20f,Per,G,Apr 22)*
Romany Ryme 100 *(21f,Crt,G,Jly 18)*
Roparta Avenue 99 *(26f,Plu,G,Apr 22)*
Rosa Fleet 106 *(22f,Tow,GS,May 18)*
Rose Of The Moon 106 *(30f,Chl,G,Nov 13)*
Roseneath 99 *(25½f,Fon,G,May 1)*
Roseville Cottage 93 *(19f,Sed,G,May 12)*
Rosquero 104 *(16½f,Ncs,S,Feb 3)*
Rossvoss 93 *(24½f,Leo,HY,Dec 27)*
Rothman 107 *(20f,Wor,G,Jly 15)*
Rouge Et Blanc 99 *(21f,Crt,GS,May 25)*
Rouquine Sauvage 101 *(16f,Lin,HY,Dec 12)*
Roxyfet 105 *(16½f,Sed,S,Nov 24)*
Royal Chief 96 *(20f,Wcn,G,Oct 25)*
Royal Macnab 107 *(20f,Mus,GS,Jan 1)*
Royal Palladium 111 *(25f,Wcn,S,Nov 7)*
Royal Regatta 117 *(21f,Asc,GS,Dec 19)*
Royale Django 117 *(24f,Sth,G,May 20)*
Royale Knight 110 *(29f,Sed,S,Mar 5)*
Royalracket 108 *(22f,Tow,GF,Apr 30)*
Royalraise 109 *(23f,Tau,GS,Nov 26)*
Royaume Bleu 99 *(24f,Fak,G,May 31)*
Ruapehu 106 *(25f,Wcn,G,May 12)*
Ruben Cotter 109 *(19½f,Chp,G,Apr 22)*
Rubi Light 91 *(20f,Pun,GY,Apr 29)*
Rule The World 117 *(34½f,Ain,S,Apr 9)*
Run Ructions Run 104 *(20f,Crl,G,Mar 26)*
Run With The Wind 104 *(20f,Per,G,Jly 12)*
Runswick Days 96 *(19f,Sed,S,Mar 27)*
Runswick Relax 109 *(19f,Sed,S,Mar 15)*
Runswick Royal 99 *(24f,Per,G,Jun 7)*
Rupert Bear 102 *(15f,Wet,S,Feb 23)*
Russborough 104 *(20½f,Ban,S,Mar 31)*
Russe Blanc 105 *(29f,War,HY,Jan 16)*
Russian Bolero 98 *(19½f,Str,GS,Sep 5)*
Russian Regent 110 *(25f,Ain,G,Oct 25)*
Rusty Nail 90 *(25½f,Fon,S,Aug 25)*
Rydon Pynes 108 *(23f,Tau,GS,Nov 26)*

Sa Suffit 95 *(19f,Sed,GS,Jan 31)*
Sabroclair 98 *(16½f,Tow,G,Nov 5)*
Sacre Malta 99 *(20f,Sth,GS,Apr 15)*
Saddle Pack 96 *(15½f,Hex,G,Jun 13)*
Saddlers Deal 100 *(15½f,Hex,HY,May 9)*
Safari Journey 94 *(16f,Cat,GS,Mar 1)*
Saffron Prince 102 *(16f,Sth,G,Mar 21)*
Saffron Wells 105 *(20½f,Kem,GS,Nov 23)*
Sail And Return 106 *(22½f,Str,G,Jun 16)*
Saint Are 112 *(24f,Don,G,Feb 24)*
Saint Breiz 103 *(20f,Wcn,S,Dec 3)*
Saint Raph 105 *(23f,Tau,G,Apr 20)*
Saint Roque 110 *(23f,Tau,GS,Nov 26)*
Saints And Sinners 106 *(20f,Per,G,Apr 21)*
Salubrious 107 *(21f,Asc,S,Jan 23)*
Salut Honore 98 *(24f,Mar,S,Feb 21)*
Sam Winner 110 *(25f,Chl,HY,Jan 30)*
Sambremont 93 *(26f,Chl,G,Mar 17)*
Sametegal 113 *(20f,Nby,S,Mar 5)*
Samingarry 110 *(25f,Ain,G,May 15)*
Samtheman 94 *(20f,Lud,G,Oct 22)*
Sand Artist 95 *(23f,Wor,G,Aug 19)*
Sands Cove 106 *(24f,Mar,S,Nov 5)*
Sandy Beach 110 *(23f,Tau,GS,Dec 10)*
Sandynow 95 *(20½f,Ban,G,Aug 21)*
Santa's Secret 106 *(16f,Sth,GS,Feb 28)*
Saphir Du Rheu 108 *(20f,Crl,GS,Nov 1)*
Saroque 109 *(23½f,Ncs,S,Nov 28)*
Sausalito Sunrise 113 *(27½f,Chl,GS,Nov 14)*
Savello 114 *(17f,Kel,GS,Apr 2)*
Scarlet Fire 99 *(24f,Hex,G,May 2)*
Scimon Templar 101 *(15½f,Ayr,HY,Jan 2)*
Scorpions Sting 101 *(20f,Mus,GS,Nov 27)*
Scotswell 102 *(26f,Sed,S,Mar 6)*
Sea Wall 105 *(16f,Lin,HY,Dec 12)*
Seabass 106 *(21½f,Fai,HY,Jan 30)*
Seamus Mor 98 *(24f,San,S,Mar 11)*
Sean Airgead 94 *(15½f,Hex,HY,May 9)*
Sedgemoor Express 106 *(24f,Kem,G,May 4)*
Seebright 107 *(26f,Nby,G,Apr 2)*
Seeyouatmidnight 115 *(23½f,Kel,HY,Dec 6)*
Sego Success 111 *(24f,Don,S,Dec 12)*
Seldom Inn 108 *(23½f,Kel,G,Oct 24)*
Sendiym 102 *(19f,Sed,G,Sep 29)*
Senor Alco 97 *(26f,Sed,GF,Apr 30)*
Sergeant Dick 92 *(21f,Nab,GS,May 19)*
Sergeant Pink 107 *(17f,Mar,G,May 17)*
Sergeant Thunder 94 *(16½f,Wor,GF,Jun 6)*
Set List 106 *(20f,Wor,GF,Sep 8)*
Settledoutofcourt 100 *(24½f,Crl,GS,Mar 20)*
Seventeen Black 96 *(16½f,Sed,GS,Feb 25)*
Seventh Hussar 98 *(16f,Lin,HY,Dec 1)*
Seventh Sky 110 *(24f,San,GS,Nov 8)*
Sew On Target 112 *(19½f,Wet,S,Feb 6)*
Sgt Bull Berry 95 *(24f,Don,G,Nov 28)*
Sgt Reckless 90 *(17f,Asc,G,Oct 31)*
Shadow Catcher 108 *(20f,Per,GS,Sep 24)*
Shadows Lengthen 108 *(24f,Per,G,Apr 21)*
Shady Glen 97 *(26f,Sed,GF,Sep 3)*
Shady Lane 109 *(16½f,Wor,GF,Jun 11)*
Shady Sadie 93 *(21½f,Wet,G,May 28)*
Shah Of Persia 105 *(24f,Sth,G,Oct 22)*
Shanahan's Turn 90 *(25f,Chl,GS,Mar 15)*

Shaneshill 116 *(24½f,Chl,G,Mar 16)*
Shangani 101 *(20f,San,S,Mar 12)*
Shantou Flyer 109 *(24½f,Chl,G,Oct 23)*
Shantou Magic 106 *(21f,Nab,GS,Oct 9)*
Shantou Tiger 97 *(25½f,Fon,G,Oct 2)*
Sharp Rise 98 *(19f,Sed,G,May 12)*
Shimla Dawn 109 *(20f,Crl,G,Nov 1)*
Shine A Diamond 105 *(15½f,Hex,GS,Oct 10)*
Shockingtimes 105 *(21½f,Mar,S,Nov 19)*
Shotavodka 110 *(24f,Don,G,Feb 24)*
Shotgun Paddy 111 *(27½f,Chl,GS,Nov 14)*
Showboater 103 *(17½f,Fon,S,Nov 25)*
Shrapnel 99 *(16f,Sth,GS,Jun 15)*
Shubaat 105 *(23½f,Kel,G,Oct 24)*
Shuil Royale 112 *(26f,Utt,G,Jun 28)*
Shutthefrontdoor 102 *(34½f,Ain,S,Apr 9)*
Si C'Etait Vrai 96 *(24f,Asc,GS,Apr 3)*
Sidbury Hill 103 *(20f,Wcn,G,Apr 4)*
Silent Cliche 99 *(25½f,Fon,G,May 1)*
Silent Snow 94 *(23½f,Kel,GS,May 6)*
Silk Hall 104 *(21f,Crt,GS,Aug 29)*
Silmi 99 *(21f,Crt,GS,May 25)*
Silsol 114 *(20f,Crl,HY,Nov 9)*
Silver Dragon 101 *(26f,Sed,HY,Dec 4)*
Silver Eagle 101 *(23½f,Hun,GS,Apr 18)*
Silver Man 110 *(26f,Utt,G,Jun 28)*
Silver Roque 101 *(19f,Mar,G,May 8)*
Silver Tassie 109 *(20f,Ncs,S,Apr 8)*
Silvergrove 103 *(24f,Kem,S,Feb 12)*
Silviniaco Conti 123 *(21f,Asc,S,Feb 20)*
Simply Ned 115 *(17f,Leo,HY,Dec 27)*
Simply The West 111 *(22f,Tow,GS,May 18)*
Simply Wings 106 *(20f,Lei,HY,Feb 18)*
Sin Bin 103 *(26f,Nab,GF,Apr 30)*
Sir Abbot 102 *(17f,Leo,S,Jan 24)*
Sir Des Champs 108 *(24f,Leo,HY,Dec 28)*
Sir Lynx 93 *(24½f,War,S,May 9)*
Sir Mattie 105 *(24f,Ban,G,Jly 31)*
Sir Note 106 *(17f,Mar,S,Mar 28)*
Sir Valentino 110 *(16f,Lud,S,Dec 16)*
Sirabad 105 *(20½f,Kem,GS,Dec 26)*
Sire Collonges 112 *(30f,Chl,GS,Dec 11)*
Sire De Grugy 113 *(15½f,San,G,Apr 23)*
Sizing Gold 93 *(22f,Pun,HY,Dec 6)*
Sizing Granite 118 *(17f,Fai,Y,Mar 29)*
Sizing John 119 *(16f,Chl,GS,Mar 15)*
Sizing Sahara 93 *(21f,Fak,GS,Dec 20)*
Skating Home 92 *(26f,Nab,G,Sep 28)*
Sky Watch 102 *(26f,Plu,G,Nov 2)*
Skylander 104 *(20f,Hex,G,Oct 2)*
Sleep In First 99 *(16f,Utt,G,Jly 24)*
Sleepy Haven 101 *(15f,Wet,S,Dec 5)*
Slidecheck 96 *(17f,Plu,HY,Jan 18)*
Smad Place 125 *(25f,Chl,HY,Jan 30)*
Smart Exit 104 *(23½f,Chp,HY,Nov 18)*
Smoking Jacket 98 *(16f,Lei,G,Dec 3)*
Smooth Stepper 112 *(23½f,Ncs,S,Nov 28)*
Snowell 94 *(16f,Fak,GS,Oct 28)*
So Bazaar 105 *(16½f,Sed,G,Sep 29)*
So Fine 100 *(24f,Asc,GS,Apr 3)*
Soaring High 91 *(21½f,Fai,HY,Jan 30)*
Solar Impulse 113 *(16f,Chl,G,Mar 18)*
Solita 110 *(17f,Fai,Y,Mar 27)*
Soll 102 *(26f,Ain,S,Dec 5)*
Solstice Son 108 *(25f,Chl,G,Apr 14)*
Solway Bay 97 *(24f,Mus,S,Jan 20)*
Solway Legend 104 *(20f,Crl,G,Oct 22)*
Solway Sam 92 *(26f,Crl,G,Mar 26)*
Somchine 104 *(20½f,Kem,G,Nov 2)*
Some Buckle 107 *(20f,San,G,Apr 23)*
Some Finish 92 *(20f,Lei,HY,Mar 1)*
Some Lad 101 *(17f,Kel,GS,Apr 2)*
Somersby 115 *(16f,Chl,GS,Nov 15)*
Somerset Lias 104 *(23f,Tau,GS,Dec 10)*
Son Of Suzie 107 *(30f,Ban,HY,Mar 2)*
Sonny The One 109 *(23f,Tau,HY,Feb 2)*
Sonofagun 105 *(24f,Don,G,Feb 24)*
Sound Investment 113 *(20½f,Chl,GS,Nov 14)*
Souriyan 108 *(20f,Utt,G,Oct 4)*
Southfield Royale 115 *(24f,Don,HY,Dec 12)*
Southfield Theatre 111 *(29f,San,G,Apr 23)*
Southfield Vic 108 *(19f,Exe,HY,Feb 14)*
Spanish Fleet 96 *(20f,Ncs,S,Feb 3)*
Spanish Optimist 90 *(19f,Exe,G,Apr 21)*
Spartilla 101 *(21f,Fak,S,Jan 1)*
Special Agent 103 *(20f,Hun,S,Jan 29)*
Special Catch 109 *(16½f,Ncs,HY,Dec 10)*
Special Tiara 117 *(16f,Chl,G,Mar 16)*
Special Wells 103 *(20f,Crl,G,Nov 1)*
Speckled Wood 104 *(21f,Pun,GY,May 1)*
Speed Master 109 *(26f,Utt,G,Jun 28)*
Speedy Bruere 104 *(20f,Sth,G,Jun 9)*
Speedy Tunes 96 *(20f,Sth,G,Jun 9)*
Spending Time 101 *(25f,Wcn,S,Dec 3)*
Spirit Of Shankly 111 *(24½f,Tow,S,Mar 17)*
Spirit River 97 *(24f,Ban,G,Jly 31)*
Splash Of Ginge 109 *(20½f,Chl,GS,Nov 14)*
Spookydooky 103 *(23f,Hay,HY,Dec 19)*
Sporting Boy 107 *(21f,Nab,G,Jun 12)*
Sportsreport 105 *(17f,Plu,S,Mar 14)*
Spring Heeled 110 *(27½f,Chl,GS,Nov 14)*
Spring Over 100 *(24f,Hex,HY,Mar 17)*
Spring Steel 91 *(16f,Sth,GF,Aug 16)*
Sprinter Sacre 125 *(15½f,San,G,Apr 23)*
Squire Trelawney 100 *(20f,Wcn,G,Oct 25)*
St Dominick 104 *(24f,Exe,HY,Nov 22)*
St Johns Point 105 *(23f,Wor,GS,Oct 21)*
St Maxime 100 *(24f,Per,G,Jly 1)*
Stafford Charlie 97 *(20f,Wor,GF,Jly 23)*
Standing Ovation 113 *(21f,Nab,GS,Aug 22)*
Star Presenter 107 *(16f,Cat,S,Jan 27)*
Starkie 99 *(16½f,Nby,GS,Mar 4)*
Steel Summit 108 *(25f,Wcn,G,May 7)*
Stellar Notion 98 *(20½f,Kem,S,Jan 25)*
Stephen Hero 108 *(21½f,Mar,G,Jun 5)*
Sterling Gent 94 *(24f,Ffo,G,Jun 4)*
Still Believing 102 *(24f,Utt,G,May 2)*
Stilletto 110 *(20f,Lei,HY,Feb 18)*
Stilo Blue Native 96 *(16½f,Ncs,HY,Mar 19)*
Stormbay Bomber 95 *(16f,Lei,GS,Dec 9)*
Storming Strumpet 105 *(21f,Chl,G,Apr 14)*
Straidnahanna 110 *(25f,Cat,S,Feb 15)*
Street Entertainer 110 *(20f,Wor,GF,Jun 24)*
Streets Of Promise 105 *(23½f,Ncs,HY,Mar 8)*
Strike Fast 102 *(26f,Sed,S,May 5)*
Strobe 98 *(20½f,Ban,G,Aug 21)*
Strollawaynow 97 *(24f,War,S,Dec 10)*
Strongly Suggested 110 *(16½f,Wor,G,Jly 28)*
Strongpoint 108 *(20f,Per,G,Jun 7)*
Strumble Head 106 *(24f,Ban,G,Jly 31)*
Sub Lieutenant 108 *(20f,Fai,SH,Nov 29)*
Sublime Talent 102 *(16f,Utt,G,Jly 24)*
Subtle Grey 109 *(23½f,Chp,HY,Jan 9)*
Such A Legend 112 *(16f,Utt,G,May 2)*
Sudski Star 100 *(21f,Crt,G,Jun 28)*
Summery Justice 106 *(24f,San,GS,Feb 6)*
Sumos Novios 103 *(21½f,Fai,HY,Jan 30)*
Sun Cloud 108 *(24f,Hay,S,Nov 21)*
Sun Wild Life 106 *(26f,Nab,S,Apr 5)*
Sunny Ledgend 101 *(20f,Tow,HY,Jan 7)*
Sunsetstorise 106 *(21½f,Fai,HY,Jan 30)*
Supapowers 106 *(26f,Nab,G,Sep 28)*
Super Collider 102 *(15½f,Hex,HY,May 9)*
Super Duty 97 *(29f,San,GS,Dec 5)*
Superior Command 92 *(17f,Kel,S,Mar 13)*
Supreme Asset 103 *(17½f,Ban,HY,Mar 2)*
Suprise Vendor 102 *(15½f,Hex,HY,Apr 18)*
Surf And Turf 107 *(16½f,Wor,GF,Jun 24)*
Susie Sheep 105 *(22½f,Utt,G,Jun 17)*
Susquehanna River 103 *(24f,Ffo,GF,Jun 18)*
Swaledale Lad 105 *(17f,Crt,GS,Jly 20)*
Swing Hard 106 *(20f,Crl,S,Mar 10)*
Swizzler 93 *(19f,Don,S,Mar 4)*
Sylvan Legend 103 *(20f,Utt,GF,Jly 7)*

Table Bluff 101 *(16f,Sth,G,Jun 2)*
Tachbury 91 *(21f,Fon,G,Jun 9)*
Tahiti Pearl 97 *(19f,Sed,GF,Apr 30)*
Take A Bow 105 *(24f,Sth,G,Aug 27)*
Take The Crown 95 *(16f,Lei,G,Dec 3)*
Take The Mick 101 *(23½f,Chp,HY,Mar 12)*
Tales Of Milan 90 *(29f,San,GS,Dec 5)*
Tango De Juilley 101 *(21f,Chl,G,Mar 17)*
Tangolan 105 *(20f,Hun,GS,Aug 31)*
Tanner Hill 93 *(24f,Fak,GS,Dec 20)*
Taquin Du Seuil 112 *(20f,War,S,Feb 13)*
Tara Road 111 *(19½f,Chp,G,Oct 11)*
Tarraco 92 *(24f,Exe,HY,Nov 22)*
Tea Caddy 104 *(19½f,Chp,HY,Feb 5)*
Tea For Two 115 *(20f,San,GS,Feb 6)*
Ted Spread 104 *(16½f,Nab,GS,Oct 9)*
Ted Veale 117 *(16f,Pun,Y,Apr 30)*
Teddy Tee 96 *(24f,Ban,HY,Nov 28)*
Teddy's Reflection 102 *(20f,Sth,G,Jun 2)*
Teenage Dream 103 *(19f,Sed,GS,Nov 10)*
Tell Us More 108 *(19f,Leo,HY,Dec 28)*
Temple Lord 102 *(20f,Sth,G,Jun 2)*
Tennis Cap 110 *(20f,Per,G,Apr 21)*
Tenor Nivernais 119 *(21f,Asc,S,Nov 20)*
Teochew 92 *(26f,Sed,S,Oct 29)*
That's The Deal 91 *(21f,Fak,G,Mar 18)*
Thatildee 103 *(24f,Hex,GS,Nov 6)*
The Absent Mare 100 *(16f,Per,S,May 13)*
The Admiral Benbow 97 *(25f,Pun,G,May 16)*
The Backup Plan 104 *(19f,Sed,G,Sep 29)*
The Bay Bandit 99 *(16½f,Nab,G,May 27)*
The Bishop 101 *(24f,Hex,HY,Mar 17)*
The Brock Again 106 *(16f,Wcn,HY,Feb 4)*
The Cat's Away 96 *(26f,Plu,G,May 10)*
The Cider Maker 104 *(26f,Plu,GS,Feb 29)*
The Clock Leary 105 *(15½f,San,S,Feb 19)*
The Cobbler Swayne 110 *(20f,Mus,G,Nov 5)*
The Druids Nephew 113 *(26f,Don,S,Mar 5)*
The Game Changer 119 *(16f,Ain,GS,Apr 9)*
The Giant Bolster 111 *(25f,Chl,HY,Jan 30)*
The Green Ogre 105 *(17f,Plu,GS,Feb 29)*
The Grey Taylor 109 *(16½f,Don,GS,Dec 29)*
The Happy Warrior 104 *(21f,Nab,S,May 7)*
The Informant 96 *(16f,Lin,HY,Dec 1)*
The Italian Yob 106 *(21f,Ffo,G,Oct 17)*
The Job Is Right 108 *(24½f,Leo,HY,Dec 27)*
The Jugopolist 90 *(16f,Sth,S,Apr 15)*
The Last Bridge 90 *(29f,War,G,Mar 23)*
The Last Samuri 117 *(26f,Don,S,Mar 5)*
The Mooch 107 *(17f,Leo,S,Jan 24)*
The Mumper 104 *(19f,Mar,S,Feb 21)*
The Omen 95 *(21f,Crt,GS,Aug 29)*
The Orange Rogue 103 *(20f,Ncs,S,Nov 28)*
The Package 105 *(26f,Utt,G,Jun 28)*
The Purchaser 100 *(24f,Mar,G,Jun 19)*
The Ramblin Kid 111 *(23½f,Ncs,S,Nov 28)*
The Romford Pele 111 *(27½f,Chl,GS,Nov 14)*
The Saint James 111 *(17½f,Ban,HY,Dec 11)*
The Shropshire Lad 92 *(20½f,Ban,G,Aug 21)*
The Society Man 103 *(25½f,Crt,G,Jun 28)*
The Tourard Man 98 *(24f,Exe,S,Nov 3)*
The Wee Midget 100 *(21f,Fon,GS,Aug 13)*
The Wexfordian 96 *(16f,Cat,GS,Mar 1)*
The Winkler 103 *(20f,Fai,HY,Jan 10)*
The Yank 103 *(16f,Sth,G,Aug 27)*
The Young Master 113 *(29f,San,G,Apr 23)*
Theatre Guide 114 *(24f,Kem,GS,Feb 27)*
Theatrical Star 93 *(25f,Chl,G,Oct 24)*
Thedrinkymeister 101 *(24f,Ban,S,Mar 31)*
Theflyingportrait 101 *(19f,Sed,S,Mar 15)*
Theinval 107 *(20½f,Ban,G,Oct 27)*
Thekingofconnemara 103 *(24f,Fai,SH,Jan 20)*
Themanfrom Minella 109 *(22f,Tow,GS,May 18)*
Thepartysover 98 *(17½f,Fon,HY,Feb 18)*
Thinger Licht 109 *(21f,Fon,GS,Feb 28)*
Third Act 100 *(17½f,Fon,GS,Jun 3)*
Third Intention 115 *(19½f,Chp,G,Oct 11)*
Thomas Brown 110 *(21f,Asc,S,Dec 18)*
Thomas Crapper 111 *(20f,Nby,G,Apr 2)*
Thomas Wild 108 *(28f,Chl,GS,Apr 13)*
Thoonavolla 104 *(20f,Sth,G,Mar 21)*
Thoresby 92 *(21½f,Mar,G,May 8)*
Three Faces West 108 *(20f,Hun,HY,Jan 15)*
Three Musketeers 114 *(20f,Chl,G,Mar 17)*
Throthethatch 107 *(17f,Kel,S,Nov 7)*
Thunder And Roses 110 *(25f,Fai,HY,Feb 20)*
Tikkandemickey 105 *(20f,Hex,HY,Nov 13)*
Tikkapick 92 *(23f,Tau,HY,Jan 23)*
Time Is Tickin 95 *(25½f,Fon,GS,Jun 3)*
Tindaro 103 *(20f,Sth,GF,Aug 16)*
Tinker Time 95 *(25½f,Lud,S,Dec 2)*
Tiny Dancer 100 *(25f,Cat,GS,Dec 2)*
Tipsy Dara 103 *(20f,Crl,S,Mar 10)*
Tipsy Gypsy 90 *(16½f,Hun,GS,Aug 31)*
Tiquer 94 *(16f,Utt,HY,Dec 31)*
To Begin 100 *(23f,Tau,G,Apr 20)*
Toast And Jam 95 *(20f,Utt,GF,Jly 7)*
Toby Lerone 104 *(20f,Lei,HY,Mar 11)*
Toe To Toe 91 *(16½f,Wor,G,Jly 28)*
Toledo Gold 99 *(17f,Crt,GS,Jly 20)*
Tolkeins Tango 104 *(19½f,Chp,HY,Nov 18)*
Tom Bach 94 *(24f,Ffo,HY,Nov 8)*
Tom Neary 90 *(20½f,Kem,GS,Feb 27)*
Tomorrow's Legend 103 *(17f,Kel,S,Nov 7)*
Too Much Too Soon 92 *(17f,Asc,S,Dec 18)*
Too Scoops 102 *(16f,War,S,Apr 4)*
Toomdeely 90 *(21f,Leo,S,Feb 28)*
Toowoomba 104 *(20f,War,S,Dec 10)*
Top Billing 102 *(20f,Crl,G,Mar 26)*
Top Cat Dj 91 *(24f,Mus,S,Jan 20)*
Top Cat Henry 110 *(21f,Str,G,Oct 17)*
Top Chief 94 *(21f,Fon,G,Sep 6)*
Top Dancer 96 *(24f,Ffo,G,May 23)*
Top Gamble 122 *(17f,Fai,Y,Mar 29)*
Top Wood 105 *(23½f,Chp,HY,Dec 5)*
Topper Thornton 104 *(24f,Per,G,Apr 20)*
Tornado In Milan 107 *(16f,Chp,HY,Mar 12)*
Total Assets 102 *(19f,Sed,GS,Nov 10)*
Total Submission 100 *(21½f,Wet,S,Apr 1)*
Tour D'Argent 94 *(17½f,Ban,G,Jly 31)*
Tour Des Champs 108 *(28½f,Plu,S,Mar 27)*
Town Mouse 110 *(19½f,Str,G,Aug 20)*
Town Pond 103 *(25f,Pun,G,May 16)*
Trafalgar 91 *(24f,Kem,G,May 13)*
Traffic Fluide 111 *(17f,Asc,S,Jan 23)*
Trafficker 104 *(24f,Ban,G,May 1)*
Trapper Peak 101 *(23f,Wor,G,Oct 14)*
Treacy Hotels Boy 96 *(20f,Wcn,HY,Nov 19)*
Treat Yourself 103 *(17f,Leo,S,Jan 24)*
Tregaro 106 *(20f,Sth,G,Sep 2)*
Treliver Manor 98 *(25f,Cat,S,Jan 27)*
Tribal Dance 99 *(21f,Fon,G,Oct 3)*
Trillerin Minella 109 *(21½f,Mar,G,May 17)*
Triolo D'Alene 114 *(20½f,Kem,S,Jan 9)*
Triple Chief 103 *(17f,Plu,S,Mar 27)*
Troika Steppes 106 *(23f,Lei,G,Dec 3)*
Trojan Star 100 *(16½f,Hun,G,Oct 4)*
Trouble In Paris 100 *(20f,Hex,GS,Nov 6)*
Troubled 101 *(24f,Fak,G,May 31)*
Truckers Highway 106 *(20f,Utt,HY,Jan 30)*
Trust Thomas 105 *(15½f,Ayr,HY,Feb 16)*
Try It Sometime 96 *(21f,Ffo,S,Apr 10)*
Tullamore Dew 110 *(24½f,Crl,HY,Dec 13)*
Tulpar 90 *(21f,Leo,S,Feb 28)*
Tulsa Jack 106 *(29f,Fai,YS,Mar 28)*
Turban 113 *(25f,Fai,HY,Feb 20)*
Turn Over Sivola 100 *(16f,Chl,G,Oct 24)*
Twelve Roses 107 *(20½f,Chl,GS,Mar 15)*
Twinlight 105 *(16f,Pun,SH,Jan 31)*
Twirling Magnet 107 *(26f,Utt,G,Jun 28)*
Twojayslad 103 *(24f,Mar,G,Jun 19)*

Ubak 107 *(20f,San,GS,Feb 6)*
Ubaltique 107 *(15½f,Ayr,GS,Apr 16)*
Ucello Conti 110 *(24½f,Leo,HY,Dec 27)*
Ueueteotl 105 *(24f,Don,G,Nov 27)*
Uhlan Bute 107 *(20f,Lud,S,Mar 3)*
Ulck Du Lin 110 *(16½f,Nab,GS,Mar 26)*
Ulis De Vassy 109 *(16f,Utt,G,Jun 28)*
Ultimatum Du Roy 104 *(26f,Utt,HY,May 6)*
Ultragold 111 *(15½f,Ayr,GS,Apr 16)*
Umberto D'Olivate 104 *(31f,Exe,GS,Apr 12)*
Un Anjou 107 *(16f,War,GS,May 20)*
Un De Sceaux 121 *(16f,Pun,Y,Apr 30)*
Un Noble 110 *(20f,Ncs,S,Apr 8)*
Un Temps Pour Tout 114 *(25f,Ain,GS,Apr 8)*
Uncle Junior 98 *(30f,Chl,G,Mar 16)*
Under The Phone 106 *(24f,Don,GS,Feb 11)*
Under The Red Sky 102 *(21f,Crl,S,Mar 10)*
Unic De Bersy 107 *(25f,Pun,HY,Jan 9)*
Union Jack D'Ycy 107 *(24f,Ban,HY,Nov 28)*
Union Saint 107 *(19f,Exe,G,Mar 22)*
Unioniste 111 *(23½f,Kel,S,Mar 13)*
Unique De Cotte 95 *(20f,Wcn,HY,Feb 4)*
Universal Soldier 100 *(27½f,Str,G,May 30)*
Uno Valoroso 108 *(16f,Cat,S,Jan 14)*
Unzing 90 *(22f,Pun,HY,Dec 6)*
Up For An Oscar 99 *(21½f,Mar,S,Nov 19)*
Upazo 106 *(16f,Pun,Y,Apr 30)*
Upbeat Cobbler 101 *(24½f,Tow,S,Mar 17)*
Upepito 108 *(19½f,Wet,G,Oct 14)*
Upham Atom 99 *(31f,Exe,GS,Apr 12)*
Upsilon Bleu 107 *(17f,Kel,GS,Apr 2)*
Upswing 112 *(27½f,Chl,GS,Nov 14)*
Uranna 98 *(20f,Fai,YS,Mar 28)*
Urano 99 *(26f,Nby,S,Nov 28)*
Urban Gale 102 *(24f,Sth,GS,Nov 9)*
Urcalin 109 *(24f,War,G,Oct 1)*
Uriah Heep 101 *(20f,Wor,GF,Jun 6)*
Usa 101 *(16f,Pun,Y,Apr 30)*
Ut Majeur Aulmes 111 *(16½f,Nab,GS,Mar 26)*

Val D'Arc 101 *(16f,Utt,HY,Dec 31)*
Valadom 107 *(30f,Chl,G,Nov 13)*
Valco De Touzaine 112 *(21f,Nab,GS,Aug 22)*
Valid Point 107 *(23f,Lei,GS,Dec 9)*
Valleyofmilan 106 *(25½f,Crt,G,Aug 31)*
Valseur Du Granval 96 *(16f,Tau,HY,Feb 23)*
Valseur Lido 115 *(21f,Chl,G,Mar 17)*
Vaniteux 118 *(16½f,Don,G,Jan 30)*
Vautour 122 *(21f,Asc,GS,Nov 21)*
Vazaro Delafayette 107 *(20f,Hun,S,Feb 25)*
Veauce De Sivola 92 *(24f,Fak,G,Mar 18)*
Vedettariat 100 *(21½f,Fai,HY,Feb 20)*
Velator 103 *(26f,Nab,GF,Apr 30)*
Velvet Maker 110 *(17f,Leo,S,Jan 24)*
Vendredi Trois 106 *(23f,Tau,G,Nov 12)*
Venetian Lad 105 *(20f,Plu,G,May 10)*
Venez Horace 95 *(20f,Hun,GS,Nov 1)*
Vengeur De Guye 108 *(15f,Wet,HY,Nov 25)*
Venitien De Mai 106 *(29f,Fai,YS,Mar 28)*
Vent Nivernais 90 *(19f,Mar,S,Nov 19)*
Verano 104 *(20f,Sth,G,May 12)*
Verko 106 *(21f,Sed,GS,Feb 25)*
Veroce 103 *(24f,Mar,S,Feb 21)*
Very Intense 97 *(20½f,Kem,G,Apr 19)*
Very Live 103 *(17f,Plu,HY,Feb 1)*
Very Noble 96 *(20½f,Kem,G,Nov 2)*
Vesperal Dream 109 *(20f,Per,G,Jun 7)*
Vesuvhill 103 *(24f,Mar,G,May 17)*
Vibrato Valtat 116 *(17½f,Exe,S,Nov 3)*
Vic De Touzaine 108 *(20f,Lei,HY,Mar 11)*
Vice Et Vertu 102 *(20f,Utt,S,Nov 14)*
Vicente 113 *(24½f,Chl,GS,Nov 14)*
Viconte Du Noyer 111 *(16f,Ain,GS,Apr 7)*
Vics Canvas 113 *(34½f,Ain,S,Apr 9)*
Victors Serenade 99 *(24f,Ffo,GS,Mar 20)*
Vieux Lion Rouge 113 *(22f,Tow,GS,May 18)*
Vikekhal 114 *(19f,Fon,G,Oct 3)*
Village Vic 115 *(21f,Chl,S,Dec 12)*
Vincent Row 94 *(21½f,Fai,SH,Apr 5)*
Vinnie The Fish 105 *(17f,Crt,GS,Jly 20)*
Vinny Gambini 91 *(17f,Kel,HY,Dec 29)*
Vino Griego 110 *(24f,San,GS,Nov 8)*
Vintage Star 103 *(26f,Crl,GS,Nov 1)*
Vintage Vinnie 105 *(23f,Wor,G,Sep 25)*
Violet Dancer 112 *(16f,War,S,Feb 13)*
Virak 112 *(23½f,Ncs,S,Nov 28)*
Virtuose Du Chenet 95 *(16f,Utt,HY,Dec 31)*
Vision De La Vie 100 *(24f,Mus,S,Feb 8)*
Vision Des Champs 108 *(15½f,San,GS,Dec 4)*
Viva Steve 110 *(24f,Kem,GS,Dec 27)*
Vivaccio 107 *(19½f,Chp,HY,Mar 28)*
Vivaldi Collonges 110 *(25½f,War,S,Feb 13)*
Vodka Wells 109 *(15½f,Hex,G,Jun 21)*
Voix D'Eau 115 *(21f,Chl,GS,Apr 13)*
Volcanic 108 *(22½f,Utt,G,Jly 24)*
Volcanic Jack 96 *(19f,Mar,G,Jly 5)*
Volio Vincente 97 *(24½f,War,S,May 9)*
Volnay De Thaix 110 *(20f,San,G,Apr 23)*
Voyage A New York 103 *(24f,Per,G,Apr 20)*
Vyta Du Roc 113 *(24½f,Chl,G,Mar 16)*

Waddingtown Hero 102 *(21f,Utt,G,May 2)*
Wadswick Court 105 *(19f,Fon,GS,Oct 21)*
Wak A Turtle 102 *(20f,Wor,GF,Jly 1)*
Wakanda 113 *(23½f,Ncs,S,Nov 28)*
Wakhan 91 *(19f,Sed,S,Nov 24)*
Walden Prince 106 *(16½f,Hun,G,Oct 4)*
Waldorf Salad 111 *(21f,Chl,HY,Jan 30)*
Walk In The Mill 106 *(16f,Lin,S,Nov 10)*

Walk To Freedom 100 *(19f,Leo,S,Jan 17)*
Waltz Darling 97 *(19f,Don,G,Nov 27)*
Waltz Legend 109 *(26f,Sed,S,Apr 9)*
Warden Hill 107 *(26f,Chl,G,Apr 14)*
Warrantor 105 *(20f,Wcn,S,Nov 7)*
Weather Babe 111 *(22½f,Utt,G,Jly 24)*
Webbswood 96 *(21f,Str,G,Jun 16)*
Wellforth 91 *(24f,Ban,S,Mar 31)*
Welsh Bard 91 *(21f,Crt,G,Jly 18)*
West Council 90 *(21½f,Fai,SH,Apr 5)*
West End 99 *(22½f,Str,G,Aug 20)*
West Of The Edge 108 *(27½f,Mar,S,Dec 26)*
West Ship Master 100 *(21½f,Fai,SH,Apr 5)*
West Wizard 90 *(20½f,Kem,GS,Feb 27)*
Westend Theatre 100 *(20f,Hex,S,Mar 29)*
Western Jo 96 *(21½f,Mar,S,Apr 10)*
Westerner Point 107 *(17f,Fai,Y,Mar 27)*
Westwire Toby 101 *(26f,Sed,S,May 5)*
What A Good Night 111 *(24f,Ban,S,Nov 11)*
What A Laugh 110 *(21f,Str,G,Oct 17)*
What A Warrior 100 *(24f,Asc,G,Oct 31)*
What Happens Now 96 *(20½f,Kem,G,Apr 19)*
What Larks 106 *(23f,Tau,GS,Dec 10)*
What's For Tea 93 *(26f,Plu,G,May 10)*
Whatareudoingtome 94 *(21½f,Fai,HY,Jan 30)*
Whats Happening 95 *(25f,Chl,G,Oct 24)*
Whats Left 106 *(24f,Exe,G,Oct 8)*
Whats On The Menu 101 *(24f,Fai,SH,Jan 20)*
Whats Up Woody 102 *(20f,Hex,S,Mar 29)*
Where'd Ya Hide It 95 *(21f,Fon,GS,Aug 13)*
Whiskey Chaser 104 *(24f,Ban,S,Mar 16)*
Whispering Harry 98 *(16½f,Nby,G,Apr 2)*
Who Am I 101 *(20f,Wor,GF,Jly 23)*
Wiesentraum 100 *(24f,Fak,G,Oct 16)*
Wild Bill 106 *(24f,Don,G,Nov 27)*
Wild Rover 97 *(23f,Tau,HY,Dec 30)*
William Money 90 *(26f,Kel,G,Oct 24)*
Willie Hall 105 *(15½f,Ayr,HY,Jan 19)*
Willoughby Hedge 107 *(24f,Don,GS,Feb 11)*
Willow's Saviour 110 *(16f,War,GS,Nov 4)*
Wilton Milan 112 *(19½f,Chp,G,Oct 11)*
Wing Mira 90 *(22½f,Utt,HY,May 6)*
Winged Crusader 100 *(24f,War,S,Feb 26)*
Winged Express 99 *(16f,Chp,S,Feb 27)*
Wings Attract 109 *(19f,Don,G,Nov 28)*
Wings Of Smoke 109 *(20f,Wor,GF,Jun 6)*
Winston Churchill 106 *(19½f,Chp,HY,Nov 18)*
Winter Alchemy 103 *(23½f,Kel,GS,May 6)*
Wish In A Well 93 *(20f,War,HY,Dec 31)*
Wishfull Thinking 110 *(20f,Ain,G,Oct 25)*
Withoutdefavourite 100 *(20f,Utt,G,Sep 20)*
Withy Mills 101 *(19f,Exe,G,Apr 21)*
Witness In Court 111 *(20f,Per,G,Apr 21)*
Witness Of Fashion 103 *(21½f,Fai,HY,Jan 30)*
Wizards Bridge 111 *(23½f,Ncs,S,Nov 28)*
Wolf Hall 90 *(16f,Sth,G,Jun 2)*
Wolf Sword 101 *(21½f,Wet,S,Apr 1)*
Wonderful Charm 98 *(26f,Chl,S,Dec 11)*
Wood Yer 105 *(24f,Ban,HY,Apr 16)*
Woodford County 107 *(29½f,Chp,HY,Jan 9)*
Workbench 111 *(17½f,Fon,G,Oct 2)*
Wounded Warrior 113 *(25f,Pun,GY,Apr 28)*
Wrath Of Titans 105 *(29f,Fai,YS,Mar 28)*
Wuff 107 *(20f,Wcn,S,Jan 21)*
Wychwoods Brook 109 *(23f,Tau,HY,Jan 13)*
Wyck Hill 100 *(32½f,Ncs,GS,Feb 27)*

Xaarcet 97 *(24f,Per,G,Jly 1)*
Xenophon 101 *(24½f,Tow,GF,Oct 7)*

Ya Hafed 103 *(26f,Plu,G,Nov 2)*
Yabadabadoo 101 *(16½f,Hun,G,Oct 4)*
Yorkist 107 *(16f,Mus,S,Feb 7)*
Youm Jamil 102 *(16f,Sth,G,Sep 29)*
Young Cheddar 108 *(26f,Nab,GS,May 19)*
Young Palm 100 *(15½f,Ayr,HY,Jan 19)*
Your Busy 103 *(21f,Leo,S,Feb 28)*

Zabana 111 *(19f,Leo,HY,Dec 28)*
Zama Zama 103 *(16f,Lud,G,Oct 22)*
Zamdy Man 108 *(17f,Plu,S,Dec 14)*
Zarawi 111 *(19f,Fon,G,Oct 3)*
Zarzal 106 *(16f,Chp,HY,Mar 12)*
Zayfire Aramis 90 *(16f,Lin,HY,Mar 7)*
Ziga Boy 114 *(24f,Don,G,Jan 30)*

HURDLES

A Bold Move 93 *(21f,War,GS,Apr 21)*
A Cor Et A Cri 102 *(21f,Kem,G,May 4)*
A Great View 108 *(16f,Pun,HY,Dec 6)*
A Hairy Koala 95 *(21½f,Wcn,GF,Oct 16)*
A Hare Breath 111 *(21f,Kem,S,Jan 25)*
A Little Bit Dusty 103 *(17f,Mar,G,May 17)*
A Little Magic 107 *(16f,War,G,Sep 22)*
A Plein Temps 104 *(23f,Exe,GS,Apr 12)*
A Shade Of Bay 104 *(21f,Utt,G,May 16)*
A Sizing Network 99 *(16f,Pun,Y,Apr 30)*
A Toi Phil 115 *(18f,Leo,HY,Dec 26)*
A Touch Of Sass 94 *(21f,Tow,S,Dec 17)*
A Vos Gardes 103 *(20f,Ain,G,Oct 25)*
Aalim 111 *(23f,Mar,G,Jly 5)*
Aaly 92 *(26f,Fon,G,Oct 3)*
Aaman 95 *(16f,Sth,GS,Feb 28)*
Abbreviate 108 *(20f,Sth,S,Nov 9)*
Abidjan 105 *(19½f,Don,GS,Dec 11)*
Ablazing 98 *(16f,Lud,GS,Apr 5)*
Abolitionist 100 *(24f,Pun,Y,Apr 30)*
Abricot De L'Oasis 109 *(21f,Kem,G,Mar 19)*
Absolute 98 *(17f,Sed,G,Oct 12)*
Absolutlyfantastic 105 *(22f,Str,GF,Jly 19)*
Abundantly 101 *(19f,Fon,S,Nov 6)*
Abyaat 104 *(16½f,Tau,GS,Dec 10)*
Academy General 93 *(17f,Nab,GS,Jun 12)*
Acadian 93 *(19½f,Chp,G,Mar 24)*
Acajou Des Bieffes 91 *(16½f,Tau,HY,Feb 2)*
Acapella Bourgeois 115 *(20f,Fai,Y,Mar 27)*
Acapulco Bay 102 *(16f,Tow,G,May 11)*
According To Harry 92 *(23f,Exe,HY,Dec 17)*
According To Trev 98 *(24f,Chl,S,Dec 11)*
Ace Of Marmalade 98 *(17f,Mar,G,Jun 19)*
Acertain Circus 109 *(20f,Wet,G,May 21)*
Aces Over Eights 102 *(19f,Fon,S,Nov 6)*
Act Four 102 *(16f,Chp,G,Apr 22)*
Act Now 93 *(19f,War,S,May 9)*
Act Of Supremacy 105 *(16f,Fak,GS,Oct 28)*
Actinpieces 108 *(20f,San,HY,Feb 19)*
Adam Du Breteau 94 *(23½f,Utt,G,Sep 9)*
Admiral Blake 102 *(23f,Exe,S,Mar 30)*
Adrakhan 106 *(17f,Mar,G,Oct 17)*
Adrien Du Pont 117 *(16f,Chp,HY,Jan 9)*
Aengus 106 *(22f,Fai,YS,Mar 28)*
Aerlite Supreme 107 *(21½f,Wcn,S,Dec 26)*
Affaire D'Honneur 109 *(16f,Kem,GS,Dec 27)*
Aficionado 108 *(20f,Wor,GF,Jun 6)*
African Gold 100 *(23½f,Asc,GS,Apr 3)*
After Eight Sivola 110 *(19f,Fon,G,Oct 3)*
After Hours 107 *(16f,Hay,HY,Dec 19)*
After Rain 101 *(16f,Leo,S,Jan 17)*
Age Of Discovery 91 *(15f,Wcn,G,May 7)*
Age Of Glory 99 *(16f,Hex,G,May 2)*
Agenor 98 *(17f,Ban,G,Aug 21)*
Agent Louise 100 *(27f,Sed,S,Mar 27)*
Agha Des Mottes 91 *(16f,Wor,G,May 22)*
Agrapart 119 *(17f,Ain,S,Dec 5)*
Ah Littleluck 110 *(20f,Fai,HY,Dec 19)*
Ahhdehken 93 *(24f,Per,S,May 13)*
Aiaam Al Namoos 100 *(25f,Ain,G,May 15)*
Aigle De La See 101 *(24½f,Ayr,S,Apr 15)*
Aimin For Anna 104 *(18f,Fai,SH,Apr 5)*
Air Horse One 102 *(20f,Utt,S,Mar 19)*
Air Of Glory 96 *(16f,Wor,GS,Sep 2)*
Airpur Desbois 102 *(20f,Wor,G,Aug 19)*
Aka Doun 98 *(23f,Exe,GS,Mar 8)*
Akavit 108 *(16f,San,S,Feb 6)*
Akinspirit 97 *(16f,Sth,G,Aug 27)*
Aklan 94 *(20f,Pun,GY,Apr 29)*
Akula 105 *(16f,Hun,GS,Nov 1)*
Al Alfa 110 *(21½f,Nab,G,Sep 18)*
Al Guwair 99 *(19f,Fon,GS,Aug 13)*
Alanjou 90 *(23½f,Asc,GS,Dec 19)*
Albert D'Olivate 111 *(21f,Kem,S,Feb 12)*
Albert Herring 93 *(16f,War,GS,Nov 4)*
Alberta 102 *(15f,Wcn,S,Apr 4)*
Alcala 108 *(21½f,Wcn,S,Dec 26)*
Alchimix 91 *(17f,Crl,S,Mar 10)*
Alco Sivola 100 *(16f,Wor,G,Sep 25)*
Aldeburgh 97 *(16f,Hun,S,Mar 6)*
Alderley Heights 97 *(23f,Exe,G,Apr 21)*
Alfiboy 92 *(16f,Kem,G,May 4)*
Alhamareer 100 *(17f,Mar,HY,Feb 9)*
Aliandy 99 *(16f,Cat,S,Jan 1)*
Alibi De Sivola 111 *(16f,Chp,S,Nov 4)*
Alices Man 91 *(20f,Pun,HY,Feb 17)*
Alizee De Janeiro 106 *(16f,Kel,HY,Dec 6)*
All Force Majeure 101 *(26½f,Nab,G,Jun 12)*
All Hell Let Loose 101 *(20f,Pun,HY,Jan 9)*
All In The Head 104 *(20f,Fai,SH,Jan 20)*
All Kings 102 *(23f,Exe,G,Apr 21)*
All Riled Up 102 *(19f,Tow,GF,Oct 7)*
All Set To Go 110 *(16½f,Tau,G,Mar 21)*
All Summer Long 103 *(20f,Pun,HY,Jan 9)*
All Together 99 *(16f,Fak,G,May 31)*
All You Need 99 *(16f,Leo,HY,Feb 6)*
All Yours 116 *(15f,Wcn,S,Nov 7)*
Alla Svelta 100 *(16f,Wor,G,Jly 15)*
Allbarnone 107 *(24f,Chl,GS,Apr 13)*
Allblak Des Places 115 *(16f,Fai,HY,Dec 19)*
Allchilledout 95 *(21½f,Nab,S,Apr 18)*
Allee Bleue 109 *(16f,Hun,S,Mar 28)*
Allelu Alleluia 98 *(16f,Chp,G,Apr 22)*
Allez Encore 104 *(16f,Lud,S,Dec 2)*
Allnecessaryforce 99 *(19f,Mar,S,Nov 5)*
Allysson Monterg 110 *(15½f,Lei,HY,Dec 3)*
Almaas 92 *(16½f,Str,G,May 17)*
Almagest 104 *(17f,Nab,GS,Jly 27)*
Almost Gemini 106 *(20f,Sed,GS,Feb 25)*
Along Came Theo 93 *(19f,Crl,HY,Dec 13)*
Aloomomo 109 *(19f,Asc,S,Feb 20)*
Alottarain 103 *(16f,Wor,G,Jly 15)*
Alpha Des Obeaux 114 *(20f,Fai,S,Nov 29)*
Alternatif 91 *(23f,Hay,S,May 9)*
Altesse De Guye 111 *(24f,Chl,GS,Apr 13)*
Altior 120 *(16f,Kem,GS,Dec 26)*
Alto Des Mottes 95 *(23f,Hex,HY,May 9)*
Alto Esqua 104 *(20f,Fai,Y,Mar 27)*
Altruism 108 *(16f,Hay,G,Mar 23)*
Always Lion 109 *(21f,Lud,GS,Nov 12)*
Always Managing 101 *(21½f,Nab,GS,Aug 12)*
Always On The Run 99 *(20f,Wor,GF,Jun 6)*
Always Resolute 102 *(16f,Cat,S,Dec 28)*
Always Tipsy 100 *(23f,Kel,GS,Apr 11)*
Alwaystheoptimist 102 *(16½f,Str,G,May 30)*
Alyasan 94 *(16f,Hun,G,Oct 13)*
Alys Rock 98 *(16f,Sth,S,Nov 17)*
Alzammaar 109 *(24f,Lud,GS,Apr 19)*
Amanto 104 *(16½f,Tau,G,Nov 12)*
Amber Flush 102 *(25f,Hun,G,Oct 4)*
Ambion Lane 100 *(18½f,Exe,HY,Feb 14)*
Ambion Wood 104 *(21½f,Wcn,S,Dec 26)*
American 115 *(22f,Asc,GS,Nov 21)*
American Life 99 *(26f,War,HY,Dec 31)*
American Spin 95 *(24f,Sth,G,Jun 9)*
Ami Desbois 102 *(24½f,Don,G,Jan 30)*
Amidon 94 *(19f,Asc,G,Oct 31)*
Amigo 92 *(26½f,Str,G,May 29)*
Amilliontimes 92 *(20f,Per,G,Jun 7)*
Amir Pasha 93 *(17f,Sed,GF,Apr 30)*
Amiral Collonges 108 *(23½f,Asc,GS,Dec 19)*
Amour D'Or 103 *(21½f,Nab,GS,Oct 9)*
Amtired 97 *(17f,Sed,G,May 12)*
Amuse Me 104 *(20f,Crl,G,Oct 22)*
An Capall Mor 96 *(20f,Per,G,Jly 1)*
An Poc Ar Buile 92 *(23f,Hex,G,Jun 21)*
An Tarbh Og 95 *(20f,Utt,G,Sep 20)*
Analifet 111 *(18f,Pun,S,May 2)*
Ancient Sands 100 *(16f,Leo,HY,Dec 27)*
Anda De Grissay 96 *(19½f,Chp,HY,Mar 12)*
Andhaar 92 *(24f,Per,GS,Sep 23)*
Angel Face 91 *(20½f,Plu,GS,Nov 2)*
Anginola 94 *(20f,Wcn,G,May 7)*
Angus Glens 107 *(20f,Ain,G,Jun 12)*
Angus Milan 93 *(16f,Fai,Y,Mar 27)*
Anibale Fly 97 *(16f,Leo,S,Feb 28)*
Ann's Lottery 100 *(21½f,Nab,GF,Apr 30)*
Annaluna 98 *(24f,Lud,G,Oct 7)*
Annaroe 105 *(22f,Str,G,Jun 30)*
Annie Power 116 *(18f,Pun,S,May 2)*
Announcement 102 *(17f,Mar,G,Oct 5)*
Anomaly 105 *(17f,Nab,GS,Aug 12)*
Another Bygones 95 *(20f,Per,GF,Sep 7)*
Another Cobbler 99 *(16f,Tow,G,Nov 5)*
Another Dimension 98 *(24f,Wet,G,May 21)*
Another For Joe 92 *(16f,Kel,G,Oct 24)*
Another Frontier 100 *(21f,Lud,HY,Jan 12)*
Another Journey 106 *(17f,Ban,G,May 1)*
Another Mattie 108 *(24f,Ncs,HY,Mar 19)*
Antartica De Thaix 115 *(20½f,Nby,G,Apr 2)*
Anteros 110 *(24f,Chl,HY,Jan 1)*
Antilope Du Seuil 90 *(20f,Per,G,Jun 7)*
Antiphony 103 *(16f,Sth,G,Mar 21)*
Anton Dolin 102 *(16f,Lud,S,Feb 3)*
Antony 107 *(19f,Fon,G,Oct 3)*
Apache Outlaw 94 *(19f,Tau,S,Mar 3)*
Apachee Prince 93 *(16f,Hex,G,Jun 21)*
Apple Of Our Eye 115 *(21f,Lud,GS,Nov 23)*
Apple's Jade 119 *(17f,Ain,S,Apr 7)*
Applesandpierres 97 *(20f,Wor,GF,Jun 24)*
Appletree Lane 102 *(17f,Crl,G,Mar 26)*
April Dusk 107 *(20f,Utt,S,Nov 14)*
Apterix 111 *(16f,Hay,G,Mar 26)*
Aqalim 115 *(24f,Wet,S,Oct 31)*
Aqua Dude 105 *(20f,Sth,S,Mar 29)*
Arabian Oasis 94 *(17f,Mar,S,Apr 10)*
Aramadyh 101 *(16f,Plu,HY,Feb 15)*
Arbre De Vie 111 *(21f,Chl,G,Mar 16)*
Arcamante 94 *(19½f,Mus,GS,Nov 27)*
Archie Rice 104 *(21½f,Fon,G,Jun 9)*
Archipeligo 97 *(15½f,Mus,GS,Jan 4)*
Archive 102 *(16f,Pun,G,May 16)*
Arctic Court 106 *(24½f,Ayr,S,Apr 15)*
Arctic Dixie 97 *(23½f,Utt,G,Jun 17)*
Arctic Fire 116 *(20f,Fai,S,Nov 29)*
Arctic Gold 100 *(19f,Asc,S,Feb 20)*
Ardamir 106 *(17f,Don,G,Feb 24)*
Ardesia 99 *(17f,Crt,GS,Jly 20)*
Ardmay 104 *(17f,Sed,G,Sep 29)*
Ardview Boy 107 *(16f,Fai,Y,Mar 27)*
Are They Your Own 106 *(16½f,Chl,G,Oct 23)*
Aregra 95 *(24f,Sth,GF,Aug 16)*
Argante 99 *(16f,Nby,HY,Feb 13)*
Argot 105 *(16f,Utt,HY,Jan 30)*
Aristo Du Plessis 111 *(15½f,Mus,GS,Jan 1)*
Arkwrisht 98 *(25f,Ain,S,Apr 8)*
Armchair Theatre 105 *(16f,Lud,GS,Nov 23)*
Arpege D'Alene 111 *(25f,Ain,S,Apr 9)*
Arquebusier 97 *(16f,Tow,HY,Jan 7)*
Arryzona 91 *(16f,Hun,S,Nov 10)*
Art Of Payroll 105 *(16f,Leo,HY,Feb 6)*
Art Of Synergy 108 *(16f,Fai,Y,Mar 27)*
Arthamint 92 *(16f,Utt,S,Oct 30)*
Arthur Burrell 90 *(21½f,Exe,S,Nov 11)*
Arthur Mc Bride 92 *(21f,Tow,G,Nov 5)*
Arthur's Gift 92 *(19½f,Chp,G,Sep 30)*
Arthur's Queen 97 *(17f,Nab,GS,Jly 27)*
Arthurs Secret 104 *(16f,Wet,GS,Mar 22)*
Artifice Sivola 99 *(16f,Kem,G,Apr 19)*
Arty Campbell 103 *(17f,Nab,GS,Aug 22)*
Arzal 105 *(16f,Hay,GS,May 9)*
Ascendant 101 *(25f,Hun,GS,Jan 29)*
Ascot De Bruyere 90 *(16f,Utt,S,Mar 19)*
Ascotdeux Nellerie 104 *(16f,Lud,G,Mar 24)*
Ash Park 105 *(17f,Crl,S,Mar 10)*
Ashbrittle 98 *(21f,War,S,May 9)*
Ashes Of Love 102 *(22f,Pun,HY,Feb 17)*
Ashoka 93 *(15½f,Mus,S,Feb 7)*
Ashtown 98 *(20f,Utt,G,Sep 9)*
Ask Vic 100 *(20f,Pun,S,May 2)*
Asknotwhat 104 *(16f,Plu,G,May 10)*
Astaroland 103 *(17f,Nab,G,Jly 19)*
Asthuria 107 *(20f,Fai,Y,Mar 27)*
Aston Cantlow 105 *(16f,San,HY,Feb 19)*
Astre De La Cour 99 *(16f,Pun,GY,Apr 28)*
Astrowolf 103 *(19f,Fon,G,May 1)*
Astrum 103 *(16f,Hex,HY,May 9)*
At First Light 113 *(20½f,Nby,G,Apr 2)*
At Fishers Cross 112 *(25f,Ain,S,Apr 9)*
At The Doubble 107 *(20f,Crl,G,Nov 1)*
At The Top 99 *(16f,Sth,S,Dec 1)*
Athou Du Nord 106 *(16f,Utt,S,Nov 14)*
Atirelarigo 104 *(21f,Kem,S,Feb 12)*
Atlanta Ablaze 97 *(21f,Kem,G,Apr 19)*
Atlantic Gold 108 *(21f,War,G,Oct 1)*
Attention Please 99 *(21f,Wet,S,Oct 30)*
Attention Seaker 106 *(16f,Hex,GS,Oct 10)*
Attribution 109 *(16f,Pun,HY,Jan 9)*
Auckland De Re 106 *(21½f,Wcn,HY,Nov 19)*
Auenwirbel 99 *(17f,Chl,S,Dec 11)*
Aughcarra 97 *(16½f,Str,G,Aug 20)*
Auld Fyffee 97 *(16f,Utt,S,Jly 26)*
Aurillac 103 *(16f,Chp,HY,Feb 5)*
Aurore D'Estruval 102 *(20f,Chl,GS,Mar 15)*
Australia Day 108 *(19f,Mar,G,Aug 2)*
Authorative 101 *(19f,Str,G,Sep 14)*
Authorized Too 111 *(16f,Plu,S,Nov 16)*
Auto Mac 102 *(16f,Utt,GF,Jly 7)*
Automated 111 *(16½f,Ain,S,Apr 9)*
Aux Ptits Soins 103 *(24f,Chl,G,Mar 17)*
Avant Tout 111 *(21f,Chl,G,Mar 16)*
Avel Vor 96 *(17f,Nab,GS,Jly 3)*
Aviador 101 *(19f,Tow,S,Feb 17)*
Aviator 110 *(23f,Mar,G,Jly 5)*
Avidity 112 *(20f,Wet,G,May 21)*
Avispa 107 *(20½f,Nby,G,Apr 2)*
Away For Slates 111 *(19½f,Mus,GS,Jan 1)*
Awaywiththegreys 98 *(23½f,Chp,HY,Jan 9)*
Awesome Rosie 104 *(15f,Wcn,S,Dec 26)*
Ayla's Emperor 105 *(17f,Nab,S,Apr 18)*
Aza Run 90 *(15½f,Lei,HY,Jan 26)*
Azure Glamour 103 *(17f,Sed,S,Mar 15)*
Azzuri 100 *(15½f,Mus,GS,Feb 7)*

Babbling Stream 105 *(16f,Fai,YS,Mar 28)*
Baby Bach 109 *(19f,Crl,G,Mar 26)*
Baby Jake 107 *(16f,Wor,S,Aug 23)*
Baby King 107 *(16f,Hay,S,Nov 21)*
Baby Ticker 92 *(19f,Crl,HY,Feb 22)*
Bacchanel 98 *(21f,War,S,Apr 4)*
Bachasson 113 *(16f,Fai,S,Nov 29)*
Back By Midnight 102 *(16f,Utt,G,Oct 15)*
Baden 99 *(17f,Chl,S,Dec 11)*
Badged 98 *(20f,Per,S,May 13)*
Badger Wood 92 *(15f,Wcn,S,Dec 26)*
Bagging Turf 103 *(19f,Tow,S,Feb 4)*
Baily Cloud 107 *(16f,Leo,HY,Dec 27)*
Bako De La Saulaie 93 *(18f,Kel,GS,Apr 11)*
Balko Des Flos 106 *(25f,Ain,S,Apr 8)*
Ball D'Arc 112 *(16½f,Ain,S,Apr 8)*
Ballagh 109 *(16f,San,S,Dec 5)*
Ballinalacken 96 *(21f,Lud,GS,Nov 23)*
Ballinure 99 *(16f,Hun,G,Oct 13)*
Ballinvegga 103 *(19f,Crl,G,Mar 26)*
Ballochmyle 96 *(25f,Hun,GS,Nov 1)*
Bally Legend 101 *(26f,Fon,G,Oct 2)*
Ballyarthur 103 *(19½f,Hun,G,Oct 13)*
Ballybane 105 *(19½f,Chp,HY,Jan 9)*
Ballybrowney Ella 104 *(22f,Pun,HY,Feb 17)*
Ballycamp 106 *(16f,Utt,G,May 2)*
Ballycash 91 *(17f,Ban,S,Mar 31)*
Ballycross 109 *(25f,Ain,S,Apr 9)*
Ballydine 116 *(22f,Str,S,Oct 29)*
Ballyglasheen 110 *(16f,Hay,GS,May 9)*
Ballyheigue Bay 101 *(23½f,Asc,GS,Apr 3)*
Ballyhenry 105 *(21f,Kem,S,Feb 12)*
Ballykan 107 *(24f,Wet,G,May 28)*
Ballyoisin 106 *(16f,Pun,G,May 16)*
Ballyoptic 112 *(20f,Utt,S,Mar 19)*
Ballypoint 106 *(19f,War,S,Feb 26)*
Ballyrath 97 *(20f,Utt,G,Sep 20)*
Ballyrock 93 *(23½f,Chp,HY,Jan 9)*
Ballythomas 101 *(24f,Sth,G,May 20)*
Ballyvoque 95 *(20f,Hex,G,Jun 21)*
Ballywilliam 107 *(19½f,Chp,S,Nov 4)*
Balmusette 105 *(19½f,Don,GS,Dec 11)*
Baltic Storm 108 *(16f,Lud,GS,Apr 5)*
Band Of Thunder 98 *(24f,Sth,G,May 20)*
Bandon Roc 93 *(21f,War,S,Dec 10)*
Bangkok Pete 101 *(23½f,Asc,S,Feb 20)*
Bantam 113 *(17f,Chl,G,Mar 17)*
Banyu 109 *(16½f,Tau,G,Mar 21)*
Baoulet Delaroque 112 *(21f,Chl,G,Mar 16)*
Bar A Mine 94 *(21f,Lud,S,Dec 2)*
Baraboy 102 *(17f,Sed,S,May 5)*
Baradari 113 *(23f,Hay,S,Nov 21)*

Barafundle 102 *(25f,Crl,HY,Dec 13)*
Baraka De Thaix 107 *(16f,Ffo,HY,Dec 14)*
Baratineur 107 *(16f,Plu,S,Feb 29)*
Baraymi 90 *(16f,Wet,HY,Jan 26)*
Baraza 98 *(17f,Ban,S,Nov 11)*
Bare Necessities 105 *(16f,Hun,GS,Aug 31)*
Barenice 107 *(20f,Wet,HY,Jan 16)*
Barista 103 *(16f,Utt,HY,Dec 18)*
Barizan 111 *(16f,Hay,GS,May 9)*
Barnacle Bill 95 *(16f,Fai,HY,Feb 20)*
Barnahash Rose 99 *(16f,Leo,S,Jan 17)*
Barney Dwan 108 *(17f,Sed,HY,Dec 26)*
Barneys Honour 108 *(16f,Fak,G,May 5)*
Baron Alco 110 *(21f,Chl,G,Mar 16)*
Baron Du Plessis 91 *(19f,Tau,G,Mar 21)*
Barra Rotha 94 *(19f,Mar,S,Nov 5)*
Barranco Valley 111 *(18½f,Nab,GS,Oct 9)*
Barters Hill 115 *(19½f,Hun,GS,Nov 1)*
Barton Antix 108 *(21½f,Wcn,GF,Oct 16)*
Barton Rose 101 *(19f,Str,GS,Oct 29)*
Bassarabad 104 *(19½f,Chp,HY,Nov 18)*
Batavir 108 *(24f,Chl,GS,Apr 13)*
Baths Well 95 *(20f,Utt,G,Jly 24)*
Battle Dust 117 *(24f,Sth,S,Nov 17)*
Battle Of Shiloh 101 *(21f,Lud,HY,Jan 12)*
Battlecat 105 *(16f,Ffo,G,May 23)*
Battling Boru 95 *(16f,Pun,Y,Apr 30)*
Bay Fortuna 91 *(20f,Sth,G,May 12)*
Bay Sly 98 *(16f,Lud,S,Feb 3)*
Bayley's Dream 105 *(21f,War,G,Oct 1)*
Baysbrown 96 *(17f,Sed,G,Oct 12)*
Baywing 109 *(20f,Crl,HY,Nov 9)*
Be Bop Boru 106 *(24f,Ffo,G,Jun 4)*
Be My Witness 99 *(20f,Utt,G,Jun 17)*
Be Seeing You 98 *(20f,Per,GS,Sep 24)*
Be The Hero 105 *(16f,Fai,SH,Apr 5)*
Beallandendall 108 *(16f,Lud,GS,Apr 5)*
Bear's Affair 106 *(20f,Chl,GS,Apr 13)*
Beat The Tide 103 *(20f,Wor,G,Aug 19)*
Beatabout The Bush 95 *(16f,Wet,S,Oct 30)*
Beatu 103 *(16f,Cat,GS,Mar 1)*
Beau Bay 104 *(17f,Ban,S,Mar 31)*
Beau Lake 99 *(16f,Hay,S,Nov 21)*
Beau Mome 96 *(16f,Fai,Y,Mar 27)*
Beau Phil 92 *(18½f,Nab,GS,Mar 26)*
Beauboreen 100 *(21f,War,S,Mar 13)*
Beaumont's Party 101 *(17f,Sed,S,Nov 24)*
Beautiful Gem 103 *(17f,Ain,S,Dec 5)*
Becauseshesaidso 103 *(20f,Crl,G,Nov 1)*
Beckwith Star 92 *(20f,Fai,S,Nov 29)*
Bedale 96 *(18f,Fon,GS,Aug 13)*
Bedouin Bay 94 *(22f,Str,GF,Jly 19)*
Beechroad Ally 99 *(16f,Kel,G,Oct 24)*
Beer Goggles 104 *(27f,Sed,S,Mar 6)*
Beggars Cross 107 *(21f,War,S,Apr 4)*
Behind The Wire 103 *(20f,Sth,G,Mar 21)*
Behind Time 95 *(19f,Tau,HY,Jan 23)*
Being Global 104 *(21f,Hun,GS,Dec 6)*
Bekkensfirth 104 *(16f,Wor,G,Oct 8)*
Bel Ami Rich 90 *(24f,Tau,GS,Dec 10)*
Belami Des Pictons 92 *(16f,War,S,Mar 13)*
Belcanto 101 *(16f,Ffo,G,Oct 17)*
Bell Weir 101 *(20f,Per,G,Apr 22)*
Bella 108 *(16f,Lud,S,Dec 2)*
Belle Fortune 108 *(20f,Fai,SH,Jan 20)*
Bello Conti 111 *(21f,Chl,G,Mar 16)*
Bellow Mome 111 *(16f,Pun,HY,Feb 17)*
Bells 'N' Banjos 92 *(21½f,Fon,S,Nov 25)*
Bells Of Ailsworth 105 *(21½f,Nab,GS,Jly 3)*
Bellshill 111 *(25f,Ain,S,Apr 8)*
Ben Cee Pee M 104 *(20f,Sth,G,Oct 22)*
Ben Dundee 101 *(16f,Leo,HY,Dec 27)*
Benarty Hill 99 *(24f,Per,G,Apr 20)*
Benbecula 97 *(18f,Fon,G,May 1)*
Bendomingo 93 *(16f,War,G,Mar 23)*
Beneficial Joe 94 *(19½f,Don,GS,Dec 29)*
Benefits Well 95 *(20f,Utt,G,Jly 24)*
Benissimo 106 *(21f,War,GS,May 20)*
Bennachie 104 *(19f,War,GS,May 4)*
Benny's Secret 93 *(18f,Kel,GS,Mar 21)*
Bennys King 102 *(16f,Chp,HY,Mar 12)*
Bentelimar 105 *(16f,Leo,S,Jan 17)*
Bentons Lad 92 *(20f,Sth,G,Oct 22)*
Benzanno 96 *(16f,War,GS,May 4)*
Benzel 98 *(16½f,Tau,S,Mar 14)*
Berea Boru 106 *(24f,Ffo,GF,Jun 18)*
Berea Venture 101 *(20f,Utt,G,May 16)*
Berkshire Downs 106 *(17f,Crl,HY,Dec 13)*
Berland 106 *(16f,Asc,GS,Apr 3)*
Bernisdale 92 *(16f,Fak,GS,Feb 19)*
Berry De Carjac 100 *(17f,Exe,G,Apr 21)*
Bertalus 106 *(24½f,Ayr,HY,Feb 16)*
Bertie Moon 104 *(16½f,Ncs,HY,Mar 8)*
Bertielicious 92 *(17f,Sed,HY,Dec 4)*
Bescot Springs 103 *(23f,Kel,HY,Dec 29)*
Bestwork 99 *(16f,Chp,G,Apr 22)*
Betsy Boo Boo 90 *(19f,Fon,S,Nov 15)*
Better Days 92 *(16f,San,HY,Feb 19)*
Beware The Bear 109 *(20f,Utt,GS,Oct 30)*
Beyondtemptation 107 *(20f,Hex,HY,Apr 18)*
Bibi D'Eole 98 *(17f,Don,S,Mar 4)*
Bidourey 101 *(16½f,Chl,GS,Nov 15)*
Big Chief Benny 110 *(19½f,Don,GS,Jan 29)*
Big Generator 108 *(20f,Sth,GS,Sep 2)*
Big McIntosh 106 *(15½f,Mus,G,Nov 6)*
Big Night Out 91 *(16f,Wor,G,Jun 21)*
Big Water 100 *(20f,Crl,GS,Nov 1)*
Bigbadjohn 110 *(20½f,Nby,GS,Apr 1)*
Bigindie 100 *(16f,Utt,G,Sep 20)*
Bigirononhiship 100 *(21f,Wet,HY,Feb 6)*
Bigmartre 109 *(19f,Fon,S,Nov 25)*
Bigpipenotobacee 98 *(20f,Sth,S,Mar 29)*
Bilbrook Blaze 101 *(19f,Asc,G,Oct 31)*
Billy Billy 95 *(18f,Fai,HY,Jan 10)*
Billy Congo 102 *(26f,Fon,G,May 24)*
Billy Dutton 107 *(23f,Hay,G,Mar 26)*
Billy My Boy 101 *(17f,Nab,GS,Jun 12)*
Billy No Name 108 *(20½f,Plu,HY,Feb 15)*
Billy's Hope 101 *(20f,Fai,Y,Mar 27)*
Bim Bam Boum 101 *(19f,Tau,HY,Dec 30)*
Bindon Mill 95 *(18½f,Exe,S,Feb 26)*
Birch Hill 91 *(24½f,Ayr,S,Apr 15)*
Biretta 104 *(16f,Tow,G,Nov 5)*
Bishop Wulstan 105 *(16f,Ffo,HY,Dec 14)*
Bishops Court 101 *(21½f,Wcn,GS,Apr 17)*
Bishopslough 105 *(16f,Leo,S,Jan 17)*
Bitofapuzzle 96 *(20f,Chl,GS,Mar 15)*
Bivouac 94 *(16f,Chp,G,Oct 10)*
Black Corton 98 *(17f,Exe,G,Apr 21)*
Black Hawk 91 *(16f,Lud,GS,Nov 23)*
Black Iceman 90 *(16f,Wor,GF,Jun 11)*
Black Jack Rover 106 *(24f,Wet,G,May 28)*
Black Kettle 92 *(21f,War,G,Oct 1)*
Black Lily 96 *(23½f,Fak,S,Nov 17)*
Black Narcissus 94 *(20½f,Lei,HY,Jan 26)*
Black Sam The Man 97 *(20f,Wor,G,Sep 25)*
Black Spot On 94 *(22f,Fai,YS,Mar 28)*
Black Zero 110 *(22f,Fai,YS,Mar 28)*
Blackadder 95 *(16f,Chp,S,Apr 9)*
Blackfire 91 *(17f,Exe,G,Apr 21)*
Blackwater King 103 *(20f,Utt,S,Nov 22)*
Blackwell Synergy 104 *(23½f,Utt,S,Jly 26)*
Bladoun 104 *(17f,Exe,GS,Mar 8)*
Blair Perrone 98 *(16f,Pun,GY,Apr 28)*
Blake Dean 99 *(25½f,Cat,S,Dec 15)*
Blandfords Gunner 91 *(18½f,Nab,GF,Apr 30)*
Blast Martha 93 *(21f,Sed,GF,Apr 30)*
Blast Of Koeman 102 *(16f,Pun,HY,Jan 9)*
Blayney Queen 95 *(15½f,Mus,G,Nov 6)*
Blazer 112 *(21f,Chl,G,Mar 16)*
Blazing West 103 *(16f,Fai,HY,Dec 19)*
Bletchley Castle 101 *(16f,Utt,G,Jun 17)*
Bleu Et Noir 103 *(17f,Mar,G,Oct 17)*
Bleu Et Rouge 114 *(16½f,Ain,S,Apr 8)*
Bloody Mary 114 *(17f,Chl,G,Mar 17)*
Blue April 106 *(16f,Fak,GS,Oct 28)*
Blue Atlantic 105 *(21½f,Wcn,G,Apr 4)*
Blue Bear 102 *(20½f,Plu,G,May 10)*
Blue Buttons 100 *(20f,Utt,S,Mar 19)*
Blue Cannon 95 *(24f,Per,G,Sep 8)*
Blue Cove 99 *(27f,Sed,S,Feb 9)*
Blue Hell 91 *(17f,Chl,G,Mar 18)*
Blue Prairie 95 *(19½f,Hun,GS,Jan 29)*
Blue Rambler 108 *(19½f,Mus,S,Feb 8)*
Blue Top 96 *(16f,Chp,S,Nov 4)*
Boa Island 99 *(23f,Exe,G,Apr 21)*
Board Of Trade 113 *(20½f,Nby,S,Nov 27)*
Bob Lewis 102 *(23f,Wor,G,Aug 19)*
Bob's Legend 99 *(16f,Hex,G,Jun 21)*
Bobble Emerald 101 *(21f,Lud,GS,Apr 19)*
Bobby Dove 98 *(16f,Utt,G,Oct 4)*
Bobcatbilly 94 *(21f,Kem,G,May 4)*
Bobonyx 96 *(20f,Wor,G,Jly 15)*
Bobowen 90 *(16f,Hex,G,May 2)*
Bobs Lady Tamure 107 *(16½f,Ncs,GS,Feb 27)*
Bobs Worth 113 *(20f,Ain,S,Nov 7)*
Bog War 100 *(16f,Pun,Y,Apr 30)*
Bogoss Du Perret 100 *(17f,Nab,G,May 27)*
Bohemian Rhapsody 106 *(20f,Sth,G,May 12)*
Boher Lad 96 *(19½f,Hun,GS,Aug 31)*
Boherna Lady 107 *(19f,Tow,GF,Oct 7)*
Boite 107 *(16½f,Ain,S,Apr 9)*
Bold Bid 98 *(16f,Leo,HY,Dec 27)*
Bold Conquest 106 *(24f,Utt,G,May 2)*
Bold Duke 109 *(16f,Chp,S,Feb 27)*
Bold Henmie 96 *(16f,Hun,G,Oct 13)*
Bold Runner 104 *(21½f,Wcn,GS,Apr 17)*
Bold Sir Brian 93 *(23f,Hay,S,Nov 21)*
Boldbob 99 *(16f,Cat,S,Feb 15)*
Bolister 96 *(16f,Plu,HY,Jan 18)*
Bollin Ace 106 *(20f,Wet,GS,Oct 30)*
Bollin Beauty 103 *(20f,Sth,G,Aug 27)*
Bolton Blue 92 *(20f,Per,G,Apr 22)*
Bon Enfant 102 *(19f,Fon,S,Nov 6)*
Bondi Mist 92 *(15f,Wcn,GF,May 12)*
Bonne Question 104 *(16f,Hun,GS,Feb 25)*
Bonnet's Vino 104 *(23½f,Fak,GS,Dec 20)*
Bonobo 104 *(20½f,Nby,S,Mar 5)*
Bonvilston Boy 96 *(16f,Lud,S,Dec 16)*
Boolavard King 103 *(16f,Sth,S,Dec 1)*
Bop Along 98 *(27f,Sed,GS,Apr 19)*
Borak 101 *(16f,Utt,G,Oct 15)*
Border Breaker 97 *(23f,Mar,G,Jun 5)*
Bored Or Bad 96 *(20f,Sth,G,Mar 21)*
Boris Boru 99 *(24f,Per,G,Apr 20)*
Born Survivor 110 *(21f,War,HY,Jan 16)*
Born To Benefit 95 *(16f,Wor,GS,May 7)*
Boruma 108 *(19½f,Don,GS,Dec 11)*
Boss Des Mottes 107 *(16f,Chp,G,Oct 10)*
Bostin 91 *(21f,Kem,G,May 13)*
Boston Blue 94 *(20½f,Lei,HY,Dec 3)*
Boston De La Roche 104 *(16f,Hay,G,Mar 23)*
Bouggietopieces 91 *(22f,Crt,GS,Aug 29)*
Bound Hill 98 *(18½f,Exe,HY,Feb 14)*
Bountiful Sin 97 *(16f,Plu,S,Nov 16)*
Bourdello 90 *(18½f,Exe,S,Nov 11)*
Bourne 96 *(25f,Hun,G,Oct 13)*
Bouvreuil 100 *(16½f,Chl,GS,Nov 15)*
Bowdler's Magic 105 *(20f,Fak,GS,Oct 28)*
Bowie 106 *(19f,Mar,G,Jun 5)*
Box Office 106 *(20f,Ain,G,Oct 25)*
Braavos 109 *(17f,Ain,S,Dec 5)*
Bracing 101 *(24½f,Ayr,G,Oct 26)*
Brain Power 107 *(15½f,Mus,GS,Feb 7)*
Braize 103 *(16f,Pun,HY,Feb 17)*
Bramble Brook 99 *(16f,Lud,S,Dec 16)*
Brand Ambassador 99 *(22f,Fai,YS,Mar 28)*
Brass Monkey 101 *(20f,Sth,G,Jun 2)*
Brave Deed 106 *(18½f,Exe,S,Nov 3)*
Brave Helios 99 *(25f,Ain,G,Jun 12)*
Brave Jaq 107 *(16f,Plu,S,Nov 16)*
Brave Richard 100 *(16f,San,S,Dec 5)*
Brave Spartacus 107 *(17f,Crt,G,Jun 28)*
Bravo Riquet 90 *(19f,Tow,S,Mar 17)*
Breaking Bits 103 *(16f,Utt,G,Sep 20)*
Breath Of Blighty 105 *(16f,Hun,GS,Jan 29)*
Briac 96 *(21f,Kem,S,Feb 12)*
Brian Boranha 101 *(17f,Mar,S,Mar 13)*
Bridal Suite 97 *(25f,Hun,S,Dec 26)*
Briery Belle 106 *(20f,Chl,G,Apr 14)*
Briery Queen 116 *(20½f,Nby,G,Apr 2)*
Brigadier Miller 101 *(16f,Wet,S,Oct 30)*
Brigadoon 101 *(16f,Hun,GS,Aug 31)*
Bright Light 92 *(20f,Wcn,G,May 7)*
Bright Prospect 107 *(19½f,Mus,GS,Jan 1)*
Brin D'Avoine 92 *(15f,Wcn,HY,Feb 4)*
Brinestine 97 *(17f,Mar,G,May 8)*
Bringerofthedawn 104 *(18f,Fai,SH,Apr 5)*
Brise Vendeenne 106 *(21½f,Wcn,HY,Feb 4)*
Britanio Bello 100 *(16f,Lud,S,Feb 3)*
Broad Spectrum 98 *(20½f,Ncs,S,Apr 8)*
Brod Na Heireann 107 *(22f,Str,S,Oct 29)*
Bronco Billy 100 *(19f,Crl,HY,Dec 13)*
Brook 92 *(21½f,Wcn,S,Jan 21)*
Brother Bennett 95 *(16½f,Tau,G,Apr 20)*
Brother Tedd 111 *(21f,Kem,G,Nov 2)*
Brotherly Company 108 *(16½f,Tau,G,Mar 21)*
Broughton 114 *(16f,Chp,G,Oct 11)*
Broughtons Bandit 103 *(24f,Per,G,Jly 2)*
Brown Bear 97 *(16f,Chp,S,Nov 4)*
Broxbourne 103 *(24f,Chl,G,Mar 17)*
Bruce Almighty 105 *(21f,Wet,S,Oct 30)*
Brunello 97 *(19f,Crl,GS,May 7)*
Bryden Boy 107 *(19½f,Ban,HY,Mar 2)*
Buche De Noel 99 *(21f,Kem,G,Apr 19)*
Buck Magic 98 *(21f,Kem,G,May 4)*
Buckboru 97 *(18½f,Exe,S,Nov 3)*
Buckled 104 *(19½f,Don,GS,Dec 11)*
Buckontupence 94 *(23f,Mar,GS,Apr 21)*
Buckwheat 108 *(16½f,Ain,G,Jun 12)*
Buiseness Sivola 104 *(16f,Pun,S,May 2)*
Bulletproof 107 *(17f,Exe,G,Oct 8)*
Bumble Bay 99 *(17f,Nab,G,Sep 28)*
Bun Doran 92 *(16f,Nby,S,Nov 27)*
Bunclody 98 *(16f,Tow,GF,Apr 30)*
Burgas 104 *(20f,Fai,SH,Jan 20)*
Burgess Dream 92 *(21½f,Fon,S,Nov 15)*
Burgundy Betty 96 *(25f,Hun,GS,Nov 1)*
Burnt Sienna 99 *(20f,Hex,G,May 26)*
Bus Named Desire 97 *(20f,Wor,G,Jly 15)*
Businessmoney Judi 100 *(20f,Utt,G,Jun 17)*
Buster Dan Dan 96 *(24f,Leo,HY,Dec 28)*
Busy Baro 95 *(16f,Tow,S,Dec 17)*
Butlergrove King 94 *(23f,Wor,G,Jly 15)*
Buttercup 98 *(21f,War,S,Jan 28)*
Buveur D'Air 119 *(16½f,Ain,S,Apr 8)*
Buy Back Bob 103 *(16f,Hun,GF,May 26)*
Buy Me Out 96 *(17f,Nab,GS,Aug 12)*
Byerley Beag 94 *(24f,Pun,G,May 16)*
Byron Blue 107 *(24f,Sth,GF,Aug 16)*
Byron Flyer 101 *(17f,Nab,S,Apr 5)*

Cab On Times 93 *(20f,Sth,G,Mar 21)*
Cabin Fever 91 *(16½f,Str,G,Aug 20)*
Cacheofgold 91 *(16f,Pun,Y,Apr 30)*
Cactus Valley 105 *(16f,Wet,S,Apr 17)*
Cadgers Hole 101 *(20f,Wet,GS,Mar 22)*
Cadore 102 *(16f,Kel,GS,May 6)*
Caged Lightning 102 *(17f,Sed,GS,Feb 25)*
Cahill 95 *(16f,Hun,G,Oct 4)*
Cahirconree 93 *(16f,Fai,HY,Jan 30)*
Cailleach Annie 97 *(23f,Exe,G,Mar 22)*
Caitys Joy 107 *(19f,Tow,S,Feb 4)*
Caius Marcius 103 *(16½f,Ncs,HY,Mar 8)*
Calculated Risk 105 *(16f,Ffo,HY,Feb 21)*
Caledon Craic 104 *(24f,Per,G,Jly 1)*
Caledonia 109 *(24½f,Ayr,S,Apr 15)*
Calibre Style 99 *(20f,Fai,SH,Jan 20)*
Calin Du Brizais 100 *(20f,Fak,GS,Oct 28)*
Calivigny 105 *(24½f,Ayr,S,Nov 11)*
Call It Magic 91 *(20f,Leo,HY,Dec 29)*
Call It On 106 *(24f,Wet,S,Nov 14)*
Call Me Kate 101 *(23f,Mar,G,Aug 15)*
Call Me Pj 91 *(16f,Pun,Y,Apr 30)*
Call The Cops 106 *(21f,Chl,G,Mar 16)*
Call To Order 99 *(17f,Don,GS,Dec 11)*
Calton Entry 97 *(16f,Kel,GF,Oct 4)*
Camakasi 90 *(16½f,Tau,G,Mar 21)*
Camborne 101 *(17f,Hun,S,Nov 10)*
Camillas Wish 99 *(24½f,Ayr,HY,Jan 2)*
Camlann 103 *(16f,Leo,HY,Dec 28)*
Campeador 109 *(16f,Leo,HY,Dec 26)*
Camping Ground 108 *(20f,Chl,HY,Jan 1)*
Canadian Diamond 107 *(16½f,Tau,GS,Dec 10)*
Canarbino Girl 100 *(19f,Tow,GF,Oct 7)*
Candelita 93 *(16f,Lud,G,May 10)*
Candlestick 106 *(18f,Fai,SH,Apr 5)*
Canicallyouback 102 *(16f,Wor,G,Jly 28)*
Cannon Fodder 112 *(23½f,Asc,S,Jan 23)*
Canny Tom 94 *(20f,Fai,SH,Apr 5)*
Cape Caster 106 *(17f,Chl,S,Dec 11)*
Cappielow Park 101 *(17f,Chl,S,Dec 11)*
Cappuccino Man 91 *(16f,Pun,HY,Feb 17)*
Captain Barbossa 95 *(16f,Leo,HY,Dec 27)*
Captain Brown 107 *(17f,Crt,GS,Aug 29)*
Captain Chaos 107 *(16f,Utt,S,Nov 14)*
Captain Conan 100 *(16f,Hay,HY,Jan 23)*
Captain Flash 99 *(20f,Utt,HY,Dec 31)*
Captain McGinley 94 *(20½f,Plu,HY,Jan 3)*
Captain Mowbray 91 *(16f,Cat,GS,Mar 1)*
Captain Redbeard 110 *(19f,Crl,S,Mar 10)*
Captain Sharpe 90 *(16½f,Ncs,HY,Dec 10)*
Captain Swift 95 *(17f,Mar,G,Jun 5)*
Captainofindustry 105 *(24f,Tau,GS,Nov 26)*
Captainofthefleet 108 *(24f,Pun,Y,Apr 30)*
Caraline 101 *(17f,Sed,HY,Dec 4)*
Card Game 106 *(17f,Sed,GS,Jan 31)*
Cardinal Palace 108 *(17f,Ain,G,Jun 12)*
Cardinal Walter 110 *(15½f,Mus,S,Feb 7)*
Carhue 94 *(21½f,Nab,GF,Apr 30)*
Carhue Princess 100 *(19f,Tow,GF,Oct 7)*
Carinena 104 *(20f,Per,G,Apr 20)*
Carlo Rocks 100 *(24f,Sth,HY,Mar 7)*
Carn Rock 101 *(25f,Ain,G,Oct 25)*
Carnaross 101 *(17f,Sed,GF,Sep 3)*
Carole Rose 94 *(24f,Pun,G,May 16)*
Carqalin 94 *(17f,Exe,GS,Apr 12)*
Carre Noir 103 *(21½f,Nab,S,Apr 8)*
Carrigeen Lantana 97 *(16f,Utt,G,Jun 11)*
Carry On Sydney 97 *(21½f,Nab,S,Apr 18)*
Carthage 99 *(16f,Cat,GS,Mar 1)*
Cash Injection 101 *(23f,Exe,G,May 5)*
Cashanova 99 *(16f,Kem,GS,Dec 26)*
Cashelard Lady 115 *(18f,Fai,HY,Jan 30)*
Casimir Road 91 *(16f,Pun,Y,Apr 30)*
Casper King 106 *(16f,Lud,S,Dec 16)*
Cassells Rock 106 *(20f,Pun,GY,Apr 29)*
Cassie 100 *(16f,Lud,GS,Nov 23)*
Castle Conflict 104 *(24f,Ffo,G,Jun 4)*
Castlemorris King 91 *(17f,Chl,G,Apr 13)*
Casual Approach 101 *(21f,Chl,G,Oct 23)*
Catcharose 90 *(15f,Wcn,G,May 12)*
Catcher On The Go 97 *(17f,Nab,GS,Aug 12)*
Catcheragain 93 *(22f,Pun,HY,Feb 17)*
Catchin Time 103 *(16f,Utt,HY,Dec 31)*
Catchthemoonlight 97 *(16f,Hex,G,May 26)*
Catherines Well 105 *(19½f,Don,GS,Dec 29)*
Catkin Copse 93 *(21½f,Fon,G,Jun 3)*
Ceann Sibheal 105 *(26f,War,G,Mar 23)*
Cearys 90 *(16f,Wor,GF,Sep 8)*
Celestial Magic 103 *(16f,Chp,S,Apr 9)*
Celestino 91 *(15½f,Mus,S,Feb 8)*
Celldomfed 108 *(16f,Chp,G,Apr 22)*
Celtic Agent 104 *(16f,Wet,S,Apr 17)*
Celtic Artisan 100 *(16f,Hun,GF,May 26)*
Celtic Flames 93 *(20f,Hex,GS,Oct 10)*
Celtic Monarch 92 *(16f,Hex,G,Jun 6)*
Central Flame 108 *(26f,Kel,GS,Apr 2)*
Centurius 100 *(16f,San,HY,Feb 19)*
Cerca Trova 101 *(16f,Fai,SH,Jan 20)*
Cest Notre Gris 99 *(16f,Pun,S,Nov 15)*
Ch'Tibello 105 *(16f,Asc,G,Oct 31)*
Chakisto 92 *(17f,Ban,S,Mar 16)*
Chalk It Down 113 *(20f,Wet,G,May 21)*
Chamonix 90 *(16f,Pun,G,May 16)*
Champagne At Tara 111 *(20f,Ain,S,Apr 8)*
Champagne Chaser 93 *(21f,Hun,S,Mar 6)*
Champagne Express 94 *(21f,Chl,GS,Nov 14)*
Champagne George 102 *(19f,Fon,GS,Apr 1)*
Champagne James 103 *(23f,Hay,HY,Feb 20)*
Champagne Present 105 *(26f,Fon,G,Oct 2)*
Champagne Ransom 104 *(16f,Wor,GS,Sep 2)*
Champayne Ginger 93 *(20f,Pun,HY,Feb 17)*
Champers On Ice 115 *(20½f,Nby,S,Nov 27)*
Champion Court 101 *(20f,Wor,G,Jun 21)*
Champoleon 100 *(24f,Pun,G,May 16)*
Changeofluck 97 *(26f,War,G,Sep 22)*
Changing The Guard 106 *(16f,Kel,GF,Sep 16)*
Chankillo 101 *(17f,Nab,G,May 27)*
Chantara Rose 105 *(21f,War,G,Mar 23)*
Charbel 113 *(15½f,Mus,GS,Feb 7)*
Charlie Cook 108 *(19½f,Don,G,Jan 30)*
Charlie Wingnut 103 *(20f,Sed,GS,Feb 25)*
Charlie's Oscar 98 *(20f,Fak,G,Oct 16)*
Charmix 106 *(19f,Nby,S,Dec 16)*
Chartbreaker 108 *(21f,Kem,G,Apr 19)*
Chase End Charlie 97 *(19½f,Don,S,Jan 8)*
Chasma 101 *(20f,Sed,S,Feb 9)*
Chasse En Mer 102 *(20f,Hex,G,May 26)*

Chaz Michaels 90 (15½f,Mus,GS,Jan 4)
Chebsey Beau 105 (17f,Crt,GS,Aug 29)
Chef D'Oeuvre 109 (21½f,Fon,HY,Feb 18)
Cheltenian 111 (17f,Chl,HY,Jan 30)
Cherry Bomb 95 (19f,Crl,HY,Feb 10)
Cherry Tiger 91 (16f,Hun,GF,May 26)
Cheshire Prince 91 (16f,Wet,G,May 28)
Chic Name 115 (16f,Chp,HY,Jan 9)
Chic Theatre 105 (17f,Don,G,Feb 24)
Chief Brody 95 (16f,Ffo,HY,Dec 14)
Chieftain's Choice 107 (17f,Don,HY,Dec 12)
Childrens List 105 (25f,Ain,S,Apr 9)
Chilly Miss 96 (17f,Crt,G,Jly 18)
Chitu 109 (19½f,Mus,GS,Nov 27)
Chocca Wocca 106 (17f,Chl,G,Mar 17)
Christmas Twenty 103 (21f,Wet,S,Apr 1)
Church Field 105 (23f,Mar,G,Aug 2)
Churchtown Champ 103 (24f,Tau,HY,Jan 13)
Cinder Rua 103 (24½f,Ayr,HY,Jan 19)
Circus Star 105 (16f,Wet,S,Dec 5)
City Supreme 106 (19½f,Don,G,Jan 30)
Claire Pet 97 (16f,Fai,HY,Dec 19)
Clan Chief 96 (16½f,Ncs,HY,Dec 19)
Clan Des Obeaux 114 (17f,Chl,HY,Jan 30)
Clan Legend 104 (16½f,Ncs,HY,Dec 10)
Clan William 97 (20f,Sth,G,Oct 22)
Clara Peggotty 103 (16f,Sth,HY,Mar 7)
Classic Tune 94 (21f,Hun,GS,Apr 18)
Claude Carter 103 (16f,Kel,G,Oct 24)
Clayton 107 (16f,Plu,HY,Feb 1)
Clean Sheet 107 (17f,Chl,HY,Jan 30)
Clemency 107 (16f,Ffo,G,Oct 17)
Clic Work 94 (19f,Nby,G,Apr 2)
Cliff House 104 (16f,Pun,GY,Apr 28)
Clock On Tom 101 (16f,Wor,S,Aug 23)
Clonbanan Lad 105 (20f,Pun,GY,Apr 29)
Clondaw Banker 104 (16½f,Chl,G,Oct 23)
Clondaw Cian 113 (19f,Fon,S,Nov 25)
Clondaw Court 100 (20f,Fai,S,Nov 29)
Clondaw Fonz 90 (21f,Hun,GS,Feb 25)
Clondaw Kaempfer 90 (19f,Crl,HY,Feb 22)
Clondaw Warrior 110 (20f,Pun,S,May 2)
Cloonacool 113 (17f,Mar,G,Sep 26)
Close Touch 99 (16f,Nby,GS,Apr 1)
Closer To Home 101 (18½f,Exe,G,Mar 22)
Closest Friend 104 (17f,Mar,GS,Apr 21)
Closing Ceremony 107 (24f,Wet,S,Oct 31)
Cloudy Copper 96 (25f,Crl,S,Mar 10)
Cloudy Dream 108 (19½f,Don,G,Nov 28)
Cloudy Joker 96 (16f,Sth,G,Oct 22)
Clyne 108 (16f,Ffo,HY,Dec 14)
Cobra De Mai 105 (19f,Nby,G,Apr 2)
Cochinillo 104 (20f,Utt,S,Nov 22)
Cocker 98 (19f,Fon,GS,Apr 1)
Coco Des Champs 105 (16f,Ffo,G,Oct 17)
Coco Shambhala 93 (19f,Fon,S,Dec 8)
Coeur Joyeux 97 (20f,Fai,HY,Dec 19)
Coeur Tantre 92 (19f,Tau,G,Mar 21)
Cogryhill 99 (24f,Fai,HY,Dec 19)
Cole Harden 106 (24f,Chl,G,Mar 17)
Colin's Brother 99 (24f,Lud,GS,Apr 19)
Colla Pier 113 (16f,Nby,S,Nov 28)
College Boy 99 (20f,Fai,S,Nov 29)
Colley Row 100 (20f,Wor,G,Jly 15)
Collodi 116 (16½f,Str,G,Jun 16)
Columbanus 102 (15f,Wcn,HY,Nov 19)
Combustible Kate 100 (25f,Hun,GF,May 26)
Come On Annie 106 (17f,Nab,S,May 7)
Come On Harriet 94 (20f,Fak,G,May 5)
Comical Red 91 (24f,Tau,S,Mar 14)
Commeragh Trix 98 (18f,Fai,HY,Jan 10)
Commissioned 117 (17f,Crt,G,Jun 28)
Conas Taoi 92 (23½f,Fak,G,May 31)
Coney Island 112 (24f,Fai,Y,Mar 29)
Connetable 114 (16f,San,S,Feb 6)
Conquer Gold 101 (24½f,Ayr,HY,Jan 19)
Consortium 98 (16f,Hun,G,Oct 4)
Consul De Thaix 113 (17f,Chl,HY,Jan 30)
Coo Star Sivola 112 (16½f,Chl,G,Mar 16)
Cool Baranca 100 (19½f,Mus,G,Nov 6)
Cool Macavity 105 (16f,Plu,G,Sep 20)
Cool Runnings 90 (20½f,Mar,G,May 8)
Cool Sky 111 (16f,Chp,G,Oct 11)
Coolaghknock Glebe 108 (20f,Fai,HY,Feb 20)
Coole Craft 100 (16f,Fai,SH,Jan 20)
Coolking 101 (26f,War,S,Feb 26)
Cooper 108 (16f,Wet,S,Oct 30)
Cooper's Friend 104 (20½f,Plu,S,Nov 16)
Coozan George 106 (24f,Sth,S,Nov 17)
Copt Hill 100 (17f,Sed,S,Mar 27)
Copy That 103 (16f,Leo,HY,Dec 27)
Cor Wot An Apple 91 (16f,Plu,S,Feb 29)
Cornborough 92 (16f,Kel,HY,Dec 6)
Cornish Beau 101 (19f,Fon,GS,Aug 13)
Corri Lindo 100 (16f,Fai,Y,Mar 27)
Cosmic Statesman 101 (16f,Cat,S,Dec 15)
Cosmic Tigress 99 (17f,Sed,G,Sep 29)
Cotillion 105 (20½f,Mar,HY,Jan 22)
Cotswold Road 95 (24f,Tau,GS,Dec 10)
Cottersrock 112 (21f,Kem,G,Apr 19)
Cotton King 94 (19f,Fon,G,May 1)
Cottonwool Baby 97 (21f,Kem,G,Apr 19)
Cougar Kid 93 (16½f,Tau,HY,Feb 2)
Count Salazar 106 (23f,Mar,G,Aug 2)
Counterfeiter 90 (16f,Nby,G,Apr 2)
Countersign 95 (17f,Mar,G,Sep 26)
Courageous Cry 90 (18f,Leo,HY,Dec 26)
Court Challenge 102 (20f,Fai,HY,Jan 10)
Court Dismissed 93 (17f,Ban,G,May 16)
Court King 100 (16f,Ffo,HY,Dec 14)
Court Minstrel 105 (19½f,Chp,G,Oct 10)
Cousin Guillaume 95 (16f,Wor,G,Jly 28)
Cousin Khee 107 (16f,Utt,G,Sep 20)
Cowslip 101 (25f,Ain,G,May 15)
Crack Away Jack 107 (24f,Sth,G,Jun 9)
Cracked Rear View 113 (19½f,Don,S,Mar 5)
Cradle Mountain 110 (16f,Fai,HY,Jan 10)
Crafty Power 108 (18f,Leo,S,Feb 28)
Craiganee 104 (18½f,Exe,HY,Jan 1)
Craigdancer 102 (20f,Wet,G,May 28)
Crazy 94 (16f,Sth,HY,Mar 7)
Crazy Jack 105 (21f,Wet,G,Oct 14)
Createur 104 (17f,Exe,G,Oct 8)
Crickel Wood 105 (16f,War,GS,Nov 4)
Crin Au Vent 102 (15f,Wcn,HY,Feb 4)
Crinkle Crags 96 (19½f,Mus,S,Feb 17)
Crockery 98 (21f,Kem,S,Feb 12)
Crookstown 106 (19½f,Don,G,Nov 28)
Cropley 105 (21½f,Wcn,GS,Apr 17)
Crosspark 118 (24f,Sth,S,Nov 17)
Crowd Control 97 (21f,Lud,HY,Jan 12)
Crown Of Gold 106 (16f,Fai,Y,Mar 27)
Cruachan 100 (20½f,Ncs,HY,Dec 10)
Cruise In Style 102 (17f,Nab,G,May 27)
Cry Fury 103 (16f,Chp,G,Apr 22)
Cucklington 94 (17f,Exe,GS,Apr 12)
Culture De Sivola 107 (17f,Ain,S,Dec 5)
Cumbrian Farmer 99 (20f,Wet,G,May 28)
Curious Carlos 101 (16f,Utt,S,May 6)
Cusheen Bridge 106 (20f,Sth,G,Oct 22)
Cut The Corner 112 (20f,Wet,G,May 21)
Cyrius Moriviere 98 (16f,Hun,GS,Dec 6)

Dadsintrouble 104 (15f,Wcn,S,Apr 4)
Dainty Diva 99 (16f,Tow,G,May 11)
Daizy 93 (20f,Sth,G,Jly 12)
Dakota Grey 106 (17f,Crl,HY,Feb 10)
Dalaki 103 (16f,Fak,S,Jan 1)
Dalby Spook 102 (20½f,Ncs,S,Apr 8)
Dalia Pour Moi 114 (20f,Wet,G,Oct 14)
Daliance 105 (19½f,Hun,S,Jan 15)
Daliyan 90 (16f,Pun,Y,Apr 30)
Damefirth 105 (16½f,Chl,G,Oct 23)
Damut 93 (24f,Fai,HY,Dec 19)
Dan Emmett 106 (24f,Ncs,HY,Mar 19)
Danceintothelight 108 (19½f,Mus,S,Feb 17)
Dancing Meadows 107 (20f,Per,G,Jly 2)
Dandy Duke 95 (20f,Utt,HY,Dec 8)
Daneking 101 (20f,Pun,S,May 2)
Danielle's Journey 101 (17f,Chl,G,Mar 17)
Dante's Way 103 (20f,Sth,G,Mar 21)
Danvinnie 99 (19f,Fon,S,Nov 6)
Daphiglote 91 (20f,Fak,S,Feb 8)
Dardanella 91 (20f,Ain,G,Jun 12)
Dare To Achieve 100 (17f,Ain,G,Jun 12)
Darebin 102 (16f,Plu,S,Mar 27)
Daring Exit 92 (24f,Wet,G,May 21)
Daring Indian 94 (20f,Wcn,G,May 7)
Dark Flame 102 (21f,Kem,G,Oct 18)
Dark Spirit 112 (23½f,Asc,S,Jan 23)
Darkestbeforedawn 98 (25f,Hun,S,Dec 26)
Darnitnev 98 (20f,Utt,G,May 16)
Darsi Dancer 103 (27f,Sed,GS,Oct 12)
Dartford Warbler 107 (20f,Utt,G,Sep 20)
Darwins Theory 100 (16f,Kem,S,Feb 12)
Dashing Oscar 100 (17f,Ban,G,Oct 27)
Daulys Anthem 93 (16f,Sth,S,Nov 9)
Daveron 101 (19f,Str,G,Oct 17)
David John 102 (17f,Sed,GS,Oct 12)
Davids Jewel 93 (24f,Pun,G,May 16)
Dawn Commander 107 (23f,Mar,G,Jly 5)
Dawnieriver 95 (20f,Wcn,G,May 7)
Daydreamer 102 (19f,Mar,G,Jly 5)
Days Of Heaven 102 (15½f,Mus,S,Feb 7)
Daytripper 108 (16f,Hex,S,Mar 29)
Dazinski 99 (19f,War,G,Apr 21)
De Bennette 95 (20f,Pun,HY,Feb 17)
De Benno 102 (20f,Fai,S,Nov 29)
De Boitron 103 (16f,Hay,S,Nov 21)
De Faoithesdream 97 (16½f,Tau,HY,Feb 2)
Deadly Approach 94 (16f,Fak,G,Mar 18)
Deadly Move 103 (19½f,Don,S,Mar 5)
Dear Darling 92 (20f,Wor,GF,Jun 6)
Deauville Dancer 100 (17f,Don,GS,Dec 11)
Debdebdeb 104 (20f,Chl,G,Apr 14)
Debt To Society 93 (26f,War,G,Mar 23)
Decimus 105 (26½f,Nab,GS,Jly 3)
Dedigout 110 (20f,Fai,YS,Mar 28)
Deebaj 118 (16½f,Str,S,Mar 5)
Deep Resolve 95 (16f,Kel,HY,Dec 6)
Deep Trouble 104 (21f,Kem,S,Jan 9)
Deepsand 91 (16f,Kem,S,Feb 12)
Definite Earl 93 (16f,Leo,HY,Dec 28)
Definite Future 99 (19f,War,G,Apr 21)
Definite Outcome 112 (21f,War,HY,Jan 16)
Definite Soldier 92 (21f,Chl,GS,Nov 15)
Definitely Better 107 (16f,Sth,HY,Mar 7)
Definitly Grey 96 (17f,Don,G,Feb 24)
Definitly Red 110 (23f,Hay,S,Nov 21)
Degenerous 100 (20f,Per,G,Apr 20)
Degooch 104 (19½f,Don,G,Jan 30)
Deja Bougg 104 (16f,Hun,GS,Feb 25)
Delgany Demon 110 (24f,Sth,GS,Feb 28)
Dell' Arca 103 (16f,Pun,GY,May 1)
Della Sun 94 (20f,Utt,G,Sep 20)
Delusionofgrandeur 106 (25½f,Cat,S,Jan 1)
Demographic 107 (21½f,Wcn,GF,Oct 16)
Denboy 101 (16f,Chp,G,Apr 22)
Denton Carnival 93 (17f,Mar,S,Nov 5)
Deny 91 (16f,Cat,S,Mar 9)
Deputy Commander 106 (20f,Utt,HY,Apr 2)
Deputy Dan 113 (24½f,Asc,GS,Dec 19)
Deputy Marshall 93 (16f,Leo,HY,Dec 28)
Derksen 91 (19½f,Don,GS,Jan 29)
Derryfadda 95 (27f,Sed,GF,Aug 27)
Descaro 98 (16½f,Str,G,Aug 20)
Descartes 92 (16f,Asc,G,Oct 31)
Desert Island Dusk 101 (20f,Per,G,Apr 22)
Desert Queen 114 (22f,Asc,GS,Nov 21)
Desert Recluse 109 (16½f,Str,G,Aug 27)
Desertmore Hill 98 (19½f,Don,G,Jan 30)
Desilvano 90 (25f,Chl,GS,Nov 14)
Desoto County 108 (16f,Leo,S,Jan 17)
Desroches 91 (20f,Sth,G,Aug 27)
Destiny Awaits 102 (24½f,Ayr,G,Oct 26)
Destiny's Gold 104 (16½f,Tau,G,Apr 20)
Detroit Blues 105 (20f,Utt,G,Sep 9)
Devilment 116 (16½f,Chl,G,Oct 24)
Devon River 96 (15½f,Mus,G,Nov 5)
Dexcite 109 (16f,Chp,G,Oct 10)
Dhaular Dhar 94 (15½f,Mus,G,Nov 5)
Diamond Cauchois 104 (20f,Fai,HY,Feb 20)
Diamond D'Amour 101 (20f,Wet,HY,Nov 25)
Diamond King 113 (21f,Chl,G,Mar 16)
Diamond Rock 97 (17f,Ban,S,Mar 16)
Diego Du Charmil 113 (16½f,Chl,G,Mar 16)
Different Gravey 116 (19f,Asc,S,Feb 20)
Ding Ding 98 (16f,Plu,S,Nov 16)
Dino Mite 105 (19f,Mar,G,Aug 2)
Dire Straits 106 (19f,Mar,G,Jly 5)
Direct Flo 97 (22f,Str,G,Jun 30)
Directional 99 (16f,Utt,G,Jun 11)
Discay 103 (16f,Chp,G,Oct 11)
Discoverie 102 (16f,Cat,S,Jan 1)
Dispour 96 (19½f,Hun,G,Oct 4)
Disputed 109 (16f,Plu,S,Mar 27)
Distant Rain 100 (16f,Chp,HY,Mar 12)
Distant Sound 96 (19f,Tow,S,Mar 17)
Divine Port 101 (20f,Wet,HY,Jan 16)
Divine Spear 103 (17f,Don,G,Feb 24)
Do We Like Him 104 (19f,Fon,G,May 1)
Doctor Look Here 104 (18½f,Exe,S,Nov 3)
Doitforthevillage 94 (19f,Fon,S,Nov 15)
Dollar And A Dream 109 (16f,Fai,Y,Mar 27)
Dolly Diamond 96 (21f,Tow,G,Nov 5)
Dolores Delightful 110 (23½f,Asc,GS,Apr 3)
Dominada 103 (16f,Utt,G,Jun 11)
Domtaline 103 (19f,Mar,S,Dec 26)
Don Padeja 104 (16½f,Str,G,Jly 12)
Don't Be Late 93 (20½f,Mar,G,Jly 18)
Don't Touch It 114 (18f,Leo,HY,Dec 26)
Don'tdropmein 102 (19½f,Chp,S,Nov 4)
Donna's Diamond 110 (26f,Kel,GS,Apr 2)
Donna's Pride 100 (19½f,Don,GS,Dec 29)
Dontupsettherhythm 91 (22f,Crt,GS,May 25)
Dormouse 107 (16f,Lin,HY,Dec 21)
Double Silver 93 (21f,Lud,G,May 10)
Double W's 110 (16f,Hay,G,Mar 23)
Doubly Clever 110 (16½f,Chl,G,Mar 16)
Douvan 106 (16f,Pun,GY,Apr 28)
Dovils Date 101 (16½f,Ain,G,Jun 12)
Down Time 96 (17f,Sed,GS,Feb 25)
Downtown Boy 107 (19f,Mar,G,Aug 2)
Doyly Carte 96 (20f,Wet,G,May 21)
Dr Cuddles 103 (19f,Mar,S,Nov 5)
Dr Dalwhinny 91 (17f,Crt,G,Jun 26)
Dr Irv 92 (21f,Wet,G,Oct 14)
Dr Robin 109 (24f,Sth,G,Jly 12)
Dr Waluigi 90 (20f,Fai,HY,Jan 30)
Draco 109 (18f,Leo,S,Feb 28)
Draco's Code 105 (16f,Plu,S,Dec 14)
Dragon City 100 (19½f,Don,G,Nov 27)
Dragon De La Tour 94 (19f,Fon,S,Nov 15)
Dragon's Den 108 (19f,Fon,G,Oct 3)
Dragoon Guard 90 (16½f,Tau,S,Mar 14)
Draytonian 107 (16f,War,S,Apr 4)
Dream Berry 103 (17f,Mar,S,Apr 10)
Dream Bolt 104 (16f,Wor,G,Sep 25)
Dreamisi 95 (26f,Fon,G,Jun 3)
Dresden 109 (16f,Chp,G,Oct 11)
Driftashore 96 (23½f,Fak,G,May 5)
Drifter 104 (20f,Per,GF,Sep 7)
Driftwood Haze 104 (22f,Ffo,GS,Mar 20)
Drombeg West 104 (16f,Tow,GF,Apr 30)
Drop A Gear 101 (21f,Wet,S,Oct 30)
Dropzone 101 (21½f,Fon,G,Jun 9)
Drum Valley 102 (21½f,Fon,S,Oct 21)
Drumcliff 102 (16f,Fai,YS,Mar 28)
Drumhart 104 (20f,Per,G,Jly 2)
Drumlang 103 (19½f,Ban,G,Oct 27)
Drumlee Lad 104 (19½f,Don,S,Mar 4)
Drumlee Sunset 110 (20f,Chl,GS,Apr 13)
Drummond 105 (16f,Chp,G,Sep 30)
Drumviredy 99 (15f,Wcn,S,Dec 26)
Dry Ol'Party 103 (16f,Wor,G,Jly 15)
Dubai Celebrity 93 (17f,Crl,HY,Feb 10)
Dubai Devils 106 (19½f,Ban,HY,Mar 2)
Dubai Prince 110 (17f,Nab,G,Jun 23)
Dubai Shen 102 (19f,Crl,G,Mar 26)
Dubawi Island 110 (21½f,Wcn,S,Dec 26)
Dubh Eile 111 (20f,Ain,G,May 15)
Dueling Banjos 100 (21f,Kem,G,Nov 2)
Duhallowcountry 92 (16f,Hex,G,May 2)
Duke Arcadio 97 (21f,Kem,S,Feb 12)
Duke Cass 93 (16f,Fai,SH,Apr 5)
Duke Des Champs 111 (19f,Mar,HY,Dec 3)
Duke Of Medina 109 (17f,Chl,HY,Jan 30)
Duke Of Sonning 108 (16f,Hun,GS,Nov 1)
Duke Street 110 (16f,San,G,Apr 23)
Duke's Affair 98 (20f,Utt,G,Oct 15)
Dukes Den 102 (21f,Lud,HY,Jan 4)
Dumbarton 101 (22f,Crt,G,May 27)
Dun Scaith 101 (20f,Sth,G,Jun 9)
Dunmallet Belle 92 (19f,War,G,Sep 22)
Dusk Till Dawn 98 (20f,Utt,G,Sep 9)
Dusky Bob 99 (27f,Sed,S,Mar 6)
Dusky Legend 115 (17f,Chl,G,Mar 17)
Dutch Canyon 99 (20f,Per,G,Apr 22)
Dylan's Storm 99 (16f,Wor,GS,Sep 2)
Dylanseoghan 101 (21f,Kem,S,Feb 12)
Dynamic Drive 109 (16f,Kel,GF,Oct 4)
Dynamic Idol 97 (23½f,Fak,G,May 31)
Dynamic Ranger 105 (16f,Hun,GS,Aug 31)
Dysios 95 (16f,Pun,GY,Apr 28)

Eamon An Cnoic 100 (16f,Lud,GS,Apr 19)
Earcomesthedream 101 (24f,Utt,HY,May 6)
Eardisland 101 (16f,Wor,G,May 28)
Earls Quarter 95 (19f,Mar,G,Jun 5)
Easily Pleased 95 (19f,Fon,G,Jun 9)
East Hill 94 (21½f,Wcn,G,Oct 25)
Easter Day 107 (25f,Chl,GS,Nov 14)
Eastern Magic 99 (19½f,Hun,GS,Nov 1)
Eastview Boy 104 (16½f,Ncs,HY,Mar 8)
Easy Beesy 96 (21f,War,S,May 9)
Easy Street 97 (23f,Exe,G,Apr 21)
Ebadani 101 (19f,Tau,G,Apr 7)
Ebazan 94 (20f,Sth,GS,Jun 15)
Ebony Empress 105 (24f,Utt,G,May 16)
Ebony Express 101 (16½f,Chl,GS,Nov 15)
Echo Brava 97 (16f,Plu,S,Dec 14)
Echo Springs 104 (20f,Ain,S,Nov 7)
Eco Warrior 99 (17f,Ban,S,Mar 16)
Eddiemaurice 106 (15f,Wcn,S,Jan 21)
Eddy 100 (18½f,Nab,G,Jun 12)
Edlomond 100 (16½f,Tau,GS,Dec 10)
Edvardo 98 (20f,Fai,SH,Apr 5)
Egmont 99 (16f,Utt,S,Jly 26)
Egret 98 (19f,Crl,HY,Nov 29)
Eight Till Late 103 (20f,Pun,GY,Apr 29)
El Bandit 103 (21f,War,G,Mar 23)
El Beau 106 (16f,Hay,G,Mar 26)
El Indio 97 (25f,Hun,S,Dec 26)
El Massivo 104 (16½f,Str,G,Jly 12)
El Toreros 102 (19f,Fon,GS,Aug 13)
Element Quartet 96 (24f,Sth,G,May 20)
Elkstone 101 (17f,Exe,G,Apr 21)
Ellistrin Belle 96 (17f,Sed,GS,Nov 10)
Elusive Ivy 106 (16f,Fai,Y,Mar 27)
Emerging Force 116 (19f,Fon,S,Nov 15)
Emerging Talent 109 (17f,Exe,HY,Jan 1)
Eminent Poet 101 (16f,Tow,HY,Jan 7)
Emperor Commodos 104 (17f,Don,G,Nov 27)
Empty Marmalades 92 (19f,Fon,G,May 1)
Empty The Tank 104 (16f,Sth,GS,Sep 2)
Endeavor 105 (16f,Kel,GF,Oct 4)
Ennisnag 106 (21½f,Wcn,GF,Oct 16)
Ennistown 107 (24f,Chl,S,Dec 12)
Entry To Evrywhere 94 (16f,Plu,S,Dec 14)
Enzani 98 (16f,Fai,Y,Mar 27)
Ephraim 108 (22f,Asc,GS,Nov 21)
Epic Warrior 105 (24f,Sth,GS,Sep 2)
Epsom Flyer 101 (20½f,Plu,G,Apr 22)
Equity Swap 95 (16f,Pun,Y,Apr 30)
Erlkonig 94 (21f,Chl,GS,Nov 14)
Etania 90 (23½f,Utt,G,Sep 20)
Ever So Much 106 (20f,Utt,G,Sep 20)
Exemplary 104 (21f,Kem,G,May 13)
Exiles Return 90 (17f,Exe,GS,Apr 12)
Exit Seven 102 (16f,Fai,HY,Dec 19)
Exitas 100 (15f,Wcn,S,Jan 21)
Expedite 112 (19½f,Hun,S,Dec 26)
Experimentalist 104 (20f,Wor,G,Jly 28)
Extreme Appeal 95 (18f,Fon,S,Dec 8)
Extreme Impact 96 (20½f,Plu,S,Nov 16)
Exxaro 101 (21f,Chl,G,Oct 23)
Eyes Of A Tiger 100 (17f,Mar,S,Mar 13)

Face Value 108 (22f,Fai,YS,Mar 28)
Fact Of The Matter 100 (20f,Utt,S,Mar 19)
Factor Fifty 104 (19½f,Hun,G,Oct 4)
Faerie Reel 104 (17f,Don,S,Mar 4)
Fagan 106 (15½f,Mus,S,Dec 7)
Fainne An Lae 97 (20f,Fai,HY,Jan 10)
Fair Dilemma 97 (16½f,Str,G,Sep 5)
Fair Loch 106 (16f,Hun,GS,Nov 1)
Fair To Middling 90 (19f,Mar,G,Oct 5)

Fairy Alisha 102 *(16f,Wor,GS,Sep 2)*
Fairy Theatre 93 *(20f,Hex,GS,Oct 10)*
Fairytale Theatre 106 *(23½f,Asc,S,Jan 23)*
Faithful Mount 103 *(19f,War,GS,May 4)*
Falcarragh 100 *(20½f,Mar,HY,Dec 3)*
Falcon Crest 108 *(16f,Leo,HY,Dec 27)*
Falcon's Reign 90 *(16f,Wet,S,Apr 17)*
Fantasy King 98 *(17f,Crt,GS,Aug 29)*
Farewelltocheyenne 98 *(16f,Hex,S,Mar 29)*
Farriers Gold 92 *(24f,Pun,G,May 16)*
Fashion Icon 93 *(17f,Exe,G,May 5)*
Fast Scat 100 *(16f,Lud,G,Oct 22)*
Fatcatinthehat 99 *(16f,Hay,HY,Dec 19)*
Father Edward 103 *(20f,Wor,GF,Jun 6)*
Father Probus 90 *(24f,Sth,S,Dec 1)*
Faugheen 126 *(16f,Kem,GS,Dec 26)*
Fauve 95 *(16f,Wor,G,Jly 6)*
Favorite Girl 106 *(17f,Don,S,Mar 4)*
Fearsome Fred 94 *(24f,Sth,GS,Sep 2)*
Feast Of Fire 100 *(26f,War,G,Sep 22)*
Federici 101 *(16f,Leo,HY,Feb 6)*
Feel The Air 104 *(16f,Hex,GS,Oct 10)*
Fenlon's Hill 94 *(16f,Fai,Y,Mar 27)*
Fergall 106 *(16f,Hay,GS,May 9)*
Fethard Player 111 *(17f,Chl,G,Mar 18)*
Fibre Optic 95 *(17f,Sed,GS,Feb 25)*
Fiddler's Flight 101 *(17f,Sed,HY,Dec 26)*
Fields Of Glory 105 *(16f,Hun,S,Mar 6)*
Fifi L'Amour 96 *(16f,Fak,S,Feb 8)*
Fifteen Kings 90 *(16f,Hex,HY,Nov 13)*
Fighter Jet 100 *(24f,Chl,G,Oct 23)*
Fighting Days 98 *(16f,Fai,Y,Mar 27)*
Filatore 96 *(23½f,Chp,HY,Jan 9)*
Film Director 105 *(17f,Mar,G,Oct 17)*
Fin D'Espere 94 *(20½f,Plu,S,Dec 14)*
Finaghy Ayr 102 *(24½f,Ayr,S,Nov 11)*
Final Fling 93 *(20½f,Ncs,S,Apr 8)*
Final Nudge 112 *(21½f,Wcn,HY,Nov 19)*
Fine Jewellery 93 *(16f,Utt,HY,Apr 2)*
Fine Tune 93 *(16f,Plu,HY,Jan 3)*
Fingerontheswitch 108 *(24½f,Don,G,Feb 24)*
Fingers Crossed 95 *(16f,San,HY,Feb 19)*
Fingertips 109 *(19f,Asc,S,Feb 20)*
Finish The Story 102 *(27f,Sed,GS,Oct 12)*
Finnegan's Garden 93 *(21f,War,GS,May 20)*
Fionn Mac Cul 105 *(19f,Crl,HY,Feb 22)*
Fire 98 *(16f,Utt,S,Nov 14)*
Fire In Soul 90 *(20f,Fai,Y,Mar 27)*
Fire Tower 99 *(20f,Utt,G,May 16)*
First Avenue 97 *(19½f,Lin,HY,Dec 12)*
First Fandango 98 *(23f,Wor,G,Jly 28)*
First Of Never 98 *(17f,Sed,S,May 5)*
First Post 98 *(16f,Leo,HY,Dec 28)*
Firsty 100 *(19f,Asc,GS,Apr 3)*
Fishing Bridge 95 *(23f,Exe,GS,Mar 8)*
Fitzwilly 90 *(19f,Nby,S,Nov 28)*
Five In A Row 99 *(23f,Hex,GS,Oct 10)*
Fixe Le Kap 109 *(16f,Hay,HY,Feb 20)*
Fizzlestix 95 *(16f,Hun,GS,Nov 1)*
Fizzy Dancer 96 *(21f,Lud,G,Oct 22)*
Flamenco Lad 102 *(18½f,Nab,GS,Oct 9)*
Flash Crash 92 *(19f,Str,GS,Oct 29)*
Flashjack 113 *(15½f,Lei,HY,Dec 3)*
Flashman 109 *(16f,Plu,GS,Nov 2)*
Flaviana 95 *(20f,Fai,SH,Apr 5)*
Fleet Dawn 91 *(20f,Wor,GS,May 7)*
Flemensbay 95 *(24f,Utt,G,May 16)*
Flemensfirthleader 109 *(17f,Sed,GS,Feb 25)*
Flemensmix 107 *(19½f,Don,GS,Dec 11)*
Flementime 101 *(20f,Chl,G,Apr 14)*
Flemerina 94 *(16f,Sth,GF,Aug 16)*
Flemi Two Toes 104 *(25f,Hun,S,Dec 26)*
Flintham 110 *(26f,War,HY,Jan 16)*
Flobury 92 *(16f,Wet,S,Feb 23)*
Floresco 109 *(16f,Hay,G,Mar 26)*
Florida Calling 95 *(24f,Tau,GS,Dec 10)*
Florrie Boy 104 *(20f,Per,G,Apr 21)*
Flower Power 106 *(20f,Sth,G,Aug 27)*
Flugzeug 102 *(24½f,Kem,S,Jan 25)*
Fluspar 106 *(16f,Fai,Y,Mar 27)*
Flute Bowl 109 *(19f,Fon,S,Nov 6)*
Flying Angel 113 *(16f,San,S,Mar 12)*
Flying Jack 96 *(16f,Hex,S,Mar 29)*
Flying Light 109 *(20f,Wor,GF,Jun 6)*
Follow The Tracks 97 *(23f,Exe,G,Apr 21)*
Foot The Bill 93 *(25½f,Cat,S,Dec 15)*
Footpad 113 *(16f,Leo,SH,Feb 6)*
Footstepsintherain 92 *(17f,Ban,G,Aug 21)*
For 'N' Against 105 *(21½f,Fon,GS,Aug 13)*
For Good Measure 107 *(16f,Utt,HY,Dec 8)*
For Goodness Sake 105 *(16½f,Str,S,Mar 5)*
For Instance 101 *(21f,Tow,G,Nov 5)*
Forest Bihan 107 *(17f,Don,HY,Dec 12)*
Forever Field 101 *(16f,Kem,GS,Nov 23)*
Forever Gold 111 *(22f,Fai,YS,Mar 28)*
Forgiving Glance 111 *(17f,Ain,S,Dec 5)*
Fort Carson 104 *(17f,Exe,G,Apr 21)*
Fort Smith 106 *(20f,Ain,S,Dec 5)*
Fort Worth 109 *(24f,Chl,GS,Apr 13)*
Fortunata Fashions 97 *(21½f,Exe,GS,Nov 3)*
Fortunate George 107 *(21½f,Wcn,G,Apr 4)*
Forty Crown 97 *(24f,Wet,S,Dec 5)*
Fou Et Sage 100 *(16½f,Chl,G,Oct 24)*
Fouburg 93 *(17f,Don,HY,Dec 12)*
Foundry Square 105 *(24f,Lud,GS,Apr 19)*
Fountains Blossom 104 *(24f,Tau,GS,Nov 26)*
Fountains Flypast 103 *(20f,Utt,G,May 2)*
Fountains Windfall 101 *(16½f,Tau,HY,Jan 23)*
Fourth Act 101 *(21½f,Wcn,GF,Oct 16)*
Foxcub 105 *(19½f,Ban,S,Nov 11)*
Foxtail Hill 99 *(16½f,Str,G,May 30)*
Francis Of Assisi 117 *(15f,Wcn,S,Nov 7)*
Franciscan 96 *(16f,Kel,GF,Sep 16)*
Frank N Fair 101 *(21½f,Fon,HY,Apr 15)*
Fred Le Macon 104 *(16f,Utt,G,Jun 11)*
Freddies Portrait 98 *(25½f,Cat,S,Dec 15)*
Frederic 106 *(15½f,Mus,GS,Jan 1)*
French Seventyfive 103 *(24f,Sth,G,Jly 12)*
Fresh By Nature 107 *(24f,Sth,S,Nov 9)*
Frightened Rabbit 106 *(19f,Mar,S,Jan 22)*
Frodon 110 *(17f,Chl,HY,Jan 30)*
From Frost 106 *(22f,Crt,G,Jun 26)*
Fromthetop 91 *(24f,Utt,HY,May 6)*
Frontier Vic 103 *(24f,Per,G,Apr 20)*
Frontline 105 *(16f,Pun,GY,Apr 28)*
Frosty Steel 102 *(16f,Chp,S,Nov 4)*
Frozen Over 106 *(16f,Lud,G,May 10)*
Full Blast 101 *(15f,Wcn,GF,Oct 16)*
Full Ov Beans 92 *(21f,War,G,Oct 1)*
Full Shift 103 *(20f,Pun,S,May 2)*
Fureys Cross 92 *(22f,Pun,HY,Feb 17)*
Fuse Wire 102 *(18½f,Nab,G,Jun 12)*
Future Security 98 *(17f,Ban,G,May 1)*
Fuzzy Logic 107 *(19½f,Chp,G,Sep 30)*

Gabrial The Great 90 *(15f,Wcn,S,Dec 3)*
Gabriel Brandy 95 *(15½f,Mus,G,Nov 5)*
Gabriella Rose 96 *(22f,Asc,GS,Nov 21)*
Gala Ball 110 *(16f,Nby,S,Mar 5)*
Galactic Power 90 *(19f,Mar,G,Jun 5)*
Galizzi 105 *(16½f,Chl,G,Nov 13)*
Gallic Destiny 107 *(19f,Fon,G,Jun 9)*
Galuppi 94 *(16f,Fak,S,Nov 17)*
Galveston 102 *(20f,Sth,G,Mar 21)*
Gambol 102 *(16f,Hun,GS,Aug 31)*
Ganbei 105 *(26f,Kel,GS,Mar 21)*
Gangster 106 *(24f,Fai,HY,Dec 19)*
Garde Fou 98 *(26½f,Nab,S,Apr 5)*
Garde Ville 93 *(16f,Utt,HY,Apr 2)*
Gardiners Hill 91 *(16f,Chp,S,Nov 4)*
Gars Bar Dine 97 *(18f,Fai,SH,Apr 5)*
Gaye Memories 95 *(24f,Utt,G,May 16)*
General Ginger 99 *(16f,Kem,G,May 13)*
General Girling 101 *(21½f,Fon,S,Nov 15)*
General Mahler 105 *(16f,Cat,GS,Mar 1)*
General Principle 104 *(16f,Fai,YS,Mar 28)*
Generous Bond 93 *(24f,Pun,G,May 16)*
Generous Jack 99 *(16f,Plu,HY,Feb 1)*
Generous Pet 98 *(20½f,Ncs,HY,Mar 8)*
George Fernbeck 95 *(27f,Sed,GS,Apr 19)*
Georgian King 101 *(23½f,Utt,GF,Jly 7)*
Georgie Lad 105 *(23f,Ban,G,Oct 27)*
Georgieshore 102 *(16f,Utt,HY,Dec 18)*
Get Home Now 95 *(20½f,Mar,G,May 17)*
Get Involved 96 *(23f,Exe,G,Mar 22)*
Get Ready Freddy 90 *(19½f,Lin,HY,Dec 21)*
Getoutwhenyoucan 90 *(24f,Leo,S,Jan 17)*
Gevrey Chambertin 109 *(26½f,Nab,GS,Oct 9)*
Ghost River 96 *(19½f,Chp,S,Feb 27)*
Gibralfaro 104 *(17f,Chl,G,Mar 18)*
Gilzean 104 *(24f,Wet,S,Nov 14)*
Gin And Tonic 106 *(16f,Fak,G,Oct 16)*
Ginger Fizz 105 *(16f,Sth,GS,Jun 15)*
Gingili 97 *(17f,Sed,G,May 12)*
Ginny's Tonic 93 *(19f,Fon,S,Dec 8)*
Gioia Di Vita 110 *(17f,Mar,G,Jly 18)*
Girly Girl 110 *(23½f,Fak,S,Jan 28)*
Gitane Du Berlais 110 *(20f,Chl,GS,Mar 15)*
Give Him A Glance 95 *(19f,War,G,Apr 21)*
Give Me A Break 101 *(24f,Pun,Y,Apr 30)*
Giveagirlachance 101 *(16f,Wor,GS,May 7)*
Giveitachance 99 *(25f,Hun,GS,Nov 1)*
Glacial Rock 100 *(20f,Per,S,May 13)*
Glenariff 93 *(19½f,Chp,S,Apr 9)*
Glenarm 96 *(19f,Mar,HY,Jan 22)*
Glendermot 93 *(24f,Tau,HY,Feb 2)*
Glengra 93 *(23f,Exe,GS,Apr 21)*
Global Bonus 101 *(21f,Hun,GS,Apr 18)*
Global Dream 95 *(15½f,Lei,HY,Feb 3)*
Global Thrill 104 *(16f,Chp,S,Feb 27)*
Go Long 113 *(17f,Don,G,Nov 27)*
Go Odee Go 100 *(20½f,Mar,G,Jly 18)*
Goal 102 *(16½f,Tau,GS,Dec 10)*
Going For Broke 106 *(18½f,Nab,GS,Oct 9)*
Going Nowhere Fast 92 *(16f,Wor,GS,May 7)*
Golan Lodge 107 *(24f,Fai,Y,Mar 29)*
Golans Choice 99 *(23f,Kel,HY,Dec 29)*
Gold Chain 103 *(20f,Per,G,Apr 20)*
Gold Present 99 *(21f,Kem,G,Mar 19)*
Goldan Jess 109 *(25½f,Crt,G,Aug 31)*
Golden Bird 102 *(22f,Asc,GS,Nov 21)*
Golden Investment 99 *(19½f,Ban,HY,Mar 2)*
Golden Sparkle 109 *(24½f,Ayr,S,Apr 15)*
Golden Spear 94 *(16f,Pun,Y,Apr 30)*
Goldie Horn 92 *(16f,Wor,S,Aug 23)*
Goldray 103 *(16f,Hun,GS,Apr 18)*
Gone Forever 100 *(25f,Ain,G,Oct 25)*
Gone Viral 95 *(16f,Hun,GS,Feb 25)*
Good As Gold 105 *(16f,Leo,S,Jan 17)*
Good Of Luck 112 *(16½f,Str,G,Jly 12)*
Good Value 102 *(19f,War,GS,May 4)*
Good Vibration 106 *(17f,Sed,GS,Nov 10)*
Goodbye Dancer 109 *(21f,Kem,G,Mar 19)*
Goodoldhonkytonk 97 *(21f,Lud,GS,Nov 23)*
Goodwood Mirage 103 *(16½f,Chl,GS,Nov 15)*
Gores Island 103 *(19f,Tau,G,Apr 7)*
Gorey Lane 97 *(21f,War,S,Mar 13)*
Gorman 92 *(19f,War,S,May 9)*
Gorsky Island 98 *(26f,War,GS,Nov 4)*
Goulane Davina 95 *(16f,Leo,S,Jan 17)*
Gowell 91 *(21½f,Fon,G,Mar 19)*
Graasten 104 *(16f,Plu,S,Feb 29)*
Graceful Legend 100 *(19f,Tow,S,Feb 4)*
Grammar 94 *(17f,Sed,G,Oct 12)*
Grams And Ounces 105 *(16½f,Str,G,Aug 20)*
Gran Cavallo 106 *(20f,Pun,HY,Feb 17)*
Gran Maestro 114 *(17f,Mar,G,Jly 18)*
Grand Enterprise 99 *(16f,Lud,S,Dec 16)*
Grand Introduction 104 *(24f,Sth,S,Dec 1)*
Grand Vintage 106 *(22f,Crt,GS,May 25)*
Grandasowt 105 *(16f,Lin,HY,Mar 7)*
Grandmaster George 96 *(17f,Exe,HY,Dec 4)*
Grange Hall 103 *(16f,Hex,HY,May 9)*
Grape Tree Flame 100 *(21f,War,S,Feb 13)*
Great Field 111 *(18f,Leo,S,Feb 28)*
Great Fighter 105 *(19f,Str,G,Oct 17)*
Great Hall 100 *(16f,Hun,G,Oct 13)*
Great Link 103 *(20½f,Mar,HY,Jan 22)*
Grecian Tiger 93 *(24f,Leo,HY,Dec 28)*
Green And White 90 *(17f,Crt,G,Jun 26)*
Grexit 95 *(16f,Kel,S,Mar 13)*
Grey Life 101 *(20f,Sed,GS,Feb 25)*
Grey Monk 99 *(27f,Sed,S,Oct 29)*
Grimley Girl 106 *(17f,Mar,GS,Apr 21)*
Grisedenuit 101 *(16½f,Str,S,Mar 5)*
Grissom 93 *(18½f,Nab,S,May 7)*
Groomed 92 *(24f,Sth,G,Jun 9)*
Grumeti 110 *(24f,Wet,S,Oct 31)*
Guanciale 94 *(16f,Chp,S,Nov 4)*
Guantoshol 107 *(15f,Wcn,HY,Feb 4)*
Guaracha 103 *(16f,Lud,S,Dec 2)*
Guard of Honour 103 *(16½f,Str,G,May 17)*
Guards Chapel 105 *(21f,Hun,GS,Dec 6)*
Gud Day 101 *(19f,Tow,S,Mar 17)*
Guitar Pete 97 *(24f,Chl,HY,Jan 30)*
Guiting Power 94 *(19½f,Hun,S,Dec 26)*
Gully's Edge 111 *(24½f,Ayr,S,Apr 15)*
Gunner Fifteen 105 *(19f,Hay,S,Nov 21)*
Gunner Lindley 101 *(16f,Hex,GS,Nov 6)*
Gunnery Sergeant 106 *(16f,Fai,S,Nov 29)*
Gurkha Brave 109 *(16f,Hex,G,Jun 6)*
Gwafa 110 *(16f,Hun,GS,Feb 25)*
Gwencily Berbas 114 *(20f,Fai,S,Nov 29)*
Gwili Spar 95 *(19f,War,GS,May 4)*

Ha'penny Woods 91 *(23f,Kel,G,Oct 24)*
Haatefina 98 *(17f,Mar,G,Oct 5)*
Hada Men 91 *(20f,Hex,S,Mar 29)*
Haddington Road 96 *(24f,Pun,G,May 16)*
Hadfield 110 *(16f,Wor,GS,Sep 2)*
Hail The Brave 90 *(18f,Kel,HY,Dec 29)*
Hainan 107 *(25½f,Cat,GS,Feb 5)*
Halling's Wish 103 *(16f,Plu,G,Sep 20)*
Hallstatt 93 *(16f,Utt,GS,Oct 30)*
Hammersly Lake 113 *(17f,Mar,G,Jly 18)*
Handazan 103 *(19f,War,S,May 9)*
Handiwork 103 *(16f,Hay,GS,May 9)*
Handmaid 104 *(22f,Crt,G,Jun 26)*
Handpicked 95 *(21f,Lud,GS,Apr 5)*
Handsome Dan 104 *(23f,Mar,G,Aug 15)*
Handsome Horace 100 *(21½f,Nab,GF,Apr 30)*
Handsome Sam 97 *(20½f,Lei,HY,Dec 9)*
Handy Andy 102 *(21½f,Fon,GS,Apr 1)*
Hannah Just Hannah 105 *(16f,Chp,G,Apr 22)*
Hannah's Princess 108 *(18½f,Exe,S,Feb 26)*
Hansupfordetroit 94 *(23½f,Chp,HY,Jan 9)*
Happy Diva 108 *(19f,Tow,G,Nov 5)*
Hargam 122 *(16f,Kem,GS,Dec 26)*
Harley Rebel 100 *(16f,San,S,Mar 12)*
Harristown 99 *(25f,Ain,G,May 15)*
Harry Hunt 103 *(24f,Wet,S,Nov 14)*
Harrys Whim 95 *(23f,Mar,G,Aug 2)*
Hartforth 102 *(25f,Crl,HY,Dec 13)*
Hartside 106 *(16f,Wet,GS,Mar 22)*
Harvey Logan 101 *(20f,Fai,S,Nov 29)*
Harvey's Hope 105 *(16f,Hex,G,May 2)*
Hassadin 101 *(25f,Hun,G,Oct 4)*
Hassle 98 *(19f,Str,G,Oct 17)*
Hastrubal 97 *(16f,Lud,GS,Apr 5)*
Hatch Hall 100 *(16f,Fai,Y,Mar 27)*
Hatton Springs 95 *(17f,Sed,S,Oct 29)*
Haughtons Bridge 92 *(21½f,Nab,GS,Aug 12)*
Haut Bages 104 *(16f,Lud,GS,Apr 5)*
Haverstock 109 *(16f,Plu,G,Oct 19)*
Hawaii Five Nil 106 *(16f,Wor,G,Jun 21)*
Hawdyerwheesht 107 *(16f,Wor,G,Jly 6)*
Hawk Gold 101 *(16f,Plu,GS,Nov 2)*
Hawk High 107 *(17f,Chl,G,Mar 18)*
Hawkhurst 112 *(22f,Str,S,Oct 29)*
Haymount 112 *(20f,Fai,Y,Mar 27)*
Hazy Tom 97 *(20f,Ain,G,May 15)*
Hazzaat 105 *(20f,Wor,G,Jly 28)*
Head To The Stars 92 *(19½f,Hun,S,Dec 26)*
Heading To First 99 *(16f,Hun,GF,May 26)*
Hear The Chimes 105 *(16f,Lud,S,Feb 3)*
Heart O Annandale 102 *(24f,Per,G,Apr 20)*
Heath Hunter 107 *(16f,Hay,G,Mar 26)*
Heavenly Brook 98 *(24f,Sth,S,Nov 9)*
Hedley Lamarr 111 *(20f,Chl,GS,Apr 13)*
Heilan Rebel 90 *(18f,Kel,GS,Apr 11)*
Helamis 101 *(16f,Chp,HY,Nov 18)*
Hell's Kitchen 113 *(20½f,Nby,S,Mar 4)*
Henllan Harri 104 *(20f,Utt,G,May 2)*
Henri Parry Morgan 110 *(24f,Sth,G,Jun 9)*
Henry Higgins 111 *(16f,Leo,S,Jan 17)*
Henry Oliver 101 *(17f,Nab,G,May 27)*
Hepijeu 102 *(19f,Str,GS,Jly 30)*
Herbert Park 107 *(21½f,Wcn,S,Dec 26)*
Here's Herbie 110 *(19f,Tau,HY,Jan 23)*
Herecomesnelson 91 *(17f,Crl,HY,Nov 29)*
Herecomesthetruth 103 *(19f,Fon,GS,Aug 13)*
Heresmynumber 101 *(16f,Fak,GS,Oct 28)*
Herewego Herewego 99 *(16f,Nby,G,Apr 2)*
Herminator 103 *(16f,Leo,HY,Dec 28)*
Hermosa Vaquera 98 *(16f,Plu,G,May 10)*
Herons Heir 107 *(16f,Lud,GS,Apr 5)*
Hes Our Vinnie 95 *(22f,Pun,HY,Feb 17)*
Hey Bob 102 *(17f,Sed,S,Mar 27)*
Hi Bronco 100 *(21½f,Fon,G,May 1)*
Hi Dancer 99 *(17f,Sed,GS,Oct 12)*
Hi Note 95 *(19f,Fon,G,Jun 9)*
Hi Tide 95 *(16f,Wor,G,Jun 21)*
Hidden Justice 104 *(19½f,Don,GS,Dec 11)*
Higgs Boson 97 *(24f,Per,G,Apr 20)*
High Counsel 96 *(20f,Utt,G,Sep 9)*
High Fair 99 *(20f,Hex,G,May 26)*
Highbury High 101 *(21½f,Fon,HY,Apr 15)*
Highland Life 93 *(21f,Lud,G,Oct 22)*
Highpower 106 *(23f,Wor,G,Aug 19)*
Highsalvia Cosmos 104 *(16f,Plu,S,Nov 30)*
Highway Storm 96 *(23f,Exe,HY,Dec 17)*
Hija 99 *(21½f,Nab,GS,Oct 9)*
Hill Fort 108 *(16f,Chp,S,Apr 9)*
Hillview Lad 100 *(20f,Wet,GS,Mar 22)*
Hinxworth 91 *(21f,Kem,S,Feb 12)*
Hit The Highway 114 *(19f,Fon,S,Nov 15)*
Hitman Hearns 104 *(16f,Cat,S,Jan 1)*
Hogan's Alley 98 *(16f,Pun,HY,Jan 9)*
Holbrook Park 102 *(21f,War,GS,Apr 21)*
Hold Court 94 *(20f,Sth,G,Jly 12)*
Hold The Fort 100 *(16f,Utt,G,Sep 20)*
Hollies Pearl 107 *(16f,Fak,S,Feb 8)*
Hollow Bay 100 *(21f,Lud,GS,Apr 5)*
Holly Bush Henry 109 *(15½f,Mus,S,Jan 20)*
Hollywood All Star 99 *(16f,Kem,S,Jan 9)*
Home Farm 103 *(18f,Leo,S,Feb 28)*
Home For Tea 104 *(19½f,Mus,S,Feb 17)*
Honey Pound 105 *(19f,Str,G,Oct 17)*
Honkytonktennessee 99 *(17f,Nab,GS,Jly 3)*
Honour A Promise 100 *(16f,Tow,GF,Apr 30)*
Honourable Gent 98 *(16f,Hex,G,Sep 18)*
Hope's Wishes 105 *(16f,Hun,GS,Feb 25)*
Hopefordebest 94 *(19½f,Hun,S,Dec 26)*
Horace Hazel 104 *(26½f,Nab,GS,Jly 3)*
Horizontal Speed 110 *(24f,Chl,HY,Jan 1)*
Horsted Valley 103 *(26f,Fon,G,May 24)*
Houston Dynimo 103 *(23f,Exe,G,May 5)*
Howaboutnever 108 *(20½f,Nby,S,Mar 5)*
Howwrongcanyoube 103 *(24f,Ffo,GF,Jun 18)*
Hubal 97 *(16f,Cat,S,Dec 15)*
Huehuecoytle 95 *(20f,Sed,GS,Apr 19)*
Hunt Ball 106 *(23½f,Fak,G,May 15)*
Hunters Belt 106 *(19½f,Mus,S,Feb 17)*
Hunters Hoof 112 *(20f,Ain,G,Oct 25)*
Hurricane Darwin 105 *(16f,Fai,HY,Jan 30)*
Hurricane Fly 116 *(24f,Pun,Y,Apr 30)*
Hurricane Higgins 96 *(17f,Ain,G,May 15)*
Hurricane Hollow 107 *(17f,Mar,G,Jly 18)*
Hurricane Rita 103 *(22f,Crt,GS,May 25)*
Hydrant 90 *(16f,Wet,S,Feb 23)*

I Just Know 99 *(20f,Wet,GS,Oct 30)*
I'dliketheoption 103 *(16f,Utt,G,Jun 17)*
I'llhavealook 101 *(21½f,Nab,GS,Jly 27)*
I'm In Charge 105 *(21½f,Wcn,GF,Oct 16)*
I'm Oscar 96 *(17f,Exe,HY,Dec 4)*
Ibis Du Rheu 111 *(20f,Chl,G,Mar 18)*
Icanmotor 97 *(20f,Utt,G,Jun 17)*
Ice Cold Soul 100 *(18f,Leo,HY,Dec 26)*
Ice Konig 98 *(17f,Nab,G,May 27)*
Ice Tres 100 *(17f,Nab,S,May 7)*
Iconic Star 95 *(21f,Lud,S,Dec 16)*
Identity Thief 118 *(16f,Leo,HY,Dec 29)*
Idlewild 96 *(16½f,Str,GS,Jly 30)*
If In Doubt 114 *(25f,Ain,S,Apr 9)*
Ifandbutwhynot 100 *(16½f,Ncs,S,Apr 8)*
Iffjack 90 *(16f,Pun,G,May 16)*
Iftiraaq 106 *(15½f,Lei,HY,Dec 3)*
Iguacu 109 *(16½f,Str,G,Jun 16)*
Ikrapol 93 *(16f,Tow,S,Mar 17)*
Iktiview 97 *(23f,Wor,G,Aug 19)*
Il Presidente 95 *(21f,War,G,Apr 21)*
Imada 105 *(19½f,Hun,S,Dec 26)*
Impeccability 98 *(16f,Sth,S,Nov 17)*
Imperial Plan 92 *(17f,Mar,G,Jly 5)*
Imperial Presence 108 *(16f,Lud,GS,Apr 5)*
Imperial Prince 106 *(19½f,Mus,S,Feb 17)*

Improved 111 *(19½f,Don,S,Mar 5)*
Improver 94 *(16f,Leo,HY,Dec 26)*
Improvisation 109 *(16f,Hun,GF,May 26)*
Impulsive American 109 *(19½f,Mus,S,Feb 17)*
In On The Act 97 *(16½f,Str,G,Sep 5)*
In The Crowd 95 *(22f,Str,G,Jun 30)*
In The Hold 93 *(21½f,Fon,HY,Feb 18)*
Indepub 92 *(24f,Per,S,May 13)*
Indian Brave 94 *(17f,Exe,GS,Apr 12)*
Indian Court 108 *(16f,Pun,HY,Jan 9)*
Indian Fairy 92 *(20f,Pun,HY,Jan 9)*
Indian Icon 100 *(16f,Pun,GY,Apr 28)*
Indian Stream 105 *(16f,Wor,G,Jun 21)*
Iniciar 93 *(17f,Crl,GS,Mar 20)*
Iniesta 99 *(16f,Kem,GS,Nov 23)*
Inishturk Lad 98 *(20f,Pun,HY,Feb 17)*
Ink Master 105 *(16f,Wor,G,Oct 8)*
Innis Shannon 101 *(20f,Hex,S,Mar 29)*
Innocent Touch 107 *(15½f,Mus,G,Nov 5)*
Innoko 99 *(16f,Wor,GS,May 7)*
Instant Karma 107 *(16f,Fak,G,Mar 18)*
Intense Tango 101 *(17f,Don,G,Jan 30)*
Invicta Lake 106 *(25f,Hun,GS,Jan 29)*
Invictus 99 *(17f,Sed,GS,Feb 25)*
Iora Glas 107 *(27f,Sed,S,Oct 29)*
Irish Octave 92 *(19f,War,HY,Dec 31)*
Iron Butterfly 105 *(19½f,Don,S,Jan 8)*
Irondale Express 105 *(16f,Wor,G,Jly 15)*
Irving 122 *(15f,Wcn,S,Nov 7)*
Isaac Bell 100 *(16f,Hun,G,Oct 13)*
Isaacstown Lad 111 *(26f,Kel,GS,Apr 2)*
Isabellesprincess 97 *(21½f,Nab,GS,Oct 9)*
Isdaal 98 *(16f,Wor,GS,May 7)*
Isla Fernandos 93 *(16f,Sth,S,Mar 29)*
Island Heights 108 *(23f,Hay,S,Nov 20)*
Island Villa 93 *(16½f,Str,G,Oct 17)*
Istimraar 105 *(19f,Fon,G,Oct 3)*
It Is I 94 *(20f,Wor,GF,Jly 23)*
It's A Mans World 98 *(16f,Hun,GS,Nov 1)*
It's A Steal 97 *(19f,Fon,GS,Apr 1)*
It's Oscar 102 *(16f,Fak,S,Jan 28)*
Its A Long Road 104 *(21½f,Wcn,S,Jan 21)*
Its'afreebee 115 *(16f,Hay,HY,Jan 23)*
Itsaboutime 94 *(19f,Fon,S,Nov 25)*
Itshard To No 106 *(17f,Ban,S,Nov 11)*
Itsnowcato 106 *(16f,Plu,S,Nov 16)*
Ittirad 109 *(16f,Utt,G,Jun 28)*
Ivan Grozny 115 *(16½f,Ain,S,Apr 9)*
Ivanhoe 104 *(16f,Hun,S,Mar 6)*
Ivanovich Gorbatov 114 *(17f,Chl,G,Mar 18)*
Ivebeenthinking 104 *(20f,Utt,G,Jun 17)*
Ivor's Queen 92 *(16f,Chp,G,Mar 24)*
Ivy Gate 93 *(21f,Wet,GS,Mar 22)*
Izbushka 104 *(23½f,Fak,S,Jan 1)*
Izzy Piccolina 92 *(19f,Tow,GF,Oct 7)*

Jaboltiski 109 *(16f,Hun,GS,Nov 1)*
Jac The Legend 108 *(27f,Sed,S,Oct 29)*
Jack Henri 100 *(19½f,Don,GS,Jan 29)*
Jackfield 96 *(24½f,Kem,S,Jan 25)*
Jackies Solitaire 94 *(20f,Ain,G,Jun 12)*
Jackofhearts 104 *(20f,Per,GS,Sep 24)*
Jajamcool 105 *(16f,Plu,HY,Jan 18)*
Jaleo 111 *(16f,Cat,GS,Dec 2)*
Jalingo 111 *(16½f,Str,G,Jly 12)*
Jamhoori 100 *(16f,Plu,G,Apr 22)*
Jansboy 103 *(21f,Chl,GS,Nov 15)*
Jarlath 103 *(16½f,Tau,G,Mar 21)*
Jarob 96 *(16f,Leo,S,Feb 28)*
Jasani 102 *(20f,Wet,GS,Mar 22)*
Jaune Et Bleue 98 *(17f,Chl,G,Mar 17)*
Jaunty Thor 104 *(17f,Ban,S,Mar 16)*
Java Rose 96 *(20f,Utt,GF,Jly 7)*
Jayo Time 106 *(20½f,Plu,G,May 10)*
Jazz Thyme 101 *(20f,Sth,G,Aug 27)*
Jean Fleming 106 *(24f,Lud,G,Oct 7)*
Jeans Lady 90 *(20f,Wor,GF,Jun 6)*
Jebril 107 *(16f,Pun,GY,Apr 28)*
Jebulani 98 *(17f,Sed,GF,Apr 30)*
Jellied Eel Jack 100 *(20f,Wet,GS,Mar 22)*
Jennies Jewel 114 *(23½f,Asc,S,Jan 23)*
Jennys Surprise 90 *(25f,War,GS,May 20)*
Jer's Girl 116 *(17f,Ain,S,Dec 5)*
Jessber's Dream 112 *(20f,San,HY,Feb 19)*
Jester Jet 98 *(19½f,Chp,HY,Mar 12)*
Jet Master 105 *(19f,Hay,S,Nov 21)*
Jethro 94 *(16f,Fak,G,Mar 18)*
Jetson 111 *(24f,Pun,Y,Apr 30)*
Jetstream Jack 109 *(19½f,Mus,S,Feb 8)*
Jett 106 *(16f,Fai,YS,Mar 28)*
Jewellery 95 *(20f,Hex,G,May 26)*
Jezki 117 *(24f,Pun,Y,Apr 30)*
Jigsaw Financial 99 *(20f,Sth,GF,Aug 16)*
Jimmy Shan 99 *(24f,Sth,GS,Sep 2)*
Jimmy Two Times 107 *(20f,Pun,S,May 2)*
Jinsha Lake 96 *(16f,San,S,Dec 4)*
Jodies Miss 112 *(20f,Fai,SH,Jan 20)*
John Biscuit 96 *(15f,Wcn,HY,Nov 19)*
John Constable 108 *(16f,Nby,S,Nov 26)*
Johnny Go 106 *(20f,Per,GS,Sep 24)*
Johnny Og 98 *(16f,Wor,G,Sep 25)*
Join The Clan 112 *(25f,Ain,S,Apr 9)*
Join The Navy 102 *(21f,War,S,Mar 13)*
Jokers And Rogues 108 *(17f,Sed,GS,Feb 25)*
Jolly Roger 96 *(17f,Chl,G,Apr 13)*
Jolly's Cracked It 112 *(16f,Asc,GS,Dec 19)*
Jonniesofa 104 *(25½f,Cat,S,Jan 1)*
Jonny Delta 107 *(15½f,Mus,S,Feb 17)*
Jopaan 92 *(19f,Tow,S,Feb 17)*
Joshua Lane 106 *(16f,Leo,HY,Feb 6)*
Jovial Joey 108 *(19f,Crl,G,Mar 26)*
Jully Les Buxy 94 *(24f,Tau,G,Mar 21)*
Jumpandtravel 104 *(20f,Crl,HY,Nov 9)*
Jumps Road 102 *(20½f,Plu,HY,Feb 15)*
Jury Duty 109 *(24f,Fai,Y,Mar 29)*
Just A Feeling 91 *(21f,Lud,G,Mar 24)*
Just A Normal Day 110 *(26½f,Nab,GS,Oct 9)*
Just Awake 99 *(24f,Per,G,Jly 2)*
Just Bee 91 *(16f,Hex,G,May 2)*
Just Bill 91 *(19½f,Lin,HY,Mar 7)*
Just Cause 113 *(22f,Fai,YS,Mar 28)*
Just Georgie 107 *(20f,Wet,S,Feb 23)*
Just Skittles 90 *(24f,Lud,G,Nov 2)*
Just So Cool 104 *(16f,Utt,HY,Jan 30)*
Just When 100 *(16f,San,HY,Mar 11)*
Justanother Muddle 97 *(19½f,Lin,S,Nov 10)*
Justatenner 102 *(16f,Utt,S,Mar 19)*
Justforjames 110 *(20f,Pun,HY,Feb 17)*

Kabjoy 91 *(16f,Pun,Y,Apr 30)*
Kaddys Girl 90 *(21f,Lud,GS,Apr 19)*
Kahdian 94 *(21½f,Wcn,GS,Apr 17)*
Kala Brandy 97 *(20f,Pun,HY,Jan 9)*
Kalane 106 *(18f,Pun,S,May 2)*
Kalanisi Glen 91 *(22f,Asc,GS,Nov 21)*
Kalifourchon 108 *(20f,Sth,GF,Aug 16)*
Kalimantan 90 *(21f,Lud,G,May 10)*
Kalkir 109 *(16f,Leo,S,Jan 17)*
Kalmbeforethestorm 109 *(26½f,Nab,GS,Oct 9)*
Kalondra 92 *(20f,Fak,GS,Dec 20)*
Kamaloka 107 *(17f,Ain,S,Dec 5)*
Kamool 101 *(21f,Hun,GS,Jan 29)*
Kanturk Bank 91 *(24f,Tau,HY,Jan 13)*
Kap Jazz 105 *(21½f,Wcn,S,Dec 3)*
Kapstadt 117 *(16½f,Str,G,Jun 16)*
Kara Tara 104 *(19f,Crl,G,Mar 26)*
Karens Lad 97 *(16f,Plu,HY,Feb 1)*
Karezak 115 *(16½f,Chl,G,Oct 24)*
Karinga Dancer 105 *(18f,Fon,G,Mar 19)*
Karisma King 101 *(16f,Utt,S,Nov 14)*
Karl Marx 102 *(21½f,Wcn,G,May 12)*
Kasakh Noir 109 *(17f,Mar,HY,Feb 9)*
Kastani Beach 104 *(16f,San,HY,Mar 11)*
Katie T 105 *(18f,Pun,S,May 2)*
Katie Too 109 *(21f,War,HY,Dec 31)*
Kauto Riko 94 *(16f,Hay,HY,Dec 30)*
Kavestorm 91 *(21½f,Fon,G,Jun 9)*
Kayf Blanco 112 *(16f,San,S,Feb 6)*
Kayf Charmer 106 *(16f,Utt,HY,Apr 2)*
Kayf Moss 93 *(23½f,Chp,HY,Jan 9)*
Kayf Willow 106 *(21½f,Nab,GS,Oct 9)*
Kayflin 92 *(16f,Plu,HY,Feb 1)*
Kayfton Pete 104 *(21f,Hun,GS,Dec 6)*
Kayla 97 *(16f,Wor,GF,Sep 8)*
Kaysersberg 108 *(21f,Kem,G,Nov 2)*
Kazlian 101 *(19f,Tau,GS,Mar 14)*
Keep Calm 101 *(19½f,Don,GS,Dec 11)*
Keep To The Beat 108 *(17f,Crt,G,Jun 26)*
Keep Up 100 *(16f,Cat,S,Dec 15)*
Kellys Brow 99 *(20f,Utt,G,May 24)*
Kelsey 112 *(19f,Tow,S,Feb 17)*
Keltic Rhythm 104 *(21f,Kem,G,May 13)*
Keltus 106 *(21f,Kem,GS,Dec 26)*
Kelvingrove 106 *(23f,Mar,G,Jly 5)*
Kenobe Star 98 *(16f,Hun,GS,Nov 1)*
Kentford Heiress 102 *(21½f,Nab,GS,Aug 12)*
Kentford Myth 105 *(19½f,Chp,HY,Mar 12)*
Kentucky Star 109 *(24f,Chl,GS,Apr 13)*
Keppel Isle 106 *(16f,Plu,GS,Nov 2)*
Keppols Queen 110 *(20f,Chl,GS,Mar 15)*
Kerisper 111 *(20f,Chl,GS,Apr 13)*
Kerrow 108 *(21f,Lud,GS,Nov 12)*
Key To Milan 102 *(17f,Nab,G,Jly 19)*
Keychain 100 *(19f,Fon,GS,Aug 13)*
Kheskianto 96 *(16f,Fak,G,Oct 16)*
Khezerabad 99 *(16f,Kem,GS,Feb 27)*
Kid Valentine 111 *(20f,Wet,G,Oct 14)*
Kie 105 *(17f,Mar,G,Jly 18)*
Kiera Royale 92 *(16f,Leo,S,Jan 17)*
Kilas Girl 103 *(25½f,Cat,S,Feb 15)*
Kilcooley 120 *(24f,Wet,S,Oct 31)*
Kilcrea Vale 101 *(19f,Asc,S,Jan 23)*
Kilcross Boy 103 *(22f,Str,G,Jun 30)*
Kilcullen Flem 96 *(20f,Wor,G,Sep 25)*
Kilfinichen Bay 107 *(24f,Ffo,GF,Jun 18)*
Kilkishen 108 *(18½f,Nab,GS,Oct 9)*
Killaro Boy 99 *(20f,Fai,SH,Apr 5)*
Killultagh Vic 108 *(24f,Pun,GY,Apr 29)*
Kilmainham 90 *(20½f,Ncs,S,Apr 8)*
Kilquiggan 94 *(26f,Kel,GS,Mar 21)*
Kilronan Castle 104 *(19f,Crl,GS,Apr 3)*
Kilrush 90 *(23f,Exe,G,Apr 21)*
Kilty Caul 107 *(16f,Tow,G,Nov 5)*
Kincora Fort 106 *(21f,Kem,G,May 13)*
Kind Of Easy 103 *(23f,Kel,HY,Dec 29)*
King Alfonso 105 *(16f,War,GS,May 20)*
King Boru 104 *(26f,War,G,Sep 22)*
King Kayf 104 *(21f,Kem,GS,Feb 27)*
King Muro 108 *(16f,Lud,GS,Apr 5)*
King Of Strings 107 *(16f,Hex,G,May 2)*
King Of The Picts 97 *(20f,Pun,S,May 2)*
King Simba 103 *(16f,Hun,GS,Apr 18)*
King's Chorister 99 *(17f,Sed,S,Feb 9)*
King's Realm 93 *(16f,Wet,G,May 28)*
King's Request 99 *(21f,Kem,G,May 13)*
King's Road 94 *(16f,Plu,GS,Nov 2)*
King's Song 90 *(24f,Lud,G,Nov 2)*
Kingfisher Creek 99 *(19f,Tau,S,Mar 3)*
Kings Bayonet 111 *(16f,Hay,G,Mar 26)*
Kings Cross 91 *(19f,Asc,G,Oct 31)*
Kings Folly 103 *(19½f,Mus,GS,Nov 27)*
Kings Lad 104 *(21f,Kem,G,Apr 19)*
Kings River 94 *(16f,Utt,GS,Oct 30)*
Kingsmere 100 *(24f,Chl,G,Apr 14)*
Kingussie 97 *(16f,Tow,S,Dec 17)*
Kisumu 100 *(16f,Cat,GS,Mar 1)*
Kit Casey 92 *(23½f,Chp,HY,Mar 12)*
Kk Lexion 99 *(17f,Don,G,Feb 24)*
Kleitomachos 100 *(24f,Tau,GS,Dec 10)*
Knight Bachelor 105 *(20½f,Plu,G,Apr 22)*
Knight In Purple 94 *(16f,Wet,G,May 28)*
Knight ofthe Realm 105 *(23½f,Asc,GS,Dec 19)*
Knight's Parade 91 *(19f,Str,GS,Oct 29)*
Knockara Beau 110 *(24f,Chl,HY,Jan 1)*
Knockgraffon 102 *(20f,Ain,G,Oct 25)*
Knocklayde Sno Cat 100 *(24½f,Ayr,HY,Jan 19)*
Knocklong 94 *(24f,Sth,G,Sep 29)*
Kodicil 103 *(19f,Mar,G,Jun 5)*
Kolaphos 90 *(24f,Pun,Y,Apr 30)*
Kublai 105 *(21f,Lud,GS,Nov 23)*
Kuda Huraa 103 *(20f,Sth,G,Oct 22)*
Kudu Country 97 *(18f,Fon,S,Nov 15)*
Kumbeshwar 93 *(20f,Per,G,Aug 22)*
Kyles Faith 103 *(20f,Wor,G,Jly 28)*

L Frank Baum 95 *(19f,Tow,S,Mar 17)*
L Stig 99 *(17f,Crt,S,May 27)*
L'Aigle Royal 107 *(21f,Wet,G,Oct 14)*
La Dama De Hierro 105 *(16f,Hex,GS,Oct 10)*
Label Des Obeaux 114 *(22f,Asc,GS,Nov 21)*
Lac Leman 106 *(15½f,Mus,GS,Jan 4)*
Lac Sacre 105 *(16f,Ffo,HY,Dec 14)*
Lackamon 102 *(24f,Ncs,HY,Mar 19)*
Ladies Dancing 106 *(16f,Wor,GF,Jly 23)*
Lady A 90 *(26f,Fon,G,Oct 3)*
Lady Busanda 92 *(17f,Sed,GS,Oct 12)*
Lady Clitico 90 *(16f,Hay,G,Mar 23)*
Lady From Geneva 107 *(21½f,Wcn,GF,Oct 16)*
Lady Of Lamanver 117 *(20½f,Nby,G,Apr 2)*
Lady Of Longstone 107 *(19f,Hay,G,Mar 26)*
Lady Persephone 96 *(16f,Utt,GS,Oct 30)*
Lady Yeats 110 *(16f,Hex,GS,Oct 10)*
Lagostovegas 104 *(16f,Leo,HY,Dec 27)*
Laid Back Luke 101 *(16f,Fai,HY,Jan 30)*
Lake Chapala 97 *(16f,Fak,S,Jan 28)*
Lake View Lad 108 *(20f,Wet,HY,Feb 12)*
Lakeshore Lady 105 *(16f,Tow,G,Nov 5)*
Lamanver Alchemy 99 *(21f,War,HY,Dec 31)*
Lamblord 101 *(17f,Exe,G,Apr 21)*
Lamool 114 *(20f,Ain,G,Jun 12)*
Landau 94 *(20f,Pun,GY,Apr 29)*
Landecker 103 *(23f,Kel,GS,Apr 11)*
Landmeafortune 98 *(17f,Sed,S,Nov 24)*
Landscape 96 *(16f,Hun,S,Jan 6)*
Lapalala 104 *(17f,Nab,GS,Mar 26)*
Laser Blazer 102 *(15f,Wcn,GF,Oct 16)*
Last Echo 93 *(16f,Chp,HY,Nov 18)*
Last Encounter 102 *(24f,Fai,HY,Dec 19)*
Last Supper 104 *(20f,Ain,S,Dec 5)*
Late Night Deed 91 *(24f,Pun,G,May 16)*
Late Night Lily 110 *(19½f,Hun,S,Dec 26)*
Late Shipment 93 *(17f,Nab,S,Apr 5)*
Laudatory 112 *(17f,Mar,G,Jly 18)*
Laugharne 100 *(19f,Fon,GS,Apr 1)*
Laughingalltheway 91 *(16f,Chp,G,Sep 30)*
Laughton Park 105 *(20½f,Plu,S,Nov 16)*
Laurium 111 *(20f,Chl,GS,Apr 13)*
Lava Lamp 107 *(20f,Wor,GF,Jun 6)*
Lawless Island 102 *(21½f,Fon,G,Jun 3)*
Lawsons Thorns 96 *(23f,Mar,G,Jun 5)*
Layerthorpe 95 *(16f,Wor,GS,Sep 2)*
Le Grand Chene 101 *(24f,Per,G,Jly 12)*
Le Legro 97 *(19½f,Don,G,Jan 30)*
Le Prezien 114 *(16f,Hay,HY,Jan 23)*
Le Vagabond 96 *(16f,Leo,HY,Dec 26)*
Leaderofthedance 106 *(21f,Lud,G,Oct 22)*
Leaders Questions 103 *(20f,Pun,HY,Jan 9)*
Leading Score 105 *(19½f,Mus,GS,Nov 27)*
Lean Burn 96 *(16f,Utt,HY,Apr 2)*
Leath Acra Mor 102 *(25f,Hun,S,Dec 26)*
Leave At Dawn 105 *(24f,Leo,HY,Dec 26)*
Leaving Las Vegas 91 *(17f,Ban,S,Dec 11)*
Lee Side Lady 102 *(20f,Fak,S,Feb 8)*
Leg Lock Luke 95 *(16f,Chp,HY,Mar 28)*
Legacy Gold 111 *(20f,Chl,GS,Mar 15)*
Legend Lady 104 *(16f,Fak,GS,Oct 28)*
Legion D'Honneur 95 *(17f,Exe,HY,Nov 22)*
Leith Hill Lad 97 *(21f,War,S,Dec 10)*
Leney Cottage 100 *(27f,Sed,S,Feb 9)*
Leoncavallo 108 *(17f,Mar,G,Sep 26)*
Let's Dance 111 *(16f,Leo,SH,Feb 6)*
Letbeso 94 *(26f,War,S,Feb 13)*
Lets High Five It 98 *(20f,Fai,SH,Jan 20)*
Lets Hope So 104 *(16f,Hun,GS,Apr 18)*
Lettheriverrundry 101 *(17f,Exe,GS,Apr 12)*
Levelling 101 *(16f,Hun,GS,Apr 18)*
Leviathan 106 *(16f,Asc,S,Nov 20)*
Lexi's Boy 95 *(20½f,Nby,S,Mar 5)*
Lexington Bay 97 *(22f,Crt,GS,May 25)*
Libby Mae 92 *(20f,Sed,GS,Jan 31)*
Libeccio 106 *(17f,Exe,GS,Apr 12)*
Lieutenant Colonel 112 *(24f,Pun,Y,Apr 30)*
Life Of A Luso 97 *(26½f,Nab,GS,Jly 3)*
Lifeboat Mona 108 *(21½f,Wcn,HY,Feb 4)*
Lifetime 99 *(19f,War,GS,May 4)*
Lift The Latch 112 *(16f,Pun,HY,Jan 9)*
Lift The Lid 94 *(16½f,Tau,HY,Feb 2)*
Light Well 105 *(21½f,Wcn,S,Jan 21)*
Lightentertainment 98 *(21½f,Fon,S,Oct 21)*
Lil Rockerfeller 114 *(16½f,Chl,G,Oct 24)*
Lilac Tree 113 *(17f,Nab,GS,Jly 27)*
Lilly Of The Moor 99 *(26½f,Nab,S,Apr 5)*
Lilly's Legend 102 *(24f,Wet,G,May 21)*
Lilshane 97 *(16f,Leo,S,Feb 28)*
Lily Little Legs 93 *(25f,Hun,GS,Aug 31)*
Lily Waugh 109 *(21½f,Wcn,S,Nov 7)*
Lilywhite Gesture 92 *(21f,Lud,S,Feb 3)*
Lime Street 96 *(17f,Ban,S,Dec 11)*
Limini 120 *(18f,Fai,HY,Jan 30)*
Limpopo Tom 92 *(19f,Str,G,Jly 19)*
Lincoln County 101 *(20f,Crl,G,Oct 15)*
Lindsay's Dream 101 *(16f,Plu,G,May 10)*
Lined With Silver 92 *(16f,Chp,S,Nov 18)*
Linguine 112 *(16f,Hun,S,Nov 10)*
Lions Charge 94 *(15f,Wcn,G,May 12)*
Lip Service 110 *(16f,Pun,HY,Feb 17)*
Lisbon 105 *(16f,Kel,GF,Sep 16)*
Lisclogher Lad 96 *(20f,Fai,S,Nov 29)*
Listen And Learn 106 *(24f,Ffo,GF,Jun 18)*
Little Boy Boru 107 *(21½f,Wcn,S,Dec 26)*
Little Bruce 95 *(19f,Crl,S,Mar 10)*
Little Buxted 93 *(16f,Plu,HY,Feb 1)*
Little James 94 *(24f,Sth,S,Dec 1)*
Little Mix 100 *(19f,Tow,GS,May 18)*
Little Roxy 90 *(20½f,Plu,G,Oct 19)*
Little Windmill 100 *(20f,Utt,G,Jly 15)*
Loch Garman 94 *(16½f,Tau,GS,Nov 26)*
Lochalsh 105 *(16½f,Str,G,Jun 16)*
Lochnagar 101 *(16½f,Tau,HY,Feb 2)*
Lochnell 105 *(24½f,Ayr,HY,Jan 2)*
Lockedoutaheaven 97 *(16f,Hex,G,Jun 21)*
Lolli 107 *(16f,Wor,G,Jly 15)*
Long Dog 114 *(16f,Fai,S,Nov 29)*
Long House Hall 112 *(21f,Chl,G,Mar 16)*
Long Lunch 102 *(16f,Hay,S,Nov 21)*
Long Way Back 112 *(20f,Pun,HY,Feb 17)*
Looking For Mick 92 *(18½f,Nab,GS,Oct 9)*
Looking Well 98 *(25f,Ain,G,May 15)*
Looks Like Power 101 *(21f,Lud,GS,Nov 23)*
Lookslikerainted 95 *(18½f,Exe,G,Mar 22)*
Looksnowtlikebrian 98 *(19f,Tau,GS,Mar 14)*
Lord Ballim 98 *(16f,Chp,S,Nov 4)*
Lord Ben 98 *(16f,Leo,HY,Dec 27)*
Lord Golan 104 *(16f,Wet,GS,Mar 22)*
Lord Landen 93 *(20f,Per,G,Apr 22)*
Lord Of The Island 101 *(16f,Chp,HY,Mar 12)*
Lord Usher 92 *(23f,Kel,GS,May 6)*
Lord Wishes 108 *(21f,Wet,G,Oct 14)*
Lords Park Star 93 *(19½f,Hun,S,Dec 26)*
Los Nadis 103 *(20f,Per,G,Aug 22)*
Lost In Newyork 90 *(19f,Mar,S,Mar 28)*
Lots Of Memories 103 *(24f,Pun,Y,Apr 30)*
Lou Vert 102 *(16½f,Tau,HY,Feb 2)*
Lough Derg Cruise 91 *(16f,Hex,G,Sep 18)*
Lough Derg Island 105 *(16f,Utt,HY,Apr 2)*
Lough Kent 103 *(17f,Chl,G,Apr 13)*
Lough Salt 102 *(20f,Wet,S,Feb 23)*
Louie The Second 90 *(16f,Pun,G,May 16)*
Louloumills 93 *(20f,Sed,S,Feb 9)*
Love The Leader 100 *(20½f,Plu,G,Oct 19)*
Lovely Bubbly 102 *(16f,Plu,G,Apr 22)*
Loves Destination 105 *(16f,San,HY,Mar 11)*
Low Key 109 *(21f,Kem,G,Nov 2)*
Lowcarr Motion 105 *(21f,Wet,S,Apr 1)*
Lower Hope Dandy 98 *(20½f,Nby,S,Dec 29)*
Loyaute 103 *(24f,Lud,G,Oct 7)*
Lucie Rie 95 *(16f,Cat,S,Jan 14)*
Lucky Buttons 92 *(20f,Per,G,Jly 2)*
Lucky Dottie 99 *(16f,Kem,G,May 4)*
Lucky Jim 105 *(17f,Nab,S,May 7)*
Luckyinmilan 102 *(22f,Pun,HY,Feb 17)*
Lunar Flow 103 *(23f,Exe,S,Mar 30)*
Lyreen Legend 95 *(24f,Leo,HY,Dec 28)*
Lyrical Theatre 91 *(16f,Pun,Y,Apr 30)*
Lyssio 98 *(19f,Fon,GS,Aug 13)*

Ma Du Fou 108 *(17f,Ban,S,Dec 11)*
Ma Filleule 101 *(19f,Nby,S,Nov 28)*
Mac Bertie 107 *(20f,Sth,GF,Aug 16)*
Mac N Cheese 105 *(20f,Wet,HY,Nov 25)*
Maccabees 96 *(24½f,Kem,S,Jan 25)*
Macnicholson 109 *(16f,Pun,GY,Apr 28)*
Mad About The Boy 91 *(22f,Asc,S,Dec 18)*
Mad For Road 105 *(17f,Crt,G,Jun 26)*
Mad Jack Mytton 107 *(17f,Chl,S,Dec 11)*
Mad Moll 94 *(21½f,Fon,S,Apr 15)*

Mad Money 98 *(17f,Mar,G,Aug 2)*
Madam Lilibet 91 *(24½f,Ayr,S,Nov 11)*
Madame Allsorts 93 *(24f,Per,S,May 13)*
Madame Trigger 92 *(16f,Utt,GS,Oct 30)*
Maestro Royal 102 *(18f,Fon,G,Mar 19)*
Maggie Blue 106 *(24½f,Crl,G,Oct 15)*
Magheral Express 102 *(23f,Wor,G,Jly 15)*
Magic Dancer 95 *(16f,Hun,S,Mar 28)*
Magic Magnolia 99 *(16f,War,GS,May 20)*
Magic Money 101 *(19f,War,G,Sep 22)*
Magic Music Man 106 *(16f,Lud,GS,Nov 23)*
Magnolia Ridge 90 *(16f,Wet,S,Apr 1)*
Mahlers Spirit 93 *(19½f,Hun,S,Dec 26)*
Mahlers Star 106 *(16f,Tow,S,Feb 4)*
Maid Of Milan 101 *(19½f,Don,S,Mar 4)*
Maid Of Tuscany 105 *(16f,Fak,G,Oct 16)*
Majestic Sun 108 *(16f,Plu,G,Oct 19)*
Major Ivan 107 *(23f,Hay,S,Nov 20)*
Major Milborne 91 *(23½f,Fak,GS,Feb 19)*
Make Me A Fortune 104 *(19f,Mar,S,Mar 28)*
Makethedifference 113 *(16f,Chp,G,Oct 11)*
Malanos 103 *(16f,Kem,G,May 4)*
Malibu Rock 112 *(21f,Kem,S,Feb 12)*
Malibu Sun 102 *(20f,Sth,G,Oct 22)*
Mall Dini 106 *(24f,Leo,HY,Dec 28)*
Maller Tree 100 *(20f,Sth,G,Jun 9)*
Malt Gem 100 *(24f,Leo,HY,Dec 28)*
Man From Seville 106 *(16f,Sth,GS,Feb 28)*
Man Of God 104 *(20½f,Ncs,S,Apr 8)*
Man Of Leisure 105 *(20f,Wor,G,Aug 19)*
Manballandall 104 *(20f,Hex,S,Mar 29)*
Mandy's Boy 100 *(18f,Fon,GS,Aug 13)*
Mango Cap 104 *(17f,Crl,HY,Dec 13)*
Manhattan Mead 105 *(16f,Plu,S,Nov 30)*
Manhattan Swing 112 *(17f,Mar,G,Jly 18)*
Mantou 107 *(19f,Fon,G,Sep 6)*
Maoi Chinn Tire 90 *(17f,Ban,G,Oct 1)*
Maputo 115 *(16f,Kem,G,Oct 18)*
Maraweh 98 *(24f,Per,G,Jly 2)*
Marchese Marconi 110 *(20f,Fai,YS,Mar 28)*
Marcus Antonius 102 *(15½f,Mus,S,Feb 17)*
Mardale 114 *(16f,Hex,GS,Oct 10)*
Marden Court 106 *(19f,Fon,G,May 1)*
Maria's Choice 102 *(18f,Plu,S,Nov 16)*
Marju's Quest 106 *(16f,Wor,S,Aug 23)*
Marlee Massie 108 *(20½f,Ncs,HY,Dec 10)*
Marlpit Oak 99 *(21½f,Nab,GS,Jly 3)*
Marquis Of Carabas 105 *(16f,Sth,G,Oct 22)*
Marracudja 110 *(16f,Kem,GS,Dec 26)*
Marshgate Lane 97 *(17f,Sed,G,Oct 12)*
Martello Tower 108 *(24f,Leo,HY,Dec 28)*
Marvellous Monty 99 *(21f,Lud,GS,Apr 5)*
Massini's Lady 90 *(23f,Hex,HY,Mar 17)*
Massini's Trap 105 *(18f,Leo,S,Feb 28)*
Master Appeal 91 *(16f,Pun,Y,Apr 30)*
Master Benjamin 106 *(22f,Str,S,Oct 29)*
Master Burbidge 97 *(16f,Ffo,HY,Dec 14)*
Master Cardor Visa 98 *(21½f,Fon,G,May 1)*
Master Dan 94 *(19f,Mar,G,May 8)*
Master Jake 107 *(16f,Hex,HY,Nov 13)*
Master Murphy 91 *(27f,Sed,S,May 5)*
Master Rajeem 91 *(23f,Mar,G,Jun 5)*
Master Ruffit 104 *(24½f,Ayr,HY,Feb 16)*
Masterful Act 95 *(19f,Str,G,Jly 19)*
Masterofdeception 102 *(25f,Ain,G,May 15)*
Masterplan 108 *(22f,Asc,S,Dec 18)*
Matchaway 95 *(17f,Ban,S,Mar 31)*
Matorico 114 *(16f,Hun,S,Nov 10)*
Mawaqeet 105 *(20f,Sth,GF,Aug 16)*
Max Forte 110 *(23½f,Asc,GS,Apr 3)*
Max The Minister 90 *(19f,Nby,GS,Apr 1)*
Maxanisi 108 *(16f,Chp,S,Nov 18)*
Maxie T 109 *(19f,Crl,HY,Feb 22)*
May Be Some Time 106 *(19f,Tau,GS,Mar 14)*
May Hay 104 *(16½f,Ncs,HY,Dec 19)*
May's Boy 98 *(17f,Crt,G,Jly 18)*
Maybe I Wont 107 *(20½f,Ncs,HY,Dec 10)*
Maybell 93 *(19f,Str,S,Mar 5)*
Maypole Lass 104 *(24f,Utt,G,May 16)*
Mazovian 92 *(21f,Lud,GS,Apr 19)*
McCabe Creek 109 *(19½f,Don,G,Jan 30)*
McKinley 102 *(20f,San,G,Apr 23)*
Mckenzie's Friend 112 *(16f,Plu,S,Nov 16)*
Mcvicar 100 *(16½f,Ncs,HY,Mar 8)*
Me Voila 92 *(16f,Sth,G,Mar 21)*
Meadow Cross 90 *(16f,Fak,GS,Oct 28)*
Meadowcroft Boy 102 *(15½f,Mus,G,Nov 6)*
Measureofmydreams 97 *(20f,Pun,S,May 2)*
Medicine Hat 98 *(19½f,Don,GS,Dec 11)*
Medieval Bishop 97 *(20f,Utt,G,Sep 20)*
Meet The Legend 112 *(18f,Kel,S,Mar 13)*
Melbourne Lady 101 *(20f,Pun,HY,Feb 17)*
Melodic Rendezvous 118 *(15f,Wcn,S,Nov 7)*
Meme's Horse 102 *(18½f,Nab,S,Apr 18)*
Memory Of Light 99 *(16½f,Tau,G,Apr 7)*
Mercers Court 108 *(21½f,Fon,G,Jun 3)*
Mercoeur 105 *(16f,Hex,G,Jun 13)*
Mere Anarchy 104 *(16f,Hay,G,Mar 23)*
Messire Des Obeaux 108 *(16f,Hay,HY,Feb 20)*
Mexican Border 94 *(18½f,Exe,S,Nov 3)*
Mia's Storm 95 *(21f,War,S,Jan 28)*
Miami Present 110 *(16f,Fak,GS,Oct 28)*
Mick The Boyo 92 *(20f,Fai,HY,Jan 10)*
Micks Lad 92 *(16f,War,G,Mar 23)*
Midnight Cowboy 107 *(21f,Kem,S,Jan 25)*
Midnight Folie 90 *(21f,Lud,GS,Apr 19)*
Midnight Game 100 *(20½f,Mar,G,Jly 18)*
Midnight Gem 102 *(21f,Lud,G,Oct 22)*
Midnight Gypsy 90 *(16f,Wor,G,Jly 15)*
Midnight Jade 91 *(21f,Lud,HY,Jan 4)*
Midnight Jazz 105 *(18½f,Exe,S,Feb 26)*
Midnight Mint 105 *(19f,War,G,Sep 22)*
Midnight Sapphire 104 *(21½f,Nab,GS,Oct 9)*
Midnight Sequel 98 *(21½f,Fon,G,May 1)*
Midnight Shot 111 *(16f,Utt,G,May 2)*
Midnight Silver 108 *(16f,Tow,G,Nov 5)*
Midnight Target 107 *(17f,Ban,S,Mar 16)*
Midnight Theatre 103 *(22f,Pun,HY,Feb 17)*
Midnight Tour 113 *(17f,Ban,S,Mar 16)*
Midtech Star 100 *(19½f,Don,GS,Dec 11)*
Midtech Valentine 101 *(16f,Hun,GS,Feb 25)*
Might Bite 113 *(21f,Kem,G,Mar 19)*
Mighty Concorde 107 *(16f,Leo,HY,Feb 6)*
Mighty Leader 107 *(21f,Lud,S,Mar 3)*
Mighty Mambo 92 *(16f,Hun,GF,May 26)*
Mighty Minnie 102 *(24f,Utt,G,May 16)*
Mighty Missile 109 *(17f,Ban,G,Jly 31)*
Mighty Mobb 102 *(26f,Fon,G,May 24)*
Mighty Whitey 108 *(17f,Sed,GF,Sep 3)*
Mijhaar 105 *(24f,Chl,G,Oct 23)*
Milan Bound 111 *(26½f,Nab,GS,Oct 9)*
Milan Of Crystal 94 *(16½f,Str,G,Oct 17)*
Milborough 104 *(20f,Crl,GS,Nov 1)*
Mile House 107 *(20f,Wor,GF,Jly 1)*
Miles To Milan 108 *(19f,Tau,HY,Jan 23)*
Millanisi Boy 107 *(19½f,Chp,HY,Jan 9)*
Millicent Silver 106 *(23½f,Utt,S,Oct 30)*
Milly Baloo 105 *(19f,Mar,HY,Jan 22)*
Milord 102 *(21f,Tow,G,Nov 5)*
Min 114 *(16f,Pun,HY,Jan 9)*
Minden March 99 *(19½f,Don,G,Nov 27)*
Mine Now 103 *(24f,Pun,Y,Apr 30)*
Minella Awards 114 *(20½f,Nby,S,Nov 27)*
Minella Bliss 101 *(24f,Lud,G,Nov 2)*
Minella Charmer 108 *(20½f,Plu,HY,Jan 3)*
Minella Daddy 113 *(23½f,Fak,S,Jan 28)*
Minella Experience 106 *(20f,Sth,G,Mar 21)*
Minella Hero 102 *(24f,Wet,G,May 21)*
Minellacelebration 104 *(23½f,Asc,GS,Dec 19)*
Minellaforleisure 109 *(17f,Chl,G,Apr 13)*
Miner's Lamp 109 *(16½f,Str,G,Jun 16)*
Mini Muck 93 *(19f,War,GS,Nov 18)*
Ministerofinterior 102 *(20f,Fak,S,Mar 28)*
Minkie Moon 95 *(16f,Hex,G,Jun 21)*
Minmore Grey 91 *(21½f,Wcn,GF,Oct 16)*
Minnie Milan 106 *(24f,Utt,G,May 16)*
Minority Interest 100 *(21½f,Fon,G,Jun 9)*
Minstrel Royal 99 *(22f,Asc,S,Dec 18)*
Minstrels Gallery 109 *(17f,Don,HY,Dec 12)*
Miracle Cure 93 *(19f,War,GS,May 4)*
Miradane 90 *(18f,Leo,HY,Dec 26)*
Misfits 95 *(16½f,Ncs,HY,Mar 8)*
Miss Crick 98 *(19½f,Don,S,Mar 4)*
Miss Dinamic 99 *(17f,Crt,G,Jun 28)*
Miss Estela 103 *(17f,Exe,GS,Apr 12)*
Miss Fortywinks 96 *(16f,Sth,GS,Jun 15)*
Miss Gotaway 101 *(25½f,Cat,S,Feb 15)*
Miss Joeking 102 *(16f,Hex,GS,Nov 6)*
Miss Lamorna 92 *(19f,Tow,GF,Oct 7)*
Miss Mackie 102 *(17f,Crl,G,Mar 26)*
Miss Macnamara 103 *(17f,Crt,GS,Aug 29)*
Miss Mash 102 *(16f,Lud,GS,Nov 23)*
Miss Mayfair 99 *(25f,Hun,GS,Aug 31)*
Miss Minx 96 *(16f,Tow,G,Nov 5)*
Miss Oscarose 95 *(21½f,Wcn,S,Dec 3)*
Miss Ranger 103 *(16f,Cat,S,Dec 15)*
Miss Sassypants 106 *(16f,Sth,GS,Jun 15)*
Miss Serious 109 *(24f,Sth,GF,Aug 16)*
Miss Tiger Lily 92 *(16f,Wor,GF,Sep 8)*
Miss Tiggy 100 *(21f,Kel,HY,Dec 6)*
Miss Tongabezi 101 *(21f,War,G,Mar 23)*
Mission Complete 98 *(23f,Mar,G,Aug 15)*
Missy Tata 111 *(16½f,Chl,G,Mar 16)*
Mist The Boat 100 *(24f,Lud,G,Nov 2)*
Mister Dick 93 *(16f,Chp,G,Apr 22)*
Mister Don 94 *(16f,Hex,HY,Nov 13)*
Mister Fizz 110 *(21½f,Nab,GS,Aug 22)*
Mister Hendre 97 *(15½f,Mus,GS,Jan 4)*
Mister Jones 98 *(16f,Hex,G,May 26)*
Mister Kalanisi 105 *(19f,Str,S,Mar 5)*
Mister Kit 92 *(17f,Crl,GS,Apr 3)*
Mister Miyagi 107 *(20f,Chl,GS,Apr 13)*
Mistress Mole 99 *(19f,War,G,Sep 22)*
Mix N Match 102 *(16f,Utt,G,Jun 11)*
Mixboy 108 *(17f,Crl,HY,Feb 22)*
Mixchievous 90 *(16f,Chp,S,Nov 18)*
Mo Chailin 110 *(16f,Cat,S,Mar 9)*
Mo Rouge 93 *(23f,Mar,G,Aug 15)*
Modeligo 108 *(16f,Utt,G,Jun 11)*
Modem 96 *(16f,Fai,Y,Mar 29)*
Modus 100 *(19f,Tau,HY,Dec 30)*
Mogestic 103 *(21½f,Exe,HY,Dec 17)*
Moidore 105 *(19½f,Don,GS,Jan 29)*
Molko Jack 97 *(16f,Utt,HY,Dec 31)*
Molly Milan 92 *(20½f,Ncs,HY,Mar 19)*
Mollyanna 93 *(20f,Wor,G,Jly 28)*
Mon Successeur 98 *(16½f,Chl,G,Nov 13)*
Monbeg Dolly 95 *(20f,Sed,S,Mar 15)*
Monbeg Gold 106 *(23f,Exe,S,Nov 11)*
Monbeg Rose 106 *(16f,Pun,SH,Jan 31)*
Mondello 94 *(16f,Chp,S,Nov 18)*
Mondlicht 103 *(20f,Crl,HY,Nov 9)*
Mondo Cane 101 *(16f,Sth,G,Mar 21)*
Monetaire 103 *(20f,Pun,S,May 2)*
Monetary Fund 95 *(23f,Ban,G,Oct 27)*
Money Maid 90 *(20f,Sth,S,Dec 1)*
Monkerty Tunkerty 116 *(24f,Sth,S,Nov 17)*
Monkhouse 104 *(20f,Sth,G,Mar 21)*
Monsart 95 *(16f,Hun,S,Mar 28)*
Monsieur Gibraltar 101 *(16f,Kem,GS,Dec 27)*
Mont Choisy 106 *(20f,Wor,G,Oct 14)*
Mont Royale 106 *(20f,Sth,G,Jun 2)*
Montbazon 104 *(16f,Nby,GS,Apr 1)*
Montdragon 110 *(19f,War,GS,May 4)*
Monte Wildhorn 105 *(17f,Nab,GS,Jun 12)*
Monty's Revenge 92 *(23f,Wor,G,Aug 19)*
Moon Arc 95 *(15½f,Mus,G,Nov 6)*
Moon Over Germany 107 *(16f,Fai,YS,Mar 28)*
Moon Trip 98 *(16f,Plu,GS,Nov 2)*
Moonlit Theatre 94 *(16f,Fai,SH,Apr 5)*
Moonlone Lane 103 *(15½f,Mus,GS,Jan 4)*
Moontripper 92 *(16f,Chp,G,Mar 24)*
Moorlands Mist 97 *(23½f,Chp,HY,Jan 9)*
Mootabar 91 *(21f,Wet,S,Feb 23)*
More Buck's 105 *(23f,Exe,G,May 5)*
More Madness 99 *(23f,Hex,HY,Mar 17)*
Moreece 98 *(16f,Utt,HY,Apr 2)*
Morello Royale 104 *(20f,Chl,GS,Mar 15)*
Morestead Screamer 106 *(26f,Fon,G,Oct 2)*
Morga 103 *(16f,Pun,GY,Apr 28)*
Morito Du Berlais 110 *(25f,Chl,GS,Nov 14)*
Morning Herald 101 *(21f,Kem,G,Apr 19)*
Morning Run 108 *(17f,Don,G,Jan 30)*
Morning Symphony 97 *(20½f,Mar,G,Aug 2)*
Morning Time 105 *(19½f,Mus,S,Feb 17)*
Morning With Ivan 98 *(17f,Crt,GS,Jly 20)*
Morthanalegend 104 *(17f,Exe,HY,Dec 4)*
Moscow Me 95 *(16f,Wor,G,Sep 25)*
Moscow Presents 105 *(27f,Sed,GS,Apr 19)*
Moss On The Mill 100 *(21f,Lud,GS,Nov 23)*
Moss Street 90 *(16½f,Tau,G,Apr 20)*
Mother Meldrum 108 *(17f,Exe,G,Mar 22)*
Motion To Strike 100 *(16f,Hex,HY,Mar 18)*
Motts Cross 98 *(23f,Exe,G,Apr 21)*
Moulin Rouge 99 *(17f,Nab,G,Jun 12)*
Mount Beckham 101 *(16f,Fai,Y,Mar 27)*
Mount Haven 107 *(21f,Lud,HY,Jan 4)*
Mount Shamsan 94 *(16f,Plu,S,Dec 14)*
Mount Vesuvius 100 *(17f,Nab,G,May 27)*
Mountain Eagle 109 *(19f,Tau,HY,Jan 23)*
Mountain Fighter 100 *(16f,Fak,G,May 31)*
Mountain Of Mourne 105 *(19½f,Chp,HY,Nov 18)*
Mountain Tunes 103 *(23½f,Utt,HY,Apr 2)*
Mountainside 105 *(17f,Nab,GS,Aug 22)*
Moveable Asset 92 *(16f,Wor,G,Jly 6)*
Movie Legend 105 *(16f,Utt,S,Nov 14)*
Moyhree 96 *(22f,Pun,HY,Feb 17)*
Moyode Wood 102 *(23f,Mar,G,Aug 15)*
Mr Banks 96 *(21f,War,GS,Apr 21)*
Mr Boss Man 100 *(16½f,Ain,S,Apr 9)*
Mr Caffrey 105 *(17f,Exe,G,Mar 22)*
Mr Cardle 101 *(25f,Hun,GF,May 26)*
Mr Diablo 99 *(16f,Pun,GY,Apr 28)*
Mr Fickle 103 *(16f,Lin,S,Nov 10)*
Mr Fitzroy 103 *(18f,Fon,S,Nov 15)*
Mr Jalfrazy 90 *(16f,Tow,S,Dec 17)*
Mr Kit Cat 100 *(17f,Exe,GS,Apr 12)*
Mr Kite 90 *(19f,Tau,G,Apr 7)*
Mr Lando 108 *(16f,Kem,G,May 4)*
Mr Mafia 100 *(23f,Wor,G,Aug 19)*
Mr McGuiness 99 *(16f,Utt,G,Oct 4)*
Mr Medic 92 *(19½f,Chp,G,Mar 24)*
Mr Mix 117 *(19f,Tau,HY,Jan 23)*
Mr Moonshine 110 *(23f,Hay,HY,Feb 20)*
Mr Morocco 90 *(16f,Cat,S,Dec 15)*
Mr Shantu 109 *(24f,Chl,G,Oct 23)*
Mr Snoozy 100 *(19½f,Don,S,Mar 4)*
Mrs Burbidge 95 *(20f,Wor,GF,Jly 23)*
Mrs Grass 98 *(19f,Crl,GS,May 7)*
Mrs Mac Veale 97 *(16f,Pun,GY,Apr 28)*
Mrsrobin 99 *(21f,War,HY,Dec 31)*
Muffins For Tea 101 *(16½f,Tau,S,Mar 14)*
Muhtaris 109 *(20f,Chl,GS,Apr 13)*
Mulligan's Man 92 *(16f,Utt,S,Oct 30)*
Mullinavat 96 *(19f,Mar,G,Jly 5)*
Multi Grain 101 *(15½f,Mus,G,Nov 6)*
Multiview 100 *(22f,Str,G,Jun 30)*
Murchu 93 *(23½f,Utt,G,Sep 9)*
Murray Mount 104 *(19½f,Ban,G,Oct 27)*
Murrayana 112 *(25f,Ain,S,Apr 9)*
Mustadrik 101 *(24f,Per,GS,Sep 24)*
Mustmeetalady 115 *(20f,Wet,G,Oct 14)*
Muthabir 102 *(17f,Don,G,Nov 27)*
Muwalla 103 *(16f,Kel,GF,Oct 4)*
Mwangaza 93 *(16f,Hex,G,Jun 21)*
My Escapade 107 *(17f,Crl,G,Mar 26)*
My Lad Percy 99 *(24f,Chl,G,Oct 23)*
My Legal Lady 103 *(21½f,Nab,GS,May 19)*
My Little Cracker 103 *(16f,Hex,HY,Mar 17)*
My Lord 102 *(16½f,Tau,G,Apr 20)*
My Manekineko 98 *(16½f,Ain,S,Apr 9)*
My Mistress 94 *(16f,Hun,GS,Apr 18)*
My Painter 90 *(15½f,Mus,GS,Jan 4)*
My Renaissance 98 *(16f,Sth,GS,Sep 2)*
My Simon 93 *(16f,Pun,HY,Jan 9)*
My Tent Or Yours 112 *(16½f,Chl,GS,Mar 15)*
Mydor 111 *(22f,Fai,YS,Mar 28)*
Myrtle Drive 99 *(16f,Cat,GS,Mar 1)*
Myska 109 *(16½f,Tau,HY,Dec 30)*
Mystery Code 111 *(17f,Ain,S,Dec 5)*
Mystic Princess 95 *(15½f,Mus,GS,Jan 4)*
Mystic Sky 105 *(17f,Mar,GS,Apr 21)*
Mystical Knight 97 *(21f,War,S,Feb 13)*
Mystifiable 101 *(18½f,Exe,G,Oct 8)*
Myztique 102 *(18f,Fai,HY,Jan 10)*

Na Trachtalai Abu 94 *(24f,Pun,G,May 16)*
Nabhan 102 *(16f,San,G,Apr 23)*
Nabucco 109 *(19f,Mar,G,Jly 5)*
Naburn 103 *(20½f,Ncs,S,Apr 8)*
Nafaath 111 *(17f,Sed,S,Nov 24)*
Nakadam 99 *(24½f,Ayr,HY,Jan 2)*
Nam Hai 98 *(16f,Sth,S,Dec 1)*
Nambour 114 *(20f,Fai,Y,Mar 27)*
Nancy's Trix 101 *(25½f,Cat,S,Feb 15)*
Nansaroy 106 *(16f,Chp,S,Nov 18)*
Nathans Pride 94 *(18f,Fon,G,Mar 19)*
Native Display 112 *(16f,Plu,G,Oct 19)*
Native Optimist 105 *(24f,Wet,S,Dec 5)*
Native Robin 90 *(21½f,Wcn,G,Oct 25)*
Nautical Nitwit 104 *(20f,Sth,G,Oct 22)*
Navanman 99 *(23½f,Fak,S,Feb 8)*
Near To Tears 94 *(15½f,Mus,G,Nov 27)*
Nebula Storm 103 *(16f,Fak,G,Oct 16)*
Needless Shouting 100 *(18f,Fon,HY,Dec 26)*
Nellie The Elegant 99 *(16f,Fak,G,Oct 16)*
Nellies Quest 102 *(16f,Wor,GS,May 7)*
Neptune Equester 105 *(26f,Kel,S,Nov 7)*
Nesterenko 107 *(19f,Str,G,Oct 17)*
Net Work Rouge 103 *(26f,War,GS,Nov 4)*
Neumond 102 *(22f,Asc,GS,Nov 21)*
Never Equalled 116 *(16f,Ffo,HY,Dec 14)*
Never Never 101 *(19½f,Mus,GS,Jan 1)*
Never Said That 103 *(24f,Pun,Y,Apr 30)*
Never Says Never 107 *(16f,Lin,HY,Dec 1)*
Never Up 101 *(20f,Ain,G,Jun 12)*
Neverushacon 101 *(16f,Pun,HY,Dec 6)*
New Horizons 104 *(21f,Kem,G,May 13)*
New Street 101 *(16f,Hay,S,Nov 21)*
New Vennture 104 *(17f,Ain,S,Dec 5)*
New Youmzain 99 *(20f,Wet,G,May 28)*
Newberry New 103 *(16f,Fai,HY,Feb 20)*
Neworld 102 *(16f,Lud,S,Dec 2)*
Newsworthy 103 *(19½f,Don,GS,Feb 11)*
Newton Geronimo 105 *(16½f,Tau,G,Apr 20)*
Newton Martini 100 *(23f,Wor,G,Aug 19)*
Newtown Lad 104 *(16f,Hex,HY,Apr 18)*
Newyearsresolution 100 *(23f,Hex,HY,Mar 17)*
Next Bend 90 *(16f,Fai,Y,Mar 27)*
Niamh Machine 93 *(24f,Pun,G,May 16)*
Nice Vintage 103 *(16f,Fai,HY,Dec 19)*
Nicely Indeed 95 *(17f,Chl,S,Dec 11)*
Nicholascopernicus 101 *(16f,Hun,GS,Apr 18)*
Nichols Canyon 119 *(16f,Leo,HY,Dec 29)*
Nick Brody 106 *(16f,Pun,HY,Feb 17)*
Nicki's Nipper 101 *(17f,Sed,S,Mar 15)*
Nicky Nutjob 97 *(19f,Tow,G,May 11)*
Night Generation 91 *(16f,Fai,HY,Dec 19)*
Night In Milan 96 *(27f,Sed,S,Oct 29)*
Nightline 104 *(23f,Ban,G,Oct 27)*
Nine Altars 104 *(16f,Kel,S,Apr 2)*
Ninepointsixthree 99 *(17f,Exe,GS,Apr 12)*
No Ceiling 102 *(19½f,Mus,S,Feb 17)*
No Comment 105 *(16f,Wet,HY,Jan 26)*
No Heretic 97 *(16f,Nby,G,Apr 2)*
No Likey 99 *(20f,Utt,G,Sep 9)*
No More Heroes 99 *(24f,Pun,GY,Apr 29)*
No Planning 92 *(23f,Hay,S,May 9)*
No Secrets 102 *(24f,Pun,Y,Apr 30)*
No Win No Fee 94 *(17f,Nab,GS,Jly 27)*
Nobel Leader 104 *(16f,Sth,GS,Feb 28)*
Noble Friend 105 *(19f,Fon,G,Sep 6)*
Noble Ned 101 *(21f,Kem,S,Jan 25)*
Noble Reach 98 *(17f,Mar,G,Oct 17)*
Nobody Home 94 *(20f,Fai,S,Nov 29)*
Norfolk Sound 97 *(17f,Crl,G,Mar 26)*
Norman The Red 101 *(21½f,Fon,HY,Feb 18)*
Norse Legend 102 *(23½f,Asc,GS,Apr 3)*
Norse Light 100 *(16f,Hun,GS,Apr 18)*
North Hill 97 *(16f,Hun,GS,Feb 25)*
North Hill Harvey 114 *(16½f,Ain,S,Apr 8)*
North London 91 *(21½f,Nab,GS,Aug 12)*
Northandsouth 101 *(17f,Don,S,Mar 4)*
Northern Meeting 103 *(16½f,Str,G,Oct 17)*
Not For Burning 110 *(22f,Fai,YS,Mar 28)*
Notebook 102 *(16f,Cat,S,Jan 27)*
Notnowsam 101 *(20f,Sth,G,May 12)*
Nouailhas 94 *(19f,Tow,G,May 11)*
Now This Is It 100 *(21f,Wet,G,Oct 14)*
Number One London 101 *(16f,Utt,G,Jly 15)*
Nuts Well 105 *(16½f,Ncs,HY,Mar 19)*
Nyanza 99 *(16f,War,GS,May 20)*

O Ceallaigh 96 *(16f,Leo,HY,Dec 27)*
O O Seven 113 *(16f,San,S,Dec 5)*
Oak Vintage 101 *(19f,Crl,HY,Feb 22)*
Occasionally Yours 107 *(20f,Fak,G,May 31)*

Oceane 107 (16½f,Chl,GS,Nov 14)
Octagon 108 (16f,Hex,HY,May 9)
Oculist 109 (20f,Ain,G,Jun 12)
Ofcoursewecan 95 (21½f,Wcn,G,May 7)
Officer Drivel 95 (16f,Fak,G,Mar 18)
Officer Hoolihan 105 (19f,Str,S,Mar 5)
Officieux 98 (16f,Leo,HY,Feb 6)
Ogaritmo 99 (16f,Sth,GS,Jun 15)
Oh Land Abloom 98 (20½f,Mar,G,May 8)
Old Guard 119 (16f,Kem,GS,Dec 26)
Old Magic 104 (17f,Ban,S,Mar 16)
Old Pride 104 (21f,Lud,GS,Nov 23)
Oldgrangewood 101 (19f,Mar,GS,Nov 19)
Oliver's Gold 110 (16½f,Str,G,Jly 12)
Olofi 111 (15f,Wcn,S,Nov 7)
Olympiad 94 (20f,Ain,G,Jun 12)
Olympian Boy 94 (21½f,Nab,S,Mar 26)
Omgnotanother 94 (16f,Utt,S,Nov 22)
Omid 103 (24½f,Crl,G,Oct 15)
On Demand 91 (15f,Wcn,S,Dec 26)
On The Bridge 110 (26½f,Nab,GS,Oct 9)
On Your Max 98 (20f,Wor,G,Aug 19)
One Big Love 104 (21f,Kem,G,May 4)
One Cool Boy 100 (16f,Hun,GS,Apr 18)
One Cool Scorpion 98 (20f,Ain,S,Nov 7)
One For Harry 111 (20f,Crl,GS,Nov 1)
One For Hocky 101 (23f,Mar,G,Aug 2)
One More Go 95 (16f,Sth,S,Dec 1)
One Style 111 (16f,Chp,S,Apr 9)
One Track Mind 113 (23f,Hay,HY,Feb 20)
Onefitzall 111 (20f,Utt,GS,Oct 30)
Oneida Tribe 101 (21f,Kem,S,Jan 25)
Oneofapear 99 (17f,Mar,G,Jun 19)
Ongenstown Lad 106 (22f,Crt,G,Jun 26)
Only Gorgeous 105 (21½f,Fon,G,Jun 3)
Onwiththeparty 95 (22f,Asc,S,Dec 18)
Open Eagle 115 (21f,War,HY,Jan 16)
Optical High 102 (27f,Sed,GS,Oct 12)
Optimistic Bias 108 (24f,Sth,GS,Feb 28)
Orby's Man 105 (24f,Utt,G,May 2)
Orchard Boy 92 (20½f,Mar,S,Apr 10)
Orchard Road 98 (17f,Sed,GS,Jan 31)
Ordensritter 100 (24f,Lud,G,Nov 2)
Ordinary World 101 (16f,Pun,G,May 16)
Orpheus Valley 93 (20f,Fai,S,Nov 29)
Orsm 96 (25f,Hun,G,Oct 13)
Orthodox Lad 103 (16f,War,GS,Nov 4)
Oscar Baby 90 (21½f,Fon,G,Jun 3)
Oscar Blue 104 (23f,Hay,S,Nov 20)
Oscar Chimes 93 (24f,Pun,G,May 16)
Oscar Jane 111 (16f,Plu,G,Oct 19)
Oscar Leney 90 (23½f,Utt,GF,Jly 7)
Oscar O'Scar 101 (20f,Wet,HY,Jan 26)
Oscar Prairie 102 (17f,Exe,HY,Nov 22)
Oscar Sam 97 (24f,Chl,G,Mar 17)
Oscar's Passion 91 (20f,Fai,HY,Feb 20)
Oscarteea 105 (19f,Hay,S,Nov 21)
Osgood 105 (19f,Fon,GS,Aug 13)
Osorios Trial 100 (16f,Utt,G,Jun 11)
Ossie's Dancer 108 (20½f,Plu,G,May 10)
Oulamayo 92 (16f,Plu,GS,Nov 2)
Our Chief 93 (21f,Kem,G,May 4)
Our Duke 114 (20f,Fai,Y,Mar 27)
Our Folly 104 (22f,Str,G,Sep 14)
Our Kaempfer 105 (24f,Chl,G,Mar 17)
Our Kylie 110 (17f,Crl,G,Mar 26)
Our Mick 97 (24f,Utt,G,May 2)
Our Phylli Vera 92 (17f,Sed,S,Oct 29)
Our Thomas 105 (17f,Don,G,Feb 24)
Our Three Sons 102 (16f,Plu,G,Apr 22)
Ourmanmassini 99 (16f,Plu,G,Apr 22)
Out Of The Mist 103 (16f,Utt,GS,Oct 30)
Out Sam 106 (20f,Crl,GS,Nov 1)
Outlander 111 (20f,Pun,GY,May 1)
Outrath 104 (16f,Plu,S,Nov 30)
Outspoken 114 (16f,Fai,HY,Dec 19)
Over And Above 99 (24f,Wet,G,May 21)
Over The Air 104 (23f,Wor,G,Aug 19)
Over To Midnight 90 (16f,Lud,G,Mar 24)
Overtheedge 109 (16f,Wet,S,Apr 17)
Overtown Express 114 (18½f,Exe,HY,Feb 14)
Owen Glendower 91 (19½f,Chp,HY,Mar 28)
Owen Na View 100 (16f,Hex,G,Jun 21)
Owner Occupier 98 (19f,Fon,GS,Aug 13)
Oyster Shell 102 (17f,Nab,G,Jun 23)
Ozzie The Oscar 106 (16½f,Tau,S,Mar 14)
Ozzy Thomas 105 (16½f,Chl,G,Oct 23)

Pack The Punch 95 (20f,Pun,GY,Apr 29)
Pack Your Bags 93 (20f,Fai,HY,Dec 19)
Paddocks Lounge 101 (20f,Utt,G,Jly 15)
Paddy The Deejay 101 (21f,Lud,GS,Apr 5)
Paddy's Field 108 (19f,Mar,S,Jan 22)
Paddys Runner 107 (16f,Kem,GS,Nov 23)
Padge 99 (23f,Exe,HY,Feb 14)
Padova 98 (16f,Chp,S,Nov 4)
Padre Tito 97 (20f,Wor,GF,Jun 6)
Pain Au Chocolat 110 (15f,Wcn,S,Feb 20)
Pakman 107 (16f,Fai,Y,Mar 27)
Palm Grey 105 (20½f,Mar,HY,Dec 3)
Palmaria 90 (18½f,Exe,S,Nov 11)
Paloma's Prince 97 (19f,War,G,Apr 21)
Pandorica 111 (17f,Nab,G,Jun 12)
Pandy Wells 94 (21f,Tow,G,Nov 5)
Panis Angelicus 99 (19f,Str,GS,Jly 30)
Pantxoa 98 (23f,Mar,G,Jly 5)
Paolozzi 98 (16f,Sth,G,Jun 9)
Park House 93 (20f,Wet,G,May 28)
Parles Pond 103 (19f,Crl,GS,May 7)
Part And Parcel 94 (23f,Wor,G,Aug 19)
Party Palace 105 (17f,Nab,S,May 7)
Party Rock 113 (20f,Ain,S,Apr 8)
Pass On The Mantle 91 (20½f,Mar,GS,Apr 21)
Pass The Time 111 (20f,Chl,GS,Mar 15)
Patricktom Boru 98 (23f,Wor,GF,Jly 1)
Pattara 102 (19½f,Hun,GS,Aug 31)
Pauls Conn 91 (21½f,Nab,G,May 27)
Pawn Star 101 (20f,Sth,S,Apr 15)
Pay Your Way 94 (16f,Utt,S,Oct 30)
Peace And Co 112 (16f,San,S,Feb 6)
Peaceful Gardens 94 (21½f,Nab,G,Jun 23)
Pearl Castle 109 (15½f,Mus,GS,Jan 1)
Pegasus Walk 97 (20f,Wet,G,May 28)
Peggy Do 94 (21½f,Nab,GS,May 19)
Pekanheim 105 (16f,Hex,G,May 26)
Pemba 106 (16f,War,GS,Nov 4)
Pembridge 95 (16f,Chp,S,Nov 4)
Pembroke House 96 (16f,Tow,GF,Apr 30)
Penglai Pavilion 112 (16f,Hex,G,Jun 13)
Penn Lane 95 (20f,Sth,HY,Dec 13)
Pennywell 100 (21f,Wet,S,Apr 1)
Perceus 96 (16f,Hun,S,Jan 15)
Perennial 96 (17f,Crt,G,Jun 26)
Perfect Poison 98 (19½f,Don,G,Nov 27)
Perfect Summer 101 (17f,Exe,G,Mar 22)
Perform 104 (20f,Ain,G,Oct 25)
Periquest 106 (21f,Hun,GS,Dec 6)
Perseid 99 (16f,Wet,S,Apr 1)
Pershing 108 (17f,Ban,G,Jly 31)
Persian Breeze 100 (16f,Hun,GS,Feb 25)
Persian Herald 99 (16f,Hex,HY,May 9)
Personable 95 (16½f,Str,G,Jun 30)
Perspicace 102 (17f,Exe,G,Apr 21)
Peter Silver 93 (21f,War,G,Apr 21)
Peter The Mayo Man 105 (17f,Ban,S,Mar 16)
Peterpanopirateman 90 (20f,Wet,HY,Nov 25)
Peters Grey 106 (16f,Kel,GS,May 6)
Petethepear 110 (23f,Hay,G,Mar 26)
Petit Mouchoir 118 (16½f,Ain,S,Apr 8)
Petite Parisienne 109 (16f,Pun,S,May 2)
Petite Power 98 (21f,Kem,S,Feb 12)
Petrou 103 (17f,Ban,S,Dec 11)
Phantom Prince 105 (20f,Pun,GY,Apr 29)
Phar Island 104 (16f,Pun,HY,Jan 9)
Phare Isle 105 (23f,Mar,G,Jly 5)
Philharmonic Hall 108 (17f,Sed,S,Nov 24)
Pied Du Roi 105 (16f,Tow,G,May 11)
Pilansberg 92 (16f,Kem,GS,Feb 27)
Pilgrims Bay 108 (21½f,Wcn,S,Jan 21)
Pilgrims Rest 104 (16f,Ffo,HY,Dec 14)
Pillard 102 (19f,Nby,G,Apr 2)
Pine Creek 97 (20f,Ain,G,Oct 25)
Pine Warbler 97 (20½f,Lei,HY,Dec 28)
Pineau De Re 110 (25f,Crl,HY,Dec 13)
Pink Coat 100 (16f,Pun,GY,Apr 28)
Pink Play 106 (16f,Wet,S,Feb 6)
Pink Tara 104 (16f,Tow,G,Nov 5)
Pinkie Brown 103 (16f,Asc,GS,Apr 3)
Pinnacle Panda 107 (24½f,Don,G,Feb 24)
Pinotage 99 (17f,Sed,GS,Oct 12)
Pistol 110 (19f,Crl,HY,Feb 22)
Pithivier 99 (20f,Sth,S,Nov 17)
Pivot Bridge 106 (16f,Pun,GY,Apr 28)
Pixie Cut 96 (22f,Crl,GS,Jly 20)
Pixiepot 105 (20f,Crl,HY,Nov 9)
Planetoid 104 (18f,Fon,GS,Apr 15)
Playhara 101 (20f,Ain,G,May 15)
Pleasant Company 109 (20f,Pun,S,May 2)
Plinth 110 (16f,Leo,HY,Dec 29)
Pobbles Bay 109 (26f,War,HY,Jan 16)
Poet Mark 94 (17f,Mar,S,Nov 5)
Poetic Lord 97 (16f,Wet,GS,Mar 22)
Poetic Presence 95 (16f,Chp,HY,Nov 18)
Poetic Verse 110 (19f,Mar,G,Aug 2)
Point The Way 109 (20½f,Mar,HY,Feb 9)
Poker School 109 (21f,Kem,GS,Feb 27)
Polamco 103 (24f,Chl,G,Oct 23)
Polarbrook 106 (19½f,Don,GS,Dec 11)
Polarisation 106 (16f,San,S,Dec 4)
Policy Breach 95 (20f,Sth,HY,Dec 13)
Politeness 101 (16f,Kel,GS,May 6)
Political Quiz 106 (16f,Sth,G,Oct 22)
Politologue 111 (17f,Exe,HY,Feb 14)
Polly Peachum 105 (20f,Chl,GS,Mar 15)
Polo The Mumm 102 (17f,Nab,GS,Jly 27)
Polstar 105 (15f,Wcn,G,Oct 25)
Pomme 96 (17f,Don,GS,Dec 11)
Poppies Milan 101 (24f,Per,G,Jly 2)
Popping Along 105 (19f,Fon,S,Aug 25)
Port Navas 92 (23f,Exe,G,Apr 21)
Posh Frock 91 (24f,Pun,G,May 16)
Positive Approach 107 (24f,Fai,Y,Mar 29)
Potters Corner 111 (20f,Wet,G,Oct 14)
Potters Legend 107 (25f,Ain,S,Apr 8)
Potters Midnight 97 (16f,Sth,S,Nov 17)
Pougne Bobbi 110 (16f,Chp,HY,Feb 5)
Poulanassy 107 (17f,Sed,GS,Nov 10)
Powderonthebonnet 101 (23½f,Utt,G,Jly 24)
Prairie Hawk 94 (20f,Wor,GF,Jly 23)
Prairie Town 110 (17f,Chl,HY,Jan 30)
Precious Ground 104 (23f,Exe,GS,Mar 8)
Premier Bond 112 (16f,San,S,Dec 5)
Preseli Rock 115 (16f,Ffo,HY,Dec 14)
Presence Felt 104 (25f,Hun,G,Oct 13)
Present Man 109 (21½f,Wcn,HY,Nov 19)
Present Times 90 (16½f,Tau,HY,Feb 2)
Present View 103 (20f,Sth,S,Mar 29)
Presented 100 (24½f,Crl,G,Oct 15)
Presenting Arms 108 (16f,Kem,GS,Nov 23)
Presenting Junior 91 (20f,Hex,GS,Nov 6)
Presenting Rose 106 (16f,Kel,HY,Dec 29)
Presenting Streak 103 (22f,Str,G,Sep 14)
Pret A Thou 102 (19f,Tow,S,Mar 17)
Pretty Miss Mahler 99 (19f,Crl,HY,Feb 22)
Pretty Rose 99 (19f,War,G,Sep 22)
Prettyasapicture 99 (16f,Wor,GS,Sep 2)
Pride Of The Braid 100 (16f,Leo,S,Jan 17)
Primo Capitano 102 (24f,Ffo,G,Jun 4)
Prince Khurram 107 (17f,Ban,G,Jly 31)
Prince Kup 103 (16f,Leo,HY,Dec 28)
Prince Mahler 103 (16f,Chp,S,Nov 4)
Prince Of Pirates 100 (20f,Wet,G,May 28)
Prince Of Poets 103 (17f,Exe,G,Oct 8)
Prince Of Scars 112 (24f,Leo,HY,Dec 28)
Prince Of Steal 111 (16f,Fak,S,Feb 8)
Prince Pippin 102 (19f,Tow,G,May 11)
Princely Conn 94 (20f,Pun,S,May 2)
Princess Lir 99 (20f,Pun,HY,Jan 9)
Princess Roania 95 (20f,Utt,G,Jly 24)
Princess Tara 106 (20f,Per,G,Apr 20)
Princeton Royale 108 (23½f,Utt,G,Oct 4)
Private Jones 94 (16f,Utt,G,Jly 24)
Professeur Emery 96 (17f,Ban,S,Mar 31)
Profit Commission 97 (21½f,Wcn,G,May 7)
Promanco 106 (19f,Fon,G,Oct 3)
Proofreader 102 (16½f,Tau,GS,Nov 26)
Protek Des Flos 115 (17f,Chl,HY,Jan 30)
Proud Times 94 (19f,Tow,S,Mar 17)
Prouts Pub 108 (18f,Fon,HY,Dec 26)
Prussian Eagle 105 (18f,Leo,S,Feb 28)
Ptit Zig 111 (24f,Chl,HY,Jan 30)
Pull The Chord 107 (17f,Exe,S,Nov 11)
Pulling Power 98 (21f,Lud,S,Dec 16)
Pulpitarian 98 (22f,Crt,GS,May 25)
Pure Science 109 (23½f,Utt,S,Nov 22)
Purple 'n Gold 106 (16½f,Str,G,Jly 12)
Purple Bay 103 (16½f,Ncs,S,Nov 28)
Push Me 106 (17f,Sed,GF,Sep 3)
Pyromaniac 94 (16f,Pun,GY,May 1)
Pyrshan 108 (24f,Sth,GS,Feb 28)

Qasser 105 (16½f,Tau,G,Nov 12)
Qatea 93 (16f,Cat,S,Dec 15)
Qewy 110 (21f,Chl,G,Mar 16)
Quadriller 91 (18½f,Nab,G,Jun 23)
Qualando 108 (16½f,Tau,HY,Feb 23)
Quantum Of Solace 102 (16f,Hun,GS,Apr 18)
Que Sera 101 (16f,Tow,S,Dec 17)
Quebec 95 (16½f,Chl,G,Oct 23)
Queen Alphabet 112 (17f,Mar,G,Sep 26)
Queen Spud 104 (20f,Fak,G,May 5)
Queens Wild 90 (24f,Pun,Y,Apr 30)
Quel Elite 108 (25f,Crl,HY,Dec 13)
Quench Tara 92 (16f,Wor,G,Jun 21)
Querry Horse 106 (17f,Mar,GS,Apr 21)
Quest Magic 100 (17f,Crt,S,May 27)
Quick Brew 103 (16f,Hex,G,Oct 2)
Quick Decisson 108 (17f,Nab,S,May 7)
Quiet Candid 93 (17f,Mar,GS,Apr 21)
Quieto Sol 92 (18½f,Exe,G,Mar 22)
Quill Art 100 (17f,Don,S,Mar 4)
Quincy Des Pictons 100 (19½f,Ban,HY,Mar 2)
Quincy Magoo 95 (21f,Kem,G,Oct 18)
Quinto 103 (20f,Crl,G,Nov 1)

Racing Europe 104 (21f,Wet,G,Oct 14)
Rafafie 107 (15f,Wcn,S,Jan 21)
Ragdollianna 110 (16f,Plu,G,Oct 19)
Raid Stane 98 (25½f,Crt,GF,Jun 26)
Raifteiri 94 (16f,Hex,G,Jun 21)
Railway Tommy 103 (20f,Pun,GY,Apr 29)
Railway Vic 91 (17f,Nab,G,Sep 18)
Rainbow Haze 103 (23f,Wor,G,Aug 19)
Rainman 96 (16f,Tow,GF,Apr 30)
Rainy City 106 (19½f,Don,GS,Jan 29)
Raise A Spark 105 (16f,Utt,G,May 2)
Raktiman 93 (20f,Utt,G,May 2)
Rally 94 (25f,Ain,G,May 15)
Rashaan 109 (16f,Leo,HY,Dec 26)
Rathnaleen Girl 96 (18f,Fai,SH,Apr 5)
Rathpatrick 104 (24f,Chl,G,Mar 17)
Rayadour 92 (24f,Wet,S,Nov 14)
Raymond Reddington 95 (20½f,Ncs,S,Apr 8)
Rayvin Black 114 (15f,Wcn,S,Feb 20)
Razzle Dazzle 'Em 98 (16f,Fak,GS,Feb 19)
Rebekah Rabbit 100 (19f,War,HY,Dec 31)
Rebel Benefit 90 (20f,Wor,GF,Jun 24)
Reblis 102 (19½f,Lin,HY,Nov 24)
Red Devil Boys 109 (19½f,Don,GS,Dec 11)
Red Devil Lads 93 (23f,Ban,S,Mar 31)
Red Devil Star 106 (18f,Fon,GS,Apr 15)
Red Hammer 96 (16f,Hun,S,Mar 28)
Red Hanrahan 111 (21½f,Fon,S,Apr 15)
Red Hott Robbie 103 (16f,War,HY,Jan 16)
Red Infantry 103 (21f,War,G,Mar 23)
Red Mystique 98 (17f,Crl,HY,Dec 13)
Red Orator 95 (16f,Kem,GS,Dec 26)
Red Red Rover 93 (19½f,Chp,G,Mar 24)
Red Riverman 96 (16f,Kem,G,Oct 18)
Red Skipper 92 (16f,Lud,G,May 10)
Red Tornado 114 (16½f,Str,S,Mar 5)
Redclue 102 (25½f,Crt,GF,Jun 26)
Redera 107 (16½f,Chl,GS,Nov 15)
Redkalani 102 (20½f,Ncs,HY,Dec 10)
Redpender 94 (16½f,Ncs,HY,Dec 10)
Regal Diamond 106 (20f,Utt,G,Jly 15)
Regal One 92 (20f,Wor,G,Jly 28)
Regal Park 93 (20f,Utt,GF,Jly 7)
Regal Ways 107 (16f,Cat,S,Mar 9)
Regulation 108 (15f,Wcn,GF,Oct 16)
Rejaah 105 (16f,Lud,G,Mar 24)
Remember Forever 90 (23f,Exe,G,Apr 21)
Rendl Beach 104 (21½f,Wcn,S,Jan 21)
Rene's Girl 105 (20½f,Nby,G,Apr 2)
Renneti 110 (16f,Asc,GS,Dec 19)
Renoyr 95 (18f,Kel,HY,Dec 29)
Rest And Be 110 (17f,Nab,G,Jun 12)
Restraint Of Trade 105 (17f,Mar,G,Jly 18)
Retrieve The Stick 105 (16f,Hex,HY,May 9)
Retro Valley 95 (17f,Nab,GS,Aug 22)
Return Flight 104 (20f,Wet,HY,Jan 16)
Return Spring 110 (23½f,Asc,GS,Apr 3)
Returntovendor 100 (20f,Fai,SH,Apr 5)
Rev Up Ruby 104 (25½f,Crt,GS,Jly 20)
Reve De Sivola 117 (24½f,Asc,GS,Dec 19)
Reyno 104 (16f,Lud,S,Feb 3)
Rhymers Stone 100 (16f,Cat,S,Feb 15)
Rhythm Of Sound 94 (19f,Crl,S,Mar 10)
Richardofdoccombe 94 (18½f,Nab,S,May 7)
Riddlestown 111 (20f,Sth,G,Mar 21)
Right Step 100 (16f,Kem,GS,Nov 23)
Rinnagree Rosie 101 (20½f,Ncs,HY,Dec 10)
Rioja Day 95 (19½f,Mus,GS,Nov 27)
Rior 102 (26½f,Nab,G,Jun 12)
Risk A Fine 106 (23f,Exe,G,May 5)
Rivabodiva 107 (16f,Hex,GS,Oct 10)
Rival D'Estruval 101 (21f,Wet,G,Oct 14)
River Dancing 97 (21½f,Fon,G,May 1)
River Maigue 108 (20f,Ain,G,May 15)
Riviera Sun 105 (20f,Pun,GY,Apr 29)
Road To Freedom 106 (23½f,Fak,S,Jan 28)
Road To Gold 108 (20f,Wet,HY,Jan 16)
Road To Respect 108 (24f,Fai,Y,Mar 29)
Road To Rome 110 (17f,Ban,S,Mar 16)
Roadie Joe 108 (16f,War,G,Sep 22)
Robbie Rabbit 107 (24f,Utt,S,May 6)
Robert's Star 102 (19½f,Chp,S,Nov 4)
Robertstown 101 (17f,Don,HY,Dec 12)
Robin Of Locksley 108 (21f,Lud,GS,Nov 12)
Robin Thyme 115 (20f,Pun,HY,Feb 17)
Robinesse 104 (18½f,Exe,HY,Dec 17)
Robins Reef 114 (17f,Chl,G,Mar 17)
Robinshill 103 (20f,Sth,G,Mar 21)
Robinsson 101 (21f,Tow,G,Nov 5)
Roc D'Apsis 91 (20f,Ain,G,Jun 12)
Rock A Doodle Doo 97 (16½f,Ncs,HY,Mar 19)
Rock Gone 107 (20½f,Plu,HY,Feb 15)
Rock N Rhythm 97 (16f,Kem,G,May 4)
Rock Of Leon 104 (19f,Str,G,Oct 17)
Rock On Oscar 107 (19½f,Don,GS,Feb 11)
Rock On Rocky 106 (16f,Chp,G,Oct 11)
Rock On Ruby 115 (24f,Wet,S,Oct 31)
Rock On The Moor 111 (20f,Chl,GS,Mar 15)
Rock On Westie 98 (18f,Fai,SH,Apr 5)
Rock Relief 107 (20½f,Ncs,HY,Dec 10)
Rock The Kasbah 110 (19f,Hay,S,Nov 21)
Rockabilly Riot 104 (16f,Kel,GF,Oct 4)
Rockawango 90 (17f,Don,S,Dec 12)
Rocklim 97 (26f,Kel,GS,Mar 21)
Rocknrobin 90 (16½f,Tau,HY,Feb 2)
Rockweiller 92 (16f,Wor,GS,May 7)
Rocky Rebel 102 (20f,Sth,G,May 12)
Rocky Stone 99 (27f,Sed,S,Feb 9)
Rocky Two 101 (17f,Sed,G,Sep 29)
Rogue Trader 106 (24f,Pun,Y,Apr 30)
Roja Dove 106 (16f,Utt,G,Jly 15)
Roll It Out 108 (22f,Fai,YS,Mar 28)
Roll Of Thunder 101 (16f,Hex,G,Jun 21)
Roll The Dough 95 (21½f,Exe,S,Nov 11)
Rolling Dough 102 (19f,War,GS,May 4)
Rolling Dylan 109 (18½f,Exe,HY,Feb 14)
Rolling Maul 104 (26f,War,HY,Jan 16)
Rolling Thunder 102 (19½f,Mus,S,Feb 17)
Romain De Senam 112 (16½f,Chl,G,Mar 16)
Roman Flight 111 (16½f,Str,G,May 30)
Roman Gold 103 (16f,Pun,HY,Dec 6)
Romany Ryme 105 (24f,Per,G,Jly 1)
Romeo Americo 92 (16½f,Tau,GS,Nov 26)
Romeo Is Bleeding 99 (22f,Ffo,GS,Mar 20)
Romulus Du Donjon 111 (19f,Fon,G,May 1)
Ronaldinho 105 (17f,Crt,GS,Jly 20)
Rons Dream 111 (25f,Chl,GS,Nov 14)
Rose Red 101 (16f,Utt,GF,Jly 7)
Rose Revived 93 (16f,Sth,GS,Feb 28)
Rosie Alice 103 (18f,Fai,HY,Jan 30)
Rosygo 96 (18½f,Exe,G,Mar 22)
Round Robin 100 (21f,Lud,GS,Nov 23)

Round Tower 107 *(19½f,Mus,GS,Nov 27)*
Roxyfet 102 *(17f,Sed,S,Mar 6)*
Royal Battalion 105 *(18f,Fon,GS,Aug 13)*
Royal Caviar 112 *(16f,Fai,YS,Mar 28)*
Royal Chief 100 *(24f,Tau,GS,Dec 10)*
Royal Guardsman 103 *(19f,Nby,S,Nov 28)*
Royal Irish Hussar 106 *(20f,Ain,G,May 15)*
Royal Milan 105 *(19½f,Don,GS,Dec 29)*
Royal Salute 97 *(18f,Fon,GS,Apr 1)*
Royal Skies 105 *(16f,Wor,GF,Jly 23)*
Royal Vacation 109 *(16½f,Tau,HY,Feb 23)*
Royale Django 98 *(23f,Wor,G,Jly 28)*
Royale Knight 99 *(23½f,Asc,S,Feb 20)*
Royale's Legacy 103 *(21½f,Fon,G,Jun 3)*
Royalraise 109 *(21½f,Fon,G,Jun 3)*
Roycano 108 *(24½f,Ayr,S,Apr 15)*
Ruacana 109 *(21½f,Wcn,S,Dec 26)*
Ruaraidh Hugh 110 *(19f,Tow,G,May 11)*
Ruby Rambler 111 *(16f,Tow,G,Nov 5)*
Ruddy Article 105 *(21½f,Nab,G,Jly 19)*
Rude And Crude 99 *(16f,Hun,S,Jan 6)*
Ruler Of All 107 *(16f,Utt,G,Jun 28)*
Rum And Butter 101 *(21½f,Nab,GS,Aug 22)*
Rumble Of Thunder 105 *(20f,Sth,GS,Sep 2)*
Run Ructions Run 100 *(24½f,Ayr,S,Apr 15)*
Running Brook 96 *(16f,Kel,G,May 24)*
Running Wolf 94 *(20f,Sth,G,Mar 21)*
Runswick Relax 100 *(17f,Sed,S,Nov 24)*
Rupert Lamb 106 *(16f,Pun,GY,Apr 28)*
Rushvale 105 *(20f,Utt,S,Nov 14)*
Russian Bill 108 *(24f,Leo,HY,Dec 28)*
Russian Royale 105 *(17f,Mar,G,Oct 5)*
Rustamabad 102 *(16f,Sth,G,Sep 29)*
Ryalex 91 *(18f,Kel,GS,Mar 21)*
Rydon Pynes 110 *(26½f,Nab,GS,Oct 9)*
Rye House 100 *(16f,Lud,G,Oct 7)*
Ryedale Racer 98 *(20f,Hex,GS,Nov 6)*
Ryeolliean 112 *(16f,Plu,G,May 10)*

Sa Suffit 105 *(19f,Crl,HY,Feb 22)*
Sacre Malta 96 *(19f,Tow,S,Mar 17)*
Sacred Square 102 *(16f,Lud,S,Dec 2)*
Saddlers Encore 109 *(21½f,Wcn,S,Dec 26)*
Sadma 110 *(16f,Plu,G,Oct 19)*
Saffron Wells 98 *(19½f,Chp,G,Oct 10)*
Sahara Haze 95 *(21f,Lud,GS,Apr 5)*
Sailors Warn 106 *(17f,Sed,GF,Sep 3)*
Saint Charles 95 *(16f,Nby,S,Mar 5)*
Saint Elm 90 *(17f,Ban,G,Jly 31)*
Saint John Henry 94 *(26f,War,S,Feb 13)*
Saint Lino 106 *(21f,Lud,HY,Jan 4)*
Sainte Ladylime 111 *(15f,Wcn,S,Mar 2)*
Sakhee's City 106 *(19f,Mar,S,Jan 22)*
Salmanazar 110 *(23½f,Asc,GS,Apr 3)*
Sam Lord 94 *(27f,Sed,S,May 5)*
Sam Red 104 *(20f,Fai,HY,Feb 20)*
Sambulando 97 *(16f,Utt,G,May 16)*
Samedi Soir 104 *(20f,Hex,G,May 26)*
Samoset 107 *(17f,Mar,G,May 17)*
Samtu 104 *(17f,Sed,GS,Feb 25)*
San Benedeto 109 *(16f,Kem,G,Oct 18)*
San Telm 108 *(24f,Chl,G,Apr 14)*
Sanaija 93 *(16f,Utt,GS,Oct 30)*
Sandford Castle 103 *(17f,Exe,HY,Jan 1)*
Sandy Beach 96 *(16½f,Tau,G,Nov 12)*
Sandygate 110 *(19f,Fon,G,May 1)*
Sandymount Duke 108 *(16f,Pun,G,May 16)*
Sandynow 94 *(26f,Fon,G,May 24)*
Saphir Du Rheu 109 *(24½f,Asc,GS,Dec 19)*
Sarpech 103 *(16f,Sth,G,Mar 21)*
Sartorial Elegance 106 *(21½f,Fon,GS,Apr 1)*
Satanic Beat 108 *(16f,War,G,Oct 1)*
Satellite 112 *(16f,Chp,S,Apr 9)*
Saucysioux 90 *(20½f,Plu,HY,Jan 18)*
Save The Bees 94 *(16½f,Chl,G,Oct 23)*
Savello 105 *(16½f,Chl,G,Oct 23)*
Saver 90 *(20f,Wet,G,May 28)*
Savingforvegas 99 *(21f,War,S,Jan 28)*
Say My Name 100 *(23f,Exe,S,Nov 3)*
Scales 98 *(16f,Lud,S,Feb 3)*
Scartare 94 *(16f,Wor,G,Jly 28)*
Sceau Royal 116 *(17f,Chl,S,Dec 12)*
School For Scandal 91 *(19f,Str,G,Sep 5)*
Scoglio 104 *(19f,Mar,G,Jun 5)*
Scoir Mear 93 *(20f,Fai,SH,Apr 5)*
Scoop The Pot 106 *(21f,Chl,GS,Nov 15)*
Scooping 99 *(18½f,Leo,S,Feb 28)*
Scooter Boy 99 *(16f,Hun,S,Jan 15)*
Scoppio Del Carro 105 *(16f,Lud,S,Dec 2)*
Score Card 103 *(16f,Lud,G,Mar 24)*
Scorpions Sting 104 *(17f,Sed,G,May 12)*
Scrafton 97 *(17f,Crt,GS,May 25)*
Sea Beat 92 *(20f,Pun,GY,Apr 29)*
Sea Lord 108 *(20f,Ain,G,May 15)*
Sea The Springs 102 *(19f,War,GS,May 4)*
Sea Wall 109 *(16½f,Tau,HY,Feb 2)*
Seacon Beg 95 *(19f,Str,G,Sep 5)*
Sealous Scout 109 *(24f,Per,GS,Sep 23)*
Sean Airgead 104 *(20f,Kem,G,Oct 2)*
Sean Ban 109 *(17f,Crl,HY,Feb 22)*
Searching 99 *(16f,San,S,Feb 6)*
Seaviper 98 *(23½f,Asc,GS,Apr 3)*
Sebastian Beach 95 *(22f,Asc,S,Dec 18)*
Sebs Sensei 108 *(16f,Plu,G,May 10)*
Secret Door 105 *(16f,Wet,S,Feb 6)*
See Double You 106 *(20f,Hex,S,Mar 29)*
See The Legend 95 *(24f,Per,G,Apr 20)*
See The Rock 105 *(19f,Mar,S,Nov 5)*
Seeking Susan 102 *(20f,Fai,SH,Jan 20)*
Seeyouallincoppers 106 *(16½f,Per,S,May 14)*
Seldom Inn 99 *(24f,Ncs,HY,Mar 19)*
Semper Invicta 96 *(22f,Asc,S,Dec 18)*
Sempre Medici 113 *(17f,Chl,S,Dec 12)*
Sendiym 99 *(17f,Crt,S,May 27)*
Separate Shadows 103 *(19f,Crl,GS,May 7)*
Serenity Now 105 *(15½f,Mus,S,Feb 17)*
Serienschock 97 *(25f,Ain,S,Apr 9)*
Seskinane 103 *(20f,Pun,GY,Apr 29)*
Set In My Ways 98 *(16f,Lud,S,Feb 3)*
Set List 100 *(20f,Utt,G,May 16)*
Set The Trend 107 *(16½f,Str,G,May 17)*
Seven Kingdoms 104 *(16f,San,S,Feb 6)*
Sevenballs Of Fire 105 *(24½f,Ayr,S,Apr 15)*
Seventeen Black 104 *(16f,Hex,G,May 26)*
Seymour Eric 93 *(25½f,Cat,GS,Mar 1)*
Seymour Legend 94 *(22f,Str,GF,May 17)*
Seymour Star 101 *(19½f,Ban,HY,Mar 2)*
Sgt Bull Berry 100 *(24f,Sth,GF,Aug 16)*
Sgt Reckless 106 *(21f,Chl,G,Mar 16)*
Shabra's Bertolini 92 *(16f,Pun,Y,Apr 30)*
Shadagann 96 *(16f,Pun,G,May 16)*
Shadarpour 106 *(21f,Chl,GS,Nov 15)*
Shaddaii 95 *(19½f,Hun,GS,Feb 25)*
Shades Of Midnight 112 *(26f,Kel,GS,Apr 2)*
Shadow Blue 106 *(16½f,Tau,GS,Dec 10)*
Shady Lane 105 *(16f,Sth,GS,Jun 15)*
Shah Of Persia 98 *(21½f,Nab,G,Jun 23)*
Shaiyzar 97 *(16f,Sth,G,Oct 22)*
Shake Devaney 91 *(16f,Plu,HY,Feb 1)*
Shaky Gift 105 *(23½f,Fak,GS,Dec 20)*
Shalambar 102 *(16f,War,GS,May 4)*
Shalianzi 107 *(19f,Fon,GS,Aug 13)*
Shamiran 107 *(20f,Pun,GY,Apr 29)*
Shammick Boy 107 *(21f,Kem,G,Apr 19)*
Shanandoa 90 *(15f,Wcn,S,Mar 2)*
Shaneshill 105 *(24f,Pun,GY,Apr 29)*
Shannak 110 *(22f,Fai,YS,Mar 28)*
Shanroe Society 98 *(16f,Kel,GS,May 6)*
Shanroe Street 101 *(19½f,Mus,S,Feb 17)*
Shantou Ed 99 *(20f,Pun,S,May 2)*
Shantou Flyer 96 *(20f,Pun,GY,Apr 29)*
Shantou Tiger 105 *(25½f,Cat,GS,Feb 5)*
Shantou Village 113 *(21f,Chl,G,Nov 13)*
Sharp Rise 109 *(18f,Kel,GS,Apr 11)*
Sharpasaknife 113 *(20f,Wet,HY,Jan 16)*
She'llbeallright 90 *(16f,Pun,HY,Feb 17)*
She's Late 97 *(16f,Kem,S,Feb 12)*
Shear Rock 107 *(19f,Mar,G,Jun 5)*
Sheer Poetry 100 *(18½f,Nab,G,Jun 12)*
Shine Away 95 *(16f,Utt,S,Nov 22)*
Shininstar 97 *(16f,Lud,GS,Apr 19)*
Shinooki 90 *(25½f,Cat,S,Mar 9)*
Shoofly Milly 101 *(24½f,Kem,S,Jan 25)*
Short Takes 100 *(17f,Ban,G,May 1)*
Shot In The Dark 101 *(19f,Str,G,May 29)*
Shotavodka 110 *(20f,Crl,GS,Nov 1)*
Shouldavboughtgold 90 *(26f,War,GS,Nov 4)*
Shout It Aloud 109 *(17f,Nab,GS,Jly 27)*
Shrewd 112 *(15½f,Mus,S,Feb 7)*
Shutter Island 93 *(16f,Pun,Y,Apr 30)*
Shwaiman 103 *(23½f,Fak,G,May 5)*
Siberian Vixen 103 *(20f,Fai,HY,Feb 20)*
Side Saddle 113 *(20f,Fai,SH,Jan 20)*
Sign Manual 91 *(19½f,Ban,G,May 1)*
Sign Of A Victory 107 *(16f,Kem,GS,Dec 26)*
Significant Move 100 *(16f,Utt,GF,Jly 7)*
Sikandar 110 *(16f,San,G,Apr 23)*
Silent Movie 101 *(16f,Utt,G,Jun 28)*
Silent Wish 92 *(22f,Pun,HY,Feb 17)*
Silk Hall 91 *(22f,Crt,G,Jly 18)*
Silsol 113 *(26f,Kel,GS,Apr 2)*
Silver Concorde 97 *(16f,Leo,HY,Dec 27)*
Silver Dixie 95 *(16f,War,G,Sep 22)*
Silver Duke 108 *(15½f,Mus,GS,Jan 1)*
Silver Shuffle 94 *(20f,Ain,G,Oct 25)*
Silviniaco Conti 109 *(21f,Kem,G,Nov 2)*
Simarthur 101 *(24½f,Crl,G,Oct 15)*
Simmply Sam 110 *(20½f,Ncs,S,Apr 8)*
Simon Squirrel 112 *(18½f,Nab,GS,Oct 9)*
Simonsig 112 *(20f,Ain,S,Nov 7)*
Simple Assignment 104 *(16f,Tow,G,May 11)*
Simply A Legend 109 *(21f,Kem,G,Mar 19)*
Sinakar 100 *(16f,Cat,GS,Mar 1)*
Sinbad The Sailor 101 *(23f,Ban,G,Oct 27)*
Singlefarmpayment 112 *(24f,Chl,HY,Jan 1)*
Sinndar's Man 94 *(20f,Utt,G,Jly 24)*
Sir Chauvelin 110 *(15½f,Mus,G,Nov 6)*
Sir Dylan 102 *(20f,Wcn,G,May 7)*
Sir Ector 106 *(20f,Pun,GY,Apr 29)*
Sir Frank Morgan 93 *(19f,Fon,G,Jun 9)*
Sir Hubert 94 *(16f,Plu,HY,Jan 18)*
Sir Ivan 110 *(21½f,Wcn,S,Dec 26)*
Sir Mangan 110 *(25f,Chl,GS,Nov 14)*
Sir Note 103 *(16f,Utt,G,Jun 11)*
Sir Safir 104 *(16f,Wet,S,Nov 14)*
Sir Scorpion 93 *(16f,Leo,S,Feb 28)*
Sir Valentino 102 *(16½f,Tau,GS,Nov 26)*
Sir Vinski 100 *(24f,Wet,HY,Feb 6)*
Sirabad 98 *(19f,Asc,S,Feb 20)*
Sirius Star 96 *(19f,Mar,S,Mar 28)*
Sirop De Menthe 107 *(16f,Hun,GS,Nov 21)*
Sirpertan 100 *(15½f,Mus,S,Dec 7)*
Sizing Codelco 107 *(16f,Pun,GY,Apr 28)*
Sizing John 102 *(16f,Pun,GY,Apr 28)*
Sizing Tennessee 97 *(17f,Chl,G,Mar 18)*
Skint 105 *(21f,Hun,GS,Dec 6)*
Sky Khan 110 *(20f,Chl,G,Mar 18)*
Sky Lino 98 *(16f,Kem,S,Feb 12)*
Sky Watch 97 *(20f,Wor,G,Jly 28)*
Skyfire 90 *(17f,Mar,G,May 8)*
Skylander 104 *(24f,Per,G,Sep 8)*
Sleep Easy 122 *(16½f,Str,S,Mar 5)*
Sleep In First 105 *(16½f,Ain,G,Jun 12)*
Sleeping City 104 *(17f,Nab,GS,Aug 22)*
Sleepy Haven 91 *(16f,Hay,GS,May 9)*
Slidecheck 102 *(15f,Wcn,S,Mar 2)*
Slipper Satin 99 *(20f,Hex,G,May 26)*
Slowmotion 106 *(16f,Fai,YS,Mar 28)*
Smadynium 104 *(16f,Kel,HY,Dec 6)*
Smart Catch 105 *(16f,San,HY,Feb 19)*
Smart Ruler 107 *(17f,Crt,G,Jun 28)*
Smart Talk 112 *(16f,Hex,GS,Oct 10)*
Smoking Big Cigars 94 *(20f,Fai,S,Nov 29)*
Smugglers Lane 91 *(17f,Mar,G,Jun 19)*
Snake Eyes 96 *(16f,Pun,GY,May 1)*
Snapping Turtle 107 *(27f,Sed,S,Oct 29)*
Sneaking Budge 96 *(16f,San,HY,Jan 2)*
Snippetydoodah 102 *(21½f,Fon,HY,Apr 15)*
Snow Falcon 112 *(20f,Fai,S,Nov 29)*
Snowball 101 *(21f,Hun,S,Nov 10)*
Snowed In 103 *(19½f,Mus,S,Feb 17)*
Snuker 102 *(27f,Sed,S,Feb 9)*
So Fine 106 *(25f,Hun,GS,Jan 29)*
So Satisfied 108 *(19½f,Mus,GS,Jan 1)*
So Young 100 *(18f,Leo,S,Feb 28)*
Solidago 102 *(19f,War,HY,Dec 31)*
Solita 99 *(16f,Leo,HY,Feb 6)*
Solomn Grundy 103 *(19f,Mar,S,Mar 28)*
Solstice Star 113 *(17f,Chl,HY,Jan 30)*
Solway Bay 100 *(24f,Per,G,Sep 8)*
Solway Dandy 101 *(20f,Per,G,Jly 12)*
Solway Prince 104 *(23½f,Utt,GF,Jly 7)*
Solway Sam 103 *(24½f,Ayr,S,Nov 11)*
Solway Trigger 97 *(27f,Sed,GS,Oct 12)*
Some Are Lucky 109 *(20f,Sth,G,Mar 21)*
Some Article 110 *(16f,Pun,GY,Apr 28)*
Some Buckle 104 *(17f,Chl,S,Dec 11)*
Some Kinda Lama 106 *(20½f,Nby,S,Mar 4)*
Some Plan 110 *(16f,Asc,GS,Dec 19)*
Somerset Jem 98 *(21½f,Wcn,S,Mar 2)*
Song Light 111 *(16f,Hay,GS,May 9)*
Song Of The Night 92 *(19½f,Hun,S,Dec 26)*
Song Saa 97 *(20f,Per,G,Apr 20)*
Songsmith 107 *(20f,Sth,GS,Sep 2)*
Sonneofpresenting 106 *(19½f,Hun,S,Dec 26)*
Sort It Out 111 *(20f,Pun,S,May 2)*
Sound Investment 99 *(19½f,Chp,G,Oct 10)*
Soupy Soups 103 *(19f,Fon,S,Nov 15)*
Souriyan 97 *(24f,Chl,G,Apr 14)*
Southfield Vic 106 *(24f,Chl,G,Apr 14)*
Sovinnie 100 *(23f,Wor,G,Aug 19)*
Spa's Dancer 104 *(16f,Lud,GS,Nov 23)*
Space Cadet 108 *(24f,Fai,Y,Mar 29)*
Space Oddity 104 *(16½f,Tau,G,Apr 20)*
Space Ship 103 *(15½f,Mus,G,Nov 6)*
Space Walker 97 *(19f,War,GS,Nov 18)*
Spanish Fleet 92 *(20f,Wet,HY,Jan 16)*
Spanish Fork 95 *(25f,Hun,GF,May 26)*
Special Agent 93 *(21f,Kem,G,Apr 19)*
Speed Master 101 *(26½f,Str,G,May 29)*
Spencer Lea 104 *(23½f,Asc,GS,Apr 3)*
Spendajennie 97 *(19½f,Don,GS,Dec 29)*
Spending Time 97 *(25f,Hun,G,Oct 13)*
Speredek 105 *(23f,Exe,GS,Mar 8)*
Spice Fair 110 *(19f,Tau,HY,Jan 23)*
Spider Web 93 *(16f,Pun,HY,Jan 9)*
Spifer 93 *(20f,Per,G,Apr 20)*
Spiker The Biker 95 *(27f,Sed,S,Mar 27)*
Spin Cast 91 *(17f,Nab,G,Sep 18)*
Spirit River 97 *(22f,Crt,G,Jun 26)*
Spiritofchartwell 93 *(23f,Wor,G,Aug 19)*
Spitz 94 *(19½f,Don,GS,Dec 11)*
Sporting Milan 97 *(21f,War,GS,Apr 21)*
Spring Steel 95 *(20½f,Mar,G,Jun 19)*
Springhill Lad 98 *(26f,War,G,Mar 23)*
Squouateur 112 *(25f,Ain,S,Apr 9)*
St Dominick 106 *(21½f,Nab,GS,May 19)*
St Lewis 91 *(16f,Sth,GS,Feb 28)*
St Quintin 99 *(20f,Utt,G,Sep 9)*
St Saviour 112 *(16f,Lud,HY,Jan 4)*
Stafford Jo 103 *(16f,Chp,G,Apr 22)*
Stage One 102 *(19½f,Don,G,Nov 28)*
Stags Leap 107 *(22f,Crt,G,Jun 26)*
Staker Wallace 104 *(16f,Pun,SH,Jan 31)*
Stand Clear 100 *(24f,Sth,G,Jly 12)*
Stand To Reason 106 *(16½f,Str,G,Jly 30)*
Standing Ovation 101 *(23½f,Utt,G,Sep 9)*
Stanley 95 *(17f,Crt,GS,Aug 29)*
Stanley Bridge 96 *(17f,Crt,S,May 27)*
Star Foot 107 *(17f,Mar,S,Mar 13)*
Star Of Angels 99 *(20f,Fai,SH,Apr 5)*
Star Of Salford 101 *(16f,Wor,G,Jly 15)*
Star Trouper 96 *(16½f,Tau,GS,Nov 26)*
Starchitect 110 *(20f,Ain,S,Apr 8)*
Starluck 104 *(16f,Asc,S,Nov 20)*
Stars Over The Sea 105 *(16½f,Chl,G,Oct 24)*
Start Me Up 91 *(26f,War,G,Sep 22)*
Starving Marvin 110 *(16f,San,HY,Feb 19)*
Stay In My Heart 103 *(22f,Str,G,Jun 30)*
Stay Tuned 93 *(16½f,Str,G,May 17)*
Steady Major 99 *(16f,Fai,HY,Jan 10)*
Steel City 103 *(16f,San,HY,Feb 19)*
Steel Gold 102 *(24f,Sth,G,Jly 12)*
Stephanie Frances 109 *(16f,Kem,G,Oct 18)*
Stephen Hero 101 *(21f,Tow,G,Nov 5)*
Stepover 93 *(19f,Mar,S,Feb 21)*
Steps And Stairs 96 *(24f,Sth,GF,Aug 16)*
Sterling Gent 98 *(21½f,Sed,GF,Apr 30)*
Sternrubin 112 *(16f,Asc,GS,Dec 19)*
Still Believing 108 *(24f,Lud,G,Oct 7)*
Stilletto 105 *(19f,Hay,S,Nov 21)*
Stonebrook 98 *(20f,Pun,S,May 2)*
Stonegate 90 *(16f,Plu,GS,Nov 2)*
Stoneham 101 *(16f,Kel,S,Apr 2)*
Stopped Out 94 *(16f,Wet,S,Dec 5)*
Storm Alert 99 *(23f,Ban,G,Oct 27)*
Storm Forecast 109 *(16f,Hex,S,Mar 29)*
Storm In September 94 *(16f,Pun,HY,Jan 9)*
Storm Of Swords 103 *(16f,Wor,G,May 22)*
Storm To Pass 94 *(20f,Utt,G,Jun 17)*
Stormbay Bomber 105 *(17f,Ban,G,Oct 1)*
Storming Strumpet 105 *(16f,Tow,G,Nov 5)*
Stout Cortez 95 *(19f,Mar,HY,Dec 3)*
Stowaway Shark 111 *(24f,Fai,Y,Mar 29)*
Strait Run 102 *(17f,Sed,S,Mar 27)*
Strawberry Hill 90 *(24½f,Kem,S,Jan 25)*
Street Entertainer 109 *(16½f,Per,S,May 14)*
Strongpoint 107 *(15½f,Mus,GS,Jan 1)*
Stuccodor 107 *(16f,Pun,HY,Jan 9)*
Stylish Chap 101 *(22f,Crt,GS,May 25)*
Sub Lieutenant 102 *(24f,Pun,GY,Apr 29)*
Subordinate 91 *(16½f,Tau,G,Mar 21)*
Sudden Wish 106 *(16½f,Str,G,May 17)*
Sugar Baron 102 *(21f,Kem,GS,Dec 26)*
Suit Yourself 108 *(17f,Crl,HY,Dec 13)*
Sukiyaki 98 *(22f,Str,GF,May 17)*
Sultana Belle 101 *(20f,Hex,G,May 26)*
Summer Sounds 101 *(19½f,Don,GS,Dec 11)*
Summer Storm 105 *(17f,Sed,GS,Nov 10)*
Summers King 92 *(16f,Fai,SH,Jan 20)*
Summit Point 91 *(16f,Fai,SH,Jan 20)*
Sun Cloud 101 *(24f,Per,GS,Sep 23)*
Sun Quest 91 *(20f,Wcn,G,May 7)*
Sunblazer 90 *(17f,Nab,GF,Apr 30)*
Sunny West 93 *(23f,Kel,G,Oct 24)*
Sunrae Shadow 90 *(20f,Fai,S,Nov 29)*
Sunshine Buddy 104 *(19f,Tow,G,May 11)*
Sunshine Corner 109 *(16f,Plu,HY,Jan 18)*
Supasundae 105 *(16½f,Chl,GS,Mar 15)*
Super Collider 93 *(16f,Wet,S,Apr 17)*
Super Lunar 94 *(20½f,Ncs,S,Apr 8)*
Super Scorpion 107 *(16f,Wor,G,Oct 8)*
Superb Story 113 *(17f,Chl,G,Mar 18)*
Superciliary 105 *(18f,Fon,S,Dec 8)*
Superfection 98 *(17f,Mar,HY,Feb 9)*
Superman De La Rue 91 *(18½f,Exe,G,Mar 22)*
Supernoverre 106 *(16f,Utt,G,Jun 11)*
Supply And Demand 101 *(16f,Utt,S,Nov 14)*
Supreme Hope 97 *(16f,Chp,S,Nov 4)*
Suprise Vendor 106 *(16f,Kel,GS,May 6)*
Surf In September 102 *(19f,Str,G,Aug 20)*
Surtee Du Berlais 105 *(16½f,Tau,HY,Dec 30)*
Sussex Road 97 *(16f,Utt,HY,Dec 18)*
Sutton Place 113 *(16f,Fai,YS,Mar 28)*
Sutton Storm 92 *(21½f,Nab,GS,Aug 12)*
Swaledale Lad 91 *(17f,Sed,GF,Sep 3)*
Swamp Fox 111 *(16f,Fai,HY,Jan 10)*
Swampfire 105 *(16f,Utt,G,Jly 15)*
Swansea Mile 112 *(16f,Kem,G,Oct 18)*
Sweeping Rock 98 *(16f,War,GS,Nov 4)*
Sweet Cherry 108 *(16f,Pun,HY,Feb 17)*
Sweet Midnight 90 *(16f,Utt,HY,Dec 18)*
Sweet Summer 99 *(19f,War,GS,May 4)*
Sweet World 101 *(17f,Nab,G,Sep 18)*
Swincombe Toby 105 *(16f,War,GS,Nov 4)*
Swnymor 97 *(21f,Kem,GS,Dec 26)*
Sword Of The Lord 99 *(16f,War,GS,Nov 4)*
Sybarite 102 *(24f,Chl,GS,Apr 13)*
Sydney De Baune 90 *(16f,Chp,HY,Mar 12)*
Sykes 107 *(25f,Ain,G,Oct 25)*
Symphony Of Pearls 101 *(16f,Utt,G,Jun 11)*

Tachbury 94 *(22f,Str,G,Jly 30)*
Tactical Manoeuvre 94 *(17f,Nab,S,Apr 5)*
Taglietelle 113 *(20f,Fai,S,Nov 29)*
Tagrita 100 *(21½f,Wcn,S,Mar 2)*
Tahira 106 *(16f,Utt,GS,Jly 26)*
Taj Badalandabad 111 *(23½f,Asc,GS,Apr 3)*
Take A Break 102 *(16f,Kem,GS,Dec 26)*
Takingrisks 107 *(23f,Kel,HY,Dec 29)*
Tales Of Milan 96 *(25f,Hun,G,Oct 13)*
Talk Of The South 101 *(26f,War,G,Mar 23)*
Tamarillo Grove 104 *(16f,Chp,S,Apr 9)*
Tambura 107 *(25f,Plu,S,Nov 30)*
Tanarpino 106 *(19f,Mar,HY,Jan 22)*
Tandem 93 *(16f,Pun,GY,May 1)*
Tanerko Emery 103 *(20f,Ain,G,May 15)*
Tangolan 105 *(19f,Str,G,Sep 14)*

Tanit River 105 (19½f,Ban,HY,Mar 2)
Tantalized 102 (20f,Utt,G,Jun 17)
Tantamount 106 (25f,Ain,G,Oct 25)
Tap Night 100 (20f,Crl,GS,Nov 1)
Tapaculo 112 (19½f,Chp,HY,Dec 5)
Tara Bridge 104 (16f,Lin,HY,Dec 12)
Tara Flow 109 (15½f,Lei,HY,Jan 26)
Tara Mac 107 (19f,Crl,GS,May 7)
Tara Mist 100 (21½f,Wcn,S,Nov 7)
Tara Point 105 (20f,Chl,GS,Mar 15)
Tara Tavey 102 (23f,Exe,G,May 5)
Tara The Tiger 103 (19f,Crl,HY,Feb 10)
Tara's Rainbow 97 (19½f,Don,G,Nov 27)
Tarabiyn 96 (20f,Pun,GY,Apr 29)
Taradrewe 101 (21½f,Fon,G,Sep 6)
Taroum 96 (20f,Wcn,G,May 7)
Tarvini 92 (24f,Sth,GS,Jun 15)
Taste The Wine 105 (16f,Chp,G,Sep 30)
Taweyla 107 (17f,Don,S,Mar 4)
Tawseef 99 (24f,Leo,HY,Dec 28)
Tayarat 94 (22f,Crt,G,Jun 26)
Taylor 99 (19f,Fon,G,Sep 6)
Tayto Park 106 (16f,Fai,Y,Mar 27)
Tb Broke Her 91 (20f,Pun,HY,Jan 9)
Tea For Two 102 (23f,Hay,S,Nov 21)
Tea In Transvaal 116 (16f,Nby,S,Nov 28)
Tea Time Fred 99 (21½f,Nab,S,Apr 18)
Teak 107 (23f,Mar,G,Jly 5)
Ted's Lad 99 (20f,Sth,G,Mar 21)
Teescomponents Max 100 (16f,Utt,GF,Jly 7)
Tekthelot 108 (16f,Hex,G,Jun 6)
Template 102 (16½f,Tau,G,Nov 12)
Temple Lord 100 (24f,Sth,G,Jly 12)
Temple Tiger 102 (20f,Wet,GS,Mar 22)
Tempo Mac 105 (17f,Crt,G,Jly 18)
Ten Sixty 107 (20½f,Nby,S,Nov 27)
Ten Times Better 107 (18f,Fai,HY,Jan 30)
Ten Trees 100 (17f,Sed,S,Mar 27)
Tenby Jewel 102 (17f,Exe,G,Oct 8)
Tennessee Bird 103 (16f,Utt,G,Jun 11)
Teo Vivo 109 (19½f,Mus,GS,Jan 1)
Teochew 104 (20f,Hex,G,Oct 2)
Tercel 104 (17f,Nab,G,May 27)
Terminal 106 (24f,Sth,S,Nov 9)
Tesseract 91 (16f,Leo,HY,Dec 26)
Teviot Prince 92 (20f,Utt,G,Sep 9)
Texas Forever 93 (16f,Hay,G,Mar 23)
Thady Quil 101 (21f,War,G,Apr 21)
Thankyou Very Much 105 (16f,Wet,GS,Mar 22)
That's A Wrap 95 (20f,Fai,SH,Apr 5)
Thatchers Gold 95 (17f,Exe,GS,Apr 12)
Thats My Rabbit 105 (20f,Utt,HY,Dec 31)
The Absent Mare 106 (17f,Crt,G,Jun 26)
The Artful Cobbler 107 (20½f,Lei,HY,Feb 3)
The Barbury Queen 100 (16f,Tow,G,Nov 5)
The Big Dipper 98 (24f,Sth,G,Sep 29)
The Big Mare 91 (16½f,Tau,HY,Feb 2)
The Boss's Dream 108 (26f,War,S,Jan 28)
The Brock Inn 108 (16f,Fai,Y,Mar 27)
The Bugler 97 (16f,Sth,S,Nov 17)
The Clonlisk Bug 99 (20f,Utt,G,Sep 9)
The Coffee Hunter 101 (16f,Lud,HY,Jan 4)
The Compeller 102 (15½f,Mus,G,Nov 6)
The Conn 94 (19f,Crl,G,Mar 26)
The Dutchman 112 (18f,Kel,S,Mar 13)
The Eaglehaslanded 111 (24f,Chl,G,Apr 14)
The Fresh Prince 99 (16f,Kel,S,Mar 13)
The Fugitive 99 (16f,Plu,S,Dec 14)
The Game Changer 109 (16f,Pun,GY,Apr 28)
The Game Is A Foot 107 (20½f,Plu,G,May 10)
The Geegeez Geegee 106 (20½f,Plu,S,Nov 16)
The Gipper 113 (16f,Chp,S,Nov 4)
The Govaness 111 (23½f,Asc,S,Jan 23)
The Ice Factor 106 (16f,Hex,G,May 2)
The Jazz Singer 93 (20f,Per,G,Apr 20)
The Job Is Right 108 (25f,Chl,GS,Nov 14)
The Kings Assassin 103 (26½f,Nab,GS,Jly 3)
The Kvilleken 99 (17f,Mar,G,Aug 2)
The Last Bar 99 (19f,Mar,S,Jan 22)
The Last Bridge 96 (26f,Fon,G,Jun 3)
The Last Leg 105 (23f,Mar,G,Aug 2)
The Late Shift 101 (20f,Wet,GS,Mar 22)
The Lion Man 93 (19f,War,S,May 9)
The Liquidator 96 (19½f,Chp,G,Oct 10)
The Living Beauty 101 (20f,Pun,HY,Jan 9)
The Missus 103 (16f,Chp,G,Mar 24)
The Mulcare Rover 94 (20f,Fai,SH,Apr 5)
The New One 122 (16f,Kem,GS,Dec 26)
The Organist 106 (15½f,Lei,HY,Jan 26)
The Pierre Lark 91 (17f,Ban,S,Mar 31)
The Plan Man 109 (16f,Hay,GS,May 9)
The Road Ahead 106 (20f,Ain,G,May 15)
The Romford Pele 111 (21f,Chl,G,Mar 16)
The Saint James 98 (20f,Pun,S,May 2)
The Selector 98 (21½f,Fon,G,May 1)
The Tailgater 104 (19½f,Hun,S,Dec 26)
The Toft 95 (16f,Hex,GS,Oct 10)
The Tourard Man 106 (23½f,Asc,GS,Apr 3)
The Unit 104 (17f,Don,G,Feb 24)
The Venerable Bede 94 (16f,San,HY,Feb 19)
The Wee Midget 100 (26f,Fon,G,Jun 3)
The Westener Boy 93 (24f,Leo,HY,Dec 28)
The Winking Prawn 101 (21½f,Nab,G,Sep 18)
The Yank 91 (16f,Utt,G,Jly 24)
The Young Master 100 (24f,Chl,HY,Jan 30)
Theatre Act 94 (20f,Sed,S,Mar 15)
Theatre Flame 110 (16f,Chp,S,Feb 27)
Theatre Goer 106 (24½f,Don,G,Feb 24)
Theatrical Style 106 (17f,Ban,HY,Mar 2)
Thegreendalerocket 98 (24f,Tau,GS,Dec 10)
Theinval 109 (21f,Chl,G,Mar 16)
Theionlady 97 (17f,Nab,G,May 27)
Thekingofconnemara 93 (24f,Leo,HY,Dec 28)
Theo 96 (20f,Fai,SH,Apr 5)
Theo's Charm 109 (16f,Plu,S,Dec 14)
Theophilus 97 (20f,Pun,HY,Jan 9)
Thepartysover 97 (21½f,Exe,HY,Dec 17)
There Is No Point 93 (17f,Ban,G,May 16)
Theredballoon 101 (16f,Sth,G,Oct 22)
Theturnofthesun 104 (16f,Leo,HY,Dec 28)
Thinger Licht 90 (20½f,Mar,G,Jly 5)
Think Of Me 90 (21f,Tow,G,Nov 5)
Thirsty Work 92 (16f,Fai,HY,Jan 30)
This Thyne Jude 98 (16f,Hex,HY,Mar 17)
Thistlecrack 120 (24½f,Asc,GS,Dec 19)
Thomas Edison 103 (16f,Pun,S,Nov 15)
Thomas Hobson 116 (21f,War,HY,Jan 16)
Thorpe 100 (16½f,Per,S,May 14)
Thousand Stars 110 (24f,Pun,Y,Apr 30)
Three Colours Red 100 (17f,Mar,HY,Feb 9)
Three Kingdoms 106 (21f,Chl,G,Mar 16)
Three Of A Kind 93 (19f,Mar,S,Mar 13)
Three Stars 99 (16½f,Ain,S,Apr 8)
Three Ways 107 (19f,Str,S,Mar 5)
Three Wise Men 110 (16f,Fai,Y,Mar 27)
Threebarmymen 98 (16f,Kem,G,Apr 19)
Thunder Sheik 113 (16f,Hay,G,Mar 26)
Thunder Zone 103 (16f,Pun,S,May 2)
Thundering Home 98 (16f,San,HY,Feb 19)
Thyne For Gold 95 (16f,Lud,S,Dec 16)
Tickenwolf 101 (20f,Crl,G,Oct 22)
Tickity Bleue 100 (18f,Fon,S,Dec 8)
Tidal Way 91 (20f,Sth,G,May 12)
Tidestream 97 (17f,Exe,G,Apr 21)
Tiger Feat 100 (16f,Plu,G,May 10)
Tiger O'Toole 93 (20½f,Mar,G,May 17)
Tiger Roll 103 (25f,Ain,S,Apr 9)
Tiger Twenty Two 105 (19f,Mar,G,Jly 5)
Tighe Beithe 93 (20f,Fai,HY,Dec 19)
Tigris River 106 (16f,Leo,S,Jan 17)
Tijori 104 (19½f,Chp,G,Sep 30)
Tikkandemickey 99 (16f,Hex,G,May 2)
Tikkapick 104 (21½f,Wcn,GS,Apr 17)
Timon's Tara 108 (20½f,Nby,G,Apr 2)
Tinseltown 103 (20f,Sth,G,Jun 9)
Tiny Dancer 93 (20f,Sed,S,Mar 15)
Tipped Up Harry 91 (16f,Pun,Y,Apr 30)
Tipperairy 95 (19½f,Don,GS,Jan 29)
Tippmanboy 107 (16f,Cat,S,Dec 28)
Tir Dubh 103 (23f,Mar,G,Aug 15)
Tiradia 105 (19½f,Hun,G,Oct 4)
Tish Hall 95 (15½f,Mus,G,Nov 5)
Titans Approach 103 (21f,Wet,S,Oct 30)
Titch Strider 101 (21½f,Wcn,G,May 12)
Tjongejonge 104 (24f,Lud,GS,Apr 19)
To Begin 107 (21f,War,GS,May 20)
Toarmandowithlove 96 (20½f,Ncs,HY,Mar 8)
Toast And Jam 94 (19f,Tow,S,Mar 17)
Tobefair 95 (23f,Wor,GF,Jly 1)
Toby Lerone 102 (21f,Tow,G,Nov 5)
Tocororo 113 (16f,Fai,HY,Jan 10)
Toe To Toe 97 (16f,Utt,GF,Jly 7)
Tokyo Brown 95 (17f,Crt,GS,Jly 20)
Tokyo Javilex 102 (27f,Sed,GS,Oct 12)
Tomahawk Wood 106 (20½f,Ncs,S,Apr 8)
Tombstone 111 (16f,Leo,HY,Dec 27)
Tomkevi 95 (19f,Cat,S,Jan 27)
Tommy Silver 112 (16f,San,G,Apr 23)
Tomngerry 103 (21f,Wet,HY,Feb 6)
Tongie 94 (18f,Leo,HY,Dec 26)
Too Many Chiefs 101 (19f,Crl,HY,Feb 22)
Too Scoops 92 (17f,Ban,G,May 16)
Toola Boola 96 (17f,Sed,S,Oct 29)
Top And Drop 98 (16f,Plu,HY,Feb 15)
Top Billing 102 (23f,Hay,HY,Feb 20)
Top Notch 116 (16½f,Ncs,S,Nov 28)
Top Set 92 (19½f,Hun,S,Dec 26)
Top Spin 101 (21f,War,G,Oct 1)
Top Wood 107 (26f,Kel,GS,Apr 2)
Topolski 92 (23f,Mar,G,Jun 5)
Topper Thornton 103 (20f,Per,G,Jun 7)
Toptempo 90 (16½f,Str,G,Oct 17)
Torero 102 (16f,Plu,S,Dec 14)
Tornado In Milan 111 (19f,Tau,HY,Jan 23)
Total Recall 107 (22f,Fai,YS,Mar 28)
Total Submission 96 (20½f,Nby,S,Mar 5)
Totalize 108 (16½f,Chl,GS,Nov 15)
Touch Back 109 (24f,Ncs,HY,Mar 19)
Tour De Ville 102 (16f,Chp,G,Apr 22)
Towerburn 97 (16f,Hex,G,May 2)
Towering 112 (19f,Fon,G,May 1)
Town Mouse 94 (16f,Lud,GS,Apr 5)
Townshend 106 (20f,Fai,HY,Feb 20)
Tradewinds 107 (24f,Ncs,HY,Mar 19)
Traditional Dancer 91 (16f,Fai,HY,Jan 30)
Trafficker 98 (23½f,Utt,G,Jun 17)
Trakeur 96 (21½f,Wcn,G,May 7)
Transient Bay 104 (23½f,Utt,HY,Apr 2)
Trapper Peak 95 (20f,Fak,S,Jan 1)
Travertine 100 (16f,Hun,S,Jan 6)
Treaty Girl 97 (21½f,Fon,G,Mar 19)
Trespassers Will 104 (19½f,Hun,GS,Jan 29)
Tricky 101 (17f,Nab,GS,Aug 22)
Tried And Tested 96 (19½f,Chp,G,Sep 30)
Triple Chief 99 (16½f,Tau,GS,Dec 10)
Triple Eight 103 (17f,Ban,G,Oct 1)
Triumph Davis 98 (25½f,Crt,GF,Jun 26)
Trojan Star 94 (16f,Kem,G,May 13)
Troll D'Oudairies 97 (24f,Pun,G,May 16)
Trooper Royal 91 (20f,Wet,GS,Mar 22)
Troubled Soul 99 (16½f,Str,G,Oct 17)
Try Catch Me 95 (20½f,Plu,G,Oct 19)
Ttebbob 111 (24f,Pun,Y,Apr 30)
Tubacurry Tornado 100 (22f,Pun,HY,Feb 17)
Tuffstuff 100 (16f,Plu,HY,Jan 18)
Tullow Tonic 103 (16f,Tow,G,Nov 5)
Tully East 108 (16f,Leo,HY,Dec 27)
Turtle Cask 108 (20½f,Ncs,S,Apr 8)
Turtle Watch 112 (16f,Kel,GS,May 6)
Twelve Strings 99 (19f,Tow,GS,May 18)
Twenty Eight Guns 102 (20f,Sth,S,Apr 15)
Twentytwo's Taken 102 (17f,Exe,HY,Mar 30)
Twin Barrels 103 (17f,Ban,HY,Mar 2)
Twiss's Hill 101 (22f,Pun,HY,Feb 17)
Two Taffs 106 (16f,Kem,GS,Dec 27)
Tyrone Tiger 103 (20f,Fai,SH,Apr 5)

Uaintseenothingyet 107 (20f,Fai,SH,Jan 20)
Ubak 115 (25f,Ain,S,Apr 9)
Ubaldo Des Menhies 105 (20f,Sth,G,Jun 9)
Ugly Bug 96 (23f,Exe,HY,Nov 22)
Ullswater 101 (16f,Utt,G,Oct 4)
Umoristic 97 (16f,Wor,G,Jun 21)
Un Ace 108 (25f,Chl,GS,Nov 14)
Un Beau Roman 97 (16f,Kem,GS,Dec 27)
Un Prophete 102 (16f,Cat,S,Jan 14)
Unanimite 109 (20f,Wet,G,May 21)
Unbuckled 103 (21f,Lud,GS,Apr 5)
Uncle Tone 103 (23f,Wor,G,Jly 15)
Undressed 94 (20f,Pun,GY,Apr 29)
Unefille De Guye 94 (21½f,Nab,G,Jun 23)
Unex Modigliani 98 (16f,Hun,S,Mar 6)
Unify 95 (16½f,Tau,G,Apr 7)
Union Dues 105 (16f,Pun,HY,Jan 9)
Unison 111 (15f,Wcn,HY,Feb 4)
Unknown Legend 105 (24f,Sth,G,May 20)
Unowhatimeanharry 112 (24f,Chl,S,Dec 12)
Until Forever 99 (21½f,Wcn,G,May 7)
Until The Man 98 (16½f,Str,G,Aug 20)
Until Winning 99 (20f,Fak,G,Oct 16)
Up For An Oscar 101 (24f,Utt,G,May 2)
Up For Review 110 (24f,Per,G,Apr 20)
Up Four It 97 (18f,Plu,S,Nov 16)
Up To Al 90 (24f,Tau,GS,Dec 10)
Upsilon Bleu 106 (15½f,Mus,GS,Jan 1)
Uptake 106 (20f,Fai,SH,Apr 5)
Upthemsteps 91 (25f,Hun,GS,Apr 18)
Upton Wood 101 (21½f,Wcn,G,May 12)
Uranna 93 (16f,Pun,Y,Apr 30)
Urano 106 (20f,Chl,G,Mar 18)
Uranox 90 (21½f,Fon,G,Jun 9)
Urban Dusk 93 (22f,Crt,GS,Jly 20)
Urban Gale 92 (27f,Sed,S,May 5)
Urban Kode 102 (20f,Per,GF,Sep 7)
Urban Storm 100 (24f,Sth,G,May 20)
Urcalin 108 (21f,Kem,G,May 4)
Ustica 107 (21½f,Nab,GS,May 19)

Vaihau 100 (27f,Sed,S,Oct 29)
Vaillant Creek 106 (21f,Lud,S,Mar 3)
Valbucca 92 (16f,Fai,HY,Dec 19)
Valco De Touzaine 107 (20f,Wor,GF,Jun 6)
Valhalla 107 (23f,Exe,GS,Apr 12)
Valleyofmilan 99 (23½f,Utt,G,Oct 4)
Valseur Du Granval 95 (17f,Ban,S,Nov 11)
Value At Risk 111 (20f,Fai,YS,Mar 28)
Valyssa Monterg 107 (24½f,Ayr,S,Apr 15)
Van Mildert 102 (17f,Crt,S,May 27)
Vancouverite 109 (17f,Sed,G,Oct 12)
Varom 104 (21½f,Wcn,S,Dec 3)
Veinard 104 (16f,Hex,S,Mar 29)
Velvet Cognac 97 (21½f,Wcn,G,May 7)
Velvet Edge 90 (16f,Plu,G,Apr 22)
Vendor 111 (15½f,Mus,S,Feb 7)
Vendredi Trois 100 (25f,Hun,G,Oct 13)
Vent Nivernais 99 (16f,Fak,S,Feb 8)
Venue 101 (15½f,Mus,S,Feb 17)
Verano 105 (20½f,Plu,S,Nov 16)
Vercingetorix 105 (16f,Asc,GS,Dec 19)
Vering 100 (15f,Wcn,S,Mar 2)
Verko 95 (23f,Hay,S,May 26)
Verni 103 (16f,Utt,HY,Dec 31)
Verona Opera 99 (17f,Crl,G,Mar 26)
Vertueux 91 (17f,Mar,S,Dec 26)
Very Extravagant 103 (16f,Nby,S,Nov 28)
Very First Time 106 (16½f,Ncs,HY,Mar 8)
Very Intense 100 (23½f,Fak,S,Jan 1)
Very Noble 100 (16f,Kem,S,Feb 12)
Verygoodverygood 91 (19½f,Chp,G,Apr 22)
Vexillum 102 (17f,Sed,GF,Sep 3)
Via Volupta 103 (16f,Sth,S,Nov 17)
Vic De Touzaine 102 (19½f,Chp,S,Nov 4)
Vicenzo Mio 105 (21f,Kem,GS,Feb 27)
Vicky's Charm 106 (19½f,Chp,HY,Mar 12)
Viconte Du Noyer 104 (16f,Pun,GY,Apr 28)
Vics Canvas 93 (23f,Hay,S,Nov 21)
Victor Hewgo 103 (24f,Ncs,HY,Mar 19)
Victor Leudorum 91 (23½f,Utt,G,Oct 4)
Victory Mill 112 (20f,Fai,HY,Dec 19)
Viens Chercher 109 (16f,Hay,S,Nov 20)
Vieux Lille 113 (16f,Hay,HY,Jan 23)
Vif Argent 95 (20f,Wor,GS,May 7)
Vigil 113 (18f,Leo,HY,Dec 26)
Vinciaettis 111 (16f,Chp,HY,Mar 28)
Vinegar Hill 95 (23f,Mar,HY,Dec 3)
Vinnie Trenta 97 (20f,Wor,G,Jly 15)
Vintage Clouds 108 (16f,Hay,HY,Dec 30)
Violoniste 103 (20f,Sth,S,Apr 15)
Virgilio 111 (20f,Ain,G,May 15)
Virnon 99 (16f,Hay,HY,Dec 19)
Visible Light 110 (20f,Sth,G,Mar 21)
Vita Nuova 90 (20f,Fai,SH,Jan 20)
Viva Rafa 95 (17f,Exe,GS,Apr 12)
Vivacissimo 106 (16½f,Str,G,Jun 30)
Vivant Poeme 113 (21½f,Fon,G,Jun 3)
Vivas 105 (19f,War,G,Apr 21)
Vive La France 94 (16f,Pun,Y,Apr 30)
Vive Le Roi 100 (17f,Ban,S,Mar 31)
Vocaliser 91 (16f,War,GS,Nov 4)
Vodka 'n Tonic 100 (20f,Sth,G,May 12)
Vodka Island 90 (24f,Lud,GS,Nov 23)
Vodka Red 103 (16½f,Ncs,HY,Dec 10)
Vodka Wells 108 (16f,Hex,G,Jun 6)
Voix Du Reve 112 (16f,San,G,Apr 23)
Volcanic 105 (23f,Hay,G,Mar 26)
Volcanic Jack 98 (17f,Crt,G,Jun 28)
Volnay De Thaix 108 (21f,Chl,G,Mar 16)
Vosne Romanee 108 (17f,Chl,G,Apr 13)
Vote Of Confidence 90 (20f,Fai,S,Nov 29)
Vroum Vroum Mag 116 (23½f,Asc,S,Jan 23)
Vulcanite 105 (20f,Ain,G,May 15)

W Six Times 101 (24½f,Ayr,S,Apr 15)
Wabanaki 94 (16f,Hay,HY,Dec 30)
Wade Harper 109 (18½f,Nab,GS,Oct 9)
Wait A Second 104 (20f,Sth,GF,Aug 16)
Wait For Me 110 (17f,Chl,G,Mar 18)
Waiting Patiently 107 (19½f,Don,G,Nov 28)
Wake Your Dreams 100 (19f,Crl,GS,Apr 3)
Walk On Al 98 (21f,Wet,G,Oct 14)
Walk To Freedom 102 (20f,Pun,GY,Apr 29)
Walkami 102 (16f,Sth,S,Dec 1)
Walking In The Air 112 (20½f,Nby,S,Mar 4)
Walser 100 (16f,Hex,G,May 2)
Walter De La Mare 99 (19f,War,GS,May 4)
Walter White 97 (16½f,Tau,G,Nov 12)
Waltz Legend 91 (24½f,Ayr,HY,Jan 19)
War On The Rocks 96 (16½f,Str,G,Oct 17)
War Singer 109 (16f,War,GS,May 20)
War Sound 113 (16f,Hay,GS,May 9)
Warrant Officer 103 (19f,Str,G,Aug 20)
Warriors Tale 100 (24f,Chl,G,Mar 17)
Warsaw Pact 102 (21½f,Exe,HY,Dec 17)
Water Sprite 112 (17f,Chl,G,Mar 17)
Waterclock 108 (20f,Wet,HY,Jan 16)
Waterlord 97 (16f,Hun,GS,Dec 6)
Waterville Rock 99 (16f,Pun,HY,Jan 9)
Watt Broderick 107 (16f,War,G,Oct 1)
Waxies Dargle 112 (21f,Chl,G,Mar 16)
Wazowski 102 (19f,Crl,G,Mar 26)
Weapon Of Choice 102 (16f,Wet,GS,Mar 22)
Weather Babe 108 (23f,Exe,G,May 5)
Welcome Bach 98 (21½f,Nab,S,Apr 18)
Welcome Ben 104 (20f,Per,G,Jly 2)
Welcometothejungle 109 (20f,Sth,G,Aug 27)
Well Rewarded 98 (21½f,Nab,G,Sep 18)
Wellforth 94 (23½f,Utt,S,Nov 22)
Wells De Lune 96 (18f,Fon,GS,Feb 28)
Welluptoscratch 102 (16f,Plu,G,Apr 22)
Welsh Shadow 111 (16f,Hay,S,Nov 20)
Werenearlyoutofit 101 (20f,Wor,G,Jly 28)
Wes Hardin 101 (16f,Pun,S,Nov 15)
West Approach 108 (24f,Chl,S,Dec 12)
West End 107 (24f,Sth,G,Jly 12)
West Hill Legend 96 (17f,Exe,G,Mar 22)
West Of The Edge 97 (16f,San,HY,Mar 11)
West Wizard 107 (21f,Kem,G,May 4)
Westend Prince 96 (15f,Wcn,S,Apr 4)
Westend Star 99 (20f,Chl,G,Mar 18)
Westerly Breeze 97 (23f,Wor,GF,Jly 1)
Western Boy 92 (16f,Pun,GY,Apr 28)
Western Breeze 99 (20f,Wet,G,May 28)
Western Cape 101 (22f,Asc,S,Dec 18)
Western Diva 99 (16½f,Str,G,May 30)
Western Goose 94 (20f,Wor,GF,Sep 8)
Western Jo 95 (21f,Wet,G,Oct 14)
Western Miller 104 (20f,Crl,G,Oct 22)
Western Rules 104 (16f,Kel,HY,Feb 18)
Western Sunrise 106 (17f,Nab,GS,Mar 26)
Western Way 107 (26f,Fon,G,Oct 2)
Western Xpress 93 (19½f,Chp,G,Sep 30)
Westren Warrior 111 (21f,Kem,S,Jan 9)
Weststreet 104 (24f,Sth,HY,Dec 13)
Weybridge Light 102 (20f,Fak,G,May 31)
Weyburn 107 (20f,Sth,G,Mar 21)
What A Game 93 (27f,Sed,S,Mar 27)
What A Jewel 108 (20f,Sth,G,Aug 27)

What A Laugh 99 *(16f,Wor,G,Oct 8)*
What A Moment 107 *(16f,San,S,Dec 5)*
What A Scorcher 98 *(16f,Wor,GS,May 7)*
What A Steel 105 *(20f,Hex,G,Oct 2)*
What Happens Now 101 *(17f,Sed,HY,Dec 26)*
What Kept You 95 *(21f,War,G,Apr 21)*
What's The Scoop 100 *(21f,Kem,S,Feb 12)*
Whataknight 106 *(21½f,Wcn,HY,Nov 19)*
Whatdoesthefoxsay 101 *(19f,Hay,G,Mar 26)*
Whatsforuwontgobyu 107 *(16f,Leo,HY,Dec 28)*
Whatsthatallabout 97 *(16f,Chp,S,Apr 9)*
Whatsupjack 96 *(21f,Sed,GF,Apr 30)*
Whatthebutlersaw 91 *(20f,Wor,GS,May 7)*
Where's Tiger 103 *(17f,Sed,G,Oct 12)*
While You Wait 103 *(16f,Utt,G,Sep 20)*
Whipcord 95 *(17f,Exe,G,Apr 21)*
Whisper 101 *(24f,Chl,G,Mar 17)*
Whispering Harry 105 *(16f,Chp,S,Feb 27)*
Whispering Speed 97 *(23½f,Fak,S,Feb 8)*
Whispering Storm 106 *(16f,Chp,G,Apr 22)*
Whistle Dixie 112 *(18f,Fai,HY,Jan 30)*
Whiteout 107 *(20f,Chl,G,Mar 18)*
Whitsundays 98 *(21f,Lud,GS,Nov 23)*
Who Am I 98 *(24f,Ffo,G,Jun 4)*
Who Dares Wins 113 *(17f,Chl,HY,Jan 30)*
Who Owns Me 97 *(24f,Wet,S,Dec 5)*
Who You For 106 *(21f,War,G,Oct 1)*
Who's Micky Brown 106 *(15f,Wcn,HY,Feb 4)*
Who's That 96 *(16f,Leo,S,Feb 28)*
Wholestone 111 *(22f,Str,S,Oct 29)*
Whos De Baby 98 *(17f,Ban,S,Mar 16)*
Wicked Games 103 *(19f,Crl,HY,Feb 22)*
Wicked Spice 101 *(24f,Pun,Y,Apr 30)*
Wicked Willy 103 *(21f,War,S,Apr 4)*
Wicklewood 92 *(19f,Tow,G,May 11)*
Wicklow Brave 116 *(16f,Pun,S,Nov 15)*
Wilberdragon 102 *(16f,Nby,S,Nov 26)*
Wilcos Mo Chara 101 *(20f,Fai,S,Nov 29)*
Wild And Wonderful 92 *(16f,Fai,SH,Apr 5)*
Wild Ginger 91 *(19½f,Don,GS,Dec 29)*
Wild Rover 94 *(20½f,Nby,S,Nov 26)*
Wild West Wind 104 *(23f,Exe,GS,Apr 12)*
Wilde Blue Yonder 91 *(20f,San,G,Apr 23)*
Will O'The West 107 *(19f,War,S,Feb 26)*
Willem 108 *(21f,Kem,G,Apr 19)*
William H Bonney 106 *(16f,Plu,S,Nov 30)*
William Of Orange 108 *(16f,Cat,S,Jan 14)*
Willshebetrying 91 *(16f,Plu,HY,Jan 18)*
Willy Brennan 94 *(16f,Hun,G,Oct 13)*
Wily Fox 95 *(25f,Ain,G,Jun 12)*
Wind Of Hope 101 *(20f,Per,S,May 13)*
Windsor Park 108 *(16f,Leo,HY,Dec 29)*
Windy Writer 104 *(16f,Sth,GS,Feb 28)*
Winged Express 102 *(20f,Sth,G,May 12)*
Wings Attract 105 *(20f,Fak,G,Oct 16)*
Winner Massagot 111 *(16f,Asc,S,Nov 20)*
Winning Spark 107 *(19f,Tau,HY,Jan 23)*
Winning Ticket 103 *(16f,Chp,G,Apr 22)*
Winter Alchemy 99 *(25f,Hun,S,Dec 26)*
Winter Escape 103 *(16f,Kem,GS,Feb 27)*
Winter Lion 106 *(15½f,Mus,G,Nov 5)*
Wintered Well 104 *(21f,Hun,GS,Jan 29)*
Winterfell 105 *(16f,War,GS,Nov 18)*
Wintour Leap 103 *(16f,Wor,GS,Sep 2)*
Wishfull Dreaming 108 *(16f,Wor,G,Oct 8)*
Wishing Wind 96 *(21f,Lud,GS,Apr 5)*
Wojciech 96 *(20f,Wcn,G,May 7)*
Wolf Of Windlesham 113 *(16f,San,G,Apr 23)*
Wolf Shield 91 *(24f,Wet,S,Nov 14)*
Wolf Sword 102 *(20f,Wet,G,Oct 14)*
Wolfcatcher 108 *(17f,Mar,HY,Feb 9)*
Wolftrap 105 *(16f,Chp,G,Apr 22)*
Woodford Island 107 *(22f,Asc,S,Dec 18)*
Woodland Opera 97 *(16f,Leo,HY,Dec 27)*
Woodland Walk 102 *(19f,Hay,G,Mar 26)*
Work In Progress 111 *(20f,Ain,G,Oct 25)*
Worldor 103 *(16f,Utt,G,Sep 9)*
Wotzizname 104 *(23f,Exe,GS,Apr 12)*
Wyfield Rose 102 *(24f,Per,G,Apr 20)*
Wymeswold 103 *(17f,Sed,G,May 12)*

Xsquared 100 *(16f,Pun,GY,Apr 28)*

Y A Bon 92 *(21½f,Nab,G,Jun 23)*
Yaha Fizz 98 *(16f,Fai,Y,Mar 27)*
Yala Enki 112 *(21f,Kem,S,Jan 9)*
Yanworth 115 *(21f,Chl,G,Mar 16)*
Yasir 101 *(19f,Mar,HY,Jan 22)*
Yes Daddy 109 *(16f,Chp,G,Oct 11)*
Yes I Did 110 *(20f,Sed,S,Feb 9)*
Yes Sir Brian 107 *(16f,Fai,HY,Jan 30)*
Yesyoucan 94 *(19f,Mar,G,Jun 5)*
Yorkhill 116 *(21f,Chl,G,Mar 16)*
You Say What 107 *(23f,Exe,GS,Mar 8)*
You've Been Mowed 102 *(20f,Fak,G,May 5)*
Younevercall 104 *(21f,Hun,GS,Apr 18)*
Young Dillon 100 *(20f,Sth,S,Nov 9)*
Young Lou 106 *(19f,Tow,S,Feb 17)*
Youngdocgallagher 93 *(23½f,Utt,GF,Jly 7)*

Zabana 113 *(24f,Pun,Y,Apr 30)*
Zaidiyn 110 *(15½f,Mus,S,Feb 7)*
Zaidpour 109 *(24f,Pun,Y,Apr 30)*
Zakety Zak 93 *(17f,Sed,S,Mar 27)*
Zamdy Man 101 *(17f,Chl,G,Mar 18)*
Zanstra 111 *(21f,Kem,S,Feb 12)*
Zante 103 *(16f,Plu,G,Apr 22)*
Zara Hope 95 *(19½f,Chp,S,Apr 9)*
Zarawi 106 *(16f,Plu,G,May 10)*
Zarib 118 *(15f,Wcn,S,Nov 7)*
Zarzal 111 *(17f,Mar,G,May 17)*
Zephyr 92 *(20f,Wor,GF,Jly 1)*
Zephyros Bleu 107 *(21½f,Wcn,S,Jan 21)*
Zero Grand 103 *(16½f,Tau,HY,Feb 2)*
Zero Visibility 99 *(16f,Plu,S,Nov 30)*
Zeroeshadesofgrey 96 *(24f,Chl,S,Dec 11)*
Ziggerson Hill 90 *(21½f,Wcn,G,Apr 4)*
Zip Wire 90 *(16f,Wor,G,Oct 8)*
Zip Wyatt 90 *(20f,Pun,HY,Feb 17)*
Zubayr 102 *(16f,Kem,GS,Feb 27)*
Zulu Oscar 110 *(16f,Kem,GS,Dec 27)*

NH FLAT RACE

A Rated 96 *(16f,Pun,SH,Jan 31)*
A Touch Of Sass 96 *(16f,Sth,G,Jly 12)*
Ablazing 91 *(16f,Utt,G,Jun 17)*
Above Board 92 *(16f,Chp,G,Oct 11)*
Acajou Des Bieffes 100 *(17f,Nab,GS,Oct 9)*
Actinpieces 97 *(17f,Ban,G,May 16)*
Aintree My Dream 108 *(16f,War,S,Apr 4)*
Air Horse One 95 *(16½f,Chl,G,Oct 24)*
Airpur Desbois 92 *(17f,Nab,GS,Jly 27)*
Alexander The Grey 99 *(16f,Sth,S,Dec 1)*
Alf 'N' Dor 103 *(17f,Mar,G,May 8)*
Alice Pink 102 *(16f,Ffo,S,Apr 10)*
Alizee Javilex 110 *(16f,Lud,G,Oct 7)*
Allycat 98 *(17f,Sed,G,May 12)*
Altior 95 *(16f,Pun,GY,Apr 29)*
Alyasan 96 *(16½f,Str,G,Jun 30)*
Amalfi Doug 96 *(16f,Sth,G,Oct 22)*
Amber Alert 99 *(16½f,Tau,GS,Mar 14)*
Amber Spyglass 93 *(16½f,Str,G,Sep 5)*
Ami Desbois 95 *(16f,Utt,HY,Nov 14)*
Amirr 105 *(18f,Fon,GS,Aug 13)*
Ange Des Malberaux 96 *(16f,Kel,GS,May 6)*
Annihilate 92 *(16f,Pun,SH,Jan 31)*
Another Sunshine 92 *(16f,Lud,S,Dec 2)*
Antartica De Thaix 92 *(15f,Wcn,S,Dec 3)*
Anti Cool 91 *(16f,Tow,G,May 11)*
Any Drama 107 *(17f,Ain,S,Apr 8)*
Apache Outlaw 108 *(17f,Ban,S,Dec 11)*
Arian 93 *(16f,Tow,S,Feb 4)*
Arthur Burrell 104 *(17f,Nab,GS,Oct 9)*
Asian Ali 97 *(16f,Wor,G,May 28)*
Atlanta Ablaze 93 *(16f,Tow,S,Dec 17)*
Atomix 107 *(16f,Cat,S,Dec 15)*
Augusta Kate 103 *(17f,Ain,S,Apr 7)*
Aurillac 103 *(16½f,Chl,GS,Nov 15)*
Australasia 93 *(16f,Hex,G,Jun 13)*
Avellino 104 *(16f,Fai,HY,Jan 30)*
Avenir D'Une Vie 99 *(16½f,Chl,G,Mar 16)*
Avichi 91 *(16f,Fai,HY,Dec 19)*
Awesome Rosie 94 *(16f,Wor,G,May 22)*
Azzerti 100 *(16f,War,S,Apr 4)*

Baby Bee Jay 92 *(17f,Ban,G,May 16)*
Bacardys 113 *(17f,Ain,S,Apr 8)*
Bacchanel 101 *(16f,Utt,HY,Nov 14)*
Badbad Leroy Brown 100 *(17f,Ban,HY,Apr 16)*
Bags Groove 91 *(16f,Nby,S,Mar 5)*
Ballinure 104 *(16f,War,GS,May 20)*
Ballyandy 110 *(16f,Wor,GS,Oct 21)*
Ballybrowneybridge 93 *(16f,Lud,S,Dec 2)*
Ballycash 95 *(17f,Don,S,Mar 5)*
Ballyhill 100 *(16f,Lud,G,Mar 24)*
Ballymalin 104 *(16f,Tow,S,Feb 4)*
Bandsman 109 *(16f,Lud,G,Mar 24)*
Banjo Girl 91 *(16f,Wet,S,Apr 17)*
Banks O' Houxty 101 *(16f,Kel,G,May 24)*
Bardd 97 *(16f,Hun,S,Mar 28)*
Bare Necessities 92 *(16½f,Str,G,Jun 30)*
Barney Dwan 100 *(16f,Kel,GF,Sep 16)*
Baron De Ligniere 94 *(16f,War,S,May 9)*
Bastien 93 *(16f,War,G,Mar 23)*
Battleford 112 *(17f,Ain,S,Apr 8)*
Baysbrown 93 *(16f,Kel,G,May 24)*
Be Daring 101 *(16f,Cat,S,Dec 15)*
Beau Du Brizais 91 *(16f,War,G,Mar 23)*
Beggar's Wishes 90 *(16f,Utt,HY,Dec 8)*
Belcanto 101 *(16f,Sth,G,Jun 2)*
Bells On Sunday 100 *(16f,Chp,HY,Mar 28)*
Bellshill 100 *(16f,Pun,GY,Apr 29)*
Bendomingo 107 *(16f,Wor,G,May 28)*
Beni Light 92 *(15f,Wcn,S,Apr 4)*
Bentworth Boy 91 *(16f,Chp,G,Oct 11)*
Bering Upsun 90 *(16f,Wet,HY,Feb 6)*
Bestiarius 92 *(16½f,Ncs,HY,Mar 8)*
Bestwork 93 *(17f,Mar,G,May 8)*
Betameche 113 *(16f,Wet,S,Apr 1)*
Better Getalong 96 *(16f,Hun,S,Dec 26)*
Big Chief Benny 99 *(15f,Wcn,S,Nov 7)*
Big Meadow 102 *(16f,Utt,S,Mar 19)*
Bigpipenotobacee 90 *(16f,Kem,S,Feb 12)*
Billy Bronco 108 *(16f,Tow,HY,Jan 7)*
Bilzic 103 *(16f,Sth,G,Oct 22)*
Bindon Mill 100 *(17f,Nab,GS,May 19)*
Biretta 105 *(17f,Nab,GS,Oct 9)*
Bitter Virtue 91 *(16f,Wor,G,May 22)*
Black Country Boy 96 *(16f,Nby,G,Apr 2)*
Black Kettle 95 *(16f,Sth,GS,Sep 2)*
Black Mischief 101 *(16f,Utt,S,Mar 19)*
Black Warrior 90 *(16f,Leo,S,Jan 24)*
Blackdown Hills 93 *(16f,Wor,G,May 28)*
Blakerigg 90 *(16½f,Ncs,HY,Mar 8)*
Bleu Et Noir 96 *(17f,Nab,GS,May 19)*
Blood Crazed Tiger 90 *(16f,Fai,S,Nov 29)*
Blow By Blow 101 *(16f,Fai,YS,Mar 28)*
Blu Cavalier 104 *(16f,Lud,G,Mar 24)*
Blu Passione 90 *(16f,Sth,G,Jun 2)*
Blue Comet 92 *(16f,Chp,S,Nov 4)*
Boatswain 97 *(16f,Utt,HY,Dec 8)*
Bol D'Air 92 *(15f,Wcn,S,Nov 7)*
Bollin Beauty 95 *(16f,Sth,G,Jly 12)*
Bonvilston Boy 97 *(17f,Mar,G,May 8)*
Boogie Life 97 *(16f,Kel,G,May 24)*
Book At Bedtime 91 *(16f,Sth,G,Mar 21)*
Boudry 103 *(16f,Tow,S,Feb 4)*
Boy In A Bentley 95 *(16f,Tow,G,May 11)*
Boyhood 97 *(15½f,Mus,S,Feb 17)*
Brahms De Clermont 92 *(16½f,Tau,G,Apr 7)*
Brake Hill 96 *(17f,Ain,G,May 15)*
Braqueur D'Or 99 *(16f,Lud,G,Mar 24)*
Brave Richard 105 *(17f,Mar,G,May 8)*
Breakdown Cover 97 *(16f,Hex,S,Mar 29)*
Breath Of Blighty 101 *(17f,Ban,G,Oct 27)*
Briac 103 *(18f,Fon,S,Nov 6)*
Bright Tomorrow 95 *(16f,Pun,SH,Jan 31)*
Bruce Of Crionaich 92 *(16f,Utt,G,Jun 17)*
Bun Doran 105 *(16f,Chp,S,Nov 4)*
Burlington Bert 100 *(16f,War,S,May 9)*
Burst Ya Bubble 97 *(15f,Wcn,GS,Apr 17)*
Burtredgipandgump 97 *(17f,Sed,G,May 12)*
Byron Flyer 103 *(17f,Mar,G,May 8)*

Caius Marcius 97 *(16½f,Chl,GS,Nov 15)*
Cajun Fiddle 97 *(16f,Wet,HY,Nov 25)*
Call To Order 105 *(16f,Utt,HY,Nov 14)*
Calling Des Blins 102 *(16f,Utt,HY,Apr 2)*
Canton Prince 99 *(16f,Lud,G,Mar 24)*
Capitaine 110 *(15f,Wcn,GS,Apr 17)*
Captain Bocelli 106 *(17f,Mar,G,May 8)*
Captain Buck's 96 *(16½f,Tau,G,Apr 7)*
Captain Flash 92 *(16f,War,GS,May 20)*
Captain Moirette 102 *(16f,Wet,S,Apr 1)*
Carole's Vigilante 91 *(17f,Crl,HY,Nov 9)*
Cash Again 111 *(16f,Nby,G,Apr 2)*
Casper King 105 *(17f,Mar,G,May 8)*
Castello Sforza 101 *(16½f,Chl,G,Mar 16)*
Catching Shadows 90 *(16f,Kel,GS,May 6)*
Champagne George 102 *(18f,Fon,S,Nov 6)*
Champagne To Go 108 *(16f,Wet,S,Apr 17)*
Champers On Ice 95 *(18f,Pun,GY,Apr 29)*
Chap 103 *(17f,Ain,G,May 15)*
Charbel 97 *(16f,Pun,GY,Apr 29)*
Chase End Charlie 106 *(17f,Ban,G,Oct 27)*
Chef D'Oeuvre 94 *(16f,San,S,Nov 8)*
Chelsea Flyer 98 *(15f,Wcn,S,Nov 7)*
Chilli Romance 94 *(16f,Tow,S,Dec 17)*
Christmas Twenty 102 *(16f,Sth,GS,Sep 2)*
Cinderfella 100 *(16f,Chp,S,Apr 9)*
Classic Tune 108 *(17f,Ban,S,Dec 11)*
Clondaw Bisto 109 *(18f,Plu,HY,Feb 1)*
Clondaw Cian 107 *(17f,Nab,GS,Oct 9)*
Clondaw Westie 95 *(16f,Nby,G,Apr 2)*
Cloudy Dream 93 *(17f,Crl,G,Oct 15)*
Coeur Blimey 100 *(16½f,Chl,G,Mar 16)*
Colin's Sister 104 *(16½f,Chl,GS,Nov 14)*
Commeragh Trix 99 *(16f,Fai,HY,Dec 19)*
Compadre 94 *(16½f,Chl,G,Mar 16)*
Copper Kay 110 *(17f,Nab,GS,Oct 9)*
Cor Wot An Apple 91 *(16f,Wor,GF,Jun 6)*
Costante Via 102 *(16½f,Tau,GS,Mar 14)*
Count Meribel 90 *(15f,Wcn,S,Apr 4)*
Coup De Pinceau 103 *(16f,Lud,GS,Apr 19)*
Court Baloo 90 *(16f,Kel,G,May 24)*
Crazy Penguin 104 *(16f,Wor,GS,Oct 21)*
Crimson Ark 96 *(16f,Wor,G,Sep 25)*
Criq Rock 115 *(17f,Ban,G,Oct 27)*
Crockery 99 *(16f,Chp,S,Nov 4)*
Cruiseaweigh 103 *(15f,Wcn,GS,Apr 17)*

Dalton Glance 93 *(17f,Chl,G,Apr 14)*
Dandy Bridge 90 *(16f,Fai,HY,Dec 19)*
Danmurphysdoor 102 *(16f,Kel,GS,May 6)*
Dante's Way 108 *(16f,Kel,GS,May 6)*
Daytime Ahead 93 *(16f,Kem,S,Feb 12)*
Death Duty 100 *(16f,Fai,YS,Mar 28)*
Debece 102 *(17f,Mar,S,Mar 28)*
Definately Vinnie 94 *(15f,Wcn,GF,May 12)*
Derrydoon 92 *(15½f,Mus,GS,Jan 4)*
Desert Retreat 108 *(16f,Chp,G,Sep 30)*
Desert Sensation 95 *(15½f,Mus,S,Feb 17)*
Deshan 92 *(16f,Wor,G,May 28)*
Disko 98 *(16f,Pun,GY,Apr 29)*
Divine Spear 100 *(16f,Tow,G,May 11)*
Dixie Lee 92 *(16f,Fai,SH,Jan 20)*
Djarkalin 91 *(15f,Wcn,S,Apr 4)*
Don't Touch It 102 *(16f,Pun,G,May 16)*
Donttellthemissis 98 *(16f,Sth,G,Jly 12)*
Dothraki Raider 95 *(16f,Lud,GS,Apr 19)*
Down The Line 96 *(16f,Kel,GS,May 6)*
Dr West 95 *(16f,Hex,S,Mar 29)*
Drama King 99 *(16f,Nby,G,Apr 2)*
Dreambaby 90 *(16½f,Chl,GS,Nov 14)*
Druids Lodge 101 *(16f,Tow,S,Feb 4)*
Drumcliff 95 *(16½f,Tau,GS,Dec 10)*
Dubai Angel 107 *(16f,Kel,GF,Sep 16)*
Dubai Devils 104 *(15½f,Mus,S,Dec 7)*
Dubai Shen 94 *(15½f,Mus,S,Feb 17)*
Due East 105 *(16f,Sth,GS,Sep 2)*

Eamon An Cnoic 100 *(16f,Ffo,GS,Mar 20)*
Eastview Boy 91 *(16f,Wet,HY,Feb 6)*
Eaton Hill 104 *(16f,Ffo,HY,Mar 31)*
El Vasco 96 *(16f,Pun,G,May 16)*
Eloped 98 *(16f,Lud,G,Mar 24)*
Emperor Sakhee 91 *(16f,Hex,G,Jun 6)*
Epic Warrior 92 *(16f,Wor,GF,Jun 11)*
Ethelwyn 94 *(17f,Ban,G,May 16)*
Evening Stanley 102 *(17f,Mar,G,May 8)*

Fact Of The Matter 109 *(16f,Chp,G,Sep 30)*
Faheem 93 *(16f,Kem,S,Feb 12)*
Fairy Theatre 93 *(16f,Kel,G,May 24)*
Fenlon's Hill 98 *(15½f,Mus,GS,Jan 4)*
First Figaro 100 *(16½f,Chl,G,Mar 16)*
Fisherman Frank 101 *(16f,Wor,G,Aug 19)*
Fit The Brief 103 *(16½f,Tau,GS,Mar 14)*
Fizzy Dancer 103 *(16f,Lud,G,Oct 7)*
Flints Legacy 103 *(16f,Chp,S,Apr 9)*
Fly Du Charmil 102 *(16f,Nby,S,Nov 26)*
For Instance 103 *(16f,War,GS,May 20)*
Fountains Windfall 92 *(18f,Plu,S,Nov 16)*
Frankly Speaking 99 *(17f,Don,G,Feb 24)*
Freeway Space 103 *(16f,Fai,HY,Jan 30)*
Full Irish 97 *(16f,San,S,Nov 8)*

G For Ginger 95 *(15f,Wcn,S,Apr 4)*
Galveston 98 *(16f,Utt,G,Jun 17)*
Gayebury 91 *(17f,Exe,HY,Jan 1)*
General Bux 91 *(16f,San,S,Nov 8)*
General Mahler 91 *(15½f,Mus,GS,Jan 4)*
Geordie Des Champs 105 *(16f,Ffo,HY,Mar 31)*
Get Rhythm 104 *(16f,Sth,S,Mar 29)*
Goaheadmakemyday 99 *(16f,Fai,HY,Jan 30)*
Gold Doubloons 97 *(16f,Fai,HY,Jan 30)*
Golden Birthday 94 *(16f,Kem,S,Feb 12)*
Golden Gate Bridge 99 *(13f,Exe,GF,Oct 20)*
Golden Thread 100 *(16f,Sth,GS,Sep 2)*
Good Thyne Tara 103 *(16f,Fai,HY,Jan 30)*
Graceful Legend 94 *(16f,Tow,S,Dec 17)*
Grand Coureur 97 *(16f,Lud,GS,Apr 19)*
Grand Introduction 102 *(16f,Sth,G,Oct 22)*
Grand Turina 94 *(16f,Chp,HY,Mar 28)*
Groundunderrepair 97 *(17f,Don,G,Feb 24)*
Gully's Edge 91 *(16f,Kel,GS,May 6)*
Gulshanigans 98 *(16f,Nby,G,Apr 2)*

Harvey 90 *(16f,Tow,S,Dec 17)*
Hastrubal 107 *(16f,Utt,HY,Dec 18)*
Heilan Rebel 93 *(17f,Sed,S,Nov 24)*
Hello Jazz 99 *(15f,Wcn,GF,May 12)*
Helmsley Lad 90 *(17f,Don,G,Nov 27)*
Hey Up Ashey 92 *(16f,Sth,G,Oct 22)*
High Bridge 114 *(16f,Cat,S,Dec 15)*
High Hopper 94 *(17f,Mar,G,May 8)*
Hitherjacques Lady 105 *(17f,Chl,G,Apr 14)*
Hoke Colburn 91 *(16f,War,G,Mar 23)*
Holbrook Park 97 *(16f,War,HY,Dec 31)*
Honey Brown 94 *(16f,Sth,G,Jly 12)*
Hoo Bally Diva 100 *(16½f,Tau,GS,Mar 14)*
Hurricane Dylan 101 *(16f,Ffo,HY,Mar 31)*

Iconic Image 94 *(16f,Pun,SH,Jan 31)*
Iconic Star 97 *(16f,Fak,GS,Oct 28)*
Ilovemints 100 *(17f,Ban,S,Mar 31)*
Imperial Eloquence 101 *(16f,Hex,S,Mar 29)*
Improved 90 *(16f,Utt,G,Jly 15)*
Indian Brave 103 *(16f,Wor,GS,Oct 21)*
Indy Five 100 *(16f,Chp,S,Apr 9)*
Informationisking 105 *(16f,Tow,S,Feb 4)*
Inner Loop 97 *(13f,Exe,GF,Oct 20)*
Instingtive 101 *(16f,Chp,HY,Feb 5)*
Island Rendezvous 96 *(16f,Chp,S,Nov 4)*
Isle Of Ewe 100 *(16f,Hex,S,Mar 29)*

Jack Dillinger 97 *(16f,Leo,S,Jan 24)*
Jackblack 102 *(16f,Wor,GS,Oct 21)*
Jacksey's Well 96 *(17f,Ban,S,Dec 11)*
Jazz Thyme 94 *(16½f,Str,GF,Jly 19)*
Jebs Gamble 91 *(18f,Fon,S,Nov 6)*
Jenkins 116 *(16f,Nby,G,Apr 2)*
Jennifer Eccles 95 *(18f,Fon,G,Oct 3)*
Jessber's Dream 92 *(17f,Ain,G,Oct 25)*
Jessie Webster 91 *(17f,Ain,G,Oct 25)*

Jethro 102 *(16f,Kel,GF,Sep 16)*
Joe Farrell 96 *(16f,Wor,GF,Jly 1)*
Johanos 93 *(17f,Mar,S,Mar 28)*
Johnny Go 99 *(16f,Hex,HY,May 9)*
Josie Jump 95 *(17f,Nab,GS,Jly 27)*
Jot'em Down 101 *(16f,Tow,S,Feb 4)*
Junior Package 107 *(16f,Sth,GS,Sep 2)*
Just A Feeling 91 *(16f,Tow,GF,Apr 30)*
Justatenner 92 *(15f,Wcn,S,Nov 7)*

Kaddys Girl 90 *(16f,Tow,GF,Apr 30)*
Kafella 91 *(16f,Hun,S,Mar 6)*
Kahaleesi 96 *(17f,Chl,G,Apr 14)*
Kalaniti 96 *(17f,Ain,G,Oct 25)*
Kara Tara 102 *(17f,Mar,G,May 8)*
Katy P 102 *(17f,Chl,G,Apr 14)*
Kayf Grace 112 *(16f,Fak,S,Mar 28)*
Kayla 92 *(16f,Tow,GF,Apr 30)*
Keep Up Keira 95 *(16f,Lud,S,Dec 2)*
Keeper Hill 107 *(16f,Wet,S,Apr 1)*
Kelka 105 *(16f,Wet,S,Apr 17)*
Kendari King 98 *(17f,Mar,G,Jun 19)*
Kilronan Castle 93 *(17f,Ban,G,Oct 1)*
King Uther 105 *(18f,Plu,HY,Feb 1)*
Kir Royal 97 *(16f,Nby,S,Nov 26)*
Knight To Open 92 *(18f,Fon,S,Nov 6)*

La Bague Au Roi 100 *(17f,Ain,G,Oct 25)*
Lady Beaufort 97 *(16f,Kel,HY,Feb 18)*
Lady Cardinal 91 *(16f,Chp,G,Sep 30)*
Lady Markby 95 *(17f,Nab,S,Apr 18)*
Lady Of Llanarmon 100 *(16f,Lud,S,Dec 2)*
Lakeside Castle 91 *(16f,Leo,S,Jan 24)*
Lamanver Alchemy 102 *(16f,Lud,G,Oct 7)*
Lamanver Odyssey 104 *(16½f,Tau,GS,Mar 14)*
Laser Light 102 *(16f,Tow,S,Feb 17)*
Last Summer 110 *(16f,Wor,G,May 28)*
Lastbutnotleast 96 *(17f,Sed,S,Mar 6)*
Late Night Lily 99 *(18f,Fon,S,Oct 21)*
Laval Noir 100 *(16f,Hun,S,Mar 28)*
Le Coeur Net 92 *(16f,Ffo,GS,Mar 20)*
Le Dauphin 103 *(16f,Nby,G,Apr 2)*
Leith Hill Lad 95 *(17f,Ain,G,May 15)*
Let's Tango 92 *(16f,Nby,G,Apr 2)*
Lets Go Dutchess 93 *(16½f,Tau,G,Nov 12)*
Lieutenant Gruber 101 *(16f,Lud,G,Mar 24)*
Lilbourne Legacy 93 *(16f,Wor,G,Aug 19)*
Lime Street 97 *(16f,Chp,S,Nov 4)*
Limos 102 *(16f,Kel,GS,May 6)*
Lincoln County 97 *(17f,Nab,G,Jly 19)*
Lip Service 98 *(16f,Pun,G,May 16)*
Lisheen Prince 93 *(16½f,Chl,GS,Nov 15)*
Listen To The Man 95 *(16f,San,S,Mar 12)*
Lithic 109 *(16f,Sth,S,Dec 1)*
Little Miss Poet 97 *(17f,Ain,S,Apr 7)*
Llantara 93 *(16f,Tow,S,Dec 17)*
Loch Garman Aris 110 *(16f,Utt,HY,Dec 18)*
Loch Linnhe 98 *(16f,Cat,S,Jan 14)*
London Prize 97 *(16f,Wor,GF,Jun 6)*
Looksnowtlikebrian 97 *(16f,Sth,G,Oct 22)*
Lord Bryan 99 *(16f,War,GS,May 20)*
Lord Westy 92 *(16f,Sth,G,Oct 22)*
Lough Salt 96 *(16f,Sth,S,Dec 1)*
Louis' Vac Pouch 98 *(15f,Wcn,GS,Apr 17)*
Lucky Pass 101 *(16f,Fai,S,Nov 29)*

Magna Cartor 90 *(16f,Utt,G,Jly 24)*
Mahler Bay 96 *(16f,Cat,S,Dec 15)*
Mahlerdramatic 107 *(16f,Sth,GS,Sep 2)*
Manhattan Spring 99 *(17f,Ain,S,Apr 8)*
Mankala 103 *(16f,Nby,G,Apr 2)*
Manton Boy 97 *(17f,Ban,G,Oct 27)*
Mardale 105 *(16f,Kel,GF,Sep 16)*
Marley Joe 95 *(16f,Wor,G,Aug 19)*
Marquis Of Carabas 102 *(16f,Wor,G,May 28)*
Martha's Benefit 94 *(16f,Sth,G,Jun 2)*
Master Majic 93 *(15f,Wcn,GS,Apr 17)*
Matchaway 110 *(17f,Ban,S,Dec 11)*
Mcgregor's Cottage 94 *(17f,Sed,HY,Dec 4)*
Mckenzie's Friend 97 *(16f,War,S,May 9)*
Meet The Legend 111 *(16f,Kel,GF,Sep 16)*
Melrose Boy 97 *(15f,Wcn,GS,Apr 17)*
Menace 104 *(18f,Fon,GS,Aug 13)*
Meribel Millie 101 *(17f,Chl,G,Apr 14)*
Micklegate Run 94 *(16f,Hex,G,Jun 13)*
Midnight Cowboy 92 *(16f,San,S,Nov 8)*
Midnight Gem 92 *(17f,Ban,G,May 16)*
Midnight Glory 104 *(17f,Chl,G,Apr 14)*
Midnight Gypsy 91 *(16f,Wor,GF,Jun 6)*
Midnight Jitterbug 99 *(17f,Don,G,Feb 24)*
Midnight Maestro 102 *(17f,Don,S,Mar 5)*
Midnight Merlot 91 *(16f,Kem,S,Feb 12)*
Midnight Target 93 *(16f,Lud,S,Dec 2)*
Midnight Tune 95 *(18f,Fon,S,Oct 21)*
Midnight Velvet 94 *(17f,Ain,G,Oct 25)*
Minella Charmer 91 *(16½f,Tau,G,Nov 12)*
Minella For Me 103 *(15f,Wcn,GS,Apr 17)*
Misfits 96 *(15½f,Mus,GS,Jan 4)*
Miss Maiden Over 100 *(17f,Chl,G,Apr 14)*
Miss Mash 91 *(16f,Lud,G,Oct 7)*
Miss Mobot 103 *(16½f,Chl,GS,Nov 14)*
Miss Yeats 90 *(16f,Wet,HY,Nov 25)*
Misterton 107 *(16f,War,S,Apr 4)*
Mo Chailin 98 *(16f,Cat,GS,Dec 2)*
Modus 98 *(16f,Pun,GY,Apr 29)*
Monkey Rum 97 *(15f,Wcn,GF,May 12)*
Monsieur Darsi 96 *(16f,Chp,S,Nov 4)*
Mont Choisy 98 *(16f,Wor,GF,Jun 11)*
Moon Jet 97 *(17f,Don,G,Feb 24)*
Moontripper 99 *(16f,Wor,G,Aug 19)*
More Than Two 90 *(17f,Ban,S,Mar 31)*
Morning Herald 96 *(16½f,Chl,GS,Nov 14)*
Mortens Leam 100 *(16f,Wet,S,Apr 1)*
Mount Mizooka 90 *(17f,Sed,S,Mar 15)*
Move To The Groove 96 *(16f,Cat,S,Jan 14)*
Movewiththetimes 104 *(15f,Wcn,GS,Apr 17)*
Mr Banks 90 *(16f,Hun,S,Dec 26)*
Mr Big Shot 106 *(16f,Utt,S,Mar 19)*
Mr Fenton 93 *(16f,Chp,HY,Dec 5)*
Mr Kite 103 *(17f,Mar,G,Jun 19)*
Mr Witmore 106 *(15½f,Mus,S,Dec 7)*
Ms Parfois 107 *(16f,Utt,HY,Apr 2)*
Muffins For Tea 96 *(16f,Chp,HY,Feb 5)*
Mullinavat 90 *(16f,Hex,G,Jun 13)*
Mustang On 93 *(17f,Don,G,Feb 24)*
Mutdula 95 *(16f,Cat,S,Dec 15)*
Muthabir 93 *(16f,Utt,G,Jun 17)*
My Khaleesi 90 *(16f,Hun,GS,Feb 11)*
My Liege 94 *(15f,Wcn,S,Dec 26)*
Myrtle Drive 90 *(17f,Ban,G,May 16)*
Mystical Knight 108 *(16f,War,HY,Dec 31)*
Myztique 109 *(15½f,Mus,S,Dec 7)*

Nambour 90 *(16f,Pun,S,May 2)*
Nampararoo 95 *(17f,Ban,G,Oct 1)*
Naranja 93 *(17f,Mar,GS,Apr 21)*
Native Princess 104 *(16f,Sth,G,Jun 2)*
Nerual 94 *(16f,Fai,HY,Dec 19)*
New Member 105 *(16f,Lud,G,Mar 24)*
New Providence 98 *(16f,Wor,G,May 28)*
New To This Town 90 *(16½f,Chl,G,Mar 16)*
Nicely Indeed 107 *(18f,Fon,GS,Aug 13)*
Nobel Leader 92 *(17f,Mar,GS,Nov 19)*
Not Another Muddle 94 *(18f,Fon,S,Nov 25)*
Notre Ami 98 *(15f,Wcn,GS,Apr 17)*
Nuts Well 107 *(16f,Kel,GS,May 6)*

Officer Hoolihan 102 *(16f,Wor,G,May 28)*
Oh So Gigolo 93 *(18f,Fon,GS,Aug 13)*
Ok Corral 94 *(16f,Pun,Y,Apr 30)*
One Cool Scorpion 101 *(17f,Nab,GS,May 19)*
Only For Love 97 *(16½f,Tau,G,Apr 7)*
Only Gorgeous 92 *(17f,Ain,G,May 15)*
Only Orvieto 111 *(17f,Sed,S,Mar 15)*
Onthewesternfront 100 *(16f,Kem,S,Feb 12)*
Orchard Park 93 *(17f,Ban,HY,Mar 2)*
Our Dancing Dandy 113 *(17f,Ban,HY,Apr 16)*
Our Reward 106 *(17f,Nab,GS,Oct 9)*
Ozzie The Oscar 91 *(16½f,Tau,GS,Dec 10)*

Paddling 99 *(16f,Cat,S,Dec 15)*
Paddy's Field 96 *(16f,War,S,May 9)*
Pampanini 93 *(17f,Nab,S,Apr 18)*
Paper Roses 109 *(17f,Sed,S,Mar 15)*
Patience Tony 96 *(16f,Cat,S,Feb 15)*
Peace N' Milan 98 *(16f,Fai,HY,Dec 19)*
Pearlita 93 *(17f,Chl,G,Apr 14)*
Penn Lane 106 *(16f,Utt,HY,Nov 14)*
Peppay Le Pugh 104 *(17f,Mar,G,May 8)*
Petethepear 104 *(16f,Chp,G,Sep 30)*
Petite Power 96 *(17f,Ain,G,May 15)*
Phobiaphiliac 94 *(16f,Kem,S,Feb 12)*
Pick Up Trix 93 *(16f,Ffo,S,Apr 10)*
Picknick Park 95 *(17f,Ban,HY,Apr 16)*
Pikarnia 91 *(17f,Sed,G,May 12)*
Pilgrims Bay 94 *(16f,Utt,G,Jun 17)*
Pinnacle Panda 99 *(17f,Ain,G,May 15)*
Piton Pete 96 *(16f,Hun,S,Mar 6)*
Point The Way 96 *(16½f,Chl,GS,Nov 15)*
Pollyogan 94 *(18f,Fon,S,Oct 21)*
Poppy Kay 104 *(16f,Lud,S,Dec 2)*
Positively Dylan 98 *(16f,Chp,HY,Dec 5)*
Post War 95 *(16f,Chp,S,Apr 9)*
Postbridge 101 *(16f,Fak,GS,Oct 28)*
Potters Legend 105 *(16f,Fak,GS,Oct 28)*
Potters Point 105 *(16f,Pun,G,May 16)*
Pougne Bobbi 103 *(16f,War,GS,May 20)*
Preseli Rock 102 *(16f,Chp,S,Nov 4)*
Presenting Percy 98 *(16f,Pun,SH,Jan 31)*
Presenting Streak 97 *(17f,Mar,G,Jun 19)*
Pretty Rose 95 *(16f,Sth,G,Jly 12)*
Pride Of Lecale 109 *(16f,Chp,HY,Feb 5)*
Prince Of Poets 102 *(17f,Mar,G,May 8)*
Prince Of Steal 100 *(16f,Sth,S,Dec 1)*
Princess Roania 103 *(16f,Sth,G,Jun 2)*
Puddle Jumper 90 *(16½f,Ncs,HY,Dec 10)*
Pulling Power 102 *(16½f,Chl,GS,Nov 14)*
Pure Vision 101 *(16f,Nby,S,Nov 26)*
Purple Genie 92 *(13f,Exe,GF,Oct 20)*
Push Ahead 100 *(17f,Ain,G,May 15)*
Pylonthepressure 96 *(16f,Pun,GY,Apr 29)*

Quieto Sol 102 *(17f,Mar,G,May 8)*
Quinto 96 *(17f,Ain,G,May 15)*

Raised On Grazeon 100 *(16f,Cat,S,Feb 15)*
Randy Pike 95 *(16f,Kel,HY,Feb 18)*
Rather Be 106 *(17f,Don,G,Feb 24)*
Rebel Collins 109 *(16f,Sth,GS,Sep 2)*
Red Infantry 102 *(16f,War,S,Jan 28)*
Red Six 94 *(16f,Ffo,GS,Mar 20)*
Reilly's Minor 105 *(16f,War,S,Jan 28)*
Reivers Lad 91 *(17f,Crl,S,Mar 10)*
Ridgeway Flyer 110 *(16f,Lud,G,Mar 24)*
River Arrow 92 *(17f,Ban,S,Mar 31)*
River Dun 95 *(16f,Cat,GS,Dec 2)*
River Of Intrigue 100 *(16f,War,S,Apr 4)*
Roadie Joe 104 *(16f,Wor,G,Aug 19)*
Rob Robin 93 *(16½f,Tau,G,Nov 12)*
Robin Roe 96 *(16f,War,G,Mar 23)*
Robinesse 99 *(16½f,Chl,GS,Nov 14)*
Rock Chick Supremo 90 *(17f,Ain,G,Oct 25)*
Rodneythetrotter 108 *(16f,Wor,GS,Oct 21)*
Rolling Dylan 93 *(15f,Wcn,S,Dec 3)*
Rolling Thunder 95 *(17f,Sed,HY,Dec 26)*
Rollo's Reflection 97 *(16f,Wor,GF,Jun 11)*
Roxy Belle 92 *(17f,Chl,G,Apr 14)*
Royal Supremo 95 *(16f,War,G,Mar 23)*
Royalzaro 109 *(17f,Ban,G,Oct 27)*
Run Bob Run 102 *(16f,Chp,G,Sep 30)*
Russian Approval 94 *(13f,Exe,GF,Oct 20)*
Rustamabad 94 *(16f,Wor,G,Aug 19)*
Ryedale Racer 103 *(16f,Hex,HY,May 9)*

Sam Fairyann 90 *(15½f,Mus,GS,Jan 4)*
Sam Spinner 110 *(16f,Wet,S,Apr 1)*
Sam's Adventure 111 *(16f,Wet,HY,Feb 6)*
Sammy B 102 *(15½f,Mus,GS,Jan 4)*
Sartorial Elegance 103 *(17f,Ban,G,Oct 27)*
Savingforvegas 98 *(16f,Wet,HY,Nov 25)*
Savoy Court 110 *(16f,Ffo,GS,Mar 20)*
Scarlett Peak 103 *(17f,Mar,G,May 8)*
Scarteen 97 *(17f,Mar,GS,Nov 19)*
Scooter Boy 90 *(16f,Chp,S,Nov 4)*
Scorpion Princess 93 *(16f,Sth,G,Mar 21)*
Seelateralligator 92 *(17f,Mar,GS,Apr 21)*
Shambougg 107 *(16f,War,S,Jan 28)*
Shan't Agree 98 *(16f,War,GS,May 20)*
Shattered Love 101 *(17f,Ain,S,Apr 7)*
She's Otto 93 *(16f,Fai,SH,Jan 20)*
Shout It Aloud 94 *(15f,Wcn,GF,May 12)*
Show On The Road 98 *(16½f,Tau,G,Apr 7)*
Shrewd Tactics 106 *(16f,War,S,Jan 28)*
Sidbury Fair 96 *(16f,Utt,HY,Apr 2)*
Sir Antony Browne 101 *(16f,Kem,S,Feb 12)*
Sir Will 97 *(16f,Chp,S,Nov 4)*
Sister Sibyl 95 *(16f,Tow,S,Dec 17)*
Sliabh Donn 91 *(16f,Fai,HY,Dec 19)*
Smart Talk 99 *(16f,Hex,HY,May 9)*
Smoking Dixie 98 *(16f,Lud,GS,Apr 19)*
Snag List 104 *(16½f,Chl,GS,Nov 14)*
Snow Leopardess 107 *(17f,Don,G,Feb 24)*
Some Are Lucky 90 *(16½f,Chl,G,Oct 24)*
Some Tank 93 *(16f,Pun,G,May 16)*
Speedalong 94 *(15f,Wcn,GS,Apr 17)*
Speronimo 90 *(15f,Wcn,GS,Apr 17)*
Spirit Of Hale 95 *(17f,Ban,S,Dec 11)*
Spirit Of Kayf 101 *(16f,Wet,HY,Feb 6)*
St Quintin 98 *(16f,Wor,G,May 28)*
Stand By Me 98 *(17f,Nab,GS,May 19)*
Stealing Mix 98 *(15f,Wcn,GS,Apr 17)*
Stickee Fingers 97 *(16f,Sth,G,Jun 2)*
Still Together 96 *(16f,Wor,G,Sep 25)*
Storm Forecast 100 *(17f,Sed,S,Nov 24)*
Stowaway Magic 101 *(16f,Kem,S,Feb 12)*
Sue Be It 97 *(16f,Lud,GS,Apr 19)*
Summer Name 98 *(16f,Nby,G,Apr 2)*
Sungai Long 103 *(16f,Cat,S,Jan 14)*
Sunni May 98 *(16f,Fai,YS,Mar 28)*
Sunshine Corner 92 *(16½f,Chl,GS,Nov 14)*
Sweet'N'Chic 92 *(18f,Fon,S,Oct 21)*
Sweetlittlekitty 95 *(16f,Chp,HY,Mar 28)*

Tanarpino 102 *(17f,Ban,G,Oct 27)*
Tara Potter 99 *(16f,Wor,G,Aug 19)*
Tara View 100 *(17f,Chl,G,Apr 14)*
Tara Well 96 *(16f,Utt,HY,Dec 31)*
Tara's Honour 102 *(16f,Lud,G,Oct 7)*
Teals Lad 92 *(16f,Sth,GS,Sep 2)*
Tearsofclewbay 104 *(16f,Utt,HY,Dec 31)*
Ted's Lad 97 *(16f,Sth,G,Oct 22)*
Templeross 115 *(16f,Utt,HY,Dec 18)*
Terra Firma 94 *(15f,Wcn,GF,May 12)*
The Clonlisk Bug 99 *(16f,Wor,G,Aug 19)*
The Drone 101 *(16½f,Str,GF,May 17)*
The Linksman 99 *(16f,Wor,GS,Oct 21)*
The Minch 112 *(17f,Ain,S,Apr 8)*
The Missus 91 *(17f,Don,G,Nov 27)*
The Model County 94 *(16f,Chp,HY,Dec 5)*
The Nipper 106 *(17f,Ban,G,May 16)*
The Organist 90 *(16½f,Per,S,May 14)*
The Pierre Lark 92 *(17f,Ban,HY,Mar 2)*
The Poodle Faker 101 *(16f,Nby,G,Apr 2)*
The Tailgater 99 *(16f,Cat,GS,Dec 2)*
The Unit 94 *(16½f,Chl,GS,Nov 15)*
The White Duke 100 *(16f,Sth,GS,Sep 2)*
The Worlds End 105 *(16f,Chp,S,Apr 9)*
Theatre Rouge 96 *(16½f,Tau,GS,Mar 14)*
Theatre Territory 105 *(16½f,Chl,GS,Nov 14)*
Thehossbehind 92 *(16f,Wor,GF,Jun 6)*
Thisulldaeus 92 *(16f,Kel,GS,May 6)*
Thomas Shelby 96 *(16f,Kem,S,Feb 12)*
Three Ways 109 *(16f,Utt,HY,Dec 18)*
Throckley 95 *(16f,Kel,GF,Sep 16)*
Tickanrun 98 *(16f,Kel,GS,May 6)*
Tiger Mountain 93 *(16f,Hex,S,Mar 29)*
Tilinisi 100 *(16f,Sth,G,Jly 12)*
Time Is Money 100 *(15f,Wcn,GF,May 12)*
Timing'severything 91 *(16f,Pun,GY,Apr 28)*
Tinted Rose 101 *(16f,Lud,G,Mar 24)*
Tobouggaloo 101 *(16½f,Chl,GS,Nov 14)*
Tolethorpe 102 *(16f,Hun,S,Mar 6)*
Tommy Rapper 109 *(16f,Ffo,GS,Mar 20)*
Tomnbill 91 *(15f,Wcn,GF,May 12)*
Tomngerry 104 *(16f,Cat,S,Jan 14)*
Top Priority 108 *(16½f,Str,GF,May 17)*
Touch Kick 96 *(15f,Wcn,S,Apr 4)*
Tour De Ville 99 *(16f,Wor,S,Aug 23)*
Trans Express 103 *(17f,Ban,G,Oct 27)*
Tullow Tonic 95 *(16f,Lud,G,Oct 7)*
Turcagua 95 *(16½f,Chl,G,Mar 16)*
Twist On Ginge 103 *(17f,Ban,HY,Apr 16)*

Utility 103 *(16f,Utt,HY,Dec 8)*

Vaillant Nonantais 107 *(16½f,Str,GF,May 17)*
Very First Time 98 *(16f,Cat,S,Feb 15)*
Very Much So 100 *(16½f,Chl,G,Mar 16)*
Vieux Lille 101 *(15f,Wcn,S,Nov 7)*
Village Mystic 99 *(16f,Leo,S,Jan 24)*
Vinciaettis 97 *(18f,Plu,S,Nov 16)*
Violets Girl 97 *(16½f,Str,GF,Jly 19)*
Viva Rafa 95 *(16½f,Str,G,Jun 30)*
Vivas 94 *(18f,Fon,G,Oct 3)*
Vive Le Roi 95 *(16f,Wor,G,Sep 25)*

Walkami 93 *(16½f,Tau,G,Nov 12)*
Walt 92 *(16f,Kem,S,Feb 12)*
War On The Rocks 93 *(16½f,Str,G,Jun 30)*
Washed Ashore 103 *(17f,Mar,G,May 8)*
Water Willow 97 *(13f,Exe,GF,Oct 20)*
Waterlord 102 *(16½f,Chl,GS,Nov 15)*
Way Of The World 101 *(16f,Ffo,HY,Mar 31)*
Welluptoscratch 90 *(18f,Plu,G,May 10)*
Wenyerreadyfreddie 99 *(17f,Don,S,Mar 5)*
West Torr 96 *(16f,Ffo,HY,Mar 31)*
Westend Story 101 *(16½f,Chl,G,Mar 16)*
Westerbee 99 *(17f,Chl,G,Apr 14)*
Western Cape 107 *(16f,Sth,G,Oct 22)*
Western Miller 102 *(16f,Wor,G,Sep 25)*
Western Sunrise 92 *(16f,Wor,G,May 22)*
Western Wave 98 *(16f,Tow,S,Feb 17)*
Weyburn 94 *(16f,Sth,G,Oct 22)*
What A Diva 100 *(16f,Tow,HY,Jan 7)*
What Happens Now 95 *(17f,Sed,S,Nov 24)*
Whatsthatallabout 94 *(16½f,Tau,GS,Mar 14)*
Which One Is Which 106 *(16½f,Chl,GS,Nov 14)*
Whiskey No Ice 95 *(16f,Pun,G,May 16)*
Who You For 112 *(16f,Sth,GS,Sep 2)*
Wholestone 104 *(16f,Wor,G,Sep 25)*
Whoshotwho 99 *(16f,Kem,S,Feb 12)*
Wicked Willy 91 *(16f,Ffo,GS,Mar 20)*
Widow On The Run 94 *(17f,Nab,S,Apr 18)*
Wilde Oak 95 *(17f,Nab,GS,Jly 27)*
Will O'The West 93 *(16f,War,S,May 9)*
William H Bonney 104 *(18f,Fon,S,Nov 6)*
Willoughby Court 110 *(17f,Ain,S,Apr 8)*
Winter Garden 95 *(17f,Ain,G,May 15)*
Winter Soldier 99 *(16f,Utt,G,Jun 17)*
Without Limites 92 *(16f,Pun,HY,Feb 17)*
Work Du Breteau 90 *(16f,Pun,G,May 16)*
Wylde Magic 108 *(16f,Sth,S,Mar 29)*

Yes I Did 108 *(16f,Lud,G,Oct 7)*
Yorkhill 96 *(16f,Pun,Y,Apr 30)*
You Say What 95 *(16f,Utt,HY,Dec 8)*

Zakety Zak 91 *(16f,Kel,G,May 24)*
Zandino 104 *(16½f,Str,GF,May 17)*
Zipple Back 91 *(17f,Ain,S,Apr 8)*

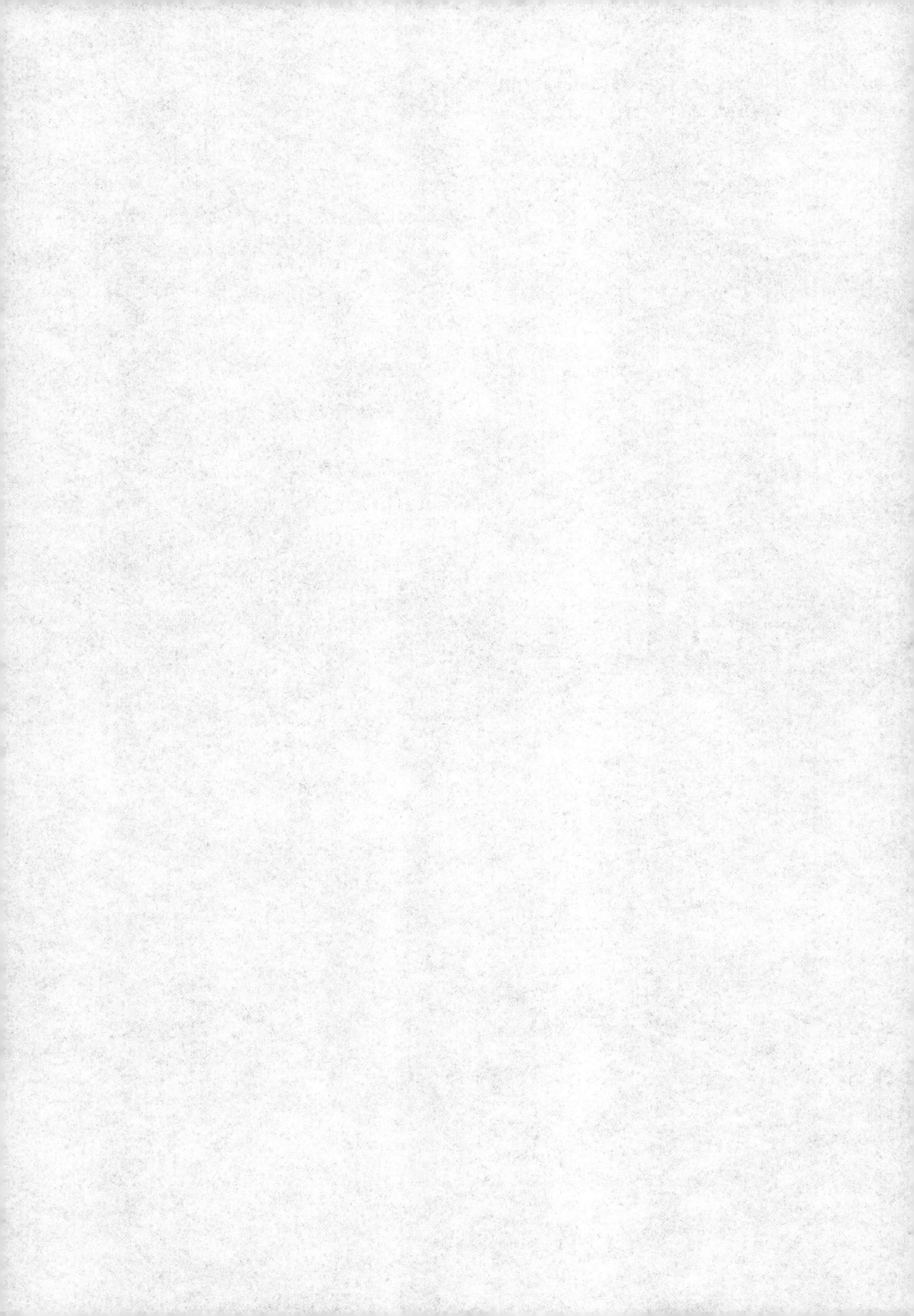